12/29/16 Ingram $34.95

THE WORLD ALMANAC®

AND BOOK OF FACTS

2017

WORLD ALMANAC BOOKS

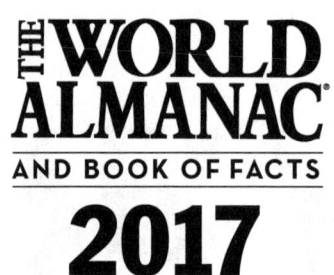

THE WORLD ALMANAC
AND BOOK OF FACTS
2017

Senior Editor: Sarah Janssen
Editor: M. L. Liu **Associate Editor:** Shmuel Ross
Index Editor: Nan Badgett
Contributors: Emily J. Dolbear, Jennifer Dunham, Robert Famighetti, Marshall Gerometta, Jacqueline Laks Gorman, Richard Hantula, Michael J. Kaufman, Marc Kissel, Donhae Koo, John Mastroberardino, William A. McGeveran Jr., Janet M. Olson, Shannon O'Toole, John Rosenthal, Helene Salmon, Peter J. Schmidtke, George W. Smith, Edward A. Thomas, Valerie J. Weber, Lori P. Wiesenfeld, Dale Williams

Production: Newgen North America
Design and Production, Year in Pictures: QBS Learning
Design, Cover: Takeshi Takahashi
Photo Research: Edward A. Thomas

For Infobase Learning:
Editorial Director: Laurie E. Likoff
Project Editor: Edward A. Thomas

Front cover: Shutterstock (unless otherwise noted); AP Images: Beyoncé. **Back cover:** Shutterstock (unless otherwise noted); AP Images: Louisiana flooding, Michelle and Barack Obama; NASA, ESA, and M. Livio (STScI): Science & Technology background. **Interior pages:** Photos are AP Images unless otherwise noted. **Jimmy Carter Library and Museum:** Carter, 528. **Everett Collection:** *The People v. O.J. Simpson*, Ray Mickshaw / © FX, 812; Roger Ailes, Derek Storm, 813. **Gerald R. Ford Presidential Library and Museum:** Ford, 528. **Hillary for America:** Clinton, 12. **IN.gov:** Pence, 13. **Lyndon Baines Johnson Library and Museum:** Vietnam War protesters, 492; Johnson, 527. **Library of Congress:** 465; slaves, 468; 470; 471; 489; U.S presidents, unless otherwise noted, 521-29; 648; 661. **National Archives and Records Administration:** 472; 494; 504; 506; Grant, 524; 664; Mandela and Clinton, William J. Clinton Presidential Library, 669. **NASA:** Kelly, 816. **National Park Service:** Tubman, 813. **Newscom:** Brussels bombing, Ketevan Kardava/Georgian/ZUMA Press, 194; Zika, Antonio Lacerda/EPA, 195; Erdogan, Depo Photos/ZUMA Press, 196; Hiroshima, Kyodo, 197; Congress, John Lewis/ZUMA Press, 198; Trail of Tears, Picture History, 468; hobbit skull, Peter Brown/KRT, 647; Martin Luther, akg-images, 655; Popes, Eric Vandeville/ABACA, 674; Serena Williams, Kyodo, 809; Ali, Staff/Mirrorpix, 814; Prince, Columbia Records/ZUMA Press, 815; Garry Shandling, face to face/ZUMA Press, 815. **Richard Nixon Library and Museum:** Nixon resignation, 493. **The Peabody Awards:** Morley Safer, 815. **Ronald Reagan Presidential Library and Museum:** Reagan inauguration, 495. **Shutterstock:** Trump, 13; 650; 651; 653; 656; 673; Pokémon Go, 812; Natalie Cole, 814; Doris Roberts, 815; Sea World, 816. **SpaceX:** Falcon 9 rocket, 816. **Supreme Court of the U.S.:** Scalia, 815. **SXS, the Simulating eXtreme Spacetimes project (www.black-holes.org):** black holes, 816. **Michael Thaidigsmann:** Peres, 814. **U.S. Dept. of Agriculture:** Louisiana flooding, 200. **U.S. Air Force:** 496. **U.S. Army:** Afghanistan surge, Spc. Mary L. Gonzalez, CJTF-101 Public Affairs, 671. **U.S. Senate:** Kaine, 12. **U.S. Strategic Bombing Survey:** Hiroshima, 665. **Univ. of Virginia:** Jefferson, 466. **White House:** Garland and Obama, Chuck Kennedy, 199; bin Laden operation, Pete Souza, 500; George W. Bush, Eric Draper, 529; Obama, Pete Souza, 530; Nancy Reagan, 815. **White House Historical Society:** Madison, 521.

World Almanac® Books
An imprint of Infobase Learning
132 West 31st Street
New York, NY 10001

Hardcover	International Standard Serial Number	Paperback
ISBN-13: 978-1-60057-206-7	0084-1382	ISBN-13: 978-1-60057-205-0
ISBN-10: 1-60057-206-5		ISBN-10: 1-60057-205-7

The World Almanac® and Book of Facts is distributed to the trade by Simon & Schuster, and in paperback and hardcover to schools and libraries at special discounts by Infobase Learning. For further information, contact (800) 322-8755 or visit www.Infobase.com.

You can find The World Almanac® and Book of Facts online at www.worldalmanac.com.
Email: almanac@infobaselearning.com

The World Almanac® and Book of Facts 2017
Book printed and bound by LSC Communications, Kendallville, IN
Date printed: November 2016
Printed in the United States of America
LSC 10 9 8 7 6 5 4 3 2 1

CONTENTS

2016: SPECIAL FEATURES AND YEAR IN REVIEW

2016: YEAR IN PICTURES

THE WORLD ALMANAC
AND BOOK OF FACTS 2017

Top 10 News Topics of 2016

1. Trump Elected 45th U.S. President. In an upset victory Nov. 8 that defied pre-election polls, Republican presidential candidate Donald J. Trump defeated Democrat Hillary Clinton, the first female presidential nominee of a major party. A real-estate executive who had never held elected office, Trump campaigned on issues including cracking down on undocumented immigration and revising or ending international trade agreements. Winning non-urban and non-college-educated white voters by large margins, Trump built a clear majority in the Electoral College, capturing key swing states such as Florida, Ohio, and Pennsylvania, all states that had twice voted for outgoing Democratic Pres. Barack Obama. Republicans retained majorities in the House of Representatives and Senate, putting the presidency and both houses of Congress in Republican control for the first time since 2006.

2. Lone-Wolf Terrorism Raises Security Concerns. So-called lone-wolf terrorist attacks, by people apparently inspired by but not directly affiliated with Islamist extremist groups, killed scores of victims and concerned security officials because of the difficulty of identifying and tracking potential attackers. In Nice, France, on July 14, a Tunisian-born man seemingly inspired by ISIS drove a truck through a Bastille Day crowd, killing 86; he was fatally shot by police. In the deadliest U.S. attack, at an Orlando, FL, gay nightclub June 12, a U.S.-born man of Afghan descent who had declared allegiance to ISIS fatally shot 49 people; he was killed by police. On Sept. 17, bombs apparently planted by an Afghanistan-born man with U.S. citizenship exploded in New Jersey and New York City; 31 people were injured in New York. The suspect, arrested after a shootout Sept. 19, was apparently inspired both by ISIS and by al-Qaeda.

3. Middle East Civil Wars Continue as Offensives Make Gains Against ISIS. In the Middle East and SW Asia, civil wars and the fight against ISIS claimed thousands of lives in 2016. Syria's civil war entered its sixth year, as Pres. Bashar al-Assad's forces battled a range of Arab and Kurdish rebel groups. Government and Russian airstrikes on rebel-held areas of Aleppo caused widespread destruction and civilian deaths. By Oct., some 11 million Syrians were refugees or internally displaced. ISIS lost some territory it had controlled in Syria, largely to Kurdish and other rebels supported by U.S.-led airstrikes. By mid-2016, ISIS had lost almost half the territory it had seized in Iraq, as a result of government and militia offensives supported by a U.S.-led air campaign and several thousand U.S. troops training and advising Iraqi forces. A resurgent Taliban fought government forces for control of many areas of Afghanistan in 2016, and an ISIS-affiliated group controlled parts of eastern Afghanistan. As of midyear, some 9,800 U.S. troops and 6,000 from allied nations supported Afghan government forces. Saudi-led airstrikes caused high civilian casualties in Yemen's civil war, principally between Shiite Houthi rebels and Saudi-backed government forces.

4. Immigration Concerns Contribute to UK "Brexit" Vote. In a June 23 referendum, United Kingdom voters approved by a narrow margin their country's leaving the 28-nation European Union. If the British exit ("Brexit") is completed, the UK would be the first country to withdraw from the EU. Conservative Prime Min. David Cameron, who had opposed Brexit, stepped down and was replaced, July 13, by Theresa May. Opinion polls found that concern about immigration—from other EU countries and elsewhere—was an important consideration for many UK voters who favored Brexit. The referendum came at a time when Europe was experiencing a large-scale movement of refugees and other migrants from the Middle East, SW Asia, and Africa and a concurrent rise in anti-immigration sentiment. By early Nov., more than 335,000 migrants had arrived in 2016, following more than 1 mil in 2015.

5. Justice Scalia Dies; 8-Member Court Hands Down Key Decisions. Associate Justice Antonin Scalia, a member of the Supreme Court for almost 30 years and one of its leading judicial conservatives, died Feb. 13. Pres. Barack Obama, Mar. 16, nominated U.S. Court of Appeals judge Merrick Garland to succeed Scalia, but with Senate Republican leaders refusing to consider a nominee, an eight-member Court heard and ruled on cases. A 4-4 tie vote, in a decision announced June 23, left standing a lower court's ruling blocking an executive order issued by Pres. Obama to provide work permits and safety from deportation for millions of undocumented immigrants. In a 5-3 ruling, June 27, the Court struck down Texas legislation tightening regulation of abortion clinics, finding that it placed an "undue burden" on a woman's right to an abortion.

6. Police Shootings of African Americans and Attacks on Police Take Many Lives. Fatal shootings of African Americans by police officers—incidents often captured on video by police cameras or bystanders—continued to raise questions about excessive force and racial bias, and appear to have led to attacks on police. On July 6, black motorist Philando Castile was fatally shot by Hispanic officer Jeronimo Yanez during a traffic stop near St. Paul, MN. A day earlier, African-American Alton Sterling was fatally shot while being held on the ground by two white police officers in Baton Rouge, LA. On July 17 in Baton Rouge, Gavin Long, an African-American veteran, shot 6 police officers, killing 3, before being fatally shot by police. After a peaceful protest against police brutality in Dallas, TX, July 7, African-American gunman Micah Johnson fatally shot 5 police officers before being killed by police. In Tulsa, OK, Sept. 16, unarmed black motorist Terence Crutcher was fatally shot by white officer Betty Jo Shelby; she was charged with manslaughter Sept. 22. In Charlotte, NC, Sept. 20, Keith L. Scott was fatally shot by officer Brentley Vinson; both men were black.

7. Lead Contaminates Water Supply in Flint, MI. On Jan. 16, Pres. Barack Obama declared a federal state of emergency in Flint, MI, and its surrounding area, in relation to lead contamination in the municipal water supply, triggering federal funds and FEMA assistance to provide residents with safe drinking water. High blood levels of lead, especially in children, can cause learning disabilities and other serious medical problems. Lead contamination of the water supply began after the city, Apr. 25, 2014, started using Flint River water as a cost-saving measure. The river water, not treated with anti-corrosion additives, caused lead to leach out of old pipes and enter the water supplied to the majority-black city's almost 100,000 people. By July 2016, nine current or former state or city employees had been indicted on criminal charges of misconduct, conspiracy, and neglect of duty. The EPA stated, June 23, 2016, that Flint tap water—if properly filtered—was safe to drink, but many residents continued to rely on bottled water.

8. Zika Virus Outbreak Spreads Through the Americas. By Oct. 2016, an outbreak of mosquito-borne Zika virus infections that began in 2015 had spread to 64 countries and territories, including 47 in the Americas and Caribbean—the most heavily affected region. The World Health Organization reported more than 650,000 confirmed or suspected Western Hemisphere cases. Brazil accounted for almost 300,000. In the U.S. by late Oct., some 180 cases were traced to local mosquitoes in southern Florida. Zika most often produces mild or no symptoms, but if a pregnant woman is infected, her child may suffer from microcephaly or other severe birth defects. By late Oct., WHO reported more than 2,200 confirmed cases of Zika-related congenital birth defects, about 93% of them in Brazil.

9. UN Climate Accord Is Ratified as Evidence Grows That Climate Change Is Affecting Weather. An agreement to combat climate change, concluded by more than 190 nations at a Dec. 2015 UN conference in Paris, came into force on Nov. 4, 2016, following ratification by at least 55 nations accounting for at least 55% of global greenhouse-gas emissions. The goal of the agreement is to hold down the rise in average global temperatures by the end of the century to less than 2°C (3.6°F). Ratification came as many scientists were seeing growing signs of a climate-change effect on weather events. In Aug., torrential rains caused widespread flooding in Louisiana, leaving at least 13 dead. A study reported Sept. 7 concluded that, as a result of climate change, such extreme weather in the central Gulf Coast region was likely to occur at least 40% more often than in the period before 1900.

10. Cubs Are Champions; U.S. Athletes Star at the Olympics. With a dramatic 8-7 victory in 10 innings, Nov. 2, the Chicago Cubs defeated the Cleveland Indians, 4 games to 3, in baseball's World Series—the first championship for the Cubs since 1908. Earlier in the year, amid concerns about security and Brazil's Zika virus outbreak, Rio de Janeiro hosted (without major incidents) the 2016 Summer Olympics, Aug. 5-21. The U.S. won the most gold and total medals, 46 and 121, respectively. Russia won 56 medals (19 gold) despite the fact that more than 100 Russian athletes were barred due to state-sponsored doping. U.S. swimmer Michael Phelps won 5 gold medals and 1 silver in Rio to bring his record medal total to 28 (23 gold). U.S. gymnast Simone Biles won 5 medals, including 4 gold.

THE WORLD
AT A GLANCE

World's most populous country . . . . China, 1.37 billion population in 2016 *(p. 730)*

World's most populous urban area. . . . . Tokyo, Japan, 38.1 million population in 2016 *(p. 729)*

World's wealthiest person. . . . . American Bill Gates, $75.0 billion net worth as of Mar. 1, 2016 *(p. 80)*

Most-visited U.S. social networking website. . . . . Facebook, 207.4 million unique visitors in June 2016 *(p. 328)*

Most-used U.S. search engine . . . . Google, 10.5 billion searches (64.4% of all searches) in June 2016 *(p. 328)*

U.S. airline that carried the most passengers. . . . . American Airlines, 146.8 million passengers in 2015 *(p. 121)*

World's busiest airport by passenger traffic . . . .Hartsfield-Jackson Atlanta Intl. Airport, 101.5 million passengers in 2015 *(p. 121)*

Top U.S. state by traveler spending . . . . California, $124.2 billion in 2014 *(p. 119)*

World's most-visited amusement park . . . . . . Magic Kingdom at Walt Disney World, Florida, 20.5 million visitors in 2015 *(p. 122)*

Nations with the most days off of work per year. . . . . Austria and Malta, 38 days off *(p. 734)*

Most popular recording artist by digital sales . . . . Rihanna, 108.0 million units sold as of Aug. 23, 2016 *(p. 285)*

All-time highest grossing American movie. . . . . *Star Wars: Episode VII—The Force Awakens* (2015), $936.7 million as of Aug. 31, 2016 *(p. 276)*

Most pirated movie. . . . . *Deadpool*, 42.4 million torrent downloads in Jan.-June 2016 *(p. 276)*

Surprising Facts

The number of refugees in the world increased from 8.7 million in 2005 to 16.1 million in 2015. The number of internally displaced persons (IDPs) increased even more steeply, from 6.6 million in 2005 to 37.5 million in 2015. *(p. 735)*

The U.S. hosted more international migrants than any other country in 2015, with 46.6 million, up from 34.8 million in 2000. Germany hosted 12.0 million international migrants in 2015, up from 9.0 million in 2000. *(p. 734)*

In 1950, the U.S. produced 75.7% of the world's motor vehicles manufactured that year; by 2015, that number had dropped to 13.3% (up from a low of 9.5% in 2009). *(p. 112)*

The average amount of student loan debt held by Americans graduating in 2014 with a bachelor's degree was $28,950, up from $18,550 for Americans graduating 10 years earlier. *(p. 416)*

21.7% of female high school students reported being bullied electronically in 2015; the rate for high school boys was 9.7%. *(p. 411)*

Americans paid an average of 25.6% of their gross wage earnings in income tax and Social Security contributions in 2015; Belgians, who had some of the highest personal-income tax rates, paid 42.0%. *(p. 733)*

Among the 50 most populous nations, the U.S. has long led in spending on health expenses, at $9,403 per capita in 2014. Germany came closest to matching U.S. spending, at $5,411 per capita. *(p. 174)*

U.S. workers with professional degrees had a lower unemployment rate (1.5%) and higher median weekly earnings ($1,730) than workers with any other level of education in 2015 (including those with doctoral degrees). *(p. 138)*

Employed U.S. women's earnings were equal to 72.0% of men's earnings in 2015. Women's earnings came closest to matching men's in the construction industry, where their earnings were 95.1% of men's, but women made up only 9.2% of construction industry employees. *(p. 138)*

Milestone Birthdays, 2017

100
Zsa Zsa Gabor, Feb. 6
I.M. Pei, Apr. 26

90
Leontyne Price, Feb. 10
Sidney Poitier, Feb. 20
Harry Belafonte, Mar. 1
Neil Simon, July 4
Roger Moore, Oct. 14
Vin Scully, Nov. 29

80
Philip Glass, Jan. 31
Warren Beatty, Mar. 30
Colin Powell, Apr. 5
George Takei, Apr. 20
Jack Nicholson, Apr. 22
Madeleine Albright, May 15
Morgan Freeman, June 1
Bill Cosby, July 12
Dustin Hoffman, Aug. 8
Jane Fonda, Dec. 21

70
Nolan Ryan, Jan. 31
Mike Krzyzewski, Feb. 13
Mitt Romney, Mar. 12
Glenn Close, Mar. 19
Elton John, Mar. 25
David Letterman, Apr. 12
Kareem Abdul-Jabbar, Apr. 16
Larry David, July 2
O.J. Simpson, July 9
Arnold Schwarzenegger, July 30
Stephen King, Sept. 21
Hillary Clinton, Oct. 26
Ted Danson, Dec. 29

60
Katie Couric, Jan. 7
Vanna White, Feb. 18
John Turturro, Feb. 28
Spike Lee, Mar. 20
Daniel Day-Lewis, Apr. 29

60
Frances McDormand, June 23
Melanie Griffith, Aug. 9
Denis Leary, Aug. 18
Ray Romano, Dec. 21
Matt Lauer, Dec. 30

50
Benicio del Toro, Feb. 19
Tim McGraw, May 1
Anderson Cooper, June 3
Nicole Kidman, June 20
Will Ferrell, July 16
Vin Diesel, July 18
Matt LeBlanc, July 25
Deion Sanders, Aug. 9
Ty Burrell, Aug. 22
Louis C.K., Sept. 12
Faith Hill, Sept. 21
Keith Urban, Oct. 26
Jimmy Kimmel, Nov. 13
Jamie Foxx, Dec. 13

40
Kerry Washington, Jan. 31
Chris Martin, Mar. 2
Michael Fassbender, Apr. 2
John Oliver, Apr. 23
Kanye West, June 8
Ludacris, Sept. 11
Tom Hardy, Sept. 15
John Mayer, Oct. 16
Maggie Gyllenhaal, Nov. 16

30
Ronda Rousey, Feb. 1
Michael B. Jordan, Feb. 9
Ellen Page, Feb. 21
Novak Djokovic, May 22
Kendrick Lamar, June 17
Zac Efron, Oct. 18
Frank Ocean, Oct. 28

21
Lorde, Nov. 7

STATISTICAL SPOTLIGHT

Approval Ratings of Pres. Barack Obama, 2009-16

Source: Gallup poll on the question, "Do you approve or disapprove of the way Barack Obama is handling his job as president?"

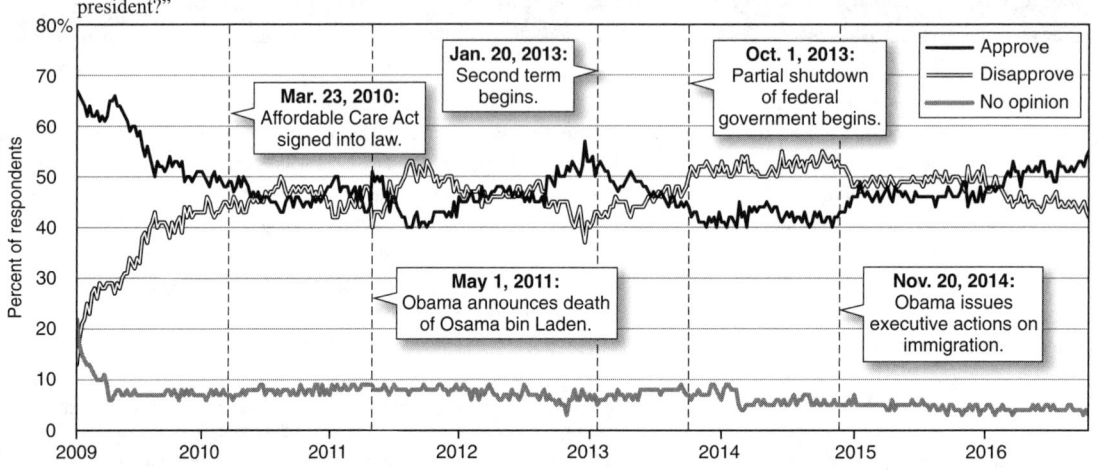

Unemployment, Underemployment, and Gross Domestic Product, 1995-2016

Source: Current Population Survey, Bureau of Labor Statistics, U.S. Dept. of Labor; Bureau of Economic Analysis, U.S. Dept. of Commerce, via Federal Reserve Bank of St. Louis

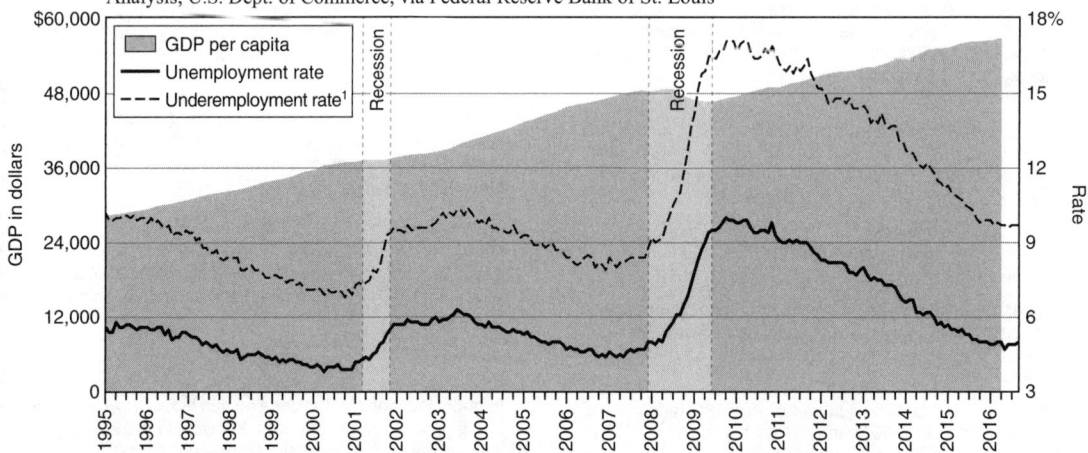

(1) Unemployment rate combined with a) those who currently are neither working nor looking for work but indicate that they want and are available for a job and have looked for work sometime in the past 12 months and b) those employed part time who want and are available for full-time work but have had to settle for a part-time schedule.

Net Productivity and Workers' Hourly Compensation, 1948-2015

Source: Economic Policy Institute (EPI), based on U.S. Bureau of Economic Analysis and U.S. Bureau of Labor Statistics data

This graph shows the cumulative percent change since 1948 in net productivity and hourly compensation in the U.S. Net productivity is the growth of goods and services produced minus depreciation per hour worked. Hourly compensation is average wages and benefits for private-sector production and nonsupervisory workers, who make up around 80% of private payroll employment. The two data series began to diverge in the 1970s, with productivity increasing more rapidly than compensation.

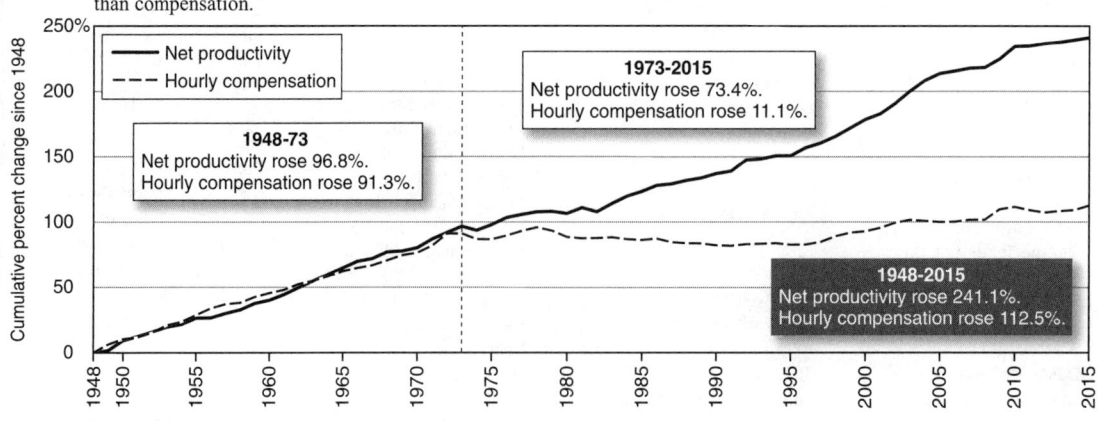

Refugees and Migrants Arriving in Europe by Country of Origin, 2016

Source: United Nations High Commissioner for Refugees (UNHCR)

90,000
80,000
70,000
60,000
50,000
40,000
30,000
20,000
10,000
0
Number
78,572 (27.8%)
40,791 (14.4%)
25,092 (8.9%)
22,347 (7.9%)
15,057 (5.3%)
8,811 (3.1%)
8,544 (3.0%)
8,116 (2.9%)
8,094 (2.9%)
67,192 (23.8%)
Syria
Afghanistan
Iraq
Nigeria
Eritrea
Pakistan
Côte d'Ivoire
Guinea
Gambia
All other nationalities

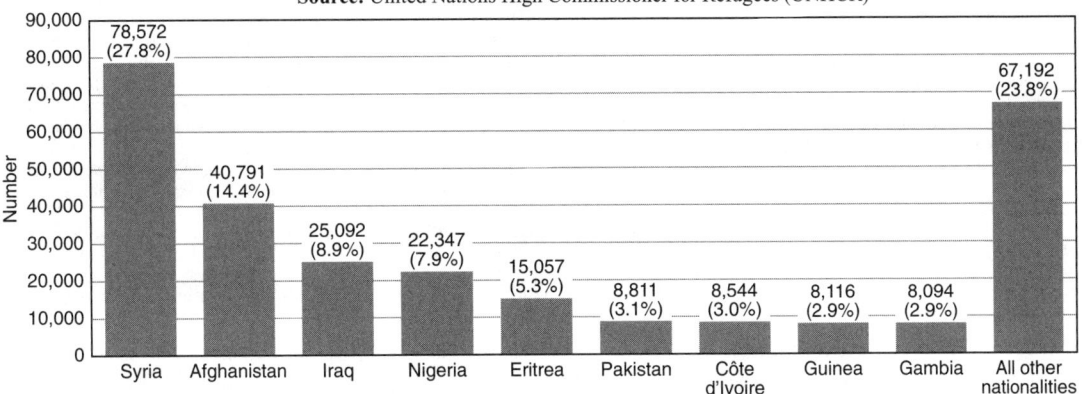

Note: Number of persons arriving in Greece, Italy, and Spain by the Mediterranean Sea, Jan.-Aug. 2016; should not be considered final. Number originating in country as percentage of total sea arrivals shown in parentheses.

Countries With Active Zika Virus Transmission, 2016

Source: Centers for Disease Control and Prevention, U.S. Dept. of Health and Human Services; European Centre for Disease Prevention and Control; Pan American Health Organization; World Health Organization (WHO)

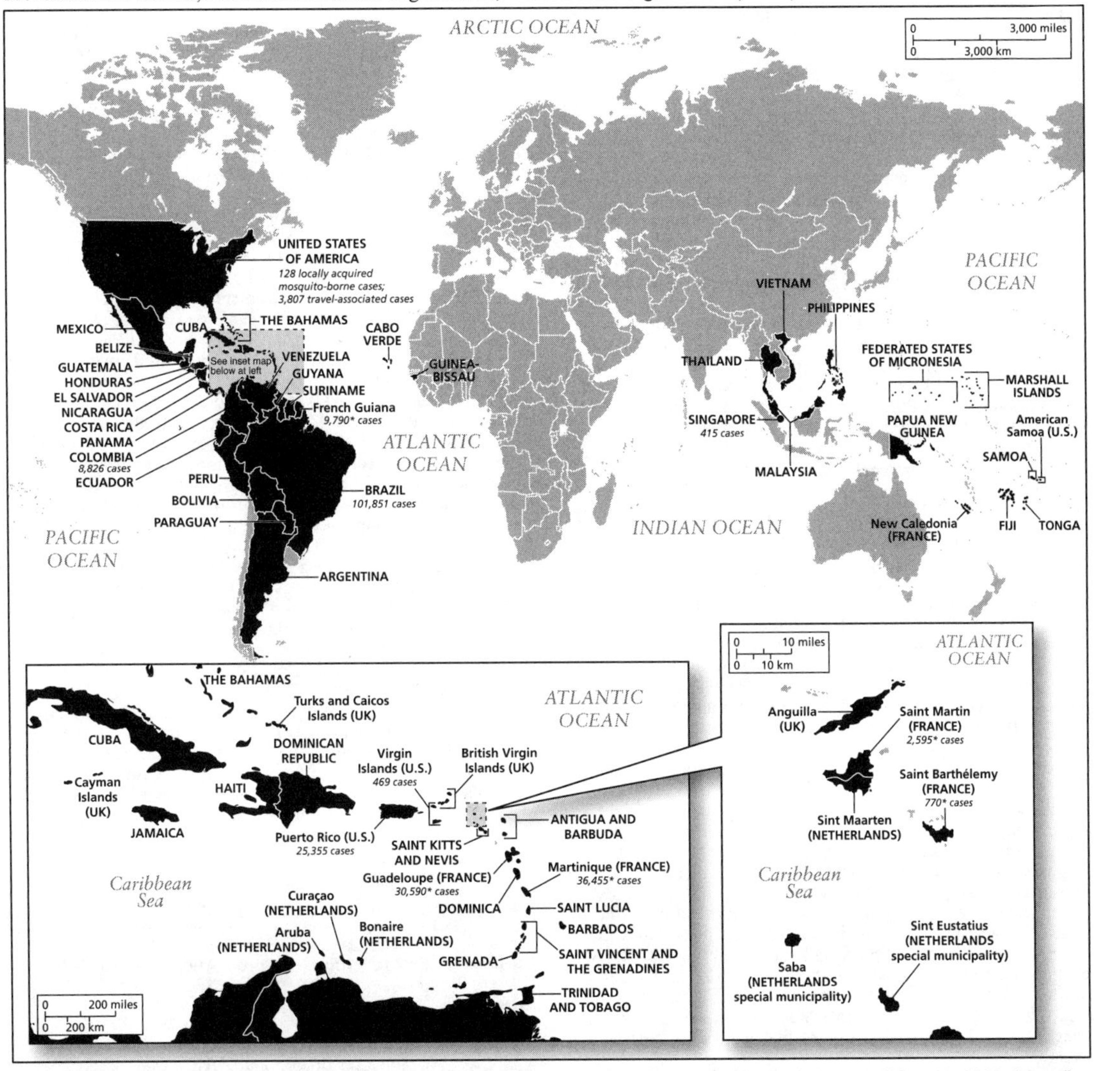

ARCTIC OCEAN
0 3,000 miles
0 3,000 km
UNITED STATES OF AMERICA
128 locally acquired mosquito-borne cases; 3,807 travel-associated cases
MEXICO
BELIZE
GUATEMALA
HONDURAS
EL SALVADOR
NICARAGUA
COSTA RICA
PANAMA
COLOMBIA
8,826 cases
ECUADOR
CUBA
THE BAHAMAS
See inset map below at left
VENEZUELA
GUYANA
SURINAME
French Guiana
9,790* cases
CABO VERDE
GUINEA-BISSAU
PERU
BOLIVIA
PARAGUAY
BRAZIL
101,851 cases
ARGENTINA
PACIFIC OCEAN
ATLANTIC OCEAN
INDIAN OCEAN
VIETNAM
PHILIPPINES
THAILAND
SINGAPORE
415 cases
MALAYSIA
PACIFIC OCEAN
FEDERATED STATES OF MICRONESIA
MARSHALL ISLANDS
PAPUA NEW GUINEA
American Samoa (U.S.)
SAMOA
New Caledonia (FRANCE)
FIJI
TONGA
THE BAHAMAS
Turks and Caicos Islands (UK)
ATLANTIC OCEAN
CUBA
DOMINICAN REPUBLIC
Cayman Islands (UK)
HAITI
JAMAICA
Virgin Islands (U.S.)
469 cases
British Virgin Islands (UK)
Puerto Rico (U.S.)
25,355 cases
SAINT KITTS AND NEVIS
ANTIGUA AND BARBUDA
Guadeloupe (FRANCE)
30,590* cases
Martinique (FRANCE)
36,455* cases
Caribbean Sea
Curaçao (NETHERLANDS)
DOMINICA
SAINT LUCIA
Aruba (NETHERLANDS)
Bonaire (NETHERLANDS)
BARBADOS
GRENADA
SAINT VINCENT AND THE GRENADINES
TRINIDAD AND TOBAGO
0 200 miles
0 200 km
0 10 miles
0 10 km
ATLANTIC OCEAN
Anguilla (UK)
Saint Martin (FRANCE)
2,595* cases
Saint Barthélemy (FRANCE)
770* cases
Sint Maarten (NETHERLANDS)
Caribbean Sea
Saba (NETHERLANDS special municipality)
Sint Eustatius (NETHERLANDS special municipality)

Note: Countries shaded black had recent active transmission (sporadic or widespread) of the Zika virus as of Oct. 13, 2016. According to WHO, 67 countries and territories have reported evidence of mosquito-borne Zika virus transmission since 2015. Transmission may only occur in part of a country. Number of cases is included for selected countries. * = Cases suspected but not yet confirmed.

ELECTION, 2016

Trump Wins the Presidency; GOP Retains Control of Congress

On Nov. 8, 2016, in an upset that defied nearly all predictions by polls and pundits, real estate billionaire Donald Trump (R) defeated former first lady, U.S. senator (D, NY), and Sec. of State Hillary Clinton (D) to win the White House. Trump was set to become the first-ever U.S. president who had no experience serving either in elected office or the military. Riding an unexpectedly strong wave of anti-establishment populism, he captured close battleground states won by Pres. Barack Obama in 2012, including Florida, Ohio, Pennsylvania, and Iowa; these were enough to offset more expected wins by Clinton in the battleground states of Nevada, Colorado, and Virginia. Trump made inroads in the Midwest Rust Belt—where strong union support had typically gone to Democratic candidates in presidential elections—and swept through the South and much of the West, while Clinton carried the traditionally blue states of the Northeast and West Coast.

Republicans also retained control of both houses of Congress, giving them important leverage. At the same time, the election left the country sharply divided between supporters of the two major candidates and left some uncertainty as to how the country would come together and forge a path ahead.

The GOP ticket, with Indiana Gov. Mike Pence as the vice-presidential candidate, was slightly behind in the popular vote, with 59.9 mil (47.4%) as of Nov. 11, versus 60.3 mil (47.7%) for the Democratic ticket, with Virginia Sen. Tim Kaine as Clinton's running mate. Gary Johnson, the Libertarian Party nominee, won about 4 mil votes, while Jill Stein, the Green Party candidate, received about 1 mil. Independent conservative Evan McMullin, who was on the ballot in only 11 states, also gained some support, especially in his home state of Utah.

The Trump Victory

Exit polls showed that white voters preferred Trump over Clinton, 58%-37%, especially those without a college degree (67%-28%). Trump won the male vote by a 53%-41% margin, while women voted for Clinton, 54%-42%, a similar margin to Barack Obama's in 2012. Clinton earned 88% of the African-American vote, down from 93% for Obama in 2012, and 65% of the Hispanic vote, down from Obama's 71% share. Voters aged 18-29 favored Clinton, 55%-37%, while those 65 years old or older voted for Trump, 53%-45%.

Party breakdown was a key factor in support for each candidate. Clinton won among Democrats, 89%-9%, while Trump won among Republicans, 90%-7%. Independents went for Trump by a margin of 48%-42%. He won the white evangelical Christian vote, 81%-16%.

In the early hours Nov. 9, Trump gave a victory speech in which he called on Americans to "bind the wounds of division" and "come together as one united people." Clinton gave a concession speech later that morning in which she called on supporters to give Trump "an open mind and a chance to lead."

Super PACs—which, based on the 2010 *Citizens United* Supreme Court decision can raise and spend unlimited money from corporations, unions, and individuals—took in more than $1.6 bil for all 2016 campaigns, a record. While Democrats had decried the court decision, they made use of a wide coordinated network of super PACs to outspend Republicans on ads. The Democrats also claimed elaborate grassroots outreach. But the Republican National Committee had worked since 2012 to build up its own ground game, of significance given Trump's own minimal campaign structure. In the end Clinton suffered from decreased turnout in crucial minority areas.

Trump vs. Clinton

Exit polls found that 23% of American voters were "angry" over how the U.S. government was working, and another 46% "dissatisfied." Trump's outsider campaign embodied the promise that he would shake up politics as usual and "make America great again," restoring job growth he said was hindered by bad trade deals, over-regulation, Obamacare, and other factors. Also pledging a restoration of "law and order," he singled out the issue of violence against police and called for building a wall along the U.S.-Mexico border to stem illegal immigration, which he linked to increased crime. He also said he would suspend admission of Muslim refugees, later amended to those from "terror-prone regions," claiming that better vetting was needed to protect against terrorism.

At the same time, Pres. Barack Obama's approval ratings were positive for most of 2016, and they were over 85% among Democrats. Clinton defined herself as building on Obama's legacy, rather than breaking with it, and called upon him and other Democratic surrogates to help engage her base. Portraying Trump's vision of change as negative and divisive, she presented herself as a champion for "everyday Americans." She stressed issues such as equal pay and abortion rights, and appealed to minorities, acknowledging police violence as an issue and advocating a path to citizenship for undocumented immigrants. She portrayed Trump as temperamentally unfit to be president and decried his attitude toward women—especially after the early Oct. release of a 2005 video in which Trump, using crude language, boasted of sexual advances that were characterized as assault.

However, Clinton had personal vulnerabilities of her own, including persistent questions surrounding her use of a private server for email, the deletion of some emails later found to be government-related, and her handling of classified emails as secretary of state, which FBI Dir. James Comey in July called "extremely careless" but not indictable. While both Clinton and Trump were widely considered untrustworthy and had high unfavorability ratings in late poll averages (54% for Clinton, 59% for Trump), Clinton had an advantage over Trump in perceived qualifications (55%-37% in a late ABC News/*Washington Post* poll) and personality and temperament (57%-34%).

Fall Campaign

For a year prior to the fall campaign, national polls showed Trump behind Clinton. Republicans hoped he would "pivot" to focus more on his policy agenda. At the first of three presidential debates, Sept. 26, seen by a record 84 mil TV viewers, he was on the defensive over topics such as his promotion of the "birther" movement and his refusal to release his tax returns. Soon afterward, leaked pages from his 1995 personal income tax returns showed he had reported a nearly $1 bil loss, which he could have used to avoid paying personal income taxes for 18 years.

On Oct. 7, the *Washington Post* made public the video with his lewd boasts to *Access Hollywood* host Billy Bush. Trump apologized but called the issue a distraction and contrasted himself with former Pres. Bill Clinton, whom Trump said had actually abused women while Hillary Clinton shamed the victims. The apology seemed insufficient to many, and some GOP candidates for office, including Sen. John McCain (AZ), said they would now not vote for him. House Speaker Paul Ryan (R, WI) said he would not defend Trump and would concentrate on trying to elect Republicans to Congress. In addition, more than a dozen women accused Trump of improper sexual advances. Polls found that most Americans believed the accusations, which he denounced as lies. Exit polls on Nov. 8 indicated that 7 out of 10 voters were bothered by his attitude toward women.

On the same day the video became public, WikiLeaks began releasing texts of emails hacked from the account of Clinton campaign chair John Podesta. These provided fuel for allegations of possible "pay for play" influence obtained by corporations and foreign countries that made contributions to the Clinton Foundation. Also an issue were differences, at least in tone, between what Hillary Clinton said in highly paid speeches to Wall Street interests and what she said in public. Her campaign, citing intelligence assessments, blamed the hacks on the Russian government and generally did not challenge the authenticity of specific emails.

The remaining presidential debates, on Oct. 9 and Oct. 19, were angry confrontations between the candidates—who did not even shake hands at the start. Trump denounced Clinton as a crooked politician who belonged in jail, and Clinton impugned Trump's character for his treatment of women and disparagement of Muslims, Hispanic immigrants, and others. Among less personally charged issues, they differed over the U.S. Supreme

Balance of Power, 2016
(as of Nov. 11, 2016)

Party	Senate Before	Senate After	House Before	House After	Governors Before	Governors After
Dem.	44	46	186	193	18	15
Rep.	54	51	246	239	31	33
Ind.	2[1]	2[1]	—	—	1	1

Note: One Senate seat (LA), four House seats (two each in CA, LA), and one governorship (NC) were undecided. (1) Both independent senators were expected to continue caucusing with the Democrats.

Court, with Trump promising pro-life, pro-Second Amendment justices of a "conservative bent." They also sparred over the Iran nuclear deal and the Syrian civil war. Trump's stated admiration for Russian Pres. Vladimir Putin's leadership style led Clinton to label him as Putin's "puppet."

Polls showed that a majority of viewers believed that Clinton won the debates, and while post-debate fact checkers found some of her assertions untruthful, they found far more of Trump's remarks to be untrue, including, for example, his claim that he (unlike Clinton) had opposed the Iraq war from the beginning.

More helpful to Trump, the FBI investigation into Clinton's use of email was temporarily reopened—at least in the eyes of the general public—when FBI Dir. Comey, Oct. 28, controversially disclosed that the agency had turned up more emails from an unrelated investigation. After an expedited examination, Comey announced, Nov. 6, that there was still no evidence to justify an indictment. Exit polls found that 6 in 10 voters were bothered by Clinton's use of email.

Paths to Nomination

Both had high name recognition going into 2016, but Hillary Clinton and Donald Trump trod two very different paths to nomination by their respective parties.

After losing the Democratic presidential nomination to Obama in 2008, the former first lady and senator spent four years serving as his secretary of state. She was the preferred choice of the party establishment well before she announced her expected candidacy, in an Apr. 12, 2015, video. She raised substantial funds, and two potential rivals for the nomination, Sen. Elizabeth Warren (D, MA) and Vice Pres. Joe Biden, declined to run. Only four candidates besides Clinton made the cut in Oct. 2015 for the first of 10 Democratic debates. Two of them never gained enough traction to be invited to another debate. Former Maryland Gov. Martin O'Malley appeared in a few but ended his campaign after the Iowa caucuses in Feb. That left Sen. Bernie Sanders (I, VT).

Sanders attracted enthusiasm from progressives and young voters generally, as he tapped into dissatisfaction with politics as usual. Critical of international trade deals and economic inequality, he attacked Clinton for big donations from and paid speeches to Wall Street. He raised funds mostly from small donations and, unlike Clinton and others, did not have a super PAC that he authorized and raised money for. However, separate super PACs spent money on ads in his support.

When Sanders announced, the RealClearPolitics average of national polls put Clinton ahead of him, 62% to 6%. But he nearly won the Feb. 1, 2016, Iowa Democratic caucuses and went on to defeat Clinton in the Feb. 9 New Hampshire primary, 60%-38%. His popularity and the anti-establishment mood behind it were a jolt to the Clinton campaign.

Clinton won the South Carolina primary, Feb. 27, and on Mar. 1, Super Tuesday, won in Massachusetts and by landslides in six Southern states, aided by her popularity among African Americans. Sanders won four states on Super Tuesday by wide margins and upset Clinton in the Michigan open primary Mar. 8. After a number of Clinton wins, he had a string of victories. But she won the New York primary, Apr. 19, by 14 points, and Sanders's momentum declined. Despite an encouraging victory, May 3, in the Indiana primary, he never fully recovered, as Clinton accumulated elected delegates; she also led in superdelegates (appointed delegates who could vote for the candidate of their choice). Sanders pinned his last hopes on the June 7 California primary, where he campaigned heavily but lost; Clinton by then had the nomination clinched.

On the Republican side, the outsider staged a takeover. Though he had never held public office, Trump was a widely known media personality before he announced for president on June 16, 2015. After the GOP loss in the 2012 presidential election, the Republican National Committee had compiled an "autopsy" report, setting forth a strategy for winning back the White House; it stressed outreach to women and minorities. But many voters were more angry about economic stagnation in their communities than concerned about party outreach. Encouraged by far-right media, they chafed at the party elite as ineffectual and decried international trade deals (which the party traditionally supported) and any compromise on illegal immigration. Trump aligned himself with these disaffected Republicans and others who shared this perspective. He hit the campaign trail drawing on his star power and populist message to energize huge crowds.

A total of 17 candidates qualified for the first of 12 GOP debates in Aug. 2015. By then Trump was well ahead of all his rivals in polls. But it was widely believed he would self-destruct, leaving one of them to break out, and there were fears he might then run as an independent. In Sept. 2015, Republican National Committee chair Reince Priebus got Trump, along with his rivals, to sign a pledge to support the eventual nominee.

Several GOP candidates dropped out before 2016, and others gave up after the Iowa caucuses or New Hampshire primary, leaving just six contenders. While Trump finished behind Texas Sen. Ted Cruz in Iowa, he won in New Hampshire and South Carolina. He went on to win the bulk of the remaining contests as his rivals dropped off.

Electoral Votes for President, 2016

Electoral votes based on the 2010 Census were in force beginning with the 2012 elections.

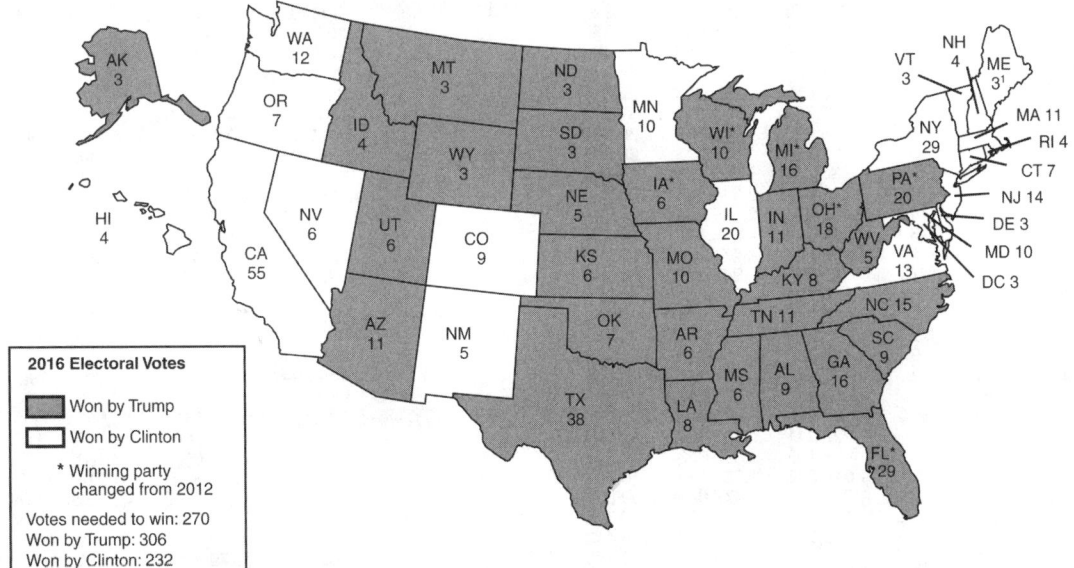

2016 Electoral Votes

■ Won by Trump
□ Won by Clinton

* Winning party changed from 2012

Votes needed to win: 270
Won by Trump: 306
Won by Clinton: 232

Note: Two states (MI, NH) had not yet been called for either candidate. Map reflects vote as of Nov. 11, 2016. (1) Trump was awarded one of Maine's four electoral votes; the other three went to Clinton.

Among them, former Florida Gov. Jeb Bush was the clearest establishment candidate. He came from a political dynasty and had backing from big donors. Bush's rhetoric was positive in tone, but he tried to discredit Trump on immigration and other issues. Trump tied the Bush name to the Sept. 11, 2001, terrorist attacks and to the Iraq war and successfully labeled Bush as "low energy." Bush bowed out in Feb. after placing a distant fourth in South Carolina.

Retired neurosurgeon Ben Carson, like Trump a political novice, failed to gain ground in debates and dropped out after Super Tuesday. Sen. Marco Rubio (FL) brought a Hispanic background and relative youth to the race, along with a critique of Obama foreign policy. He faltered after repeating scripted remarks in a Feb. 6 debate then engaged in a war of personal insults with Trump; he left the race after finishing a distant second in his home state's Mar. 15 primary, having won just three states.

Cruz—a freshman Tea Party senator whose 2013 push to defund Obamacare had led to an unpopular government shutdown and angered congressional leadership in his own party—started out seeking common ground with Trump, whose delegates he hoped to pick up, but relations eventually soured, and they sharply attacked each other. Cruz won the Iowa caucuses, but placed third in New Hampshire, behind Trump and

Ohio Gov. John Kasich. He failed to make headway against Trump in the South, and his social conservatism was unpopular in the Northeast. In all he won 11 contests.

Kasich promoted his government experience but won only one primary—in his home state—and dropped out following the May 3 Indiana primary. In Mar. he had renounced his pledge to support Trump, as had Cruz, and he did not attend the party convention even though it was held in his home state. (Neither the two living Republican ex-presidents nor the last two GOP presidential nominees attended.) Cruz gave a convention speech in which he conspicuously failed to endorse the nominee. But he endorsed Trump in Sept., even though he had previously called Trump a "pathological liar."

As tallied by The Green Papers, Trump in the primaries earned some 14 mil votes, or 45% of all GOP votes. Clinton earned 55% of the Democratic vote, or nearly 17 mil, while Sanders drew 13 mil, or 43%. Turnout was relatively high for primaries—a record high for Republicans. At the Republican National Convention, held July 18-21 in Cleveland, Trump won votes from 1,725 delegates, or 70% of the total; Cruz earned the biggest share of the rest (484, or 20%). At the Democratic National Convention, held July 25-28 in Philadelphia, Clinton received 2,842 delegate votes (60% of the total) while Sanders, who ultimately endorsed Clinton, drew 1,865 votes (39%).

Electoral and Popular Vote, 2012 and 2016

Source: 2016 results, © Associated Press; all rights reserved; preliminary as of Nov. 11, 2016. 2012 results, Federal Election Commission

	2016					2012					
	Electoral vote		Popular vote			Electoral vote		Popular vote			
State	Clinton	Trump	Clinton	Trump	Johnson	Obama	Romney	Obama	Romney	Johnson	State
AL	0	9	718,084	1,306,925	43,869	0	9	795,696	1,255,925	12,328	AL
AK	0	3	93,007	130,415	14,593	0	3	122,640	164,676	7,392	AK
AZ	0	11	933,655	1,017,166	79,874	0	11	1,025,232	1,233,654	32,100	AZ
AR	0	6	378,729	677,904	29,518	0	6	394,409	647,744	16,276	AR
CA	55	0	5,491,633	2,970,914	282,115	55	0	7,854,285	4,839,958	143,221	CA
CO	9	0	1,212,209	1,137,455	129,451	9	0	1,323,102	1,185,243	35,545	CO
CT	7	0	884,432	668,266	48,051	7	0	905,083	634,892	12,580	CT
DE	3	0	235,581	185,103	14,751	3	0	242,584	165,484	3,882	DE
DC	3	0	260,223	11,553	4,501	3	0	267,070	21,381	2,083	DC
FL	0	29	4,485,745	4,605,515	206,007	29	0	4,237,756	4,163,447	44,726	FL
GA	0	16	1,837,300	2,068,623	123,641	0	16	1,773,827	2,078,688	45,324	GA
HI	4	0	266,827	128,815	15,949	4	0	306,658	121,015	3,840	HI
ID	0	4	189,677	407,199	28,256	0	4	212,787	420,911	9,453	ID
IL	20	0	2,977,498	2,118,179	204,491	20	0	3,019,512	2,135,216	56,229	IL
IN	0	11	1,031,953	1,556,220	133,856	0	11	1,152,887	1,420,543	50,111	IN
IA	0	6	650,790	798,923	57,322	6	0	822,544	730,617	12,926	IA
KS	0	6	414,788	656,009	53,648	0	6	440,726	692,634	20,456	KS
KY	0	8	628,834	1,202,942	53,749	0	8	679,370	1,087,190	17,063	KY
LA	0	8	779,535	1,178,004	37,950	0	8	809,141	1,152,262	18,157	LA
ME[1]	3	1	354,873	334,838	37,764	4	0	401,306	292,276	9,352	ME[1]
MD	10	0	1,497,951	873,646	71,107	10	0	1,677,844	971,869	30,195	MD
MA	11	0	1,964,768	1,083,069	136,784	11	0	1,921,290	1,188,314	30,920	MA
MI	0	16	2,267,798	2,279,221	173,023	16	0	2,564,569	2,115,256	7,774	MI
MN	10	0	1,366,676	1,322,891	112,944	10	0	1,546,167	1,320,225	35,098	MN
MS	0	6	462,001	678,457	13,789	0	6	562,949	710,746	6,676	MS
MO	0	10	1,054,889	1,585,753	96,404	0	10	1,223,796	1,482,440	43,151	MO
MT	0	3	174,521	274,120	27,264	0	3	201,839	267,928	14,165	MT
NE[1]	0	5	273,858	485,819	37,615	0	5	302,081	475,064	11,109	NE[1]
NV	6	0	537,753	511,319	37,299	6	0	531,373	463,567	10,968	NV
NH	4	0	348,126	345,598	30,530	4	0	369,561	329,918	8,212	NH
NJ	14	0	2,021,756	1,535,513	68,695	14	0	2,125,101	1,477,568	21,045	NJ
NM	5	0	380,724	315,875	73,669	5	0	415,335	335,788	27,788	NM
NY	29	0	4,143,874	2,640,570	161,836	29	0	4,485,741	2,490,431	47,256	NY
NC	0	15	2,162,074	2,339,603	127,794	0	15	2,178,391	2,270,395	44,515	NC
ND	0	3	93,526	216,133	21,351	0	3	124,827	188,163	5,231	ND
OH	0	18	2,317,001	2,771,984	168,599	18	0	2,827,709	2,661,437	49,493	OH
OK	0	7	419,788	947,934	83,334	0	7	443,547	891,325	—	OK
OR	7	0	934,631	742,506	86,306	7	0	970,488	754,175	24,089	OR
PA	0	20	2,844,705	2,912,941	142,653	20	0	2,990,274	2,680,434	49,991	PA
RI	4	0	237,811	173,504	14,111	4	0	279,677	157,204	4,388	RI
SC	0	9	849,469	1,143,611	48,715	0	9	865,941	1,071,645	16,321	SC
SD	0	3	117,442	227,701	20,845	0	3	145,039	210,610	5,795	SD
TN	0	11	867,110	1,517,402	70,084	0	11	960,709	1,462,330	18,623	TN
TX	0	38	3,867,816	4,681,590	282,524	0	38	3,308,124	4,569,843	88,580	TX
UT	0	6	237,241	397,004	27,735	0	6	251,813	740,600	12,572	UT
VT	3	0	178,179	95,053	10,047	3	0	199,239	92,698	3,487	VT
VA	13	0	1,916,845	1,731,156	116,600	13	0	1,971,820	1,822,522	31,216	VA
WA	12	0	1,285,942	877,031	99,091	12	0	1,755,396	1,290,670	42,202	WA
WV	0	5	187,457	486,198	22,798	0	5	238,269	417,655	6,302	WV
WI	0	10	1,382,210	1,409,467	106,442	10	0	1,620,985	1,410,966	20,439	WI
WY	0	3	55,949	174,248	13,285	0	3	69,286	170,962	5,326	WY
Total	**232**	**306**	**60,275,264**	**59,937,885**	**4,102,629**	**332**	**206**	**65,915,795**	**60,933,504**	**1,275,971**	**Total**

— = Not listed on state's ballot. **Note:** Two states (MI, NH) had not yet been called for either candidate. (1) Maine and Nebraska are the only two states that allow electoral votes to be split between candidates.

Congressional Contests

Prior to the election, Democrats had hopes of winning control of the Senate because Republicans had 24 seats to defend, while they had only 10. The Democrats needed a net gain of 4-5 seats (depending on the party of the vice president, who breaks tie votes). In the end, while they lost no seats of their own, they managed to pick up only two from Republicans.

In one Democratic pickup, Sen. Mark Kirk, elected in blue-state Illinois in the 2010 Republican wave, lost to U.S. Rep. Tammy Duckworth (D), an Asian-American Iraq War veteran. In the other, moderate New Hampshire first-term Sen. Kelly Ayotte (R) lost her seat to Gov. Maggie Hassan (D).

Democrats had hoped to gain an open seat in Indiana, for which former Sen. Evan Bayh (D) was persuaded to run. But Bayh was branded as a Washington insider and lost to Rep. Todd Young (R), a conservative who had won his House seat in the 2010 Republican wave. Also a target was Wisconsin Sen. Ron Johnson (R). Dismissed as a long shot until late in the campaign, he managed to outpoll former Sen. Russ Feingold (D), a progressive whose seat he had won in 2010. And in Pennsylvania, first-term Sen. Pat Toomey (R), considered highly vulnerable, outpolled Democrat Kate McGinty.

Among other Republicans who held on, Sen. Rob Portman (R) waged a strong campaign to defeat Gov. Ted Strickland (D) in Ohio. In North Carolina, Sen. Richard Burr (R), a powerful committee chair, outpolled former state Rep. Deborah Ross (D), onetime head of the state's ACLU chapter. In Missouri, Sen. Roy Blunt (R), another committee chair, survived a challenge from Missouri Sec. of State Jason Kander (D), an Afghanistan War veteran who, in a campaign ad supporting background checks for gun sales, assembled an automatic rifle while blindfolded. Sen. Marco Rubio, who ran for reelection in Florida after having dropped out of the presidential race, defeated Rep. Patrick Murphy (D), who had criticized him for absenteeism and not serving on the state's behalf. Sen. John McCain (AZ), the GOP presidential nominee in 2008, easily held onto his seat.

Republicans had hoped to pick up the open seat in Nevada, where Senate Democratic Leader Harry Reid was retiring, but his chosen candidate, Catherine Cortez Masto, a former state attorney general, defeated Rep. Joe Heck (R), a physician and retired Army general, to become the first Latina U.S. senator.

Democrats fell far short of the 30 new seats needed to win control of the U.S. House, but they did score some gains. For example, veteran Rep. John L. Mica (R, FL) lost to Stephanie Murphy (D), a young former national defense specialist, and former Florida Gov. Charlie Crist, who had switched parties since his days as governor and was running as a Democrat, defeated incumbent Rep. David Jolly (R). On the other hand, Reps. Barbara Comstock (VA) and Carlos Curbelo (FL), Republican moderates for whom House Speaker Paul Ryan had campaigned heavily, won reelection. And veteran Rep. Darrell Issa (R, CA), a major target for Democrats, appeared poised to win reelection after an unexpectedly tough battle against retired Marine Col. Doug Applegate, though the race was still too close to call as of Nov. 11. In Texas, veteran Rep. Lamar Smith, chair of the House science committee and a climate-change skeptic, easily fought off a challenge from Democrat Tom Wakely.

Statehouses and Ballot Issues

There were eight governorships currently held by Democrats and four held by Republicans on 2016 ballots. Of these 12, Republicans won six and Democrats five, with one race, in North Carolina, too close to call as of Nov. 15.

More than 160 measures appeared on statewide ballots in 2016. Voters in three states—California, Massachusetts, and Nevada—agreed on legalizing recreational use of marijuana, while medical marijuana won approval in Arkansas, Florida, Montana, and North Dakota. Colorado voters approved assisted suicide for the terminally ill. California voters rejected a proposal to repeal the death penalty, and Nebraska voters voted to repeal a death penalty ban. Gun control measures were approved in California, Nevada, and Washington but rejected in Maine. And voters in Arizona, Colorado, Maine, and Washington agreed to a higher minimum wage.

Campaign Trail Quotes, 2016

"Please clap."
—Former Florida governor and GOP primary contender Jeb Bush, after an applause line fell flat at a New Hampshire campaign event, Feb. 2.

"Here's what I know. Donald Trump is a phony, a fraud. His promises are as worthless as a degree from Trump University."
—Former Massachusetts governor and 2012 GOP pres. nominee Mitt Romney, in a Mar. 3 speech in Salt Lake City, UT.

"Although we did not find clear evidence that Secretary Clinton or her colleagues intended to violate laws governing the handling of classified information, there is evidence that they were extremely careless in their handling of very sensitive, highly classified information."
—FBI Director James Comey, July 5, on probe over Hillary Clinton's use of a private email server as secretary of state.

"Together, we continue the fight to create a government which represents all of us, and not just the one percent."
—Sen. Bernie Sanders, July 12, at a rally in Portsmouth, NH, where he endorsed Hillary Clinton, while not yet formally dropping out of the race.

"I have visited the laid-off factory workers, and the communities crushed by our horrible and unfair trade deals. … I am your voice."
—Donald Trump accepting nomination at the Republican Natl. Convention, July 21.

"There has never been a man or woman—not me, not Bill, nobody—more qualified than Hillary Clinton to serve as president of the United States of America."
—Pres. Barack Obama at the Democratic Natl. Convention, July 27.

"Go look at the graves of brave patriots who died defending the United States of America. You will see all faiths, genders, and ethnicities. You have sacrificed nothing and no one."
—Attorney and Muslim immigrant Khizr Khan, whose son was killed in Iraq, addressing Trump's comments about Muslim immigrants before the DNC, July 28.

"A man you can bait with a tweet is not a man we can trust with nuclear weapons."
—Hillary Clinton in her July 28 acceptance speech at the DNC.

"What is Aleppo?"
—Libertarian presidential nominee Gary Johnson, in a flub during his appearance on MSNBC's *Morning Joe*, Sept. 8.

"To just be grossly generalistic, you could put half of Trump's supporters into what I call the basket of deplorables. Right? The racist, sexist, homophobic, xenophobic, Islamophobic—you name it."
—Hillary Clinton, Sept. 9, at a New York City fundraiser. She later apologized and qualified the remark.

"And, Hillary, I'd just ask you this. You've been doing this for 30 years. Why are you just thinking about these solutions right now?"
—Donald Trump in first presidential debate, Sept. 26.

"I think Donald just criticized me for preparing for this debate. And, yes, I did. And you know what else I prepared for? I prepared to be president. And I think that's a good thing."
—Hillary Clinton, in Sept. 26 debate.

"I have brilliantly used those laws."
—Donald Trump, referring to tax laws, after the *New York Times*, Oct. 1, reported on leaked pages allegedly from his 1995 personal income tax returns showing he had declared a $916 mil loss, which by law could have enabled him to avoid paying income tax for 18 years.

"Politics is like sausage being made. … [Y]ou need both a public and a private position."
—Hillary Clinton in a paid Apr. 2013 speech to a real estate trade organization obtained by WikiLeaks and made public Oct. 7.

"You know I'm automatically attracted to beautiful [women]—I just start kissing them. It's like a magnet. Just kiss. I don't even wait. And when you're a star they let you do it. … Grab them by the pussy. You can do anything."
—Donald Trump, in a 2005 conversation with an *Access Hollywood* host recorded on an open microphone and first published by the *Washington Post*, Oct. 7.

"I don't think you understood what was—this was locker room talk. I'm not proud of it. I apologize to my family. I apologize to the American people."
—Donald Trump in second presidential debate, Oct. 9.

"The election is absolutely being rigged by the dishonest and distorted media pushing Crooked Hillary—but also at many polling places—SAD."
—Donald Trump, in a tweet, Oct. 16.

Profiles of Presidential Nominees, 2016

Democratic Nominee for President: Hillary Clinton

Born: Hillary Diane Rodham, Oct. 26, 1947, Chicago, IL, to parents Hugh E. Rodham, Dorothy (Howell) Rodham. **Education:** BA (political science), Wellesley Coll., 1969; JD, Yale Law School, 1973. **Career:** attorney, Children's Defense Fund, 1973-74, and U.S. House Judiciary Committee, 1974; assistant prof., Univ. of Arkansas Law School, 1974-77, 1979-80; attorney, then partner, Rose Law Firm, Little Rock, AR, 1977-92; Arkansas first lady, 1979-81, 1983-93; U.S. first lady, 1993-2001; U.S. senator (NY), 2001-09; U.S. sec. of state, 2009-13. **Net worth:** $11.3-$52.7 mil (*Forbes* est., $45 mil). **Religion:** Methodist. **Family:** married Bill Clinton (b. 1946), 1975; children: Chelsea (b. 1980).

Hillary Clinton grew up in the Chicago suburb of Park Ridge, where she was active in her church youth group and social causes. She supported Sen. Barry Goldwater (R, AZ) in the 1964 presidential campaign and headed a Young Republicans chapter early on at Wellesley, but she soon joined the Democratic Party and campaigned for antiwar Sen. Eugene McCarthy (D, MN) in the 1968 presidential primaries. Elected president of student government and chosen as the school's first-ever student commencement speaker, she made national news by criticizing Sen. Edward Brooke (R, MA), who had characterized "coercive protest" as unnecessary in the speech he gave before hers. While at Yale, she served on the board of the *Yale Review of Law and Social Action* and volunteered at the Yale Child Study Center; she also spent a summer in Washington, DC, researching migrant issues for a Senate subcommittee. In 1972 she campaigned for presidential candidate Sen. George McGovern (D, SD).

After serving as a staff attorney in the 1974 Watergate impeachment inquiry, Hillary moved to Arkansas, where she married Bill Clinton—whom she had met at Yale—and joined the prominent Rose Law Firm. She chaired the state's Education Standards Committee and served on boards of several corporations and nonprofits. During her husband's 1992 presidential campaign, she gained national recognition once she appeared with him on *60 Minutes*, as he answered questions about an alleged 12-year sexual relationship with another woman. After an opponent in the primaries charged that state money was being funneled to her law firm, she remarked that she could instead have "stayed home and baked cookies"—a remark some took as depreciating stay-at-home mothers. Critics also questioned some of her financial dealings, including a venture in commodities trading.

As U.S. first lady, Hillary Clinton had an office in the West Wing and, early on, headed a task force on health-care reform. But the task force's deliberations were controversially closed to the public, and Congress rejected its recommendations. Clinton is generally given credit for having pushed the passage of a 1997 measure providing health insurance for low-income children.

A special prosecutor was appointed to investigate Hillary and Bill Clinton in connection with illegal actions by their partners in a failed real estate development project known as Whitewater. Clinton also drew some criticism for her role in the firing of staff members from the White House travel office ("Travelgate"). She stood by her husband when he was impeached and acquitted in relation to his testimony regarding an affair with White House intern Monica Lewinsky. Clinton published *It Takes a Village: And Other Lessons Children Teach Us* (1996), about child rearing, and *Living History* (2003), about her White House years.

In 2000, she ran for a vacant U.S. Senate seat in New York and won by a double-digit margin. She supported the U.S.-led invasion of Afghanistan and, in what she eventually called a mistake, voted to give Pres. George W. Bush authority for a possible invasion of Iraq. In 2006 she was easily reelected.

Clinton amassed significant financial support for the 2008 presidential race, in which she was an early favorite. But despite winning some important primaries, she lost the nomination to then-Sen. Barack Obama (IL). Appointed as his secretary of state, she served for the duration of Obama's first term, visiting a record 112 countries. *Hard Choices*, a memoir of her experiences as secretary, was published in 2014. Clinton's supporters often cite her marshaling of support for international sanctions against Iran. Critics fault her for having advocated U.S. intervention in Libya and for U.S. security failures in Benghazi, Libya, where four Americans were killed in a 2012 terrorist attack.

In 2015 it was revealed that she had used a private email address and server while secretary, raising concerns over security and transparency. In July 2016 FBI Director James Comey reported no basis for an indictment but stated that she had been "extremely careless" in her handling of classified material. Critics also charged that contributions by foreign donors to the family's Clinton Foundation raised conflict-of-interest issues.

In Apr. 2015 Clinton announced that she would again seek the presidency. Her only serious competition for the nomination was Sen. Bernie Sanders (I, VT), a self-described democratic socialist. Sanders's populist campaign caught fire, and he criticized Clinton in particular for her highly paid speeches to Wall Street interests. Clinton argued she had always acted independently and presented herself as a realistic progressive with a record of experience. By June 7 she had amassed a convincing delegate lead, and on July 26 at the Democratic National Convention, she became the first woman ever nominated for president by a major party.

Democratic Nominee for Vice President: Tim Kaine

Born: Timothy Michael Kaine, Feb. 26, 1958, St. Paul, MN, to parents Albert A. Kaine Jr., Mary Kathleen (Burns) Kaine. **Education:** BA (economics), Univ. of Missouri, 1979; JD, Harvard Law School, 1983. **Career:** clerk, U.S. Court of Appeals, 11th Circuit, Macon, GA, 1983-84; practicing attorney in Richmond, VA, beginning 1984; adjunct faculty, Univ. of Richmond Law School, 1987-93; City Council member, Richmond, VA, 1994-2001; mayor of Richmond, 1998-2001; Virginia lieutenant governor, 2002-06; Virginia governor, 2006-10; chairman, Democratic Natl. Committee, 2009-11; U.S. senator (D, VA), 2013-present. **Net worth:** $1.45 mil (est.). **Religion:** Roman Catholic. **Family:** married Anne Holton (b. 1958), 1984; children: Nat (b. 1990), Woody (b. 1992), Annella (b. 1995).

The oldest of three sons, Tim Kaine grew up near Kansas City, MO. He attended a Jesuit boys' prep school, where he joined the debating society and was student government president. Kaine finished college in three years, graduating summa cum laude, and went on to Harvard Law School, where he met his future wife, Anne Holton, daughter of former Virginia Gov. Linwood Holton (R). Kaine took a year off from Harvard to work with Jesuit missionaries in Honduras on a project teaching vocational skills to young men.

After graduation and a legal clerkship, Kaine settled with his wife in Richmond, VA, where she worked as a legal aid attorney (later a judge, then state secretary of education). He began his government career on the Richmond City Council and was later elected mayor. In 2005, he campaigned successfully for governor, presenting himself as a leader guided by family values and faith.

In office during a major recession, Kaine kept unemployment below the national average, but, unable to get Republican support for tax increases, he championed unpopular cuts in programs and services. Kaine gave the Democratic response to Pres. George W. Bush's 2006 State of the Union address and was vetted as a possible Obama running mate in 2008; the next year he was selected to chair the Democratic National Committee.

Elected to the U.S. Senate in 2012, Kaine earned generally high ratings from liberal and labor groups although he was pro-free-trade and supported fast-track trade authority for voting on the Trans-Pacific Partnership. Though expressing personal opposition to abortion and to public funding for abortions, he earned a 100% pro-choice rating from Planned Parenthood. On July 22, 2016, Clinton announced his selection as her running mate. Generally moderate in tone, and self-described as boring, he has had good relations with Senate colleagues on both sides of the aisle.

Republican Nominee for President: Donald Trump

Born: Donald John Trump, June 14, 1946, Queens, NY, to parents Frederick C. Trump, Mary (MacLeod) Trump. **Education:** Fordham Univ., 1964-66; BS (economics and real estate), Wharton School of Finance, Univ. of Penn., 1968. **Career:** worked in family company, from late 1960s; received control of the business in 1971; star and coproducer of NBC's *The Apprentice* and *Celebrity Apprentice*, 2004-15. **Net worth:** $3.0 bil (Bloomberg est.); $3.7 bil (Forbes est.); $10 bil (Trump est.). **Religion:** Presbyterian. **Family:** married Ivana Marie Zelníčková (b. 1949), 1977; children: Donald Jr. (b. 1977), Ivanka (b. 1981), Eric (b. 1984); div. 1992; married Marla Maples (b. 1963), 1993; daughter: Tiffany (b. 1993); div. 1999; married Melania Knauss (b. 1970), 2005; son: Barron (b. 2006).

Donald Trump grew up in Queens, NY, the fourth of five children. His father made a small fortune developing apartment complexes in New York City's outer boroughs. At age 13 Trump was sent to a military boarding school, where he rose to student leadership positions.

After graduating from the Wharton School, Trump worked full-time for his father's real estate development enterprise. In 1973 the Justice Dept. sued Trump and his father for racial discrimination in housing; the suit was settled with a monitoring arrangement and no admission of guilt. Meanwhile, drawing on tax concessions from the city, Trump spearheaded an expansion into Manhattan. His first big success was the transformation of the crumbling Commodore Hotel into the Grand Hyatt (in partnership with owners of the Hyatt chain); it opened in 1980. Trump Tower, a Manhattan high-rise that contained Trump Organization offices and Trump's penthouse residence, opened in 1983.

In Atlantic City during the 1980s, Trump teamed up with Holiday Inn to build the Trump Plaza casino, bought a Hilton hotel that became Trump's Castle, and acquired what became the Trump Taj Mahal. These enterprises, from which he eventually separated, went into bankruptcies, and Trump sustained personal losses. (Leaked tax returns in fall 2016 showed he declared a $916-mil loss in 1995, potentially enabling him to avoid paying income taxes for years.) But Trump's fortunes rebounded; Trump Organization today owns or has stakes in an array of properties and business enterprises around the world.

Trump co-authored several business-advice books, starting with *Trump: The Art of the Deal* (1987). He became more widely known in the early 2000s for his reality TV series *The Apprentice* and *Celebrity Apprentice*. He also licensed his name to various enterprises, products, and services, including Trump Univ. (now defunct), a for-profit company that ran a real estate and entrepreneurial training program and became an object of litigation for alleged false claims it had made.

Trump has changed political party registration several times, and he explored running for president as a third-party candidate in 2000; he did not run but set forth an economically conservative agenda in *The America We Deserve* (2000). Trump was a conspicuous "birther," questioning whether Pres. Barack Obama was a native-born citizen eligible for the presidency.

On June 16, 2015, Trump announced his candidacy for the presidency, presenting himself as a skilled negotiator and job creator. He described the U.S. as a "dumping ground for everybody else's problems," crippled by trade deals and illegal immigration, which he blamed for job losses, drugs, and crime. He promised to build a wall across the U.S.-Mexican border and have Mexico pay for it. In Dec. 2015, following a deadly attack in San Bernardino, CA, by a Muslim married couple, he advocated a temporary ban on all Muslim immigration to the U.S.—a proposal he later qualified in different ways.

Trump's suspicion of free trade and his stands on some other issues clashed with traditional conservative positions, and from the start he generated controversy for inflammatory remarks. For example, in summer 2015 he said he did not consider Sen. John McCain (R, AZ) a war hero for having been imprisoned and tortured in Vietnam, and he taunted Fox News journalist Megyn Kelly with comments taken by many as disrespectful to women. But many of his supporters welcomed what they deemed a repudiation of political correctness. Later, in fall 2016, details of Trump's crude private remarks about women and alleged sexual advances became public.

In the nomination battle, Trump positioned himself as an anti–government-as-usual outsider and stood out in a field of 17 mostly more experienced and less flamboyant competitors. After a loss in the Iowa caucuses, he won the next three contests and a majority of those on Super Tuesday, Mar. 1. Following Trump's landslide victory in the May 3 Indiana primary, his last GOP opponents dropped out, and he was nominated at the Republican National Convention on July 19.

Republican Nominee for Vice President: Mike Pence

Born: Michael Richard Pence, June 7, 1959, Columbus, IN, to parents Edward J. Pence Jr., Nancy Jane (Cawley) Pence. **Education:** BA (history), Hanover College, 1981; JD, Indiana Univ. School of Law, 1986. **Career:** attorney in private practice, 1986-91; pres., Indiana Policy Review Foundation, 1991-93; host, syndicated radio talk show, 1992-99, and morning TV talk show, 1995-99; U.S. representative (R, IN), 2001-13; chair, House Republican Conference, 2009-11; Indiana governor, 2013-present. **Net worth:** negative, aside from defined benefits pension valued at $500,000-$1 mil. **Religion:** Evangelical Christian. **Family:** married Karen Pence (b. 1958), 1985; children: Michael, Charlotte, Audrey.

One of six children born to a middle-class Catholic family, Mike Pence grew up as an admirer of Pres. John F. Kennedy and volunteered for the county Democratic party. In college he became a conservative and converted to evangelical Christianity.

After law school, Pence worked as an attorney and entered politics as a Republican precinct committeeman. He made unsuccessful runs for Congress in 1988 and 1990, later publishing an article in which he regretted having used attack ads rather than emphasizing his conservative message. Meanwhile, he aired his political opinions as a radio and TV talk show host in Indiana.

Elected to Congress in 2000, he has described himself as "a Christian, a conservative, and a Republican, in that order." Diverging from Pres. George W. Bush, he voted against the No Child Left Behind bill (2001), the Medicare prescription drug expansion (2003), and the bank bailout (2008). In 2011 he supported a federal government shutdown unless funding for Planned Parenthood could be cut off. He failed in a 2006 challenge to Rep. John Boehner (OH) for the House speakership, but two years later was chosen as Republican conference chair.

As governor of Indiana, Pence signed into law tax and spending cuts that created a budget surplus. He expanded a voucher program for nonpublic schools and signed legislation to remove Indiana from Common Core but then substituted similar state academic standards. In 2015 he signed a broadly worded Religious Freedom Restoration Act, which appeared to authorize denial of services to LGBT individuals. The law damaged his popularity and led to boycotts; soon afterward he signed an amendment designed to protect LGBT minorities from being denied services. In 2016 he signed a bill to prohibit abortions in cases of fetal disability, but a federal judge blocked the measure.

Pence initially supported Sen. Ted Cruz (TX) for the GOP presidential nomination. In naming Pence as his choice for vice president, Trump stressed a need for party unity, while also praising Pence's record as governor. In order to run, Pence was required by state law to drop his bid for reelection.

Members of the 115th Congress: U.S. Senate

Source: © Associated Press; all rights reserved. 2016 results are preliminary as of Nov. 9, 2016.

51 Republicans, 46 Democrats, 2 independents (who caucus with Democrats). Results in one race were still pending and are listed in italics. Boldface denotes the 2016 election winner. * = Incumbent. Third-party or independent candidates receiving fewer than 50,000 votes are not necessarily listed.

Terms are for six years and end Jan. 3 of the year preceding the senator's name in the following table. Annual salary: $174,000; President Pro Tempore, Majority Leader, and Minority Leader: $193,400. To be eligible to serve in the Senate, a person must be at least 30 years old, a U.S. citizen for at least nine years, and a resident of the state from which elected.

D = Democrat; R = Republican; DFL = Dem.-Farmer-Labor; Ind. = Independent; LB = Libertarian; NPL = Nonpartisan League.

Term ends	Senator/candidate (party); service from	2016 election results
Alabama		
2021	Jeff Sessions (R); 1/7/1997	
2023	**Richard Shelby* (R); 1/6/1987**	1,319,742
	Ron Crumpton (D)	736,615
Alaska		
2021	Dan Sullivan (R); 1/6/2015	
2023	**Lisa Murkowski* (R); 12/20/2002**	110,226
	Joe Miller (LB)	73,876
	Ray Metcalfe (D)	27,830
Arizona		
2019	Jeff Flake (R); 1/3/2013	
2023	**John McCain* (R); 1/6/1987**	999,900
	Ann Kirkpatrick (D)	775,804
	Gary Swing (Green)	103,408
Arkansas		
2021	Tom Cotton (R); 1/6/2015	
2023	**John Boozman (R); 1/5/2011**	657,856
	Conner Eldridge (D)	397,078
California		
2019	Dianne Feinstein (D); 11/10/1992	
2023	**Kamala Harris (D)**	4,857,345
	Loretta Sanchez (D)	2,911,570
Colorado		
2021	Cory Gardner (R); 1/6/2015	
2023	**Michael Bennet* (D); 1/22/2009**	1,151,443
	Darryl Glenn (R)	1,079,285
	Lily Williams (LB)	78,847
Connecticut		
2019	Christopher S. Murphy (D); 1/3/2013	
2023	**Richard Blumenthal* (D); 1/5/2011**	911,005
	Dan Carter (R)	513,361
Delaware		
2019	Thomas R. Carper (D); 1/3/2001	
2021	Christopher Coons (D); 11/15/2010	
Florida		
2019	Bill Nelson (D); 1/3/2001	
2023	**Marco Rubio* (R); 1/5/2011**	4,818,789
	Patrick Murphy (D)	4,101,582
	Paul Stanton (LB)	195,910
	Bruce Nathan (Ind.)	52,219
Georgia		
2021	David Perdue (R); 1/6/2015	
2023	**Johnny Isakson* (R); 1/4/2005**	2,108,067
	Jim Barksdale (D)	1,562,626
	Allen Buckley (LB)	159,714
Hawaii		
2019	Mazie K. Hirono (D); 1/3/2013	
2023	**Brian Schatz* (D); 12/26/2012**	289,298
	John Carroll (R)	87,270
Idaho		
2021	Jim Risch (R); 1/6/2009	
2023	**Mike Crapo* (R); 1/6/1999**	427,016
	Jerry Sturgill (D)	180,462
Illinois		
2021	Richard J. Durbin (D); 1/7/1997	
2023	**Tammy Duckworth (D)**	2,905,794
	Mark Kirk* (R); 11/29/2010	2,147,509
	Kenton McMillen (LB)	171,869
	Scott Summers (Green)	113,849
Indiana		
2019	Joe Donnelly (D); 1/3/2013	
2023	**Todd Young (R)**	1,414,500
	Evan Bayh (D)	1,148,917
	Lucy Brenton (LB)	148,681
Iowa		
2021	Joni Ernst (R); 1/6/2015	
2023	**Chuck Grassley* (R); 1/5/1981**	921,957
	Patty Judge (D)	549,130

Term ends	Senator/candidate (party); service from	2016 election results
Kansas		
2021	Pat Roberts (R); 1/7/1997	
2023	**Jerry Moran* (R); 1/5/2011**	715,362
	Patrick Wiesner (D)	367,596
	Robert Garrard (LB)	63,280
Kentucky		
2021	Mitch McConnell (R); 1/3/1985	
2023	**Rand Paul* (R); 1/5/2011**	1,090,061
	Jim Gray (D)	813,224
Louisiana		
2021	Bill Cassidy (R); 1/6/2015	
2023[1]	*John Kennedy (R)*	*482,380*
	Foster Campbell (D)	*337,682*
Maine		
2019	Angus King (Ind.); 1/3/2013	
2021	Susan M. Collins (R); 1/7/1997	
Maryland		
2019	Benjamin L. Cardin (D); 1/4/2007	
2023	**Chris Van Hollen (D)**	1,488,845
	Kathy Szeliga (R)	898,902
	Margaret Flowers (Green)	78,752
Massachusetts		
2019	Elizabeth A. Warren (D); 1/3/2013	
2021	Ed Markey (D); 7/16/2013	
Michigan		
2019	Debbie Stabenow (D); 1/3/2001	
2021	Gary Peters (D); 1/6/2015	
Minnesota		
2019	Amy Klobuchar (DFL); 1/4/2007	
2021	Al Franken (DFL); 7/7/2009	
Mississippi		
2019	Roger F. Wicker (R); 12/31/2007	
2021	Thad Cochran (R); 12/27/1978	
Missouri		
2019	Claire McCaskill (D); 1/4/2007	
2023	**Roy Blunt* (R); 1/5/2011**	1,370,240
	Jason Kander (D)	1,283,222
	Jonathan Dine (LB)	67,067
Montana		
2019	Jon Tester (D); 1/4/2007	
2021	Steve Daines (R); 1/6/2015	
Nebraska		
2019	Deb Fischer (R); 1/3/2013	
2021	Ben Sasse (R); 1/6/2015	
Nevada		
2019	Dean Heller (R); 5/9/2011	
2023	**Catherine Cortez Masto (D)**	520,658
	Joe Heck (R)	494,427
New Hampshire		
2021	Jeanne Shaheen (D); 1/6/2009	
2023	**Maggie Hassan (D)**	353,978
	Kelly Ayotte* (R); 1/5/2011	353,262
New Jersey		
2019	Robert Menendez (D); 1/18/2006	
2021	Cory Booker (D); 10/31/2013	
New Mexico		
2019	Martin Heinrich (D); 1/3/2013	
2021	Tom Udall (D); 1/6/2009	
New York		
2019	Kirsten E. Gillibrand (D); 1/27/2009	
2023	**Charles Schumer* (D); 1/6/1999**	4,693,947
	Wendy Long (R)	1,831,172
	Robin Wilson (Green)	100,372
North Carolina		
2021	Thom Tillis (R); 1/6/2015	
2023	**Richard Burr* (R); 1/4/2005**	2,371,186
	Deborah Ross (D)	2,102,696
	Sean Haugh (LB)	165,319

Term ends	Senator/candidate (party); service from	2016 election results
North Dakota		
2019	Heidi Heitkamp (D-NPL); 1/3/2013	
2023	**John Hoeven* (R); 1/5/2011**	**267,964**
	Eliot Glassheim (D-NPL)	57,976
Ohio		
2019	Sherrod Brown (D); 1/4/2007	
2023	**Rob Portman* (R); 1/5/2011**	**3,048,467**
	Ted Strickland (D)	1,929,873
	Tom Connors (Ind.)	89,977
	Joseph DeMare (Green)	84,521
	Scott Rupert (Ind.)	74,682
Oklahoma		
2021	James M. Inhofe (R); 11/21/1994	
2023	**James Lankford* (R); 1/6/2015**	**979,728**
	Mike Workman (D)	355,389
Oregon		
2021	Jeff Merkley (D); 1/6/2009	
2023	**Ron Wyden* (D); 2/6/1996**	**1,012,359**
	Mark Callahan (R)	600,615
	Shanti Lewallen (Working Families)	54,195
	Steven Reynolds (Ind.)	53,181
Pennsylvania		
2019	Bob Casey Jr. (D); 1/4/2007	
2023	**Pat Toomey* (R); 1/5/2011**	**2,893,260**
	Katie McGinty (D)	2,793,356
	Edward Clifford (LB)	230,508
Rhode Island		
2019	Sheldon Whitehouse (D); 1/4/2007	
2021	Jack Reed (D); 1/7/1997	
South Carolina		
2021	Lindsey Graham (R); 1/7/2003	
2023	**Tim Scott* (R); 1/3/2013**	**1,199,552**
	Thomas Dixon (D)	713,291
South Dakota		
2021	Mike Rounds (R); 1/6/2015	
2023	**John Thune* (R); 1/4/2005**	**265,374**
	Jay Williams (D)	104,091

Term ends	Senator/candidate (party); service from	2016 election results
Tennessee		
2019	Bob Corker (R); 1/4/2007	
2021	Lamar Alexander (R); 1/7/2003	
Texas		
2019	Ted Cruz (R); 1/3/2013	
2021	John Cornyn (R); 12/2/2002	
Utah		
2019	Orrin G. Hatch (R); 1/5/1977	
2023	**Mike Lee* (R); 1/5/2011**	**501,773**
	Misty Snow (D)	206,311
Vermont		
2019	Bernard Sanders (Ind.); 1/4/2007	
2023	**Patrick Leahy* (D); 1/3/1975**	**191,737**
	Scott Milne (R)	103,217
Virginia		
2019	Timothy M. Kaine (D); 1/3/2013	
2021	Mark Warner (D); 1/6/2009	
Washington		
2019	Maria Cantwell (D); 1/3/2001	
2023	**Patty Murray* (D); 1/3/1993**	**1,216,070**
	Chris Vance (R)	784,476
West Virginia		
2019	Joe Manchin III (D); 11/15/2010	
2021	Shelley Moore Capito (R); 1/6/2015	
Wisconsin		
2019	Tammy Baldwin (D); 1/3/2013	
2023	**Ron Johnson* (R); 1/5/2011**	**1,477,367**
	Russ Feingold (D)	1,379,070
	Phil Anderson (LB)	87,176
Wyoming		
2019	John Barrasso (R); 6/22/2007	
2021	Michael B. Enzi (R); 1/7/1997	

(1) No candidate won the required majority; top two vote recipients (shown) were to meet in a runoff scheduled Dec. 9, 2016.

Members of the 115th Congress: U.S. House of Representatives

Source: © Associated Press; all rights reserved. 2016 results are preliminary as of Nov. 9, 2016.

239 Republicans, 193 Democrats. Results in four races were still pending and are listed in italics. Boldface denotes the 2016 election winner. * = Incumbent; ** = Incumbent in another district. Third-party or independent candidates receiving fewer than 10,000 votes are not necessarily listed. Only the top two vote recipients are listed for Louisiana districts.

Terms are for two years ending on Jan. 3, 2019. Annual salary, $174,000; Majority Leader and Minority Leader, $196,400; Speaker of the House, $223,500. To be eligible to serve in the House, a person must be at least 25 years of age, a U.S. citizen for at least seven years, and a resident of the state from which elected.

D = Democrat; R = Republican; DFL = Dem.-Farmer-Labor; Ind. = Independent; LB = Libertarian; NPA = No party affiliation; NPL = Nonpartisan League; NPP = No party preference; RF = Reform.

Dist.	Representative/candidate (party)	2016 election results
Alabama		
1	**Bradley Byrne* (R)**	**Unopposed**
2	**Martha Roby* (R)**	**134,450**
	Nathan Mathis (D)	111,640
3	**Mike Rogers* (R)**	**190,724**
	Jesse Smith (D)	93,567
4	**Robert B. Aderholt* (R)**	**Unopposed**
5	**Mo Brooks* (R)**	**204,791**
	Will Boyd (D)	101,577
6	**Gary Palmer (R)**	**240,897**
	David Putman (D)	81,296
7	**Terri A. Sewell* (D)**	**Unopposed**
Alaska		
	Don Young* (R)	**124,581**
	Steve Lindbeck (D)	90,180
	Jim McDermott (LB)	24,978
Arizona		
1	**Tom O'Halleran (D)**	**110,894**
	Paul Babeu (R)	93,004
	Ray Parrish (Green)	12,326
2	**Martha McSally* (R)**	**149,184**
	Matt Heinz (D)	113,715
3	**Raúl M. Grijalva* (D)**	**Unopposed**
4	**Paul A. Gosar* (R)**	**159,601**
	Mikel Weisser (D)	63,327

Dist.	Representative/candidate (party)	2016 election results
5	**Andy Biggs (R)**	**141,669**
	Talia Fuentes (D)	82,844
6	**David Schweikert* (R)**	**146,772**
	W. John Williamson (D)	91,839
7	**Ruben Gallego* (D)**	**81,169**
	Eve Nunez (R)	27,799
8	**Trent Franks* (R)**	**154,465**
	Mark Salazar (Green)	70,931
9	**Kyrsten Sinema* (D)**	**117,597**
	Dave Giles (R)	74,303
Arkansas		
1	**Rick Crawford* (R)**	**183,068**
	Mark West (LB)	56,240
2	**French Hill* (R)**	**176,100**
	Dianne Curry (D)	111,049
	Chris Hayes (LB)	14,287
3	**Steve Womack* (R)**	**214,268**
	Steve Isaacson (LB)	62,793
4	**Bruce Westerman* (R)**	**179,980**
	Kerry Hicks (LB)	62,900
California		
1	**Doug LaMalfa* (R)**	**130,026**
	Jim Reed (D)	90,915
2	**Jared Huffman* (D)**	**154,411**
	Dale Mensing (R)	47,490

Dist.	Representative/candidate (party)	2016 election results
3	**John Garamendi* (D)**	**102,237**
	Eugene Cleek (R)	69,563
4	**Tom McClintock* (R)**	**146,704**
	Robert Derlet (D)	88,690
5	**Mike Thompson* (D)**	**147,902**
	Carlos Santamaria (R)	44,223
6	**Doris O. Matsui* (D)**	**102,272**
	Robert Evans (R)	34,383
7	*Ami Bera* (D)*	*86,794*
	Scott Jones (R)	*84,700*
8	**Paul Cook* (R)**	**104,091**
	Rita Ramirez (D)	60,496
9	**Jerry McNerney* (D)**	**80,187**
	Tony Amador (R)	60,509
10	**Jeff Denham* (R)**	**80,668**
	Michael Eggman (D)	73,246
11	**Mark DeSaulnier* (D)**	**137,649**
	Roger Petersen (R)	54,942
12	**Nancy Pelosi* (D)**	**185,039**
	Preston Picus (NPP)	41,618
13	**Barbara Lee* (D)**	**166,145**
	Sue Caro (R)	17,774
14	**Jackie Speier* (D)**	**149,847**
	Angel Cardenas (R)	35,246
15	**Eric Swalwell* (D)**	**120,387**
	Danny Turner (R)	43,910
16	**Jim Costa* (D)**	**57,545**
	Johnny Tacherra (R)	46,371
17	**Ro Khanna (D)**	**83,968**
	Mike Honda* (D)	56,561
18	**Anna G. Eshoo* (D)**	**145,727**
	Richard Fox (R)	57,587
19	**Zoe Lofgren* (D)**	**105,493**
	Burt Lancaster (D)	37,995
20	**Jimmy Panetta (D)**	**102,696**
	Casey Lucius (R)	42,871
21	**David G. Valadao* (R)**	**48,308**
	Emilio Huerta (D)	34,171
22	**Devin Nunes* (R)**	**97,376**
	Louie Campos (D)	44,845
23	**Kevin McCarthy* (R)**	**118,744**
	Wendy Reed (D)	49,432
24	**Salud Carbajal (D)**	**114,270**
	Justin Fareed (R)	98,214
25	**Steve Knight* (R)**	**94,552**
	Bryan Caforio (D)	79,533
26	**Julia Brownley* (D)**	**118,096**
	Rafael Dagnesses (R)	80,321
27	**Judy Chu* (D)**	**112,421**
	Jack Orswell (R)	56,013
28	**Adam B. Schiff* (D)**	**140,287**
	Lenore Solis (R)	40,106
29	**Tony Cárdenas* (D)**	**84,292**
	Richard Alarcón (D)	28,115
30	**Brad Sherman* (D)**	**133,150**
	Mark Reed (R)	50,448
31	**Pete Aguilar* (D)**	**77,399**
	Paul Chabot (R)	63,602
32	**Grace F. Napolitano* (D)**	**80,977**
	Roger Hernández (D)	49,567
33	**Ted Lieu* (D)**	**144,541**
	Kenneth Wright (R)	73,433
34	**Xavier Becerra* (D)**	**81,188**
	Adrienne Edwards (D)	21,954
35	**Norma J. Torres* (D)**	**79,813**
	Tyler Fischella (R)	31,804
36	**Raul Ruiz* (D)**	**92,785**
	Jeff Stone (R)	60,883
37	**Karen Bass* (D)**	**121,168**
	Chris Wiggins (D)	26,456
38	**Linda T. Sánchez* (D)**	**112,704**
	Ryan Downing (R)	48,365
39	**Ed Royce* (R)**	**104,247**
	Brett Murdock (D)	75,477
40	**Lucille Roybal-Allard* (D)**	**73,336**
	Roman Gonzalez (NPP)	28,593

Dist.	Representative/candidate (party)	2016 election results
41	**Mark Takano* (D)**	**75,154**
	Doug Shepherd (R)	44,942
42	**Ken Calvert* (R)**	**95,714**
	Tim Sheridan (D)	64,004
43	**Maxine Waters* (D)**	**109,327**
	Omar Navarro (R)	35,081
44	**Nanette Barragán (D)**	**61,828**
	Isadore Hall (D)	58,983
45	**Mimi Walters* (R)**	**127,705**
	Ron Varasteh (D)	86,894
46	**Lou Correa (D)**	**67,798**
	Bao Nguyen (D)	28,784
47	**Alan Lowenthal* (D)**	**102,295**
	Andy Whallon (R)	60,191
48	**Dana Rohrabacher* (R)**	**126,485**
	Suzanne Savary (D)	88,461
49	*Darrell E. Issa* (R)*	*93,684*
	Doug Applegate (D)	*89,704*
50	**Duncan Hunter* (R)**	**102,773**
	Patrick Malloy (D)	57,250
51	**Juan Vargas* (D)**	**70,363**
	Juan Hidalgo Jr. (R)	27,469
52	**Scott Peters* (D)**	**100,296**
	Denise Gitsham (R)	76,943
53	**Susan A. Davis* (D)**	**106,187**
	James Veltmeyer (R)	54,439
Colorado		
1	**Diana DeGette* (D)**	**172,623**
	Charles "Casper" Stockham (R)	71,594
2	**Jared Polis* (D)**	**233,300**
	Nicholas Morse (R)	152,724
	Richard Longstreth (LB)	22,444
3	**Scott R. Tipton* (R)**	**185,238**
	Gail Schwartz (D)	137,600
	Gaylon Kent (LB)	16,225
4	**Ken Buck* (R)**	**231,884**
	Bob Seay (D)	113,365
	Bruce Griffith (LB)	16,623
5	**Doug Lamborn* (R)**	**222,169**
	Misty Plowright (D)	109,573
	Mike McRedmond (LB)	24,320
6	**Mike Coffman* (R)**	**162,208**
	Morgan Carroll (D)	133,963
	Norm Olsen (LB)	14,473
7	**Ed Perlmutter* (D)**	**160,804**
	George Athanasopoulos (R)	117,061
	Martin Buchanan (LB)	12,489
Connecticut		
1	**John B. Larson* (D)**	**188,286**
	Matthew Corey (R)	100,976
2	**Joe Courtney* (D)**	**195,738**
	Daria Novak (R)	104,846
3	**Rosa L. DeLauro* (D)**	**203,989**
	Angel Cadena (R)	94,533
4	**Jim Himes* (D)**	**133,630**
	John Shaban (R)	101,053
5	**Elizabeth Esty* (D)**	**174,349**
	Clay Cope (R)	129,279
Delaware		
	Lisa Blunt Rochester (D)	**233,542**
	Hans Reigle (R)	172,290
Florida		
1	**Matt Gaetz (R)**	**254,280**
	Steven Specht (D)	113,586
2	**Neal Dunn (R)**	**230,724**
	Walter Dartland (D)	102,459
3	**Ted Yoho* (R)**	**193,261**
	Ken McGurn (D)	135,688
	Tom Wells (NPA)	12,438
4	**John Rutherford (R)**	**286,018**
	David Bruderly (D)	112,253
5	**Al Lawson (D)**	**193,019**
	Glo Smith (R)	107,682
6	**Ron DeSantis* (R)**	**213,180**
	Bill McCullough (D)	150,677

Dist.	Representative/candidate (party)	2016 election results
7	Stephanie Murphy (D)	181,021
	John L. Mica* (R)	170,945
8	Bill Posey* (R)	246,247
	Corry Westbrook (D)	126,944
	Bill Stinson (NPA)	16,921
9	Darren Soto (D)	194,647
	Wayne Liebnitzky (R)	144,106
10	Val Demings (D)	196,949
	Thuy Lowe (R)	106,777
11	Daniel Webster* (R)	256,571
	Dave Koller (D)	123,676
	Bruce Ray Riggs (NPA)	11,873
12	Gus M. Bilirakis* (R)	253,347
	Robert Tager (D)	115,909
13	Charlie Crist (D)	184,371
	David W. Jolly* (R)	170,964
14	Kathy Castor* (D)	194,851
	Christine Quinn (R)	120,584
15	Dennis A. Ross* (R)	182,498
	Jim Lange (D)	134,945
16	Vern Buchanan* (R)	230,187
	Jan Schneider (D)	154,854
17	Tom Rooney* (R)	208,906
	April Freeman (D)	115,631
	John Sawyer (NPA)	13,326
18	Brian Mast (R)	201,010
	Randy Perkins (D)	161,325
	Carla Spalding (NPA)	12,451
19	Francis Rooney (R)	238,975
	Robert Neeld (D)	123,625
20	Alcee L. Hastings* (D)	220,452
	Gary Stein (R)	54,079
21	Lois Frankel* (D)	208,999
	Paul Spain (R)	117,273
22	Ted Deutch* (D)	197,396
	Andrea Leigh McGee (D)	137,691
23	Debbie Wasserman Schultz* (D)	180,979
	Joe Kaufman (R)	129,400
24	Frederica S. Wilson* (D)	Unopposed
25	Mario Diaz-Balart* (R)	157,748
	Alina Valdes (D)	95,008
26	Carlos Curbelo* (R)	148,445
	Joe Garcia (D)	115,348
	Jose Peixoto (D)	16,491
27	Ileana Ros-Lehtinen* (R)	157,763
	Scott Fuhrman (D)	129,548

Georgia

Dist.	Representative/candidate (party)	2016 election results
1	Buddy Carter (R)	Unopposed
2	Sanford D. Bishop Jr.* (D)	146,201
	Greg Duke (R)	93,383
3	Drew Ferguson (R)	206,930
	Angela Pendley (D)	95,736
4	Henry "Hank" Johnson* (D)	214,278
	Victor Armendariz (R)	69,075
5	John Lewis* (D)	241,773
	Douglas Bell (R)	44,032
6	Tom Price* (R)	191,792
	Rodney Stooksbury (D)	119,536
7	Rob Woodall* (R)	173,638
	Rashid Malik (D)	113,593
8	Austin Scott* (R)	169,914
	James Harris (D)	80,962
9	Doug Collins* (R)	Unopposed
10	Jody Hice* (R)	Unopposed
11	Barry Loudermilk* (R)	216,772
	Don Wilson (D)	104,401
12	Rick W. Allen* (R)	158,705
	Patricia "Tricia" McCracken (D)	98,870
13	David Scott* (D)	Unopposed
14	Tom Graves* (R)	Unopposed

Hawaii

Dist.	Representative/candidate (party)	2016 election results
1	Colleen Hanabusa (D)	135,069
	Shirlene Ostrov (R)	42,569
2	Tulsi Gabbard* (D)	163,484
	Angela Kaaihue (R)	38,098

Idaho

Dist.	Representative/candidate (party)	2016 election results
1	Raúl R. Labrador* (R)	216,389
	James Piotrowski (D)	101,569
2	Mike Simpson* (R)	208,887
	Jennifer Martinez (D)	97,250
	Anthony Tompkins (Constitution)	25,575

Illinois

Dist.	Representative/candidate (party)	2016 election results
1	Bobby L. Rush* (D)	221,551
	August "O'Neill" Deuser (R)	80,161
2	Robin L. Kelly* (D)	228,695
	John Morrow (R)	58,517
3	Daniel Lipinski* (D)	Unopposed
4	Luis V. Gutiérrez* (D)	Unopposed
5	Mike Quigley* (D)	201,983
	Vince Kolber (R)	82,930
	Rob Sherman (Green)	13,867
6	Peter J. Roskam* (R)	205,746
	Amanda Howland (D)	140,023
7	Danny K. Davis* (D)	232,322
	Jeffrey Leef (R)	44,242
8	Raja Krishnamoorthi (D)	141,080
	Pete DiCianni (R)	101,871
9	Jan Schakowsky* (D)	203,776
	Joan McCarthy Lasonde (R)	105,900
10	Brad Schneider (D)	147,299
	Robert Dold* (R)	133,383
11	Bill Foster* (D)	157,659
	Tonia Khouri (R)	105,762
12	Mike Bost* (R)	169,233
	C.J. Baricevic (D)	123,754
	Paula Bradshaw (Green)	18,713
13	Rodney Davis* (R)	186,791
	Mark Wicklund (D)	125,932
14	Randy Hultgren* (R)	197,962
	Jim Walz (D)	134,362
15	John Shimkus* (R)	Unopposed
16	Adam Kinzinger* (R)	Unopposed
17	Cheri Bustos* (D)	170,746
	Patrick Harlan (R)	113,141
18	Darin LaHood* (R)	247,893
	Junius Rodriguez (D)	95,474

Indiana

Dist.	Representative/candidate (party)	2016 election results
1	Peter J. Visclosky* (D)	207,206
	Donna Dunn (LB)	46,994
2	Jackie Walorski* (R)	164,272
	Lynn Coleman (D)	102,326
	Ron Cenkush (LB)	10,594
3	Jim Banks (R)	201,216
	Tommy Schrader (D)	65,908
	Pepper Snyder (LB)	19,782
4	Todd Rokita* (R)	193,272
	John Dale (D)	91,153
	Steven Mayoras (LB)	14,758
5	Susan Brooks* (R)	221,087
	Angela Demaree (D)	123,250
	Matthew Wittlief (LB)	15,276
6	Luke Messer* (R)	203,089
	Barry Welsh (D)	78,264
	Rich Turvey (LB)	12,254
7	André Carson* (D)	156,591
	Catherine "Cat" Ping (R)	93,663
	Drew Thompson (LB)	11,346
8	Larry Bucshon* (R)	187,569
	Ron Drake (D)	93,130
	Andrew Horning (LB)	13,630
9	Trey Hollingsworth (R)	169,414
	Shelli Yoder (D)	125,355
	Russell Brooksbank (LB)	16,960

Iowa

Dist.	Representative/candidate (party)	2016 election results
1	Rod Blum* (R)	205,615
	Monica Vernon (D)	175,977
2	Dave Loebsack* (D)	197,802
	Christopher Peters (R)	170,529
3	David Young* (R)	208,240
	Jim Mowrer (D)	154,754
	Bryan Holder (LB)	15,327
4	Steve King* (R)	225,842
	Kim Weaver (D)	142,018

Kansas

Dist.	Representative/candidate (party)	2016 election results
1	Roger Marshall (R)	166,051
	Alan LaPolice (Ind.)	66,218
	Kerry Burt (LB)	18,415
2	Lynn Jenkins* (R)	177,727
	Britani Potter (D)	94,386
	James Bales (LB)	18,685

Dist.	Representative/candidate (party)	2016 election results
3	**Kevin Yoder* (R)**	**170,490**
	Jay Sidie (D)	134,915
	Steven Hohe (LB)	26,716
4	**Mike Pompeo* (R)**	**163,406**
	Daniel Giroux (D)	78,822
	Miranda Allen (Ind.)	18,358
Kentucky		
1	**James Comer (R)**	**216,957**
	Samuel Gaskins (D)	81,710
2	**Brett Guthrie* (R)**	**Unopposed**
3	**John A. Yarmuth* (D)**	**212,388**
	Harold Bratcher (R)	122,085
4	**Thomas Massie* (R)**	**233,922**
	Calvin Sidle (D)	94,064
5	**Harold "Hal" Rogers* (R)**	**Unopposed**
6	**Garland "Andy" Barr* (R)**	**202,093**
	Nancy Jo Kemper (D)	128,760
Louisiana		
1	**Steve Scalise* (R)**	**243,575**
	Lee Ann Dugas (D)	41,816
2	**Cedric L. Richmond* (D)**	**198,169**
	Kip Holden (D)	57,083
3[1]	*Scott Angelle (R)*	*91,374*
	Clay Higgins (R)	*84,809*
4[1]	*Marshall Jones (D)*	*80,558*
	Mike Johnson (R)	*70,556*
5	**Ralph Abraham* (R)**	**208,504**
	Billy Burkette (R)	47,106
6	**Garret Graves* (R)**	**207,453**
	Richard Lieberman (D)	49,352
Maine		
1	**Chellie Pingree* (D)**	**216,726**
	Mark Holbrook (R)	157,302
2	**Bruce Poliquin* (R)**	**183,167**
	Emily Cain (D)	151,386
Maryland		
1	**Andy Harris* (R)**	**229,135**
	Joe Werner (D)	94,776
	Matt Beers (LB)	14,207
2	**C.A. Dutch Ruppersberger* (D)**	**172,324**
	Pat McDonough (R)	92,099
	Kristin Kasprzak (LB)	12,530
3	**John P. Sarbanes* (D)**	**194,362**
	Mark Plaster (R)	106,627
4	**Anthony Brown (D)**	**218,215**
	George McDermott (R)	63,674
5	**Steny H. Hoyer* (D)**	**223,582**
	Mark Arness (R)	98,768
	Jason Summers (LB)	10,033
6	**John Delaney* (D)**	**167,229**
	Amie Hoeber (R)	123,611
7	**Elijah E. Cummings* (D)**	**211,962**
	Corrogan R. Vaughn (R)	61,854
8	**Jamie Raskin (D)**	**191,671**
	Dan Cox (R)	115,200
Massachusetts		
1	**Richard E. Neal* (D)**	**232,066**
	Frederick Mayock (Ind.)	56,875
	Thomas Simmons (LB)	27,010
2	**Jim McGovern* (D)**	**Unopposed**
3	**Niki Tsongas* (D)**	**234,361**
	Ann Wofford (R)	106,882
4	**Joseph P. Kennedy III* (D)**	**261,356**
	David Rosa (R)	111,890
5	**Katherine M. Clark* (D)**	**Unopposed**
6	**Seth Moulton* (D)**	**Unopposed**
7	**Michael E. Capuano* (D)**	**Unopposed**
8	**Stephen F. Lynch* (D)**	**263,362**
	William Burke (R)	100,497
9	**Bill Keating* (D)**	**209,911**
	Mark Alliegro (R)	127,199
	Paul Harrington (Ind.)	26,086
Michigan		
1	**Jack Bergman (R)**	**200,618**
	Lon Johnson (D)	144,047
	Diane Bostow (LB)	13,345
2	**Bill Huizenga* (R)**	**213,095**
	Dennis Murphy (D)	110,077

Dist.	Representative/candidate (party)	2016 election results
3	**Justin Amash* (R)**	**203,069**
	Douglas Smith (D)	128,159
	Ted Gerrard (U.S. Taxpayers)	10,374
4	**John Moolenaar* (R)**	**194,569**
	Debra Wirth (D)	101,275
5	**Daniel T. Kildee* (D)**	**195,076**
	Al Hardwick (R)	111,908
6	**Fred Upton* (R)**	**192,862**
	Paul Clements (D)	119,871
	Lorence Wenke (LB)	16,239
7	**Tim Walberg* (R)**	**183,549**
	Gretchen Driskell (D)	133,697
	Ken Proctor (LB)	16,402
8	**Mike Bishop* (R)**	**205,617**
	Suzanna Shkreli (D)	143,775
9	**Sander M. Levin* (D)**	**199,620**
	Christopher Morse (R)	128,907
10	**Paul Mitchell (R)**	**214,164**
	Frank Accaviti (D)	109,875
	Lisa Gioia (LB)	10,582
11	**Dave Trott* (R)**	**198,433**
	Anil Kumar (D)	150,431
	Kerry Bentivolio (Ind.)	16,487
12	**Debbie Dingell* (D)**	**210,922**
	Jeff Jones (R)	95,823
13	**John Conyers Jr.* (D)**	**194,758**
	Jeff Gorman (R)	39,242
14	**Brenda Lawrence* (D)**	**243,437**
	Howard Klausner (R)	58,091
Minnesota		
1	**Tim Walz* (DFL)**	**169,080**
	Jim Hagedorn (R)	166,533
2	**Jason Lewis (R)**	**172,345**
	Angie Craig (DFL)	164,622
	Paula Overby (Independence)	28,508
3	**Erik Paulsen* (R)**	**223,076**
	Terri Bonoff (DFL)	169,237
4	**Betty McCollum* (DFL)**	**202,238**
	Greg Ryan (R)	120,743
	Susan Pendergast Sindt (Legal Marijuana)	27,100
5	**Keith Ellison* (DFL)**	**249,955**
	Frank Drake (R)	80,660
	Dennis Schuller (Legal Marijuana)	30,758
6	**Tom Emmer* (R)**	**235,531**
	David Snyder (DFL)	123,122
7	**Collin C. Peterson* (DFL)**	**173,545**
	Dave Hughes (R)	156,896
8	**Rick Nolan* (DFL)**	**179,108**
	Stewart Mills (R)	177,083
Mississippi		
1	**Trent Kelly* (R)**	**201,696**
	Jacob Owens (D)	81,640
2	**Bennie G. Thompson* (D)**	**178,419**
	John Bouie II (R)	77,832
3	**Gregg Harper* (R)**	**200,004**
	Dennis Quinn (D)	91,665
4	**Steven M. Palazzo* (R)**	**170,804**
	Mark Gladney (D)	72,766
	Richard McCluskey (LB)	13,978
Missouri		
1	**Lacy Clay* (D)**	**231,604**
	Steven Bailey (R)	61,252
	Robb Cunningham (LB)	13,954
2	**Ann Wagner* (R)**	**238,826**
	Bill Otto (D)	153,331
	Jim Higgins (LB)	11,621
3	**Blaine Luetkemeyer* (R)**	**248,880**
	Kevin Miller (D)	102,484
	Dan Hogan (LB)	11,906
4	**Vicky Hartzler* (R)**	**225,034**
	Gordon Christensen (D)	92,385
	Mark Bliss (LB)	14,355
5	**Emanuel Cleaver* (D)**	**185,494**
	Jacob Turk (R)	122,367
6	**Sam Graves* (R)**	**236,938**
	David Blackwell (D)	98,588
7	**Billy Long* (R)**	**228,001**
	Genevieve Williams (D)	92,390
	Benjamin Brixey (LB)	17,706
8	**Jason T. Smith* (R)**	**229,648**
	Dave Cowell (D)	69,949

Dist.	Representative/candidate (party)	2016 election results
Montana		
	Ryan Zinke* (R)	259,173
	Denise Juneau (D)	181,620
	Rick Breckenridge (LB)	14,400
Nebraska		
1	**Jeff Fortenberry* (R)**	187,258
	Daniel Wik (D)	81,939
2	**Don Bacon (R)**	134,291
	Brad Ashford* (D)	128,739
3	**Adrian Smith* (R)**	Unopposed
Nevada		
1	**Dina Titus* (D)**	116,045
	Mary Perry (R)	54,053
	Reuben D'Silva (Ind.)	13,806
2	**Mark E. Amodei* (R)**	182,452
	H. D. "Chip" Evans (D)	115,395
3	**Jacky Rosen (D)**	146,653
	Danny Tarkanian (R)	142,726
	Warren Markowitz (Independent Amer.)	11,580
4	**Ruben Kihuen (D)**	128,680
	Cresent Hardy* (R)	118,220
	Steve Brown (LB)	10,184
New Hampshire		
1	**Carol Shea-Porter (D)**	161,765
	Frank Guinta* (R)	156,953
	Shawn O'Connor (Ind.)	34,356
2	**Ann McLane Kuster* (D)**	173,945
	Jim Lawrence (R)	158,696
	John Babiarz (Ind.)	16,773
New Jersey		
1	**Donald Norcross* (D)**	156,020
	Bob Patterson (R)	98,559
2	**Frank A. LoBiondo* (R)**	166,145
	David Cole (D)	103,438
3	**Tom MacArthur* (R)**	176,966
	Frederick LaVergne (D)	114,534
4	**Chris Smith* (R)**	193,901
	Lorna Phillipson (D)	100,344
5	**Joshua Gottheimer (D)**	156,628
	Scott Garrett* (R)	146,428
6	**Frank Pallone Jr.* (D)**	146,234
	Brent Sonnek-Schmelz (R)	82,252
7	**Leonard Lance* (R)**	177,253
	Peter Jacob (D)	138,791
8	**Albio Sires* (D)**	120,557
	Agha Khan (R)	29,400
9	**Bill Pascrell Jr.* (D)**	151,823
	Hector Castillo (R)	61,384
10	**Donald M. Payne Jr.* (D)**	179,082
	David Pinckney (R)	24,628
11	**Rodney P. Frelinghuysen* (R)**	183,416
	Joseph Wenzel (D)	121,195
12	**Bonnie Watson Coleman (D)**	160,851
	Steven Uccio (R)	83,049
New Mexico		
1	**Michelle Lujan Grisham* (D)**	179,380
	Richard Priem (R)	96,061
2	**Steve Pearce* (R)**	141,832
	Merrie Lee Soules (D)	84,362
3	**Ben Ray Luján* (D)**	167,842
	Michael Romero (R)	100,518
New York		
1	**Lee M. Zeldin* (R)**	174,682
	Anna Throne-Holst (D)	121,640
2	**Peter T. King* (R)**	171,915
	DuWayne Gregory (D)	103,643
3	**Thomas Suozzi (D)**	156,315
	Jack Martins (R)	142,023
4	**Kathleen M. Rice* (D)**	173,796
	David Gurfein (R)	118,821
5	**Gregory W. Meeks* (D)**	184,179
	Michael O'Reilly (R)	28,030
6	**Grace Meng* (D)**	126,018
	Danniel Maio (R)	47,278
7	**Nydia M. Velázquez* (D)**	158,972
	Allan Romaguera (R)	16,255
8	**Hakeem S. Jeffries* (D)**	199,747
	Daniel Cavanagh (Conservative)	14,468
9	**Yvette D. Clarke* (D)**	200,266
	Alan Bellone (Conservative)	16,617
10	**Jerrold Nadler* (D)**	170,286
	Philip Rosenthal (R)	49,530

Dist.	Representative/candidate (party)	2016 election results
11	**Dan Donovan* (R)**	134,366
	Richard Reichard (D)	78,066
12	**Carolyn B. Maloney* (D)**	219,165
	Robert Ardini (R)	44,981
13	**Adriano Espaillat (D)**	187,382
	Tony Evans (R)	14,501
14	**Joseph Crowley* (D)**	134,603
	Frank Spotorno (R)	28,332
15	**José E. Serrano* (D)**	150,058
	Alejandro Vega (R)	5,606
16	**Eliot L. Engel* (D)**	143,723
	Derickson Lawrence (People's Choice)	6,522
17	**Nita M. Lowey* (D)**	Unopposed
18	**Sean Patrick Maloney* (D)**	142,146
	Phil Oliva (R)	116,597
19	**John Faso (R)**	152,681
	Zephyr Teachout (D)	126,508
20	**Paul Tonko* (D)**	183,804
	Joe Vitollo (R)	87,057
21	**Elise Stefanik* (R)**	164,792
	Mike Derrick (D)	73,024
	Matthew Funiciello (Green)	11,394
22	**Claudia Tenney (R)**	120,777
	Kim Myers (D)	103,955
	Martin Babinec (RF)	32,303
23	**Thomas Reed* (R)**	149,439
	John Plumb (D)	108,163
24	**John Katko* (R)**	169,418
	Colleen Deacon (D)	108,485
25	**Louise Slaughter* (D)**	169,179
	Mark W. Assini (R)	134,285
26	**Brian Higgins* (D)**	193,515
	Shelly Schratz (R)	66,688
27	**Chris Collins* (R)**	207,389
	Diana Kastenbaum (D)	99,051
North Carolina		
1	**G. K. Butterfield* (D)**	237,938
	H. Powell Dew (R)	100,633
2	**George Holding** (R)**	219,342
	John McNeil (D)	167,299
3	**Walter B. Jones* (R)**	214,850
	Ernest Reeves (D)	104,007
4	**David E. Price* (D)**	275,501
	Sue Googe (R)	128,331
5	**Virginia Foxx* (R)**	204,943
	Josh Brannon (D)	145,597
6	**Mark Walker* (R)**	205,973
	Pete Glidewell (D)	141,480
7	**David Rouzer* (R)**	209,933
	J. Wesley Casteen (D)	134,344
8	**Richard Hudson* (R)**	187,909
	Thomas Mills (D)	131,428
9	**Robert Pittenger* (R)**	191,660
	Christian Cano (D)	137,335
10	**Patrick T. McHenry* (R)**	219,589
	Andy Millard (D)	128,114
11	**Mark Meadows* (R)**	229,130
	Rick Bryson (D)	127,972
12	**Alma Adams* (D)**	232,451
	Leon Threatt (R)	114,242
13	**Ted Budd (R)**	196,736
	Bruce Davis (D)	153,691
North Dakota		
	Kevin Cramer* (R)	233,248
	Chase Iron Eyes (D-NPL)	80,188
	Robert J. "Jack" Seaman (LB)	23,456
Ohio		
1	**Steve Chabot* (R)**	205,283
	Michele Young (D)	139,279
2	**Brad Wenstrup* (R)**	215,265
	William Smith (D)	107,859
3	**Joyce Beatty* (D)**	189,536
	John Adams (R)	88,040
4	**Jim Jordan* (R)**	205,669
	Janet Garrett (D)	96,334
5	**Bob Latta* (R)**	240,036
	James Neu (D)	98,045
6	**Bill Johnson* (R)**	209,177
	Michael Lorentz (D)	86,938
7	**Bob Gibbs* (R)**	194,146
	Roy Rich (D)	87,602
	Dan Phillip (Ind.)	21,062

Dist.	Representative/candidate (party)	2016 election results
8	**Warren Davidson* (R)**	219,453
	Steven Fought (D)	85,313
	Derrick Hendricks (Green)	13,371
9	**Marcy Kaptur* (D)**	187,926
	Donald Larson (R)	86,311
10	**Mike Turner* (R)**	210,256
	Robert Klepinger (D)	105,947
	Tom McMasters (Ind.)	10,463
11	**Marcia Fudge* (D)**	233,285
	Beverly Goldstein (R)	58,066
12	**Pat Tiberi* (R)**	243,970
	Ed Albertson (D)	109,455
	Joe Manchik (Green)	12,848
13	**Tim Ryan* (D)**	203,430
	Richard Morckel (R)	97,312
14	**David P. Joyce* (R)**	214,618
	Michael Wager (D)	127,547
15	**Steve Stivers* (R)**	216,186
	Scott Wharton (D)	110,272
16	**Jim Renacci* (R)**	221,495
	Keith Mundy (D)	117,296

Oklahoma

Dist.	Representative/candidate (party)	2016 election results
1	**Jim Bridenstine* (R)**	Unopposed
2	**Markwayne Mullin* (R)**	189,612
	Joshua Harris-Till (D)	62,307
	John McCarthy (Ind.)	16,618
3	**Frank D. Lucas* (R)**	227,276
	Frankie Robbins (D)	63,008
4	**Tom Cole* (R)**	203,942
	Christina Owen (D)	76,380
	Sevier White (LB)	12,548
5	**Steve Russell* (R)**	160,012
	Al McAffrey (D)	103,122
	Zachary Knight (LB)	17,084

Oregon

Dist.	Representative/candidate (party)	2016 election results
1	**Suzanne Bonamici* (D)**	206,796
	Brian Heinrich (R)	129,396
	Kyle Sheahan (LB)	10,876
2	**Greg Walden* (R)**	242,607
	James Crary (D)	92,147
3	**Earl Blumenauer* (D)**	249,220
	David Walker (Ind.)	69,886
	David Delk (Progressive)	23,765
4	**Peter A. DeFazio* (D)**	216,442
	Art Robinson (R)	155,271
	Mike Beilstein (Pacific Green)	11,807
5	**Kurt Schrader* (D)**	178,330
	Colm Willis (R)	143,807
	Marvin Sandnes (Pacific Green)	10,578

Pennsylvania

Dist.	Representative/candidate (party)	2016 election results
1	**Robert A. Brady* (D)**	237,882
	Deborah Williams (R)	51,516
2	**Dwight Evans (D)**	310,770
	James Jones (R)	33,911
3	**Mike Kelly* (R)**	Unopposed
4	**Scott Perry* (R)**	216,772
	Joshua Burkholder (D)	111,158
5	**Glenn W. Thompson* (R)**	200,627
	Kerith Strano Taylor (D)	97,686
6	**Ryan A. Costello* (R)**	203,671
	Mike Parrish (D)	151,800
7	**Patrick Meehan* (R)**	219,314
	Mary Ellen Balchunis (D)	147,808
8	**Brian Fitzpatrick (R)**	206,607
	Steve Santarsiero (D)	172,571
9	**Bill Shuster* (R)**	183,798
	Art Halvorson (D)	105,958
10	**Tom Marino* (R)**	207,796
	Michael Molesevich (D)	87,865
11	**Lou Barletta* (R)**	194,653
	Mike Marsicano (D)	110,925
12	**Keith J. Rothfus* (R)**	217,362
	Erin McClelland (D)	133,448
13	**Brendan Boyle (D)**	Unopposed
14	**Mike Doyle* (D)**	252,709
	Lenny McAllister (R)	87,334
15	**Charles W. Dent* (R)**	184,562
	Rick Daugherty (D)	120,233
	Paul Rizzo (LB)	11,310
16	**Lloyd Smucker (R)**	167,698
	Christina Hartman (D)	132,969
	Shawn House (LB)	10,408
17	**Matthew Cartwright* (D)**	155,766
	Matt Connolly (R)	133,719
18	**Tim Murphy* (R)**	Unopposed

Rhode Island

Dist.	Representative/candidate (party)	2016 election results
1	**David N. Cicilline* (D)**	116,899
	H. Russell Taub (R)	64,268
2	**Jim Langevin* (D)**	120,243
	Rhue Reis (R)	64,495
	Jeffrey Johnson (Ind.)	14,937

South Carolina

Dist.	Representative/candidate (party)	2016 election results
1	**Mark Sanford* (R)**	179,270
	Dimitri Cherny (D)	112,727
	Michael Grier (LB)	11,117
2	**Joe Wilson* (R)**	169,650
	Arik Bjorn (D)	93,599
	Eddie McCain (American)	10,917
3	**Jeff Duncan* (R)**	196,793
	Hosea Cleveland (D)	72,990
4	**Trey Gowdy* (R)**	197,235
	Chris Fedalei (D)	91,106
5	**Mick Mulvaney* (R)**	175,139
	Fran Person (D)	114,936
6	**James E. Clyburn* (D)**	157,953
	Laura Sterling (R)	66,911
7	**Tom Rice* (R)**	170,826
	Mal Hyman (D)	110,378

South Dakota

Dist.	Representative/candidate (party)	2016 election results
	Kristi L. Noem* (R)	237,019
	Paula Hawks (D)	132,759

Tennessee

Dist.	Representative/candidate (party)	2016 election results
1	**Phil Roe* (R)**	196,562
	Alan Bohms (D)	38,513
	Robert Franklin (Ind.)	15,605
2	**John J. Duncan, Jr* (R)**	212,313
	Stuart Starr (D)	00,070
3	**Chuck Fleischmann* (R)**	176,410
	Melody Shekari (D)	76,664
4	**Scott DesJarlais* (R)**	165,594
	Steven Reynolds (D)	89,018
5	**Jim Cooper* (D)**	170,729
	Stacy Snyder (R)	102,220
6	**Diane Black* (R)**	202,038
	David Kent (D)	61,940
	David Ross (Ind.)	20,241
7	**Marsha Blackburn* (R)**	196,940
	Tharon Chandler (D)	63,947
	Leonard Ladner (Ind.)	11,693
8	**David Kustoff (R)**	193,353
	Rickey Hobson (D)	70,426
9	**Steve Cohen* (D)**	169,911
	Wayne Alberson (R)	40,580

Texas

Dist.	Representative/candidate (party)	2016 election results
1	**Louie Gohmert* (R)**	192,066
	Shirley J. McKellar (D)	62,635
2	**Ted Poe* (R)**	168,524
	Pat Bryan (D)	100,077
3	**Sam Johnson* (R)**	193,063
	Adam Bell (D)	108,780
	Scott Jameson (LB)	10,408
4	**John Ratcliffe* (R)**	215,705
	Cody Wommack (LB)	29,437
5	**Jeb Hensarling* (R)**	136,739
	Ken Ashby (LB)	35,396
6	**Joe Barton* (R)**	159,031
	Ruby Faye Woolridge (D)	106,325
7	**John Culberson* (R)**	143,369
	James Cargas (D)	111,774
8	**Kevin Brady* (R)**	Unopposed
9	**Al Green* (D)**	151,884
	Jeff Martin (R)	36,454
10	**Michael T. McCaul* (R)**	178,926
	Tawana Cadien (D)	119,728
	Bill Kelsey (LB)	13,174
11	**Mike Conaway* (R)**	201,476
	Nicholas Landholt (LB)	23,613
12	**Kay Granger* (R)**	196,040
	Bill Bradshaw (D)	75,811
	Ed Colliver (LB)	10,566
13	**Mac Thornberry* (R)**	192,563
	Calvin DeWeese (LB)	14,301
14	**Randy Weber* (R)**	160,340
	Michael Cole (D)	98,815
15	**Vicente Gonzalez (D)**	101,566
	Tim Westley (R)	66,706
16	**Beto O'Rourke* (D)**	148,027
	Jaime Perez (LB)	17,144
17	**Bill Flores* (R)**	149,157
	William Matta (D)	86,352

Dist.	Representative/candidate (party)	2016 election results
18	**Sheila Jackson Lee* (D)**	**149,928**
	Lori Bartley (R)	48,248
19	**Jodey Arrington (R)**	**175,980**
	Troy Bonar (LB)	17,339
20	**Joaquin Castro* (D)**	**149,522**
	Jeffrey Blunt (LB)	29,023
21	**Lamar Smith* (R)**	**202,523**
	Tom Wakely (D)	129,253
	Mike Loewe (LB)	14,698
22	**Pete Olson* (R)**	**181,663**
	Mark Gibson (D)	123,462
23	**Will Hurd* (R)**	**109,816**
	Pete P. Gallego (D)	106,049
	Ruben Corvalan (LB)	10,717
24	**Kenny Marchant* (R)**	**154,218**
	Jan McDowell (D)	107,756
25	**Roger Williams* (R)**	**180,577**
	Kathi Thomas (D)	116,551
	Loren Schneiderman (LB)	12,092
26	**Michael C. Burgess* (R)**	**210,212**
	Eric Mauck (D)	93,908
	Mark Boler (LB)	12,730
27	**Blake Farenthold* (R)**	**141,722**
	Roy Barrera (D)	87,931
28	**Henry Cuellar* (D)**	**104,554**
	Zeffen Hardin (R)	55,640
29	**Gene Green* (D)**	**95,508**
	Julio Garza (R)	31,619
30	**Eddie Bernice Johnson* (D)**	**169,905**
	Charles Lingerfelt (R)	41,365
31	**John R. Carter* (R)**	**165,678**
	Mike Clark (D)	103,543
	Scott Ballard (LB)	14,638
32	**Pete Sessions* (R)**	**162,212**
	Ed Rankin (LB)	43,297
	Gary Stuard (Green)	22,692
33	**Marc Veasey* (D)**	**92,856**
	Mark Mitchell (R)	33,134
34	**Filemon Vela* (D)**	**104,513**
	Rey Gonzalez Jr. (R)	62,240
35	**Lloyd Doggett* (D)**	**124,161**
	Susan Narvaiz (R)	62,212
36	**Brian Babin (R)**	**203,779**
	Hal Ridley (Green)	25,911
Utah		
1	**Rob Bishop* (R)**	**117,839**
	Peter Clemens (D)	53,235
	Craig Bowden (LB)	10,478
2	**Chris Stewart* (R)**	**109,992**
	Charlene Albarran (D)	62,438
3	**Jason Chaffetz* (R)**	**150,326**
	Stephen Tryon (D)	51,465
4	**Mia Love* (R)**	**92,521**
	Doug Owens (D)	74,880
Vermont		
	Peter Welch* (D)	**263,245**
	Erica Clawson (Liberty Union)	29,317
Virginia		
1	**Robert J. Wittman* (R)**	**220,843**
	Matt Rowe (D)	129,582
	Gail Parker (Ind.)	12,081
2	**Scott Taylor (R)**	**172,586**
	Shaun Brown (D)	106,989
3	**Bobby Scott* (D)**	**196,497**
	Marty Williams (R)	98,223
4	**Donald McEachin (D)**	**191,937**
	Michael Wade (R)	143,260

Dist.	Representative/candidate (party)	2016 election results
5	**Tom Garrett (R)**	**206,572**
	Jane Dittmar (D)	147,655
6	**Bob Goodlatte* (R)**	**223,389**
	Kai Degner (D)	111,499
7	**David Brat* (R)**	**217,472**
	Eileen Bedell (D)	158,714
8	**Donald S. Beyer Jr.* (D)**	**245,775**
	Charles Hernick (R)	98,123
	Julio Gracia (Ind.)	14,617
9	**H. Morgan Griffith* (R)**	**212,391**
	Derek Kitts (D)	87,769
10	**Barbara Comstock* (R)**	**203,983**
	LuAnn Bennett (D)	181,975
11	**Gerry Connolly* (D)**	**Unopposed**
Washington		
1	**Suzan DelBene* (D)**	**121,565**
	Robert Sutherland (R)	90,990
2	**Rick Larsen* (D)**	**132,584**
	Marc Hennemann (R)	70,922
3	**Jaime Herrera Beutler* (R)**	**123,868**
	Jim Moeller (D)	86,700
4	**Dan Newhouse* (R)**	**70,133**
	Clint Didier (R)	51,122
5	**Cathy McMorris Rodgers* (R)**	**117,287**
	Joseph Pakootas (D)	83,812
6	**Derek Kilmer* (D)**	**134,390**
	Todd Bloom (R)	81,493
7	**Pramila Jayapal (D)**	**136,547**
	Brady Piñero Walkinshaw (D)	102,341
8	**Dave Reichert* (R)**	**110,088**
	Tony Ventrella (D)	78,478
9	**Adam Smith* (D)**	**130,129**
	Doug Basler (R)	44,948
10	**Denny Heck* (D)**	**105,987**
	Jim Postma (R)	72,065
West Virginia		
1	**David B. McKinley* (R)**	**162,339**
	Mike Manypenny (D)	73,025
2	**Alex Mooney* (R)**	**140,153**
	Mark Hunt (D)	100,551
3	**Evan Jenkins* (R)**	**137,133**
	Matt Detch (D)	46,809
	Zane Lawhorn (LB)	16,644
Wisconsin		
1	**Paul Ryan* (R)**	**230,063**
	Ryan Solen (D)	106,857
2	**Mark Pocan* (D)**	**275,016**
	Peter Theron (R)	125,033
3	**Ron Kind* (D)**	**Unopposed**
4	**Gwen Moore* (D)**	**220,389**
	Robert Raymond (Ind.)	33,496
	Andy Craig (LB)	32,184
5	**Jim Sensenbrenner* (R)**	**260,702**
	Khary Penebaker (D)	114,469
	John Arndt (LB)	15,324
6	**Glenn Grothman* (R)**	**203,920**
	Sarah Lloyd (D)	132,908
	Jeff Dahlke (Ind.)	20,690
7	**Sean P. Duffy* (R)**	**222,833**
	Mary Hoeft (D)	137,910
8	**Mike Gallagher (R)**	**227,732**
	Tom Nelson (D)	135,648
Wyoming		
	Liz Cheney (R)	**156,040**
	Ryan Greene (D)	75,419
	Daniel Cummings (Constitution)	10,381

(1) No candidate won the required majority; top two vote recipients (shown) were to meet in a runoff scheduled Dec. 9, 2016.

Nonvoting Members of Congress

Delegate/candidate (party)	2016 election results
American Samoa	
Aumua Amata Coleman Radewagen* (R)	8,923
Vaitinasa Salu Hunkin-Finau (No party)	1,581
Paepaetele Mapu S. Jamias (No party)	978
Meleagi Suitonu-Chapman (No party)	181
Tim Jones (No party)	171
District of Columbia	
Eleanor Holmes Norton* (D)	244,711
Martin Moulton (LB)	17,272
Natale Stracuzzi (DC Statehood Green)	13,358
Guam	
Madeleine Z. Bordallo* (D)	**18,263**
Felix Camacho (R)	15,564

Delegate/candidate (party)	2016 election results
Northern Mariana Islands	
Gregorio Kilili Camacho Sablan* (D)	13,820
Puerto Rico—Resident Commissioner[1]	
Jennifer González (New Progressive Party)	707,200
Héctor Ferrer Rios (Popular Democratic Party)	685,454
Hugo Rodríguez Díaz (Puerto Rican Independence Party)	39,064
Mariana Nogales Molinelli (Working People's Party)	18,692
Virgin Islands	
Stacey E. Plaskett* (D)	**13,958**

(1) The resident commissioner of Puerto Rico is the only member of the U.S. House of Representatives who serves a four-year term.

Governors of the 50 States

Source: © Associated Press; all rights reserved. 2016 results are preliminary as of Nov. 9, 2016.

15 Democrats, 33 Republicans, 1 independent; results of one race were still pending and are listed in italics. Boldface denotes the 2016 election winner. * = Incumbent. Third-party or independent candidates receiving fewer than 50,000 votes are not necessarily listed. Governors of states not holding elections in Nov. 2016 are shown for reference. Unless otherwise noted, terms are for four years—with the exception of two-year terms for governors of New Hampshire and Vermont—ending in Jan. of year listed. D = Democrat; R = Republican; DFL = Dem.-Farmer-Labor; Ind. = Independent; LB = Libertarian.

Term expires	Governor	2016 election results	Term expires	Governor	2016 election results
Alabama			**Nebraska**		
2019	Robert Bentley (R)		2019	Pete Ricketts (R)	
Alaska			**Nevada**		
Dec. 2018	Bill Walker (Ind.)		2019	Brian Sandoval (R)	
Arizona			**New Hampshire**		
2019	Doug Ducey (R)		2019	**Chris Sununu (R)**	353,427
Arkansas				Colin Van Ostern (D)	337,141
2019	Asa Hutchinson (R)		**New Jersey**		
California			2018	Chris Christie (R)	
2019	Jerry Brown (D)		**New Mexico**		
Colorado			2019	Susana Martinez (R)	
2019	John Hickenlooper (D)		**New York**		
Connecticut			2019	Andrew Cuomo (D)	
2019	Dan Malloy (D)		**North Carolina**		
Delaware			2021	*Roy Cooper (D)*	*2,281,155*
2021	**John Carney (D)**	248,402		*Pat McCrory* (R)*	*2,276,383*
	Colin Bonini (R)	166,849		*Lon Cecil (LB)*	*101,028*
Florida			**North Dakota**		
2019	Rick Scott (R)		Dec. 2020	**Doug Burgum (R)**	259,071
Georgia				Marvin Nelson (D)	65,693
2019	Nathan Deal (R)		**Ohio**		
Hawaii			2019	John Kasich (R)	
Dec. 2018	David Ige (D)		**Oklahoma**		
Idaho			2019	Mary Fallin (R)	
2019	C. L. "Butch" Otter (R)		**Oregon**[1]		
Illinois			2019	**Kate Brown* (D)**	899,529
2019	Bruce Rauner (R)			Bud Pierce (R)	780,317
Indiana			**Pennsylvania**		
2021	**Eric Holcomb (R)**	1,387,933	2019	Tom Wolf (D)	
	John Gregg (D)	1,225,987	**Rhode Island**		
	Rex Bell (LB)	86,050	2019	Gina Raimondo (D)	
Iowa			**South Carolina**		
2019	Terry Branstad (R)		2019	Nikki Haley (R)	
Kansas			**South Dakota**		
2019	Sam Brownback (R)		2019	Dennis Daugaard (R)	
Kentucky			**Tennessee**		
Dec. 2019	Matt Bevin (R)		2019	Bill Haslam (R)	
Louisiana			**Texas**		
2020	John Bel Edwards (D)		2019	Greg Abbott (R)	
Maine			**Utah**		
2019	Paul LePage (R)		2021	**Gary Herbert* (R)**	495,610
Maryland				Mike Weinholtz (D)	217,136
2019	Larry Hogan (R)		**Vermont**		
Massachusetts			2019	**Phil Scott (R)**	165,756
2019	Charlie Baker (R)			Sue Minter (D)	138,753
Michigan			**Virginia**		
2019	Rick Snyder (R)		2018	Terry McAuliffe (D)	
Minnesota			**Washington**		
2019	Mark Dayton (DFL)		2021	**Jay Inslee* (D)**	1,124,030
Mississippi				Bill Bryant (R)	873,686
2020	Phil Bryant (R)		**West Virginia**		
Missouri			2021	**Jim Justice (D)**	344,965
2021	**Eric Greitens (R)**	1,424,730		Bill Cole (R)	298,418
	Chris Koster (D)	1,261,110	**Wisconsin**		
Montana			2019	Scott Walker (R)	
2021	**Steve Bullock* (D)**	226,400	**Wyoming**		
	Greg Gianforte (R)	214,899	2019	Matt Mead (R)	

(1) Secretary of State Kate Brown became governor Feb. 18, 2015, following four-term Gov. John Kitzhaber's resignation. Results shown are for special election to fill the position for the term's final two years.

Governors of U.S. Commonwealths and Territories

Term expires	Governor	2016 election results	Term expires	Governor	2016 election results
American Samoa			**Puerto Rico**		
2021	**Lolo Matalasi Moliga* (Ind.)**	7,235	2021	**Ricardo Rosselló Nevares (New Progressive Party)**	649,791
	Faoa Aitofele Sunia (Ind.)	4,305		David Bernier (Popular Democratic Party)	605,710
	Tuika Tuika (Ind.)	484		Alexandra Lúgaro (Ind.)	172,941
Guam				Manuel Cidre (Ind.)	89,069
2019	Eddie Baza Calvo (R)			María de Lourdes Santiago (Puerto Rican Independence Party)	33,179
Northern Mariana Islands					
2019	Eloy S. Inos (R/Covenant)				
Virgin Islands					
2019	Kenneth Mapp (Ind.)				

Presidential Election Results by State and County, 2016

Alabama

County	2016		2012	
	Clinton (D)	Trump (R)	Obama (D)	Romney (R)
Autauga	5,908	18,110	6,363	17,379
Baldwin	17,463	69,431	18,424	66,016
Barbour	4,848	5,431	5,912	5,550
Bibb	1,874	6,733	2,202	6,132
Blount	2,150	22,808	2,970	20,757
Bullock	3,530	1,139	4,061	1,251
Butler	3,716	4,891	4,374	5,087
Calhoun	13,197	32,803	15,511	30,278
Chambers	5,763	7,803	6,871	7,626
Cherokee	1,524	8,809	2,132	7,506
Chilton	2,909	15,068	3,397	13,932
Choctaw	3,109	4,102	3,786	4,152
Clarke	5,712	7,109	6,334	7,470
Clay	1,234	5,230	1,777	4,817
Cleburne	684	5,738	971	5,272
Coffee	4,194	15,825	4,925	14,666
Colbert	7,296	16,718	9,166	13,936
Conecuh	3,069	3,413	3,555	3,439
Coosa	1,780	3,376	2,191	3,049
Covington	2,379	13,222	3,158	12,153
Crenshaw	1,663	4,511	2,050	4,331
Cullman	3,730	32,734	5,052	28,999
Dale	4,408	13,798	5,286	13,108
Dallas	12,826	5,784	14,612	6,288
De Kalb	3,682	21,779	5,239	18,331
Elmore	8,436	27,619	8,954	26,253
Escambia	4,698	10,282	5,489	9,287
Etowah	10,350	32,132	12,803	29,130
Fayette	1,358	6,705	1,817	6,054
Franklin	2,197	9,466	3,171	7,567
Geneva	1,522	9,967	2,039	9,175
Greene	4,006	838	4,521	804
Hale	4,772	3,172	5,411	3,210
Henry	2,286	5,623	3,083	5,628
Houston	10,547	30,567	12,367	29,270
Jackson	3,663	16,643	5,822	14,439
Jefferson	151,581	130,614	159,876	141,683
Lamar	1,035	5,819	1,646	5,457
Lauderdale	9,877	27,735	12,511	23,911
Lawrence	3,611	10,732	5,069	8,874
Lee	20,987	34,321	21,381	32,194
Limestone	9,340	28,824	9,829	25,295
Lowndes	4,882	1,751	5,747	1,756
Macon	7,237	1,394	9,045	1,331
Madison	62,435	89,199	62,015	90,884
Marengo	5,607	5,224	6,167	5,336
Marion	1,432	11,273	2,249	9,697
Marshall	4,913	29,217	6,299	25,867
Mobile	68,429	91,087	78,760	94,893
Monroe	4,310	5,771	4,914	5,741
Montgomery	58,669	33,928	63,085	38,332
Morgan	11,216	37,392	13,439	35,391
Perry	3,823	1,403	4,568	1,506
Pickens	3,972	5,454	4,455	5,124
Pike	5,039	7,681	6,035	7,963
Randolph	2,290	7,697	3,078	7,224
Russell	9,577	9,210	10,500	8,278
St. Clair	5,550	31,579	5,801	29,031
Shelby	22,927	72,846	20,051	71,436
Sumter	4,739	1,581	5,421	1,586
Talladega	12,108	20,596	13,905	19,246
Tallapoosa	5,271	12,967	6,319	12,396
Tuscaloosa	31,746	47,701	32,048	45,748
Walker	4,486	24,208	6,557	21,651
Washington	2,366	6,031	2,976	5,761
Wilcox	4,329	1,737	4,868	1,679
Winston	871	9,225	1,286	8,312
Totals	**717,138**	**1,303,576**	**795,696**	**1,255,925**

All candidates, 2016: Trump, R, 1,303,576; Clinton, D, 717,138; Johnson, Ind., 43,731; Stein, Ind., 9,274.

Alaska

	2016		2012	
	Clinton (D)	Trump (R)	Obama (D)	Romney (R)
Totals	92,013	129,786	122,640	164,676

All candidates, 2016: Trump, R, 129,786; Clinton, D, 92,013; Johnson, LB, 14,524; Stein, Green, 4,394; Castle, Const., 3,070; De La Fuente, NPA, 959.

Arizona

County	2016		2012	
	Clinton (D)	Trump (R)	Obama (D)	Romney (R)
Apache	11,891	5,217	17,147	8,250
Cochise	15,291	25,036	18,546	29,497
Coconino	25,308	16,573	29,257	21,220
Gila	6,295	12,342	7,697	13,455
Graham	3,194	7,348	3,609	8,076
Greenlee	1,092	1,892	1,310	1,592
La Paz	1,318	3,381	1,880	3,714
Maricopa	500,424	540,943	602,288	749,885
Mohave	15,536	51,312	19,533	49,168
Navajo	15,362	18,165	16,945	19,884
Pima	182,028	137,992	201,251	174,779
Pinal	29,546	44,432	44,306	62,079
Santa Cruz	7,769	2,556	9,486	4,235
Yavapai	28,312	55,534	33,918	64,468
Yuma	18,336	20,586	18,059	23,352
Totals	**861,702**	**943,309**	**1,025,232**	**1,233,654**

All candidates, 2016: Trump, R, 943,309; Clinton, D, 861,702; Johnson, LB, 72,183; Stein, Green, 22,734.

Arkansas

County	2016		2012	
	Clinton (D)	Trump (R)	Obama (D)	Romney (R)
Arkansas	1,939	3,825	2,455	3,897
Ashley	2,408	5,338	2,859	4,867
Baxter	4,163	14,655	5,172	13,688
Benton	27,894	60,751	22,636	54,646
Boone	2,925	12,225	3,772	11,159
Bradley	1,317	2,163	1,449	2,134
Calhoun	636	1,554	660	1,458
Carroll	3,334	6,773	3,696	6,125
Chicot	2,350	1,716	2,649	1,670
Clark	3,606	4,398	3,811	4,343
Clay	1,999	3,779	1,738	3,225
Cleburne	2,101	9,454	2,620	8,693
Cleveland	723	2,460	845	2,313
Columbia	3,140	5,456	3,557	5,790
Conway	2,655	4,844	3,005	4,514
Craighead	10,474	22,798	10,527	20,350
Crawford	4,476	16,655	4,881	15,145
Crittenden	8,368	6,953	9,487	6,998
Cross	1,995	4,577	2,279	4,269
Dallas	1,165	1,507	1,337	1,665
Desha	2,227	1,915	2,443	1,896
Drew	2,364	3,967	2,630	3,887
Faulkner	14,525	29,170	13,621	26,722
Franklin	1,376	5,034	1,726	4,631
Fulton	1,067	3,470	1,452	2,949
Garland	12,283	26,053	13,804	26,014
Grant	1,407	5,160	1,468	4,829
Greene	3,056	10,698	4,000	9,071
Hempstead	2,371	4,391	2,468	4,284
Hot Spring	3,137	8,153	3,830	7,097
Howard	1,350	3,155	1,471	2,892
Independence	2,878	9,925	3,281	8,728
Izard	1,111	4,042	1,524	3,575
Jackson	1,583	3,262	2,095	3,072
Jefferson	15,721	9,231	17,470	9,520
Johnson	2,421	6,072	2,799	5,064
Lafayette	1,028	1,750	1,173	1,713
Lawrence	1,263	4,064	1,788	3,536
Lee	1,735	1,229	2,107	1,280
Lincoln	1,252	2,455	1,425	2,199
Little River	1,397	3,604	1,552	3,385
Logan	1,712	5,737	2,009	5,079
Lonoke	5,638	19,902	5,625	17,880
Madison	1,587	4,917	2,099	4,263
Marion	1,377	5,077	2,037	4,774
Miller	4,273	11,293	4,518	10,622
Mississippi	5,621	6,988	6,467	6,603
Monroe	1,298	1,400	1,583	1,585
Montgomery	735	2,573	920	2,369
Nevada	1,156	2,001	1,314	1,996
Newton	699	2,875	993	2,508
Ouachita	4,320	5,347	4,633	5,521
Perry	1,035	2,979	1,187	2,581

County	2016 Clinton (D)	Trump (R)	2012 Obama (D)	Romney (R)
Phillips	4,292	2,443	5,202	2,598
Pike	684	3,150	851	2,847
Poinsett	1,878	3,149	2,390	4,974
Polk	1,210	6,606	1,556	5,955
Pope	4,818	15,694	5,126	14,763
Prairie	812	2,503	880	2,153
Pulaski	89,377	61,182	87,248	68,984
Randolph	1,425	4,508	2,046	3,701
St. Francis	4,031	3,195	4,910	3,368
Saline	13,247	35,852	12,869	32,963
Scott	507	2,378	897	2,631
Searcy	601	2,955	814	2,699
Sebastian	12,184	28,769	13,092	29,169
Sevier	1,075	3,281	1,042	3,136
Sharp	1,472	5,405	2,092	4,921
Stone	1,189	4,081	1,356	3,776
Union	5,667	10,201	6,196	10,699
Van Buren	1,547	5,382	1,832	4,365
Washington	32,296	40,418	28,236	39,688
White	5,157	21,038	5,765	20,011
Woodruff	1,117	1,344	1,340	1,227
Yell	1,472	4,600	1,722	4,042
Totals	**378,729**	**677,904**	**394,409**	**647,744**

All candidates, 2016: Trump, R, 677,904; Clinton, D, 378,729; Johnson, LB, 29,618; McMullin, Better for Amer., 13,120; Stein, Green, 9,887; Hedges, Ind., 4,684; Castle, Const., 4,567; Kahn, Ind., 3,404.

California

County	2016 Clinton (D)	Trump (R)	2012 Obama (D)	Romney (R)
Alameda	300,185	59,384	469,684	108,182
Alpine	318	211	389	236
Amador	3,420	6,069	6,830	10,281
Butte	31,638	35,354	42,669	44,479
Calaveras	6,225	10,126	8,670	12,365
Colusa	1,832	2,709	2,314	3,601
Contra Costa	201,936	76,743	290,824	136,517
Del Norte	2,997	4,370	3,791	4,614
El Dorado	28,026	37,286	35,166	50,973
Fresno	82,863	79,858	129,129	124,490
Glenn	1,766	3,405	3,301	5,632
Humboldt	19,596	10,883	34,457	18,825
Imperial	14,331	5,607	25,136	12,777
Inyo	2,499	3,328	3,422	4,340
Kern	64,980	95,064	89,495	126,618
Kings	9,077	13,158	12,979	17,671
Lake	6,240	5,752	13,163	9,200
Lassen	1,614	5,219	3,053	7,296
Los Angeles	1,601,382	525,308	2,216,903	885,333
Madera	13,283	19,221	16,018	22,852
Marin	64,333	13,127	99,896	30,880
Mariposa	2,568	4,317	3,498	5,140
Mendocino	6,905	3,571	23,193	9,658
Merced	21,856	18,486	33,005	27,581
Modoc	798	2,413	1,111	2,777
Mono	2,551	1,989	2,733	2,285
Monterey	47,387	19,580	82,920	37,390
Napa	20,454	9,335	35,870	19,526
Nevada	16,199	14,686	24,663	24,986
Orange	395,801	356,892	512,440	582,332
Placer	43,915	55,212	66,818	99,921
Plumas	3,224	5,079	4,026	5,721
Riverside	228,731	219,359	329,063	318,127
Sacramento	186,237	114,359	300,503	202,514
San Benito	6,751	4,358	11,276	7,343
San Bernardino	220,853	188,080	305,109	262,358
San Diego	390,531	269,422	626,957	536,726
San Francisco	228,211	26,461	301,723	47,076
San Joaquin	71,349	56,194	114,121	86,071
San Luis Obispo	46,965	39,263	61,258	59,967
San Mateo	152,134	37,996	206,085	72,756
Santa Barbara	72,605	38,973	94,129	64,606
Santa Clara	307,240	90,285	450,818	174,843
Santa Cruz	60,529	14,523	90,805	24,047
Shasta	15,533	35,256	25,819	48,067
Sierra	582	1,030	653	1,056
Siskiyou	5,252	8,392	8,046	11,077
Solano	73,858	38,945	96,783	52,092
Sonoma	116,027	37,421	153,942	54,784
Stanislaus	51,171	52,567	77,724	73,459
Sutter	7,599	10,947	12,192	18,122
Tehama	4,737	10,468	7,934	14,235
Trinity	1,876	2,409	2,674	2,716
Tulare	23,663	33,372	41,752	56,956
Tuolumne	7,075	10,614	9,998	13,880
Ventura	136,848	97,516	170,929	147,958
Yolo	34,460	13,178	48,715	23,368
Yuba	5,115	8,869	7,711	11,275
Totals	**5,476,131**	**2,963,999**	**7,854,285**	**4,839,958**

All candidates, 2016: Clinton, D, 5,476,131; Trump, R, 2,963,999; Johnson, LB, 281,193; Stein, Green, 152,159; La Riva, Peace/Freedom, 38,102.

Colorado

County	2016 Clinton (D)	Trump (R)	2012 Obama (D)	Romney (R)
Adams	64,628	55,993	100,649	70,972
Alamosa	3,168	3,031	3,811	2,705
Arapahoe	132,014	97,841	153,905	125,588
Archuleta	2,489	4,234	2,679	3,872
Baca	278	1,716	467	1,559
Bent	581	1,166	815	1,075
Boulder	114,294	34,867	125,091	49,981
Broomfield	19,530	14,272	16,966	15,008
Chaffee	4,773	5,283	5,086	5,070
Cheyenne	127	905	172	889
Clear Creek	2,585	2,426	3,119	2,430
Conejos	1,753	1,885	2,213	1,835
Costilla	1,109	581	1,340	446
Crowley	336	1,069	535	924
Custer	797	2,059	868	1,788
Delta	4,048	11,584	4,622	10,915
Denver	154,599	38,366	222,018	73,111
Dolores	227	936	334	859
Douglas	67,045	100,178	61,094	104,397
Eagle	12,000	9,152	12,792	9,411
El Paso	105,807	176,506	111,819	170,952
Elbert	3,056	11,536	3,603	10,266
Fremont	5,275	15,066	6,704	13,174
Garfield	10,068	11,551	11,305	12,535
Gilpin	1,634	1,564	1,892	1,346
Grand	3,319	4,467	3,684	4,253
Gunnison	4,882	3,123	5,044	3,341
Hinsdale	197	339	229	353
Huerfano	1,631	1,875	1,953	1,646
Jackson	171	628	216	600
Jefferson	142,929	122,040	159,296	144,197
Kiowa	91	726	118	677
Kit Carson	526	2,894	838	2,785
La Plata	15,300	12,471	15,489	12,794
Lake	1,600	1,264	1,839	1,098
Larimer	82,143	73,080	92,747	82,376
Las Animas	2,614	3,656	3,445	3,263
Lincoln	399	1,873	552	1,687
Logan	1,843	7,272	2,712	6,179
Mesa	20,216	45,955	23,846	47,472
Mineral	237	344	291	344
Moffat	874	5,293	1,330	4,695
Montezuma	3,920	7,771	4,542	7,401
Montrose	4,510	11,623	6,138	13,552
Morgan	3,128	8,104	3,912	6,602
Otero	1,719	2,988	3,647	4,382
Ouray	1,690	1,337	1,646	1,481
Park	3,351	6,035	3,862	5,236
Phillips	436	1,791	588	1,637
Pitkin	7,239	2,522	6,849	3,024
Prowers	1,173	3,508	1,519	3,230
Pueblo	27,945	27,746	42,551	31,894
Rio Blanco	403	2,497	568	2,724
Rio Grande	1,985	3,060	2,478	2,918
Routt	7,487	5,149	7,547	5,469
Saguache	1,345	1,109	1,865	964
San Juan	265	215	266	212
San Miguel	2,960	1,030	2,992	1,154
Sedgwick	267	1,015	419	881
Summit	9,502	5,064	9,347	5,571
Teller	3,547	9,580	4,333	8,702
Washington	289	2,284	468	2,076
Weld	41,721	69,308	49,050	63,775
Yuma	701	3,755	987	3,490
Totals	**1,117,428**	**1,067,559**	**1,323,102**	**1,185,243**

All candidates, 2016: Clinton, D, 1,117,428; Trump, R, 1,067,559; Johnson, LB, 115,958; Stein, Green, 28,763; McMullin, unaff., 24,331; Castle, Const., 9,940; Keniston, Veterans, 8,448; Smith, unaff., 1,530; De La Fuente, Amer. Delta, 908; Kopitke, Independent Amer., 905; Maldonado, unaff., 704; Maturen, Amer. Solidarity, 679; Scott, unaff., 643; Silva, Nutrition, 579; Hoefling, America's Party, 565; La Riva, Socialism/Liberation, 403; Kennedy, Soc. Workers, 368; Kotlikoff, unaff., 338; Lyttle, Nonviolent/Pacifist, 301; Atwood, Approval Voting, 287; Soltysik, Soc. USA, 207; Hedges, Prohib., 147.

Connecticut

City	2016 Clinton (D)	Trump (R)	2012 Obama (D)	Romney (R)
Bridgeport	32,035	6,596	32,135	5,168
Bristol	12,476	12,739	14,146	10,004
Danbury	15,668	11,393	15,290	10,590
East Hartford	13,285	5,220	14,149	4,556
Enfield	8,548	9,238	10,152	7,709
Fairfield	17,859	12,024	15,283	14,357
Glastonbury	11,049	7,531	10,135	8,809
Greenwich	16,253	11,096	13,079	16,456
Haddam	2,141	2,556	19,181	7,482
Hartford	27,425	2,276	31,735	2,138
Manchester	15,132	8,358	15,565	7,961
Meriden	12,788	8,661	14,886	6,880
Middletown	12,957	7,124	13,834	6,105
Milford	13,596	13,386	13,668	11,462
New Britain	15,433	6,046	16,052	4,783
New Haven	34,577	4,483	39,865	4,430
Norwalk	24,229	12,288	22,369	12,773
Shelton	8,001	12,051	8,362	10,327
Southington	9,890	12,383	10,727	10,452
Stamford	34,148	16,223	29,623	17,473
Stratford	13,729	10,534	13,483	9,324
Wallingford	10,651	10,940	11,560	9,259
Waterbury	19,866	12,836	20,957	11,050
West Hartford	20,215	7,131	21,069	10,511
West Haven	12,477	7,774	14,286	5,789
Windsor	11,370	4,013	11,463	4,305
Other	458,634	433,366	452,047	404,734
Totals	**884,432**	**668,266**	**905,083**	**634,892**

All candidates, 2016: Clinton, D, 884,432; Trump, R, 668,266; Johnson, LB, 48,051; Stein, Green, 22,793.

Delaware

County	2016 Clinton (D)	Trump (R)	2012 Obama (D)	Romney (R)
Kent	33,347	36,989	35,527	32,135
New Castle	162,905	85,507	167,082	81,230
Sussex	39,329	62,607	39,975	52,119
Totals	**235,581**	**185,103**	**242,584**	**165,484**

All candidates, 2016: Clinton, D, 235,581; Trump, R, 185,103; Johnson, LB, 14,751; Stein, Green, 6,100.

District of Columbia

	2016 Clinton (D)	Trump (R)	2012 Obama (D)	Romney (R)
Totals	**260,223**	**11,553**	**267,070**	**21,381**

All candidates, 2016: Clinton, D, 260,223; Trump, R, 11,553; Johnson, LB, 4,501; Stein, DC Green, 3,995.

Florida

County	2016 Clinton (D)	Trump (R)	2012 Obama (D)	Romney (R)
Alachua	75,370	46,584	69,699	48,797
Baker	2,112	10,294	2,311	8,975
Bay	21,689	62,010	22,051	56,876
Bradford	2,924	8,913	3,325	8,219
Brevard	119,525	181,620	122,993	159,300
Broward	546,956	258,521	508,312	244,101
Calhoun	1,236	4,647	1,664	4,366
Charlotte	33,421	60,196	35,906	47,996
Citrus	22,765	54,377	28,460	44,662
Clay	27,768	74,898	25,759	70,022
Collier	60,941	105,297	51,698	96,520
Columbia	7,599	20,359	8,462	18,429
De Soto	3,761	6,744	4,174	5,587
Dixie	1,270	5,822	1,798	5,052
Duval	203,627	210,061	196,737	211,615
Escambia	57,114	88,370	58,185	88,711
Flagler	21,985	33,804	23,207	26,969
Franklin	1,738	4,119	1,845	3,570
Gadsden	14,994	6,721	15,770	6,630
Gilchrist	1,457	6,740	1,885	5,917
Glades	1,271	2,996	1,603	2,344
Gulf	1,715	5,320	2,014	4,995
Hamilton	1,899	3,439	2,228	3,138
Hardee	2,147	5,238	2,463	4,696
Hendry	4,610	6,192	4,751	5,355
Hernando	30,843	57,703	37,830	44,938
Highlands	14,708	29,285	16,148	25,915
Hillsborough	306,422	265,928	286,467	250,186
Holmes	852	7,476	1,264	6,919
Indian River	28,997	48,564	27,492	43,450
Jackson	6,383	14,231	7,342	13,418
Jefferson	3,537	3,930	3,945	3,808

County	2016 Clinton (D)	Trump (R)	2012 Obama (D)	Romney (R)
Lafayette	515	2,795	687	2,668
Lake	62,597	101,888	61,799	87,643
Lee	124,725	191,141	110,157	154,163
Leon	91,372	53,559	90,881	55,805
Levy	5,091	13,758	6,119	12,054
Liberty	651	2,542	942	2,301
Madison	3,526	4,849	4,176	4,474
Manatee	71,066	101,681	66,503	85,627
Marion	61,958	107,710	66,831	93,043
Martin	30,158	53,182	30,107	48,183
Miami-Dade	623,006	333,666	541,440	332,981
Monroe	18,949	21,885	19,404	19,234
Nassau	10,849	34,221	10,251	29,929
Okaloosa	23,711	71,788	23,421	70,168
Okeechobee	3,953	9,342	4,856	7,328
Orange	327,160	193,843	273,665	188,589
Osceola	85,287	50,252	67,239	40,592
Palm Beach	371,411	270,762	349,651	247,398
Pasco	89,998	141,943	98,263	112,427
Pinellas	233,135	238,602	239,104	213,258
Polk	117,182	157,216	114,622	131,577
Putnam	9,920	21,873	11,667	19,326
St. Johns	43,037	88,633	35,190	78,513
St. Lucie	66,811	70,246	65,869	56,202
Santa Rosa	18,398	65,126	17,768	58,186
Sarasota	97,676	124,098	95,119	110,504
Seminole	105,611	109,265	96,445	109,943
Sumter	22,631	52,722	19,524	40,646
Suwannee	3,955	14,281	4,751	12,672
Taylor	2,149	6,923	2,764	6,249
Union	1,014	4,567	1,339	3,980
Volusia	108,793	142,763	114,748	117,490
Wakulla	4,348	10,507	5,175	9,290
Walton	6,861	25,695	6,671	21,490
Washington	2,261	8,630	2,820	8,038
Totals	**4,481,401**	**4,602,353**	**4,237,756**	**4,163,447**

All candidates, 2016: Trump, R, 4,602,353; Clinton, D, 4,481,401; Johnson, LB, 205,651; Stein, Green, 63,911; Castle, Const., 16,352; De La Fuente, RF, 9,056.

Georgia

County	2016 Clinton (D)	Trump (R)	2012 Obama (D)	Romney (R)
Appling	1,434	5,492	1,758	5,233
Atkinson	696	1,873	930	1,938
Bacon	607	3,356	791	3,093
Baker	650	775	794	785
Baldwin	7,965	7,691	8,483	7,589
Banks	684	6,130	780	5,354
Barrow	6,580	21,105	6,028	18,725
Bartow	8,204	29,879	8,396	26,876
Ben Hill	2,098	3,734	2,512	3,396
Berrien	1,041	5,408	1,273	4,843
Bibb	34,383	22,589	38,585	25,623
Bleckley	1,094	3,717	1,269	3,587
Brantley	619	5,561	939	4,964
Brooks	2,504	3,679	3,138	3,554
Bryan	4,010	10,513	3,707	9,560
Bulloch	8,812	14,476	9,593	14,174
Burke	4,730	4,491	5,405	4,301
Butts	2,566	6,717	2,968	6,306
Calhoun	1,178	829	1,298	883
Camden	5,914	12,287	6,377	11,343
Candler	1,023	2,661	1,157	2,344
Carroll	12,422	29,983	12,688	28,280
Catoosa	4,769	20,860	5,365	17,858
Charlton	1,004	2,950	1,197	2,527
Chatham	58,998	43,649	60,246	47,204
Chattahoochee	593	746	729	735
Chattooga	1,612	6,457	2,232	5,452
Cherokee	25,203	80,611	19,841	76,514
Clarke	27,889	11,757	25,431	13,815
Clay	697	566	862	537
Clayton	75,908	11,740	81,479	14,164
Clinch	685	1,724	852	1,598
Cobb	159,416	152,602	133,124	171,722
Coffee	4,090	9,575	5,057	9,248
Colquitt	3,460	9,892	3,973	9,243
Columbia	18,863	43,060	16,451	41,765
Cook	1,752	4,175	2,042	3,935
Coweta	16,572	42,513	15,168	39,653
Crawford	1,419	3,632	1,706	3,368
Crisp	2,835	4,539	3,167	4,182
Dade	965	5,047	1,411	4,471
Dawson	1,444	9,880	1,241	8,847
Decatur	4,104	6,009	4,591	5,824

County	2016 Clinton (D)	Trump (R)	2012 Obama (D)	Romney (R)
DeKalb	239,131	47,531	238,224	64,392
Dodge	1,836	5,021	2,442	5,214
Dooly	1,860	1,941	2,285	1,985
Dougherty	23,224	10,227	26,295	11,449
Douglas	30,971	24,803	28,441	26,241
Early	2,165	2,552	2,765	2,557
Echols	156	1,006	173	917
Effingham	4,851	17,865	4,947	15,596
Elbert	2,507	5,269	3,181	4,859
Emanuel	2,433	5,330	2,927	5,100
Evans	1,130	2,404	1,268	2,268
Fannin	1,920	9,622	2,028	7,857
Fayette	23,255	35,034	19,736	38,075
Floyd	9,127	24,045	9,640	22,733
Forsyth	23,427	69,801	14,571	65,908
Franklin	1,243	7,054	1,499	6,114
Fulton	281,875	110,372	255,470	137,124
Gilmer	1,955	10,465	1,958	8,926
Glascock	138	1,235	176	1,135
Glynn	11,738	21,482	11,950	20,893
Gordon	3,176	15,171	3,440	13,197
Grady	2,930	6,012	3,419	5,924
Greene	3,194	5,488	3,201	5,071
Gwinnett	165,063	146,463	132,509	159,855
Habersham	2,483	13,184	2,301	12,166
Hall	16,153	51,681	12,999	47,481
Hancock	2,695	841	3,308	769
Haralson	1,474	9,579	1,789	8,446
Harris	4,002	11,931	4,145	11,197
Hart	2,583	7,285	2,870	6,517
Heard	743	3,370	948	3,160
Henry	49,902	45,641	43,761	46,774
Houston	21,397	33,897	22,702	34,662
Irwin	890	2,711	1,141	2,538
Jackson	4,469	21,754	4,238	19,135
Jasper	1,544	4,353	1,845	4,136
Jeff Davis	901	4,102	1,275	3,996
Jefferson	3,809	3,057	4,261	2,999
Jenkins	1,108	1,892	1,488	1,887
Johnson	1,136	2,519	1,305	2,440
Jones	3,960	8,304	4,274	7,744
Lamar	2,267	5,183	2,602	4,899
Lanier	805	1,984	1,114	1,820
Laurens	6,737	12,401	7,513	11,950
Lee	3,166	10,641	3,196	10,314
Liberty	9,531	6,125	10,457	5,565
Lincoln	1,271	2,759	1,586	2,807
Long	1,356	2,623	1,442	2,306
Lowndes	14,614	21,308	17,470	21,327
Lumpkin	2,216	9,613	2,055	8,647
Macon	2,705	1,540	3,211	1,545
Madison	2,423	9,195	2,494	8,443
Marion	1,213	1,921	1,412	1,733
McDuffie	3,699	5,432	4,044	5,475
McIntosh	2,298	3,482	2,864	3,409
Meriwether	3,800	5,216	4,331	4,856
Miller	622	1,888	852	1,905
Mitchell	3,492	4,272	4,081	4,155
Monroe	3,570	8,821	3,785	8,361
Montgomery	847	2,668	1,135	2,662
Morgan	2,658	6,559	2,753	6,186
Murray	1,799	10,340	2,542	8,443
Muscogee	39,602	26,901	42,573	27,510
Newton	21,936	20,907	21,851	20,982
Oconee	5,253	12,885	4,421	13,098
Oglethorpe	1,829	4,622	1,914	4,251
Paulding	18,004	44,646	15,825	40,846
Peach	5,083	5,405	6,148	5,287
Pickens	1,977	11,651	1,975	10,547
Pierce	903	6,301	1,124	5,667
Pike	1,239	7,273	1,356	6,668
Polk	2,863	11,006	3,615	9,811
Pulaski	1,104	2,436	1,219	2,444
Putnam	2,745	6,516	2,926	6,215
Quitman	461	575	612	510
Rabun	1,443	6,287	1,559	5,754
Randolph	1,597	1,270	1,770	1,271
Richmond	48,707	24,441	52,560	25,845
Rockdale	23,206	13,463	22,023	15,716
Schley	401	1,472	448	1,286
Screven	2,300	3,305	2,774	3,287
Seminole	1,186	2,343	1,478	2,245
Spalding	9,347	15,636	9,898	14,911
Stephens	1,835	7,682	2,131	7,221
Stewart	1,220	805	1,323	745
Sumter	5,520	5,275	6,375	5,378
Talbot	2,001	1,196	2,265	1,202
Taliaferro	545	349	636	323
Tattnall	1,678	5,092	1,897	4,706
Taylor	1,295	2,062	1,572	1,948
Telfair	1,313	2,449	1,805	2,480
Terrell	2,267	1,872	2,544	1,834
Thomas	7,138	11,225	7,653	11,156
Tift	3,892	8,680	4,660	9,185
Toombs	2,338	6,612	2,746	6,524
Towns	1,206	5,377	1,273	4,876
Treutlen	860	1,808	1,074	1,652
Troup	9,597	15,643	10,547	15,179
Turner	1,243	2,094	1,510	2,028
Twiggs	1,970	2,034	2,270	1,907
Union	1,962	9,849	2,139	8,773
Upson	3,471	7,288	3,959	7,230
Walker	4,213	18,938	5,274	16,247
Walton	8,279	31,093	8,148	29,036
Ware	3,436	8,508	3,900	7,941
Warren	1,313	991	1,529	990
Washington	4,187	4,138	4,714	4,035
Wayne	2,039	8,147	2,596	7,557
Webster	471	630	582	601
Wheeler	646	1,421	772	1,366
White	1,672	9,751	1,671	8,651
Whitfield	7,925	21,514	7,210	19,305
Wilcox	852	2,006	1,060	2,053
Wilkes	1,844	2,569	2,087	2,635
Wilkinson	1,893	2,332	2,181	2,246
Worth	2,015	6,144	2,487	5,869
Totals	**1,834,537**	**2,066,200**	**1,773,827**	**2,078,688**

All candidates, 2016: Trump, R, 2,066,200; Clinton, D, 1,834,537; Johnson, LB, 124,638.

Hawaii

County	2016 Clinton (D)	Trump (R)	2012 Obama (D)	Romney (R)
Hawaii	40,484	17,209	47,224	14,753
Honolulu	163,621	84,142	204,349	88,461
Kauai	16,456	7,574	18,641	6,121
Maui	31,292	12,723	36,052	11,602
Overseas	NA	NA	392	78
Totals	**251,853**	**121,648**	**306,658**	**121,015**

All candidates, 2016: Clinton, D, 251,853; Trump, R, 121,648; Johnson, LB, 14,854; Stein, Green, 11,608; Castle, Const., 4,191.

Idaho

County	2016 Clinton (D)	Trump (R)	2012 Obama (D)	Romney (R)
Ada	75,676	93,748	77,137	97,554
Adams	415	1,556	577	1,413
Bannock	10,342	17,180	13,214	21,010
Bear Lake	255	2,203	302	2,489
Benewah	780	3,101	1,164	2,596
Bingham	2,924	10,907	3,822	13,440
Blaine	6,416	3,340	5,992	3,939
Boise	777	2,673	1,053	2,284
Bonner	1,052	1,578	6,500	11,367
Bonneville	8,930	26,699	9,903	32,276
Boundary	933	3,789	1,225	3,138
Butte	160	914	258	1,001
Camas	110	410	159	402
Canyon	13,140	36,332	19,866	44,369
Caribou	271	2,275	386	2,608
Cassia	1,036	5,949	1,098	7,154
Clark	44	203	66	235
Clearwater	704	2,852	1,032	2,541
Custer	427	1,777	530	1,744
Elmore	1,814	5,816	2,513	5,227
Franklin	385	3,901	325	5,195
Fremont	651	4,091	810	4,907
Gem	1,229	5,980	1,957	5,311
Gooding	930	3,743	1,287	3,696
Idaho	1,196	6,441	1,708	5,921

County	2016 Clinton (D)	2016 Trump (R)	2012 Obama (D)	2012 Romney (R)
Jefferson	976	8,436	1,303	9,895
Jerome	2,117	7,347	1,699	4,804
Kootenai	16,264	44,449	18,851	39,381
Latah	8,093	7,255	8,306	7,589
Lemhi	733	3,011	960	3,029
Lewis	270	1,202	396	1,173
Lincoln	360	1,184	469	1,141
Madison	1,201	8,941	832	13,445
Minidoka	1,167	4,887	1,390	5,442
Nez Perce	4,828	10,699	6,451	9,967
Oneida	184	1,531	217	1,838
Owyhee	591	3,052	833	2,794
Payette	892	4,306	2,271	6,004
Power	699	1,666	982	1,870
Shoshone	1,384	3,297	2,277	2,699
Teton	2,157	2,161	1,926	2,458
Twin Falls	6,844	21,063	7,541	19,773
Valley	1,913	2,906	2,095	2,664
Washington	776	3,283	1,104	3,128
Totals	**182,046**	**388,134**	**212,787**	**420,911**

All candidates, 2016: Trump, R, 388,134; Clinton, D, 182,046; McMullin, Ind., 45,193; Johnson, LB, 27,038; Stein, Ind., 7,964; Castle, Ind., 4,215; Copeland, Const., 2,219; De La Fuente, Ind., 1,313.

Illinois

County	2016 Clinton (D)	2016 Trump (R)	2012 Obama (D)	2012 Romney (R)
Adams	7,376	21,957	9,648	20,416
Alexander	1,262	1,496	1,965	1,487
Bond	2,066	4,884	3,020	4,095
Boone	8,952	12,261	9,883	11,096
Brown	475	1,776	787	1,513
Bureau	6,010	9,264	8,134	8,164
Calhoun	739	1,719	1,080	1,440
Carroll	2,437	4,428	3,665	3,555
Cass	1,617	3,216	2,053	2,707
Champaign	49,694	33,235	40,831	35,312
Christian	3,982	10,522	5,494	8,885
Clark	1,873	5,620	2,591	5,144
Clay	1,014	5,009	1,584	4,190
Clinton	3,939	12,394	5,596	10,524
Coles	5,642	11,298	9,262	11,631
Cook	1,527,618	439,513	1,488,537	495,542
Crawford	1,969	6,146	2,858	5,585
Cumberland	1,028	4,200	1,641	3,509
DeKalb	20,348	19,051	21,207	18,934
DeWitt	1,907	5,072	2,601	4,579
Douglas	1,946	5,695	2,430	5,334
DuPage	222,499	164,355	199,460	195,046
Edgar	1,778	5,634	2,565	5,132
Edwards	432	2,777	754	2,405
Effingham	3,071	13,613	3,861	12,501
Fayette	1,814	7,363	2,853	5,951
Ford	1,410	4,474	1,656	4,229
Franklin	4,711	13,101	7,254	10,267
Fulton	6,118	8,482	8,328	6,632
Gallatin	656	1,942	1,029	1,492
Greene	1,202	4,139	2,023	3,451
Grundy	8,021	13,417	9,451	11,343
Hamilton	800	3,205	1,269	2,566
Hancock	1,744	5,713	3,650	5,271
Hardin	419	1,650	742	1,535
Henderson	1,151	2,153	1,978	1,541
Henry	8,835	13,962	12,332	11,583
Iroquois	2,496	9,728	3,413	9,120
Jackson	11,619	10,889	13,319	9,864
Jasper	924	3,973	1,436	3,514
Jefferson	4,408	11,681	6,089	9,811
Jersey	2,673	7,737	3,667	6,039
Jo Daviess	4,452	6,113	5,667	5,534
Johnson	1,135	4,644	1,572	3,963
Kane	99,389	82,087	90,332	88,335
Kankakee	18,908	25,081	21,595	23,136
Kendall	23,392	24,152	22,471	24,047
Knox	9,939	10,658	13,451	9,408
Lake	168,186	108,608	153,757	129,764
LaSalle	19,277	26,269	23,073	23,256
Lawrence	1,288	4,517	2,011	3,857
Lee	5,499	8,597	6,937	8,059
Livingston	4,005	10,197	5,020	9,753
Logan	3,301	8,167	3,978	7,844
Macon	18,211	26,782	22,780	25,309
Macoupin	6,532	14,194	9,464	10,946

County	2016 Clinton (D)	2016 Trump (R)	2012 Obama (D)	2012 Romney (R)
Madison	50,336	70,295	58,922	60,608
Marion	4,231	11,677	6,225	9,248
Marshall	1,784	3,776	2,455	3,290
Mason	2,008	4,051	2,867	3,265
Massac	1,555	4,844	2,092	4,278
McDonough	5,278	6,789	5,967	6,147
McHenry	59,827	71,117	59,797	71,598
McLean	35,918	37,081	31,883	39,947
Menard	1,808	4,230	2,100	3,948
Mercer	3,061	4,800	4,507	3,876
Monroe	5,522	12,614	6,215	10,888
Montgomery	3,490	8,616	5,058	6,776
Morgan	4,693	9,060	5,806	7,972
Moultrie	1,476	4,453	2,144	3,784
Ogle	8,025	14,344	9,514	13,422
Peoria	37,436	35,299	40,209	36,774
Perry	2,433	6,816	3,819	5,507
Piatt	2,633	5,623	3,090	5,413
Pike	1,412	5,749	2,278	4,860
Pope	374	1,678	650	1,512
Pulaski	817	1,583	1,389	1,564
Putnam	1,143	1,762	1,559	1,502
Randolph	3,421	9,992	5,759	8,290
Richland	1,579	5,736	2,362	4,756
Rock Island	32,258	26,969	39,157	24,934
St. Clair	60,180	53,479	67,285	50,125
Saline	2,551	8,248	3,701	6,806
Sangamon	40,731	49,823	42,107	50,225
Schuyler	1,074	2,523	1,727	2,069
Scott	528	1,965	910	1,587
Shelby	2,279	8,209	3,342	6,843
Stark	748	1,777	1,095	1,528
Stephenson	7,531	10,845	10,165	10,512
Tazewell	20,568	38,620	24,438	35,335
Union	2,389	5,780	3,137	4,957
Vermilion	9,876	18,582	12,878	16,892
Wabash	1,146	4,039	1,590	3,478
Warren	2,983	4,267	4,044	3,618
Washington	1,446	5,566	2,450	4,792
Wayne	1,048	6,963	1,514	5,988
White	1,412	5,639	2,188	4,731
Whiteside	11,005	12,597	14,833	10,448
Will	146,230	129,726	144,229	128,969
Williamson	8,539	21,503	10,647	17,909
Winnebago	52,595	53,922	61,732	55,138
Woodford	5,068	13,180	5,572	12,961
Totals	**2,974,634**	**2,115,017**	**3,019,512**	**2,135,216**

All candidates, 2016: Clinton, D, 2,974,634; Trump, R, 2,115,017; Johnson, LB, 204,226; Stein, Green, 74,016.

Indiana

County	2016 Clinton (D)	2016 Trump (R)	2012 Obama (D)	2012 Romney (R)
Adams	2,802	9,642	3,806	8,937
Allen	55,222	83,801	60,036	84,613
Bartholomew	9,841	20,637	10,625	18,083
Benton	860	2,579	1,159	2,329
Blackford	1,243	3,349	1,927	2,711
Boone	10,181	19,654	8,328	18,808
Brown	2,518	5,015	3,060	4,332
Carroll	1,891	6,273	2,635	4,999
Cass	3,758	9,697	5,371	8,443
Clark	14,028	24,110	20,807	25,450
Clay	2,306	8,528	3,460	7,096
Clinton	2,819	8,530	3,308	6,338
Crawford	1,323	3,013	2,041	2,421
Daviess	1,800	8,545	2,437	7,638
Dearborn	4,883	18,110	6,528	15,394
Decatur	2,121	8,488	2,941	7,119
DeKalb	3,941	12,054	5,419	10,587
Delaware	18,100	24,217	22,654	21,251
Dubois	5,389	13,365	6,522	11,654
Elkhart	20,667	41,810	24,399	42,378
Fayette	2,223	6,783	3,555	5,045
Floyd	13,939	21,427	14,812	19,878
Fountain	1,476	5,661	2,237	4,664
Franklin	1,967	8,665	2,909	7,424
Fulton	1,960	6,010	2,621	5,317
Gibson	3,720	11,079	4,928	9,487
Grant	7,029	17,009	9,589	15,151
Greene	2,929	10,275	4,350	8,457

County	2016 Clinton (D)	Trump (R)	2012 Obama (D)	Romney (R)
Hamilton	57,214	87,299	43,796	90,747
Hancock	8,901	25,050	9,319	22,796
Harrison	4,776	12,993	6,607	10,640
Hendricks	22,595	48,326	21,112	44,312
Henry	5,124	13,895	7,613	10,838
Howard	11,215	23,675	15,135	20,327
Huntington	3,506	11,649	4,596	10,862
Jackson	3,843	12,857	5,838	10,419
Jasper	3,329	9,382	4,672	7,955
Jay	1,889	5,697	3,063	4,645
Jefferson	4,325	8,538	5,728	7,096
Jennings	1,638	6,470	3,821	6,120
Johnson	17,318	45,456	17,260	39,513
Knox	3,772	11,077	5,228	9,612
Kosciusko	6,311	23,909	6,862	22,558
LaGrange	2,080	7,025	2,898	6,231
Lake	116,896	75,565	130,897	68,431
LaPorte	19,725	22,619	24,107	18,615
Lawrence	4,210	14,034	5,779	11,622
Madison	18,595	32,376	24,407	26,769
Marion	209,920	129,028	216,336	136,509
Marshall	4,798	12,286	6,137	11,260
Martin	881	3,695	1,351	3,262
Miami	2,766	9,975	4,222	8,174
Monroe	34,183	20,527	33,436	22,481
Montgomery	3,362	11,051	4,271	9,824
Morgan	6,037	23,671	7,969	19,591
Newton	1,403	4,074	2,212	3,291
Noble	3,904	10,108	5,229	10,680
Ohio	686	2,118	994	1,759
Orange	2,048	5,800	2,939	4,617
Owen	1,946	6,151	2,823	5,062
Parke	1,441	4,863	2,110	4,234
Perry	3,062	4,556	4,316	3,403
Pike	1,297	4,398	2,125	3,627
Porter	33,531	38,719	37,252	34,406
Posey	3,515	8,393	4,533	7,430
Pulaski	1,327	3,854	1,899	3,366
Putnam	3,356	10,637	4,507	9,005
Randolph	2,446	7,515	3,769	6,218
Ripley	2,471	9,806	3,241	7,484
Rush	1,525	5,292	2,221	4,633
St. Joseph	52,247	52,019	56,460	52,578
Scott	2,642	6,074	3,998	4,539
Shelby	4,247	12,718	5,359	10,978
Spencer	2,861	6,572	4,026	5,515
Starke	2,489	6,367	3,809	4,738
Steuben	3,741	10,127	4,853	8,547
Sullivan	2,113	6,138	3,191	4,902
Switzerland	930	2,558	1,437	1,872
Tippecanoe	27,207	30,711	26,711	28,757
Tipton	1,587	5,589	2,432	4,773
Union	715	2,445	1,018	2,022
Vanderburgh	28,296	40,422	31,725	39,389
Vermillion	2,081	4,511	2,979	3,426
Vigo	15,922	21,924	19,712	19,369
Wabash	3,018	9,819	3,973	8,644
Warren	839	2,896	1,324	2,377
Warrick	9,086	19,133	8,793	15,351
Washington	2,636	8,204	3,909	6,533
Wayne	8,322	16,028	10,591	14,321
Wells	2,585	9,999	3,436	9,256
White	2,563	6,813	3,637	5,970
Whitley	3,379	11,357	4,420	10,258
Totals	**1,023,609**	**1,547,249**	**1,152,887**	**1,420,543**

All candidates, 2016: Trump, R, 1,547,249; Clinton, D, 1,023,609; Johnson, LB, 133,021.

Iowa

County	2016 Clinton (D)	Trump (R)	2012 Obama (D)	Romney (R)
Adair	1,127	2,456	1,790	2,114
Adams	565	1,393	1,028	1,108
Allamakee	2,409	4,072	3,553	3,264
Appanoose	1,813	4,031	2,951	3,161
Audubon	1,079	2,135	1,611	1,802
Benton	4,672	8,226	6,862	6,940
Black Hawk	32,006	27,382	39,821	26,235
Boone	5,517	7,458	7,512	6,556
Bremer	5,349	7,199	6,763	6,405

County	2016 Clinton (D)	Trump (R)	2012 Obama (D)	Romney (R)
Buchanan	3,966	5,504	5,911	4,450
Buena Vista	2,851	4,895	3,700	4,554
Butler	2,163	4,918	3,329	4,106
Calhoun	1,396	3,466	2,238	2,891
Carroll	3,305	6,627	4,947	5,601
Cass	1,946	4,755	2,858	4,217
Cedar	3,578	5,275	4,972	4,529
Cerro Gordo	9,840	11,583	13,316	10,128
Cherokee	1,676	4,188	2,634	3,662
Chickasaw	2,264	3,739	3,554	2,836
Clarke	1,463	2,706	2,189	2,124
Clay	2,246	5,870	3,385	4,951
Clayton	3,236	5,309	4,806	4,164
Clinton	10,079	11,249	15,141	9,432
Crawford	1,985	4,608	3,066	3,595
Dallas	15,662	19,288	16,576	20,988
Davis	976	2,721	1,520	2,138
Decatur	1,201	2,296	1,791	1,947
Delaware	2,956	5,688	4,616	4,636
Des Moines	8,178	9,479	11,888	8,136
Dickinson	3,051	6,743	4,095	5,912
Dubuque	22,774	23,384	28,768	21,280
Emmet	1,356	3,121	2,099	2,507
Fayette	3,666	5,591	5,732	4,492
Floyd	3,177	4,371	4,680	3,472
Franklin	1,490	3,153	2,266	2,823
Fremont	959	2,401	1,637	1,972
Greene	1,688	2,819	2,375	2,380
Grundy	1,847	4,516	2,635	4,215
Guthrie	1,720	3,000	2,569	3,171
Hamilton	2,715	4,450	3,782	3,991
Hancock	1,582	3,972	2,521	3,317
Hardin	2,774	5,231	4,075	4,670
Harrison	2,123	4,892	3,136	4,065
Henry	2,897	5,764	4,460	5,035
Howard	1,674	2,611	2,768	1,795
Humboldt	1,251	3,564	1,972	3,099
Ida	792	2,655	1,321	2,286
Iowa	3,070	5,193	4,144	4,569
Jackson	3,837	5,821	5,907	4,177
Jasper	7,108	10,556	10,257	8,877
Jefferson	3,702	3,738	4,798	3,436
Johnson	49,942	20,993	50,666	23,698
Jones	3,779	5,718	5,534	4,721
Keokuk	1,265	3,385	2,303	2,843
Kossuth	4,694	5,607	3,850	4,937
Lee	6,195	8,762	10,714	7,785
Linn	58,071	47,827	68,581	47,622
Louisa	1,643	3,060	2,452	2,420
Lucas	1,236	2,873	1,987	2,254
Lyon	917	5,188	1,423	4,978
Madison	2,666	5,336	3,630	4,638
Mahaska	2,606	7,404	4,213	6,448
Marion	5,469	10,940	7,507	9,828
Marshall	7,550	8,910	10,257	8,472
Mills	2,080	5,050	2,848	4,216
Mitchell	1,879	3,180	2,831	2,643
Monona	1,244	3,115	2,101	2,557
Monroe	1,053	2,635	1,731	2,026
Montgomery	1,312	3,431	1,922	3,001
Muscatine	8,284	9,549	11,323	8,168
O'Brien	1,314	5,735	1,969	5,266
Osceola	552	2,528	912	2,230
Page	1,801	4,875	2,613	4,348
Palo Alto	1,395	3,079	2,139	2,660
Plymouth	2,878	9,659	4,164	8,597
Pocahontas	962	2,692	1,523	2,396
Polk	119,671	93,421	128,465	96,096
Pottawattamie	15,306	24,421	19,644	21,860
Poweshiek	4,272	4,936	5,357	4,424
Ringgold	753	1,820	1,186	1,368
Sac	1,269	3,692	2,122	3,094
Scott	40,302	39,083	50,652	38,251
Shelby	1,649	4,340	2,469	3,911
Sioux	2,289	14,761	2,700	14,407
Story	25,085	19,111	26,192	19,668
Tama	3,194	4,968	4,768	4,098
Taylor	755	2,108	1,262	1,683
Union	1,920	3,521	3,043	2,813
Van Buren	843	2,524	1,402	2,064

County	2016 Clinton (D)	Trump (R)	2012 Obama (D)	Romney (R)
Wapello	5,591	8,710	8,663	6,789
Warren	10,371	14,773	12,551	13,052
Washington	3,938	6,170	5,115	5,562
Wayne	719	2,069	1,251	1,583
Webster	6,293	10,049	9,537	8,469
Winnebago	1,920	3,437	2,903	2,906
Winneshiek	5,238	5,332	6,256	4,622
Woodbury	16,102	24,627	22,302	21,841
Worth	1,523	2,443	2,350	1,744
Wright	1,890	3,790	2,836	3,349
Totals	**652,437**	**798,302**	**822,544**	**730,617**

All candidates, 2016: Trump, R, 798,302; Clinton, D, 652,437; Johnson, LB, 57,380; McMullin, unaff., 12,242; Stein, Green, 11,180; Castle, Const., 7,283; Vacek, Legal Marijuana, 2,301; Kahn, New Ind., 2,174; De La Fuente, RF, 477; La Riva, Socialism/Liberation, 323.

Kansas

County	2016 Clinton (D)	Trump (R)	2012 Obama (D)	Romney (R)
Allen	1,398	3,575	1,869	3,316
Anderson	665	2,386	944	2,276
Atchison	1,946	3,977	2,567	3,917
Barber	281	1,822	482	1,772
Barton	1,823	7,766	2,297	7,874
Bourbon	1,306	4,314	1,996	4,102
Brown	850	2,860	1,076	2,829
Butler	6,489	18,781	7,282	18,157
Chase	313	964	358	875
Chautauqua	236	1,552	280	1,304
Cherokee	1,959	6,017	2,930	5,456
Cheyenne	188	1,172	233	1,159
Clark	118	813	174	805
Clay	665	2,831	834	2,788
Cloud	744	2,856	974	2,954
Coffey	719	2,990	898	2,903
Comanche	102	705	143	767
Cowley	3,436	8,016	4,319	8,081
Crawford	5,064	8,394	6,826	7,708
Decatur	178	1,220	266	1,218
Dickinson	1,582	5,905	2,020	5,832
Doniphan	584	2,601	902	2,414
Douglas	30,089	14,308	29,267	17,401
Edwards	208	1,033	298	1,059
Elk	160	1,048	281	1,049
Ellis	2,669	8,311	3,057	8,399
Ellsworth	515	1,933	702	1,930
Finney	3,006	6,155	2,682	6,219
Ford	2,032	4,994	2,600	5,602
Franklin	2,829	7,025	3,694	6,984
Geary	2,569	4,116	3,332	4,372
Gove	149	1,127	176	1,168
Graham	185	1,013	256	1,056
Grant	427	1,755	456	1,811
Gray	257	1,651	324	1,603
Greeley	83	523	113	543
Greenwood	484	2,146	478	1,590
Hamilton	114	690	163	693
Harper	388	1,950	550	1,759
Harvey	5,006	8,503	5,373	8,588
Haskell	228	1,011	215	1,159
Hodgeman	124	845	179	868
Jackson	1,489	3,888	1,901	3,527
Jefferson	2,483	5,112	2,977	4,827
Jewell	180	1,204	229	1,235
Johnson	125,214	133,022	110,526	158,401
Kearny	224	1,048	268	1,097
Kingman	594	2,507	733	2,397
Kiowa	111	855	163	976
Labette	2,234	5,232	3,117	4,742
Lane	104	684	172	739
Leavenworth	10,064	17,387	11,357	17,059
Lincoln	214	1,168	289	1,165
Linn	721	3,377	1,170	3,177
Logan	149	1,124	197	1,126
Lyon	4,456	6,354	5,111	6,470
Marion	1,177	3,928	1,385	3,889
Marshall	1,060	3,250	1,469	3,195
McPherson	3,183	8,407	3,449	8,545
Meade	206	1,390	258	1,428
Miami	3,949	9,839	4,712	9,858
Mitchell	469	2,216	584	2,327
Montgomery	2,557	8,466	3,501	8,630
Morris	586	1,790	718	1,773

County	2016 Clinton (D)	Trump (R)	2012 Obama (D)	Romney (R)
Morton	145	970	189	1,072
Nemaha	714	4,066	1,000	3,930
Neosho	1,464	4,340	2,050	4,272
Ness	160	1,216	218	1,209
Norton	277	1,808	398	1,878
Osage	1,730	4,713	2,268	4,427
Osborne	231	1,437	324	1,479
Ottawa	424	2,261	558	2,295
Pawnee	567	1,872	718	1,836
Phillips	296	2,200	382	2,135
Pottawatomie	2,191	7,451	2,335	6,804
Pratt	769	2,824	980	2,771
Rawlins	160	1,209	190	1,223
Reno	6,670	15,100	8,085	15,718
Republic	370	1,993	477	2,134
Rice	668	2,652	911	2,676
Riley	8,892	9,817	8,977	11,507
Rooks	273	1,999	361	2,038
Rush	227	1,177	367	1,166
Russell	454	2,544	593	2,553
Saline	6,084	13,367	7,040	13,840
Scott	232	1,832	277	1,728
Sedgwick	66,716	101,319	71,977	106,506
Seward	1,491	3,025	1,490	3,617
Shawnee	33,074	35,260	36,975	37,782
Sheridan	126	1,186	168	1,154
Sherman	340	2,043	577	1,976
Smith	295	1,635	358	1,624
Stafford	303	1,485	404	1,385
Stanton	132	580	143	605
Stevens	215	1,564	252	1,749
Sumner	2,039	6,844	2,658	6,260
Thomas	467	2,832	598	2,788
Trego	193	1,211	291	1,261
Wabaunsee	773	2,358	918	2,256
Wallace	45	711	68	719
Washington	378	2,136	524	2,316
Wichita	139	765	157	821
Wilson	550	2,747	1,636	5,650
Woodson	270	1,063	380	1,035
Wyandotte	29,346	15,520	34,302	15,496
Totals	**413,482**	**655,034**	**440,726**	**692,634**

All candidates, 2016: Trump, R, 655,034; Clinton, D, 413,482; Johnson, LB, 53,476; Stein, Ind., 22,628.

Kentucky

County	2016 Clinton (D)	Trump (R)	2012 Obama (D)	Romney (R)
Adair	1,323	6,637	1,660	5,841
Allen	1,349	6,466	1,808	5,184
Anderson	2,634	8,242	3,315	6,822
Ballard	816	3,161	1,189	2,647
Barren	4,275	13,483	5,400	10,922
Bath	1,361	3,082	1,770	2,275
Bell	1,720	7,764	2,224	7,127
Boone	15,026	39,082	15,629	35,922
Bourbon	2,791	5,569	3,075	4,692
Boyd	6,021	13,591	7,776	10,884
Boyle	4,281	8,040	4,471	7,703
Bracken	705	2,711	1,147	2,029
Breathitt	1,537	3,991	1,562	3,318
Breckinridge	1,960	6,484	2,825	5,025
Bullitt	8,255	26,210	9,971	21,306
Butler	947	4,428	1,293	3,716
Caldwell	1,260	4,507	1,852	3,904
Calloway	4,749	10,367	5,317	9,440
Campbell	14,658	25,050	15,080	24,240
Carlisle	432	2,094	750	1,835
Carroll	1,106	2,588	1,629	1,999
Carter	2,276	7,587	3,383	5,279
Casey	767	5,482	1,086	4,904
Christian	7,188	14,108	8,252	13,475
Clark	4,706	10,710	5,228	9,931
Clay	752	5,861	1,111	6,176
Clinton	547	3,809	752	3,569
Crittenden	617	3,290	960	2,839
Cumberland	459	2,502	599	2,216
Daviess	14,163	28,907	16,208	25,092
Edmonson	979	4,135	1,374	3,232
Elliott	740	2,000	1,186	1,126
Estill	1,108	4,236	1,356	3,749
Fayette	69,776	56,890	62,080	60,795
Fleming	1,348	4,861	1,911	3,780
Floyd	4,015	11,993	4,733	9,784

County	2016 Clinton (D)	Trump (R)	2012 Obama (D)	Romney (R)
Franklin	10,717	11,819	11,535	11,345
Fulton	774	1,549	1,022	1,425
Gallatin	749	2,443	1,238	1,758
Garrard	1,453	5,904	1,661	5,310
Grant	1,910	7,268	2,810	5,664
Graves	3,308	12,671	4,547	10,699
Grayson	1,959	8,219	2,744	6,404
Green	832	4,372	1,165	3,634
Greenup	4,146	11,546	6,027	8,855
Hancock	1,244	2,788	1,833	2,212
Hardin	13,944	26,970	15,214	23,357
Harlan	1,372	9,129	1,830	8,652
Harrison	2,031	5,435	2,471	4,556
Hart	1,730	5,320	2,283	4,257
Henderson	6,707	12,159	8,091	10,296
Henry	1,828	4,944	2,530	3,940
Hickman	449	1,657	686	1,431
Hopkins	4,310	15,277	5,789	13,681
Jackson	482	4,889	612	4,365
Jefferson	190,824	143,758	186,181	148,423
Jessamine	6,144	15,474	6,001	14,233
Johnson	1,250	8,043	1,723	7,095
Kenton	24,213	42,958	24,920	41,389
Knott	1,245	4,357	1,420	4,130
Knox	1,761	9,885	2,484	8,467
LaRue	1,278	4,799	1,733	3,911
Laurel	3,440	20,592	3,905	18,151
Lawrence	1,045	4,816	1,520	3,995
Lee	444	2,151	595	1,977
Leslie	400	4,015	433	4,439
Letcher	1,542	7,293	1,702	6,811
Lewis	785	4,363	1,342	3,326
Lincoln	1,865	7,338	2,582	6,416
Livingston	887	3,570	1,346	3,089
Logan	2,755	7,778	3,469	6,899
Lyon	1,045	2,789	1,373	2,412
Madison	11,793	23,431	11,512	21,128
Magoffin	1,172	3,824	1,433	3,391
Marion	2,679	5,122	3,418	3,800
Marshall	3,672	12,322	5,022	10,402
Martin	363	3,503	574	3,180
Mason	1,970	4,944	2,592	4,197
McCracken	9,134	20,774	10,062	19,979
McCreary	664	5,012	1,069	4,564
McLean	988	3,381	1,432	2,705
Meade	3,026	8,660	4,122	6,606
Menifee	700	2,010	1,048	1,484
Mercer	2,395	7,740	2,966	6,820
Metcalfe	976	3,491	1,425	2,676
Monroe	601	4,278	936	3,762
Montgomery	3,158	7,856	3,701	6,398
Morgan	1,006	3,628	1,369	3,021
Muhlenberg	3,272	9,393	4,771	7,762
Nelson	6,434	13,430	7,611	10,673
Nicholas	787	1,957	948	1,583
Ohio	2,080	7,942	2,987	6,470
Oldham	10,268	20,469	9,240	20,179
Owen	1,142	3,745	1,501	2,971
Owsley	256	1,474	283	1,279
Pendleton	1,164	4,604	1,859	3,556
Perry	2,136	8,158	2,047	8,040
Pike	4,277	19,740	5,646	17,590
Powell	1,272	3,513	1,620	2,766
Pulaski	4,208	22,900	4,976	20,714
Robertson	222	759	340	579
Rockcastle	915	5,609	1,097	5,028
Rowan	3,295	5,174	3,438	4,035
Russell	1,093	6,863	1,445	6,346
Scott	7,713	15,052	7,532	12,679
Shelby	6,276	13,196	6,634	11,790
Simpson	2,144	5,077	2,650	4,355
Spencer	1,921	7,196	2,549	5,726
Taylor	2,553	8,320	3,285	7,551
Todd	1,042	3,612	1,403	3,247
Trigg	1,587	4,928	2,115	4,520
Trimble	879	2,771	1,355	2,133
Union	1,331	4,701	1,942	3,955
Warren	16,966	28,673	16,805	26,384
Washington	1,420	4,013	1,669	3,495
Wayne	1,431	6,370	1,855	5,289
Webster	1,240	4,397	1,765	3,607
Whitley	2,067	11,312	2,683	10,232
Wolfe	753	1,804	976	1,542

County	2016 Clinton (D)	Trump (R)	2012 Obama (D)	Romney (R)
Woodford	4,958	7,697	4,883	7,219
Totals	**628,914**	**1,203,081**	**679,370**	**1,087,190**

All candidates, 2016: Trump, R, 1,203,081; Clinton, D, 628,914; Johnson, LB, 53,747; McMullin, Ind., 22,651; Stein, Green, 13,988; De La Fuente, Amer. Delta, 1,240.

Louisiana

Parish	2016 Clinton (D)	Trump (R)	2012 Obama (D)	Romney (R)
Acadia	5,638	21,159	6,560	19,931
Allen	2,106	6,867	2,617	6,495
Ascension	16,471	36,135	16,349	33,856
Assumption	3,931	6,714	4,754	6,083
Avoyelles	5,032	11,163	6,077	10,670
Beauregard	2,393	12,238	2,828	11,112
Bienville	3,129	3,756	3,490	3,641
Bossier	12,638	35,451	12,956	34,988
Caddo	53,448	48,977	58,042	52,459
Calcasieu	26,293	54,182	28,359	51,850
Caldwell	788	3,822	1,016	3,640
Cameron	323	3,256	408	3,260
Catahoula	1,322	3,479	1,408	2,744
Claiborne	2,717	3,585	3,014	3,649
Concordia	3,272	5,474	3,833	5,450
DeSoto	5,163	8,067	5,553	7,353
East Baton Rouge	102,711	84,620	102,656	92,292
East Carroll	1,838	1,059	2,478	1,508
East Feliciana	4,235	5,569	4,648	5,397
Evangeline	4,208	10,357	5,330	10,181
Franklin	2,506	6,514	2,921	6,294
Grant	1,181	7,406	1,422	7,082
Iberia	10,698	20,903	12,132	20,892
Iberville	8,324	7,320	9,548	7,271
Jackson	2,139	5,169	2,305	5,132
Jefferson	73,540	100,292	70,384	102,536
Jefferson Davis	3,080	10,775	3,484	10,014
Lafayette	32,726	68,191	31,768	64,992
Lafourche	8,423	31,958	9,623	28,592
LaSalle	605	5,835	764	5,726
Lincoln	7,102	10,761	7,956	10,739
Livingston	6,950	48,797	7,451	45,513
Madison	2,744	1,927	3,154	2,000
Morehouse	5,155	6,502	5,888	6,591
Natchitoches	7,143	8,965	7,942	9,077
Orleans	133,833	24,267	126,722	28,003
Ouachita	24,420	41,712	26,645	40,948
Plaquemines	3,347	6,900	3,599	6,471
Pointe Coupee	4,764	6,789	5,436	6,548
Rapides	18,318	36,814	20,045	37,193
Red River	1,938	2,391	2,253	2,483
Richland	3,157	6,286	3,387	5,846
Sabine	1,703	7,877	2,194	7,738
St. Bernard	4,957	10,232	5,059	8,501
St. Charles	8,558	16,620	8,896	15,937
St. Helena	3,353	2,497	3,780	2,529
St. James	6,418	5,456	7,059	5,209
St. John the Baptist	12,658	7,569	13,179	7,620
St. Landry	17,208	21,966	19,668	21,475
St. Martin	8,266	16,872	9,422	15,653
St. Mary	8,050	14,353	9,450	13,885
St. Tammany	27,716	90,914	25,728	84,723
Tangipahoa	16,869	33,933	17,722	31,590
Tensas	1,329	1,180	1,564	1,230
Terrebonne	10,664	31,900	12,074	29,503
Union	2,691	7,972	3,075	7,561
Vermilion	4,745	19,807	5,720	18,910
Vernon	2,665	13,471	3,173	12,150
Washington	5,690	12,552	6,466	11,798
Webster	6,259	11,538	6,802	11,400
West Baton Rouge	5,382	6,926	5,692	6,922
West Carroll	715	3,970	853	3,628
West Feliciana	2,247	3,390	2,441	3,257
Winn	1,643	4,605	1,919	4,541
Totals	**779,535**	**1,178,004**	**809,141**	**1,152,262**

All candidates, 2016: Trump, R, 1,178,004; Clinton, D, 779,535; Johnson, LB, 37,950; Stein, Green, 14,018; McMullin, other, 8,546; Castle, Const., 3,128; Keniston, Veterans, 1,880; Hoefling, other, 1,581; Kotlikoff, other, 1,046; Jacob, other, 748; Kennedy, Soc. Workers, 480; La Riva, Socialism/Liberation, 446; White, other, 369.

Maine

City	2016 Clinton (D)	Trump (R)	2012 Obama (D)	Romney (R)
Auburn	5,296	5,324	6,503	4,462
Augusta	4,396	3,805	5,220	3,351
Bangor	8,146	5,993	8,781	5,788
Biddeford	5,605	3,729	6,618	3,047
Brunswick	7,991	3,646	7,900	3,670
Gorham	4,995	3,945	5,123	3,742
Lewiston	8,189	7,301	9,624	5,796
Portland	28,505	6,786	29,810	8,346
Saco	5,904	4,067	6,179	3,569
Sanford	4,438	4,733	5,588	3,701
Scarborough	5,193	4,051	6,351	5,187
South Portland	9,901	3,945	9,958	4,104
Westbrook	2,307	1,196	5,528	3,053
Other	240,724	261,321	288,123	234,460
Totals	341,590	319,842	401,306	292,276

All candidates, 2016: Clinton, D, 341,590; Trump, R, 319,842; Johnson, LB, 36,119; Stein, Green, 13,482.

Maryland

County	2016 Clinton (D)	Trump (R)	2012 Obama (D)	Romney (R)
Allegany	6,665	20,025	9,805	19,230
Anne Arundel	116,074	114,509	126,635	126,832
Baltimore	189,437	131,009	220,322	154,908
Calvert	16,669	24,680	20,529	23,952
Caroline	3,747	8,999	4,970	8,098
Carroll	24,314	55,593	27,939	56,761
Cecil	12,651	27,579	16,557	24,806
Charles	46,063	24,163	48,774	25,178
Dorchester	5,695	7,938	7,257	7,976
Frederick	51,891	56,472	55,146	58,798
Garrett	2,252	10,189	3,124	9,743
Harford	43,803	74,261	49,729	72,911
Howard	93,808	44,792	91,393	57,758
Kent	4,178	4,598	4,842	4,870
Montgomery	309,761	82,985	323,400	123,353
Prince George's	313,627	29,290	347,938	35,734
Queen Anne's	7,316	16,211	8,556	15,823
St. Mary's	15,786	26,889	19,711	26,797
Somerset	3,484	5,056	5,240	5,042
Talbot	7,865	10,098	8,808	11,339
Washington	19,193	38,842	25,042	36,074
Wicomico	16,327	20,832	19,635	21,764
Worcester	8,783	15,910	11,014	15,951
City				
Baltimore	178,562	22,726	221,478	28,171
Totals	1,497,951	873,646	1,677,844	971,869

All candidates, 2016: Clinton, D, 1,497,951; Trump, R, 873,646; Johnson, LB, 71,107; Stein, Green, 31,966.

Massachusetts

City	2016 Clinton (D)	Trump (R)	2012 Obama (D)	Romney (R)
Arlington	20,159	4,625	18,850	6,694
Boston	216,754	37,756	200,190	48,985
Brockton	25,075	8,707	25,262	8,710
Brookline	23,913	3,137	22,277	5,880
Cambridge	44,835	3,262	43,515	5,476
Fall River	17,272	10,792	21,878	7,390
Framingham	20,277	7,031	18,499	8,978
Haverhill	15,104	11,809	15,592	11,894
Lawrence	19,689	3,517	18,278	3,462
Lowell	23,186	10,495	22,771	10,643
Lynn	21,841	9,174	23,124	8,512
Malden	15,759	5,536	15,010	5,730
Medford	20,037	7,561	18,874	8,359
New Bedford	20,749	10,319	25,253	7,550
Newton	35,395	7,644	32,099	12,154
Peabody	14,385	12,029	15,027	11,622
Pittsfield	13,767	4,736	15,648	4,057
Plymouth	15,323	14,168	15,233	14,347
Quincy	25,298	13,297	24,849	14,850
Somerville	32,903	4,064	28,853	4,885
Springfield	38,235	10,890	43,869	10,515
Waltham	17,103	7,494	15,906	8,856
Weymouth	15,278	11,951	15,166	12,362
Worcester	42,534	17,634	42,210	17,949
Other	1,205,770	842,504	1,183,057	928,454
Totals	1,960,641	1,080,132	1,921,290	1,188,314

All candidates, 2016: Clinton, D, 1,960,641; Trump, R, 1,080,132; Johnson, LB, 136,471; Stein, Green, 46,819.

Michigan

County	2016 Clinton (D)	Trump (R)	2012 Obama (D)	Romney (R)
Alcona	1,732	4,201	2,472	3,571
Alger	1,663	2,585	2,212	2,330
Allegan	17,932	33,812	20,806	31,123
Alpena	4,877	9,090	6,549	7,298
Antrim	4,448	8,469	5,107	7,917
Arenac	2,238	4,704	3,669	4,057
Baraga	1,156	2,158	1,574	1,866
Barry	9,109	19,197	11,491	16,655
Bay	21,641	28,327	27,877	24,911
Benzie	4,108	5,539	4,685	5,075
Berrien	29,496	38,646	33,465	38,209
Branch	4,740	11,025	6,913	10,035
Calhoun	24,154	31,489	29,267	28,333
Cass	7,270	14,241	9,591	12,659
Charlevoix	5,137	8,674	5,939	8,000
Cheboygan	4,302	8,680	5,831	7,286
Chippewa	5,378	9,120	7,100	8,278
Clare	4,250	8,507	6,338	6,988
Clinton	16,490	21,635	18,191	20,650
Crawford	2,110	4,354	2,994	3,744
Delta	6,431	11,112	8,330	9,534
Dickinson	3,923	8,580	4,952	7,688
Eaton	24,534	27,608	27,913	26,197
Emmet	6,972	10,617	7,225	10,253
Genesee	102,744	84,174	128,978	71,808
Gladwin	3,794	8,124	5,760	6,661
Gogebic	2,925	4,019	4,058	3,444
Grand Traverse	20,780	26,839	20,875	26,534
Gratiot	5,665	9,878	7,610	8,241
Hillsdale	4,799	14,094	7,106	11,727
Houghton	6,018	8,475	6,801	8,196
Huron	4,579	10,629	6,518	8,806
Ingham	80,015	44,346	80,847	45,306
Ionia	8,206	16,374	11,018	14,315
Iosco	4,344	8,344	6,242	6,909
Iron	2,004	3,675	2,687	3,224
Isabella	11,404	12,338	13,038	10,800
Jackson	25,795	39,793	32,301	36,298
Kalamazoo	67,142	51,031	69,051	52,662
Kalkaska	2,279	6,213	3,272	4,901
Kent	138,567	147,959	133,408	155,925
Keweenaw	527	814	582	774
Lake	1,939	3,159	2,752	2,487
Lapeer	12,734	30,037	18,796	23,734
Leelanau	6,774	7,239	6,576	7,483
Lenawee	16,750	26,428	21,776	22,351
Livingston	34,378	65,665	37,216	60,083
Luce	681	1,756	991	1,580
Mackinac	2,085	3,740	2,652	3,397
Macomb	176,238	224,589	208,016	191,913
Manistee	4,979	6,915	6,473	5,737
Marquette	16,042	14,646	18,115	13,606
Mason	5,281	8,505	6,856	7,580
Mecosta	5,827	10,305	7,515	9,176
Menominee	3,539	6,704	5,242	5,564
Midland	15,655	23,877	17,450	23,919
Missaukee	1,565	5,386	2,274	4,665
Monroe	26,859	43,255	36,310	35,593
Montcalm	7,874	16,907	11,430	13,621
Montmorency	1,286	3,498	2,049	2,928
Muskegon	36,640	35,962	44,436	30,884
Newaygo	6,212	15,174	8,728	12,457
Oakland	342,976	289,127	349,002	296,514
Oceana	3,973	7,228	5,063	6,239
Ogemaw	3,030	6,827	4,791	5,437
Ontonagon	1,172	2,060	1,586	1,906
Osceola	2,705	7,336	3,981	6,141
Oscoda	1,044	2,843	1,657	2,308
Otsego	3,556	8,266	4,681	7,011
Ottawa	46,276	90,456	42,737	88,166
Presque Isle	2,400	4,486	3,192	3,794
Roscommon	4,287	8,141	6,198	6,701
Saginaw	44,395	45,469	54,381	42,720
St. Clair	24,553	49,067	33,983	39,271
St. Joseph	7,529	14,886	10,112	12,978
Sanilac	4,873	13,446	7,212	10,963
Schoolcraft	1,369	2,556	1,865	2,142
Shiawassee	12,547	19,232	17,197	15,962
Tuscola	7,493	17,421	11,425	14,240
Van Buren	13,258	17,890	16,290	16,141
Washtenaw	128,025	50,335	120,890	56,412
Wayne	512,240	225,462	595,846	213,814
Wexford	4,436	10,000	6,184	8,450
Totals	2,261,153	2,275,770	2,564,569	2,115,256

All candidates, 2016: Trump, R, 2,275,770; Clinton, D, 2,261,153; Johnson, LB, 172,793; Stein, Green, 51,420; Castle, U.S. Taxpayers, 16,112; Soltysik, Natural Law, 2,233.

Minnesota

County	2016 Clinton (D)	Trump (R)	2012 Obama (D)	Romney (R)
Aitkin	3,134	5,516	4,412	4,533
Anoka	75,611	93,474	88,614	93,430
Becker	5,208	10,880	6,829	9,204
Beltrami	8,688	10,783	11,818	9,637
Benton	5,640	12,872	8,173	10,849
Big Stone	921	1,607	1,345	1,385
Blue Earth	14,428	15,667	18,164	14,916
Brown	3,763	8,708	5,630	7,938
Carlton	8,460	8,160	11,389	6,586
Carver	21,514	29,063	20,745	31,155
Cass	4,949	9,982	6,858	8,957
Chippewa	1,978	3,764	3,083	2,967
Chisago	9,281	18,444	12,524	16,227
Clay	12,953	13,531	15,208	12,920
Clearwater	1,100	2,925	1,753	2,359
Cook	1,912	1,156	1,993	1,221
Cottonwood	1,678	3,679	2,433	3,316
Crow Wing	10,982	22,287	14,760	19,415
Dakota	107,666	97,921	116,255	109,516
Dodge	3,102	6,527	4,487	5,522
Douglas	6,227	13,966	8,653	11,884
Faribault	2,153	4,659	3,407	4,104
Fillmore	3,876	6,277	5,713	4,913
Freeborn	6,041	8,808	9,326	6,969
Goodhue	9,446	14,041	12,212	12,986
Grant	1,104	2,063	1,647	1,748
Hennepin	429,273	191,767	423,982	240,073
Houston	4,145	5,616	5,201	4,951
Hubbard	3,432	7,269	4,676	6,622
Isanti	5,656	13,635	8,024	11,675
Itasca	9,015	12,920	12,852	10,501
Jackson	1,492	3,609	2,268	3,044
Kanabec	2,327	5,230	3,593	4,328
Kandiyohi	7,266	12,785	9,805	11,240
Kittson	823	1,349	1,241	1,095
Koochiching	2,306	3,569	3,451	2,841
Lac Qui Parle	1,301	2,294	1,974	1,938
Lake	3,077	2,932	4,043	2,610
Lake of the Woods	553	1,540	859	1,306
Le Sueur	4,623	9,182	6,753	7,715
Lincoln	860	1,930	1,429	1,595
Lyon	3,825	7,259	5,465	6,594
Mahnomen	930	991	1,276	871
Marshall	1,225	3,208	1,998	2,569
Martin	2,733	7,062	4,054	6,657
McLeod	4,980	12,155	6,968	11,069
Meeker	3,192	8,104	4,969	6,913
Mille Lacs	3,709	8,340	5,829	6,951
Morrison	3,637	12,925	6,153	10,159
Mower	7,444	8,826	11,129	6,938
Murray	1,295	2,974	2,160	2,504
Nicollet	7,886	8,436	9,652	8,214
Nobles	2,733	5,299	3,793	4,581
Norman	1,264	1,699	1,730	1,384
Olmsted	36,266	35,668	39,338	36,832
Otter Tail	9,338	20,932	12,165	18,860
Pennington	2,146	4,000	3,024	3,305
Pine	4,580	8,191	6,750	6,845
Pipestone	1,127	3,338	1,725	2,826
Polk	4,712	8,979	6,773	7,615
Pope	2,106	3,794	2,981	3,142
Ramsey	176,599	70,656	184,938	86,800
Red Lake	540	1,141	928	978
Redwood	1,887	5,138	3,008	4,570
Renville	2,117	4,890	3,394	4,149
Rice	14,437	15,428	17,054	14,384
Rock	1,373	3,091	1,946	2,810
Roseau	1,856	5,451	2,772	4,409
St. Louis	57,769	44,631	73,378	39,131
Scott	28,502	39,948	29,712	40,323
Sherburne	13,299	31,049	17,597	27,848
Sibley	1,954	5,193	2,916	4,693
Stearns	25,575	47,618	33,551	43,015
Steele	6,239	11,198	8,706	9,903
Stevens	2,116	2,800	2,742	2,766
Swift	1,689	2,962	2,751	2,248
Todd	2,783	8,485	4,819	6,719
Traverse	631	1,050	943	861
Wabasha	3,866	6,989	5,415	6,049

County	2016 Clinton (D)	Trump (R)	2012 Obama (D)	Romney (R)
Wadena	1,681	4,824	2,492	4,143
Waseca	2,838	5,967	4,370	5,116
Washington	67,086	64,429	70,203	69,137
Watonwan	1,814	2,768	2,494	2,517
Wilkin	893	2,129	1,258	1,884
Winona	11,366	12,122	14,980	11,480
Wright	20,336	43,274	25,741	40,466
Yellow Medicine	1,524	3,327	2,465	2,806
Totals	**1,363,862**	**1,321,125**	**1,546,167**	**1,320,225**

All candidates, 2016: Clinton, D, 1,363,862; Trump, R, 1,321,125; Johnson, LB, 112,781; McMullin, Ind., 53,024; Stein, Green, 36,923; Vacek, Legal Marijuana, 11,276; Castle, Const., 9,443; Kennedy, Soc. Workers, 1,668; De La Fuente, Amer. Delta, 1,428.

Mississippi

County	2016 Clinton (D)	Trump (R)	2012 Obama (D)	Romney (R)
Adams	6,921	5,125	9,061	6,293
Alcorn	2,609	11,616	3,511	11,111
Amite	2,688	4,282	3,242	4,414
Attala	2,847	4,288	3,927	5,126
Benton	1,704	2,239	2,051	2,041
Bolivar	8,410	4,251	10,582	4,701
Calhoun	1,884	4,360	2,586	4,412
Carroll	1,648	3,774	2,007	3,960
Chickasaw	3,340	3,756	4,378	3,994
Choctaw	1,000	2,515	1,428	2,812
Claiborne	2,523	414	4,838	625
Clarke	2,556	5,088	3,111	5,049
Clay	5,695	4,136	6,712	4,291
Coahoma	5,954	2,094	7,792	2,712
Copiah	6,203	5,576	7,749	6,282
Covington	3,267	5,423	3,878	5,405
DeSoto	19,892	42,155	21,575	43,559
Forrest	10,666	14,292	13,272	16,574
Franklin	1,471	2,685	1,726	2,735
George	1,013	8,652	1,359	8,376
Greene	956	4,309	1,325	4,531
Grenada	3,774	5,158	5,288	5,986
Hancock	2,911	12,338	3,917	12,964
Harrison	20,679	39,710	23,119	39,470
Hinds	65,727	24,813	76,112	29,664
Holmes	5,820	1,151	7,812	1,435
Humphreys	2,652	924	3,903	1,293
Issaquena	395	298	479	302
Itawamba	1,022	7,961	1,706	7,393
Jackson	13,087	31,204	17,299	35,747
Jasper	4,016	3,555	5,097	4,193
Jefferson	3,337	489	3,951	468
Jefferson Davis	3,703	2,462	4,267	2,507
Jones	7,258	18,596	9,211	20,687
Kemper	2,827	1,778	3,239	1,789
Lafayette	7,968	10,872	8,091	11,075
Lamar	5,044	18,493	5,494	19,101
Lauderdale	10,910	17,574	13,814	18,700
Lawrence	2,181	4,072	2,468	4,192
Leake	3,579	4,775	4,079	4,863
Lee	9,635	21,695	12,563	22,415
Leflore	6,677	2,757	9,119	3,587
Lincoln	4,458	10,550	5,471	10,839
Lowndes	11,545	13,124	13,388	13,518
Madison	18,358	25,607	20,722	28,507
Marion	3,572	7,697	4,393	8,237
Marshall	7,944	6,525	9,650	6,473
Monroe	5,485	10,107	7,056	9,723
Montgomery	1,775	2,334	2,675	2,947
Neshoba	2,668	7,613	3,089	7,837
Newton	2,549	5,929	3,319	6,394
Noxubee	4,330	1,181	4,920	1,325
Oktibbeha	7,851	7,671	9,095	8,761
Panola	7,300	7,371	9,079	7,629
Pearl River	2,919	15,530	4,366	17,549
Perry	1,140	3,678	1,527	4,137
Pike	7,636	7,748	9,650	8,181
Pontotoc	2,123	9,442	2,804	9,448

County	2016		2012		County	2016		2012	
	Clinton (D)	Trump (R)	Obama (D)	Romney (R)		Clinton (D)	Trump (R)	Obama (D)	Romney (R)
Prentiss	2,009	7,513	2,817	7,075	Holt	346	1,926	551	1,725
Quitman	2,303	998	2,837	1,116	Howard	1,279	3,277	1,723	3,017
Rankin	13,741	46,168	14,988	48,444	Howell	2,880	13,888	4,395	11,544
Scott	3,999	5,742	5,031	6,089	Iron	933	3,173	1,669	2,252
Sharkey	1,235	619	1,782	737	Jackson	163,723	114,777	78,283	93,199
Simpson	3,640	6,709	4,723	7,424	Jasper	10,565	35,058	12,809	31,349
Smith	1,506	5,380	1,979	6,049	Jefferson	31,546	68,973	41,564	53,978
Stone	1,400	4,810	2,003	5,420	Johnson	5,924	13,702	7,667	12,763
Sunflower	6,186	2,559	8,199	2,929	Knox	379	1,413	698	1,205
Tallahatchie	3,311	2,437	3,959	2,499	Laclede	2,543	12,834	4,093	10,934
Tate	3,804	7,385	4,933	7,332	Lafayette	4,047	10,977	5,655	9,803
Tippah	1,808	7,182	2,317	6,717	Lawrence	2,898	13,084	4,017	11,421
Tishomingo	990	7,117	1,643	6,133	Lewis	933	3,343	1,508	2,677
Tunica	2,577	840	3,475	883	Lincoln	5,561	18,111	7,734	14,332
Union	1,969	9,161	2,742	8,498	Linn	1,239	4,084	2,041	3,344
Walthall	2,597	3,757	3,422	4,051	Livingston	1,265	4,879	1,906	4,006
Warren	7,795	8,506	10,786	10,457	Macon	1,518	5,794	2,309	4,701
Washington	9,847	4,541	13,981	5,651	Madison	1,005	4,102	1,588	3,227
Wayne	3,493	5,957	4,148	6,111	Maries	794	3,559	1,299	3,165
Webster	999	3,949	1,190	3,992	Marion	2,993	9,418	4,031	7,923
Wilkinson	2,826	1,305	3,412	1,415	McDonald	1,329	6,599	1,920	5,694
Winston	3,778	4,874	4,607	5,168	Mercer	216	1,486	353	1,255
Yalobusha	2,574	3,366	3,030	3,276	Miller	1,750	9,285	2,651	8,099
Yazoo	4,988	4,300	6,603	4,941	Mississippi	1,458	3,600	1,858	2,997
Totals	**457,569**	**668,987**	**562,949**	**710,746**	Moniteau	1,237	5,344	1,608	4,704
					Monroe	853	3,159	1,398	2,564
					Montgomery	1,118	4,124	1,740	3,490
					Morgan	1,768	6,757	2,773	5,733
					New Madrid	1,933	5,270	2,814	4,284
					Newton	4,988	20,546	6,425	18,181
					Nodaway	2,529	6,379	3,172	5,593
					Oregon	865	3,668	1,419	2,886

All candidates, 2016: Trump, R, 668,987; Clinton, D, 457,569; Johnson, LB, 13,658; Castle, Const., 3,856; Stein, Green, 3,589; De La Fuente, Amer. Delta, 696; Hedges, Prohib., 679.

Missouri

County	2016		2012		County	2016		2012	
	Clinton (D)	Trump (R)	Obama (D)	Romney (R)		Clinton (D)	Trump (R)	Obama (D)	Romney (R)
Adair	3,495	6,019	4,219	5,651	Osage	998	5,845	1,473	5,329
Andrew	2,045	6,665	2,649	5,457	Ozark	724	3,639	1,261	3,080
Atchison	541	2,059	756	1,902	Pemiscot	1,946	3,964	2,671	3,598
Audrain	2,567	6,981	3,539	6,186	Perry	1,520	6,907	2,184	5,669
Barry	2,710	11,427	3,667	9,832	Pettis	4,322	12,792	5,904	10,842
Barton	795	4,958	1,230	4,418	Phelps	4,761	12,699	5,798	11,895
Bates	1,617	6,000	2,557	5,020	Pike	1,806	5,274	2,582	4,577
Benton	2,024	7,212	2,925	6,069	Platte	18,915	24,975	19,175	25,618
Bollinger	705	4,827	1,213	4,095	Polk	2,630	10,435	3,580	9,252
Boone	41,072	36,146	39,847	37,404	Pulaski	2,918	9,870	4,199	9,092
Buchanan	12,010	21,315	15,594	18,660	Putnam	352	1,936	587	1,673
Butler	3,036	13,647	4,363	12,248	Ralls	1,138	3,969	1,736	3,231
Caldwell	837	3,231	1,312	2,721	Randolph	2,283	7,529	3,031	6,667
Callaway	4,988	13,052	6,071	11,745	Ray	3,088	7,103	4,275	5,815
Camden	4,706	16,721	6,458	15,092	Reynolds	540	2,402	1,157	1,931
Cape Girardeau	8,468	26,939	9,728	25,370	Ripley	830	4,520	1,396	3,743
Carroll	745	3,480	1,154	3,072	St. Charles	68,225	120,899	71,838	110,784
Carter	436	2,323	754	1,978	St. Clair	936	3,501	1,460	3,019
Cass	14,816	33,006	17,044	30,912	St. Francois	6,250	17,467	8,829	13,248
Cedar	1,010	5,019	1,537	4,376	St. Louis Co.	280,866	199,081	297,097	224,742
Chariton	888	2,948	1,339	2,402	Ste. Genevieve	2,540	5,495	3,813	4,055
Christian	8,505	30,941	9,813	27,473	Saline	2,787	5,977	3,790	5,104
Clark	724	2,458	1,398	1,730	Schuyler	354	1,505	697	1,174
Clay	45,182	57,328	47,310	56,191	Scotland	365	1,525	643	1,246
Clinton	2,572	7,058	3,688	5,931	Scott	3,574	13,168	5,122	11,623
Cole	10,907	24,610	12,005	24,490	Shannon	776	2,966	1,302	2,262
Cooper	1,932	5,623	2,474	4,887	Shelby	606	2,524	966	2,188
Crawford	1,824	7,724	2,951	6,434	Stoddard	1,873	11,077	3,153	9,496
Dade	637	3,184	939	2,895	Stone	2,886	13,149	3,923	11,787
Dallas	1,271	5,895	2,122	4,992	Sullivan	526	1,884	908	1,610
Daviess	730	2,763	1,125	2,290	Taney	4,367	18,240	5,479	15,746
DeKalb	824	3,540	1,194	3,056	Texas	1,728	8,875	2,871	7,618
Dent	978	5,599	1,585	4,883	Vernon	1,706	6,526	2,580	5,758
Douglas	984	5,486	1,710	4,649	Warren	3,915	11,109	5,219	9,150
Dunklin	2,360	8,026	3,636	6,850	Washington	1,926	7,047	3,417	5,071
Franklin	12,339	35,420	16,347	29,396	Wayne	946	4,640	1,813	3,790
Gasconade	1,519	5,670	2,099	4,895	Webster	3,173	12,829	4,409	10,708
Gentry	605	2,304	937	1,988	Worth	195	808	341	664
Greene	42,400	77,387	46,219	76,900	Wright	1,166	6,703	1,953	5,830
Grundy	780	3,462	1,212	3,030	City St. Louis	101,487	20,281	118,780	22,943
Harrison	574	2,965	984	2,624	**Totals**	**1,054,889**	**1,585,753**	**1,223,796**	**1,482,440**
Henry	2,356	7,072	3,606	6,229					
Hickory	1,016	3,539	1,733	2,835					

All candidates, 2016: Trump, R, 1,585,753; Clinton, D, 1,054,889; Johnson, LB, 96,404; Stein, Green, 25,086; Castle, Const., 12,966.

Montana

County	2016 Clinton (D)	Trump (R)	2012 Obama (D)	Romney (R)
Beaverhead	1,115	3,243	1,371	3,289
Big Horn	2,061	1,833	2,882	1,667
Blaine	1,187	1,259	1,616	1,178
Broadwater	566	2,329	764	2,152
Carbon	1,824	3,729	2,146	3,533
Carter	70	677	96	678
Cascade	7,130	9,610	15,232	18,345
Chouteau	729	1,676	978	1,758
Custer	1,172	3,638	1,833	3,373
Daniels	167	729	237	740
Dawson	786	3,298	1,219	3,029
Deer Lodge	2,018	1,736	2,860	1,448
Fallon	154	1,276	237	1,128
Fergus	1,196	4,235	1,640	4,257
Flathead	13,233	30,079	13,892	28,309
Gallatin	18,235	17,882	21,961	24,358
Garfield	34	653	66	622
Glacier	3,076	1,598	2,924	1,415
Golden Valley	71	365	110	351
Granite	469	1,185	533	1,107
Hill	2,350	3,446	3,403	3,164
Jefferson	1,975	4,099	2,272	4,055
Judith Basin	232	867	337	854
Lake	4,703	7,453	5,805	7,135
Lewis and Clark	13,605	15,660	15,620	16,803
Liberty	205	695	257	702
Lincoln	2,040	6,720	0,652	6,057
Madison	1,175	3,280	1,289	3,130
McCone	154	858	223	745
Meagher	191	728	269	670
Mineral	515	1,322	700	1,216
Missoula	25,555	18,016	32,824	22,652
Musselshell	331	1,961	492	1,833
Park	2,838	4,326	3,783	4,709
Petroleum	30	276	49	240
Phillips	315	1,715	471	1,688
Pondera	737	1,786	975	1,673
Powder River	127	880	170	833
Powell	549	2,017	888	1,806
Prairie	100	555	167	520
Ravalli	6,166	14,673	7,285	14,307
Richland	669	3,885	1,002	3,510
Roosevelt	1,504	1,722	2,086	1,514
Rosebud	969	2,211	1,422	2,004
Sanders	1,211	4,268	1,720	3,980
Sheridan	476	1,237	665	1,207
Silver Bow	8,545	6,252	10,857	5,430
Stillwater	904	3,630	1,248	3,337
Sweet Grass	398	1,580	475	1,594
Teton	803	2,152	1,082	2,113
Toole	399	1,495	582	1,440
Treasure	59	350	114	319
Valley	886	2,697	1,385	2,337
Wheatland	179	698	272	693
Wibaux	55	460	98	421
Yellowstone	21,117	38,675	26,403	40,500
Totals	**157,360**	**253,675**	**201,839**	**267,928**

All candidates, 2016: Trump, R, 253,675; Clinton, D, 157,360; Johnson, LB, 24,305; Stein, Green, 6,682; De La Fuente, Amer. Delta, 1,364.

Nebraska

County	2016 Clinton (D)	Trump (R)	2012 Obama (D)	Romney (R)
Adams	3,272	9,205	4,062	8,316
Antelope	381	2,717	571	2,596
Arthur	16	237	30	227
Banner	18	355	55	346
Blaine	30	273	29	268
Boone	414	2,299	615	2,138
Box Butte	953	3,550	1,692	2,869
Boyd	128	978	188	873
Brown	153	1,380	224	1,302
Buffalo	4,690	14,424	5,365	13,570
Burt	928	2,360	1,291	2,029
Butler	690	3,068	1,045	2,738
Cass	3,461	8,388	4,367	7,556
Cedar	572	3,533	958	3,278
Chase	171	1,621	254	1,584
Cherry	317	2,623	436	2,557
Cheyenne	702	3,610	1,084	3,449
Clay	470	2,373	667	2,232
Colfax	857	2,171	969	2,051
Cuming	712	3,095	1,031	2,876
Custer	635	4,616	1,083	4,296
Dakota	2,904	4,028	2,922	3,094
Dawes	785	2,559	1,132	2,478
Dawson	2,116	5,935	2,199	5,460
Deuel	120	809	215	763
Dixon	556	2,041	870	1,745
Dodge	4,451	9,736	5,673	8,995
Douglas	105,207	102,151	106,456	113,220
Dundy	89	823	176	792
Fillmore	610	2,100	807	2,007
Franklin	250	1,345	384	1,112
Frontier	161	1,106	271	1,007
Furnas	304	1,915	423	1,782
Gage	2,930	6,333	3,903	5,513
Garden	153	869	242	829
Garfield	121	819	149	769
Gosper	165	792	230	734
Grant	20	367	30	322
Greeley	210	911	340	820
Hall	6,142	14,139	7,161	12,646
Hamilton	873	3,763	1,146	3,600
Harlan	213	1,702	354	1,395
Hayes	30	471	51	470
Hitchcock	158	1,216	274	1,178
Holt	522	4,275	882	3,922
Hooker	40	355	59	330
Howard	544	2,284	914	1,890
Jefferson	831	2,387	1,195	2,166
Johnson	560	1,348	790	1,225
Kearney	550	2,519	773	2,349
Keith	560	3,203	928	3,044
Keya Paha	39	458	80	393
Kimball	227	1,317	395	1,235
Knox	715	3,181	1,059	2,885
Lancaster	60,533	60,456	62,015	62,434
Lincoln	2,878	11,992	4,450	10,728
Logan	32	400	68	356
Loup	48	323	62	290
Madison	2,663	10,518	3,485	10,062
McPherson	14	257	41	237
Merrick	601	2,914	925	2,490
Morrill	282	1,788	455	1,681
Nance	280	1,257	481	1,106
Nemaha	765	2,068	1,128	2,012
Nuckolls	348	1,709	568	1,574
Otoe	2,017	4,833	2,561	4,258
Pawnee	279	970	400	899
Perkins	160	1,202	238	1,135
Phelps	571	3,832	880	3,400
Pierce	382	3,052	637	2,707
Platte	2,612	10,864	3,148	10,061
Polk	411	2,019	528	1,890
Red Willow	638	4,212	952	3,891
Richardson	798	2,684	1,191	2,443
Rock	70	687	103	672
Saline	1,630	2,849	2,289	2,557
Sarpy	27,704	44,649	26,671	43,213
Saunders	2,509	7,486	3,307	6,770
Scotts Bluff	3,151	9,952	4,327	9,648
Seward	1,881	5,451	2,386	5,003
Sheridan	286	2,192	390	2,021
Sherman	338	1,143	552	927
Sioux	77	602	101	624
Stanton	417	2,173	614	1,949
Thayer	490	1,993	728	1,874
Thomas	30	344	42	360
Thurston	911	1,013	1,247	939
Valley	337	1,770	498	1,657
Washington	2,606	7,374	3,132	6,899
Wayne	828	2,675	1,074	2,493

County	Clinton (D) 2016	Trump (R)	Obama (D) 2012	Romney (R)
Webster	306	1,320	442	1,258
Wheeler	62	377	93	345
York	1,181	4,686	1,373	4,874
Totals	**273,858**	**485,819**	**302,081**	**475,064**

All candidates, 2016: Trump, R, 485,819; Clinton, D, 273,858; Johnson, LB, 37,615; Stein, petitioning cand., 8,346.

Nevada

County	Clinton (D) 2016	Trump (R)	Obama (D) 2012	Romney (R)
Churchill	2,210	7,828	2,961	7,061
Clark	401,068	319,571	389,936	289,053
Douglas	8,453	17,406	9,297	16,276
Elko	3,400	13,542	3,511	12,014
Esmeralda	65	329	92	317
Eureka	74	723	107	663
Humboldt	1,386	4,521	1,737	3,810
Lander	403	1,828	534	1,580
Lincoln	285	1,671	400	1,691
Lyon	6,146	16,005	7,380	13,520
Mineral	637	1,179	863	1,080
Nye	5,095	13,320	6,320	10,566
Pershing	430	1,403	632	1,167
Storey	752	1,616	920	1,321
Washoe	97,032	94,529	95,409	88,453
White Pine	707	2,723	983	2,601
City				
Carson City	9,610	13,125	10,291	12,394
Totals	**537,753**	**511,319**	**531,373**	**463,567**

All candidates, 2016: Clinton, D, 537,753; Trump, R, 511,319; Johnson, LB, 37,299; None of these candidates, 28,824; Castle, Independent Amer., 5,254; De La Fuente, no party, 2,541.

New Hampshire

City	Clinton (D) 2016	Trump (R)	Obama (D) 2012	Romney (R)
Bedford	5,851	6,816	4,713	7,990
Concord	12,884	7,776	14,218	7,325
Derry	6,825	9,237	7,612	8,350
Dover	10,118	6,015	9,724	6,162
Durham	6,501	2,450	5,074	2,217
Exeter	5,514	3,286	5,194	3,614
Hanover	6,561	926	5,469	1,727
Hudson	5,306	7,220	5,451	6,683
Keene	7,932	3,831	8,718	3,613
Londonderry	5,968	7,338	5,690	7,323
Manchester	24,700	21,414	26,227	20,942
Merrimack	6,405	7,397	6,832	7,750
Nashua	22,428	17,391	23,413	17,658
Portsmouth	8,911	3,632	8,848	4,088
Rochester	5,219	7,655	7,493	6,816
Salem	6,068	9,312	6,026	8,285
Windham	3,507	4,825	2,964	5,224
Other	196,118	218,858	215,895	204,151
Totals	**346,816**	**345,379**	**369,561**	**329,918**

All candidates, 2016: Clinton, D, 346,816; Trump, R, 345,379; Johnson, LB, 30,311; Stein, Green, 6,228; De La Fuente, Amer. Delta, 672.

New Jersey

County	Clinton (D) 2016	Trump (R)	Obama (D) 2012	Romney (R)
Atlantic	54,175	47,741	65,600	46,522
Bergen	209,251	163,220	212,754	169,070
Burlington	107,485	79,085	126,377	87,401
Camden	117,308	59,716	153,682	69,476
Cape May	18,626	28,237	21,657	25,781
Cumberland	26,051	23,328	34,055	20,658
Essex	231,031	62,059	236,618	64,406
Gloucester	66,355	66,949	74,013	59,456
Hudson	148,009	44,911	153,108	42,369
Hunterdon	28,797	38,565	26,876	38,687
Mercer	93,721	42,604	104,377	47,355
Middlesex	164,887	108,981	190,555	107,310
Monmouth	121,004	151,184	133,145	147,513
Morris	102,343	116,672	100,146	124,947
Ocean	81,845	170,103	102,300	146,474
Passaic	112,608	71,488	115,926	64,523
Salem	11,766	16,256	14,719	14,334
Somerset	83,839	64,640	74,592	66,603
Sussex	23,771	46,216	26,104	40,625
Union	132,590	62,437	139,752	68,314

County	Clinton (D) 2016	Trump (R)	Obama (D) 2012	Romney (R)
Warren	14,730	26,217	18,745	25,744
Totals	**1,950,192**	**1,490,609**	**2,125,101**	**1,477,568**

All candidates, 2016: Clinton, D, 1,950,192; Trump, R, 1,490,609; Johnson, LB, 66,041; Stein, Green, 35,001; Castle, Const., 5,601; Kennedy, Soc. Workers, 2,046; De La Fuente, Amer. Delta, 1,723; Moorehead, Workers World, 1,625; La Riva, Socialism/Liberation, 1,581.

New Mexico

County	Clinton (D) 2016	Trump (R)	Obama (D) 2012	Romney (R)
Bernalillo	141,960	93,874	150,739	106,408
Catron	425	1,444	560	1,494
Chaves	5,359	12,349	6,604	13,088
Cibola	3,721	3,179	4,961	2,998
Colfax	2,118	2,569	2,828	2,699
Curry	2,776	7,560	4,022	9,251
De Baca	192	617	287	586
Doña Ana	37,535	25,082	37,139	27,322
Eddy	5,008	13,124	6,142	12,583
Grant	6,226	5,251	7,090	5,358
Guadalupe	962	591	1,488	557
Harding	156	311	260	327
Hidalgo	780	906	995	899
Lea	3,877	12,306	4,080	12,548
Lincoln	2,318	5,859	2,942	5,961
Los Alamos	5,443	3,329	5,191	4,796
Luna	3,195	3,478	3,583	3,670
McKinley	13,162	4,893	15,841	5,546
Mora	1,533	662	1,955	595
Otero	6,033	11,756	6,829	12,451
Quay	1,016	2,208	1,383	2,202
Rio Arriba	9,534	3,583	11,465	3,397
Roosevelt	1,445	3,865	1,727	4,043
San Juan	12,820	27,869	15,855	28,849
San Miguel	7,249	2,302	8,850	2,303
Sandoval	27,405	25,748	27,236	24,387
Santa Fe	49,956	14,198	50,872	15,500
Sierra	1,600	2,998	1,964	2,928
Socorro	3,275	2,592	4,058	2,722
Taos	10,550	2,706	11,978	2,730
Torrance	1,770	3,695	2,428	3,529
Union	318	1,214	472	1,236
Valencia	10,810	13,175	13,511	12,825
Totals	**380,527**	**315,293**	**415,335**	**335,788**

All candidates, 2016: Clinton, D, 380,527; Trump, R, 315,293; Johnson, LB, 73,604; Stein, Green, 9,722; McMullin, Better for Amer., 5,705; Castle, Const., 1,487; La Riva, Socialism/Liberation, 1,174; De La Fuente, Amer. Delta, 465.

New York

County	Clinton (D) 2016	Trump (R)	Obama (D) 2012	Romney (R)
Albany	74,775	44,227	87,556	45,064
Allegany	4,473	11,712	6,139	10,390
Bronx[1]	318,403	34,424	339,211	29,967
Broome	35,212	38,077	41,970	37,641
Cattaraugus	8,717	18,668	12,649	16,569
Cayuga	12,202	16,194	17,007	13,454
Chautauqua	17,176	29,042	23,812	27,971
Chemung	12,394	19,025	16,797	17,612
Chenango	5,943	11,024	9,116	9,713
Clinton	13,446	13,181	18,961	11,115
Columbia	13,123	12,756	16,221	12,225
Cortland	7,976	9,207	10,482	8,695
Delaware	5,825	11,012	8,304	9,938
Dutchess	56,874	58,163	65,312	56,025
Erie	192,065	173,817	237,356	169,675
Essex	6,760	7,275	9,784	6,647
Franklin	6,517	7,636	9,894	5,740
Fulton	5,770	12,448	8,607	10,814
Genesee	6,946	15,986	9,601	14,607
Greene	6,370	11,546	9,030	11,174
Hamilton	752	1,795	1,128	1,932
Herkimer	7,289	15,664	11,273	13,282
Jefferson	12,289	19,947	17,099	18,122
Kings (Brooklyn)[1]	595,086	133,653	604,443	124,551
Lewis	2,828	6,916	4,724	5,651
Livingston	10,478	17,112	11,705	14,448

County	2016 Clinton (D)	2016 Trump (R)	2012 Obama (D)	2012 Romney (R)
Madison	10,548	14,901	13,871	13,622
Monroe	174,063	123,871	193,501	133,362
Montgomery	5,961	10,579	8,493	9,334
Nassau	307,326	275,479	302,695	259,308
New York (Manhattan)[1]	515,481	58,935	502,674	89,559
Niagara	32,888	49,223	43,986	43,240
Oneida	30,749	48,490	40,468	44,530
Onondaga	102,915	78,277	122,254	78,831
Ontario	20,040	24,237	23,087	23,820
Orange	63,037	72,129	73,315	65,367
Orleans	4,113	10,402	5,787	8,594
Oswego	15,614	25,870	23,515	19,980
Otsego	9,285	12,284	12,117	11,461
Putnam	17,363	25,241	19,512	24,083
Queens[1]	473,389	138,550	470,732	118,589
Rensselaer	30,039	31,933	37,408	29,113
Richmond (Staten Island)[1]	67,561	95,612	78,181	74,223
Rockland	63,454	57,148	65,657	57,363
St. Lawrence	14,659	18,450	21,353	15,138
Saratoga	46,546	51,088	52,957	50,382
Schenectady	30,870	27,268	36,844	26,568
Schoharie	3,777	8,173	5,427	7,467
Schuylor	2,761	5,179	3,674	4,281
Seneca	5,175	6,719	7,004	5,889
Steuben	11,215	25,091	15,787	21,954
Suffolk	276,953	328,403	304,079	282,131
Sullivan	10,983	14,626	15,268	12,705
Tioga	6,832	10,528	8,930	12,117
Tompkins	25,555	9,647	27,244	11,107
Ulster	39,884	32,806	47,752	29,759
Warren	11,366	14,284	14,806	14,119
Washington	8,238	12,770	11,523	11,085
Wayne	11,896	20,893	16,635	20,060
Westchester	156,621	81,033	240,785	143,122
Wyoming	3,585	11,884	5,661	10,348
Yates	3,219	5,180	4,488	4,798
Totals	4,053,670	2,589,690	4,485,741	2,490,431

(1) Borough of New York City.
All candidates, 2016: Clinton, D, 4,053,670; Trump, R, 2,589,690; Johnson, LB, 159,147; Stein, Green, 98,149.

North Carolina

County	2016 Clinton (D)	2016 Trump (R)	2012 Obama (D)	2012 Romney (R)
Alamance	29,268	38,235	28,875	38,170
Alexander	3,750	13,826	4,611	12,253
Alleghany	1,300	3,789	1,583	3,390
Anson	5,785	4,480	7,019	4,166
Ashe	3,476	9,353	4,116	8,242
Avery	1,670	6,226	1,882	5,766
Beaufort	8,699	14,478	9,435	13,977
Bertie	5,837	3,476	6,695	3,387
Bladen	7,021	8,511	8,062	7,748
Brunswick	23,117	42,440	22,038	34,743
Buncombe	74,937	55,339	70,625	54,701
Burke	10,930	25,741	13,701	22,267
Cabarrus	35,048	53,224	32,849	49,557
Caldwell	8,403	26,499	10,898	23,229
Camden	1,266	3,527	1,508	3,109
Carteret	9,806	26,228	10,301	24,775
Caswell	4,549	5,758	5,348	5,594
Catawba	21,050	48,062	24,069	44,538
Chatham	20,953	17,012	18,361	16,665
Cherokee	2,809	10,711	3,378	9,278
Chowan	2,965	3,983	3,556	3,891
Clay	1,352	4,395	1,579	3,973
Cleveland	14,896	28,394	17,062	25,793
Columbus	8,991	14,177	11,050	12,941
Craven	17,481	27,556	18,763	26,928
Cumberland	70,523	50,593	75,792	50,666
Currituck	2,879	9,070	3,562	7,496
Dare	7,079	11,283	7,393	10,248
Davidson	17,328	52,870	20,624	49,383
Davie	5,228	15,502	5,735	14,687
Duplin	8,196	12,151	9,033	11,416
Durham	118,783	27,879	111,224	33,769
Edgecombe	16,152	8,219	18,310	8,546
Forsyth	92,488	74,793	92,323	79,768
Franklin	12,811	16,320	13,436	14,603
Gaston	30,982	61,467	33,171	56,138
Gates	2,371	2,851	2,786	2,564
Graham	761	3,260	1,119	2,750
Granville	12,827	13,500	13,598	12,405
Greene	3,570	4,358	3,778	4,411
Guilford	147,949	97,461	146,365	104,789
Halifax	15,642	8,954	17,176	8,763
Harnett	16,452	27,278	17,331	25,565
Haywood	10,414	18,844	11,833	15,633
Henderson	19,664	35,535	18,642	32,994
Hertford	6,886	3,081	7,843	3,007
Hoke	9,608	7,676	10,076	6,819
Hyde	956	1,275	1,163	1,193
Iredell	24,441	54,164	26,076	49,299
Jackson	7,564	9,706	8,095	8,254
Johnston	28,153	54,082	27,290	48,427
Jones	2,041	2,941	2,352	2,837
Lee	10,380	13,625	10,801	13,158
Lenoir	11,752	13,354	13,948	13,980
Lincoln	9,836	28,653	11,024	25,267
Macon	4,841	12,035	5,712	10,835
Madison	3,899	6,735	4,484	5,404
Martin	5,814	5,874	6,583	5,995
McDowell	4,645	14,517	6,031	11,775
Mecklenburg	292,258	154,303	272,262	171,668
Mitchell	1,585	6,225	1,838	5,806
Montgomery	4,108	7,070	4,706	6,404
Moore	16,148	30,273	16,505	29,495
Nash	23,024	23,142	24,313	23,842
New Hanover	50,219	54,665	48,668	53,385
Northampton	6,113	3,556	7,232	3,483
Onslow	17,156	36,342	18,490	32,243
Orange	50,106	18,373	53,901	21,539
Pamlico	2,427	4,225	2,647	4,061
Pasquotank	8,455	8,082	10,282	7,633
Pender	9,086	17,317	9,632	14,617
Perquimans	2,291	4,143	2,759	3,822
Person	7,772	11,116	8,418	10,496
Pitt	40,967	35,191	41,843	36,214
Polk	3,715	6,738	4,013	6,236
Randolph	13,074	49,156	14,773	45,160
Richmond	8,290	10,199	9,904	9,332
Robeson	18,377	20,294	24,988	17,510
Rockingham	14,057	26,463	16,351	25,227
Rowan	19,208	42,388	22,650	38,775
Rutherford	7,451	21,694	9,374	18,954
Sampson	10,486	14,761	11,566	14,422
Scotland	7,279	6,212	8,215	5,831
Stanly	7,008	21,788	8,431	19,904
Stokes	4,645	16,976	6,018	15,237
Surry	7,438	23,495	9,112	19,923
Swain	2,186	3,557	2,618	2,976
Transylvania	6,520	10,441	6,826	9,634
Tyrrell	705	968	837	930
Union	34,051	66,265	32,473	61,107
Vance	12,168	7,304	13,323	7,429
Wake	298,353	193,607	267,262	211,596
Warren	6,668	3,302	6,978	3,140
Washington	3,490	2,560	3,833	2,622
Watauga	13,953	13,521	13,002	13,861
Wayne	21,520	27,360	23,314	27,641
Wilkes	6,596	23,613	8,148	20,515
Wilson	19,527	17,410	20,875	17,954
Yadkin	3,140	13,815	3,957	12,578
Yancey	3,181	6,367	3,981	5,278
Totals	2,162,074	2,339,603	2,178,391	2,270,395

All candidates, 2016: Trump, R, 2,339,603; Clinton, D, 2,162,074; Johnson, LB, 127,794.

North Dakota

County	2016 Clinton (D)	2016 Trump (R)	2012 Obama (D)	2012 Romney (R)
Adams	216	904	328	918
Barnes	1,597	3,156	2,394	2,964
Benson	842	927	1,235	868
Billings	58	492	89	472
Bottineau	734	2,482	1,183	2,280
Bowman	227	1,445	414	1,280
Burke	118	879	230	769
Burleigh	10,865	32,499	14,122	27,951
Cass	31,291	39,738	34,712	36,855
Cavalier	476	1,356	818	1,195

County	2016 Clinton (D)	Trump (R)	2012 Obama (D)	Romney (R)
Dickey	551	1,656	853	1,610
Divide	243	860	385	733
Dunn	356	1,753	508	1,506
Eddy	354	790	486	634
Emmons	215	1,672	383	1,435
Foster	348	1,240	607	1,030
Golden Valley	99	793	162	742
Grand Forks	10,828	16,325	14,032	15,060
Grant	187	1,098	334	1,025
Griggs	298	847	536	771
Hettinger	168	1,032	313	1,000
Kidder	179	1,106	393	870
LaMoure	500	1,475	740	1,377
Logan	112	867	232	810
McHenry	474	1,991	943	1,678
McIntosh	233	1,095	459	1,035
McKenzie	696	3,661	927	2,458
McLean	1,070	3,827	1,670	3,141
Mercer	616	3,715	1,166	3,152
Morton	3,077	11,319	4,469	8,680
Mountrail	1,211	2,551	1,403	1,962
Nelson	536	1,025	767	865
Oliver	119	827	281	693
Pembina	681	2,204	1,253	1,899
Pierce	431	1,433	660	1,465
Ramsey	1,505	3,216	2,164	2,665
Ransom	836	1,209	1,343	1,009
Renville	200	978	398	851
Richland	2,064	4,759	3,198	4,229
Rolette	2,097	1,210	3,353	1,092
Sargent	693	1,088	1,075	879
Sheridan	94	644	163	642
Sioux	758	256	900	225
Slope	42	361	83	341
Stark	1,745	9,718	2,812	8,521
Steele	361	537	518	498
Stutsman	2,484	6,706	3,585	5,685
Towner	305	733	516	623
Traill	1,239	2,263	1,811	1,996
Walsh	1,166	2,991	1,985	2,656
Ward	5,792	18,601	8,441	16,230
Wells	419	1,793	673	1,654
Williams	1,722	10,033	2,322	7,184
Totals	**93,528**	**216,136**	**124,827**	**188,163**

All candidates, 2016: Trump, R, 216,136; Clinton, D, 93,528; Johnson, LB, 21,352; Stein, Green, 3,769; Castle, Const., 1,825; De La Fuente, Amer. Delta, 364.

Ohio

County	2016 Clinton (D)	Trump (R)	2012 Obama (D)	Romney (R)
Adams	2,293	8,445	3,976	6,865
Allen	12,815	29,858	17,914	29,502
Ashland	5,659	17,169	8,281	15,519
Ashtabula	15,191	22,755	23,803	18,298
Athens	15,552	10,816	18,307	8,543
Auglaize	3,825	18,130	5,831	17,169
Belmont	8,652	20,729	14,156	16,758
Brown	4,270	14,257	7,107	11,916
Butler	56,700	104,441	62,388	105,176
Carroll	3,124	9,067	5,543	7,315
Champaign	4,488	12,314	7,044	11,045
Clark	22,666	34,311	31,297	31,820
Clermont	26,096	65,960	30,458	64,208
Clinton	3,943	13,466	5,791	12,009
Columbiana	12,273	31,086	19,821	25,251
Coshocton	3,908	10,381	6,940	8,390
Crawford	4,518	13,265	7,507	11,852
Cuyahoga	383,974	179,894	447,273	190,660
Darke	4,395	19,698	6,826	18,108
Defiance	5,282	11,478	7,732	10,176
Delaware	39,584	55,660	37,292	60,194
Erie	15,692	19,301	21,793	16,952
Fairfield	24,150	43,163	29,890	41,034
Fayette	2,672	7,763	4,249	6,620
Franklin	335,961	192,328	346,373	215,997

County	2016 Clinton (D)	Trump (R)	2012 Obama (D)	Romney (R)
Fulton	5,981	13,419	9,073	11,738
Gallia	2,564	9,567	4,557	7,750
Geauga	17,165	29,577	19,659	30,589
Greene	28,023	47,506	32,256	49,819
Guernsey	4,286	11,164	7,450	8,993
Hamilton	207,587	169,972	219,927	193,326
Hancock	9,419	23,777	12,564	22,443
Hardin	2,870	8,541	4,619	7,489
Harrison	1,663	5,021	2,950	4,019
Henry	3,690	9,136	5,658	8,257
Highland	3,436	13,005	6,054	11,413
Hocking	3,713	8,282	6,157	6,285
Holmes	1,766	8,578	2,608	8,702
Huron	7,080	15,930	11,006	13,060
Jackson	3,142	9,618	5,166	7,904
Jefferson	9,483	20,668	15,385	17,034
Knox	7,959	18,563	10,470	17,266
Lake	45,056	62,627	57,680	58,744
Lawrence	6,849	18,240	10,744	14,651
Licking	26,360	49,346	34,201	45,503
Logan	4,537	15,586	7,062	13,633
Lorain	64,958	65,346	81,464	59,405
Lucas	107,363	74,102	136,616	69,940
Madison	4,662	11,319	6,845	10,342
Mahoning	56,188	52,808	77,059	42,641
Marion	7,748	16,563	12,504	14,265
Medina	31,582	53,811	38,785	50,418
Meigs	2,157	6,869	4,027	5,895
Mercer	3,335	17,200	4,745	16,561
Miami	12,832	36,311	16,383	34,606
Monroe	1,647	4,781	3,035	3,548
Montgomery	117,661	120,766	137,139	124,841
Morgan	1,711	4,315	2,814	3,179
Morrow	3,711	11,722	5,933	9,865
Muskingum	10,926	23,588	17,002	19,264
Noble	1,201	4,441	2,131	3,563
Ottawa	8,136	12,389	11,503	10,538
Paulding	2,068	6,359	3,538	5,354
Perry	4,072	9,978	7,033	7,627
Pickaway	6,325	16,482	9,684	14,037
Pike	3,443	7,669	5,684	5,685
Portage	31,463	38,978	39,453	35,242
Preble	4,323	15,376	6,211	13,535
Putnam	2,874	14,704	4,318	13,721
Richland	15,629	35,805	22,687	33,867
Ross	9,905	17,833	14,569	15,008
Sandusky	9,733	16,045	14,541	13,755
Scioto	8,841	19,742	15,077	15,492
Seneca	7,237	14,559	11,353	13,243
Shelby	4,143	18,148	6,343	17,142
Stark	66,581	96,345	89,432	88,581
Summit	129,922	109,531	153,041	111,001
Trumbull	42,130	48,152	61,672	38,279
Tuscarawas	11,895	26,105	18,407	22,242
Union	7,530	17,601	8,805	16,289
Van Wert	2,667	10,328	4,029	9,585
Vinton	1,332	3,799	2,436	2,856
Warren	33,036	75,947	32,909	76,564
Washington	7,841	19,901	11,651	17,284
Wayne	14,670	31,622	19,808	30,251
Williams	4,287	11,706	7,266	10,047
Wood	26,440	31,734	32,802	29,704
Wyandot	2,484	7,346	4,137	6,180
Totals	**2,317,001**	**2,771,984**	**2,827,709**	**2,661,437**

All candidates, 2016: Trump, R, 2,771,984; Clinton, D, 2,317,001; Johnson, Ind., 168,599; Stein, Green, 44,310; Duncan, Ind., 23,501.

Oklahoma

County	2016 Clinton (D)	Trump (R)	2012 Obama (D)	Romney (R)
Adair	1,374	4,753	2,127	4,381
Alfalfa	216	1,931	322	1,761
Atoka	795	4,068	1,243	3,538
Beaver	176	1,987	244	2,062
Beckham	958	6,287	1,417	5,508
Blaine	711	2,884	992	2,824

County	2016 Clinton (D)	Trump (R)	2012 Obama (D)	Romney (R)
Bryan	2,793	10,449	3,681	9,520
Caddo	2,418	6,473	3,164	5,687
Canadian	11,666	39,969	10,537	35,625
Carter	4,002	13,751	4,908	12,214
Cherokee	5,455	9,992	6,144	8,162
Choctaw	1,064	4,202	1,494	3,572
Cimarron	70	962	115	1,082
Cleveland	38,790	62,469	34,771	59,116
Coal	411	1,892	649	1,710
Comanche	11,439	19,153	12,521	17,664
Cotton	424	2,054	657	1,796
Craig	1,249	4,279	1,747	3,559
Creek	5,834	21,539	7,128	18,986
Custer	2,102	7,818	2,359	7,446
Delaware	3,306	11,796	4,196	10,080
Dewey	222	1,964	301	1,792
Ellis	155	1,610	226	1,575
Garfield	4,391	15,998	4,733	15,177
Garvin	1,852	8,243	2,559	6,925
Grady	3,878	17,293	4,786	14,833
Grant	287	1,827	393	1,675
Greer	323	1,482	488	1,344
Harmon	224	714	264	659
Harper	131	1,307	173	1,261
Haskell	882	3,697	1,175	3,069
Hughes	961	3,387	1,370	2,838
Jackson	1,473	5,969	1,954	5,965
Jefferson	365	1,905	605	1,634
Johnston	782	3,081	1,137	2,649
Kay	3,734	12,168	4,627	11,499
Kingfisher	783	5,151	898	4,870
Kiowa	766	2,593	1,106	2,316
Latimer	797	3,094	1,170	2,628
Le Flore	3,245	13,346	4,662	11,177
Lincoln	2,423	10,838	3,273	9,553
Logan	4,239	13,613	4,724	12,314
Love	735	2,920	1,034	2,436
Major	310	2,940	446	2,700
Marshall	1,095	4,202	1,396	3,744
Mayes	3,423	11,550	4,823	9,637
McClain	2,893	13,151	3,194	11,112
McCurtain	1,799	8,642	2,440	7,635
McIntosh	2,122	5,501	2,779	4,509
Murray	1,086	4,173	1,540	3,606
Muskogee	7,969	15,029	9,952	13,404
Noble	901	3,707	1,143	3,488
Nowata	742	3,321	1,244	2,832
Okfuskee	943	2,791	1,256	2,335
Oklahoma	112,661	141,429	106,982	149,728
Okmulgee	4,379	8,926	5,432	7,731
Osage	5,593	12,559	6,704	11,242
Ottawa	2,584	7,627	3,509	6,466
Pawnee	1,341	4,716	1,813	4,232
Payne	8,785	16,644	9,198	16,481
Pittsburg	3,704	12,740	4,831	10,841
Pontotoc	3,633	10,420	3,947	8,945
Pottawatomie	6,005	17,826	7,188	16,250
Pushmataha	748	3,581	1,043	3,087
Roger Mills	151	1,546	272	1,402
Rogers	7,895	30,893	9,148	27,553
Seminole	2,067	5,612	2,600	4,856
Sequoyah	3,061	10,888	4,193	9,578
Stephens	3,084	14,166	3,939	12,908
Texas	855	4,615	862	4,930
Tillman	657	1,944	906	1,815
Tulsa	87,663	143,985	82,744	145,062
Wagoner	6,711	22,967	7,791	20,900
Washington	5,047	15,810	5,532	15,668
Washita	588	3,851	822	3,494
Woods	521	2,945	671	2,727
Woodward	871	6,329	1,133	5,945
Totals	**419,788**	**947,934**	**443,547**	**891,325**

All candidates, 2016: Trump, R, 947,934; Clinton, D, 419,788; Johnson, Ind., 83,334.

Oregon

County	2016 Clinton (D)	Trump (R)	2012 Obama (D)	Romney (R)
Baker	1,781	6,160	2,369	5,702
Benton	28,431	13,030	27,776	14,991
Clackamas	90,187	79,062	95,493	88,592
Clatsop	8,899	7,794	9,861	7,249
Columbia	9,959	12,967	12,004	10,772
Coos	10,355	17,699	12,845	14,673
Crook	2,591	8,388	3,104	6,790
Curry	4,253	7,157	4,625	6,598
Deschutes	25,182	26,251	36,961	42,463
Douglas	13,891	34,112	17,145	30,776
Gilliam	221	632	371	639
Grant	732	3,187	853	2,926
Harney	682	2,904	832	2,607
Hood River	6,359	3,223	6,058	3,429
Jackson	43,550	53,083	44,468	49,020
Jefferson	2,892	5,337	3,301	4,642
Josephine	13,223	26,582	14,953	23,673
Klamath	7,080	20,170	8,302	18,898
Lake	628	3,001	770	2,808
Lane	100,497	66,218	102,652	62,509
Lincoln	12,300	9,901	13,401	8,686
Linn	17,456	32,683	20,378	28,944
Malheur	2,213	7,141	2,759	6,851
Marion	48,803	54,336	56,376	60,190
Morrow	1,004	2,698	1,202	2,532
Multnomah	263,522	60,905	274,887	75,302
Polk	15,741	18,333	16,292	17,819
Sherman	202	726	319	678
Tillamook	5,701	6,486	6,293	5,684
Umatilla	7,466	16,775	8,584	15,499
Union	3,221	8,378	3,973	7,636
Wallowa	1,097	2,825	1,253	2,804
Wasco	4,634	5,721	5,211	5,229
Washington	137,818	75,903	135,291	93,974
Wheeler	152	581	266	545
Yamhill	18,635	22,589	19,260	22,045
Totals	**911,358**	**722,938**	**970,488**	**754,175**

All candidates, 2016: Clinton, D, 911,358; Trump, R, 722,938; Johnson, LB, 83,180; Stein, Pacific Green, 43,304.

Pennsylvania

County	2016 Clinton (D)	Trump (R)	2012 Obama (D)	Romney (R)
Adams	14,077	31,249	15,091	26,767
Allegheny	363,017	257,488	352,687	262,039
Armstrong	6,849	22,676	9,045	20,142
Beaver	30,225	46,081	37,055	42,344
Bedford	3,613	19,455	4,788	16,702
Berks	75,169	93,094	83,011	54,702
Blair	13,093	37,224	16,276	33,319
Bradford	6,263	17,957	8,624	14,410
Bucks	165,861	163,873	160,521	156,579
Butler	26,834	61,388	28,550	59,761
Cambria	17,646	40,419	24,249	35,163
Cameron	469	1,495	724	1,359
Carbon	8,917	18,714	11,580	13,504
Centre	36,555	35,099	34,176	34,001
Chester	140,188	115,582	124,311	124,840
Clarion	4,256	12,545	5,056	10,828
Clearfield	7,700	23,909	11,121	20,347
Clinton	4,533	9,701	5,734	7,303
Columbia	8,502	17,387	10,937	14,236
Crawford	10,215	23,912	13,883	20,901
Cumberland	44,282	65,649	44,367	64,809
Dauphin	64,287	60,620	64,965	57,450
Delaware	169,169	106,559	171,792	110,853
Elk	3,637	9,704	5,463	7,579
Erie	54,820	57,168	68,036	49,025
Fayette	17,826	34,388	21,971	26,018
Forest	626	1,680	896	1,383
Franklin	17,322	49,554	18,995	43,260
Fulton	904	5,676	1,310	4,814
Greene	4,157	10,394	5,852	8,428
Huntingdon	4,487	14,369	5,409	11,979
Indiana	11,468	24,920	14,473	21,257
Jefferson	3,437	14,533	4,787	13,048
Juniata	1,810	8,234	2,547	6,862

County	2016 Clinton (D)	Trump (R)	2012 Obama (D)	Romney (R)
Lackawanna	51,593	48,102	61,838	35,085
Lancaster	90,066	137,145	88,481	130,669
Lawrence	13,933	25,323	17,513	21,047
Lebanon	17,860	38,804	19,900	35,872
Lehigh	77,087	70,285	78,283	66,874
Luzerne	51,454	77,508	64,307	58,325
Lycoming	12,926	35,475	15,203	30,658
McKean	3,802	11,159	5,297	9,545
Mercer	17,631	30,034	24,232	25,925
Mifflin	3,563	14,050	4,273	11,939
Monroe	31,930	31,706	35,221	26,867
Montgomery	251,063	160,803	233,356	174,381
Montour	2,851	5,274	3,053	4,652
Northampton	65,936	71,384	67,606	61,446
Northumberland	9,184	24,418	13,072	19,518
Perry	4,416	15,114	5,685	13,120
Philadelphia	560,542	105,418	588,806	96,467
Pike	9,247	16,035	10,210	12,786
Potter	1,300	6,247	1,897	5,231
Schuylkill	16,724	43,937	24,546	32,278
Snyder	3,991	11,710	4,687	10,073
Somerset	7,367	27,347	9,436	23,984
Sullivan	756	2,318	1,034	1,868
Susquehanna	5,065	13,295	6,935	10,800
Tioga	3,642	12,928	5,357	11,342
Union	6,138	10,605	6,109	9,896
Venango	5,889	15,254	7,945	13,815
Warren	4,828	12,032	6,995	10,010
Washington	34,436	58,941	40,345	53,230
Wayne	6,398	15,269	8,396	12,896
Westmoreland	59,506	116,427	63,722	103,932
Wyoming	3,573	8,375	5,061	6,587
York	67,428	126,933	73,191	113,304
Totals	**2,844,339**	**2,912,351**	**2,990,274**	**2,680,434**

All candidates, 2016: Trump, R, 2,912,351; Clinton, D, 2,844,339; Johnson, LB, 142,623; Stein, Green, 48,998; Castle, Const., 20,887.

Rhode Island

City	2016 Clinton (D)	Trump (R)	2012 Obama (D)	Romney (R)
Barrington	4,248	2,121	5,557	3,836
Bristol	4,764	3,514	6,359	3,707
Coventry	6,484	8,791	9,122	6,969
Cranston	17,176	14,660	21,388	13,008
Cumberland	7,954	6,985	9,291	7,106
East Providence	10,775	6,641	14,095	5,752
Johnston	5,214	7,160	7,503	5,417
Lincoln	4,776	5,039	6,028	4,866
Newport	5,441	2,334	6,174	2,959
North Kingstown	6,827	5,532	7,847	6,451
North Providence	7,244	6,559	9,613	5,404
Pawtucket	14,463	5,805	18,155	5,228
Portsmouth	4,103	3,412	5,017	4,165
Providence	41,596	7,087	43,885	7,335
Smithfield	3,875	4,800	5,293	4,681
South Kingstown	7,460	4,138	8,611	4,720
Warwick	18,394	17,303	24,448	15,027
West Warwick	5,171	5,450	6,956	4,332
Westerly	3,470	3,558	6,071	4,382
Woonsocket	5,968	5,183	7,985	4,114
Other	39,960	39,457	50,279	37,745
Totals	**225,363**	**165,529**	**279,677**	**157,204**

All candidates, 2016: Clinton, D, 225,363; Trump, R, 165,529; Johnson, LB, 13,416; Stein, Green, 5,732; De La Fuente, Amer. Delta, 592.

South Carolina

County	2016 Clinton (D)	Trump (R)	2012 Obama (D)	Romney (R)
Abbeville	3,712	6,742	4,543	5,981
Aiken	25,426	45,981	25,322	44,042
Allendale	2,722	788	3,297	838
Anderson	21,040	56,109	22,405	48,709
Bamberg	3,886	2,197	4,624	2,194

County	2016 Clinton (D)	Trump (R)	2012 Obama (D)	Romney (R)
Barnwell	4,395	4,888	5,188	4,659
Beaufort	29,577	39,986	29,848	42,687
Berkeley	30,492	44,223	28,542	38,475
Calhoun	3,569	3,785	4,045	3,707
Charleston	89,048	75,233	81,487	77,629
Cherokee	6,089	15,165	7,231	13,314
Chester	6,582	7,272	7,891	6,367
Chesterfield	7,125	9,576	7,958	8,490
Clarendon	7,635	7,246	9,091	7,071
Colleton	7,616	9,083	8,475	8,443
Darlington	13,866	14,973	15,457	14,434
Dillon	5,832	5,637	7,523	5,427
Dorchester	17,470	27,046	23,445	32,531
Edgefield	4,491	6,842	4,967	6,512
Fairfield	6,936	4,024	7,777	3,999
Florence	26,630	29,498	28,614	28,961
Georgetown	13,234	17,334	14,163	16,526
Greenville	73,338	125,595	68,070	121,685
Greenwood	10,633	16,881	11,972	16,348
Hampton	5,163	3,483	5,834	3,312
Horry	36,731	83,819	38,885	72,127
Jasper	7,789	6,100	5,757	4,169
Kershaw	10,293	17,464	11,259	16,324
Lancaster	13,718	23,598	13,419	19,333
Laurens	8,845	16,770	10,318	14,746
Lee	5,170	2,789	5,977	2,832
Lexington	35,143	79,866	34,148	76,662
Marion	8,522	5,434	9,688	5,164
Marlboro	5,928	4,257	6,100	3,676
McCormick	2,479	2,651	2,653	2,467
Newberry	6,212	10,011	6,913	9,260
Oconee	7,979	24,096	8,550	21,611
Orangeburg	26,258	11,909	30,720	12,022
Pickens	10,327	36,096	11,156	33,474
Richland	70,415	36,777	103,989	53,105
Saluda	2,809	5,525	3,328	5,135
Spartanburg	39,888	76,101	41,461	66,969
Sumter	24,024	18,733	27,589	19,274
Union	4,727	7,058	5,796	6,584
Williamsburg	9,949	4,863	11,335	4,824
York	41,230	66,245	39,131	59,546
Totals	**804,943**	**1,119,749**	**865,941**	**1,071,645**

All candidates, 2016: Trump, R, 1,119,749; Clinton, D, 804,943; Johnson, LB, 47,698; McMullin, Ind., 20,242; Stein, Green, 12,602; Castle, Const., 5,550; Skewes, American, 3,140.

South Dakota

County	2016 Clinton (D)	Trump (R)	2012 Obama (D)	Romney (R)
Aurora	340	974	556	804
Beadle	1,912	4,455	2,881	4,230
Bennett	412	666	548	626
Bon Homme	704	2,105	1,167	1,830
Brookings	4,879	6,748	5,827	6,220
Brown	5,452	9,613	7,250	8,321
Brule	571	1,565	824	1,499
Buffalo	296	171	472	166
Butte	693	3,355	1,002	3,073
Campbell	105	704	153	616
Charles Mix	935	2,382	1,483	2,230
Clark	398	1,139	713	1,067
Clay	2,608	2,109	2,955	2,147
Codington	3,174	7,764	4,588	6,696
Corson	535	588	648	515
Custer	1,093	3,165	1,335	3,062
Davison	2,355	5,157	3,042	4,757
Day	974	1,627	1,497	1,320
Deuel	570	1,366	941	1,175
Dewey	887	723	1,207	663
Douglas	214	1,338	332	1,334
Edmunds	380	1,433	622	1,264
Fall River	821	2,511	1,140	2,258
Faulk	204	858	331	765
Grant	970	2,381	1,493	2,034
Gregory	391	1,600	599	1,507
Haakon	77	936	138	940
Hamlin	555	2,051	921	1,803
Hand	334	1,391	575	1,242

County	2016 Clinton (D)	Trump (R)	2012 Obama (D)	Romney (R)
Hanson	424	1,497	760	1,627
Harding	38	694	82	638
Hughes	2,449	5,174	2,786	5,219
Hutchinson	692	2,517	923	2,451
Hyde	125	543	189	531
Jackson	323	722	426	661
Jerauld	264	648	452	538
Jones	69	450	108	490
Kingsbury	703	1,680	1,092	1,451
Lake	2,314	4,038	2,724	3,419
Lawrence	3,356	7,411	3,973	7,025
Lincoln	8,076	15,499	7,982	13,611
Lyman	369	977	605	933
Marshall	754	1,056	1,061	889
McCook	623	1,794	905	1,655
McPherson	192	892	272	921
Meade	2,223	8,441	2,928	7,566
Mellette	238	402	375	381
Miner	281	706	479	636
Minnehaha	30,610	42,043	34,674	40,342
Moody	1,042	1,729	1,429	1,535
Oglala Lakota	2,504	241	2,937	188
Pennington	14,074	29,804	15,125	28,232
Perkins	188	1,333	319	1,205
Potter	215	1,069	339	1,029
Roberts	1,539	2,142	2,302	1,883
Sanborn	241	819	389	688
Spink	919	1,854	1,300	1,670
Stanley	329	1,148	435	1,063
Sully	137	679	186	613
Todd	1,505	487	1,976	498
Tripp	462	2,069	737	1,905
Turner	961	2,937	1,411	2,715
Union	2,227	5,288	2,782	4,698
Walworth	457	1,896	671	1,731
Yankton	3,301	5,654	4,226	5,495
Ziebach	352	368	439	314
Totals	**117,415**	**227,576**	**145,039**	**210,610**

All candidates, 2016: Trump, R, 227,576; Clinton, D, 117,415; Johnson, LB, 20,839; Castle, Const., 4,159.

Tennessee

County	2016 Clinton (D)	Trump (R)	2012 Obama (D)	Romney (R)
Anderson	9,010	19,201	10,122	18,968
Bedford	3,384	11,455	4,211	10,034
Benton	1,474	4,715	2,258	3,850
Bledsoe	896	3,621	1,267	3,022
Blount	12,085	37,385	12,934	35,441
Bradley	7,070	29,761	8,037	27,422
Campbell	2,248	9,860	3,328	8,604
Cannon	1,126	4,006	1,564	3,309
Carroll	2,323	7,731	3,475	7,225
Carter	3,453	16,897	4,789	15,503
Cheatham	3,877	11,295	4,659	10,268
Chester	902	3,827	1,624	4,684
Claiborne	1,831	8,589	2,433	7,617
Clay	707	2,140	1,037	1,747
Cocke	1,980	9,791	2,804	8,459
Coffee	4,741	14,409	5,870	13,023
Crockett	1,302	3,977	1,669	3,783
Cumberland	5,202	20,410	6,261	18,653
Davidson	148,473	84,365	143,120	97,622
Decatur	894	3,580	1,303	2,874
DeKalb	1,566	5,164	2,174	4,143
Dickson	4,718	13,213	6,233	11,296
Dyer	2,815	10,175	3,757	9,921
Fayette	5,865	13,046	6,688	12,689
Fentress	1,100	6,032	1,561	5,243
Franklin	4,372	11,526	5,603	10,262
Gibson	5,255	13,779	6,564	12,883
Giles	2,915	7,964	3,760	6,915
Grainger	1,154	6,618	1,668	5,470
Greene	4,211	18,538	6,225	17,245
Grundy	998	3,626	1,643	2,516
Hamblen	4,075	15,839	5,234	14,522
Hamilton	55,260	78,661	58,836	79,933
Hancock	322	1,842	475	1,527
Hardeman	2,757	2,752	5,482	4,865
Hardin	1,622	8,012	2,467	7,886
Hawkins	3,502	16,611	5,088	14,382

County	2016 Clinton (D)	Trump (R)	2012 Obama (D)	Romney (R)
Haywood	3,704	3,010	4,569	2,960
Henderson	1,796	8,118	2,517	7,421
Henry	3,061	9,483	4,339	8,193
Hickman	1,823	5,685	2,698	4,758
Houston	865	2,180	1,400	1,579
Humphreys	1,967	4,928	2,905	3,833
Jackson	1,129	3,229	1,739	2,383
Jefferson	3,490	14,760	4,232	13,038
Johnson	988	5,400	1,483	4,611
Knox	62,861	105,724	59,399	109,707
Lake	577	1,357	884	1,163
Lauderdale	3,656	4,884	4,011	4,616
Lawrence	2,821	12,419	4,237	10,770
Lewis	890	3,579	1,447	3,117
Lincoln	2,550	10,375	3,290	9,803
Loudon	4,916	17,588	5,058	16,707
Macon	1,071	6,260	1,552	5,260
Madison	15,438	21,321	18,367	21,993
Marion	2,829	7,680	3,953	6,272
Marshall	2,848	8,167	3,725	6,832
Maury	10,026	23,781	11,825	20,708
McMinn	3,507	14,673	4,609	12,967
McNairy	1,847	7,839	2,645	7,015
Meigs	856	3,337	1,163	2,734
Monroe	3,184	13,361	4,372	11,731
Montgomery	21,686	32,320	24,499	30,245
Moore	496	2,325	705	2,053
Morgan	1,053	5,429	1,725	4,669
Obion	2,425	9,525	3,321	8,814
Overton	1,943	6,055	2,805	4,775
Perry	597	2,167	992	1,578
Pickett	536	2,019	712	1,712
Polk	1,252	5,097	1,856	4,108
Putnam	6,847	18,981	7,802	17,254
Rhea	1,942	8,650	2,628	7,802
Roane	4,833	15,863	6,018	14,724
Robertson	6,634	19,393	8,290	17,643
Rutherford	36,627	64,428	36,414	60,846
Scott	934	6,044	1,452	5,117
Sequatchie	1,051	4,434	1,489	3,541
Sevier	6,293	28,610	7,418	25,984
Shelby	206,640	114,948	232,443	135,649
Smith	1,688	5,485	2,470	4,495
Stewart	1,222	3,864	2,069	2,963
Sullivan	11,910	45,577	15,321	43,562
Sumner	18,153	50,105	18,579	46,003
Tipton	5,779	16,893	7,133	16,672
Trousdale	943	2,099	1,240	1,612
Unicoi	1,260	5,666	1,913	5,032
Union	1,010	5,024	1,478	4,282
Van Buren	539	1,820	875	1,386
Warren	3,535	9,535	4,752	8,010
Washington	13,003	34,179	14,325	32,808
Wayne	717	5,034	1,163	4,253
Weakley	2,770	9,001	3,548	8,605
White	1,842	7,657	2,795	6,197
Williamson	30,992	68,160	25,142	69,850
Wilson	14,356	39,304	14,695	36,109
Totals	**865,693**	**1,515,242**	**960,709**	**1,462,330**

All candidates, 2016: Trump, R, 1,515,242; Clinton, D, 865,693; Johnson, Ind., 70,041; Stein, Ind., 15,903; Smith, Ind., 7,237; De La Fuente, Ind., 4,057; Kennedy, Ind., 2,864.

Texas

County	2016 Clinton (D)	Trump (R)	2012 Obama (D)	Romney (R)
Anderson	3,358	13,165	3,813	12,262
Andrews	836	3,925	795	3,639
Angelina	7,538	21,666	7,834	20,303
Aransas	2,458	7,730	2,704	6,830
Archer	394	3,785	525	3,600
Armstrong	70	924	98	828
Atascosa	4,635	8,598	5,133	7,461
Austin	2,319	9,637	2,252	9,265
Bailey	397	1,343	466	1,339
Bandera	1,726	8,159	1,864	7,426
Bastrop	10,555	16,314	9,864	14,033
Baylor	191	1,267	267	1,297
Bee	3,443	4,743	3,452	4,356
Bell	37,608	51,780	35,512	49,574
Bexar	319,191	240,161	264,856	241,617
Blanco	1,244	4,212	1,220	3,638

County	2016 Clinton (D)	Trump (R)	2012 Obama (D)	Romney (R)	County	2016 Clinton (D)	Trump (R)	2012 Obama (D)	Romney (R)
Borden	31	330	32	324	Hamilton	479	3,056	591	2,918
Bosque	1,277	6,325	1,367	5,885	Hansford	171	1,730	159	1,788
Bowie	8,831	24,913	10,196	24,869	Hardeman	249	1,207	302	1,176
Brazoria	43,075	72,653	34,421	70,862	Hardin	2,779	19,600	3,359	17,746
Brazos	23,041	38,662	17,477	37,209	Harris	706,471	544,960	587,044	586,073
Brewster	1,869	2,073	1,765	1,976	Harrison	7,130	18,712	8,456	17,512
Briscoe	91	625	117	578	Hartley	172	1,727	184	1,708
Brooks	1,937	613	1,886	507	Haskell	314	1,403	553	1,424
Brown	1,621	12,010	1,904	11,895	Hays	33,117	33,730	25,537	31,661
Burleson	1,491	5,316	1,705	4,671	Hemphill	181	1,460	192	1,298
Burnet	3,785	14,595	3,674	12,843	Henderson	5,649	23,574	6,106	21,231
Caldwell	4,663	6,516	4,791	6,021	Hidalgo	118,713	48,581	97,969	39,865
Calhoun	2,118	4,638	2,410	4,144	Hill	2,535	10,075	2,752	9,132
Callahan	568	4,858	751	4,378	Hockley	1,257	5,793	1,486	5,546
Cameron	59,319	29,432	49,975	26,099	Hood	4,001	21,367	3,843	18,409
Camp	1,260	3,201	1,428	2,881	Hopkins	2,508	10,704	2,777	9,836
Carson	249	2,617	292	2,451	Houston	1,978	6,205	2,265	5,880
Cass	2,250	9,182	2,924	8,763	Howard	1,768	6,635	2,110	6,453
Castro	526	1,413	630	1,470	Hudspeth	324	503	379	471
Chambers	2,939	13,278	2,790	11,787	Hunt	6,301	23,866	6,671	21,011
Cherokee	3,466	12,896	3,875	12,094	Hutchinson	854	7,039	1,045	6,804
Childress	253	1,802	320	1,665	Irion	90	660	112	668
Clay	536	4,376	740	4,266	Jack	314	2,973	303	2,580
Cochran	190	679	256	649	Jackson	904	4,266	1,070	3,906
Coke	140	1,265	179	1,218	Jasper	2,582	10,578	3,423	9,957
Coleman	387	3,177	442	3,012	Jeff Davis	422	694	440	719
Collin	139,837	200,395	101,415	196,888	Jefferson	42,404	42,828	44,668	43,242
Collingsworth	145	983	177	962	Jim Hogg	1,635	430	1,301	356
Colorado	1,977	6,323	2,029	6,026	Jim Wells	6,688	5,411	6,492	4,598
Comal	14,166	44,996	11,450	39,318	Johnson	10,976	44,370	10,496	37,661
Comanche	788	4,300	890	3,944	Jones	935	4,815	1,226	4,262
Concho	148	885	194	793	Karnes	1,144	2,959	1,325	2,825
Cooke	1,447	7,060	2,246	11,951	Kaufman	10,265	29,537	9,472	24,846
Coryell	5,057	12,212	5,158	11,220	Kendall	3,633	15,663	3,043	14,508
Cottle	84	486	180	555	Kenedy	99	84	82	84
Crane	299	1,047	275	985	Kent	59	360	66	335
Crockett	372	980	480	957	Kerr	4,665	17,658	4,338	17,274
Crosby	468	1,180	639	1,132	Kimble	206	1,697	217	1,667
Culberson	454	280	568	295	King	5	149	5	139
Dallam	222	1,258	253	1,248	Kinney	457	936	522	880
Dallas	458,845	261,865	405,571	295,813	Kleberg	4,713	4,364	4,754	4,058
Dawson	835	2,636	1,019	2,591	Knox	247	1,078	332	1,160
Deaf Smith	1,185	2,911	1,239	3,042	La Salle	1,125	870	965	669
Delta	400	1,836	454	1,524	Lamar	3,579	14,546	4,181	12,826
Denton	110,000	169,175	80,978	157,579	Lamb	770	3,040	998	3,058
DeWitt	1,161	5,510	1,467	5,122	Lampasas	1,479	6,371	1,479	5,621
Dickens	128	755	216	793	Lavaca	1,170	7,339	1,428	6,796
Dimmit	2,173	974	2,141	762	Lee	1,372	4,996	1,632	4,507
Donley	190	1,225	226	1,287	Leon	909	6,391	1,062	5,814
Duval	2,783	1,316	3,331	980	Liberty	4,851	18,856	5,202	17,323
Eastland	776	6,008	970	5,444	Limestone	1,748	5,747	2,208	5,288
Ector	10,225	24,976	8,118	24,010	Lipscomb	135	1,159	119	1,044
Edwards	302	741	232	642	Live Oak	739	3,450	919	3,154
El Paso	145,509	54,567	112,952	57,150	Llano	1,825	8,283	1,822	7,610
Ellis	16,197	44,807	13,881	39,574	Loving	4	57	9	54
Erath	2,159	11,205	1,965	10,329	Lubbock	27,956	65,566	26,271	63,469
Falls	1,682	3,438	2,033	3,356	Lynn	403	1,546	506	1,439
Fannin	2,123	9,536	2,486	8,161	Madison	881	3,349	967	3,028
Fayette	2,127	8,648	2,315	8,106	Marion	1,156	2,968	1,495	2,733
Fisher	403	1,265	512	1,094	Martin	266	1,453	248	1,368
Floyd	435	1,473	551	1,523	Mason	353	1,656	380	1,565
Foard	113	383	140	348	Matagorda	3,357	8,147	3,980	8,040
Fort Bend	134,475	117,212	101,144	116,126	Maverick	10,397	2,816	8,303	2,171
Franklin	665	3,583	751	3,446	McCulloch	480	2,546	537	2,419
Freestone	1,461	5,995	1,850	5,646	McLennan	27,046	48,245	25,694	47,903
Frio	1,401	1,232	2,376	1,559	McMullen	40	454	67	431
Gaines	597	3,907	535	3,484	Medina	4,624	12,054	4,784	11,079
Galveston	45,503	73,566	39,511	69,059	Menard	153	681	171	665
Garza	224	1,223	279	1,263	Midland	9,993	36,896	8,286	35,689
Gillespie	2,286	10,445	2,055	10,306	Milam	2,042	6,340	2,636	5,481
Glasscock	34	553	44	526	Mills	242	1,949	279	1,882
Goliad	973	2,618	1,127	2,294	Mitchell	353	1,780	538	1,756
Gonzales	1,567	4,580	1,777	4,216	Montague	885	7,526	1,116	6,549
Gray	699	6,495	886	6,443	Montgomery	45,744	150,188	32,920	137,969
Grayson	10,276	35,274	10,670	30,936	Moore	1,096	3,974	964	3,968
Gregg	11,623	28,693	12,398	28,742	Morris	1,425	3,443	1,858	3,232
Grimes	2,194	7,065	2,339	6,141	Motley	40	571	55	538
Guadalupe	18,308	36,495	15,744	33,117	Nacogdoches	6,822	14,751	6,465	13,925
Hale	2,090	6,347	2,243	6,490	Navarro	3,998	11,984	4,350	10,847
Hall	164	891	265	832	Newton	978	2,961	1,677	4,112

County	2016 Clinton (D)	Trump (R)	2012 Obama (D)	Romney (R)
Nolan	1,029	3,551	1,216	3,282
Nueces	49,102	50,704	45,772	48,966
Ochiltree	274	2,628	253	2,719
Oldham	78	850	71	790
Orange	5,716	25,385	6,800	23,366
Palo Pinto	1,700	8,222	1,811	7,393
Panola	1,835	8,445	2,211	7,950
Parker	8,329	46,433	7,853	39,243
Parmer	848	1,911	529	2,011
Pecos	1,551	2,463	1,591	2,512
Polk	7,123	26,587	4,859	14,071
Potter	7,620	19,499	7,126	18,918
Presidio	1,458	652	1,282	504
Rains	619	3,919	761	3,279
Randall	8,340	43,379	7,574	41,447
Reagan	167	709	158	676
Real	262	1,382	277	1,236
Red River	1,148	3,924	1,482	3,549
Reeves	1,659	1,417	1,655	1,188
Refugio	1,034	1,830	998	1,663
Roberts	20	524	33	468
Robertson	2,203	4,665	2,798	4,419
Rockwall	9,633	28,396	8,120	27,113
Runnels	452	3,241	519	3,104
Rusk	3,935	14,675	4,451	13,924
Sabine	614	3,992	807	3,727
San Augustine	907	2,620	1,193	2,469
San Jacinto	2,034	8,050	2,410	7,107
San Patricio	7,825	13,004	7,856	12,005
San Saba	293	2,025	323	1,905
Schleicher	209	819	221	787
Scurry	733	4,403	838	4,124
Shackelford	103	1,378	131	1,218
Shelby	1,757	7,171	2,322	6,879
Sherman	96	807	121	908
Smith	22,128	58,631	21,456	57,331
Somervell	540	3,206	613	2,871
Starr	9,246	2,218	10,260	1,547
Stephens	348	3,033	475	2,892
Sterling	70	549	31	459
Stonewall	135	555	160	507
Sutton	313	1,075	369	1,110
Swisher	462	1,671	579	1,655
Tarrant	287,411	345,100	253,071	348,920
Taylor	10,047	33,172	9,750	32,904
Terrell	140	287	184	358
Terry	424	1,295	1,059	2,602
Throckmorton	84	715	109	700
Titus	2,538	6,405	2,648	6,084
Tom Green	9,117	27,376	9,294	26,878
Travis	306,475	126,750	232,788	140,152
Trinity	1,154	4,737	1,614	4,537
Tyler	1,243	6,601	1,668	5,910
Upshur	2,378	13,198	2,971	12,015
Upton	284	961	333	953
Uvalde	3,863	4,828	3,825	4,529
Val Verde	6,920	5,856	6,285	5,635
Van Zandt	NA	NA	3,084	15,794
Victoria	8,843	21,253	8,802	19,692
Walker	6,085	12,878	6,252	12,140
Waller	5,744	10,525	6,514	9,244
Ward	780	2,541	841	2,366
Washington	3,381	10,944	3,381	10,857
Webb	27,404	8,471	37,597	11,078
Wharton	4,238	10,149	4,235	9,750
Wheeler	194	2,087	232	1,878
Wichita	8,752	27,609	10,525	29,812
Wilbarger	807	3,166	971	2,956
Willacy	3,416	1,541	3,600	1,416
Williamson	84,252	104,029	61,875	97,006
Wilson	4,790	13,991	4,821	12,218
Winkler	420	1,403	398	1,311
Wise	3,412	20,655	3,221	17,207
Wood	2,624	15,681	3,056	14,351
Yoakum	426	1,797	409	1,698
Young	873	6,587	992	6,225
Zapata	2,056	1,028	2,527	997
Zavala	2,633	692	3,042	574
Totals	**3,848,617**	**4,651,955**	**3,308,124**	**4,569,843**

All candidates, 2016: Trump, R, 4,651,955; Clinton, D, 3,848,617; Johnson, LB, 281,516; Stein, Green, 70,958.

Utah

County	2016 Clinton (D)	Trump (R)	2012 Obama (D)	Romney (R)
Beaver	258	1,800	346	2,174
Box Elder	1,814	10,324	1,984	17,101
Cache	5,435	12,385	6,244	35,039
Carbon	1,673	5,055	2,275	5,090
Daggett	76	327	94	406
Davis	19,458	39,047	21,889	96,861
Duchesne	NA	NA	581	5,698
Emery	NA	NA	569	3,777
Garfield	352	1,577	308	1,832
Grand	NA	NA	1,727	1,996
Iron	NA	NA	2,148	14,200
Juab	434	2,750	451	3,448
Kane	627	1,720	744	2,522
Millard	410	3,672	431	4,478
Morgan	NA	NA	403	4,114
Piute	NA	NA	74	697
Rich	104	786	83	915
Salt Lake	117,667	82,590	146,147	223,811
San Juan	1,143	2,073	2,139	3,074
Sanpete	979	6,081	980	8,406
Sevier	545	5,002	738	7,207
Summit	8,188	5,413	8,072	8,884
Tooele	3,595	7,823	4,524	14,268
Uintah	733	7,223	997	10,421
Utah	22,934	84,863	17,281	156,950
Wasatch	NA	NA	2,191	7,220
Washington	8,369	33,472	8,337	44,698
Wayne	NA	NA	215	1,089
Weber	18,819	30,561	19,841	54,224
Totals	**213,613**	**344,544**	**251,813**	**740,600**

All candidates, 2016: Trump, R, 344,544; Clinton, D, 213,613; McMullin, unaff., 156,849; Johnson, LB, 24,435; Stein, Green, 5,171; Castle, Const., 4,927; Giordani, Independent Amer., 1,883; De La Fuente, unaff., 504; Moorehead, unaff., 357; Kennedy, unaff., 345.

Vermont

City	2016 Clinton (D)	Trump (R)	2012 Obama (D)	Romney (R)
Bennington	3,361	1,949	4,503	1,753
Brattleboro	4,347	858	4,621	915
Burlington	14,519	2,082	14,326	2,592
Colchester	4,456	2,425	4,618	2,551
Essex	6,715	3,013	6,630	3,640
Hartford	3,190	1,303	3,356	1,417
Montpelier	3,696	492	3,694	700
Rutland	3,495	2,734	4,252	2,430
Shelburne	3,376	941	3,076	1,403
South Burlington	7,246	2,059	6,513	2,748
Williston	3,508	1,481	3,329	1,697
Other	120,165	75,688	140321	70852
Totals	**178,074**	**95,025**	**199,239**	**92,698**

All candidates, 2016: Clinton, D, 178,074; Trump, R, 95,025; Johnson, LB, 10,042; Stein, Green, 6,742; De La Fuente, Ind., 1,063; La Riva, Liberty Union, 323.

Virginia

County	2016 Clinton (D)	Trump (R)	2012 Obama (D)	Romney (R)
Accomack	6,737	8,582	7,655	8,213
Albemarle	33,297	19,232	29,757	23,297
Alleghany	2,165	4,873	3,403	3,595
Amelia	2,150	4,704	2,490	4,331
Amherst	4,986	9,643	5,900	8,876
Appomattox	2,023	5,714	2,453	5,340
Arlington	91,879	20,155	81,269	34,474
Augusta	8,168	26,152	9,451	23,624
Bath	603	1,548	894	1,274
Bedford	9,733	30,578	10,209	26,679
Bland	453	2,572	735	2,144
Botetourt	4,492	13,369	5,452	12,479
Brunswick	4,472	3,044	4,994	2,968
Buchanan	1,721	7,292	3,094	6,436
Buckingham	3,128	3,969	3,750	3,569
Campbell	6,597	19,442	7,595	17,695
Caroline	6,425	7,143	7,276	6,151
Carroll	2,590	10,653	3,685	8,736
Charles City	2,244	1,381	2,772	1,396
Charlotte	2,153	3,479	2,503	3,311
Chesterfield	80,993	84,938	77,694	90,934
Clarke	3,053	4,657	3,239	4,296

County	2016 Clinton (D)	Trump (R)	2012 Obama (D)	Romney (R)
Craig	541	2,139	830	1,757
Culpeper	7,744	13,341	8,285	11,580
Cumberland	2,032	2,693	2,422	2,538
Dickenson	1,335	4,932	2,473	4,274
Dinwiddie	5,765	7,447	6,550	6,875
Essex	2,541	2,657	3,016	2,602
Fairfax	354,486	157,547	315,273	206,773
Fauquier	12,960	22,110	13,965	21,034
Floyd	2,300	5,289	2,732	4,673
Fluvanna	5,751	7,018	5,893	6,678
Franklin	7,254	18,560	9,090	16,718
Frederick	11,920	26,069	12,690	22,858
Giles	1,949	5,930	2,730	4,660
Gloucester	5,399	13,087	6,764	12,137
Goochland	4,884	8,374	4,676	8,448
Grayson	1,407	5,593	2,068	4,801
Greene	2,923	5,943	3,290	5,569
Greensville	2,558	1,736	3,135	1,766
Halifax	6,890	9,698	7,766	8,694
Hanover	19,360	39,592	18,294	39,940
Henrico	93,649	59,636	89,594	70,449
Henry	8,199	15,207	10,317	13,984
Highland	371	958	459	924
Isle of Wight	7,673	11,971	8,761	11,802
James City	19,091	21,284	17,879	22,843
King and Queen	1,451	2,059	1,745	1,865
King George	4,002	7,338	4,477	6,604
King William	2,752	5,963	3,344	5,466
Lancaster	2,862	3,520	3,149	3,753
Lee	1,614	7,522	2,583	6,847
Loudoun	99,909	69,633	82,479	75,292
Louisa	6,208	10,507	6,953	9,215
Lunenburg	2,226	3,206	2,684	2,969
Madison	2,202	4,418	2,639	3,869
Mathews	1,563	3,515	1,807	3,488
Mecklenburg	6,571	8,283	6,921	7,973
Middlesex	2,107	3,668	2,370	3,619
Montgomery	20,015	19,455	19,903	20,006
Nelson	3,677	4,150	4,171	3,947
New Kent	3,545	8,117	3,555	7,246
Northampton	3,255	2,686	3,741	2,676
Northumberland	2,830	5,089	3,191	4,310
Nottoway	2,829	3,712	3,344	3,409
Orange	5,955	10,511	6,870	9,244
Page	2,514	7,824	3,724	6,344
Patrick	1,768	6,454	2,417	5,622
Pittsylvania	9,195	21,742	10,858	19,263
Powhatan	4,057	11,875	4,088	11,200
Prince Edward	4,590	4,099	5,132	3,952
Prince George	6,419	9,157	6,991	8,879
Prince William	83,093	54,065	103,331	74,458
Pulaski	4,170	10,314	5,292	8,920
Rappahannock	1,741	2,532	1,980	2,311
Richmond	1,347	2,213	1,574	2,160
Roanoke	16,747	30,857	18,711	31,624
Rockbridge	3,506	6,671	4,088	5,898
Rockingham	9,361	25,269	10,065	24,186
Russell	2,328	9,516	3,718	8,180
Scott	1,579	8,242	2,395	7,439
Shenandoah	5,269	14,078	6,469	12,538
Smyth	2,661	9,746	4,171	8,379
Southampton	3,595	5,035	4,437	4,733
Spotsylvania	23,279	33,742	25,165	31,844
Stafford	27,879	33,900	27,182	32,480
Surry	2,069	1,785	2,576	1,671
Sussex	2,874	2,055	3,358	2,021
Tazewell	2,895	15,160	3,661	13,843
Warren	5,165	11,762	6,452	9,869
Washington	5,480	18,979	7,076	18,141
Westmoreland	3,723	4,331	4,295	3,731
Wise	2,687	11,983	3,760	11,076
Wythe	2,765	10,044	3,783	8,324
York	12,989	18,823	13,183	20,204
City				
Alexandria	57,147	13,241	52,199	20,249
Bristol	1,832	4,884	2,492	4,780
Buena Vista	693	1,432	919	1,564
Charlottesville	17,865	2,951	16,510	4,844
Chesapeake	52,554	53,988	55,052	53,900
Colonial Heights	2,367	5,681	2,544	5,941

City	2016 Clinton (D)	Trump (R)	2012 Obama (D)	Romney (R)
Covington	914	1,349	1,319	975
Danville	11,051	7,306	12,218	7,763
Emporia	1,529	792	1,793	886
Fairfax	7,363	3,695	6,651	4,775
Falls Church	5,810	1,323	5,015	2,147
Franklin	2,516	1,421	2,833	1,496
Fredericksburg	6,690	3,731	7,131	4,060
Galax	680	1,603	900	1,332
Hampton	41,030	17,802	46,966	18,640
Harrisonburg	10,100	6,232	8,654	6,565
Hopewell	4,722	3,885	5,179	3,739
Lexington	1,514	766	1,486	1,146
Lynchburg	14,787	17,979	15,948	19,806
Manassas	8,395	5,934	8,478	6,463
Manassas Park	3,218	1,732	2,879	1,699
Martinsville	3,531	2,149	3,855	2,312
Newport News	40,997	23,650	51,100	27,230
Norfolk	51,429	19,785	62,687	23,147
Norton	383	1,021	566	895
Petersburg	12,005	1,448	14,283	1,527
Poquoson	1,609	5,088	1,679	5,312
Portsmouth	25,262	11,913	32,501	12,858
Radford	2,923	2,637	2,732	2,520
Richmond	74,640	14,254	75,921	20,050
Roanoke	23,403	16,045	24,134	14,991
Salem	4,212	7,225	4,760	7,299
Staunton	5,329	5,129	5,728	5,272
Suffolk	23,012	17,206	24,267	17,820
Virginia Beach	76,744	84,389	94,299	99,291
Waynesboro	3,762	4,798	3,840	4,790
Williamsburg	5,199	1,921	4,903	2,682
Winchester	5,161	4,786	5,094	4,946
Totals	**1,912,740**	**1,728,707**	**1,971,820**	**1,822,522**

All candidates, 2016: Clinton, D, 1,912,740; Trump, R, 1,728,707; Johnson, LB, 115,867; McMullin, Ind., 59,623; Stein, Green, 27,256.

Washington

County	2016 Clinton (D)	Trump (R)	2012 Obama (D)	Romney (R)
Adams	841	2,157	1,540	3,171
Asotin	2,768	4,998	4,003	5,654
Benton	15,454	27,189	28,145	49,461
Chelan	6,528	8,831	13,112	18,402
Clallam	12,331	12,012	18,580	18,437
Clark	71,663	67,218	93,382	92,951
Columbia	482	1,359	645	1,568
Cowlitz	10,511	12,887	22,726	20,746
Douglas	1,755	3,336	5,166	9,425
Ferry	960	1,927	1,294	1,995
Franklin	3,460	5,627	8,398	13,748
Garfield	268	797	336	913
Grant	6,021	14,947	8,950	17,852
Gray's Harbor	8,533	9,691	15,960	11,914
Island	17,540	14,627	21,478	19,605
Jefferson	10,805	5,019	12,739	6,405
King	459,920	132,243	668,004	275,700
Kitsap	44,680	32,563	67,277	52,846
Kittitas	5,224	7,136	7,949	9,782
Klickitat	2,311	3,031	4,598	5,316
Lewis	4,548	9,377	12,664	20,452
Lincoln	1,091	3,570	1,673	4,063
Mason	9,747	10,780	14,764	12,761
Okanogan	2,630	4,048	7,108	9,221
Pacific	3,900	4,444	5,711	4,499
Pend Oreille	1,609	3,641	2,508	3,952
Pierce	100,162	83,219	186,430	148,467
San Juan	5,516	2,018	7,125	3,111
Skagit	16,369	13,926	28,688	25,071
Skamania	1,618	2,086	2,628	2,687
Snohomish	108,205	72,210	188,516	133,016
Spokane	62,946	71,411	102,295	115,285
Stevens	3,477	8,463	7,762	13,691
Thurston	47,784	32,167	74,037	49,287
Wahkiakum	729	1,135	1,094	1,119
Walla Walla	4,960	6,875	9,768	14,648
Whatcom	44,711	30,574	57,089	42,703
Whitman	2,866	2,596	8,037	8,507
Yakima	13,849	20,584	33,217	42,239
Totals	**1,118,772**	**750,719**	**1,755,396**	**1,290,670**

All candidates, 2016: Clinton, D, 1,118,772; Trump, R, 750,719; Johnson, LB, 78,748; Stein, Green, 26,346; Castle, Const., 8,603; Kennedy, Soc. Workers, 2,362; La Riva, Socialism/Liberation, 1,664.

West Virginia

County	2016 Clinton (D)	Trump (R)	2012 Obama (D)	Romney (R)
Barbour	1,213	4,509	1,768	3,824
Berkeley	12,287	28,210	14,275	22,156
Boone	1,783	6,483	2,790	5,467
Braxton	1,570	3,516	1,998	2,725
Brooke	2,549	6,574	4,005	5,060
Cabell	11,306	19,648	13,568	17,985
Calhoun	456	2,023	818	1,319
Clay	566	2,289	931	1,971
Doddridge	360	2,347	575	2,130
Fayette	4,246	10,263	5,419	8,350
Gilmer	537	1,889	840	1,595
Grant	510	4,338	718	3,783
Greenbrier	2,126	6,110	4,710	7,930
Hampshire	1,576	6,646	2,299	5,523
Hancock	3,247	8,870	4,627	7,226
Hardy	1,249	4,544	1,482	3,536
Harrison	7,675	18,687	9,732	15,876
Jackson	2,648	8,959	3,854	7,408
Jefferson	9,458	13,144	10,398	11,258
Kanawha	27,985	43,464	32,480	41,364
Lewis	1,336	5,245	1,736	4,375
Lincoln	1,435	5,257	2,227	4,383
Logan	2,082	9,866	3,469	8,222
Marion	6,926	14,592	8,959	12,054
Marshall	2,894	9,565	4,484	8,135
Mason	2,069	7,597	3,778	5,741
McDowell	1,429	4,614	2,109	3,959
Mercer	4,689	17,362	5,432	15,450
Mineral	2,019	8,957	2,885	7,833
Mingo	1,365	7,070	2,428	6,191
Monongalia	14,568	18,278	13,826	16,831
Monroe	1,089	4,337	1,455	3,616
Morgan	1,568	5,718	2,363	4,513
Nicholas	1,821	7,169	2,664	5,898
Ohio	5,452	11,077	6,786	10,768
Pendleton	726	2,388	1,074	2,095
Pleasants	620	2,342	955	1,825
Pocahontas	924	2,474	1,303	2,182
Preston	2,462	9,501	2,931	7,889
Putnam	5,784	17,455	7,256	16,032
Raleigh	6,362	21,835	7,739	20,614
Randolph	2,724	7,583	3,342	6,160
Ritchie	490	3,376	768	2,921
Roane	1,220	3,772	1,939	2,982
Summers	1,186	3,444	1,621	2,981
Taylor	1,483	4,701	1,941	3,840
Tucker	750	2,557	880	2,176
Tyler	505	2,967	890	2,314
Upshur	1,763	6,971	2,158	5,939
Wayne	3,334	11,077	4,931	8,688
Webster	554	2,284	947	1,710
Wetzel	1,348	4,461	2,217	3,473
Wirt	383	1,903	676	1,427
Wood	8,327	25,168	11,230	22,183
Wyoming	1,061	6,527	1,583	5,769
Totals	**186,095**	**482,809**	**238,269**	**417,655**

All candidates, 2016: Trump, R, 482,809; Clinton, D, 186,095; Johnson, LB, 22,598; Stein, Mountain, 8,015; Castle, Const., 3,751.

Wisconsin

County	2016 Clinton (D)	Trump (R)	2012 Obama (D)	Romney (R)
Adams	3,493	5,798	5,542	4,644
Ashland	4,136	3,428	5,399	2,820
Barron	7,881	13,595	10,890	11,443
Bayfield	4,953	4,125	6,033	3,603
Brown	53,358	67,192	62,526	64,836
Buffalo	2,531	4,049	3,570	3,364
Burnett	2,948	5,412	3,986	4,550
Calumet	9,634	15,345	11,489	14,539
Chippewa	10,495	16,031	15,237	15,322
Clark	4,225	8,645	6,172	7,412
Columbia	13,525	14,160	17,175	13,026
Crawford	3,426	3,844	4,629	3,067
Dane	217,506	71,270	216,071	83,644
Dodge	13,968	26,643	18,762	25,211
Door	8,026	8,584	9,357	8,121
Douglas	11,342	9,657	14,863	7,705
Dunn	9,025	11,487	11,316	10,224
Eau Claire	27,271	23,301	30,666	23,256
Florence	666	1,897	953	1,645
Fond du Lac	17,391	31,044	22,379	30,355
Forest	1,583	2,787	2,425	2,172
Grant	10,047	12,347	13,594	10,255
Green	9,121	8,693	11,206	7,857

County	2016 Clinton (D)	Trump (R)	2012 Obama (D)	Romney (R)
Green Lake	2,700	6,210	3,793	5,782
Iowa	6,669	4,809	8,105	4,287
Iron	1,273	2,090	1,784	1,790
Jackson	3,821	4,907	5,298	3,900
Jefferson	16,559	23,409	20,158	23,517
Juneau	4,100	7,188	6,242	5,411
Kenosha	35,770	36,025	44,867	34,977
Kewaunee	3,593	6,616	5,153	5,747
La Crosse	32,402	26,384	36,693	25,751
Lafayette	3,288	3,977	4,536	3,314
Langlade	3,260	6,436	4,573	5,816
Lincoln	5,370	8,400	7,563	7,455
Manitowoc	14,563	23,234	20,403	21,604
Marathon	26,476	39,010	32,363	36,617
Marinette	6,243	12,995	9,882	10,619
Marquette	2,808	4,712	4,014	3,992
Menominee	1,003	269	1,191	179
Milwaukee	288,986	126,091	332,438	154,924
Monroe	7,047	11,442	9,515	9,675
Oconto	5,886	13,255	8,865	10,741
Oneida	8,103	11,677	10,452	10,917
Outagamie	38,117	51,579	45,659	47,372
Ozaukee	20,167	30,458	19,159	36,077
Pepin	1,345	2,228	1,876	1,794
Pierce	8,380	11,260	10,235	10,397
Polk	7,568	13,864	10,073	12,094
Portage	18,524	17,310	22,075	16,615
Price	2,671	4,562	3,887	3,884
Racine	42,506	46,620	53,008	49,347
Richland	3,577	4,021	4,969	3,573
Rock	39,336	31,483	49,219	30,517
Rusk	2,171	4,564	3,397	3,676
St. Croix	17,496	26,123	19,910	25,503
Sauk	16,050	15,871	18,736	12,838
Sawyer	2,846	4,625	4,486	4,442
Shawano	6,056	12,742	9,000	11,022
Sheboygan	22,636	32,368	27,918	34,072
Taylor	2,398	6,589	3,763	5,601
Trempealeau	5,645	7,370	7,605	5,707
Vernon	6,351	6,994	8,044	5,942
Vilas	4,769	8,169	5,951	7,749
Walworth	18,706	28,848	22,552	29,006
Washburn	3,283	5,404	4,447	4,699
Washington	20,854	51,729	23,166	54,765
Waukesha	79,198	145,519	78,779	162,798
Waupaca	8,303	16,013	11,578	14,002
Waushara	3,802	7,669	5,335	6,562
Winnebago	37,054	43,447	45,449	42,122
Wood	14,232	21,502	18,581	19,704
Totals	**1,380,512**	**1,407,401**	**1,620,985**	**1,407,966**

All candidates, 2016: Trump, R, 1,407,401; Clinton, D, 1,380,512; Johnson, LB, 106,292; Stein, Green, 30,957; Castle, Const., 12,177; Moorehead, Workers World, 1,786; De La Fuente, Amer. Delta, 1,561.

Wyoming

County	2016 Clinton (D)	Trump (R)	2012 Obama (D)	Romney (R)
Albany	6,888	7,601	7,458	7,866
Big Horn	594	4,067	868	4,285
Campbell	1,324	15,778	2,163	14,953
Carbon	1,279	4,409	2,110	4,148
Converse	668	5,520	1,089	5,043
Crook	271	3,347	426	3,109
Fremont	4,200	11,167	5,333	11,075
Goshen	924	4,418	1,458	4,178
Hot Springs	400	1,939	523	1,895
Johnson	638	3,477	749	3,363
Laramie	11,572	24,844	14,295	23,904
Lincoln	1,105	6,779	1,287	7,144
Natrona	6,573	23,523	8,961	22,132
Niobrara	115	1,116	200	1,022
Park	2,535	11,115	2,927	11,234
Platte	719	3,437	1,223	3,136
Sheridan	2,926	10,266	3,618	10,267
Sublette	644	3,409	767	3,472
Sweetwater	3,233	12,153	4,774	11,428
Teton	7,313	3,920	6,213	4,858
Uinta	1,202	6,154	1,628	6,615
Washakie	532	2,911	794	3,014
Weston	294	2,898	422	2,821
Totals	**55,949**	**174,248**	**69,286**	**170,962**

All candidates, 2016: Trump, R, 174,248; Clinton, D, 55,949; Johnson, LB, 13,285; Stein, Ind., 2,512; Castle, Const., 2,038; De La Fuente, Ind., 710.

Nov. 1, 2015, to Oct. 31, 2016

The Chronology of Events reports the top National, International, and General news stories, month by month.

November 2015

National

Obama Signs Budget, Defense Bills—Pres. Barack Obama Nov. 2 signed federal budget legislation—passed by Congress in late Oct. following weeks of negotiations—that increased the country's $18.1-tril debt-ceiling through Mar. 2017, averting a Nov. 3 default deadline. The deal raised sequestration caps (in place since 2011) by $80 bil in discretionary spending over two years, forestalling projected 52% hikes in some Medicare premiums that would have affected about 16 mil beneficiaries. The bill also boosted emergency war spending to fund operations against ISIS and terrorists in Afghanistan by $32 bil over two years.

After criticizing provisions that would make it more difficult to close the U.S. prison in Guantánamo Bay, Cuba, Obama Nov. 25 signed a $607-bil 2016 defense appropriations bill passed earlier in Nov. by the House (370-58) and Senate (91-3). The bill raised service members' pay, reformed the military's retirement system, called for the development of gender-neutral employment standards, and allowed commanders discretion to permit personal guns on military bases in the U.S.

Domestic Growth in Jobs, Wages; U.S. Fines Takata; Other Developments—The U.S. Dept. of Labor reported Nov. 6 that 271,000 jobs had been added to the U.S. economy in Oct., the largest monthly gain in 2015. The monthly unemployment rate for Oct. slipped to 5.0% from 5.1% in Sept. The Dow Jones industrial average held steady after a bullish Oct. and finished Nov. at 17,719.92, up 0.3%, while the S&P 500 closed Nov. at 2,080.41, up 0.1% for the month. The Nasdaq composite index finished at 5,108.67, up 1.1%.

The U.S. Dept. of Transportation's Natl. Highway Transportation Authority Nov. 3 fined Japanese auto parts maker Takata a record $200 mil (of which $130 mil was deferred pending Takata's anticipated cooperation with regulators) for failing to promptly disclose air bag defects linked to at least 8 deaths and 100 injuries worldwide. Officials gave Takata until the end of 2019 to make repairs on some 19 mil existing vehicles. Auto manufacturers Ford, Honda, Mazda, Nissan, and Toyota pledged not to use Takata air bag inflators in new models.

New York-based Pfizer and Dublin, Ireland-based Allergan agreed Nov. 22 on a $160-bil merger that would create the world's largest drug maker if approved by shareholders and regulators. According to the terms of the agreement, pharmaceutical giant Pfizer would move its headquarters to Ireland post-merger, allowing it to avoid paying U.S. taxes on profits earned abroad. If approved, the deal would create the largest-ever tax inversion.

Obama Rejects Keystone XL Pipeline—Pres. Obama Nov. 6 announced that he was rejecting a Canadian energy company's request to build a 1,179-mi oil pipeline known as Keystone XL between Alberta oil sands and Nebraska. The pipeline would have transported up to 830,000 barrels of crude oil daily between Canada and refineries in the U.S. The proposal, which for seven years had undergone regulatory scrutiny by a number of federal agencies, had pitted environmental activists and mostly Democratic lawmakers against oil companies and mostly Republican legislators. Although Obama cited the Keystone XL's potential to hamper U.S. efforts against climate change, the U.S. Dept. of State in 2014 concluded that the pipeline's direct environmental impact would have been limited.

Racially Charged Protests Unseat University President—Univ. of Missouri system Pres. Tim Wolfe and the chancellor of its main Columbia campus, R. Bowen Loftin, announced their resignations from the university's leadership Nov. 9 after weeks of intensifying protests. Demonstrators accused the administration of ignoring issues important to the flagship campus's community and, in particular, of being dismissive of racial incidents on campus, where the student body was 7% black. Heightening national attention paid to the protesters and adding consequence to the movement, members of the school's Div. I football team (nearly half of whom are black) threatened Nov. 7 to strike as long as Wolfe remained in office.

International

Turkey's Ruling Party Regains Majority—Turkey's governing Justice and Development Party (AKP) scored an unexpected victory in Nov. 1 snap elections, winning back the parliamentary majority it lost in June voting. Called by Turkish Pres. Recep Tayyip Erdogan after his AKP party failed to form a coalition in parliament, the new election, participated in by about 85% of the electorate, handed the AKP 316 of 550 parliamentary seats—up 58 seats from the June results. Many international observers said the election campaign was flawed, and some alleged the AKP took advantage of pre-election unrest—including double suicide bombings at an Ankara peace rally that killed about 100 people in Oct.—to unnecessarily silence opposition candidates.

China, Taiwan Leaders Hold Historic Meeting—Chinese Pres. Xi Jinping and Pres. Ma Ying-jeou of Taiwan met in Singapore Nov. 7 for the first direct talks between the leaders of the two governments since 1945, four years before Chiang Kai-shek's nationalists fled after defeat by Mao Zedong's communists. Although the meeting did not produce a significant accord, Xi—while still not formally recognizing Taiwan's sovereignty—embraced Ma's proposal of establishing the first telephone hotline between the two governments. Other summit topics included Chinese missiles located across from Taiwan and Taiwan's pursuit of membership in international organizations.

Opposition Wins Big in Myanmar Elections; Mine Landslide Kills Over 100—Nobel Peace Prize laureate Aung San Suu Kyi's National League for Democracy (NLD) won an absolute majority of seats up for vote in both houses of Myanmar's national parliament in Nov. 8 voting participated in by 80% of eligible voters. The ruling military-proxy Union Solidarity and Development Party (USDP) won just 41 seats to the NLD's 390; other parties netted 60 seats. Myanmar's constitution, drafted under military rule in 2008, sets aside 25% of parliamentary seats for unelected military representatives and disqualifies Suu Kyi from becoming president. Nevertheless, as party leader, Suu Kyi implied that she would serve "above the president" selected by parliament. While international observers found the election peaceful and the results credible, hundreds of thousands of minority Muslim Rohingya in the majority-Buddhist country were excluded from voting because they are not considered full citizens. Outgoing Pres. Thein Sein said he would transfer rule peacefully, and the new parliament was sworn in Feb. 1, 2016.

Authorities in northern Myanmar recovered the bodies of at least 113 migrant workers at a jade mine dump site after an early-morning landslide Nov. 21 buried their makeshift camp.

ISIS Bombings Kill Scores in Lebanese Capital—Perpetrating the deadliest terrorist attack on Beirut since 1990, two suicide bombers Nov. 12 killed at least 43 and wounded 239 others in the Lebanese city's mostly Shiite Bourj al-Barajneh neighborhood. (The body of a third bomber—apparently killed by one of the blasts before he could detonate his own explosives—was later found.) The Sunni extremist group known as the Islamic State of Iraq and Syria (ISIS) called the action a strike against Hezbollah, the Lebanon-based Shiite militant organization.

Terrorists Target France, Killing Over 100; Other Developments—ISIS claimed responsibility for coordinated attacks that rocked Paris and surrounding areas in France the night of Nov. 13, killing 130 people from at least 17 nations and wounding more than 350 others. The deadliest attacks in Western Europe since 2004, when bombings in

Spain killed 191, began north of the French capital outside a packed sports stadium. A suicide bomber—prevented from entering the stadium by a security check—killed himself and one other person. Within minutes, gunmen carried out drive-by shootings at five restaurants and bars in multiple Paris neighborhoods, killing 39. The greatest mass casualties were sustained at Paris's Bataclan concert hall, where three shooters indiscriminately fired on some 1,500 occupants. Following a more than two-hour standoff with police, one of the attackers was shot, and two others detonated explosives, bringing the Bataclan death toll (not including assailants) to 89.

Within hours, French Pres. François Hollande closed France's borders and declared a state of emergency, allowing police to carry out hundreds of warrantless raids. ISIS in a Nov. 14 social media post linked the attacks with France's nearly 7-week-old air campaign against ISIS militants in Syria, which France sharply escalated Nov. 15. Hollande also activated a never-before-used European Union mutual defense clause mandating member nation assistance, which all 28 countries accepted. Authorities said most of the seven suspected assailants that died in the attacks—six of whom were French citizens—had ties to Belgium, prompting raids and related arrests there. Police killed Belgian-Moroccan alleged ringleader Abdelhamid Abaaoud and two accomplices during a Nov. 18 raid in a Paris suburb.

French, Belgian, and other European officials remained vigilant for further attacks, canceling some high-profile events and closing schools and subways in Brussels for four days. In the U.S., reports that one of the suspects had a Syrian passport (later determined to be a forgery) led to heightened anti-refugee rhetoric. The Republican-controlled U.S. House Nov. 19 voted 289-137 to pass a symbolic measure halting Syrian and Iraqi refugee resettlement in the country.

Extremists Raid Mali Hotel—Heavily armed militants Nov. 20 attacked a luxury hotel in the Malian capital of Bamako, killing at least 20 people and holding dozens hostage. Responding security personnel killed two gunmen during a siege that exceeded seven hours. The Mali-based, al-Qaeda-linked group Al-Mourabitoun said it staged the attack with another al-Qaeda affiliate, but the unaffiliated Malian Islamic extremist group Massina Liberation Front also claimed responsibility. The attack may have been carried out in retaliation against France's 2013 intervention in northern Mali, which Islamic militants and anti-government Tuareg rebels had seized following a military coup d'état in 2012.

Buenos Aires Mayor Captures Argentinean Presidency—Argentine voters ended 12 years of leftist rule Nov. 22 when they chose Buenos Aires mayor Mauricio Macri as president over outgoing Pres. Cristina Fernández de Kirchner's handpicked successor, Buenos Aires province Gov. Daniel Scioli. The center-right Macri, of the Republican Proposal Party, defeated the Peronist Front for Victory's Scioli, 51.4%-48.6%, in the country's first-ever presidential runoff, in which 80.9% of the electorate participated. Macri campaigned on distancing Argentina's foreign policy from Iran and Venezuela and on boosting the economy, which was plagued by deficits and an inflation rate as high as 26%. Macri was sworn in Dec. 10.

Turkey Shoots Down Russian Jet; Russia Blames October Airliner Disaster on Terrorism—Turkish fighter planes downed a Russian fighter jet Nov. 24 near the Turkey-Syria border, marking the first time since 1952 that a NATO member state shot down a Russian plane. Syrian rebels reportedly fatally shot the pilot after he ejected from the plane, but the plane's navigator was safely recovered by Syrian government forces. Russia denied Turkey's charge that its plane had violated Turkish airspace, and the incident strained relations between the two countries, which were both engaged in independent airstrike campaigns in Syria. Turkey said its pilots had issued 10 warnings before firing on the jet, and the U.S. State Dept. confirmed the Russian aircraft had briefly entered Turkish airspace.

Russian officials Nov. 17 said they had identified traces of explosives in the wreckage of a Russian airliner that crashed Oct. 31, killing all 224 on the flight, which crashed en route from Egypt to Russia. Russia sharply escalated its military campaign in Syria, coordinating attacks with France against ISIS's self-proclaimed capital of Raqqa. Critics alleged Russian airstrikes—purportedly targeting ISIS in Syria since late Sept. 2015—had instead mostly hit non-ISIS anti-Assad rebels and ethnic Turkish areas.

General

Kansas City Royals Win World Series—The Kansas City Royals won the World Series over the New York Mets in a decisive Game 5 victory on Nov. 2 at New York's Citi Field. Play extended into a 12th inning, during which Kansas City scored five runs to secure a 7-2 victory. The Royals, who were defeated in the 2014 World Series, claimed the expansion franchise's second Series victory. A 14-inning Game 1, which the Royals finally won, 5-4, was kicked off with the first World Series inside-the-park home run since 1929 by Royals shortstop Alcides Escobar. Royals catcher Salvador Pérez was named the World Series MVP.

Global Track and Field Body Bans Russian Athletes—The world's governing body for track and field, the Intl. Assn. of Athletics Federations (IAAF), Nov. 13 suspended the All-Russia Athletic Federation for an indefinite period. Four days earlier, the World Anti-Doping Agency (WADA) alleged that the chief of Russia's anti-doping lab had concealed positive test results and destroyed more than 1,400 samples in what was effectively a state-supported doping program. Russian athletes would be consequently barred from all international track and field events, including the 2016 Olympics.

UFC Star Rousey Suffers First Defeat—Underdog fighter Holly Holm routed then-undefeated Ultimate Fighting Championship star and defending women's bantamweight champion Ronda Rousey Nov. 15 at Etihad Stadium in Melbourne, Australia. Holm knocked out Rousey with a kick to the head, ending the match 59 sec. into the second round. Rousey, an Olympic bronze medalist in judo who had attained celebrity status as a mixed martial arts fighter and actress, landed about half as many blows as Holm, a world champion boxer, in the first five-minute round.

Pope Francis Visits Africa—In his last international trip during a whirlwind travel year, Pope Francis Nov. 25-30 visited Africa for the first time. The leader of the world's 1.25 bil Roman Catholics first landed in Kenya, where he celebrated mass before a crowd of some 400,000 in Nairobi Nov. 26 and spoke against "new forms of colonialism" and corruption from a slum and a sports stadium Nov. 27 before departing for Uganda. Francis became the first pope in recent history to visit an active war zone when he arrived in the Central African Republic Nov. 29. Christian and Muslim militias have clashed within the nation since Mar. 2013.

Shooting Kills Three at Colorado Clinic—Armed with a semi-automatic rifle, a 57-year-old man Nov. 27 fatally shot three—including a police officer—and wounded nine at a Planned Parenthood clinic in Colorado Springs, CO. Police engaged in a five-hour standoff with the shooter, later identified as Robert L. Dear Jr., before he surrendered. In an outburst during a Dec. 9 court appearance, the alleged gunman declared he was guilty and called himself a "warrior for the babies."

December 2015
National

California Shooting Kills 14 in Act of Terrorism, Provoking Debate—A California married couple, Syed Rizwan Farook and Tashfeen Malik, fatally shot 14 people and injured 21 at a Dec. 2 holiday party for employees of the San Bernardino County Dept. of Public Health, which employed the U.S.-born Farook. After the shooting, the couple fled in an SUV; they were killed in a shootout with police later that day. The Pakistan-born Malik had posted a Facebook message declaring the couple's allegiance to the leader of the Sunni extremist group Islamic State of Iraq and Syria (ISIS), and Pres. Barack Obama declared the attack an act of terrorism. Although ISIS praised the attackers, the FBI believed the couple had planned the attack alone. A friend of Farook's, Enrique Marquez Jr., was indicted Dec. 30 on federal charges of conspiring to carry out other attacks.

Obama during a Dec. 6 address repeated calls for increased gun control, said the U.S. would continue airstrikes against ISIS, and urged against anti-Muslim discrimination. Among other Republican lawmakers and candidates criticizing Obama as soft on terrorism, Republican presidential candidate Donald Trump Dec. 7 called for a ban on Muslims entering the U.S.

Justice Dept. Investigates Chicago Police—In the midst of a national protest movement against police racial bias, the U.S. Justice Dept. announced Dec. 7 it had launched a civil rights investigation into the Chicago Police Dept. (CPD). Two weeks earlier, city officials publicly released police dashcam video footage that appeared to show white CPD officer Jason Van Dyke fatally shooting black teenager Laquan McDonald without cause in Oct. 2014. Van Dyke was charged with first-degree murder of the 17-year-old McDonald hours before the video was released on a judge's order. Weeks of protests followed, with demonstrators questioning the timing of the indictment and video release and calling for the resignation of Chicago Mayor Rahm Emanuel. Emanuel Dec. 1 ousted the CPD superintendent and in late Dec. announced other reform measures, which included increasing the department's supply of stun guns and de-escalation training.

A Cuyahoga County, OH, grand jury Dec. 29 decided not to charge two white police officers in the fatal shooting of black 12-year-old Tamir Rice in Cleveland in Nov. 2014. The officer who shot Rice said he thought the boy's pellet gun was a real firearm.

Fed Raises Interest Rates for First Time in Seven Years; Other Economic, Business News—Capping months of speculation, the Federal Reserve Dec. 16 raised its key interest rates from the near-zero levels it had held for seven years. Although the rate increase to a range of 0.25%-0.50% was slight, the change signaled the Federal Reserve's confidence in the economy's recovery from the Great Recession, more than five years after its official end in June 2009. Stock markets rose following the announcement, but the Dow Jones industrial average was down 1.7% for the month, closing Dec. 31 at 17,425.03, down 2.2% for the calendar year. The S&P 500 closed at 2,043.94, dropping 1.8% from Nov. and 0.7% for the year. The Nasdaq composite index closed 2015 at 5,007.41, down 2.0% for the month but up 5.7% over 2014.

The U.S. Dept. of Labor's Dec. 4 report showed that the Nov. 2015 unemployment rate held steady from Oct. at 5.0% and that the economy had added 211,000 jobs. The Bureau of Economic Analysis Dec. 22 released revised figures for third quarter 2015 reporting that real GDP grew by 2.0%, compared to a 3.9% increase the previous quarter.

DuPont and Dow Chemical Co. announced Dec. 11 that they would merge in an estimated $130-bil deal that, if approved by regulators, would precede the combined company's split into three separate publicly traded companies.

Democratic Presidential Contenders Clash Over Data Breach; Candidates Exit Republican Race—The Democratic Natl. Committee Dec. 17 briefly barred the presidential campaign of Sen. Bernie Sanders (D, VT) from accessing the DNC's voter information database after it was revealed that Sanders aides had exploited a technical glitch to improperly view information gathered by the presidential campaign of former Sec. of State Hillary Clinton. Sanders's campaign Dec. 18 sued the DNC, claiming the ban was excessive, but a deal to restore access was reached before a hearing took place.

Republican presidential candidates Sen. Lindsey Graham (SC) and former New York Gov. George Pataki both ended their campaigns in Dec. Their departures, along with Louisiana Gov. Bobby Jindal's Nov. exit, left 12 Republican candidates in the running.

Obama Signs Major Spending, Education Acts; Military Opens All Roles to Women—Pres. Barack Obama signed into law a combined $1.8-tril spending and tax relief legislative package Dec. 18. Newly installed House Speaker Paul Ryan (R, WI) persuaded 149 other Republicans to support the legislation, resulting in a Dec. 18 vote of 316-113 on the spending bill, which followed a 318-109 vote the day before in support of the tax cuts. The Senate Dec. 18 passed both bills, 65-33. Lawmakers increased spending by $66 bil over caps set by the so-called sequester that took effect in 2013. Proposals defunding Planned Parenthood and banning Syrian refugees were rejected from the final package, but other controversial measures, like increasing scrutiny of some visa applicants and repealing a 40-year-old U.S.-produced crude oil export ban, were included.

Pres. Obama Dec. 10 signed the Every Student Succeeds Act to replace the 2001 No Child Left Behind Act, which governed public schools nationwide (and technically expired in 2007). Passed by the House Dec. 2 (359-64) and the Senate Dec. 9 (85-12), the new education regulations retained mandatory testing requirements but returned to states the ability to consider other factors when assessing school performance.

Defense Sec. Ash Carter Dec. 3 said that all U.S. military occupations, including combat positions, would be open to women meeting the requirements beginning in Jan. 2016.

International

Burkina Faso Holds Historic Election—Officials in Burkina Faso Dec. 1 announced that former Prime Min. Roch Marc Christian Kaboré was the victor of late-Nov. presidential voting considered to be the nation's first democratic election in decades. Kaboré, founder of the center-left People's Movement for Progress (MPP) party, had pledged to fight corruption and secured 53.5% of votes cast by about 60% of registered voters. The election sought to replace the interim government imposed by the military since Pres. Blaise Compaoré resigned in Oct. 2014 after a sometimes-violent popular uprising. Compaoré, who took power in a 1987 coup, had incited public anger when he tried to amend the constitution to extend his rule. Kaboré was sworn in Dec. 29.

Opposition Unseats Socialists in Venezuela—In Venezuelan parliamentary elections Dec. 6, an opposition coalition of 27 parties known as the Democratic Unity Roundtable (MUD) ended 17 years of socialist control. MUD candidates and their indigenous allies (for whom three seats are reserved) captured 112 of 167 seats, while the United Socialist Party of Venezuela (PSUV) and its allies won 55 seats. The opposition campaigned against Pres. Nicolás Maduro's leadership, which it held responsible for triple-digit inflation and food shortages. Upholding socialist accusations of voting irregularities, Venezuela's Supreme Court Dec. 30 rejected three newly elected opposition lawmakers (and one socialist lawmaker), in a move seemingly intended to deprive MUD of a two-thirds supermajority.

Syrian Rebels Abandon Homs; UK Launches Anti-ISIS Airstrikes—Rebels resisting the government of Syrian Pres. Bashar al-Assad began evacuating a suburb of the city of Homs Dec. 9 under a United Nations-supported cease-fire. Syrian government forces likewise lifted their nearly three-year siege. The rebels' departure marked the return of governmental control over the city, where some of the first anti-regime protests were held in 2011. The deal allowed civilian residents to receive food assistance for the first time in almost a year. Syrian opposition representatives from about a dozen armed rebel factions agreed to new peace talks in Jan. 2016, but Assad appeared to limit the potential of the negotiations when he said Dec. 11 that he would not meet with those he deemed "terrorist groups."

Britain Dec. 3 launched its first airstrikes against ISIS in Syria, joining the year-long, U.S.-led air campaign there. Germany's parliament the next day voted to send some 1,200 troops to serve in a noncombat role in Syria, expanding upon the nation's support of Kurdish fighters. The UN in mid-Dec. said that Russian airstrikes, which began Sept. 30, 2015, at Assad's request, had hindered aid supply routes and targeted civilians.

Political Violence Kills Scores in Burundi—Violence at three military sites in and near the nation's capital left at least

87 people dead, Dec. 11-12. Government officials said almost all of the dead had been assailants, but residents claimed security forces executed numerous unarmed young men and left bodies in the streets. Pres. Pierre Nkurunziza rejected an African Union plan to deploy peacekeepers. The United Nations announced Dec. 15 that some 400 people had been killed and about 235,000 had fled or been internally displaced since Apr. Observers feared the political unrest would return Burundi to ethnic conflict, which killed about 300,000 people, 1993-2006.

Nations Approve Landmark Climate Accord—Officials representing 196 parties reached a historic agreement Dec. 12 to reduce the greenhouse gases linked to global climate change. Coming at the end of a two-week summit in Paris, the UN-sponsored deal included developing nations such as China and India, which had been exempt from the 1997 Kyoto Protocol. Participating nations agreed to review their emissions-reduction goals every five years and to report their progress towards limiting the average global temperature increase over preindustrial levels to below 2°C (3.6°F). A nonbinding part of the agreement urged wealthy nations to provide financing to help poorer countries meet emissions targets.

Saudi Women Participate in First Elections—For the first time, women in Saudi Arabia Dec. 12 both ran and voted in elections for the country's 2,106 open municipal council seats. Their participation was a milestone in the conservative kingdom, the last country (other than Vatican City) to grant women the right to vote. An estimated 11% of the 1.3 mil Saudis who voted were women, and 20 women won seats.

European Union Continues to Grapple With Migrant Influx—Addressing her center-right Christian Democratic Union's party congress Dec. 14, German Chancellor Angela Merkel appeared to back off Germany's open-door refugee policy when she said she hoped to noticeably reduce the number of migrants entering the country. Merkel Nov. 3 had proposed a plan to register migrants at European Union borders so they could be evenly distributed throughout the EU. But multiple member nations continued to resist pro-migrant initiatives; some 2,000 Dutch protesters in mid-Dec. rioted over a proposed migrant center. The UN Refugee Agency and International Organization for Migration estimated that some 1 mil refugees and migrants entered Europe in 2015.

Iraqi Forces Retake Ramadi, Sinjar; Other Developments—Iraqi government forces Dec. 28 retook control of central Ramadi, the capital of Iraq's Anbar province and the largest urban area Iraqi forces had liberated without help from Kurdish rebel forces or Iran-linked Shiite Muslim militias. Kurdish forces known as the Peshmerga had liberated the northern Iraqi city of Sinjar in Nov. U.S. Defense Sec. Ash Carter in early Dec. said the U.S. was preparing a roughly 200-member special operations force to launch anti-ISIS raids. In a statement Dec. 14, Pres. Barack Obama indicated that ISIS had lost about 40% of the populated territory it once occupied in Iraq. A Dept. of Defense spokesperson said, Dec. 29, that the coalition had conducted more than 150 airstrikes in Iraq in Dec.

Military Allegedly Kills Hundreds in Nigeria; Other Developments—The U.S. State Dept. Dec. 16 called for an investigation into clashes the previous weekend between the Nigerian military and a Shiite group said to have left hundreds dead in Zaria. The military alleged that fighting began when the minority sect, known as the Islamic Movement in Nigeria, attempted to assassinate the army chief of staff. A Human Rights Watch report issued Dec. 22 estimated a death toll of at least 300, but military leaders denied the killings.

Nigeria was also grappling with the ongoing violence from the Sunni extremist group Boko Haram, which killed some 6,100 in 2015 according to the Council on Foreign Relations. Bombings and shooting attacks killed at least 50 people Dec. 27-28 in the northeastern city of Maiduguri. Two female suicide bombers Dec. 28 killed at least 30 people at a Madagali market.

More than 100 people in rural Nnewi were killed Dec. 24 when a tanker truck exploded, injuring those waiting at a gas station.

General

Timbers Win MLS Championship Amid Controversy—The Portland Timbers defeated the Columbus Crew, 2-1, before a sellout crowd Dec. 6 at Mapfre Stadium in Columbus, OH, to win their first MLS title. The Timbers claimed the lead after just 27 seconds—the fastest first goal in MLS Cup history—when the Crew's goalkeeper tried to dribble around Portland's Diego Valeri, who deflected it for a score; he was later named the match's MVP. Seven minutes into play, Portland doubled their lead on a diving header by Rodney Wallace. The controversial second goal came several passes after Portland continued to play a ball which was out of bounds by almost all accounts but was never called out by officials.

SpaceX Achieves Reusable Rocket; Japanese Spacecraft Achieves Venus Orbit—The private aerospace company SpaceX made history Dec. 21 when a rocket it had launched from Cape Canaveral, FL, landed back on Earth after reaching space orbit. The safe return of the first stage of the company's reusable *Falcon 9* rocket was seen as a key step in lowering the cost of future space travel.

Japan's national space agency Dec. 7 announced its unmanned Venus Climate Orbiter *Akatsuki* had entered orbit around Venus. It was the first Japanese probe to achieve orbit around another planet.

Floods, Tornadoes Kill Dozens in U.S.—Severe weather killed at least 43 across seven states over several days beginning Dec. 22. Twelve tornadoes left 11 dead in the Dallas, TX, area; tornadoes killed 11 more in Mississippi and Tennessee. The weather system, caused in part by El Niño, inundated a swath of the central U.S., including southern Illinois and central Missouri, where at least 24 died in flooded roadways. Pres. Barack Obama Jan. 2 declared a state of emergency in Missouri, where the Mississippi River at Cape Girardeau crested at nearly 49 ft, exceeding the previous flood record set in 1993.

New Chemical Elements Added to Periodic Table—The International Union of Pure and Applied Chemistry (IUPAC) announced Dec. 30 they had officially verified synthetic elements 113, 115, 117, and 118, discovered in recent years by scientists in Japan, Russia, and the U.S., completing the seventh row of the periodic table.

January 2016

National

Presidential Actions on Gun Control Draw Republican Criticism—In an emotional address attended by family members of people killed in recent shootings, Pres. Barack Obama Jan. 5 announced new executive orders aimed at reducing gun violence and chastised Congress for not passing gun control legislation. Under revised guidelines from the U.S. Bureau of Alcohol, Tobacco, Firearms, and Explosives (ATF), resources allotted to background checks for gun purchasers would expand, including those devoted to gun show purchases and internet sales. Although many noted the relatively limited reach of the actions, the new guidelines faced legal challenges and drew rebuke from congressional Republicans and candidates for the GOP presidential nomination.

Obama Delivers Final State of the Union—In his final State of the Union address, Pres. Obama Jan. 12 reflected on his tenure and called on lawmakers to confront large problems. Though he touted his economic record and foreign policy achievements, including renewed relations with Cuba and the Iran nuclear accord, he lamented failing to transform rancorous Washington partisanship.

South Carolina Gov. Nikki Haley delivered the Republican response, stressing her party's frustrations with a broken system of government and their efforts to fix it.

Flint Water Crisis Rocks Michigan—Pres. Obama declared a federal state of emergency in Flint, MI, and its surrounding county Jan. 16 in response to a lead-contaminated water crisis in the cash-strapped city, located about 70 mi northwest of Detroit. The state managers of Flint's finances switched the municipal water source from Lake Huron to the Flint River in Apr. 2014, after which residents of the majority-black city noted issues with the water's color, scent, and taste. In spite of initial assurances from local and state authorities that the water was safe, repeated tests found it was contaminated with lead, which was leaching from the pipes after exposure to untreated, corrosive water. Flint restored its connection to Detroit's water system in Oct. 2015, but analysis continued to find unsafe lead levels.

Flint residents in Nov. 2015 filed a class-action lawsuit against city and state officials for not treating the river water with anti-corrosives, which might have prevented lead from leaching into the supply. Some called for the resignation of Michigan's Gov. Rick Snyder (R), who did not publicly acknowledge a problem until Sept. 2015, seven months after a federal Environmental Protection Agency employee discussed independent evidence of high lead levels. Snyder declared a state of emergency in Genesee County Jan. 5 and called in the state National Guard to aid bottled water distribution. Documents released in late Feb. showed that by Mar. 2015, the governor's staff was aware of Legionnaires' disease cases with possible links to the water; at least nine died. The U.S. Dept. of Justice was investigating.

Oil Prices Fall to 12-Year Low; Job Growth Continues; Other Economic News—Prices for U.S. benchmark West Texas Intermediate crude oil fell below $27 per barrel Jan. 20, for the lowest prices in more than 12 years. An estimated 250,000 oil industry-related jobs had been lost globally since oil value began declining in mid-2014.

The job market elsewhere remained strong, as the Labor Dept. reported Jan. 8 that the economy had added 292,000 jobs in Dec., bringing the 2015 total to 2.65 mil. The Dec. unemployment rate held steady at 5.0%.

The impact of the oil price decline and China's stock crash was felt on Wall Street, as the Dow Jones industrial average finished the month at 16,466.30, down 5.5% from Dec. 31, while the S&P 500 closed Jan. at 1,940.24, losing 5.1%, from the month before. The Nasdaq composite index finished at 4,613.95, down 7.9%.

Texas Grand Jury Declines to Indict Planned Parenthood—A Houston, TX, grand jury tasked with investigating allegations that women's health services provider Planned Parenthood participated in illegal fetal tissue sales declined Jan. 25 to charge the organization. The grand jury's investigation was in response to highly publicized undercover videos released in the summer of 2015. While declining to indict Planned Parenthood, the jury indicted the two video creators for creating fake driver licenses, a felony; one was also charged with attempting to purchase human organs, a misdemeanor. Planned Parenthood had been subject to investigation by several congressional committees and 11 states related to the video footage, but thus far had been cleared of wrongdoing.

FBI Clashes With Occupiers of Federal Land—An armed takeover of the Malheur National Wildlife Refuge headquarters in eastern Oregon began Jan. 2 when activist Ammon Bundy demanded the federal government release two Oregon ranchers recently imprisoned for arson on federal lands. Bundy also later called for the refuge to be turned over to local entities. On Jan. 26, authorities arrested Bundy and five others at a traffic stop north of the refuge. Two of the armed militants were shot, one fatally, after they reportedly refused to surrender. Three others were arrested separately the same day. The last four holdouts occupying the refuge surrendered Feb. 11.

International

North Korea Claims Detonation of H-Bomb, Launches Satellite—North Korea Jan. 6 announced it had carried out its first test of a hydrogen bomb. The claim was quickly disputed by U.S. officials, who said the 5.1 magnitude earthquake detected in the communist stronghold's northeast was far less powerful than a hydrogen bomb would cause. Regardless, the consensus of the international community was to denounce the country's fourth nuclear test since 2006. Crucial North Korean ally China said it would seek a denuclearized Korean

peninsula, and the U.S. House of Representatives Jan. 12 voted 418-2 to pass a measure to expand economic sanctions against North Korea. The Senate unanimously passed the measure Feb. 10.

North Korea Feb. 7 launched a three-stage rocket, bringing its second satellite into orbit. The UN Security Council condemned the move as a violation of UN resolutions banning North Korea from furthering technology to launch intercontinental ballistic missiles. North Korea insisted the rocket and satellite launch were in pursuit of peaceful objectives.

Stocks Crash in China, Furthering Investor Anxieties—Trading on China's primary stock exchange halted for the day Jan. 7 just 29 min. after opening as Chinese Securities Index 300 losses reached 7%. The sell-off and subsequent automatic shutdown—the second in a week—was attributed to investors' concerns that China was devaluing its yuan currency too quickly. In reaction, financial markets tumbled globally—the Dow Jones industrial average dropped 392 points Jan. 7, and Europe's DAX and FTSE experienced similar losses. Chinese regulators announced that the new rules that had provided for the automatic shutdowns would be suspended with the start of trading Jan. 8.

Zika Virus Outbreak Hits Central, South America—The U.S.'s Centers for Disease Control and Prevention Jan. 15 advised pregnant women to avoid visiting at least 14 Latin American countries and territories where reports of infection with the mosquito-borne Zika virus were increasing. The virus, which typically causes no symptoms in infected people, seemed to be associated with babies born with microcephaly and other birth defects. (The CDC confirmed the link Apr. 13.) Brazil, the nation hardest hit by the outbreak, declared a nationwide public health emergency in Nov. 2015 and by Jan. 30 reported some 4,000 suspected cases of microcephaly since Oct. 2015, compared to 150 in all of 2014.

The World Health Organization Feb. 1 declared a global health emergency, projecting some 4 mil Zika cases worldwide, and health officials in several affected nations cautioned women against pregnancy.

Amid Conflicts, Sanctions Against Iran Are Lifted—The U.S., European Union, and UN eased economic sanctions against Iran Jan. 16 in accordance with the terms of a landmark multinational nuclear deal agreed upon in 2015. Besides allowing Iran to export oil to Europe and access global financial markets, the pact restored Iran's access to some $100 bil in frozen assets. The U.S. continued to embargo most Iranian goods, including oil. Hours before the sanctions were lifted, the U.S. and Iran carried out a prisoner exchange, trading seven Iranians for five U.S. citizens, including *Washington Post* reporter Jason Rezaian.

Two weeks earlier, Sunni-led Saudi Arabia executed prominent Shiite cleric Nimr al-Nimr and 46 others Jan. 2, igniting condemnation from Iran and other majority Shiite states. Amnesty International called al-Nimr's trial "political and grossly unfair" and said the conviction was aimed at crushing dissent. Protesters in Tehran, Iran's capital, ransacked and set ablaze the Saudi embassy, prompting Saudi Arabia to cut diplomatic ties. Within a week, Sunni allies Bahrain, Sudan, Djibouti, and Somalia severed diplomatic relations with Iran, and other nations, including Qatar and the UAE, downgraded their diplomatic relationships. Iran Jan. 12 held 10 U.S. sailors from two boats that had illegally entered its waters. The sailors were released the next day.

Nationalists Lose Power in Taiwan—Taiwanese voters Jan. 16 decisively elected Tsai Ing-wen their first female president and handed the Nationalist Party (KMT) its first parliamentary defeat since the KMT government fled mainland China. Participated in by a record-low 66% of eligible voters, the election gave Tsai's pro-independence Democratic Progressive Party (DPP) 68 of 113 legislative seats, while the KMT took 35 seats, down from 64. Tsai, who won 56% of the vote to the KMT candidate's 31%, had campaigned primarily on boosting Taiwan's sagging economy.

Moldova Affirms Prime Minister as Protesters Storm Parliament—Moldova's parliament ended months of political impasse when it voted Jan. 20 to install a new pro-European government led by compromise candidate Pavel Filip, despite an opposition party boycott of the vote. Moldovans remained split over seeking European Union membership or closer ties with Moscow, and thousands of demonstrators from opposition groups rushed parliament following Filip's appointment. Already one of Eastern Europe's poorest countries, Moldova was confronted with a financial crisis after the 2010-14 disappearance of $1 bil (one-eighth of the country's GDP) from its banks.

ISIS Attacks Kill Scores as Syrian Peace Talks Begin—United Nations-mediated peace talks aimed at ending the nearly five-year-old civil war between the government of Syrian Pres. Bashar al-Assad and rebel fighters began Jan. 29 in Geneva, Switzerland. Though it controlled roughly one-fourth of the territory in Iraq and Syria, the Sunni extremist group known as the Islamic State or ISIS was not invited to take part in the talks. Representatives from assorted opposition groups met with a UN envoy but said they would not negotiate with Syrian government delegates.

ISIS Jan. 16-17 reportedly killed at least 85 civilians and some 50 Syrian government soldiers in one of the last Syrian-controlled districts of Deir ez-Zor city, Syria; ISIS forces also kidnapped at least 400 additional civilians in the assault's wake. A triple suicide bombing claimed by ISIS killed more than 70 people near a Shia shrine in the Syrian capital of Damascus, Jan. 31.

General

Two Elected to Baseball Hall of Fame—The Baseball Writers' Assn. of America elected sluggers Ken Griffey Jr. and Mike Piazza to the National Baseball Hall of Fame Jan. 6. Griffey, a 13-time All-Star and 10-time Gold Glove award-winner over 22 seasons, was chosen in his first ballot with a record 99.3% of the vote. The outfielder, who hit 630 career home runs primarily with Seattle and Cincinnati, became the first-ever No. 1 draft pick to be elected to the Hall. Twelve-time All-Star Piazza was chosen with 83% of the vote in his fourth year of eligibility, after a 16-season career during which he hit 427 home runs, with an MLB-record 396 as a catcher.

Mexico Recaptures Drug Kingpin—Almost six months after his second escape from a maximum security prison, Mexican security forces Jan. 8 apprehended Joaquín "El Chapo" Guzmán, the notorious leader of the country's Sinaloa drug cartel, following a raid that killed five. A Mexican official said American actor Sean Penn's Oct. 2, 2015, interview with Guzmán, published in *Rolling Stone* magazine days after his capture, played a role in their investigation.

'Bama Captures College Football Championship—The Univ. of Alabama Crimson Tide won its fourth title in seven years when it edged the Clemson Univ. Tigers, 45-40, at Univ. of Phoenix Stadium in Glendale, AZ, Jan. 11. Tight end O.J. Howard, the game's offensive MVP, caught five passes for 208 yards and quarterback Jake Coker completed 16 of 25 passes for two touchdowns and 335 yards. Alabama head coach Nick Saban claimed his fifth national title.

Evidence Suggests Ninth Planet—Scientists at Caltech Jan. 20 announced evidence, published in the *Astronomical Journal*, of a giant, icy planet in our solar system. Although they had not observed it directly, researchers said "Planet Nine" had a mass about 10 times that of Earth and a highly elliptical orbit—about 20 times farther from the Sun than Neptune, on average—that takes some 10,000 to 20,000 Earth years to complete.

Snowstorm Paralyzes East Coast—A slow-moving snowstorm hit the eastern U.S. Jan. 23-24, killing at least 50 people in 12 states. Parts of West Virginia and Maryland received more than three feet of snow, and both New York City and Washington, DC, banned travel on all city roads.

Kerber, Djokovic Win at Australian Open; Match-Fixing Scandal Surfaces—No. 7-seed Angelique Kerber of Germany upset defending Australian Open champion Serena Williams (6-4, 3-6, 6-4) in a 2 hr., 8-min. match at Rod Laver Arena in Melbourne Jan. 30 for her first Grand Slam title. The following night, Serbian Novak Djokovic won his third straight Grand Slam title when he bested Andy Murray of Scotland (6-1, 7-5, 7-6) to become the first man in the Open era to win six Australian Open titles.

The BBC and Buzzfeed Jan. 17 published reports of suspected match-fixing in professional tennis believed to have taken place over the past decade. Leaked documents appeared to show that world tennis authorities failed to take action after a 2008 probe revealed evidence that players accepted money to manipulate matches to benefit gambling operations in Russia and Italy. At least 16 unnamed players—all of whom had reportedly ranked in the top 50—were implicated.

February 2016
National

Supreme Court's Scalia Dies, Prompting Political Battle—U.S. Supreme Court Associate Justice Antonin Scalia was found dead at a Texas hunting lodge Feb. 13, leaving a vacancy on the nation's highest court. A conservative Reagan nominee confirmed in 1986, Scalia established himself as a staunch originalist, known for his rhetorical flourishes in opinions and dissents based on his interpretation of the Constitution's original meaning. Senate Majority Leader Mitch McConnell (R, KY) Feb. 13 called for deferring the nomination to fill the vacancy until after the 2016 presidential race. In response that same day, Pres. Barack Obama said he planned to "fulfill my constitutional responsibilities to nominate a successor in due time."

Supreme Court Associate Justice Clarence Thomas Feb. 29 broke a noted decade-long streak of asking no questions during oral arguments with a series of queries at a hearing on a relatively low-profile case on the gun rights of those convicted on domestic violence charges.

Apple Fights iPhone Court Order; Other Economic News—The global computing giant Apple said it would not comply with a Feb. 16 court ruling that ordered it to help the FBI unlock a password-protected Apple iPhone used by one of the two people accused of fatally shooting 14 in San Bernardino, CA, in Dec. 2015. Apple executives cited concerns that creating a back door for investigators could allow hackers to exploit other customers' data. The case stirred debate over tech companies' responsibilities regarding consumer privacy rights and national security.

The Labor Dept. reported Feb. 5 that 151,000 jobs had been added in the U.S. in Jan.; the Jan. unemployment rate fell slightly to 4.9%. Stock markets were mostly flat for the month, with the Dow Jones industrial average finishing at 16,516.50, up 0.3% from Jan., and the S&P 500 closing Feb. at 1,932.23, down 0.4% from the month before. The Nasdaq composite index finished at 4,557.95, down 1.2%.

Obama Proposes Guantánamo Prison Shutdown—Pres. Obama Feb. 23 submitted to Congress a plan to shutter the U.S. military's prison in Guantánamo Bay, Cuba, and transfer its remaining high-risk detainees with alleged terrorist links to domestic facilities. The plan was opposed by many in Congress, who noted that the defense appropriations bill signed by Obama in Nov. 2015 banned detainee transfers to the U.S. The Guantánamo facility at the time of Obama's proposal held 91 detainees, of whom 35 were slated for repatriation or removal abroad. Obama cited closure savings of up to $85 mil per year after an initial $290-$475 mil upgrade to U.S. facilities.

Trump, Clinton Lead After Early Presidential Contests; Other Campaign Developments—Divisive real estate tycoon Donald Trump's status as front-runner for the Republican presidential nomination was solidified Feb. 23 when he secured his third straight state victory, emerging from the Nevada caucuses with 45.9% of the vote, followed distantly by Florida Sen. Marco Rubio (23.9%) and Texas Sen. Ted Cruz (21.4%). He had previously won by similarly significant margins in New Hampshire Feb. 9

and South Carolina Feb. 20. Cruz was the narrow winner of the Iowa caucuses Feb. 1, claiming 27.6% of the vote over Trump's 24.3% and Rubio's 23.1%. Trump revealed a divide between voters and GOP leaders favoring more conventional Republican candidates such as former Florida Gov. Jeb Bush, who ended his campaign after South Carolina's primary. By the end of Feb., the GOP field—at one point 17 candidates strong—had narrowed to five, with New Jersey Gov. Chris Christie suspending his campaign Feb. 10 and endorsing Trump Feb. 26.

In the Democratic race, former Sec. of State, U.S. senator (D, NY), and first lady Hillary Clinton narrowly edged Sen. Bernie Sanders (I, VT) in the Iowa caucuses Feb. 1, winning 49.9% of votes to 49.6% for Sanders. Former Maryland Gov. Martin O'Malley ended his campaign that same night. Sanders easily won primary voting Feb. 9 in his neighboring state of New Hampshire, 60.4%-38.0%, but Clinton won Nevada, 52.6%-47.3%, and South Carolina, 73.5%-26.0%.

The State Dept. Feb. 29 made public the last batch of Hillary Clinton's emails—more than 52,000 in total—ordered released by a federal judge from the private email server she used to send official messages while serving as secretary of state.

International

Boko Haram Targets Refugees in Nigeria—Two female suicide bombers killed at least 58 people and injured scores more Feb. 9 at a camp for displaced persons in the northeastern Nigerian town of Dikwa. A third would-be bomber who did not detonate her explosives reportedly said that Boko Haram was behind the attacks and had others planned. The attacks were believed to be in retaliation for recent raids on Boko Haram strongholds; the week prior, government security forces raided three villages held by the militants, killing more than 100 combatants and rescuing more than 1,000 captives. Boko Haram has killed more than 20,000 and displaced millions since it launched a military campaign in 2009 to create an Islamic caliphate under Sharia law. The group Jan. 30 killed at least 80 people in a raid on Dalori, a village outside the northern Borno state capital.

Austrian Migrant Cap Provokes Ire; French Police Actions Spark Migrant Uprising—Europe's response to the ongoing refugee crisis continued to be divisive, with Austria Feb. 16 announcing it would accept just 80 asylum claims per day and allow no more than 3,200 refugees per day to transit through the country to other EU destinations. The EU's European Commission warned Austria it was violating EU and international law, and an official for Germany, which accommodated some 1.1 mil refugees in 2015, declared the action unacceptable. Croatia, Hungary, Macedonia, and Slovenia also took actions to greatly limit refugee entrance. Greece by late Feb. had recalled its ambassador to Austria, as officials feared a bottleneck of asylum seekers would form in their own resource-strapped country.

Clashes between French police and migrants living in a makeshift camp in Calais known as the Jungle erupted Feb. 29 when authorities tried to evict refugees, some of whom set dwellings on fire. The government had ordered the removal of some 1,000 migrants who had refused official accommodation in favor of awaiting relocation to the UK.

Jamaican Voters Reject Austerity Government—Jamaicans narrowly elected the opposition Jamaican Labour Party (JLP) in a Feb. 25 general election viewed as a referendum on the cost-saving measures put in place by Prime Min. Portia Simpson-Miller and the ruling People's National Party (PNP). Pledging to decrease taxes and spur job growth, incoming Prime Min. Andrew Holness helped the JLP capture 50.1% of the vote and 32 of 63 parliamentary seats (up from just 21). The PNP, which won 31 seats with 49.7% of the vote, had previously enacted spending cuts and wage freezes mandated by the Intl. Monetary Fund (IMF) bailout it accepted in 2013. Just 47.7% of the electorate participated in the nation's lowest election turnout since 1983.

U.S., Russia Mediate Syrian Cease-Fire; Other Developments—An internationally brokered cease-fire agreement went into effect Feb. 27 in Syria, where nearly five years of bloody fighting between the regime of Syrian Pres. Bashar al-Assad and multifactional rebels opposed to his rule had killed hundreds of thousands. Although fighting continued post-truce, a decrease in violence was noted; the lull was used to deliver humanitarian assistance in many areas for the first time in years. Syrian forces and almost 100 rebel groups acceded to the cease-fire, but the agreement included neither the al-Qaeda-linked al-Nusra Front or the Islamic State of Iraq and Syria (ISIS), which continued to be the target of U.S. and Russian airstrikes. An early round of peace talks had been suspended in Geneva, Switzerland, in early Feb. Despite international pressure, Turkish Prime Min. Ahmet Davutoglu in mid-Feb. said his country's forces would not stop striking Kurdish militias in Aleppo and elsewhere near the Syria-Turkey border. ISIS claimed responsibility for bomb blasts in Homs and Damascus that killed at least 140 people, Feb. 21.

General

Scores Die in Taiwan Earthquake—A 6.4 magnitude earthquake struck southern Taiwan Feb. 6, killing 117 and injuring about 550 others in heavily populated Tainan. All but two of the reported deaths occurred when a 17-story apartment building collapsed. Within days, three executives were charged with negligence for their role in the construction of the collapsed building.

Denver Defeats Carolina in Super Bowl 50; Rams Bring Football Back to Los Angeles; New NFL Hall of Famers—Peyton Manning and the Denver Broncos overcame the Cam Newton-led Carolina Panthers, 24-10, at Levi's Stadium in Santa Clara, CA, to win Super Bowl 50 on Feb. 7. After scoring on a field goal early in the first quarter, the Broncos maintained their lead, despite veteran quarterback Peyton Manning suffering five sacks and completing just 13 of 23 throws for 141 yards. Broncos linebacker Von Miller was named the Super Bowl MVP; he was credited with 5 solo tackles, 2.5 sacks, and 2 forced fumbles. Playing his final career game (he officially retired Mar. 7), the 39-year-old Manning became the oldest quarterback to win an NFL championship, his second. The broadcast, which included a halftime show featuring Coldplay, Beyoncé, and Bruno Mars, was watched by an average 111.9 mil viewers, down slightly from the 2015 audience.

NFL team owners voted Jan. 12 to allow the St. Louis Rams franchise to move to the Los Angeles area—where they were located 1946-94—beginning with the 2016 season. The Chargers were given a year to decide whether to stay in San Diego, where they were negotiating for a new stadium, or move and share space with the Rams.

The Pro Football Hall of Fame elected eight new members Feb. 6, including quarterback Brett Favre. Chosen in his first year of eligibility, the longtime Green Bay Packer ended 20 seasons as the NFL's career leader in passing completions, yards, and touchdowns. Other new members included wide receiver Marvin Harrison, linebacker Kevin Greene, tackle Orlando Pace, coach Tony Dungy, owner Edward DeBartolo Jr., and the late quarterback Ken Stabler and guard Dick Stanfel.

Einstein's Gravitational Waves Detected—Researchers Feb. 11 announced in the journal *Physical Review Letters* the first direct observation of the ripples in space-time known as gravitational waves, which had been predicted a century earlier by Albert Einstein's general theory of relativity. The international team of researchers, led by Caltech and MIT scientists, used one installation in Livingston, LA, and one in Hanford, WA—together known as the Laser Interferometer Gravitational-Wave Observatory (LIGO)—to detect waves from the collision of two black holes about 1.3 bil light years away.

Pope and Russian Orthodox Leader Hold Historic Meeting—Pope Francis and Patriarch Kirill met in Cuba Feb. 12, marking the first modern visit between the heads of the Roman Catholic and Russian Orthodox churches. In a joint declaration, the two regretted their churches' lack of unity since the Great Schism in 1054 and called for action in areas where Christians were facing persecution, notably the Middle East and North Africa.

Alabama Shakes, Lamar, Swift Win Big at Grammy Awards—Hip-hop artist Kendrick Lamar won five Grammy Awards, and pop star Taylor Swift and rock band Alabama Shakes each won three at the ceremony held in Los Angeles, CA, on Feb. 15. Swift won album of the year and best pop vocal album for *1989*, and also received best music video for "Bad Blood," featuring Lamar, who claimed best rap performance, best rap song, best rap/sung collaboration, and best rap album for *To Pimp a Butterfly*. "Don't Wanna Fight" by Alabama Shakes won best rock performance as well as best rock song, and their album *Sound & Color* was voted best alternative album.

Uber Driver Commits Kalamazoo Shooting Spree—A driver for the mobile app-based taxi service Uber reportedly confessed to shooting eight people, six fatally, Feb. 20 in Kalamazoo, MI. Jason Brian Dalton allegedly carried out the attacks over a five-hour span at an apartment complex, restaurant parking lot, and car dealership in between fares. Seemingly targeting victims at random, the 45-year-old Dalton allegedly told investigators the Uber app had taken control and made him "like a puppet."

Hamlin Wins Photo-Finish Daytona 500—Denny Hamlin won the Daytona 500 Feb. 21 in Daytona Beach, FL, edging Martin Truex Jr. by about half a foot. The 0.01-sec. margin of victory was the closest in the race's 58-year history and marked the first win there for both Hamlin and Toyota. After leading most of the race, Hamlin surrendered first place to teammate Matt Kenseth with 41 laps remaining and later slipped to fifth position amid other lead changes. On the backstretch of the final lap, a near spinout slowed Kenseth and set up Hamlin for the win.

Spotlight **and** ***The Revenant*** **Win at Oscars; Lack of Diversity in Nominees Prompts Criticism**—The journalism drama *Spotlight* received the Oscar for best picture at the 88th Academy Awards ceremony in Los Angeles, CA, Feb. 28, with its writers, Tom McCarthy and Josh Singer, also claiming the award for best original screenplay. Hollywood veteran Leonardo DiCaprio won his first-ever Oscar for best actor (after four previous acting nominations) in the historical adventure *The Revenant*, which also brought Alejandro G. Iñárritu the best director award for the second straight year. Brie Larson received the award for best actress in *Room*. Swedish actress Alicia Vikander won best supporting actress for *The Danish Girl*, and British stage star Mark Rylance claimed best supporting actor for *Bridge of Spies*. Post-apocalyptic epic *Mad Max: Fury Road* earned six statuettes, the most of any film.

With 34.4 mil viewers tuned in, it was the least-watched Oscars ceremony since 2008. Second-time host Chris Rock focused his opening monologue on the lack of racial diversity among the acting nominees. The board of the Academy of Motion Picture Arts and Sciences Jan. 22 unanimously approved sweeping membership changes aimed at doubling its voting women and minority members by 2020.

March 2016

National

Trump, Clinton Extend Delegate Leads; Violence Percolates at Trump Rallies—Real estate titan Donald Trump broadened his advantage in the race for the Republican presidential nomination, winning seven Super Tuesday primaries held Mar. 1 and 10 more states by the month's end. Sen. Ted Cruz (TX) claimed three Super Tuesday victories and Sen. Marco Rubio (FL) claimed one. Trump's victories included Rubio's delegate-rich home state of Florida, bringing his delegate count to 757, with 478 pledged to Cruz. Rubio suspended his campaign after the Mar. 15 Florida voting; neurosurgeon Dr. Ben Carson, who had not won any states, dropped out Mar. 4.

Former Sec. of State Hillary Clinton won eight Democratic state primaries and caucuses Mar. 1 over Sen. Bernie Sanders (I, VT), who won four. By Mar. 26, Clinton and Sanders had each won nine more states, but Clinton's lead in the pledged delegate count had increased to 1,261 over Sanders's 1,043.

Despite solid front-runner status, Trump continued to attract controversy on the campaign trail. A 78-year-old Trump supporter was charged with assault for punching a protester at a North Carolina Trump rally Mar. 9. A woman assigned to report on Donald Trump's campaign by the conservative news organization Breitbart accused Trump's campaign manager, Corey Lewandowski, of forcibly grabbing and pulling her Mar. 8. Lewandowski was charged with misdemeanor battery in Jupiter, FL, Mar. 29, but charges were dropped Apr. 14. St. Louis police Mar. 11 arrested 31 people accused of general peace disturbance at a Trump event there; that same day, the candidate canceled a Chicago rally amid fighting between supporters and protesters that injured two police officers.

U.S. Job Growth Continues; Markets Recover; Other Developments—The Labor Dept. reported Mar. 4 that 242,000 jobs had been added to the U.S. economy in Feb. The unemployment rate held steady at 4.9%—its lowest level since Mar. 2008—and the so-called underemployment rate, which includes part-time employees and discouraged job-seekers, was 9.7%.

U.S. stocks regained some earlier losses, with the Dow Jones industrial average finishing Mar. at 17,685.09, up 7.1% from the month before, and the S&P 500 closing at 2,059.74, gaining 6.6% from Feb. The Nasdaq composite index finished at 4,869.85, up 6.8%. The Bureau of Economic Analysis's final revised figure for the fourth quarter of 2015 showed Mar. 25 that real U.S. GDP grew by 1.4%, down from 2.0% in the third quarter.

Chesapeake Energy co-founder and fracking pioneer Aubrey McClendon was killed in a single-car crash in Oklahoma Mar. 2, one day after he was charged with conspiring to fix bids on oil/natural gas leases.

Obama Nominates Scalia Replacement; Supreme Court Upholds Union Rights—Pres. Barack Obama Mar. 16 nominated longtime Washington, DC, Circuit Court judge Merrick Garland to the U.S. Supreme Court seat vacated by the sudden death in Feb. 2016 of Associate Justice Antonin Scalia. Despite the 63-year-old Garland's reputation as a respected moderate liberal, Senate Majority Leader Mitch McConnell (R, KY) and other GOP lawmakers said they would not consider any Obama nominee.

Delivering its first significant split verdict since Scalia's passing, the Supreme Court Mar. 29 deadlocked 4-4 over a case challenging the right of teacher, police, and other public sector unions to collect fees from nonmembers. The tie vote left standing a lower court's ruling upholding the fees.

Obama Makes Historic Visit to Cuba—Pres. Obama visited Cuba Mar. 20-22, furthering the thaw in U.S.-Cuban relations that began in Dec. 2014. The first sitting U.S. president to visit Cuba since 1928, Obama met separately with Cuban Pres. Raúl Castro and political dissidents. Both leaders celebrated the reconciliatory steps their countries had taken, but Obama voiced concerns with Cuba's handling of dissent, and Castro criticized the U.S.'s lack of universal health care access and renewed calls for the U.S. to end the embargo of Cuba and close its military prison in Guantánamo Bay.

FBI Cracks Accused Shooter's iPhone, Ends Case Against Apple—Ending a more than month-long stalemate, the U.S. Justice Dept. Mar. 28 dropped its demand that U.S.-based computer giant Apple help unlock an iPhone used by one of two people believed to have fatally shot 14 people in San Bernardino, CA, in late 2015. The FBI reportedly paid contractors to access the data without the aid of Apple, which had argued that creating a master key to allow such access could then be exploited by hackers. Unmoved by a federal court order compelling it to assist investigators, Apple argued the government lacked the authority to require the company to write new software to unlock the phone. The development left unresolved the debate weighing national security interests against the need to securely encrypt data.

International

UN Hits North Korea With Tougher Sanctions—The United Nations Security Council responded Mar. 2 to recent nuclear provocations by North Korea by imposing its strictest economic sanctions ever on the communist country. The nation performed its fourth nuclear test since 2006 in Jan. 2016, and launched a long-range rocket that delivered a satellite into space in Feb. 2016. The UN resolution—which had the crucial support of China, North Korea's primary trading partner—included a requirement that member countries search all passing cargo vessels to or from North Korea. The U.S. and South Korea Mar. 7 began their annual joint military exercises, and North Korea threatened preemptive nuclear strikes against the U.S. Pres. Barack Obama Mar. 16 levied more new sanctions, opposed by China, that froze assets of foreigners carrying out business within large sectors of North Korea's economy.

Chinese Economic Growth Slows; EU Acts to Stimulate Economy—Chinese Prime Min. Li Keqiang outlined the government's economic plan before China's parliament, Mar. 5, projecting a growth rate of 6.5%-7.0% in 2016. The rate of GDP growth in the world's second-largest economy was less than half of China's recent peak annual rate of 14.2% in 2007. The decline in growth was seen as a possible challenge to (or symptom of) Chinese Pres. Xi Jinping's long-term plan to move the country toward a consumer- and service-driven economy.

The European Central Bank (ECB) Mar. 10 announced measures aimed at jump-starting sluggish economic growth in the 19-country eurozone, including expanding an existing bond-buying program and decreasing main interest rates.

Bombing Kills 37 in Turkey's Capital; Other Developments—A car bomb killed at least 37 people and injured another 120 in a commercial district of Ankara, Turkey, Mar. 13. The government quickly launched retaliatory airstrikes at separatist Kurdistan Workers' Party (PKK) camps in Iraq. Turkish airstrikes against PKK targets had been ongoing since July 2015 and claimed at least 67 lives Mar. 9. Four days after the bombing, the Kurdistan Freedom Falcons (TAK)—a splinter faction of the PKK—claimed responsibility. The TAK had also claimed responsibility for a Feb. 17 military convoy bombing in Ankara that killed at least 28 people.

Hundreds protested Turkish Pres. Recep Tayyip Erdogan's Mar. 4 closure of the country's widest circulated newspaper, *Zaman*, which reopened Mar. 6 under new management and with a markedly more pro-government tone.

Russia Announces Syrian Troop Withdrawal; Other Developments—Russian Pres. Vladimir Putin Mar. 14 ordered the removal of the "main part" of Russia's military forces from Syria. Since late Sept. 2015, Russian forces served there in tacit support of Syrian Pres. Bashar al-Assad in his ongoing battle against multifactional Sunni and Kurdish rebel groups. Putin's surprise announcement came the same day a second round of UN-mediated, indirect peace talks began in Geneva, Switzerland. Putin asserted that Russian airstrikes and ground offensives had achieved their goals, which some believed to be a reference to victories over U.S.-supported rebels in northern Syria. By Mar. 27, Syrian government forces backed by Russian air support retook the ancient central city of Palmyra, controlled by the Sunni extremist group known as the Islamic State or ISIS since May 2015.

Relatively low levels of violence since a Feb. truce had allowed some access to areas of Syria that had been unreachable by humanitarian aid workers for months or even years. According to the Syrian Center for Policy Research, since Mar. 2011, about 470,000 people had been killed, 3.1 mil had fled as refugees, 1.2 mil had migrated to other countries, and 6.4 mil had been displaced within Syria.

EU, Turkey Finalize Refugee Deal—In the midst of Europe's largest refugee crisis since World War II, the European Union and Turkey Mar. 18 reached an agreement intended to help stem the flow of mostly Syrian, African, and South Asian refugees and other migrants, more than 1 mil of whom reached Europe in 2015. In exchange for expedited consideration for EU membership and visa-less travel within Europe for Turkish citizens, Turkey said it would accept all asylum seekers landing in Greece beginning Mar. 20. In return, the EU agreed to pay 6 bil euro ($6.8 bil), which would partially help Turkey support some 2.7 mil already living in its refugee camps.

To provide relief to tens of thousands of migrants crowded into Greek camps, the EU Mar. 2 proposed a $760-mil emergency aid package requiring the approval of member countries.

ISIS Bombers Strike Brussels—Suicide bombings Mar. 22 at Zaventem airport and a subway station in Brussels, Belgium, killed 35 (including three bombers) and injured more than 300 others. ISIS claimed credit for the coordinated attacks, which came four days after Brussels police arrested Salah Abdeslam, believed to be the sole surviving suspect involved in the Nov. 2015 attacks in and around Paris, France. In the wake of the attacks, authorities suspended public transportation in Brussels and Belgian Prime Min. Charles Michel called for three days of mourning.

Police carried out an extensive search for a man suspected of aiding the subway bomber and another thought to have handled an unexploded suitcase bomb found at the airport; both were arrested Apr. 8. Investigators discovered links between the Paris and Brussels attacks, including DNA from one of the deceased Brussels airport bombers found on explosives used in Paris. Belgian authorities drew criticism for their failure to detect an apparently extensive local terror network, with Turkish officials claiming they had deported and warned Belgium about one of the two Belgian-born brothers who had detonated themselves in the attack.

Karadzic Convicted of Bosnian War Crimes—Former Bosnian Serb leader Radovan Karadzic was found guilty and sentenced to 40 years in prison Mar. 24 for crimes against humanity, war crimes, and genocide during the 1992-95 Bosnian war. He was convicted by a tribunal in The Hague, Netherlands, on 10 of 11 counts, including a charge related to the killing of more than 8,000 Muslims in Srebrenica. In hiding for more than a decade before his 2008 arrest, Karadzic was the senior-most figure to be successfully prosecuted for the campaign of attempted ethnic cleansing in the former Yugoslavia. Karadzic was expected to appeal the verdict.

Park Bombing Kills Scores in Lahore—A suicide bombing Mar. 27 in a crowded park in Lahore, Pakistan, killed some 70 people including at least 29 children. Jamaat-ul-Ahrar, a splinter group of the Pakistani Taliban, claimed responsibility for the attack and said it had intentionally targeted Christians on the Easter Sunday. Officials Mar. 28 announced they would launch a paramilitary crackdown against extremists in Punjab, the majority Muslim province where the attack took place. It was the group's fifth major bombing since Dec. 2015.

Myanmar Swears in Nonmilitary Government—For the first time since 1962, Myanmar Mar. 30 inaugurated a civilian president. Pres. Htin Kyaw of the National League for Democracy (NLD) was expected to serve as a proxy for NLD leader and former longtime political prisoner Aung San Suu Kyi, who was constitutionally barred from serving as president. The NLD overwhelmingly defeated the military-backed Union Solidarity and Development Party in Nov. 2015 elections, but the military constitutionally retained one-quarter of parliamentary seats, tempering the NLD's victory. Suu Kyi was sworn into several cabinet positions, including foreign minister, on Mar. 30. In early Apr., she became state counselor, a newly created position that allowed her to work in both legislative and executive capacities.

Suu Kyi pledged that the new government would include more minorities and work to establish peace between warring militias and the military, but she refused to recognize the majority-Buddhist Myanmar's persecuted Muslim Rohingya population as citizens.

General

Astronaut Returns After Nearly a Year in Space; Other Space Developments—NASA commander Scott Kelly touched down in Kazakhstan Mar. 2 after 340 days aboard the International Space Station (ISS), the longest space mission in U.S. history. Kelly and Russian cosmonaut Mikhail Kornienko had launched Mar. 27, 2015, with the ambitious goal of spending nearly a year in space. The mission gave Kelly a U.S.-record 520 days in space (over four flights). To assess the physical and psychological effects of extended space habitation, researchers compared Kelly with his Earth-bound identical twin, retired astronaut Mark Kelly.

NASA Mar. 3 announced its Hubble Space Telescope had detected the most distant galaxy yet at 13.4 bil light years away, in the direction of Ursa Major.

Sharapova Banned From Court; Other Doping Developments—The Intl. Tennis Assn. announced Mar. 7 that it would provisionally suspend five-time Grand Slam singles champion Maria Sharapova after revealing she had tested positive for the prohibited performance-enhancing drug meldonium in late Jan. The Russian Sharapova, who had taken the drug since 2006, claimed she had "made a huge mistake" in failing to realize meldonium had been banned since Jan. 1, 2016, by the World Anti-Doping Association (WADA). WADA decided Apr. 13 to lift suspensions on athletes able to prove they had last taken meldonium before Jan. 1; it was unclear whether this would impact Sharapova, who on June 7 was given a two-year suspension. (The Court of Arbitration for Sport (CAS) reduced the suspension to 15 months Oct. 4.)

CAS Mar. 24 upheld the Intl. Assn. of Athletics Federations' (IAAF) disqualifying of six world championship medal-winning Russian track-and-field athletes' results for varying periods between 2009 and 2013. Russia's athletics federation was banned from international competition over widespread corruption and doping accusations in Nov. 2015; the ban was upheld in an IAAF meeting June 17.

Women's National Soccer Team Brings Equal Pay Suit—Five players on the 2015 World Cup-champion U.S. women's national soccer team filed a wage discrimination complaint Mar. 30 with the federal Equal Employment Opportunity Commission against the U.S. Soccer Federation (USSF). The complaint cited data from USSF's 2015 financial report showing team members were paid less than their male counterparts despite generating more in revenue than the men's team.

April 2016

National

Inversion Crackdown Dashes Pfizer-Allergan Merger; Banks' Living Wills Fail; Other Economic Developments—The U.S. Treasury Dept. Apr. 4 imposed new restrictions that sought to limit tax-avoidant corporate inversions, wherein a U.S. corporation moves its headquarters overseas through a merger with a foreign-owned entity. The new restrictions would ignore any foreign acquisitions of U.S. assets made three years prior to an inversion deal in assessing the proportion of foreign ownership. Two days later, U.S. pharmaceutical giant Pfizer terminated a planned $160-bil merger with Ireland-based Allergan that would have been the largest corporate inversion in history.

Federal regulators Apr. 13 declared that five of eight major U.S. banks—including JPMorgan Chase, Wells Fargo, and Bank of America—had failed to create acceptable "living wills," or plans to wind down operations under bankruptcy without a public bailout. The living wills were mandated by reforms passed in the wake of the 2007-09 recession and financial crisis. The U.S. Justice Dept. announced Apr. 11 that Goldman Sachs would pay $5.1 bil to settle charges it knowingly sold investors faulty mortgage-backed securities that contributed to the crisis.

Once-heralded blood-testing startup Theranos acknowledged Apr. 18 that it was under federal investigation for misleading investors about the effectiveness of its minimally invasive technology. *Forbes* estimates June 1 revised the value of the company to $800 mil from $9 bil.

The Labor Dept. Apr. 1 reported that the U.S. economy had added 215,000 jobs in Mar. while the unemployment rate rose slightly to 5.0% from 4.9% in Feb., an uptick attributed to more people joining the labor force. The Dow Jones industrial average finished Apr. at 17,773.6, up 0.5% from the month before, while the S&P 500 closed at 2,065.30, gaining 0.3% from Mar. The Nasdaq composite index finished at 4,775.36, down 1.9%.

North Carolina Bathroom Bill Controversy Continues; Obama Administration Weighs In—North Carolina Gov. Pat McCrory (R) Apr. 12 issued an executive order amending a controversial state law widely criticized as limiting the civil rights of lesbian, gay, bisexual, and transgender (LGBT) people. McCrory's order expanded protections for state workers but left untouched a provision requiring that individuals use public bathrooms that correspond with the sex listed on their birth certificate. The law superseded local anti-discrimination ordinances and its passage on Mar. 23 garnered nearly immediate backlash, with companies such as PayPal and Deutsche Bank nixing planned expansions there.

McCrory's executive action failed to allay the federal Justice Dept., which filed a civil rights lawsuit against the state May 9. In a May 13 letter signed by top officials in the Justice and Education Depts., the Obama administration issued "significant guidance" to public schools nationwide, directing them to allow transgender students to use bathrooms and other facilities matching their gender identity. By May 25, Texas and 10 other states had sued over the directive, which did not carry the force of law but tacitly threatened the loss of federal education funding for noncompliant states or municipalities.

Three Indicted in Flint Water Crisis—Michigan's attorney general Apr. 20 filed the first criminal charges related to widespread lead contamination in the municipal water of Flint, MI. Two of the three indicted were state employees whose charges included conspiracy and tampering with evidence and test results. A city administrator was also charged. Flint switched its water supply to the cheaper yet highly corrosive Flint River in Apr. 2014 and told residents the water was safe for nearly 18 months afterward in spite of evidence to the contrary.

Tubman Named First African-American Woman on U.S. Currency—The U.S. Treasury Dept. Apr. 20 announced that abolitionist Harriet Tubman would become the first African-American woman to appear on U.S. currency with the redesign of the $20 bill. Tubman would be added to the bill's front, and current subject Pres. Andrew Jackson would be moved to the back. In further diversification of U.S. currency portraits, officials also announced the addition of five women voting-rights activists to the back of the $10 bill. Civil rights leader Martin Luther King Jr., first lady Eleanor Roosevelt, and African-American opera singer Marian Anderson will be added to the back of the $5 note.

Former House Speaker Sentenced—Former U.S. House Speaker Dennis Hastert (R, IL) was sentenced Apr. 27 to 15 months in federal prison. Hastert had pleaded guilty to evading financial reporting requirements on $1.7 mil he paid to a man he allegedly sexually abused decades earlier when he was a high school wrestling coach and teacher and his accuser was a 14-year-old student. Hastert served for 20 years in the House and as speaker, 1999-2007.

International

Leaked "Panama Papers" Expose Tax Evasions by World Leaders—An international network of investigative journalists reported in multiple press outlets Apr. 3 the first findings from a trove of 11.5 mil documents leaked from the Panamanian law firm Mossack Fonseca that linked dozens of politicians and public officials to offshore shell companies and trusts that could be used to mask unlawful tax evasion. Two days later, Iceland Prime Min. Sigmundur Gunnlaugsson resigned over allegations stemming from the leaks. UK Prime Min. David Cameron also faced major criticism over his father's offshore fund, from which Cameron admitted he benefited until 2010, when he sold his stake. Other leaders directly named in the so-called Panama Papers included Argentine Pres. Mauricio Macri, King Salman of Saudi Arabia, and Ukrainian Pres. Petro Poroshenko. Investigations of the documents by journalists and law enforcement were ongoing in dozens of countries.

EU Begins Migrant Deportations—Facing a continuing influx of unauthorized refugees and other migrants, the European Union Apr. 4 began sending newly arrived migrants in Greece to Turkey under a controversial deal reached in Mar., for which Turkey received expedited EU-membership consideration and $6.8 bil in aid. Some Syrian refugees already in Turkey who qualified for asylum would be resettled in EU states. Critics said the agreement violated asylum seekers' rights and questioned whether increasingly authoritarian Turkey could provide safe haven.

The Italian coast guard rescued 1,850 migrants Apr. 11, the same week up to 500 refugees traveling from Libya were feared to have drowned after their boat capsized in the Mediterranean. In late Apr., Austria approved a law allowing it to directly reject most asylum seekers—including those from Syria—at its border.

Rival Libyan Government Steps Aside—Libya's Government of National Salvation—one of two competing militia-backed governments that had withheld support from the Government of National Accord (GNA), a United Nations-approved unity government—disbanded Apr. 5. The remaining rival government, the relatively secular House of Representatives, headquartered in eastern Libya, continued to resist the GNA, which by the end of the month controlled a majority of state agencies in Tripoli. Libya had been plagued by internal conflict since the 2011 ouster of longtime dictator Muammar al-Qaddafi.

Truce Aims to Abate Yemen Conflict; AQAP City Seized; Other Yemeni Developments—A shaky cease-fire between Yemen's exiled government led by Abd Rabbuh Mansur Hadi and Iran-allied Houthi rebels went into effect Apr. 10 and mostly held throughout the month. Houthis, in cooperation with other forces loyal to Yemeni Pres. Ali Abdullah Saleh, had seized the national capital of Sanaa and much of western Yemen beginning in 2014. Violence increased further in Mar. 2015 after a pro-Hadi military alliance headed by Saudi Arabia joined the conflict, in which al-Qaeda in the Arabian Peninsula (AQAP) was also believed to be an active participant. The regional chaos had enabled AQAP to expand its holdings in southern Yemen throughout 2015, but more than 800 AQAP fighters were believed to have been killed in a successful attempt Apr. 25 to seize its local stronghold, the port city of Al Mukalla, by pro-Hadi government forces working with the Saudi coalition.

The United Nations in Mar. 2016 had warned the nation was on the brink of famine, and Houthi rebels and pro-Hadi officials Apr. 26 approved an agenda for UN-backed peace talks. According to the UN, fighting in Yemen had killed more than 6,400 people since Mar. 2015.

Voters Hobble South Korean Ruling Party—The conservative party of South Korean Pres. Park Geun-hye unexpectedly lost its parliamentary majority in general elections held Apr. 13. Voters handed the progressive Minjoo party 123 of 300 parliamentary seats, while Park's Saenuri won 122, down from an outright-majority of 152, and the centrist People's Party, which had split from Minjoo, won 38. A 20-year-high 58% of voters had participated in the election, widely viewed as a referendum on Park, whom opponents blamed for a sluggish economy. Park, constitutionally barred from seeking a second five-year term in 2017 elections, said legislative gridlock prevented reforms she claimed would have boosted growth.

New Unity Government in South Sudan—Former South Sudanese Vice Pres. and rebel leader Riek Machar was sworn into his old office Apr. 26 in Juba as part of an Intergovernmental Authority on Development (IGAD)-mediated peace agreement. The nation had erupted in civil war in July 2013, when South Sudanese Pres. Salva Kiir fired his cabinet, including Machar, whom he accused of organizing a coup. The conflict, which displaced an estimated 2.3 mil, was drawn along ethnic lines and violence had continued beyond the IGAD-accord signing in Aug. 2015.

Brazil Impeaches President Amid Widespread Protests—The lower house of Brazil's parliament impeached Pres. Dilma Rousseff by a 367-137 vote Apr. 17. Rousseff was accused of concealing the size of the nation's budget deficit ahead of her 2014 reelection, among other corruption allegations. The parliamentary action followed anti-government protests in Mar. that drew some 3 mil Brazilians. The nation was in the throes of its worst recession in decades, and protesters also objected to the alleged involvement of Rousseff's ally and predecessor Luiz Inácio Lula da Silva and

dozens of other politicians in a kickback scheme with the oil giant Petrobras. Backing the lower house, the Senate May 12 voted 55-22 to suspend Rousseff for up to 180 days pending further action.

Taliban Commits Deadliest Attack in Kabul Since 2011; Other Afghan Developments—An attack on Afghanistan's capital claimed by the Taliban killed at least 64 people and wounded nearly 350 more Apr. 19. The Kabul assault, which followed a violent winter, began when a suicide bomber detonated a truck bomb at a government compound. Security forces several days earlier repelled a Taliban assault on Kunduz, reportedly killing some 40 militants attempting to seize the strategic northern provincial capital. Taliban officials Apr. 12 had announced the beginning of their annual springtime offensive and signaled the group's disinterest in restarting stalled peace talks.

The U.S. Dept. of Defense Apr. 29 released a report declaring the U.S. bombing of a Doctors Without Borders hospital in Kunduz that killed at least 42 people in Oct. was committed in error and was not a war crime. The Pentagon disciplined 16 people related to the attack with punishments that included suspension and removal of command.

Nations Sign Paris Climate Deal—Delegates from 175 countries signed the climate-focused Paris Agreement, drafted in Dec. 2015, on Apr. 22 in New York, NY. The agreement aimed to limit global warming to well below 2°C (3.6°F) above pre-industrial levels. It required ratification by 55% of countries that account for at least 55% of global emissions to take effect.

Human Rights Panel Questions Official Government Story on Missing Mexican Students—An international panel appointed by the Inter-American Commission on Human Rights (IACHR) released a report Apr. 24 denouncing Mexico's investigation into the Sept. 2014 disappearance of 43 students from Iguala, in the southwestern state of Guerrero. Mexican officials said that police passed the students off to a drug cartel, which killed and incinerated them, but the IACHR panel cast doubt on the government's conclusions.

General

Villanova, UConn Win NCAA Basketball Tournaments in Historic Fashion—The second-seed Villanova Univ. Wildcats edged the top-ranked Univ. of North Carolina Tar Heels, 77-74, to win the school's second NCAA basketball championship Apr. 4 at NRG Stadium in Houston, TX. A North Carolina three-pointer tied the game with less than 5 sec. remaining, but Wildcat Kris Jenkins countered with the first three-point, game-winning "buzzer beater" in national championship history. Villanova guard Ryan Arcidiacono, who had 16 points and two assists—including the pass that set up Jenkins's game-winner—was named the most outstanding player of the Final Four.

In the women's tournament final Apr. 5, the Univ. of Connecticut routed the Syracuse Univ. Orange, 82-51, at Bankers Life Fieldhouse in Indianapolis, IN. It was the fourth straight title for UConn, and Huskies Moriah Jefferson, Breanna Stewart, and Morgan Tuck became the only players in NCAA basketball history to win four championships. Stewart was designated most outstanding player of the Final Four a record fourth time, with 24 points, 10 rebounds, and 6 assists. The victory gave UConn head coach Geno Auriemma a record 11th title.

Willett Wins Masters Tournament—Danny Willett became the first Brit to win the Masters Tournament in two decades, upsetting defending champ Jordan Spieth Apr. 10 at Augusta Natl. Golf Club in Augusta, GA. The surprise victor trailed Spieth by five shots at the end of the final round's front nine but gained the lead after Spieth quadruple bogeyed the 12th hole. Willett finished 5-under 283, 3 strokes ahead of Spieth and Lee Westwood, for his first major victory.

NBA Season Win Record Falls; Bryant Retires—The Golden State Warriors set a new NBA record for regular season wins when they defeated the Memphis Grizzlies, 125-104, Apr. 13 at Oakland's Oracle Arena for their 73rd win. The previous record was held by the 1995-96 Chicago Bulls.

That same day, 37-year-old L.A. Lakers guard Kobe Bryant, the NBA's third all-time leading scorer, played the last game of his 20-year career, scoring 60 points in a 101-96 victory against the Utah Jazz.

Ecuadorian Earthquake Kills Hundreds—The northern coast of Ecuador was struck Apr. 16 by a magnitude 7.8 earthquake that killed at least 661 people and displaced some 28,000 others. The quake's epicenter was offshore, and cities Pedernales, Manta, and Portoviejo were hardest hit. The earthquake was deadliest to strike Ecuador since 1987, when about 1,000 were killed in a magnitude 7.2 earthquake.

Courts Affirm NFL Concussion Settlement, Uphold Brady Suspension—A federal appeals court Apr. 18 upheld an estimated $1-bil settlement between the NFL and former players who are afflicted with or may in the future suffer from football-associated brain injuries. The agreement covered more than 20,000 retired players, who each stood to gain up to $5 mil. Some criticized the deal's failure to cover current players or apply to mood and behavioral disorders.

A federal appeals court ruled Apr. 25 that New England Patriots quarterback Tom Brady must serve a four-game suspension imposed by the NFL over allegations he was "generally aware" of a scheme to illegally deflate footballs in the Jan. 2015 AFC championship game.

May 2016

National

Trump Rivals Depart GOP Presidential Race; Clinton Moves Forward—Real estate magnate Donald Trump all but secured the Republican nomination for president May 3 after winning the Indiana primary. Sen. Ted Cruz (TX), Trump's nearest opponent in delegates, and Ohio Gov. John Kasich had entered into an unprecedented yet shaky public alliance, with each pledging not to campaign in certain states, in an ultimately unsuccessful last ditch effort to compete. Cruz suspended his campaign May 3, and Kasich, who had won only his home state, dropped out May 4. Underscoring GOP concerns over Trump's general election viability, House Speaker Paul Ryan (R, WI) May 5 said he was "just not ready" to endorse Trump. Unopposed in the rest of the month's primaries, Trump by late May tallied 1,239 total delegates, two more than was needed to claim the nomination.

Despite May primary victories limited to Guam, Kentucky, and Washington, former Sec. of State Hillary Clinton held a commanding delegate lead, keeping her on track to clinch the Democratic Party's presidential nomination. Sen. Bernie Sanders (I, VT) defeated Clinton in Indiana May 3 and also scored wins in West Virginia (May 10) and Oregon (May 17). The State Dept.'s inspector general May 25 released a report concluding Clinton's usage of a private email server during her tenure in the Obama administration violated agency rules. The report rebuked Clinton's failure to turn over all state business-related emails prior to resigning and criticized former Sec. of State Colin Powell's similar use of a private email account.

Former Republican New Mexico Gov. Gary Johnson won the Libertarian Party presidential nomination May 29, with former Massachusetts Gov. Bill Weld as his running mate.

Puerto Rico Debt Crisis Escalates—Puerto Rico Gov. Alejandro García Padilla issued an executive order suspending $370 mil in bond payments due May 2 so that the government could continue covering essential services. The default was the island's third since 2015; Puerto Rico's status as a U.S. territory prevented it from seeking federal bankruptcy protection or Intl. Monetary Fund assistance. After weeks of negotiations, the U.S. House of Representatives June 9 voted 297-127 to allow Puerto Rico to restructure its $72 bil debt. According to the Treasury Dept., 45% of Puerto Rico's 3.5 mil residents, most of whom are U.S. citizens by birth, lived in poverty, compared with 16% nationally. The crisis was expected to further deepen July 1, when $1.9 bil more in bond payments was due.

Takata Expands Air Bag Recall; U.S. Revamps Overtime Rules; Other Economic News—Japan's Takata Corp. May 4 recalled 35-40 mil more defective air bag inflators that were linked to at least 10 deaths in the U.S. In combination with Takata's earlier 28.8 mil recalls, the air bags were the largest-ever safety recall in the U.S.

The White House May 17 announced that an additional 4.2 mil salaried workers would be eligible for overtime pay under a new Labor Dept. rule effective Dec. 1. The income eligibility threshold for salaried employees increased for the first time since 2004, from $23,660 to $47,476 annually.

Facebook founder and CEO Mark Zuckerberg met May 18 with prominent conservatives over complaints his site suppressed conservative news content in its trending topics. Facebook May 23 said an internal investigation detected no such favoritism, but it revamped the feature to minimize potential risk.

The Labor Dept. May 6 reported that the U.S. economy added 160,000 jobs in Apr., a downturn from Mar. The Dow Jones industrial average finished May at 17,787.20, up 0.1% from the month before, while the S&P 500 closed at 2,096.95, gaining 1.5% from Apr. The Nasdaq composite index finished at 4,948.05, gaining 3.6%.

International

Turkish Prime Minister Steps Down—Prime Min. Ahmet Davutoglu of Turkey's ruling Justice and Development Party (AKP) announced his resignation May 5 over a reported rift with Pres. Recep Tayyip Erdogan, the former AKP leader, who continued to urge lawmakers to expand his mostly ceremonial role to that of a stronger executive. In contrast to Erdogan, Davutoglu favored resuming peace talks with the Kurdistan Workers' Party (PKK), Kurdish separatists waging a 32-year-old rebellion, even as Turkey's military prosecuted a strong counterinsurgency campaign against them. The AKP May 22 unanimously approved Davutoglu's replacement, staunch Erdogan ally Binali Yildirim.

Davutoglu's departure threatened the agreement he had brokered with the European Union to take in more of Europe's refugees. Under the agreement, signed in Mar. 2016, Turkey had pledged to soften antiterrorism laws allegedly used by Erdogan's government to muzzle dissent. After it failed to do so, the EU June 15 delayed granting Turkish citizens visa-free travel throughout Europe.

North Korea Holds First Party Congress Since 1980—North Korea's ruling communist Workers' Party convened its first congress in 36 years May 6-9 in Pyongyang. Held at the behest of 32-year-old autocrat Kim Jong Un, the congress appeared to yield no significant policy developments but was widely viewed by international observers as an opportunity for Kim to further consolidate his rule over the politically isolated nation. Declaring that North Korea was a "responsible nuclear power" and would only use nuclear weapons in response to a foreign threat, Kim called on the country to develop nuclear energy as part of a five-year economic plan.

Hardliner Claims Filipino Presidency—With over 6 mil more votes than his nearest competitor, hardliner Rodrigo Duterte easily won the Philippines' presidential election May 9 over the Liberal Party's Mar Roxas—the candidate endorsed by Pres. Benigno Aquino III, who was constitutionally prohibited from seeking a second six-year term—and four other official candidates. The longtime mayor of Davao City, Duterte had earned comparison to U.S. presumptive Republican presidential nominee Donald Trump through bombastic comments including pledging to issue security forces shoot-to-kill orders for suspected criminals. Critics accused Duterte of overseeing death squads that had killed over 1,000 people, including children and minor criminals.

Boxing legend Manny Pacquiao won a Philippine Senate seat in the day's elections, which saw a record 81% turnout.

Deadly ISIS Bombings Rock Baghdad; Other Iraq Developments—Three bombings in Baghdad killed at least 90 people and injured 165 others May 11, in what was the deadliest day of attacks in Iraq in 2016. The Sunni extremist group Islamic State of Iraq and Syria (ISIS) claimed responsibility for the May 11 attacks and other deadly bombings in May. Three explosions May 17 killed at least another 69 in Shiite neighborhoods in Baghdad, and two car bombings had killed 32 in the southern city of Samawa May 1. In spite of the civilian losses, Iraqi officials May 11 said U.S.-backed security forces had retaken about two-thirds of territory seized by ISIS in northern and western Iraq since 2014. U.S. Sec. of State John Kerry had been positive but less optimistic in public statements in Apr., claiming ISIS had lost 40% of its territory. Iraqi Prime Min. Haider al-Abadi May 22 announced the start of an offensive to liberate Fallujah, a major city held by ISIS since Jan. 2014.

Venezuelan Opposition Protests Amid Economic Hardship—Venezuelan Pres. Nicolás Maduro Moros declared a 60-day state of emergency May 13, saying that it was aimed at "the external and foreign aggressions" against the oil-rich country, which was mired in recession amidst plummeting global oil prices and 2016 inflation forecast at 500% by the IMF. Maduro's decree, the third of its kind since Jan., permitted the government to seize idle factories and empowered security forces to distribute and sell food, at a shortage throughout Venezuela. Maduro's opponents in parliament decried the emergency measure, but the country's supreme court ruled it constitutional. Activists who blamed the country's economic woes on Maduro, the socialist successor to Hugo Chávez, continued to call for his ouster and thousands of demonstrators thronged the capital of Caracas. Opposition lawmakers May 2 had submitted a petition signed by 1.85 mil people requesting a recall referendum against Maduro.

U.S. Kills Taliban Chief; Other Afghanistan Developments—The Afghan Taliban confirmed May 25 that its leader, Akhtar Muhammad Mansour, was killed by a U.S. drone strike May 21. The strike, which targeted Mansour's moving vehicle in Pakistan near the Afghan border, was hailed by U.S. Pres. Barack Obama and officials who said Mansour had been planning assaults on U.S. targets in Kabul.

The foreign ministers of nearly 40 nations agreed May 20 to extend their country's participation in NATO's Resolute Support mission to train and assist Afghan forces beyond 2016. The U.S. formally marked the end of its 13-year war in Afghanistan in Dec. 2014 but contributed over 6,950 of the current mission's 12,800 troops.

Obama Visits Hiroshima on Final Asia Trip; Other Developments—More than 70 years after the U.S. dropped two atomic bombs on Japan, Pres. Barack Obama May 27 became the first sitting U.S. president to visit Hiroshima, a city devastated by one of the bombs. As expected, Obama did not apologize for the action but instead laid a wreath at the Hiroshima Peace Memorial and advocated for global nuclear disarmament before an audience that included survivors and relatives of the bombing's victims.

Obama traveled to Vietnam and Japan May 21-28 on his 10th and likely final presidential trip to Asia. In Hanoi May 23, he declared the U.S. would fully end its arms embargo against Vietnam, parts of which were first imposed in 1975, a move protested by human rights groups. He attended a G-7 summit in Ise-Shima, Japan, May 26-27, where Obama and other leaders of the world's seven most industrialized democratic nations (not including Russia, suspended from the G-8 in 2014) discussed China's maritime aggression, North Korea's nuclear actions, and Europe's refugee crisis.

General

Wildfire Prompts Canadian Province's Largest-Ever Evacuation—A fast-moving wildfire in northeastern Alberta, Canada, forced the evacuation by May 3 of all 88,000 residents of the oil-boom city of Fort McMurray and surrounding areas. The blaze destroyed an estimated 2,400 buildings and cut daily oil production by some 1 mil barrels. Alberta authorities declared a state of emergency May 4, roughly two weeks before the fire spread into neighboring Saskatchewan province. The fire, which was Canada's most expensive natural disaster ever, was thought to have been started by human activity in very dry conditions.

Long-Shot Team Wins Soccer Title—The underdog Leicester City Football Club secured England's Premier League soccer championship May 2 after nearest rival Tottenham blew a 2-0 lead against London's Chelsea to end its match in a draw. Leicester City's title came after the club fought off relegation to a lower league the previous season,

which they rallied to finish 14th out of 20 teams. Leicester City lost only three games over the course of the season, which they began with 5,000-to-1 odds of winning a title.

Nyquist Wins Kentucky Derby; Exaggerator Clinches Preakness—Three-year-old bay colt Nyquist surged past Gun Runner in the final stretch and held off hard-charging second-place finisher Exaggerator by 1¼ lengths to win the 142nd Kentucky Derby in 2:01.31 May 7 at Churchill Downs in Louisville, KY. It was the second Derby victory for Mexican jockey Mario Gutierrez. Exaggerator dashed Nyquist's Triple Crown bid May 21 at the 141st Preakness Stakes at a muddy Pimlico Race Course in Baltimore, MD. The Derby-winner led three-quarters of the race until Exaggerator and jockey Kent Desormeaux overtook him on the final stretch to finish 3½ lengths ahead of second-place finisher Cherry Wine. Nyquist came in third.

Nearly 1,300 Planets Discovered—NASA May 10 announced researchers had used its Kepler space telescope to discover 1,284 new planets. The scientists said that nine of these were likely rocky worlds like Earth with surface temperatures that would allow liquid water to exist. The discovery more than doubled the total number of planets located by the telescope since its 2009 launch.

Egyptian Airliner Crashes, Killing Scores—EgyptAir Flight 804 plunged into the Mediterranean Sea May 19, killing all 66 people onboard. Debris from the Airbus A320, which was en route from Paris to Cairo, was found floating about 180 mi north of Alexandria, Egypt, and parts of the plane were located on the seafloor between Crete and the Egyptian coast nearly a month later. The exact cause of the crash remained a mystery; although a mayday call was not issued, automated flight data showed smoke in multiple areas of the plane shortly before it lost radar contact at 37,000 ft. Egyptian officials said the cause was most likely terrorism, though they did not provide evidence to support their claim.

Drug Resistant Superbug Reaches U.S.—According to a study published May 26 in an Amer. Society for Microbiology journal, scientists for the first time found a person in the U.S. carrying *E. coli* bacteria resistant to the last-resort antibiotic colistin. Although the Pennsylvania woman's bacterial strain was ultimately treatable by different antibiotics, researchers feared the bacteria's colistin-resistant gene could spread to bacteria already invulnerable to all other antibiotics.

Rossi Victorious at Indianapolis 500—Rookie Alexander Rossi won the 100th Indy 500 at Indianapolis Motor Speedway May 29 in a stunning finale that saw the 24-year-old long shot run out of gas and coast to victory. Rossi gambled that his fuel would hold out after front-runners Colombian Carlos Muñoz and Josef Newgarden pitted with four and five laps remaining, respectively. The race included multiple accidents, including a three-car pit mishap that threw then-contenders Ryan Hunter-Reay and Townsend Bell out of contention.

June 2016
National

Clinton Clinches Democratic Presidential Nomination; Trump Campaign Missteps Draw Attention—The Associated Press announced June 6 that former Sec. of State Hillary Clinton had won the Puerto Rico primary June 5 and secured the required number of pledged delegates to be named the presumptive Democratic nominee over Vermont Sen. Bernie Sanders. Clinton continued to accrue delegates with wins in four more contests during the month, including California and New Jersey June 7, but Sanders vowed to take his populist message to the party convention.

After two years of investigation, the House Select Committee on Benghazi June 28 released its final report, which found no new evidence of wrongdoing by then-Sec. of State Clinton after 2012 attacks killed four at the American consulate in Benghazi, Libya.

Presumptive Republican nominee Donald Trump June 2 received the endorsement of House Speaker Paul Ryan (R, WI). That same day, Trump told the *Wall Street Journal* that U.S. District Judge Gonzalo Curiel had an "absolute conflict" and could not be impartial in presiding over fraud suits against Trump University, his real estate training program, because Trump had pledged to build a wall between the U.S. and Mexico and Curiel, an Indiana-born American, had Mexican heritage. After Trump refused to disavow the claim, Ryan joined many critics of the statement in labeling it racist but did not withdraw his endorsement.

Shooter Kills Scores at Orlando Nightclub; Gun Control Filibuster Draws Notice—A gunman killed 49 mostly Hispanic victims and injured at least 53 others June 12 at Pulse, a gay nightclub in Orlando, FL. Armed with a semi-automatic rifle and a handgun, the shooter, Omar Mateen, fired indiscriminately into crowds before exchanging shots with an armed off-duty police officer who was working as a security guard. After retreating to a bathroom, where he took hostages, the shooter phoned police and declared his allegiance to the Sunni extremist group Islamic State in Iraq and Syria (ISIS). Police broke a three-hour standoff by ramming through an outside wall, and Mateen, who emerged and fired at police, was shot and killed. The attack set a grim new record for the deadliest act by a single shooter in modern U.S. history.

ISIS claimed the U.S.-born Mateen as a member, but investigators did not uncover tangible ties to the group. The FBI revealed it had investigated Mateen twice since 2013 but had concluded he was not a threat. His Afghanistan-born father told NBC News that his son had reacted angrily towards gay people. Some early reports suggested he may have used a gay dating app and previously visited Pulse, but FBI investigators found no evidence that could independently verify those reports.

Pres. Barack Obama responded to the shooting by reiterating earlier calls for gun control. Sen. Chris Murphy (D, CT) June 15 led a nearly 15-hour filibuster in an attempt to force votes on expanding background checks for gun purchases and banning those on the FBI's terrorism "watch list" from buying guns. The Senate June 20 rejected both measures. U.S. Rep. John Lewis (D, GA) and 170 other House Democrats held a 25-hour-long sit-in June 22-23 demanding a vote on gun-control legislation.

Short-Handed Supreme Court Ends Term on Abortion, Immigration, Affirmative Action—Missing a ninth vote since the death of Associate Justice Antonin Scalia in Feb. 2016, the U.S. Supreme Court concluded its 2015-16 term June 27 with a 5-3 decision in *Whole Woman's Health v. Hellerstedt*, ruling that a Texas law placed an "undue burden" on women's access to abortions. Writing for the majority, Justice Stephen Breyer argued that mandating that doctors who performed abortions obtain hospital admitting privileges and that clinics upgrade to hospital-style facility regulations did not further Texas's "legitimate interest in protecting women's health."

In *U.S. v. Texas*, the Court June 23 voted 4-4 on the question of affirming or overturning a lower court's ruling blocking enforcement of Pres. Barack Obama's Nov. 2014 executive action deferring deportation of certain undocumented immigrants. With no vote to break the justices' tie, the lower court's opinion was upheld but did not hold precedential value.

The Court in a 4-3 decision in *Fisher v. University of Texas* June 23 upheld Univ. of Texas-Austin's race-conscious admissions criteria. In his majority opinion, Justice Anthony Kennedy rejected the argument that the university denying admission to a white applicant while accepting a less qualified minority student violated the 14th Amendment right to equal protection. Associate Justice Elena Kagan, who had participated in early stages of the case as solicitor general, recused herself from the decision.

VW Reaches $15-Billion Settlement Over Emissions Scandal; Job Growth Drops; Other Business News—Volkswagen agreed June 28 to pay $14.7 bil to settle government allegations that many of its VW and Audi diesel vehicles for model-years 2009-15 cheated U.S. emissions tests and actually released up to 40 times the legally permissible levels of pollutants. More than $10 bil of the settlement was set aside to buy back or repair 475,000 affected U.S. vehicles and pay owners $5,100-$10,000 each for lost value.

The Labor Dept. reported June 3 that the economy had added just 38,000 jobs in May, over 120,000 fewer than predicted, for the worst monthly job growth since Sept. 2010. Despite poor growth, May's unemployment rate dropped to 4.7% from 5.0% in Apr., attributed to some half-million people leaving the workforce. According to the Bureau of Economic Analysis's final revised figures for the first quarter of 2016 released in June, real GDP grew by 1.1%, compared with 1.4% in the fourth quarter of 2015. The Dow Jones industrial average finished June at 17,929.99, up 0.8% from the month before while the S&P 500 closed at 2,098.86, gaining 0.1% from May. The Nasdaq composite index finished at 4,842.67, losing 2.1%.

In what would be its largest acquisition ever, software giant Microsoft June 13 announced plans to purchase the professional networking site LinkedIn for $26.2 bil.

International

Fujimori Loses Cliffhanger Election in Peru—Peru's tightest presidential race in five decades ended June 10 after Keiko Fujimori, daughter of jailed former Pres. Alberto Fujimori, conceded victory to economist Pedro Pablo Kuczynski. Voters chose Kuczynski 50.1%-49.9% June 5, two months after Fujimori's center-right Popular Force party easily won general voting, securing 73 of 130 congressional seats to 18 won by Kuczynski's center-right Peruvians for Change. Fujimori had promised she would not pardon her father, who was imprisoned for crimes against humanity, but thousands branded her as corrupt and authoritarian at demonstrations leading up to voting.

U.S. Diplomats Advocate Direct Action Against Assad; Other Syria Developments—A U.S. State Dept. memo, made public June 16, called for targeted airstrikes against Pres. Bashar al-Assad's regime in Syria, which had repeatedly violated a late-Feb. cease-fire with U.S.-backed rebels aimed at finding a resolution to the five-year-old civil war. The memo—signed by 51 mostly mid-level State Dept. diplomats—sharply criticized other aspects of the Obama administration's Syria policy, which focused on arming anti-Assad rebels and airstrikes on ISIS targets.

Colombia, FARC Sign Historic Cease-Fire—Colombian Pres. Juan Manuel Santos and the head of the guerilla group Revolutionary Armed Forces of Colombia (FARC) June 23 signed a cease-fire deal aimed at ending 52 years of armed conflict. Finalized with the Aug. 23 signing of a broader peace deal subject to a popular referendum set for Oct., the agreement called for FARC to disarm and demobilize its estimated 7,000 soldiers, many of whom were kidnapped as children. FARC, which formed in 1964, initially sought a revolution to establish a Marxist government but became known for its terrorism, drug trafficking, and kidnappings of foreigners, journalists, and high-profile Colombians. The conflict killed some 220,000 people and displaced 5-7 mil.

UK Votes to Leave European Union—In a historic June 23 referendum, voters in the United Kingdom elected to leave the 28-country European Union—the first member country to do so—after a 42-year membership in the EU and its predecessors. Drawing 72% of the electorate—more than any UK-wide vote since 1992—the 51.9%-48.1% result surprised many despite pre-vote polling showing a nearly even split on the issue. The regional differences were stark; while Scotland and Northern Ireland both strongly voted to remain, those in economically distressed areas of England and Wales, along with rural and older voters, were thought to have tipped the scales in favor of "Brexit." EU proponents argued in favor of open access to European markets and warned of economic ruin, while "vote leave" campaigners criticized high EU membership fees and regulations, with some vilifying Eastern Europeans and other immigrants. At the height of heated Brexit campaign rhetoric, Labour Party MP and "remain" supporter Jo Cox was fatally shot and stabbed June 16 by a man who reportedly shouted "Britain first."

Conservative UK Prime Min. David Cameron announced June 24 he would resign so that someone who supported Brexit would be in charge of the transition. Global markets rattled by the uncertain future fell dramatically, with world stocks losing $2.8 tril June 24, the largest one-day global decline in history; Standard & Poor's downgraded Britain's credit rating June 27 from AAA to AA. Despite the immediate economic fallout, within days far-right lawmakers in other EU nations, including France and the Netherlands, demanded their own EU opt-out referendums.

Iraqi Forces Defeat ISIS in Fallujah—Iraq's army declared Fallujah "fully liberated" from ISIS militants June 26, five weeks after Iraqi troops and Shiite-dominated militias launched a major offensive to reclaim the mostly minority Sunni city, held by militants since Jan. 2014. The liberation was aided by U.S.-led airstrikes, including one coalition bombing that killed 47 militants, according to an Iraqi officer. The United Nations said that more than 85,000 people who had fled Fallujah and surrounding areas since the start of the offensive remained in overcrowded desert camps. Located about 40 mi west of Baghdad, Fallujah was the site in late 2004 of the U.S.'s deadliest confrontation during the Iraq War, with nearly 100 U.S. military deaths there.

Istanbul Airport Attack Kills Dozens—Three attackers laid siege to Istanbul Atatürk Airport June 28, killing at least 45 and injuring more than 230 others. After opening fire at a security checkpoint outside the terminal, the attackers reportedly detonated explosives, killing themselves. Turkish officials said the men were from Russia, Uzbekistan, and Kyrgyzstan, and had likely acted under ISIS direction. The assault brought attention to the large numbers of Russians—estimated at 5,000-7,000—believed to be involved with ISIS. It was the eighth suicide bombing and deadliest major attack in Turkey in 2016, all of which its government blamed on ISIS or Kurdish separatists. In the past year, Turkey had granted the U.S. access to its Incirlik Air Base, from which the U.S. was staging anti-ISIS airstrikes, and had stepped up its own offensives against Kurdish separatists.

General

Muguruza and Djokovic Take French Open Titles—No. 4-ranked Spaniard Garbiñe Muguruza defeated 2015 French Open champion Serena Williams (7-5, 6-4) June 4 at Roland Garros in Paris, France. The upset victory marked the 22-year-old Muguruza's first Grand Slam title. The next day, No. 1-seed Novak Djokovic of Serbia bested No. 2-ranked Scotsman Andy Murray (3-6, 6-1, 6-2, 6-4) to achieve a career Grand Slam and become the first man since 1969 to win four straight Grand Slam singles titles.

Creator Wins Belmont Stakes—Creator, a 16-1 longshot, won the 148th Belmont Stakes June 11 at Belmont Park in Elmont, NY. Ridden by Puerto Rican-born jockey Irad Ortiz Jr., the 3-year-old gray colt surged in the final stretch to catch Destin by a nose and finish the 1½-mi race in 2:28.51. Exaggerator, the winner of the Preakness Stakes, finished 14 lengths behind the leader in 11th place.

Pittsburgh Penguins Hoist Stanley Cup—The Pittsburgh Penguins defeated the San Jose Sharks, 3-1, June 12 at San Jose's SAP Center to win the NHL's Stanley Cup in six games. It was the fourth championship for Pittsburgh; Penguins captain Sidney Crosby scored 19 points in 24 postseason games to win the Conn Smythe Trophy as the most valuable player in the playoffs.

The NHL's commissioner June 22 announced the league would add a 31st team in Las Vegas for the 2017-18 season.

Russian Track Team Banned From Rio; Other Doping Developments—The Intl. Association of Athletics Federations (IAAF) banned Russia's entire track and field team June 17 from the upcoming Summer Olympics in Rio de Janeiro, Brazil, claiming that Russia had not adequately addressed allegations of state-sponsored doping. IAAF's unanimous vote extended an existing ban on Russian track athletes from international competition, which the governing body enacted in Nov. 2015 after a damning World Anti-Doping Agency (WADA) report. Despite the ban, the IAAF said individual athletes who "show that they are not tainted by

the Russian system" could apply for permission to compete in the Summer Games. The Intl. Olympic Committee July 24 said eligibility decisions on Russian athletes would be made by the federations governing each sport.

Cleveland Defeats Golden State to Win NBA Title—The Cleveland Cavaliers won Game 7, 93-89, over the Golden State Warriors June 19 at Oracle Arena in Oakland, CA, to claim the NBA Finals championship. LeBron James led the Cavaliers comeback from a 3-games-to-1 deficit—unprecedented in NBA Finals history—to defeat the defending champion Warriors, who had set an NBA season record for wins in 2016. James scored 27 points with 11 rebounds and 11 assists in the final game and was unanimously named Finals MVP. Defeated by the Warriors in the previous year's Finals, the Cavaliers' win marked the first championship for a Cleveland major pro sports team in 52 years.

Johnson Takes Golf's U.S. Open—Dustin Johnson won the 116th U.S. Open golf tournament June 19 at Oakmont Country Club in Oakmont, PA. Johnson began the final 18 holes four shots down before rallying with three birdies. Despite officials levying a controversial, post-round penalty stroke against Johnson for allegedly moving his ball on the 5th hole, he finished atop the leaderboard with a 4-under-par 276, three shots ahead of Jim Furyk, Scott Piercy, and Shane Lowry.

Flooding Turns Deadly in West Virginia, Texas—Flash flooding struck West Virginia June 23, killing at least 23 people, mostly in Greenbrier County. Gov. Earl Ray Tomblin declared a state of emergency in 44 counties, some of which received 8-10 in. of rain in 6-8 hours. Pres. Barack Obama June 25 declared the state a disaster area.

Nine U.S. Army soldiers stationed at Fort Hood, TX, drowned June 2-3 when their vehicle overturned at a flooded low-water crossing near Lake Belton. Southern and central Texas experienced record flooding that had killed at least nine others May 27-31.

Panama Opens Canal Expansion—Panama inaugurated a $5.3-bil expansion of its 50-mi-long Panama Canal June 26. Nearly a decade in the making, the 102-year-old canal's enlarged locks and wider and deeper channels allow for transit of larger ships. But it aimed to increase the canal's shipping capacity and efficiency just as international trade was slumping, raising concerns about its viability.

July 2016

National

More Police Killings of Black Men Spark Protests—Video footage posted online showed police officers in Baton Rouge, LA, fatally shooting 37-year-old black man Alton Sterling July 5 despite his having been pinned on the ground by two officers. Promising transparency, Louisiana Gov. John Bel Edwards (D) said federal officials would investigate Sterling's death. On July 6, an officer shot and killed 32-year-old black motorist Philando Castile in Falcon Heights, MN, a St. Paul suburb. Castile's girlfriend, Diamond Reynolds—who was a passenger in the car and live-streamed footage of the aftermath—said the officer shot Castile as he was reaching into his pocket for identification on the officer's instruction. Castile had told the officer he had a licensed weapon in the car.

Large-scale protests assembled in Minnesota and Louisiana in the wake of the shootings. By July 13, 41 demonstrators were arrested for blocking traffic in Minnesota, and 21 St. Paul police officers were reportedly injured by objects thrown by protesters. In Baton Rouge, police arrested 102 on July 9, including prominent Black Lives Matter activist DeRay Mckesson.

Baltimore prosecutors July 27 dropped charges against the three remaining officers facing trial in the death of Freddie Gray, who was killed in 2015 in police custody. Three other officers had already been acquitted.

Gunmen Target Police in Multiple Attacks—A lone black gunman fatally shot five officers and wounded nine others July 7 following an otherwise peaceful anti-police brutality protest in Dallas, TX. A 4½-hour standoff with the 25-year-old shooter, identified as Army veteran Micah

Johnson, ended when police detonated a bomb-equipped robot, killing him. Officials said the shooter was motivated to kill white officers in the wake of highly publicized police shootings of black men that same week in Minnesota and Louisiana.

A 29-year-old black man shot and killed three officers (one of whom was black) and wounded three others July 17 in Baton Rouge, LA, before he was fatally shot by police. Law enforcement officials said the shooter, identified as Gavin Long, was armed with two rifles and one handgun and described the attack as a targeted ambush.

Job Growth Rebounds; Other Economic News— The U.S. Labor Dept. reported July 8 that 287,000 jobs had been added to the economy in June, a sharp increase from the previous month's dismal jobs report, though the unemployment rate rose to 4.9% from 4.7% in May. Wall Street reacted with optimism, with markets gaining steadily throughout the month. The Dow Jones industrial average finished July at 18,432.24, up 2.8% from the month before while the S&P 500 closed at 2,173.60, gaining 3.6% from June. The Nasdaq composite index finished at 5,162.13, gaining 6.6%.

French yogurt producer Danone announced a $10.4-bil plan July 7 to acquire WhiteWave Foods, which makes Silk soy milk, Horizon Organic milk, and other products.

Republican Convention Nominates Trump, Pence; Democrats Nominate Clinton, Kaine; Other Presidential Race Developments—Meeting July 18-21 at Quicken Loans Arena in Cleveland, OH, the Republican National Convention formally nominated real estate mogul Donald Trump for president and Indiana Gov. Mike Pence for vice president. Trump had named Pence, a former six-term congressman, his running mate July 15. Trump formally accepted the nomination July 21, in a 75-min. speech that painted a chaotic and economically dismal portrait of America. Declaring himself the "law-and-order" candidate, Trump claimed that murder rates were on the rise and repeated his signature promise to build a wall between the U.S. and Mexico. Trump's wife, Melania Trump, and primary opponent Sen. Ted Cruz (TX) garnered significant attention earlier in the week: commentators noted that Melania's speech possibly plagiarized sections of first lady Michelle Obama's 2008 convention speech, and Cruz was booed after refusing to endorse Trump in his speech addressing the convention. Many nationally prominent Republicans—including host state Gov. John Kasich and both of the party's living former presidents—were notably absent from the convention.

The Democratic National Convention convened July 25-28 at Wells Fargo Center in Philadelphia, PA, where it nominated former first lady and Sec. of State Hillary Clinton for president and Virginia Sen. Tim Kaine for vice president. Ahead of rousing convention speeches by Pres. Obama and Michelle Obama, populist primary contender Sen. Bernie Sanders (I, VT) urged delegates to back Clinton. In his speech July 27, Kaine reached out to disaffected Republicans and emphasized his long career in public service. The first woman to be nominated for president by a major political party, Clinton spoke on the final day of the convention and attempted to refute Trump's dark assessment of America even as she portrayed him as a threat to national security. Other speakers that night included Khizr Khan, the father of a Muslim-American soldier killed while serving as an Army Reserve officer in Iraq, who castigated Trump's anti-Muslim immigration proposals and questioned his level of sacrifice. Trump criticized Khan, drawing backlash across the political spectrum.

The website WikiLeaks July 22 leaked hacked Democratic National Committee (DNC) emails purportedly showing bias by DNC officials against Sanders. DNC chair Rep. Debbie Wasserman Schultz (FL) resigned in response. Attorney Gen. Loretta Lynch announced in early July that the Justice Dept. would not press charges in relation to Clinton's use of a private email server while serving as secretary of state, even as FBI Dir. James Comey said Clinton and her aides were "extremely careless" in their handling of information. Comey also reported that of 30,000 emails Clinton turned over, 110 contained classified information, contradicting her earlier claims. Trump July 27 appeared to call on Russian hackers to locate emails Clinton had deleted.

Would-Be Reagan Assassin Freed—Saying that continued treatment was "no longer clinically warranted or beneficial," a federal judge July 27 granted full-time release to 61-year-old John Hinckley Jr., who in 1981 shot then-Pres. Ronald Reagan and three others. Hinckley was found not guilty by reason of insanity in 1982 and confined in a Washington, DC, mental health treatment facility. He was released Sept. 10.

International

ISIS Appears to Expand Targets as Ramadan Ends; Other Developments—Terror attacks by the Sunni extremist group the Islamic State of Iraq and Syria were widespread during the month, including a suicide truck bombing in Baghdad July 3 that killed at least 292 people and marked the city's deadliest attack since 2003. ISIS had called for increased bloodshed during the Islamic month of Ramadan, which ended July 5, and was also linked to a July 1-2 attack by Bangladeshi militants that left 20 mostly foreign hostages dead at a Dhaka café and a bombing in Saudi Arabia that killed four people at the Prophet's Mosque July 4 in the holy city of Medina. An explosion July 23 killed at least 80 at a protest of mainly Shiite demonstrators in Kabul, Afghanistan. If confirmed as the work of ISIS, which claimed responsibility, the Kabul bombings would represent the group's first terror assault in Afghanistan's capital. A grenade explosion at a nightclub near Kuala Lumpur June 28 left eight injured and was thought to be ISIS's first successful attack in Malaysia.

U.S. Defense Sec. Ash Carter July 11 announced the U.S. would send 560 more troops to Iraq to help fight ISIS, bringing the total number there to some 4,650. According to UK-based Syrian Observatory for Human Rights, U.S.-led coalition anti-ISIS airstrikes killed at least 56 civilians—including 11 children—July 19 outside Manbij in northern Syria.

Mediterranean Migrant Drownings Persist—Political and economic refugees and migrants from Syria and elsewhere attempting to reach northern Europe via the Mediterranean Sea continued to perish in large numbers, with the International Organization for Migration reporting an estimated 3,127 deaths in 2016 through the end of July, compared to a record high 3,765 in all of 2015 (1,971 in 2015 by the end of July). According to the IOM, some 238,220 migrants had entered Europe by sea in 2016 as of July 10—most of whom arrived in Italy and Greece—compared to 141,944 who arrived during the first six months of 2015. Amid ongoing drownings, rescue teams continued to pick up migrants arriving in overloaded and unseaworthy vessels; on July 5 alone, the Italian coast guard reportedly saved about 4,500 people between Italy and Libya.

China Loses Maritime Dispute Case—An international tribunal in The Hague, Netherlands, July 12 rejected China's contentious claims to disputed islands, reefs, and waters in the South China Sea. The tribunal also ruled that Mischief Reef, on which China had recently constructed an artificial island with a military airstrip, was in Philippine waters. The tribunal said China had constructed artificial islands, failed to prevent Chinese fishing in the Philippines' "exclusive economic zone," and interfered with Philippine fishing and oil exploration. Chinese president Xi Jinping rejected the tribunal's legally binding ruling, which lacked any enforcement mechanism.

UK Leadership in Transition in Brexit Vote's Wake—Theresa May of the Conservative Party became prime minister of the United Kingdom July 13 in the aftermath of the Brexit referendum results, which led to the resignation of Prime Min. David Cameron. May said the next week that she would not formally initiate the UK's departure from the EU before the end of 2016. The nation's first female prime minister since Margaret Thatcher (1979-90), May removed five of Cameron's cabinet members and appointed, among others, former London mayor and staunch Brexit supporter Boris Johnson as foreign minister and Liz Truss as justice secretary and Lord Chancellor, the first woman to hold the latter position.

Truck Attack Kills Scores in France; ISIS Backers Kill French Priest—Using a 19-ton truck as a weapon, a Tunisian-born man in Nice, France, killed 86 people and injured more than 300 others July 14 when he drove more than a mile on a closed seaside road through crowds gathered to celebrate Bastille Day. The 31-year-old attacker, Mohamed Lahouaiej-Bouhlel, reportedly fired on police before he was shot dead. Just hours before the attack, French Pres. François Hollande said he planned to lift a state of emergency put in place after 130 people were killed in attacks in and around Paris in Nov. 2015; he quickly reversed himself, ordering the nationwide deployment of 10,000 soldiers and suggesting France would expand airstrikes against ISIS in Syria and Iraq. Although ISIS claimed responsibility for the truck rampage, no direct link was found between the group and Lahouaiej-Bouhlel, a Tunisan-born legal French resident. Authorities July 21 charged five people with helping Lahouaiej-Bouhlel—a longtime sufferer of mental health problems, according to his family—plan the attack. An additional nine suspects were arrested in Aug. and Sept.

ISIS also claimed responsibility for a July 26 attack on a Catholic church in northern France. Two attackers were shot dead by police after they took six people hostage, including a priest, whom they killed.

Turkish Coup Attempt Fails; Government Suppresses Opposition—Saying its demands included reinstating democracy, a faction of Turkey's military late July 15 attempted to topple the government of Turkey's Islamist Pres. Recep Tayyip Erdogan. Coup supporters blocked bridges and seized military vehicles and aircraft as well as airports, army bases, and multiple media outlets. Erdogan evaded capture and appealed to the public, including by appearing on TV via a FaceTime call. Tens of thousands of anti-coup demonstrators assembled in the streets of Istanbul and Ankara, where they encountered tanks and were reportedly fired on. Coup leaders surrendered by early morning, but at least 265 people were killed during the attempted coup, including 161 civilians and police officers.

In the aftermath, Erdogan declared a state of emergency and ordered the detention of large numbers of suspected anti-government plotters and sympathizers; by July's end, some 15,000 people had been detained (including about 10,000 from the military), and more than 45,000 removed from their jobs. Although Pres. Barack Obama and other leaders voiced support for Turkey's democratically elected government in response to the undemocratic seizure of power that the coup attempt represented, the U.S. and other Western countries had expressed alarm over Turkey's treatment of dissenters even before the recent round of purges.

General

Williams and Murray Take Wimbledon Championships—Top-ranked Serena Williams defeated No. 4-seed Angelique Kerber of Germany in straight sets (7-5, 6-3) at the women's final of the Wimbledon Championships in London July 9. It was Williams' seventh Wimbledon win as well as her 22nd Grand Slam singles title, which tied the Open-era record held by Steffi Graf. The next day, Scotland's No. 2-seed Andy Murray beat Canadian 6th-seeded Milos Raonic (6-4, 7-6, 7-6) to claim the men's title.

Stenson, Jutanugarn Win Golf British Opens; Walker Claims PGA Title—Henrik Stenson of Sweden clinched the 145th British Open golf championship at Royal Troon Golf Club in Troon, Scotland, July 17. Trading the lead multiple times in the final round with American Phil Mickelson, the 40-year-old No. 6-ranked Stenson birdied four of the last five holes to finish at 20-under-264, three strokes ahead of Mickelson.

Jimmy Walker won the 98th PGA Championship at a muddy Baltusrol Golf Club in Springfield, NJ, July 31. The 37-year-old American opened the closing round with nine straight pars and shot three birdies to finish at 14-under-266, one shot ahead of 2015 PGA Championship winner Jason Day of Australia.

Ariya Jutanugarn of Thailand shot 16-under-272 to win the 41st Women's British Open July 31 at Woburn Golf Club in Milton Keynes, England. Jutanugarn finished three strokes ahead of both American Mo Martin and South Korea's Mirim Lee.

British Racer Wins Third Tour de France—Kenyan-born Brit Chris Froome won the 103rd Tour de France, his third victory in four years July 24. The 31-year-old Froome completed the 2,088-mi course in Paris in 89 hr., 4 min., 48 sec. Frenchman Romain Bardet finished 4 min., 5 sec. behind Froome. Slovakia's Peter Sagan claimed the green jersey as the race's best sprinter for the fifth straight year.

Fox News Chief Resigns Amid Scandal—Fox News Channel chair and CEO Roger Ailes resigned July 21 amid a lawsuit filed by ex-*Fox & Friends* morning show host Gretchen Carlson, alleging the 76-year-old executive had sexually harassed her and retaliated when her overtures were rebuffed. Other women, including prominent anchor Megyn Kelly, made similar claims to investigators.

Fox News Channel's parent company Sept. 6 agreed to settle with Carlson for $20 mil and a public apology. Ailes received $40 mil from the company as part of his negotiated exit agreement.

Aviation Stunts and Tragedy Draw Headlines—*Solar Impulse 2* became the first aircraft to fly around the world on solar power alone when it landed July 26 in Abu Dhabi, United Arab Emirates. The Swiss-engineered plane completed its 25,000-mi journey in 17 legs over a 16-month span.

Pro skydiver Luke Aikins jumped out of an airplane 25,000 ft above California's Simi Valley July 30 with neither a parachute nor a wingsuit and landed without incident in a 10,000-sq-ft net at 120 mph.

A hot air balloon crashed July 30 south of Austin, TX, killing the pilot and all 15 passengers in what was the deadliest-ever U.S. ballooning accident. The craft is believed to have collided with power lines, causing the balloon's gondola to catch fire.

August 2016
National

Milwaukee Police Shooting Sparks Violence; Justice Dept. Releases Baltimore Report, Announces Private Prison Phaseout—Riots shook parts of Milwaukee, WI, Aug. 13-15 after a black police officer fatally shot 23-year-old Sylville Smith, an armed black man who fled a traffic stop. Although the city's police chief said the officer's body camera footage showed the suspect turned toward the officer with a gun in his hand, he declined to make the video public. About 100 demonstrators gathered in the city's Sherman Park neighborhood, where violence broke out. Multiple police cars and at least six businesses were set on fire, and other businesses were looted. Wisconsin Gov. Scott Walker (R) declared a state of emergency Aug. 14. At least eight police officers were injured in the unrest, and 31 people were arrested.

In a report released by the U.S. Dept. of Justice Aug. 10, federal investigators found that Baltimore Police Dept. officers routinely unlawfully stopped and employed excessive force against black residents, though illegal guns and drugs were more often found on whites.

The Justice Dept. Aug. 18 announced a strategy to eliminate its use of privately operated facilities to house inmates of the Federal Bureau of Prisons. According to an internal audit released the week prior, private prisons, which house about 12% of federal prisoners, had more incidents of violence, lockdowns, and inappropriate solitary confinement than other federal facilities.

Audit Uncovers Army Bookkeeping Blunders—The U.S. Dept. of Defense's Inspector General reported that the U.S. Army committed $6.5 tril in accounting errors in 2015, according to a highly critical Pentagon report made public by Reuters Aug. 19. The DOD partially attributed the erroneous general fund adjustments to employees' failure to detect and fix software and system glitches, but the inspector also accused personnel of falsifying data on a large scale to balance their books and conceal an accounting system in disarray.

EU Slaps Apple With Hefty Tax Bill; EpiPen Price Controversy; Other Economic News—The European Union Aug. 30 ordered tech giant Apple to pay up to $14.5 bil in back taxes to Ireland's government, alleging Apple had received tax breaks from the Irish government that were against EU regulations. Apple said it would appeal the record penalty.

Parents and lawmakers voiced outrage over pharmaceutical maker Mylan's decision to raise the price of its EpiPen, a drug-delivery device that treats severe symptoms of allergic reactions, from a little over $100 per two-pack in 2009 to more than $600 in May 2016. The Senate Sept. 7 opened an investigation into the markup.

The Labor Dept. reported Aug. 5 that July's unemployment rate held steady at 4.9% and the economy added 255,000 jobs. Stock indexes were buoyed by the report, and the Nasdaq composite index closed that day at a record-high 5,221.12. The Nasdaq ended the month at 5,213.22, gaining 1.0%. The Dow Jones industrial average finished the month at 18,400.88, down 0.2% from July while the S&P 500 closed at 2,170.95, a 0.1% monthly drop. Domestic new home sales surged in July to an annual rate of 654,000 units, the highest level since 2007 and up 31.3% from July 2015.

International

Thailand Supports New Constitution; Unknown Bombings Strike—Thai voters approved a military-drafted constitution in an Aug. 7 referendum that delivered tacit approval to the military junta that took power from the country's corruption-tainted government in a bloodless coup in May 2014. Of the 59.4% of the electorate who voted, 61.4% approved the constitution, paving the way for general elections by the end of 2017. The constitution limited the ability of a single party to win a parliamentary majority. A second measure narrowly approved by voters empowered the military government to appoint the entire 250-seat national senate, which would then have a role in electing the prime minister.

Bombings struck five Thai provinces Aug. 11-12 mostly in southern tourist areas including Phuket and Hua Hin, killing four people and injuring dozens. Investigators ruled out international terrorism; some blamed the attacks on dissidents critical of the military regime.

Syrian Siege of Aleppo Continues; U.S. Kills ISIS Second-in-Command; Other Developments—Syria's civil war between the regime of Bashar al-Assad and rebels continued its deadly course, with the UK-based Syrian Observatory for Human Rights Aug. 14 reporting 327 civilians were killed—including 76 children—in the besieged northern city of Aleppo and its surrounding area in the month's first two weeks. A photo of a bloodied and dust-covered 5-year-old, recently rescued from the aftermath of a regime or Russian airstrike there, went viral online in mid-Aug., drawing renewed Western attention to the 5½-year-old conflict. Highlighting the dire conditions, an envoy said the United Nations had received reports of 44 attacks in July on Syrian medical facilities. For the first time in the war, government warplanes bombed far-northern, Kurdish-held parts of al-Hasakah.

The Pentagon said U.S. airstrikes killed Abu Mohammad al-Adnani, reportedly the Sunni extremist Islamic State of Iraq and Syria's (ISIS) top spokesman, in a late Aug. strike in Aleppo province. Capping a two-month offensive, the U.S.-backed Syrian Democratic Forces—an alliance of mostly Kurdish and Arab forces focused primarily on defeating ISIS—Aug. 12 took full control of the strategic northern Syrian city of Manbij.

The Associated Press Aug. 30 reported it had documented 72 mass graves—17 in Syria—containing thousands of ISIS victims, many of them Yazidi.

UN Admits Role in Haitian Cholera Epidemic—The United Nations Aug. 18 acknowledged the part its aid workers played in an ongoing cholera epidemic in Haiti that has killed some 10,000 people since 2010, an admission viewed by many critics as long overdue. The results of the

UN investigation had been leaked to the *New York Times* and published a day earlier. Non-UN experts had earlier alleged Nepalese peacekeepers, sent to Haiti following a catastrophic earthquake, brought the intestinal bacterial disease and unknowingly spread it through fecal waste that leaked directly into a river.

Philippine Anti-Drug Campaign Kills Thousands—Philippine Pres. Rodrigo Duterte's self-proclaimed war against drugs, in which he called on citizens to participate by killing addicts, claimed the lives of nearly 2,000 traffickers, drug users, and others July 1-Aug. 20, according to the country's national police, who reportedly carried out close to 900 of the killings during that period. The United Nations and human rights groups condemned the campaign, which began even before Duterte took office. The brash-speaking Duterte's bloody crusade created a rift with the U.S., a longtime ally. The White House canceled a planned meeting in early Sept. between Pres. Barack Obama and Duterte after he insulted Obama and warned other countries against denouncing the killings.

ISIS-Linked Terror Hits Turkey, Yemen; U.S. Bombs ISIS in Libya—A suicide bombing killed 53 people at a Kurdish wedding in southern Turkey, Aug. 20. Blamed on ISIS by Turkish Pres. Recep Tayyip Erdogan, the attack followed at least five others in the first half of 2016 and was reportedly carried out by a boy believed to be 12-14 years old. A car bombing nine days later, claimed by ISIS, killed at least 54 people in the southern port city of Aden in civil war-torn Yemen, where the ISIS continued to attack mostly Shiite targets. The U.S. Aug. 1 expanded its anti-ISIS air campaign to Libya's coastal city of Sirte at the request of the country's interim government.

Attacks Target Kabul's American Univ., Pakistan Hospital—Adding to a spike in violence in the Afghan capital of Kabul, at least three suspected Taliban militants attacked the American Univ. of Afghanistan Aug. 24, killing 13 people, including three police and seven students. Police ended the 9-hour siege, fatally shooting two of the gunmen; a third was killed when he detonated a bomb. The university was viewed by many as a symbol of cooperation between the U.S. and Afghanistan.

A Taliban faction and ISIS separately claimed responsibility for a suicide bombing that killed at least 72 people—mostly lawyers—Aug. 8 at a hospital in the southwestern Pakistani city of Quetta.

Brazil's Senate Impeaches President—Brazil's Senate voted 61-20 to impeach Dilma Rousseff Aug. 31 over charges that her administration illegally borrowed state bank funds to attempt to lessen the country's deficit ahead of 2014 elections, when she was running for reelection. Rousseff, the country's first woman president, had been suspended from office May 12. Oil-rich Brazil continued to suffer from a deep recession fueled by slumping oil prices. Protests and accusations of corruption plagued Rousseff during most of her second term, and although she had not been charged, she was linked to the pay-for-play scandal involving the state-run oil company Petrobras that had engulfed many lawmakers belonging to Rousseff's Workers' Party, in power since 2002. Interim Pres. Michel Temer, of the more conservative Brazilian Democratic Movement Party, was himself implicated in the awarding of Petrobras contracts in exchange for campaign contributions.

General

Zika Virus Prompts Miami Travel Warning; Other Developments—The U.S. Centers for Disease Control and Prevention Aug. 1 warned pregnant women and their partners against traveling to a specific Miami neighborhood after at least 14 people there were diagnosed with the Zika virus, which can be spread by mosquitoes; infections in pregnant women have been linked to the birth defect microcephaly. It was thought to be the first time the CDC urged avoidance of a continental U.S. destination due to a health risk and came amid a Zika outbreak first detected in May 2015 in Brazil, where more than 1,700 microcephaly cases had been confirmed. The U.S. Aug. 12 declared a state of emergency in

Puerto Rico in response to nearly 2,000 new Zika cases in the past week and 10,690 since Dec.

XXXI Summer Olympics Held in Rio de Janeiro, Brazil—More than 11,500 athletes from 206 nations and dependencies competed in 306 medal events at the XXXI Summer Olympic Games, hosted Aug. 5-21 by Rio de Janeiro, Brazil. Rio reportedly spent at least $12 bil preparing for the Games, drawing criticism from residents, as the nation was hit in 2015-16 with its worst recession in 25 years.

The U.S. dominated the medal count, with a total of 121 medals: 46 gold, 37 silver, and 38 bronze. China was second overall, with 70 medals: 26 gold, 18 silver, and 26 bronze. An ongoing doping scandal disqualified 118 of 389 Russian athletes. Notably, the Rio Games were the first to include a refugee team, composed of 10 displaced athletes. Marking the return of golf as an Olympic sport after a 112-year absence, the 2016 Games were also the first to feature men's and women's rugby sevens.

Already the most decorated Olympian ever, 31-year-old American swimmer Michael Phelps came out of retirement to claim five gold medals and one silver, elevating his career total medal tally to 28; his victory in the 200-m individual medley was the first time a swimmer won the same event at four successive Olympics. Jamaican track sprinter Usain Bolt became the first man to win three consecutive 100-m and 200-m Olympic titles; he also won a third straight gold in the men's 4x100-m relay. Other American stars included swimmer Katie Ledecky, who won four gold medals and one silver, and gymnast Simone Biles, who captured gold in the all-around, vault, and floor competitions and helped the U.S. women's team win its second straight Olympic title. Simone Manuel tied for gold in the 100-m freestyle, becoming the first African-American woman to win an individual Olympic medal in swimming.

In the final week of the Games, American swimmer Ryan Lochte created an international scandal after he falsely said he and three other swimmers had been robbed at gunpoint. Brazilian investigators said armed security guards took $50 from the swimmers after one or more of them allegedly vandalized a gas station. Lochte Sept. 8 was suspended from sanctioned competition for 10 months.

Flooding Devastates Louisiana—As much as two feet of rain fell on parts of Louisiana in the 48 hours ending Aug. 13, bringing catastrophic flooding that killed 13 people in the southern part of the state. Louisiana Gov. John Bel Edwards (D) declared a state of emergency Aug. 12, and Pres. Barack Obama Aug. 14 issued a major disaster declaration that later extended to 20 parishes. The unincorporated city of Watson, 15 mi northeast of Baton Rouge, received 31.39 in. of rain Aug. 16. Edwards estimated damages of more than $8.7 bil, and the Federal Emergency Management Agency reported 63,000 families were receiving housing assistance by Sept. 9.

Nearest Potentially Livable Planet Found—Queen Mary University of London scientists in the journal *Nature* Aug. 24 reported a rocky planet 1.3 times the mass of Earth with a potential to hold liquid water orbiting Proxima Centauri, the nearest star to the Sun. Although Proxima b's discovery marked the closest known potentially habitable planet, it was still 4.2 light-years from Earth. Previously, the closest-known comparable planet was 14 light-years away.

Deadly Earthquake Strikes Italy—A magnitude 6.2 earthquake struck a mountainous region in central Italy Aug. 24, killing at least 290 people and affecting more than two dozen towns and villages. Most victims were located in hardest-hit Amatrice, which was preparing to host a food festival about 65-mi northeast of Rome. Despite more than 470 aftershocks within 30 hours of the quake, rescuers digging through rubble reportedly freed at least 238 people. The quake was Italy's deadliest since a 2009 tremor killed over 300.

September 2016

National

Wells Fargo Admits Massive Consumer Fraud; Scope of Yahoo Data Breach Startles; Other Economic News—Regulators ordered U.S. banking giant Wells Fargo to pay $185 mil in fines Sept. 8 after investigators revealed its employees had opened about 1.5 mil banking accounts and applied for some 565,000 credit cards in the names of current customers without their knowledge. Appearing before House lawmakers later in the month, Wells Fargo CEO John G. Stumpf apologized and said he was forgoing at least $41 mil in pay; the bank dropped its sales incentive program, which Stumpf said had been abused, and fired 5,300 employees implicated in the scam. (Stumpf formally resigned Oct. 12.) Included in the fine was $100 mil levied by the Consumer Financial Protection Bureau, the agency's largest ever penalty.

Marking what was said to be the largest-ever data breach in history, internet giant Yahoo Sept. 22 acknowledged that a late 2014 hack—by what it alleged was a "state-sponsored actor"—resulted in the theft of at least 500 mil users' account data.

Agricultural giant Monsanto Sept. 14 agreed to a $66 bil buyout by Germany-based Bayer, pending regulatory approval. For-profit ITT Technical Institute abruptly closed Sept. 6, affecting about 35,000 students nationwide. Less than two weeks earlier, the U.S. Dept. of Education sanctioned the 50-year-old educational institution over its recruiting and accounting practices and barred it from enrolling students accepting federal financial aid.

The Labor Dept. reported Sept. 2 that the economy added 151,000 jobs in Aug., a moderate slowdown from strong growth over the previous two months, and the unemployment rate remained at 4.9% for the third straight month. According to the Bureau of Economic Analysis's final scheduled estimate for the second quarter of 2016, real GDP increased by an annual rate of 1.4% compared to 0.8% in the first quarter. The Dow Jones industrial average finished Sept. at 18,308.15, down 0.5% from Aug., while the S&P 500 closed at 2,168.27, a 0.1% decrease from the month before. The Nasdaq composite index finished at 5,312.00, gaining 1.9%.

White House Interrupts Dakota Pipeline Construction—The Obama administration responded Sept. 9 to several months of protests by the Standing Rock Sioux Tribe of North Dakota and South Dakota by temporarily halting further construction of an oil pipeline within 20 mi of Lake Oahe, in North Dakota. The tribe and their supporters argued the pipeline—slated to run underneath the lake upstream of tribal land—could impact drinking water and destroy sacred sites. Thousands of protesters—many of whom were members of dozens of other American Indian tribes from across the country—demonstrated at an encampment about 45 mi south of Bismarck, ND. Video footage in early Sept. showed private security officers threatening demonstrators with dogs; some protesters alleged they were bitten and attacked with pepper spray. The adminstration's stop-work order came the same day a federal judge rejected the tribe's injunction request. If completed, the Dakota Access pipeline would span nearly 1,200 mi from North Dakota to Illinois.

Apparent Terrorist Acts Strike New York, New Jersey, Minnesota—A homemade bomb exploded near a dumpster in New York City's Chelsea neighborhood Sept. 17, injuring 31 people. Police discovered a second, undetonated bomb four blocks away. Authorities Sept. 19 apprehended 28-year-old Afghan-born Ahmad Khan Rahami following a shootout in Linden, NJ, that left two officers with minor injuries. Injured by multiple shots, Rahami was directly linked to the Chelsea bombing along with an earlier pipe bomb explosion that same morning in Seaside Park, NJ, in which no one was injured. Rahami had traveled to Pakistan (2011) and Afghanistan (2013-14), but authorities did not immediately link him to any terrorist groups. FBI officials had twice interviewed Rahami's father, Mohammad Rahami, in connection with the father's concerns that his son was a terrorist, but Rahami himself was not interviewed at that time.

The Sunni extremist group known as the Islamic State of Iraq and Syria claimed responsibility for a mass stabbing in a St. Cloud, MN, shopping mall Sept. 17 that injured 10 people. An off-duty officer shot and killed the lone perpetrator, who was a Somali-American U.S. citizen born in Kenya. The FBI was investigating the attack as a potential act of terrorism.

North Carolina Police Shooting Sparks Protests; Tulsa Officer Indicted for Killing Black Motorist—Continuing a trend of outrage over alleged injustice by police against African Americans, hundreds of demonstrators Sept. 20 took to the streets of Charlotte, NC, hours after an officer fatally shot 43-year-old Keith Lamont Scott. Police said Scott exited his vehicle with a firearm, which they said they had recovered, but Scott's wife said he was not armed. Multiple demonstrations in Charlotte demanding the release of police videos turned aggressive that same night, with protesters reportedly looting several tractor-trailer trucks on an interstate roadway shut down by the protests. The next evening, police used tear gas on protesters in uptown Charlotte. One person was shot by another civilian; 44 protesters were arrested and four officers reported injuries. Gov. Pat McCrory (R) declared a state of emergency, initiating deployment of National Guard troops. Protests were largely peaceful Sept. 22-24, despite police releasing two videos Sept. 24 that Scott's family and other observers said did not justify his death or confirm he was armed. Additional footage released early Oct. also did not show a weapon.

Tulsa police officer Betty Shelby was charged Sept. 22 in the shooting death six days earlier of unarmed black motorist Terence Crutcher in Tulsa, OK. Although video footage did not show the shooting, it captured Crutcher ignoring Shelby's commands as he walked away from her with both hands in the air. The county's district attorney said Shelby, a white woman, overreacted when she fired without having detected any weapon.

Presidential Nominees Face Off in Debate—Former Sec. of State Hillary Clinton (D) and real estate mogul Donald Trump (R) met Sept. 26 at Hofstra University in Hempstead, NY, in the first presidential debate between the 2016 major party nominees. Trump appeared to score points on trade policy, citing his opposition to the 12-nation Trans-Pacific Partnership, which Clinton supported in its early stages, but frequently seemed unprepared, with few policy details or anecdotes when discussing other topics. He neglected to attack Clinton with many campaign talking points and raised her use of a private email server for State Dept. correspondence only once. He dodged moderator Lester Holt's inquiries regarding his tax returns and his crusade to prove Obama was not a U.S. citizen. A seemingly well-rehearsed Clinton questioned Trump's claim that he had not supported the Iraq War, derided his lack of an apparent plan to combat ISIS, and said his economic plan would benefit only wealthy Americans. She also addressed Trump's assertion that she didn't have the "stamina" to serve as president, and called out past negative statements Trump had made about women. By the end of Sept., RealClearPolitics's national polling data average gave Clinton a slight lead, 47.5%-44.4%.

Congress Overrides Obama Veto; U.S. to Admit More Refugees—Congress Sept. 28 overwhelmingly voted to override Pres. Barack Obama's veto of legislation permitting families of victims of the Sept. 11, 2001, terror attacks to sue the Saudi government, which they suspected of supporting the 15 of 19 hijackers known to be Saudi Arabian nationals. Obama argued the Justice Against Sponsors of Terrorism Act would set a dangerous precedent for allowing countries to sue American military members and other officials in foreign courts. Approved 97-1 in the Senate and 348-77 in the House, the override was Congress's first during Obama's presidency. Just one day later, House Speaker Paul Ryan (R, WI) and Senate Majority Leader Mitch McConnell (R, KY) echoed Obama's objections to the bill and called for changes, arguing Obama did not raise his concerns effectively enough. By the date of the override, no direct evidence had been uncovered linking the Saudi government to the attackers.

White House officials Sept. 14 announced it would boost by nearly 30% the number of refugees it allowed into the country in 2017, to 110,000, of which nearly 40,000 would be from the Near East and South Asia region, including civil war-torn Syria.

International

Workers Strike Across India—Initiating what was thought to be the largest labor strike in human history, an estimated 150-180 mil public sector employees throughout India went on a day-long strike Sept. 2. The 10 trade unions staging the strike objected to government policies boosting privatization and called for a doubling of the minimum wage and guaranteed health care and social security.

Protesters Win Hong Kong Legislature Seats—Pro-independence candidates from newly-forged opposition parties gained a foothold in Hong Kong's 70-seat legislature in Sept. 4 elections. The elections were the first since protests demanding greater electoral freedom shut down areas of the Chinese territory for 79 days in late 2014. Pro-China candidates won 40 seats, but six seats were claimed by so-called localist candidates seeking greater self-determination or outright independence, including Nathan Law, a leader of the 2014 protests. The youngest candidate ever elected to the former British colony's legislature, 23-year-old Law and others had protested China's insistence on central government approval of candidates for Hong Kong's 2017 election of a chief executive.

North Korea Conducts Fifth Nuclear Test; Flooding Devastates Country—Continuing to defy United Nations resolutions, North Korea conducted its fifth and largest-to-date underground nuclear test on Sept. 9, the 68th anniversary of the country's founding. Confirmed by North Korea's state-run news service, the blast was unofficially estimated by a South Korean military official to have packed an explosive yield equal to 10 kilotons of TNT. A U.S. expert, however, estimated the blast at 20-30 kilotons. According to North Korea, the test—its second of the year—showed it was capable of producing a functioning nuclear warhead, though skeptics expressed doubts that the country had mastered the technology required.

Severe flooding in northeastern regions of North Korea affected by Typhoon Lionrock killed at least 133 people and left nearly 400 others missing. According to the United Nations, the disaster displaced more than 107,000 North Koreans; 140,000 received food aid.

Syrian Cease-Fire Collapses—A U.S.-Russian brokered cease-fire set to officially begin Sept. 12 in Syria collapsed, dashing United Nations plans to transport much-needed humanitarian aid to some 275,000 civilians trapped in besieged, rebel-held areas of Aleppo, Syria's largest city. U.S. officials blamed Russia or the regime for Sept. 19 airstrikes on an aid convoy outside of Aleppo that killed 20 people, which Russia denied. The Syrian government charged that U.S. airstrikes that reportedly killed more than 60 Syrian troops two days earlier, during the cease-fire, were not intended against ISIS militants, as U.S. officials claimed. Numerous violations by both the regime of Pres. Bashar al-Assad and anti-government rebels further dismantled the truce, the first since a partial cease-fire in Feb.

Russian and Syrian warplanes Sept. 19 began an assault against eastern Aleppo that included use of bunker-buster bombs and incendiary weapons and attacks on medical facilities, which UN Sec. Gen. Ban Ki-moon denounced as possible war crimes. According to UK-based Syrian Observatory for Human Rights, at least 3,686 people were killed in the Syrian conflict in Sept., including 1,228 civilians.

General

Pope Canonizes Mother Teresa—Nineteen years after her death, Nobel Peace Prize winner Mother Teresa was canonized Sept. 4 in a mass led by Pope Francis at the Vatican. Born in 1910 in present-day Macedonia as Anjezë Gonxhe Bojaxhiu, she joined a Catholic order in 1928 and taught for 17 years in India before devoting her life to serve the country's poor and infirm; she formed her own order to that end by 1950. Her canonization was criticized by some who argued her institutions were overly evangelical, misused funds, and provided substandard medical care.

Kerber and Wawrinka Victorious at U.S. Open—German Angelique Kerber held off Karolina Pliskova (6-3, 4-6, 6-4) of the Czech Republic to win her second Grand Slam and first U.S. Open title Sept. 10 at Billie Jean King Natl. Tennis Center in New York City. The No. 10-seed Pliskova two days earlier overcame injured six-time Open champion Serena Williams in two sets. On Sept. 11, No. 3-seed Stan Wawrinka of Switzerland defeated top-ranked defending champion Novak Djokovic of Serbia (6-7, 6-4, 7-5, 6-3) in a grueling, 3 hr., 55 min. match, winning his third career major and first U.S. Open.

Study Finds Sugar Industry Manipulated Research— The sugar industry influenced scientists in the 1960s to minimize the possible link between added dietary sugars and heart disease, according to a report in the Sept. 12 issue of *JAMA Internal Medicine*. Backing their claim, the Univ. of California, San Francisco, researchers included internal documents from the Sugar Research Foundation (now the Sugar Association) showing it paid Harvard scientists to publish a survey of studies that highlighted evidence linking saturated fat to coronary disease while downplaying similar or stronger evidence on sugar's link.

Game of Thrones, *The People v. O.J. Simpson* **Win Big at Emmys—** HBO's epic *Game of Thrones* won the Emmy for outstanding drama series for the second year in a row at the 68th Primetime Emmy Awards Sept. 18 in Los Angeles, CA. With 38 awards over six seasons, the fantasy series surpassed *Frasier* as the winningest fictional television show in Emmy history. FX's *The People v. O.J. Simpson* won five awards, the most at the ceremony, including best limited series. Perennial favorite *Veep* claimed best comedy series as star Julia Louis-Dreyfus picked up a record-breaking sixth Emmy for lead actress in a comedy series. Rami Malek won outstanding lead actor in a drama series for his role in USA's *Mr. Robot*, and Tatiana Maslany was awarded best dramatic actress for BBC America's sci-fi thriller *Orphan Black*.

New Jersey Train Crash Injures Scores— A NJ Transit commuter train crashed into Hoboken Terminal in Hoboken, NJ, Sept. 29, killing a 34-year-old woman on the platform and injuring more than 100 passengers. The crash revived calls for use of positive train control (PTC), which can automatically prevent some incidents caused by operator error or another problem.

October 2016

National

October Surprises Jar Presidential Campaigns as Nominees Face Off in Debates— In the final month of the 2016 presidential race, the campaigns of Donald Trump (R) and Hillary Clinton (D) experienced significant setbacks. The *Washington Post* Oct. 7 made public 2005 video footage it obtained of Trump (mostly off camera) bragging to an NBC *Access Hollywood* host about kissing and groping women without their permission. Some prominent Republicans, including 2008 presidential nominee Sen. John McCain (AZ) and House Speaker Paul Ryan (WI), backed away from Trump in the aftermath. Although Trump apologized and said the conversation was "locker room talk," by the end of Oct., more than 10 women came forward claiming that Trump had sexually harassed them. Portions of Trump's 1995 tax records, leaked to the *New York Times* and published Oct. 1, revealed he had declared a $916 mil business loss that could have permitted him to avoid federal income taxes for up to 18 years. Though legal, Trump's use of the tax loophole was seized upon by Clinton as unpatriotic.

The website WikiLeaks Oct. 7 began to release thousands of emails apparently hacked from John Podesta, chair of Democratic presidential nominee Hillary Clinton's campaign. One memo, describing allegedly separate fundraising activities by the same people to raise money for both the Clinton Foundation and Bill Clinton's for-profit goals, raised suspicions of a conflict of interest, while others revealed that CNN contributor and interim Democratic National Committee chair Donna Brazile had leaked Clinton two questions, one for a primary debate Mar. 6 and the second for a town hall meeting Mar. 13. Further straining tense relations with Russia, the Dept. of Homeland Security and the Office of the Director of National Intelligence Oct. 7 formally accused the Russian government of orchestrating cyberattacks against U.S. persons and organizations, including the Democratic National Committee.

Vice presidential candidates Virginia Sen. Tim Kaine (D) and Indiana Gov. Mike Pence (R) squared off Oct. 4 in their only scheduled debate at Longwood Univ. in Farmville, VA. Clinton and Trump met for a second debate Oct. 9 in a combative town hall at Washington Univ. in St. Louis, MO. Trump said he would appoint a special prosecutor to investigate Clinton over her past email use if elected president, and Clinton criticized Trump's treatment of women and tax return secrecy. At their final debate Oct. 19 at the Univ. of Nevada in Las Vegas, Trump and Clinton engaged somewhat more substantively, in particular highlighting their differences over abortion and gun control. Nonetheless, Trump made headlines by refusing to say he would accept the election results, after repeating his claim the election was "rigged."

FBI Dir. James Comey Oct. 28 informed Congress the FBI had found emails "that appear to be pertinent" to its completed investigation of Clinton's use of a private email server while serving as secretary of state. The messages had been found on a computer belonging to Clinton aide Huma Abedin's estranged husband, former Rep. Anthony Weiner (D, NY), who was under investigation on an unrelated case. Critics of Comey's letter in both parties, including Pres. Barack Obama and two GOP former attorneys general, argued Comey had erred in commenting on an active investigation so close to the election.

National polling averages by RealClearPolitics showed fluctuating support for the candidates leading up to Nov. 8 voting. The average Oct. 1 had Clinton with 43.7% support, 2.6 points ahead of Trump; she increased her margin to 7.1 points ahead of Trump Oct. 17-18. By Nov. 1, the race had again tightened considerably, with Clinton leading Trump 45.3%-43.1%, or 2.2 points.

AT&T and Time Warner Propose Mega-Merger; Samsung Yanks Flagship Phone; Economy Maintains Moderate Growth— Telecommunications giant AT&T agreed Oct. 22 to acquire Time Warner, owner of media giants HBO and CNN, for about $85.4 bil. The deal, which would produce a company capable of both producing and distributing news and entertainment content, would require approval from federal antitrust regulators and perhaps the FCC. Numerous lawmakers expressed concern over media consolidation and its potential to raise prices and limit competition. The day before, British American Tobacco proposed a $47 bil buyout of Reynolds American that would create the world's largest publicly traded tobacco company ahead of current leader Philip Morris Intl. Samsung discontinued its flagship Galaxy Note 7 Oct. 11 after multiple reports surfaced of the smartphones—even the replacement model sent in a month-old recall—spontaneously catching fire, which the company initially attributed to faulty batteries from one of its suppliers. Days later, Samsung expanded its recall to 1.9 mil devices

The Labor Dept. reported Oct. 7 that the economy added 156,000 jobs in Sept., less than expected but a sign of continuing modest gains nonetheless. Unemployment, meanwhile, ticked up to 5.0% from its three-month-old rate of 4.9%, reflecting more people in the labor force. The Dow Jones industrial average finished Oct. at 18,142.42, down 0.9% from Sept., and the S&P 500 closed at 2,126.15, a 1.9% drop from the month before. The Nasdaq composite index finished Oct. at 5,189.14, dropping 2.3% for the month.

Hundreds Arrested Protesting Dakota Access Pipeline; Armed Oregon Sanctuary Occupiers Acquitted— Months of demonstrations on federal land south of Bismarck, ND, aimed at halting oil pipeline construction upstream of the Standing Rock Indian Reservation further intensified, with over 140 protestors arrested Oct. 27. Some 200 police officers and National Guard personnel used pepper spray and armored vehicles to clear an offshoot encampment of demonstrators located on private property; at least two protesters were taken into custody after firing shots. Police Oct. 22 had arrested 83 on charges that included rioting and assaulting an officer. A federal court Oct. 9 allowed work to continue within 20 mi of Lake Oahe while it considered the tribe's appeal of a Sept. court ruling that allowed further construction on the nearly 1,200-mi-long pipeline. The Army Corps of Engineers continued to provisionally prohibit pipeline construction on federal land under and bordering the lake.

Brothers Ammon and Ryan Bundy and five others were acquitted Oct. 27 of charges related to their highly publicized 41-day armed takeover of a federal wildlife sanctuary the previous winter. Critics of the decision contrasted the acquittal of the armed protesters with current treatment of the largely unarmed, mostly American Indian protesters at Standing Rock. Ammon and Ryan Bundy—and their father, Cliven—still faced federal charges over a 2014 standoff near their Nevada ranch.

International

Colombia Defeats FARC Peace Deal—In referendum voting Oct. 2, Colombians unexpectedly scrapped a peace agreement signed earlier in 2016 between the Colombian government and Colombian government and the Marxist Revolutionary Armed Forces of Colombia (FARC), the FARC, who in five decades had contributed to violence that killed about 220,000 people and displaced some 5-7 mil. Just 37% of the electorate participated in the referendum, which rejected the deal by the slimmest of margins (50.2%). Critics argued the agreement was too lenient on the former FARC; under its terms, violent offenders would receive only light sentences, and it also provided disarmed rebels with stipends and other financial support. Voters in some regions—including the nation's capital—approved the historic deal, but it was strongly rejected in the central urban areas less affected by FARC. Awarded the Nobel Peace Prize later that week for his efforts at mediation with FARC and other groups, Colombian Pres. Juan Manuel Santos vowed to maintain a nearly five-week-old cease-fire

U.S.-Russia Syrian Peace Talks Collapse—The U.S. halted negotiations with Russia over Syria's bloody 5½-year-old civil war Oct. 3, accusing accused Russia and the regime of Syrian Pres. Bashar al-Assad of repeatedly violating a week-long cease-fire in Sept. Russian Pres. Vladimir Putin broke a plutonium-disposal treaty with the U.S. the same day. Already strained over allegations of Russian state-sponsored hacking, U.S.-Russian relations had further deteriorated two weeks earlier after the U.S. blamed Russia for airstrikes that struck a convoy attempting to bring humanitarian aid to some 250,000 civilians trapped in rebel-occupied eastern Aleppo. U.S. officials also alleged that Russian and Syrian aircraft had intentionally targeted medical facilities, including Aleppo's primary trauma hospital, which could be considered a war crime. The Syrian government and Russian forces declared a unilateral cease-fire for Oct. 20 and urged civilians to evacuate Aleppo, but bombing resumed Oct. 23.

Poland Rejects Abortion Ban—Facing widespread opposition, Poland's parliament voted Oct. 6, 352-58, to reject a bill criminalizing all abortions except when the mother's life is at risk. Some 115,000 mostly female demonstrators had gathered throughout the country three days earlier in protest of the proposed legislation. Poland, which has an overwhelmingly Roman Catholic population, had already outlawed abortions in most cases.

Saudi Airstrikes Kill Scores of Yemeni Mourners—A Saudi-led coalition bombed a funeral hall in Yemen's capital of Sanaa Oct. 8, killing at least 140 people. The Saudi military said the strikes were intended to target rebel Houthi leaders but were executed based on "wrong information." Widely condemned, the funeral attack produced one of the largest single-incident death tolls in Yemen since the Saudi coalition began airstrikes in opposition to the rebel Houthi government in Mar. 2015. The U.S., which contributed arms, logistical assistance, and midair refueling to the coalition, said it might reconsider its support. In apparent retribution, Houthi-controlled areas twice fired missiles at a U.S. Navy destroyer, prompting its forces to destroy three radar installations, the U.S.'s first direct involvement in Yemen's civil war. A UN official estimated in Aug. 2016 that some 10,000 people had died in the conflict since Mar. 2015.

King of Thailand Dies After 70-Year Rule—The world's longest-reigning living monarch, King Bhumibol Adulyadej of Thailand, died Oct. 13 at age 88. Though he exercised limited powers, the king was widely revered and was noted by political analysts to have had a stabilizing effect on the fractious country, serving through 17 constitutions and at least 10 coups; Thailand at the time of King Bhumibol's death remained under military rule following a 2014 takeover. The next day, Thailand began an official one-year mourning period, and thousands lined his funeral procession route to Bangkok's Grand Palace. Crown Prince Maha Vajiralongkorn was expected to be the king's successor.

Iraq Launches Mosul Offensive—About 30,000 Iraqi security, Kurdish peshmerga, and Sunni tribal forces initiated a campaign Oct. 17 to liberate the strategic northern Iraqi city of Mosul, held by the Sunni extremist group known as the Islamic State, or ISIS, since June 2014. Mosul, the country's second largest city, was thought to be ISIS's last remaining major Iraq stronghold. According to U.S. officials, the campaign, backed by U.S. airstrikes, by late Oct. retook at least 40 villages on the city's outskirts. According to Iraqi intelligence, ISIS militants executed 284 men and boys in Mosul Oct. 20-21, and the United Nations reported the group abducted tens of thousands of civilians there to use as so-called human shields. Iraqi Prime Min. Haider al-Abadi Oct. 22 declined Turkey's offer to contribute troops to the operation.

France Closes Migrant "Jungle" Camp; Other Migrant Crisis News—French authorities Oct. 24 began clearing an informal encampment in Calais known as the Jungle, estimated to be inhabited by 6,000-10,000 mostly Afghan and African refugees and migrants trying to reach England. The migrants, who had received minimal official assistance from France and had relied on aid groups, were bused to retention centers where they could apply for asylum in France. Authorities said housing had been established for some 12,000 migrants to be dispersed throughout the country, but many camp residents sought to remain in place.

Some 6,000 migrants bound for Europe on about 40 overloaded boats were rescued off the Libyan coast Oct. 3, marking one of the largest single-day rescues of the current migration crisis. According to the International Organization for Migration, at least 3,930 asylum seekers drowned attempting to cross the Mediterranean in 2016 (through Oct. 26), well over the number drowned during the same period in 2015 despite fewer attempting the journey. More than 332,000 people reached Europe by late Oct., compared to nearly 729,000 at that point in 2015.

Lebanon Elects President, Breaking Deadlock—Lebanon's parliament elected former general Michel Aoun as president Oct. 31, with 83 of 127 votes, ending a stalemate that had left the geopolitically precarious country without a leader for more than two years. Marking the country's shift away from Sunni power-center Saudi Arabia, Aoun's election was seen as a clear victory for his ally Hezbollah, the Iran-backed Shiite militia and political party, which also supported the neighboring regime of Syrian Pres. Bashar al-Assad. Though largely ceremonial, Lebanon's president appoints cabinet members and has some impact over foreign affairs. Sensing its waning power there, Saudi Arabia in Feb. 2016 suspended $3 bil in military aid to Lebanon and withdrew its ambassador in Sept.

General

Strong Hurricane Lashes Haiti, U.S.—Hurricane Matthew struck southwestern Haiti early Oct. 4 with 145-mph winds and flood-inducing rains, killing at least 550 people. The Category 4 storm—the strongest to hit Haiti since 1964—left some 1.4 mil in need of aid; the UN Oct. 10 appealed for $120 bil in emergency aid. Matthew also impacted the Dominican Republic, Cuba, The Bahamas, and other Caribbean countries, killing at least five people.

U.S. officials ordered some 2 mil people to evacuate coastal areas from Florida to North Carolina as Matthew approached. Beginning Oct. 6, it moved up the Atlantic coast offshore, producing a heavy storm surge and making landfall as a Category 1 hurricane Oct. 8, southeast of McClellanville, SC, with 75-mph winds. Matthew killed at least 48 people in the U.S., including 28 in southeastern North Carolina, where some motorists were swept away after more than a foot of rain flooded roads. Goldman Sachs estimated U.S. damage at $10 bil.

Sparks Capture WNBA Championship—The Los Angeles Sparks held off the defending champion Minnesota Lynx, 77-76, in Game 5 Oct. 20 at Target Center in Minneapolis, MN, to claim the Women's National Basketball Association title. It was Los Angeles's first championship since 2002 and third overall and capped the first postseason in which the best teams faced off without regard to conference. Lynx forward Candace Parker was named MVP, with 28 points and 12 rebounds in Game 5. The Finals officiating was widely criticized; the league admitted to errors late in both Games 4 and 5 that may have changed the outcome.

OBITUARIES

(Nov. 1, 2015-Oct. 31, 2016)

A

Adam, Ken, 95, British production designer best known for his James Bond film sets and the *Chitty Chitty Bang Bang* (1968) car; London, Eng., UK, Mar. 10, 2016.

Adelman, Bob, 85, photographer who vividly captured the 1960s Civil Rights era; Miami Beach, FL, Mar. 19, 2016.

Albee, Edward, 88, Pulitzer Prize-winning playwright whose work, including *Who's Afraid of Virginia Woolf?* (1962), explored modern relationships; Montauk, NY, Sept. 16, 2016.

Ali, Muhammad, 74, three-time heavyweight champion boxer and activist known for championing civil rights and his eloquence and verbosity; Scottsdale, AZ, June 3, 2016.

Anderson, Arthur, 93, actor best known for commercial voice work as Lucky Charms cereal's leprechaun character; New York, NY, Apr. 9, 2016.

Antar, Eddie, 68, businessman who created the Crazy Eddie New York-area chain of electronics stores, which collapsed amid fraud charges; Sept. 10, 2016.

Arquette, Alexis, 47, actress, singer, and transgender activist; Beverly Hills, CA, Sept. 11, 2016.

Asawa, Brian, 49, Japanese-American opera countertenor; Mission Hills, CA, Apr. 18, 2016.

Atkins, Doug, 85, Hall of Fame defensive end (1953-69) who appeared in eight Pro Bowls; Knoxville, TN, Dec. 30, 2015.

Aylwin, Patricio, 97, first democratically elected president of Chile (1990-94) after the Pinochet dictatorship; Santiago, Chile, Apr. 19, 2016.

B

Babbitt, Natalie, 84, children's author known for *Tuck Everlasting* (1975); Hamden, CT, Oct. 31, 2016.

Babenco, Héctor, 70, Argentinian-born Brazilian film director best known for *Kiss of the Spider Woman* (1985); São Paulo, Brazil, July 13, 2016.

Backer, Bill, 89, advertising executive who created Coca-Cola campaigns, including "I'd Like to Buy the World a Coke" (1971); Warrantor, VA, May 13, 2016.

Baker, Kenny, 81, British actor who played robot R2-D2 in six Star Wars movies; Preston, Eng., UK, Aug. 13, 2016.

Barbieri, Gato, 83, Argentinean-born Grammy Award-winning saxophonist; New York, NY, Apr. 2, 2016.

Barris, George, 89, car customizer known for creating the Batmobile for TV's *Batman* (1966-68) and the Munster Koach for *The Munsters* (1964-66); Encino, CA, Nov. 5, 2015.

Bathgate, Andy, 83, Hall of Fame Canadian hockey player mostly with the NY Rangers; Brampton, ON, Canada, Feb. 26, 2016.

Bedford, Brian, 80, Tony Award-winning British actor known for performing Shakespeare and Chekhov; Santa Barbara, CA, Jan. 13, 2016.

Beranek, Lou, 102, acoustics expert whose company Bolt, Beranek and Newman (BNN) helped develop ARPANET; Westwood, MA, Oct. 10, 2016.

Berg, Delmer, 100, last known living veteran of the Abraham Lincoln Brigade, Americans who fought in the Spanish Civil War; Columbia, CA, Feb. 28, 2016.

Berger, Samuel R. "Sandy," 70, national security adviser to Pres. Bill Clinton (1997-2001); Washington, DC, Dec. 2, 2015.

Berrigan, Daniel, 94, Jesuit priest and poet whose antiwar activism during the Vietnam War led to his imprisonment; Bronx, NY, Apr. 30, 2016.

Bhumibol Adulyadej, 88, King of Thailand (1946-2016) who served as a stabilizing force alongside a series of governments; Bangkok, Thailand, Oct. 13, 2016.

Boulez, Pierre, 90, Grammy Award-winning French composer and conductor who promoted 20th century music; Baden-Baden, Germany, Jan. 5, 2016.

Boutros-Ghali, Boutros, 93, Egyptian diplomat; first African and first Arab UN secretary-general (1992-96); Cairo, Egypt, Feb. 16, 2016.

Bowie, David, 69, British singer-songwriter who continually reinvented his career, from "Space Oddity" (1969) to number-one singles "Fame" (1975) and "Let's Dance" (1983) and collaborations with Queen and Brian Eno; New York, NY, Jan. 10, 2016.

Bradshaw, John, 82, self-help guru who popularized the search for one's "inner child"; Houston, TX, May 8, 2016.

Brand, Oscar, 96, Canadian-born folk singer-songwriter; hosted "Folksong Festival" radio program for more than 70 years; Great Neck, NY, Sept. 30, 2016.

Breen, Bobby, 87, Canadian-born child actor who appeared in RKO films of the late 1930s; Pompano Beach, FL, Sept. 19, 2016.

Brookner, Anita, 87, British writer best known for her Man Booker Prize-winning novel *Hotel du Lac* (1984); Mar. 10, 2016.

Brown, Eric, 97, British Navy test pilot who broke many records, including flying 487 different types of aircrafts; Redhill, Eng., UK, Feb. 21, 2016.

Bumpers, Dale, 90, U.S. senator (D, AR, 1975-99); delivered defense closing argument during Pres. Bill Clinton's Senate impeachment trial (1999); Little Rock, AR, Jan. 1, 2016.

C

Caldwell, Bettye, 91, educator and advocate for early childhood education; St. Louis, MO, Apr. 17, 2016.

Canary, David, 77, Emmy Award-winning actor known for *Bonanza* (1967-73) and *All My Children* (1984-2011, 2013); Wilton, CT, Nov. 16, 2015.

Carr, Charmian, 73, actress known for role as Liesl in *The Sound of Music* film (1965); Woodland Hills, CA, Sept. 17, 2016.

Cáslavská, Vera, 74, Czech Olympic gold medal-winning gymnast who protested the Soviet Union's invasion of Czechoslovakia at the 1968 Olympics; Prague, Czech Republic, Aug. 30, 2016.

Chalabi, Ahmed, 71, Iraqi politician who opposed Saddam Hussein and influenced the U.S. decision to go to war; Baghdad, Iraq, Nov. 3, 2015.

Chyna (Joanie Laurer), 46, professional wrestler (WWF, now WWE) and actress; Redondo Beach, CA, Apr. 20, 2016.

Cianci, Vincent "Buddy," 74, mayor of Providence, RI (1975-84, 1991-2002); he was forced out of office twice due to felony convictions; Providence, RI, Jan. 28, 2016.

Cimino, Michael, 77, Academy Award-winning director best known for *The Deer Hunter* (1978); Los Angeles, CA, July 2, 2016.

Clark, Guy, 74, Grammy Award-winning country singer-songwriter best known for "L.A. Freeway" (1975) and "Desperados Waiting for a Train" (1975); Nashville, TN, May 17, 2016.

Clark, Wesley A., 88, physicist credited with designing the first minicomputer; Brooklyn, NY, Feb. 22, 2016.

Cole, Natalie, 65, Grammy Award-winning R&B and jazz singer best known for "Unforgettable" (1991), a duet with her late father, Nat King Cole; Los Angeles, CA, Dec. 31, 2015.

Collins, Bud, 86, International Tennis Hall of Fame journalist and TV sportscaster who provided colorful commentary on the sport for nearly 50 years; Brookline, MA, Mar. 4, 2016.

Conrad, Tony, 76, avant-garde filmmaker and composer as part of the NYC art scene in the 1960s; Cheektowaga, NY, Apr. 9, 2016.

Conroy, Pat, 70, best-selling author known for *The Great Santini* (1976) and *The Prince of Tides* (1986); Beaufort, SC, Mar. 4, 2016.

Courrèges, André, 92, French fashion designer credited with modernizing couture; Neuilly-sur-Seine, France, Jan. 7, 2016.

Cronin, James, 84, Nobel Prize-winning physicist who researched matter and anti-matter; St. Paul, MN, Aug. 25, 2016.

Crouch, Jan, 78, televangelist who co-founded the Trinity Broadcasting Network (1973); Orlando, FL, May 31, 2016.

Cunningham, Bill, 87, *NY Times* photographer known for candid street fashion images; New York, NY, June 25, 2016.

D

Davidson, Gordon, 83, Tony Award-winning director who led the Center Theatre Group in Los Angeles; Los Angeles, CA, Oct. 2, 2016.

Davies, Peter Maxwell, 81, British avant-garde composer and conductor; Orkney Islands, Scotland, UK, Mar. 14, 2016.

Davis, Jack, 91, cartoonist who was a founding artist for humor magazine *Mad* (1952); St. Simons Island, GA, July 27, 2016.

de Filippis, Maria Teresa, 89, Italian race car driver; first woman to compete in a Formula 1 world championship grand prix; Scanzorosciate, Lombardy, Italy, Jan. 9, 2016.

DeHaven, Gloria, 91, actress who appeared in 1940s MGM musicals; Las Vegas, NV, July 30, 2016

Dial, Thornton, 87, African-American outsider artist whose paintings and sculptures used found materials; McCalla, AL, Jan. 25, 2016.

Dinoire, Isabelle, 49, French woman known as the first to undergo a partial face transplant (2005); France, Apr. 22, 2016.

Dobbs, Mattiwilda, 90, operatic soprano; first African American to sing a principal role at La Scala; Atlanta, GA, Dec. 8, 2015.

Doda, Carol, 78, performer who popularized topless dancing beginning in 1964; San Francisco, CA, Nov. 9, 2015.

Drake, Larry, 67, Emmy Award-winning actor known for TV drama *L.A. Law* (1987-94); Los Angeles, CA, Mar. 17, 2016.

Duke, Patty, 69, Oscar-winning actress in *The Miracle Worker* (1962); also known for dual roles in an eponymous sitcom (1963-66); Coeur d'Alene, ID, Mar. 29, 2016.

Duncan, Lois, 82, writer of young adult suspense novels, best known for *I Know What You Did Last Summer* (1973); Bradenton, FL, June 15, 2016.

Dunn, Katherine, 70, novelist known for *Geek Love* (1989), an unlikely bestseller about a family of sideshow freaks; Portland, OR, May 11, 2016.

E

Ebeling, Bob, 89, aerospace engineer whose warnings about the safety of space shuttle *Challenger* went unheeded in 1986; Brigham City, UT, Mar. 21, 2016.

Eco, Umberto, 84, Italian philosopher and novelist best known for *The Name of the Rose* (1983); Milan, Italy, Feb. 19, 2016.

Elliott, Bob, 92, comedian on radio and TV as half of the comedy duo Bob and Ray; Cundy's Harbor, ME, Feb. 2, 2016.

Engelberger, Joseph, 90, engineer who co-founded the world's first industrial robotics manufacturer; Newtown, CT, Dec. 1, 2015.

F

Fawcett, Jane, 95, British codebreaker who decrypted a message that led to the 1941 sinking of the German battleship *Bismarck*; Oxford, Eng., UK, May 21, 2016.

Feek, Joey, 40, country music singer; half of the husband-and-wife duo Joey + Rory; Alexandria, IN, Mar. 4, 2016.

Fernández, José, 24, Cuban-born pitcher for the Miami Marlins whose storied escape from Cuba, talent, and personality made him a fan favorite; Miami Beach, FL, Sept. 25, 2016.

Ferré, Rosario, 77, Puerto Rican writer whose work reflected on the island's history and identity; San Juan, Puerto Rico, Feb. 18, 2016.

Ferzetti, Gabriele, 90, Italian actor best known for Michelangelo Antonioni's *L'Avventura* (1960); Rome, Italy, Dec. 2, 2015.

Finkel, Fyvush, 93, Emmy Award-winning actor best known for *Picket Fences* (1982-96) and *Boston Public* (2000-04); began his career in Yiddish theater; New York, NY, Aug. 14, 2016.

Fischer, Artur, 96, German inventor who held over 1,100 patents, including for the first synchronized camera flash; Waldachtal, Germany, Jan. 27, 2016.

Fo, Dario, 90, Nobel Prize-winning Italian playwright whose work often satirized the Catholic church and Italian life; Milan, Italy, Oct. 13, 2016.

Ford, Rob, 46, Canadian mayor of Toronto (2010-14) whose tenure included admission of smoking crack cocaine; Toronto, ON, Canada, Mar. 22, 2016.

Ford, Robert, 91, British commander in N. Ireland whose troops fatally shot 13 unarmed protesters in what became known as Bloody Sunday (1972); Nov. 24, 2015.

Forster, Margaret, 77, British writer best known for her novel *Georgy Girl* (1965); London, England, UK, Feb. 8, 2016.

Fortnum, Peggy, 96, British illustrator who first drew the Paddington Bear character; Colchester, Eng., UK, Mar. 28, 2016.

Francis-McBarnette, Yvette, 89, Jamaican-born pediatrician who used antibiotics to help battle childhood sickle cell anemia; Alexandria, VA, Mar. 28, 2016.

Frey, Glenn, 67, singer-songwriter; founding member of rock band the Eagles (1971); New York, NY, Jan. 18, 2016.

Friedman, Greta Zimmer, 92, one of several women who claimed to be kissed by a sailor in Eisenstaedt's famous V-J Day photo; Richmond, VA, Sept. 8, 2016.

G

Gabriel, Juan, 66, Mexican singer and songwriter known for dramatic performance style; Santa Monica, CA, Aug. 28, 2016.

Galanos, James, 92, fashion designer known for dressing elite clientele, including first lady Nancy Reagan; West Hollywood, CA, Oct. 30, 2016.

Garagiola, Joe, 90, MLB catcher who had a successful later career as a sportscaster; Scottsdale, AZ, Mar. 23, 2016.

Gilkey, David, 50, NPR photojournalist killed in a Taliban attack; Helmand Province, Afghanistan, June 5, 2016.

Gomelsky, Giorgio, 81, music impresario who helped launch the Rolling Stones and the Yardbirds; Bronx, NY, Jan. 13, 2016.

Goody, Gordon, 86, British businessman believed to have been the mastermind of the UK's so-called Great Train Robbery (1963); Mojácar, Spain, Jan. 29, 2016.

Grant, Toni, 73, psychologist known for a call-in radio show; Beverly Hills, CA, Mar. 27, 2016.

Green, Dennis, 67, NFL coach who led the Minnesota Vikings to the playoffs (1998); San Diego, CA, July 21, 2016.

Greenberg, Jack, 91, lawyer and civil rights activist who led the NAACP Legal Defense and Educational Fund; co-counsel on *Brown v. Board of Education*; New York, NY, Oct. 12, 2016.

Grimes, Tammy, 82, Tony Award-winning actress best known for *The Unsinkable Molly Brown* (1960); Englewood, NJ, Oct. 30, 2016.

Gross, Michael C., 70, producer, artist, and designer known for the *Ghostbusters* (1984) logo; Oceanside, CA, Nov. 16, 2015.

Grove, Andrew S., 79, Hungarian-born businessman who led Intel; Los Altos, CA, Mar. 21, 2016.

Gutfreund, John, 86, CEO who made Salomon Brothers a profitable investment firm in the 1980s but resigned amid scandal; New York, NY, Mar. 9, 2016.

H

Hadid, Zaha, 65, Pritzker Prize-winning Iraqi-born British architect whose iconic works included the London Aquatics Centre (2012); Miami, FL, Mar. 31, 2016.

Haggard, Merle, 79, country singer-songwriter whose hits, including "Mama Tried" (1968) and "Okie From Muskogee" (1969), propelled him from San Quentin prison to the Country Music Hall of Fame; Palo Cedro, CA, Apr. 6, 2016.

Haggerty, Dan, 73, actor best known in the title role of *The Life and Times of Grizzly Adams* film (1974) and TV series (1977-78); Burbank, CA, Jan. 15, 2016.

Hamilton, Dorothy Cann, 67, founder and CEO of the International Culinary Center (fmr. French Culinary Institute); Cape Breton Island, NS, Canada; Sept. 16, 2016.

Hamner, Earl, Jr., 92, writer and TV producer whose novel *Spencer's Mountain* (1961) inspired *The Waltons* (1972-81); Los Angeles, CA, Mar. 24, 2016.

Hanson, Curtis, 71, Academy Award-winning film director and screenwriter best known for his film noir *L.A. Confidential* (1997); Los Angeles, CA, Sept. 20, 2016.

Harrington, Pat, Jr., 86, Emmy-winning actor best known for his role on CBS sitcom *One Day at a Time* (1975-84); Los Angeles, CA, Jan. 6, 2016.

Harrison, Jim, 78, poet and novelist known for *Legends of the Fall* (1979); Patagonia, AZ, Mar. 26, 2016.

Hartman, Thomas J., 69, Roman Catholic priest who with Rabbi Marc Gellman comprised "The God Squad" in a syndicated column and on radio and TV; Uniondale, NY, Feb. 16, 2016.

Hasegawa, Goro, 83, Japanese inventor credited with creating the board game Othello (1973); Kashiwa, Japan, June 20, 2016.

Hayden, Tom, 76, antiwar and civil rights activist who later served as a member of the California senate (1992-2000); Santa Monica, CA, Oct. 23, 2016.

Heldt, Margaret, 98, beautician who invented the beehive hairstyle (1960); Elmhurst, IL, June 10, 2016.

Hendrickson, Richard, 103, farmer who recorded the weather twice daily as a National Weather Service volunteer for 85 years; Westhampton, NY, Jan. 9, 2016.

Herr, Michael, 76, writer whose reporting in *Dispatches* (1977) documented those serving in the Vietnam War; Delhi, NY, June 23, 2016.

Hill, Steven, 94, actor best known as a NY district attorney on *Law & Order* (1990-2000); New York, NY, Aug. 23, 2016.

Hirsch, Charles, 79, forensic pathologist who as chief medical examiner of NYC (1989-2013) helped identify victims of the World Trade Center terrorist attack in 2001; Westwood, NJ, Apr. 8, 2016.

Hofsiss, Jack, 65, Tony Award-winning director best known for *The Elephant Man* (1979); New York, NY, Sept. 13, 2016.

Howard, Ken, 71, Emmy and Tony Award-winning actor known for *The White Shadow* (1978-81) and later as Screen Actors Guild president (2009-16); Valencia, CA, Mar. 23, 2016.

Howe, Gordie, 88, Hall of Fame Canadian hockey player who established many records including the longest pro career (1946-71, 1973-80), mostly with the Detroit Red Wings; Sylvania, OH, June 10, 2016.

Huddleston, David, 85, character actor best known for *The Big Lebowski* (1998); Santa Fe, NM, Aug. 2, 2016.

Hutcherson, Bobby, 75, legendary jazz vibraphonist who was a staple of the Blue Note label; Montara, CA, Aug. 15, 2016.

I

Irvin, Monte, 96, Hall of Fame outfielder with the Giants (1949-55) and Cubs (1956) after establishing his career in the Negro League (1937-42, 1945-48); Houston, TX, Jan. 11, 2016.

J

Jackson, Anne, 90, Obie-winning stage actress who frequently performed with husband Eli Wallach; New York, NY, Apr. 12, 2016.

Jaffe, Shirley, 93, abstract artist known for using colorful geometric forms; Louveciennes, France, Sept. 29, 2016.

Jaffrey, Saeed, 86, Indian-born actor known for roles in *Gandhi* (1982) and *My Beautiful Laundrette* (1985); London, Eng., UK, Nov. 15, 2015.

James, Sonny, 87, country music singer-songwriter known for "Young Love" (1956); Nashville, TN, Feb. 22, 2016.

K

Kagan, Vladimir, 88, German-born modern furniture designer; Palm Beach, FL, Apr. 7, 2016.

Kallen, Kitty, 94, Swing-era singer known for "Bésame Mucho" (1944) and "Little Things Mean a Lot" (1954); Cuernavaca, Mexico, Jan. 7, 2016.

Kantner, Paul, 74, singer-songwriter and guitarist; co-founder of rock bands Jefferson Airplane and Jefferson Starship; San Francisco, CA, Jan. 28, 2016.

Karimov, Islam, 78, president of post-Soviet Uzbekistan (1991-2016), known for repressing opposition; Tashkent, Uzbekistan, Sept. 2, 2016.

Kelly, Ellsworth, 92, painter and sculptor whose abstract art used geometric shapes and vivid colors; Spencertown, NY, Dec. 27, 2015.

Kennedy, George, 91, Academy Award-winning actor best known for *Cool Hand Luke* (1967); Middleton, ID, Feb. 28, 2016.

Kertész, Imre, 86, Nobel Prize-winning Hungarian writer, whose work was based on his experiences as a Holocaust survivor; Budapest, Hungary, Mar. 31, 2016.

Kiarostami, Abbas, 76, Palme d'Or-winning Iranian film director known for documentary-style fictional films, including *Taste of Cherry* (1997); Paris, France, July 4, 2016.

Kiley, Robert, 80, transportation executive who helped modernize transit systems in Boston, New York, and London; Chilmark, MA, Aug. 9, 2016.

Kilmister, Ian "Lemmy," 70, British singer and bassist for heavy metal band Motörhead; Los Angeles, CA, Dec. 28, 2015.

Kim Young-sam, 87, South Korean president (1993-98) who pushed reforms; Seoul, South Korea, Nov. 22, 2015.

Kimsey, Jim, 76, cofounder of internet provider America Online (AOL); McLean, VA, Mar. 1, 2016.

King, Florence, 80, writer and conservative columnist known for work in the *National Review*; Fredericksburg, VA, Jan. 6, 2016.

Kinsella, W(illiam) P(atrick), 81, Canadian novelist whose *Shoeless Joe* (1982) was adapted into the movie *Field of Dreams* (1989); Hope, BC, Canada, Sept. 16, 2016.

Kiplinger, Austin, 97, publisher who with his father co-founded *Kiplinger's Personal Finance* magazine (1947); Rockville, MD, Nov. 20, 2015.

Kives, Philip, 87, Canadian businessman who founded the company K-tel, marketing products on TV; Winnipeg, MB, Can., Apr. 27, 2016.

Kohn, Walter, 93, Austrian-born Nobel Prize-winning theoretical physicist; Santa Barbara, CA, Apr. 19, 2016.

Kono, Tommy, 85, Japanese-American Olympic gold medal-winning weightlifter who held numerous world records; Honolulu, HI, Apr. 24, 2016.

L

LaHaye, Tim, 90, evangelical Christian minister who co-authored the best-selling Left Behind series of apocalyptic fiction; San Diego, CA, July 25, 2016.

Lane, Mark, 89, lawyer and author whose *Rush to Judgment* (1966) suggested that Pres. Kennedy's death was a conspiracy; Charlottesville, VA, May 10, 2016.

Lazarus, Mell, 89, cartoonist who created the comic strips "Miss Peach" and "Momma"; Los Angeles, CA, May 24, 2016.

Lee, (Nelle) Harper, 89, Pulitzer Prize-winning author of *To Kill a Mockingbird* (1960); her *Go Set a Watchman* was the best-selling novel of 2015 amid controversy; Monroeville, AL, Feb. 19, 2016.

Lemon, Meadowlark, 83, Hall of Fame Harlem Globetrotter known as the "Clown Prince of Basketball"; Scottsdale, AZ, Dec. 27, 2015.

Lewis, Guy V., 93, Hall of Fame basketball coach for Univ. of Houston (1956-86); Kyle, TX, Nov. 26, 2015.

Loggia, Robert, 85, actor best known for *Scarface* (1983); Los Angeles, CA, Dec. 4, 2015.

Louis, Murray, 89, performer and choreographer who added comic elements to dance; New York, NY, Feb. 1, 2016.

Lovellette, Clyde, 86, Hall of Fame basketball player who won NCAA and NBA championships and Olympic gold; North Manchester, IN, Mar. 9, 2016.

Lundgren, Gillis, 86, Swedish industrial designer who created furniture for Ikea; Feb. 25, 2016.

M

Mack, Lonnie, 74, singer and guitarist who created an influential blues-rock hybrid sound; Nashville, TN, Apr. 21, 2016.

Mandelli, Mariuccia, 90, Italian fashion designer credited with the invention of hot pants; Milan, Italy, Dec. 6, 2015.

Marriner, Neville, 92, British conductor who founded the Academy of St. Martin in the Fields chamber orchestra (1958); London, Eng., UK, Oct. 2, 2016.

Mars, Forrest, Jr., 84, executive who developed his family's business into one of the world's largest candy companies (M&Ms, Snickers); Seattle, WA, July 26, 2016.

Marshall, Garry, 81, TV and film producer known for his sitcoms—*Happy Days* (1974-84), *Laverne & Shirley* (1976-83), and *Mork & Mindy* (1978-82)—and for directing *Pretty Woman* (1990); Burbank, CA, July 19, 2016.

Martin, George, 90, Grammy Award-winning British music producer who signed the Beatles in 1962 and produced much of their music; Wiltshire, Eng., UK, Mar. 8, 2016.

Masur, Kurt, 88, German music director of the Leipzig Gewandhaus Orchestra (1970-96) and New York Philharmonic (1991-2002); Greenwich, CT, Dec. 19, 2015.

Mayer, Frederick, 94, German-born Jewish-American spy who returned to Germany to gather intelligence during World War II; Charles Town, WV, Apr. 15, 2016.

McLaughlin, John, 89, political commentator and host of *The McLaughlin Group*, a public affairs TV show (1982-2016); Washington, DC, Aug. 16, 2016.

McPherson, James Alan, 72, Pulitzer Prize-winning writer who overcame poverty and segregation and represented the black experience; Iowa City, IA, July 27, 2016.

Medicine Crow, Joseph, 102, Presidential Medal of Freedom-winning American Indian historian; last living war chief of the Crow Tribe; Billings, MT, Apr. 3, 2016.

Mills, Harriet, 95, Fulbright scholar arrested in China and accused of spying (1951); Mitchellville, MD, Mar. 5, 2016.

Minsky, Marvin, 88, computer scientist considered one of the fathers of artificial intelligence; Boston, MA, Jan. 24, 2016.

Mirra, Dave, 41, BMX cyclist and rallycross racer; ESPN X Games gold medalist; Greenville, NC, Feb. 4, 2016.

Miss Cleo (Youree Dell Harris), 53, TV personality known for her Jamaican accent in commercials for a psychic phone service in the 1990s; Palm Beach, FL, July 26, 2016.

Mitchell, Edgar, 85, astronaut who became the sixth man to walk on the Moon (1971); West Palm Beach, FL, Feb. 4, 2016.

Mondavi, Peter, Sr., 101, winemaker who pioneered a process of cold fermenting white wines; St. Helena, CA, Feb. 20, 2016.

Moore, Dickie, 84, Hall of Fame Canadian hockey forward who won six Stanley Cups with the Montréal Canadiens (1953, 1956-60); Montréal, QC, Can., Dec. 19, 2015.

Morellet, François, 90, French painter and sculptor who used unusual materials; Cholet, France, May 10, 2016.

Moseley, Winston, 81, serial killer convicted of the murder of Kitty Genovese in Kew Gardens, Queens, NY (1964); Dannemora, NY, Mar. 28, 2016.

Mother Angelica (Rita Antoinette Rizzo), 92, Franciscan nun who founded the Eternal Word Television Network (EWTN); Hanceville, AL, Mar. 27, 2016.

N

Name, Billy (William Linich Jr.), 76, photographer who chronicled Andy Warhol's "Factory" studio during the 1960s; Poughkeepsie, NY, July 18, 2016.

Nathanson, E. M., 88, author of World War II novel *The Dirty Dozen* (1965); Laguna Niguel, CA, Apr. 5, 2016.

Naylor, Gloria, 66, National Book Award-winning black writer best known for *The Women of Brewster Place* (1982); Christiansted, U.S. Virgin Islands, Sept. 28, 2016.

Nederlander, James, 94, theater impresario who built the Nederlander Organization into one of the largest live theater operators in the U.S.; Southampton, NY, July 25, 2016.

Neill, Noel, 95, actress known for playing Lois Lane on the *Adventures of Superman* (1953-58); Tucson, AZ, July 3, 2016.

Neusner, Jacob, 84, scholar whose English translations of rabbinic texts furthered Judaic study at secular institutions; Rhinebeck, NY, Oct. 8, 2016.

Nixon, Agnes, 93, writer and creator of the soap operas *One Life to Live* (1968-2012) and *All My Children* (1970-2011, 2013); Rosemont, PA, Sept. 28, 2016.

Nixon, Marni, 86, singer who dubbed singing voices of actresses in *The King and I* (1956), *West Side Story* (1961), and *My Fair Lady* (1964); New York, NY, July 24, 2016.

North, Douglass, 95, Nobel Prize-winning economist known for institutional analysis; Benzonia, MI, Nov. 23, 2015.

O

O'Brian, Hugh, 91, actor known for TV series *The Life and Legend of Wyatt Earp* (1955-61); Beverly Hills, CA, Sept. 5, 2016.

Olmstead, Bert, 89, Canadian Hall of Fame hockey player who played in 11 Stanley Cup Finals (1951-60, 1962), winning 5; High River, AB, Canada, Nov. 16, 2015.

Ortman, George, 89, abstract artist whose work often included multi-dimensional canvases and geometric shapes and symbols; New York, NY, Dec. 16, 2015.

P

Palmer, Arnold, 87, professional golfer who won 7 major championships; his charisma and style made him the sport's first superstar; Pittsburgh, PA, Sept. 25, 2016.

Paxton, Gary S., 77, music producer best known for "Monster Mash" (1962); Branson, MO, July 17, 2016.

Pearlman, Lou, 62, producer who managed the Backstreet Boys and NSYNC convicted of running a Ponzi scheme (2008); Miami, FL, Aug. 19, 2016.

Peres, Shimon, 93, Polish-born Nobel Peace Prize-winning statesman who served as Israel's prime minister (1984-86, '95-'96)

and president (2007-14); Ramat Gan, Israel, Sept. 28, 2016.

Phife Dawg (Malik Taylor), 45, rapper and co-founder of pioneering hip-hop trio A Tribe Called Quest; Oakley, CA, Mar. 22, 2016.

Prince (Rogers Nelson), 57, Oscar, Golden Globe, and Grammy Award-winning singer, songwriter, and multi-instrumentalist known as an innovator and eclectic; sold more than 100 mil records, including *Purple Rain* (1984); Chanhassen, MN, Apr. 21, 2016.

Putnam, Hilary, 89, philosopher who made contributions in a variety of fields; Arlington, MA, Mar. 13, 2016.

R

Ratner, Michael, 72, human rights lawyer; won Guantánamo Bay detainees the right to challenge the validity of their detention; New York, NY, May 11, 2016.

Reagan, Nancy, 94, former actress and first lady known for elegant omnipresence during Ronald Reagan's presidency; founded the "Just Say No" drug awareness campaign; Los Angeles, CA, Mar. 6, 2016.

Rickman, Alan, 69, British film and stage actor best known as Severus Snape in the Harry Potter movie franchise; London, England, UK, Jan. 14, 2016.

Rivette, Jacques, 87, French film director and critic associated with the French New Wave; Paris, France, Jan. 29, 2016.

Roberts, Doris, 90, Emmy Award-winning actress best known for TV sitcom *Everybody Loves Raymond* (1996-2005); Los Angeles, CA, Apr. 17, 2016.

Rogers, Wayne, 82, actor best known as "Trapper" John McIntyre on TV's *M*A*S*H* (1972-75); Los Angeles, CA, Dec. 31, 2015.

Rosencrans, Robert, 89, TV executive who helped launch public affairs network C-Span; Greenwich, CT, Aug. 3, 2016.

Rowen, Henry S., 90, national security expert who resigned the presidency of RAND Corp. when the organization's copy of the Pentagon Papers was leaked to the media (1971); Menlo Park, CA, Nov. 12, 2015.

Rykiel, Sonia, 86, French designer known for knitwear and a modern approach to fashion; Paris, France, Aug. 25, 2016.

S

Safer, Morley, 84, Canadian-American TV journalist known for investigative reporting on *60 Minutes* (1970-2016); New York, NY, May 19, 2016.

Sailors, Ken, 95, basketball player credited with the invention of the jump shot; Laramie, WY, Jan. 30, 2016.

Sakato, George T. "Joe," 94, Japanese-American soldier awarded the Medal of Honor for action in World War II in 2000; last survivor of 22 Asian Americans who were denied that commendation for more than a half-century; Denver, CO, Dec. 2, 2015.

Saunders, John, 61, Canadian-born sportscaster for ABC and ESPN; Hastings-on-Hudson, NY, Aug. 10, 2016.

Scalia, Antonin, 79, U.S. Supreme Court associate justice (1986-2016); known as a conservative who followed the originalism theory of constitutional interpretation; Shafter, TX, Feb. 13, 2016.

Schaefer, Thomas, 85, military attaché who was ranking officer at the U.S. embassy in Iran when 52 Americans were taken hostage (1979-81); Scottsdale, AZ, May 31, 2016.

Schallert, William, 93, actor best known for *The Patty Duke Show* (1963-66); president of the Screen Actors Guild (1979-81); Pacific Palisades, CA, May 8, 2016.

Schanberg, Sydney, 82, Pulitzer Prize-winning journalist whose coverage of Cambodia inspired the film *The Killing Fields* (1984); Poughkeepsie, NY, July 9, 2016.

Schayes, Dolph, 87, Hall of Fame basketball player and coach for the Syracuse Nationals/Philadelphia 76ers; Syracuse, NY, Dec. 10, 2015.

Schlafly, Phyllis, 92, conservative activist who worked to prevent the ratification of the Equal Rights Amendment; Ladue, MO, Sept. 5, 2016.

Schmidt, Helmut, 96, chancellor of West Germany (1974-82) known for attempts at East-West détente; Hamburg, Germany, Nov. 10, 2015.

Scola, Ettore, 84, Italian film director and screenwriter of comedic dramas about Italian society and history; Rome, Italy, Jan. 19, 2016.

Shaffer, Peter, 90, Academy Award-winning British playwright and screenwriter known for *Equus* (1973) and *Amadeus* (1979); County Cork, Ireland, June 6, 2016.

Shandling, Garry, 66, Emmy Award-winning comedian and writer who starred in meta-sitcoms *It's Garry Shandling's Show* (1986-90) and *The Larry Sanders Show* (1992-98); Los Angeles, CA, Mar. 24, 2016.

Shapley, Lloyd, 92, Nobel Prize-winning mathematician who researched game theory; Tucson, AZ, Mar. 12, 2016.

Shepard, Jean, 82, singer-songwriter of honky-tonk country music songs who performed at the Grand Ole Opry for over 60 years; Nashville, TN, Sept. 25, 2016.

Shikler, Aaron, 93, artist who painted White House portraits of Kennedys and first lady Nancy Reagan; New York, NY, Nov. 12, 2015.

Sinatra, Frank, Jr., 72, singer-songwriter who followed in his father's footsteps; Daytona Beach, FL, Mar. 16, 2016.

Sizemore, Chris Costner, 89, patient diagnosed with multiple-personality disorder who was the inspiration for *The Three Faces of Eve* (1957); Ocala, FL, July 24, 2016.

Sloan, P.F., 70, songwriter known for "Eve of Destruction" (1965) and "Secret Agent Man" (1966); Los Angeles, CA, Nov. 15, 2015.

Smart-Grosvenor, Vertamae, 79, culinary anthropologist and NPR commentator who celebrated Gullah cuisine and culture; Bronx, NY, Sept. 3, 2016.

Smith, Richard, 84, British artist whose work ranged from Pop Art to Color Field painting styles; Patchogue, NY, Apr. 15, 2016.

Snider, Ed, 83, co-founder and longtime owner of the Philadelphia Flyers NHL team; Montecito, CA, Apr. 11, 2016.

Spitzer, Robert, 83, psychiatrist who helped develop the manual for diagnosing and classifying mental disorders; Seattle, WA, Dec. 25, 2015.

Stanley, Ralph, 89, Grammy Award-winning bluegrass singer and banjo player whose "O Death" in *O Brother, Where Art Thou?* (2000) introduced the genre to new generations; Sandy Ridge, VA, June 23, 2016.

Stigwood, Robert, 81, Australian-born producer who managed the Bee Gees and produced *Saturday Night Fever* (1977) and *Grease* (1978); London, Eng., UK, Jan. 4, 2016.

Stucky, Steven, 66, Pulitzer Prize-winning composer; resident composer for the L.A. Philharmonic (1988-2009); Ithaca, NY, Feb. 14, 2016.

Summitt, Pat, 64, Hall of Fame coach of the Univ. of Tennessee women's basketball team (1974-2012); holds record for most wins (1,098) in NCAA basketball history; Knoxville, TN, June 28, 2016.

Sutter, Joe, 95, aeronautical engineer who helped design the Boeing 747; Bremerton, WA, Aug. 30, 2016.

Swados, Elizabeth, 64, playwright and composer best known for Broadway's *Runaways* (1978); New York, NY, Jan. 5, 2016.

T

Tabei, Junko, 77, Japanese mountaineer; first woman to summit Mount Everest (1975); Kawagoe, Saitama, Japan, Oct. 20, 2016.

Taylor, Jack, 94, founder of Enterprise Rent-A-Car company; St. Louis, MO, July 2, 2016.

Temperton, Rod, 66, British songwriter known for Michael Jackson hits including "Thriller" (1982) and "Rock With You" (1979); London, Eng., UK, Sept./Oct., 2016.

Thompson, Fred, 73, U.S. senator (R, TN, 1994-2003) and actor, best known for *Die Hard 2* (1990) and *Law & Order* (2002-07); Nashville, TN, Nov. 1, 2015.

Thurmond, Nate, 74, Hall of Fame basketball center known as a great rebounder; San Francisco, CA, July 16, 2016.

Tishman, John, 90, real estate developer whose company helped build the World Trade Center and Madison Square Garden in New York City; Bedford, NY, Feb. 6, 2016.

Toffler, Alvin, 87, futurist writer whose *Future Shock* (1970) predicted the influence technology would have on society; Los Angeles, CA, June 27, 2016.

Tomita, Isao, 84, Japanese electronic musician best known for "Snowflakes Are Dancing" (1974); Tokyo, Japan, May 5, 2016.

Tomlinson, Ray, 74, computer programmer credited with creating email (1971) and selecting the "@" sign for use in an email address; Lincoln, MA, Mar. 5, 2016.

Tompkins, Douglas, 72, conservationist and co-founder of clothing brands The North Face and Esprit; Coyhaique, Chile, Dec. 8, 2015.

Toussaint, Allen, 77, R&B songwriter, producer, and performer whose compositions included "Mother-in-Law" (1961) and "Working in the Coal Mine" (1966); Madrid, Spain, Nov. 9, 2015.

Trentlage, Richard D., 87, jingle writer best known for the "The Oscar Mayer Wiener Song"; Libertyville, IL, Sept. 21, 2016.

Trudell, John, 69, activist, actor, and poet; chair of the American Indian Movement (1973-79); Santa Clara Co., CA, Dec. 8, 2015.

Turner, Kevin, 46, NFL fullback who was a lead plaintiff in a lawsuit against the NFL over the health risks of concussions; Vestavia Hills, AL, Mar. 24, 2016.

V

Vanity (Denise Matthews), 57, Canadian R&B singer and model; part of trio Vanity 6 that toured with Prince; Fremont, CA, Feb. 15, 2016.

Vee, Bobby, 73, teen idol and singer best known for the 1961 hits "Rubber Ball" and "Take Good Care of My Baby"; Rogers, MN, Oct. 24, 2016.

Vega, Alan (Boruch Alan Bermowitz), 78, artist who was part of electro-punk duo Suicide; New York, NY, July 16, 2016.

Vernon, Lillian, 88, German-born founder of eponymous company best known for its mail-order catalog; New York, NY, Dec. 14, 2015.

Vessey, John W., Jr., 94, U.S. Army general who served as chairman of the Joint Chiefs of Staff (1982-85); North Oaks, MN, Aug. 18, 2016.

Vigoda, Abe, 94, actor known for role in *The Godfather* (1972) and as Detective Fish on TV sitcom *Barney Miller* (1975-77); Woodland Park, NJ, Jan. 26, 2016.

Voinovich, George, 79, Ohio politician who served as mayor of Cleveland (1980-89), governor (1991-98), and senator (R, 1999-2011); Cleveland, OH, June 12, 2016.

W

Waas, Les, 94, adman who created the jingle for Mister Softee ice cream trucks; Warminster, PA, Apr. 19, 2016.

Wajda, Andrzej, 90, honorary Academy Award-winning Polish film director; Warsaw, Poland, Oct. 9, 2016.

Wanzer, Bobby, 94, Hall of Fame basketball guard who led the Rochester Royals to an NBA championship (1951); Pittsford, NY, Jan. 23, 2016.

Weiland, Scott, 48, singer-songwriter who fronted rock groups Stone Temple Pilots and Velvet Revolver; Bloomington, MN, Dec. 3, 2015.

Welland, Colin, 81, Academy Award-winning British screenwriter of *Chariots of Fire* (1981); London, Eng., UK, Nov. 2, 2015.

Wemba, Papa, 66, Congolese singer and musician known as the King of Rumba Rock; Abidjan, Côte d'Ivoire, Apr. 24, 2016.

Wexler, Haskell, 93, Academy Award-winning cinematographer best known for *Who's Afraid of Virginia Woolf?* (1966) and *Bound for Glory* (1976); Santa Monica, CA, Dec. 27, 2015.

White, Maurice, 74, Grammy Award-winning singer-songwriter who founded Earth, Wind & Fire; Los Angeles, CA, Feb. 4, 2016.

White, Michael, 80, Tony Award-winning Scottish-born producer best known for *The Rocky Horror Picture Show* (play, 1973; film, 1975) and *Monty Python and the Holy Grail* (1975); Ojai, CA, Mar. 7, 2016.

White, Nera, 80, basketball player who was one of the first women inducted into the Basketball Hall of Fame; Gallatin, TN, Apr. 13, 2016.

Whitfield, Mal, 91, Olympic gold medalist in 800-m run (1948, '52); also a Tuskegee airman; Washington, DC, Nov. 19, 2015.

Wiesel, Elie, 87, Romanian-born Nobel Peace Prize-winning writer and activist; *Night* (1960) documented his experiences in concentration camps during the Holocaust; New York, NY, July 2, 2016.

Wilder, Gene, 83, actor known for comic roles in *The Producers* (1967), *Young Frankenstein* (1974), and *Blazing Saddles* (1974); also known for *Willy Wonka & the Chocolate Factory* (1971); Stamford, CT, Aug. 29, 2016.

Williams, Chuck, 100, founder of kitchenware retailer Williams-Sonoma; San Francisco, CA, Dec. 5, 2015.

Wistert, Al, 95, Philadelphia Eagles tackle who helped win consecutive NFL championships (1948-49); Grants Pass, OR, Mar. 5, 2016.

Woodlawn, Holly, 69, transgender actress known for appearances in Andy Warhol films and as a subject of Lou Reed's song "Walk on the Wild Side" (1972); Los Angeles, CA, Dec. 6, 2015.

Worrell, Bernie, 72, keyboardist and synthesizer pioneer who was a founding member of Parliament-Funkadelic; Everson, WA, June 24, 2016.

Worsley, Henry, 55, British explorer who came within 30 miles of being first to cross Antarctica alone; Punta Arenas, Chile, Jan. 24, 2016.

Wright, C(arolyn) D., 67, poet whose work reflected her Ozark background; Barrington, RI, Jan. 12, 2016.

Wu, Harry, 79, Chinese human rights activist who spoke out about his detention in forced-labor prison camps; Honduras, Apr. 26, 2016.

Y

Yang Jiang, 104, Chinese author known for *Six Chapters From My Life "Downunder"* (1981), a memoir of China's Cultural Revolution; Beijing, China, May 25, 2016.

Yelchin, Anton, 27, Soviet-born American actor known as Pavel Chekov in three Star Trek franchise films (2009-16); Studio City, CA, June 19, 2016.

Young, Alan, 96, English-born Canadian-American actor known as the owner of the talking horse in the TV sitcom *Mister Ed* (1961-66); Woodland Hills, CA, May 19, 2016.

Z

Zacherle, John, 98, entertainer known for hosting horror movies on late-night TV; New York, NY, Oct. 27, 2016.

Zydeco, Buckwheat (Stanley Dural Jr.), 68, accordionist and bandleader who performed French Creole zydeco music; Lafayette, LA, Sept. 24, 2016.

CONGRESS

Key Information on the 114th Congress

The 114th Congress convened Jan. 6, 2015, with Republicans in control of both the Senate (54-44, 2 ind.) and the House (246-188, 1 vacancy) for the first time in eight years. A record 108 women were serving in Congress, of whom 20 were in the Senate and 88 (including 4 nonvoting delegates) were in the House. The 114th Congress also had a record number of Hispanic members, with 4 in the Senate and 34 (including 1 nonvoting delegate and a resident commissioner) serving in the House. Among Senate members were 2 African Americans and 1 Asian American. The House had 45 African-American members (including 2 nonvoting delegates), 13 Americans of Asian or Pacific Islander heritage (including 2 nonvoting delegates), and 2 American Indians. Two lawmakers died during the term: 56-year-old third-term Rep. Alan Nunnelee (R, MS) on Feb. 6, 2015, and 49-year-old freshman Rep. Mark Takai (D, HI), on July 20, 2016. For the first time since 1955, a new Congress convened without seating John Dingell (D, MI), who had been the House's longest continuously serving member before his retirement at the end of his 29th full term.

Pope Francis became the first pope to address a joint session of Congress on Sept. 24, 2015.

Leadership. In the Senate, where the party balance had shifted, former Minority Leader Mitch McConnell (R, KY) became majority leader, and Harry Reid (D, NV), assumed the minority leader role. Majority Whip John Cornyn (R, TX) and Minority Whip Richard Durbin (D, IL) likewise exchanged roles. John Boehner (R, OH) retained his office of speaker of the House when the 114th Congress convened, despite losing the support of 25 Republicans in the Freedom Caucus. Boehner in Sept. 2015 announced his resignation both as speaker and from Congress, effective Oct. 29, 2015. After House Majority Leader Kevin McCarthy (R, CA) abruptly withdrew his candidacy, 45-year-old Paul Ryan (R, WI) was elected to the post with 236 House votes, becoming the youngest speaker since 1875. Steve Scalise (R, LA) continued as majority whip. Other leading house members were Minority Leader Nancy Pelosi (D, CA) and Minority Whip Steny Hoyer (D, MD).

Ethics. Reelected to a third term, Rep. Michael Grimm (R, NY) resigned the day before the 114th Congress convened after pleading guilty to felony tax evasion related to his health food restaurant. Indicted on 19 other federal counts, including perjury and hiring undocumented workers, Grimm was sentenced to eight months in prison. Fourth-term Rep. Aaron Schock (R, IL) resigned on Mar. 31, 2015, amid allegations he used taxpayer funds for lavish trips, events, and office renovations and fraudulently reported vehicle mileage reimbursements. Rep. Chaka Fattah (D, PA) resigned June 23, 2016, two days after he was convicted by a federal jury on 23 corruption charges—including racketeering, money laundering, and fraud—tied to an illegal $1 mil loan to his Philadelphia mayoral campaign in 2007.

Unfinished Business. The House, Sept. 28, 2016, and Senate, Oct. 7, 2016, adjourned for the election campaign season, leaving multiple measures unpassed or unfunded. Congress's inability to fund efforts to combat Zika virus garnered widespread criticism. Congress also failed to pass military and veteran spending bills.

For Further Information. Detailed legislative information can be accessed at www.congress.gov.

Major Actions of the 114th Congress

Major actions taken by the 114th Congress through Sept. 30, 2016. Laws are identified by their Public Law (PL) number.

Medicare Reform. Medicare Access and CHIP Reauthorization Act of 2015 replaces formula for calculating Medicare payments to physicians with alternatives, including flat-fee increases over next 10 years. It also creates a merit-based incentive payment system for doctors and extends the Children's Health Insurance Plan (CHIP). Passed by the House, Mar. 26, 392-37; passed by the Senate, Apr. 14, 92-8; signed by Pres. Obama Apr. 16 (PL 114-10).

Anti-Terrorism and Privacy. USA Freedom Act of 2015 extends through 2019 key newly expired sections of the post-9/11 USA Patriot Act, reauthorizing roving wiretaps, lone-wolf surveillance, and secret court orders while ending the Natl. Security Agency's controversial bulk collection of phone data. It permits federal agencies to obtain phone data from telecom companies if "reasonable, articulable suspicion" exists. Passed by the House, May 13, 338-88; passed by the Senate, June 2, 67-32; signed by Pres. Obama, June 2 (PL 114-23).

Space Mining. Space Act of 2015 permits U.S. citizens to exploit extraterrestrial non-biological resources including water and minerals for commercial benefit. Also allows NASA astronauts to launch in private spacecraft. Passed by the Senate (as amended), Nov. 10, unanimous consent; passed by the House (as amended), Nov. 16, voice vote; signed by Pres. Obama, Nov. 25 (PL-114-90).

Roadway Updates. Fixing America's Surface Transportation (FAST) Act of 2015 provides $305 bil for FY2016-20 for highway/bridge repair and investment, congestion mitigation and air quality enhancement, safety improvements, public transportation, freight-related advances, and city planning. Passed by the House (as amended), Dec. 3, 359-65; passed by the Senate (as amended), Dec. 3, 83-16; signed by Pres. Obama, Dec. 4 (PL 114-94).

Education. Every Student Succeeds Act of 2015 retains most standardized testing of U.S. students in the No Child Left Behind Act of 2001 (officially expired in 2007) but shifts federal oversight to states. Allocates more power to states in creating goals and accountability policies and in developing intervention strategies for low-performing schools. Passed by the House (as amended), Dec. 2, 359-64; passed by the Senate (as amended), Dec. 9, 85-12; signed by Pres. Obama, Dec. 10 (PL 114-95).

Federal Spending. Consolidated Appropriations Act of 2015 authorizes $1.15 tril to fund most of federal government through Sept. 2016; trims taxes by about $680 bil over 10 years; increases NASA budget to $19.3 bil; ends 40-year ban on crude oil exports; and creates Cybersecurity Information Sharing Act. Passed in two parts (as amended) by the House, Dec. 17, 318-109, and Dec. 18, 316-113; passed by the Senate (as amended), Dec. 18, 65-33; signed by Pres. Obama, Dec. 18 (PL 114-113).

Puerto Rican Debt. Puerto Rico Oversight, Management, and Economic Stability Act of 2016 restructures Puerto Rico's debilitating $72 bil bond debt two days before it would have defaulted—for the fourth time since 2015—on about $2 bil in payments. Also establishes a federally appointed financial oversight board and exempts employers there from paying young workers the federal minimum wage. Passed by the House (as amended), June 9, 297-127; passed by the Senate (as amended), June 29, 68-30; signed by Pres. Obama, June 30 (PL 114-187).

Agriculture Aid. Global Food Security Act of 2016 allots over $7 bil to boost food production and improve nutrition in low-income countries around the world. Passed by the Senate, Apr. 20, voice vote; passed by the House, July 6, 369-53; signed by Pres. Obama, July 20 (PL 114-195).

Leadership of Selected Congressional Committees

Congressional leadership as of Sept. 30, 2016.

House
Appropriations: Hal Rogers (R, KY)
Armed Services: Mac Thornberry (R, TX)
Budget: Tom Price (R, GA)
Education and the Workforce: John Kline (R, MN)
Energy and Commerce: Fred Upton (R, MI)
Ethics: Charles Dent (R, PA)
Financial Services: Jeb Hensarling (R, TX)
Foreign Affairs: Ed Royce (R, CA)
Intelligence: Devin Nunes (R, CA)
Judiciary: Bob Goodlatte (R, VA)
Natural Resources: Rob Bishop (R, UT)
Oversight and Government Reform: Jason Chaffetz (R, UT)
Transportation and Infrastructure: Bill Shuster (R, PA)
Ways and Means: Kevin Brady (R, TX)

Senate
Appropriations: Thad Cochran (R, MS)
Armed Services: John McCain (R, AZ)
Banking, Housing, and Urban Affairs: Richard Shelby (R, AL)
Budget: Mike Enzi (R, WY)
Commerce, Science, and Transportation: John Thune (R, SD)
Energy and Natural Resources: Lisa Murkowski (R, AK)
Finance: Orrin Hatch (R, UT)
Foreign Relations: Bob Corker (R, TN)
Health, Education, Labor, and Pensions: Lamar Alexander (R, TN)
Judiciary: Chuck Grassley (R, IA)

Joint Committees
Economic: Rep. Pat Tiberi (R, OH), Sen. Daniel Coats (R, IN)
Taxation: Sen. Orrin Hatch (R, UT), Rep. Kevin Brady (R, TX)

U.S. SUPREME COURT

The U.S. Supreme Court's 2015-16 term began Oct. 5, 2015, and concluded June 27, 2016, when it adjourned for its summer recess. The justices decided 80 cases (63 of which carried signed opinions). The court operated on an $88-mil budget in 2016.

Chief Justice John G. Roberts Jr. presided over his 11th full term. The eight associate justices, by order of seniority, were Antonin Scalia, Anthony M. Kennedy, Clarence Thomas, Ruth Bader Ginsburg, Stephen G. Breyer, Samuel A. Alito Jr., Sonia Sotomayor, and Elena Kagan. Justice Scalia died Feb. 13, 2016, with more than four months remaining in the term. Pres. Barack Obama nominated appellate court judge Merrick Garland Mar. 16, 2016, to fill the seat. The Senate had not held hearings on his nomination as of Oct. 2016.

Roberts, Scalia, Thomas, and Alito tended to vote as a conservative bloc, while Ginsburg, Breyer, Sotomayor, and Kagan composed the court's liberal wing. Associate Justice Kennedy tended to be a swing vote.

Notable Supreme Court Decisions, 2015-16

Note: The columns on the right provide information on how each justice voted. Gray shading indicates a justice who was part of the majority; black, a justice who did not participate in the decision. Striped boxes indicate where the court tied and did not reach a majority opinion. MO = justice authored majority opinion; CO = justice authored concurring opinion; COJ = justice authored opinion concurring in judgment but not its reasoning; DO = justice authored dissenting opinion.

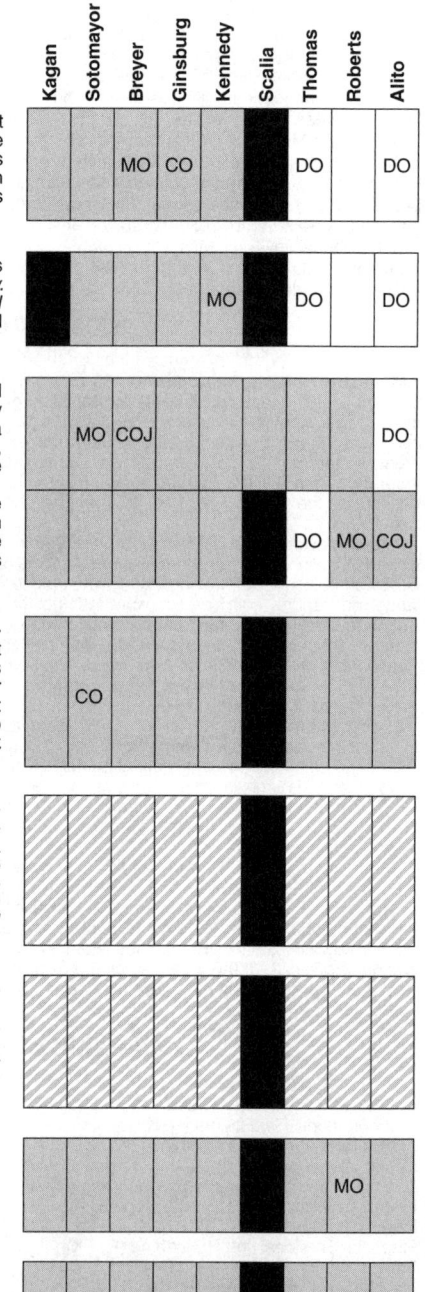

Abortion

The U.S. Supreme Court June 27 ruled, 5-3, that a Texas law that placed stringent limits on abortions violated the constitutional rights of Texas women. A Supreme Court decision in 1992 allowed states to regulate abortion only if any restrictions did not impose an "undue burden" on women attempting to obtain an abortion in the early stages of pregnancy. In *Whole Woman's Health v. Hellerstedt*, the justices ruled the Texas law did not pass the undue burden test.

Affirmative Action

The court June 23 rejected, 4-3, a challenge to the Univ. of Texas's admissions policy, which took race and ethnicity into account, among other factors, in *Fisher v. University of Texas at Austin*. The decision was frequently referred to as *Fisher II* because the Supreme Court had also ruled on the case—brought by plaintiff Abigail Fisher—in 2013, sending it back to a lower court for reevaluation.

Capital Punishment

The court Jan. 12 ruled, 8-1, that the legislation that governed Florida's capital sentencing process—which allowed judges to impose death sentences with only "advisory" input from a jury—violated the Sixth Amendment's guarantee of a trial by jury. The Supreme Court had ruled in *Ring v. Arizona* (2002) that a jury, not a judge, had to determine whether to impose the death penalty. The 2016 case was *Hurst v. Florida*.

The court May 23 ruled, 7-1, that Georgia prosecutors in the capital murder case against Timothy Foster—a black man who had been sentenced to death by an all-white jury in 1987 for the murder of an elderly white woman—had violated the Constitution when they dismissed black people from the pool of potential jurors solely because of their race. The case was *Foster v. Chatman*.

Health Care and Contraception

The justices May 16 declined to rule on the legal issues in a group of consolidated cases in which religious nonprofit organizations challenged the requirement in the 2010 Patient Protection and Affordable Care Act (ACA) that most employers provide their workers with insurance coverage for contraceptives and certain other reproductive health services. In a brief, unsigned, and unanimous opinion, the court instructed lower courts to evaluate whether a compromise between the case's two sides was possible. The consolidated cases were known by the lead case, *Zubik v. Burwell*.

Immigration

The court June 23 announced that it had deadlocked, voting 4-4 in a case addressing whether an immigration policy announced in Nov. 2014 by Pres. Obama constituted executive overreach. The tie ruling had the effect of extending a block that a federal judge in Texas had placed on the policy in Feb. 2015. Although the Supreme Court ruling set no judicial precedent and did not formally strike down the measures, the ruling made it all but certain that the policy would not be resurrected in the remaining seven months of Obama's presidency. The case was *United States v. Texas*.

Labor

The justices Mar. 29 reached a 4-4 tie in a case challenging rules that in some states compelled public employees who had opted not to join a union to nevertheless pay fees to the union in support of its collective-bargaining efforts. This left standing an earlier ruling by the U.S. 9th Circuit that allowed the California Teachers Association (CTA) to require nonmember teachers to pay so-called fair share fees because it conducted collective bargaining on their behalf. The case was *Friedrichs v. California Teachers Association*.

Official Corruption

The court June 27 ruled unanimously to void the conviction of former Virginia Gov. Bob McDonnell (R) on federal corruption charges and to send his case back to a lower court. The ruling significantly narrowed the definition of official corruption under federal law and ordered the lower court to reconsider whether prosecutors had enough evidence to retry McDonnell. The case was *McDonnell v. U.S.*

Voting Rights

The court Apr. 4 unanimously ruled that states could continue to interpret the constitutional principle of "one person, one vote" to mean that state legislative districts should be drawn so that they had equal numbers of people (as measured by the census), rather than equal numbers of eligible voters. The question had significant political ramifications because redrawing districts based on the number of eligible voters would increase the voting power of rural areas with fewer children, non-citizen immigrants, and felons. The case was *Evenwel v. Abbott*.

Decision	Kagan	Sotomayor	Breyer	Ginsburg	Kennedy	Scalia	Thomas	Roberts	Alito
Abortion			MO	CO		■	DO		DO
Affirmative Action	■				MO		DO		DO
Capital Punishment (Hurst v. Florida)	MO	COJ							DO
Capital Punishment (Foster v. Chatman)						■	DO	MO	COJ
Health Care and Contraception	CO					■			
Immigration	(tie)	(tie)	(tie)	(tie)	(tie)	■	(tie)	(tie)	(tie)
Labor	(tie)	(tie)	(tie)	(tie)	(tie)	■	(tie)	(tie)	(tie)
Official Corruption								MO	
Voting Rights				MO		■	COJ		COJ

NOTABLE QUOTES, 2016

For notable quotes from the 2016 campaign trail, see p. 11.

Around the World

"A person who thinks only about building walls, wherever they may be, and not building bridges, is not Christian."
—**Pope Francis**, when asked about Donald Trump and his proposed wall along the U.S.-Mexican border, Feb. 18.

"Terrorism is terrorism. It has no state, no nationality, no religion, no country."
—**Sheikh Mohamed Tojgani**, imam of an influential Brussels mosque, repudiating the Mar. 22 bombings of the Belgian capital's airport and subway.

"Their souls speak to us. They ask us to look inward, to take stock of who we are and what we might become."
—Pres. **Barack Obama**, while visiting Hiroshima, Japan, May 27, remembering those who died after the U.S. dropped the atomic bomb in 1945.

"[T]here is simply no need in the 21st century to be part of a federal system of government based in Brussels that is imitated nowhere else on Earth. It was a noble idea for its time. It is no longer right for this country."
—"Leave" campaign leader and UK Foreign Sec. **Boris Johnson**, after British voters approved the June 23 Brexit referendum calling for the country to leave the European Union.

"Why on the 14th of July? Because it is a celebration of freedom."
—French Pres. **François Hollande**, on truck terror attack that killed 86 people at a Bastille Day celebration, July 14, in Nice, France.

"We will continue to cleanse the virus from all state institutions."
—Turkish Pres. **Recep Tayyip Erdogan**, at a funeral for persons killed in an abortive July 15 coup; thousands were arrested.

"Son of a whore, I will curse you in that forum. We will be wallowing in the mud like pigs if you do that to me."
—Philippine Pres. **Rodrigo Duterte**, Sept. 5, publicly warning Pres. Obama not to blame his regime for extrajudicial killings; Obama canceled their scheduled meeting.

"Vladimir Putin is a strong leader in the same way that arsenic is a strong drink."
—Russian former world chess champion **Garry Kasparov**, Sept. 8, criticizing praise of Putin by Republican U.S. presidential nominee Donald Trump.

"Here, people can't believe anything. But they are always waiting for peace."
—Syrian writer **Khaled Khalifa**, chatting online with the *New York Times*, Sept. 12, as a shaky cease-fire went into effect in the Syrian civil war between the Bashar al-Assad regime and multifactional rebel forces.

National News

"First graders. … Every time I think about those kids, it gets me mad."
—Pres. **Obama**, Jan. 5, recalling the 2012 mass shooting at Sandy Hook (CT) Elementary School, as he announced executive initiatives intended to curb gun violence.

"It's one of the few regrets of my presidency—that the rancor and suspicion between the parties has gotten worse instead of better. I have no doubt a president with the gifts of Lincoln or Roosevelt might have better bridged the divide."
—Pres. **Obama** in State of the Union speech, Jan. 12.

"We disagreed now and then, but when I wrote for the Court and received a Scalia dissent … Justice Scalia nailed all the weak spots … and gave me just what I needed to strengthen the majority opinion."
—U.S. Supreme Court Associate Justice **Ruth Bader Ginsburg**, in a statement about her friend, ideological opposite, and fellow justice Antonin Scalia, following the latter's Feb. 13 death.

"Ms. Eisenstein, one question."
—Associate Justice **Clarence Thomas**, speaking from the Supreme Court bench, Feb. 29, for the first time in 10 years.

"Mommy I love you. In club they shooting … Trapp in bathroom. He's coming. I'm gonna die."
—**Eddie Justice** in text messages to his mother before he was fatally shot, with 48 others, June 12, at a nightclub in Orlando, FL.

"I think he was just black in the wrong place."
—**Valerie Castile**, in a CNN interview after her son, Philando Castile, was fatally shot July 6 by a police officer during a traffic stop in a Minnesota suburb.

"Over the past five days, I've had more people offer to buy me a coffee than I can remember."
—Cambridge (MA) Police Sgt. **Thomas Glynn**, after July incidents in which police officers were ambushed and killed in Baton Rouge, LA, and Dallas, TX.

"That is the story of this country … the story of generations of people who felt the lash of bondage … the sting of segregation, but who kept on striving and hoping … so that today I wake up every morning in a house that was built by slaves. And I watch my daughters, two beautiful, intelligent, black young women, playing with their dogs on the White House lawn."
—First lady **Michelle Obama**, in July 25 speech at the Democratic National Convention.

People and Culture

"You know, in the '60s … I'm sure there were no black nominees some of those years … And black people did not protest. … Why? Because we had real things to protest at the time … We were too busy being raped and lynched to care about who won best cinematographer."
—Actor-comedian **Chris Rock**, hosting the 88th Academy Awards, Feb. 28.

"Ladies, this year's fragrance is DEET."
—**Ismarie Morales**, nutritionist at a clinic near San Juan, PR, urging women to use mosquito repellent to avoid the Zika virus, in *NY Times*, Mar. 19.

"His life will never be the one that he dreamed about and worked so hard to achieve. That is a steep price to pay for 20 minutes of action out of his 20 plus years of life."
—**Dan Turner**, father of Stanford Univ. student Brock Turner, in a letter requesting leniency after his son was convicted of sexual assault of an unconscious woman. The judge, June 2, handed down a controversial sentence of only six months.

"You took away my worth, my privacy, my energy, my time, my intimacy, my confidence, my own voice, until today."
—Excerpt from victim's statement in the Brock Turner assault case, made public June 2.

"Love is love is love is love is love is love is love is love, cannot be killed or swept aside."
—*Hamilton* mastermind **Lin-Manuel Miranda**, June 12, paying tribute to victims of the shooting at a gay nightclub in Orlando, FL, earlier that day, as he accepted one of his musical's 11 Tony Awards.

"I gave everything that I had. I put my heart and my blood and my sweat and my tears into this game. Cleveland, this is for you!"
—**LeBron James**, June 19, after fulfilling his promise to lead the Cavaliers to the NBA championship and the city's first pro sports championship in 52 years.

"I'm not the next Usain Bolt or Michael Phelps. I'm the first Simone Biles."
—Olympic gymnast **Simone Biles** in an Aug. 11 interview after winning gold in the women's gymnastics all-around.

"I over-exaggerated that story."
—Olympic medal-winning swimmer **Ryan Lochte**, in an interview with NBC's Matt Lauer that aired Aug. 20, after claims that he and teammates had been robbed at gunpoint at a Rio de Janeiro gas station appeared to have been cover for a vandalism incident.

"I am not going to stand up to show pride in a flag for a country that oppresses black people and people of color."
—San Francisco 49ers quarterback **Colin Kaepernick**, explaining why he controversially refused to stand during the national anthem before an Aug. 26 NFL preseason game.

"I would not be unhappy were I the last cisgender male to play a female transgender on television."
—**Jeffrey Tambor**, Sept. 18, accepting an Emmy award for best actor in a comedy series for playing a transgender woman on the Amazon series *Transparent*.

"It happened: @Cubs win World Series. That's change even this South Sider can believe in. Want to come to the White House before I leave?"
—Pres. **Obama** (@POTUS) in a tweet Nov. 3, after the Chicago Cubs defeated the Cleveland Indians to end the team's 108-year-long championship drought.

Love Stinks

Love may be blind, but could it respond to smell? To investigate, artist and environmental engineer Tega Brain and New York University researcher Sam Lavigne launched a service called Smell Dating in 2016. For $25, intrepid daters were sent a white cotton T-shirt to wear for three days and nights, preferably without deodorant or other artificial scents, and then send back. The service then cut the fragrant areas of the shirts into tiny pieces and sent them out to potential partners. Participants were given ten swatches from others' shirts but not any of the usual trappings of online dating—no names, photos, or indications of height, weight, age, race, or gender. Everyone could then choose which scents appealed to them. In the event of a match, the service would provide each party with the other's contact information. As of Sept. 2016, there was a waiting list for the next round of dating.

In the Eye of the Beholder

Alvin Barr brought a clay jug adorned with a variety of ugly faces to the *Antiques Roadshow* event in Spokane, WA, in June 2015. He'd bought the jug—then covered in dirt, straw, and chicken manure—at a barn sale in Eugene, OR, for $300. Appraiser Stephen L. Fletcher stunned him with an appraisal of $30,000-$50,000, calling it "... Bizarre and wonderful. You even see a little bit of, like, Pablo Picasso going on here. It's a little difficult to identify precisely when this was made, but I think it's probably late 19th or early 20th century." But when the episode showing the appraisal aired Jan. 11, 2016, it was seen by a friend of Elizabeth "Betsy" Soule, who recognized the jug as one Soule had created as a high school student in the 1970s. *Roadshow* sheepishly downgraded its appraisal to $3,000-$5,000.

Barr was relieved at the news. "I hated it when it was $30,000 to $50,000, because who wants $30,000 to $50,000 lying around their house?" he said. "Now, it's on my table, and I love it."

Marathons Go to the Dogs

The first-ever Trackless Train Trek Half-Marathon was held Jan. 16, 2016, in Elkmont, AL. The fastest female runner, Ludivine, completed it in 1:32:56, putting her in seventh place overall. But that was an unofficial result, as Ludivine hadn't registered for the race—she was a dog. Ludivine's owner, April Hamlin, had let the 2½-year-old bloodhound out of their nearby farmhouse when the dog happened upon the start of the race and took off with the pack of runners, to Hamlin's surprise. As she told *Runner's World* magazine, "She's laid-back and friendly, so I can't believe she ran the whole half-marathon ... she's actually really lazy." Ludivine was given a medal, and the 2017 race was renamed the Hound Dog Half.

But half-marathons are relatively easy. In June, Australian ultramarathoner Dion Leonard began the Gobi March—a 155-mi, 6-stage, 7-day race across the Gobi Desert—and noticed a small, sandy-colored dog at the starting line. To his surprise, she soon joined him and stayed with him the next few days. They were first to finish the third stage, during which Leonard carried her across a river. With temperatures rising as high as 125°F, organizers took the dog by car to the finish lines of the next two stages, where she waited for Leonard. They then finished the race together. In all, the dog—now named Gobi—ran about half the course. Leonard planned to bring her to his home in Scotland once a mandated quarantine process ended.

Let's Go to the Videotape

James Meyers Jr. of Concord, NC, was pulled over Mar. 22, 2016, for having a broken taillight. The police ran his driver's license. "The officer said, 'I don't know how to tell you this, but there's a warrant out for your arrest from 2002. Apparently you rented the movie *Freddy Got Fingered* and never returned it.' I thought he was joking," Meyers said. The 37-year-old single dad was allowed to take his daughter to school and go to work but promised to turn himself in later that day. He went down to the police station, expecting that everything would be quickly ironed out, but was instead taken in handcuffs to a magistrate's office and given a court date for the next month. The rental store, J&J Video, had since closed, but the misdemeanor was still punishable by a fine of up to $200.

The news went viral online, and soon the film's star, Tom Green, tweeted, "I just saw this and I am struggling to believe it is real." Green offered to put in a good word with the court, or even to pay the fine, but the charge was dropped.

Dial-A-Swede

Sweden's tourism industry is no stranger to innovative publicity campaigns. Since 2012, the nation's official Twitter account, @Sweden, has been given over to random members of the public, one week at a time. The Swedish Tourist Association upped the ante—if not the technology required—on Apr. 6, 2016, giving anyone in the world a chance to talk to a random Swede on the phone. "The Swedish Number" allowed anyone in Sweden to volunteer to take calls, and enabled anyone outside Sweden to call in and be randomly connected to one of those volunteers. Participants were free to discuss anything they wanted. (In one amusing incident, a reporter for *Adweek* was connected to the Stockholm bureau chief of the Associated Press; both were researching news articles about the number.) In the 79 days the service was open, 193,084 calls were received from 186 countries, with roughly a third of the calls coming from the United States.

The Fugitive Is Armed

The National Aquarium of New Zealand reported Apr. 12, 2016, that Inky, an octopus who had resided at the aquarium since 2014, had hot-footed it a few months earlier. Originally brought in by a volunteer who found him while fishing, Inky was believed to have been getting adjusted to aquarium life, though a curator of exhibits noted, "We have to keep Inky amused or he will get bored."

Inky may have gotten bored. (Or perhaps he got his tentacles on an advance release of *Finding Dory*, which featured a similarly wily octopus, and was inspired.) Octopuses are notoriously intelligent, have excellent eyesight, and can squeeze their bodies through a hole the size of a coin. The staff theorized that the lid on the octopus tank was left slightly ajar; Inky squeezed out, climbed down the tank, and crossed the floor to a six-inch-wide drain, which led right to the Pacific Ocean.

Things Fall Apart

The year 2016 was not kind to Austria's Interior Ministry: its first two attempts at holding a presidential runoff election ended in failure. The first runoff, held May 22, 2016, was struck down after a legal challenge due to irregularities in, among other things, counting mail-in votes. The do-over election was set for Oct. 2, but then came Gluegate—or, as it was dubbed by a TV anchor, *Bundespräsidentenwiederholungswahlverschiebung*.

Since 2009, envelopes for mail-in ballots have featured a flap that covers voters' personal information. Voters take the cover off a built-in adhesive strip and press the flap shut after casting their vote. If the flap is reopened before the vote is counted, the ballot is invalidated. But multiple voters found that the glue wasn't sticking and the envelopes spontaneously opened after they filled their ballots out. The planned Oct. election was rescheduled for Dec. 4 with the mail-in ballots used before 2009. Meanwhile, investigations were in progress to find out why the German-manufactured glue failed and how it was applied to the 1.5 mil envelopes.

Mark My Words

The Fluxus artists of the 1960s and 1970s followed in the footsteps of Dada and later anti-artists in breaking down barriers between art and non-art and in questioning the artistic establishment. Their often playful works made use of found objects and sought to engage viewers or listeners. One of the collage works in Danish Fluxus artist Arthur Köpcke's series of "Reading/Work-Pieces" (1963-65) was on display at Nuremberg's Neues Museum in 2016. It included a crossword puzzle, headed with the instructions "insert words so it suits." On a July visit, 91-year-old German retiree Hannelore K. took those instructions to heart and filled in part of the puzzle with a ballpoint pen. The piece had been insured for almost $90,000, and the museum was required to report the defacement to legal authorities.

K.'s lawyer drafted a response noting that the incident had brought Köpcke's work to the attention of a wider public, and that the artist probably would have approved of his client's actions, which were in line with Fluxus ideals. He even suggested that K. (whose last name was not released) had created a new derivative work, to which she held the copyright.

The pen marks were successfully removed, and there were no plans to file charges.

HISTORICAL ANNIVERSARIES

1917 – 100 Years Ago

The Great War continues to rage: Germany resumes unrestricted submarine warfare against Allies Feb. 1. U.S. cuts diplomatic ties with Germany Feb. 3, formally declares war Apr. 6, and passes a law instituting a military draft May 18. The first U.S. troops arrive in Europe June 26; Germans withdraw to Hindenburg line.

Mexico ratifies a new constitution Feb. 5.

The Jones-Shafroth Act, signed into law Mar. 2, makes inhabitants of Puerto Rico U.S. citizens.

The Espionage Act is signed into law June 15 criminalizing support of U.S. enemies.

Race riots in East St. Louis, IL, beginning July 1, kill up to 200 mostly black residents and cause thousands more to flee the violence.

The UK's King George V July 17 changes the royal family's house name to Windsor from the German Saxe-Coburg and Gotha.

In Russia's October Revolution, Bolsheviks led by Vladimir Lenin overthrow the government of Aleksandr Kerensky Nov. 7.

French ammunition ship *Mont Blanc* and Belgian steamer *Imo* collide Dec. 6 in Halifax Harbor, NS, Canada, causing a massive explosion that destroys much of the city and kills over 1,900.

Art. Marc Chagall's *Bella With White Collar*, Marcel Duchamp's *Fountain*, Amedeo Modigliani's *Nu couché*.

Film. Theda Bara stars in *Cleopatra*. Buster Keaton makes film debut in Fatty Arbuckle's *The Butcher Boy*. *The Poor Little Rich Girl* and *Rebecca of Sunnybrook Farm* starring Mary Pickford.

Health and medicine. Shinobu Ishihara develops and publishes tests for red-green color blindness.

Literature. P. G. Wodehouse's *The Man With Two Left Feet*, Upton Sinclair's *King Coal*, Edith Wharton's *Summer*.

Music. The ballet *Parade*, featuring music by Erik Satie and costumes and sets by Pablo Picasso, debuts in Paris. Giacomo Puccini's opera *La Rondine* debuts in Monte Carlo; Sergei Prokofiev completes *Symphony No. 1*.

Nonfiction. The first Pulitzer Prizes are awarded. D'Arcy Wentworth Thompson's *On Growth and Form*.

Pop music. "Dixieland Jass Band One-Step/Livery Stable Blues" is considered the first commercial jazz recording. George M. Cohan's "Over There."

Science and technology. Félix d'Hérelle announces discovery of bacteriophages.

Sports. National Hockey League is established in Canada.

Theater. *Oh, Boy!*; *Maytime*; *Peter Ibbetson* starring John and Lionel Barrymore; *Why Marry?*

Miscellaneous. Accused double agent Mata Hari is arrested in Paris Feb. 13 and executed by firing squad Oct. 15. The National Civil Liberties Bureau (forerunner of the American Civil Liberties Union) is founded.

1967 – 50 Years Ago

Three NASA astronauts—Virgil "Gus" Grissom, Edward H. White II, and Roger Chaffee—die Jan. 27 in *Apollo 1* flash fire on ground at Cape Canaveral, FL.

The 25th Amendment to the U.S. Constitution, clarifying presidential succession, is ratified Feb. 10.

Antiwar march in New York City Apr. 15 draws more than 100,000 participants; a similar march in Washington, DC, Oct. 21-22, drew 100,000 participants.

Amid increasing ethnic violence, eastern Nigerian leader Odumegwu Ojukwu May 30 proclaims the traditionally Igbo region as the independent Republic of Biafra, leading to a civil war in Africa's most populous country.

Israel captures the Sinai Peninsula, Gaza Strip, West Bank, Golan Heights, and Jerusalem's Old City in the Six-Day War, June 5-10.

The U.S. Supreme Court rules unanimously that laws banning interracial marriage are unconstitutional June 12 in *Loving v. Virginia*.

U.S. Solicitor General Thurgood Marshall is nominated June 13 as first black U.S. Supreme Court justice and sworn in Oct. 2.

Riots erupt among residents of predominantly black Newark, NJ, July 12-17; 26 killed, more than 700 injured, 1,500 arrested. In Detroit, MI, July 23-27, 43 died, 7,200 arrested; 5,000 left homeless by rioting, looting, and burning in city's black neighborhoods.

An errant rocket launch sets off a fire and explosions onboard aircraft carrier USS *Forrestal*, killing 134 in the Gulf of Tonkin July 29.

Carl B. Stokes (D, Cleveland) and Richard G. Hatcher (D, Gary, IN) are elected the first black mayors of major U.S. cities Nov. 7.

Australian Prime Min. Harold Holt disappears in probable drowning while swimming near Portsea, Victoria, Dec. 17; his body is never recovered.

Art. New York's Museum of Modern Art opens first American exhibit to focus on Pablo Picasso's sculptures; a 50-ft untitled Picasso sculpture is dedicated in Chicago's Daley Plaza. Diane Arbus's *Identical Twins, Roselle, New Jersey, 1967*; David Hockney's *A Bigger Splash*.

Film. *Bonnie and Clyde* starring Warren Beatty and Faye Dunaway; *Camelot*; *Cool Hand Luke* starring Paul Newman; *The Dirty Dozen*; *The Graduate* starring Dustin Hoffman; *Guess Who's Coming to Dinner* starring Katharine Hepburn, Sidney Poitier, and Spencer Tracy; *In the Heat of the Night*; *Valley of the Dolls*; *You Only Live Twice* starring Sean Connery as James Bond.

Health and medicine. The first human heart transplant takes place in South Africa Dec. 3.

Literature. Gabriel García Márquez's *One Hundred Years of Solitude* is first published in the original Spanish; Mikhail Bulgakov's *The Master and Margarita* is published in book form for first time. S. E. Hinton's *The Outsiders*, E. L. Konigsburg's *From the Mixed-Up Files of Mrs. Basil E. Frankweiler*, Ira Levin's *Rosemary's Baby*, William Styron's *The Confessions of Nat Turner*.

Music. Steve Reich's *Piano Phase* and *Violin Phase*, Karlheinz Stockhausen's *Hymnen*, Morton Subotnick's *Silver Apples of the Moon*.

Nonfiction. First issue of *Rolling Stone* magazine is published. Martin Luther King Jr.'s *Where Do We Go From Here: Chaos or Community?*, William Manchester's *The Death of a President*, Desmond Morris's *The Naked Ape*.

Pop music. Monterey Pop Festival features The Grateful Dead, Jimi Hendrix, Janis Joplin, The Mamas and the Papas, Otis Redding, Ravi Shankar, and The Who. The Beatles' *Sgt. Pepper's Lonely Hearts Club Band* and *Magical Mystery Tour*; The Box Tops' "The Letter"; Cream's *Disraeli Gears*; The Doors' eponymous debut album; The 5th Dimension's "Up, Up and Away"; Aretha Franklin's "Respect"; The Jimi Hendrix Experience's *Are You Experienced*; Lulu's "To Sir With Love"; Scott McKenzie's "San Francisco (Be Sure to Wear Flowers in Your Hair)"; The Rolling Stones' "Let's Spend the Night Together" and "Ruby Tuesday"; *The Velvet Underground & Nico*.

Science and technology. Computer pioneer Doug Engelbart applies for a patent on the computer mouse. Jocelyn Bell and Antony Hewish discover pulsars.

Sports. Green Bay Packers defeat Kansas City Chiefs in first Super Bowl, Jan. 15, in Los Angeles. Heavyweight champion Muhammad Ali refuses Army induction and is stripped of title.

Television. The first live global satellite TV broadcast, *Our World*, is watched by an estimated 350 million people. Last episode of *The Fugitive* airs. *The Smothers Brothers Comedy Hour* and *The Carol Burnett Show* debut. The Corporation for Public Broadcasting is established.

Theater. Harold Pinter's *The Homecoming*, Tom Stoppard's *Rosencrantz and Guildenstern Are Dead*, and the musical *Hallelujah, Baby!* debut on Broadway.

Miscellaneous. The so-called Summer of Love takes place, as thousands of mostly young people convene in the Haight-Ashbury district of San Francisco and embrace a countercultural lifestyle. Lynda Bird Johnson is married at White House.

1992 – 25 Years Ago

After more than 12 years of fighting in El Salvador, the military-led government and a coalition of guerilla groups sign a peace accord Jan. 16.

Representatives of 12 member nations Feb. 7 sign the Maastricht Treaty to create the European Union and its common currency, the euro.

War breaks out in the former Yugoslavian republic of Bosnia and Herzegovina in Apr. between Bosniaks (Bosnian Muslims), Serbs, and Croats; the violence included many incidents of what was euphemistically called "ethnic cleansing."

More than 50 are killed in Los Angeles riots beginning Apr. 29 after a jury acquits four police officers in the beating—caught on video by a bystander—of Rodney King, a black motorist.

Category 5 storm Hurricane Andrew ravages South Florida and Louisiana Aug. 24-26, causing 65 deaths.

Randall Weaver surrenders Aug. 31 after 11-day standoff with federal agents at his Ruby Ridge, ID, cabin, during which his wife, son, and a federal marshal were killed.

Arkansas Gov. Bill Clinton (D) is elected the 42nd U.S. president, Nov. 3, defeating Pres. George H. W. Bush (R) and Texas businessman Ross Perot.

A UN-sanctioned military force, led by U.S. troops, arrives in Somalia Dec. 9.

Presidents of the U.S., Canada, and Mexico Dec. 17 sign the North American Free Trade Agreement (NAFTA).

Pres. George H. W. Bush Dec. 24 pardons former Defense Sec. Caspar Weinberger and five other Reagan administration officials implicated in the Iran-contra scandal.

Art. New York's Whitney Museum exhibits career retrospective of Jean-Michel Basquiat. *Agrippa* by William Gibson and Dennis Ashbaugh; Damien Hirst's *Pharmacy*; Jeff Koons's *Puppy*; Mona Hatoum's *Light Sentence*; Madonna's *Sex*.

Film. Disney's *Aladdin*; *The Bodyguard* starring Kevin Costner and Whitney Houston; *Basic Instinct* starring Michael Douglas and Sharon Stone; *Bram Stoker's Dracula* directed by Francis Ford Coppola and starring Gary Oldman, Winona Ryder, and Anthony Hopkins; *A Few Good Men* starring Tom Cruise, Demi Moore, and Jack Nicholson; *Howards End*; *A League of Their Own*; Spike Lee's *Malcolm X* starring Denzel Washington; *My Cousin Vinnie*;

Quentin Tarantino's *Reservoir Dogs*; *Scent of a Woman*; *Sister Act*; Baz Luhrmann's *Strictly Ballroom*; Clint Eastwood's *Unforgiven*.

Health and medicine. AIDS becomes the leading cause of death for men aged 25-44. Responding to safety concerns, the FDA announces a moratorium on the use of silicone breast implants.

Literature. Robert Olen Butler's *A Good Scent From a Strange Mountain*; Cormac McCarthy's *All the Pretty Horses*; Ian McEwan's *Black Dogs*; Terry McMillan's *Waiting to Exhale*; Toni Morrison's *Jazz*; Michael Ondaatje's *The English Patient*; Neil Stephenson's *Snow Crash*; Barry Unsworth's *Sacred Hunger*; Robert James Waller's *The Bridges of Madison County*.

Music. Philip Glass's *Symphony No. 1 "Low"*; Karel Goeyvaerts's *Aquarius*.

Nonfiction. Al Gore's *Earth in the Balance*; John Gray's *Men Are From Mars, Women Are From Venus*; Nick Hornby's *Fever Pitch*; Rush Limbaugh's *The Way Things Ought to Be*; David McCullough's *Truman*.

Pop music. CD unit sales overtake cassettes for first time. Boyz II Men's "End of the Road"; Eric Clapton's "Tears in Heaven" and *Unplugged*; Dr. Dre's *The Chronic*; Guns N' Roses' "November Rain"; *The Bodyguard* soundtrack feat. Whitney Houston's "I Will Always Love You"; R.E.M.'s *Automatic for the People*; Sir Mix-a-Lot's "Baby Got Back."

Science and technology. Microsoft releases the Windows 3.1 operating system.

Sports. Boxer Mike Tyson is convicted of rape in Indiana. U.S. men's basketball "Dream Team" is a highlight at Olympic Games in Barcelona.

Television. Cartoon Network is launched. Televised *Freddie Mercury Tribute Concert* has audience of up to 1 billion; Vice Pres. Dan Quayle condemns CBS sitcom character Murphy Brown for being a single parent. *Barney & Friends*, *The Larry Sanders Show*, and *Melrose Place* debut.

Theater. *Crazy for You* and *Dancing at Lughnasa* win Tony Awards. *Jelly's Last Jam* premieres.

Miscellaneous. Euro Disney (now Disneyland Paris) opens. Infamous crime boss John Gotti is convicted and sentenced to life imprisonment. After 350+ years, Vatican admits Galileo was correct about heliocentric Earth orbit. British royals Charles and Diana separate.

WORLD ALMANAC EDITORS' PICKS
2016 Time Capsule

The editors of *The World Almanac* have selected the following items as representative of the year 2016.

- Everything associated with the 2016 presidential campaign, including Hillary Clinton's complete email archives, 20 years of Donald Trump's federal income tax returns, and a pocket-sized copy of the Constitution.
- A vial of lead-contaminated water from Flint, MI, where a federal state of emergency was declared in response to the city's municipal water crisis in Jan.
- A copy of Chipotle's new food safety guidelines, updated in the wake of a series of foodborne-illness infections that prompted the fast-food chain to close its approx. 2,000 U.S. stores for four hours Feb. 8, 2016, in order to refresh employees on proper food handling.
- The U.S. Supreme Court seat vacated by the Feb. 13 death of Associate Justice Antonin Scalia and still vacant when the court convened in Oct. for the 2016 term.
- The leaked documents known collectively as the Panama Papers, the first of which were made public Apr. 3 and which documented the sometimes-illegal use of offshore corporations, such as for tax evasion.
- A Leicester City "Premier League Champions" scarf, in celebration of the team's 5,000-to-1 longshot win of the English Premier League soccer title in May.
- Lin-Manuel Miranda's ponytail, which he cut off after ending his run playing the title character in his Broadway smash-hit musical *Hamilton*, and one of the 11 Tony Awards won by the show June 12.
- Ballots from the UK's June 23 Brexit referendum, in which voters elected to withdraw from the European Union, 51.9%-48.1%.

- A lifetime supply of DEET, intended to combat Zika virus-infected mosquitoes, which by July were found to be transmitting the virus in Florida.
- A Snorlax, one of the rarer creatures players could capture in the *Pokémon Go* augmented reality game, released in the U.S. July 6.
- Mementos from the 2016 Summer Olympics held in Rio de Janeiro, Brazil, Aug. 5-21, including Michael Phelps's historic 28th career Olympic medal and the Olympic flag under which the first-ever all-refugee team marched in the opening ceremony.
- The championship rings won by the Cleveland Cavaliers in June and Chicago Cubs in Nov., ending lengthy title droughts.
- An EpiPen, the device used to treat extreme allergic reactions, whose manufacturer, Mylan, faced public scrutiny in late summer 2016 over its steep list price increases.
- Legal papers filed Sept. 19 in Los Angeles seeking to dissolve the marriage of the celebrity couple widely known as Brangelina (Angelina Jolie and Brad Pitt).
- The peace treaty between the Colombian government and rebel group FARC, intended to end decades of conflict, rejected by voters in an Oct. referendum.
- More than 1.5 million deposit accounts and 565,000 credit card accounts opened without customers' consent by Wells Fargo employees since 2011, forcing the resignation of the company's CEO Oct. 12.

ECONOMICS

U.S. Gross Domestic Product, 1930-2015

Source: Bureau of Economic Analysis, U.S. Dept. of Commerce
(in billions of current dollars)

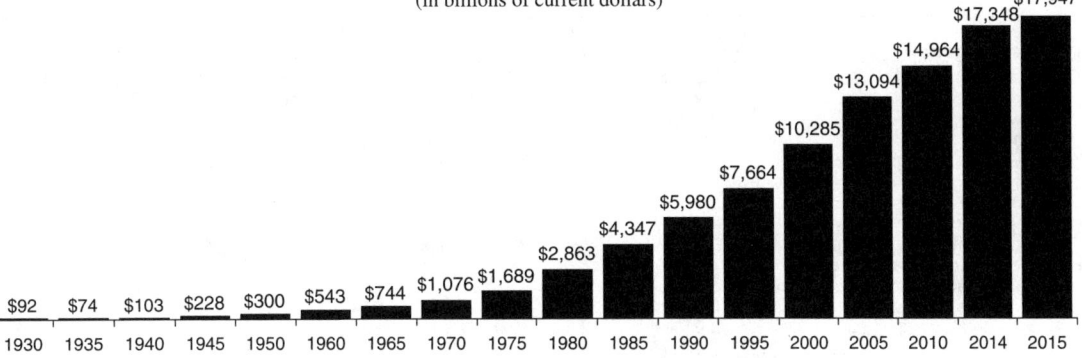

1930	$92
1935	$74
1940	$103
1945	$228
1950	$300
1960	$543
1965	$744
1970	$1,076
1975	$1,689
1980	$2,863
1985	$4,347
1990	$5,980
1995	$7,664
2000	$10,285
2005	$13,094
2010	$14,964
2014	$17,348
2015	$17,947

Tracking the U.S. Economy, 1960-2015

Source: Bureau of Economic Analysis, U.S. Dept. of Commerce
(in billions of current dollars, revised)

	1960	1970	1980	1990	2000	2010	2014	2015
Gross domestic product	$543.3	$1,075.9	$2,862.5	$5,979.6	$10,284.8	$14,964.4	$17,348.1	$17,947.0
Gross national product	546.4	1,082.3	2,896.7	6,014.3	10,321.8	15,170.3	17,611.2	18,160.6
Less: Consumption of fixed capital. . .	67.9	136.8	426.0	886.8	1,514.2	2,381.6	2,746.7	2,821.3
Equals: Net national product.	478.5	945.5	2,470.7	5,127.5	8,807.5	12,788.8	14,864.5	15,339.3
Less: Statistical discrepancy	−1.4	5.3	43.9	91.4	−99.5	49.2	−212.0	−207.0
Equals: National income	479.9	940.1	2,426.8	5,036.1	8,907.0	12,739.5	15,076.5	15,546.2
Less: Corporate profits with inventory valuation and capital consumption adjustments.	54.7	86.2	223.6	417.2	781.2	1,746.4	2,072.9	2,008.9
Taxes on production and imports less subsidies[1]	43.4	86.6	190.5	398.0	662.7	1,001.2	1,155.8	1,177.3
Contributions for government social insurance	16.4	46.4	166.2	410.1	705.8	984.1	1,159.0	1,204.0
Net interest and miscellaneous payments on assets	10.7	40.5	186.2	450.1	565.0	489.4	532.3	523.8
Business current transfer payments (net)	1.7	4.4	14.0	39.2	85.3	128.5	127.3	141.2
Current surplus of government enterprises	0.5	−1.2	−5.1	3.2	10.7	−22.9	−18.3	−16.5
Plus: Personal income receipts on assets	44.3	112.7	386.0	991.2	1,453.5	1,739.6	2,117.5	2,180.5
Personal current transfer receipts	25.7	74.7	280.1	596.9	1,087.3	2,324.7	2,529.2	2,662.7
Equals: Personal income.	422.5	864.6	2,317.5	4,906.4	8,637.1	12,477.1	14,694.2	15,350.7
Addenda:								
Gross domestic income	544.6	1,070.5	2,818.6	5,888.2	10,384.3	14,915.2	17,560.1	18,153.9
Gross national income	547.8	1,076.9	2,852.8	5,922.9	10,421.3	15,121.1	17,823.2	18,367.5

Note: Numbers may not add up to totals due to rounding. (1) Subsidies are included net of the current surplus of government enterprises.

U.S. Gross Domestic Product, 2000-15

Source: Bureau of Economic Analysis, U.S. Dept. of Commerce

	Billions of current dollars				Billions of constant (2009) dollars			
	2000	2005	2014	2015	2000	2005	2014	2015
Gross domestic product	$10,284.8	$13,093.7	$17,348.1	$17,947.0	$12,559.7	$14,234.2	$15,961.7	$16,348.9
Personal consumption expenditures	6,792.4	8,794.1	11,865.9	12,271.9	8,170.7	9,531.8	10,875.7	11,213.3
Goods.	2,452.9	3,080.3	3,948.4	3,978.8	2,588.3	3,177.2	3,731.2	3,869.6
Durable goods	912.6	1,127.2	1,280.2	1,328.7	758.3	1,046.9	1,384.1	1,466.5
Nondurable goods	1,540.3	1,953.1	2,668.2	2,650.1	1,863.6	2,132.3	2,367.8	2,430.0
Services	4,339.5	5,713.8	7,917.5	8,293.1	5,599.3	6,353.4	7,144.6	7,345.3
Gross private domestic investment.	2,033.8	2,527.1	2,860.0	3,020.6	2,375.5	2,672.6	2,717.7	2,851.9
Fixed investment.	1,979.2	2,467.5	2,782.9	2,911.4	2,316.2	2,611.0	2,633.8	2,740.2
Nonresidential	1,493.8	1,611.5	2,233.7	2,301.9	1,647.7	1,717.4	2,148.3	2,209.3
Structures	318.1	345.6	507.0	497.2	533.5	421.2	464.6	457.7
Equipment.	766.1	790.7	1,036.7	1,076.1	726.9	801.6	1,026.2	1,057.8
Intellectual property products.	409.5	475.1	690.0	728.6	426.1	495.0	659.5	696.8
Residential	485.4	856.1	549.2	609.5	637.9	872.6	486.4	529.6
Change in inventories.	54.5	59.6	77.1	109.2	66.2	64.3	68.0	97.5
Net exports of goods and services.	−375.8	−721.2	−530.0	−528.9	−477.8	−782.3	−442.5	−543.4
Exports.	1,096.8	1,308.9	2,341.9	2,253.4	1,258.4	1,381.9	2,086.4	2,110.1
Goods.	797.3	926.6	1,618.0	1,504.9	902.2	970.6	1,443.0	1,439.7
Services	299.6	382.3	723.9	748.5	354.3	410.3	642.9	668.7
Imports.	1,472.6	2,030.1	2,871.9	2,782.3	1,736.2	2,164.2	2,528.9	2,653.5
Goods.	1,251.5	1,719.4	2,388.5	2,280.6	1,455.4	1,817.9	2,076.5	2,176.1
Services	221.2	310.7	483.4	501.8	276.4	341.1	450.8	475.8
Government consumption expenditures and gross investment.	1,834.4	2,493.7	3,152.1	3,183.4	2,498.2	2,826.2	2,838.3	2,858.9
Federal	632.4	946.3	1,219.9	1,224.6	817.7	1,034.8	1,116.3	1,113.2
National defense.	391.7	608.3	748.2	740.8	512.3	665.5	689.1	680.6
Nondefense	240.7	338.1	471.6	483.9	305.4	369.4	427.0	432.2
State and local	1,202.0	1,547.4	1,932.3	1,958.8	1,689.1	1,792.3	1,720.8	1,744.3

U.S. National Income by Type, 1930-2015

Source: Bureau of Economic Analysis, U.S. Dept. of Commerce
(in billions of current dollars)

	1930	1940	1950	1970	1980	1990	2000	2010	2014	2015
NATIONAL INCOME[1]	$83.1	$91.6	$267.0	$940.1	$2,426.8	$5,036.1	$8,907.0	$12,739.5	$15,076.5	$15,546.2
Employee compensation	47.2	52.8	158.5	625.1	1,626.2	3,342.7	5,856.6	7,961.4	9,248.9	9,666.6
Wages and salaries	46.2	49.9	147.3	551.6	1,373.4	2,741.2	4,825.9	6,377.5	7,477.8	7,834.9
Government	5.2	8.5	22.6	117.2	261.5	519.0	779.8	1,191.1	1,237.2	1,268.8
Other.	41.0	41.4	124.6	434.3	1,112.0	2,222.2	4,046.1	5,186.4	6,240.5	6,566.1
Supplements to wages and salaries. . .	1.0	2.9	11.2	73.6	252.8	601.5	1,030.7	1,583.9	1,771.2	1,831.7
Employer contributions for employee pension and insurance funds	1.0	1.6	7.8	49.7	163.9	395.0	685.5	1,114.6	1,224.0	1,264.3
Employer contributions for government social insurance	0.0	1.4	3.4	23.8	88.9	206.5	345.2	469.4	547.2	567.4
Proprietors' income with inventory valuation and capital consumption adjustments	10.9	12.2	37.5	77.8	171.6	354.4	757.8	1,032.7	1,346.7	1,388.3
Farm	3.9	4.1	12.9	12.9	11.7	32.2	31.5	46.0	78.1	59.9
Nonfarm	7.0	8.2	24.6	64.9	159.9	322.3	726.3	986.7	1,268.6	1,328.4
Rental income of persons with capital consumption adjustments.	5.4	3.8	8.8	20.7	19.7	31.4	187.7	402.8	610.8	656.6
Corporate profits with inventory valuation and capital consumption adjustments	7.5	9.9	36.1	86.2	223.6	417.2	781.2	1,746.4	2,072.9	2,008.9
Taxes on corporate income	0.8	2.8	17.9	34.8	87.2	145.4	265.1	370.6	513.9	529.7
Profits after tax with inventory valuation and capital consumption adjustments	6.7	7.0	18.1	51.5	136.4	271.7	516.1	1,375.9	1,559.1	1,479.2
Net dividends	5.5	4.0	8.8	24.3	64.1	169.1	384.7	564.0	860.0	888.6
Undistributed profits with inventory valuation and capital consumption adjustments	1.2	3.0	9.3	27.2	72.3	102.7	131.4	811.9	699.0	590.6
Net interest and miscellaneous payments.	4.8	3.3	3.2	40.5	186.2	450.1	565.0	489.4	532.3	523.8

Note: Numbers may not add up to totals because of rounding and incomplete enumeration. (1) National income is the aggregate of labor and property earnings that arise in the production of goods and services. It is the sum of employee compensation, proprietors' income, rental income, adjusted corporate profits, and net interest. It measures the total factor costs of goods and services produced by the economy. Income is measured before deduction of taxes. Total national income figures include adjustments not itemized.

U.S. National Income by Industry, 2000-15

Source: Bureau of Economic Analysis, U.S. Dept. of Commerce
(in billions of current dollars)

	2000	2005	2010	2012	2013	2014	2015
National income without capital consumption adjustment.	$8,817.5	$11,338.8	$12,662.6	$14,043.0	$14,422.7	$15,036.1	$15,787.0
Domestic industries	8,780.5	11,246.3	12,456.7	13,805.5	14,172.4	14,773.0	15,573.4
Private industries	7,729.4	9,865.5	10,776.9	12,104.0	12,454.0	13,015.2	13,772.0
Agriculture, forestry, fishing, and hunting	73.8	94.0	123.1	154.3	183.1	175.8	160.2
Mining	90.7	175.0	184.7	241.6	253.6	254.6	248.7
Utilities.	137.3	162.1	188.2	167.4	179.7	179.2	186.0
Construction	470.7	648.9	523.4	587.0	619.7	667.8	724.7
Manufacturing	1,243.1	1,326.7	1,350.2	1,552.1	1,589.5	1,635.2	1,756.8
Durable goods	758.2	753.2	752.8	885.0	905.0	937.8	1,016.8
Nondurable goods	485.0	573.5	597.5	667.2	684.4	697.5	740.0
Wholesale trade	570.6	685.2	737.3	848.5	878.5	909.3	955.8
Retail trade	666.7	857.0	872.2	964.1	998.2	1,027.4	1,082.1
Transportation and warehousing	268.5	333.4	368.4	417.2	426.3	450.1	509.0
Information	306.8	423.0	442.7	495.0	540.7	554.9	592.2
Finance, insurance, real estate, rental, and leasing	1,472.6	1,969.1	2,142.5	2,411.3	2,436.3	2,618.9	2,760.0
Professional and business services[1]	1,115.7	1,428.1	1,697.4	1,913.8	1,927.3	2,013.1	2,128.1
Educational services, health care, and social assistance	689.4	988.4	1,294.8	1,395.5	1,431.8	1,486.4	1,560.8
Arts, entertainment, recreation, accommodation, and food services	340.1	437.2	483.3	551.8	577.8	609.4	657.4
Other services, except government.	283.3	337.4	368.4	404.4	411.6	433.1	450.0
Government.	1,051.0	1,380.8	1,679.8	1,701.5	1,718.3	1,757.8	1,801.4
Rest of the world	37.0	92.6	206.0	237.6	250.4	263.1	213.6

Note: Estimates based on the 2002 North American Industry Classification System (NAICS). (1) Consists of professional, scientific, and technical services; management of companies and enterprises; and administrative and waste management services.

Consumer Price Index

The Consumer Price Index (CPI) is a measure of the change in prices over time of one or more kinds of basic consumer goods and services. The overall CPI is based on the price of food, clothing, shelter, and fuels; transportation fares; charges for doctors' and dentists' services; drug prices; and the cost of other goods and services bought for day-to-day living. Since Jan. 1988, the base period for comparison has been 1982-84, which equals 100.0. The price of apparel, entertainment and recreation, and education and communication have not risen significantly, while the cost of medical care has more than quadrupled since 1982-84. The Consumer Price Index for all urban consumers (CPI-U), covers about 87% of the total U.S. population. The Bureau of Labor Statistics also publishes a separate Consumer Price Index for urban wage earners and clerical workers (CPI-W), which covers about 32% of the total U.S. population.

Distribution of U.S. Total Personal Income, 1930-2015

Source: Bureau of Economic Analysis, U.S. Dept. of Commerce
(in billions of current dollars, except for per capita figures)

Year	Personal income	Personal current taxes	Disposable personal income	Personal outlays	Personal savings	Savings as % of income[1]	Disposable personal income per capita Current dollars	Disposable personal income per capita Constant (2009) dollars
1930	$76.5	$1.6	$74.9	$71.6	$3.3	4.4%	$608	$6,411
1940	79.4	1.7	77.7	72.4	5.3	6.8	588	7,464
1950	233.9	18.9	215.0	195.0	20.0	9.3	1,417	10,033
1960	422.5	46.1	376.5	338.6	37.8	10.0	2,083	11,877
1970	864.6	103.1	761.5	665.5	96.1	12.6	3,713	16,643
1980	2,316.8	298.9	2,018.0	1,804.8	213.2	10.6	8,861	20,159
1990	4,904.5	592.7	4,311.8	3,976.3	335.4	7.8	17,235	25,556
2000	8,637.1	1,236.6	7,400.5	7,092.8	307.7	4.2	26,206	31,524
2005	10,614.0	1,213.2	9,400.8	9,157.7	243.1	2.6	31,760	34,424
2009	12,094.8	1,152.3	10,942.5	10,275.1	667.4	6.1	35,616	35,616
2010	12,477.1	1,239.3	11,237.9	10,607.9	630.0	5.6	36,274	35,684
2011	13,254.5	1,453.2	11,801.4	11,091.2	710.1	6.0	37,804	36,298
2012	13,915.1	1,511.4	12,403.7	11,457.0	946.7	7.6	39,441	37,166
2013	14,068.4	1,672.8	12,395.6	11,805.7	589.9	4.8	39,128	36,374
2014	14,694.2	1,780.2	12,913.9	12,293.7	620.2	4.8	40,453	37,077
2015	15,350.7	1,947.4	13,403.2	12,717.5	685.7	5.1	41,663	38,069

Note: Personal income minus current taxes equals disposable income; disposable income minus outlays equals savings. Figures may not add up to totals because of rounding. (1) Personal savings as a percentage of disposable personal income.

U.S. Consumer Price Index, 1915-2015

Source: Bureau of Labor Statistics, U.S. Dept. of Labor

Excluding 2009, prices as measured by the U.S. Consumer Price Index have risen steadily since World War II. What cost $1.00 in 1982-84 cost about $0.10 in 1913, $0.18 in 1945, and $2.37 in 2015.

(Annual averages of monthly figures, for all urban consumers. **1982-84 = 100.**)

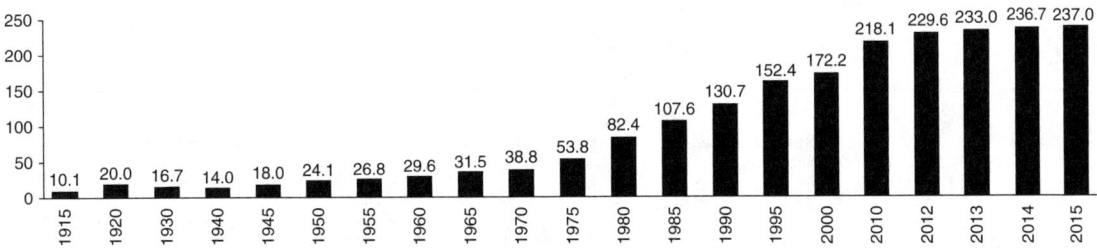

U.S. Consumer Price Index by Major Group, 1915-2015

Source: Bureau of Labor Statistics, U.S. Dept. of Labor
For all urban consumers. **1982-84 = 100**, unless otherwise noted.

Year	All items	Apparel	Food & beverages	Housing	Transpor- tation	Medical care	Entertainment & recreation[1]	Educ. & communi- cation[1]	Other goods & services
1915	10.1	15.3	—	—	—	—	—	—	—
1920	20.0	43.1	—	—	—	—	—	—	—
1930	16.7	24.2	—	—	—	—	—	—	—
1940	14.0	21.8	—	—	14.2	10.4	—	—	—
1945	18.0	31.4	—	—	15.9	11.9	—	—	—
1950	24.1	40.3	—	—	22.7	15.1	—	—	—
1955	26.8	42.9	—	—	25.8	18.2	—	—	—
1960	29.6	45.7	—	—	29.8	22.3	—	—	—
1965	31.5	47.8	—	—	31.9	25.2	—	—	—
1970	38.8	59.2	40.1	36.4	37.5	34.0	—	—	40.9
1975	53.8	72.5	60.2	50.7	50.1	47.5	—	—	53.9
1980	82.4	90.9	86.7	81.1	83.1	74.9	—	—	75.2
1985	107.6	105.0	105.6	107.7	106.4	113.5	—	—	114.5
1990	130.7	124.1	132.1	128.5	120.5	162.8	—	—	159.0
1995	152.4	132.0	148.9	148.5	139.1	220.5	94.5	92.2	206.9
2000	172.2	129.6	168.4	169.6	153.3	260.8	103.3	102.5	271.1
2005	195.3	119.5	191.2	195.7	173.9	323.2	109.4	113.7	313.4
2010	218.1	119.5	220.0	216.3	193.4	388.4	113.3	129.9	381.3
2011	224.9	122.1	227.9	219.1	212.4	400.3	113.4	131.5	387.2
2012	229.6	126.3	233.7	222.7	217.3	414.9	114.7	133.8	394.4
2013	233.0	127.4	237.0	227.4	217.4	425.1	115.3	135.9	401.0
2014	236.7	127.5	242.4	233.2	215.9	435.3	115.5	137.5	408.1
2015	237.0	125.9	246.8	238.1	199.1	446.8	115.9	138.2	414.9

— = Comparable data not available. (1) Dec. 1997 = 100. Entertainment was reclassified as Recreation in 1997. Data is not seasonally adjusted.

Consumer Price Indexes by Region and Major Cities, 1990-2015

Source: Bureau of Labor Statistics, U.S. Dept. of Labor
For all urban consumers; % change not annualized. **1982-84 = 100**, unless otherwise noted.

Region and city	1990	1995	2000	2005	2010	2012	2013	2014	2015
U.S. city average	130.7	152.4	172.2	195.3	218.1	229.6	233.0	236.7	237.0
Northeast urban	**136.3**	**159.1**	**179.4**	**207.5**	**233.9**	**245.7**	**249.0**	**252.5**	**252.2**
Boston-Brockton-Nashua, MA-NH-ME-CT	138.9	158.6	183.6	216.4	237.4	247.7	251.1	255.2	256.7
New York-Northern New Jersey-Long Island, NY-NJ-CT-PA	138.5	162.2	182.5	212.7	240.9	252.6	256.8	260.2	260.6
Philadelphia-Wilmington-Atlantic City, PA-NJ-DE-MD	135.8	158.7	176.5	204.2	227.7	238.1	240.9	244.1	243.9
Pittsburgh, PA	126.2	149.2	168.0	189.8	215.4	232.9	235.9	239.0	240.6
Midwest urban	**127.4**	**148.4**	**168.3**	**188.4**	**208.0**	**219.1**	**222.2**	**225.4**	**224.2**
Chicago-Gary-Kenosha, IL-IN-WI	131.7	153.3	173.8	194.3	212.9	222.0	224.5	228.5	227.8
Cincinnati-Hamilton, OH-KY-IN	126.5	146.2	164.8	181.6	204.7	216.3	220.0	224.1	223.3
Cleveland-Akron, OH	129.0	147.9	168.0	187.9	204.6	214.7	217.5	220.6	220.5
Detroit-Ann Arbor-Flint, MI	128.6	148.6	169.8	190.8	205.1	216.1	219.5	221.8	218.7
Kansas City, MO-KS	126.0	145.3	166.6	185.3	205.4	218.5	221.6	222.7	222.3
Milwaukee-Racine, WI	126.2	151.0	168.6	185.2	209.6	221.1	225.1	227.8	226.6
Minneapolis-St. Paul, MN-WI	127.0	147.0	170.1	193.1	211.7	224.5	228.8	232.0	230.6
St. Louis, MO-IL	128.1	145.2	163.1	186.2	203.2	214.8	218.0	220.2	219.3
South urban	**127.9**	**149.0**	**167.2**	**188.3**	**211.3**	**223.2**	**226.7**	**230.6**	**230.1**
Atlanta, GA	131.7	150.9	170.6	188.9	203.5	212.8	216.3	221.0	221.6
Dallas-Fort Worth, TX	125.1	144.9	164.7	184.7	201.6	212.2	216.0	218.4	217.5
Houston-Galveston-Brazoria, TX	120.6	139.8	154.2	175.6	194.2	204.2	207.6	213.4	213.0
Miami-Fort Lauderdale, FL	128.0	148.9	167.8	194.3	223.1	235.2	238.2	243.1	245.4
Tampa-St. Petersburg-Clearwater, FL[1]	111.7	129.7	145.7	168.5	193.5	203.6	206.8	210.8	211.6
Washington-Baltimore, DC-MD-VA-WV[2]	NA	NA	107.6	124.3	142.2	150.2	152.5	154.8	155.4
West urban	**131.5**	**153.5**	**174.8**	**198.9**	**221.2**	**232.4**	**235.8**	**240.2**	**243.0**
Anchorage, AK	118.6	138.9	150.9	171.8	195.1	205.9	212.4	215.8	216.9
Denver-Boulder-Greeley, CO	120.9	147.9	173.2	190.9	212.4	224.6	230.8	237.2	240.0
Honolulu, HI	138.1	168.1	176.3	197.8	234.9	249.5	253.9	257.6	260.2
Los Angeles-Riverside-Orange County, CA	135.9	154.6	171.6	201.8	225.9	236.6	239.2	242.4	244.6
Phoenix-Mesa, AZ[3]	NA	NA	NA	108.3	118.2	124.2	125.8	127.8	128.0
Portland-Salem, OR-WA	127.4	153.2	178.0	196.0	218.3	229.8	235.5	241.2	244.2
San Diego, CA	138.4	156.8	182.8	220.6	245.5	257.0	260.3	265.1	269.4
San Francisco-Oakland-San Jose, CA	132.1	151.6	180.2	202.7	227.5	239.6	245.0	252.0	258.6
Seattle-Tacoma-Bremerton, WA	126.8	152.3	179.2	200.2	226.7	238.7	241.6	246.0	249.4

NA = Not available. **Note:** Data is not seasonally adjusted. (1) 1987 = 100. (2) Nov. 1996 = 100. (3) Dec. 2001 = 100.

World's Wealthiest Individuals, 2016

Source: *Forbes* magazine, Mar. 1, 2016

Rank	Name, country	Source of wealth	Net worth (bil)
1.	Bill Gates, U.S.	Microsoft	$75.0
2.	Amancio Ortega, Spain	Zara	67.0
3.	Warren Buffett, U.S.	Berkshire Hathaway	60.8
4.	Carlos Slim Helú, Mexico	Telecom	50.0
5.	Jeff Bezos, U.S.	Amazon.com	45.2
6.	Mark Zuckerberg, U.S.	Facebook	44.6
7.	Larry Ellison, U.S.	Oracle	43.6
8.	Michael Bloomberg, U.S.	Bloomberg, LP	40.0
9.	Charles Koch, U.S.	Manufacturing, energy	39.6
9.	David Koch, U.S.	Manufacturing, energy	39.6
11.	Liliane Bettencourt, France	L'Oreal	36.1
12.	Larry Page, U.S.	Google	35.2
13.	Sergey Brin, U.S.	Google	34.4
14.	Bernard Arnault, France	Louis Vuitton-Moët Hennessy	34.0
15.	Jim Walton, U.S.	Wal-Mart	33.6
16.	Alice Walton, U.S.	Wal-Mart	32.3
17.	S. Robson Walton, U.S.	Wal-Mart	31.9
18.	Wang Jianlin, China	Real estate	28.7
19.	Jorge Paulo Lemann, Brazil	Beer	27.8
20.	Li Ka-shing, Hong Kong	Diversified	27.1
21.	Beate Heister and Karl Albrecht Jr., Germany	Aldi supermarkets	$25.9
22.	Sheldon Adelson, U.S.	Sands casinos	25.2
23.	George Soros, U.S.	Hedge funds	24.9
24.	Phil Knight, U.S.	Nike	24.4
25.	David Thomson, Canada	Media, publishing	23.8
26.	Steve Ballmer, U.S.	Microsoft	23.5
27.	Forrest Mars Jr., U.S.	Candy	23.4
27.	Jacqueline Mars, U.S.	Candy	23.4
27.	John Mars, U.S.	Candy	23.4
30.	Maria Franca Fissolo, Italy	Nutella, chocolates	22.1
31.	Lee Shau Kee, Hong Kong	Real estate	21.5
32.	Stefan Persson, Sweden	H&M	20.8
33.	Jack Ma, China	Alibaba	20.5
34.	Theo Albrecht Jr., Germany	Aldi, Trader Joe's	20.3
35.	Michael Dell, U.S.	Dell Computers	19.8
36.	Mukesh Ambani, India	Petrochemicals, oil, gas	19.3
37.	Leonardo Del Vecchio, Italy	Eyeglasses	18.7
38.	Susanne Klatten, Germany	BMW, pharmaceuticals	18.5
39.	Georg Schaeffler, Germany	Ball bearings	18.1
40.	Paul Allen, U.S.	Microsoft, investments	17.5

Poverty Thresholds by Family Size, 1980-2015

Source: U.S. Census Bureau, U.S. Dept. of Commerce

	1980	1990	2000	2010	2015		1980	1990	2000	2010	2015
1 person	$4,190	$6,652	$8,791	$11,137	$12,082	3 people	$6,565	$10,419	$13,740	$17,373	$18,871
Under age 65	4,290	6,800	8,959	11,344	12,331	4 people	8,414	13,359	17,604	22,315	24,257
Age 65 or older	3,949	6,268	8,259	10,458	11,367	5 people	9,966	15,792	20,815	26,442	28,741
2 people	5,363	8,509	11,235	14,216	15,391	6 people	11,269	17,839	23,533	29,904	32,542
Householder under age 65	5,537	8,794	11,589	14,676	15,952	7 people	12,761	20,241	26,750	34,019	36,998
						8 people	14,199	22,582	29,701	37,953	41,029
Householder age 65 or older	4,983	7,905	10,418	13,194	14,342	9 or more people	16,896	26,848	35,150	45,224	49,177

Note: Weighted averages; not used for computing poverty data.

Median Income by Race, Hispanic Origin, and Sex, 1948-2015

Source: Current Population Survey, U.S. Census Bureau, U.S. Dept. of Commerce

Race, Hispanic origin, and year		Male			Female		
		Number with income (thous.)	Median income Current dollars	Median income 2015 dollars	Number with income (thous.)	Median income Current dollars	Median income 2015 dollars
All races	2015	112,322	$37,138	$37,138	114,440	$23,769	$23,769
	2014	110,372	36,302	36,344	112,599	22,240	22,266
	2010	105,191	32,205	35,010	107,220	20,775	22,585
	2000	98,504	28,343	39,008	101,704	16,063	22,107
	1990	88,220	20,293	35,705	92,245	10,070	17,718
	1980	78,661	12,530	34,327	80,826	4,920	13,479
	1970	65,008	6,670	36,346	51,647	2,237	12,190
	1960	55,172	4,080	28,585	36,526	1,261	8,835
	1950	47,585	2,570	22,096	24,651	953	8,193
	1948	47,370	2,396	20,600	22,725	1,009	8,675
White	2015	90,375	39,491	39,491	89,535	24,278	24,278
	2014	89,203	37,574	37,617	88,417	22,479	22,505
	2010	86,368	34,374	37,368	85,486	20,896	22,716
	2000	83,372	29,797	41,009	84,123	16,079	22,129
	1990	76,480	21,170	37,248	78,566	10,317	18,152
	1980	69,420	13,328	36,513	70,573	4,947	13,553
	1970	58,447	7,011	38,204	45,288	2,266	12,348
	1960	49,788	4,296	30,098	32,001	1,352	9,472
	1950	NA	2,709	23,291	NA	1,060	9,113
	1948	NA	2,510	21,580	NA	1,133	9,741
White, not Hispanic	2015	74,629	42,207	42,207	75,992	25,629	25,629
	2014	73,897	41,072	41,119	75,502	24,005	24,033
	2010	72,723	37,154	40,390	73,995	21,715	23,607
	2000	72,530	31,508	43,364	75,206	16,665	22,936
	1990	69,987	21,958	38,635	72,939	10,581	18,617
	1980	65,564	13,681	37,480	67,084	4,980	13,643
Black	2015	12,955	27,396	27,396	15,710	21,514	21,514
	2014	12,539	26,433	26,463	15,383	20,938	20,962
	2010	11,433	23,086	25,097	14,212	19,548	21,251
	2000	9,905	21,343	29,374	12,461	15,881	21,857
	1990	8,820	12,868	22,641	10,687	8,328	14,653
	1980	7,387	8,009	21,941	8,596	4,580	12,547
	1970	5,844	4,157	22,652	5,844	2,063	11,242
	1960	5,384	2,260	15,834	4,525	837	5,864
	1950	NA	1,471	12,647	NA	474	4,075
	1948	NA	1,363	11,718	NA	492	4,230
Asian	2015	6,555	42,268	42,268	6,748	26,572	26,572
	2014	6,411	40,457	40,504	6,564	25,231	25,260
	2010	5,406	35,121	38,180	5,604	23,552	25,604
	2000	4,303	30,833	42,435	4,192	17,356	23,887
	1990	2,235	19,394	34,123	2,333	11,086	19,506
Hispanic	2015	17,549	28,110	28,110	15,415	18,905	18,905
	2014	17,036	26,675	26,706	14,691	17,585	17,605
	2010	15,106	22,420	24,373	12,947	16,292	17,711
	2000	11,343	19,498	26,835	9,431	12,248	16,857
	1990	6,767	13,470	23,700	5,903	7,532	13,252
	1980	3,996	9,659	26,462	3,617	4,405	12,068

NA = Not available. **Note:** Income for persons 15 years of age and over beginning in Mar. 1980; 14 years of age and over as of Mar. of the following year for previous years. Beginning in 2010, totals for White, Black, and Asian include those who identified themselves as being that race in combination with some other race. Before 2010, Asian category includes Pacific Islanders. Hispanic persons may be of any race.

Consumer Credit Outstanding, 2010-15

Source: Federal Reserve System

(in billions of dollars as of Dec. of year shown, not seasonally adjusted)

	2010	2014	2015		2010	2014	2015
TOTAL	$2,647.2	$3,318.0	$3,534.6	Credit unions	$36.3	$46.8	$49.4
Major holders				Nonfinancial business	25.5	24.0	23.2
Depository institutions	1,185.5	1,343.1	1,428.3	Pools of securitized assets[3]	31.4	28.9	23.5
Finance companies	705.0	684.1	681.1				
Credit unions	226.5	302.8	341.7	**Nonrevolving[3]**	1,807.8	2,426.5	2,596.7
Federal government[1]	363.8	846.2	949.7	Depository institutions	520.8	611.6	641.5
Nonprofit and educational institutions[2]	71.3	47.6	44.2	Finance companies	623.5	623.8	626.2
				Credit unions	190.1	256.0	292.3
Nonfinancial business	44.8	44.4	43.6	Federal government[1]	363.8	846.2	949.7
Pools of securitized assets[3]	50.3	49.8	46.0	Nonprofit and educational institutions[4]	71.3	47.6	44.2
Major types of credit, by holder				Nonfinancial business	19.3	20.4	20.4
Revolving	839.4	891.5	937.9	Pools of securitized assets[3]	19.0	20.9	22.5
Depository institutions	664.7	731.6	786.8				
Finance companies	81.5	60.3	54.9				

(1) Includes student loans originated by the Dept. of Education under the Federal Direct Loan Program and the Perkins Loan Program, as well as Federal Family Education Program loans that the government purchased under the Ensuring Continued Access to Student Loans Act. (2) Outstanding balances of pools upon which securities have been issued; these balances are no longer carried on the balance sheets of the loan originators. (3) Includes motor vehicle loans and all other loans not included in revolving credit, such as loans for mobile homes, education, boats, trailers, or vacations. These loans may be secured or unsecured. (4) Includes student loans originated under the Federal Family Education Loan Program and held by educational institutions and nonprofit organizations that are affiliated with state governments.

Financial Assets of U.S. Families, 1989-2013
Source: Survey of Consumer Finances (triennial), Federal Reserve System

Category	1989	1992	1995	1998	2001	2004	2007	2010	2013
Median net worth (thous.)	$46.9	$49.5	$57.8	$71.7	$86.6	$93.1	$120.6	$77.3	$81.2
Average net worth (thous.)	185.9	186.6	212.1	282.9	397.4	449.4	557.8	498.8	534.6
Financial assets				Percent of families holding asset					
Transaction accounts	19.0%	17.4%	13.9%	11.4%	11.4%	13.1%	10.9%	13.3%	13.3%
Certificates of deposit	10.2	8.0	5.6	4.3	3.1	3.7	4.0	3.9	2.0
Savings bonds	1.5	1.1	1.3	0.7	0.7	0.5	0.4	0.3	0.3
Bonds	10.2	8.4	6.3	4.3	4.5	5.3	4.1	4.4	3.2
Stocks	15.0	16.5	15.6	22.7	21.5	17.5	17.8	14.0	15.9
Pooled investment funds (excluding money market funds)	5.3	7.6	12.7	12.4	12.1	14.6	15.8	15.0	14.8
Retirement accounts	21.5	25.8	28.3	27.8	29.0	32.4	35.0	38.1	38.8
Cash value life insurance	6.0	5.9	7.2	6.3	5.3	2.9	3.2	2.5	2.7
Other managed assets	6.5	5.4	5.8	8.5	10.5	7.9	6.5	6.2	7.6
Other.......................	4.8	3.8	3.3	1.7	1.9	2.1	2.1	2.3	1.5
Financial assets as % of total assets	**30.5**	**31.6**	**36.8**	**40.7**	**42.2**	**35.8**	**34.0**	**37.9**	**40.8**

Persons Below Poverty Level, 1960-2015
Source: U.S. Census Bureau, U.S. Dept. of Commerce

Year	Number below poverty level (mil)					% of subgroup below poverty level					Avg. income cut-off, family of 4 at poverty level[4]
	All races[1]	Asian[2]	White	Black[2]	Hispanic[3]	All races[1]	Asian[2]	White	Black[2]	Hispanic[3]	
1960	39.9	NA	28.3	NA	NA	22.2%	NA	17.8%	NA	NA	$3,022
1970	25.4	NA	17.5	7.5	NA	12.6	NA	9.9	33.5%	NA	3,968
1980	29.3	NA	19.7	8.6	3.5	13.0	NA	10.2	32.5	25.7%	8,414
1990	33.6	0.9	22.3	9.8	6.0	13.5	12.2%	10.7	31.9	28.1	13,359
1995	36.4	1.4	24.4	9.9	8.6	13.8	14.6	11.2	29.3	30.3	15,569
2000	31.6	1.3	21.6	8.0	7.7	11.3	9.9	9.5	22.5	21.5	17,604
2005	37.0	1.5	24.9	9.5	9.4	12.6	10.9	10.6	24.7	21.8	19,971
2006	36.5	1.4	24.4	9.5	9.2	12.3	10.1	10.3	24.2	20.6	20,614
2007	37.3	1.5	25.1	9.7	9.9	12.5	10.2	10.5	24.4	21.5	21,203
2008	39.8	1.7	27.0	9.9	11.0	13.2	11.6	11.2	24.6	23.2	22,025
2009	43.6	1.9	29.8	10.6	12.4	14.3	12.4	12.3	25.9	25.3	21,954
2010	46.3	2.1	31.1	11.6	13.5	15.1	12.0	13.0	27.4	26.5	22,315
2011	46.2	2.2	30.8	11.7	13.2	15.0	12.3	12.8	27.5	25.3	23,021
2012	46.5	2.1	30.8	11.8	13.6	15.0	11.4	12.7	27.1	25.6	23,492
2013	46.3	2.4	31.3	11.1	13.4	14.8	12.5	12.9	25.3	24.7	23,834
2014	46.7	2.3	31.1	11.6	13.1	14.8	11.5	12.7	26.0	23.6	24,230
2015	43.1	2.2	28.6	10.8	12.1	13.5	11.2	11.6	23.9	21.4	24,257

NA = Not available. **Note:** Because of a change in the definition of poverty, data prior to 1980 are not directly comparable to data since 1980. (1) Includes other races not shown separately. (2) Beginning in 2002, numbers include those who identified themselves as being Asian or black in combination with some other race. For 1990-2000, Asian includes Pacific Islanders. (3) Persons of Hispanic origin may be of any race. (4) Figures for 1960-80 for nonfarm families only.

Families Below Poverty Level by Status, Race, and Sex, 1980-2015
Source: U.S. Census Bureau, U.S. Dept. of Commerce
(numbers in thousands)

Year and race	All families			Married-couple families			Male householder, no wife present			Female householder, no husband present		
		Below poverty level			Below poverty level			Below poverty level			Below poverty level	
	Total	Number	Percent	Total	Number	Percent	Total	Number	Percent	Total	Number	Percent
All races												
1980	60,309	6,217	10.3%	49,294	3,032	6.2%	1,933	213	11.0%	9,082	2,972	32.7%
1990	66,322	7,098	10.7	52,147	2,981	5.7	2,907	349	12.0	11,268	3,768	33.4
2000	73,778	6,400	8.7	56,598	2,637	4.7	4,277	485	11.3	12,903	3,278	25.4
2010	79,559	9,400	11.8	58,667	3,681	6.3	5,649	892	15.8	15,243	4,827	31.7
2013	82,316	9,645	11.7	59,643	3,394	5.7	6,497	1,048	16.1	16,176	5,203	32.2
2014	81,730	9,467	11.6	60,015	3,735	6.2	6,162	969	15.7	15,553	4,764	30.6
2015	82,199	8,589	10.4	60,258	3,245	5.4	6,311	939	14.9	15,630	4,404	28.2
White[1]												
1980	52,710	4,195	8.0	44,860	2,437	5.4	1,584	149	9.4	6,266	1,609	25.7
1990	56,803	4,622	8.1	47,014	2,386	5.1	2,277	226	9.9	7,512	2,010	26.8
2000	61,330	4,333	7.1	49,473	2,181	4.4	3,283	332	10.1	8,574	1,820	21.2
2010	63,976	6,305	9.9	50,016	2,921	5.8	4,176	563	13.5	9,784	2,822	28.8
2013	65,837	6,526	9.9	50,543	2,647	5.2	4,850	766	15.8	10,444	3,113	29.8
2014	64,945	6,310	9.7	50,489	2,944	5.8	4,448	595	13.4	10,008	2,771	27.7
2015	65,272	5,743	8.8	50,588	2,539	5.0	4,643	610	13.1	10,042	2,594	25.8
Black[1]												
1980	6,317	1,826	28.9	3,392	474	14.0	291	52	17.7	2,634	1,301	49.4
1990	7,471	2,193	29.3	3,569	448	12.6	472	97	20.6	3,430	1,648	48.1
2000	8,731	1,686	19.3	4,214	266	6.3	732	120	16.3	3,785	1,300	34.3
2010	9,571	2,311	24.1	4,267	377	8.8	916	236	25.7	4,387	1,698	38.7
2013	9,850	2,204	22.4	4,251	330	7.8	1,023	192	18.8	4,576	1,681	36.7
2014	9,909	2,265	22.9	4,488	399	8.9	1,133	270	23.9	4,289	1,596	37.2
2015	9,848	2,082	21.1	4,435	354	8.0	1,024	241	23.5	4,388	1,487	33.9

(1) Data are for one race only. The Census Bureau revised race categories in 2002, so data after 2002 are not directly comparable with data for previous years.

Poverty Rates by State, 1990-2015

Source: U.S. Census Bureau, U.S. Dept. of Commerce

The poverty rate is the proportion of the population with income below the government's official poverty level, which is the same nationwide but is adjusted each year for inflation. The poverty rate declined dramatically between 2013 and 2016, from 46.7 to 43.1 million people (or from 14.5% to 13.5% of the population). Those percentages are still higher than in 2000, when just 11.3% of the population lived below the poverty line.

State	1990	2000	2005	2010	2015	State	1990	2000	2005	2010	2015
Alabama	19.2%	13.3%	16.7%	17.2%	16.3%	Montana	16.3	14.1	13.8	14.5	11.9
Alaska	11.4	7.6	10.0	12.5	9.2	Nebraska	10.3%	8.6%	9.5%	10.2%	10.3%
Arizona	13.7	11.7	15.2	18.8	17.2	Nevada	9.8	8.8	10.6	16.6	13.0
Arkansas	19.6	16.5	13.8	15.3	16.1	New Hampshire	6.3	4.5	5.6	6.5	7.3
California	13.9	12.7	13.2	16.3	13.9	New Jersey	9.2	7.3	6.8	11.1	11.2
Colorado	13.7	9.8	11.4	12.3	9.9	New Mexico	20.9	17.5	17.9	18.3	19.7
Connecticut	6.0	7.7	9.3	8.6	9.1	New York	14.3	13.9	14.5	16.0	14.2
Delaware	6.9	8.4	9.2	12.2	11.1	North Carolina	13.0	12.5	13.1	17.4	15.3
Dist. of Columbia	21.1	15.2	21.3	19.5	16.6	North Dakota	13.7	10.4	11.2	12.6	10.7
Florida	14.4	11.0	11.1	16.0	16.2	Ohio	11.5	10.0	12.3	15.4	13.6
Georgia	15.8	12.1	14.4	18.8	18.1	Oklahoma	15.6	14.9	15.6	16.3	14.2
Hawaii	11.0	8.9	8.6	12.4	10.9	Oregon	9.2	10.9	12.0	14.3	11.9
Idaho	14.9	12.5	9.9	13.8	12.3	Pennsylvania	11.0	8.6	11.2	12.2	12.3
Illinois	13.7	10.7	11.5	14.1	10.9	Rhode Island	7.5	10.2	12.1	14.0	11.8
Indiana	13.0	8.5	12.6	16.3	13.5	South Carolina	16.2	11.1	15.0	16.9	14.3
Iowa	10.4	8.3	11.3	10.3	10.4	South Dakota	13.3	10.7	11.8	13.6	13.9
Kansas	10.3	8.0	12.5	14.5	14.2	Tennessee	16.9	13.5	14.9	16.7	14.7
Kentucky	17.3	12.6	14.8	17.7	19.5	Texas	15.9	15.5	16.2	18.4	14.7
Louisiana	23.6	17.2	18.3	21.5	18.6	Utah	8.2	7.6	9.2	10.0	9.3
Maine	13.1	10.1	12.6	12.6	12.3	Vermont	10.9	10.0	7.6	10.8	10.7
Maryland	9.9	7.4	9.7	10.9	9.6	Virginia	11.1	8.3	9.2	10.7	10.9
Massachusetts	10.7	9.8	10.1	10.9	11.5	Washington	8.9	10.8	10.2	11.6	11.4
Michigan	14.3	9.9	12.0	15.7	12.8	West Virginia	18.1	14.7	15.4	16.8	14.5
Minnesota	12.0	5.7	8.1	10.8	7.8	Wisconsin	9.3	9.3	10.2	10.1	11.4
Mississippi	25.7	14.9	20.1	22.5	19.1	Wyoming	11.0	10.8	10.6	9.6	9.8
Missouri	13.4	9.2	11.6	15.0	9.8	**United States**	**13.5**	**11.3**	**12.6**	**15.1**	**13.5**

Temporary Assistance for Needy Families (TANF), 1997-2015

Source: Office of Family Assistance, Admin. for Children and Families, U.S. Dept of Health and Human Services

State	Total TANF expenditures (mil)	Average number of monthly cash beneficiaries in 2015			State	Total TANF expenditures (mil)	Average number of monthly cash beneficiaries in 2015		
		Families	Recipients	Children			Families	Recipients	Children
Alabama	$160.6	13,590	31,774	24,448	New Jersey	$1,089.0	24,203	56,865	42,413
Alaska	74.0	3,138	8,471	5,738	New Mexico	205.4	12,018	31,120	22,694
Arizona	448.9	11,547	24,869	18,732	New York	4,972.0	111,249	382,006	183,379
Arkansas	144.3	4,861	10,855	8,040	North Carolina	483.3	12,122	23,920	19,189
California	6,273.2	448,134	1,806,069	879,626	North Dakota	38.6	1,176	2,917	2,300
Colorado	300.9	17,137	45,174	31,891	Ohio	1,006.8	60,074	113,806	96,784
Connecticut	479.0	13,144	26,274	18,784	Oklahoma	171.2	7,103	15,802	15,863
Delaware	95.0	4,533	12,789	7,472	Oregon	347.7	20,509	171,457	32,656
Dist. of Columbia	263.0	6,242	15,670	11,671	Pennsylvania	889.2	65,236	162,233	116,059
Florida	823.1	49,046	84,148	70,202	Puerto Rico	NA	10,838	29,733	18,369
Georgia	532.6	13,330	25,853	23,112	Rhode Island	148.1	4,913	11,675	8,249
Guam	NA	1,084	2,414	1,928	South Carolina	180.4	10,451	23,572	18,849
Hawaii	263.6	7,583	21,735	14,610	South Dakota	26.6	3,014	5,935	5,260
Idaho	35.2	1,861	2,735	2,642	Tennessee	246.5	37,863	88,505	66,524
Illinois	1,373.6	18,643	41,886	34,248	Texas	965.4	32,406	70,524	61,592
Indiana	233.2	8,933	18,397	16,016	Utah	78.5	3,699	9,518	6,619
Iowa	179.5	11,664	33,633	20,885	Vermont	83.2	2,795	7,688	4,418
Kansas	140.9	6,099	14,384	10,794	Virgin Islands	NA	358	1,126	766
Kentucky	254.1	25,292	50,185	40,743	Virginia	240.7	23,816	55,257	38,413
Louisiana	213.5	5,264	11,859	10,055	Washington	935.3	33,721	75,739	53,720
Maine	85.2	4,714	48,181	7,036	West Virginia	116.5	7,689	16,139	12,556
Maryland	578.9	19,323	46,493	34,664	Wisconsin	505.4	23,093	55,339	41,002
Massachusetts	974.4	36,264	140,722	45,113	Wyoming	28.0	334	675	550
Michigan	1,295.4	21,354	52,225	37,678	**1997 U.S. total**	**19,010.2**	**3,936,610**	**10,935,125**	**NA**
Minnesota	491.0	19,166	44,032	33,794	**2000 U.S. total**	**24,780.7**	**2,229,315**	**5,833,043**	**4,303,943**
Mississippi	67.8	6,966	13,972	10,752	**2005 U.S. total**	**25,580.1**	**1,901,810**	**4,495,175**	**3,428,885**
Missouri	398.4	24,569	67,268	41,506	**2010 U.S. total**	**33,255.5**	**1,847,152**	**4,364,979**	**3,280,150**
Montana	41.4	2,960	7,113	5,396	**2011 U.S. total**	**30,264.1**	**1,921,243**	**4,599,846**	**3,435,218**
Nebraska	92.0	4,612	13,417	9,092	**2012 U.S. total**	**28,867.3**	**1,876,426**	**4,476,476**	**3,351,971**
Nevada	90.8	11,115	28,802	21,059	**2013 U.S. total**	**29,147.1**	**1,751,067**	**4,102,491**	**3,091,076**
New Hampshire	42.4	2,863	13,436	4,245	**2014 U.S. total**	**29,350.9**	**1,652,996**	**3,894,213**	**2,934,582**
					2015 U.S. total	**29,203.6**	**1,333,707**	**4,176,387**	**2,370,198**

NA = Not available.

Adults Receiving TANF Funds by Employment Status, 2015

Source: Office of Family Assistance, Admin. for Children and Families, U.S. Dept of Health and Human Services

State	Adults	Employed	State	Adults	Employed	State	Adults	Employed	State	Adults	Employed
AL	7,314	41.3%	IL	7,168	62.8%	NE	1,526	48.6%	SC	4,341	31.2%
AK	2,731	32.5	IN	1,721	25.2	NV	7,585	39.5	SD	652	18.1
AZ	5,364	18.2	IA	7,670	42.8	NH	1,484	29.3	TN	23,096	29.3
AR	2,846	32.9	KS	3,647	39.8	NJ	15,025	15.6	TX	8,626	31.8
CA	279,666	26.7	KY	9,180	31.8	NM	7,866	21.0	UT	1,727	17.1
CO	13,487	50.3	LA	1,478	20.9	NY	65,550	32.5	VT	1,549	20.4
CT	7,836	28.2	ME	3,069	20.7	NC	4,604	28.8	Virgin Isls.	294	2.6
DE	1,459	27.4	MD	10,791	17.9	ND	542	48.4	VA	12,909	30.5
DC	3,992	20.8	MA	22,656	10.0	OH	16,322	23.5	WA	22,101	17.6
FL	14,333	14.1	MI	10,593	44.9	OK	2,297	5.5	WV	2,857	24.3
GA	2,725	14.4	MN	9,345	36.0	OR	13,453	9.2	WI	12,749	34.1
Guam	486	4.3	MS	3,309	20.6	PA	44,086	25.6	WY	126	12.0
HI	7,116	39.9	MO	17,530	16.9	Puerto Rico	10,149	2.5	**U.S. total**	**744,257**	**26.7**
ID	91	6.7	MT	1,714	25.1	RI	3,423	21.1			

Selected Personal Consumption Expenditures in the U.S., 1990-2015
Source: Bureau of Economic Analysis, U.S. Dept. of Commerce
(in billions of dollars)

	1990	1995	2000	2005	2010	2014	2015
Personal consumption expenditures	$3,825.6	$4,984.2	$6,792.4	$8,794.1	$10,202.2	$11,863.4	$12,283.7
Goods	1,491.3	1,815.5	2,452.9	3,080.3	3,362.8	3,970.5	4,012.1
Durable goods	497.1	635.7	912.6	1,127.2	1,070.7	1,294.8	1,355.2
Motor vehicles and parts	205.1	255.7	363.2	410.0	342.0	442.8	464.8
New motor vehicles	134.7	147.5	210.7	248.9	182.3	266.1	277.3
Net purchases of used motor vehicles	42.2	72.9	110.7	110.5	104.2	111.2	120.5
Motor vehicle parts and accessories	28.3	35.4	41.8	50.6	55.5	65.4	67.0
Furnishings, durable household equipment . .	120.9	146.7	208.1	271.3	250.4	292.1	305.1
Furniture and furnishings	69.2	83.4	121.7	160.6	148.4	173.1	181.8
Household appliances	23.7	26.6	34.1	45.1	41.7	46.9	48.0
Glassware, tableware, and household utensils	18.4	23.7	35.3	44.6	42.7	51.0	53.3
Recreational goods and vehicles	105.6	153.7	230.9	305.0	312.7	358.8	376.6
Video, audio, photo equip.	56.1	84.7	127.7	172.7	194.1	214.2	221.5
Sporting equipment, guns, ammunition	19.9	27.2	39.1	50.9	51.3	63.7	67.3
Sports and recreational vehicles	16.6	22.5	34.9	49.1	35.6	47.1	51.7
Other durable goods	65.5	79.6	110.4	141.0	165.6	201.2	208.7
Jewelry and watches	30.3	37.8	49.1	59.8	62.6	77.0	77.2
Therapeutic appliances and equipment	18.4	21.0	32.2	43.2	55.6	64.9	67.5
Nondurable goods	994.2	1,179.8	1,540.3	1,953.1	2,292.1	2,675.7	2,656.9
Food and beverages purchased for							
off-premises consumption	391.2	443.7	540.6	668.2	788.9	891.4	900.7
Food and nonalcoholic beverages	341.2	388.3	463.1	575.3	675.9	762.9	766.8
Alcoholic beverages	49.3	55.0	77.1	92.6	112.6	127.9	133.3
Clothing and footwear	195.2	231.2	280.8	310.7	320.6	370.8	379.5
Women's and girls' clothing.	94.5	108.9	132.7	149.6	152.8	175.8	180.2
Men's and boys' clothing.	57.4	72.2	85.9	86.3	84.9	98.4	100.5
Children's and infants' clothing	8.1	9.0	11.4	15.4	17.7	19.2	19.5
Other clothing materials and footwear	35.3	41.2	50.8	59.3	65.2	77.4	79.3
Gasoline and other energy goods	124.2	133.4	184.5	283.8	333.4	398.9	303.7
Other nondurable goods	283.6	371.4	534.4	690.4	849.2	1,014.6	1,073.0
Pharmaceutical and other medical products . .	59.1	85.1	159.0	248.5	334.1	428.7	465.9
Recreational items	50.9	68.9	91.9	112.6	127.7	149.4	154.9
Household supplies	54.2	70.4	86.7	102.0	108.3	121.6	124.1
Personal care products.	39.3	50.2	68.5	88.0	104.7	122.4	126.1
Tobacco	41.0	49.2	68.5	76.7	106.3	104.6	107.9
Magazines, newspapers, and stationery	36.5	46.1	56.6	58.0	62.8	82.1	89.2
Services.	2,334.3	3,168.6	4,339.5	5,713.8	6,839.4	7,892.9	8,271.6
Housing and utilities	696.5	913.7	1,198.6	1,583.6	1,909.0	2,142.8	2,233.2
Housing	570.6	756.1	1,010.5	1,332.5	1,609.7	1,823.9	1,919.9
Rental of tenant-occupied nonfarm housing	150.8	186.6	227.9	268.3	372.6	451.6	488.0
Imputed rental of owner-occupied nonfarm							
housing	412.8	559.4	768.9	1,044.3	1,214.5	1,352.2	1,410.9
Household utilities	125.9	157.6	188.1	251.1	299.3	318.9	313.3
Water supply and sanitation	27.1	39.3	50.4	61.3	78.0	86.8	88.0
Electricity	71.8	87.6	98.4	128.5	166.8	176.2	177.4
Natural gas	27.0	30.7	39.3	61.3	54.6	55.9	48.0
Health care	506.2	719.9	918.4	1,322.3	1,690.7	1,952.8	2,069.0
Outpatient services.	232.1	336.6	436.6	626.2	767.9	871.1	930.8
Physician services	134.8	177.8	229.2	333.9	402.8	452.7	484.5
Dental services	32.4	45.4	63.6	87.9	104.5	112.7	117.8
Paramedical services	64.9	113.4	143.8	204.4	260.6	306.7	328.5
Hospitals.	228.8	318.4	393.9	577.2	770.5	912.8	963.7
Nursing homes	45.3	64.8	87.9	119.0	152.3	167.9	174.4
Transportation services.	126.4	177.9	263.5	289.4	292.9	354.1	368.4
Motor vehicle services	87.2	129.1	189.3	211.8	211.9	254.2	265.5
Motor vehicle maintenance and repair	73.9	93.5	127.4	155.1	152.4	176.7	181.3
Public transportation.	39.2	48.8	74.3	77.6	81.0	99.8	102.9
Recreation services	121.8	181.1	254.4	328.9	385.1	451.6	466.3
Membership clubs, sports centers, parks,							
theaters, museums	49.7	69.5	91.9	117.9	141.8	168.6	182.3
Gambling	23.7	45.4	67.6	96.5	105.6	120.6	127.0
Food services and accommodations	262.7	316.1	408.8	530.6	617.7	753.7	808.8
Purchased meals and beverages	228.3	271.8	344.9	446.0	516.9	624.6	671.6
Accommodations	27.6	36.6	55.0	72.5	85.5	111.2	118.4
Financial services and insurance	247.4	366.4	566.3	689.6	763.2	885.7	921.1
Financial services.	135.7	212.9	360.0	417.4	473.3	553.0	578.1
Insurance	111.7	153.5	206.3	272.2	290.0	332.7	343.0
Other services	297.5	391.2	571.5	759.1	905.4	1,038.7	1,076.9
Telecommunication services	60.7	85.2	126.4	137.7	152.1	163.3	164.5
Postal and delivery services.	7.5	9.2	9.9	10.4	11.7	10.6	10.6
Internet access.	0.1	1.6	16.4	29.7	63.0	97.6	103.5
Higher education	34.7	51.9	76.8	110.9	158.3	179.2	183.8
Nursery, elementary, and secondary schools. .	14.8	19.2	24.1	29.6	35.3	40.9	42.2
Commercial and vocational schools	11.1	14.4	24.3	30.3	42.0	48.6	51.8
Professional and other services	67.7	82.8	113.0	148.4	163.3	178.8	186.0
Personal care and clothing services.	44.5	57.1	80.4	103.3	114.9	141.6	148.2
Social services and religious activities	41.2	58.1	81.1	110.2	138.9	161.5	171.0
Household maintenance.	25.4	34.5	48.6	57.9	58.6	74.3	77.1

Note: Subtotals may not add up to totals due to rounding or incomplete enumeration.

Leading U.S. Businesses, 2015

Source: *Fortune* magazine, June 15, 2016

(ranked by revenues, in millions of dollars)

Industry/company (rank)	Revenues	Industry/company (rank)	Revenues	Industry/company (rank)	Revenues
Advertising		Oracle (77)	$38,226	Kellogg (207)	$13,525
Omnicom Group (186)	$15,134	Salesforce.com (386)	6,667	Land O'Lakes (215)	13,161
Interpublic Group (355)	7,614	Symantec (400)	6,508	Hormel Foods (304)	9,264
Aerospace		**Computers, Office Equipment**		Dean Foods (336)	8,122
Boeing (24)	$96,114	Apple (3)	$233,715	Campbell Soup (337)	8,082
United Technologies (45)	61,047	HP (20)	103,355	Hershey (362)	7,387
Lockheed Martin (60)	46,132	NCR (409)	6,373	J.M. Smucker (452)	5,693
General Dynamics (88)	31,469	**Construction, Farm Machinery**		**Food Production**	
Northrop Grumman (118)	23,526	Caterpillar (59)	$47,011	Archer Daniels Midland (41)	$67,702
Raytheon (120)	23,247	Deere (97)	28,863	Tyson Foods (66)	41,373
Textron (209)	13,423	Cummins (148)	19,110	CHS (84)	34,582
L-3 Communications (245)	11,554	AGCO (360)	7,467	Leucadia National (242)	11,684
Precision Castparts (282)	10,056	Terex (396)	6,543	Ingredion (456)	5,621
Huntington Ingalls Industries (378)	7,020	**Diversified Financials**		Seaboard (460)	5,594
Spirit AeroSystems Holdings (389)	6,644	Fannie Mae (16)	$110,359	**Food Services**	
Rockwell Collins (490)	5,262	Freddie Mac (43)	63,491	McDonald's (109)	$25,413
Airlines		INTL FCStone (83)	34,693	Starbucks (146)	19,163
American Airlines Group (67)	$40,990	American Express (85)	34,441	Yum! Brands (218)	13,105
Delta Air Lines (68)	40,704	Icahn Enterprises (184)	15,272	Darden Restaurants (371)	7,164
United Continental Holdings (80)	37,864	Marsh & McLennan (222)	12,893	**Forest & Paper Products**	
Southwest Airlines (142)	19,820	Ameriprise Financial (232)	12,200	Weyerhaeuser (373)	$7,082
JetBlue Airways (405)	6,416	Voya Financial (252)	11,341	Domtar (489)	5,264
Alaska Air Group (459)	5,598	Ally Financial (298)	9,539	**General Merchandisers**	
Apparel		Arthur J. Gallagher (471)	5,392	Walmart (1)	$482,130
Nike (91)	$30,601	Navient (494)	5,197	Target (38)	73,785
VF (231)	12,377	**Diversified Outsourcing Services**		Macy's (103)	27,079
PVH (340)	8,020	Aramark (199)	$14,329	Sears Holdings (111)	25,146
Ralph Lauren (354)	7,620	ADP (248)	11,477	Dollar General (139)	20,369
Hanesbrands (448)	5,732	ABM Industries (485)	5,291	Kohl's (145)	19,204
Automotive Retailing, Services		**Electronics**		Nordstrom (197)	14,437
AutoNation (136)	$20,862	Honeywell International (75)	$38,581	J.C. Penney (228)	12,625
Penske Automotive Group (143)	19,361	Emerson Electric (128)	22,304	Dillard's (380)	6,755
CarMax (191)	14,874	Whirlpool (134)	20,891	**Health Care: Insurance &**	
Group 1 Automotive (267)	10,633	Rockwell Automation (412)	6,308	**Managed Care**	
Hertz Global Holdings (269)	10,535	Harman International Industries		UnitedHealth Group (6)	$157,107
Sonic Automotive (297)	9,624	(419)	6,155	Anthem (33)	79,157
Avis Budget Group (330)	8,502	**Energy**		Aetna (46)	60,337
Lithia Motors (346)	7,864	NRG Energy (193)	$14,674	Humana (52)	54,289
Asbury Automotive Group (393)	6,588	Williams (364)	7,360	Cigna (79)	37,876
Beverages		UGI (384)	6,691	Centene (124)	22,795
Coca-Cola (62)	$44,294	Calpine (402)	6,472	Health Net (172)	16,244
Coca-Cola Enterprises (397)	6,540	Energy Future Holdings (475)	5,370	Molina Healthcare (201)	14,178
Dr Pepper Snapple Group (413)	6,282	**Engineering, Construction**		WellCare Health Plans (202)	13,890
Constellation Brands (429)	6,028	Fluor (155)	$18,114	**Health Care: Medical Facilities**	
Chemicals		AECOM (156)	17,990	HCA Holdings (63)	$43,591
Dow Chemical (56)	$48,778	Jacobs Engineering Group (235)	12,115	Community Health Systems (125)	22,678
DuPont (101)	27,940	Peter Kiewit Sons' (314)	8,992	Tenet Healthcare (140)	20,111
PPG Industries (182)	15,330	Quanta Services (352)	7,632	DaVita HealthCare Partners	
Monsanto (189)	15,001	EMCOR Group (381)	6,723	(200)	14,210
Ecolab (206)	13,545	CH2M Hill (478)	5,362	Universal Health Services (290)	9,785
Sherwin-Williams (253)	11,339	**Entertainment**		Kindred Healthcare (372)	7,098
Praxair (262)	10,776	Walt Disney (53)	$52,465	LifePoint Health (430)	6,014
Huntsman (277)	10,299	Twenty-First Century Fox (96)	28,987	Genesis Healthcare (457)	5,619
Air Products & Chemicals (288)	9,895	Time Warner (99)	28,118	**Health Care: Pharmacies**	
Eastman Chemical (296)	9,648	CBS (203)	13,886	Express Scripts Holding (22)	$101,752
Mosaic (316)	8,895	Viacom (213)	13,268	Laboratory Corp. of America	
Celanese (453)	5,674	Live Nation Entertainment (366)	7,246	(325)	8,680
Ashland (472)	5,387	Discovery Communications		Quest Diagnostics (358)	7,493
Commercial Banks		(406)	6,394	Quintiles Transnational (447)	5,738
JPMorgan Chase & Co. (23)	$101,006	iHeartMedia (414)	6,242	Envision Healthcare Holdings	
Bank of America Corp. (26)	93,056	**Financial Data Services**		(469)	5,448
Wells Fargo (27)	90,033	Visa (204)	$13,880	**Home Equipment, Furnishings**	
Citigroup (29)	88,275	First Data (249)	11,451	Stanley Black & Decker (256)	$11,211
Goldman Sachs Group (74)	39,208	MasterCard (294)	9,667	Jarden (328)	8,604
Morgan Stanley (78)	37,897	PayPal Holdings (307)	9,248	Mohawk Industries (338)	8,072
Capital One Financial (112)	25,098	Fidelity National Information		Masco (345)	7,904
U.S. Bancorp (131)	21,494	Services (392)	6,595	Newell Brands (434)	5,972
PNC Financial Services Group		Alliance Data Systems (404)	6,440	**Homebuilders**	
(171)	16,270	Western Union (468)	5,484	D.R. Horton (260)	$10,824
Bank of New York Mellon Corp.		S&P Global (481)	5,313	Lennar (301)	9,474
(179)	15,523	Fiserv (492)	5,254	PulteGroup (433)	5,982
State Street Corp. (264)	10,760	**Food & Drug Stores**		NVR (498)	5,170
BB&T Corp. (273)	10,346	CVS Health (7)	$153,290	**Hotels, Casinos, Resorts**	
Discover Financial Services		Kroger (17)	109,830	Marriott International (195)	$14,486
(283)	10,002	Walgreens Boots Alliance (19)	103,444	Las Vegas Sands (241)	11,688
SunTrust Banks (329)	8,533	Publix Super Markets (87)	32,619	Hilton Worldwide Holdings (254)	11,272
Fifth Third Bancorp (376)	7,031	Rite Aid (107)	26,528	MGM Resorts International (309)	9,190
Regions Financial (453)	5,674	Supervalu (160)	17,820	Starwood Hotels & Resorts (444)	5,763
Citizens Financial Group (486)	5,276	Whole Foods Market (181)	15,389	Wyndham Worldwide (466)	5,536
Computer Peripherals		**Food Consumer Products**		**Household & Personal Products**	
EMC (113)	$24,704	PepsiCo (44)	$63,056	Procter & Gamble (34)	$78,756
Western Digital (194)	14,572	Mondelēz International (94)	29,636	Kimberly-Clark (151)	18,591
NetApp (422)	6,123	Kraft Heinz (153)	18,338	Colgate-Palmolive (174)	16,034
Computer Software		General Mills (161)	17,630	Estée Lauder (261)	10,780
Microsoft (25)	$93,580	ConAgra Foods (176)	15,849	Avon Products (370)	7,173

Industry/company (rank)	Revenues
HRG Group (441)	$5,816
Clorox (455)	5,666
Industrial Machinery	
General Electric (11)	$140,389
Illinois Tool Works (211)	13,405
Parker-Hannifin (224)	12,712
Dover (377)	7,029
Information Technology	
IBM (31)	$82,461
Xerox (150)	18,664
CDW (220)	12,989
Cognizant Technology Solutions (230)	12,416
Computer Sciences (233)	12,183
Booz Allen Hamilton (487)	5,275
Insurance: Life, Health (Mutual)	
New York Life Insurance (61)	$45,891
Massachusetts Mutual Life Insurance (76)	38,243
TIAA (82)	35,181
Northwestern Mutual (100)	28,111
Guardian Life Ins. Co. of America (226)	12,628
Thrivent Financial for Lutherans (318)	8,789
Western & Southern Financial Group (479)	5,356
Insurance: Life, Health (Stock)	
MetLife (40)	$69,951
Prudential Financial (50)	57,119
Aflac (135)	20,872
Lincoln National (205)	13,572
Principal Financial (236)	11,964
Unum Group (265)	10,731
Reinsurance Group of America (271)	10,418
Genworth Financial (306)	9,249
Pacific Life (326)	8,642
Mutual of Omaha Insurance (367)	7,236
Insurance: Property & Casualty (Mutual)	
State Farm Insurance Cos. (35)	$75,697
Nationwide (69)	40,222
Farmers Insurance Exchange (227)	12,626
Auto-Owners Insurance (398)	6,517
Insurance: Property & Casualty (Stock)	
Berkshire Hathaway (4)	$210,821
AIG (49)	58,327
Liberty Mutual Insurance Group (73)	39,450
Allstate (81)	35,653
Travelers Cos. (105)	26,800
USAA (114)	24,361
Progressive (137)	20,854
Hartford Financial Services Group (152)	18,377
Loews (210)	13,415
Assurant (275)	10,325
Fidelity National Financial (311)	9,132
American Family Insurance Group (332)	8,286
W.R. Berkley (368)	7,207
Erie Insurance Group (411)	6,351
American Financial Group (421)	6,145
Old Republic International (442)	5,766
Markel (476)	5,370
First American Financial (497)	5,175
Cincinnati Financial (499)	5,142
Internet Services & Retailing	
Amazon.com (18)	$107,006
Alphabet (36)	74,989
Facebook (157)	17,928
Liberty Interactive (284)	9,989
eBay (300)	9,496
Priceline Group (308)	9,224
Expedia (385)	6,672
Mail, Package, & Freight Delivery	
UPS (48)	$58,363
FedEx (58)	47,453
Medical Products & Equipment	
Abbott Laboratories (138)	$20,661
Becton Dickinson (278)	10,282
Baxter International (286)	9,968
Stryker (287)	9,946
Boston Scientific (359)	7,477
Zimmer Biomet Holdings (431)	5,998
St. Jude Medical (465)	5,541

Industry/company (rank)	Revenues
Metals	
Alcoa (126)	$22,534
Nucor (170)	16,439
United States Steel (244)	11,574
Reliance Steel & Aluminum (303)	9,351
Steel Dynamics (356)	7,594
AK Steel Holding (383)	6,693
Commercial Metals (417)	6,162
Mining, Crude Oil Production	
ConocoPhilips (90)	$30,935
Freeport-McMoRan (175)	15,877
Devon Energy (216)	13,145
Chesapeake Energy (223)	12,764
Occidental Petroleum (225)	12,699
EOG Resources (322)	8,757
Andarko Petroleum (324)	8,698
Newmont Mining (349)	7,729
Apache (388)	6,654
Marathon Oil (438)	5,861
Peabody Energy (458)	5,609
Miscellaneous	
3M (93)	$30,274
Univar (315)	8,982
A-Mark Precious Metals (426)	6,070
United Rentals (440)	5,817
Mattel (450)	5,703
Owens Corning (480)	5,350
Motor Vehicles & Parts	
General Motors (8)	$152,356
Ford Motor (9)	149,558
Johnson Controls (70)	40,204
Paccar (147)	19,115
Lear (154)	18,211
Goodyear Tire & Rubber (169)	16,443
Navistar International (281)	10,140
Autoliv (310)	9,170
Tenneco (334)	8,209
BorgWarner (339)	8,023
Oshkosh (424)	6,098
Dana Holding (428)	6,060
Visteon (470)	5,444
Network & Other Communications Equipment	
Cisco Systems (54)	$49,161
Qualcomm (110)	25,281
Corning (313)	9,111
Motorola Solutions (451)	5,695
Amphenol (462)	5,569
Oil and Gas Equipment & Services	
Halliburton (117)	$23,633
Baker Hughes (178)	15,742
National Oilwell Varco (192)	14,757
Cameron International (319)	8,782
FMC Technologies (410)	6,363
Packaging, Containers	
International Paper (127)	$22,365
Westrock (251)	11,381
Crown Holdings (321)	8,762
Ball (341)	7,997
Sealed Air (375)	7,032
Owens-Illinois (418)	6,156
Avery Dennison (435)	5,967
Packaging Corp. of America (446)	5,742
Petroleum Refining	
Exxon Mobil (2)	$246,204
Chevron (14)	131,118
Phillips 66 (30)	87,169
Valero Energy (32)	81,824
Marathon Petroleum (42)	64,566
Tesoro (98)	28,150
HollyFrontier (214)	13,238
PBF Energy (217)	13,124
Western Refining (289)	9,787
Hess (394)	6,575
Delek US Holdings (445)	5,762
Pharmaceuticals	
Johnson & Johnson (39)	$70,074
Pfizer (55)	48,851
Merck (72)	39,498
Gilead Sciences (86)	32,639
AbbVie (123)	22,859
Amgen (130)	21,662
Eli Lilly (141)	19,959
Bristol-Myers Squibb (168)	16,560
Biogen (263)	10,764
Celgene (305)	9,256

Industry/company (rank)	Revenues
Baxalta (420)	$6,149
Pipelines	
Energy Transfer Equity (65)	$42,126
Enterprise Products Partners (104)	27,028
Plains GP Holdings (121)	23,152
Kinder Morgan (198)	14,403
Oneok (348)	7,763
Targa Resources (387)	6,659
Spectra Energy (493)	5,234
Publishing, Printing	
R.R. Donnelley & Sons (255)	$11,257
News Corp. (327)	8,633
Railroads	
Union Pacific (129)	$21,813
CSX (239)	11,811
Norfolk Southern (270)	10,511
Real Estate	
CBRE Group (259)	$10,856
Jones Lang LaSalle (436)	5,966
Realogy Holdings (449)	5,706
Host Hotels & Resorts (472)	5,387
Simon Property Group (488)	5,266
Scientific, Photograph, & Control Equipment	
Danaher (133)	$20,909
Thermo Fisher Scientific (164)	16,965
Securities	
BlackRock (250)	$11,401
Franklin Resources (344)	7,949
KKR (347)	7,786
Jones Financial (382)	6,694
Charles Schwab (401)	6,501
Raymond James Financial (482)	5,308
Semiconductors	
Intel (51)	$55,355
Jabil Circuit (158)	17,914
Micron Technology (173)	16,192
Texas Instruments (219)	13,000
Applied Materials (295)	9,659
Broadcom (331)	8,394
Sanmina (408)	6,375
SanDisk (464)	5,565
Lam Research (491)	5,259
Specialty Retailers: Apparel	
TJX (89)	$30,945
Gap (177)	15,797
L Brands (234)	12,154
Ross Stores (237)	11,940
Foot Locker (361)	7,412
Burlington Stores (500)	5,130
Specialty Retailers: Other	
Costco (15)	$116,199
Home Depot (28)	88,519
Lowe's (47)	59,074
Best Buy (71)	39,745
Staples (132)	21,059
Dollar Tree (180)	15,498
Office Depot (196)	14,485
Bed Bath & Beyond (238)	11,881
Toys "R" Us (240)	11,802
Murphy USA (258)	10,885
AutoZone (280)	10,187
Advance Auto Parts (293)	9,737
CST Brands (299)	9,499
GameStop (302)	9,364
O'Reilly Automotive (342)	7,967
Dick's Sporting Goods (365)	7,271
Casey's General Stores (374)	7,052
Netflix (379)	6,780
Tractor Supply (415)	6,227
Barnes & Noble (427)	6,069
TravelCenters of America (439)	5,851
Big Lots (495)	5,191
Telecommunications	
AT&T (10)	$146,801
Verizon (13)	131,620
Comcast (37)	74,510
Time Warner Cable (116)	23,697
CenturyLink (159)	17,900
DISH Network (187)	15,069
Charter Communications (292)	9,754
Level 3 Communications (333)	8,229
Cablevision Systems (399)	6,510
Windstream Holdings (443)	5,765
Frontier Communications (461)	5,576
Telephone & Data Systems (496)	5,176

Industry/company (rank)	Revenues	Industry/company (rank)	Revenues	Industry/company (rank)	Revenues
Temporary Help		Consolidated Edison (229)	$12,554	WESCO International (357)	$7,519
ManpowerGroup (144)	$19,330	Dominion Resources (243)	11,683	LKQ (369)	7,193
Kelly Services (467)	5,518	Edison International (246)	11,524	Anixter International (391)	6,596
Tobacco		Entergy (247)	11,513	Graybar Electric (423)	6,110
Philip Morris International (106)	$26,794	Xcel Energy (257)	11,024	Lansing Trade Group (463)	5,565
Altria Group (149)	18,854	Public Service Enterprise Group		Airgas (484)	5,305
Reynolds American (266)	10,675	(272)	10,415	**Wholesalers: Electronics &**	
Transportation & Logistics		DTE Energy (274)	10,337	**Office Equipment**	
C.H. Robinson Worldwide (208)	$13,476	Sempra Energy (279)	10,231	Ingram Micro (64)	$43,026
XPO Logistics (353)	7,623	Eversource Energy (343)	7,955	Avnet (102)	27,925
Expeditors International of		PPL (350)	7,669	Tech Data (108)	26,380
Washington (390)	6,617	CenterPoint Energy (363)	7,386	Arrow Electronics (119)	23,282
Transportation Equipment		CMS Energy (403)	6,456	Synnex (212)	13,338
Trinity Industries (407)	$6,393	Ameren (425)	6,098	Insight Enterprises (474)	5,373
Harley-Davidson (432)	5,995	WEC Energy Group (437)	5,926	Essendant (477)	5,363
Trucking, Truck Leasing		NiSource (483)	5,308	**Wholesalers: Food & Grocery**	
Ryder System (395)	$6,572	**Waste Management**		Sysco (57)	$48,681
J.B. Hunt Transport Services (416)	6,188	Waste Management (221)	$12,961	US Foods Holding (122)	23,128
Utilities: Gas & Electric		Republic Services (312)	9,115	Performance Food Group (185)	15,270
Exelon (95)	$29,447	**Wholesalers, Diversified**		Core-Mark Holding (317)	8,858
Duke Energy (115)	24,002	World Fuel Services (92)	$30,380	United Natural Foods (335)	8,185
Southern (162)	17,489	NGL Energy Partners (167)	16,802	SpartanNash (351)	7,652
NextEra Energy (163)	17,486	Genuine Parts (183)	15,280	**Wholesalers: Health Care**	
American Electric Power (165)	16,900	Global Partners (276)	10,315	McKesson (5)	$181,241
PG&E Corp. (166)	16,833	W.W. Grainger (285)	9,973	AmerisourceBergen (12)	135,962
FirstEnergy (188)	15,026	HD Supply Holdings (320)	8,779	Cardinal Health (21)	102,531
AES (190)	14,963	Veritiv (323)	8,718	Henry Schein (268)	10,630
				Owens & Minor (291)	9,773

World's Largest Companies, 2015

Source: *Fortune* magazine, July 20, 2016
(ranked by 2015 revenues, in millions of dollars)

Rank	Company (2014 rank), country	Revenue	Rank	Company (2014 rank), country	Revenue
1.	Walmart (1), U.S.	$482,130	51.	BMW (56), Germany	$102,248
2.	State Grid (7), China	329,601	52.	Express Scripts Holding (66), U.S.	101,752
3.	China National Petroleum (4), China	299,271	53.	Nissan Motor (59), Japan	101,536
4.	Sinopec Group (2), China	294,344	54.	China Life Insurance (94), China	101,274
5.	Royal Dutch Shell (3), Netherlands	272,156	55.	J.P. Morgan Chase (61), U.S.	101,006
6.	Exxon Mobil (5), U.S.	246,204	56.	Gazprom (26), Russia	99,464
7.	Volkswagen (8), Germany	236,600	57.	China Railway Engineering (71), China	99,435
8.	Toyota Motor (9), Japan	236,592	58.	Petrobras (28), Brazil	97,314
9.	Apple (15), U.S.	233,715	59.	Trafigura Group (40), Singapore	97,237
10.	BP (6), UK	225,982	60.	Nippon Telegraph & Telephone (65), Japan	96,134
11.	Berkshire Hathaway (14), U.S.	210,821	61.	Boeing (85), U.S.	96,114
12.	McKesson (16), U.S.	192,487	62.	China Railway Construction (79), China	95,652
13.	Samsung Electronics (13), South Korea	177,440	63.	Microsoft (95), U.S.	93,580
14.	Glencore (10), Switzerland	170,497	64.	Bank of America Corp. (80), U.S.	93,056
15.	Industrial & Commercial Bank of China (18), China	167,227	65.	ENI (25), Italy	92,985
16.	Daimler (17), Germany	165,800	66.	Nestlé (70), Switzerland	92,285
17.	UnitedHealth Group (35), U.S.	157,107	67.	Wells Fargo (90), U.S.	90,033
18.	CVS Health (30), U.S.	153,290	68.	HSBC Holdings (81), UK	89,061
19.	EXOR Group (19), Italy	152,591	69.	Home Depot (101), U.S.	88,519
20.	General Motors (21), U.S.	152,356	70.	Citigroup (86), U.S.	88,275
21.	Ford Motor (27), U.S.	149,558	71.	Siemens (63), Germany	87,660
22.	China Construction Bank (29), China	147,910	72.	Tesco (62), UK	87,633
23.	AT&T (33), U.S.	146,801	73.	Carrefour (64), France	87,474
24.	Total (11), France	143,421	74.	Phillips 66 (23), U.S.	87,169
25.	Hon Hai Precision Industry (31), Taiwan	141,213	75.	Banco Santander (67), Spain	84,885
26.	General Electric (24), U.S.	140,389	76.	Lukoil (43), Russia	84,677
27.	China State Construction Engineering (37), China	140,159	77.	Crédit Agricole (58), France	84,099
28.	AmerisourceBergen (46), U.S.	135,962	78.	Enel (69), Italy	83,926
29.	Agricultural Bank of China (36), China	133,419	79.	Hitachi (89), Japan	83,584
30.	Verizon (41), U.S.	131,620	80.	Électricité de France (78), France	83,202
31.	Chevron (12), U.S.	131,118	81.	Dongfeng Motor Group (109), China	82,817
32.	E.ON (22), Germany	129,277	82.	IBM (82), U.S.	82,461
33.	AXA (20), France	129,250	83.	Valero Energy (34), U.S.	81,824
34.	Allianz (32), Germany	122,948	84.	Hyundai Motor (99), South Korea	81,320
35.	Bank of China (45), China	122,337	85.	Anthem (120), U.S.	79,157
36.	Honda Motor (44), Japan	121,624	86.	Procter & Gamble (100), U.S.	78,756
37.	Japan Post Holdings (38), Japan	118,762	87.	Robert Bosch (150), Germany	78,323
38.	Costco (52), U.S.	116,199	88.	BASF (76), Germany	78,147
39.	BNP Paribas (42), France	111,531	89.	Engie (73), France	77,520
40.	Fannie Mae (50), U.S.	110,359	90.	Deutsche Telekom (102), Germany	76,793
41.	Ping An Insurance (96), China	110,308	91.	China Resources National (115), China	76,574
42.	Kroger (54), U.S.	109,830	92.	SoftBank Group (110), Japan	76,469
43.	Société Générale (49), France	107,736	93.	State Farm Insurance Cos. (127), U.S.	75,697
44.	Amazon.com (88), U.S.	107,006	94.	Alphabet (124), U.S.	74,989
45.	China Mobile Communications (55), China	106,761	95.	China Southern Power Grid (113), China	74,697
46.	SAIC Motor (60), China	106,684	96.	Comcast (135), U.S.	74,510
47.	Walgreens Boots Alliance (114), U.S.	103,444	97.	Target (117), U.S.	73,785
48.	HP (53), U.S.	103,355	98.	Pemex (47), Mexico	73,514
49.	Assicurazioni Generali (48), Italy	102,567	99.	Pacific Construction Group (156), China	73,047
50.	Cardinal Health (84), U.S.	102,531	100.	Airbus Group (106), Netherlands	71,493

Top U.S. Franchises, 2016
Source: *Entrepreneur* magazine

Rank	Company (2015 rank)	Type of business	Locations[1]	Startup costs[2]
1.	Jimmy John's Sandwiches (6)	Sandwiches	2,434	$326,000-555,000
2.	Hampton by Hilton (1).	Mid-price hotels	2,122	$4.2 mil-7.8 mil
3.	Supercuts (5)	Hair salons	1,548	$144,000-294,000
4.	Servpro (7)	Insurance/disaster restoration and cleaning.	1,702	$156,000-210,000
5.	Subway (3)	Submarine sandwiches, salads	44,702	$117,000-263,000
6.	McDonald's (14)	Burgers, chicken, salads, beverages	30,197	$989,000-2.2 mil
7.	7-Eleven Inc. (10)	Convenience stores	55,944	$38,000-1.1 mil
8.	Dunkin' Donuts (11)	Coffee, doughnuts, baked goods	11,750	$217,000-1.6 mil
9.	Denny's Inc. (8).	Family restaurants	1,598	$1.2 mil-2.1 mil
10.	Anytime Fitness (2).	Fitness centers	3,097	$63,000-418,000
11.	Pizza Hut Inc. (9)	Pizza, pasta, wings.	13,248	$297,000-2.1 mil
12.	Hardee's (17)	Burgers, chicken, biscuits.	2,011	$1.3 mil-1.8 mil
13.	Jack in the Box (4)	Hamburgers	1,836	$1.3 mil-2.4 mil
14.	Ace Hardware Corp. (29)	Hardware and home improvement stores.	4,800	$239,000-1.6 mil
15.	GNC Franchising (23).	Vitamins and nutrition products	3,226	$192,000-354,000
16.	Sport Clips (36)	Men's sports-theme hair salons	1,485	$183,000-352,000
17.	The UPS Store (21)	Postal, business, print, & communications services	4,908	$168,000-354,000
18.	Taco Bell (19)	Mexican food	5,507	$1.2 mil-2.6 mil
19.	Papa Murphy's (32)	Take-and-bake pizza.	1,369	$265,000-446,000
20.	Aaron's (15)	Furniture, electronics, computer, and appliance leasing and sales	740	$276,000-783,000
21.	RE/MAX LLC (75).	Real estate	6,986	$38,000-280,000
22.	Snap-on Tools (25)	Professional tools and equipment.	5,236	$160,700-320,000
23.	Jiffy Lube Intl. Inc. (27)	Oil changes, light repairs	2,085	$219,000-400,000
24.	Jan-Pro Franchising Intl. Inc. (12) . . .	Commercial cleaning	6,975	$3,985-$51,605
25.	Cruise Planners (22).	Travel agencies.	2,257	$2,000-23,000

NA = Not available. **Note:** Franchises are ranked by a combination of factors, including financial strength and stability, growth rate, number of locations, startup costs, and whether the company provides financing. (1) Includes locations outside the U.S. but not company-owned franchises. (2) Does not include franchise fees, which vary.

Small Businesses in the U.S. Economy, 1977-2014
Source: Business Dynamics Statistics, U.S. Census Bureau

Year	Total businesses	Small businesses	Small businesses as % of total	Total employed	Small business employees	% employed by small business
1977	3,432,013	3,421,875	99.7%	66,091,813	34,519,673	52.2%
1978	3,472,195	3,461,831	99.7	69,670,354	37,226,003	53.4
1979	3,599,612	3,588,766	99.7	74,016,679	39,784,612	53.8
1980	3,608,883	3,597,797	99.7	74,749,926	39,441,701	52.8
1981	3,567,814	3,556,513	99.7	73,539,034	38,237,469	52.0
1982	3,623,736	3,611,819	99.7	74,482,225	38,761,661	52.0
1983	3,690,777	3,678,597	99.7	72,716,866	38,460,148	52.9
1984	3,838,655	3,826,450	99.7	77,386,764	41,649,922	53.8
1985	3,977,854	3,965,106	99.7	80,896,890	44,020,000	54.4
1986	4,088,356	4,074,915	99.7	83,467,839	45,579,787	54.6
1987	4,202,248	4,187,761	99.7	85,651,976	46,950,187	54.8
1988	4,200,061	4,185,483	99.7	87,414,682	47,273,081	54.1
1989	4,215,265	4,199,664	99.6	90,415,809	48,303,217	53.4
1990	4,312,888	4,297,295	99.6	92,553,401	49,405,250	53.4
1991	4,375,709	4,359,937	99.6	91,404,879	48,274,797	52.8
1992	4,398,407	4,382,381	99.6	91,685,318	48,559,676	53.0
1993	4,451,671	4,436,034	99.6	93,249,403	49,428,646	53.0
1994	4,526,571	4,510,367	99.6	94,945,113	50,335,138	53.0
1995	4,617,160	4,600,494	99.6	98,485,465	52,017,989	52.8
1996	4,694,155	4,676,975	99.6	100,344,551	52,656,815	52.5
1997	4,767,576	4,749,945	99.6	103,184,739	53,967,419	52.3
1998	4,799,956	4,782,104	99.6	106,272,897	54,754,435	51.5
1999	4,828,276	4,809,869	99.6	109,063,779	55,529,962	50.9
2000	4,840,136	4,821,350	99.6	112,607,042	56,925,603	50.6
2001	4,884,934	4,865,778	99.6	114,009,997	57,132,852	50.1
2002	4,923,438	4,904,152	99.6	111,827,416	56,576,798	50.6
2003	4,965,328	4,946,995	99.6	112,409,112	57,701,058	51.3
2004	5,041,791	5,023,270	99.6	113,707,630	58,647,695	51.6
2005	5,141,900	5,123,273	99.6	115,140,083	59,011,437	51.3
2006	5,185,814	5,166,701	99.6	118,614,800	60,480,334	51.0
2007	5,253,216	5,232,786	99.6	119,627,021	60,201,946	50.3
2008	5,204,140	5,184,058	99.6	119,780,685	59,688,492	49.8
2009	5,030,089	5,010,001	99.6	113,333,976	56,056,768	49.5
2010	4,956,460	4,937,934	99.6	110,792,627	54,863,184	49.5
2011	4,915,209	4,896,614	99.6	112,121,688	54,908,981	49.0
2012	4,991,078	4,971,340	99.6	114,761,137	56,024,730	48.8
2013	5,025,673	5,005,505	99.6	117,194,376	56,678,331	48.4
2014	5,060,326	5,039,793	99.6	119,102,910	57,525,365	48.3

Note: Small businesses are firms employing less than 500 people. Figures include only businesses with paid employees.

New Circulating and Commemorative Coins
Source: United States Mint, U.S. Dept. of the Treasury

Dollar coins. A large, unwieldy dollar coin featuring the likeness of Pres. Dwight D. Eisenhower was minted 1971-78. The smaller Susan B. Anthony dollar, minted 1979-81, marked the first time that a woman other than a mythical figure appeared on a generally circulated U.S. coin. A golden dollar coin was first minted in 2000. It depicts Sacagawea, a Shoshone woman who helped guide explorers Lewis and Clark, on the obverse. In 2007, the mint began issuing a series of golden dollar coins featuring U.S. presidents on the front and the Statue of Liberty on the back. Each included the president's name, likeness, and years of service. Four were issued each year in the order in which the presidents served. The 2015 set featured Harry S. Truman, Dwight D. Eisenhower, John F. Kennedy, and Lyndon B. Johnson. Only presidents deceased more than two years were honored, so the program ended in 2016 with coins commemorating Richard Nixon, Gerald Ford, and Ronald Reagan. The mint also issues golden dollar coins whose reverse sides celebrate the important contributions made by American Indian tribes to the development of the U.S. The 2014 coin commemorated the hospitality that ensured the success of the Lewis and Clark expedition; the 2015 coin celebrated the contribution of Mohawk iron workers; and the 2016 coin honored the Native American code talkers from World War I and World War II.

America the Beautiful quarters. In 2010, the U.S. Mint began an initiative to honor 56 national parks and other sites of national importance. Five new reverse designs appear on the quarter-dollar each year in 2010-21; the order of issuance corresponds to the order in which the featured site was first established. The 2015 coins celebrated Homestead Natl. Monument of America, NE; Kisatchie Natl. Forest, LA; Blue Ridge Parkway, NC; Bombay Hook Natl. Wildlife Refuge, DE; and Saratoga Natl. Historical Park, NY. The 2016 coins commemorated Shawnee Natl. Forest, IL; Cumberland Gap Natl. Historical Park, KY; Harpers Ferry Natl. Historical Park, WV; Theodore Roosevelt Natl. Park, ND; and Fort Moultrie at Fort Sumter Natl. Monument, SC. The 2017 coins depict Effigy Mounds Natl. Monument, IA; Frederick Douglass Natl. Historic Site, DC; Ozark Natl. Scenic Riverways, MO; Ellis Island Natl. Monument, NJ; and George Rogers Clark Natl. Historical Park, IN.

Commemorative coins. From 1892 to 1954, and again since 1982, Congress has authorized the mint to produce more than 50 different commemorative coins. Recent issues include the 2009 Louis Braille Bicentennial-Braille Literacy silver dollar, the 2014 Civil Rights Act of 1964 silver dollar, and the 2016 100th Anniversary of the Natl. Park Service coins.

Bureau of Engraving and Printing
Source: Bureau of Engraving and Printing, U.S. Dept. of the Treasury

The Bureau of Engraving and Printing manufactures the financial and other securities of the U.S. It designs and prints a variety of products, including Federal Reserve notes (bills in various denominations), Treasury securities, identification cards, naturalization certificates, and other special security documents. The bureau produces printings in denominations ranging from a 1/5-cent wine stamp to a $100,000,000 Intl. Monetary Fund special note. It also produces all hand-engraved invitations issued by the White House.

The first general circulation of paper money by the federal government dates back to 1861, prior to the establishment of the bureau, when Congress authorized the U.S. Treasury to issue non-interest-bearing demand notes, nicknamed "greenbacks" because of their color, to finance the Civil War. A portrait of Pres. Abraham Lincoln appeared on the face of the first $10 notes. By 1862, the design of U.S. currency incorporated fine-line engraving, intricate geometric lathe work patterns, a Treasury seal, and engraved signatures to aid in counterfeit deterrence. All U.S. currency issued since 1861 remain valid and redeemable at full face value.

The Bureau of Engraving and Printing began operations by 1862, originally separating and sealing bank notes that were printed by private companies. In 1877, the bureau became the sole producer of U.S. currency. The Federal Reserve Act of 1913 created the Federal Reserve as the nation's central bank and provided for currency called Federal Reserve notes. The first notes, issued the following year, were $10 notes bearing a portrait of Pres. Andrew Jackson. In 1929, the look of U.S. currency was standardized. The national motto, "In God We Trust," was added to paper money in 1957.

In 2016, the Treasury Dept. announced plans for a major overhaul of U.S. currency, including new faces on the $5, $10, and $20. Most notably, former slave and abolitionist Harriet Tubman will replace Andrew Jackson on the front of the $20 bill (Jackson will move to the back of the bill). Alexander Hamilton will remain on the front of the $10 bill, and Abraham Lincoln on the front of the $5 bill, but the reverse of both bills will be redesigned. The new $10 reverse will honor the women's suffrage movement with images of Lucretia Mott, Sojourner Truth, Susan B. Anthony, Elizabeth Cady Stanton, and Alice Paul; the $5 will commemorate historic events that took place at the Lincoln Memorial, and will feature images of Martin Luther King Jr., Marian Anderson, and Eleanor Roosevelt. Design concepts for the new bills will be unveiled in 2020, with the redesigned $10 scheduled to enter circulation first.

The Bureau of Engraving and Printing currently operates two facilities, one in Washington, DC, opened in 1914, and one in Fort Worth, TX, which began operations in 1991.

Denominations of U.S. Currency
Since 1969 the largest denomination of U.S. currency that has been issued is the $100 bill. As larger-denomination bills reach the Federal Reserve Bank, they are removed from circulation. Because some discontinued currency is expected to be in the hands of holders for many years, the description of the various denominations below is continued.

Note	Portrait	Embellishment on back	Note	Portrait	Embellishment on back
$1	George Washington	Great Seal of U.S.	$500	William McKinley	Ornate denominational marking
2	Thomas Jefferson	Signers of Declaration	1,000	Grover Cleveland	Ornate denominational marking
5	Abraham Lincoln	Lincoln Memorial	5,000	James Madison	Washington resigning as Army commander
10	Alexander Hamilton	U.S. Treasury	10,000	Salmon Chase	Embarkation of the Pilgrims
20	Andrew Jackson	White House	100,000*	Woodrow Wilson	Ornate denominational marking
50	Ulysses S. Grant	U.S. Capitol			
100	Benjamin Franklin	Independence Hall			

* = For use only in transactions between Federal Reserve System and Treasury Department.

The U.S. $1 Bill

Plate position: Shows where on the 32-note plate this bill was printed.

Serial number: Each bill has its own.

Federal Reserve Bank number: Shows which district issued the bill.

Federal Reserve seal: The name of the Federal Reserve Bank that issued the bill is printed in the seal. The letter also tells you which bank distributed the bill. Here are the number and letter codes for the 12 Federal Reserve Banks:

  1/A: Boston
  2/B: New York
  3/C: Philadelphia
  4/D: Cleveland
  5/E: Richmond
  6/F: Atlanta
  7/G: Chicago
  8/H: St. Louis
  9/I: Minneapolis
  10/J: Kansas City
  11/K: Dallas
  12/L: San Francisco

Treasury Department seal: The balancing scales represent justice. The pointed stripe across the middle has 13 stars for the original 13 colonies. The key represents authority.

Plate serial number: Shows which printing plate was used for the face of the bill.

Treasurer of the U.S. signature

Series indicator: Year note's design was first used.

Secretary of the Treasury signature

Plate serial number: Shows which plate was used for the back.

Front of the Great Seal of the United States: The bald eagle is the national bird. The shield has 13 stripes for the 13 original colonies. The eagle holds 13 arrows (symbol of war) and an olive branch with 13 olives and leaves (symbol of peace). Above the eagle is the motto "E Pluribus Unum," Latin for "out of many, one," and a constellation of 13 stars.

Reverse of the Great Seal of the United States: The pyramid symbolizes something that endures for ages. The eye, known as the Eye of Providence, probably comes from an ancient Egyptian symbol. The pyramid has 13 levels; at its base are the Roman numerals for 1776, the year of American independence. "Annuit Coeptis" is Latin for "God has favored our undertaking." "Novus Ordo Seclorum" is Latin for "a new order of the ages." Both phrases are from the works of the Roman poet Virgil.

U.S. Currency and Coin

Source: Bureau of the Fiscal Service, U.S. Dept. of the Treasury

Total Money in Circulation, 1955-2016

Date	Dollars (mil)	Per capita[1]	Date	Dollars (mil)	Per capita[1]	Date	Dollars (mil)	Per capita[1]
June 30, 1955	$30,229	$183	Sept. 30, 1985	$187,337	$782	June 30, 2011	$1,028,910	$3,302
June 30, 1960	32,064	177	Sept. 30, 1990	278,903	1,105	June 30, 2012	1,111,901	3,540
June 30, 1965	39,719	204	Sept. 30, 1995	409,272	1,553	June 30, 2013	1,193,771	3,774
June 30, 1970	54,351	265	Sept. 30, 2000	568,614	2,061	June 30, 2014	1,282,431	4,027
June 30, 1975	81,196	380	Sept. 30, 2005	766,487	2,578	June 30, 2015	1,368,622	4,260
Sept. 30, 1980	129,916	581	June 30, 2010	945,138	3,051	June 30, 2016	1,463,923	4,520

(1) Based on U.S. Census Bureau population estimates.

Money in Circulation by Denomination, 2016

Denomination	Amount in circulation	Denomination	Amount in circulation	Denomination	Amount in circulation
$1	$11,511,238,335	$50	$80,259,300,050	$10,000	$3,450,000
$2	2,277,441,422	$100	1,118,111,721,100	Fractional notes[1]	600
$5	13,671,833,960	$500	141,973,500	**Total currency**	**1,418,323,910,907**
$10	18,568,730,400	$1,000	165,317,000	**Total coins**	**45,599,166,586**
$20	173,611,139,540	$5,000	1,765,000	**Total currency and coins**	**1,463,923,077,493**

(1) Represents the value of certain partial denominations not presented for redemption.

Budget Receipts and Outlays, 1789-1940

Source: U.S. Dept. of the Treasury
(in thousands of dollars; annual statements for years ending June 30, unless otherwise noted)

Yearly average	Receipts	Outlays	Yearly average	Receipts	Outlays	Yearly average	Receipts	Outlays
1789-1800[1]	$5,717	$5,776	1866-1870	$447,301	$377,642	1906-1910	$628,507	$639,178
1801-1810[2]	13,056	9,086	1871-1875	336,830	287,460	1911-1915	710,227	720,252
1811-1820[2]	21,032	23,943	1876-1880	288,124	255,598	1916-1920	3,483,652	8,065,333
1821-1830[2]	21,928	16,162	1881-1885	366,961	257,691	1921-1925	4,306,673	3,578,989
1831-1840[2]	30,461	24,495	1886-1890	375,448	279,134	1926-1930	4,069,138	3,182,807
1841-1850[2]	28,545	34,097	1891-1895	352,891	363,599	1931-1935	2,770,973	5,214,874
1851-1860	60,237	60,163	1896-1900	434,877	457,451	1936-1940	4,960,614	10,192,367
1861-1865	160,907	683,785	1901-1905	559,481	535,559			

(1) Average for period Mar. 4, 1789, to Dec. 31, 1800. (2) Years 1801-42 end Dec. 31; average for 1841-50 is for the period Jan. 1, 1841, to June 30, 1850.

U.S. Budget Receipts and Outlays, Fiscal Years 2000-15

Source: Congressional Budget Office; *Budget of the U.S. Government*, Office of Mgmt. and Budget, Exec. Office of the President

A $236 bil surplus in 2000 turned into a $1.4 tril deficit by 2009. Since then, however, the deficit has been trimmed by nearly $1 tril. A nearly 50% increase in tax receipts over the past decade has helped the government keep pace with increased spending on national defense, Medicare, and other health and income security programs.

(in millions of current dollars; numbers may not add up to totals because of independent rounding or omitted subcategories, including some subcategories with negative values)

Function and subfunction	2000	2005	2010	2013	2014	2015
NET RECEIPTS	$2,025,191	$2,153,611	$2,162,706	$2,775,103	$3,021,487	$3,249,886
Individual income taxes	1,004,462	927,222	898,549	1,316,405	1,394,568	1,540,802
Corporation income taxes	207,289	278,282	191,437	273,506	320,731	343,797
Social insurance and retirement receipts	652,852	794,125	864,814	947,820	1,023,458	1,065,257
Employment and general retirement	620,451	747,664	815,894	887,445	955,029	1,010,427
Old-age and survivors insurance (off-budget)	411,677	493,646	539,996	575,555	628,792	658,543
Disability insurance (off-budget)	68,907	83,830	91,691	97,719	106,773	111,829
Hospital insurance	135,529	166,068	180,068	209,270	224,107	234,189
Railroad retirement/pension fund	2,688	2,284	2,285	2,791	3,032	3,336
Railroad social security equivalent account	1,650	1,836	1,854	2,110	2,325	2,530
Unemployment insurance	27,640	42,002	44,823	56,811	54,957	51,178
Other retirement	4,761	4,459	4,097	3,564	3,472	3,652
Excise taxes	68,865	73,094	66,909	84,007	93,368	98,279
Federal funds	22,692	22,547	18,256	28,330	34,240	37,759
Alcohol	8,140	8,111	9,229	9,253	9,815	9,639
Tobacco	7,221	7,920	17,160	15,083	15,562	14,453
Telephone	5,670	6,047	993	733	611	607
Transportation fuels	819	−770	−11,030	−2,681	−3,509	−3,394
Trust funds	46,173	50,547	48,653	55,677	59,128	60,520
Transportation	34,972	37,892	34,992	36,462	39,049	40,813
Airport and airway	9,739	10,314	10,612	12,854	13,513	14,268
Black lung disability	518	610	595	531	579	552
Inland waterway	101	91	74	75	82	98
Oil spill liability	182	—	476	410	436	496
Aquatic resources	342	429	580	539	569	574
Leaking underground storage tank	184	189	169	162	173	179
Tobacco assessments	—	899	937	947	1,140	49
Vaccine injury compensation	133	123	218	204	243	275
Other receipts	91,723	80,888	140,997	153,365	189,362	201,751
OUTLAYS	1,788,950	2,471,957	3,457,079	3,454,647	3,506,089	3,688,292
National defense	294,363	495,294	693,485	633,446	603,457	589,564
Department of Defense—Military	281,029	474,071	666,703	607,795	577,897	562,499
Military personnel	75,950	127,463	155,690	150,825	148,923	145,206
Operation and maintenance	105,812	188,118	275,988	259,662	244,481	247,239
Procurement	51,696	82,294	133,603	114,912	107,485	101,342
Research, development, test, and evaluation	37,602	65,694	76,990	66,892	64,928	64,124
Military construction	5,109	5,331	21,169	12,318	9,823	8,114
Family housing	3,413	3,720	3,173	1,829	1,354	1,198
Atomic energy defense activities	12,138	18,031	19,308	17,634	17,416	18,692
Defense-related activities	1,196	3,192	7,474	8,017	8,144	8,373
International affairs	17,213	34,565	45,195	46,231	46,686	48,576
International development and humanitarian assistance	6,516	17,696	19,014	22,551	23,534	24,087
International security assistance	6,387	7,895	11,363	9,954	11,381	12,907
Conduct of foreign affairs	4,708	9,148	13,557	13,038	12,859	13,246
Foreign information and exchange activities	817	1,129	1,485	1,519	1,464	1,531
International financial programs	−1,215	−1,303	−224	−831	−2,552	−3,195
General science, space, and technology	18,594	23,597	30,100	28,908	28,570	29,412
General science and basic research	6,167	8,819	11,730	12,479	12,011	11,719
Space flight, research, and supporting activities	12,427	14,778	18,370	16,429	16,559	17,693
Energy	−761	440	11,618	11,042	5,270	6,838
Energy supply	−1,818	−929	5,801	9,038	4,056	4,707
Energy conservation	666	883	4,997	1,240	910	1,187
Emergency energy preparedness	162	162	199	217	−140	449
Energy information, policy, and regulation	229	324	621	547	444	495
Natural resources and environment	25,003	27,983	43,667	38,145	36,171	36,034
Water resources	5,078	5,724	11,662	7,675	7,912	7,760
Conservation and land management	6,762	6,226	10,783	10,723	9,707	10,519
Recreational resources	2,540	2,990	3,911	3,506	3,362	3,501
Pollution control and abatement	7,395	8,065	10,841	9,624	8,634	7,241
Agriculture	36,458	26,565	21,356	29,678	24,386	18,500
Farm income stabilization	33,446	22,048	16,604	25,213	20,012	13,424
Agricultural research and services	3,012	4,517	4,752	4,465	4,374	5,076
Commerce and housing credit	3,207	7,566	−82,316	−83,199	−94,861	−37,905
Mortgage credit	−3,335	−862	35,804	−87,854	−84,300	−35,968
Postal Service	2,129	−1,223	−682	−1,839	−2,453	−1,610
Deposit insurance	−3,053	−1,371	−32,033	4,292	−13,823	−12,812
Transportation	46,853	67,894	91,972	91,673	91,938	89,533
Ground transportation	31,697	42,317	60,784	60,005	60,827	59,126
Air transportation	10,571	18,807	21,431	21,464	20,923	20,033
Water transportation	4,394	6,439	9,351	9,774	9,782	9,994
Community and regional development	10,623	26,262	23,894	32,336	20,670	20,670
Community development	5,480	5,861	9,901	7,814	7,896	7,817
Area and regional development	2,538	2,745	3,249	1,540	3,027	3,861
Disaster relief and insurance	2,605	17,656	10,744	22,982	9,747	8,992
Education, training, employment, and social services	53,764	97,555	128,598	72,808	90,615	122,061
Elementary, secondary, and vocational education	20,578	38,271	73,261	42,407	40,813	40,022
Higher education	10,115	31,442	20,908	−525	20,104	51,341
Research and general education aids	2,543	3,124	3,631	3,705	3,552	3,493

Function and subfunction	2000	2005	2010	2013	2014	2015
Training and employment	$6,777	$6,852	$9,854	$7,271	$7,013	$7,103
Social services	12,557	16,251	19,179	18,062	17,299	18,303
Health	**154,504**	**250,548**	**369,068**	**358,315**	**409,449**	**482,223**
Health care services	136,201	219,559	330,710	321,849	374,581	446,360
Health research and training	15,979	28,050	34,214	32,881	30,911	31,400
Consumer and occupational health and safety	2,324	2,939	4,144	3,585	3,957	4,463
Medicare	**197,113**	**298,638**	**451,636**	**497,826**	**511,688**	**546,202**
Income security	**253,724**	**345,847**	**622,210**	**536,511**	**513,644**	**508,843**
General retirement and disability insurance (excl. social security)	5,189	6,976	6,564	6,969	8,776	7,805
Federal employee retirement and disability	77,152	93,351	119,867	131,739	134,613	139,166
Unemployment compensation	23,012	35,435	160,145	70,729	45,717	34,978
Housing assistance	28,949	37,899	58,651	46,687	47,615	47,823
Food and nutrition assistance	32,483	50,833	95,110	109,706	102,936	104,797
Social security	**409,423**	**523,305**	**706,737**	**813,551**	**850,533**	**887,753**
Veterans benefits and services	**46,989**	**70,120**	**108,384**	**138,938**	**149,616**	**159,738**
Income security for veterans	24,907	35,767	49,163	65,890	70,906	76,360
Veterans education, training, and rehabilitation	1,285	2,790	8,089	12,893	13,506	13,383
Hospital and medical care for veterans	19,516	28,754	45,714	52,544	56,226	61,908
Veterans housing	364	860	540	1,328	2,143	743
Administration of justice	**28,499**	**40,019**	**54,383**	**52,601**	**50,457**	**51,903**
Federal law enforcement activities	12,121	19,912	28,713	27,295	26,106	26,934
Federal litigative and judicial activities	7,762	9,641	13,073	14,633	14,224	14,717
Federal correctional activities	3,707	5,862	7,748	6,892	6,751	7,049
Criminal justice assistance	4,909	4,604	4,849	3,781	3,376	3,203
General government	**13,013**	**16,997**	**23,014**	**27,737**	**26,913**	**20,969**
Legislative functions	2,227	3,460	4,100	3,729	3,568	3,760
Executive direction and management	456	569	528	478	484	510
Central fiscal operations	8,285	9,515	11,906	12,051	11,695	11,096
General property and records management	−32	472	1,194	−10	−386	−490
Central personnel management	184	101	338	372	268	81
General purpose fiscal assistance	2,084	3,333	5,082	7,852	7,643	7,266
Deductions for offsetting receipts	−2,383	−2,841	−1,721	−2,692	127	−4,782
Net interest	**222,949**	**183,986**	**196,194**	**220,885**	**228,956**	**223,181**
Undistributed offsetting receipts	**−42,581**	**−65,224**	**−82,116**	**−92,785**	**−88,044**	**−115,803**
Employer share, employee retirement (on-budget)	−30,214	−47,977	−62,100	−65,155	−63,612	−65,112
TOTAL SURPLUS/DEFICIT	**236,241**	**−318,346**	**−1,294,373**	**−679,544**	**−484,627**	**−438,406**

Federal Receipts, Outlays, and Surpluses or Deficits, 1901-2016

Source: *Budget of the U.S. Government, Fiscal Year 2016*, Office of Management and Budget, Exec. Office of the President
(in millions of current dollars)

Fiscal year	Receipts	Outlays	Surplus or deficit (−)	Fiscal year	Receipts	Outlays	Surplus or deficit (−)	Fiscal year	Receipts	Outlays	Surplus or deficit (−)
1901	$588	$525	**$63**	1940	$6,548	$9,468	−$2,920	1979	$463,302	$504,028	− $40,726
1902	562	485	**77**	1941	8,712	13,653	−4,941	1980	517,112	590,941	−73,830
1903	562	517	**45**	1942	14,634	35,137	−20,503	1981	599,272	678,241	−78,968
1904	541	584	−43	1943	24,001	78,555	−54,554	1982	617,766	745,743	−127,977
1905	544	567	−23	1944	43,747	91,304	−47,557	1983	600,562	808,364	−207,802
1906	595	570	**25**	1945	45,159	92,712	−47,553	1984	666,438	851,805	−185,367
1907	666	579	**87**	1946	39,296	55,232	−15,936	1985	734,037	946,344	−212,308
1908	602	659	−57	1947	38,514	34,496	**4,018**	1986	769,155	990,382	−221,227
1909	604	694	−89	1948	41,560	29,764	**11,796**	1987	854,288	1,004,017	−149,730
1910	676	694	−18	1949	39,415	38,835	**580**	1988	909,238	1,064,416	−155,178
1911	702	691	**11**	1950	39,443	42,562	−3,119	1989	991,105	1,143,744	−152,639
1912	693	690	**3**	1951	51,616	45,514	**6,102**	1990	1,031,958	1,252,994	−221,036
1913	714	715	—	1952	66,167	67,686	−1,519	1991	1,054,988	1,324,226	−269,238
1914	725	726	—	1953	69,608	76,101	−6,493	1992	1,091,208	1,381,529	−290,321
1915	683	746	−63	1954	69,701	70,855	−1,154	1993	1,154,335	1,409,386	−255,051
1916	761	713	**48**	1955	65,451	68,444	−2,993	1994	1,258,566	1,461,753	−203,186
1917	1,101	1,954	−853	1956	74,587	70,640	**3,947**	1995	1,351,790	1,515,742	−163,952
1918	3,645	12,677	−9,032	1957	79,990	76,578	**3,412**	1996	1,453,053	1,560,484	−107,431
1919	5,130	18,493	−13,363	1958	79,636	82,405	−2,769	1997	1,579,232	1,601,116	−21,884
1920	6,649	6,358	**291**	1959	79,249	92,098	−12,849	1998	1,721,728	1,652,458	**69,270**
1921	5,571	5,062	**509**	1960	92,492	92,191	**301**	1999	1,827,452	1,701,842	**125,610**
1922	4,026	3,289	**736**	1961	94,388	97,723	−3,335	2000	2,025,191	1,788,950	**236,241**
1923	3,853	3,140	**713**	1962	99,676	106,821	−7,146	2001	1,991,082	1,862,846	**128,236**
1924	3,871	2,908	**963**	1963	106,560	111,316	−4,756	2002	1,853,136	2,010,894	−157,758
1925	3,641	2,924	**717**	1964	112,613	118,528	−5,915	2003	1,782,314	2,159,899	−377,585
1926	3,795	2,930	**865**	1965	116,817	118,228	−1,411	2004	1,880,114	2,292,841	−412,727
1927	4,013	2,857	**1,155**	1966	130,835	134,532	−3,698	2005	2,153,611	2,471,957	−318,346
1928	3,900	2,961	**939**	1967	148,822	157,464	−8,643	2006	2,406,869	2,655,050	−248,181
1929	3,862	3,127	**734**	1968	152,973	178,134	−25,161	2007	2,567,985	2,728,686	−160,701
1930	4,058	3,320	**738**	1969	186,882	183,640	**3,242**	2008	2,523,991	2,982,544	−458,553
1931	3,116	3,577	−462	1970	192,807	195,649	−2,842	2009	2,104,989	3,517,677	−1,412,688
1932	1,924	4,659	−2,735	1971	187,139	210,172	−23,033	2010	2,162,706	3,457,079	−1,294,373
1933	1,997	4,598	−2,602	1972	207,309	230,681	−23,373	2011	2,303,466	3,603,059	−1,299,593
1934	2,955	6,541	−3,586	1973	230,799	245,707	−14,908	2012	2,449,988	3,536,951	−1,086,963
1935	3,609	6,412	−2,803	1974	263,224	269,359	−6,135	2013	2,775,103	3,454,647	−679,544
1936	3,923	8,228	−4,304	1975	279,090	332,342	−53,242	2014	3,021,487	3,506,114	−484,627
1937	5,387	7,580	−2,193	1976	298,060	371,792	−73,732	2015	3,249,886	3,688,292	−438,406
1938	6,751	6,840	−89	1977	355,559	409,218	−53,659	2016[1]	3,335,502	3,951,307	−615,805
1939	6,295	9,141	−2,846	1978	399,561	458,746	−59,185				

— = $500,000 or less. Figures in **bold** denote annual surplus. **Note:** Budget figures prior to 1933 are based on administrative budget concepts rather than unified budget concepts. Through 1976, fiscal year ends June 30; after 1976, fiscal year ends Sept. 30. Surplus or deficit column may not equal difference between figures because of rounding. (1) Estimate as of Feb. 1, 2016.

Public Debt of the U.S., 1946-2020

Source: *Budget of the U.S. Government*, Office of Management and Budget, Exec. Office of the President

Year	Debt held by public Current dollars (bil)	Debt held by public FY2015 dollars (bil)	As % of GDP	Interest on public debt as % of— Total federal outlays	Interest on public debt as % of— GDP	Year	Debt held by public Current dollars (bil)	Debt held by public FY2015 dollars (bil)	As % of GDP	Interest on public debt as % of— Total federal outlays	Interest on public debt as % of— GDP
1946	$241.9	$2,416.9	106.1%	7.6%	1.8%	2005	$4,592.2	$5,510.9	35.6%	7.7%	1.5%
1950	219.0	1,770.6	78.5	11.4	1.7	2010	9,018.9	9,796.9	60.9	6.6	1.5
1955	226.6	1,610.1	55.7	7.6	1.3	2011	10,128.2	10,783.0	65.9	7.4	1.7
1960	236.8	1,490.9	44.3	8.5	1.5	2012	11,281.1	11,794.1	70.4	6.6	1.4
1965	260.8	1,537.5	36.7	8.1	1.3	2013	11,982.7	12,316.1	72.6	7.5	1.6
1970	283.2	1,391.2	27.0	7.9	1.5	2014	12,779.9	12,914.9	74.4	7.7	1.6
1975	394.7	1,429.0	24.5	7.5	1.6	2015	13,116.7	13,116.7	73.7	7.1	1.5
1980	711.9	1,793.8	25.5	10.6	2.2	2016[1]	14,128.7	13,954.8	76.5	7.5	1.6
1985	1,507.3	2,898.7	35.3	16.2	3.6	2017[1]	14,763.0	14,320.2	76.5	8.8	1.9
1990	2,411.6	3,987.5	40.8	16.2	3.4	2018[1]	15,323.5	14,604.1	76.1	10.0	2.2
1995	3,604.4	5,259.4	47.5	15.8	3.2	2019[1]	15,982.2	14,936.5	76.1	11.1	2.4
2000	3,409.8	4,586.5	33.6	13.0	2.3	2020[1]	16,614.9	15,226.5	75.8	11.9	2.7

Note: As of end of fiscal year. Through 1976, the fiscal year ended June 30. For 1977 on, the fiscal year ended Sept. 30. (1) Estimate.

State Finances: Revenues, Taxes, Expenditures, and Debt, 2014

Source: U.S. Census Bureau, U.S. Dept. of Commerce

(in thousands of dollars)

State	Revenues Total revenue	Revenues General revenues	Revenues Intergovt. revenue	Taxes	Total expenditures	Debt at end of fiscal year
Alabama	$28,280,058	$22,948,381	$8,135,043	$9,293,754	$28,127,696	$8,907,686
Alaska	12,871,274	10,436,362	2,810,194	3,392,869	12,920,065	6,048,619
Arizona	39,053,409	29,349,780	10,951,041	13,084,043	33,231,219	14,315,828
Arkansas	23,417,228	18,058,204	6,096,896	8,936,781	20,410,423	4,533,255
California	353,368,448	230,741,509	63,516,604	138,069,870	284,555,886	156,807,868
Colorado	34,387,619	24,739,273	7,277,716	11,755,394	30,648,903	16,929,327
Connecticut	31,291,641	25,845,190	6,364,610	15,937,742	29,308,254	33,229,567
Delaware	9,298,130	7,605,276	2,101,677	3,176,169	8,786,763	5,354,253
Florida	104,127,723	76,827,084	25,801,529	35,384,350	83,274,449	36,348,245
Georgia	54,206,860	39,007,185	14,611,862	18,628,502	45,452,071	13,380,184
Hawaii	15,055,561	11,304,424	2,810,537	6,033,331	12,378,789	8,426,573
Idaho	10,511,073	7,435,715	2,531,469	3,671,715	8,449,255	3,606,305
Illinois	90,167,626	66,636,637	18,227,252	39,182,894	77,319,107	65,831,516
Indiana	39,528,798	33,259,949	11,055,684	16,846,961	35,990,274	21,120,303
Iowa	25,196,625	18,889,101	6,218,631	8,271,839	21,214,460	6,343,482
Kansas	19,012,887	15,391,445	3,975,772	7,334,481	16,920,498	6,742,696
Kentucky	31,507,525	25,268,291	9,768,931	11,103,545	29,938,181	14,829,986
Louisiana	33,275,548	25,351,939	10,214,940	9,695,281	31,803,632	18,996,129
Maine	10,528,889	8,192,598	3,028,373	3,847,181	9,258,232	5,473,870
Maryland	44,699,507	36,280,744	11,038,357	18,929,069	41,308,885	26,378,595
Massachusetts	61,746,528	49,046,286	14,165,615	25,235,726	58,304,754	74,234,582
Michigan	68,884,416	54,834,376	17,929,672	24,803,973	63,861,993	31,528,074
Minnesota	50,419,432	37,645,695	9,838,098	23,128,901	41,845,094	15,818,353
Mississippi	23,346,924	17,576,209	7,377,669	7,574,515	20,013,073	7,104,085
Missouri	38,507,812	26,676,937	10,394,689	11,240,657	30,454,270	19,041,613
Montana	8,939,148	5,977,163	2,341,686	2,655,553	7,218,707	3,402,199
Nebraska	12,112,397	9,778,806	3,094,850	4,877,401	10,046,378	1,908,707
Nevada	19,049,438	11,479,806	3,021,228	7,143,169	13,217,485	3,520,774
New Hampshire	8,261,811	5,912,732	1,853,129	2,282,507	7,344,811	8,098,921
New Jersey	65,657,635	56,558,996	16,049,091	29,679,226	69,081,342	66,089,959
New Mexico	20,421,122	15,590,791	5,558,490	5,757,432	17,720,552	6,887,017
New York	205,789,823	146,853,198	49,114,188	76,978,982	178,324,895	136,440,657
North Carolina	61,748,866	46,909,231	15,643,257	23,396,751	51,113,382	17,853,232
North Dakota	9,966,316	8,849,893	1,534,035	6,120,435	7,486,329	1,886,865
Ohio	96,424,844	62,101,141	22,350,068	27,020,625	79,239,198	33,662,042
Oklahoma	28,534,050	21,441,335	7,409,652	9,103,302	23,377,996	9,047,456
Oregon	37,665,178	24,355,892	8,791,134	9,683,640	29,413,524	14,583,105
Pennsylvania	89,537,550	70,354,934	21,868,995	34,192,869	86,985,760	47,572,612
Rhode Island	8,995,804	7,116,847	2,509,818	2,965,975	8,334,471	9,388,127
South Carolina	31,870,556	23,076,006	7,639,636	8,932,564	28,903,767	15,089,289
South Dakota	6,124,116	4,161,877	1,573,610	1,608,496	4,520,937	3,239,167
Tennessee	31,290,576	26,493,021	10,645,251	11,806,329	30,518,934	6,049,178
Texas	160,134,265	121,679,260	40,561,370	55,260,850	130,573,820	41,855,106
Utah	19,413,736	14,974,256	4,211,310	6,312,489	17,039,808	7,327,147
Vermont	6,545,351	5,771,744	1,943,173	2,962,531	6,302,744	3,291,205
Virginia	53,731,192	41,468,565	10,027,820	18,949,272	48,187,730	27,739,117
Washington	55,071,735	38,295,614	11,474,963	19,447,899	47,971,432	31,601,016
West Virginia	15,381,616	12,246,658	4,350,205	5,379,937	13,240,704	7,986,591
Wisconsin	47,260,457	32,441,479	9,255,939	16,410,925	38,583,376	22,367,764
Wyoming	7,450,967	5,780,141	2,208,034	2,263,387	5,894,985	929,532
United States	2,360,070,090	1,739,017,976	551,273,793	865,752,089	2,036,419,293	1,149,147,779

Note: Figures may not add up to totals because of rounding.

State and Local Government Receipts and Current Expenditures, 1960-2015

Source: Bureau of Economic Analysis, U.S. Dept. of Commerce
(in billions of current dollars; as of Aug. 2016)

	1960	1970	1980	1990	2000	2010	2013	2014	2015
Receipts	**$44.2**	**$118.9**	**$335.3**	**$729.6**	**$1,303.1**	**$1,998.5**	**$2,136.5**	**$2,225.0**	**$2,324.7**
Current tax receipts	37.0	91.3	230.0	519.1	893.2	1,305.6	1,479.8	1,517.5	1,562.2
Personal current taxes	4.2	14.2	48.9	122.6	236.7	297.6	372.2	383.3	409.5
Income taxes	2.5	10.9	42.6	109.6	217.4	267.1	339.2	349.9	375.5
Other.	1.7	3.3	6.3	13.0	19.4	30.5	32.9	33.4	34.0
Taxes on production and imports	31.5	73.3	166.7	374.1	621.3	960.4	1,052.2	1,075.9	1,093.3
Sales taxes	12.2	31.6	82.9	184.3	316.8	446.0	507.2	524.9	541.2
Property taxes.	16.2	36.7	68.8	161.5	254.7	435.0	449.5	455.6	462.2
Other.	3.1	5.0	15.0	28.3	49.8	79.4	95.4	95.4	90.0
Taxes on corporate income	1.2	3.7	14.5	22.5	35.2	47.7	55.5	58.3	59.4
Contributions for government social insurance	0.5	1.1	3.6	10.0	10.8	18.1	18.6	18.9	18.8
Income receipts on assets	1.3	5.2	26.3	68.5	93.9	82.6	74.3	75.7	78.0
Interest receipts	1.0	4.3	23.1	64.1	86.3	69.1	58.0	58.7	60.0
Dividends	—	—	0.1	0.2	1.4	2.3	3.7	3.8	4.3
Rents and royalties.	0.3	0.8	3.1	4.2	6.3	11.2	12.6	13.2	13.7
Current transfer receipts	4.3	20.1	76.9	126.4	299.7	612.0	571.2	621.5	673.8
Federal grants-in-aid.	3.8	18.3	69.7	104.4	233.1	505.3	450.1	494.8	532.0
From business (net)	0.2	0.6	2.5	7.1	28.6	43.4	49.6	48.7	65.9
From persons	0.3	1.2	4.7	14.9	38.0	63.2	71.5	72.8	75.5
Current surplus of government enterprises	1.2	1.3	−1.4	5.6	5.4	−19.8	−7.5	−8.6	−8.1
Expenditures.	**41.6**	**115.9**	**329.9**	**736.0**	**1,293.2**	**2,235.8**	**2,323.6**	**2,392.7**	**2,460.1**
Consumption expenditures	34.1	92.1	252.8	546.2	969.1	1,518.3	1,560.7	1,601.0	1,611.4
Government social benefit payments to persons	4.6	16.1	51.2	127.6	271.4	523.8	562.3	609.9	659.9
Interest payments	3.0	7.7	25.6	61.8	52.1	192.1	200.1	181.4	188.4
Subsidies	0.0	0.0	0.4	0.4	0.5	1.6	0.5	0.5	0.5
Net state and local government saving	**2.6**	**3.0**	**5.4**	**−6.5**	**9.9**	**−237.3**	**−187.1**	**−167.7**	**−135.4**
Social insurance funds	0.0	0.2	1.3	2.0	2.0	3.2	4.1	4.2	3.8
Other.	2.5	2.8	4.1	−8.4	7.9	−240.5	−191.2	−171.9	−139.2
Addenda:									
Total receipts.	**47.2**	**125.1**	**353.9**	**754.6**	**1,347.3**	**2,075.2**	**2,207.9**	**2,296.0**	**2,395.5**
Current receipts	44.2	118.9	335.3	729.6	1,303.1	1,998.5	2,136.5	2,225.0	2,324.7
Capital transfer receipts	3.0	6.2	18.6	25.0	44.2	76.7	71.4	71.0	70.7
Total expenditures	**52.0**	**135.4**	**364.7**	**807.2**	**1,418.5**	**2,385.5**	**2,417.6**	**2,487.8**	**2,567.8**
Current expenditures	41.6	115.9	329.9	736	1,293.2	2,235.8	2,323.6	2,392.7	2,460.1
Gross government investment	14.1	29.3	65.7	132.2	232.9	351.9	322.9	331.3	347.4
Capital transfer payments	—	—	—	0.0	0.0	0.0	0.0	0.0	0.0
Net purchases of nonproduced assets	0.9	1.1	2.2	5.7	8.6	10.6	9.6	9.9	9.8
Less: Consumption of fixed capital	4.5	10.9	33.1	66.7	116.2	212.7	238.5	246.1	249.5
Net lending or net borrowing (–)	**−4.8**	**−10.3**	**−10.8**	**−52.7**	**−71.2**	**−310.3**	**−209.7**	**−191.8**	**−172.4**

Federal Deposit Insurance Corporation (FDIC)

The Federal Deposit Insurance Corporation (FDIC) was created by Congress during the height of the Depression to maintain stability and public confidence in the nation's banking system. It covered depositors for up to $2,500 in case of bank failure in 1934; the limit today is 100 times that much, or $250,000. In its unique role as deposit insurer of banks and savings associations, and in cooperation with other federal and state regulatory agencies, the FDIC seeks to promote the safety and soundness of insured depository institutions in the U.S. financial system.

The quarterly premiums on deposit insurance are paid by the banks rather than by consumers. The amount of the premium is based on the institution's balance of insured deposits for the preceding quarter and the institution's risk to the insurance fund. In 2009, Congress permanently increased the limit that the FDIC may borrow from the U.S. Treasury from $30 bil to $100 bil.

U.S. Banks, 1935-2016

Source: *Summary of Deposits*, Federal Deposit Insurance Corp (FDIC).
Comprises all FDIC-insured commercial and savings banks, including savings and loan institutions (S&Ls).

	Number of banks				Deposits (in mil dollars)				
		Commercial banks[2]		Savings banks, total			Commercial banks[2]		Savings banks, total
Year	All banks[1]	National charter	State charter	Non-members		All deposits[1]	National charter	State charter	Non-members	
1935[3]	15,295	5,386	1,001	7,735	1,173	$45,102	$24,802	$13,653	$5,669	$978
1940	15,772	5,144	1,342	6,956	2,330	67,494	35,787	20,642	7,040	4,025
1950	16,500	4,958	1,912	6,576	3,054	171,963	84,941	41,602	19,726	25,694
1960	17,549	4,530	1,641	6,955	4,423	310,262	120,242	65,487	34,369	90,164
1970	18,205	4,621	1,147	7,743	4,694	686,901	285,436	101,512	95,566	204,367
1980	18,763	4,425	997	9,013	4,328	1,832,716	656,752	191,183	344,311	640,470
1990	15,158	3,979	1,009	7,355	2,815	3,637,292	1,558,915	397,797	693,438	987,142
1995	12,289	2,941	995	6,230	2,082	3,214,678	1,337,105	439,430	696,108	735,856
2000	10,119	2,302	996	5,180	1,622	4,003,744	1,792,773	707,562	793,275	706,461
2005	8,855	1,864	906	4,779	1,293	5,933,742	2,946,589	765,673	1,191,977	1,023,620
2008	8,441	1,585	874	4,744	1,227	7,025,791	3,596,712	857,003	1,432,614	1,132,356
2009	8,185	1,505	858	4,632	1,180	7,559,590	4,141,792	962,232	1,512,677	936,101
2010	7,821	1,427	836	4,413	1,135	7,676,878	4,305,697	1,002,425	1,464,022	891,159
2011	7,523	1,349	824	4,240	1,100	8,249,233	4,708,210	1,120,747	1,491,112	909,912
2012	7,255	1,285	836	4,101	1,023	8,947,239	5,250,842	1,220,930	1,576,616	874,850
2013	6,950	1,194	849	3,937	960	9,433,525	5,667,790	1,281,662	1,648,153	806,933
2014	6,669	1,110	860	3,789	900	10,112,716	6,089,894	1,445,246	1,729,789	807,157
2015	6,358	1,027	816	3,629	876	10,657,721	6,393,433	1,573,880	1,823,558	823,906
2016	6,068	962	794	3,482	820	11,269,167	6,786,622	1,707,675	1,908,835	867,775

Note: Figures are for the end of the year shown through 1990 and for June 30 thereafter. (1) Includes U.S. branches of foreign banks not listed separately. (3) Figures for 1935 do not include S&Ls, the data for which are not available. (2) Nonmembers are banks that are not members of the Federal Reserve System; national charter and state charter institutions are Federal Reserve members.

U.S. Bank Failures, 1934-2016

Source: Federal Deposit Insurance Corp. (FDIC)

Covers all FDIC-insured commercial and savings banks, including savings and loan institutions (S&Ls) 1980 and after. As of Oct. 1, 2016.

Year	Closed or assisted	Year	Closed or assisted	Year	Closed or assisted	Year	Closed or assisted	Year	Closed or assisted
1934	9	1970-79 . .	79	1989	534	1999	8	2009	148
1935	25	1980	22	1990	382	2000	7	2010	157
1936	69	1981	40	1991	271	2001	4	2011	92
1937	75	1982	119	1992	181	2002	11	2012	51
1938	74	1983	99	1993	50	2003	3	2013	24
1939	60	1984	106	1994	15	2004	4	2014	18
1940	43	1985	180	1995	8	2005	0	2015	8
1941	15	1986	204	1996	6	2006	0	2016	5
1942	20	1987	262	1997	1	2007	3	**Total,**	
1950-59 . .	28	1988	470	1998	3	2008	30	**1934-2016**	**4,088**
1960-69 . .	44								

Largest U.S. Bank Holding Companies, 2016

Source: National Information Center, Federal Financial Institutions Examination Council
(ranked by total assets, in millions of dollars; as of Mar. 31, 2016)

Rank	Institution name, location	Assets	Rank	Institution name, location	Assets
1.	JPMorgan Chase & Co., New York, NY	$2,423,808	21.	Fifth Third Bancorp, Cincinnati, OH	$142,430
2.	Bank of America Corp., Charlotte, NC	2,188,633	22.	United Services Auto. Assn., San Antonio, TX . .	142,123
3.	Wells Fargo & Co., San Francisco, CA	1,849,182	23.	State Farm Mutual Automobile Insurance Co.,	
4.	Citigroup Inc., New York, NY.	1,800,967		Bloomington, IL.	141,284
5.	Goldman Sachs Group, Inc., New York, NY . . .	878,102	24.	Citizens Financial Group, Inc., Providence, RI . .	140,409
6.	Morgan Stanley, New York, NY	807,497	25.	RBC USA Holdco Corp., New York, NY	139,892
7.	U.S. Bancorp, Minneapolis, MN	428,638	26.	Santander Holdings USA, Inc., Boston, MA . . .	131,099
8.	Bank of New York Mellon Corp., New York, NY	372,870	27.	BMO Financial Corp., Wilmington, DE	125,793
9.	PNC Financial Services Group, Inc.,		28.	Regions Financial Corp., Birmingham, AL	125,747
	Pittsburgh, PA	361,187	29.	M&T Bank Corp., Buffalo, NY	124,626
10.	Capital One Financial Corp., McLean, VA.	330,489	30.	MUFG Americas Holdings Corp., New York,	
11.	HSBC North America Holdings Inc., New York,			NY.	120,915
	NY.	289,057	31.	Northern Trust Corp., Chicago, IL.	117,799
12.	GE Capital Global Holdings, LLC, Norwalk, CT	287,622	32.	KeyCorp, Cleveland, OH.	98,571
13.	TD Group U.S. Holdings LLC, Wilmington, DE	274,387	33.	BancWest Corp., Honolulu, HI	96,194
14.	Teachers Insurance & Annuity Assn. of		34.	BBVA Compass Bancshares, Inc., Houston, TX	92,152
	America, New York, NY.	272,102	35.	Discover Financial Services, Riverwoods, IL . .	88,093
15.	State Street Corp., Boston, MA	243,685	36.	Synchrony Financial, Stamford, CT	81,656
16.	BB&T Corp., Winston-Salem, NC	212,405	37.	Huntington Bancshares Inc., Columbus, OH . .	72,645
17.	SunTrust Banks, Inc., Atlanta, GA	194,253	38.	Comerica Incorporated, Dallas, TX.	69,131
18.	Charles Schwab Corp., San Francisco, CA . . .	190,998	39.	CIT Group, Livingston, NJ.	67,188
19.	American Express Co., New York, NY	158,804	40.	Zions Bancorp., Salt Lake City, UT.	59,180
20.	Ally Financial Inc., Detroit, MI	156,505			

Note: Includes foreign-owned banks with a strong presence in the U.S.

Status of Top Recipients of Treasury Department "Bailout" Funds, 2016

Source: ProPublica

Since Oct. 2008, the federal government has spent more than $621 bil to bail out more than 900 institutions severely affected by the financial crisis. As of Oct. 1, 2016, the government had recouped $390 bil in loans and $303 bil in dividends, interest, and other returns, leading to an overall profit of more than $71 bil. Companies that have failed to repay the government, resulting in a loss to the taxpayers, are listed in bold italics.

(in billions of dollars, ranked by amount disbursed; as of Oct. 1, 2016)

Recipient	Disbursed	Repaid[1]	Net profit or amount outstanding[2]	Recipient	Disbursed	Repaid[1]	Net profit or amount outstanding[2]
Fannie Mae.	$116.1	$151.4	$35.2	BB&T	$3.1	$3.3	$0.2
Freddie Mac	71.3	99.1	27.8	Bank of New York Mellon . . .	3.0	3.2	0.2
AIG	67.8	72.9	5.0	*JPMorgan Chase*			
General Motors	*50.7*	*39.3*	*−11.4*	*subsidiaries . . . .*	*2.6*	*0.0*	*−2.6*
Bank of America	45.0	49.6	4.6	*Wells Fargo Bank, NA*	*2.5*	*0.0*	*−2.5*
Citigroup.	45.0	58.4	13.4	KeyCorp	2.5	2.9	0.4
JPMorgan Chase	25.0	26.7	1.7	*CIT Group*	*2.3*	*−*	*−2.3*
Wells Fargo.	25.0	27.3	2.3	Comerica Incorporated.	2.3	2.6	0.3
GMAC (now Ally Financial) . .	16.3	19.3	3.1	State Street.	2.0	2.1	0.1
Chrysler	*10.7*	*9.5*	*−1.2*	*Bank of America subsids.*			
Goldman Sachs	10.0	11.4	1.4	*(incl. Countrywide)*	*1.9*	*0.0*	*−1.9*
Morgan Stanley.	10.0	11.3	1.3	*CalHFA Mortgage*			
PNC Financial Services	7.6	8.3	0.7	*Assistance Corp.*	*1.9*	*0.0*	*−1.9*
U.S. Bancorp	6.6	6.9	0.3	RLJ Western Asset Public/			
SunTrust	4.9	5.4	0.5	Private Master Fund, L.P.	1.9	2.3	0.5
Capital One Financial Corp.	3.6	3.8	0.3	Invesco Legacy Securities			
Regions Financial Corp. . . .	3.5	4.1	0.6	Master Fund, L.P.	1.7	2.3	0.6
Wellington Management				Marshall & Ilsley	1.7	1.9	0.2
Legacy Securities PPIF				Oaktree PPIP Fund, L.P. . . .	1.7	2.0	0.3
Master Fund, LP	3.4	4.2	0.7	Blackrock PPIF, L.P.	1.6	2.0	0.4
Fifth Third Bancorp	3.4	4.0	0.6	Northern Trust.	1.6	1.7	0.1
Hartford Financial Services	3.4	4.2	0.8	Chrysler Financial Services	1.5	1.5	—
American Express	3.4	3.8	0.4	Marathon Legacy Securities			
AG GECC PPIF Master				Public-Private Investment			
Fund, L.P.	3.4	4.3	0.9	Partnership, L.P.	1.4	1.8	0.4
AllianceBernstein Legacy				Zions Bancorp.	1.4	1.7	0.3
Securities Master Fund, L.P.	3.2	3.8	0.6	Huntington Bancshares	1.4	1.6	0.2
Ocwen Loan Servicing, LLC	*3.1*	*0.0*	*−3.1*	Discover Financial Services	1.2	1.5	0.2
				Total	**621.0**	**692.9**	**71.7**

— = less than $0.1 bil. **Note:** Total includes other disbursements not shown. Figures may not add up to totals due to rounding. (1) Amounts repaid include principal, dividends, interest, warrants, and other proceeds. (2) Negative number represents outstanding debt.

Federal Reserve System

The Federal Reserve System is the central bank for the U.S. The system was established on Dec. 23, 1913, originally to give the country an elastic currency, provide facilities for discounting commercial paper, and improve the supervision of banking. Since then, the system's responsibilities have been broadened. Over the years, stability and growth of the economy, a high level of employment, stability in the purchasing power of the dollar, and reasonable balance in transactions with other countries have come to be recognized as primary objectives of governmental economic policy.

The Federal Reserve System consists of the Board of Governors, the 12 District Reserve Banks and their branch offices, and the Federal Open Market Committee. Several advisory councils help the board meet its varied responsibilities.

The hub of the system is the seven-member **Board of Governors** in Washington, DC. The members of the board are appointed by the president and confirmed by the Senate to 14-year terms. The president also appoints the chairman and vice chairman of the board from among the board members for four-year terms. As of July 2016, the board members were Janet L. Yellen, chair; Stanley Fischer, vice chair; Daniel K. Tarullo; Jerome H. Powell; and Lael Brainard. There have been two vacancies since June 2014, but Congress has stalled all nominations to the Board of Governors.

The 12 **District Reserve Banks** and their branch offices serve as the decentralized portion of the system, carrying out day-to-day operations such as circulating currency and coin and providing fiscal agency functions and payments mechanism services. The 12 are in Boston, New York, Philadelphia, Cleveland, Richmond, Atlanta, Chicago, St. Louis, Minneapolis, Kansas City, Dallas, and San Francisco.

The system's principal function is monetary policy, which it controls using three tools: reserve requirements, the discount rate, and open market operations.

Uniform **reserve requirements**, set by the board, are applied to the transaction accounts and nonpersonal time deposits of all depository institutions. Responsibility for setting the **discount rate** (the interest rate at which depository institutions can borrow money from the Reserve Banks) is shared by the Board of Governors and the Reserve Banks. Changes in the discount rate are recommended by the individual boards of directors of the Reserve Banks and are subject to approval by the Board of Governors.

The most important tool of monetary policy is **open market operations**, or the purchase and sale of government securities. Responsibility for influencing the cost and availability of money and credit through the purchase and sale of government securities lies with the **Federal Open Market Committee** (FOMC), which comprises the seven members of the Board of Governors, the president of the Federal Reserve Bank of New York, and four other Federal Reserve Bank presidents, who each serve one-year terms on a rotating basis. The committee bases its decisions on economic and financial developments and outlook, setting yearly growth objectives for key measures of money supply and credit. The decisions of the committee are carried out by the domestic trading desk of the Federal Reserve Bank of New York.

A Federal Advisory Council of banking industry representatives meets with the Federal Reserve Board four times a year to discuss business and financial conditions, as well as to make recommendations.

Website: www.federalreserve.gov

Federal Reserve Board Discount Rates, 1955-2016

The interest rate that the Federal Reserve charges its member banks to borrow money overnight is often referred to as the discount rate. On Jan. 9, 2003, the Fed divided the discount window into two categories: primary credit, for banks in sound financial condition, and secondary credit, for banks that do not qualify for primary credit. The secondary credit rate is ½ a percentage point higher than the primary credit rate. Banks typically raise or lower the rates they extend to their customers to track changes in the discount rate.

Effective date	Rate	Effective date	Rate	Effective date	Rate	Effective date	Rate	Effective date	Rate
1955		**1970**		**1979**		**1990**		**2003**	
Jan. 3	1½	Nov. 13	5¾	July 20	10	Dec. 18	6½	Jan. 9	2¼[1]
Apr. 15	1¾	Dec. 4	5½	Aug. 17	10½	**1991**		June 25	2
Aug. 5	2	**1971**		Sept. 19	11	Apr. 30	5½	**2004**	
Sept. 9	2¼	Jan. 8	5¼	Oct. 8	12	Sept. 13	5	June 30	2¼
Nov. 18	2½	Jan. 22	5	**1980**		Nov. 6	4½	Aug. 10	2½
1956		Feb. 19	4¾	Feb. 15	13	Dec. 20	3½	Sept. 21	2¾
Apr. 13	2¾	July 16	5	May 30	12	**1992**		Nov. 10	3
Aug. 24	3	Nov. 19	4¾	June 13	11	July 2	3	Dec. 14	3¼
1957		Dec. 17	4½	July 28	10	**1994**		**2005**	
Aug. 23	3½	**1973**		Sept. 26	11	May 17	3½	Feb. 2	3½
Nov. 15	3	Jan. 15	5	Nov. 17	12	Aug. 16	4	Mar. 22	3¾
1958		Feb. 26	5½	Dec. 5	13	Nov. 15	4¾	May 3	4
Jan. 24	2¾	May 4	5¾	**1981**		**1995**		June 30	4¼
Mar. 7	2¼	May 11	6	May 5	14	Feb. 1	5	Aug. 9	4½
Apr. 18	1¾	June 11	6½	Nov. 2	13	**1996**		Sept. 20	4¾
Sept. 12	2	July 2	7	Dec. 4	12	Jan. 31	5	Nov. 1	5
Nov. 7	2½	Aug. 14	7½	**1982**		**1998**		Dec. 13	5¼
1959		**1974**		July 20	11½	Oct. 15	4¾	**2006**	
Mar. 6	3	Apr. 25	8	Aug. 2	11	Nov. 17	4½	Jan. 31	5½
May 29	3½	Dec. 9	7¾	Aug. 16	10	**1999**		Mar. 28	5¾
Sept. 11	4	**1975**		Aug. 27	10	Aug. 24	4¾	May 10	6
1960		Jan. 10	7¼	Oct. 12	9½	Nov. 16	5	June 29	6¼
June 10	3½	Feb. 5	6¾	Dec. 15	8½	**2000**		**2007**	
Aug. 12	3	Mar. 19	6¼	**1984**		Feb. 2	5¼	Aug. 17	5¾
1963		May 16	6	Apr. 9	9	Mar. 21	5½	Sept.18	5¼
July 17	3½	**1976**		Nov. 21	8½	May 16	6	Nov. 1	5
1964		Jan. 19	5½	Dec. 24	8	**2001**		Dec. 12	4¾
Nov. 24	4	Nov. 22	5¼	**1985**		Jan. 3	5¾	**2008**	
1965		**1977**		May 20	7½	Jan. 31	5	Jan. 22	4
Dec. 6	4½	Aug. 31	5¾	**1986**		Mar. 20	4½	Jan. 30	3½
1967		Oct. 26	6	Mar. 7	7	Apr. 18	4	Mar. 17	3¼
Apr. 7	4	**1978**		Apr. 21	6½	May 15	3½	Mar. 18	2½
Nov. 20	4½	Jan. 9	6½	July 11	6	June 27	3¼	Apr. 30	2¼
1968		May 11	7	Aug. 21	5½	Aug. 21	3	Oct. 8	1¾
Mar. 22	5	July 3	7¼	**1987**		Sept. 17	2½	Oct. 29	1¼
Apr. 19	5½	Aug. 21	7¾	Sept. 4	6	Oct. 2	2	Dec. 16	½
Aug. 30	5¼	Sept. 22	8	**1988**		Dec. 11	1¼	**2010**	
Dec. 18	5½	Oct. 16	8½	Aug. 9	6½	**2002**		Feb. 19	¾
1969		Nov. 1	9½	**1989**		Nov. 6	¾	**2015**	
Apr. 4	6			Feb. 24	7			Dec. 17	1

Note: As of Oct. 24, 2016, rate effective Dec. 17, 2015, was unchanged. (1) Adjustment credit rate replaced with primary credit rate. See note above.

Standard & Poor's 500 Index, 1998-2016

Monthly closing levels beginning with Oct. 1998; record high daily closing was 2,190.15 on Aug. 15, 2016.

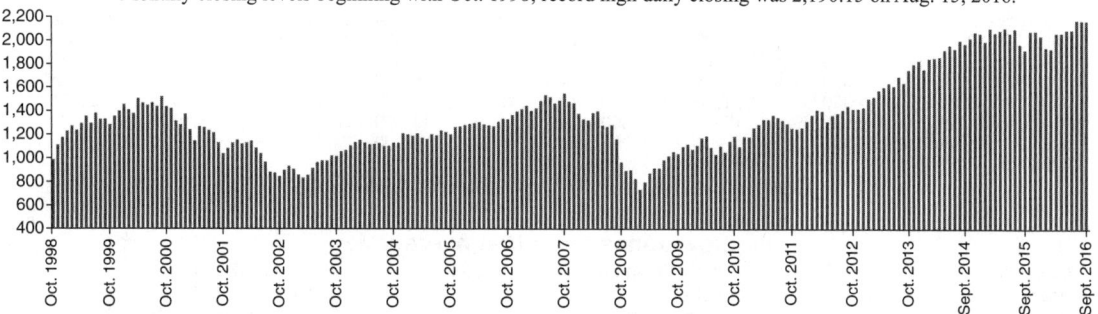

U.S. Holdings of Foreign Securities, 2006-14

Source: *U.S. Portfolio Holdings of Foreign Securities*, U.S. Dept. of the Treasury
(in billions of dollars; countries within a region ranked by 2014 figure)

	2006	2010	2012	2013	2014		2006	2010	2012	2013	2014
Europe	$3,129	$3,154	$3,562	$4,437	$4,487	Latin America and					
UK	1,076	1,001	1,139	1,344	1,300	Caribbean	$946	$1,064	$1,598	$1,715	$2,007
France	402	366	376	466	485	Cayman Islands . .	376	366	797	901	1,150
Switzerland	264	327	335	443	424	Bermuda	208	160	178	211	227
Netherlands	234	233	292	386	388	Brazil	110	235	216	180	166
Ireland	121	132	184	281	387	Mexico	108	109	157	154	166
Germany	292	299	330	391	375	Curaçao[1]	58	83	70	86	82
Sweden	102	122	122	165	165	Asia	1,166	1,342	1,426	1,608	1,757
Spain	111	87	99	133	133	Japan	596	519	521	686	689
Luxembourg	60	100	107	125	133	South Korea	124	148	175	183	178
Italy	106	66	110	124	109	Hong Kong	88	135	145	140	151
Canada	478	695	808	826	844	China (mainland) . .	75	102	92	103	133
Africa	57	99	110	103	121	India	49	91	79	86	129
South Africa	43	78	86	77	83	Taiwan	74	95	88	98	114
Australia	173	323	351	338	311	Total holdings	5,991	6,763	7,958	9,130	9,640

Note: Regional totals include countries not shown here. (1) Figures are for Netherlands Antilles prior to 2012.

Record One-Day Gains and Losses of the Dow Jones Industrial Average

Source: Dow Jones & Co., Inc.
(ranked by largest one-day losses and gains for two terms; as of Oct. 1, 2016)

Greatest % gains

Rank	Date	Close	Net chg.	% chg.
1.	3/15/1933	62.10	8.26	15.34%
2.	10/6/1931	99.34	12.86	14.87
3.	10/30/1929	258.47	28.40	12.34
4.	9/21/1932	75.16	7.67	11.36
5.	10/13/2008	9,387.61	936.42	11.08

Greatest point gains

Rank	Date	Close	Net chg.	% chg.
1.	10/13/2008	9,387.61	936.42	11.08%
2.	10/28/2008	9,065.12	889.35	10.88
3.	8/26/2015	16,285.51	619.07	3.95
4.	11/13/2008	8,835.25	552.60	6.67
5.	3/16/2000	10,630.61	499.19	4.93

Greatest % losses

Rank	Date	Close	Net chg.	% chg.
1.	10/19/1987	1,738.74	−508.00	−22.61%
2.	10/28/1929	260.64	−38.33	−12.82
3.	10/29/1929	230.07	−30.57	−11.73
4.	11/6/1929	232.13	−25.55	−9.92
5.	12/18/1899	58.27	−5.57	−8.72

Greatest point losses

Rank	Date	Close	Net chg.	% chg.
1.	9/29/2008	10,365.45	−777.68	−6.98%
2.	10/15/2008	8,577.91	−733.08	−7.87
3.	9/17/2001	8,920.70	−684.81	−7.13
4.	12/1/2008	8,149.09	−679.95	−7.70
5.	10/9/2008	8,579.19	−678.92	−7.33

Dow Jones Industrial Average, 1965-2016

Source: Dow Jones & Co., Inc.
(as of Oct. 1, 2016)

Year	Highest close		Lowest close		Year	Highest close		Lowest close	
1965	Dec. 31	969.26	June 28	840.59	2001	May 21	11,337.92	Sept. 21	8,235.81
1970	Dec. 29	842.00	May 6	631.16	2002	Mar. 19	10,635.25	Oct. 9	7,286.27
1975	July 15	881.81	Jan. 2	632.04	2003	Dec. 31	10,453.90	Mar. 11	7,524.06
1980	Nov. 20	1,000.17	Apr. 21	759.13	2004	Dec. 28	10,854.54	Oct. 25	9,749.99
1985	Dec. 16	1,553.10	Jan. 4	1,184.96	2005	Mar. 4	10,940.50	Apr. 20	10,012.36
1990	July 16	2,999.75	Oct. 11	2,365.10	2006	Dec. 27	12,510.57	Jan. 20	10,667.39
1991	Dec. 31	3,168.83	Jan. 9	2,470.30	2007	Oct. 9	14,164.53	Mar. 5	12,050.41
1992	June 1	3,413.21	Oct. 9	3,136.58	2008	Jan. 3	13,056.72	Nov. 20	7,552.29
1993	Dec. 29	3,794.33	Jan. 20	3,241.95	2009	Dec. 30	10,548.51	Mar. 9	6,547.05
1994	Jan. 31	3,978.36	Apr. 4	3,593.35	2010	Dec. 29	11,585.38	July 2	9,686.48
1995	Dec. 13	5,216.47	Jan. 30	3,832.08	2011	Apr. 29	12,810.54	Oct. 3	10,655.30
1996	Dec. 27	6,560.91	Jan. 10	5,032.94	2012	Oct. 5	13,610.15	June 4	12,101.46
1997	Aug. 6	8,259.31	Apr. 11	6,391.69	2013	Dec. 31	16,576.66	Jan. 8	13,328.85
1998	Nov. 23	9,374.27	Aug. 31	7,539.07	2014	Dec. 26	18,053.71	Feb. 3	15,372.80
1999	Dec. 31	11,497.12	Jan. 22	9,120.67	2015	May 19	18,312.39	Aug. 25	15,666.44
2000	Jan. 14	11,722.98	Mar. 7	9,796.03	2016	Aug. 15	18,636.05*	Feb. 11	15,560.18

* = Record high closing.

Milestones of the Dow Jones Industrial Average
(as of Oct. 1, 2016)

First close over—		First close over—		First close over—		First close over—		First close over—	
100	Jan. 12, 1906	3,500	May 19, 1993	6,500	Nov. 25, 1996	9,500	Jan. 6, 1999	13,000	Apr. 25, 2007
500	Mar. 12, 1956	4,000	Feb. 23, 1995	7,000	Feb. 13, 1997	10,000	Mar. 29, 1999	14,000	July 19, 2007
1,000	Nov. 14, 1972	4,500	June 16, 1995	7,500	June 10, 1997	10,500	Apr. 21, 1999	15,000	June 27, 2013
1,500	Dec. 11, 1985	5,000	Nov. 21, 1995	8,000	July 16, 1997	11,000	May 3, 1999	16,000	Nov. 21, 2013
2,000	Jan. 8, 1987	5,500	Feb. 8, 1996	8,500	Feb. 27, 1998	11,500	Jan. 7, 2000	17,000	July 3, 2014
2,500	July 17, 1987	6,000	Oct. 14, 1996	9,000	Apr. 6, 1998	12,000	Oct. 19, 2006	18,000	Dec. 23, 2014
3,000	Apr. 17, 1991								

Components of the Dow Jones Averages
(as of Oct. 1, 2016)

Dow Jones Industrial Average

- 3M Co. (MMM)
- American Express Co. (AXP)
- Apple Inc. (AAPL)
- Boeing Co. (BA)
- Caterpillar Inc. (CAT)
- Chevron Corp. (CVX)
- Cisco Systems Inc. (CSCO)
- Coca-Cola Co. (KO)
- E. I. du Pont de Nemours and Co. (DD)
- Exxon Mobil Corp. (XOM)
- General Electric Co. (GE)

- Goldman Sachs Group Inc. (GS)
- Home Depot Inc. (HD)
- Intel Corp. (INTC)
- International Business Machines Corp. (IBM)
- Johnson & Johnson (JNJ)
- JPMorgan Chase & Co. (JPM)
- McDonald's Corp. (MCD)
- Merck & Co. Inc. (MRK)
- Microsoft Corp. (MSFT)

- Nike Inc. (NKE)
- Pfizer Inc. (PFE)
- Procter & Gamble Co. (PG)
- Travelers Companies Inc. (TRV)
- United Technologies Corp. (UTX)
- UnitedHealth Group Inc. (UNH)
- Verizon Communications Inc. (VZ)
- Visa Inc. (V)
- Wal-Mart Stores Inc. (WMT)
- Walt Disney Co. (DIS)

Dow Jones Utility Average

- AES Corp. (AES)
- American Electric Power Co. Inc. (AEP)
- American Water Works Co. Inc. (AWK)
- CenterPoint Energy Inc. (CNP)
- Consolidated Edison Inc. (ED)

- Dominion Resources Inc. (D)
- Duke Energy Corp. (DUK)
- Edison International (EIX)
- Exelon Corp. (EXC)
- FirstEnergy Corp. (FE)
- NextEra Energy Inc. (NEE)

- NiSource Inc. (NI)
- PG&E Corp. (PCG)
- Public Service Enterprise Group Inc. (PEG)
- Southern Co. (SO)

Dow Jones Transportation Average

- Alaska Air Group Inc. (ALK)
- American Airlines Group Inc. (AAL)
- Avis Budget Group Inc. (CAR)
- C.H. Robinson Worldwide Inc. (CHRW)
- CSX Corp. (CSX)
- Delta Air Lines Inc. (DAL)
- Expeditors International of

Washington Inc. (EXPD)
- FedEx Corp. (FDX)
- J.B. Hunt Transport Services Inc. (JBHT)
- JetBlue Airways Corp. (JBLU)
- Kansas City Southern (KSU)
- Kirby Corp. (KEX)
- Landstar System Inc. (LSTR)

- Matson Inc. (MATX)
- Norfolk Southern Corp. (NSC)
- Ryder System Inc. (R)
- Southwest Airlines Co. (LUV)
- Union Pacific Corp. (UNP)
- United Continental Holdings (UAL)
- United Parcel Service Inc. (UPS)

Record One-Day Gains and Losses on the Nasdaq Stock Market
Source: Nasdaq Stock Market
(ranked by largest one-day losses and gains for two terms; as of Oct. 5, 2016)

	Greatest point gains			Greatest % gains			Greatest point losses			Greatest % losses	
Rank	Date	Change	Rank	Date	% change	Rank	Date	Change	Rank	Date	% change
1.	1/3/2001	324.83	1.	1/3/2001	14.17%	1.	4/14/2000	−355.49	1.	10/19/1987	−11.35%
2.	12/5/2000	274.05	2.	10/13/2008	11.81	2.	4/3/2000	−349.15	2.	4/14/2000	−9.67
3.	4/18/2000	254.41	3.	12/5/2000	10.48	3.	4/12/2000	−286.27	3.	9/29/2008	−9.14
4.	5/30/2000	254.37	4.	10/28/2008	9.53	4.	4/10/2000	−258.25	4.	10/20/1987	−9.00
5.	10/19/2000	247.04	5.	4/5/2001	8.92	5.	1/4/2000	−229.46	5.	10/26/1987	−9.00
6.	10/13/2000	242.09	6.	4/18/2001	8.12	6.	3/14/2000	−200.61	6.	12/1/2008	−8.95
7.	6/2/2000	230.88	7.	5/30/2000	7.94	7.	5/10/2000	−200.28	7.	8/31/1998	−8.56
8.	4/25/2000	228.75	8.	10/13/2000	7.87	8.	5/23/2000	−199.66	8.	10/15/2008	−8.47
9.	4/17/2000	217.87	9.	10/19/2000	7.79	9.	9/29/2008	−199.61	9.	4/3/2000	−7.64
10.	10/13/2008	194.74	10.	5/8/2002	7.78	10.	10/25/2000	−190.22	10.	1/2/2001	−7.23

Nasdaq Stock Market Closing Prices, 1971-2016
Source: Nasdaq Stock Market; as of Oct. 5, 2016

Year	High	Low	Year	High	Low	Year	High	Low	Year	High	Low
1971	114.12	99.68	1983	329.11	229.88	1995	1,072.82	740.53	2006	2,465.98	2,020.39
1972	135.15	113.65	1984	288.41	223.91	1996	1,328.45	978.17	2007	2,811.61	2,340.68
1973	136.84	88.67	1985	325.53	245.82	1997	1,748.62	1,194.39	2008	2,609.63	1,505.90
1974	96.53	54.87	1986	411.21	322.14	1998	2,200.63	1,357.09	2009	2,167.70	1,265.52
1975	88.00	60.70	1987	456.27	288.49	1999	4,090.61	2,193.13	2010	2,671.48	2,091.79
1976	97.88	78.06	1988	397.54	329.00	2000	5,048.62	2,332.78	2011	2,873.54	2,335.83
1977	105.05	93.66	1989	487.60	376.87	2001	2,892.36	1,387.06	2012	3,183.95	2,648.36
1978	139.25	99.09	1990	470.30	322.93	2002	2,059.38	1,114.11	2013	4,176.59	3,091.81
1979	152.29	117.84	1991	586.35	352.85	2003	2,009.88	1,271.47	2014	4,806.91	3,996.96
1980	208.29	124.09	1992	676.95	545.85	2004	2,178.00	1,752.00	2015	5,218.86	4,506.49
1981	223.96	170.80	1993	790.56	645.02	2005	2,273.37	1,904.18	2016	5,339.52*	4,266.84
1982	241.63	158.92	1994	803.93	691.23						

* = Record high closing, Sept. 22, 2016.

Average Yields of Treasury, Corporate, and State and Local Bonds, 1986-2016

Source: Office of Market Finance, U.S. Dept. of the Treasury; Federal Reserve System

Period	Treasury 30-year bonds[1]	New Aa corporate bonds[2]	State and local bonds[3]	Period	Treasury 30-year bonds[1]	New Aa corporate bonds[2]	State and local bonds[3]	Period	Treasury 30-year bonds[1]	New Aa corporate bonds[2]	State and local bonds[3]
1986				**1997**				**2007**			
June	7.57%	9.39%	7.87%	June	6.77%	7.71%	5.53%	June	5.20%	5.79%	4.60%
Dec.	7.37	8.87	6.87	Dec.	5.99	6.68	5.19	Dec.	4.53	5.49	4.42
1987				**1998**				**2008**			
June	8.57	9.64	7.79	June	5.70	6.43	5.12	June	4.69	5.68	4.69
Dec.	9.12	10.22	7.96	Dec.	5.06	6.13	4.98	Dec.	2.87	5.05	5.56
1988				**1999**				**2009**			
June	9.00	10.08	7.78	June	6.04	7.21	5.37	June	4.52	5.61	4.81
Dec.	9.01	10.05	7.61	Dec.	6.35	7.55	5.95	Dec.	4.49	5.26	4.21
1989				**2000**				**2010**			
June	8.27	9.24	7.02	June	5.93	7.75	5.80	June	4.13	4.88	4.36
Dec.	7.90	9.23	6.98	Dec.	5.49	7.21	5.22	Dec.	4.42	5.02	4.92
1990				**2001**				**2011**			
June	8.46	9.69	7.24	June	5.67	7.11	5.20	June	4.23	4.99	4.51
Dec.	8.24	9.55	7.09	Dec.	5.48	6.80	5.25	Dec.	2.98	3.93	3.95
1991				**2002**				**2012**			
June	8.47	9.37	7.13	June	5.65	6.57	5.09	June	2.70	3.64	3.94
Dec.	7.70	8.55	6.69	Dec.	5.01	5.93	4.85	Dec.	2.88	3.65	3.48
1992				**2003**				**2013**			
June	7.84	8.45	6.49	June	4.34	4.97	4.33	June	3.40	4.27	4.27
Dec.	7.44	8.12	6.22	Dec.	5.11	5.62	4.65	Dec.	3.89	4.62	4.73
1993				**2004**				**2014**			
June	6.81	7.48	5.63	June	5.45	6.01	5.05	June	3.42	4.25	4.35
Dec.	6.25	7.22	5.35	Dec.	4.88	5.47	4.49	Dec.	2.83	3.79	3.70
1994				**2005**				**2015**			
June	7.40	8.16	6.11	June	4.35	4.96	4.23	June	3.11	4.19	3.82
Dec.	7.87	8.66	6.80	Dec.	4.73	5.37	4.46	Dec.	2.97	3.97	3.57
1995				**2006**				**2016**			
June	6.57	7.42	5.84	June	5.15	5.89	4.60	June	2.45	3.50	3.20
Dec.	6.06	7.02	5.45	Dec.	4.68	5.32	4.11				
1996											
June	7.06	8.00	6.02								
Dec.	6.55	7.45	5.64								

(1) On Feb. 18, 2002, the U.S. discontinued the 30-year constant maturity yield and reintroduced it on Feb. 9, 2006; rates in the interim are for 20-year yields. (2) Treasury series based on 3-week moving average of reoffering yields of new corporate bonds rated Aa by Moody's Investors Service with an original maturity of at least 20 years. Treasury discontinued yield index after Jan. 31, 2003. Rates thereafter are for Moody's seasoned Aaa corporate bonds as listed by Federal Reserve. (3) Index of new reoffering yields on 20-year general obligations rated Aa by Moody's Investors Service; discontinued by Treasury Jan. 31, 2003; rates thereafter are from Bond Buyer Index of general obligation, 20 years to maturity, mixed quality state and local bonds.

Ownership of U.S. Treasury Securities, 2001-15

Source: *Treasury Bulletin, Sept. 2015*, Financial Management Service, U.S. Dept. of the Treasury

In 2001, just over 17% of U.S. treasury securities were held by foreign and international investors. By 2015, the total public debt had more than tripled, while the portion held by investors outside the U.S. had nearly doubled, to 32.5%.

(in billions of dollars)

	2001	2005	2007	2008	2009	2010	2011	2012	2013	2014	2015
Total public debt	$5,943	$8,170	$9,229	$10,700	$12,311	$14,025	$15,223	$16,433	$17,352	$18,141	$18,922
Federal Reserve and intra-governmental holdings ..	3,124	4,200	4,834	4,806	5,277	5,656	6,440	6,524	7,205	7,579	7,711
Total privately held	2,819	3,971	4,396	5,893	7,034	8,369	8,783	9,909	10,147	10,563	11,211
Depository institutions	181	129	130	105	202	319	280	348	321	514	547
U.S. savings bonds.	190	205	196	194	191	188	185	182	179	176	172
Private pension funds[1]	146	184	229	174	176	207	392	468	478	509	540
Pension funds of state and local governments.	155	154	144	130	151	154	161	173	188	177	164
Insurance companies	106	202	142	171	222	248	272	271	265	285	297
Mutual funds.	262	254	344	758	669	722	927	1,031	975	1,107	1,315
State and local governments.	328	512	648	601	586	596	561	604	586	623	687
Foreign and international ..	1,040	2,034	2,353	3,077	3,685	4,436	5,007	5,574	5,793	6,158	6,148
Other investors[2]	411	295	298	709	1,152	1,500	999	1,260	1,362	1,014	1,343

(1) Includes securities held by the Federal Employees Retirement System Thrift Savings Plan "G Fund." (2) Includes individuals, government-sponsored enterprises, brokers and dealers, bank personal trusts and estates, corporate and noncorporate businesses, and other investors.

Federal Corporate Tax Rates, 2016

Personal service corporations (used by incorporated professionals such as attorneys and doctors) pay a flat rate of 35%.

Taxable income amount	Tax rate	Taxable income amount	Tax rate
Not more than $50,000.	15%	$335,001 to $10,000,000	34%
$50,001 to $75,000.	25	$10,000,001 to $15,000,000.	35
$75,001 to $100,000.	34	$15,000,001 to $18,333,333.	38
$100,001 to $335,000.	39	More than $18,333,333	35

Characteristics of Mutual Fund Investors, 2015

Source: *The Investment Company Fact Book 2016*, Investment Company Institute

Median age of head of household	51	Married or living with a partner.	71%
Median annual household income	$87,500	Four-year college degree or more.	51%
Median household financial assets.	$200,000	Own Individual Retirement Accounts (IRAs).	61%
Median mutual fund assets.	$120,000	Hold more than half their financial assets in	
Median number of funds owned	3	mutual funds	67%
Employed	71%		

Performance of Mutual Funds by Type, 2016
Source: *Kiplinger's Personal Finance* magazine analysis of Morningstar data
(as of Aug. 31, 2016)

Fund type/fund objective	Average annual return 1-year	3-year	5-year	Fund type/fund objective	Average annual return 1-year	3-year	5-year
Large-Company				**Sector**			
Growth	6.28%	10.86%	12.89%	Equity Precious Metals	76.91%	−0.08%	−14.07%
Blend	8.76	10.00	12.89	Financial	3.35	6.96	11.86
Value	9.62	8.76	12.28	Health	−7.98	13.59	18.45
Midsize-Company				Natural Resources	5.61	−4.28	−2.62
Growth	3.37	8.14	11.43	Real Estate	21.50	14.72	12.41
Blend	5.78	8.29	11.94	Technology	15.01	14.29	13.91
Value	8.46	8.69	12.44	Utilities	12.27	8.81	9.63
Small-Company				**Multialternative**			
Growth	3.26	6.90	11.63	Multialternative Funds	0.05	1.74	2.61
Blend	7.48	7.39	11.70	**International**			
Value	9.25	7.38	11.79	Diversified Emerging Markets	10.44	1.25	−0.13
Taxable Government Bond				World Bond	6.89	2.62	1.75
Short-Term	0.88	0.97	0.61	World Stock	5.89	6.26	8.33
Intermediate-Term	3.14	2.97	1.91	**Corporate Bond**			
Long-Term	13.97	10.09	6.40	High Yield	5.91	3.91	6.23
Tax-Free Government Bond				Short-Term	1.85	1.42	1.49
Short-Term Municipal	1.97	1.56	1.33	Intermediate-Term	5.47	4.04	3.43
Intermediate-Term Municipal	5.81	5.29	4.03	Long-Term	15.37	9.61	7.21
Long-Term Municipal	7.27	7.04	5.29				

Mutual Fund Ownership, 1940-2015
Source: *The Investment Company Fact Book 2016*, Investment Company Institute

Year	Mutual funds	Mutual fund accounts (thous.)	Total net assets (bil)	Households owning mutual funds Number (thous.)	Percent of all households	Exchange-traded funds (ETFs) Number of funds	Total net assets (bil)
1940	68	296	$0.45	NA	NA	NA	NA
1950	98	939	2.53	NA	NA	NA	NA
1960	161	4,898	17.03	NA	NA	NA	NA
1970	361	10,690	47.62	NA	NA	NA	NA
1980	564	12,088	134.76	4,600	5.7%	NA	NA
1990	3,079	61,948	1,065.19	23,400	25.1	NA	NA
2000	8,155	244,705	6,964.63	48,600	45.7	80	$65.59
2005	7,977	275,479	8,891.38	50,300	44.4	204	300.82
2010	7,555	291,299	11,833.36	53,200	45.3	923	991.99
2011	7,588	272,628	11,632.35	52,900	44.1	1,134	1,048.13
2012	7,590	257,074	13,056.68	53,800	44.4	1,194	1,337.11
2013	7,715	264,848	15,050.82	56,700	46.3	1,294	1,674.62
2014	7,928	NA	15,875.27	53,200	43.3	1,411	1,974.38
2015	8,116	NA	15,651.96	53,600	43.0	1,594	2,100.44

NA = Not available. **Note:** Does not include data for funds that invest primarily in other mutual funds. Mutual fund accounts data include both individual and omnibus accounts.

CME Average Daily Volume, 2013-15
Source: CME Group, Inc.

By product	Average daily volume (thous.) 2013	2014	2015	Percent change, 2014-15	By venue	Average daily volume (thous.) 2013	2014	2015	Percent change, 2014-15
Interest Rates	5,903	7,009	6,720	−4%	Open outcry	1,040	1,176	1,139	3%
Equity Indexes	2,642	2,764	2,792	1	Electronic	10,821	11,805	12,185	3
Foreign Exchange (FX)	886	803	872	9	Privately negotiated	679	682	639	−6
Energy	1,676	1,630	1,970	21	**Total**	**12,546**	**13,663**	**13,963**	**2**
Agricultural Commodities	1,053	1,120	1,265	13					
Metals	386	337	344	2					

Note: Volume of products listed on one of the CME Group's regulated exchanges: Chicago Mercantile Exchange (CME), Board of Trade of the City of Chicago, New York Mercantile Exchange, and Commodity Exchange.

Gold Owned by the U.S., 2016
Source: *Status Report of U.S. Treasury-Owned Gold*, Bureau of the Fiscal Service, U.S. Dept. of the Treasury
(as of July 29, 2016; numbers may not add to totals due to rounding)

	Fine troy ounces	Book value		Fine troy ounces	Book value
Total Treasury-owned gold	261,498,926	$11,041,059,957	**Held by the Federal Reserve**		
Gold bullion	258,641,878	10,920,429,099	Bank	13,452,811	$568,007,257
Gold coins, blanks,			Gold bullion	13,378,981	564,890,013
miscellaneous	2,857,048	120,630,859	Federal Reserve Banks–		
Held by the U.S. Mint	248,046,116	10,473,052,701	NY vault	13,376,988	564,805,851
Denver, CO, deep storage	43,853,707	1,851,599,996	Federal Reserve Banks–display	1,993	84,162
Fort Knox, KY, deep storage	147,341,858	6,221,097,413	Gold coins	73,830	3,117,244
West Point, NY, deep storage	54,067,331	2,282,841,677	Federal Reserve Banks–		
Gold coins, blanks,			NY vault	73,452	3,101,308
miscellaneous	2,783,219	117,513,615	Federal Reserve Banks–display	377	15,936

World's Leading Gold Producers, 1980-2015

Source: *Mineral Commodity Summaries 2015*, U.S. Geological Survey, U.S. Dept. of the Interior
(ranked by 2015 production; in thousands of troy ounces)

Country	1980	1990	2000	2005	2010	2011	2012	2013	2014	2015[1]
China	225	3,215	5,787	7,234	11,092	11,639	12,957	13,825	14,468	15,754
Australia	548	7,845	9,530	8,423	8,391	8,295	8,038	8,520	8,809	9,645
Russia[2]	8,300	9,710	4,598	5,279	6,173	6,430	7,009	7,395	7,941	7,780
United States	970	9,452	11,349	8,231	7,427	7,523	7,555	7,395	6,752	6,430
Canada	1,627	5,433	5,022	3,844	2,926	3,119	3,344	3,987	4,887	4,823
Peru[3]	134	293	4,263	6,682	5,273	5,272	5,176	4,855	4,501	4,823
South Africa	21,669	19,451	13,767	9,474	6,076	5,819	5,144	5,144	4,887	4,501
Mexico	196	311	848	976	2,347	2,701	3,119	3,151	3,794	3,858
Uzbekistan	NA	NA	2,733	2,894	2,894	2,926	2,990	3,151	3,215	3,312
Ghana	353	540	2,318	2,149	2,637	2,572	2,797	2,894	2,926	2,733
Brazil	NA	NA	NA	NA	1,865	1,993	2,090	2,283	2,572	2,572
Indonesia[4]	60	360	4,006	4,200	3,858	3,087	1,897	1,961	2,218	2,411
World	39,197	70,089	82,949	79,412	82,306	85,520	86,485	90,022	96,131	96,452

(1) Estimated. (2) Figures for 1980-90 refer to the former USSR. Includes gold recovered as a byproduct but excludes secondary production. (3) Includes documented production from placer artisanal production. (4) Excludes production from "people's mines" or unauthorized small-scale mines, which may add more than 600,000 troy oz. to the total.

Prices of Precious Metals, 1990-2015

Source: *Mineral Commodity Summaries 2016*, U.S. Geological Survey, U.S. Dept. of the Interior

Year	Dollars per troy ounce			Dollars per pound			
	Platinum[1]	Gold	Silver	Copper[2]	Lead[3]	Tin[4]	Zinc[5]
1990	$467	$385	$4.82	$1.23	$0.46	$3.86	$0.75
1995	425	386	5.15	1.38	0.42	4.16	0.56
2000	549	280	5.00	0.88	0.44	3.70	0.56
2001	533	272	4.39	0.77	0.44	3.15	0.44
2002	543	311	4.62	0.76	0.44	2.92	0.39
2003	694	365	4.91	0.85	0.44	3.40	0.41
2004	849	411	6.69	1.34	0.55	5.47	0.52
2005	900	446	7.34	1.74	0.61	4.83	0.67
2006	1,144	606	11.57	3.15	0.77	5.65	1.59
2007	1,308	699	13.41	3.28	1.24	8.99	1.54
2008	1,578	874	15.00	3.19	1.20	11.29	0.89
2009	1,208	975	14.69	2.41	0.87	8.37	0.78
2010	1,616	1,228	20.20	3.48	1.09	12.40	1.02
2011	1,725	1,572	35.28	4.06	1.22	15.75	1.06
2012	1,555	1,673	31.22	3.67	1.14	12.83	0.96
2013	1,490	1,415	23.87	3.40	1.15	13.52	0.96
2014	1,388	1,269	19.37	3.18	1.06	10.23	1.07
2015[6]	1,080	1,170	16.00	2.77	0.93	7.20	0.95

(1) Average annual dealer prices. (2) U.S. producer price for cathode copper. (3) North American producer price through 2013; North American market price thereafter. (4) *Platts Metals Week* composite price through 2013, New York dealer prices thereafter. (5) *Platts Metals Week* price for North American special high grade zinc except for 1990, which shows average price for high grade zinc. (6) Estimated.

Top Brands in Selected Categories, 2015-16

Source: Information Resources, Inc., a Chicago-based marketing research company
Figures for 52-week period ending Aug. 7, 2016. Percent change represents dollar sales change in 2015-16 over same period in 2014-15.

Product	Sales	% change	Market share
Beer, domestic, total	**$9,218,116,869**	**4.0%**	
Bud Light	1,422,116,517	0.1	15.43%
Coors Light	792,488,890	1.8	8.60
Miller Lite	664,887,819	2.3	7.21
Budweiser	533,945,257	−0.4	5.79
Michelob Ultra	385,379,003	19.6	4.18
Bottled water, total	**$4,586,117,991**	**6.0%**	
Private label	1,269,896,130	3.7	27.69%
Dasani	416,155,053	3.4	9.07
Aquafina	313,312,333	4.9	6.83
Poland Spring	308,115,630	7.2	6.72
Nestlé Pure Life	296,063,498	5.7	6.46
Cat food (dry), total	**$1,050,147,408**	**−1.7%**	
Meow Mix Original Choice	73,984,004	−4.9	7.05%
Purina Cat Chow Indoor	63,260,353	−7.1	6.02
Purina Kit & Kaboodle	62,308,978	−11.4	5.93
Purina Cat Chow Naturals	60,075,004	21.4	5.72
Private label	58,649,871	−7.7	5.58
Cereal (ready-to-eat), total	**$5,721,047,109**	**−2.1%**	
Private label	518,111,222	−5.7	9.06%
General Mills Honey Nut Cheerios	321,929,691	5.9	5.63
Post Honey Bunches of Oats	274,289,424	−0.2	4.79

Product	Sales	% change	Market share
Kellogg's Frosted Flakes	$241,891,568	0.6%	4.23%
General Mills Cheerios	223,779,611	−0.5	3.91
Chocolate candy, total	**$2,692,496,434**	**0.8%**	
M&M's	348,553,552	6.9	12.95%
Hershey's	210,347,001	3.9	7.81
Reese's	129,618,451	5.1	4.81
Private label	114,793,778	−6.1	4.26
Dove Promises	112,428,470	1.5	4.18
Coffee (ground), total	**$2,619,584,034**	**−1.4%**	
Folger's	644,489,349	−2.0	24.60%
Maxwell House	333,418,837	−11.2	12.73
Starbucks	299,633,897	8.0	11.44
Private label	260,269,057	−6.8	9.94
Dunkin' Donuts	172,568,306	−5.6	6.59
Cookies, total	**$4,716,164,848**	**1.7%**	
Private label	646,940,837	−3.2	13.72%
Nabisco Oreo	493,650,243	5.3	10.47
Nabisco Chips Ahoy!	372,168,329	−1.7	7.89
Nabisco Oreo Double Stuf	169,840,631	−4.4	3.60
Nabisco BelVita	156,219,995	21.0	3.31
Disposable diapers, total	**$1,848,733,575**	**−1.0%**	
Private label	300,369,507	−10.7	16.25%
Pampers Swaddlers Sesame Beginnings	229,924,898	8.6	12.44

Product	Sales	% change	Market share
Huggies Snug & Dry			
Disney Baby..........	$221,255,457	12.1%	11.97%
Pampers Baby Dry			
Sesame Street........	174,911,091	−2.0	9.46
Luvs Ultra Leakguards....	162,480,574	−9.2	8.79
Dog food (dry), total	**$1,967,189,993**	**−2.9%**	
Purina One SmartBlend...	166,294,574	3.9	8.45%
Iams ProActive Health....	147,825,546	−1.0	7.51
Pedigree	136,148,955	0.7	6.92
Purina Dog Chow	132,891,464	−1.7	6.76
Private label...........	129,312,672	−11.4	6.57
Ice cream, total	**$4,297,721,480**	**4.7%**	
Private label...........	944,698,331	−1.7	21.98%
Häagen-Dazs...........	389,931,620	11.9	9.07
Ben & Jerry's	378,480,045	15.0	8.81
Breyer's	312,540,876	8.6	7.27
Turkey Hill	242,379,349	10.7	5.64
Pasta, total	**$1,460,305,915**	**1.8%**	
Barilla	421,182,316	2.8	28.84%
Private label...........	329,866,383	2.2	22.59
Ronzoni	95,326,314	3.3	6.53
Mueller's	60,707,115	−6.1	4.16
Creamette	49,488,319	0.3	3.39
Potato chips, total........	**$3,896,822,411**	**−0.4%**	
Lay's	1,099,521,995	0.4	28.22%
Wavy Lay's............	351,910,497	−4.8	9.03
Ruffles	331,245,373	4.9	8.50
Pringles	303,741,379	6.6	7.79
Private label...........	285,310,810	−5.7	7.32
Salsa, total.............	**$814,214,487**	**3.1%**	
Tostitos	306,975,295	4.1	37.70%
Private label...........	122,385,807	−0.9	15.03
Pace	74,687,717	0.6	9.17
Herdez	42,467,564	14.6	5.22
Chi-Chi's	35,790,966	2.2	4.40

Product	Sales	% change	Market share
Soft drinks, total	**$8,119,614,336**	**0.4%**	
Coca-Cola	1,946,835,289	0.6	23.98%
Pepsi	1,139,241,143	−3.7	14.03
Mountain Dew	741,249,008	−3.2	9.13
Dr Pepper	651,584,364	1.7	8.02
Sprite.................	622,406,862	5.1	7.67
Soft drinks (low-calorie), total	**$3,814,532,791**	**−4.6%**	
Diet Coke..............	979,396,684	−3.1	25.68%
Diet Pepsi	518,863,896	−9.6	13.60
Coca-Cola Zero	341,907,381	−1.6	8.96
Diet Mountain Dew	303,730,682	−3.7	7.96
Diet Dr Pepper..........	260,299,505	1.0	6.82
Toilet tissue, total	**$4,228,703,486**	**−0.7%**	
Private label...........	718,512,719	−2.0	16.99%
Charmin Ultra Strong.....	586,317,833	9.6	13.87
Charmin Ultra Soft.......	564,523,672	−7.6	13.35
Scott	496,358,481	0.9	11.74
Angel Soft	434,101,277	1.4	10.27
Toothpaste, total	**$1,518,534,347**	**2.4%**	
Colgate Total	98,311,746	6.6	6.47%
Sensodyne ProNamel	92,565,637	11.2	6.10
Crest 3D White..........	92,265,846	28.4	6.08
Sensodyne.............	89,473,164	13.2	5.89
Colgate Optic White.....	84,310,122	8.5	5.55
Yogurt, total.............	**$5,259,410,560**	**1.5%**	
Chobani	705,406,726	7.4	13.41%
Dannon Light & Fit.......	469,984,318	3.4	8.94
Private label...........	448,684,648	−8.5	8.53
Dannon Oikos	428,199,880	17.8	8.14
Yoplait Original..........	358,267,586	−1.7	6.81

Note: "Private label" represents the aggregated sales figures for store-branded products in that category. Total category sales include other brands not listed here.

Who Owns What: Familiar Consumer Products and Services

The following is a partial list of well-known consumer brands with their (U.S.) parent companies as of Sept. 2016. Among brands not listed are many whose parent companies have the same or a similar name (e.g., Colgate is owned by Colgate-Palmolive Co.).

ABC broadcasting: Walt Disney
Advil: Pfizer
Ajax cleanser: Colgate-Palmolive
Altoids mints: Mars
Amana appliances: Whirlpool
American Girl: Mattel
Aquafina water: PepsiCo
Arm & Hammer: Church & Dwight
Band-Aid bandages: Johnson & Johnson
Barbie dolls: Mattel
Bejeweled video game: PopCap
Ben & Jerry's ice cream: Unilever
Betty Crocker products: General Mills
Bounty paper towels: Procter & Gamble
Braun appliances: Procter & Gamble
Brita water systems: Clorox
Cadbury chocolates: Mondelēz
  International
Calphalon cookware: Newell Rubbermaid
Canada Dry ginger ale: Dr Pepper Snapple
  Group
ChapStick: Pfizer
Charmin toilet tissue: Procter & Gamble
Cheer detergent: Procter & Gamble
Cheez Whiz: Kraft Heinz
Chips Ahoy!: Mondelēz International
Claritin allergy products: Merck
Contadina tomatoes: Del Monte
Coppertone sunscreen: Bayer
Crest toothpaste: Procter & Gamble
Crisco shortening: J.M. Smucker
Dasani water: Coca-Cola
Depends adult diapers: Kimberly-Clark
Doritos chips: PepsiCo
Dove soap: Unilever

Dreyer's ice cream: Nestlé
Duracell batteries: Procter & Gamble
ESPN networks: Walt Disney
Febreze: Procter & Gamble
Fisher-Price toys: Mattel
Folger's coffee: J.M. Smucker
Formula 409 spray cleaner: Clorox
Friskies cat food: Nestlé
Frito-Lay's snacks: PepsiCo
Fruit of the Loom apparel: Berkshire
  Hathaway
Gatorade sports drinks: PepsiCo
GEICO auto insurance: Berkshire
  Hathaway
Gerber baby food: Nestlé
Gillette: Procter & Gamble
Glad products: Clorox
Glade air fresheners: S.C. Johnson
Green Giant vegetables: General Mills
Grey Poupon mustard: Kraft Heinz
Halls cough drops: Mondelēz International
Head & Shoulders shampoo: Procter &
  Gamble
Healthy Choice meals: ConAgra
Hebrew National meats: ConAgra
Hellmann's mayonnaise: Unilever
Hillshire Farm: Tyson Foods
Hot Wheels/Matchbox cars: Mattel
Hunt's tomatoes: ConAgra
I Can't Believe It's Not Butter: Unilever
Iams pet food: Mars
Irish Spring soap: Colgate-Palmolive
Ivory soap: Procter & Gamble
Jell-O: Kraft Heinz

Jennie-O turkey: Hormel
Jif peanut butter: J.M. Smucker
Jimmy Dean sausages: Tyson Foods
Jolly Rancher candy: Hershey
Keebler cookies: Kellogg Co.
KFC restaurants: Yum! Brands
Kibbles 'n Bits pet food: J.M. Smucker
Kingsford charcoal: Clorox
Kit Kat candy: Hershey
KitchenAid appliances: Whirlpool
Kiwi shoe products: S.C. Johnson
Kleenex: Kimberly-Clark
Knorr soups: Unilever
Kool-Aid: Kraft Heinz
Lea & Perrins Worcestershire sauce:
  Kraft Heinz
Lipton tea: Unilever
Listerine mouthwash: Johnson & Johnson
Maxwell House coffee: Kraft Heinz
Maytag appliances: Whirlpool
Minute Maid juices: Coca-Cola
Mr. Clean: Procter & Gamble
Monopoly board game: Hasbro
Mountain Dew soda: PepsiCo
Neosporin: Johnson & Johnson
Neutrogena soap: Johnson & Johnson
9Lives cat food: J.M. Smucker
o.b. tampons: Edgewell Personal Care
OFF! insect repellents: S.C. Johnson
Olay: Procter & Gamble
Old Navy clothing: Gap
Old Spice: Procter & Gamble
Oreo cookies: Mondelēz International
Oscar Mayer meats: Kraft Heinz
Pampers diapers: Procter & Gamble

Pantene shampoo: Procter & Gamble
Paper Mate pens: Newell Rubbermaid
Pedigree pet food: Mars
Pepperidge Farm prods.: Campbell Soup
Pepto-Bismol: Procter & Gamble
Perrier water: Nestlé
Pine-Sol cleaner: Clorox
Pizza Hut restaurants: Yum! Brands
Planters nuts: Kraft Heinz
Post-it notes: 3M
Prego pasta sauce: Campbell Soup
Pringles snacks: Kellogg Co.
Promise spread: Unilever
Purina pet foods: Nestlé
Q-tips: Unilever
Quaker Oats: PepsiCo
Raid insecticide: S.C. Johnson
Reese's candy: Hershey
Rice-A-Roni: PepsiCo

Right Guard deodorant: Henkel
Ritz crackers: Mondelēz International
Robitussin: Pfizer
Rogaine hair regrowth treatment: Johnson
  & Johnson
Saran wrap: S.C. Johnson
Schick razors: Edgewell Personal Care
Scope mouthwash: Procter & Gamble
Scotch tape: 3M
Skippy peanut butter: Hormel
Splenda artificial sweetener: Heartland
  Food Products
Sprite soda: Coca-Cola
Sudafed: Johnson & Johnson
Swanson broth: Campbell Soup
Taco Bell restaurants: Yum! Brands
Tampax tampons: Procter & Gamble
Tide detergent: Procter & Gamble
Timberland apparel: V.F. Corp.

Trident gum: Mondelēz International
Trojan condoms: Church & Dwight
Tropicana juice: PepsiCo
Twizzlers candy: Hershey
Tylenol: Johnson & Johnson
Uncle Ben's Rice: Mars
V8 vegetable juice: Campbell Soup
Vans apparel: V.F. Corp.
Vaseline: Unilever
Velveeta cheese products: Kraft Heinz
Viagra: Pfizer
Vicks cold medicines: Procter & Gamble
Visine eye drops: Johnson & Johnson
Windex cleaning products: S.C. Johnson
Wrigley's candy and gum: Mars
Xanax: Pfizer
Yoplait yogurt: General Mills
Ziploc storage bags: S.C. Johnson

U.S. Home Ownership Rates by Selected Characteristics 1995-2016
Source: U.S. Census Bureau, U.S. Dept. of Commerce

	1995	2000	2005	2010	2011	2012	2013	2014	2015	2016
Region										
Northeast	62.3%	63.4%	64.7%	64.2%	63.0%	63.7%	63.2%	62.1%	60.2%	59.2%
Midwest	68.5	72.2	73.4	70.8	70.0	69.6	69.4	69.6	68.4	67.7
South	66.5	69.2	70.4	69.1	68.2	67.4	66.5	65.9	64.9	64.8
West	59.8	61.9	63.8	61.4	60.3	59.7	59.4	59.6	58.5	57.9
Age										
Under 35 years	38.7	40.2	42.8	39.0	37.5	36.5	36.7	35.9	34.8	34.1
35-44 years	65.1	67.5	68.7	65.6	63.8	62.2	60.3	60.2	58.0	58.3
45-54 years	75.2	76.7	76.3	73.6	72.3	71.4	70.9	70.7	69.9	69.1
55-64 years	79.9	80.3	81.3	78.7	77.8	77.1	76.7	76.4	75.4	74.7
65+ years	78.1	80.3	80.3	80.4	80.8	81.6	80.9	80.1	78.5	77.9
Race/ethnicity[1]										
White alone, non-Hispanic	70.2	73.7	75.6	74.4	73.7	73.5	73.3	72.9	71.6	71.5
Black alone	42.6	46.7	48.0	46.2	44.2	43.8	42.9	43.5	43.0	41.7
Hispanic	42.2	45.4	49.2	47.8	46.6	46.5	45.9	45.8	45.4	45.1
Other	47.6	54.4	58.0	55.7	56.0	55.0	54.5	54.7	52.6	51.2
Income[2]										
Median family income or more	79.5	81.8	84.0	81.9	81.2	80.5	79.7	79.5	78.3	77.8
Below median family income	48.6	50.8	52.7	51.9	50.6	50.6	50.3	49.8	48.6	48.0
Total U.S.	**64.7**	**67.2**	**68.6**	**66.9**	**65.9**	**65.5**	**65.0**	**64.7**	**63.4**	**62.9**

Note: Figures are for 2nd quarter of year shown. Not seasonally adjusted. (1) Hispanic householders may be of any race. "Other" includes householders self-identifying as Asian, Native Hawaiian/Pacific Islander, and American Indian/Alaska Native, as well as combinations of two or more races/ethnicities. (2) Due to a change in survey methodology, data from 2010 forward are not directly comparable with prior years.

U.S. Housing Affordability, 1990-2016
Source: National Association of REALTORS®

Year[1]	Median-priced existing home	Avg. mortgage rate[2]	Monthly principal & interest payment	Payment as % of median monthly income	Year[1]	Median-priced existing home	Avg. mortgage rate[2]	Monthly principal & interest payment	Payment as % of median monthly income
1990	$92,000	10.04%	$648	22.0%	2010	$173,100	4.89%	$734	14.5%
1995	110,500	7.85	639	18.9	2011	166,200	4.67	687	13.4
2000	139,000	8.03	818	19.3	2012	177,200	3.83	663	12.7
2005	219,000	5.91	1,040	22.4	2013	197,400	4.00	754	14.1
2007	217,900	6.52	1,104	21.7	2014	208,900	4.31	828	15.1
2008	196,600	6.15	958	18.1	2015	223,900	4.03	858	15.3
2009	172,100	5.14	751	14.8	2016[2]	249,800	3.84	936	16.3

(1) 2016 figures are for June, the latest available. All other figures are annual averages. (2) All figures assume a down payment of 20% of the home price. Based on effective rate on loans closed on existing homes for the period shown.

S&P/Case-Shiller National Home Price Index, 1975-2016
Source: S&P Dow Jones Indices

This index compares the median price of existing U.S. homes over time. The baseline for comparison is Jan. 2000; all numbers before or after reflect home prices in relation to it. For example, the Jan. 2016 index of 175.3 means that home prices were 75.3% higher than they were 16 years earlier, while the Jan. 1975 index of 25.2 means prices then were 25.2% of what they were in 2000.

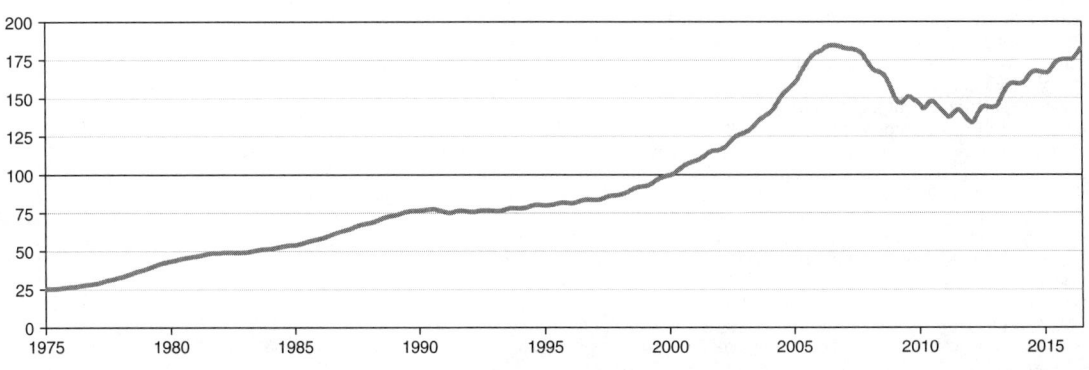

Median Price of Existing Single-Family Homes, by Metropolitan Area, 2010-16

Source: National Association of REALTORS®

Median prices are in thousands of dollars and based on all transactions within time period shown.

Metropolitan area	2010	2015	2016[1]	Metropolitan area	2010	2015	2016[1]
Akron, OH	$108.9	$118.6	$131.1	Los Angeles-Long Beach-Glendale, CA	$323.3	$476.8	$480.0
Albany-Schenectady-Troy, NY	195.7	206.3	202.7	Louisville/Jefferson County, KY-IN	134.6	154.5	164.0
Albuquerque, NM	178.7	180.8	193.5	Madison, WI	217.7	238.0	248.1
Allentown-Bethlehem-Easton, PA-NJ	224.0	182.6	185.7	Manchester-Nashua, NH	232.0	253.2	263.2
Amarillo, TX	124.7	150.3	158.3	Memphis, TN-MS-AR	120.2	147.0	160.8
Anaheim-Santa Ana-Irvine, CA	546.4	707.5	742.2	Miami-Fort Lauderdale-West Palm			
Atlanta-Sandy Springs-Marietta, GA	114.8	173.6	192.0	Beach, FL	201.9	280.0	310.0
Atlantic City-Hammonton, NJ	226.4	206.0	186.4	Milwaukee-Waukesha-West Allis, WI	205.9	220.4	230.0
Austin-Round Rock, TX	193.6	263.3	289.1	Minneapolis-St. Paul-Bloomington,			
Baltimore-Towson, MD	246.1	242.8	265.8	MN-WI	170.6	223.7	242.4
Barnstable Town, MA	326.0	362.6	367.4	Mobile, AL	121.0	123.9	133.9
Baton Rouge, LA	169.6	181.5	188.7	Montgomery, AL	129.0	136.5	145.7
Beaumont-Port Arthur, TX	125.1	138.0	143.5	Nashville-Davidson–Murfreesboro–			
Birmingham-Hoover, AL	143.0	178.5	195.2	Franklin, TN	153.8	204.2	227.0
Bismarck, ND	163.4	245.9	251.9	New Haven-Milford, CT	231.0	215.4	224.7
Bloomington, IL	157.9	154.6	153.7	New Orleans-Metairie, LA	159.7	169.7	195.9
Boise City-Nampa, ID	136.2	188.8	208.2	New York-Newark-Jersey City, NY-NJ-PA	393.7	386.8	395.4
Boston-Cambridge-Newton, MA-NH	357.3	403.9	435.8	Norwich-New London, CT	204.7	203.6	213.2
Boulder, CO	358.1	454.1	549.6	Oklahoma City, OK	145.7	149.6	154.9
Bridgeport-Stamford-Norwalk, CT	408.6	377.7	380.5	Omaha-Council Bluffs, NE-IA	137.3	159.1	169.8
Buffalo-Cheektowaga-Niagara Falls, NY	121.2	129.8	129.6	Orlando-Kissimmee-Sanford, FL	134.7	198.0	223.0
Burlington-South Burlington, VT	261.2	289.6	313.2	Palm Bay-Melbourne-Titusville, FL	103.0	162.0	185.0
Canton-Massillon, OH	90.9	119.1	128.2	Pensacola-Ferry Pass-Brent, FL	141.0	157.5	171.5
Cape Coral-Fort Myers, FL	88.9	210.0	230.0	Peoria, IL	116.9	120.7	120.5
Cedar Rapids, IA	144.7	151.5	157.0	Philadelphia-Camden-Wilmington,			
Champaign-Urbana, IL	141.9	143.1	145.2	PA-NJ-DE-MD	214.9	223.7	232.2
Charleston-North Charleston, SC	200.5	240.8	260.1	Phoenix-Mesa-Scottsdale, AZ	139.2	216.4	234.7
Charleston, WV	129.1	135.6	141.8	Pittsfield, MA	195.5	195.7	190.9
Charlotte-Concord-Gastonia, NC-SC	143.3	194.0	218.1	Portland-South Portland, ME	NA	237.3	248.8
Chattanooga, TN-GA	121.4	154.7	167.4	Portland-Vancouver-Hillsboro, OR-WA	237.3	312.1	356.7
Chicago-Naperville-Elgin, IL-IN-WI	191.4	218.9	246.4	Providence-Warwick, RI-MA	228.5	248.8	265.6
Cincinnati, OH-KY-IN	128.0	145.4	160.6	Raleigh, NC	190.4	238.2	258.8
Cleveland-Elyria, OH	114.5	125.1	138.1	Reading, PA	153.3	150.2	158.3
Colorado Springs, CO	195.5	238.6	259.3	Reno, NV	179.5	283.6	307.9
Columbia, MO	146.3	169.5	174.6	Richmond, VA	NA	227.3	240.4
Columbia, SC	142.6	153.4	165.5	Riverside-San Bernardino-Ontario, CA	179.3	290.7	315.5
Columbus, OH	136.4	164.7	181.7	Rochester, NY	118.9	134.0	134.6
Corpus Christi, TX	135.1	181.5	190.1	Rockford, IL	NA	91.4	109.0
Cumberland, MD-WV	100.3	81.1	94.9	Sacramento–Roseville–Arden-Arcade,			
Dallas-Fort Worth-Arlington, TX	143.8	207.2	232.2	CA	184.2	289.3	323.7
Davenport-Moline-Rock Island, IA-IL	112.2	121.6	125.5	St. Louis, MO-IL	131.1	158.0	170.3
Dayton, OH	103.6	121.7	138.8	Salem, OR	173.5	210.3	236.2
Deltona-Daytona Beach-Ormond				Salt Lake City, UT	206.5	255.0	276.9
Beach, FL	115.6	150.0	172.0	San Antonio-New Braunfels, TX	151.0	195.0	210.5
Denver-Aurora-Lakewood, CO	232.4	353.6	394.4	San Diego-Carlsbad, CA	385.7	542.6	589.9
Des Moines-West Des Moines, IA	150.9	181.3	187.9	San Francisco-Oakland-Hayward, CA	525.6	782.3	885.6
Detroit-Warren-Livonia, MI[2]	NA	NA	NA	San Jose-Sunnyvale-Santa Clara, CA	595.0	950.4	1,085.0
Dover, DE	193.3	191.4	204.0	Sarasota-Bradenton-North Port, FL	164.6	240.0	260.7
Durham-Chapel Hill, NC	158.3	222.9	245.7	Seattle-Tacoma-Bellevue, WA	295.7	379.7	420.5
El Paso, TX	134.3	142.1	149.3	Shreveport-Bossier City, LA	156.6	160.6	170.7
Erie, PA	107.7	118.7	115.1	Sioux Falls, SD	143.3	174.0	186.8
Eugene, OR	196.3	222.2	242.8	Spartanburg, SC	118.2	138.9	145.6
Fargo, ND-MN	NA	190.6	205.7	Spokane-Spokane Valley, WA	172.2	191.9	209.5
Gainesville, FL	161.6	182.0	203.0	Springfield, IL	124.0	121.6	143.1
Gary-Hammond, IN	122.9	141.7	150.4	Springfield, MA	190.0	197.0	201.6
Grand Rapids-Wyoming, MI	91.5	150.8	160.7	Springfield, MO	109.1	124.4	133.2
Green Bay, WI	130.4	144.3	149.2	Syracuse, NY	125.1	128.3	128.4
Greensboro-High Point, NC	129.8	151.5	159.3	Tallahassee, FL	152.8	176.5	187.3
Greenville-Anderson-Mauldin, SC	145.3	175.1	188.0	Tampa-St. Petersburg-Clearwater, FL	134.2	173.0	199.9
Gulfport-Biloxi, MS	125.0	126.7	134.1	Toledo, OH	81.5	107.3	125.1
Hartford-W. Hartford-E. Hartford, CT	235.8	221.5	236.9	Topeka, KS	107.2	119.1	129.8
Honolulu, HI	607.6	707.7	725.2	Trenton, NJ	250.7	262.3	274.9
Houston-Baytown-Sugar Land, TX	155.0	213.4	217.4	Tucson, AZ	156.6	182.9	192.5
Indianapolis-Carmel-Anderson, IN	123.3	153.2	164.3	Tulsa, OK	132.3	150.2	152.7
Jackson, MS	133.2	166.1	172.6	Virginia Beach-Norfolk-Newport News,			
Jacksonville, FL	137.7	195.0	215.0	VA-NC	205.0	209.0	223.0
Kansas City, MO-KS	141.6	170.4	188.6	Washington-Arlington-Alexandria,			
Knoxville, TN	140.9	157.2	167.7	DC-VA-MD-WV	325.3	383.4	406.9
Lansing-East Lansing, MI	84.4	128.3	139.2	Wichita, KS	118.7	132.9	138.4
Las Vegas-Henderson-Paradise, NV	138.0	216.8	242.3	Wilmington, NC	NA	211.2	225.1
Lexington-Fayette, KY	143.2	148.1	160.4	Winston-Salem, NC	NA	143.6	153.6
Lincoln, NE	133.6	156.8	162.7	Worcester, MA-CT	223.3	243.8	242.4
Little Rock-N. Little Rock-Conway, AR	132.5	135.9	140.7				

NA = Not available. (1) Second quarter figures for 2015 are preliminary. (2) $53,800 in 2011 and $63,400 in 2012.

Characteristics of American Housing Units, 2013

Source: *American Housing Survey, 2013*, U.S. Dept. of Housing and Urban Development

Characteristic	Number of homes (thous.)	% of all homes	Characteristic	Number of homes (thous.)	% of all homes
Total housing units	132,832	100.0%	**Number of bedrooms**		
Units in structure			None	1,101	0.8%
1, detached	83,392	62.8	1	15,151	11.4
1, attached	7,581	5.7	2	34,731	26.1
2-4.	10,724	8.1	3	54,731	41.2
5-9.	6,604	5.0	4 or more	27,118	20.4
10-19.	6,135	4.6	**Number of complete bathrooms**		
20-49.	4,579	3.4	None	1,510	1.1
50 or more.	5,213	3.9	1	46,130	34.7
Manufactured/mobile home/trailer	8,603	6.5	1-1/2	17,055	12.8
Cooperatives	853	0.6	2 or more	68,136	51.3
Condominiums	10,125	7.6	**Location[1]**		
Year built			Inside metropolitan statistical areas	92,772	80.1
2010-14.	2,390	1.8	Outside metropolitan statistical areas	23,080	19.9
2005-09.	7,890	5.9	Northeast	21,110	18.2
2000-04.	9,100	6.9	Midwest.	25,912	22.4
1995-99.	8,967	6.8	South.	42,951	37.1
1990-94.	7,116	5.4	West	25,879	22.3
1985-89.	8,927	6.7	**Lot size[2]**		
1980-84.	7,779	5.9	Less than 1/8 acre	16,223	16.9
1975-79.	13,760	10.4	1/8-1/4 acre.	25,008	26.0
1970-74.	10,949	8.2	1/4-1/2 acre.	16,841	17.5
1960-69.	15,145	11.4	1/2-1 acre	10,199	10.6
1950-59.	13,392	10.1	1-5 acres	20,593	21.4
1940-49.	7,836	5.9	5-10 acres	3,117	3.2
1930-39.	5,660	4.3	10+ acres	4,177	4.3
1920-29.	5,201	3.9	*Median lot size (acres) . . . .*	*0.25*	—
1919 or earlier.	8,720	6.6	**Equipment**		
Median year built	*1975*	—	Washing machine	104,458	78.6
Square footage of unit			Clothes dryer.	101,905	76.7
Less than 500	3,874	2.9	Dishwasher	86,877	65.4
500-749.	10,178	7.7	Central air conditioning	86,847	65.4
750-999.	16,028	12.1	Kitchen sink disposal	66,901	50.4
1,000-1,499.	31,319	23.6	Trash compactor	4,418	3.3
1,500-1,999.	24,446	18.4	Lacking full kitchen facilities	5,579	4.2
2,000-2,499.	15,967	12.0	**Main heating source[3]**		
2,500-2,999.	8,005	6.0	Piped gas	64,041	48.5
3,000-3,999.	7,565	5.7	Electricity	50,210	38.0
4,000 or more	4,989	3.8	Fuel oil	7,861	6.0
Not reported	10,461	7.9	Bottled gas	6,335	4.8
Median square footage.	*1,480*	—	Wood	2,388	1.8

— = Not applicable. (1) Percentages based on 115,852 occupied homes. (2) Percentages based on 96,159 1-unit structures; does not include cooperatives or condominiums. (3) Percentages based on 131,972 homes with heat. Not all heating fuels are shown here.

Fair Market Rents for Select Metropolitan Areas, 2016

Source: *Fair Market Rents 2016*, U.S. Dept. of Housing and Urban Development

Metropolitan area	0	1	2	3	4	Metropolitan area	0	1	2	3	4
Atlanta, GA	$764	$820	$949	$1,253	$1,532	Milwaukee-Waukesha, WI. . .	$596	$723	$907	$1,146	$1,266
Austin, TX	740	902	1,126	1,523	1,845	Minneapolis-St. Paul, MN-WI	656	813	1,027	1,444	1,693
Baltimore-Towson, MD	851	1,033	1,298	1,663	1,934	Nashville-Davidson, TN	661	756	925	1,228	1,433
Birmingham-Hoover, AL	613	726	840	1,134	1,250	New Orleans-Metairie, LA . .	669	787	963	1,219	1,464
Boston-Cambridge-Quincy,						New York, NY	1,293	1,357	1,571	2,021	2,224
MA-NH	1,056	1,261	1,567	1,945	2,148	Oklahoma City, OK	542	614	791	1,087	1,305
Buffalo-Niagara Falls, NY . . .	589	626	755	959	1,098	Orlando-Kissimmee, FL	748	835	1,003	1,332	1,608
Charlotte-Concord-Gastonia,						Philadelphia-Camden-					
NC-SC.	653	745	864	1,173	1,469	Wilmington, PA-NJ-DE-MD	830	1,003	1,210	1,502	1,659
Chicago-Joliet-Naperville, IL	860	1,001	1,176	1,494	1,780	Phoenix-Mesa-Scottsdale, AZ	596	735	914	1,332	1,558
Cincinnati, OH-KY-IN	509	600	787	1,102	1,297	Pittsburgh, PA	556	657	827	1,026	1,134
Cleveland-Elyria, OH	499	614	773	1,017	1,073	Portland-Vancouver, OR-WA	753	867	1,026	1,492	1,791
Columbus, OH	532	638	831	1,065	1,243	Providence-Fall River, RI-MA	655	801	972	1,206	1,452
Dallas, TX	667	796	986	1,337	1,692	Richmond, VA	795	835	966	1,276	1,557
Denver-Aurora-Lakewood,						Riverside-San Bernardino-					
CO.	775	965	1,227	1,788	2,083	Ontario, CA	798	945	1,187	1,672	2,056
Detroit-Warren-Livonia, MI . .	532	658	863	1,148	1,234	Sacramento-Roseville, CA . .	707	815	1,026	1,495	1,791
Hartford, CT	758	968	1,210	1,502	1,721	St. Louis, MO-IL	558	645	840	1,109	1,284
Honolulu, HI	1,334	1,507	1,985	2,893	3,140	Salt Lake City, UT	603	757	938	1,351	1,575
Houston, TX	684	773	948	1,291	1,650	San Antonio, TX	597	739	929	1,222	1,430
Indianapolis-Carmel, IN	552	651	809	1,084	1,230	San Diego-Carlsbad, CA . . .	1,040	1,153	1,499	2,167	2,329
Jacksonville, FL	616	787	960	1,270	1,578	San Francisco, CA	1,412	1,814	2,289	2,987	3,556
Kansas City, MO-KS.	562	721	893	1,219	1,385	San Jose-Santa Clara, CA . .	1,348	1,582	1,994	2,777	3,098
Las Vegas-Henderson, NV . .	632	781	968	1,411	1,690	San Juan-Guaynabo, PR . . .	407	456	548	736	895
Los Angeles-Long Beach, CA	947	1,154	1,490	2,009	2,227	Seattle-Bellevue, WA	1,049	1,225	1,523	2,220	2,617
Louisville, KY-IN	551	644	817	1,123	1,275	Tampa-St. Petersburg, FL. . .	668	795	992	1,319	1,575
Memphis, TN-MS-AR	602	700	827	1,128	1,309	Washington-Arlington-					
Miami-Miami Beach, FL	774	975	1,250	1,671	1,987	Alexandria, DC-VA-MD . . .	1,307	1,402	1,623	2,144	2,726

Note: Figures are projections made in the previous fiscal year. Metropolitan area may include individual cities not shown here.

TRADE

U.S. Trade With Selected Countries and Major Areas, 2015

Source: U.S. Census Bureau and U.S. Bureau of Economic Analysis, U.S. Dept. of Commerce

(in millions of dollars; top 25 countries as ranked by amount of total trade with U.S.)

Rank	Country	Total trade with U.S.	U.S. exports to	Rank[1]	U.S. imports from	Rank[1]	U.S. trade balance with	Rank[2]
1.	China[3]	$599,317	$116,072	3	$483,245	1	−$367,173	1
2.	Canada	576,765	280,609	1	296,156	3	−15,547	13
3.	Mexico	532,153	235,745	2	296,408	2	−60,663	4
4.	Japan	193,807	62,443	4	131,364	4	−68,922	3
5.	Germany	174,791	49,971	6	124,821	5	−74,850	2
6.	South Korea	115,204	43,446	7	71,759	6	−28,313	7
7.	United Kingdom	114,077	56,115	5	57,962	7	−1,848	40
8.	France	77,919	30,104	12	47,815	8	−17,712	11
9.	Taiwan	66,768	25,860	14	40,908	11	−15,048	14
10.	India	66,244	21,452	18	44,792	9	−23,340	9
11.	Italy	60,363	16,204	21	44,159	10	−27,955	8
12.	Brazil	59,119	31,651	11	27,468	17	4,182	225
13.	Netherlands	57,032	40,196	8	16,836	23	23,361	233
14.	Belgium	53,642	34,160	10	19,482	21	14,678	231
15.	Switzerland	53,582	22,185	17	31,397	15	−9,211	18
16.	Ireland	48,267	8,931	29	39,336	12	−30,405	6
17.	Singapore	46,740	28,472	13	18,268	22	10,205	229
18.	Malaysia	46,248	12,277	24	33,971	14	−21,694	10
19.	Vietnam	45,107	7,088	36	38,020	13	−30,932	5
20.	Hong Kong	43,963	37,167	9	6,796	37	30,371	234
21.	Saudi Arabia	41,820	19,739	19	22,081	19	−2,342	31
22.	Thailand	39,863	11,231	25	28,632	16	−17,401	12
23.	Israel	38,016	13,539	23	24,477	18	−10,938	16
24.	Australia	35,930	25,036	15	10,894	29	14,142	230
25.	Colombia	30,362	16,287	20	14,075	27	2,212	220

Major area/group

	Total trade with U.S.	U.S. exports to	U.S. imports from	U.S. trade balance with
North America	$1,108,918	$516,354	$592,564	−$76,209
Europe	811,892	319,675	492,217	−172,542
Euro Area	533,730	200,949	332,780	−131,831
EU	699,550	271,988	427,562	−155,573
Africa	52,515	27,135	25,380	1,756
OECD	2,295,845	984,766	1,311,080	−326,314
Pacific Rim Countries	1,201,879	370,316	831,563	−461,247
Asia-Near East	134,799	71,916	62,884	9,032
Asia-South	82,593	25,109	57,484	−32,375
ASEAN	226,831	74,872	151,959	−77,086
APEC	2,456,552	935,703	1,520,848	−585,145
South/Central America	268,408	152,533	115,875	36,658
Twenty Latin American Republics	778,424	372,783	405,641	−32,858
CAFTA-DR	52,472	28,722	23,750	4,973
Central American Common Market	40,693	21,609	19,085	2,524
NATO Allies	1,217,499	546,707	670,792	−124,084
OPEC	139,053	72,821	66,233	6,588
WORLD TOTAL	3,750,805	1,502,572	2,248,232	−745,660

Note: Figures shown are on Census Bureau basis and are not seasonally adjusted. Figures may not equal totals due to rounding. Country grouping data reflect groups at the time of reporting. (1) Rank shown is for column to the left. Ranking includes territories as well as nations. (2) Rank by size of U.S. trade deficit. Ranking includes territories as well as nations. (3) Not incl. Hong Kong, Macao, and Taiwan. *Definitions of major areas/groups used in table, as provided by source:* **North America**—Canada, Mexico. **Europe**—Albania, Andorra, Armenia, Austria, Azerbaijan, Belarus, Belgium, Bosnia-Herzegovina, Bulgaria, Croatia, Cyprus, Czech Republic, Denmark, Estonia, Faroe Isls., Finland, France, Georgia, Germany, Gibraltar, Greece, Hungary, Iceland, Ireland, Italy, Kazakhstan, Kosovo, Kyrgyzstan, Latvia, Liechtenstein, Lithuania, Luxembourg, Macedonia, Malta, Moldova, Monaco, Montenegro, Netherlands, Norway, Poland, Portugal, Romania, Russia, San Marino, Serbia, Slovakia, Slovenia, Spain, Svalbard-Jan Mayen Isl., Sweden, Switzerland, Tajikistan, Turkey, Turkmenistan, Ukraine, United Kingdom, Uzbekistan, Vatican City. **Euro Area**—Austria, Belgium, Cyprus, Estonia, Finland, France, Germany, Greece, Ireland, Italy, Latvia, Lithuania, Luxembourg, Malta, Netherlands, Portugal, Slovakia, Slovenia, Spain. **EU (European Union)**—Euro Area plus Bulgaria, Croatia, Czech Republic, Denmark, Hungary, Poland, Romania, Sweden, United Kingdom. **Africa**—Algeria, Angola, Benin, Botswana, British Indian Ocean Territories, Burkina Faso, Burundi, Cabo Verde, Cameroon, Central African Republic, Chad, Comoros, Congo (Brazzaville), Congo (Kinshasa), Côte d'Ivoire, Djibouti, Egypt, Equatorial Guinea, Eritrea, Ethiopia, French Southern and Antarctic Lands, Gabon, Gambia, Ghana, Guinea, Guinea-Bissau, Kenya, Lesotho, Liberia, Libya, Madagascar, Malawi, Mali, Mauritania, Mauritius, Mayotte, Morocco, Mozambique, Namibia, Niger, Nigeria, Réunion, Rwanda, St. Helena, São Tomé and Príncipe, Senegal, Seychelles, Sierra Leone, Somalia, South Africa, South Sudan, Sudan, Swaziland, Tanzania, Togo, Tunisia, Uganda, Western Sahara, Zambia, Zimbabwe. **OECD (Org. for Economic Cooperation and Development)**—Australia, Austria, Belgium, Canada, Chile, Czech Republic, Denmark, Estonia, Finland, France, Germany, Greece, Hungary, Iceland, Ireland, Israel, Italy, Japan, Korea (South), Luxembourg, Mexico, New Zealand, Norway, Poland, Portugal, Slovakia, Slovenia, Spain, Sweden, Switzerland, Turkey, United Kingdom. **Pacific Rim Countries**—Australia, Brunei, China, Hong Kong, Indonesia, Japan, Korea (South), Macao, Malaysia, New Zealand, Papua New Guinea, Philippines, Singapore, Taiwan. **Asia-Near East**—Bahrain, Gaza Strip Administered by Israel, Iran, Iraq, Israel, Jordan, Kuwait, Lebanon, Oman, Qatar, Saudi Arabia, Syria, United Arab Emirates, West Bank Administered by Israel, Yemen. **Asia-South**—Afghanistan, Bangladesh, India, Nepal, Pakistan, Sri Lanka. **ASEAN (Assn. of South East Asian Nations)**—Brunei, Cambodia, Indonesia, Laos, Malaysia, Myanmar, Philippines, Singapore, Thailand, Vietnam. **APEC (Asia-Pacific Economic Cooperation)**—Australia, Brunei, Canada, Chile, China, Hong Kong, Indonesia, Japan, Korea (South), Malaysia, Mexico, New Zealand, Papua New Guinea, Peru, Philippines, Russia, Singapore, Taiwan, Thailand, Vietnam. **South/Central America**—Anguilla, Antigua and Barbuda, Argentina, Aruba, Bahamas, Barbados, Belize, Bermuda, Bolivia, Brazil, British Virgin Isls., Cayman Isls., Chile, Colombia, Costa Rica, Cuba, Curaçao, Dominica, Dominican Republic, Ecuador, El Salvador, Falkland Isls., French Guiana, Grenada, Guadeloupe, Guatemala, Guyana, Haiti, Honduras, Jamaica, Martinique, Montserrat, Netherlands Antilles, Nicaragua, Panama, Paraguay, Peru, Sint Marten, St. Kitts and Nevis, St. Lucia, St. Vincent and the Grenadines, Suriname, Trinidad and Tobago, Turks and Caicos Isls., Uruguay, Venezuela. **Twenty Latin American Republics**—Argentina, Bolivia, Brazil, Chile, Colombia, Costa Rica, Cuba, Dominican Republic, Ecuador, El Salvador, Guatemala, Haiti, Honduras, Mexico, Nicaragua, Panama, Paraguay, Peru, Uruguay, Venezuela. **CAFTA-DR (Dominican Republic-Central America-U.S. Free Trade Agreement)**—Costa Rica, Dominican Republic, El Salvador, Guatemala, Honduras, Nicaragua. **Central American Common Market**—Costa Rica, El Salvador, Guatemala, Honduras, Nicaragua. **NATO (North Atlantic Treaty Org.) Allies**—Albania, Belgium, Bulgaria, Canada, Croatia, Czech Republic, Denmark, Estonia, France, Germany, Greece, Hungary, Iceland, Italy, Latvia, Lithuania, Luxembourg, Netherlands, Norway, Poland, Portugal, Romania, Slovakia, Slovenia, Spain, Turkey, United Kingdom. **OPEC (Org. of Petroleum Exporting Countries)**—Algeria, Angola, Ecuador, Gabon, Indonesia, Iran, Iraq, Kuwait, Libya, Nigeria, Qatar, Saudi Arabia, United Arab Emirates, Venezuela.

U.S. Exports and Imports by Principal Commodities, 2015
Source: U.S. Census Bureau and U.S. Bureau of Economic Analysis, U.S. Dept. of Commerce
(in millions of dollars)

Item	Exports	Imports
Total[1]	**$1,502,572**	**$2,248,232**
Manufactured goods	**1,111,607**	**1,946,296**
Agricultural commodities	**133,039**	**113,810**
Food and live animals	**97,898**	**98,662**
Live animals other than fish	717	3,286
Meat and preparations	15,998	9,988
Dairy products and birds	4,605	2,173
Fish and preparations	5,232	18,581
Cereals and preparations	22,864	8,991
Vegetables and fruits	22,066	30,164
Sugar, preparations, and honey	1,938	4,657
Coffee, tea, cocoa, and spices	3,040	13,403
Feeding stuff for animals	12,599	2,945
Miscellaneous edible products	8,841	4,475
Beverages and tobacco	**6,744**	**22,601**
Beverages	5,212	20,543
Tobacco and manufactures	1,532	2,058
Crude materials except fuels	**71,726**	**31,466**
Hides, skins, and furskins (raw)	2,436	242
Oil seeds and oleaginous fruits	20,738	1,250
Crude rubber	2,650	2,988
Cork and wood	6,579	6,947
Pulp and waste paper	8,469	3,293
Textile fibers including waste	5,998	1,446
Crude fertilizers	2,586	2,850
Metalliferous ores and metal scrap	19,236	6,839
Crude animal and vegetable materials	3,034	5,610
Mineral fuels and lubricants	**102,956**	**190,435**
Coal, coke, and briquettes	5,889	1,139
Petroleum products and preparations	85,242	177,446
Gas, natural and manufactured	11,584	9,388
Electric current	241	2,462
Animal and vegetable oils	**2,597**	**5,665**
Animal oil and fat	536	239
Fixed vegetable fats and oil, crude	1,730	5,249
Animal or vegetable fats, processed	331	176
Chemicals and related products	**195,802**	**216,155**
Organic chemicals	34,445	49,125
Inorganic chemicals	10,408	12,031
Dyeing, tanning, and coloring materials	7,289	3,829
Medicinal and pharmaceutical products	49,904	89,258
Essential oil and reinoids	$15,298	$13,852
Fertilizers	3,566	7,868
Plastics in primary forms	32,358	14,549
Plastics in nonprimary forms	12,882	9,639
Chemical materials and products	29,652	16,005
Manufactured goods by material	**109,573**	**244,140**
Leather and leather manufactures	1,217	1,427
Rubber manufactures	9,278	21,244
Cork and wood manufactures	2,107	10,306
Paper and paperboard	15,415	16,481
Textile yarn, fabrics	12,701	28,174
Nonmetallic mineral manufactures	13,702	45,039
Iron and steel	14,852	36,937
Nonferrous metals	14,311	34,506
Manufactures of metals	25,988	50,024
Machinery and transport equipment	**517,749**	**971,404**
Power-generating machinery	37,103	67,302
Specialized industrial machinery	43,679	44,917
Metalworking machinery	5,439	9,771
General industrial machinery	66,186	93,241
Office machinery	20,621	116,859
Telecommunications equipment	22,922	159,522
Electrical machinery	80,093	164,560
Road vehicles	114,708	275,772
Transport equipment	126,997	39,462
Miscellaneous manufactured articles	**120,278**	**370,183**
Prefabricated buildings	2,902	12,606
Furniture	6,464	45,539
Travel goods	592	11,511
Apparel and clothing accessories	3,347	93,617
Footwear	848	27,650
Scientific and controlling equipment	48,122	52,433
Photographic equipment	6,398	14,478
Miscellaneous manufactured articles	51,605	112,350
Miscellaneous commodities	**61,433**	**97,521**
Special transactions	8,552	67,098
Coin, including gold coin	353	1,827
Coin, other than gold	35	25
Gold, nonmonetary	20,237	11,436
Low value estimate	32,256	17,134
Re-exports	**215,818**	**NA**
Agricultural commodities	4,209	NA
Manufactured goods	204,723	NA

NA = Not applicable. **Note:** Numbers may not add up to totals due to rounding. (1) Total on Census Bureau basis; includes re-exports.

Trends in U.S. Foreign Trade, 1790-2015
Source: U.S. Census Bureau and U.S. Bureau of Economic Analysis, U.S. Dept. of Commerce
In 1790, U.S. exports and imports combined came to $43 mil, and there was a $3 mil trade deficit. The trade balance was positive for much of the 20th century, but the U.S. has had a trade deficit in every year since 1975.
(in millions of dollars)

Year	Exports	Imports	Trade balance	Year	Exports	Imports	Trade balance	Year	Exports	Imports	Trade balance
1790	$20	$23	–$3	1895	$808	$732	$76	1996	$851,602	$955,667	–$104,065
1795	48	70	–22	1900	1,394	850	545	1997	934,453	1,042,726	–108,273
1800	71	91	–20	1905	1,519	1,118	401	1998	933,174	1,099,314	–166,140
1805	96	121	–25	1910	1,745	1,557	188	1999	969,867	1,228,485	–258,617
1810	67	85	–19	1915	2,769	1,674	1,094	2000	1,075,321	1,447,837	–372,517
1815	53	113	–60	1920	8,228	5,278	2,950	2001	1,005,654	1,367,165	–361,511
1820	70	74	–5	1925	4,910	4,227	683	2002	978,706	1,397,660	–418,955
1825	91	90	1	1930	3,843	3,061	782	2003	1,020,418	1,514,308	–493,890
1830	72	63	9	1935	2,283	2,047	235	2004	1,161,549	1,771,433	–609,883
1835	115	137	–22	1940	4,021	2,625	1,396	2005	1,286,022	2,000,267	–714,245
1840	124	98	25	1945	9,806	4,159	5,646	2006	1,457,642	2,219,358	–761,716
1845	106	113	–7	1950	9,997	8,954	1,043	2007	1,653,548	2,358,922	–705,375
1850	144	174	–29	1955	14,298	11,566	2,732	2008	1,841,612	2,550,339	–708,726
1855	219	258	–39	1960	25,940	22,432	3,508	2009	1,583,053	1,966,827	–383,774
1860	334	354	–20	1965	35,285	30,621	4,664	2010	1,853,606	2,348,263	–494,658
1865	166	239	–73	1970	56,640	54,386	2,254	2011	2,127,021	2,675,646	–548,625
1870	393	436	–43	1975	132,585	120,181	12,404	2012	2,218,989	2,755,762	–536,773
1875	513	533	–20	1980	271,834	291,241	–19,407	2013	2,293,457	2,755,334	–461,876
1880	836	668	168	1985	289,070	410,950	–121,880	2014	2,376,577	2,866,754	–490,176
1885	742	578	165	1990	535,233	616,097	–80,864	2015	2,261,163	2,761,525	–500,361
1890	858	789	69	1895	794,387	890,771	–96,384				

Note: Figures shown using balance of payments basis.

World Trade Organization (WTO)
The World Trade Organization is an international body that seeks to promote free trade by eliminating barriers to trade. Founded in 1995, the WTO had grown to 164 member countries as of July 29, 2016, with 20 others, including Belarus and Iran, granted observer status. International intergovernmental organizations, such as the International Monetary Fund and the World Bank, may also be granted observer status. With the exception of Vatican City, observers must start accession negotiations within five years of becoming observers.

U.S. Trade in Goods and Services, 2015

Source: U.S. Census Bureau and U.S. Bureau of Economic Analysis, U.S. Dept. of Commerce
(top countries as ranked by amount of total trade with U.S.; in millions of dollars)

Country and category	Food and live animals	Beverages and tobacco	Crude materials, except fuels	Mineral fuels, lubricants	Chemicals	Manufactured goods	Machinery and transport equipment	Misc. manufactured	Commodities and transactions[1]	Total
China										
U.S. exports to	$7,597	$303	$24,264	$2,241	$13,808	$5,087	$52,388	$9,422	$1,033	**$116,186**
U.S. imports fr.	−5,951	−72	−2,266	−503	−16,757	−57,529	−255,564	−159,063	−4,927	**−502,689**
Trade balance	1,646	231	21,998	1,738	−2,949	−52,442	−203,176	−149,641	−3,894	**−386,503**
Canada										
U.S. exports to	21,452	2,080	6,584	21,237	31,381	34,439	124,117	28,483	9,800	**280,017**
U.S. imports fr.	−21,515	−832	−11,992	−74,702	−27,065	−38,261	−92,175	−14,157	−19,819	**−302,180**
Trade balance	−63	1,248	−5,408	−53,464	4,316	−3,822	31,943	14,326	−10,018	**−22,164**
Mexico										
U.S. exports to	14,002	524	8,014	18,597	26,324	31,310	111,473	18,223	7,288	**236,377**
U.S. imports fr.	−18,725	−4,454	−1,486	−13,986	−6,090	−19,515	−188,734	−32,960	−11,469	**−297,519**
Trade balance	−4,724	−3,930	6,528	4,611	20,234	11,795	−77,261	−14,737	−4,181	**−61,142**
Japan										
U.S. exports to	10,458	547	3,621	1,753	10,840	3,627	21,071	9,304	1,210	**62,472**
U.S. imports fr.	−671	−108	−566	−655	−8,559	−10,148	−100,286	−10,188	−3,547	**−134,776**
Trade balance	9,786	439	3,055	1,097	2,281	−6,521	−79,215	−884	−2,337	**−72,304**
Germany										
U.S. exports to	1,284	291	1,971	496	7,782	3,690	25,239	7,165	1,981	**49,947**
U.S. imports fr.	−1,281	−404	−890	−348	−23,823	−10,217	−73,994	−10,883	−4,635	**−126,494**
Trade balance	2	−113	1,081	148	−16,041	−6,527	−48,755	−3,718	−2,654	**−76,547**
South Korea										
U.S. exports to	5,464	92	2,645	1,213	6,762	2,780	19,531	4,274	676	**43,499**
U.S. imports fr.	−540	−193	−502	−3,011	−3,824	−10,584	−50,202	−3,954	−1,308	**−74,121**
Trade balance	4,925	−101	2,143	−1,798	2,938	−7,805	−30,671	320	−633	**−30,623**
United Kingdom										
U.S. exports to	1,313	548	1,717	2,338	8,378	3,929	22,971	8,854	6,278	**56,353**
U.S. imports fr.	−682	−1,956	−304	−3,714	−13,885	−3,729	−21,219	−7,453	−5,883	**−58,836**
Trade balance	630	−1,408	1,413	−1,376	−5,506	200	1,752	1,401	395	**−2,483**

Note: Figures for exports are "free alongside ship" values; figures for imports are "cost, insurance, and freight" values. Neither is directly comparable with the Census Bureau basis shown in other tables in this section. Trade balance is with U.S. and may not sum from export/import numbers due to rounding. Total includes categories not shown here. (1) Not classified elsewhere.

Foreign Exchange Rates, 1970-2015

Source: Federal Reserve Board
One U.S. dollar was worth the following amounts in each country's national currency; exchange rates are annual averages.

Nation (currency)	1970	1980	1990	2000	2005	2010	2012	2013	2014	2015
Australia (dollar)	0.898	0.877	1.280	1.720	1.311	1.087	0.965	1.033	1.107	1.329
Austria (schilling; euro)	25.880	12.945	11.370	1.083	0.803	0.754	0.778	0.753	0.752	0.901
Belgium (franc; euro)	49.680	29.237	33.418	1.083	0.803	0.754	0.778	0.753	0.752	0.901
Brazil (real)	NA	NA	NA	1.830	2.435	1.760	1.954	2.157	2.351	3.336
Canada (dollar)	1.010	1.169	1.167	1.485	1.211	1.030	1.000	1.030	1.104	1.279
China (yuan)	NA	NA	NA	8.278	8.194	6.770	6.309	6.148	6.162	6.283
Denmark (krone)	7.489	5.634	6.189	8.095	5.995	5.627	5.792	5.617	5.615	6.726
France (franc; euro)	5.520	4.225	5.445	1.083	0.803	0.754	0.778	0.753	0.752	0.901
Germany[1] (mark; euro)	3.648	1.817	1.616	1.083	0.803	0.754	0.778	0.753	0.752	0.901
Greece (drachma; euro)	30.000	42.620	158.510	365.920	0.803	0.754	0.778	0.753	0.752	0.901
Hong Kong (dollar)	NA	NA	NA	7.793	7.778	7.769	7.757	7.757	7.755	7.752
India (rupee)	7.576	7.890	17.504	45.000	44.000	45.650	53.370	58.510	61.000	64.110
Ireland (pound; euro)	2.396	2.058	1.659	1.083	0.803	0.754	0.778	0.753	0.752	0.901
Italy (lira; euro)	623.040	856.000	1,198.000	1.083	0.803	0.754	0.778	0.753	0.752	0.901
Japan (yen)	357.600	226.630	144.790	107.800	110.110	87.780	79.820	97.600	105.740	121.050
Malaysia (ringgit)	3.090	2.177	2.705	3.800	3.787	3.218	3.086	3.149	3.270	3.904
Mexico (peso[2])	NA	NA	NA	9.459	10.894	12.623	13.154	12.758	13.302	15.873
Netherlands (guilder; euro)	3.597	1.988	1.821	1.083	0.803	0.754	0.778	0.753	0.752	0.901
Norway (krone)	7.140	4.938	6.260	8.813	6.441	6.045	5.818	5.877	6.297	8.068
Portugal (escudo; euro)	28.750	50.080	142.550	1.083	0.803	0.754	0.778	0.753	0.752	0.901
Singapore (dollar)	3.080	2.141	1.813	1.725	1.664	1.363	1.249	1.251	1.257	1.375
South Korea (won)	310.570	607.430	707.760	1,130.900	1,023.750	1,155.740	1,126.160	1,094.670	1,052.290	1,130.960
Spain (peseta; euro)	69.720	71.760	101.930	1.083	0.803	0.754	0.778	0.753	0.752	0.901
Sweden (krona)	5.170	4.231	5.919	9.174	7.471	7.205	6.772	6.512	6.858	8.435
Switzerland (franc)	4.316	1.677	1.389	1.690	1.246	1.043	0.938	0.927	0.915	0.963
Taiwan (dollar)	NA	NA	NA	31.260	32.131	31.498	29.558	29.680	30.299	31.744
Thailand (baht)	21.000	20.476	25.585	40.210	40.252	31.700	31.055	30.696	32.461	34.241
United Kingdom (pound)	0.417	0.430	0.560	0.660	0.549	0.647	0.634	0.639	0.607	0.654

NA = Not available. **Note:** The euro, the European Union's single currency, replaced the national currencies in the EU nations shown above. Since 1999 (or 2001 in the case of Greece), the euro has been fixed at the following conversion rates: 13.7603 Austrian schillings, 40.3399 Belgian francs, 6.55957 French francs, 1.95583 German marks, 340.750 Greek drachmas, 0.787564 Irish pounds, 1,936.27 Italian lire, 2.20371 Netherlands guilders, 200.482 Portuguese escudos, and 166.386 Spanish pesetas. (1) West Germany before 1991. (2) Mexico re-based its currency in 1993; earlier values are not comparable.

Top U.S. Trading Partners, 1985-2015

Source: U.S. Census Bureau, U.S. Dept. of Commerce

(in millions of dollars; top five countries as ranked by amount of total trade with U.S. in 2015)

Country/category	1985	1990	1995	2000	2005	2010	2012	2013	2014	2015
China										
U.S. exports	$3,856	$4,806	$11,754	$16,185	$41,192	$91,911	$110,517	$121,746	$123,621	$116,072
U.S. imports from	3,862	15,237	45,543	100,018	243,470	364,953	425,619	440,430	468,484	483,245
Trade balance..........	–6	–10,431	–33,790	–83,833	–202,278	–273,042	–315,103	–318,684	–344,863	–367,173
Canada										
U.S. exports to	47,251	83,674	127,226	178,941	211,899	249,257	292,651	300,755	312,817	280,609
U.S. imports from	69,006	91,380	144,370	230,838	290,384	277,637	324,263	332,504	349,278	296,156
Trade balance..........	–21,755	–7,706	–17,144	–51,897	–78,486	–28,380	–31,613	–31,749	–36,461	–15,547
Mexico										
U.S. exports to	13,635	28,279	46,292	111,349	120,248	163,665	215,875	225,954	240,331	235,745
U.S. imports from	19,132	30,157	62,100	135,926	170,109	229,986	277,594	280,556	295,740	296,408
Trade balance..........	–5,497	–1,878	–15,808	–24,577	–49,861	–66,321	–61,719	–54,602	–55,408	–60,663
Japan										
U.S. exports to	22,631	48,580	64,343	64,924	54,681	60,472	69,976	65,237	66,876	62,443
U.S. imports from	68,783	89,684	123,479	146,479	138,004	120,552	146,432	138,575	134,505	131,364
Trade balance..........	–46,152	–41,105	–59,137	–81,555	–83,323	–60,080	–76,456	–73,338	–67,629	–68,922
Germany										
U.S. exports to	9,050	18,760	22,394	29,448	34,184	48,155	48,803	47,364	49,370	49,971
U.S. imports from	20,239	28,162	36,844	58,513	84,751	82,450	109,226	114,342	124,179	124,821
Trade balance..........	–11,189	–9,402	–14,450	–29,065	–50,567	–34,295	–60,423	–66,978	–74,809	–74,850

Note: Figures shown are on Census Bureau basis.

Busiest U.S. Ports, 2014

Source: U.S. Army Corps of Engineers, Dept. of the Army, U.S. Dept. of Defense

(figures in millions of short tons; ranked by total tonnage handled)

Rank	Port	Domestic	Foreign	Total	Rank	Port	Domestic	Foreign	Total
1.	South Louisiana, LA	141.6	125.8	267.4	26.	Richmond, CA	8.7	17.3	26.0
2.	Houston, TX	73.8	160.5	234.3	27.	Newport News, VA	1.0	24.7	25.7
3.	New York, NY-NJ	46.5	79.6	126.2	28.	Portland, OR	9.5	15.6	25.1
4.	Beaumont, TX	34.3	52.9	87.3	29.	Tacoma, WA	4.5	20.6	25.1
5.	Long Beach, CA	10.9	74.1	85.0	30.	Port Everglades, FL	9.5	12.9	22.4
6.	Corpus Christi, TX	40.2	44.7	84.9	31.	Seattle, WA	5.5	16.9	22.4
7.	New Orleans, LA	47.4	37.1	84.5	32.	Freeport, TX	6.3	16.1	22.3
8.	Baton Rouge, LA	42.8	26.4	69.2	33.	Charleston, SC	1.6	18.3	19.8
9.	Mobile, AL	27.5	36.8	64.3	34.	Oakland, CA	2.0	16.9	18.9
10.	Los Angeles, CA	5.8	55.2	61.0	35.	Philadelphia, PA	11.2	7.4	18.5
11.	Lake Charles, LA	28.1	28.7	56.8	36.	Paulsboro, NJ	6.9	11.0	17.9
12.	Plaquemines, LA	35.3	20.2	55.5	37.	Chicago, IL	15.4	2.1	17.5
13.	Cincinnati-Northern, KY . .	49.9	0.0	49.9	38.	Jacksonville, FL	6.5	10.8	17.3
14.	Norfolk Harbor, VA	6.0	42.0	48.0	39.	Boston, MA	5.1	11.9	17.0
15.	Texas City, TX	18.8	29.0	47.9	40.	Two Harbors, MN	14.0	0.8	14.8
16.	Huntington-Tristate, WV . .	46.4	0.0	46.4	41.	Memphis, TN	14.7	0.0	14.7
17.	St. Louis, MO-IL	38.9	0.0	38.9	42.	Honolulu, HI	13.5	1.1	14.6
18.	Duluth-Superior, MN-WI . .	28.5	8.9	37.4	43.	Detroit, MI	11.3	2.8	14.1
19.	Baltimore, MD	6.9	30.3	37.2	44.	Longview, WA	1.8	12.1	13.8
20.	Port Arthur, TX	11.0	25.7	36.7	45.	Indiana Harbor, IN	12.7	0.3	13.0
21.	Tampa, FL	22.6	12.6	35.2	46.	Cleveland, OH	11.5	1.5	13.0
22.	Savannah, GA	1.3	33.1	34.4	47.	Toledo, OH	6.3	5.0	11.3
23.	Pittsburgh, PA	31.5	0.0	31.5	48.	Matagorda, TX	3.3	7.9	11.3
24.	Pascagoula, MS	9.6	18.3	27.9	49.	San Juan, PR	4.7	6.1	10.8
25.	Valdez, AK	26.4	0.1	26.5	50.	Kalama, WA	0.5	10.2	10.7

World's Busiest Ports, 2012-14

Source: United Nations Conference on Trade and Development

(ranked by throughput volume in 2014 as measured in twenty-ft equivalent units (TEUs))

Rank, port	Volume (TEUs)			Percent change	
	2012	2013	2014[1]	2012-13	2013-14
1. Shanghai, China..........................	32,529,000	36,617,000	35,290,000	12.57%	–3.62%
2. Singapore[2]	31,649,400	32,600,000	33,869,000	3.00	3.89
3. Shenzhen, China	22,940,130	23,279,000	24,040,000	1.48	3.27
4. Hong Kong, China........................	23,117,000	22,352,000	22,200,000	–3.31	–0.68
5. Ningbo, China............................	15,670,000	17,351,000	19,450,000	10.73	12.10
6. Busan, South Korea	17,046,177	17,686,000	18,678,000	3.75	5.61
7. Guangzhou, China	14,743,600	15,309,000	16,610,000	3.83	8.50
8. Qingdao, China..........................	14,503,000	15,520,000	16,580,000	7.01	6.83
9. Dubai, United Arab Emirates...............	13,270,000	13,641,000	15,200,000	2.80	11.43
10. Tianjin, China	12,300,000	13,000,000	14,060,000	5.69	8.15
11. Rotterdam, Netherlands	11,865,916	11,621,000	12,298,000	–2.06	5.83
12. Port Klang, Malaysia	10,001,495	10,350,000	10,946,000	3.48	5.76
13. Kaohsiung, Taiwan	9,781,221	9,938,000	10,593,000	1.60	6.59
14. Dalian, China	8,064,000	10,015,000	10,130,000	24.19	1.15
15. Hamburg, Germany	8,863,896	9,258,000	9,729,000	4.45	5.09
16. Antwerp, Belgium	8,635,169	8,578,000	8,978,000	–0.66	4.66
17. Xiamen, China	7,201,700	8,008,000	8,572,000	11.20	7.04
18. Tanjung Pelepas, Malaysia	7,700,000	7,628,000	8,500,000	–0.94	11.43
19. Los Angeles, CA, U.S.	8,077,714	7,869,000	8,340,000	–2.58	5.99
20. Jakarta, Indonesia	6,100,000	6,171,000	6,053,000	1.16	–1.91
Total top 20	**284,059,418**	**296,791,000**	**310,116,000**	**4.48**	**4.49**

Note: A TEU is the size of a typical shipping container. (1) Preliminary. (2) Port of Jurong not included.

Value of Freight Shipments by Transportation Mode, 2007-13

Source: *Freight Facts and Figures 2015*, U.S. Dept. of Transportation

(value in billions of 2007 dollars)

Mode of transportation	2007 Total	Domestic	Exports	Imports	2013 Total	Domestic	Exports	Imports
Truck	$10,780	$10,225	$267	$287	$11,444	$10,841	$312	$291
Rail	512	374	45	93	577	424	54	99
Water	340	158	15	167	284	131	20	133
Air, air and truck	1,077	151	422	505	1,167	134	425	609
Multiple modes and mail	2,884	1,646	394	844	3,065	1,695	500	870
Pipeline	716	651	4	61	1,083	1,003	15	65
Other and unknown	341	252	48	41	363	270	53	40
Total	**16,651**	**13,457**	**1,196**	**1,997**	**17,983**	**14,496**	**1,380**	**2,107**

Note: Imports and exports that pass through the U.S. from a foreign origin to a foreign destination by any mode not included. 2013 data are provisional estimates. All truck, rail, water, and pipeline movements that involve more than one mode, including exports and imports that change mode at international gateways, are included in multiple modes and mail to avoid double counting.

Merchant Fleets of the World, 2015

Source: *Review of Maritime Transport, 2015*, United Nations Conference on Trade and Development

(ranked by deadweight tonnage under flag of registration as of Jan. 1, 2015)

Flag of registration	Number of ships	Percent of world total	Tonnage (thous.)	Percent of world total	Average vessel size (tons)	Tonnage change, 2014-15
Panama	8,351	9.33%	352,192	20.13%	44,052	0.91%
Liberia	3,143	3.51	203,832	11.65	65,018	0.31
Marshall Islands	2,580	2.88	175,345	10.02	67,990	13.32
Hong Kong	2,425	2.71	150,801	8.62	63,575	6.47
Singapore	3,689	4.12	115,022	6.58	33,830	8.52
Malta	1,895	2.12	82,002	4.69	43,898	8.69
Greece	1,484	1.66	78,728	4.50	63,286	4.45
The Bahamas	1,421	1.59	75,779	4.33	54,322	2.54
China	3,941	4.41	75,676	4.33	20,756	−1.28
Cyprus	1,629	1.82	33,664	1.92	32,000	3.96
Isle of Man	1,079	1.21	23,008	1.32	55,441	−2.28
Japan	5,224	5.84	22,419	1.28	5,558	7.47
Norway	1,558	1.74	20,738	1.19	15,339	−1.20
Italy	1,418	1.58	17,555	1.00	14,556	−11.22
United Kingdom	1,865	2.08	17,103	0.98	16,059	−0.35
South Korea	673	0.75	16,825	0.96	10,099	−3.13
Denmark	7,373	8.24	16,656	0.95	26,606	13.94
Indonesia	1,604	1.79	15,741	0.90	3,681	2.29
India	1,174	1.31	15,551	0.89	10,157	−1.39
Antigua and Barbuda	650	0.73	12,753	0.73	10,909	−3.45
Germany	3,561	3.98	12,693	0.73	22,230	−11.69
United States	1,613	1.80	12,683	0.73	6,089	2.59
Tanzania	1,313	1.47	11,703	0.67	46,256	−1.54
Bermuda	1,245	1.39	11,511	0.66	71,946	2.69
Malaysia	1,777	1.99	9,232	0.53	6,793	−0.95
Turkey	2,471	2.76	8,820	0.50	8,181	−2.64
Netherlands	1,412	1.58	8,651	0.49	7,536	0.34
Belgium	756	0.85	8,609	0.49	45,548	21.96
Vietnam	674	0.75	7,351	0.42	4,499	0.81
Russia	963	1.08	7,221	0.41	2,974	2.45
France	670	0.75	6,882	0.39	16,042	−8.85
Philippines	646	0.72	6,850	0.39	6,149	6.19
Kuwait	765	0.86	5,440	0.31	40,002	37.91
Thailand	749	0.84	5,070	0.29	7,636	0.86
Taiwan	586	0.66	4,829	0.28	18,431	8.05
World total	**89,464**	**100.00**	**1,749,222**	**100.00**	**22,757**	**3.54**

U.S. International Transactions, 1970-2015

Source: U.S. Bureau of Economic Analysis, U.S. Dept. of Commerce

(in millions of dollars)

	1970	1980	1990	2000	2005	2010	2014	2015[1]
CURRENT ACCOUNT								
Exports of goods and services and income payments (credits)	$68,388	$344,440	$712,128	$1,471,532	$1,895,983	$2,630,799	$3,306,574	$3,138,696
Goods	42,469	224,250	387,401	784,940	913,016	1,290,273	1,632,639	1,513,453
Services	14,171	47,585	147,833	290,381	373,006	563,333	710,565	710,165
Primary income receipts	11,748	72,605	176,894	358,822	543,982	684,915	823,353	783,077
Imports of goods and services and income payments (debits)	66,055	342,124	791,097	1,882,288	2,641,418	3,074,729	3,696,100	3,622,774
Goods	39,866	249,750	498,438	1,231,722	1,695,820	1,938,950	2,374,101	2,272,760
Services	14,519	41,492	117,660	216,115	304,448	409,313	477,428	490,613
Primary income payments	5,514	42,533	148,345	339,643	476,349	507,254	585,369	591,753
Secondary income payments (current transfers)[2]	6,156	8,349	26,654	94,808	164,801	219,212	259,202	267,647
CAPITAL ACCOUNT								
Capital transfer receipts and other credits	NA	NA	0	35	15,462	0	0	0
Capital transfer payments and other debits	NA	NA	7,220	36	2,346	157	45	45
Net U.S. acquisition of financial assets[3]	9,336	86,968	103,985	589,315	572,317	963,449	792,145	242,234
Net U.S. incurrence of liabilities[3]	7,226	62,036	162,109	1,067,016	1,273,038	1,386,345	977,421	426,036
Balance on current account	**2,331**	**2,318**	**−78,969**	**−410,756**	**−745,434**	**−443,930**	**−389,526**	**−484,078**
Balance on capital account	**NA**	**NA**	**−7,221**	**−1**	**13,116**	**−157**	**−45**	**−45**
Net lending (+) or net borrowing (−) from financial-acct. transactions[4]	2,110	24,932	−58,124	−477,701	−700,721	−436,972	−239,648	−209,203

NA = Not available or applicable. (1) Preliminary. (2) Includes U.S. government and private transfers, such as U.S. government grants and pensions, fines and penalties, withholding taxes, personal transfers (remittances), insurance-related transfers, and other current transfers. (3) Excludes financial derivatives. (4) Net lending means that U.S. residents are net suppliers of funds to foreign residents, and net borrowing means the opposite. Net lending or net borrowing can be computed from current- and capital-account transactions or from financial-account transactions.

U.S. International Direct Investments, 1990-2015

Source: U.S. Bureau of Economic Analysis, U.S. Dept. of Commerce
(in millions of dollars)

	U.S. direct investment abroad					Foreign direct investment in U.S.				
	1990	2000	2010	2014	2015	1990	2000	2010	2014	2015
All countries[1]	$430,521	$1,316,247	$3,741,910	$4,829,425	$5,040,648	$394,911	$1,256,867	$2,280,044	$2,913,304	$3,134,199
Canada	69,508	132,472	295,206	358,452	352,928	29,544	114,309	192,463	257,142	268,972
Europe[1]	**214,739**	**687,320**	**2,034,559**	**2,773,447**	**2,949,235**	**247,320**	**887,014**	**1,659,774**	**1,983,202**	**2,162,845**
Austria	1,113	2,872	11,485	16,359	17,275	625	3,007	4,532	6,962	7,116
Belgium	9,464	17,973	43,975	47,515	45,087	3,900	14,787	69,565	87,571	80,134
Czech Rep.	NA	1,228	5,268	6,554	5,831	NA	NA	65	84	107
Denmark	1,726	5,270	11,802	13,800	14,398	819	4,025	7,772	13,286	14,274
Finland	544	1,342	1,597	2,643	1,177	1,504	8,875	4,943	9,070	9,833
France	19,164	42,628	78,320	78,421	78,282	18,650	125,740	189,763	212,726	233,844
Germany	27,609	55,508	103,319	104,242	108,094	28,232	122,412	203,077	227,900	255,471
Greece	282	795	1,775	−482	−608	94	659	−41	605	631
Hungary	NA	1,920	4,237	6,086	6,398	NA	5,287	39,266	19,668	13,190
Ireland	5,894	35,903	158,851	279,730	343,382	1,340	25,523	24,097	25,184	13,455
Italy	14,063	23,484	27,137	24,328	22,499	1,524	6,576	20,142	24,082	28,648
Luxembourg	1,697	27,849	272,206	491,456	502,998	2,195	58,930	170,309	225,597	328,400
Netherlands	19,120	115,429	514,689	797,251	858,102	64,671	138,894	234,408	280,739	282,525
Norway	4,209	4,379	28,541	34,540	33,588	773	2,665	10,478	19,647	20,771
Poland	NA	3,884	13,152	11,374	11,038	29	57	4,386	NA	1,456
Portugal	897	2,664	2,612	2,089	2,042	−19	−68	204	802	937
Russia	NA	1,147	10,040	9,277	9,201	NA	118	5,689	4,892	4,561
Spain	7,868	21,236	52,390	35,738	35,794	792	5,068	43,095	58,923	61,947
Sweden	1,787	25,959	23,275	25,738	24,981	5,484	21,991	38,780	44,042	46,928
Switzerland	25,099	55,377	119,891	141,371	155,221	17,674	64,719	180,642	248,823	257,859
Turkey	522	1,826	4,155	3,700	3,661	20	188	749	624	625
UK	72,707	230,762	501,247	563,055	593,028	98,676	277,613	400,435	458,727	483,841
Latin America[1]	**71,413**	**266,576**	**752,788**	**834,197**	**847,571**	**20,168**	**53,691**	**62,130**	**119,962**	**118,796**
Argentina	2,531	17,488	11,747	13,094	13,323	420	364	464	70	10
Bahamas, The	4,004	NA	NA	NA	NA	1,535	1,254	1,753	818	1,834
Barbados	252	2,141	7,524	14,149	14,894	191	1,560	706	301	1,290
Bermuda	20,169	60,114	265,524	267,374	269,329	1,550	18,336	365	115	−5,467
Brazil	14,384	36,717	66,963	72,497	65,272	377	882	1,357	1,443	431
Chile	1,896	10,052	30,747	27,070	27,331	5	24	391	837	2,088
Colombia	1,677	3,693	6,181	7,102	6,157	55	2	382	−187	−80
Costa Rica	251	1,716	1,827	1,497	1,521	−2	2	−48	−104	−82
Curaçao[2]	−4,501	NA	NA	5,709	5,706	12,974	3,807	2,819	1,844	1,468
Dominican Rep.	529	1,143	1,432	1,213	1,357	0	79	−142	−5	−8
Ecuador	280	832	1,283	576	429	6	29	77	NA	NA
Honduras	262	399	936	741	1,175	8	−3	7	−19	−16
Mexico	10,313	39,352	85,751	89,650	92,812	575	7,462	10,970	16,567	16,597
Panama	9,289	30,758	5,156	4,616	4,055	4,188	3,819	952	2,350	2,653
Peru	599	3,130	7,196	6,445	6,859	NA	−13	182	119	113
UK isls. in Caribbean	5,929	33,451	191,680	242,142	257,256	−2,979	15,191	38,477	90,705	93,023
Venezuela	1,087	10,531	10,255	11,344	9,068	496	792	3,122	3,927	4,182
Africa[1]	**3,650**	**11,891**	**54,816**	**67,588**	**64,040**	**505**	**2,700**	**2,265**	**853**	**707**
Egypt	1,231	1,998	12,599	24,135	23,326	1	−4	−277	−84	−77
Nigeria	−401	470	5,058	4,924	5,521	−17	NA	23	14	29
South Africa	775	3,562	6,017	6,144	5,604	10	704	699	−507	−657
Middle East[1]	**3,959**	**10,863**	**34,431**	**49,400**	**48,525**	**4,425**	**6,506**	**16,808**	**16,691**	**18,468**
Israel	746	3,735	9,464	9,705	10,297	640	3,012	8,714	6,173	7,448
Saudi Arabia	1,899	3,661	7,436	9,502	10,509	1,811	NA	NA	NA	NA
UAE	409	683	4,935	15,330	15,622	99	64	747	2,840	3,008
Asia and Pacific[1]	**64,718**	**207,125**	**570,111**	**746,341**	**778,349**	**92,948**	**192,647**	**346,605**	**535,454**	**564,411**
Australia	15,110	34,838	125,421	176,881	167,401	6,542	18,775	35,632	48,856	42,301
China	354	11,140	58,996	67,500	74,560	NA	277	3,300	9,853	14,838
Hong Kong	6,055	27,447	41,264	60,466	64,049	1,511	1,493	4,440	10,524	11,102
India	372	2,379	24,666	27,140	28,335	NA	96	4,102	8,924	9,250
Indonesia	3,207	8,904	10,558	13,709	13,546	25	16	138	1,522	1,577
Japan	22,599	57,091	113,523	100,077	108,535	83,091	159,690	255,012	382,032	411,201
Korea, South	2,695	8,968	26,233	33,453	34,564	−1,009	3,110	15,746	39,923	40,130
Malaysia	1,466	7,910	11,791	15,172	13,959	56	310	338	1,154	1,279
New Zealand	3,156	4,271	6,724	7,563	7,176	157	395	584	1,047	585
Philippines	1,355	3,638	5,399	4,549	4,724	77	47	103	1,029	1,178
Singapore	3,975	24,133	102,778	206,958	228,666	1,289	5,087	21,517	20,528	19,423
Taiwan	2,226	7,836	22,188	14,778	15,005	836	3,174	4,642	6,108	6,968
Thailand	1,790	5,824	12,999	11,669	11,295	150	132	158	2,003	2,470

NA = Not available. **Note:** On a historical cost basis for comparison purposes. Direct investment in all industries. Book value of foreign direct investors' equity in, and net outstanding loans to, their U.S. affiliates. A U.S. affiliate is a U.S. business enterprise in which a single foreign direct investor owns at least 10% of the voting securities, or the equivalent. (1) Totals and subtotals include countries or territories not shown in table. (2) Curaçao figures before 2010 are for the entire Netherlands Antilles, a confederation that ended in 2010.

TRANSPORTATION AND TRAVEL

Top Motor Vehicle Producing Nations, 2015

Source: International Organization of Motor Vehicle Manufacturers (OICA)
(in thousands of units; ranked by total production)

Nation	Total motor vehicles	Cars	Light commercial vehicles[1]	% change, 2014-15[2]
China[3]	24,503	21,079	3,424	3.3%
U.S.	12,100	4,164	7,936	3.8
Japan	9,278	7,831	1,448	−5.1
Germany	6,033	5,708	325	2.1
South Korea	4,556	4,135	421	0.7
India	4,126	3,378	748	7.3
Mexico	3,565	1,968	1,597	5.9
Spain	2,733	2,219	514	13.7
Brazil	2,429	2,019	411	−22.8
Canada	2,283	889	1,395	−4.6
France	1,970	1,554	416	8.2
Thailand	1,915	772	1,143	1.9
UK	1,682	1,588	94	5.2
Russia	1,384	1,215	170	−26.6
Turkey	1,359	791	568	16.1
Czech Rep.	1,304	1,298	5	0.0
Indonesia	1,099	824	274	−15.4
Italy	1,014	663	351	45.3
Slovakia	1,000	1,000	0	3.0
Iran	982	885	97	−9.9
Poland	661	535	126	11.3
South Africa	616	341	275	8.8

Nation	Total motor vehicles	Cars	Light commercial vehicles[1]	% change, 2014-15[2]
Malaysia	615	558	56	3.3%
Argentina	534	309	225	−13.5
Hungary	495	492	4	13.2
Belgium	409	369	40	−20.8
Romania	387	387	0	−1.1
Taiwan	351	298	53	−7.4
Sweden	189	189	0	22.6
Uzbekistan	185	185	0	−24.5
Australia	173	160	13	−4.0
Portugal	157	115	41	−3.0
Slovenia	133	133	0	12.2
Austria	126	109	17	−17.4
Serbia	84	82	1	−18.9
Finland	69	69	0	53.3
Netherlands	44	42	2	40.4
Egypt	36	12	24	−15.3
Ukraine	8	6	3	−71.3
Others	833	694	139	19.1
NAFTA	**17,434**	**7,020**	**10,413**	**3.0**
Total	**90,781**	**68,540**	**22,241**	**1.1**

NAFTA = North American Free Trade Agreement. **Note:** Numbers may not add up to totals due to rounding. (1) Also includes heavy trucks, coaches, and buses. (2) Percent change in number of total motor vehicles. (3) Not including Taiwan.

World Motor Vehicle Production, 1950-2015

Source: For 1950-90, American Automobile Manufacturers Assn.; 2000-12, Automotive News Data Center and R.L. Polk; 2013-15, OICA
(in thousands of units)

Year	U.S.	Canada	Europe[1]	Japan	Other	World total	U.S. % of world total
1950	8,006	388	1,991	32	160	10,577	75.7%
1960	7,905	398	6,837	482	866	16,488	47.9
1970	8,284	1,160	13,049	5,289	1,637	29,419	28.2
1980	8,010	1,324	15,496	11,043	2,692	38,565	20.8
1990	9,783	1,928	18,866	13,487	4,496	48,554	20.1
2000	12,832	2,952	17,678	10,145	16,098	59,704	21.5
2002	12,328	2,624	17,419	10,240	16,975	59,587	20.7
2003	12,145	2,547	16,943	10,286	19,641	61,562	19.7
2004	12,021	2,698	20,850	10,512	16,573	65,654	18.3
2005	12,018	2,665	20,855	10,800	20,691	67,892	17.7
2006	11,351	2,545	21,490	11,486	23,180	70,992	16.0
2007	10,611	2,602	22,858	11,596	26,019	74,647	14.2
2008	8,503	2,046	21,608	10,969	31,224	67,602	12.6
2009	5,591	1,476	17,075	7,648	32,374	59,096	9.5
2010	7,632	2,074	19,371	9,197	35,036	73,311	10.4
2011	8,462	2,127	20,709	7,901	36,828	76,027	11.1
2012	10,142	2,454	22,324	9,448	36,714	81,082	12.5
2013	11,066	2,380	19,923	9,630	44,508	87,507	12.6
2014	11,661	2,394	20,430	9,775	45,536	89,776	12.9
2015	12,100	2,283	21,096	9,278	46,024	90,781	13.3

Note: Data may not be fully comparable across all years because they are derived from different sources. Number of units may not add up to totals due to rounding. (1) Prior to 2004, numbers exclude Eastern European production.

New and Used Passenger Cars Imported Into the U.S. by Country of Origin, 1970-2015

Source: Economic Indicators Division, U.S. Census Bureau
(in number of units)

Year	Japan	Germany[1]	Italy	UK	Sweden	France	S. Korea	Mexico	Canada	Total[2]
1970	381,338	674,945	42,523	76,257	57,844	37,114	NA	NA	692,783	2,013,420
1975	695,573	370,012	102,344	67,106	51,993	15,647	NA	0	733,766	2,074,653
1980	1,991,502	338,711	46,899	32,517	61,496	47,386	NA	1	594,770	3,116,448
1985	2,527,467	473,110	8,689	24,474	142,640	42,882	NA	13,647	1,144,805	4,397,679
1990	1,867,794	245,286	11,045	27,271	93,084	1,976	201,475	215,986	1,220,221	3,944,602
1995	1,114,360	204,932	1,031	42,450	82,593	14	131,718	462,800	1,552,691	3,624,428
2000	1,837,631	491,704	3,129	81,079	86,707	28,024	568,153	933,948	2,138,825	6,326,013
2005	1,832,534	547,191	5,377	184,716	93,736	412	730,500	693,149	1,967,985	6,564,844
2006	2,347,532	532,022	5,469	148,014	81,008	567	697,061	947,824	1,963,922	7,380,077
2007	2,300,913	466,458	5,650	108,576	92,600	1,746	676,594	889,474	1,912,744	7,220,792
2008	2,190,013	502,971	5,783	110,737	59,638	28,198	612,300	928,273	1,609,005	6,525,836
2009	1,238,773	348,093	3,067	78,999	27,017	16,900	476,912	649,740	1,164,849	4,276,163
2010	1,569,220	506,053	4,298	96,689	38,749	4,153	515,601	902,565	1,741,493	5,668,111
2011	1,421,750	537,158	5,372	95,742	26,884	3,580	587,574	953,514	1,835,819	5,673,139
2012	1,723,014	629,579	11,767	114,073	24,653	10,949	705,089	1,052,212	2,094,793	6,590,863
2013	1,722,119	657,832	14,289	115,326	21,617	12,694	759,964	1,127,375	2,009,140	6,682,557
2014	1,530,386	624,891	21,607	105,135	26,443	25,292	895,141	1,290,183	2,022,449	6,813,003
2015	1,609,597	639,838	132,316	134,367	37,789	28,024	1,065,971	1,438,840	1,969,466	7,420,310

NA = Not available. **Note:** Excludes cars assembled in U.S. foreign trade zones. (1) Figures prior to 1991 are for West Germany. (2) Includes units imported from countries not shown in table.

Passenger Car Production in U.S. Plants, 2013-15

Source: WardsAuto Group, a division of Penton
(in number of units)

	2015	2014	2013
FCA TOTAL[1]	**287,114**	**263,176**	**343,204**
Chrysler 200 Series	190,439	160,941	129,685
Chrysler Total	**190,439**	**160,941**	**129,685**
Dodge Avenger	—	18,533	121,944
Dodge Dart	96,150	83,099	88,973
Dodge Viper	525	549	1,501
Dodge Total	**96,675**	**102,181**	**212,418**
Lancia Flavia	—	54	1,101
FORD TOTAL	**550,008**	**485,349**	**553,446**
Ford C-Max	23,619	27,094	38,532
Ford Focus	237,921	235,666	292,809
Ford Fusion	41,453	45,679	29,277
Ford Mustang	165,138	95,231	88,020
Ford Taurus	74,358	73,355	93,115
Ford Total	**542,489**	**477,025**	**541,753**
Lincoln Continental	20	—	—
Lincoln MKS	7,499	8,324	11,693
Lincoln Total	**7,519**	**8,324**	**11,693**
GENERAL MOTORS TOTAL	**725,535**	**861,483**	**831,854**
Buick LaCrosse	34,399	51,473	53,484
Buick Verano	41,929	47,181	53,646
Buick Total	**76,328**	**98,654**	**107,130**
Cadillac ATS	23,411	38,254	47,650
Cadillac CTS	17,813	31,155	34,956
Cadillac ELR	375	2,468	271
Cadillac Total	**41,599**	**71,877**	**82,877**
Chevrolet Camaro	10,251	—	—
Chevrolet Corvette	40,403	39,918	15,726
Chevrolet Cruze	269,437	290,028	282,946
Chevrolet Impala	29,584	17,971	36,210
Chevrolet Malibu	181,443	216,498	189,870
Chevrolet Sonic	60,748	105,499	94,038
Chevrolet Volt	15,741	20,699	22,507
Chevrolet Total	**607,607**	**690,613**	**641,297**
Opel Ampera	1	339	550

	2015	2014	2013
HONDA TOTAL	**678,828**	**684,196**	**733,998**
Acura ILX	28,017	17,800	17,196
Acura TL	—	3,765	25,714
Acura TLX	53,224	36,947	—
Acura Total	**81,241**	**58,512**	**42,910**
Honda Accord	379,385	401,423	466,695
Honda Civic	218,202	224,261	224,393
Honda Total	**597,587**	**625,684**	**691,088**
HYUNDAI TOTAL	**384,519**	**398,851**	**399,495**
Hyundai Elantra	172,244	162,943	194,059
Hyundai Sonata	212,275	235,908	205,436
KIA MOTORS TOTAL	**109,522**	**142,561**	**133,946**
Kia Optima	109,522	142,561	133,946
MERCEDES-BENZ TOTAL	**93,505**	**40,096**	**—**
Mercedes C-Class	93,505	40,096	—
NISSAN TOTAL	**421,110**	**461,777**	**470,232**
Nissan Altima	346,530	366,472	383,818
Nissan Leaf	19,340	32,201	26,387
Nissan Maxima	55,240	58,156	48,247
Nissan Sentra	—	4,948	11,780
SUBARU TOTAL[2]	**145,845**	**148,481**	**137,803**
Subaru Legacy	66,002	55,005	40,800
Toyota Camry	79,843	93,476	97,003
TESLA TOTAL	**50,080**	**34,481**	**24,093**
Tesla Model S	50,080	34,481	24,093
TOYOTA TOTAL	**629,088**	**615,019**	**607,623**
Lexus ES	4,088	—	—
Toyota Avalon	69,087	72,277	100,096
Toyota Camry	365,399	353,428	348,970
Toyota Corolla	190,514	189,314	158,647
VOLKSWAGEN TOTAL	**87,156**	**117,628**	**133,141**
Volkswagen Passat	87,156	117,628	133,141
TOTAL CARS	**4,162,310**	**4,253,098**	**4,368,835**

— = No production. (1) Fiat Chrysler Automobiles, or FCA, was formed in 2014 when Fiat acquired the remaining shares of Chrysler Group that it did not already own. (2) SIA (Subaru of Indiana Automotive) also builds the Toyota Camry in collaboration with Toyota.

Domestic and Imported Retail Car Sales in the U.S., 1980-2015

Source: WardsAuto Group, a division of Penton
(in number of units)

	Cars			Light trucks			All vehicles		
Year	Domestic[1]	Imports	Total cars	Domestic[1]	Imports	Total light trucks	Domestic[1]	Imports	Total vehicles
1980	6,579,778	2,369,457	8,949,235	1,750,735	478,887	2,229,622	8,330,513	2,848,344	11,178,857
1985	8,204,670	2,774,517	10,979,187	3,629,080	832,186	4,461,266	12,109,999	3,615,292	15,725,291
1986	8,215,017	3,189,222	11,404,239	3,675,914	977,920	4,653,834	12,145,084	4,177,937	16,323,021
1987	7,085,279	3,106,598	10,191,877	3,791,882	921,698	4,713,580	11,144,275	4,048,671	15,192,946
1988	7,543,116	3,003,692	10,546,808	4,199,643	710,661	4,910,304	12,054,181	3,737,363	15,791,544
1989	7,098,098	2,680,419	9,778,517	4,113,441	641,387	4,754,828	11,503,384	3,341,877	14,845,261
1990	6,918,869	2,384,346	9,303,215	3,956,756	611,941	4,568,697	11,135,513	3,013,865	14,149,378
1991	6,161,573	2,023,406	8,184,979	3,605,633	538,008	4,143,641	9,975,798	2,573,725	12,549,523
1992	6,285,916	1,927,197	8,213,113	4,247,097	408,003	4,655,100	10,767,685	2,349,759	13,117,444
1993	6,741,667	1,776,192	8,517,859	5,000,482	377,639	5,378,121	12,029,051	2,169,803	14,198,854
1994	7,255,303	1,735,214	8,990,517	5,658,302	409,759	6,068,061	13,251,198	2,160,176	15,411,374
1995	7,113,902	1,506,257	8,620,159	5,705,708	402,181	6,107,889	13,192,861	1,923,464	15,116,325
1996	7,206,349	1,272,196	8,478,545	6,179,881	438,757	6,618,638	13,732,379	1,723,733	15,456,112
1997	6,862,175	1,355,305	8,217,480	6,324,758	579,483	6,904,241	13,549,251	1,948,609	15,497,860
1998	6,705,208	1,379,781	8,084,989	6,802,016	656,002	7,458,018	13,913,028	2,054,259	15,967,287
1999	6,918,781	1,718,927	8,637,708	7,480,607	775,223	8,255,830	14,901,266	2,513,462	17,414,728
2000	6,761,603	2,016,120	8,777,723	7,719,707	852,325	8,572,032	14,922,648	2,889,025	17,811,673
2001	6,254,371	2,097,629	8,352,000	7,789,089	981,280	8,770,369	14,372,624	3,099,754	17,472,378
2002	5,816,671	2,225,584	8,042,255	7,707,738	1,066,375	8,774,113	13,829,568	3,309,084	17,138,652
2003	5,472,500	2,083,051	7,555,551	7,856,322	1,227,180	9,083,502	13,638,351	3,329,091	16,967,442
2004	5,333,496	2,149,059	7,482,555	8,138,107	1,246,258	9,384,365	13,880,251	3,418,322	17,298,573
2005	5,473,450	2,186,533	7,659,983	8,072,456	1,215,315	9,287,771	14,020,528	3,423,801	17,444,329
2006	5,416,828	2,344,764	7,761,592	7,396,058	1,346,750	8,742,808	13,334,843	3,714,138	17,048,981
2007	5,197,271	2,365,063	7,562,334	7,138,803	1,388,085	8,526,888	12,687,016	3,773,299	16,460,315
2008	4,490,863	2,278,271	6,769,134	5,329,165	1,096,469	6,425,634	10,107,753	3,385,439	13,493,192
2009	3,558,283	1,843,282	5,401,565	4,116,550	884,242	5,000,792	7,867,766	2,734,277	10,602,043
2010	3,791,499	1,844,240	5,635,739	5,020,441	898,644	5,919,085	9,020,088	2,752,438	11,772,526
2011	4,142,811	1,946,897	6,089,708	5,662,578	982,443	6,645,021	10,101,024	2,939,624	13,040,918
2012	5,119,114	2,125,325	7,244,439	6,137,440	1,060,720	7,198,160	11,590,767	3,197,708	14,788,475
2013	5,432,737	2,152,604	7,585,341	6,707,097	1,239,268	7,946,365	12,480,609	3,402,834	15,883,443
2014	5,590,865	2,098,245	7,689,110	7,387,697	1,359,910	8,747,607	13,372,126	3,471,338	16,843,464
2015	5,611,411	1,913,612	7,525,023	8,080,687	1,780,337	9,861,024	14,127,239	3,708,266	17,835,505

Note: Vehicles are cars and light trucks belonging to gross vehicle weight (GWV) classes 1-3 (under 14,001 lbs). (1) Includes the U.S., Canada, and Mexico.

U.S. Vehicle Sales, 2000-15

Source: WardsAuto Group, a division of Penton

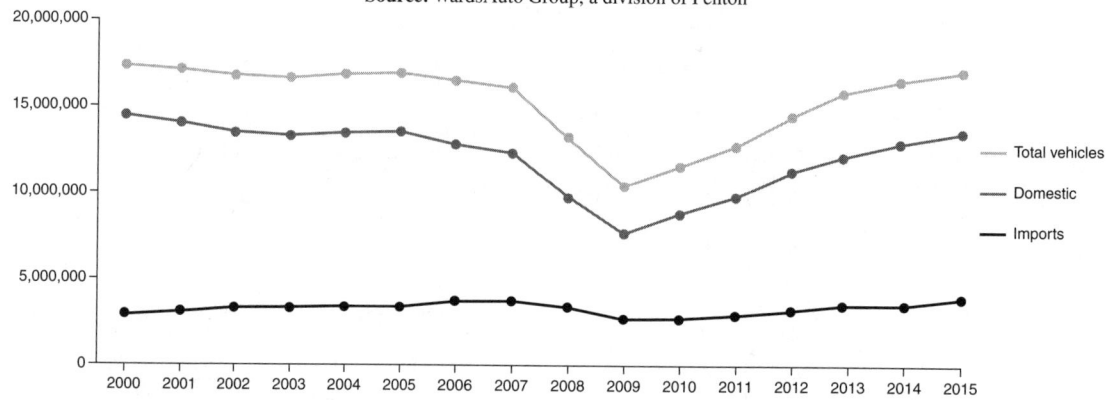

Note: Vehicles are cars and light trucks belonging to gross vehicle weight (GWV) classes 1-3 (under 14,001 lbs). Domestic sales include the U.S., Canada, and Mexico.

U.S. Sales of Hybrid and Electric Vehicles, 2000-15

Source: WardsAuto Group, a division of Penton; in number of units sold

Power type	2000	2005	2008	2009	2010	2011	2012	2013	2014	2015
Hybrid car..............	9,350	151,253	250,462	237,263	231,819	231,075	407,628	478,031	424,959	354,981
Hybrid light truck.........	0	54,575	65,226	53,477	42,286	30,432	24,170	20,023	26,872	22,606
Total hybrid............	**9,350**	**205,828**	**315,688**	**290,740**	**274,105**	**261,507**	**431,798**	**498,054**	**451,831**	**377,587**
Electric car..............	463	0	27	675	326	10,447	14,534	47,424	67,067	72,318
Electric light truck.........	0	0	0	0	0	0	192	1,096	1,184	61
Total electric...........	**463**	**0**	**27**	**675**	**326**	**10,447**	**14,726**	**48,520**	**68,251**	**72,379**
Plug-in hybrid car.........	0	0	0	0	326	7,671	38,585	49,043	55,441	41,739
Plug-in hybrid light truck....	0	0	0	0	0	0	0	0	100	2,076
Total plug-in hybrid.....	**0**	**0**	**0**	**0**	**326**	**7,671**	**38,585**	**49,043**	**55,441**	**43,815**

Top-Selling Passenger Cars in the U.S., 2012-15

Source: WardsAuto Group, a division of Penton
(ranked by number of vehicles sold)

Car	2015 sales	Car	2015 sales	Car	2015 sales
1. Toyota Camry..........	429,355	8. Chevrolet Cruze........	226,602	15. Kia Soul..............	147,133
2. Toyota Corolla..........	363,332	9. Hyundai Sonata........	213,303	16. Toyota Prius...........	146,310
3. Honda Accord..........	355,557	10. Nissan Sentra..........	203,509	17. Nissan Versa..........	144,528
4. Honda Civic...........	335,384	11. Ford Focus............	202,478	18. Volkswagen Jetta.......	131,109
5. Nissan Altima..........	333,398	12. Chevrolet Malibu........	194,854	19. Ford Mustang..........	122,349
6. Ford Fusion............	300,170	13. Chrysler 200 Series.....	177,889	20. Chevrolet Impala........	116,825
7. Hyundai Elantra........	241,706	14. Kia Optima............	159,414		

Car	2014 sales	Car	2013 sales	Car	2012 sales
1. Toyota Camry..........	428,606	1. Toyota Camry..........	408,484	1. Toyota Camry..........	404,886
2. Honda Accord..........	388,374	2. Honda Accord..........	366,678	2. Honda Accord..........	331,872
3. Toyota Corolla..........	339,498	3. Honda Civic...........	336,180	3. Honda Civic...........	317,909
4. Nissan Altima..........	335,644	4. Nissan Altima..........	320,723	4. Nissan Altima..........	302,934
5. Honda Civic...........	325,981	5. Toyota Corolla..........	302,180	5. Toyota Corolla..........	290,947
6. Ford Fusion............	306,860	6. Ford Fusion............	295,280	6. Ford Focus............	245,922
7. Chevrolet Cruze........	273,060	7. Chevrolet Cruze........	248,224	7. Ford Fusion............	241,263
8. Hyundai Elantra........	222,023	8. Hyundai Elantra........	247,912	8. Chevrolet Cruze........	237,758
9. Ford Focus............	219,634	9. Ford Focus............	234,570	9. Hyundai Sonata........	230,605
10. Hyundai Sonata........	216,936	10. Hyundai Sonata........	203,648	10. Chevrolet Malibu........	210,951

U.S. Retail Car Sales by Vehicle Size, 1985-2015

Source: WardsAuto Group, a division of Penton
(as percent of total U.S. sales)

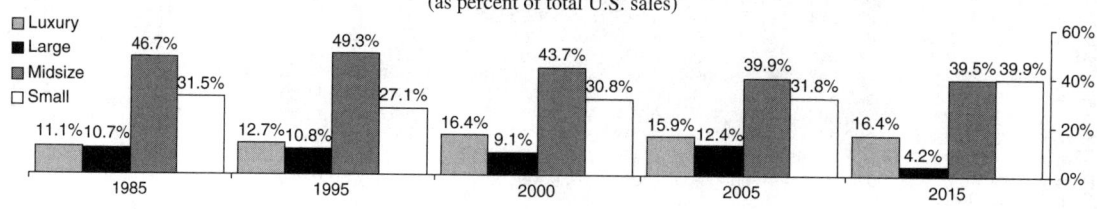

U.S. Light Truck Sales by Type, 1985-2015

Source: WardsAuto Group, a division of Penton
(as percent of total U.S. sales)

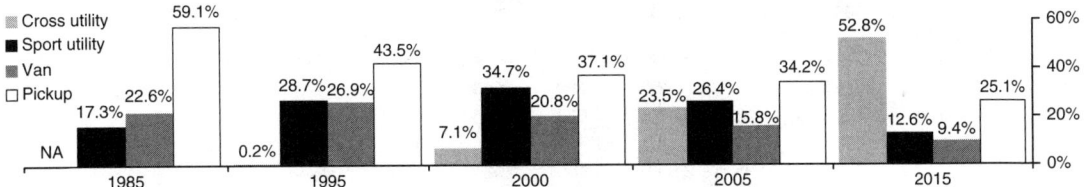

Legend: ■ Cross utility ■ Sport utility ■ Van □ Pickup

1985: NA, 17.3%, 22.6%, 59.1%
1995: 0.2%, 28.7%, 26.9%, 43.5%
2000: 7.1%, 34.7%, 20.8%, 37.1%
2005: 23.5%, 26.4%, 15.8%, 34.2%
2015: 52.8%, 12.6%, 9.4%, 25.1%

NA = Not applicable. **Note:** Comm. chassis sales (not shown) were 1.0% (for 1985), 0.7% (1995), 0.2% (2000), 0.1% (2005), 0.1% (2015).

Top-Selling Light Trucks in the U.S., 2013-15

Source: WardsAuto Group, a division of Penton
(ranked by number of vehicles sold)

Truck	2015 sales	Truck	2014 sales	Truck	2013 sales
1. Ford F-Series	725,726	1. Ford F-Series	701,102	1. Ford F-Series	713,960
2. Chevrolet Silverado	600,544	2. Chevrolet Silverado	529,755	2. Chevrolet Silverado	480,414
3. Ram Pickup	435,304	3. Ram Pickup	425,388	3. Ram Pickup	344,772
4. Honda CR-V	345,647	4. Honda CR-V	335,019	4. Honda CR-V	303,904
5. Toyota RAV4	315,412	5. Ford Escape	306,212	5. Ford Escape	295,993
6. Ford Escape	306,492	6. Toyota RAV4	267,698	6. Chevrolet Equinox	238,192
7. Nissan Rogue	287,190	7. Chevrolet Equinox	242,242	7. Toyota RAV4	218,249
8. Chevrolet Equinox	277,589	8. GMC Sierra	211,833	8. Ford Explorer	192,397
9. Ford Explorer	249,251	9. Ford Explorer	209,994	9. GMC Sierra	184,389
10. GMC Sierra	224,139	10. Nissan Rogue	199,199	10. Jeep Grand Cherokee	174,275

Most Popular Colors by Vehicle Type, 2015

Source: WardsAuto Group, a division of Penton; Axalta Coating Systems; for 2015 model year

Luxury cars/SUVs		Intermediate cars/CUVs		Compact/sports cars		Light trucks	
Color	Percent	Color	Percent	Color	Percent	Color	Percent
Black/black effect	27%	White/white pearl	29%	White/white pearl	21%	White/white pearl	33%
White/white pearl	26	Black/black effect	18	Black/black effect	21	Black/black effect	20
Gray	15	Gray	14	Gray	17	Silver	11
Silver	12	Silver	12	Silver	14	Red	11
Red	7	Red	10	Red	11	Gray	11
Blue	4	Blue	8	Blue	9	Blue	8
Beige/brown	3	Beige/brown	3	Beige/brown	4	Beige/brown	2
Yellow/gold	2	Yellow/gold	3	Yellow/gold	2	Green	1
Green	2	Green	2	Green	1	Yellow/gold	1
Other	2	Other	1	Other	<1	Other	2

U.S. Light-Duty Vehicle Fuel Efficiency, 1975-2015

Source: Natl. Vehicle and Fuel Emissions Laboratory, Office of Transportation and Air Quality, U.S. Environmental Protection Agency

Cars and light-duty trucks (SUVs, minivans, passenger vans, and pickup trucks) showed significant fuel-efficiency improvements from 1975 through 1987, when the fuel economy for both reached a high of 22 miles per gallon (mpg). The fuel economy value mainly declined, 1988-2004, but since 2005, fuel economy has generally increased, reaching a new all-time high of 24.7 mpg in 2015.

Year[1]	Cars (mpg)	Light-duty trucks (mpg)	All light-duty vehicles (mpg)	Year[1]	Cars (mpg)	Light-duty trucks (mpg)	All light-duty vehicles (mpg)
1975	13.5	11.6	13.1	2005	23.1	16.9	19.9
1980	20.0	15.8	19.2	2006	23.0	17.2	20.1
1985	23.0	17.5	21.3	2007	23.7	17.4	20.6
1990	23.3	17.4	21.2	2008	23.9	17.8	21.0
1995	23.3	17.0	20.5	2009	25.0	18.5	22.4
1998	23.0	17.1	20.1	2010	25.7	18.8	22.6
1999	22.7	16.6	19.7	2011	25.6	19.1	22.4
2000	22.5	16.8	19.8	2012	27.1	19.3	23.7
2001	22.6	16.5	19.6	2013	27.9	19.8	24.3
2002	22.8	16.5	19.5	2014	27.9	20.4	24.3
2003	23.0	16.7	19.6	2015[2]	28.4	20.7	24.7
2004	22.9	16.5	19.3				

Note: Adjusted mpg composite values (city and highway fuel efficiency combined in a 55%/45% ratio) are used for all vehicles and are intended to reflect real-world use. (1) Because of changes in methodology, mpg figures prior to 1986 are not entirely comparable with later values. (2) Preliminary.

Registered Cars in the U.S., 1900-2014

Source: Office of Highway Policy Information, Federal Highway Administration, U.S. Dept. of Transportation
(number of automobiles for public and private use)

Year	Reg. cars	Year	Reg. cars	Year	Reg. cars	Year	Reg. cars	Year	Reg. cars
1900	8,000	1945	25,796,985	1990	133,700,497	1999	132,432,044	2007	135,932,930
1905	77,400	1950	40,339,077	1991	128,299,601	2000	133,621,420	2008	137,079,843
1910	458,377	1955	52,144,739	1992	126,581,148	2001	137,633,467	2009	134,879,600
1915	2,332,426	1960	61,671,390	1993	127,327,189	2002	135,920,677	2010	130,892,240
1920	8,131,522	1965	75,257,588	1994	127,883,469	2003	135,669,897	2011	125,656,528
1925	17,481,001	1970	89,243,557	1995	128,386,775	2004	136,430,651	2012	111,289,906
1930	23,034,753	1975	106,705,934	1996	129,728,311	2005	136,568,083	2013	113,676,345
1935	22,567,827	1980	121,600,843	1997	129,748,704	2006	135,399,945	2014	113,898,845
1940	27,465,826	1985	127,885,193	1998	131,838,538				

Note: There were no publicly owned vehicles before 1925; statistics also exclude military vehicles for all years. Alaska and Hawaii data included since 1960.

Licensed Drivers by Age and Sex, 1980-2014

Source: Office of Highway Policy Information, Federal Highway Administration, U.S. Dept. of Transportation
(numbers in thousands)

Age (years)	1980 Total	1990 Total	2000 Total	2010 Male	Female	Total	2014 Male	Female	Total	% total drivers
Under 16	93	43	27	199	198	398	31	31	62	0.0%
16	1,823	1,443	1,470	608	605	1,213	509	513	1,022	0.5
17	2,790	2,132	2,331	1,025	1,004	2,028	951	930	1,881	0.9
18	3,247	2,595	2,839	1,408	1,323	2,731	1,304	1,236	2,540	1.2
19	3,542	3,037	3,077	1,641	1,546	3,187	1,540	1,446	2,986	1.4
19 and under	**11,496**	**9,249**	**9,744**	**4,880**	**4,676**	**9,556**	**4,336**	**4,155**	**8,491**	**4.0**
20	3,636	3,229	3,140	1,744	1,682	3,426	1,652	1,569	3,221	1.5
21	3,733	3,249	3,172	1,756	1,717	3,474	1,709	1,633	3,341	1.6
22	3,811	3,262	3,182	1,757	1,725	3,483	1,794	1,741	3,536	1.7
23	3,938	3,398	3,247	1,767	1,748	3,515	1,856	1,827	3,683	1.7
24	3,915	3,758	3,225	1,792	1,779	3,571	1,907	1,891	3,799	1.8
20-24	**19,032**	**16,897**	**15,966**	**8,817**	**8,651**	**17,469**	**8,918**	**8,661**	**17,579**	**8.2**
25-29	18,925	19,895	17,586	9,179	9,253	18,431	9,324	9,386	18,710	8.7
30-34	17,369	20,578	19,155	8,934	8,915	17,849	9,233	9,418	18,651	8.7
35-39	13,696	19,055	21,059	9,079	9,082	18,161	8,666	8,846	17,512	8.2
40-44	11,134	16,905	21,093	9,613	9,565	19,178	9,114	9,237	18,351	8.6
45-49	10,076	13,020	19,154	10,381	10,433	20,814	9,421	9,489	18,910	8.8
50-54	10,090	10,484	16,868	10,241	10,388	20,628	10,198	10,389	20,587	9.6
55-59	9,770	9,438	12,760	9,127	9,313	18,440	9,731	10,019	19,750	9.2
60-64	8,232	9,235	9,915	7,847	8,011	15,858	8,383	8,719	17,102	8.0
65-69	6,580	8,375	8,386	5,652	5,816	11,468	6,868	7,146	14,014	6.5
70-74	NA	NA	7,468	4,029	4,202	8,231	4,778	5,040	9,818	4.6
75-79	NA	NA	5,911	2,966	3,192	6,158	3,197	3,437	6,634	3.1
80-84	NA	NA	3,511	2,090	2,373	4,464	2,094	2,312	4,405	2.1
85 and over	**NA**	**NA**	**2,050**	**1,541**	**1,870**	**3,411**	**1,647**	**1,930**	**3,577**	**1.7**
Total..............	**145,295**	**167,015**	**190,625**	**104,374**	**105,740**	**210,115**	**105,908**	**108,185**	**214,092**	**100.0**

NA = Not available. **Note:** Numbers may not add up to totals due to rounding.

Handheld Phone and Texting Device Laws for Drivers, 2016

Source: Insurance Institute for Highway Safety; as of Aug. 2016

State	Handheld ban	Texting ban	Enforce-ment	State	Handheld ban	Texting ban	Enforce-ment	State	Handheld ban	Texting ban	Enforce-ment
AL	No[1]	Yes	P[2]	KY	No[4]	Yes	P	ND	No[4]	Yes	P
AK	No	Yes	P	LA	No[4,5,7]	Yes	P[8]	OH	No[4]	Yes	P[12]
AZ	No	No	NA	ME	No[5]	Yes	P	OK	No[5]	Yes	P
AR	No[3]	Yes	P[2]	MD	Yes	Yes	P	OR	Yes	Yes	P
CA	Yes	Yes	P[2]	MA	No[4]	Yes	P	PA	No	Yes	P
CO	No[4]	Yes	P	MI	No[5]	Yes	P	RI	No[4]	Yes	P
CT	Yes	Yes	P	MN	No[9]	Yes	P	SC	No	Yes	P
DE	Yes	Yes	P	MS	No	Yes	P	SD	No[5]	Yes	S
DC	Yes	Yes	P	MO	No	No[10]	P	TN	No[5]	Yes	P
FL	No	Yes	S	MT	No	No	NA	TX	No[4]	No[4]	P
GA	No[4]	Yes	P	NE	No[11]	Yes	S	UT	No[4]	Yes	P
HI	Yes	Yes	P	NV	Yes	Yes	P	VT	Yes	Yes	P
ID	No	Yes	P	NH	Yes	Yes	P	VA	No[4]	Yes	P[2]
IL	Yes	Yes	P	NJ	Yes	Yes	P	WA	Yes	Yes	P
IN	No[3]	Yes	P	NM	No[5]	Yes	P	WV	Yes	Yes	P
IA	No[5]	Yes	S[6]	NY	Yes	Yes	P	WI	No[5]	Yes	P
KS	No[5]	Yes	P	NC	No[4]	Yes	P	WY	No	Yes	P

NA = Not applicable. P = Officer may stop vehicle for violation (primary); S = Officer may issue citation only when vehicle is stopped for another moving violation (secondary). **Note:** Laws shown for licensed passenger car drivers. Different laws and regulations apply to school bus, municipal transit, and other mass transit operators. Different laws may apply in school zones, construction zones, or other such areas. (1) Yes for 16-year-old drivers and for 17-year-old drivers who have held an intermediate license for fewer than 6 months. (2) Secondary for cell phone use by young drivers. (3) Yes for drivers under 21 years of age. (4) Yes for drivers under 18. (5) Yes for learner's permit and intermediate license holders. (6) Primary for learner's permit and intermediate license holders. (7) Yes for drivers in the year after getting their first license. (8) Secondary for cell phone use by novice drivers. (9) Yes for learner's permit and provisional license holders in their first year after licensing. (10) Yes for drivers 21 and younger. (11) Yes for learner's permit and intermediate license holders under 18. (12) Primary for drivers younger than 18, and secondary for texting.

Selected Motor Vehicle Statistics

Source: Federal Highway Admin., U.S. Dept. of Transportation; Insurance Inst. for Highway Safety; American Petroleum Inst. Driver's license age requirements, state gas tax, and safety belt use laws (incl. laws passed, but not in effect) as of 2016. Other figures are for 2014.

STATE	Driver's license age requirements		Gas taxes (cents/ gal)[5]	Safety belt use law[6]	Licensed drivers		Reg. motor vehicles per 1,000 pop.	Fuel use per reg. motor vehicle (gal)	Annual miles driven		
	Learner's permit	Regular[1]			Per 1,000 resident pop.	Per reg. motor vehicle			Per gal used	Per reg. vehicle	Per lic. driver
Alabama	15	17	39.3	P	800	0.73	1,107	628	19.48	12,236	16,918
Alaska	14	16y, 6m	30.7	P	722	0.68	1,086	527	11.51	6,068	9,134
Arizona	15y, 6m	16y, 6m	37.4	S	725	0.88	830	619	18.11	11,208	12,829
Arkansas	14	18	40.2	P	712	0.77	937	732	16.73	12,245	16,111
California	15y, 6m	17[2]	58.8	P	639	0.89	739	615	18.87	11,603	13,414
Colorado	15	17	40.4	S	725	0.82	900	591	17.19	10,162	12,614
Connecticut	16	18[2,3,4]	56.3	P	707	0.90	797	595	18.28	10,881	12,267
Delaware	16	17[2]	41.4	P	783	0.77	1,024	529	18.95	10,021	13,104
Dist. of Columbia	16	18[4]	41.9	P	637	1.34	507	390	27.05	10,551	8,401
Florida	15	18	55.0	P	699	0.91	779	637	20.35	12,966	14,465
Georgia	15	18[2]	49.4	P	659	0.83	808	728	18.77	13,677	16,771
Hawaii	15y, 6m	17[2]	60.4	P	636	0.66	981	361	20.20	7,303	11,272
Idaho	14y, 6m	16[2]	50.4	S	690	0.64	1,078	562	16.30	9,164	14,315
Illinois	15	18[2]	49.5	P	650	0.81	807	594	17.00	10,093	12,528
Indiana	15	18	49.1	P	674	0.74	911	722	18.24	13,173	17,806
Iowa	14	17[2]	50.4	P	717	0.63	1,158	657	13.30	8,734	14,100
Kansas	14	16y, 6m	42.4	P(a)	696	0.81	876	716	16.87	12,078	15,193
Kentucky	16	17[2]	44.4	P	681	0.73	940	703	16.43	11,556	15,954
Louisiana	15	17[2]	38.4	P	712	0.87	836	760	16.34	12,414	14,566
Maine	15	16y, 9m[2]	48.4	P	766	0.86	898	823	14.55	11,971	14,036
Maryland	15y, 9m	18	51.0	P(a)	693	1.05	678	808	17.23	13,927	13,621
Massachusetts	16	18[2]	44.9	S	706	0.97	740	629	18.33	11,523	12,077
Michigan	14y, 9m	17[2]	49.9	P	711	0.88	820	682	17.56	11,984	13,820
Minnesota	15	17[2]	47.0	P	615	0.65	957	619	17.75	10,988	17,095
Mississippi	15	16y, 6m	37.2	P	661	0.96	691	1,099	17.39	19,102	19,972
Missouri	15	17y, 11m	35.7	S(b)	708	0.81	879	632	21.03	13,297	16,509
Montana	14y, 6m	16[2]	46.2	S	751	0.49	1,549	497	15.41	7,666	15,815
Nebraska	15	17	46.1	S	735	0.73	1,035	684	14.72	10,070	14,174
Nevada	15y, 6m	18[2]	52.3	S	633	0.81	789	630	17.93	11,293	14,084
New Hampshire	15y, 6m	18[2]	42.2	None	808	0.83	987	616	16.08	9,900	12,100
New Jersey	16	18[2]	32.9	P(a)	688	0.91	769	716	15.20	10,890	12,167
New Mexico	15	16y, 6m[2]	37.3	P	693	0.76	926	773	16.99	13,128	17,543
New York	16	17[2]	60.7	P	573	1.04	552	637	18.61	11,855	11,421
North Carolina	15	16y, 6m[2]	53.7	P(a)	706	0.91	792	687	19.95	13,714	15,375
North Dakota	14	16	41.4	S	713	0.62	1,177	1,026	11.76	12,072	19,925
Ohio	15y, 6m	18[2]	46.4	S	683	0.77	902	629	17.16	10,788	14,246
Oklahoma	15y, 6m	16y, 6m	35.4	P	632	0.70	907	817	16.60	13,559	19,453
Oregon	15	17[2,3]	49.5	P	702	0.83	861	593	17.07	10,126	12,425
Pennsylvania	16	17	68.7	S(b)	697	0.86	822	625	15.21	9,508	11,203
Rhode Island	16	17y, 6m[2]	52.4	P	709	0.88	820	520	17.07	8,878	10,259
South Carolina	15	16y, 6m	35.2	P	749	0.92	831	849	14.64	12,428	13,803
South Dakota	14	16	48.4	S	715	0.61	1,210	671	13.30	8,933	15,125
Tennessee	15	17	39.8	P	704	0.86	839	757	17.39	13,162	15,680
Texas	15	18	38.4	P	581	0.77	774	894	13.02	11,643	15,533
Utah	15	17[2]	47.8	P	484	0.67	731	735	17.43	12,813	19,327
Vermont	15	16y, 6m[2]	48.9	S	870	0.90	977	610	18.90	11,526	12,945
Virginia	15y, 6m	18[2]	40.7	S	693	0.82	860	703	16.08	11,311	14,038
Washington	15	17[2]	62.9	P	765	0.85	907	533	16.99	9,064	10,750
West Virginia	15	17	51.6	P	633	0.78	839	703	17.50	12,309	16,313
Wisconsin	15y, 6m	16y, 9m[2]	51.3	P	727	0.80	928	640	17.56	11,246	14,339
Wyoming	15	16y, 6m[2]	42.4	S	726	0.52	1,404	877	13.14	11,532	22,306
U.S. AVERAGE			**48.0**		**671**	**0.84**	**817**	**669**	**17.37**	**11,621**	**14,132**

Note: Most states have graduated licensing systems that phase in full driving privileges. During the learner's stage, driving generally is not permitted without adult supervision. In an intermediate stage, young licensees may be allowed to drive unsupervised under certain conditions. (1) Min. age at which all restrictions may be lifted on private passenger car operation. (2) Applicants under a specified age (typically between 17 and 19) must complete driver education. (3) Home training (CT) or more hours of supervised driving (OR) may be substituted for driver ed. (4) Learner's stage mandatory for all license applicants regardless of age. (5) Some values rounded. Includes 18.4 cents per gallon in federal excise taxes. (6) P = Officer may stop vehicle for violation (primary); S = Officer may issue seat belt citation only when vehicle is stopped for another moving violation (secondary). (a) Secondary enforcement for rear seat occupants; (b) Primary enforcement for children under a specified age.

International Tourism Receipts, 2000-15

Source: World Tourism Organization (UNWTO), © UNWTO

(in billions of U.S. dollars; ranked by most recent figures available)

Rank	Country	2000	2005	2010	2013	2014	2015*	Rank	Country	2000	2005	2010	2013	2014	2015*
1.	U.S.	$100.2	$101.5	$137.0	$172.9	$177.2	$178.3	27.	Sweden. . . .	$4.1	$6.8	$8.7	$11.5	$12.9	$12.2
2.	China[1].	16.2	29.3	45.8	51.7	105.4	114.1	28.	Belgium. . . .	6.6	9.9	11.4	13.4	13.9	11.7
3.	Spain	30.9	49.7	54.6	62.6	65.1	56.5	29.	Indonesia . .	5.0	4.5	7.0	9.1	10.3	10.7
4.	France.	33.0	44.0	47.0	56.6	57.4	45.9	30.	Saudi Arabia	NA	4.6	6.7	7.7	8.2	10.1
5.	Thailand . . .	7.5	9.6	20.1	41.8	38.4	44.6	31.	Poland.	5.7	6.3	9.6	11.3	11.2	9.7
6.	UK.	22.1	31.1	33.0	41.8	46.6	42.4	32.	New Zealand	2.9	6.5	6.5	7.4	8.4	8.9
7.	Italy.	27.5	35.4	38.8	43.9	45.5	39.7	33.	Croatia	2.8	7.4	8.1	9.5	9.9	8.8
8.	Germany. . .	18.7	29.2	34.7	41.3	43.3	36.9	34.	Russia.	3.4	5.9	8.8	12.0	11.8	8.5
9.	Hong Kong	5.9	10.3	22.2	38.9	38.4	35.9	35.	South Africa	2.7	7.5	9.1	9.2	9.3	8.2
10.	Macao.	3.2	6.9	22.2	43.0	42.6	31.3	36.	Vietnam . . .	NA	2.3	4.5	7.3	7.3	7.3
11.	Australia . . .	9.4	16.7	28.6	31.3	31.9	29.4	37.	Denmark. . .	3.7	5.3	5.9	7.0	7.6	6.6
12.	Turkey.	7.6	19.2	22.6	28.0	29.6	26.6	38.	Lebanon . . .	NA	5.5	8.0	6.5	6.5	NA
13.	Japan	3.4	6.6	13.2	15.1	18.9	25.0	39.	Dominican						
14.	India	3.5	7.5	14.5	18.4	19.7	21.0		Republic	2.9	3.5	4.2	5.1	5.6	6.2
15.	Austria	9.8	16.1	18.6	20.2	20.6	18.3	40.	Egypt	4.3	6.9	12.5	6.0	7.2	6.1
16.	Malaysia . . .	5.0	8.8	18.1	21.5	22.6	17.6	41.	Czech Rep.	3.0	4.8	7.2	7.0	6.8	6.0
17.	Mexico	8.3	11.8	12.0	13.9	16.2	17.5	42.	Morocco . . .	2.0	4.6	6.7	6.8	7.1	6.0
18.	Singapore . .	5.1	6.2	14.2	19.2	19.1	16.7	43.	Brazil.	1.8	3.9	5.3	6.5	6.8	5.8
19.	Switzerland	6.6	10.0	14.7	16.8	17.4	16.2	44.	Israel.	4.4	3.3	5.1	5.7	5.7	5.4
20.	United Arab							45.	Hungary . . .	3.8	4.1	5.6	5.4	5.9	5.3
	Emirates	1.1	3.2	8.6	12.4	14.0	16.0	46.	Philippines	2.2	2.3	2.6	4.7	5.0	5.3
21.	Canada. . . .	10.8	13.7	15.8	17.7	17.4	16.0	47.	Qatar.	0.1	0.8	0.6	3.5	4.6	5.0
22.	Greece	9.2	13.3	12.7	16.1	17.8	15.7	48.	Norway	2.2	3.5	4.7	5.6	5.6	5.0
23.	South Korea	6.8	5.8	10.3	14.6	17.8	15.3	49.	Ireland.	2.6	4.8	4.1	4.5	4.9	4.8
24.	Taiwan	3.7	5.0	8.7	12.3	14.6	14.4	50.	Argentina . .	2.9	2.7	4.9	4.3	4.6	4.4
25.	Netherlands	7.2	8.8	11.7	13.8	14.7	13.2		**World**	**495**	**706**	**986**	**1,236**	**1,295**	**1,232**
26.	Portugal . . .	5.2	7.7	10.1	12.3	13.8	12.6								

NA = Not available. * = Preliminary. (1) Not including Hong Kong and Macao.

International Tourist Arrivals by Country of Destination, 2000-15

Source: World Tourism Organization (UNWTO), © UNWTO

(visitors in millions; ranked by most recent figures available)

Rank	Country	2000	2005	2010	2013	2014	2015*	% change, 2014-15	Rank	Country	2000	2005	2010	2013	2014	2015*	% change, 2014-15
1.	France.	77.2	75.0	77.6	83.6	83.7	84.5	0.9%	28.	Sweden. . . .	3.8	4.9	5.0	11.0	10.5	NA	NA
2.	U.S.	51.2	49.2	60.0	70.0	75.0	NA	NA	29.	Taiwan	2.6	3.4	5.6	8.0	9.9	10.4	5.3%
3.	Spain	46.4	55.9	52.7	60.7	64.9	68.2	5.0	30.	Indonesia . .	5.1	5.0	7.0	8.8	9.4	10.4	10.3
4.	China[1].	31.2	46.8	55.7	55.7	55.6	56.9	2.3	31.	Denmark. . .	3.5	9.2	8.7	8.6	10.3	NA	NA
5.	Italy.	41.2	36.5	43.6	47.7	48.6	50.7	4.4	32.	Morocco . . .	4.3	5.8	9.3	10.0	10.3	10.2	−1.0
6.	Turkey.	9.6	24.2	31.4	37.8	39.8	NA	NA	33.	Portugal . . .	5.7	6.0	6.8	8.3	9.3	10.2	9.7
7.	Germany. . .	19.0	21.5	26.9	31.5	33.0	35.0	6.0	34.	United Arab							
8.	UK.	23.2	28.0	28.3	31.2	32.6	NA	NA		Emirates[2]	3.1	5.8	7.4	10.0	NA	NA	NA
9.	Mexico	20.6	21.9	23.3	24.2	29.3	32.1	9.5	35.	Switzerland	7.8	7.2	8.6	9.0	9.2	9.3	1.6
10.	Russia.	19.2	19.9	20.3	28.4	29.8	31.3	5.0	36.	Egypt	5.1	8.2	14.1	9.2	9.6	9.1	−5.1
11.	Thailand . . .	9.6	11.6	15.9	26.5	24.8	29.9	20.4	37.	South Africa	5.9	7.4	8.1	9.5	9.5	8.9	−6.8
12.	Austria	18.0	20.0	22.0	24.8	25.3	26.7	5.6	38.	Ireland.	6.6	7.3	7.1	8.3	8.8	NA	NA
13.	Hong Kong	8.8	14.8	20.1	25.7	27.8	26.7	−3.9	39.	Belgium. . . .	6.5	6.7	7.2	7.7	7.9	8.0	1.8
14.	Malaysia . . .	10.2	16.4	24.6	25.7	27.4	25.7	−6.3	40.	India	2.6	3.9	5.8	7.0	7.7	8.0	4.4
15.	Greece	13.1	14.8	15.0	17.9	22.0	23.6	7.1	41.	Vietnam . . .	2.1	3.5	5.0	7.6	7.9	7.9	0.9
16.	Japan	4.8	6.7	8.6	10.4	13.4	19.7	47.1	42.	Australia . . .	4.9	5.5	5.8	6.4	6.9	7.4	8.2
17.	Saudi Arabia	6.6	8.0	10.9	15.8	16.3	18.0	−1.5	43.	Bulgaria . . .	2.8	4.8	6.0	6.9	7.3	NA	NA
18.	Canada. . . .	19.6	18.8	16.2	16.1	16.5	17.8	7.5	44.	Brazil.	5.3	5.4	5.2	5.8	6.4	6.3	−1.9
19.	Poland.	17.4	15.2	12.5	15.8	16	16.7	4.6	45.	Slovakia . . .	1.1	6.2	5.4	NA	NA	NA	NA
20.	Netherlands	10.0	10.0	10.9	12.8	13.9	15.0	7.8	46.	Argentina . .	2.9	3.8	5.3	5.2	5.9	NA	NA
21.	Hungary . . .	3.0	10.0	9.5	10.6	12.1	14.3	17.9	47.	Dominican							
22.	Macao.	5.2	9.0	11.9	14.3	14.6	14.3	−1.8		Republic	3.0	3.7	4.1	4.7	5.1	5.6	8.9
23.	South Korea	5.3	6.0	8.8	12.2	14.2	13.2	−6.8	48.	Philippines	NA	2.6	3.5	4.8	4.8	5.4	10.9
24.	Croatia	5.3	7.7	9.1	10.9	11.6	12.7	9.1	49.	Tunisia	5.1	6.4	7.8	7.4	7.2	5.4	−25.2
25.	Ukraine. . . .	6.4	17.6	21.2	24.7	12.7	12.4	−2.2	50.	Iran	1.3	1.9	2.9	4.8	5.0	NA	NA
26.	Singapore . .	6.1	7.1	9.2	11.9	11.9	12.1	1.6		**World**	**674**	**809**	**950**	**1,088**	**1,134**	**1,184**	**4.4**
27.	Czech Rep.	4.8	9.4	8.6	10.3	10.6	11.1	5.0									

NA = Not available or not applicable. * = Preliminary. (1) Not including Hong Kong and Macao. (2) Dubai only.

World Tourism Receipts, 1990-2015

Source: World Tourism Organization (UNWTO), © UNWTO

(in billions of U.S. dollars)

Year	Receipts[1]	Year	Receipts[1]	Year	Receipts[1]	Year	Receipts[1]	Year	Receipts[1]	Year	Receipts[1]
1990	$271	1998	$457	2002	$501	2006	$766	2010	$986	2013	$1,236
1995	415	1999	475	2003	549	2007	883	2011	1,104	2014	1,295
1996	449	2000	495	2004	652	2008	967	2012	1,146	2015	1,232*
1997	449	2001	481	2005	706	2009	882				

* = Provisional. (1) Total of all transactions made by or on behalf of visitors for the duration of their visit. Does not include receipts from international passenger transport contracted from companies outside a traveler's country of residence.

International Travel to the U.S., 1990-2015

Source: National Travel and Tourism Office, Intl. Trade Admin., U.S. Dept. of Commerce; World Tourism Organization
(number of visitors in millions)

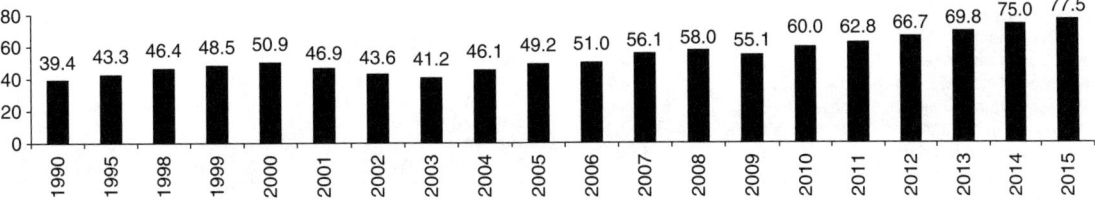

U.S. Domestic Leisure Travel Volume, 2000-15

Source: U.S. Travel Assn.
(in billions of person-trips of 50 mi or more, one-way)

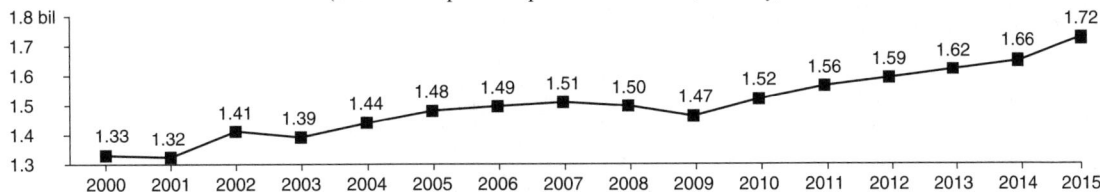

Note: Method of collecting travel data has been revised; data for earlier years have been adjusted to maintain comparability.

Top 10 U.S. States by Traveler Spending, 2014

Source: U.S. Travel Assn.
(domestic and international traveler spending within state, in billions of dollars)

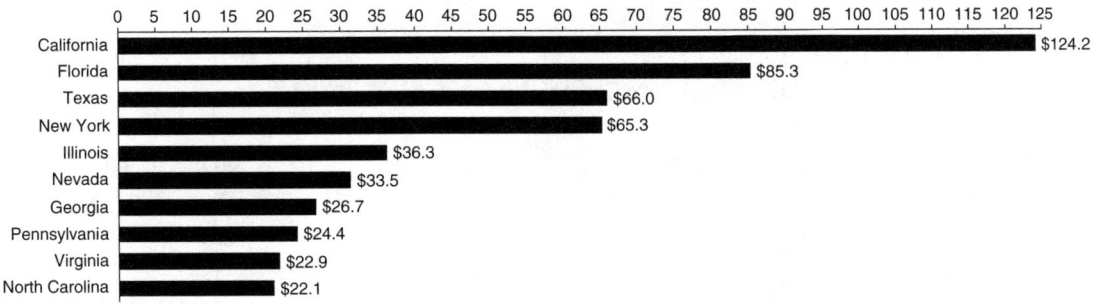

State	Spending
California	$124.2
Florida	$85.3
Texas	$66.0
New York	$65.3
Illinois	$36.3
Nevada	$33.5
Georgia	$26.7
Pennsylvania	$24.4
Virginia	$22.9
North Carolina	$22.1

International Visitors to the U.S. by Top Countries of Origin, 2014

Source: National Travel and Tourism Office, Intl. Trade Admin., U.S. Dept. of Commerce
(ranked by number of visitors)

Country of origin	Visitors	Expenditures (mil)	Expenditures per visitor	Country of origin	Visitors	Expenditures (mil)	Expenditures per visitor
1. Canada	23,013,691	$26,282	$1,142	12. India	962,133	$9,842	$10,229
2. Mexico	17,069,818	18,665	1,093	13. Colombia	881,274	NA	NA
3. United Kingdom	4,149,129	13,496	3,253	14. Spain	707,733	2,421	3,421
4. Japan	3,620,224	17,676	4,883	15. Argentina	684,788	3,277	4,785
5. Brazil	2,263,996	13,429	5,932	16. Netherlands	642,211	2,211	3,443
6. China[1]	2,189,781	24,019	10,969	17. Venezuela	616,037	3,303	5,362
7. Germany	2,056,492	7,360	3,579	18. Sweden	551,996	1,850	3,351
8. France	1,658,345	5,861	3,534	19. Switzerland	499,649	2,442	4,887
9. South Korea	1,459,938	7,799	5,342	20. Taiwan	414,269	2,107	5,086
10. Australia	1,304,172	6,180	4,739	All countries	75,021,716	220,757	2,943
11. Italy	963,540	3,260	3,383				

NA = Not available. **Note:** Expenditures include passenger fares. (1) Not including Hong Kong, Macao, and Taiwan.

Traveler Spending in the U.S., 1987-2015

Source: National Travel and Tourism Office, Intl. Trade Admin., U.S. Dept. of Commerce; U.S. Travel Assn.
(in billions of dollars by origin of traveler)

Year	Domestic	International	Year	Domestic	International	Year	Domestic	International
1987	$235	$31	1998	$425	$71	2007	$641	$97
1990	291	43	1999	458	75	2008	662	110
1991	296	48	2000	503	82	2009	606	94
1992	306	55	2001	484	72	2010	644	104
1993	323	58	2002	478	67	2011	694	119
1994	340	58	2003	496	65	2012	728	127
1995	360	63	2004	532	75	2013	751	135
1996	385	70	2005	572	82	2014	792	136
1997	406	73	2006	610	86	2015	814	133

Characteristics of U.S. Travelers Visiting Overseas Destinations, 2014

Source: Survey of Intl. Air Travelers, National Travel and Tourism Office, Intl. Trade Admin., U.S. Dept. of Commerce

Total U.S. resident travelers	30,780,000
Males (adults).	50%
Females (adults).	50%
Avg. age of males (yrs.)	45.4
Avg. age of females (yrs.)	44.0
Median annual household income	$100,000
Avg. total trip expend. per visitor (incl. airfare) . .	$2,831
Avg. international airfare.	$1,347
Avg. expend. outside the U.S. per visitor per day	$84
Purchased travel insurance	28%
Median number of nights	10

Region of residence	% of travelers
Middle Atlantic	24%
South Atlantic (incl. Florida, DC metro area)	20
Pacific (incl. California, Washington)	16
West South Central (incl. Texas).	10
East North Central (incl. Illinois, Ohio)	10
New England	7
West North Central.	5
Mountain.	5
East South Central	3

Main purpose of trip	% of travelers
Vacation/holiday	51%
Visit friends/relatives.	27
Business.	11
Education	5
Convention/conference/trade show	3
Religion/pilgrimages.	2
Health treatment.	<1

Occupation	% of travelers
Management, business, science, arts	42%
Retired	15
Service	11
Student.	10
Sales and office	7
Homemaker	5
Military/government	3
Production, transportation, material moving	3
Natural resources, construction, maintenance	3

Leisure/recreational activities[1]	% of travelers
Sightseeing.	80%
Shopping.	75
Small towns/countryside.	44
Historical locations	40
Fine dining	39
Guided tours	37
Art galleries/museums	32
Cultural/ethnic heritage sights	32
National parks/monuments.	29
Nightclubbing/dancing	23
Water sports	21
Concert/play/musical	13
Amusement/theme parks	10
Casino/gamble	9
Camping/hiking.	8
Environmental/ecological excursions	8
Sporting event	7
Golfing/tennis	4
Hunting/fishing	4
Snow sports	1

(1) Percentages based on multiple responses.

U.S. Resident Travel Abroad, 1997-2014

Source: National Travel and Tourism Office, Intl. Trade Admin., U.S. Dept. of Commerce
(numbers in thousands)

Region/country[1]	2014	2000	1997	Region/country[1]	2014	2000	1997
Total outbound[2]	**68,176**	**61,327**	**52,735**	Caribbean.	7,387	3,867	NA
Mexico	25,882	19,285	17,909	Dominican Republic	2,709	779	195
Canada.	11,515	15,189	13,401	Jamaica.	1,385	886	1,341
				Asia.	5,694	4,914	NA
Overseas subtotal[3]	**30,780**	**26,853**	**21,634**	China[4].	1,139	644	476
Europe	10,804	13,373	NA	India	1,077	457	368
United Kingdom	2,832	4,189	3,570	Central America	2,370	886	NA
France.	2,124	2,927	2,098	South America	2,278	2,095	NA
Italy.	1,908	2,148	1,471	Middle East.	1,724	1,370	NA
Germany.	1,878	2,309	1,796	Africa	893	483	NA
Spain	1,170	1,262	714	Oceania	585	1,047	NA

NA = Not available. **Note:** Visits of one or more nights. Visitation estimates for Canada and Mexico include all modes of transportation used. Estimates for all other countries are available only for air travel to that country and are based upon data from the airlines that voluntarily provided it. (1) Only individual countries that received more than 1 mil visitors in 2014 are shown. Region figures include U.S. resident travelers to all countries in region. (2) To Canada, Mexico, and overseas. (3) To all countries except Canada and Mexico. (4) Not including Hong Kong, Macao, and Taiwan.

Airline Safety, U.S. Scheduled Commercial Carriers, 1985-2015

Source: National Transportation Safety Board; Federal Aviation Administration, U.S. Dept. of Transportation

Year	Departures (mil)	Fatal accidents	Fatalities[1]	Rate of fatal accidents[2]	Year	Departures (mil)	Fatal accidents	Fatalities[1]	Rate of fatal accidents[2]
1985	6.1	4	197	0.066	2005	10.9	3	22	0.027
1990	7.8	4	11	0.051	2006	10.6	2	50	0.019
1995	8.1	1	160	0.012	2007	10.7	0	0	—
1996	7.9	3	342	0.038	2008	10.3	0	0	—
1997	9.9	3	3	0.030	2009	9.6	1	50	0.010
1998	10.5	1	1	0.009	2010	9.5	0	0	—
1999	10.9	2	12	0.018	2011	9.4	0	0	—
2000	11.1	2	89	0.018	2012	9.2	0	0	—
2001[3]	10.6	6	531	0.019	2013	9.1	0	0	—
2002	10.3	0	0	—	2014	8.9	0	0	—
2003	10.2	2	22	0.020	2015*	8.9	0	0	—
2004	10.8	1	13	0.009					

— = Not applicable. * = Preliminary. (1) Includes deaths that occurred on the ground as a result of an accident, except for fatalities resulting from the Sept. 11, 2001, terrorist attacks. (2) Per 100,000 departures. (3) The Sept. 11, 2001, terrorist attacks have been included among the number of fatal accidents but have been excluded when calculating the fatal accident rate.

U.S. Airline Statistics, 1995-2015

Source: Airlines for America
(in millions, except where otherwise noted)

	1995	2000	2005	2010	2011	2012	2013	2014	2015
Passengers enplaned[1] . . .	547.8	666.1	738.6	720.5	730.8	736.7	743.2	762.1	798.4
Revenue passenger miles[1,2]	540.7	692.8	779.0	798.0	814.4	823.2	840.4	862.1	902.4
Available seat miles[1,3] . . .	807.1	957.0	1,003.3	972.6	992.7	994.5	1,011.2	1,033.8	1,077.2
Cargo revenue ton miles[1,2]	16,921	23,888	28,039	27,885	28,123	27,790	26,441	27,236	26,619
% of seating utilized[1]	67.0%	72.4%	77.6%	82.1%	82.0%	82.8%	83.1%	83.4%	83.8%
Passenger revenue[4]	$70,132	$94,307	94,340	$104,431	$114,820	$116,909	$121,332	$127,445	$126,880
Net profit[4]	$2,001	$2,238	–$28,647	$2,245	$525	$131	$12,183	$7,446	$25,596
Total employment[5]	546.6	739.6	619.6	564.4	577.3	584.5	584	589.1	605.3

(1) Scheduled service only. (2) One fare-paying passenger or one ton of revenue cargo transported one mile. (3) One seat transported one mile. (4) Passenger carriers only. (5) Figures are of avg. full-time equivalents (FTE), i.e., the number of full-time employees that could have been employed if the reported number of hours worked by part-time employees had been worked by full-time employees. In this table, part-time employees are treated as 0.5 FTEs.

Top 25 U.S. Passenger Airlines, 2015

Source: Airlines for America
(in millions; ranked by number of passengers enplaned in scheduled service)

	Airline	Passengers		Airline	Passengers		Airline	Passengers		Airline	Passengers
1.	American Airlines	146.8	8.	Alaska Airlines . .	22.9	16.	Allegiant Air.	9.6	22.	Compass Airlines	5.0
2.	Southwest Airlines	144.6	9.	Spirit Airlines	17.6	17.	PSA Airlines	9.1	23.	GoJet Airlines[1] . .	4.4
3.	Delta Air Lines. . .	137.9	10.	Republic Airlines	14.0	18.	Horizon Air	7.9	24.	Trans States	
4.	United Airlines. . .	95.0	11.	Frontier Airlines. .	13.1	19.	Shuttle America	7.8		Airlines	3.0
5.	JetBlue Airways. .	35.1	12.	Envoy Air.	12.3	20.	Virgin America . .	7.0	25.	Piedmont Airlines	2.9
6.	SkyWest Airlines	30.1	13.	Mesa Airlines . . .	11.4	21.	Air Wisconsin				
7.	ExpressJet		14.	Hawaiian Airlines	10.5		Airlines	6.3			
	Airlines	26.0	15.	Endeavor Air. . . .	10.3						

Note: Includes domestic and international passengers on U.S. airlines. (1) Doing business as United Express.

Top North American Airports by Passenger Traffic, 2015

Source: *2015 World Annual Traffic Report*, Airports Council Intl.

City/airport name (airport code)	Total passengers[1]
1. Hartsfield-Jackson Atlanta Intl. (ATL)	101,491,106
2. Chicago O'Hare Intl. (ORD)	76,949,504
3. Los Angeles Intl. (LAX)	74,937,004
4. Dallas/Ft. Worth Intl. (DFW)	64,074,762
5. New York John F. Kennedy Intl. (JFK)	56,827,154
6. Denver Intl. (DEN).	54,014,502
7. San Francisco Intl. (SFO)	50,057,887
8. Charlotte Douglas Intl. (CLT).	44,876,627
9. Miami Intl. (MIA).	44,350,247
10. Phoenix Sky Harbor Intl. (PHX)	44,003,840
11. Las Vegas McCarran Intl. (LAS).	43,965,471
12. Houston George Bush Intercontinental (IAH) . .	43,023,224
13. Seattle-Tacoma Intl. (SEA).	42,340,537
14. Toronto Pearson Intl. (YYZ)	41,036,847
15. Orlando Intl. (MCO)	38,727,749
16. Mexico City Intl. (MEX)	38,433,288
17. Newark Liberty Intl. (EWR)	37,494,704
18. Minneapolis/St. Paul Intl. (MSP)	36,582,854
19. Boston Logan Intl. (BOS).	33,515,905
20. Detroit Metropolitan Wayne County (DTW) . . .	33,440,112
21. Philadelphia Intl. (PHL)	31,444,403
22. New York LaGuardia (LGA)	28,437,668
23. Ft. Lauderdale-Hollywood Intl. (FLL)	26,941,671
24. Baltimore/Washington Intl. Thurgood Marshall (BWI)	23,823,532
25. Ronald Reagan Washington National (DCA) . . .	23,012,191

Top World Airports by Passenger Traffic, 2015

Source: *2015 World Annual Traffic Report*, Airports Council Intl.

City/airport name (country; airport code)	Total passengers[1]
1. Beijing Capital Intl. (China; PEK)	89,938,628
2. Dubai Intl. (United Arab Emirates; DXB)	78,014,841
3. Tokyo Haneda Intl. (Japan; HND)	75,573,106
4. London Heathrow (UK; LHR)	74,989,795
5. Hong Kong Intl. (China; HKG).	68,283,407
6. Paris Charles de Gaulle (France; CDG)	65,766,986
7. Istanbul Atatürk Intl. (Turkey; IST)	61,346,229
8. Frankfurt Intl. (Germany; FRA)	61,032,022
9. Shanghai Pudong Intl. (China; PVG)	60,098,073
10. Amsterdam Schiphol (Netherlands; AMS)	58,284,864
11. Singapore Changi (Singapore; SIN)	55,449,000
12. Guangzhou Baiyun Intl. (China; CAN)	55,201,915
13. Jakarta Soekarno-Hatta Intl. (Indonesia; CGK). .	54,089,062
14. Bangkok Suvarnabhumi (Thailand; BKK)	52,902,110
15. Seoul Incheon Intl. (South Korea; ICN)	49,412,750
16. Kuala Lumpur Intl. (Malaysia; KUL)	48,938,424
17. Madrid-Barajas (Spain; MAD).	46,779,554
18. Delhi Indira Gandhi Intl. (India; DEL)	45,981,773
19. Chengdu Shuangliu Intl. (China; CTU)	42,244,842
20. Munich (Germany; MUC)	40,981,522
21. Mumbai Chhatrapati Shivaji Intl. (India; BOM) . .	40,637,377
22. Rome Leonardo da Vinci-Fiumicino (Italy; FCO) . .	40,422,156
23. London Gatwick (UK; LGW)	40,269,087
24. Sydney Intl. (Australia; SYD)	39,915,674
25. Shenzhen Baoan Intl. (China; SZX)	39,721,619

Note: World list excludes North American airports and airports that do not participate in Airports Council Intl.'s Airport Traffic Statistics collection. (1) Arriving and departing passengers and direct transit passengers counted once.

Busiest Amtrak Stations, 2015

Source: Amtrak National Fact Sheet, Amtrak; ranked by total ridership

Station	Tickets from	Tickets to	Total ridership	Station	Tickets from	Tickets to	Total ridership
New York, NY	5,113,115	5,076,406	10,189,521	Providence, RI	337,204	353,548	690,752
Washington, DC	2,481,112	2,490,016	4,971,128	BWI Airport, MD	332,425	337,184	669,609
Philadelphia, PA	2,074,791	2,063,986	4,138,777	Newark, NJ	322,200	319,146	641,346
Chicago, IL	1,651,653	1,643,977	3,295,630	Seattle, WA	304,719	300,113	604,832
Los Angeles, CA	842,731	746,660	1,589,391	Milwaukee, WI	298,641	295,435	594,076
Boston South Station,				Emeryville, CA	293,061	294,865	587,926
MA.	783,284	760,885	1,544,169	Boston Back Bay, MA	292,605	285,798	578,403
Sacramento, CA	521,953	505,060	1,027,013	Portland, OR.	277,643	283,953	561,596
Baltimore, MD.	497,343	496,378	993,721	Lancaster, PA	271,522	269,730	541,252
Albany-Rensselaer,				Bakersfield, CA	255,697	258,187	513,884
NY.	412,818	412,535	825,353	Harrisburg, PA.	255,433	253,252	508,685
San Diego, CA	392,836	380,661	773,497	Route 128, MA	225,930	218,740	444,670
Wilmington, DE.	349,606	350,735	700,341	Irvine, CA	195,185	226,551	421,736
New Haven, CT	352,005	346,651	698,656				

Top Travel Websites, 2016

Source: comScore Media Metrix, Inc.; ranked by number of visitors

Rank	Website	Visitors[1]	Rank	Website	Visitors[1]
1.	TripAdvisor Inc.	79,459	12.	American Airlines	11,052
2.	Expedia Inc.	63,257	13.	Delta Airlines.	11,017
3.	Priceline.com Inc.	31,244	14.	Lyft, Inc.	9,955
4.	Uber	25,586	15.	Fareportal Media Group	9,590
5.	Southwest Airlines Co.	21,398	16.	Time Inc. Affluent Media Group	9,096
6.	United Airlines.	13,637	17.	InterContinental Hotels Group	8,520
7.	USAToday Travel	13,058	18.	Disney Parks & Travel.	8,013
8.	Marriott	12,951	19.	MSN Travel	7,397
9.	Kayak.com Network	11,880	20.	Enterprise Rent-A-Car Company	7,028
10.	Airbnb Sites	11,675	**Total travel audience[2].**		**178,736**
11.	Hilton Worldwide.	11,446	**Total internet audience[2]**		**257,754**

(1) Number of unique visitors, in thousands, who visited website at least once in June 2016. (2) Audience comprises all persons older than 2 years of age, at U.S. home/work locations.

Most Visited Amusement/Theme Parks, 2015

Source: Themed Entertainment Association

(visitors in thousands)

	North America			World	
Rank	Park, location	Visitors	Rank	Park, location	Visitors
1.	Magic Kingdom[1], Lake Buena Vista, FL	20,492	1.	Tokyo Disneyland, Tokyo, Japan	16,600
2.	Disneyland, Anaheim, CA	18,278	2.	Universal Studios Japan, Osaka, Japan	13,900
3.	Epcot[1], Lake Buena Vista, FL	11,798	3.	Tokyo Disney Sea, Tokyo, Japan	13,600
4.	Disney's Animal Kingdom[1], Lake Buena Vista, FL	10,922	4.	Disneyland Park at Disneyland Paris, Marne-la-Vallée, France	10,360
5.	Disney's Hollywood Studios[1], Lake Buena Vista, FL	10,828	5.	Chimelong Ocean Kingdom, Hengqin, China	7,486
6.	Universal Studios[2], Orlando, FL	9,585	6.	Everland, Gyeonggi-Do, South Korea	7,423
7.	Disney's California Adventure, Anaheim, CA	9,383	7.	Ocean Park, Hong Kong.	7,387
8.	Islands of Adventure[2], Orlando, FL.	8,792	8.	Lotte World, Seoul, South Korea.	7,310
9.	Universal Studios Hollywood, Universal City, CA	7,097	9.	Hangzhou Songcheng Park, Hangzhou, China.	7,289
10.	SeaWorld Florida, Orlando, FL.	4,777	10.	Hong Kong Disneyland, Hong Kong	6,800

Note: World list excludes North American parks. (1) Located at Walt Disney World. (2) Located at Universal Orlando.

Record-Breaking Roller Coasters

Source: UltimateRollerCoaster.com; speed measured in mph, length and height in ft

Steel-Tracked Roller Coasters

Fastest	Roller coaster	Theme park, location
149.1 mph	Formula Rossa	Ferrari World Abu Dhabi, United Arab Emirates
128	Kingda Ka	Six Flags Great Adventure, Jackson, NJ
120	Top Thrill Dragster	Cedar Point, Sandusky, OH
106.9	Dodonpa	Fuji-Q High Land, Fujiyoshida-shi, Japan
100	Tower of Terror	Dreamworld, Gold Coast, Australia
100	Superman: Escape From Krypton	Six Flags Magic Mountain, Valencia, CA

Tallest		
456 ft	Kingda Ka	Six Flags Great Adventure, Jackson, NJ
420	Top Thrill Dragster	Cedar Point, Sandusky, OH
415	Superman: Escape From Krypton	Six Flags Magic Mountain, Valencia, CA
377.3	Tower of Terror II	Dreamworld, Gold Coast, Australia
325	Fury 325	Carowinds, Charlotte, NC

Largest drop		
418 ft	Kingda Ka	Six Flags Great Adventure, Jackson, NJ
400	Top Thrill Dragster	Cedar Point, Sandusky, OH
328.1	Superman: Escape From Krypton	Six Flags Magic Mountain, Valencia, CA
328.1	Tower of Terror.	Dreamworld, Gold Coast, Australia

Longest		
8,133.2 ft	Steel Dragon 2000	Nagashima Spa Land, Mie, Japan
7,442	The Ultimate	Lightwater Valley, UK
6,708.7	Fujiyama	Fuji-Q High Land, Fujiyoshida-shi, Japan
6,602	Fury 325	Carowinds, Charlotte, NC

Wood-Tracked Roller Coasters

Fastest	Roller coaster	Theme park, location
73 mph	Lightning Rod	Dollywood, Pigeon Forge, TN
72	Goliath	Six Flags Great America, Gurnee, IL
70.2	Wildfire	Kolmarden Wildlife Park, Norrköping, Sweden
70	El Toro	Six Flags Great Adventure, Jackson, NJ
68.4	Colossos	Heide Park, Soltau, Germany

Tallest		
196.8 ft	Colossos.	Heide Park, Soltau, Germany
187	Wildfire	Kolmarden Wildlife Park, Norrköping, Sweden
183.8	T Express	Everland, Yongin, S. Korea
181	El Toro	Six Flags Great Adventure, Jackson, NJ
165	Goliath	Six Flags Great America, Gurnee, IL

Largest drop		
180 ft	Goliath.	Six Flags Great America, Gurnee, IL
176	El Toro.	Six Flags Great Adventure, Jackson, NJ
165	Lightning Rod	Dollywood, Pigeon Forge, TN
162	Outlaw Run	Silver Dollar City, Branson, MO
160.8	Wildfire	Kolmarden Wildlife Park, Norrköping, Sweden

Longest		
7,359 ft	The Beast	Kings Island, Cincinnati, OH
6,442	The Voyage	Holiday World & Splashin' Safari, Santa Claus, IN
5,577.4	White Cyclone	Nagashima Spa Land, Mie, Japan
5,427	Mean Streak	Cedar Point, Sandusky, OH
5,383	T Express	Everland, Yongin, S. Korea

Passports, Health Regulations, and Travel Warnings for Foreign Travel

Source: Bureau of Consular Affairs, U.S. Dept. of State; Centers for Disease Control and Prevention (CDC), U.S. Dept. of Health and Human Services; World Health Organization (WHO); Transportation Security Administration (TSA), U.S. Dept. of Homeland Security

Passports, Visas

Passports are issued by the Dept. of State to U.S. citizens and nationals to provide documentation for foreign travel. As of Oct. 2016, the fees for a new passport book and passport card for persons ages 16 and over total $165; provided certain criteria are met, these can be renewed for $140. For a passport book alone, fees are $135 for a new passport and $110 for passport renewal.

In July 2008, the U.S. government began issuing passport cards. Travelers arriving by land or sea from Canada, Mexico, the Caribbean, and Bermuda may present a passport card to enter the U.S. Passport cards may not be used for air travel, however. The fees for a new passport card for persons ages 16 and over total $55.

A U.S. passport is often sufficient for U.S. citizens to gain admission for a limited stay in another country. Some countries also require an entry visa. Each country has its own specific guidelines concerning length and purpose of visit, among other considerations. Visitors may need to provide proof of sufficient funds for their intended stay, onward/return tickets, and/or at least six months remaining validity on their U.S. passports.

All persons traveling by air outside of the U.S. (excluding direct travel to and from a U.S. territory) are required to present a passport or other valid document upon reentering the U.S.

For up-to-date passport and international travel information, visit the Consular Affairs website (travel.state. gov) or call the National Passport Information Center at 1-877-4USA-PPT (1-877-487-2778).

Health Regulations

Under WHO regulations, first instituted in 1969, member countries agree to abide by resolutions meant to contain the spread of disease. For example, some countries require travelers to provide proof of vaccination against yellow fever before entering.

Detailed information can be found in *Health Information for International Travel*, or the "yellow book," published every two years by the CDC. The book is written primarily for health care providers but may be of use to other travelers. The CDC also issues travel notices on outbreaks, health precautions, and health warnings. For current notices and more on travelers' health, visit wwwnc. cdc.gov/travel/.

WHO publishes a more technical guide, *International Travel and Health*, which can be found online at www. who.int/ith/.

Travel Warnings and Alerts

The State Dept. issues travel warnings as recommendations that Americans avoid travel to certain countries. Long-term conditions in such countries may be dangerous or unstable; an embassy closure or limited personnel may reduce the U.S. government's ability to assist U.S. citizens. As of Oct. 2016, travel warnings were in effect for the following countries: Afghanistan, Algeria, The Bahamas, Bangladesh, Burkina Faso, Burundi, Cameroon, Central African Republic, Chad, Colombia, Dem. Rep. of the Congo, El Salvador, Eritrea, Ethiopia, Haiti, Honduras, Iran, Iraq, Israel (incl. West Bank and Gaza), Kenya, North Korea, Lebanon, Libya, Mali, Mauritania, Mexico, Niger, Nigeria, Pakistan, Philippines, Saudi Arabia, Somalia, South Sudan, Sudan, Syria, Tunisia, Turkey, Ukraine, Venezuela, and Yemen.

The department issues travel alerts when it has concerns about short-term conditions—natural disasters, terrorist attacks, anniversaries of attacks, election-related demonstrations, and regional sporting events, among others. For the latest travel warnings and alerts, see travel. state.gov.

Summary of TSA Regulations

Airplane carry-ons. TSA promotes the "3-1-1" rule regarding carry-on items. Containers with liquids, gels, aerosols, creams, or pastes must hold **3.4** oz or less; these containers should be packed inside a single **1**-quart, clear plastic, resealable bag; and this **1** bag must be X-rayed when going through security. Exceptions to the 3-1-1 rule include medication, baby formula and food, and breast milk. Travelers must declare any exceptions at security.

Security checkpoint identification. Adult travelers (18 years of age and over) must present a photo ID. Acceptable documents include a U.S. passport or passport card; foreign government-issued passport; state-issued driver's license; permanent resident card; or U.S. military ID, among others.

Screening process. Travelers may wear loose fitting or religious garments (incl. head coverings) through security. They may be subject to additional screening if clothing could conceal prohibited items. Travelers may request a private area if selected for personal screening. Travelers will be screened by someone of the same gender.

Disability-related permitted carry-on items:

- Wheelchairs, scooters
- Crutches, canes, and walkers
- Portable oxygen concentrators (though not permitted by all airlines)
- Canes, Braille note-takers
- Medications and associated supplies
- Service animals

Permitted carry-on items:

- Disposable razors
- Eye drops and saline solution (amounts greater than 3.4 oz must be declared)
- Nail clippers, tweezers
- Scissors with pointed tips and blades shorter than 4 inches
- Mobile phones
- Strollers (must be inspected at security)
- Beverages (any size) purchased after security screening
- Musical instruments (must undergo screening; must fit into overhead bin or under seats; some airlines may allow purchase of seat for an instrument)

Prohibited carry-on items:

- Knives (except for plastic or round-bladed butter knives), incl. knives that are religious objects
- Baseball bats, golf clubs
- Flare guns
- Firearms or realistic firearm replicas, ammunition, firearm parts
- Hammers, screwdrivers, wrenches, pliers, and other tools more than 7 in. in length
- Brass knuckles
- Lighter fluid
- Liquid bleach, turpentine, paint thinner
- Spray paint
- Self-defense sprays

For complete travel information, visit www.tsa.gov/travel.

Number and Acreage of Farms by State, 2000, 2015

Source: National Agricultural Statistics Service, U.S. Dept. of Agriculture

State	No. of farms (thous.) 2015	No. of farms (thous.) 2000	Acreage in farms (mil) 2015	Acreage in farms (mil) 2000	Acreage per farm 2015	Acreage per farm 2000	State	No. of farms (thous.) 2015	No. of farms (thous.) 2000	Acreage in farms (mil) 2015	Acreage in farms (mil) 2000	Acreage per farm 2015	Acreage per farm 2000
AL.....	42.7	47.0	8.8	9.0	206	191	NE.....	48.7	46.1	45.2	46.1	928	887
AK.....	0.8	0.6	0.8	0.9	1,107	1,569	NV.....	4.2	3.1	6.0	6.4	1,419	2,065
AZ.....	19.5	10.7	26.0	26.9	1,333	2,518	NH	4.4	3.3	0.5	0.4	107	133
AR.....	43.5	48.0	13.8	14.6	317	304	NJ.....	9.1	9.7	0.7	0.8	79	86
CA.....	77.5	83.1	25.5	28.0	329	337	NM	24.7	18.0	43.2	44.9	1,749	2,494
CO	34.2	30.0	31.7	31.6	927	1,060	NY.....	35.5	37.5	7.2	7.7	203	205
CT.....	6.0	4.2	0.4	0.4	73	86	NC	48.8	55.5	8.3	9.2	170	166
DE.....	2.5	2.6	0.5	0.6	200	215	ND	30.0	30.8	39.2	39.4	1,307	1,279
FL.....	47.3	44.0	9.5	10.4	200	238	OH	74.4	79.0	14.0	14.8	188	187
GA	40.5	49.1	9.3	10.9	230	223	OK	78.0	84.5	34.2	33.8	438	401
HI	7.0	5.5	1.1	1.4	160	251	OR	34.6	40.0	16.4	17.3	474	433
ID	24.4	24.5	11.8	11.9	484	486	PA.....	57.9	59.0	7.7	7.7	133	130
IL	73.6	77.0	26.9	27.5	365	357	RI	1.3	0.8	0.1	0.1	56	75
IN	57.7	63.4	14.7	15.2	255	240	SC	24.4	24.2	5.0	4.9	205	203
IA	87.5	94.0	30.5	32.5	349	346	SD	31.3	32.4	43.3	44.0	1,383	1,358
KS.....	60.4	64.5	46.0	47.5	762	736	TN	67.3	88.0	10.9	11.8	162	134
KY.....	76.4	90.0	13.0	13.7	170	152	TX	242.0	228.3	130.0	130.9	537	573
LA.....	26.9	29.0	7.8	8.0	288	277	UT	18.1	15.5	11.0	11.6	608	747
ME	8.2	7.1	1.5	1.4	177	190	VT	7.3	6.6	1.3	1.3	171	192
MD	12.2	12.4	2.0	2.1	166	172	VA	44.7	48.5	8.1	8.7	181	180
MA	7.8	6.1	0.5	0.5	67	89	WA	36.0	37.0	14.7	15.6	408	420
MI.....	51.5	53.0	10.0	10.2	193	192	WV	20.9	20.8	3.6	3.6	172	173
MN	73.6	81.0	25.9	27.9	352	344	WI	68.9	77.5	14.4	16.0	209	206
MS	36.7	42.0	10.8	11.2	294	266	WY	11.6	9.2	30.4	34.5	2,621	3,750
MO	97.1	109.0	28.3	30.2	291	277	**U.S.**	**2,067.0**	**2,166.8**	**912.0**	**945.1**	**441**	**436**
MT	27.5	27.8	59.7	59.3	2,171	2,133							

Supplemental Nutrition Assistance Program (SNAP), 1969-2015

Source: Food and Nutrition Service (FNS), U.S. Dept. of Agriculture

Fiscal year	Avg. participation (thous.)	Avg. monthly benefit per person	Total benefits (mil)	All other costs (mil)[1]	Total costs (mil)	Fiscal year	Avg. participation (thous.)	Avg. monthly benefit per person	Total benefits (mil)	All other costs (mil)[1]	Total costs (mil)
1969	2,878	$6.63	$228.8	$21.7	$250.5	2003	21,250	$83.94	$21,404.3	$2,412.0	$23,816.3
1970	4,340	10.55	549.7	27.2	576.9	2004	23,811	86.16	24,618.9	2,480.1	27,099.0
1975	17,064	21.40	4,385.5	233.2	4,618.7	2005	25,628	92.89	28,567.9	2,504.2	31,072.1
1980	21,082	34.47	8,720.9	485.6	9,206.5	2006	26,549	94.75	30,187.4	2,715.7	32,903.1
1985	19,899	44.99	10,743.6	959.6	11,703.2	2007	26,316	96.18	30,373.3	2,800.3	33,173.5
1990	20,049	58.78	14,142.8	1,304.5	15,447.3	2008	28,223	102.19	34,608.4	3,031.3	37,639.6
1995	26,619	71.27	22,764.1	1,856.3	24,620.4	2009	33,490	125.31	50,359.9	3,260.0	53,619.9
1996	25,543	73.21	22,440.1	1,890.9	24,331.0	2010	40,302	133.79	64,702.2	3,581.3	68,283.5
1997	22,858	71.27	19,548.9	1,958.7	21,507.6	2011	44,709	133.85	71,810.9	3,875.6	75,686.5
1998	19,791	71.12	16,890.5	2,097.8	18,988.3	2012	46,609	133.41	74,619.3	3,790.3	78,409.7
1999	18,183	72.27	15,769.4	2,051.5	17,820.9	2013	47,636	133.07	76,066.3	3,804.5	79,870.8
2000	17,194	72.62	14,983.3	2,070.7	17,054.0	2014	46,664	125.01	69,998.8	4,076.0	74,074.8
2001	17,318	74.81	15,547.4	2,242.0	17,789.4	2015	45,767	126.83	69,655.5	4,324.1	73,979.6
2002	19,096	79.67	18,256.2	2,380.8	20,637.0						

(1) Includes the federal share of state administrative expenses, nutrition education, and employment and training programs, in addition to other federal costs (e.g., benefit and retailer redemption and monitoring, payment accuracy, EBT [electronic benefit transfer] systems, program evaluation and modernization, program access, health and nutrition pilot projects).

U.S. Federal Food Assistance Programs, 1990-2015

Source: Food and Nutrition Service (FNS), U.S. Dept. of Agriculture

(in millions of dollars; for fiscal years ending on Sept. 30)

Program	1990	1995	2000	2005	2010	2012	2013	2014	2015
Supplemental Nutrition Assistance Program (SNAP)[1]	$15,491	$24,620	$17,054	$31,073	$68,284	$78,410	$79,871	$74,075	$73,980
Puerto Rico nutrition assistance[2]	937	1,131	1,268	1,495	2,001	2,001	2,001	1,903	1,951
Natl. school lunch[3]	3,834	5,160	6,149	8,031	10,880	11,578	12,221	12,658	13,006
School breakfast[3,4]	596	1,048	1,393	1,927	2,859	3,277	3,514	3,685	3,893
WIC (Women, Infants, and Children)[5]. ..	2,122	3,440	3,982	4,994	6,690	6,801	6,492	6,335	6,167
Summer food service[6]	164	237	267	267	359	398	428	465	489
Child and adult care[7]	813	1,464	1,683	2,111	2,638	2,854	2,994	3,132	3,307
Special milk[4]......................	19	17	15	16	12	12	11	11	10
Nutrition for the elderly (NSIP)[8]	142	148	137	4	3	3	3	2	3
Food distrib. to Indian reserv.[9]	66	65	76	76	95	97	100	110	119
Commodity supplemental food prog.[9]. . .	85	99	98	156	165	209	203	198	193
Food distrib. to charitable insts.[10]	104	64	2	4	1	0	0	0	0
Emergency food assistance (TEFAP)[11]. .	334	135	225	373	631	444	693	629	525
Total	**24,707**	**37,628**	**32,349**	**50,527**	**94,618**	**106,084**	**108,531**	**103,203**	**103,643**

Note: 2015 data are preliminary. All data subject to revision by the FNS. (1) Formerly known as the Food Stamp Program. Includes benefits and admin. expenses. (2) Provides benefits analogous to SNAP. (3) Nine-month averages (summer months excluded). (4) Cash payments based on federal reimbursement rates to states. (5) Includes food benefits, nutrition services and admin. funds, Farmers' Market Nutrition Program, infrastructure, breastfeeding promotion and peer counseling, program evaluation, and technical assistance. (6) Includes cash payments, commodity costs, and admin. costs for services similar to natl. school lunch and breakfast programs. (7) Includes cash payments, entitlement and bonus commodities, cash-in-lieu of commodities, sponsor admin. costs, start-up costs, and audits. (8) For 2003 and on, program administered by the Agency on Aging; FNS costs limited to value of commodities distributed. (9) Includes cost of commodities and distrib. and admin. expenses. (10) Includes summer camps. (11) Includes cost of commodities to hunger relief orgs. (e.g., food banks, soup kitchens) and admin. expenses.

U.S. Cost of Food, 2016

Source: Center for Nutrition Policy and Promotion (CNPP), U.S. Dept. of Agriculture (USDA)

Age-gender group	Weekly cost[1]				Monthly cost[1]			
	Thrifty plan	Low-cost plan	Mod.-cost plan	Liberal plan	Thrifty plan	Low-cost plan	Mod.-cost plan	Liberal plan
Individual child[2]								
1 year.............	$21.70	$28.90	$32.70	$39.90	$93.90	$125.10	$141.80	$173.00
2-3 years...........	23.70	30.20	36.40	44.30	102.60	130.90	157.60	192.10
4-5 years...........	24.80	31.20	38.80	47.30	107.60	135.10	167.90	205.10
6-8 years...........	31.70	44.30	53.00	62.80	137.40	192.10	229.70	272.30
9-11 years..........	35.70	47.50	61.40	71.50	154.60	205.80	266.10	309.90
Individual male[2]								
12-13 years	38.50	54.70	68.60	80.40	167.00	236.90	297.20	348.40
14-18 years.........	39.70	55.50	70.80	81.20	171.90	240.50	306.90	351.90
19-50 years.........	42.60	55.10	69.20	85.20	184.70	238.80	299.80	369.40
51-70 years	38.90	52.00	64.70	78.10	168.60	225.20	280.20	338.50
71+ years	39.20	51.40	63.60	79.10	169.80	222.60	275.80	342.90
Individual female[2]								
12-13 years	38.50	47.00	56.60	69.50	167.00	203.70	245.20	301.30
14-18 years	37.80	47.10	57.20	70.40	163.90	203.90	247.70	305.00
19-50 years	37.70	47.70	59.10	75.30	163.50	206.70	255.90	326.20
51-70 years	37.40	46.50	58.00	69.90	162.00	201.30	251.20	302.90
71+ years	36.30	45.90	57.00	68.90	157.30	198.90	247.20	298.40
2-person family								
19-50 years	88.40	113.10	141.10	176.60	383.10	490.10	611.20	765.10
51-70 years	83.90	108.30	134.90	162.80	363.70	469.10	584.60	705.50
4-person family[3] with 2 children ages—								
2-3 and 4-5 years....	128.90	164.20	203.40	252.20	558.40	711.60	881.20	1,092.80
6-8 and 9-11 years....	147.80	194.70	242.70	294.90	640.20	843.40	1,051.50	1,277.80

Note: As of June 2016. The official USDA food plans represent a nutritious diet at four different cost levels. The nutritional bases are the 1997-2005 Dietary Reference Intakes, 2005 Dietary Guidelines for Americans, and 2005 MyPyramid food intake recommendations. In addition to cost, differences among plans are in specific foods and quantities of foods. Another basis of the food plans is that all meals and snacks are prepared at home. For specific foods and quantities, see *Thrifty Food Plan, 2006* and *The Low-Cost, Moderate-Cost, and Liberal Food Plans, 2007* from the CNPP. All four food plans are based on 2001-02 data and updated to current dollars using the consumer price index for specific food items. (1) All costs are rounded to nearest 10 cents. (2) The costs given are for individuals in 4-person families. (3) Defined as a couple, 19-50 years old, and two children.

U.S. Household Food Security by Selected Characteristics, 2015

Source: Economic Research Service, U.S. Dept. of Agriculture

(in thousands of households)

	Total[1]	Food secure		With low food security		With very low food security	
		No.	%	No.	%	No.	%
All households...........................	125,164	109,315	87.3%	9,540	7.7%	6,309	5.0%
Household composition							
With children under 18 years old	38,978	32,519	83.4	4,557	11.7	1,902	4.9
With children under 6 years old	16,995	14,129	83.1	2,146	12.7	720	4.2
Married-couple families...................	25,232	22,670	89.8	1,923	7.7	639	2.5
Female head, no spouse...................	10,117	7,052	69.7	2,109	20.9	956	9.4
Male head, no spouse....................	3,133	2,432	77.6	443	14.2	258	8.2
Other household with child[2]................	496	366	73.8	82	16.5	48	9.7
With no children under 18 years old............	86,187	76,796	89.1	4,983	5.8	4,408	5.1
More than one adult......................	51,357	46,976	91.5	2,504	4.8	1,877	3.7
Women living alone......................	18,954	16,169	85.3	1,413	7.5	1,372	7.2
Men living alone.........................	15,876	13,652	86.0	1,065	6.7	1,159	7.3
With elderly.............................	35,265	32,340	91.7	1,789	5.1	1,136	3.2
Elderly living alone......................	13,137	11,932	90.8	657	5.0	548	4.2
Race/ethnicity							
White, non-Hispanic.....................	83,931	75,563	90.0	4,759	5.7	3,609	4.3
Black, non-Hispanic.....................	15,734	12,357	78.5	2,127	13.6	1,250	7.9
Other, non-Hispanic.....................	8,695	7,803	89.7	521	6.0	371	4.3
Hispanic[3]	16,803	13,592	80.9	2,132	12.7	1,079	6.4
Area of residence[4]							
Inside metropolitan area	106,990	93,947	87.8	7,843	7.3	5,200	4.9
In principal cities[5].....................	36,809	31,606	85.9	3,240	8.8	1,963	5.3
Not in principal cities	53,585	48,023	89.6	3,304	6.2	2,258	4.2
Outside metropolitan area.................	18,175	15,369	84.6	1,697	9.3	1,109	6.1

Note: Low food security households report food acquisition problems and reduced diet quality but typically few, if any, indications of reduced food intake. The very low food security category identifies households in which the food intake of one or more members was reduced and eating patterns disrupted because of insufficient money and resources for food. (1) Totals exclude households of unknown food security status. Exclusions represented 0.3% of all households in 2015. (2) Households with children in complex living arrangements, e.g., children of other relatives or unrelated roommate. (3) Hispanics may be of any race. (4) Based on 2013 Office of Management and Budget delineations of metropolitan areas. (5) Households within incorporated areas of the largest cities in each metropolitan area. Residence in or out of principal cities unknown for about 16% of households in metropolitan statistical areas.

U.S. Adoption of Genetically Modified Crops, 2000-16

Source: Economic Research Service, U.S. Dept of Agriculture

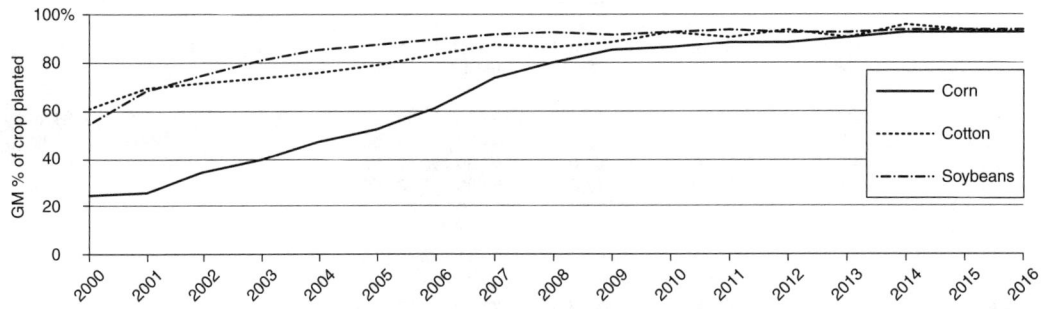

U.S. Annual Per Capita Consumption of Selected Foods, 1970-2014

Source: Economic Research Service, U.S. Dept. of Agriculture; Distilled Spirits Council of the U.S.; Beer Institute; Wine Institute
(fruits and vegetables in pounds, beverages in gallons)

	1970	1990	2014	% change, 1970-2014		1970	1990	2014	% change, 1970-2014
Fresh fruit	100.9	117.0	135.9	34.7%	**Fresh vegetables**	144.4	163.9	171.2	18.6%
Apples	17.2	19.8	18.9	9.9	Bell peppers	2.0	5.4	9.8	390.0
Avocados	0.5	1.4	6.5	1,200.0	Broccoli	0.5	3.1	6.1	1,120.0
Bananas	17.4	24.3	27.9	60.3	Cabbage	8.1	7.8	6.2	−23.5
Grapes	2.9	7.9	7.7	165.5	Carrots	5.8	8.0	8.2	41.4
Melons	21.4	24.6	22.1	3.3	Celery	6.8	6.7	5.1	−25.0
Oranges	16.2	12.4	9.4	−42.0	Cucumbers	2.6	4.3	6.8	161.5
Peaches/nectarines	5.8	5.5	3.3	−43.1	Garlic	0.4	1.1	1.6	300.0
Pears	1.9	3.3	2.9	52.6	Head lettuce	20.8	25.8	13.5	−35.1
Pineapples	0.7	2.0	7.2	928.6	Onions	9.5	14.2	17.2	81.1
Strawberries	1.7	3.2	7.9	364.7	Potatoes	59.3	44.9	32.2	−44.0
Canned vegetables	93.0	110.3	93.2	0.2	Sweet corn	7.2	6.2	7.0	−2.8
Green peas	0.9	1.9	0.7	−22.2	Tomatoes	10.3	13.2	17.4	68.9
Snap beans	1.1	3.7	2.8	154.5	**Beverages**				
Sweet corn	14.3	10.9	5.8	−59.4	Bottled water	NA	8.8	30.8[1]	NA
Tomatoes	62.1	75.3	67.2	8.2	Carbonated soft drinks	24.3	46.2	NA	NA
Frozen vegetables	43.7	66.7	66.1	51.3	Regular	22.2	35.6	NA	NA
Broccoli	1.0	2.2	2.6	160.0	Diet	2.1	10.7	NA	NA
Carrots	1.4	2.3	1.2	−14.3	Coffee	33.4	26.8	25.7	−23.1
Green peas	1.9	2.2	1.6	−15.8	Fruit juice	5.5	7.4	5.8	5.5
Potatoes	28.5	46.4	46.3	62.5	Beer	18.5	23.9	20.1	8.6
Sweet corn	5.7	8.6	7.7	35.1	Wine	1.3	2.1	2.8	115.4
					Distilled spirits	1.8	1.5	1.6	−11.1

NA = Not available. **Note:** All figures are rounded; percent change is calculated based on unrounded original data. Per capita consumption based on total population. Alcoholic beverage consumption would be higher if based on legal drinking age population. (1) As of 2012 (most recent figure available).

U.S. Meat Production and Consumption, 1940-2016

Source: Economic Research Service, U.S. Dept. of Agriculture
(in millions of pounds)

Year	Beef Prod.	Beef Cons.	Veal Prod.	Veal Cons.	Lamb and mutton Prod.	Lamb and mutton Cons.	Pork Prod.	Pork Cons.	All red meats[1] Prod.	All red meats[1] Cons.	All poultry[2] Prod.	All poultry[2] Cons.
1940	7,175	7,257	981	981	876	873	10,044	9,701	19,076	18,812	NA	NA
1950	9,534	9,529	1,230	1,206	597	596	10,714	10,390	22,075	21,721	3,174	3,097
1960	14,728	15,465	1,109	1,118	769	857	13,905	14,057	30,511	31,497	6,310	6,168
1970	21,684	23,451	588	613	551	669	14,699	14,957	37,522	39,689	10,193	9,981
1980	21,643	23,560	400	420	318	351	16,617	16,838	38,978	41,170	14,173	13,525
1990	22,743	24,030	327	325	363	397	15,354	16,025	38,787	40,778	23,468	22,152
1995	25,222	25,534	319	319	285	346	17,849	17,768	43,675	43,967	30,393	25,944
2000	26,888	27,338	225	225	234	354	18,952	18,643	46,299	46,560	36,073	30,508
2009	25,965	26,904	147	147	177	339	22,999	19,839	49,274	47,227	41,673	34,116
2010	26,304	26,392	145	150	168	317	22,437	19,072	49,039	45,931	43,058	35,201
2011	26,195	25,545	136	137	153	295	22,758	18,384	49,232	44,363	43,513	35,548
2012	25,913	25,752	125	123	161	299	23,253	18,604	49,439	44,779	43,523	34,870
2013	25,720	25,483	117	119	161	324	23,187	19,095	49,174	45,020	44,159	35,630
2014	24,252	24,686	100	98	161	340	22,843	19,069	47,345	44,192	44,827	36,379
2015	23,760	24,771	88	88	159	343	24,517	20,656	48,520	45,872	45,769	38,785
2016*	25,026	25,584	NA	NA	NA	NA	24,923	20,819	50,187	46,867	47,073	39,847

NA = Not available. * = Projected. (1) Includes beef, veal, lamb and mutton, and pork. May not add up to totals because of rounding. (2) Includes broilers, turkeys, and mature chicken.

U.S. Annual Per Capita Consumption of Meat and Dairy, 1910-2014

Source: Economic Research Service, U.S. Dept. of Agriculture

(in pounds per capita per year, unless otherwise noted)

Meat	1910	1930	1950	1970	1990	2000	2010	2012	2013	2014	% change, 1910-2014
Beef	48.5	33.7	44.6	79.6	63.9	64.5	56.7	54.5	53.5	51.5	6.2%
Chicken	11.0	11.1	14.3	27.4	42.4	54.2	58.0	56.6	57.6	58.7	433.6
Fish/shellfish	11.2	10.2	11.9	11.7	14.9	15.2	15.8	14.2	14.3	14.5	29.5
Pork	38.2	41.1	43.0	48.1	46.4	47.8	44.4	42.5	43.4	43.1	12.8
Red meat	96.0	83.6	95.8	131.9	112.2	113.7	102.1	97.9	97.9	95.4	−0.6
Dairy											
Butter	18.4	17.6	10.9	5.4	4.3	4.5	4.9	5.5	5.5	5.5	−70.1
Cheese, American	2.8	3.2	5.5	7.0	11.1	12.7	13.3	13.2	13.3	13.5	382.1
Cheese, other	1.5	1.5	2.2	4.4	13.5	16.9	19.4	20.0	20.1	20.4	1,260.0
Ice cream	1.9	9.3	16.4	16.7	14.8	15.6	13.5	12.8	12.7	12.2	542.1
Milk, skim/lower fat (gallons)	7.1	5.0	2.9	5.8	15.2	14.6	14.8	14.3	13.8	13.1	84.5
Milk, whole (gallons)	25.2	28.2	34.2	25.3	10.5	8.2	5.7	5.4	5.4	5.3	−79.0

U.S. Organic Farmland and Animals, 1995-2011

Source: Economic Research Service, U.S. Dept. of Agriculture

Crop	1995	2000	Organic acreage[1] 2004	2005	2008	2011	% change, 1995-2011	% change, 2005-11	Total U.S. farmland[2]
Total cropland	638,500	1,218,905	1,452,353	1,723,271	2,655,382	3,084,989	383.2%	79.0%	370,653,755
Grains									
Corn	32,650	77,912	99,111	130,672	194,637	234,470	618.1	79.4	93,600,000
Wheat	120,820	206,474	214,244	293,824	415,902	344,644	185.3	17.3	60,433,000
Oats	13,250	29,771	42,616	46,465	57,374	62,015	368.0	33.5	3,760,000
Barley	17,150	41,904	26,629	39,271	46,954	63,903	272.6	62.7	4,020,000
Rice	8,400	26,870	22,173	26,428	49,638	48,533	477.8	83.6	2,761,000
Beans									
Soybeans	47,200	136,071	114,239	122,217	125,621	132,411	180.5	8.3	63,631,000
Dry beans	NA	14,010	7,642	10,561	16,465	28,656	NA	171.3	1,526,900
Dry peas & lentils	5,900	10,144	15,893	17,757	16,987	17,887	203.2	0.7	571,000
Hay & silage	84,100	231,207	356,590	411,342	793,442	785,970	834.6	91.1	61,625,000
All vegetables	NA	62,342	86,822	98,525	177,049	147,446	NA	49.7	2,045,020
All fruits	NA	43,481	80,707	97,277	121,066	131,498	NA	35.2	3,839,300
Other crops									
Cotton	32,850	15,027	9,213	9,537	15,377	12,030	−63.4	26.1	10,830,300
Peanuts	NA	2,085	9,514	11,940	16,776	13,258	NA	11.0	1,230,000
Potatoes	NA	5,433	7,300	6,581	8,273	13,258	NA	101.5	1,148,800
Trees for maple syrup	10,200	11,965	13,357	12,247	31,340	43,831	329.7	257.9	NA
Fallow land	NA	57,688	116,582	198,650	194,428	271,644	NA	36.7	37,968,749
Total pasture & rangeland	276,300	557,167	1,592,756	2,331,158	2,160,577	2,298,130	731.8	−1.4	473,212,960
Total farmland	914,800	1,776,073	3,045,109	4,054,429	4,815,959	5,383,119	488.4	32.8	843,866,715

Animal	1995	2000	Number of organic animals[1] 2004	2005	2008	2011	% change, 2000-11	% change, 2005-11	Total U.S. animals
Total livestock	NA	56,028	157,253	196,506	475,829	492,353	778.8%	150.6%	167,512,858
Beef cows	NA	13,829	36,662	36,113	63,680	106,181	667.8	194.0	32,834,801
Milk cows	NA	38,196	74,840	87,082	249,766	254,771	567.0	192.6	9,266,574
Other cows[3]	NA	NA	36,598	58,822	144,817	113,114	NA	92.3	54,246,483
Hogs & pigs	NA	1,724	4,883	10,018	10,111	12,373	617.7	23.5	65,110,000
Sheep & lambs	NA	2,279	4,270	4,471	7,455	5,914	159.5	32.3	6,055,000
Total poultry	NA	3,159,050	7,304,566	13,757,270	15,518,075	37,028,242	1,072.1	169.2	9,632,362,000
Layer hens	NA	1,113,746	1,787,901	2,415,056	5,538,011	6,663,278	498.3	175.9	377,492,000
Broilers	NA	1,924,807	4,769,104	10,405,879	9,015,984	28,644,354	1,388.2	175.3	8,882,000,000
Turkeys	NA	9,138	164,292	144,086	398,531	504,315	5,418.9	250.0	262,460,000
Other/ unclassified	NA	111,359	583,269	792,249	565,549	1,216,295	992.2	53.5	110,410,000

NA = Not available. (1) Based on information from USDA-accredited state and private organic certifiers. (2) Total acreage of organic and nonorganic land used for agricultural purposes. (3) Includes breeding stock, replacement heifers, and unclassified cows.

Livestock on Farms in the U.S., 1900-2016

Source: National Agricultural Statistics Service, U.S. Dept. of Agriculture

(in thousands as of Jan. 1, unless otherwise noted)

Year	All cattle[1]	Milk cows	Sheep and lambs	Hogs and pigs[2]	Year	All cattle[1]	Milk cows	Sheep and lambs	Hogs and pigs[2]
1900	59,739	16,544	48,105	51,055	1995	102,755	9,487	8,886	57,150
1910	58,993	19,450	50,239	48,072	2000	98,199	9,183	7,036	59,335
1920	70,400	21,455	40,743	60,159	2005	95,838	9,005	6,135	60,975
1930	61,003	23,032	51,565	55,705	2006	96,702	9,063	6,230	61,449
1940	68,309	24,940	52,107	61,165	2007	97,003	9,132	6,165	62,490
1950	77,963	23,853	29,826	58,937	2008	96,035	9,257	5,950	66,963
1955	96,592	23,462	31,582	50,474	2009	94,521	9,333	5,747	66,768
1960	96,236	19,527	33,170	59,026	2010	93,881	9,086	5,620	65,327
1965	109,000	16,981	25,127	56,106	2011	100,000	9,200	5,480	64,625
1970	112,369	12,091	20,423	57,046	2012	90,769	9,230	5,365	66,361
1975	132,028	11,220	14,515	54,693	2013	89,300	9,218	5,335	66,373
1980	111,242	10,758	12,699	67,318	2014	88,526	9,208	5,245	64,775
1985	109,582	10,777	10,716	54,073	2015	89,143	9,307	5,280	66,145
1990	95,816	10,015	11,358	53,788	2016	91,988	9,315	5,320	68,869

(1) For 1970 and on, includes milk cows and heifers that have calved. (2) As of Dec. 1 of preceding year.

Production of Principal U.S. Crops, 1990-2015

Source: National Agricultural Statistics Service, U.S. Dept. of Agriculture

Year	Corn for grain (1,000 bu)	Oats (1,000 bu)	Barley (1,000 bu)	Sorghum for grain (1,000 bu)	All wheat (1,000 bu)	Rye (1,000 bu)	Flaxseed (1,000 bu)	Cotton (upland) (1,000 b)	Cottonseed (1,000 t)
1990	7,934,028	357,654	422,196	573,303	2,729,778	10,176	3,812	15,505.4	5,968.5
1995	7,373,876	162,027	359,562	460,373	2,182,591	10,064	2,211	17,532.2	6,848.7
2000	9,915,051	149,545	318,728	470,526	2,232,460	8,386	10,730	16,799.2	6,435.6
2004	11,807,086	115,695	279,743	453,654	2,158,245	8,255	10,368	22,505.1	8,242.1
2005	11,114,082	114,878	211,896	392,933	2,104,690	7,537	19,695	23,259.7	8,172.1
2006	10,534,868	93,638	180,165	277,538	1,812,036	7,193	11,019	20,822.4	7,347.9
2007	13,037,875	90,430	210,110	497,445	2,051,088	6,311	5,896	18,355.1	6,588.7
2008	12,091,648	89,135	240,193	472,342	2,499,164	7,979	5,716	12,384.5	4,300.3
2009	13,091,862	93,081	227,323	382,983	2,218,061	6,993	7,423	11,787.6	4,148.8
2010	12,446,865	81,190	180,268	345,625	2,206,916	7,431	9,056	17,600.0	6,098.1
2011	12,359,612	53,649	155,780	214,443	1,999,347	6,326	2,791	14,722.0	5,370.0
2012	10,755,111	61,486	218,990	247,742	2,252,307	6,542	5,798	16,534.0	5,666.0
2013	13,828,964	64,642	216,745	392,331	2,134,979	7,626	3,356	12,275.0	4,203.0
2014	14,215,532	70,232	181,542	432,575	2,026,310	7,189	6,368	15,753.0	5,125.0
2015	13,601,198	89,535	214,297	596,751	2,051,752	11,496	10,095	12,508.0	4,153.0

Year	Tobacco (1,000 lb)	All hay (1,000 t)	Beans, dry edible (1,000 cwt)	Peas, dry edible (1,000 cwt)	Peanuts[1] (1,000 lb)	Soybeans[2] (1,000 bu)	Potatoes (1,000 cwt)	Sweet potatoes (1,000 cwt)
1990	1,626,380	146,212	32,379	2,372	3,602,770	1,925,947	402,110	12,594
1995	1,268,538	154,166	30,812	4,765	4,247,455	2,176,814	443,606	12,906
2000	1,052,999	151,921	26,409	3,474	3,265,505	2,757,810	513,621	13,794
2004	881,973	158,247	17,788	11,419	4,288,200	3,123,686	456,041	16,112
2005	645,015	151,017	26,772	14,003	4,869,860	3,063,237	423,926	15,730
2006	727,347	142,336	24,247	13,203	3,464,250	3,188,247	441,348	16,248
2007	787,653	146,901	25,586	16,287	3,672,250	2,667,117	444,875	18,070
2008	800,504	146,270	25,558	12,270	5,162,400	2,967,007	415,055	18,443
2009	822,581	147,700	25,427	17,137	3,691,650	3,359,011	432,601	19,469
2010	718,190	145,624	31,801	14,221	4,156,840	3,329,181	404,273	23,845
2011	598,252	131,216	19,890	5,625	3,658,590	3,093,524	429,647	26,964
2012	762,709	117,072	31,925	11,002	6,753,880	3,042,044	464,970	26,482
2013	723,579	135,002	24,576	15,620	4,173,170	3,357,984	434,652	24,785
2014	876,415	139,923	28,910	17,155	5,188,665	3,927,090	442,170	29,584
2015	711,236	134,388	30,121	18,283	6,213,790	3,929,885	440,498	31,016

Year	Rice (1,000 cwt)	Sugarcane (1,000 t)	Sugar beets (1,000 t)	Pecans[3] (1,000 lb)	Apples (1,000 t)	Grapes (1,000 t)	Peaches (1,000 t)	Oranges[4] (1,000 bx)	Grapefruit[4] (1,000 bx)
1990	156,088	28,136	27,513	205,000	4,828	5,660	1,121	184,415	49,300
1995	173,871	30,944	27,954	268,000	5,293	5,922	1,150	263,605	71,050
2000	190,872	36,114	32,541	209,850	5,291	7,688	1,276	299,760	66,980
2004	232,362	29,013	30,021	185,800	5,220	6,240	1,307	294,620	52,540
2005	223,235	26,606	27,433	280,250	4,853	7,814	1,185	216,500	25,640
2006	193,736	29,564	34,064	207,300	4,912	6,378	1,010	210,750	30,600
2007	198,388	29,969	31,834	387,305	4,545	7,057	1,127	177,280	39,900
2008	203,733	27,603	26,881	202,080	4,817	7,319	1,135	234,376	37,900
2009	219,850	30,432	29,783	302,020	4,853	7,307	1,104	210,709	32,025
2010	243,104	27,360	32,034	293,740	4,646	7,471	1,150	192,835	30,400
2011	184,941	29,224	28,896	269,700	4,713	7,448	1,072	204,949	30,360
2012	199,939	32,227	35,224	302,300	4,496	7,531	968	206,119	27,650
2013	189,953	30,761	32,789	266,330	5,216	8,632	904	189,893	28,950
2014	222,215	30,424	31,285	264,150	5,907	7,884	853	155,977	25,200
2015	192,343	32,549	35,278	254,290	5,002	7,677	847	147,252	20,950

b = bale; bu = bushel; bx = box; cwt = hundred weight; lb = pound; t = ton. **Note:** Some 2015 figures are preliminary estimates. (1) Harvested for nuts. (2) Harvested for beans. (3) Utilized production only. (4) Crop year ending in year cited.

Animal Products: Average Prices Received by U.S. Farmers, 1940-2015

Source: National Agricultural Statistics Service, U.S. Dept. of Agriculture

Figures represent dollars per 100 lb for veal calves, beef cattle, hogs, lambs, milk (wholesale), and sheep; dollars per head for milk cows; cents per lb for broilers, chickens, turkeys, and wool; and cents per dozen for eggs. Weighted calendar year prices for livestock and livestock products other than wool. For 1943-63, wool prices were weighted on marketing year basis. The marketing year was changed in 1964 from a calendar year to a Dec.-Nov. basis for broilers, chickens, eggs, and hogs.

Year	Broilers	Calves (veal)	Cattle (beef)	Chickens (excl. broilers)	Eggs	Hogs	Lambs[1]	Milk	Milk cows	Sheep[1]	Turkeys	Wool
1940	17.3	8.83	7.56	13.0	18.0	5.39	8.10	1.82	61	3.95	15.2	28.4
1950	27.4	26.30	23.30	22.2	36.3	18.00	25.10	3.89	198	11.60	32.8	62.1
1960	16.9	22.90	20.40	12.2	36.1	15.30	17.90	4.21	223	5.61	25.4	42.0
1970	13.6	34.50	27.10	9.1	39.1	22.70	26.40	5.71	332	7.51	22.6	35.4
1980	27.7	76.80	62.40	11.0	56.3	38.00	63.60	13.05	1,190	21.30	41.3	88.1
1990	32.6	95.60	74.60	9.3	70.9	53.70	55.50	13.74	1,160	23.20	39.4	80.0
2000	33.6	104.00	68.60	5.7	61.8	42.30	79.80	12.40	1,340	34.30	40.7	33.0
2003	34.6	102.00	79.70	4.9	73.2	37.20	94.40	12.55	1,340	34.90	36.1	73.0
2004	44.6	119.00	85.80	5.8	71.4	49.30	101.00	16.13	1,580	38.80	42.0	80.0
2005	43.6	135.00	89.70	6.5	54.0	50.20	110.00	15.19	1,770	45.10	44.9	71.0
2006	36.3	133.00	87.20	5.8	58.2	46.00	95.50	12.96	1,730	35.20	47.9	68.0
2007	43.6	119.00	89.90	5.6	88.5	46.60	98.50	19.21	1,830	31.00	52.3	87.0
2008	45.8	110.00	89.10	6.6	109.0	47.00	99.60	18.45	1,950	27.20	56.5	99.0
2009	45.7	105.00	80.30	7.2	81.7	41.60	99.60	12.93	1,390	32.50	50.0	79.0

Year	Broilers	Calves (veal)	Cattle (beef)	Chickens (excl. broilers)	Eggs	Hogs	Lambs[1]	Milk	Milk cows	Sheep[1]	Turkeys	Wool
2010	48.2	117.00	92.20	8.1	85.7	54.10	125.00	16.35	1,330	49.70	61.5	115.0
2011	46.6	142.00	113.00	8.7	95.6	65.30	NA	20.25	1,420	NA	68.2	167.0
2012	50.0	168.00	122.00	8.8	101.1	64.20	NA	18.56	1,430	NA	72.1	153.0
2013	60.6	181.00	125.00	9.5	107.2	67.20	NA	20.12	1,380	NA	66.5	145.0
2014	63.7	261.00	152.00	10.1	122.1	76.50	NA	24.07	1,830	NA	73.5	146.0
2015	53.8	247.00	147.00	10.3	168.0	55.30	NA	17.21	1,990	NA	81.1	145.0

NA = Not available. (1) Prices not calculated after 2010.

Crops: Average Prices Received by U.S. Farmers, 1940-2015

Source: National Agricultural Statistics Service, U.S. Dept. of Agriculture

Figures represent cents per lb for apples, cotton, and peanuts; dollars per bushel for barley, corn, oats, soybeans, and wheat; dollars per 100 lb for potatoes, rice, and sorghum; and dollars per ton for cottonseed and baled hay. Weighted crop year prices. The marketing year is described as follows: apples, June-May; barley, hay, oats, potatoes, and wheat, July-June; cotton, cottonseed, peanuts, and rice, Aug.-July; soybeans, Sept.-Aug.; and corn and sorghum grain, Oct.-Sept.

Year	Apples	Barley	Corn	Cotton-seed	Cotton (upland)*	Hay	Oats	Peanuts	Pota-toes	Rice	Sor-ghum	Soy-beans	Wheat
1940	NA	0.39	0.62	21.70	9.8	9.78	0.30	3.7	0.85	1.80	0.87	0.89	0.67
1950	NA	1.19	1.52	86.60	39.9	21.10	0.79	10.9	1.50	5.09	1.88	2.47	2.00
1960	2.7	0.84	1.00	42.50	30.1	21.70	0.60	10.0	2.00	4.55	1.49	2.13	1.74
1970	6.5	0.97	1.33	56.40	21.9	26.10	0.62	12.8	2.21	5.17	2.04	2.85	1.33
1980	12.1	2.86	3.11	129.00	74.4	71.00	1.79	25.1	6.55	12.80	5.25	7.57	3.91
1990	20.9	2.14	2.28	121.00	67.1	80.60	1.14	34.7	6.08	6.68	3.79	5.74	2.61
2000	17.8	2.11	1.85	105.00	49.8	84.60	1.10	27.4	5.08	5.61	3.37	4.54	2.62
2003	29.4	2.83	2.42	117.00	61.8	85.50	1.48	19.3	5.89	8.08	4.26	7.34	3.40
2004	21.8	2.48	2.06	107.00	41.6	92.00	1.48	18.9	5.67	7.33	3.19	5.74	3.40
2005	24.4	2.53	2.00	96.00	47.7	98.20	1.63	17.3	7.06	7.65	3.33	5.66	3.42
2006	31.7	2.85	3.04	111.00	46.5	110.00	1.87	17.7	7.33	9.96	5.88	6.43	4.26
2007	28.8	4.02	4.20	162.00	59.3	128.00	2.63	20.5	7.51	12.80	7.28	10.10	6.48
2008	23.2	5.37	4.06	223.00	47.8	152.00	3.15	23.0	9.09	16.80	5.72	9.97	6.78
2009	23.1	4.66	3.55	158.00	62.9	108.00	2.02	21.7	8.25	14.40	5.75	9.59	4.87
2010	25.1	3.86	5.18	161.00	81.5	114.00	2.52	22.5	9.20	12.70	8.96	11.30	5.70
2011	30.3	5.35	6.22	260.00	88.3	178.00	3.49	31.8	9.41	14.50	10.70	12.50	7.24
2012	37.1	6.43	6.89	252.00	72.5	191.00	3.89	30.1	8.63	15.10	11.30	14.40	7.77
2013	30.3	6.06	4.46	246.00	77.9	176.00	3.75	24.9	9.71	16.30	7.64	13.00	6.87
2014	25.7	5.30	3.70	194.00	61.3	172.00	3.21	22.0	8.88	13.40	7.20	10.10	5.99
2015[1]	34.2	5.50	3.60	227.00	59.3	151.00	2.20	19.0	8.74	12.90	5.90	8.80	5.00

* = Beginning in 1964, 480-lb net weight bales. NA = Not available. (1) Preliminary data.

World Meat Production, 2000, 2013

Source: UN Food and Agriculture Organization; in thousands of metric tons; ranked by top producers in 2013

Rank	Top beef producers Country	2000	2013	Rank	Top pork producers Country	2000	2013	Rank	Top poultry producers Country	2000	2013
1.	U.S.	12,298	11,698	1.	China[1]	35,694	52,733	1.	U.S.	16,416	20,085
2.	Brazil	6,579	9,675	2.	U.S.	8,597	10,510	2.	China[1]	11,890	18,265
3.	China[1]	4,988	6,730	3.	Germany	3,982	5,494	3.	Brazil	6,125	12,915
4.	Argentina	2,718	2,822	4.	Spain	2,905	3,431	4.	Russia	775	3,463
5.	India	2,237	2,577	5.	Brazil	2,600	3,280	5.	Mexico	1,868	2,846
6.	Australia	1,988	2,318	6.	Vietnam	1,409	3,218	6.	India	904	2,358
7.	Mexico	1,409	1,807	7.	Russia	1,569	2,816	7.	Iran	815	1,967
8.	Pakistan	886	1,646	8.	France	2,312	2,121	8.	Indonesia	818	1,872
9.	Russia	1,894	1,633	9.	Canada	1,640	1,977	9.	Argentina	1,000	1,826
10.	France	1,528	1,400	10.	Poland	1,923	1,745	10.	Turkey	661	1,771
11.	Germany	1,304	1,106	11.	Philippines	1,213	1,681	11.	France	2,221	1,743
12.	Canada	1,263	1,056	12.	Italy	1,479	1,625	12.	UK	1,513	1,662
13.	Turkey	359	870	13.	Denmark	1,625	1,589	13.	Poland	589	1,652
14.	Egypt	544	862	14.	Japan	1,256	1,309	14.	South Africa	821	1,504
15.	Italy	1,153	854	15.	Mexico	1,030	1,284	15.	Thailand	1,149	1,470
16.	South Africa	625	851	16.	Netherlands	1,623	1,282	16.	Germany	790	1,457
17.	Colombia	745	848	17.	Belgium	1,042	1,131	17.	Japan	1,195	1,450
18.	UK	705	847	18.	South Korea	916	1,007	18.	Malaysia	714	1,360
19.	Uzbekistan	390	813	19.	Thailand	693	967	19.	Venezuela	693	1,276
20.	Indonesia	386	586	20.	Taiwan	921	887	20.	Colombia	504	1,276
21.	Spain	651	581	21.	UK	899	833	21.	Canada	1,065	1,254
22.	New Zealand	572	564	22.	Ukraine	676	748	22.	Italy	1,092	1,233
23.	Ireland	577	518	23.	Indonesia	413	743	23.	Peru	542	1,203
24.	Venezuela	429	516	24.	Myanmar	123	621	24.	Spain	987	1,200
25.	Japan	530	508	25.	Chile	261	550	25.	Myanmar	248	1,196
	Africa	4,312	6,084		Africa	769	1,304		Africa	2,955	5,030
	Asia	12,858	17,694		Asia	44,041	64,449		Asia	22,899	38,561
	Central America	1,766	2,264		Central America	1,140	1,464		Central America	2,371	3,703
	Europe	11,768	10,152		Europe	25,377	27,122		Europe	11,866	18,149
	North America	13,561	12,754		North America	10,237	12,487		North America	17,480	21,339
	Oceania	2,581	2,901		Oceania	489	498		Oceania	767	1,297
	South America	11,846	15,618		South America	3,774	5,371		South America	9,733	20,020
	World total	**58,916**	**67,706**		**World total**	**86,036**	**113,035**		**World total**	**68,562**	**108,669**

(1) Not including Hong Kong or Macao.

World Corn, Rice, and Wheat Production, 2000, 2014

Source: UN Food and Agriculture Organization; in millions of metric tons; ranked by top producers in 2014

	Top corn producers				Top rice producers				Top wheat producers		
Rank	Country	2000	2014	Rank	Country	2000	2014	Rank	Country	2000	2014
1.	U.S.	251.9	361.1	1.	China	189.8	208.2	1.	China	99.6	126.2
2.	China	106.2	215.8	2.	India	127.5	157.2	2.	India	76.4	94.5
3.	Brazil	31.9	79.9	3.	Indonesia	51.9	70.8	3.	Russia	34.5	59.7
4.	Argentina	16.8	33.0	4.	Bangladesh	37.6	52.2	4.	U.S.	60.6	55.4
5.	Ukraine	3.8	28.5	5.	Vietnam	32.5	45.0	5.	France	37.4	39.0
6.	India	12.0	23.7	6.	Thailand	25.8	32.6	6.	Canada	26.5	29.3
7.	Mexico	17.6	23.3	7.	Myanmar	21.3	26.4	7.	Germany	21.6	27.8
8.	Indonesia	9.7	19.0	8.	Philippines	12.4	19.0	8.	Pakistan	21.1	26.0
9.	France	16.0	18.5	9.	Brazil	11.1	12.2	9.	Australia	22.1	25.3
10.	South Africa	11.4	15.0	10.	Japan	11.9	10.5	10.	Ukraine	10.2	24.1
11.	Romania	4.9	12.0	11.	U.S.	8.7	10.0	11.	Turkey	21.0	19.0
12.	Canada	7.0	11.5	12.	Cambodia	4.0	9.3	12.	United Kingdom	16.7	16.6
13.	Russia	1.5	11.3	13.	Pakistan	7.2	7.0	13.	Argentina	16.1	13.9
14.	Nigeria	4.1	10.8	14.	Nigeria	3.3	6.7	14.	Kazakhstan	9.1	13.0
15.	Hungary	5.0	9.3	15.	Egypt	6.0	6.0	15.	Poland	8.5	11.6
16.	Italy	10.1	9.2	16.	South Korea	7.2	5.6	16.	Egypt	6.6	9.3
17.	Serbia	NA	8.0	17.	Nepal	4.2	5.0	17.	Iran	8.1	8.7
18.	Philippines	4.5	7.8	18.	Laos	2.2	4.0	18.	Romania	4.5	7.6
19.	Ethiopia	2.7	7.2	19.	Madagascar	2.5	4.0	19.	Italy	7.5	7.1
20.	Tanzania	2.0	6.7	20.	Sri Lanka	2.9	3.4	20.	Uzbekistan	3.5	7.0
21.	Turkey	2.3	6.0	21.	Peru	1.9	2.9	21.	Spain	7.3	6.5
22.	Egypt	6.5	5.8	22.	Malaysia	2.1	2.6	22.	Brazil	1.7	6.3
23.	Vietnam	2.0	5.2	23.	North Korea	1.7	2.6	23.	Czech Republic	4.1	5.4
24.	Germany	3.3	5.1	24.	Tanzania	0.8	2.6	24.	Afghanistan	1.5	5.4
25.	Thailand	4.5	4.8	25.	Iran	2.0	2.6	25.	Bulgaria	2.8	5.3
	Africa	44.3	77.6		Africa	17.5	31.2		Africa	14.3	26.1
	Asia	149.1	304.1		Asia	545.5	667.3		Asia	254.5	315.7
	Central America	20.3	26.9		Central America	1.2	1.3		Central America	3.5	3.7
	Europe	63.5	129.4		Europe	3.2	4.0		Europe	183.6	249.1
	North America	258.8	372.6		North America	8.7	10.0		North America	87.2	84.7
	Oceania	0.6	0.6		Oceania	1.1	0.8		Oceania	22.4	25.7
	South America	55.4	126.1		South America	20.4	24.9		South America	20.2	24.0
	World total	**592.5**	**1,038.3**		**World total**	**598.9**	**741.0**		**World total**	**585.7**	**729.0**

NA = Not available.

Value of U.S. Agricultural Exports and Imports, 1978-2015

Source: Economic Research Service, U.S. Dept. of Agriculture

(in billions of dollars, unless otherwise noted)

Year[1]	Agric. trade surplus	Agric. exports	% of all exports	Agric. imports	% of all imports	Year[1]	Agric. trade surplus	Agric. exports	% of all exports	Agric. imports	% of all imports
1978	$13.4	$27.3	21%	$13.9	8%	1999	$11.8	$49.1	8%	$37.3	4%
1980	23.2	40.5	19	17.3	7	2000	11.9	50.8	7	38.9	3
1983	18.5	34.8	18	16.3	7	2001	13.7	52.7	8	39.0	3
1984	19.1	38.0	18	18.9	6	2002	12.4	53.3	8	41.0	4
1985	11.5	31.2	15	19.7	6	2003	10.3	56.0	9	45.7	4
1986	5.4	26.3	13	20.9	6	2004	9.7	62.4	9	52.7	4
1987	7.2	27.9	12	20.7	5	2005	4.8	62.5	8	57.7	4
1988	14.3	35.3	12	21.0	5	2006	4.6	68.6	8	64.0	3
1989	18.1	39.7	12	21.6	5	2007	12.2	82.2	8	70.1	4
1990	16.6	39.5	11	22.9	5	2008	35.6	114.9	10	79.3	4
1991	16.4	39.3	10	22.9	5	2009	22.9	96.3	10	73.4	5
1992	18.3	43.1	10	24.8	5	2010	29.6	108.5	10	79.0	4
1993	17.7	42.9	10	25.1	4	2011	43.0	137.5	11	94.5	4
1994	19.2	46.2	10	27.0	4	2012	32.5	135.9	10	103.4	5
1995	26.0	56.3	10	30.3	4	2013	37.3	141.1	10	103.9	5
1996	26.8	60.3	10	33.5	4	2014	43.1	152.3	11	109.2	5
1997	21.7	57.3	9	35.7	4	2015	25.7	139.7	10	114.0	5
1998	16.8	53.7	8	36.8	4						

(1) Fiscal year (Oct.-Sept.).

Crop Consumption Per Capita in Selected Nations, 1980-2011

Source: UN Food and Agriculture Organization

(in kilograms per capita per year, unless otherwise noted)

	Corn				Rice				Wheat			
Country	1980	1990	2011	% change, 1980-2011	1980	1990	2011	% change, 1980-2011	1980	1990	2011	% change, 1980-2011
Afghanistan	33	24	3	−92.4%	20	17	16	−16.8%	162	140	162	0.2%
Argentina	6	5	10	65.0	3	6	8	212.0	115	114	103	−9.9
Australia	2	4	5	121.7	8	8	11	42.1	81	70	70	−13.4
Bangladesh	0	0	0	NA	144	159	173	19.7	29	21	17	−39.7
Brazil	22	22	24	9.5	39	41	34	−12.8	50	44	54	7.9
Canada	4	3	19	421.6	3	5	10	185.3	76	78	70	−8.8
China	5	4	7	51.0	76	81	79	4.6	59	77	63	7.7
Congo Republic	5	3	4	−23.4	2	5	20	1,064.7	33	33	40	20.8
Cuba	0	0	24	NA	51	47	64	25.1	78	74	52	−33.5
Egypt	49	57	63	30.2	26	31	40	49.6	129	151	146	13.0
France	2	13	11	533.3	4	4	6	62.9	96	92	106	11.4
Germany	3	6	10	212.9	2	2	3	57.9	69	67	85	24.5
India	8	8	7	−17.5	64	78	72	12.4	45	41	59	31.2
Indonesia	24	29	34	43.5	125	131	133	6.4	10	9	24	142.3
Iran	1	1	3	316.7	30	30	29	−1.7	154	164	152	−1.1
Iraq	0	3	0	NA	31	37	30	−2.9	144	185	140	−3.3
Israel	12	23	17	46.1	6	8	9	53.3	138	124	122	−11.6

Country	Corn 1980	Corn 1990	Corn 2011	Corn % change, 1980-2011	Rice 1980	Rice 1990	Rice 2011	Rice % change, 1980-2011	Wheat 1980	Wheat 1990	Wheat 2011	Wheat % change, 1980-2011
Italy	5	3	4	−16.0%	5	5	5	13.0%	174	149	146	−16.2%
Japan	15	19	11	−24.7	59	53	43	−26.7	44	44	49	11.0
Kenya	114	88	77	−32.4	2	1	10	329.2	20	23	34	70.5
Korea, North	43	56	45	6.3	71	70	75	4.9	32	22	23	−26.3
Korea, South	2	13	13	700.0	138	97	86	−37.8	49	48	52	5.3
Mexico	118	124	116	−1.8	5	4	6	21.3	42	42	34	−20.4
New Zealand	1	3	4	200.0	2	4	7	191.7	78	69	76	−3.2
Nigeria	6	33	31	409.8	15	21	30	104.8	16	3	25	57.1
Pakistan	7	6	14	113.4	23	14	12	−44.9	114	128	114	0.0
Philippines	22	19	31	40.5	97	94	119	22.7	17	20	15	−12.5
Russia	NA	NA	1	NA	NA	NA	5	NA	NA	NA	131	NA
Saudi Arabia	12	13	22	93.9	33	18	37	12.0	88	104	91	3.4
South Africa	120	108	100	−16.5	4	8	17	288.6	56	57	61	7.7
Thailand	5	5	10	117.4	137	114	112	−18.6	4	4	12	195.0
Turkey	9	21	18	110.6	4	7	10	182.9	210	223	174	−17.3
Ukraine	NA	NA	12	NA	NA	NA	4	NA	NA	NA	106	NA
United Arab Emirates	1	1	1	−22.2	43	34	50	16.5	63	65	96	52.5
UK	3	3	3	−9.4	2	3	7	263.2	82	82	97	17.7
U.S.	8	13	13	58.2	4	7	8	92.3	70	81	80	13.2
Venezuela	55	54	57	3.4	21	13	27	28.2	50	51	55	8.5
Vietnam	7	7	11	58.2	128	133	145	13.2	17	3	9	−47.6
Africa	37	41	43	16.7	15	17	23	57.4	48	48	49	3.8
Asia	8	9	10	26.3	76	82	78	2.0	54	61	63	17.0
Central America	107	113	103	−4.6	8	7	10	33.3	38	38	34	−10.6
Europe	4	5	7	94.6	5	4	5	−2.0	118	117	108	−8.5
North America	8	12	13	74.7	4	7	8	102.6	71	81	79	10.9
Oceania	2	4	5	136.8	9	10	13	50.6	79	69	70	−11.2
South America	22	23	26	19.0	30	32	30	0.0	58	53	58	0.2
World per capita consumption	**13**	**15**	**18**	**36.2**	**49**	**54**	**54**	**9.8**	**65**	**68**	**65**	**0.8**

NA = Not available or not applicable. **Note:** All figures are rounded. Percent change based on unrounded raw data.

Meat Consumption Per Capita in Selected Nations, 1980-2011

Source: UN Food and Agriculture Organization

(in kilograms per capita per year, unless otherwise noted)

Country	Beef 1980	Beef 1990	Beef 2011	Beef % change, 1980-2011	Pork 1980	Pork 1990	Pork 2011	Pork % change, 1980-2011	Poultry 1980	Poultry 1990	Poultry 2011	Poultry % change, 1980-2011
Afghanistan	5	7	5	−5.9%	NA	NA	NA	NA	1	1	3	188.9%
Argentina	85	64	55	−35.4	10	4	9	−5.3%	11	11	35	215.2
Australia	53	47	41	−22.8	15	18	23	58.2	21	24	45	116.8
Bangladesh	2	1	1	−13.3	0	0	0	NA	1	1	1	133.3
Brazil	23	28	39	73.8	8	7	13	57.5	10	14	41	302.0
Canada	40	36	30	−26.1	35	28	24	−29.5	22	28	37	67.9
China	0	1	5	1,100.0	12	20	36	200.8	2	3	13	652.9
Congo Republic	4	1	3	−25.0	1	2	3	257.1	2	5	22	1,015.0
Cuba	15	13	6	−58.4	5	10	19	306.4	9	12	17	81.9
Egypt	7	8	13	88.6	0	0	0	NA	4	5	12	205.3
France	33	33	25	−22.3	38	34	34	−10.7	16	21	23	44.4
Germany	23	22	13	−41.7	60	60	54	−11.0	10	11	18	85.6
India	2	2	1	−43.5	0	1	0	−25.0	0	1	2	800.0
Indonesia	2	2	3	38.9	1	3	3	150.0	1	3	7	483.3
Iran	6	6	6	−6.5	0	0	0	NA	6	7	26	346.6
Iraq	5	7	3	−43.5	0	0	0	NA	9	11	14	67.4
Israel	13	14	28	111.5	3	2	3	0.0	35	39	70	97.5
Italy	26	27	22	−17.9	25	32	40	61.0	18	20	18	0.0
Japan	5	8	9	80.0	14	15	21	51.9	10	14	19	89.1
Kenya	12	9	11	−7.6	0	0	0	NA	2	1	1	−75.0
Korea, North	2	2	1	−50.0	10	11	5	−51.6	2	3	2	−19.0
Korea, South	3	6	15	461.5	8	13	31	296.2	3	6	16	556.0
Mexico	11	14	16	50.9	18	9	14	−22.5	6	10	30	368.3
New Zealand	57	39	48	−17.1	12	14	19	68.7	10	17	36	269.8
Nigeria	5	2	2	−57.4	1	1	2	200.0	2	2	2	0.0
Pakistan	5	6	9	79.2	0	0	0	NA	1	2	4	633.3
Philippines	3	2	4	57.1	9	12	18	110.3	5	4	11	129.2
Russia	NA	NA	16	NA	NA	NA	23	NA	NA	NA	23	NA
Saudi Arabia	6	5	6	−1.6	NA	NA	NA	NA	24	29	48	100.8
South Africa	20	17	16	−19.8	3	4	5	50.0	8	15	35	346.2
Thailand	6	6	3	−55.2	6	6	13	128.6	7	9	12	78.3
Turkey	3	7	10	221.9	0	0	0	NA	6	8	19	233.3
Ukraine	NA	NA	9	NA	NA	NA	18	NA	NA	NA	22	NA
United Arab Emirates	14	13	5	−63.1	NA	NA	NA	NA	43	39	39	−9.2
UK	23	21	19	−17.2	26	25	27	1.1	14	19	31	126.5
U.S.	47	43	37	−21.8	33	28	28	−15.5	26	39	51	94.7
Venezuela	22	18	20	−8.6	6	5	7	18.3	17	13	45	159.8
Vietnam	2	2	7	278.9	5	10	34	549.1	2	3	16	766.7
Africa	7	6	6	−12.5	1	1	1	100.0	3	3	6	148.0
Asia	2	3	4	120.0	6	9	15	144.3	2	3	9	327.3
Central America	10	12	14	35.6	14	8	12	−17.6	6	9	27	365.5
Europe	23	25	15	−35.0	32	35	35	7.8	12	15	22	85.5
North America	47	43	36	−22.3	33	28	28	−16.6	26	38	50	92.3
Oceania	50	43	39	−22.1	14	17	22	58.1	18	22	42	135.2
South America	28	27	31	11.3	7	6	11	50.0	9	12	35	275.0
World per capita consumption	**11**	**10**	**9**	**−11.3**	**12**	**13**	**16**	**31.4**	**6**	**8**	**14**	**148.3**

NA = Not available or not applicable. **Note:** All figures are rounded. Percent change based on unrounded raw data.

World Capture of Fish, Crustaceans, and Mollusks, 2005-14

Source: UN Food and Agriculture Organization
(in thousands of metric tons; ranked by 2014 captures)

Country	2005	2007	2010	2013	2014	Country	2005	2007	2010	2013	2014
China	14,589	14,659	15,415	16,275	17,107	Chile	4,328	3,819	2,680	1,771	2,175
Indonesia	4,685	5,030	5,374	6,038	6,437	Thailand	2,814	2,305	1,811	1,825	1,770
U.S.	4,893	4,768	4,387	5,142	4,976	South Korea ..	1,647	1,870	1,722	1,593	1,728
India	3,691	3,859	4,689	4,645	4,719	Bangladesh...	1,334	1,494	1,727	1,550	1,591
Russia.......	3,198	3,476	4,070	4,348	4,226	Mexico	1,319	1,470	1,527	1,616	1,520
Myanmar.....	1,732	2,244	3,063	3,787	4,083	Malaysia	1,214	1,386	1,433	1,489	1,464
Japan	4,334	4,298	4,067	3,656	3,661	Morocco	1,026	879	1,136	1,253	1,365
Peru	9,388	7,211	4,302	5,854	3,573	Spain	855	820	975	987	1,110
Vietnam	1,988	2,075	2,414	2,804	2,919	Iceland	1,665	1,399	1,061	1,367	1,077
Philippines ...	2,270	2,500	2,612	2,332	2,351	**World total[1]** ..	**92,474**	**90,793**	**89,130**	**92,669**	**93,445**
Norway	2,393	2,380	2,680	2,079	2,302						

(1) Includes nations not shown.

World Aquaculture Production, 2005-14

Source: UN Food and Agriculture Organization; ranked by 2014 production volume

Country	Metric tons (thous.) 2005	2007	2010	2013	2014	Value (mil) 2005	2007	2010	2013	2014
China	28,121	31,415	36,734	43,550	45,469	$30,204	$44,756	$58,822	$70,037	$73,286
India	2,967	3,112	3,786	4,551	4,881	3,763	4,984	7,339	10,358	10,768
Indonesia	1,197	1,393	2,305	3,974	4,254	1,999	2,462	4,895	8,992	8,888
Vietnam	1,437	2,085	2,671	3,207	3,397	2,931	4,028	6,312	6,804	7,173
Bangladesh.........	882	946	1,309	1,860	1,957	1,246	1,523	2,840	4,414	4,853
Norway	662	842	1,020	1,248	1,332	2,136	2,999	5,087	6,897	7,068
Chile	724	780	701	1,033	1,215	3,229	4,866	3,753	7,525	10,276
Egypt	540	636	920	1,098	1,137	792	1,193	1,680	2,089	2,025
Myanmar............	485	605	851	929	962	959	778	956	1,715	1,868
Thailand	1,304	1,370	1,286	998	935	1,741	2,139	2,817	2,960	2,636
Philippines	557	710	745	815	788	794	1,234	1,563	1,977	1,880
Japan	746	770	718	609	657	3,012	2,995	4,091	3,642	3,633
Brazil...............	258	289	411	477	562	445	595	1,307	1,322	1,532
South Korea	437	606	476	402	480	1,195	1,577	1,482	1,455	1,660
U.S.	514	526	497	421	426	896	957	1,023	1,166	1,143
Ecuador	139	171	273	332	368	610	763	1,250	1,763	1,961
Taiwan	305	316	310	344	340	969	991	1,116	1,326	1,369
Iran	112	159	220	325	320	320	449	638	957	967
Nigeria	56	85	201	279	313	159	241	576	799	894
Spain	219	282	252	224	282	308	391	520	509	562
World total[1]	**44,298**	**49,941**	**58,973**	**70,261**	**73,784**	**65,754**	**90,205**	**119,854**	**151,758**	**160,152**

Note: Does not include production of aquatic plants or marine mammals. (1) Includes nations not shown.

U.S. Commercial Landings of Fish and Shellfish, 1990-2014

Source: Natl. Marine Fisheries Service, Natl. Oceanic and Atmospheric Admin., U.S. Dept. of Commerce

Year	Landings for human food Weight (mil lbs)	Value (mil)	Landings for industrial purposes[1] Weight (mil lbs)	Value (mil)	Total Weight (mil lbs)	Value (mil)
1990	7,041	$3,366	2,363	$156	9,404	$3,522
1995	7,667	3,625	2,121	145	9,788	3,770
2000	6,912	3,398	2,157	152	9,069	3,550
2002	7,205	2,940	2,192	152	9,397	3,092
2003	7,521	3,185	1,986	157	9,507	3,347
2004	7,794	3,611	1,889	145	9,683	3,756
2005	7,997	3,825	1,710	117	9,707	3,942
2006	7,842	3,911	1,641	113	9,483	4,024
2007	7,490	4,015	1,819	177	9,309	4,192
2008	6,633	4,231	1,692	152	8,325	4,383
2009	6,198	3,733	1,833	158	8,031	3,891
2010	6,526	4,356	1,705	164	8,231	4,520
2011	7,909	5,108	1,949	181	9,858	5,289
2012	7,477	4,923	2,157	180	9,634	5,103
2013	8,043	5,268	1,827	198	9,870	5,466
2014	7,828	5,256	1,658	192	9,486	5,448

Note: Does not include products of aquaculture, except oysters and clams. Landings reported in round (live) weight for all items except univalve and bivalve mollusks (e.g., clams, oysters, and scallops), which are reported in weight of meats (excluding the shell). (1) Processed into meal, oil, solubles, and shell products or used as bait or animal food.

U.S. Domestic Landings by Region, 2005, 2014

Source: Natl. Marine Fisheries Service, Natl. Oceanic and Atmospheric Admin., U.S. Dept. of Commerce

Region	2005 Weight (thous. lbs)	Value (thous.)	2014[1] Weight (thous. lbs)	Value (thous.)
New England	684,090	$971,663	642,669	$1,999,490
Middle Atlantic[2].......................	199,937	221,505	601,105	470,802
Chesapeake[2]	508,953	218,933	NA	NA
South Atlantic	122,422	125,117	103,756	184,788
Gulf.................................	1,196,355	620,987	1,204,765	989,399
Pacific Coast (incl. Alaska)	6,950,647	1,700,927	6,884,305	2,480,874
Great Lakes[3].........................	16,732	12,434	15,878	21,015
Hawaii...............................	28,139	70,811	33,474	101,249
Total	**9,707,275**	**3,942,376**	**9,485,952**	**5,447,617**

NA = Not available. **Note:** Landings reported in round (live) weight for all items except univalve and bivalve mollusks (e.g., clams, oysters, scallops), which are reported in weight of meats (excluding the shell). (1) Preliminary. (2) Chesapeake Region states (Maryland and Virginia) included with Middle Atlantic in 2014. (3) Data for the Great Lakes states lag by one year (i.e., figures are for 2004 and 2013).

EMPLOYMENT

Employment and Unemployment in the U.S., 1900-2015
Source: Bureau of Labor Statistics, U.S. Dept. of Labor
(civilian labor force, persons 16 years of age and older unless otherwise noted; annual averages, in thousands)

Year	Employed	Unemployed Number	Unemployed Rate	Year	Employed	Unemployed Number	Unemployed Rate	Year	Employed	Unemployed Number	Unemployed Rate
1900[1] ...	26,956	1,420	5.0%	1988	114,968	6,701	5.5%	2002	136,485	8,378	5.8%
1910[1] ...	34,599	2,150	5.9	1989	117,342	6,528	5.3	2003	137,736	8,774	6.0
1920[1] ...	39,208	2,132	5.2	1990	118,793	7,047	5.6	2004	139,252	8,149	5.5
1930[1] ...	44,183	4,340	8.9	1991	117,718	8,628	6.8	2005	141,730	7,591	5.1
1940[1] ...	47,520	8,120	14.6	1992	118,492	9,613	7.5	2006	144,427	7,001	4.6
1950	58,918	3,288	5.3	1993	120,259	8,940	6.9	2007	146,047	7,078	4.6
1955	62,170	2,852	4.4	1994	123,060	7,996	6.1	2008	145,362	8,924	5.8
1960	65,778	3,852	5.5	1995	124,900	7,404	5.6	2009	139,877	14,265	9.3
1965	71,088	3,366	4.5	1996	126,708	7,236	5.4	2010	139,064	14,825	9.6
1970	78,678	4,093	4.9	1997	129,558	6,739	4.9	2011	139,869	13,747	8.9
1975	85,846	7,929	8.5	1998	131,463	6,210	4.5	2012	142,469	12,506	8.1
1980	99,303	7,637	7.1	1999	133,488	5,880	4.2	2013	143,929	11,460	7.4
1985	107,150	8,312	7.2	2000	136,891	5,692	4.0	2014	146,305	9,617	6.2
1986	109,597	8,237	7.0	2001	136,933	6,801	4.7	2015	148,834	8,296	5.3
1987	112,440	7,425	6.2								

Note: Because of revisions in population controls, data for a given year may not be strictly comparable to other years. **Other unemployment rates (1905-45)**, persons 14 years of age and older: 1905, 4.3%; 1915, 8.5%; 1925, 3.2%; 1935, 20.3%; 1936, 16.9%; 1937, 14.3%; 1938, 19.0%; 1939, 17.2%; 1945, 1.9%. (1) Persons 14 years of age and older.

Unemployment Rate and Benefits Data by State, 2015
Source: Employment and Training Admin., U.S. Dept. of Labor; state programs only

State/ terr.	Unemployment rate	Monetarily eligible claimants	Number of first payments	Number of final payments	Initial claims	Benefits paid	Average weekly benefit	Employers subject to state law
AL	6.1%	104,330	65,204	23,843	181,795	$193,011,490	$215.94	86,137
AK	6.5	43,010	26,792	11,863	64,475	105,349,193	266.30	18,139
AZ	6.1	130,905	82,567	36,051	219,781	274,771,314	222.61	125,363
AR	5.2	91,599	57,641	19,908	151,880	199,804,902	303.14	68,642
CA	6.2	940,459	1,012,256	505,194	2,418,356	5,002,422,432	306.37	1,279,051
CO	3.9	119,666	92,374	41,656	146,094	498,053,035	389.86	159,983
CT	5.6	133,673	120,404	42,399	204,683	610,525,454	356.20	100,179
DE	4.9	27,684	16,493	6,271	43,015	70,494,507	252.81	27,596
DC	6.9	24,033	21,295	9,334	18,556	101,891,871	297.74	32,064
FL	5.4	252,818	194,170	104,684	458,450	506,254,750	235.35	506,005
GA	5.9	246,483	165,308	64,847	404,746	381,811,169	275.69	218,415
HI	3.6	30,682	22,974	6,862	67,162	134,765,140	441.54	31,198
ID	4.1	38,254	30,082	9,102	74,067	95,331,101	298.13	49,112
IL	5.9	348,270	326,431	109,554	607,139	1,668,096,568	339.23	312,293
IN	4.8	141,671	97,213	25,146	211,511	323,850,368	368.95	126,836
IA	3.7	112,413	92,606	23,634	164,567	383,492,606	368.95	76,595
KS	4.2	96,713	59,694	27,000	130,769	182,792,774	364.66	70,484
KY	5.4	119,227	59,899	20,367	194,307	278,840,929	305.78	91,495
LA	6.3	114,046	57,062	18,594	138,027	225,657,589	214.95	98,636
ME	4.4	36,217	30,004	8,928	55,919	109,257,406	299.84	42,818
MD	5.2	135,837	107,255	41,591	215,970	518,453,443	328.69	141,129
MA	5.0	215,298	189,738	71,899	314,714	1,337,302,685	452.77	207,248
MI	5.4	306,756	242,223	84,571	477,888	865,000,455	286.90	209,836
MN	3.7	167,763	122,686	40,541	233,172	665,030,239	409.14	129,683
MS	6.5	59,250	36,346	11,180	98,439	94,002,427	203.11	54,763
MO	5.0	160,109	103,654	39,631	291,156	316,356,339	247.30	150,049
MT	4.1	34,714	24,082	8,301	57,307	94,026,072	314.47	38,996
NE	3.0	38,187	23,732	8,133	58,381	80,684,593	300.18	58,104
NV	6.7	96,810	71,275	30,353	154,860	343,438,284	320.56	63,185
NH	3.4	25,929	17,437	3,471	40,648	67,164,110	303.54	41,371
NJ	5.6	332,822	294,169	130,692	519,127	1,864,448,628	410.17	230,772
NM	6.6	45,842	33,423	13,051	63,034	156,162,543	320.89	46,359
NY	5.3	632,995	459,372	161,501	1,012,836	2,156,162,570	316.83	519,633
NC	5.7	188,502	108,235	58,511	235,638	266,314,827	235.81	206,176
ND	2.7	37,320	27,636	10,337	33,547	171,448,825	498.47	26,180
OH	4.9	277,535	196,409	53,112	421,790	897,885,679	341.82	221,481
OK	4.2	87,145	59,805	24,482	109,009	330,258,629	368.67	86,839
OR	5.7	142,069	94,121	32,133	267,292	510,365,347	348.18	119,095
PA	5.1	444,669	391,726	114,367	1,030,468	1,993,415,473	376.30	303,483
PR	12.0	82,672	70,241	35,663	105,484	151,142,486	117.60	48,995
RI	6.0	38,529	31,551	10,081	66,960	154,006,422	333.52	33,574
SC	6.0	114,793	56,329	19,203	177,908	166,876,468	252.34	104,846
SD	3.1	10,852	5,932	873	13,863	24,858,981	302.04	26,874
TN	5.8	134,504	94,077	32,998	227,188	284,129,956	225.63	117,710
TX	4.5	676,381	482,925	200,362	888,703	2,565,147,952	384.52	509,791
UT	3.5	57,079	37,992	10,672	73,522	152,608,391	369.65	75,287
VT	3.7	21,140	16,928	3,043	34,388	63,747,366	328.51	21,908
VA	4.4	151,293	85,956	37,844	195,881	375,786,642	299.28	207,937
VI	NA	2,212	2,177	1,077	2,525	9,867,845	329.22	3,522
WA	5.7	217,627	162,883	46,560	380,404	891,604,680	416.77	219,794
WV	6.7	62,521	51,734	14,539	78,135	221,970,034	300.67	35,907
WI	4.6	225,922	152,641	37,457	427,128	527,504,474	295.97	137,072
WY	4.2	22,746	16,092	4,832	26,616	86,397,204	401.65	22,531
U.S.	**5.3**	**8,399,976**	**6,501,251**	**2,508,298**	**14,289,280**	**32,033,733,268**	**328.65**	**7,941,164**

NA = Not available.

U.S. Unemployment Duration by Industry and Occupation, 2015
Source: Bureau of Labor Statistics, U.S. Dept. of Labor

Occupation	Total	Number of unemployed persons (thous.) Less than 5 weeks	5 to 14 weeks	15 to 26 weeks	27 weeks and over	Weeks of unemployment Average (mean) duration	Median duration
Management, professional, and related.................	1,504	426	416	220	442	32.3	11.8
Management, business, and financial operations	602	144	160	97	202	36.4	14.3
Professional and related	902	282	256	123	241	29.5	10.2
Service	1,855	563	504	275	513	28.3	11.1
Sales and office	1,792	492	492	288	521	29.5	12.3
Sales and related............................	909	249	252	142	267	29.2	12.2
Office and administrative support.................	883	243	240	146	254	29.9	12.4
Natural resources, construction, and maintenance	1,058	329	293	171	265	27.4	10.7
Farming, fishing, and forestry.....................	132	48	44	19	21	18.6	8.6
Construction and extraction.......................	701	221	190	117	173	27.5	10.8
Installation, maintenance, and repair................	225	60	59	35	71	32.1	13.0
Production, transportation, and material moving...........	1,182	342	332	176	331	27.9	11.5
Production	513	145	144	76	149	30.0	11.8
Transportation and material moving	668	197	188	100	183	26.3	11.2
Industry[1]							
Agriculture and related industries.................	161	54	53	27	27	18.3	9.4
Mining, quarrying, and oil and gas extraction	87	31	28	12	15	18.2	8.4
Construction.....................................	636	196	177	103	161	27.4	10.7
Manufacturing....................................	683	189	183	110	202	31.5	12.7
Durable goods	413	115	109	67	123	32.4	12.8
Nondurable goods	270	74	75	43	79	30.1	12.4
Wholesale and retail trade	1,146	308	317	185	336	29.9	12.6
Transportation and utilities.........................	315	95	85	46	90	25.8	11.4
Information	111	30	27	13	40	41.3	13.3
Financial activities	255	59	66	48	82	33.7	15.2
Professional and business services..................	915	239	247	148	281	31.0	13.0
Education and health services......................	1,074	325	306	153	289	29.2	10.4
Leisure and hospitality	1,132	369	323	159	281	25.7	9.9
Other services	342	96	90	50	105	31.6	12.5
Public administration	145	36	35	26	47	34.8	15.0
No previous work experience......................	879	242	259	130	248	28.5	11.8
Total unemployed[2]............................	**8,296**	**2,399**	**2,302**	**1,267**	**2,328**	**29.2**	**11.6**

Note: Persons 16 years of age and older. (1) Includes wage and salary workers only. (2) Includes persons whose last job was in the U.S. Armed Forces.

Persons Not in the U.S. Labor Force, 2015
Source: Bureau of Labor Statistics, U.S. Dept. of Labor

The Labor Dept.'s unemployment rate, based on its household survey, shows the number of people out of work as a percentage of adults age 16 and older in the labor force. That rate excludes the millions of adults considered to be not in the labor force.

(in thousands)

	Number	Age in years 16 to 24	25 to 54	55 and over	Sex Men	Women
Total not in the labor force	93,671	17,367	23,957	52,347	37,481	56,190
Do not want a job now[1]...............	87,589	15,525	21,344	50,719	34,681	52,907
Want a job[1]........................	6,082	1,842	2,612	1,628	2,799	3,283
Did not search for work in previous year	3,454	1,030	1,357	1,067	1,507	1,947
Searched in previous year but not previous four weeks[2]	2,628	812	1,256	561	1,292	1,336
Not available to work now	673	287	307	79	277	395
Available to work now	1,956	525	949	482	1,015	941
Reason not currently looking[3]						
Discouraged over job prospects[4]........	664	159	316	189	404	261
Reasons other than discouragement.....	1,291	366	632	293	611	680
Family responsibilities	216	23	138	55	64	153
In school or training	212	154	51	7	106	107
Ill health or disability..............	168	16	77	75	84	84
Other[5]........................	695	174	366	155	358	337

(1) Includes some persons who are not asked if they want a job. (2) Persons who had a job in the prior 12 months must have searched since the end of that job to be considered unemployed. (3) Of those available to work now. (4) Includes believing no work is available, not being able to find work, lacking necessary schooling or training, thought of as too young or old by employers, and other types of discrimination. (5) Includes those who did not actively look for work in the prior four weeks for such reasons as child-care and transportation problems, as well as a small number for which reason for nonparticipation was not ascertained.

U.S. Displaced Workers, 2016
Source: Bureau of Labor Statistics, U.S. Dept. of Labor

	Number (thous.)	Reason for job loss (% distrib.) Plant or company closed down or moved	Insufficient work	Position or shift abolished
Total displaced workers...........	3,191	37.4%	25.6%	37.1%
Age: 20 to 24 years...............	71	NA	NA	NA
25 to 54 years...............	2,023	37.4	27.4	35.2
55 to 64 years...............	853	36.4	22.8	40.8
65 years and over............	245	33.9	23.7	42.4
Sex: Men.........................	1,773	37.2	29.0	33.8
Women....................	1,419	37.5	21.3	41.1
Race: White	2,573	37.2	25.9	36.9
Black......................	394	35.4	27.7	36.9
Asian......................	145	45.9	21.3	32.8
Hispanic or Latino...........	423	45.3	24.4	30.3

NA = Not available. **Note:** As of Jan. 2016. Displaced workers are persons age 20 or older who lost or left jobs they had held for at least three years. Workers in this table were displaced between Jan. 2013 and Dec. 2015. Hispanic or Latino persons may be of any race.

U.S. Unemployment Rates by Selected Characteristics, 1995-2016

Source: Bureau of Labor Statistics, U.S. Dept. of Labor

	1995	2000	2005	2010	2012	2013	2014	2015 Jan.	2015 June	2015 Yr.	2016 Jan.	2016 June
Total (all civilian workers)	5.6%	4.0%	5.1%	9.6%	8.1%	7.4%	6.2%	6.1%	5.5%	5.3%	5.3%	5.1%
Men, 20 years and older	4.8	3.3	4.4	9.8	7.5	7.0	5.7	6.0	4.6	4.9	5.1	4.3
Women, 20 years and older	4.9	3.6	4.6	8.0	7.3	6.5	5.6	5.2	4.9	4.8	4.7	4.6
Both sexes, 16 to 19 years	17.3	13.1	16.6	25.9	24.0	22.9	19.6	19.2	21.4	16.9	16.5	19.2
White	4.9	3.5	4.4	8.7	7.2	6.5	5.3	5.3	4.8	4.6	4.7	4.5
Black	10.4	7.6	10.0	16.0	13.8	13.1	11.3	10.7	9.8	9.6	9.1	8.8
Asian	—	3.6	4.0	7.5	5.9	5.2	5.0	4.1	4.1	3.8	3.7	3.7
Hispanic or Latino (any race)	9.3	5.7	6.0	12.5	10.3	9.1	7.4	7.5	6.8	6.6	6.6	6.0
Married men, spouse present	3.3	—	—	6.8	4.9	4.3	3.4	2.9	2.8	2.8	2.6	2.6
Married women, spouse present	3.9	—	—	5.9	5.3	4.6	3.8	3.3	3.2	3.1	3.0	3.2
Women who maintain families, spouse absent	8.0	5.9	7.8	12.3	11.4	10.2	8.6	8.1	7.8	7.4	7.1	7.3
Occupation												
Management, professional, and related	2.4	1.8	2.3	4.7	4.1	3.6	3.1	2.9	2.9	2.5	2.3	2.8
Service	7.5	5.2	6.4	10.3	9.1	8.6	7.3	7.6	6.3	6.7	6.4	5.7
Sales and office	5.0	3.8	4.8	9.0	7.7	7.2	6.0	5.5	5.0	5.1	5.3	4.4
Natural resources, constr., and maintenance	—	5.3	6.5	16.1	11.5	9.8	8.0	9.9	6.2	7.2	8.6	5.5
Production, transp., and material moving	—	5.1	6.5	12.8	9.8	9.1	7.4	7.2	6.0	6.3	6.9	5.9
Industry												
Nonagricultural private wage and salary workers	5.8	4.1	5.2	9.9	7.9	7.2	5.9	6.0	5.0	5.1	5.2	4.4
Mining	5.2	4.4	3.1	9.4	6.0	5.8	4.7	6.0	8.9	8.6	8.1	11.5
Construction	11.5	6.2	7.4	20.6	13.9	11.3	8.9	9.8	6.3	7.3	8.5	4.6
Manufacturing	4.9	3.5	4.9	10.6	7.3	6.6	4.9	5.2	3.9	4.3	4.3	3.7
Durable goods	4.4	3.2	4.6	11.2	7.2	6.3	4.7	4.9	3.6	4.1	4.4	3.8
Nondurable goods	5.7	4.0	5.3	9.6	7.5	7.1	5.2	5.8	4.4	4.6	4.2	3.4
Wholesale and retail trade	6.5	4.3	5.4	9.5	8.1	7.3	6.1	6.2	5.7	5.5	6.0	4.7
Transportation and utilities	4.5	3.4	4.1	8.4	6.9	6.6	5.7	5.2	4.5	4.4	5.1	4.0
Information	—	3.2	5.0	9.7	7.6	6.2	5.2	4.4	3.9	3.9	4.6	4.7
Financial activities	3.3	2.4	2.9	6.9	5.1	4.5	4.0	3.0	2.5	2.6	3.1	2.2
Professional and business services	—	4.8	6.2	10.8	8.9	8.3	6.9	6.8	5.2	5.6	5.6	4.7
Education and health services	—	2.5	3.4	5.8	5.5	4.9	4.2	4.0	4.2	3.6	3.2	3.6
Leisure and hospitality	—	6.6	7.8	12.2	10.4	10.0	8.6	9.4	7.5	7.9	7.7	6.6
Other services	8.4	3.9	4.8	8.5	7.2	6.9	5.7	6.1	4.3	5.2	5.2	5.4
Agriculture and related private wage and salary workers	11.1	9.0	8.3	13.9	12.4	10.1	9.4	13.3	7.6	9.4	13.0	8.6
Government workers	2.9	2.1	2.6	4.4	4.3	4.0	3.2	2.8	3.3	2.7	2.4	3.6
Self-employed and unpaid family workers	—	2.1	2.7	5.9	5.4	5.3	4.4	4.7	3.6	3.9	4.0	3.8

— = Not available. **Note:** All monthly rates are unadjusted, except for married men and women, which are seasonally adjusted.

U.S. Workers by Industry and Type, 2005, 2015

Source: Bureau of Labor Statistics, U.S. Dept. of Labor

(in thousands)

	2005 Total employed	2005 Private industry workers	2005 Govt. workers	2005 Self-employed workers	2015 Total employed	2015 Private industry workers[1]	2015 Govt. workers	2015 Self-employed workers
Mining[2]	624	609	4	11	917	895	1	21
Construction	11,197	8,895	458	1,830	9,935	7,938	385	1,603
Manufacturing	16,253	15,839	80	327	15,338	14,962	81	288
Durable goods	10,333	10,057	62	209	9,709	9,472	65	169
Nondurable goods	5,919	5,782	18	118	5,629	5,489	17	119
Wholesale and retail trade	21,405	20,031	102	1,251	20,320	19,333	101	870
Wholesale trade	4,579	4,354	10	213	3,635	3,491	7	134
Retail trade	16,825	15,678	92	1,038	16,686	15,841	94	736
Transportation and utilities	7,360	5,377	1,537	442	7,726	6,019	1,307	397
Transportation and warehousing	6,184	4,543	1,195	442	6,459	5,082	977	397
Utilities	1,176	834	342	—	1,267	937	330	—
Information	3,402	3,083	193	126	2,988	2,660	167	161
Financial activities	10,203	9,187	228	785	10,087	9,238	218	625
Finance and insurance	7,035	6,584	140	309	7,081	6,702	146	232
Real estate and rental and leasing	3,168	2,603	88	476	3,005	2,536	72	393
Professional and business services	14,294	11,923	402	1,957	17,409	14,984	473	1,944
Professional and technical services	8,584	7,208	218	1,154	10,625	9,275	283	1,065
Management, administrative, and waste services	5,709	4,715	184	803	6,784	5,709	190	879
Education and health services	29,174	17,752	10,340	1,071	33,678	22,127	10,475	1,069
Educational services	12,264	3,379	8,688	197	13,601	4,630	8,765	207
Health care and social assistance	16,910	14,373	1,652	874	20,077	17,497	1,710	862
Hospitals	5,719	4,959	747	13	6,698	5,971	716	11
Health services, except hospitals	8,332	7,508	449	368	10,165	9,263	472	424
Social assistance	2,860	1,907	456	493	3,213	2,263	522	427
Leisure and hospitality	12,071	10,931	453	674	13,821	12,687	429	698
Arts, entertainment, and recreation	2,765	1,951	395	415	3,184	2,380	360	443
Accommodation and food services	9,306	8,981	57	259	10,637	10,307	69	255
Other services	7,020	5,946	31	1,036	7,264	6,236	35	988
Other services, except private households	6,208	5,134	31	1,036	6,466	5,438	35	988
Private households	812	812	—	—	798	798	—	—
Public administration	6,530	—	6,530	—	6,928	—	6,928	—

— = No data or data that do not meet publication criteria. (1) Includes self-employed workers whose businesses are incorporated. (2) For 2015, includes quarrying and oil and gas extraction.

U.S. Occupations Projected to Grow Most, 2014-24

Source: Employment Projections Program, Bureau of Labor Statistics, U.S. Dept. of Labor
(numbers in thousands)

Occupation	Employment 2014	Employment 2024	Change, 2014-24 Number	Change, 2014-24 Percent	Median annual wage, 2015
Total, all occupations.............................	150,539.9	160,328.8	9,788.9	6.5%	$36,200
Personal care aides	1,768.4	2,226.5	458.1	25.9	20,980
Registered nurses...............................	2,751.0	3,190.3	439.3	16.0	67,490
Home health aides	913.5	1,261.9	348.4	38.1	21,920
Food preparation/serving, including fast food.............	3,159.7	3,503.2	343.5	10.9	18,910
Retail salespersons	4,624.9	4,939.1	314.2	6.8	21,780
Nursing assistants	1,492.1	1,754.1	262.0	17.6	25,710
Customer service representatives	2,581.8	2,834.8	252.9	9.8	31,720
Cooks, restaurant	1,109.7	1,268.7	158.9	14.3	23,100
General and operations managers..................	2,124.1	2,275.2	151.1	7.1	97,730
Construction laborers	1,159.1	1,306.5	147.4	12.7	31,910
Accountants and auditors.........................	1,332.7	1,475.1	142.4	10.7	67,190
Medical assistants	591.3	730.2	138.9	23.5	30,590
Janitors and cleaners, except maids and housekeepers	2,360.6	2,496.9	136.3	5.8	23,440
Software developers, applications	718.4	853.7	135.3	18.8	98,260
Laborers and freight, stock, and material movers, hand......	2,441.3	2,566.4	125.1	5.1	25,010
Supervisors of office and admin. support workers	1,466.1	1,587.3	121.2	8.3	52,630
Computer systems analysts	567.8	686.3	118.6	20.9	85,800
Licensed practical and vocational nurses...............	719.9	837.2	117.3	16.3	43,170
Maids and housekeeping cleaners....................	1,457.7	1,569.4	111.7	7.7	20,740

U.S. Occupations Projected to Decline Most, 2014-24

Source: Employment Projections Program, Bureau of Labor Statistics, U.S. Dept. of Labor
(numbers in thousands)

Occupation	Employment 2014	Employment 2024	Change, 2014-24 Number	Change, 2014-24 Percent	Median annual wage, 2015
Total, all occupations	150,539.9	160,328.8	9,788.9	6.5%	$36,200
Bookkeeping, accounting, and auditing clerks	1,760.3	1,611.5	−148.7	−8.4	37,250
Cooks, fast food	524.4	444.0	−80.4	−15.3	19,080
Postal service mail carriers.........................	297.4	219.4	−78.1	−26.2	58,280
Executive secretaries and executive administrative assistants	776.6	732.0	−44.6	−5.7	53,370
Farmworkers and laborers, crop, nursery, and greenhouse ...	470.2	427.3	−42.9	−9.1	19,770
Sewing machine operators...........................	153.9	112.2	−41.7	−27.1	22,550
Tellers..	520.5	480.5	−40.0	−7.7	26,410
Postal service mail sorters, processors, and processing machine operators	117.6	78.0	−39.7	−33.7	56,740
Cutting, punching, and press machine setters, operators, and tenders, metal and plastic.........................	192.2	152.7	−39.5	−20.6	31,280
Switchboard operators, including answering service	112.4	75.4	−37.0	−32.9	27,440
Molding, coremaking, and casting machine setters, operators, and tenders, metal and plastic	129.5	97.2	−32.3	−25.0	29,340
Computer programmers	328.6	302.2	−26.5	−8.0	79,530
Printing press operators	173.0	151.4	−21.6	−12.5	35,240

Projected Employment by Typical Entry-Level Education, 2014-24

Source: Employment Projections Program, Bureau of Labor Statistics, U.S. Dept. of Labor

Typical entry-level education	Employment, 2014 Number (thous.)	Employment, 2014 Percent distribution	% change in employment, 2014-24	Median annual wage, 2015
Total, all occupations......................	150,539.9	100.0%	6.5%	$36,200
Doctoral or professional degree	4,111.5	2.7	12.2	100,490
Master's degree	2,518.8	1.7	13.8	66,420
Bachelor's degree........................	31,848.6	21.2	8.2	70,400
Associate's degree	3,458.2	2.3	8.7	50,230
Postsecondary nondegree award	9,090.7	6.0	11.5	35,660
Some college, no degree	3,785.8	2.5	0.5	33,870
High school diploma or equivalent	54,927.4	36.5	3.9	36,210
No formal educational credential	40,799.0	27.1	6.9	21,420

Note: The occupational employment and growth rates shown include projected growth in all jobs 2014-24, not just entry-level jobs. Entry-level education reflects 2014 requirements—BLS does not project changes in educational requirements.

Highest Average Weekly Wages by County, 2015

Source: Bureau of Labor Statistics, U.S. Dept. of Labor

County	Avg. weekly wage	% change, 2014-15	County	Avg. weekly wage	% change, 2014-15
Santa Clara, CA	$2,335	9.3%	Fairfax, VA...................	$1,618	2.5%
New York, NY	2,235	0.8	Morris, NJ...................	1,601	5.2
San Mateo, CA	2,095	−2.3	Somerset, NJ	1,576	1.0
San Francisco, CA	1,961	6.4	Middlesex, MA	1,563	5.3
Suffolk, MA..................	1,943	5.0	Alexandria City, VA	1,487	1.4
Washington, DC	1,756	3.4	Lake, IL.....................	1,450	9.8
Fairfield, CT	1,735	3.5	Westchester, NY..............	1,449	2.0
Arlington, VA.................	1,686	2.4			

Note: Figures shown are for the 4th quarter, from among the 343 largest U.S. counties, which comprise 72.5% of total covered workers. Cameron County, TX, recorded the lowest average weekly earnings among the largest counties, with an average of $649. It was followed by Horry County, SC ($653); Hidalgo County, TX ($661); Webb County, TX ($706); Harrison County, MS ($729); Osceola County, FL ($730); Lake County, FL ($738); Yakima County, WA ($740); El Paso County, TX ($743); Marion County, FL ($749); and Pasco County, FL ($749). Data include all workers covered by state and federal unemployment insurance programs.

Federal Minimum Hourly Wage Rates

Source: Bureau of Labor Statistics, U.S. Dept. of Labor; as of July 19, 2016

Effective date	Minimum wage	% avg. earnings[1]	In 2016 dollars	Effective date	Minimum wage	% avg. earnings[1]	In 2016 dollars
Oct. 24, 1938	$0.25	40%	$4.27	Jan. 1, 1978	$2.65	43%	$9.80
Oct. 24, 1939	0.30	48	5.20	Jan. 1, 1979	2.90	43	9.63
Oct. 24, 1945	0.40	39	5.36	Jan. 1, 1980	3.10	43	9.07
Jan. 25, 1950	0.75	52	7.50	Jan. 1, 1981	3.35	42	8.88
Mar. 1, 1956	1.00	51	8.86	Apr. 1, 1990	3.80	35	7.01
Sept. 3, 1961	1.15	50	9.27	Apr. 1, 1991	4.25	38	7.52
Sept. 3, 1963	1.25	51	9.85	Oct. 1, 1996	4.75	37	7.30
Feb. 1, 1967	1.40	49	10.10	Sept. 1, 1997	5.15	39	7.73
Feb. 1, 1968	1.60	53	11.08	July 24, 2007	5.85	34	6.80
May 1, 1974	2.00	45	9.78	July 24, 2008	6.55	37	7.33
Jan. 1, 1975	2.10	43	9.41	July 24, 2009	7.25	40	8.15
Jan. 1, 1976	2.30	44	9.74				

Note: Before 1961, the minimum wage applied primarily to employees engaged in, or producing goods for, interstate commerce. Coverage was added 1961-64 primarily to employees in large retail and service enterprises and to local transit, construction, and gas station employees. Coverage was added 1966-77 (at reduced rates) to farm workers; federal, state, and local government employees; workers in various retail and service trades; and certain domestic workers. Starting in 1978, the minimum wage applied equally to all covered, nonexempt workers. Exceptions apply under specific circumstances to workers with disabilities, full-time students, persons under age 20 in their first 90 consecutive calendar days of employment, tipped employees, and student-learners. (1) Percent of gross hourly earnings of production workers in manufacturing.

Fatal Occupational Injuries, 2014

Source: Census of Fatal Occupational Injuries, Bureau of Labor Statistics, U.S. Dept. of Labor, in cooperation with other agencies

Event or exposure	Fatalities Number	%	Event or exposure	Fatalities Number	%
Total.	4,679	100%	Contact with objects and equipment	708	15%
Transportation incidents	1,891	40	Struck by object or equipment	498	11
Roadway, involving motorized land vehicles	1,075	23	Struck by falling object or equipment	240	5
Collision with other vehicles	566	12	Struck by flying object.	21	—
Collision with object other than vehicle	294	6	Caught in or compressed by equipment or objects	131	3
Noncollision.	211	5	Caught in running equipment or machinery . . .	104	2
Jackknifed or overturned.	178	4	Struck, caught, or crushed in collapsing		
Nonroadway.	246	5	structure, equipment, or material	74	2
Jackknifed or overturned.	127	3			
Pedestrian vehicular incidents	313	7	**Falls, slips, trips**	793	17
Rail vehicle incidents.	55	1	Fall to lower level	647	14
Water vehicle incidents.	53	1	Fall on same level.	129	3
Aircraft incidents.	135	3	**Exposure to harmful substances or environments**	390	8
Violence by persons or animals	749	16	Exposure to electricity	156	3
Homicides.	403	9	Exposure to temperature extremes	26	1
Shooting	307	7	Exposure to other harmful substances.	180	4
Stabbing	39	1	Inhalation of harmful substance	59	1
Self-inflicted injury—intentional	271	6	**Fires and explosions**	137	3

— = Less than 0.5%. Note: Category totals may include subcategories not shown. Percentages show incidence rate per total fatalities.

U.S. Occupational Injuries and Illnesses Involving Days Away From Work, 2014

Source: Bureau of Labor Statistics, U.S. Dept. of Labor

Characteristic	Illnesses/ injuries[2]	Percent of days-away-from-work cases[1] involving—							Median days away from work
		1 day	2 days	3-5 days	6-10 days	11-20 days	21-30 days	31 days or more	
Total	916,440	13.9%	10.7%	17.1%	11.8%	11.3%	6.3%	29.0%	9
Male	560,970	13.7	10.0	16.6	11.6	11.4	6.6	30.1	10
Female	348,720	14.1	11.9	18.0	12.2	11.1	5.7	27.0	7
Occupation(s)									
Management.	20,510	13.9	13.4	18.1	14.6	10.5	7.6	21.7	7
Business, financial operations	6,560	15.9	15.2	14.3	6.2	13.3	5.5	29.6	9
Computer and mathematical.	2,100	21.4	14.3	13.8	16.2	9.5	7.1	17.1	6
Architecture, engineering	3,580	10.9	14.2	9.2	7.8	10.1	5.3	42.2	16
Life, physical, social science	2,240	10.7	18.8	24.1	13.4	9.4	5.8	17.9	5
Community, social services.	7,010	17.4	13.7	19.8	12.1	11.0	4.7	21.1	5
Legal	980	3.1	30.6	7.1	29.6	5.1	2.0	22.4	10
Education, training, library	9,890	20.7	15.1	18.4	12.0	12.5	3.6	17.6	5
Arts, design, entertainment, sports, media.	5,740	15.9	9.4	19.2	13.9	14.5	7.0	20.0	7
Health care practitioners	51,060	14.9	11.0	18.5	13.0	10.8	7.2	24.6	7
Health care support	55,200	13.6	13.2	20.2	14.1	10.0	5.1	23.8	6
Protective service	9,270	13.1	12.8	15.5	11.7	11.2	6.0	29.6	8
Food preparation, serving	69,690	15.9	13.2	21.0	12.9	11.1	4.7	21.2	5
Building and grounds cleaning, maintenance	58,570	13.4	10.7	18.1	13.8	11.1	5.7	27.1	8
Personal care, service.	26,090	13.3	15.9	21.9	12.5	9.6	5.2	21.7	5
Sales.	55,460	15.7	9.9	16.7	11.4	12.2	5.3	28.7	9
Office and administrative support . .	70,750	14.3	10.2	16.1	9.8	11.9	6.0	31.7	10
Farming, fishing, forestry.	14,780	13.9	13.4	20.8	12.6	10.2	6.2	22.9	6
Construction, extraction	73,460	14.0	9.8	15.9	9.9	9.7	8.3	32.5	11
Installation, maintenance, repair . . .	81,730	13.5	8.5	16.4	11.7	12.5	6.7	30.7	10
Production.	104,980	15.4	10.7	16.2	11.3	11.5	6.2	28.6	8
Transportation, material moving . . .	182,800	11.0	8.3	14.8	11.5	11.6	6.8	35.9	14

(1) Cases include those that resulted in days away from work. (2) Number of nonfatal occupational injuries and illnesses involving days away from work for private industry workers; excludes farms with fewer than 11 employees.

Civilian Employment of the Executive Branch, 1940-2014

Source: U.S. Office of Personnel Management

(numbers in thousands)

Year	Total executive branch	Dept. of Defense	Total employees	Agricul- ture	HHS, Education, Social Sec.[1]	Homeland Sec.	Interior	Justice	Transpor- tation	Treasury	Veterans Affairs	Other
					Civilian agencies/depts.							
1940	699	256	443	98	9	18	46	11	NA	45	40	176
1945	3,370	2,635	736	82	11	20	45	19	NA	84	65	409
1950	1,439	753	686	84	13	20	66	20	NA	76	188	219
1955	1,860	1,187	673	86	40	21	54	24	NA	65	178	206
1960	1,808	1,047	761	99	62	21	56	24	NA	62	172	265
1965	1,901	1,034	867	113	87	21	71	27	NA	74	167	307
1970	2,203	1,219	983	118	112	23	75	33	62	84	169	308
1975	2,149	1,042	1,107	121	147	31	80	47	69	101	213	297
1980	2,161	960	1,201	129	163	40	77	48	66	102	228	346
1985	2,252	1,107	1,145	122	147	40	80	55	56	110	247	286
1990	2,250	1,034	1,216	123	129	49	78	71	61	132	248	326
1995	2,012	802	1,210	113	132	56	76	87	58	128	264	297
2000	1,778	651	1,127	104	126	70	74	98	58	113	220	265
2004	1,882	644	1,238	111	130	153	77	104	57	111	236	257
2005	1,872	649	1,224	108	131	147	76	105	56	108	235	258
2006	1,880	653	1,227	105	129	154	72	107	54	107	239	260
2007	1,888	651	1,237	103	129	159	72	107	54	104	254	254
2008	1,960	670	1,289	104	132	172	76	109	55	106	274	261
2009	2,094	737	1,357	104	139	180	75	113	57	109	297	283
2010	2,133	773	1,360	107	144	183	70	118	58	110	305	265
2011	2,146	774	1,372	104	143	194	77	117	58	108	314	257
2012	2,104	730	1,374	99	143	191	77	117	57	112	323	255
2013	2,087	729	1,355	95	139	192	71	116	55	112	323	252
2014	2,079	723	1,356	94	141	186	70	114	55	112	340	244

NA = Not available. HHS = Health and Human Services. **Note:** End-of-fiscal-year count; U.S. Postal Service excluded. (1) Estimated, 1940-50.

Median Earnings by Industry and Sex, 2015

Source: American Community Survey, U.S. Census Bureau, U.S. Dept. of Commerce

Industry	Total	% men	% women	Total	Men	Women	Women's as % of men's
	Employed			**Median earnings**			
Total	150,534,773	52.6%	47.4%	$34,656	$40,699	$29,319	72.0%
Agriculture; forestry, fishing and hunting; mining	2,906,158	80.2	19.8	32,630	36,955	21,406	57.9
Arts, entertainment, recreation; accommodation, food services	14,756,511	48.6	51.4	16,153	19,058	13,899	72.9
Construction	9,622,525	90.8	9.2	36,272	36,427	34,642	95.1
Educational services; health care, social assistance . . .	34,510,561	25.7	74.3	35,506	44,404	32,195	72.5
Finance, insurance; real estate, rental, leasing.	9,822,476	46.0	54.0	47,740	61,033	41,069	67.3
Information	3,155,281	59.3	40.7	50,587	58,416	40,581	69.5
Manufacturing	15,470,595	71.3	28.7	42,223	47,186	33,867	71.8
Professional, scientific, management; administrative, waste management services	17,009,744	57.9	42.1	41,900	50,763	35,124	69.2
Other services, except public administration	7,343,926	46.7	53.3	23,410	31,120	18,487	59.4
Public administration.	6,860,152	55.6	44.4	51,852	60,564	44,748	73.9
Retail trade	17,301,650	50.8	49.2	21,734	26,473	17,945	67.8
Transportation, warehousing; utilities	7,682,950	76.0	24.0	42,308	46,371	34,996	75.5
Wholesale trade	4,092,244	70.1	29.9	42,365	46,632	36,279	77.8

Note: For the civilian employed population 16 years of age and over including workers not employed full-time.

Unemployment Rates and Earnings by Education, 2015

Source: Bureau of Labor Statistics, U.S. Dept. of Labor

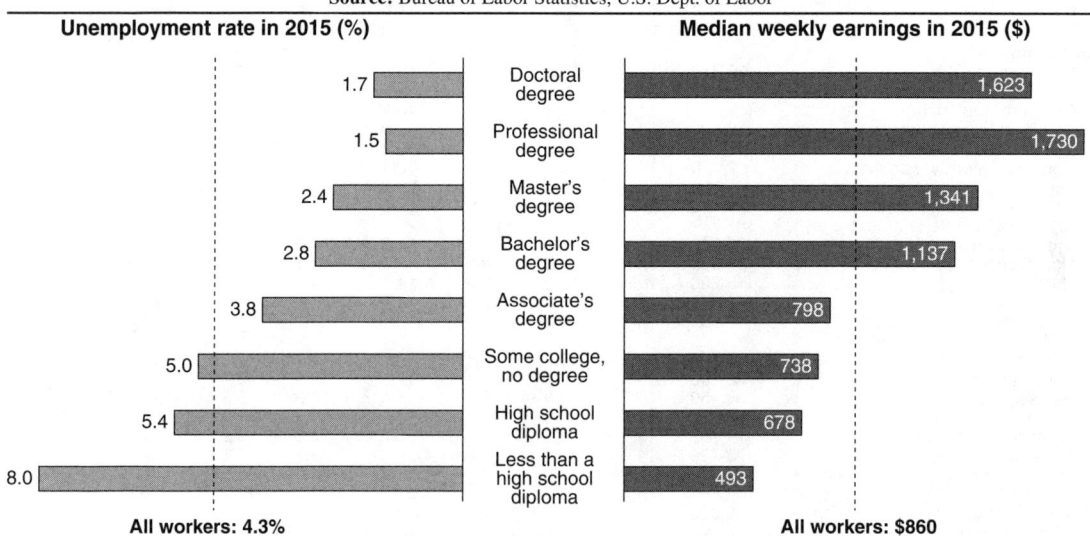

	Unemployment rate in 2015 (%)	Median weekly earnings in 2015 ($)
Doctoral degree	1.7	1,623
Professional degree	1.5	1,730
Master's degree	2.4	1,341
Bachelor's degree	2.8	1,137
Associate's degree	3.8	798
Some college, no degree	5.0	738
High school diploma	5.4	678
Less than a high school diploma	8.0	493

All workers: 4.3% — **All workers: $860**

Note: Data are for persons age 25 and over. Earnings are for full-time wage and salary workers.

U.S. Median Weekly Earnings, 2016

Source: Bureau of Labor Statistics, U.S. Dept. of Labor

AGE, RACE, AND ETHNICITY	Total Number of workers (thous.)	Total Median weekly earnings	Men Number of workers (thous.)	Men Median weekly earnings	Women Number of workers (thous.)	Women Median weekly earnings
All workers, by age						
16 years and over	111,166	$824	62,045	$909	49,121	$744
16 to 24 years	10,140	492	5,724	505	4,415	470
16 to 19 years	1,298	404	730	422	568	390
20 to 24 years	8,842	505	4,995	516	3,847	489
25 years and over	101,026	880	56,320	967	44,706	777
25 to 54 years	78,468	865	44,133	944	34,336	774
25 to 34 years	27,500	753	15,589	791	11,911	710
35 to 44 years	25,270	943	14,406	1,024	10,863	845
45 to 54 years	25,699	948	14,137	1,063	11,562	829
55 years and over	22,558	928	12,188	1,049	10,370	785
55 to 64 years	18,532	935	9,877	1,054	8,655	795
65 years and over	4,026	898	2,311	1,032	1,715	736
White						
16 years and over	86,638	854	49,241	941	37,397	759
16 to 24 years	7,961	500	4,612	510	3,349	483
25 years and over	78,677	907	44,629	997	34,049	797
25 to 54 years	60,196	893	34,539	971	25,657	799
55 years and over	18,481	959	10,090	1,114	8,392	791
Black						
16 years and over	13,954	677	6,838	704	7,116	646
16 to 24 years	1,239	423	626	462	612	408
25 years and over	12,716	708	6,212	731	6,504	684
25 to 54 years	10,302	698	5,058	718	5,244	675
55 years and over	2,413	771	1,154	819	1,260	739
Asian						
16 years and over	7,085	1,021	3,963	1,147	3,122	907
16 to 24 years	392	519	212	520	180	515
25 years and over	6,693	1,063	3,751	1,190	2,942	945
25 to 54 years	5,436	1,114	3,029	1,249	2,407	982
55 years and over	1,257	885	722	943	535	833
Hispanic[1]						
16 years and over	18,956	618	11,718	652	7,238	581
16 to 24 years	2,455	476	1,510	481	945	461
25 years and over	16,501	658	10,208	692	6,294	605
25 to 54 years	14,173	650	8,821	683	5,351	602
55 years and over	2,329	705	1,386	767	942	624
OCCUPATION						
Managerial, professional, and related	46,153	1,174	22,304	1,405	23,848	1,019
Management, business, and financial	19,031	1,260	10,191	1,441	8,840	1,073
Professional and related	27,122	1,138	12,114	1,377	15,009	994
Service	15,275	512	7,703	564	7,572	480
Sales and office	23,712	688	9,535	775	14,177	645
Sales and related	9,872	730	5,446	882	4,426	580
Office and administrative support	13,840	673	4,088	695	9,751	666
Natural resources, construction, and maintenance	10,935	771	10,491	778	444	552
Farming, fishing, and forestry	898	543	699	570	199	459
Construction and extraction	5,935	784	5,818	786	117	685
Installation, maintenance, and repair	4,102	819	3,973	818	128	848
Production, transportation, and material moving	15,092	663	12,012	708	3,080	532
Production	8,105	662	5,983	722	2,122	535
Transportation and material moving	6,986	664	6,028	694	958	528

Note: Not seasonally adjusted; figures are median usual weekly earnings of full-time wage and salary workers for second quarter 2016. Total includes races not shown here. (1) May be of any race.

Average Hours and Earnings of U.S. Production Workers, 1969-2015

Source: Bureau of Labor Statistics, U.S. Dept. of Labor
(annual averages)

Year	Weekly hours	Hourly earnings	Weekly earnings	Year	Weekly hours	Hourly earnings	Weekly earnings	Year	Weekly hours	Hourly earnings	Weekly earnings
1969	37.5	$3.22	$120.70	1985	34.9	$8.74	$304.62	2001	34.0	$14.54	$493.74
1970	37.0	3.40	125.79	1986	34.7	8.93	309.78	2002	33.9	14.96	506.54
1971	36.7	3.63	133.22	1987	34.7	9.14	317.39	2003	33.7	15.37	517.76
1972	36.9	3.90	143.87	1988	34.6	9.44	326.48	2004	33.7	15.68	528.81
1973	36.9	4.14	152.59	1989	34.5	9.80	338.34	2005	33.8	16.12	544.00
1974	36.4	4.43	161.61	1990	34.3	10.20	349.63	2006	33.9	16.75	567.06
1975	36.0	4.73	170.29	1991	34.1	10.51	358.46	2007	33.8	17.42	589.18
1976	36.1	5.06	182.65	1992	34.2	10.77	368.20	2008	33.6	18.06	607.42
1977	35.9	5.44	195.58	1993	34.3	11.05	378.89	2009	33.1	18.61	615.96
1978	35.8	5.88	210.29	1994	34.5	11.34	391.17	2010	33.4	19.05	636.19
1979	35.6	6.34	225.69	1995	34.3	11.65	400.04	2011	33.6	19.44	652.89
1980	35.2	6.85	241.07	1996	34.3	12.04	413.25	2012	33.7	19.74	665.65
1981	35.2	7.44	261.53	1997	34.5	12.51	431.86	2013	33.7	20.13	677.73
1982	34.7	7.87	273.10	1998	34.5	13.01	448.59	2014	33.7	20.61	694.91
1983	34.9	8.20	286.43	1999	34.3	13.49	463.15	2015	33.7	21.04	709.13
1984	35.1	8.49	298.26	2000	34.3	14.02	480.99				

Note: Data refer to production workers in natural resources, mining, and manufacturing; construction workers; and nonsupervisory workers in the service industries.

Elderly in U.S. Labor Force, 1890-2015

Source: U.S. Census Bureau, U.S. Dept. of Commerce

(percent of persons age 65 and older who participated in the labor force; 1910 figures not available)

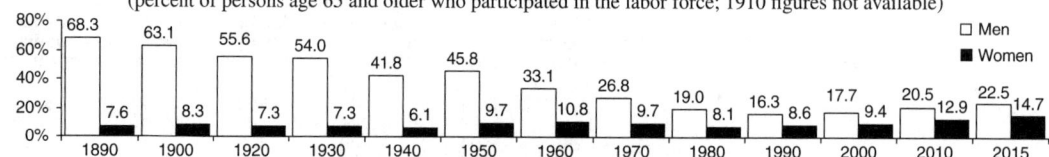

	1890	1900	1920	1930	1940	1950	1960	1970	1980	1990	2000	2010	2015
Men	68.3	63.1	55.6	54.0	41.8	45.8	33.1	26.8	19.0	16.3	17.7	20.5	22.5
Women	7.6	8.3	7.3	7.3	6.1	9.7	10.8	9.7	8.1	8.6	9.4	12.9	14.7

U.S. Union Membership, 1930-2015

Source: Bureau of Labor Statistics, U.S. Dept. of Labor

(numbers in thousands)

Year	Total employed[1]	% in union	Union members[2]	Year	Total employed[1]	% in union	Union members[2]	Year	Total employed[1]	% in union	Union members[2]
1930	29,424	11.6%	3,401	1975	76,945	25.5%	19,611	2008	129,377	12.4%	16,098
1935	27,053	13.2	3,584	1980	90,564	21.9	19,843	2009	124,490	12.3	15,327
1940	32,376	26.9	8,717	1985	94,521	18.0	16,996	2010	124,073	11.9	14,715
1945	40,394	35.5	14,322	1990	103,905	16.1	16,740	2011	125,187	11.8	14,764
1950	45,222	31.5	14,267	1995	110,038	14.9	16,360	2012	127,577	11.3	14,366
1955	50,675	33.2	16,802	2000	120,786	13.5	16,258	2013	129,110	11.3	14,528
1960	54,234	31.4	17,049	2005	125,889	12.5	15,685	2014	131,431	11.1	14,576
1965	60,815	28.4	17,299	2006	128,237	12.0	15,359	2015	133,743	11.1	14,795
1970	70,920	27.3	19,381	2007	129,767	12.1	15,670				

(1) Prior to 1985, total labor force figure, which includes unemployed persons. From 1985 on, does not include self-employed workers. (2) From 1930 to 1980, includes dues-paying members of traditional trade unions, regardless of employment status; after 1980, includes employed only. From 1985 on, includes members of employee associations similar to a union.

Median Weekly Earnings of U.S. Workers by Union Affiliation, 2000, 2015

Source: Bureau of Labor Statistics, U.S. Dept. of Labor

Sex and age	2000				2015			
	Total	Union members[1]	Represented by unions[2]	Non-union	Total	Union members[1]	Represented by unions[2]	Non-union
Total, 16 years and older ..	**$576**	**$696**	**$691**	**$542**	**$809**	**$980**	**$975**	**$776**
16 to 24 years..........	361	437	436	355	487	616	605	482
25 years and older	611	709	705	592	860	997	994	831
25 to 34 years........	550	627	624	529	735	886	882	716
35 to 44 years........	631	716	712	614	900	1,050	1,048	870
45 to 54 years........	671	755	752	639	923	1,029	1,024	899
55 to 64 years........	617	727	723	592	927	1,020	1,017	904
65 years and older	442	577	565	422	873	961	963	852
Men, 16 years and older...	**646**	**739**	**737**	**620**	**895**	**1,017**	**1,014**	**869**
16 to 24 years..........	376	458	457	370	510	655	633	505
25 years and older	700	753	752	682	947	1,041	1,038	927
25 to 34 years........	603	678	675	591	770	888	889	756
35 to 44 years........	731	776	774	718	983	1,093	1,094	963
45 to 54 years........	777	801	799	769	1,040	1,107	1,110	1,023
55 to 64 years........	738	755	757	729	1,064	1,084	1,082	1,059
65 years and older	537	613	613	514	1,003	1,010	998	1,005
Women, 16 years and older	**491**	**616**	**613**	**472**	**726**	**928**	**921**	**697**
16 to 24 years..........	342	406	405	339	450	567	565	443
25 years and older	515	627	623	497	761	944	940	736
25 to 34 years........	493	579	578	483	690	884	876	667
35 to 44 years........	520	605	604	506	804	1,002	1,001	764
45 to 54 years........	565	697	692	522	799	958	950	768
55 to 64 years........	505	659	647	481	784	937	934	759
65 years and older	378	485	484	365	740	894	905	718

Note: Data refer to the sole or principal job of full-time wage and salary workers. Excludes self-employed workers regardless of whether or not their businesses are incorporated. (1) Includes members of an employee association similar to a union. (2) Includes members of a labor union as well as those whose jobs are covered by a union or an employee-association contract.

Work Stoppages (Strikes and Lockouts) in the U.S., 1950-2015

Source: Bureau of Labor Statistics, U.S. Dept. of Labor; involving 1,000 workers or more

Year	No.	Workers (thous.)	Days idle (thous.)	Year	No.	Workers (thous.)	Days idle (thous.)	Year	No.	Workers (thous.)	Days idle (thous.)
1950	424	1,698	30,390	1986	69	533	11,861	2001	29	99	1,151
1955	363	2,055	21,180	1987	46	174	4,481	2002	19	46	660
1960	222	896	13,260	1988	40	118	4,381	2003	14	129	4,091
1965	268	999	15,140	1989	51	452	16,996	2004	17	171	3,344
1970	381	2,468	52,761	1990	44	185	5,926	2005	22	100	1,736
1975	235	965	17,563	1991	40	392	4,584	2006	20	70	2,688
1976	231	1,519	23,962	1992	35	364	3,989	2007	21	189	1,265
1977	298	1,212	21,258	1993	35	182	3,981	2008	15	72	1,954
1978	219	1,006	23,774	1994	45	322	5,021	2009	5	13	124
1979	235	1,021	20,409	1995	31	192	5,771	2010	11	45	302
1980	187	795	20,844	1996	37	273	4,889	2011	19	113	1,020
1981	145	729	16,908	1997	29	339	4,497	2012	19	148	1,131
1982	96	656	9,061	1998	34	387	5,116	2013	15	55	290
1983	81	909	17,461	1999	17	73	1,996	2014	11	34	200
1984	62	376	8,499	2000	39	394	20,419	2015	12	47	740
1985	54	324	7,079								

Note: Numbers cover stoppages that began in the year indicated. Workers are counted more than once if they are involved in more than one stoppage during the year. For work stoppages ongoing at the end of a calendar year, days idle include only the days for the calendar year.

ENERGY

U.S. Energy Overview, 1960-2015

Source: *Monthly Energy Review*, Aug. 2016, Energy Information Administration (EIA), U.S. Dept. of Energy; in quadrillion Btu

	1960	1970	1980	1985	1990	1995	2000	2005	2010	2014	2015
Production	42.80	63.50	67.23	67.80	70.70	71.17	71.33	69.43	74.72	87.28	87.99
Fossil fuels	39.87	59.19	59.01	57.54	58.56	57.54	57.37	55.04	58.22	69.37	70.07
Coal[1]	10.82	14.61	18.60	19.33	22.49	22.13	22.74	23.19	22.04	20.29	17.95
Natural gas (dry)	12.66	21.67	19.91	16.98	18.33	19.08	19.66	18.56	21.81	26.55	27.93
Crude oil[2]	14.93	20.40	18.25	18.99	15.57	13.89	12.36	10.97	11.59	18.43	19.72
Natural gas plant liquids (NGPL)	1.46	2.51	2.25	2.24	2.17	2.44	2.61	2.33	2.78	4.10	4.47
Nuclear electric power	0.01	0.24	2.74	4.08	6.10	7.08	7.86	8.16	8.43	8.34	8.34
Renewable energy	2.93	4.08	5.49	6.18	6.04	6.56	6.10	6.23	8.07	9.58	9.57
Conventional hydroelectric power[3]	1.61	2.63	2.90	2.97	3.05	3.21	2.81	2.70	2.54	2.47	2.39
Biomass[4]	1.32	1.43	2.48	3.02	2.74	3.10	3.01	3.10	4.32	4.85	4.72
Geothermal energy	—	0.01	0.11	0.20	0.17	0.15	0.16	0.18	0.21	0.21	0.22
Solar	NA	NA	NA	—	0.06	0.07	0.07	0.06	0.08	0.32	0.43
Wind	NA	NA	NA	—	0.03	0.03	0.06	0.18	0.92	1.73	1.82
Imports	4.19	8.34	15.80	11.78	18.82	22.26	28.97	34.71	29.87	23.24	23.73
Coal	0.01	—	0.03	0.05	0.07	0.24	0.31	0.76	0.48	0.25	0.25
Natural gas	0.16	0.85	1.01	0.95	1.55	2.90	3.87	4.45	3.83	2.76	2.78
All petroleum prods.[5]	4.00	7.47	14.66	10.61	17.12	18.88	24.53	29.25	25.36	19.95	20.35
Electricity[6]	0.02	0.02	0.09	0.16	0.06	0.15	0.17	0.15	0.15	0.23	0.26
Exports	1.48	2.63	3.69	4.20	4.75	4.51	4.01	4.56	8.18	12.27	12.93
Coal	1.02	1.94	2.42	2.44	2.77	2.32	1.53	1.27	2.10	2.43	1.85
Natural gas	0.01	0.07	0.05	0.06	0.09	0.16	0.25	0.74	1.15	1.53	1.80
All petroleum prods.[5]	0.43	0.55	1.16	1.66	1.82	1.99	2.15	2.44	4.78	8.16	9.14
Electricity[6]	—	0.01	0.01	0.02	0.06	0.01	0.05	0.07	0.07	0.04	0.03
Consumption	45.09	67.84	78.12	76.49	84.49	91.03	98.81	100.28	97.44	98.41	97.36
Fossil fuels	42.14	63.52	69.83	66.09	72.33	77.26	84.73	85.79	80.89	80.34	79.24
Coal	9.84	12.26	15.42	17.48	19.17	20.09	22.58	22.80	20.83	18.00	15.57
Natural gas[7]	12.39	21.80	20.24	17.70	19.60	22.67	23.82	22.57	24.58	27.49	23.31
Petroleum[8]	19.92	29.52	34.20	30.92	33.55	34.44	38.26	40.39	35.49	34.88	35.37
Nuclear electric power	0.01	0.24	2.74	4.08	6.10	7.08	7.86	8.16	8.43	8.34	8.34
Renewable energy	2.93	4.08	5.49	6.18	6.04	6.56	6.11	6.24	8.03	9.54	9.56
Conventional hydroelectric power[3]	1.61	2.63	2.90	2.97	3.05	3.21	2.81	2.70	2.54	2.47	2.39
Biomass[4]	1.32	1.43	2.48	3.02	2.74	3.10	3.01	3.12	4.27	4.81	4.70
Geothermal energy	—	0.01	0.11	0.20	0.17	0.15	0.16	0.18	0.21	0.21	0.22
Solar	NA	NA	NA	—	0.06	0.07	0.07	0.06	0.08	0.32	0.43
Wind	NA	NA	NA	—	0.03	0.03	0.06	0.02	0.92	1.72	1.82

NA = Not available. — = Less than 0.005 quadrillion Btu. **Note:** Numbers may not add up to totals because of rounding. (1) Incl. waste coal supplied beginning in 1989 and refuse recovery beginning in 2001. (2) Incl. lease condensate. (3) Starting in 1990, pumped storage was removed and expanded coverage of industrial use of hydroelectric power was included. (4) Category known as "wood, waste, and alcohol" for years prior to 2000. Includes wood, waste, and alcohol fuels (ethanol blended into motor gasoline). Ethanol is included in both Petroleum and Biomass categories but is only counted once in totals. (5) Imports incl. crude oil for the Strategic Petroleum Reserve, which began in 1977. Imports/exports excl. biofuels. (6) Small amts. transmitted across borders with Canada and Mexico. (7) Incl. supplemental gaseous fuels. (8) Petroleum products supplied, incl. natural gas plant liquids and crude oil burned as fuel.

World's Largest Energy Producers and Consumers, 1980-2013

Source: Energy Information Administration (EIA), U.S. Dept. of Energy

(primary energy in quadrillion Btu; ranked by top producers/consumers in 2013)

Production	1980	1990	1995	2000	2005	2010	2011	2012	2013
1. China	18.12	29.37	34.88	38.47	63.28	86.53	94.56	97.33	99.88
2. United States	67.18	70.71	71.17	71.33	69.43	74.76	77.96	79.16	81.75
3. Russia	NA	NA	41.42	41.70	51.05	53.92	54.86	55.60	54.54
4. Saudi Arabia	22.43	15.92	20.66	21.59	26.06	25.35	26.72	27.94	27.60
5. Canada	10.28	13.41	16.83	18.13	18.88	18.37	18.86	19.13	18.94
6. Indonesia	4.23	5.30	6.95	7.44	8.47	13.78	15.80	16.96	16.00
7. India	3.14	6.83	9.48	9.83	11.94	15.71	16.15	16.18	14.90
8. Iran	3.94	7.67	9.35	10.40	13.12	14.61	14.79	13.63	13.03
9. Brazil	1.90	3.76	4.47	6.36	7.66	9.47	9.91	9.76	9.69
10. Qatar	1.20	1.20	1.51	2.83	4.23	8.10	9.53	9.55	9.62
Consumption	**1980**	**1990**	**1995**	**2000**	**2005**	**2010**	**2011**	**2012**	**2013**
1. China	17.94	28.29	34.44	41.11	72.65	99.73	108.24	113.04	116.72
2. United States	78.07	84.49	91.03	98.82	100.19	97.48	96.90	94.49	97.24
3. Russia	NA	NA	27.82	26.17	27.95	30.25	30.66	31.85	30.52
4. India	3.97	7.80	11.38	13.29	16.59	23.70	23.31	24.44	25.43
5. Japan	15.55	18.69	20.98	22.43	22.44	22.13	20.85	20.34	20.37
6. Canada	9.86	10.96	12.17	13.01	13.58	13.55	13.86	13.79	14.19
7. Germany	NA	NA	14.31	14.18	14.06	13.99	13.40	13.57	13.78
8. Brazil	4.01	5.76	6.99	8.50	9.25	11.43	11.89	12.27	12.57
9. South Korea	1.76	3.83	6.37	8.02	9.27	10.95	11.21	11.28	11.35
10. France	8.47	9.14	10.06	10.84	11.37	11.01	10.77	10.62	10.81

NA = Not available.

U.S. Energy Consumption by Source, 1949-2015

Source: *Monthly Energy Review*, Aug. 2016, Energy Information Administration (EIA), U.S. Dept. of Energy

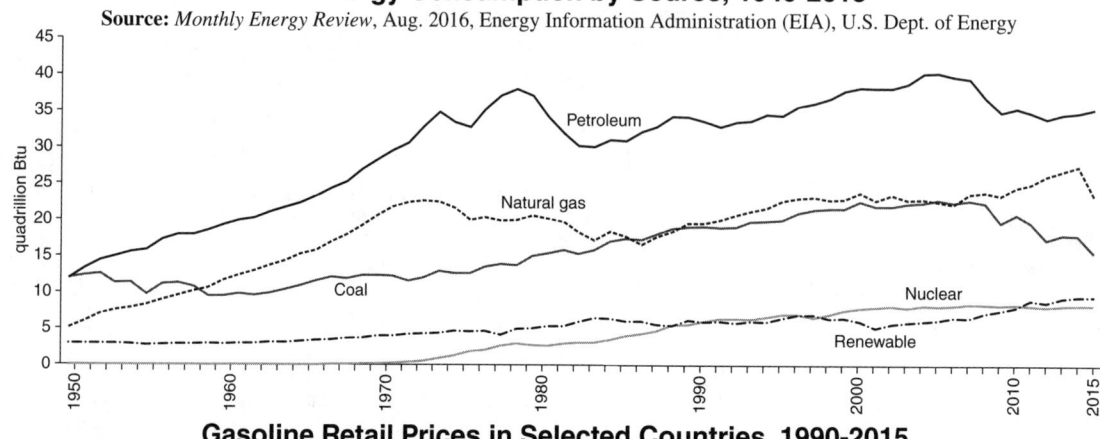

Gasoline Retail Prices in Selected Countries, 1990-2015

Source: *Energy Prices and Taxes*, International Energy Agency
(average price in dollars per gallon, including taxes)

Country	1990	1995	2000	2004	2005	2006	2007	2008	2009	2010	2011	2012	2013	2014	2015
Regular unleaded															
Australia	NA	$1.93	$1.93	$2.73	$3.22	$3.52	$3.86	$4.47	$3.79	$4.35	$5.60	$5.60	$5.30	$5.00	$3.63
Canada...........	$1.85	1.51	1.85	2.35	2.88	3.26	3.60	4.09	3.14	3.79	4.77	4.81	4.69	4.39	3.22
China	NA	NA	NA	1.48	1.70	2.12	2.31	3.10	3.26	3.71	NA	NA	NA	NA	NA
Germany..........	2.65	3.97	3.44	5.26	5.64	6.02	6.89	7.76	6.81	7.12	NA	NA	NA	NA	NA
Japan	3.14	4.43	3.63	3.94	4.28	4.47	4.50	5.75	4.85	5.72	6.93	6.97	6.06	5.83	4.32
Korea, South.......	2.04	2.95	4.16	4.50	5.26	5.91	6.21	5.83	4.69	5.60	6.59	6.66	6.66	6.59	5.07
Mexico	1.02	1.10	2.01	2.04	2.23	2.31	2.42	2.46	2.12	2.46	2.80	2.95	3.37	3.60	3.14
Taiwan	2.46	2.23	2.16	2.46	2.76	3.07	3.22	3.52	3.03	3.56	4.05	NA	NA	NA	NA
United States	1.17	1.10	1.48	1.85	2.27	2.57	2.80	3.26	2.35	2.76	3.52	3.63	3.52	3.37	2.42
Premium unleaded															
France...........	$3.63	$4.28	$3.79	$5.00	$5.45	$5.87	$6.59	$7.50	$6.36	$6.74	$7.91	$7.61	$7.72	$7.46	$5.68
Germany..........	2.76	4.09	3.56	5.34	5.75	6.13	6.97	7.76	6.81	7.12	8.21	8.03	8.03	7.72	5.87
Italy.............	4.58	4.01	3.79	5.30	5.75	6.09	6.74	7.65	6.47	6.85	8.18	8.71	8.78	8.59	6.47
Mexico	NA	NA	2.23	2.38	2.57	2.73	2.95	3.03	2.65	2.95	3.14	3.14	3.56	3.79	3.37
South Africa	NA	NA	1.78	2.57	3.07	3.41	3.63	4.13	3.22	4.09	NA	NA	NA	NA	NA
Spain	NA	3.26	2.84	4.09	4.50	4.85	5.38	6.13	5.26	5.83	6.97	6.93	7.19	6.97	5.15
Thailand	NA	1.25	1.36	1.78	2.23	2.76	3.22	4.01	4.13	4.85	NA	NA	NA	NA	NA
United Kingdom	2.84	3.22	4.58	5.56	5.98	6.36	7.15	7.42	5.87	6.85	8.10	8.14	7.95	7.95	6.44
United States	NA	1.21	1.59	1.97	2.38	2.69	2.91	3.37	2.46	2.91	3.63	3.75	3.67	3.56	2.65

NA = Not available. **Note:** Premium unleaded refers to fuels with a research octane number of 95.

Average U.S. Gasoline Prices, 1950-2015

Source: *Monthly Energy Review*, Aug. 2016; *Short-Term Energy Outlook*, Aug. 2016; Energy Information Administration (EIA), U.S. Dept. of Energy

(in dollars per gallon, including taxes; constant dollars is price in Aug. 2015 dollars)

Year	Leaded regular	Unleaded regular	Unleaded premium	All types[1]	Constant dollars, unleaded regular[2]	Year	Leaded regular	Unleaded regular	Unleaded premium	All types[1]	Constant dollars, unleaded regular[2]
1950	$0.27	NA	NA	NA	NA	1997	NA	$1.23	$1.42	$1.29	$1.80
1955	0.29	NA	NA	NA	NA	1998	NA	1.06	1.25	1.12	1.52
1960	0.31	NA	NA	NA	NA	1999	NA	1.17	1.36	1.22	1.64
1965	0.31	NA	NA	NA	NA	2000	NA	1.51	1.69	1.56	2.08
1970	0.36	NA	NA	NA	NA	2001	NA	1.46	1.66	1.53	1.94
1975	0.57	NA	NA	NA	NA	2002	NA	1.36	1.56	1.44	1.80
1980	1.19	$1.25	NA	$1.22	$3.64	2003	NA	1.59	1.78	1.64	2.04
1985	1.12	1.20	$1.34	1.20	2.61	2004	NA	1.88	2.07	1.92	2.36
1986	0.86	0.93	1.09	0.93	2.08	2005	NA	2.30	2.49	2.34	2.80
1987	0.90	0.95	1.09	0.96	1.95	2006	NA	2.59	2.81	2.64	3.07
1988	0.90	0.95	1.11	0.96	1.86	2007	NA	2.80	3.03	2.85	3.25
1989	1.00	1.02	1.20	1.06	1.78	2008	NA	3.27	3.52	3.32	3.64
1990	1.15	1.16	1.35	1.22	1.75	2009	NA	2.35	2.61	2.40	2.63
1991	NA	1.14	1.32	1.20	1.75	2010	NA	2.79	3.05	2.84	3.07
1992	NA	1.13	1.32	1.19	1.84	2011	NA	3.53	3.79	3.58	3.77
1993	NA	1.11	1.30	1.17	3.64	2012	NA	3.64	3.92	3.70	3.80
1994	NA	1.11	1.31	1.17	2.61	2013	NA	3.53	3.84	3.58	3.62
1995	NA	1.15	1.34	1.21	2.08	2014	NA	3.37	3.71	3.42	3.42
1996	NA	1.23	1.41	1.29	1.95	2015	NA	2.45	2.87	2.51	2.46

NA = Not applicable. **Note:** Until unleaded gas became available in 1976, leaded was the only type used in automobiles. (1) Includes types of motor gasoline not shown separately. Includes gasohol starting in 1985. (2) Base prices vary slightly from unleaded regular column at left.

Energy Consumption, Total and Per Capita, by State, 2014

Source: State Energy Data System, Energy Information Administration (EIA), U.S. Dept. of Energy

Total Consumption				Consumption per Capita			
Rank, state	Btu (tril)	Rank, state	Btu (tril)	Rank, state	Btu (mil)	Rank, state	Btu (mil)
1. Texas	12,899.5	27. Arizona	1,422.6	1. Louisiana	920.5	27. Maine	308.6
2. California	7,620.1	28. Maryland	1,400.6	2. Wyoming	916.7	28. Pennsylvania	305.0
3. Louisiana	4,279.4	29. Mississippi	1,155.5	3. North Dakota	864.9	29. Delaware	292.8
4. Florida	4,121.7	30. Kansas	1,132.4	4. Alaska	818.3	30. Virginia	291.8
5. Illinois	4,042.3	31. Arkansas	1,114.4	5. Iowa	495.9	31. Michigan	290.6
6. Pennsylvania	3,902.4	32. Oregon	987.1	6. Texas	478.1	32. Washington	284.8
7. Ohio	3,809.6	33. Nebraska	864.3	7. South Dakota	459.2	33. Georgia	282.4
8. New York	3,742.9	34. Utah	798.0	8. Nebraska	459.0	34. Colorado	275.8
9. Indiana	2,931.6	35. West Virginia	752.9	9. Indiana	444.3	35. Wash., DC	271.2
10. Michigan	2,881.5	36. Connecticut	750.0	10. Oklahoma	433.0	36. Utah	271.0
11. Georgia	2,851.0	37. New Mexico	679.1	11. West Virginia	407.3	37. New Jersey	261.8
12. North Carolina	2,554.8	38. Nevada	660.3	12. Alabama	404.1	38. North Carolina	257.0
13. Virginia	2,430.2	39. North Dakota	640.1	13. Kentucky	401.3	39. Oregon	248.6
14. New Jersey	2,340.2	40. Alaska	603.1	14. Montana	394.3	40. Maryland	234.4
15. Tennessee	2,194.5	41. Wyoming	535.6	15. Kansas	390.1	41. New Hampshire	233.5
16. Washington	2,011.9	42. Idaho	519.9	16. Mississippi	386.0	42. Nevada	232.6
17. Alabama	1,958.2	43. Maine	410.5	17. Arkansas	375.6	43. Vermont	223.2
18. Minnesota	1,912.1	44. Montana	403.4	18. Minnesota	350.4	44. Massachusetts	212.8
19. Missouri	1,903.8	45. South Dakota	391.9	19. South Carolina	338.0	45. Arizona	211.4
20. Wisconsin	1,868.9	46. New Hampshire	310.1	20. Tennessee	335.2	46. Connecticut	208.6
21. Kentucky	1,770.7	47. Hawaii	281.2	21. Ohio	328.5	47. Florida	207.1
22. Oklahoma	1,679.9	48. Delaware	274.0	22. New Mexico	325.6	48. Hawaii	198.0
23. South Carolina	1,632.1	49. Rhode Island	204.5	23. Wisconsin	324.5	49. California	196.4
24. Iowa	1,541.9	50. Wash., DC	178.9	24. Idaho	318.0	50. Rhode Island	193.8
25. Colorado	1,477.2	51. Vermont	139.9	25. Missouri	314.0	51. New York	189.5
26. Massachusetts	1,437.6	**United States**	**98,385.2**	26. Illinois	313.8	**United States**	**308.5**

Note: U.S. total includes 17.4 trillion Btu of net exports of coal coke that is not allocated to the states.

U.S. Production of Crude Oil by State, 2015

Source: *Petroleum Supply Annual 2015*, Energy Information Administration (EIA), U.S. Dept. of Energy

Oil production in North Dakota nearly quadrupled, 2010-15, through the use of hydraulic fracturing, or fracking, a process by which water, sand, and chemicals are injected at high pressure to create fractures in shale rock, releasing the oil within.

(in thousands of barrels)

Rank, state	Total	Rank, state	Total	Rank, state	Total	Rank, state	Total
1. Texas	1,262,011	9. Louisiana	63,311	17. West Virginia	8,282	25. South Dakota	1,631
2. North Dakota	428,550	10. Kansas	44,618	18. Pennsylvania	7,369	26. Tennessee	342
3. California	201,738	11. Utah	36,970	19. Arkansas	6,536	27. New York	341
4. Alaska	176,240	12. Montana	28,641	20. Michigan	6,449	28. Nevada	281
5. Oklahoma	157,770	13. Ohio	26,330	21. Nebraska	2,956	29. Missouri	138
6. New Mexico	149,403	14. Mississippi	24,926	22. Kentucky	2,862	30. Arizona	37
7. Colorado	119,239	15. Alabama	9,734	23. Indiana	2,219	31. Virginia	15
8. Wyoming	87,537	16. Illinois	9,521	24. Florida	2,208	**U.S. total**	**3,442,205**

Note: One barrel is equal to 42 U.S. gallons. U.S. total includes 562,630 thousand barrels of federal offshore oil production.

Fracking in the U.S.

Hydraulic fracturing, more commonly known as fracking, is a process by which water, sand, and chemicals are injected at high pressure to create fractures in shale rock, releasing the oil and/or natural gas within. Enormous shale deposits in Pennsylvania, California, and other parts of North America have inspired predictions that the U.S. could some day be a net energy exporting nation. However, more recent estimates from the U.S. Dept. of Energy have significantly reduced the amount of oil that can realistically be derived from some of those shale deposits. Fracking also involves numerous environmental concerns, including pollution of groundwater, massive use of freshwater in drought-prone areas, and effects on seismicity in earthquake-prone areas. Vermont and New York have both banned fracking within their borders, while Connecticut has prohibited the storage or handling of fracking waste.

Shale Dry Gas Production in the U.S., 2000-16

Source: *Shale in the U.S.*, Energy Information Administration (EIA), U.S. Dept. of Energy

(production in billions of cubic ft per day)

Site name (primary location)	2000	2005	2010	2011	2012	2013	2014	2015	2016
Marcellus (PA, WV, OH, NY)	—	—	0.6	2.3	5.1	8.0	11.8	15.1	16.0
Eagle Ford (TX)	0	0	0.1	0.6	1.7	2.8	3.6	4.8	4.8
Haynesville (LA, TX)	0.1	0.1	2.4	5.3	7.2	5.8	4.0	3.6	3.8
Utica (OH, PA, WV)	0	0	0	0	—	0.1	0.7	2.0	3.6
Barnett (TX)	0.2	0.9	4.0	4.5	4.9	4.6	4.1	3.9	3.4
Fayetteville (AR)	0	—	1.8	2.4	2.7	2.8	2.8	2.6	2.2
Woodford (OK)	—	—	1.0	1.2	1.2	1.7	1.6	1.9	2.0
Bakken (ND)	—	—	0.1	0.1	0.3	0.5	0.6	0.9	1.0
Antrim (MI, IN, OH)	0.5	0.4	0.3	0.3	0.3	0.3	0.3	0.2	0.2
Other U.S. shale locations	1.4	1.4	1.8	1.9	2.3	2.8	3.5	4.5	5.7
Total	**2.2**	**2.8**	**12.0**	**18.7**	**25.8**	**29.4**	**32.9**	**39.6**	**44.0**

— = Less than 100 million cubic feet per day. **Note:** Figures are monthly averages of production per day estimates as of Jan. 1 of year shown.

U.S. Petroleum Trade, 1955-2015

Source: *Monthly Energy Review*, Aug. 2016, Energy Information Administration (EIA), U.S. Dept. of Energy
(in thousands of barrels per day; average for the year)

Year	Imports from Persian Gulf[1]	Total imports	Total exports	Net imports[2]	Petroleum products supplied[3]	Year	Imports from Persian Gulf[1]	Total imports	Total exports	Net imports[2]	Petroleum products supplied[3]
1955	NA	1,248	368	880	8,455	2004	2,493	13,145	1,048	12,097	20,731
1960	326	1,815	202	1,613	9,797	2005	2,334	13,714	1,165	12,549	20,802
1965	359	2,468	187	2,281	11,512	2006	2,211	13,707	1,317	12,390	20,687
1970	184	3,419	259	3,161	14,697	2007	2,163	13,468	1,433	12,036	20,680
1975	1,165	6,056	209	5,846	16,322	2008	2,370	12,915	1,802	11,114	19,498
1980	1,519	6,909	544	6,365	17,056	2009	1,689	11,691	2,024	9,667	18,771
1985	311	5,067	781	4,286	15,726	2010	1,711	11,793	2,353	9,441	19,180
1990	1,966	8,018	857	7,161	16,988	2011	1,861	11,436	2,986	8,450	18,882
1995	1,573	8,835	949	7,886	17,725	2012	2,156	10,598	3,205	7,393	18,490
2000	2,488	11,459	1,040	10,419	19,701	2013	2,009	9,859	3,621	6,237	18,961
2001	2,761	11,871	971	10,900	19,649	2014	1,875	9,241	4,176	5,065	19,106
2002	2,269	11,530	984	10,546	19,761	2015	1,507	9,401	4,750	4,561	19,395
2003	2,501	12,264	1,027	11,238	20,034						

NA = Not available. **Note:** U.S. exports include shipments to U.S. territories; imports include receipts from U.S. territories. Numbers may not add up to totals because of rounding. (1) Bahrain, Iran, Iraq, Kuwait, Qatar, Saudi Arabia, United Arab Emirates, and the Neutral Zone between Kuwait and Saudi Arabia. (2) Total imports minus total exports. (3) Includes domestic production and imports minus change in stocks, refinery imports, and exports.

World Fossil Fuel Reserves

Source: International Energy Statistics Database, Energy Information Administration (EIA), U.S. Dept. of Energy

	Crude oil (bil barrels), 2015	Natural gas (tril cu ft), 2015	Coal (mil short tons), 2011		Crude oil (bil barrels), 2015	Natural gas (tril cu ft), 2015	Coal (mil short tons), 2011
North America[1] ..	**219.8**	**422.1**	**267,411**	**Middle East**	**808.1**	**2,818.2**	**1,237**
Canada	172.5	71.8	7,255	Bahrain	0.1	3.3	NA
Greenland	0.0	0.0	202	Iran	157.8	1,201.4	1,237
Mexico........	9.8	16.5	1,335	Iraq	144.2	111.5	NA
United States[1] ..	36.5	338.3	258,619	Israel	0.0	7.0	NA
Central & South				Kuwait	104.0	63.5	NA
America	**329.4**	**274.3**	**16,139**	Oman	5.2	24.9	NA
Argentina......	2.4	11.1	606	Qatar	25.2	871.6	NA
Bolivia	0.2	9.9	1	Saudi Arabia ...	268.3	294.3	NA
Brazil	15.3	16.2	7,308	Syria	2.5	8.5	NA
Chile	0.2	3.5	171	UAE..........	97.8	215.1	NA
Colombia......	2.4	6.4	7,436	Yemen	3.0	16.9	NA
Cuba	0.1	2.5	NA	**Africa**	**126.5**	**604.1**	**35,069**
Ecuador.......	8.8	0.2	26	Algeria........	12.2	159.1	65
Peru..........	0.7	15.0	49	Angola........	9.0	9.7	NA
Trinidad &				Congo, Dem.			
Tobago......	0.7	12.2	NA	Rep.........	0.2	0.0	97
Venezuela	298.4	197.1	528	Congo Rep.....	1.6	3.2	NA
Europe	**11.7**	**130.9**	**90,743**	Egypt.........	4.4	77.2	18
Albania	0.2	0.0	875	Libya	48.4	53.2	NA
Bosnia & Herz.	0.0	0.0	3,145	Mozambique ...	0.0	100.0	234
Bulgaria.......	0.0	0.2	2,608	Namibia	0.0	2.2	NA
Czech Republic	0.0	0.1	1,160	Niger	0.2	NA	77
Germany	0.0	3.4	44,697	Nigeria........	37.1	180.5	209
Greece........	0.0	0.0	3,329	South Africa....	0.0	NA	33,241
Hungary.......	0.0	0.3	1,830	Sudan[2]........	5.0	3.0	NA
Italy	0.5	2.0	55	Swaziland	0.0	0.0	159
Macedonia.....	0.0	0.0	366	Tanzania	0.0	0.2	220
Montenegro	0.0	0.0	157	Zimbabwe	0.0	0.0	553
Netherlands....	0.1	31.7	NA	**Asia & Oceania** ..	**46.0**	**534.5**	**317,827**
Norway	5.5	72.4	6	Afghanistan	0.0	1.8	73
Poland........	0.1	3.0	6,024	Australia	1.2	30.4	84,217
Romania	0.6	3.7	321	Bangladesh	0.0	8.5	323
Serbia	0.1	1.7	14,783	Brunei	1.1	13.8	NA
Slovakia.......	0.0	0.5	289	China.........	24.6	164.0	126,215
Slovenia.......	0.0	0.0	246	India.........	5.7	50.4	66,800
Spain.........	0.2	0.1	584	Indonesia......	3.7	103.4	30,883
Turkey	0.3	0.2	9,592	Japan.........	0.0	0.7	383
United Kingdom	3.0	8.5	251	Korea, North ...	0.0	0.0	661
Eurasia........	**118.9**	**2,178.0**	**251,364**	Korea, South ...	NA	0.3	139
Armenia.......	0.0	0.0	180	Laos..........	0.0	0.0	554
Azerbaijan.....	7.0	35.0	NA	Malaysia	4.0	83.0	4
Belarus	0.2	0.1	110	Mongolia	NA	0.0	2,778
Georgia	0.0	0.3	222	Myanmar......	0.1	10.0	2
Kazakhstan	30.0	85.0	37,038	New Zealand ...	0.1	1.4	629
Kyrgyzstan.....	0.0	0.2	895	Pakistan.......	0.4	24.7	2,282
Russia	80.0	1,688.2	173,074	Philippines.....	0.1	3.5	348
Tajikistan	0.0	0.2	413	Thailand.......	0.5	8.4	1,366
Turkmenistan...	0.6	265.0	NA	Vietnam........	4.4	24.7	165
Ukraine	0.4	39.0	37,339	**World[1]**	**1,655.6**	**6,927.5**	**979,791**
Uzbekistan.....	0.6	65.0	2,094				

NA = Not reported separately but included in regional and world totals. **Note:** Regional and world totals may include countries not shown. Proved reserves only. Some countries omitted for lack of appreciable reserves. (1) U.S. figures for crude oil and natural gas are from 2013, the latest year available. (2) Includes South Sudan.

U.S. Crude Oil Imports by Selected Countries, 1975-2015

Source: *Petroleum Supply Annual*, Energy Information Administration (EIA), U.S. Dept. of Energy

The United States' dependence on foreign oil continues to decline thanks to increased U.S. production of crude oil, natural gas, and domestic biofuels like ethanol and biodiesel. Imports stood at just 7.3 mil barrels a day in 2015, down from more than 10.1 mil barrels per day a decade ago. And imports from the Oil Producing and Exporting Countries (OPEC) declined to 2.7 mil barrels daily, the lowest amount since 1987. In 2015, approximately 24% of the petroleum consumed by the United States was imported from foreign countries, the lowest level since 1970. Since 2005, Canada has been the largest supplier of U.S. oil, responsible for nearly 40% of all U.S. oil imports. Imports from Canada exceeded those from all OPEC countries combined in 2015. In 1995-2016, sanctions prohibited the U.S. from importing oil from Iran.

(in thousands of barrels per day; ranked by 2015 imports)

Country	1975	1980	1985	1990	1995	2000	2005	2010	2014	2015
Canada	600	199	468	643	1,040	1,348	1,633	1,970	2,882	3,169
*Saudi Arabia	701	1,250	132	1,195	1,260	1,523	1,445	1,082	1,159	1,051
*Venezuela	395	156	306	666	1,151	1,223	1,241	912	733	779
Mexico	70	507	715	689	1,027	1,313	1,556	1,152	781	688
Colombia	0	0	0	140	207	318	156	338	294	370
*Iraq	2	28	46	514	0	620	527	415	369	229
*Ecuador[1]	0	0	0	0	96	125	276	210	213	225
*Kuwait	4	27	4	79	213	263	227	195	309	206
Brazil	0	1	0	0	0	5	94	255	145	189
*Angola[2]	71	37	104	236	360	295	456	383	139	124
Chad	NA	NA	NA	NA	NA	NA	74	18	61	72
*Nigeria	746	841	280	784	621	875	1,077	983	58	57
*Indonesia[3]	379	314	292	98	64	36	19	33	20	34
Russia[4]	0	0	0	1	14	7	199	269	18	28
Argentina	NA	NA	NA	NA	44	53	56	29	29	16
Azerbaijan	NA	NA	NA	NA	NA	NA	NA	55	23	13
United Kingdom	0	173	278	155	341	291	224	120	10	11
Australia	0	0	21	47	16	49	10	10	2	10
Norway	12	144	31	96	258	302	119	25	9	9
Vietnam	NA	NA	NA	NA	1	9	31	12	10	9
Congo Republic	NA	NA	NA	NA	20	42	25	70	4	8
Guatemala	NA	NA	NA	NA	8	18	11	11	7	8
*Gabon[5]	NA	NA	NA	NA	229	143	127	47	16	7
Trinidad and Tobago	115	115	98	76	62	56	64	45	5	7
Peru	NA	NA	NA	NA	21	4	4	14	9	6
Equatorial Guinea	NA	NA	NA	NA	NA	6	68	50	4	5
*Algeria	264	456	84	63	27	1	228	328	6	3
*Libya	223	548	0	0	0	0	44	43	5	3
Non-OPEC countries[1,2,3,5]	NA	NA	NA	NA	3,660	4,526	5,310	4,661	4,339	4,672
OPEC countries[1,2,3,5]	3,211	3,864	1,312	3,514	3,570	4,544	4,816	4,553	3,005	2,679
Persian Gulf countries[6]	1,121	1,508	244	1,801	1,479	2,409	2,207	1,694	1,851	1,488
TOTAL	4,105	5,263	3,201	5,894	7,230	9,071	10,126	9,213	7,344	7,351

* = OPEC member. NA = Not available. **Note:** Subtotals and totals include countries not shown here. (1) Ecuador suspended its OPEC membership Dec. 1992-Nov. 2007. Imports from Ecuador in 1993-2007 appear in non-OPEC totals. (2) Angola became a member of OPEC as of 2007 and is not included in OPEC totals from before that year. (3) Indonesia withdrew from OPEC, 2009-15. Imports for 2009-15 appear in non-OPEC totals. (4) May include oil from USSR states before 1992. (5) Gabon withdrew from OPEC as of Dec. 31, 1994, but rejoined in July 2016. Imports for 1995-2015 appear in non-OPEC totals. (6) Bahrain, Iran, Iraq, Kuwait, Qatar, Saudi Arabia, and United Arab Emirates.

U.S. Coal Production and Consumption, 1950-2015

Source: *Monthly Energy Review*, Aug. 2016; *Annual Coal Report, 2014*; Energy Information Administration (EIA); U.S. Dept. of Energy

(in thousand short tons)

	Coal production[1]			Coal consumption				
Year	Surface mining	Underground mining	Total production	Residential	Commercial	Industrial	Electric power[2]	Total consumption
1950	139,388	421,000	560,388	51,562	63,021	224,637	91,871	494,102
1960	141,745	292,584	434,329	24,159	16,789	177,402	176,685	398,081
1970	272,131	340,530	612,661	9,024	7,090	186,637	320,182	523,231
1975	361,174	293,467	654,641	2,823	6,587	147,244	405,962	562,640
1980	492,192	337,508	829,700	1,355	5,097	127,004	569,274	702,730
1985	532,838	350,800	883,638	1,711	6,068	116,429	693,841	818,049
1990	604,529	424,546	1,029,076	1,345	5,379	115,207	782,567	904,498
1995	636,725	396,249	1,032,974	755	5,052	106,067	850,230	962,104
2000	699,953	373,659	1,073,612	454	3,673	94,147	985,821	1,084,095
2005	762,887	368,612	1,131,498	378	4,342	83,774	1,037,485	1,125,978
2010	745,357	337,155	1,084,368	339	3,081	70,381	975,052	1,048,514
2011	748,372	345,606	1,095,628	307	2,793	67,671	932,484	1,002,948
2012	672,748	342,387	1,016,458	NA	2,045	63,589	823,551	889,185
2013	641,191	341,685	984,482	NA	1,951	64,529	857,962	924,442
2014	643,721	354,704	1,000,049	NA	1,887	64,243	851,602	917,731
2015	NA	NA	NA	NA	1,503	58,182	739,689	799,375

NA = Not available. (1) A small amount of refuse recovery has been included in coal production figures since 2001. (2) Electricity-only and combined-heat-and-power (CHP) plants whose primary business is to sell electricity or electricity and heat to the public. Through 1988, data are for electric utilities only; beginning in 1989, data are for electric utilities and independent power producers.

World Nuclear Power Summary, 2015

Source: *Nuclear Power Reactors in the World*, International Atomic Energy Agency (IAEA); as of Dec. 31, 2015

Country	Reactors in operation No. of units	Reactors in operation Total MW(e)	Reactors under construction No. of units	Reactors under construction Total MW(e)	Nuclear electricity supplied in 2015 TW(e).h[1]	Nuclear electricity supplied in 2015 % of nation's total	Total operating experience[2] Years	Total operating experience[2] Months
Argentina	3	1,632	1	25	6.5	4.8%	76	2
Armenia	1	375	—	—	2.6	34.5	41	8
Belgium	7	5,913	—	—	24.8	37.5	275	7
Brazil	2	1,884	1	1,245	13.9	2.8	49	3
Bulgaria	2	1,926	—	—	14.7	31.3	159	3
Canada	19	13,524	—	—	95.6	16.6	693	6
China	31	26,774	24	24,128	161.2	3.0	209	2
Czech Republic	6	3,930	—	—	25.3	32.5	146	10
Finland	4	2,752	1	1,600	22.3	33.7	147	4
France	58	63,130	1	1,630	419.0	76.3	2,048	4
Germany	8	10,799	—	—	86.8	14.1	816	7
Hungary	4	1,889	—	—	15.0	52.7	122	2
India	21	5,308	6	3,907	34.6	3.5	439	6
Iran	1	915	—	—	3.2	1.3	4	4
Japan	43	40,290	2	2,650	4.3	0.5	1,739	0
Korea, South	24	21,733	4	5,420	157.2	31.7	474	0
Mexico	2	1,440	—	—	11.2	6.8	47	11
Netherlands	1	482	—	—	3.9	3.7	71	0
Pakistan	3	690	2	630	4.3	4.4	64	8
Romania	2	1,300	—	—	10.7	17.3	27	11
Russia	35	25,443	8	6,582	182.8	18.6	1,191	4
Slovakia	4	1,814	2	880	14.1	55.9	156	7
Slovenia	1	688	—	—	5.4	38.0	34	3
South Africa	2	1,860	—	—	11.0	4.7	62	3
Spain	7	7,121	—	—	54.8	20.3	315	1
Sweden	10	9,648	—	—	54.5	34.3	432	6
Switzerland	5	3,333	—	—	22.2	33.5	204	11
Taiwan	6	5,052	2	2,600	35.1	16.3	206	1
Ukraine	15	13,107	2	1,900	82.4	56.5	458	6
United Kingdom	15	8,918	—	—	63.9	18.9	1,559	7
United States	99	99,185	5	5,633	798.0	19.5	4,111	4
TOTAL	**441**	**382,855**	**67**	**66,428**	**2,441.3**	**—**	**16,536**	**7**

— = Not applicable. MW(e) = Megawatt electricity. (1) 1 terawatt-hour [TW(e).h] = 106 megawatt-hour [MW(e).h]. For an average power plant, 1 TW(e).h = 0.39 megaton of coal equivalent (input) and 0.23 megaton of oil equivalent (input). (2) Total includes shutdown plants for countries not listed here: Italy (80 years, 8 months), Kazakhstan (25 years, 10 months), and Lithuania (43 years, 6 months).

Nations Most Reliant on Nuclear Energy, 2015

Source: *Nuclear Power Reactors in the World*, International Atomic Energy Agency (IAEA)
(nuclear electricity generation as % of total electricity generated within country)

Rank	Country	Nuclear share	Rank	Country	Nuclear share	Rank	Country	Nuclear share	Rank	Country	Nuclear share
1.	France	76.3%	9.	Finland	33.7%	17.	Russia	18.6%	25.	Pakistan	4.4%
2.	Ukraine	56.5	10.	Switzerland	33.5	18.	Romania	17.3	26.	Netherlands	3.7
3.	Slovakia	55.9	11.	Czech Republic	32.5	19.	Canada	16.6	27.	India	3.5
4.	Hungary	52.7	12.	Korea, South	31.7	20.	Taiwan	16.3	28.	China	3.0
5.	Slovenia	38.0	13.	Bulgaria	31.3	21.	Germany	14.1	29.	Brazil	2.8
6.	Belgium	37.5	14.	Spain	20.3	22.	Mexico	6.8	30.	Iran	1.3
7.	Armenia	34.5	15.	United States	19.5	23.	Argentina	4.8	31.	Japan	0.5
8.	Sweden	34.3	16.	United Kingdom	18.9	24.	South Africa	4.7			

U.S. Nuclear Reactors and Power Plant Operations, 1953-2015

Source: *Monthly Energy Review*, Aug. 2016, Energy Information Administration (EIA), U.S. Dept. of Energy

Years	Ordered[1]	Canceled	Construction permits issued[2]	Low-power licenses issued[3]	Full-power licenses issued[4]	Shutdown[5]	Operable units[6]	Capacity factor[6,7]	Nuclear electricity generation (bil net kWh)[6]	Nuclear share of domestic electricity generation[6]
1953-59	14	0	8	2	2	0	2	NA	0.2	NA
1960-64	7	0	12	13	12	2	13	NA	3.3	0.3%
1965-69	81	0	50	8	9	4	17	NA	13.9	1.0
1970-74	143	16	59	41	41	5	55	47.8%	114.0	6.1
1975-79	13	43	48	17	17	3	69	58.4	255.2	11.3
1980-84	0	54	0	24	19	1	87	56.3	327.6	13.5
1985-89	0	7	0	24	28	4	111	62.2	529.4	17.8
1990-94	0	2	0	2	3	3	109	73.8	640.4	19.7
1995-99	0	2	0	1	1	6	104	85.3	728.3	19.7
2000-04	0	0	0	0	0	0	104	90.1	788.5	19.9
2005-09	0	0	0	0	0	0	104	90.3	798.9	20.2
2010-15	0	0	0	0	0	5	99	92.2	797.2	19.5
Total	**259**	**124**	**177**	**132**	**132**	**32**	**NA**	**NA**	**NA**	**NA**

NA = Not applicable. **Note:** The permit/license categories shown here are historic. The Nuclear Regulatory Commission anticipates 16 or more new combined license applications under current regulations over the next few years—the first of which was submitted in Sept. 2007—which may amount to 25 or more new reactor units. (1) Order placed by a utility or government agency for a nuclear steam supply system. (2) Permits issued in a given period, not extant permits. (3) Permission to conduct testing but not operate at full power. (4) Permission to operate at full power. (5) Permanently ceased operation. (6) As of the end of the designated period. (7) The ratio of electric energy produced to the amount that could be produced at continuous full-power operation.

U.S. Nuclear Reactors Generating the Most Electricity, 2015

Source: U.S. Nuclear Statistics Database, Energy Information Administration (EIA), U.S. Dept. of Energy
(in thousand net megawatt-hours)

Rank	Reactor, location	Electricity generated	Capacity[1]	Rank	Reactor, location	Electricity generated	Capacity[1]
1.	Grand Gulf-1, Port Gibson, MS	11,714,588	94.9%	14.	South Texas-2, Bay City, TX	10,127,479	90.3%
2.	Palo Verde-1, Wintersburg, AZ	11,611,012	101.1	15.	Byron-2, Byron, IL	10,041,586	100.9
3.	Nine Mile Point-2, Scriba, NY	11,051,693	97.0	16.	Limerick-1, Limerick, PA	10,014,943	102.1
4.	Talen Susquehanna-1, Salem Township, PA	10,903,513	98.8	17.	Braidwood-1, Braceville, IL	9,994,362	96.9
5.	Peach Bottom-2, Delta, PA	10,759,975	97.6	18.	PSEG Salem-1, Salem, NJ	9,748,411	95.1
6.	Millstone-3, Waterford, CT	10,653,010	99.3	19.	Braidwood-2, Braceville, IL	9,745,649	96.6
7.	Comanche Peak-1, Glen Rose, TX	10,604,708	100.5	20.	Diablo Canyon-2, Avila Beach, CA	9,715,715	99.2
8.	Palo Verde-3, Wintersburg, AZ	10,507,132	91.4	21.	Talen Susquehanna-2, Salem Township, PA	9,687,747	87.8
9.	Callaway-1, Fulton, MO	10,440,082	99.9	22.	Browns Ferry-3, Athens, AL	9,623,053	99.4
10.	Palo Verde-2, Wintersburg, AZ	10,407,451	90.4	23.	Seabrook-1, Seabrook, NH	9,484,204	86.9
11.	McGuire-1, Huntersville, NC	10,188,919	102.2	24.	Perry-1, Perry, OH	9,482,845	87.3
12.	LaSalle-1, Marseilles, IL	10,154,572	102.1	25.	Browns Ferry-1, Athens, AL	9,455,321	98.1
13.	Vogtle-2, Waynesboro, GA	10,142,539	100.5				

(1) The ratio of power generated to the maximum potential generation expressed as a percentage.

Renewable Energy Sources

Source: U.S. Dept. of Energy

Concern over the environmental impact of burning fossil fuels has helped spur interest in alternative fuels that are less polluting. And because the supply of fossil fuels is finite and diminishing, there is interest in "renewable" sources that do not deplete existing supplies. However, renewable energy sources still make up only a small share of U.S. domestic energy production (about 11% in 2015). The main reason for this is their relatively higher cost (in some cases two to four times that of power obtained from traditional fuels). The following are the major renewable energy sources available.

Biomass is plant-derived material usable as an energy source. It includes wood energy crops such as hybrid poplars and willow trees, agricultural crops including soybeans and corn, and animal and other wastes. Biomass is one of the two most common renewable energy sources in the U.S. today, along with hydropower. Biomass such as wood can be burned to produce heat and generate electricity. Agricultural crops can be chemically converted into fuels such as ethanol and biodiesel; these are the only known renewable liquid energy sources and may one day replace petroleum and fossil-fuel-produced diesel. But bringing ethanol and biodiesel into wide use would require more energy-efficient methods of production and transportation. Overall, biomass fuels burn much cleaner than fossil fuels, though biomass fuels still produce carbon dioxide and other pollutants.

Geothermal energy is generated from heat inside of the Earth. This form of energy is both clean and renewable. The technology has caught on in countries with substantial geothermal activity such as Iceland, where it accounted for 66% of primary energy use in 2015. In the U.S., the best sources for geothermal power are in the West and in Hawaii, where there are many heated underground lakes. Large-scale access would require drilling. A major goal in this field is to find a way to harness energy directly from magma (molten rock material), which has great potential because of its high temperatures.

Hydrogen is the third most abundant element on Earth. It does not naturally occur on Earth as a pure gas or liquid but is always combined with other elements (such as oxygen, to form water, or carbon, to form methane). If hydrogen is to be used for energy, it must be separated from these other elements. That can be achieved through methods involving heat, photosynthesis, sunlight, or electricity.

Hydrogen batteries, or fuel cells, were used by NASA's space shuttles. Within a fuel cell, a chemical reaction occurs in which electrons are released from hydrogen atoms. These electrons flow through an external circuit as electricity. The hydrogen atoms' protons combine with oxygen (and some of the electrons in the electric current) to produce heat and water suitable for drinking. Fuel cells do not run down but work as long as hydrogen is supplied. Some experts think hydrogen will be the power source of the future. An infrastructure would need to be created for safe and cost-effective transportation and storage of hydrogen.

Hydropower, or hydroelectric power, is generated by water flowing through turbines. Along with biomass fuels, it is one of the two most common renewable energy sources in the U.S. today. A dam on a river is a common hydropower producer. No harmful greenhouse gases are produced, but the dams needed to generate power can harm river ecosystems. Researchers are working on turbine technologies to maximize use of hydropower and reduce adverse environmental effects.

Ocean energy can be generated in two ways. Thermal ocean energy uses heat that the ocean absorbs from the sun to power generators, sometimes producing drinkable desalinated water as a byproduct. Mechanical ocean energy is generated by the movement of tides and waves through turbines. In both cases, power generation is not very efficient with current technology. Much more research is needed. Mechanical ocean energy requires the building of large dams or breakwater-type structures called tidal barrages, which could harm coastal ecosystems.

Solar energy is generated using heat and light from the sun. Solar energy is an increasingly common source of electricity. Photovoltaic (PV) solar cells are made of semiconducting materials that can directly convert sunlight to electricity without producing any harmful waste. Arrays of mirrors can concentrate the sun's rays onto PV panels, making solar collectors more efficient. Sunlight can also be used to heat water directly. According to the Dept. of Energy, homes incorporating solar heating designs can save as much as 50% on heating bills. The downside to solar energy is that it depends heavily on a range of factors including location, time of year, and weather.

Wind energy uses wind turbines to produce energy. They are perched on high towers, usually 100 ft tall or higher, and often placed in large groups ("farms"). Farmers and homeowners sometimes use standalone turbines to generate supplemental electricity. Tax credits for wind energy producers and government incentives for homeowners have significantly lowered the price of wind power. But some object to wind farms because of their appearance or the noise the turbines make. Wind power raises few other environmental problems, but the turbines can pose a danger to birds. In addition, because weather is involved, consistent energy generation can be a challenge.

CRIME

Crime in the U.S., 1990-2014

Source: *Crime in the United States, 2014*, Federal Bureau of Investigation (FBI), U.S. Dept. of Justice

Reported offenses are classified as **violent crimes** if they involve force or the threat of force: murder and nonnegligent manslaughter, rape, robbery, and aggravated assault. The following offenses are considered **property crimes**: burglary, larceny-theft, motor vehicle theft, and arson (excluded from this table).

		Violent crime					Property crime			
Year	Population[1]	All violent crimes	Murder and nonnegligent manslaughter	Rape[2]	Robbery	Aggravated assault[3]	All property crimes	Burglary	Larceny-theft[4]	Motor vehicle theft
NUMBER OF OFFENSES										
1990	249,464,396	1,820,127	23,438	102,555	639,271	1,054,863	12,655,486	3,073,909	7,945,670	1,635,907
1995	262,803,276	1,798,792	21,606	97,470	580,509	1,099,207	12,063,935	2,593,784	7,997,710	1,472,441
2000	281,421,906	1,425,486	15,586	90,178	408,016	911,706	10,182,584	2,050,992	6,971,590	1,160,002
2005	296,507,061	1,390,745	16,740	94,347	417,438	862,220	10,174,754	2,155,448	6,783,447	1,235,859
2007	301,621,157	1,422,970	17,128	92,160	447,324	866,358	9,882,212	2,190,198	6,591,542	1,100,472
2008	304,059,724	1,394,461	16,465	90,750	443,563	843,683	9,774,152	2,228,887	6,586,206	959,059
2009	307,006,550	1,325,896	15,399	89,241	408,742	812,514	9,337,060	2,203,313	6,338,095	795,652
2010	309,330,219	1,251,248	14,722	85,593	369,089	781,844	9,112,625	2,168,459	6,204,601	739,565
2011	311,587,816	1,206,005	14,661	84,175	354,746	752,423	9,052,743	2,185,140	6,151,095	716,508
2012	313,873,685	1,217,057	14,856	85,141	355,051	762,009	9,001,992	2,109,932	6,168,874	723,186
2013	316,497,531	1,168,298	14,319	82,109	345,093	726,777	8,651,892	1,932,139	6,019,465	700,288
2014	318,857,056	1,165,383	14,249	84,041	325,802	741,291	8,277,829	1,729,806	5,858,496	689,527
PERCENT CHANGE: NUMBER OF OFFENSES										
2013-14		−0.2%	−0.5%	2.4%	−5.6%	2.0%	−4.3%	−10.5%	−2.7%	−1.5%
2010-14		−6.9	−3.2	−1.8	−11.7	−5.2	−9.2	−20.2	−5.6	−6.8
2005-14		−16.2	−14.9	−10.9	−22.0	−14.0	−18.6	−19.7	−13.6	−44.2
RATE PER 100,000 RESIDENTS										
1990		729.6	9.4	41.1	256.3	422.9	5,073.1	1,232.2	3,185.1	655.8
1995		684.5	8.2	37.1	220.9	418.3	4,590.5	987.0	3,043.2	560.3
2000		506.5	5.5	32.0	145.0	324.0	3,618.3	728.8	2,477.3	412.2
2005		469.0	5.6	31.8	140.8	290.8	3,431.5	726.9	2,287.8	416.8
2007		471.8	5.7	30.6	148.3	287.2	3,276.4	726.1	2,185.4	364.9
2008		458.6	5.4	29.8	145.9	277.5	3,214.6	733.0	2,166.1	315.4
2009		431.9	5.0	29.1	133.1	264.7	3,041.3	717.7	2,064.5	259.2
2010		404.5	4.8	27.7	119.3	252.8	2,945.9	701.0	2,005.8	239.1
2011		387.1	4.7	27.0	113.9	241.5	2,905.4	701.3	1,974.1	230.0
2012		387.8	4.7	27.1	113.1	242.8	2,868.0	672.2	1,965.4	230.4
2013		369.1	4.5	25.9	109.0	229.6	2,733.6	610.5	1,901.9	221.3
2014		365.5	4.5	26.4	102.2	232.5	2,596.1	542.5	1,837.3	216.2
PERCENT CHANGE: RATE PER 100,000 RESIDENTS										
2013-14		−1.0%	−1.2%	1.6%	−6.3%	1.2%	−5.0%	−11.1%	−3.4%	−2.3%
2010-14		−9.6	−6.1	−4.7	−14.4	−8.0	−11.9	−22.6	−8.4	−9.6
2005-14		−22.1	−20.8	−17.2	−27.4	−20.1	−24.3	−25.4	−19.7	−48.1

(1) U.S. Census Bureau estimates for July 1 of each year except for 1990, 2000, and 2010, which show Apr. 1 decennial census counts. (2) The FBI revised its definition of rape in 2012 for data collection from 2013 on. For comparison purposes, however, figures for rape after 2012 refer to the legacy definition of rape: "carnal knowledge of a female forcibly and against her will." That definition does not include statutory rape, other types of sexual offenses, or sexual attacks on males, which were considered aggravated assaults or sex offenses, depending on circumstances and extent of injuries. (3) Attack upon another with the intent of doing serious bodily harm; usually accompanied by the use of a weapon or other means likely to produce death or great bodily harm. (4) The unlawful taking of another's property not involving force or fraud (e.g., theft of motor vehicle parts, shoplifting). Excludes crimes such as embezzlement and check fraud.

Violent Crime Rates in the U.S., 1976-2014

Source: *Crime in the United States*, 1995, 2000, and 2014 editions, Federal Bureau of Investigation (FBI), U.S. Dept. of Justice

After rising during much of the 1980s, the violent crime rate has dropped sharply. Overall, the 2014 rate was half what it was in 1990, and the rates of murder and robbery have dropped even more precipitously. Crime rate is the number of reported offenses per 100,000 residents.

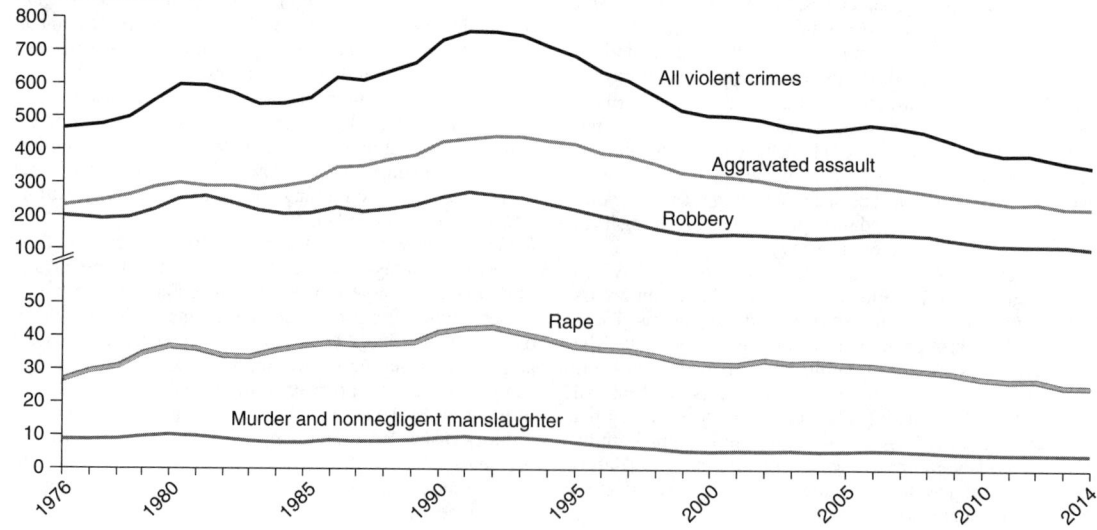

U.S. Crime Rates by Region, Geographic Division, and State, 2014

Source: *Crime in the United States, 2014*, Federal Bureau of Investigation (FBI), U.S. Dept. of Justice

(per 100,000 residents, as estimated by U.S. Census Bureau for July 1 of year)

	Violent crime				Property crime[1]			
	All violent crimes	Murder and nonnegligent manslaughter	Rape[2]	Robbery	Aggravated assault[3]	All property crimes	Burglary	Larceny-theft[4]	Motor vehicle theft
Total U.S.[5]	375.7	4.5	36.6	102.2	232.5	2,596.1	542.5	1,837.3	216.2
Northeast...........	322.5	3.3	26.8	104.6	187.8	1,817.5	322.7	1,390.5	104.3
New England	287.2	1.9	30.7	72.4	182.0	1,902.4	360.8	1,418.3	123.3
Connecticut........	236.9	2.4	21.7	87.8	125.0	1,920.4	332.4	1,418.1	169.9
Maine	127.8	1.6	36.5	22.9	66.9	1,986.4	378.2	1,548.2	60.1
Massachusetts	391.4	2.0	32.3	89.5	267.6	1,857.1	370.1	1,364.5	122.5
New Hampshire	196.1	0.9	44.8	40.5	110.0	1,962.7	313.7	1,584.4	64.6
Rhode Island.......	219.2	2.4	34.2	50.1	132.5	2,173.6	457.1	1,542.8	173.7
Vermont	99.3	1.6	17.6	11.2	68.9	1,524.4	324.6	1,160.8	38.9
Middle Atlantic	334.9	3.8	25.4	115.9	189.8	1,787.5	309.2	1,380.7	97.6
New Jersey........	261.2	3.9	14.3	117.5	125.6	1,734.1	354.8	1,248.3	131.0
New York..........	381.8	3.1	27.5	121.8	229.4	1,718.2	257.2	1,381.4	79.7
Pennsylvania.......	314.1	4.8	29.9	105.8	173.5	1,931.7	357.5	1,472.2	102.0
Midwest	342.2	4.3	41.2	90.2	206.4	2,383.3	488.5	1,713.0	181.8
East North Central	350.6	4.7	41.4	102.8	201.8	2,331.0	494.5	1,664.4	172.0
Illinois	370.0	5.3	32.3	118.8	213.7	2,075.9	388.2	1,552.2	135.5
Indiana	365.3	5.0	33.1	104.5	222.6	2,649.4	559.3	1,880.0	210.1
Michigan	427.3	5.4	63.3	80.9	277.7	2,043.9	445.9	1,384.5	213.5
Ohio	284.9	4.0	43.5	110.0	127.4	2,799.1	680.0	1,963.6	155.4
Wisconsin	290.3	2.9	29.1	88.0	170.4	2,088.3	368.5	1,547.6	172.3
West North Central	323.7	3.5	41.0	62.4	216.9	2,499.7	474.9	1,821.2	203.5
Iowa	273.5	1.9	36.3	33.6	201.6	2,093.8	464.4	1,495.8	133.6
Kansas	348.6	3.1	48.6	46.9	250.0	2,735.2	545.0	1,952.4	237.8
Minnesota	229.1	1.6	36.7	67.6	123.3	2,297.5	380.7	1,763.5	153.3
Missouri..........	442.9	6.6	39.2	92.2	304.8	2,906.5	581.5	2,055.3	269.8
Nebraska.........	280.4	2.9	45.8	55.4	176.2	2,523.5	422.5	1,864.1	236.8
North Dakota.......	265.1	3.0	48.4	23.4	190.3	2,110.3	366.1	1,539.5	204.7
South Dakota	326.5	2.3	55.1	23.4	245.7	1,863.9	330.3	1,415.5	118.0
South[5]	422.0	5.5	37.3	107.5	271.7	3,009.8	668.7	2,130.8	210.3
South Atlantic[5]	422.0	5.6	34.2	110.4	271.8	2,997.6	648.0	2,151.8	197.8
Delaware..........	489.1	5.8	41.3	135.6	306.4	2,982.0	616.5	2,230.1	135.4
District of Columbia[5]	1,244.4	15.9	71.6	530.7	626.1	5,182.5	526.0	4,082.3	574.1
Florida............	540.5	5.8	43.0	125.2	366.4	3,415.5	719.9	2,481.5	214.0
Georgia...........	377.3	5.7	30.2	123.0	218.4	3,281.2	756.9	2,258.4	266.0
Maryland..........	446.1	6.1	27.1	159.7	253.2	2,507.5	468.7	1,819.6	219.2
North Carolina......	329.5	5.1	24.3	84.6	215.4	2,873.1	798.2	1,937.8	137.1
South Carolina	497.7	6.4	42.8	82.7	365.8	3,460.3	759.9	2,433.4	267.0
Virginia...........	196.2	4.1	27.7	51.5	112.9	1,930.3	277.7	1,560.5	92.1
West Virginia.......	302.0	4.0	27.3	35.2	235.5	2,034.7	484.9	1,447.3	102.5
East South Central	416.1	5.7	37.4	94.3	278.7	2,877.6	712.3	1,986.8	178.5
Alabama	427.4	5.7	41.3	96.9	283.4	3,177.6	819.0	2,149.5	209.1
Kentucky..........	211.6	3.6	32.6	75.6	99.8	2,246.9	526.7	1,577.1	143.2
Mississippi........	278.5	8.6	35.3	81.2	153.4	2,921.2	813.3	1,956.9	150.9
Tennessee	608.4	5.7	38.6	110.9	453.2	3,060.6	712.2	2,156.0	192.4
West South Central	424.8	5.2	42.4	109.2	268.0	3,094.2	681.0	2,167.1	246.1
Arkansas..........	480.1	5.6	59.4	69.1	346.0	3,338.0	835.7	2,313.5	188.8
Louisiana..........	514.7	10.3	29.6	122.5	352.4	3,458.8	824.5	2,421.6	212.7
Oklahoma	406.0	4.5	45.8	78.6	277.0	2,990.7	760.9	1,956.9	272.9
Texas	405.9	4.4	42.3	115.7	243.6	3,019.4	627.8	2,137.3	254.3
West.............	372.0	3.9	38.5	102.7	226.9	2,710.3	554.4	1,815.6	340.4
Mountain	380.4	3.8	51.8	82.3	242.4	2,806.3	563.4	1,991.8	251.1
Arizona	399.9	4.7	50.2	92.8	252.1	3,197.5	647.1	2,289.1	261.3
Colorado..........	309.1	2.8	56.7	56.7	192.8	2,530.1	438.2	1,857.1	234.8
Idaho.............	212.2	2.0	37.3	12.5	160.5	1,854.8	393.3	1,359.9	101.6
Montana	323.7	3.6	52.9	19.8	247.4	2,472.9	351.2	1,922.1	199.6
Nevada	635.6	6.0	47.8	209.7	372.1	2,625.4	772.3	1,494.3	358.7
New Mexico	597.4	4.8	70.7	100.0	421.8	3,542.3	887.3	2,353.4	301.6
Utah	215.6	2.3	49.4	44.6	119.4	2,878.5	391.4	2,239.1	248.0
Wyoming..........	195.5	2.7	29.8	9.1	153.9	1,964.7	289.1	1,572.4	103.2
Pacific	368.2	3.9	32.5	111.8	220.0	2,667.5	550.3	1,736.9	380.2
Alaska...........	635.8	5.6	104.7	85.4	440.2	2,760.0	427.6	2,096.4	236.0
California..........	396.1	4.4	29.7	125.5	236.6	2,441.1	522.3	1,527.4	391.3
Hawaii............	259.2	1.8	31.3	78.0	148.1	3,050.0	547.9	2,228.9	273.3
Oregon	232.3	2.0	36.7	52.7	140.8	2,879.0	434.0	2,204.6	240.5
Washington........	285.2	2.5	38.2	79.9	164.7	3,706.1	783.0	2,489.1	434.0
Puerto Rico	236.2	19.2	1.6	145.7	69.7	1,285.7	339.2	815.8	130.7

Note: Offense totals are based on all reporting agencies and estimates for unreported areas. Figures may not add up to totals due to rounding. (1) Data for arson, considered a property crime, are not included in this table. (2) Beginning in 2013, the FBI expanded the definition of rape to include "penetration, no matter how slight, of the vagina or anus with any body part or object, or oral penetration by a sex organ of another person, without the consent of the victim." The new definition, which applies to people of any gender, updated the 80-year-old historical definition of rape, which was "carnal knowledge of a female forcibly and against her will." (3) Attack upon another with the intent of doing serious bodily harm; usually accompanied by the use of a weapon or other means likely to produce death or great bodily harm. (4) The unlawful taking of another's property not involving force or fraud (e.g., theft of motor vehicle parts, shoplifting). Excludes crimes such as embezzlement and check fraud. (5) Includes offenses reported by National Zoological Park Police and Washington Metro Transit Police.

Crime Rates in the Largest U.S. Metropolitan Areas, 2014

Source: *Crime in the United States, 2014*, Federal Bureau of Investigation, U.S. Dept. of Justice
(per 100,000 population, as estimated by U.S. Census Bureau for July 1 of year)

Memphis was the U.S. metropolitan statistical area (MSA) with the highest rate of violent crime in 2014, with more than 1,000 violent crimes per 100,000 people. It is not shown in the table below, which includes only the 30 largest MSAs; among them, Las Vegas MSA had the highest violent crime rate. San Juan, PR, had the highest murder rate, with more than 23 homicides per 100,000 residents. Among MSAs with populations over 2 mil, Portland, OR, had the lowest overall violent crime rate (258.7), while Minneapolis, MN, had the lowest murder rate (1.8).

| Metropolitan statistical area (MSA) | MSA pop. (mil.) | Violent crime | | | | | Property crime | | | |
		All violent crimes	Murder and nonnegligent manslaughter	Rape	Robbery	Aggravated assault	All property crimes	Burglary	Larceny-theft	Motor vehicle theft
Atlanta-Sandy Springs-Roswell, GA	5.6	398.4	6.1	20.4	154.0	217.9	3,231.3	725.9	2,170.4	334.9
Baltimore-Columbia-Towson, MD	2.8	588.5	9.6	20.4	222.5	336.0	2,793.5	528.2	2,010.8	254.5
Charlotte-Concord-Gastonia, NC-SC	2.4	392.2	4.5	22.3	99.4	266.0	2,822.1	601.2	2,080.7	140.2
Chicago-Naperville-Elgin, IL-IN-WI	9.5	380.1	6.3	28.2	143.3	202.2	2,135.4	361.7	1,605.9	167.9
Cincinnati, OH-KY-IN	2.1	267.3	4.6	36.7	112.6	113.4	2,957.9	637.6	2,187.7	132.6
Columbus, OH	2.0	294.9	4.8	53.9	127.3	108.9	3,097.9	718.0	2,189.3	190.6
Denver-Aurora-Lakewood, CO	2.8	331.2	2.8	54.9	75.0	198.5	—	—	1,891.6	292.5
Detroit-Warren-Dearborn, MI	4.3	529.4	8.7	44.9	125.5	350.3	2,203.7	467.1	1,353.0	383.5
Houston-The Woodlands-Sugar Land, TX	6.5	567.4	5.8	33.2	232.2	296.1	3,208.1	688.6	2,132.6	387.0
Indianapolis-Carmel-Anderson, IN	2.0	646.3	7.9	38.7	209.4	390.3	3,243.4	783.5	2,118.1	341.8
Kansas City, MO-KS	2.1	482.1	6.6	54.4	113.2	307.9	3,017.2	627.9	1,991.0	398.3
Las Vegas-Henderson-Paradise, NV	2.1	743.0	6.6	48.0	268.3	420.0	2,791.8	869.2	1,506.1	416.4
Los Angeles-Long Beach-Anaheim, CA	13.3	368.9	4.4	21.6	136.6	206.2	2,050.4	402.8	1,324.6	323.0
Miami-Fort Lauderdale-West Palm Beach, FL	5.9	595.2	7.1	37.3	188.2	362.7	3,888.9	716.8	2,881.7	290.4
Minneapolis-St. Paul-Bloomington, MN-WI	3.5	261.8	1.8	33.7	94.3	131.9	2,496.5	402.3	1,915.8	178.4
New York-Newark-Jersey City, NY-NJ-PA	20.1	371.4	3.1	16.6	135.3	216.3	—	220.8	—	100.8
Orlando-Kissimmee-Sanford, FL	2.3	685.4	6.8	62.5	154.4	461.8	4,012.5	976.0	2,789.2	247.3
Philadelphia-Camden-Wilmington, PA-NJ-DE-MD	6.1	459.6	7.0	34.3	179.6	238.7	2,331.3	432.0	1,741.9	157.4
Pittsburgh, PA	2.4	287.2	5.4	15.4	84.1	182.3	1,819.6	346.9	1,400.5	72.1
Portland-Vancouver-Hillsboro, OR-WA	2.3	258.7	2.0	33.2	68.8	154.8	2,898.3	430.2	2,171.6	296.5
Riverside-San Bernardino-Ontario, CA	4.4	327.5	4.6	20.6	99.0	203.3	2,617.1	673.7	1,499.9	443.5
Sacramento-Roseville-Arden-Arcade, CA	2.2	410.6	4.0	24.5	115.9	266.3	2,474.9	552.3	1,579.4	343.2
St. Louis, MO-IL	2.8	429.8	8.8	35.8	103.4	281.8	2,449.2	470.4	1,765.0	213.8
San Antonio-New Braunfels, TX	2.3	404.9	5.8	59.4	87.1	252.6	4,197.6	729.5	3,105.8	362.2
San Diego-Carlsbad, CA	3.3	325.2	2.3	23.4	83.1	216.4	1,813.5	336.6	1,186.3	290.6
San Francisco-Oakland-Hayward, CA	4.6	498.1	4.6	27.8	225.7	240.0	3,370.0	573.0	2,194.4	602.6
San Juan-Carolina-Caguas, Puerto Rico	2.2	283.5	23.5	0.6	190.2	69.2	1,425.4	336.9	906.8	181.7
Seattle-Tacoma-Bellevue, WA	3.7	327.3	2.7	32.7	110.2	181.8	4,189.4	840.4	2,784.0	565.0
Tampa-St. Petersburg-Clearwater, FL	2.9	447.5	5.5	36.3	98.0	307.7	3,236.4	669.7	2,360.8	206.0
Washington-Arlington-Alexandria, DC-VA-MD-WV	6.0	316.6	3.7	23.6	123.2	166.0	2,111.6	260.0	1,666.6	185.0

— = The FBI determined that the data were underreported.

Criminal Victimization, 2005-14

Source: *Criminal Victimization, 2014*, Bureau of Justice Statistics, U.S. Dept. of Justice

A crime committed against an individual or single household counts as one **victimization**. Because a personal crime may involve more than one victim, the number of victimizations may be greater than the number of personal crime incidents.

Victimization rates measure the frequency with which victimizations occurred. Personal crime victimization rates are based on the number of victimizations per 1,000 persons in the total population age 12 and over.

| Type of crime | Number of victimizations | | | Rate per 1,000 persons | | |
	2005	2013	2014	2005	2013	2014
Violent crime[1]	6,947,800	6,126,420	5,359,570	28.4	23.2	20.1
Rape/sexual assault	207,760	300,170	284,350	0.8	1.1	1.1
Robbery	769,150	645,650	664,210	3.1	2.4	2.5
Assault	5,970,890	5,180,610	4,411,010	24.4	19.6	16.5
Aggravated assault	1,281,490	994,220	1,092,090	5.2	3.8	4.1
Simple assault	4,689,400	4,186,390	3,318,920	19.2	15.8	12.4
Domestic violence[2]	1,242,290	1,116,090	1,109,880	5.1	4.2	4.2
Intimate partner violence[3]	816,010	748,080	634,610	3.3	2.8	2.4
Stranger violence	2,829,600	2,098,170	2,166,130	11.6	7.9	8.1
Violent crime involving injury	1,759,210	1,603,960	1,375,950	7.2	6.1	5.2
Serious violent crime[4]	2,258,400	1,940,030	2,040,650	9.2	7.3	7.7
Serious domestic violence[2]	425,270	464,730	400,030	1.7	1.8	1.5
Serious intimate partner violence[3]	311,480	360,820	265,890	1.3	1.4	1.0
Serious stranger violence	1,096,480	737,940	930,690	4.5	2.8	3.5
Serious violent crime involving weapons	1,659,030	1,174,370	1,306,900	6.8	4.4	4.9
Serious violent crime involving injury	824,800	739,210	692,470	3.4	2.8	2.6

Note: Details may not add up to totals due to rounding. (1) Includes rape or sexual assault, robbery, aggravated assault, and simple assault but excludes murder because victimization data are based on interviews with victims. (2) Victimization by intimate partners and family members. (3) Victimization by current or former spouses, boyfriends, or girlfriends. (4) Includes rape or sexual assault, robbery, and aggravated assault.

Prison Population by State, 2000-14

Source: *Prisoners in 2014*, Bureau of Justice Statistics, U.S. Dept. of Justice

The prison population decreased slightly in 2014. As of Dec. 31, 2014, 1,561,525 prisoners were under the jurisdiction, or legal authority, of state (86.5%) or federal (13.5%) correctional authorities, down from 1,576,950 prisoners the previous year. North Dakota's prison population increased the most (9.0%), followed by Nebraska (8.3%), Hawaii (4.2%), and Arkansas (3.7%). Jails, which are locally operated, typically hold persons awaiting trial or sentencing as well as those sentenced to one year or less.

Jurisdiction	2000	2013	2014	% change, 2013-14	Jurisdiction	2000	2013	2014	% change, 2013-14
U.S. total	1,391,261	1,576,950	1,561,525	-1.0%	Missouri	27,543	31,537	31,942	1.3%
Federal[1]	145,416	215,866	210,567	-2.5	Montana	3,105	3,642	3,699	1.6
State	1,245,845	1,361,084	1,350,958	-0.7	Nebraska	3,895	5,026	5,441	8.3
Alabama	26,332	32,381	31,771	-1.9	Nevada[4]	10,063	NA	12,537	NA
Alaska[2,3]	4,173	5,081	5,216	NA	New Hampshire	2,257	3,018	2,963	-1.8
Arizona	26,510	41,177	42,259	2.6	New Jersey	29,784	22,452	21,590	-3.8
Arkansas	11,915	17,235	17,874	3.7	New Mexico	5,342	6,931	7,021	1.3
California	163,001	135,981	136,088	0.1	New York	70,199	53,550	52,518	-1.9
Colorado	16,833	20,371	20,646	1.3	North Carolina	31,266	36,922	37,096	0.5
Connecticut[3,5]	18,355	17,563	16,636	NA	North Dakota	1,076	1,576	1,718	9.0
Delaware[3]	6,921	7,004	6,955	-0.7	Ohio	45,833	51,729	51,519	-0.4
Florida	71,319	103,028	102,870	-0.2	Oklahoma	23,181	27,547	27,650	0.4
Georgia	44,232	54,004	52,949	-2.0	Oregon	10,580	15,517	15,075	-2.8
Hawaii[3]	5,053	5,632	5,866	4.2	Pennsylvania	36,847	51,422	50,694	-1.4
Idaho	5,535	8,242	8,117	-1.5	Rhode Island[3]	3,286	3,361	3,359	-0.1
Illinois	45,281	48,653	48,278	-0.8	South Carolina	21,778	22,060	21,401	-3.0
Indiana	20,125	29,913	29,271	-2.1	South Dakota	2,616	3,682	3,608	-2.0
Iowa	7,955	8,697	8,838	1.6	Tennessee	22,166	28,521	28,769	0.9
Kansas[5]	8,344	9,763	9,663	NA	Texas	166,719	168,280	166,043	-1.3
Kentucky	14,919	21,030	21,657	3.0	Utah	5,637	7,077	7,026	-0.7
Louisiana	35,207	39,299	38,030	-3.2	Vermont[3]	1,697	2,078	1,979	-4.8
Maine	1,679	2,173	2,242	3.2	Virginia	30,168	36,982	37,544	1.5
Maryland	23,538	21,335	21,011	-1.5	Washington	14,915	17,984	18,120	0.8
Massachusetts	10,722	10,950	10,713	-2.2	West Virginia	3,856	6,824	6,896	1.1
Michigan	47,718	43,759	43,390	-0.8	Wisconsin	20,754	22,471	22,597	NA
Minnesota	6,238	10,289	10,637	3.4	Wyoming	1,680	2,310	2,383	3.2
Mississippi	20,241	21,969	18,793	-14.5					

NA = Not available. (1) Includes inmates held in nonsecure privately operated community corrections facilities and juveniles held in contract facilities. Prisoners sentenced under Washington, DC's criminal code are housed in federal facilities. (2) Alaska did not submit 2014 data; jurisdiction totals were obtained from a report to the state legislature. (3) Prisons and jails form one integrated system. Data includes total jail and prison population. (4) Nevada did not submit 2013 data; state is not reflected in that year's totals. (5) State has changed reporting methodology, so 2014 counts are not comparable to those published for earlier years.

Death Penalty by State, 1930-2013

Source: *Capital Punishment, 2013*, Bureau of Justice Statistics, U.S. Dept. of Justice

In 2013, states executed a total of 39 inmates; Texas executed 41% of the total. Since 2000, the death row population has decreased every year, but the composition has changed little: 98% were male, 56% were white, and 42% were black.

On May 27, 2015, the Nebraska legislature outlawed capital punishment, overriding the governor's veto. That lowered to 32 the number of states that authorize the death penalty (the federal government also issues capital sentences). Nebraska's decision followed on the heels of similar repeals in Maryland (for offenses committed after May 2, 2013), Connecticut (for crimes after Apr. 25, 2012), Illinois (on July 1, 2011), and New Mexico (for crimes after July 1, 2009). Alaska, Hawaii, Maine, Michigan, Minnesota, North Dakota, Rhode Island, and Wisconsin do not have the death penalty and did not execute anyone after 1930; they are not shown here.

All death penalty states authorized lethal injection as a method of execution. Eight also permit electrocution; three permit the gas chamber or inhalation of lethal gas, three hanging, and two (Oklahoma and Utah) authorize firing squads.

Jurisdiction	Prisoners under sentence of death, year-end 2013[3]	Executions[1,2] 2013	Executions[1,2] 1930-2013	Executions[1,2] 1977-2013	Jurisdiction	Prisoners under sentence of death, year-end 2013[3]	Executions[1,2] 2013	Executions[1,2] 1930-2013	Executions[1,2] 1977-2013
U.S. total	2,979	39	5,218[4]	1,359[4]	Montana	2	0	9	3
Federal	56	0	36	3	Nebraska	11	0	7	3
State	2,923	39	5,182	1,356	Nevada	81	0	41	12
Alabama	190	1	191	56	New Hampshire	1	0	1	0
Arizona	122	2	74	36	New Jersey	—	—	74	0
Arkansas	37	0	145	27	New Mexico	2	0	9	1
California	735	0	305	13	New York	0	0	329	0
Colorado	3	0	48	1	North Carolina	151	0	306	43
Connecticut	10	0	22	1	Ohio	136	3	224	52
Delaware	17	0	28	16	Oklahoma	48	6	168	108
Florida	398	7	251	81	Oregon	34	0	21	2
Georgia	82	1	419	53	Pennsylvania	190	0	155	3
Idaho	12	0	6	3	South Carolina	45	0	205	43
Illinois	—	—	102	12	South Dakota	3	0	4	3
Indiana	14	0	61	20	Tennessee	75	0	99	6
Iowa	—	—	18	0	Texas	273	16	805	508
Kansas	9	0	15	0	Utah	8	0	20	7
Kentucky	33	0	106	3	Vermont	—	—	4	0
Louisiana	84	0	161	28	Virginia	7	1	202	110
Maryland	5	0	73	5	Washington	9	0	52	5
Massachusetts	—	—	27	0	West Virginia	—	—	40	0
Mississippi	50	0	175	21	Wyoming	1	0	8	1
Missouri	45	2	132	70					

— = Not available or applicable. (1) Figures do not include persons held under Armed Forces jurisdiction with a military death sentence for murder. (2) Data do not include 160 executions carried out by military authorities between 1930 and 1961. (3) As of mid-2015, Connecticut, Maryland, Nebraska, and New Mexico continue to hold prisoners on death row for crimes committed before each state repealed capital punishment. (4) Total includes 40 executions performed under the jurisdiction of the District of Columbia when capital punishment was legal there.

U.S. Prison Population, 1925-2014

Source: *Prisoners* series, Bureau of Justice Statistics, U.S. Dept. of Justice

As recently as 1970, the U.S. had fewer than 200,000 people behind bars nationwide, or less than 1 in 1,000 residents. That number rose steadily throughout the 1970s, '80s, and '90s, reaching an all-time high of more than 1.6 mil prisoners in 2009. The imprisonment rate has declined steadily since its all-time high of 506 prisoners per 100,000 residents in 2007.

Year[1]	Prisoners	Imprison-ment rate	Year[1]	Prisoners	Imprison-ment rate	Year[1]	Prisoners	Imprison-ment rate
1925	91,669	79	1970	196,429	96	2010	1,613,803	500
1930	129,453	104	1980	329,821	138	2011	1,598,968	492
1940	173,706	131	1990	773,919	295	2012	1,570,397	480
1950	166,123	109	2000	1,394,231	470	2013	1,576,950	477
1960	212,953	117	2005	1,525,910	492	2014[2]	1,561,525	471

Note: Imprisonment rate is per 100,000 U.S. residents. (1) Data for 1940-70 include all adult felons serving sentences in state and federal institutions. In 1977, the Bureau of Justice Statistics began to include persons incarcerated in private prisons, local jails, and other facilities not in the state's physical custody. Figures may not be directly comparable. (2) Includes figures imputed for Alaska, which did not submit timely data.

Prison Situation Under Correctional Authorities' Jurisdiction, 2014

Source: *Prisoners in 2014*, Bureau of Justice Statistics, U.S. Dept. of Justice

Largest prison populations		Imprisonment rate of sentenced prisoners		% change in prison population, 2013-14		Prison population as % of maximum prison capacity	
Jurisdiction	Number	Jurisdiction	Rate[1]	Jurisdiction	% change	Jurisdiction	% max. capacity
U.S. total	1,561,525	U.S. total	471	U.S. total	−1.0%	U.S. total	NA
Federal[2,3]	210,567	Federal[2,3]	60	Federal[2,3]	−2.5	Federal[2]	128.0%
State	1,350,958	State	412	State	−0.7	State	NA
1. Texas	166,043	1. Louisiana	816	1. North Dakota	9.0	1. Illinois	150.4
2. California	136,088	2. Oklahoma	700	2. Nebraska	8.3	2. Ohio	131.9
3. Florida	102,870	3. Alabama	633	3. Hawaii[4]	4.2	3. Massachusetts	130.1
4. Georgia	52,949	4. Arkansas	599	4. Arkansas	3.7	4. Nebraska[5]	127.7
5. New York	52,518	5. Mississippi	597	5. Minnesota	3.4	5. Delaware[5]	119.1
6. Ohio	51,519	6. Arizona	593	6. Maine	3.2	6. Colorado	115.1
7. Pennsylvania	50,694	7. Texas	584	7. Wyoming	3.2	7. Iowa[6]	112.8
8. Illinois	48,278	8. Missouri	526	8. Kentucky	3.0	8. Hawaii	112.4
9. Michigan	43,390	9. Georgia	517	9. Arizona	2.6	9. Idaho[5,6]	106.9
10. Arizona	42,259	10. Florida	513	10. Iowa	1.6	10. Kansas	103.3
11. Louisiana	38,030	11. Idaho	489	11. Montana	1.6	11. Louisiana[6]	103.3
12. Virginia	37,544	12. Kentucky	474	12. Virginia	1.5	12. Oklahoma	102.6
13. North Carolina	37,096	13. Virginia	449	13. Colorado	1.3	13. Washington	102.6
14. Missouri	31,942	14. Ohio	444	14. Missouri	1.3	14. Minnesota	101.3
15. Alabama	31,771	15. Indiana	442	15. New Mexico	1.3	15. Pennsylvania	101.2
16. Indiana	29,271	16. Delaware[4]	440	16. West Virginia	1.1	16. New York	101.0
17. Tennessee	28,769	17. Michigan	437	17. Tennessee	0.9	17. Missouri[5]	100.7
18. Oklahoma	27,650	18. Tennessee	437	18. Washington	0.8	18. Montana	100.5
19. Wisconsin	22,597	19. Nevada	434	19. North Carolina	0.5	19. New Hampshire[5]	100.0
20. Kentucky	21,657	20. South Carolina	429	20. Oklahoma	0.4	20. Kentucky	99.6

NA = Not applicable. **Note:** Excludes jail population unless otherwise noted. (1) Prisoners sentenced to more than one year. Rates are per 100,000 population, based upon U.S. Census Bureau population estimates. (2) Federal totals include prisoners sentenced under DC's criminal code. (3) Includes inmates held in nonsecure privately operated community corrections facilities and juveniles held in contract facilities. (4) Prisons and jails form one integrated system. Data includes total jail and prison population. (5) State defines capacity in a way that differs from standard definition. (6) Excludes inmates in community-based work release facilities.

Imprisonment Rate by Gender, Race, Hispanic Origin, and Age, 2014

Source: *Prisoners in 2014*, Bureau of Justice Statistics, U.S. Dept. of Justice

(number of prisoners sentenced to more than one year per 100,000 of each group in the U.S. resident population)

Age	All prisoners	Male				Age	Female			
		Total[1]	White	Black	Hispanic		Total[1]	White	Black	Hispanic
Total[2]	471	890	465	2,724	1,091	Total[2]	65	53	109	64
18-19	169	317	102	1,072	349	18-19	14	8	32	17
20-24	746	1,365	584	3,868	1,521	20-24	96	72	152	94
25-29	1,055	1,912	958	5,434	2,245	25-29	170	150	244	165
30-34	1,161	2,129	1,111	6,412	2,457	30-34	185	163	264	174
35-39	1,067	1,982	1,029	6,122	2,272	35-39	155	138	229	137
40-44	904	1,689	942	5,105	1,933	40-44	132	119	213	107
45-49	758	1,417	815	4,352	1,602	45-49	111	90	203	94
50-54	567	1,081	633	3,331	1,320	50-54	72	57	128	67
55-59	358	698	400	2,178	978	55-59	37	27	72	42
60-64	212	422	252	1,265	680	60-64	20	15	37	25
65 or older	72	158	109	418	299	65 or older	5	4	8	7

Note: Rates are based on U.S. Census Bureau population estimates. Hispanics may be of any race but are not included in white and black populations here. (1) Includes racial categories not shown here. (2) Includes persons under age 18.

Prisoners and Incarceration Rates by Nation, 2005-13

Source: *Adults Held in Prisons, Penal Institutions or Correctional Institutions* (2015), United Nations Office on Drugs and Crime

The U.S. imprisons more residents than any other nation in the world, both in terms of total prisoners and in its imprisonment rate, or the number of prisoners per 100,000 residents. The following table lists the 25 countries with the highest incarceration rates in 2013. Numbers and rates include jail populations.

Country	Total number of prisoners					Incarceration rate				
	2005	2010	2011	2012	2013	2005	2010	2011	2012	2013
United States	2,179,600	2,259,800	2,232,900	2,221,600	2,211,200	973.1	953.1	931.6	917.3	904.1
El Salvador	12,525	24,662	25,367	27,033	26,848	359.1	652.9	659.8	689.8	671.7
Russia.	804,489	812,281	751,209	698,013	673,930	699.3	692.1	641.0	597.6	579.7
Guyana.	1,439	2,160	2,019	1,986	1,998	326.7	484.1	447.8	435.9	433.1
Mongolia.	6,948	7,344	7,929	8,058	8,004	433.6	402.8	427.3	426.4	416.2
Barbados	—	910	1,060	1,045	908	—	424.9	490.7	479.7	413.5
Costa Rica	8,271	10,541	12,154	13,257	13,457	290.4	324.2	365.1	389.6	387.2
Uruguay	—	8,700	9,070	9,418	9,448	—	354.7	367.2	378.5	377.0
Lithuania.	7,958	8,981	9,790	9,617	9,172	308.3	362.4	397.1	391.2	373.6
Colombia	66,829	84,444	100,451	113,884	120,032	244.3	277.4	323.4	359.4	371.5
Kazakhstan.	43,572	54,688	49,156	45,175	41,936	418.8	489.9	436.1	396.8	364.8
Trinidad and Tobago	3,566	2,927	4,074	3,531	3,447	379.3	294.1	406.6	350.6	340.9
Peru	33,010	—	—	—	67,597	192.7	—	—	—	339.8
Mexico	205,621	219,027	230,943	224,969	246,334	300.7	289.9	299.5	285.7	306.4
Latvia	7,342	6,692	—	6,062	5,090	408.5	388.5	—	356.4	301.1
Azerbaijan.	17,803	19,159	17,587	17,821	20,599	309.0	294.8	265.3	263.9	300.0
Singapore	14,453	12,782	12,405	12,361	12,805	418.9	320.8	302.8	293.6	296.3
Estonia	3,349	3,350	3,371	3,250	3,090	315.0	317.0	320.2	309.8	295.5
Botswana	4,679	6,678	4,466	—	3,573	436.7	574.8	379.4	—	295.2
Turkey.	55,293	118,701	126,270	134,019	143,500	123.9	241.8	252.6	263.3	276.9
Poland.	77,607	77,522	78,467	81,306	76,596	256.7	249.8	252.2	260.7	245.1
Liechtenstein	130	76	71	60	68	471.9	262.2	242.6	203.0	227.9
Algeria	39,544	48,506	49,582	49,567	59,744	181.8	195.1	195.6	191.6	226.4
Paraguay	6,281	6,197	7,161	7,916	9,233	184.9	159.5	179.8	194.0	220.9
Argentina	43,689	58,917	60,106	61,192	64,109	165.2	208.4	209.9	211.0	218.3

— = Not available. **Note:** Data is not available for all nations. Use caution when making comparisons between countries because of the differences in each country's legal definitions of offenses and the differences in methods of counting and reporting.

Law Enforcement Officers and Civilian Employees, 2014

Source: *Crime in the United States, 2014*; *Law Enforcement Officers Killed and Assaulted, 2014*; Federal Bureau of Investigation (FBI); U.S. Dept. of Justice

As of Oct. 31, 2014, 12,656 city, county, state, college and university, and tribal agencies around the country collectively employed 889,212 full-time law enforcement workers. About two-thirds of these employees were sworn officers. The FBI defines a sworn law enforcement officer as a person who ordinarily carries a firearm and badge, has full arrest powers, and is paid from government funds specifically dedicated to law enforcement. Civilians (e.g., clerks, radio dispatchers, correctional officers) made up the remainder.

Altogether, they provided service to an estimated 268 mil people around the country, meaning there were 3.4 full-time law enforcement employees and 2.3 sworn officers per 1,000 residents.

The great majority of sworn officers (88.1%) were male, while females made up 60.1% of civilian employees. Not surprisingly, the most populous state, California, employed the greatest number of full-time law enforcement workers (118,491). The nation's capital, Washington, DC, had the highest rate, with 7.7 full-time law enforcement employees for every 1,000 residents in its population.

Nationwide, 51 law enforcement officers were killed feloniously in the line of duty in 2014, nearly twice the number in 2013, but down from 72 in 2011. Of that number, 11 died while responding to disturbance calls, 9 were fatally injured during traffic pursuits or stops, 7 were ambushed, and another 7 died while investigating suspicious persons or circumstances. All but four of the officers killed were white (two were black, two were Asian or Pacific Islander), and 46 were killed with firearms, even though 39 of those officers were wearing body armor. Handguns were responsible for a majority (33) of officer murders.

Sentenced Prisoners by Offense and Selected Characteristics, 2013

Source: *Prisoners in 2014*, Bureau of Justice Statistics, U.S. Dept. of Justice

	All inmates[1]	Male	Female	White[2]	Black[2]	Hispanic
Total number of sentenced inmates	1,325,305	1,233,724	91,581	468,600	497,000	274,200
	Percent of total in category (by most serious offense)					
All violent crimes	53.2%	54.0%	37.0%	47.8%	56.8%	59.0%
Murder and non-negligent manslaughter	12.5	12.6	11.0	9.6	14.0	14.2
Manslaughter	1.0	1.3	3.0	1.5	0.8	1.1
Rape/sexual assault	13.0	13.0	2.0	16.7	8.0	13.6
Robbery	14.0	14.0	9.0	8.0	20	13.5
Aggravated/simple assault	10.0	10.0	9.0	8.8	10.9	13.0
Other.	3.1	3.0	4.0	3.2	3.5	3.7
All property crimes	19.3	19.0	28.0	25.0	16.4	13.5
Burglary.	10.5	10.7	7.6	12.4	9.7	8.3
Larceny-theft	3.8	3.0	9.0	5.7	4.0	2.1
Motor vehicle theft	0.8	1.0	0.8	1.1	1.0	1.0
Fraud.	2.0	2.0	8.0	3.1	2.0	1.0
Other.	2.0	2.0	3.0	2.9	1.3	1.2
Drug offenses[3]	15.7	15.1	24.0	14.5	16.1	14.5
Public-order offenses[4]	11.0	11.2	9.2	11.9	10.3	12.2
Other[5]	0.8	0.8	1.3	0.7	0.4	0.5

Note: Counts based on state prisoners with a sentence of more than one year. Details may not add up to totals due to rounding and missing offense data. (1) Total includes inmates of other races not shown separately. (2) Excludes inmates of Hispanic origin and inmates of two or more races. (3) Includes trafficking and other offenses. (4) Includes weapons, drunk driving, and court offenses; commercialized vice, morals, and decency offenses; liquor law violations; and other public-order offenses. (5) Includes juvenile offenses and other unspecified offense categories.

Arrests by Race and Hispanic Origin, 2014

Source: *Crime in the United States, 2014*, Federal Bureau of Investigation, U.S. Dept. of Justice

Each instance in which a person is arrested, cited, or summoned for an offense is counted as one arrest. The figures below therefore do not represent the number of individuals arrested but the number of times persons were arrested, as an individual may be arrested multiple times in one year. Arrest estimates are based on statistics from law enforcement agencies that reported 12 months of arrest data.

Offense charged	Total[1]	White	Black or African- American	American Indian or Alaska Native	Asian	Hawaiian or Other Pacific Islander	Total[2]	Hispanic
Total arrests	8,730,665	69.4%	27.8%	1.6%	1.1%	0.1%	6,541,125	18.9%
Violent crime.	390,233	59.4	37.7	1.4	1.4	0.2	306,376	24.0
Murder and nonnegligent manslaughter. . .	8,230	46.3	51.3	1.0	1.3	0.1	6,045	21.6
Rape[3]	16,326	67.2	29.9	1.3	1.4	0.2	11,508	27.2
Robbery	74,077	42.3	55.9	0.8	0.8	0.1	55,913	20.5
Aggravated assault.	291,600	63.7	33.1	1.5	1.5	0.2	232,910	24.8
Property crime	1,218,747	68.8	28.4	1.5	1.2	0.1	924,100	16.8
Burglary	186,794	67.6	30.2	0.9	1.1	0.2	152,261	20.1
Larceny-theft.	971,199	69.1	28.0	1.6	1.2	0.1	725,373	15.5
Motor vehicle theft	53,456	66.5	30.7	1.2	1.3	0.3	40,946	25.6
Arson	7,298	73.1	23.4	1.9	1.3	0.2	5,520	18.5
Other assaults[4]	853,887	65.4	31.9	1.6	1.1	0.1	639,100	17.9
Forgery and counterfeiting	44,336	63.8	34.0	0.6	1.5	0.1	34,657	16.2
Fraud	109,576	66.1	31.8	1.0	1.0	0.1	88,004	10.0
Embezzlement	12,678	61.9	35.6	0.7	1.7	0.1	10,325	10.3
Stolen property; buying, receiving, possessing	69,912	65.5	32.2	0.9	1.2	0.1	54,153	19.6
Vandalism.	154,755	70.1	27.0	1.8	1.0	0.1	122,943	19.0
Weapons; carrying, possessing, etc.	109,891	57.3	40.7	0.7	1.2	0.1	81,630	23.5
Prostitution and commercialized vice	37,030	53.7	41.8	0.5	3.9	0.1	28,546	19.3
Sex offenses (except rape and prostitution). .	43,125	72.5	24.3	1.5	1.6	0.1	31,963	25.6
Drug abuse violations.	1,216,225	68.9	29.1	0.8	1.1	0.1	910,629	20.9
Gambling	4,363	35.8	58.9	0.4	4.4	0.6	2,059	19.6
Offenses against the family and children	79,075	64.4	32.9	1.9	0.7	—	51,746	11.7
Driving under the influence.	863,598	83.7	13.0	1.4	1.8	0.1	646,288	23.5
Liquor laws	246,304	80.2	14.5	3.9	1.3	0.1	173,195	15.6
Drunkenness	327,325	80.9	15.7	2.1	1.1	0.1	305,049	23.8
Disorderly conduct	338,636	63.0	33.9	2.3	0.7	0.1	207,465	13.1
Vagrancy	21,577	68.7	28.3	2.1	0.8	0.1	16,903	15.7
All other offenses (except traffic)	2,546,822	67.8	29.5	1.7	0.9	0.1	1,876,766	17.2
Suspicion	1,057	52.7	44.7	1.4	1.2	0.0	157	4.5
Curfew and loitering law violations	41,513	51.4	46.2	1.1	1.1	0.2	29,071	24.6

— = Less than one-tenth of 1%. (1) Total arrests reporting race. Includes racial categories not shown, so percentages may not add up to 100. (2) Total arrests reporting Hispanic origin, which may be of any race. Not all agencies provide ethnicity data. Not directly comparable with race data. (3) The rape data are aggregate totals based on both the legacy and revised Uniform Crime Reporting definitions. (4) Simple assaults, where no weapons were used and where the victim did not sustain serious injury (e.g., stalking).

Gun Violence Incidents and Deaths, 2014-15

Source: Gun Violence Archive, as of Aug. 2016

The Gun Violence Archive is an independent data collection and research group with no affiliation with any advocacy organization. Since 2013, it has maintained an online archive of gun violence incidents, which it collects daily from more than 1,500 media, law enforcement, government, and commercial sources.

	2014	2015		2014	2015
Total gun violence incidents	51,829	53,351	Defensive uses.	1,592	1,303
Deaths, total	12,594	13,467	Accidental shootings.	1,606	1,963
Injuries, total	23,024	27,021	**Officer-involved incidents**		
Mass shootings[1]	277	332	Officer shot or killed	260	319
Home invasions	2,613	2,364	Subject/suspect shot or killed	1,778	1,912

(1) Four or more people shot during a single event, not including shooter.

Firearm Violence, 1993-2011

Source: *Firearm Violence, 1993-2011*, Bureau of Justice Statistics, U.S. Dept. of Justice

The number of homicides due to firearms declined by nearly 40% in the two decades after Congress passed the Brady Handgun Violence Prevention Act in 1993. The Brady Act required licensed dealers to conduct background checks on individuals seeking to purchase firearms. As of Dec. 31, 2012 (the latest point at which data were available), federal, state, and local authorities had denied more than 2.4 mil of 148 mil applications to purchase firearms; the most common reason for denial was a previous felony conviction or indictment.

	Homicides				Nonfatal victimizations			
Year	By handgun	By other type of firearm[1]	Total	Rate[2]	By handgun	By other type of firearm	Total	Rate[3]
1993	NA	NA	18,253	7.0	NA	NA	1,529,700	730
1995	12,090	2,670	15,551	5.8	1,240,200	132,800	1,193,200	550
2000	8,020	2,190	10,801	3.8	555,800	65,300	610,200	270
2005	8,550	2,840	12,352	4.2	410,600	56,200	503,500	210
2010	6,920	3,030	11,078	3.6	382,100	26,700	415,000	160
2011	7,230	2,690	11,101	3.6	389,400	49,700	467,300	180

NA = Not available. **Note:** Numbers may not add up to totals because of small differences in sample sizes. (1) Includes shotguns and rifles. (2) Per 100,000 persons. (3) Per 100,000 persons age 12 or older.

Hate Crimes by Offense Type and Bias Motivation, 2014

Source: *Hate Crime Statistics, 2014*, Federal Bureau of Investigation (FBI), U.S. Dept. of Justice

Hate crimes are defined as crimes in which victims are chosen because of one or more personal characteristics, such as race, ethnicity, or religion. Congress enacted the Hate Crime Statistics Act of 1990, which led to the collection of hate crime data as part of the FBI's Uniform Crime Report (UCR) program beginning in 1992. Not all agencies that participate in the UCR program submit hate crime data, so the data presented is not representative of the nation as a whole.

Bias motivation	Total incidents	Crimes against persons				Crimes against property					Total crimes against society[3]
		Aggravated assault	Simple assault	Intimidation	Other[1]	Robbery	Burglary	Larceny-theft	Destruction/ damage/vandalism	Other[2]	
Total offenses	6,418	770	1,514	1,745	19	122	162	239	1,694	100	53
Single-bias incidents	6,385	767	1,507	1,738	19	121	160	237	1,684	99	53
Race	3,081	404	684	971	9	56	91	123	667	48	28
Anti-white	701	96	185	168	4	30	27	70	84	17	20
Anti-black	1,955	265	421	701	4	17	24	17	491	11	4
Anti-American Indian/Alaska Native	142	10	23	25	1	5	13	28	21	14	2
Anti-Asian, Native Hawaiian, or Pacific Islander	172	17	38	44	0	3	27	6	32	5	0
Anti-multiple races, group	111	16	17	33	0	1	0	2	39	1	2
Religion	1,092	37	129	194	1	4	25	30	637	23	12
Anti-Jewish	635	4	65	93	0	1	8	5	451	4	4
Anti-Catholic	67	0	4	5	0	0	3	8	40	5	2
Anti-Protestant	28	1	2	4	0	0	3	4	12	1	1
Anti-Islamic (Muslim)	178	20	36	64	0	3	2	2	45	3	3
Anti-other religion	120	9	13	15	0	0	6	6	60	10	1
Anti-multiple religions, group	51	0	8	11	1	0	2	3	25	0	1
Anti-atheism/agnosticism/etc.	13	3	1	2	0	0	1	2	4	0	0
Sexual orientation	1,178	171	397	306	2	36	20	20	216	6	4
Anti-gay (male)	683	108	259	166	1	24	14	4	102	4	1
Anti-lesbian	168	23	40	66	0	5	2	4	27	0	1
Anti-lesbian, gay, bisexual, or transgender (mixed group)	278	36	88	66	1	7	3	3	74	0	0
Anti-heterosexual	18	0	4	5	0	0	0	4	5	0	0
Anti-bisexual	31	4	6	3	0	0	1	5	8	2	2
Ethnicity	790	122	238	215	5	19	13	28	138	8	4
Anti-Hispanic or Latino	376	56	99	124	2	14	8	4	63	4	2
Anti-other ethnicity/national origin	414	66	139	91	3	5	5	24	75	4	2
Disability	95	5	24	22	1	1	5	12	14	9	2
Anti-physical	26	2	6	8	0	0	0	3	1	6	0
Anti-mental	69	3	18	14	1	1	5	9	13	3	2
Gender	40	5	8	14	1	1	2	2	3	1	3
Anti-male	12	1	1	8	0	0	2	0	0	0	0
Anti-female	28	4	7	6	1	1	0	2	3	1	3
Gender identity	109	23	27	16	0	4	4	22	9	4	0
Anti-transgender	69	18	21	16	0	3	1	5	4	1	0
Anti-gender non-conforming	40	5	6	0	0	1	3	17	5	3	0
Multiple-bias incidents[4]	33	3	7	7	0	1	2	2	10	1	0

(1) Includes murder, nonnegligent manslaughter, rape, and additional offenses not shown here in detail. (2) Includes arson, motor vehicle theft, and additional offenses not shown here in detail. (3) Includes drug or narcotic offenses, gambling and prostitution offenses, and weapon law violations where society as a whole is considered the victim. (4) Incidents in which one or more offense types are motivated by two or more biases.

Notable Assassinations Since 1865

1865—Apr. 14: U.S. Pres. Abraham Lincoln shot by John Wilkes Booth, well-known actor with Confederate sympathies, at Ford's Theater in Washington, DC; died Apr. 15.

1881—Mar. 13: Alexander II of Russia. **July 2:** U.S. Pres. James A. Garfield shot by Charles J. Guiteau, disappointed office seeker, in Washington, DC; died Sept. 19.

1894—June 24: French Pres. Sadi Carnot by Sante Caserio, Italian anarchist, in Lyon.

1898—Sept. 10: Empress Elizabeth of Austria stabbed by Luigi Luccheni, Italian anarchist.

1900—July 29: Umberto I, king of Italy, by an anarchist.

1901—Sept. 6: U.S. Pres. William McKinley shot by Leon Czolgosz, anarchist, in Buffalo, NY; died Sept. 14.

1908—Feb. 1: King Carlos I of Portugal and his son Luís Filipe, in Lisbon.

1913—Feb. 23: Mexican Pres. Francisco I. Madero and Vice Pres. José María Pino Suárez. **Mar. 18:** King George of Greece, by an anarchist.

1914—June 28: Archduke Franz Ferdinand of Austria-Hungary and his wife shot by Gavrilo Princip, Serb nationalist, in Sarajevo, Bosnia.

1916—Dec. 30: Grigory Rasputin, Russian mystic and court figure, by group of aristocrats.

1918—July 12: Grand Duke Michael of Russia, at Perm. **July 16:** Nicholas II, former (abdicated) czar of Russia; his wife, Czarina Alexandra; their son, Czarevitch Alexis; their daughters, Grand Duchesses Olga, Tatiana, Marie, Anastasia; and 4 members of household executed by Bolsheviks at Ekaterinburg.

1920—May 20: Mexican Pres. Gen. Venustiano Carranza, in Tlaxcalantongo.

1922—Aug. 22: Michael Collins, Irish revolutionary, in West Cork. **Dec. 16:** Polish Pres. Gabriel Narutowicz in Warsaw.

1923—July 20: Gen. Francisco "Pancho" Villa, ex-rebel leader, in Parral, Mexico.

1928—July 17: Gen. Alvaro Obregon, president-elect of Mexico, in San Angel.

1932—May 6: French Pres. Paul Doumer shot by Russian émigré, Pavel Gorgulov, in Paris.

1934—July 25: Austrian Chancellor Engelbert Dollfuss by Nazis, in Vienna.

1935—Sept. 8: Sen. Huey P. Long, former Louisiana governor, shot by Dr. Carl Austin Weiss, son-in-law of political opponent, in Baton Rouge; died Sept. 10.

1940—Aug. 20: Leon Trotsky (Lev Bronstein), exiled Soviet commissar of war, fatally wounded with ice ax by Soviet agent nr. Mexico City.

1948—Jan. 30: Leader of movement for Indian independence Mohandas K. Gandhi (Mahatma) shot by Hindu fanatic in New Delhi. **Sept. 17:** Count Folke Bernadotte, UN mediator for Palestine, by Jewish extremists in Jerusalem.

1951—July 20: Jordanian King Abdullah ibn Hussein. **Oct. 16:** Prime Min. Liaquat Ali Khan of Pakistan shot, in Rawalpindi.
1956—Sept. 21: Pres. Anastasio Somoza of Nicaragua shot in Leon by a young poet; died Sept. 29.
1957—July 26: Guatemalan Pres. Carlos Castillo Armas, in Guatemala City by one of his guards.
1958—July 14: King Faisal of Iraq, Crown Prince Abdullah, and **July 15,** Prem. Nuri as-Said, by rebels in Baghdad.
1959—Sept. 25: Prime Min. Solomon Bandaranaike of Ceylon (Sri Lanka), by Buddhist monk in Colombo.
1961—Jan. 17: First elected prime min. of the Congo, Patrice Lumumba, in Katanga Prov. by political rivals. **May 30:** Dominican dictator Rafael Leónidas Trujillo Molina, nr. Ciudad Trujillo.
1963—June 12: Medgar Evers, NAACP's Mississippi field secretary, shot by Byron De La Beckwith in Jackson, MS. **Nov. 2:** Pres. Ngo Dinh Diem of South Vietnam and his brother, Ngo Dinh Nhu, in military coup. **Nov. 22:** U.S. Pres. John F. Kennedy shot while riding in motorcade through downtown Dallas, TX; accused assassin Lee Harvey Oswald murdered by nightclub owner Jack Ruby while awaiting trial.
1965—Jan. 21: Iranian Prem. Hassan Ali Mansour, in Tehran. **Feb. 21:** Malcolm X, black nationalist leader, shot by 3 men linked to Nation of Islam at New York City rally.
1966—Sept. 6: Prime Min. Hendrik F. Verwoerd of South Africa stabbed to death in parliament at Cape Town.
1968—Apr. 4: Rev. Martin Luther King Jr. fatally shot in Memphis, TN; James Earl Ray convicted of crime. **June 5:** Sen. Robert F. Kennedy (D, NY) shot in Los Angeles; died June 6. Sirhan Sirhan convicted of crime.
1971—Nov. 28: Jordanian Prime Min. Wasfi Tal by Palestinian guerrillas, in Cairo, Egypt.
1973—Mar. 2: U.S. Amb. Cleo A. Noel Jr., U.S. Charge d'Affaires George C. Moore, and Belgian Charge d'Affaires Guy Eid by Palestinian guerrillas, in Khartoum, Sudan. **Dec. 20:** Spanish Prem. Luis Carrero Blanco in car bombing by Basque separatist group ETA, in Madrid.
1974—Aug. 19: U.S. Amb. to Cyprus, Rodger P. Davies, by sniper's bullet in Nicosia.
1975—Feb. 11: Pres. Richard Ratsimandrava of Madagascar shot in Antananarivo. **Mar. 25:** Saudi Arabian King Faisal shot by nephew Prince Musad Abdel Aziz, in Riyadh. **Aug. 15:** Bangladesh Pres. Sheik Mujibur Rahman killed in coup.
1976—Feb. 13: Nigerian head of state, Gen. Murtala Ramat Mohammed, by self-styled young revolutionaries.
1977—Mar. 16: Kamal Jumblat, Lebanese Druse chieftain, shot nr. Beirut. **Mar. 18:** Rep. of the Congo Pres. Marien Ngouabi shot in Brazzaville.
1978—May 9: Former Italian Prem. Aldo Moro killed by Red Brigades terrorists who had abducted him Mar. 16 in Rome and held him hostage. **July 9:** Former Iraqi Prem. Abdul Razak Al-Naif shot in London.
1979—Aug. 27: Lord Mountbatten, WWII hero, and 2 others when a bomb exploded on his fishing boat off coast of Co. Sligo, Ireland. IRA claimed responsibility. **Oct. 26:** S. Korean Pres. Park Chung Hee and 6 bodyguards fatally shot by Kim Jae Kyu, head of S. Korean intelligence agency.
1980—Apr. 12: Liberian Pres. William R. Tolbert, in military coup. **Sept. 17:** Former Nicaraguan Pres. Anastasio Somoza Debayle shot in Paraguay.
1981—Oct. 6: Egyptian Pres. Anwar al-Sadat shot by commandos while reviewing military parade in Cairo; 7 others killed, 28 wounded.
1982—Sept. 14: Lebanese Pres.-elect Bashir Gemayel killed by bomb in east Beirut.
1983—Aug. 21: Philippine opposition leader Benigno Aquino Jr. shot at Manila Intl. Airport.
1984—Oct. 31: Indian Prime Min. Indira Gandhi shot by 2 Sikh bodyguards in New Delhi.
1986—Feb. 28: Swedish Prime Min. Olof Palme shot on Stockholm street; case still unsolved.
1987—June 1: Lebanese Prem. Rashid Karami killed when bomb exploded aboard helicopter.

1988—Apr. 16: PLO military chief Khalil Wazir (Abu Jihad) gunned down by Israeli commandos in Tunisia.
1989—Aug. 18: Colombian pres. candidate Luis Carlos Galán killed by Medellín cartel drug traffickers at campaign rally in Bogotá. **Nov. 22:** Lebanese Pres. Rene Moawad killed when bomb exploded next to his motorcade.
1990—Mar. 22: Colombian pres. candidate Bernardo Jaramillo Ossa shot at airport in Bogotá.
1991—May 21: Former Indian Prime Min. Rajiv Gandhi killed by bomb during election rally in Madras.
1992—June 29: Algerian Pres. Mohammed Boudiaf shot in Annaba.
1993—May 1: Sri Lankan Pres. Ranasinghe Premadasa killed by bomb in Colombo.
1994—Apr. 6: Burundian Pres. Cyprien Ntaryamira and Rwandan Pres. Juvénal Habyarimana killed with 8 others when their plane was shot down, precipitating Rwandan genocide.
1995—Nov. 4: Israeli Prime Min. Yitzhak Rabin shot by Yigal Amir, Jewish extremist, at peace rally in Tel Aviv.
1996—Oct. 2: Andrei Lukanov, former Bulgarian prime min., shot outside home by unidentified assailant.
1998—Apr. 26: Guatemalan Roman Catholic Bishop Juan Gerardi Conedera, human rights champion, found beaten to death in Guatemala City.
1999—Apr. 9: Niger Pres. Ibrahim Bare Mainassara ambushed and killed by dissident soldiers. **Oct. 27:** Armenian Prime Min. Vazgen Sarkissian, along with 7 others, shot during session of parliament.
2001—Jan. 16: Dem. Rep. of the Congo Pres. Laurent Kabila shot to death by bodyguard at pres. palace in Kinshasa. **June 1:** Nepal's King Birendra, Queen Aiswarya, and 7 other royals fatally shot by Crown Prince Dipendra, who also killed himself.
2002—July 6: Afghan Vice Pres. Haji Abdul Qadir shot outside his office in Kabul.
2003—Mar. 12: Serbian Prime Min. Zoran Djindjic shot by paramilitary snipers outside govt. headquarters in Belgrade.
2004—Feb. 13: Former Chechen Pres. Zelimkhan Yandarbiyev killed after car exploded in Qatar. **Mar. 22:** Sheik Ahmed Yassin, spiritual leader of Hamas, by Israeli missile attack in Gaza City. **May 9:** Chechen Pres. Akhmad Kadyrov by bomb at WWII memorial service in Grozny. **Nov. 2:** Filmmaker Theo van Gogh, critic of Islam and great-grandnephew of painter Vincent van Gogh, shot and stabbed by Muslim militant in Amsterdam.
2005—Jan. 4: Baghdad Gov. Ali al-Haidari gunned down by insurgents in Baghdad, Iraq.
2007—Aug. 2: *Oakland Post* editor Chauncey Bailey, who was investigating financial status of Your Black Muslim Bakery, shot in Oakland, CA. **Dec. 27:** Benazir Bhutto, former Pakistani prime min. and first female elected leader of a Muslim state, by bomb and gunman later linked to then-Pres. Pervez Musharraf.
2008—Feb. 12: Imad Mughniyeh, top Hezbollah commander and reputed mastermind of the 1983 bombing of U.S. embassy in Beirut, by car bomb in Damascus, Syria. Mughniyeh had been on FBI's Most Wanted Terrorist list. **Oct. 23:** Ivo Pukanic, editor-in-chief of Croatian political newspaper *Nacional*, killed in Zagreb when bomb exploded nr. his car.
2009—Mar. 2: Guinea-Bissau's longtime Pres. João Bernardo Vieira shot by army troops outside his home in Bissau. **May 31:** Dr. George Tiller, one of the few doctors in the U.S. to perform abortions late in pregnancy, shot to death in his Wichita, KS, church by anti-abortion activist.
2011—Sept. 20: Burhanuddin Rabbani, leader of Afghanistan's High Peace Council and a former pres., killed in his Kabul home by assassin with explosives hidden in his turban.
2012—Jan. 11: Iranian nuclear scientist Mostafa Ahmadi Roshan killed by car bomb.
2014—Sept. 1: U.S. airstrikes killed Ahmed Abdi Godane, leader of Somalia-based Islamist militant group al-Shabab.
2015—Feb. 27: Boris Y. Nemtsov, Russian opposition leader and former first deputy prime minister, shot near Red Square.
2016—June 16: UK Labour MP Jo Cox shot and stabbed in West Yorkshire by far-right assailant.

Notable Assassination Attempts Since 1912

1912—Oct. 14: Former U.S. Pres. Theodore Roosevelt shot and wounded by mentally ill man in Milwaukee, WI.
1933—Feb. 15: In Miami, FL, anarchist Joseph Zangara shot at Pres.-elect Franklin D. Roosevelt, but a woman seized Zangara's arm; bullet fatally wounded Chicago Mayor Anton J. Cermak, who died Mar. 6.
1944—July 20: Adolf Hitler injured when bomb, planted by German officer, exploded in his headquarters; one aide killed, 12 injured.
1950—Nov. 1: In attempt to assassinate Pres. Harry Truman, 2 members of Puerto Rican nationalist movement—Griselio

Torresola and Oscar Collazo—tried to shoot their way into Blair House, across the street from White House. Torresola killed. Pvt. Leslie Coffelt, White House policeman, fatally shot.
1970—Nov. 27: Pope Paul VI unharmed by knife-wielding assailant who attempted to attack him in airport in Manila, Philippines.
1972—May 15: Alabama Gov. George Wallace seriously wounded when shot in Laurel, MD, by fame-seeking Arthur Bremer.
1975—Sept. 5: Pres. Gerald R. Ford unharmed when Secret Service agent grabbed pistol aimed at him by Lynette

"Squeaky" Fromme, follower of cult leader Charles Manson, in Sacramento, CA. **Sept. 22:** Pres. Ford unharmed when bystander grabbed arm of Sara Jane Moore as she fired upon Ford in San Francisco.

1980—May 29: Civil rights leader Vernon E. Jordan Jr. shot and wounded in Ft. Wayne, IN.

1981—Mar. 30: Pres. Ronald Reagan, along with Press Sec. James Brady, Secret Service agent Timothy J. McCarthy, and Wash., DC, policeman Thomas Delahanty shot and seriously wounded by John W. Hinckley Jr. in DC. **May 13:** Pope John Paul II and 2 bystanders shot and wounded by Mehmet Ali Agca, escaped Turkish prisoner, in St. Peter's Square, Vatican City.

1982—May 12: Pope John Paul II wounded by ultra-conservative priest wielding bayonet, in Fatima, Portugal.

1984—Oct. 12: British Prime Min. Margaret Thatcher unharmed when a bomb, said to have been planted by the IRA, exploded at the Grand Hotel in Brighton, Eng., during a Party conference; 4 died, incl. a member of Parliament.

1986—Sept. 7: Chilean Pres. Gen. Augusto Pinochet Ugarte unharmed after motorcade was attacked by rebels.

1995—June 26: Egyptian Pres. Hosni Mubarak unharmed when shots fired on his motorcade in Addis Ababa, Ethiopia; 4 died, incl. 2 Ethiopian police officers.

1997—Feb. 12: Colombian Pres. Ernesto Samper Pizano unharmed when bomb exploded on runway in Barranquilla as his plane was preparing to land. **Apr. 30:** Tajik Pres. Imamali Rakhmanov injured when a grenade was thrown at him.

1998—Feb. 9: Georgian Pres. Eduard A. Shevardnadze unharmed when gunmen fired on his motorcade in Tbilisi.

2002—July 14: French Pres. Jacques Chirac unharmed after Maxime Brunerie, gunman with ties to neo-Nazi groups, fired at his open-top vehicle during Bastille Day parade in Paris. **Sept. 5:** Afghan Pres. Hamid Karzai unharmed after militant shot at car in Kandahar. **Nov. 25:** Turkmenistan Pres.

Saparmurat Niyazov unharmed after gunmen opened fire on his motorcade in Ashgabat.

2003—Dec. 14: Pakistani Pres. Pervez Musharraf unharmed after bomb detonated on bridge in Rawalpindi seconds after his motorcade crossed.

2004—Mar. 19: Taiwanese Pres. Chen Shui-bian shot while campaigning in motorcade; minor injuries. **July 13:** Separatists bombed motorcade of Sergei Abramov, Chechnya's acting pres. **Sept. 5:** Ukrainian opposition presidential candidate Viktor Yushchenko, who later won office, fell ill after meeting; diagnosed with dioxin poisoning. **Sept. 16:** Rocket fired at helicopter carrying Afghan Pres. Hamid Karzai, nr. Gardez.

2005—Mar. 15: Kosovo Pres. Ibrahim Rugova survived bombing of his motorcade as it traveled through Pristina.

2008—Feb. 11: Pres. José Ramos-Horta shot in attack led by fugitive former army official in Dili, Timor-Leste. Ambush of Prime Min. Xanana Gusmão's motorcade a short time later unsuccessful. **Apr. 27:** Afghan Pres. Hamid Karzai unharmed after Taliban fired on military parade in Kabul where Karzai was in attendance.

2011—Jan. 8: U.S. Rep. Gabrielle Giffords (D, AZ) severely wounded by lone gunman at public meeting nr. Arizona supermarket; 6 others killed, including a federal judge. **June 3:** Yemeni Pres. Ali Abdullah Saleh survived presidential palace bombing.

2012—May 18: Taliban killed 7 in assassination attempt on governor of the Afghanistan prov. of Farah. **Sept. 12:** Hassan Sheik Mohamud survived suicide bombing attack on his home 2 days after being elected Somalia's president.

2013—Apr. 29: Syrian Prime Min. Wael Nader al-Halqi survived car bombing of his motorcade in Damascus.

2015—Sept. 28: Maldives Pres. Abdulla Yameen survived explosion on his speedboat. Parliament Nov. 5 impeached Vice Pres. Ahmed Adeeb for alleged role in the explosion.

Notable U.S. Kidnappings Since 1924

Bobby Franks, 14, in Chicago, May 21, 1924, by 2 youths from wealthy families—Richard Loeb, 18, and Nathan Leopold, 19—who killed boy. Demand for $10,000 ignored. Loeb killed in prison; Leopold paroled 1958.

Charles A. Lindbergh Jr., 20 months old, nr. Hopewell, NJ, Mar. 1, 1932; found dead May 12. Ransom of $50,000 paid to man identified as Bruno Richard Hauptmann, 35, paroled German convict who entered U.S. illegally. Hauptmann convicted, electrocuted in Trenton, NJ, prison, Apr. 3, 1936.

William A. Hamm Jr., 39, brewing company pres. in St. Paul, MN, June 15, 1933, by Karpis-Barker gang. $100,000 paid. Alvin Karpis given life sentence, paroled in 1969.

Charles F. Urschel, in Oklahoma City, July 22, 1933. Released July 31 after $200,000 paid. George "Machine Gun" Kelly and 5 others sentenced to life.

Brooke L. Hart, 22, in San Jose, CA. Thomas Thurmond and John Holmes arrested after demanding $40,000. When Hart's body was found in San Francisco Bay, Nov. 26, 1933, a mob forced its way into jail and lynched the 2 kidnappers.

June Robles, 6, abducted in Tucson, AZ, Apr. 25, 1934. Missing for 19 days after ransom note sent to parents. Found alive in iron cage buried in desert. No arrests ever made.

George Weyerhaeuser, 9, of Weyerhaeuser lumber company, in Tacoma, WA, May 24, 1935. Returned home June 1 after $200,000 paid. Kidnappers given 20 to 60 years.

Robert C. Greenlease, 6, son of wealthy car dealer, taken from Kansas City, MO, school Sept. 28, 1953; held for $600,000. Body found Oct. 7. Bonnie Brown Heady and Carl A. Hall pleaded guilty, were executed.

Lee Crary, 8, in Everett, WA, Sept. 22, 1957; $10,000 ransom not paid. Crary escaped after 3 days and led police to George E. Collins, who was convicted.

Adolph Coors III, 45, brewing company heir, near Morrison, CO, Feb. 9, 1960. Wife received ransom note but no further word. Body found Sept. 11. Kidnapper caught, convicted, sentenced to life in prison.

Frank Sinatra Jr., 19, from hotel room in Lake Tahoe, CA, Dec. 8, 1963. Released Dec. 11 after his father paid $240,000 ransom. Three men sentenced to prison.

Barbara Jane Mackle, 20, abducted Dec. 17, 1968, from Atlanta, GA, motel; found unharmed 3 days later, buried in coffin-like box 18 in. underground, after her father paid $500,000 ransom. Gary Steven Krist sentenced to life, Ruth Eisenmann-Schier to 7 years.

Virginia Piper, 49, abducted July 27, 1972, from her home in suburban Minneapolis, MN; found unharmed nr. Duluth 2 days later after husband, retired banker, paid $1 mil ransom.

J. Paul Getty III, 17, grandson of the oil billionaire, disappeared July 10, 1973, in Rome, Italy. Ransom of $2.8 mil paid after abductors sent one of Getty's ears to an Italian newspaper with a warning that other parts of his body would be mutilated. Released Dec. 15.

Patricia "Patty" Hearst, 19, taken from her Berkeley, CA, apartment Feb. 4, 1974; "Symbionese Liberation Army" captors demanded her father, publisher Randolph Hearst, give millions to area poor. Patty implicated in San Francisco bank holdup, Apr. 15. The FBI, Sept. 18, 1975, captured her and others. She was convicted of bank robbery, Mar. 20, 1976; released from prison under executive clemency, Feb. 1, 1979. In 1978, William and Emily Harris were sentenced to 10 years to life for the kidnapping; both were paroled in 1983.

J. Reginald Murphy, 40, an editor of *Atlanta Constitution* (GA), kidnapped Feb. 20, 1974; freed Feb. 22 after newspaper paid $700,000 ransom. William A. H. Williams later convicted.

Jack Teich, Kings Point, NY, steel executive, seized Nov. 12, 1974; released Nov. 19 after payment of $750,000.

Adam Walsh, 6, abducted from Hollywood, FL, dept. store, July 27, 1981. Severed head found 2 weeks later. John Walsh, Adam's father, became active in raising awareness about missing children. Case officially closed in 2008; drifter who had died in prison while serving life sentences for murder found responsible.

Terry Anderson, 37, Middle East bureau chief for Associated Press, in Beirut, Lebanon, by members of Islamic fundamentalist group Hezbollah on Mar. 16, 1985. Freed Dec. 4, 1991. Anderson had been held hostage with **William Buckley**, 55, CIA station chief in Beirut who was kidnapped Mar. 16, 1984, and died in captivity.

Jacob Wetterling, 11, kidnapped Oct. 22, 1989, nr. his home in St. Joseph, MN, by armed man. Federal legislation named for Wetterling passed in 1994, requiring states to set up registries of offenders convicted of sexually violent crimes or crimes against children. Wetterling's remains found in 2016 after his kidnapper confessed (as part of a plea) to having killed the boy.

Jaycee Dugard, 11, kidnapped nr. her home in South Lake Tahoe, CA, June 10, 1991; held for 18 years by Nancy and Philip Garrido, who fathered 2 girls with Dugard during her captivity. Dugard, along with her 11- and 15-year-old daughters, was reunited with her family Aug. 27, 2009, after police arrested the Garridos.

Sidney J. Reso, oil company exec., seized Apr. 29, 1992; died May 3. Arthur D. Seale—former security official at oil company—and his wife, Irene, arrested June 19. Arthur sentenced to life in prison; Irene sentenced to 20-year prison term.

Polly Klaas, 12, Petaluma, CA, abducted at knife point, Oct. 1, 1993, during slumber party at her home. Police arrested Richard Allen Davis on Nov. 30; he led them to her body, found Dec. 4 in wooded area of Cloverdale, CA. Davis found guilty June 18, 1996, and sentenced to death Sept. 26.

Amber Hagerman, 9, abducted Jan. 13, 1996, while riding her bicycle in Arlington, TX, found dead five days later. Her murder, which remains unsolved, led to the creation of the AMBER Alert (America's Missing: Broadcast Emergency Response), used to broadcast child abductions over the nation's Emergency Alert System.

Tionda Z. Bradley, 10, and sister **Diamond Yvette Bradley**, 3, went missing July 6, 2001, in Chicago. Note left by Tionda at home stated the 2 girls were going to the store and playground. Disappearance still unsolved.

Daniel Pearl, 38, reporter for *Wall Street Journal*, abducted Jan. 23, 2002, while investigating links between al-Qaeda and British-born "shoe-bomber" Richard Reid. Beheaded Feb. 1, 2002; act captured on videotape. British-born militant Ahmad Omar Saeed Sheikh and 3 others convicted July 15, 2002, of kidnapping and murder by judge in Hyderabad. In 2007, while in captivity at Guantanamo Bay, Cuba, Khalid Sheikh Mohammed, mastermind of the Sept. 11 attacks, admitted to murdering Pearl.

Elizabeth Smart, 14, abducted from her home in Salt Lake City, UT, June 5, 2002, by Brian D. Mitchell, and forced to live with Mitchell and wife Wanda for 9 months in various U.S. cities; found walking down street with captors in Sandy, UT, 15 mi from Smart family home, Mar. 12, 2003.

Michelle Knight, 21, abducted Aug. 23, 2002; **Amanda Berry**, 17, seized Apr. 21, 2003; and **Gina DeJesus**, 14, kidnapped Apr. 2, 2004. All 3 women escaped from the Cleveland, OH, home of Ariel Castro, May 6, 2013, after a decade in captivity during which Berry gave birth to a daughter.

Jill Carroll, 28, freelance journalist on assignment for *Christian Science Monitor*, seized in Baghdad by group called the Revenge Brigade, Jan. 7, 2006. She was released Mar. 30; 4 Iraqis arrested in connection with her kidnapping.

Steve Centanni, 60, Fox News reporter released Aug. 26, 2006 (along with a colleague), after being held hostage for 13 days by Palestinian militant group Holy Jihad Brigades. The group had demanded U.S. release of all Muslims in its prisons.

Reigh Storrow Mills, 7, abducted July 27, 2008, by her father, Christian Gerhartsreiter (alias Clark Rockefeller); reunited with her mother Aug. 2, 2008, by FBI agents who took Gerhartsreiter into custody.

Felix Batista, 55, Cuban-American security expert who negotiated the release of numerous kidnapping victims, abducted in Mexico, Dec. 10, 2008. Still missing.

Jessica Buchanan, 32, aid worker for Danish Refugee Council, taken hostage by Somali pirates Oct. 25, 2011; rescued by U.S. Navy SEALs Jan. 25, 2012.

James Foley, 39, freelance journalist, taken hostage during civil war in Syria's Idlib province, Nov. 22, 2012. Sunni extremist group the Islamic State in Iraq and Syria (ISIS) released video Aug. 19, 2014, showing execution of Foley.

Richard Engel, 39, NBC News foreign correspondent in Syria and his crew held captive, Dec. 13, 2012; freed by rebel militia 5 days later.

Hannah Anderson, 16, abducted Aug. 3, 2013, by James DiMaggio, a family friend who killed her mother and brother at his California home before fleeing with her to Idaho; freed Aug. 10 when FBI agents shot and killed DiMaggio.

Madyson Middleton, 8, reported missing July 26, 2015, from Santa Cruz, CA, arts center; found dead July 27. A 15-year-old neighbor was charged with her rape and murder.

Long Ma, 71, cabdriver kidnapped Jan. 22, 2016, by three escapees from an Orange County (CA) jail who forced him, at gunpoint, to drive to San Jose and enable them to obtain motel rooms and cash. Released Jan. 29 when one escapee surrendered.

Notable Terrorist Incidents Worldwide Since 1971

Source: U.S. Dept. of State; *Facts On File World News Digest*; World Almanac research

Selected noteworthy incidents, excluding most assassinations, kidnappings, and military targets. Does not include all incidents in Iraq or Afghanistan, 2001-present; see also Chronology of the Year's Events.

1971—Mar. 1: Senate wing of U.S. Capitol Building in Wash., DC, bombed by Weather Underground; no deaths.

1972—July 21: "Bloody Friday." Provisional IRA exploded 20+ bombs across Belfast, N. Ireland; 9 killed, hundreds injured. **Sept. 5:** Palestinian group Black September killed 2 Israeli athletes and seized 9 others at Olympic Village in Munich, W. Germany, during Summer Olympics; 9 hostages, 5 militants, 1 Ger. officer died in botched rescue.

1973—Dec. 17: Palestinian gunmen attacked Rome airport and bombed plane on tarmac; hijacked Lufthansa plane with 5 Italian hostages to Athens, Greece, then to Kuwait; 31 killed in all.

1974—June 17: Houses of Parliament in London, England, bombed by Provisional IRA; 11 injured.

1975—Jan. 27: Puerto Rican FALN nationalists bombed Fraunces Tavern in New York City; 4 killed, 53 injured. **Jan. 29:** U.S. State Dept. building in Wash., DC, bombed by Weather Underground; no deaths.

1976—June 27: Palestinian and Baader-Meinhof militants forced Air France jet to land in Entebbe, Uganda. Israeli army rescued 103 hostages from airport terminal in battle with terrorists and Ugandan troops, July 3-4; 32 killed in all.

1978—Mar. 11: Palestinian militants shot civilians and hijacked bus with hostages from Haifa to Tel Aviv, Israel. Bus exploded during firefight with police at a roadblock; 38 killed.

1979—Nov. 4: Iranian radicals seized U.S. embassy in Tehran, taking 66 Americans hostage. 52 were held until Jan. 20, 1981. **Nov. 20:** 200 Islamic terrorists seized Grand Mosque in Mecca, Saudi Arabia, and held hundreds of pilgrims hostage. Saudi forces retook mosque Dec. 4; about 250 died.

1980—Feb. 1: Members of leftist guerrilla group April 19 Movement (M-19) seized Dominican Republic embassy in Bogota, Colombia; 80 hostages taken, 18 held until Apr. 27.

1983—Apr. 18: Hezbollah suicide truck bomb at U.S. embassy in Beirut, Lebanon, killed 63. **Oct. 9:** N. Korean agents ambushed a S. Korean govt. delegation in Rangoon, Burma, killing 21. **Oct. 23:** Hezbollah suicide truck bombings of U.S. and French military bases, Beirut, Lebanon; 242 Americans, 58 French killed.

1984—Sept. 20: U.S. embassy annex nr. Beirut, Lebanon, bombed, killing approx. 20. **Sept. 20:** In worst bioterrorism attack in U.S. history, members of Rajneesh cult poisoned an Oregon salsa bar with salmonella, sickening 751.

1985—Apr. 12: Bomb blast at restaurant nr. U.S. air base in Torrejon, Spain; 18 killed. **June 14:** Hezbollah members hijacked TWA Flight 847 with 153 passengers and crew to Beirut, Lebanon; 39 held for 17 days, 1 U.S. Navy sailor killed. **June 23:** Air India Flight 182 destroyed by bomb off coast of Ireland; 329 killed. Blamed on Sikh terrorists. **Oct. 7:** Four Palestinians hijacked Italian cruise ship *Achille Lauro*; 1 passenger killed. **Nov. 23:** EgyptAir Flight 648 from Athens, Greece, to Cairo hijacked to Malta by Palestinian group Abu Nidal; 60 killed in rescue. **Dec. 27:** Palestinian militants opened fire at El-Al airline counters at Rome and Vienna airports; 19 killed.

1986—Apr. 5: Nightclub in Berlin, W. Germany, bombed; 3 killed, incl. 2 U.S. service personnel, 200+ hurt. 3 Libyan embassy workers in Germany convicted.

1987—Apr. 17: Bomb in Sri Lankan capital killed 100+; blamed on Tamil rebels who, 4 days later, attacked Sinhalese travelers on highway, killing 127. **June 19:** Basque group ETA bombed supermarket garage in Barcelona; 21 killed, 45 injured. **Nov. 29:** Bomb planted by N. Korean agents exploded on Korean Air Lines Flight 858 over Indian Ocean; 115 killed.

1988—Dec. 21: Pan Am Flight 103 exploded over Lockerbie, Scotland, killing all 259 aboard and 11 on ground; Libya took responsibility for bombing in Aug. 2003.

1989—Sept. 19: French UTA Flight 722 from Congo Republic to Paris destroyed by bomb in midair over Niger; 170 killed.

1992—Mar. 17: Israeli embassy in Buenos Aires, Argentina, bombed; 28 killed, 200+ injured. Hezbollah suspected.

1993—Feb. 26: Truck bomb exploded in World Trade Center garage in New York City; 6 killed. Blast later linked to al-Qaeda. **Mar. 12-19:** At least 11 bombs ripped through Bombay and Calcutta, India; 300+ killed.

1994—Feb. 25: U.S.-born Israeli settler Baruch Goldstein opened fire in mosque in Hebron, West Bank; about 30 Muslim worshippers killed. **July 18:** Buenos Aires, Argentina, Jewish center bombed; 87 killed. Blamed on Hezbollah.

1995—Mar. 20: Twelve killed and over 5,000 injured when Japanese Aum Shinri-kyu cult members released sarin nerve gas in several Tokyo subway cars. **Apr. 19:** Murrah Federal Building in Oklahoma City bombed, killing 168 and injuring 500+. Timothy McVeigh and Terry Nichols convicted. McVeigh executed in 2001; Nichols sentenced to life in prison. **Nov. 13:** U.S. military compound in Riyadh, Saudi Arabia, bombed by Islamic Movement of Change; 7 killed.

1996—Jan. 31: Tamil Tigers drove explosives-laden truck into Central Bank in Colombo, Sri Lanka; 90 killed. **June 25:** Bomb-laden fuel truck exploded outside Khobar Towers, U.S. military complex in Dhahran, Saudi Arabia; killed 19. **July 27:** Bomb exploded at Centennial Olympic Park in Atlanta, GA, during Summer Games; killed 2, injured 100+. Extremist Eric Robert Rudolph sentenced to life in prison, 2005. **Dec. 3:** Bomb exploded on subway train in Paris; 4 killed, 86 injured.

1997—Nov. 17: Gamaa al-Islamiya militants killed 58 tourists and 4 Egyptians in Valley of the Kings nr. Luxor, Egypt.

1998—Aug. 7: U.S. embassies in Nairobi, Kenya, and Dar-es-Salaam, Tanzania, bombed; 257 people killed. Al-Qaeda blamed. **Aug. 15:** IRA car bomb exploded outside courthouse in Omagh, N. Ireland; killed 29, injured 300+. **Oct. 18:** National Liberation Army of Colombia blew up Ocensa oil pipeline; about 71 killed, 100+ injured.

1999—Sept. 9-16: Three buildings bombed in Moscow and Volgodonsk, Russia; about 300 killed. Chechen rebels blamed.

2000—Oct. 12: Small boat assisting in docking of U.S.S. *Cole* exploded while alongside it in Aden, Yemen; 17 U.S. sailors killed, 39 injured. Blamed on al-Qaeda.

2001—Sept. 11: 19 al-Qaeda terrorists hijacked 4 U.S. domestic flights, including 2 planes that crashed into New York City's World Trade Center towers and 1 into Pentagon. Total dead minus hijackers: 2,977; deadliest terrorist attack yet on U.S. soil. **Sept.-Nov. 7:** Letters tainted with deadly anthrax bacteria mailed through U.S. postal system killed 5, sickened 17; investigation concluded in 2010 that microbiologist Bruce Ivins, who committed suicide in 2008, was responsible.

2002—Mar. 27: Suicide bombing at hotel in Netanya, Israel, during Passover celebration; 27 killed. **Oct. 12:** Resort in Bali, Indonesia, bombed; 202 dead. Jemaah Islamiah blamed. **Oct. 23:** Chechen guerrillas seized theater in Moscow, held 700+ hostages. Russian authorities gassed theater; most guerrillas and about 128 hostages killed. **Dec. 27:** Chechen rebels plowed truck bomb into pro-Russian govt. headquarters in Grozny, Chechnya; 80 killed, 152 injured.

2003—May 12-13: Al-Qaeda militants detonated car bombs at 3 residential complexes used by Westerners in Riyadh, Saudi Arabia; 34 killed. **May 16:** Five explosions in Casablanca, Morocco; 44 killed, 100+ wounded. Blamed on al-Qaeda. **Aug. 19:** UN headquarters in Baghdad bombed by truck; 22 killed, incl. UN envoy to Iraq. **Aug. 25:** 2 bombs exploded in taxis in Mumbai, India; 46 killed, 100+ injured. Islamic militants suspected. **Nov. 15:** Two synagogues in Istanbul, Turkey, bombed; 25 killed. **Nov. 20:** British consulate and offices of British bank HSBC bombed in Istanbul, Turkey; 27 killed. Blamed on al-Qaeda. **Dec. 5:** Suicide bombing on commuter train in Yessentuki, Russia; 44 killed, 150 injured. Blamed on Chechen rebels.

2004—Feb. 6: Bomb exploded in Moscow subway; 39 killed, 130 injured. Chechen rebels blamed. **Mar. 11:** Al-Qaeda cell bombed 4 commuter trains during morning rush hour in Madrid, Spain; 191 killed, about 1,200 injured. **May 29:** Al-Qaeda militants stormed foreigner compound in Khobar, Saudi Arabia, taking hostages; 22 killed. **Aug. 24:** Chechen suicide bombers caused near-simultaneous crash of two Russian passenger planes in diff. parts of Russia; 90 killed. **Sept. 1:** Chechen militants seized school in Beslan, in North Ossetia, Russia; held 1,000+ hostage for 3 days before Russian troops stormed school. About 330 killed, incl. 27 hostage-takers.

2005—July 7: Four bombs exploded on 3 separate subways and 1 bus in central London, Eng.; 52 killed, about 700 injured. **July 23:** Three car bombs explode nr. resorts at Sharm el Sheik, Egypt; about 90 killed. **Nov. 9:** 3 suicide bombings targeted hotels in Amman, Jordan; killed 56+, injured about 100. Al-Qaeda in Iraq took responsibility.

2006—July 11: 8 explosions struck 7 different trains and 1 station of public commuter rail system in Mumbai, India; 207 killed, 700+ wounded. Lashkar-e-Qahhar (Army of Terror) claimed responsibility.

2007—Feb. 19: Train traveling between New Delhi and border with Pakistan caught fire, 68 killed; Indian ministers blamed Muslim militants for trying to disrupt peace talks between India and Pakistan. **Dec. 11:** Two coordinated car bombs went off outside govt. building and UN office building in Algiers, Algeria; 41 killed, incl. 17 UN employees, 170 wounded.

2008—Sept. 20: Suicide bomber in truck set off explosion outside of Marriott Hotel in Islamabad, Pakistan. Hotel was popular among foreigners, wealthy residents and was located nr. prime min.'s house and parliament building; 53 killed, 271 wounded. **Nov. 26-29:** Series of attacks and bombings on luxury hotels and high-profile targets in Mumbai, India; 171 killed, 300 injured.

2009—Feb. 20: Suicide bomber targeted Shiite funeral in Dera Ismail Khan, Pakistan; 30 killed, 50+ wounded. **Dec. 25:** Umar Farouk Abdulmutallab, 23-year-old Nigerian, failed to blow up a Northwest Airlines flight from Amsterdam to Detroit with bomb hidden in his underpants.

2010—Jan. 1: Taliban suicide bomber killed more than 100 on a playground in NW Pakistan. **Mar. 29:** Two female Chechen separatists detonated suicide bombs at two landmark subway stations in Moscow, killing at least 40. **July 9:** Suicide bombers targeted tribal elders in Mohmand, Pakistan, killing more than 100. **July 11:** Several bombs exploded simultaneously in Kampala, Uganda, killing more than 70 people who had gathered to watch the broadcast of the World Cup final.

2011—Jan. 24: Suicide bomber killed 35 in Moscow's Domodedovo Airport, location chosen to maximize deaths of foreigners. **July 22:** Anders Behring Breivik, right-wing Norwegian extremist, set off a bomb in van outside govt. buildings in Oslo, then massacred dozens of young people at a summer camp on Tyrifjorden Lake, bringing death toll to 77.

2012—Jan. 21: Series of attacks by Islamist extremist group Boko Haram killed more than 185 in Kano, Nigeria. **May 21:** Suicide bomber claimed by al-Qaeda in the Arabian Peninsula (AQAP) killed more than 100 soldiers, wounded 200 during military parade rehearsal nr. Yemeni presidential palace. **Sept. 11:** Terrorists stormed U.S. embassy in Benghazi, Libya, killing 4 Americans, including U.S. Amb. J. Christopher Stevens.

2013—Apr. 15: Two bombs exploded nr. Boston Marathon finish line, killing 3 and injuring 264; 4-day search ended in death of suspect Tamerlan Tsarnaev and capture of his brother, Dzhokhar, a naturalized Chechen immigrant. **Sept. 21:** Al-Shabab, a Somali militant group, killed up to 70 people and wounded at least 175 at a Nairobi, Kenya, shopping mall.

2014—Apr.-May: Islamist extremist group Boko Haram kidnapped more than 250 girls from schools in Nigeria; killed more than 150 villagers in town of Gamboru. **Dec. 15:** Nine Taliban gunmen attacked military-affiliated school in Peshawar, Pakistan, executing about 150 people including 132 children.

2015—Jan. 7: Gunmen stormed Paris offices of *Charlie Hebdo*, a satirical newspaper, killing 12. Two days later, French police killed suspects, brothers who identified themselves as belonging to AQAP. **Mar. 18:** Gunmen killed 21 tourists and a police officer at Tunisia's National Bardo Museum. Several terrorist groups claimed credit. **Apr. 2:** Al-Shabab militants killed 147 students at Kenya's Garissa Univ. after separating Christian and Muslim students. **June 17:** Lone white-supremacist gunman killed 9, incl. a state senator, in a historically black church in Charleston, SC. **Oct. 31:** Terrorists downed a Russian charter flight shortly after takeoff from Egypt's Sharm el-Sheikh resort, killing all 224 onboard. An Egyptian affiliate of the Sunni extremist group the Islamic State in Iraq and Syria (ISIS) said it smuggled a bomb in a soda can onto the plane. **Nov. 13:** Series of coordinated suicide bombings and other attacks by ISIS on Paris cafes, a soccer stadium, and the popular Bataclan concert hall killed 137 (incl. 7 attackers); wounded 350+. **Dec. 2:** A heavily armed married couple opened fire on the husband's coworkers at a holiday party for San Bernardino (CA) County Health Dept., killing 14, wounding 21.

2016—March 22: Three explosions in Brussels, two at the airport and one at a busy subway station, killed 35 people (incl. 3 bombers) and injured 300+. ISIS claimed credit; investigators linked perpetrators to Nov. 2015 Paris attacks. **June 12:** Lone gunman killed 49 people and wounded 53 at a gay nightclub in Orlando, FL. **July 7:** A heavily armed man shot and killed five police officers and wounded seven other officers and two civilians in downtown Dallas, TX.

MILITARY AFFAIRS

Chairmen of the Joint Chiefs of Staff, 1949-2016

Chairman	Service	Chairman	Service
Gen. of the Army Omar N. Bradley, USA	8/16/1949-8/15/1953	Adm. William J. Crowe Jr., USN	10/1/1985-9/30/1989
Adm. Arthur W. Radford, USN.	8/15/1953-8/15/1957	Gen. Colin L. Powell, USA.	10/1/1989-9/30/1993
Gen. Nathan F. Twining, USAF.	8/15/1957-9/30/1960	Gen. John M. Shalikashvili, USA.	10/25/1993-9/30/1997
Gen. Lyman L. Lemnitzer, USA.	10/1/1960-9/30/1962	Gen. Henry H. Shelton, USA.	9/30/1997-9/30/2001
Gen. Maxwell D. Taylor, USA	10/1/1962-7/1/1964	Gen. Richard B. Myers, USAF.	10/1/2001-9/30/2005
Gen. Earle G. Wheeler, USA.	7/3/1964-7/2/1970	Gen. Peter Pace, USMC	9/30/2005-9/30/2007
Adm. Thomas H. Moorer, USN	7/2/1970-7/1/1974	Adm. Michael G. Mullen, USN.	10/1/2007-9/30/2011
Gen. George S. Brown, USAF.	7/1/1974-6/20/1978	Gen. Martin E. Dempsey, USA	10/1/2011-9/25/2015
Gen. David C. Jones, USAF	6/21/1978-6/18/1982	Gen. Joseph F. Dunford Jr., USMC.	9/25/2015-
Gen. John W. Vessey Jr., USA.	6/18/1982-9/30/1985		

Chief Commanding Officers of the U.S. Military

Chairman, Joint Chiefs of Staff: Gen. Joseph F. Dunford Jr. (USMC)
Vice Chairman: Gen. Paul J. Selva (USAF)

Date of rank is date when the individual achieved his or her current rank. While serving in any of these positions, or as commander of a unified or specified combatant command, basic pay is $21,147.30 per month. Officers hold positions listed as of Sept. 1, 2016.

Army

Chief of Staff (CSA)	Date of rank
Milley, Mark A.	Aug. 15, 2014
Other Generals	
Abrams, Robert B.	Aug. 10, 2015
Allyn, Daniel	Apr. 26, 2013
Brooks, Vincent K.	July 2, 2013
Brown, John B.	May 4, 2016
Grass, Frank J.	Sept. 7, 2012
Nicholson, John W., Jr.	Mar. 3, 2016
Perkins, David G.	Mar. 14, 2014
Rodriguez, David M.	Aug. 15, 2011
Scaparrotti, Curtis M.	Oct. 2, 2013
Thomas, Raymond A., III	Mar. 30, 2016
Via, Dennis L.	Aug. 7, 2012
Votel, Joseph L., III	Aug. 28, 2014

Air Force

Chief of Staff (CSAF or AF/CC)	Date of rank
Goldfein, David L.	Aug. 17, 2005
Other Generals	
Carlisle, Herbert J.	Aug. 3, 2012
Everhart, Carlton D., II	Aug. 11, 2015
Hyten, John E.	Aug. 15, 2014
Lengyel, Joseph L.	Aug. 3, 2016
McDew, Darren W.	May 5, 2014
O'Shaughnessy, Terrence J.	July 12, 2016
Pawlikowski, Ellen M.	June 8, 2015
Rand, Robin.	Oct. 10, 2013
Robinson, Lori J.	Oct. 16, 2014
Selva, Paul J.	Nov. 30, 2012
Wilson, Stephen W.	July 22, 2016
Wolters, Tod D.	Aug. 11, 2016

Navy

Chief of Naval Operations (CNO)	Date of rank
Richardson, John M. (submariner)	July 26, 2012
Other Admirals	
Caldwell, James F. (submariner).	Aug. 14, 2015
Davidson, Philip S. (surface warfare)	Dec. 19, 2014
Haney, Cecil D. (surface warfare).	Jan. 20, 2012
Harris, Harry B., Jr. (aviator)	Oct. 16, 2013
Howard, Michelle J. (surface warfare).	July 1, 2014
Moran, William F. (aviator)	May 31, 2016
Rogers, Michael S. (information warfare)	Mar. 31, 2014
Swift, Scott H. (aviator)	May 27, 2015
Tidd, Kurt W. (surface warfare)	Jan. 14, 2016

Marine Corps

Commandant of the Marine Corps (CMC)	Date of rank
Neller, Robert B.	Sept. 24, 2015
Other Generals	
Dunford, Joseph F.	Oct. 23, 2010
Waldhauser, Thomas D.	July 18, 2016
Walters, Glenn M.	Aug. 2, 2016

Coast Guard

Commandant, with rank of Admiral	Date of rank
Zukunft, Paul F.	May 30, 2014
Vice Commandant, with rank of Vice Admiral	
Michel, Charles D.	May 1, 2014

Commanders of the Unified Combatant Commands

U.S. European Command, Stuttgart-Vaihingen, Germany:
Gen. Curtis M. Scaparrotti (U.S. Army)
U.S. Pacific Command, Honolulu, Hawaii:
Adm. Harry B. Harris Jr. (USN)
U.S. Special Operations Command, MacDill AFB, Florida:
Gen. Raymond A. Thomas III (U.S. Army)
U.S. Transportation Command, Scott AFB, Illinois:
Gen. Darren W. McDew (USAF)
U.S. Central Command, MacDill AFB, Florida:
Gen. Joseph L. Votel III (U.S. Army)

U.S. Southern Command, Doral, Florida:
Adm. Kurt W. Tidd (USN)
U.S. Northern Command, Peterson AFB, Colorado:
Gen. Lori J. Robinson (USAF)
U.S. Strategic Command, Offutt AFB, Nebraska:
Adm. Cecil D. Haney (USN)
U.S. Africa Command, Kelley Barracks, Stuttgart, Germany:
Gen. Thomas D. Waldhauser (USMC)

North Atlantic Treaty Organization (NATO) International Commands

NATO Headquarters: Chairman, NATO Military Committee:
Gen. Petr Pavel (Czech Army)
ACO Subordinate Commands:
Joint Force Command Brunssum (JFC Brunssum):
Gen. Salvatore Farina (Italian Army), Commander
Joint Force Command Naples (JFC Naples): Adm. Michelle
Howard (USN), Commander

Strategic Commands:
Allied Command Operations (ACO): Gen. Curtis M. Scaparrotti (U.S. Army), Supreme Allied Commander, Europe
Allied Command Transformation (ACT): Gen. Denis Mercier (French Air Force), Supreme Allied Commander Transformation

Directors of the Central Intelligence Agency, 1946-2016

In 1942, Pres. Franklin D. Roosevelt established the Office of Strategic Services (OSS); it was disbanded in 1945. In 1946, Pres. Harry Truman established the Central Intelligence Group (CIG) to operate under the National Intelligence Authority (NIA). A 1947 law replaced the NIA with the National Security Council (NSC) and the CIG with the Central Intelligence Agency (CIA).

Director	Served	Appointed by President	Director	Served	Appointed by President
Adm. Sidney W. Souers	1946	Truman	William J. Casey	1981-1987	Reagan
Gen. Hoyt S. Vandenberg	1946-1947	Truman	William H. Webster	1987-1991	Reagan
Adm. Roscoe H. Hillenkoetter	1947-1950	Truman	Robert M. Gates	1991-1993	Bush, G. H. W.
Gen. Walter Bedell Smith	1950-1953	Truman	R. James Woolsey	1993-1995	Clinton
Allen W. Dulles	1953-1961	Eisenhower	John M. Deutch	1995-1997	Clinton
John A. McCone	1961-1965	Kennedy	George J. Tenet.	1997-2004	Clinton
Adm. William F. Raborn Jr.	1965-1966	Johnson, L. B.	Porter Goss	2004-2006	Bush, G. W.
Richard Helms.	1966-1973	Johnson, L. B.	Gen. Michael V. Hayden	2006-2009	Bush, G. W.
James R. Schlesinger	1973	Nixon	Leon E. Panetta.	2009-2011	Obama
William E. Colby	1973-1976	Nixon	Gen. David H. Petraeus.	2011-2012	Obama
George H. W. Bush	1976-1977	Ford	John O. Brennan	2013-	Obama
Adm. Stansfield Turner	1977-1981	Carter			

U.S. Army and Air Force Units

Army Units. Squad: In infantry, usually 8-16 enlisted personnel under a sergeant or staff sergeant. **Platoon:** In infantry, 3 squads under a lieutenant. **Company:** Headquarters and 3-5 platoons under a captain. (Company-size unit in the artillery is a battery; in the cavalry, a troop.) **Battalion:** 3-6 companies under a lieutenant colonel. (Battalion-size unit in the cavalry is a squadron.) **Brigade:** Three or more battalions under a colonel. (Brigade-size unit in the cavalry and rangers is a regiment; in the special forces, a group.) **Division:** 3 brigades with combat support and combat service support units under a major general. **Corps:** 2-5 divisions with corps troops under a lieutenant general. **Army:** 2-5 corps with operational and support responsibilities under a general.

Air Force Units. Flight: Numerically designated flights are the lowest level unit. They are used primarily where there is a need for small mission elements to be incorporated into an organized unit. **Squadron:** The basic unit. Designates specific operational or support capability like mission units in operational commands. **Group:** Flexible unit composed of 2 or more squadrons whose functions may be operational, support, or administrative in nature. **Wing:** Primary group with supporting groups on a distinct mission with significant scope such as combat, flying training, or airlift. **Numbered Air Force (NAF):** Normally operationally oriented, the numbered air force is designed for the control of subordinate units with the same mission and/or geographical location. **Major Command (MAJCOM):** A major subdivision with full staff that manages a major segment of the USAF mission. Major command is composed of 3 or more numbered air forces.

U.S. Military Personnel Strength on Active Duty Worldwide, 2015

Source: U.S. Dept. of Defense

(as of Sept. 30, 2015)

Area	Personnel	Area	Personnel	Area	Personnel
TOTAL WORLDWIDE[1]	**1,301,443**	**EUROPE**		**EAST ASIA AND PACIFIC**	
		Belgium	1,210	Australia	175
U.S. TERRITORIES AND		Germany	36,691	British Indian Ocean Territory	
SPEC. LOCATIONS		Greece	373	(Diego Garcia)	488
U.S., 48 contiguous states	1,075,505	Greenland	145	Japan	52,060
Alaska	17,838	Italy	11,425	South Korea	24,889
Guam	5,666	Netherlands	362	Philippines	29
Hawaii	46,764	Portugal	457	Singapore	189
Puerto Rico	152	Spain	2,503	Thailand	304
Regional total[2]	1,145,932	Turkey	1,581	Regional total[2]	**78,294**
		United Kingdom	8,920	**NORTH AFRICA, NEAR EAST, AND**	
OTHER WESTERN HEMISPHERE		Regional total[2]	**64,479**	**SOUTH ASIA**	
Canada	133			Afghanistan[3]	14,542
Colombia	52	**SUB-SAHARAN AFRICA**		Bahrain	3,419
Cuba (Guantánamo)	668	South Africa	236	Egypt	250
Haiti	5	Regional total[2]	**404**	Iraq[3]	2,679
Honduras	395			Qatar	593
Regional total[2]	**1,577**	**FORMER SOVIET UNION**		Saudi Arabia	315
		Total	87	United Arab Emirates	391
				Regional total[2,4]	**5,146**

(1) Includes undistributed personnel. (2) Most countries and areas with fewer than 100 assigned U.S. military members not listed; regional totals include personnel stationed in countries and areas not shown. (3) Includes troops in surrounding areas and deployed Reserve/National Guard as of Mar. 31, 2015; more recent figures not publicly available. (4) Excludes troops deployed to Afghanistan/Iraq.

U.S. Army Personnel on Active Duty, 1940-2016

Source: Dept. of the Army, U.S. Dept. of Defense

(as of midyear, except where noted)

Date	Total strength[1]	Commissioned officers			Warrant officers[3]		Enlisted personnel		
		Total	Male	Female[2]	Male	Female	Total	Male	Female
1940	267,767	17,563	16,624	939	763	—	249,441	249,441	—
1942	3,074,184	203,137	190,662	12,475	3,285	—	2,867,762	2,867,762	—
1943	6,993,102	557,657	521,435	36,222	21,919	—	6,413,526	6,358,200	55,325
1944	7,992,868	740,077	692,351	47,726	36,893	10	7,215,888	7,144,601	71,287
1945	8,266,373	835,403	772,511	62,892	56,216	44	7,374,710	7,283,930	90,780
1946	1,889,690	257,300	240,658	16,642	9,826	18	1,622,546	1,605,847	16,699
1950	591,487	67,784	63,375	4,409	4,760	22	518,921	512,370	6,551
1955	1,107,606	111,347	106,196	5,151	10,552	48	985,659	977,943	7,716
1960	871,348	91,056	86,832	4,224	10,141	39	770,112	761,833	8,279
1965	967,049	101,812	98,029	3,783	10,285	23	854,929	846,409	8,520
1970	1,319,735	143,704	138,469	5,235	23,005	13	1,153,013	1,141,537	11,476
1975	781,316	89,756	85,184	4,572	13,214	22	678,324	640,621	37,703
1980 (Sept. 30)	772,661	85,339	77,843	7,496	13,265	113	673,944	612,593	61,351
1985 (Sept. 30)	776,244	94,103	83,563	10,540	15,296	288	666,557	598,639	67,918
1990 (Mar. 31)	746,220	91,330	79,520	11,810	15,177	470	639,713	567,015	72,698
1995	521,036	72,646	62,250	10,396	12,053	599	435,807	377,832	57,975
2000	471,633	66,344	56,391	9,953	10,608	781	393,900	333,947	59,953
2005 (Sept. 30)	492,728	69,174	57,675	11,499	11,506	976	406,923	346,194	57,354
2006 (Sept. 30)	505,402	68,742	57,318	11,424	11,931	1,035	419,353	361,528	57,825
2007 (Sept. 30)	522,017	70,657	58,854	11,803	13,844	1,160	433,109	374,989	58,120
2008 (Sept. 30)	539,170	72,650	60,357	12,293	13,428	1,246	451,846	392,163	59,683
2009 (Sept. 30)	553,044	75,337	63,146	12,191	13,815	1,348	457,980	398,579	59,401
2010 (Sept. 30)	566,045	78,588	64,952	13,636	14,106	1,434	467,248	406,871	60,377
2011 (Sept. 30)	565,463	81,395	67,140	14,255	14,373	1,472	463,605	403,381	60,224
2012 (Sept. 30)	550,064	82,538	68,021	14,517	14,401	1,484	447,075	389,646	57,429
2013 (Sept. 30)	532,043	82,916	68,219	14,697	14,229	1,489	428,923	373,263	55,660
2014 (Dec. 31)	498,642	81,184	66,615	14,569	13,965	1,455	397,690	344,897	52,793
2015 (Dec. 31)	482,264	78,586	64,223	14,363	14,998	1,421	384,301	331,620	52,681
2016	474,472	78,742	64,253	14,489	14,714	1,391	376,432	324,117	52,315

— = Not applicable. **Note:** Represents strength of active Army, including Philippine Scouts (1940-46), ret. Regular Army personnel on extended active duty, and National Guard and Reserve personnel on extended active duty; excl. those (e.g. U.S. Military Academy cadets, contract surgeons, and National Guard and Reserve personnel) not on extended active duty. (1) Includes categories not listed, e.g., West Point cadets. Data for 1940-46 include personnel in the Army Air Forces and its predecessors (Air Service and Air Corps). (2) Includes Army Nurse Corps for all years, Women's Army Corps (1942-78), and Medical Specialists Corps (1949 and after). (3) Act of Congress approved Apr. 27, 1926, directed the appointment as warrant officers of field clerks still in active service. Includes flight officers as follows: 1943, 5,700; 1944, 13,615; 1945, 31,117; 1946, 2,580.

U.S. Navy Personnel on Active Duty, 1940-2016
Source: U.S. Dept. of Defense
(as of midyear, except where noted)

Year	Officers	Nurses[1]	Enlisted	Officer candidates[1]	Total[2]	Year	Officers	Nurses[1]	Enlisted	Officer candidates[1]	Total[2]
1940	13,162	442	144,824	2,569	160,997	2005	54,039	—	305,368	—	363,858
1945	320,293	11,086	2,988,207	61,231	3,380,817	2006	53,209	—	295,773	—	353,496
1950	42,687	1,964	331,860	5,037	381,538	2007 (Sept.)	51,385	—	281,772	—	337,547
1960	67,456	2,103	544,040	4,385	617,984	2008	52,184	—	276,346	—	331,785
1970	78,488	2,273	605,899	6,000	692,660	2009	52,233	—	274,858	—	331,637
1980	63,100	—	464,100	—	527,200	2010	53,071	—	273,609	—	330,065
1990 (Sept.)	74,429	—	530,133	—	604,562	2011	53,620	—	270,425	—	328,648
1995 (May)	61,075	—	402,626	—	463,701	2012 (Mar.)	52,558	—	263,928	—	320,961
1997	57,341	—	340,616	—	397,957	2013 (Feb.)	52,450	—	260,581	—	317,464
1998 (Sept.)	55,007	—	326,196	—	381,203	2014	54,852	—	265,622	—	323,792
1999	55,726	—	322,372	—	378,098	2015	54,770	—	268,408	—	326,504
2000 (Oct.)	53,698	—	320,212	—	373,910	2016	54,973	—	271,100	—	330,556

— = Not applicable. (1) Starting in 1980, "Nurses" are included with "Officers," and "Officer candidates" are included with "Enlisted." (2) May include categories not shown, e.g., midshipmen.

U.S. Air Force Personnel on Active Duty, 1918-2016
Source: U.S. Dept. of Defense
(as of midyear, except where noted)

Year[1]	Total	Year[1]	Total	Year[1]	Total	Year[1]	Total	Year[1]	Total	Year[1]	Total
1918	195,023	1944	2,372,292	1986	608,200	1995	400,051	2005	358,705	2011	333,729
1920	9,050	1945	2,282,259	1990	535,233	1996	389,400	2006	352,620	2012[2]	332,709
1930	13,531	1950	411,277	1991	510,432	1997	378,681	2007	340,596	2013[3]	334,157
1940	51,165	1960	814,213	1992	470,315	1998	363,479	2008	328,771	2014	328,791
1941	152,125	1970	791,078	1993	444,351	1999	357,929	2009	334,009	2015	312,195
1942	764,415	1980	557,969	1994	426,327	2000	357,777	2010	337,505	2016	315,786
1943	2,197,114										

(1) Prior to 1950, data are for U.S. Army Air Corps and Air Service of the Signal Corps. (2) In Mar. (3) In Feb.

U.S. Marine Corps Personnel on Active Duty, 1940-2016
Source: U.S. Dept. of Defense
(as of midyear, except where noted)

Year	Officers	Enlisted	Total	Year	Officers	Enlisted	Total	Year	Officers	Enlisted	Total
1940	1,800	26,545	28,345	1995	18,017	153,929	171,946	2008	20,137	172,903	193,040
1945	37,067	437,613	474,680	1996	18,146	154,141	172,287	2009	21,031	183,243	204,274
1950	7,254	67,025	74,279	1997	18,089	154,240	172,329	2010	21,680	179,446	201,126
1960	16,203	154,418	170,621	1998	17,984	154,648	172,632	2011	22,281	178,546	200,827
1970	24,941	234,796	259,737	1999	17,892	155,250	173,142	2012 (Mar.)	22,253	176,174	198,427
1980	18,198	170,271	188,469	2000	17,897	154,744	172,641	2013 (Feb.)	21,907	173,222	195,129
1990	19,958	176,694	196,652	2005	19,118	159,113	178,231	2014	21,507	169,327	190,834
1993	18,878	161,205	180,083	2006	19,218	159,705	178,923	2015	21,144	163,144	184,587
1994	18,430	159,949	178,379	2007	19,456	162,085	181,541	2016	20,827	162,543	183,370

U.S. Coast Guard Personnel on Active Duty, 1970-2016
Source: U.S. Dept. of Defense
(as of midyear, except where noted)

Year	Officers	Cadets	Enlisted	Total	Year	Officers	Cadets	Enlisted	Total
1970	5,512	653	31,524	37,689	2008	8,282	1,005	33,137	42,424
1980	6,463	877	32,041	39,381	2009	8,497	993	34,024	43,514
1985	6,775	733	31,087	38,595	2010	8,678	744	33,713	43,135
1990	6,475	820	29,860	37,308	2011	8,659	1,053	33,615	43,327
1995	7,489	841	28,401	36,731	2012 (Mar.)	8,316	988	33,758	43,062
2000	7,154	863	27,695	35,712	2013 (Jan.)	8,376	1,010	32,971	42,357
2005	7,908	1,006	31,900	40,814	2014	8,572	676	31,233	40,481
2006	8,032	1,004	32,001	40,639	2015	8,550	623	30,896	40,069
2007	8,231	720	32,314	41,265	2016	8,550	623	30,896	40,069

Women in the U.S. Armed Forces
Source: U.S. Dept. of Defense; U.S. Census Bureau, U.S. Dept. of Commerce; U.S. Coast Guard, U.S. Dept. of Homeland Security
    Women in the Army, Navy, Air Force, Marines, and Coast Guard are fully integrated with male personnel. All enlisted jobs were opened to women when the draft ended June 30, 1973. Admission to service academies began in 1976. Under rules instituted in 1993, women were allowed to fly combat aircraft and serve aboard warships. By the mid-1990s, 80% of all jobs and more than 90% of all career fields had been opened to women. A woman first achieved the rank of four-star general in 2009. In Apr. 2010, the Navy announced that women would be placed on submarine crews by Jan. 2012. The Pentagon in 2013 lifted its ban on women serving in direct ground combat units. In Aug. 2015, the first two women graduated from the Army's Ranger School.

Women Active Duty Troops, 2016

Service	% women
Army	14.6%
Navy	18.8
Marines	8.0
Air Force	19.4
Coast Guard	17.1

Women on Active Duty, All DOD[1] Services, 1973-2016

Year	% women	Year	% women
1973	2.5%	2000	14.4%
1975	4.6	2005	14.6
1981	8.9	2010	14.5
1987	10.2	2012	14.6
1993	11.6	2015	15.6
1997	13.6	2016	15.9

Women Veterans by Period of Service, 2016

Period of service[2]	% of women vets
Gulf War era[3]	58.7%
Vietnam era	12.2
Korean War	2.3
World War II	1.8
Peacetime only	24.9

Note: Numbers on active duty are as of Sept. 30 in previous years and June 30 in 2016. (1) Does not include Coast Guard. (2) Includes women who served in multiple periods. (3) Includes women who served both pre- and post-9/11 but not in peacetime only.

Average Age and Length of Service of Active Enlisted Personnel, 1973-2014

Source: U.S. Dept. of Defense

Year	Avg. age	Avg. months of service	Year	Avg. age	Avg. months of service	Year	Avg. age	Avg. months of service
1973	25.0	69.8	1988	26.3	76.7	2001	27.0	84.4
1974	25.0	69.6	1989	26.4	78.0	2002	27.1	84.1
1975	24.9	68.2	1990	26.7	81.8	2003	27.0	83.3
1976	24.9	67.6	1991	27.0	84.8	2004	27.0	82.6
1977	24.9	66.5	1992	27.1	86.4	2005	27.1	83.2
1978	25.0	67.3	1992	27.1	86.4	2006	27.1	82.0
1979	25.1	67.7	1993	27.2	87.7	2007	27.1	81.0
1980	25.0	66.5	1994	27.3	89.6	2008	27.1	80.3
1981	25.1	67.1	1995	27.4	89.3	2009	27.2	80.4
1982	25.4	68.6	1996	27.4	89.6	2010	27.3	80.9
1983	25.6	70.0	1997	27.4	89.2	2011	27.4	81.1
1984	25.7	71.1	1998	27.3	88.4	2012	27.4	NA
1985	25.8	72.3	1999	27.3	87.3	2013	27.3	NA
1986	25.9	73.1	2000	27.1	85.5	2014	27.3	NA
1987	26.1	74.8						

NA = Not available.

Monthly Military Pay Scale, 2016

Source: U.S. Dept. of Defense
(effective Jan. 1, 2016; salaries rounded to nearest dollar)

	Cumulative years of service														
	<2	2	3	4	6	8	10	12	14	16	18	20	22	24	26
Commissioned officers															
O-10	NA	NA	NA	NA	NA	NA	NA	NA	NA	NA	NA	16,072	16,151	16,487	17,072
O-9	NA	NA	NA	NA	NA	NA	NA	NA	NA	NA	NA	14,057	14,260	14,552	15,062
O-8	9,946	10,272	10,488	10,549	10,819	11,269	11,374	11,802	11,925	12,293	12,827	13,319	13,647	13,647	13,647
O-7	8,264	8,648	8,826	8,967	9,223	9,476	9,768	10,059	10,351	11,269	12,044	12,044	12,044	12,044	12,106
O-6	6,267	6,885	7,337	7,337	7,365	7,681	7,722	7,722	8,161	8,937	9,393	9,848	10,107	10,369	10,878
O-5	5,225	5,886	6,293	6,370	6,624	6,776	7,110	7,356	7,673	8,159	8,389	8,617	8,876	8,876	8,876
O-4	4,508	5,218	5,567	5,644	5,967	6,314	6,746	7,082	7,315	7,449	7,527	7,527	7,527	7,527	7,527
O-3	3,964	4,493	4,849	5,287	5,541	5,819	5,998	6,294	6,448	6,448	6,448	6,448	6,448	6,448	6,448
O-2	3,425	3,900	4,492	4,644	4,739	4,739	4,739	4,739	4,739	4,739	4,739	4,739	4,739	4,739	4,739
O-1	2,972	3,094	3,740	3,740	3,740	3,740	3,740	3,740	3,740	3,740	3,740	3,740	3,740	3,740	3,740
Commissioned officers with over 4 years of active duty service as enlisted member or warrant officer															
O-3E	NA	NA	NA	5,287	5,541	5,819	5,998	6,294	6,543	6,687	6,881	6,881	6,881	6,881	6,881
O-2E	NA	NA	NA	4,644	4,739	4,890	5,145	5,342	5,489	5,489	5,489	5,489	5,489	5,489	5,489
O-1E	NA	NA	NA	3,740	3,994	4,142	4,292	4,441	4,644	4,644	4,644	4,644	4,644	4,644	4,644
Warrant officers															
W-5	NA	NA	NA	NA	NA	NA	NA	NA	NA	NA	NA	7,283	7,652	7,928	8,232
W-4	4,096	4,406	4,532	4,657	4,871	5,083	5,298	5,621	5,904	6,173	6,394	6,609	6,925	7,184	7,480
W-3	3,740	3,896	4,056	4,109	4,276	4,606	4,949	5,111	5,298	5,490	5,837	6,071	6,210	6,359	6,562
W-2	3,310	3,623	3,719	3,785	4,000	4,334	4,499	4,662	4,861	5,016	5,157	5,326	5,437	5,525	5,525
W-1	2,906	3,218	3,302	3,480	3,690	4,000	4,144	4,346	4,545	4,702	4,845	5,021	5,021	5,021	5,021
Enlisted members															
E-9	NA	NA	NA	NA	NA	NA	4,949	5,061	5,202	5,368	5,536	5,805	6,032	6,271	6,637
E-8	NA	NA	NA	NA	NA	4,051	4,230	4,341	4,474	4,618	4,878	5,009	5,234	5,358	5,664
E-7	2,816	3,074	3,191	3,347	3,469	3,678	3,796	4,005	4,179	4,298	4,424	4,473	4,637	4,725	5,061
E-6	2,436	2,680	2,798	2,914	3,034	3,303	3,409	3,612	3,674	3,720	3,773	3,773	3,773	3,773	3,773
E-5	2,231	2,381	2,497	2,614	2,798	2,990	3,148	3,166	3,166	3,166	3,166	3,166	3,166	3,166	3,166
E-4	2,046	2,150	2,267	2,382	2,483	2,483	2,483	2,483	2,483	2,483	2,483	2,483	2,483	2,483	2,483
E-3	1,847	1,963	2,082	2,082	2,082	2,082	2,082	2,082	2,082	2,082	2,082	2,082	2,082	2,082	2,082
E-2	1,757	1,757	1,757	1,757	1,757	1,757	1,757	1,757	1,757	1,757	1,757	1,757	1,757	1,757	1,757
E-1[1]	1,567	1,567	1,567	1,567	1,567	1,567	1,567	1,567	1,567	1,567	1,567	1,567	1,567	1,567	1,567

NA = Not applicable. **Note:** Basic pay rate for Academy cadets/midshipmen and ROTC members/applicants is $1,041. See Dept. of Defense Financial Management Regulations for details on pay-scale limitations and eligibility requirements. **Over 30 years**—O-10: $17,925; O-9: 15,816; O-8: 13,989; O-7: 12,348; O-6: 11,095; W-5: 8,645; W-4: 7,630; E-9: 6,968; E-8: 5,778. **Over 34 years**—O-10: $18,821; O-9: 16,607; O-8: 14,339; W-5: 9,076; E-9: 7,317. **Over 38 years**—O-10: $19,763; O-9: 17,437; W-5: 9,531; E-9: 7,683. (1) Applicable to E-1 with 4 months or more of active duty. Basic pay for an E-1 with less than 4 months of active duty is $1,449.

U.S. Veteran Population, 2016

Source: U.S. Dept. of Veterans Affairs
(projected population, in thousands, as of Sept. 30)

Period of service	Vet. pop.	Period of service	Vet. pop.
Total peacetime veterans[1]	**5,263.8**	Total Vietnam War era[3]	6,953.0
Service between Vietnam War era and Gulf War era	3,333.9	Vietnam War era with no other wartime service	6,424.3
Service between Korean War and Vietnam War	1,848.5	Vietnam War era with service in Korea	148.3
Service between WWII and Korean War	74.4	Vietnam War era with service in Korea and WWII	23.0
Pre-WWII service	7.0	Total Gulf War era[3]	7,468.1
Total wartime veterans[2]	**16,104.4**	Gulf War era pre-9/11 with service in Vietnam era	303.3
Total World War II[3]	695.6	Gulf War era pre-9/11, post-9/11, and with service	
WWII only	619.8	in Vietnam War era	54.1
Total Korean War[3]	1,592.2	Gulf War era pre-9/11	2,766.9
Korean War with no other wartime service	1,368.1	Gulf War era pre-9/11 and post-9/11	1,358.3
Korean War with service in WWII	52.8	Gulf War era post-9/11	2,985.5
		TOTAL VETERANS IN CIVILIAN LIFE	**21,368.2**

Note: Figures are for U.S. veterans worldwide. Includes those who served on active duty in Army, Navy, Air Force, Marines, Coast Guard, uniformed Public Health Service and NOAA, and reservists called to federal active duty. Excludes those dishonorably discharged, those whose only active duty was training, and those currently on active duty. (1) Veterans with both wartime and peacetime service are counted only as "wartime veterans." (2) Veterans serving in more than one period are counted only once in total. (3) Total includes veterans who also served in other periods.

African American Service in U.S. Wars

Source: U.S. Dept. of Defense; U.S. Census Bureau, U.S. Dept. of Commerce

American Revolution. About 5,000 served in the Continental Army, mostly in integrated units, some in all-black combat units.

Civil War. Some 180,000 served in 163 units of the Union Army's U.S. Colored Troops, and 200,000 worked in service units—10% of the Union Army in all; about 37,000 died, 31,000 wounded.

World War I. 350,000-400,000 served in the armed forces, 100,000 in France. Some 40,000 fought.

World War II. Some 1 mil served in the armed forces—8% of all troops—mostly in Army service units; all-black fighter and bomber Army Air Force units and infantry divisions gave distinguished service.

Korean War. More than 600,000 served in the military; 3,075 lost their lives in combat. By 1954, armed forces were completely desegregated.

Vietnam War. 274,937 served in the armed forces (1965-74)— 9.8% of all troops; 7,243 were killed in combat.

Persian Gulf War. About 104,000 served in the Kuwaiti theater—20% of all U.S. troops; 66 died in combat.

Operation Enduring Freedom/Freedom's Sentinel. 194 military deaths and 1,417 wounded in Afghanistan and elsewhere.

Operation Iraqi Freedom/Operation New Dawn/Operation Inherent Resolve. 449 military deaths and 2,766 wounded.

Outlays for Individual Payments to Veterans, 1940-2017

Source: White House Office of Management and Budget
(in millions of dollars)

Year	Total	Compen-sation	Pen-sions	Hospital, medical	Edu-cation	Insurance & burial	Year	Total	Compen-sation	Pen-sions	Hospital, medical	Edu-cation	Insurance & burial
1940	$574	$244	$185	$69	—	$76	2006	$71,139	$31,000	$3,547	$31,888	$3,354	$1,350
1950	8,613	1,533	476	764	$2,739	3,101	2007	73,726	31,064	3,376	34,485	3,456	1,345
1960	5,300	2,049	1,263	931	392	665	2008	84,463	36,266	3,790	39,409	3,634	1,364
1970	8,883	2,980	2,255	1,798	1,002	848	2009	94,985	40,490	4,161	44,637	4,328	1,369
1980	21,153	7,446	3,585	6,513	2,421	1,188	2010	106,454	43,498	4,359	48,506	8,773	1,318
1990	28,801	10,735	3,594	12,281	791	1,400	2011	122,524	52,780	4,664	52,681	11,112	1,287
2000	46,835	20,777	2,969	20,090	1,636	1,363	2012	119,574	50,058	4,537	53,002	10,734	1,243
2001	46,187	18,587	2,760	21,730	1,763	1,347	2013	136,120	59,393	5,173	55,091	13,220	1,230
2002	52,621	22,429	3,166	23,465	2,241	1,320	2014	145,452	64,360	5,251	58,932	13,729	1,166
2003	57,407	24,705	3,229	25,568	2,574	1,331	2015	153,521	69,725	5,299	63,667	13,605	1,225
2004	62,567	26,307	3,334	28,556	2,978	1,392	2016*	169,982	80,246	6,112	67,356	15,129	1,139
2005	69,824	30,888	3,663	30,650	3,254	1,369	2017*	171,351	78,729	6,025	70,181	15,296	1,120

— = Not available. * = Estimate. **Note:** Compensation is service-connected; pension is not.

Veterans Health Administration Characteristics, 2002-14

Source: U.S. Dept. of Veterans Affairs

Fiscal year	Total enrollees[1] (mil)	Outpatient visits[2] (mil)	Inpatient admissions (thous.)	Fiscal year	Total enrollees[1] (mil)	Outpatient visits[2] (mil)	Inpatient admissions (thous.)
2002	6.8	46.5	564.7	2009	8.1	74.9	662.0
2003	7.1	49.8	567.3	2010	8.3	80.2	682.3
2004	7.3	54.0	589.8	2011	8.6	79.8	692.1
2005	7.7	57.5	585.8	2012	8.8	83.6	703.5
2006	7.9	59.1	568.9	2013	8.9	86.4	694.7
2007	7.8	62.3	589.0	2014	9.1	92.4	707.4
2008	7.8	67.7	641.4				

(1) Includes non-enrolled veteran patients. (2) Includes fee visits.

Employment Status of Veterans With Service-Connected Disabilities, 2015

Source: Bureau of Labor Statistics, U.S. Dept. of Labor; as of Aug. 2015

Veteran status, presence of disability, and period of service	Employed (thous.) Total	Men	Women	Unemployed (thous.) Total	Men	Women	Unemployment rate (%) Total	Men	Women	Not in labor force (thous.) Total	Men	Women
Total veterans	10,121	8,932	1,189	472	408	64	4.5%	4.4%	5.1%	10,576	9,830	746
With service-connected disability	1,866	1,616	249	106	94	12	5.4	5.5	4.6	2,337	2,146	191
Without service-connected disability	7,987	7,069	918	362	314	48	4.3	4.3	5.0	7,961	7,440	520
Gulf War era, total	5,536	4,702	833	268	213	55	4.6	4.3	6.2	1,255	975	280
With service-connected disability	1,368	1,145	223	83	76	6	5.7	6.2	2.8	583	478	105
Without service-connected disability	4,040	3,443	596	182	137	45	4.3	3.8	7.0	617	459	158
Gulf War era II	2,812	2,368	443	148	125	23	5.0	5.0	5.0	649	480	170
With service-connected disability	816	672	144	48	42	5	5.5	5.9	3.6	317	258	59
Without service-connected disability	1,916	1,619	297	96	82	14	4.8	4.8	4.5	292	197	94
Gulf War era I	2,724	2,334	390	120	89	32	4.2	3.7	7.5	606	496	110
With service-connected disability	552	473	79	35	34	1	5.9	6.7	1.4	266	220	46
Without service-connected disability	2,123	1,825	299	86	55	31	3.9	2.9	9.3	326	262	64
WWII, Korean War, and Vietnam era	2,072	1,990	83	92	92	NA	4.2	4.4	NA	6,688	6,456	232
With service-connected disability	207	201	6	13	13	NA	6.1	6.2	NA	1,451	1,405	46
Without service-connected disability	1,779	1,707	72	78	78	NA	4.2	4.4	NA	5,062	4,884	178
Other service periods	2,513	2,240	273	113	103	9	4.3	4.4	3.3	2,633	2,400	234
With service-connected disability	291	271	20	10	4	6	3.4	1.6	NA	303	263	40
Without service-connected disability	2,168	1,918	251	103	99	4	4.5	4.9	1.4	2,281	2,097	184

NA = Not available. **Note:** Veterans in survey were on active duty in the U.S. Armed Forces during these periods of service: Gulf War era II (Sept. 2001-present), Gulf War era I (Aug. 1990-Aug. 2001), Vietnam era (Aug. 1964-Apr. 1975), Korean War (July 1950-Jan. 1955), World War II (Dec. 1941-Dec. 1946), and other service periods. Veterans who served in more than one wartime period are classified in the most recent period only. A service-connected disability is a health condition or impairment caused or made worse by military service.

Nations With Largest Armed Forces, 2016

Source: *The Military Balance 2016*, International Institute for Strategic Studies, published by Routledge Journals, Taylor & Francis, UK
(ranked by active-duty troop strength as of 2016; all other data as of Nov. 2015)

Rank	Country	Troop strength Active troops (thous.)	Troop strength Reserve troops (thous.)	Defense expend. (mil)	Tanks (MBT) (army only)	Navy Cruisers/ frigates/ destroyers	Navy Sub- marines	Combat aircraft (air force only) FGA	Combat aircraft (air force only) FTR
1.	China	2,333	510	$145,832	6,540	54F/19D*	61	626	842
2.	United States	1,381	841	597,503	2,384	22C/4F/62D*	71	868	275
3.	India	1,346	1,155	47,956	2,974+	13F/13D*	14	729	62
4.	North Korea	1,190	600	—	3,500+	3F	73	30	401+
5.	Russia	798	2,000	51,605	2,700	6C/10F/18D*	63	357	320
6.	Pakistan	644	0	7,456	2,561+	10F	8	192	210
7.	South Korea	628	4,500	33,460	2,418+	3C/14F/6D	23	314	174
8.	Iran	523	350	NA	1,663+	0	29	110	184+
9.	Turkey	511	379	8,347	2,504	18F	13	311	53
10.	Vietnam	482	5,000	4,033[1]	1,270	2F	6	101	0
11.	Egypt	439	479	6,394	2,170	8F/1D	4	325	62
12.	Myanmar	406	0	2,245	185+	4F	0	0	88
13.	Indonesia	396	400	7,587	40	11F	2	24	22
14.	Thailand	361	200	5,374	293	9F*	0	12	78
15.	Brazil	335	1,340	24,260	393	10F/3D*	5	49	57
16.	Colombia	297	35	9,865	0	4F	4	19	0
17.	Mexico	277	82	6,051	0	6F	0	0	8
18.	Japan	247	56	41,013	688	2C/9F/33D*	18	147	201
19.	Sudan	244	0	1,892[1]	465	0	0	4	22
20.	Saudi Arabia	227	0	81,853	730	4F/3D	0	192	81
21.	Taiwan	215	1,657	10,257	565	4C/22F	4	128	288
22.	France	209	28	46,751	200	11F/11D*	10	177	40
23.	Ukraine	204	900	3,916	788	1F	0	34	122
24.	Eritrea	202	120	78[1]	270	0	0	10	6
25.	Morocco	196	150	3,298	434	5F/1D	0	49	22
26.	South Sudan	185	0	1,346	80+	0	0	0	0
27.	Germany	179	32	36,686	306	8F/7D	5	86	129
28.	Israel	177	465	18,597	500	0	4	251	143

— = Not available. * = Navy with aircraft carrier(s), as follows: Brazil 1, China 1, France 1, India 2, Italy 1, Japan 3, Russia 1, Thailand 1, U.S. 10. FGA = Fighter, ground attack. FTR = Fighter. MBT = Main battle tank. (1) As of 2013.

Budget for Global War on Terror Operations, 2001-14

Source: Congressional Research Service, Library of Congress
(in billions of dollars)

	2001/02[1]	2003	2004	2005	2007	2008	2010	2012	2013	2014	Total 2001-14
Total: war designated funding	$35.8	$74.4	96.0	$108.4	$169.7	$195.2	$165.4	$129.7	$99.9	$95.2	$1,608.9
Dept. of Defense.	35.0	70.7	74.3	103.6	164.0	188.7	154.6	115.3	87.5	85.4	1,498.7
Foreign aid and diplomacy[2]	0.8	3.8	21.7	4.8	5.0	5.4	8.9	11.5	9.2	6.0	92.7
Veterans Affairs medical. . . .	0.0	0.0	0.0	0.0	0.7	1.0	1.9	2.9	3.2	3.7	17.6
Total: war designated funding not war-related	**0.0**	**0.0**	**0.0**	**6.6**	**7.3**	**12.1**	**6.4**	**8.6**	**6.6**	**12.8**	**81.3**
Dept. of Defense.	0.0	0.0	0.0	6.6	7.3	12.1	6.4	5.4	1.9	10.2	70.9
Foreign aid and diplomacy[2]	0.0	0.0	0.0	0.0	0.0	0.0	0.0	3.2	4.6	2.6	10.4
Op. Iraqi Freedom/New Dawn	**0.0**	**51.0**	**76.7**	**79.1**	**130.8**	**143.9**	**64.8**	**20.3**	**7.7**	**4.8**	**814.6**
Dept. of Defense.	0.0	48.0	57.1	77.1	127.1	140.3	59.9	13.5	4.9	1.1	753.1
Foreign aid and diplomacy[2]	0.0	3.0	19.5	2.0	3.2	2.7	3.3	4.7	0.7	1.4	48.6
Veterans Affairs medical. . . .	0.0	0.0	0.0	0.0	0.6	0.9	1.6	2.1	2.1	2.3	12.9
Op. Enduring Freedom[3]	**22.8**	**17.4**	**15.4**	**20.7**	**31.1**	**39.0**	**94.1**	**100.6**	**85.6**	**77.4**	**685.6**
Dept. of Defense.	22.0	16.7	13.2	17.9	29.2	36.1	88.2	96.3	80.6	74.0	647.3
Foreign aid and diplomacy[2]	0.8	0.7	2.2	2.8	1.9	2.7	5.6	3.5	3.9	2.0	33.6
Veterans Affairs medical. . . .	0.0	0.0	0.0	0.0	0.1	0.1	0.3	0.8	1.1	1.4	4.7
Op. Noble Eagle[4].	**13.0**	**6.0**	**4.0**	**2.0**	**0.5**	**0.2**	**0.1**	**0.2**	**0.1**	**0.1**	**27.4**

(1) Fiscal year (FY) 2001 and FY2002 funds combined because most were obligated in FY2002 after the Sept. 11, 2001, attacks at the end of FY2001, on Sept. 30, 2001. (2) Includes monies for reconstruction, development and humanitarian aid, embassy operations, counternarcotics, initial training of the Afghan and Iraqi armies, foreign military sales credits, and Economic Support Funds. (3) Covers Afghanistan (officially ended Dec. 2014) and other Global War on Terror operations, ranging from the Philippines to Djibouti, that began immediately after the Sept. 11, 2001, attacks. (4) Dept. of Defense funds that rebuilt the Pentagon and provided higher security at U.S. military bases and other homeland security, including combat air patrol.

Leading Purchasers of U.S. Defense Articles and Services

Source: Congressional Research Service, Library of Congress

Worldwide deliveries, 2004-07 Rank	Country	Value	Rank	Country	Value	Worldwide deliveries, 2008-11 Rank	Country	Value	Rank	Country	Value
1.	Israel.	$5.7 bil	6.	South Korea . . .	$2.5 bil	1.	Saudi Arabia . .	$5.9 bil	6.	Iraq	$2.6 bil
2.	Egypt	5.2 bil	7.	Japan	2.4 bil	2.	Egypt	3.9 bil	7.	Japan	2.5 bil
3.	Saudi Arabia . . .	4.3 bil	8.	Poland	1.9 bil	3.	Israel.	3.8 bil	8.	South Korea . . .	2.5 bil
4.	Taiwan	4.3 bil	9.	Australia	1.7 bil	4.	Australia	2.9 bil	9.	Greece	2.1 bil
5.	Greece	2.8 bil	10.	UK.	1.6 bil	5.	Taiwan	2.9 bil	10.	Turkey.	2.0 bil

Note: Total dollar value of all U.S. defense articles and services actually delivered to top 10 purchasers worldwide. Figures include government-to-government sales through the Foreign Military Sales system (which accounts for the overwhelming majority of U.S. conventional arms deliveries) concluded in calendar years listed, as well as commercially licensed exports concluded in pertinent fiscal years.

U.S. Foreign Military Financing, 2005-15

Source: Defense Security Cooperation Agency, U.S. Dept. of Defense

Listed are grants extended to foreign governments in a fiscal year to pay for military equipment and services. May be from the U.S. Dept. of Defense (DOD) or, for specific countries, negotiated directly with U.S. commercial suppliers with DOD approval.

(in thousands of U.S. dollars)

	2005	2010	2015		2005	2010	2015
Western Hemisphere	$108,155	$89,720	$48,550	**Europe**	$220,274	$151,696	$146,150
Colombia	99,200	55,000	27,000	Bosnia and			
El Salvador	1,488	1,000	1,600	Herzegovina	8,480	4,000	4,000
Honduras	1,492	1,514	3,100	Bulgaria	6,944	9,000	5,000
Mexico	0	5,250	4,675	Croatia	0	2,500	3,500
Near East and				Czech Republic . . .	5,952	6,000	2,127
South Asia	4,541,843	4,666,797	4,886,776	Georgia	11,904	16,000	30,000
Afghanistan	396,800	0	0	Kosovo	NA	2,500	4,400
Bahrain	18,847	19,000	7,500	Macedonia	5,208	4,000	4,000
Egypt	1,289,600	1,300,000	1,300,000	Moldova	990	750	11,250
Israel	2,202,240	2,775,000	3,100,000	Poland	76,470	47,000	9,000
Jordan	304,352	300,000	385,000	Romania	13,412	12,999	5,400
Lebanon	0	0	84,117	Turkey	33,728	0	0
Oman	19,840	8,847	4,000	Ukraine	2,976	11,000	47,000
Pakistan	298,000	248,000	0	**Africa**	49,453	45,370	52,950
Yemen	10,420	12,500	0	Djibouti	4,468	2,000	710
East Asia and				Liberia	2,976	6,000	2,500
Pacific	36,537	59,100	77,250	Morocco	15,128	9,000	12,000
Indonesia	0	20,000	14,000	Tunisia	10,407	18,000	30,000
Mongolia	2,778	4,500	2,000	**World total**	4,956,262	5,015,952	5,211,901
Philippines	29,760	29,000	50,000				
Vietnam	0	2,000	10,750				

NA = Not available. **Note:** Regional subtotals include countries not listed.

Defense Contracts, 2015

Source: U.S. Dept. of Defense

Listed are the 50 companies or organizations receiving the largest dollar volume of prime contract awards from the U.S. Dept. of Defense during fiscal year 2015 (Oct. 1, 2014-Sept. 30, 2015).

(in millions of U.S. dollars)

Rank Contractor	Contracts awarded[1]	% of total	Rank Contractor	Contracts awarded[1]	% of total
1. Lockheed Martin Corp.	$29,388.8	10.52%	28. CACI International Inc.	$1,255.6	0.45%
2. Raytheon Co.	12,346.1	4.42	29. Cerberus Capital Management L.P. . .	1,197.9	0.43
3. The Boeing Co.	12,170.0	4.36	30. Hewlett-Packard Co.	1,143.2	0.41
4. General Dynamics Corp.	11,521.4	4.13	31. Leidos Holdings, Inc.	1,142.5	0.41
5. Northrop Grumman Corp.	7,273.2	2.60	32. Alliant Techsystems Inc.	1,096.3	0.39
6. United Technologies Corp.	6,698.6	2.40	33. Atlantic Diving Supply Inc.	1,080.1	0.39
7. L-3 Communications Holdings Inc. . .	5,048.8	1.81	34. Massachusetts Institute of Tech.	967.6	0.35
8. Bae Systems PLC	4,353.6	1.56	35. Sierra Nevada Corp.	926.7	0.33
9. Humana Inc.	3,553.9	1.27	36. MacAndrews & Forbes Holdings Inc. . .	918.0	0.33
10. Huntington Ingalls Industries Inc.	3,081.0	1.10	37. Honeywell International Inc.	901.8	0.32
11. Bechtel Group Inc.	2,916.5	1.04	38. Cardinal Health Inc.	895.0	0.32
12. Health Net Inc.	2,765.0	0.99	39. Vectrus Systems Corp.	892.8	0.32
13. UnitedHealth Group Inc.	2,632.9	0.94	40. Royal Dutch Shell PLC	878.5	0.31
14. Boeing Company, The	2,421.5	0.87	41. The Bahrain Petroleum Company		
15. General Atomic Technologies Corp. . .	2,303.6	0.82	B.S.C. (Closed)	865.0	0.31
16. Northrop Grumman Systems Corp. . .	2,249.1	0.81	42. Austal Ltd.	846.0	0.30
17. McKesson Corp.	2,143.5	0.77	43. The Aerospace Corp.	840.4	0.30
18. Bell Boeing Joint Project Office	2,043.6	0.73	44. Fluor Corp.	778.5	0.28
19. AmerisourceBergen Corp.	1,854.0	0.66	45. Exxon Mobil Corp.	770.8	0.28
20. United Launch Alliance LLC	1,723.4	0.62	46. Rockwell Collins Inc.	767.1	0.27
21. Booz Allen Hamilton Holding Corp. . .	1,703.9	0.61	47. Johns Hopkins University	760.0	0.27
22. Textron Inc.	1,585.4	0.57	48. The MITRE Corp.	755.1	0.27
23. Saic Gemini Inc.	1,507.3	0.54	49. Jacobs Engineering Group Inc.	717.1	0.26
24. General Electric Co.	1,504.0	0.54	50. Alion Science and Tech. Corp.	690.2	0.25
25. Oshkosh Corp.	1,406.4	0.50	Other	129,462.9	46.35
26. Computer Sciences Corp.	1,285.5	0.46	**Total**	**279,301.8**	
27. Harris Corp.	1,271.9	0.46			

NA = Not available. **Note:** Contractors listed more than once represent different company locations or facilities. (1) Amounts include contracts awarded to subsidiaries of each company.

Arms Transfer Agreements With the World by Supplier, 2007-14

Source: Congressional Research Service, Library of Congress

(in millions of current U.S. dollars)

Supplier	2007	2008	2009	2010	2011	2012	2013	2014	2007-14
United States	$22,618	$35,206	$20,723	$19,631	$65,372	$24,201	$26,304	$36,223	$250,278
Russia	9,300	5,600	15,200	8,200	8,200	18,200	10,300	10,200	85,200
France	2,200	6,600	9,900	2,000	6,300	2,900	3,400	4,400	37,700
United Kingdom	9,800	200	1,500	1,600	700	5,700	3,400	300	23,200
China	2,500	2,200	3,100	1,900	3,200	3,400	4,200	2,200	22,700
Germany	1,900	3,900	5,400	200	200	5,000	9,300	900	26,800
Italy	2,400	4,300	1,700	1,600	1,600	1,900	3,100	1,300	17,900
All other European	6,700	5,400	7,000	4,600	3,700	10,100	5,000	10,700	53,200
All others	2,900	3,300	5,300	2,500	3,500	6,300	5,100	4,300	33,200
Total	**60,318**	**66,706**	**69,823**	**42,231**	**92,772**	**77,701**	**70,104**	**71,823**	**551,478**

Note: All data are for the calendar year given except for U.S. MAP (Military Assistance Program), IMET (International Military Education, and Training), and Excess Defense Article data, which are included with the particular fiscal year. All amounts given include the values of all categories of weapons, spare parts, construction, all associated services, military assistance, excess defense articles, and training programs. Statistics for foreign countries are based upon estimated selling prices. All foreign data are rounded to the nearest $100 mil.

Personal Salutes and Honors

The U.S. **national salute**, 21 guns, is also the salute to a national flag. U.S. independence is commemorated by the salute to the Union—one gun for each state—fired at noon July 4, at all military posts provided with suitable artillery.

A 21-gun salute on arrival and departure, with 4 ruffles and flourishes, is rendered to the **president**, to a former president, and to a president-elect. The national anthem or "Hail to the Chief," as appropriate, is played for the president, and the national anthem for the others. A 21-gun salute on arrival and departure, with 4 ruffles and flourishes, also is rendered to the **sovereign or chief of state of a foreign country** or a member of a reigning royal family, and the national anthem of his or her country is played. The music is considered an inseparable part of the salute and immediately follows the ruffles and flourishes without pause. For the Honors March, generals receive the "General's March," admirals receive the "Flag Officer's March," and all others receive the 32-bar medley of "The Stars and Stripes Forever."

| | SALUTE (IN GUNS) | | Ruffles and | |
GRADE, TITLE, OR OFFICE	Arriving	Leaving	flourishes	Music
Vice President of U.S.	19	—	4	Hail, Columbia
Speaker of the House.	19	—	4	Honors March
U.S. or foreign ambassador in country to which accredited	19	—	4	Natl. anthem of official
Premier or prime minister.	19	—	4	Natl. anthem of official
Secretary of Defense, Army, Navy, or Air Force	19	19	4	Honors March
Other cabinet members, Senate president pro tempore, governor, or chief justice of U.S.	19	—	4	Honors March
Chairman, Joint Chiefs of Staff.	19	19	4	Honors March
Army chief of staff, chief of naval operations, Air Force chief of staff, Marine commandant.	19	19	4	Honors March
General of the Army, general of the Air Force, fleet admiral	19	19	4	Honors March
Generals, admirals	17	17	4	Honors March
Assistant secretaries of Defense, Army, Navy, or Air Force.	17	17	4	Honors March
Chair of a committee of Congress	17	—	4	Honors March

Medal of Honor

Source: Congressional Medal of Honor Society; U.S. Army, U.S. Dept. of Defense
(as of Aug. 25, 2016)

The Medal of Honor is the highest military award for bravery that can be given to any individual in the U.S. On Dec. 21, 1861, Pres. Abraham Lincoln signed a bill to create the Navy Medal of Honor. Lincoln, on July 14, 1862, approved a resolution providing for the presentation of Medals of Honor to enlisted men of the Army and Voluntary Forces. The law was amended on Mar. 3, 1863, so that officers as well as enlisted men were eligible. The first Army Medals of Honor were awarded on Mar. 25, 1863; the first Navy medals went to sailors and Marines on Apr. 3, 1863.

The Medal of Honor is awarded in the name of Congress to a person who, while a member of the armed forces, distinguishes himself or herself conspicuously by gallantry and intrepidity at the risk of life above and beyond the call of duty while engaged in an action against any enemy of the U.S.; while engaged in military operations involving conflict with an opposing foreign force; or while serving with friendly foreign forces engaged in an armed conflict against an opposing armed force in which the U.S. is not a belligerent party.

The deed performed must have been one of personal bravery or self-sacrifice so conspicuous as to clearly distinguish the individual above his or her comrades and must have involved risk of life. Incontestable proof of the performance of service is required, and each recommendation for award of this decoration is considered on the standard of extraordinary merit.

Prior to World War I, the 2,625 Army Medal of Honor awards up to that time were reviewed to determine which met new stringent criteria. The Army removed 911 names from the list, most of them former members of a Civil War volunteer infantry group who had been induced to extend their enlistments when they were promised the medal. However, the medal was restored to Dr. Mary Walker in 1977 and to Buffalo Bill Cody and seven other Indian scouts in 1989.

Seven African American soldiers were awarded Medals of Honor for service in World War II (six of them posthumously) in Jan. 1997. Previously, no black soldier had received the medal for World War II service; an Army inquiry begun in 1993 concluded that the prevailing political climate and Army practices of the time had prevented proper recognition of heroism on the part of black soldiers in that war. In 1996, Congress authorized a review of Asian American and Pacific Islander recipients of the Distinguished Service Cross whose award should be upgraded. Twenty-two Asian Americans received the Medal of Honor for World War II service in June 2000.

In one of the largest Medal of Honor ceremonies in U.S. history, Pres. Barack Obama Mar. 18, 2014, awarded 24 mostly Hispanic, Jewish, and African-American veterans with the nation's highest military decoration for valor displayed in World War II, the Korean War, and Vietnam. The recipients, three of whom were alive to receive the award, had been found deserving following a congressionally mandated review of the records of service members who may have been overlooked due to discrimination.

Medal of Honor Recipients From Recent Conflicts

Honoree	Rank	Branch of service	Date of action	Date of award
Somalia Campaign				
Gordon, Gary I.*	Master Sgt.	U.S. Army	10/3/1993	5/23/1994
Shughart, Randall D.*	Sgt. First Class	U.S. Army	10/3/1993	5/23/1994
War in Iraq				
Dunham, Jason L.*	Corporal	USMC	4/14/2004	1/11/2007
McGinnis, Ross A.*	Pvt. First Class	U.S. Army	12/4/2006	6/5/2008
Monsoor, Michael A.*	Petty Officer Second Class	U.S. Navy	9/29/2006	4/8/2008
Smith, Paul R.*	Sgt. First Class	U.S. Army	4/4/2003	4/5/2005
War in Afghanistan				
Byers, Edward C., Jr.	Chief	U.S. Navy	12/8-9/2012	2/29/2016
Carpenter, William Kyle	Lance Cpl.	USMC	11/21/2010	6/19/2014
Carter, Ty M.	Specialist	U.S. Army	10/3/2009	8/26/2013
Giunta, Salvatore A.	Specialist	U.S. Army	10/25/2007	11/16/2010
Groberg, Florent A.	Capt.	U.S. Army	8/8/2012	11/12/2015
Meyer, Dakota	Sgt.	USMC	9/8/2009	9/15/2011
Miller, Robert J.*	Staff Sgt.	U.S. Army	1/25/2008	10/6/2010
Monti, Jared C.*	Sgt. First Class	U.S. Army	6/21/2006	9/17/2009
Murphy, Michael P.*	Lt.	U.S. Navy	6/28/2005	10/22/2007
Petry, Leroy A.	Staff Sgt.	U.S. Army	5/26/2008	7/12/2011
Pitts, Ryan M.	Sgt.	U.S. Army	7/13/2008	7/21/2014
Romesha, Clinton L.	Staff Sgt.	U.S. Army	10/3/2009	2/11/2013
Swenson, William D.	Capt.	U.S. Army	9/8/2009	10/15/2013
White, Kyle J.	Sgt.	U.S. Army	11/9/2007	5/13/2014

* = Awarded posthumously.

Other Selected Awards

Source: The Institute of Heraldry, U.S. Army; Navy Department Awards Web Service; Air Force Personnel Center

Distinguished Service Cross

Established by Congress July 9, 1918, on recommendation of Gen. John J. "Black Jack" Pershing, and awarded for extraordinary heroism not justifying the award of a Medal of Honor. The act or acts of heroism must have been so notable and have involved risk of life so extraordinary as to set the individual apart from his or her comrades.

Silver Star

Third-highest military combat honor. An earlier version of this award, the Citation Star, was established by Congress on July 19, 1918, and retroactively awarded to soldiers for "gallantry in action," back to the Spanish-American War. The Silver Star medal replaced the Citation Star in 1932 and is awarded for gallantry in action which, while of a lesser degree than that required for award of the Distinguished Service Cross, must nevertheless have been performed with marked distinction.

Legion of Merit

Established by Congress on July 20, 1942, and awarded to individuals who have distinguished themselves by exceptionally meritorious conduct in the performance of outstanding services. There are different designs depending on the level of command of the award recipient.

Distinguished Flying Cross

Established by Congress July 2, 1926, and awarded for heroism or extraordinary achievement while participating in aerial flight. Awards are made only to recognize single acts of heroism or extraordinary achievement, not sustained operational activities against an armed enemy. Initial awards were given to persons who made record-breaking long-distance and endurance flights or who set altitude records. The first DFC was awarded to Cpt. Charles A. Lindbergh on May 31, 1927. DFCs were awarded retroactively to Orville and Wilbur Wright.

Soldier's Medal

Established by Congress July 2, 1926, to recognize acts of heroism not involving actual conflict with an enemy. The same degree of heroism is required as for the award of the Distinguished Flying Cross. The performance must have involved personal hazard or danger and the voluntary risk of life under conditions not involving conflict with an armed enemy. Awards are not made solely on the basis of having saved a life.

Bronze Star

Established by executive order Feb. 4, 1944, largely to raise the morale of ground troops in WWII, on the recommendation of Gen. George C. Marshall. It is awarded to any person who, while serving in any capacity in or with the U.S. military, distinguishes himself or herself by heroic or meritorious achievement or service not involving participation in aerial flight.

Purple Heart

The original Purple Heart, designated as the Badge of Military Merit, was established by Gen. George Washington on Aug. 7, 1782. Following the American Revolution, the badge fell into disuse until 1932, the 200th anniversary of Washington's birth. During WWII, the Order of the Purple Heart was awarded for both wounds received in action and for meritorious service. Following the introduction of the Legion of Merit, the Purple Heart was awarded only for combat wounds. Today, it is awarded to any armed forces member who, while serving with the U.S. Armed Services, has been wounded or killed, or who has died or may hereafter die after being wounded in action against an enemy of the U.S. or in an armed conflict in which the U.S. or friendly foreign forces are engaged; as the result of an act of any hostile foreign force; as a result of an international terrorist attack against the U.S. or a friendly foreign nation; or as a result of military operations outside the U.S. as part of a peacekeeping force. Wounds must be inflicted directly by enemy action, including while held as a prisoner of war or while being taken captive.

Air Medal

Authorized by Pres. Franklin D. Roosevelt on May 11, 1942, and awarded for heroism or meritorious achievement while participating in aerial flight. Awards may be made to recognize single acts of merit or heroism or for meritorious service. Awards are not made to individuals who use air transportation solely for the purpose of moving between points in a combat zone.

Army Commendation

Established Dec. 18, 1945, and awarded for heroism, meritorious achievement, or meritorious service. It may also be awarded to a member of the armed forces of a friendly foreign nation who distinguishes him- or herself by an act of heroism, extraordinary achievement, or meritorious service.

U.S. Military Awards in Selected Wars and Conflicts

Source: U.S. Army Human Resources Command, U.S. Dept. of Defense; Congressional Medal of Honor Society

Award	Civil War	WWI	WWII	Korea	Vietnam	Gulf War	Afghanistan[1]	Iraq[2]
Medal of Honor	1,523	122	473	146	260	0	14	4
Distinguished Service Cross	NA	6,428	4,427	715	840	0	16	15
Silver Star	NA	NA	73,654	10,061	21,634	75	378	377
Legion of Merit	NA	NA	20,273	NA	10,356	158	220	140
Distinguished Flying Cross	NA	NA	126,318	NA	21,697	108	216	118
Soldier's Medal	NA	NA	12,485	581	5,402	43	64	111
Bronze Star (total)[3]	NA	NA	395,380	30,359	719,968	28,857	68,514	112,420
Purple Heart	NA	NA	NA	NA	220,516	504	9,163	22,462
Air Medal (total)[3]	NA	NA	1,166,471	0	1,039,124	6,399	17,079	22,433
Army Commendation (total)[3]	NA	NA	0	0	837,037	81,979	178,035	390,894

NA = Not available or applicable. **Note:** Numbers for the individual decorations shown here represent only those awards that were properly processed and reported to Dept. of the Army Headquarters. The actual number of individual decorations awarded under combat conditions, when award approval authority is delegated to field commanders, cannot be stated with absolute certainty. Numbers here reflect the current statistics recorded by the Military Awards Branch, as of Dec. 31, 2015, except for MOH, which was reported by the Congressional Medal of Honor Society as of Aug. 31, 2016. (1) Operation Enduring Freedom and Operation Freedom's Sentinel. May include awards for actions related to operations but occurring outside of Afghanistan. (2) Operation Iraqi Freedom, Operation New Dawn, and Operation Inherent Resolve. May include awards for actions related to operations but occurring in other nations, including Syria. (3) Includes awards for valor/heroism and for meritorious service or achievement.

Federal Service Academies

U.S. Military Academy, West Point, NY. Founded 1802. Awards BS degree and Army commission for a 5-year service obligation. **Website:** www.usma.edu

U.S. Naval Academy, Annapolis, MD. Founded 1845. Awards BS degree and Navy or Marine Corps commission for a 5-year service obligation. **Website:** www.usna.edu

U.S. Air Force Academy, Colorado Springs, CO. Founded 1954. Awards BS degree and Air Force commission for a 6-year service obligation. **Website:** www.usafa.edu

U.S. Coast Guard Academy, New London, CT. Founded 1876. Awards BS degree and Coast Guard commission for a 5-year service obligation. **Website:** www.cga.edu

U.S. Merchant Marine Academy, Kings Point, NY. Founded 1943. Awards BS degree; a license as a deck, engineer, or dual officer; and a U.S. Naval Reserve commission. Service obligations vary according to options taken by the graduate. **Website:** www.usmma.edu

U.S. Army, Navy, Air Force, Marine Corps, and Coast Guard Insignia

Source: Dept. of the Army, Dept. of the Navy, Dept. of the Air Force, U.S. Dept. of Defense; U.S. Coast Guard, U.S. Dept. of Homeland Security

Army

General of the Armies—Gen. John J. Pershing (1860-1948), the only person to have held this rank while living, was authorized to prescribe his own insignia but never wore in excess of four stars. Congress established the rank in 1799 to be bestowed on George Washington; Washington was finally promoted to the rank by joint resolution of Congress, approved by Pres. Gerald Ford, Oct. 19, 1976.

General of the Army—Five silver stars fastened together in a circle and the coat of arms of the U.S. in gold color metal with shield and crest enameled. Reserved for wartime use only.

Rank	Insignia
General of the Army*	Five silver stars
General	Four silver stars
Lieutenant General	Three silver stars
Major General	Two silver stars
Brigadier General	One silver star
Colonel	Silver eagle
Lieutenant Colonel	Silver oak leaf
Major	Gold oak leaf
Captain	Two silver bars
First Lieutenant	One silver bar
Second Lieutenant	One gold bar

Warrant Officers

Grade Five—Silver bar with enamel black line.
Grade Four—Silver bar with 4 enamel black squares.
Grade Three—Silver bar with 3 enamel black squares.
Grade Two—Silver bar with 2 enamel black squares.
Grade One—Silver bar with 1 enamel black square.

Noncommissioned Officers

Sergeant Major of the Army (E-9)—Three chevrons above 3 arcs, with a U.S. coat of arms centered on the chevrons, flanked by 2 stars—1 star on each side of the eagle. Also distinctive red-and-white shield collar insignia.

Command Sergeant Major (E-9)—Three chevrons above 3 arcs with a 5-pointed star with a wreath around the star between the chevrons and arcs.

Sergeant Major (E-9)—Three chevrons above 3 arcs with a 5-pointed star between the chevrons and arcs.

First Sergeant (E-8)—Three chevrons above 3 arcs with a lozenge between the chevrons and arcs.

Master Sergeant (E-8)—Three chevrons above 3 arcs.

Sergeant First Class (E-7)—Three chevrons above 2 arcs.

Staff Sergeant (E-6)—Three chevrons above 1 arc.

Sergeant (E-5)—Three chevrons.

Corporal (E-4)—Two chevrons.

Specialists

Specialist (E-4)—Eagle device only.

Other Enlisted

Private First Class (E-3)—One chevron above 1 arc.

Private (E-2)—One chevron.

Private (E-1)—None.

*Rank reserved for wartime use only.

Air Force

Insignia for Air Force officers are identical to those of the Army. Insignia for enlisted personnel are worn on both sleeves and consist of 1 star and an appropriate number of rockers. Chevrons appear above 5 rockers for the top three noncommissioned officer ranks, as follows (in ascending order): Master Sergeant, 1 chevron; Senior Master Sergeant, 2 chevrons; Chief Master Sergeant, 3 chevrons. The insignia of the Chief Master Sergeant of the Air Force has 3 chevrons and a wreath around the star design. General of the Air Force is reserved for wartime use only.

Navy

The following stripes are worn on the lower sleeves of the Service Dress Blue uniform. They are of gold embroidery.

Rank	Insignia
Fleet Admiral*	1 two inch with 4 one-half inch
Admiral	1 two inch with 3 one-half inch
Vice Admiral	1 two inch with 2 one-half inch
Rear Admiral (upper half)	1 two inch with 1 one-half inch
Rear Admiral (lower half)	1 two inch
Captain	4 one-half inch
Commander	3 one-half inch
Lieutenant Commander	2 one-half inch with 1 one-quarter inch between
Lieutenant	2 one-half inch
Lieutenant (jr. grade)	1 one-half inch with 1 one-quarter inch above
Ensign	1 one-half inch
Warrant Officer W-5	½" stripe under ⅛" blue strip with 1 break
Warrant Officer W-4	½" stripe with 1 break
Warrant Officer W-3	½" stripe with 2 breaks, 2" apart
Warrant Officer W-2	½" stripe with 3 breaks, 2" apart

Enlisted personnel (noncommissioned petty officers)—Rating badge worn on the upper left sleeve consisting of a spread eagle, appropriate number of chevrons, and centered specialty mark.

*Rank reserved for wartime use only.

Marine Corps

Marine Corps' distinctive cap and collar ornament is the Marine Corps emblem—a combination of the American eagle, a globe, and an anchor. Marine Corps and Army officer insignia are similar. Marine Corps enlisted insignia, although basically similar to the Army's, feature crossed rifles beneath the chevrons. Marine Corps enlisted rank insignia are as follows:

Sergeant Major of the Marine Corps (E-9)—Same as Sergeant Major (below) but with Marine Corps emblem in the center with a 5-pointed star on both sides of the emblem.

Sergeant Major (E-9)—Three chevrons above 4 rockers with a 5-pointed star in the center.

Master Gunnery Sergeant (E-9)—Three chevrons above 4 rockers with a bursting bomb insignia in the center.

First Sergeant (E-8)—Three chevrons above 3 rockers with a diamond in the middle.

Master Sergeant (E-8)—Three chevrons above 3 rockers with crossed rifles in the middle.

Gunnery Sergeant (E-7)—Three chevrons above 2 rockers with crossed rifles in the middle.

Staff Sergeant (E-6)—Three chevrons above 1 rocker with crossed rifles in the middle.

Sergeant (E-5)—Three chevrons above crossed rifles.

Corporal (E-4)—Two chevrons above crossed rifles.

Lance Corporal (E-3)—One chevron above crossed rifles.

Private First Class (E-2)—One chevron.

Private (E-1)—None.

Coast Guard

Coast Guard insignia follow Navy custom, with certain minor changes such as the officer cap insignia. The Coast Guard shield is worn on both sleeves of officers and on the right sleeve of all enlisted personnel.

U.S. Armed Forces Contact Information

Additional information on all the U.S. Armed Forces branches, as well as many other related organizations, can be accessed through the official website of the Dept. of Defense: www.defense.gov.

Army—Office of the Chief of Public Affairs, Media Relations Division—MRD, 1500 Army Pentagon, Washington, DC 20310-1500. **Website:** www.army.mil

Navy—Chief of Information, 1200 Navy Pentagon, Washington, DC 20350-1200. **Website:** www.navy.mil

Air Force—Office of Public Affairs, 1690 Air Force Pentagon, Washington, DC 20330-1690. **Website:** www.af.mil

Marine Corps—Marine Corps Headquarters, Division of Public Affairs, 3000 Marine Corps, Pentagon, Washington, DC 20350-3000. **Website:** www.usmc.mil

Coast Guard—Commandant (CG-09222), Attn: Chief of Media Relations, U.S. Coast Guard, 2100 2nd St. SW, Stop 7362, Washington, DC 20593-7362. **Website:** www.uscg.mil

Casualties in Principal Wars of the U.S.

Source: U.S. Dept. of Defense; U.S. Coast Guard, U.S. Dept. of Homeland Security

Data prior to World War I are based on incomplete records in many cases. Casualty data are confined to dead and wounded personnel and, therefore, exclude personnel captured or missing in action who were subsequently returned to military control.

	Branch of service	Number serving	CASUALTIES Battle deaths	Other deaths	Wounds not mortal[1]	Total[2]
Revolutionary War	Total	—	4,435	—	6,188	10,623
1775-83	Army	184,000	4,044	—	6,004	10,048
	Navy	to	342	—	114	456
	Marines	250,000[13]	49	—	70	119
War of 1812	Total	286,730[14]	2,260	—	4,505	6,765
1812-15	Army	—	1,950	—	4,000	5,950
	Navy	—	265	—	439	704
	Marines	—	45	—	66	111
Mexican War	Total	78,718[14]	1,733	11,550	4,152	17,435
1846-48	Army	—	1,721	11,550	4,102	17,373
	Navy	—	1	—	3	4
	Marines	—	11	—	47	58
	Coast Guard[8] . .	71 off.	—	—	—	—
Civil War						
1861-65						
Union forces[3]	Total	2,213,363	140,414	224,097	281,881	646,392
	Army	2,128,948[14]	138,154	221,374	280,040	639,568
	Navy	84,415	2,112	2,411	1,710	6,233
	Marines	(in Navy total)	148	312	131	591
	Coast Guard[8] . .	219 off.	1	—	—	1
Confederate forces (estimate)[3]	Total	—	74,524	59,297	—	133,821
	Army	600,000	—	—	—	—
	Navy	to	—	—	—	—
	Marines	1,500,000	—	—	—	—
Spanish-American War	Total	306,760	385	2,061	1,662	4,108
1898	Army[9]	280,564	369	2,061	1,594	4,024
	Navy	22,875	10	—	47	57
	Marines	3,321	6	—	21	27
	Coast Guard[8] . .	660	0	—	—	—
World War I	Total	4,734,991	53,402	63,114	204,002	320,518
Apr. 6, 1917-Nov. 11, 1918	Army[10]	4,057,101	50,510	55,868	193,663	300,041
	Navy	599,051	431	6,856	819	8,106
	Marines	78,839	2,461	390	9,520	12,371
	Coast Guard . . .	8,835	111	81	—	192
World War II[4]	Total	16,112,566	291,557	113,842	670,846	1,076,245
Dec. 7, 1941-Dec. 31, 1946	Army[11]	11,260,000	234,874	83,400	565,861	884,135
	Navy[12]	4,183,466	36,950	25,664	37,778	100,392
	Marines	669,100	19,733	4,778	67,207	91,718
	Coast Guard . . .	241,093	574	1,343	—	1,917
Korean War[5]	Total	5,720,000	33,739	2,835	103,284	139,858
June 25, 1950-July 27, 1953	Army	2,834,000	27,731	2,125	77,596	107,452
	Navy	1,177,000	503	154	1,576	2,233
	Marines	424,000	4,267	242	23,744	28,253
	Air Force	1,285,000	1,238	314	368	1,920
	Coast Guard . . .	44,143	—	—	—	—
Vietnam War[6]	Total	8,744,000	47,434	10,786	153,303	211,523
Aug. 4, 1964-Jan. 27, 1973	Army	4,368,000	30,963	7,261	96,802	135,026
	Navy	1,842,000	1,631	935	4,178	6,744
	Marines	794,000	13,095	1,749	51,392	66,236
	Air Force	1,740,000	1,745	841	931	3,517
	Coast Guard . . .	8,000	7	2	60	69
Persian Gulf War	Total	2,225,000	148	235	467	850
1991	Army	782,000	98	126	354	578
	Navy	669,000	6	50	12	68
	Marines	213,000	24	44	92	160
	Air Force	561,000	20	15	9	44
	Coast Guard . . .	400	—	—	—	—
Iraq War[7]	Total	269,363[15]	3,519	965	32,248	36,732
Mar. 19, 2003-Dec. 15, 2011	Army	99,664[15]	2,574	722	22,522	25,818
	Navy	61,018[15]	63	45	647	756
	Marines	66,166[15]	852	171	8,626	9,649
	Air Force	42,515[15]	29	27	452	508
	Coast Guard . . .	1,250[15]	1	—	1	2

— = Not available. Off. = Officers. **Note:** As of Aug. 2016, there were 1,843 battle deaths, 503 non-hostile deaths, and 20,090 wounded in Op. Enduring Freedom (Oct. 7, 2001-Dec. 31, 2014), mostly in Afghanistan and the Persian Gulf area; 12 battle deaths, 12 non-hostile deaths, and 120 wounded in Operation Freedom's Sentinel (Jan. 1, 2015-) in Afghanistan; 3 battle deaths, 19 non-hostile deaths, and 16 wounded in Operation Inherent Resolve (Aug. 8, 2014-) against ISIS in Iraq and Syria. (1) Marine Corps data for Iraq War, World War II, Spanish-American War, and prior wars represent the number of individuals wounded, whereas all other data in this column represent the total number (incidence) of wounds. (2) Totals for all branches do not include categories for which no data are listed. (3) From the final report of the Provost Marshal General, 1863-66. Authoritative statistics for the Confederate forces are not available. In addition, an estimated 26,000-31,000 Confederate personnel died in Union prisons. New estimates published in *Civil War History* in 2012 recalculated the death toll for both sides and determined that it was 20% higher than previously thought, at 750,000. (4) Data are for Dec. 1, 1941, through Dec. 31, 1946, when hostilities were officially terminated by presidential proclamation; few battle deaths or wounds not mortal were incurred after Japanese acceptance of Allied peace terms on Aug. 14, 1945. Numbers serving Dec. 1, 1941-Aug. 31, 1945: Total—14,903,213; Army—10,420,000; Navy—3,883,520; Marine Corps—599,693. (5) As a result of an ongoing Dept. of Defense review of available Korean War casualty record information, updates have been made to previously reported figures for battle deaths and other deaths. (6) Number serving Aug. 5, 1964-Jan. 27, 1973 (date of cease-fire). Includes casualties incurred in Mayaguez incident. Wounds not mortal exclude 150,341 persons not requiring hospital care. (7) Military deaths during the invasion phase, which ended Apr. 30, 2003, totaled 115 combat-related and 23 other. (8) Then known as the U.S. Revenue Cutter Services, predecessor to the U.S. Coast Guard. (9) Number serving Apr. 1-Aug. 31, 1898, while dead and wounded data are for May 1-Aug. 31, 1898. Active hostilities ceased on Aug. 13, 1898, but the U.S. and Spain did not exchange ratifications of the treaty of peace until Apr. 11, 1899. (10) Includes Army Air Forces battle deaths and wounds not mortal, as well as casualties suffered by American forces in northern Russia to Aug. 25, 1919, and in Siberia to Apr. 1, 1920. Other deaths cover Apr. 1, 1917-Dec. 31, 1918. (11) Includes Army Air Forces. (12) Battle deaths and wounds not mortal include casualties incurred in Oct. 1941 due to hostile action. (13) Estimated. (14) As reported by Commissioner of Pensions in his Annual Report for Fiscal Year 1903. (15) Number serving as of Mar. 31, 2003, i.e., does not include numbers of troops deployed since then.

Timeline of Major Wars Since 1066

Norman Conquest 1066-71	William I, duke of Normandy, landed on the English coast near Hastings on Sept. 28, 1066, and defeated Harold II, Saxon king of England, at Battle of Hastings Oct. 14. William crowned king Dec. 25 in Westminster Abbey. Most revolts were suppressed by 1071. **Conquest linked England's interests with those of the continent and led to its rise as a powerful monarchy.**
Crusades 1095-1270/1291	Military expeditions undertaken by **Western European Christians**, usually at the behest of the **papacy**, to recover **Jerusalem** and other Biblical places of pilgrimage from **Muslim** control. In the long term, stimulated trade and flow of ideas between East and West. Pope Urban II called Nov. 27, 1095, for the **First Crusade**; Crusaders took Jerusalem on July 15, 1099, massacred inhabitants, and founded four temporary states: Antioch, Edessa, Jerusalem, and Tripoli. The failed **Second Crusade** was prompted by Muslims' capture of Edessa in 1144. Jerusalem was captured by Ayyubid sultan Saladin on Oct. 2, 1187, leading to the **Third Crusade**, which involved the Holy Roman emperor, Frederick I (Barbarossa); the French king, Philip II (Augustus); and the English king, Richard I (Lion-Heart) but did not lead to a Crusader victory. The **Fourth Crusade** sacked Constantinople on Apr. 13, 1204. The **Fifth Crusade** began with capture of Damietta in Egypt (1219) but failed at Cairo. A **Sixth Crusade** led to the Treaty of Jaffa in 1229, giving Jerusalem to the Crusaders until 1244, when its seizure by the Khwarezmians led to the launch of a **Seventh Crusade**. The last crusade abruptly ended when its leader, French King Louis IX, died in 1270. The last major Crusader stronghold, Acre, was lost on May 18, 1291.
Hundred Years War 1337-1453	Series of armed conflicts over rival claims to the French throne, broken by a number of truces and peace treaties. Edward III declared self king of France in 1338 and invaded, with victories at Crécy (1346) and Poitiers (1356). **Treaty of Brétigny** signed May 8, 1360, but French king Charles V renewed fighting in 1369. Truce from 1396 until **Henry V** of England invaded in 1415 and **defeated French army at Agincourt**, capturing land north of Loire River, including Paris. **Treaty of Troyes** in 1420 made Henry VI heir of both thrones. The siege of French stronghold Orléans, lifted in 1429 with help from **Joan of Arc**, turned tide in favor of French, who won last battle (1453). **War ended English claims to France, paved way for French absolute monarchy.**
Wars of the Roses 1455-85	Series of dynastic civil wars for the throne in England fought by the **rival houses of Lancaster and York**. Richard, third duke of York, in conflict with the Lancastrian King **Henry VI**, won victories at St. Albans (1455) and Northampton (1460); Richard died at battle of Wakefield on Dec. 30, 1460, before coronation, leaving his son to become King Edward IV. Henry VI imprisoned in Tower of London, 1465. Edward died in 1483; his brother became **Richard III** after usurping throne from Edward V, nephew. Henry Tudor defeated Richard III at the Battle of Bosworth Field (1485). As Henry VII, he married Edward IV's daughter Elizabeth, 1486, **uniting the houses**.
Thirty Years' War 1618-48	A series of religious and political conflicts involving **most countries of Western Europe**; majority of fighting in Germany, devastating it. Protestants stormed Hapsburg palace in the "Defenestration of Prague" (May 23, 1618). Major conflicts included defeat of King Christian IV of Denmark and Norway by Catholic League (1626); victories by Lutheran King Gustav II Adolph of Sweden at Breitenfeld (1631) and Lützen (1632). France, under cardinal and statesman **Richelieu**, chief minister of King Louis XIII, declared war on the Hapsburgs in May 1635; defeated Austro-Bavarian army (Aug. 3, 1645), leading to Truce of Ulm. **Peace of Westphalia** signed at Münster on Oct. 24, 1648, bringing peace by recognizing the rulers' sovereignty within their lands and their right to determine the religious beliefs of their subjects.
English Civil Wars 1638-60	Series of conflicts between followers of King Charles (Cavaliers) and of Parliament (Roundheads), over divine right of king versus Parliament's right to control national finances. Presbyterian Scots, allied with Parliament, rioted and in 1640 occupied the northern counties of England. **Oliver Cromwell**, second in command of Parliament's New Model Army, destroyed the king's army at Battle of Naseby (June 14, 1645); first civil war ended May 1646 when Charles surrendered to the Scots. Charles later allied with Scots but was defeated by Cromwell at Preston Aug. 17-19, 1648, and executed Jan. 30, 1649. Parliament abolished monarchy and House of Lords. Cromwell suppressed Irish and Scottish rebellions, was briefly succeeded by son Richard after death (1658). **Charles II restored to the throne** by the "Long Parliament," May 1660.
War of the Spanish Succession 1701-14	War fought by the Grand Alliance (originally England, Netherlands, Denmark, and Austria; later also Portugal), against coalition of France, Spain, and a number of small Italian and German principalities to preserve balance of power after death of Spanish king Charles II. Opened with invasion of Italy, via Venice, by an Austrian army under Prince Eugène of Savoy in May 1701. French forced to withdraw from Netherlands and Italy in 1706 and were finally defeated in 1709 in bloodiest battle of the war at French village of Malplaquet. Treaties of Rastatt and Baden signed in 1714; **Austria given control of Spanish Netherlands, and peace settled between Austria and France.**
War of the Austrian Succession 1740-48	Conflict over rival claims for the **hereditary dominions of the Habsburg family**, following death (1740) of Charles VI, Holy Roman emperor and archduke of Austria. An alliance of Bavaria, France, Spain, Sardinia, Prussia, and Saxony fought against Austria, allied with Holland and Great Britain. King Frederick the Great of Prussia captured Silesia from Austria in the First (1740-42) and Second (1744-45) Silesian Wars. British king George II defeated French army at Battle of Dettingen am Main (June 27, 1743). French conquered Austrian Netherlands (1745-46). Treaty of Aix-la-Chapelle Oct. 18, 1748, **restored most original borders; Prussia became significant force.**
Seven Years' War 1756-63	Worldwide conflicts fought for **control of Germany** and for **supremacy in colonial N America and India**. French defeated British Gen. Edward Braddock in Battle of Monongahela in 1754, leading to formal declaration of **French-Indian War**, May 1756. Frederick II of Prussia invaded Saxony on Aug. 29, 1756; defeated French at Rossbach (1757), Austrians at Leuthen (1757), Russians at Zorndorf (1758). By 1760, British conquered French Canada. Peter III of Russia signed armistice with Prussia, 1762. Treaty of Paris signed Feb. 10, 1763; Peace of Hubertusburg Feb. 15, 1763, between Prussia and Austria. **England emerged as leading world naval power.**
American Revolution 1775-83	Conflict between Great Britain and 13 British colonies in eastern N America. George Washington took command of the Continental Army, July 2, 1775, and King George III declared colonies traitors on Aug. 23. **Declaration of Independence of colonies adopted July 4, 1776.** France recognized the colonies' independence Feb. 6, 1778, followed by Spain on June 21, 1779; both pledged support. French fleet drove British fleet under Adm. Thomas Graves from Chesapeake Bay on Sept. 5, 1781. French and Americans laid siege to Yorktown, VA, Sept. 28-Oct. 19, forcing British Gen. Cornwallis to surrender. **Treaty of Paris** (Sept. 3, 1783) recognized U.S. independence.
Wars of French Revolution and Napoleonic Wars 1792-1815	Large-scale wars fought between France and two multinational coalitions. France declared war on the Austrian part of the Holy Roman Empire, Apr. 20, 1792. Newly created French Republic declared war on monarchs of Britain and Holland, Feb. 1, 1793, and of Spain, Mar. 7. **Napoleon Bonaparte** defeated Austria in N Italy (1796-97), captured Egypt from Britain (1798-99; Battle of the Pyramids, July 21, 1798), and became First Consul after coup d'état of Nov. 9-10, 1799. French Grande Armée later swept through Europe using innovative and aggressive tactics. French navy defeated by British under Adm. Horatio Nelson at **Trafalgar** (Oct. 21, 1805), but Napoleon defeated Austro-Russian forces at Austerlitz (Dec. 2) and controlled most of Europe except Russia and Great Britain by 1808. France suffered its first major defeat by Austria at Aspern-Essling, May 21-22, 1809. **Napoleon invaded Russia**, captured Moscow Sept. 14, 1812, but fled the bitter Russian winter and abandoned Germany after defeat at Leipzig, Oct. 16-19, 1813. Paris captured by Allied armies Mar. 30-31, 1814. Napoleon exiled to Elba May 4 but returned for "Hundred Days" reign, Mar. 20-June 28, 1815; **final defeat at Waterloo** by British and Prussian troops (June 18). The **Bourbon monarchy was restored under Louis XVIII**, and Britain, Prussia, Russia, and Austria maintained European peace.

Crimean War
1853-56

Conflict between **Russia** and coalition of **Great Britain, France, Sardinia, and Turkey for influence over Balkans** and the straits between the Black Sea and Mediterranean. Russia destroyed Turkish fleet at Sinope on Nov. 30, 1853. Britain and France declared war in Mar. 1854 and with Turkish troops defeated Russians at Battle of Alma River, Sept. 20. Lord Lucan of Britain prevented Russia from capturing Balaklava on Oct. 25 ("Charge of the Light Brigade" led by Lord Cardigan). Siege of Sevastopol ended when Russia evacuated Sept. 8, 1855. Treaty of Paris signed Mar. 30, 1856; **curbed Russian expansion and loosened European power alignments**.

American Civil War
1861-65

Conflict between the U.S. (the Union) and 11 secessionist Southern states, organized as the Confederate States of America. Union garrison at Fort Sumter in harbor of Charleston, SC, surrendered to Brig. Gen. Pierre Beauregard (Apr. 12-13, 1861). 22,000 Confederates under Beauregard repelled 35,000 Union troops under Gen. Irvin McDowell along Bull Run stream near Manassas, VA (July 21). The *Merrimack* (renamed the *Virginia*) battled the *Monitor* Mar. 9, 1862. In **Battle of Antietam**, MD (Sept. 17), some 12,000 Northerners and 12,700 Southerners were killed or wounded. Pres. Abraham Lincoln announced **Emancipation Proclamation** on Sept. 22. Confederate Gen. Robert E. Lee's forces numbering 75,000 battled 88,000 Union troops under Gen. George Meade at **Gettysburg**, PA, July 1-3, 1863; Lee's army forced back across the Potomac River. Lee surrendered to Ulysses S. Grant at **Appomattox Court House** in Virginia (Apr. 9, 1865). **The Union was preserved and slavery abolished.**

Franco-Prussian War
1870-71

German states led by Prussia defeated France, seizing Alsace and part of Lorraine. French defeated in several major battles, culminating at **Sedan** Sept. 1, 1870, when Prussian forces decisively defeated the French army and captured emperor Napoleon III. Prussian king crowned William I, emperor of unified Germany, Jan 18, 1871. **France surrendered** Jan. 28. Final treaty signed May 10; set the stage for later **German imperialistic expansion**.

Spanish-American War
1898

War waged by the U.S. to **liberate Cuba from Spanish rule.** A mysterious explosion, blamed on Spain by American newspapers, sank the U.S. battleship *Maine* in Havana's harbor (Feb. 15, 1898), killing 260. The U.S. called for Spain's withdrawal from Cuba, and Spain declared war (Apr. 24). William Rufus Shafter led 17,000 U.S. troops from Daiquirí to Santiago de Cuba, taking **San Juan Hill** with help of the Rough Riders under Teddy Roosevelt. Santiago de Cuba surrendered July 17. The Treaty of Paris (Dec. 10, 1898) provided for the **independence of Cuba** and the cession by Spain to the U.S. of **Puerto Rico, Guam, and for a $20 mil payment, the Philippine Islands**.

World War I
1914-18

Local European war that grew into a global war involving 32 nations: the Allies and the Associated Powers—28 nations including Great Britain, France, Russia, Italy, and the U.S.—versus the Central Powers of Germany, Austria-Hungary, Turkey, and Bulgaria. Archduke Francis Ferdinand of Austria assassinated in Sarajevo, Bosnia (June 28, 1914). Germany invaded France through Belgium; advance on Paris halted by the French under Gen. Joseph Jacques Césaire Joffre at the **First Battle of the Marne**, Sept. 5-12. Germany checked the Russian army at the Battle of Tannenberg, Aug. 26-30. The British suffered 57,470 casualties (19,240 dead) in the opening day of the **First Battle of the Somme** (July 1-Nov. 18, 1916), first of 12 battles that forced Germany back to Hindenburg Line. **U.S. declared war on Germany Apr. 6, 1917.** Russian involvement ended when Bolshevik party seized power on Nov. 7; signed armistice Dec. 15. German offensive halted by U.S. and French troops at **Second Battle of the Marne** (July 15-Aug. 5, 1918), turning point of the war. Allied counteroffensive broke the Hindenburg Line, and an armistice was signed Nov. 11.

World War II
1939-45

Global military conflict stemming from European unrest after World War I and Japan's aggressive expansion into Asia and the Pacific. **War in Europe:** Nazi-Soviet nonaggression pact (Aug. 23, 1939) freed Germany and the Soviet Union to attack Poland in Sept. **Britain and France declared war on Germany** Sept. 3. German forces raced through Europe (Apr.-June 1940), captured Paris June 14. **Italy declared war on France and Britain** June 10. German-Italian campaigns won the Balkans and N Africa by June 1941. U.S. entered war Dec. 1941. Three million Axis troops invaded Russia June 22, 1941, but Russian counterthrusts stopped the German advance (**Stalingrad**, Aug. 20, 1942-Feb. 2, 1943), and Allies took N Africa (Nov. 8, 1942-May 13, 1943), Italy (July 10, 1943-May 2, 1945). Normandy invaded on **D-Day**, June 6, 1944; Paris liberated Aug. 25. Leaders at Yalta Conference (Feb. 4-11, 1945) discussed defeat and division of Germany into four. Adolf Hitler committed suicide Apr. 30. **Germany surrendered unconditionally** May 7. **War in the Pacific:** Japan invaded China (July 7, 1937), joined alliance with Germany and Italy (Sept. 27, 1940), and signed nonaggression pact with Russia (Apr. 13, 1941); attacked Hawaii's Pearl Harbor, Dec. 7, 1941; U.S. declared war on Japan Dec. 8. **Battle of Midway** (June 4-7, 1942) repulsed Japanese advance. Marines landed on Guadalcanal Aug. 7. U.S. Navy defeated Japanese fleet at **Leyte Gulf**, Oct. 23-26, 1944. B-29 bombing raids on Japan began in Nov. Marines invaded Iwo Jima (Feb. 19-Mar. 16, 1945) with heavy casualties, then Okinawa (Apr. 1-June 21). **U.S. atom bombs dropped** on Hiroshima (Aug. 6) and Nagasaki (Aug. 9) and Soviet invasion of Manchuria (Aug. 8) **forced Japan to agree, on Aug. 14, to surrender**; formal surrender on Sept. 2.

Korean War
1950-53

Military struggle fought on the Korean Peninsula between the Democratic Peoples' Republic of Korea (N Korea) and the Republic of Korea (S Korea) that developed into an international war involving China allied with N Korea against the U.S. and other nations under the UN flag. DPRK army crossed the 38th parallel and invaded S Korea (June 25, 1950), entering Seoul (June 26). Amphibious assault launched at **Inchon** by Gen. Douglas MacArthur (Sept. 15) helped U.S. forces rout DPRK close to Yalu River by Nov. 24. Chinese counterattack retook Seoul (Jan. 4, 1951) but were forced back to the 38th parallel by Apr. 22. Armistice was signed (July 27, 1953) by the UN, DPRK, and China, but not ROK, **leaving the peninsula partitioned at about the 38th parallel**.

Vietnam War
1959-75

Struggle primarily in S Vietnam that widened into a war between S Vietnam supported mainly by the U.S. and N Vietnam supported by the USSR and China. Viet Minh, led by Communist leader Ho Chi Minh, formed the Democratic Republic of Vietnam (Sept. 2, 1945). Colonial power France withdrew after fortress at Dien Bien Phu fell (May 8, 1954). Pres. John F. Kennedy pledged U.S. commitment to S Vietnamese independence Dec. 14, 1961. USS *Maddox* destroyer damaged in **Gulf of Tonkin** (Aug. 2, 1964), prompting Congress to increase involvement. Regular bombing of N Vietnam began (Feb. 24, 1965), and the first U.S. combat ground forces arrived (Mar. 6). N Vietnamese Army siege of **Khe Sanh** (Jan. 21-Apr. 7, 1968) and the **"Tet"** offensive (Jan. 30) aimed to cause insurrection in the S. **My Lai Massacre** by U.S. soldiers of civilians (Mar. 16, 1968) created scandal, fueled U.S. disaffection with war. U.S. forces peaked at 543,400 in Apr. 1969. NVA **"Easter Offensive"** (Mar. 30, 1972) rebuffed, and U.S. responded with aerial bombings in May and Dec. U.S. withdrew after ceasefire, Jan. 1973. **NVA offensive captured Saigon, Apr. 30, 1975, and unified Vietnam under Communist rule.**

Persian Gulf Wars
1991, 2003-10

Conflicts fought principally between Iraq and the U.S. concerning Iraq's influence in the Middle East and its development of weapons of mass destruction. **First Gulf War:** Iraq under dictator Saddam Hussein invaded Kuwait Aug. 2, 1990, and annexed it; UN Security Council ordered Iraqi forces to withdraw by Jan. 15, 1991. Beginning Jan. 17, a U.S.-led multinational force (**Operation Desert Storm**) bombed military targets in Iraq and Kuwait. A coordinated air-land offensive (**Operation Desert Sabre**, begun Feb. 24) retook Kuwait City Feb. 26, and permanent cease-fire was signed on Apr. 6. Iraq was ordered to pay reparations to Kuwait, reveal locations of biological and chemical weapons, and eliminate weapons of mass destruction. **Second Gulf War:** The U.S. and UK mistakenly asserted that Iraq was still producing WMDs and posed an imminent threat. The UN passed Resolution 1441, Nov. 8, 2002, warning Iraq of "serious consequences" if it failed to cooperate fully and unconditionally with UN weapons inspectors. Iraq rejected a Mar. 17, 2003, U.S. ultimatum demanding Hussein and his sons leave Iraq. U.S. launched **Operation Iraqi Freedom** Mar. 19, 2003, with support from UK and other allies, but without full UN Security Council support. Baghdad fell Apr. 9, and major combat operations declared over May 1. Hussein was captured Dec. 13, 2003, but guerrilla opposition to U.S. troops and insurgent violence continued. U.S. combat operations in Iraq formally ended Aug. 31, 2010.

HEALTH

U.S. Health Expenditures, 1960-2014

Source: *Health, United States, 2015*, National Center for Health Statistics, CDC, U.S. Dept. of Health and Human Services

Type of national health expenditure	1960	1970	1980	1990	2000	2012	2013	2014
					Amount in billions			
National health expenditures (total)	$27.2	$74.6	$255.3	$721.4	$1,369.7	$2,799.0	$2,879.9	$3,031.3
					Percent distribution			
Health consumption expenditures	90.8%	89.9%	92.2%	93.4%	93.9%	94.5%	94.7%	94.9%
Personal health care.	85.5	84.6	85.0	85.3	84.8	84.7	84.8	84.6
Hospital care.	33.0	36.4	39.4	34.7	30.3	32.3	32.4	32.1
Professional services	29.1	26.5	25.3	28.7	28.3	26.8	26.7	26.4
Physician and clinical services	20.4	19.2	18.7	22.0	21.1	20.1	20.0	19.9
Other professional services.	1.4	1.0	1.4	2.4	2.7	2.8	2.8	2.8
Dental services	7.3	6.3	5.2	4.4	4.5	3.9	3.8	3.7
Other health, residential, personal care	1.6	1.7	3.3	3.3	4.7	4.9	5.0	5.0
Home health care[1].	0.2	0.3	0.9	1.7	2.4	2.7	2.8	2.7
Nursing care facilities and continuing care retirement communities[1]	3.0	5.4	6.0	6.2	6.2	5.3	5.2	5.1
Retail outlet sales of medical products . .	18.5	14.2	10.1	10.6	13.0	12.7	12.7	13.2
Prescription drugs	9.8	7.4	4.7	5.6	8.8	9.3	9.2	9.8
Durable medical equipment.	2.7	2.3	1.6	1.9	1.8	1.6	1.6	1.5
Other nondurable medical products. .	6.0	4.5	3.8	3.1	2.3	1.9	1.9	1.9
Government administration.	0.2	1.0	1.1	1.0	1.2	1.2	1.3	1.3
Net cost of health insurance	3.7	2.5	3.6	4.4	4.7	5.9	6.0	6.4
Government public health activities[2]	1.4	1.8	2.5	2.8	3.1	2.7	2.7	2.6
Investment.	**9.2**	**10.1**	**7.8**	**6.6**	**6.1**	**5.5**	**5.3**	**5.1**
Research[3]	2.6	2.6	2.1	1.8	1.9	1.7	1.6	1.5
Structures and equipment.	6.7	7.5	5.7	4.8	4.2	3.7	3.7	3.6
		Average annual percent change from previous year shown						
National health expenditures.	—	10.6%	13.1%	10.9%	6.6%	6.1%	2.9%	5.3%
Health consumption expenditures	—	10.5	13.4	11.1	6.7	6.2	3.1	5.5
Personal health care	—	10.5	13.2	11.0	6.6	6.1	2.9	5.0
Hospital care	—	11.7	14.0	9.6	5.2	6.7	3.5	4.1
Professional services.	—	9.6	12.6	12.4	6.5	5.7	2.4	4.4
Physician and clinical services	—	9.9	12.8	12.7	6.2	5.7	2.5	4.6
Other professional services.	—	6.3	17.0	17.4	7.8	6.4	3.5	5.2
Dental services	—	9.0	11.0	9.0	7.0	4.8	1.5	2.8
Other health, residential, personal care	—	11.5	20.5	11.0	10.4	6.6	4.7	4.1
Home health care[1].	—	14.5	26.9	18.1	9.9	7.5	3.3	4.8
Nursing care facilities and continuing care retirement communities[1]	—	17.4	14.2	11.4	6.6	4.7	1.3	3.6
Retail outlet sales of medical products. .	—	7.7	9.4	11.4	8.8	6.0	2.6	9.6
Prescription drugs	—	7.5	8.2	12.8	11.6	6.5	2.4	12.2
Durable medical equipment.	—	9.0	8.8	13.0	6.2	4.7	2.8	3.2
Other nondurable medical products. .	—	7.4	11.4	8.6	3.5	4.5	3.5	2.4
Government administration.	—	30.0	14.1	10.0	9.0	5.8	8.5	10.7
Net cost of health insurance	—	6.4	17.2	13.0	7.4	8.1	5.3	12.4
Government public health activities[2]	—	13.8	16.9	12.0	8.0	4.9	0.7	3.1
Investment.	—	**11.6**	**10.2**	**9.1**	**5.8**	**5.2**	**−0.5**	**0.9**
Research[3]	—	10.9	10.8	8.9	7.2	5.5	−4.1	−2.0
Structures and equipment.	—	11.9	10.0	9.2	5.3	5.1	1.2	2.2

— = Not applicable. **Note:** Numbers may not add up to totals because of rounding. (1) In freestanding facilities only. Additional services of this type provided in hospital-based facilities are considered hospital care. (2) Includes health care services delivered by government public health agencies. (3) Excludes research and development expenditures of drug companies and other mfrs. and providers of medical equipment and supplies. They are included in the expenditure class in which a product falls.

Health Coverage for Persons Under 65, 1984-2014

Source: *Health, United States, 2015*, National Center for Health Statistics, CDC, U.S. Dept. of Health and Human Services

	Private insurance[1]				Medicaid[1,2]				Not covered[3]			
	1984[4]	2000	2010	2014	1984[4]	2000	2010	2014	1984[4]	2000	2010	2014
						Percent of population						
Total.	76.8%	71.5%	61.7%	63.7%	6.8%	9.5%	16.9%	19.6%	14.5%	17.0%	18.2%	13.3%
Age												
Under 18 years	72.6	66.6	54.1	53.7	11.9	19.6	36.4	39.4	13.9	12.6	7.8	5.4
18-44 years.	76.5	70.5	60.0	64.3	5.1	5.6	10.9	13.8	17.1	22.4	27.1	19.7
45-64 years.	83.3	78.7	71.3	71.7	3.4	4.5	6.8	9.9	9.6	12.6	15.7	11.8
Race and Hispanic origin												
White only, non-Hispanic	82.4	79.5	72.0	73.7	3.7	6.1	11.0	13.0	11.9	12.5	13.7	9.7
Black only, non-Hispanic.	58.2	56.0	45.1	48.0	20.7	21.0	30.0	33.4	19.7	19.5	20.7	13.5
Hispanic, any race	55.7	47.8	36.8	41.2	13.3	15.5	28.6	31.3	29.5	35.6	32.0	25.5
Percent of poverty level												
Below 100%	32.2	25.2	16.0	17.4	33.0	38.4	50.8	56.5	33.9	34.2	30.3	23.0
100%-199%	70.3	50.1	34.8	38.2	5.3	16.2	28.5	34.0	21.8	31.0	32.4	23.4
200%-399%	89.3	78.1	70.7	73.6	0.8	4.0	8.4	9.9	7.6	15.4	17.4	12.6
400% or more	95.4	91.9	89.9	91.5	0.2	0.9	2.0	2.2	3.2	5.9	5.6	3.8
Geographic region												
Northeast	80.5	76.3	68.2	67.7	8.6	10.6	17.9	21.4	10.2	12.2	12.4	9.3
Midwest.	80.6	78.8	66.7	68.7	7.4	8.0	17.3	18.6	11.3	12.3	14.1	10.3
South.	74.3	66.8	57.5	59.4	5.1	9.4	16.0	18.7	17.7	20.5	21.9	16.9
West	71.9	66.5	58.9	62.9	7.0	10.4	17.1	20.9	18.2	20.7	20.6	13.3

Note: Data based on household interviews of a sample of the civilian noninstitutionalized population. Totals incl. groups not shown separately. (1) Incl. persons who also had another type of coverage in addition. (2) Incl. other public assistance, such as a state-sponsored health plan or Children's Health Insurance Program (CHIP). (3) Incl. persons not covered by private insurance, Medicaid or other public assistance, Medicare, or military plans. (4) Because of questionnaire redesign and different tabulating methods, data for 1984 are not strictly comparable with later years.

Spending on Health in the 50 Most Populous Countries, 2014

Source: Global Health Expenditure Database, World Health Organization

Country	As % of GDP	Per capita[1]	Country	As % of GDP	Per capita[1]	Country	As % of GDP	Per capita[1]	Country	As % of GDP	Per capita[1]
Afghanistan...	8.2%	$57	France......	11.5%	$4,959	Morocco	5.9%	$190	Sudan.......	8.4%	$130
Algeria	7.2	362	Germany.....	11.3	5,411	Mozambique..	7.0	42	Tanzania	5.6	52
Angola	3.3	179	Ghana.......	3.6	58	Myanmar.....	2.3	20	Thailand	6.5	360
Argentina	4.8	605	India	4.7	75	Nepal	5.8	40	Turkey.......	5.4	568
Bangladesh...	2.8	31	Indonesia ...	2.8	99	Nigeria	3.7	118	Uganda......	7.2	52
Brazil........	8.3	947	Iran.........	6.9	351	Pakistan	2.6	36	Ukraine......	7.1	203
Canada......	10.4	5,292	Iraq.........	5.5	292	Peru	5.5	359	UK..........	9.1	3,935
China	5.5	420	Italy.........	9.2	3,258	Philippines ...	4.7	135	U.S.	17.1	9,403
Colombia	7.2	569	Japan	10.2	3,703	Poland.......	6.4	910	Uzbekistan ...	5.8	124
Congo, Dem. Rep. of the..	4.3	19	Kenya	5.7	78	Russia.......	7.1	893	Venezuela....	5.3	873
Egypt	5.6	178	Korea, South..	7.4	2,060	Saudi Arabia..	4.7	1,147	Vietnam	7.1	142
Ethiopia.....	4.9	27	Malaysia	4.2	456	South Africa ..	8.8	570	Yemen.......	5.6	80
			Mexico	6.3	677	Spain	9.0	2,658	World[2]	9.9	1,058

(1) At average exchange rate. (2) Includes other nations not shown.

Population Not Covered by Health Insurance by State, 1990-2015

Source: American Community Survey and Current Population Survey, U.S. Census Bureau, U.S. Dept. of Commerce
(numbers in thousands)

	1990 No. not covered	1990 % pop. not covered	2000 No. not covered	2000 % pop. not covered	2015 No. not covered	2015 % pop. not covered		1990 No. not covered	1990 % pop. not covered	2000 No. not covered	2000 % pop. not covered	2015 No. not covered	2015 % pop. not covered
AL	710	17.4%	547	12.5%	484	10.1%	MT	115	14.0%	144	16.1%	119	11.6%
AK	77	15.4	108	17.4	106	14.9	NE	138	8.5	134	7.9	154	8.2
AZ	547	15.5	853	16.4	728	10.8	NV	201	16.5	321	15.7	351	12.3
AR	421	17.4	373	14.1	278	9.5	NH	107	9.9	97	7.9	83	6.3
CA	5,683	19.1	5,956	17.5	3,317	8.6	NJ	773	10.0	857	10.2	771	8.7
CO	495	14.7	559	12.9	433	8.1	NM	339	22.2	415	23.0	224	10.9
CT	226	6.9	300	8.9	211	6.0	NY	2,176	12.1	2,730	14.5	1,381	7.1
DE	96	13.9	66	8.5	54	5.9	NC	883	13.8	964	12.1	1,103	11.2
DC	109	19.2	71	12.8	25	3.8	ND	40	6.3	61	9.8	57	7.8
FL	2,376	18.0	2,591	16.2	2,662	13.3	OH	1,123	10.3	1,101	9.8	746	6.5
GA	971	15.3	1,126	13.9	1,388	13.9	OK	574	18.6	587	17.4	533	13.9
HI	81	7.3	95	7.9	55	4.0	OR	360	12.4	398	11.6	280	7.0
ID	159	15.2	198	15.4	180	11.0	PA	1,218	10.1	915	7.6	802	6.4
IL	1,272	10.9	1,474	12.0	900	7.1	RI	105	11.1	71	6.9	59	5.7
IN	587	10.7	608	10.1	628	9.6	SC	550	16.2	426	10.7	523	10.9
IA	225	8.1	233	8.1	155	5.0	SD	81	11.6	80	10.8	86	10.2
KS	272	10.8	256	9.6	261	9.1	TN	673	13.7	603	10.7	667	10.3
KY	480	13.2	509	12.7	261	6.0	TX	3,569	21.1	4,555	22.0	4,615	17.1
LA	797	19.7	736	16.8	546	11.9	UT	156	9.0	243	10.8	311	10.5
ME	139	11.2	131	10.4	111	8.4	VT	54	9.5	44	7.4	24	3.8
MD	601	12.7	473	9.0	389	6.6	VA	996	15.7	670	9.6	746	9.1
MA	530	9.1	450	7.1	189	2.8	WA	557	11.4	767	13.1	468	6.6
MI	865	9.4	767	7.8	597	6.1	WV	249	13.8	239	13.4	108	6.0
MN	389	8.9	393	8.0	245	4.5	WI	321	6.7	378	7.1	323	5.7
MS	531	19.9	368	13.2	372	12.7	WY	58	12.5	71	14.7	66	11.5
MO	665	12.7	474	8.6	583	9.8	**U.S.**	**34,719**	**13.9**	**36,586**	**13.1**	**29,758**	**9.4**

Persons Not Covered by Health Insurance by Selected Characteristics, 2015

Source: Annual Social and Economic Supplement, Current Population Survey, U.S. Census Bureau, U.S. Dept. of Commerce
(numbers in thousands)

Race and Hispanic origin[1]	Number not covered	% of pop. specified at left	Nativity	Number not covered	% of pop. specified at left
White........................	21,454	8.7%	Native	21,150	7.7%
White, not Hispanic	13,100	6.7	Foreign born.................	7,815	18.1
Black.......................	4,627	11.1	Naturalized citizen...........	1,750	8.7
Amer. Indian and Alaska Native	762	17.7	Not a citizen	6,066	26.4
Asian.......................	1,360	7.5	**Marital status**		
Native Hawaiian and other Pacific Islander	114	9.8	Married.....................	9,432	7.3
Two or more races...........	648	8.5	Widowed....................	571	3.8
Hispanic (any race)...........	9,235	16.2	Divorced....................	3,062	12.0
Age			Separated...................	992	18.8
Under 65 years	28,460	10.5	Never married...............	14,909	10.3
Under 18 years	3,866	5.2	**Household income**		
Under 6 years	1,442	6.1	Less than $25,000...........	7,713	14.8
6 to 11 years	1,149	4.6	$25,000 to $49,999..........	8,151	12.5
12 to 17 years	1,276	5.0	$50,000 to $74,999..........	5,308	9.6
18 to 24 years	3,915	13.1	$75,000 and over	7,793	5.3
25 to 34 years	7,128	16.3	**Work experience[2]**		
35 to 44 years	5,489	13.7	Worked during the year	17,758	10.9
45 to 54 years	4,449	10.5	Full-time....................	13,703	10.5
55 to 64 years	3,613	8.8	Part-time....................	4,055	12.1
65 years and older	505	1.1	Did not work last year	8,032	8.5
			Total.........................	**28,966**	**9.1**

(1) Numbers are for one race alone unless otherwise noted. (2) Does not include persons under 15 years of age.

Health Insurance Marketplace Plan Enrollment by Selected Characteristics

Source: Office of the Asst. Sec. for Planning and Evaluation, U.S. Dept. of Health and Human Services
(cumulative enrollment-related activity for Nov. 1, 2015-Feb. 1, 2016; as of Mar. 8, 2016)

	Marketplace total		State marketplaces[1]		Federal marketplace[2]	
	Number[3]	Percent	Number[3]	Percent	Number[3]	Percent
Number who have selected a plan	12,681,874	NA	3,055,892	NA	9,625,982	NA
By known age	12,680,684	100.0%	3,054,755	100.0%	9,625,929	100.0%
0 to 34 years of age	4,594,172	36.2	1,034,133	33.9	3,560,039	37.0
Under 18 years of age................	1,068,631	8.4	184,459	6.0	884,172	9.2
18 to 34 years of age.................	3,525,541	27.8	849,674	27.8	2,675,867	27.8
18 to 25 years of age.............	1,370,048	10.8	302,571	9.9	1,067,477	11.1
26 to 34 years of age.............	2,155,493	17.0	547,103	17.9	1,608,390	16.7
35 to 44 years of age	2,043,932	16.1	488,281	16.0	1,555,651	16.2
45 to 54 years of age	2,682,762	21.2	672,105	22.0	2,010,657	20.9
55 to 64 years of age	3,262,215	25.7	830,590	27.2	2,431,625	25.3
65 years of age and older.............	97,603	0.8	29,646	1.0	67,957	0.7
Age unknown	1,190	NA	1,137	NA	53	NA
By known financial assistance status[4].....	12,598,526	100.0	2,972,544	100.0	9,625,982	100.0
With financial assistance................	10,510,141	83.4	2,327,082	78.3	8,183,059	85.0
Without financial assistance	2,088,385	16.6	645,462	21.7	1,442,923	15.0
Financial assistance status unknown	83,516	NA	83,516	NA	0	NA

NA = Not applicable. **Note:** Figures may not add up to totals due to rounding. (1) For states implementing their own marketplaces, known as state-based marketplaces. (2) For states with marketplaces supported or fully run by the Dept. of Health and Human Services, or the federally facilitated marketplace. (3) Includes individuals whether or not a first premium payment has been made. (4) Advance premium tax credit with or without cost-sharing reduction.

Federal Health Insurance Marketplace Average Monthly Premiums, 2016

Source: Office of the Asst. Sec. for Planning and Evaluation, U.S. Dept. of Health and Human Services

(based on enrollment-related activity for Nov. 1, 2015-Feb. 1, 2016; as of Mar. 8, 2016)

In the 38 states with health insurance marketplaces supported or fully run by the federal government, 85% of those who selected a plan chose one with advance premium tax credits based on projected income. Comparable data for state marketplaces are not available.

State	Avg. premium after tax credits	Avg. premium before tax credits	Avg. tax credit	Avg. % reduction in premium after tax credits	State	Avg. premium after tax credits	Avg. premium before tax credits	Avg. tax credit	Avg. % reduction in premium after tax credits
Alabama	$102	$410	$308	75%	New Hampshire ..	$155	$396	$241	61%
Alaska.........	126	863	737	85	New Jersey......	161	484	323	67
Arizona........	120	324	204	63	New Mexico[1].....	127	332	205	62
Arkansas.......	122	409	286	70	North Carolina ...	98	497	399	80
Delaware.......	150	477	328	69	North Dakota	142	405	262	65
Florida........	84	386	302	78	Ohio	164	405	240	59
Georgia........	98	385	287	75	Oklahoma.......	80	376	296	79
Hawaii[1]	118	389	270	70	Oregon[1]	142	392	250	64
Illinois	152	385	233	61	Pennsylvania.....	145	396	251	63
Indiana	156	415	259	63	South Carolina ...	97	406	309	76
Iowa	122	425	303	71	South Dakota	110	416	306	74
Kansas........	106	352	246	70	Tennessee	104	400	296	74
Louisiana	86	448	362	81	Texas	87	344	257	75
Maine	103	428	325	76	Utah	84	271	187	69
Michigan.......	143	382	239	63	Virginia	93	366	273	75
Mississippi	91	388	297	76	West Virginia.....	155	542	387	71
Missouri	94	407	313	77	Wisconsin	125	455	330	73
Montana	115	421	306	73	Wyoming........	117	571	454	80
Nebraska	105	400	295	74	**Total**	**106**	**396**	**290**	**73**
Nevada[1]	107	372	265	71					

(1) State-based marketplace using the HealthCare.gov platform.

Health Care Visits by Selected Characteristics, 1997-2014

Source: Natl. Health Interview Survey, Natl. Ctr. for Health Statistics, CDC, U.S. Dept. of Health and Human Services

	Zero visits			1-3 visits			4-9 visits			10 or more visits		
	1997	2010	2014	1997	2010	2014	1997	2010	2014	1997	2010	2014
Characteristic						Percent distribution						
All persons[1]...............	16.5%	15.6%	15.3%	46.2%	45.4%	50.4%	23.6%	25.8%	22.8%	13.7%	13.2%	11.5%
Age												
Under 6 years	5.0	3.7	4.3	44.9	48.9	55.6	37.0	36.8	32.4	13.0	10.6	7.7
6-17 years	15.3	10.4	9.7	58.7	59.1	66.3	19.3	23.6	18.5	6.8	6.9	5.5
18-44 years	21.7	24.2	23.2	46.7	43.9	48.7	19.0	20.6	17.9	12.6	11.3	10.2
45-64 years	16.9	14.8	15.0	42.9	42.8	46.8	24.7	26.1	24.2	15.5	16.4	14.0
65-74 years	9.8	6.3	6.4	36.9	36.1	39.2	31.6	35.7	35.0	21.6	21.9	19.4
75 years and over	7.7	4.1	4.4	31.8	31.0	33.7	33.8	38.0	36.4	26.6	27.0	25.5
Sex												
Male.....................	21.3	20.4	19.7	47.1	46.4	51.0	20.6	22.7	20.1	11.0	10.5	9.3
Female..................	11.8	10.9	11.1	45.4	44.4	49.9	26.5	28.8	25.4	16.3	15.9	13.6
Race and Hispanic origin												
White only, not Hispanic....	14.7	13.2	13.2	46.6	45.3	50.1	24.4	27.1	24.0	14.3	14.4	12.7
Black only, not Hispanic....	16.9	15.6	14.6	46.1	47.3	52.2	23.1	24.9	23.0	13.8	12.2	10.2
Hispanic, any race........	24.9	23.5	21.8	42.3	43.2	47.6	20.3	22.6	20.9	12.5	10.7	9.6
Health insurance status[2]												
Insured continuously	14.1	12.1	12.6	49.2	48.6	54.3	23.6	26.2	22.3	13.0	13.0	10.8
Uninsured, up to 12 mos. ..	18.9	18.5	20.8	46.0	47.8	50.7	20.8	22.0	19.3	14.4	11.6	9.3
Uninsured 12+ mos........	39.0	43.8	44.2	41.4	39.7	42.1	13.2	12.6	10.6	6.4	3.9	3.0

Note: Totals include visits to hospital emergency departments, doctor offices, and clinics as well as home visits by a health care professional. (1) Includes persons of races not shown separately and of unknown health insurance status. (2) In 12 months prior to interview, for persons under age 65 only.

Reasons Given by Patients for Physician Office Visits, 2012

Source: National Ambulatory Medical Care Survey, National Center for Health Statistics, Centers for Disease Control and Prevention, U.S. Dept. of Health and Human Services

Rank	Reason	Number of visits (thous.)	% of all visits	Rank	Reason	Number of visits (thous.)	% of all visits
1.	Progress visit, not otherwise specified	74,103	8.0%	12.	Counseling, not otherwise specified	12,987	1.4%
2.	General medical examination	70,435	7.6	13.	Symptoms referable to throat	12,895	1.4
3.	Postoperative visit	28,829	3.1	14.	Skin rash	12,511	1.3
4.	Cough	25,853	2.8	15.	Stomach and abdominal pain,		
5.	Medication, other and unspecified				cramps, and spasms	12,284	1.3
	kinds	18,282	2.0	16.	For other and unspecified test results	12,115	1.3
6.	Prenatal examination, routine	15,964	1.7	17.	Diabetes mellitus	11,706	1.3
7.	Knee symptoms	14,608	1.6	18.	Fever	10,902	1.2
8.	Gynecological examination	14,402	1.6	19.	Hypertension	10,546	1.1
9.	Well-baby examination	13,838	1.5	20.	Earache, or ear infection	9,701	1.0
10.	Low back symptoms	13,335	1.4		**All other reasons**	520,102	56.0
11.	Back symptoms	13,232	1.4		**All visits**	928,630	100.0

Note: Numbers of visits to office-based patient care physicians may not add to totals because of rounding.

Visits to Physician Offices and Hospital Outpatient and Emergency Departments, 1995-2012

Source: National Ambulatory Medical Care Survey and National Hospital Ambulatory Medical Care Survey, National Center for Health Statistics, Centers for Disease Control and Prevention, U.S. Dept. of Health and Human Services

(number of visits per 100 persons)

Sex and age	All places[1]			Physician offices[2]				Hospital outpatient depts.			Hospital emergency depts.		
	1995	2000	2011	1995	2000	2011	2012	1995	2000	2011	1995	2000	2011
Total	334	374	400	271	304	314	292	26	31	40	37	40	45
Male	290	325	354	232	261	280	254	21	26	32	37	38	42
Under 18 years	273	302	372	209	231	294	236	25	29	37	40	41	41
18-44 years	190	203	208	139	148	145	140	14	17	20	37	38	43
45-54 years	275	316	322	229	260	250	251	20	26	34	26	30	38
55-64 years	351	428	430	300	367	351	343	26	32	45	25	30	34
65-74 years	508	614	655	445	539	566	505	29	38	52	34	36	37
75 years and over	711	771	869	616	670	758	685	34	42	49	61	59	62
Female	377	420	444	309	345	348	328	31	35	48	37	41	48
Under 18 years	277	285	341	217	221	265	229	25	29	38	35	35	39
18-44 years	336	377	393	265	298	286	281	31	33	47	40	46	59
45-54 years	400	451	459	339	384	364	340	32	36	53	29	31	41
55-64 years	446	529	520	382	453	436	413	38	45	54	26	31	31
65-74 years	603	692	707	534	609	611	556	36	46	60	32	37	37
75 years and over	666	763	790	571	645	657	660	34	49	61	61	69	72

Note: Data based on reporting by a sample of survey respondents. (1) Incl. visits to physician offices, hospital outpatient departments, and hospital emergency departments. (2) 2011 data incl. visits to community health centers; 2012 data excl. such visits. (Prior to 2006, visits to community health centers were not included in survey.)

Most Frequently Mentioned Drugs at Office Visits, 2012

Source: National Ambulatory Medical Care Survey, National Center for Health Statistics, Centers for Disease Control and Prevention, U.S. Dept. of Health and Human Services

Rank	Therapeutic drug category[1]	No. of mentions (thous.)	% of total[2]	Rank	Therapeutic drug category[1]	No. of mentions (thous.)	% of total[2]
1.	Analgesics	262,846	11.4%	11.	Bronchodilators	69,229	3.0%
2.	Antihyperlipidemic agents	120,042	5.2	12.	Proton pump inhibitors	67,025	2.9
3.	Antidepressants	108,730	4.7	13.	Immunostimulants	63,651	2.8
4.	Anxiolytics, sedatives, and hypnotics	92,053	4.0	14.	Diuretics	56,142	2.4
5.	Antidiabetic agents	82,027	3.5	15.	ACE[3] inhibitors	56,121	2.4
6.	Antiplatelet agents	76,915	3.3	16.	Antihistamines	53,603	2.3
7.	Beta-adrenergic blocking agents	75,543	3.3	17.	Adrenal cortical steroids	48,994	2.1
8.	Dermatological agents	74,862	3.2	18.	Vitamin and mineral combinations	45,736	2.0
9.	Anticonvulsants	73,315	3.2	19.	Thyroid hormones	44,682	1.9
10.	Vitamins	72,218	3.1	20.	Minerals and electrolytes	43,026	1.9

Note: A mention is a documentation in a patient's record of a drug provided, prescribed, or continued at a visit to a nonfederal office-based patient care physician. (1) Based on the Multum Lexicon second-level therapeutic drug category. (2) Based on an estimated 2,310,812,000 drug mentions at office visits in 2012. (3) Angiotensin-converting enzyme.

U.S. Organ Transplants

Source: Organ Procurement and Transplantation Network (OPTN), United Network for Organ Sharing (UNOS)

Waiting List, July 2016

Type of transplant	Registered candidates	% of total
Any organ	120,052	—
Kidney	99,519	82.9%
Liver	14,652	12.2
Heart	4,110	3.4
Kidney-pancreas	1,885	1.6
Lung	1,427	1.2
Pancreas	973	0.8
Intestine	270	0.2
Heart-lung	42	0.03

Note: Waiting list as of July 15, 2016.

Transplants Performed, 2015

Type of transplant	Number	% of total
Any organ	30,969	—
Kidney	17,878	57.7%
Liver	7,127	23.0
Heart	2,804	9.1
Lung	2,057	6.6
Kidney-pancreas	719	2.3
Pancreas	228	0.7
Intestine	141	0.5
Heart-lung	15	0.05

Drug Use in the General U.S. Population, 2014

Source: Substance Abuse and Mental Health Services Administration (SAMHSA), U.S. Dept. of Health and Human Services

According to the 2014 results of SAMHSA's annual survey on drug use and health, an estimated 130.3 mil Americans 12 years of age and older (or 49.2% of that population) had used an illicit drug at least once in their lifetimes. Of that number, an estimated 80.1 mil (30.2% of persons 12 and older) had used an illicit drug other than marijuana at least once in their lives. About 16.7% of the 12-and-older population had used an illicit drug in the previous year; 10.2% had used one in the month prior to their participation in the survey. The rate of current illicit drug use (i.e., within the past month) in 2014 was 12.8% for men and 7.7% for women.

SAMHSA's Drug Abuse Warning Network (DAWN) reported 2.5 mil drug abuse or misuse-related visits to hospital emergency departments in 2011, the last year for which DAWN data is available. Just over half (51%) of all visits involved illicit drugs, with the highest rates for cocaine and marijuana. About 25% of all visits associated with drug misuse or abuse also involved alcohol.

Illicit Drug Use Among Persons Age 12 or Older, 2005-14

Source: National Survey on Drug Use and Health, Substance Abuse and Mental Health Services Admin. (SAMHSA), U.S. Dept. of Health and Human Services

(numbers in thousands)

	2005 No.	%	2010 No.	%	2011 No.	%	2012 No.	%	2013 No.	%	2014 No.	%
Used in lifetime												
Illicit drugs[1]	112,085	46.1	119,508	47.1	121,078	47.0	124,808	48.0	127,458	48.6	130,332	49.2
Illicit drugs other than marijuana[1]	71,822	29.5	76,203	30.0	75,447	29.3	78,034	30.0	78,076	29.8	80,119	30.2
Used in past month												
Illicit drugs[1]	19,720	8.1	22,622	8.9	22,454	8.7	23,863	9.2	24,573	9.4	26,983	10.2
Illicit drugs other than marijuana[1]	8,963	3.7	9,017	3.6	8,020	3.1	8,883	3.4	8,665	3.3	8,719	3.3
Used in past year												
Illicit drugs[1]	35,041	14.4	38,806	15.3	38,287	14.9	41,479	16.0	41,591	15.9	44,157	16.7
Marijuana and hashish	25,375	10.4	29,206	11.5	29,739	11.5	31,513	12.1	32,952	12.6	35,124	13.2
Illicit drugs other than marijuana[1]	20,109	8.3	20,576	8.1	18,959	7.4	21,267	8.2	19,868	7.6	19,719	7.4
Cocaine	5,523	2.3	4,499	1.8	3,857	1.5	4,671	1.8	4,182	1.6	4,553	1.7
Crack	1,381	0.6	871	0.3	625	0.2	921	0.4	632	0.2	773	0.3
Heroin	379	0.2	618	0.2	620	0.2	669	0.3	681	0.3	914	0.3
Hallucinogens	3,809	1.6	4,517	1.8	4,069	1.6	4,306	1.7	4,430	1.7	4,250	1.6
LSD	563	0.2	874	0.3	880	0.3	1,057	0.4	1,111	0.4	1,290	0.5
PCP	164	0.1	95	0.0	119	0.0	172	0.1	90	0.0	90	0.0
Ecstasy	1,960	0.8	2,645	1.0	2,422	0.9	2,610	1.0	2,588	1.0	2,342	0.9
Inhalants	2,187	0.9	2,030	0.8	1,861	0.7	1,693	0.7	1,533	0.6	1,617	0.6
Nonmedical use of psychotherapeutics[2]	15,346	6.3	16,031	6.3	14,657	5.7	16,666	6.4	15,348	5.8	14,966	5.6
Pain relievers	11,815	4.9	12,213	4.8	11,143	4.3	12,489	4.8	11,082	4.2	10,337	3.9
OxyContin®	1,226	0.5	1,869	0.7	1,623	0.6	1,477	0.6	1,442	0.5	1,237	0.5
Tranquilizers	5,249	2.2	5,581	2.2	5,109	2.0	6,073	2.3	5,269	2.0	5,202	2.0
Stimulants	3,088	1.3	2,887	1.1	2,700	1.0	3,317	1.3	3,492	1.3	3,715	1.4
Methamphetamine	NA	NA	959	0.4	1,033	0.4	1,155	0.4	1,186	0.5	1,301	0.5
Sedatives	750	0.3	907	0.4	526	0.2	590	0.2	639	0.2	775	0.3

NA = Not available. (1) Illicit drugs include marijuana/hashish, cocaine (including crack), heroin, hallucinogens, inhalants, or prescription-type psychotherapeutics used nonmedically. (2) Includes the nonmedical use of pain relievers, tranquilizers, stimulants, or sedatives but not over-the-counter drugs.

Lifetime Prevalence of Drug Use in 12th Graders, 1975-2015

Source: Monitoring the Future study, Univ. of Michigan Inst. for Social Research; Natl. Inst. on Drug Abuse, Natl. Insts. of Health

(percent who have ever used)

Drug	1975	1980	1985	1990	1995	2000	2005	2010	2011	2012	2013	2014	2015	2014-15 change
Any illicit drug[1]	55.2%	65.4%	60.6%	47.9%	48.4%	54.0%	50.4%	48.2%	49.9%	49.1%	49.8%	49.1%	48.9%	−0.1%
Marijuana/hashish	47.3	60.3	54.2	40.7	41.7	48.8	44.8	43.8	45.5	45.2	45.5	44.4	44.7	0.3
Inhalants[2]	—	17.3	18.1	18.5	17.8	14.6	11.9	9.0	8.1	7.9	6.9	6.5	5.7	−0.8
Nitrites	—	11.1	7.9	2.1	1.5	0.8	1.1	—	—	—	—	—	—	—
Hallucinogens[3]	—	15.6	12.1	9.7	13.1	13.6	9.3	8.6	8.3	7.5	7.6	6.3	6.4	0.0
LSD	11.3	9.3	7.5	8.7	11.7	11.1	3.5	4.0	4.0	3.8	3.9	3.7	4.3	0.6
PCP	—	9.6	4.9	2.8	2.7	3.4	2.4	1.8	2.3	1.6	1.3	—	—	—
Ecstasy (MDMA)	—	—	—	—	—	11.0	5.4	7.3	8.0	7.2	7.1	7.9	5.9	−2.0
Cocaine	9.0	15.7	17.3	9.4	6.0	8.6	8.0	5.5	5.2	4.9	4.5	4.6	4.0	−0.5
Crack	—	—	—	3.5	3.0	3.9	3.5	2.4	1.9	2.1	1.8	1.8	1.7	0.0
Heroin (with and without a needle)	2.2	1.1	1.2	1.3	1.6	2.4	1.5	1.6	1.4	1.1	1.0	1.0	0.8	−0.2
Narcotics other than heroin[4]	9.0	9.8	10.2	8.3	7.2	10.6	12.8	13.0	13.0	12.2	11.1	9.5	8.4	−1.0
Amphetamines[4]	22.3	26.4	26.2	17.5	15.3	15.6	13.1	11.1	12.2	12.0	13.8	12.1	10.8	−1.2
Methamphetamine	—	—	—	—	—	7.9	4.5	2.3	2.1	1.7	1.5	1.9	1.0	−0.9
Crystal meth	—	—	—	2.7	3.9	4.0	4.0	1.8	2.1	1.7	2.0	1.3	1.2	−0.1
Sedatives (barbiturates)[4]	18.2	14.9	11.8	7.5	7.6	9.3	11.0	7.5	7.0	6.9	7.5	6.8	5.9	−1.0
Methaqualone[4]	8.1	9.5	6.7	2.3	1.2	0.8	1.3	0.4	0.6	0.8	—	—	—	—
Tranquilizers[4]	17.0	15.2	11.9	7.2	7.1	8.9	9.9	8.5	8.7	8.5	7.7	7.4	6.9	−0.5
Alcohol	90.4	93.2	92.2	89.5	80.7	80.3	75.1	71.0	70.0	69.4	68.2	66.0	64.0	−2.0
Cigarettes	73.6	71.0	68.8	64.4	64.2	62.5	50.0	42.2	40.0	39.5	38.1	34.4	31.1	−3.3
Smokeless tobacco	—	—	—	—	30.9	23.1	17.5	17.6	16.9	17.4	17.2	15.1	13.2	−1.9
Steroids[4]	—	—	—	2.9	2.3	2.5	2.6	2.0	1.8	1.8	2.1	1.9	2.3	0.4

— = Not available. **Note:** Because of changes to question wording, some data may not be directly comparable to data from previous years. (1) Includes marijuana, LSD, other hallucinogens, crack, other cocaine, or heroin; or any use of narcotics other than heroin, amphetamines, sedatives (barbiturates), or tranquilizers not under a doctor's orders. (2) Not adjusted for underreporting of amyl and butyl nitrites. (3) Not adjusted for underreporting of PCP. (4) Includes only drug use not under a doctor's orders.

Cigarette Use in the U.S., 1985-2014

Source: National Survey on Drug Use and Health, Substance Abuse and Mental Health Services Admin. (SAMHSA), U.S. Dept. of Health and Human Services

(percentage of persons age 12 or older, unless otherwise noted, reporting use in the month prior to the survey)

	1985	2000	2005	2010	2012	2013	2014		1985	2000	2005	2010	2012	2013	2014
Total	38.7	24.9	24.9	23.0	22.1	21.3	20.8	**Race/Hispanic origin**							
Sex								White, not Hispanic	38.9	25.9	26.0	24.3	23.7	22.7	22.3
								Black, not Hispanic	38.0	23.3	24.5	22.6	23.0	23.0	22.5
Male	43.4	26.9	27.4	25.4	24.6	23.6	23.2	Hispanic, any race	40.0	20.7	22.1	20.1	16.8	16.8	16.7
Female	34.5	23.1	22.5	20.7	19.8	19.0	18.6	**Education[2]**							
Age								Non-HS graduate . .	37.3	32.4	34.8	34.3	33.7	33.6	31.2
12-17 years.	29.4	13.4	10.8	8.3	6.6	5.6	4.9	HS graduate	37.0	31.1	31.8	29.6	29.4	27.7	28.6
18-25 years.	47.4	38.3	39.0	34.2	31.8	30.6	28.4	Some college	32.6	27.7	28.1	25.8	25.5	25.5	24.8
26 years or older[1] . .	45.7	24.2	24.3	22.8	22.4	21.6	18.6	College graduate. . .	23.0	13.9	13.8	12.8	11.5	11.2	10.9

HS = High school. (1) Persons age 26 to 34 only in 1985. (2) Persons age 18 or older.

Daily Use of Cigarettes by 8th, 10th, and 12th Graders, 1995-2015

Source: Monitoring the Future study, Univ. of Michigan Inst. for Social Research; Natl. Inst. on Drug Abuse, Natl. Insts. of Health

(percent who smoked daily in last 30 days)

	8th grade						10th grade						12th grade					
	1995	2000	2005	2010	2015	% change, 2010-15	1995	2000	2005	2010	2015	% change, 2010-15	1995	2000	2005	2010	2015	% change, 2010-15
Total	9.3	7.4	4.0	2.9	1.3	−55.2%	16.3	14.0	7.5	6.6	3.0	−54.5%	21.6	20.6	13.6	10.7	5.5	−48.6%
Sex																		
Male	9.2	7.0	3.9	3.5	1.1	−68.6	16.3	13.7	7.2	7.2	2.8	−61.1	21.7	20.9	14.6	12.3	6.6	−46.3
Female	9.2	7.5	4.0	2.3	1.4	−39.1	16.1	14.1	7.7	5.9	2.8	−52.5	20.8	19.7	11.9	8.7	3.9	−55.2
College plans																		
None or under 4 yrs.	22.5	21.7	14.4	12.8	5.9	−53.9	32.7	28.8	19.2	19.1	10.8	−43.5	33.7	31.7	24.9	21.6	14.1	−34.7
Complete 4 yrs.	7.5	5.6	2.9	2.0	0.9	−55.0	13.3	11.6	5.9	5.0	2.0	−60.0	17.4	16.6	10.5	8.2	3.5	−57.3
Region																		
Northeast . . .	9.2	6.9	3.2	2.4	0.7	−70.8	15.8	14.1	7.6	5.7	2.7	−52.6	22.5	22.8	13.3	10.3	5.4	−47.6
Midwest	11.0	9.0	4.8	3.3	1.6	−51.5	17.6	16.3	8.6	7.3	2.8	−61.6	25.7	23.6	16.3	12.5	6.6	−47.2
South	9.4	7.8	5.0	3.8	1.5	−60.5	19.3	15.7	8.8	7.9	3.6	−54.4	21.7	19.4	15.4	12.3	6.1	−50.4
West	7.0	4.9	2.4	1.4	1.1	−21.4	9.4	7.8	4.0	4.4	2.3	−47.7	14.5	16.9	7.6	6.7	3.5	−47.8
Parental education[1]																		
Some HS or less	15.8	13.1	7.8	4.2	1.7	−59.5	20.0	18.9	9.9	10.0	5.2	−48.0	21.3	22.8	11.7	8.9	7.2	−19.1
Some or completed HS.	11.3	11.3	6.3	4.8	1.9	−60.4	21.6	17.6	11.1	10.1	4.6	−54.5	24.6	22.9	18.3	13.9	7.8	−43.9
Completed HS or some college. . . .	9.4	6.7	4.3	2.8	1.6	−42.9	17.0	14.2	7.9	7.1	3.4	−52.1	21.6	21.2	14.4	11.6	5.8	−50.0
Some or completed college. . . .	7.2	3.9	2.2	1.9	0.8	−57.9	12.6	11.5	5.2	3.9	2.1	−46.2	19.7	18.6	11.7	8.7	3.7	−57.5
Completed college or higher	5.7	4.1	1.4	1.0	0.4	−60.0	10.3	9.8	4.4	3.1	1.0	−67.7	18.5	15.2	8.1	6.1	3.1	−49.2
Race/Hispanic origin[2]																		
White	10.5	9.0	4.6	3.2	1.4	−56.3	17.6	17.7	9.1	7.4	3.5	−52.7	23.9	25.7	17.1	13.5	7.3	−45.9
Black.	2.8	3.2	2.1	1.9	0.9	−52.6	4.7	5.2	3.9	3.5	2.1	−40.0	6.1	8.0	5.6	5.3	4.1	−22.6
Hispanic	9.2	7.1	3.1	2.3	1.0	−56.5	9.9	8.8	5.9	4.4	2.1	−52.3	11.6	15.7	7.7	5.7	3.7	−35.1

HS = High school; **Note:** Figures may not add up to totals because of rounding. (1) Avg. highest level of education attained by respondent's mother and father. (2) For each of these groups, data for the specified year and previous year have been combined to increase sample size and thus provide more stable estimates.

Tobacco Use by High School and Middle School Students, 2015

Source: Centers for Disease Control and Prevention (CDC), U.S. Dept. of Health and Human Services

Between 2011 and 2015, high school and middle school students increased their current use of e-cigarettes and hookahs, but decreased use of more traditional products, such as cigarettes and cigars, resulting in no change in overall tobacco use. Use is defined here as use of a product on at least one day in the past 30 days.

	High school students using tobacco				Middle school students using tobacco			
Tobacco product	Female	Male	All students	Estimated no. of users[1]	Female	Male	All students	Estimated no. of users[1]
Electronic cigarettes	12.8%	19.0%	16.0%	2,390,000	4.8%	5.9%	5.3%	620,000
Cigarettes	7.7	10.7	9.3	1,370,000	2.2	2.3	2.3	260,000
Cigars	5.6	11.5	8.6	1,270,000	1.4	1.8	1.6	180,000
Hookah	6.9	7.4	7.2	1,040,000	2.0	1.9	2.0	220,000
Smokeless tobacco	1.8	10.0	6.0	900,000	1.1	—	1.8	210,000
Pipe tobacco.	0.7	1.4	1.0	150,000	—	—	0.4	40,000
Bidis	0.4	0.9	0.6	90,000	—	—	0.2	20,000
Any tobacco product use	20.3	30.0	25.3	3,820,000	6.4	8.3	7.4	880,000
2+ tobacco product use[2]	9.6	16.2	13.0	1,960,000	3.1	3.5	3.3	390,000

— = Not available. (1) Rounded down to nearest 10,000. (2) Use of two or more of the tobacco products listed here on at least one day in the past 30 days.

Alcohol Use by 8th and 12th Graders, 1980-2015

Source: Monitoring the Future study, Univ. of Michigan Inst. for Social Research; Natl. Inst. on Drug Abuse, Natl. Insts. of Health

	1980	1990	1995	2000	2005	2010	2012	2013	2014	2015	% change, 2014-15
Alcohol use[1]					Percent using in the month before the survey						
All 8th graders	—	—	24.6%	22.4%	17.1%	13.8%	11.0%	10.2%	9.0%	9.7%	7.8%
Male	—	—	25.0	22.5	16.2	13.2	10.3	9.3	8.2	9.1	11.0
Female	—	—	24.0	22.0	17.9	14.3	11.6	11.2	9.5	9.9	4.2
White..........	—	—	25.4	24.7	17.9	13.9	10.7	9.5	9.0	8.9	−1.1
Black..........	—	—	18.7	16.0	14.9	11.8	10.0	9.7	8.8	8.2	−6.8
Hispanic	—	—	32.4	26.7	20.6	18.1	17.5	14.3	11.2	10.4	−7.1
All 12th graders ...	72.0%	57.1%	51.3	50.0	47.0	41.2	41.5	39.2	37.4	35.3	−5.6
Male	77.4	61.3	55.7	54.0	50.7	44.2	43.8	41.8	37.4	36.0	−3.7
Female	66.8	52.3	47.0	46.1	43.3	37.9	38.8	36.3	37.1	35.0	−5.7
White..........	75.4	63.8	54.5	55.1	52.3	45.4	43.8	43.6	42.5	40.9	−3.8
Black..........	47.6	35.8	35.2	30.0	29.0	31.4	29.6	28.4	25.9	24.0	−7.3
Hispanic	63.6	49.1	48.7	51.2	43.3	40.1	39.8	39.0	37.0	36.3	−1.9
Heavy alcohol use[2]				Percent heavily using in the two weeks before the survey							
All 8th graders	—	—	12.3%	11.7%	8.4%	7.2%	5.1%	5.1%	4.1%	4.6%	12.2%
Male	—	—	12.5	11.7	8.2	6.5	4.6	4.5	3.5	4.6	31.4
Female	—	—	12.1	11.3	8.6	7.8	5.5	5.7	4.6	4.6	0.0
White..........	—	—	12.1	13.0	9.0	7.1	4.9	4.2	4.2	4.0	−4.8
Black..........	—	—	8.3	7.3	6.1	5.3	4.3	4.5	4.4	4.1	−6.8
Hispanic	—	—	18.4	16.0	12.1	10.8	9.9	7.8	5.7	5.4	−5.3
All 12th graders ...	41.2%	32.2%	29.8	30.0	27.1	23.2	23.7	22.1	19.4	17.2	−11.3
Male	52.1	39.1	36.9	36.7	32.6	28.0	27.2	26.1	22.3	19.3	−13.5
Female	30.5	24.4	23.0	23.5	21.6	18.4	19.7	18.1	16.6	14.9	−10.2
White..........	44.3	36.6	32.3	34.6	32.5	27.6	25.7	25.6	23.8	21.2	−10.9
Black..........	17.7	14.4	14.9	11.5	11.3	13.1	11.3	12.5	11.3	9.8	−13.3
Hispanic	33.1	25.6	26.6	31.0	23.9	22.1	21.8	22.4	20.4	18.5	−9.3

— = Not available. **Note:** To derive percentages for each race/ethnicity subgroup, data for the specified year and previous year have been combined to increase sample size and thus provide more stable estimates. (1) In 1993, the alcohol question was changed slightly to indicate that a "drink" is defined as "more than a few sips." (2) Five or more drinks in a row.

Acquired Immune Deficiency Syndrome (AIDS)

Source: Centers for Disease Control and Prevention (CDC), U.S. Dept. of Health and Human Services

AIDS (Acquired Immune Deficiency Syndrome) is caused by the human immunodeficiency virus (HIV). HIV kills or disables crucial immune cells, progressively destroying the body's ability to fight disease.

HIV is commonly spread through unprotected sexual contact with an infected partner's semen or vaginal fluids. It is also spread through contact with infected blood. Where modern screening techniques are used, it is rare to contract HIV from transfusion or organ/tissue transplants. But it can be contracted when intravenous drug users share syringes and similar equipment with others. A woman can also transmit HIV to her child during pregnancy or delivery or through breastfeeding. With treatment, a woman can reduce her transmission rate from about 20% to 1%-2%. There is no evidence HIV can spread through saliva or casual contact such as shaking hands or the sharing of food utensils, towels and bedding, or toilet seats.

Some people experience flu-like symptoms within a few weeks of being infected with HIV. Even when symptoms are not present, HIV is active in the body, multiplying, infecting, and killing crucial CD4+ T cells, also known as T-lymphocytes or T-helper cells, which signal other immune cells to perform their functions.

The term AIDS applies to the final stage of HIV infection. According to the official case definition issued by the CDC, an HIV-infected person with fewer than 200 CD4+ T cells per cubic millimeter of blood can be said to have AIDS. (Healthy adults usually have 500-1,600 per cubic millimeter.) An HIV-infected person, regardless of T cell count, can also be diagnosed with AIDS if he or she develops one of 20+ opportunistic illnesses that occur when the immune system is so ravaged by HIV that the body cannot fight off certain bacteria, viruses, and microbes.

Months or years prior to the onset of AIDS, people may experience such symptoms as swollen glands, lack of energy, fevers and sweats, and skin rashes. People diagnosed with AIDS may develop infections of the intestinal tract, lungs, brain, eyes, and other organs and become severely debilitated. They also are prone to developing certain cancers, such as Kaposi sarcoma, cervical cancer, and lymphoma. Children with AIDS may have delayed development or fail to thrive.

HIV is primarily detected by testing a person's blood for the presence of antibodies (disease-fighting proteins of the immune system) to HIV. In very rare cases, HIV antibodies may take more than six months after exposure to reach detectable levels. But in 97% of infected individuals, the antibodies are detectable in the first three months. Rapid HIV tests can provide preliminary results in 30 minutes or less. There are also two home HIV tests available.

Patients receiving antiretroviral (ARV) therapy typically take a combination of drugs. Taking more than one drug reduces the chance of the virus becoming resistant to any single one. While these drugs extend the period between HIV infection and the development of serious illness, they do not prevent the spread of the disease to others and can have severe side effects.

In 1987, a drug called zidovudine (commonly known as AZT) became the first approved treatment for HIV disease. Since then, the U.S. Food and Drug Administration has approved approximately 35 drugs to treat people living with HIV/AIDS. These drugs belong in different classes: Nucleoside Reverse Transcriptase Inhibitors (NRTIs), Non-Nucleoside Reverse Transcriptase Inhibitors (NNRTIs), Protease Inhibitors (PIs), Fusion Inhibitors, Entry Inhibitors, Integrase Inhibitors (INSTIs), and Pharmacokinetic Enhancers. Each class of drug attacks the virus at a different point in its life cycle. Patients generally take three different ARVs from two different classes.

There are also fixed-dose combinations of drugs. These are not a separate class of HIV medications but combinations of two or more medications, with specific fixed doses from one or more different classes, combined into a single pill.

Since there is no vaccine or cure for AIDS, the best way to prevent HIV is to avoid activities that carry a risk. The CDC recommends abstinence, mutual monogamy with an uninfected partner, limiting the number of sexual partners, never sharing needles, and using condoms correctly and consistently. Pre-exposure prophylaxis, or PrEP, is a prevention option for people who do not have HIV but are at high risk of getting HIV. It is meant to be used consistently, as a pill taken every day, and to be used with other prevention options. PrEP has been shown to greatly reduce the risk of HIV infection. PEP, or post-exposure prophylaxis, is the use of ARVs after a single high-risk event to stop HIV from making copies of itself and spreading throughout the body. PEP must be started no more than 72 hours after the exposure to HIV, and it is not always effective.

New AIDS Diagnoses in the U.S., by Transmission Category, 1985-2014

Source: *HIV Surveillance Report, 2014*; National Center for HIV/AIDS, Viral Hepatitis, STD, and TB Prevention; CDC

Transmission category	All years[1]	1985	1990	2000	2005	2010	2012	2013	2014
All males 13 years of age and older	954,875	7,504	36,193	30,251	27,436	21,161	19,324	19,130	15,624
Male-to-male sexual contact	586,385	5,348	23,658	13,648	16,824	14,448	13,664	13,785	11,277
Injection drug use	187,372	1,103	6,923	5,554	4,350	2,072	1,649	1,477	1,268
Male-to-male sexual contact and injection drug use	85,290	661	2,943	1,587	2,085	1,431	1,166	1,005	782
Heterosexual contact[2]	84,200	32	715	2,537	3,920	3,092	2,728	2,730	2,211
Other[3]	11,627	—	—	—	256	118	117	133	85
All females 13 years of age and older	246,372	524	4,547	9,979	9,799	7,105	6,353	6,075	5,168
Injection drug use	90,413	287	2,347	2,545	2,724	1,469	1,205	1,089	913
Heterosexual contact[2]	149,980	119	1,538	4,025	6,856	5,502	5,039	4,839	4,150
Other[3]	5,979	—	—	—	219	133	109	147	106
All children, under 13 years of age	9,588	—	—	—	55	21	10	8	104
Perinatal	8,715	—	—	—	50	15	8	8	92
Other[3]	874	—	—	—	5	6	2	0	12

— = Not available. **Note:** Table shows diagnoses of persons with an HIV infection at stage 3 (AIDS). The definition of AIDS cases for reporting purposes was expanded in 1985, 1987, and 1993. The 2008 HIV case definitions were used to classify cases diagnosed in 2010-13; the 2014 definitions were used to classify 2014 cases. (1) Includes number of diagnoses for years not shown, from the beginning of the epidemic (1981) through 2014. (2) Heterosexual contact with a person known to have or be at high risk for HIV infection. (3) Includes hemophilia, blood transfusion, perinatal exposure (for persons 13 and older), and risk factor not reported or not identified.

New HIV Diagnoses in the U.S., 2010-14

Source: National Center for HIV/AIDS, Viral Hepatitis, STD, and TB Prevention; Centers for Disease Control and Prevention (CDC)

Characteristic	Number of diagnoses					Diagnoses per 100,000 resident pop.				
	2010	2011	2012	2013	2014	2010	2011	2012	2013	2014
All persons	44,940	43,510	43,165	42,566	44,073	14.5	14.0	13.7	13.4	13.8
Male, 13 years and over	34,871	34,146	34,259	34,034	35,571	27.9	27.0	26.9	26.4	27.4
Female, 13 years and over	9,831	9,166	8,656	8,340	8,328	7.5	6.9	6.5	6.2	6.1
Age diagnosed										
Under 13 years	238	198	250	191	174	0.4	0.4	0.5	0.4	0.3
13-14 years	43	45	46	43	35	0.5	0.5	0.6	0.5	0.4
15-19 years	2,118	2,068	1,964	1,792	1,828	9.6	9.5	9.2	8.5	8.7
20-24 years	7,245	7,311	7,489	7,483	7,868	33.4	33.0	33.1	32.7	34.3
25-29 years	6,520	6,563	6,777	7,151	7,870	30.8	30.8	31.7	33.1	35.8
30-34 years	5,639	5,455	5,729	5,574	6,026	28.1	26.6	27.4	26.2	28.0
35-39 years	5,171	4,622	4,374	4,288	4,662	25.8	23.6	22.4	21.8	23.4
40-44 years	5,361	4,971	4,646	4,257	4,196	25.6	23.6	22.1	20.4	20.4
45-49 years	4,972	4,758	4,527	4,268	4,021	22.0	21.5	20.8	20.1	19.3
50-54 years	3,602	3,487	3,377	3,235	3,242	16.1	15.4	14.9	14.3	14.4
55-59 years	2,132	2,072	2,019	2,184	2,166	10.8	10.2	9.7	10.3	10.1
60-64 years	1,091	1,111	1,106	1,170	1,069	6.4	6.2	6.2	6.5	5.8
65 years and over	810	848	861	930	914	2.0	2.0	2.0	2.1	2.0
Hispanic origin/race										
Not Hispanic or Latino										
White	12,135	11,738	11,752	11,581	12,025	6.1	5.9	5.9	5.9	6.1
Black	20,987	20,064	19,581	19,252	19,540	55.2	52.3	50.5	49.2	49.4
Amer. Indian or Alaska Native	177	163	193	186	222	7.8	7.1	8.4	8.0	9.5
Asian	727	802	848	859	1,046	4.9	5.3	5.4	5.3	6.2
Native Hawaiian or other Pac. Islander	58	58	60	56	58	11.7	11.4	11.6	10.6	10.6
Multiple race	1,565	1,456	1,358	1,246	982	27.7	25.0	22.6	20.1	15.4
Hispanic or Latino, any race	9,291	9,230	9,372	9,386	10,201	18.3	17.8	17.7	17.3	18.4

Note: Data shown are for the 50 states and DC. They are estimates of the min. number of persons for whom HIV infection has been diagnosed (during 2010-14) and reported to the CDC as of July 31, 2015. Totals were calculated independent of subpopulation values; therefore, sums of values may not equal totals. Because of a change in case definition, HIV diagnoses prior to 2014 are not strictly comparable to those in 2014.

U.S. Deaths of Persons With HIV Ever Classified as AIDS, 1981-2013

Source: *HIV Surveillance Report, 2014*; National Center for HIV/AIDS, Viral Hepatitis, STD, and TB Prevention; CDC

Age at death	Number	% of total	Transmission category	Number	% of total
Under 13 years	4,998	0.7%	Male adult or adolescent	547,251	81.3%
13-14 years	296	0.0	Male-to-male sexual contact	317,564	47.1
15-19 years	1,318	0.2	Injection drug use	132,455	19.7
20-24 years	9,967	1.5	Male-to-male sexual contact and		
25-29 years	47,389	7.0	injection drug use	51,413	7.6
30-34 years	102,708	15.2	Heterosexual contact[2]	36,648	5.4
35-39 years	129,198	19.2	Perinatal	419	0.1
40-44 years	123,245	18.3	Other[3]	8,751	1.3
45-49 years	96,371	14.3	Female adult or adolescent	121,289	18.0
50-54 years	66,507	9.9	Injection drug use	57,596	8.6
55-59 years	41,777	6.2	Heterosexual contact[2]	59,511	8.8
60-64 years	24,673	3.7	Perinatal	527	0.1
65 years and over	25,091	3.7	Other[3]	3,656	0.5
Race/ethnicity			Child (under 13 years old at death)	4,998	0.7
American Indian/Alaska Native	1,919	0.3	Perinatal	4,534	0.7
Asian[1]	3,462	0.5	Other[3]	464	0.1
Black/African American	277,059	41.1	**Region of residence**		
Hispanic/Latino (any race)	103,819	15.4	Northeast	211,694	31.4
Native Hawaiian/other Pac. Islander	361	0.1	Midwest	68,733	10.2
White	274,206	40.7	South	260,531	38.7
Multiple races	12,710	1.9	West	132,529	19.7
			Total[4]	673,538	

Note: Deaths of persons with diagnosed HIV infection may be due to any cause. Number of deaths are cumulative from the beginning of the epidemic, in 1981. Figures are estimated and calculated independently, so they may not add up to totals. (1) Includes "Asian/Pacific Islander" legacy cases. (2) Heterosexual contact with a person known to have or to be at high risk for HIV infection. (3) Includes hemophilia, blood transfusion, and risk factor not reported or not identified.

Allergies and Asthma

Source: Asthma and Allergy Foundation of America

An estimated one in five Americans suffers from allergies. People with allergies have immune systems that overreact to a foreign protein substance ("allergen") that is eaten, breathed into the lungs, injected, or touched. Common allergens include plant pollens, dust mites, or animal dander; plants such as poison ivy; certain drugs, such as penicillin; and foods such as eggs, milk, wheat, nuts, or seafood.

The tendency to develop allergies is usually inherited. While allergies typically manifest in childhood, they can show up at any age. Food allergies and eczema (patches of dry skin) are common allergies among infants. Older children and adults may develop allergic rhinitis, or hay fever, in reaction to an inhaled allergen. Allergic rhinitis symptoms include nasal congestion, runny nose, and sneezing.

People with allergies should avoid contact with an allergen, if feasible. Medications, such as antihistamines and nasal steroids, may be used to decrease an allergic reaction. Other effective allergy treatments include decongestants, eye drops, and ointments. There are also treatments aimed at gradually desensitizing a patient to an allergen.

Some allergy sufferers also have asthma. Asthma, which can develop at any age, is a chronic inflammation disease affecting the passageways that carry air into and out of the lungs. About 24 mil Americans have asthma. During an asthma attack, these symptoms are exacerbated. The airways narrow even more and fill with mucus. A person may experience wheezing, difficulty breathing, tightening of the chest, and coughing. Exposure to an allergen can set off an attack. Asthma can become life-threatening if not controlled in its early stages. The following symptoms may be indicative of an emergency: the patient shows no improvement minutes after initial treatment; struggles to breathe while hunched over with chest and neck pulled in; has trouble walking or talking; and develops gray or blue lips or fingernails.

Tobacco smoke, cold air, and expressing strong emotion can also trigger an asthma attack, as can respiratory infections or physical exercise. An accurate diagnosis by a physician is important. Although there is no cure for asthma or allergies, they can be controlled through lifestyle changes and medications (including quick-relief and long-term control).

Website: www.aafa.org

Persons With Asthma, 2014

Source: National Health Interview Survey, Centers for Disease Control and Prevention, U.S. Dept. of Health and Human Services

	Number (thous.)	Percent
Total	24,009	7.7%
Child (under age 18)	6,292	8.6
Adult	17,717	7.4
Age		
0-4 years	849	4.3
5-14 years	4,244	10.3
15-19 years	1,912	9.1
20-24 years	1,890	8.9
25-34 years	3,133	7.5
35-64 years	8,897	7.3
65+ years.................	3,084	6.9
Sex		
Males....................	9,659	6.3
Under age 18............	3,770	10.1
Age 18 and over..........	5,889	5.1
Females..................	14,350	9.0
Under age 18............	2,522	7.0
Age 18 and over..........	11,828	9.6
Race/ethnicity		
White, non-Hispanic......	14,852	7.6
Black, non-Hispanic.......	3,760	9.9
Other non-Hispanic	1,746	7.0
Hispanic (any race)	3,651	6.7
Puerto Rican	817	16.5
Mexican/Mexican American . .	1,952	5.7

Note: Includes only those with a current diagnosis of asthma. Numbers may not add up to totals due to rounding.

Alzheimer's Disease

Source: Alzheimer's Association

Alzheimer's disease, the most common form of dementia, is a progressive, degenerative brain disease in which nerve cells deteriorate and die. The most common early symptom is forgetting newly learned information. As the disease advances, it leads to disorientation and mood/behavior changes; confusion about events, time, and place; suspicions about family, friends, and caregivers; more serious memory loss; and difficulty speaking, swallowing, and walking.

The rate of progression of Alzheimer's varies, ranging from 4 to 20 years. The average length of time from onset of symptoms until death is eight years. As they become progressively debilitated, affected individuals grow increasingly susceptible to infections of the lungs, urinary tract, and other organs.

Alzheimer's disease affects an estimated 5.4 mil Americans, striking men and women of all races and ethnicities. Almost two-thirds of all Americans living with Alzheimer's are women. Although most people are older than age 65 when diagnosed with Alzheimer's, younger-onset, or early-onset, cases occur in people in their 40s and 50s. An estimated 11% of the U.S. population over age 65 and 32% over age 85 have Alzheimer's.

Diagnosis involves a comprehensive evaluation that may include a complete health history, physical examination, neurological and mental status assessments, and other tests. Skilled health care professionals can generally diagnose Alzheimer's with more than 90% accuracy. Depression, drug interactions, nutritional imbalances, and infections such as AIDS, meningitis, and syphilis can cause similar symptoms. Other forms of dementia, such as those associated with Huntington's disease, Parkinson's disease, frontotemporal dementia, and vascular disease, can also appear to be Alzheimer's. Absolute confirmation of a diagnosis requires a brain biopsy or autopsy.

Treatments for cognitive and behavioral symptoms are available, but no intervention has yet been developed to prevent Alzheimer's or reverse its course. The U.S. Food and Drug Administration has approved six drugs that temporarily slow worsening of symptoms for about six to twelve months. They are effective for only about half of the individuals who take them. Some research suggests that risk factors for heart disease, such as high blood pressure, elevated cholesterol, diabetes, and excess body weight, may increase a person's risk of developing Alzheimer's. Staying physically and mentally active and socially connected may be associated with a lower risk for the disease.

Providing care for people with Alzheimer's is physically and psychologically demanding. About 60%-70% of affected individuals live at home, where family or friends tend to them without pay. In the disease's advanced stages, many individuals require long-term residential care. Nearly half of all nursing home residents in the U.S. have Alzheimer's.

The U.S. cost of diagnosing, treating, and providing long-term care for Alzheimer's patients is estimated to be $236 bil in 2016. People with Alzheimer's need a safe, stable environment and a regular daily schedule offering appropriate stimulation. Physical exercise and social interaction are important, as are proper nutrition and adequate pain management. Security is also a consideration, because many people with Alzheimer's tend to wander. An identification bracelet with the person's name, address, and condition can help ensure the safe return of an individual who wanders.

Website: www.alz.org

Warning Signs of Alzheimer's Disease

- Memory loss that disrupts daily life
- Challenges in planning or solving problems
- Difficulty completing familiar tasks at home, at work, or at leisure
- Confusion with time or place
- Trouble understanding visual images and spatial relationships
- New problems with words in speaking or writing
- Misplacing things and losing the ability to retrace steps
- Decreased or poor judgment
- Withdrawal from work or social activities
- Changes in mood and personality

Arthritis

Source: Arthritis Foundation; Centers for Disease Control and Prevention (CDC), U.S. Dept. of Health and Human Services

The term arthritis refers to more than 100 different diseases that cause pain, aching, stiffness, and swelling in or around the joints. The condition is usually chronic. The CDC estimates that nearly 53 mil adults in the United States report being told by a doctor that they have arthritis. There were an estimated 100 mil ambulatory care visits in 2010 and an estimated 6.7 mil hospitalizations in 2011 with a principal diagnosis of arthritis and other rheumatic conditions. The cause for most types of arthritis is unknown; scientists are studying the roles played by genetics, lifestyle, and environment.

Symptoms may develop gradually or suddenly. A visit to the doctor is indicated when pain, stiffness, swelling in a joint, or difficulty in moving a joint persists for three days or more. To diagnose arthritis, the doctor records the patient's symptoms and examines his or her joints, looking for any swelling or limited movement. In addition, the doctor checks for other signs often seen with arthritis, such as rashes, mouth sores, or eye involvement. The doctor may test blood, urine, or joint fluid, or take X-rays of the joints.

Of the three most prevalent forms of arthritis, **osteoarthritis** is the most common, affecting approximately 31 mil Americans. It usually occurs after age 40. In patients with osteoarthritis, also called degenerative arthritis, the protective cartilage of joints is lost and changes occur in the bone, leading to pain and stiffness. The joints most commonly affected are the lower back, hips, knees, hands, and feet.

Fibromyalgia, another common arthritis condition, affects about 5 mil Americans. People suffering from fibromyalgia experience widespread pain, abnormal pain processing, sleep disturbance, fatigue, and psychological distress. Other symptoms include morning stiffness, tingling or numbness in hands and feet, headaches, or problems with thinking and memory. More women than men are afflicted with this type of arthritis.

Rheumatoid arthritis, which affects an estimated 1.5 mil in the U.S., is one of the most serious and disabling forms of the disease. In this type—which is also more common and more degenerative in women—inflammation of the joints leads to cartilage and bone damage. The hands, wrists, feet, knees, ankles, and elbows can be affected.

Other forms of arthritis and related conditions include lupus, gout, psoriatic arthritis, and Sjögren's syndrome. Bursitis and tendinitis, which may result from injuring or overusing a joint, are also related.

Medications that relieve pain and swelling, such as analgesics, anti-inflammatory drugs, biologic response modifiers, glucocorticoids, and antirheumatic drugs, can be used to treat arthritis. They also tend to slow the disease process. Most treatment programs call for exercise, use of heat or cold, and joint-protection techniques, such as avoidance of excess stress on the joints, the use of assistive devices, and weight loss and control. In some cases, surgery may help.

Website: www.arthritis.org

Attention Deficit Hyperactivity Disorder (ADHD)

Source: Centers for Disease Control and Prevention; Natl. Institute of Mental Health

Attention deficit hyperactivity disorder, or ADHD, is one of the most common neurodevelopmental disorders of childhood. It is usually first diagnosed in childhood and often lasts into adulthood. Children with ADHD may have trouble paying attention, controlling impulsive behaviors, or be overly active.

Signs and Symptoms of ADHD

- Daydreaming a lot
- Forgetting or losing things a lot
- Squirming or fidgeting
- Talking too much
- Making careless mistakes or taking unnecessary risks
- Having a hard time resisting temptation or taking turns
- Having difficulty getting along with others

There are three different types of ADHD, depending on which types of symptoms are strongest in the individual. A person who is **predominantly inattentive** is easily distracted or forgets details of daily routines. Someone who is **predominantly hyperactive-impulsive** may fidget and talk a lot and find it hard to sit still for long. In the third type, **combined presentation**, the individual displays symptoms of the first two types equally. The cause of ADHD is unknown, but current research shows that genetics plays an important role.

The average age of onset is 7 years old. ADHD affects about 4.1% of American adults age 18 years and older in a given year. The disorder affects 9% of American children age 13 to 18 years. Boys are four times more at risk than girls. Studies show that the number of children being diagnosed with ADHD is increasing, but it is unclear why. Rates of ADHD diagnosis increased an average of 3% per year from 1997 to 2006 and an average of 5% per year from 2003 to 2011. In addition, a 2013 survey found that in 2011, 11% of children aged 4-17 years had ever received an ADHD diagnosis and that 8.8% currently had ADHD.

In most cases, ADHD is treated with a combination of medication and behavior therapy. Stimulants are the most widely used medication. Nonstimulants, approved for treating ADHD in 2003, have fewer side effects than stimulants and can last up to 24 hours.

Breast Cancer

Source: American Cancer Society, Inc.

In 2016, an estimated 246,660 women and 2,600 men in the U.S. will be newly diagnosed with breast cancer, and about 40,450 women and 440 men will die from it. In 2016, more than 3.5 mil women were living with a history of breast cancer, the second biggest cause of cancer death for women in the U.S. (lung cancer ranks first). But mortality rates have been declining, especially among younger women, probably because of earlier detection and improved treatment.

The risk for breast cancer increases with age. It is higher for women with a personal or family history of cancer (particularly breast cancer), a long menstrual history (menstrual periods that started early and ended later in life), physical inactivity, recent use of birth control pills, use of menopausal hormone therapy containing estrogen and progestin, and in those who have no children or had no live birth until age 30 or older. Other risk factors include alcohol consumption and being overweight or obese. Inherited mutations such as in the BRCA1 and BRCA2 genes greatly increase risk, but these probably account for 5% to 10% of all breast cancers. By far the majority of women who develop breast cancer have no family history of it.

Breast cancer often manifests first as an abnormality on a mammogram X-ray. Physical symptoms that show up later, which may be detectable by a woman or her doctor, include a breast lump and, less commonly, persistent changes to the breast, such as thickening, swelling, distortion, tenderness, skin irritation, redness, scaliness, or nipple abnormalities, such as ulceration, retraction, or spontaneous discharge. Breast pain is more likely to be caused by benign conditions and is not a common early symptom of breast cancer.

Studies show that early detection increases survival and treatment options. Although most detected breast lumps are noncancerous, any suspicious lump should be biopsied.

Treatment for breast cancer may involve breast-conserving surgery (removal of the tumor and surrounding tissue), mastectomy (surgical removal of the breast), radiation therapy, chemotherapy, hormone therapy, and/or targeted therapy. The five-year survival rate for female invasive breast cancer patients has improved from 75% in the mid-1970s to 89% today. The five-year survival for women diagnosed with localized breast cancer (cancer that has not spread to lymph nodes or other locations outside the breast) is 99%.

Website: www.cancer.org

Prostate Cancer

Source: Prostate Cancer Foundation; American Cancer Society, Inc.

The prostate is a male gland located between the bladder and scrotum that secretes seminal fluid. Prostate cancer is the most common non-skin cancer in the U.S., and the second-most common cause, after lung cancer, of cancer deaths in American men. In 2016, an estimated 180,890 men will be diagnosed with prostate cancer, and about 26,120 will die from the disease. An estimated 3.3 mil men in the U.S. were living with a history of prostate cancer at the start of 2016.

The exact cause of prostate cancer is unknown. The most identifiable risk factors are age, family history, and race. About 6 in 10 cases of prostate cancer are diagnosed in men 65 years of age and older, and the chances of developing the disease rise dramatically with age. Having a single first-degree relative with a history of prostate cancer more than doubles a man's risk of developing the disease, and those with several affected relatives have a much higher risk. African-American men are much more likely to develop prostate cancer than non-Hispanic white men and are more than twice as likely to die from it. The cause for this disparity remains unclear.

Usually, the disease has no symptoms in its early stages. As the disease advances, a man may experience weak or interrupted urine flow; inability to urinate or difficulty starting or stopping the urine flow; the need to urinate frequently, especially at night; blood in the urine; or pain or burning with urination. Advanced prostate cancer commonly spreads to the bones, which can cause pain in the hips, spine, ribs, or other areas.

The American Cancer Society recommends that once they reach 50, men at average risk of prostate cancer should speak with their health care provider about the benefits and limitations of prostate-specific antigen (PSA) testing. African-American men or those with a family history of the disease should be aware of their screening options beginning at age 40 or 45. Men under 40 seldom get prostate cancer.

Prostate cancer treatment may include surgery, radiation, hormonal therapy, chemotherapy, or some combination. If caught early on, while tumor cells are localized within the prostate, the five-year relative survival rate approaches 100%.

Websites: www.pcf.org; www.cancer.org

Skin Cancer

Source: American Cancer Society, Inc.

Skin cancer is generally divided into two main classes, **nonmelanomas** and **melanomas**, affecting different types of skin cells. Melanoma is the most dangerous type of skin cancer because it can easily spread to other parts of the body. Although skin cancer is the most common type of cancer diagnosed in the U.S., melanoma accounts for less than 2% of all skin cancers. The exact causes of melanoma are unclear, but risk factors include overexposure to UV light, multiple or unusual moles, fair skin, family or personal history of skin cancers, history of severe sunburns, and occupational exposure to certain compounds.

Melanomas generally look like abnormal moles on the surface of the skin. Abnormal moles differ from regular skin cells and may be a sign of skin cancer. An irregular mole should be examined by a doctor as soon as possible.

If caught early, melanoma is highly curable. The overall five-year survival rate for melanoma is 92%. For localized melanoma, the five-year survival rate is 98%; survival rates for regional and distant stage diseases are 63% and 17%, respectively. About 84% of melanomas are diagnosed at a localized stage.

Treatment may include simple removal of the melanoma; amputation if the cancer is found on a finger or toe; or chemotherapy, immunotherapy, and/or radiation if the melanoma has spread to other parts of the body.

Warning Signs of Abnormal Moles

- **A**symmetry: one half does not match the other half
- **B**order: edges are irregular, ragged, notched, or blurred
- **C**olor: not uniform; may be shades of brown or black, and patches of pink, red, blue, or white
- **D**iameter: moles wider than ¼ inch are abnormal (however, melanomas can be smaller)
- **E**volving: mole changes size, shape, or color

Website: www.cancer.org

Cancer Risk Factors

Source: American Cancer Society, Inc., www.cancer.org

Alcohol: Alcohol consumption increases the risk of cancers of the mouth, pharynx, larynx, esophagus, liver, colorectum, breast, and possibly pancreas. Alcohol consumption combined with tobacco use increases the risk of cancers of the mouth, pharynx, larynx, and esophagus far more than either drinking or smoking alone.

Diet and physical activity: Overweight and obesity are associated with increased risk for developing many cancers, including cancers of the breast in postmenopausal women, colon and rectum, endometrium, kidney, pancreas, and esophagus. Overweight and obesity may also be associated with increased risk of aggressive prostate cancer, non-Hodgkin lymphoma, multiple myeloma, and cancers of the liver, cervix, ovary, and gallbladder. It's not yet known for certain how diet, nutrition intake, and the amount and distribution of body fat factor into the development of certain cancers.

Environmental hazards: Exposure to various chemicals (including benzene, asbestos, vinyl chloride, arsenic, and aflatoxin) increases risk of various cancers. Risk of lung cancer from asbestos is greatly increased among smokers.

Estrogen: Menopausal hormone therapy (MHT, formerly called hormone replacement therapy) without the use of progestin can increase the risk of endometrial and ovarian cancer. Combining progestin with estrogen MHT may help minimize that risk. Studies, however, suggest that use of MHT increases the risk of breast cancer. The benefits and risks of the use of estrogen should be discussed carefully with one's doctor.

HPV infection: There are three vaccines (Gardasil, Gardasil 9, and Cervarix) approved for use in females ages 9-26 for the prevention of the most common types of HPV infection that cause cervical cancer. Gardasil and Gardasil 9 are also approved for use in males ages 9-26 for the prevention of anal and penile cancers, and the prevention of anal, vaginal, and vulvar cancers (and precancers) in women.

Radiation: Excessive exposure to ionizing radiation can increase cancer risk. Medical and dental X-rays are adjusted to deliver the lowest dose possible without sacrificing image quality. Excessive radon exposure in the home may increase lung cancer risk, especially in cigarette smokers.

Smokeless tobacco: Use of chewing tobacco, snuff, snus, and other tobacco products that are not smoked causes oral, esophageal, stomach, and pancreatic cancers. The excess risk of cancer of the cheek and gum is especially high among long-term snuff users.

Smoking: The risk of developing lung cancer is about 25 times higher for current male smokers and nearly 26 times higher for current female smokers than for those who have never smoked. Tobacco use is responsible for 30% of all cancer deaths and about 80% of lung cancer deaths in the U.S. Smoking increases the risk of the following types of cancer: lung, larynx, oral cavity, nose and sinuses, pharynx, esophagus, stomach, pancreas, cervix, kidney, bladder, ovary, colorectum, and acute myeloid leukemia.

Sunlight: Many of the 5.4 mil skin cancers diagnosed annually in the U.S. could have been prevented by protection from the sun's rays and avoiding indoor tanning. Epidemiological evidence shows that sun exposure is a major factor in the development of melanoma and that incidence rates are increasing worldwide.

Screening Guidelines for Early Detection of Cancer

Cancer site	Population	Test or procedure	Frequency
Breast	Women, age 40+	Mammography	The American Cancer Society no longer recommends regular breast self-exams or clinical breast exams; research has not found that they reduce the risk of dying from breast cancer. Women should be familiar with how their breasts look and feel and report any changes to a health care professional. At age 40: begin annual mammography if desired. For ages 45-54: annual mammograms. For ages 55-74: mammograms every two years or yearly. There is currently insufficient evidence for the benefits of screening at age 75 and older; women in good health with at least a 10-year life expectancy can choose to continue screening.
Cervix	Women, ages 21-65	Pap test, HPV DNA test	All women should begin screening at age 21. Women ages 21-29 should have a Pap test every 3 years. For ages 30-65, the preferred screening method is a Pap test combined with an HPV test every 5 years. Another option is to get a Pap test alone every 3 years. Women age 65 or over who have had regular screenings in the previous 10 years and no serious precancers in the past 20 should consult a physician; health history may allow them to stop cervical cancer screening. Women who have had a total hysterectomy may stop screening. Women should not be screened annually by any method at any age.
Colorectal	Men and women, age 50+	High-sensitivity guaiac-based fecal occult blood test (FOBT) **or** high-sensitivity fecal immunochemical test (FIT) **or**	Annual, starting at age 50, for people with average risk. Testing at home with adherence to manufacturer's recommendation for collection techniques and number of samples is recommended. An FOBT or FIT done with a stool sample collected during a digital rectal examination in a health care setting is not sufficient for screening.
		Stool DNA test (sDNA), **or**	Every 3 years, starting at age 50.
		Flexible sigmoidoscopy (FSIG), **or**	Every 5 years, starting at age 50. FSIG can be performed alone, or consideration can be given to performing a high-sensitivity FOBT or FIT every three years when done in combination with FSIG.
		Double contrast barium enema (DCBE), **or**	Every 5 years, starting at age 50.
		CT colonography, **or**	Every 5 years, starting at age 50.
		Colonoscopy	Every 10 years, starting at age 50. A colonoscopy should also be done if any of the above tests is positive.
Endometrial	Women, at menopause	Women at average risk should be informed about risks and symptoms of endometrial cancer and strongly encouraged to report any unexpected bleeding or spotting to their physicians.	
Lung	Current or former smokers, ages 55-74	Low dose CT scan (LDCT)	Apparently healthy patients with a history of heavy smoking (at least one pack per day over 30 years, or two packs per day over 15 years, etc.), whether they currently smoke or have quit within the past 15 years, should discuss with a clinician the potential benefits, limitations, and harms associated with lung-cancer screening.
Prostate	Men, age 50+	Digital rectal examination (DRE) and prostate-specific antigen test (PSA)	Men should talk with their health care provider at age 50 about whether to be screened for prostate cancer given the potential benefits, risks, and uncertainties associated with screening. African Americans—who have a higher rate of prostate cancer—should have this talk at age 45. Men with a close relative who had prostate cancer before age 65 should also have this talk at age 45; those with two or more such close relatives should have the talk at age 40.

New U.S. Cancer Cases and Deaths for Leading Sites, 2016

Source: *Cancer Facts & Figures 2016*, American Cancer Society, Inc.

The following estimates exclude basal cell and squamous cell skin cancers, also referred to as nonmelanoma skin cancers, and in situ carcinomas (i.e., noninvasive cancers), except of the urinary bladder. In 2016, an estimated 61,000 cases of carcinoma in situ of the female breast and 68,480 cases of melanoma in situ are expected to be diagnosed. An est. 5.4 mil cases of basal cell and squamous cell skin cancer were diagnosed among 3.3 mil people in 2012, according to a recent study.

Estimated New Cases

Both sexes		Male		Female	
Breast	249,260	Prostate	180,890	Breast	246,660
Lung and bronchus	224,390	Lung and bronchus	117,920	Lung and bronchus	106,470
Prostate	180,890	Colon and rectum	70,820	Colon and rectum	63,670
Colon and rectum	134,490	Urinary bladder	58,950	Uterine corpus	60,050
Urinary bladder	76,960	Melanoma—skin	46,870	Thyroid	49,350
Melanoma—skin	76,380	Non-Hodgkin lymphoma	40,170	Non-Hodgkin lymphoma	32,410
Non-Hodgkin lymphoma	72,580	Kidney and renal pelvis	39,650	Melanoma—skin	29,510
Thyroid	64,300	Oral cavity and pharynx	34,780	Leukemia	26,050
Kidney and renal pelvis	62,700	Leukemia	34,090	Pancreas	25,400
Leukemia	60,140	Liver and intrahepatic bile duct	28,410	Kidney and renal pelvis	23,050
All sites	**1,685,210**	**All sites**	**841,390**	**All sites**	**843,820**

Estimated Deaths

Both sexes		Male		Female	
Lung and bronchus	158,080	Lung and bronchus	85,920	Lung and bronchus	72,160
Colon and rectum	49,190	Prostate	26,120	Breast	40,450
Pancreas	41,780	Colon and rectum	26,020	Colon and rectum	23,170
Breast	40,890	Pancreas	21,450	Pancreas	20,330
Liver and intrahepatic bile duct	27,170	Liver and intrahepatic bile duct	18,280	Ovary	14,240
Prostate	26,120	Leukemia	14,130	Uterine corpus	10,470
Leukemia	24,400	Esophagus	12,720	Leukemia	10,270
Non-Hodgkin lymphoma	20,150	Urinary bladder	11,820	Liver and intrahepatic bile duct	8,890
Urinary bladder	16,390	Non-Hodgkin lymphoma	11,520	Non-Hodgkin lymphoma	8,630
Brain and other nervous system	16,050	Brain and other nervous system	9,440	Brain and other nervous system	6,610
All sites	**595,690**	**All sites**	**314,290**	**All sites**	**281,400**

U.S. Cancer Survival Rates by Year of Diagnosis, 1960-2012
Source: SEER (Surveillance, Epidemiology, and End Results) Cancer Statistics Review 1975-2013, National Cancer Institute, National Institutes of Health

Year of diagnosis	All races % total	All races % male	All races % female	White % total	White % male	White % female	Black % total	Black % male	Black % female
1960-63	—	—	—	39%	—	—	27%	—	—
1970-73	—	—	—	43	—	—	31	—	—
1975-77	48.9%	41.7%	55.9%	49.8	42.7%	56.5%	39.0	32.7%	46.2%
1978-80	49.0	43.1	54.9	50.0	44.3	55.6	39.0	33.3	45.6
1981-83	50.2	45.2	55.1	51.3	46.6	56.0	38.8	34.2	44.4
1984-86	52.4	47.2	57.6	53.6	48.6	58.5	40.2	35.5	45.5
1987-89	55.3	51.1	59.6	56.7	52.8	60.6	43.0	38.9	47.7
1990-92	59.9	59.1	60.9	61.4	60.8	62.0	47.8	47.6	48.2
1993-95	61.3	60.8	61.8	62.4	62.0	62.8	52.8	54.4	50.6
1996-98	63.3	63.0	63.6	64.3	64.0	64.7	55.2	57.9	52.1
1999-2001	66.0	66.3	65.7	67.2	67.5	66.8	57.9	61.0	54.3
2002-05	67.2	67.8	66.6	68.5	69.0	67.9	59.5	63.2	55.5
2006-12	69.0	69.3	68.6	70.0	70.3	69.7	62.7	65.6	59.5

— = Statistic could not be calculated. **Note:** The geographic areas of surveillance may vary for different years. Rates are five-year relative (estimated) survival rates for all invasive cancer sites; based on follow-up of patients into 2013.

U.S. Cancer Survival Rates by Age at Diagnosis, 2006-12
Source: SEER (Surveillance, Epidemiology, and End Results) Cancer Statistics Review, 1975-2013, National Cancer Institute, National Institutes of Health

Age at diagnosis	All races % total	All races % male	All races % female	White % total	White % male	White % female	Black % total	Black % male	Black % female
Under age 45..........	82.0%	77.4%	84.9%	83.5%	79.2%	86.3%	71.2%	65.7%	74.4%
Ages 45-54	73.8	68.6	78.2	75.1	69.6	79.7	64.6	63.3	65.8
Ages 55-64	70.5	70.1	70.9	71.4	70.8	72.1	63.7	66.2	59.8
Under age 65..........	73.8	70.9	76.7	74.9	71.8	78.0	65.3	65.3	65.4
Ages 65-74	66.7	69.5	62.7	67.2	69.7	63.7	61.3	66.6	53.4
Ages 65 and older	59.5	63.3	55.0	59.9	63.3	56.0	54.5	61.5	46.4
Ages 75 and older	51.6	55.1	48.3	52.2	55.1	49.4	44.2	51.3	38.5

Note: Rates are five-year relative (estimated) survival rates for all invasive cancer sites; based on follow-up of patients into 2013.

Depression
Source: National Institute of Mental Health (NIMH), National Institutes of Health, U.S. Dept. of Health and Human Services

Depression is a serious illness that affects thoughts, feelings, and the ability to function in everyday life. It strikes all age groups and often goes unrecognized or is inadequately treated. The NIMH estimates that in 2014, about 15.7 mil adults age 18 and older (or 6.7% of the adult population) in the U.S. had at least one major depressive episode. Over the same 12-month period, 9.3% of persons aged 18 to 25 years experienced at least one major depressive episode versus 5.2% of those 50 or older. More women than men reported suffering from major depression, with 8.2% of women and 4.8% of men having experienced a major depressive episode in 2014.

Available treatments can alleviate symptoms, and with awareness growing, more people with depression are seeking help. But many depressed people—and those around them—still fail to realize that they have an illness or could benefit from medical help.

Symptoms and Types of Depression
- Persistent sad, anxious, or "empty" feelings
- Feelings of hopelessness or pessimism
- Feelings of guilt, worthlessness, or helplessness
- Irritability, restlessness
- Loss of interest in activities or hobbies once pleasurable, including sex
- Fatigue and decreased energy
- Difficulty concentrating, remembering, or making decisions
- Insomnia, early-morning wakefulness, or excessive sleeping
- Overeating or appetite loss
- Thoughts of suicide or suicide attempts
- Aches or pains, headaches, cramps, or digestive problems that do not ease even with treatment

A diagnosis of **major depressive disorder** (or **clinical depression**) is made if an individual reports experiencing five or more of these symptoms in the same two-week period.

Bipolar disorder (or **manic-depressive illness**) is a distinct illness from depression. But it is characterized by episodes of major depression alternating with periods of mania, when a person experiences a persistent, abnormally elevated mood, accompanied by feelings of inflated self-esteem, less need for sleep, increased talkativeness, racing thoughts, distractibility, agitation, and excessive involvement in pleasurable activities that have a high potential for painful consequences.

Treatments for Depression
A variety of medicines are used to treat depression. These drugs influence the functioning of certain neurotransmitters in the brain, primarily serotonin and norepinephrine. Older drugs—tricyclic antidepressants (TCAs) and monoamine oxidase inhibitors (MAOIs)—affect the functioning of both of these neurotransmitters. But they can have strong side effects or, in the case of MAOIs, require dietary restrictions. Newer medications, such as selective serotonin reuptake inhibitors (SSRIs), have fewer side effects.

NIMH research has shown that certain types of psychotherapy, particularly cognitive-behavioral therapy (CBT) and interpersonal therapy (IPT), can help relieve depression. CBT helps patients change the negative thinking and behaving patterns often associated with depression. IPT focuses patients on working through personal relationships that may contribute to depression. Studies of adults have shown that a combination of psychotherapy and antidepressant medication is most effective in treating moderate-to-severe depression.

Electroconvulsive therapy (ECT) has been found effective in treating some cases of severe depression, particularly those that have not responded to other forms of treatment. ECT involves producing a seizure in the brain of a patient under general anesthesia by applying electrical stimulation through electrodes placed on the scalp. Memory loss and other cognitive problems, though common side effects, are typically short-lived.

Website: www.nimh.nih.gov

Diabetes

Source: American Diabetes Association; Centers for Disease Control and Prevention, U.S. Dept. of Health and Human Services

Diabetes is a chronic disease in which the body does not produce or properly use the hormone **insulin**. Insulin is needed to convert sugar, starches, and other foods into energy. Both genetics and environment appear to play roles in the onset of diabetes. This disease, which has no cure, was the seventh leading cause of death in the U.S. in 2014, with 76,488 deaths (2.9% of total deaths). In 2012, the most recent year for which figures are available, an est. 29.1 mil Americans had diabetes, 8.1 mil of whom were undiagnosed.

The American Diabetes Association supports studies proving that detection at an earlier stage and modest lifestyle changes, such as eating better and exercising more, will help prevent or delay complications.

There are two major types of diabetes:

Type 1 (formerly known as insulin-dependent or juvenile diabetes). The body does not produce insulin; the disease is usually diagnosed in children and young adults. People with type 1 diabetes must take daily insulin to stay alive.

Type 2 (formerly known as non-insulin dependent or adult-onset diabetes). The body does not produce enough or cannot properly use insulin. It is the most common form of the disease (90%-95% of diabetes cases in people over age 20) and often begins later in life.

Prediabetes

In 2012, 86 mil Americans age 20 and older had prediabetes, the state that occurs when a person's blood glucose levels are higher than normal but not high enough for a diagnosis of diabetes. According to the Centers for Disease Control and Prevention, 15%-30% of people with prediabetes will develop type 2 diabetes within five years unless lifestyle changes are made.

Complications From Diabetes

People often have diabetes for many years before it is diagnosed. During that time, serious complications may develop. Potential complications include the following:

Blindness. Diabetes is the leading cause of new cases of blindness in people ages 20-74. Each year, 12,000 to 24,000 people lose their eyesight because of diabetes.

Kidney disease. About 30% of patients with type 1 diabetes and 10%-40% of those with type 2 diabetes eventually suffer from kidney failure. In 2011, a total of 49,677 people in the U.S. initiated treatment for kidney failure due to diabetes.

Amputations. Diabetes is the most frequent cause for nontraumatic lower-limb amputations. The risk of a leg amputation is 15-40 times greater for a person with diabetes than for the average American. In 2010, approximately 73,000 lower-limb amputations were performed as a result of complications brought on by diabetes.

Heart disease and stroke. People with diabetes are about 1.7 times more likely to die of heart disease. They are 1.5 times more likely to suffer a stroke.

Common Diabetes Symptoms

- Frequent urination
- Thirst
- Hunger
- Extreme fatigue
- Blurry vision
- Cuts/bruises that are slow to heal
- Weight loss, even with increased caloric intake (type 1)
- Tingling, pain, or numbness in the hands/feet (type 2)

Gestational Diabetes

Gestational diabetes is a form of diabetes that affects about 18% of pregnant women. Usually there are no symptoms, or the symptoms are mild. Because the condition usually appears around the 24th week, it is recommended that all pregnant women receive a glucose tolerance test between the 24th and 28th week. Pregnancy hormones can cause insulin resistance, making blood glucose levels rise. The goal of treatment is to keep blood glucose levels within normal limits, mainly through diet and exercise; treatment may also include daily blood glucose testing and insulin injections. Women with gestational diabetes tend to have larger babies at birth, which can increase the chance of problems at the time of delivery. Glucose levels usually return to normal after delivery, but odds of recurrence in future pregnancies and development of type 2 diabetes later in life increase.

Website: www.diabetes.org

Eating Disorders

Source: National Institute of Mental Health, National Institutes of Health, U.S. Dept. of Health and Human Services

Eating disorders involve serious disturbances in eating behavior, usually in the forms of extreme and unhealthy reduction of food intake or severe overeating. They are not due to a lifestyle choice or a failure of will; rather, they are real and treatable medical illnesses in which certain behavior patterns get out of control. The main types are anorexia nervosa, bulimia nervosa, and binge-eating disorder (technically categorized with "eating disorders not otherwise specified"). These disorders usually develop in adolescence or early adulthood and often occur with other illnesses such as depression, substance abuse, and anxiety disorders. They are much more common among females; about 5%-10% of anorexia patients, 20% of bulimia patients, and 40% of binge eaters are male.

If not treated, eating disorders can lead to serious complications, including heart conditions and kidney failure, which may result in death.

Anorexia nervosa affects an estimated 0.6% of the U.S. adult population and 0.9% of all females. Symptoms include resistance to maintaining weight at minimally healthy levels, intense fear of gaining weight, exaggerated importance of body weight or shape in one's self image, and infrequent or absent menstrual periods. Anorexics see themselves as overweight even when they are dangerously thin. In response, they avoid food and take other extreme measures to lose weight, such as exercising compulsively or purging by means of vomiting or laxatives and enemas. While some anorexics fully recover after a single episode, others may relapse frequently or experience chronic deterioration.

Bulimia nervosa affects an estimated 0.6% of the U.S. adult population. It is characterized by recurrent uncontrolled binge-eating episodes followed by what is believed to be compensatory behavior to prevent weight gain, such as self-induced vomiting, use of laxatives or diuretics, exercising excessively, or fasting. Persons with bulimia can weigh within the normal range for their age and height, but they still fear gaining weight and are intensely dissatisfied with their bodies. They often perform their behaviors in secret, feeling shame when they binge and relief when they purge.

Binge-eating disorder affects an estimated 2.8% of the U.S. adult population. As with bulimia, a binge-eating disorder involves episodes of excessive eating during which the sufferer may feel a complete lack of control. But individuals with this disorder do not compensate by purging, exercising, or fasting. Many are thus overweight or obese, and the shame they feel can lead to further binge-eating.

Eating disorder sufferers may not admit they are ill. Early diagnosis and a comprehensive treatment program are essential to recovery. Some patients may need immediate hospitalization. For anorexia, treatment usually follows three established steps: weight restoration, usually in an inpatient hospital setting; treatment of any accompanying psychological disturbances, including the use of medications; and achieving long-term remission or recovery by reducing or eliminating negative thoughts and behaviors.

Heart and Blood Vessel Disease

Source: American Heart Assn.; Natl. Ctr. for Chronic Disease Prevention and Health Promotion, Centers for Disease Control and Prevention; Natl. Heart, Blood, and Lung Inst., Natl. Insts. of Health, U.S. Dept. of Health and Human Services

Warning Signs of Heart Attack

- Chest discomfort. Most heart attacks involve discomfort in the center of the chest that lasts more than a few minutes or that goes away and then returns. It can feel like uncomfortable pressure, squeezing, fullness, or pain.
- Discomfort in other areas of the upper body. Symptoms can include pain or discomfort in one or both arms, the back, neck, jaw, or stomach.
- Shortness of breath. This feeling may occur with or without chest discomfort.
- Other signs may include breaking out in a cold sweat, nausea, or lightheadedness.

The American Heart Association advises immediate action at onset of symptoms, as more than half of heart attack victims die within an hour of symptoms first manifesting. Call 9-1-1. Get to a hospital right away.

Warning Signs of Stroke

- Sudden numbness or weakness of the face, arm, or leg, especially on one side of the body.
- Sudden confusion, trouble speaking, or understanding.
- Sudden trouble seeing in one or both eyes.
- Sudden trouble walking, dizziness, loss of balance or coordination.
- Sudden severe headache with no known cause.

Prompt treatment of a stroke can be a major factor in controlling the effects. If you have one or more stroke symptoms that last more than a few minutes, call 9-1-1 or the emergency medical service number immediately so an ambulance, ideally one with advanced life support, can be sent for you quickly.

Major Modifiable Risk Factors

High blood pressure. High blood pressure, or hypertension, increases the risk of stroke, heart attack, kidney failure, and congestive heart failure. It affects men and women of all races, ethnic origins, and ages. Obesity, physical inactivity, and an unhealthy diet can contribute to this often symptomless disease. Individuals should have a blood pressure reading at least once every two years or more often if advised by a physician.

A blood pressure reading consists of two measurements, with one value written above the other, such as 122/78 mmHg (millimeters of mercury). The upper number (systolic pressure) represents the amount of pressure in the arteries when the heart contracts (beats) and pushes blood through the circulatory system. The lower number (diastolic pressure) represents the pressure in the arteries between beats, when the heart is resting. According to National Institutes of Health (NIH) guidelines, a blood pressure reading below 120/80 is considered normal, while readings from 120/80 to 139/89 are considered prehypertension.

There are two stages of high blood pressure:
Stage 1 is 140-159 (systolic) over 90-99 (diastolic);
Stage 2 is 160+ (systolic) over 100+ (diastolic).

The diagnosis can be based on either the systolic or the diastolic reading.

High blood pressure usually cannot be cured, but it can be controlled in a variety of ways, including lifestyle modifications and medication. Treatment always should be at the direction and under the supervision of a physician. The treatment goal for patients with hypertension is blood pressure below 140/90. Individuals with hypertension and diabetes or chronic kidney disease should aim for blood pressure lower than 130/80.

High blood cholesterol. Cholesterol is a waxy fat-like substance found in all cells of the body. It is produced by the body and also comes in some foods. The body needs some cholesterol, but excess levels increase the risk of heart disease. High cholesterol in itself usually does not cause symptoms, so many people are unaware that they have a problem.

There are two major kinds of cholesterol: LDL (low-density lipoprotein), often called "bad" cholesterol, leads to narrowing of the arteries. HDL (high-density lipoprotein), known as "good" cholesterol, helps reduce that risk.

NIH guidelines classify total cholesterol levels (determined by a blood test) of less than 200 mg/dl as desirable, 200-239 as borderline high, and 240 and higher as high. About 13% of Americans have a cholesterol level of 240 mg/dl or higher. LDL levels of less than 100 mg/dl are considered optimal, 130-159 as borderline high, 160-189 as high, and 190 and higher as very high. For HDL, levels of 60 mg/dl and higher are considered protective against heart disease, while levels under 40 mg/dl are considered a risk factor.

As with high blood pressure, high blood cholesterol can be controlled by lifestyle changes and medication and should be treated by a physician.

Triglycerides, another form of fat in the blood, can also raise the risk of heart disease. Levels that are borderline high (150-199 mg/dl) or high (200 or more) may need treatment.

Diabetes. Diabetes is a major risk factor for heart disease; at least 65% of people with diabetes mellitus die of some form of heart disease or stroke.

Smoking. Cigarette smokers are two to four times more likely to develop coronary heart disease (CHD). Smoking is also associated with the risk of sudden cardiac death.

Obesity. Using a body mass index (BMI) of 25 and higher for overweight and 30 and higher for obesity, about 70% of Americans aged 20 and over are either overweight or obese, and about 36% are obese.

Physical inactivity. A sedentary lifestyle is a risk factor for CHD. The risk increase is comparable to that observed for high blood cholesterol, high blood pressure, or cigarette smoking.

Women and Cardiovascular Disease

The American Heart Association reports that heart disease, stroke, and other cardiovascular diseases are the number one cause of death in American women. (Cancer is the second leading cause.) Nearly one in three women died of some form of cardiovascular disease in 2013. Because heart disease was long viewed as a "man's" disease, many of the major cardiovascular studies were conducted only on men. Recent attention has been directed toward understanding the influence of gender on cardiovascular disease risk and prevention, but important gaps in knowledge remain.

Women often present some of the same classic symptoms of heart attack as men, such as chest pain that spreads to the shoulders and arms. But women may more often report atypical chest pain, abdominal pain, difficulty breathing (dyspnea), nausea/vomiting, and back or jaw pain. Another problem in **diagnosis** is that women tend to have heart attacks later in life than men, so symptoms may be masked by other age-related diseases such as arthritis or osteoporosis. Even certain diagnostic tests and procedures such as the exercise stress test may not be as accurate in women, with the result that the disease process leading to heart attack or stroke may not be detected early on, with potentially serious consequences.

Website: www.heart.org

Common Infectious Diseases

Source: National Institutes of Health, Centers for Disease Control and Prevention, U.S. Dept. of Health and Human Services; World Health Organization

The following is a list of major infectious diseases. It is meant to be used for reference purposes only and not as a tool for diagnosis. Statistics may appear uneven because of the different reporting methods used by the various agencies and because not all diseases are surveyed in the same year.

Chicken pox

(*Varicella simplex*) Usually nonthreatening viral disease commonly associated with children. In adults, the disease can be serious. **Transmission:** highly contagious. Transmitted by direct contact with rash, coughing, or sneezing of infected persons. **Symptoms:** blister-like rash, discomfort, high fever. Infected people may develop shingles later in life. **Vaccine:** available since 1995. **Treatment:** none; antibiotics in some severe cases. **Annual U.S. cases:** before 1995, about 4 mil, mostly children; 13,447 reported in 2012.

Chlamydia

(*Chlamydia trachomatis*) One of the most widely spread sexually transmitted diseases (STDs). **Transmission:** sexually transmitted. **Symptoms:** about 70% of those infected show no symptoms. In women, vaginal discharge, infection of the cervix and urinary tract; can cause pelvic inflammatory disease. In men, infection of urinary tract and epididymitis (inflammation of testicular duct); can also infect the throat, rectum, and eyes. **Treatment:** curable with antibiotics. **Annual U.S. cases:** 1,441,789 in 2014.

Common cold

(More than 200 different viruses) An upper respiratory viral infection. **Transmission:** touching one's nose, eyes, or mouth after touching something contaminated by the virus; inhalation of airborne virus. **Symptoms:** irritated nose or scratchy throat, sneezing and watery green or yellow nasal discharge, coughing, muscle aches, headaches, postnasal drip, decreased appetite. **Treatment:** no cure. Over-the-counter remedies can relieve symptoms; effectiveness of antiviral drugs uncertain. **Est. annual U.S. cases:** about 1 bil.

Gonorrhea

(*Neisseria gonorrhoeae*) Common bacterial STD. **Transmission:** sexually transmitted. **Symptoms:** in men, discomfort in urethra, yellow or green discharge, burning during urination. In women, pelvic pain, bleeding associated with intercourse, burning during urination, yellow or bloody discharge. **Treatment:** highly curable with antibiotics. **Annual U.S. cases:** 350,062 in 2014.

Hepatitis

A viral disease that causes inflammation of the liver. In the U.S., five forms are endemic: A, B, C, D, and E. Forms A, B, and C are the most common. **Symptoms:** all forms have generally similar symptoms including jaundice, fatigue, abdominal pain, loss of appetite, nausea, mild flu-like symptoms. Many cases cause no symptoms. In extreme cases, liver transplants may be necessary.

Hepatitis A (*Hepatovirus picornaviridae*). **Transmission:** consuming food or water contaminated with feces from infected persons. **Vaccine:** effective; travelers are advised to not drink tap water in countries where disease is common. **Treatment:** disease usually resolves on its own; alcohol consumption should be avoided. **Est. annual U.S. cases:** 2,500 infections in 2014; 1,239 acute lab-confirmed cases reported in 2014.

Hepatitis B (*Orthohepadnavirus hepadnaviridae*). **Transmission:** unsterilized needle sharing; contaminated blood transfusions; sexual contact. **Vaccine:** highly effective. **Treatment:** for chronic cases, drug treatment is necessary. For acute cases, disease usually resolves itself. Severe cases treated with lamivudine. **Est. annual U.S. cases:** 19,200 infections in 2014; 2,953 acute lab-confirmed cases reported in 2014.

Hepatitis C (*Hepacivirus flavinviridae*). **Transmission:** unsterilized needle sharing; contaminated blood transfusions; sexual contact. **Vaccine:** none. **Treatment:** chronic cases treated with drugs, which eliminates virus in about 50% of patients. For acute cases, treatment recommended if disease

present after two to three months. **Est. annual U.S. cases:** 30,500 infections in 2014; 2,194 acute lab-confirmed cases reported in 2014.

HPV

(More than 100 strains of human papillomavirus) Common viral infection; leading cause of cervical cancer. **Transmission:** sexually transmitted. **Symptoms:** most of those infected have no symptoms but can still transmit virus. In some cases, genital warts and precancerous bumps on anus, cervix or vulva, or penis. **Vaccine:** Gardasil and Cervarix. **Treatment:** while there is no cure, a healthy immune system can usually fight off HPV on its own. Women with HPV should have a Pap smear and pelvic exam every six months. **Est. annual U.S. cases:** 14 mil new cases; approximately 79 mil currently infected with HPV.

Influenza

(Various influenza viruses) Highly contagious viral respiratory infection. **Transmission:** airborne; contact with face after touching infected surface. **Symptoms:** chills, fatigue, fever, headaches, sore throat, sinus congestion, coughing. ("Stomach flu" is not influenza.) **Vaccine:** yearly vaccinations recommended; available as injection or nasal spray. **Treatment:** antiviral drugs; disease normally runs its course in a matter of days. **Est. annual U.S. cases:** 5%-20% of population; more than 200,000 flu-related hospitalizations, 3,000-49,000 flu-related deaths depending on severity of season.

Lyme disease

(*Borrelia burgdorferi*) Bacterial inflammatory disease, first identified 1975 in Old Lyme, CT. Concentrated heavily in the Northeast and upper Midwest U.S. usually in areas with large deer populations. **Transmission:** bite from infected blacklegged (or deer) tick. Mice and deer are most common tick hosts. **Symptoms:** mimic those of other diseases. Flu-like symptoms: fatigue, stiff neck, joints. Skin rash may appear at site of tick bite. **Treatment:** antibiotics in early stages; anti-inflammatory drugs to relieve symptoms. Without treatment, long-term complications (some fatal) involving joints, heart, and nervous system. **Annual U.S. cases:** from 9,895 reported cases in 1992 to 25,359 confirmed and 8,102 probable cases in 2014.

Malaria

(*Plasmodium* parasite) Infectious disease known from as early as 2700 BCE. Virtually eradicated in developed countries; still a major killer in tropical regions. **Transmission:** bite from infected mosquito. **Symptoms:** high fever, shaking chills, heavy sweating, headaches, fatigue, enlarged spleen. If left untreated, organ damage and death. **Treatment:** antimalarial drugs, including chloroquine, for treatment and prevention. **Annual cases:** 1,727 (2 congenital) in the U.S. in 2013; worldwide in 2013, an estimated 198 mil cases and 584,000 deaths, mostly young children in sub-Saharan Africa.

Measles

(*Rubeola* virus) Once-common viral infection; occurs sporadically in U.S. **Transmission:** airborne transmission by infected persons. **Symptoms:** itchy and raised rash, sore throat, cough, pink eye, high fever. In rare cases, encephalitis, seizures, permanent deafness, death. **Vaccine:** highly effective. **Treatment:** no specific treatment; symptoms relieved with bed rest, acetaminophen, humidified air. **Annual U.S. cases:** 188 in 2015.

Mumps

(Mumps virus) Acute and contagious viral infection. **Transmission:** direct contact with mucus or saliva of infected persons. **Symptoms:** painful, visible swelling of the salivary or parotid glands in the face. Chills, headaches, fever, painful swallowing. In some cases, inflammation of testes, pancreas, ovaries. In severe cases, brain swelling and symptoms ranging from nausea and drowsiness to seizures and permanent deafness. **Vaccine:** MMR (measles, mumps, and rubella) vaccine is effective. **Treatment:** no specific treatment; symptoms may be relieved by applying ice or heat to swollen glands. **Annual U.S. cases:** 1,223 in 2014.

Peptic ulcer

(Most from *Helicobacter pylori* [*H. pylori*] bacteria; also overuse of aspirin or other anti-inflammatory drugs) Weakening of the stomach's protective mucous coating, allowing stomach acid and bacteria to irritate stomach lining. **Transmission:** *H. pylori* may be transmitted through food and water. **Symptoms:** indigestion; bloating; dull, transient abdominal pain or discomfort; nausea; vomiting. **Treatment:** antibiotics, acid-suppressing drugs. **Est. annual U.S. cases:** about 20% of the population under 40 years of age and half of those over 60 may be infected with *H. pylori*. An estimated 500,000 to 850,000 develop peptic ulcers each year.

Pertussis or Whooping cough

(*Bordetella pertussis* or *B. parepertussis*) Upper respiratory bacterial infection. **Transmission:** airborne transmission by infected persons; highly contagious. **Symptoms:** initially, mild cold-like symptoms, fever, diarrhea, difficulty breathing; later, violent coughing with characteristic "whooping" sound when patient tries to breathe between coughs, vomiting. In severe cases, apnea, pneumonia, seizures, encephalopathy. **Vaccine:** available as part of Tdap (tetanus, diphtheria, pertussis) combination vaccine. **Treatment:** antibiotics in early cases; otherwise, disease must run its course. **Annual U.S. cases:** 32,971 in 2014.

Salmonella or Salmonellosis

(*Salmonella enteritidis*) Bacterial infection. **Transmission:** eating foods contaminated by feces carrying the bacteria or eating undercooked meats or raw eggs contaminated by bacteria. Contact with feces of infected animal or pet. **Symptoms:** fever, diarrhea, abdominal cramps 12 to 72 hours after infection. **Treatment:** no standard treatment. Runs its course in four to seven days. Antibiotics in severe cases. **Annual U.S. cases:** 47,735 lab-confirmed infections in 2013.

Shigellosis

(Four species of *Shigella*: *boydii*, *dysenteriae*, *flexneri*, and *sonnei*) Bacterial infection and a form of dysentery, an intestinal disease. **Transmission:** consuming food contaminated by infected feces or eating vegetables grown in fields containing contaminated sewage. Swimming in contaminated water. **Symptoms:** watery or bloody diarrhea one to four days after infection, high fever, vomiting, painful bowel movements. In extreme cases, seizures in children, intestinal perforation. **Treatment:** mild infection allowed to run its course; replacement of fluids and salts lost through excessive diarrhea. Antibiotics in severe cases. Although severe

diarrhea is symptomatic, antidiarrheal medicines may make illness worse. **Annual U.S. cases:** 12,729 in 2013.

Syphilis

(*Treponema pallidum*) Bacterial infection known since ancient times that spread rampantly throughout Europe in the Middle Ages. **Transmission:** sexually transmitted. **Symptoms:** primary stage: painless sore, called a chancre, where bacteria enters the body; usually heals in 3 to 12 weeks with or without treatment. Without treatment, disease enters secondary stage: skin rash as chancre is healing or weeks after it is healed. Without treatment, enters tertiary stage: mouth sores, fever, fatigue, loss of appetite, weight loss, hair loss, jaundice, syphilitic meningitis, aortal aneurysms, lesions, damage to nervous system, heart, and eyes. Most infected do not progress beyond primary or secondary stage. **Treatment:** curable with antibiotics (mostly penicillin). **Annual U.S. cases:** 63,450 (19,999 primary and secondary) in 2014.

Tetanus or Lockjaw

(*Clostridium tetani*) Bacterial infection. **Transmission:** bacteria, found in soil, entering body through broken skin. **Symptoms:** muscle stiffness and spasms or "locking" of muscles of the jaw, neck, and limbs. **Vaccine:** four forms of immunization. **Treatment:** tetanus immune globulin to fight infection. With treatment, less than 10% of cases are fatal. **Annual U.S. cases:** 25 in 2014.

Tuberculosis

(*Mycobacterium tuberculosis*) Bacterial infection that primarily affects the lungs. **Transmission:** airborne transmission by persons with active TB infection. **Symptoms:** weight loss, fever, cough with discharge (sometimes with bloody sputum), night sweats, growing shortness of breath over time, chest pains. **Vaccine/treatment:** BCG (Bacille Calmette Guerin) vaccine only effective in protecting young children and used where TB is prevalent. Not recommended by health experts for use in the U.S. because of the low risk of infection and its variable effectiveness. **Annual U.S. cases:** 9,421 in 2014.

Yellow fever

(Yellow fever virus, in *flavivirus* group) Viral infection endemic in tropical areas of Africa and Central and South America. **Transmission:** bite from mosquito carrying the virus. **Symptoms:** headaches, muscle aches, fever, jaundice (yellowing skin), nausea and vomiting, kidney failure, severe generalized pain. In severe cases, shock, coma, and death. **Vaccine:** available, safe, and effective. **Treatment:** symptoms treated until disease runs its course. **Annual cases:** none in the U.S.; an estimated 200,000 new cases and 30,000 deaths worldwide.

U.S. Reported Cases and Deaths From Vaccine-Preventable Diseases, 1950-2013

Source: Centers for Disease Control and Prevention, U.S. Dept. of Health and Human Services

Year	Diphtheria Cases	Diphtheria Deaths	Tetanus Cases	Tetanus Deaths	Pertussis Cases	Pertussis Deaths	Polio (paralytic) Cases	Polio (paralytic) Deaths	Measles Cases	Measles Deaths	Mumps Cases	Mumps Deaths	Rubella Cases	Rubella Deaths
1950	5,796	410	486	336	120,718	1,118	33,300	1,904	319,124	468	NR		NR	
1960	918	69	368	231	14,809	118	3,190	230	441,703	380	NR	42	NR	12
1970	435	30	148	79	4,249	12	33	7	47,351	89	104,953	16	56,552	31
1980	3	1	95	28	1,730	11	9	2	13,506	11	8,576	2	3,904	1
1990	4	1	64	11	4,570	12	6	0	27,786	64	5,292	1	1,125	8
2000	1	0	35	5	7,867	12	0	0	86	1	338	2	176	0
2001	2	0	37	5	7,580	17	0	0	116	1	266	0	23	2
2002	1	0	25	5	9,771	18	0	0	44	0	270	1	18	0
2003	1	1	20	4	11,647	11	0	0	56	1	231	0	7	0
2004	0	0	34	4	25,827	16	0	0	37	0	258	0	10	1
2005	0	0	27	1	25,616	31	1[1]	0	66	NA	314	0	11	0
2006	0	0	41	4	15,632	9	0	0	55	0	6,584	1	11	0
2007	0	0	28	5	10,454	9	0	0	43	0	800	0	11	1
2008	0	0	19	3	13,278	20	0	0	140	0	454	2	16	0
2009	0	0	18	6	16,858	15	1[1]	0	71	NA	1,991	2	3	2
2010	0	0	26	3	27,550	26	0	0	63	NA	2,612	2	5	2
2011	0	NA	36	NA	18,719	NA	0	NA	220	NA	404	NA	4	NA
2012	1	NA	37	NA	48,277	NA	0	NA	55	NA	229	NA	9	NA
2013	0	NA	26	NA	28,639	NA	1[1]	NA	187	NA	584	NA	9	NA

NA = Not available. NR = Not nationally reportable. (1) Vaccine-associated/derived paralytic polio.

Dietary Requirements

The Food and Nutrition Board of the National Academy of Sciences' Health and Medicine Division, in reports published between 1997 and 2010, established **Dietary Reference Intakes (DRIs)**. DRIs establish daily consumption values for vitamins and elements (often called minerals) that aim to optimize health, not just guard against nutritional deficiencies, at all stages of life.

There are four DRI categories. The **Recommended Dietary Allowance (RDA)** gives intake values that meet the nutrient requirements of almost all (97%-98%) healthy individuals in a specified group. The **Estimated Average Requirement (EAR)** specifies the average daily nutrient intake level estimated to meet the requirement of half the healthy individuals in a specified group. **Adequate Intake (AI)** values are given when there is inadequate scientific evidence to calculate an RDA. For healthy breastfed infants, the AI is the mean intake; for other life stage groups, the AI is thought to cover the needs of all group individuals, but lack of data or uncertainty in the data prevents the percentage of individuals covered from being specified with confidence. The **Tolerable Upper Intake Level (UL)** designates the maximum intake amount that is unlikely to pose a risk of adverse health effects in almost all healthy individuals in a group. RDAs and AIs may both be used as individual intake goals.

Estimated Calorie Requirements

Source: *2015-2020 Dietary Guidelines for Americans*, U.S. Dept. of Agriculture and U.S. Dept. of Health and Human Services

Estimated amount of calories, rounded to the nearest 200, needed to maintain energy balance by sex, for various age groups and levels of physical activity. In adults, calorie needs generally decrease with age.

	Age (years)	Sedentary[1]	Moderately active[2]	Active[3]		Age (years)	Sedentary[1]	Moderately active[2]	Active[3]
Female[4]	2-3	1,000	1,000-1,200	1,000-1,400	Male	2-3	1,000	1,000-1,400	1,000-1,400
	4-8	1,200-1,400	1,400-1,600	1,400-1,800		4-8	1,200-1,400	1,400-1,600	1,600-2,000
	9-13	1,400-1,600	1,600-2,000	1,800-2,200		9-13	1,600-2,000	1,800-2,200	2,000-2,600
	14-18	1,800	2,000	2,400		14-18	2,000-2,400	2,400-2,800	2,800-3,200
	19-30	1,800-2,000	2,000-2,200	2,400		19-30	2,400-2,600	2,600-2,800	3,000
	31-50	1,800	2,000	2,200		31-50	2,200-2,400	2,400-2,600	2,800-3,000
	51+	1,600	1,800	2,000-2,200		51+	2,000-2,200	2,200-2,400	2,400-2,800

Note: Based on Estimated Energy Requirements (EER) equations, using reference heights (average) and reference weights (healthy) for each age-sex group. For children and adolescents, reference height and weight vary. For adults, the reference man is 5 ft 10 in. tall and weighs 154 lbs. The reference woman is 5 ft 4 in. tall and weighs 126 lbs. (1) Engaging only in the light activities associated with ordinary day-to-day life. (2) Includes physical activity equivalent to walking 1.5-3 mi per day at 3-4 mph. (3) Includes physical activity equivalent to walking more than 3 mi per day at 3-4 mph. (4) Excludes women who are pregnant or breastfeeding.

Understanding Food Components

Proteins, composed of amino acids, are essential to good nutrition. They build, maintain, and repair the body. Best sources: eggs, milk, fish, meat, poultry, soybeans, nuts. High-quality proteins such as eggs, milk, or fish supply all eight amino acids needed in a diet. Plant-sourced foods can be combined to meet protein needs as well.

Fats provide energy by furnishing calories to the body. They also help the body absorb vitamins A, D, E, and K. Best sources of polyunsaturated and monounsaturated fats: vegetable/plant oils, nuts. Concentrated sources of saturated fats: meats, cheeses, butter, cream, egg yolks, lard.

Carbohydrates are the most important source of energy for the body. The digestive system changes carbohydrates into glucose, which the body uses for energy for cells, tissues, and organs. The body stores extra sugar in the liver and muscles. Best sources: grains, legumes, potatoes, vegetables, fruits.

Fiber is the portion of plant foods that our bodies cannot digest. There are two basic types: insoluble and soluble. Insoluble fibers help move food materials through the digestive tract; soluble fibers tend to slow them down. Both types absorb water, thus preventing and treating constipation. Soluble fibers may also be helpful in reducing blood cholesterol levels. Best sources: beans, bran, fruits, whole grains, vegetables.

Water dissolves and transports other nutrients throughout the body, aiding in the processes of digestion, absorption, circulation, and excretion. It helps regulate body temperature.

Vitamins

Vitamin A promotes good eyesight; helps keep skin and mucous membranes resistant to infection. Best sources: liver, sweet potatoes, carrots, kale, cantaloupe, turnip greens, collard greens, broccoli, fortified milk.

Vitamin B_1 (thiamine) prevents beriberi. Essential to carbohydrate metabolism and nervous system health. Best sources: eggs, enriched bread and flour, nuts, seeds, organ meats, whole grains.

Vitamin B_2 (riboflavin) protects the skin, mouth, eyes, and mucous membranes. Essential to growth, red blood cell production, and energy metabolism. Best sources: dairy products, meat, poultry, broccoli, spinach, eggs, nuts.

Vitamin B_6 (pyridoxine) is important in the regulation of the central nervous system and in protein metabolism. Best sources: whole grains, meat, fish, nuts, avocado, bananas.

Vitamin B_{12} (cobalamin) is needed to form red blood cells. Best sources: meat, shellfish, poultry, eggs, dairy products.

Niacin maintains health of skin, nerves, and the digestive system. Best sources: poultry, nuts, fish, eggs.

Folic acid (folacin) is required for new cell formation, growth, and reproduction and for important chemical reactions in body cells. Best sources: leafy green vegetables, fruits, dried beans, peas, nuts, enriched bread, cereals.

Other B vitamins include biotin and pantothenic acid.

Vitamin C (ascorbic acid) maintains collagen, a protein necessary for the formation of skin, ligaments, and bones. Helps heal wounds and mend fractures. Best sources: citrus fruits and juices, cantaloupe, broccoli, Brussels sprouts, potatoes and sweet potatoes, tomatoes, cabbage.

Vitamin D is important for bone development. Best sources: sunlight, milk products, tuna, salmon, oysters.

Vitamin E (tocopherol) helps protect red blood cells. Best sources: vegetable oils, wheat germ, whole grains, eggs, peanuts, margarine, green leafy vegetables.

Vitamin K is necessary for formation of prothrombin, which helps blood to clot. Also made by intestinal bacteria. Best dietary sources: green leafy vegetables, tomatoes.

Minerals

Calcium works with phosphorus to build and maintain bones and teeth. Best sources: dairy, leafy green vegetables.

Phosphorus's main function is in the formation of bones and teeth, but it performs more functions than any other mineral and plays a part in nearly every chemical reaction in the body. Best sources: cheese, milk, meats, poultry, fish, tofu.

Iron is necessary for the formation of myoglobin, a reservoir of oxygen for muscle tissue, and hemoglobin, which transports oxygen within blood. Best sources: lean meats, beans, green leafy vegetables, shellfish, whole grains.

Other minerals include chloride, chromium, cobalt, copper, fluoride, iodine, magnesium, manganese, molybdenum, potassium, selenium, sodium, sulfur, zinc.

Understanding Food Label Claims

Source: Center for Food Safety and Applied Nutrition, U.S. Food and Drug Admin. (FDA), U.S. Dept. of Health and Human Services; Food Safety and Inspection Service, Agricultural Marketing Service, U.S. Dept. of Agriculture (USDA)

Nutrition Packaging Terms

Manufacturers can make certain claims on processed food labels only if they meet the definitions specified here.

SUGAR. Sugar free: less than 0.5 g per serving; **No added sugars; Without added sugars:** no sugars or sugar-containing ingredients added during processing; must state if food is not "low calorie" or "reduced calorie"; **Unsweetened; No added sweeteners:** remain as factual statements; **Reduced sugar:** at least 25% less sugar than reference food.

FAT. Fat free: less than 0.5 g of fat per serving; **Saturated fat free:** less than 0.5 g of saturated fat and less than 0.5 g of trans fatty acids per serving; **Low fat:** 3 g or less per serving and, if the serving is 30 g or less or 2 tbs or less, per 50 g of the food; **Low saturated fat:** 1 g or less per serving and not more than 15% of calories from saturated fat; **Reduced fat; Less fat:** at least 25% less per serving than reference food.

FIBER. High fiber: 5 g or more per serving (must also meet low-fat definition or state level of total fat); **Good source of fiber:** 2.5 g to 4.9 g per serving; **More fiber; Added fiber:** at least 2.5 g more per serving than reference food.

SODIUM. Sodium free: less than 5 mg per serving; **Low sodium:** 140 mg or less per serving and, if the serving is 30 g or less or 2 tbs or less, per 50 g of the food; **Very low sodium:** 35 mg or less per serving and, if the serving is 30 g or less or 2 tbs or less, per 50 g of the food; **Reduced sodium; Less sodium:** at least 25% less per serving than reference food.

CALORIES. Calorie free: less than 5 calories per serving; **Low calorie:** 40 calories or less per serving; if the serving is 30 g or less or 2 tbs or less, 40 calories or less per 50 g of the food; **Reduced calories; Fewer calories:** at least 25% fewer calories than reference food.

CHOLESTEROL. Cholesterol free: less than 2 mg of cholesterol and 2 g or less of saturated fat per serving; **Low cholesterol:** 20 mg or less of cholesterol and 2 g or less of saturated fat per serving and, if the serving is 30 g or less or 2 tbs or less, per 50 g of the food; **Reduced cholesterol; Less cholesterol:** at least 25% less than reference food.

Other Packaging Terms

The FDA allows food producers and marketers to use language on their packaging that advertises the health benefits and production methods of their products. Products marked "certified" have been formally evaluated for class, grade, or other quality characteristics by the USDA's Food Safety and Inspection Service. Below are some common packaging terms and their meanings.

Organic: Produced by farmers who use environmentally friendly methods to raise their crops or animals. Before a product can be labeled organic, the farm where the food is grown must pass a special inspection by a USDA official. Organic foods must be produced without irradiation, sewage sludge, synthetic fertilizers, prohibited pesticides, and genetically modified organisms.

Foods that contain 100% organic ingredients may advertise "100 percent certified organic" on the front of the packaging along with the USDA organic seal. Foods with at least 95% organic ingredients may be called "organic" and may place the official seal on their packaging. Products with at least 70% organic ingredients may advertise "made with organic" prominently on the front of the package that the item contains organic ingredients. Products with less than 70% organic ingredients may not make any organic claims on the front of the package but may list organic ingredients on the side panel.

Natural: The FDA has not developed a definition for use of the term *natural* or its derivatives. However, the agency has not objected to the use of the term if the food does not contain added color, artificial flavors, or synthetic substances.

Free range or **free roaming:** Producers must demonstrate to the USDA that the poultry has been allowed access to the outside.

Fresh poultry: Whole poultry and cuts that have never been below 26°F.

Frozen poultry: Temperature of raw, frozen poultry is 0°F or below.

Gluten free: Products with a gluten limit of 20 parts per million.

Halal and **Zabiah Halal:** Produced in federally inspected meat packing plants and handled in accordance with Islamic law and under Islamic authority.

Kosher: Meat and poultry products prepared under rabbinical supervision.

No hormones added: Hormones are not allowed in the raising of hogs or poultry, so those products may not make this claim. If sufficient documentation is provided to the USDA, this term may appear on packages of beef.

No antibiotics added: Claim may be made on a package (red meat and poultry) if sufficient documentation is provided to the USDA showing that the animals were raised without antibiotics.

Dietary Guidelines for Americans, 2015: Key Recommendations

Source: *2015-2020 Dietary Guidelines for Americans*, U.S. Dept. of Agriculture and U.S. Dept. of Health and Human Services

The federal government revises its dietary guidelines every five years. The most recent edition aims to help Americans establish a healthy eating pattern that meets nutrient needs over time at an appropriate calorie level. All foods and beverages consumed should be accounted for.

Healthy eating patterns include a variety from the following food groups:

- **Vegetables** from the five subgroups: dark green, red and orange, legumes (beans and peas), starchy, and other.
- **Fruits**, especially whole fruits.
- **Grains**, at least half of which should be whole grains. Choose refined grains that are enriched.
- Fat-free or low-fat **dairy**, including milk, yogurt, and cheese. Those who cannot or choose not to consume dairy should eat foods, such as fortified soy beverages, that provide the same nutrients.
- A variety of **protein foods**, including seafood, lean meats and poultry, eggs, nuts, seeds, and soy products. Legumes (beans and peas) can be considered vegetables or proteins but should be counted in one group only.
- **Oils**, which should replace solid fats where possible.

- Potassium, dietary fiber, calcium, and vitamin D are underconsumed in American diets, which affects public health.
- Not enough iron is consumed by young children and women who could become or are pregnant.

Dietary components to limit:

- Less than 2,300 mg per day of **sodium**. Adults with prehypertension and hypertension may benefit from consuming less than 1,500 mg of sodium per day.
- Less than 10% of daily calories from **saturated fats**; replace with monounsaturated and polyunsaturated fats.
- Less than 10% of daily calories from **added sugars**.
- As little as possible of **trans fats**.
- **Alcohol** in moderation, if at all—up to one drink per day for women and two drinks per day for men.

Top 10 Calorie Sources in American Diets

Source: National Health and Nutrition Examination Survey, National Center for Health Statistics, CDC, U.S. Dept. of Health and Human Services

Rank All Americans (ages 2+)	Rank Children and adolescents (ages 2-18)	Rank All adults (ages 19+)
1. Grain-based desserts	1. Grain-based desserts	1. Grain-based desserts
2. Yeast breads	2. Pizza	2. Yeast breads
3. Chicken dishes	3. Soda/energy/sports drinks	3. Chicken dishes
4. Soda/energy/sports drinks	4. Yeast breads	4. Soda/energy/sports drinks
5. Pizza	5. Chicken dishes	5. Alcoholic beverages
6. Alcoholic beverages	6. Pasta dishes	6. Pizza
7. Pasta dishes	7. Reduced-fat milk	7. Tortillas, burritos, tacos
8. Tortillas, burritos, tacos	8. Dairy desserts	8. Pasta dishes
9. Beef dishes	9. Potato/corn/other chips	9. Beef dishes
10. Dairy desserts	10. Ready-to-eat cereals	10. Dairy desserts

Note: Data are drawn from analyses of usual dietary intakes conducted by the Natl. Cancer Institute. Foods and beverages consumed were divided into 97 categories and ranked according to calorie contribution to the diet. Average total daily calorie intake was 2,157 overall, 2,027 for children and adolescents (ages 2-18), and 2,199 for adults (ages 19+).

Weight Guidelines for Adults

Source: National Center for Health Statistics, CDC, U.S. Dept. of Health and Human Services

Guidelines on identification, evaluation, and treatment of overweight and obesity in adults were released in June 1998 by the National Heart, Lung, and Blood Institute (NHLBI), in cooperation with the National Institute of Diabetes and Digestive and Kidney Diseases (NIDDK). The guidelines, based on research into risk factors contributing to heart disease, stroke, and other conditions, define overweight and obese in terms of **body mass index (BMI)**. BMI, based on a person's weight and height, can be an indicator of total body fat. A BMI of 25-29 is said to indicate **overweight**; a BMI of 30 or higher indicates **obesity**. Calculate your BMI at www.nhlbi.nih.gov/health/educational/lose_wt/BMI/bmicalc.htm. Waist circumference can also be used as a screening tool. Men with a waist circumference of more than 40 inches and non-pregnant women with a waist circumference of more than 35 inches may have a higher risk of developing obesity-related conditions. BMI and waist circumference are screening tools, not diagnostics; a healthcare provider should be consulted to evaluate risk and diagnose disease. Factors such as high blood pressure, cholesterol levels, and family medical history may increase a person's risk of developing an obesity-related disease.

The National Center for Health Statistics notes that in 2011-14, 34.9% of American adults (ages 20 and over) were obese. Over the past four decades, childhood obesity rates in America have more than tripled, and in 2011-14, 17% of children and adolescents (ages 2-19) were obese. Based on directly measured weight and height, between 1988-94 and 2011-14, the proportion of adults ages 20 years and over who were obese rose by 59%, from 22.9%. During the same period, obesity increased by 54.9% in children ages 6-11, from 11.3% to 17.5%, and by 95.2% in adolescents ages 12-19, from 10.5% to 20.5%.

A high prevalence of overweight and obesity is a public health concern because excess body fat, particularly abdominal fat, has been associated with type 2 diabetes, hypertension, dyslipidemia, cardiovascular disease, stroke, gallbladder disease, respiratory dysfunction, gout, osteoarthritis, and certain kinds of cancers.

Adults Meeting U.S. Fitness Guidelines, 1998-2014

Source: National Health Interview Survey, National Center for Health Statistics, CDC, U.S. Dept. of Health and Human Services

Characteristic	% meeting aerobic activity guidelines					% meeting muscle-strengthening guidelines				
	1998	2000	2005	2010	2014	1998	2000	2005	2010	2014
Sex and age										
Men, ages 18-44.	51.5%	53.6%	50.0%	59.0%	60.8%	27.2%	26.3%	28.7%	35.6%	35.4%
Men, ages 45-54.	44.3	45.2	42.6	50.7	48.9	18.8	18.0	19.2	24.8	24.5
Men, ages 55-64.	38.3	38.9	38.4	46.0	44.7	12.9	13.8	15.7	22.9	20.7
Men, ages 65-74.	38.5	41.8	38.3	40.7	45.6	12.0	12.2	14.5	20.6	21.5
Men, age 75+	26.1	30.7	28.6	32.3	35.2	9.5	10.1	12.4	14.5	15.3
Women, ages 18-44	40.0	42.0	43.1	48.5	52.7	17.9	17.9	19.8	22.1	23.4
Women, ages 45-54	36.1	39.1	38.1	44.7	46.7	13.7	16.1	19.8	20.4	20.4
Women, ages 55-64	32.5	33.5	34.1	38.6	44.2	10.3	12.4	15.9	17.5	18.3
Women, ages 65-74	26.2	32.6	30.2	31.8	39.7	7.8	10.5	13.3	15.6	16.8
Women, age 75+	14.0	16.8	18.8	18.3	23.2	5.7	6.7	6.7	10.8	11.4
Race or Hispanic origin[1]										
White, not Hispanic.	43.1	45.7	45.7	51.5	53.7	18.7	19.3	22.5	26.3	26.7
Black, not Hispanic.	30.4	31.7	29.1	37.3	43.6	15.6	16.0	15.7	21.6	23.3
Amer. Indian or AK Native. .	39.7	29.7	41.6	42.0	44.1	18.2	13.9	20.5	16.7	27.9
Asian.	37.1	41.7	37.5	44.2	47.5	17.2	17.2	16.9	21.9	19.5
Two or more races	—	43.9	41.1	50.2	50.5	—	22.2	23.6	30.4	24.8
Hispanic or Latino.	29.1	30.8	28.5	36.2	41.3	12.7	11.9	12.9	18.1	19.0
Geographic region										
Northeast	39.6	45.3	43.3	46.9	48.6	17.5	20.0	21.6	24.3	24.9
Midwest	42.0	43.5	43.5	46.1	48.9	18.2	19.3	21.9	24.7	24.3
South	35.3	37.3	36.5	45.0	48.7	15.0	15.1	17.6	22.0	23.2
West.	46.7	46.9	44.4	52.0	54.5	22.3	19.7	21.3	27.5	27.1

— = Not available. **Note:** Measures of physical activity reflect the federal 2008 Physical Activity Guidelines for Americans, which recommend that for substantial health benefits, adults perform at least 150 minutes a week of moderate-intensity, or 75 minutes a week of vigorous-intensity aerobic physical activity, or an equivalent combination of moderate- and vigorous-intensity activity. Aerobic activity should be performed in episodes of at least 10 min., preferably spread throughout the week. The guidelines also recommend that adults perform muscle-strengthening activities that are moderate or high intensity and involve all major muscle groups on two or more days a week. (1) Persons reporting only one race, unless otherwise noted. Persons of Hispanic origin may be of any race.

2016 YEAR IN PICTURES

WORLD

BASTILLE DAY ATTACK In what investigators called an act of terrorism, a cargo truck driver plowed into crowds during Bastille Day celebrations in Nice, France, July 14, 2016, killing 86 people and injuring hundreds.

CIVIL WAR'S CIVILIAN TOLL In spite of several attempts at cease-fires, the civil war in Syria passed its bloody fifth birthday in 2016 and continued to claim casualties, as civilian death toll estimates climbed past 400,000.

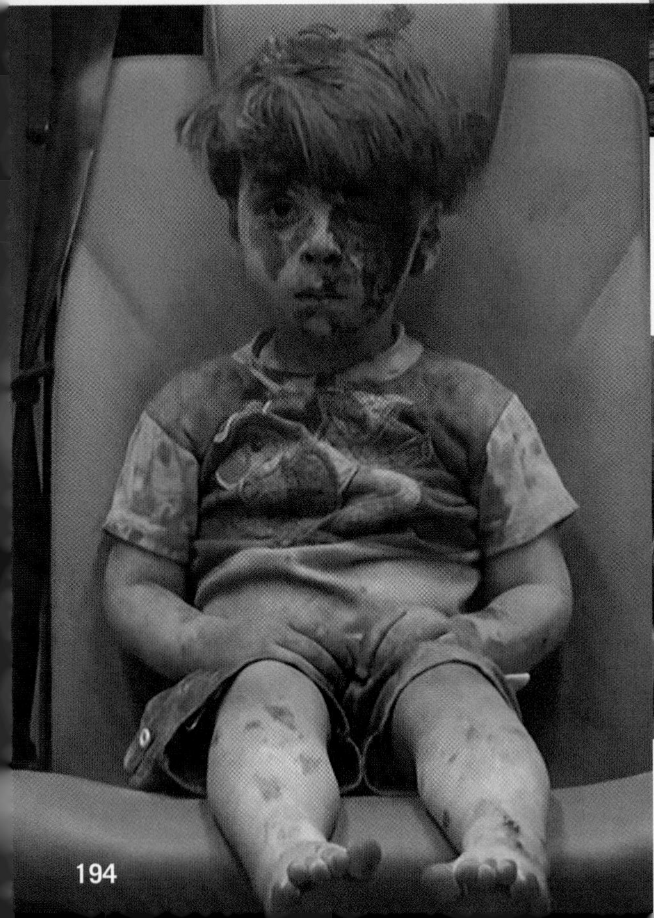

RISKY VOYAGE As hundreds of thousands of refugees and migrants attempted to reach Europe via narrowing routes in 2016, many boarded unseaworthy or overcrowded vessels for the Mediterranean crossing and required rescue.

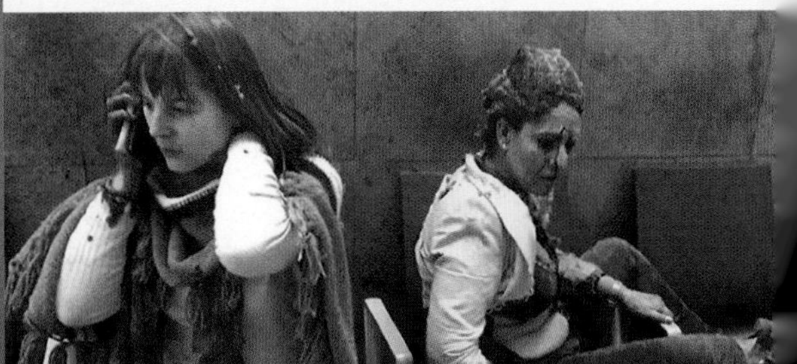

TERROR IN BRUSSELS ISIS took responsibility for three coordinated suicide bombings Mar. 22, 2016, that killed 32 others at a train station and airport in Brussels, Belgium.

FIGHT FOR FALLUJAH Iraqi forces battled the Sunni extremist group known as ISIS for control of Fallujah, retaking the city June 26, 2016.

NUCLEAR THREAT North Korea's nuclear test Sept. 9, 2016—believed to be its fifth since 2006—was widely condemned by the international community.

UK'S BREAKAWAY In a June 23, 2016, referendum on whether to leave or remain in the European Union, UK voters supported Brexit, 52%-48%, causing a parliamentary leadership shake-up that introduced new Prime Min. Theresa May.

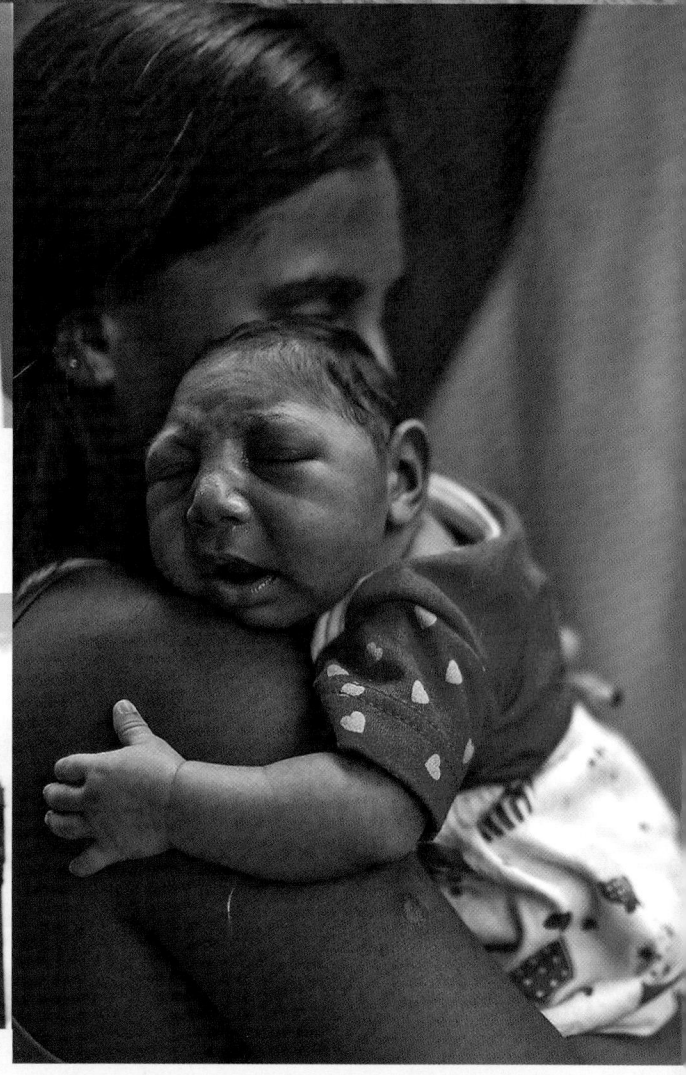

ZIKA'S COST The 2015-16 Zika virus outbreak caused a surge in infants born with microcephaly and other severe birth defects, especially in Brazil, where the outbreak of the mosquito-borne virus was first detected.

WORLD

DISASTER HITS HAITI Hurricane Matthew made landfall in Haiti as a Category 4 storm Oct. 4, 2016, killing hundreds and inflicting massive damage on the natural disaster-stricken and cholera-ravaged nation.

DEFLECTED COUP Turkish Pres. Recep Tayyip Erdogan used FaceTime to communicate with the media and the public and ultimately defeated an attempted military coup d'état July 15-16, 2016.

SON DAKİKA

Cumhurbaşkanı Erdoğan açıklama yapıyor

izleyicitemsilcisi@cnnturk.com.tr

ALEVLER YÜKSELDİ   AA: GÜVENİLİR KAYNAKLAR, GENELKURMAY BAŞKA

SON DAKİKA

CRISIS IN CARACAS Anger in Venezuela over a spiraling economy and ongoing food scarcity erupted into protests; an estimated 1 million demonstrated in Caracas in opposition to Pres. Nicolás Maduro Sept. 1, 2016.

DUTERTE'S DRUG WAR BEGINS Rodrigo Duterte was sworn in as president of the Philippines June 30, 2016; he encouraged violence and killings against alleged drug dealers and addicts by police and vigilantes.

HISTORIC TRUCE After 52 years of conflict and more than 220,000 killed, Colombian Pres. Juan Manuel Santos (left) and Revolutionary Armed Forces of Colombia (FARC) leader Timoleón Jiménez (right), agreed to a cease-fire deal in Havana, Cuba, June 23, 2016, though obstacles to peace remained.

DILMA DEPOSED Brazilian Pres. Dilma Rousseff called the Senate's Aug. 31, 2016, vote to formally impeach and remove her from office a "coup against the people."

WAR AND PEACE U.S. Pres. Barack Obama met with atomic bombing survivors during his May 27, 2016, visit to Hiroshima, Japan; he was the first sitting American president to view the site.

AMATRICE QUAKE DEVASTATES A 6.2 magnitude earthquake struck central Italy Aug. 24, 2016, causing severe damage in Amatrice and killing 298.

THE DEMOCRATIC NOMINEES Former Sec. of State Hillary Clinton became the first woman to win the presidential nomination of a major party when she accepted the Democratic nomination July 28, 2016, alongside her running mate, Sen. Tim Kaine (D, VA).

THE REPUBLICAN NOMINEES Emerging triumphant from a 17-candidate primary battle, New York real estate tycoon Donald Trump accepted the Republican presidential nomination July 21, 2016, with his vice presidential pick, Indiana Gov. Mike Pence.

CONGRESS SITS IN House and Senate Democrats, led by U.S. Rep. John Lewis (GA), staged a sit-in on the floor of the House of Representatives June 22-23, 2016, to demand a vote on certain gun control measures.

GOLD STAR SCANDAL Khizr (right) and Ghazala Khan, parents of a Muslim U.S. Army captain who died while serving in Iraq, appeared before the Democratic convention July 28, 2016, setting off an emotionally charged public exchange with Republican nominee Donald Trump, who had previously called for a ban on Muslim immigration to the U.S.

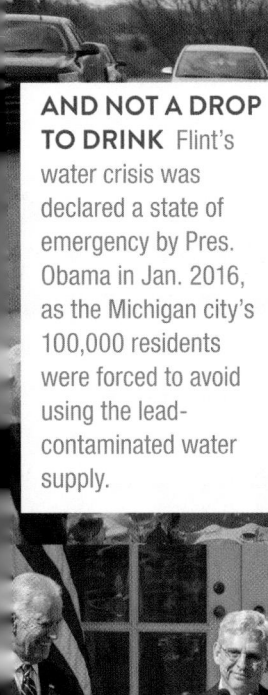

AND NOT A DROP TO DRINK Flint's water crisis was declared a state of emergency by Pres. Obama in Jan. 2016, as the Michigan city's 100,000 residents were forced to avoid using the lead-contaminated water supply.

SUPREME NOMINEE Pres. Barack Obama Mar. 16, 2016, nominated appellate court judge Merrick Garland to replace the late U.S. Supreme Court Associate Justice Antonin Scalia; the Senate judiciary committee declined to hold hearings on his nomination.

AFTERMATH OF A MASS SHOOTING A shooter June 12, 2016, at Pulse nightclub—a gay club hosting its Latin Night—in Orlando, FL, killed 49 people, most of them gay and Latino.

DALLAS TRAGEDY A black Army Reserve veteran—reportedly angry about recent police shootings—targeted and killed five police officers July 7, 2016, at the end of an otherwise peaceful Black Lives Matter-organized protest in Dallas, TX.

BLACK LIVES MATTER New rounds of protests erupted following a number of deaths of black men caught on video in 2016, including that of Alton Sterling (in mural, left), a 37-year-old shot dead by police July 5, 2016, while appearing in video footage to be subdued on the ground.

NATIONAL

WATER, WATER EVERYWHERE As much as two feet of rain fell in 48 hours on parts of southern Louisiana in Aug. 2016, causing historic flooding in 20 parishes and damages estimated at more than $8.7 billion.

OVERSTAYED WELCOME An armed group, led by activist Ammon Bundy, occupied Malheur National Wildlife Refuge Jan.-Feb. 2016, in protest of federal land management policies.

WE DON'T CARE

LIVING HISTORY Opening ceremonies for the Smithsonian National Museum of African American History and Culture Sept. 24, 2016, in Washington, DC, included the Bonner family, whose 99-year-old matriarch, Ruth Bonner, was the daughter of a former slave.

BATHROOM BILL BATTLE A North Carolina bill signed into law Mar. 23, 2016, required people to use public facilities according to the sex they were assigned at birth, a problem for transgender individuals, sparking legal challenges.

Obesity Among Adults in the U.S., 2015

Source: National Health Interview Survey, National Center for Health Statistics, CDC, U.S. Dept. of Health and Human Services

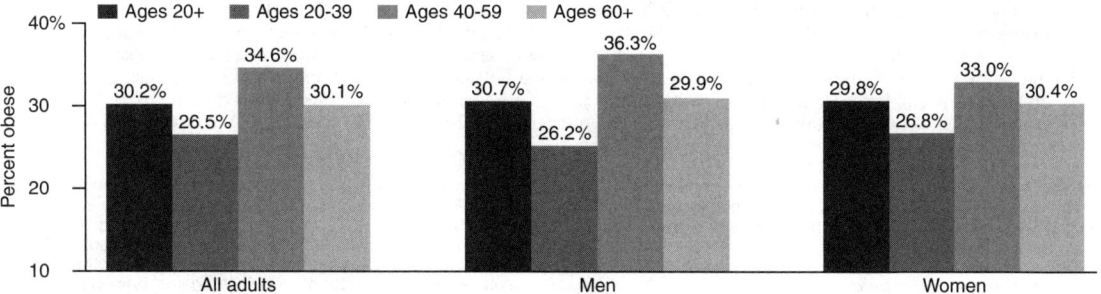

Overweight and Obesity Among U.S. Adults, 1960-2014

Source: National Health Examination Survey and National Health and Nutrition Examination Survey, NCHS, CDC, U.S. Dept. of Health and Human Services

(as percent of adults age 20-74 in 1960-80 and age 20 and over for all other years shown here)

Survey period	Total			Men			Women		
	Overweight	Obesity	Extreme obesity	Overweight	Obesity	Extreme obesity	Overweight	Obesity	Extreme obesity
1960-62	31.5%	13.4%	0.9%	38.7%	10.7%	0.3*	24.7%	15.8%	1.4%
1971-74	32.7	14.5	1.3	41.7	12.1	0.6	24.3	16.6	2.0
1976-80	32.1	15.0	1.4	39.9	12.7	0.4	24.9	17.0	2.2
1988-94	32.6	23.2	3.0	40.3	20.5	1.8	25.1	25.9	4.1
1999-2000	33.6	30.9	5.0	39.2	27.7	3.3	28.0	34.0	6.6
2001-02	34.4	31.2	5.4	41.5	28.3	3.9	27.3	34.1	6.8
2003-04	33.4	32.9	5.1	39.4	31.7	3.0	27.3	34.0	7.3
2005-06	32.2	35.1	6.2	39.7	33.8	4.3	24.7	36.3	7.9
2007-08	33.6	34.3	6.0	39.4	32.5	4.4	27.9	36.2	7.6
2009-10	32.7	36.1	6.6	38.0	35.9	4.6	27.5	36.1	8.5
2011-12	33.3	35.3	6.6	37.3	33.9	4.5	29.5	36.6	8.6
2013-14	31.9	38.2	8.1	38.2	35.5	5.7	25.8	41.0	10.5

* = Estimate is considered unreliable.

Obesity Among Children and Adolescents in the U.S., 1988-2014

Source: National Health and Nutrition Examination Survey, National Center for Health Statistics, CDC, U.S. Dept. of Health and Human Services

Age/sex/poverty level	1988-94	1999-2002	2001-04	2003-06	2005-08	2007-10	2009-12	2011-14
				Percent of population				
2-5 years								
Both sexes	7.2%	10.3%	12.4%	12.5%	10.5%	11.1%	10.2%	8.9%
Boys	6.2	10.0	13.1	12.8	9.8	11.9	12.0	9.2
Girls	8.2	10.6	11.7	12.2	11.2	10.2	8.4	8.6
Percent of poverty level[1]								
Below 100%	9.7	10.9	14.4	14.3	12.3	13.2	12.3	11.6
100%-199%	7.3	13.8*	13.3	12.7	10.0	11.8	11.6	10.2
200%-399%	5.6	7.6*	13.6	11.9	11.6	13.9	11.0	7.7*
400% or more	—	—	—	10.0*	—	5.8*	5.0*	—
6-11 years								
Both sexes	11.3	15.9	17.5	17.0	17.4	18.8	17.9	17.5
Boys	11.6	16.9	18.7	18.0	18.7	20.7	18.3	17.6
Girls.	11.0	14.7	16.3	15.8	16.0	16.9	17.4	17.5
Percent of poverty level[1]								
Below 100%	11.4	19.1	20.0	22.0	21.5	22.2	24.6	21.5
100%-199%	11.1	16.4	18.4	19.2	22.2	20.7	18.5	20.4
200%-399%	11.7	15.3	18.2	16.7	16.8	18.9	15.8	15.7
400% or more	—	12.9*	11.4	9.2*	9.5*	12.5*	12.2*	12.2*
12-19 years								
Both sexes	10.5	16.0	17.0	17.6	17.9	18.2	19.4	20.5
Boys	11.3	16.7	17.9	18.2	18.7	19.4	20.0	20.1
Girls	9.7	15.3	16.0	16.8	17.0	16.9	18.9	21.0
Percent of poverty level[1]								
Below 100%	15.8	19.8	18.2	19.3	23.1	24.3	23.2	22.4
100%-199%	11.2	15.1	17.0	18.4	19.8	20.1	22.5	25.7
200%-399%	9.4	15.7	19.0	19.3	17.2	16.3	17.9	19.7
400% or more	—	13.9	13.2	12.6	14.0	14.0	13.8	13.7*

* = Estimates are considered unreliable. — = Estimate not available/considered unreliable. **Note:** Obesity is defined as body mass index (BMI) at or above sex- and age-specific 95th percentile from 2000 CDC growth charts. (1) Ratio of family's household income to contemporary federal poverty guidelines.

Basic First Aid

Source: Courtesy of the American National Red Cross, www.redcross.org. All rights reserved in all countries.

Note: This information is not intended to be a substitute for formal training. It is recommended that you contact your local American Red Cross chapter to sign up for a First Aid/CPR/AED (automated external defibrillator) course.

In an emergency, it is important to get medical assistance as soon as possible, but knowing what to do until a doctor or other trained person gets to the scene can save a life, especially in cases of severe bleeding, choking, poisoning, and shock.

People with special medical problems, such as diabetes, cardiovascular disease, epilepsy, or allergies, are urged to wear some sort of emblem identifying the problem as a safeguard against receiving medication that might be harmful or even fatal. Emblems can be obtained from MedicAlert Foundation, 5226 Pirrone Ct., Salida, CA 95368; (800) 432-5378; www.medicalert.org.

Animal bite: Call 9-1-1 or the local emergency number if the wound is bleeding seriously or if you suspect the animal might have rabies. Control any bleeding. Wash minor wounds with soap under running water and apply antibiotic ointment and a dressing. When possible, proper authorities should test the animal for rabies.

Asphyxiation: Call 9-1-1 or the local emergency number.

Bleeding: Use a barrier between your hand and the wound to help prevent infection. Cover wound with a sterile dressing. Apply direct pressure until bleeding stops. Cover compress with a bandage. Call 9-1-1 or the local emergency number if bleeding is severe.

Burn: Check for life-threatening conditions. If the burn is mild, with skin unbroken and no blisters, flush with cold running water for at least 20 minutes. Gently wash with soap and water and pat dry. Apply a thin layer of antibiotic ointment. Apply a loose, sterile dry dressing to prevent infection. If the burn is severe, call 9-1-1 or the local emergency number. Care for shock (see separate entry). Keep the person from getting chilled or overheated until advanced medical assistance arrives. Do not try to clean a severe burn or break blisters.

Chemical in eye: Call 9-1-1 or the local emergency number. Turn the person's head to the side so that the affected eye is lower than the unaffected eye. Flush the affected eye with large amounts of water for at least 20 minutes.

Choking: See **First Aid for Choking** below.

Convulsions (seizures): Remove nearby objects that might cause injury. Protect the person's head by placing a thin folded towel or item of clothing under it. Roll him or her on one side to drain fluids from the mouth. Do not place anything between the person's teeth. Stay with the person until he or she is fully conscious. If convulsions do not stop, get medical attention immediately.

Cut (minor): Use a clean barrier between your hand and the wound to prevent infection. Apply direct pressure for a few minutes to control any bleeding. Wash the wound thoroughly with soap and water and apply a thin layer of antibiotic ointment or a microthin film dressing. Cover the wound with a sterile dressing and a bandage.

Foreign object in eye: If an object is impaled in someone's eye, do not remove it. If not impaled, try to remove the object by having the person blink several times. If the object doesn't come out, gently flush the eye with saline solution or water. Do not rub the eye. If the object still doesn't come out, the person should receive professional medical attention.

Frostbite: Handle the frostbitten area gently. Do not rub. If there is no danger of the affected area refreezing, soak it in warm water (not warmer than 105°F). Do not allow the frostbitten area to touch the side of the water container. Keep the frostbitten part in the water until normal color returns and it feels warm. Loosely bandage the area with dry, sterile dressings. If fingers or toes are frostbitten, put cotton or gauze between them. Do not break any blisters. Call 9-1-1 or seek emergency help as soon as possible.

Heart attack and stroke: See **Heart and Blood Vessel Disease** earlier in chapter.

Heat stroke: Remove the person from the heat. Loosen any tight clothing. Immerse person in cold water until he or she becomes alert. If a large enough source of water is not available, drench the person with cold water and fan constantly. If the person is conscious, have him or her slowly drink some cool water. Call 9-1-1 if the person's condition does not improve.

Hypothermia: Call 9-1-1 or the local emergency number. For mild hypothermia, cover all exposed skin. Replace wet clothes with something dry. If the person is alert, give him or her simple carbohydrates to eat and warm, nonalcoholic and decaffeinated liquids to drink. Apply heat pads or other heat sources if available but do not place against bare skin.

Loss of limb: Call 9-1-1 or the local emergency number and care for any life-threatening conditions. If a limb is severed, it is important to properly protect the limb so that it can possibly be reattached. After the victim is cared for, the limb should be wrapped in sterile gauze and placed in a plastic bag. Place bag in a larger bag or container of an ice and water slurry, not ice alone. Be sure the limb is taken to the hospital with the person.

Poisoning: Care for any life-threatening conditions. Call the National Capital Poison Center (800-222-1222), 9-1-1, or the local emergency number and follow their directions. Do not give the person any food or drink or induce vomiting unless specified to do so by medical professionals.

Shock (injury-related): Monitor breathing and consciousness. Have the person lie down and keep him or her as comfortable as possible. Maintain an open airway. Give sips of cool water if he or she can tolerate fluids. Elevate his or her legs about 12 inches unless you suspect injuries to the head or lower extremities. Maintain normal body temperature. If the weather is cold or damp, place blankets or extra clothing over and under the person; if the weather is hot, provide shade.

Snakebite: Call 9-1-1 or the local emergency number. Gently wash the injury. Splint bitten extremities, and keep the area at approximately the level of the heart. Keep the person calm. Do not cut, suck, apply a constricting band, or apply cold to a bite from a pit viper (such as a rattlesnake, copperhead, or cottonmouth). For a bite from an elapid snake, such as a coral snake, apply an elastic roller bandage after washing the wound.

Sprains and strains: Splint any injured bone or joint that the person cannot use.

Sting from bee or wasp: If possible, remove the stinger by scraping it away with your finger or a plastic card (like a credit card) or using tweezers. If you use tweezers, grasp the stinger, not the venom sac. Wash the area with soap and water. Cover it to keep it clean. Apply cold to the area. Call 9-1-1 or the local emergency number immediately if the wound does not stop swelling, the person collapses, or he or she is known to be allergic to the sting.

Unconsciousness: Call 9-1-1 or the local emergency number immediately. Do not move the person if a spinal injury is suspected.

First Aid for Choking

The recommended first aid for a conscious choking victim who is unable to speak, cough, or breathe is to deliver a series of five blows to the back and five thrusts to the abdomen. Have another person call 9-1-1 or the local emergency number. Obtain consent from the victim to treat him or her. Lean the victim forward and apply five blows to his or her back with the heel of your hand. If the victim is still choking, stand or kneel behind the victim and wrap your arms around his or her waist. Make a fist with one hand and place the thumb side against the middle of the person's abdomen, just above the navel and well below the lower tip of the breastbone. Grasp your fist in your other hand and quickly thrust upwards into the abdomen five times. Continue back blows and abdominal thrusts until the object is dislodged, and the person can breathe or cough forcefully, or the person loses consciousness.

VITAL STATISTICS

Births and Deaths in the U.S., 1960-2015

Source: National Center for Health Statistics (NCHS), CDC, U.S. Dept. of Health and Human Services

Year	BIRTHS Total number	Rate	DEATHS Total number	Rate	Year	BIRTHS Total number	Rate	DEATHS Total number	Rate
1960	4,257,850	23.7	1,711,982	9.5	2004	4,112,052	14.0	2,397,615	8.2
1970	3,731,386	18.4	1,921,031	9.5	2005	4,138,349	14.0	2,448,017	8.3
1980	3,612,258	15.9	1,989,841	8.8	2006	4,265,555	14.2	2,426,264	8.1
1990	4,092,994	16.7	2,148,463	8.6	2007	4,316,233	14.3	2,423,712	8.0
1995	3,899,589	14.6	2,312,132	8.7	2008	4,247,694	14.0	2,471,984	8.1
1996	3,891,494	14.4	2,314,690	8.6	2009	4,130,665	13.5	2,437,163	7.9
1997	3,880,894	14.2	2,314,245	8.5	2010	3,999,386	13.0	2,468,435	8.0
1998	3,941,553	14.3	2,337,256	8.5	2011	3,953,590	12.7	2,515,458	8.1
1999	3,959,417	14.2	2,391,399	8.6	2012	3,952,841	12.6	2,543,279	8.1
2000	4,058,814	14.4	2,403,351	8.5	2013	3,932,181	12.4	2,596,993	8.2
2001	4,025,933	14.1	2,416,425	8.5	2014	3,988,076	12.5	2,626,418	8.2
2002	4,021,726	13.9	2,443,387	8.5	2015[1]	3,998,000	12.5	2,688,000	8.4
2003	4,089,950	14.1	2,448,288	8.4					

Note: Rates are per 1,000 population; population counts are enumerated as of Apr. 1 for decennial census years and estimated as of July 1 for all other years. Beginning in 1970, statistics exclude births and deaths among nonresidents of the U.S. (1) Provisional; based on events occurring in the U.S. regardless of place of residence.

Marriage and Divorce Rates in the U.S., 1920-2014

Source: National Center for Health Statistics (NCHS), CDC, U.S. Dept. of Health and Human Services

(Per 1,000 total population. Rates for 2000-14 may exclude data and populations from nonreporting states. Some data are provisional.)

The U.S. marriage rate dipped during the Depression and peaked sharply just after World War II; the trend after that has been more gradual. The divorce rate generally rose from the 1920s through 1981, when it peaked at 5.3 per 1,000 population, before declining somewhat. The graph below shows marriage and divorce rates since 1920.

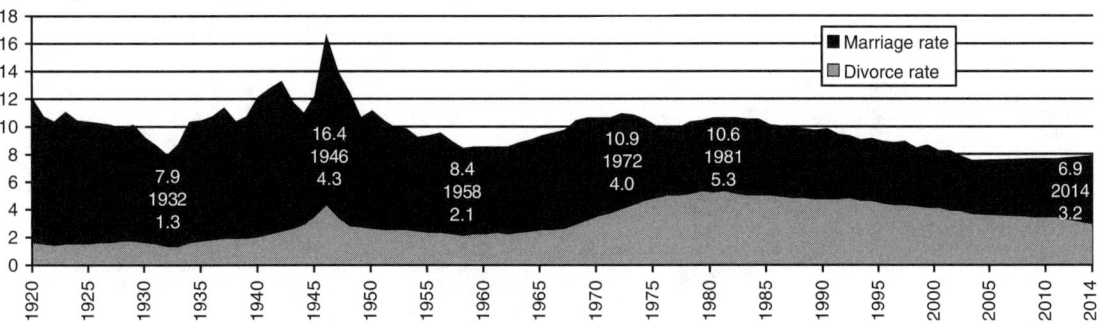

U.S. Median Age at First Marriage, 1890-2015

Source: U.S. Census Bureau, U.S. Dept. of Commerce

Year[1]	Men	Women	Year[1]	Men	Women	Year[1]	Men	Women	Year[1]	Men	Women
1890	26.1	22.0	1950	22.8	20.3	1985	25.5	23.3	2011	28.4	26.4
1900	25.9	21.9	1960	22.8	20.3	1990	26.1	23.9	2012	28.6	26.6
1910	25.1	21.6	1965	22.8	20.6	1995	26.9	24.5	2013	29.0	26.6
1920	24.6	21.2	1970	23.2	20.8	2000	26.8	25.1	2014	29.3	27.0
1930	24.3	21.3	1975	23.5	21.1	2005	27.1	25.3	2015	29.2	27.1
1940	24.3	21.5	1980	24.7	22.0	2010	28.2	26.1			

(1) Figures for 1947 and on are based on Current Population Survey data; earlier figures based on decennial censuses.

Divorce Rates by State, 2014

Source: National Center for Health Statistics (NCHS), CDC, U.S. Dept. of Health and Human Services

(per 1,000 population, estimated as of July 1)

State	Divorce rate	State	Divorce rate	State	Divorce rate
Alabama	3.8	Louisiana	2.3	Ohio	3.2
Alaska	4.0	Maine	3.6	Oklahoma	4.5
Arizona	3.9	Maryland	2.5	Oregon	3.4
Arkansas	4.8	Massachusetts	2.7	Pennsylvania	2.7
California	NA	Michigan	3.0	Rhode Island	2.8
Colorado	3.9	Minnesota	NA	South Carolina	2.9
Connecticut	2.6	Mississippi	3.4	South Dakota	2.8
Delaware	3.3	Missouri	3.3	Tennessee	3.8
District of Columbia	2.6	Montana	3.4	Texas	2.7
Florida	4.0	Nebraska	3.1	Utah	3.1
Georgia	NA	Nevada	5.3	Vermont	3.5
Hawaii	NA	New Hampshire	3.5	Virginia	3.5
Idaho	4.2	New Jersey	2.8	Washington	3.6
Illinois	2.2	New Mexico	3.6	West Virginia	4.2
Indiana	NA	New York	2.8	Wisconsin	2.7
Iowa	1.5	North Carolina	3.4	Wyoming	4.6
Kansas	3.0	North Dakota	2.8	**United States**	**3.2**
Kentucky	3.8				

NA = Not available. **Note:** Rates based on provisional counts of divorce including annulments and, for certain areas, divorce petitions filed or legal separations.

Birth Rates and Fertility Rates by Age of Mother, 1950-2015

Source: National Center for Health Statistics (NCHS), CDC, U.S. Dept. of Health and Human Services

Live births per 1,000 women by age of mother

Year	Birth rate[1]	Fertility rate[2]	10-14 years	15-19 years	15-17 years	18-19 years	20-24 years	25-29 years	30-34 years	35-39 years	40-44 years	45-49 years[3]
1950	24.1	106.2	1.0	81.6	40.7	132.7	196.6	166.1	103.7	52.9	15.1	1.2
1960	23.7	118.0	0.8	89.1	43.9	166.7	258.1	197.4	112.7	56.2	15.5	0.9
1970	18.4	87.9	1.2	68.3	38.8	114.7	167.8	145.1	73.3	31.7	8.1	0.5
1980	15.9	68.4	1.1	53.0	32.5	82.1	115.1	112.9	61.9	19.8	3.9	0.2
1990	16.7	70.9	1.4	59.9	37.5	88.6	116.5	120.2	80.8	31.7	5.5	0.2
1995	14.6	64.6	1.3	56.0	35.5	87.7	107.5	108.8	81.1	34.0	6.6	0.3
2000	14.4	65.9	0.9	47.7	26.9	78.1	109.7	113.5	91.2	39.7	8.0	0.5
2001	14.1	65.3	0.8	45.3	24.7	76.1	106.2	113.4	91.9	40.6	8.1	0.5
2002	13.9	64.8	0.7	43.0	23.2	72.8	103.6	113.6	91.5	41.4	8.3	0.5
2003	14.1	66.1	0.6	41.6	22.4	70.7	102.6	115.6	95.1	43.8	8.7	0.5
2004	14.0	66.3	0.7	41.1	22.1	70.0	101.7	115.5	95.3	45.4	8.9	0.5
2005	14.0	66.7	0.7	40.5	21.4	69.9	102.2	115.5	95.8	46.3	9.1	0.6
2006	14.2	68.5	0.6	41.9	22.0	73.0	105.9	116.7	97.7	47.3	9.4	0.6
2007	14.3	69.5	0.6	42.5	22.1	73.9	106.3	117.5	99.9	47.5	9.5	0.6
2008	14.0	68.6	0.6	41.5	21.7	70.6	103.0	115.1	99.3	46.9	9.8	0.7
2009	13.5	66.2	0.5	37.9	19.6	64.0	96.2	111.5	97.5	46.1	10.0	0.7
2010	13.0	64.1	0.4	34.2	17.3	58.2	90.0	108.3	96.5	45.9	10.2	0.7
2011	12.7	63.2	0.4	31.3	15.4	54.1	85.3	107.2	96.5	47.2	10.3	0.7
2012	12.6	63.0	0.4	29.4	14.1	51.4	83.1	106.5	97.3	48.3	10.4	0.7
2013	12.4	62.5	0.3	26.5	12.3	47.1	80.7	105.5	98.0	49.3	10.4	0.8
2014	12.5	62.9	0.3	24.2	10.9	43.8	79.0	105.8	100.8	51.0	10.6	0.8
2015[4]	12.5	62.5	0.2	22.3	9.9	40.7	76.9	104.3	101.4	51.7	11.0	0.8

(1) Live births per 1,000 population. (2) Live births per 1,000 women 15-44 years of age. (3) Beginning in 1997, rate computed by relating births to women age 45 and over to women 45-49 years of age. (4) Preliminary.

Cesarean Delivery Rates by State, 2000-15

Source: National Center for Health Statistics (NCHS), CDC, U.S. Dept. of Health and Human Services

State	2000	2010	2013	2015[1]	Percent change, 2000-15	State	2000	2010	2013	2015[1]	Percent change, 2000-15
Alabama	26.3%	35.3%	35.8%	35.2%	33.8%	Missouri	22.3%	31.9%	31.1%	30.4%	36.3%
Alaska	17.0	21.5	24.0	23.0	35.3	Montana	19.0	30.3	29.7	29.7	56.3
Arizona	18.6	27.0	27.4	27.6	48.4	Nebraska	22.5	31.1	30.3	31.1	38.2
Arkansas	26.3	34.8	34.4	32.3	22.8	Nevada	21.7	34.8	34.9	34.6	59.4
California	23.4	33.0	33.2	32.3	38.0	New Hampshire	21.0	30.4	30.1	30.8	46.7
Colorado	18.3	25.9	26.0	25.9	41.5	New Jersey	27.3	38.4	38.4	36.6	34.1
Connecticut	21.6	35.1	34.8	34.0	57.4	New Mexico	17.1	22.8	24.3	24.3	42.1
Delaware	24.8	33.9	31.5	32.0	29.0	New York	24.6	34.5	34.3	33.8	37.4
District of Columbia	22.6	33.0	34.2	31.8	40.7	North Carolina	23.0	30.8	30.4	29.3	27.4
Florida	24.9	37.8	37.7	37.3	49.8	North Dakota	20.6	27.7	28.6	27.5	33.5
Georgia	22.5	33.8	34.2	33.6	49.3	Ohio	20.0	30.7	31.1	30.4	52.0
Hawaii	14.6	27.2	25.2	25.9	77.4	Oklahoma	21.0	34.7	33.8	32.4	54.3
Idaho	18.3	24.8	24.9	24.4	33.3	Oregon	19.4	29.4	28.0	27.1	39.7
Illinois	20.9	31.1	31.7	31.0	48.3	Pennsylvania	21.7	31.3	31.3	30.1	38.7
Indiana	21.5	30.3	30.5	29.6	37.7	Rhode Island	21.9	33.0	31.3	30.8	40.6
Iowa	20.8	30.3	30.8	29.8	43.3	South Carolina	25.2	35.0	35.0	33.7	33.7
Kansas	22.2	30.5	30.2	29.6	33.3	South Dakota	22.8	26.6	25.5	25.7	12.7
Kentucky	23.6	35.4	36.6	34.4	45.8	Tennessee	24.8	34.2	34.0	33.1	33.5
Louisiana	26.6	39.6	38.9	37.5	41.0	Texas	24.7	35.1	35.2	34.4	39.3
Maine	22.8	29.8	30.0	29.4	28.9	Utah	16.8	23.1	22.4	22.8	35.7
Maryland	24.1	34.5	35.1	34.9	44.8	Vermont	17.3	27.5	27.3	25.5	47.4
Massachusetts	23.3	33.0	31.5	31.5	35.2	Virginia	23.1	34.3	33.7	32.9	42.4
Michigan	21.9	32.6	32.6	32.0	46.1	Washington	20.6	29.5	28.3	27.5	33.5
Minnesota	19.4	27.1	26.9	26.5	36.6	West Virginia	25.4	36.0	35.9	34.8	37.0
Mississippi	28.2	37.0	38.5	38.0	34.8	Wisconsin	17.5	26.0	26.2	26.2	49.7
						Wyoming	19.4	27.9	28.9	27.3	40.7
						United States	**22.8**	**32.7**	**32.7**	**32.0**	**40.4**

Note: The cesarean rate is the percentage of all live births by cesarean delivery. (1) Preliminary.

Use of Infertility Services by Selected Characteristics, 2006-10

Source: National Center for Health Statistics (NCHS), CDC, U.S. Dept. of Health and Human Services

Characteristic	Total[1]	Age in years				Prior live births		Current fertility problems[2]	
		25-29	30-34	35-39	40-44	None	One or more	Yes	No
Number of women (thous.)	40,912	10,535	9,188	10,538	10,652	10,340	30,572	5,791	35,121
				Percent					
Any infertility service	16.8%	12.5%	14.4%	20.7%	19.3%	14.4%	17.6%	41.0%	12.8%
Any medical help to get pregnant	12.5	7.7	11.1	16.4	14.5	13.6	12.1	36.3	8.6
Advice	9.4	6.2	7.8	13.3	9.9	11.4	8.7	28.9	6.1
Tests on either partner	7.3	3.3	6.3	10.4	9.0	8.5	6.9	27.4	4.0
Ovulation drugs	5.8	2.4	5.5	8.6	6.5	5.6	5.8	19.5	3.5
Surgery or treatment of blocked tubes	1.3	0.3	0.5	2.0	2.3	1.8	1.1	3.2	1.0
Artificial insemination	1.7	0.3	0.9	2.9	2.8	2.3	1.5	7.4	0.8
Assisted reproductive technology	0.7	NA	0.2	1.5	0.9	0.9	0.6	3.1	0.3
Any medical help to prevent miscarriage	6.8	6.1	5.7	8.1	7.3	2.7	8.2	12.8	5.8

NA = Not available. Note: Data is for women or their partners who have ever used service shown. Respondents could report one or more types of medical help, so sum of figures will not equal totals. From interviews conducted 2006-10. (1) Women aged 25-44. (2) Impaired fecundity (physical difficulty in either getting pregnant or carrying a pregnancy to live birth) or 12-month infertility at time of interview.

Numbers of Multiple Births in the U.S., 1990-2014

Source: National Center for Health Statistics (NCHS), CDC, U.S. Dept. of Health and Human Services

Year	Twins	Triplets	Quadruplets	Quintuplets[1]	Year	Twins	Triplets	Quadruplets	Quintuplets[1]
1990	93,865	2,830	185	13	2007	138,961	5,967	369	91
1995	96,736	4,551	365	57	2008	138,660	5,877	345	46
2000	118,916	6,742	506	77	2009	137,217	5,905	355	80
2001	121,246	6,885	501	85	2010	132,562	5,153	313	37
2002	125,134	6,898	434	69	2011	131,269	5,137	239	41
2003	128,665	7,110	468	85	2012	131,024	4,598	276	45
2004	132,219	6,750	439	86	2013	132,324	4,364	270	66
2005	133,122	6,208	418	68	2014	135,336	4,233	246	47
2006	137,085	6,118	355	67					

(1) Quintuplets and other multiple births of five or more.

Origin Countries for U.S. Foreign Adoptions, 2000-15

Source: Annual Report on Intercountry Adoption, Bureau of Consular Affairs, U.S. Dept. of State; Office of Immigration Statistics, U.S. Dept. of Homeland Security

(ranked by fiscal year 2015 adoptions)

Country	2015	2014	2013	2012	2011	2010	2009	2008	2007	2005	2000
China[2]	2,354	2,040	2,306	2,697	2,589	3,401	2,990	3,852	5,453	7,906	5,053
Ethiopia	335	716	993	1,568	1,727	2,513	2,221	1,666	1,255	441	95
South Korea	318	370	138	627	736	863	1,106	1,038	939	1,630	1,794
Ukraine	303	521	438	395	632	445	605	487	606	821	659
Uganda	202	201	276	238	207	62	69	55	54	17	1
Bulgaria	185	183	160	125	75	40	15	5	20	30	214
Congo, Dem. Rep. of the	168	230	313	240	133	41	21	9	10	11	1
Colombia	153	172	159	195	216	235	237	308	310	291	246
Philippines	150	172	178	125	230	214	292	279	265	271	173
Haiti	143	464	388	154	33	133[1]	336	300	190	234	131
Total[3]	5,648	6,441	7,094	8,668	9,320	11,059[1]	12,782	17,229	19,741	22,710	18,120

(1) Does not reflect approx. 1,090 Haitian children admitted as part of the Special Humanitarian Parole following the 2010 earthquake in Haiti. (2) Not incl. adoptions from Hong Kong. (3) Includes countries not shown.

Leading Causes of Infant Death in the U.S., 2014

Source: National Vital Statistics System, National Center for Health Statistics, CDC, U.S. Dept. of Health and Human Services

Cause of death	Number	Percent of total deaths	Mortality rate[1]
Congenital malformations, deformations, and chromosomal abnormalities	4,746	20.4%	119.0
Disorders related to short gestation and low birth weight, not elsewhere classified	4,173	18.0	104.6
Newborn affected by maternal complications of pregnancy	1,574	6.8	39.5
Sudden infant death syndrome	1,545	6.7	38.7
Accidents (unintentional injuries)	1,161	5.0	29.1
Newborn affected by complications of placenta, cord, and membranes	965	4.2	24.2
Bacterial sepsis[2] of newborn	544	2.3	13.6
Respiratory distress of newborn	460	2.0	11.5
Diseases of the circulatory system	444	1.9	11.1
Neonatal hemorrhage	441	1.9	11.1
All other causes	7,162	30.9	—
All causes	**23,215**	**100.0**	**582.1**

— = Not available. (1) Deaths of infants under 1 year of age per 100,000 live births. (2) Toxic condition resulting from the spread of bacteria.

Nonmarital Childbearing in the U.S., 1970-2014

Source: National Center for Health Statistics (NCHS), CDC, U.S. Dept. of Health and Human Services

	1970	1975	1980	1985	1990	1995	2000	2005	2010	2012	2013	2014
Live births to unmarried mothers (thous.)	399	448	666	828	1,165	1,254	1,347	1,527	1,633	1,610	1,596	1,605
Race/Hispanic origin of mother	Percent of live births to unmarried mothers											
All races and origins	10.7%	14.3%	18.4%	22.0%	28.0%	32.2%	33.2%	36.9%	40.8%	40.7%	40.6%	40.2%
White	5.5	7.1	11.2	14.7	20.4	25.3	27.1	31.7	35.9	35.9	35.8	35.7
Black	37.5	49.5	56.1	61.2	66.5	69.9	68.5	69.3	72.1	71.6	71.0	70.4
American Indian or Alaska Native	22.4	32.7	39.2	46.8	53.6	57.2	58.4	63.5	65.6	66.9	66.4	65.7
Asian or Pacific Islander	—	—	7.3	9.5	13.2	16.3	14.8	16.2	17.0	17.0	17.0	16.4
Hispanic origin (select states)[1,2]	—	—	23.6	29.5	36.7	40.8	42.7	48.0	53.4	53.5	53.2	52.9
Maternal age	Percent distribution of live births to unmarried mothers											
Under 20 years	50.1%	52.1%	40.8%	33.8%	30.9%	30.9%	28.0%	23.1%	20.1%	17.1%	15.4%	13.9%
20-24 years	31.8	29.9	35.6	36.3	34.7	34.5	37.4	38.3	36.8	36.9	36.8	36.1
25 years and over	18.1	18.0	23.5	29.9	34.4	34.7	34.6	38.7	43.1	46.1	47.9	50.0
Race/Hispanic origin of mother	Live births per 1,000 unmarried women 15-44 years of age[3]											
All races and origins	26.4	24.5	29.4	32.8	43.8	44.3	44.0	47.2	47.5	45.3	44.3	43.9
White[4]	13.9	12.4	18.1	22.5	32.9	37.0	38.2	43.2	44.5	42.1	40.8	40.6
Black[4]	95.5	84.2	81.1	77.0	90.5	74.5	70.5	67.2	65.3	62.6	61.7	61.5
Hispanic origin (select states)[1,2]	—	—	—	89.6	88.7	87.2	96.2	80.6	72.6	69.9	68.5	

— = Not available. (1) Hispanic origin data prior to 1995 is not directly comparable with data for more recent years due to differences in reporting area. (2) Hispanics may be of any race. (3) Rates computed by dividing births to unmarried mothers, regardless of mother's age, by the pop. of unmarried women 15-44 years of age. (4) For 1970 and 1975, birth rates are by race of child.

Number, Ratio, and Rate of Legal Abortions in U.S., 1970-2012

Source: *Abortion Surveillance—United States, 2012*, Centers for Disease Control and Prevention, U.S. Dept. of Health and Human Services

Year	Legal abortions	Ratio[1]	Rate[2]	Year	Legal abortions	Ratio[1]	Rate[2]	Year	Legal abortions	Ratio[1]	Rate[2]
1970	193,491	52	5	1993	1,330,414	333	23	2003	848,163	245	16
1971	485,816	137	11	1994	1,267,415	321	21	2004	839,226	241	16
1972	586,760	180	13	1995	1,210,883	311	20	2005	820,151	236	16
1973	615,831	196	14	1996	1,225,937	315	21	2006	852,385	237	16
1974	763,476	242	17	1997	1,186,039	306	20	2007	827,609	229	16
1975	854,853	272	18	1998	884,273	270	17	2008	825,564	232	16
1980	1,297,606	359	25	1999	861,789	261	17	2009	789,217	227	15
1990	1,429,247	344	24	2000	857,475	251	16	2010	765,651	227	15
1991	1,388,937	338	24	2001	853,485	249	16	2011	730,322	219	14
1992	1,359,146	334	23	2002	854,122	250	16	2012	699,202	210	13

Note: After 1998, reporting area varies. (1) Number of abortions per 1,000 live births. (2) Number of abortions per 1,000 women aged 15-44 years.

Reported U.S. Abortions by Age, Race, and Marital Status, 2012

Source: *Abortion Surveillance—United States, 2012*, Centers for Disease Control and Prevention, U.S. Dept. of Health and Human Services

Characteristic	White No.	%	Black No.	%	Other No.	%	Total, all races No.	%
Age[1]								
Under 15 years..................	466	0.3%	638	0.6%	81	0.3%	1,185	0.4%
15-19 years.....................	17,079	12.5	13,165	12.2	2,363	10.1	32,607	12.2
20-24 years.....................	45,923	33.7	37,370	34.6	6,651	28.3	89,944	33.6
25-29 years.....................	33,697	24.7	27,896	25.8	5,929	25.3	67,522	25.2
30-34 years.....................	21,263	15.6	17,857	16.5	4,433	18.9	43,553	16.3
35-39 years.....................	12,528	9.2	8,412	7.8	2,822	12.0	23,762	8.9
40 years and over...............	5,408	4.0	2,711	2.5	1,189	5.1	9,308	3.5
Total.........................	**136,364**	**100.0**	**108,049**	**100.0**	**23,468**	**100.0**	**267,881**	**100.0**
Marital status[2]								
Married.......................	19,775	16.7	6,924	8.0	5,556	27.4	32,255	14.3
Unmarried.....................	98,462	83.3	79,438	92.0	14,721	72.6	192,621	85.7
Total.........................	**118,237**	**100.0**	**86,362**	**100.0**	**20,277**	**100.0**	**224,876**	**100.0**

Note: The CDC requests data annually from the central health agencies of 52 reporting areas (all states, DC, and NYC). Reporting is voluntary. Data exclude areas that did not report, did not report by characteristic, or did not meet reporting standards. (1) Data from 30 reporting areas; excludes 22 (AZ, CA, CT, DC, FL, HI, IL, KY, ME, MD, MA, NE, NV, NH, NM, NY, NYC, PA, TX, VT, WA, WY). (2) Data from 27 reporting areas; excludes 25 (AZ, CA, CT, DC, FL, GA, HI, IL, KY, ME, MD, MA, NE, NV, NH, NM, NY, NYC, PA, RI, TX, VT, WA, WI, WY).

Adult Transgender Population by State

Source: "How Many Adults Identify as Transgender in the United States?" (2016), The Williams Institute, UCLA School of Law

Rank	State	Population	Percent	Rank	State	Population	Percent
1.	Hawaii.................	8,450	0.78%	27.	Colorado..............	20,850	0.53%
2.	California	218,400	0.76	28.	Rhode Island	4,250	0.51
3.	New Mexico	11,750	0.75	29.	New York..............	78,600	0.51
4.	Georgia................	55,650	0.75	30.	Illinois	49,750	0.51
5.	Texas	125,350	0.66	31.	Maine	5,350	0.50
6.	Florida	100,300	0.66	32.	Maryland..............	22,300	0.49
7.	Oregon	19,750	0.65	33.	Alaska................	2,700	0.49
8.	Oklahoma.............	18,350	0.64	34.	Ohio	39,950	0.45
9.	Delaware..............	4,550	0.64	35.	Pennsylvania..........	43,800	0.44
10.	Tennessee	31,200	0.63	36.	New Jersey............	30,100	0.44
11.	Washington............	32,850	0.62	37.	Connecticut...........	12,400	0.44
12.	Arizona...............	30,550	0.62	38.	Wisconsin.............	19,150	0.43
13.	Nevada	12,700	0.61	39.	New Hampshire	4,500	0.43
14.	Mississippi	13,650	0.61	40.	Michigan..............	32,900	0.43
15.	Alabama...............	22,500	0.61	41.	Kansas	9,300	0.43
16.	North Carolina	44,750	0.60	42.	West Virginia	6,100	0.42
17.	Louisiana	20,900	0.60	43.	Idaho.................	4,750	0.41
18.	Arkansas..............	13,400	0.60	44.	Nebraska	5,400	0.39
19.	Vermont	3,000	0.59	45.	Utah	7,200	0.36
20.	Minnesota.............	24,250	0.59	46.	South Dakota	2,150	0.34
21.	South Carolina	21,000	0.58	47.	Montana	2,700	0.34
22.	Massachusetts	29,900	0.57	48.	Wyoming..............	1,400	0.32
23.	Indiana	27,600	0.56	49.	Iowa	7,400	0.31
24.	Virginia	34,500	0.55	50.	North Dakota	1,650	0.30
25.	Missouri	25,050	0.54		Washington, DC	14,550	2.77
26.	Kentucky..............	17,700	0.53		**United States...........**	**1,397,150**	**0.58**

Sexual Behavior With Opposite-Sex and Same-Sex Partners, 2011-13
Source: National Survey of Family Growth, National Center for Health Statistics (NCHS), U.S. Dept. of Health and Human Services

Characteristic	Number (thous.)	Opposite-sex sexual contact[1]	Vaginal intercourse with opposite-sex partner	Oral sex with opposite-sex partner	Anal sex with opposite-sex partner	Same-sex sexual contact[2]
		Percent of selected pop. at left who have had any—				
All women aged 18-44	**55,271**	**95.3%**	**94.2%**	**86.2%**	**35.9%**	**17.4%**
Age						
18-24 years...................	14,269	85.6	81.7	77.3	28.4	19.4
25-44 years...................	41,002	98.7	98.5	89.3	38.5	16.7
25-34 years...............	20,790	98.3	98.0	89.8	39.0	20.0
35-44 years...............	20,212	99.1	99.1	88.7	38.0	13.1
Marital/cohabiting status						
Currently married	23,191	100.0	100.0	91.2	37.5	10.9
Currently cohabiting	9,032	100.0	100.0	90.3	42.2	23.9
Never married, not cohabiting......	17,499	85.2	81.5	76.4	27.8	20.1
Formerly married, not cohabiting ...	5,549	100.0	100.0	89.0	44.4	25.0
Education[3]						
No H.S. diploma or equiv.	4,904	99.2	99.1	72.6	24.4	15.2
H.S. diploma or equiv.	11,891	98.6	97.6	87.3	40.8	20.6
Some college, no bachelor's.......	14,851	97.7	97.5	92.2	42.9	22.2
Bachelor's degree or higher	15,446	96.8	96.1	91.5	36.2	12.2
Race/Hispanic origin						
White, not Hispanic..............	31,880	95.4	93.9	91.9	40.5	19.6
Black, not Hispanic..............	7,581	96.3	95.6	82.7	27.5	19.4
Hispanic, any race	10,811	95.8	95.5	77.7	32.3	11.2
All men aged 18-44	**54,685**	**93.5**	**92.0**	**87.4**	**42.3**	**6.2**
Age						
18-24 years...................	14,718	83.5	79.9	77.6	29.3	6.6
25-44 years...................	39,967	97.2	96.5	91.0	47.0	6.0
25-34 years...............	20,453	95.6	94.6	90.1	49.3	6.0
35-44 years...............	19,514	98.9	98.5	92.0	44.8	6.0
Marital/cohabiting status						
Currently married	21,298	100.0	100.0	93.4	45.4	3.9
Currently cohabiting	8,157	100.0	100.0	94.7	57.0	5.4
Never married, not cohabiting......	21,793	83.7	79.9	77.4	30.8	8.9
Formerly married, not cohabiting ...	3,438	100.0	100.0	97.3	60.4	5.2
Education[3]						
No H.S. diploma or equiv.........	5,890	97.0	97.0	80.2	45.0	3.7
H.S. diploma or equiv............	13,473	96.9	96.9	90.9	50.4	5.4
Some college, no bachelor's.......	14,002	96.6	94.2	92.7	47.1	7.5
Bachelor's degree or higher	13,007	95.2	94.8	91.7	38.5	6.6
Race/Hispanic origin						
White, not Hispanic..............	31,423	93.7	92.0	91.0	44.1	6.9
Black, not Hispanic..............	6,304	96.3	95.4	90.4	35.4	5.3
Hispanic, any race	11,292	93.3	92.4	78.6	40.4	6.2

H.S. = High school. **Note:** Totals include those of other or multiple race and origin groups not shown separately. (1) Includes vaginal, oral, or anal sex. (2) For women, includes oral sex or any sexual experience with same-sex (female) partners. For men, includes oral or anal sex with male partners. (3) Persons aged 22-44 at time of interview only.

Sexual Orientation Among U.S. Adults, 2014
Source: *National Health Interview Survey, 2014*, National Center for Health Statistics (NCHS), U.S. Dept. of Health and Human Services

Sexual orientation	Gay or lesbian[1]		Straight[2]		Bisexual	
	Number (thous.)	% of group	Number (thous.)	% of group	Number (thous.)	% of group
Overall	3,756	1.6%	226,434	97.6%	1,720	0.7%
Sex						
Men..................	2,097	1.9	109,351	97.7	441	0.4
Women................	1,659	1.4	117,083	97.6	1,279	1.1
Age						
18-44 years.............	1,963	1.8	105,589	97.0	1,268	1.2
45-64 years.............	1,451	1.8	77,919	97.8	332	0.4
65 years and older	342	0.8	42,926	98.9	120	0.3[3]

Note: Percent distributions may not equal 100 due to rounding. (1) Response option provided was "gay" for men and "gay or lesbian" for women. (2) Response option provided was "straight, that is, not gay" for men and "straight, that is, not gay or lesbian" for women. (3) Does not meet standards of reliability or precision.

Contraceptive Use in the U.S. by Age, Hispanic Origin, and Race, 2011-13

Source: National Survey of Family Growth, National Center for Health Statistics (NCHS), U.S. Dept. of Health and Human Services

	All women	All women using contraception	Age group (years)			Hispanic origin and race			
						Hispanic, any race	Non-Hispanic White, single race	Non-Hispanic Black, single race	All other races
			15-24	25-34	35-44				
Total number (in thousands)	60,887	37,586	9,421	14,011	14,155	6,894	22,652	4,917	3,124
					Percent distribution				
Using contraception[1]	**61.7%**	100.0%	100.0%	100.0%	100.0%	100.0%	100.0%	100.0%	100.0%
Female sterilization.	15.5	25.1	1.6	21.7	44.2	32.9	21.4	36.8	16.7
Male sterilization.	5.1	8.2	*	3.8	17.9	3.5	11.9	1.5	2.3
Pill.	16.0	25.9	47.3	25.0	12.4	19.0	29.0	17.0	32.0
Long-acting reversible contraception	7.2	11.6	10.5	16.5	7.6	15.1	11.4	8.6	10.6
Intrauterine device.	6.4	10.3	7.6	15.1	7.4	13.2	10.5	6.5	9.1
Implant.	0.8	1.3	2.9	1.4	*	1.9	0.9	2.1	1.5
Injectable (Depo-Provera).	2.8	4.5	8.5	4.8	1.6	2.1	2.4	3.1	4.7
Contraceptive ring or patch	1.6	2.6	4.2	3.1	1.0	4.7	3.1	10.0	6.0
Condom	9.4	15.3	21.4	17.1	9.4	15.0	14.2	16.3	22.0
Periodic abstinence— calendar rhythm	0.7	1.2	—	—	—	—	—	—	—
Periodic abstinence— natural family planning	0.1	0.2	—	—	—	—	—	—	—
Withdrawal	3.0	4.8	4.7	6.0	3.7	6.4	4.5	5.1	3.3
Other methods	0.3	0.5	1.7	1.9	2.2	1.4	2.1	1.7	2.4
Not using contraception[2]	**38.3%**	—	—	—	—	—	—	—	—
Pregnant or postpartum	5.0	—	—	—	—	—	—	—	—
Seeking pregnancy	4.5	—	—	—	—	—	—	—	—
Never had intercourse.	10.8	—	—	—	—	—	—	—	—
No intercourse in 3 months before interview.	8.2	—	—	—	—	—	—	—	—
Had intercourse in 3 months before interview.	6.9	—	—	—	—	—	—	—	—

— = Not available or applicable. * = Figure does not meet standards of reliability or precision. **Note:** Percentages may not add to 100 due to rounding. (1) Does not include the diaphragm contraceptive method because figure does not meet reliability/precision standards. (2) Includes reasons for nonuse not shown.

Child Care Arrangements of Young Children, 1991-2012

Source: *Digest of Education Statistics*, National Center for Education Statistics, U.S. Dept. of Education

	1991	1995	1999	2001	2005	2012
			Number in thousands			
All 3- to 5-year-olds[1]	8,402	9,222	8,518	8,551	9,066	8,244
			Percent of total			
Nonparental arrangements[2]	69.0%	74.1%	76.9%	73.9%	73.7%	77.9%
Center-based programs[3]	52.8	55.1	59.7	56.4	57.2	60.6
Relative care	16.9	19.4	22.8	22.8	22.6	26.2
Nonrelative care	14.8	16.9	16.1	14.0	11.6	13.3
Parental care only	31.0	25.9	23.1	26.1	26.3	22.1

(1) 3- to 5-year-old children not yet enrolled in kindergarten. (2) Total percentage of children who participated in nonparental arrangements. Each child is counted only once, even if he or she participated in more than one type of nonparental care; percentages may not add up to 100. (3) Includes day care centers, nursery schools, prekindergartens, preschools, and Head Start programs.

Sexual Activity of U.S. High School Students, 2015

Source: *Youth Risk Behavior Surveillance—United States, 2015*, Centers for Disease Control and Prevention, U.S. Dept. of Health and Human Services

Race/ethnicity	Ever had sexual intercourse			First sexual intercourse before age 13			Currently sexually active[1]			Condom use during last sexual intercourse[2]		
	Female	Male	Total	Female	Male	Total	Female	Male	Total	Female	Male	Total
White, non-Hispanic . .	40.3%	39.5%	39.9%	1.6%	3.5%	2.5%	31.4%	29.1%	30.3%	55.9%	58.1%	56.8%
Black, non-Hispanic . .	37.4	58.8	48.5	4.3	12.1	8.3	25.7	40.0	33.1	46.7	73.6	63.4
Hispanic, any race . . .	39.8	45.1	42.5	3.1	6.8	5.0	30.1	30.5	30.3	48.3	62.5	55.6
Grade												
9	20.7	27.3	24.1	2.5	4.6	3.6	14.0	17.3	15.7	56.7	63.3	60.5
10	33.5	37.9	35.7	2.7	6.8	4.7	24.7	26.4	25.5	54.0	65.6	59.9
11	48.2	51.2	49.6	1.6	4.8	3.2	36.7	34.5	35.5	52.9	62.5	57.7
12	57.2	59.0	58.1	1.7	5.5	3.6	46.5	45.4	46.0	48.8	57.4	52.9
Total	**39.2**	**43.2**	**41.2**	**2.2**	**5.6**	**3.9**	**29.8**	**30.3**	**30.1**	**52.0**	**61.5**	**56.9**

(1) Sexual intercourse during the 3 months before the survey. (2) Among the 30.1% who were currently sexually active. (3) Non-Hispanic.

Risk Behaviors in U.S. High School Students, 2015

Source: *Youth Risk Behavior Surveillance—United States, 2015*, Centers for Disease Control and Prevention, U.S. Dept. of Health and Human Services

		Rarely or never wore a seat belt[1]			Rarely or never wore a bicycle helmet[2]			Rode with a driver who had been drinking alcohol[3]		
		Female	Male	Total	Female	Male	Total	Female	Male	Total
Race/	White, non-Hispanic	3.5%	5.3%	4.4%	75.3%	77.5%	76.4%	17.5%	17.7%	17.7%
ethnicity	Black, non-Hispanic	7.6	12.4	10.1	82.6	91.6	88.2	21.2	20.6	21.1
	Hispanic, any race	6.3	6.8	6.5	90.3	90.0	90.1	27.3	25.3	26.2
Grade	9	5.5	7.0	6.3	78.3	80.2	79.4	21.3	19.1	20.2
	10	4.5	7.6	6.0	81.9	80.4	81.1	18.4	19.0	18.7
	11	4.1	7.1	5.8	78.5	85.4	82.3	20.1	20.4	20.6
	12	5.1	6.1	5.6	82.1	84.9	83.5	21.0	19.9	20.4
Total		**4.9**	**7.2**	**6.1**	**80.1**	**82.4**	**81.4**	**20.2**	**19.6**	**20.0**

(1) When riding in a car driven by someone else. (2) Among the 68.0% of students who had ridden a bicycle during the 12 months before the survey. (3) In a car or other vehicle one or more times during the 30 days before the survey.

Risky Driving Behaviors by U.S. High School Students, 2015

Source: *Youth Risk Behavior Surveillance–United States, 2015*, Centers for Disease Control and Prevention, U.S. Dept. of Health and Human Services

		Drove when drinking alcohol[1]			Texted or emailed while driving[2]		
		Female	Male	Total	Female	Male	Total
Race/	White, non-Hispanic	5.4%	9.4%	7.4%	45.3%	45.0%	45.2%
ethnicity	Black, non-Hispanic	5.1	8.3	6.9	33.1	33.0	32.8
	Hispanic, any race	8.0	10.7	9.4	28.2	42.2	35.8
Grade	9	5.5	5.7	5.6	14.4	17.4	15.9
	10	2.2	8.2	5.3	24.7	25.2	25.0
	11	6.8	10.3	8.7	45.1	50.1	47.9
	12	8.0	11.7	9.9	60.8	61.9	61.4
Total		**6.0**	**9.5**	**7.8**	**40.4**	**42.4**	**41.5**

(1) Among the 61.4% of students who had driven a car or other vehicle one or more times during the 30 days before the survey. (2) Among the 61.3% of students who had driven a car or other vehicle on at least one day during the 30 days before the survey.

U.S. Motor Vehicle Crashes

Source: National Safety Council (NSC); Natl. Highway Traffic Safety Admin. (NHTSA)

An estimated 35,398 people in the U.S. were killed in motor vehicle crashes in 2014, up 0.1% from the total for 2013. The number of licensed drivers (212.8 mil) and vehicle miles driven (3.04 tril) increased slightly in 2014; the death rate per 100 mil vehicle miles dropped 2% to 1.16.

Motor vehicle deaths per 10,000 registered vehicles was 1.37 in 2014. In comparison, the death rate was 1.38 in 2013 and 1.85 in 2004, which represents a 25% decrease over 10 years. The number of fatalities per 100,000 population declined 27% between 2004 and 2014 but only decreased 1% from 2013 to 2014.

Male drivers were involved in about 6 mil crashes in 2014, whereas female drivers were in 3.3 mil. Male drivers were also involved in 74% of fatal crashes, or about 32,402, compared with 11,214 incidents involving female drivers.

In 2014, 9,967 motor vehicle traffic fatalities (31%) involved an alcohol-impaired (blood alcohol concentration of 0.08 or greater) driver or motorcycle operator.

Seat belt use was 89% in 2015. The least likely seat belt users were occupants of pickup trucks (81%) and those traveling in light traffic (79%). In 2014, the most recent year for which data was available, seat belts and child restraints saved an estimated 13,054 lives among passenger vehicle occupants; frontal air bags saved an estimated 2,396 more lives. Women used safety belts (89%) more often than men (84%).

Crashes	Deaths	Injuries
All motor vehicle crashes	35,398	4,100,000
Collision between motor vehicles	13,900	3,150,000
Collision with fixed object	10,700	520,000
Collision with pedestrian	6,300	145,000
Noncollision accidents (e.g., rollovers)	3,300	150,000
Collision with pedalcycle	1,000	120,000
Collision with railroad train	144	1,000
Other (mostly collisions with animals). .	100	14,000

Note: NSC numbers are rounded and preliminary.

Improper Driving Reported in U.S. Crashes, 2000-14

Source: National Safety Council (NSC)

	Percent of fatal crashes			Percent of injury crashes			Percent of all crashes		
Type	2014	2005	2000	2014	2005	2000	2014	2005	2000
Improper driving	**57.9%**	**62.7%**	**61.6%**	**62.7%**	**62.7%**	**60.3%**	**60.4%**	**58.5%**	**57.8%**
Speed too fast or unsafe.	15.1	18.1	23.7	13.5	15.0	16.3	12.1	12.7	13.6
Right of way	11.1	12.2	18.6	19.0	17.5	19.9	13.8	14.3	20.1
Failed to yield	7.6	8.0	10.1	13.8	12.5	12.5	10.5	10.8	12.7
Disregarded signal	1.6	1.4	4.6	3.3	2.5	3.6	2.0	1.7	5.3
Passed stop sign.	1.9	2.8	3.8	2.0	2.5	1.3	1.3	1.8	2.2
Drove left of center	6.1	8.0	8.2	1.4	2.2	1.1	1.0	1.6	1.0
Made improper turn	3.2	4.5	0.7	3.5	4.2	2.0	3.5	4.5	2.4
Improper overtaking	1.1	1.4	0.9	1.0	0.6	0.6	1.1	0.8	0.9
Followed too closely	1.0	1.0	0.5	7.6	6.8	4.3	8.2	8.7	5.7
Other improper driving	20.3	17.5	9.0	16.7	16.4	16.1	20.7	15.9	14.1
No improper driving stated	**42.1**	**37.3**	**38.4**	**37.3**	**37.3**	**39.7**	**39.6**	**41.5**	**42.2**

Note: Based on reports from state traffic authorities. When a driver was under the influence of alcohol or drugs, the crash was considered a result of the driver's physical condition, not a driving error. Percents may not add up to totals due to rounding.

U.S. Passenger Deaths and Death Rates, 1999-2013
Source: National Safety Council (NSC)

Year	Light duty vehicles[1] Deaths	Rate[4]	Vans, SUVs, pickup trucks[1] Deaths	Rate[4]	Buses[2] Deaths	Rate[4]	Railroad passenger trains Deaths	Rate[4]	Scheduled airlines[3] Deaths	Rate[4]
1999	20,851	0.84	11,295	0.76	40	0.07	14	0.10	23	0.005
2000	20,689	0.81	11,545	0.76	3	0.01	4	0.03	94	0.02
2001	20,310	0.78	11,736	0.76	11	0.02	3	0.02	273	0.06
2002	20,564	0.78	12,278	0.78	36	0.06	7	0.05	0	0.00
2003	19,723	0.74	12,551	0.78	30	0.05	3	0.02	23	0.005
2004	19,183	0.71	12,678	0.75	27	0.05	3	0.02	13	0.002
2005	18,509	0.68	13,043	0.76	43	0.07	16	0.10	20	0.003
2006	17,792	0.66	12,723	0.72	15	0.02	2	0.01	51	0.01
2007	29,075	0.66	NA	NA	18	0.03	5	0.03	0	0.00
2008	25,457	0.59	NA	NA	50	0.08	24	0.13	0	0.00
2009	23,441	0.53	NA	NA	21	0.04	3	0.02	49	0.01
2010	22,271	0.50	NA	NA	28	0.05	3	0.02	0	0.00
2011	21,221	0.48	NA	NA	35	0.06	6	0.03	0	0.00
2012	21,669	0.49	NA	NA	25	0.04	5	0.02	0	0.00
2013	21,127	0.47	NA	NA	28	0.04	6	0.03	5	0.001

NA = Not available. (1) From 2007 on, light duty vehicles includes passenger cars, light trucks, vans, and SUVs, which are shown separately in previous years. Drivers of light duty vehicles are considered passengers. Includes taxi passengers. (2) Excludes school buses. (3) Excludes charter, cargo, and on-demand services and deaths due to suicide/sabotage. (4) Deaths per 100 mil passenger miles.

U.S. Death Rates for Suicide at Selected Ages, 1960-2014
Source: *Health, United States, 2015*, National Center for Health Statistics (NCHS), CDC, U.S. Dept. of Health and Human Services
(deaths per 100,000 resident population)

Age	2014 Both sexes	Male	Female	2000 Both sexes	Male	Female	1980 Both sexes	Male	Female	1960 Both sexes	Male	Female
15-24 years	11.5	18.2	4.6	10.2	17.1	3.0	12.3	20.2	4.3	5.2	8.2	2.2
25-44 years	15.8	24.3	7.2	13.4	21.3	5.4	15.6	24.0	7.7	12.2	17.9	6.6
45-64 years	19.5	29.7	9.8	13.5	21.3	6.2	15.9	23.7	8.9	22.0	34.4	10.2
65 years and older	16.6	31.4	5.0	15.2	31.1	4.0	17.6	35.0	6.1	24.5	44.0	8.4
All ages[1]	13.0	20.7	5.8	10.4	17.7	4.0	12.2	19.9	5.7	12.5	20.0	5.6

(1) Incl. ages not shown separately here.

U.S. Fires, 2015
Source: National Fire Protection Association

Fires
- Public fire departments responded to 1,345,500 fires in 2015, an increase of 3.7% from 2014.
- Every 23 seconds, a fire department responds to a fire somewhere in the United States.
- There were 501,500 structure fires in 2015, a slight increase of 1.5% from 2014. Of those fires, 73% (365,500 fires) occurred in homes.
- Fires in highway vehicles increased 3.9% from the previous year, totaling 174,000 in 2015.
- There were 639,500 fires in outside and other properties, a significant increase of 4.8% from 2014.

Intentionally set fires
- There were an estimated 23,000 intentionally set structure fires in 2015, a significant increase of 21.1% from 2014.
- Intentionally set structure fires are believed to have resulted in 205 civilian deaths in 2015, a significant increase of 30.6% from the year before. Property damage from intentionally set structure fires totaled $460 mil, a significant decrease of 25.0% from the 2014 figure.

Civilian deaths
- There were an estimated 3,280 civilian fire deaths in 2015. This was a 0.2% increase from the year before.
- The number of civilian fire deaths that occurred in home structure fires decreased 6.7% to 2,560, and fires in the home caused 78% of all fire deaths.
- Fires caused an average of one civilian death every 2 hours and 40 minutes.

Civilian injuries
- There were an estimated 15,700 civilian fire injuries reported in 2015, a 0.5% decrease from 2014. Nationwide, a civilian was injured in a fire every 33½ minutes; a civilian fire injury occurred in a home fire every 47½ minutes.
- Home structure fires were the site of 11,075 civilian fire injuries in 2015. Non-home structure fires accounted for 1,925 civilian injuries.

Property damage
- Direct property damage from fires amounted to an estimated $14.3 bil* in 2015, an increase of 23.2% from 2014. Structure fires accounted for $10.3 bil of property damage.
- Property loss associated with home fires came to $7.0 bil for 2015.

* = Includes two major California wildfires (Valley Fire resulting in $1.5 bil and the Butte Fire resulting in $450 mil).

Leading Causes of Death in the U.S., 2014
Source: National Vital Statistics System, National Center for Health Statistics, CDC, U.S. Dept. of Health and Human Services

	Number	% of total deaths	Death rate[1]		Number	% of total deaths	Death rate[1]
All causes	2,626,418	100.0%	724.6	6. Alzheimer's disease	93,541	3.6	25.4
1. Heart disease	614,348	23.4	167.0	7. Diabetes	76,488	2.9	20.9
2. Cancer	591,699	22.5	161.2	8. Influenza and pneumonia	55,227	2.1	15.1
3. Chronic lower respiratory diseases	147,101	5.6	40.5	9. Kidney disease	48,146	1.8	13.2
4. Unintentional injuries	136,053	5.2	40.5	10. Suicide	42,773	1.6	13.0
5. Stroke	133,103	5.1	36.5	All other causes (residual)	687,939	26.2	—

— = Not available. (1) Per 100,000 U.S. population.

Drug-Induced Deaths in the U.S., 2014

Source: National Vital Statistics System, National Center for Health Statistics, CDC, U.S. Dept. of Health and Human Services

Numbers include deaths from poisoning and medical conditions caused by use of legal or illegal drugs regardless of intent (accident, suicide, homicide, or undetermined).

State	Number	Rate[1]	State	Number	Rate[1]	State	Number	Rate[1]	State	Number	Rate[1]
Alabama	800	16.5	Indiana	1,233	18.7	Nebraska	140	7.4	South Carolina	726	15.0
Alaska.	127	17.2	Iowa	273	8.8	Nevada	555	19.5	South Dakota. .	70	8.2
Arizona	1,274	18.9	Kansas	349	12.0	New Hampshire	348	26.2	Tennessee . . .	1,330	20.3
Arkansas.	377	12.7	Kentucky.	1,128	25.6	New Jersey . . .	1,303	14.6	Texas	2,727	10.1
California	4,816	12.4	Louisiana	810	17.4	New Mexico . .	559	26.8	Utah	617	21.0
Colorado	917	17.1	Maine	227	17.1	New York.	2,510	12.7	Vermont	90	14.4
Connecticut. . .	639	17.8	Maryland.	1,095	18.3	North Carolina	1,435	14.4	Virginia	1,002	12.0
Delaware.	204	21.8	Massachusetts	1,402	20.8	North Dakota. .	48	6.5	Washington. . .	1,058	15.0
Florida	2,804	14.1	Michigan	2,048	20.7	Ohio	2,832	24.4	West Virginia. .	646	34.9
Georgia.	1,268	12.6	Minnesota. . . .	586	10.7	Oklahoma	809	20.9	Wisconsin	874	15.2
Hawaii.	174	12.3	Mississippi . . .	361	12.1	Oregon	617	15.5	Wyoming.	112	19.2
Idaho.	218	13.3	Missouri	1,107	18.3	Pennsylvania. .	2,829	22.1	Wash., DC . . .	106	16.1
Illinois	1,736	13.5	Montana	145	14.2	Rhode Island. .	253	24.0	**U.S.**	**49,714**	**15.6**

(1) Number of deaths due to drug-induced causes per 100,000 population.

Principal Types of Accidental Deaths in the U.S., 1970-2014

Source: *Injury Facts®, 2016 Edition*, National Safety Council; National Center for Health Statistics, U.S. Dept. of Health and Human Services

Year[1]	Total[2]	Motor vehicle	Falls	Poisoning	Choking: Inhalation of food, object	Drowning	Fires, flames, smoke	Mechanical suffocation	Firearms
1970	NA	54,633	16,926	5,299	2,753	7,860	6,718	NA	2,406
1980	105,718	53,172	13,294	4,331	3,249	7,257	5,822	NA	1,955
1985	93,457	45,901	12,001	5,170	3,551	5,316	4,938	NA	1,649
1990	91,983	46,814	12,313	5,803	3,303	4,685	4,175	NA	1,416
1995	93,320	43,363	13,986	9,072	3,185	4,350	3,761	NA	1,225
2000	97,900	43,354	13,322	12,757	4,313	3,482	3,377	1,335	776
2005	117,809	45,343	19,656	23,617	4,386	3,582	3,197	1,514	789
2007	123,706	43,945	22,631	29,846	4,344	3,443	3,286	1,653	613
2008	121,902	39,790	24,013	31,116	4,366	3,548	2,912	1,759	592
2009	118,046	36,216	24,792	31,758	4,370	3,517	2,756	1,569	554
2010	120,859	35,332	26,009	33,041	4,570	3,782	2,782	1,595	606
2011	126,438	35,303	27,483	36,280	4,708	3,556	2,746	1,534	591
2012	127,792	36,415	28,756	36,332	4,634	3,551	2,464	1,604	548
2013	130,557	35,398	30,208	38,851	4,864	3,391	2,760	1,737	505
2014[3]	136,053	35,398	31,959	42,032	4,816	3,406	2,701	1,764	586
Deaths per 100,000 population									
1970	NA	26.8	8.3	2.6	1.4	3.9	3.3	NA	1.2
1980	46.5	23.4	5.9	1.9	1.4	3.2	2.6	NA	0.9
1985	39.3	19.3	5.0	2.2	1.5	2.2	2.1	NA	0.7
1990	36.9	18.8	4.9	2.3	1.3	1.9	1.7	NA	0.6
1995	35.5	16.5	5.3	3.4	1.2	1.7	1.4	NA	0.5
2000	35.6	15.7	4.8	4.6	1.6	1.3	1.2	0.5	0.3
2005	39.7	15.3	6.6	8.0	1.5	1.2	1.1	0.5	0.3
2007	41.1	14.6	7.5	9.9	1.4	1.1	1.1	0.5	0.2
2008	40.0	13.1	7.9	10.2	1.4	1.2	1.0	0.6	0.2
2009	38.5	11.8	8.1	10.3	1.4	1.1	0.9	0.5	0.2
2010	39.0	11.4	8.4	10.7	1.5	1.2	0.9	0.5	0.2
2011	40.6	11.3	8.8	11.6	1.5	1.1	0.9	0.5	0.2
2012	40.7	11.6	9.2	11.6	1.5	1.1	0.8	0.5	0.2
2013	41.3	11.2	9.6	12.3	1.5	1.1	0.9	0.5	0.2
2014[3]	42.7	11.1	10.0	13.2	1.5	1.1	0.8	0.6	0.2

NA = Not available. **Note:** All figures include on-the-job deaths. (1) Data after 1999 are not comparable with earlier data because of classification changes. (2) Total incl. other accidental deaths not shown in detail here. (3) Preliminary.

Deaths in the U.S. Involving Firearms by Age and Sex, 2013

Source: *Injury Facts®, 2016 Edition*, National Safety Council

Type and sex	All ages	Under 5	5-14	15-19	20-24	25-44	45-64	65-74	75 or older
Total firearms deaths	33,677	82	327	2,057	4,130	11,563	9,927	2,840	2,751
Male	28,831	57	246	1,847	3,651	9,894	8,161	2,461	2,514
Female	4,846	25	81	210	479	1,669	1,766	379	237
Unintentional.	506	30	39	55	53	130	139	35	25
Male	441	24	31	51	49	113	118	34	21
Female	65	6	8	4	4	17	21	1	4
Suicide.	21,190	—	138	740	1,471	5,850	7,873	2,557	2,561
Male	18,254	—	116	650	1,288	4,955	6,574	2,268	2,403
Female	2,936	—	22	90	183	895	1,299	289	158
Homicide.	11,230	51	142	1,217	2,490	5,223	1,738	223	146
Male	9,466	32	93	1,104	2,210	4,500	1,315	140	72
Female	1,764	19	49	113	280	723	423	83	74
Legal intervention.	469	0	1	19	78	251	106	10	4
Male	448	0	1	18	77	243	96	9	4
Female	21	0	0	1	1	8	10	1	0
Undetermined[1]	282	1	7	26	38	109	71	15	15
Male	222	1	5	24	27	83	58	10	14
Female	60	0	2	2	11	26	13	5	1

— = Not applicable. (1) The intention of the death (unintentional, suicide, or homicide) could not be determined.

U.S. Infant Mortality Rates by Race and Sex, 1960-2014

Source: National Center for Health Statistics (NCHS), CDC, U.S. Dept. of Health and Human Services
(deaths of infants under 1 year old per 1,000 live births)

Year[1]	All races[2] Both sexes	Male	Female	White Both sexes	Male	Female	Black Both sexes	Male	Female
1960	26.0	29.3	22.6	22.9	26.0	19.6	44.3	49.1	39.4
1970	20.0	22.4	17.5	17.8	20.0	15.4	32.7	36.2	29.0
1980	12.6	13.9	11.2	10.9	12.1	9.5	22.2	24.2	20.2
1990	9.2	10.3	8.1	7.6	8.5	6.6	18.0	19.6	16.3
1995	7.6	8.3	6.8	6.3	7.0	5.6	15.1	16.3	13.9
1996	7.3	8.0	6.6	6.1	6.7	5.4	14.7	16.0	13.3
1997	7.2	8.0	6.5	6.0	6.7	5.4	14.2	15.5	12.8
1998	7.2	7.8	6.5	6.0	6.5	5.4	14.3	15.8	12.8
1999	7.1	7.7	6.4	5.8	6.4	5.2	14.6	15.9	13.2
2000	6.9	7.6	6.2	5.7	6.2	5.1	14.1	15.5	12.6
2001	6.9	7.5	6.1	5.7	6.2	5.1	14.0	15.5	12.5
2002	7.0	7.6	6.3	5.8	6.4	5.1	14.4	15.4	13.3
2003	6.9	7.6	6.1	5.7	6.4	5.1	14.0	15.5	12.4
2004	6.8	7.5	6.1	5.7	6.2	5.1	13.8	15.2	12.3
2005	6.9	7.6	6.2	5.7	6.3	5.1	13.7	15.2	12.3
2006	6.7	7.3	6.0	5.6	6.1	5.0	13.3	14.4	12.2
2007	6.8	7.4	6.1	5.6	6.2	5.1	13.2	14.5	11.9
2008	6.6	7.2	6.0	5.6	6.1	5.0	12.7	13.9	11.5
2009	6.4	7.0	5.8	5.3	5.8	4.8	12.6	14.1	11.2
2010	6.2	6.7	5.6	5.2	5.7	4.7	11.6	12.7	10.5
2011	6.1	6.6	5.5	5.1	5.5	4.7	11.5	12.6	10.4
2012	6.0	6.5	5.4	5.1	5.5	4.7	11.2	12.3	10.0
2013	6.0	6.5	5.4	5.1	5.6	4.5	11.2	12.0	10.4
2014	5.8	6.3	5.3	4.9	5.4	4.5	11.1	12.0	10.1

(1) Number of live births is tabulated according to mother's race (1980 and on) or parents' race (before 1980) stated on birth certificate.
(2) Incl. races not shown.

Years of Life Expected at Birth in U.S., 1900-2014

Source: National Center for Health Statistics (NCHS), CDC, U.S. Dept. of Health and Human Services

Year[3]	All races[1] Both sexes	Male	Female	White Both sexes	Male	Female	Black[2] Both sexes	Male	Female
1900	47.3	46.3	48.3	47.6	46.6	48.7	33.0	32.5	33.5
1950	68.2	65.6	71.1	69.1	66.5	72.2	60.8	59.1	62.9
1960	69.7	66.6	73.1	70.6	67.4	74.1	63.6	61.1	66.3
1970	70.8	67.1	74.7	71.7	68.0	75.6	64.1	60.0	68.3
1980	73.7	70.0	77.4	74.4	70.7	78.1	68.1	63.8	72.5
1990	75.4	71.8	78.8	76.1	72.7	79.4	69.1	64.5	73.6
1995	75.8	72.5	78.9	76.5	73.4	79.6	69.6	65.2	73.9
2000	76.8	74.1	79.3	77.3	74.7	79.9	71.8	68.2	75.1
2001	77.0	74.3	79.5	77.5	74.9	80.0	72.0	68.5	75.3
2002	77.0	74.4	79.6	77.5	74.9	80.1	72.2	68.7	75.4
2005	77.6	75.0	80.1	78.0	75.5	80.5	73.0	69.5	76.2
2006	77.8	75.2	80.3	78.3	75.8	80.7	73.4	69.9	76.7
2007	78.1	75.5	80.6	78.5	76.0	80.9	73.8	70.3	77.0
2008	78.2	75.6	80.6	78.5	76.1	80.9	74.3	70.9	77.3
2009	78.5	76.0	80.9	78.8	76.4	81.2	74.7	71.4	77.7
2010	78.7	76.2	81.0	78.9	76.5	81.3	75.1	71.8	78.0
2011	78.7	76.3	81.1	79.0	76.6	81.3	75.3	72.2	78.2
2012	78.8	76.4	81.2	79.1	76.7	81.4	75.5	72.3	78.4
2013	78.8	76.4	81.2	79.1	76.7	81.4	75.5	72.3	78.4
2014	78.8	76.4	81.2	79.0	76.7	81.4	75.6	72.5	78.4

(1) Includes races not shown. (2) Data for 1900-60 are for the nonwhite pop. (3) Data prior to 1950 does not include all states.

U.S. Life Expectancy at Selected Ages, 2014

Source: National Center for Health Statistics (NCHS), CDC, U.S. Dept. of Health and Human Services

Exact age in years	All races[1] Both sexes	Male	Female	White Both sexes	Male	Female	Black Both sexes	Male	Female
0	78.8	76.4	81.2	79.0	76.7	81.4	75.6	72.5	78.4
1	78.3	75.9	80.6	78.4	76.1	80.7	75.4	72.3	78.2
5	74.4	72.0	76.7	74.5	72.2	76.8	71.5	68.5	74.3
10	69.4	67.0	71.7	69.5	67.2	71.8	66.6	63.5	69.4
15	64.5	62.1	66.8	64.6	62.3	66.9	61.7	58.6	64.4
20	59.6	57.3	61.9	59.7	57.5	61.9	56.8	53.8	59.5
25	54.8	52.6	57.0	54.9	52.8	57.1	52.2	49.3	54.7
30	50.1	48.0	52.1	50.2	48.1	52.2	47.5	44.8	49.9
35	45.4	43.3	47.3	45.5	43.5	47.4	42.9	40.2	45.1
40	40.7	38.7	42.6	40.8	38.8	42.7	38.3	35.8	40.5
45	36.1	34.2	37.9	36.2	34.3	38.0	33.8	31.3	35.9
50	31.6	29.8	33.3	31.7	29.9	33.4	29.5	27.1	31.5
55	27.3	25.6	28.9	27.4	25.7	29.0	25.4	23.1	27.3
60	23.3	21.7	24.7	23.3	21.7	24.7	21.6	19.5	23.3
65	19.3	18.0	20.5	19.3	18.0	20.5	18.2	16.3	19.6
70	15.6	14.4	16.6	15.6	14.4	16.6	14.9	13.3	16.0
75	12.2	11.2	13.0	12.2	11.2	12.9	11.8	10.5	12.7
80	9.2	8.3	9.7	9.1	8.3	9.7	9.1	8.1	9.7
85	6.6	5.9	7.0	6.5	5.9	6.9	6.9	6.0	7.3
90	4.6	4.1	4.8	4.5	4.0	4.7	5.1	4.5	5.3
95	3.2	2.9	3.3	3.1	2.8	3.2	3.8	3.4	3.8
100	2.3	2.1	2.3	2.2	2.0	2.2	2.9	2.6	2.8

(1) Includes races not shown.

NOTED PERSONALITIES

Widely Known Americans of the Present

Political leaders, journalists, other prominent living persons. As of Oct. 2016. Excludes most who fall in categories listed elsewhere in Noted Personalities, such as Writers of the Present and Entertainment Personalities of the Present. Includes some figures who are active in American life but are not U.S. citizens.

Sheldon Adelson, b 8/4/1933 (Dorchester, MA), Las Vegas Sands founder, CEO.

Roger Ailes, b 5/15/1940 (Warren, OH), former TV exec.

Madeleine K. Albright, b 5/15/1937 (Prague, Czech.), former sec. of state.

Edwin "Buzz" Aldrin, b 1/20/1930 (Montclair, NJ), former astronaut, second person to walk on the Moon.

Samuel A. Alito Jr., b 4/1/1950 (Trenton, NJ), Supreme Court justice.

Paul Allen, b 1/21/1953 (Seattle, WA), cofounder of Microsoft.

Marin Alsop, b 10/16/1956 (New York, NY), Baltimore Symphony musical dir.

Christiane Amanpour, b 1/12/1958 (London, Eng., UK), TV journalist.

Marc Andreessen, b 7/9/1971 (New Lisbon, IA), co-author of web browser Mosaic, cofounder of Netscape.

David Axelrod, b 2/22/1955 (New York, NY), political strategist; former sr. adviser to Pres. Obama.

F. Lee Bailey, b 6/10/1933 (Waltham, MA), attorney.

Russell Baker, b 8/14/1925 (Morrisonville, VA), columnist.

Steve Ballmer, b 3/24/1956 (Detroit, MI), former Microsoft CEO; L.A. Clippers owner.

Mike Barnicle, b 8/24/1944 (Fitchburg, MA), columnist.

Mary Barra, b 12/24/1961 (Waterford, MI), General Motors CEO.

Dave Barry, b 7/3/1947 (Armonk, NY), humorist.

Max Baucus, b 12/11/1941 (Helena, MT), U.S. amb. to China, former senator (D, MT).

Gary Bauer, b 5/4/1946 (Covington, KY), domestic policy adviser to Pres. Reagan; founder, Campaign for Working Families.

Glenn Beck, b 2/10/1964 (Mount Vernon, WA), political commentator.

Chris Berman, b 5/10/1955 (Greenwich, CT), sportscaster.

Ben Bernanke, b 12/13/1953 (Augusta, GA), former Federal Reserve chair.

Carl Bernstein, b 2/14/1944 (Washington, DC), journalist; with Bob Woodward cracked Watergate scandal.

Jeff Bezos, b 1/12/1964 (Albuquerque, NM), founder and CEO of Amazon.com.

Jill Biden, b 6/5/1951 (Hammonton, NJ), English college professor, wife of U.S. vice pres. Joe Biden.

Joseph R. Biden Jr., b 11/20/1942 (Scranton, PA), U.S. vice pres.; former sen. (D, DE).

Lloyd Blankfein, b 9/20/1954 (Bronx, NY), CEO and chairman of Goldman Sachs.

Wolf Blitzer, b 3/22/1948 (Augsburg, Germany), TV journalist.

Harold Bloom, b 7/11/1930 (New York, NY), literary critic.

Michael R. Bloomberg, b 2/14/1942 (Brighton, MA), former NYC mayor, financial information/media entrepreneur.

John Boehner, b 11/17/1949 (Cincinnati, OH), former U.S. rep. (R, OH) and speaker of the House.

Charles F. Bolden, b 8/19/1946 (Columbia, SC), NASA head.

Cory Booker, b 4/27/1969 (Washington, DC), U.S. sen. (D, NJ), former Newark mayor.

Barbara Boxer, b 11/11/1940 (Brooklyn, NY), U.S. senator (D, CA).

Donna Brazile, b 12/15/1959 (Kenner, LA), political analyst.

L. Paul Bremer III, b 9/30/1941 (Hartford, CT), diplomat, former top U.S. civilian administrator in Iraq.

John O. Brennan, b 9/22/1955 (North Bergen, NJ), CIA director.

Jimmy Breslin, b 10/17/1930 (Jamaica, Queens, NY), columnist, author.

Stephen Breyer, b 8/15/1938 (San Francisco, CA), U.S. Supreme Court justice.

Sergey Brin, b 8/21/1973 (Moscow, Russia), cofounder of Google.

Roslyn M. Brock, b 5/30/1965 (Fort Pierce, FL), NAACP chair.

Tom Brokaw, b 2/6/1940 (Webster, SD), TV journalist, retired anchor.

David Brooks, b 8/11/1961 (Toronto, ON, Can.), columnist, political commentator.

Aaron Brown, b 11/10/1948 (Hopkins, MN), broadcast journalist.

Jerry (Edmund G.) Brown Jr., b 4/7/1938 (San Francisco, CA), CA gov. (D, 1975-83, 2011-), former pres. candidate.

Frank Bruni, b 10/31/1964 (White Plains, NY), columnist.

Pat Buchanan, b 11/2/1938 (Washington, DC), journalist, former pres. candidate (R).

Warren Buffett, b 8/30/1930 (Omaha, NE), investor, leading philanthropist.

Barbara Bush, b 6/8/1925 (Flushing, Queens, NY), former first lady.

Barbara Bush, b 11/25/1981 (Dallas, TX), daughter of former Pres. George W. Bush.

George H. W. Bush, b 6/12/1924 (Milton, MA), former U.S. president.

George W. Bush, b 7/6/1946 (New Haven, CT), former U.S. president.

Jeb Bush, b 2/11/1953 (Midland, TX), FL gov. (R); 2016 pres. contender.

Laura Bush, b 11/4/1946 (Midland, TX), former first lady.

Tucker Carlson, b 5/16/1969 (San Francisco, CA), journalist, TV commentator.

Ben Carson, b 9/18/1951 (Detroit, MI), neurosurgeon; 2016 pres. contender (R).

Jimmy Carter, b 10/1/1924 (Plains, GA), former U.S. president; 2002 Nobel Peace Prize winner.

Rosalynn Carter, b 8/18/1927 (Plains, GA), former first lady.

James Carville Jr., b 10/25/1944 (Fort Benning, GA), TV political analyst.

Steve Case, b 8/21/1958 (Honolulu, HI), former AOL Time Warner chair.

Joaquin Castro, b 9/16/1974 (San Antonio, TX), U.S. rep. (D, TX).

Julian Castro, b 9/16/1974 (San Antonio, TX), housing and urban development sec., former San Antonio mayor.

Dick Cheney, b 1/30/1941 (Lincoln, NE), former U.S. vice president.

Lynne Cheney, b 8/14/1941 (Casper, WY), political commentator, wife of former U.S. vice pres. Dick Cheney.

Brian Chesky, b 8/29/1981 (Niskayuna, NY), Airbnb founder, CEO.

Noam Chomsky, b 12/7/1928 (Philadelphia, PA), linguist, activist.

Chris Christie, b 9/6/1962 (Newark, NJ), NJ gov. (R); 2016 pres. contender.

Connie Chung, b 8/20/1946 (Washington, DC), former TV journalist.

James R. Clapper Jr., b 1941, director of national intelligence.

Bill Clinton, b 8/19/1946 (Hope, AR), former U.S. president.

Chelsea Clinton, b 2/27/1980 (Little Rock, AR), daughter of former pres. Bill Clinton and Hillary Rodham Clinton.

Hillary Rodham Clinton, b 10/26/1947 (Chicago, IL), former sec. of state, U.S. sen. (D, NY), first lady; 2016 presidential nominee (D).

Kate Clinton, b 11/9/1947 (Buffalo, NY), political humorist.

Kenneth Cole, b 3/23/1954 (Brooklyn, NY), fashion designer.

Gail Collins, b 11/25/1945 (Cincinnati, OH), newspaper columnist, writer.

Jason Collins, b 12/2/1978 (Northridge, CA), first openly gay active NBA player.

James Comey, b 12/14/1960 (Yonkers, NY), FBI director.

Tim Cook, b 11/1/1960 (Robertdale, AZ), CEO of Apple, Inc.

Anderson Cooper, b 6/3/1967 (New York, NY), TV news anchor.

Bob Corker, b 8/24/52 (Orangeburg, SC), U.S. sen. (R, TN).

John Cornyn, b 2/2/1952 (Houston, TX), U.S. sen. (R, TX), majority whip.

Bob Costas, b 3/22/1952 (Astoria, Queens, NY), TV sports journalist.

Ann Coulter, b 12/8/1961 (New Canaan, CT), political commentator, author.

Katie Couric, b 1/7/1957 (Arlington, VA), TV and online journalist.

Candy Crowley, b 12/12/1948 (Kalamazoo, MI), TV journalist.

Ted Cruz, b 12/22/1970 (Calgary, AB, Can.), U.S. sen. (R, TX); 2016 pres. contender.

Mark Cuban, b 7/31/1958 (Pittsburgh, PA), entrepreneur, Dallas Mavericks (NBA) owner.

Andrew Cuomo, b 12/6/1957 (New York, NY), NY gov. (D), former state atty. gen.

Ann Curry, b 11/19/1956 (Guam), former *Today* show news anchor.

Bill de Blasio, b 5/8/1961 (New York, NY), NYC mayor (D).

Michael Dell, b 2/23/1965 (Houston, TX), founder, chairman, and CEO of Dell computers.

Alan Dershowitz, b 9/1/1938 (Brooklyn, NY), attorney, political commentator.

Barry Diller, b 2/2/1942 (San Francisco, CA), media exec.

Jamie Dimon, b 3/13/1956 (New York, NY), chairman, CEO of JPMorgan Chase.

Lou Dobbs, b 9/24/1945 (Childress, TX), TV journalist.

James Dobson, b 4/21/1936 (Shreveport, LA), evangelical Christian leader, founder of Focus on the Family.

Christopher Dodd, b 5/27/1944 (Willimantic, CT), Motion Picture Assn. of America chair/CEO; former U.S. sen. (D, CT).

Timothy Dolan, b 2/6/1950 (St. Louis, MO), Rom. Cath. cardinal, archbishop of NY.

Elizabeth Hanford Dole, b 7/29/1936 (Salisbury, NC), former U.S. sen. (R, NC), Red Cross pres., cabinet member.

Robert Dole, b 7/22/1923 (Russell, KS), former U.S. Senate majority leader (R, KS), 1996 pres. nominee.

Sam Donaldson, b 3/11/1934 (El Paso, TX), former TV journalist.

Jack Dorsey, b 11/19/1976 (St. Louis, MO), Twitter cofounder.

Maureen Dowd, b 1/14/1952 (Washington, DC), columnist.

Elizabeth Drew, b 11/16/1935 (Cincinnati, OH), journalist.

Matt Drudge, b 10/27/1966 (Takoma Park, MD), Internet journalist.

Michael S. Dukakis, b 11/3/1933 (Brookline, MA), former MA gov. (D), 1988 pres. nominee.

Dick Durbin, b 11/21/1944 (East St. Louis, IL), U.S. Senate minority whip (D, IL).

Josh Earnest, b 5/2/1977 (Kansas City, MO), White House press secretary.

Bernard Ebbers, b 8/27/1941 (Edmonton, AB, Can.), former WorldCom CEO; jailed for fraud.

Marian Wright Edelman, b 6/6/1939 (Bennettsville, SC), pres. and founder of Children's Defense Fund.

John Edwards, b 6/10/1953 (Seneca, SC), former U.S. sen. (D, NC), 2004 vice-pres. nominee, 2008 pres. contender.

Michael Eisner, b 3/7/1942 (Mt. Kisco, NY), former Disney Co. CEO.

Lawrence J. Ellison, b 8/17/1944 (New York, NY), Oracle Corp. cofounder.

Rahm Emanuel, b 11/29/1959 (Chicago, IL), Chicago mayor; former White House chief of staff, U.S. rep. (D, IL).

Myrlie Evers-Williams, b 3/17/1933 (Vicksburg, MS), civil rights activist.

Louis Farrakhan, b 5/11/1933 (Roxbury, MA), Nation of Islam leader.

Dianne Feinstein, b 6/22/1933 (San Francisco, CA), U.S. sen. (D, CA).

Larry Fink, b 11/2/1952 (Los Angeles, CA), BlackRock CEO.

Carly (Carleton) S. Fiorina, b 9/6/1954 (Austin, TX), former Hewlett-Packard CEO, 2016 pres. contender (R).

Larry Flynt, b 11/1/1942 (Lakeville, KY), publisher.

Steve (Malcolm) Forbes Jr., b 7/18/1947 (Morristown, NJ), publisher, former pres. contender.

Tom Ford, b 8/27/1961 (Austin, TX), fashion designer.

Barney Frank, b 3/31/1940 (Bayonne, NJ), attorney, former U.S. rep. (D, MA).

Al Franken, b 5/21/1951 (New York, NY), U.S. sen. (D, MN); humorist.

Thomas Friedman, b 7/20/1953 (Minneapolis, MN), journalist, author.

Bill Gates, b 10/28/1955 (Seattle, WA), software pioneer; Microsoft exec.

Henry Louis Gates Jr., b 9/16/1950 (Keyser, WV), African American studies scholar.

Melinda Gates, b 8/15/1964 (Dallas, TX), philanthropist.

Robert M. Gates, b 9/25/1943 (Wichita, KS), former sec. of defense; Boy Scouts of America pres.

David Geffen, b 2/21/1943 (Brooklyn, NY), entertainment exec.

Timothy Geithner, b 8/18/1961 (New York, NY), former Treasury secretary.

Charles Gibson, b 3/4/1943 (Evanston, IL), TV journalist, former host of ABC's *World News*.

Gabrielle Giffords, b 6/8/1970 (Tucson, AZ), former U.S. rep. (D, AZ); shot in 2011 assassination attempt.

Kirsten Gillibrand, b 12/9/1966 (Albany, NY), U.S. sen. (D, NY), attorney.

Newt Gingrich, b 6/17/1943 (Harrisburg, PA), former House speaker (R, GA), 2012 pres. contender.

Ruth Bader Ginsburg, b 3/15/1933 (Brooklyn, NY), U.S. Supreme Court justice.

Rudolph Giuliani, b 5/28/1944 (Brooklyn, NY), former NYC mayor (R).

Ira Glass, b 3/3/1959 (Baltimore, MD), radio host.

John Glenn, b 7/18/1921 (Cambridge, OH), former U.S. sen. (D, OH), astronaut.

Alberto Gonzales, b 8/4/1955 (San Antonio, TX), former U.S. attorney general.

Roger Goodell, b 2/19/1959 (Jamestown, NY), NFL commissioner.

Ellen Goodman, b 4/11/1941 (Newton, MA), columnist.

Doris Kearns Goodwin, b 1/4/1943 (Brooklyn, NY), historian, TV commentator.

Berry Gordy, b 11/28/1929 (Detroit, MI), Motown record label founder.

Al Gore Jr., b 3/31/1948 (Washington, DC), former U.S. sen. (D, TN), vice pres., 2000 pres. nominee; 2007 Nobel Peace Prize winner.

Billy Graham, b 11/7/1918 (Charlotte, NC), evangelist.

(William) Franklin Graham III, b 7/14/1952 (Asheville, NC), evangelist, son of Billy Graham.

Lindsey Graham, b 7/9/1955 (Central, SC), U.S. sen. (R, SC); 2016 pres. contender.

Temple Grandin, b 8/29/1947 (Boston, MA), animal behavioral scientist, autism activist.

Jeff Greenfield, b 6/10/1943 (New York, NY), TV journalist.

Alan Greenspan, b 3/6/1926 (New York, NY), former Federal Reserve chairman.

Jenna Bush Hager, b 11/25/1981 (Dallas, TX), daughter of former Pres. George W. Bush.

Nikki Haley, b 1/20/1972 (Bamberg, SC), SC gov. (R).

Pete Hamill, b 6/24/1935 (Brooklyn, NY), journalist, author.

Sean Hannity, b 12/30/1961 (New York, NY), radio and TV host, author, political commentator.

Kamala Harris, b 10/20/1964 (Oakland, CA), atty. gen. (CA); U.S. Senate candidate (D).

Reed Hastings, b 10/8/1960 (Boston, MA), founder, pres., CEO and board chair, Netflix, Inc.

Orrin Hatch, b 3/22/1934 (Homestead Park, PA), U.S. sen. (R, UT) and Senate pres. pro tempore.

Carla Hayden, b 8/10/1952 (Tallahassee, FL), librarian of U.S. Congress.

Hugh Hefner, b 4/9/1926 (Chicago, IL), publisher.

Tommy Hilfiger, b 3/24/1951 (Elmira, NY), fashion designer.

Anita Hill, b 7/30/1956 (Morris, OK), legal scholar; complainant against Supreme Court justice Clarence Thomas.

Paris Hilton, b 2/17/1981 (New York, NY), heiress, actress.

Perez Hilton, b 3/23/1978 (Miami, FL), gossip columnist.

James P. Hoffa, b 5/19/1941 (Detroit, MI), Teamsters Union head.

Eric Holder Jr., b 1/21/1951 (Bronx, NY), former U.S. atty. gen.

Lester Holt, b 3/8/1959 (San Francisco, CA), TV journalist.

David Horowitz, b 1/10/1939 (New York, NY), consumer advocate, columnist, author.

Steny H. Hoyer, b 6/14/1939 (New York, NY), House minority whip (D, MD).

Mike Huckabee, b 8/24/1955 (Hope, AR), former AR gov. (R), minister, TV host; pres. contender (2008, '16).

Dolores Huerta, 4/10/1930 (Dawson, NM), labor activist.

Arianna Huffington, b 7/15/1950 (Athens, Greece), political commentator.

H. Wayne Huizenga, b 12/29/1939 (Evergreen Park, IL), entrepreneur, sports exec.

Brit Hume, b 6/22/1943 (Washington, DC), TV journalist on FOX.

Lee Iacocca, b 10/15/1924 (Allentown, PA), former auto exec. (Ford, Chrysler).

Carl Icahn, b 2/16/1936 (Brooklyn, NY), financier.

Gwen Ifill, b 9/29/1955 (Queens, NY), TV journalist, moderator on PBS.

Bob Iger, b 2/10/1951 (Oceanside, NY), Walt Disney Co. CEO.

Don Imus, b 7/23/1940 (Riverside, CA), talk-show host.

Patricia Ireland, b 10/19/1945 (Oak Park, IL), feminist leader.

Jesse Jackson, b 10/8/1941 (Greenville, SC), civil rights leader, former pres. contender (D).

Marc Jacobs, b 4/9/1964 (New York, NY), fashion designer.

Valerie Jarrett, b 11/14/1956 (Shiraz, Iran), sr. adviser to Pres. Obama.

Bobby Jindal, b 6/10/1971 (Baton Rouge, LA), former LA gov. (R); 2016 pres. contender.

Jasper Johns, b 5/15/1930 (Augusta, GA), painter, printmaker.

Robert L. Johnson, b 4/8/1946 (Hickory, MS), Black Entertainment Television founder.

Vernon E. Jordan Jr., b 8/15/1935 (Atlanta, GA), attorney, former pres. adviser, civil rights leader.

Elena Kagan, b 4/28/1960 (New York, NY), U.S. Supreme Court justice.

Tim Kaine, b 2/26/1958 (St. Paul, MN), U.S. sen. (D, VA), 2016 vice-pres. nominee.

Travis Kalanick, b 8/6/1976 (Los Angeles, CA), Uber cofounder and CEO.

Donna Karan, b 10/2/1948 (Forest Hills, Queens, NY), fashion designer.

John Kasich, b 5/13/1952 (McKees Rocks, PA), OH gov. (R); 2016 pres. contender.

Jeffrey Katzenberg, b 12/21/1950 (New York, NY), entertainment exec.

Garrison Keillor, b 8/7/1942 (Anoka, MN), author, broadcaster.

Mark Kelly, b 2/21/1964 (Orange, NJ), U.S. Navy capt., former NASA shuttle commander.

Megyn Kelly, b 11/18/1970 (Syracuse, NY), TV commentator, host.

Anthony M. Kennedy, b 7/23/1936 (Sacramento, CA), U.S. Supreme Court justice.

John Kerry, b 12/11/1943 (Aurora, CO), sec. of state, former U.S. sen. (D, MA), 2004 pres. nominee.

Larry King, b 11/19/1933 (Brooklyn, NY), TV talk-show host.

Michael Kinsley, b 3/9/1951 (Detroit, MI), editor, political commentator.

Henry Kissinger, b 5/27/1923 (Furth, Germany), former sec. of state.

Calvin Klein, b 11/19/1942 (Bronx, NY), fashion designer.

Philip H. Knight, b 2/24/1938 (Portland, OR), founder and chairman of the board of Nike.

Charles G. Koch, b 5/3/1940 (Wichita, KS), Koch Industries exec., philanthropist.

David H. Koch, b 11/1/1935 (Wichita, KS), Koch Industries exec., philanthropist.

Sarah Koenig, b 7/9/1969 (New York, NY), radio journalist.

Ted Koppel, b 2/8/1940 (Lancashire, Eng., UK), former TV journalist.

Michael Kors, b 8/9/1959 (Merrick, NY), fashion designer.

Larry Kramer, b 6/25/1935 (Bridgeport, CT), AIDS activist, writer.

Charles Krauthammer, b 3/13/1950 (New York, NY), columnist.

Nicholas D. Kristof, b 4/27/1959 (Chicago, IL), columnist, author.

William Kristol, b 12/23/1952 (New York, NY), editor, columnist.

Steve Kroft, b 8/22/1945 (Kokomo, IN), TV journalist.

Paul Krugman, b 2/28/1953 (Albany, NY), economist, columnist.
Brian Lamb, b 10/9/1941 (Lafayette, IN), cable TV exec., journalist.
Wayne LaPierre Jr., b 11/8/1949 (Schenectady, NY), National Rifle Assn. exec. VP.
Matt Lauer, b 12/30/1957 (New York, NY), TV journalist.
Ralph Lauren, b 10/14/1939 (Bronx, NY), fashion designer.
Bernard F. Law, b 11/4/1931 (Torreon, Mexico), cardinal archbishop emeritus of Boston.
Patrick Leahy, b 3/31/1940 (Montpelier, VT), U.S. sen. (D, VT).
Norman Lear, b 7/27/1922 (New Haven, CT), TV producer, political activist.
Jim Lehrer, b 5/19/1934 (Wichita, KS), TV journalist, author.
Annie Leibovitz, b 10/2/1949 (Waterbury, CT), photographer.
Jacob Lew, b 8/29/1955 (New York, NY), sec. of treasury, former White House chief of staff.
Monica Lewinsky, b 7/23/1973 (San Francisco, CA), former White House intern.
Joseph Lieberman, b 2/24/1942 (Stamford, CT), former U.S. sen. (I, CT), 2000 vice-pres. nominee (D).
Rush Limbaugh, b 1/12/1951 (Cape Girardeau, MO), radio talk-show host.
Shannon Lucid, b 1/14/1943 (Shanghai, China), NASA scientist, astronaut.
Loretta Lynch, b 5/21/1959 (Greensboro, NC), U.S. atty. gen.
Rachel Maddow, b 4/1/1973 (Castro Valley, CA), TV/radio host, political commentator.
Bernie Madoff, b 4/29/1938 (Queens, NY), financier who swindled investors; sentenced to 150 years in prison.
Rob Manfred, b 9/28/1958 (Rome, NY), MLB commissioner.
Chelsea (fmr. Bradley) Manning, b 12/17/1987 (Crescent, OK), Army pvt. convicted on espionage charges for providing classified information to WikiLeaks.
Susana Martinez, b 7/14/1959 (El Paso, TX), NM gov. (R).
Mary Matalin, b 8/19/1953 (Chicago, IL), political commentator.
Chris Matthews, b 12/17/1945 (Philadelphia, PA), TV journalist.
Marissa Mayer, b 5/30/1975 (Wausau, WI), Yahoo! CEO.
John McCain, b 8/29/1936 (Panama Canal Zone), U.S. sen. (R, AZ), 2008 Republican pres. candidate.
Kevin McCarthy, b 1/26/1965 (Bakersfield, CA), U.S. rep. (R, CA), House majority leader.
Mitch McConnell, b 2/20/1942 (Tuscumbia, AL), U.S. sen. (R, KY) majority leader.
David McCullough, b 7/7/1933 (Pittsburgh, PA), historian, biographer.
Denis McDonough, b 12/2/1969 (Stillwater, MN), White House chief of staff.
Dr. Phil McGraw, b 9/1/1950 (Vinita, OK), talk-show host, motivational speaker, author.
Lorne Michaels, b 11/17/44 (Toronto, ON, Canada), creator and producer of *Saturday Night Live*.
Kate Michelman, b 8/4/1942 (NJ), activist.
Kate Millett, b 9/14/1934 (St. Paul, MN), author, feminist.
George Mitchell, b 8/20/1933, (Waterville, ME), former spec. envoy for Middle East peace, U.S. Sen. majority leader (D, ME), diplomat, Disney Co. chair.
Walter Mondale, b 1/5/1928 (Ceylon, MN), former vice pres., U.S. sen. (D, MN), 1984 pres. nominee.
Ernest Moniz, b 12/22/1944 (Fall River, MA), energy sec., nuclear physicist.
Michael Moore, b 4/23/1954 (Davison, MI), activist, documentary filmmaker, author.
Bill Moyers, b 6/5/1934 (Hugo, OK), TV journalist, author.
Robert S. Mueller III, b 8/7/1944 (New York, NY), former FBI director.
David Muir, b 11/8/1973 (Syracuse, NY), TV news anchor.
Rupert Murdoch, b 3/11/1931 (Melbourne, Vic., Austral.), media exec.

Vivek Murthy, b 7/10/1977 (Huddersfield, Eng., UK), U.S. surgeon gen.
Ralph Nader, b 2/27/1934 (Winsted, CT), consumer advocate, independent pres. cand. (1996, 2000, '04, '08).
Janet Napolitano, b 11/29/1957 (New York, NY), Univ. of Calif. pres.; former homeland security sec., AZ gov. (D).
Craig Newmark, b 12/6/1952 (Morristown, NJ), founder of Craigslist.com.
Peggy Noonan, b 9/7/1950 (Brooklyn, NY), columnist, speechwriter.
Oliver North, b 10/7/1943 (San Antonio, TX), talk-show host, former Natl. Sec. Council aide, figure in Iran-contra scandal.
Eleanor Holmes Norton, b 6/13/1937 (Washington, DC), U.S. House delegate for Washington, DC (D).
Barack Obama, b 8/4/1961 (Honolulu, HI), U.S. president, former U.S. sen. (D, IL).
Michelle Obama, b 1/17/1964 (Chicago, IL), first lady, lawyer.
Soledad O'Brien, b 9/19/1966 (Smithtown, NY), TV journalist.
Sandra Day O'Connor, b 3/26/1930 (El Paso, TX), former Supreme Court justice.
Keith Olbermann, b 1/27/1959 (New York, NY), political commentator, former ESPN/MSNBC host.
Todd Oldham, b 11/22/1961 (Corpus Christi, TX), fashion designer.
Martin O'Malley, b 1/18/63 (Bethesda, MD), former MD gov. (D); 2016 pres. contender.
Bill O'Reilly, b 9/10/1949 (New York, NY), TV commentator, host.
Suze Orman, b 5/5/1951 (Chicago, IL), financial advisor; TV host.
Joel Osteen, b 3/5/1963 (Houston, TX), televangelist, author.
Michael Ovitz, b 12/14/1946 (Encino, CA), entertainment exec.
Clarence Page, b 6/2/1947 (Dayton, OH), journalist, TV commentator.
Lawrence Page, b 3/26/1973 (East Lansing, MI), cofounder of Google.
Camille Paglia, b 4/2/1947 (Endicott, NY), scholar, author.
Sarah Palin, b 2/11/1964 (Sandpoint, ID), former AK gov. (R), 2008 vice-pres. nominee.
Leon E. Panetta, b 6/28/1938 (Monterey, CA), former sec. of defense, CIA director, White House chief of staff, U.S. rep. (D, CA).
Sean Parker, b 12/3/1979 (Herndon, VA), cofounder of Napster, Facebook.
George Pataki, b 6/24/1945 (Peekskill, NY), former NY gov. (R); 2016 pres. contender.
Rand Paul, b 1/7/1963 (Pittsburgh, PA), U.S. sen. (R, KY); 2016 pres. contender.
Ron Paul, b 8/20/1935 (Pittsburgh, PA), physician, former U.S. rep. (R, TX), pres. contender (2008, '12).
Jane Pauley, b 10/31/1950 (Indianapolis, IN), TV journalist.
Nancy Pelosi, b 3/26/1940 (Baltimore, MD), U.S. rep. (D, CA), House minority leader, former House speaker.
Mike Pence, 6/7/1959 (Columbus, IN), IN gov. (R), 2016 vice-pres. nominee.
Ross Perot, b 6/27/1930 (Texarkana, TX), entrepreneur, independent and Reform pres. candidate (1992, '96).
Rick Perry, b 3/4/1950 (Paint Creek, TX), TX gov. (R), pres. contender (2012, '16).
David Petraeus, b 11/7/1952 (Cornwall-on-Hudson, NY), former CIA director, U.S. Forces Afghanistan cmdr., CENTCOM cmdr.
Colin Powell, b 4/5/1937 (New York, NY), former sec. of state, natl. security adviser, Joint Chiefs of Staff chairman.
Samantha Power, b 9/21/1970 (Dublin, Ire.), U.S. ambassador to UN.
Reince Priebus, b 3/18/1972 (Kenosha, WI), Rep. Natl. Committee chair.
Dan Quayle, b 2/4/1947 (Indianapolis, IN), former U.S. vice pres., U.S. sen. (R, IN).
Anna Quindlen, b 7/8/1953 (Philadelphia, PA), author, columnist.
Martha Raddatz, b 1953 (Idaho Falls, ID), TV journalist.

Jorge Ramos, b 3/15/1958 (Mexico City, Mex.), TV journalist.
Dan Rather, b 10/31/1931 (Wharton, TX), TV journalist, retired anchor.
Sumner Redstone, b 5/27/1923 (Boston, MA), media executive.
Ralph Reed Jr., b 6/24/1961 (Portsmouth, VA), political adviser.
Robert B. Reich, b 6/24/1946 (Scranton, PA), economist, author, former labor sec.
Harry Reid, b 12/2/1939 (Searchlight, NV), U.S. Sen. minority leader (D, NV).
Janet Reno, b 7/21/1938 (Miami, FL), former U.S. attorney gen.
Condoleezza Rice, b 11/14/1954 (Birmingham, AL), former sec. of state, former natl. security adviser.
Susan Rice, b 11/17/1964 (Washington, DC), national security adviser, former U.S. ambassador to UN.
Frank Rich, b 6/2/1949 (Washington, DC), essayist, columnist.
Cecile Richards, b 1957 (Waco, TX), pres. of Planned Parenthood.
Tom Ridge, b 8/26/1945 (Munhall, PA), former homeland security sec., PA gov. (R).
Geraldo Rivera, b 7/4/1943 (New York, NY), TV journalist.
Cokie Roberts, b 12/27/1943 (New Orleans, LA), TV journalist.
John G. Roberts, b 1/27/1955 (Buffalo, NY), Supreme Court chief justice.
Robin Roberts, b 11/23/1960 (Tuskegee, AL), *Good Morning America* co-host.
Pat Robertson, b 3/22/1930 (Lexington, VA), religious broadcasting exec., former pres. contender (R).
Eugene Robinson, b 3/12/1954 (Orangeburg, SC), columnist.
V. Gene Robinson, b 5/29/1947 (Lexington, KY), first openly gay Episcopal bishop (retired).
David Rockefeller, b 6/12/1915 (New York, NY), banker.
Al Roker, b 8/20/1954 (Queens, NY), TV weather person.
Mitt Romney, b 3/12/1947 (Detroit, MI), 2012 pres. nominee, former MA gov. (R).
Charlie Rose, b 1/5/1942 (Henderson, NC), TV journalist.
Karl Rove, b 12/25/1950 (Denver, CO), former adviser to Pres. G. W. Bush, political commentator.
Marco Rubio, b 5/28/1971 (Miami, FL), U.S. sen. (R, FL), 2016 pres. contender.
Donald Rumsfeld, b 7/9/1932 (Chicago, IL), former sec. of defense.
Edward Ruscha, b 12/16/1937 (Omaha, NE), artist.
Paul Ryan, b 1/29/1970 (Janesville, WI), 2012 vice-pres. nominee, U.S. rep. (R, WI) and speaker of the House.
Sheryl Sandberg, b 8/28/1969 (Washington, DC), Facebook exec.
Bernie Sanders, b 9/8/1941 (New York, NY), U.S. sen. (I, VT); 2016 Dem. pres. contender.
Rick Santorum, b 5/10/1958 (Winchester, VA), former U.S. sen. (R, PA); pres. contender (2012, '16).
Diane Sawyer, b 12/22/1945 (Glasgow, KY), TV journalist.
Stephen Scalise, b 10/6/1965 (New Orleans, LA), U.S. rep. (R, LA), House majority whip.
Bob Schieffer, b 2/25/1937 (Austin, TX), TV journalist.
Caroline Kennedy Schlossberg, b 11/27/1957 (New York, NY), ambassador to Japan, author, daughter of Pres. Kennedy.
Eric Schmidt, b 4/27/1955 (Washington, DC), former Google CEO.
Charles Schumer, b 11/23/1950 (Brooklyn, NY), U.S. sen. (D, NY).
Arnold Schwarzenegger, b 7/30/1947 (Thal, Styria, Austria), actor, former CA gov. (R).
Willard Scott, b 3/7/1934 (Alexandria, VA), former TV weather person.
Kathleen Sebelius, b 5/15/1958 (Cincinnati, OH), former health and human services sec., KS gov. (D).

Richard Serra, b 11/2/1939 (San Francisco, CA), sculptor.

Al Sharpton, b 10/3/1954 (Brooklyn, NY), activist, civil rights leader, TV personality.

Will Shortz, b 8/26/1952 (Crawfordsville, IN), puzzle editor.

Maria Shriver, b 11/6/1955 (Chicago, IL), TV journalist, former CA first lady.

George P. Shultz, b 12/13/1920 (New York, NY), former sec. of state, other cabinet posts.

Michelangelo Signorile, b 12/19/1960 (Brooklyn, NY), journalist, author.

Adam Silver, b 4/25/1962 (Rye, NY), NBA commissioner.

Nate Silver, b 1/13/1978 (E. Lansing, MI), statistician.

Russell Simmons, b 10/4/1957 (Queens, NY), music producer.

O. J. Simpson, b 7/9/1947 (San Francisco, CA), former NFL star, murder defendant.

Harry Smith, b 8/21/1951 (Lansing, IL), TV journalist.

Liz Smith, b 2/2/1923 (Ft. Worth, TX), gossip columnist.

Edward Snowden, b 6/21/1983 (Elizabeth City, NC), computer specialist accused of leaking classified information about U.S. and UK govt. surveillance.

George Soros, b 8/12/1930 (Budapest, Hung.), financier, philanthropist.

Sonia Sotomayor, b 6/25/1954 (Bronx, NY), U.S. Supreme Court justice.

Kate Spade, b 1962 (Kansas City, MO), fashion designer.

Steven Spielberg, b 12/18/1946 (Cincinnati, OH), movie director, producer.

Eliot Spitzer, b 6/10/1959 (Bronx, NY), former NY gov. (D); resigned after involvement with prostitutes exposed.

Lesley Stahl, b 12/16/1941 (Swampscott, MA), TV journalist.

Shelby Steele, b 1/1/1946 (Chicago, IL), scholar, critic.

Ben Stein, b 11/25/1944 (Washington, DC), attorney, columnist, TV personality.

Gloria Steinem, b 3/25/1934 (Toledo, OH), author, feminist.

Frank Stella, b 5/12/1936 (Malden, MA), painter.

George Stephanopoulos, b 2/10/1961 (Fall River, MA), TV journalist, *Good Morning America* co-host; former pres. adviser.

Howard Stern, b 1/12/1954 (Roosevelt, NY), radio talk-show host.

John Paul Stevens, b 4/20/1920 (Chicago, IL), former Supreme Court justice.

Martha Stewart, b 8/3/1941 (Nutley, NJ), homemaking adviser, entrepreneur, TV personality.

Biz Stone, b 3/10/1974 (Boston, MA), cofounder of Twitter.

Chesley Sullenberger III, b 1/23/1951 (Denison, TX), pilot who safely landed a passenger jet in the Hudson River.

Andrew Sullivan, b 8/10/1963 (Eng., UK), political commentator and blogger.

Arthur Ochs Sulzberger Jr., b 9/22/1951 (Mt. Kisco, NY), newspaper publisher.

Lawrence H. Summers, b 11/30/1954 (New Haven, CT), economist; former Natl. Economic Council dir., Harvard Univ. pres., sec. of treasury.

George Tenet, b 1/5/1953 (Flushing, Queens, NY), former CIA director.

Clarence Thomas, b 6/23/1948 (Savannah, GA), U.S. Supreme Court justice.

Chuck Todd, b 4/8/1972 (Miami, FL), TV journalist, *Meet the Press* moderator.

Richard Trumka, b 7/24/1949 (Waynesburg, PA), pres. of AFL-CIO.

Donald Trump, b 6/14/1946 (Jamaica, Queens, NY), real estate exec., TV personality; 2016 pres. nominee (R).

Ted Turner, b 11/19/1938 (Cincinnati, OH), TV exec., philanthropist.

Neil deGrasse Tyson, b 10/5/1958 (New York, NY), astrophysicist, director of NYC's Hayden Planetarium, author, TV host.

Urvashi Vaid, b 10/8/1958 (New Delhi, India), LGBT rights activist.

Gloria Vanderbilt, b 2/20/1924 (New York, NY), fashion designer, heiress.

Greta Van Susteren, b 6/11/1954 (Appleton, WI), attorney, TV journalist.

Jesse Ventura, b 7/15/1951 (Minneapolis, MN), former wrestler, MN gov. (I).

Meredith Vieira, b 12/30/1953 (Providence, RI), TV personality.

Paul Volcker, b 9/5/1927 (Cape May, NJ), economist, former Federal Reserve chairman.

Diane von Fürstenberg, b 12/31/1946 (Brussels, Belgium), fashion designer.

Jimmy Wales, b 8/8/1966 (Huntsville, AL), cofounder of Wikipedia.

Scott Walker, b 11/2/1967 (Colorado Springs, CO), WI gov. (R), 2016 pres. contender.

Barbara Walters, b 9/25/1929 (Boston, MA), TV journalist.

Alexander Wang, b 5/17/1984 (San Francisco, CA), fashion designer.

Vera Wang, b 6/27/1949 (New York, NY), fashion designer.

Elizabeth Warren, b 6/22/1949 (Oklahoma City, OK), U.S. sen. (D, MA).

Rick Warren, b 1/28/1954 (San Jose, CA), evangelical Christian pastor, founder of Saddleback Church, author.

Debbie Wasserman Schultz, b 9/27/1966 (Forest Hills, NY), U.S. rep. (D, FL), former Dem. Natl. Committee chair.

James Watson, b 4/6/1928 (Chicago, IL), biochemist, DNA pioneer, co-winner of the 1962 Nobel Prize in Physiology/Medicine.

Andrew Weil, b 6/8/1942 (Philadelphia, PA), health adviser.

Harvey Weinstein, b 3/19/1952 (Flushing, Queens, NY), movie exec.

Jack Welch, b 11/19/1935 (Peabody, MA), former General Electric CEO.

Jann Wenner, b 1/7/1946 (New York, NY), publisher, founder of *Rolling Stone*.

Cornel West, b 6/23/1953 (Tulsa, OK), African American scholar, critic.

Ruth Westheimer, b 6/4/1928 (Frankfurt am Main, Germany), human sexuality expert.

Mary Jo White, b 12/27/1947 (Kansas City, MO), Securities and Exchange Commission chair.

Meg Whitman, b 8/4/1956 (Cold Spring Harbor, NY), 2010 CA gubernatorial candidate (R), former eBay CEO; HP CEO.

George Will, b 5/4/1941 (Champaign, IL), journalist, author.

Brian Williams, b 5/5/1959 (Ridgewood, NJ), TV journalist.

Evan Williams, b 3/31/1972 (Clarks, NE), Twitter cofounder.

Jody Williams, b 10/9/1950 (Brattleboro, VT), peace activist, 1997 Nobel Peace Prize winner.

Edie (Edith) Windsor, b 6/20/1929 (Philadelphia, PA), LGBT activist.

Oprah Winfrey, b 1/29/1954 (Kosciusko, MS), TV and media personality, entrepreneur, actress.

Anna Wintour, b 11/3/1949 (London, Eng., UK), *Vogue editor.*

Susan Wojcicki, b 7/5/1968 (CA), CEO of YouTube.

Bob Woodward, b 3/26/1943 (Geneva, IL), journalist; with Carl Bernstein cracked Watergate scandal.

Steve Wozniak, b 8/11/1950 (Sunnyvale, CA), inventor, cofounder of Apple.

Steve Wynn, b 1/27/1942 (New Haven, CT), casino developer.

Chuck Yeager, b 2/13/1923 (Myra, WV), test pilot, first to break sound barrier.

Janet Yellen, b 8/13/1946 (New York, NY), Federal Reserve chair.

Paula Zahn, b 2/24/1956 (Omaha, NE), TV journalist.

Mark Zuckerberg, b 5/14/1984 (Dobbs Ferry, NY), founder of Facebook.

Mortimer Zuckerman, b 6/4/1937 (Montréal, QC, Can.), publisher, columnist.

Widely Known World Personalities of the Present

Living non-Americans only. Generally excludes current heads of state or government (see Nations of the World) and excludes most others covered elsewhere, such as in Widely Known Americans, Writers, and Entertainment or Sports Personalities.

Mahmoud Abbas (Abu Mazen), b 3/26/1935 (Safed, Palestine [now Israel]), president of the Palestinian National Authority.

Gerry Adams, b 10/6/1948 (Belfast, N. Ireland, UK), Sinn Fein leader.

Mahmoud Ahmadinejad, b 10/28/1956 (Garmsar, Iran), former Iranian pres.

Albert II, b 6/6/1934 (Brussels, Belgium), former king (1993-2013).

Prince Andrew (Duke of York), b 2/19/1960 (London, Eng., UK), second son of Queen Elizabeth II.

Kofi Annan, b 4/8/1938 (Kumasi, Ghana), former UN sec.-gen.; 2001 Nobel laureate.

Princess Anne (Princess Royal), b 8/15/1950 (London, Eng., UK), daughter of Queen Elizabeth II.

Michael Arad, b 1969 (London, Eng., UK), designer of the Natl. 9/11 Memorial in NYC.

Oscar Arias Sánchez, b 9/13/1941 (Heredia, Costa Rica), former Costa Rican pres., peace negotiator, 1987 Nobel Peace laureate.

Giorgio Armani, b 7/30/1934 (Piacenza, Italy), fashion designer.

Hanan Ashrawi, b 10/8/1946 (Nablus, Israel), Palestinian activist.

Julian Assange, b 7/3/1971 (Townsville, Qld., Austral.), founder of WikiLeaks media org.

Ban Ki-moon, b 6/13/1944 (Umsong, [now] South Korea), UN sec.-gen.

Ehud Barak, b 2/12/1942 (Mishmar Ha-Sharon Kibbutz, Israel), former Israeli min. of defense, prime min.

Beatrix, b 1/31/1938 (Baarn, Netherlands), former Dutch queen (1980-2013).

Benedict XVI (Joseph Ratzinger), b 4/16/1927 (Marktl am Inn, Germany), pope emeritus of Rom. Cath. Church, elected 2005, resigned 2013.

Boris Berezovsky, b 1/23/1946 (Moscow, USSR), businessman, politician.

Tim Berners-Lee, b 6/8/1955 (London, Eng., UK), World Wide Web inventor.

Liliane Bettencourt, b 10/21/1922 (Paris, France), L'Oreal principal shareholder; world's richest woman.

Tony Blair, b 5/6/1953 (Edinburgh, Scot., UK), former British prime min.

Hans Blix, b 6/28/1928 (Uppsala, Swed.), former UN weapons inspector.

Bono (Paul David Hewson), b 5/20/1960 (Glasnevin, Dublin, Ire.), musician, social activist, philanthropist.

Fernando Botero, b 4/19/1932 (Medellín, Colombia), artist.

Richard Branson, b 7/18/1950 (S. London, Eng., UK), British Virgin Records and Airways founder.

Gordon Brown, b 2/20/1951 (Glasgow, Scot., UK), former British prime min.

Tina Brown, b 11/21/1953 (Maidenhead, Eng., UK), journalist, author.

Carla Bruni, b 12/23/1967 (Turin, Italy), former first lady of France; musician, actress, model.

Gisele Bündchen, b 7/20/1980 (Horizontina, Rio Grande do Sul, Braz.), model and UN Goodwill ambassador.

Mark Burnett, b 7/17/1960 (Myland, Eng., UK), reality TV producer.

Rhonda Byrne, b 3/12/1951 (Australia), author, TV writer and producer.

David Cameron, b 10/9/1966 (London, Eng., UK), former British prime min.

Kim Campbell, b 3/10/1947 (Port Alberni, BC, Can.), former Canadian prime min.

Pierre Cardin, b 7/7/1922 (San Biaggio di Callalta, Italy), fashion designer.

Magnus Carlsen, b 11/30/1990 (Tonsberg, Norway), world chess champion.

Princess Caroline, b 1/23/1957 (Monte Carlo, Monaco), Monaco royal (eldest daughter of Prince Rainier and Princess Grace).

Fidel Castro, b 8/13/1926 (Birán, Cuba), former prime min., pres. of Cuba.

Catherine (Kate) Middleton (Duchess of Cambridge), b 1/9/1982 (Reading, Eng., UK), wife of Prince William.

Prince Charles (of Wales), b 11/14/1948 (London, Eng., UK), eldest son of Queen Elizabeth II; heir to British throne.

Princess Charlotte Elizabeth Diana (of Cambridge), b 5/2/2015 (London, Eng., UK), daughter of Prince William and Catherine.

Chen Guangcheng, b 11/12/1971 (Dongshigu, China), civil rights activist.

Yao Chen, b 10/5/1979 (Nanping, Fujian, China), actress, microblogger.

Jacques Chirac, b 11/29/1932 (Paris, France), former French pres.

Deepak Chopra, b 1946 (New Delhi, India), writer, alternative medicine advocate.

Jean Chrétien, b 1/11/1934 (Shawinigan, QC, Can.), former Canadian prime min.

Christo (Javacheff), b 6/13/1935 (Gabrovo, Bulg.), artist.

Joe (Charles Joseph) Clark, b 6/5/1939 (High River, AB, Can.), former Canadian prime min.

King Constantine II, b 6/2/1940 (Psychiko, Greece), former king of Greece.

Simon Cowell, b 10/7/1959 (Brighton, East Sussex, Eng., UK), music exec., TV producer, former *American Idol* host.

Dalai Lama, 14th (Tenzin Gyatso), b 7/6/1935 (Taktser, Amdo, Tibet), Buddhist leader; 1989 Nobel Peace Prize laureate.

Richard Dawkins, b 3/26/1941 (Nairobi, Kenya), ethologist, evolutionary biologist, author.

F. W. (Frederik Willem) de Klerk, b 3/18/1936 (Johannesburg, S. Afr.), former S. African pres.; 1993 Nobel Peace Prize winner.

Mario Draghi, b 9/3/1947 (Rome, Italy), European Central Bank pres.

Shirin Ebadi, b 6/21/1947 (Hamadan, Iran), human rights activist, 2003 Nobel Peace Prize winner.

Prince Edward (Earl of Essex), b 3/10/1964 (London, Eng., UK), third son of Queen Elizabeth II.

Mohamed ElBaradei, b 6/17/1942 (Cairo, Egypt), former director general of the International Atomic Energy Agency (IAEA); 2005 Nobel Peace Prize winner.

Sarah Ferguson, b 10/15/1958 (London, Eng., UK), Duchess of York, ex-wife of Prince Andrew.

Francis (Jorge Mario Bergoglio), b 12/17/1936 (Buenos Aires, Argentina), pope of Rom. Cath. Church.

John Galliano, b 11/28/1960 (Gibraltar, UK), fashion designer.

Prince George Alexander Louis (of Cambridge), b 7/22/2013 (London, Eng., UK), son of Prince William and Catherine.

Wael Ghonim, b 12/23/1980 (Cairo, Egypt), computer engineer and Internet activist.

Valery Giscard d'Estaing, b 2/2/1926 (Koblenz, Ger.), former French pres.

Jane Goodall, b 4/3/1934 (London, Eng., UK), anthropologist, primatologist.

Mikhail Gorbachev, b 3/2/1931 (Privolnoye, USSR), former Soviet pres.; 1990 Nobel Peace Prize winner.

Jürgen Habermas, b 6/18/1929 (Dusseldorf, Ger.), philosopher.

Stephen Harper, b 4/30/1959 (Toronto, ON, Can.), former Canadian prime min.

Stephen Hawking, b 1/8/1942 (Oxford, Eng., UK), physicist, author.

Prince Henry (Harry) (of Wales), b 9/15/1984 (London, Eng., UK), son of Prince Charles and Diana.

Damien Hirst, b 6/7/1965 (Bristol, Eng., UK), artist.

David Hockney, b 7/9/1937 (Bradford, Eng., UK), artist.

Hu Jintao, b 12/21/1942 (Shanghai, China), former pres. of China.

Jiang Zemin, b 8/17/1926 (Yangzhou, Jiangsu Prov., China), former pres. of China.

Boris Johnson, b 6/19/1964 (New York, NY), British foreign minister.

Juan Carlos I, b 1/5/1938 (Rome, Italy), former king of Spain (1975-2014).

Hamid Karzai, b 12/24/1957 (Kandahar, Afghanistan), former pres. of Afghanistan.

Garry Kasparov, b 4/13/1963 (Baku, Azerbaijan, USSR), former world chess champion; Russian pro-democracy leader.

Ayatollah Ali Khamenei, b 7/17/1939 (Mashhad, Iran), Supreme Leader, cleric; former president of Iran.

Helmut Kohl, b 4/3/1930 (Ludwigshafen, Ger.), former German chancellor.

Hans Küng, b 3/19/1928 (Sursee, Switz.), Rom. Cath. theologian.

Christine Lagarde, b 1/1/1956 (Paris, Fr.), Intl. Monetary Fund managing dir.

Karl Lagerfeld, b 9/10/1938 (Hamburg, Ger.), fashion designer.

Richard Leakey, b 12/19/1944 (Nairobi, Kenya), anthropologist, paleontologist, conservationist.

Jean-Marie Le Pen, b 6/20/1928 (La Trinité-sur-Mer, Fr.), French right-wing politician.

Marine Le Pen, b 8/5/1968 (Neuilly-sur-Seine, Fr.), head of France's National Front.

Tzipi Livni, b 7/5/1958 (Tel Aviv, Isr.), attorney, Israeli politician.

John Major, b 3/29/1943 (Wimbledon, Eng., UK), former British prime min.

Nouri al-Malaki, b 7/1/1950 (Iraq), former prime min. of Iraq.

Imelda Marcos, b 7/2/1929 (Manila, Philip.), former first lady of the Philippines.

Paul Martin, b 8/28/1938 (Windsor, ON, Can.), former prime min. of Canada.

Peter Max, b 10/19/1937 (Berlin, Ger.), artist, designer.

Stella McCartney, b 9/13/1971 (London, Eng., UK), fashion designer.

Angela Merkel, b 7/17/1954 (Hamburg, Ger.), first woman chancellor of Germany.

Jean-Marie Messier, b 12/13/1956 (Grenoble, Fr.), former CEO of Vivendi Universal.

Empress Michiko, b 10/20/1934 (Tokyo, Japan), empress of Japan.

Maryam Mirzakhani, b 5/1977 (Tehran, Iran), mathematician.

Mohammed Morsi, b 8/8/1951 (Edwa, Egypt), first democratically elected pres. of Egypt; deposed July 2013.

Kate Moss, b 1/16/1974 (Addiscombe, Surrey, Eng., UK), model.

Hosni Mubarak, b 5/4/1928 (Kafre al-Musailha, Egypt), deposed Egyptian president.

Brian Mulroney, b 3/20/1939 (Baie-Comeau, QC, Can.), former Canadian prime min.

Renhō Murata, b 11/28/1968 (Tokyo, Japan), first woman leader of Japan's Democratic Party.

Elon Musk, 6/28/1971 (Pretoria, S. Afr.), SpaceX and Tesla CEO.

Prince Naruhito, b 2/23/1960 (Tokyo, Japan), crown prince of Japan.

Hassan Nasrallah, b 8/31/1960 (Qarantina, Lebanon), sec.-gen. of Hezbollah.

Queen Noor (Lisa Halaby), b 8/23/1951 (Washington, DC), American-born widow of Jordan's King Hussein.

Ehud Olmert, b 9/30/1945 (Binyamina, Palestine), former prime min. of Israel.

Daniel Ortega Saavedra, b 11/11/1945 (La Libertad, Nicar.), Nicaraguan pres., Sandinista leader.

Camilla Parker-Bowles (Duchess of Cornwall), b 7/17/1947 (London, Eng., UK), wife of Prince Charles.

Javier Perez de Cuellar, b 1/19/1920 (Lima, Peru), former UN sec.-gen.

Prince Philip (Duke of Edinburgh), b 6/10/1921 (Corfu, Greece), husband of Queen Elizabeth II.

Gerhard Richter, b 2/9/1932 (Dresden, Ger.), artist.

Mary Robinson, b 5/21/1944 (Ballina, Co. Mayo, Ire.), former Irish pres., former UN High Commissioner for Human Rights.

Arundhati Roy, b 11/24/1961 (Shillong, Meghalaya, India), author, political activist.

Ségolène Royal, b 9/22/1953 (Dakar, Senegal), French socialist politician.

Muqtada al-Sadr, b 8/12/1973? (Najaf, Iraq), extremist Shiite cleric.

Nicolas Sarkozy, b 1/28/1955 (Paris, France), former French pres.

Gerhard Schröder, b 4/7/1944 (Mossenburg, Ger.), former German chancellor.

Ayatollah Ali al-Sistani, b 8/4/1930 (Mashhad, Iran), major Iraqi Shiite religious leader.

Carlos Slim Helú, b 1/28/1940 (Mexico City, Mex.), founder Grupo Carso; former chairman of Telmex, América Móvil.

Princess Stephanie, b 2/1/1965 (Monte Carlo, Monaco), youngest child of Prince Rainier and Princess Grace.

Dominique Strauss-Kahn, b 4/25/1949 (Neuilly-sur-Seine, France), former Intl. Monetary Fund managing dir.

Aung San Suu Kyi, b 6/19/1945 (Rangoon, Myanmar), political activist, 1991 Nobel Peace Prize winner; de facto Myanmar govt. leader.

Valentina Tereshkova, b 3/6/1937 (Maslennikovo, Russia, USSR), first woman in space.

John Napier Turner, b 6/7/1929 (Richmond, Surrey, Eng., UK), former Canadian prime min.

Desmond Tutu, b 10/7/1931 (Klerksdorp, Transvaal, S. Afr.), former S. African archbishop; 1984 Nobel Peace Prize winner.

Lech Walesa, b 9/29/1943 (Popowo, Pol.), Solidarity leader, former pres. of Poland; 1983 Nobel Peace Prize winner.

Justin Welby, b 1/6/1956 (London, Eng., UK), archbishop of Canterbury.

Prince William (Duke of Cambridge), b 6/21/1982 (London, Eng., UK), eldest son of Prince Charles and Diana; 2nd in line to British throne.

Rowan Williams, b 6/14/1950 (Ystradgynlais, Wales, UK), former archbishop of Canterbury.

Malala Yousafzai, b 7/12/1997 (Mingora, Pakistan), education activist, 2014 Nobel Peace Prize winner.

Muhammad Yunus, b 6/28/1940 (Chittagong, Bangladesh), economist, 2006 Nobel Peace Prize winner.

Mohammad Javad Zarif, b 1/8/1960 (Tehran, Iran), Irani minister of foreign affairs.

Ayman al-Zawahiri, b 6/19/1951 (Cairo, Egypt), reputed high-ranking al-Qaeda leader.

Architects

Alvar Aalto, 1898-1976, Säynätsalo, Jyväskylä, Finland; Vuoksenniska Church, Vuoksenniska, Finland.

Max Abramovitz, 1908-2004, Avery Fisher Hall, New York, NY; U.S. Steel Bldg., Pittsburgh, PA.

Tadao Ando, b 1941, Modern Art Museum, Ft. Worth, TX; Stone Hill Center, MA.

Michael Arad, b 1969, World Trade Center Memorial, New York, NY.

Henry Bacon, 1866-1924, Lincoln Memorial, Washington, DC.

Benjamin Banneker, 1731-1806, African American inventor, astronomer,

mathematician; helped design and lay out Washington, DC.

Pietro Belluschi, 1899-1994, Juilliard School, Lincoln Center, Pan Am Bldg. (now MetLife Bldg.) with Walter Gropius, New York, NY.

Marcel Breuer, 1902-81, Whitney Museum of American Art (with Hamilton Smith), New York, NY.

Charles Bulfinch, 1763-1844, State House, Boston, MA; Capitol (part), Wash., DC.

Gordon Bunshaft, 1909-90, Lever House, New York, NY; Hirshhorn Museum, Washington, DC.

Daniel H. Burnham, 1846-1912, Union Station, Washington, DC; Flatiron Bldg., New York, NY.

Irwin Chanin, 1892-1988, theaters, skyscrapers, New York, NY.

David Childs, b 1941, Washington Mall Master Plan/Constitution Gardens, Washington, DC; One World Trade Center, New York, NY.

Lucio Costa, 1902-98, master plan for city of Brasilia, Brazil (with Oscar Niemeyer).

Ralph Adams Cram, 1863-1942, Cath. of St. John the Divine, New York, NY; U.S. Military Acad. (part), West Point, NY.

Norman Foster, b 1935, Commerzbank Headquarters, Frankfurt-am-Main, Ger.; London Millennium Bridge, 30 St. Mary Axe ("The Gherkin"), London, Eng., UK.

James Ingo Freed, 1930-2005, Holocaust Memorial Museum, Washington, DC; Jacob K. Javits Center, New York, NY.

R. Buckminster Fuller, 1895-1983, U.S. Pavilion (geodesic domes), Expo 67, Montreal, QC, Can.

Frank O. Gehry, b 1929, Guggenheim Museum, Bilbao, Spain; Experience Music Project, Seattle, WA; Walt Disney Concert Hall, Los Angeles, CA.

Cass Gilbert, 1859-1934, Custom House, Woolworth Bldg., New York, NY; Supreme Court Bldg., Washington, DC.

Bertram G. Goodhue, 1869-1924, Capitol, Lincoln, NE; St. Thomas's Church, St. Bartholomew's Church, New York, NY.

Michael Graves, 1934-2015, Portland Bldg., Portland, OR; Humana Bldg., Louisville, KY.

Walter Gropius, 1883-1969, Pan Am Bldg. (now MetLife Bldg.) (with Pietro Belluschi), New York, NY.

Zaha Hadid, 1950-2016, Rosenthal Center for Contemporary Art, Cincinnati, OH; London Aquatics Centre, Eng., UK.

Lawrence Halprin, 1916-2009, Ghirardelli Sq., San Francisco, CA; Nicollet Mall, Minneapolis, MN; FDR Memorial, Wash., DC.

Peter Harrison, 1716-75, Touro Synagogue, Redwood Library, Newport, RI.

Wallace K. Harrison, 1895-1981, Metropolitan Opera House, Lincoln Center, New York, NY.

Thomas Hastings, 1860-1929, NY Public Library (with John Carrère), Frick Mansion, New York, NY.

James Hoban, 1762-1831, White House, Washington, DC.

Raymond Hood, 1881-1934, Rockefeller Center (part), Daily News Bldg., New York, NY; Tribune Tower, Chicago, IL.

Richard M. Hunt, 1827-95, Metropolitan Museum (part), New York, NY; Biltmore Estate, Asheville, NC.

Helmut Jahn, b 1940, United Airlines Terminal, O'Hare Airport, Chicago, IL.

William Le Baron Jenney, 1832-1907, Home Insurance Bldg. (demolished 1931), Chicago, IL.

Philip C. Johnson, 1906-2005, AT&T Bldg. (now 550 Madison Ave.), New York, NY; Transco (now Williams) Tower, Houston, TX.

Albert Kahn, 1869-1942, General Motors Bldg., Detroit, MI.

Louis Kahn, 1901-74, Salk Laboratory, La Jolla, CA; Yale Art Gallery, New Haven, CT.

Rem Koolhaas, b 1944, Seattle Central Library, Seattle, WA.

Christopher Grant LaFarge, 1862-1938, Roman Catholic Chapel, West Point, NY.

Benjamin H. Latrobe, 1764-1820, Capitol (part), Washington, DC; State Capitol Bldg., Richmond, VA.

Le Corbusier (Charles-Edouard Jeanneret), 1887-1965, Salvation Army Hostel, Swiss Dormitory, Paris, France; master plan for cities of Algiers and Buenos Aires.

William Lescaze, 1896-1969, Philadelphia Savings Fund Society, PA; Borg-Warner Bldg., Chicago, IL.

Daniel Libeskind, b 1946, primary architect for the rebuilding of World Trade Center site, New York, NY.

Maya Lin, b 1959, Vietnam Veterans Mem., Washington, DC.

Charles Rennie Mackintosh, 1868-1928, Glasgow School of Art; Hill House, Helensburgh, Scot., UK.

Bernard R. Maybeck, 1862-1957, Hearst Hall, Univ. of CA, Berkeley; First Church of Christ Scientist, Berkeley, CA.

Charles F. McKim, 1847-1909, Boston Public Library; Columbia Univ. (part), New York, NY.

Charles M. McKim, b 1920, KUHT-TV Transmitter Bldg., Lutheran Church of the Redeemer, Houston, TX.

Richard Meier, b 1934, Getty Center Museum, Los Angeles, CA; High Museum of Art, Atlanta, GA.

Ludwig Mies van der Rohe, 1886-1969, Seagram Bldg. (with Philip C. Johnson), New York, NY; National Gallery, Berlin, Ger.

Robert Mills, 1781-1855, Washington Monument, Washington, DC.

Charles Moore, 1925-93, Sea Ranch, nr. San Francisco, CA; Piazza d'Italia, New Orleans, LA.

Julia Morgan, 1872-1957, San Simeon, CA.

John Nash, 1752-1835, Buckingham Palace, London, Eng., UK.

Richard J. Neutra, 1892-1970, Mathematics Park, Princeton, NJ; Orange Co. Courthouse, Santa Ana, CA.

Oscar Niemeyer, 1907-2012, government buildings, Brasilia Palace Hotel, Brasilia, Braz.

Gyo Obata, b 1923, Natl. Air and Space Museum, Smithsonian Inst., Washington, DC; Dallas-Ft. Worth Airport, TX.

Frederick L. Olmsted, 1822-1903, Central Park, New York, NY; Fairmount Park, Philadelphia, PA.

I(eoh) M(ing) Pei, b 1917, East Wing, Natl. Gallery of Art, Washington, DC; Pyramid, The Louvre, Paris, Fr.; Rock & Roll Hall of Fame and Museum, Cleveland, OH.

Cesar Pelli, b 1926, World Financial Center, Carnegie Hall Tower, New York, NY; Petronas Twin Towers, Malaysia.

William Pereira, 1909-85, Cape Canaveral, FL; Transamerica Pyramid, San Francisco, CA.

Renzo Piano, b 1937, Pompidou Centre, Paris, Fr.; New York Times Bldg., New York, NY; The Shard, London.

John Russell Pope, 1874-1937, National Gallery, Jefferson Memorial, Wash., DC.

John Portman, b 1924, Peachtree Center, Atlanta, GA.

George Browne Post, 1837-1913, NY Stock Exchange, New York, NY; Capitol, Madison, WI.

James Renwick Jr., 1818-95, Grace Church, St. Patrick's Cathedral, New York, NY; Smithsonian Institution (Castle), Washington, DC.

Henry H. Richardson, 1838-86, Trinity Church, Boston, MA.

Kevin Roche, b 1922, Oakland Museum, Oakland, CA; Fine Arts Center, Univ. of Massachusetts, Amherst, MA.

James Gamble Rogers, 1867-1947, Columbia-Presbyterian Medical Ctr., New York, NY; Northwestern Univ., Evanston, IL.

John Wellborn Root, 1887-1963, Palmolive Bldg., Chicago, IL; Hotel Statler, Wash., DC.

Paul Rudolph, 1918-97, Jewitt Art Center, Wellesley College, MA; Art & Architecture Bldg., Yale Univ., New Haven, CT.

Eero Saarinen, 1910-61, Gateway to the West Arch, St. Louis, MO; TWA Flight Center, JFK Airport, New York, NY.

Kazuyo Sejima, b 1956, 21st Century Museum of Contemporary Art (with Ryue Nishizawa), Kanazawa, Japan.

Louis Skidmore, 1897-1962, Atomic Energy Commission town site, Oak Ridge, TN; Terrace Plaza Hotel, Cincinnati, OH.

Norma Merrick Sklarek, 1928-2012, Terminal One, Los Angeles International Airport, CA.

Clarence S. Stein, 1882-1975, Temple Emanu-El, New York, NY.

Edward Durell Stone, 1902-78, interior of Radio City Music Hall, Museum of Modern Art, New York, NY.

Louis H. Sullivan, 1856-1924, Auditorium Bldg., Chicago, IL.

Kenzo Tange, 1913-2005, Hiroshima Peace Park, 1964 Tokyo Olympic stadiums, Japan.

Richard Upjohn, 1802-78, Trinity Church, New York, NY.

Max O. Urbahn, 1912-95, Vehicle Assembly Bldg., Cape Canaveral, FL.

Joern Utzon, 1918-2008, Sydney Opera House, NSW, Australia.

William Van Alen, 1883-1954, Chrysler Building, New York, NY.

Robert Venturi, b 1925, Gordon Wu Hall, Princeton, NJ; Mielparque Nikko Kirifuri Resort, Japan.

Ralph T. Walker, 1889-1973, NY Telephone Bldg. (now Verizon Bldg.), New York, NY; IBM Research Lab, Poughkeepsie, NY.

Wang Shu, 1963, Ningbo Museum, China.

Roland A. Wank, 1898-1970, Cincinnati Union Terminal, OH; head architect, 1933-44, Tennessee Valley Authority.

Stanford White, 1853-1906, Washington Arch in Washington Square Park, first Madison Square Garden, New York, NY.

Christopher Wren, 1632-1723, St. Paul's Cathedral, London, Eng., UK.

Frank Lloyd Wright, 1867-1959, Imperial Hotel, Tokyo, Jpn.; Guggenheim Museum, New York, NY; Kaufmann "Fallingwater" house, Mill Run, PA; Taliesin West, Scottsdale, AZ.

Thomas Wright, b 1957, Burj Al Arab hotel, Dubai, UAE.

William Wurster, 1895-1973, Ghirardelli Sq., San Francisco, CA.

Minoru Yamasaki, 1912-86, World Trade Center (destroyed 2001), New York, NY.

Artists, Photographers, and Sculptors of the Past

Artists are painters unless otherwise indicated.

Berenice Abbott, 1898-1991, (U.S.) photographer. Documentary of New York City, *Changing New York* (1939).

Ansel Easton Adams, 1902-84, (U.S.) photographer. Landscapes of the American Southwest.

Washington Allston, 1779-1843, (U.S.) landscapist. *Belshazzar's Feast*.

Albrecht Altdorfer, 1480-1538, (Ger.) landscapist.

Fra Angelico, c. 1400-55, (It.) Renaissance muralist. *Madonna of the Linen Drapers' Guild*.

Diane Arbus, 1923-71, (U.S.) photographer. Disturbing images.

Alexsandr Archipenko, 1887-1964, (U.S.) sculptor. *Boxing Match, Medranos*.

Jean Arp, 1887-1966, (Fr.) sculptor and painter. Founder of Dada movement.

Richard Artschwager, 1923-2013, (U.S.) painter and sculptor. *Table With Pink Tablecloth*.

Eugène Atget, 1856-1927, (Fr.) photographer. Paris life.

John James Audubon, 1785-1851, (U.S.) *Birds of America*.

Richard Avedon, 1923-2004, (U.S.) fashion and celebrity photographer.

Hans Baldung-Grien, 1484-1545, (Ger.) *Todentanz*.

Ernst Barlach, 1870-1938, (Ger.) Expressionist sculptor. *Man Drawing a Sword*.

Frédéric-Auguste Bartholdi, 1834-1904, (Fr.) sculptor. *Liberty Enlightening the World* (Statue of Liberty).

Fra Bartolommeo, 1472-1517, (It.) *Vision of St. Bernard*.

Romare Bearden, 1911-88, (U.S.) collage and other media. *The Visitation*.

Aubrey Beardsley, 1872-98, (Br.) illustrator. *Salome, Lysistrata, Morte d'Arthur, Volpone*.

Cecil Beaton, 1904-80, (Br.) fashion and celebrity photographer.

Max Beckmann, 1884-1950, (Ger.) Expressionist. *The Descent From the Cross*.

Gentile Bellini, 1426-1507, (It.) Renaissance. *Procession in St. Mark's Square*.

Giovanni Bellini, 1428-1516, (It.) Renaissance. *St. Francis in Ecstasy*.

Jacopo Bellini, 1400-70, (It.) Renaissance. *Crucifixion*.

George Wesley Bellows, 1882-1925, (U.S.) sports artist, portraitist, landscapist. *Stag at Sharkey's, Edith Clavell*.

Thomas Hart Benton, 1889-1975, (U.S.) American regionalist. *Threshing Wheat, Arts of the West*.

Ruth Bernhard, 1905-2006, (Ger.-U.S.) photographer. Black-and-white studies of female nudes.

Gianlorenzo Bernini, 1598-1680, (It.) Baroque sculptor. *The Assumption*.

Albert Bierstadt, 1830-1902, (U.S.) landscapist. *The Rocky Mountains, Mount Corcoran*.

George Caleb Bingham, 1811-79, (U.S.) American frontier. *Fur Traders Descending the Missouri*.

William Blake, 1757-1827, (Br.) engraver. *Book of Job, Songs of Innocence, Songs of Experience*.

Rosa Bonheur, 1822-99, (Fr.) Realist. *The Horse Fair*.

Pierre Bonnard, 1867-1947, (Fr.) Intimist. *The Breakfast Room, Girl in a Straw Hat*.

Gutzon Borglum, 1867-1941, (U.S.) sculptor. Mt. Rushmore Memorial.

Hieronymus Bosch, 1450-1516, (Flem.) religious allegories. *The Crowning With Thorns*.

Sandro Botticelli, 1444-1510, (It.) Renaissance. *Birth of Venus, Adoration of the Magi, Guiliano de'Medici*.

Louise Bourgeois, 1911-2010, (Fr.) sculptor. *Maman*.

Margaret Bourke-White, 1904-71, (U.S.) photographer, photojournalist. WWII, USSR, rural South during the Depression.

Mathew Brady, c. 1823-96, (U.S.) photographer. Civil War.

Constantin Brancusi, 1876-1957, (Romania-Fr.) Nonobjective sculptor. *Flying Turtle, The Kiss*.

Georges Braque, 1882-1963, (Fr.) Cubist. *Violin and Palette*.

Pieter Bruegel the Elder, c. 1525-69, (Flem.) Renaissance. *The Peasant Dance, Hunters in the Snow, Magpie on the Gallows*.

Pieter Bruegel the Younger, 1564-1638, (Flem.) Baroque. *Village Fair, The Crucifixion*.

Edward Burne-Jones, 1833-98, (Br.) Pre-Raphaelite artist-craftsman. *The Mirror of Venus*.

Alexander Calder, 1898-1976, (U.S.) sculptor. *Lobster Trap and Fish Tail*.

Julia Margaret Cameron, 1815-79, (Br.) photographer, prominent portraitist.

Robert Capa (Endre Friedmann), 1913-54, (Hung.-U.S.) photographer, war photojournalist. Invasion of Normandy.

Michelangelo Merisi da Caravaggio, 1573-1610, (It.) Baroque. *The Supper at Emmaus*.

Emily Carr, 1871-1945, (Can.) landscapist. *Blunden Harbour, Big Raven, Rushing Sea of Undergrowth*.

Carlo Carrà, 1881-1966, (It.) Metaphysical school. *Lot's Daughters, The Enchanted Room*.

Leonora Carrington, 1917-2011, (Br.) Surrealist. *The Inn of the Dawn Horse (Self-Portrait)*.

Henri Cartier-Bresson, 1908-2004, (Fr.) photographer. *Imagenes à la sauvette*.

Mary Cassatt, 1844-1926, (U.S.) Impressionist. *The Cup of Tea, Woman Bathing, The Boating Party*.

George Catlin, 1796-1872, (U.S.) American Indian life. *Gallery of Indians, Buffalo Dance*.

Benvenuto Cellini, 1500-71, (It.) Mannerist sculptor, goldsmith. *Perseus and Medusa*.

Paul Cézanne, 1839-1906, (Fr.) Post-Impressionist. *Card Players, Mont-Sainte-Victoire With Large Pine Trees*.

Marc Chagall, 1887-1985, (Russ.) Jewish life and folklore. *I and the Village, The Praying Jew*.

John Chamberlain, 1927-2011, (U.S.) sculptor of automobile metal.

Jean Simeon Chardin, 1699-1779, (Fr.) still lifes. *The Kiss, The Grace*.

Giorgio de Chirico, 1888-1978, (It.) founded the Metaphysical school. *Enigma of an Autumn Night*.

Frederick Church, 1826-1900, (U.S.) Hudson River school. *Niagara, Andes of Ecuador*.

Giovanni Cimabue, 1240-1302, (It.) Byzantine mosaicist. *Madonna Enthroned With St. Francis*.

Claude (Lorrain) (Claude Gellée), 1600-82, (Fr.) Ideal-landscapist. *The Enchanted Castle*.

Thomas Cole, 1801-48, (U.S.) Hudson River school. *The Ox-Bow, In the Catskills*.

John Constable, 1776-1837, (Br.) landscapist. *Salisbury Cathedral From the Bishop's Grounds*.

John Singleton Copley, 1738-1815, (U.S.) portraitist. *Samuel Adams, Watson and the Shark*.

Lovis Corinth, 1858-1925, (Ger.) Expressionist. *Apocalypse*.

Jean-Baptiste-Camille Corot, 1796-1875, (Fr.) landscapist. *Souvenir de Mortefontaine, Pastorale*.

Correggio, 1494-1534, (It.) Renaissance muralist. *Mystic Marriages of St. Catherine*.

Gustave Courbet, 1819-77, (Fr.) Realist. *The Artist's Studio*.

Lucas Cranach the Elder, 1472-1553, (Ger.) Protestant Reformation portraitist. *Luther*.

Bill Cunningham, 1929-2016, (U.S.) fashion photographer.

Imogen Cunningham, 1883-1976, (U.S.) photographer, portraitist. *Plants*.

Nathaniel Currier, 1813-88, and **James M. Ives**, 1824-95, (both U.S.) lithographers. *A Midnight Race on the Mississippi, American Forest Scene—Maple Sugaring*.

John Steuart Curry, 1897-1946, (U.S.) Americana, murals. *Baptism in Kansas*.

Edward S. Curtis, 1868-1952, (U.S.) photographer. *The North American Indian*.

Salvador Dalí, 1904-89, (Sp.) Surrealist. *Persistence of Memory, The Crucifixion*.

Honoré Daumier, 1808-79, (Fr.) caricaturist. *The Third-Class Carriage*.

Jacques-Louis David, 1748-1825, (Fr.) Neoclassicist. *The Oath of the Horatii*.

Arthur Davies, 1862-1928, (U.S.) Romantic landscapist. *Unicorns, Leda and the Dioscuri*.

Edgar Degas, 1834-1917, (Fr.) Realist/Impressionist. *The Ballet Class*.

Willem de Kooning, 1904-97, (Neth.-U.S.) Abstract Expressionist. *Excavation, Woman I, Door to the River*.

Eugène Delacroix, 1798-1863, (Fr.) Romantic. *Massacre at Chios, Liberty Leading the People*.

Paul Delaroche, 1797-1856, (Fr.) historical themes. *Children of Edward IV*.

Luca Della Robbia, 1400-82, (It.) Renaissance terra-cotta. *Cantoria (singing gallery)*, Florence cathedral.

Donatello, 1386-1466, (It.) Renaissance sculptor. *David, Gattamelata*.

Aaron Douglas, 1899-79, (U.S.) Harlem Renaissance illustrator and muralist.

Jean Dubuffet, 1902-85, (Fr.) painter, sculptor, printmaker. *Group of Four Trees*.

Marcel Duchamp, 1887-1968, (Fr.) Dadaist. *Nude Descending a Staircase, No. 2*.

Raoul Dufy, 1877-1953, (Fr.) Fauvist. *Chateau and Horses*.

Asher Brown Durand, 1796-1886, (U.S.) Hudson River school. *Kindred Spirits*.

Albrecht Dürer, 1471-1528, (Ger.) Renaissance painter, engraver, woodcuts. *St. Jerome in His Study, Melencolia I*.

Anthony van Dyck, 1599-1641, (Flem.) Baroque portraitist. *Portrait of Charles I Hunting*.

Thomas Eakins, 1844-1916, (U.S.) Realist. *The Gross Clinic*.

Alfred Eisenstaedt, 1898-1995, (Ger.-U.S.) photographer, photojournalist. Famous photo, V-J Day, Aug. 14, 1945.

Peter Henry Emerson, 1856-1936, (Br.) photographer. Promoted photography as an independent art form.

Jacob Epstein, 1880-1959, (Br.) religious and allegorical sculptor. *Genesis, Ecce Homo*.

Erté (Romain de Tiertoff), 1892-1990, (Fr.) painter, fashion and stage designer.

Walker Evans, 1903-75, (U.S.) photographer. Documented Great Depression.

Jan van Eyck, c. 1390-1441, (Flem.) naturalistic panels. *Adoration of the Lamb*.

Horst Faas, 1933-2012, (Ger.) Vietnam War photographer.

Roger Fenton, 1819-69, (Br.) photographer. Crimean War.

Anselm Feuerbach, 1829-80, (Ger.) Romantic Classicist. *Judgment of Paris, Iphigenia*.

John Bernard Flannagan, 1895-1942, (U.S.) animal sculptor. *Triumph of the Egg*.

Jean-Honoré Fragonard, 1732-1806, (Fr.) Rococo. *The Swing*.

Helen Frankenthaler, 1928-2011, (U.S.) Abstract Expressionist. *Mountains and Sea*.

Daniel Chester French, 1850-1931, (U.S.) sculptor. *The Minute Man of Concord*; seated *Lincoln*, Lincoln Memorial, Washington, DC.

Lucian Freud, 1922-2011, (Ger.-Br.) portraitist. *Girl With Roses*.

Caspar David Friedrich, 1774-1840, (Ger.) Romantic landscapist. *Man and Woman Gazing at the Moon*.

Thomas Gainsborough, 1727-88, (Br.) portraitist. *The Blue Boy, The Watering Place, The Parish Clerk*.

Alexander Gardner, 1821-82, (U.S.) photographer. Civil War, railroad construction, Great Plains Indians.

Paul Gauguin, 1848-1903, (Fr.) Post-Impressionist. *The Tahitians, Spirit of the Dead Watching*.

Lorenzo Ghiberti, 1378-1455, (It.) Renaissance sculptor. "Gates of Paradise" baptistery doors, Florence, It.

Alberto Giacometti, 1901-66, (Switz.) attenuated sculptures of solitary figures. *Man Pointing*.

Giorgione, c. 1477-1510, (It.) Renaissance. *The Tempest*.

Giotto di Bondone, 1267-1337, (It.) Renaissance. *Presentation of Christ in the Temple*.

François Girardon, 1628-1715, (Fr.) Baroque sculptor of classical themes. *Apollo Tended by the Nymphs*.

Edward Gorey, 1925-2000, (U.S.) illustrator. *The Doubtful Guest*.

Arshile Gorky, 1905-48, (U.S.) Surrealist. *The Liver Is the Cock's Comb*.

Francisco de Goya y Lucientes, 1746-1828, (Sp.) painter, printmaker. *The Naked Maja, The Disasters of War* (etchings).

El Greco (Domenikos Theotokopoulos), 1541-1614, (Gr.-Sp.) painter, sculptor. *View of Toledo, Assumption of the Virgin*.

Horatio Greenough, 1805-52, (U.S.) Neoclassical sculptor.

Matthias Grünewald, 1480-1528, (Ger.) mystical religious themes. *The Resurrection*.

Frans Hals, c. 1580-1666, (Neth.) portraitist. *Laughing Cavalier, Gypsy Girl*.

Richard Hamilton, 1922-2011, (Br.) Pop Art. *Just What Is It That Makes Today's Homes So Different, So Appealing?*

Austin Hansen, 1910-96, (U.S.) photographer. Harlem, NY, life.

Childe Hassam, 1859-1935, (U.S.) Impressionist. *Southwest Wind, July 14 Rue Daunon*.

Edward Hicks, 1780-1849, (U.S.) folk. *The Peaceable Kingdom*.

Lewis Wickes Hine, 1874-1940, (U.S.) photographer. Studies of immigrants, children in industry.

Hans Hofmann, 1880-1966, (U.S.) early Abstract Expressionist. *Spring, The Gate*.

William Hogarth, 1697-1764, (Br.) caricaturist. *The Rake's Progress*.

Katsushika Hokusai, 1760-1849, (Jpn.) printmaker. *Crabs*.

Hans Holbein the Elder, 1460-1524, (Ger.) late Gothic. *Presentation of Christ in the Temple*.

Hans Holbein the Younger, 1497-1543, (Ger.) portraitist. *Henry VIII, The French Ambassadors*.

Winslow Homer, 1836-1910, (U.S.) naturalist, marine themes. *Marine Coast, High Cliff*.

Edward Hopper, 1882-1967, (U.S.) realistic urban scenes. *Nighthawks, House by the Railroad*.

Horst P. Horst, 1906-99, (Ger.) fashion, celebrity photographer.

Jean-Auguste-Dominique Ingres, 1780-1867, (Fr.) Classicist. *Valpincon Bather*.

George Inness, 1825-94, (U.S.) luminous landscapist. *Delaware Water Gap*.

William Henry Jackson, 1843-1942, (U.S.) photographer. American West, building of Union Pacific Railroad.

Jeanne-Claude (Javacheff), 1935-2009, (Moroc.), created large-scale, temporary installations in public places with her husband, Christo.

Donald Judd, 1928-94, (U.S.) sculptor, major Minimalist.

Frida Kahlo, 1907-54, (Mex.) folkloric stylist. *Self-Portrait With Monkey*.

Wassily Kandinsky, 1866-1944, (Russ.) Abstractionist. *Capricious Forms*, *Improvisation 28 (second version)*.

Ellsworth Kelly, 1923-2015, (U.S.) painter, sculptor. *Red Blue Green*.

Paul Klee, 1879-1940, (Switz.) Abstractionist. *Twittering Machine*, *Pastoral*, *Death and Fire*.

Gustav Klimt, 1862-1918, (Austria) cofounder of Vienna Secession Movement. *The Kiss*.

Oscar Kokoschka, 1886-1980, (Austria) Expressionist. *View of Prague*, *Harbor of Marseilles*.

Kathe Kollwitz, 1867-1945, (Ger.) printmaker, social justice themes. *The Peasant War*.

Gaston Lachaise, 1882-1935, (U.S.) figurative sculptor. *Standing Woman*.

John La Farge, 1835-1910, (U.S.) muralist. *Red and White Peonies*, *The Ascension*.

Sir Edwin (Henry) Landseer, 1802-73, (Br.) painter, sculptor. *Shoeing*, *Rout of Comus*.

Dorothea Lange, 1895-1965, (U.S.) photographer. Great Depression, migrant farm workers.

Fernand Léger, 1881-1955, (Fr.) Machine art. *The Cyclists*.

Saul Leiter, 1923-2013, (U.S) photographer.

Leonardo da Vinci, 1452-1519, (It.) Renaissance. *Mona Lisa*, *Last Supper*, *The Annunciation*.

Emanuel Leutze, 1816-68, (U.S.) historical themes. *Washington Crossing the Delaware*.

Roy Lichtenstein, 1923-97, (U.S.) Pop Art.

Jacques Lipchitz, 1891-1973, (Fr.) Cubist sculptor. *Harpist*.

Filippino Lippi, 1457-1504, (It.) Renaissance. *Adoration of the Magi*.

Fra Filippo Lippi, 1406-69, (It.) Renaissance. *Coronation of the Virgin*, *Madonna and Child With Angels*.

Morris Louis, 1912-62, (U.S.) Abstract Expressionism. *Signa*, *Stripes*, *Alpha-Phi*.

René Magritte, 1898-1967, (Belg.) Surrealist. *The Descent of Man*, *The Betrayal of Images*.

Aristide Maillol, 1861-1944, (Fr.) sculptor. *L'Harmonie*.

Édouard Manet, 1832-83, (Fr.) forerunner of Impressionism. *Luncheon on the Grass*, *Olympia*.

Andrea Mantegna, 1431-1506, (It.) Renaissance frescoes. *Triumph of Caesar*.

Robert Mapplethorpe, 1946-89, (U.S.) photographer.

Franz Marc, 1880-1916, (Ger.) Expressionist. *Blue Horses*.

John Marin, 1870-1953, (U.S.) Expressionist seascapes. *Maine Island*.

Reginald Marsh, 1898-1954, (U.S.) satire. *Tattoo and Haircut*.

Agnes Martin, 1912-2004, (U.S.) abstract artist. *Night Sea*.

Masaccio, 1401-28, (It.) Renaissance. *The Tribute Money*.

Henri Matisse, 1869-1954, (Fr.) Fauvist. *Woman With the Hat*.

John McCracken, 1934-2011, (U.S.) Minimalist sculptor.

Michelangelo Buonarroti, 1475-1564, (It.) Renaissance. *Pietà*, *David*, *Moses*, *The Last Judgment*, Sistine Chapel ceiling.

Jean-Francois Millet, 1814-75, (Fr.) peasants. *The Gleaners*, *The Man With a Hoe*.

Joan Miró, 1893-1983, (Sp.) exuberant colors, playful images. Catalan landscape, *Dutch Interior*.

Amedeo Modigliani, 1884-1920, (It.) figurative paintings, sculptures. *Reclining Nude*.

Piet Mondrian, 1872-1944, (Neth.) Abstractionist. *Composition With Red, Yellow and Blue*.

Claude Monet, 1840-1926, (Fr.) Impressionist. *The Bridge at Argenteuil*, *Haystacks*, *Bridge Over a Pond of Water Lillies*.

Henry Moore, 1898-1986, (Br.) sculptor of large-scale, abstract works. *Reclining Figure* (several).

Gustave Moreau, 1826-98, (Fr.) Symbolist. *The Apparition*, *Dance of Salome*.

James Wilson Morrice, 1865-1924, (Can.) landscapist. *The Ferry, Quebec*, *Venice, Looking Over the Lagoon*.

William Morris, 1834-96, (Br.) decorative artist, leader of Arts and Crafts movement.

Grandma Moses (Anna Mary Robertson Moses), 1860-1961, (U.S.) folk. *Out for the Christmas Tree*, *Catching the Thanksgiving Turkey*.

Edvard Munch, 1863-1944, (Nor.) Expressionist. *The Cry*.

Bartolome Murillo, 1618-82, (Sp.) Baroque religious artist. *Vision of St. Anthony*, *The Two Trinities*.

Elizabeth Murray, 1940-2007, (U.S.) abstract colors. *Kitchen Party*.

Eadweard Muybridge, 1830-1904, (Br.-U.S.) photographer. Studies of motion, *Animal Locomotion*.

Nadar (Gaspar-Félix Tournachon), 1820-1910, (Fr.) photographer, caricaturist, portraitist. Invented photo-essay.

LeRoy Neiman, 1921-2012, (U.S.) sports expressionist painter.

Arnold Newman, 1918-2006, (U.S.) portrait photographer.

Barnett Newman, 1905-70, (U.S.) Abstract Expressionism. *Stations of the Cross*.

Isamu Noguchi, 1904-88, (U.S.) abstract sculptor, designer. *Kouros*, *BirdC(MU)*, sculptural gardens.

Kenneth Noland, 1924-2010, (U.S.) Color Field, abstract.

Georgia O'Keeffe, 1887-1986, (U.S.) Southwest motifs. *Cow's Skull: Red, White, and Blue*; *The Shelton With Sunspots*.

José Clemente Orozco, 1883-1949, (Mex.) frescoes. *House of Tears*, *Pre-Columbian Golden Age*.

Timothy H. O'Sullivan, 1840-82, (U.S.) Civil War photographer.

Gordon Parks, 1912-2006, (U.S.) African American photographer, filmmaker. *Life* photographer, 1948-68.

Charles Willson Peale, 1741-1827, (U.S.) Amer. Revolutionary portraitist. *The Staircase Group*, U.S. presidents.

Rembrandt Peale, 1778-1860, (U.S.) portraitist. *Thomas Jefferson*.

Irving Penn, 1917-2009, (U.S.) portraitist, fashion photographer.

Pietro Perugino, 1446-1523, (It.) Renaissance. *Delivery of the Keys to St. Peter*.

Pablo Picasso, 1881-1973, (Sp.) painter, sculptor. *Guernica*, *Dove*, *Head of a Woman*, *Head of a Bull*, *Metamorphosis*.

Piero della Francesca, c. 1415-92, (It.) Renaissance. *Duke of Urbino*, *Flagellation of Christ*.

Camille Pissarro, 1830-1903, (Fr.) Impressionist. *Boulevard des Italiens, Morning, Sunlight*; *Bather in the Woods*.

Jackson Pollock, 1912-56, (U.S.) Abstract Expressionism. *Autumn Rhythm*.

Nicolas Poussin, 1594-1665, (Fr.) Baroque pictorial classicism. *St. John on Patmos*.

Maurice B. Prendergast, c. 1860-1924, (U.S.) Postimpressionist watercolorist. *Umbrellas in the Rain*.

Pierre-Paul Prud'hon, 1758-1823, (Fr.) Romanticist. *Crime Pursued by Vengeance and Justice*.

Pierre Cecile Puvis de Chavannes, 1824-98, (Fr.) muralist. *The Poor Fisherman*.

Raphael Sanzio, 1483-1520, (It.) Renaissance. *Disputa*, *School of Athens*, *Sistine Madonna*.

Robert Rauschenberg, 1925-2008, (U.S.) printmaker. *Combine*, *Bed*, *Revolvers*, *Outpost*.

Man Ray (Emmanuel Radnitsky), 1890-1976, (U.S.) Dadaist and Surrealist. *Observing Time*, *The Lovers*, *Marquis de Sade*.

Odilon Redon, 1840-1916, (Fr.) Symbolist painter, lithographer. *In the Dream*, *Vase of Flowers*.

Rembrandt van Rijn, 1606-69, (Neth.) painter, printmaker. *The Bridal Couple*, *The Night Watch*.

Frederic Remington, 1861-1909, (U.S.) painter, sculptor. Portrayer of the American West, *Bronco Buster*.

Pierre-Auguste Renoir, 1841-1919, (Fr.) Impressionist. *The Luncheon of the Boating Party*, *Dance in the Country*.

Joshua Reynolds, 1723-92, (Br.) portraitist. *Mrs. Siddons as the Tragic Muse*.

Herb Ritts, 1952-2002, (U.S.) photographer. Nudes, celebrities.

Diego Rivera, 1886-1957, (Mex.) frescoes. *The Fecund Earth*.

Larry Rivers, 1923-2002, (U.S.) painter, sculptor, often realistic. Dutch Masters series.

Henry Peach Robinson, 1830-1901, (Br.) a leader of "high art" photography.

Norman Rockwell, 1894-1978, (U.S.) painter, illustrator. *Saturday Evening Post* covers.

Auguste Rodin, 1840-1917, (Fr.) sculptor. *The Thinker*.

Milton Rogovin, 1909-2011, (U.S.) documentary photographer.

Willy Ronis, 1910-2009, (Fr.) photographer. Postwar Paris.

Joe Rosenthal, 1911-2006, (U.S.) photojournalist; photographed six Marines raising the U.S. flag over Iwo Jima in WWII.

Mark Rothko, 1903-70, (U.S.) Abstract Expressionist. *Light, Earth and Blue*.

Georges Rouault, 1871-1958, (Fr.) Expressionist. *Three Judges*.

Henri Rousseau, 1844-1910, (Fr.) primitive exotic themes. *The Snake Charmer*.

Theodore Rousseau, 1812-67, (Switz.-Fr.) landscapist. *Under the Birches, Evening*.

Peter Paul Rubens, 1577-1640, (Flem.) Baroque. *Mystic Marriage of St. Catherine*.

Jacob van Ruisdael, c. 1628-82, (Neth.) landscapist. *Jewish Cemetery*.

Charles M. Russell, 1866-1926, (U.S.) Western life.

Salomon van Ruysdael, c. 1600-70, (Neth.) landscapist. *River With Ferry-Boat*.

Albert Pinkham Ryder, 1847-1917, (U.S.) seascapes, allegories. *Toilers of the Sea*.

Augustus Saint-Gaudens, 1848-1907, (U.S.) memorial statues. *Farragut*, *Mrs. Henry Adams (Grief)*.

Niki de Saint Phalle, 1930-2002, (Fr.) paintings, sculptures, prints, large public installations.

Andrea Sansovino, 1460-1529, (It.) Renaissance sculptor. *Baptism of Christ*.

Jacopo Sansovino, 1486-1570, (It.) Renaissance sculptor. *St. John the Baptist*.

John Singer Sargent, 1856-1925, (U.S.) Edwardian society portraitist. *The Wyndham Sisters*, *Madame X*.

Andrea del Sarto, 1486-1530, (It.) frescoes. *Madonna of the Harpies*.

George Segal, 1924-2000, (U.S.) sculptor. Life-sized figures realistically depicting daily life.

Georges Seurat, 1859-91, (Fr.) Pointillist. *Sunday Afternoon on the Island of La Grande Jatte*.

Gino Severini, 1883-1966, (It.) Futurist and Cubist. *Dynamic Hieroglyph of the Bal Tabarin*.

Ben Shahn, 1898-1969, (U.S.) social and political themes. Sacco and Vanzetti series, *Seurat's Lunch*, *Handball*.

Charles Sheeler, 1883-1965, (U.S.) abstractionist.

David Alfaro Siqueiros, 1896-1974, (Mex.) political muralist. *March of Humanity*.

David Smith, 1906-65, (U.S.) welded metal sculpture. *Hudson River Landscape*, *Zig*, *Cubi* series.

Edward Steichen, 1879-1973, (U.S.) photographer. Credited with transforming photography into an art form.

Alfred Stieglitz, 1864-1946, (U.S.) photographer, editor. Helped create acceptance of photography as art.

Paul Strand, 1890-1976, (U.S.) photographer. People, nature, landscapes.

Gilbert Stuart, 1755-1828, (U.S.) portraitist. George Washington, Thomas Jefferson, James Madison.

Thomas Sully, 1783-1872, (U.S.) portraitist. *Col. Thomas Handasyd Perkins*, *The Passage of the Delaware*.

William Henry Fox Talbot, 1800-77, (Br.) photographer. *Pencil of Nature*, early photographically illustrated book.

Cy Twombly, 1928-2011, (U.S.) painter and sculptor. *Leda and the Swan*.
Paolo Uccello, 1397-1475, (It.) Gothic-Renaissance. *The Rout of San Romano*.
Maurice Utrillo, 1883-1955, (Fr.) Impressionist. *Sacre-Coeur de Montmartre*.
Vincent van Gogh, 1853-90, (Neth.) *The Starry Night, L'Arlesienne, Bedroom at Arles, Self-Portrait*.
John Vanderlyn, 1775-1852, (U.S.) Neoclassicist. *Ariadne Asleep on the Island of Naxos*.
Diego Velázquez, 1599-1660, (Sp.) Baroque. *Las Meninas, Portrait of Juan de Pareja*.
Jan Vermeer, 1632-75, (Neth.) interior genre subjects. *Young Woman With a Water Jug*.
Paolo Veronese, 1528-88, (It.) devotional themes, vastly peopled canvases. *The Temptation of St. Anthony*.
Andrea del Verrocchio, 1435-88, (It.) sculptor. *Colleoni*.
Maurice de Vlaminck, 1876-1958, (Fr.) Fauvist landscapist. *Red Trees*.

George Tames, 1919-94, (U.S.) photographer. Presidents, political leaders.
Yves Tanguy, 1900-55, (Fr.) Surrealist. *Rose of the Four Winds; Mama, Papa Is Wounded!*
Giovanni Battista Tiepolo, 1696-1770, (It.) Rococo frescoes. *The Crucifixion*.
Jacopo Tintoretto, 1518-94, (It.) Mannerist. *The Last Supper*.
Titian (Tiziano Vecellio), c. 1488-1576, (It.) Renaissance. *Venus and the Lute Player, The Bacchanal*.
Jose Rey Toledo, 1916-94, (U.S.) Native American life. Tribal dances.
George Tooker, 1920-2011, (U.S.) Magic Realist. *Subway*.
Henri de Toulouse-Lautrec, 1864-1901, (Fr.) Postimpressionist. *At the Moulin Rouge*.
John Trumbull, 1756-1843, (U.S.) historical themes. *The Declaration of Independence*.
Deborah Turbeville, 1937-2013, (U.S.) fashion photographer.
J(oseph) M(allord) W(illiam) Turner, 1775-1851, (Br.) Romantic landscapist. *Snow Storm*.

Andy Warhol, 1928-87, (U.S.) Pop Art. *Campbell's Soup Cans, Marilyn Diptych*.
Antoine Watteau, 1684-1721, (Fr.) Rococo "scenes of gallantry." *The Embarkation for Cythera*.
George Frederic Watts, 1817-1904, (Br.) painter and sculptor. Grandiose allegorical themes. *Hope*.
Benjamin West, 1738-1820, (U.S.) realistic historical themes. *Death of General Wolfe*.
Edward Weston, 1886-1958, (U.S.) photographer. Landscapes of American West.
James Abbott McNeill Whistler, 1834-1903, (U.S.) *Arrangement in Grey and Black No. 1 (Portrait of the Artist's Mother)*.
Archibald M. Willard, 1836-1918, (U.S.) murals. *The Spirit of '76*.
Grant Wood, 1891-1942, (U.S.) Midwestern regionalist. *American Gothic, Daughters of Revolution*.
Andrew Wyeth, 1917-2009, (U.S.), regionalist. *Christina's World*.
Ossip Zadkine, 1890-1967, (Russ.) School of Paris sculptor. *The Destroyed City, Musicians, Christ*.

Business Leaders and Philanthropists of the Past

Giovanni Agnelli, 1921-2003, (It.) industrialist; principal shareholder of Fiat.
Karl Albrecht, 1920-2014, and **Theo Albrecht**, 1922-2010, (both Ger.) cofounders of Aldi supermarkets.
Walter Annenberg, 1908-2002, (U.S.) publisher, founder of *TV Guide*, philanthropist.
Elizabeth Arden (F. N. Graham), 1884-1966, (U.S.) Canadian-born founder of cosmetics empire.
Philip D. Armour, 1832-1901, (U.S.) industrialist; streamlined meatpacking.
Brooke Astor, 1902-2007, (U.S.) philanthropist; pres. of Vincent Astor Foundation.
John Jacob Astor, 1763-1848, (U.S.) German-born fur trader, banker, real estate magnate; at death, richest in U.S.
Francis W. Ayer, 1848-1923, (U.S.) ad industry pioneer.
August Belmont, 1816-90, (U.S.) German-born financier.
James B. (Diamond Jim) Brady, 1856-1917, (U.S.) financier, philanthropist, legendary bon vivant.
Adolphus Busch, 1839-1913, (U.S.) German-born businessman; established brewery empire.
Asa Candler, 1851-1929, (U.S.) founded Coca-Cola Co.
Andrew Carnegie, 1835-1919, (U.S.) Scottish-born industrialist, philanthropist; founded Carnegie Steel Co.
Tom Carvel, 1908-89, (Gr.-U.S.) founded ice cream chain.
William Colgate, 1783-1857, (Br.-U.S.) businessman, philanthropist; founded soap-making empire.
Jay Cooke, 1821-1905, (U.S.) financier.
Peter Cooper, 1791-1883, (U.S.) industrialist, inventor, philanthropist; founded Cooper Union college (1859).
Ezra Cornell, 1807-74, (U.S.) businessman, philanthropist; headed Western Union.
Erastus Corning, 1794-1872, (U.S.) financier; headed New York Central Railroad.
Charles Crocker, 1822-88, (U.S.) railroad builder, financier.
Samuel Cunard, 1787-1865, (Can.) pioneered transatlantic steam navigation.
Marcus Daly, 1841-1900, (U.S.) Irish-born copper magnate.
W. Edwards Deming, 1900-93, (U.S.) quality-control expert who revolutionized Japanese manufacturing.
Walt Disney, 1901-66, (U.S.) pioneer in cinema animation; built entertainment empire.
Herbert H. Dow, 1866-1930, (U.S.) founder of chemical co.
Anthony Drexel, 1826-93, (U.S.) banker, philanthropist, university founder.
James Duke, 1856-1925, (U.S.) founded American Tobacco, Duke Univ.
Eleuthere I. du Pont, 1771-1834, (Fr.-U.S.) gunpowder manufacturer; founded one of the largest business empires.
Thomas C. Durant, 1820-85, (U.S.) railroad official, financier.

William C. Durant, 1861-1947, (U.S.) industrialist; formed General Motors.
George Eastman, 1854-1932, (U.S.) inventor; manufacturer of photographic equipment.
Marshall Field, 1834-1906, (U.S.) merchant; founded Chicago's largest department store.
Harvey Firestone, 1868-1938, (U.S.) founded tire company.
Avery Fisher, 1906-94, (U.S.) industrialist, philanthropist; founded Fisher Electronics.
Henry M. Flagler, 1830-1913, (U.S.) financier; helped form Standard Oil, developed FL as resort state.
Malcolm Forbes, 1919-90, (U.S.) magazine publisher.
Henry Ford, 1863-1947, (U.S.) automaker; developed first popular low-priced car.
Henry Ford II, 1917-87, (U.S.) headed auto company founded by grandfather.
Henry C. Frick, 1849-1919, (U.S.) steel and coke magnate; had prominent role in development of U.S. Steel.
Jakob Fugger (Jakob the Rich), 1459-1525, (Ger.) headed leading banking, trading house in 16th-cent. Europe.
Alfred C. Fuller, 1885-1973, (U.S.) Canadian-born businessman; founded brush company.
Elbert H. Gary, 1846-1927, (U.S.) chaired board of U.S. Steel, 1903-27.
Jean Paul Getty, 1892-1976, (U.S.) founded oil empire.
Amadeo Giannini, 1870-1949, (U.S.) founded Bank of America.
Stephen Girard, 1750-1831, (U.S.) French-born financier, philanthropist; richest man in U.S. at time of death.
Leonard H. Goldenson, 1905-99, (U.S.) turned ABC into major TV network.
Jay Gould, 1836-92, (U.S.) railroad magnate, financier.
Hetty Green, 1834-1916, (U.S.) financier, the "witch of Wall St."; richest woman in U.S. in her day.
William Gregg, 1800-67, (U.S.) launched textile industry in the South.
Meyer Guggenheim, 1828-1905, (U.S.) Swiss-born merchant, philanthropist; built merchandising, mining empires.
Armand Hammer, 1898-1990, (U.S.) headed Occidental Petroleum, promoted U.S.-Soviet ties.
Elliot Handler, 1916-2011, (U.S.) cofounder of Mattel; introduced the Barbie doll.
Edward H. Harriman, 1848-1909, (U.S.) railroad financier; headed Union Pacific.
Henry J. Heinz, 1844-1919, (U.S.) founded food company.
Harry (1909-97) and **Leona Helmsley**, 1920-2007, (U.S.) real estate magnates, philanthropists.
Milton Snavely Hershey, 1857-1945, (U.S.) chocolate co. founder, philanthropist.

James J. Hill, 1838-1916, (U.S.) Canadian-born railroad magnate, financier; founded Great Northern Railway.
Conrad N. Hilton, 1888-1979, (U.S.) hotel chain founder.
Howard Hughes, 1905-76, (U.S.) industrialist, aviator, filmmaker.
H. L. Hunt, 1889-1974, (U.S.) oil magnate.
Collis P. Huntington, 1821-1900, (U.S.) railroad magnate.
Henry E. Huntington, 1850-1927, (U.S.) railroad builder, philanthropist.
Walter L. Jacobs, 1898-1985, (U.S.) founder of the first rental car agency.
Steve Jobs, 1955-2011, (U.S.) Apple cofounder and exec.; Pixar exec.
Howard Johnson, 1896-1972, (U.S.) founded restaurants.
John H. Johnson, 1918-2005, (U.S.) built publishing empire based on *Ebony* and *Jet*.
Samuel Curtis Johnson, 1928-2004, (U.S.) headed S.C. Johnson & Sons.
Henry J. Kaiser, 1882-1967, (U.S.) industrialist; built empire in steel, aluminum.
Minor C. Keith, 1848-1929, (U.S.) railroad magnate; founded United Fruit Co.
Will K. Kellogg, 1860-1951, (U.S.) businessman, philanthropist; founded breakfast food co.
Kirk Kerkorian, 1917-2015, (U.S.) private equity magnate; real estate developer.
Richard King, 1825-85, (U.S.) cattle farmer; founded King Ranch in Texas.
John W. Kluge, 1914-2010, (Ger.-U.S.) Metromedia chair; philanthropist.
William S. Knudsen, 1879-1948, (U.S.) Danish-born auto industry executive.
Samuel H. Kress, 1863-1955, (U.S.) businessman, art collector, philanthropist; founded "dime store" chain.
Ray A. Kroc, 1902-84, (U.S.) original CEO of McDonald's Corp.; oversaw company's vast expansion.
Alfred Krupp, 1812-87, (Ger.) armaments magnate.
Estée Lauder, 1908-2004, (U.S.) cofounder of Estée Lauder companies.
Kenneth L. Lay, 1942-2006, (U.S.), former CEO of Enron; indicted on fraud charges.
William Levitt, 1907-94, (U.S.) industrialist; "suburb maker."
Thomas Lipton, 1850-1931, (Scot.) merchant; tea empire.
James McGill, 1744-1813, (Scot.-Can.) funded Montréal's McGill Univ.
Andrew W. Mellon, 1855-1937, (U.S.) financier, industrialist, philanthropist.
Charles E. Merrill, 1885-1956, (U.S.) financier; developed firm of Merrill Lynch.
J(ohn) P(ierpont) Morgan, 1837-1913, (U.S.) most powerful figure in finance and industry at turn of 20th cent.
Akio Morita, 1921-99, (Jpn.) cofounded Sony Corp.
Malcolm Muir, 1885-1979, (U.S.) created *Business Week* magazine; headed *Newsweek*, 1937-61.

Roy Neuberger, 1903-2010, (U.S.) financier, art patron.
Samuel Newhouse, 1895-1979, (U.S.) publishing and broadcasting magnate.
Jean Nidetch, 1923-2015, (U.S.) Weight Watchers cofounder.
Aristotle Onassis, 1906-75, (Gr.) shipping magnate.
William S. Paley, 1901-90, (U.S.) built CBS communications empire.
Frederick D. Patterson, 1901-88, (U.S.) founder of United Negro College Fund, 1944.
George Peabody, 1795-1869, (U.S.) merchant, financier, philanthropist.
James C. Penney, 1875-1971, (U.S.) businessman; developed department store.
Frank Perdue, 1920-2005, (U.S.) founder of Perdue Farms, chicken-processing co.
William C. Procter, 1862-1934, (U.S.) headed soap co.
John D. Rockefeller, 1839-1937, (U.S.) industrialist; established Standard Oil.
John D. Rockefeller Jr., 1874-1960, (U.S.) philanthropist; provided land for UN.
Laurance S. Rockefeller, 1910-2004, (U.S.) philanthropist, conservationist.
Meyer A. Rothschild, 1743-1812, (Ger.) founded international banking house.
Thomas Fortune Ryan, 1851-1928, (U.S.) financier; a founder of American Tobacco.
Edmond J. Safra, 1932-99, (U.S.) banker.
David Sarnoff, 1891-1971, (U.S.) broadcasting pioneer; established first radio network, NBC.

Richard Sears, 1863-1914, (U.S.) founded mail-order co.
Werner von Siemens, 1816-92, (Ger.) industrialist, inventor.
Alfred P. Sloan, 1875-1966, (U.S.) industrialist, philanthropist; headed General Motors.
A. Leland Stanford, 1824-93, (U.S.) railroad official, philanthropist; founded university.
Frank Stanton, 1908-2006, (U.S.) president of CBS network, 1946-71.
Nathan Straus, 1848-1931, (U.S.) German-born merchant, philanthropist; headed Macy's dept. stores.
Levi Strauss, c. 1829-1902, (U.S.) pants manufacturer.
Clement Studebaker, 1831-1901, (U.S.) wagon, carriage maker.
Gustavus Swift, 1839-1903, (U.S.) pioneer meatpacker.
Gerard Swope, 1872-1957, (U.S.) industrialist, economist; headed General Electric.
Dave Thomas, 1932-2002, (U.S.) Wendy's restaurant chain founder.
James Walter Thompson, 1847-1928, (U.S.) ad exec., founder of ad agency.
Alice Tully, 1902-93, (U.S.) philanthropist, arts patron.
Theodore N. Vail, 1845-1920, (U.S.) organized Bell Telephone system, headed AT&T.
Cornelius Vanderbilt, 1794-1877, (U.S.) financier; established steamship, railroad empires.

Lillian Vernon, 1927-2015, (Ger.-U.S.) catalog merchant, philanthropist.
Henry Villard, 1835-1900, (U.S.) German-born railroad executive, financier.
Charles R. Walgreen, 1873-1939, (U.S.) founded drugstore chain.
Madame C. J. Walker, 1867-1919, (U.S.) African-American hair care entrepreneur, philanthropist.
DeWitt Wallace, 1889-1981, and **Lila Wallace**, 1889-1984, (both U.S.) cofounders of *Reader's Digest* magazine.
Sam Walton, 1918-92, (U.S.) founder of Wal-Mart stores.
John Wanamaker, 1838-1922, (U.S.) department-store merchandising pioneer.
Aaron Montgomery Ward, 1843-1913, (U.S.) established first mail-order firm.
Thomas J. Watson, 1874-1956, (U.S.) IBM head, 1914-56.
George Westinghouse, 1846-1914, (U.S) inventor, manufacturer; organized Westinghouse Electric Co., 1886.
John Hay Whitney, 1905-82, (U.S.) publisher, sportsman, philanthropist.
Chuck Williams, 1915-2015, (U.S.) Williams-Sonoma founder.
Charles E. Wilson, 1890-1961, (U.S.) auto exec., public official.
Frank W. Woolworth, 1852-1919, (U.S.) created five-and-dime chain.
William Wrigley Jr., 1861-1932, (U.S.) founded Wrigley chewing gum co.

American Cartoonists

Reviewed by Lucy Shelton Caswell, Professor and Curator, Cartoon Research Library, Ohio State University.

Scott Adams, b 1957, Dilbert.
Charles Addams, 1912-88, macabre cartoons.
Brad Anderson, 1924-2015, Marmaduke.
Sergio Aragonés, b 1937, (Span.-Mex.) *Mad* magazine.
Peter Arno, 1904-68, *The New Yorker*.
Tex Avery, 1908-80, animator; Bugs Bunny, Porky Pig.
George Baker, 1915-75, The Sad Sack.
Carl Barks, 1901-2000, Donald Duck comic books.
Alison Bechdel, b 1960, graphic novelist.
C. C. Beck, 1910-89, Captain Marvel.
Dave Berg, 1920-2002, *Mad* magazine.
Jim Berry, 1932-2015, Berry's World.
Herb Block (Herblock), 1909-2001, political cartoonist.
George Booth, b 1926, *The New Yorker*.
Berkeley Breathed, b 1957, Bloom County.
Dik Browne, 1917-89, Hi & Lois, Hagar the Horrible.
Marjorie Buell, 1904-93, Little Lulu.
Ernie Bushmiller, 1905-82, Nancy.
Milton Caniff, 1907-88, Terry & the Pirates, Steve Canyon.
Al Capp, 1909-79, Li'l Abner.
Roz Chast, b 1954, *The New Yorker*.
Gene Colan, 1926-2011, *Daredevil*.
Paul Conrad, 1924-2010, political cartoonist.
Roy Crane, 1901-77, Captain Easy, Buz Sawyer.
R(obert) Crumb, b 1943, underground cartoonist.
Shamus Culhane, 1908-96, animator.
Jay N. "Ding" Darling, 1876-1962, political cartoonist.
Jack Davis, 1924-2016, *Mad* magazine.
Jim Davis, b 1945, Garfield.
Billy DeBeck, 1890-1942, Barney Google.
Rudolph Dirks, 1877-1968, The Katzenjammer Kids.
Walt Disney, 1901-66, produced animated cartoons; created Mickey Mouse, Donald Duck.
Steve Ditko, b 1927, Spider-Man.
Mort Drucker, b 1929, *Mad* magazine.
Will Eisner, 1917-2005, The Spirit.
Jules Feiffer, b 1929, political cartoonist.
Bud Fisher, 1884?-1954, Mutt & Jeff.
Ham Fisher, 1900-55, Joe Palooka.
Max Fleischer, 1883-1972, Betty Boop.
Hal Foster, 1892-1982, Tarzan, Prince Valiant.
Fontaine Fox, 1884-1964, Toonerville Folks.
Isadore "Friz" Freleng, 1905-95, animator; Yosemite Sam, Porky Pig, Sylvester and Tweety Bird.
Rube Goldberg, 1883-1970, Boob McNutt.
Chester Gould, 1900-85, Dick Tracy.
Harold Gray, 1894-1968, Little Orphan Annie.
Matt Groening, b 1954, Life in Hell, The Simpsons.

Cathy Guisewite, b 1950, Cathy.
Bill Hanna, 1910-2001, and **Joe Barbera**, 1911-2006, animators; Tom & Jerry, Yogi Bear, Flintstones.
Oliver Harrington, 1912-95, Bootsie.
Johnny Hart, 1931-2007, B.C., Wizard of Id.
Alfred Harvey, 1913-94, created Casper the Friendly Ghost.
Jimmy Hatlo, 1898-1963, Little Iodine.
John Held Jr., 1889-1958, Jazz Age.
George Herriman, 1881-1944, Krazy Kat.
Harry Hershfield, 1885-1974, Abie the Agent.
Stephen Hillenburg, b 1961, SpongeBob SquarePants.
Al Hirschfeld, 1903-2003, *NY Times* theater caricaturist.
Burne Hogarth, 1911-96, Tarzan.
Helen Hokinson, 1900-49, *The New Yorker*.
Nicole Hollander, b 1939, Sylvia.
Lynn Johnston, b 1947, (Can.) For Better or For Worse.
Oliver Johnston, 1912-2008, Disney animator.
Chuck Jones, 1912-2002, animator; Bugs Bunny, Porky Pig; created Road Runner, Wile E. Coyote.
Mike Judge, b 1962, Beavis and Butt-Head, King of the Hill.
Bob Kane, 1916-98, Batman.
Bil Keane, 1922-2011, The Family Circus.
Walt Kelly, 1913-73, Pogo.
Hank Ketcham, 1920-2001, Dennis the Menace.
Ted Key, 1912-2008, Hazel.
Frank King, 1883-1969, Gasoline Alley.
Jack Kirby, 1917-94, Fantastic Four, The Incredible Hulk.
Rollin Kirby, 1875-1952, political cartoonist.
B(ernard) Kliban, 1935-90, cat books.
Edward Koren, b 1935, *The New Yorker*.
John Kricfalusi, b 1955, Ren & Stimpy.
Joe Kubert, 1926-2012, Sgt. Rock.
Harvey Kurtzman, 1924-93, *Mad* magazine.
Walter Lantz, 1900-94, Woody Woodpecker.
Gary Larson, b 1950, The Far Side.
Mell Lazarus, 1927-2016, Momma, Miss Peach.
Stan Lee, b 1922, Marvel Comics.
David Levine, 1926-2009, *NY Review of Books* caricatures.
Seth MacFarlane, b 1973, Family Guy.
Jeff MacNelly, 1947-2000, political cartoonist; Shoe.
Doug Marlette, 1949-2007, political cartoonist; Kudzu.
Don Martin, 1931-2000, *Mad* magazine.
Bill Mauldin, 1921-2003, political cartoonist.
Winsor McCay, 1872-1934, Little Nemo.
John T. McCutcheon, 1870-1949, political cartoonist.
Dwayne McDuffie, 1962-2011, *Justice League*.

Aaron McGruder, b 1974, The Boondocks.
George McManus, 1884-1954, Bringing Up Father.
Dale Messick, 1906-2005, Brenda Starr.
Norman Mingo, 1896-1980, Alfred E. Neuman.
Bob Montana, 1920-75, Archie.
Dick Moores, 1909-86, Gasoline Alley.
Willard Mullin, 1902-78, sports cartoonist; Dodgers' "Brooklyn Bum," "Mets Kid."
Randall Munroe, b 1984, xkcd.
Russell Myers, b 1938, Broom Hilda.
Thomas Nast, 1840-1902, political cartoonist; Republican elephant, Democratic donkey.
Pat Oliphant, b 1935, political cartoonist.
Frederick Burr Opper, 1857-1937, Happy Hooligan.
Richard Outcault, 1863-1928, Yellow Kid, Buster Brown.
Brant Parker, 1920-2007, Wizard of Id.
Trey Parker, b 1969, animator, co-creator of South Park.
Harvey Pekar, 1939-2010, American Splendor.
Mike Peters, b 1943, Mother Goose & Grimm.
George Price, 1901-95, *The New Yorker*.
Antonio Prohias, 1921-98, Spy vs. Spy.
Alex Raymond, 1909-56, Flash Gordon, Jungle Jim.
Forrest (Bud) Sagendorf, 1915-94, Popeye.
Art Sansom, 1920-91, The Born Loser.
Charles Schulz, 1922-2000, Peanuts.
Elzie C. Segar, 1894-1938, Popeye.
Joe Shuster, 1914-92, and **Jerry Siegel**, 1914-96, Superman.
Sidney Smith, 1887-1935, The Gumps.
Otto Soglow, 1900-75, Little King.
Art Spiegelman, b 1948, Raw, Maus.
William Steig, 1907-2003, *The New Yorker*.
Matt Stone, b 1971, animator, co-creator of South Park.
James Swinnerton, 1875-1974, Little Jimmy, Canyon Kiddies.
Paul Szep, b 1941, political cartoonist.
Paul Terry, 1887-1971, animator of Mighty Mouse.
Bob Thaves, 1924-2006, Frank and Ernest.
James Thurber, 1894-61, *The New Yorker*.
Garry Trudeau, b 1948, Doonesbury.
Jim Unger, 1937-2012, Herman.
Mort Walker, b 1923, Beetle Bailey.
Bill Watterson, b 1958, Calvin and Hobbes.
Russ Westover, 1887-1966, Tillie the Toiler.
Signe Wilkinson, b 1950, political cartoonist.
Frank Willard, 1893-1958, Moon Mullins.
J. R. Williams, 1888-1957, The Willets Family, Out Our Way.
Gahan Wilson, b 1930, *The New Yorker*.
Tom Wilson, 1931-2011, Ziggy.
Art Young, 1866-1943, political cartoonist.
Chic Young, 1901-73, Blondie.

Economists, Educators, Historians, and Social Scientists of the Past

For psychologists, see Scientists of the Past.

Brooks Adams, 1848-1927, (U.S.) historian, political theoretician; *The Law of Civilization and Decay*.

Henry Adams, 1838-1918, (U.S.) historian, autobiographer; *The Education of Henry Adams*.

Stephen Ambrose, 1936-2002, (U.S.) historian; *Eisenhower*.

Francis Bacon, 1561-1626, (Eng.) philosopher, essayist, statesman; championed observation and induction.

George Bancroft, 1800-91, (U.S.) historian; 10-volume *History of the United States*.

Jack Barbash, 1910-94, (U.S.) labor economist; helped create the AFL-CIO.

Henry Barnard, 1811-1900, (U.S.) public school reformer.

Charles A. Beard, 1874-1948, (U.S.) historian; *The Economic Basis of Politics*.

(St.) Bede (the Venerable), c. 673-735, (Br.) scholar, historian; *Ecclesiastical History of the English People*.

Daniel Bell, 1919-2011, (U.S.) sociologist; *The End of Ideology*.

Ruth Benedict, 1887-1948, (U.S.) anthropologist; studied Indian tribes of the Southwest.

Sir Isaiah Berlin, 1909-97, (Br.) philosopher, historian; *The Age of Enlightenment*.

Leonard Bloomfield, 1887-1949, (U.S.) linguist; *Language*.

Franz Boas, 1858-1942, (U.S.) German-born anthropologist; studied American Indians.

Van Wyck Brooks, 1886-1963, (U.S.) historian; critic of New England culture, especially literature.

Edmund Burke, 1729-97, (Ire.) British parliamentarian and political philosopher; *Reflections on the Revolution in France*.

James MacGregor Burns, 1918-2014, (U.S.) historian, political scientist.

Nicholas Murray Butler, 1862-1947, (U.S.) educator; headed Columbia Univ., 1902-45; Nobel Peace Prize, 1931.

Joseph Campbell, 1904-87, (U.S.) author, editor, teacher; wrote books on mythology, folklore.

Thomas Carlyle, 1795-1881, (Scot.) historian, critic; *Sartor Resartus*, *Past and Present*, *The French Revolution*.

(Charles) Bruce Catton, 1899-1978, (U.S.) historian; *A Stillness at Appomattox*.

Edward Channing, 1856-1931, (U.S.) historian; 6-volume *History of the United States*.

Henry Steele Commager, 1902-98, (U.S.) historian, educator; *The Growth of the American Republic*.

John R. Commons, 1862-1945, (U.S.) economist, labor historian; *Legal Foundations of Capitalism*.

James B. Conant, 1893-1978, (U.S.) educator, diplomat; *The American High School Today*.

Benedetto Croce, 1866-1952, (It.) philosopher, statesman, historian; *Philosophy of the Spirit*.

Bernard A. De Voto, 1897-1955, (U.S.) historian; wrote trilogy on American West, edited Mark Twain manuscripts.

Melvil Dewey, 1851-1931, (U.S.) devised decimal system of library-book classification.

Donald Herbert Donald, 1920-2009, (U.S.) Pulitzer Prize-winning Civil War and Lincoln historian.

St. Clair Drake, 1911-90, (U.S.) sociologist, black studies pioneer; *Black Metropolis* (1945), with Horace R. Cayton.

W(illiam) E(dward) B(urghardt) Du Bois, 1868-1963, (U.S.) historian, sociologist; NAACP founder, 1909.

Will(iam), 1885-1981, (U.S.) and **Ariel Durant**, 1898-1981, (Ukraine) historians; *The Story of Civilization*.

Emile Durkheim, 1858-1917, (Fr.) a founder of modern sociology; *The Rules of Sociological Method*.

Jean Baptiste Point du Sable, c. 1750-1818, (U.S.) pioneer trader and first settler of Chicago, 1779.

Charles Eliot, 1834-1926, (U.S.) educator, Harvard president.

Friedrich Engels, 1820-95, (Ger.) political writer; with Marx wrote the *Communist Manifesto*.

Irving Fisher, 1867-1947, (U.S.) economist; contributed to the development of modern monetary theory.

John Fiske, 1842-1901, (U.S.) historian and lecturer; popularized Darwinian theory of evolution.

Charles Fourier, 1772-1837, (Fr.) utopian socialist.

John Hope Franklin, 1915-2009, (U.S.) historian; *From Slavery to Freedom: A History of African Americans*.

Sir James George Frazer, 1854-1941, (Br.) anthropologist; studied myth in religion; *The Golden Bough*.

Milton Friedman, 1912-2006, (U.S.) economist.

Paul Fussell, 1924-2012, (U.S.) literary historian; *The Great War and Modern Memory*.

John Kenneth Galbraith, 1908-2006, (Can.-U.S.) economist, author, professor, former amb. to India.

Peter Gay, 1923-2015, (Ger.-U.S.) cultural historian; *The Enlightenment: An Interpretation*.

Giovanni Gentile, 1875-1944, (It.) philosopher, educator; reformed Italian educational system.

Henry George, 1839-97, (U.S.) economist, reformer; led single-tax movement.

Edward Gibbon, 1737-94, (Br.) historian; *The History of the Decline and Fall of the Roman Empire*.

Andrew Greeley, 1928-2013, (U.S.) Rom. Cath. priest; sociologist.

Francesco Guicciardini, 1483-1540, (It.) historian; *Storia d'Italia*, principal historical work of the 16th cent.

Thomas Hobbes, 1588-1679, (Eng.) philosopher, political theorist; *Leviathan*.

Richard Hofstadter, 1916-70, (U.S.) historian; *The Age of Reform*.

Charles Hamilton Houston, 1895-1950, (U.S.) African American lawyer, Howard University instructor; champion of minority rights.

Samuel Huntington, 1927-2008, (U.S.), political scientist, Harvard University professor; *The Clash of Civilizations*.

Alfred Kahn, 1917-2010, (U.S.) economist; deregulated the U.S. airline industry.

John Keegan, 1934-2012, (Br.) war historian; *The Face of Battle*.

George F. Kennan, 1904-2005, (U.S.) diplomat, historian; main architect of U.S. Cold War "containment" strategy.

John Maynard Keynes, 1883-1946, (Br.) economist; principal advocate of deficit spending.

Alfred Kinsey, 1894-1956, (U.S.) zoologist; pioneering human sex researcher.

Russell Kirk, 1918-94, (U.S.), social philosopher; *The Conservative Mind*.

Alfred L. Kroeber, 1876-1960, (U.S.) cultural anthropologist; studied Indians of North and South America.

Elisabeth Kubler-Ross, 1926-2004, (Switz.) psychiatrist, author; *On Death and Dying*.

Christopher Lasch, 1932-94, (U.S.) social critic, historian; *The Culture of Narcissism*.

James L. Laughlin, 1850-1933, (U.S.) economist; helped establish Federal Reserve System.

Margaret Leech, 1893-1974, (U.S.) historian; *Reveille in Washington, 1860-1865*.

Lucien Lévy-Bruhl, 1857-1939, (Fr.) philosopher; studied the psychology of primitive societies; *Primitive Mentality*.

John Locke, 1632-1704, (Eng.) philosopher, political theorist; *Two Treatises of Government*.

Thomas B. Macaulay, 1800-59, (Br.) historian, statesman.

Niccolò Machiavelli, 1469-1527, (It.) writer, statesman; *The Prince*.

Bronislaw Malinowski, 1884-1942, (Pol.) considered the father of social anthropology.

Thomas R. Malthus, 1766-1834, (Br.) economist; *Essay on the Principle of Population*.

Horace Mann, 1796-1859, (U.S.) pioneered modern public school system.

Karl Mannheim, 1893-1947, (Hung.) sociologist, historian; *Ideology and Utopia*.

Harriet Martineau, 1802-76, (Eng.) writer, feminist; *Society in America*.

Karl Marx, 1818-83, (Ger.) political theorist, proponent of Communism; *Communist Manifesto*, *Das Kapital*.

Benjamin Mays, 1895-1984, (U.S.) minister, educator, civil rights leader; headed Morehouse College, 1940-67.

Giuseppe Mazzini, 1805-72, (It.) political philosopher.

William H. McGuffey, 1800-73, (U.S.) his *Reader* was a mainstay of 19th-cent. U.S. public education.

George H. Mead, 1863-1931, (U.S.) philosopher, social psychologist.

Margaret Mead, 1901-78, (U.S.) cultural anthropologist; popularized field; *Coming of Age in Samoa*.

Alexander Meiklejohn, 1872-1964, (U.S.) Br.-born educator; championed academic freedom and experimental curricula.

James Mill, 1773-1836, (Scot.) philosopher, historian, economist; a proponent of utilitarianism.

John Stuart Mill, 1806-73, (Eng.) philosopher, economist; *Utilitarianism*. Eldest son of James Mill.

Perry G. Miller, 1905-63, (U.S.) historian; interpreted 17th-cent. New England.

Theodor Mommsen, 1817-1903, (Ger.) historian; *The History of Rome*.

Ashley Montagu, 1905-99, (Eng.) anthropologist; *The Natural Superiority of Women*.

Charles-Louis Montesquieu, 1689-1755, (Fr.) social philosopher; *The Spirit of Laws*.

Maria Montessori, 1870-1952, (It.) educator, physician; started Montessori method of student self-motivation.

Samuel Eliot Morison, 1887-1976, (U.S.) historian; chronicled voyages of early explorers.

Lewis Mumford, 1895-1990, (U.S.) sociologist, critic; *The Culture of Cities*.

Gunnar Myrdal, 1898-1987, (Swed.) economist, social scientist; *Asian Drama: An Inquiry Into the Poverty of Nations*.

Allan Nevins, 1890-1971, (U.S.) historian, biographer; *The Ordeal of the Union*.

José Ortega y Gasset, 1883-1955, (Sp.) philosopher; advocated control by elite; *The Revolt of the Masses*.

Elinor Ostrom, 1933-2012, (U.S.) political economist.

Robert Owen, 1771-1858, (Br.) political philosopher, reformer; pioneer in cooperative movement.

Thomas Paine, 1737-1809, (Br.-U.S.) political theorist, writer; *Common Sense*.

Vilfredo Pareto, 1848-1923, (It.) economist, sociologist.

Francis Parkman, 1823-93, (U.S.) historian; *France and England in North America*.

Elizabeth P. Peabody, 1804-94, (U.S.) education pioneer; founded first kindergarten in U.S., 1860.

William Prescott, 1796-1859, (U.S.) early American historian; *The Conquest of Peru*.

Pierre Joseph Proudhon, 1809-65, (Fr.) social theorist; father of anarchism; *The Philosophy of Property*.

François Quesnay, 1694-1774, (Fr.) economic theorist.

Robert V. Remini, 1921-2013, (U.S.) historian; *The Life of Andrew Jackson*.

David Ricardo, 1772-1823, (Br.) economic theorist; advocated free international trade.

David Riesman, 1909-2002, (U.S.) sociologist; co-author, *The Lonely Crowd*.

Jacqueline de Romilly, 1913-2010, (Fr.) scholar of Greek civilization and language.

Theodore Roszak, 1933-2011, (U.S.) historian; *The Making of a Counter Culture*.

Jean-Jacques Rousseau, 1712-78, (Fr.) social philosopher; the father of romantic sensibility; *Confessions*.

Paul Samuelson, 1915-2009, (U.S.) economist, famed for modern mathematical approach to economics.

Edward Sapir, 1884-1939, (Ger.-U.S.) anthropologist; studied ethnology and linguistics of American Indian groups.

Ferdinand de Saussure, 1857-1913, (Switz.) a founder of modern linguistics.

Arthur Schlesinger Jr., 1917-2007, (U.S.) historian, author; *The Imperial Presidency*.

Joseph Schumpeter, 1883-1950, (Czech.-U.S.) economist, sociologist.

Elizabeth Seton, 1774-1821, (U.S.) nun; est. parochial school education in U.S., first native-born American saint.

Georg Simmel, 1858-1918, (Ger.) sociologist, philosopher; helped establish German sociology.

Robert Sklar, 1936-2011, (U.S.) film scholar.

Adam Smith, 1723-90, (Br.) economist; advocated laissez-faire economy, free trade; *The Wealth of Nations*.

Jared Sparks, 1789-1866, (U.S.) historian, educator, editor; *The Library of American Biography*.

Oswald Spengler, 1880-1936, (Ger.) philosopher, historian; *The Decline of the West*.

Leo Steinberg, 1920-2011, (Russ.-U.S.) art historian.

William G. Sumner, 1840-1910, (U.S.) social scientist, economist; laissez-faire economy, Social Darwinism.

Hippolyte Taine, 1828-93, (Fr.) historian, basis of naturalistic school; *The Origins of Contemporary France*.

A(lan) J(ohn) P(ercivale) Taylor, 1906-90, (Br.) historian; *The Origins of the Second World War*.

Nikolaas Tinbergen, 1907-88, (Neth.-Br.) ethologist; pioneer in study of animal behavior.

Alexis de Tocqueville, 1805-59, (Fr.) political scientist, historian; *Democracy in America*.

Francis E. Townsend, 1867-1960, (U.S.) led old-age pension movement, 1933.

Arnold Toynbee, 1889-1975, (Br.) historian; *A Study of History*, sweeping analysis of hist. of civilizations.

George Trevelyan, 1876-1962, (Br.) historian, statesman. Favored "literary" over "scientific" history; *History of England*.

Henri Troyat, 1911-2007, (Russ.-Fr.), biographies of major figures in Russian history.

Frederick J. Turner, 1861-1932, (U.S.) historian, educator; *The Frontier in American History*.

Thorstein B. Veblen, 1857-1929, (U.S.) economist, social philosopher; *The Theory of the Leisure Class*.

Giovanni Vico, 1668-1744, (It.) historian, biographer; regarded by many as first modern historian; *New Science*.

Izaak Walton, 1593-1683, (Eng.) biographer; political-philosophical study of fishing, *The Compleat Angler*.

Booker T. Washington, 1856-1915, (U.S.) founder, 1881, and first pres. of Tuskegee Institute; *Up From Slavery*.

Sidney J., 1859-1947, and **Beatrice Webb**, 1858-1943, (both Br.) leading figures in Fabian Society and Labor Party.

Max Weber, 1864-1920, (Ger.) sociologist; *The Protestant Ethic and the Spirit of Capitalism*.

Walter White, 1893-1955, (U.S.) exec. sec., NAACP, 1931-55.

Roy Wilkins, 1901-81, (U.S.) exec. director, NAACP, 1955-77.

Emma Hart Willard, 1787-1870, (U.S.) pioneered higher education for women.

James Q. Wilson, 1931-2012, (U.S.) political scientist; co-authored broken windows theory.

Carter G. Woodson, 1875-1950, (U.S.) historian; founded Assn. for the Study of Negro Life and History.

C. Vann Woodward, 1908-99, (U.S.) historian; *The Strange Career of Jim Crow*.

Howard Zinn, 1922-2010, (U.S.) historian; *A People's History of the United States*.

American Journalists of the Past

Reviewed by Dean Mills, Dean, Missouri School of Journalism.

See also Business Leaders and Philanthropists, American Cartoonists, and Writers of the Past.

Franklin P. Adams (F.P.A.), 1881-1960, humorist; wrote column "The Conning Tower."

Joseph W. Alsop, 1910-89, and **Stewart Alsop**, 1914-74, Washington-based political analysts, columnists.

Jack Anderson, 1922-2006, muckraking Washington, DC, syndicated columnist.

Brooks Atkinson, 1894-1984, theater critic.

Robert L. Bartley, 1937-2003, editorial-page editor for *Wall Street Journal*.

James Gordon Bennett, 1795-1872, editor and publisher; founded *NY Herald*.

James Gordon Bennett, 1841-1918, succeeded father, financed expeditions, founded afternoon paper.

Nellie Bly (Elizabeth Cochrane), 1864?-1922, pioneer woman journalist, investigative reporter; noted for series on trip around the world.

Elias Boudinot, c. 1803-39, founding editor of first Native American newspaper in U.S., *Cherokee Phoenix* (1828-34).

Benjamin Bradlee, 1921-2014, (U.S.) *Washington Post* exec. editor.

Ed Bradley, 1941-2006, TV journalist (*60 Minutes*).

Andrew Breitbart, 1969-2012, conservative commentator and blogger.

David Brinkley, 1920-2003, co-anchor of NBC's *Huntley-Brinkley Report*, host of ABC's *This Week With David Brinkley*.

Arthur Brisbane, 1864-1936, editor; helped introduce "yellow journalism" with sensational, simply written articles.

David Broder, 1929-2011, political journalist for *The Washington Post*.

Joyce Brothers, 1927-2013, psychologist, columnist.

Heywood Broun, 1888-1939, author, columnist; founded American Newspaper Guild.

Helen Gurley Brown, 1922-2012, author; editor-in-chief of *Cosmopolitan* magazine (1965-97).

Art Buchwald, 1925-2007, journalist, humorist, syndicated columnist.

William F. Buckley Jr., 1925-2008, columnist and commentator; founder of *National Review*.

Herb Caen, 1916-97, longtime columnist for *San Francisco Chronicle* and *Examiner*.

John Campbell, 1653-1728, published *Boston News-Letter*, first continuing newspaper in the American colonies.

Jimmy Cannon, 1909-73, syndicated sports columnist.

John Chancellor, 1927-96, NBC reporter, anchor.

Harry Chandler, 1864-1944, *Los Angeles Times* publisher (1917-41); made it a dominant force.

Otis Chandler, 1928-2006, *Los Angeles Times* publisher (1960-80).

Marquis Childs, 1903-90, reporter and columnist for *St. Louis Post-Dispatch* and United Feature syndicate.

Craig Claiborne, 1920-2000, *NY Times* food editor and critic; key in internationalizing American tastes.

Alexander Cockburn, 1941-2012, left-wing journalist.

Charles Collingwood, 1917-85, CBS news correspondent.

Alistair Cooke, 1908-2004, Brit. journalist, TV narrator; naturalized American citizen, "Letter From America" series.

Howard Cosell, 1920-95, TV and radio sportscaster.

Gardner Cowles, 1861-1946, founded newspaper chain.

Judith Crist, 1922-2012, film critic.

Walter Cronkite, 1916-2009, CBS evening news anchor, TV journalist.

Evelyn Cunningham, 1916-2010, African American civil rights reporter.

Cyrus Curtis, 1850-1933, publisher of *Saturday Evening Post*, *Ladies' Home Journal*, *Country Gentleman*.

John Charles Daly, 1914-91, war correspondent, TV journalist; Voice of America head.

Charles Anderson Dana, 1819-97, editor, publisher; made *NY Sun* famous for its news reporting.

Elmer (Holmes) Davis, 1890-1958, *NY Times* editorial writer, radio commentator.

Richard Harding Davis, 1864-1916, war correspondent, travel writer, fiction writer.

Benjamin Day, 1810-89, published *NY Sun* beginning in 1833, introducing penny press to the U.S.

Dorothy Dix (Elizabeth Meriwether Gilmer), 1861-1951, reporter; pioneer of the advice column genre.

Finley Peter Dunne, 1867-1936, humorist, social critic; wrote "Mr. Dooley" columns.

Roger Ebert, 1942-2013, film critic.

Mary Baker Eddy, 1821-1910, founded Christian Science movement and *Christian Science Monitor*.

Rowland Evans Jr., 1921-2001, Washington columnist.

Fanny Fern (Sara Willis Parton), 1811-72, newspaper columnist, author.

Marshall Field III, 1893-1956, retail magnate, *Chicago Sun* founder.

Doris Fleeson, 1901-70, war correspondent, columnist.

Benjamin Franklin, 1706-90, publisher of *Poor Richard's Almanack*.

James Franklin, 1697-1735, printer, pioneer journalist; publisher of *New England Courant* and *Rhode Island Gazette*.

Fred W. Friendly, 1915-98, radio, TV reporter, producer, executive; collaborator with Edward R. Murrow.

Margaret Fuller, 1810-50, social reformer, transcendentalist, critic and foreign correspondent for *NY Tribune*.

Frank E. Gannett, 1876-1957, founded newspaper chain.

Mary Ellen Garber, 1916-2008, sports journalist.

William Lloyd Garrison, 1805-79, abolitionist; publisher of *The Liberator*.

Jack Germond, 1928-2013, political reporter.

Edwin Lawrence Godkin, 1831-1902, founder of *The Nation*, editor of *NY Evening Post*.

Katharine Graham, 1917-2001, *Washington Post* publisher.

Sheilah Graham, 1904-89, Hollywood gossip columnist.

Horace Greeley, 1811-72, editor, politician; founded *NY Tribune*.

Meg Greenfield, 1930-99, *Newsweek* columnist, *Washington Post* editorial page editor.

Gilbert Hovey Grosvenor, 1875-1966, longtime editor of *National Geographic* magazine.

John Gunther, 1901-70, *Chicago Daily News* foreign correspondent, author.

David Halberstam, 1934-2007, journalist, sports reporter, author; *The Best and the Brightest*, *Summer of '49*.

Sarah Josepha Buell Hale, 1788-1879, first female magazine editor; *Ladies' Magazine*, later *Godey's Lady's Book*.

Paul Harvey, 1918-2009, radio broadcaster and commentator.

William Randolph Hearst, 1863-1951, founder of Hearst newspaper chain, one of the pioneers of yellow journalism.

Gabriel Heatter, 1890-1972, radio commentator.

John Hersey, 1914-98, foreign correspondent for *Time*, *Life*, and *The New Yorker*; author.

Marguerite Higgins, 1920-66, reporter, war correspondent.

Christopher Hitchens, 1949-2011, columnist and literary critic.

Hedda Hopper, 1885-1966, Hollywood gossip columnist.

Roy Howard, 1883-1964, editor, executive; Scripps-Howard papers and United Press (later United Press International).

Chet (Chester Robert) Huntley, 1911-74, co-anchor of NBC's *Huntley-Brinkley Report*.

Ada Louise Huxtable, 1921-2013, architecture critic.

Ralph Ingersoll, 1900-85, editor; *Fortune*, *Time*, *Life* exec.

Molly Ivins, 1944-2007, author, syndicated political columnist.

Peter Jennings, 1938-2005, ABC correspondent, anchor.

Pauline Kael, 1919-2001, film critic.

H. V. (Hans von) Kaltenborn, 1878-1965, radio commentator, reporter.

Murray Kempton, 1917-97, reporter, columnist for magazines and newspapers, including *NY Post*.

Dorothy Kilgallen, 1913-65, crime reporter, columnist.

James J. Kilpatrick, 1920-2010, political columnist, author and television personality.

John S. Knight, 1894-1981, editor, publisher; founded Knight newspaper group, which merged into Knight-Ridder.

Joseph Kraft, 1942-86, foreign policy columnist.

Irving Kristol, 1920-2009, columnist, commentator.

Arthur Krock, 1886-1974, *NY Times* political writer, Washington bureau chief.

Charles Kuralt, 1934-97, TV anchor; host of CBS "On the Road" featuring stories about life in the U.S.

Ann Landers (Eppie Lederer), 1918-2002, advice columnist.

David Lawrence, 1888-1973, reporter, columnist, publisher; founded *U.S. News & World Report*.

Frank Leslie, 1821-80, engraver, publisher of newspapers and magazines, notably *Leslie's Illustrated Newspaper*.

Anthony Lewis, 1927-2013, legal journalist.

Alexander Liberman, 1912-99, editorial director for Condé Nast magazines.

A(bbott) J(oseph) Liebling, 1904-63, foreign correspondent, critic; principally with *The New Yorker*.

Walter Lippmann, 1889-1974, political analyst, social critic, columnist, author.

Peter Lisagor, 1915-76, Washington bureau chief, *Chicago Daily News*; broadcast commentator.

David Ross Locke, 1833-88, humorist, satirist under pseudonym P.V. Nasby; owned *Toledo (Ohio) Blade*.

Elijah Parish Lovejoy, 1802-37, abolitionist editor in St. Louis and in Alton, IL; killed by proslavery mob.

Clare Booth Luce, 1903-87, war correspondent for *Life*, diplomat, playwright.

Henry R. Luce, 1898-1967, founded *Time*, *Fortune*, *Life*, *Sports Illustrated*.

Dwight Macdonald, 1906-82, reporter, social critic.

Don Marquis, 1878-1937, humor columnist for *NY Sun* and *NY Tribune*; wrote "Archy and Mehitabel" stories.

Nancy Hicks Maynard, 1946-2008, African American publisher, journalist.

Robert Maynard, 1937-97, first African American editor and then owner of major U.S. paper, the *Oakland Tribune*.

C(harles) K(enny) McClatchy, 1858-1936, founder of McClatchy newspaper chain.

Sarah McClendon, 1910-2003, veteran White House correspondent.

Samuel McClure, 1857-1949, founder (1893) of *McClure's Magazine*, famous for its investigative reporting.

Anne O'Hare McCormick, 1889-1954, foreign correspondent; first woman on *NY Times* editorial board.

Robert R. McCormick, 1880-1955, editor, publisher, executive of *Chicago Tribune* and *NY Daily News*.

Ralph McGill, 1893-1969, crusading editor, publisher of *Atlanta Constitution*.

Mary McGrory, 1918-2004, Washington columnist.

O(scar) O(dd) McIntyre, 1884-1938, feature writer, syndicated columnist on everyday life in New York City.

John McLaughlin, 1927-2016, TV journalist.

Joseph Medill, 1823-99, longtime editor of the *Chicago Tribune*.

H(enry) L(ouis) Mencken, 1880-1956, reporter, editor, columnist with *Baltimore Sun* papers; anti-establishment viewpoint.

Edwin Meredith, 1876-1928, founder of magazine company.

Frank A. Munsey, 1854-1925, owner, editor, and publisher of newspapers and magazines, including *Munsey's Magazine*.

Edward R. Murrow, 1908-65, broadcast reporter, exec.; reported from Britain in WWII; hosted *See It Now*, *Person to Person*.

Allen Neuharth, 1924-2013, *USA Today* founder.

Edwin Newman, 1919-2010, NBC news correspondent.

Louella Parsons, 1881-1972, Hollywood gossip columnist.

Ethel L. Payne, 1911-91, African American civil rights reporter.

Daniel Pearl, 1963-2002, American journalist; kidnapped and murdered in Pakistan.

Drew (Andrew Russell) Pearson, 1897-1969, investigative reporter, columnist.

(James) Westbrook Pegler, 1894-1969, reporter, columnist.

Shirley Povich, 1905-98, sports columnist.

Joseph Pulitzer, 1847-1911, *NY World* publisher; founded Columbia Journalism School, Pulitzer Prizes.

Joseph Pulitzer II, 1885-1955, longtime *St. Louis Post-Dispatch* editor, publisher; built it into major paper.

Ernie Pyle, 1900-45, reporter, war correspondent; killed in WWII.

William Raspberry, 1935-2012, public affairs columnist.

Henry Raymond, 1820-69, cofounder, editor, *NY Times*.

Harry Reasoner, 1923-91, ABC and CBS news reporter, anchor.

John Reed, 1887-1920, reporter; foreign correspondent famous for coverage of Bolshevik Revolution; buried at the Kremlin.

Whitelaw Reid, 1837-1912, longtime editor, *NY Tribune*.

James Reston, 1909-95, *NY Times* political reporter, columnist.

Frank Reynolds, 1923-83, ABC reporter, anchor.

(Henry) Grantland Rice, 1880-1954, sportswriter.

Jacob Riis, 1849-1914, reporter, photographer; exposed slum conditions in *How the Other Half Lives*.

Max Robinson, 1939-88, first African American to anchor network news (ABC), 1978.

Andy Rooney, 1919-2011, radio and TV commentator (*60 Minutes*).

A. M. Rosenthal, 1922-2006, reporter, editor for *NY Times* (1943-99).

Harold Ross, 1892-1951, founder, editor, *The New Yorker*.

Carl T. Rowan, 1925-2000, reporter, columnist, author.

Mike Royko, 1932-97, Chicago newspaper columnist; wrote *Boss*, biography of Mayor Richard J. Daley (1902-76).

Louis Rukeyser, 1933-2006, TV journalist, financial analyst; hosted *Wall Street Week* on public television.

(Alfred) Damon Runyon, 1884-1946, sportswriter, columnist; stories collected in *Guys and Dolls*.

Tim Russert, 1950-2008, TV journalist; moderator of *Meet the Press* (NBC).

John B. Russwurm, 1799-1851, cofounded (1827) nation's first black newspaper, *Freedom's Journal*, in New York, NY.

Morley Safer, 1931-2016, TV journalist (*60 Minutes*).

William Safire, 1929-2009, Pulitzer Prize-winning columnist, *NY Times*.

Adela Rogers St. Johns, 1894-1988, reporter, sportswriter for Hearst newspapers.

Pierre Salinger, 1925-2004, press sec. under Pres. Kennedy and Johnson, foreign correspondent.

Harrison Salisbury, 1908-93, reporter, foreign correspondent; Soviet specialist.

Andrew Sarris, 1928-2012, film critic, *Village Voice*.

Daniel Schorr, 1916-2010, broadcast and print journalist.

E(dward) W(illis) Scripps, 1854-1926, founded first large U.S. newspaper chain, pioneered syndication.

Eric Sevareid, 1912-92, war correspondent, radio newscaster, CBS commentator.

Anthony Shadid, 1968-2012, foreign correspondent.

Randy Shilts, 1951-94, journalist; author of *And the Band Played On*.

William L. Shirer, 1904-93, broadcaster, foreign correspondent; wrote *The Rise and Fall of the Third Reich*.

Howard K. Smith, 1914-2002, ABC news reporter, anchor.

Red (Walter) Smith, 1905-82, sportswriter.

Edgar P. Snow, 1905-71, correspondent; expert on Chinese Communist movement.

Tony Snow, 1955-2008, columnist, radio/TV journalist, White House press sec.

Tom Snyder, 1936-2007, television journalist.

Lawrence Spivak, 1900-94, co-creator, moderator, producer of *Meet the Press*.

(Joseph) Lincoln Steffens, 1866-1936, muckraking journalist.

I(sidor) F(einstein) Stone, 1907-89, one-man editor of *I. F. Stone's Weekly*.

Arthur Hays Sulzberger, 1891-1968, longtime publisher of *NY Times* (1935-61).

Arthur Ochs "Punch" Sulzberger, 1926-2012, long-time publisher of *NY Times* (1963-92).

C(yrus) L(eo) Sulzberger, 1912-93, *NY Times* foreign correspondent, columnist.

David Susskind, 1920-87, TV producer, public affairs talk-show host (*Open End*).

John Cameron Swayze, 1906-95, early TV newscaster (NBC).

Herbert Bayard Swope, 1882-1958, war correspondent, editor of *NY World*.

Ida Tarbell, 1857-1944, muckraking journalist.

Helen Thomas, 1920-2013, White House correspondent, 1959-2010.

Isaiah Thomas, 1750-1831, printer, publisher; cofounder of revolutionary journal, *Massachusetts Spy*.

Lowell Thomas, 1892-1981, radio newscaster, world traveler.

Dorothy Thompson, 1894-1961, foreign correspondent, columnist, radio commentator.

Hunter S. Thompson, 1937-2005, political journalist, author; *Fear and Loathing on the Campaign Trail* (1972).

Kenneth Thompson, 1923-2006, Canadian media magnate; owned Toronto *Globe and Mail* newspaper.

Abigail Van Buren (Pauline Phllips), 1918-2013, advice columnist.

Mike Wallace, 1918-2012, TV journalist (*60 Minutes*).

Ida Bell Wells-Barnett, 1862-1931, African American reporter, editor, anti-lynching crusader.

William Allen White, 1868-1944, newspaper editor, publisher.

Tom Wicker, 1926-2011, *NY Times* political reporter, columnist.

Walter Winchell, 1897-1972, reporter, columnist, broadcaster of celebrity news.

John Peter Zenger, 1697-1746, printer, journalist; acquitted in precedent-setting libel suit (1735).

Military and Naval Leaders of the Past

Reviewed by Alan C. Aimone, U.S. Military Academy Library.

Alexander the Great, 356-323 BCE, (Maced.) conquered Persia and much of the world known to Europeans.

Harold Alexander, 1891-1969, (Br.) led Allied invasion of Italy, 1943, WWII.

Ethan Allen, 1738-89, (U.S.) headed Green Mountain Boys; captured Ft. Ticonderoga, 1775, Amer. Rev.

Edmund Allenby, 1861-1936, (Br.) in Boer War, WWI; led Egyptian expeditionary force, 1917-18.

Benedict Arnold, 1741-1801, (U.S.) victorious at Saratoga; tried to betray West Point to British, Amer. Rev.

Henry "Hap" Arnold, 1886-1950, (U.S.) commanded Army Air Force in WWII.

Ashurnasirpal II, 884-859 BCE, (Assyria) king; began Assyrian conquest of Middle East.

John Barry, 1745-1803, (U.S.) won numerous sea battles during Amer. Rev.

Pierre Beauregard, 1818-93, (U.S.) Confed. general; ordered bombardment of Ft. Sumter that began Civil War.

Belisarius, c. 505-565, (Byzant.) won remarkable victories for Byzantine emperor Justinian I.

Gebhard von Blücher, 1742-1819, (Ger.) helped defeat Napoleon at Waterloo.

Simón Bolívar, 1783-1830, (Venez.) S. Amer. revolutionary who liberated much of the continent from Spanish rule.

Napoleon Bonaparte, 1769-1821, (Fr.) defeated Russia and Austria at Austerlitz, 1805; invaded Russia, 1812; defeated at Waterloo, 1815.

Edward Braddock, 1695-1755, (Br.) commanded forces in French and Indian War.

Omar N. Bradley, 1893-1981, (U.S.) headed U.S. ground troops in Normandy invasion, 1944, WWII.

John Burgoyne, 1722-92, (Br.) general; defeated at Saratoga, Amer. Rev.

Julius Caesar, 100-44 BCE, (Rom.) general and politician; conquered northern Gaul, overthrew Roman government.

Charlemagne, 742-814, (Fr.) king of the Franks, Holy Roman Emperor; conquered most of Western Europe.

Claire Lee Chennault, 1893-1958, (U.S.) headed Flying Tigers in WWII.

El Cid (Rodrigo Díaz de Vivar), 1040-99, (Sp.) renowned knight; captured Valencia (1094), hero of "Song of Cid" epic.

Mark W. Clark, 1896-1984, (U.S.) helped plan N African invasion in WWII; commander of UN forces, Korean War.

Karl von Clausewitz, 1780-1831, (Prus.) military theorist.

Lucius D. Clay, 1897-1978, (U.S.) led Berlin airlift, 1948-49.

Henry Clinton, 1738-95, (Br.) commander of forces in Amer. Rev., 1778-81.

Cochise, c. 1815-74, (Amer. Ind.) chief of Chiricahua band of Apache Indians in Southwest U.S.

Charles Cornwallis, 1738-1805, (Br.) victorious at Brandywine, 1777; surrendered at Yorktown, Amer. Rev.

Hernán Cortés, 1485-1547, (Sp.) led Spanish conquistadors in the defeat of the Aztec empire, 1519-28.

Crazy Horse, 1849-77, (Amer. Ind.) Sioux war chief victorious at Battle of Little Bighorn.

George Armstrong Custer, 1839-76, (U.S.) army officer defeated and killed at Battle of Little Bighorn.

Benjamin O. Davis Jr., 1912-2002, (U.S.) leader of WWII black aviators; first African American general in U.S. Air Force.

Benjamin O. Davis Sr., 1877-1970, (U.S.) first African American general in U.S. Army, 1940.

Moshe Dayan, 1915-81, (Isr.) directed campaigns in the 1967, 1973 Arab-Israeli wars.

Stephen Decatur, 1779-1820, (U.S.) naval hero of Barbary wars, War of 1812.

Anton Denikin, 1872-1947, (Russ.) led White forces in Russian civil war.

George Dewey, 1837-1917, (U.S.) destroyed Spanish fleet at Manila, 1898, Span.-Amer. War.

Karl Doenitz, 1891-1980, (Ger.) submarine cmdr. in chief and naval cmdr., WWII; last pres. of Third Reich.

Jimmy Doolittle, 1896-1993, (U.S.) led 1942 air raid on Tokyo and other Japanese cities in WWII.

Hugh Dowding, 1882-1970, (Br.) headed RAF Fighter Command, 1936-40, WWII.

Jubal Early, 1816-94, (U.S.) Confed. general; led raid on Washington, DC, 1864, Civil War.

Dwight D. Eisenhower, 1890-1969, (U.S.) commanded Allied forces in Europe, WWII.

Erich von Falkenhayn, 1861-1922, (Ger.) minister of war, general, commander at Verdun in WWI.

David Farragut, 1801-70, (U.S.) Union admiral; captured New Orleans, Mobile Bay, Civil War.

John Arbuthnot Fisher, 1841-1920, (Br.) WWI admiral; naval reformer.

Ferdinand Foch, 1851-1929, (Fr.) headed victorious Allied armies, 1918, WWI.

Nathan Bedford Forrest, 1821-77, (U.S.) Confed. general; led raids against Union supply lines, Civil War.

Frederick the Great, 1712-86, (Prus.) led Prussia in Seven Years' War.

Horatio Gates, 1728-1806, (U.S.) commanded army at Saratoga, Amer. Rev.

Genghis Khan, 1162-1227, (Mongol) unified Mongol tribes, subjugated much of Asia, 1206-21.

Geronimo, 1829-1909, (Amer. Ind.) leader of Chiricahua band of Apache Indians.

Vo Nguyen Giap, 1911?-2013, (Viet.) commanded People's Army of Vietnam against U.S.

Charles G. Gordon, 1833-85, (Br.) led forces in China, Crimean War; killed at Khartoum.

Ulysses S. Grant, 1822-85, (U.S.) headed Union army, Civil War, 1864-65; forced Robert E. Lee's surrender, 1865.

Nathanael Greene, 1742-86, (U.S.) defeated British in Southern campaign, 1780-81, Amer. Rev.

Heinz Guderian, 1888-1954, (Ger.) tank theorist; led panzer tank forces in Poland, France, Russia, WWII.

Gustavus Adolphus, 1594-1632, (Swed.) king, military tactician, reformer; led forces in Thirty Years' War.

Douglas Haig, 1861-1928, (Br.) led British armies in France, 1915-18, WWI.

William F. Halsey, 1882-1959, (U.S.) defeated Japanese fleet at Leyte Gulf, 1944, WWII.

Hannibal, 247-183 BCE, (Carthage) invaded Rome, crossing Alps, in Second Punic War, 218-201 BCE.

Sir Arthur Travers Harris, 1895-1984, (Br.) led Britain's WWII bomber command.

Paul von Hindenburg, 1847-1934, (Ger.) chief of general staff, WWI; second pres. of Weimar Republic.

Richard Howe, 1726-99, (Br.) commanded navy in Amer. Rev., 1776-78; June 1 victory against French, 1794.

William Howe, 1729-1814, (Br.) commanded forces in Amer. Rev., 1776-78.

Isaac Hull, 1773-1843, (U.S.) sunk British frigate *Guerriere*, War of 1812.

Thomas "Stonewall" Jackson, 1824-63, (U.S.) Confed. general; led Shenandoah Valley campaign, Civil War.

Daniel James Jr., 1920-78, (U.S.) first black 4-star general, 1975; commander, N. American Air Defense Command.

Joseph Joffre, 1852-1931, (Fr.) headed Allied armies; won Battle of the Marne, 1914, WWI.

John Paul Jones, 1747-92, (U.S.) commanded *Bonhomme Richard* in victory over *Serapis*, Amer. Rev., 1779.

Chief Joseph, c. 1840-1904, (Amer. Ind.) chief of the Nez Percé; forced by U.S. army to retreat and surrender.

Stephen Kearny, 1794-1848, (U.S.) headed Army of the West in Mexican War.

Albert Kesselring, 1885-1960, (Ger.) field marshal who led the defense of Italy in WWII.

Ernest J. King, 1878-1956, (U.S.) key WWII naval strategist.

Horatio H. Kitchener, 1850-1916, (Br.) led forces in Boer War, victorious at Khartoum, organized army in WWI.

Henry Knox, 1750-1806, (U.S.) general in Amer. Rev.; first sec. of war under U.S. Constitution.

Lavrenti Kornilov, 1870-1918, (Russ.) commander-in-chief, 1917; led counterrevolutionary march on Petrograd.

Thaddeus Kosciusko, 1746-1817, (Pol.) aided Amer. Rev.

Walter Krueger, 1881-1967, (U.S.) led Sixth Army in WWII in Southwest Pacific.

Mikhail Kutuzov, 1745-1813, (Russ.) fought at Borodino, Napol. Wars, 1812; abandoned Moscow, forced French retreat.

Marquis de Lafayette, 1757-1834, (Fr.) fought in, secured French aid for Amer. Rev.

T(homas) E. Lawrence (of Arabia), 1888-1935, (Br.) organized revolt of Arabs against Turks in WWI.

William Daniel Leahy, 1875-1959, (U.S.) chief of staff to Pres. Roosevelt in WWII, Fleet Admiral.

Henry (Light-Horse Harry) Lee, 1756-1818, (U.S.) cavalry officer in Amer. Rev.

Robert E. Lee, 1807-70, (U.S.) Confed. general; defeated at Gettysburg, Civil War; surrendered to Grant, 1865.

Curtis LeMay, 1906-90, (U.S.) Air Force cmdr. in WWII, Korean War, Vietnam War.

Lyman Lemnitzer, 1899-1988, (U.S.) WWII hero; later general, chairman of Joint Chiefs of Staff.

James Longstreet, 1821-1904, (U.S.) aided Lee at Gettysburg, Civil War.

Erich Ludendorff, 1865-1937, (Ger.) general; victor at Tannenberg, WWI.

Douglas MacArthur, 1880-1964, (U.S.) commanded forces in SW Pacific in WWII; headed occupation forces in Japan, 1945-51; UN commander in Korean War.

Carl Gustaf Mannerheim, 1867-1951, (Fin.) army officer and pres. of Finland, 1944-46.

Erich von Manstein, 1887-1973, (Ger.) served WWI, WWII; planned invasion of France (1940); convicted of war crimes.

Francis Marion, 1733-95, (U.S.) led guerrilla actions in South Carolina during Amer. Rev.

Duke of Marlborough, 1650-1722, (Br.) led forces against Louis XIV in War of the Spanish Succession.

George C. Marshall, 1880-1959, (U.S.) chief of staff in WWII; authored Marshall Plan.

Maurice, Count of Nassau, 1567-1625, (Neth.) military innovator; led forces in Thirty Years' War.

George B. McClellan, 1826-85, (U.S.) Union general; commanded Army of the Potomac, 1861-62, Civil War.

George Meade, 1815-72, (U.S.) commanded Union forces at Gettysburg, Civil War.

Doris "Dorie" Miller, 1919-43, (U.S.) Navy hero of Pearl Harbor attack; first African American awarded Navy Cross.

Billy Mitchell, 1879-1936, (U.S.) WWI air-power advocate; court-martialed for insubordination, later vindicated.

Helmuth von Moltke, 1800-91, (Ger.) victorious in Austro-Prussian, Franco-Prussian wars.

Louis de Montcalm, 1712-59, (Fr.) headed troops in Canada, French and Indian War; defeated at Quebec, 1759.

Bernard Law Montgomery, 1887-1976, (Br.) stopped German offensive at Alamein, 1942, WWII; helped plan Normandy invasion.

Daniel Morgan, 1736-1802, (U.S.) victorious at Cowpens, 1781, Amer. Rev.

Louis Mountbatten, 1900-79, (Br.) Supreme Allied Commander of SE Asia, 1943-46, WWII.

Joachim Murat, 1767-1815, (Fr.) led cavalry at Marengo, Austerlitz, and Jena, Napoleonic Wars.

Horatio Nelson, 1758-1805, (Br.) naval cmdr.; destroyed French fleet at Trafalgar.

Michel Ney, 1769-1815, (Fr.) commanded forces in Switz., Austria, Russ., Napoleonic Wars; defeated at Waterloo.

Chester Nimitz, 1885-1966, (U.S.) cmdr. of naval forces in Pacific in WWII.

George S. Patton, 1885-1945, (U.S.) led assault on Sicily, 1943, Third Army invasion of Europe, WWII.

Oliver Perry, 1785-1819, (U.S.) won Battle of Lake Erie in War of 1812.

John Pershing, 1860-1948, (U.S.) commanded Mexican border campaign, 1916; Amer. Expeditionary Force, WWI.

Henri Philippe Pétain, 1856-1951, (Fr.) defended Verdun, 1916; headed Vichy government in WWII.

George E. Pickett, 1825-75, (U.S.) Confed. general famed for "charge" at Gettysburg, Civil War.

Charles Portal, 1893-1971, (Br.) chief of staff, Royal Air Force, 1940-45; led in Battle of Britain.

Manfred Freiherr von Richthofen (Red Baron), 1892-1918, (Ger.) WWI flying ace, led elite fighter squadron.

Hyman Rickover, 1900-86, (U.S.) father of nuclear navy.

Matthew Bunker Ridgway, 1895-1993, (U.S.) commanded Allied ground forces in Korean War.

Erwin Rommel, 1891-1944, (Ger.) headed Afrika Korps, WWII.

Gerd von Rundstedt, 1875-1953, (Ger.) supreme cmdr. in West, 1942-45, WWII.

Saladin, 1138-93, (Kurdish Muslim) recaptured Jerusalem from Crusaders.

Aleksandr Samsonov, 1859-1914, (Russ.) led invasion of E Prussia, WWI; defeated at Tannenberg, 1914.

Antonio López de Santa Anna, 1794-1876, (Mex.) defeated Texans at the Alamo; defeated in Mexican War.

Maurice, Count of Saxe, 1696-1750, (Fr.) general, noted tactician; War of Austrian Succession, War of Pol. Succession.

H. Norman Schwarzkopf, 1934-2012, (U.S.) army general; led Persian Gulf War, 1991.

Scipio Africanus the Elder, 234?-183 BCE, (Rom.) hero of Second Punic War; defeated Hannibal, invaded N Africa.

Winfield Scott, 1786-1866, (U.S.) hero of War of 1812; headed forces in Mexican War, took Mexico City.

Philip Sheridan, 1831-88, (U.S.) Union cavalry officer; headed Army of the Shenandoah, 1864-65, Civil War.

William T. Sherman, 1820-91, (U.S.) Union general; sacked Atlanta during "march to the sea," 1864, Civil War.

Sitting Bull, c. 1831-90, (Amer. Ind.) Hunkpapa Sioux chief; victorious at Battle of the Little Big Horn.

Carl Spaatz, 1891-1974, (U.S.) directed strategic bombing against Germany, later Japan, in WWII.

Raymond Spruance, 1886-1969, (U.S.) victorious at Midway Island, 1942, WWII.

Joseph W. Stilwell, 1883-1946, (U.S.) headed forces in the China, Burma, India theater in WWII.

J.E.B. Stuart, 1833-64, (U.S.) Confed. cavalry commander, Civil War.

Sun Tzu, 6th? cent. BCE, (China) general; author of *The Art of War*.

Aleksandr Suvorov, 1729-1800, (Russ.) commanded Allied Russian and Austrian armies, Russo-Turkish War.

Tamerlane, 1336-1405, (Turkoman Mongol) conqueror; established empire from India to Mediterranean Sea.

Tecumseh, 1768-1813, (Amer. Ind.) Shawnee chief; led Indian confederation opposing colonists.

George H. Thomas, 1816-70, (U.S.) saved Union army at Chattanooga, 1863; won at Nashville, 1864, Civil War.

Semyon Timoshenko, 1895-1970, (USSR) defended Moscow, Stalingrad, WWII; led winter offensive, 1942-43.

Alfred von Tirpitz, 1849-1930, (Ger.) responsible for submarine blockade in WWI.

Henri de la Tour d'Auvergne, Viscount of Turenne, 1611-75, (Fr.) marshal; Thirty Years' War, Fronde, War of Devolution.

Sebastien Le Prestre de Vauban, 1633-1707, (Fr.) innovative military engineer, theorist.

Jonathan M. Wainwright, 1883-1953, (U.S.) forced to surrender on Corregidor, Philippines, 1942, WWII.

George Washington, 1732-99, (U.S.) led Continental army, 1775-83, Amer. Rev.

Archibald Wavell, 1883-1950, (Br.) commanded forces in N and E Africa, SE Asia in WWII.

Anthony Wayne, 1745-96, (U.S.) captured Stony Point, NY, 1779, Amer. Rev.

Duke of Wellington, 1769-1852, (Br.) defeated Napoleon at Waterloo, 1815.

William Westmoreland, 1914-2005, (U.S.) commanded forces in Vietnam, 1964-68.

William I (The Conqueror), 1027-87, (Br.) victor, Battle of Hastings, 1066; became first Norman king of England.

James Wolfe, 1727-59, (Br.) captured Quebec from French, 1759, French and Indian War.

Isoroku Yamamoto, 1884-1943, (Jpn.) cmdr. in chief of Japanese fleet, naval planner before and during WWII.

Georgi Zhukov, 1895-1974, (Russ.) defended Moscow, 1941; led assault on Berlin, 1945, WWII.

Philosophers and Religious Figures of the Past

Excludes biblical figures and popes (see Religion chapter). For Greeks and Romans, see also Historical Figures chapter.

Lyman Abbott, 1835-1922, (U.S.) clergyman, reformer; advocate of Christian Socialism.

Pierre Abelard, 1079-1142, (Fr.) philosopher, theologian, teacher; used dialectic method to support Christian beliefs.

Felix Adler, 1851-1933, (U.S.) German-born founder of the Ethical Culture Soc.

Mortimer Adler, 1902-2001, (U.S.) philosopher; helped create "Great Books" program.

(St.) Anselm, c. 1033-1109, (It.) philosopher-theologian, church leader; "ontological argument" for God's existence.

(St.) Thomas Aquinas, 1225-74, (It.) pre-eminent medieval philosopher-theologian; *Summa Theologica*.

Aristotle, 384-322 BCE, (Gr.) pioneering wide-ranging philosopher, logician, ethician, naturalist.

(St.) Augustine, 354-430, (N Africa) philosopher, theologian, bishop; *Confessions*, *City of God*, *On the Trinity*.

J. L. Austin, 1911-60, (Br.) ordinary-language philosopher.

Averroes (Ibn Rushd), 1126-98, (Sp.) Islamic philosopher, physician.

Avicenna (Ibn Sina), 980-1037, (Iran) Islamic philosopher, scientist.

A(lfred) J(ules) Ayer, 1910-89, (Br.) philosopher, logical positivist; *Language, Truth, and Logic*.

Roger Bacon, c. 1214-94, (Eng.) philosopher, scientist.

Bahá'u'lláh (Mirza Husayn Ali), 1817-92, (Pers.) founder of Bahá'í faith.

Karl Barth, 1886-1968, (Switz.) theologian; a leading force in 20th-cent. Protestantism.

Thomas à Becket, 1118-70, (Eng.) archbishop of Canterbury; opposed Henry II, murdered by king's men.

(St.) Benedict, c. 480-547, (It.) founded the Benedictines.

Jeremy Bentham, 1748-1832, (Br.) philosopher, reformer; enunciated utilitarianism.

Henri Bergson, 1859-1941, (Fr.) philosopher of evolution.

George Berkeley, 1685-1753, (Ire.) idealist philosopher, bishop.

John Biddle, 1615-62, (Eng.) founder of English Unitarianism.

Jakob Boehme, 1575-1624, (Ger.) theosophist, mystic.

Dietrich Bonhoeffer, 1906-45, (Ger.) Lutheran theologian, pastor; executed as opponent of Nazis.

William Brewster, 1567-1644, (Eng.) *Mayflower* passenger, Plymouth Colony leader.

Emil Brunner, 1889-1966, (Switz.) Protestant theologian.

Giordano Bruno, 1548-1600, (It.) philosopher, pantheist.

Martin Buber, 1878-1965, (Ger.) Jewish philosopher, theologian; *I and Thou*.

Buddha (Siddhartha Gautama), c. 563-c. 483 BCE, (India) philosopher; founded Buddhism.

John Calvin, 1509-64, (Fr.) theologian; a key figure in the Protestant Reformation.

Rudolph Carnap, 1891-1970, (U.S.) German-born analytic philosopher; a founder of logical positivism.

William Ellery Channing, 1780-1842, (U.S.) clergyman; early spokesman for Unitarianism.

Auguste Comte, 1798-1857, (Fr.) philosopher; originated positivism.

Confucius, 551-479 BCE, (China) founder of Confucianism.

John Cotton, 1584-1652, (Eng.) Puritan theologian.

Thomas Cranmer, 1489-1556, (Eng.) Anglican churchman; wrote much of *Book of Common Prayer*.

Jacques Derrida, 1930-2004, (Fr.) deconstructionist philosopher.

René Descartes, 1596-1650, (Fr.) philosopher, mathematician; "father of modern philosophy"; *Discourse on Method*, *Meditations on First Philosophy*.

John Dewey, 1859-1952, (U.S.) philosopher, educator; instrumentalist theory of knowledge, progressive education.

Denis Diderot, 1713-84, (Fr.) philosopher, encyclopedist.

John Duns Scotus, c. 1266-1308, (Scot.) Franciscan philosopher, theologian.

Mary Baker Eddy, 1821-1910, (U.S.) founder of Christian Science; *Science and Health*.

Jonathan Edwards, 1703-58, (U.S.) preacher, theologian; "Sinners in the Hands of an Angry God."

(Desiderius) Erasmus, c. 1466-1536, (Neth.) Renaissance humanist; *On the Freedom of the Will*.

Jerry Falwell, 1933-2007, (U.S.) TV evangelist, religious commentator.

Johann Fichte, 1762-1814, (Ger.) idealist philosopher.

Michel Foucault, 1926-84, (Fr.) structuralist philosopher, historian.

George Fox, 1624-91, (Br.) founder of Society of Friends (Quakers).

(St.) Francis of Assisi, 1182-1226, (It.) espoused voluntary poverty, founded Franciscans.

al-Ghazali, 1058-1111, (Iran) Islamic philosopher.

Billy James Hargis, 1925-2004, (U.S.) anti-Communist televangelist; founder of the Church of the Christian Crusade.

Georg W. F. Hegel, 1770-1831, (Ger.) idealist philosopher; *Phenomenology of Mind*.

Martin Heidegger, 1889-1976, (Ger.) existentialist philosopher; affected many fields; *Being and Time*.

Johann G. Herder, 1744-1803, (Ger.) philosopher, cultural historian; a founder of German Romanticism.

Thomas Hobbes, 1588-1679, (Eng.) philosopher, political theorist; *Leviathan.*

David Hume, 1711-76, (Scot.) empiricist philosopher; *Enquiry Concerning Human Understanding.*

Jan Hus, 1369-1415, (Czech.) religious reformer.

Edmund Husserl, 1859-1938, (Ger.) philosopher; founded the phenomenological movement.

Thomas Huxley, 1825-95, (Br.) philosopher, educator.

William Ralph Inge, 1860-1954, (Br.) theologian; explored mystic aspects of Christianity.

William James, 1842-1910, (U.S.) philosopher, psychologist, pragmatist; studied religious experience.

Karl Jaspers, 1883-1969, (Ger.) existentialist philosopher.

Joan of Arc, 1412-31, (Fr.) national heroine, a patron saint of France; key figure in the Hundred Years' War.

Immanuel Kant, 1724-1804, (Ger.) philosopher; founder of modern critical philosophy; *Critique of Pure Reason.*

Thomas à Kempis, c. 1380-1471, (Ger.) monk, devotional writer; *Imitation of Christ* attributed to him.

Soren Kierkegaard, 1813-55, (Den.) religious philosopher, pre-existentialist; *Either/Or, The Sickness Unto Death.*

John Knox, 1505-72, (Scot.) leader of Protestant Reformation in Scotland.

Lao-Tzu, 604-531 BCE, (China) philosopher; considered the founder of the Taoist religion.

Gottfried von Leibniz, 1646-1716, (Ger.) rationalistic philosopher, logician, mathematician.

John Locke, 1632-1704, (Eng.) political theorist, empiricist philosopher; *Essay Concerning Human Understanding.*

(St.) Ignatius Loyola, 1491-1556, (Sp.) founder of the Jesuits; *Spiritual Exercises.*

Martin Luther, 1483-1546, (Ger.) leader of the Protestant Reformation; founded Lutheran church.

Jean-Francois Lyotard, 1924-98, (Fr.) postmodern philosopher, lecturer; *The Post-Modern Condition.*

Maimonides, 1135-1204, (Sp.) major Jewish philosopher.

Gabriel Marcel, 1889-1973, (Fr.) Rom. Cath. existentialist philosopher, dramatist.

Jacques Maritain, 1882-1973, (Fr.) neo-Thomist philosopher.

Cotton Mather, 1663-1728, (U.S.) defender of orthodox Puritanism; founded Yale, 1701.

Aimee Semple McPherson, 1890-1944, (Can.) Pentecostal evangelist.

Philipp Melanchthon, 1497-1560, (Ger.) theologian, humanist; an important voice in the Reformation.

Maurice Merleau-Ponty, 1908-61, (Fr.) existentialist philosopher; *Phenomenology of Perception.*

Thomas Merton, 1915-68, (U.S.) Trappist monk, spiritual writer; *The Seven Storey Mountain.*

Dwight Moody, 1837-99, (U.S.) evangelist.

Rev. Sun Myung Moon, 1920-2012, (N. Kor.) Unification Church founder.

G(eorge) E(dward) Moore, 1873-1958, (Br.) philosopher; *Principia Ethica*, "A Defense of Common Sense."

Muhammad, c. 570-632, (Arab.) prophet of Islam.

Elijah Muhammad, 1897-1975, (U.S.) founder of Black Muslim group, Nation of Islam.

Heinrich Muhlenberg, 1711-87, (Ger.) organized the Lutheran Church in America.

John H. Newman, 1801-90, (Br.) Rom. Cath. convert, cardinal; led Oxford Movement; *Apologia pro Vita Sua.*

Reinhold Niebuhr, 1892-1971, (U.S.) Protestant theologian.

Richard Niebuhr, 1894-1962, (U.S.) Protestant theologian.

Friedrich Nietzsche, 1844-1900, (Ger.) philosopher; *The Birth of Tragedy, Beyond Good and Evil, Thus Spake Zarathustra.*

Robert Nozick, 1938-2002, (U.S.) political philosopher; *Anarchy, State, and Utopia.*

Blaise Pascal, 1623-62, (Fr.) philosopher, mathematician; *Pensées.*

(St.) Patrick, c. 389-c. 461, (Br.) brought Christianity to Ireland.

Norman Vincent Peale, 1898-1993, (U.S.) minister, author; *The Power of Positive Thinking.*

C(harles) S. Peirce, 1839-1914, (U.S.) philosopher, logician; originated concept of pragmatism, 1878.

Plato, c. 428-347 BCE, (Gr.) philosopher; wrote Socratic dialogues; argued for immortality of soul, indep. reality of ideas or forms; *Republic, Meno, Phaedo, Apology.*

Plotinus, 205-70, (Rom.) a founder of neo-Platonism; *Enneads.*

W(illard) V(an) O(rman) Quine, 1908-2001, (U.S.) philosopher, logician; "On What There Is."

John Rawls, 1922-2002, (U.S.) political philosopher; *A Theory of Justice.*

Oral Roberts, 1918-2009, (U.S.) televangelist, university founder.

Moishe Rosen, 1932-2010, (U.S.) Jews for Jesus founder.

Josiah Royce, 1855-1916, (U.S.) idealist philosopher.

Bertrand Russell, 1872-1970, (Br.) philosopher, logician; one of the founders of modern logic; prolific popular writer.

Charles T. Russell, 1852-1916, (U.S.) founder of Jehovah's Witnesses.

Gilbert Ryle, 1900-76, (Br.) analytic philosopher; *The Concept of Mind.*

George Santayana, 1863-1952, (U.S.) philosopher, writer, critic; *The Sense of Beauty, The Realms of Being.*

Jean-Paul Sartre, 1905-80, (Fr.) philosopher, novelist, playwright; *Nausea, No Exit, Being and Nothingness.*

Friedrich von Schelling, 1775-1854, (Ger.) philosopher of romantic movement.

Friedrich Schleiermacher, 1768-1834, (Ger.) theologian; a founder of modern Protestant theology.

Arthur Schopenhauer, 1788-1860, (Ger.) philosopher; *The World as Will and Idea.*

Robert Schuller, 1926-2015, (U.S.) evangelist; Crystal Cathedral founder.

Albert Schweitzer, 1875-1965, (Ger.) theologian, social philosopher, medical missionary.

Joseph Smith, 1805-44, (U.S.) founded Latter-Day Saints (Mormon) movement, 1830.

Socrates, 469-399 BCE, (Gr.) philosopher immortalized by Plato.

Herbert Spencer, 1820-1903, (Br.) philosopher of evolution.

Herbert Spiegel, 1914-2009, (U.S.) psychiatrist who popularized hypnosis.

Baruch de Spinoza, 1632-77, (Neth.) rationalist philosopher; *Ethics.*

John Stott, 1921-2011, (Br.) evangelical Anglican cleric.

Billy Sunday, 1862-1935, (U.S.) evangelist.

Daisetz Teitaro Suzuki, 1870-1966, (Jpn.) Buddhist scholar.

Emanuel Swedenborg, 1688-1772, (Swed.) philosopher, mystic; *Principia.*

Pierre Teilhard de Chardin, 1881-1955, (Fr.) Jesuit priest, paleontologist, philosopher-theologian; *The Divine Milieu.*

(St.) Therese of Lisieux, 1873-97, (Fr.) Carmelite nun ("Little Flower"), revered for everyday sanctity; *The Story of a Soul.*

Paul Tillich, 1886-1965, (U.S.) German-born philosopher, theologian; brought depth psychology to Protestantism.

John Wesley, 1703-91, (Br.) theologian, evangelist; founded Methodism.

Alfred North Whitehead, 1861-1947, (Br.) philosopher, mathematician; *Process and Reality.*

William of Occam, c. 1285-c. 1349, (Eng.) medieval scholastic philosopher, nominalist.

Roger Williams, c. 1603-83, (U.S.) clergyman; championed religious freedom and separation of church and state.

Ludwig Wittgenstein, 1889-1951, (Austria) philosopher; major influence on contemporary language philosophy; *Tractatus Logico-Philosophicus, Philosophical Investigations.*

John Woolman, 1720-72, (U.S.) Quaker social reformer, abolitionist, writer; *The Journal.*

John Wycliffe, 1320-84, (Eng.) theologian, reformer.

(St.) Francis Xavier, 1506-52, (Sp.) Jesuit missionary; "Apostle of the Indies."

Brigham Young, 1801-77, (U.S.) Mormon leader after Joseph Smith's death; colonized Utah.

Huldrych Zwingli, 1484-1531, (Switz.) theologian; led Swiss Protestant Reformation.

Political Leaders of the Past

U.S. presidents, vice presidents, Supreme Court justices, and signers of the Declaration of Independence listed elsewhere. See also Historical Figures.

Abu Bakr, 573-634, (Arab.) Muslim leader, first caliph, chosen successor to Muhammad.

Dean Acheson, 1893-1971, (U.S.) sec. of state; architect of Cold War foreign policy.

Samuel Adams, 1722-1803, (U.S.) patriot; Boston Tea Party firebrand.

Konrad Adenauer, 1876-1967, (Ger.) first West German chancellor.

Emilio Aguinaldo, 1869-1964, (Philip.) revolutionary; fought against Spain and the U.S.

Corazon Aquino, 1933-2009, (Philip.) pres. of the Philippines, 1986-92.

Akbar, 1542-1605, Mogul emperor of India.

Carl Albert, 1908-2000, (U.S.) House rep. (D, OK), Speaker, 1971-76.

Salvador Allende Gossens, 1908-73, (Chile) Marxist pres., 1970-73; ousted and died in coup.

Idi Amin, 1925-2003, (Uganda) Ugandan ruler, 1971-79; blamed for hundreds of thousands of deaths.

Yasir Arafat, 1929-2004, (Egypt) leader of the Palestine Liberation Organization (PLO).

Herbert H. Asquith, 1852-1928, (Br.) Liberal prime min.; instituted major social reforms.

Hafez al Assad, 1930-2000, (Syr.) pres. of Syria, 1970-2000.

Atahualpa, 1500?-33, (Inca) ruling chief of Peru.

Kemal Atatürk, 1881-1938, (Turk.) founded modern Turkey.

Clement Attlee, 1883-1967, (Br.) Labour party leader, prime min.; enacted natl. health care system, nationalized many industries.

Stephen F. Austin, 1793-1836, (U.S.) led Texas colonization.

Mikhail Bakunin, 1814-76, (Russ.) revolutionary; leading exponent of anarchism.

Arthur J. Balfour, 1848-1930, (Br.) foreign sec. under Lloyd George; issued Balfour Declaration backing Zionism.

Bernard M. Baruch, 1870-1965, (U.S.) financier, govt. adviser.

Fulgencio Batista y Zaldívar, 1901-73, (Cub.) Cuban pres., 1940-44, 1952-59; overthrown by Castro.

Lord Beaverbrook, 1879-1964, (Br.) financier, statesman, newspaper owner.

Menachem Begin, 1913-92, (Isr.) Israeli prime min.; shared 1978 Nobel Peace Prize.

Ahmed Ben Bella, 1918-2012, (Alg.) first Algerian pres., 1963-65.

Eduard Benes, 1884-1948, (Czech.) pres. during interwar and post-WWII eras.

David Ben-Gurion, 1886-1973, (Isr.) first prime min. of Israel, 1948-53, 1955-63.

Thomas Hart Benton, 1782-1858, (U.S.) MO senator; championed agrarian interests and westward expansion.

Aneurin Bevan, 1897-1960, (Br.) Labour party leader.

Ernest Bevin, 1881-1951, (Br.) Labour party leader, foreign minister; helped lay foundation for NATO.

Benazir Bhutto, 1953-2007, (Pak.) Pakistan prime min.; first elected woman leader of a majority-Muslim country.

Otto von Bismarck, 1815-98, (Ger.) statesman known as the Iron Chancellor; uniter of Germany, 1870.

James G. Blaine, 1830-93, (U.S.) Republican politician, diplomat; influential in Pan-American movement.

Léon Blum, 1872-1950, (Fr.) socialist leader, writer; headed first Popular Front government.

William E. Borah, 1865-1940, (U.S.) isolationist senator (R, ID); helped block U.S. membership in League of Nations.

Cesare Borgia, 1476-1507, (It.) soldier, politician; Italian Renaissance figure who partly inspired Machiavelli's *The Prince*.

P. W. Botha, 1916-2006, (S. Afr.) S. African president, prime min.

Boutros Boutros-Ghali, 1922-2016, (Egypt) UN sec.-gen.

Tom Bradley, 1917-98, (U.S.) first African American mayor of L.A.

Willy Brandt, 1913-92, (Ger.) statesman, chancellor of West Germany, 1969-74; promoted East/West peace, *Ostpolitik*.

Leonid Brezhnev, 1906-82, (USSR) Soviet leader, 1964-82.

Aristide Briand, 1862-1932, (Fr.) foreign min.; chief architect of Locarno Pact and anti-war Kellogg-Briand Pact.

William Jennings Bryan, 1860-1925, (U.S.) Democratic, populist leader, orator; three times lost race for presidency.

Ralph Bunche, 1904-71, (U.S.) first black person to win the Nobel Peace Prize, 1950; undersecretary of the UN, 1950.

Robert Byrd, 1917-2010, (U.S.) longest serving U.S. senator (D, WV).

John C. Calhoun, 1782-1850, (U.S.) political leader; champion of states' rights and a symbol of the Old South.

James Callaghan (Baron Callaghan), 1912-2005, (Br.) Labour party politician, prime min., 1976-79.

Robert Castlereagh, 1769-1822, (Br.) foreign sec.; guided Grand Alliance against Napoleon.

Camillo Benso Cavour, 1810-61, (It.) statesman; largely responsible for uniting Italy under the House of Savoy.

Nicolae Ceausescu, 1918-89, (Rom.) Communist leader, head of state, 1967-89; executed.

Austen Chamberlain, 1863-1937, (Br.) statesman; helped finalize Locarno Treaties, both 1925.

Neville Chamberlain, 1869-1940, (Br.) Conservative prime min. whose appeasement of Hitler led to Munich Pact.

Hugo Chávez, 1954-2013, (Venez.) socialist Venezuelan pres., 1999-2013.

Chiang Kai-shek, 1887-1975, (China) Nationalist Chinese pres. whose govt. was driven from mainland to Taiwan.

Madame Chiang Kai-shek (Mayling Soong), 1898-2003, (China) highly influential wife of Nationalist Chinese leader Chiang Kai-shek.

Shirley Chisholm, 1924-2005, (U.S.) first black woman elected to U.S. House (1968, D, NY); pres. contender, 1972.

Warren Christopher, 1925-2011, (U.S.) secretary of state, diplomat.

Winston Churchill, 1874-1965, (Br.) prime min., soldier, author; guided Britain through WWII.

Galeazzo Ciano, 1903-44, (It.) Fascist foreign minister; helped create Rome-Berlin Axis; executed by Benito Mussolini.

Henry Clay, 1777-1852, (U.S.) "The Great Compromiser"; one of the most influential pre-Civil War political leaders.

Georges Clemenceau, 1841-1929, (Fr.) twice prem.; Woodrow Wilson's antagonist at Paris Peace Conference after WWI.

DeWitt Clinton, 1769-1828, (U.S.) political leader; responsible for promoting the Erie Canal.

Robert Clive, 1725-74, (Br.) first administrator of Bengal; laid foundation for British Empire in India.

Jean Baptiste Colbert, 1619-83, (Fr.) statesman; influential under Louis XIV; created the French navy.

Bettino Craxi, 1934-2000, (It.) Italy's first post-WWII Socialist prem.

David Crockett, 1786-1836, (U.S.) frontiersman, congressman; died defending the Alamo.

Oliver Cromwell, 1599-1658, (Br.) Lord Protector of England; led parliamentary forces during Civil War.

Mario Cuomo, 1932-2015, NY governor (D), 1983-94.

Curzon of Kedleston, 1859-1925, (Br.) viceroy of India, foreign sec.; major force in post-WWI world.

Édouard Daladier, 1884-1970, (Fr.) Radical Socialist politician, arrested by Vichy, interned by Germans until 1945.

Richard J. Daley, 1902-76, (U.S.) Chicago mayor, 1955-76.

Georges Danton, 1759-94, (Fr.) leading French Rev. figure.

Jefferson Davis, 1808-89, (U.S.) pres. of the Confederacy.

Charles G. Dawes, 1865-1951, (U.S.) statesman, banker; advanced plan to stabilize post-WWI German finances.

William L. Dawson, 1886-1970, (U.S.) U.S. rep. (D, IL); first black chair of a standing U.S. House committee.

Alcide De Gasperi, 1881-1954, (It.) prime min.; founder of Christian Democratic party.

Charles De Gaulle, 1890-1970, (Fr.) general, statesman; first pres. of the Fifth Republic.

Deng Xiaoping, 1904-97, (China) "paramount leader" of China; backed economic modernization.

Eamon De Valera, 1882-1975, (Ire.-U.S.) statesman; led fight for Irish independence.

Thomas E. Dewey, 1902-71, (U.S.) NY governor (R); twice lost in try for presidency.

Ngo Dinh Diem, 1901-63, (Viet.) South Vietnamese pres.; assassinated in government takeover.

Everett M. Dirksen, 1896-1969, (U.S.) Senate Republican minority leader, orator.

Benjamin Disraeli, 1804-81, (Br.) prime min.; considered founder of modern Conservative party.

Anatoly Dobrynin, 1919-2010, (Russ.) diplomat and Soviet amb. to U.S. (1962-86).

Engelbert Dollfuss, 1892-1934, (Austria) chancellor; assassinated by Austrian Nazis.

Andrea Doria, 1466-1560, (It.) Genoese admiral, statesman; called "Father of Peace" and "Liberator of Genoa."

Stephen A. Douglas, 1813-61, (U.S.) Democratic leader, orator; ran against Lincoln for IL sen. seat, presidency.

Alexander Dubcek, 1921-92, (Czech.) statesman whose attempted liberalization was crushed, 1968.

John Foster Dulles, 1888-1959, (U.S.) sec. of state under Eisenhower; Cold War policy maker.

Lawrence Eagleburger, 1930-2011, (U.S.) diplomat and foreign policy advisor.

Abba Eban, 1915-2002, (Isr.) diplomat; foreign min., 1966-74.

Friedrich Ebert, 1871-1925, (Ger.) Social Democratic movement leader; first pres., Weimar Republic, 1919-25.

Sir Anthony Eden, 1897-1977, (Br.) foreign sec., prime min. during Suez invasion of 1956.

Ludwig Erhard, 1897-1977, (Ger.) economist, West German chancellor; led nation's economic rise after WWII.

King Fahd, 1923-2005, (Saudi Arabia) monarch from 1982 but inactive after 1995 stroke; encouraged U.S. relations.

Geraldine Ferraro, 1935-2011, (U.S.) U.S. rep. (D, NY), vice-pres. nominee.

João Baptista de Figueiredo, 1918-99, (Braz.) pres. of Brazil; restored nation's democracy after military rule.

Hamilton Fish, 1808-93, (U.S.) sec. of state; successfully mediated disputes with Great Britain, Latin America.

James V. Forrestal, 1892-1949, (U.S.) sec. of navy, first sec. of defense.

Francisco Franco, 1892-1975, (Sp.) leader of rebel forces during Spanish Civil War, longtime ruler of Spain.

Benjamin Franklin, 1706-90, (U.S.) printer, publisher, author, inventor, scientist, diplomat.

Louis de Frontenac, 1620-98, (Fr.) governor of New France (Canada); encouraged explorations, fought Iroquois.

J. William Fulbright, 1905-95, (U.S.) U.S. senator (D, AR); leading figure in U.S. foreign policy during Cold War years.

Hugh Gaitskell, 1906-63, (Br.) Labour party leader; major force in reversing its stand for unilateral disarmament.

Albert Gallatin, 1761-1849, (U.S.) sec. of treasury; instrumental in negotiating end of War of 1812.

Léon Gambetta, 1838-82, (Fr.) statesman, politician; one of the founders of the Third Republic.

Indira Gandhi, 1917-84, (India) daughter of Jawaharlal Nehru; prime min. of India, 1966-77, 1980-84; assassinated.

Mohandas K. Gandhi, 1869-1948, (India) political leader, ascetic; led movement against British rule; assassinated.

Giuseppe Garibaldi, 1807-82, (It.) patriot, soldier; a leader in the Risorgimento, Italian unification movement.

William E. Gladstone, 1809-98, (Br.) prime min.; dominant force of Liberal party 1868-94.

Paul Joseph Goebbels, 1897-1945, (Ger.) Nazi propagandist; master of mass psychology.

Barry Goldwater, 1909-98, (U.S.) conservative U.S. senator (R, AZ), 1964 pres. nominee.

Klement Gottwald, 1896-1953, (Czech.) Communist leader; ushered Communism into his country.

Alexander Hamilton, 1755-1804, (U.S.) first treasury sec.; champion of strong central government.

Dag Hammarskjöld, 1905-61, (Swed.) statesman; UN sec.-general.

King Hassan II, 1929-99, (Moroc.) ruler of Morocco, 1962-99.

Vaclav Havel, 1936-2011, (Czech.) first president of Czech Republic, 1989-92.

John Hay, 1838-1905, (U.S.) sec. of state; primarily associated with Open Door Policy toward China.

Sir Edward Heath, 1916-2005, (Br.) Conservative prime min., 1970-74; promoted European unity.

Jesse Helms, 1921-2008, (U.S.) conservative U.S. senator (R, NC).

Patrick Henry, 1736-99, (U.S.) major Revolutionary War figure, orator.

Édouard Herriot, 1872-1957, (Fr.) Radical Socialist leader; twice prem., pres. of National Assembly.

Theodor Herzl, 1860-1904, (Hung.) founded modern Zionism.

Heinrich Himmler, 1900-45, (Ger.) head of Nazi SS and Gestapo.

Paul von Hindenburg, 1847-1934, (Ger.) field marshal, WWI; second pres. of Weimar Republic, 1925-34.

Adolf Hitler, 1889-1945, (Ger.) dictator; built Nazism, launched WWII, presided over the Holocaust.

Ho Chi Minh, 1890-1969, (Viet.) N. Vietnamese pres., Vietnamese Communist leader.

Harry L. Hopkins, 1890-1946, (U.S.) New Deal administrator; closest adviser to Franklin D. Roosevelt during WWII.

Edward M. House, 1858-1938, (U.S.) diplomat; confidential adviser to Woodrow Wilson.

Samuel Houston, 1793-1863, (U.S.) leader of struggle for Texas independence.

Cordell Hull, 1871-1955, (U.S.) sec. of state, 1933-44; initiated reciprocal trade to lower tariffs, helped organize UN.

Hubert H. Humphrey, 1911-78, (U.S.) U.S. senator (D, MN), vice pres., pres. candidate.

King Hussein, 1935-99, (Jordan) peacemaker; ruler of Jordan, 1952-99.

Saddam Hussein, 1937-2006, (Iraq) Iraqi ruler; put to death for crimes against humanity.

Muhammad Ali Jinnah, 1876-1948, (Pak.) founder, first gov.-gen. of Pakistan.

Barbara Jordan, 1936-96, (U.S.) U.S. rep. (D, TX), orator, educator; first black woman to win a seat in the TX state senate, 1966.

Benito Juarez, 1806-72, (Mex.) rallied his country against foreign threats; sought to create democratic, federal republic.

Constantine Karamanlis, 1907-98, (Gr.) Greek prime min.; restored democracy, later president.

Frank B. Kellogg, 1856-1937, (U.S.) sec. of state; negotiated Kellogg-Briand Pact to outlaw war.

Jack Kemp, 1935-2009, (U.S.) sec. of HUD, U.S. rep. (R, NY), football player.

Edward M. Kennedy, 1932-2009, (U.S.) senator (D, MA); championed progressive causes.

Robert F. Kennedy, 1925-68, (U.S.) attorney general, U.S. sen. (D, NY); assassinated while seeking presidency.

Aleksandr Kerensky, 1881-1970, (Russ.) headed provisional government after Feb. 1917 revolution.

Ayatollah Ruhollah Khomeini, 1900-89, (Iran), religious-political leader; spearheaded overthrow of Shah, 1979.

Nikita Khrushchev, 1894-1971, (USSR) prem., first sec. of Communist party; initiated de-Stalinization.

Kim Dae-jung, 1925-2009, (Korea) S. Korean dissident, opposition leader, pres.; 2000 Nobel Peace Prize winner.

Kim Il Sung, 1912-94, (Korea) N. Korean dictator, 1948-94.

Kim Jong Il, 1942-2011, (Korea) N. Korean dictator, 1994-2011.

Edward I. Koch, 1924-2013, (U.S.) New York City mayor, 1978-89.

Lajos Kossuth, 1802-94, (Hung.) principal figure in 1848 Hungarian revolution.

Pyotr Kropotkin, 1842-1921, (Russ.) anarchist; championed the peasants but opposed Bolshevism.

Kublai Khan, c. 1215-94, (Mongol) emperor; founder of Yuan dynasty in China.

Béla Kun, 1886-c. 1939, (Hung.) member of Third Communist International; tried to foment worldwide revolution.

Robert M. LaFollette, 1855-1925, (U.S.) WI public official; leader of progressive movement.

Fiorello La Guardia, 1882-1947, (U.S.) New York City reform mayor, 1933-45.

Pierre Laval, 1883-1945, (Fr.) politician; Vichy foreign min.; executed for treason.

Andrew Bonar Law, 1858-1923, (Can.) Conservative party politician, British prime min.; led opposition to Irish home rule.

Vladimir Ilyich Lenin (Ulyanov), 1870-1924, (Russ.) revolutionary; founded Bolshevism; Soviet leader, 1917-24.

Ferdinand de Lesseps, 1805-94, (Fr.) diplomat, engineer; conceived idea of Suez Canal.

Rene Levesque, 1922-87, (Can.) prem. of Quebec, 1976-85; led unsuccessful separatist campaign.

Trygve Lie, 1896-1968, (Nor.) first UN sec.-gen.

Maxim Litvinov, 1876-1951, (Pol.-Russ.) revolutionary, commissar of foreign affairs; favored cooperation with West.

Liu Shaoqi, c. 1898-1969, (China) Communist leader; fell from grace during Cultural Revolution.

David Lloyd George, 1863-1945, (Br.) Liberal party prime min.; laid foundations for modern welfare state.

Henry Cabot Lodge, 1850-1924, (U.S.) U.S. senator (R, MA); led opposition to participation in League of Nations.

Huey P. Long, 1893-1935, (U.S.) Louisiana political demagogue, governor, U.S. senator (D); assassinated.

Rosa Luxemburg, 1871-1919, (Ger.) revolutionary; leader of the German Social Democratic party and Spartacus party.

J. Ramsay MacDonald, 1866-1937, (Br.) first Labour party prime min. of Great Britain.

Harold Macmillan, 1895-1986, (Br.) prime min. of Great Britain, 1957-63.

Makarios III, 1913-77, (Cyprus) Greek Orthodox archbishop; first pres. of Cyprus.

Nelson Mandela, 1918-2013, (S. Afr.) anti-apartheid leader; first black pres. of S. Africa, 1994-99.

Wilma Mankiller, 1945-2010, (U.S.) first female chief of the Cherokee Nation.

Mao Zedong, 1893-1976, (China) chief Chinese Marxist theorist, revolutionary, political leader; led revolution establishing his nation as Communist state.

Jean Paul Marat, 1743-93, (Fr.) revolutionary, politician; identified with radical Jacobins; assassinated.

Thurgood Marshall, 1908-93, (U.S.) first black U.S. solicitor general, 1965; first black justice of U.S. Supreme Court, 1967-91.

José Martí, 1853-95, (Cub.) patriot, poet; independence leader.

Jan Masaryk, 1886-1948, (Czech.) foreign min.; died under mysterious circumstances, allegedly committed suicide following Communist coup.

Thomas G. Masaryk, 1850-1937, (Czech.) statesman, philosopher; first pres. of Czechoslovakia.

Jules Mazarin, 1602-61, (Fr.) cardinal, statesman; prime min. under Louis XIII and queen regent Anne of Austria.

Giuseppe Mazzini, 1805-72, (It.) reformer dedicated to Risorgimento movement for renewal of Italy.

Tom Mboya, 1930-69, (Kenya) political leader; instrumental in securing independence for Kenya.

Eugene McCarthy, 1916-2005, (U.S.) political leader, author; 1968 Dem. presidential contender.

Joseph R. McCarthy, 1908-57, (U.S.) senator (R, WI); extremist in searching out alleged Communists and pro-Communists.

George McGovern, 1922-2012, (U.S.) liberal senator (D, SD), 1972 pres. nominee.

Cosimo I de' Medici, 1519-74, (It.) Duke of Florence, grand duke of Tuscany.

Lorenzo de' Medici (the Magnificent), 1449-92, (It.) merchant prince; a towering figure in Italian Renaissance.

Catherine de Médicis, 1519-89, (Fr.) queen consort of Henry II, regent of France; influential in Catholic-Huguenot wars.

Golda Meir, 1898-1978, (Isr.) a founder of the state of Israel; prime min., 1969-74.

Klemens W. N. L. Metternich, 1773-1859, (Austria) statesman; arbiter of post-Napoleonic Europe.

Slobodan Milosevic, 1941-2006, (Serb./Yugo.) former Yugoslav pres.; tried for genocide, crimes against humanity.

François Mitterrand, 1916-96, (Fr.) pres. of France, 1981-95.

Mobutu Sese Seko, 1930-97, (Zaire) longtime ruler of Zaire (now Dem. Rep. of Congo), 1965-97; exiled after rebellion.

Guy Mollet, 1905-75, (Fr.) socialist politician, resistance leader.

Henry Morgenthau Jr., 1891-1967, (U.S.) sec. of treasury; fundraiser for New Deal and U.S. WWII activities.

Gouverneur Morris, 1752-1816, (U.S.) statesman, diplomat, financial expert; helped plan decimal coinage.

Daniel Patrick Moynihan, 1927-2003, (U.S.) senator (D, NY), diplomat, social scientist, author.

Benito Mussolini, 1883-1945, (It.) leader of the Italian fascist state; assassinated.

Imre Nagy, c. 1896-1958, (Hung.) Communist prem.; assassinated after Soviets crushed 1956 uprising.

Gamal Abdel Nasser, 1918-70, (Egypt) leader of Arab unification, second Egyptian pres.

Jawaharlal Nehru, 1889-1964, (India) prime min.; guided India through its early years of independence.

Kwame Nkrumah, 1909-72, (Ghana) first prime min., 1957-60; pres., 1960-66, of Ghana.

Frederick North, 1732-92, (Br.) prime min.; his policies led to loss of American colonies.

Julius K. Nyerere, 1922-99, (Tanz.) founding father; first pres., 1962-85, of Tanzania.

Daniel O'Connell, 1775-1847, (Ire.) nationalist political leader; known as The Liberator.

Omar, c. 581-644, (Arab.) Muslim leader; second caliph, led Islam to become an imperial power.

Thomas P. (Tip) O'Neill Jr., 1912-94, (U.S.) U.S. rep. (D, MA), speaker of the House, 1977-86.

Ignace Paderewski, 1860-1941, (Pol.) statesman, pianist, composer, briefly prime min.; ardent patriot.

Ian Paisley, 1926-2014, (Ire.) Unionist Party leader who agreed to power sharing in N. Ireland.

Viscount Palmerston, 1784-1865, (Br.) Whig-Liberal prime min., foreign min.; embodied British nationalism.

Andreas George Papandreou, 1919-96, (Gr.) leftist politician; served as prem., 1981-89, 1993-96.

Georgios Papandreou, 1888-1968, (Gr.) Republican politician; served three times as prime min.

Franz von Papen, 1879-1969, (Ger.) politician; major role in overthrow of Weimar Republic and rise of Hitler.

Charles Stewart Parnell, 1846-1891, (Ire.) nationalist leader; "uncrowned king of Ireland."

Lester Pearson, 1897-1972, (Can.) diplomat, Liberal party leader, prime min.

Robert Peel, 1788-1850, (Br.) reformist prime min.; founder of Conservative party.

Shimon Peres, 1922-2016, (Isr.) Israel prime min., 1984-86, '95-'96; president, 2007-14.

Frances Perkins, 1882-1965, (U.S.) first female cabinet member (sec. of labor).

Eva (Evita) Perón, 1919-52, (Arg.) highly influential second wife of Juan Perón.

Juan Perón, 1895-1974, (Arg.) dynamic pres. of Argentina, 1946-55, 1973-74.

Joseph Pilsudski, 1867-1935, (Pol.) statesman; instrumental in reestablishing Polish state in the 20th cent.

Charles Pinckney, 1757-1824, (U.S.) founding father; his Pinckney plan largely incorporated into Constitution.

Christian Pineau, 1905-95, (Fr.) leader of French Resistance during WWII; French foreign min., 1956-58.

Augusto Pinochet (Ugarte), 1915-2006, (Chile) former Chilean ruler; indicted for human rights abuses while in office.

William Pitt the Elder, 1708-78, (Br.) statesman; the "Great Commoner," transformed Britain into imperial power.

William Pitt the Younger, 1759-1806, (Br.) prime min. during French Revolutionary wars.

Georgi Plekhanov, 1857-1918, (Russ.) revolutionary, social philosopher; called "father of Russian Marxism."

Raymond Poincaré, 1860-1934, (Fr.) French pres.; advocated harsh punishment of Germany after WWI.

Pol Pot, 1925-98, (Camb.) leader of Khmer Rouge; ruled Cambodia, 1975-79; responsible for mass deaths.

Georges Pompidou, 1911-74, (Fr.) Gaullist political leader; pres., 1969-74.

Grigori Potemkin, 1739-91, (Russ.) field marshal; favorite of empress Catherine II.

Adam Clayton Powell Jr., 1908-72, (U.S.) civil rights leader; U.S. rep. (D, NY), 1945-69.

Muammar al-Qaddafi, 1942-2011, (Libya) Libyan ruler, 1969-2011.

Yitzhak Rabin, 1922-95, (Isr.) military, political leader; prime min. of Israel, 1974-77, 1992-95; assassinated.

Joseph H. Rainey, 1832-87, (U.S.) first black person elected to U.S. House (1869), from SC.

Edmund Randolph, 1753-1813, (U.S.) attorney; prominent in drafting, ratification of Constitution.

John Randolph, 1773-1833, (U.S.) Southern planter; strong advocate of states' rights.

Jeannette Rankin, 1880-1973, (U.S.) pacifist; first woman member of U.S. Congress (R, MT).

Walter Rathenau, 1867-1922, (Ger.) industrialist, statesman.

Sam Rayburn, 1882-1961, (U.S.) U.S. rep. (D, TX) for 47 years, House speaker for 17.

Hiram R. Revels, 1822-1901, (U.S.) first African-American U.S. senator (R); elected in MS, served 1870-71.

Paul Reynaud, 1878-1966, (Fr.) statesman; prem. in 1940 at time of France's defeat by Germany.

Syngman Rhee, 1875-1965, (Korea) first pres. of S. Korea.

Cecil Rhodes, 1853-1902, (Br.) imperialist, industrial magnate; established Rhodes scholarships in his will.

Ann Richards, 1933-2006, (U.S.) former TX gov.

Cardinal de Richelieu, 1585-1642, (Fr.) statesman, known as "red eminence"; chief minister to Louis XIII.

Maximilien Robespierre, 1758-94, (Fr.) leading figure in French Revolution and Reign of Terror.

Nelson Rockefeller, 1908-79, (U.S.) Republican governor of NY, 1959-73; U.S. vice pres., 1974-77.

Eleanor Roosevelt, 1884-1962, (U.S.) influential first lady, humanitarian, UN diplomat.

Elihu Root, 1845-1937, (U.S.) lawyer, statesman, diplomat; leading Republican supporter of the League of Nations.

Dean Rusk, 1909-95, (U.S.) statesman; sec. of state, 1961-69.

John Russell, 1792-1878, (Br.) Liberal prime min. during the Irish potato famine.

Anwar al-Sadat, 1918-81, (Egypt) pres., 1970-81; promoted peace with Israel; Nobel laureate; assassinated.

António de Oliveira Salazar, 1889-1970, (Port.) longtime dictator.

José de San Martin, 1778-1850, ([now] Arg.) S. Amer. revolutionary; protector of Peru.

Eisaku Sato, 1901-75, (Jpn.) prime min.; presided over Japan's post-WWII emergence as major world power.

Abdul Aziz Ibn Saud, c. 1880-1953, (Saudi Arabia) king of Saudi Arabia, 1932-53.

Helmut Schmidt, 1918-2015, (Ger.) German chancellor, 1974-82.

Robert Schuman, 1886-1963, (Fr.) statesman; founded European Coal and Steel Community.

Carl Schurz, 1829-1906, (U.S.) German-American political leader, journalist, orator, dedicated reformer.

Kurt Schuschnigg, 1897-1977, (Austria) chancellor; unsuccessful in stopping Austria's annexation by Germany.

William H. Seward, 1801-72, (U.S.) antislavery activist; as U.S. sec. of state purchased Alaska.

Carlo Sforza, 1872-1952, (It.) foreign min., anti-Fascist.

Yitzhak Shamir, 1915-2012, (Isr.) prime min. of Israel, 1983-84, 1986-92.

Ariel Sharon, 1928-2014, (Isr.) prime min. of Israel, 2001-06.

Eduard Shevardnadze, 1928-2014, (Geo.) Georgian pres., 1995-2003.

Norodom Sihanouk, 1922-2012, (Camb.) king of Cambodia (1941-55, 1993-2004).

Sitting Bull, c. 1831-90, (Amer. Ind.) Sioux leader in Battle of Little Bighorn against George A. Custer, 1876.

Alfred E. Smith, 1873-1944, (U.S.) NY Democratic governor; first Roman Catholic to run for president.

Margaret Chase Smith, 1897-1995, (U.S.) U.S. rep., senator (R, ME); first woman elected to both houses of Congress.

Jan C. Smuts, 1870-1950, (S. Afr.) statesman, philosopher, soldier, prime min.

Paul Henri Spaak, 1899-1972, (Belg.) statesman, socialist leader.

Joseph Stalin, 1879-1953, (USSR) Soviet dictator, 1924-53; instituted forced collectivization, massive purges, and labor camps, causing millions of deaths.

Edwin M. Stanton, 1814-69, (U.S.) sec. of war, 1862-68.

Alexander Stephens, 1812-83, (U.S.) vice pres. of the Confederacy.

Edward R. Stettinius Jr., 1900-49, (U.S.) industrialist; sec. of state who coordinated aid to WWII allies.

Adlai E. Stevenson, 1900-65, (U.S.) Democratic leader, diplomat, governor (IL), presidential candidate.

Henry L. Stimson, 1867-1950, (U.S.) statesman; served in five administrations, foreign policy adviser in 1930s and 1940s.

Carl Stokes, 1927-96, (U.S.) first black mayor of a major American city (Cleveland, 1967-72).

Suharto, 1921-2008, (Indon.) former longtime Indonesian ruler.

Sukarno, 1901-70, (Indon.) dictatorial first pres. of the Indonesian republic.

Sun Yat-sen, 1866-1925, (China) revolutionary; leader of Kuomintang political party, regarded as father of modern China.

Robert A. Taft, 1889-1953, (U.S.) conservative Senate leader (OH); called "Mr. Republican."

Charles de Talleyrand, 1754-1838, (Fr.) statesman, diplomat; the major force of the Congress of Vienna of 1814-15.

U Thant, 1909-74, (Burma) statesman, UN sec.-general.

Margaret Thatcher, 1925-2013, (Br.) conservative British prime min., 1979-90; first woman UK prime min.

Norman M. Thomas, 1884-1968, (U.S.) social reformer; six times Socialist party presidential candidate.

Josip Broz Tito, 1892-1980, (Yugo.) pres. of Yugoslavia from 1953; WWII guerrilla chief, postwar rival of Stalin.

Palmiro Togliatti, 1893-1964, (It.) major Italian Communist leader.

Hideki Tojo, 1885-1948, (Jpn.) statesman, soldier; prime min. during most of WWII.

François Toussaint L'Ouverture, c. 1744-1803, (Haiti) patriot, martyr; thwarted French colonial aims.

Leon Trotsky, 1879-1940, (Russ.) revolutionary; founded Red Army, expelled from party in conflict with Stalin; assassinated.

Pierre Elliott Trudeau, 1919-2000, (Can.) longtime liberal prime min. of Canada, 1968-79, 1980-84; achieved native Canadian constitution.

Rafael L. Trujillo Molina, 1891-1961, (Dom. Rep.) dictator of Dominican Republic, 1930-61; assassinated.

Moise K. Tshombe, 1919-69, (Congo) pres. of secessionist Katanga prov., prem. of Congo (now Dem. Rep. of the Congo).

William M. Tweed, 1823-78, (U.S.) political boss of Tammany Hall, New York City's Democratic political machine.

Walter Ulbricht, 1893-1973, (Ger.) Communist leader of German Democratic Republic.

Arthur H. Vandenberg, 1884-1951, (U.S.) senator (R, MI); proponent of bipartisan anti-Communist foreign policy.

Eleutherios Venizelos, 1864-1936, (Gr.) most prominent Greek statesman of early 20th cent.

Hendrik F. Verwoerd, 1901-66, (S. Afr.) prime min.; rigorously applied apartheid policy despite protest.

Kurt Waldheim, 1918-2007, (Austria) UN sec.-gen., Austrian pres.

George Wallace, 1919-98, (U.S.) former segregationist governor of Alabama, pres. candidate.

Robert Walpole, 1676-1745, (Br.) statesman; generally considered Britain's first prime min.

Harold Washington, 1922-87, (U.S.) first black mayor of Chicago.

Robert C. Weaver, 1907-97, (U.S.) first African American appointed to cabinet; sec. of Housing and Urban Development.

Daniel Webster, 1782-1852, (U.S.) orator, politician; advocate of business interests during Jacksonian agrarianism.

Caspar Weinberger, 1917-2006, (U.S.) business exec., former defense sec., other cabinet posts.

Chaim Weizmann, 1874-1952, (Russ.-Isr.) Zionist leader, scientist; first Israeli pres.

Kevin White, 1929-2012, (U.S.) Boston mayor, 1967-84.

Wendell L. Willkie, 1892-1944, (U.S.) Republican who tried to unseat Franklin D. Roosevelt when he ran for his third term.

Harold Wilson, 1916-95, (Br.) Labour party leader; prime min., 1964-70, 1974-76.

Boris Yeltsin, 1931-2007, (Russ.) first freely elected pres. of post-Soviet Russia.

Coleman A. Young, 1918-97, (U.S.) first African-American mayor of Detroit, 1974-93.

Emiliano Zapata, c. 1879-1919, (Mex.) revolutionary; major influence on modern Mexico.

Todor Zhivkov, 1911-98, (Bulg.) Communist ruler of Bulgaria from 1954 until ousted in a 1989 coup.

Zhou Enlai, 1898-1976, (China) diplomat, prime min.; a leading figure of the Chinese Communist party.

Scientists of the Past

Revised by Peter Barker, Prof. and Chair, Dept. of the History of Science, Univ. of Oklahoma.
For pre-modern scientists, see also Philosophers and Religious Figures of the Past and the Historical Figures chapter.

Albertus Magnus, c. 1200-80, (Ger.) theologian, philosopher; helped found medieval study of natural science.

Alhazen (Ibn al-Haytham), c. 965-c. 1040, mathematician, astronomer, optical theorist.

Andre-Marie Ampère, 1775-1836, (Fr.) mathematician, chemist; founder of electrodynamics.

Neil Armstrong, 1930-2012, (U.S.) astronaut, first man to walk on the Moon.

John V. Atanasoff, 1903-95, (U.S.) physicist; co-invented Atanasoff-Berry electronic digital computer (1939-41).

Amedeo Avogadro, 1776-1856, (It.) chemist, physicist; proposed that equal volumes of gas contain equal numbers of molecules, permitting determination of molecular weights.

John Bardeen, 1908-91, (U.S.) double Nobel laureate in physics (transistor, 1956; superconductivity, 1972).

A. H. Becquerel, 1852-1908, (Fr.) physicist; discovered radioactivity in uranium (1896).

Alexander Graham Bell, 1847-1922, (U.S.) inventor; first to patent and commercially exploit the telephone (1876).

Daniel Bernoulli, 1700-82, (Switz.) mathematician; developed fluid dynamics and kinetic theory of gases.

Clifford Berry, 1918-63, (U.S.) collaborated with John V. Atanasoff on the ABC electronic digital computer (1939-41).

Jöns Jakob Berzelius, 1779-1848, (Swed.) chemist; developed modern chemical symbols and formulas.

Henry Bessemer, 1813-98, (Br.) engineer; invented Bessemer steel-making process.

Hans Bethe, 1906-2005, (Ger.-U.S.) physicist; won Nobel Prize in 1967 for describing how stars generate energy.

Bruno Bettelheim, 1903-90, (Austria-U.S.) psychoanalyst; studied disturbed children; *Uses of Enchantment* (1976).

Louis Blériot, 1872-1936, (Fr.) engineer; monoplane pioneer, first English Channel flight (1909).

Franz Boas, 1858-1942, (Ger.-U.S.) founded modern anthropology; studied Pacific Coast tribes.

Niels Bohr, 1885-1962, (Den.) atomic and nuclear physicist; founded quantum mechanics.

Norman Borlaug, 1914-2009, (U.S.) plant pathologist and geneticist; father of "green" (agricultural) revolution.

Max Born, 1882-1970, (Ger.) atomic and nuclear physicist; helped develop quantum mechanics.

Satyendranath Bose, 1894-1974, (India) physicist; forerunner of modern quantum theory for integral-spin particles.

Louis de Broglie, 1892-1987, (Fr.) physicist; proposed quantum wave-particle duality.

Robert Bunsen, 1811-99, (Ger.) chemist; pioneered spectroscopic analysis; discovered rubidium, caesium.

Luther Burbank, 1849-1926, (U.S.) naturalist; developed plant breeding into a modern science.

Vannevar Bush, 1890-1974, (U.S.) electrical engineer; developed differential analyzer, an early analogue computer; headed WWII Office of Scientific Res. and Dev.

Marvin Camras, 1916-95, (U.S.) inventor, electrical engineer; invented magnetic tape recording.

Alexis Carrel, 1873-1944, (Fr.) surgeon, biologist; developed methods of suturing blood vessels, transplanting organs.

Rachel Carson, 1907-64, (U.S.) marine biologist, environmentalist; *Silent Spring* (1962).

George Washington Carver, 1864-1943, (U.S.) chemist and botanist; promoted alternative crops.

James Chadwick, 1891-1974, (Br.) physicist; discovered the neutron (1932); led Brit. team on Manhattan Project in U.S.

Eugenie Clark, 1922-2015, (U.S.) ichthyologist and oceanographer.

Albert Claude, 1898-1983, (Belg.-U.S.) a founder of modern cell biology; determined role of mitochondria.

Samuel Cohen, 1921-2010, (U.S.) physicist who invented the neutron bomb.

Barry Commoner, 1917-2012, biologist; noted environmentalist.

Nicolaus Copernicus, 1473-1543, (Pol.) first modern astronomer to propose Sun as center of the planets' motions.

Jacques Yves Cousteau, 1910-97, (Fr.) oceanographer; co-inventor, with Emile Gagnan (Fr.), of the Aqualung (1943).

Seymour Cray, 1925-96, (U.S.) computer industry pioneer; developed supercomputers.

Francis Crick, 1916-2004, (Br.) biophysicist; co-discoverer of genetic code; shared 1962 Nobel Prize in Physiology/Medicine.

Marie, 1867-1934, (Pol.-Fr.) and **Pierre Curie**, 1859-1906, (Fr.) physical chemists; pioneer investigators of radioactivity; discovered radium and polonium (1898).

Gottlieb Daimler, 1834-1900, (Ger.) engineer, inventor; pioneer automobile manufacturer.

John Dalton, 1766-1844, (Br.) chemist, physicist; formulated atomic theory, made first table of atomic weights.

Charles Darwin, 1809-82, (Br.) naturalist; established theory of organic evolution; *Origin of Species* (1859).

Lee De Forest, 1873-1961, (U.S.) inventor of triode; pioneer in wireless telegraphy, sound pictures, television.

Pierre-Gilles de Gennes, 1932-2007, (Fr.) physicist whose research aided development of liquid-crystal display (LCD); awarded 1991 Nobel Prize for Physics.

Max Delbrück, 1906-81, (Fr.-Ger.-U.S.) founded molecular biology.

Rudolf Diesel, 1858-1913, (Ger.) mechanical engineer; patented Diesel engine (1892).

Theodosius Dobzhansky, 1900-75, (Russ.-U.S.) biologist; reconciled genetics and natural selection.

Christian Doppler, 1803-53, (Austria) physicist; showed change in wave frequency caused by motion of source, now known as Doppler effect.

J. Presper Eckert Jr., 1919-95, (U.S.) co-inventor, with John W. Mauchly, of the ENIAC computer (1943-45).

Thomas A. Edison, 1847-1931, (U.S.) inventor; held more than 1,000 patents, including incandescent electric lamp.

Robert Edwards, 1925-2013, (Br.) physiologist; pioneered in vitro fertilization.

Paul Ehrlich, 1854-1915, (Ger.) medical researcher in immunology and bacteriology; pioneered antitoxin production.

Albert Einstein, 1879-1955, (Ger.-U.S.) theoretical physicist; founded relativity theory.

John F. Enders, 1897-1985, (U.S.) virologist; helped discover vaccines against polio, measles, mumps, and chicken pox.

Erik Erikson, 1902-94, (U.S.) psychoanalyst, author; theory of developmental stages of life; *Childhood and Society* (1950).

Leonhard Euler, 1707-83, (Switz.) mathematician, physicist; pioneer of calculus, revived ideas of Fermat.

Gabriel Fahrenheit, 1686-1736, (Ger.) physicist; improved thermometers and introduced Fahrenheit temperature scale.

Michael Faraday, 1791-1867, (Br.) chemist, physicist; discovered electrical induction and invented dynamo (1831).

Philo T. Farnsworth, 1906-71, (U.S.) inventor; built first television system (San Francisco, 1928).

Pierre de Fermat, 1601-65, (Fr.) mathematician; founded modern theory of numbers.

Enrico Fermi, 1901-54, (It.-U.S.) nuclear physicist; demonstrated first controlled chain reaction (Chicago, 1942).

Richard Feynman, 1918-88, (U.S.) theoretical physicist, author; founder of Quantum Electrodynamics (QED).

Alexander Fleming, 1881-1955, (Br.) bacteriologist; discovered penicillin (1928).

Dian Fossey, 1932-85, (U.S.) primatologist.

Jean B. J. Fourier, 1768-1830, (Fr.) introduced Fourier Series, method of analysis in math and physics.

Sigmund Freud, 1856-1939, (Austria) psychiatrist; founder of psychoanalysis; *Interpretation of Dreams* (1901).

Erich Fromm, 1900-80, (U.S.) psychoanalyst; *Man for Himself* (1947).

Galileo Galilei, 1564-1642, (It.) physicist; used telescope to vindicate Copernicus, founded modern science of motion.

Carl Friedrich Gauss, 1777-1855, (Ger.) mathematician; completed work of Fermat and Euler in number theory.

Josiah W. Gibbs, 1839-1903, (U.S.) theoretical physicist, chemist; founded chemical thermodynamics.

Robert H. Goddard, 1882-1945, (U.S.) physicist; invented liquid fuel rocket (1926).

George W. Goethals, 1858-1928, (U.S.) chief engineer who completed Panama Canal (1907-14).

William C. Gorgas, 1854-1920, (U.S.) physician; pioneer in prevention of yellow fever and malaria.

Stephen Jay Gould, 1941-2002, (U.S.) paleontologist, evolutionary biologist, writer.

Ernest Haeckel, 1834-1919, (Ger.) zoologist, evolutionist; early Darwinist, introduced concept of "ecology."

Otto Hahn, 1879-1968, (Ger.) chemist; with Lise Meitner discovered nuclear fission (1938).

Edmund Halley, 1656-1742, (Br.) astronomer; predicted return of 1682 comet (Halley's Comet) in 1759.

William Harvey, 1578-1657, (Br.) physician, anatomist; discovered circulation of the blood (1628).

Werner Heisenberg, 1901-76, (Ger.) physicist; developed matrix mechanics and uncertainty principle (1927).

Hermann von Helmholtz, 1821-94, (Ger.) physicist, physiologist; formulated principle of conservation of energy.

William Herschel, 1738-1822, (Ger.-Br.) astronomer; discovered Uranus (1781).

Heinrich Hertz, 1857-94, (Ger.) physicist; discovered radio waves and photo-electric effect (1886-87).

David Hilbert, 1862-1943, (Ger.) mathematician; contributed to algebra, calculus, and foundational studies (formalism).

Albert Hofmann, 1906-2008, (Switz.) chemist; inventor of LSD.

Edwin P. Hubble, 1889-1953, (U.S.) astronomer; discovered observational evidence of expanding universe.

Alexander von Humboldt, 1769-1859, (Ger.) naturalist; explored Central, S. America, ideated ecology.

Edward Jenner, 1749-1823, (Br.) physician; pioneered vaccination, introduced term "virus."

James Joule, 1818-89, (Br.) physicist; found relation between heat and mechanical energy (conservation of energy).

Carl Jung, 1875-1961, (Switz.) psychiatrist; founder of analytical psychology.

Ernest Everett Just, 1883-1941, (U.S.) marine biologist; studied egg development; *Biology of Cell Surfaces* (1941).

Johannes Kepler, 1571-1630, (Ger.) astronomer; discovered laws of planetary motion.

Al-Khwarizmi, early 9th cent., (Arab.) mathematician; regarded as founder of algebra.

Robert Koch, 1843-1910, (Ger.) bacteriologist; isolated bacterial causes of tuberculosis and other diseases.

Georges Köhler, 1946-95, (Ger.) immunologist; with César Milstein, developed monoclonal antibody technique.

Willem Kolff, 1911-2009, (Neth.-U.S.) physician, biomedical engineer; developed first practical kidney dialysis machine; considered the "father of artificial organs."

Jacques Lacan, 1901-81, (Fr.) influential psychoanalyst.

Joseph Lagrange, 1736-1813, (Fr.) geometer, astronomer; showed that gravity of Earth and Moon cancel, creating stable points in space around them.

Jean B. Lamarck, 1744-1829, (Fr.) naturalist; forerunner of Darwin in evolutionary theory.

Pierre Simon de Laplace, 1749-1827, (Fr.) astronomer, physicist; proposed nebular origin for solar system.

Lewis H. Latimer, 1848-1928, (U.S.) African American scientist; associate of Edison; supervised installation of first electric street lighting in New York City.

Antoine Lavoisier, 1743-94, (Fr.) a founder of modern chemistry.

Ernest O. Lawrence, 1901-58, (U.S.) physicist; invented the cyclotron.

Louis, 1903-72, and **Mary Leakey**, 1913-96, (both Br.) early hominid paleoanthropologists; discovered remains in Africa.

Anton van Leeuwenhoek, 1632-1723, (Neth.) founder of microscopy.

Jerome Lejeune, 1927-94, (Fr.) geneticist; discovered chromosomal cause of Down syndrome (1959).

Claude Levi-Strauss, 1908-2009, (Belg.-Fr.) cultural anthropologist, sociologist, philosopher.

Kurt Lewin, 1890-1947, (Ger.-U.S.) social psychologist; studied human motivation and group dynamics.

Justus von Liebig, 1803-73, (Ger.) founded quantitative organic chemistry.

Joseph Lister, 1827-1912, (Br.) physician; pioneered antiseptic surgery.

Hendrik Lorentz, 1853-1928, (Neth.) physicist; developed electron theory of matter, contributed to relativity theory.

Konrad Lorenz, 1903-89, (Austria) ethologist; pioneer in study of animal behavior.

Bernard Lovell, 1913-2012, (Br.) physicist and radio astronomer.

Percival Lowell, 1855-1916, (U.S.) astronomer; predicted the existence of Pluto.

Louis, 1864-1948, and **Auguste Lumière**, 1862-1954, (both Fr.) invented cinematograph, made first motion picture (1895).

Theodore H. Maiman, 1927-2007, (U.S.) physicist; invented the first workable laser, which he displayed in 1960.

Guglielmo Marconi, 1874-1937, (It.) physicist; developed wireless telegraphy.

John W. Mauchly, 1907-80, (U.S.) co-inventor, with J. Presper Eckert Jr., of computer ENIAC (1943-45).

James Clerk Maxwell, 1831-79, (Br.) physicist; unified electricity and magnetism, electromagnetic theory of light.

Maria Goeppert Mayer, 1906-72, (Ger.-U.S.) physicist; developed shell model of atomic nuclei.

Barbara McClintock, 1902-92, (U.S.) geneticist; showed that some genetic elements are mobile.

Lise Meitner, 1878-1968, (Austria) co-discoverer, with Otto Hahn, of nuclear fission (1938).

Gregor J. Mendel, 1822-84, (Austria) botanist, monk; his experiments became the foundation of modern genetics.

Dmitri Mendeleyev, 1834-1907, (Russ.) chemist; established Periodic Table of the Elements.

Bruce R. Merrifield, 1921-2006, (U.S.) chemist; discovered how to synthesize proteins quickly and efficiently.

Franz Mesmer, 1734-1815, (Ger.) physician; introduced hypnotherapy.

Albert A. Michelson, 1852-1931, (U.S.) physicist; invented interferometer.

Robert A. Millikan, 1868-1953, (U.S.) physicist; measured electronic charge.

Thomas Hunt Morgan, 1866-1945, (U.S.) geneticist, embryologist; established role of chromosomes in heredity.

John F. Nash Jr., 1928-2015, (U.S.) mathematician; Nobel Prize winner (1994) for work on game theory.

Isaac Newton, 1642-1727, (Br.) natural philosopher; discovered laws of gravitation, motion; with Gottfried Wilhelm von Leibniz, founded calculus.

Robert N. Noyce, 1927-90, (U.S.) invented microchip.

J. Robert Oppenheimer, 1904-67, (U.S.) physicist; scientific director of Manhattan Project.

Wilhelm Ostwald, 1853-1932, (Ger.) chemist, philosopher; main founder of modern physical chemistry.

Louis Pasteur, 1822-95, (Fr.) chemist; showed that germs cause disease and fermentation; originated pasteurization.

Linus C. Pauling, 1901-94, (U.S.) chemist; studied chemical bonds; campaigned for nuclear disarmament.

Jean Piaget, 1896-1980, (Switz.) psychologist; four-stage theory of intellectual development in children.

Max Planck, 1858-1947, (Ger.) physicist; introduced quantum hypothesis (1900).

Jules Henri Poincaré, 1854-1912, (Fr.) mathematician; founded algebraic topology, many other discoveries.

Walter S. Reed, 1851-1902, (U.S.) Army physician; proved mosquitoes transmit yellow fever.

Theodor Reik, 1888-1969, (Austria-U.S.) psychoanalyst; major Freudian disciple.

Sally Ride, 1951-2012, (U.S.) astronaut, 1st U.S. woman in space.

Bernhard Riemann, 1826-66, (Ger.) mathematician; developed non-Euclidean geometry used by Einstein.

Norbert Rillieux, 1806-94, (U.S.) African American inventor of a vacuum pan evaporator (1846); revolutionized sugar-refining industry.

Wilhelm Roentgen, 1845-1923, (Ger.) physicist; discovered X-rays (1895).

Carl Rogers, 1902-87, (U.S.) psychotherapist, author; originated nondirective therapy.

Ernest Rutherford, 1871-1937, (Br.) physicist; pioneer investigator of radioactivity, identified the atomic nucleus.

Albert B. Sabin, 1906-93, (Russ.-U.S.) developed oral polio live-virus vaccine.

Carl Sagan, 1934-96, (U.S.) astronomer, author.

Jonas Salk, 1914-95, (U.S.) developed first successful polio vaccine, widely used in U.S. after 1955.

Allan Sandage, 1926-2010, (U.S.) astronomer; refined the Hubble Constant, a measure of the universe's expansion.

Frederick Sanger, 1918-2013, (Br.) biochemist; detailed molecular structure of insulin.

Giovanni Schiaparelli, 1835-1910, (It.) astronomer; reported canals on Mars.

Erwin Schrödinger, 1887-1961, (Austria) physicist; developed wave equation for quantum systems.

Glenn T. Seaborg, 1912-99, (U.S.) chemist; Nobel Prize winner (1951); co-discoverer of plutonium.

Harlow Shapley, 1885-1972, (U.S.) astronomer; mapped galactic clusters and position of Sun in our galaxy.

Norman E. Shumway, 1923-2006, (U.S.) surgeon; performed world's first successful heart-lung transplant.

B. F. Skinner, 1904-90, (U.S.) psychologist; leading advocate of behaviorism.

Richard E. Smalley, 1943-2005, (U.S.) chemist; with three other scientists, discovered buckminsterfullerenes, a previously unknown class of carbon molecules.

Roger W. Sperry, 1913-94, (U.S.) neurobiologist; established different functions of right and left sides of brain.

Benjamin Spock, 1903-98, (U.S.) pediatrician, child care expert; *Common Sense Book of Baby and Child Care*.

Charles P. Steinmetz, 1865-1923, (Ger.-U.S.) electrical engineer; developed basic ideas on alternating current.

Ernst Stuhlinger, 1913-2008, (Ger.) rocket scientist; electric propulsion for NASA in early space age.

Leo Szilard, 1898-1964, (Hung.-U.S.) physicist; helped on Manhattan Project, later opposed nuclear weapons.

Edward Teller, 1908-2003, (Hung.-U.S.) physicist; aided on Manhattan Project, had key role in development of H-bomb.

Nikola Tesla, 1856-1943, (Serb.-U.S.) invented electrical devices including AC dynamos, transformers, and motors.

William Thomson (Lord Kelvin), 1824-1907, (Br.) physicist; aided in success of transatlantic telegraph cable (1865); proposed Kelvin absolute temperature scale.

Alan Turing, 1912-54, (Br.) mathematician; helped develop basis for computers.

James Van Allen, 1914-2006, (U.S.) physicist; discovered the presence of radiation belts around Earth (Van Allen belts).

Rudolf Virchow, 1821-1902, (Ger.) pathologist; pioneered the modern theory that diseases affect the body through cells.

Alessandro Volta, 1745-1827, (It.) physicist; electricity pioneer.

Wernher von Braun, 1912-77, (Ger.-U.S.) developed rockets for warfare and space exploration.

John von Neumann, 1903-57, (Hung.-U.S.) mathematician; originated game theory; basic design for modern computers.

Alfred Russell Wallace, 1823-1913, (Br.) naturalist; proposed concept of evolution independently of Darwin.

John B. Watson, 1878-1958, (U.S.) psychologist; a founder of behaviorism.

James E. Watt, 1736-1819, (Br.) mechanical engineer, inventor; invented modern steam engine (1765).

Alfred L. Wegener, 1880-1930, (Ger.) meteorologist, geophysicist; postulated continental drift.

Norbert Wiener, 1894-1964, (U.S.) mathematician; founder of cybernetics.

Daniel Hale Williams, 1858-1931, (U.S.) African American surgeon; performed one of first two open-heart operations (1893).

Sewall Wright, 1889-1988, (U.S.) evolutionary theorist; helped found population genetics.

Wilhelm Wundt, 1832-1920, (Ger.) founder of experimental psychology.

Qian Xuesen, 1911-2009, (China) rocket scientist; helped found Jet Propulsion Lab, father of China's space program.

Rosalyn Yalow, 1921-2011, (U.S.) physicist; co-developer of radioimmunoassay.

Ferdinand von Zeppelin, 1838-1917, (Ger.) soldier, aeronaut, airship designer.

Social Reformers, Activists, and Humanitarians of the Past

Ralph David Abernathy, 1926-90, (U.S.) black civil rights activist; pres., 1968, Southern Christian Leadership Conf.

Jane Addams, 1860-1935, (U.S.) cofounder of Hull House; won Nobel Peace Prize, 1931.

Susan B. Anthony, 1820-1906, (U.S.) a leader in temperance, antislavery, and woman suffrage movements.

Thomas Barnardo, 1845-1905, (Br.) social reformer; pioneer in care of destitute children.

Clara Barton, 1821-1912, (U.S.) organized American Red Cross.

Daisy Bates, 1914-99, (U.S.) black civil rights leader who fought for integration; advocate for the "Little Rock 9" during Arkansas desegregation crisis in 1957.

Henry Ward Beecher, 1813-87, (U.S.) clergyman, abolitionist.

Peter Benenson, 1921-2005, (Br.) activist; founded Amnesty International, 1961.

Mary McLeod Bethune, 1875-1955, (U.S.) black educator, civil rights activist; adviser to FDR and Truman; founder, pres., Bethune-Cookman College.

Elizabeth Blackwell, 1821-1910, (Br.) first female physician in the U.S.

Amelia Bloomer, 1818-94, (U.S.) suffragette, social reformer.

Julian Bond, 1940-2015, (U.S.) civil rights leader, NAACP chair, 1998-2015.

Yelena Bonner, 1923-2011, (Russ.) human rights activist in former Soviet Union.

William Booth, 1829-1912, (Br.) founded Salvation Army.

James Brady, 1940-2014, (U.S.) gun control advocate; Reagan press sec.

John Brown, 1800-59, (U.S.) abolitionist who led murder of five pro-slavery men; hanged.

Frances Xavier (Mother) Cabrini, 1850-1917, (It.-U.S.) nun; founded charitable institutions; first American canonized as a saint, 1946.

Stokely Carmichael (Kwame Ture), 1941-98, (Trinidad-U.S.) black power activist; major proponent of Pan-Africanism; prime min. of Black Panthers.

Carrie Chapman Catt, 1859-1947, (U.S.) suffragette.

Cesar Chavez, 1927-93, (U.S.) labor leader; helped establish United Farm Workers of America.

Eldridge Cleaver, 1935-98, (U.S.) revolutionary social critic; former minister of information for Black Panthers; *Soul on Ice.*

Clarence Darrow, 1857-1938, (U.S.) lawyer; defender of underdog, opponent of capital punishment.

Ossie Davis, 1917-2005, (U.S.) black civil rights activist, actor, director.

Dorothy Day, 1897-1980, (U.S.) founder of Catholic Worker movement.

Eugene V. Debs, 1855-1926, (U.S.) labor leader; led Pullman Strike, 1894; fourtime Socialist presidential candidate.

Vine Deloria Jr., 1933-2005, (U.S.) Native American activist, author; *Custer Died for Your Sins.*

Dorothea Dix, 1802-87, (U.S.) crusader for mentally ill.

Thomas Dooley, 1927-61, (U.S.) "jungle doctor"; noted for efforts to supply medical aid to developing countries.

Marjory Stoneman Douglas, 1890-1998, (U.S.) writer, environmentalist; campaigned to save Florida Everglades.

Frederick Douglass, 1817-95, (U.S.) slave, author, editor, orator, diplomat; edited abolitionist weekly *The North Star.*

Andrea Dworkin, 1946-2005, (U.S.) radical feminist, antipornography crusader.

Medgar Evers, 1925-63, (U.S.) black civil rights leader; campaigned to register black voters; assassinated.

James Farmer, 1920-99, (U.S.) black civil rights leader; founded Congress of Racial Equality (CORE).

Betty Friedan, 1921-2006, (U.S.) author, feminist; *The Feminine Mystique.*

Millard Fuller, 1935-2009, (U.S.) founder of Habitat for Humanity.

William Lloyd Garrison, 1805-79, (U.S.) abolitionist.

Miep Gies, 1909-2010, (Neth.) protector of Anne Frank and her family during WWII.

Emma Goldman, 1869-1940, (Russ.-U.S.) published anarchist *Mother Earth*; birth-control advocate.

Samuel Gompers, 1850-1924, (U.S.) labor leader; first pres. of the American Federation of Labor (AFL).

Juliette Gordon Low, 1860-1927, (U.S.) Girl Scouts founder.

Prince Hall, 1735-1807, (U.S.) activist; founded black Freemasonry; served in American Revolutionary War.

Michael Harrington, 1928-89, (U.S.) exposed poverty in affluent U.S. in *The Other America,* 1963.

Dorothy Height, 1912-2010, (U.S.) civil rights activist; pres. of the National Council of Negro Women, 1957-97.

Sidney Hillman, 1887-1946, (U.S.) labor leader; helped organize CIO.

Benjamin Hooks, 1925-2010, (U.S.) civil rights activist; exec. dir. NAACP, 1977-92.

Samuel G. Howe, 1801-76, (U.S.) social reformer; changed public attitudes toward the blind, deaf, mentally challenged.

Franklin Kameny, 1925-2011, (U.S.) gay rights activist.

Helen Keller, 1880-1968, (U.S.) crusader for better treatment for the disabled; deaf and blind herself.

Jack Kevorkian, 1928-2011, (U.S.) pathologist; assisted-suicide activist.

Coretta Scott King, 1927-2006, (U.S.) black civil rights leader; wife of Rev. Martin Luther King Jr.

Rev. Martin Luther King Jr., 1929-68, (U.S.) civil rights leader; led 1955-56 Montgomery, AL, boycott; founder, pres., Southern Christian Leadership Conference, 1957; Nobel peace laureate, 1964; assassinated.

Maggie Kuhn, 1905-95, (U.S.) founded Gray Panthers, 1970.

William Kunstler, 1919-95, (U.S.) civil liberties attorney.

John L. Lewis, 1880-1969, (U.S.) labor leader; headed United Mine Workers, 1920-60.

Belva Lockwood, 1830-1917, (U.S.) lawyer; first woman to argue before U.S. Supreme Court.

Almena Lomax, 1915-2011, (U.S.) civil rights activist; journalist who founded *The Los Angeles Tribune.*

Clara Luper, 1923-2011, (U.S.) civil rights activist.

Wangari Maathai, 1940-2011, (Kenya), environmental activist; 2004 Nobel Peace Prize winner.

Robert Macauley, 1923-2010, (U.S.) founder of AmeriCares.

Malcolm X (Little), 1925-65, (U.S.) Black Muslim, black nationalist leader; promoted black pride; assassinated.

Russell Means, 1939-2012, (U.S.) American Indian activist.

Karl Menninger, 1893-1990, (U.S.) with brother William, founded Menninger Clinic and Menninger Foundation.

Lucretia Mott, 1793-1880, (U.S.) reformer, pioneer feminist.

Philip Murray, 1886-1952, (U.S.) Scottish-born labor leader.

Huey P. Newton, 1942-89, (U.S.) cofounded Black Panther Party, 1966.

Florence Nightingale, 1820-1910, (Br.) founder of modern nursing.

Emmeline Pankhurst, 1858-1928, (Br.) suffragette.

Rosa Parks,1913-2005, (U.S.) black civil rights activist; her actions sparked 1955-56 Montgomery, AL, bus boycott.

A. Philip Randolph, 1889-1979, (U.S.) organized Brotherhood of Sleeping Car Porters, 1925; an organizer of 1941 and 1963 March on Washington movements.

Walter Reuther, 1907-70, (U.S.) labor leader; headed United Auto Workers.

Jacob Riis, 1849-1914, (U.S.) crusader for urban reforms.

Paul Robeson, 1898-1976, (U.S.) actor, singer, black civil rights activist.

Bayard Rustin, 1910-87, (U.S.) an organizer of the 1963 March on Washington; exec. dir., A. Philip Randolph Institute.

Margaret Sanger, 1883-1966, (U.S.) social reformer; pioneered the birth-control movement.

Phyllis Schlafly, 1924-2016, (U.S.) anti-Equal Rights Amendment activist.

Earl of Shaftesbury (A. A. Cooper), 1801-85, (Br.) social reformer.

Eunice Kennedy Shriver, 1921-2009, (U.S.) cofounder of Special Olympics for mentally challenged athletes.

Sargent Shriver, 1915-2011, (U.S.) founding director of Peace Corps; founder of Job Corps, Head Start.

Fred Shuttlesworth, 1922-2011, (U.S.) civil rights activist.

Albertina Sisulu, 1918-2011, (S. Africa), anti-apartheid activist.

Elizabeth Cady Stanton, 1815-1902, (U.S.) woman suffrage pioneer.

Lucy Stone, 1818-93, (U.S.) feminist, abolitionist.

Mother Teresa of Calcutta, 1910-97, (Alban.) nun; founded order to care for sick, dying poor; 1979 Nobel Peace Prize; canonized 2016.

Willard Townsend, 1895-1957, (U.S.) organized the United Transport Service Employees (Red Caps), 1935.

Sojourner Truth (Isabella Baumfree), 1797-1883, (U.S.) preacher, abolitionist; worked for black educ. opportunity.

Harriet Tubman, 1823-1913, (U.S.) prominent figure in the Underground Railroad; nurse, spy for Union Army in the Civil War.

Nat Turner, 1800-31, (U.S.) slave who led the most significant of more than 200 slave revolts in U.S., in Southampton, VA; hanged.

Philip Vera Cruz, 1905-94, (Philip.-U.S.) helped found the United Farm Workers Union.

Edgar Wayburn, 1906-2010, (U.S.) conservationist; Sierra Club pres.

Elie Wiesel, 1928-2016, (Rom.-U.S.) Holocaust survivor, author, and activist; 1986 Nobel Peace Prize.

William Wilberforce, 1759-1833, (Br.) social reformer; prominent in struggle to abolish slave trade.

Frances E. Willard, 1839-98, (U.S.) temperance, women's rights leader.

Mary Wollstonecraft, 1759-97, (Br.) *Vindication of the Rights of Women.*

Victoria Woodhull, 1838-1927, (U.S.) suffragist, first woman to run for president (1872).

Sports Personalities of the Past and Present

Henry (Hank) Aaron, b 1934, Milwaukee-Atlanta outfielder; hit record 755 home runs, led NL 4 times; record 2,297 RBI.

Kareem Abdul-Jabbar, b 1947, Milwaukee, L.A. Lakers center; MVP 6 times; all-time leading NBA scorer, 38,387 pts.

Andre Agassi, b 1970, tennis player; won Wimbledon (1992); U.S. Open ('94, '99), Austral. Open ('95, 2000-01, '03), French Open ('99).

Troy Aikman, b 1966, quarterback; led Dallas Cowboys to Super Bowl wins in 1993-94, '96; Super Bowl MVP, 1993.

Ben Ainslie, b 1977, (Br.) most decorated Olympic sailor; gold, 2000, '04, '08, '12. silver, 1996.

Michelle Akers, b 1966, soccer player; led U.S. to victory in World Cup (1991, '99).

Amy Alcott, b 1956, golfer; 33 career wins (5 majors); inducted into Hall of Fame, 1999.

Grover Cleveland "Pete" Alexander, 1887-1950, pitcher; won 373 NL games; pitched 16 shutouts, 1916.

Muhammad Ali, 1942-2016, 3-time heavyweight champion, activist.

Fernando Alonso, b 1981, (Sp.) Formula 1 racer; youngest ever to win a World Grand Prix championship, 2005; defended title, 2006.

Morten Andersen, b 1960, (Den.) kicker; NFL's career points leader, with 2,544 (1982-2007).

Gary Anderson, b 1959, (S. Afr.) kicker; NFL's 2nd in career points, with 2,434.

Sparky Anderson, 1934-2010, first manager to win World Series in the NL (Cincinnati, 1975-76) and AL (Detroit, 1984).

Mario Andretti, b 1940, (It.) race-car driver; won Daytona 500 (1967), Indy 500 (1969); Formula 1 world title (1978).

Earl Anthony, 1938-2001, bowler; won record 6 PBA Championships (1973-75, '81-'83), 43 career PBA tournaments.

Eddie Arcaro, 1916-97, only jockey to win racing's Triple Crown twice, 1941, '48; rode to 4,779 wins in his career.

Lance Armstrong, b 1971, cyclist; record 7-time winner of Tour de France (1999-2005); stripped of victories in 2012 for use of performance-enhancing drugs.

Arthur Ashe, 1943-93, tennis player; won U.S. Open (1968); Wimbledon (1975).

Evelyn Ashford, b 1957, sprinter; won 100m gold (1984) and silver (1988); member of 5 U.S. Olympic teams.

Red Auerbach, 1917-2006, coached Boston to 9 NBA titles.

Geno Auriemma, b 1954, (It.) UConn women's basketball coach; record-holder for number of NCAA basketball titles.

Tracy Austin, b 1962, tennis player; youngest to win U.S. Open (age 16 in 1979).

Victoria Azarenka, b 1989, (Belarus) tennis player; won Austral. Open (2012-13).

Ernie Banks, 1931-2015, Chicago Cubs slugger; hit 512 NL homers; twice MVP.

Roger Bannister, b 1929, (Br.) physician; ran 1st sub-4-min. mile, May 6, 1954 (3 min., 59.4 sec.).

Charles Barkley, b 1963, NBA MVP, 1993; 4th player ever to surpass 20,000 pts., 10,000 rebounds, 4,000 assists.

Rick Barry, b 1944, NBA scoring leader, 1967; ABA scoring leader, 1969.

Sammy Baugh, 1914-2008, Washington Redskins quarterback; held numerous records upon retirement after 16 seasons.

Elgin Baylor, b 1934, L.A. Lakers forward; 11-time all-star.

Bob Beamon, b 1946, Olympic long jump gold medalist, 1968; world record jump of 29 ft 2½ in. stood until 1991.

Boris Becker, b 1967, (Ger.) tennis star; won U.S. Open 1989; Wimbledon champ 1985-86, '89.

David Beckham, b 1975, (Br.) soccer star; joined L.A. Galaxy, 2007-12, with record-breaking $250-mil contract.

Bill Belichick, b 1952, NFL coach; led New England Patriots to 4 Super Bowl wins (2001, '03-'04, '14); best all-time post-season coaching record.

Jean Béliveau, 1931-2014, (Can.) Montréal Canadiens center; scored 507 goals; twice MVP.

Johnny Bench, b 1947, Cincinnati Reds catcher; twice MVP; led league in home runs twice, RBIs 3 times.

Patty Berg, 1918-2006, 80+ golf tournament wins; AP Woman Athlete of the Year 3 times.

Chris Berman, b 1955, sportscaster, anchor for ESPN and ABC Sports.

Yogi Berra, 1925-2015, Yankee catcher (1946-63); 3-time MVP.

Abebe Bikila, 1932-73, (Eth.) runner; won consecutive Olympic marathon gold medals in 1960 (barefoot), '64.

Simone Biles, b 1997, gymnast; won 3 Olympic gold medals, including all-around and team (2016).

Matt Biondi, b 1965, swimmer; won 5 golds, 1988 Olympics.

Larry Bird, b 1956, Boston Celtics forward (1979-92); NBA MVP, 1984-86; 1998 coach of the year with Indiana Pacers.

Bonnie Blair, b 1964, speed skater; won 5 individual gold medals in 3 Olympics (1988, '92, '94).

George Blanda, 1927-2010, quarterback, kicker; 26 years as active player, scored 2,002 career points.

Fanny Blankers-Koen, 1918-2004, (Neth.) track star; won 4 golds in 1948 Olympics.

Wade Boggs, b 1958, AL batting champ, 1983, '85-'88; reached 3,000 career hits, 1999 (3,010).

Usain Bolt, b 1986, (Jam.) Olympic sprinter, gold medalist, 2008, '12, '16; world record for men's 100-m, 200-m runs.

Barry Bonds, b 1964, outfielder; hit record 73 homers, 2001; NL MVP, 1990, '92-'93, 2001-04; 1st all-time in HRs (762); indicted in steroid scandal, 2007.

Björn Borg, b 1956, (Swed.) led Sweden to first Davis Cup, 1975; 6-time French Open, 5-time Wimbledon champion.

Ray Bourque, b 1960, (Can.) Boston defenseman,1979-2000; 5-time Norris Trophy winner; won Stanley Cup with Colorado, 2001.

Bill Bradley, b 1943, All-American at Princeton; led NY Knicks to 2 NBA titles (1970, '73); U.S. senator, 1979-97.

Donald Bradman, 1908-2001, (Austral.) widely regarded as greatest cricketer ever; set several batting records.

Terry Bradshaw, b 1948, quarterback; led Pittsburgh to 4 Super Bowl wins, 1975-76, '79-'80; NFL MVP, 1978.

Tom Brady, b 1977, quarterback; led New England to 4 Super Bowl titles, 2002, '04-'05, '15; Super Bowl MVP, 2002, '04, '15; NFL MVP, 2007, '10.

Drew Brees, b 1979, New Orleans Saints quarterback; Super Bowl MVP, 2010.

Christine Brennan, b 1958, sports journalist for *USA Today*, radio and TV commentator specializing in figure skating.

George Brett, b 1953, Kansas City Royals infielder; led AL in batting, 1976, '80, '90; MVP, 1980.

Lou Brock, b 1939, St. Louis Cardinals outfielder; stole NL single-season record 118 bases, 1974; led NL 8 times.

Jim Brown, b 1936, Cleveland fullback; 12,312 career yds; NFL MVP 1957-58, '65.

Paul Brown, 1908-91, football team owner, coach; led eponymous Cleveland Browns to 3 NFL championships.

Bob Bryan and **Mike Bryan**, b 1978, doubles tennis players; won 16 Grand Slam doubles titles (2003-14); Olympic gold, 2012.

Kobe Bryant, b 1978, NBA guard; won 3 titles with Lakers (2000-02); leading NBA scorer, 2006, '07; NBA MVP, 2008; NBA Finals MVP, 2010; Olympic gold medal winner (2008, '12).

Paul "Bear" Bryant, 1913-83, college football coach with 323 wins; led Alabama to 6 national titles (1961, '64-'65, '73, '78-'79).

Sergei Bubka, b 1963, (Ukr.) pole vaulter; first to clear 20 ft; gold medal, 1988 Olympics.

Don Budge, 1915-2000, won numerous amateur and pro tennis titles; Grand Slam, 1938.

Reggie Bush, b 1985, NFL running back; helped USC to 2 national titles (2003-04; '04 vacated).

Dick Butkus, b 1942, Chicago Bears linebacker; NFL defensive player of the year (1969-70).

Dick Button, b 1929, figure skater; won 1948, '52 Olympic gold medals; world titleholder, 1948-52.

Miguel Cabrera, b 1983, (Venez.) 9-time All-Star; won AL triple crown (2012); AL MVP 2013.

Walter Camp, 1859-1925, Yale football player, coach, athletic director; established many rules for modern football.

Roy Campanella, 1921-93, Hall of Fame catcher for the Brooklyn Dodgers (1948-57); 3-time NL MVP.

Earl Campbell, b 1955, NFL running back; MVP 1978-79.

Jose Canseco, b 1964, outfielder; led Oakland A's to the World Series, 1988; wrote book about steroids in baseball, 2005.

Eric Cantona, b 1966, (Fr.) soccer star; Manchester United (1992-97).

Rod Carew, b 1945, AL infielder; 7 batting titles, 1977 MVP.

Steve Carlton, b 1944, NL pitcher; won 20 games 6 times, Cy Young winner 4 times; 4,136 career strikeouts.

Pete Carroll, b 1951, football coach; NCAA champion (2003, '04); won Super Bowl XLIX.

Billy Casper, 1931-2015, PGA Player of the Year 2 times; U.S. Open champ twice.

Tamika Catchings, b 1979, Indiana Fever forward; 4-time Olympic gold medalist; WNBA MVP, 2011.

Tracy Caulkins, b 1963, swimmer; 3-time Olympic gold medalist.

Wilt Chamberlain, 1936-99, center; 7-time NBA leading scorer, 4-time MVP; scored 100 pts. in a game, 1962.

Bobby Clarke, b 1949, (Can.) Philadelphia Flyers center; led team to 2 Stanley Cup championships; MVP 3 times.

Roger Clemens, b 1962, pitcher; 1986 AL MVP; only 7-time Cy Young winner (1986-87, '91, '97-'98, 2001, '04); twice recorded record 20 Ks in a game; 354 wins, 4,672 Ks (3rd all-time); accused of lying to Congress about steroids, 2010.

Roberto Clemente, 1934-72, Pittsburgh Pirates outfielder; won 4 batting titles; MVP, 1966; 3,000 career hits; killed in plane crash.

Kim Clijsters, b 1983, (Belg.) tennis player; U.S. Open winner (2005, '09-'10); Austral. Open (2011).

Ty Cobb, 1886-1961, Detroit Tigers outfielder; record .367 lifetime batting average, 12 batting titles.

Sebastian Coe, b 1956, (Br.) runner; won Olympic 1,500m gold medal and 800m silver medal in both 1980, '84.

Nadia Comaneci, b 1961, (Rom.) gymnast; won 3 gold medals, achieved 7 perfect scores, 1976 Olympics; 9 Olympic medals overall.

Maureen Connolly, 1934-69, won tennis Grand Slam, 1953; AP Woman Athlete of the Year 3 times.

Jimmy Connors, b 1952, tennis player; 8 Grand Slam singles titles.

Alberto Contador, b 1982, (Sp.) cyclist; won Tour de France 2007, '09; stripped of 2010 title because of doping offense.

Cynthia Cooper, b 1963, basketball; 4-time MVP of WNBA finals; 2-time league MVP for the Houston Comets.

James J. Corbett, 1866-1933, heavyweight champion, 1892-97; credited with being the first "scientific" boxer.

Angel Cordero Jr., b 1942, jockey; leading money winner, 1976, '82-'83; rode 3 Kentucky Derby winners.

Margaret Smith Court, b 1942, (Austral.) tennis great; won 24 Grand Slam events.

Bob Cousy, b 1928, Boston guard; 6 NBA titles, 1957 MVP.

Sidney Crosby, b 1987, (Can.) hockey player; Art Ross, Hart Trophies (2007, '14), Olympic gold medal (2010, '14).

Mark Cuban, b 1958, Dallas Mavericks owner; known for outspokenness.

Stephen Curry, b 1988, NBA point guard; NBA MVP, 2015, '16.

Bjoern Daehlie, b 1967, (Nor.) cross-country skier; won record 8 Winter Olympic gold medals.

Lindsay Davenport, b 1976, tennis player; won Olympic gold, 1996; U.S. Open, 1998; Wimbledon, 1999; Austral. Open, 2000.

Al Davis, 1929-2011, Oakland Raiders owner, former coach.

Oscar De La Hoya, b 1973, won IBF lightweight (1995); WBC super lightweight (1996); welterweight (1997-99, 2000) titles.

Donna de Varona, b 1947, swimmer; won 2 Olympic golds, 1964; 1st female sportscaster at a major network, 1965.

Dizzy Dean, 1910-74, pitcher; St. Louis Cardinals' "Gashouse Gang" in the '30s.

Mary Decker Slaney, b 1958, runner; has held 6 separate American records from the 800m to 10,000m.

Frank Deford, b 1938, sr. contributing writer for *Sports Illustrated*; author, commentator.

Jack Dempsey, 1895-1983, heavyweight champ, 1919-26.

Gail Devers, b 1966, Olympic 100m gold medalist (1992, '96).

Joe DiMaggio, 1914-99, NY Yankees outfielder; hit safely in record 56 consecutive games, 1941; AL MVP 3 times.

Novak Djokovic, b 1987, (Serb.) tennis player; 12 Grand Slam singles titles.

Landon Donovan, b 1982, soccer forward; all-time leading U.S. men's intl. goal scorer with 57; MLS MVP, 2009.

Tony Dorsett, b 1954, Heisman winner who led the Dallas Cowboys to an NFL title in his rookie year, 1977.

Gabrielle Douglas, b 1995, gymnast; Olympic gold in all-around (2012), team (2012, '16).

Tim Duncan, b 1976, San Antonio center; 3-time NBA Finals MVP, 1999, 2003, '05; NBA MVP, 2002, '03.

duPont, Margaret Osborne, 1918-2012, tennis player; 6-time Grand Slam singles champion.

Roberto Duran, b 1951, (Pan.) boxer; held titles at 3 weights; lost 1980 "no mas" fight to Sugar Ray Leonard.

Kevin Durant, b 1988, NBA forward; NBA MVP, 2014; Olympic gold medalist, 2012, '16.

Leo Durocher, 1905-91, manager; won 3 NL pennants (Brooklyn, 1941; NY Giants, 1951, '54), 1954 World Series.

Dale Earnhardt Jr., b 1974, stock car racer; Daytona 500 winner (2004, '14).

Dale Earnhardt Sr., 1951-2001, 7-time NASCAR Winston Cup champ; died in a last-lap crash at 2001 Daytona 500.

Ashton Eaton, b 1988, Olympic decathlon gold medalist, 2012, '16.

Stefan Edberg, b 1966, (Swed.) tennis player; U.S. Open (1991-92), Wimbledon (1988, '90), Austral. Open (1985, '87).

Gertrude Ederle, 1905-2003, first woman to swim English Channel; broke existing men's record, 1926.

Teresa Edwards, b 1964, 5-time basketball Olympian; gold medalist, 1984, '88, '96, 2000; bronze medalist, 1992.

Hicham El Guerrouj, b 1974, (Morocco) runner; holds world records in mile (3:43.13) and 1,500m (3:26); won gold medals in 1,500m and 5,000m, 2004 Olympics.

John Elway, b 1960, quarterback; led Denver Broncos to 2 Super Bowl wins, 1998-99; NFL MVP, 1987; Super Bowl MVP, 1999.

Roy Emerson, b 1936 (Austral.), tennis player; 12-time Grand Slam singles and 16-time Grand Slam doubles champion.

Julius "Dr. J" Erving, b 1950, 3-time ABA MVP, 1981 NBA MVP.

Phil Esposito, b 1942, (Can.) NHL scoring leader 5 times.

Janet Evans, b 1971, 4 Olympic swimming golds, 1988, '92.

Lee Evans, b 1947, Olympic 400m gold medalist in 1968 with 43.86-sec. world record not broken until 1988.

Chris Evert, b 1954, 6-time U.S. Open tennis champ, 3-time Wimbledon champ.

Ray Ewry, 1873-1937, track-and-field star; won 8 Olympic gold medals (1900, '04, '08).

Nick Faldo, b 1957, (Br.) golfer; won Masters, British Open 3 times each.

Juan Manuel Fangio, 1911-95 (Arg.), 5-time World Grand Prix driving champ (1951, '54-'57).

Marshall Faulk, b 1973, 2000 NFL MVP; scored then-record 26 TDs, 2001; 3-time Off. Player of the Year (1999-2001).

Brett Favre, b 1969, quarterback; led Green Bay to Super Bowl win, 1997; NFL MVP, 1995-97.

Roger Federer, b 1981, (Switz.) tennis player; 17 Grand Slam singles titles (1st all-time).

Bob Feller, 1918-2010, Cleveland Indians pitcher; won 266 games; pitched 3 no-hitters, 12 one-hitters.

Rollie Fingers, b 1946, pitcher; 341 career saves; AL MVP, Cy Young, 1981; World Series MVP, 1974.

Peggy Fleming, b 1948, world figure skating champion, 1966-68; gold medalist, 1968 Olympics.

Whitey Ford, b 1928, NY Yankees pitcher; won record 10 World Series games.

George Foreman, b 1949, heavyweight champion, 1973-74, '94-'95; at 45, oldest to win a heavyweight title; gold medalist, 1968 Olympics.

Dick Fosbury, b 1947, high jumper; won 1968 Olympic gold medal; developed the "Fosbury Flop."

Jimmie Foxx, 1907-67, Red Sox, Athletics slugger; MVP 3 times; triple crown, 1933.

A. J. Foyt, b 1935, won Indy 500 4 times; U.S. Auto Club champ 7 times.

Dario Franchitti, b 1973, (Scot.) 3-time Indy 500 winner, 2007, '10, '12.

Missy Franklin, b 1995, swimmer; 5-time Olympic gold medalist (2012, '16).

Joe Frazier, 1944-2011, heavyweight champion, 1970-73; gold medalist, 1964 Olympics.

Walt Frazier, b 1945, Hall of Fame guard for NY Knicks' NBA championship teams (1970, '73).

Chris Froome, b 1985, (Kenya) 3-time Tour de France winner (2013, '15, '16).

Peter Gammons, b 1945, sportswriter, broadcaster; named to Baseball Hall of Fame.

Lou Gehrig, 1903-41, NY Yankees 1st baseman; MVP, 1927, '36; triple crown, 1934; AL record 184 RBIs, 1931; played in 2,130 straight games (1925-39), a record that stood until 1995.

Althea Gibson, 1927-2003, 2-time U.S. Nationals and Wimbledon champ.

Bob Gibson, b 1935, St. Louis Cardinals pitcher; won Cy Young twice; struck out 3,117 batters.

Josh Gibson, 1911-47, Hall of Fame catcher; known as "Babe Ruth of the Negro Leagues"; credited with as many as 84 homers in 1 season, about 800 in his career.

Marc Girardelli, b 1963, (Lux.) skier; won 5 World Cup titles.

Raúl González, b 1977, (Sp.) soccer player; led Real Madrid to 3 Champions League titles (1998, 2000, '02).

Jeff Gordon, b 1971, race-car driver; youngest to win NASCAR title 4 times (1995, '97-'98, 2001).

Steffi Graf, b 1969, (Ger.) tennis player; 22 Grand Slam singles titles (2nd all-time).

Otto Graham, 1921-2003, Cleveland quarterback; 4-time all-pro.

Red Grange, 1903-91, All-American at Univ. of Illinois, 1923-25; played for Chicago Bears, 1925-35.

"Mean" Joe Greene, b 1946, Pittsburgh Steelers lineman; twice NFL outstanding defensive player.

Wayne Gretzky, b 1961, (Can.) top scorer in NHL history with record 894 goals, 1,963 assists, 2,857 pts.; MVP, 1980-87, '89.

Bob Griese, b 1945, All-Pro quarterback; led Miami Dolphins to 17-0 season, 1972, 2 Super Bowl titles, 1973-74.

Ken Griffey Jr., b 1969, Hall of Fame outfielder; led AL in homers 1994, '97-'99; 1997 AL MVP; 10 gold gloves.

Archie Griffin, b 1954, Ohio State running back; only 2-time winner of the Heisman Trophy (1974-75).

Florence Griffith Joyner, 1959-98, sprinter; won 3 gold medals at 1988 Olympics; world and Olympic record for 100m.

Lefty Grove, 1900-75, pitcher; won 300 AL games.

Vladimir Guerrero, b 1975, (Dom. Rep.) right fielder; 2004 AL MVP award.

Janet Guthrie, b 1938, 1st woman driver in Indy 500 (1977).

Tony Gwynn, 1960-2014, 8-time NL batting champ (1984, '87-'89, '94-'97); 3,141 career hits.

Walter Hagen, 1892-1969, golfer; 5 PGA, 4 British Open titles.

Mika Hakkinen, b 1968, (Fin.) Formula One racing driver; Formula One champion, 1998-99.

George Halas, 1895-1983, founder/player/coach of Chicago Bears; won 6 NFL championships as coach.

Roy Halladay, b 1977, pitcher; Cy Young, 2003, '10; pitched perfect game, 2010.

Dorothy Hamill, b 1956, figure skater; Olympic gold medalist, 1976.

Scott Hamilton, b 1958, U.S. and world figure skating champion, 1981-84; Olympic gold medalist, 1984.

Mia Hamm, b 1972, soccer player; led U.S. teams to World Cup victories (1991, '99) and Olympic gold (1996, 2004).

Franco Harris, b 1950, running back; 4 Super Bowls with Steelers (1975-76, '79-'80); 1,000+ yds in a season 8 times.

Marvin Harrison, b 1972, Indianapolis Colts wide receiver; NFL record for single-season receptions (143), 2002.

Bill Hartack, 1932-2007, jockey; rode 5 Kentucky Derby winners.

Dominik Hasek, b 1965, (Czech.) NHL goaltender; won Vezina Trophy, 1994-95, '97-'99, 2001; NHL MVP, 1997-98.

John Havlicek, b 1940, Boston Celtics forward; scored 26,395 career pts.

Eric Heiden, b 1958, speed skater; won 5 Olympic golds, 1980.

Rickey Henderson, b 1958, outfielder; 1990 AL MVP; record 130 stolen bases, 1982; all-time leader in steals, runs.

Sonja Henie, 1912-69, (Nor.) world champion figure skater, 1927-36; Olympic gold medalist, 1928, '32, '36.

Martina Hingis, b 1980, (Switz.) won Austral. and U.S. Opens, Wimbledon; youngest number one player (16 yrs., 6 mos.), 1997.

Ben Hogan, 1912-97, golfer; won 4 U.S. Open titles, 2 PGA Championships, 2 Masters.

Santonio Holmes, b 1984, wide receiver; Super Bowl MVP, 2009.

Evander Holyfield, b 1962, 4-time heavyweight champion.

Rogers Hornsby, 1896-1963, NL 2nd baseman; batted record .424, 1924; twice won triple crown.

Paul Hornung, b 1935, Green Bay Packers running back, placekicker; scored record 176 pts., 1960.

Gordie Howe, 1928-2016, (Can.) hockey forward; NHL MVP 6 times; scored 801 goals in 26 NHL seasons.

Carl Hubbell, 1903-88, NY Giants pitcher; 20-game winner 5 consecutive seasons, 1933-37.

Bobby Hull, b 1939, (Can.) NHL all-star 10 times; MVP, 1965-66.

Brett Hull, b 1964, (Can.) St. Louis Blues forward; led NHL in goals, 1990-92; MVP, 1991.

Catfish Hunter, 1946-99, pitched perfect game, 1968; 20-game winner 5 times.

Don Hutson, 1913-97, Packers receiver; caught 99 TD passes; 2-time NFL MVP.

Juli Inkster, b 1960, Hall of Fame golfer; won 7 career major titles.

Bo Jackson, b 1962, NFL running back (1987-90) and MLB outfielder (1986-91, '93-'94); 1985 Heisman Trophy winner.

Phil Jackson, b 1945, won 11 NBA titles as coach of Bulls and Lakers; 1970, '73 title as player with NY Knicks.

Reggie Jackson, b 1946, slugger; led AL in home runs 4 times; MVP, 1973; hit 5 World Series home runs, 1977.

"Shoeless" Joe Jackson, 1889-1951, outfielder; 3rd highest career batting average (.356); one of the "Black Sox" banned for allegedly throwing 1919 World Series.

Jaromír Jágr, b 1972, (Czech.) hockey player; NHL MVP, 1999; Art Ross Trophy (leading scorer), 1995, 1998-2001.

LeBron James, b 1984, NBA forward; Olympic gold medalist (2008, '12); NBA MVP, 2009, '10, '12, '13.

Ron Jaworski, b 1951, former NFL quarterback (1974-89); NFL analyst on ESPN.

Sally Jenkins, b 1960, sports journalist and writer for *Washington Post*.

Caitlyn (fmr. Bruce) Jenner, b 1949, Olympic decathlon gold medalist, 1976; came out as a transgender woman in 2015.

Lynn Jennings, b 1960, runner; 3-time World, 9-time U.S. cross country champ; bronze (10,000m), 1992 Olympics.

Derek Jeter, b 1974, shortstop; led NY Yankees to 5 World Series titles; World Series MVP, 2000.

Earvin "Magic" Johnson, b 1959, NBA MVP, 1987, '89, '90; playoff MVP, 1980, '82, '87; 4th in career assists.

Jack Johnson, 1878-1946, heavyweight champion, 1908-15.

Jimmie Johnson, b 1975, 5-time NASCAR Sprint Cup Series champ, 2006-10, '13; Daytona 500 winner, 2006.

Michael Johnson, b 1967, 4-time Olympic gold medalist (1992, '96, 2000); longtime world and Olympic record-holder.

Randy Johnson, b 1963, 5-time Cy Young winner; strikeout leader, 1992-95, 1999-2002, '04; 4,875 strikeouts (2nd all-time); pitched perfect game, 2004.

Walter Johnson, 1887-1946, Washington Senators pitcher; won 417 games; record 110 shutouts.

Bobby Jones, 1902-71, won golf's Grand Slam, 1930; U.S. amateur champ 5 times, U.S. Open champ 4 times.

Cobi Jones, b 1970, soccer player; most U.S. national team appearances with 164.

David "Deacon" Jones, 1938-2013, 5-time All-Pro with L.A. Rams (1965-69); "sack" specialist credited with inventing the term.

Marion Jones, b 1975, multi-event Olympic medalist; stripped of medals in 2007 after admitting use of PEDs.

Roy Jones Jr., b 1969, light heavyweight champ, 1999-2004.

Michael Jordan, b 1963, guard; leading NBA scorer, 1987-93, '96-'98; MVP, 1988, '91-'92, '96, '98; playoff MVP, 1991-93, '96-'98; ESPN Athlete of the Century.

Dorothy Kamenshek, 1925-2010, led Rockford (IL) Peaches to 4 All-American Girls Baseball League titles in the 1940s.

Jackie Joyner-Kersee, b 1962, Olympic gold medalist in heptathlon (1988, '92), long jump (1988).

Clayton Kershaw, b 1988, pitcher; NL Cy Young winner (2011, '13, '14).

Harmon Killebrew, 1936-2011, Minnesota Twins slugger; led AL in home runs 6 times; 573 lifetime.

Jean Claude Killy, b 1943, (Fr.) skier; 3 Olympic golds, 1968.

Kim Yu-na, b 1990, (S. Kor.) figure skater; Olympic medal winner (gold, 2010; silver, 2014) world champion, 2009, '13.

Ralph Kiner, 1922-2014, Pittsburgh Pirates slugger; led NL in home runs 7 consecutive years, 1946-52.

Billie Jean King, b 1943, U.S. singles champ 4 times; Wimbledon champ 6 times; beat Bobby Riggs, 1973.

Peter King, b 1957, senior writer for *Sports Illustrated*.

Bob Knight, b 1940, ESPN studio analyst, ret. basketball coach; led Indiana to NCAA men's title in 1976, '81, '87.

Olga Korbut, b 1955, (Belarus) gymnast; 4 Olympic gold medals, (1972, '76).

Sandy Koufax, b 1935, 3-time Cy Young winner; lowest ERA in NL, 1962-66; pitched 4 no-hitters, 1 perfect game.

Jack Kramer, 1921-2009, world's number one tennis player, 1946-53; first at Wimbledon to compete in shorts.

Ingrid Kristiansen, b 1956, (Nor.) only runner to have held world records in 5,000m, 10,000m, and marathon.

Julie Krone, b 1963, winningest female jockey; first woman to ride a winner in a Triple Crown race (Belmont, 1993).

Mike Krzyzewski, b 1947, basketball coach; 5 NCAA championships with Duke; led 3 Olympic gold medal teams (2008, '12, '16).

Petra Kvitová, b 1990, (Czech.) tennis player; won Wimbledon, 2011, '14.

Michelle Kwan, b 1980, figure skater; 9 U.S., 5 World titles; silver medalist at 1998 Olympics, bronze in 2002.

Guy Lafleur, b 1951, (Can.) 3-time NHL scoring leader; 1977-78 MVP.

Alexi Lalas, b 1970, soccer player; first modern-era American to play in Italian League Serie A.

Kenesaw Mountain Landis, 1866-1944, 1st commissioner of baseball (1920-44); banned the 8 "Black Sox" involved in fixing 1919 World Series.

Tom Landry, 1924-2000, Dallas Cowboys head coach, 1960-88; won 2 Super Bowls (1972, '78); 3rd in career wins (270).

Dick "Night Train" Lane, 1928-2002, Hall of Fame defensive back; intercepted an NFL season record 14 passes (1952).

Don Larsen, b 1929, as NY Yankee, pitched only World Series perfect game, Oct. 8, 1956—2-0 win over Brooklyn.

Rod Laver, b 1938, (Austral.) won tennis Grand Slam, 1962, '69; Wimbledon champ 4 times.

Katie Ledecky, b 1997, swimmer; Olympic medalist, incl. 5 gold (2012, '16).

Mario Lemieux, b 1965, (Can.) 6-time NHL leading scorer; MVP, 1988, '93, '96; playoff MVP, 1991-92.

Greg Lemond, b 1961, cyclist; 3-time Tour de France winner (1986, '89-'90); first American to win the event.

Ivan Lendl, b 1960, (Czech.) 8 Grand Slam tennis titles, including U.S. Open, 1985-87.

Sugar Ray Leonard, b 1956, boxer; held titles in 5 different weight classes.

Lisa Leslie, b 1972, L.A. Sparks center; 3-time WNBA MVP (2001, '04, '06).

Carl Lewis, b 1961, track-and-field star; won 9 Olympic gold medals in sprinting and long jump.

Lennox Lewis, b 1965, (Br.) heavyweight champ, 1994, 1997-2004; Olympic gold medalist, 1998.

Ray Lewis, b 1975, linebacker for the Baltimore Ravens; Super Bowl MVP, 2001.

Li Na, b 1982, (China) tennis player; won French Open, 2011, Austral. Open 2014.

Tim Lincecum, b 1984, pitcher; NL Cy Young winner, 2008-09.

Tara Lipinski, b 1982, youngest figure skater to win U.S., world championships, 1997, and Winter Olympic gold, 1998.

Carli Lloyd, b 1982, soccer midfielder; Olympic gold medalist (2008, '12); World Cup champion (2015).

Ryan Lochte, b 1984, swimmer; 12-time Olympic medalist, incl. 6 gold (2004, '08, '12, '16).

Vince Lombardi, 1913-70, Green Bay Packers coach; led team to 5 NFL championships, 2 Super Bowl victories.

Nancy Lopez, b 1957, Hall of Fame golfer; 4-time LPGA Player of the Year, 3-time winner of the LPGA Championship.

Greg Louganis, b 1960, won Olympic gold medals in both springboard and platform diving, 1984, '88.

Joe Louis, 1914-81, heavyweight champion, 1937-49.

Sid Luckman, 1916-98, Chicago Bears quarterback; led team to 4 NFL championships; MVP, 1943.

Evan Lysacek, b 1985, figure skater; world champion, 2009; Olympic gold winner, 2010.

Connie Mack, 1862-1956, Philadelphia Athletics manager, 1901-50; won 9 pennants, 5 championships.

John Madden, b 1936, won Super Bowl as coach of Oakland Raiders (1977); former NFL TV analyst.

Greg Maddux, b 1966, Hall of Fame pitcher; won 4 Cy Young awards, 1992-95; 355 career wins.

Karl Malone, b 1963, Utah Jazz, L.A. Lakers forward; MVP, 1997, '99; 14-time All-Star; 36,928 career pts. (2nd all-time).

Moses Malone, 1955-2015, NBA center; MVP, 1979, '82, '83.

Eli Manning, b 1981, NY Giants quarterback; Super Bowl MVP, 2008, '12.

Peyton Manning, b 1976, quarterback; most NFL MVP awards, 2003-04, '08-'09, '13; Super Bowl MVP, 2007; single-season passing yards record (5,477), 2013.

Mickey Mantle, 1931-95, NY Yankees outfielder; triple crown, 1956; 18 World Series home runs; MVP 3 times.

Diego Maradona, b 1960, (Arg.) soccer player; led Argentina to World Cup, 1986.

Pete Maravich, 1947-88, guard; scored NCAA record 44.2 ppg during collegiate career; led NBA in scoring, 1977.

Rocky Marciano, 1923-69, heavyweight champion, 1952-56; retired undefeated.

Dan Marino, b 1961, Miami quarterback; NFL record single-season yards passing (5,084), 1984.

Roger Maris, 1934-85, NY Yankees outfielder; hit AL record 61 home runs, 1961, record held 37 years; MVP, 1960-61.

Marta (Marta Vieira da Silva), b 1986, (Braz.) soccer forward; FIFA World Player of the Year, 2006-10.

Curtis Martin, b 1973, Jets running back; 5-time Pro-Bowler; 4th in all-time rushing yards with 14,101.

Eddie Mathews, 1931-2001, Milwaukee-Atlanta Braves 3rd baseman; hit 512 career home runs.

Christy Mathewson, 1880-1925, pitcher; won 373 games.

Bob Mathias, 1930-2006, decathlon gold, 1948, '52 Olympics.

Misty May-Treanor, b 1977, beach volleyball player; 3-time Olympic gold medalist with Kerri Walsh Jennings (2004, '08, '12).

Willie Mays, b 1931, NY-S.F. Giants center fielder; hit 660 home runs, led NL 4 times; had 3,283 hits; twice MVP.

Willie McCovey, b 1938, S.F. Giants slugger; hit 521 home runs; led NL 3 times; MVP, 1969.

John McEnroe, b 1959, U.S. Open tennis champ (1979-81, '84); Wimbledon champ (1981, '83-'84).

John McGraw, 1873-1934, NY Giants manager; led team to 10 pennants, 3 championships.

Mark McGwire, b 1963, hit then-record 70 home runs in 1998; 583 career home runs (10th); admitted career steroid use, 2010.

Rory McIlroy, b 1989, (N. Ire.) golfer; won U.S. Open, 2011; won PGA Championship, 2012, '14; British Open, 2014.

Tamara McKinney, b 1962, 1st U.S. skier to win overall Alpine World Cup championship (1983).

Andrea Mead Lawrence, 1932-2009, skier; first woman to win 2 gold medals in alpine skiing at one Olympics (1952).

Lionel Messi, b 1987, (Arg.) forward for FC Barcelona; FIFA World Player of the Year, 2009-10.

Mark Messier, b 1961, (Can.) center; NHL MVP, 1990, '92; Conn Smythe Trophy, 1984.

Debbie Meyer, b 1952, 1st swimmer to win 3 individual Olympic golds (1968).

Al Michaels, b 1944, *NBC Sunday Night Football* announcer; 5-time Outstanding Sports Personality Emmy winner.

Phil Mickelson, b 1970, golfer; 5 career major titles.

George Mikan, 1924-2005, Minn. Lakers center; considered the best basketball player of first half of 20th cent.

Stan Mikita, b 1940, (Czech.) Chicago Blackhawks center; led NHL in scoring 4 times; MVP twice.

Billy Mills, b 1938, runner; upset winner of the 1964 Olympic 10,000m; only American man ever to win the event.

Joe Montana, b 1956, S.F. 49ers quarterback; Super Bowl MVP, 1982, '85, '90.

Archie Moore, 1913-98, light-heavyweight champ, 1952-62.

Howie Morenz, 1902-37, (Can.) Montréal Canadiens forward; considered best hockey player of first half of 20th cent.

Edwin Moses, b 1955, undefeated in 122 consecutive 400m hurdles races, 1977- 87; Olympic gold medalist, 1976, '84.

Shirley Muldowney, b 1940, 1st woman to race Natl. Hot Rod Assn. Top Fuel dragsters; 3-time NHRA points champ.

Andy Murray, b 1987, (Br.) tennis player; 3-time Grand Slam singles champion; Olympic gold medal in men's singles (2012, '16).

Eddie Murray, b 1956, 3rd player with both 3,000+ hits and 500+ home runs.

Stan Musial, 1920-2013, St. Louis Cardinals star; won 7 NL batting titles; MVP 3 times.

Rafael Nadal, b 1986, (Sp.) tennis player; 14-time Grand Slam singles champion; Olympic gold medal in men's singles (2008).

Bronko Nagurski, 1908-90, (Can.) Chicago Bears fullback and tackle; gained more than 4,000 yds rushing.

Joe Namath, b 1943, Jets quarterback; 1969 Super Bowl MVP.

Rosie Napravnik, b 1988, jockey.

Steve Nash, b 1974, (Can.) Phoenix Suns point guard; NBA MVP, 2005, '06.

Martina Navratilova, b 1956, (Czech.) tennis player; won 18 Grand Slam singles titles.

Byron Nelson, 1912-2006, won 11 consecutive golf tournaments in 1945; twice Masters and PGA titlist.

Ernie Nevers, 1903-76, Stanford football star; selected as best college fullback to play between 1919 and 1969.

Paula Newby-Fraser, b 1962, ([now] Zimbabwe) 8-time Ironman Triathlon world champ.

John Newcombe, b 1944, (Austral.) tennis player; 7 Grand Slam singles and 17 Grand Slam men's doubles titles.

Jack Nicklaus, b 1940, PGA Player of the Year, 1967, '72; leading money winner 8 times; won 18 majors (6 Masters).

Chuck Noll, 1932-2014, Pittsburgh Steelers coach; won 4 Super Bowls.

Dirk Nowitzki, b 1978, (Ger.) NBA forward; led Mavericks to NBA title, 2011; NBA MVP, 2007.

Paavo Nurmi, 1897-1973, (Fin.) distance runner; won 9 Olympic gold medals, 1920, '24, '28.

Lorena Ochoa, b 1981, (Mex.) LPGA Player of the Year, 2006-09, money leader 2006-08.

Al Oerter, 1936-2007, discus thrower; won gold medal at 4 consecutive Olympics, 1956, '60, '64, '68.

Apolo Ohno, b 1982, short-track speed skater; most decorated U.S. Winter Olympic athlete with 2 gold, 2 silver, 4 bronze (2002, '06, '10).

Hakeem Olajuwon, b 1963, (Nigeria) Houston center; NBA MVP, 1994, playoff MVP, 1994-95; career blocked shots leader (3,830).

Barney Oldfield, 1878-1946, pioneer auto racer; was first to drive a car 60 mph, 1903.

Shaquille O'Neal, b 1972, center; led L.A. Lakers to NBA titles, 2000-02, and Miami Heat to NBA title, 2006; Finals MVP 2000-02; NBA MVP 2000.

Bobby Orr, b 1948, (Can.) Boston Bruins defenseman; 8-time Norris Trophy winner; led NHL in scoring twice, assists 5 times.

Mel Ott, 1909-58, NY Giants right fielder; hit 511 home runs; led NL 6 times.

Alexander Ovechkin, b 1985, (Russ.) hockey player; NHL MVP, 2008, '09, '13.

Jesse Owens, 1913-80, track-and-field athlete; 4 1936 Olympic golds.

Terrell Owens, b 1973, wide receiver.

Satchel Paige, 1906-82, pitcher; starred in Negro Leagues, 1924-48; entered major leagues at age 42.

Arnold Palmer, 1929-2016, golf's first $1 mil winner; won 4 Masters, 2 British Opens.

Jim Palmer, b 1945, Baltimore Orioles pitcher; won Cy Young award 3 times; 20-game winner 8 times.

Inbee Park, b 1988, (S. Kor.) golfer; 2nd ever to win first 3 majors.

Candace Parker, b 1986, L.A. Sparks forward; first woman to dunk in an NCAA tournament game; WNBA MVP (2008, '13); gold medalist (2008, '12).

Joe Paterno, 1926-2012, Penn St. football coach; national title-winner, 1982, '86; most wins in NCAA Div. I coaching history (409); legacy complicated by child sex abuse scandal at Penn St.

Danica Patrick, b 1982, race car driver; 1st woman to lead Indy 500 and to win NASCAR Sprint Cup series pole.

Floyd Patterson, 1935-2006, 2-time heavyweight champion; first to ever regain the title after losing it.

Walter Payton, 1954-99, Chicago Bears running back; 2nd most rushing yards in NFL history; top NFC rusher, 1976-80.

Pelé (Edson Arantes do Nascimento), b 1940, (Braz.) soccer player; led Brazil to 3 World Cups (1958, '62, '70); scored 1,281 goals.

Bob Pettit, b 1932, first NBA player to score 20,000 pts.; twice NBA scoring leader.

Richard Petty, b 1937, NASCAR national champ 7 times; 7-time Daytona 500 winner.

Michael Phelps, b 1985, Olympic swimmer; record-holder, most Olympic medals (28) and gold medals (23) won by a single athlete.

Oscar Pistorius, b 1986, (S. Afr.) sprinter; 1st double-leg amputee to compete in Olympics, 2012; convicted (2015) of murder in girlfriend's death.

Jacques Plante, 1929-86, (Can.) NHL goaltender; 7 Vezina trophies; first goalie to wear mask in a game.

Gary Player, b 1935, (S. Afr.) golfer; won 3 Masters, 3 British Opens, 2 PGA Championships, and U.S. Open.

Mike Powell, b 1963, track-and-field athlete; holds world record for long jump (29 ft 4.5 in.).

Steve Prefontaine, 1951-75, runner; 1st to win 4 NCAA titles in same event (5,000m, 1970-73).

Kirby Puckett, 1960-2006, Minnesota Twins center fielder (1984-95); led team to World Series titles in 1987, '91.

Albert Pujols, b 1980, MLB slugger; NL MVP, 2005, '08-'09.

Paula Radcliffe, b 1973, British runner; set marathon world record of 2:15:25 in London, 2003.

Manny Ramirez, b 1972, (Dom. Rep.) outfielder; 2004 World Series MVP; suspended for violating MLB performance-enhancing drug policy, 2009, '11.

Willis Reed, b 1942, NY Knicks center; MVP, 1970; playoff MVP, 1970, '73.

Mary Lou Retton, b 1968, gymnast; won all-around gold medal at 1984 Olympics; also won 2 silvers, 2 bronzes.

Jerry Rice, b 1962, receiver; 1989 Super Bowl MVP; NFL record for career touchdowns (208), receptions (1,549).

Maurice Richard, 1921-2000, (Can.) Montréal Canadiens forward; scored 544 regular season goals, 82 playoff goals.

Branch Rickey, 1881-1965, MLB exec. helped break baseball's color barrier, 1947; initiated farm system, 1919.

Cal Ripken Jr., b 1960, Baltimore shortstop; AL MVP, 1983, '91; most consecutive games played (2,632).

Mariano Rivera, b 1969, (Pan.) relief pitcher; helped NY Yankees to 5 World Series titles; World Series MVP, 1999; all-time MLB leader in regular season and postseason saves.

Oscar Robertson, b 1938, NBA guard; averaged career 25.7 pts. per game; MVP, 1964.

Brooks Robinson, b 1937, Baltimore Orioles 3rd baseman; played in 4 World Series; MVP, 1964; 16 gold gloves.

Frank Robinson, b 1935, MVP in both NL and AL; triple crown, 1966; 586 career home runs; first black manager in majors.

Jackie Robinson, 1919-72, broke baseball's color barrier with Brooklyn Dodgers, 1947; NL MVP, 1949.

Sugar Ray Robinson, 1921-89, boxer; middleweight champion 5 times; welterweight champion, 1946-51.

Knute Rockne, 1888-1931, Notre Dame football coach, 1918-31; revolutionized game by stressing forward pass.

Aaron Rodgers, b 1983, Green Bay quarterback; led Packers to victory in Super Bowl XLV; Super Bowl MVP, 2011; NFL MVP, 2011, '14.

Bill Rodgers, b 1947, runner; won Boston and New York City marathons 4 times each between 1975 and 1980.

Alex Rodriguez, b 1975, MLB infielder; AL MVP in 2003, '05, '07; 14-time All Star; admitted steroid use 2001-03; suspended 162 games for PED use, 2013-14.

Juan "Chi Chi" Rodriguez, b 1935, champion golfer; 8 PGA tour wins, 22 Champions tour wins.

Ben Roethlisberger, b 1982, Pittsburgh Steelers quarterback; youngest QB to win Super Bowl, 2005.

Ronaldinho (Ronaldo de Assis Moreira), b 1980, (Braz.) soccer midfielder; FIFA World Player of the Year, 2004, '05.

Ronaldo (Ronaldo Luiz Nazario de Lima), b 1976, (Braz.) soccer forward; led Brazil to 2002 World Cup title; 3-time FIFA world player of the year, 1996-97.

Cristiano Ronaldo, b 1985, (Port.) soccer forward; FIFA player of the year, 2008; UEFA career scoring leader (94).

Art Rooney, 1901-88, NFL owner; bought Pittsburgh Pirates in 1933, renamed Steelers, 1940.

Pete Rose, b 1941, won 3 NL batting titles; hit in 44 consecutive games, 1978; most career hits, 4,256; banned for gambling, 1989; admitted betting on his team, 2004.

Ken Rosewall, b 1934, (Austral.) tennis player; 8 Grand Slam singles titles.

Ronda Rousey, b 1987, judoka and mixed martial arts fighter.

Patrick Roy, b 1965, (Can.) Montréal-Colorado goalie; only 3-time NHL playoffs MVP, 1986, '93, 2001.

Wilma Rudolph, 1940-94, sprinter; won 3 1960 Olympic golds.

Adolph Rupp, 1901-77, NCAA basketball coach; led Kentucky to 4 national titles, 1948-49, '51, '58.

Bill Russell, b 1934, Boston Celtics center; led team to 11 NBA titles; MVP 5 times; first black coach of major pro sports team.

Babe Ruth, 1895-1948, NY Yankees outfielder; hit 60 home runs, 1927, 714 lifetime (3rd all-time); led AL 12 times.

Johnny Rutherford, b 1938, auto racer; won 3 Indy 500s.

Nolan Ryan, b 1947, pitcher; holds season (383), career (5,714) strikeout records; won 324 games (7 no-hitters).

Pete Sampras, b 1971, tennis player; 14 Grand Slam singles wins (2nd-most all-time).

Joan Benoit Samuelson, b 1957, won 1st Olympic women's marathon (1984), Boston Marathon (1979, '83).

Barry Sanders, b 1968, rushed for 2,053 yds in 1997; led NFL in rushing, 1990, '94, '96-'97.

Deion Sanders, b 1967, NFL cornerback (1989-2000, '04-'05) and MLB outfielder (1989-95, '97, 2005).

Gale Sayers, b 1943, Chicago running back; twice led NFL in rushing.

Mike Schmidt, b 1949, Phillies 3rd baseman; led NL in home runs 8 times; 548 lifetime; NL MVP, 1980-81, '86.

Michael Schumacher, b 1969, (Ger.) race-car driver; 7-time Formula 1 world champ (1994-95, 2000-04).

Tom Seaver, b 1944, pitcher; won NL Cy Young award 3 times; won 311 major league games.

Monica Seles, b 1973, (Yugo.) tennis player; won 9 Grand Slam singles titles; stabbed on court by spectator, 1993.

Maria Sharapova, b 1987, (Russ.) tennis player; won Wimbledon (2004), U.S. Open (2006), Austral. Open (2008), French Open (2012, '14); Olympic silver, 2012.

Patty Sheehan, b 1956, Hall of Fame golfer; 3 LPGA Championships (1983-84, '93).

Willie Shoemaker, 1931-2003, jockey; rode 4 Kentucky Derby, 5 Belmont Stakes winners.

Frank Shorter, b 1947, runner; only American to win men's Olympic marathon (1972) since 1908; silver medalist (1976).

Don Shula, b 1930, all-time winningest NFL coach (347 games).

Bill Simmons, b 1969, columnist; podcast, TV host; Grantland and theringer.com founder.

O. J. Simpson, b 1947, running back; rushed for 2,003 yds, 1973; AFC leading rusher 4 times; acquitted of murder, 1995; jailed after being found guilty of robbery and kidnapping, 2008.

Dean Smith, 1931-2015, retired basketball coach; 879 Division I wins; led North Carolina to 2 NCAA titles (1982, '93).

Emmitt Smith, b 1969, running back; NFL and Super Bowl MVP, 1993; rushed for career record 18,355 yds.

Conn Smythe, 1895-1980, (Can.) won 7 Stanley Cups as Toronto GM (1929-61); playoff MVP award named in his honor.

Sam Snead, 1912-2002, PGA and Masters champ 3 times each; record 82 PGA tournament victories.

Annika Sorenstam, b 1970, (Swed.) golfer; set LPGA 18-hole record of 59 (−13), 72-hole record of 27-under-par, 2001; won 10 LPGA majors, including career Grand Slam.

Sammy Sosa, b 1968, (Dom. Rep.) MLB slugger; NL MVP, 1998; 1st to hit 60+ HR 3 times (1998-99, 2001).

Warren Spahn, 1921-2003, pitcher; won 363 NL games; 20-game winner 13 times; Cy Young winner, 1957.

Tris Speaker, 1888-1958, AL outfielder; batted .345 over 22 seasons; hit record 792 career doubles.

Jordan Spieth, b 1993, golfer; won Masters, 2015; U.S. Open, 2015.

Mark Spitz, b 1950, swimmer; won 7 golds at 1972 Olympics.

Amos Alonzo Stagg, 1862-1965, football innovator; Univ. of Chicago football coach for 41 years, 5 undefeated seasons.

Bart Starr, b 1934, Green Bay Packers quarterback; led team to 5 NFL titles, 2 Super Bowl victories.

Roger Staubach, b 1942, Dallas Cowboys quarterback; leading NFC passer 5 times.

George Steinbrenner, 1930-2010, NY Yankees owner.

Casey Stengel, 1890-1975, managed Yankees to 10 pennants, 7 World Series wins between 1949 and 1960.

Jackie Stewart, b 1939, (Scot.) auto racer; 27 Grand Prix wins.

John Stockton, b 1962, Utah Jazz guard; NBA career leader in assists, steals; NBA assists leader, 1988-96.

Picabo Street, b 1971, skier; 2-time World Cup downhill champion (1995-96); Olympic super G gold medalist, 1998.

Louise Suggs, 1923-2015, golfer; U.S. Women's Open champ, 1949, '52; 11 major victories.

John L. Sullivan, 1858-1918, last bareknuckle heavyweight champion, 1882-92.

Pat Summerall, 1930-2013, NFL kicker, radio and TV sportscaster who announced 26 Super Bowls.

Pat Summitt, 1952-2016, women's basketball coach; led Tennessee Lady Vols to 8 NCAA titles (1987, '89, '91, '96-'98, 2007-08); all-time winningest NCAA coach.

Ichiro Suzuki, b 1973, (Jpn.) outfielder; AL MVP, 2001; single-season hits record (262), 2004; career (Japan-U.S.) hits leader since 2013; 3,000th U.S. hit, 2016.

Sheryl Swoopes, b 1971, guard/forward; 1st 3-time WNBA MVP (2000, '02, '05); Olympic gold medalist (1996, 2000, '04).

Fran Tarkenton, b 1940, Minnesota, NY Giants quarterback; 342 career TD passes; 1975 Player of the Year.

Diana Taurasi, b 1982, WNBA guard; 4-time Olympic gold medalist; WNBA MVP, 2009.

Lawrence Taylor, b 1959, linebacker; led NY Giants to 2 Super Bowl titles; played in 10 Pro Bowls.

Daley Thompson, b 1958, (Br.) decathlete; Olympic gold medalist in 1980, '84.

Jenny Thompson, b 1973, swimmer; 12 Olympic medals (8 gold) in 1992, '96, 2000, '04.

Bobby Thomson, 1923-2010, MLB utility player known for pennant-clinching "Shot Heard 'Round the World" for the NY Giants, 1951.

Jim Thorpe, 1888-1953, football All-American, 1911-12; won pentathlon and decathlon, 1912 Olympics.

Bill Tilden, 1893-1953, won 7 U.S. tennis titles, 3 Wimbledon.

Y. A. Tittle, b 1926, NY Giants quarterback; MVP, 1961, '63.

Alberto Tomba, b 1966, (It.) skier; 5 Olympic alpine medals (3 golds, 2 silver) in 1988, '92, '94.

LaDainian "L.T." Tomlinson, b 1979, running back; NFL record for rushing touchdowns (28).

Joe Torre, b 1940, former MLB player; managed L.A. Dodgers, NY Yankees, St. Louis, Atlanta, and NY Mets.

Lee Trevino, b 1939, golfer; won U.S., British Open twice.

Bryan Trottier, b 1956, (Can.) Islanders, Penguins center for 6 Stanley Cup champs.

Mike Trout, b 1991, MLB player; AL MVP, 2014.

Gene Tunney, 1897-1978, heavyweight champion, 1926-28.

Mike Tyson, b 1966, undisputed heavyweight champ, 1987-90; at 20, youngest to win a heavyweight title (WBC, 1986).

Wyomia Tyus, b 1945, Olympic 100m gold medalist, 1964, '68.

Johnny Unitas, 1933-2002, Baltimore Colts quarterback; passed for more than 40,000 yds; MVP, 1957, '67.

Al Unser, b 1939, Indy 500 winner 4 times.

Bobby Unser, b 1934, Indy 500 winner 3 times.

Norm Van Brocklin, 1926-83, quarterback; passed for game record 554 yds, 1951; MVP, 1960.

Amy Van Dyken, b 1973, swimmer; first American woman to win 4 gold medals in one Olympics (1996).

Justin Verlander, b 1983, pitcher; won AL MVP and Cy Young, 2011.

Michael Vick, b 1980, quarterback; suspended and convicted (2007) of illegal dog fighting, gambling activities.

Lasse Viren, b 1949, (Fin.) runner; Olympic 5,000m and 10,000m gold medalist in 1972, '76.

Lindsey Vonn, b 1984; skier, Olympic gold, 2010; 4 World Cup titles 2008-10, '12.

Dwyane Wade, b 1982, guard; led Miami Heat to NBA title, 2006, '12-'13; finals MVP, 2006; NBA scoring title, 2009.

Honus Wagner, 1874-1955, Pittsburgh Pirates shortstop; 8 NL batting titles.

Grete Waitz, 1953-2011, (Nor.) 9-time winner of the New York City Marathon (1978-80, '82-'86, '88).

"Jersey" Joe Walcott, 1914-94, boxer; became heavyweight champion at age 37, 1951-52.

Kerri Walsh Jennings, b 1978, beach volleyball player; 3-time Olympic gold medalist with Misty May-Treanor (2004, '08, '12).

Bill Walton, b 1952, center; led Portland Trail Blazers to 1977 NBA title; MVP, 1978; NBA TV commentator.

Abby Wambach, b 1980, soccer player; 2 gold medals in Olympics (2004, '12); all-time intl.-competition goal scorer.

Kurt Warner, b 1971, quarterback; NFL MVP, 1999, 2001; Super Bowl MVP, 2000.

Gerry "Bubba" Watson, b 1978, golfer; won Masters, 2012, '14.

Tom Watson, b 1949, golfer; 6-time PGA Player of the Year; won 5 British Opens, 2 Masters, U.S. Open.

Stan Wawrinka, b 1985, (Switz.) tennis player; won Austral. Open (2014), French Open (2015), U.S. Open (2016).

Karrie Webb, b 1974, (Austral.) golfer; youngest woman (26 yrs., 6 mos.) to win career Grand Slam, 1999-2001.

Johnny Weissmuller, 1903-84, swimmer; won 52 national championships, 5 Olympic gold medals; set 67 world records.

Jerry West, b 1938, L.A. Lakers guard; had career average 27 pts. per game; first team all-star 10 times.

Dan Wheldon, 1978-2011, (Br.) race-car driver; 2-time Indy 500 winner (2005, '11).

Byron "Whizzer" White, 1917-2002, running back; led NCAA in scoring and rushing at Colorado, 1937; led NFL in rushing twice, 1938, '40; Supreme Court justice, 1962-93.

Shaun White, b 1986, snowboarder/skateboarder, Olympic gold medalist in halfpipe (2006, '10).

Kathy Whitworth, b 1939, 7-time LPGA Player of the Year (1966-69, '71-'73); 88 tour wins, most on LPGA or PGA tour.

Michelle Wie, b 1989, golfer; in 2002 became youngest-ever qualifier for LPGA event; turned pro at age 15.

Bradley Wiggins, b 1980, (Br.) cyclist; Tour de France winner, 2012; 8 Olympic medals (5 gold) over 5 Games.

Michael Wilbon, b 1958, commentator/analyst for ESPN.

Lenny Wilkens, b 1937, 2nd winningest coach in NBA history; Hall of Fame player and coach.

Serena Williams, b 1981, tennis player; 22-time Grand Slam singles champion; Olympic gold medals in singles (2012) and doubles (2000, '08, '12) with sister Venus.

Ted Williams, 1918-2002, Boston Red Sox outfielder; won 6 batting titles, 2 triple crowns; hit .406 in 1941.

Venus Williams, b 1980, tennis player; 7-time Grand Slam singles champion; Olympic gold medals in singles (2000) and doubles with sister Serena (2000, '08, '12).

Helen Wills Moody, 1905-98, tennis star; won U.S. Open 7 times, Wimbledon 8 times.

Katarina Witt, b 1965, (Ger.) figure skater; won Olympic gold medal, 1984, '88; world champ, 1984-85, '87-'88.

John Wooden, 1910-2010, UCLA basketball coach; 10 NCAA titles.

Tiger Woods, b 1975, golfer; youngest to win career Grand Slam, at age 24 (1997-2000); 14 career major titles.

Mickey Wright, b 1935, golfer; won LPGA and U.S. Open championship 4 times; 82 career wins, including 13 majors.

Eric Wynalda, b 1969, soccer; scored 1st goal in major league soccer history (1996).

Kristi Yamaguchi, b 1971, figure skater; won national, world, Olympic titles, in 1992.

Yao Ming, b 1980, (China) center for Houston Rockets; 8-time NBA All-Star.

Carl Yastrzemski, b 1939, Boston Red Sox slugger; won 3 batting titles; triple crown, 1967.

Cy Young, 1867-1955, pitcher; won record 511 games.

Steve Young, b 1961, 49ers quarterback; led NFL in passing, 1991-94, '96-'97; NFL MVP, 1992, '94; Super Bowl MVP, 1995.

Babe Didrikson Zaharias, 1911-56, all-around athlete; 3 track-and-field medals (2 golds), 1932 Olympics; won 10 golf majors; also played baseball; 6-time AP Female Athlete of the Year.

Emil Zátopek, 1922-2000, (Czech.) runner; won 3 gold medals at 1952 Olympics (5,000m, 10,000m, marathon).

Zinedine Zidane, b 1972, (Fr.) soccer midfielder; led France to 1998 World Cup title; named top player in 2006; 3-time FIFA world player of the year (1998, 2000, '03).

Writers of the Present

Name	Birthplace	Birthdate
Richard Adams	Newbury, England, UK	5/9/1920
Chimamanda Ngozi Adichie	Enugu, Nigeria	9/15/1977
Mitch Albom	Passaic, NJ	5/23/1958
Elizabeth Alexander	New York, NY	5/30/1962
Sherman Alexie	Wellpinit, WA	10/7/1966
Isabel Allende	Lima, Peru	8/2/1942
Dorothy Allison	Greenville, SC	4/11/1949
Martin Amis	Oxford, England, UK	8/25/1949
Piers Anthony	Oxford, England, UK	8/6/1934
Jeffrey Archer	Somerset, England, UK	4/15/1940
John Ashbery	Rochester, NY	7/28/1927
Margaret Atwood	Ottawa, ON, Canada	11/18/1939
David Auburn	Chicago, IL	11/30/1969
Jean Auel	Chicago, IL	2/18/1936
Paul Auster	Newark, NJ	2/3/1947
Alan Ayckbourn	Hampstead, England, UK	4/12/1939
Nicholson Baker	New York, NY	1/7/1957
David Baldacci	Richmond, VA	8/5/1960
Russell Banks	Newton, MA	3/28/1940
John Barth	Cambridge, MD	5/27/1930
Ann Beattie	Washington, DC	9/8/1947
Alan Bennett	Leeds, England, UK	5/9/1934
John Berendt	Syracuse, NY	12/5/1939
Elizabeth Berg	St. Paul, MN	12/2/1948
Judy Blume	Elizabeth, NJ	2/12/1938
T. Coraghessan Boyle	Peekskill, NY	12/2/1948
Barbara Taylor Bradford	Leeds, England, UK	5/10/1933
Christopher Bram	Buffalo, NY	2/22/1952
Geraldine Brooks	Sydney, NSW, Australia	9/14/1955
Dan Brown	Exeter, NH	6/22/1964
Rita Mae Brown	Hanover, PA	11/28/1944
Christopher Buckley	New York, NY	9/28/1952
James Lee Burke	Houston, TX	12/5/1936
Augusten Burroughs	Pittsburgh, PA	10/23/1965
Robert Olen Butler	Granite City, IL	1/20/1945
A. S. Byatt	Sheffield, England, UK	8/24/1936
Ethan Canin	Ann Arbor, MI	7/19/1960
Peter Carey	Bacchus-Marsh, Victoria, Australia	5/7/1943
Robert A. Caro	New York, NY	10/30/1935
Caleb Carr	New York, NY	8/2/1955
Michael Chabon	Washington, DC	5/24/1963
Tracy Chevalier	Washington, DC	10/19/1962
Sandra Cisneros	Chicago, IL	12/20/1954
Mary Higgins Clark	Bronx, NY	12/24/1927
Beverly Cleary	McMinnville, OR	4/12/1916
Ta-Nehisi Coates	Baltimore, MD	9/30/1975
Harlan Coben	Newark, NJ	1/4/1962
Paulo Coelho	Rio de Janeiro, Brazil	8/24/1947
J(ohn) M(axwell) Coetzee	Capetown, South Africa	2/9/1940
Billy Collins	New York, NY	3/22/1941
Suzanne Collins	Hartford, CT	8/10/1962
Robin Cook	New York, NY	5/4/1940
Patricia Cornwell	Miami, FL	6/9/1956
Michael Cunningham	Cincinnati, OH	11/6/1952
Clive Cussler	Aurora, IL	7/15/1931
Don DeLillo	Bronx, NY	11/20/1936
Nelson DeMille	Jamaica, Queens, NY	8/23/1943
Junot Díaz	Santo Domingo, Dominican Republic	12/31/1968
Joan Didion	Sacramento, CA	12/5/1934
Annie Dillard	Pittsburgh, PA	4/30/1945
Anthony Doerr	Cleveland, OH	10/27/1973
Emma Donoghue	Dublin, Ireland	10/24/1969
Rita Dove	Akron, OH	8/28/1952
Roddy Doyle	Dublin, Ireland	5/8/1958
Carol Ann Duffy	Glasgow, Scotland, UK	12/23/1955
Jennifer Egan	Chicago, IL	9/7/1962
Dave Eggers	Boston, MA	3/12/1970
Bret Easton Ellis	Los Angeles, CA	3/7/1964
James Ellroy	Los Angeles, CA	3/4/1948
Louise Erdrich	Little Falls, MN	6/7/1954
Laura Esquivel	Mexico City, Mexico	9/30/1950
Jeffrey Eugenides	Detroit, MI	3/8/1960
Janet Evanovich	South River, NJ	4/22/1943
Lawrence Ferlinghetti	Yonkers, NY	3/24/1919
Helen Fielding	Morley, Yorkshire, Eng., UK	2/19/1958
Fannie Flagg	Birmingham, AL	9/21/1944
Gillian Flynn	Kansas City, MO	2/24/1971
Ken Follett	Cardiff, Wales, UK	6/5/1949
Richard Ford	Jackson, MS	2/16/1944
Frederick Forsyth	Ashford, England, UK	8/25/1938
Paula Fox	New York, NY	4/22/1923
Jonathan Franzen	Western Springs, IL	8/17/1959
Michael Frayn	London, England, UK	9/8/1933
Charles Frazier	Asheville, NC	11/4/1950
Neil Gaiman	Portchester, England, UK	11/10/1960
Ernest J. Gaines	Oscar, LA	1/15/1933
Malcolm Gladwell	Fareham, Hampshire, Eng., UK	9/3/1963
Robert Goddard	Fareham, Hampshire, Eng., UK	11/13/1954
Gail Godwin	Birmingham, AL	6/18/1937
William Goldman	Highland Park, IL	8/12/1931
Mary Gordon	Far Rockaway, NY	12/8/1949
Sue Grafton	Louisville, KY	4/24/1940
Shirley Ann Grau	New Orleans, LA	7/8/1929
John Green	Indianapolis, IN	8/24/1977
John Grisham	Jonesboro, AR	2/8/1955
John Guare	New York, NY	2/5/1938
Pete Hamill	Brooklyn, NY	6/24/1935
David Handler	Los Angeles, CA	9/14/1952
Paul Harding	Wenham, MA	12/19/1967
David Hare	St. Leonards, Sussex, Eng., UK	6/5/1947
Robert Hass	San Francisco, CA	3/1/1941
Mark Helprin	New York, NY	6/28/1947
Carl Hiaasen	Plantation, FL	3/12/1953
Laura Hillenbrand	Fairfax, VA	5/15/1967
S. E. Hinton	Tulsa, OK	7/22/1948
Alice Hoffman	New York, NY	3/16/1952
Alan Hollinghurst	Stroud, Gloucestershire, England, UK	5/26/1954
Khaled Hosseini	Kabul, Afghanistan	3/4/1965
John Irving	Exeter, NH	3/2/1942
Walter Isaacson	New Orleans, LA	5/20/1952
Kazuo Ishiguro	Nagasaki, Japan	11/8/1954
John Jakes	Chicago, IL	3/31/1932
E. L. James	London, England, UK	7/3/1963
Elfriede Jelinek	Müzzuschlag, Austria	10/20/1946
Ha Jin	Liaoning, China	2/21/1956
Edward P. Jones	Washington, DC	10/5/1950
Erica Jong	New York, NY	3/26/1942
Sebastian Junger	Boston, MA	1/17/1962
Jan Karon	Lenoir, NC	3/14/1937
Garrison Keillor	Anoka, MN	8/7/1942
Thomas Keneally	Sydney, NSW, Australia	10/7/1935
William Kennedy	Albany, NY	1/16/1928
Sue Monk Kidd	Sylvester, GA	8/12/1948
Jamaica Kincaid	St. John's, Antigua and Barbuda	5/25/1949
Stephen King	Portland, ME	9/21/1947
Barbara Kingsolver	Annapolis, MD	4/8/1955
Maxine Hong Kingston	Stockton, CA	10/27/1940
Dean Koontz	Everett, PA	7/9/1945
Ted Kooser	Ames, IA	4/25/1939
Jon Krakauer	Brookline, MA	4/12/1954
Larry Kramer	Bridgeport, CT	6/25/1935
Judith Krantz	New York, NY	1/9/1928
Milan Kundera	Brno, Czechoslovakia	4/1/1929
Tony Kushner	New York, NY	7/16/1956
Jhumpa Lahiri	London, England, UK	7/11/1967
Erik Larson	Brooklyn, NY	1/3/1954
John Le Carré	Poole, England, UK	10/19/1931
Jean Marie Gustave Le Clézio	Nice, France	4/13/1940
Ursula K. Le Guin	Berkeley, CA	10/21/1929
David Leavitt	Pittsburgh, PA	6/23/1961
Jonathan Lethem	Brooklyn, NY	2/19/1964
David Lodge	South London, England, UK	1/28/1935
Alison Lurie	Chicago, IL	9/3/1926
Gregory Maguire	Albany, NY	6/9/1954
David Malouf	Brisbane, Qld., Australia	3/20/1934
Thomas Mallon	Glen Cove, NY	11/2/1951
David Mamet	Chicago, IL	11/30/1947
Hilary Mantel	Derbyshire, England, UK	7/6/1952
Yann Martel	Salamanca, Spain	6/25/1963
George R. R. Martin	Bayonne, NJ	9/20/1948
Bobbie Ann Mason	nr. Mayfield, KY	5/1/1940
Armistead Maupin	Washington, DC	4/13/1944
Cormac McCarthy	Providence, RI	7/20/1933
David McCullough	Pittsburgh, PA	7/7/1933
Alice McDermott	Brooklyn, NY	6/27/1953
Ian McEwan	Aldershot, England, UK	6/21/1948
Thomas McGuane	Wyandotte, MI	12/11/1939
Jay McInerney	Hartford, CT	1/13/1955
Terry McMillan	Port Huron, MI	10/18/1951
Larry McMurtry	Wichita Falls, TX	6/3/1936
Terrence McNally	St. Petersburg, FL	11/3/1939
John McPhee	Princeton, NJ	3/8/1931
W(illiam) S(tanley) Merwin	New York, NY	9/30/1927
Stephenie Meyer	Hartford, CT	12/24/1973
Steven Millhauser	New York, NY	8/3/1943
Toni Morrison	Lorain, OH	2/18/1931

Name	Birthplace	Birthdate	Name	Birthplace	Birthdate
Walter Mosley	Los Angeles, CA	1/12/1952	Salman Rushdie	Bombay, India	6/19/1947
Andrew Motion	London, England, UK	10/26/1952	Richard Russo	Johnstown, NY	7/15/1949
Bharati Mukherjee	Calcutta, India	7/27/1940	Alice Sebold	Madison, WI	9/6/1963
Herta Müller	Nitzkydorf, Banat, Romania	8/17/1953	David Sedaris	Johnson City, NY	12/26/1956
Alice Munro	Wingham, ON, Canada	7/10/1931	Vikram Seth	Calcutta, India	6/20/1952
Haruki Murakami	Kyoto, Japan	1/12/1949	John Patrick Shanley	Bronx, NY	10/13/1950
V. S. Naipaul	Chaguanas, Trinidad and Tobago	8/17/1932	Sam Shepard	Ft. Sheridan, IL	11/5/1943
Joyce Carol Oates	Lockport, NY	6/16/1938	Lionel Shriver	Gastonia, NC	5/18/1957
Edna O'Brien	Tuamgraney, Ireland	12/15/1930	Anne Rivers Siddons	Atlanta, GA	1/9/1936
Tim O'Brien	Austin, MN	10/1/1946	Neil Simon	Bronx, NY	7/4/1927
Kenzaburo Oe	Uchiko, Japan	1/31/1935	Jane Smiley	Los Angeles, CA	9/26/1949
Michael Ondaatje	Colombo, Sri Lanka	9/12/1943	Zadie Smith	London, Eng., UK	10/25/1975
Cynthia Ozick	New York, NY	4/17/1928	Wole Soyinka	Abeokuta, Nigeria	7/13/1934
Orhan Pamuk	Istanbul, Turkey	6/7/1952	Nicholas Sparks	Omaha, NE	12/31/1965
Suzan-Lori Parks	Fort Knox, KY	5/10/1963	Danielle Steel	New York, NY	8/14/1947
Ann Patchett	Los Angeles, CA	12/2/1963	R(obert) L(awrence) Stine	Columbus, OH	10/8/1943
James Patterson	Newburgh, NY	3/22/1947	Kathryn Stockett	Jackson, MS	1969
Jodi Picoult	New York, NY	5/19/1966	Tom Stoppard	Zlin, Czechoslovakia	7/3/1937
Marge Piercy	Detroit, MI	3/31/1936	Elizabeth Strout	Portland, ME	1/6/1956
Robert Pinsky	Long Branch, NJ	10/20/1940	Amy Tan	Oakland, CA	2/19/1952
Michael Pollan	New York, NY	2/6/1955	Donna Tartt	Greenwood, MS	12/23/1963
Richard Powers	Evanston, IL	6/18/1957	Paul Theroux	Medford, MA	4/10/1941
Richard Price	Bronx, NY	10/12/1949	Calvin Trillin	Kansas City, MO	12/5/1935
E. Annie Proulx	Norwich, CT	8/22/1935	Scott F. Turow	Chicago, IL	4/12/1949
Philip Pullman	Norwich, England, UK	10/19/1946	Anne Tyler	Minneapolis, MN	10/25/1941
Thomas Pynchon	Glen Cove, NY	5/8/1937	Mario Vargas Llosa	Arequipa, Peru	3/28/1936
David Rabe	Dubuque, IA	3/10/1940	Paula Vogel	Washington, DC	11/16/1951
Ishmael Reed	Chattanooga, TN	2/22/1938	Sarah Vowell	Muskogee, OK	12/27/1969
Anne Rice	New Orleans, LA	10/4/1941	Derek Walcott	Castries, Saint Lucia	1/23/1930
Mary Roach	Etna, NH	3/20/1959	Alice Walker	Eatonton, GA	2/9/1944
Nora Roberts	Silver Spring, MD	10/10/1950	Joseph Wambaugh	East Pittsburgh, PA	1/22/1937
Marilynne Robinson	Sandpoint, IL	11/26/1943	Edmund White	Cincinnati, OH	1/13/1940
Philip Roth	Newark, NJ	3/19/1933	Tom Wolfe	Richmond, VA	3/2/1931
Veronica Roth	New York, NY	8/19/1988	Tobias Wolff	Birmingham, AL	6/19/1945
J. K. Rowling	Chipping Sodbury, Eng., UK	7/31/1965	Herman Wouk	New York, NY	5/27/1915
Norman Rush	San Francisco, CA	10/24/1933	Yevgeny Yevtushenko	Zima, Russia	7/18/1933

Writers of the Past

See also Journalists, and Greeks and Romans in Historical Figures chapter.

Chinua Achebe, 1930-2013, (Nigeria) novelist. *Things Fall Apart*.

Alice Adams, 1926-99, (U.S.) novelist, short-story writer. *Superior Woman*.

James Agee, 1909-55, (U.S.) novelist. *A Death in the Family*.

S(hmuel) Y(osef) Agnon, 1888-1970, (Isr.) Hebrew novelist. *Only Yesterday*.

Conrad Aiken, 1889-1973, (U.S.) poet, critic. *Ushant*.

Anna Akhmatova, 1889-1966, (Russ.) poet. *Requiem*.

Edward Albee, 1928-2016, (U.S.) playwright. *Who's Afraid of Virginia Woolf?*

Louisa May Alcott, 1832-88, (U.S.) novelist. *Little Women*.

Sholom Aleichem, 1859-1916, (Russ.) Yiddish writer. *Tevye's Daughters*, *The Old Country*.

Vicente Aleixandre, 1898-1984, (Sp.) poet. *La destrucción o el amor*, *Dialogolos del conocimiento*.

Horatio Alger, 1832-99, (U.S.) "rags-to-riches" books.

Jorge Amado, 1912-2001, (Brazil) novelist. *Dona Flor and Her Two Husbands*, *The Violent Land*.

Eric Ambler, 1909-98, (Br.) suspense novelist. *A Coffin for Dimitrios*.

Kingsley Amis, 1922-95, (Br.) novelist, critic. *Lucky Jim*.

Hans Christian Andersen, 1805-75, (Den.) author of fairy tales. *The Ugly Duckling*.

Maxwell Anderson, 1888-1959, (U.S.) playwright. *What Price Glory?*, *High Tor*, *Winterset*, *Key Largo*.

Sherwood Anderson, 1876-1941, (U.S.) short-story writer. "Death in the Woods," *Winesburg, Ohio*.

Maya Angelou, 1928-2014, (U.S.) poet, memoirist. *I Know Why the Caged Bird Sings*.

Reinaldo Arenas, 1943-90, (Cuba) short-story writer, novelist. *Before Night Falls*.

Ludovico Ariosto, 1474-1533, (It.) poet. *Orlando Furioso*.

Matthew Arnold, 1822-88, (Br.) poet, critic. "Thrysis," "Dover Beach," "Culture and Anarchy."

Isaac Asimov, 1920-92, (U.S.) versatile writer, espec. of science fiction. *I Robot*.

Miguel Angel Asturias, 1899-1974, (Guat.) novelist. *El Señor Presidente*.

Louis Auchincloss, 1917-2010, (U.S.) novelist, memoirist, short-story writer. *The Rector of Justin*.

W(ystan) H(ugh) Auden, 1907-73, (Br.) poet, playwright, literary critic. "The Age of Anxiety."

Jane Austen, 1775-1817, (Br.) novelist. *Pride and Prejudice*, *Sense and Sensibility*, *Emma*, *Mansfield Park*.

Ba Jin (Li Yaotang), 1904-2005, (China) novelist of pre-revolutionary China.

Isaac Babel, 1894-1941, (Russ.) short-story writer, playwright. *Odessa Tales*, *Red Cavalry*.

James Baldwin, 1924-87, (U.S.) author, playwright. *The Fire Next Time*, *Blues for Mister Charlie*.

Honoré de Balzac, 1799-1850, (Fr.) novelist. *Le Père Goriot*, *Cousine Bette*, *Eugénie Grandet*.

James M. Barrie, 1860-1937, (Br.) playwright, novelist. *Peter Pan*, *Dear Brutus*, *What Every Woman Knows*.

Charles Baudelaire, 1821-67, (Fr.) poet. *Les Fleurs du Mal*.

L(yman) Frank Baum, 1856-1919, (U.S.) *Wizard of Oz* series.

Simone de Beauvoir, 1908-86, (Fr.) novelist, essayist. *The Second Sex*, *Memoirs of a Dutiful Daughter*.

Samuel Beckett, 1906-89, (Ire.) novelist, playwright. *Waiting for Godot*, *Endgame* (plays); *Murphy*, *Watt*, *Molloy* (novels).

Brendan Behan, 1923-64, (Ire.) playwright. *The Quare Fellow*, *The Hostage*, *Borstal Boy*.

Saul Bellow, 1915-2005, (U.S.) novelist. *The Adventures of Augie March*, *Humboldt's Gift*.

Robert Benchley, 1889-1945, (U.S.) humorist.

Stephen Vincent Benét, 1898-1943, (U.S.) poet, novelist. *John Brown's Body*.

Jan Berenstain, 1923-2012, and **Stan Berenstain**, 1923-2005, (both U.S.) co-writers and illustrators of Berenstain Bears series of children's books.

Thomas Berger, 1924-2014, (U.S.) novelist. *Little Big Man*.

John Berryman, 1914-72, (U.S.) poet. *Homage to Mistress Bradstreet*.

Ambrose Bierce, 1842-1914, (U.S.) short-story writer, journalist. *In the Midst of Life*, *The Devil's Dictionary*.

Maeve Binchy, 1940-2012, (Ire.) novelist, short-story writer, *Circle of Friends*, *Tara Road*.

Elizabeth Bishop, 1911-79, (U.S.) poet. *North and South—A Cold Spring*.

William Blake, 1757-1827, (Br.) poet, artist. *Songs of Innocence*, *Songs of Experience*.

Aleksandr Blok, 1880-1921, (Russ.) poet. "The Twelve," "The Scythians."

Enid Blyton, 1897-1968, (Br.) children's writer. Famous Five series.

Giovanni Boccaccio, 1313-75, (It.) poet. *Decameron*.

Heinrich Böll, 1917-85, (Ger.) novelist, short-story writer. *Group Portrait With Lady*.

Jorge Luis Borges, 1900-86, (Arg.) short-story writer, poet, essayist. *Labyrinths*.

James Boswell, 1740-95, (Scot.) biographer. *The Life of Samuel Johnson*.

Pierre Boulle, 1913-94, (Fr.) novelist. *The Bridge Over the River Kwai*, *Planet of the Apes*.

Paul Bowles, 1910-99, (U.S.) novelist, short-story writer. *The Sheltering Sky*.

Ray Bradbury, 1920-2012, (U.S.) novelist, short-story writer. *Fahrenheit 451*, *The Martian Chronicles*.

Anne Bradstreet, c. 1612-72, (U.S.) poet. *The Tenth Muse Lately Sprung Up in America*.

Bertolt Brecht, 1898-1956, (Ger.) dramatist, poet. *The Threepenny Opera*, *Mother Courage and Her Children*.

Joseph Brodsky, 1940-96, (Russ.-U.S.) poet. *A Part of Speech, Less Than One, To Urania.*

Charlotte Brontë, 1816-55, (Br.) novelist. *Jane Eyre.*

Emily Brontë, 1818-48, (Br.) novelist. *Wuthering Heights.*

Sterling A. Brown, 1901-89, (U.S.) poet, literature professor. *Southern Road.*

William Wells Brown, 1815-84, (U.S.) writer, memoirist; first novel by an African American, *Clotel*, 1853.

Elizabeth Barrett Browning, 1806-61, (Br.) poet. *Sonnets From the Portuguese, Aurora Leigh.*

Robert Browning, 1812-89, (Br.) poet. "My Last Duchess," "Fra Lippo Lippi," *The Ring and the Book.*

Pearl S. Buck, 1892-1973, (U.S.) novelist. *The Good Earth.*

Charles Bukowski, 1920-94, (U.S.) novelist, poet. *Ham on Rye, Women.*

Mikhail Bulgakov, 1891-1940, (Russ.) novelist, playwright. *The Heart of a Dog, The Master and Margarita.*

John Bunyan, 1628-88, (Br.) writer. *Pilgrim's Progress.*

Anthony Burgess, 1917-93, (Br.) author. *A Clockwork Orange.*

Frances Hodgson Burnett, 1849-1924, (Br.-U.S.) novelist. *The Secret Garden.*

Robert Burns, 1759-96, (Scot.) poet. "Flow Gently, Sweet Afton," "My Heart's in the Highlands," "Auld Lang Syne."

Edgar Rice Burroughs, 1875-1950, (U.S.) writer; created Tarzan, John Carter.

William S. Burroughs, 1914-97, (U.S.) novelist. *Naked Lunch.*

George Gordon, Lord Byron, 1788-1824, (Br.) poet. *Don Juan, Childe Harold, Manfred, Cain.*

Pedro Calderon de la Barca, 1600-81, (Sp.) playwright. *Life Is a Dream.*

Hortense Calisher, 1911-2009, (U.S.) novelist, short-story writer. *False Entry.*

Italo Calvino, 1923-85, (It.) novelist, short-story writer. *If on a Winter's Night a Traveler.*

Luís Vaz de Camões, 1524?-80 (Port.) poet. *The Lusiads.*

Albert Camus, 1913-60, (Fr.) writer. *The Stranger, The Fall.*

Elias Canetti, 1905-94, (Bulg.) novelist, essayist. *Auto-Da-Fe.*

Karel Capek, 1890-1938, (Czech.) playwright, novelist, essayist. *R.U.R. (Rossum's Universal Robots).*

Truman Capote, 1924-84, (U.S.) author. *Other Voices, Other Rooms; Breakfast at Tiffany's; In Cold Blood.*

Lewis Carroll (Charles Dodgson), 1832-98, (Br.) writer, mathematician. *Alice's Adventures in Wonderland.*

Barbara Cartland 1901-2000, (Br.) romance novelist.

Giacomo Casanova, 1725-98, (It.) adventurer, memoirist.

Willa Cather, 1873-1947, (U.S.) novelist. *O Pioneers!, My Ántonia, Death Comes for the Archbishop.*

Constantine Cavafy, 1863-1933, (Gr.) poet. "Ithaka," "Sensual Pleasures."

Camilo Jose Cela, 1916-2001, (Sp.) novelist. *The Family of Pascual Duarte, The Hive.*

Miguel de Cervantes Saavedra, 1547-1616, (Sp.) novelist, dramatist, poet. *Don Quixote.*

Raymond Chandler, 1888-1959, (U.S.) writer of detective fiction. Philip Marlowe series.

Geoffrey Chaucer, c. 1340-1400, (Br.) poet. *The Canterbury Tales, Troilus and Criseyde.*

John Cheever, 1912-82, (U.S.) novelist, short-story writer. *The Wapshot Scandal,* "The Country Husband."

Anton Chekhov, 1860-1904, (Russ.) short-story writer, dramatist. *Uncle Vanya, The Cherry Orchard, The Three Sisters.*

Charles Waddell Chesnutt, 1858-1932, (U.S.) author known for his short stories. *The Conjure Woman.*

G(ilbert) K(eith) Chesterton, 1874-1936, (Br.) critic, novelist, relig. apologist. Father Brown series of mysteries.

Kate Chopin, 1851-1904, (U.S.) writer. *The Awakening.*

Agatha Christie, 1890-1976, (Br.) mystery writer; created Miss Marple, Hercule Poirot. *And Then There Were None, Murder on the Orient Express, Murder of Roger Ackroyd.*

Tom Clancy, 1947-2013, novelist. *The Hunt for Red October.*

Arthur C. Clarke, 1917-2008, (Br.) science-fiction writer. *2001: A Space Odyssey.*

James Clavell, 1924-94, (Br.-U.S.) novelist. *Shogun, King Rat.*

Jean Cocteau, 1889-1963, (Fr.) writer, visual artist, filmmaker. *The Beauty and the Beast, Les Enfants Terribles.*

Samuel Taylor Coleridge, 1772-1834, (Br.) poet, critic. "Kubla Khan," "The Rime of the Ancient Mariner."

(Sidonie) Colette, 1873-1954, (Fr.) novelist. *Claudine, Gigi.*

Wilkie Collins, 1824-89, (Br.) novelist. *The Moonstone.*

Evan S. Connell, 1924-2013, (Br.) novelist, short-story writer. *Mrs. Bridge.*

Joseph Conrad, 1857-1924, (Br.) novelist. *Lord Jim, Heart of Darkness, The Secret Agent.*

Pat Conroy, 1945-2016, (U.S.) novelist. *The Prince of Tides, The Great Santini.*

James Fenimore Cooper, 1789-1851, (U.S.) novelist. *Leatherstocking Tales, The Last of the Mohicans.*

Pierre Corneille, 1606-84, (Fr.) dramatist. *Medeé, Le Cid.*

Hart Crane, 1899-1932, (U.S.) poet. "The Bridge."

Stephen Crane, 1871-1900, (U.S.) novelist, short-story writer. *The Red Badge of Courage,* "The Open Boat."

Harry Crews, 1935-2012, (U.S.) novelist. *A Feast of Snakes.*

Michael Crichton, 1942-2008, (U.S.) writer. *The Andromeda Strain, Jurassic Park.*

Countee Cullen, 1903-46, (U.S.) poet, prominent in the Harlem Renaissance of the 1920s. *The Black Christ.*

E. E. Cummings, 1894-1962, (U.S.) poet. *Tulips and Chimneys.*

Roald Dahl, 1916-90, (Br.-U.S.) writer. *Charlie and the Chocolate Factory, James and the Giant Peach.*

Gabriele D'Annunzio, 1863-1938, (It.) poet, novelist, dramatist. *The Child of Pleasure, The Intruder, The Victim.*

Dante Alighieri, 1265-1321, (It.) poet. *The Divine Comedy.*

Robertson Davies, 1913-95, (Can.) novelist, playwright, essayist. Salterton, Deptford, and Cornish trilogies.

Daniel Defoe, 1660-1731, (Br.) writer. *Robinson Crusoe, Moll Flanders, Journal of the Plague Year.*

Philip K. Dick, 1928-82, (U.S.) science-fiction writer. *Do Androids Dream of Electric Sheep?*

Charles Dickens, 1812-70, (Br.) novelist. *David Copperfield, Oliver Twist, Great Expectations, A Tale of Two Cities.*

James Dickey, 1923-97, (U.S.) poet, novelist. *Deliverance.*

Emily Dickinson, 1830-86, (U.S.) poet. "Because I could not stop for Death …," "Success is counted sweetest …"

Isak Dinesen (Karen Blixen), 1885-1962, (Den.) author. *Out of Africa, Seven Gothic Tales, Winter's Tales.*

E(dgar) L(awrence) Doctorow, 1931-2015, (U.S.) novelist. *Ragtime, Billy Bathgate.*

John Donne, 1573-1631, (Br.) poet. *Songs and Sonnets.*

José Donoso, 1924-96, (Chile) surreal novelist and short-story writer. *The Obscene Bird of Night.*

John Dos Passos, 1896-1970, (U.S.) novelist. *U.S.A.*

Fyodor Dostoyevsky, 1821-81, (Russ.) novelist. *Crime and Punishment, The Brothers Karamazov, The Possessed.*

Arthur Conan Doyle, 1859-1930, (Br.) novelist. Sherlock Holmes mystery stories.

Theodore Dreiser, 1871-1945, (U.S.) novelist. *An American Tragedy, Sister Carrie.*

John Dryden, 1631-1700, (Br.) poet, dramatist, critic. *All for Love, Mac Flecknoe, Absalom and Achitophel.*

Alexandre Dumas (père), 1802-70, (Fr.) novelist, dramatist. *The Three Musketeers, The Count of Monte Cristo.*

Alexandre Dumas (fils), 1824-95, (Fr.) dramatist, novelist. *La Dame aux Camélias, Le Demi-Monde.*

Paul Laurence Dunbar, 1872-1906, (U.S.) poet, novelist. *Lyrics of Lowly Life.*

Lawrence Durrell, 1912-90, (Br.) novelist, poet. *Alexandria Quartet.*

Umberto Eco, 1932-2016, (It.) novelist. *The Name of the Rose.*

Ilya G. Ehrenburg, 1891-1967, (Russ.) writer. *The Thaw.*

George Eliot (Mary Ann or Marian Evans), 1819-80, (Br.) novelist. *Silas Marner, Middlemarch.*

T(homas) S(tearns) Eliot, 1888-1965, (Br.) poet, critic. *The Waste Land,* "The Love Song of J. Alfred Prufrock."

Stanley Elkin, 1930-95, (U.S.) novelist, short-story writer. *George Mills.*

Ralph Ellison, 1914-94, (U.S.) writer. *Invisible Man.*

Ralph Waldo Emerson, 1803-82, (U.S.) poet, essayist. "Brahma," "Nature," "The Over-Soul," "Self-Reliance."

James T. Farrell, 1904-79, (U.S.) novelist. *Studs Lonigan.*

Howard Fast, 1914-2003, (U.S.) novelist. *Spartacus, The Immigrants.*

William Faulkner, 1897-1962, (U.S.) novelist. *Sanctuary; Light in August; The Sound and the Fury; Absalom, Absalom!*

Edna Ferber, 1887-1968, (U.S.) novelist, short-story writer, playwright. *So Big, Cimarron, Show Boat.*

Henry Fielding, 1707-54, (Br.) novelist. *Tom Jones.*

F(rancis) Scott Fitzgerald, 1896-1940, (U.S.) short-story writer, novelist. *The Great Gatsby, Tender Is the Night.*

Gustave Flaubert, 1821-80, (Fr.) novelist. *Madame Bovary.*

Ian Fleming, 1908-64, (Br.) novelist. James Bond spy thrillers: *Dr. No, Goldfinger.*

Horton Foote, 1916-2009, (U.S.) playwright, screenwriter. *The Trip to Bountiful.*

Ford Madox Ford, 1873-1939, (Br.) novelist, critic, poet. *The Good Soldier.*

C(ecil) S(cott) Forester, 1899-1966, (Br.) writer. Horatio Hornblower books.

E(dward) M(organ) Forster, 1879-1970, (Br.) novelist. *A Passage to India, Howards End.*

Anatole France, 1844-1924, (Fr.) writer. *Penguin Island, My Friend's Book, The Crime of Sylvestre Bonnard.*

Dick Francis, 1920-2010, (Br.) crime novelist.

Marilyn French, 1929-2009, (U.S.) novelist. *The Women's Room.*

Brian Friel, 1929-2015, (N. Ire.) playwright. *Dancing at Lughnasa.*

Robert Frost, 1874-1963, (U.S.) poet. "Birches," "Fire and Ice," "Stopping by Woods on a Snowy Evening."

Carlos Fuentes, 1928-2012, (Pan.) novelist, essayist. *The Old Gringo.*

William Gaddis, 1922-98, (U.S.) novelist. *The Recognitions.*

John Galsworthy, 1867-1933, (Br.) novelist, dramatist. *The Forsyte Saga.*

Federico García Lorca, 1898-1936, (Sp.) poet, dramatist. *Blood Wedding.*

Gabriel García Márquez, 1927-2014, (Col.) novelist. *One Hundred Years of Solitude.*

Erle Stanley Gardner, 1889-1970, (U.S.) mystery writer; created Perry Mason.

Jean Genet, 1911-86, (Fr.) playwright, novelist. *The Maids*.

Kahlil Gibran, 1883-1931, (Leban.-U.S.) mystical novelist, essayist, poet. *The Prophet*.

André Gide, 1869-1951, (Fr.) writer. *The Immoralist*, *The Pastoral Symphony*, *Strait Is the Gate*.

Allen Ginsberg, 1926-97, (U.S.) Beat poet. "Howl."

Jean Giraudoux, 1882-1944, (Fr.) novelist, dramatist. *Electra*, *The Madwoman of Chaillot*, *Ondine*, *Tiger at the Gate*.

Johann Wolfgang von Goethe, 1749-1832, (Ger.) poet, dramatist, novelist. *Faust*, *Sorrows of Young Werther*.

Nikolai Gogol, 1809-52, (Russ.) short-story writer, dramatist, novelist. *Dead Souls*, *The Inspector General*.

William Golding, 1911-93, (Br.) novelist. *Lord of the Flies*.

Oliver Goldsmith, 1728-74, (Br.-Ire.) dramatist, novelist. *The Vicar of Wakefield*, *She Stoops to Conquer*.

Nadine Gordimer, 1923-2014, (S. Afr.) novelist. *Burger's Daughter*.

Maxim Gorky, 1868-1936, (Russ.) dramatist, novelist. *The Lower Depths*.

Günter Grass, 1927-2015, (Ger.) novelist, poet. *The Tin Drum*.

Robert Graves, 1895-1985, (Br.) poet, classical scholar, novelist. *I, Claudius*; *The White Goddess*.

Thomas Gray, 1716-71, (Br.) poet. "Elegy Written in a Country Churchyard," "The Progress of Poesy."

Julien Green, 1900-98, (U.S.-Fr.) expatriate American novelist. *Moira*, *Each Man in His Darkness*.

Graham Greene, 1904-91, (Br.) novelist. *The Power and the Glory*, *The Heart of the Matter*, *The Ministry of Fear*.

Zane Grey, 1872-1939, (U.S.) writer of Western stories.

Jakob Grimm, 1785-1863, philologist, folklorist; with brother **Wilhelm Grimm**, 1786-1859, (both Ger.) collected *Grimm's Fairy Tales*.

Alex Haley, 1921-92, (U.S.) author. *Roots*.

Dashiell Hammett, 1894-1961, (U.S.) detective-story writer; created Sam Spade. *The Maltese Falcon*.

Jupiter Hammon, c. 1720-1800, (U.S.) poet; first African American to have his works published, 1761.

Knut Hamsun, 1859-1952, (Nor.) novelist. *Hunger*.

Lorraine Hansberry, 1930-65, (U.S.) playwright. *A Raisin in the Sun*.

Thomas Hardy, 1840-1928, (Br.) novelist, poet. *The Return of the Native*, *Tess of the D'Urbervilles*, *Jude the Obscure*.

E. Lynn Harris, 1955-2009, (U.S.) novelist. *Invisible Life*, *Basketball Jones*.

Joel Chandler Harris, 1848-1908, (U.S.) writer. Uncle Remus stories.

Jim Harrison, 1937-2016, (U.S.) novelist and essayist. *Legends of the Fall*.

Moss Hart, 1904-61, (U.S.) playwright. *Once in a Lifetime*, *You Can't Take It With You*, *The Man Who Came to Dinner*.

Bret Harte, 1836-1902, (U.S.) short-story writer, poet. *The Luck of Roaring Camp*.

Jaroslav Hasek, 1883-1923, (Czech.) writer, playwright. *The Good Soldier Schweik*.

Vaclav Havel, 1936-2011, (Czech.) essayist, poet, playwright. *The Power of the Powerless*.

John Hawkes, 1925-98, (U.S.) experimental fiction writer. *The Goose on the Grave*, *Blood Oranges*.

Nathaniel Hawthorne, 1804-64, (U.S.) novelist, short-story writer. *The Scarlet Letter*, "Young Goodman Brown."

Seamus Heaney, 1939-2013, (Ire.) poet. *Death of a Naturalist*.

Heinrich Heine, 1797-1856, (Ger.) poet. *Book of Songs*.

Robert Heinlein, 1907-88, (U.S.) science-fiction writer. *Stranger in a Strange Land*.

Joseph Heller, 1923-99, (U.S.) novelist. *Catch-22*.

Lillian Hellman, 1905-84, (U.S.) playwright, memoirist. *The Little Foxes*, *An Unfinished Woman*, *Pentimento*.

Ernest Hemingway, 1899-1961, (U.S.) novelist, short-story writer. *A Farewell to Arms*, *For Whom the Bell Tolls*.

O. Henry (W. S. Porter), 1862-1910, (U.S.) short-story writer. "The Gift of the Magi."

George Herbert, 1593-1633, (Br.) poet. "The Altar," "Easter Wings."

Zbigniew Herbert, 1924-98, (Pol.) poet. "Apollo and Marsyas."

Robert Herrick, 1591-1674, (Br.) poet. "To the Virgins to Make Much of Time."

John Hersey, 1914-93, (U.S.) novelist, journalist. *Hiroshima*, *A Bell for Adano*.

Hermann Hesse, 1877-1962, (Ger.) novelist, poet. *Death and the Lover*, *Steppenwolf*, *Siddhartha*.

Oscar Hijuelos, 1951-2013, (U.S.) novelist. *The Mambo Kings Play Songs of Love*.

Tony Hillerman, 1925-2008, (U.S.) novelist. *Dance Hall of the Dead*.

James Hilton, 1900-54, (Br.) novelist. *Lost Horizon*.

Chester Himes, 1909-84, (U.S.) novelist. *Cotton Comes to Harlem*.

Oliver Wendell Holmes, 1809-94, (U.S.) poet, novelist. *The Autocrat of the Breakfast-Table*.

Gerard Manley Hopkins, 1844-89, (Br.) poet. "Pied Beauty," "God's Grandeur."

A(lfred) E. Housman, 1859-1936, (Br.) poet. *A Shropshire Lad*.

William Dean Howells, 1837-1920, (U.S.) novelist, critic. *The Rise of Silas Lapham*.

Langston Hughes, 1902-67, (U.S.) poet, lyric writer, author; a major influence in 1920s Harlem Renaissance.

Ted Hughes, 1930-98, (Br.) British poet laureate, 1984-98. *Crow*, *The Hawk in the Rain*.

Victor Hugo, 1802-85, (Fr.) poet, dramatist, novelist. *Notre Dame de Paris*, *Les Misérables*.

Zora Neale Hurston, 1903-60, (U.S.) novelist, folklorist. *Their Eyes Were Watching God*, *Mules and Men*.

Aldous Huxley, 1894-1963, (Br.) writer. *Brave New World*.

Henrik Ibsen, 1828-1906, (Nor.) dramatist, poet. *A Doll's House*, *Ghosts*, *The Wild Duck*, *Hedda Gabler*.

William Inge, 1913-73, (U.S.) playwright. *Picnic*; *Come Back, Little Sheba*; *Bus Stop*.

Eugene Ionesco, 1910-94, (Fr.) surrealist dramatist. *The Bald Soprano*, *The Chairs*.

Washington Irving, 1783-1859, (U.S.) writer. "Rip Van Winkle," "The Legend of Sleepy Hollow."

Christopher Isherwood, 1904-86, (Br.) novelist, playwright. *The Berlin Stories*.

Shirley Jackson, 1919-65, (U.S.) short-story writer. "The Lottery."

Henry James, 1843-1916, (U.S.) novelist, short-story writer, critic. *The Portrait of a Lady*, *The Ambassadors*, *Daisy Miller*.

P(hyllis) D(orothy) James, 1920-2014, (Br.) mystery novelist.

Robinson Jeffers, 1887-1962, (U.S.) poet, dramatist. *Tamar and Other Poems*, *Medea*.

James Weldon Johnson, 1871-1938, (U.S.) poet, novelist, diplomat; lyricist for *Lift Every Voice and Sing*.

Samuel Johnson, 1709-84, (Br.) author, scholar, critic. *Dictionary of the English Language*, *Vanity of Human Wishes*.

Ben Jonson, 1572-1637, (Br.) dramatist, poet. *Volpone*.

James Joyce, 1882-1941, (Ire.) writer. *Ulysses*, *Dubliners*, *A Portrait of the Artist as a Young Man*, *Finnegans Wake*.

Ernst Junger, 1895-1998, (Ger.) novelist, essayist. *The Peace*, *On the Marble Cliff*.

Franz Kafka, 1883-1924, (Austria-Hung./Czech.) novelist, short-story writer. *The Trial*, *The Castle*, "The Metamorphosis."

George S. Kaufman, 1889-1961, (U.S.) playwright. *The Man Who Came to Dinner*, *You Can't Take It With You*.

Yasunari Kawabata, 1899-1972, (Jpn.) novelist. *The Sound of the Mountains*.

Nikos Kazantzakis, 1883-1957, (Gr.) novelist. *Zorba the Greek*, *A Greek Passion*.

Alfred Kazin, 1915-98 (U.S.) author, critic, teacher. *On Native Grounds*.

John Keats, 1795-1821, (Br.) poet. "Ode on a Grecian Urn," "Ode to a Nightingale," "La Belle Dame Sans Merci."

Jack Kerouac, 1922-69, (U.S.) author, Beat poet. *On the Road*, *The Dharma Bums*, "Mexico City Blues."

Joyce Kilmer, 1886-1918, (U.S.) poet. "Trees."

Galway Kinnell, 1927-2014, (U.S.) poet.

Rudyard Kipling, 1865-1936, (Br.) author, poet. "The White Man's Burden," "Gunga Din," *The Jungle Book*.

Maxine Kumin, 1925-2014, (U.S.) poet, author. *Up Country: Poems of New England*.

Jean de la Fontaine, 1621-95, (Fr.) poet. *Fables choisies* (Selected Fables).

Pär Lagerkvist, 1891-1974, (Swed.) poet, dramatist, novelist. *Barabbas*, *The Sybil*.

Selma Lagerlöf, 1858-1940, (Swed.) novelist. *Jerusalem*, *The Ring of the Lowenskolds*.

Alphonse de Lamartine, 1790-1869, (Fr.) poet, novelist, statesman. *Méditations poétiques*.

Charles Lamb, 1775-1834, (Br.) essayist. *Specimens of English Dramatic Poets*, *Essays of Elia*.

Louis L'Amour, 1908-88, (U.S.) Western author, screenwriter. *Hondo*, *The Cherokee Trail*.

Giuseppe di Lampedusa, 1896-1957, (It.) novelist. *The Leopard*.

William Langland, c. 1332-1400, (Br.) poet. *Piers Plowman*.

Ring Lardner, 1885-1933, (U.S.) short-story writer, humorist.

Steig Larsson, 1954-2004, (Swed.) novelist. *The Girl With the Dragon Tattoo*.

Arthur Laurents, 1917-2011, (U.S.) playwright and director. *West Side Story*.

D(avid) H(erbert) Lawrence, 1885-1930, (Br.) novelist. *Sons and Lovers*, *Women in Love*, *Lady Chatterley's Lover*.

Halldór Laxness, 1902-98, (Iceland) novelist. *Iceland's Bell*.

Harper Lee, 1926-2016, (U.S.) novelist. *To Kill a Mockingbird*.

Madeleine L'Engle, 1918-2007, (U.S.) novelist of young adult fiction. *A Wrinkle in Time*.

Elmore Leonard, 1925-2013, (U.S.) novelist. *Get Shorty*.

Mikhail Lermontov, 1814-41, (Russ.) novelist, poet. "Demon," *Hero of Our Time*.

Alain-René Lesage, 1668-1747, (Fr.) novelist. *Gil Blas de Santillane*.

Doris Lessing, 1919-2013, (Br.) writer. *The Golden Notebook*.

Gotthold Lessing, 1729-81, (Ger.) dramatist, philosopher, critic. *Miss Sara Sampson*, *Minna von Barnhelm*.

Ira Levin, 1929-2007, (U.S.) novelist, playwright. *Deathtrap*.

C(live) S(taples) Lewis, 1898-1963, (Br.) critic, novelist, religious writer. *Allegory of Love*; *The Lion, the Witch and the Wardrobe*; *Out of the Silent Planet*.

Sinclair Lewis, 1885-1951, (U.S.) novelist. *Babbitt*, *Main Street*, *Arrowsmith*, *Dodsworth*.

Li Po, 701-762, (China) poet. "Song Before Drinking," "She Spins Silk."

Vachel Lindsay, 1879-1931, (U.S.) poet. *General William Booth Enters Into Heaven*, *The Congo*.

Hugh Lofting, 1886-1947, (Br.) writer. Dr. Doolittle series.

Jack London, 1876-1916, (U.S.) novelist, journalist. *Call of the Wild*, *The Sea-Wolf*, *White Fang*.

Henry Wadsworth Longfellow, 1807-82, (U.S.) poet. *Evangeline*, *The Song of Hiawatha*.

Lope de Vega, 1562-1635, (Sp.) playwright. *Noche de San Juan*, *Maestro de Danzar*.

H(oward) P(hillips) Lovecraft, 1890-1937, (U.S.) novelist, short-story writer. "At the Mountains of Madness."

Amy Lowell, 1874-1925, (U.S.) poet, critic. "Lilacs."

James Russell Lowell, 1819-91, (U.S.) poet, editor. *Poems*, *The Biglow Papers*.

Robert Lowell, 1917-77, (U.S.) poet. "Lord Weary's Castle."

Joaquim Maria Machado de Assis, 1839-1908, (Brazil) novelist, poet. *The Posthumous Memoirs of Bras Cubas*.

Archibald MacLeish, 1892-1982, (U.S.) poet. *Conquistador*.

Naguib Mahfouz, 1911-2006, (Egypt) novelist; first Arabic-language writer to win the Nobel Prize for Literature. *Cairo Trilogy*.

Norman Mailer, 1923-2007, (U.S.) novelist, essayist, journalist. *The Naked and the Dead*.

Bernard Malamud, 1914-86, (U.S.) short-story writer, novelist. "The Magic Barrel," *The Assistant*, *The Fixer*.

Stéphane Mallarmé, 1842-98, (Fr.) poet. *Poésies*.

Sir Thomas Malory, c. 1410-71, (Br.) writer. *Morte d'Arthur*.

Andre Malraux, 1901-76, (Fr.) novelist. *Man's Fate*.

Osip Mandelstam, 1891-1938, (Russ.) poet. *Stone, Tristia*.

Thomas Mann, 1875-1955, (Ger.) novelist, essayist. *Buddenbrooks*, *The Magic Mountain*, "Death in Venice."

Katherine Mansfield, 1888-1923, (Br.) short-story writer. "Bliss."

Christopher Marlowe, 1564-93, (Br.) dramatist, poet. *Tamburlaine the Great*, *Dr. Faustus*, *The Jew of Malta*.

Andrew Marvell, 1621-78, (Br.) poet. "To His Coy Mistress."

John Masefield, 1878-1967, (Br.) poet. "Sea Fever," "Cargoes," *Salt Water Ballads*.

Edgar Lee Masters, 1869-1950, (U.S.) poet, biographer. *Spoon River Anthology*.

Peter Matthiessen, 1927-2014, (U.S.) novelist. *The Snow Leopard*.

W(illiam) Somerset Maugham, 1874-1965, (Br.) author. *Of Human Bondage*, *The Moon and Sixpence*.

Guy de Maupassant, 1850-93, (Fr.) novelist, short-story writer. "A Life," "Bel-Ami," "The Necklace."

François Mauriac, 1885-1970, (Fr.) novelist, dramatist. *Viper's Tangle*, *The Kiss to the Leper*.

Vladimir Mayakovsky, 1893-1930, (Russ.) poet, dramatist. *The Cloud in Trousers*.

Mary McCarthy, 1912-89, (U.S.) critic, novelist, memoirist. *Memories of a Catholic Girlhood*.

Frank McCourt, 1930-2009, (U.S.) memoirist. *Angela's Ashes*, *'Tis*, *Teacher Man*.

Carson McCullers, 1917-67, (U.S.) novelist. *The Heart Is a Lonely Hunter*, *Member of the Wedding*.

Colleen McCullough, 1937-2015, (Austral.) novelist. *The Thorn Birds*.

Herman Melville, 1819-91, (U.S.) novelist, poet. *Moby-Dick*, *Typee*, *Billy Budd*, *Omoo*.

George Meredith, 1828-1909, (Br.) novelist, poet. *The Ordeal of Richard Feverel*, *The Egoist*.

Prosper Mérimée, 1803-70, (Fr.) author. *Carmen*.

James Merrill, 1926-95, (U.S.) poet. *Divine Comedies*.

James Michener, 1907-97, (U.S.) novelist. *Tales of the South Pacific*.

Edna St. Vincent Millay, 1892-1950, (U.S.) poet. *The Harp Weaver and Other Poems*.

Arthur Miller,1915-2005, (U.S.) playwright. *The Crucible*, *After the Fall*, *Death of a Salesman*.

Henry Miller, 1891-1980, (U.S.) erotic novelist. *Tropic of Cancer*.

A(lan) A(lexander) Milne, 1882-1956, (Br.) author. *Winnie-the-Pooh*.

Czeslaw Milosz, 1911-2004, (Pol.) essayist, poet. "Esse," "Encounter."

John Milton, 1608-74, (Br.) poet, writer. *Paradise Lost*, *Comus*, *Lycidas*, *Areopagitica*.

Mishima Yukio (Hiraoka Kimitake) 1925-70, (Jpn.) writer. *Confessions of a Mask*.

Gabriela Mistral, 1889-1957, (Chile) poet. *Sonnets of Death*.

Margaret Mitchell, 1900-49, (U.S.) novelist. *Gone With the Wind*.

Jean Baptiste Molière, 1622-73, (Fr.) dramatist. *Tartuffe*, *Le Misanthrope*, *Le Bourgeois Gentilhomme*.

Ferenc Molnár, 1878-1952, (Hung.) dramatist, novelist. *Liliom*, *The Guardsman*, *The Swan*.

Michel de Montaigne, 1533-92, (Fr.) essayist. *Essais*.

Eugenio Montale, 1896-1981, (It.) poet.

Brian Moore, 1921-99, (Ire.-U.S.) novelist. *The Lonely Passion of Judith Hearne*.

Clement C. Moore, 1779-1863, (U.S.) poet, educator. "A Visit From Saint Nicholas."

Marianne Moore, 1887-1972, (U.S.) poet.

Alberto Moravia, 1907-90, (It.) novelist, short-story writer. *The Time of Indifference*.

Sir Thomas More, 1478-1535, (Br.) writer, statesman, saint. *Utopia*.

Wright Morris, 1910-98, (U.S.) novelist. *My Uncle Dudley*.

Murasaki Shikibu, c. 978-1026, (Jpn.) novelist. *The Tale of Genji*.

Iris Murdoch, 1919-99, (Br.) novelist, philosopher. *The Sea, the Sea*.

Alfred de Musset, 1810-57, (Fr.) poet, dramatist. *La Confession d'un Enfant du Siècle*.

Vladimir Nabokov, 1899-1977, (Russ.-U.S.) novelist. *Lolita*, *Pale Fire*.

R. K. Narayan, 1906-2001, (India) novelist. *The Guide*.

Ogden Nash, 1902-71, (U.S.) poet of light verse.

Irène Némirovsky, 1903-42, (Ukraine) novelist. *David Golder*, *Suite Française*.

Pablo Neruda, 1904-73, (Chile) poet. *Twenty Love Poems and One Song of Despair*, *Toward the Splendid City*.

Patrick O'Brian, 1914-2000, (Br.) historical novelist. *Master and Commander*, *Blue at the Mizzen*.

Sean O'Casey, 1884-1964, (Ire.) dramatist. *Juno and the Paycock*, *The Plough and the Stars*.

Flannery O'Connor, 1925-64, (U.S.) novelist, short-story writer. *Wise Blood*, "A Good Man Is Hard to Find."

Frank O'Connor (Michael Donovan), 1903-66, (Ire.) short-story writer. "Guests of a Nation."

Clifford Odets, 1906-63, (U.S.) playwright. *Waiting for Lefty*, *Awake and Sing*, *Golden Boy*, *The Country Girl*.

John O'Hara, 1905-70, (U.S.) novelist, short-story writer. *From the Terrace*, *Appointment in Samarra*, *Pal Joey*.

Omar Khayyam, c. 1028-1122, (Per.) poet. *Rubaiyat*.

Eugene O'Neill, 1888-1953, (U.S.) playwright. *Emperor Jones*, *Anna Christie*, *Long Day's Journey Into Night*.

George Orwell (Eric Arthur Blair), 1903-50, (Br.) novelist, essayist. *Animal Farm*, *Nineteen Eighty-Four*.

John Osborne, 1929-95, (Br.) dramatist, novelist. *Look Back in Anger*, *The Entertainer*.

Wilfred Owen, 1893-1918, (Br.) poet. "Dulce et Décorum Est."

Grace Paley, 1922-2007, (U.S.) short-story writer, poet. *The Little Disturbances of Man*.

Dorothy Parker, 1893-1967, (U.S.) poet, short-story writer. *Enough Rope*, *Laments for the Living*.

Robert B. Parker, 1932-2010, (U.S.) crime novelist. "Spenser" novels.

Boris Pasternak, 1890-1960, (Russ.) poet, novelist. *Doctor Zhivago*.

Alan Paton, 1903-88, (S. Africa) novelist. *Cry, the Beloved Country*.

Octavio Paz, 1914-98, (Mex.) poet, essayist. *The Labyrinth of Solitude*, *They Shall Not Pass!*, *The Sun Stone*.

Samuel Pepys, 1633-1703, (Br.) public official, diarist.

S(idney) J(oseph) Perelman, 1904-79, (U.S.) humorist. *The Road to Miltown*, *Under the Spreading Atrophy*.

Charles Perrault, 1628-1703, (Fr.) writer. *Tales From Mother Goose* (*Sleeping Beauty*, *Cinderella*).

Petrarch (Francesco Petrarca), 1304-74, (It.) poet. *Africa*, *Trionfi*, *Canzoniere*.

Harold Pinter, 1930-2008, (Br.) playwright. *The Birthday Party*, *The Caretaker*, *The Homecoming*.

Luigi Pirandello, 1867-1936, (It.) novelist, dramatist. *Six Characters in Search of an Author*.

Sylvia Plath, 1932-63, (U.S.) author, poet. *The Bell Jar*.

Edgar Allan Poe, 1809-49, (U.S.) poet, short-story writer, critic. "Annabel Lee," "The Raven," "The Purloined Letter."

Alexander Pope, 1688-1744, (Br.) poet. *The Rape of the Lock*, *The Dunciad*, *An Essay on Man*.

Katherine Anne Porter, 1890-1980, (U.S.) novelist, short-story writer. *Ship of Fools*.

Chaim Potok, 1929-2002, (U.S.) novelist. *The Chosen*.

Ezra Pound, 1885-1972, (U.S.) poet. *Cantos*.

Anthony Powell, 1905-2000, (Br.) novelist. *A Dance to the Music of Time* series.

Terry Pratchett, 1948-2015 (Br.) fantasy novelist. *Discworld* series.

Reynolds Price, 1933-2011, (U.S.) novelist, short-story writer, poet. *A Long and Happy Life*.

J(ohn) B(oynton) Priestley, 1894-1984, (Br.) novelist, dramatist. *The Good Companions*.

Marcel Proust, 1871-1922, (Fr.) novelist. *Remembrance of Things Past*.

Aleksandr Pushkin, 1799-1837, (Russ.) poet, novelist. *Boris Godunov*, *Eugene Onegin*.

Mario Puzo, 1920-99, (U.S.) novelist. *The Godfather*.

François Rabelais, 1495-1553, (Fr.) writer. *Gargantua*.

Jean Racine, 1639-99, (Fr.) dramatist. *Andromaque*, *Phèdre*, *Bérénice*, *Britannicus*.

David Rakoff, 1964-2012, (Can.-U.S.) essayist. *Fraud*, *Don't Get Too Comfortable*.

Ayn Rand, 1905-82, (Russ.-U.S.) novelist, moral theorist. *The Fountainhead*, *Atlas Shrugged*.

Terence Rattigan, 1911-77, (Br.) playwright. *Separate Tables*, *The Browning Version*.

Erich Maria Remarque, 1898-1970, (Ger.-U.S.) novelist. *All Quiet on the Western Front*.

Mary Renault, 1905-83, (Br.) novelist. *The Last of the Wine*.

Ruth Rendell, 1930-2015, (Br.) novelist. Chief Inspector Reginald Wexford mysteries.

Adrienne Rich, 1929-2012, (U.S.) poet. *Diving Into the Wreck: Poems, 1971-1972*.

Samuel Richardson, 1689-1761, (Br.) novelist. *Pamela; or Virtue Rewarded*.

Rainer Maria Rilke, 1875-1926, (Ger.) poet. *Life and Songs*, *Duino Elegies*, *Poems From the Book of Hours*.

Arthur Rimbaud, 1854-91, (Fr.) poet. *A Season in Hell*.

Harold Robbins, 1916-97, (U.S.) novelist, *The Carpetbaggers*.

Edwin Arlington Robinson, 1869-1935, (U.S.) poet. "Richard Cory," "Miniver Cheevy," *Merlin*.

Theodore Roethke, 1908-63, (U.S.) poet. *Open House*, *The Waking*, *The Far Field*.

Romain Rolland, 1866-1944, (Fr.) novelist, biographer. *Jean-Christophe*.

Pierre de Ronsard, 1524-85, (Fr.) poet. *Sonnets pour Hélène*, *La Franciade*.

Christina Rossetti, 1830-94, (Br.) poet. "When I Am Dead, My Dearest."

Dante Gabriel Rossetti, 1828-82, (Br.) poet, painter. "The Blessed Damozel."

Edmond Rostand, 1868-1918, (Fr.) poet, dramatist. *Cyrano de Bergerac*.

Damon Runyon, 1880-1946, (U.S.) short-story writer, journalist. *Guys and Dolls, Blue Plate Special*.

John Ruskin, 1819-1900, (Br.) critic, social theorist. *Modern Painters, The Seven Lamps of Architecture*.

Oliver Sacks, 1933-2015, (Br.) neurologist, writer. *The Man Who Mistook His Wife for a Hat*.

François Sagan (Françoise Quoirez), 1935-2004, (Fr.) novelist. *Bonjour Tristesse*.

Antoine de Saint-Exupéry, 1900-44, (Fr.) writer. *Wind, Sand and Stars; The Little Prince*.

Saki (or H[ector] H[ugh] Munro), 1870-1916, (Br.) writer. *The Chronicles of Clovis*.

J. D. Salinger, 1919-2010, (U.S.) novelist. *The Catcher in the Rye*.

George Sand (Amandine Lucie Aurore Dupin), 1804-76, (Fr.) novelist. *Indiana, Consuelo*.

Carl Sandburg, 1878-1967, (U.S.) poet. *The People, Yes; Chicago Poems; Smoke and Steel; Harvest Poems*.

Jose Saramago, 1922-2010, (Port.) novelist. *Blindness*.

William Saroyan, 1908-81, (U.S.) playwright, novelist. *The Time of Your Life, The Human Comedy*.

Nathalie Sarraute, 1900-99, (Fr.) Nouveau Roman novelist. *Tropismes*.

May Sarton, 1914-95, (Belg.-U.S.) poet, novelist. *Encounter in April, Anger*.

Dorothy L. Sayers, 1893-1957, (Br.) mystery writer; created Lord Peter Wimsey.

Richard Scarry, 1920-94, (U.S.) author of children's books. *Richard Scarry's Best Story Book Ever*.

Friedrich von Schiller, 1759-1805, (Ger.) dramatist, poet, historian. *Don Carlos, Maria Stuart, Wilhelm Tell*.

Sir Walter Scott, 1771-1832, (Scot.) novelist, poet. *Ivanhoe*.

Gil Scott-Heron, 1949-2011, (U.S.) poet. "The Revolution Will Not Be Televised."

Jaroslav Seifert, 1902-86, (Czech.) poet.

Maurice Sendak, 1928-2012, (U.S.) children's book author and illustrator. *Where the Wild Things Are*.

Dr. Seuss (Theodor Seuss Geisel), 1904-91, (U.S.) children's book author and illustrator. *The Cat in the Hat*.

William Shakespeare, 1564-1616, (Br.) dramatist, poet. *Romeo and Juliet, Hamlet, King Lear, Julius Caesar*, sonnets.

Karl Shapiro, 1913-2000, (U.S.) poet. "Elegy for a Dead Soldier."

George Bernard Shaw, 1856-1950, (Ire.-Br.) playwright, critic. *St. Joan, Pygmalion, Major Barbara, Man and Superman*.

Sidney Sheldon, 1917-2007, (U.S.) screenwriter, novelist. *Rage of Angels, Memories of Midnight*.

Mary Wollstonecraft Shelley, 1797-1851, (Br.) novelist, feminist. *Frankenstein, The Last Man*.

Percy Bysshe Shelley, 1792-1822, (Br.) poet. *Prometheus Unbound, Adonais*, "Ode to the West Wind," "To a Skylark."

Richard B. Sheridan, 1751-1816, (Br.) dramatist. *The Rivals, School for Scandal*.

Robert Sherwood, 1896-1955, (U.S.) playwright, biographer. *The Petrified Forest, Abe Lincoln in Illinois*.

Mikhail Sholokhov, 1906-84, (Russ.) writer. *The Silent Don*.

Shel Silverstein, 1932-99, (U.S.) poet, writer. *The Giving Tree, Where the Sidewalk Ends*.

Georges Simenon (Georges Sims), 1903-89, (Belg.-Fr.) mystery writer; created Inspector Maigret.

Upton Sinclair, 1878-1968, (U.S.) novelist. *The Jungle*.

Isaac Bashevis Singer, 1904-91, (Pol.-U.S.) novelist, short-story writer, in Yiddish. *The Magician of Lublin*.

C(harles) P(ercy) Snow, 1905-80, (Br.) novelist, scientist. *Strangers and Brothers, Corridors of Power*.

Aleksandr Solzhenitsyn, 1918-2008, (Russ.) novelist, dramatist. *One Day in the Life of Ivan Denisovich*.

Susan Sontag, 1933-2004, (U.S.) critic, essayist, novelist. *Notes on Camp, The Volcano Lover, In America*.

Stephen Spender, 1909-95, (Br.) poet, critic, novelist. *Twenty Poems*, "Elegy for Margaret."

Edmund Spenser, 1552-99, (Br.) poet. *The Faerie Queene*.

Mickey Spillane, 1918-2006, (U.S.) novelist; Mike Hammer detective novels. *The Killing Man*.

Johanna Spyri, 1827-1901, (Switz.) children's author. *Heidi*.

Christina Stead, 1903-83, (Austral.) novelist, short-story writer. *The Man Who Loved Children*.

Richard Steele, 1672-1729, (Br.) essayist, playwright; began the *Tatler* and *Spectator*. *The Conscious Lovers*.

Gertrude Stein, 1874-1946, (U.S.) writer. *Three Lives*.

John Steinbeck, 1902-68, (U.S.) novelist. *The Grapes of Wrath, Of Mice and Men, The Winter of Our Discontent*.

Stendhal (Marie Henri Beyle), 1783-1842, (Fr.) novelist. *The Red and the Black, The Charterhouse of Parma*.

Laurence Sterne, 1713-68, (Br.) novelist. *Tristram Shandy*.

Wallace Stevens, 1879-1955, (U.S.) poet. *Harmonium, The Man With the Blue Guitar, Notes Toward a Supreme Fiction*.

Robert Louis Stevenson, 1850-94, (Br.) novelist, poet, essayist. *Treasure Island, A Child's Garden of Verses*.

Mary Stewart, 1916-2014, (Br.) fantasy novelist. Merlin series.

Bram Stoker, 1847-1912, (Br.) writer. *Dracula*.

Rex Stout, 1886-1975, (U.S.) mystery writer; created Nero Wolfe.

Harriet Beecher Stowe, 1811-96, (U.S.) novelist. *Uncle Tom's Cabin*.

Lytton Strachey, 1880-1932, (Br.) biographer, critic. *Eminent Victorians, Queen Victoria, Elizabeth and Essex*.

Mark Strand, 1934-2014, (Can.-U.S.) poet. *Blizzard of One*.

August Strindberg, 1849-1912, (Swed.) dramatist, novelist. *The Father, Miss Julie, The Creditors*.

William Styron, 1925-2006, (U.S.) novelist, essayist. *The Confessions of Nat Turner, Sophie's Choice, Darkness Visible: A Memoir of Madness*.

Jonathan Swift, 1667-1745, (Br.) satirist, poet. *Gulliver's Travels*, "A Modest Proposal."

Algernon C. Swinburne, 1837-1909, (Br.) poet, dramatist. *Atalanta in Calydon*.

John M. Synge, 1871-1909, (Ire.) poet, dramatist. *Riders to the Sea, The Playboy of the Western World*.

Wislawa Szymborska, 1923-2012, (Pol.) poet. "Cat in an Empty Apartment."

Rabindranath Tagore, 1861-1941, (India) author, poet. *Sadhana, The Realization of Life, Gitanjali*.

Booth Tarkington, 1869-1946, (U.S.) novelist. *The Magnificent Ambersons*.

Peter Taylor, 1917-94, (U.S.) novelist. *A Summons to Memphis*.

Sara Teasdale, 1884-1933, (U.S.) poet. *Helen of Troy and Other Poems, Rivers to the Sea*.

Alfred, Lord Tennyson, 1809-92, (Br.) poet. *Idylls of the King, In Memoriam*, "The Charge of the Light Brigade."

William Makepeace Thackeray, 1811-63, (Br.) novelist. *Vanity Fair, Henry Esmond, Pendennis*.

Dylan Thomas, 1914-53, (Wales) poet. *Under Milk Wood, A Child's Christmas in Wales*.

Hunter S. Thompson, 1937-2005, (U.S.) author, journalist. *Hell's Angels, Fear and Loathing in Las Vegas*.

Henry David Thoreau, 1817-62, (U.S.) writer, philosopher, naturalist. *Walden*, "Civil Disobedience."

James Thurber, 1894-1961, (U.S.) humorist. "The Secret Life of Walter Mitty," *My Life and Hard Times*.

J(ohn) R(onald) R(euel) Tolkien, 1892-1973, (Br.) writer. *The Hobbit*, Lord of the Rings trilogy.

Leo Tolstoy, 1828-1910, (Russ.) novelist, short-story writer. *War and Peace, Anna Karenina*, "The Death of Ivan Ilyich."

Lionel Trilling, 1905-75, (U.S.) critic, author, teacher. *The Liberal Imagination*.

Anthony Trollope, 1815-82, (Br.) novelist. *The Warden, Barchester Towers*, the Palliser novels.

Ivan Turgenev, 1818-83, (Russ.) novelist, short-story writer. *Fathers and Sons, First Love, A Month in the Country*.

Amos Tutuola, 1920-97, (Nigeria) novelist. *The Palm-Wine Drunkard, My Life in the Bush of Ghosts*.

Mark Twain (Samuel Clemens), 1835-1910, (U.S.) novelist, humorist. *The Adventures of Huckleberry Finn*.

Sigrid Undset, 1881-1949, (Nor.) novelist. *Kristin Lavransdatter*.

John Updike, 1932-2009, (U.S.) novelist, literary critic. *Rabbit is Rich, The Witches of Eastwick*.

Paul Valéry, 1871-1945, (Fr.) poet, critic. *La Jeune Parque, The Graveyard by the Sea*.

Paul Verlaine, 1844-96, (Fr.) Symbolist poet. *Songs Without Words*.

Jules Verne, 1828-1905, (Fr.) novelist. *Twenty Thousand Leagues Under the Sea*.

Gore Vidal, 1925-2012, (U.S.) novelist. *The City and the Pillar*.

François Villon, 1431-c. 1463, (Fr.) poet. *The Lays, The Grand Testament*.

Voltaire (F. M. Arouet), 1694-1778, (Fr.) writer of "philosophical romances"; philosopher, historian. *Candide*.

Kurt Vonnegut Jr., 1922-2007, (U.S.) novelist, essayist. *Cat's Cradle, Slaughterhouse-Five, Breakfast of Champions*.

David Foster Wallace, 1962-2008, (U.S.) novelist, essayist. *Infinite Jest, A Supposedly Fun Thing I'll Never Do Again*.

Robert Penn Warren, 1905-89, (U.S.) novelist, poet, critic. *All the King's Men*.

Wendy Wasserstein, 1950-2006, (U.S.) playwright. *The Heidi Chronicles*.

Evelyn Waugh, 1903-66, (Br.) novelist. *The Loved One, Brideshead Revisited, A Handful of Dust*.

H(erbert) G(eorge) Wells, 1866-1946, (Br.) novelist. *The Time Machine, The Invisible Man, The War of the Worlds*.

Eudora Welty, 1909-2001, (U.S.) Southern short-story writer, novelist. "Why I Live at the P.O.," "The Ponder Heart."

Rebecca West, 1893-1983, (Br.) novelist, critic, journalist. *Black Lamb and Grey Falcon*.

Edith Wharton, 1862-1937, (U.S.) novelist. *The Age of Innocence, The House of Mirth, Ethan Frome*.

Phillis Wheatley, c. 1753-84, (U.S.) poet; 2nd American woman and first black woman to be published, 1770.

E(lwyn) B(rooks) White, 1899-1985, (U.S.) essayist, novelist. *Charlotte's Web, Stuart Little*.

Patrick White, 1912-90, (Austral.) novelist. *The Tree of Man*.

T(erence) H(anbury) White, 1906-64, (Br.) author. *The Once and Future King, A Book of Beasts*.

Walt Whitman, 1819-92, (U.S.) poet. *Leaves of Grass*.

John Greenleaf Whittier, 1807-92, (U.S.) poet, journalist. *Snow-Bound*.

Elie Wiesel, 1928-2016, (Rom.) memoirist, novelist. *Night*.

Oscar Wilde, 1854-1900, (Ire.) novelist, playwright. *The Picture of Dorian Gray, The Importance of Being Earnest*.

Laura Ingalls Wilder, 1867-1957, (U.S.) novelist. Little House on the Prairie series of children's books.

Thornton Wilder, 1897-1975, (U.S.) playwright. *Our Town, The Skin of Our Teeth, The Matchmaker.*

Tennessee Williams, 1911-83, (U.S.) playwright. *A Streetcar Named Desire, Cat on a Hot Tin Roof, The Glass Menagerie.*

William Carlos Williams, 1883-1963, (U.S.) poet, physician. *The Tempers, Al Que Quiere! Paterson,* "This Is Just to Say."

Edmund Wilson, 1895-1972, (U.S.) critic, novelist. *Axel's Castle, To the Finland Station.*

Lanford Wilson, 1937-2011, (U.S.) playwright. *Talley's Folly, Fifth of July.*

P(elham) G(renville) Wodehouse, 1881-1975, (Br.-U.S.) humorist. "Jeeves" novels, *Anything Goes.*

Thomas Wolfe, 1900-38, (U.S.) novelist. *Look Homeward, Angel; You Can't Go Home Again.*

Virginia Woolf, 1882-1941, (Br.) novelist, essayist. *Mrs. Dalloway, To the Lighthouse, A Room of One's Own.*

William Wordsworth, 1770-1850, (Br.) poet. "Tintern Abbey," "Ode: Intimations of Immortality," *The Prelude.*

Richard Wright, 1908-60, (U.S.) novelist, short-story writer. *Native Son, Black Boy, Uncle Tom's Children.*

Elinor Wylie, 1885-1928, (U.S.) poet. *Nets to Catch the Wind.*

William Butler Yeats, 1865-1939, (Ire.) poet, playwright. "The Second Coming," *The Wild Swans at Coole.*

Frank Yerby, 1916-91, (U.S.) first best-selling African American novelist. *The Foxes of Harrow.*

Émile Zola, 1840-1902, (Fr.) novelist. *Nana, Thérèsè Raquin.*

Poets Laureate

There is no record of the origin of the office of Poet Laureate of England. Henry III (1216-72) reportedly had a Versificator Regis, or King's Poet, paid 100 shillings per year. Other poets said to have filled the role include Geoffrey Chaucer (d 1400), Edmund Spenser (d 1599), Ben Jonson (d 1637), and Sir William d'Avenant (d 1668). The first official English poet laureate was John Dryden, appointed 1668, for life (as was customary). Then came Thomas Shadwell, in 1689; Nahum Tate, 1692; Nicholas Rowe, 1715; Rev. Laurence Eusden, 1718; Colley Cibber, 1730; William Whitehead, 1757; Rev. Thomas Warton, 1785; Henry James Pye, 1790; Robert Southey, 1813; William Wordsworth, 1843; Alfred, Lord Tennyson, 1850; Alfred Austin, 1896; Robert Bridges, 1913; John Masefield, 1930; C. Day Lewis, 1968; Sir John Betjeman, 1972; Ted Hughes, 1984; Andrew Motion, 1999; and Carol Ann Duffy, 2009.

In the U.S., appointment is by the Librarian of Congress to a term of one year, which may be renewed: Robert Penn Warren, appointed 1986; Richard Wilbur, 1987; Howard Nemerov, 1988; Mark Strand, 1990; Joseph Brodsky, 1991; Mona Van Duyn, 1992; Rita Dove, 1993; Robert Hass, 1995; Robert Pinsky, 1997; Stanley Kunitz, 2000; Billy Collins, 2001; Louise Gluck, 2003; Ted Kooser, 2004; Donald Hall, 2006; Charles Simic, 2007; Kay Ryan, 2008; W. S. Merwin, 2010; Philip Levine, 2011; Natasha Trethewey, 2012; Charles Wright, 2014; Juan Felipe Herrera, 2015.

Composers of Classical and Avant Garde Music

John Adams, b 1947, (U.S.) *Nixon in China, The Death of Klinghoffer.*

Milton Babbitt, 1916-2011, (U.S.) serial and electronic music.

Carl Philipp Emanuel Bach, 1714-88, (Ger.) cantatas, passions, numerous keyboard and instrumental works.

Johann Christian Bach, 1735-82, (Ger.) concertos, operas, sonatas. Known as the "English" Bach.

Johann Sebastian Bach, 1685-1750, (Ger.) *St. Matthew Passion, The Well-Tempered Clavier.*

Samuel Barber, 1910-81, (U.S.) *Adagio for Strings, Vanessa.*

Béla Bartók, 1881-1945, (Hung.) *Concerto for Orchestra, The Miraculous Mandarin.*

Amy Beach (Mrs. H. H. A. Beach), 1867-1944, (U.S.) *The Year's at the Spring, Fireflies, The Chambered Nautilus.*

Ludwig van Beethoven, 1770-1827, (Ger.) concertos (*Emperor*), sonatas (*Moonlight, Pathétique*), 9 symphonies.

Vincenzo Bellini, 1801-35, (It.) *I Puritani, La Sonnambula, Norma.*

Alban Berg, 1885-1935, (Austria) *Wozzeck, Lulu.*

Hector Berlioz, 1803-69, (Fr.) *Damnation of Faust, Symphonie Fantastique, Requiem.*

Leonard Bernstein, 1918-90, (U.S.) *Chichester Psalms, Jeremiah Symphony, Mass.*

Georges Bizet, 1838-75, (Fr.) *Carmen, Pearl Fishers.*

Ernest Bloch, 1880-1959, (Switz.-U.S.) *Macbeth* (opera), *Schelomo, Voice in the Wilderness.*

Luigi Boccherini, 1743-1805, (It.) chamber music and guitar pieces.

Alexander Borodin, 1833-87, (Russ.) *Prince Igor, In the Steppes of Central Asia, Polovtzian Dances.*

Pierre Boulez, 1925-2016, (Fr.) *Le Visage nuptial, Edats/Multiple, Domaines.*

Johannes Brahms, 1833-97, (Ger.) *Liebeslieder Waltzes, Acad. Festival Overture,* chamber music, 4 symphonies.

Henry Brant, 1913-2008, (Can.) spatial music.

Benjamin Britten, 1913-76, (Br.) *Peter Grimes, Turn of the Screw, A Ceremony of Carols, War Requiem.*

Anton Bruckner, 1824-96, (Austria) 9 symphonies.

Dietrich Buxtehude, 1637-1707, (Den.) organ works, vocal music.

William Byrd, 1543-1623, (Br.) masses, motets.

John Cage, 1912-92, (U.S.) *Winter Music, Fontana Mix.*

Elliott Carter, 1908-2012, (U.S.) *Second String Quartet, Third String Quartet.*

Emmanuel Chabrier, 1841-94, (Fr.) *Le Roi Malgré Lui, España.*

Gustave Charpentier, 1860-1956, (Fr.) *Louise.*

Frédéric Chopin, 1810-49, (Pol.) mazurkas, waltzes, etudes, nocturnes, polonaises, sonatas.

Aaron Copland, 1900-90, (U.S.) *Appalachian Spring, Fanfare for the Common Man, Lincoln Portrait.*

John Corigliano, b 1938, (U.S.) *Symphony No. 2.*

Paul Creston, 1906-85, (U.S.) *Walt Whitman.*

Claude Debussy, 1862-1918, (Fr.) *Pelleas et Melisande, La Mer, Prelude to the Afternoon of a Faun.*

David Del Tredici, b 1937, (U.S.) *Child Alice, In Memory of a Summer Day.*

Gaetano Donizetti, 1797-1848, (It.) *Elixir of Love, Lucia di Lammermoor, Daughter of the Regiment.*

Paul Dukas, 1865-1935, (Fr.) *Sorcerer's Apprentice.*

Antonín Dvořák, 1841-1904, (Czech.) *Songs My Mother Taught Me, Symphony in E Minor (From the New World).*

Edward Elgar, 1857-1934, (Br.) *Enigma Variations, Pomp and Circumstance.*

Manuel de Falla, 1876-1946, (Sp.) *El Amor Brujo, La Vida Breve, The Three-Cornered Hat.*

Gabriel Fauré, 1845-1924, (Fr.) *Requiem, Elègie for Cello and Piano.*

Cesar Franck, 1822-90, (Belg.) *Symphony in D minor, Violin Sonata.*

George Gershwin, 1898-1937, (U.S.) *Rhapsody in Blue, An American in Paris, Porgy and Bess.*

Philip Glass, b 1937, (U.S.) *Einstein on the Beach, The Voyage.*

Mikhail Glinka, 1804-57, (Russ.) *A Life for the Tsar, Ruslan and Ludmilla.*

Christoph W. Gluck, 1714-87, (Ger.) *Alceste, Iphigènie en Tauride.*

Henryk Gorecki, 1933-2010, (Pol.) Symphony no. 3 (*Symphony of Sorrowing Songs*).

Charles Gounod, 1818-93, (Fr.) *Faust, Romeo and Juliet.*

Percy Grainger, 1882-1961, (Austral.) *Country Gardens.*

Edvard Grieg, 1843-1907, (Nor.) *Peer Gynt Suite,* Concerto in A minor for piano.

George Frideric Handel, 1685-1759, (Ger.-Br.) *Messiah, Water Music.*

Howard Hanson, 1896-1981, (U.S.) Symphonies No. 1 (*Nordic*) and No. 2 (*Romantic*).

Roy Harris, 1898-1979, (U.S.) symphonies.

(Franz) Joseph Haydn, 1732-1809, (Austria) symphonies (*Clock, London, Toy*), chamber music, oratorios.

Hildegard von Bingen, 1098-1179, (Ger.) *Ordo virtutum.*

Paul Hindemith, 1895-1963, (U.S.) *Mathis der Maler.*

Gustav Holst, 1874-1934, (Br.) *The Planets.*

Arthur Honegger, 1892-1955, (Fr.) *Judith, Le Roi David, Pacific 231.*

Alan Hovhaness, 1911-2000, (U.S.) symphonies, *Magnificat.*

Engelbert Humperdinck, 1854-1921, (Ger.) *Hansel and Gretel.*

Charles Ives, 1874-1954, (U.S.) *Concord Sonata,* symphonies.

Aram Khachaturian, 1903-78, (Russ.) ballets, piano pieces, *Sabre Dance.*

Zoltán Kodaly, 1882-1967, (Hung.) *Háry János, Psalmus Hungaricus.*

Fritz Kreisler, 1875-1962, (Austria) *Caprice Viennois, Tambourin Chinois.*

Edouard Lalo, 1823-92, (Fr.) *Symphonie Espagnole.*

David Lang, b 1957, (U.S.) *The Little Match Girl Passion.*

Morten Lauridsen, b 1943, (U.S.) *Lux Aeterna.*

Ruggero Leoncavallo, 1857-1919, (It.) *Pagliacci.*

György Ligeti, 1923-2006, (Rom.) *Atmosphères, Requiem.*

Franz Liszt, 1811-86, (Hung.) 20 Hungarian rhapsodies, symphonic poems.

Edward MacDowell, 1861-1908, (U.S.) *To a Wild Rose.*

Gustav Mahler, 1860-1911, (Austria) *Das Lied von der Erde;* 9 complete symphonies.

Pietro Mascagni, 1863-1945, (It.) *Cavalleria Rusticana.*

Jules Massenet, 1842-1912, (Fr.) *Manon, Le Cid*, *Thaïs*.

Felix Mendelssohn, 1809-47, (Ger.) *A Midsummer Night's Dream*, *Songs Without Words*, violin concerto.

Gian Carlo Menotti, 1911-2007, (It.-U.S.) *The Medium*, *The Consul*, *Amahl and the Night Visitors*.

Olivier Messiaen, 1908-1992, (Fr.) *Apparition de l'Église Éternelle*.

Claudio Monteverdi, 1567-1643, (It.) opera, masses, madrigals.

Wolfgang Amadeus Mozart, 1756-91, (Austria) chamber music, concertos, operas (*Magic Flute*, *Marriage of Figaro*), 41 symphonies.

Modest Mussorgsky, 1839-81, (Russ.) *Boris Godunov*, *Pictures at an Exhibition*.

Carl Nielsen, 1865-1931, (Den.) *Saul og David*.

Jacques Offenbach, 1819-80, (Fr.) *Tales of Hoffmann*.

Carl Orff, 1895-1982, (Ger.) *Carmina Burana*.

Johann Pachelbel, 1653-1706, (Ger.) *Canon and Fugue in D major*.

Ignacy Paderewski, 1860-1941, (Pol.) *Minuet in G*.

Niccolò Paganini, 1782-1840, (It.) *Caprices for violin solo*.

Giovanni Palestrina, c. 1525-94, (It.) masses, madrigals.

Arvo Pärt, b 1935, (Eston.) sacred music. *Fratres*, *Cantus in memoriam Benjamin Britten*, *Tabula Rasa*.

Krzysztof Penderecki, b 1933, (Pol.) *Psalmus*, *Polymorphia*, *De natura sonoris*.

Francis Poulenc, 1899-1963, (Fr.) *Dialogues des Carmélites*.

Mel Powell, 1923-98, (U.S.) *Duplicates: A Concerto for Two Pianos and Orchestra*, *Cantilena Concertante*.

Sergei Prokofiev, 1891-1953, (Russ.) *Classical Symphony*, *Love for Three Oranges*, *Peter and the Wolf*.

Giacomo Puccini, 1858-1924, (It.) *La Boheme*, *Manon Lescaut*, *Tosca*, *Madama Butterfly*.

Henry Purcell, 1659-95, (Br.) *Dido and Aeneas*.

Sergei Rachmaninoff, 1873-1943, (Russ.) concertos, preludes (Prelude in C sharp minor), symphonies.

Maurice Ravel, 1875-1937, (Fr.) *Boléro*, *Daphnis et Chloè*, *Piano Concerto in D for Left Hand Alone*.

Steve Reich, b 1936, (U.S.) *Double Sextet*, *Three Tales*.

Nikolai Rimsky-Korsakov, 1844-1908, (Russ.) *Golden Cockerel*, *Scheherazade*, *Flight of the Bumblebee*.

Gioacchino Rossini, 1792-1868, (It.) *Barber of Seville*, *Otello*, *William Tell*.

John Rutter, b 1945, (Br.) *Magnificat*, *Requiem*.

Camille Saint-Saëns, 1835-1921, (Fr.) *Carnival of Animals (The Swan)*, *Samson and Delilah*, *Danse Macabre*.

Alessandro Scarlatti, 1660-1725, (It.) cantatas, oratorios, operas.

Domenico Scarlatti, 1685-1757, (It.) harpsichord works.

Alfred Schnittke, 1934-98 (Russ.-Ger.) *Life With an Idiot*.

Arnold Schoenberg, 1874-1951, (Austria) *Pelleas and Melisande*, *Pierrot Lunaire*, *Verklärte Nacht*.

Franz Schubert, 1797-1828, (Austria) chamber music (*Trout Quintet*), lieder, symphonies ("Unfinished").

Robert Schumann, 1810-56, (Ger.) *Die Frauenliebe und Leben*, *Träumerei*.

Dmitri Shostakovich, 1906-75, (Russ.) symphonies, *Lady Macbeth of the District Mzensk*.

Jean Sibelius, 1865-1957, (Fin.) *Finlandia*.

Bedrich Smetana, 1824-84, (Czech.) *The Bartered Bride*.

Karlheinz Stockhausen, 1928-2008, (Ger.) *Kontra-Punkte*, *Kontakte for Electronic Instruments*.

Richard Strauss, 1864-1949, (Ger.) *Salome*, *Elektra*, *Der Rosenkavalier*, *Thus Spake Zarathustra*.

Igor Stravinsky, 1882-1971, (Russ.) *Noah and the Flood*, *The Rake's Progress*, *The Rite of Spring*.

Toru Takemitsu, 1930-96, (Jpn.) *Requiem for Strings*, *Dorian Horizon*.

Thomas Tallis, c. 1505-85, (Br.) anthems, motets.

Peter I. Tchaikovsky, 1840-93, (Russ.) *Nutcracker*, *Swan Lake*, *The Sleeping Beauty*.

Georg Philipp Telemann, 1681-1767, (Ger.) church music, orchestral suites, chamber music.

Virgil Thomson, 1859-1989, (U.S.) opera, film music, *Four Saints in Three Acts*.

Dmitri Tiomkin, 1894-1979, (Russ.-U.S.) film scores, including *High Noon*.

Sir Michael Tippett, 1905-98, (Br.) *A Child of Our Time*, *The Midsummer Marriage*, *The Knot Garden*.

Michael Torke, b 1961, (U.S.) *Bright Blue Music*, *Ecstatic Orange*.

Eric Whitacre, b 1970, (U.S.) *Cloudburst*.

Ralph Vaughan Williams, 1872-1958, (Br.) *Fantasia on a Theme by Thomas Tallis*, symphonies, vocal music.

Giuseppe Verdi, 1813-1901, (It.) *Aida*, *Rigoletto*, *Don Carlo*, *Il Trovatore*, *La Traviata*, *Falstaff*, *Macbeth*.

Heitor Villa-Lobos, 1887-1959, (Braz.) *Bachianas Brasileiras*.

Antonio Vivaldi, 1678-1741, (It.) Concerto grossos (*The Four Seasons*).

Richard Wagner, 1813-83, (Ger.) *Rienzi*, *Tannhäuser*, *Lohengrin*, *Tristan und Isolde*.

William Walton, 1902-83, (Br.) *Façade*, *Belshazzar's Feast*.

Carl Maria von Weber, 1786-1826, (Ger.) *Der Freischutz*.

Composers of Operettas, Musicals, and Popular Music

Richard Adler, 1921-2012, (U.S.) *Pajama Game*; *Damn Yankees*.

Milton Ager, 1893-1979, (U.S.) "I Wonder What's Become of Sally"; "Hard-Hearted Hannah"; "Ain't She Sweet?"

Leroy Anderson, 1908-75, (U.S.) "Sleigh Ride"; "Blue Tango"; "Syncopated Clock."

Paul Anka, b 1941, (Can.) "My Way"; *Tonight Show* theme.

Harold Arlen, 1905-86, (U.S.) "Stormy Weather"; "Over the Rainbow"; "Blues in the Night"; "That Old Black Magic."

Burt Bacharach, b 1928, (U.S.) "Raindrops Keep Fallin' on My Head"; "Walk on By"; "What the World Needs Now Is Love."

Ernest Ball, 1878-1927, (U.S.) "Mother Machree"; "When Irish Eyes Are Smiling."

John Barry, 1933-2011, (U.S.) *Born Free*; *Lion in Winter*; *Out of Africa*.

Irving Berlin, 1888-1989, (U.S.) *Annie Get Your Gun*; *Call Me Madam*; "God Bless America"; "White Christmas."

Leonard Bernstein, 1918-90, (U.S.) *On the Town*; *Wonderful Town*; *Candide*; *West Side Story*.

Eubie Blake, 1883-1983, (U.S.) *Shuffle Along*; "I'm Just Wild About Harry."

Jerry Bock, 1928-2010, (U.S.) *Mr. Wonderful*; *Fiorello*; *Fiddler on the Roof*; *The Rothschilds*.

Carrie Jacobs Bond, 1862-1946, (U.S.) "I Love You Truly."

Nacio Herb Brown, 1896-1964, (U.S.) "Singing in the Rain"; "You Were Meant for Me"; "All I Do Is Dream of You."

Hoagy Carmichael, 1899-1981, (U.S.) "Stardust"; "Georgia on My Mind"; "Old Buttermilk Sky."

James Cleveland, 1931-91, (U.S.) composer, musician, singer; first black gospel artist to appear at Carnegie Hall.

George M. Cohan, 1878-1942, (U.S.) "Give My Regards to Broadway"; "You're a Grand Old Flag"; "Over There."

Cy Coleman, 1929-2004, (U.S.) *Sweet Charity*; "Witchcraft."

John Frederick Coots, 1895-1985, (U.S.) "Santa Claus Is Coming to Town"; "You Go to My Head"; "For All We Know."

Noël Coward, 1899-1973, (Br.) *Bitter Sweet*; "Mad Dogs and Englishmen"; "Mad About the Boy."

Neil Diamond, b 1941, (U.S.) "I'm a Believer"; "Sweet Caroline."

Walter Donaldson, 1893-1947, (U.S.) "My Buddy"; "Carolina in the Morning"; "Makin' Whoopee."

Vernon Duke, 1903-69, (U.S.) "April in Paris."

Bob Dylan, b 1941, (U.S.) "Blowin' in the Wind"; "Like a Rolling Stone."

Gus Edwards, 1879-1945, (U.S.) "School Days"; "By the Light of the Silvery Moon"; "In My Merry Oldsmobile."

Sherman Edwards, 1919-81, (U.S.) "See You in September"; "Wonderful! Wonderful!"

Duke Ellington, 1899-1974, (U.S.) "Sophisticated Lady"; "Satin Doll"; "It Don't Mean a Thing"; "Solitude."

Sammy Fain, 1902-89, (U.S.) "I'll Be Seeing You"; "Love Is a Many-Splendored Thing."

Fred Fisher, 1875-1942, (U.S.) "Peg O' My Heart"; "Chicago."

Stephen Collins Foster, 1826-64, (U.S.) "My Old Kentucky Home"; "Old Folks at Home"; "Beautiful Dreamer."

Rudolf Friml, 1879-1972, (Czech.-U.S.) *The Firefly*; *Rose Marie*; *Vagabond King*; *Bird of Paradise*.

John Gay, 1685-1732, (Br.) *The Beggar's Opera*.

George Gershwin, 1898-1937, (U.S.) "Someone to Watch Over Me"; "I've Got a Crush on You"; "Embraceable You."

Morton Gould, 1913-96, (U.S.) "Fall River Suite"; "Holocaust Suite"; "Spirituals for Orchestra"; "Stringmusic."

Ferde Grofe, 1892-1972, (U.S.) "Grand Canyon Suite."

Marvin Hamlisch, 1944-2012, (U.S.) "The Way We Were"; "Nobody Does It Better"; *A Chorus Line*.

Ray Henderson, 1896-1970, (U.S.) *George White's Scandals*; "That Old Gang of Mine"; "Five Foot Two, Eyes of Blue."

Victor Herbert, 1859-1924, (Ire.-U.S.) *Mlle. Modiste*; *Babes in Toyland*; *The Red Mill*; *Naughty Marietta*; *Sweethearts*.

Jerry Herman, b 1931, (U.S.) *Hello, Dolly!*; *Mame*.

Brian Holland, b 1941, **Lamont Dozier**, b 1941, **Eddie Holland**, b 1939, (all U.S.) "Heat Wave"; "Stop! In the Name of Love"; "Baby, I Need Your Loving."

Rupert Holmes, b 1947, (Br.-U.S.) *The Mystery of Edwin Drood*; *Curtains*.

James Horner, 1953-2015, (U.S.) *Titanic*; "Somewhere Out There"; "My Heart Will Go On."

Antonio Carlos Jobim, 1927-94, (Brazil) "The Girl From Ipanema"; "Desafinado"; "One Note Samba."

Billy Joel (William Martin), b 1949, (U.S.) "Just the Way You Are"; "Honesty"; "Piano Man."

Elton John, b 1947, (Br.) *The Lion King*; "Candle in the Wind"; "Your Song."

Scott Joplin, 1868-1917, (U.S.) *Maple Leaf Rag*; *Treemonisha*.

John Kander, b 1927, (U.S.) *Cabaret*; *Chicago*; *Funny Lady*.

Jerome Kern, 1885-1945, (U.S.) *Sally*; *Sunny*; *Show Boat*.

Carole King, b 1942, (U.S.) "Will You Love Me Tomorrow?"; "Natural Woman"; "One Fine Day"; "Up on the Roof."

Burton Lane, 1912-97, (U.S.) *Finian's Rainbow*.

Jonathan Larson, 1960-96, (U.S.) *tick, tick... BOOM!*; *Rent*.

Franz Lehar, 1870-1948, (Hung.) *Merry Widow*.

Jerry Leiber, 1933-2011, and **Mike Stoller**, b 1933, (both U.S.) "Hound Dog"; "Searchin'"; "Yakety Yak"; "Love Me Tender."

Mitch Leigh, 1928-2014, (U.S.) *Man of La Mancha*.

John Lennon, 1940-80, and **Paul McCartney**, b 1942, (both Br.) "I Want to Hold Your Hand"; "She Loves You."

Jay Livingston, 1915-2001, (U.S.) "Mona Lisa"; "Que Sera, Sera."

Andrew Lloyd Webber, b 1948, (Br.) *Jesus Christ Superstar*; *Evita*; *Cats*; *The Phantom of the Opera*.

Frank Loesser, 1910-69, (U.S.) *Guys and Dolls*; *Where's Charley?*; *The Most Happy Fella*; *How to Succeed in Business*....

Frederick Loewe, 1901-88, (Austria-U.S.) *Brigadoon*; *Paint Your Wagon*; *My Fair Lady*; *Camelot*.

Robert Lopez, b 1975, (U.S.) *Avenue Q*; *The Book of Mormon*; *Frozen*.

Henry Mancini, 1924-94, (U.S.) "Moon River"; "Days of Wine and Roses"; "Pink Panther Theme."

Barry Mann, b 1939, and **Cynthia Weil**, b 1937, (both U.S.) "You've Lost That Loving Feeling."

Hugh Martin, 1914-2011, (U.S.) "Have Yourself a Merry Little Christmas"; "The Trolley Song."

Jimmy McHugh, 1894-1969, (U.S.) "Don't Blame Me"; "I'm in the Mood for Love"; "I Feel a Song Coming On."

Alan Menken, b 1949, (U.S.) *Little Shop of Horrors*; *Beauty and the Beast*.

Joseph Meyer, 1894-1987, (U.S.) "If You Knew Susie"; "California, Here I Come"; "Crazy Rhythm."

Lin-Manuel Miranda, b 1980, (U.S.) *In the Heights*; *Hamilton*.

Willie Nelson, b 1933, (U.S.) "Crazy"; "On the Road Again."

Chauncey Olcott, 1858-1932, (U.S.) "Mother Machree."

Jerome "Doc" Pomus, 1925-91, (U.S.) "Save the Last Dance for Me"; "A Teenager in Love."

Cole Porter, 1891-1964, (U.S.) *Anything Goes*; *Kiss Me Kate*; *Can Can*; *Silk Stockings*.

Smokey Robinson, b 1940, (U.S.) "Shop Around"; "My Guy"; "My Girl"; "Get Ready."

Richard Rodgers, 1902-79, (U.S.) *Oklahoma!*; *Carousel*; *South Pacific*; *The King and I*; *The Sound of Music*.

Sigmund Romberg, 1887-1951, (Hung.) *Maytime*; *The Student Prince*; *Desert Song*; *Blossom Time*.

Harold Rome, 1908-93, (U.S.) *Pins and Needles*; *Call Me Mister*; *Wish You Were Here*; *Fanny*; *Destry Rides Again*.

Vincent Rose, 1880-1944, (U.S.) "Avalon"; "Whispering"; "Blueberry Hill."

Harry Ruby, 1895-1974, (U.S.) "Three Little Words"; "Who's Sorry Now?"

Arthur Schwartz, 1900-84, (U.S.) *The Band Wagon*; "Dancing in the Dark"; "By Myself"; "That's Entertainment."

Steven Schwartz, b 1948, (U.S.) *Godspell*; *Pippin*; *Wicked*.

Neil Sedaka, b 1939, (U.S.) "Breaking Up Is Hard to Do."

Marc Shaiman, b 1959, (U.S.) *Hairspray*.

Paul Simon, b 1942, (U.S.) "Sounds of Silence"; "I Am a Rock"; "Mrs. Robinson"; "Bridge Over Troubled Waters."

Stephen Sondheim, b 1930, (U.S.) *A Little Night Music*; *Company*; *Sweeney Todd*; *Sunday in the Park With George*.

John Philip Sousa, 1854-1932, (U.S.) *El Capitan*; "Stars and Stripes Forever."

Oskar Straus, 1870-1954, (Austrian) *Chocolate Soldier*.

Johann Strauss, 1825-99, (Austrian) *Gypsy Baron*; *Die Fledermaus*; waltzes: Blue Danube; Artist's Life.

Charles Strouse, b 1928, (U.S.) *Bye Bye, Birdie*; *Annie*.

Jule Styne, 1905-94, (Br.-U.S.) *Gentlemen Prefer Blondes*; *Bells Are Ringing*; *Gypsy*; *Funny Girl*.

Arthur S. Sullivan, 1842-1900, (Br.) *H.M.S. Pinafore*; *Pirates of Penzance*; *The Mikado*.

Deems Taylor, 1885-1966, (U.S.) *Peter Ibbetson*.

Harry Tobias, 1905-94, (U.S.) *I'll Keep the Lovelight Burning*.

Egbert van Alstyne, 1882-1951, (U.S.) "In the Shade of the Old Apple Tree"; "Memories"; "Pretty Baby."

Jimmy Van Heusen, 1913-90, (U.S.) "Moonlight Becomes You"; "Swinging on a Star"; "All the Way"; "Love and Marriage."

Albert von Tilzer, 1878-1956, (U.S.) "I'll Be With You in Apple Blossom Time"; "Take Me Out to the Ball Game."

Harry von Tilzer, 1872-1946, (U.S.) "Only a Bird in a Gilded Cage"; "Wait 'til the Sun Shines, Nellie."

Fats Waller, 1904-43, (U.S.) "Honeysuckle Rose"; "Ain't Misbehavin'."

Harry Warren, 1893-1981, (U.S.) "You're My Everything"; "We're in the Money"; "I Only Have Eyes for You."

Jimmy Webb, b 1946, (U.S.) "Up, Up and Away"; "By the Time I Get to Phoenix"; "Didn't We?"; "Wichita Lineman."

Kurt Weill, 1900-50, (Ger.-U.S.) *Threepenny Opera*; *Lady in the Dark*; *Knickerbocker Holiday*; *One Touch of Venus*.

Percy Wenrich, 1887-1952, (U.S.) "When You Wore a Tulip"; "Moonlight Bay"; "Put On Your Old Gray Bonnet."

Richard A. Whiting, 1891-1938, (U.S.) "Till We Meet Again"; "Sleepytime Gal"; "Beyond the Blue Horizon"; "My Ideal."

Frank Wildhorn, b 1959, (U.S.) *Jekyll and Hyde*; *Victor/Victoria*; *The Civil War*.

John Williams, b 1932, (U.S.) *Jaws*; *E.T.*; *Star Wars* series; *Raiders of the Lost Ark* series.

Meredith Willson, 1902-84, (U.S.) *The Music Man*.

Stevie Wonder, b 1950, (U.S.) "You Are the Sunshine of My Life"; "Signed, Sealed, Delivered, I'm Yours."

Vincent Youmans, 1898-1946, (U.S.) *Two Little Girls in Blue*; *Wildflower*; *No, No, Nanette*; *Hit the Deck*; *Rainbow*; *Smiles*.

Lyricists

Howard Ashman, 1950-91, (U.S.) *Little Shop of Horrors*; *The Little Mermaid*.

Johnny Burke, 1908-84, (U.S.) "Misty"; "Imagination."

Irving Caesar, 1895-1996, (U.S.) "Swanee"; "Tea for Two"; "Just a Gigolo."

Sammy Cahn, 1913-93, (U.S.) "High Hopes"; "Love and Marriage"; "The Second Time Around"; "It's Magic."

Leonard Cohen, b 1934, (Can.) "Suzanne"; "Hallelujah."

Betty Comden, 1917-2006, and **Adolph Green**, 1915-2002, (both U.S.) "The Party's Over"; "New York, New York."

Hal David, 1921-2012, (U.S.) "What the World Needs Now Is Love."

Buddy De Sylva, 1895-1950, (U.S.) "When Day Is Done"; "Look for the Silver Lining"; "April Showers."

Howard Dietz, 1896-1983, (U.S.) "Dancing in the Dark"; "That's Entertainment."

Al Dubin, 1891-1945, (U.S.) "Tiptoe Through the Tulips"; "Lullaby of Broadway."

Fred Ebb, 1936-2004, (U.S.) *Cabaret*; *Zorba*; *Woman of the Year*; *Chicago*.

Ray Evans, 1915-2007, (U.S.) "Mona Lisa"; "Que Sera, Sera."

Dorothy Fields, 1905-74, (U.S.) "On the Sunny Side of the Street"; "Don't Blame Me"; "The Way You Look Tonight."

Ira Gershwin, 1896-1983, (U.S.) "The Man I Love"; "S'Wonderful"; "Embraceable You."

William S. Gilbert, 1836-1911, (Br.) *H.M.S. Pinafore*; *Pirates of Penzance*.

Gerry Goffin, 1939-2014, (U.S.) "Will You Love Me Tomorrow"; "Take Good Care of My Baby"; "Up on the Roof."

Mack Gordon, 1905-59, (Pol.-U.S.) "You'll Never Know"; "The More I See You"; "Chattanooga Choo-Choo."

Oscar Hammerstein II, 1895-1960, (U.S.) *Ol' Man River*; *Oklahoma!*; *Carousel*.

E. Y. (Yip) Harburg, 1898-1981, (U.S.) "Brother, Can You Spare a Dime"; "April in Paris"; "Over the Rainbow."

Sheldon Harnick, b 1924, (U.S.) *Fiddler on the Roof*; *She Loves Me*.

Lorenz Hart, 1895-1943, (U.S.) "Isn't It Romantic"; "Blue Moon"; "Lover"; "Manhattan"; "My Funny Valentine."

DuBose Heyward, 1885-1940, (U.S.) "Summertime."

Gus Kahn, 1886-1941, (U.S.) "Memories"; "Ain't We Got Fun."

Alan J. Lerner, 1918-86, (U.S.) *Brigadoon*; *My Fair Lady*; *Camelot*; *Gigi*; *On a Clear Day You Can See Forever*.

Johnny Mercer, 1909-76, (U.S.) "Blues in the Night"; "Come Rain or Come Shine"; "Laura"; "That Old Black Magic."

Bob Merrill, 1921-98, (U.S.) "People"; "(How Much Is That) Doggie in the Window."

Jack Norworth, 1879-1959, (U.S.) "Take Me Out to the Ball Game"; "Shine On Harvest Moon."

Mitchell Parish, 1901-93, (U.S.) "Stardust"; "Stairway to the Stars."

Andy Razaf, 1895-1973, (U.S.) "Honeysuckle Rose"; "Ain't Misbehavin."

Leo Robin, 1900-84, (U.S.) "Thanks for the Memory"; "Diamonds Are a Girl's Best Friend."

Robert Sherman, 1925-2012, (U.S.) *Mary Poppins*, *The Jungle Book*.

Bernie Taupin, b 1947 (Br.) "Rocket Man"; "Your Song."

Paul Francis Webster, 1907-84, (U.S.) "Secret Love"; "The Shadow of Your Smile"; "Love Is a Many-Splendored Thing."

Jack Yellen, 1892-1991, (U.S.) "Ain't She Sweet"; "Happy Days Are Here Again."

Blues and Jazz Artists of the Past

Julian "Cannonball" Adderley, 1928-75, alto sax.

Nat Adderley, 1931-2000, cornet.

Henry "Red" Allen, 1908-67, trumpet.

Louis "Satchmo" Armstrong, 1901-71, trumpet, singer, bandleader.

Albert Ayler, 1936-70, tenor sax, alto sax.

Mildred Bailey, 1907-51, singer.

Chet Baker, 1929-88, trumpet, singer.

Ray Barretto, 1930-2006, conga drummer.

William "Count" Basie, 1904-84, bandleader, piano, composer.

Sidney Bechet, 1897-1959, soprano sax, clarinet.

Bix Beiderbecke, 1903-31, cornet, composer, piano.

Rowland "Bunny" Berigan, 1908-42, trumpet.

Barney Bigard, 1906-80, clarinet.

Eubie Blake, 1883-1983, composer, piano.

Art Blakey, 1919-90, drums, bandleader.

Jimmy Blanton, 1921-42, bass.

Charles "Buddy" Bolden, 1877-1931, cornet, pioneer bandleader.

Lester Bowie, 1941-99, trumpet, composer, bandleader.

Michael Brecker, 1949-2007, saxophone.

Big Bill Broonzy, 1893-1958, blues singer, guitar.

Clarence "Gatemouth" Brown, 1924-2005, guitar, singer.

Clifford Brown, 1930-56, trumpet.

Ray Brown, 1926-2002, bass.

Dave Brubeck, 1920-2012, piano, bandleader.

Don Byas, 1912-72, tenor sax.

Charlie Byrd, 1925-99, guitar; popularized bossa nova.

Cab Calloway, 1907-94, bandleader, singer.

Harry Carney, 1910-74, baritone sax, clarinet.
Benny Carter, 1907-2003, alto sax.
Betty Carter, 1930-98, jazz singer.
Sidney "Big Sid" Catlett, 1910-51, drums.
Adolphus Anthony "Doc" Cheatham, 1905-97, trumpet.
Don Cherry, 1936-95, trumpet.
Charlie Christian, 1916-42, guitar.
Terry Clark, 1920-2015, trumpet.
Kenny "Klook" Clarke, 1914-85, drums.
Buck Clayton, 1911-91, trumpet.
Al Cohn, 1925-88, tenor sax.
Nat "King" Cole, 1919-65, piano, singer.
William "Cozy" Cole, 1909-81, drums.
Alice Coltrane, 1937-2007, piano, composer.
John Coltrane, 1926-67, tenor sax, soprano sax, composer.
Eddie Condon, 1905-73, guitar, bandleader.
Tadd Dameron, 1917-65, piano, composer.
Eddie "Lockjaw" Davis, 1921-86, tenor sax.
Miles Davis, 1926-91, trumpet, composer.
Wild Bill Davison, 1906-89, cornet.
Blossom Dearie, 1924-2009, singer.
Paul Desmond, 1924-77, alto sax.
Vic Dickenson, 1906-84, trombone.
Willie Dixon, 1915-92, composer, bass.
Johnny Dodds, 1892-1940, clarinet.
Warren "Baby" Dodds, 1898-1959, drums.
Eric Dolphy, 1928-64, alto sax, bass clarinet, flute.
Jimmy Dorsey, 1904-57, alto sax, bandleader.
Tommy Dorsey, 1905-56, trombone, bandleader.
Billy Eckstine, 1914-93, singer, bandleader.
Harry "Sweets" Edison, 1915-99, trumpet.
David "Honeyboy" Edwards, 1915-2011, guitar, singer.
Roy Eldridge, 1911-89, trumpet, singer.
Duke Ellington, 1899-1974, piano, bandleader, composer.
Bill Evans, 1929-80, piano.
Gil Evans, 1912-88, composer, arranger, piano.
Art Farmer, 1928-99, trumpet, flugelhorn.
Maynard Ferguson, 1926-2006, trumpet, bandleader.
Ella Fitzgerald, 1917-96, singer.
Tommy Flanagan, 1930-2001, piano.
Pete Fountain, 1930-2016, clarinetist.
Erroll Garner, 1921-77, piano, composer.
Stan Getz, 1927-91, tenor sax.
Dizzy Gillespie, 1917-93, trumpet, composer, singer.
Benny Goodman, 1909-86, clarinet, bandleader.
Dexter Gordon, 1923-90, tenor sax.
Stéphane Grappelli, 1908-97, violin.
Bobby Hackett, 1915-76, trumpet, cornet.
Lionel Hampton, 1908-2002, vibraphone, bandleader.
W. C. Handy, 1873-1958, composer.
Jimmy Harrison, 1900-31, trombone.
Coleman Hawkins, 1904-69, tenor sax.
Percy Heath, 1923-2005, bass.
Fletcher Henderson, 1898-1952, bandleader, arranger.
Woody Herman, 1913-87, clarinet, alto sax, bandleader.
Jay C. Higginbotham, 1906-73, trombone.
Ruiz Hilton, 1952-2006, piano, composer.
Earl "Fatha" Hines, 1903-83, piano.
Milt Hinton, 1910-2000, bass.
Al Hirt, 1922-99, trumpet.
Johnny Hodges, 1906-70, alto sax.
Billie Holiday, 1915-59, singer.
John Lee Hooker, 1917-2001, blues guitar, singer.
Sam "Lightnin'" Hopkins, 1912-82, blues singer, guitar.
Shirley Horn, 1934-2005, piano, singer.
Howlin' Wolf (Chester Burnett), 1910-76, blues singer, harmonica, guitar.

Alberta Hunter, 1895-1984, singer.
Mahalia Jackson, 1911-72, gospel singer.
Milt Jackson, 1923-99, vibraphone.
Elmore James, 1918-63, blues singer, guitar.
Etta James, 1938-2012, blues singer.
"Blind" Lemon Jefferson, 1897-1929, blues singer, guitar.
J. J. Johnson, 1924-2001, trombone.
James P. Johnson, 1891-1955, piano, composer.
Robert Johnson, 1912-38, blues singer, guitar.
William "Bunk" Johnson, 1879-1949, trumpet.
Elvin Jones, 1927-2004, drums.
Jo Jones, 1911-85, drums.
Philly Joe Jones, 1923-85, drums.
Thad Jones, 1923-86, cornet, bandleader, composer.
Scott Joplin, 1868-1917, ragtime composer.
Louis Jordan, 1908-75, singer, alto sax.
Stan Kenton, 1911-79, bandleader, composer, piano.
Barney Kessel, 1923-2004, guitar.
Albert King, 1923-92, blues guitar.
B. B. King, 1925-2015, blues guitar, singer.
John Kirby, 1908-52, bandleader, bass.
Rahsaan Roland Kirk, 1936-77, saxophone, composer.
Gene Krupa, 1909-73, drums, bandleader.
Scott LaFaro, 1936-61, bass.
Lead Belly (Huddie Ledbetter), 1888-1949, folk and blues singer, guitar.
Peggy Lee, 1920-2002, singer.
John Lewis, 1920-2001, piano, Modern Jazz Quartet founder.
Mel Lewis, 1929-90, drums, bandleader.
Jimmie Lunceford, 1902-47, bandleader.
Machito (Frank Grillo), 1908-84, Latin percussion, singer, bandleader.
Shelly Manne, 1920-84, drums, bandleader.
Jackie McLean, 1931-2006, saxophone, composer.
Jimmy McPartland, 1907-91, trumpet.
Marian McPartland, 1918-2013, pianist.
Carmen McRae, 1920-94, singer.
Glenn Miller, 1904-44, trombone, bandleader.
Charles Mingus, 1922-79, bass, composer, bandleader.
Thelonious Monk, 1917-82, piano, composer.
Wes Montgomery, 1925-68, guitar.
James Moody, 1925-2010, saxophone.
Ferdinand "Jelly Roll" Morton, 1885-1941, composer, piano.
Bennie Moten, 1894-1935, piano, bandleader.
Gerry Mulligan, 1927-96, baritone sax, composer.
Theodore "Fats" Navarro, 1923-50, trumpet.
Red Nichols, 1905-65, cornet, bandleader.
Red Norvo, 1908-99, vibraphone, xylophone, bandleader.
Anita O'Day, 1919-2006, singer.
Arturo "Chico" O'Farrill, 1921-2001, Latin composer, arranger.
King Oliver, 1885-1938, cornet, bandleader.
Sy Oliver, 1910-88, arranger, composer.
Edward "Kid" Ory, 1886-1973, trombone, bandleader.
Johnny Otis, 1921-2012, blues singer.
Oran "Hot Lips" Page, 1908-54, trumpet, singer.
Charlie "Bird" Parker, 1920-55, alto sax, composer.
Joe Pass, 1929-94, guitar.
Art Pepper, 1925-82, alto sax.
Pinetop Perkins, 1913-2011, piano.
Oscar Peterson, 1925-2007, piano.
Oscar Pettiford, 1922-60, bass.
Earl "Bud" Powell, 1924-66, piano.
Chano Pozo, 1915-48, percussionist, singer.

Louis Prima, 1911-78, singer, bandleader.
Tito Puente, 1923-2000, Latin percussion, bandleader.
Gertrude "Ma" Rainey, 1886-1939, blues singer.
Lou Rawls, 1933-2006, singer.
Dewey Redman, 1931-2006, tenor sax.
Don Redman (Robert Rodney Chudnick), 1900-64, composer, arranger.
Django Reinhardt, 1910-53, guitar.
Buddy Rich, 1917-87, drums.
Max Roach, 1924-2007, drums, composer.
Red Rodney (Robert Chudnick), 1927-94, trumpet.
Jimmy Rowles, 1918-96, piano.
Jimmy Rushing, 1903-72, blues and jazz singer.
Charles "Pee Wee" Russell, 1906-69, clarinet.
Artie Shaw, 1910-2004, swing-era bandleader, clarinet.
George Shearing, 1919-2011, piano.
Nina Simone (Eunice Waymon), 1933-2003, singer.
John "Zoot" Sims, 1925-85, tenor sax.
Zutty Singleton, 1898-1975, drums.
Bessie Smith, 1894-1937, blues singer.
Clarence "Pinetop" Smith, 1904-29, piano, singer, boogie woogie pioneer.
Willie "The Lion" Smith, 1897-1973, piano, composer.
Francis "Muggsy" Spanier, 1906-67, cornet.
Edward "Sonny" Stitt, 1924-82, tenor sax, alto sax.
Billy Strayhorn, 1915-67, composer, piano, Duke Ellington collaborator.
Sun Ra (Herman Blount), 1915?-93, bandleader, piano, composer.
Art Tatum, 1910-56, piano.
Art Taylor, 1929-95, drums.
Billy Taylor, 1921-2010, piano.
Jack Teagarden, 1905-64, trombone, singer.
Mel Tormé, 1925-99, singer ("The Velvet Fog").
Dave Tough, 1908-48, drums.
Lennie Tristano, 1919-78, piano, composer.
Joe Turner, 1911-85, blues singer.
Sarah Vaughan, 1924-90, singer.
Joe Venuti, 1903-78, violin.
Aaron "T-Bone" Walker, 1910-75, blues guitar.
Thomas "Fats" Waller, 1904-43, piano, singer, composer.
Dinah Washington (Ruth Jones), 1924-63, singer.
Grover Washington Jr., 1943-99, pop-jazz sax, composer.
Ethel Waters, 1896-1977, jazz and blues singer.
Muddy Waters (McKinley Morganfield), 1915-83, blues singer, songwriter.
Julius Watkins, 1921-77, French horn.
William "Chick" Webb, 1902-39, bandleader, drums.
Ben Webster, 1909-73, tenor sax.
Junior Wells (Amos Blackmore), 1934-98, blues singer, harmonica.
Paul Whiteman, 1890-1967, bandleader.
Margaret Whiting, 1924-2011, singer.
Charles "Cootie" Williams, 1910-85, trumpet, bandleader.
Joe Williams, 1918-99, singer.
Mary Lou Williams, 1910-81, piano, composer.
Tony Williams, 1945-97, drums.
John Lee "Sonny Boy" Williamson, 1914-48, blues singer, harmonica.
Sonny Boy Williamson (Aleck "Rice" Miller), 1900?-65, blues singer, harmonica.
Teddy Wilson, 1912-86, piano.
Kai Winding, 1922-83, trombone.
Jimmy Yancey, 1894-1951, piano.
Lester "Pres" Young, 1909-59, tenor sax.

Country Music Artists of the Past and Present

Roy Acuff, 1903-92, fiddler, singer, songwriter; "Wabash Cannon Ball."

Alabama (Jeff Cook, b 1949; Teddy Gentry, b 1952; Mark Herndon, b 1955; Randy Owen, b 1949); "Feels So Right."

Jason Aldean, b 1977, singer; "Don't You Wanna Stay."

James "Whispering Bill" Anderson, b 1937, singer, songwriter; "Make Mine Night Time."

Eddy Arnold, 1918-2008, singer, guitarist, known as the "Tennessee Plowboy."

Chet Atkins, 1924-2001, guitarist, composer, producer; helped create the "Nashville sound."

Gene Autry, 1907-98, first great singing movie cowboy; "Back in the Saddle Again."

Clint Black, b 1962, singer, songwriter; "Killin' Time."

Garth Brooks, b 1962, singer, songwriter; "Friends in Low Places."

Brooks & Dunn (Kix Brooks, b 1955; Ronnie Dunn, b 1953); "Hard Workin' Man."

Luke Bryan, b 1976, singer, songwriter; "Someone Else Calling You Baby."

Boudleaux, 1920-87, and **Felice Bryant**, 1925-2003, songwriting team; "Hey Joe."

Glen Campbell, b 1936, singer, guitarist; "Gentle on My Mind."

Mary Chapin Carpenter, b 1958, singer, songwriter; "I Feel Lucky."

Carter Family (original members A. P., 1891-1960; "Mother" Maybelle, 1909-78; Sara, 1898-1979); "Wildwood Flower."

Johnny Cash, 1932-2003, singer, songwriter; "I Walk the Line," "Ring of Fire," "Folsom Prison Blues."

Kenny Chesney, b 1968, guitarist, singer, songwriter; "You Had Me From Hello."

Roy Clark, b 1933, guitarist, banjoist, singer, co-host of *Hee Haw*; "Yesterday, When I Was Young."

Patsy Cline, 1932-63, singer; "Walkin' After Midnight," "Crazy," "Sweet Dreams."

Billy Ray Cyrus, b 1961, singer, songwriter; "Achy Breaky Heart."

Charlie Daniels, b 1936, guitarist, fiddler; "The Devil Went Down to Georgia."

Jimmy Dean, 1928-2010, singer; "Big Bad John."

John Denver, 1943-97, singer, songwriter; "Rocky Mountain High."

Dixie Chicks (Natalie Maines, b 1974; Emily Erwin Robison, b 1972; Martie Seidel, b 1969); "Wide Open Spaces."

Dale Evans, 1912-2001, singer, actress, married Roy Rogers.

Sara Evans, b 1971, singer, songwriter; "Born to Fly."

Flatt & Scruggs (Lester Flatt, 1914-79; Earl Scruggs, 1924-2012), guitar-banjo duo and soloists; "Foggy Mountain Breakdown."

Red Foley, 1910-68, singer; "Chattanoogie Shoe Shine Boy."

Tennessee Ernie Ford, 1919-91, singer, TV host; "Sixteen Tons."

William "Lefty" Frizzell, 1928-75, singer, guitarist; "Long Black Veil."

Vince Gill, b 1957, singer, songwriter; "When I Call Your Name."

Merle Haggard, 1937-2016, singer, songwriter; "Okie From Muskogee."

Emmylou Harris, b 1947, singer, songwriter, folk-country crossover artist; "If I Could Only Win Your Love."

Hunter Hayes, b 1991, singer; "Wanted."

Faith Hill, b 1967, singer, songwriter; "Breathe."

Alan Jackson, b 1958, singer, songwriter; "Where Were You (When the World Stopped Turning)."

Waylon Jennings, 1937-2002, singer, songwriter, "outlaw country" pioneer; "Luckenbach, Texas."

George Jones, 1931-2013, singer; "He Stopped Loving Her Today."

The Judds (Naomi, b 1946; Wynonna, b 1964), mother-daughter duo; Wynonna also a solo act.

Toby Keith, b 1961, singer, songwriter, guitarist; "Should've Been a Cowboy."

Alison Krauss, b 1971, bluegrass fiddler, singer, bandleader; "When You Say Nothing at All."

Kris Kristofferson, b 1936, singer, songwriter, actor; "Me and Bobby McGee."

Lady Antebellum (Dave Haywood, b 1982; Charles Kelley, b 1981; Hillary Scott, b 1984); "I Run to You."

Miranda Lambert, b 1983, singer, guitarist; "The House That Built Me."

Louvin Brothers (Charlie, 1927-2011; Ira, 1924-65), singers; "If I Could Only Win Your Love."

Patty Loveless, b 1957, singer, songwriter; "How Can I Help You Say Goodbye."

Lyle Lovett, b 1957, singer, songwriter, bandleader, actor; "Cowboy Man."

Loretta Lynn, b 1932, singer; "Coal Miner's Daughter."

Barbara Mandrell, b 1948, singer; "I Was Country When Country Wasn't Cool."

Kathy Mattea, b 1959, singer, songwriter; "Eighteen Wheels and a Dozen Roses."

Martina McBride, b 1966, singer, songwriter; "Independence Day."

Reba McEntire, b 1955, singer, songwriter, actress; "Whoever's in New England."

Tim McGraw, b 1967, singer; "It's Your Love," "I Like It, I Love It."

Roger Miller, 1936-92, singer, songwriter; "King of the Road."

Ronnie Milsap, b 1944, singer, songwriter; "There's No Gettin' Over Me."

Bill Monroe, 1911-96, singer, songwriter, mandolin player; "father of bluegrass music"; "Mule Skinner Blues."

Anne Murray, b 1945, singer; "You Needed Me."

Willie Nelson, b 1933, singer, songwriter, actor; "On the Road Again."

Mark O'Connor, b 1961, fiddler, country-classical crossover composer.

Buck Owens, 1929-2006, singer, guitarist; "Act Naturally."

Brad Paisley, b 1972, singer, songwriter; "Whiskey Lullaby," "When I Get Where I'm Going."

Dolly Parton, b 1946, singer, songwriter, actress; "Here You Come Again," "9 to 5."

Johnny Paycheck (Don Lytle), 1938-2003, singer, guitarist; "Take This Job and Shove It."

Minnie Pearl, 1912-96, comedienne, Grand Ole Opry star.

Kellie Pickler, b 1986, singer, songwriter.

Ray Price, 1926-2013, country singer, guitarist, songwriter; "Crazy Arms."

Charley Pride, b 1938, singer, first African American country star; "Kiss an Angel Good Mornin'."

Eddie Rabbit, 1941-98, singer, songwriter; "I Love a Rainy Night."

Rascal Flatts (Jay DeMarcus, b 1971; Gary LeVox, b 1970; Joe Don Rooney, b 1975); "Life Is a Highway."

Jim Reeves, 1923-64, singer, songwriter; "Four Walls."

Charlie Rich, 1932-95, singer, songwriter called the "Silver Fox"; "The Most Beautiful Girl."

LeAnn Rimes, b 1982, singer; "Blue."

Tex Ritter, 1905-74, singer, songwriter; "Jingle, Jangle, Jingle."

Marty Robbins, 1925-82, singer, songwriter; "A White Sport Coat and a Pink Carnation."

Jimmie Rodgers, 1897-1933, singer, songwriter; "T for Texas."

Kenny Rogers, b 1938, singer, songwriter; "The Gambler."

Roy Rogers (Leonard Slye), 1911-98, singer, actor, "King of the Cowboys," sang with Sons of the Pioneers.

Fred Rose, 1898-1954, songwriter, singer, producer; "Blue Eyes Cryin' in the Rain."

Blake Shelton, b 1976, singer; "Home."

Ricky Skaggs, b 1954, singer, songwriter, bandleader; "Don't Cheat in Our Hometown."

Ralph Stanley, 1927-2016, singer, banjo player; "Man of Constant Sorrow."

George Strait, b 1952, singer, bandleader; "Ace in the Hole."

Sugarland (Kristian Bush, b 1970; Jennifer Nettles, b 1974); "Stay."

Taylor Swift, b 1989, singer, songwriter; "You Belong With Me."

Lonnie "Mel" Tillis, b 1932, singer, songwriter, bandleader; "I Ain't Never."

Merle Travis, 1917-83, singer, guitarist, songwriter; "Divorce Me C.O.D."

Randy Travis, b 1959, singer, songwriter; "Forever and Ever, Amen."

Ernest Tubb, 1914-84, singer, songwriter, guitarist; "Walking the Floor Over You."

Josh Turner, b 1977, singer; "Why Don't We Just Dance."

Shania Twain, b 1965, singer, songwriter; "You're Still the One."

Conway Twitty, 1933-93, singer, songwriter; "Hello Darlin'."

Carrie Underwood, b 1983, singer, songwriter; *American Idol* winner.

Keith Urban, b 1967, guitarist, singer, songwriter; "It's a Love Thing."

Porter Wagoner, 1927-2007, singer, songwriter, guitarist; "Soul of a Convict."

Kitty Wells (Ellen Deason), 1919-2012, singer, songwriter; "It Wasn't God Who Made Honky-Tonk Angels."

Dottie West, 1932-91, singer, songwriter; "Here Comes My Baby."

Hank Williams Jr., b 1949, singer, songwriter; "Bocephus"; "All My Rowdy Friends (Have Settled Down)."

Hank Williams Sr., 1923-53, singer, songwriter; "Your Cheatin' Heart."

Bob Wills, 1905-75, Western Swing fiddler, singer, bandleader, songwriter; "New San Antonio Rose."

Lee Ann Womack, b 1966, singer, songwriter; "I Hope You Dance."

Tammy Wynette, 1942-98, singer; "Stand By Your Man."

Trisha Yearwood, b 1964, singer, songwriter; "How Do I Live."

Dwight Yoakam, b 1957, singer, songwriter, actor; "Ain't That Lonely Yet."

Zac Brown Band (Coy Bowles, b 1979; Zac Brown, b 1978; Clay Cook, Jimmy De Martini, Chris Fryar, b 1970; John Driskell Hopkins, b 1971); "Chicken Fried."

Dance Figures of the Past

Alvin Ailey, 1931-89, (U.S.) modern dancer, choreographer; melded modern dance and Afro-Caribbean techniques.

Frederick Ashton, 1904-88, (Br.) ballet choreographer; director of Great Britain's Royal Ballet, 1963-70.

Fred Astaire, 1899-1987, dancer, actor; teamed with dancer/actress **Ginger Rogers**, 1911-95, (both U.S.) in movie musicals.

George Balanchine, 1904-83, (Russ.-U.S.) ballet choreographer, teacher; most influential exponent of neoclassical style; founded, with Lincoln Kirstein, School of American Ballet and New York City Ballet.

Pina Bausch, 1940-2009, (Ger.) modern dance choreographer influencing the Tanztheater style of dance.

Carlo Blasis, 1795-1878, (It.) ballet dancer, choreographer, writer; his teaching methods are standards of classical dance.

August Bournonville, 1805-79, (Den.) ballet dancer, choreographer, teacher; exuberant, light style.

Fernando Bujones, 1955-2005, (Cuba-U.S.) ballet dancer.

Gisella Caccianza, 1914-98, (U.S.) ballerina; charter member of Balanchine's American Ballet.

Irene, 1893-1969, (U.S.) and **Vernon Castle**, 1887-1918, (Br.) husband-and-wife ballroom dancers.

Enrico Cecchetti, 1850-1928, (It.) ballet dancer, leading dancer of Russia's Imperial Ballet; his technique was basis for Britain's Imperial Soc. of Teachers of Dancing.

Gower, 1921-80, dancer, choreographer, director; with wife **Marge Champion**, b 1923, (both U.S.) choreographed, danced in Broadway musicals and films.

John Cranko, 1927-73, (S. Afr.) choreographer; created narrative ballets based on literary works.

Merce Cunningham, 1919-2009, (U.S.) dancer, choreographer of avant-garde dance.

Alexandra Danilova, 1903-97, (Russ.) ballerina; noted teacher at the School of American Ballet.

Agnes de Mille, 1905-93, (U.S.) ballerina, choreographer; known for using American themes, she choreographed the ballet *Rodeo* and the musical *Oklahoma!*

Dame Ninette De Valois, 1898-2001, (Br.) choreographer, founding director of London's Royal Ballet; *The Rake's Progress*.

Sergei Diaghilev, 1872-1929, (Russ.) impresario; founded Les Ballet Russes; saw ballet as art unifying dance, drama, music, and decor.

Isadora Duncan, 1877-1927, (U.S.) expressive dancer who united free movement with serious music; one of the founders of modern dance.

Katherine Dunham, 1910-2006, (U.S.) dancer, choreographer; internationally known for African, Caribbean, and African American dance forms.

Fanny Elssler, 1810-84, (Austria) ballerina of the Romantic era; known for dramatic skill, sensual style.

Michel Fokine, 1880-1942, (Russ.) ballet dancer, choreographer, teacher; rejected strict classicism in favor of dramatically expressive style.

Margot Fonteyn, 1919-91, (Br.) prima ballerina, Royal Ballet of Great Britain; famed performance partner of Rudolf Nureyev.

Bob Fosse, 1927-87, (U.S.) jazz dancer, choreographer, director; Broadway musicals and film.

Serge Golovine, 1924-98, (Fr.) ballet dancer with Grand Ballet du Marquis de Cuevas, choreographer.

Martha Graham, 1894-1991, (U.S.) modern dancer, choreographer; created and codified her own dramatic technique.

Melissa Hayden, 1923-2006, (Can.) ballet dancer.

Martha Hill, 1900-95, (U.S.) educator; leading figure in modern dance. Founded American Dance Festival.

Gregory Hines, 1946-2003, (U.S.) tapdance innovator; master of improvisation.

Doris Humphrey, 1895-1958, (U.S.) modern dancer, choreographer, writer, teacher.

Michael Jackson, 1958-2009, (U.S.) singer and dancer who perfected the "moonwalk."

Robert Joffrey, 1930-88, ballet dancer, choreographer; cofounded with **Gerald Arpino**, 1928-2008, (both U.S.) the Joffrey Ballet.

Kurt Jooss, 1901-79, (Ger.) choreographer, teacher; created expressionist works using modern and classical techniques.

Tamara Karsavina, 1885-1978, (Russ.) prima ballerina of Russia's Imperial Ballet and Diaghilev's Ballets Russes; partner of Nijinsky.

Nora Kaye, 1920-87, (U.S.) ballerina with Metropolitan Opera Ballet and Ballet Theater (now American Ballet Theatre).

Gene Kelly, 1912-96, (U.S.) dancer, actor in movie musicals.

Michael Kidd, 1915-2003, (U.S.) dancer, film and theater choreographer.

Lincoln Kirstein, 1907-96 (U.S.) brought ballet as an art form to U.S.; founded, with George Balanchine, School of American Ballet and New York City Ballet.

Serge Lifar, 1905-86, (Russ.-Fr.) prem. danseur, choreographer; director of dance at Paris Opera, 1930-45, 1947-58.

José Limón, 1908-72, (Mex.-U.S.) modern dancer, choreographer, teacher; developed technique based on Humphrey.

Catherine Littlefield, 1908-51, (U.S.) ballerina, choreographer, teacher; pioneer of American ballet.

Kenneth MacMillan, 1929-92, (Br.) dancer, choreographer; directed Royal Ballet of Great Britain, 1970-77.

Dame Alicia Markova, 1910-2004, (Br.) ballerina known for title role in *Giselle*; helped popularize ballet in U.S. and Britain.

Léonide Massine, 1896-1979, (Russ.-U.S.) ballet dancer, choreographer; known for his "symphonic ballet."

Fayard Nicholas, 1914-2006, tap dancer, choreographer, actor; together with brother **Harold Nicholas**, 1921-2000, (both U.S.) formed the Nicholas Brothers.

Vaslav Nijinsky, 1890-50, (Russ.) prem. danseur, choreographer; leading member of Diaghilev's Ballets Russes. His ballets were revolutionary for their time.

Alwin Nikolais, 1910-93, (U.S.) modern choreographer; created dance theater utilizing mixed media effects.

Jean-George Noverre, 1727-1810, (Fr.) ballet choreographer, teacher, writer; "Shakespeare of the Dance."

Rudolf Nureyev, 1938-93, (Russ.) prem. danseur, choreographer; leading male dancer of his generation; director of dance at Paris Opera, 1983-89.

Ruth Page, 1899-1991, (U.S.) ballerina, choreographer; danced, directed ballet at Chicago Lyric Opera.

Anna Pavlova, 1881-1931, (Russ.) prima ballerina; toured with her own company to world acclaim.

Marius Petipa, 1818-1910, (Fr.) ballet dancer, choreographer; ballet master of the Imperial Ballet; established Russian classicism as leading style of late 19th cent.

Roland Petit, 1924-2011, (Fr.) dancer, choreographer; founder of Les Ballets de Paris.

Pearl Primus, 1919-95, (Trinidad-U.S.) modern dancer, choreographer, scholar; combined African, Caribbean, and African American styles.

Jerome Robbins, 1918-98, (U.S.) choreographer, director, dancer; *The King and I, West Side Story, Fiddler on the Roof*.

Bill "Bojangles" Robinson, 1878-1949, (U.S.) famed tap dancer; called "King of Tapology" on stage and screen.

Ruth St. Denis, 1877-1968, (U.S.) influential interpretive dancer, choreographer, teacher.

Ted Shawn, 1891-1972, (U.S.) modern dancer, choreographer; formed dance company and school with Ruth St. Denis; established Jacob's Pillow Dance Festival.

Marie Taglioni, 1804-84, (It.) ballerina, teacher; in title role of *La Sylphide* established image of the ethereal ballerina.

Maria Tallchief, 1925-2013, (U.S.) prima ballerina, 1st of Amer. Indian descent.

Glen Tetley, 1926-2007, (U.S.) dancer, choreographer, ballet director; fused elements of modern dance with ballet.

Antony Tudor, 1908-87, (Br.) choreographer, teacher; exponent of the "psychological ballet."

Galina Ulanova, 1910-98, (Russ.) revered ballerina with Bolshoi Ballet.

Agrippina Vaganova, 1879-1951, (Russ.) ballet teacher, director called "queen of variations"; codified Soviet ballet technique.

Mary Wigman, 1886-1973, (Ger.) modern dancer, choreographer, teacher; influenced European expressionist dance.

Opera Singers of the Past

Licia Albanese, 1909-2014, (It.) soprano.
Frances Alda, 1879-1952, (N.Z.) soprano.
Pasquale Amato, 1878-1942, (It.) baritone.
Marian Anderson, 1897-1993, (U.S.) contralto.
Charles Anthony, 1929-2012, (U.S.) tenor.
Jussi Björling, 1911-60, (Swed.) tenor.
Lucrezia Bori, 1887-1960, (It.) soprano.
Maria Callas, 1923-77, (U.S.) soprano.
Emma Calvé, 1858-1942, (Fr.) soprano.
Enrico Caruso, 1873-1921, (It.) tenor.
Feodor Chaliapin, 1873-1938, (Russ.) bass.

Lili Chookasian, 1921-2012, (U.S.) contralto.
Boris Christoff, 1914-93, (Bulg.) bass.
Franco Corelli, 1921-2003, (It.) tenor.
Hughes Cuenod, 1902-2010, (Switz.) tenor.
Victoria De Los Angeles, 1923-2005, (Sp.) soprano.
Giuseppe De Luca, 1876-1950, (It.) baritone.
Fernando De Lucia, 1860-1925, (It.) tenor.
Edouard De Reszke, 1853-1917, (Pol.) bass.

Jean De Reszke, 1850-1925, (Pol.) tenor.
Emmy Destinn, 1878-1930, (Czech.) soprano.
Mattiwilda Dobbs, 1925-2015, (U.S.) coloratura soprano.
Emma Eames, 1865-1952, (U.S.) soprano.
(Carlo Broschi) Farinelli, 1705-82, (It.) castrato.
Geraldine Farrar, 1882-1967, (U.S.) soprano.
Eileen Farrell, 1920-2002, (U.S.) soprano.
Kathleen Ferrier, 1912-53, (Eng.) contralto.

Dietrich Fischer-Dieskau, 1925-2012, (Ger.) baritone.
Kirsten Flagstad, 1895-1962, (Nor.) soprano.
Olive Fremstad, 1871-1951, (Swed.-U.S.) soprano.
Amelita Galli-Curci, 1882-1963, (It.) soprano.
Mary Garden, 1874-1967, (Br.) soprano.
Nicolai Ghiaurov, 1929-2004, (Bulg.) bass.
Beniamino Gigli, 1890-1957, (It.) tenor.
Tito Gobbi, 1913-84, (It.) baritone.
Giulia Grisi, 1811-69, (It.) soprano.
Frieda Hempel, 1885-1955, (Ger.) soprano.
Jerome Hines, 1921-2003, (U.S.) bass.
Hans Hotter, 1909-2003, (Ger.) bass-baritone.
Maria Jeritza, 1887-1982, (Czech.) soprano.
Sena Jurinac, 1921-2011, (Yugo.) soprano.
Alexander Kipnis, 1891-1978, (Russ.-U.S.) bass.
Dorothy Kirsten, 1910-92, (U.S.) soprano.
Alfredo Kraus, 1927-99, (Sp.) tenor.
Luigi Lablache, 1794-1858, (It.) bass.
Lilli Lehmann, 1848-1929, (Ger.) soprano.
Lotte Lehmann, 1888-1976, (Ger.-U.S.) soprano.
Jenny Lind, 1820-87, (Swed.) soprano.
Cornell MacNeil, 1922-2011, (U.S.) baritone.
Maria Malibran, 1808-36, (Sp.) mezzo-soprano.
Giovanni Martinelli, 1885-1969, (It.) tenor.
John McCormack, 1884-1945, (Ire.) tenor.

Nellie Melba, 1861-1931, (Austral.) soprano.
Lauritz Melchior, 1890-1973, (Den.) tenor.
Robert Merrill, 1919-2004, (U.S.) baritone.
Zinka Milanov, 1906-89, (Yugo.) soprano.
Patrice Munsel, 1925-2015, (U.S.) coloratura soprano.
Patricia Neway, 1919-2012, (U.S.) soprano.
Birgit Nilsson, 1918-2005, (Swed.) soprano.
Lillian Nordica, 1857-1914, (U.S.) soprano.
Magda Olivero, 1910-2014, (It.) soprano.
Giuditta Pasta, 1797-1865, (It.) soprano.
Adelina Patti, 1843-1919, (It.) soprano.
Luciano Pavarotti, 1935-2007, (It.) tenor.
Peter Pears, 1910-86, (Eng.) tenor.
Jan Peerce, 1904-84, (U.S.) tenor.
Ezio Pinza, 1892-1957, (It.) bass.
Lily Pons, 1898-1976, (Fr.) soprano.
Rosa Ponselle, 1897-1981, (U.S.) soprano.
Hermann Prey, 1929-98, (Ger.) baritone.
Margaret Price, 1941-2011, (U.K.) soprano.
Regina Resnik, 1922-2013, (U.S.) soprano turned mezzo-soprano.
Elisabeth Rethberg, 1894-1976, (Ger.) soprano.
Giovanni Battista Rubini, 1794-1854, (It.) tenor.
Leonie Rysanek, 1926-98, (Austria) soprano.
Dorothy Sarnoff, 1914-2008, (U.S.) soprano.
Bidú Sayão, 1902-99, (Braz.) soprano.
Friedrich Schorr, 1888-1953, (Hung.) bass-baritone.
Elisabeth Schwarzkopf, 1915-2006, (Ger.) soprano.

Marcella Sembrich, 1858-1935, (Pol.) soprano.
Cesare Siepi, 1923-2010, (It.) bass.
Beverly Sills, 1929-2007, (U.S.) soprano.
Elisabeth Söderström, 1927-2009, (Swed.) soprano.
Eleanor Steber, 1914-90, (U.S.) soprano.
Risë Stevens, 1913-2013, (U.S.) mezzo-soprano.
Joan Sutherland, 1926-2010, (Austral.) soprano.
Ferrucio Tagliavini, 1913-95, (It.) tenor.
Renata Tebaldi, 1922-2004 (It.) soprano.
Luisa Tetrazzini, 1871-1940, (It.) soprano.
Lawrence Tibbett, 1896-1960, (U.S.) baritone.
Giorgio Tozzi, 1923-2011, (U.S.) bass-baritone.
Tatiana Troyanos, 1938-93, (U.S.) mezzo-soprano.
Richard Tucker, 1913-75, (U.S.) tenor.
Shirley Verrett, 1931-2010, (U.S.) mezzo-soprano.
Pauline Viardot, 1821-1910, (Fr.) mezzo-soprano.
Jon Vickers, 1926-2015, (Can.) tenor.
William Warfield, 1920-2002, (U.S.) bass-baritone.
Leonard Warren, 1911-60, (U.S.) baritone.
Ljuba Welitsch, 1913-96, (Bulg.) soprano.
Camilla Williams, 1919-2012, (U.S.) soprano.
Wolfgang Windgassen, 1914-74, (Ger.) tenor.

Rock and Roll, Rhythm and Blues, and Rap Artists

Titles in quotation marks are singles; others are albums. * = Inducted into Rock and Roll Hall of Fame as performer between 1986 and 2016; year is in parentheses.

*ABBA (2010): "Dancing Queen"
Paula Abdul: "Straight Up"
*AC/DC (2003): "Back in Black"
Bryan Adams: "Cuts Like a Knife"
Adele: "Rolling in the Deep"
*Aerosmith (2001): "Sweet Emotion"
Christina Aguilera: "What a Girl Wants"
Alice in Chains: "Heaven Beside You"
*The Allman Brothers Band (1995): "Ramblin' Man"
*The Animals (1994): "House of the Rising Sun"
Paul Anka: "Lonely Boy"
Fiona Apple: "Criminal"
Frankie Avalon: "Venus"
Iggy Azalea: "Fancy"
The B-52s: "Love Shack"
Bachman Turner Overdrive: "Takin' Care of Business"
Backstreet Boys: "I Want It That Way"
Bad Company: "Can't Get Enough"
Erykah Badu: "On and On"
*La Vern Baker (1991): "I Cried a Tear"
*Hank Ballard[1] and the Midnighters (1990): "Work With Me, Annie"
*The Band (1994): "The Weight"
Barenaked Ladies: "One Week"
*The Beach Boys (1988): "Good Vibrations"
*Beastie Boys (2012): "(You Gotta) Fight for Your Right (to Party)"
*The Beatles (1988): *Sgt. Pepper's Lonely Hearts Club Band*
Beck: "Loser"
*Jeff Beck (2009): "Escape"
*The Bee Gees (1997): "Stayin' Alive"
Pat Benatar: "Hit Me With Your Best Shot"
*Chuck Berry (1986): "Johnny B. Goode"
Beyoncé: "Crazy in Love"
The Big Bopper: "Chantilly Lace"
Björk: "Human Behavior"
The Black Crowes: "Hard to Handle"
Black Eyed Peas: *Elephunk*
*Black Sabbath (2006): "Paranoid"
*Bobby "Blue" Bland (1992): "Turn On Your Love Light"
Mary J. Blige: *My Life*
Blind Faith: "Can't Find My Way Home"
Blink-182: "All the Small Things"
*Blondie (2006): "Heart of Glass"
Blood, Sweat, and Tears: "Spinning Wheel"
Blues Traveler: "Run-Around"
Gary "U.S." Bonds: "Quarter to Three"
Bon Jovi: "Livin' on a Prayer"
*Booker T. and the M.G.'s (1992): "Green Onions"
Boston: "More Than a Feeling"
*David Bowie (1996): "Space Oddity"

Boyz II Men: "I'll Make Love to You"
Toni Braxton: "Un-Break My Heart"
Chris Brown: "Kiss Kiss"
*James Brown (1986): "Papa's Got a Brand New Bag"
*Ruth Brown (1993): "Lucky Lips"
*Jackson Browne (2004): "Doctor My Eyes"
*Buffalo Springfield (1997): "For What It's Worth"
Jimmy Buffett: "Margaritaville"
*Solomon Burke (2001): "Over and Over (Huggin' and Lovin')"
*The Paul Butterfield Blues Band (2015): "Born in Chicago"
*The Byrds (1991): "Turn! Turn! Turn!"
Mariah Carey: "Vision of Love"
The Carpenters: "(They Long to Be) Close to You"
The Cars: "Shake It Up"
*Johnny Cash (1992): "I Walk the Line"
*Ray Charles (1986): "Georgia on My Mind"
*Cheap Trick (2016): "Surrender"
Chubby Checker: "The Twist"
*Chicago (2016): "Saturday in the Park"
*Eric Clapton (2000): "Layla"
Kelly Clarkson: "Since U Been Gone"
*The Clash (2003): "Rock the Casbah"
*Jimmy Cliff (2010): "I Can See Clearly Now"
*The Coasters (1987): "Yakety Yak"
*Eddie Cochran (1987): "Summertime Blues"
Joe Cocker: "With a Little Help From My Friends"
*Leonard Cohen (2008): "Suzanne"
Coldplay: "Clocks"
Collective Soul: "The World I Know"
Phil Collins: "Against All Odds"
*Sam Cooke (1986): "You Send Me"
Coolio: "Gangsta's Paradise"
*Alice Cooper (2011): "School's Out"
*Elvis Costello and the Attractions (2003): "Alison"
Counting Crows: "Mr. Jones"
*Cream (1993): "Sunshine of Your Love"
Creed: "Arms Wide Open"
*Creedence Clearwater Revival (1993): "Proud Mary"
*Crosby, Stills, and Nash (1997): "Suite: Judy Blue Eyes"
Sheryl Crow: "All I Want to Do"
The Crystals: "Da Doo Ron Ron"
The Cure: "Boys Don't Cry"
Daft Punk: "Get Lucky"
Danny and the Juniors: "At the Hop"
*Bobby Darin (1990): "Splish Splash"
Daughtry: "It's Not Over"

*The Dave Clark Five (2008): "Glad All Over"
Dave Matthews Band: "Don't Drink the Water"
*Miles Davis (2006): *Bitches Brew*
Spencer Davis Group: "Gimme Some Lovin'"
*Deep Purple (2016): "Smoke on the Water"
Def Leppard: "Photograph"
*The Dells (2004): "Oh, What a Night"
Depeche Mode: "Strange Love"
Destiny's Child: "Survivor"
*Neil Diamond (2011): "Cracklin' Rosie"
*Bo Diddley (1987): "Who Do You Love?
*Dion[1] and the Belmonts (1989): "A Teenager in Love"
Celine Dion: "Because You Loved Me"
Dire Straits: "Money for Nothing"
DMX: "What's My Name"
*Fats Domino (1986): "Blueberry Hill"
*Donovan (2012): "Mellow Yellow"
The Doobie Brothers: "What a Fool Believes"
*The Doors (1993): "Light My Fire"
Dr. Dre: "Nothin' But a 'G' Thang"
*Dr. John (2011): "Right Place, Wrong Time"
Drake: "Hotline Bling"
*The Drifters (1988): "Save the Last Dance for Me"
Duran Duran: "Hungry Like the Wolf"
*Bob Dylan (1988): "Like a Rolling Stone"
*The Eagles (1998): "Hotel California"
*Earth, Wind, and Fire (2000): "Shining Star"
*Duane Eddy (1994): "Rebel-Rouser"
Missy Elliott: "Sock It 2 Me"
Eminem: "The Real Slim Shady"
En Vogue: "Hold On"
The Eurythmics: "Sweet Dreams (Are Made of This)"
Everclear: "Father Of Mine"
*The Everly Brothers (1986): "Wake Up, Little Susie"
50 Cent (Curtis Jackson): *Get Rich or Die Tryin'*
The Five Satins: "In the Still of the Night"
Roberta Flack: "The First Time Ever I Saw Your Face"
*The Flamingos (2001): "I Only Have Eyes for You"
*Fleetwood Mac (1998): *Rumours*
The Foo Fighters: "I'll Stick Around"
Foreigner: "Double Vision"
*The Four Seasons (1990): "Sherry"
*The Four Tops (1990): "I Can't Help Myself (Sugar Pie, Honey Bunch)"
*Aretha Franklin (1987): "Respect"
fun.: "We Are Young"

Nelly Furtado: "I'm Like a Bird"
*Peter Gabriel (2014): "Shock the Monkey"
*Gamble (Kenny) and Huff (Leon) (2008): "If You Don't Know Me by Now"
*Marvin Gaye (1987): "I Heard It Through the Grapevine"
*Genesis (2010): "No Reply at All"
Goo Goo Dolls: "Iris"
Grand Funk Railroad: "We're an American Band"
*Grandmaster Flash and the Furious Five (2007): "The Message"
*The Grateful Dead (1994): "Uncle John's Band"
*Al Green (1995): "Let's Stay Together"
*Green Day (2015): "Boulevard of Broken Dreams"
The Guess Who: "American Woman"
*Guns N' Roses (2012): "Sweet Child o' Mine"
*Buddy Guy (2005): A Man and His Blues
*Bill Haley[1] and His Comets (1987): "Rock Around the Clock"
*Hall (Darryl) and Oates (John) (2014): "Kiss on My List"
*George Harrison (2004): "My Sweet Lord"
*Isaac Hayes (2002): "Theme From 'Shaft'"
*Heart (2013): "Barracuda"
*Jimi Hendrix (1992): "Purple Haze"
Lauryn Hill: "Doo-Wop (That Thing)"
*The Hollies (2010): "Long Cool Woman (In a Black Dress)"
*Buddy Holly (1986): "Peggy Sue"
*John Lee Hooker (1991): "Boogie Chillen"
Hootie and the Blowfish: Cracked Rear View
Whitney Houston: "I Will Always Love You"
*The Impressions (1991): "For Your Precious Love"
Indigo Girls: "Closer to Fine"
INXS: "Need You Tonight"
*The Isley Brothers (1992): "It's Your Thing"
Ja Rule: Venni, Vetti, Vecci
*The Jackson Five (1997): "ABC"
Janet Jackson: Rhythm Nation
*Michael Jackson (2001): Thriller
*Etta James (1993): "At Last"
Tommy James and the Shondells: "Crimson and Clover"
Jane's Addiction: "Jane Says"
Jay and the Americans: "This Magic Moment"
Jay Z: "99 Problems"
*Jefferson Airplane (1996): "White Rabbit"
Jethro Tull: Aqualung
*Joan Jett and the Blackhearts (2015): "I Love Rock 'n' Roll"
Jewel: "You Were Meant for Me"
*Billy Joel (1999): "Piano Man"
*Elton John (1994): "Candle in the Wind"
*Little Willie John (1996): "Sleep"
Norah Jones: Come Away With Me
*Janis Joplin (1995): "Me and Bobby McGee"
Journey: "Don't Stop Believin' "
K.C. and the Sunshine Band: "Get Down Tonight"
R. Kelly: "I Can't Sleep Baby (If I)"
Alicia Keys: "Fallin'"
Kid Rock: "Cowboy"
*B. B. King (1987): "The Thrill Is Gone"
Carole King: Tapestry
*The Kinks (1990): "You Really Got Me"
*Kiss (2014): "Rock 'n' Roll All Night"
*Gladys Knight and the Pips (1996): "Midnight Train to Georgia"
Korn: "Blind"
Lenny Kravitz: "Are You Gonna Go My Way?"
Lady Gaga: "Poker Face"
*Led Zeppelin (1995): "Stairway to Heaven"
*Brenda Lee (2002): "I'm Sorry"
John Legend: "Ordinary People"
*John Lennon (1994): "Imagine"
*Jerry Lee Lewis (1986): "Whole Lotta Shakin' Going On"
Lil' Kim: "No Matter What They Say"
Lil Wayne: Tha Block Is Hot
Limp Bizkit: "Break Stuff"
Linkin Park: "One Step Closer"
*Little Anthony and the Imperials (2009): "Tears on My Pillow"
*Little Richard (1986): "Tutti Frutti"
*Little Walter (2008): "Juke"
LL Cool J: "Mama Said Knock You Out"
Jennifer Lopez: "Love Don't Cost a Thing"

*Darlene Love (2011): "He's a Rebel"
*The Lovin' Spoonful (2000): "Summer in the City"
Ludacris: "Money Maker"
*Frankie Lymon and the Teenagers (1993): "Why Do Fools Fall in Love?"
*Lynyrd Skynyrd (2006): "Free Bird"
*Madonna (2008): "Material Girl"
*The Mamas and the Papas (1998): "Monday, Monday"
Marilyn Manson: "Beautiful People"
*Bob Marley (1994): Exodus
Maroon 5: Songs About Jane
Bruno Mars: "Just the Way You Are"
*Martha and the Vandellas (1995): "Dancin' in the Streets"
The Marvelettes: "Please, Mr. Postman"
Matchbox 20: "Push"
John Mayer: "Daughters"
*Curtis Mayfield (1999): "Superfly"
*Paul McCartney (1999): "Band on the Run"
Don McLean: "American Pie"
*Clyde McPhatter (1987): "A Lover's Question"
Meat Loaf: "Paradise by the Dashboard Light"
*John (Cougar) Mellencamp (2008): "Jack and Diane"
Men at Work: "Who Can It Be Now?"
*Metallica (2009): "Enter Sandman"
George Michael: "Faith"
*Steve Miller (2016): "Take the Money and Run"
Nicki Minaj: Pink Friday.
*Joni Mitchell (1997): "Both Sides Now"
Moby: "Bodyrock"
The Monkees: "I'm a Believer"
Moody Blues: "Nights in White Satin"
*The Moonglows (2000): "Blue Velvet"
Alanis Morissette: "Ironic"
*Van Morrison (1993): "Brown-Eyed Girl"
Mötley Crüe: "Live Wire"
Motörhead: "Ace of Spades"
Jason Mraz: "I'm Yours"
Mumford & Sons: "Little Lion Man"
Nelly: Country Grammar
*Ricky Nelson (1987): "Hello, Mary Lou"
Nine Inch Nails: "Closer"
*Nirvana (2014): Nevermind
No Doubt: Rock Steady
The Notorious B.I.G.: "Mo Money Mo Problems"
NSYNC: "Bye, Bye, Bye"
Ted Nugent: "Stranglehold"
*N.W.A. (2016): "Straight Outta Compton"
*The O'Jays (2005): "Back Stabbers"
One Direction: "What Makes You Beautiful"
*Roy Orbison (1987): "Oh, Pretty Woman"
Ozzy Osbourne: "Crazy Train"
OutKast: Speakerboxxx/The Love Below
*Parliament/Funkadelic (1997): "One Nation Under a Groove"
Pearl Jam: "Jeremy"
*Carl Perkins (1987): "Blue Suede Shoes"
Katy Perry: "Firework"
Peter, Paul, and Mary: "Leaving on a Jet Plane"
*Tom Petty and the Heartbreakers (2002): "Refugee"
Liz Phair: Exile in Guyville
Phish: "Sample in a Jar"
*Wilson Pickett (1991): "Land of 1,000 Dances"
Pink: Missundaztood
*Pink Floyd (1996): The Wall
*Gene Pitney (2002): "Only Love Can Break a Heart"
*The Platters (1990): "The Great Pretender"
The Pointer Sisters: "I'm So Excited"
*The Police (2003): "Every Breath You Take"
Iggy Pop: "Lust for Life"
*Elvis Presley (1986): "Love Me Tender"
*The Pretenders (2005): "Back on the Chain Gang"
*Lloyd Price (1998): "Stagger Lee"
*Prince (The Artist) (2004): "Purple Rain"
*Public Enemy (2013): "Fight the Power"
Puff Daddy and the Family: No Way Out
*Queen (2001): "Bohemian Rhapsody"
Radiohead: OK Computer
Rage Against the Machine: "Bulls on Parade"
*Bonnie Raitt (2000): "Something to Talk About"
*The Ramones (2002): "I Wanna Be Sedated"

*Red Hot Chili Peppers (2012): "Under the Bridge"
*Otis Redding (1989): "(Sittin' on) The Dock of the Bay"
*Jimmy Reed (1991): "Ain't That Loving You, Baby?"
*Lou Reed (2015): "Walk on the Wild Side"
*R.E.M. (2007): "Losing My Religion"
REO Speedwagon: "Can't Fight This Feeling"
Busta Rhymes: "What's It Gonna Be?"
*The Righteous Brothers (2003): "You've Lost That Lovin' Feelin' "
Rihanna: "Umbrella"
Johnny Rivers: "Poor Side of Town"
*Smokey Robinson[1] and the Miracles (1987): "Shop Around"
*The Rolling Stones (1989): "Satisfaction"
*The Ronettes (2007): "Be My Baby"
*Linda Ronstadt (2014): "You're No Good"
Diana Ross: "I'm Coming Out"
*Run-D.M.C. (2009): "Raisin' Hell"
*Rush (2013): "Tom Sawyer"
Sade: "Smooth Operator"
Salt-N-Pepa: "Shoop"
*Sam and Dave (1992): "Soul Man"
*Santana (1998): "Black Magic Woman"
Seal: "Kiss From a Rose"
Neil Sedaka: "Breaking Up Is Hard to Do"
*Bob Seger (2004): "Old Time Rock & Roll"
*Sex Pistols (2006): "Anarchy in the UK"
Shakira: "Whenever, Wherever"
Tupac Shakur: "How Do U Want It"
*Del Shannon (1999): "Runaway"
Ed Sheeran: "Thinking Out Loud"
*The Shirelles (1996): "Soldier Boy"
Carly Simon: "You're So Vain"
*Paul Simon (2001): "50 Ways to Leave Your Lover"
*Simon and Garfunkel (1990): "Bridge Over Troubled Water"
*Percy Sledge (2005): "When a Man Loves a Woman"
*Sly and the Family Stone (1993): "Everyday People"
Smashing Pumpkins: "Today"
*Patti Smith (2007): "Because the Night"
Sam Smith: "Stay With Me"
Will Smith: "Gettin' Jiggy With It"
The Smiths: "This Charming Man"
Snoop Dogg (a.k.a. Snoop Lion, Snoopzilla): "Gin and Juice"
Sonic Youth: "Bull in the Heather"
Soundgarden: "Black Hole Sun"
Britney Spears: "Hit Me Baby One More Time"
Spice Girls: "Wannabe"
*Dusty Springfield (1999): "I Only Want to Be With You"
*Bruce Springsteen (1999): "Born to Run"
*Staple Singers (1999): "I'll Take You There"
*Steely Dan (2001): "Rikki Don't Lose That Number"
Gwen Stefani: "Hollaback Girl"
Steppenwolf: "Born to Be Wild"
*Cat Stevens (2014): "Wild World"
*Rod Stewart (1994): "Maggie Mae"
Sting: "If You Love Somebody, Set Them Free"
Stone Temple Pilots: "Plush"
*The Stooges (2010): "I Wanna Be Your Dog"
Styx: "Come Sail Away"
The Sugar Hill Gang: "Rapper's Delight"
*Donna Summer (2013): "Bad Girls"
*The Supremes (1988): "Stop! In the Name of Love"
*Talking Heads (2002): "Once in a Lifetime"
*James Taylor (2001): "You've Got a Friend"
*The Temptations (1989): "My Girl"
Robin Thicke: "Blurred Lines"
Three Dog Night: "Joy to the World"
Justin Timberlake: "SexyBack"
TLC: "Waterfalls"
*Traffic (2004): Traffic
*Big Joe Turner (1987): "Shake, Rattle & Roll"
*Ike and Tina Turner (1991): "Proud Mary"
The Turtles: "Happy Together"
*U2 (2005): "With or Without You"
Usher: "You Make Me Wanna"
*Ritchie Valens (2001): "La Bamba"
*Van Halen (2007): "Running With the Devil"
*Stevie Ray Vaughan & Double Trouble (2015): "Change It"
*The Velvet Underground (1996): "Sweet Jane"
*The Ventures (2008): "Walk, Don't Run"

*Gene Vincent (1998): "Be-Bop-A-Lula"
*Tom Waits (2011): "Downtown Train"
The Wallflowers: "One Headlight"
Dionne Warwick: "I Say a Little Prayer"
*Muddy Waters (1987): "I Can't Be Satisfied"
Mary Wells: "My Guy"
Kanye West: "Gold Digger"
The White Stripes: "Seven Nation Army"
Whitesnake: "Here I Go Again"

*The Who (1990): *Tommy*
Pharrell Williams: "Happy"
*Jackie Wilson (1987): "That's Why"
*Bill Withers (2015): "Lean on Me"
*Bobby Womack (2009): "Lookin' for a Love"
*Stevie Wonder (1989): "You Are the Sunshine of My Life"
Wu-Tang Clan: "Protect Ya Neck"

*The Yardbirds (1992): "For Your Love"
Yes: "Roundabout"
*Neil Young (1995): "Down by the River"
*The Young Rascals/The Rascals (1997): "Good Lovin'"
*Frank Zappa[1]/Mothers of Invention (1995): *Hot Rats*
*ZZ Top (2004): "Legs"

(1) Only individual performer is in Rock and Roll Hall of Fame.

Entertainment Personalities of the Present

Living actors, musicians, dancers, singers, producers, directors, and radio-TV performers.

Name	Birthplace	Birthdate	Name	Birthplace	Birthdate
Abdul, Paula	San Fernando, CA	6/19/1962	Atkins, Sharif	Pittsburgh, PA	1/29/1975
Abraham, F. Murray	Pittsburgh, PA	10/24/1939	Atkinson, Rowan	Newcastle upon Tyne, Eng., UK	1/6/1955
Abrams, J(effrey) J(acob)	New York, NY	6/27/1966			
Adams, Amy	Vicenza, Italy	8/20/1974	Auberjonois, Rene	New York, NY	6/1/1940
Adams, Bryan	Kingston, ON, Canada	11/5/1959	Austin, Patti	New York, NY	8/10/1948
Adams, Yolanda	Houston, TX	8/27/1961	Avalon, Frankie	Philadelphia, PA	9/18/1940
Adele	London, England, UK	5/5/1988	Aykroyd, Dan	Ottawa, ON, Canada	7/1/1952
Adjani, Isabelle	Paris, France	6/27/1955	Azalea, Iggy	Sydney, NSW, Australia	6/7/1990
Ad-Rock	South Orange, NJ	10/31/1966	Azaria, Hank	Forest Hills, Queens, NY	4/25/1964
Aduba, Uzo	Boston, MA	2/10/1981	Aznavour, Charles	Paris, France	5/22/1924
Affleck, Ben	Berkeley, CA	8/15/1972	Babyface	Indianapolis, IN	4/10/1959
Affleck, Casey	Falmouth, MA	8/12/1975	Baccarin, Morena	Rio de Janeiro, Brazil	6/2/1979
Aghdashloo, Shohreh	Tehran, Iran	5/11/1952	Bacon, Kevin	Philadelphia, PA	7/8/1958
Aguilera, Christina	Staten Island, NY	12/18/1980	Badalucco, Michael	Brooklyn, NY	12/20/1954
Aiello, Danny	New York, NY	6/20/1933	Bader, Diedrich	Alexandria, VA	12/24/1966
Aiken, Clay	Raleigh, NC	11/30/1978	Badu, Erykah	Dallas, TX	2/26/1971
Aimée, Anouk	Paris, France	4/27/1932	Baez, Joan	Staten Island, NY	1/9/1941
Alba, Jessica	Pomona, CA	4/28/1981	Baio, Scott	Brooklyn, NY	9/22/1960
Alberghetti, Anna Maria	Pesaro, Italy	5/15/1936	Baker, Anita	Toledo, OH	1/26/1958
Albert, Marv	Brooklyn, NY	6/12/1941	Baker, Carroll	Johnstown, PA	5/28/1931
Alda, Alan	New York, NY	1/28/1936	Baker, Diane	Hollywood, CA	2/25/1938
Alexander, Jane	Boston, MA	10/28/1939	Baker, Joe Don	Groesbeck, TX	2/12/1936
Alexander, Jason	Newark, NJ	9/23/1959	Baker, Kathy	Midland, TX	6/8/1950
Allen, Debbie	Houston, TX	1/16/1950	Baker, Simon	Launceston, Tas., Australia	7/30/1969
Allen, Joan	Rochelle, IL	8/20/1956	Bakula, Scott	St. Louis, MO	10/9/1954
Allen, Karen	Carrollton, IL	10/5/1951	Baldwin, Alec	Massapequa, NY	4/3/1958
Allen, Kris	Jacksonville, AR	6/21/1985	Baldwin, Daniel	Massapequa, NY	10/5/1960
Allen, Marty	Pittsburgh, PA	3/23/1922	Baldwin, Stephen	Massapequa, NY	5/12/1966
Allen, Tim	Denver, CO	6/13/1953	Baldwin, William	Massapequa, NY	2/21/1963
Allen, Woody	Bronx, NY	12/1/1935	Bale, Christian	Pembrokeshire, Wales, UK	1/30/1974
Alley, Kirstie	Wichita, KS	1/12/1951	Ballard, Kaye	Cleveland, OH	11/20/1926
Allman, Gregg	Nashville, TN	12/8/1947	Ballas, Mark	Houston, TX	5/24/1986
Alpert, Herb	Los Angeles, CA	3/31/1935	Bana, Eric	Melbourne, Vic., Australia	8/9/1968
Almodóvar, Pedro	Calzada de Calatrava, Spain	9/24/1949	Banderas, Antonio	Málaga, Spain	8/10/1960
Ambrose, Lauren	New Haven, CT	2/20/1978	Banks, Elizabeth	Pittsfield, MA	2/10/1974
Ames, Ed	Malden, MA	7/9/1927	Banks, Jonathan	Washington, DC	1/31/1947
Amos, John	Newark, NJ	12/27/1939	Banks, Tyra	Los Angeles, CA	12/4/1973
Amos, Tori	Newton, NC	8/22/1963	Baranski, Christine	Buffalo, NY	5/2/1952
Anderson, Anthony	Los Angeles, CA	8/15/1970	Barbeau, Adrienne	Sacramento, CA	6/11/1945
Anderson, Gillian	Chicago, IL	8/9/1968	Bardem, Javier	Las Palmas, Canary Islands, Spain	3/1/1969
Anderson, Harry	Newport, RI	10/14/1952			
Anderson, Ian	Dunfermline, Scotland, UK	8/10/1947	Bardot, Brigitte	Paris, France	9/28/1934
Anderson, Loni	St. Paul, MN	8/5/1946?	Barker, Bob	Darrington, WA	12/12/1923
Anderson, Louie	St. Paul, MN	3/24/1953	Barkin, Ellen	Bronx, NY	4/16/1955
Anderson, Melissa Sue	Berkeley, CA	9/26/1962	Barrie, Barbara	Chicago, IL	5/23/1931
Anderson, Pamela	Ladysmith, BC, Canada	7/1/1967	Barrino, Fantasia	High Point, NC	6/30/1984
Anderson, Richard	Long Branch, NJ	8/8/1926	Barrymore, Drew	Los Angeles, CA	2/22/1975
Anderson, Richard Dean	Minneapolis, MN	1/23/1950	Bartoli, Cecilia	Rome, Italy	6/4/1966
Anderson, Wes	Houston, TX	5/1/1969	Barton, Misha	London, England, UK	1/24/1986
Andersson, Bibi	Stockholm, Sweden	11/11/1935	Baryshnikov, Mikhail	Riga, Latvia	1/28/1948
André 3000	Atlanta, GA	5/27/1975	Basinger, Kim	Athens, GA	12/8/1953
Andress, Ursula	Bern, Switzerland	3/19/1936	Bass, Lance	Laurel, MS	5/4/1979
Andrews, Julie	Walton-on-Thames, Surrey, England, UK	10/1/1935	Bassett, Angela	New York, NY	8/16/1958
			Bassey, Shirley	Cardiff, Wales, UK	1/8/1937
Andrews, Naveen	London, England, UK	1/17/1969	Batali, Mario	Yakima, WA	9/9/1960
Aniston, Jennifer	Sherman Oaks, CA	2/11/1969	Bateman, Jason	Rye, NY	1/14/1969
Anka, Paul	Ottawa, ON, Canada	7/30/1941	Bateman, Justine	Rye, NY	2/19/1966
Ann-Margret	Stockholm, Sweden	4/28/1941	Bates, Kathy	Memphis, TN	6/28/1948
Ansari, Aziz	Columbia, SC	2/23/1983	Batt, Bryan	New Orleans, LA	3/1/1963
Anthony, Marc	New York, NY	9/16/1968	Battle, Kathleen	Portsmouth, OH	8/13/1948
Apatow, Judd	Syosset, NY	12/6/1967	Baxter, Meredith	South Pasadena, CA	6/21/1947
Apple, Fiona	New York, NY	9/13/1977	Bean, Orson	Burlington, VT	7/22/1928
Applegate, Christina	Los Angeles, CA	11/25/1971	Bean, Sean	Sheffield, England, UK	4/17/1959
Archer, Anne	Los Angeles, CA	8/24/1947	Beatty, Ned	Louisville, KY	7/6/1937
Arkin, Adam	Brooklyn, NY	8/19/1956	Beatty, Warren	Richmond, VA	3/30/1937
Arkin, Alan	New York, NY	3/26/1934	Beauvais, Garcelle	St. Marc, Haiti	11/26/1966
Armisen, Fred	Hattiesburg, MS	12/4/1966	Beck	Los Angeles, CA	7/8/1970
Arnaz, Desi, Jr.	Hollywood, CA	1/19/1953	Beck, Jeff	Wallington, Surrey, Eng., UK	6/24/1944
Arnaz, Lucie	Hollywood, CA	7/17/1951	Beckham, Victoria	Hertfordshire, England, UK	4/17/1974
Arnett, Will	Toronto, ON, Canada	5/4/1970	Beckinsale, Kate	London, England, UK	7/26/1973
Arnold, Tom	Ottumwa, IA	3/6/1959	Bedelia, Bonnie	New York, NY	3/25/1948
Arquette, David	Winchester, VA	9/8/1971	Begley, Ed, Jr.	Los Angeles, CA	9/16/1949
Arquette, Patricia	Chicago, IL	4/8/1968	Behar, Joy	Brooklyn, NY	10/7/1942
Arquette, Rosanna	New York, NY	8/10/1959	Belafonte, Harry	New York, NY	3/1/1927
Arroyo, Martina	New York, NY	2/2/1937	Bell, Art	Camp Lejeune, NC	6/17/1945
Ashanti (Douglas)	Glen Cove, NY	10/13/1980	Bell, Kristen	Huntington Woods, MI	7/18/1980
Ashley, Elizabeth	Ocala, FL	8/30/1939	Bello, Maria	Norristown, PA	4/18/1967
Asner, Ed	Kansas City, KS	11/15/1929	Belmondo, Jean-Paul	Neuilly-sur-Seine, France	4/9/1933
Assante, Armand	New York, NY	10/4/1949	Belushi, Jim	Chicago, IL	6/15/1954
Astin, John	Baltimore, MD	3/30/1930	Belzer, Richard	Bridgeport, CT	8/4/1944
Astin, Sean	Santa Monica, CA	2/25/1971	Benanti, Laura	Kinnelon, NJ	7/15/1979
Atkins, Eileen	London, England, UK	6/16/1934	Benatar, Pat	Brooklyn, NY	1/10/1953

Name	Birthplace	Birthdate
Benedict, Dirk	Helena, MT	3/1/1945
Benigni, Roberto	Misericordia, Italy	10/27/1952
Bening, Annette	Topeka, KS	5/29/1958
Benjamin, Richard	New York, NY	5/22/1938
Bennett, Alan	Leeds, England, UK.	5/9/1934
Bennett, Tony	Astoria, Queens, NY	8/3/1926
Benson, George	Pittsburgh, PA	3/22/1943
Benson, Robby	Dallas, TX	1/21/1956
Berenger, Tom	Chicago, IL	5/31/1950
Bergen, Candice	Beverly Hills, CA	5/9/1946
Bergeron, Tom	Haverhill, MA	5/6/1955
Berman, Shelley	Chicago, IL	2/3/1925
Bernard, Crystal	Garland, TX	9/30/1961
Bernhard, Sandra	Flint, MI	6/6/1955
Bernsen, Corbin	North Hollywood, CA	9/7/1954
Berry, Chuck	St. Louis, MO.	10/18/1926
Berry, Halle	Cleveland, OH	8/14/1966
Berry, Ken	Moline, IL	11/3/1933
Bertinelli, Valerie	Wilmington, DE	4/23/1960
Bertolucci, Bernardo	Parma, Italy	3/16/1940
Best, Eve	London, England, UK	7/31/1971
Bettany, Paul	London, England, UK	5/27/1971
Bialik, Mayim	San Diego, CA	12/12/1975
Bichir, Demián	Mexico City, Mexico	8/1/1963
Bieber, Justin	Stratford, ON, Canada	3/1/1994
Biel, Jessica	Ely, MN	3/3/1982
Big Boi	Savannah, GA	2/1/1975
Bigelow, Kathryn	San Carlos, CA	11/27/1951
Biggs, Jason	Pompton Plains, NJ	5/12/1978
Bilson, Rachel	Los Angeles, CA	8/25/1981
Binoche, Juliette	Paris, France	3/9/1964
Birch, Thora	Beverly Hills, CA	3/11/1982
Birney, David	Washington, DC	4/23/1939
Bisset, Jacqueline	Weybridge, England, UK	9/13/1944
Björk (Gudmundsdottir)	Reykjavik, Iceland	11/21/1965
Black, Clint	Long Branch, NJ	2/4/1962
Black, Jack	Santa Monica, CA	4/7/1969
Black, Lewis	Washington, DC	8/30/1948
Blades, Ruben	Panama City, Panama	7/16/1948
Blair, Linda	St. Louis, MO.	1/22/1959
Blake, Robert	Nutley, NJ	9/18/1933
Blanchett, Cate	Melbourne, Vic., Australia	5/14/1969
Bledsoe, Tempestt	Chicago, IL	8/1/1973
Bleeth, Yasmine	New York, NY	6/14/1968
Blethyn, Brenda	Ramsgate, Kent, Eng., UK	2/20/1946
Blige, Mary J.	Bronx, NY	1/11/1971
Bloom, Claire	London, England, UK	2/15/1931
Bloom, Orlando	Canterbury, England, UK	1/13/1977
Bloom, Rachel	Manhattan Beach, CA	4/3/1987
Blunt, Emily.	London, England, UK	2/23/1983
Blyth, Ann	Mt. Kisco, NY.	8/16/1928
Bochco, Steven	New York, NY	12/16/1943
Bocelli, Andrea	Lajatico, Italy	9/22/1958
Bogdanovich, Peter	Kingston, NY	7/30/1939
Bogosian, Eric	Woburn, MA	4/24/1953
Bologna, Joseph	Brooklyn, NY	12/30/1934
Bolton, Michael	New Haven, CT	2/26/1953
Bomer, Matt	Spring, TX	10/11/1977
Bon Jovi, Jon	Sayreville, NJ.	3/2/1962
Bonet, Lisa	San Francisco, CA	11/16/1967
Bonham Carter, Helena	London, England, UK	5/26/1966
Bonneville, Hugh	London, England, UK	11/10/1963
Bono	Dublin, Ireland	5/10/1960
Boone, Debby	Hackensack, NJ.	9/22/1956
Boone, Pat	Jacksonville, FL	6/1/1934
Boreanaz, David	Buffalo, NY	5/16/1969
Bosco, Philip	Jersey City, NJ.	9/26/1930
Bostwick, Barry	San Mateo, CA	2/24/1945
Bosworth, Kate	Los Angeles, CA	1/2/1983
Bottoms, Timothy	Santa Barbara, CA.	8/30/1951
Bourdain, Anthony	Leonia, NJ	6/25/1956
Bow Wow	Columbus, OH	3/9/1987
Bowen, Julie	Baltimore, MD	3/3/1970
Bowles, Peter	London, England, UK	10/16/1936
Boxleitner, Bruce	Elgin, IL	5/12/1950
Boy George	Bexleyheath, England, UK.	6/14/1961
Boyle, Danny	Manchester, England, UK	10/20/1956
Boyle, Lara Flynn	Davenport, IA	3/24/1970
Boyle, Susan	Blackburn, Scotland, UK	4/1/1961
Bracco, Lorraine	Brooklyn, NY	10/2/1955
Brady, Wayne	Orlando, FL	6/2/1972
Braff, Zach	South Orange, NJ	4/6/1975
Branagh, Kenneth	Belfast, N. Ireland, UK	12/10/1960
Brand, Russell	Grays, Essex, UK	6/4/1975
Brandauer, Klaus Maria	Steiermark, Austria	6/22/1944
Brandy (Norwood)	McComb, MS.	2/11/1979
Bratt, Benjamin	San Francisco, CA.	12/16/1963
Braugher, Andre	Chicago, IL	7/1/1962
Braxton, Toni	Severn, MD	10/7/1966
Bremner, Ewen	Edinburgh, Scotland, UK	1/23/1972
Brendon, Nicholas	Los Angeles, CA	4/12/1971
Brenneman, Amy	Glastonbury, CT.	6/22/1964
Bridges, Beau	Los Angeles, CA	12/9/1941
Bridges, Jeff	Los Angeles, CA	12/4/1949
Brightman, Sarah	Berkhamsted, England, UK	8/14/1960
Brimley, Wilford	Salt Lake City, UT	9/27/1934
Brinkley, Christie	Monroe, MI	2/2/1954
Britton, Connie	Boston, MA	3/6/1967
Broadbent, Jim	Lincolnshire, England, UK	5/24/1949
Broderick, Matthew	New York, NY	3/21/1962
Brody, Adam	San Diego, CA	12/15/1979
Brody, Adrien	New York, NY	4/14/1973
Brolin, James	Los Angeles, CA	7/18/1940
Brolin, Josh	Los Angeles, CA	2/12/1968
Brooks, Albert	Beverly Hills, CA	7/22/1947
Brooks, Garth	Tulsa, OK	2/7/1962
Brooks, James L.	North Bergen, NJ.	5/9/1940
Brooks, Mel.	Brooklyn, NY	6/28/1926
Brosnan, Pierce	Navan, Co. Meath, Ireland	5/16/1953
Brown, Blair	Washington, DC	4/23/1946
Brown, Bobby	Roxbury, MA	2/5/1969
Brown, Bryan	Panania, NSW, Australia	6/23/1947
Brown, Chris	Tappahannock, VA	5/5/1989
Brown, Foxy	Brooklyn, NY	9/6/1979
Browne, Jackson	Heidelberg, Germany	10/9/1948
Bryan, Luke	Leesburg, GA	7/17/1976
Bryson, Peabo	Greenville, SC	4/13/1951
Bublé, Michael	Burnaby, BC, Canada	9/9/1975
Buckley, Betty	Big Spring, TX	7/3/1947
Buffett, Jimmy	Pascagoula, MS	12/25/1946
Bujold, Geneviève	Montreal, QC, Canada	7/1/1942
Bullock, Sandra	Arlington, VA	7/26/1964
Bumbry, Grace	St. Louis, MO.	1/4/1937
Bündchen, Gisele	Horizontina, Brazil	7/20/1980
Burghoff, Gary	Bristol, CT	5/24/1943
Burke, Cheryl	San Francisco, CA.	5/3/1984
Burke, Delta	Orlando, FL	7/30/1956
Burnett, Carol	San Antonio, TX.	4/26/1933
Burns, Edward	Woodside, Queens, NY	1/29/1968
Burrell, Ty	Grants Pass, OR	8/22/1967
Burstyn, Ellen	Detroit, MI	12/7/1932
Burton, LeVar	Landstuhl, Germany	2/16/1957
Burton, Tim	Burbank, CA	8/25/1958
Buscemi, Steve	Brooklyn, NY	12/13/1957
Busey, Gary	Goose Creek, TX.	6/29/1944
Busfield, Timothy	Lansing, MI	6/12/1957
Butler, Brett	Montgomery, AL	1/30/1958
Butler, Dan	Fort Wayne, IN.	12/2/1954
Butler, Gerard	Glasgow, Scotland, UK	11/13/1969
Butz, Norbert Leo	St. Louis, MO.	1/30/1967
Buzzi, Ruth	Westerly, RI	7/24/1936
Bynes, Amanda	Thousand Oaks, CA	4/3/1986
Byrne, David	Dumbarton, Scotland, UK	5/14/1952
Byrne, Gabriel	Dublin, Ireland	5/12/1950
Byrne, Rose	Sydney, NSW, Australia	7/24/1979
Caan, James.	Bronx, NY	3/26/1940
Caballe, Montserrat	Barcelona, Spain	4/12/1933
Cage, Nicolas	Long Beach, CA	1/7/1964
Cain, Dean	Mt. Clemens, MI	7/31/1966
Caine, Michael	London, England, UK	3/14/1933
Caldwell, Zoe	Hawthorn, Vic., Australia	9/14/1933
Callies, Sarah Wayne	LaGrange, IL	6/1/1977
Callow, Simon	London, England, UK	6/15/1949
Cameron, James	Kapuskasing, ON, Canada.	8/16/1954
Cameron, Kirk.	Panorama City, CA	10/12/1970
Campanella, Joseph	New York, NY	11/21/1927
Campbell, Bruce	Royal Oak, MI	6/22/1958
Campbell, Glen.	Delight, AR	4/22/1936
Campbell, Naomi	South London, Eng., UK	5/22/1970
Campbell, Neve	Guelph, ON, Canada	10/3/1973
Campion, Jane	Waikanae, New Zealand	4/30/1954
Cannavale, Bobby	Union City, NJ	5/3/1971
Cannon, Dyan	Tacoma, WA	1/4/1937
Cannon, Nick	San Diego, CA.	10/8/1980
Caplan, Lizzy	Los Angeles, CA	6/30/1982
Capshaw, Kate	Ft. Worth, TX.	11/3/1953
Cara, Irene	New York, NY	3/18/1959
Cardellini, Linda	Redwood City, CA	6/25/1975
Cardinale, Claudia	Tunis, Tunisia	4/15/1938
Carell, Steve	Concord, MA.	8/16/1962
Carey, Drew	Cleveland, OH.	5/23/1958
Carey, Mariah	Huntington, NY	3/27/1970
Cariou, Len	St. Boniface, MB, Canada	9/30/1939
Carlton, Vanessa	Milford, PA.	8/16/1980
Carlyle, Robert	Glasgow, Scotland, UK	4/14/1961
Carmen, Eric.	Cleveland, OH.	8/11/1949
Caron, Leslie.	Boulogne, France	7/1/1931
Carpenter, John	Carthage, NY	1/16/1948
Carpenter, Mary Chapin	Princeton, NJ.	2/21/1958
Carr, Vikki	El Paso, TX	7/19/1941
Carreras, Jose	Barcelona, Spain	12/5/1946
Carrere, Tia	Honolulu, HI	1/2/1967
Carrey, Jim	Newmarket, ON, Canada.	1/17/1962
Carroll, Diahann	Bronx, NY	7/17/1935
Carroll, Pat	Shreveport, LA	5/5/1927
Carter, Jack	Brooklyn, NY	6/24/1923
Carter, Jim	Harrogate, Yorkshire, England, UK	8/19/1948
Carter, Lynda	Phoenix, AZ.	7/24/1951
Carter, Nick	Jamestown, NY	1/28/1980
Carter, Ron	Ferndale, MI	5/4/1937
Cartwright, Nancy	Kettering, OH.	10/25/1957

Name	Birthplace	Birthdate
Caruso, David	Forest Hills, Queens, NY	1/17/1956
Carvey, Dana	Missoula, MT.	6/2/1955
Cash, Rosanne	Memphis, TN.	5/24/1955
Cassidy, David	New York, NY	4/12/1950
Castellaneta, Dan	Chicago, IL	10/29/1957
Castle-Hughes, Keisha	Donnybrook, WA, Australia	3/24/1990
Cates, Phoebe	New York, NY	7/16/1963
Cattrall, Kim	Liverpool, England, UK	8/21/1956
Cavanagh, Tom	Ottawa, ON, Canada	10/26/1963
Cavett, Dick	Gibbon, NE	11/19/1936
Caviezel, Jim	Mount Vernon, WA.	9/26/1968
Cavill, Henry	Jersey, Channel Islands, UK	5/5/1983
Cedric the Entertainer	Jefferson City, MO	4/24/1964
Cera, Michael	Brampton, ON, Canada	6/7/1988
Chalke, Sarah	Ottawa, ON, Canada	8/27/1976
Chamberlain, Richard	Beverly Hills, CA	3/31/1934
Chambers, Justin	Springfield, OH	7/11/1970
Chan, Jackie	Hong Kong	4/7/1954
Chandler, Kyle	Buffalo, NY	9/17/1965
Channing, Carol	Seattle, WA	1/31/1921
Channing, Stockard	New York, NY	2/13/1944
Chaplin, Geraldine	Santa Monica, CA	7/31/1944
Chapman, Tracy	Cleveland, OH	3/30/1964
Chappelle, Dave	Washington, DC	8/24/1973
Charles, Josh	Baltimore, MD	9/15/1971
Charo	Murcia, Spain	1/15/1951?
Chase, Chevy	New York, NY	10/8/1943
Chasez, JC (Joshua)	Washington, DC	8/8/1976
Chastain, Jessica	Sacramento, CA	3/29/1977
Cheadle, Don	Kansas City, MO	11/29/1964
Checker, Chubby	Spring Gulley, SC	10/3/1941
Chen, Julie	New York, NY	1/6/1970
Chenoweth, Kristin	Broken Arrow, OK	7/24/1968
Cher	El Centro, CA.	5/20/1946
Chesney, Kenny	Lutrelle, TN	3/26/1968
Chianese, Dominic	Bronx, NY	2/24/1931
Chiba, Sonny	Fukuoka, Kyushu, Japan	1/23/1939
Chiklis, Michael	Lowell, MA.	8/30/1963
Chlumsky, Anna	Chicago, IL	12/3/1980
Chmerkovskiy, Maksim	Odessa, Ukraine	1/17/1980
Cho, Margaret	San Francisco, CA.	12/5/1968
Chong, Thomas	Edmonton, AB, Canada	5/24/1938
Chow Yun-Fat	Lamma Island, Hong Kong	5/18/1955
Christensen, Hayden	Vancouver, BC, Canada	4/19/1981
Christie, Julie	Chukua, Assam, India	4/14/1940
Christopher, William	Evanston, IL	10/20/1932
Chuck D	Roosevelt, NY	8/1/1960
Church, Charlotte	Llandaff, Cardiff, Wales, UK	2/21/1986
Church, Thomas Haden	El Paso, TX	6/17/1960
Clapp, Gordon	North Conway, NH	9/24/1948
Clapton, Eric	Ripley, Surrey, England, UK	3/30/1945
Clark, Petula	Epson, Surrey, England, UK	11/15/1932
Clark, Roy	Meherrin, VA	4/15/1933
Clarkson, Kelly	Burleson, TX	4/24/1982
Clarkson, Patricia	New Orleans, LA	12/29/1959
Clay, Andrew Dice	Brooklyn, NY	9/29/1957
Cleese, John	Weston-super-Mare, Eng., UK	10/27/1939
Clooney, George	Lexington, KY	5/6/1961
Close, Glenn	Greenwich, CT	3/19/1947
Coen, Ethan	St. Louis Park, MN.	9/21/1957
Coen, Joel	St. Louis Park, MN.	11/29/1954
Cohen, Andy	St. Louis, MO.	6/2/1968
Cohen, Leonard	Montreal, QC, Canada	9/21/1934
Cohen, Sacha Baron	London, England, UK	10/13/1971
Colbert, Stephen	Washington, DC	5/13/1964
Cole, Gary	Park Ridge, IL	9/20/1956
Coleman, Dabney	Austin, TX	1/3/1932
Colfer, Chris	Fresno, CA	5/27/1990
Collette, Toni	Blacktown, NSW, Australia	11/1/1972
Collins, Joan	London, England, UK	5/23/1933
Collins, Judy	Seattle, WA	5/1/1939
Collins, Pauline	Exmouth, England, UK	9/3/1940
Collins, Phil	London, England, UK	1/30/1951
Collins, Stephen	Des Moines, IA	10/1/1947
Columbus, Chris	Spangler, PA	9/10/1958?
Colvin, Shawn	Vermillion, SD	1/10/1956
Combs, Sean	New York, NY	11/4/1969
Connelly, Jennifer	Round Top, NY	12/12/1970
Connery, Sean	Edinburgh, Scotland, UK	8/25/1930
Connick, Harry, Jr.	New Orleans, LA	9/11/1967
Connolly, Kevin	Patchogue, NY	3/5/1974
Connors, Mike	Fresno, CA	8/15/1925
Conrad, Robert	Chicago, IL	3/1/1935
Conroy, Frances	Monroe, GA.	11/13/1953
Constantine, Michael	Reading, PA.	5/22/1927
Conti, Tom	Paisley, Scotland, UK.	11/22/1941
Conway, Tim	Willoughby, OH	12/15/1933
Cook, Barbara	Atlanta, GA	10/25/1927
Cook, David	Houston, TX	12/20/1982
Coolidge, Rita	Nashville, TN.	5/1/1945
Coolio	Compton, CA.	8/1/1963
Cooper, Alice	Detroit, MI	2/4/1948
Cooper, Bradley	Philadelphia, PA	1/5/1975
Cooper, Chris	Kansas City, MO	7/9/1951
Copeland, Misty	Kansas City, MO	9/10/1982
Copperfield, David	Metuchen, NJ	9/16/1956

Name	Birthplace	Birthdate
Coppola, Francis Ford	Detroit, MI	4/7/1939
Coppola, Sofia	New York, NY	5/14/1971
Corbett, John	Wheeling, WV	5/9/1961
Corbin, Barry	Lamesa, TX.	10/16/1940
Corden, James	Hillingdon, England, UK	8/22/1978
Corea, Chick	Chelsea, MA	6/12/1941
Corgan, Billy	Elk Grove, IL	3/17/1967
Cornell, Chris	Seattle, WA	7/20/1964
Corwin, Jeff	Norwell, MA.	7/11/1967
Cosby, Bill	Philadelphia, PA	7/12/1937
Cosgrove, Miranda	Los Angeles, CA	5/14/1993
Costas, Bob	Astoria, Queens, NY	3/22/1952
Costello, Elvis	London, England, UK	8/25/1954
Costner, Kevin	Compton, CA.	1/18/1955
Cotillard, Marion	Paris, France	9/30/1975
Cowell, Simon	London, England, UK	10/7/1959
Cox, Brian	Dundee, Scotland, UK	6/1/1946
Cox, Courteney	Birmingham, AL	6/15/1964
Cox, Laverne	Mobile, AL	5/29/1984?
Cox, Ronny	Cloudcroft, NM.	7/23/1938
Coyote, Peter	New York, NY	10/10/1941
Craig, Daniel	Chester, England, UK	3/2/1968
Cranston, Bryan	San Fernando Valley, CA	3/7/1956
Crawford, Cindy	DeKalb, IL	2/20/1966
Crawford, Michael	Salisbury, England, UK	1/19/1942
Criss, Darren	San Francisco, CA.	2/5/1987
Cromwell, James	Los Angeles, CA	1/27/1940
Crosby, David	Los Angeles, CA	8/14/1941
Cross, Ben	London, England, UK	12/16/1947
Cross, Marcia	Marlborough, MA.	3/25/1962
Crouse, Lindsay	New York, NY	5/12/1948
Crow, Sheryl	Kennett, MO	2/11/1962
Crowe, Cameron	Palm Springs, CA	7/13/1957
Crowe, Russell	Wellington, New Zealand	4/7/1964
Crudup, Billy	Manhasset, NY	7/8/1948
Cruise, Tom	Syracuse, NY	7/3/1962
Cruz, Penelope	Madrid, Spain	4/28/1974
Cryer, Jon	New York, NY	4/16/1965
Crystal, Billy	Long Beach, NY	3/14/1948
Cuarón, Alfonso	Mexico City, Mexico	11/28/1961
Culkin, Macaulay	New York, NY	8/26/1980
Cullum, John	Knoxville, TN	3/2/1930
Cumberbatch, Benedict	London, England, UK	7/19/1976
Cumming, Alan	Aberfeldy, Perthshire, Scotland, UK	1/27/1965
Cuoco, Kaley	Camarillo, CA	11/30/1985
Curry, Tim	Grappenhall, Cheshire, England, UK	4/19/1946
Curtin, Jane	Cambridge, MA	9/6/1947
Curtis, Jamie Lee	Los Angeles, CA	11/22/1958
Cusack, Joan	New York, NY	10/11/1962
Cusack, John	Evanston, IL	6/28/1966
Cyrus, Billy Ray	Flatwoods, KY.	8/25/1961
Cyrus, Miley	Nashville, TN.	11/23/1992
Dafoe, Willem	Appleton, WI	7/22/1955
Dahl, Arlene	Minneapolis, MN.	8/11/1925
Dale, Jim	Rothwell, England, UK.	8/15/1935
Dalton, Timothy	Colwyn Bay, Wales, UK	3/21/1946
Daltrey, Roger	London, England, UK	3/1/1944
Daly, Carson	Santa Monica, CA	6/22/1973
Daly, Timothy	New York, NY	3/1/1956
Daly, Tyne	Madison, WI	2/21/1946
Damon, Matt	Cambridge, MA.	10/8/1970
Damone, Vic	Brooklyn, NY.	6/12/1928
Dane, Eric	San Francisco, CA.	11/9/1972
Danes, Claire	New York, NY	4/12/1979
D'Angelo	Richmond, VA	2/11/1974
D'Angelo, Beverly	Columbus, OH.	11/15/1954
Daniels, Anthony	Salisbury, England, UK	2/21/1946
Daniels, Charlie	Wilmington, NC	10/28/1936
Daniels, Jeff	Athens, GA	2/19/1955
Daniels, Lee	Philadelphia, PA	12/24/1959
Daniels, William	Brooklyn, NY	3/31/1927
Danner, Blythe	Rosemont, PA	2/3/1943
Danson, Ted	San Diego, CA.	12/29/1947
Danza, Tony	Brooklyn, NY	4/21/1951
Darby, Kim	Hollywood, CA.	7/8/1948
Daughtry, Chris	Roanoke Rapids, NC	12/26/1979
David, Larry	Brooklyn, NY	7/2/1947
Davidson, John	Pittsburgh, PA	12/13/1941
Davis, Clifton	Chicago, IL	10/4/1945
Davis, Geena	Wareham, MA	1/21/1956
Davis, Hope	Englewood, NJ	3/23/1964
Davis, Judy	Perth, WA, Australia	4/23/1955
Davis, Kristin	Boulder, CO.	2/24/1965
Davis, Mac	Lubbock, TX	1/21/1942
Davis, Viola	Saint Matthews, SC	8/11/1965
Dawber, Pam	Farmington Hills, MI.	10/18/1951
Dawson, Rosario	New York, NY	5/9/1979
Day, Doris	Cincinnati, OH.	4/3/1924
Day-Lewis, Daniel	London, England, UK	4/29/1957
De Havilland, Olivia	Tokyo, Japan.	7/1/1916
De Mornay, Rebecca	Santa Rosa, CA	8/29/1962
De Niro, Robert	New York, NY	8/17/1943
De Rossi, Portia	Melbourne, Vic., Australia	1/31/1973
DeGeneres, Ellen	Metairie, LA.	1/26/1958

Name	Birthplace	Birthdate
DeGraw, Gavin	Middletown, NY	2/4/1977
Del Toro, Benicio	Santurce, Puerto Rico	2/19/1967
Delaney, Kim	Philadelphia, PA	11/29/1961
Delany, Dana	New York, NY	3/13/1956
Delon, Alain	Sceaux, France	11/8/1935
Demme, Jonathan	Baldwin, NY	2/22/1944
Dempsey, Patrick	Lewiston, ME	1/13/1966
Dench, Judi	York, England, UK	12/9/1934
Deneuve, Catherine	Paris, France	10/22/1943
Dennehy, Brian	Bridgeport, CT	7/9/1938
DePalma, Brian	Newark, NJ	9/11/1940
Depardieu, Gerard	Chateauroux, France	12/27/1948
Depp, Johnny	Owensboro, KY	6/9/1963
Derek, Bo	Long Beach, CA	11/20/1956
Dern, Bruce	Winnetka, IL	6/4/1936
Dern, Laura	Santa Monica, CA	2/10/1967
Deschanel, Zooey	Los Angeles, CA	1/17/1980
Devine, Loretta	Houston, TX	8/21/1949
DeVito, Danny	Neptune, NJ	11/17/1944
DeWitt, Joyce	Wheeling, WV	4/23/1949
Dey, Susan	Pekin, IL	12/10/1952
Diamond, Neil	Brooklyn, NY	1/24/1941
Diaz, Cameron	San Diego, CA	8/30/1972
Diaz, Guillermo	New Jersey	3/22/1975
DiCaprio, Leonardo	Hollywood, CA	11/11/1974
Dick, Andy	Charleston, SC	12/21/1965
Dickinson, Angie	Kulm, ND	9/30/1931
Diesel, Vin	New York, NY	7/18/1967
Diggs, Taye	Newark, NJ	1/2/1972
Dillahunt, Garret	Castro Valley, CA	11/24/1964
Dillman, Bradford	San Francisco, CA	4/14/1930
Dillon, Kevin	Mamaroneck, NY	8/19/1965
Dillon, Matt	New Rochelle, NY	2/18/1964
Dinklage, Peter	Morristown, NJ	6/11/1969
DioGuardi, Kara	Scarsdale, NY	12/9/1970
Dion, Celine	Charlemagne, QC, Canada	3/30/1968
Djalili, Omid	London, England, UK	9/30/1965
Dobrev, Nina	Sofia, Bulgaria	1/9/1989
Dobson, Kevin	Jackson Heights, Queens, NY	3/18/1943
Dockery, Michelle	Barking, Essex, Eng., UK	12/15/1981
Doherty, Shannen	Memphis, TN	4/12/1971
Dolenz, Mickey	Los Angeles, CA	3/8/1945
Domingo, Placido	Madrid, Spain	1/21/1941
Domino, Fats	New Orleans, LA	2/26/1928
Donahue, Phil	Cleveland, OH	12/21/1935
Donen, Stanley	Columbia, SC	4/13/1924
D'Onofrio, Vincent	Brooklyn, NY	6/30/1959
Donovan (Leitch)	Glasgow, Scotland, UK	5/10/1946
Donovan, Tate	New York, NY	9/25/1963
Dorn, Michael	Luling, TX	12/9/1952
Dotrice, Roy	Guernsey, Channel Isls., UK	5/26/1923
Douglas, Kirk	Amsterdam, NY	12/9/1916
Douglas, Michael	New Brunswick, NJ	9/25/1944
Dourdan, Gary	Philadelphia, PA	12/11/1966
Dovolani, Tony	Pristina, Kosovo	7/17/1973
Dow, Tony	Hollywood, CA	4/13/1945
Down, Lesley-Anne	London, England, UK	3/17/1954
Downey, Robert, Jr.	New York, NY	4/4/1965
Downey, Roma	Derry, N. Ireland, UK	5/6/1960
Downs, Hugh	Akron, OH	2/14/1921
Drake	Toronto, ON, Canada	10/24/1986
Drescher, Fran	Flushing, Queens, NY	9/30/1957
Dreyfuss, Richard	Brooklyn, NY	10/29/1947
Driver, Adam	San Bernardino, CA	11/19/1983
Driver, Minnie	London, England, UK	1/31/1970
Dryer, Fred	Hawthorne, CA	7/6/1946
Duchovny, David	New York, NY	8/7/1960
Duff, Hilary	Houston, TX	9/28/1987
Duff (Aimee Anne)	Bangor, Gwynedd, Wales, UK	6/23/1984
Duffy, Julia	Minneapolis, MN	6/27/1951
Duffy, Patrick	Townsend, MT	3/17/1949
Duhamel, Josh	Minot, ND	11/14/1972
Dujardin, Jean	Rueil-Malmaison, France	6/19/1972
Dukakis, Olympia	Lowell, MA	6/20/1931
Dullea, Keir	Cleveland, OH	5/30/1936
Dunaway, Faye	Bascom, FL	1/14/1941
Duncan, Lindsay	Edinburgh, Scotland, UK	11/7/1950
Duncan, Sandy	Henderson, TX	2/20/1946
Dunham, Lena	New York, NY	5/13/1986
Dunne, Griffin	New York, NY	6/8/1955
Dunst, Kirsten	Point Pleasant, NJ	4/30/1982
Dussault, Nancy	Pensacola, FL	6/30/1936
Dutton, Charles S.	Baltimore, MD	1/30/1951
Duvall, Robert	San Diego, CA	1/5/1931
Duvall, Shelley	Houston, TX	7/7/1949
Dylan, Bob	Duluth, MN	5/24/1941
Dylan, Jakob	New York, NY	12/9/1969
Dzundza, George	Rosenheim, Germany	7/19/1945
Eads, George	Fort Worth, TX	3/1/1967
Easton, Sheena	Bellshill, Scotland, UK	4/27/1959
Eastwood, Clint	San Francisco, CA	5/31/1930
Ebersole, Christine	Chicago, IL	2/21/1953
Eckhart, Aaron	Cupertino, CA	3/12/1968
Eden, Barbara	Tucson, AZ	8/23/1931
Edwards, Anthony	Santa Barbara, CA	7/19/1962
Efron, Zac	San Luis Obispo, CA	10/18/1987
Ehle, Jennifer	Winston-Salem, NC	12/29/1969
Eikenberry, Jill	New Haven, CT	1/21/1947
Eisenberg, Jesse	Bayside, NY	10/5/1983
Ejiofor, Chiwetel	London, England, UK	7/10/1974
Ekland, Britt	Stockholm, Sweden	10/6/1942
Elba, Idris	London, England, UK	9/6/1972
Electra, Carmen	Cincinnati, OH	4/20/1972
Elfman, Jenna	Los Angeles, CA	9/30/1971
Elizondo, Hector	New York, NY	12/22/1936
Elliott, Chris	New York, NY	5/31/1960
Elliott, Missy	Portsmouth, VA	7/1/1971
Elliott, Sam	Sacramento, CA	8/9/1944
Elvira	Manhattan, KS	9/17/1951
Emerson, Michael	Cedar Rapids, IA	9/7/1954
Eminem	St. Joseph, MO	10/17/1972
Enberg, Dick	Mt. Clemens, MI	1/9/1935
Englund, Robert	Glendale, CA	6/6/1949
Enya	Gweedore, Ireland	5/17/1961
Epps, Omar	Brooklyn, NY	7/23/1973
Estefan, Gloria	Havana, Cuba	9/1/1957
Estevez, Emilio	New York, NY	5/12/1962
Estrada, Erik	New York, NY	3/16/1949
Etheridge, Melissa	Leavenworth, KS	5/29/1961
Evans, Chris	Framingham, MA	6/13/1981
Evans, Linda	Hartford, CT	11/18/1942
Evans, Robert	New York, NY	6/29/1930
Everett, Rupert	Norfolk, England, UK	5/29/1959
Everly, Don	Brownie, KY	2/1/1937
Evigan, Greg	South Amboy, NJ	10/14/1953
Fabares, Shelley	Santa Monica, CA	1/19/1944
Fabian	Philadelphia, PA	2/6/1943
Fabio (Lanzoni)	Milan, Italy	3/15/1959
Fabolous	Brooklyn, NY	11/18/1977
Facinelli, Peter	Queens, NY	11/26/1973
Fairchild, Morgan	Dallas, TX	2/3/1950
Faison, Donald	New York, NY	6/22/1974
Falana, Lola	Philadelphia, PA	9/11/1942
Falco, Edie	Brooklyn, NY	7/5/1963
Fallon, Jimmy	Brooklyn, NY	9/19/1974
Fanning, Dakota	Conyers, GA	2/23/1994
Fargo, Donna	Mt. Airy, NC	11/10/1949
Faris, Anna	Baltimore, MD	11/29/1976
Farmiga, Vera	Clifton, NJ	8/6/1973
Farr, Jamie	Toledo, OH	7/1/1934
Farrell, Colin	Dublin, Ireland	5/31/1976
Farrell, Mike	St. Paul, MN	2/6/1939
Farrell, Perry	Bayside, Queens, NY	3/29/1959
Farrell, Suzanne	Cincinnati, OH	8/16/1945?
Farrelly, Bobby	Cumberland, RI	6/17/1958
Farrelly, Peter	Phoenixville, PA	12/17/1956
Farrow, Mia	Los Angeles, CA	2/9/1945
Fassbender, Michael	Heidelberg, Germany	4/2/1977
Fatone, Joey	Brooklyn, NY	1/28/1977
Feinstein, Michael	Columbus, OH	9/7/1956
Feldman, Corey	Los Angeles, CA	7/16/1971
Feldon, Barbara	Bethel Park, PA	3/12/1933
Feldshuh, Tovah	New York, NY	12/27/1952
Feliciano, Jose	Lares, Puerto Rico	9/10/1945
Fenn, Sherilyn	Detroit, MI	2/1/1965
Fergie	Hacienda Heights, CA	3/27/1975
Ferguson, Craig	Glasgow, Scotland, UK	5/17/1962
Ferguson, Jesse Tyler	Missoula, MT	10/22/1975
Ferrara, Jerry	Brooklyn, NY	11/29/1979
Ferrell, Conchata	Charleston, WV	3/28/1943
Ferrell, Will	Irvine, CA	7/16/1967
Ferrera, America	Los Angeles, CA	4/18/1984
Feuerstein, Mark	New York, NY	6/8/1971
Fey, Tina	Upper Darby, PA	5/18/1970
Field, Sally	Pasadena, CA	11/6/1946
Fiennes, Joseph	Salisbury, England, UK	5/27/1970
Fiennes, Ralph	Suffolk, England, UK	12/22/1962
Fierstein, Harvey	Brooklyn, NY	6/6/1954
50 Cent	Jamaica, Queens, NY	7/6/1976
Fillion, Nathan	Edmonton, AB, Canada	3/27/1971
Fincher, David	Denver, CO	8/28/1962
Finney, Albert	Salford, England, UK	5/9/1936
Fiorentino, Linda	Philadelphia, PA	3/9/1960
Firth, Colin	Grayshott, England, UK	9/10/1960
Firth, Peter	Bradford, Yorkshire, Eng., UK	10/27/1953
Fischer, Jenna	Ft. Wayne, IN	3/7/1974
Fishburne, Laurence	Augusta, GA	7/30/1961
Fisher, Carrie	Beverly Hills, CA	10/21/1956
Flack, Roberta	Black Mountain, NC	2/10/1939
Flanagan, Fionnula	Dublin, Ireland	12/10/1941
Flavor Flav	Roosevelt, NY	3/16/1959
Fleetwood, Mick	Redruth, Cornwall, Eng., UK	6/24/1942
Fleming, Rhonda	Hollywood, CA	8/10/1923
Fletcher, Louise	Birmingham, AL	7/22/1934
Flockhart, Calista	Freeport, IL	11/11/1964
Florek, Dann	Flat Rock, MI	5/1/1950
Fogerty, John	Berkeley, CA	5/28/1945
Foley, Dave	Etobicoke, ON, Canada	1/4/1963
Foley, Scott	Kansas City, KS	7/15/1972

Name	Birthplace	Birthdate
Fonda, Bridget	Los Angeles, CA	1/27/1964
Fonda, Jane	New York, NY	12/21/1937
Fonda, Peter	New York, NY	2/23/1940
Ford, Faith	Alexandria, LA	9/14/1964
Ford, Harrison	Chicago, IL	7/13/1942
Forman, Milos	Caslav, Czechoslovakia	2/18/1932
Forte, Will	Alameda Co., CA	6/17/1970
Foster, Jodie	Los Angeles, CA	11/19/1962
Foster, Sutton	Statesboro, GA	3/18/1975
Fox, James	London, England, UK	5/19/1939
Fox, Jorja	New York, NY	7/7/1968
Fox, Matthew	Abington, PA	7/14/1966
Fox, Megan	Rockwood, TN	5/16/1986
Fox, Michael J.	Edmonton, AB, Canada	6/9/1961
Fox, Vivica A.	South Bend, IN	7/30/1964
Foxworth, Robert	Houston, TX	11/1/1941
Foxworthy, Jeff	Atlanta, GA	9/6/1958
Foxx, Jamie	Terrell, TX	12/13/1967
Frampton, Peter	Kent, England, UK	4/22/1950
Francis, Connie	Newark, NJ	12/12/1938
Franco, Dave	Palo Alto, CA	6/12/1985
Franco, James	Palo Alto, CA	4/19/1978
Franken, Al	New York, NY	5/21/1951
Franklin, Aretha	Memphis, TN	3/25/1942
Franz, Dennis	Maywood, IL	10/28/1944
Fraser, Brendan	Indianapolis, IN	12/3/1968
Freeman, Martin	Aldershot, Hampshire, Eng., UK	9/8/1971
Freeman, Morgan	Memphis, TN	6/1/1937
French, Dawn	Holyhead, Wales, UK	10/11/1957
Fricker, Brenda	Dublin, Ireland	2/17/1945
Friedkin, William	Chicago, IL	8/29/1939
Froggatt, Joanne	Littlebeck, North Yorkshire, England, UK	8/21/1980
Fry, Stephen	London, England, UK	8/24/1957
Fuentes, Daisy	Havana, Cuba	11/17/1966
Fuller, Robert	Troy, NY	7/29/1934
Furlong, Edward	Pasadena, CA	8/2/1977
Furtado, Nelly	Victoria, BC, Canada	12/2/1978
Gabor, Zsa Zsa	Budapest, Hungary	2/6/1917
Gabriel, Peter	Surrey, England, UK	2/13/1950
Gaines, Boyd	Atlanta, GA	5/11/1953
Galecki, Johnny	Bree, Belgium	4/30/1975
Galifianakis, Zach	Wilkesboro, NC	10/1/1969
Gallagher, Peter	Armonk, NY	8/19/1955
Gallo, Vincent	Buffalo, NY	4/11/1961
Galway, James	Belfast, N. Ireland, UK	12/8/1939
Garber, Victor	London, ON, Canada	3/16/1949
Garcia, Andy	Havana, Cuba	4/12/1956
Garfield, Andrew	Los Angeles, CA	8/20/1983
Garfunkel, Art	Forest Hills, Queens, NY	11/5/1941
Garlin, Jeff	Chicago, IL	6/5/1962
Garner, Jennifer	Houston, TX	4/17/1972
Garofalo, Janeane	Newton, NJ	9/28/1964
Garr, Teri	Lakewood, OH	12/11/1944
Garrett, Brad	Woodland Hills, CA	4/14/1960
Garth, Jennie	Urbana, IL	4/3/1972
Gatlin, Larry	Seminole, TX	5/2/1948
Gavin, John	Los Angeles, CA	4/8/1931
Gayle, Crystal	Paintsville, KY	1/9/1951
Gaynor, Mitzi	Chicago, IL	9/4/1931
Geary, Anthony	Coalville, UT	5/29/1947
Gedda, Nicolai	Stockholm, Sweden	7/11/1925
Gellar, Sarah Michelle	New York, NY	4/14/1977
Gere, Richard	Philadelphia, PA	8/31/1949
Gervais, Ricky	Reading, England, UK	6/25/1961
Giannini, Giancarlo	La Spezia, Italy	8/1/1942
Gibb, Barry	Isle of Man, England, UK	9/1/1946
Gibbons, Leeza	Hartsville, SC	3/26/1957
Gibbs, Marla	Chicago, IL	6/14/1931
Gibson, Debbie	Brooklyn, NY	8/31/1970
Gibson, Mel	Peekskill, NY	1/3/1956
Gibson, Thomas	Charleston, SC	7/3/1962
Gifford, Kathie Lee	Neuilly-sur-Seine, France	8/16/1953
Gilbert, Melissa	Los Angeles, CA	5/8/1964
Gilbert, Sara	Santa Monica, CA	1/29/1975
Gilberto, Astrud	Salvador, Brazil	3/30/1940
Gill, Vince	Norman, OK	4/12/1957
Gillette, Anita	Baltimore, MD	8/16/1936
Gilley, Mickey	Natchez, MS	3/9/1936
Gilliam, Terry	Minneapolis, MN	11/22/1940
Gilmour, David	Cambridge, England, UK	3/6/1946
Gilpin, Peri	Waco, TX	5/27/1961
Gilsig, Jessalyn	Montreal, QC, Canada	11/30/1971
Givens, Robin	New York, NY	11/27/1964
Glaser, Paul Michael	Cambridge, MA	3/25/1943
Gleeson, Brendan	Belfast, N. Ireland, UK	11/29/1955?
Glenn, Scott	Pittsburgh, PA	1/26/1941
Gless, Sharon	Los Angeles, CA	5/31/1943
Glover, Crispin	New York, NY	4/20/1964
Glover, Danny	San Francisco, CA	7/22/1947
Glover, John	Kingston, NY	8/7/1944
Glover, Julian	London, England, UK	3/27/1935
Glover, Savion	Newark, NJ	11/19/1973
Godard, Jean-Luc	Paris, France	12/3/1930
Goldberg, Whoopi	New York, NY	11/13/1955

Name	Birthplace	Birthdate
Goldblum, Jeff	Pittsburgh, PA	10/22/1952
Goldthwait, Bobcat	Syracuse, NY	5/26/1962
Goldwyn, Tony	Los Angeles, CA	5/20/1960
Gomez, Selena	Grand Prairie, TX	7/22/1992
Gooding, Cuba, Jr.	Bronx, NY	1/2/1968
Goodman, John	Affton, MO	6/20/1952
Goodman, Len	London, England, UK	4/25/1944
Gordon-Levitt, Joseph	Los Angeles, CA	2/17/1981
Gosling, Ryan	London, ON, Canada	11/12/1980
Gosselaar, Mark-Paul	Panorama City, CA	3/1/1974
Gossett, Louis, Jr.	Brooklyn, NY	5/27/1936
Gould, Elliott	Brooklyn, NY	8/29/1938
Grace, Topher	New York, NY	7/12/1978
Graham, Heather	Milwaukee, WI	1/29/1970
Grammer, Kelsey	St. Thomas, U.S. Virgin Isls.	2/21/1955
Grande, Ariana	Boca Raton, FL	6/26/1993
Grant, Amy	Augusta, GA	11/25/1960
Grant, Hugh	London, England, UK	9/9/1960
Grant, Lee	New York, NY	10/31/1927?
Gray, Linda	Santa Monica, CA	9/12/1940
Gray, Macy	Canton, OH	9/6/1969
Green, Al	Forrest City, AR	4/13/1946
Green, Cee Lo	Atlanta, GA	5/30/1974
Green, Seth	Philadelphia, PA	2/8/1974
Green, Tom	Pembroke, ON, Canada	7/30/1971
Greene, Shecky	Chicago, IL	4/8/1926
Greenfield, Max	Dobbs Ferry, NY	9/4/1980
Greenwood, Bruce	Noranda, QC, Canada	8/12/1956
Gregory, Cynthia	Los Angeles, CA	7/8/1946
Gregory, Dick	St. Louis, MO	10/12/1932
Grenier, Adrian	Santa Fe, NM	7/10/1976
Grey, Jennifer	New York, NY	3/26/1960
Grey, Joel	Cleveland, OH	4/11/1932
Grier, David Alan	Detroit, MI	6/30/1955
Grier, Pam	Winston-Salem, NC	5/26/1949
Gries, Jon	Glendale, CA	6/17/1957
Griffin, Kathy	Oak Park, IL	11/4/1961
Griffith, Melanie	New York, NY	8/9/1957
Griffiths, Rachel	Melbourne, Vic., Australia	12/18/1968
Grimes, Tammy	Lynn, MA	1/30/1934
Grint, Rupert	Walton-at-Stone, Hertfordshire, Eng., UK	8/24/1988
Groban, Josh	Los Angeles, CA	2/27/1981
Grodin, Charles	Pittsburgh, PA	4/21/1935
Groff, Jonathan	Lancaster, PA	3/26/1985
Grohl, David	Warren, OH	1/14/1969
Gross, Michael	Chicago, IL	6/21/1947
Guest, Christopher	New York, NY	2/5/1948
Guillaume, Robert	St. Louis, MO	11/30/1927
Gumbel, Greg	New Orleans, LA	5/3/1946
Gunn, Anna	Santa Fe, NM	8/11/1968
Gunn, Tim	Washington, DC	7/29/1953
Guthrie, Arlo	Brooklyn, NY	7/10/1947
Guttenberg, Steve	Brooklyn, NY	8/24/1958
Guy, Buddy	Lettsworth, LA	7/30/1936
Guy, Jasmine	Boston, MA	3/10/1964
Gyllenhaal, Jake	Los Angeles, CA	12/19/1980
Gyllenhaal, Maggie	New York, NY	11/16/1977
Hackman, Gene	San Bernardino, CA	1/30/1930
Hader, Bill	Tulsa, OK	6/7/1978
Hagerty, Julie	Cincinnati, OH	6/15/1955
Haid, Charles	San Francisco, CA	6/2/1943
Hale, Barbara	DeKalb, IL	4/18/1922
Hale, Tony	West Point, NY	9/30/1970
Hall, Anthony Michael	West Roxbury, MA	4/14/1968
Hall, Arsenio	Cleveland, OH	2/12/1955
Hall, Daryl	Pottstown, PA	10/11/1946
Hall, Deidre	Milwaukee, WI	10/31/1947
Hall, Michael C.	Raleigh, NC	2/1/1971
Hall, Monty	Winnipeg, MB, Canada	8/25/1921
Hall, Tom T.	Olive Hill, KY	5/25/1936
Halliwell, Geri	Watford, England, UK	8/6/1972
Hamill, Mark	Oakland, CA	9/25/1951
Hamilton, George	Memphis, TN	8/12/1939
Hamilton, Linda	Salisbury, MD	9/26/1956
Hamlin, Harry	Pasadena, CA	10/30/1951
Hamm, Jon	St. Louis, MO	3/10/1971
Hammer, Armie	Los Angeles, CA	8/28/1986
Hammer (M.C.)	Oakland, CA	3/30/1963
Hammond, Darrell	Melbourne, FL	10/8/1955
Hancock, Herbie	Chicago, IL	4/12/1940
Handler, Chelsea	Livingston, NJ	2/25/1975
Hanks, Colin	Sacramento, CA	11/24/1977
Hanks, Tom	Concord, CA	7/9/1956
Hannah, Daryl	Chicago, IL	12/3/1960
Hannigan, Alyson	Washington, DC	3/24/1974
Hanson, Curtis	Reno, NV	3/24/1945
Hanson, Isaac	Tulsa, OK	11/17/1980
Hanson, Taylor	Tulsa, OK	3/14/1983
Hanson, Zac	Tulsa, OK	10/22/1985
Harden, Marcia Gay	La Jolla, CA	8/14/1959
Hardy, Tom	London, England, UK	9/15/1977
Harewood, Dorian	Dayton, OH	8/6/1950
Hargitay, Mariska	Los Angeles, CA	1/23/1964
Harmon, Angie	Highland Park, TX	8/10/1972
Harmon, Mark	Burbank, CA	9/2/1951

Name	Birthplace	Birthdate
Harper, Ben	Claremont, CA	10/28/1969
Harper, Tess	Mammoth Spring, AR	8/15/1950
Harper, Valerie	Suffern, NY	8/22/1939
Harrelson, Woody	Midland, TX	7/23/1961
Harris, Barbara	Evanston, IL	7/25/1935
Harris, Ed	Tenafly, NJ	11/28/1950
Harris, Emmylou	Birmingham, AL	4/2/1947
Harris, Neil Patrick	Albuquerque, NM	6/15/1973
Harris, Rosemary	Ashby, England, UK	9/19/1927?
Harris, Steve	Chicago, IL	12/3/1965
Harrison, Gregory	Avalon, CA	5/31/1950
Harry, Deborah	Miami, FL	7/1/1945
Hart, Kevin	Philadelphia, PA	7/3/1980
Hart, Mary	Madison, SD	11/8/1950
Hart, Melissa Joan	Smithtown, NY	4/18/1976
Hartley, Mariette	New York, NY	6/21/1940
Hartman, David	Pawtucket, RI	5/19/1935
Hartman Black, Lisa	Houston, TX	6/1/1956
Hartnett, Josh	San Francisco, CA	7/21/1978
Harvey, P. J.	Yeovil, Somerset, Eng., UK	10/9/1969
Harvey, Steve	Welch, WV	11/23/1956
Hasselbeck, Elisabeth	Cranston, RI	5/28/1977
Hasselhoff, David	Baltimore, MD	7/17/1952
Hatcher, Teri	Sunnyvale, CA	12/8/1964
Hatfield, Juliana	Wiscasset, ME	7/27/1967
Hathaway, Anne	Brooklyn, NY	11/12/1982
Hauer, Rutger	Breukelen, Netherlands	1/23/1944
Hawke, Ethan	Austin, TX	11/6/1970
Hawn, Goldie	Washington, DC	11/21/1945
Hayek, Salma	Coatzacoalcos, Mexico	9/2/1966
Hayes, Hunter	Breaux Bridge, LA	9/9/1991
Hayes, Sean	Glen Ellyn, IL	6/26/1970
Haynes, Roy	Roxbury, MA	3/13/1925
Hays, Robert	Bethesda, MD	7/24/1947
Haysbert, Dennis	San Mateo, CA	6/2/1955
Head, Anthony	Camden Town, Eng., UK	2/20/1954
Heard, John	Washington, DC	3/7/1945
Hearn, George	St. Louis, MO	6/18/1934
Heaton, Patricia	Bay Village, OH	3/4/1958
Heche, Anne	Aurora, OH	5/25/1969
Heder, Jon	Fort Collins, CO	10/26/1977
Hedren, Tippi	New Ulm, MN	1/19/1930?
Heigl, Katherine	Washington, DC	11/24/1978
Helberg, Simon	Los Angeles, CA	12/9/1980
Helfgott, David	Melbourne, Vic., Australia	5/19/1947
Helgenberger, Marg	Fremont, NE	11/16/1958
Helmond, Katherine	Galveston, TX	7/5/1928?
Helms, Ed	Atlanta, GA	1/24/1974
Hemingway, Mariel	Mill Valley, CA	11/22/1961
Hemsworth, Chris	Melbourne, Vic., Australia	8/11/1983
Hemsworth, Liam	Melbourne, Vic., Australia	1/13/1990
Henderson, Florence	Dale, IN	2/14/1934
Hendricks, Christina	Knoxville, TN	5/3/1975
Henley, Don	Gilmer, TX	7/22/1947
Henner, Marilu	Chicago, IL	4/6/1952
Hennessy, Jill	Edmonton, AB, Canada	11/25/1968
Henry, Buck	New York, NY	12/9/1930
Henson, Taraji P.	Washington, DC	9/11/1970
Herman, Pee-Wee	Peekskill, NY	8/27/1952
Hershey, Barbara	Hollywood, CA	2/5/1948
Hesseman, Howard	Lebanon, OR	2/27/1940
Hetfield, James	Downey, CA	8/3/1963
Hewitt, Jennifer Love	Waco, TX	2/21/1979
Hicks, Catherine	Scottsdale, AZ	8/6/1951
Hiddleston, Tom	London, England, UK	2/9/1981
Higgins, John Michael	Boston, MA	2/12/1963
Hightower, Chelsie	Las Vegas, NV	7/21/1989
Hill, Dulé	Orange, NJ	5/3/1975
Hill, Faith	Jackson, MS	9/21/1967
Hill, Jonah	Los Angeles, CA	12/20/1983
Hill, Lauryn	South Orange, NJ	5/26/1975
Hillerman, John	Denison, TX	12/20/1932
Hilton, Paris	New York, NY	2/17/1981
Hines, Cheryl	Miami Beach, FL	9/21/1965
Hirsch, Emile	Palms, CA	3/13/1985
Hirsch, Judd	Bronx, NY	3/15/1935
Hodgman, John	Cambridge, MA	6/3/1971
Hoffman, Dustin	Los Angeles, CA	8/8/1937
Hogan, Hulk	Augusta, GA	8/11/1953
Hogan, Paul	Lightning Ridge, NSW, Australia	10/8/1939
Holbrook, Hal	Cleveland, OH	2/17/1925
Holliday, Polly	Jasper, AL	7/2/1937
Holliman, Earl	Delhi, LA	9/11/1928
Holloway, Josh	San Jose, CA	7/20/1969
Holly, Lauren	Bristol, PA	10/28/1963
Holm, Ian	Ilford, England, UK	9/12/1931
Holmes, Katie	Toledo, OH	12/18/1978
Hopkins, Anthony	Port Talbot, South Wales, UK	12/31/1937
Hopkins, Bo	Greenville, SC	2/2/1942
Hopkins, Telma	Louisville, KY	10/28/1948
Horne, Marilyn	Bradford, PA	1/16/1934
Hornsby, Bruce	Williamsburg, VA	11/23/1954
Horsley, Lee	Muleshoe, TX	5/15/1955
Hough, Derek	Salt Lake City, UT	5/17/1985
Hough, Julianne	Salt Lake City, UT	7/20/1988
Hounsou, Djimon	Cotonou, Benin	4/24/1964
Howard, Clint	Burbank, CA	4/20/1959
Howard, Ron	Duncan, OK	3/1/1954
Howard, Terrence	Chicago, IL	3/11/1969
Howell, C. Thomas	Van Nuys, CA	12/7/1966
Howes, Sally Ann	St. John's Wood, London, England, UK	7/20/1930
Hudgens, Vanessa	Salinas, CA	12/14/1988
Hudson, Jennifer	Chicago, IL	9/12/1981
Hudson, Kate	Los Angeles, CA	4/19/1979
Huffman, Felicity	Bedford, NY	12/9/1962
Hughley, D. L.	Los Angeles, CA	3/6/1963
Hulce, Tom	Detroit, MI	12/6/1953
Humperdinck, Engelbert	Madras, India	5/2/1936
Humphries, Barry	Melbourne, Vic., Australia	2/17/1934
Hunt, Bonnie	Chicago, IL	9/22/1964
Hunt, Helen	Culver City, CA	6/15/1963
Hunt, Linda	Morristown, NJ	4/2/1945
Hunter, Holly	Conyers, GA	3/20/1958
Hunter, Tab	New York, NY	7/11/1931
Hurley, Elizabeth	Hampshire, England, UK	6/10/1965
Hurt, John	Chesterfield, England, UK	1/22/1940
Hurt, Mary Beth	Marshalltown, IA	9/26/1948
Hurt, William	Washington, DC	3/20/1950
Huston, Anjelica	Santa Monica, CA	7/8/1951
Hutcherson, Josh	Union, KY	10/12/1992
Hutton, Lauren	Charleston, SC	11/17/1943
Hutton, Timothy	Malibu, CA	8/16/1960
Hyman, Earle	Rocky Mount, NC	10/11/1926
Ian, Janis	Bronx, NY	4/7/1951
Ice Cube	Los Angeles, CA	6/15/1969
Ice-T	Newark, NJ	2/16/1958
Idle, Eric	S. Shields, England, UK	3/29/1943
Idol, Billy	Middlesex, England, UK	11/30/1955
Iglesias, Enrique	Madrid, Spain	5/8/1975
Iglesias, Julio	Madrid, Spain	9/23/1943
Iler, Robert	New York, NY	3/2/1985
Iman	Mogadishu, Somalia	7/25/1955
Imbruglia, Natalie	Sydney, NSW, Australia	2/4/1975
Imperioli, Michael	Mount Vernon, NY	3/26/1966
Imus, Don	Riverside, CA	7/23/1940
Iñárritu, Alejandro G.	Mexico City, Mexico	8/15/1963
Ingram, James	Akron, OH	2/16/1952
Innes, Laura	Pontiac, MI	8/16/1957?
Ireland, Kathy	Glendale, CA	3/20/1963
Irons, Jeremy	Cowes, Isle of Wight, Eng., UK	9/19/1948
Irving, Amy	Palo Alto, CA	9/10/1953
Irving, George S.	Springfield, MA	11/1/1922
Irwin, Bill	Santa Monica, CA	4/11/1950
Isaac, Oscar	Guatemala	1/5/1980
Ivanek, Željko	Ljubljana, Yugo. (Slovenia)	8/15/1957
Ivey, Judith	El Paso, TX	9/4/1951
Ivory, James	Berkeley, CA	6/7/1928
Izzard, Eddie	Aden, Yemen	2/7/1962
Ja Rule	Hollis, Queens, NY	2/29/1976
Jackée (Harry)	Winston-Salem, NC	8/14/1956
Jackman, Hugh	Sydney, NSW, Australia	10/12/1968
Jackson, Cheyenne	Newport, WA	7/12/1975
Jackson, Glenda	Birkenhead, England, UK	5/9/1936
Jackson, Janet	Gary, IN	5/16/1966
Jackson, Jermaine	Gary, IN	12/11/1954
Jackson, Jonathan	Orlando, FL	5/11/1982
Jackson, Joshua	Vancouver, BC, Canada	6/11/1978
Jackson, Kate	Birmingham, AL	10/29/1948
Jackson, La Toya	Gary, IN	5/29/1956
Jackson, Peter	Wellington, New Zealand	10/31/1961
Jackson, Samuel L.	Washington, DC	12/21/1948
Jacobi, Derek	London, England, UK	10/22/1938
Jagger, Mick	Dartford, England, UK	7/26/1943
James, Kevin	Mineola, NY	4/26/1965
Jamison, Judith	Philadelphia, PA	5/10/1943
Janis, Conrad	New York, NY	2/11/1928
Janney, Allison	Dayton, OH	11/19/1959
Janssen, Famke	Amsterdam, Netherlands	11/5/1965
Jardine, Al	Lima, OH	9/3/1942
Jarmusch, Jim	Akron, OH	1/22/1953
Jarreau, Al	Milwaukee, WI	3/12/1940
Jarrett, Keith	Allentown, PA	5/8/1945
Jay Z	Brooklyn, NY	12/4/1969
Jeffreys, Anne	Goldsboro, NC	1/26/1923
Jenkins, Richard	DeKalb, IL	5/4/1947
Jenner, Caitlyn	Mount Kisco, NY	10/28/1949
Jenner, Kris	San Diego, CA	11/5/1955
Jepsen, Carly Rae	Mission, BC, Canada	11/21/1985
Jett, Joan	Philadelphia, PA	9/22/1958
Jewel (Kilcher)	Payson, UT	5/23/1974
Jewison, Norman	Toronto, ON, Canada	7/21/1926
Jillette, Penn	Greenfield, MA	3/5/1955
Jillian, Ann	Cambridge, MA	1/29/1950
Joel, Billy	Bronx, NY	5/9/1949
Johansson, Scarlett	New York, NY	11/22/1984
John, Elton	Pinner, Middlesex, Eng., UK	3/25/1947

Name	Birthplace	Birthdate
Johns, Glynis	Durban, South Africa	10/5/1923
Johnson, Arte	Benton Harbor, MI	1/20/1929
Johnson, Beverly	Buffalo, NY	10/13/1952
Johnson, Don	Flatt Creek, MO	12/15/1949
Johnson, Dwayne "The Rock"	Hayward, CA	5/2/1972
Johnston, Bruce	Los Angeles, CA	6/24/1942
Johnston, Kristen	Washington, DC	9/20/1967
Jolie, Angelina	Los Angeles, CA	6/4/1975
Jonas, Joe	Casa Grande, AZ	8/15/1989
Jonas, Kevin	Teaneck, NJ	11/5/1987
Jonas, Nick	Dallas, TX	9/16/1992
Jones, Angus T.	Austin, TX	10/8/1993
Jones, Bill T.	Bunnell, FL	2/15/1952
Jones, Cherry	Paris, TN	11/21/1956
Jones, Gemma	London, England, UK	12/4/1942
Jones, Grace	Spanish Town, Jamaica	5/19/1948
Jones, Jack	Hollywood, CA	1/14/1938
Jones, James Earl	Arkabutla, MS	1/17/1931
Jones, John Paul	Sidcup, England, UK	1/3/1946
Jones, January	Sioux Falls, SD	1/5/1978
Jones, Mick	London, England, UK	6/26/1955
Jones, Norah	New York, NY	3/30/1979
Jones, Quincy	Chicago, IL	3/14/1933
Jones, Shirley	Charleroi, PA	3/31/1934
Jones, Star	Badin, NC	3/24/1962
Jones, Tom	Pontypridd, Wales, UK	6/7/1940
Jones, Tommy Lee	San Saba, TX	9/15/1946
Jonze, Spike	Rockville, MD	10/22/1969
Jordan, Michael B.	Santa Ana, CA	2/9/1987
Jovovich, Milla	Kiev, Ukraine	12/17/1975
Judd, Ashley	Granada Hills, CA	4/19/1968
Judd, Naomi	Ashland, KY	1/11/1946
Judd, Wynonna	Ashland, KY	5/30/1964
Kaczmarek, Jane	Milwaukee, WI	12/21/1955
Kaling, Mindy	Cambridge, MA	6/24/1979
Kanaly, Steve	Burbank, CA	3/14/1946
Kane, Carol	Cleveland, OH	6/18/1952
Kaplan, Gabe	Brooklyn, NY	3/31/1945
Kardashian, Khloe	Los Angeles, CA	6/27/1984
Kardashian, Kim	Los Angeles, CA	10/21/1980
Kardashian, Kourtney	Los Angeles, CA	4/18/1979
Karlen, John	New York, NY	5/28/1940
Karn, Richard	Seattle, WA	2/17/1956
Katic, Stana	Hamilton, ON, Canada	4/26/1978
Kattan, Chris	Sherman Oaks, CA	10/19/1970
Kavner, Julie	Burbank, CA	9/7/1951
Kaye, Judy	Phoenix, AZ	12/11/1948
Kazan, Lainie	New York, NY	5/15/1940
Keach, Stacy	Savannah, GA	6/2/1941
Keaton, Diane	Santa Ana, CA	1/5/1946
Keaton, Michael	Coraopolis, PA	9/5/1951
Keener, Catherine	Miami, FL	3/23/1959
Keillor, Garrison	Anoka, MN	8/7/1942
Keitel, Harvey	Brooklyn, NY	5/13/1939
Keith, David	Knoxville, TN	5/8/1954
Keith, Penelope	Sutton, Surrey, Eng., UK	4/2/1940
Kellerman, Sally	Long Beach, CA	6/2/1937
Kelly, Minka	Los Angeles, CA	6/24/1980
Kelly, R(obert)	Chicago, IL	1/8/1967
Kemper, Ellie	Kansas City, MO	5/2/1980
Kendrick, Anna	Portland, ME	8/9/1985
Kennedy, Jamie	Upper Darby, PA	5/25/1970
Kenny G	Seattle, WA	6/5/1956
Kent, Allegra	Santa Monica, CA	8/11/1937
Keoghan, Phil	Christchurch, New Zealand	5/31/1967
Kercheval, Ken	Wolcottville, IN.	7/15/1935
Kerns, Joanna	San Francisco, CA	2/12/1953
Kesha	Los Angeles, CA	3/1/1987
Keys, Alicia	New York, NY	1/25/1981
Khalifa, Wiz	Minot, ND	9/8/1987
Khan, Chaka	Great Lakes, IL	3/23/1953
Kid Rock	Romeo, MI	1/17/1971
Kidder, Margot	Yellowknife, NT, Canada	10/17/1948
Kidman, Nicole	Honolulu, HI	6/20/1967
Kilborn, Craig	Kansas City, KS.	8/24/1962
Kilmer, Val	Los Angeles, CA	12/31/1959
Kim, Daniel Dae	Pusan, South Korea	8/4/1968
Kimmel, Jimmy	Brooklyn, NY	11/13/1967
King, Carole	Brooklyn, NY	2/9/1942
King, Gayle	Chevy Chase, MD	12/28/1954?
King, Larry	Brooklyn, NY	11/19/1933
King, Perry	Alliance, OH	4/30/1948
King, Regina	Los Angeles, CA	1/15/1971
Kingsley, Ben	Scarborough, England, UK	12/31/1943
Kingston, Alex	London, England, UK	3/11/1963
Kinnear, Greg	Logansport, IN.	6/17/1963
Kinney, Kathy	Stevens Point, WI	11/3/1954
Kinski, Nastassja	Berlin, W. Germany	1/24/1960
Kirkland, Gelsey	Bethlehem, PA.	12/29/1952
Kirkpatrick, Chris	Clarion, PA	10/17/1971
Kirshner, Mia	Toronto, ON, Canada	1/25/1975
Kitsch, Taylor	Kelowna, BC, Canada	4/8/1981
Klein, Robert	Bronx, NY	2/8/1942
Kline, Kevin	St. Louis, MO.	10/24/1947
Klum, Heidi	Bergish-Gladbach, Germany	6/1/1973

Name	Birthplace	Birthdate
Knight, Gladys	Atlanta, GA	5/28/1944
Knight, Shirley	Goessel, KS	7/5/1936
Knight, T. R.	Minneapolis, MN	3/26/1973
Knight, Wayne	New York, NY	8/7/1955
Knightley, Keira	Teddington, England, UK	3/26/1985
Knopfler, Mark	Glasgow, Scotland, UK	8/12/1949
Knowles, Beyoncé	Houston, TX	9/4/1981
Knoxville, Johnny	Knoxville, TN	3/11/1971
Konitz, Lee	Chicago, IL	10/13/1927
Kopell, Bernie	Brooklyn, NY	6/21/1933
Kotto, Yaphet	New York, NY	11/15/1937
Krakowski, Jane	Parsippany, NJ.	10/11/1968
Krasinski, John	Newton, MA.	10/20/1979
Krause, Peter	Alexandria, MN	8/12/1965
Kressley, Carson	Allentown, PA	11/11/1969
Kretschmann, Thomas	Dessau, E. Germany	9/8/1962
Kristofferson, Kris	Brownsville, TX	6/22/1936
Kudrow, Lisa	Encino, CA	7/30/1963
Kunis, Mila	Kiev, Ukraine	8/14/1983
Kurtz, Swoosie	Omaha, NE	9/6/1944
Kutcher, Ashton	Cedar Rapids, IA	2/7/1978
Kwan, Nancy	Hong Kong	5/19/1939
LaBelle, Patti	Philadelphia, PA	5/24/1944
LaBeouf, Shia	Los Angeles, CA	6/11/1986
Lachey, Nick	Harlan, KY.	11/9/1973
Ladd, Cheryl	Huron, SD	7/12/1951
Ladd, Diane	Meridian, MS.	11/29/1932
Lady Gaga	New York, NY	3/28/1986
Lagasse, Emeril	Fall River, MA	10/15/1959
Lahti, Christine	Birmingham, MI	4/4/1950
Laine, Cleo	Southall, England, UK	10/28/1927
Lake, Ricki	Hastings-on-Hudson, NY.	9/21/1968
Lamar, Kendrick	Compton, CA.	6/17/1987
Lamas, Lorenzo	Santa Monica, CA	1/20/1958
Lambert, Adam	Indianapolis, IN	1/29/1982
Lambert, Christopher	Great Neck, NY	3/29/1957
Lambert, Miranda	Longview, TX.	11/10/1983
Landau, Martin	Brooklyn, NY	6/20/1928
Landis, John	Chicago, IL	8/3/1950
Lane, Diane	New York, NY	1/22/1965
Lane, Nathan	Jersey City, NJ.	2/3/1956
lang, k.d.	Consort, AB, Canada	11/2/1961
Lang, Stephen	Jamaica Estates, Queens, NY	7/11/1952
Lange, Jessica	Cloquet, MN	4/20/1949
Langella, Frank	Bayonne, NJ	1/1/1938
Lansbury, Angela	London, England, UK	10/16/1925
LaPaglia, Anthony	Adelaide, SA, Australia	1/31/1959
Larroquette, John	New Orleans, LA.	11/25/1947
Larson, Brie	Sacramento, CA	10/1/1989
LaSalle, Eriq	Hartford, CT	6/23/1962
Lauper, Cyndi	Ozone Park, Queens, NY	6/22/1953
Laurie, Hugh	Oxford, England, UK	6/11/1959
Laurie, Piper	Detroit, MI	1/22/1932
Lautner, Taylor	Grand Rapids, MI	2/11/1992
Lavigne, Avril	Belleville, ON, Canada.	9/27/1984
Lavin, Linda	Portland, ME	10/15/1937
Law, Jude	London, England, UK	12/29/1972
Lawless, Lucy	Mount Albert, New Zealand	3/29/1968
Lawrence, Carol	Melrose Park, IL	9/5/1934
Lawrence, Jennifer	Louisville, KY.	8/15/1990
Lawrence, Joey	Montgomery, PA	4/20/1976
Lawrence, Martin	Frankfurt, Germany	4/16/1965
Lawrence, Vicki	Brooklyn, NY	7/8/1935
Leach, Robin	Inglewood, CA.	3/26/1949
Leachman, Cloris	London, England, UK	8/29/1941
Lear, Norman	Des Moines, IA	4/30/1926
Learned, Michael	New Haven, CT	7/27/1922
Leary, Denis	Washington, DC.	4/9/1939
LeBlanc, Matt	Worcester, MA	8/18/1957
LeBon, Simon	Newton, MA.	7/25/1967
Lee, Ang	Bushey, England, UK	10/27/1958
Lee, Brenda	Pingtung, Taiwan	10/23/1954
Lee, Jason	Lithonia, GA.	12/11/1944
Lee, Michele	Huntington Beach, CA	4/25/1970
Lee, Spike	Los Angeles, CA	6/24/1942
Leeves, Jane	Atlanta, GA	3/20/1957
Legend, John	Ilford, England, UK.	4/18/1961
Legrand, Michel	Springfield, OH	12/28/1978
Leguizamo, John	Paris, France	2/24/1932
Leibman, Ron	Bogotá, Colombia	7/22/1964
Leigh, Jennifer Jason	New York, NY	10/11/1937
Leighton, Laura	Hollywood, CA	2/5/1962
Lennox, Annie	Iowa City, IA.	7/24/1968
Leno, Jay	Aberdeen, Scotland, UK.	12/25/1954
Leo, Melissa	New Rochelle, NY	4/28/1950
Leonard, Robert Sean	New York, NY.	9/14/1960
Leoni, Tea	Westwood, NJ	2/28/1969
Leto, Jared	New York, NY	2/25/1966
Letterman, David	Bossier City, LA.	12/26/1971
Levin, Harvey	Indianapolis, IN	4/12/1947
Levine, Adam	Los Angeles, CA	9/2/1960
Levine, James	Los Angeles, CA	3/18/1979
Levine, Ted	Cincinnati, OH.	6/23/1943
Levinson, Barry	Bellaire, OH.	5/29/1957
	Baltimore, MD	4/6/1942

Name	Birthplace	Birthdate
Levy, Eugene	Hamilton, ON, Canada	12/17/1946
Lewis, Damian	London, Eng., UK	2/11/1971
Lewis, Huey	New York, NY	7/5/1950
Lewis, Jason	Newport Beach, CA	6/25/1971
Lewis, Jerry	Newark, NJ	3/16/1926
Lewis, Jerry Lee	Ferriday, LA	9/29/1935
Lewis, Juliette	Los Angeles, CA	6/21/1973
Lewis, Leona	London, England, UK	4/3/1985
Lewis, Richard	Brooklyn, NY	6/29/1947
Li, Jet	Beijing, China	4/26/1963
Light, Judith	Trenton, NJ	2/9/1949
Lightfoot, Gordon	Orillia, ON, Canada	11/17/1938
Lil' Kim	Brooklyn, NY	7/11/1975
Lil' Romeo	New Orleans, LA	8/19/1989
Lil Wayne	New Orleans, LA	9/27/1982
Lilly, Evangeline	Fort Saskatchewan, AB, Can.	8/3/1979
Lincoln, Andrew	London, England, UK	9/14/1973
Linden, Hal	Bronx, NY	3/20/1931
Ling, Lisa	Sacramento, CA	8/30/1973
Linn-Baker, Mark	St. Louis, MO.	6/17/1954
Linney, Laura	New York, NY	2/5/1964
Liotta, Ray.	Newark, NJ	12/18/1954
Lithgow, John	Rochester, NY	10/19/1945
Little, Rich	Ottawa, ON, Canada	11/26/1938
Little Richard.	Macon, GA	12/5/1932
Littrell, Brian	Lexington, KY	2/20/1975
Liu, Lucy	Jackson Heights, Queens, NY	12/2/1968
Lively, Blake	Tarzana, CA.	8/25/1987
LL Cool J	St. Albans, Queens, NY	1/14/1968
Lloyd, Christopher.	Stamford, CT.	10/22/1938
Lloyd Webber, Andrew	London, England, UK	3/22/1948
Locke, Sondra	Shelbyville, TN.	5/28/1944
Lockhart, June	New York, NY	6/25/1925
Locklear, Heather	Westwood, CA.	9/25/1961
Loggins, Kenny	Everett, WA	1/7/1948
Lohan, Lindsay	New York, NY	7/2/1986
Lollobrigida, Gina	Subiaco, Italy	7/4/1927
Lonergan, Kenneth	New York, NY	10/16/1962
Long, Nia	Brooklyn, NY	10/30/1970
Long, Shelley	Ft. Wayne, IN.	8/23/1949
Longoria, Eva	Corpus Christi, TX	3/15/1975
Lopez, George	Mission Hills, CA	4/23/1961
Lopez, Jennifer.	Bronx, NY	7/24/1969
Lopez, Mario.	San Diego, CA	10/10/1973
Lorde	Takapuna, New Zealand	11/7/1996
Loren, Sophia	Rome, Italy	9/20/1934
Loring, Gloria	New York, NY	12/10/1946
Louis C.K.	Washington, DC	9/12/1967
Louis-Dreyfus, Julia	New York, NY	1/13/1961
Lovato, Demi.	Dallas, TX	8/20/1992
Love, Courtney	San Francisco, CA	7/9/1964
Love, Mike	Baldwin Hills, CA	3/15/1941
Loveless, Patty	Pikeville, KY	1/4/1957
Lovett, Lyle	Klein, TX	11/1/1957
Lovitz, Jon	Tarzana, CA.	7/21/1957
Lowe, Rob.	Charlottesville, VA	3/17/1964
Lucas, George	Modesto, CA	5/14/1944
Lucci, Susan.	Scarsdale, NY	12/23/1946
Luckinbill, Laurence	Ft. Smith, AR	11/21/1934
Ludacris	Champaign, IL.	9/11/1977
Ludwig, Christa.	Berlin, Germany	3/16/1924
Luhrmann, Baz	Sydney, NSW, Australia	9/17/1962
LuPone, Patti	Northport, NY	4/21/1949
Lynch, David	Missoula, MT.	1/20/1946
Lynch, Jane	Dolton, IL.	7/14/1960
Lynley, Carol	New York, NY	2/13/1942
Lynn, Loretta.	Butcher Hollow, KY	4/14/1932
Lynn, Vera.	London, England, UK	3/20/1917
Lynne, Shelby.	Quantico, VA	10/22/1968
Ma, Yo-Yo.	Paris, France	10/7/1955
Macchio, Ralph.	Huntington, NY	11/4/1961
MacDonald, Kelly	Glasgow, Scotland, UK	2/23/1976
MacDowell, Andie	Gaffney, SC	4/21/1958
MacFarlane, Seth	Kent, CT	10/26/1973
MacGowan, Shane	Tunbridge, Kent, Eng., UK	12/25/1957
MacGraw, Ali.	Pound Ridge, NY.	4/1/1939
Macklemore	Seattle, WA	6/19/1983
MacLachlan, Kyle	Yakima, WA.	2/22/1959
MacLaine, Shirley	Richmond, VA	4/24/1934
MacLeod, Gavin	Mt. Kisco, NY.	2/28/1931
MacNicol, Peter	Dallas, TX	4/10/1954
MacPherson, Elle	Sydney, NSW, Australia	3/29/1964
Macy, Bill.	Revere, MA	5/18/1922
Macy, William H.	Miami, FL	3/13/1950
Madden, John.	Austin, MN.	4/10/1936
Madigan, Amy.	Chicago, IL.	9/11/1950
Madonna (Ciccone)	Bay City, MI	8/16/1958
Madsen, Michael	Chicago, IL	9/25/1959
Maguire, Tobey.	Santa Monica, CA	6/27/1975
Maher, Bill.	New York, NY	1/20/1956
Mahoney, John	Blackpool, Lancashire, England, UK	6/20/1940
Majors, Lee.	Wyandotte, MI	4/23/1939
Makarova, Natalia	Leningrad, Russia	11/21/1940

Name	Birthplace	Birthdate
Malek, Rami	Los Angeles, CA	5/12/1981
Malick, Terrence	Ottawa, IL	11/30/1943
Malick, Wendie	Buffalo, NY	12/13/1950
Malina, Joshua	New York, NY	1/17/1966
Malkovich, John	Christopher, IL.	12/9/1953
Malone, Dorothy	Chicago, IL	1/30/1925
Mamet, David	Chicago, IL	11/30/1947
Manchester, Melissa	Bronx, NY	2/15/1951
Mandel, Howie	Toronto, ON, Canada	11/29/1955
Mandrell, Barbara	Houston, TX	12/25/1948
Mangione, Chuck	Rochester, NY	11/29/1940
Manheim, Camryn	Caldwell, NJ	3/8/1961
Manilow, Barry	Brooklyn, NY	6/17/1943
Mann, Aimee.	Richmond, VA	8/9/1960
Manoff, Dinah	New York, NY	1/25/1958
Manson, Marilyn	Canton, OH	1/5/1969
Mantegna, Joe	Chicago, IL	11/13/1947
Mantello, Joe	Rockford, IL	12/27/1962
Mara, Kate	Bedford, NY.	2/27/1983
Mara, Rooney	Bedford, NY.	4/17/1985
Marcil, Vanessa	Indio, CA	10/15/1969
Margulies, Julianna	Spring Valley, NY	6/8/1966
Marie, Constance	Hollywood, CA.	9/9/1965
Marin, Cheech	Los Angeles, CA	7/13/1946
Marinaro, Ed	New York, NY	3/31/1950
Mars, Bruno	Honolulu, HI	10/8/1985
Marsalis, Branford.	Breaux Bridge, LA	8/26/1960
Marsalis, Wynton	New Orleans, LA	10/18/1961
Marsh, Jean	London, England, UK	7/1/1934
Marshall, Penny	Bronx, NY	10/15/1942
Marshall, Peter	Huntington, WV	3/30/1926
Martin, Chris.	Devon, England, UK	3/2/1977
Martin, Jesse L.	Rocky Mount, VA	1/18/1969
Martin, Kellie	Riverside, CA.	10/16/1975
Martin, Ricky.	San Juan, Puerto Rico	12/24/1971
Martin, Steve	Waco, TX.	8/14/1945
Martindale, Margo.	Jacksonville, TX.	7/18/1951
Martins, Peter	Copenhagen, Denmark	10/27/1946
Maslany, Tatiana	Regina, SK, Canada	9/22/1985
Mason, Jackie.	Sheboygan, WI	6/9/1931
Mason, Marsha.	St. Louis, MO.	4/3/1942
Masterson, Christopher	Long Island, NY.	1/22/1980
Masterson, Mary Stuart	New York, NY	6/28/1966
Mastrantonio, Mary Elizabeth	Lombard, IL.	11/17/1958
Masur, Richard	New York, NY	11/20/1948
Mathers, Jerry	Sioux City, IA	6/2/1948
Matheson, Tim	Glendale, CA.	12/31/1947
Mathis, Johnny	Gilmer, TX.	9/30/1935
Matlin, Marlee.	Morton Grove, IL	8/24/1965
Matthews, Dave	Johannesburg, South Africa	1/9/1967
May, Elaine.	Philadelphia, PA	4/21/1932
Mayer, John.	Bridgeport, CT.	10/16/1977
Mays, Jayma	Bristol, TN	7/16/1979
Mazar, Debi	Jamaica, Queens, NY	8/13/1964
McAdams, Rachel.	London, ON, Canada.	11/17/1978
McArdle, Andrea	Abington, PA	11/5/1963
McAvoy, James	Glasgow, Scotland, UK	4/21/1979
McBride, Patricia	Teaneck, NJ	8/23/1942
McCallum, David.	Glasgow, Scotland, UK	9/19/1933
McCarthy, Andrew.	Westfield, NJ	11/29/1962
McCarthy, Jenny	Chicago, IL	11/1/1972
McCarthy, Melissa	Plainfield, IL.	8/26/1970
McCartney, Paul	Liverpool, England, UK	6/18/1942
McCarver, Tim	Memphis, TN.	10/16/1941
McConaughey, Matthew	Uvalde, TX.	11/4/1969
McCoo, Marilyn.	Jersey City, NJ.	9/30/1943
McCormack, Eric	Toronto, ON, Canada.	4/18/1963
McCormack, Mary	Plainsfield, NJ	2/8/1969
McCrane, Paul	Philadelphia, PA	1/19/1961
McCreery, Scotty	Garner, NC	10/9/1993
McDaniel, James	Washington, DC	3/25/1958
McDermott, Dylan	Waterbury, CT.	10/26/1961
McDiarmid, Ian	Carnoustie, Tayside, Scot., UK	4/17/1944?
McDonald, Audra	Berlin, Germany	7/3/1970
McDonnell, Mary	Wilkes-Barre, PA	4/28/1952
McDormand, Frances	Chicago, IL	6/23/1957
McDowell, Malcolm.	Leeds, England, UK.	6/13/1943
McEntire, Reba.	McAlester, OK	3/28/1955
McFerrin, Bobby	New York, NY	3/11/1950
McGillis, Kelly	Newport Beach, CA.	7/9/1957
McGovern, Elizabeth	Evanston, IL	7/18/1961
McGovern, Maureen	Youngstown, OH	7/27/1949
McGraw, Tim.	Delhi, LA	5/1/1967
McGregor, Ewan.	Crieff, Scotland, UK.	3/31/1971
McHale, Joel.	Rome, Italy	11/20/1971
McHale, Kevin.	Plano, TX.	6/14/1988
McKean, Michael	New York, NY	10/17/1947
McKechnie, Donna	Pontiac, MI	11/16/1942
McKellen, Ian	Burnley, England, UK.	5/25/1939
McKenzie, Ben	Austin, TX	9/12/1978
McKidd, Kevin	Elgin, Scotland, UK	8/9/1973
McKinnon, Kate	Sea Cliff, NY	1/6/1984
McLachlan, Sarah.	Halifax, NS, Canada	1/28/1968
McLean, A. J.	West Palm Beach, FL	1/9/1978

Name	Birthplace	Birthdate
McNichol, Kristy	Los Angeles, CA	9/11/1962
McRaney, Gerald	Collins, MS	8/19/1947
McQueen, Steve	London, England, UK	10/9/1969
McQueen, Steven R.	Los Angeles, CA	7/13/1988
McShane, Ian	Blackburn, England, UK.	9/29/1942
Meat Loaf	Dallas, TX	9/27/1947
Meester, Leighton	Marco Island, FL	4/9/1986
Mehta, Zubin	Bombay, India	4/29/1936
Mellencamp, John	Seymour, IN	10/7/1951
Meloni, Christopher	Washington, DC	4/2/1961
Mendes, Sam	Redding, England, UK.	8/1/1965
Mendes, Sergio	Niteroi, Brazil	2/11/1941
Menzel, Idina	Syosset, NY.	5/30/1971
Merchant, Natalie	Jamestown, NY	10/26/1963
Merkerson, S. Epatha	Saginaw, MI.	11/28/1952
Merrill, Dina	New York, NY	12/9/1925
Messing, Debra	Brooklyn, NY	8/15/1968
Metcalf, Laurie	Carbondale, IL	6/16/1955
Meyers, Seth	Bedford, NH.	12/28/1973
Michael, George	London, England, UK	6/25/1963
Michaels, Al	Brooklyn, NY	11/12/1944
Michaels, Bret	Butler, PA	3/15/1963
Michaels, Lorne	Toronto, ON, Canada.	11/17/1944
Michele, Lea	Bronx, NY	8/29/1986
Midler, Bette	Honolulu, HI	12/1/1945
Midori (Goto)	Osaka, Japan	10/25/1971
Mike D	Brooklyn, NY	11/20/1965
Milano, Alyssa	Brooklyn, NY	12/19/1972
Miles, Sarah	Ingatestone, England, UK	12/31/1941
Miles, Vera	nr. Boise City, OK.	8/23/1930
Miller, Dennis	Pittsburgh, PA	11/3/1953
Miller, Jonny Lee	Kingston Upon Thames, England, UK	11/15/1972
Miller, Penelope Ann	Santa Monica, CA	1/13/1964
Mills, Donna	Chicago, IL	12/11/1943
Mills, Hayley	London, England, UK	4/18/1946
Milnes, Sherrill	Downers Grove, IL.	1/10/1935
Milsap, Ronnie	Robinsville, NC	1/16/1944
Mimieux, Yvette	Hollywood, CA.	1/8/1942
Minaj, Nicki	St. James, Trinidad and Tobago	12/8/1982
Ming-Na (Wen)	Coloane Island, Macao	11/20/1963
Minnelli, Liza	Los Angeles, CA	3/12/1946
Minogue, Kylie	Melbourne, Vic., Australia	5/28/1968
Miranda, Lin-Manuel	New York, NY	1/16/1980
Mirren, Helen	London, England, UK	7/26/1945
Mitchell, Brian Stokes	Seattle, WA	10/31/1957
Mitchell, Elizabeth	Los Angeles, CA	3/27/1970
Mitchell, Jerry	Paw Paw, MI	1/15/1960
Mitchell, Joni	Fort McLeod, AB, Canada	11/7/1943
Moby	New York, NY	9/11/1965
Modine, Matthew	Loma Linda, CA.	3/22/1959
Moffat, Donald	Plymouth, England, UK.	12/26/1930
Molina, Alfred	London, England, UK	5/24/1953
Moll, Richard	Pasadena, CA	1/13/1943
Moloney, Janel	Woodland Hills, CA	10/3/1969
Monaghan, Dominic	Berlin, Germany	12/8/1976
Monica (Arnold)	College Park, GA.	10/24/1980
Mo'Nique	Woodlawn, MD	12/11/1967
Moore, Demi	Roswell, NM	11/11/1962
Moore, Julianne	Fort Bragg, NC	12/3/1960
Moore, Mandy	Nashua, NH.	4/10/1984
Moore, Mary Tyler	Brooklyn, NY.	12/29/1936
Moore, Melba	New York, NY	10/29/1945
Moore, Michael	Flint, MI	4/23/1954
Moore, Roger	London, England, UK	10/14/1927
Moore, Terry	Los Angeles, CA	1/7/1929
Morales, Esai	Brooklyn, NY	10/1/1962
Moranis, Rick	Toronto, ON, Canada.	4/18/1953
Moreau, Jeanne	Paris, France	1/23/1928
Moreno, Rita	Humacao, Puerto Rico.	12/11/1931
Morgan, Jeffrey Dean	Seattle, WA	4/22/1966
Morgan, Piers	Guildford, Surrey, UK.	3/30/1965
Morgan, Tracy	Bronx, NY	11/10/1968
Moriarty, Michael	Detroit, MI	4/5/1941
Morris, Garrett	New Orleans, LA	2/1/1937
Morissette, Alanis	Ottawa, ON, Canada	6/1/1974
Morrison, Matthew	Fort Ord, CA	10/30/1978
Morrison, Van	Belfast, N. Ireland, UK	8/31/1945
Morrissey (Steven Patrick)	Manchester, England, UK	5/22/1959
Morrow, Rob	New Rochelle, NY	9/21/1962
Morse, David	Beverly, MA	10/11/1953
Morse, Robert	Newton, MA.	5/18/1931
Mortensen, Viggo	New York, NY	10/20/1958
Mortimer, Emily	London, England, UK	12/1/1971
Morton, Joe	New York, NY	10/18/1947
Morton, Samantha	Nottingham, England, UK	5/13/1977
Moses, William	Los Angeles, CA	11/17/1959
Moss, Carrie-Anne	Vancouver, BC, Canada.	8/21/1967
Moss, Elisabeth	Los Angeles, CA	7/24/1982
Moss, Kate	Croydon, Surrey, Eng., UK.	1/16/1974
Moyer, Stephen	Brentwood, UK	10/11/1969
Moynahan, Bridget	Binghamton, NY	4/28/1971
Mueller-Stahl, Armin	Tilsit, E. Prussia	12/17/1930
Muldaur, Diana	Brooklyn, NY	8/19/1938
Mulgrew, Kate	Dubuque, IA	4/29/1955

Name	Birthplace	Birthdate
Mull, Martin	Chicago, IL	8/18/1943
Mullally, Megan	Los Angeles, CA	11/12/1958
Mullan, Peter	Peterhead, Scotland, UK	11/2/1959
Mulligan, Carey	London, England, UK	5/28/1985
Mulroney, Dermot	Alexandria, VA	10/31/1963
Muniz, Frankie	Wood-Ridge, NJ	12/5/1985
Murphy, Ben	Jonesboro, AR	3/6/1942
Murphy, Donna	Corona, Queens, NY	3/7/1958
Murphy, Eddie	Brooklyn, NY	4/3/1961
Murphy, Michael	Los Angeles, CA	5/5/1938
Murray, Anne	Springhill, NS, Canada	6/20/1945
Murray, Bill	Wilmette, IL	9/21/1950
Murray, Don	Hollywood, CA.	7/31/1929
Musburger, Brent	Portland, OR	5/26/1939
Muti, Riccardo	Naples, Italy.	7/28/1941
Myers, Mike	Scarborough, ON, Canada	5/25/1963
Nabors, Jim	Sylacauga, AL	6/12/1930
Nagra, Parminder	Leicester, England, UK	10/5/1975
Nash, Graham	Blackpool, England, UK.	2/2/1942
Nash, Niecy	Palmdale, CA.	2/23/1970
Naughton, James	Middletown, CT	12/6/1945
Navarro, Dave	Santa Monica, CA	6/7/1967
Nealon, Kevin	St. Louis, MO.	11/18/1953
Neeson, Liam	Ballymena, N. Ireland, UK	6/7/1952
Neff, Lucas	Chicago, IL	11/7/1985
Neill, Sam	Ulster, N. Ireland, UK	9/14/1947
Nelligan, Kate	London, ON, Canada.	3/16/1951
Nelly	Austin, TX	11/2/1974
Nelson, Craig T.	Spokane, WA.	4/4/1944
Nelson, Judd.	Portland, ME.	11/28/1959
Nelson, Tracy	Santa Monica, CA	10/25/1963
Nelson, Willie	Abbott, TX.	4/30/1933
Nero, Peter	Brooklyn, NY	5/22/1934
Nesmith, Michael	Houston, TX	12/30/1942
Neuwirth, Bebe	Newark, NJ	12/31/1958
Neville, Aaron	New Orleans, LA	1/24/1941
Newhart, Bob	Oak Park, IL	9/5/1929
Newman, Randy	New Orleans, LA	11/28/1943
Newton, Wayne	Norfolk, VA	4/3/1942
Newton-John, Olivia	Cambridge, England, UK.	9/26/1948
Nicholas, Denise	Detroit, MI	7/12/1944
Nicholson, Jack	Neptune, NJ	4/22/1937
Nicks, Stevie	Phoenix, AZ.	5/26/1948
Nighy, Bill	Caterham, Surrey, Eng., UK	12/12/1949
Nixon, Cynthia	New York, NY	4/9/1966
Noah, Trevor	Soweto, South Africa	2/20/1984
Nolan, Christopher	London, England, UK	7/30/1970
Nolte, Nick	Omaha, NE	2/8/1941
Noone, Peter	Manchester, England, UK	11/5/1947
Norman, Jessye	Augusta, GA	9/15/1945
Norris, Chuck	Ryan, OK.	3/10/1940
Northam, Jeremy	Cambridge, England, UK.	12/1/1961
Norton, Edward.	Boston, MA	8/18/1969
Noth, Christopher	Madison, WI	11/13/1954
Novak, Kim	Chicago, IL	2/13/1933
Nuyen, France	Marseilles, France	7/31/1939
Nyong'o, Lupita	Mexico City, Mexico	3/1/1983
Oates, John	New York, NY	4/7/1949
O'Brien, Conan	Brookline, MA	4/18/1963
O'Brien, Margaret	San Diego, CA	1/15/1937
Ocean, Billy	Fyzabad, Trinidad and Tobago	1/21/1950
Ocean, Frank	Long Beach, CA	10/28/1987
O'Connor, Sinead	Glenageary, Ireland	12/8/1966
Odenkirk, Bob.	Berwyn, IL	10/22/1962
O'Donnell, Chris	Winnetka, IL	6/26/1970
O'Donnell, Rosie	Commack, NY	3/21/1962
O'Grady, Gail	Detroit, MI	1/23/1963
Oh, Sandra	Nepean, ON, Canada	7/20/1971
O'Hara, Catherine	Toronto, ON, Canada.	3/4/1954
O'Hare, Denis	Kansas City, MO	1/17/1962
Oka, Masi	Tokyo, Japan.	12/27/1974
Oldman, Gary	South London, Eng., UK	3/21/1958
Olin, Ken	Chicago, IL	7/30/1954
Olin, Lena	Stockholm, Sweden.	3/22/1955
Oliver, Jamie	Clavering, England, UK	5/27/1975
Oliver, John	Birmingham, England, UK.	4/23/1977
Olmos, Edward James	E. Los Angeles, CA	2/24/1947
Olsen, Ashley	Sherman Oaks, CA	6/13/1986
Olsen, Mary-Kate	Sherman Oaks, CA	6/13/1986
Olson, Nancy	Milwaukee, WI	7/14/1928
Olyphant, Timothy.	Honolulu, HI	5/20/1968
O'Malley, Mike	Boston, MA	10/31/1966
O'Neal, Ryan	Los Angeles, CA	4/20/1941
O'Neal, Tatum	Los Angeles, CA	11/5/1963
O'Neill, Ed.	Youngstown, OH	4/12/1946
Ontkean, Michael	Vancouver, BC, Canada.	1/24/1946
O'Quinn, Terry	Newbury, MI	7/15/1952
Orlando, Tony	New York, NY	4/3/1944
Ormond, Julia	Epsom, England, UK.	1/4/1965
Osbourne, Jack	London, England, UK	11/8/1985
Osbourne, Kelly	London, England, UK	10/27/1984
Osbourne, Ozzy	Birmingham, England, UK.	12/3/1948
Osbourne, Sharon	London, England, UK	10/9/1952
Osment, Haley Joel	Los Angeles, CA	4/10/1988

Name	Birthplace	Birthdate	Name	Birthplace	Birthdate
Osmond, Donny	Ogden, UT	12/9/1957	Potts, Annie	Nashville, TN	10/28/1952
Osmond, Marie	Ogden, UT	10/13/1959	Povich, Maury	Washington, DC	1/17/1939
O'Toole, Annette	Houston, TX	4/1/1951	Powell, Jane	Portland, OR	4/1/1929
Owen, Clive	Keresley, England, UK	10/3/1964	Powers, Stefanie	Hollywood, CA	11/2/1942
Oyelowo, David	Oxford, England, UK	4/1/1976	Pratt, Chris	Virginia, MN.	6/21/1979
Oz, Frank	Herford, England, UK	5/25/1944	Prentiss, Paula	San Antonio, TX	3/4/1939
Ozawa, Seiji	Shenyang, China	9/1/1935	Prepon, Laura	Watchung, NJ	3/7/1980
Pacino, Al	New York, NY	4/25/1940	Presley, Priscilla	Brooklyn, NY	5/24/1945
Packer, Billy	Wellsville, NY	2/25/1940	Pressly, Jaime	Kinston, NC	7/30/1977
Page, Ellen	Halifax, NS, Canada	2/21/1987	Previn, Andre	Berlin, Germany	4/6/1929
Page, Jimmy	Heston, England, UK	1/9/1944	Price, Leontyne	Laurel, MS.	2/10/1927
Paget, Debra	Denver, CO	8/19/1933	Price, Molly	North Plainfield, NJ	12/15/1966
Paige, Janis	Tacoma, WA	9/16/1922	Pride, Charley	Sledge, MS	3/18/1938
Paisley, Brad	Glen Dale, WV	10/28/1972	Priestley, Jason	Vancouver, BC, Canada	8/28/1969
Palin, Michael	Sheffield, England, UK	5/5/1943	Prince, Faith	Augusta, GA	8/5/1957
Palmer, Geoffrey	London, England, UK	6/4/1927	Principal, Victoria	Fukuoka, Japan	1/3/1950
Palminteri, Chazz	Bronx, NY	5/15/1951	Probst, Jeff	Wichita, KS	11/4/1962
Paltrow, Gwyneth	Los Angeles, CA	9/27/1972	Proctor, Emily	Raleigh, NC.	10/8/1968
Panettiere, Hayden	Palisades, NY	8/21/1989	Pryce, Jonathan	Holywell, N. Wales, UK	6/1/1947
Panjabi, Archie	Edgware, England, UK	5/31/1972	Puck, Wolfgang	St. Veit, Austria	1/8/1949
Pantoliano, Joe	Hoboken, NJ	9/12/1951	Pulliam, Keshia Knight	Newark, NJ	4/9/1979
Papas, Irene	Chiliomodi, Greece	9/3/1926	Pullman, Bill	Hornell, NY	12/17/1953
Paquin, Anna	Winnipeg, MB, Canada	7/24/1982	Purcell, Sarah	Richmond, IN	10/8/1948
Parker, Alan	Islington, England, UK	2/14/1944	Purefoy, James	Taunton, England, UK	6/3/1964
Parker, Jameson	Baltimore, MD	11/18/1947	Quaid, Dennis	Houston, TX	4/9/1954
Parker, Mary-Louise	Fort Jackson, SC	8/2/1964	Quaid, Randy	Houston, TX	10/1/1950
Parker, Sarah Jessica	Nelsonville, OH	3/25/1965	Queen Latifah	Newark, NJ	3/18/1970
Parsons, Estelle	Marblehead, MA	11/20/1927	Quinn, Aidan	Chicago, IL	3/8/1959
Parsons, Jim	Houston, TX	3/24/1973	Quinn, Colin	Brooklyn, NY	6/6/1959
Parton, Dolly	Sevierville, TN	1/19/1946	Quinn, Martha	Albany, NY.	5/11/1959
Pasdar, Adrian	Pittsfield, MA	4/30/1965	Quinto, Zachary	Pittsburgh, PA	6/2/1977
Patinkin, Mandy	Chicago, IL	11/30/1952	Rachins, Alan	Cambridge, MA	10/3/1942
Patric, Jason	Flushing, Queens, NY	6/17/1966	Radcliffe, Daniel	London, England, UK	7/23/1989
Pattinson, Robert	London, England, UK	5/13/1986	Radnor, Josh	Columbus, OH.	7/29/1974
Patton, Will	Charleston, SC	6/14/1954	Rae, Charlotte	Milwaukee, WI	4/22/1926
Paul, Aaron	Emmett, ID	8/27/1979	Raffi (Cavoukian)	Cairo, Egypt.	7/8/1948
Paul, Adrian	London, England, UK	5/29/1959	Raitt, Bonnie	Burbank, CA	11/8/1949
Paulson, Sarah	Tampa, FL	12/17/1975	Ramey, Samuel	Colby, KS.	3/28/1942
Paxton, Bill	Fort Worth, TX	5/17/1955	Ramirez, Efren	Los Angeles, CA	10/2/1973
Pearce, Guy	Ely, England, UK	10/5/1967	Ramirez, Sara	Mazatlan, Mexico.	8/31/1975
Peet, Amanda	New York, NY	1/11/1972	Rampling, Charlotte	Sturmer, MA	2/5/1946
Penn, Kal	Montclair, NJ	4/23/1977	Rancic, Giuliana	Naples, Italy.	8/17/1975
Penn, Sean	Burbank, CA	8/17/1960	Randolph, Joyce	Detroit, MI	10/21/1924
Pepper, Barry	Campbell River, BC, Can.	4/4/1970	Raphael, Sally Jessy	Easton, PA.	2/25/1935
Perez, Rosie	Brooklyn, NY	9/6/1964	Rashad, Phylicia	Houston, TX	6/19/1948
Perkins, Elizabeth	Flushing, Queens, NY	11/18/1960	Ratzenberger, John	Bridgeport, CT.	4/6/1947
Perlman, Itzhak	Tel Aviv, Israel	8/31/1945	Raver, Kim	New York, NY	3/15/1969
Perlman, Rhea	Brooklyn, NY	3/31/1948	Ray, Rachael	Glen Falls, NY	8/25/1968
Perlman, Ron	New York, NY	4/13/1950	Reddy, Helen	Melbourne, Vic., Australia	10/25/1941
Perrine, Valerie	Galveston, TX	9/3/1943	Redford, Robert	Santa Monica, CA	8/18/1936
Perry, Katy	Santa Barbara, CA.	10/25/1984	Redgrave, Vanessa	London, England, UK	1/30/1937
Perry, Luke	Mansfield, OH	10/11/1965	Redmayne, Eddie	London, England, UK	1/6/1982
Perry, Matthew	Williamstown, MA	8/19/1969	Reed, Rex	Ft. Worth, TX	10/2/1938
Perry, Tyler	New Orleans, LA	9/13/1969	Reese, Della	Detroit, MI	7/6/1931
Persoff, Nehemiah	Jerusalem, Israel	8/2/1919	Reeves, Keanu	Beirut, Lebanon	9/2/1964
Pesci, Joe	Newark, NJ	2/9/1943	Reeves, Martha	Eufaula, AL	7/18/1941
Peters, Bernadette	Ozone Park, Queens, NY	2/28/1948	Regalbuto, Joe	New York, NY	8/24/1949
Peters, Roberta	Bronx, NY	5/4/1930	Reid, Tara	Wyckoff, NJ	11/8/1975
Petersen, Wolfgang	Emden, Germany	3/14/1941	Reid, Tim	Norfolk, VA	12/19/1944
Petty, Lori	Chattanooga, TN	3/23/1963	Reid, Vernon	London, England, UK	8/22/1958
Petty, Tom	Gainesville, FL	10/20/1950	Reilly, John C.	Chicago, IL	5/24/1965
Pfeiffer, Michelle	Santa Ana, CA	4/29/1958	Reiner, Carl	Bronx, NY	3/20/1922
Phair, Liz	New Haven, CT	4/17/1967	Reiner, Rob.	Bronx, NY	3/6/1947
Philbin, Regis	New York, NY	8/25/1931	Reinhold, Judge	Wilmington, DE	5/21/1957
Phillippe, Ryan	New Castle, DE	9/10/1974	Reinking, Ann	Seattle, WA	11/10/1949
Phillips, Lou Diamond	Subic Bay, Philippines	2/17/1962	Reiser, Paul	New York, NY	3/30/1957
Phillips, Mackenzie	Alexandria, VA	11/10/1959	Reitman, Ivan	Komarno, Czechoslovakia	10/26/1946
Phillips, Michelle	Long Beach, CA	6/4/1944	Remini, Leah	Brooklyn, NY	6/15/1970
Phillips, Phillip	Leesburg, GA	9/20/1990	Renner, Jeremy	Modesto, CA	1/7/1971
Phillips, Sian	Bettws, Wales, UK.	5/14/1934	Reynolds, Burt	Waycross, GA	2/11/1936
Phoenix, Joaquin	San Juan, Puerto Rico.	10/28/1974	Reynolds, Debbie	El Paso, TX	4/1/1932
Pierce, David Hyde	Albany, NY.	4/3/1959	Reynolds, Ryan	Vancouver, BC, Canada.	10/23/1976
Pike, Rosamund	London, England, UK	1/27/1979	Reznor, Trent	Mercer, PA.	5/17/1965
Pinchot, Bronson	New York, NY	5/20/1959	Rhames, Ving	New York, NY	5/12/1959
Pink	Doylestown, PA	9/8/1979	Rhimes, Shonda	Chicago, IL	1/13/1970
Pinkett Smith, Jada	Baltimore, MD	9/18/1971	Rhymes, Busta	Brooklyn, NY	5/20/1972
Pirner, Dave	Green Bay, WI	4/16/1964	Rhys, Matthew	Cardiff, Wales, UK	11/4/1974
Piscopo, Joe	Passaic, NJ	6/17/1951	Rhys Meyers, Jonathan	Dublin, Ireland	7/27/1977
Pitbull	Miami, FL	1/15/1981	Ribisi, Giovanni	Los Angeles, CA	12/17/1974
Pitt, Brad	Shawnee, OK	12/18/1963	Ricci, Christina	Santa Monica, CA	2/12/1980
Piven, Jeremy	New York, NY	7/26/1965	Richards, Denise	Downers Grove, IL.	2/17/1971
Plant, Robert	W. Bromwich, England, UK	8/20/1948	Richards, Keith	Dartford, Kent, Eng., UK	12/18/1943
Plimpton, Martha	New York ,NY	11/16/1970	Richards, Michael	Culver City, CA	7/24/1949
Plowright, Joan	Brigg, England, UK	10/28/1929	Richardson, Kevin	Lexington, KY	10/3/1971
Plummer, Amanda	New York, NY	3/23/1957	Richardson, Miranda	Lancashire, England, UK.	3/3/1958
Plummer, Christopher	Toronto, ON, Canada.	12/13/1927	Richardson, Patricia	Bethesda, MD	2/23/1951
Poehler, Amy	Newton, MA.	9/16/1971	Richie, Lionel	Tuskegee, AL.	6/20/1949
Poitier, Sidney	Miami, FL	2/20/1927	Richie, Nicole	Berkeley, CA	9/21/1981
Polanski, Roman	Paris, France	8/18/1933	Richter, Andy	Grand Rapids, MI	10/28/1966
Pompeo, Ellen	Everett, MA	11/10/1969	Rickles, Don	Jackson Heights, Queens, NY	5/8/1926
Pop, Iggy	Muskegon, MI	4/21/1947			
Portman, Natalie	Jerusalem, Israel	6/9/1981	Riegert, Peter	New York, NY	4/11/1947
Posey, Parker	Baltimore, MD	11/8/1968	Rigg, Diana	Doncaster, England, UK	7/20/1938
Post, Markie	Palo Alto, CA	11/4/1950	Rihanna	St. Michael, Barbados	2/20/1988
Potente, Franka	Dulmen bei Munster, Germany	7/22/1974	Riley, Amber	Long Beach, CA	2/15/1986
			Rimes, LeAnn	Jackson, MS	8/28/1982

Name	Birthplace	Birthdate
Ringwald, Molly	Roseville, CA	2/18/1968
Ripa, Kelly	Stratford, NJ	10/2/1970
Rivera, Chita	Washington, DC	1/23/1933
Rivera, Geraldo	New York, NY	7/4/1943
Robbins, Tim	W. Covina, CA	10/16/1958
Roberts, Eric	Biloxi, MS	4/18/1956
Roberts, Julia	Smyrna, GA	10/28/1967
Roberts, Tony	New York, NY	10/22/1939
Robinson, Smokey	Detroit, MI	2/19/1940
Rock, Chris	Andrews, SC	2/7/1965
Rodgers, Jimmie	Camas, WA	9/18/1933
Rodriguez, Johnny	Sabinal, TX	12/10/1951
Rodriguez, Michelle	Bexar County, TX	7/12/1978
Rogan, Joe	Newark, NJ	8/11/1967
Rogen, Seth	Vancouver, BC, Canada	4/15/1982
Rogers, Kenny	Houston, TX	8/21/1938
Rogers, Mimi	Coral Gables, FL	1/27/1956
Rohm, Elisabeth	Dusseldorf, Germany	4/28/1973
Rollins, Henry	Washington, DC	2/13/1961
Rollins, Sonny	New York, NY	9/7/1930
Romano, Ray	Forest Hills, Queens, NY	12/21/1957
Romijn, Rebecca	Berkeley, CA	11/6/1972
Ronan, Saoirse	New York, NY	4/12/1994
Ronson, Mark	London, England, UK	9/4/1975
Ronstadt, Linda	Tucson, AZ	7/15/1946
Root, Stephen	Sarasota, FL	11/17/1951
Rose, Axl	Lafayette, IN	2/6/1962
Rose Marie	New York, NY	8/15/1923
Roseanne	Salt Lake City, UT	11/3/1952
Ross, Charlotte	Winnetka, IL	1/21/1968
Ross, Diana	Detroit, MI	3/26/1944
Ross, Katharine	Hollywood, CA	1/29/1940
Ross, Marion	Albert Lea, MN	10/25/1928
Ross, Tracee Ellis	Los Angeles, CA	10/29/1972
Rossdale, Gavin	London, England, UK	10/30/1965
Rossellini, Isabella	Rome, Italy	6/18/1952
Rossum, Emmy	New York, NY	9/12/1986
Roth, David Lee	Bloomington, IN	10/10/1955
Roth, Tim	London, England, UK	5/14/1961
Rotten, Johnny	London, England, UK	1/31/1956
Roundtree, Richard	New Rochelle, NY	7/9/1942
Rourke, Mickey	Schenectady, NY	9/16/1952
Routh, Brandon	Des Moines, IA	10/9/1979
Routledge, Patricia	Birkenhead, England, UK	2/17/1929
Rowan, Kelly	Ottawa, ON, Canada	10/26/1965
Rowlands, Gena	Cambria, WI	6/19/1930
Rubinstein, John	Beverly Hills, CA	12/8/1946
Rudd, Paul	Passaic, NJ	4/6/191969
Rudner, Rita	Miami, FL	9/17/1955?
Rudolph, Maya	Gainesville, FL	7/27/1972
Ruehl, Mercedes	Jackson Heights, Queens, NY	2/28/1948
Ruffalo, Mark	Kenosha, WI	11/22/1967
RuPaul	San Diego, CA	11/17/1960
Rupp, Debra Jo	Glendale, CA	2/24/1951
Rush, Barbara	Denver, CO	1/4/1927
Rush, Geoffrey	Toowoomba, Qld., Australia	7/6/1951
Russell, Keri	Fountain Valley, CA	3/23/1976
Russell, Kurt	Springfield, MA	3/17/1951
Russell, Leon	Lawton, OK	4/2/1941
Russell, Mark	Buffalo, NY	8/23/1932
Russell, Theresa	San Diego, CA	3/20/1957
Russo, Rene	Burbank, CA	2/17/1954
Ruttan, Susan	Oregon City, OR	9/16/1950
Ryan, Meg	Fairfield, CT	11/19/1961
Ryan, Roz	Detroit, MI	7/7/1951
Rydell, Bobby	Philadelphia, PA	4/26/1942
Ryder, Winona	Winona, MN	10/29/1971
Rylance, Mark	Ashford, England, UK	1/18/1960
Sabato, Antonio, Jr.	Rome, Italy	2/29/1972
Sade (Adu)	Ibadan, Nigeria	1/16/1959
Sagal, Katey	Hollywood, CA	1/19/1954
Saget, Bob	Philadelphia, PA	5/17/1956
Sagnier, Ludivine	La Celle-St.-Cloud, France	7/3/1979
Sahl, Mort	Montreal, QC, Canada	5/11/1927
Saint, Eva Marie	Newark, NJ	7/4/1924
St. James, Susan	Hollywood, CA	8/14/1946
St. John, Jill	Los Angeles, CA	8/19/1940
St. Patrick, Mathew	Philadelphia, PA	3/17/1968
Sajak, Pat	Chicago, IL	10/26/1946
Saldana, Zoë	Passaic, NJ	6/19/1978
Salling, Mark	Dallas, TX	8/17/1982
Salonga, Lea	Manila, Philippines	2/22/1971
Samberg, Andy	Berkeley, CA	8/18/1978
Samms, Emma	London, England, UK	8/28/1960
San Giacomo, Laura	Hoboken, NJ	11/14/1962
Sandler, Adam	Brooklyn, NY	9/9/1966
Sands, Julian	West Yorkshire, Eng., UK	1/15/1958
Santana, Carlos	Autlan, Mexico	7/20/1947
Sara, Mia	Brooklyn, NY	6/19/1967
Sarandon, Susan	New York, NY	10/4/1946
Sartain, Gailard	Tulsa, OK	9/18/1946
Savage, Ben	Highland Park, IL	9/13/1980
Savage, Fred	Highland Park, IL	7/9/1976
Sawa, Devon	Vancouver, BC, Canada	9/7/1978
Saxon, John	Brooklyn, NY	8/5/1936
Sayles, John	Schenectady, NY	9/28/1950
Scacchi, Greta	Milan, Italy	2/18/1960

Name	Birthplace	Birthdate
Scaggs, Boz	Canton, OH	6/8/1944
Scales, Prunella	Sutton Abinger, Eng., UK	6/22/1932
Scalia, Jack	Brooklyn, NY	11/10/1951
Schiff, Richard	Bethesda, MD	5/27/1955
Schiffer, Claudia	Rheinbach, Germany	8/25/1970
Schneider, John	Mt. Kisco, NY	4/8/1960
Schneider, Rob	San Francisco, CA	10/31/1963
Schreiber, Liev	San Francisco, CA	10/4/1967
Schroder, Rick	Staten Island, NY	4/13/1970
Schumer, Amy	New York, NY	6/1/1981
Schwarzenegger, Arnold	Thal, Austria	7/30/1947
Schwimmer, David	Astoria, Queens, NY	11/2/1966
Sciorra, Annabella	Wethersfield, CT	3/24/1964
Scolari, Peter	New Rochelle, NY	9/12/1954
Scorsese, Martin	Flushing, Queens, NY	11/17/1942
Scott, Ridley	South Shields, England, UK	11/30/1937
Scott, Seann William	Cottage Grove, MN	10/3/1976
Scott Thomas, Kristin	Redruth, England, UK	5/24/1960
Scotto, Renata	Savona, Italy	2/24/1934
Scully, Vin	Bronx, NY	11/29/1927
Seacrest, Ryan	Atlanta, GA	12/24/1974
Seagal, Steven	Lansing, MI	4/10/1951
Secor, Kyle	Tacoma, WA	5/31/1957
Sedaka, Neil	Brooklyn, NY	3/13/1939
Sedgwick, Kyra	New York, NY	8/19/1965
Segal, George	Great Neck, NY	2/13/1934
Segel, Jason	Los Angeles, CA	1/18/1980
Seidelman, Susan	Abington, PA	12/11/1952
Seinfeld, Jerry	Brooklyn, NY	4/29/1954
Sellecca, Connie	Bronx, NY	5/25/1955
Selleck, Tom	Detroit, MI	1/29/1945
Severinsen, Doc	Arlington, OR	7/7/1927
Sevigny, Chloë	Springfield, MA	11/18/1974
Sewell, Rufus	Twickenham, Middlesex, England, UK	10/29/1967
Seyfried, Amanda	Allentown, PA	12/3/1985
Seymour, Jane	Hillingdon, England, UK	2/15/1951
Shackelford, Ted	Oklahoma City, OK	6/23/1946
Shaffer, Paul	Thunder Bay, ON, Canada	11/28/1949
Shakira (Mebarak Ripoll)	Barranquilla, Colombia	2/2/1977
Shalhoub, Tony	Green Bay, WI	10/9/1953
Shannon, Molly	Shaker Heights, OH	9/16/1964
Shatner, William	Montreal, QC, Canada	3/22/1931
Shaughnessy, Charles	London, England, UK	2/9/1955
Shaver, Helen	St. Thomas, ON, Canada	2/24/1951
Shawkat, Alia	Riverside, CA	4/18/1989
Shea, John	North Conway, NH	4/14/1949
Shearer, Harry	Los Angeles, CA	12/23/1943
Sheedy, Ally	New York, NY	6/13/1962
Sheen, Charlie	Los Angeles, CA	9/3/1965
Sheen, Martin	Dayton, OH	8/3/1940
Sheen, Michael	Newport, Wales, UK	2/5/1969
Sheeran, Ed	Hebden Bridge, West Yorkshire, Eng., UK	2/17/1991
Sheindlin, Judy	Brooklyn, NY	10/21/1942
Shelley, Carole	London, England, UK	8/16/1939
Shelton, Blake	Ada, OK	6/18/1976
Shepard, Sam	Ft. Sheridan, IL	11/5/1943
Shepherd, Cybill	Memphis, TN	2/18/1950
Shepherd, Sherri	Chicago, IL	4/22/1967
Sheridan, Nicollette	Worthing, England, UK	11/21/1963
Shields, Brooke	New York, NY	5/31/1965
Shire, Talia	Lake Success, NY	4/25/1946
Short, Martin	Hamilton, ON, Canada	3/26/1950
Shortz, Will	Crawfordsville, IN	8/26/1952
Show, Grant	Detroit, MI	2/27/1962
Shue, Andrew	South Orange, NJ	2/20/1967
Shue, Elisabeth	Wilmington, DE	10/6/1963
Shyamalan, M. Night	Pondicherry, India	8/6/1970
Sidibe, Gabourey	Brooklyn, NY	5/6/1983
Sigler, Jamie-Lynn	Jericho, NY	5/15/1981
Sikking, James B.	Los Angeles, CA	3/5/1934
Silverman, Jonathan	Beverly Hills, CA	8/5/1966
Silverman, Sarah	Bedford, NH	12/1/1970
Silverstone, Alicia	San Francisco, CA	10/4/1976
Simmons, Gene	Haifa, Israel	8/25/1949
Simmons, Henry	Stamford, CT	7/1/1970
Simmons, Richard	New Orleans, LA	7/12/1948
Simon, Carly	New York, NY	6/25/1945
Simon, Paul	Newark, NJ	10/13/1941
Simpson, Ashlee	Waco, TX	10/3/1984
Simpson, Jessica	Abilene, TX	7/10/1980
Sinatra, Nancy	Jersey City, NJ	6/8/1940
Sinbad	Benton Harbor, MI	11/10/1956
Singleton, John	Los Angeles, CA	1/6/1968
Sinise, Gary	Blue Island, IL	3/17/1955
Sirico, Tony	Brooklyn, NY	7/29/1942
Sisto, Jeremy	Grass Valley, CA	10/6/1974
Sizemore, Tom	Detroit, MI	9/29/1961
Skerritt, Tom	Detroit, MI	8/25/1933
Slater, Christian	New York, NY	8/18/1969
Slater, Helen	Massapequa, NY	12/15/1963
Slattery, John	Boston, MA	8/13/1962
Slezak, Erika	Hollywood, CA	8/5/1946

Name	Birthplace	Birthdate
Slick, Grace	Evanston, IL	10/30/1939
Smirnoff, Karina	Kharkiv, Ukraine	1/2/1978
Smirnoff, Yakov	Odessa, Ukraine	1/24/1951
Smith, Allison	New York, NY	12/9/1969
Smith, Jaclyn	Houston, TX	10/26/1945
Smith, Jaden	Malibu, CA.	7/8/1998
Smith, Keely	Norfolk, VA	3/9/1928
Smith, Kevin	Red Bank, NJ	8/2/1970
Smith, Maggie	Ilford, England, UK	12/28/1934
Smith, Patti	Chicago, IL	12/30/1946
Smith, Robert	Blackpool, England, UK	4/21/1959
Smith, Sam	London, England, UK	5/19/1992
Smith, Will	Philadelphia, PA	9/25/1968
Smith, Willow	Los Angeles, CA	10/31/2000
Smits, Jimmy	Brooklyn, NY	7/9/1955
Smothers, Dick	Governor's Island, NY	11/20/1938
Smothers, Tom	Governor's Island, NY	2/2/1937
Smulders, Cobie	Vancouver, BC, Canada	4/3/1982
Snipes, Wesley	Orlando, FL	7/31/1962
Snooki (Nicole Polizzi)	Santiago, Chile	11/23/1987
Snoop Dogg (aka Snoop Lion, Snoopzilla)	Long Beach, CA	10/20/1971
Soderbergh, Steven	Atlanta, GA	1/14/1963
Soloway, Jill	Chicago, IL	9/26/1965
Somerhalder, Ian	Covington, LA	12/8/1978
Somers, Suzanne	San Bruno, CA.	10/16/1946
Sommer, Elke	Berlin, Germany	11/5/1940
Sorbo, Kevin	Mound, MN	9/24/1958
Sorvino, Mira	Tenafly, NJ.	9/28/1967
Sorvino, Paul	Brooklyn, NY	4/13/1939
Soul, David	Chicago, IL	8/28/1943
Spacek, Sissy	Quitman, TX	12/25/1949
Spacey, Kevin	South Orange, NJ	7/26/1959
Spade, David	Birmingham, MI	7/22/1964
Spader, James	Boston, MA	2/7/1960
Spalding, Esperanza	Portland, OR	10/18/1984
Spano, Joe	San Francisco, CA	7/7/1946
Sparks, Jordin	Phoenix, AZ.	12/22/1989
Spears, Britney	Kentwood, LA	12/2/1981
Spears, Jamie-Lynn	McComb, MS.	4/4/1991
Spector, Phil	Bronx, NY	12/26/1940
Spelling, Tori	Los Angeles, CA	5/16/1973
Spencer, Octavia	Montgomery, AL	5/25/1972
Spielberg, Steven	Cincinnati, OH	12/18/1946
Spiner, Brent	Houston, TX	2/2/1949
Springer, Jerry	London, England, UK	2/13/1944
Springfield, Rick	Sydney, NSW, Australia	8/23/1949
Springsteen, Bruce	Long Branch, NJ	9/23/1949
Spurlock, Morgan	Parksburg, WV.	11/7/1970
Stahl, Nick	Harlingen, TX	12/5/1979
Stallone, Sylvester	New York, NY	7/6/1946
Stamos, John	Cypress, CA	8/19/1963
Stamp, Terence	Stepney, England, UK	7/22/1938
Stanton, Harry Dean	West Irvine, KY	7/14/1926
Starr, Ringo.	Liverpool, England, UK	7/7/1940
Steenburgen, Mary	Newport, AR	2/8/1953
Stefani, Gwen	Fullerton, CA.	10/3/1969
Stein, Ben	Washington, DC	11/25/1944
Stern, Daniel	Bethesda, MD	8/28/1957
Stern, Howard	Roosevelt, NY	1/12/1954
Sternhagen, Frances	Washington, DC	1/13/1930
Stevens, Andrew	Memphis, TN	6/10/1955
Stevens, Cat (Yusef Islam)	London, England, UK	7/21/1948
Stevens, Connie	Brooklyn, NY	8/8/1938
Stevens, Stella	Yazoo City, MS	10/1/1936
Stevenson, Parker	Philadelphia, PA	6/4/1952
Stewart, French	Albuquerque, NM.	2/20/1964
Stewart, Jon	New York, NY	11/28/1962
Stewart, Kristen	Los Angeles, CA	4/9/1990
Stewart, Patrick	Mirfield, England, UK.	7/13/1940
Stewart, Rod	London, England, UK	1/10/1945
Stiers, David Ogden	Peoria, IL.	10/31/1942
Stiles, Julia	New York, NY	3/28/1981
Stiller, Ben	New York, NY	11/30/1965
Stiller, Jerry	Brooklyn, NY	6/8/1927
Stills, Stephen	Dallas, TX	1/3/1945
Sting	Newcastle upon Tyne, England, UK	10/2/1951
Stipe, Michael	Decatur, GA.	1/4/1960
Stockwell, Dean	North Hollywood, CA	3/5/1936
Stoltz, Eric	Whittier, CA	9/30/1961
Stone, Dee Wallace	Kansas City, KS.	12/14/1948
Stone, Emma	Scottsdale, AZ.	11/6/1988
Stone, Oliver	New York, NY	9/15/1946
Stone, Sharon	Meadville, PA.	3/10/1958
Stonestreet, Eric	Kansas City, KS.	9/9/1971
Stookey, Paul	Baltimore, MD	12/30/1937
Storch, Larry	New York, NY	1/8/1923
Stowe, Madeleine	Eagle Rock, CA.	8/18/1958
Strahan, Michael	Houston, TX	11/21/1971
Strait, George	Pearsall, TX.	5/18/1952
Strasser, Robin	New York, NY	5/7/1945
Stratas, Teresa	Toronto, ON, Canada.	5/26/1938
Strathairn, David	San Francisco, CA	1/26/1949
Strauss, Peter	Croton-on-Hudson, NY	2/20/1947
Streep, Meryl	Summit, NJ	6/22/1949
Streisand, Barbra	Brooklyn, NY	4/24/1942
Stringfield, Sherry	Colorado Springs, CO	6/24/1967
Stroman, Susan	Wilmington, DE	10/17/1954
Struthers, Sally	Portland, OR	7/28/1948
Studdard, Ruben	Frankfurt, Germany	9/12/1978
Styles, Harry	Holmes Chapel, Cheshire, Eng., UK	2/1/1994
Suchet, David	London, England, UK	5/2/1946
Sudeikis, Jason	Fairfax, VA	9/18/1975
Sullivan, Erik Per	Worcester, MA.	7/12/1991
Sullivan, Susan	New York, NY	11/18/1942
Sunjata, Daniel	Evanston, IL	12/30/1971
Sutherland, Donald	St. John, NB, Canada	7/17/1934
Sutherland, Kiefer	London, England, UK	12/21/1966
Suvari, Mena	Newport, RI	2/9/1979
Swank, Hilary	Lincoln, NE	7/30/1974
Swift, Taylor	Wyomissing, PA.	12/13/1989
Swinton, Tilda	London, England, UK	11/5/1960
Swit, Loretta	Passaic, NJ	11/4/1937
Sykes, Wanda	Portsmouth, VA	3/7/1964
Szmanda, Eric	Milwaukee, WI	7/24/1975
T, Mr.	Chicago, IL	5/21/1952
Takei, George	Los Angeles, CA	4/20/1937
Tamblyn, Amber	Santa Monica, CA	5/14/1983
Tamblyn, Russ	Los Angeles, CA	12/30/1934
Tambor, Jeffrey	San Francisco, CA.	7/8/1944
Tarantino, Quentin	Knoxville, TN	3/27/1963
Tatum, Channing	Cullman, AL.	4/26/1980
Tautou, Audrey	Beaumont, France	8/9/1976?
Taylor, Buck	Hollywood, CA.	5/13/1938
Taylor, James	Boston, MA	3/12/1948
Taylor, Lili	Glencoe, IL	2/20/1967
Taylor, Paul	Englewood, PA	7/29/1930
Taylor, Rip	Washington, DC	1/13/1934
Taymor, Julie	Newton, MA.	12/15/1952
Te Kanawa, Kiri	Gisborne, New Zealand.	3/6/1944
Teller	Philadelphia, PA	2/14/1948
Tennant, David	Bathgate, West Lothian, Scotland, UK	4/18/1971
Tennant, Victoria	London, England, UK	9/30/1950
Tennille, Toni.	Montgomery, AL	5/8/1940
Tesh, John	Garden City, NY.	7/9/1952
Tharp, Twyla	Portland, IN	7/1/1941
The Weeknd	Toronto, ON, Canada.	2/16/1990
Theron, Charlize	Benoni, South Africa	8/7/1975
Thicke, Alan	Kirkland Lake, ON, Canada	3/1/1947
Thicke, Robin	Los Angeles, CA	3/10/1977
Thiessen, Tiffani	Long Beach, CA	1/23/1974
Thomas, Jay	Kermit, TX	7/12/1948
Thomas, Jonathan Taylor	Bethlehem, PA.	9/8/1981
Thomas, Marlo	Deerfield, MI	11/21/1937
Thomas, Michael Tilson	Hollywood, CA.	12/21/1944
Thomas, Philip Michael	Columbus, OH.	5/26/1949
Thomas, Richard	New York, NY	6/13/1951
Thomas, Sean Patrick	Wilmington, DE	12/17/1970
Thompson, Emma	London, England, UK	4/15/1959
Thompson, Jack	Sydney, NSW, Australia	8/31/1940
Thompson, Kenan	Atlanta, GA	5/10/1978
Thompson, Lea	Rochester, MN.	5/31/1961
Thorne-Smith, Courtney	San Francisco, CA.	11/8/1967
Thornton, Billy Bob	Hot Springs, AR.	8/4/1955
Thurman, Uma	Boston, MA	4/29/1970
Tiegs, Cheryl	Breckenridge, MN	9/25/1947
Tierney, Maura	Boston, MA	2/3/1965
Tillis, Mel.	Tampa, FL	8/8/1932
Tilly, Jennifer	Harbor City, CA	9/16/1958
Tilly, Meg.	Long Beach, CA	2/14/1960
Timberlake, Justin.	Memphis, TN.	1/31/1981
Tisdale, Ashley	West Deal, NJ	7/2/1985
Tomei, Marisa	Brooklyn, NY	12/4/1964
Tomlin, Lily	Detroit, MI	9/1/1939
Tonioli, Bruno	Ferrara, Italy	11/25/1955
Tork, Peter	Washington, DC	2/13/1942
Torn, Rip	Temple, TX	2/6/1931
Townsend, Robert	Chicago, IL	2/6/1957
Townshend, Peter.	Chiswick, England, UK	5/19/1945
Travanti, Daniel J.	Kenosha, WI	3/7/1940
Travis, Nancy	Astoria, Queens, NY	9/21/1961
Travis, Randy	Marshville, NC	5/4/1959
Travolta, John	Englewood, NJ	2/18/1954
Trebek, Alex	Sudbury, ON, Canada	7/22/1940
Tripplehorn, Jean	Tulsa, OK	6/10/1963
Tritt, Travis	Marietta, GA	2/9/1963
Tucci, Stanley	Peekskill, NY	1/11/1960
Tucker, Chris	Decatur, GA.	8/31/1972
Tucker, Michael	Baltimore, MD	2/6/1944
Tucker, Tanya	Seminole, TX.	10/10/1958
Tune, Tommy	Wichita Falls, TX	2/28/1939
Turlington, Christy	Walnut Creek, CA	1/2/1969
Turner, Janine	Lincoln, NE	12/6/1962
Turner, Kathleen	Springfield, MO	6/19/1954
Turner, Tina	Nutbush, TN	11/26/1939
Turturro, John	Brooklyn, NY	2/28/1957

Name	Birthplace	Birthdate
Tveit, Aaron	Middletown, NY	10/21/1983
Twain, Shania	Windsor, ON, Canada	8/28/1965
Twiggy (Lawson)	London, England, UK	9/19/1949
Tyler, Liv	New York, NY	7/1/1977
Tyler, Steven	Yonkers, NY	3/26/1948
Tyson, Cicely	New York, NY	12/19/1924
Uecker, Bob	Milwaukee, WI	1/26/1934
Uggams, Leslie	New York, NY	5/25/1943
Ullman, Tracey	Slough, England, UK	12/30/1959
Ullmann, Liv	Tokyo, Japan	12/16/1938
Ulrich, Skeet	Lynchburg, VA	1/20/1970
Underwood, Blair	Tacoma, WA	8/25/1964
Underwood, Carrie	Muskogee, OK	3/10/1983
Urban, Keith	Whangarei, North Island, New Zealand	10/26/1967
Urie, Michael	Dallas, TX	8/8/1980
Usher (Raymond IV)	Dallas, TX	10/14/1978
Vaccaro, Brenda	Brooklyn, NY	11/18/1939
Valley, Mark	Ogdensburg, NY	12/24/1964
Valli, Frankie	Newark, NJ	5/3/1934
Van Ark, Joan	New York, NY	6/16/1943
Van Damme, Jean-Claude	Brussels, Belgium	10/18/1960
Van Der Beek, James	Cheshire, CT	3/8/1977
Van Doren, Mamie	Rowena, SD	2/6/1931
Van Dyke, Dick	West Plains, MO	12/13/1925
Van Dyke, Jerry	Danville, IL	7/27/1931
Van Halen, Eddie	Nijmegen, Netherlands	1/26/1955
Van Peebles, Mario	Mexico City, Mexico	1/15/1957
Van Sant, Gus	Louisville, KY	7/24/1952
Van Zandt, Steven	Winthrop, MA	11/22/1950
VanCamp, Emily	Port Perry, ON, Canada	5/12/1986
Vance, Courtney B.	Detroit, MI	3/12/1960
Vardalos, Nia	Winnipeg, MB, Canada	9/24/1962
Vaughn, Robert	New York, NY	11/22/1932
Vaughn, Vince	Minneapolis, MN	3/28/1970
Vedder, Eddie	Evanston, IL	12/23/1964
Vega, Alexa	Miami, FL	8/27/1988
Ventimiglia, Milo	Anaheim, CA	7/8/1977
Vereen, Ben	Miami, FL	10/10/1946
Vergara, Sofia	Barranquilla, Colombia	7/10/1972
Vieira, Meredith	Providence, RI	12/30/1953
Vikander, Alicia	Gothenburg, Sweden	10/3/1988
Villella, Edward	Long Island, NY	10/1/1936
Vincent, Jan-Michael	Denver, CO	7/15/1944
Vinton, Bobby	Canonsburg, PA	4/16/1935
Visnjic, Goran	Sibenik, Yugo. (Croatia)	9/9/1972
Vitale, Dick	East Rutherford, NJ	6/9/1939
Voight, Jon	Yonkers, NY	12/29/1938
Von Stade, Frederica	Somerville, NJ	6/1/1945
Von Sydow, Max	Lund, Sweden	4/10/1929
Von Trier, Lars	Copenhagen, Denmark	4/30/1956
Wagner, Jack	Washington, MO	10/3/1959
Wagner, Lindsay	Los Angeles, CA	6/22/1949
Wagner, Robert	Detroit, MI	2/10/1930
Wahl, Ken	Chicago, IL	10/31/1954
Wahlberg, Donnie	Dorchester, MA	8/17/1969
Wahlberg, Mark	Dorchester, MA	6/5/1971
Wain, Bea	Bronx, NY	4/30/1917
Waits, Tom	Pomona, CA	12/7/1949
Walden, Robert	New York, NY	9/25/1943
Walken, Christopher	Astoria, Queens, NY	3/31/1943
Walker, Clint	Hartford, IL	5/30/1927
Wallis, Quvenzhané	Houma, LA	8/23/2008
Walsh, Kate	San Jose, CA	10/13/1967
Walter, Jessica	Brooklyn, NY	1/31/1941
Waltz, Christoph	Vienna, Austria	10/4/1956
Warburton, Patrick	Paterson, NJ	11/14/1964
Ward, Fred	San Diego, CA	12/30/1942
Ward, Sela	Meridian, MS	7/11/1956
Warfield, Marsha	Chicago, IL	3/5/1954
Warner, Malcolm-Jamal	Jersey City, NJ	8/18/1970
Warren, Lesley Ann	New York, NY	8/16/1946
Warwick, Dionne	East Orange, NJ	12/12/1940
Washington, Denzel	Mt. Vernon, NY	12/28/1954
Washington, Isaiah	Houston, TX	8/3/1963
Washington, Kerry	Bronx, NY	1/31/1977
Wasikowska, Mia	Canberra, Australia	10/14/1989
Watanabe, Ken	Koide, Niigata, Japan	10/21/1959
Waters, John	Baltimore, MD	4/22/1946
Waters, Roger	Great Bookham, Eng., UK	9/6/1943
Waterston, Sam	Cambridge, MA	11/15/1940
Watson, Emily	London, England, UK	1/14/1967
Watson, Emma	Paris, France	4/15/1990
Watts, Naomi	Shoreham, England, UK	9/28/1968
Wayans, Damon	New York, NY	9/4/1960
Wayans, Keenen Ivory	Brooklyn, NY	6/8/1958
Wayans, Marlon	New York, NY	7/23/1972
Wayans, Shawn	New York, NY	1/19/1971
Weathers, Carl	New Orleans, LA	1/14/1948
Weaver, Fritz	Pittsburgh, PA	1/19/1926
Weaver, Sigourney	New York, NY	10/8/1949
Weir, Peter	Sydney, NSW, Australia	8/21/1944
Weisz, Rachel	London, England, UK	3/7/1971
Weitz, Bruce	Norwalk, CT	5/27/1943

Name	Birthplace	Birthdate
Welch, Raquel	Chicago, IL	9/5/1940
Weld, Tuesday	New York, NY	8/27/1943
Weller, Peter	Stevens Point, WI	6/24/1947
Welling, Tom	Putnam Valley, NY	4/26/1977
Wendt, George	Chicago, IL	10/17/1948
Wentz, Pete	Wilmette, IL	6/5/1979
West, Adam	Walla Walla, WA	9/19/1928
West, Kanye	Atlanta, GA	6/8/1977
West, Shane	Baton Rouge, LA	6/10/1978
Wettig, Patricia	Cincinnati, OH	12/4/1951
Whalley, Joanne	Manchester, England, UK	8/25/1964
Wheaton, Wil	Burbank, CA	7/29/1972
Whitaker, Forest	Longview, TX	7/15/1961
White, Betty	Oak Park, IL	1/17/1922
White, Jack	Detroit, MI	7/9/1975
White, Jaleel	Pasadena, CA	11/27/1976
White, Vanna	N. Myrtle Beach, SC	2/18/1957
Whitford, Bradley	Madison, WI	10/10/1959
Wiest, Dianne	Kansas City, MO	3/28/1948
Wiig, Kristen	Canandaigua, NY	8/22/1973
Wilde, Olivia	New York, NY	3/10/1984
Wilkinson, Tom	Leeds, England, UK	12/12/1948
Williams, Armstrong	Marion, SC	2/5/1959
Williams, Barry	Santa Monica, CA	9/30/1954
Williams, Billy Dee	New York, NY	4/6/1937
Williams, Cindy	Van Nuys, CA	8/22/1947
Williams, Hal	Columbus, OH	12/14/1938
Williams, Hank, Jr.	Shreveport, LA	5/26/1949
Williams, JoBeth	Houston, TX	12/6/1948
Williams, Kimberly	Rye, NY	9/14/1971
Williams, Lucinda	Lake Charles, LA	1/26/1953
Williams, Michelle	Kalispell, MT	9/9/1980
Williams, Montel	Baltimore, MD	7/3/1956
Williams, Paul	Omaha, NE	9/19/1940
Williams, Pharrell	Virginia Beach, VA	4/5/1973
Williams, Treat	Rowayton, CT	12/1/1951
Williams, Vanessa	Millwood, NY	3/18/1963
Williamson, Kevin	New Bern, NC	3/14/1965
Willis, Bruce	Idar-Oberstein, W. Germany	3/19/1955
Wilmore, Larry	Los Angeles, CA	10/30/1961
Wilson, Brian	Inglewood, CA	6/20/1942
Wilson, Cassandra	Jackson, MS	12/4/1955
Wilson, Chandra	Houston, TX	8/27/1969
Wilson, Demond	Valdosta, GA	10/13/1946
Wilson, Luke	Dallas, TX	9/21/1971
Wilson, Nancy	Chillicothe, OH	2/20/1937
Wilson, Owen	Dallas, TX	11/18/1968
Wilson, Rainn	Seattle, WA	1/20/1966
Wilson, Rebel	Sydney, NSW, Australia	2/3/1980
Winfrey, Oprah	Kosciusko, MS	1/29/1954
Winger, Debra	Cleveland, OH	5/16/1955
Winkler, Henry	New York, NY	10/30/1945
Winningham, Mare	Phoenix, AZ	5/16/1959
Winslet, Kate	Reading, England, UK	10/5/1975
Winwood, Steve	Birmingham, England, UK	5/12/1948
Withers, Jane	Atlanta, GA	4/12/1926
Witherspoon, Reese	New Orleans, LA	3/22/1976
Witt, Alicia	Worcester, MA	8/21/1975
Wolf, Scott	Boston, MA	6/4/1968
Wonder, Stevie	Saginaw, MI	5/13/1950
Wong, Faye	Beijing, China	8/8/1969
Woo, John	Guangzhou, China	5/1/1946
Wood, Elijah	Cedar Rapids, IA	1/28/1981
Woodard, Alfre	Tulsa, OK	11/8/1952
Woodley, Shailene	Simi Valley, CA	11/15/1991
Woods, James	Vernal, UT	4/18/1947
Woodward, Joanne	Thomasville, GA	2/27/1930
Wopat, Tom	Lodi, WI	9/9/1951
Worthington Sam	Godalming, Surrey, Eng., UK	8/2/1976
Wright, Jeffrey	Washington, DC	12/7/1965
Wright, Max	Detroit, MI	8/2/1943
Wright, Robin	Dallas, TX	4/8/1966
Wright, Steven	New York, NY	12/6/1955
Wyle, Noah	Hollywood, CA	6/4/1971
Wyman, Bill	London, England, UK	10/24/1936
Yankovic, Weird Al	Lynwood, CA	10/23/1959
Yanni (Chrysomallis)	Kalamata, Greece	11/14/1954
Yarrow, Peter	New York, NY	5/31/1938
Yearwood, Trisha	Monticello, GA	9/19/1964
Yoakam, Dwight	Pikesville, KY	10/23/1956
York, Michael	Fulmer, England, UK	3/27/1942
Young, Burt	New York, NY	4/30/1940
Young, Neil	Toronto, ON, Canada	11/12/1945
Young, Sean	Louisville, KY	11/20/1959
Zane, Billy	Chicago, IL	2/24/1966
Zeffirelli, Franco	Florence, Italy	2/12/1923
Zellweger, Renée	Katy, TX	4/25/1969
Zemeckis, Robert	Chicago, IL	5/14/1952
Zerbe, Anthony	Long Beach, CA	5/20/1936
Zeta-Jones, Catherine	Swansea, Wales, UK	9/25/1969
Zhang, Ziyi	Beijing, China	2/9/1979
Zimbalist, Stephanie	New York, NY	10/8/1956
Zimmer, Kim	Grand Rapids, MI	2/2/1955
Zukerman, Pinchas	Tel Aviv, Israel	7/16/1948
Zuniga, Daphne	Berkeley, CA	10/28/1962

Entertainment Personalities of the Past

See also other lists for some deceased entertainers not included here.

Name	Born	Died	Name	Born	Died	Name	Born	Died
Aaliyah (Haughton)	1979	2001	Barrymore, Maurice	1848	1905	Brady, Alice	1892	1939
Abbado, Claudio	1933	2014	Barthelmess, Richard	1895	1963	Brando, Marlon	1924	2004
Abbott, Bud	1895	1974	Bartholomew, Freddie	1924	1992	Branigan, Laura	1957	2004
Abbott, George	1887	1995	Barty, Billy	1924	2000	Brazzi, Rossano	1916	1994
Acuff, Roy	1903	1992	Basehart, Richard	1914	1984	Brennan, Eileen	1932	2013
Adams, Don	1923	2005	Basie, Count	1904	1984	Brennan, Walter	1894	1974
Adams, Edie	1927	2008	Bates, Alan	1934	2003	Brenner, David	1936	2014
Adams, Joey	1911	1999	Bavier, Frances	1902	1989	Brent, George	1904	1979
Adams, Maude	1872	1953	Baxter, Anne	1923	1985	Brett, Jeremy	1935	1995
Adler, Jacob P.	1855	1926	Baxter, Warner	1889	1951	Brewer, Teresa	1931	2007
Adoree, Renee	1898	1933	Beaumont, Hugh	1909	1982	Brice, Fanny	1891	1951
Agar, John	1921	2002	Beavers, Louise	1902	1962	Bridges, Lloyd	1913	1998
Aherne, Brian	1902	1986	Beery, Noah, Jr.	1913	1994	Broderick, Helen	1891	1959
Ailey, Alvin	1931	1989	Beery, Noah, Sr.	1884	1946	Bronson, Charles	1921	2003
Akins, Claude	1918	1994	Beery, Wallace	1885	1949	Brooks, Foster	1912	2001
Albert, Eddie	1906	2005	Begley, Ed	1901	1970	Brooks, Louise	1906	1985
Albertson, Frank	1909	1964	Bel Geddes, Barbara	1922	2005	Brown, Clarence	1890	1987
Albertson, Jack	1907	1981	Bellamy, Ralph	1904	1991	Brown, James	1933	2006
Alda, Robert	1914	1986	Belushi, John	1949	1982	Brown, Joe E.	1892	1973
Allen, Fred	1894	1956	Benaderet, Bea	1906	1968	Brown, Johnny Mack	1904	1974
Allen, Gracie	1906	1964	Bendix, William	1906	1964	Brown, Les	1912	2001
Allen, Mel	1913	1996	Bennett, Constance	1904	1965	Browne, Roscoe Lee	1925	2007
Allen, Peter	1944	1992	Bennett, Joan	1910	1990	Browning, Tod	1882	1962
Allen, Steve	1921	2000	Bennett, Michael	1943	1987	Brubeck, Dave	1920	2012
Allgood, Sara	1883	1950	Benny, Jack	1894	1974	Bruce, Lenny	1925	1966
Allyson, June	1917	2006	Berg, Gertrude	1899	1966	Bruce, Nigel	1895	1953
Altman, Robert	1925	2006	Bergen, Edgar	1903	1978	Bruce, Virginia	1910	1982
Ameche, Don	1908	1993	Bergen, Polly	1930	2014	Brynner, Yul	1915	1985
Ames, Leon	1903	1993	Bergman, Ingmar	1918	2007	Buchanan, Edgar	1903	1979
Amsterdam, Morey	1908	1996	Bergman, Ingrid	1915	1982	Buchholz, Horst	1933	2003
Anderson, G. M. "Bronco Billy"	1882	1971	Berkeley, Busby	1895	1976	Buñuel, Luis	1900	1983
Anderson, Judith	1897	1992	Berle, Milton	1908	2002	Buono, Victor	1938	1982
Anderson, Lynn	1947	2015	Berlin, Irving	1888	1989	Burke, Billie	1885	1970
Anderson, Marian	1897	1993	Bernardi, Herschel	1923	1986	Burnette, Smiley	1911	1967
Andre the Giant	1946	1993	Bernhardt, Sarah	1844	1923	Burns, George	1896	1996
Andrews, Dana	1909	1992	Bernstein, Leonard	1918	1990	Burr, Raymond	1917	1993
Andrews, Laverne	1913	1967	Berry, Jan	1941	2004	Burton, Richard	1925	1984
Andrews, Maxene	1916	1995	Bessell, Ted	1939	1996	Busch, Mae	1897	1946
Andrews, Patty	1918	2013	Bickford, Charles	1889	1967	Bushman, Francis X.	1883	1966
Angeli, Pier	1932	1971	Big Bopper, The	1930	1959	Buttons, Red	1919	2006
Antonioni, Michelangelo	1912	2007	Bikel, Theodore	1924	2015	Byington, Spring	1893	1971
Arbuckle, Fatty (Roscoe)	1887	1933	Billingsley, Barbara	1915	2010	Cabot, Bruce	1904	1972
Archerd, Army	1922	2009	Bing, Rudolf	1902	1997	Cabot, Sebastian	1918	1977
Arden, Eve	1908	1990	Bishop, Joey	1918	2007	Caesar, Sid	1922	2014
Arlen, Richard	1900	1976	Bitzer, Billy	1872	1944	Cagney, James	1899	1986
Arliss, George	1868	1946	Bixby, Bill	1934	1993	Caldwell, Sarah	1924	2006
Armstrong, Louis	1901	1971	Black, Karen	1939	2013	Calhern, Louis	1895	1956
Arnaz, Desi	1917	1986	Blackstone, Harry, Jr.	1934	1997	Calhoun, Rory	1922	1999
Arness, James	1923	2011	Blackstone, Harry, Sr.	1885	1965	Callas, Charlie	1927	2011
Arnold, Eddy	1918	2008	Blaine, Vivian	1921	1995	Callas, Maria	1923	1977
Arnold, Edward	1890	1956	Blake, Amanda	1931	1989	Calloway, Cab	1907	1994
Arquette, Cliff	1905	1974	Blake, Eubie	1883	1983	Cambridge, Godfrey	1933	1976
Arthur, Beatrice	1922	2009	Blanc, Mel	1908	1989	Campbell, Mrs. Patrick	1865	1940
Arthur, Jean	1900	1991	Blocker, Dan	1928	1972	Candy, John	1950	1994
Arzner, Dorothy	1897	1979	Blondell, Joan	1909	1979	Cantinflas	1911	1993
Ashcroft, Peggy	1907	1991	Blondin, Charles	1824	1897	Cantor, Eddie	1892	1964
Astaire, Fred	1899	1987	Blore, Eric	1887	1959	Capra, Frank	1897	1991
Astor, Mary	1906	1987	Blue, Ben	1901	1975	Carey, Harry	1878	1947
Atkins, Chet	1924	2001	Blyden, Larry	1925	1975	Carey, Harry, Jr.	1921	2012
Attenborough, Richard	1923	2014	Bogarde, Dirk	1921	1999	Carey, Macdonald	1913	1994
Atwill, Lionel	1885	1946	Bogart, Humphrey	1899	1957	Carle, Frankie	1903	2001
Auer, Mischa	1905	1967	Boland, Mary	1880	1965	Carlin, George	1937	2008
Aumont, Jean-Pierre	1911	2001	Boles, John	1895	1969	Carlisle Hart, Kitty	1910	2007
Austin, Gene	1900	1972	Bolger, Ray	1904	1987	Carney, Art	1918	2003
Autry, Gene	1907	1998	Bond, Ward	1903	1960	Carpenter, Karen	1950	1983
Axton, Hoyt	1938	1999	Bondi, Beulah	1888	1981	Carradine, David	1936	2009
Ayres, Lew	1908	1996	Bono, Sonny	1935	1998	Carradine, John	1906	1988
Bacall, Lauren	1924	2014	Boone, Richard	1917	1981	Carrillo, Leo	1880	1961
Backus, Jim	1913	1989	Booth, Edwin	1833	1893	Carroll, Leo G.	1892	1972
Bailey, Pearl	1918	1990	Booth, John Wilkes	1838	1865	Carroll, Madeleine	1906	1987
Bain, Conrad	1923	2013	Booth, Junius Brutus	1796	1852	Carson, Jack	1910	1963
Bainter, Fay	1892	1968	Booth, Shirley	1898	1992	Carson, Johnny	1925	2005
Baker, Josephine	1906	1975	Borge, Victor	1909	2000	Carter, Benny	1907	2003
Balanchine, George	1904	1983	Borgnine, Ernest	1917	2012	Carter, Dixie	1939	2010
Ball, Lucille	1911	1989	Borzage, Frank	1893	1962	Carter, Nell	1948	2003
Balsam, Martin	1919	1996	Bosley, Tom	1927	2010	Caruso, Enrico	1873	1921
Bancroft, Anne	1931	2005	Bow, Clara	1905	1965	Casals, Pablo	1876	1973
Bankhead, Tallulah	1902	1968	Bowes, Maj. Edward	1874	1946	Cash, Johnny	1932	2003
Bara, Theda	1885?	1955	Bowie, David	1947	2016	Cash, June Carter	1929	2003
Barnett, Etta Moten	1902	2004	Bowman, Lee	1914	1979	Cass, Peggy	1924	1999
Barnum, Phineas T.	1810	1891	Boxcar Willie	1931	1999	Cassavetes, John	1929	1989
Barrett, Syd	1946	2006	Boyd, Stephen	1928	1977	Cassidy, Jack	1927	1976
Barry, Gene	1919	2009	Boyd, William	1898	1972	Castle, Irene	1893	1969
Barrymore, Ethel	1879	1959	Boyer, Charles	1899	1978	Castle, Vernon	1887	1918
Barrymore, John	1882	1942	Boyle, Peter	1935	2006	Chaliapin, Feodor	1873	1938
Barrymore, Lionel	1878	1954	Bracken, Eddie	1915	2002	Champion, Gower	1919	1980

Name	Born	Died
Chandler, Jeff	1918	1961
Chaney, Lon	1883	1930
Chaney, Lon, Jr.	1905	1973
Chapin, Harry	1942	1981
Chaplin, Charles	1889	1977
Chapman, Graham	1941	1989
Charisse, Cyd	1921	2008
Charles, Ray	1930	2004
Chase, Ilka	1905	1978
Chatterton, Ruth	1893	1961
Cherrill, Virginia	1908	1996
Chevalier, Maurice	1888	1972
Child, Julia	1912	2004
Clair, René	1898	1981
Clark, Dick	1929	2012
Clayburgh, Jill	1944	2010
Clayton, Jan	1917	1983
Clemons, Clarence	1942	2011
Cliburn, Van	1934	2013
Clift, Montgomery	1920	1966
Cline, Patsy	1932	1963
Clooney, Rosemary	1928	2002
Clyde, Andy	1892	1967
Cobain, Kurt	1967	1994
Cobb, Lee J.	1911	1976
Coburn, Charles	1877	1961
Coburn, James	1928	2002
Coca, Imogene	1908	2001
Cocker, Joe	1944	2014
Coco, James	1930	1987
Cody, Buffalo Bill	1846	1917
Cody, Iron Eyes	1907	1999
Cohan, George M.	1878	1942
Cohen, Myron	1902	1986
Colbert, Claudette	1903	1996
Cole, Nat "King"	1919	1965
Cole, Natalie	1950	2015
Coleman, Gary	1968	2010
Coleman, Ornette	1930	2015
Collins, Gary	1938	2012
Collins, Ray	1890	1965
Colman, Ronald	1891	1958
Columbo, Russ	1908	1934
Comden, Betty	1917	2006
Como, Perry	1912	2001
Conniff, Ray	1916	2002
Connors, Chuck	1921	1992
Conrad, William	1920	1994
Conried, Hans	1917	1982
Conte, Richard	1911	1975
Convy, Bert	1933	1991
Conway, Tom	1904	1967
Coogan, Jackie	1914	1984
Cook, Elisha, Jr.	1904	1995
Cooke, Alistair	1908	2004
Cooke, Sam	1931	1964
Cooper, Gary	1901	1961
Cooper, Gladys	1888	1971
Cooper, Jackie	1922	2011
Copland, Aaron	1900	1990
Corby, Ellen	1913	1999
Corelli, Franco	1921	2003
Corey, Jeff	1914	2002
Corio, Ann	1914	1999
Corley, Pat	1930	2006
Cornelius, Don	1936	2012
Cornell, Katharine	1893	1974
Correll, Charles	1890	1972
Costello, Dolores	1905	1979
Costello, Lou	1906	1959
Cotten, Joseph	1905	1994
Coward, Noel	1899	1973
Cox, Wally	1924	1973
Crabbe, Buster	1908	1983
Crain, Jeanne	1925	2003
Crane, Bob	1928	1978
Craven, Wes	1939	2015
Crawford, Broderick	1911	1986
Crawford, Joan	1904	1977
Crenna, Richard	1926	2003
Crews, Laura Hope	1880	1942
Crisp, Donald	1880	1974
Crisp, Quentin	1908	1999
Croce, Jim	1942	1973
Cronyn, Hume	1911	2003
Crosby, Bing	1903	1977
Crothers, Scatman	1910	1986

Name	Born	Died
Cruz, Celia	1925	2003
Cugat, Xavier	1900	1990
Cukor, George	1899	1983
Cullen, Bill	1920	1990
Culp, Robert	1930	2010
Cummings, Constance	1910	2005
Cummings, Robert	1908	1990
Curtis, Ken	1916	1991
Curtis, Tony	1925	2010
Curtiz, Michael	1888	1962
Cushing, Peter	1913	1994
Da Silva, Howard	1909	1986
Dailey, Dan	1915	1978
Dandridge, Dorothy	1923	1965
Dangerfield, Rodney	1921	2004
Daniell, Henry	1894	1963
Daniels, Bebe	1901	1971
Darin, Bobby	1936	1973
Darnell, Linda	1923	1965
Darwell, Jane	1879	1967
Davenport, Harry	1866	1949
Davies, Marion	1897	1961
Davis, Ann B.	1926	2014
Davis, Bette	1908	1989
Davis, Joan	1907	1961
Davis, Ossie	1917	2005
Davis, Sammy, Jr.	1925	1990
Dawson, Richard	1932	2012
Day, Dennis	1917	1988
Day, Laraine	1920	2007
De Carlo, Yvonne	1922	2007
De Laurentiis, Dino	1919	2010
de Mille, Agnes	1905	1993
De Mille, Cecil B.	1881	1959
De Wilde, Brandon	1942	1972
De Wolfe, Billy	1907	1974
Dean, James	1931	1955
Dean, Jimmy	1928	2010
Dearie, Blossom	1924	2009
Dee, Frances	1907	2004
Dee, Ruby	1922	2014
Dee, Sandra	1942	2005
Defore, Don	1917	1993
DeFranco, Buddy	1923	2014
DeHaven, Gloria	1925	2016
Dekker, Albert	1905	1968
Del Rio, Dolores	1905	1983
DeLuise, Dom	1933	2009
Demarest, William	1892	1983
Dennis, Sandy	1937	1992
Denny, Reginald	1891	1967
Denver, Bob	1935	2005
Denver, John	1943	1997
Derek, John	1926	1998
DeSica, Vittorio	1901	1974
Devine, Andy	1905	1977
Dewhurst, Colleen	1924	1991
Diamond, Selma	1920	1985
Diddley, Bo	1928	2008
Dietrich, Marlene	1901	1992
Diller, Phyllis	1917	2012
Disney, Walt	1901	1966
Dix, Richard	1894	1949
Dmytryk, Edward	1908	1999
Donahue, Troy	1936	2001
Donat, Robert	1905	1958
Donlevy, Brian	1901	1972
Dors, Diana	1931	1984
Dorsey, Jimmy	1904	1957
Dorsey, Tommy	1905	1956
Douglas, Melvyn	1901	1981
Douglas, Paul	1907	1959
Dove, Billie	1900	1998
Downey, Morton, Jr.	1933	2001
Doyle, David	1929	1997
Drake, Alfred	1914	1992
Draper, Ruth	1884	1956
Dressler, Marie	1869	1934
Drew, Ellen	1915	2003
Drew, Mrs. John	1820	1897
Dru, Joanne	1923	1996
Duchin, Eddy	1909	1951
Duff, Howard	1917	1990
Duggan, Andrew	1923	1988
Duke, Patty	1946	2016
Dumbrille, Douglass	1890	1974

Name	Born	Died
Dumont, Margaret	1889	1965
Duncan, Isadora	1878	1927
Duncan, Michael Clarke	1957	2012
Dunham, Katherine	1910	2006
Dunn, James	1905	1967
Dunne, Irene	1898	1990
Dunnock, Mildred	1901	1991
Durante, Jimmy	1893	1980
Durbin, Deanna	1921	2013
Durning, Charles	1923	2012
Duryea, Dan	1907	1968
Duse, Eleanora	1858	1924
Dvorak, Ann	1912	1979
Dysart, Richard	1929	2015
Eagels, Jeanne	1894	1929
Ebert, Roger	1942	2013
Ebsen, Buddy	1908	2003
Eckstine, Billy	1914	1993
Eddy, Nelson	1901	1967
Edelman, Herb	1933	1996
Edwards, Blake	1922	2010
Edwards, Cliff	1895	1971
Edwards, Ralph	1913	2005
Edwards, Vince	1928	1996
Egan, Richard	1923	1987
Eisenstein, Sergei	1898	1948
Ekberg, Anita	1931	2015
Elam, Jack	1916	2003
Ellington, Duke	1899	1974
Elliot, Cass	1941	1974
Elliott, Bob	1923	2016
Elliott, Denholm	1922	1992
Ellis, Mary	1897	2003
Elman, Mischa	1891	1967
Ephron, Nora	1941	2012
Errol, Leon	1881	1951
Evans, Dale	1912	2001
Evans, Edith	1888	1976
Evans, Maurice	1901	1989
Everett, Chad	1936?	2012
Everly, Phil	1939	2014
Ewell, Tom	1909	1994
Fadiman, Clifton	1904	1999
Fairbanks, Douglas	1883	1939
Fairbanks, Douglas, Jr.	1909	2000
Falk, Peter	1927	2011
Farentino, James	1938	2012
Farina, Dennis	1944	2013
Farley, Chris	1964	1997
Farmer, Frances	1913	1970
Farnsworth, Richard	1920	2000
Farnum, Dustin	1874	1929
Farnum, William	1876	1953
Farrar, Geraldine	1882	1967
Farrell, Charles	1901	1990
Farrell, Eileen	1920	2002
Fassbinder, Rainer Werner	1946	1982
Fawcett, Farrah	1947	2009
Faye, Alice	1915	1998
Fazenda, Louise	1895	1962
Feld, Fritz	1900	1993
Feldman, Marty	1933	1982
Fell, Norman	1924	1998
Fellini, Federico	1920	1993
Fenneman, George	1919	1997
Ferrer, Jose	1912	1992
Ferrer, Mel	1917	2008
Fetchit, Stepin	1898	1985
Fiedler, Arthur	1894	1979
Fiedler, John	1925	2005
Fields, Gracie	1898	1979
Fields, Totie	1930	1978
Fields, W. C.	1879	1946
Finch, Peter	1916	1977
Fine, Larry	1902	1975
Fisher, Eddie	1928	2010
Fiske, Minnie Maddern	1865	1932
Fitzgerald, Barry	1888	1961
Fitzgerald, Ella	1917	1996
Fitzgerald, Geraldine	1913	2005
Fleischer, Richard	1916	2006
Fleming, Art	1924	1995
Fleming, Victor	1889	1949
Flynn, Errol	1909	1959
Flynn, Joe	1925	1974
Foch, Nina	1924	2008
Fogelberg, Dan	1951	2007

Name	Born	Died	Name	Born	Died	Name	Born	Died
Foley, Red	1910	1968	Goodman, Benny	1909	1986	Hayworth, Rita	1918	1987
Fonda, Henry	1905	1982	Gorcey, Leo	1917	1969	Head, Edith	1897	1981
Fontaine, Frank	1920	1978	Gordon, Gale	1906	1995	Healy, Ted	1896	1937
Fontaine, Joan	1917	2013	Gordon, Ruth	1896	1985	Heckart, Eileen	1919	2001
Fontanne, Lynn	1887	1983	Gorme, Eydie	1932	2013	Heflin, Van	1910	1971
Fonteyn, Margot	1919	1991	Gorshin, Frank	1934	2005	Heifetz, Jascha	1901	1987
Ford, Glenn	1916	2006	Gosden, Freeman	1899	1982	Held, Anna	1873	1918
Ford, John	1895	1973	Gottschalk, Louis	1829	1869	Helm, Levon	1940	2012
Ford, Paul	1901	1976	Gould, Glenn	1932	1982	Hemingway, Margaux	1955	1996
Ford, Tennessee Ernie	1919	1991	Gould, Harold	1923	2010	Hemmings, David	1941	2003
Forrest, Helen	1917	1999	Gould, Morton	1913	1996	Hemsley, Sherman	1938	2012
Forsythe, John	1918	2010	Goulet, Robert	1933	2007	Henderson, Skitch	1918	2005
Fosse, Bob	1927	1987	Grable, Betty	1916	1973	Hendrix, Jimi	1942	1970
Foster, Phil	1914	1985	Graham, Martha	1894	1991	Henie, Sonja	1912	1969
Foster, Preston	1901	1970	Graham, Virginia	1912	1998	Henreid, Paul	1908	1992
Foxx, Redd	1922	1991	Grahame, Gloria	1925	1981	Henson, Jim	1936	1990
Foy, Eddie	1856	1928	Granger, Farley	1925	2011	Hepburn, Audrey	1929	1993
Franchi, Sergio	1926	1990	Granger, Stewart	1913	1993	Hepburn, Katharine	1907	2003
Franciosa, Anthony	1928	2006	Grant, Cary	1904	1986	Herrmann, Edward	1943	2014
Francis, Anne	1930	2011	Granville, Bonita	1923	1988	Hersholt, Jean	1886	1956
Francis, Arlene	1907	2001	Grapewin, Charley	1869	1956	Heston, Charlton	1923	2008
Francis, Kay	1905	1968	Graves, Peter	1926	2010	Hewett, Christopher	1922	2001
Franciscus, James	1934	1991	Gray, Dolores	1924	2002	Hickey, William	1928	1997
Frankenheimer, John	1930	2002	Gray, Spalding	1941	2004	Hickson, Joan	1906	1998
Franklin, Bonnie	1944	2013	Grayson, Kathryn	1922	2010	Hildegarde	1906	2005
Frann, Mary	1943	1998	Greco, Jose	1918	2000	Hill, Arthur	1922	2006
Frawley, William	1887	1966	Green, Adolph	1915	2002	Hill, Benny	1925	1992
Frederick, Pauline	1885	1938	Greene, Lorne	1915	1987	Hill, George Roy	1921	2002
Freed, Alan	1921	1965	Greenstreet, Sydney	1879	1954	Hiller, Wendy	1912	2003
Freeman, Al, Jr.	1934	2012	Greenwood, Charlotte	1890	1978	Hines, Gregory	1946	2003
Freeman, Mona	1926	2014	Gregory, James	1911	2002	Hines, Jerome	1921	2003
French, Victor	1934	1989	Griffin, Merv	1925	2007	Hingle, Pat	1924	2009
Friganza, Trixie	1870	1955	Griffith, Andy	1926	2012	Hirt, Al	1922	1999
Froman, Jane	1907	1980	Griffith, David Wark	1874	1948	Hitchcock, Alfred	1899	1980
Frost, David	1939	2013	Griffith, Hugh	1912	1980	Ho, Don	1930	2007
Funicello, Annette	1942	2013	Griffiths, Richard	1947	2013	Hodiak, John	1914	1955
Funt, Allen	1914	1999	Grizzard, George	1928	2007	Hoffman, Philip Seymour	1967	2014
Furness, Betty	1916	1994	Guardino, Harry	1925	1995	Holden, William	1918	1981
Gabin, Jean	1904	1976	Guinness, Sir Alec	1914	2000	Holder, Geoffrey	1930	2014
Gable, Clark	1901	1960	Guthrie, Woody	1912	1967	Holiday, Billie	1915	1959
Gabor, Eva	1920	1995	Gwenn, Edmund	1875	1959	Holliday, Judy	1921	1965
Gandolfini, James	1961	2013	Gwynne, Fred	1926	1993	Holloway, Sterling	1905	1992
Garagiola, Joe	1926	2016	Hackett, Buddy	1924	2003	Holly, Buddy	1936	1959
Garbo, Greta	1905	1990	Hackett, Joan	1934	1983	Holm, Celeste	1919	2012
Garcia, Jerry	1942	1995	Hagen, Uta	1919	2004	Holt, Jack	1888	1951
Gardenia, Vincent	1922	1992	Haggard, Merle	1937	2016	Holt, Tim	1918	1973
Gardner, Ava	1922	1990	Hagman, Larry	1931	2012	Homolka, Oscar	1898	1978
Garfield, John	1913	1952	Haines, William	1900	1973	Hooker, John Lee	1917	2001
Garland, Beverly	1926	2008	Hale, Alan, Jr.	1918	1990	Hoon, Shannon	1967	1995
Garland, Judy	1922	1969	Hale, Alan, Sr.	1892	1950	Hope, Bob	1903	2003
Garner, James	1928	2014	Haley, Bill	1925	1981	Hopkins, Miriam	1902	1972
Garrett, Betty	1919	2011	Haley, Jack	1899	1979	Hopper, Dennis	1936	2010
Garson, Greer	1904	1996	Hall, Huntz	1919	1999	Hopper, DeWolf	1858	1935
Gassman, Vittorio	1922	2000	Hall, Jon	1915	1979	Hopper, Hedda	1885	1966
Gaye, Marvin	1939	1984	Hamilton, Margaret	1902	1985	Hopper, William	1915	1970
Gaynor, Janet	1906	1984	Hammerstein, Oscar	1847	1919	Horowitz, Vladimir	1904	1989
Gazzara, Ben	1930	2012	Hammerstein, Oscar, II	1895	1960	Horne, Lena	1917	2010
Gebel-Williams, Gunther	1934	2001	Hampton, Lionel	1908	2002	Horton, Edward Everett	1886	1970
Geer, Will	1902	1978	Hardwicke, Cedric	1893	1964	Hoskins, Bob	1942	2014
George, Gladys	1904	1954	Hardy, Oliver	1892	1957	Houdini, Harry	1874	1926
Gershwin, George	1898	1937	Harlow, Jean	1911	1937	Houseman, John	1902	1988
Getty, Estelle	1923	2008	Harrington, Pat, Jr.	1929	2016	Houston, Whitney	1963	2012
Ghostley, Alice	1926	2007	Harris, Julie	1925	2013	Howard (Horwitz), Curly	1903	1952
Gibb, Andy	1958	1988	Harris, Phil	1904	1995	Howard, Ken	1944	2016
Gibb, Maurice	1949	2003	Harris, Richard	1930	2002	Howard, Leslie	1890	1943
Gibb, Robin	1949	2012	Harrison, George	1943	2001	Howard (Horwitz), Moe	1897	1975
Gibson, Henry	1935	2009	Harrison, Rex	1908	1990	Howard (Horwitz), Shemp	1895	1955
Gibson, Hoot	1892	1962	Hart, William S.	1864	1946	Howard, Trevor	1916	1988
Gielgud, John	1904	2000	Hartman, Phil	1948	1998	Hudson, Rock	1925	1985
Gifford, Frank	1930	2015	Harvey, Laurence	1928	1973	Hughes, Bernard	1915	2006
Gilbert, Billy	1894	1971	Harvey, Paul	1918	2009	Hughes, John	1950	2009
Gilbert, John	1895	1936	Harwell, Ernie	1918	2010	Hull, Henry	1890	1977
Gilford, Jack	1907	1990	Hatfield, Bobby	1940	2003	Hull, Josephine	1886	1957
Gillespie, Dizzy	1917	1993	Havens, Richie	1941	2013	Hunter, Jeffrey	1926	1969
Gillette, William	1853	1937	Havoc, June	1912	2010	Hunter, Kim	1922	2002
Gingold, Hermione	1897	1987	Hawkins, Jack	1910	1973	Hunter, Ross	1920	1996
Gish, Dorothy	1898	1968	Hawkins, Screamin' Jay	1929	2000	Hussey, Ruth	1911	2005
Gish, Lillian	1893	1993	Hawks, Howard	1896	1977	Huston, John	1906	1987
Giulini, Carlo Maria	1914	2005	Hawthorne, Nigel	1929	2001	Huston, Walter	1884	1950
Gleason, Jackie	1916	1987	Hayakawa, Sessue	1890	1973	Hutchence, Michael	1960	1997
Gleason, James	1886	1959	Hayden, Sterling	1916	1986	Hutton, Betty	1921	2007
Gluck, Alma	1884	1938	Hayes, Gabby	1885	1969	Hutton, Jim	1934	1979
Gobel, George	1919	1991	Hayes, Helen	1900	1993	Hyde-White, Wilfrid	1903	1991
Goddard, Paulette	1905?	1990	Hayes, Isaac	1942	2008	Ingram, Rex	1895	1969
Godfrey, Arthur	1903	1983	Hayward, Leland	1902	1971	Ireland, Jill	1936	1990
Godunov, Alexander	1949	1995	Hayward, Louis	1909	1985	Ireland, John	1915	1992
Goldwyn, Samuel	1882	1974	Hayward, Susan	1917	1975	Irving, Henry	1838	1905

Name	Born	Died	Name	Born	Died	Name	Born	Died
Ives, Burl	1909	1995	Kinski, Klaus	1926	1991	Lombardo, Guy	1902	1977
Irwin, Steve	1962	2006	Kirby, Bruno	1949	2006	Long, Richard	1927	1974
Iturbi, Jose	1895	1980	Kirby, George	1923	1995	Lopes, Lisa	1971	2002
Jack, Wolfman	1938	1995	Kirby, Durward	1912	2000	Lopez, Vincent	1895	1975
Jackson, Anne	1926	2016	Kitt, Eartha	1927	2008	Lord, Jack	1920	1998
Jackson, Joe	1875	1942	Klemperer, Werner	1920	2000	Lorne, Marion	1888	1968
Jackson, Mahalia	1911	1972	Klugman, Jack	1922	2012	Lorre, Peter	1904	1964
Jackson, Michael	1958	2009	Knievel, Evel	1938	2007	Loudon, Dorothy	1925	2003
Jackson, Milt	1923	1999	Knight, Ted	1923	1986	Lowe, Edmund	1890	1971
Jaeckel, Richard	1926	1997	Knotts, Don	1924	2006	Loy, Myrna	1905	1993
Jaffe, Sam	1891	1984	Korman, Harvey	1927	2008	Lubitsch, Ernst	1892	1947
Jagger, Dean	1903	1991	Kostelanetz, Andre	1901	1980	Ludden, Allen	1918	1981
Jam Master Jay	1965	2002	Kovacs, Ernie	1919	1962	Lugosi, Bela	1882	1956
James, Dennis	1917	1997	Kramer, Stanley	1913	2001	Lukas, Paul	1894	1971
James, Etta	1938	2012	Kruger, Otto	1885	1974	Lumet, Sidney	1924	2011
James, Harry	1916	1983	Kubrick, Stanley	1928	1999	Lunt, Alfred	1892	1977
James, Rick	1948	2004	Kulp, Nancy	1921	1991	Lupino, Ida	1918	1995
Janis, Elsie	1889	1956	Kurosawa, Akira	1910	1998	Lymon, Frankie	1942	1968
Jannings, Emil	1886	1950	Kyser, Kay	1906	1985	Lynde, Paul	1926	1982
Janssen, David	1930	1980	Ladd, Alan	1913	1964	Maazel, Lorin	1930	2014
Jenkins, Allen	1900	1974	Lahr, Bert	1895	1967	Mac, Bernie	1957	2008
Jennings, Waylon	1937	2002	Laine, Frankie	1913	2007	MacArthur, James	1937	2010
Jessel, George	1898	1981	Lake, Arthur	1905	1987	MacCorkindale, Simon	1952	2010
Jeter, Michael	1952	2003	Lake, Veronica	1919	1973	MacDonald, Jeanette	1903	1965
Johnson, Ben	1918	1996	LaLanne, Jack	1914	2011	Mack, Ted	1904	1976
Johnson, Celia	1908	1982	Lamarr, Hedy	1913	2000	MacKenzie, Gisele	1927	2003
Johnson, Chic	1892	1962	Lamas, Fernando	1915	1982	MacLane, Barton	1902	1969
Johnson, J.J.	1924	2001	Lamour, Dorothy	1914	1996	MacMurray, Fred	1908	1991
Johnson, Robert	1911	1938	Lancaster, Burt	1913	1994	MacNee, Patrick	1922	2015
Johnson, Van	1916	2008	Lanchester, Elsa	1902	1986	MacRae, Gordon	1921	1986
Jolson, Al	1886	1950	Landis, Carole	1919	1948	Macready, George	1909	1973
Jones, Brian	1942	1969	Landon, Michael	1936	1991	Madison, Guy	1922	1996
Jones, Buck	1889	1942	Lane, Priscilla	1917	1995	Magnani, Anna	1908	1973
Jones, Carolyn	1933	1983	Lang, Fritz	1890	1976	Mancini, Henry	1924	1994
Jones, Charlie	1930	2008	Langdon, Harry	1884	1944	Main, Marjorie	1890	1975
Jones, Davy	1945	2012	Lange, Hope	1931	2003	Malden, Karl	1912	2009
Jones, Dean	1931	2015	Langford, Frances	1914	2005	Malle, Louis	1932	1995
Jones, Elvin	1927	2004	Langtry, Lillie	1853	1929	Mamoulian, Rouben	1897	1987
Jones, George	1931	2013	Lanza, Mario	1921	1959	Mankiewicz, Joseph	1909	1993
Jones, Henry	1912	1999	LaRue, Lash (Alfred)	1917	1996	Mann, Herbie	1930	2003
Jones, Jennifer	1919	2009	Lauder, Harry	1870	1950	Mansfield, Jayne	1932	1967
Jones, Spike	1911	1965	Laughton, Charles	1899	1962	Mantovani, Annunzio	1905	1980
Joplin, Janis	1943	1970	Laurel, Stan	1890	1965	Marais, Jean	1913	1998
Joplin, Scott	1868	1917	Lawford, Peter	1923	1984	March, Fredric	1897	1975
Jordan, Richard	1937	1993	Lawrence, Florence	1886	1938	March, Hal	1920	1970
Jory, Victor	1902	1982	Lawrence, Gertrude	1898	1952	Marchand, Nancy	1928	2000
Joslyn, Allyn	1905	1981	Lean, David	1908	1991	Markova, Alicia	1910	2004
Jourdan, Louis	1921	2015	Ledger, Heath	1979	2008	Marley, Bob	1945	1981
Julia, Raul	1940	1994	Lee, Anna	1913	2004	Marriner, Neville	1924	2016
Jump, Gordon	1932	2003	Lee, Bernard	1908	1981	Marshall, E. G.	1910?	1998
Jurado, Katy	1924	2002	Lee, Bruce	1940	1973	Marshall, Garry	1934	2016
Jurgens, Curt	1915	1982	Lee, Canada	1907	1952	Marshall, Herbert	1890	1966
Kahn, Madeline	1942	1999	Lee, Christopher	1922	2015	Martin, Barney	1923	2005
Kane, Helen	1904	1966	Lee, Gypsy Rose	1914	1970	Martin, Dean	1917	1995
Kanin, Garson	1912	1999	Lee, Peggy	1920	2002	Martin, Dick	1922	2008
Karloff, Boris	1887	1969	LeGallienne, Eva	1899	1991	Martin, Mary	1913	1990
Karns, Roscoe	1893	1970	Leigh, Janet	1927	2004	Martin, Ross	1920	1981
Karras, Alex	1935	2012	Leigh, Vivien	1913	1967	Martin, Tony	1913	2012
Kasem, Casey	1932	2014	Leighton, Margaret	1922	1976	Marvin, Lee	1924	1987
Kaufman, Andy	1949	1984	Lemmon, Jack	1925	2001	Marx, Harpo (Arthur)	1888	1964
Kaye, Danny	1913	1987	Lennon, John	1940	1980	Marx, Zeppo (Herbert)	1901	1979
Kaye, Stubby	1918	1997	Lenya, Lotte	1898	1981	Marx, Groucho (Julius)	1890	1977
Kazan, Elia	1909	2003	Leonard, Eddie	1870	1941	Marx, Chico (Leonard)	1887	1961
Kean, Charles	1811	1868	Leonard, Sheldon	1907	1997	Marx, Gummo (Milton)	1893	1977
Kean, Mrs. Charles	1806	1880	Leone, Sergio	1929	1989	Mason, James	1909	1984
Kean, Edmund	1787	1833	LeRoy, Mervyn	1900	1987	Massey, Raymond	1896	1983
Keaton, Buster	1895	1966	Leslie, Joan	1925	2015	Mastroianni, Marcello	1924	1996
Keel, Howard	1919	2004	Levant, Oscar	1906	1972	Masur, Kurt	1927	2015
Keeler, Ruby	1910	1993	Levene, Sam	1905	1980	Matthau, Walter	1920	2000
Keeshan, Bob (Captain			Levenson, Sam	1911	1980	Mature, Victor	1913	1999
Kangaroo)	1927	2004	Lewis, Al	1923	2006	Maxwell, Marilyn	1921	1972
Keith, Brian	1921	1997	Lewis, Joe E.	1902	1971	Mayer, Louis B.	1885	1957
Kellaway, Cecil	1893	1973	Lewis, Shari	1934	1998	Mayfield, Curtis	1942	1999
Kelley, DeForest	1920	1999	Lewis, Ted	1892	1971	Mayo, Virginia	1920	2005
Kelly, Emmett	1898	1979	Liberace	1919	1987	Mazurki, Mike	1909	1990
Kelly, Gene	1912	1996	Lillie, Beatrice	1894	1989	Mazursky, Paul	1930	2014
Kelly, Grace	1929	1982	Lincoln, Elmo	1889	1952	MCA (Adam Yauch)	1964	2012
Kelly, Jack	1927	1992	Lind, Jenny	1820	1887	McCambridge, Mercedes	1916	2004
Kelly, Patsy	1910	1981	Lindfors, Viveca	1920	1995	McCarey, Leo	1898	1969
Kennedy, Arthur	1914	1990	Lindley, Audra	1918	1997	McCarthy, Kevin	1914	2010
Kennedy, Edgar	1890	1948	Linkletter, Art	1912	2010	McCartney, Linda	1941	1998
Kennedy, George	1925	2016	Linville, Larry	1939	2000	McClanahan, Rue	1934	2010
Kerr, Deborah	1921	2007	Little, Cleavon	1939	1992	McClure, Doug	1935	1995
Kibbee, Guy	1886	1956	Llewelyn, Desmond	1914	1999	McCormack, John	1884	1945
Kiel, Richard	1939	2014	Lloyd, Harold	1893	1971	McCrary, Tex	1910	2003
Kilbride, Percy	1888	1964	Lloyd, Marie	1870	1922	McCrea, Joel	1905	1990
Kiley, Richard	1922	1999	Lockhart, Gene	1891	1957	McDaniel, Hattie	1895	1952
King, Alan	1927	2004	Loggia, Robert	1930	2015	McDowall, Roddy	1928	1998
King, B. B.	1925	2015	Lom, Herbert	1917	2012	McFarland, Spanky (George)	1928	1993
King, Henry	1896	1982	Lombard, Carole	1908	1942	McGoohan, Patrick	1928	2009

Name	Born	Died	Name	Born	Died	Name	Born	Died
McGuire, Al	1931	2001	Munsel, Patrice	1925	2016	Parker, Fess	1925	2010
McGuire, Dorothy	1916	2001	Munshin, Jules	1915	1970	Parker, Jean	1915	2005
McHugh, Frank	1898	1981	Murnau, F. W.	1888	1931	Parks, Bert	1914	1992
McIntire, John	1907	1991	Murphy, Audie	1924	1971	Parks, Larry	1914	1975
McLaglen, Victor	1886	1959	Murphy, Brittany	1977	2009	Pasternack, Josef A.	1881	1940
McMahon, Ed	1923	2009	Murphy, George	1902	1992	Pastor, Tony (vaudevillian)	1837	1908
McNeill, Don	1907	1996	Murray, Arthur	1895	1991	Pastor, Tony (bandleader)	1907	1969
McPartland, Marian	1918	2013	Murray, Kathryn	1906	1999	Patrick, Gail	1911	1980
McQueen, Butterfly	1911	1995	Murray, Mae	1889	1965	Patti, Adelina	1843	1919
McQueen, Steve	1930	1980	Nagel, Conrad	1897	1970	Patti, Carlotta	1840	1889
Meader, Vaughn	1936	2004	Naish, J. Carroll	1900	1973	Paul, Les	1915	2009
Meadows, Audrey	1924	1996	Naldi, Nita	1898	1961	Pavarotti, Luciano	1935	2007
Meadows, Jayne	1919	2015	Nance, Jack	1943	1996	Pavlova, Anna	1885	1931
Meara, Anne	1929	2015	Natwick, Mildred	1908	1994	Paycheck, Johnny	1938	2003
Meek, Donald	1880	1946	Nazimova, Alla	1879	1945	Payne, John	1912	1989
Meeker, Ralph	1920	1988	Neal, Patricia	1926	2010	Pearl, Minnie	1912	1996
Melba, Nellie	1861	1931	Negri, Pola	1897	1987	Peck, Gregory	1916	2003
Méliès, Georges	1861	1938	Nelson, David	1936	2011	Peckinpah, Sam	1925	1984
Menjou, Adolphe	1890	1963	Nelson, Ed	1928	2014	Peerce, Jan	1904	1984
Menken, Helen	1902	1966	Nelson, Harriet (Hilliard)	1909	1994	Pendergrass, Teddy	1950	2010
Menuhin, Yehudi	1916	1999	Nelson, Ozzie	1906	1975	Penn, Arthur	1922	2010
Mercer, Marian	1935	2011	Nelson, Rick	1940	1985	Penn, Chris	1965	2006
Mercouri, Melina	1925	1994	Nesbit, Evelyn	1884	1967	Penner, Joe	1905	1941
Mercury, Freddie	1946	1991	Nettleton, Lois	1927	2008	Peppard, George	1928	1994
Meredith, Burgess	1909	1997	Newley, Anthony	1931	1999	Perkins, Anthony	1932	1992
Merman, Ethel	1908	1984	Newman, Edwin	1919	2010	Perkins, Carl	1932	1998
Merrick, David	1911	2000	Newman, Paul	1925	2008	Perkins, Marlin	1905	1986
Merrill, Gary	1915	1990	Nicholas, Fayard	1914	2006	Peters, Brock	1927	2005
Milestone, Lewis	1895	1980	Nicholas, Harold	1924	2000	Peters, Jean	1926	2000
Mifune, Toshiro	1920	1997	Nichols, Mike	1931	2014	Peters, Susan	1921	1952
Milland, Ray	1905	1986	Nielsen, Leslie	1926	2010	Peterson, Oscar	1925	2007
Miller, Ann	1923	2004	Nijinsky, Vaslav	1890	1950	Phillips, John	1935	2001
Miller, Glenn	1904	1944	Nilsson, Anna Q.	1888	1974	Phoenix, River	1970	1993
Miller, Marilyn	1898	1936	Nimoy, Leonard	1931	2015	Piaf, Edith	1915	1963
Miller, Mitch	1911	2010	Niven, David	1910	1983	Pickens, Slim	1919	1983
Miller, Roger	1936	1992	Nolan, Lloyd	1902	1985	Pickett, Wilson	1941	2006
Mills, Donald	1915	1999	Normand, Mabel	1894	1930	Pickford, Mary	1892	1979
Mills, Harry	1913	1982	North, Sheree	1933	2005	Picon, Molly	1898	1992
Mills, Herbert	1912	1989	Notorious B.I.G.	1972	1997	Pidgeon, Walter	1897	1984
Mills, John	1889	1967	Novarro, Ramon	1899	1968	Pinza, Ezio	1892	1957
Mills, Sir John	1908	2005	Nureyev, Rudolf	1938	1993	Pitney, Gene	1941	2006
Milner, Martin	1931	2015	Oakie, Jack	1903	1978	Pitts, Zasu	1898	1963
Mineo, Sal	1939	1976	Oakley, Annie	1860	1926	Plato, Dana	1964	1999
Miner, Jan	1917	2004	Oates, Warren	1928	1982	Pleasence, Donald	1919	1995
Minghella, Anthony	1954	2008	Oberon, Merle	1911	1979	Pleshette, Suzanne	1937	2008
Mingus, Charles	1922	1979	O'Brian, Hugh	1925	2016	Pollack, Sydney	1934	2008
Minnelli, Vincente	1903	1986	O'Brien, Edmond	1915	1985	Pons, Lily	1904	1976
Miranda, Carmen	1909	1955	O'Brien, Pat	1899	1983	Ponselle, Rosa	1897	1981
Mitchell, Thomas	1892	1962	O'Connell, Arthur	1908	1981	Ponti, Carlo	1912	2007
Mitchum, Robert	1917	1997	O'Connell, Helen	1921	1993	Porter, Edwin S.	1870	1941
Mix, Tom	1880	1940	O'Connor, Carroll	1924	2001	Postlethwaite, Pete	1946	2011
Moffo, Anna	1932	2006	O'Connor, Donald	1925	2003	Poston, Tom	1921	2007
Molinaro, Al	1919	2015	O'Connor, Una	1880	1959	Powell, Dick	1904	1963
Monroe, Marilyn	1926	1962	Odetta (Holmes)	1930	2008	Powell, Eleanor	1912	1982
Monroe, Vaughn	1911	1973	O'Hara, Maureen	1920	2015	Powell, William	1892	1984
Montalban, Ricardo	1920	2009	O'Herlihy, Daniel	1919	2005	Power, Tyrone	1914	1958
Montand, Yves	1921	1991	O'Keefe, Dennis	1908	1968	Preminger, Otto	1905	1986
Monteith, Cory	1982	2013	Oland, Warner	1880	1938	Presley, Elvis	1935	1977
Montez, Maria	1917	1951	Olcott, Chauncey	1860	1932	Preston, Billy	1946	2006
Montgomery, Elizabeth	1933	1995	Oliveira, Manoel de	1908	2015	Preston, Robert	1918	1987
Montgomery, George	1916	2000	Oliver, Edna May	1883	1942	Price, Ray	1926	2013
Montgomery, Robert	1904	1981	Olivier, Laurence	1907	1989	Price, Vincent	1911	1993
Moody, Ron	1924	2015	Olsen, Merlin	1940	2010	Prima, Louis	1911	1978
Moore, Clayton	1914	1999	Olsen, Ole	1892	1963	Prince	1958	2016
Moore, Colleen	1900	1988	O'Neal, Ron	1937	2004	Prinze, Freddie	1954	1977
Moore, Dudley	1935	2002	O'Neill, James	1849	1920	Prosky, Robert	1930	2008
Moore, Garry	1915	1993	Ophüls, Max	1902	1957	Provine, Dorothy	1937	2010
Moore, Grace	1898	1947	Orbach, Jerry	1935	2004	Prowse, Juliet	1936	1996
Moorehead, Agnes	1906	1974	Orbison, Roy	1936	1988	Pryor, Richard	1940	2005
Moreland, Mantan	1902	1973	Ormandy, Eugene	1899	1985	Puente, Tito	1923	2000
Morgan, Dennis	1910	1994	O'Shea, Milo	1926	2013	Pyle, Denver	1920	1997
Morgan, Frank	1890	1949	O'Sullivan, Maureen	1911	1998	Quayle, Anthony	1913	1989
Morgan, Harry	1915	2011	O'Toole, Peter	1932	2013	Questel, Mae	1908	1998
Morgan, Helen	1900	1941	Ouspenskaya, Maria	1876	1949	Quinn, Anthony	1915	2001
Morgan, Henry	1915	1994	Owen, Reginald	1887	1972	Quintero, José	1924	1999
Morita, Pat	1932	2005	Owens, Buck	1929	2006	Rabb, Ellis	1930	1998
Morley, Robert	1908	1992	Paar, Jack	1918	2004	Rabbit, Eddie	1941	1998
Morris, Chester	1901	1970	Paderewski, Ignace	1860	1941	Radner, Gilda	1946	1989
Morris, Greg	1934	1996	Page, Bettie	1923	2008	Rafferty, Gerry	1947	2011
Morris, Howard	1919	2005	Page, Geraldine	1924	1987	Raft, George	1895	1980
Morris, Wayne	1914	1959	Page, Patti	1927	2013	Rainer, Luise	1910	2014
Morrison, Jim	1943	1971	Pakula, Alan	1928	1998	Rains, Claude	1889	1967
Morrow, Vic	1929	1982	Palance, Jack	1919	2006	Raitt, John	1917	2005
Morton, Jelly Roll	1885	1941	Pallette, Eugene	1889	1954	Ralston, Esther	1902	1994
Mostel, Zero	1915	1977	Palmer, Betsy	1926	2015	Ramis, Harold	1944	2014
Mowbray, Alan	1897	1969	Palmer, Lilli	1914	1986	Ramone, Dee Dee	1952	2002
Mulhare, Edward	1923	1997	Palmer, Robert	1949	2003	Ramone, Joey	1951	2001
Mulligan, Gerry	1927	1996	Pangborn, Franklin	1894	1958	Ramone, Johnny	1948	2004
Mulligan, Richard	1932	2000	Pardo, Don	1918	2014	Ramone, Tommy	1949	2014
Muni, Paul	1895	1967	Parker, Eleanor	1922	2013			

Name	Born	Died	Name	Born	Died	Name	Born	Died
Rampal, Jean-Pierre	1922	2000	Rowan, Dan	1922	1987	Silverheels, Jay	1912	1980
Randall, Tony	1920	2004	Rubinstein, Artur	1887	1982	Silvers, Phil	1912	1985
Randolph, John	1915	2004	Rubenstein, Zelda	1933	2010	Sim, Alastair	1900	1976
Rathbone, Basil	1892	1967	Ruggles, Charles	1886	1970	Simmons, Jean	1929	2010
Ratoff, Gregory	1897	1960	Russell, Harold	1914	2002	Simone, Nina	1933	2003
Rawls, Lou	1933	2006	Russell, Jane	1921	2011	Sinatra, Frank	1915	1998
Ray, Aldo	1926	1991	Russell, Ken	1927	2011	Sinclair, Madge	1938	1995
Ray, Johnnie	1927	1990	Russell, Lillian	1861	1922	Singleton, Penny	1908	2003
Ray, Nicholas	1911	1979	Russell, Nipsey	1923	2005	Sirk, Douglas	1900	1987
Rayburn, Gene	1917	1999	Russell, Rosalind	1911	1976	Siskel, Gene	1946	1999
Raye, Martha	1916	1994	Rutherford, Ann	1917	2012	Sjostrom, Victor	1879	1960
Raymond, Gene	1908	1998	Rutherford, Margaret	1892	1972	Skelton, Red	1913	1997
Reagan, Ronald	1911	2004	Ryan, Irene	1903	1973	Skinner, Otis	1858	1942
Redding, Otis	1941	1967	Ryan, Robert	1909	1973	Sledge, Percy	1940	2015
Redgrave, Corin	1939	2010	Sabu (Dastagir)	1924	1963	Smith, Alexis	1921	1993
Redgrave, Lynn	1943	2010	St. Cyr, Lili	1917	1999	Smith, Bessie	1894?	1937
Redgrave, Michael	1908	1985	St. Denis, Ruth	1877	1968	Smith, Buffalo Bob	1917	1998
Reed, Donna	1921	1986	Sakall, S. Z.	1883	1955	Smith, C. Aubrey	1863	1948
Reed, Jerry	1937	2008	Saks, Gene	1921	2015	Smith, Elliott	1969	2003
Reed, Lou	1942	2013	Sale (Chic), Charles	1885	1936	Smith, Kate	1907	1986
Reed, Oliver	1938	1999	Sales, Soupy	1926	2009	Snodgress, Carrie	1946	2004
Reed, Robert	1932	1992	Sanders, George	1906	1972	Snow, Hank	1914	1999
Rees, Roger	1944	2015	Sanford, Isabel	1917	2004	Snyder, Tom	1936	2007
Reeve, Christopher	1952	2004	Sargent, Dick	1933	1994	Solti, George	1912	1997
Reeves, George	1914	1959	Sarrazin, Michael	1940	2011	Sondergaard, Gale	1899	1985
Reeves, Steve	1926	2000	Savalas, Telly	1924	1994	Sothern, Ann	1909	2001
Reid, Wallace	1891	1923	Schallert, William	1922	2016	Sousa, John Philip	1854	1932
Reilly, Charles Nelson	1931	2007	Scheider, Roy	1935	2008	Sparks, Ned	1884	1957
Reinhardt, Max	1873	1943	Schell, Maria	1926	2005	Spelling, Aaron	1923	2006
Remick, Lee	1935	1991	Schell, Maximilian	1930	2014	Spencer, John	1946	2005
Renaldo, Duncan	1904	1980	Schenkel, Chris	1923	2005	Sperber, Wendie Jo	1958	2005
Rennie, Michael	1909	1971	Schiavelli, Vincent	1948	2005	Springfield, Dusty	1939	1999
Renoir, Jean	1894	1979	Schildkraut, Joseph	1896	1964	Stack, Robert	1919	2003
Rettig, Tommy	1941	1996	Schipa, Tito	1888	1965	Stafford, Jo	1917	2008
Reynolds, Marjorie	1921	1997	Schlesinger, John	1926	2003	Stander, Lionel	1908	1994
Rich, Charlie	1932	1995	Schnabel, Artur	1882	1951	Stang, Arnold	1918	2009
Richardson, Ian	1934	2007	Schneider, Maria	1952	2011	Stanley, Kim	1925	2001
Richardson, Natasha	1963	2009	Schneider, Romy	1938	1982	Stanwyck, Barbara	1907	1990
Richardson, Ralph	1902	1983	Schwartzkopf, Elizabeth	1915	2006	Stapleton, Jean	1923	2013
Rickman, Alan	1946	2016	Scofield, Paul	1922	2008	Stapleton, Maureen	1925	2006
Riddle, Nelson	1921	1985	Scott, George C.	1927	1999	Steiger, Rod	1925	2002
Riefenstahl, Leni	1902	2003	Scott, Gordon	1926	2007	Sterling, Jan	1921	2004
Ripperton, Minnie	1947	1979	Scott, Hazel	1920	1981	Stern, Isaac	1920	2001
Ritchard, Cyril	1898	1977	Scott, Lizabeth	1922	2015	Stevens, Craig	1918	2000
Ritter, John	1948	2003	Scott, Martha	1914	2003	Stevens, George	1904	1975
Ritter, Tex	1905	1974	Scott, Randolph	1898	1987	Stevens, Inger	1934	1970
Ritter, Thelma	1905	1969	Scott, Stuart	1965	2015	Stevens, Mark	1916	1994
Ritz, Al	1901	1965	Scott, Zachary	1914	1965	Stevens, Risë	1913	2013
Ritz, Harry	1906	1986	Scott-Heron, Gil	1949	2011	Stevenson, McLean	1929	1996
Ritz, Jimmy	1903	1985	Scott-Siddons, Mrs.	1843	1896	Stewart, James	1908	1997
Rivers, Joan	1933	2014	Seberg, Jean	1938	1979	Stickney, Dorothy	1896	1998
Roach, Hal	1892	1992	Seeger, Pete	1919	2014	Stokowski, Leopold	1882	1977
Roach, Max	1924	2007	Seeley, Blossom	1892	1974	Stone, Fred	1873	1959
Robards, Jason	1922	2000	Segovia, Andres	1893	1987	Stone, Lewis	1879	1953
Robbins, Jerome	1918	1998	Seldes, Marian	1928	2014	Stone, Milburn	1904	1980
Robbins, Marty	1925	1982	Selena (Quintanilla)	1971	1995	Storm, Gale	1922	2009
Roberts, Doris	1925	2016	Sellers, Peter	1925	1980	Straight, Beatrice	1918	2001
Roberts, Pernell	1928	2010	Selznick, David O.	1902	1965	Strasberg, Lee	1901	1982
Roberts, Rachel	1927	1980	Sennett, Mack	1880	1960	Strasberg, Susan	1938	1999
Robertson, Cliff	1925	2011	Señor Wences	1896	1999	Stritch, Elaine	1925	2014
Robertson, Dale	1923	2013	Serling, Rod	1924	1975	Strode, Woody	1914	1994
Robeson, Paul	1898	1976	Shakur, Tupac	1971	1996	Strummer, Joe	1952	2002
Robinson, Bill	1878	1949	Shandling, Garry	1949	2016	Stuart, Gloria	1910	2010
Robinson, Edward G.	1893	1973	Shankar, Ravi	1920	2012	Stuarti, Enzo	1919	2005
Robson, Flora	1902	1984	Sharif, Omar	1932	2015	Sturges, Preston	1898	1959
Roche, Eugene	1928	2004	Shaw, Artie	1910	2004	Sullavan, Margaret	1911	1960
Rochester (Eddie Anderson)	1905	1977	Shaw, Robert (actor)	1927	1978	Sullivan, Barry	1912	1994
Roddenberry, Gene	1921	1991	Shaw, Robert (conductor)	1916	1999	Sullivan, Ed	1902	1974
Rodgers, Jimmie	1897	1933	Shawn, Ted	1891	1972	Sullivan, Francis L.	1903	1956
Rogers, Buddy	1904	1999	Shean, Al	1868	1949	Sumac, Yma	1922	2008
Rogers, Fred	1928	2003	Shearer, Moira	1926	2006	Summer, Donna	1948	2012
Rogers, Ginger	1911	1995	Shearer, Norma	1902	1983	Summerville, Slim	1892	1946
Rogers, Roy	1911	1998	Shearing, George	1919	2011	Sutherland, Joan	1926	2010
Rogers, Wayne	1933	2015	Sheppard, Bob	1910	2010	Swanson, Gloria	1899	1983
Rogers, Will	1879	1935	Sheridan, Ann	1915	1967	Swarthout, Gladys	1904	1969
Rohmer, Éric	1920	2010	Shore, Dinah	1917	1994	Swayze, Patrick	1952	2009
Roland, Gilbert	1905	1994	Short, Bobby	1924	2005	Sweet, Blanche	1896	1986
Rolle, Esther	1920?	1998	Shubert, Lee	1875	1953	Switzer, Carl "Alfalfa"	1927	1959
Rollins, Howard	1950	1996	Shull, Richard B.	1929	1999	Talbot, Lyle	1902	1996
Roman, Ruth	1924	1999	Siddons, Sarah	1755	1831	Tallchief, Maria	1925	2013
Romero, Cesar	1907	1994	Sidney, Sylvia	1910	1999	Talmadge, Constance	1900	1973
Rooney, Mickey	1920	2014	Siegel, Don	1912	1991	Talmadge, Norma	1893	1957
Rose, Billy	1899	1966	Signoret, Simone	1921	1985	Tamiroff, Akim	1899	1972
Rossellini, Roberto	1906	1977	Sills, Beverly	1929	2007	Tandy, Jessica	1909	1994
Rostropovich, Mstislav	1927	2007	Silver, Ron	1946	2009	Tanguay, Eva	1878	1947

Name	Born	Died	Name	Born	Died	Name	Born	Died
Tati, Jacques	1908	1982	Vera-Ellen (Rohe)	1926	1981	Wilding, Michael	1912	1979
Taylor, Billy	1921	2010	Verdon, Gwen	1925	2000	Williams, Andy	1927	2012
Taylor, Deems	1885	1966	Verrett, Shirley	1931	2010	Williams, Bert	1874	1922
Taylor, Dub	1907	1994	Vickers, Jon	1926	2015	Williams, Esther	1921	2013
Taylor, Elizabeth	1932	2011	Vidor, King	1894	1982	Williams, Guy	1924	1989
Taylor, Estelle	1899	1958	Vigoda, Abe	1921	2016	Williams, Hank, Sr.	1923	1953
Taylor, Laurette	1887	1946	Villechaize, Herve	1943	1993	Williams, Robin	1951	2014
Taylor, Robert	1911	1969	Vincent, Gene	1935	1971	Williamson, Nicol	1936	2011
Taylor, Rod	1930	2015	Vicious, Sid	1957	1979	Wills, Bob	1905	1975
Temple Black, Shirley	1928	2014	Von Stroheim, Erich	1885	1957	Wills, Chill	1902	1978
Terry, Ellen	1847	1928	Von Zell, Harry	1906	1981	Wilson, Carl	1946	1998
Thalberg, Irving	1899	1936	Waite, Ralph	1928	2014	Wilson, Dennis	1944	1983
Thaw, John	1942	2002	Walker, Junior	1942	1995	Wilson, Dooley	1894	1953
Thaxter, Phyllis	1919	2012	Walker, Nancy	1922	1992	Wilson, Elizabeth	1921	2015
Thigpen, Lynne	1948	2003	Walker, Robert	1918	1951	Wilson, Flip	1933	1998
Thomas, Danny	1912	1991	Wallace, Marcia	1942	2013	Wilson, Jackie	1934	1984
Thompson, Sada	1927	2011	Wallach, Eli	1915	2014	Wilson, Marie	1917	1972
Thorndike, Sybil	1882	1976	Wallenda, Karl	1905	1978	Windom, William	1923	2012
Thulin, Ingrid	1926	2004	Walsh, J. T.	1943	1998	Windsor, Marie	1919	2000
Tierney, Gene	1920	1991	Walsh, Raoul	1887	1980	Winehouse, Amy	1983	2011
Tiny Tim	1932	1996	Walston, Ray	1914	2001	Winfield, Paul	1941	2004
Todd, Michael	1909	1958	Walter, Bruno	1876	1962	Winter, Johnny	1944	2014
Todd, Richard	1919	2009	Ward, Simon	1941	2012	Winters, Jonathan	1925	2013
Tomlinson, David	1917	2000	Warden, Jack	1920	2006	Winters, Shelley	1920	2006
Tone, Franchot	1905	1968	Waring, Fred	1900	1984	Wise, Robert	1914	2005
Torme, Mel	1925	1999	Warner, H. B.	1876	1958	Wiseman, Joseph	1918	2009
Toscanini, Arturo	1867	1957	Warrick, Ruth	1915	2005	Wong, Anna May	1907	1961
Tracy, Lee	1898	1968	Washington, Dinah	1924	1963	Wood, Ed	1924	1978
Tracy, Spencer	1900	1967	Waters, Ethel	1896	1977	Wood, Natalie	1938	1981
Travers, Henry	1874	1965	Waters, Muddy	1913?	1983	Wood, Peggy	1892	1978
Travers, Mary	1936	2009	Waxman, Al	1935	2001	Wood, Sam	1884	1949
Treacher, Arthur	1894	1975	Wayne, David	1914	1995	Woodard, Edward	1930	2009
Tree, Herbert Beerbohm	1853	1917	Wayne, John	1907	1979	Wooley, Sheb	1921	2003
Trevor, Claire	1909	2000	Weaver, Dennis	1924	2006	Woolley, Monty	1888	1963
Truex, Ernest	1890	1973	Webb, Clifton	1891	1966	Worth, Irene	1916	2002
Truffaut, Francois	1932	1984	Webb, Jack	1920	1982	Wray, Fay	1907	2004
Tucker, Forrest	1919	1986	Weems, Ted	1901	1963	Wright, Teresa	1918	2005
Tucker, Richard	1913	1975	Weiland, Scott	1967	2015	Wyatt, Jane	1910	2006
Tucker, Sophie	1884	1966	Weissmuller, Johnny	1904	1984	Wyler, William	1902	1981
Turner, Big Joe	1911	1985	Welk, Lawrence	1903	1992	Wyman, Jane	1914?	2007
Turner, Ike	1931	2008	Welles, Orson	1915	1985	Wynette, Tammy	1942	1998
Turner, Lana	1920?	1995	Wellman, William	1896	1975	Wynn, Ed.	1886	1966
Turpin, Ben	1869	1940	Wells, Kitty	1919	2012	Wynn, Keenan	1916	1986
Twitty, Conway	1933	1993	Werner, Oskar	1922	1984	York, Dick	1928	1992
Urich, Robert	1946	2002	West, Mae	1893	1980	York, Susannah	1939	2011
Ustinov, Peter	1921	2004	Weston, Jack	1924	1996	Young, Alan	1919	2016
Valens, Ritchie	1941	1959	Whale, James	1889	1957	Young, Clara Kimball	1890	1960
Valentino, Rudolph	1895	1926	White, Barry	1944	2003	Young, Gig	1913	1978
Vallee, Rudy	1901	1986	White, Jesse	1919	1997	Young, Loretta	1913	2000
Van, Bobby	1928	1980	White, Pearl	1889	1938	Young, Robert	1907	1998
Van Cleef, Lee	1925	1989	Whiteman, Paul	1891	1967	Young, Roland	1887	1953
Van Fleet, Jo	1922	1996	Whiting, Margaret	1924	2011	Youngman, Henny	1906	1998
Van Patten, Dick	1928	2015	Whitmore, James	1921	2009	Zanuck, Darryl F.	1902	1979
Vance, Vivian	1912	1979	Whitty, May	1865	1948	Zappa, Frank	1940	1993
Vandross, Luther	1951	2005	Wickes, Mary	1910	1995	Zevon, Warren	1947	2003
Varney, Jim	1949	2000	Widmark, Richard	1914	2008	Ziegfeld, Florenz	1869	1932
Vaughan, Sarah	1924	1990	Wilde, Cornel	1915	1989	Zimbalist, Efrem, Jr.	1918	2014
Veidt, Conrad	1893	1943	Wilder, Billy	1906	2002	Zinneman, Fred	1907	1997
Velez, Lupe	1908	1944	Wilder, Gene	1933	2016	Zukor, Adolph	1873	1976

Original Names of Selected Entertainers

Adele: Adele Laurie Blue Adkins
Ad-Rock: Adam Horovitz
Clay Aiken: Clayton Grissom
Alan Alda: Alphonso D'Abruzzo
Jason Alexander: Jay Greenspan
Woody Allen: Allen Konigsberg
André 3000: Andre Benjamin
Julie Andrews: Julia Wells
Criss Angel: Christopher Sarantakos
Beatrice Arthur: Bernice Frankel
Fred Astaire: Frederick Austerlitz
Babyface: Kenneth Edmonds
Lauren Bacall: Betty Joan Perske
Erykah Badu: Erica Wright
Eric Bana: Eric Banadinovich
Anne Bancroft: Anna Maria Italiano
Theda Bara: Theodosia Goodman
Beck: Bek David Campbell
Pat Benatar: Patricia Andrejewski
Tony Bennett: Anthony Benedetto
Jack Benny: Benjamin Kubelsky
Milton Berle: Mendel Berlinger
Irving Berlin: Israel Baline
Sarah Bernhardt: Henriette-Rosine Bernard

Jello Biafra: Eric Reed Boucher
Big Boi: Antwan Patton
The Big Bopper: Jiles Perry "J.P." Richardson
Robert Blake: Michael James Vijencio Gubitosi
Jon Bon Jovi: John Francis Bongiovi
Bono: Paul Hewson
David Bowie: David Robert Jones
Boy George: George Alan O'Dowd
Fanny Brice: Fanny Borach
Charles Bronson: Charles Buchinski
Albert Brooks: Albert Einstein
Mel Brooks: Melvin Kaminsky
Foxy Brown: Inga Marchand
George Burns: Nathan Birnbaum
Ellen Burstyn: Edna Gilhooley
Richard Burton: Richard Jenkins
Red Buttons: Aaron Chwatt
Nicolas Cage: Nicholas Coppola
Michael Caine: Maurice Micklewhite
Maria Callas: Maria Kalogeropoulos
Jackie Chan: Chan Kwong-Sung
Cyd Charisse: Tula Finklea

Ray Charles: Ray Charles Robinson
Charo: María Rosario Pilar Martínez Molina Baeza
Chubby Checker: Ernest Evans
Cher: Cherilyn Sarkisian
Chuck D: Carlton Ridenhour
Patsy Cline: Virginia Patterson Hensley
Claudette Colbert: Lily Chauchoin
Coolio: Artis Leon Ivey Jr.
Alice Cooper: Vincent Furnier
David Copperfield: David Kotkin
Howard Cosell: Howard Cohen
Elvis Costello: Declan McManus
Lou Costello: Louis Cristillo
Peter Coyote: Peter Cohon
Joan Crawford: Lucille LeSueur
Quentin Crisp: Denis Pratt
Tom Cruise: Thomas Cruise Mapother IV
Tony Curtis: Bernard Schwartz
Miley Cyrus: Destiny Hope Cyrus
D'Angelo: Michael D'Angelo Archer
Rodney Dangerfield: Jacob Cohen
Bobby Darin: Walden Robert Cassotto
Doris Day: Doris von Kappelhoff

Yvonne De Carlo: Peggy Middleton
Portia de Rossi: Amanda Lee Rogers
Sandra Dee: Alexandra Zuck
John Denver: Henry John Deutschendorf Jr.
Bo Derek: Mary Cathleen Collins
Danny DeVito: Daniel Michaeli
Angie Dickinson: Angeline Brown
Bo Diddley: Elias Bates
Vin Diesel: Mark Vincent
Phyllis Diller: Phyllis Driver
Divine: Harris Glenn Milstead
DMX: Earl Simmons
Troy Donahue: Merle Johnson Jr.
Kirk Douglas: Issur Danielovitch
Drake: Aubrey Drake Graham
Bob Dylan: Robert Zimmerman
Barbara Eden: Barbara Huffman
Elvira: Cassandra Peterson
Eminem: Marshall Mathers
Enya: Eithne Ni Bhraonian
Dale Evans: Frances Smith
Chad Everett: Raymon Cramton
Fabian: Fabian Anthony Forte
Fabolous: John David Jackson
Douglas Fairbanks: Douglas Ullman
Morgan Fairchild: Patsy McClenny
Jamie Farr: Jameel Farah
Fergie: Stacy Ferguson
Stepin Fetchit: Lincoln Perry
W. C. Fields: William Claude Dukenfield
50 Cent: Curtis Jackson
Flavor Flav: William Drayton
Joan Fontaine: Joan de Havilland
Jodie Foster: Alicia Christian Foster
Jamie Foxx: Eric Bishop
Redd Foxx: John Sanford
Arlene Francis: Arlene Kazanjian
Connie Francis: Concetta Franconero
Greta Garbo: Greta Gustafsson
Judy Garland: Frances Gumm
James Garner: James Bumgarner
Crystal Gayle: Brenda Gail Webb
George Gershwin: Jacob Gershowitz
Kathie Lee Gifford: Kathie Epstein
Whoopi Goldberg: Caryn Johnson
Cary Grant: Archibald Leach
Lee Grant: Lyova Rosenthal
Robert Guillaume: Robert Williams
Buddy Hackett: Leonard Hacker
Hammer: Stanley Kirk Burrell
Jean Harlow: Harlean Carpenter
Helen Hayes: Helen Brown
Susan Hayward: Edythe Marrener
Rita Hayworth: Margarita Cansino
Pee-Wee Herman: Paul Reubenfeld
Charlton Heston: John Charles Carter
Perez Hilton: Mario Armando
    Lavandeira Jr.
Hulk Hogan: Terry Gene Bollea
Billie Holiday: Eleanora Fagan
Judy Holliday: Judith Tuvim
Bob Hope: Leslie Townes Hope
Harry Houdini: Erik Weisz
Howlin' Wolf: Chester Burnett
Rock Hudson: Roy Scherer Jr. (later
    Fitzgerald)
Engelbert Humperdinck: Arnold Dorsey
Kim Hunter: Janet Cole
Ice Cube: O'Shea Jackson
Ice-T: Tracy Morrow
Billy Idol: William Broad
Etta James: Jamesetta Hawkins
Ja Rule: Jeffrey Atkins
Jay-Z: Shawn Carter
Elton John: Reginald Dwight
Al Jolson: Asa Yoelson
Jennifer Jones: Phylis Isley
Tom Jones: Thomas Woodward
Spike Jonze: Adam Spiegel
Wynonna Judd: Christina Ciminella
Boris Karloff: William Henry Pratt

Diane Keaton: Diane Hall
Michael Keaton: Michael Douglas
Kesha: Kesha Rose Sebert
Alicia Keys: Alicia Augello Cook
Chaka Khan: Yvette Stevens
Kid Rock: Robert Ritchie
Carole King: Carole Klein
Larry King: Larry Zeiger
Ben Kingsley: Krishna Banji
Ted Knight: Tadewurz Wladziu Konopka
Cheryl Ladd: Cheryl Stoppelmoor
Lady Gaga: Stefani Germanotta
Veronica Lake: Constance Ockleman
Kendrick Lamar: Kendrick Lamar
    Duckworth
Hedy Lamarr: Hedwig Kiesler
Dorothy Lamour: Mary Leta Dorothy Slaton
Michael Landon: Eugene Orowitz
Mario Lanza: Alfredo Cocozza
Queen Latifah: Dana Owens
Stan Laurel: Arthur Jefferson
Brenda Lee: Brenda Mae Tarpley
Gypsy Rose Lee: Rose Louise Hovick
Peggy Lee: Norma Egstrom
Janet Leigh: Jeanette Morrison
Vivien Leigh: Vivian Hartley
Huey Lewis: Hugh Cregg
Jerry Lewis: Joseph Levitch
Lil' Kim: Kimberly Denise Jones
Little Richard: Richard Penniman
LL Cool J: James Todd Smith
Carole Lombard: Jane Peters
Lorde: Ella Yelich-O'Connor
Sophia Loren: Sophia Scicolone
Peter Lorre: Laszlo Lowenstein
Louis C.K.: Louis Szekely
Myrna Loy: Myrna Williams
Bela Lugosi: Bela Ferenc Blasko
Moms Mabley: Loretta Mary Aiken
Macklemore: Ben Haggerty
Shirley MacLaine: Shirley Beaty
Elle Macpherson: Eleanor Gow
Madonna: Madonna Louise Veronica
    Ciccone
Lee Majors: Harvey Lee Yeary
Karl Malden: Mladen Sekulovich
Barry Manilow: Barry Alan Pincus
Jayne Mansfield: Vera Jane Palmer
Marilyn Manson: Brian Warner
Bruno Mars: Peter Gene Hernandez
Dean Martin: Dino Crocetti
Ricky Martin: Enrique Jose Martin Morales
MCA: Adam Yauch
Meat Loaf: Marvin Lee Aday
Freddie Mercury: Farrokh Bulsara
Ethel Merman: Ethel Zimmermann
George Michael: Georgios Panayiotou
Mike D: Michael Diamond
Nicki Minaj: Onika Tanya Maraj
Helen Mirren: Ilynea Lydia Mironoff
Joni Mitchell: Roberta Joan Anderson
Moby: Richard Melville Hall
Mo'Nique: Monique Imes
Marilyn Monroe: Norma Jean Mortenson
    (later Baker)
Yves Montand: Ivo Livi
Demi Moore: Demetria Guynes
Rita Moreno: Rosita Alverio
Harry Morgan: Harry Bratsburg
Morrissey: Steven Patrick Morrissey
Mr. T: Lawrence Tureaud
Paul Muni: Mehilem Weisenfreund
Nelly: Cornell Haynes Jr.
Mike Nichols: Michael Igor Peschowsky
Chuck Norris: Carlos Ray Norris
Notorious B.I.G.: Christopher Wallace
Hugh O'Brian: Hugh Krampke
Maureen O'Hara: Maureen FitzSimons
Jack Palance: Vladimir Palanuik
Minnie Pearl: Sarah Ophelia Cannon
Katy Perry: Kathryn Hudson

Bernadette Peters: Bernadette Lazzara
Joaquin Phoenix: Joaquin Bottom
Edith Piaf: Edith Gassion
Slim Pickens: Louis Lindley
Mary Pickford: Gladys Smith
Pink: Alecia Moore
Pitbull: Armando Christian Pérez
Iggy Pop: James Newell Osterberg
Natalie Portman: Natalie Hershlag
Prince: Prince Rogers Nelson
Dee Dee Ramone: Douglas Colvin
Joey Ramone: Jeffrey Hyman
Johnny Ramone: John Cummings
Tommy Ramone: Tom Erdelyi
Tony Randall: Leonard Rosenberg
Della Reese: Delloreese Patricia Early
Busta Rhymes: Trevor Smith Jr.
Joan Rivers: Joan Sandra Molinsky
Edward G. Robinson: Emmanuel
    Goldenberg
The Rock: Dwayne Johnson
Ginger Rogers: Virginia McMath
Roy Rogers: Leonard Franklin Slye
Mickey Rooney: Joe Yule Jr.
Johnny Rotten: John Lydon
Lillian Russell: Helen Leonard
Meg Ryan: Margaret Hyra
Winona Ryder: Winona Horowitz
Sade: Helen Folsade Abu
Soupy Sales: Milton Supman
Susan Sarandon: Susan Tomaling
Seal: Seal Henry Olusegun Olumide
    Adeola Samuel
Jane Seymour: Joyce Frankenberg
Omar Sharif: Michael Shalhoub
Charlie Sheen: Carlos Irwin Estevez
Martin Sheen: Ramon Estevez
Talia Shire: Talia Coppola
Beverly Sills: Belle Silverman
Phil Silvers: Philip Silversmith
Gene Simmons: Chaim Witz
Sinbad: David Adkins
Anna Nicole Smith: Vickie Lynn Hogan
Snoop Dogg (a.k.a. Snoop Lion,
    Snoopzilla)**:** Calvin Broadus
Barbara Stanwyck: Ruby Stevens
Jean Stapleton: Jeanne Murray
Ringo Starr: Richard Starkey
Cat Stevens: Stephen Demetre Georgiou
Connie Stevens: Concetta Ingolia
Jon Stewart: Jonathan Stuart Leibowitz
Sting: Gordon Sumner
Joe Strummer: John Graham Mellor
Donna Summer: La Donna Gaines
Rip Taylor: Charles Elmer Taylor Jr.
Robert Taylor: Spangler Brugh
The Weeknd: Abel Makkonen Tesfaye
Danny Thomas: Muzyad Yakhoob (later
    Amos Jacobs)
Tiny Tim: Herbert Khaury
Rip Torn: Elmore Rual Torn Jr.
Randy Travis: Randy Traywick
Tina Turner: Annie Mae Bullock
Shania Twain: Eileen Regina Edwards
Twiggy: Lesley Hornby
Conway Twitty: Harold Lloyd Jenkins
Steven Tyler: Stephen Tallarico
Rudolph Valentino: Rudolpho
    D'Antonguolla
Frankie Valli: Frank Castelluccio
Eddie Vedder: Edward Louis Seversen III
Sid Vicious: John Simon Ritchie
John Wayne: Marion Morrison
Raquel Welch: Raquel Tejada
Gene Wilder: Jerome Silberman
Shelley Winters: Shirley Schrift
Stevie Wonder: Stevland Morris
Jane Wyman: Sarah Jane Mayfield
Loretta Young: Gretchen Michaels Young
Buckwheat Zydeco: Stanley Dural Jr.

ARTS AND MEDIA

Some Notable Movies, Sept. 2015-Aug. 2016

Film (rating)	Stars	Director(s)
Alice Through the Looking Glass (PG)	Johnny Depp, Mia Wasikowska, Helena Bonham Carter	James Bobin
The Angry Birds Movie (PG)	Animated. Jason Sudeikis, Josh Gad, Maya Rudolph, Bill Hader	Clay Kaytis, Fergal Reilly
Anomalisa (R)	David Thewlis, Jennifer Jason Leigh, Tom Noonan	Duke Johnson, Charlie Kaufman
Bad Moms (R)	Mila Kunis, Kathryn Hahn, Kristen Bell	Jon Lucas, Scott Moore
Barbershop: The Next Cut (PG-13)	Ice Cube, Cedric the Entertainer, Regina Hall, Anthony Anderson	Malcolm D. Lee
Batman v. Superman: Dawn of Justice (PG-13)	Ben Affleck, Henry Cavill, Amy Adams, Jesse Eisenberg	Zack Snyder
Ben-Hur (PG-13)	Jack Huston, Toby Kebbell, Rodrigo Santoro, Morgan Freeman	Timur Bekmambetov
The BFG (PG)	Mark Rylance, Ruby Barnhill, Penelope Wilton, Bill Hader	Steven Spielberg
The Big Short (R)	Christian Bale, Steve Carell, Ryan Gosling	Adam McKay
Black Mass (R)	Johnny Depp, Benedict Cumberbatch, Dakota Johnson	Scott Cooper
The Boss (R)	Melissa McCarthy, Kristen Bell, Peter Dinklage, Kathy Bates	Ben Falcone
Bridge of Spies (PG-13)	Tom Hanks, Mark Rylance, Amy Ryan, Alan Alda	Steven Spielberg
Brooklyn (PG-13)	Saoirse Ronan, Emory Cohen, Domhnall Gleeson, Jim Broadbent	John Crowley
Café Society (PG-13)	Steve Carell, Jesse Eisenberg, Blake Lively, Kristen Stewart	Woody Allen
Captain America: Civil War (PG-13)	Chris Evans, Robert Downey Jr., Scarlett Johansson	Anthony Russo, Joe Russo
Carol (R)	Cate Blanchett, Rooney Mara, Kyle Chandler, Sarah Paulson	Todd Haynes
Central Intelligence (PG-13)	Dwayne Johnson, Kevin Hart, Amy Ryan, Aaron Paul	Rawson Marshall Thurber
Chi-Raq (R)	Nick Cannon, Wesley Snipes, Teyonah Parris, Jennifer Hudson	Spike Lee
Concussion (PG-13)	Will Smith, Alec Baldwin, Albert Brooks	Peter Landesman
Creed (PG-13)	Michael B. Jordan, Sylvester Stallone, Tessa Thompson	Ryan Coogler
The Danish Girl (R)	Eddie Redmayne, Alicia Vikander	Tom Hooper
Deadpool (R)	Ryan Reynolds, Morena Baccarin, T.J. Miller	Tim Miller
The Divergent Series: Allegiant (PG-13)	Shailene Woodley, Theo James, Jeff Daniels	Robert Schwentke
Don't Think Twice (R)	Keegan-Michael Key, Gillian Jacobs, Mike Birbiglia, Chris Gethard	Mike Birbiglia
Everest (PG-13)	Jason Clarke, Ang Phula Sherpa, Thomas M. Wright	Baltasar Kormákur
Finding Dory (PG)	Animated. Ellen DeGeneres, Albert Brooks, Ed O'Neill, Ty Burrell	Andrew Stanton, Angus MacLane
Florence Foster Jenkins (PG-13)	Meryl Streep, Hugh Grant, Simon Helberg	Stephen Frears
45 Years (R)	Charlotte Rampling, Tom Courtenay	Andrew Haigh
Ghostbusters (PG-13)	Melissa McCarthy, Kristen Wiig, Kate McKinnon, Leslie Jones	Paul Feig
The Good Dinosaur (PG)	Animated. Jeffrey Wright, Frances McDormand	Peter Sohn
Goosebumps (PG)	Animated. Jack Black, Dylan Minnette, Odeya Rush	Rob Letterman
Grandma (R)	Lily Tomlin, Julia Garner, Marcia Gay Harden, Sam Elliott	Paul Weitz
Hail, Caesar! (PG-13)	Josh Brolin, George Clooney, Ralph Fiennes, Scarlett Johansson	Ethan Coen, Joel Coen
The Hateful Eight (R)	Samuel L. Jackson, Kurt Russell, Jennifer Jason Leigh	Quentin Tarantino
Hotel Transylvania 2 (PG)	Animated. Adam Sandler, Andy Samberg, Selena Gomez	Genndy Tartakovsky
The Hunger Games: Mockingjay Part 2 (PG-13)	Jennifer Lawrence, Josh Hutcherson, Liam Hemsworth	Francis Lawrence
Independence Day: Resurgence (PG-13)	Liam Hemsworth, Jeff Goldblum, Jessie T. Usher, Bill Pullman	Roland Emmerich
The Intern (PG-13)	Robert De Niro, Anne Hathaway, Rene Russo	Nancy Meyers
Jason Bourne (PG-13)	Matt Damon, Tommy Lee Jones, Julia Stiles, Alicia Vikander	Paul Greengrass
Joy (PG-13)	Jennifer Lawrence, Robert De Niro, Bradley Cooper	David O. Russell
The Jungle Book (PG)	Neel Sethi, Bill Murray, Ben Kingsley, Idris Elba, Lupita Nyong'o	Jon Favreau
Kung Fu Panda 3 (PG)	Animated. Jack Black, Bryan Cranston, Dustin Hoffman, Angelina Jolie, J.K. Simmons, Jackie Chan	Alessandro Carloni, Jennifer Yuh
The Legend of Tarzan (PG-13)	Alexander Skarsgård, Margot Robbie, Christoph Waltz	David Yates
The Light Between Oceans (PG-13)	Michael Fassbender, Alicia Vikander, Rachel Weisz	Derek Cianfrance
London Has Fallen (R)	Gerard Butler, Aaron Eckhart, Morgan Freeman, Angela Bassett	Babak Najafi
The Martian (PG-13)	Matt Damon, Jessica Chastain, Kristen Wiig, Chiwetel Ejiofor	Ridley Scott
Me Before You (PG-13)	Emilia Clarke, Sam Claflin	Thea Sharrock
Money Monster (R)	George Clooney, Julia Roberts	Jodie Foster
My Big Fat Greek Wedding 2 (PG-13)	Nia Vardalos, John Corbett, Lainie Kazan, Michael Constantine	Kirk Jones
Neighbors 2: Sorority Rising (R)	Zac Efron, Rose Byrne, Seth Rogen, Chloë Grace Moretz	Nicholas Stoller
The Night Before (R)	Joseph Gordon-Levitt, Seth Rogen, Lizzy Caplan, Mindy Kaling	Jonathan Levine
Now You See Me 2 (PG-13)	Mark Ruffalo, Woody Harrelson, Jesse Eisenberg, Lizzy Caplan	Jon M. Chu
The Peanuts Movie (G)	Animated. Noah Schnapp, Bill Melendez, Hadley Belle Miller	Steve Martino
Pete's Dragon (PG)	Wes Bentley, Bryce Dallas Howard, Robert Redford, Karl Urban	David Lowery
The Revenant (R)	Leonardo DiCaprio, Tom Hardy, Will Poulter	Alejandro G. Iñárritu
Ride Along 2 (PG-13)	Ice Cube, Kevin Hart, Tika Sumpter, Benjamin Bratt, Olivia Munn	Tim Story
Room (R)	Brie Larson, Jacob Tremblay, Joan Allen, William H. Macy	Lenny Abrahamson
Sausage Party (R)	Animated. Seth Rogen, Kristen Wiig, Jonah Hill, Bill Hader	Greg Tiernan, Conrad Vernon
The Secret Life of Pets (PG)	Animated. Louis C.K., Eric Stonestreet, Kevin Hart, Ellie Kemper	Yarrow Cheney, Chris Renaud
Sicario (R)	Emily Blunt, Josh Brolin, Benicio Del Toro, Victor Garber	Denis Villeneuve
Sisters (R)	Amy Poehler, Tina Fey, Maya Rudolph	Jason Moore
Son of Saul (R)	Géza Röhrig, Levente Molnár, Urs Rechn	László Nemes
Spectre (PG-13)	Daniel Craig, Christoph Waltz, Léa Seydoux	Sam Mendes
Spotlight (R)	Mark Ruffalo, Michael Keaton, Rachel McAdams, Liev Schreiber	Tom McCarthy
Star Trek Beyond (PG-13)	Chris Pine, Zachary Quinto, Zoe Saldana, John Cho, Idris Elba	Justin Lin
Star Wars: Episode VII — The Force Awakens (PG-13)	Harrison Ford, Carrie Fisher, Daisy Ridley, John Boyega, Mark Hamill	J. J. Abrams
Steve Jobs (R)	Michael Fassbender, Kate Winslet, Seth Rogen, Jeff Daniels	Danny Boyle
Suicide Squad (PG-13)	Will Smith, Margot Robbie, Jared Leto, Viola Davis	David Ayer
10 Cloverfield Lane (PG-13)	John Goodman, Mary Elizabeth Winstead, John Gallagher Jr.	Dan Trachtenberg
13 Hours: The Secret Soldiers of Benghazi (R)	John Krasinski, Pablo Schreiber, James Badge Dale	Michael Bay
Trumbo (R)	Bryan Cranston, Diane Lane, Helen Mirren	Jay Roach
Truth (R)	Cate Blanchett, Robert Redford, Topher Grace, Elisabeth Moss	James Vanderbilt
A Walk in the Woods (R)	Robert Redford, Nick Nolte, Emma Thompson, Mary Steenburgen	Ken Kwapis
A War (R)	Pilou Asbæk, Tuva Novotny, Dar Salim	Tobias Lindholm
War Dogs (R)	Jonah Hill, Miles Teller	Todd Phillips
Weiner (R)	Documentary. Anthony Weiner, Huma Abedin	Elyse Steinberg, Josh Kriegman
Wiener-Dog (R)	Ellen Burstyn, Danny DeVito, Greta Gerwig, Julie Delpy	Todd Solondz
Winter on Fire (NR)	Documentary. Bishop Agapit, Serhii Averchenko	Evgeny Afineevsky
X-Men: Apocalypse (PG-13)	James McAvoy, Michael Fassbender, Jennifer Lawrence	Bryan Singer
Zootopia (PG)	Animated. Ginnifer Goodwin, Jason Bateman, Idris Elba	Byron Howard, Rich Moore, Jared Bush

50 Top-Grossing Movies, 2015
Source: Rentrak Corporation

Rank	Title	Gross (mil)	Rank	Title	Gross (mil)
1.	Jurassic World	$652.3	26.	The Good Dinosaur	$110.7
2.	Star Wars: Episode VII—The Force Awakens	652.0	27.	Trainwreck	110.2
3.	Avengers: Age of Ultron	459.0	28.	Creed	99.4
4.	Inside Out	356.5	29.	Tomorrowland	93.4
5.	Furious 7	353.0	30.	Get Hard	90.4
6.	American Sniper	348.6	31.	Terminator Genisys	89.8
7.	Minions	336.0	32.	Taken 3	89.3
8.	The Hunger Games: Mockingjay Part 2	269.6	33.	Maze Runner: The Scorch Trials	81.6
9.	The Martian	225.3	34.	Ted 2	81.5
10.	Cinderella	201.2	35.	Goosebumps	79.1
11.	Spectre	197.1	36.	Pixels	78.7
12.	Mission: Impossible–Rogue Nation	195.0	37.	Paddington	76.2
13.	Pitch Perfect 2	184.3	38.	The Intern	75.6
14.	Ant-Man	180.2	39.	Paul Blart: Mall Cop 2	71.0
15.	Home	177.4	40.	Bridge of Spies	70.4
16.	Hotel Transylvania 2	168.5	41.	The Imitation Game	68.4
17.	Fifty Shades of Grey	166.2	42.	War Room	67.8
18.	The SpongeBob Movie: Sponge Out of Water	163.0	43.	Magic Mike XXL	66.0
19.	Straight Outta Compton	161.2	44.	The Visit	65.2
20.	San Andreas	155.2	45.	Daddy's Home	64.7
21.	Mad Max: Fury Road	153.6	46.	The Wedding Ringer	64.5
22.	The Divergent Series: Insurgent	130.2	47.	Black Mass	62.6
23.	Kingsman: The Secret Service	128.3	48.	Vacation	58.9
24.	The Peanuts Movie	128.2	49.	The Perfect Guy	57.0
25.	Spy	110.8	50.	The Hobbit: The Battle of the Five Armies	56.2

Note: Box-office grosses in the U.S. and Canada Jan. 1, 2015-Dec. 31, 2015; some films had 2014 release dates.

All-Time Top-Grossing American Movies
Source: Rentrak Corporation

Rank	Title (original release date)	Gross (mil)	Rank	Title (original release date)	Gross (mil)
1.	Star Wars: Episode VII—The Force Awakens (2015)	$936.7	25.	The Lord of the Rings: The Return of the King (2003)	$377.0
2.	Avatar (2009)	760.5	26.	Spider-Man 2 (2004)	373.4
3.	Jurassic World (2015)	652.3	27.	The Passion of the Christ (2004)	370.3
4.	The Avengers (2012)	623.4	28.	Despicable Me 2 (2013)	368.1
5.	Titanic (1997)	600.8	29.	The Jungle Book (2016)	363.7
6.	The Dark Knight (2008)	533.3	30.	Deadpool (2016)	363.1
7.	Finding Dory (2016)	479.8	31.	Jurassic Park (1993)	357.1
8.	Star Wars: Episode I—The Phantom Menace (1999)	474.5	32.	Inside Out (2015)	356.5
9.	Star Wars (1977)	461.0	33.	The Secret Life of Pets (2016)	354.6
10.	Avengers: Age of Ultron (2015)	459.0	34.	Furious 7 (2015)	353.0
11.	The Dark Knight Rises (2012)	448.1	35.	Transformers: Dark of the Moon (2011)	352.4
12.	Shrek 2 (2004)	436.7	36.	American Sniper (2014)	350.1
13.	E.T. the Extra-Terrestrial (1982)	435.0	37.	The Lord of the Rings: The Two Towers (2002)	341.7
14.	The Hunger Games: Catching Fire (2013)	424.7	38.	Zootopia (2016)	341.3
15.	Pirates of the Caribbean: Dead Man's Chest (2006)	423.3	39.	Finding Nemo (2003)	339.7
16.	Toy Story 3 (2010)	415.0	40.	The Hunger Games: Mockingjay Part 1 (2014)	337.1
17.	Iron Man 3 (2013)	409.0	41.	Spider-Man 3 (2007)	336.5
18.	The Hunger Games (2012)	408.0	42.	Minions (2015)	336.0
19.	Captain America: Civil War (2016)	407.9	43.	Alice in Wonderland (2010)	334.2
20.	Spider-Man (2002)	403.7	44.	Guardians of the Galaxy (2014)	333.2
21.	Transformers: Revenge of the Fallen (2009)	402.1	45.	Batman v. Superman: Dawn of Justice (2016)	330.4
22.	Frozen (2013)	400.7	46.	Forrest Gump (1994)	330.3
23.	Harry Potter and the Deathly Hallows: Part 2 (2011)	381.0	47.	Shrek the Third (2007)	322.7
24.	Star Wars: Episode III—Revenge of the Sith (2005)	380.3	48.	Transformers (2007)	319.2
			49.	Iron Man (2008)	318.6
			50.	Harry Potter and the Sorcerer's Stone (2001)	317.6

Note: Box-office grosses in the U.S. and Canada through Aug. 31, 2016, in absolute dollars. Rising ticket prices favor newer films. Revenues from re-releases are included.

Most Pirated Movies, 2015-16
Source: Excipio

(ranked by number of torrent downloads worldwide)

Rank	2015 Film (release date)	Downloads	Rank	2016 Film (release date)	Downloads
1.	Avengers: Age of Ultron (2015)	49,105,576	1.	Deadpool (2016)	42,389,711
2.	Furious 7 (2015)	48,910,613	2.	The Revenant (2015)	35,512,568
3.	Interstellar (2014)	48,145,489	3.	Spectre (2015)	24,916,186
4.	Mad Max: Fury Road (2015)	40,171,287	4.	The Martian (2015)	24,491,240
5.	Jurassic World (2015)	40,128,305	5.	Star Wars: Episode VII—The Force Awakens (2015)	23,969,182
6.	Fifty Shades of Grey (2015)	38,238,841	6.	Kung Fu Panda 3 (2016)	21,919,825
7.	The Hobbit: The Battle of the Five Armies (2014)	37,574,923	7.	The Hateful Eight (2015)	21,288,556
8.	American Sniper (2014)	36,765,207	8.	Batman v. Superman: Dawn of Justice (2016)	19,758,839
9.	Terminator Genisys (2015)	35,898,025	9.	Zootopia (2016)	19,117,782
10.	Big Hero 6 (2014)	33,108,816	10.	Creed (2015)	17,328,502

Note: 2016 data is for Jan.-June.

Best American Movies of All Time

Source: American Film Institute

First unveiled in 1998 based on ballots sent to 1,500 individuals, mostly from the film world, in 1997. Updated in 2007 (the version shown here) to include newly eligible films and reflect shifting cultural perspectives. Criteria for judging included historical significance, cultural impact, critical recognition and awards, and popularity. The year each film was first released is in parentheses.

1. Citizen Kane (1941)
2. The Godfather (1972)
3. Casablanca (1942)
4. Raging Bull (1980)
5. Singin' in the Rain (1952)
6. Gone With the Wind (1939)
7. Lawrence of Arabia (1962)
8. Schindler's List (1993)
9. Vertigo (1958)
10. The Wizard of Oz (1939)
11. City Lights (1931)
12. The Searchers (1956)
13. Star Wars (1977)
14. Psycho (1960)
15. 2001: A Space Odyssey (1968)
16. Sunset Boulevard (1950)
17. The Graduate (1967)
18. The General (1927)
19. On the Waterfront (1954)
20. It's a Wonderful Life (1946)
21. Chinatown (1974)
22. Some Like It Hot (1959)
23. The Grapes of Wrath (1940)
24. E.T. the Extra-Terrestrial (1982)
25. To Kill a Mockingbird (1962)
26. Mr. Smith Goes to Washington (1939)
27. High Noon (1952)
28. All About Eve (1950)
29. Double Indemnity (1944)
30. Apocalypse Now (1979)
31. The Maltese Falcon (1941)
32. The Godfather Part II (1974)
33. One Flew Over the Cuckoo's Nest (1975)
34. Snow White and the Seven Dwarfs (1937)
35. Annie Hall (1977)
36. The Bridge on the River Kwai (1957)
37. The Best Years of Our Lives (1946)
38. The Treasure of the Sierra Madre (1948)
39. Dr. Strangelove (1964)
40. The Sound of Music (1965)
41. King Kong (1933)
42. Bonnie and Clyde (1967)
43. Midnight Cowboy (1969)
44. The Philadelphia Story (1940)
45. Shane (1953)
46. It Happened One Night (1934)
47. A Streetcar Named Desire (1951)
48. Rear Window (1954)
49. Intolerance (1916)
50. The Lord of the Rings: The Fellowship of the Ring (2001)

National Film Registry, 2015

Source: National Film Registry, Library of Congress

The National Film Registry adds 25 "culturally, historically, or aesthetically significant" American films annually.

Being There (1979)
Black and Tan (1929)
Dracula (Spanish language version) (1931)
Dream of a Rarebit Fiend (1906)
Eadweard Muybridge, Zoopraxographer (1975)
Edison Kinetoscopic Record of a Sneeze (1894)
A Fool There Was (1915)
Ghostbusters (1984)
Hail the Conquering Hero (1944)
Humoresque (1920)
Imitation of Life (1959)
The Inner World of Aphasia (1968)
John Henry and the Inky-Poo (1946)
L.A. Confidential (1997)
The Mark of Zorro (1920)
The Old Mill (1937)
Our Daily Bread (1934)
Portrait of Jason (1967)
Seconds (1966)
The Shawshank Redemption (1994)
Sink or Swim (1990)
The Story of Menstruation (1946)
Symbiopsychotaxiplasm: Take One (1968)
Top Gun (1986)
Winchester '73 (1950)

Movie Theaters, 1946-2015

Source: Motion Picture Association of America (MPAA); Rentrak Corporation

Year	Box office (mil)	Admissions (mil)	Admissions per week (mil)	Screens	Avg. ticket price	Films produced	Films released
1946	$1,692.0	4,067.3	78.2	NA	$0.42	NA	400
1950	1,379.0	3,017.5	58.0	NA	0.46	NA	483
1955	1,204.0	2,072.3	39.9	NA	0.58	NA	319
1960	984.4	1,304.5	25.1	NA	0.76	NA	248
1965	1,041.8	1,031.5	19.8	NA	1.01	NA	279
1970	1,429.2	920.6	17.7	NA	1.55	279	306
1975	2,114.8	1,032.8	19.9	15,030	2.03	258	233
1980	2,748.5	1,021.5	19.6	17,590	2.69	214	233
1985	3,749.4	1,056.1	20.3	21,147	3.55	264	470
1990	5,021.8	1,188.6	22.9	23,689	4.22	346	410
1995	5,269.0	1,211.0	23.3	27,805	4.35	631	411
2000	7,468.0	1,383.0	26.6	37,396	5.39	683	475
2001	8,125.0	1,438.0	27.7	36,764	5.65	611	454
2002	9,272.0	1,599.0	30.8	35,280	5.80	546	475
2003	9,165.0	1,521.0	29.3	35,786	6.03	593	455
2004	9,215.0	1,484.0	28.5	36,594	6.21	611	489
2005	8,832.0	1,376.0	26.5	38,852	6.41	920	507
2006	9,138.0	1,395.0	26.8	38,415	6.55	928	594
2007	9,629.0	1,400.0	26.9	38,974	6.88	789	611
2008	9,791.0	1,364.0	26.2	38,834	7.18	773	638
2009	10,543.6	1,415.0	27.2	39,233	7.50	751	558
2010	10,741.0	1,341.0	25.8	39,547	7.89	795	563
2011	10,186.1	1,285.0	24.7	39,641	7.93	818	609
2012	10,774.5	1,358.0	26.0	39,918	7.96	476[1]	677
2013	10,919.7	1,340.0	25.8	42,814	8.13	455[1]	659
2014	10,357.4	1,267.6	24.4	43,265	8.17	481[1]	707
2015	11,097.7	1,321.0	25.4	43,661	8.43	501[1]	708

NA = Not available. (1) Non-MPAA members with est. budget under $1 mil were not tracked.

Top Film Websites, 2016

Source: comScore Media Metrix, Inc.; ranked by number of visitors

Rank	Website	Visitors[1]	Rank	Website	Visitors[1]
1.	IMDb	63,606	11.	Moviefone	7,145
2.	Fandango sites	52,873	12.	Disney Movies	6,629
3.	Yahoo Movies	14,684	13.	Regal Entertainment	6,398
4.	Playwire Media—Now Playing Entertainment	11,890	14.	Hollywood.com sites	6,129
5.	MSN Movies	10,413	15.	AMC Entertainment Inc.	5,798
6.	CinemaBlend.com	10,296	16.	Insticator.com	5,590
7.	Moviepilot Network	8,975	17.	Cinemark.com	5,468
8.	Putlocker.is	8,236	18.	MovieGoer Network	5,279
9.	ScreenRant.com	7,555	19.	Nflxext.com	5,047
10.	Lucasfilm Ltd.	7,389	20.	ComplexMovies	4,340

(1) Number of persons age 2 and older, in thousands, who visited the media property (including website/apps) at least once from any U.S. location in June 2016. Mobile users under age 18 are not measured.

Most Popular Movie DVDs, 2015

Source: Rentrak Corporation

Top Rentals, 2015

Rank	Movie	Rank	Movie
1.	The Equalizer (2014)	11.	A Walk Among the Tombstones (2014)
2.	Fury (2014)	12.	Jurassic World
3.	Get Hard	13.	San Andreas
4.	Interstellar (2014)	14.	Paul Blart: Mall Cop 2
5.	Gone Girl (2014)	15.	American Sniper (2014)
6.	Big Hero 6 (2014)	16.	Taken 3 (2014)
7.	The Hunger Games: Mockingjay Part 1 (2014)	17.	Focus
		18.	The Maze Runner (2014)
8.	Lucy (2014)	19.	Kingsman: The Secret Service (2014)
9.	The Wedding Ringer		
10.	John Wick (2014)	20.	The Divergent Series: Insurgent

Top-Selling DVDs, 2015

Rank	Movie	Rank	Movie
1.	Jurassic World	11.	Home
2.	Minions	12.	Pitch Perfect 2
3.	Furious 7	13.	Interstellar (2014)
4.	Big Hero 6 (2014)	14.	Cinderella
5.	Inside Out	15.	Mad Max: Fury Road
6.	Avengers: Age of Ultron	16.	Ant-Man
7.	American Sniper (2014)	17.	San Andreas
8.	The Hobbit: The Battle of the Five Armies (2014)	18.	Paddington (2014)
		19.	Kingsman: The Secret Service (2014)
9.	The Hunger Games: Mockingjay Part 1 (2014)	20.	The Divergent Series: Insurgent
10.	Fifty Shades of Grey		

Note: Includes Blu-ray format titles. Top rentals include units rented in U.S. brick-and-mortar, subscription-by-mail, and kiosk channels. Top-selling DVDs exclude units sold into rental and online channels. Movies released in 2015 unless otherwise noted.

Top-Selling Video Games, 2015

Source: The NPD Group/Retail Tracking Service

U.S. consumers spent $17.0 bil on video game content in 2015: $7.2 bil on physical software and other physical formats (including rental/used content) and $9.9 bil on content in digital formats. Spending decreased 2% on physical content, but digital content spending grew 22%.

Rank	Game (console)	Rank	Game (console)
1.	Call of Duty: Black Ops III (360, PC, PS3, PS4, XBO)*	6.	NBA 2K16 (360, PS3, PS4, XBO)*
2.	Madden NFL 16 (360, PS3, PS4, XBO)*	7.	Minecraft (360, PS3, PS4, XBO)
3.	Fallout 4 (PC, PS4, XBO)*	8.	Mortal Kombat X (PS4, XBO)*
4.	Star Wars Battlefront 2015 (PC, PS4, XBO)*	9.	FIFA 16 (360, PS3, PS4, XBO)*
5.	Grand Theft Auto V (360, PC, PS3, PS4, XBO)*	10.	Call of Duty: Advanced Warfare (360, PC, PS3, PS4, XBO)*

* = Includes bundled, collector's, or game-of-the-year editions, except those bundled with hardware. 360 = Microsoft Xbox 360; PC = personal computer; PS3 = PlayStation 3; PS4 = PlayStation 4; XBO = Microsoft Xbox One.

Film and TV Content Ratings

The Motion Picture Association of America (MPAA) established a ratings system in 1968. It was revised in 1984 and in 1990. The MPAA, Natl. Cable Television Assn., and Natl. Assn. of Broadcasters developed the TV ratings system in 1997, in accordance with the Telecommunications Act of 1996; it was implemented in Oct. 1997.

Film Ratings

G: General Audience. All ages admitted. Does not contain themes, language, nudity, sex, or violence that the MPAA ratings board believes would offend parents whose younger children see the film. Does not necessarily denote a certificate of approval nor children's movie. No nudity, sex scenes, or drug use depicted.

PG: Parental Guidance Suggested. Some material may not be suited for children. The MPAA ratings board recommends that parents determine whether the content of the film is appropriate for their children. The film may contain more mature themes, some profanity, violence, or brief nudity. No drug use depicted.

PG-13: Parents Strongly Cautioned. Some material may be inappropriate for children under 13. The MPAA urges more strongly that parents vet the movie to see if its content is appropriate for their children. Any movie depicting drug use or more than brief nudity is automatically rated at least PG-13. Violence is permitted, though it is generally not both realistic or extreme and persistent violence. The single use of one sexually-derived expletive rates a PG-13; more than one use requires at least an R rating.

R: Restricted. Under 17 requires accompanying parent or adult guardian. Movies given R ratings contain some adult material, defined as adult themes or activity, hard language, intense or persistent violence, sexually-oriented nudity, or drug abuse.

NC-17: No One 17 and Under Admitted. The ratings board considers NC-17 films those that most parents would consider too adult for children under 17. An NC-17 rating does not mean the film is obscene or pornographic. The rating can be based on violence, sex, aberrational behavior, drug abuse, or any other element that most parents would consider too adult for children.

TV Ratings

TV-Y: All Children. Program designed to be acceptable for children of all ages. Its themes and elements are designed for a very young audience.

TV-Y7: Directed to Older Children. Program designed for children ages 7 and older, and more appropriate for those who have the skills to distinguish between make-believe and reality. May include mild fantasy/comedic violence. Programs with more than mild fantasy violence are denoted TV-Y7-FV.

TV-G: General Audience. Program not necessarily designed for children, but most parents would find it suitable for all ages. Little or no violence, no strong language, and little or no sexual dialogue or situations.

TV-PG: Parental Guidance Suggested. Program might contain material that parents would consider inappropriate for children, such as an adult theme or one or more of the following: suggestive dialogue (D), infrequent coarse language (L), some sexual situations (S), or moderate violence (V).

TV-14: Parents Strongly Cautioned. Program contains material that many parents would consider inappropriate for children under 14, such as one or more of the following: intensely suggestive dialogue (D), strong coarse language (L), intense sexual situations (S), or intense violence (V).

TV-MA: Mature Audience Only. Program specifically designed for adults and may be unsuitable for children under 17. Contains one or more of the following: crude indecent language (L), explicit sexual activity (S), or graphic violence (V).

Opera: Most Produced Works, 2015-16

Source: OPERA America

Work, composer	Productions	Work, composer	Productions	Work, composer	Productions
Madama Butterfly, Giacomo Puccini	17	*La traviata*, Giuseppe Verdi	13	*Tosca*, Giacomo Puccini	12
La bohème, Giacomo Puccini	16	*The Barber of Seville*, Gioachino Rossini	12	*Turandot*, Giacomo Puccini	12
Carmen, Georges Bizet	16			*Macbeth*, Giuseppe Verdi	11
Don Giovanni, Wolfgang Amadeus Mozart	14	*The Magic Flute*, Wolfgang Amadeus Mozart	12		

Note: Scheduled productions of a given work (not individual performances) during the 2015-16 season (generally Oct.-Sept.) by members of OPERA America and Opera.ca.

Longest-Running Broadway Shows
Source: The Broadway League, New York, NY

Rank	Title (run)[1]	Performances[2]	Rank	Title (run)[1]	Performances[2]	Rank	Title (run)[1]	Performances[2]
1.	*The Phantom of the Opera (1988-)	11,782	17.	Life With Father (1939-47)	3,224	34.	South Pacific (1949-54)	1,925
2.	*Chicago (revival) (1996-)	8,107	18.	Tobacco Road (1933-41)	3,182	35.	The Magic Show (1974-78)	1,920
3.	*The Lion King (1997-)	7,705	19.	Hello, Dolly! (1964-70)	2,844	36.	Aida (2000-04)	1,852
4.	Cats (1982-2000)	7,485	20.	My Fair Lady (1956-62)	2,717	37.	Gemini (1977-81)	1,819
5.	Les Misérables (1987-2003)	6,680	21.	Hairspray (2002-09)	2,642	38.	Deathtrap (1978-82)	1,793
6.	A Chorus Line (1975-90)	6,137	22.	Mary Poppins (2006-13)	2,619	39.	Harvey (1944-49)	1,775
7.	Oh! Calcutta! (revival) (1976-89)	5,959	23.	Avenue Q (2003-09)	2,534	40.	Dancin' (1978-82)	1,774
8.	Mamma Mia! (2001-15)	5,758	24.	The Producers (2001-07)	2,502	41.	La Cage aux Folles (1983-87)	1,761
9.	Beauty and the Beast (1994-2007)	5,461	25.	Cabaret (revival) (1998-2004)	2,377	42.	Hair (1968-72)	1,750
10.	*Wicked (2003-)	5,238		Annie (1977-83)	2,377	43.	The Wiz (1975-79)	1,672
11.	Rent (1996-2008)	5,123	27.	Rock of Ages (2009-15)	2,328	44.	Born Yesterday (1946-49)	1,642
12.	*Jersey Boys (2005-)	4,370		Man of La Mancha (1965-71)	2,328	45.	Crazy for You (1992-96)	1,622
13.	Miss Saigon (1991-2001)	4,092	29.	Abie's Irish Rose (1922-27)	2,327	46.	Ain't Misbehavin' (1978-82)	1,604
14.	42nd Street (1980-89)	3,486	30.	Oklahoma! (1943-48)	2,212	47.	The Best Little Whorehouse in Texas (1978-82)	1,584
15.	Grease (1972-80)	3,388	31.	*The Book of Mormon (2011-)	2,160	48.	Spamalot (2005-09)	1,575
16.	Fiddler on the Roof (1964-72)	3,242	32.	Smokey Joe's Café (1995-2000)	2,036	49.	Mary, Mary (1961-64)	1,572
			33.	Pippin (1972-77)	1,944	50.	Evita (1979-83)	1,567

* = Still running as of Sept. 1, 2016. (1) Unless noted, listings reflect a play's first run on Broadway. (2) Number of performances through May 22, 2016.

Broadway Season Statistics, 1959-2016
Source: The Broadway League, New York, NY

Season	Gross (mil $)	Attendance (mil)	Playing weeks	New productions	Avg. ticket price	Season	Gross (mil $)	Attendance (mil)	Playing weeks	New productions	Avg. ticket price
1959-1960	$46	7.9	1,156	58	$5.82	2006-2007	$939	12.3	1,509	35	$76.28
1964-1965	51	8.2	1,250	67	6.20	2007-2008	938	12.3	1,560	36	76.45
1969-1970	53	7.1	1,047	62	7.46	2008-2009	943	12.2	1,548	43	77.61
1974-1975	57	6.6	1,101	54	8.64	2009-2010	1,020	11.9	1,464	39	85.79
1979-1980	146	9.6	1,540	61	15.21	2010-2011	1,081	12.5	1,588	42	86.27
1984-1985	209	7.3	1,078	33	28.47	2011-2012	1,139	12.3	1,522	41	92.38
1989-1990	282	8.0	1,070	39	35.07	2012-2013	1,139	11.6	1,430	46	98.44
1994-1995	406	9.0	1,120	33	44.91	2013-2014	1,269	12.2	1,496	44*	103.93
1999-2000	603	11.4	1,460	37	52.99	2014-2015	1,365	13.1	1,626	37	104.20
2004-2005	769	11.5	1,494	39	66.70	2015-2016	1,373	13.3	1,648	39	103.11
2005-2006	862	12.0	1,501	39	71.83						

* = Includes one return engagement.

Notable U.S. Museums

This unofficial list of some of the largest museums in the U.S., by budget, was compiled with the assistance of the American Association of Museums, a national association representing the concerns of the museum community. Association members also include zoos, aquariums, arboretums, botanical gardens, and planetariums, but these are not included in *The World Almanac* listings.

Museum	City	State	Museum	City	State
American Museum of Natural History	New York	NY	Franklin Institute	Philadelphia	PA
Amon Carter Museum of Western Art	Ft. Worth	TX	The Frick Collection	New York	NY
The Art Institute of Chicago	Chicago	IL	J. Paul Getty Museum	Los Angeles	CA
Boston Children's Museum	Boston	MA	Solomon R. Guggenheim Museum of Art	New York	NY
Brooklyn Museum of Art	Brooklyn	NY	Harvard University Art Museums	Cambridge	MA
Busch-Reisinger Museum	Cambridge	MA	Henry F. DuPont Winterthur Museum	Winterthur	DE
California Academy of Sciences	San Francisco	CA	Henry Ford Museum/Greenfield Village	Dearborn	MI
California Science Center	Los Angeles	CA	High Museum of Art	Atlanta	GA
Carnegie Museums of Pittsburgh	Pittsburgh	PA	Houston Museum of Natural Science	Houston	TX
Children's Museum of Indianapolis	Indianapolis	IN	Jamestown-Yorktown Foundation	Williamsburg	VA
Cincinnati Art Museum	Cincinnati	OH	Jewish Museum	New York	NY
Cincinnati Museum Center	Cincinnati	OH	L.A. County Museum of Art	Los Angeles	CA
Cleveland Museum of Art	Cleveland	OH	Liberty Science Center, Liberty State Park	Jersey City	NJ
Colonial Williamsburg	Williamsburg	VA	Maryland Science Center	Baltimore	MD
Corning Museum of Glass	Corning	NY	Mashantucket Pequot Museum and Research Center	Mashantucket	CT
Crystal Bridges Museum of American Art	Bentonville	AR	Metropolitan Museum of Art	New York	NY
Dallas Museum of Art	Dallas	TX	Milwaukee Public Museum	Milwaukee	WI
Denver Art Museum	Denver	CO	Minneapolis Institute of Arts	Minneapolis	MN
Denver Museum of Nature and Science	Denver	CO	Museum of African American History	Detroit	MI
Detroit Institute of Arts	Detroit	MI	Museum of the American West	Los Angeles	CA
Exploratorium	San Francisco	CA	Museum of Contemporary Art	Los Angeles	CA
The Field Museum	Chicago	IL	Museum of Fine Arts	Boston	MA
Fine Arts Museums of San Francisco	San Francisco	CA			

Museum	City	State
Museum of Fine Arts	Houston	TX
Museum of Modern Art	New York	NY
Museum of New Mexico	Santa Fe	NM
Museum of Science	Boston	MA
Museum of Science and Industry	Chicago	IL
Musical Instrument Museum	Phoenix	AZ
Mystic Seaport Museum	Mystic	CT
National Air and Space Museum	Washington	DC
National Baseball Hall of Fame and Museum, Inc.	Cooperstown	NY
National Constitution Center	Philadelphia	PA
National Gallery of Art	Washington	DC
National Museum of American History	Washington	DC
National Museum of the American Indian	Washington	DC
National Museum of Natural History	Washington	DC
Nelson-Atkins Museum of Art	Kansas City	MO
New-York Historical Society	New York	NY

Museum	City	State
New York State Museum	Albany	NY
Peabody Essex Museum	Salem	MA
Philadelphia Museum of Art	Philadelphia	PA
Rock and Roll Hall of Fame and Museum, Inc.	Cleveland	OH
St. Louis Science Center	St. Louis	MO
San Diego Museum of Art	San Diego	CA
San Francisco Museum of Modern Art	San Francisco	CA
Science Museum of Minnesota	St. Paul	MN
Toledo Museum of Art	Toledo	OH
U.S. Holocaust Memorial Museum	Washington	DC
Univ. of Pennsylvania Museum of Archaeology and Anthropology	Philadelphia	PA
Virginia Museum of Fine Arts	Richmond	VA
Wadsworth Atheneum	Hartford	CT
Walker Art Center	Minneapolis	MN
Whitney Museum of American Art	New York	NY

Characteristics of Public Libraries by State, 2014

Source: Public Libraries Survey, Institute of Museum and Library Services

State	Libraries[1]	Operating revenue[2] (thous.)	Library visits		Circulation[3]		Internet use[4]	
			Total (thous.)	Per capita	Total (thous.)	Per capita	Total (thous.)	Per capita
AL	218	$100,345	17,002	3.7	20,494	4.5	4,335	0.9
AK	79	37,651	3,477	5.3	4,778	7.3	767	1.2
AZ	90	168,412	27,610	4.1	43,672	6.6	8,255	1.2
AR	58	74,794	10,974	4.2	14,390	5.4	1,970	0.7
CA	184	1,354,978	164,300	4.3	222,789	5.8	35,001	0.9
CO	113	283,933	32,979	6.4	64,674	12.5	7,394	1.4
CT	182	187,948	20,979	6.1	29,741	8.7	4,289	1.3
DE	21	25,667	3,835	4.1	6,181	6.7	623	0.7
DC	1	54,189	4,231	6.4	3,939	6.0	1,051	1.6
FL	82	505,833	75,554	3.9	116,693	6.0	19,076	1.0
GA	63	201,271	29,490	2.9	39,002	3.8	13,141	1.3
HI	1	33,963	4,875	3.5	6,465	4.6	723	0.5
ID	102	51,685	8,730	6.4	14,334	10.6	1,878	1.4
IL	623	801,990	72,590	6.2	114,148	9.8	13,884	1.2
IN	237	333,051	35,441	5.8	77,210	12.7	7,226	1.2
IA	534	121,677	18,030	5.9	27,848	9.1	3,417	1.1
KS	318	120,993	13,925	5.6	25,029	10.0	3,164	1.3
KY	119	176,636	19,284	4.4	30,480	6.9	4,551	1.0
LA	68	238,886	17,242	3.7	20,838	4.5	5,276	1.1
ME	228	43,790	6,834	5.9	9,287	8.1	1,197	1.0
MD	24	305,466	27,794	4.8	58,308	10.0	6,495	1.1
MA	368	285,560	42,010	6.4	63,104	9.6	7,279	1.1
MI	388	396,217	50,126	5.1	83,817	8.5	10,825	1.1
MN	137	211,189	24,566	4.5	54,128	10.0	5,442	1.0
MS	52	51,750	9,191	3.1	8,066	2.7	2,523	0.8
MO	149	243,607	29,518	5.4	55,686	10.2	6,376	1.2
MT	82	27,101	4,703	4.8	5,942	6.0	1,913	1.9
NE	263	55,738	8,329	5.4	13,157	8.5	2,129	1.4
NV	21	89,935	10,525	3.8	21,042	7.5	2,737	1.0
NH	219	57,973	7,493	6.5	10,423	9.0	989	0.9
NJ	281	468,689	45,302	5.3	58,086	6.7	9,683	1.1
NM	87	47,784	7,323	4.5	9,194	5.6	2,083	1.3
NY	756	1,341,672	106,454	5.5	143,089	7.4	22,261	1.1
NC	80	212,601	35,106	3.6	52,849	5.4	7,806	0.8
ND	73	18,243	2,175	3.4	3,977	6.1	576	0.9
OH	251	757,967	82,495	7.2	183,629	15.9	20,037	1.7
OK	117	113,580	13,687	4.3	21,854	6.9	3,619	1.1
OR	129	201,073	21,638	5.8	57,133	15.2	3,882	1.0
PA	455	343,877	44,792	3.6	66,394	5.3	8,544	0.7
RI	48	46,930	6,026	5.7	7,162	6.8	1,425	1.4
SC	42	130,553	18,179	3.9	26,021	5.6	4,481	1.0
SD	112	25,259	3,915	5.1	5,764	7.6	1,475	1.9
TN	186	112,098	19,528	3.1	26,176	4.1	5,268	0.8
TX	548	487,114	73,033	3.0	113,233	4.7	17,512	0.7
UT	72	104,528	17,650	6.1	37,211	13.0	2,946	1.0
VT	155	21,439	3,702	6.4	4,364	7.6	635	1.1
VA	91	277,591	37,406	4.6	74,613	9.2	7,246	0.9
WA	62	401,115	41,281	6.0	83,745	12.2	10,539	1.5
WV	97	39,073	5,368	2.9	6,262	3.4	1,075	0.6
WI	381	228,511	32,854	5.7	60,411	10.5	6,037	1.1
WY	23	32,104	3,667	6.3	4,914	8.4	905	1.6
U.S.	**9,070**	**$12,054,030**	**1,423,217**	**4.6**	**2,311,745**	**7.5**	**321,962**	**1.1**

(1) Includes central libraries only. (2) Some operating revenues may be estimated. (3) The total annual circulation of all library materials of all types, including renewals. (4) Total number of sessions accessing the internet using the library's devices.

Top 25 Public Libraries in the U.S by Holdings, 2012

Source: American Library Association (ALA)

Rank	Library name	Print materials	Electronic books	Audio and video	Total holdings
1.	New York Public Library, The Branch Libraries, NY	20,889,337	262,444	2,080,901	23,232,682
2.	Boston Public Libraries, MA	8,947,271	20,198	168,144	9,135,613
3.	Detroit Public Library, MI	6,870,782	982	245,137	7,116,901
4.	Los Angeles Public Library, CA	6,301,338	37,077	582,658	6,921,073
5.	County of Los Angeles Public Library, CA	5,367,967	16,593	948,541	6,333,101
6.	Public Library of Cincinnati and Hamilton County, OH	4,772,281	125,076	930,374	5,827,731
7.	Chicago Public Library, IL	5,032,111	11,016	365,282	5,408,409
8.	San Diego Public Library, CA	4,883,416	56,052	439,889	5,379,357
9.	Queens Borough Public Library, NY	4,481,261	27,192	497,674	5,006,127
10.	Hennepin County Library, MN	4,274,219	78,062	301,126	4,653,407
11.	King County Library System, WA	3,623,876	98,948	712,035	4,434,859
12.	Dallas Public Library, TX	4,131,672	10,153	249,993	4,391,818
13.	Hawaii State Public Library System, HI	3,393,557	11,688	415,035	3,820,280
14.	Cleveland Public Library, OH	3,283,319	79,089	358,892	3,721,300
15.	Broward County Libraries Division, FL	2,764,321	115,810	783,553	3,663,684
16.	Miami-Dade Public Library System, FL	3,294,232	30,002	253,858	3,578,092
17.	Brooklyn Public Library, NY	3,179,126	43,994	275,428	3,498,548
18.	Free Library of Philadelphia, PA	2,811,962	146,656	489,465	3,448,083
19.	Allen County Public Library, IN	2,996,595	28,220	230,980	3,255,795
20.	San Francisco Public Library, CA	2,723,178	19,170	360,927	3,103,275
21.	Las Vegas-Clark County Library District, NV	2,222,341	79,921	646,349	2,948,611
22.	Houston Public Library, TX	2,682,526	19,736	225,749	2,928,011
23.	Jacksonville Public Library, FL	2,342,818	31,502	498,316	2,872,636
24.	Cuyahoga County Public Library, OH	1,756,053	109,887	900,195	2,766,135
25.	Mid-Continent Public Library (Kansas City metro area), MO	2,367,164	7,805	382,825	2,757,794

Most Challenged Books, 2015

Source: Office for Intellectual Freedom, American Library Association (ALA)

A challenge is a formal, written complaint filed with a library or school requesting that materials be removed because of content or appropriateness. The common reasons given for challenges follow each book's title and author.

1. *Looking for Alaska*, John Green: Offensive language, sexually explicit, and unsuited for age group.
2. *Fifty Shades of Grey*, E. L. James: Sexually explicit, unsuited to age group, and other ("poorly written," "concerns that a group of teenagers will want to try it").
3. *I Am Jazz*, Jessica Herthel and Jazz Jennings: Inaccurate, homosexuality, sex education, religious viewpoint, and unsuited for age group.
4. *Beyond Magenta: Transgender Teens Speak Out*, Susan Kuklin: Anti-family, offensive language, homosexuality, sex education, political viewpoint, religious viewpoint, unsuited for age group, and other ("wants to remove from collection to ward off complaints").
5. *The Curious Incident of the Dog in the Night-Time*, Mark Haddon: Offensive language, religious viewpoint, unsuited for age group, and other ("profanity and atheism").
6. *The Holy Bible*: Religious viewpoint.
7. *Fun Home*, Alison Bechdel: Violence and other ("graphic images").
8. *Habibi*, Craig Thompson: Nudity, sexually explicit, and unsuited for age group.
9. *Nasreen's Secret School: A True Story From Afghanistan*, Jeanette Winter: Religious viewpoint, unsuited to age group, and violence.
10. *Two Boys Kissing*, David Levithan: Homosexuality and other ("condones public displays of affection").

Best-Selling U.S. Magazines, 2016

Source: Audit Bureau of Circulations (ABC)

General magazines, exclusive of comics; also excludes magazines that failed to file reports to ABC. Based on total average paid and verified circulation during the six months ending June 30, 2016; ranked by paid circulation size.

Publication	Paid circ.	Publication	Paid circ.	Publication	Paid circ.
1. AARP The Magazine	23,144,225	18. Glamour	2,297,755	34. InStyle	1,745,697
2. AARP The Bulletin	22,700,945	19. Redbook	2,221,487	35. Rachael Ray Every Day	1,735,930
3. Better Homes and		20. Taste of Home	2,217,616	36. Golf Digest	1,640,948
Gardens	7,645,364	21. ESPN The Magazine	2,138,762	37. Money	1,577,860
4. Game Informer Magazine	6,353,075	22. American Rifleman	2,131,072	38. TV Guide Magazine	1,571,537
5. AAA Living	4,898,168	23. FamilyFun Magazine	2,124,620	39. Guideposts	1,529,725
6. Good Housekeeping	4,315,026	24. Martha Stewart Living	2,119,341	40. Bon Appétit	1,516,975
7. Family Circle	4,056,156	25. Parents	2,078,090	41. Prevention	1,512,798
8. People	3,418,555	26. Real Simple	2,038,429	42. Entertainment Weekly	1,511,979
9. Woman's Day	3,275,962	27. Seventeen	2,000,585	43. Women's Health	1,511,791
10. National Geographic	3,147,721	28. American Legion		44. Self	1,491,431
11. Sports Illustrated	3,057,042	Magazine	1,993,065	45. Rolling Stone	1,467,971
12. Time	3,032,581	29. Us Weekly	1,956,591	46. Golf Magazine	1,417,816
13. Cosmopolitan	3,011,848	30. Men's Health	1,852,715	47. Country Living	1,411,880
14. Southern Living	2,828,450	31. Smithsonian	1,840,077	48. Health	1,363,422
15. Reader's Digest	2,662,066	32. Cooking Light	1,793,587	49. HGTV Magazine	1,337,770
16. Shape	2,521,203	33. Food Network Magazine	1,790,032	50. Allrecipes	1,333,122
17. O, The Oprah Magazine	2,398,130				

Best-Selling Digital Replica U.S. Magazines, 2016

Source: Audit Bureau of Circulations (ABC)

General magazines, exclusive of comics; also excludes magazines that failed to file reports to ABC. Based on total average paid and verified circulation during the six months ending June 30, 2016; ranked by paid circulation size.

Publication	Paid circ.	Publication	Paid circ.	Publication	Paid circ.
1. Game Informer Magazine	2,456,163	17. Backpacker	99,621	34. Weight Watchers	72,014
2. Maxim	244,614	18. Popular Science	98,569	35. Automobile Magazine	68,103
3. National Geographic	192,117	19. Prevention	97,309	36. Vanity Fair	67,070
4. Star Magazine	166,238	20. New Yorker	96,835	37. Runner's World	65,691
5. Nylon	143,025	21. Cosmopolitan	96,151	38. Fast Company	64,463
6. Better Homes and Gardens	139,504	22. O, The Oprah Magazine	95,813	39. Rachael Ray Every Day	64,428
7. Men's Health	137,439	23. Food Network Magazine	92,292	40. Popular Photography	62,703
8. Shape	121,883	24. HGTV Magazine	83,768	41. Scientific American	62,614
9. Bloomberg BusinessWeek	120,949	25. Vegetarian Times	83,365	42. Outside	62,111
10. Motor Trend	118,429	26. Family Circle	83,300	43. Rolling Stone	61,651
11. Vanidades	110,544	27. EatingWell	83,179	44. Time	60,116
12. Women's Health	106,314	28. Martha Stewart Living	77,330	45. FamilyFun Magazine	59,421
13. OK! Weekly	104,067	29. Us Weekly	76,057	46. Parents	59,068
14. ESPN The Magazine	102,655	30. People	75,943	47. Allrecipes	58,568
15. Yoga Journal	102,029	31. Clean Living	74,175	48. Entrepeneur	57,650
16. Hot Rod Magazine	101,786	32. Ski Magazine	74,107	49. Out	56,667
		33. Real Simple	73,636	50. Reader's Digest	56,447

Some Notable New Books, 2016

Source: Reference and User Services Association, American Library Association (ALA)

Fiction
In the Country: Stories, Mia Alvar
The Sellout: A Novel, Paul Beatty
Did You Ever Have a Family, Bill Clegg
Delicious Foods: A Novel, James Hannaham
Black River: A Novel, S. M. Hulse
Fortune Smiles: Stories, Adam Johnson
The Prophets of Eternal Fjord: A Novel, Kim Leine, translated by Martin Aitken
The Tsar of Love and Techno: Stories, Anthony Marra
The Sympathizer: A Novel, Viet Thanh Nguyen
This Is the Life: A Novel, Alex Shearer
The Book of Aron, Jim Shepard
A Little Life, Hanya Yanagihara

Poetry
Bastards of the Reagan Era, Reginald Dwayne Betts
Conflict Resolution for Holy Beings: Poems, Joy Harjo

Nonfiction
The Interstellar Age: Inside the Forty-Year Voyager Mission, Jim Bell
Give Us the Ballot: The Modern Struggle for Voting Rights in America, Ari Berman
The End of Plenty: The Race to Feed a Crowded World, Joel K. Bourne Jr.
Between the World and Me, Ta-Nehisi Coates
The Gay Revolution: The Story of the Struggle, Lillian Faderman
Romantic Outlaws: The Extraordinary Lives of Mary Wollstonecraft and Her Daughter, Mary Shelley, Charlotte Gordon
Dead Wake: The Last Crossing of the Lusitania, Erik Larson
The Wright Brothers, David McCullough
The Soul of an Octopus: A Surprising Exploration into the Wonder of Consciousness, Sy Montgomery
M Train, Patti Smith
Nagasaki: Life After Nuclear War, Susan Southard
Stalin's Daughter: The Extraordinary and Tumultuous Life of Svetlana Alliluyeva, Rosemary Sullivan

Best-Selling Books, 2015

Source: Publishers Weekly; Nielsen BookScan

Hardcover Fiction
1. *Go Set a Watchman*, Harper Lee
2. *The Girl on the Train*, Paula Hawkins
3. *Rogue Lawyer*, John Grisham
4. *See Me*, Nicholas Sparks
5. *The Nightingale*, Kristin Hannah
6. *The Bazaar of Bad Dreams: Stories*, Stephen King
7. *The Girl in the Spider's Web*, David Lagercrantz
8. *Cross Justice*, James Patterson
9. *The Guilty*, David Baldacci
10. *Tricky Twenty-Two*, Janet Evanovich

Hardcover Nonfiction
1. *Killing Reagan*, Bill O'Reilly and Martin Dugard
2. *The Pioneer Woman Cooks: Dinnertime*, Ree Drummond
3. *The Wright Brothers*, David McCullough
4. *Guinness World Records 2016*
5. *Between the World and Me*, Ta-Nehisi Coates
6. *The 20/20 Diet*, Phil McGraw
7. *Thomas Jefferson and the Tripoli Pirates*, Brian Kilmeade and Don Yaeger
8. *Humans of New York: Stories*, Brandon Stanton
9. *The Whole30*, Melissa Hartwig and Dallas Hartwig
10. *Why Not Me?* Mindy Kaling

Mass Market Fiction
1. *Gray Mountain: A Novel*, John Grisham
2. *The Martian*, Andy Weir
3. *The Escape*, David Baldacci
4. *Deadline: A Virgil Flowers Novel*, John Sanford
5. *Cold Cold Heart*, Tami Hoag
6. *Hope to Die*, James Patterson
7. *Invisible*, James Patterson and David Ellis
8. *The Burning Room: A Harry Bosch Novel*, Michael Connelly
9. *Pegasus: A Novel*, Danielle Steel
10. *Havana Storm: A Dirk Pitt Novel*, Clive Cussler

Trade Paperback
1. *Grey: Fifty Shades of Grey as Told by Christian*, E. L. James
2. *Paper Towns*, John Green
3. *Secret Garden: An Inky Treasure Hunt and Coloring Book*, Johanna Basford
4. *Enchanted Forest: An Inky Quest & Coloring Book*, Johanna Basford
5. *The Martian*, Andy Weir
6. *The Boys in the Boat: Nine Americans and Their Epic Quest for Gold at the 1936 Berlin Olympics*, Daniel James Brown
7. *Lost Ocean: An Inky Adventure and Coloring Book for Adults*, Johanna Basford
8. *Laugh-Out-Loud Jokes for Kids*, Rob Elliott
9. *Miss Peregrine's Home for Peculiar Children*, Ransom Riggs
10. *Looking for Alaska*, John Green

Children's and Young Adult Hardcover
1. *Old School (Diary of a Wimpy Kid Series #10)*, Jeff Kinney
2. *The Isle of the Lost: A Descendants Novel*, Melissa de la Cruz
3. *What Pet Should I Get?*, Dr. Seuss
4. *Dork Diaries 10: Tales From a Not-So-Perfect Pet Sitter*, Rachel Renée Russell
5. *Magnus Chase and the Gods of Asgard, Book 1: The Sword of Summer*, Rick Riordan
6. *Dork Diaries 9: Tales from a Not-So-Dorky Drama Queen*, Rachel Renée Russell
7. *Harry Potter and the Sorcerer's Stone: The Illustrated Edition*, J. K. Rowling and Jim Kay
8. *The Day the Crayons Came Home*, Drew Daywalt and Oliver Jeffers
9. *Twilight Tenth Anniversary/Life and Death Dual Edition*, Stephenie Meyer
10. *Descendants: Mal's Spell Book*, Disney Book Group

Note: Hardcover and mass market bestsellers include frontlist/2015 releases only. Trade paperback bestsellers are for overall 2015 sales of paperback editions for titles first published in any year.

U.S. Daily Newspapers, 2015

Source: *Editor & Publisher International Data Book*
(ranked by circulation as of Sept. 30, 2015)

Rank	Newspaper	Circulation	Rank	Newspaper	Circulation
1.	McLean (VA) *USA Today*	3,981,877	27.	San Diego (CA) *Union-Tribune*	208,448
2.	New York (NY) *Wall Street Journal*	2,285,084	28.	San Francisco (CA) *Chronicle*	206,868
3.	New York (NY) *Times*	2,100,822	29.	Springfield (MA) *Republican*	194,292
4.	San Jose (CA) *Mercury News*	651,418	30.	Phoenix (AZ) *Republic*	188,467
5.	Los Angeles (CA) *Times*	615,664	31.	Tampa (FL) *Tribune*	180,461
6.	New York (NY) *Post*	487,762	32.	Orlando (FL) *Sentinel*	173,542
7.	Melville (NY) *Newsday*	460,149	33.	Seattle (WA) *Times*	167,995
8.	Santa Ana (CA) *Orange County Register*	456,376	34.	Miama (FL) *Herald*	166,272
9.	Woodland Hills (CA) *Daily News*	448,234	35.	Woodland Park (NJ) *Herald News*	152,167
10.	New York (NY) *Daily News*	441,618	36.	Los Angeles (CA) *La Opinión*	151,793
11.	Washington (DC) *Post*	436,601	37.	Ft. Lauderdale (FL) *South Florida Sun-Sentinel*	147,934
12.	Chicago (IL) *Tribune*	390,517			
13.	Las Vegas (NV) *Review-Journal*	364,326	38.	Sacramento (CA) *Bee*	144,399
14.	St. Petersburg (FL) *Tampa Bay Times*	317,270	39.	Clinton (PA) *Pittsburgh Post-Gazette*	140,987
15.	Denver (CO) *Post*	295,082	40.	St. Paul (MN) *Pioneer Press*	139,403
16.	Minneapolis (MN) *Star Tribune*	288,315	41.	Little Rock (AR) *Democrat-Gazette*	135,267
17.	Chicago (IL) *Sun-Times*	269,687	42.	Portland (OR) *Oregonian*	133,703
18.	Dallas (TX) *Morning News*	258,667	43.	Henderson (NV) *Las Vegas Sun*	127,648
19.	Cleveland (OH) *Plain Dealer*	251,509	44.	Buffalo (NY) *News*	127,502
20.	Philadelphia (PA) *Inquirer*	249,921	45.	Milwaukee (WI) *Journal Sentinel*	127,367
21.	Boston (MA) *Globe*	243,986	46.	Riverside (CA) *Press-Enterprise*	124,051
22.	Houston (TX) *Chronicle*	237,549	47.	Kansas City (MO) *Star*	122,094
23.	Silver City (NM) *Sun-News*	230,687	48.	Norfolk (VA) *Virginian-Pilot*	120,091
	Albuquerque (NM) *Daily Lobo*	230,687	49.	Detroit (MI) *Free Press*	117,325
25.	Austin (TX) *American-Statesman*	226,049	50.	Walnut Creek (CA) *Tri-Valley Times*	113,068
26.	Newark (NJ) *Star-Ledger*	213,890			

Note: Excludes newspapers for which no average weekday circulation number was available.

Paid U.S. Newspaper Circulation, 1940-2015

Source: *Editor & Publisher International Data Book*
(circulation figures in thousands as of Sept. 30, 2015)

Year	Number of daily newspapers			Circulation of daily newspapers			Sunday newspapers	
	Morning	Evening	Total	Morning	Evening	Total	Number	Circulation
1940	380	1,498	1,878	16,114	25,018	41,132	525	32,371
1950	322	1,450	1,772	21,266	32,563	53,829	549	46,582
1960	312	1,459	1,763	24,029	34,853	58,882	563	47,699
1970	334	1,429	1,748	25,934	36,174	62,108	586	49,217
1980	387	1,388	1,745	29,414	32,787	62,202	736	54,676
1990	559	1,084	1,611	41,311	21,017	62,328	863	62,635
2000	766	727	1,480	46,772	9,000	55,773	917	59,421
2005	817	645	1,452	46,122	7,222	53,345	914	55,270
2006	833	614	1,437	45,441	6,888	52,329	907	53,179
2007	867	565	1,422	44,548	6,194	50,742	907	51,246
2008	872	546	1,408	42,758	5,840	48,598	902	49,115
2009	869	528	1,397	40,796	5,482	46,278	919	46,850
2011	931	451	1,382	40,321	4,100	44,421	900	48,510
2012	985	442	1,427	38,723	4,709	43,432	981	48,821
2013	980	444	1,395	36,795	3,737	40,712	934	43,292
2014	953	402	1,331	36,765	3,655	40,420	923	42,751
2015	972	389	1,350	31,620	3,280	34,900	904	40,013

Canadian Daily Newspapers, 2015

Source: *Editor & Publisher International Data Book*
(ranked by circulation as of Sept. 30, 2015)

Rank	Newspaper	Circulation	Rank	Newspaper	Circulation
1.	Toronto (ON) *Globe and Mail*	222,575	6.	Calgary (AB) *Herald*	101,012
2.	Toronto (ON) *Star*	171,674	7.	Montréal (QC) *La Presse*	92,762
3.	Montréal (QC) *Le Journal de Montréal*	171,560	8.	Edmonton (AB) *Journal*	89,595
4.	Vancouver (BC) *Sun*	125,623	9.	Bedford (NS) *Chronicle Herald*	88,893
5.	Vancouver (BC) *Province*	104,562	10.	Toronto (ON) *Sun*	86,462

Top Newspaper Websites, 2016

Source: comScore Media Metrix, Inc.
(ranked by number of visitors, in thousands)

Rank	Website	Visitors[1]	Rank	Website	Visitors[1]
1.	The New York Times	74,723	12.	Cox Media Group-Newspaper	15,493
2.	WashingtonPost.com	71,201	13.	Lee Enterprises, Inc.	14,045
3.	Mail Online	71,053	14.	Berkshire Hathaway Media Group	10,995
4.	T-365-Tribune Newspapers	64,941	15.	A. H. Belo	9,075
5.	Hearst Newspapers	42,075	16.	BostonGlobe.com sites	9,063
6.	The Guardian	41,818	17.	Miami Herald sites	8,132
7.	NY Post Network	32,661	18.	Sun-Times Media/Chicago Region-Wide Network (CRWN)	8,130
8.	Telegraph Media Group	21,272			
9.	MediaNews Group	21,173	19.	Michigan.com sites	7,439
10.	Independent.co.uk	20,084	20.	Philly.com sites	7,321
11.	Mirror Online	17,656			

(1) Number of persons age 2 and older, in thousands, who visited the media property (including website/apps) at least once from any U.S. location in June 2016. Mobile users under age 18 are not measured.

Top News/Information Websites, 2016
Source: comScore Media Metrix, Inc.
(ranked by number of visitors, in thousands)

Rank Website	Visitors[1]	Rank Website	Visitors[1]
1. Yahoo-ABC News Network	136,879	11. Mail Online	71,053
2. CNN Network	136,147	12. T365-Tribune Newspapers	64,941
3. The Weather Company	119,988	13. Fox News Digital Network	64,470
4. NBC News Digital	110,508	14. AccuWeather sites	51,424
5. USA Today Network	107,352	15. About	49,164
6. CBS News	90,854	16. Frankly Inc. (formerly WorldNow)	43,619
7. Huffington Post Media Group	90,264	17. Advance Digital	42,100
8. Buzzfeed.com	77,798	18. Hearst Newspapers	42,075
9. New York Times Digital	74,855	19. The Guardian	41,818
10. WashingtonPost.com	71,201	20. BBC sites	40,597

(1) Number of persons age 2 and older, in thousands, who visited the media property (including website/apps) at least once from any U.S. location in June 2016. Mobile users under age 18 are not measured.

National Recording Registry, 2015
Source: Library of Congress

Each year since 2002, the National Recording Registry at the Library of Congress adds 25 recordings showcasing the "range and diversity of American recorded sound heritage."

"Let Me Call You Sweetheart" (single), Columbia Quartette (The Peerless Quartet) (1911)
"Wild Cat Blues" (single), Clarence Williams' Blue Five (1923)
"Statesboro Blues" (single), Blind Willie McTell (1928)
"Bonaparte's Retreat," W.H. Stepp (1937)
"Vic and Sade," episode: "Decoration Day" (May 28, 1937)
Mahler Symphony No. 9, Vienna Philharmonic Orchestra, Bruno Walter, conductor (1938)
"Carousel of American Music," George M. Cohan, Irving Berlin, Johnny Mercer, Arthur Freed, Shelton Brooks, Hoagy Carmichael, others (Sept. 24, 1940)
The Marshall Plan Speech, George C. Marshall (June 5, 1947)
"Destination Freedom" episodes: "A Garage in Gainesville" and "Execution Awaited" (Sept. 25 and Oct. 2, 1949)
A Streetcar Named Desire (original soundtrack), Alex North, composer (1951)
"Cry Me a River" (single), Julie London (1955)

"Mack the Knife" (singles), Louis Armstrong (1956), Bobby Darin (1959)
Radio coverage of fourth quarter of Wilt Chamberlin's 100-point game (Philadelphia Warriors vs. New York Knicks), Bill Campbell, announcer (Mar. 2, 1962)
A Love Supreme, John Coltrane (1964)
It's My Way, Buffy Sainte-Marie (1964)
"Where Did Our Love Go" (single), The Supremes (1964)
"People Get Ready" (single), The Impressions (1965)
"Mama Tried" (single), Merle Haggard (1968)
Abraxas, Santana (1970)
Class Clown, George Carlin (1972)
Robert and Clara Schumann Complete Piano Trios, The Beaux Arts Trio (1972)
"Piano Man" (single), Billy Joel (1973)
Bogalusa Boogie, Clifton Chenier (1976)
"I Will Survive" (single), Gloria Gaynor (1978)
Master of Puppets, Metallica (1986)

U.S. Commercial Radio Stations by Format, 2006-16
Source: Inside Radio (www.insideradio.com)
(as of July 2016; ranked by 2016 numbers)

Primary format	2006	2007	2008	2009	2010	2011	2012	2013	2014	2015	2016
1. Country	2,034	2,032	2,024	1,996	1,996	1,988	2,013	2,042	2,049	2,105	2,126
2. News/Talk	1,335	1,363	1,367	1,414	1,436	1,453	1,498	1,465	1,415	1,364	1,353
3. Spanish	705	781	799	801	806	812	816	835	847	856	877
4. Classic Hits	425	468	519	572	624	656	664	681	743	799	871
5. Sports	530	560	595	634	661	677	690	737	783	789	781
6. Adult Contemporary	660	664	668	627	635	609	595	604	599	607	608
7. Top 40	485	473	470	482	492	522	557	573	578	578	585
8. Classic Rock	455	456	474	479	482	478	479	482	486	486	488
9. Hot Adult Contemporary	375	377	372	408	421	434	419	423	461	465	463
10. Oldies	729	712	702	665	642	622	598	568	488	409	351
11. Religion (Teaching, Variety)	313	288	298	327	324	332	343	343	325	316	321
12. Rock	279	281	288	295	296	302	295	297	303	306	307
13. Black Gospel	266	252	244	242	233	226	217	210	211	217	215
14. Contemporary Christian	150	151	136	156	165	167	165	172	158	168	172
15. Adult Standards	369	372	359	328	270	253	242	227	221	193	169
Total stations	11,038	11,161	11,224	11,310	11,360	11,351	11,415	11,403	11,396	11,314	11,390

Note: Totals include stations that are changing or did not report format, as well as formats not listed here.

Top-Selling Albums of All Time
Source: Recording Industry Assn. of America (RIAA)
(Sales figures represent RIAA multi-platinum certifications; albums ranked by latest sales certification. As of Aug. 23, 2016.)

Rank Title, artist	Unit sales (mil)	Rank Title, artist	Unit sales (mil)
1. *Thriller*, Michael Jackson	32.0	15. *The Beatles 1967-1970*, The Beatles	17.0
2. *Eagles/Their Greatest Hits 1971-1975*, Eagles	29.0	16. *The Bodyguard* (soundtrack), Whitney Houston	17.0
3. *Greatest Hits Volume I & Volume II*, Billy Joel	23.0	17. *Jagged Little Pill*, Alanis Morissette	16.0
4. *Led Zeppelin IV*, Led Zeppelin	23.0	18. *Hotel California*, Eagles	16.0
5. *The Wall*, Pink Floyd	23.0	19. *Cracked Rear View*, Hootie & the Blowfish	16.0
6. *Back in Black*, AC/DC	22.0	20. *Physical Graffiti*, Led Zeppelin	16.0
7. *Double Live*, Garth Brooks	21.0	21. *Metallica*, Metallica	16.0
8. *Rumours*, Fleetwood Mac	20.0	22. *Saturday Night Fever* (soundtrack), Bee Gees	15.0
9. *Come on Over*, Shania Twain	20.0	23. *Legend*, Bob Marley and the Wailers	15.0
10. *The Beatles*, The Beatles	19.0	24. *Born in the U.S.A.*, Bruce Springsteen	15.0
11. *Appetite for Destruction*, Guns N' Roses	18.0	25. *Greatest Hits*, Journey	15.0
12. *Boston*, Boston	17.0	26. *Dark Side of the Moon*, Pink Floyd	15.0
13. *Greatest Hits*, Elton John	17.0	27. *Supernatural*, Santana	15.0
14. *No Fences*, Garth Brooks	17.0	28. *The Beatles 1962-1966*, The Beatles	15.0

Top-Selling Artists by Digital Sales

Source: Recording Industry Assn. of America (RIAA)

(Sales figures represent RIAA-confirmed digital units sold. As of Aug. 23, 2016.)

Artist	Unit sales (mil)	Artist	Unit sales (mil)	Artist	Unit sales (mil)	Artist	Unit sales (mil)
Rihanna	108.0	Carrie Underwood	30.0	Macklemore and Ryan Lewis	22.5	Fun.	17.0
Taylor Swift	97.5	Adele	28.0	Blake Shelton	22.0	The Fray	17.0
Katy Perry	83.5	Nicki Minaj	26.0	The Black Eyed Peas	22.0	Fergie	16.5
Lady Gaga	59.0	Jason Aldean	26.0	Tim McGraw	19.5	Luke Bryan	16.5
Justin Bieber	51.0	Fall Out Baby	24.5	Ed Sheeran	19.5	Sam Smith	16.5
Kanye West	48.0	Florida Georgia Line	24.5	Meghan Trainor	19.0	Miley Cyrus	16.0
Flo Rida	41.0	Wiz Khalifa	24.0	Imagine Dragons	19.0	Selena Gomez & the Scene	15.0
Drake	39.0	The Weeknd	23.0	Ariana Grande	18.5	Maroon 5	15.0
Bruno Mars	38.0	Beyoncé	23.0	LMFAO	18.0	Kenny Chesney	15.0
Eminem	34.0	Jason Derulo	22.5			Lady Antebellum	14.5
Lil Wayne	32.0						

Multi-Platinum and Platinum Awards for Recorded Music, 2015-16

Source: Recording Industry Assn. of America (RIAA)

To be certified platinum, an **album** must sell 1 mil units (LPs, CDs, or digital) with a manufacturer's dollar volume of at least $2 mil based on one-third of the suggested retail list price for each copy sold. To achieve multi-platinum status, an album must reach minimum total sales of at least 2 mil units with a manufacturer's dollar volume of at least $4 mil based on one-third of the list price. RIAA began including streaming in their platinum and multi-platinum award formulas in 2016; 1,500 streams count as the equivalent of ten track sales or one album sale. **Digital singles** must sell 1 mil units to achieve a platinum award and 2 mil to achieve a multi-platinum award. For digital singles award formulas, 150 streams equal one download sold.

Awards listed here are for albums and digital singles (released Sept. 2014-Aug. 2016) that were certified Sept. 2015-Aug. 2016. Number in parentheses represents millions sold. Alphabetized by artist name.

Albums, Multi-Platinum

25, Adele (8)
Purpose, Justin Bieber (3)
If You're Reading This It's Too Late, Drake (2)
Views, Drake (2)
Montevallo, Sam Hunt (2)
The Pinkprint, Nicki Minaj (2)
That's Christmas to Me, Pentatonix (2)
Anti, Rihanna (2)
Beauty Behind the Madness, The Weeknd (3)
Title, Meghan Trainor (2)

Albums, Platinum

Lemonade, Beyoncé
Dark Sky Paradise, Big Sean
X, Chris Brown
Kill the Lights, Luke Bryan
2014 Forest Hills Drive, J. Cole
What a Time to Be Alive, Drake & Future
American Beauty/American Psycho, Fall Out Boy
Fetty Wap, Fetty Wap
Anything Goes, Florida Georgia Line
DS2, Future
When It's Dark Out, G-Eazy
Hozier, Hozier
To Pimp a Butterfly, Kendrick Lamar
Queen of the Clouds, Tove Lo
Handwritten, Shawn Mendes
Made in the A.M., One Direction
Hoy Más Fuerte, Gerardo Ortiz
SremmLife, Rae Sremmurd
Traveller, Chris Stapleton
T R A P S O U L, Bryson Tiller
Blurryface, Twenty One Pilots
Greatest Hits: Decade Number 1, Carrie Underwood
Fifty Shades of Grey soundtrack, various artists
Hamilton cast recording, various artists

Digital Singles, Platinum and Multi-Platinum

"Hello" (6), Adele
"Ay Vamos" (10), "Bobo," "Ginza" (10), J Balvin
"I'll Show You," "Love Yourself" (2), "Sorry" (5), "What Do You Mean?" (5), Justin Bieber
"Blessings" (2), "I Don't F**k With You" (3), Big Sean
"Burning House," Cam
"Here" (2), Alessia Cara
"Don't Let Me Down" (2), "Roses" (2), The Chainsmokers
"Andas en Mi Cabeza," Chino & Nacho
"I Bet," Ciara

"Adventure of a Lifetime," Coldplay
"No Role Modelz," "Wet Dreamz," J. Cole
"Hide Away," Daya
"Want to Want Me" (2), Jason Derulo
"Panda," Desiigner
"The Sound of Silence," Disturbed
"Middle," DJ Snake feat. Bipolar Sunshine
"You Know You Like It" (2), DJ Snake & AlunaGeorge
"Cake by the Ocean" (2), DNCE
"Energy" (2), "Hotline Bling" (5), "Jumpman" (3), Drake
"Centuries" (4), "Immortals," "Irresistible," "Uma Thurman" (2), Fall Out Boy
"Lejos De Aqui" (3), Farruko
"My Way," Fetty Wap
"Work From Home" (2), Fifth Harmony feat. Ty Dolla $ign
"Worth It" (3), Fifth Harmony feat. Kid Ink
"G.D.F.R." (3), "My House" (3), Flo Rida
"Sippin' on Fire," "Sun Daze," Florida Georgia Line
"F*ck Up Some Commas," Future
"Where Ya At," Future feat. Drake
"Low Life," Future feat. The Weeknd
"Really Really," "2 Phones" (2), Kevin Gates
"Me, Myself & I" (3), G-Eazy & Bebe Rexha
"Good for You" (3), Selena Gomez feat. A$AP Rocky
"Hands to Myself," "Same Old Love" (2), Selena Gomez
"On My Mind," Ellie Goulding
"Dangerous Woman," "Focus," Ariana Grande
"Hey Mama" (2), David Guetta feat. Nicki Minaj, Bebe Rexha, Afrojack
"How Deep Is Your Love," Calvin Harris & Disciples
"House Party" (2), Sam Hunt
"Hit the Quan," iLoveMemphis
"I Bet My Life," Imagine Dragons
"Buy Me a Boat," Chris Janson
"Oui," "Planez," Jeremih
"Classic Man," Jidenna feat. Roman GianArthur
"Close," Nick Jonas feat. Tove Lo
"See You Again" (6), Wiz Khalifa feat. Charlie Puth
"Ex's & Oh's" (2), Elle King
"Say It," Tory Lanez
"Never Forget You," Zara Larsson & MNEK
"Girl Crush" (2), Little Big Town
"Confident," "Cool for the Summer," Demi Lovato
"7 Years" (3), Lukas Graham
"Downtown," Macklemore & Ryan Lewis feat. Eric Nally, Melle Mel, Kool Moe Dee, Grandmaster Caz
"Lean On" (4), Major Lazer feat. MØ & DJ Snake

"Something Big," "Stitches" (4), Shawn Mendes
"I Know What You Did Last Summer," Shawn Mendes & Camila Cabello
"R.I.C.O.," Meek Mill
"The Night Is Still Young," Nicki Minaj
"Picky," Joey Montana
"The Fix," Nelly feat. Jeremih
"Coco," O.T. Genasis
"Break Up With Him," Old Dominion
"Fight Song" (3), "Stand By You," Rachel Platten
"I Took a Pill in Ibiza" (2), Mike Posner
"White Iverson" (2), Post Malone
"One Call Away" (2), Charlie Puth
"Marvin Gaye" (2), Charlie Puth feat. Meghan Trainor
"Locked Away," R. City feat. Adam Levine
"Come Get Her," "No Type" (3), "This Could Be Us," "Throw Sum Mo," Rae Sremmurd
"Crash and Burn," "Die a Happy Man" (2), Thomas Rhett
"Flex (Ooh, Ooh, Ooh)" (2), Rich Homie Quan
"Bitch Better Have My Money" (2), "Needed Me" (2), "Work" (3), Rihanna
"Lost Boy," Ruth B
"Antidote," Travis Scott
"Photograph" (2), "Thinking Out Loud" (7), Ed Sheeran
"Sangria," Blake Shelton
"Watch Me (Whip/Nae Nae)" (5), Silentó
"Youth," Troye Sivan
"Where Are Ü Now" (3), Skrillex & Diplo
"Slow Motion," Trey Songz
"Tennessee Whiskey," Chris Stapleton
"Love Myself," Hailee Steinfeld
"Bad Blood" (4), "Out of the Woods," "Style" (3), "Wildest Dreams" (2), Taylor Swift
"You Should Be Here," Cole Swindell
"Don't" (2), "Exchange," Bryson Tiller
"Can't Stop the Feeling!," Justin Timberlake
"Lips Are Movin" (4), "No," Meghan Trainor
"Like I'm Gonna Lose You" (2), Meghan Trainor feat. John Legend
"Nasty Freestyle," T-Wayne
"Ride," "Stressed Out" (4), "Tear in My Heart," Twenty One Pilots
"Acquainted," "Can't Feel My Face" (5), "Earned It (Fifty Shades of Grey)" (5), "In the Night," "The Hills" (7), The Weeknd
"Renegades," X Ambassadors
"Down in the DM," Yo Gotti
"I'm Comin' Over," Chris Young
"Best Friend," Young Thug
"Pillowtalk" (2), Zayn
"I Want You to Know," Zedd feat. Selena Gomez

Top-Grossing North American Concert Tours, 1985-2015

Source: Pollstar

Rank Artist (year)	Total gross[1]	Cities/ shows	Rank Artist (year)	Total gross[1]	Cities/ shows
1. Taylor Swift (2015)	$199.4	41/62	14. Taylor Swift (2013)	$112.7	47/66
2. The Rolling Stones (2005)	162.0	38/42	15. The Rolling Stones (2015)	109.7	14/14
3. U2 (2011)	156.0	21/25	16. U2 (2001)	109.7	56/80
4. U2 (2005)	138.9	43/78	17. Bon Jovi (2010)	108.2	38/51
5. The Rolling Stones (2006)	138.5	35/39	18. Bon Jovi (2013)	107.3	58/62
6. Madonna (2012)	133.7	31/45	19. Madonna (2008)	105.3	19/30
7. The Police (2007)	133.2	41/54	20. Bruce Springsteen & The E Street Band (2012)	104.7	42/52
8. One Direction (2014)	127.2	21/31	21. Pink Floyd (1994)	103.5	39/59
9. U2 (2009)	123.0	16/20	22. Paul McCartney (2002)	103.3	43/53
10. The Rolling Stones (1994)	121.2	43/60	23. The Rolling Stones (1989)	98.0	33/60
11. Kenny Chesney (2015)	116.4	56/59	24. Taylor Swift (2011)	97.7	59/80
12. Bruce Springsteen & The E Street Band (2003)	115.9	30/47	25. Kenny Chesney and Tim McGraw (2012)	96.5	22/23
13. Garth Brooks (2015)	114.9	23/120			

(1) In millions. Not adjusted for inflation.

Sales of Recorded Music and Music Videos, by Units Shipped and Value, 2000-15

Source: Recording Industry Assn. of America

(in millions, net after returns)

	2000	2005	2009	2010	2011	2012	2013	2014	2015	% change, 2014-15
Physical units shipped...	1,079.2	748.7	309.2	233.0	222.0	182.9	187.2	161.7	144.2	−10.8%
Dollar value	$14,323.7	11,195.0	4,555.9	3,438.7	3,170.9	2,584.3	2,444.8	2,251.3	2,024.0	−10.1
Compact discs (CDs) ...	942.5	705.4	292.9	253.0	240.8	198.2	172.2	142.8	122.9	−13.9
Dollar value	$13,214.5	10,520.2	4,274.1	3,389.4	3,100.7	2,485.6	2,123.5	1,832.6	1,520.8	−17.0
Cassettes	76.0	2.5	—	—	—	—	—	—	—	—
Dollar value	$626.0	13.1	—	—	—	—	—	—	—	—
LPs/EPs	2.2	1.0	3.2	4.2	5.5	6.9	9.4	13.2	16.9	28.3
Dollar value	$27.7	14.2	60.2	88.9	119.4	160.7	210.7	314.9	416.2	32.2
CD singles	34.2	2.8	0.9	1.0	1.3	1.1	0.6	1.0	0.4	−59.5
Dollar value	$142.7	10.9	3.1	2.9	3.5	3.2	2.4	3.8	1.2	−67.5
Vinyl singles	4.8	2.3	0.3	0.3	0.4	0.4	0.3	0.5	0.5	4.1
Dollar value	$26.3	13.2	2.5	2.3	4.6	4.7	3.0	5.9	6.1	2.8
Music videos[1]	18.2	33.8	11.8	9.1	7.7	6.0	4.7	4.1	3.3	−20.4
Dollar value	$281.9	602.2	212.0	177.6	151.0	116.6	104.7	91.2	73.2	−19.8
Digital formats[2]	—	383.1	1,236.8	1,283.4	1,454.7	1,521.4	1,458.0	1,325.1	1,135.8	−14.3
Dollar value	—	$503.6	2,030.7	2,232.9	2,628.3	2,852.9	2,822.6	2,574.9	2,327.1	−9.6
Download albums	—	13.6	76.4	85.8	103.9	116.7	118.0	117.6	109.4	−7.0
Dollar value	—	$135.7	763.4	872.4	1,070.8	1,204.8	1,232.1	1,150.9	1,090.7	−5.2
Download singles	—	366.9	1,138.3	1,177.4	1,332.3	1,392.2	1,327.9	1,199.1	1,021.0	−14.9
Dollar value	—	$363.3	1,220.3	1,317.4	1,522.4	1,623.6	1,567.6	1,407.8	1,226.9	−12.8
Music videos	—	1.9	20.4	18.4	16.3	10.5	8.4	6.8	3.2	−52.8
Dollar value	—	$3.7	40.6	36.6	32.4	20.8	16.7	13.6	6.4	−52.8
Mobile formats[3]	—	170.0	305.8	188.5	115.4	69.3	39.4	26.6	21.9	−17.7
Dollar value	—	$421.6	728.8	448.0	276.2	166.9	98.0	66.3	54.6	−17.7
Subscription formats[4]	—	1.3	1.2	1.5	1.8	3.4	6.2	7.7	10.8	40.2
Dollar value	—	$149.2	213.1	212.4	359.2	570.8	639.2	800.1	1,218.9	52.3
Digital performances & streaming[5]	—	$27.4	155.5	249.2	292.0	462.0	590.4	773.4	802.6	3.8
On-demand streaming (ad supported)	—	—	—	—	—	$170.9	220.0	294.8	385.1	30.6
Total units[6]	1,079.2	1,301.8	1,851.8	1,739.6	1,824.9	1,803.3	1,684.6	1,513.4	1,302.0	−14.0
Total value	$14,323.7	12,296.9	7,683.9	6,995.0	7,133.1	7,015.7	7,004.8	6,950.5	7,015.9	0.9

— = Not available or not applicable. (1) Includes DVD videos. (2) Includes kiosk singles and albums. (3) Includes master ringtones, ringbacks, music videos, full-length downloads, and other mobile music. (4) Weighted annual average. (5) Estimated payments in dollars to performers and copyright holders for digital radio services under statutory licenses. (6) Includes albums and singles; excludes subscriptions and royalties.

Top Basic Cable TV Networks, 2015

Source: SNL Kagan, an offering of S&P Global Market Intelligence

Rank	Network (year began)	Subscribers (mil)	Rank	Network (year began)	Subscribers (mil)
1.	C-SPAN (1979)	98.7	11.	A&E (1994)	93.8
2.	Food Network (1993)	95.2	12.	AMC (1984)	93.6
3.	Discovery Channel (1985)	94.6	13.	HLN (1982)	93.6
4.	USA (1980)	94.5	14.	HGTV (1994)	93.6
5.	TBS (1976)	94.5	15.	TNT (1988)	93.2
6.	CNN (1980)	94.3	16.	FX (1994)	92.8
7.	Cartoon Network (1992)	94.2	17.	TLC (1980)	92.7
8.	History Channel (1995)	94.2	18.	E! (1987)	92.6
9.	Disney Channel (1983)	94.0	19.	Fox News (1996)	92.6
10.	Lifetime Television (1994)	94.0	20.	Syfy (1992)	92.5

U.S. Television Set Owners, 2016

Source: Nielsen Media Research, July 2016

Of the 116.4 mil U.S. households that owned at least one TV set in 2016—

83.6% had 2 or more TV sets	2.1% had a VCR	84.0% received basic cable
32.2% had 4 or more TV sets	75.4% had a DVD player	50.6% received premium cable
	50.3% had a DVR	

U.S. Households With Cable Television, 1980-2016

Source: Nielsen Media Research

Year[1]	Subscribers[2] (mil)	As % of house-holds with TVs	Year[1]	Subscribers[2] (mil)	As % of house-holds with TVs	Year[1]	Subscribers[2] (mil)	As % of house-holds with TVs
1980	17.7	22.6%	2001	81.5	79.8%	2009	103.0	89.7%
1985	38.7	45.3	2002	87.8	83.8	2010	104.1	90.6
1990	53.9	58.6	2003	88.4	82.9	2011	104.8	90.4
1990	62.1	65.1	2004	92.4	85.3	2012	103.6	90.3
1996	63.6	66.3	2005	94.0	85.7	2013	103.3	90.5
1997	65.1	67.2	2006	95.0	86.2	2014	103.7	89.6
1998	65.9	67.2	2007	94.5	83.8	2015	100.2	86.0
1999	76.4	76.9	2008	99.7	88.2	2016	97.8	84.0
2000	78.6	77.9						

(1) After 1998, figures include wired-cable households as well as households that receive TV programming via alternate delivery systems (including satellite receivers, SMATV, and MMDS). (2) Households that subscribe to basic cable service.

Selected Reality TV Show Winners, 2000-16

Numbers in parentheses represent the season, edition, or cycle of the show. As of Sept. 2016.

The Amazing Race. Debuted Aug. 2001 on CBS. Rob Frisbee & Brennan Swain (1); Chris Luca & Alex Boylan (2); Flo Pesenti & Zach Behr (3); Reichen Lehmkuhl & Chip Arndt (4); Chip & Kim McAllister (5); Freddy Holliday & Kendra Bentley (6); Uchenna & Joyce Agu (7); The Linz Family (8); B. J. Averell & Tyler Mac-Niven (9); Tyler Denk & James Branaman (10); All-Stars: Eric Sanchez & Danielle Turner (11); TK Erwin & Rachel Morales (12); Nick & Starr Spangler (13); Tammy & Victor Jih (14); Meghan Rickey & Cheyne Whitney (15); Dan & Jordan Pious (16); Natalie Strand & Katherine Chang (17); LaKisha & Jennifer Hoffman (18); Ernie Halvorsen & Cindy Chiang (19); Rachel Brown & Dave Brown Jr. (20); Josh Kilmer-Purcell & Brent Ridge (21); Bates & Anthony Battaglia (22); Jason Case & Amy Diaz (23); David & Connor O'Leary (24); Amy DeJong & Maya Warren (25); Laura Pierson & Tyler Adams (26); Kelsey Gerckens & Joey Buttitta (27); Dana Borriello & Matt Steffanina (28).

American Idol. Debuted July 2002 on FOX. Kelly Clarkson (1); Ruben Studdard (2); Fantasia Barrino (3); Carrie Underwood (4); Taylor Hicks (5); Jordin Sparks (6); David Cook (7); Kris Allen (8); Lee DeWyze (9); Scotty McCreery (10); Phillip Phillips (11); Candice Glover (12); Caleb Johnson (13); Nick Fradiani (14); Trent Harmon (15).

America's Got Talent. Debuted June 2006 on NBC. Bianca Ryan (1); Terry Fator (2); Neil E. Boyd (3); Kevin Skinner (4); Michael Grimm (5); Landau Eugene Murphy Jr. (6); Olate Dogs (7); Kenichi Ebina (8); Mat Franco (9); Paul Zerdin (10); Grace VanderWaal (11).

America's Next Top Model. Debuted May 2003 on UPN. Adrianne Curry (1); Yoanna House (2); Eva Pigford (3); Naima Mora (4); Nicole Linkletter (5); Danielle Evans (6); CariDee English (7); Jaslene Gonzalez (8); Saleisha Stowers (9); Whitney Thompson (10); McKey Sullivan (11); Teyona Anderson (12); Nicole Fox (13); Krista White (14); Ann Ward (15); Brittani Kline (16); Lisa D'Amato (17); Sophie Sumner (18); Laura James (19); Jourdan Miller (20); Keith Carlos (21); Nyle DiMarco (22).

The Apprentice. Debuted Jan. 2004 on NBC. Bill Rancic (1); Kelly Perdew (2); Kendra Todd (3); Randal Pinkett (4); Sean Yazbeck (5); Stefani Schaeffer (6); Brandy Kuentzel (7). *Celebrity Apprentice:* Piers Morgan (1); Joan Rivers (2); Bret Michaels (3); John Rich (4); Arsenio Hall (5); Trace Adkins (6); Leeza Gibbons (7).

The Bachelor. Debuted Mar. 2002 on ABC. Alex Michel chose Amanda Marsh (1); Aaron Buerge chose Helene Eksterowicz (2); Andrew Firestone chose Jen Schefft (3); Bob Guiney chose Estella Gardinier (4); Jesse Palmer chose Jessica Bowlin (5); Byron Velvick chose Mary Delgado (6); Charlie O'Connell chose Sarah Brice (7); Travis Stork chose Sarah Stone (8); Lorenzo Borghese chose Jennifer Wilson (9); Andy Baldwin chose Tessa Horst (10); Brad Womack chose no one (11); Matt Grant chose Shayne Lamas (12); Jason Mesnick chose Melissa Rycroft (13); Jake Pavelka chose Vienna Girardi (14); Brad Womack chose Emily Maynard (15); Ben Flajnik chose Courtney Robertson (16); Sean Lowe chose Catherine Giudici (17); Juan Pablo Galavis chose Nikki Ferrell (18); Chris Soules chose Whitney Bischoff (19); Ben Higgins chose Lauren Bushnell (20).

The Bachelorette. Debuted Jan. 2003 on ABC. Trista Rehn chose Ryan Sutter (1); Meredith Phillips chose Ian McKee (2); Jen Schefft chose Jerry Ferris (3); DeAnna Pappas chose Jesse Csincsak (4); Jillian Harris chose Ed Swiderski (5); Ali Fedotowsky chose Roberto Martinez (6); Ashley Hebert chose J. P. Rosenbaum (7); Emily Maynard chose Jef Holm (8); Desiree Hartsock chose Chris Siegfried (9); Andi Dorfman chose Josh Murray (10); Kaitlyn Bristowe chose Shawn Booth (11); JoJo Fletcher chose Jordan Rodgers (12).

Big Brother. Debuted July 2000 on CBS. Eddie McGee (1); Will Kirby (2); Lisa Donahue (3); Jun Song (4); Drew Daniel (5); Maggie Ausburn (6); Mike Malinto (7); Dick Donato (8); Adam Jasinski (9); Dan Gheesling (10); Jordan Lloyd (11); Hayden Moss (12); Rachel Reilly (13); Ian Terry (14); Andy Herren (15); Derrick Levasseur (16); Steve Moses (17); Nicole Franzel (18).

The Biggest Loser. Debuted Oct. 2004 on NBC. Ryan Benson (1); Matt Hoover (2); Erik Chopin (3); Bill Germanakos (4); Ali Vincent (5); Michelle Aguilar (6); Helen Phillips (7); Danny Cahill (8); Michael Ventrella (9); Patrick House (10); Olivia Ward (11); John Rhode (12); Jeremy Britt (13); Danni Allen (14); Rachel Frederickson (15); Toma Dobrosavljevic (16); Roberto Hernandez (17).

Dancing With the Stars. Debuted June 2005 on ABC. Kelly Monaco & Alex Mazo (1); Drew Lachey & Cheryl Burke (2); Emmitt Smith & Cheryl Burke (3); Apolo Anton Ohno & Julianne Hough (4); Helio Castroneves & Julianne Hough (5); Kristi Yamaguchi & Mark Ballas (6); Brooke Burke & Derek Hough (7); Shawn Johnson & Mark Ballas (8); Donny Osmond & Kym Johnson (9); Nicole Scherzinger & Derek Hough (10); Jennifer Grey & Derek Hough (11); Hines Ward & Kym Johnson (12); J.R. Martinez & Karina Smirnoff (13); Donald Driver & Peta Murgatroyd (14); All-Stars: Melissa Rycroft & Tony Dovolani (15); Kellie Pickler & Derek Hough (16); Amber Riley & Derek Hough (17); Meryl Davis & Maksim Chmerkovskiy (18); Alfonso Ribeiro & Witney Carson (19); Rumer Willis & Val Chmerkovskiy (20); Bindi Irwin & Derek Hough (21); Nyle DiMarco & Peta Murgatroyd (22).

Hell's Kitchen. Debuted Mar. 2005 on FOX. Michael Wray (1); Heather West (2); Rock Harper (3); Christina Machamer (4); Danny Veltri (5); Dave Levey (6); Holli Ugalde (7); Nona Sivley (8); Paul Niedermann (9); Christina Wilson (10); Ja'Nel Witt (11); Scott Commings (12); La Tasha McCutchen (13); Meghan Gill (14); Ariel Malone (15).

Project Runway. Debuted Dec. 2004 on Bravo. Jay McCarroll (1); Chloe Dao (2); Jeffrey Sebelia (3); Christian Siriano (4); Leanne Marshall (5); Irina Shabayeva (6); Seth Aaron Henderson (7); Gretchen Jones (8); Anya Ayoung-Chee (9); Dmitry Sholokhov (10); Michelle Lesniak Franklin (11); Dom Streater (12); Sean Kelly (13); Ashley Nell Tipton (14). *All-Stars:* Mondo Guerra (1); Anthony Ryan Auld (2); Seth Aaron Henderson (3); Dmitry Sholokhov (4); Dom Streater (5).

So You Think You Can Dance. Debuted July 2005 on FOX. Nick Lazzarini (1); Benji Schwimmer (2); Sabra Johnson (3); Joshua Allen (4); Jeanine Mason (5); Russell Ferguson (6); Lauren Froderman (7); Melanie Moore (8); Eliana Girard & Chehon Wespi-Tschopp (9); DuShaunt "Fik-Shun" Stegall & Amy Yakima (10); Ricky Ubeda (11); Gaby Diaz (12); Leon "Kida" Burns (13).

Survivor. Debuted May 2000 on CBS. Borneo: Richard Hatch (1); Outback: Tina Wesson (2); Africa: Ethan Zohn (3); Marquesas: Vecepia Towery (4); Thailand: Brian Heidik (5); The Amazon: Jenna Morasca (6); Pearl Islands: Sandra Diaz-Twine (7); All-Stars: Amber Brkich (8); Vanuatu: Chris Daugherty (9); Palau: Tom Westman (10); Guatemala: Danni Boatwright (11); Panama: Aras Baskauskas (12); Cook Islands: Yul Kwon (13); Fiji: Earl Cole (14); China: Todd Herzog (15); Micronesia: Parvati Shallow (16); Gabon: Robert Crowley (17); Tocantins: James "JT" Thomas (18); Samoa: Natalie White (19); Heroes vs. Villains: Sandra Diaz-Twine (20); Nicaragua: Jud Birza (21); Redemption Island: Rob Mariano (22); South Pacific: Sophie Clarke (23); One World: Kim Spradlin (24); Philippines: Denise Stapley (25); Caramoan—Fans vs. Favorites: John Cochran (26); Blood vs. Water: Tyson Apostol (27); Cagayan: Tony Vlachos (28); San Juan del Sur: Natalie Anderson (29); Worlds Apart: Mike Holloway (30); Cambodia: Second Chance: Jeremy Collins (31); Kaoh Rong: Michele Fitzgerald (32).

Top Chef. Debuted Mar. 2006 on Bravo. Harold Dieterle (1); Ilan Hall (2); Hung Huynh (3); Stephanie Izard (4); Hosea Rosenberg (5); Michael Voltaggio (6); Kevin Sbraga (7); Richard Blais (8); Paul Qui (9); Kristen Kish (10); Nicholas Elmi (11); Mei Lin (12); Jeremy Ford (13). *Top Chef Masters:* Rick Bayless (1); Marcus Samuelsson (2); Floyd Cardoz (3); Chris Cosentino (4); Douglas Keane (5).

The Voice. Debuted Apr. 2011 on NBC. Javier Colon (1); Jermaine Paul (2); Cassadee Pope (3); Danielle Bradbery (4); Tessanne Chin (5); Josh Kaufman (6); Craig Wayne Boyd (7); Sawyer Fredericks (8); Jordan Smith (9); Alisan Porter (10).

Average U.S. Television Viewing Time, 2015-16

Source: Nielsen Media Research; viewing time given in hours:minutes

Group	Age	Total per week	M-F 7-10 AM	M-F 10 AM-4 PM	M-Sun. 8-11 PM	M-F 11:30 PM-1 AM	Sat. 7 AM-1 PM	Sun. 1-7 PM
Men	18+	33:34	2:00	4:31	7:55	1:36	1:02	1:54
	18-24	16:11	0:44	2:15	3:35	0:56	0:25	0:55
	25-54	29:07	1:35	3:28	7:02	1:33	0:55	1:42
	55+	46:35	3:06	6:56	10:49	1:54	1:25	2:33
Female	18+	38:07	2:32	5:54	8:42	1:47	1:08	1:49
	18-24	18:23	0:57	2:55	4:00	0:60	0:30	0:52
	25-54	32:57	2:08	4:44	7:37	1:40	1:00	1:36
	55+	50:57	3:32	8:20	11:34	2:10	1:31	2:22
Children	2-11	21:06	1:27	3:12	4:17	0:42	0:60	1:10
Teens	12-17	15:31	0:40	1:32	3:45	0:45	0:32	0:53
All viewers[1]		32:18	2:02	4:40	7:25	1:29	1:02	1:41

Note: For viewing period Sept. 21, 2015-May 29, 2016. Includes DVR playback. (1) Ages 2+.

Highest-Rated Prime-Time Television Programs, 2015-16

Source: Nielsen Media Research

Data are for regularly scheduled network programs Sept. 21, 2015-May 25, 2016 (unless otherwise noted). Ranked by average audience percentages, or ratings, which are estimates of the percentage of all TV-owning households watching a particular program live or on DVR within seven days of broadcast. Audience share percentages are estimates of the percentage of those watching TV at a certain time that are tuned in to a particular program.

Rank	Program, network	Avg. audience	Audience share	Rank	Program, network	Avg. audience	Audience share
1.	NCIS, CBS	12.8%	21.26%	26.	Survivor[4], CBS	6.6%	11.30%
2.	The Big Bang Theory, CBS	12.5	21.35	27.	Code Black, CBS	6.6	12.08
3.	Empire, FOX	10.2	16.82	28.	Chicago Med, NBC	6.5	10.86
4.	NCIS: New Orleans, CBS	9.4	15.38	29.	Life in Pieces, CBS	6.5	10.59
5.	Dancing With the Stars[1], ABC	8.9	14.35	30.	Shades of Blue, NBC	6.5	11.92
6.	Blue Bloods, CBS	8.4	15.76	31.	Limitless, CBS	6.3	11.37
7.	The Voice[2], NBC	8.2	13.27	32.	The Bachelor[5], ABC	6.3	10.11
8.	The X-Files, FOX	8.2	13.32	33.	Modern Family, ABC	6.2	10.29
9.	The Voice-Tuesday[2], NBC	7.9	13.13	34.	Castle, ABC	6.2	11.11
10.	Grey's Anatomy, ABC	7.9	13.65	35.	Mom, CBS	6.2	10.35
11.	Criminal Minds, CBS	7.8	12.84	36.	Supergirl, CBS	6.1	9.72
12.	Madame Secretary, CBS	7.8	12.62	37.	Criminal Minds: Beyond Borders, CBS	6.1	11.23
13.	60 Minutes, CBS	7.7	13.05	38.	Person of Interest, CBS	6.0	10.84
14.	Scorpion, CBS	7.6	12.08	39.	Chicago P.D., NBC	5.9	10.74
15.	Scandal, ABC	7.6	12.67	40.	Elementary, CBS	5.9	10.88
16.	The Blacklist, NBC	7.3	12.11	41.	Law and Order: SVU, NBC	5.7	9.55
17.	How to Get Away With Murder, ABC	7.2	13.03	42.	Angel From Hell, CBS	5.7	9.50
18.	Little Big Shots, NBC	7.2	12.27	43.	Mysteries of Laura, NBC	5.6	9.48
19.	NCIS: Los Angeles, CBS	7.1	12.66	44.	CSI: Cyber, CBS	5.6	10.41
20.	Blindspot, NBC	7.1	12.70	45.	The Odd Couple, CBS	5.6	9.72
21.	The Good Wife, CBS	7.1	11.71	46.	Mike & Molly, CBS	5.5	9.14
22.	Hawaii Five-0, CBS	7.0	12.64	47.	Quantico, ABC	5.4	9.68
23.	Chicago Fire, NBC	7.0	12.60	48.	2 Broke Girls, CBS	5.2	8.73
24.	American Idol-Wednesday[3], FOX	6.9	11.59	49.	The Middle, ABC	5.1	8.90
25.	American Idol-Thursday[3], FOX	6.7	11.22	50.	The Catch, ABC	5.1	9.27

(1) Mar. 21-May 24, 2016. (2) Feb. 29-May 24, 2016. (3) Jan. 6-Apr. 7, 2016. (4) Feb. 17-May 18, 2016. (5) Jan. 4-Mar. 14, 2016.

Highest-Rated Syndicated Programs, 2015-16

Source: Nielsen Media Research

Average audience percentages, or ratings, are estimates of the percentage of all TV-owning households watching a program live or on DVR within seven days of broadcast, Sept. 21, 2015-Aug. 14, 2016.

Rank	Program	Avg. audience	Rank	Program	Avg. audience
1.	Judge Judy	7.3%	14.	The Closer	2.9%
2.	Litton's Weekend Adventure	7.0	15.	Live With Kelly	2.9
3.	Family Feud	6.7	16.	Family Guy (weekend)	2.8
4.	Wheel of Fortune	6.5	17.	Two and a Half Men	2.7
5.	Jeopardy	6.2	18.	Wheel of Fortune (weekend)	2.6
6.	The Big Bang Theory	5.7	19.	The Ellen DeGeneres Show	2.5
7.	Law & Order: Special Victims Unit (weekend)	4.6	20.	Hot Bench	2.4
8.	The Big Bang Theory (weekend)	3.8	21.	Modern Family (weekend)	2.4
9.	Modern Family	3.2	22.	Blue Bloods	2.2
10.	Entertainment Tonight	3.1	23.	Family Guy	2.2
11.	Dr. Phil Show	3.1	24.	2 Broke Girls	2.0
12.	Family Feud (weekend)	2.9	25.	Mike & Molly	2.0
13.	Inside Edition	2.9			

Highest-Rated Basic Cable Programs, 2015-16

Source: Nielsen Media Research

Data are for regularly scheduled basic cable programs Sept. 21, 2015-Aug. 14, 2016; excludes children's series, miniseries, movies, and news events. Average audience percentages, or ratings, are estimates of the percentage of all TV-owning households watching a program live or on DVR within seven days of broadcast.

Rank	Program, channel	Avg. audience	Rank	Program, channel	Avg. audience
1.	The Walking Dead, AMC	10.2%	16.	The Haves and the Have Nots, OWN	2.5%
2.	Fear the Walking Dead, AMC	4.9	17.	Project Runway, Lifetime	2.4
3.	The People v. O.J. Simpson, FX	4.7	18.	The Last Ship, TNT	2.4
4.	Rizzoli & Isles, TNT	4.0	19.	Love & Hip Hop Atlanta, VH1	2.3
5.	American Horror Story, FX	3.8	20.	Alaska: The Last Frontier, Discovery	2.3
6.	Major Crimes, TNT	3.7	21.	Real Housewives of Beverly Hills, Bravo	2.2
7.	Talking Dead, AMC	3.4	22.	The Librarians, TNT	2.2
8.	Gold Rush Alaska, Discovery	3.3	23.	Love & Hip Hop New York, VH1	2.2
9.	Into the Badlands, AMC	3.3	24.	Suits, USA	2.2
10.	Better Call Saul, AMC	3.0	25.	Love & Hip Hop Hollywood, VH1	2.2
11.	Fixer Upper, HGTV	2.8	26.	Real Housewives of Orange County, Bravo	2.2
12.	Alaskan Bush People, Discovery	2.8	27.	Greenleaf, OWN	2.2
13.	Vikings, History	2.7	28.	The O'Reilly Factor, Fox News Channel	2.1
14.	Real Housewives of Atlanta, Bravo	2.6	29.	Preacher, AMC	2.1
15.	Curse of Oak Island, History	2.5	30.	Keeping Up With the Kardashians, E!	2.1

Highest-Rated Premium Cable Programs, 2015-16

Source: Nielsen Media Research

Average audience percentages, or ratings, are estimates of the percentage of all TV-owning households watching a program live or on DVR within seven days of broadcast, Sept. 21, 2015-Aug. 14, 2016.

Highest-Rated Series

Rank	Program, channel	Avg. audience
1.	Game of Thrones, HBO	6.1%
2.	Power, Starz	1.8
3.	Homeland, Showtime	1.7
4.	Shameless, Showtime	1.7
5.	Ray Donovan, Showtime	1.5
6.	Ballers, HBO	1.5
7.	Silicon Valley, HBO	1.4
8.	Last Week Tonight With John Oliver, HBO	1.4
9.	Billions, Showtime	1.4
10.	Outlander, Starz	1.3
11.	Real Time With Bill Maher, HBO	1.2
12.	The Night Of, HBO	1.2
13.	The Affair, Showtime	1.0
14.	Vice Principals, HBO	1.0
15.	Veep, HBO	1.0

Highest-Rated Movies

Rank	Program, channel	Avg. audience
1.	Straight Outta Compton, HBO	0.4%
2.	The Godfather Epic, HBO	0.4
3.	The Bourne Ultimatum, HBO	0.4
4.	The Martian, HBO	0.4
5.	Ted 2, HBO	0.4
6.	San Andreas, HBO	0.4
7.	American Sniper, HBO	0.4
8.	Kingsman: The Secret Service, HBO	0.4
9.	Fifty Shades of Grey, HBO	0.4
10.	The Intern, HBO	0.4
11.	Independence Day, HBO	0.3
12.	Jurassic World, HBO	0.3
13.	Brooklyn, HBO	0.3
14.	Furious 7, HBO	0.3
15.	Black Mass, HBO	0.3

All-Time Most Watched Television Programs

Source: Nielsen Media Research, Jan. 1961-Aug. 2016

Estimates exclude unsponsored or joint network telecasts (e.g., presidential addresses) and programs under 30 minutes long. Ranked by number of TV-owning households tuned in to the program. (Rating is percentage of all TV-owning households tuned in.)

Rank	Program	Telecast date	Network	Rating	Avg. audience (thous.)
1.	Super Bowl XLIX	2/1/2015	NBC	48.1%	55,948
2.	Super Bowl 50	2/7/2016	CBS	47.1	54,775
3.	Super Bowl XLVIII	2/2/2014	FOX	47.1	54,585
4.	Super Bowl XLVI	2/5/2012	NBC	47.0	53,910
5.	Super Bowl XLV	2/6/2011	FOX	46.1	53,435
6.	Super Bowl XLVII	2/3/2013	CBS	46.7	53,363
7.	Super Bowl XLIV	2/7/2010	CBS	45.2	51,873
8.	Super Bowl XLVII Delay	2/3/2013	CBS	44.5	50,861
9.	M*A*S*H (last episode)	2/28/1983	CBS	60.2	50,150
10.	Super Bowl XLII	2/3/2008	FOX	43.2	48,721
11.	Super Bowl XLIII	2/1/2009	NBC	42.0	48,139
12.	Super Bowl XLI	2/4/2007	CBS	42.7	47,535
13.	Super Bowl XL	2/5/2006	ABC	41.6	45,869
14.	XVII Winter Olympics (Women's figure skating)	2/23/1994	CBS	48.5	45,690
15.	Super Bowl XXXIX	2/6/2005	FOX	41.1	45,080
16.	Super Bowl XXXVIII	2/1/2004	CBS	41.4	44,910
17.	Super Bowl XXX	1/28/1996	NBC	46.0	44,150
18.	Super Bowl XXXII	1/25/1998	NBC	44.5	43,630
19.	Super Bowl XXXIV	1/30/2000	ABC	43.3	43,620
20.	Super Bowl XXXVII	1/26/2003	ABC	40.7	43,430
21.	Super Bowl XXVIII	1/30/1994	NBC	45.5	42,860
22.	Super Bowl XXXVI	2/3/2002	FOX	40.4	42,660
23.	Cheers (last episode)	5/20/1993	NBC	45.5	42,360
24.	Super Bowl XXXI	1/26/1997	FOX	43.3	42,000
25.	Super Bowl XXVII	1/31/1993	NBC	45.1	41,990
26.	XVII Winter Olympics (Women's figure skating)	2/25/1994	CBS	44.1	41,540
27.	Super Bowl XX	1/26/1986	NBC	48.3	41,490
28.	Dallas ("Who Shot J.R.?" episode)	11/21/1980	CBS	53.3	41,470
29.	Super Bowl XXXV	1/28/2001	CBS	40.4	41,270

Highest-Rated Television Programs by Season, 1950-2016

Source: Nielsen Media Research; regular series programs, Sept.-May season

Rating is percentage of all TV-owning households tuned in to the program. Data prior to 1988-89 exclude Alaska and Hawaii.

Season	Program	Rating	TV-owning households (thous.)	Season	Program	Rating	TV-owning households (thous.)
1950-51	Texaco Star Theatre	61.6%	10,320	1983-84	Dallas	25.7%	83,800
1951-52	Godfrey's Talent Scouts	53.8	15,300	1984-85	Dynasty	25.0	84,900
1952-53	I Love Lucy	67.3	20,400	1985-86	Cosby Show	33.8	85,900
1953-54	I Love Lucy	58.8	26,000	1986-87	Cosby Show	34.9	87,400
1954-55	I Love Lucy	49.3	30,700	1987-88	Cosby Show	27.8	88,600
1955-56	$64,000 Question	47.5	34,900	1988-89	Roseanne	25.5	90,400
1956-57	I Love Lucy	43.7	38,900	1989-90	Roseanne	23.4	92,100
1957-58	Gunsmoke	43.1	41,920	1990-91	Cheers	21.6	93,100
1958-59	Gunsmoke	39.6	43,950	1991-92	60 Minutes	21.7	92,100
1959-60	Gunsmoke	40.3	45,750	1992-93	60 Minutes	21.6	93,100
1960-61	Gunsmoke	37.3	47,200	1993-94	Home Improvement	21.9	94,200
1961-62	Wagon Train	32.1	48,555	1994-95	Seinfeld	20.5	95,400
1962-63	Beverly Hillbillies	36.0	50,300	1995-96	E.R.	22.0	95,900
1963-64	Beverly Hillbillies	39.1	51,600	1996-97	E.R.	21.2	97,000
1964-65	Bonanza	36.3	52,700	1997-98	Seinfeld	22.0	98,000
1965-66	Bonanza	31.8	53,850	1998-99	E.R.	17.8	99,400
1966-67	Bonanza	29.1	55,130	1999-2000	Who Wants to Be a Millionaire	18.6	100,800
1967-68	Andy Griffith	27.6	56,670	2000-01	Survivor II	17.4	102,200
1968-69	Rowan & Martin's Laugh-In	31.8	58,250	2001-02	Friends	15.3	105,500
1969-70	Rowan & Martin's Laugh-In	26.3	58,500	2002-03	CSI	16.3	106,700
1970-71	Marcus Welby, M.D.	29.6	60,100	2003-04	CSI	15.9	108,400
1971-72	All in the Family	34.0	62,100	2004-05	CSI	16.5	106,900
1972-73	All in the Family	33.3	64,800	2005-06	American Idol-Tuesday	17.6	110,200
1973-74	All in the Family	31.2	66,200	2006-07	American Idol-Wednesday	17.3	112,800
1974-75	All in the Family	30.2	68,500	2007-08	American Idol-Tuesday	15.5	113,050
1975-76	All in the Family	30.1	69,600	2008-09	American Idol-Wednesday	14.4	114,900
1976-77	Happy Days	31.5	71,200	2009-10	American Idol-Tuesday	13.7	114,900
1977-78	Laverne & Shirley	31.6	72,900	2010-11	American Idol-Wednesday	14.5	115,900
1978-79	Laverne & Shirley	30.5	74,500	2011-12	NCIS	12.3	114,700
1979-80	60 Minutes	28.2	76,300	2012-13	NCIS	13.5	114,200
1980-81	Dallas	31.2	79,900	2013-14	NCIS	12.6	115,800
1981-82	Dallas	28.4	81,500	2014-15	The Big Bang Theory	11.6	116,400
1982-83	60 Minutes	25.5	83,300	2015-16	NCIS	12.8	116,400

All-Time Highest-Rated Television Programs

Source: Nielsen Media Research, Jan. 1961-Aug. 2016

Estimates exclude unsponsored or joint network telecasts (e.g., presidential addresses) and programs under 30 minutes long. Ranked by rating (percentage of all TV-owning households tuned in to the program). Average audience is number of TV-owning households tuned in.

Rank	Program	Telecast date	Network	Rating	Avg. audience (thous.)
1.	M*A*S*H (last episode)	2/28/1983	CBS	60.2%	50,150
2.	Dallas ("Who Shot J.R.?" episode)	11/21/1980	CBS	53.3	41,470
3.	Roots-Pt. 8	1/30/1977	ABC	51.1	36,380
4.	Super Bowl XVI	1/24/1982	CBS	49.1	40,020
5.	Super Bowl XVII	1/30/1983	NBC	48.6	40,480
6.	XVII Winter Olympics (Women's figure skating)	2/23/1994	CBS	48.5	45,690
7.	Super Bowl XX	1/26/1986	NBC	48.3	41,490
8.	Super Bowl XLIX	2/1/2015	NBC	48.1	55,948
9.	Gone With the Wind-Pt. 1	11/7/1976	NBC	47.7	33,960
10.	Gone With the Wind-Pt. 2	11/8/1976	NBC	47.4	33,750
11.	Super Bowl XII	1/15/1978	CBS	47.2	34,410
12.	Super Bowl 50	2/7/2016	CBS	47.1	54,775
13.	Super Bowl XLVIII	2/2/2014	FOX	47.1	54,585
14.	Super Bowl XIII	1/21/1979	NBC	47.1	35,090
15.	Super Bowl XLVI	2/5/2012	NBC	47.0	53,910
16.	Super Bowl XLVII	2/3/2013	CBS	46.7	53,363
17.	Bob Hope Christmas Show	1/15/1970	NBC	46.6	27,260
18.	Super Bowl XIX	1/20/1985	ABC	46.4	39,390
19.	Super Bowl XVIII	1/22/1984	CBS	46.4	38,880
20.	Super Bowl XIV	1/20/1980	CBS	46.3	35,330
21.	Super Bowl XLV	2/6/2011	FOX	46.1	53,435
22.	Super Bowl XXX	1/28/1996	NBC	46.0	44,150
23.	ABC Sunday Night Movie (The Day After)	11/20/1983	ABC	46.0	38,550
24.	Roots-Pt. 6	1/28/1977	ABC	45.9	32,680
25.	The Fugitive (last episode)	8/29/1967	ABC	45.9	25,700
26.	Super Bowl XXI	1/25/1987	CBS	45.8	40,030
27.	Roots-Pt. 5	1/27/1977	ABC	45.7	32,540
28.	Super Bowl XXVIII	1/30/1994	NBC	45.5	42,860
29.	Cheers (last episode)	5/20/1993	NBC	45.5	42,360
30.	The Ed Sullivan Show (first live U.S. TV appearance of The Beatles)	2/9/1964	CBS	45.3	23,240

AWARDS — MEDALS — PRIZES

Alfred B. Nobel Prizes, 1901-2016

Alfred B. Nobel (1833-96) bequeathed $9 mil, the interest on which was to be distributed yearly to those judged to have most benefited humankind in chemistry, literature, promotion of peace, physics, and physiology or medicine. Prizes were first awarded in 1901. The prize in economics, funded by Sweden's central bank, was first awarded in 1969. Each prize is now worth 8 mil Swedish kronor (about $930,000). If year is omitted, no award was given. The Royal Swedish Academy selects prize winners for chemistry, economics, and physics; the Nobel Assembly at Karolinska Institutet, physiology or medicine; the Swedish Academy, literature; and the Norwegian Nobel Committee, the peace prize. The 2016 Nobel Prizes were announced Oct. 3-13. Winners sharing a prize are generally listed in alphabetical order, except when the awarding body has given a larger proportion of a shared prize to one or more recipients.

Nobel Prizes, 2016

Chemistry: Bernard L. Feringa, Neth.; Jean-Pierre Sauvage, France; and J. Fraser Stoddart, UK-U.S. shared the prize for "design and synthesis of molecular machines."

Economics: Oliver Hart, U.S., and Bengt Holmström, Fin.-U.S., split the prize for their work on contract theory.

Literature: American songwriter Bob Dylan was awarded the prize "for having created new poetic expressions within the great American song tradition."

Medicine: Yoshinori Ohsumi, Japan, claimed the prize for his work in autophagy, or how a cell recycles its content.

Peace: Colombian Pres. Juan Manuel Santos was awarded the prize for his efforts to end his country's 50-year civil war.

Physics: The committee awarded half the prize to David J. Thouless, UK-U.S., and half to F. Duncan M. Haldane and J. Michael Kosterlitz, both UK-U.S., for their studies of unusual states of matter using advanced mathematics.

Physics

1901	Wilhelm C. Röntgen, Ger.
1902	Hendrik A. Lorentz, Pieter Zeeman, Neth.
1903	Antoine Henri Becquerel, Pierre Curie, Fr.; Marie Curie, Pol.-Fr.
1904	Lord Rayleigh (John W. Strutt), UK
1905	Philipp E. A. von Lenard, Ger.
1906	Sir Joseph J. Thomson, UK
1907	Albert A. Michelson, U.S.
1908	Gabriel Lippmann, Fr.
1909	Carl F. Braun, Ger.; Guglielmo Marconi, Ital.
1910	Johannes D. van der Waals, Neth.
1911	Wilhelm Wien, Ger.
1912	Nils G. Dalén, Swed.
1913	Heike Kamerlingh Onnes, Neth.
1914	Max von Laue, Ger.
1915	Sir William H. Bragg, William L. Bragg, UK
1917	Charles G. Barkla, UK
1918	Max K. E. L. Planck, Ger.
1919	Johannes Stark, Ger.
1920	Charles E. Guillaume, Fr.-Switz.
1921	Albert Einstein, Ger.-U.S.
1922	Niels Bohr, Den.
1923	Robert A. Millikan, U.S.
1924	Karl M. G. Siegbahn, Swed.
1925	James Franck, Gustav Hertz, Ger.
1926	Jean B. Perrin, Fr.
1927	Arthur H. Compton, U.S.; Charles T. R. Wilson, UK
1928	Owen W. Richardson, UK
1929	Prince Louis-Victor de Broglie, Fr.
1930	Sir Chandrasekhara V. Raman, India
1932	Werner Heisenberg, Ger.
1933	Paul A. M. Dirac, UK; Erwin Schrödinger, Austria
1935	Sir James Chadwick, UK
1936	Carl D. Anderson, U.S.; Victor F. Hess, Austria
1937	Clinton J. Davisson, U.S.; Sir George P. Thomson, UK
1938	Enrico Fermi, Ital.-U.S.
1939	Ernest O. Lawrence, U.S.
1943	Otto Stern, U.S.
1944	Isidor Isaac Rabi, U.S.
1945	Wolfgang Pauli, U.S.-Austria
1946	Percy W. Bridgman, U.S.
1947	Sir Edward V. Appleton, UK
1948	Patrick M. S. Blackett, UK
1949	Hideki Yukawa, Jpn.
1950	Cecil F. Powell, UK
1951	Sir John D. Cockcroft, UK; Ernest T. S. Walton, Ire.
1952	Felix Bloch, Edward M. Purcell, U.S.
1953	Frits Zernike, Neth.
1954	Max Born, UK; Walter Bothe, Ger.
1955	Polykarp Kusch, Willis E. Lamb, U.S.
1956	John Bardeen, Walter H. Brattain, William Shockley, U.S.
1957	Tsung-Dao Lee, Chen Ning Yang, U.S.-China
1958	Pavel Cherenkov, Il'ja Frank, Igor Y. Tamm, USSR
1959	Owen Chamberlain, Emilio G. Segre, U.S.
1960	Donald A. Glaser, U.S.
1961	Robert Hofstadter, U.S.; Rudolf L. Mossbauer, Ger.
1962	Lev D. Landau, USSR
1963	Maria Goeppert-Mayer, Eugene P. Wigner, U.S.; J. Hans D. Jensen, Ger.
1964	Nicolay G. Basov, Aleksandr M. Prokhorov, USSR; Charles H. Townes, U.S.
1965	Sin-Itiro Tomonaga, Jpn.; Julian S. Schwinger, Richard P. Feynman, U.S.
1966	Alfred Kastler, Fr.
1967	Hans A. Bethe, U.S.
1968	Luis W. Alvarez, U.S.
1969	Murray Gell-Mann, U.S.
1970	Hannes Alfvén, Swed.; Louis Néel, Fr.
1971	Dennis Gabor, UK
1972	John Bardeen, Leon N. Cooper, John R. Schrieffer, U.S.
1973	Brian D. Josephson, UK; Leo Esaki, Jpn.; Ivar Giaever, U.S.
1974	Antony Hewish, Sir Martin Ryle, UK
1975	Aage Bohr, Den.; Ben Mottelson, U.S.-Den.; Leo James Rainwater, U.S.
1976	Burton Richter, Samuel C. C. Ting, U.S.
1977	Philip W. Anderson, John H. van Vleck, U.S.; Sir Nevill F. Mott, UK
1978	Pyotr Kapitsa, USSR; Arno Penzias, Robert Wilson, U.S.
1979	Sheldon L. Glashow, Steven Weinberg, U.S.; Abdus Salam, Pakistan
1980	James W. Cronin, Val L. Fitch, U.S.
1981	Nicolaas Bloembergen, Arthur Schawlow, U.S.; Kai M. Siegbahn, Swed.
1982	Kenneth G. Wilson, U.S.
1983	Subramanyan Chandrasekhar, William A. Fowler, U.S.
1984	Carlo Rubbia, Ital.; Simon van der Meer, Neth.
1985	Klaus von Klitzing, Ger.
1986	Ernest Ruska, Gerd Binnig, Ger.; Heinrich Rohrer, Switz.
1987	J. Georg Bednorz, Ger.; K. Alex Müller, Switz.
1988	Leon M. Lederman, Melvin Schwartz, Jack Steinberger, U.S.
1989	Norman F. Ramsey, U.S.; Hans G. Dehmelt, Ger.-U.S.; Wolfgang Paul, Ger.
1990	Jerome I. Friedman, Henry W. Kendall, U.S.; Richard E. Taylor, Can.
1991	Pierre-Gilles de Gennes, Fr.
1992	Georges Charpak, Pol.-Fr.
1993	Russell A. Hulse, Joseph H. Taylor, U.S.
1994	Bertram N. Brockhouse, Can.; Clifford G. Shull, U.S.
1995	Martin Perl, Frederick Reines, U.S.
1996	David M. Lee, Douglas D. Osheroff, Robert C. Richardson, U.S.
1997	Steven Chu, William D. Phillips, U.S.; Claude Cohen-Tannoudji, Fr.
1998	Robert B. Laughlin, U.S.; Horst L. Störmer, Ger.-U.S; Daniel C. Tsui, China-U.S.
1999	Gerardus 't Hooft, Martinus J. G. Veltman, Neth.
2000	Jack S. Kilby, U.S.; Herbert Kroemer, Ger.-U.S.; Zhores I. Alferov, Russ.
2001	Eric A. Cornell, Carl E. Wieman, U.S.; Wolfgang Ketterle, Ger.
2002	Raymond Davis Jr., Riccardo Giacconi, U.S.; Masatoshi Koshiba, Jpn.
2003	Alexei A. Abrikosov, Vitaly L. Ginzburg, Russ.; Anthony J. Leggett, UK
2004	David J. Gross, H. David Politzer, Frank Wilczek, U.S.
2005	Roy J. Glauber, John L. Hall, U.S.; Theodor W. Hänsch, Ger.
2006	John C. Mather, George F. Smoot, U.S.
2007	Albert Fert, Fr.; Peter Grünberg, Ger.
2008	Yoichiro Nambu, U.S.; Makoto Kobayashi, Toshihide Maskawa, Jpn.
2009	Charles K. Kao, U.S.-UK; Willard S. Boyle, U.S.-Can.; George E. Smith, U.S.
2010	Andre Geim, Russ.-Neth.; Konstantin Novoselov, Russ.-UK
2011	Saul Perlmutter, Adam G. Riess, U.S.; Brian P. Schmidt, Austral.-U.S.
2012	Serge Haroche, Fr.; David J. Wineland, U.S.
2013	François Englert, Belg.; Peter W. Higgs, UK
2014	Isamu Akasaki, Hiroshi Amano, Jpn.; Shuji Nakamura, Jpn.-U.S.
2015	Takaaki Kajita, Jpn.; Arthur B. McDonald, Can.
2016	David J. Thouless, UK-U.S.; F. Duncan M. Haldane, J. Michael Kosterlitz, UK-U.S.

Chemistry

1901 Jacobus H. van 't Hoff, Neth.	1956 Sir Cyril N. Hinshelwood, UK;	1993 Kary B. Mullis, U.S.;
1902 Emil Fischer, Ger.	Nikolay N. Semenov, USSR	Michael Smith, UK-Can.
1903 Svante A. Arrhenius, Swed.	1957 Lord (Alexander R.) Todd, UK	1994 George A. Olah, U.S.
1904 Sir William Ramsay, UK	1958 Frederick Sanger, UK	1995 Paul Crutzen, Neth.;
1905 Adolf von Baeyer, Ger.	1959 Jaroslav Heyrovsky, Czech.	Mario Molina, Mex.-U.S.;
1906 Henri Moissan, Fr.	1960 Willard F. Libby, U.S.	Sherwood Rowland, U.S.
1907 Eduard Buchner, Ger.	1961 Melvin Calvin, U.S.	1996 Robert F. Curl Jr.,
1908 Ernest Rutherford, UK	1962 John C. Kendrew, Max F. Perutz, UK	Richard E. Smalley, U.S.;
1909 Wilhelm Ostwald, Ger.	1963 Giulio Natta, Ital.; Karl Ziegler, Ger.	Sir Harold W. Kroto, UK
1910 Otto Wallach, Ger.	1964 Dorothy C. Hodgkin, UK	1997 Paul D. Boyer, U.S.; John E. Walker,
1911 Marie Curie, Pol.-Fr.	1965 Robert B. Woodward, U.S.	UK; Jens C. Skou, Den.
1912 Victor Grignard, Paul Sabatier, Fr.	1966 Robert S. Mulliken, U.S.	1998 Walter Kohn, U.S.;
1913 Alfred Werner, Switz.	1967 Manfred Eigen, Ger.; Ronald G. W.	John A. Pople, UK
1914 Theodore W. Richards, U.S.	Norrish, George Porter, UK	1999 Ahmed H. Zewail, U.S.
1915 Richard M. Willstätter, Ger.	1968 Lars Onsager, U.S.	2000 Alan J. Heeger, U.S.;
1918 Fritz Haber, Ger.	1969 Derek H. R. Barton, UK;	Alan G. MacDiarmid, N.Z.-U.S.;
1920 Walther H. Nernst, Ger.	Odd Hassel, Nor.	Hideki Shirakawa, Jpn.
1921 Frederick Soddy, UK	1970 Luis F. Leloir, Arg.	2001 K. Barry Sharpless, U.S.;
1922 Francis W. Aston, UK	1971 Gerhard Herzberg, Can.	William S. Knowles, U.S.;
1923 Fritz Pregl, Austria	1972 Christian B. Anfinsen, Stanford	Ryoji Noyori, Jpn.
1925 Richard A. Zsigmondy, Ger.	Moore, William H. Stein, U.S.	2002 John B. Fenn, U.S.;
1926 Theodor Svedberg, Swed.	1973 Ernst Otto Fischer, Ger.;	Koichi Tanaka, Jpn.;
1927 Heinrich O. Wieland, Ger.	Geoffrey Wilkinson, UK	Kurt Wüthrich, Switz.
1928 Adolf O. R. Windaus, Ger.	1974 Paul J. Flory, U.S.	2003 Peter Agre,
1929 Sir Arthur Harden, UK;	1975 John Cornforth, Austral.-UK;	Roderick MacKinnon, U.S.
Hans von Euler-Chelpin, Swed.	Vladimir Prelog, Bosnia-Switz.	2004 Aaron Ciechanover, Avram Hershko,
1930 Hans Fischer, Ger.	1976 William N. Lipscomb, U.S.	Isr.; Irwin Rose, U.S.
1931 Friedrich Bergius, Carl Bosch, Ger.	1977 Ilya Prigogine, Belg.	2005 Yves Chauvin, Fr.; Robert H.
1932 Irving Langmuir, U.S.	1978 Peter Mitchell, UK	Grubbs, Richard R. Schrock, U.S.
1934 Harold C. Urey, U.S.	1979 Herbert C. Brown, U.S.;	2006 Roger D. Kornberg, U.S.
1935 Frédéric Joliot, Irène Joliot-Curie, Fr.	Georg Wittig, Ger.	2007 Gerhard Ertl, Ger.
1936 Peter J. W. Debye, Neth.	1980 Paul Berg, Walter Gilbert, U.S.;	2008 Martin Chalfie, Osamu Shimomura,
1937 Walter N. Haworth, UK;	Frederick Sanger, UK	Roger Y. Tsien, U.S.
Paul Karrer, Switz.	1981 Kenichi Fukui, Jpn.;	2009 Venkatraman Ramakrishnan, UK;
1938 Richard Kuhn, Ger.	Roald Hoffmann, U.S.	Thomas A. Steitz, U.S.;
1939 Adolf F. J. Butenandt, Ger.;	1982 Aaron Klug, UK-Lith.	Ada E. Yonath, Isr.
Leopold Ruzicka, Switz.	1983 Henry Taube, Can.	2010 Richard F. Heck, U.S.; Ei-ichi
1943 George de Hevesy, Hung.	1984 Robert Bruce Merrifield, U.S.	Negishi, Jpn.-U.S.; Akira Suzuki, Jpn.
1944 Otto Hahn, Ger.	1985 Herbert A. Hauptman,	2011 Dan Shechtman, Isr.
1945 Artturi I. Virtanen, Fin.	Jerome Karle, U.S.	2012 Brian K. Kobilka,
1946 James B. Sumner, John H.	1986 Dudley Herschbach, Yuan T. Lee,	Robert J. Lefkowitz, U.S.
Northrop, Wendell M. Stanley, U.S.	U.S.; John C. Polanyi, Can.	2013 Martin Karplus, Austria-U.S.;
1947 Sir Robert Robinson, UK	1987 Donald J. Cram,	Michael Levitt, S. Afr.-U.S.;
1948 Arne W. K. Tiselius, Swed.	Charles J. Pedersen, U.S.;	Arieh Warshel, Isr.-U.S.;
1949 William F. Giauque, U.S.	Jean-Marie Lehn, Fr.	2014 Eric Betzig, William E. Moerner,
1950 Kurt Alder, Otto P. H. Diels, Ger.	1988 Johann Deisenhofer, Robert Huber,	U.S.; Stefan W. Hell, Ger.
1951 Edwin M. McMillan,	Hartmut Michel, Ger.	2015 Tomas Lindahl, Swed.-UK;
Glenn T. Seaborg, U.S.	1989 Sidney Altman,	Paul Modrich, U.S.;
1952 Archer J. P. Martin,	Thomas R. Cech, U.S.	Aziz Sancar, Turk.-U.S.
Richard L. M. Synge, UK	1990 Elias James Corey, U.S.	2016 Bernard L. Feringa, Neth.;
1953 Hermann Staudinger, Ger.	1991 Richard R. Ernst, Switz.	Jean-Pierre Sauvage, France;
1954 Linus C. Pauling, U.S.	1992 Rudolph A. Marcus, Can.-U.S.	J. Fraser Stoddart, UK-U.S.
1955 Vincent du Vigneaud, U.S.		

Physiology or Medicine

1901 Emil A. von Behring, Ger.	1934 George R. Minot, William P. Murphy,	1958 George W. Beadle, Edward L.
1902 Sir Ronald Ross, UK	G. H. Whipple, U.S.	Tatum, Joshua Lederberg, U.S.
1903 Niels R. Finsen, Den.	1935 Hans Spemann, Ger.	1959 Arthur Kornberg,
1904 Ivan P. Pavlov, Russ.	1936 Sir Henry H. Dale, UK;	Severo Ochoa, U.S.
1905 Robert Koch, Ger.	Otto Loewi, U.S.	1960 Sir Frank Macfarlane Burnet,
1906 Camillo Golgi, Ital.;	1937 Albert Szent-Gyorgyi, Hung.-U.S.	Austral.; Peter B. Medawar, UK
Santiago Ramón y Cajal, Spain	1938 Corneille J. F. Heymans, Belg.	1961 Georg von Békésy, U.S.
1907 Charles L. A. Laveran, Fr.	1939 Gerhard Domagk, Ger.	1962 Francis H. C. Crick,
1908 Paul Ehrlich, Ger.;	1943 Henrik C. P. Dam, Den.;	Maurice H. F. Wilkins, UK;
Ilya Mechnikov, Fr.	Edward A. Doisy, U.S.	James D. Watson, U.S.
1909 Emil T. Kocher, Switz.	1944 Joseph Erlanger,	1963 Sir John C. Eccles, Austral.;
1910 Albrecht Kossel, Ger.	Herbert S. Gasser, U.S.	Alan L. Hodgkin,
1911 Allvar Gullstrand, Swed.	1945 Ernst B. Chain, Sir Alexander	Andrew F. Huxley, UK
1912 Alexis Carrel, Fr.	Fleming, Sir Howard W. Florey, UK	1964 Konrad E. Bloch, U.S.;
1913 Charles R. Richet, Fr.	1946 Hermann J. Muller, U.S.	Feodor Lynen, Ger.
1914 Robert Bárány, Austria	1947 Carl F. Cori, Gerty T. Cori, U.S.;	1965 François Jacob, André Lwoff,
1919 Jules Bordet, Belg.	Bernardo A. Houssay, Arg.	Jacques Monod, Fr.
1920 Schack A. S. Krogh, Den.	1948 Paul H. Müller, Switz.	1966 Charles B. Huggins,
1922 Archibald V. Hill, UK;	1949 Walter R. Hess, Switz.;	Peyton Rous, U.S.
Otto F. Meyerhof, Ger.	Antonio Egas Moniz, Port.	1967 Ragnar Granit, Swed.;
1923 Frederick G. Banting, Can.;	1950 Philip S. Hench, Edward C. Kendall,	Haldan Keffer Hartline,
John J. R. Macleod, UK	U.S.; Tadeus Reichstein, Switz.	George Wald, U.S.
1924 Willem Einthoven, Neth.	1951 Max Theiler, U.S.	1968 Robert W. Holley,
1926 Johannes A. G. Fibiger, Den.	1952 Selman A. Waksman, U.S.	H. Gobind Khorana,
1927 Julius Wagner-Jauregg, Austria	1953 Hans A. Krebs, UK;	Marshall W. Nirenberg, U.S.
1928 Charles J. H. Nicolle, Fr.	Fritz A. Lipmann, U.S.	1969 Max Delbrück, Alfred D. Hershey,
1929 Christiaan Eijkman, Neth.;	1954 John F. Enders, Frederick C.	Salvador Luria, U.S.
Sir Frederick G. Hopkins, UK	Robbins, Thomas H. Weller, U.S.	1970 Julius Axelrod, U.S.;
1930 Karl Landsteiner, U.S.	1955 Axel H. T. Theorell, Swed.	Sir Bernard Katz, UK;
1931 Otto H. Warburg, Ger.	1956 André F. Cournand,	Ulf von Euler, Swed.
1932 Edgar D. Adrian,	Dickinson W. Richards, U.S.;	1971 Earl W. Sutherland Jr., U.S.
Sir Charles S. Sherrington, UK	Werner Forssmann, Ger.	1972 Gerald M. Edelman, U.S.;
1933 Thomas H. Morgan, U.S.	1957 Daniel Bovet, Ital.	Rodney R. Porter, UK

Year		Year		Year	
1973	Konrad Lorenz, Austria; Nikolaas Tinbergen, UK; Karl von Frisch, Ger.	1986	Stanley Cohen, U.S.; Rita Levi-Montalcini, Ital.-U.S.	2002	Sydney Brenner, John E. Sulston, UK; H. Robert Horvitz, U.S.
1974	Albert Claude, Lux.-U.S.; Christian de Duve, Belg.; George Emil Palade, Rom.-U.S.	1987	Susumu Tonegawa, Jpn.	2003	Paul C. Lauterbur, U.S.; Sir Peter Mansfield, UK
1975	David Baltimore, Howard Temin, U.S.; Renato Dulbecco, Ital.-U.S.	1988	Sir James W. Black, UK; Gertrude B. Elion, George H. Hitchings, U.S.	2004	Richard Axel, Linda B. Buck, U.S.
		1989	J. Michael Bishop, Harold E. Varmus, U.S.	2005	Barry J. Marshall, J. Robin Warren, Austral.
1976	Baruch S. Blumberg, Daniel Carleton Gajdusek, U.S.	1990	Joseph E. Murray, E. Donnall Thomas, U.S.	2006	Andrew Z. Fire, Craig C. Mello, U.S.
1977	Rosalyn S. Yalow, Roger Guillemin, Andrew V. Schally, U.S.	1991	Edwin Neher, Bert Sakmann, Ger.	2007	Mario R. Capecchi, Oliver Smithies, U.S.; Sir Martin J. Evans, UK
1978	Werner Arber, Switz.; Daniel Nathans, Hamilton O. Smith, U.S.	1992	Edmond H. Fisher, Edwin G. Krebs, U.S.	2008	Harald zur Hausen, Ger.; Françoise Barré-Sinoussi, Luc Montagnier, Fr.
		1993	Richard J. Roberts, UK; Phillip A. Sharp, U.S.		
1979	Allan M. Cormack, U.S.; Godfrey N. Hounsfield, UK	1994	Alfred G. Gilman, Martin Rodbell, U.S.	2009	Elizabeth H. Blackburn, Carol W. Greider, Jack W. Szostak, U.S.
1980	Baruj Benacerraf, George Snell, U.S.; Jean Dausset, Fr.	1995	Edward B. Lewis, Eric F. Wieschaus, U.S.; Christiane Nüsslein-Volhard, Ger.	2010	Robert G. Edwards, UK
1981	Roger W. Sperry, David H. Hubel, Torsten N. Wiesel, U.S.	1996	Peter C. Doherty, Austral.; Rolf M. Zinkernagel, Switz.	2011	Bruce A. Beutler, U.S.; Jules A. Hoffmann, Fr.; Ralph M. Steinman, Can.-U.S.
1982	Sune K. Bergström, Bengt I. Samuelsson, Swed.; John R. Vane, UK	1997	Stanley B. Prusiner, U.S.	2012	John B. Gurdon, UK; Shinya Yamanaka, Jpn.-U.S.
		1998	Robert F. Furchgott, Louis J. Ignarro, Ferid Murad, U.S.	2013	James E. Rothman, Randy W. Schekman, U.S.; Thomas C. Südhof, Ger.-U.S.
1983	Barbara McClintock, U.S.	1999	Günter Blobel, U.S.		
1984	Niels K. Jerne, UK-Den.; Georges J. F. Köhler, Ger.; César Milstein, UK-Arg.	2000	Arvid Carlsson, Swed.; Paul Greengard, U.S.; Eric R. Kandel, Austria-U.S.	2014	John O'Keefe, U.S.-UK; May-Britt Moser, Edvard I. Moser, Nor.
		2001	Leland H. Hartwell, U.S.; R. Timothy (Tim) Hunt, Sir Paul M. Nurse, UK	2015	William C. Campbell, Ire.-U.S.; Satoshi Omura, Jpn.; Youyou Tu, China
1985	Michael S. Brown, Joseph L. Goldstein, U.S.			2016	Yoshinori Ohsumi, Jpn.

Literature

Year		Year		Year	
1901	Rene F. A. Sully Prudhomme, Fr.	1945	Gabriela Mistral, Chile	1979	Odysseus Elytis, Greece
1902	Theodor Mommsen, Ger.	1946	Hermann Hesse, Ger.-Switz.	1980	Czeslaw Milosz, Pol.-U.S.
1903	Bjørnstjerne Bjørnson, Nor.	1947	André Gide, Fr.	1981	Elias Canetti, Bulg.-UK
1904	José Echegaray y Eizaguirre, Spain; Fréderic Mistral, Fr.	1948	T. S. Eliot, UK	1982	Gabriel García Márquez, Colombia
1905	Henryk Sienkiewicz, Pol.	1949	William Faulkner, U.S.	1983	William Golding, UK
1906	Giosuè Carducci, Ital.	1950	Bertrand Russell, UK	1984	Jaroslav Siefert, Czech.
1907	Rudyard Kipling, UK	1951	Pär F. Lagerkvist, Swed.	1985	Claude Simon, Fr.
1908	Rudolf C. Eucken, Ger.	1952	François Mauriac, Fr.	1986	Wole Soyinka, Nigeria
1909	Selma Lagerlöf, Swed.	1953	Sir Winston Churchill, UK	1987	Joseph Brodsky, USSR-U.S.
1910	Paul J. L. Heyse, Ger.	1954	Ernest Hemingway, U.S.	1988	Naguib Mahfouz, Egypt
1911	Maurice Maeterlinck, Belg.	1955	Halldór K. Laxness, Ice.	1989	Camilo José Cela, Spain
1912	Gerhart Hauptmann, Ger.	1956	Juan Ramón Jiménez, Spain	1990	Octavio Paz, Mex.
1913	Rabindranath Tagore, India	1957	Albert Camus, Fr.	1991	Nadine Gordimer, S. Afr.
1915	Romain Rolland, Fr.	1958	Boris L. Pasternak, USSR (declined)	1992	Derek Walcott, St. Lucia
1916	Verner von Heidenstam, Swed.			1993	Toni Morrison, U.S.
1917	Karl A. Gjellerup, Henrik Pontoppidan, Den.	1959	Salvatore Quasimodo, Ital.	1994	Kenzaburo Oe, Jpn.
		1960	Saint-John Perse, Fr.	1995	Seamus Heaney, Ire.
1919	Carl F. G. Spitteler, Switz.	1961	Ivo Andric, Yugo.	1996	Wislawa Szymborska, Pol.
1920	Knut Hamsun, Nor.	1962	John Steinbeck, U.S.	1997	Dario Fo, Ital.
1921	Anatole France, Fr.	1963	Giorgos Seferis, Greece	1998	Jose Saramago, Por.
1922	Jacinto Benavente, Spain	1964	Jean-Paul Sartre, Fr. (declined)	1999	Günter Grass, Ger.
1923	William Butler Yeats, Ire.	1965	Mikhail Sholokhov, USSR	2000	Gao Xingjian, China-Fr.
1924	Wladyslaw S. Reymont, Pol.	1966	Shmuel Yosef Agnon, Isr.; Nelly Sachs, Swed.	2001	Sir V. S. Naipaul, UK
1925	George Bernard Shaw, Ire.-UK			2002	Imre Kertész, Hung.
1926	Grazia Deledda, Ital.	1967	Miguel Angel Asturias, Guat.	2003	J. M. Coetzee, S. Afr.
1927	Henri Bergson, Fr.	1968	Yasunari Kawabata, Jpn.	2004	Elfriede Jelinek, Austria
1928	Sigrid Undset, Nor.	1969	Samuel Beckett, Ire.	2005	Harold Pinter, UK
1929	Thomas Mann, Ger.	1970	Aleksandr I. Solzhenitsyn, USSR	2006	Orhan Pamuk, Turk.
1930	Sinclair Lewis, U.S.	1971	Pablo Neruda, Chile	2007	Doris Lessing, UK
1931	Erik A. Karlfeldt, Swed.	1972	Heinrich Böll, Ger.	2008	Jean-Marie Gustave Le Clézio, Fr.
1932	John Galsworthy, UK	1973	Patrick White, Austral.	2009	Herta Müller, Ger.
1933	Ivan A. Bunin, USSR	1974	Eyvind Johnson, Harry Edmund Martinson, Swed.	2010	Mario Vargas Llosa, Peru
1934	Luigi Pirandello, Ital.			2011	Tomas Tranströmer, Swed.
1936	Eugene O'Neill, U.S.	1975	Eugenio Montale, Ital.	2012	Mo Yan, China
1937	Roger Martin du Gard, Fr.	1976	Saul Bellow, U.S.	2013	Alice Munro, Can.
1938	Pearl S. Buck, U.S.	1977	Vicente Aleixandre, Spain	2014	Patrick Modiano, Fr.
1939	Frans E. Sillanpää, Fin.	1978	Isaac Bashevis Singer, U.S.	2015	Svetlana Alexievich, Belarus
1944	Johannes V. Jensen, Den.			2016	Bob Dylan, U.S.

Peace

Year		Year		Year	
1901	Jean H. Dunant, Switz.; Frédéric Passy, Fr.	1908	Klas P. Arnoldson, Swed.; Fredrik Bajer, Den.	1919	Woodrow Wilson, U.S.
				1920	Léon V. A. Bourgeois, Fr.
1902	Élie Ducommun, Charles A. Gobat, Switz.	1909	Auguste M. F. Beernaert, Belg.; Paul H. B. B. d'Estournelles de Constant, Fr.	1921	Karl H. Branting, Swed.; Christian L. Lange, Nor.
1903	Sir William R. Cremer, UK			1922	Fridtjof Nansen, Nor.
1904	Institute of International Law, Belg.	1910	Permanent Intl. Peace Bureau	1925	Sir Austen Chamberlain, UK; Charles G. Dawes, U.S.
1905	Baroness Bertha von Suttner, Austria	1911	Tobias M. C. Asser, Neth.; Alfred H. Fried, Austria		
				1926	Aristide Briand, Fr.; Gustav Stresemann, Ger.
1906	Theodore Roosevelt, U.S.	1912	Elihu Root, U.S.		
1907	Ernesto T. Moneta, Ital.; Louis Renault, Fr.	1913	Henri La Fontaine, Belg.	1927	Ferdinand E. Buisson, Fr.; Ludwig Quidde, Ger.
		1917	Intl. Committee of the Red Cross		

1929 Frank B. Kellogg, U.S.	1970 Norman E. Borlaug, U.S.	1995 Joseph Rotblat, Pol.-UK;
1930 Nathan Söderblom, Swed.	1971 Willy Brandt, Ger.	Pugwash Conferences, Can.
1931 Jane Addams,	1973 Henry Kissinger, U.S.;	1996 Bishop Carlos Ximenes Belo,
Nicholas Murray Butler, U.S.	Le Duc Tho, N. Viet. (Tho declined)	José Ramos-Horta, Timor-Leste
1933 Sir Norman Angell, UK	1974 Seán MacBride, Ire.;	1997 Jody Williams, U.S.;
1934 Arthur Henderson, UK	Eisaku Sato, Jpn.	Intl. Campaign to Ban Landmines
1935 Carl von Ossietzky, Ger.	1975 Andrei Sakharov, USSR	1998 John Hume, David Trimble, N. Ire.
1936 Carlos Saavedra Lamas, Arg.	1976 Mairead Corrigan,	1999 Médecins Sans Frontières
1937 Lord Robert Cecil, UK	Betty Williams, N. Ire.	(Doctors Without Borders), Fr.
1938 Nansen Intl. Office for Refugees	1977 Amnesty International, UK	2000 Kim Dae Jung, S. Kor.
1944 Intl. Committee of the Red Cross	1978 Anwar al-Sadat, Egypt;	2001 UN; Kofi Annan, Ghana
1945 Cordell Hull, U.S.	Menachem Begin, Isr.	2002 Jimmy Carter, U.S.
1946 Emily G. Balch, John R. Mott, U.S.	1979 Mother Teresa of Calcutta,	2003 Shirin Ebadi, Iran
1947 Friends Service Council, UK; Amer.	Alb.-India	2004 Wangari Maathai, Kenya
Friends Service Committee, U.S.	1980 Adolfo Pérez Esquivel, Arg.	2005 Mohamed ElBaradei, Egypt;
1949 Lord John Boyd Orr of Brechin, UK	1981 Office of UN High Commissioner	Intl. Atomic Energy Agency, Austria
1950 Ralph J. Bunche, U.S.	for Refugees	2006 Muhammad Yunus,
1951 Léon Jouhaux, Fr.	1982 Alfonso García Robles, Mex.;	Grameen Bank, Bangl.
1952 Albert Schweitzer, Fr.	Alva Myrdal, Swed.	2007 Intergovernmental Panel on Climate
1953 George C. Marshall, U.S.	1983 Lech Walesa, Pol.	Change, Switz.;
1954 Office of UN High Commissioner	1984 Bishop Desmond Tutu, S. Afr.	Albert Arnold Gore Jr., U.S.
for Refugees	1985 Intl. Physicians for the Prevention	2008 Martti Ahtisaari, Fin.
1957 Lester B. Pearson, Can.	of Nuclear War, U.S.	2009 Barack H. Obama, U.S.
1958 Georges Pire, Belg.	1986 Elie Wiesel, Rom.-U.S.	2010 Liu Xiaobo, China
1959 Philip J. Noel-Baker, UK	1987 Oscar Arias Sánchez, Costa Rica	2011 Leymah Gbowee,
1960 Albert J. Lutuli, S. Afr.	1988 UN Peacekeeping Forces	Ellen Johnson Sirleaf, Liberia;
1961 Dag Hammarskjöld, Swed.	1989 Dalai Lama (Tenzin Gyatso), Tibet	Tawakkol Karman, Yemen
1962 Linus C. Pauling, U.S.	1990 Mikhail S. Gorbachev, USSR	2012 European Union
1963 Intl. Committee of the Red Cross,	1991 Aung San Suu Kyi, Burma	2013 Organization for the Prohibition of
League of Red Cross Societies	1992 Rigoberta Menchú Tum, Guat.	Chemical Weapons (OPCW)
1964 Martin Luther King Jr., U.S.	1993 Frederik W. de Klerk,	2014 Kailash Satyarthi, India;
1965 UN Children's Fund (UNICEF)	Nelson Mandela, S. Afr.	Malala Yousafzai, Pakistan
1968 René Cassin, Fr.	1994 Yasser Arafat, Pal.; Shimon Peres,	2015 National Dialogue Quartet, Tunisia
1969 Intl. Labor Organization, Switz.	Yitzhak Rabin, Isr.	2016 Juan Manuel Santos, Colombia

Nobel Memorial Prize in Economic Sciences

1969 Ragnar Frisch, Nor.;	1988 Maurice Allais, Fr.	2003 Robert F. Engle, U.S.;
Jan Tinbergen, Neth.	1989 Trygve Haavelmo, Nor.	Clive W. J. Granger, UK
1970 Paul A. Samuelson, U.S.	1990 Harry M. Markowitz,	2004 Finn E. Kydland, Nor.;
1971 Simon Kuznets, U.S.	Merton H. Miller,	Edward C. Prescott, U.S.
1972 Kenneth J. Arrow, U.S.;	William F. Sharpe, U.S.	2005 Robert J. Aumann, Isr.-U.S.;
John R. Hicks, UK	1991 Ronald H. Coase, UK-U.S.	Thomas C. Schelling, U.S.
1973 Wassily Leontief, U.S.	1992 Gary S. Becker, U.S.	2006 Edmund S. Phelps, U.S.
1974 Gunnar Myrdal, Swed.;	1993 Robert W. Fogel,	2007 Leonid Hurwicz, Eric S. Maskin,
Friedrich A. von Hayek, Austria	Douglass C. North, U.S.	Roger B. Myerson, U.S.
1975 Leonid Kantorovich, USSR;	1994 John C. Harsanyi, John F. Nash,	2008 Paul Krugman, U.S.
Tjalling C. Koopmans, Neth.-U.S.	U.S.; Reinhard Selten, Ger.	2009 Elinor Ostrom,
1976 Milton Friedman, U.S.	1995 Robert E. Lucas Jr., U.S.	Oliver E. Williamson, U.S.
1977 James E. Meade, UK;	1996 James A. Mirrlees, UK;	2010 Peter A. Diamond, Dale T.
Bertil Ohlin, Swed.	William Vickrey, Can.-U.S.	Mortensen, U.S.; Christopher A.
1978 Herbert A. Simon, U.S.	1997 Robert C. Merton, U.S.;	Pissarides, Cyprus-UK
1979 Sir Arthur Lewis, UK;	Myron S. Scholes, Can.-U.S.	2011 Thomas J. Sargent,
Theodore W. Schultz, U.S.	1998 Amartya Sen, India	Christopher A. Sims, U.S.
1980 Lawrence R. Klein, U.S.	1999 Robert A. Mundell, Can.	2012 Alvin E. Roth, Lloyd S. Shapley, U.S.
1981 James Tobin, U.S.	2000 James J. Heckman,	2013 Eugene F. Fama, Lars Peter
1982 George J. Stigler, U.S.	Daniel L. McFadden, U.S.	Hansen, Robert J. Shiller, U.S.
1983 Gerard Debreu, Fr.-U.S.	2001 George A. Akerlof, A. Michael	2014 Jean Tirole, Fr.
1984 Richard Stone, UK	Spence, Joseph E. Stiglitz, U.S.	2015 Angus Deaton, UK-U.S.
1985 Franco Modigliani, Ital.-U.S.	2002 Daniel Kahneman, U.S.-Isr.;	2016 Oliver Hart, U.S.; Bengt Holmström,
1986 James M. Buchanan, U.S.	Vernon L. Smith, U.S.	Fin.-U.S.
1987 Robert M. Solow, U.S.		

Pulitzer Prizes in Journalism, Letters, and Music, 1917-2016

Endowed by Joseph Pulitzer (1847-1911), publisher of the *New York World*, in a bequest to Columbia Univ. and awarded annually, in years shown, for work published the previous year. Prizes are currently $10,000 in each category except Public Service (in Journalism), for which a gold medal is given. The prize board began considering submissions from online-only publications in 2009.

Pulitzer Prizes in Journalism, 2016

Public Service: Associated Press, for investigation of labor abuses tied to the American seafood supply.

Breaking News Reporting: *L.A. Times* staff, for reporting on the shooting in San Bernardino, CA, and the subsequent terrorism investigation.

Investigative Reporting: Leonora LaPeter Anton and Anthony Cormier, *Tampa Bay Times*, and Michael Braga, *Sarasota Herald-Tribune*, for collaborative reporting on violence and neglect in Florida's mental hospitals.

Explanatory Reporting: T. Christian Miller, ProPublica, and Ken Armstrong, The Marshall Project, for examination and exposé of law enforcement's failures in rape investigations.

Local Reporting: Michael LaForgia, Cara Fitzpatrick, and Lisa Gartner, *Tampa Bay Times*, for exposing school board culpability in turning some county schools into "failure factories."

National Reporting: *Washington Post* staff, for initiative in creating a national database to show how often and why police shoot to kill and who the victims are likely to be.

International Reporting: Alissa J. Rubin, *NY Times*, for accounts giving voice to Afghan women.

Feature Writing: Kathryn Schulz, *New Yorker*, for scientific narrative on the rupturing Cascadia fault line.

Commentary: Farah Stockman, *Boston Globe*, for columns on the legacy of busing and its effect on education in Boston.

Criticism: Emily Nussbaum, *New Yorker*, for television reviews.

Editorial Writing: John Hackworth and Brian Gleason, Sun Newspapers (Charlotte Harbor, FL), for editorials demanding truth and change after a deadly assault of an inmate by corrections officers.

Editorial Cartooning: Jack Ohman, *Sacramento Bee* (CA), for cartoons that convey wry, rueful perspectives.

Breaking News Photography: Mauricio Lima, Sergey Ponomarev, Tyler Hicks, and Daniel Etter, *NY Times*, and Thomson Reuters photography staff, for coverage of the refugee crisis.

Feature Photography: Jessica Rinaldi, *Boston Globe*, for story of a boy who strives to find his footing after abuse.

Pulitzer Prizes in Letters, 1918-2016

Other Pulitzer Prize Winners, 2016: Biography/autobiography: William Finnegan, *Barbarian Days: A Surfing Life*. History (U.S.): T. J. Stiles, *Custer's Trials: A Life on the Frontier of a New America*. Poetry: Peter Balakian, *Ozone Journal*.

Fiction

1918 Ernest Poole, *His Family*
1919 Booth Tarkington, *The Magnificent Ambersons*
1921 Edith Wharton, *The Age of Innocence*
1922 Booth Tarkington, *Alice Adams*
1923 Willa Cather, *One of Ours*
1924 Margaret Wilson, *The Able McLaughlins*
1925 Edna Ferber, *So Big*
1926 Sinclair Lewis, *Arrowsmith* (refused)
1927 Louis Bromfield, *Early Autumn*
1928 Thornton Wilder, *The Bridge of San Luis Rey*
1929 Julia Peterkin, *Scarlet Sister Mary*
1930 Oliver La Farge, *Laughing Boy*
1931 Margaret Ayer Barnes, *Years of Grace*
1932 Pearl S. Buck, *The Good Earth*
1933 T. S. Stribling, *The Store*
1934 Caroline Miller, *Lamb in His Bosom*
1935 Josephine W. Johnson, *Now in November*
1936 Harold L. Davis, *Honey in the Horn*
1937 Margaret Mitchell, *Gone With the Wind*
1938 John P. Marquand, *The Late George Apley*
1939 Marjorie Kinnan Rawlings, *The Yearling*
1940 John Steinbeck, *The Grapes of Wrath*
1942 Ellen Glasgow, *In This Our Life*
1943 Upton Sinclair, *Dragon's Teeth*
1944 Martin Flavin, *Journey in the Dark*
1945 John Hersey, *A Bell for Adano*
1947 Robert Penn Warren, *All the King's Men*
1948 James A. Michener, *Tales of the South Pacific*
1949 James Gould Cozzens, *Guard of Honor*
1950 A. B. Guthrie Jr., *The Way West*
1951 Conrad Richter, *The Town*
1952 Herman Wouk, *The Caine Mutiny*
1953 Ernest Hemingway, *The Old Man and the Sea*
1955 William Faulkner, *A Fable*
1956 MacKinlay Kantor, *Andersonville*
1958 James Agee, *A Death in the Family*
1959 Robert Lewis Taylor, *The Travels of Jaimie McPheeters*
1960 Allen Drury, *Advise and Consent*
1961 Harper Lee, *To Kill a Mockingbird*
1962 Edwin O'Connor, *The Edge of Sadness*
1963 William Faulkner, *The Reivers*
1965 Shirley Ann Grau, *The Keepers of the House*
1966 Katherine Anne Porter, *Collected Stories*
1967 Bernard Malamud, *The Fixer*
1968 William Styron, *The Confessions of Nat Turner*
1969 N. Scott Momaday, *House Made of Dawn*
1970 Jean Stafford, *Collected Stories*
1972 Wallace Stegner, *Angle of Repose*
1973 Eudora Welty, *The Optimist's Daughter*
1975 Michael Shaara, *The Killer Angels*
1976 Saul Bellow, *Humboldt's Gift*
1978 James Alan McPherson, *Elbow Room*
1979 John Cheever, *The Stories of John Cheever*
1980 Norman Mailer, *The Executioner's Song*
1981 John Kennedy Toole, *A Confederacy of Dunces*
1982 John Updike, *Rabbit Is Rich*
1983 Alice Walker, *The Color Purple*
1984 William Kennedy, *Ironweed*
1985 Alison Lurie, *Foreign Affairs*
1986 Larry McMurtry, *Lonesome Dove*
1987 Peter Taylor, *A Summons to Memphis*
1988 Toni Morrison, *Beloved*
1989 Anne Tyler, *Breathing Lessons*
1990 Oscar Hijuelos, *The Mambo Kings Play Songs of Love*
1991 John Updike, *Rabbit at Rest*
1992 Jane Smiley, *A Thousand Acres*
1993 Robert Olen Butler, *A Good Scent From a Strange Mountain*
1994 E. Annie Proulx, *The Shipping News*
1995 Carol Shields, *The Stone Diaries*
1996 Richard Ford, *Independence Day*
1997 Steven Millhauser, *Martin Dressler: The Tale of an American Dreamer*
1998 Philip Roth, *American Pastoral*
1999 Michael Cunningham, *The Hours*
2000 Jhumpa Lahiri, *Interpreter of Maladies*
2001 Michael Chabon, *The Amazing Adventures of Kavalier & Clay*

2002 Richard Russo, *Empire Falls*
2003 Jeffrey Eugenides, *Middlesex*
2004 Edward P. Jones, *The Known World*
2005 Marilynne Robinson, *Gilead*
2006 Geraldine Brooks, *March*
2007 Cormac McCarthy, *The Road*
2008 Junot Díaz, *The Brief Wondrous Life of Oscar Wao*
2009 Elizabeth Strout, *Olive Kitteridge*
2010 Paul Harding, *Tinkers*
2011 Jennifer Egan, *A Visit From the Goon Squad*
2013 Adam Johnson, *The Orphan Master's Son*
2014 Donna Tartt, *The Goldfinch*
2015 Anthony Doerr, *All the Light We Cannot See*
2016 Viet Thanh Nguyen, *The Sympathizer*

Drama

1918 Jesse Lynch Williams, *Why Marry?*
1920 Eugene O'Neill, *Beyond the Horizon*
1921 Zona Gale, *Miss Lulu Bett*
1922 Eugene O'Neill, *Anna Christie*
1923 Owen Davis, *Icebound*
1924 Hatcher Hughes, *Hell-Bent Fer Heaven*
1925 Sidney Howard, *They Knew What They Wanted*
1926 George Kelly, *Craig's Wife*
1927 Paul Green, *In Abraham's Bosom*
1928 Eugene O'Neill, *Strange Interlude*
1929 Elmer Rice, *Street Scene*
1930 Marc Connelly, *The Green Pastures*
1931 Susan Glaspell, *Alison's House*
1932 George S. Kaufman, Morrie Ryskind, and Ira Gershwin, *Of Thee I Sing*
1933 Maxwell Anderson, *Both Your Houses*
1934 Sidney Kingsley, *Men in White*
1935 Zoe Akins, *The Old Maid*
1936 Robert E. Sherwood, *Idiot's Delight*
1937 George S. Kaufman and Moss Hart, *You Can't Take It With You*
1938 Thornton Wilder, *Our Town*
1939 Robert E. Sherwood, *Abe Lincoln in Illinois*
1940 William Saroyan, *The Time of Your Life*
1941 Robert E. Sherwood, *There Shall Be No Night*
1943 Thornton Wilder, *The Skin of Our Teeth*
1945 Mary Chase, *Harvey*
1946 Russel Crouse and Howard Lindsay, *State of the Union*
1948 Tennessee Williams, *A Streetcar Named Desire*
1949 Arthur Miller, *Death of a Salesman*
1950 Richard Rodgers, Oscar Hammerstein II, and Joshua Logan, *South Pacific*
1952 Joseph Kramm, *The Shrike*
1953 William Inge, *Picnic*
1954 John Patrick, *The Teahouse of the August Moon*
1955 Tennessee Williams, *Cat on a Hot Tin Roof*
1956 Frances Goodrich and Albert Hackett, *The Diary of Anne Frank*
1957 Eugene O'Neill, *Long Day's Journey Into Night*
1958 Ketti Frings, *Look Homeward, Angel*
1959 Archibald MacLeish, *J. B.*
1960 George Abbott, Jerome Weidman, Sheldon Harnick, and Jerry Bock, *Fiorello!*
1961 Tad Mosel, *All the Way Home*
1962 Frank Loesser and Abe Burrows, *How to Succeed in Business Without Really Trying*
1965 Frank D. Gilroy, *The Subject Was Roses*
1967 Edward Albee, *A Delicate Balance*
1969 Howard Sackler, *The Great White Hope*
1970 Charles Gordone, *No Place to Be Somebody*
1971 Paul Zindel, *The Effect of Gamma Rays on Man-in-the-Moon Marigolds*
1973 Jason Miller, *That Championship Season*
1975 Edward Albee, *Seascape*
1976 Michael Bennett, James Kirkwood, Nicholas Dante, Marvin Hamlisch, and Edward Kleban, *A Chorus Line*
1977 Michael Cristofer, *The Shadow Box*
1978 Donald L. Coburn, *The Gin Game*
1979 Sam Shepard, *Buried Child*
1980 Lanford Wilson, *Talley's Folly*
1981 Beth Henley, *Crimes of the Heart*
1982 Charles Fuller, *A Soldier's Play*

1983 Marsha Norman, *'night, Mother*
1984 David Mamet, *Glengarry Glen Ross*
1985 Stephen Sondheim and James Lapine, *Sunday in the Park With George*
1987 August Wilson, *Fences*
1988 Alfred Uhry, *Driving Miss Daisy*
1989 Wendy Wasserstein, *The Heidi Chronicles*
1990 August Wilson, *The Piano Lesson*
1991 Neil Simon, *Lost in Yonkers*
1992 Robert Schenkkan, *The Kentucky Cycle*
1993 Tony Kushner, *Angels in America: Millennium Approaches*
1994 Edward Albee, *Three Tall Women*
1995 Horton Foote, *The Young Man From Atlanta*
1996 Jonathan Larson, *Rent*
1998 Paula Vogel, *How I Learned to Drive*
1999 Margaret Edson, *Wit*
2000 Donald Margulies, *Dinner With Friends*
2001 David Auburn, *Proof*
2002 Suzan-Lori Parks, *Topdog/Underdog*
2003 Nilo Cruz, *Anna in the Tropics*
2004 Doug Wright, *I Am My Own Wife*
2005 John Patrick Shanley, *Doubt, a parable*
2007 David Lindsay-Abaire, *Rabbit Hole*
2008 Tracy Letts, *August: Osage County*
2009 Lynn Nottage, *Ruined*
2010 Tom Kitt and Brian Yorkey, *Next to Normal*
2011 Bruce Norris, *Clybourne Park*
2012 Quiara Alegría Hudes, *Water by the Spoonful*
2013 Ayad Akhtar, *Disgraced*
2014 Annie Baker, *The Flick*
2015 Stephen Adly Guirgis, *Between Riverside and Crazy*
2016 Lin-Manuel Miranda, *Hamilton*

General Nonfiction

1962 Theodore H. White, *The Making of the President 1960*
1963 Barbara W. Tuchman, *The Guns of August*
1964 Richard Hofstadter, *Anti-Intellectualism in American Life*
1965 Howard Mumford Jones, *O Strange New World*
1966 Edwin Way Teale, *Wandering Through Winter*
1967 David Brion Davis, *The Problem of Slavery in Western Culture*
1968 Will and Ariel Durant, *Rousseau and Revolution*
1969 Norman Mailer, *The Armies of the Night*; Rene Jules Dubos, *So Human an Animal: How We Are Shaped by Surroundings and Events*
1970 Eric H. Erikson, *Gandhi's Truth*
1971 John Toland, *The Rising Sun*
1972 Barbara W. Tuchman, *Stilwell and the American Experience in China, 1911-1945*
1973 Frances FitzGerald, *Fire in the Lake: The Vietnamese and the Americans in Vietnam*; Robert Coles, *Children of Crisis, Vols. II and III*
1974 Ernest Becker, *The Denial of Death*
1975 Annie Dillard, *Pilgrim at Tinker Creek*
1976 Robert N. Butler, *Why Survive? Being Old in America*
1977 William W. Warner, *Beautiful Swimmers*
1978 Carl Sagan, *The Dragons of Eden*
1979 Edward O. Wilson, *On Human Nature*
1980 Douglas R. Hofstadter, *Gödel, Escher, Bach: An Eternal Golden Braid*
1981 Carl E. Schorske, *Fin-de-Siècle Vienna: Politics and Culture*
1982 Tracy Kidder, *The Soul of a New Machine*
1983 Susan Sheehan, *Is There No Place on Earth for Me?*
1984 Paul Starr, *Social Transformation of American Medicine*
1985 Studs Terkel, *The Good War*
1986 Joseph Lelyveld, *Move Your Shadow*; J. Anthony Lukas, *Common Ground*

1987 David K. Shipler, *Arab and Jew: Wounded Spirits in a Promised Land*
1988 Richard Rhodes, *The Making of the Atomic Bomb*
1989 Neil Sheehan, *A Bright Shining Lie: John Paul Vann and America in Vietnam*
1990 Dale Maharidge and Michael Williamson, *And Their Children After Them*
1991 Bert Holldobler and Edward O. Wilson, *The Ants*
1992 Daniel Yergin, *The Prize: The Epic Quest for Oil, Money, and Power*
1993 Garry Wills, *Lincoln at Gettysburg*
1994 David Remnick, *Lenin's Tomb: The Last Days of the Soviet Empire*
1995 Jonathan Weiner, *The Beak of the Finch: A Story of Evolution in Our Time*
1996 Tina Rosenberg, *The Haunted Land: Facing Europe's Ghosts After Communism*
1997 Richard Kluger, *Ashes to Ashes: America's Hundred-Year Cigarette War, the Public Health, and the Unabashed Triumph of Philip Morris*
1998 Jared Diamond, *Guns, Germs, and Steel: The Fates of Human Societies*
1999 John McPhee, *Annals of the Former World*
2000 John W. Dower, *Embracing Defeat: Japan in the Wake of World War II*
2001 Herbert P. Bix, *Hirohito and the Making of Modern Japan*
2002 Diane McWhorter, *Carry Me Home: Birmingham, Alabama: The Climactic Battle of the Civil Rights Revolution*
2003 Samantha Power, *A Problem From Hell: America and the Age of Genocide*
2004 Anne Applebaum, *Gulag: A History*
2005 Steve Coll, *Ghost Wars*
2006 Caroline Elkins, *Imperial Reckoning: The Untold Story of Britain's Gulag in Kenya*
2007 Lawrence Wright, *The Looming Tower: Al-Qaeda and the Road to 9/11*
2008 Saul Friedländer, *The Years of Extermination: Nazi Germany and the Jews, 1939-1945*
2009 Douglas A. Blackmon, *Slavery by Another Name: The Re-Enslavement of Black Americans From the Civil War to World War II*
2010 David E. Hoffman, *The Dead Hand: The Untold Story of the Cold War Arms Race and Its Dangerous Legacy*
2011 Siddhartha Mukherjee, *The Emperor of All Maladies: A Biography of Cancer*
2012 Stephen Greenblatt, *The Swerve: How the World Became Modern*
2013 Gilbert King, *Devil in the Grove: Thurgood Marshall, the Groveland Boys, and the Dawn of a New America*
2014 Dan Fagin, *Toms River: A Story of Science and Salvation*
2015 Elizabeth Kolbert, *The Sixth Extinction: An Unnatural History*
2016 Joby Warrick, *Black Flags: The Rise of ISIS*

Special Citation in Letters

1944 Richard Rodgers and Oscar Hammerstein II, for *Oklahoma!*
1957 Kenneth Roberts, for his historical novels
1960 *The Armada*, by Garrett Mattingly
1961 *American Heritage Picture History of the Civil War*
1973 *George Washington, Vols. I-IV*, by James Thomas Flexner
1977 Alex Haley, for *Roots*
1978 E. B. White
1984 Theodor Seuss Geisel (Dr. Seuss)
1992 Art Spiegelman, for *Maus*
2006 Edmund S. Morgan
2007 Ray Bradbury

Pulitzer Prizes in Music, 1943-2016

1943 William Schuman, *Secular Cantata No. 2, A Free Song*
1944 Howard Hanson, *Symphony No. 4, Op. 34*
1945 Aaron Copland, *Appalachian Spring*
1946 Leo Sowerby, *The Canticle of the Sun*
1947 Charles Ives, *Symphony No. 3*
1948 Walter Piston, *Symphony No. 3*
1949 Virgil Thomson, *Louisiana Story*
1950 Gian-Carlo Menotti, *The Consul*
1951 Douglas Moore, *Giants in the Earth*
1952 Gail Kubik, *Symphony Concertante*
1954 Quincy Porter, *Concerto for Two Pianos and Orchestra*
1955 Gian-Carlo Menotti, *The Saint of Bleecker Street*

1956 Ernest Toch, *Symphony No. 3*
1957 Norman Dello Joio, *Meditations on Ecclesiastes*
1958 Samuel Barber, *Vanessa*
1959 John LaMontaine, *Concerto for Piano and Orchestra*
1960 Elliott Carter, *Second String Quartet*
1961 Walter Piston, *Symphony No. 7*
1962 Robert Ward, *The Crucible*
1963 Samuel Barber, *Piano Concerto No. 1*
1966 Leslie Bassett, *Variations for Orchestra*
1967 Leon Kirchner, *Quartet No. 3*
1968 George Crumb, *Echoes of Time and the River*
1969 Karel Husa, *String Quartet No. 3*

1970 Charles Wuorinen, *Time's Encomium*
1971 Mario Davidovsky, *Synchronisms No. 6*
1972 Jacob Druckman, *Windows*
1973 Elliott Carter, *String Quartet No. 3*
1974 Donald Martino, *Notturno*
1975 Dominick Argento, *From the Diary of Virginia Woolf*
1976 Ned Rorem, *Air Music*
1977 Richard Wernick, *Visions of Terror and Wonder*
1978 Michael Colgrass, *Deja Vu for Percussion and Orchestra*
1979 Joseph Schwantner, *Aftertones of Infinity*
1980 David Del Tredici, *In Memory of a Summer Day*
1982 Roger Sessions, *Concerto for Orchestra*
1983 Ellen Taaffe Zwilich, *Symphony No. 1*
1984 Bernard Rands, *Canti del Sole*
1985 Stephen Albert, *Symphony, RiverRun*
1986 George Perle, *Wind Quintet IV*
1987 John Harbison, *The Flight Into Egypt*
1988 William Bolcom, *12 New Etudes for Piano*
1989 Roger Reynolds, *Whispers Out of Time*
1990 Mel Powell, *Duplicates: A Concerto for Two Pianos and Orchestra*
1991 Shulamit Ran, *Symphony*
1992 Wayne Peterson, *The Face of the Night, The Heart of the Dark*
1993 Christopher Rouse, *Trombone Concerto*
1994 Gunther Schuller, *Of Reminiscences and Reflections*
1995 Morton Gould, *Stringmusic*
1996 George Walker, *Lilacs for Voice and Orchestra*
1997 Wynton Marsalis, *Blood on the Fields*
1998 Aaron Jay Kernis, *String Quartet No. 2 (musica instrumentalis)*

1999 Melinda Wagner, *Concerto for Flute, Strings, and Percussion*
2000 Lewis Spratlan, *Life is a Dream, Opera in Three Acts: Act II, Concert Version*
2001 John Corigliano, *Symphony No. 2 for String Orchestra*
2002 Henry Brant, *Ice Field*
2003 John Adams, *On the Transmigration of Souls*
2004 Paul Moravec, *Tempest Fantasy*
2005 Steven Stucky, *Second Concerto for Orchestra*
2006 Yehudi Wyner, *Piano Concerto: "Chiavi in Mano"*
2007 Ornette Coleman, *Sound Grammar*
2008 David Lang, *The Little Match Girl Passion*
2009 Steve Reich, *Double Sextet*
2010 Jennifer Higdon, *Violin Concerto*
2011 Zhou Long, *Madame White Snake*
2012 Kevin Puts, *Silent Night: Opera in Two Acts*
2013 Caroline Shaw, *Partita for 8 Voices*
2014 John Luther Adams, *Become Ocean*
2015 Julia Wolfe, *Anthracite Fields*
2016 Henry Threadgill, *In for a Penny, In for a Pound*

Special Citation in Music

1974 Roger Sessions
1976 Scott Joplin
1982 Milton Babbitt
1985 William Schuman
1998 George Gershwin
1999 Edward Kennedy "Duke" Ellington
2006 Thelonious Monk
2007 John Coltrane
2008 Bob Dylan
2010 Hank Williams

Man Booker Prize for Fiction, 1969-2016

The Booker Prize for fiction, established in 1968 and renamed the Man Booker Prize in 2002, is £50,000, awarded annually to the author of the best new full-length novel written in English. Award-winning authors were required to be a citizen of the UK, the Commonwealth, or Ireland until 2014, the first year in which all English-language novels published in Britain were considered.

Year Author, book

1969 P. H. Newby, *Something to Answer For*
1970 Bernice Rubens, *The Elected Member*
1971 V. S. Naipaul, *In a Free State*
1972 John Berger, *G*
1973 J. G. Farrell, *The Siege of Krishnapur*
1974 Nadine Gordimer, *The Conservationist*; Stanley Middleton, *Holiday*
1975 Ruth Prawer Jhabvala, *Heat and Dust*
1976 David Storey, *Saville*
1977 Paul Scott, *Staying On*
1978 Iris Murdoch, *The Sea, the Sea*
1979 Penelope Fitzgerald, *Offshore*
1980 William Golding, *Rites of Passage*
1981 Salman Rushdie, *Midnight's Children*[1]
1982 Thomas Keneally, *Schindler's Ark*
1983 J. M. Coetzee, *Life and Times of Michael K*
1984 Anita Brookner, *Hotel du Lac*
1985 Keri Hulme, *The Bone People*
1986 Kingsley Amis, *The Old Devils*
1987 Penelope Lively, *Moon Tiger*
1988 Peter Carey, *Oscar and Lucinda*
1989 Kazuo Ishiguro, *The Remains of the Day*
1990 A. S. Byatt, *Possession*
1991 Ben Okri, *The Famished Road*
1992 Michael Ondaatje, *The English Patient*; Barry Unsworth, *Sacred Hunger*
1993 Roddy Doyle, *Paddy Clarke Ha Ha Ha*

Year Author, book

1994 James Kelman, *How Late It Was, How Late*
1995 Pat Barker, *The Ghost Road*
1996 Graham Swift, *Last Orders*
1997 Arundhati Roy, *The God of Small Things*
1998 Ian McEwan, *Amsterdam*
1999 J. M. Coetzee, *Disgrace*
2000 Margaret Atwood, *The Blind Assassin*
2001 Peter Carey, *True History of the Kelly Gang*
2002 Yann Martel, *Life of Pi*
2003 DBC Pierre, *Vernon God Little*
2004 Alan Hollinghurst, *The Line of Beauty*
2005 John Banville, *The Sea*
2006 Kiran Desai, *The Inheritance of Loss*
2007 Anne Enright, *The Gathering*
2008 Aravind Adiga, *The White Tiger*
2009 Hilary Mantel, *Wolf Hall*
2010 Howard Jacobson, *The Finkler Question*
2011 Julian Barnes, *The Sense of an Ending*
2012 Hilary Mantel, *Bring up the Bodies*
2013 Eleanor Catton, *The Luminaries*
2014 Richard Flanagan, *The Narrow Road to the Deep North*
2015 Marlon James, *A Brief History of Seven Killings*
2016 Paul Beatty, *The Sellout*

(1) Rushdie's *Midnight's Children* also won the Booker of Bookers prize in 1993 and the Best of the Booker prize in 2008.

Newbery Medal, 1922-2016

The Newbery Medal is awarded annually by the Association for Library Service to Children, a division of the American Library Association, to the most distinguished contribution to American children's literature published in the previous year.

Year Book, author

1922 *The Story of Mankind*, Hendrik Willem van Loon
1923 *The Voyages of Dr. Dolittle*, Hugh Lofting
1924 *The Dark Frigate*, Charles Boardman Hawes
1925 *Tales From Silver Lands*, Charles J. Finger
1926 *Shen of the Sea*, Arthur Bowie Chrisman
1927 *Smoky, the Cowhorse*, Will James
1928 *Gay-Neck: The Story of a Pigeon*, Dhan Gopal Mukerji
1929 *The Trumpeter of Krakow*, Eric P. Kelly
1930 *Hitty, Her First Hundred Years*, Rachel Field
1931 *The Cat Who Went to Heaven*, Elizabeth Coatsworth
1932 *Waterless Mountain*, Laura Adams Armer
1933 *Young Fu of the Upper Yangtze*, Elizabeth Foreman Lewis
1934 *Invincible Louisa*, Cornelia Meigs

Year Book, author

1935 *Dobry*, Monica Shannon
1936 *Caddie Woodlawn*, Carol Ryrie Brink
1937 *Roller Skates*, Ruth Sawyer
1938 *The White Stag*, Kate Seredy
1939 *Thimble Summer*, Elizabeth Enright
1940 *Daniel Boone*, James Daugherty
1941 *Call It Courage*, Armstrong Sperry
1942 *The Matchlock Gun*, Walter D. Edmonds
1943 *Adam of the Road*, Elizabeth Janet Gray
1944 *Johnny Tremain*, Esther Forbes
1945 *Rabbit Hill*, Robert Lawson
1946 *Strawberry Girl*, Lois Lenski
1947 *Miss Hickory*, Carolyn Sherwin Bailey

Year	Book, author
1948	*The Twenty-One Balloons*, William Pène du Bois
1949	*King of the Wind*, Marguerite Henry
1950	*The Door in the Wall*, Marguerite de Angeli
1951	*Amos Fortune, Free Man*, Elizabeth Yates
1952	*Ginger Pye*, Eleanor Estes
1953	*Secret of the Andes*, Ann Nolan Clark
1954	*… And Now Miguel*, Joseph Krumgold
1955	*The Wheel on the School*, Meindert DeJong
1956	*Carry On, Mr. Bowditch*, Jean Lee Latham
1957	*Miracles on Maple Hill*, Virginia Sorensen
1958	*Rifles for Watie*, Harold Keith
1959	*The Witch of Blackbird Pond*, Elizabeth George Speare
1960	*Onion John*, Joseph Krumgold
1961	*Island of the Blue Dolphins*, Scott O'Dell
1962	*The Bronze Bow*, Elizabeth George Speare
1963	*A Wrinkle in Time*, Madeleine L'Engle
1964	*It's Like This, Cat*, Emily Cheney Neville
1965	*Shadow of a Bull*, Maia Wojciechowska
1966	*I, Juan de Pareja*, Elizabeth Borton de Trevino
1967	*Up a Road Slowly*, Irene Hunt
1968	*From the Mixed-Up Files of Mrs. Basil E. Frankweiler*, E. L. Konigsburg
1969	*The High King*, Lloyd Alexander
1970	*Sounder*, William H. Armstrong
1971	*The Summer of the Swans*, Betsy Byars
1972	*Mrs. Frisby and the Rats of NIMH*, Robert C. O'Brien
1973	*Julie of the Wolves*, Jean Craighead George
1974	*The Slave Dancer*, Paula Fox
1975	*M. C. Higgins, the Great*, Virginia Hamilton
1976	*The Grey King*, Susan Cooper
1977	*Roll of Thunder, Hear My Cry*, Mildred D. Taylor
1978	*Bridge to Terabithia*, Katherine Paterson
1979	*The Westing Game*, Ellen Raskin
1980	*A Gathering of Days*, Joan Blos
1981	*Jacob Have I Loved*, Katherine Paterson
1982	*A Visit to William Blake's Inn: Poems for Innocent and Experienced Travelers*, Nancy Willard

Year	Book, author
1983	*Dicey's Song*, Cynthia Voigt
1984	*Dear Mr. Henshaw*, Beverly Cleary
1985	*The Hero and the Crown*, Robin McKinley
1986	*Sarah, Plain and Tall*, Patricia MacLachlan
1987	*The Whipping Boy*, Sid Fleischman
1988	*Lincoln: A Photobiography*, Russell Freedman
1989	*Joyful Noise: Poems for Two Voices*, Paul Fleischman
1990	*Number the Stars*, Lois Lowry
1991	*Maniac Magee*, Jerry Spinelli
1992	*Shiloh*, Phyllis Reynolds Naylor
1993	*Missing May*, Cynthia Rylant
1994	*The Giver*, Lois Lowry
1995	*Walk Two Moons*, Sharon Creech
1996	*The Midwife's Apprentice*, Karen Cushman
1997	*The View From Saturday*, E. L. Konigsburg
1998	*Out of the Dust*, Karen Hesse
1999	*Holes*, Louis Sachar
2000	*Bud, Not Buddy*, Christopher Paul Curtis
2001	*A Year Down Yonder*, Richard Peck
2002	*A Single Shard*, Linda Sue Park
2003	*Crispin: The Cross of Lead*, Avi
2004	*The Tale of Despereaux*, Kate DiCamillo
2005	*Kira-Kira*, Cynthia Kadohata
2006	*Criss Cross*, Lynne Rae Perkins
2007	*The Higher Power of Lucky*, Susan Patron
2008	*Good Masters! Sweet Ladies! Voices From a Medieval Village*, Laura Amy Schlitz
2009	*The Graveyard Book*, Neil Gaiman
2010	*When You Reach Me*, Rebecca Stead
2011	*Moon Over Manifest*, Clare Vanderpool
2012	*Dead End in Norvelt*, Jack Gantos
2013	*The One and Only Ivan*, Katherine Applegate
2014	*Flora & Ulysses: The Illuminated Adventures*, Kate DiCamillo
2015	*The Crossover*, Kwame Alexander
2016	*Last Stop on Market Street*, Matt de la Peña

Caldecott Medal, 1938-2016

The Caldecott Medal is awarded annually by the Association for Library Service to Children, a division of the American Library Association, to the illustrator of the most distinguished American picture book for children.

Year	Book, illustrator
1938	*Animals of the Bible*, Dorothy P. Lathrop
1939	*Mei Li*, Thomas Handforth
1940	*Abraham Lincoln*, Ingri and Edgar Parin d'Aulaire
1941	*They Were Strong and Good*, Robert Lawson
1942	*Make Way for Ducklings*, Robert McCloskey
1943	*The Little House*, Virginia Lee Burton
1944	*Many Moons*, Louis Slobodkin
1945	*Prayer for a Child*, Elizabeth Orton Jones
1946	*The Rooster Crows*, Maude and Miska Petersham
1947	*The Little Island*, Leonard Weisgard
1948	*White Snow, Bright Snow*, Roger Duvoisin
1949	*The Big Snow*, Berta and Elmer Hader
1950	*Song of the Swallows*, Leo Politi
1951	*The Egg Tree*, Katherine Milhous
1952	*Finders Keepers*, Nicolas, pseud. (Nicholas Mordvinoff)
1953	*The Biggest Bear*, Lynd Ward
1954	*Madeline's Rescue*, Ludwig Bemelmans
1955	*Cinderella, or the Little Glass Slipper*, Marcia Brown
1956	*Frog Went A-Courtin'*, Feodor Rojankovsky
1957	*A Tree Is Nice*, Marc Simont
1958	*Time of Wonder*, Robert McCloskey
1959	*Chanticleer and the Fox*, Barbara Cooney
1960	*Nine Days to Christmas*, Marie Hall Ets
1961	*Baboushka and the Three Kings*, Nicolas Sidjakov
1962	*Once a Mouse*, Marcia Brown
1963	*The Snowy Day*, Ezra Jack Keats
1964	*Where the Wild Things Are*, Maurice Sendak
1965	*May I Bring a Friend?*, Beni Montresor
1966	*Always Room for One More*, Nonny Hogrogian
1967	*Sam, Bangs, and Moonshine*, Evaline Ness
1968	*Drummer Hoff*, Ed Emberley
1969	*The Fool of the World and the Flying Ship*, Uri Shulevitz
1970	*Sylvester and the Magic Pebble*, William Steig
1971	*A Story A Story*, Gail E. Haley
1972	*One Fine Day*, Nonny Hogrogian
1973	*The Funny Little Woman*, Blair Lent
1974	*Duffy and the Devil*, Margot Zemach
1975	*Arrow to the Sun*, Gerald McDermott
1976	*Why Mosquitoes Buzz in People's Ears*, Leo and Diane Dillon
1977	*Ashanti to Zulu: African Traditions*, Leo and Diane Dillon
1978	*Noah's Ark*, Peter Spier
1979	*The Girl Who Loved Wild Horses*, Paul Goble

Year	Book, illustrator
1980	*Ox-Cart Man*, Barbara Cooney
1981	*Fables*, Arnold Lobel
1982	*Jumanji*, Chris Van Allsburg
1983	*Shadow*, Marcia Brown
1984	*The Glorious Flight: Across the Channel With Louis Bleriot*, Alice and Martin Provensen
1985	*Saint George and the Dragon*, Trina Schart Hyman
1986	*The Polar Express*, Chris Van Allsburg
1987	*Hey, Al*, Richard Egielski
1988	*Owl Moon*, John Schoenherr
1989	*Song and Dance Man*, Stephen Grammell
1990	*Lon Po Po: A Red-Riding Hood Story From China*, Ed Young
1991	*Black and White*, David Macaulay
1992	*Tuesday*, David Wiesner
1993	*Mirette on the High Wire*, Emily Arnold McCully
1994	*Grandfather's Journey*, Allen Say
1995	*Smoky Night*, David Diaz
1996	*Officer Buckle and Gloria*, Peggy Rathmann
1997	*Golem*, David Wisniewski
1998	*Rapunzel*, Paul O. Zelinsky
1999	*Snowflake Bentley*, Mary Azarian
2000	*Joseph Had a Little Overcoat*, Simms Taback
2001	*So You Want to be President?*, David Small
2002	*The Three Pigs*, David Wiesner
2003	*My Friend Rabbit*, Eric Rohmann
2004	*The Man Who Walked Between the Towers*, Mordicai Gerstein
2005	*Kitten's First Full Moon*, Kevin Henkes
2006	*The Hello, Goodbye Window*, Chris Raschka
2007	*Flotsam*, David Wiesner
2008	*The Invention of Hugo Cabret*, Brian Selznick
2009	*The House in the Night*, Beth Krommes
2010	*The Lion & the Mouse*, Jerry Pinkney
2011	*A Sick Day for Amos McGee*, Erin E. Stead
2012	*A Ball for Daisy*, Chris Raschka
2013	*This Is Not My Hat*, Jon Klassen
2014	*Locomotive*, Brian Floca
2015	*The Adventures of Beekle: The Unimaginary Friend*, Dan Santat
2016	*Finding Winnie: The True Story of the World's Most Famous Bear*, Sophie Blackall

National Book Awards, 1950-2015

The National Book Awards (known as American Book Awards 1980-86) are administered by the National Book Foundation and have been given annually since 1950. The prizes, each valued at $10,000, are awarded to U.S. citizens for works published in the U.S. In some years, multiple awards were given for nonfiction in various categories; in such cases, the history and biography (if any) or biography winner is listed. Selected additional awards in nonfiction are listed in footnotes.

Other National Book Awards, 2015: Poetry: Robin Coste Lewis, *Voyage of the Sable Venus*. Young People's Literature: Neal Shusterman, *Challenger Deep*. Distinguished Contribution to American Letters: Don DeLillo. Literarian Award: James Patterson.

Fiction

Year	Author, book	Year	Author, book
1950	Nelson Algren, *The Man With the Golden Arm*	1983	Alice Walker, *The Color Purple*
1951	William Faulkner, *The Collected Stories*	1984	Ellen Gilchrist, *Victory Over Japan*
1952	James Jones, *From Here to Eternity*	1985	Don DeLillo, *White Noise*
1953	Ralph Ellison, *Invisible Man*	1986	E. L. Doctorow, *World's Fair*
1954	Saul Bellow, *The Adventures of Augie March*	1987	Larry Heinemann, *Paco's Story*
1955	William Faulkner, *A Fable*	1988	Pete Dexter, *Paris Trout*
1956	John O'Hara, *Ten North Frederick*	1989	John Casey, *Spartina*
1957	Wright Morris, *The Field of Vision*	1990	Charles Johnson, *Middle Passage*
1958	John Cheever, *The Wapshot Chronicle*	1991	Norman Rush, *Mating*
1959	Bernard Malamud, *The Magic Barrel*	1992	Cormac McCarthy, *All the Pretty Horses*
1960	Philip Roth, *Goodbye, Columbus*	1993	E. Annie Proulx, *The Shipping News*
1961	Conrad Richter, *The Waters of Kronos*	1994	William Gaddis, *A Frolic of His Own*
1962	Walker Percy, *The Moviegoer*	1995	Philip Roth, *Sabbath's Theater*
1963	J. F. Powers, *Morte d'Urban*	1996	Andrea Barrett, *Ship Fever and Other Stories*
1964	John Updike, *The Centaur*	1997	Charles Frazier, *Cold Mountain*
1965	Saul Bellow, *Herzog*	1998	Alice McDermott, *Charming Billy*
1966	Katherine Anne Porter, *The Collected Stories*	1999	Ha Jin, *Waiting*
1967	Bernard Malamud, *The Fixer*	2000	Susan Sontag, *In America*
1968	Thornton Wilder, *The Eighth Day*	2001	Jonathan Franzen, *The Corrections*
1969	Jerzy Kosinski, *Steps*	2002	Julia Glass, *Three Junes*
1970	Joyce Carol Oates, *Them*	2003	Shirley Hazzard, *The Great Fire*
1971	Saul Bellow, *Mr. Sammler's Planet*	2004	Lily Tuck, *The News From Paraguay*
1972	Flannery O'Connor, *The Complete Stories*	2005	William T. Vollmann, *Europe Central*
1973	John Barth, *Chimera*	2006	Richard Powers, *The Echo Maker*
1974	Thomas Pynchon, *Gravity's Rainbow*	2007	Denis Johnson, *Tree of Smoke*
1974	Isaac Bashevis Singer, *A Crown of Feathers*	2008	Peter Matthiessen, *Shadow Country*
1975	Robert Stone, *Dog Soldiers*	2009	Colum McCann, *Let the Great World Spin*
1976	William Gaddis, *JR*	2010	Jaimy Gordon, *Lord of Misrule*
1977	Wallace Stegner, *The Spectator Bird*	2011	Jesmyn Ward, *Salvage the Bones*
1978	Mary Lee Settle, *Blood Ties*	2012	Louise Erdrich, *The Round House*
1979	Tim O'Brien, *Going After Cacciato*	2013	James McBride, *The Good Lord Bird*
1980	William Styron, *Sophie's Choice*	2014	Phil Klay, *Redeployment*
1981	Wright Morris, *Plains Song*	2015	Adam Johnson, *Fortune Smiles: Stories*
1982	John Updike, *Rabbit Is Rich*		

Nonfiction

Year	Author, book	Year	Author, book
1950	Ralph L. Rusk, *Ralph Waldo Emerson*	1975	Richard B. Sewall, *The Life of Emily Dickinson*[6]
1951	Newton Arvin, *Herman Melville*	1976	David Brion Davis, *The Problem of Slavery in the Age of Revolution, 1770-1823*
1952	Rachel Carson, *The Sea Around Us*		
1953	Bernard A. De Voto, *The Course of an Empire*	1977	W. A. Swanberg, *Norman Thomas: The Last Idealist*[7]
1954	Bruce Catton, *A Stillness at Appomattox*	1978	W. Jackson Bate, *Samuel Johnson*
1955	Joseph Wood Krutch, *The Measure of Man*	1979	Arthur M. Schlesinger Jr., *Robert Kennedy and His Times*
1956	Herbert Kubly, *An American in Italy*	1980	Tom Wolfe, *The Right Stuff*
1957	George F. Kennan, *Russia Leaves the War*	1981	Maxine Hong Kingston, *China Men*
1958	Catherine Drinker Bowen, *The Lion and the Throne*	1982	Tracy Kidder, *The Soul of a New Machine*
1959	J. Christopher Herold, *Mistress to an Age: A Life of Madame De Stael*	1983	Fox Butterfield, *China: Alive in the Bitter Sea*
1960	Richard Ellman, *James Joyce*	1984	Robert V. Remini, *Andrew Jackson and the Course of American Democracy, 1833-1845*
1961	William L. Shirer, *The Rise and Fall of the Third Reich*		
1962	Lewis Mumford, *The City in History: Its Origins, Its Transformations, and Its Prospects*	1985	J. Anthony Lukas, *Common Ground: A Turbulent Decade in the Lives of Three American Families*
		1986	Barry Lopez, *Arctic Dreams*
1963	Leon Edel, *Henry James, Vol. II: The Conquest of London* and *Vol. III: The Middle Years*	1987	Richard Rhodes, *The Making of the Atom Bomb*
		1988	Neil Sheehan, *A Bright Shining Lie: John Paul Vann and America in Vietnam*
1964	William H. McNeill, *The Rise of the West: A History of the Human Community*		
		1989	Thomas L. Friedman, *From Beirut to Jerusalem*
1965	Louis Fisher, *The Life of Lenin*	1990	Ron Chernow, *The House of Morgan: An American Banking Dynasty and the Rise of Modern Finance*
1966	Arthur M. Schlesinger Jr., *A Thousand Days: John F. Kennedy in the White House*		
1967	Peter Gay, *The Enlightenment, An Interpretation, Vol. I: The Rise of Modern Paganism*	1991	Orlando Patterson, *Freedom*
		1992	Paul Monette, *Becoming a Man: Half a Life Story*
1968	George F. Kennan, *Memoirs: 1925-1950*[1]	1993	Gore Vidal, *United States: Essays 1952-1992*
1969	Winthrop D. Jordan, *White Over Black: American Attitudes Toward the Negro, 1550-1812*[2]	1994	Sherwin B. Nuland, *How We Die: Reflections on Life's Final Chapter*
1970	T. Harry Williams, *Huey Long*[3]	1995	Tina Rosenberg, *The Haunted Land: Facing Europe's Ghosts After Communism*
1971	James MacGregor Burns, *Roosevelt: The Soldier of Freedom*		
1972	Joseph P. Lash, *Eleanor and Franklin: The Story of Their Relationship, Based on Eleanor Roosevelt's Private Papers*	1996	James Carroll, *An American Requiem: God, My Father, and the War That Came Between Us*
		1997	Joseph J. Ellis, *American Sphinx: The Character of Thomas Jefferson*
1973	James Thomas Flexner, *George Washington, Vol. IV: Anguish and Farewell, 1793-1799*[4]	1998	Edward Ball, *Slaves in the Family*
		1999	John W. Dower, *Embracing Defeat: Japan in the Wake of World War II*
1974	John Clive, *Macaulay, The Shaping of the Historian*; Douglas Day, *Malcolm Lowry: A Biography*[5]	2000	Nathaniel Philbrick, *In the Heart of the Sea: The Tragedy of the Whaleship Essex*

Year	Author, book	Year	Author, book
2001	Andrew Solomon, *The Noonday Demon: An Atlas of Depression*	2008	Annette Gordon-Reed, *The Hemingses of Monticello: An American Family*
2002	Robert A. Caro, *Master of the Senate: The Years of Lyndon Johnson*	2009	T. J. Stiles, *The First Tycoon: The Epic Life of Cornelius Vanderbilt*
2003	Carlos Eire, *Waiting for Snow in Havana: Confessions of a Cuban Boy*	2010	Patti Smith, *Just Kids*
2004	Kevin Boyle, *Arc of Justice: A Saga of Race, Civil Rights, and Murder in the Jazz Age*	2011	Stephen Greenblatt, *The Swerve: How the World Became Modern*
2005	Joan Didion, *The Year of Magical Thinking*	2012	Katherine Boo, *Behind the Beautiful Forevers: Life, Death, and Hope in a Mumbai Undercity*
2006	Timothy Egan, *The Worst Hard Time: The Untold Story of Those Who Survived the Great American Dust Bowl*	2013	George Packer, *The Unwinding: An Inner History of the New America*
2007	Tim Weiner, *Legacy of Ashes: The History of the CIA*	2014	Evan Osnos, *Age of Ambition: Chasing Fortune, Truth, and Faith in the New China*
		2015	Ta-Nehisi Coates, *Between the World and Me*

(1) Science, Philosophy, & Religion: Jonathan Kozol, *Death at an Early Age*. (2) Arts & Letters: Norman Mailer, *The Armies of the Night: History as a Novel, the Novel as History*. (3) Arts & Letters: Lillian Hellman, *An Unfinished Woman: A Memoir*. (4) Contemp. Affairs: Frances FitzGerald, *Fire in the Lake: The Vietnamese and the Americans in Vietnam*. (5) Arts & Letters: Pauline Kael, *Deeper Into the Movies*. (6) Arts & Letters: Roger Shattuck, *Marcel Proust*; Lewis Thomas, *The Lives of a Cell: Notes of a Biology Watcher*. (7) Contemp. Thought: Bruno Bettelheim, *The Uses of Enchantment: The Meaning and Importance of Fairy Tales*.

Journalism Awards, 2016

National Magazine Awards, by American Society of Magazine Editors and Columbia Univ. Graduate School of Journalism, honoring excellence in print and on digital platforms. Magazine of the Year: *The Atlantic*. General Excellence: News, Sports, and Entertainment: *New York*; Literature, Science, and Politics: *Oxford American*; Service and Lifestyle: *Lucky Peach*; Special Interest: *Hollywood Reporter*. Columns and Commentary: *Intercept*. Design: *Wired*. Essays and Criticism: *Esquire*. Feature Photography: *Politico*. Feature Writing: *New Yorker*. Fiction: *Zoetrope: All-Story*. Leisure Interests: *Eater*. Magazine Section: *New York*. Multimedia: *New York*. Personal Service: *FamilyFun*. Photography: *California Sunday Magazine*. Public Interest: *BuzzFeed News*. Reporting: *Matter*. Single-Topic Issue: *Bloomberg Businessweek*. Video: *Vice News*. Website: *New York*.

George Foster Peabody Awards, by Univ. of Georgia, awarded to the best in electronic media. Listed alphabetically by media outlet. *Black-ish*, ABC. *Transparent*, Amazon Video. "European Migrant Crisis"/"A New Life in Europe"/"The Year of Migration," BBC. *Katie Morag*, CBeebies. *Going Clear: Scientology and the Prison of Belief; How to Dance in Ohio; The Jinx: The Life and Deaths of Robert Durst; The Leftovers; Night Will Fall; "The Killing Fields," Real Sports With Bryant Gumbel*, HBO. *UnREAL*, Lifetime. *Beasts of No Nation; Marvel's Jessica Jones; Master of None; What Happened, Miss Simone?*, Netflix. "Secret Mustard Gas Experiments," NPR News. *Independent Lens: India's Daughter; POV: Don't Tell Anyone (No Le Digas a Nadie); Wolf Hall*, PBS. "Desperate Journey," *PBS NewsHour*, PBS/WETA-TV. "ISIS in Afghanistan," *Frontline*, PBS/WGBH. *Listen to Me Marlon*, Showtime. *Deutschland 83*, Sundance-TV. "The Case for School Desegregation Today," *This American Life*. *Do Not Track*, Upian, National Film Board of Canada, Arte, Bayerischer Rundfunk, CBC/Radio-Canada. *Mr. Robot*, USA Network. "The LaQuan McDonald Investigation," WMAQ-TV (Chicago). *Meet the Composer*, WQXR.org (NYC). "Burning Questions: WTAE Investigates Fire Response Times," WTAE-TV (Pittsburgh). "911: Lost on the Line," WXIA-TV (Atlanta).

Scripps Howard Awards, by Scripps Howard Foundation. Breaking News: *Post and Courier* staff (Charleston, SC). Business/Economics Reporting: *Wall Street Journal* staff. Community Journalism: *Post and Courier* staff (Charleston, SC). Digital Innovation: Stephen Stirling, *NJ Advance Media*. Distinguished Service to the First Amendment: Todd Wallack, *Boston Globe*. Environmental Reporting: Neela Banerjee, John H. Cushman Jr., David Hasemyer, Lisa Song, *InsideClimate News*. Human Interest Storytelling: N. R. Kleinfield, *NY Times*. Investigative Reporting: Aram Roston and Jeremy Singer-Vine, *BuzzFeed News*. Opinion: Nancy Kaffer, *Detroit Free Press*. Photojournalism: Carolyn Cole, *L.A. Times*. Public Service Reporting: Alison Young, Nick Penzenstadler, Tom Vanden Brook, and others, *USA Today* Network. Radio In-Depth Coverage: Aleem Maqbool, BBC News. TV/Cable In-Depth Local Coverage: KNXV-TV (Phoenix, AZ). TV/Cable In-Depth Natl. and Intl. Coverage: Dan Edge, *Frontline*, WGBH-PBS. Topic of the Year: Rachel Aviv, *New Yorker*.

Miscellaneous Book Awards, 2016

Bollingen Prize for American Poetry, by the Yale Univ. Library, $150,000 (biennial, awarded in 2015): Nathaniel Mackey.

Coretta Scott King Awards, by American Library Assn., for African American authors and illustrators of outstanding books for children and young adults. Author: Rita Williams-Garcia, *Gone Crazy in Alabama*. Illustrator: Bryan Collier, *Trombone Shorty*. New talent: Ronald L. Smith (author) and Ekua Holmes (illustrator).

Costa Book Awards. Book of the Year (formerly Whitbread Award): *The Lie Tree*, Frances Hardinge.

Edgar Awards, by the Mystery Writers of America. Novel: *Let Me Die in His Footsteps*, Lori Roy. First Novel: *The Sympathizer*, Viet Thanh Nguyen. Paperback Original: *The Long and Faraway Gone*, Lou Berney. Fact Crime: *Whipping Boy: The Forty-Year Search for My Twelve-Year-Old Bully*, Allen Kurzweil. Critical/Biographical: *The Golden Age of Murder*, Martin Edwards. Short Story: "Obits," *Bazaar of Bad Dreams*, Stephen King. Juvenile: *Footer Davis Probably Is Crazy*, Susan Vaught. Young Adult: *A Madness So Discreet*, Mindy McGinnis. TV Episode: "Gently With the Women," *George Gently*, Peter Flannery. Robert L. Fish Award: "Chung Ling Soo's Greatest Trick," Russell W. Johnson, *Ellery Queen Mystery Magazine*. Grand Master: Walter Mosley. Raven Award: Margaret Kinsman, Sisters in Crime. Ellery Queen Award: Janet Rudolph, founder of Mystery Readers Intl. Simon & Schuster-Mary Higgins Clark Award: *Little Pretty Things*, Lori Rader-Day.

Golden Kite Awards, by the Society of Children's Book Writers and Illustrators. Fiction: *Challenger Deep*, Neal Shusterman. Nonfiction: *Enchanted Air: Two Cultures, Two Wings: A Memoir*, Margarita Engle. Middle Grade/Young Reader Fiction: *The Detective's Assistant*, Kate Hannigan. Picture Book Text: *Boats for Papa*, Jessixa Bagley. Picture Book Illustration: *Marvelous Cornelius*, John Parra.

Hugo Awards, by the World Science Fiction Society (WSFS). Novel: *The Fifth Season*, N. K. Jemisin. Novella: *Binti*, Nnedi Okorafor. Novelette: "Folding Beijing," Hao Jingfang (trans. by Ken Liu). Short Story: "Cat Pictures Please," Naomi Kritzer. Graphic Story: *The Sandman: Overture*, Neil Gaiman, art by J. H. Williams III. Dramatic Presentation, long form: *The Martian*, Drew Goddard. Dramatic Presentation, short form: "AKA Smile," *Jessica Jones*, Netflix. (No award given in two standard categories.)

Lincoln Prize, by Gettysburg College and the Gilder Lehrman Inst. of American History, $50,000: Martha Hodes, *Mourning Lincoln*.

National Book Critics Circle Awards. Fiction: Paul Beatty, *The Sellout*. Nonfiction: Sam Quinones, *Dreamland: The True Story of America's Opiate Epidemic*. Autobiography: Margo Jefferson, *Negroland: A Memoir*. Biography: Charlotte Gordon, *Romantic Outlaws: The Extraordinary Lives of Mary Wollstonecraft and Her Daughter Mary Shelley*. Criticism: Maggie Nelson, *The Argonauts*. Poetry: Ross Gay, *Catalogue of Unabashed Gratitude*. John Leonard Prize: Kirstin Valdez Quade, *Night at the Fiestas*. Ivan Sandrof Lifetime Achievement Award: Wendell Berry. Nona Balakian Citation for Excellence in Reviewing: Carlos Lozada.

Nebula Awards, by the Science Fiction and Fantasy Writers of America. Novel: *Uprooted*, Naomi Novik. Novella: *Binti*, Nnedi Okorafor. Novelette: "Our Lady of the Open Road," Sarah Pinsker. Short Story: "Hungry Daughters of Starving Mothers," Alyssa Wong. Ray Bradbury Award: *Mad Max: Fury Road*. Andre Norton Award: *Updraft*, Fran Wilde.

PEN/Faulkner Award, for fiction, $15,000: James Hannaham, *Delicious Foods*.

Printz Award, for young adult literature: *Bone Gap*, Laura Ruby.

Spingarn Medal, 1915-2016

The Spingarn Medal has been awarded annually in most years since 1915 by the National Assn. for the Advancement of Colored People for outstanding achievement by an African American.

1915 Ernest E. Just	1942 A. Philip Randolph	1967 Edward W. Brooke	1992 Barbara Jordan
1916 Charles Young	1943 William H. Hastie	1968 Sammy Davis Jr.	1993 Dorothy I. Height
1917 Harry T. Burleigh	1944 Charles Drew	1969 Clarence M. Mitchell Jr.	1994 Maya Angelou
1918 William S. Braithwaite	1945 Paul Robeson	1970 Jacob Lawrence	1995 John Hope Franklin
1919 Archibald H. Grimké	1946 Thurgood Marshall	1971 Leon H. Sullivan	1996 A. Leon Higginbotham Jr.
1920 W. E. B. Du Bois	1947 Dr. Percy L. Julian	1972 Gordon Parks	1997 Carl T. Rowan
1921 Charles S. Gilpin	1948 Channing H. Tobias	1973 Wilson C. Riles	1998 Myrlie Evers-Williams
1922 Mary B. Talbert	1949 Ralph J. Bunche	1974 Damon Keith	1999 Earl G. Graves Sr.
1923 George W. Carver	1950 Charles H. Houston	1976 Henry (Hank) Aaron	2000 Oprah Winfrey
1924 Roland Hayes	1951 Mabel K. Staupers	1977 Alvin Ailey	2001 Vernon E. Jordan Jr.
1925 James W. Johnson	1952 Harry T. Moore	1977 Alex Haley	2002 John Lewis
1926 Carter G. Woodson	1953 Paul R. Williams	1979 Andrew Young	2003 Constance Baker Motley
1927 Anthony Overton	1954 Theodore K. Lawless	1979 Rosa L. Parks	2004 Robert L. Carter
1928 Charles W. Chesnutt	1955 Carl Murphy	1980 Dr. Rayford W. Logan	2005 Oliver W. Hill
1929 Mordecai W. Johnson	1956 Jack R. Robinson	1981 Coleman Young	2006 Dr. Benjamin S. Carson
1930 Henry A. Hunt	1957 Martin Luther King Jr.	1982 Dr. Benjamin E. Mays	2007 John Conyers Jr.
1931 Richard B. Harrison	1958 Daisy Bates and the	1983 Lena Horne	2008 Ruby Dee
1932 Robert R. Moton	Little Rock Nine	1985 Thomas Bradley	2009 Julian Bond
1933 Max Yergan	1959 Duke Ellington	1985 Bill Cosby	2010 Cicely Tyson
1934 William T. B. Williams	1960 Langston Hughes	1986 Dr. Benjamin L. Hooks	2011 Frankie Muse Freeman
1935 Mary McLeod Bethune	1961 Kenneth B. Clark	1987 Percy E. Sutton	2012 Harry Belafonte
1936 John Hope	1962 Robert C. Weaver	1988 Frederick D. Patterson	2013 Jessye Norman
1937 Walter White	1963 Medgar W. Evers	1989 Jesse Jackson	2014 Quincy Jones
1939 Marian Anderson	1964 Roy Wilkins	1990 L. Douglas Wilder	2015 Sidney Poitier
1940 Louis T. Wright	1965 Leontyne Price	1991 Gen. Colin L. Powell	2016 Nathaniel R. Jones
1941 Richard Wright	1966 John H. Johnson		

Miss America Winners, 1921-2017

Year	Winner, hometown	Year	Winner, hometown
1921	Margaret Gorman, Washington, DC	1974	Rebecca Ann King, Denver, Colorado
1922-23	Mary Campbell, Columbus, Ohio	1975	Shirley Cothran, Denton, Texas
1924	Ruth Malcolmson, Philadelphia, Pennsylvania	1976	Tawney Elaine Godin, Saratoga Springs, New York
1925	Fay Lamphier, Oakland, California	1977	Dorothy Kathleen Benham, Edina, Minnesota
1926	Norma Smallwood, Tulsa, Oklahoma	1978	Susan Perkins, Columbus, Ohio
1927	Lois Delander, Joliet, Illinois	1979	Kylene Barker, Roanoke, Virginia
1933	Marion Bergeron, West Haven, Connecticut	1980	Cheryl Prewitt, Ackerman, Mississippi
1935	Henrietta Leaver, Pittsburgh, Pennsylvania	1981	Susan Powell, Elk City, Oklahoma
1936	Rose Coyle, Philadelphia, Pennsylvania	1982	Elizabeth Ward, Russellville, Arkansas
1937	Bette Cooper, Bertrand Island, New Jersey	1983	Debra Maffett, Anaheim, California
1938	Marilyn Meseke, Marion, Ohio	1984[1]	Suzette Charles, Mays Landing, New Jersey
1939	Patricia Donnelly, Detroit, Michigan	1985	Sharlene Wells, Salt Lake City, Utah
1940	Frances Marie Burke, Philadelphia, Pennsylvania	1986	Susan Akin, Meridian, Mississippi
1941	Rosemary LaPlanche, Los Angeles, California	1987	Kellye Cash, Memphis, Tennessee
1942	Jo-Caroll Dennison, Tyler, Texas	1988	Kaye Lani Rae Rafko, Monroe, Michigan
1943	Jean Bartel, Los Angeles, California	1989	Gretchen Carlson, Anoka, Minnesota
1944	Venus Ramey, Washington, DC	1990	Debbye Turner, Columbia, Missouri
1945	Bess Myerson, New York, New York	1991	Marjorie Vincent, Oak Park, Illinois
1946	Marilyn Buferd, Los Angeles, California	1992	Carolyn Suzanne Sapp, Honolulu, Hawaii
1947	Barbara Walker, Memphis, Tennessee	1993	Leanza Cornett, Jacksonville, Florida
1948	BeBe Shopp, Hopkins, Minnesota	1994	Kimberly Aiken, Columbia, South Carolina
1949	Jacque Mercer, Litchfield, Arizona	1995	Heather Whitestone, Birmingham, Alabama
1951	Yolande Betbeze, Mobile, Alabama	1996	Shawntel Smith, Muldrow, Oklahoma
1952	Coleen Kay Hutchins, Salt Lake City, Utah	1997	Tara Dawn Holland, Overland Park, Kansas
1953	Neva Jane Langley, Macon, Georgia	1998	Kate Shindle, Evanston, Illinois
1954	Evelyn Margaret Ay, Ephrata, Pennsylvania	1999	Nicole Johnson, Roanoke, Virginia
1955	Lee Meriwether, San Francisco, California	2000	Heather Renee French, Maysville, Kentucky
1956	Sharon Ritchie, Denver, Colorado	2001	Angela Perez Baraquio, Honolulu, Hawaii
1957	Marian McKnight, Manning, South Carolina	2002	Katie Harman, Gresham, Oregon
1958	Marilyn Van Derbur, Denver, Colorado	2003	Erika Harold, Urbana, Illinois
1959	Mary Ann Mobley, Brandon, Mississippi	2004	Ericka Dunlap, Orlando, Florida
1960	Lynda Lee Mead, Natchez, Mississippi	2005	Deidre Downs, Birmingham, Alabama
1961	Nancy Fleming, Montague, Michigan	2006	Jennifer Berry, Tulsa, Oklahoma
1962	Maria Fletcher, Asheville, North Carolina	2007	Lauren Nelson, Lawton, Oklahoma
1963	Jacquelyn Mayer, Sandusky, Ohio	2008	Kirsten Haglund, Farmington Hills, Michigan
1964	Donna Axum, El Dorado, Arkansas	2009	Katie Stam, Seymour, Indiana
1965	Vonda Kay Van Dyke, Phoenix, Arizona	2010	Caressa Cameron, Fredricksburg, Virginia
1966	Deborah Irene Bryant, Overland Park, Kansas	2011	Teresa Scanlan, Gering, Nebraska
1967	Jane Anne Jayroe, Laverne, Oklahoma	2012	Laura Kaeppeler, Kenosha, Wisconsin
1968	Debra Dene Barnes, Moran, Kansas	2013	Mallory Hytes Hagen, Brooklyn, New York
1969	Judith Anne Ford, Belvidere, Illinois	2014	Nina Davuluri, Syracuse, New York
1970	Pamela Anne Eldred, Birmingham, Michigan	2015	Kira Kazantsev, New York, New York
1971	Phyllis Ann George, Denton, Texas	2016	Betty Cantrell, Warner Robins, Georgia
1972	Laurie Lea Schaefer, Bexley, Ohio	2017	Savvy Shields, Fayetteville, Arkansas
1973	Terry Anne Meeuwsen, DePere, Wisconsin		

Note: Since the 1950 pageant, winners have been crowned Miss America of the following year (e.g., Miss America 1951 competed in 1950). (1) Miss New York, Vanessa Williams, resigned July 23, 1984.

Tony (Antoinette Perry) Awards, 2016

Play: *The Humans*, Stephen Karam
Musical: *Hamilton*
Book of a musical: *Hamilton*, Lin-Manuel Miranda
Original score: *Hamilton*, Lin-Manuel Miranda
Play revival: *A View From the Bridge*
Musical revival: *The Color Purple*
Actor, play: Frank Langella, *The Father*
Actress, play: Jessica Lange, *Long Day's Journey Into Night*
Actor, musical: Leslie Odom Jr., *Hamilton*
Actress, musical: Cynthia Erivo, *The Color Purple*
Featured actor, play: Reed Birney, *The Humans*
Featured actress, play: Jayne Houdyshell, *The Humans*
Featured actor, musical: Daveed Diggs, *Hamilton*
Featured actress, musical: Renée Elise Goldsberry, *Hamilton*
Direction, play: Ivo Van Hove, *A View From the Bridge*
Direction, musical: Thomas Kail, *Hamilton*
Choreography: Andy Blankenbuehler, *Hamilton*

Orchestrations: Alex Lacamoire, *Hamilton*
Scenic design, play: David Zinn, *The Humans*
Scenic design, musical: David Rockwell, *She Loves Me*
Costume design, play: Clint Ramos, *Eclipsed*
Costume design, musical: Paul Tazewell, *Hamilton*
Lighting design, play: Natasha Katz, *Long Day's Journey Into Night*
Lighting design, musical: Howell Binkley, *Hamilton*
Regional theatre: Paper Mill Playhouse, Millburn, NJ
Special Tony Award: National Endowment for the Arts, Miles Wilkin
Special Tony Award, lifetime achievement: Sheldon Harnick, Marshall W. Mason
Isabelle Stevenson Award: Brian Stokes Mitchell
Tony Honors for Excellence in the Theatre: Seth Gelblum, Joan Lader, Sally Ann Parsons

Tony Awards, 1948-2016

Year	Play	Musical	Year	Play	Musical
1948	*Mister Roberts*	No award	1984	*The Real Thing*	*La Cage aux Folles*
1949	*Death of a Salesman*	*Kiss Me Kate*	1985	*Biloxi Blues*	*Big River*
1950	*The Cocktail Party*	*South Pacific*	1986	*I'm Not Rappaport*	*The Mystery of Edwin Drood*
1951	*The Rose Tattoo*	*Guys and Dolls*	1987	*Fences*	*Les Miserables*
1952	*The Fourposter*	*The King and I*	1988	*M. Butterfly*	*Phantom of the Opera*
1953	*The Crucible*	*Wonderful Town*	1989	*The Heidi Chronicles*	*Jerome Robbins' Broadway*
1954	*The Teahouse of the August Moon*	*Kismet*	1990	*The Grapes of Wrath*	*City of Angels*
1955	*The Desperate Hours*	*The Pajama Game*	1991	*Lost in Yonkers*	*The Will Rogers Follies*
1956	*The Diary of Anne Frank*	*Damn Yankees*	1992	*Dancing at Lughnasa*	*Crazy for You*
1957	*Long Day's Journey Into Night*	*My Fair Lady*	1993	*Angels in America: Millennium Approaches*	*Kiss of the Spider Woman*
1958	*Sunrise at Campobello*	*The Music Man*	1994	*Angels in America: Perestroika*	*Passion*
1959	*J.B.*	*Redhead*			
1960	*The Miracle Worker*	*Fiorello!* and *The Sound of Music*	1995	*Love! Valour! Compassion!*	*Sunset Boulevard*
1961	*Becket*	*Bye, Bye Birdie*	1996	*Master Class*	*Rent*
1962	*A Man for All Seasons*	*How to Succeed in Business Without Really Trying*	1997	*The Last Night of Ballyhoo*	*Titanic*
			1998	*Art*	*The Lion King*
1963	*Who's Afraid of Virginia Woolf?*	*A Funny Thing Happened on the Way to the Forum*	1999	*Side Man*	*Fosse*
			2000	*Copenhagen*	*Contact*
1964	*Luther*	*Hello, Dolly!*	2001	*Proof*	*The Producers*
1965	*The Subject Was Roses*	*Fiddler on the Roof*	2002	*Edward Albee's The Goat or Who Is Sylvia?*	*Thoroughly Modern Millie*
1966	*Marat/Sade*	*Man of La Mancha*			
1967	*The Homecoming*	*Cabaret*	2003	*Take Me Out*	*Hairspray*
1968	*Rosencrantz and Guildenstern Are Dead*	*Hallelujah, Baby!*	2004	*I Am My Own Wife*	*Avenue Q*
			2005	*Doubt*	*Monty Python's Spamalot*
1969	*The Great White Hope*	*1776*	2006	*The History Boys*	*Jersey Boys*
1970	*Borstal Boy*	*Applause*	2007	*The Coast of Utopia*	*Spring Awakening*
1971	*Sleuth*	*Company*	2008	*August: Osage County*	*In the Heights*
1972	*Sticks and Bones*	*Two Gentlemen of Verona*	2009	*God of Carnage*	*Billy Elliot, The Musical*
1973	*That Championship Season*	*A Little Night Music*	2010	*Red*	*Memphis*
1974	*The River Niger*	*Raisin*	2011	*War Horse*	*The Book of Mormon*
1975	*Equus*	*The Wiz*	2012	*Clybourne Park*	*Once*
1976	*Travesties*	*A Chorus Line*	2013	*Vanya and Sonia and Masha and Spike*	*Kinky Boots*
1977	*The Shadow Box*	*Annie*			
1978	*Da*	*Ain't Misbehavin'*	2014	*All the Way*	*A Gentleman's Guide to Love & Murder*
1979	*The Elephant Man*	*Sweeney Todd*			
1980	*Children of a Lesser God*	*Evita*	2015	*The Curious Incident of the Dog in the Night-Time*	*Fun Home*
1981	*Amadeus*	*42nd Street*			
1982	*The Life and Adventures of Nicholas Nickelby*	*Nine*	2016	*The Humans*	*Hamilton*
1983	*Torch Song Trilogy*	*Cats*			

Selected Daytime Emmy Awards, 2016

Drama: *General Hospital*, ABC
Game show: *The Price Is Right*, CBS
Entertainment news show: *Extra*, synd.
Entertainment program, Spanish language: *SuperLatina With Gaby Natale*, SuperLatina + AGANAR media + Vme TV
Morning show: *CBS Sunday Morning*, CBS
Morning show, Spanish language: *Café CNN*, CNN
Talk show, entertainment: *The Talk*, CBS
Talk show, informative: *The Chew*, ABC

Lead actress: Mary Beth Evans, *Days of Our Lives*, NBC
Lead actor: Tyler Christopher, *General Hospital*, ABC
Game show host: Craig Ferguson, *Celebrity Name Game*, synd.
Talk show host, entertainment: Kelly Ripa and Michael Strahan, *Live! With Kelly and Michael*, synd.
Talk show host, informative: Dr. Mehmet Oz, *The Dr. Oz Show*, synd.

Selected Prime-Time Emmy Awards, 2016

Drama series: *Game of Thrones*, HBO
Comedy series: *Veep*, HBO
Limited series: *The People v. O.J. Simpson*, FX
TV movie: *Sherlock: The Abominable Bride*, PBS
Variety talk series: *Last Week Tonight With John Oliver*, HBO
Variety sketch series: *Key & Peele*, Comedy Central
Lead actor, drama: Rami Malek, *Mr. Robot*, USA
Lead actress, drama: Tatiana Maslany, *Orphan Black*, BBC America
Lead actor, comedy: Jeffrey Tambor, *Transparent*, Amazon
Lead actress, comedy: Julia Louis-Dreyfus, *Veep*, HBO
Lead actor, limited series: Courtney B. Vance, *The People v. O.J. Simpson*, FX

Lead actress, limited series: Sarah Paulson, *The People v. O.J. Simpson*, FX
Sup. actor, drama: Ben Mendelsohn, *Bloodline*, Netflix
Sup. actress, drama: Maggie Smith, *Downton Abbey*, PBS
Sup. actor, comedy: Louis Anderson, *Baskets*, HBO
Sup. actress, comedy: Kate McKinnon, *Saturday Night Live*, NBC
Sup. actor, limited series: Sterling K. Brown, *The People v. O.J. Simpson*, FX
Sup. actress, limited series: Regina King, *American Crime*, ABC
Reality-competition program: *The Voice*, NBC

Prime-Time Emmy Awards, 1952-2016

The Academy of Television Arts and Sciences presented the first Emmy Awards in 1949. Through the years, award categories have changed, but since 1952, the Academy has given out an outstanding comedy and drama award annually.

Year	Comedy	Drama	Year	Comedy	Drama
1952	*Red Skelton Show*, NBC	*Studio One*, CBS	1981	*Taxi*, ABC	*Hill Street Blues*, NBC
1953	*I Love Lucy*, CBS	*Robert Montgomery Presents*, NBC	1982	*Barney Miller*, ABC	*Hill Street Blues*, NBC
			1983	*Cheers*, NBC	*Hill Street Blues*, NBC
1954	*I Love Lucy*, CBS	*The U.S. Steel Hour*, ABC	1984	*Cheers*, NBC	*Hill Street Blues*, NBC
1955	*Make Room for Daddy*, ABC	*The U.S. Steel Hour*, ABC	1985	*The Cosby Show*, NBC	*Cagney & Lacey*, CBS
1956	*Phil Silvers Show*, CBS	*Producers' Showcase*, NBC	1986	*Golden Girls*, NBC	*Cagney & Lacey*, CBS
1957	*Phil Silvers Show*, CBS	"Requiem for a Heavyweight," CBS[1]	1987	*Golden Girls*, NBC	*L.A. Law*, NBC
			1988	*The Wonder Years*, ABC	*thirtysomething*, ABC
1958	*Phil Silvers Show*, CBS	*Gunsmoke*, CBS	1989	*Cheers*, NBC	*L.A. Law*, NBC
1959[2]	*Jack Benny Show*, CBS	2 awards[3]	1990	*Murphy Brown*, CBS	*L.A. Law*, NBC
1960	*Art Carney Special*, NBC	*Playhouse 90*, CBS	1991	*Cheers*, NBC	*L.A. Law*, NBC
1961	*Jack Benny Show*, CBS	*Hallmark Hall of Fame: Macbeth*, NBC	1992	*Murphy Brown*, CBS	*Northern Exposure*, CBS
			1993	*Seinfeld*, NBC	*Picket Fences*, CBS
1962	*Bob Newhart Show*, CBS	*The Defenders*, CBS	1994	*Frasier*, NBC	*Picket Fences*, CBS
1963	*Dick Van Dyke Show*, CBS	*The Defenders*, CBS	1995	*Frasier*, NBC	*NYPD Blue*, ABC
1964	*Dick Van Dyke Show*, CBS	*The Defenders*, CBS	1996	*Frasier*, NBC	*ER*, NBC
1965	*Dick Van Dyke Show*, CBS	*Hallmark Hall of Fame: The Magnificent Yankee*, NBC	1997	*Frasier*, NBC	*Law & Order*, NBC
			1998	*Frasier*, NBC	*The Practice*, ABC
1966	*Dick Van Dyke Show*, CBS	*The Fugitive*, ABC	1999	*Ally McBeal*, FOX	*The Practice*, ABC
1967	*The Monkees*, NBC	*Mission: Impossible*, CBS	2000	*Will & Grace*, NBC	*The West Wing*, NBC
1968	*Get Smart*, NBC	*Mission: Impossible*, CBS	2001	*Sex and the City*, HBO	*The West Wing*, NBC
1969	*Get Smart*, NBC	*NET Playhouse*, NET	2002	*Friends*, NBC	*The West Wing*, NBC
1970	*My World and Welcome to It*, NBC	*Marcus Welby, M.D.*, ABC	2003	*Everybody Loves Raymond*, CBS	*The West Wing*, NBC
1971	*All in the Family*, CBS	*The Bold Ones: The Senator*, NBC	2004	*Arrested Development*, FOX	*The Sopranos*, HBO
			2005	*Everybody Loves Raymond*, CBS	*Lost*, ABC
1972	*All in the Family*, CBS	*Masterpiece Theatre: Elizabeth R*, PBS	2006	*The Office*, NBC	*24*, FOX
1973	*All in the Family*, CBS	*The Waltons*, CBS	2007	*30 Rock*, NBC	*The Sopranos*, HBO
1974	*M*A*S*H*, CBS	*Masterpiece Theatre: Upstairs, Downstairs*; PBS	2008	*30 Rock*, NBC	*Mad Men*, AMC
			2009	*30 Rock*, NBC	*Mad Men*, AMC
1975	*Mary Tyler Moore Show*, CBS	*Masterpiece Theatre: Upstairs, Downstairs*; PBS	2010	*Modern Family*, ABC	*Mad Men*, AMC
1976	*Mary Tyler Moore Show*, CBS	*Police Story*, NBC	2011	*Modern Family*, ABC	*Mad Men*, AMC
1977	*Mary Tyler Moore Show*, CBS	*Masterpiece Theatre: Upstairs, Downstairs*; PBS	2012	*Modern Family*, ABC	*Homeland*, Showtime
			2013	*Modern Family*, ABC	*Breaking Bad*, AMC
1978	*All in the Family*, CBS	*The Rockford Files*, NBC	2014	*Modern Family*, ABC	*Breaking Bad*, AMC
1979	*Taxi*, ABC	*Lou Grant*, CBS	2015	*Veep*, HBO	*Game of Thrones*, HBO
1980	*Taxi*, ABC	*Lou Grant*, CBS	2016	*Veep*, HBO	*Game of Thrones*, HBO

(1) Best single program of the year; shown on *Playhouse 90*, which was named best new series. (2) Beginning in 1959, Emmys were awarded for work in the season encompassing the previous and current year. (3) *Playhouse 90* (CBS) was best dramatic series of one hour or longer, *Alcoa-Goodyear Theatre* (NBC) of less than one hour.

Golden Globe Awards, 2016

The Hollywood Foreign Press Association (then the Hollywood Foreign Correspondents Association) presented its first awards for achievement in film in 1944; television was considered for the first time in 1955.

Film

Drama: *The Revenant*
Comedy/musical: *The Martian*
Actress, drama: Brie Larson, *Room*
Actor, drama: Leonardo DiCaprio, *The Revenant*
Actress, comedy/musical: Jennifer Lawrence, *Joy*
Actor, comedy/musical: Matt Damon, *The Martian*
Supporting actress: Kate Winslet, *Steve Jobs*
Supporting actor: Sylvester Stallone, *Creed*
Director: Alejandro G. Iñárritu, *The Revenant*
Screenplay: Aaron Sorkin, *Steve Jobs*
Animated film: *Inside Out*
Foreign-language film: *Son of Saul*, Hungary
Original score: Ennio Morricone, *The Hateful Eight*
Original song: "Writing's on the Wall," *Spectre*, Sam Smith and Jimmy Napes
Cecil B. DeMille Award: Denzel Washington

Television

Series, drama: *Mr. Robot*, USA
Series, comedy/musical: *Mozart in the Jungle*, Amazon
Miniseries or made-for-TV movie: *Wolf Hall*, PBS
Actress, drama: Taraji P. Henson, *Empire*, Fox
Actor, drama: Jon Hamm, *Mad Men*, AMC
Actress, comedy/musical: Rachel Bloom, *Crazy Ex-Girlfriend*, The CW
Actor, comedy/musical: Gael García Bernal, *Mozart in the Jungle*, Amazon
Actress, miniseries/TV movie: Lady Gaga, *American Horror Story: Hotel*, FX
Actor, miniseries/TV movie: Oscar Isaac, *Show Me a Hero*, HBO
Supporting actress: Maura Tierney, *The Affair*, Showtime
Supporting actor: Christian Slater, *Mr. Robot*, USA

Selected People's Choice Awards, 2016

The People's Choice Awards, sponsored by Procter & Gamble, were first presented in 1975. The nominees and awards were initially selected by a Gallup Poll. Since 2005, winners have been selected by Internet voting.

Digital

Social media celebrity: Britney Spears
Social media star: Matt Bellassai
Mobile game: *Candy Crush Saga*
Video game: *Super Smash Bros.*
YouTube star: Connor Franta

Film

Movie: *Furious 7*
Actor: Channing Tatum
Actress: Sandra Bullock
Action movie: *Furious 7*
Comedy: *Pitch Perfect 2*
Drama: *The Martian*
Family movie: *Minions*
Thriller: *Taken 3*

Music

Album: *Title*, Meghan Trainor
Song: "What Do You Mean?," Justin Bieber
Male artist: Ed Sheeran

Female artist: Taylor Swift
Group: Fifth Harmony

Television

Show: *The Big Bang Theory*
Network comedy: *The Big Bang Theory*
Network drama: *Grey's Anatomy*
Cable comedy: *It's Always Sunny in Philadelphia*
Cable drama: *Pretty Little Liars*
Premium cable show: *Homeland*
Animated show: *The Simpsons*
Competition show: *The Voice*
Streaming series: *Orange Is the New Black*
Comedic actor: Jim Parsons, *The Big Bang Theory*
Comedic actress: Melissa McCarthy, *Mike & Molly*
Dramatic actor: Taylor Kinney, *Chicago Fire*
Dramatic actress: Ellen Pompeo, *Grey's Anatomy*
Daytime host: Ellen DeGeneres
Daytime hosting team: *The Talk*
Late-night talk show host: Jimmy Fallon

Academy Awards (Oscars), 1927-2015

Year	Picture	Actor	Actress	Supporting actor[1]	Supporting actress[1]	Director
1927 -28	Wings	Emil Jannings The Way of All Flesh	Janet Gaynor Seventh Heaven	NA	NA	Frank Borzage Seventh Heaven; Lewis Milestone Two Arabian Knights
1928 -29	Broadway Melody	Warner Baxter In Old Arizona	Mary Pickford Coquette	NA	NA	Frank Lloyd The Divine Lady
1929 -30	All Quiet on the Western Front	George Arliss Disraeli	Norma Shearer The Divorcee	NA	NA	Lewis Milestone All Quiet on the Western Front
1930 -31	Cimarron	Lionel Barrymore Free Soul	Marie Dressler Min and Bill	NA	NA	Norman Taurog Skippy
1931 -32	Grand Hotel	Fredric March Dr. Jekyll and Mr. Hyde; Wallace Beery The Champ	Helen Hayes The Sin of Madelon Claudet	NA	NA	Frank Borzage Bad Girl
1932 -33	Cavalcade	Charles Laughton The Private Life of Henry VIII	Katharine Hepburn Morning Glory	NA	NA	Frank Lloyd Cavalcade
1934	It Happened One Night	Clark Gable It Happened One Night	Claudette Colbert It Happened One Night	NA	NA	Frank Capra It Happened One Night
1935	Mutiny on the Bounty	Victor McLaglen The Informer	Bette Davis Dangerous	NA	NA	John Ford The Informer
1936	The Great Ziegfeld	Paul Muni Story of Louis Pasteur	Luise Rainer The Great Ziegfeld	Walter Brennan Come and Get It	Gale Sondergaard Anthony Adverse	Frank Capra Mr. Deeds Goes to Town
1937	Life of Emile Zola	Spencer Tracy Captains Courageous	Luise Rainer The Good Earth	Joseph Schildkraut Life of Emile Zola	Alice Brady In Old Chicago	Leo McCarey The Awful Truth
1938	You Can't Take It With You	Spencer Tracy Boys Town	Bette Davis Jezebel	Walter Brennan Kentucky	Fay Bainter Jezebel	Frank Capra You Can't Take It With You
1939	Gone With the Wind	Robert Donat Goodbye, Mr. Chips	Vivien Leigh Gone With the Wind	Thomas Mitchell Stage Coach	Hattie McDaniel Gone With the Wind	Victor Fleming Gone With the Wind
1940	Rebecca	James Stewart The Philadelphia Story	Ginger Rogers Kitty Foyle	Walter Brennan The Westerner	Jane Darwell The Grapes of Wrath	John Ford The Grapes of Wrath
1941	How Green Was My Valley	Gary Cooper Sergeant York	Joan Fontaine Suspicion	Donald Crisp How Green Was My Valley	Mary Astor The Great Lie	John Ford How Green Was My Valley
1942	Mrs. Miniver	James Cagney Yankee Doodle Dandy	Greer Garson Mrs. Miniver	Van Heflin Johnny Eager	Teresa Wright Mrs. Miniver	William Wyler Mrs. Miniver
1943	Casablanca	Paul Lukas Watch on the Rhine	Jennifer Jones The Song of Bernadette	Charles Coburn The More the Merrier	Katina Paxinou For Whom the Bell Tolls	Michael Curtiz Casablanca
1944	Going My Way	Bing Crosby Going My Way	Ingrid Bergman Gaslight	Barry Fitzgerald Going My Way	Ethel Barrymore None But the Lonely Heart	Leo McCarey Going My Way
1945	The Lost Weekend	Ray Milland The Lost Weekend	Joan Crawford Mildred Pierce	James Dunn A Tree Grows in Brooklyn	Anne Revere National Velvet	Billy Wilder The Lost Weekend
1946	The Best Years of Our Lives	Fredric March The Best Years of Our Lives	Olivia de Havilland To Each His Own	Harold Russell The Best Years of Our Lives	Anne Baxter The Razor's Edge	William Wyler The Best Years of Our Lives
1947	Gentleman's Agreement	Ronald Colman A Double Life	Loretta Young The Farmer's Daughter	Edmund Gwenn Miracle on 34th Street	Celeste Holm Gentleman's Agreement	Elia Kazan Gentleman's Agreement
1948	Hamlet	Laurence Olivier Hamlet	Jane Wyman Johnny Belinda	Walter Huston Treasure of Sierra Madre	Claire Trevor Key Largo	John Huston Treasure of Sierra Madre
1949	All the King's Men	Broderick Crawford All the King's Men	Olivia de Havilland The Heiress	Dean Jagger Twelve O'Clock High	Mercedes McCambridge All the King's Men	Joseph L. Mankiewicz Letter to Three Wives
1950	All About Eve	Jose Ferrer Cyrano de Bergerac	Judy Holliday Born Yesterday	George Sanders All About Eve	Josephine Hull Harvey	Joseph L. Mankiewicz All About Eve
1951	An American in Paris	Humphrey Bogart The African Queen	Vivien Leigh A Streetcar Named Desire	Karl Malden A Streetcar Named Desire	Kim Hunter A Streetcar Named Desire	George Stevens A Place in the Sun
1952	The Greatest Show on Earth	Gary Cooper High Noon	Shirley Booth Come Back, Little Sheba	Anthony Quinn Viva Zapata!	Gloria Grahame The Bad and the Beautiful	John Ford The Quiet Man
1953	From Here to Eternity	William Holden Stalag 17	Audrey Hepburn Roman Holiday	Frank Sinatra From Here to Eternity	Donna Reed From Here to Eternity	Fred Zinnemann From Here to Eternity

Year	Picture	Actor	Actress	Supporting actor[1]	Supporting actress[1]	Director
1954	On the Waterfront	Marlon Brando *On the Waterfront*	Grace Kelly *The Country Girl*	Edmond O'Brien *The Barefoot Contessa*	Eva Marie Saint *On the Waterfront*	Elia Kazan *On the Waterfront*
1955	Marty	Ernest Borgnine *Marty*	Anna Magnani *The Rose Tattoo*	Jack Lemmon *Mister Roberts*	Jo Van Fleet *East of Eden*	Delbert Mann *Marty*
1956	Around the World in 80 Days	Yul Brynner *The King and I*	Ingrid Bergman *Anastasia*	Anthony Quinn *Lust for Life*	Dorothy Malone *Written on the Wind*	George Stevens *Giant*
1957	The Bridge on the River Kwai	Alec Guinness *The Bridge on the River Kwai*	Joanne Woodward *The Three Faces of Eve*	Red Buttons *Sayonara*	Miyoshi Umeki *Sayonara*	David Lean *The Bridge on the River Kwai*
1958	Gigi	David Niven *Separate Tables*	Susan Hayward *I Want to Live*	Burl Ives *The Big Country*	Wendy Hiller *Separate Tables*	Vincente Minnelli *Gigi*
1959	Ben-Hur	Charlton Heston *Ben-Hur*	Simone Signoret *Room at the Top*	Hugh Griffith *Ben-Hur*	Shelley Winters *Diary of Anne Frank*	William Wyler *Ben-Hur*
1960	The Apartment	Burt Lancaster *Elmer Gantry*	Elizabeth Taylor *Butterfield 8*	Peter Ustinov *Spartacus*	Shirley Jones *Elmer Gantry*	Billy Wilder *The Apartment*
1961	West Side Story	Maximilian Schell *Judgment at Nuremberg*	Sophia Loren *Two Women*	George Chakiris *West Side Story*	Rita Moreno *West Side Story*	Jerome Robbins and Robert Wise *West Side Story*
1962	Lawrence of Arabia	Gregory Peck *To Kill a Mockingbird*	Anne Bancroft *The Miracle Worker*	Ed Begley *Sweet Bird of Youth*	Patty Duke *The Miracle Worker*	David Lean *Lawrence of Arabia*
1963	Tom Jones	Sidney Poitier *Lilies of the Field*	Patricia Neal *Hud*	Melvyn Douglas *Hud*	Margaret Rutherford *The V.I.P.s*	Tony Richardson *Tom Jones*
1964	My Fair Lady	Rex Harrison *My Fair Lady*	Julie Andrews *Mary Poppins*	Peter Ustinov *Topkapi*	Lila Kedrova *Zorba the Greek*	George Cukor *My Fair Lady*
1965	The Sound of Music	Lee Marvin *Cat Ballou*	Julie Christie *Darling*	Martin Balsam *A Thousand Clowns*	Shelley Winters *A Patch of Blue*	Robert Wise *The Sound of Music*
1966	A Man for All Seasons	Paul Scofield *A Man for All Seasons*	Elizabeth Taylor *Who's Afraid of Virginia Woolf?*	Walter Matthau *The Fortune Cookie*	Sandy Dennis *Who's Afraid of Virginia Woolf?*	Fred Zinnemann *A Man for All Seasons*
1967	In the Heat of the Night	Rod Steiger *In the Heat of the Night*	Katharine Hepburn *Guess Who's Coming to Dinner*	George Kennedy *Cool Hand Luke*	Estelle Parsons *Bonnie and Clyde*	Mike Nichols *The Graduate*
1968	Oliver!	Cliff Robertson *Charly*	Katharine Hepburn *The Lion in Winter*; Barbra Streisand *Funny Girl*	Jack Albertson *The Subject Was Roses*	Ruth Gordon *Rosemary's Baby*	Sir Carol Reed *Oliver!*
1969	Midnight Cowboy	John Wayne *True Grit*	Maggie Smith *The Prime of Miss Jean Brodie*	Gig Young *They Shoot Horses, Don't They?*	Goldie Hawn *Cactus Flower*	John Schlesinger *Midnight Cowboy*
1970	Patton	George C. Scott *Patton* (refused)	Glenda Jackson *Women in Love*	John Mills *Ryan's Daughter*	Helen Hayes *Airport*	Franklin Schaffner *Patton*
1971	The French Connection	Gene Hackman *The French Connection*	Jane Fonda *Klute*	Ben Johnson *The Last Picture Show*	Cloris Leachman *The Last Picture Show*	William Friedkin *The French Connection*
1972	The Godfather	Marlon Brando *The Godfather* (refused)	Liza Minnelli *Cabaret*	Joel Grey *Cabaret*	Eileen Heckart *Butterflies Are Free*	Bob Fosse *Cabaret*
1973	The Sting	Jack Lemmon *Save the Tiger*	Glenda Jackson *A Touch of Class*	John Houseman *The Paper Chase*	Tatum O'Neal *Paper Moon*	George Roy Hill *The Sting*
1974	The Godfather Part II	Art Carney *Harry and Tonto*	Ellen Burstyn *Alice Doesn't Live Here Anymore*	Robert DeNiro *The Godfather Part II*	Ingrid Bergman *Murder on the Orient Express*	Francis Ford Coppola *The Godfather Part II*
1975	One Flew Over the Cuckoo's Nest	Jack Nicholson *One Flew Over the Cuckoo's Nest*	Louise Fletcher *One Flew Over the Cuckoo's Nest*	George Burns *The Sunshine Boys*	Lee Grant *Shampoo*	Milos Forman *One Flew Over the Cuckoo's Nest*
1976	Rocky	Peter Finch *Network*	Faye Dunaway *Network*	Jason Robards *All the President's Men*	Beatrice Straight *Network*	John G. Avildsen *Rocky*
1977	Annie Hall	Richard Dreyfuss *The Goodbye Girl*	Diane Keaton *Annie Hall*	Jason Robards *Julia*	Vanessa Redgrave *Julia*	Woody Allen *Annie Hall*
1978	The Deer Hunter	Jon Voight *Coming Home*	Jane Fonda *Coming Home*	Christopher Walken *The Deer Hunter*	Maggie Smith *California Suite*	Michael Cimino *The Deer Hunter*
1979	Kramer vs. Kramer	Dustin Hoffman *Kramer vs. Kramer*	Sally Field *Norma Rae*	Melvyn Douglas *Being There*	Meryl Streep *Kramer vs. Kramer*	Robert Benton *Kramer vs. Kramer*
1980	Ordinary People	Robert DeNiro *Raging Bull*	Sissy Spacek *Coal Miner's Daughter*	Timothy Hutton *Ordinary People*	Mary Steenburgen *Melvin and Howard*	Robert Redford *Ordinary People*
1981	Chariots of Fire	Henry Fonda *On Golden Pond*	Katharine Hepburn *On Golden Pond*	John Gielgud *Arthur*	Maureen Stapleton *Reds*	Warren Beatty *Reds*
1982	Gandhi	Ben Kingsley *Gandhi*	Meryl Streep *Sophie's Choice*	Louis Gossett Jr. *An Officer and a Gentleman*	Jessica Lange *Tootsie*	Richard Attenborough *Gandhi*
1983	Terms of Endearment	Robert Duvall *Tender Mercies*	Shirley MacLaine *Terms of Endearment*	Jack Nicholson *Terms of Endearment*	Linda Hunt *The Year of Living Dangerously*	James L. Brooks *Terms of Endearment*

Year	Picture	Actor	Actress	Supporting actor[1]	Supporting actress[1]	Director
1984	*Amadeus*	F. Murray Abraham *Amadeus*	Sally Field *Places in the Heart*	Haing S. Ngor *The Killing Fields*	Peggy Ashcroft *A Passage to India*	Milos Forman *Amadeus*
1985	*Out of Africa*	William Hurt *Kiss of the Spider Woman*	Geraldine Page *The Trip to Bountiful*	Don Ameche *Cocoon*	Anjelica Huston *Prizzi's Honor*	Sydney Pollack *Out of Africa*
1986	*Platoon*	Paul Newman *The Color of Money*	Marlee Matlin *Children of a Lesser God*	Michael Caine *Hannah and Her Sisters*	Dianne Wiest *Hannah and Her Sisters*	Oliver Stone *Platoon*
1987	*The Last Emperor*	Michael Douglas *Wall Street*	Cher *Moonstruck*	Sean Connery *The Untouchables*	Olympia Dukakis *Moonstruck*	Bernardo Bertolucci *The Last Emperor*
1988	*Rain Man*	Dustin Hoffman *Rain Man*	Jodie Foster *The Accused*	Kevin Kline *A Fish Called Wanda*	Geena Davis *The Accidental Tourist*	Barry Levinson *Rain Man*
1989	*Driving Miss Daisy*	Daniel Day-Lewis *My Left Foot*	Jessica Tandy *Driving Miss Daisy*	Denzel Washington *Glory*	Brenda Fricker *My Left Foot*	Oliver Stone, *Born on the Fourth of July*
1990	*Dances With Wolves*	Jeremy Irons *Reversal of Fortune*	Kathy Bates *Misery*	Joe Pesci *Goodfellas*	Whoopi Goldberg *Ghost*	Kevin Costner *Dances With Wolves*
1991	*The Silence of the Lambs*	Anthony Hopkins *The Silence of the Lambs*	Jodie Foster *The Silence of the Lambs*	Jack Palance *City Slickers*	Mercedes Ruehl *The Fisher King*	Jonathan Demme *The Silence of the Lambs*
1992	*Unforgiven*	Al Pacino *Scent of a Woman*	Emma Thompson *Howards End*	Gene Hackman *Unforgiven*	Marisa Tomei *My Cousin Vinny*	Clint Eastwood *Unforgiven*
1993	*Schindler's List*	Tom Hanks *Philadelphia*	Holly Hunter *The Piano*	Tommy Lee Jones *The Fugitive*	Anna Paquin *The Piano*	Steven Spielberg *Schindler's List*
1994	*Forrest Gump*	Tom Hanks *Forrest Gump*	Jessica Lange *Blue Sky*	Martin Landau *Ed Wood*	Dianne Wiest, *Bullets Over Broadway*	Robert Zemeckis *Forrest Gump*
1995	*Braveheart*	Nicolas Cage *Leaving Las Vegas*	Susan Sarandon *Dead Man Walking*	Kevin Spacey *The Usual Suspects*	Mira Sorvino *Mighty Aphrodite*	Mel Gibson *Braveheart*
1996	*The English Patient*	Geoffrey Rush *Shine*	Frances McDormand *Fargo*	Cuba Gooding Jr. *Jerry Maguire*	Juliette Binoche *The English Patient*	Anthony Minghella *The English Patient*
1997	*Titanic*	Jack Nicholson *As Good As It Gets*	Helen Hunt *As Good As It Gets*	Robin Williams *Good Will Hunting*	Kim Basinger *L.A. Confidential*	James Cameron *Titanic*
1998	*Shakespeare in Love*	Roberto Benigni *Life Is Beautiful*	Gwyneth Paltrow *Shakespeare in Love*	James Coburn *Affliction*	Judi Dench *Shakespeare in Love*	Steven Spielberg *Saving Private Ryan*
1999	*American Beauty*	Kevin Spacey *American Beauty*	Hilary Swank *Boys Don't Cry*	Michael Caine, *The Cider House Rules*	Angelina Jolie *Girl, Interrupted*	Sam Mendes *American Beauty*
2000	*Gladiator*	Russell Crowe *Gladiator*	Julia Roberts *Erin Brockovich*	Benicio Del Toro *Traffic*	Marcia Gay Harden *Pollock*	Steven Soderbergh *Traffic*
2001	*A Beautiful Mind*	Denzel Washington *Training Day*	Halle Berry *Monster's Ball*	Jim Broadbent *Iris*	Jennifer Connelly *A Beautiful Mind*	Ron Howard *A Beautiful Mind*
2002	*Chicago*	Adrien Brody *The Pianist*	Nicole Kidman *The Hours*	Chris Cooper *Adaptation*	Catherine Zeta-Jones, *Chicago*	Roman Polanski *The Pianist*
2003	*The Lord of the Rings: The Return of the King*	Sean Penn *Mystic River*	Charlize Theron *Monster*	Tim Robbins *Mystic River*	Renée Zellweger *Cold Mountain*	Peter Jackson *The Lord of the Rings: The Return of the King*
2004	*Million Dollar Baby*	Jamie Foxx *Ray*	Hilary Swank *Million Dollar Baby*	Morgan Freeman *Million Dollar Baby*	Cate Blanchett *The Aviator*	Clint Eastwood *Million Dollar Baby*
2005	*Crash*	Philip Seymour Hoffman *Capote*	Reese Witherspoon *Walk the Line*	George Clooney *Syriana*	Rachel Weisz *The Constant Gardener*	Ang Lee *Brokeback Mountain*
2006	*The Departed*	Forest Whitaker, *The Last King of Scotland*	Helen Mirren *The Queen*	Alan Arkin *Little Miss Sunshine*	Jennifer Hudson *Dreamgirls*	Martin Scorsese *The Departed*
2007	*No Country for Old Men*	Daniel Day-Lewis *There Will Be Blood*	Marion Cotillard *La Vie en Rose*	Javier Bardem *No Country for Old Men*	Tilda Swinton *Michael Clayton*	Joel Coen and Ethan Coen, *No Country for Old Men*
2008	*Slumdog Millionaire*	Sean Penn *Milk*	Kate Winslet *The Reader*	Heath Ledger *The Dark Knight*	Penelope Cruz, *Vicky Cristina Barcelona*	Danny Boyle *Slumdog Millionaire*
2009	*The Hurt Locker*	Jeff Bridges *Crazy Heart*	Sandra Bullock *The Blind Side*	Christoph Waltz *Inglourious Basterds*	Mo'Nique *Precious*	Kathryn Bigelow *The Hurt Locker*
2010	*The King's Speech*	Colin Firth *The King's Speech*	Natalie Portman *Black Swan*	Christian Bale *The Fighter*	Melissa Leo *The Fighter*	Tom Hooper *The King's Speech*
2011	*The Artist*	Jean Dujardin *The Artist*	Meryl Streep *The Iron Lady*	Christopher Plummer, *Beginners*	Octavia Spencer *The Help*	Michel Hazanavicius *The Artist*
2012	*Argo*	Daniel Day-Lewis *Lincoln*	Jennifer Lawrence *Silver Linings Playbook*	Christoph Waltz *Django Unchained*	Anne Hathaway *Les Misérables*	Ang Lee *Life of Pi*
2013	*12 Years a Slave*	Matthew McConaughey *Dallas Buyers Club*	Cate Blanchett *Blue Jasmine*	Jared Leto *Dallas Buyers Club*	Lupita Nyong'o *12 Years a Slave*	Alfonso Cuarón *Gravity*
2014	*Birdman*	Eddie Redmayne *The Theory of Everything*	Julianne Moore *Still Alice*	J. K. Simmons *Whiplash*	Patricia Arquette *Boyhood*	Alejandro G. Iñárritu *Birdman*
2015	*Spotlight*	Leonardo DiCaprio *The Revenant*	Brie Larson *Room*	Mark Rylance *Bridge of Spies*	Alicia Vikander *The Danish Girl*	Alejandro G. Iñárritu *The Revenant*

(1) Award not given until 1936.

Other Academy Award Winners, 2015

Animated film: *Inside Out*
Cinematography: *The Revenant*
Costume design: *Mad Max: Fury Road*
Documentary feature: *Amy*
Film editing: *Mad Max: Fury Road*
Foreign language film: *Son of Saul*, Hungary
Makeup and hairstyling: *Mad Max: Fury Road*
Original score: *The Hateful Eight*, Ennio Morricone
Original song: "Writing's on the Wall," *Spectre*, Sam Smith and Jimmy Napes

Production design: *Mad Max: Fury Road*
Screenplay, adapted: *The Big Short*, Charles Randolph and Adam McKay
Screenplay, original: *Spotlight*, Josh Singer and Tom McCarthy
Short films: *Bear Story* (animated), *A Girl in the River: The Price of Forgiveness* (documentary), *Stutterer* (live action)
Sound editing: *Mad Max: Fury Road*
Sound mixing: *Mad Max: Fury Road*
Visual effects: *Ex Machina*

Other Film Awards, 2016

British Academy of Film and Television Awards (BAFTAs)

Best film: The Revenant
Outstanding British film: Brooklyn
Director: Alejandro G. Iñárritu, The Revenant
Original screenplay: Tom McCarthy, Josh Singer, Spotlight
Adapted screenplay: Adam McKay, Charles Randolph, The Big Short
Film not in English: Wild Tales, Argentina
Animated film: Inside Out
Actor: Leonardo DiCaprio, The Revenant
Actress: Brie Larson, Room
Supporting actor: Mark Rylance, Bridge of Spies
Supporting actress: Kate Winslet, Steve Jobs

Canadian Screen Awards

Motion picture: Room
Actor: Jacob Tremblay, Room
Actress: Brie Larson, Room
Supporting actor: Nick Serino, Sleeping Giant
Supporting actress: Joan Allen, Room
Director: Lenny Abrahamson, Room

Cannes International Film Festival Awards

Palme d'Or: I, Daniel Blake, UK
Grand Prix: Juste la fin du monde [It's Only the End of the World], Canada/France
Best director ex-aequo: Cristian Mungiu, Bacalaureat [Graduation], Romania; Olivier Assayas, Personal Shopper, France
Best screenplay: Asghar Farhadi, Forushande [The Salesman], France/Iran
Best actress: Jaclyn Jose, Ma' Rosa, Philippines
Best actor: Shahab Hosseini, Forushande [The Salesman], France/Iran
Jury Prize: American Honey, Andrea Arnold, UK
Palme d'Or, short film: Timecode, Juanjo Gimenez, Spain

Director's Guild of America Awards

Feature film: Alejandro G. Iñárritu, The Revenant
Documentary: Matthew Heineman, Cartel Land

TV movie/miniseries: Dee Rees, Bessie
TV series (drama): David Nutter, Game of Thrones, "Mother's Mercy"
TV series (comedy): Chris Addison, Veep, "Election Night"

Sundance Film Festival Awards

U.S. Grand Jury Prize: The Birth of a Nation (drama); Weiner (doc.)
World Cinema Jury Prize: Sand Storm, Israel (drama); Sonita, Germany/Iran/Switzerland (doc.)
U.S. Audience Award: The Birth of a Nation (drama); Jim: The James Foley Story (doc.)
World Cinema Audience Award: Between Sea and Land, Colombia (drama); Sonita, Germany/Iran/Switzerland (doc.)
NEXT Audience Award: First Girl I Loved
U.S. Directing: Dan Kwan, Daniel Scheinert, Swiss Army Man (drama); Roger Ross Williams, Life, Animated (doc.)
World Cinema Directing: Felix van Groeningen, Belgica, Belgium/France/Netherlands (drama); Michal Marczak, All These Sleepless Nights, Poland (doc.)
Waldo Salt Screenwriting Award: Chad Hartigan, Morris From America
Alfred P. Sloan Feature Film Prize: Embrace of the Serpent

Toronto International Film Festival

People's Choice Award: La La Land
People's Choice Documentary Award: I Am Not Your Negro
People's Choice Midnight Madness Award: Free Fire
Canadian Feature Film: Those Who Make Revolution Halfway Only Dig Their Own Graves [Ceux qui font les révolutions à moitié n'ont fait que se creuser un tombeau]
Canadian Short Film: Mutants
Canadian First Feature Film: Old Stone [Lao Shi]
International Critics' Prize (FIPRESCI Prize) for Discovery: Kati Kati
FIPRESCI Prize for Special Presentations: I Am Not Madame Bovary
NETPAC Award: In Between [Bar Bahar]
Platform Prize: Jackie
Short Film: Imago

Academy of Country Music Awards, 2016

Entertainer of the year: Jason Aldean
Male vocalist: Chris Stapleton
Female vocalist: Miranda Lambert
Vocal duo: Florida Georgia Line
Vocal group: Little Big Town
New male vocalist: Chris Stapleton
New female vocalist: Kelsea Ballerini

New vocal duo/group: Old Dominion
Album: Traveller, Chris Stapleton
Record (single): "Die a Happy Man," Thomas Rhett
Song: "Nobody to Blame," Chris Stapleton
Vocal event: "Smokin' and Drinkin'," Miranda Lambert feat. Little Big Town
Video: "Mr. Misunderstood," Eric Church

Selected Grammy Awards, 2015

Source: National Academy of Recording Arts and Sciences
For albums released Oct. 1, 2014-Sept. 30, 2015, awarded in Feb. 2016.

Record of the year (single): "Uptown Funk," Mark Ronson feat. Bruno Mars
Album of the year: 1989, Taylor Swift
Song of the year: "Thinking Out Loud," Ed Sheeran (Ed Sheeran and Amy Wadge, songwriters)
New artist: Meghan Trainor
Pop performance, solo: "Thinking Out Loud," Ed Sheeran
Pop performance, duo/group: "Uptown Funk," Mark Ronson feat. Bruno Mars
Pop album, traditional vocal: The Silver Lining: The Songs of Jerome Kern, Tony Bennett and Bill Charlap
Pop album, vocal: 1989, Taylor Swift
Dance recording: "Where Are Ü Now," Skrillex and Diplo with Justin Bieber
Dance/electronic album: Skrillex and Diplo Present Jack Ü, Skrillex and Diplo
Contemporary instrumental album: Sylva, Snarky Puppy and Metropole Orkest
Rock performance: "Don't Wanna Fight," Alabama Shakes
Metal performance: "Cirice," Ghost
Rock song: "Don't Wanna Fight," Alabama Shakes (Alabama Shakes, songwriters)
Rock album: Drones, Muse
Alternative music album: Sound & Color, Alabama Shakes
R&B performance: "Earned It (Fifty Shades of Grey)," The Weeknd
R&B performance, traditional: "Little Ghetto Boy," Lalah Hathaway
R&B song: "Really Love," D'Angelo and the Vanguard (D'Angelo and Kendra Foster, songwriters)
R&B album: Black Messiah, D'Angelo and the Vanguard

Urban contemporary album: Beauty Behind the Madness, The Weeknd
Rap performance: "Alright," Kendrick Lamar
Rap/sung collaboration: "These Walls," Kendrick Lamar feat. Bilal, Anna Wise, and Thundercat
Rap song: "Alright," Kendrick Lamar (Kendrick Duckworth, Kawan Prather, Mark Anthony Spears, Pharrell Williams, songwriters)
Rap album: To Pimp a Butterfly, Kendrick Lamar
Country performance, solo: "Traveller," Chris Stapleton
Country performance, duo/group: "Girl Crush," Little Big Town
Country song: "Girl Crush," Little Big Town (Hillary Lindsey, Lori McKenna, Liz Rose, songwriters)
Country album: Traveller, Chris Stapleton
Jazz album, instrumental: Past Present, John Scofield
Jazz album, vocal: For One to Love, Cécile McLorin Salvant
Americana album: Something More Than Free, Jason Isbell
Blues album: Born to Play Guitar, Buddy Guy
Latin pop album: A Quien Quiera Escuchar, Ricky Martin
New age album: Grace, Paul Avgerinos
Comedy album: Live at Madison Square Garden, Louis C.K.
Spoken word album: A Full Life: Reflections at Ninety, Jimmy Carter
Soundtrack album, compilation: Glen Campbell: I'll Be Me, Julian Raymond, compilation producer
Soundtrack album, score: Birdman, Antonio Sanchez
Song, visual media: "Glory," Selma, Common and John Legend (Lonnie Lynn, Che Smith, John Stephens, songwriters)
Music video: "Bad Blood," Taylor Swift feat. Kendrick Lamar
Music film: Amy, Asif Kapadia, director

Grammy Awards, 1958-2015

Record of the Year (single)	Year	Album of the Year
Domenico Modugno, "Nel Blu Dipinto Di Blu (Volare)"	1958	Henry Mancini, *The Music From Peter Gunn*
Bobby Darin, "Mack the Knife"	1959	Frank Sinatra, *Come Dance With Me*
Percy Faith, "Theme From a Summer Place"	1960	Bob Newhart, *Button Down Mind*
Henry Mancini, "Moon River"	1961	Judy Garland, *Judy at Carnegie Hall*
Tony Bennett, "I Left My Heart in San Francisco"	1962	Vaughn Meader, *The First Family*
Henry Mancini, "The Days of Wine and Roses"	1963	Barbra Streisand, *The Barbra Streisand Album*
Stan Getz and Astrud Gilberto, "The Girl From Ipanema"	1964	Stan Getz and João Gilberto, *Getz/Gilberto*
Herb Alpert, "A Taste of Honey"	1965	Frank Sinatra, *September of My Years*
Frank Sinatra, "Strangers in the Night"	1966	Frank Sinatra, *A Man and His Music*
5th Dimension, "Up, Up and Away"	1967	The Beatles, *Sgt. Pepper's Lonely Hearts Club Band*
Simon and Garfunkel, "Mrs. Robinson"	1968	Glen Campbell, *By the Time I Get to Phoenix*
5th Dimension, "Aquarius/Let the Sunshine In"	1969	Blood, Sweat & Tears, *Blood, Sweat & Tears*
Simon and Garfunkel, "Bridge Over Troubled Water"	1970	Simon and Garfunkel, *Bridge Over Troubled Water*
Carole King, "It's Too Late"	1971	Carole King, *Tapestry*
Roberta Flack, "The First Time Ever I Saw Your Face"	1972	George Harrison and Friends, *The Concert for Bangla Desh*
Roberta Flack, "Killing Me Softly With His Song"	1973	Stevie Wonder, *Innervisions*
Olivia Newton-John, "I Honestly Love You"	1974	Stevie Wonder, *Fulfillingness' First Finale*
Captain & Tennille, "Love Will Keep Us Together"	1975	Paul Simon, *Still Crazy After All These Years*
George Benson, "This Masquerade"	1976	Stevie Wonder, *Songs in the Key of Life*
Eagles, "Hotel California"	1977	Fleetwood Mac, *Rumours*
Billy Joel, "Just the Way You Are"	1978	Bee Gees, *Saturday Night Fever*
The Doobie Brothers, "What a Fool Believes"	1979	Billy Joel, *52nd Street*
Christopher Cross, "Sailing"	1980	Christopher Cross, *Christopher Cross*
Kim Carnes, "Bette Davis Eyes"	1981	John Lennon and Yoko Ono, *Double Fantasy*
Toto, "Rosanna"	1982	Toto, *Toto IV*
Michael Jackson, "Beat It"	1983	Michael Jackson, *Thriller*
Tina Turner, "What's Love Got to Do With It"	1984	Lionel Richie, *Can't Slow Down*
USA for Africa, "We Are the World"	1985	Phil Collins, *No Jacket Required*
Steve Winwood, "Higher Love"	1986	Paul Simon, *Graceland*
Paul Simon, "Graceland"	1987	U2, *The Joshua Tree*
Bobby McFerrin, "Don't Worry, Be Happy"	1988	George Michael, *Faith*
Bette Midler, "Wind Beneath My Wings"	1989	Bonnie Raitt, *Nick of Time*
Phil Collins, "Another Day in Paradise"	1990	Quincy Jones, *Back on the Block*
Natalie Cole, with Nat "King" Cole, "Unforgettable"	1991	Natalie Cole, with Nat "King" Cole, *Unforgettable*
Eric Clapton, "Tears in Heaven"	1992	Eric Clapton, *Unplugged*
Whitney Houston, "I Will Always Love You"	1993	Whitney Houston, *The Bodyguard*
Sheryl Crow, "All I Wanna Do"	1994	Tony Bennett, *MTV Unplugged*
Seal, "Kiss From a Rose"	1995	Alanis Morissette, *Jagged Little Pill*
Eric Clapton, "Change the World"	1996	Celine Dion, *Falling Into You*
Shawn Colvin, "Sunny Came Home"	1997	Bob Dylan, *Time Out of Mind*
Celine Dion, "My Heart Will Go On"	1998	Lauryn Hill, *The Miseducation of Lauryn Hill*
Santana feat. Rob Thomas, "Smooth"	1999	Santana, *Supernatural*
U2, "Beautiful Day"	2000	Steely Dan, *Two Against Nature*
U2, "Walk On"	2001	Various artists, *O Brother, Where Art Thou?*
Norah Jones, "Don't Know Why"	2002	Norah Jones, *Come Away With Me*
Coldplay, "Clocks"	2003	OutKast, *Speakerboxxx/The Love Below*
Ray Charles and Norah Jones, "Here We Go Again"	2004	Ray Charles and various artists, *Genius Loves Company*
Green Day, "Boulevard of Broken Dreams"	2005	U2, *How to Dismantle an Atomic Bomb*
Dixie Chicks, "Not Ready to Make Nice"	2006	Dixie Chicks, *Taking the Long Way*
Amy Winehouse, "Rehab"	2007	Herbie Hancock, *River: The Joni Letters*
Robert Plant and Alison Krauss, "Please Read the Letter"	2008	Robert Plant and Alison Krauss, *Raising Sand*
Kings of Leon, "Use Somebody"	2009	Taylor Swift, *Fearless*
Lady Antebellum, "Need You Now"	2010	Arcade Fire, *The Suburbs*
Adele, "Rolling in the Deep"	2011	Adele, *21*
Gotye, "Somebody That I Used to Know"	2012	Mumford & Sons, *Babel*
Daft Punk feat. Pharrell Williams and Nile Rodgers, "Get Lucky"	2013	Daft Punk, *Random Access Memories*
Sam Smith, "Stay With Me"	2014	Beck, *Morning Phase*
Mark Ronson feat. Bruno Mars, "Uptown Funk"	2015	Taylor Swift, *1989*

MTV Video Music Awards, 2016

Video of the year: "Formation," Beyoncé
Best new artist: DNCE
Female video: "Hold Up," Beyoncé
Male video: "This Is What You Came For," Calvin Harris feat. Rihanna
Electronic video: "How Deep Is Your Love," Calvin Harris and Disciples
Hip-hop video: "Hotline Bling," Drake
Pop video: "Formation," Beyoncé
Rock video: "Heathens," Twenty One Pilots
Breakthrough long-form video: *Lemonade*, Beyoncé

Song of the summer: "All in My Head," Fifth Harmony feat. Fetty Wap
Collaboration: "Work From Home," Fifth Harmony feat. Ty Dolla $ign
Art direction: "Blackstar," David Bowie
Choreography: "Formation," Beyoncé
Cinematography: "Formation," Beyoncé
Direction: "Formation," Beyoncé
Editing: "Formation," Beyoncé
Visual effects: "Up&Up," Coldplay

SCIENCE

Science and Technology News, 2016

The following were some of the more newsworthy developments in science and technology in the past year.

Life on Earth Earlier Than Thought

Hopes for the presence of life elsewhere in the universe were bolstered by recent findings on Earth. Previous evidence suggested that life did not arise on Earth (which is generally thought to have formed a little more than 4.5 bil years ago) until about 3.8 bil years ago, after volcanic activity had eased and the surface became more stable. But some form of life may have existed as many as 300 mil years earlier, according to a report by UCLA and Stanford researchers published in the Nov. 24, 2015, issue of the journal *Proceedings of the National Academy of Sciences* (available online from Oct. 19). The researchers discovered a "chemofossil"—a specific mixture of carbon isotopes that is ordinarily associated with biological processes—in a 4.1-bil-year-old zircon grain found in Western Australia. As zircons form, they can capture materials in their immediate environment. The zircon grains are durable and can preserve the captured materials. In this case, the carbon seemed to have come from some sort of living organisms. The study suggested that life arose rather quickly on Earth, despite the harsh conditions that must have prevailed. "The faster life arises on Earth," said one of the researchers, "the more varied and possibly extreme are the conditions in which it can do so elsewhere and be sustained."

Milestone Win for A.I.

After computers demonstrated marked prowess in chess, many humans consoled themselves with the thought that artificial-intelligence (AI) researchers would find Go, a more complex board game, too difficult a challenge. But less than two decades after an IBM system's 1997 defeat of Russian world chess champion Garry Kasparov, the Google program AlphaGo overpowered the European Go champion, five games to none, in Oct. 2015, and then one of the world's best players, South Korean Lee Sedol, four games to one, in Mar. 2016. Google computer scientists described their project in the Jan. 28 issue of *Nature*.

Google's DeepMind division sought to develop software that could act intuitively, using neural networks, reminiscent of the brain. AlphaGo learned how to play by analyzing millions of moves of superior human players and by playing against itself millions of times, thereby acquiring a sense of which patterns of moves tend to be more successful. Brute-force calculation of all possible future outcomes was not feasible. AlphaGo instead relied on so-called Monte Carlo tree search, looking at a random sample of more promising moves to see how they play out. Following its Mar. victory, AlphaGo received an honorary "9-dan professional" ranking (the highest level) from the Korean Baduk [Go] Association. The win spotlighted the potential for applying AI in the future to a wide variety of complex planning situations.

Zika Epidemic

The Zika virus, first isolated in Africa in 1947, causes an infection that attracted little notice for decades because there tends to be only mild symptoms (such as fever, rash, joint pain, red eyes, muscle pain, and headache), if any. But sizable outbreaks were noted in Micronesia in 2007 (an estimated 5,000 infections) and in French Polynesia in 2013-14 (affecting possibly more than 30,000 people), with some cases involving the nervous system disorder Guillain-Barré syndrome.

The virus first appeared in the Americas in 2015; Brazilian health officials put the number of suspected cases of infection as high as 1.3 mil. Evidence began mounting that in pregnant women the illness could lead to fetal abnormalities, such as the brain-development disorder microcephaly. In Feb. 2016, the World Health Organization declared the Zika epidemic a Public Health Emergency of International Concern. By the following month, the virus had turned up in at least 33 countries and territories in the Americas, including the U.S. According to the U.S. Centers for Disease Control and Prevention (CDC), reported cases of Zika in the U.S. (excluding territories) in 2015-16, as of Sept. 14, totaled 3,176, nearly all associated with travel abroad; 8 instances of Guillain-Barré syndrome were recorded. U.S. territories reported 17,629 cases, most of them locally acquired; Guillain-Barré cases totaled 34.

Zika is spread most often by infected mosquitoes of the genus *Aedes*. It can also spread from a pregnant woman to her fetus and through sexual contact. There currently is no vaccine or specific treatment for the infection. The CDC recommends taking steps to avoid mosquito bites and advises pregnant women not to travel to regions with active Zika virus transmission.

Gravitational Waves Detected, at Last

One hundred years ago, Albert Einstein predicted the existence of gravitational waves. Not until a century later did scientists finally succeed in directly observing them. Einstein's general theory of relativity attributed gravity to a curving of the fabric of space-time caused by the presence of mass. Masses undergoing acceleration should disturb this fabric, producing ripples, or waves. According to Einstein, this gravitational "radiation" would likely be quite weak, even for very large masses and extremely high acceleration. Confirmation at last came in the first half of 2016 when researchers twice reported detecting gravitational waves. In both cases, the waves seemed to result from a cataclysmic collision of huge black holes. Both collisions occurred more than 1 bil light-years from Earth—which is to say they took place more than 1 bil years ago.

In both cases, the gravitational-wave "signal" was observed by two large and extremely sensitive detectors located in Louisiana and Washington State that together make up the Laser Interferometer Gravitational-Wave Observatory (LIGO). The two observations, made on Sept. 14 and Dec. 26, 2015, were reported in the Feb. 12 and June 17, 2016, issues of *Physical Review Letters*.

Weird State of Matter

Four states of matter are commonly known: solid, liquid, gas, and plasma. Some four decades ago, scientists predicted that a state called quantum spin liquid could exist in certain magnetic materials. A team of researchers reported the first successful observation of this state in real life in the July issue of the journal *Nature Materials*, published online on Apr. 4, 2016.

As many materials cool, their electrons tend to align—that is, their spins become oriented in the same direction. In a quantum spin liquid, however, the electrons' spins interact in such a way that they do not align. Just like in a liquid, disorder reigns—hence the name of the state. The electrons in this "liquid" behave as if they were split into smaller entities. Since they do not actually fragment, these smaller entities (pairs of so-called Majorana fermions) are referred to as quasi-particles. In the new research, scientists took a graphene-like material called alpha-ruthenium chloride and bombarded it with neutrons, thereby exciting the electrons. The pattern they observed in the neutrons bouncing off the material fit the pattern predicted for a quantum spin liquid containing Majorana fermions. Commentators speculated that such Majorana fermions might someday find application as building blocks for powerful quantum computers.

Exoplanets Galore

Astronomers did not succeed in confirming the existence of any extrasolar planets—planets orbiting a star other than the Sun—until the final decade of the 20th century. The pace of discovery stepped up following NASA's 2009 launch of the *Kepler* space observatory, and 2016 turned out to be a boom year for the *Kepler* mission. NASA announced in May 2016 that 1,284 candidate discoveries had been confirmed as planets, more than doubling the total number known. As of Sept. 15, the confirmed planets in NASA's Exoplanet Archive totaled 3,388. At about the same time, 3,530 were listed in another team's Extrasolar Planets Encyclopaedia, which uses slightly different confirmation criteria.

Most of the exoplanets known to astronomers are much more massive than Earth because their size makes them easier to detect. But researchers reported in the Aug. 25 issue of the science journal *Nature* the discovery of an apparently almost Earth-sized planet right next door to our solar system. It circles our closest neighbor—a mere 4.2 light-years away—the red dwarf star Proxima Centauri. The planet seemed to lie in a "habitable zone" relative to its star. In other words, liquid water, necessary for life as we know it, might be able to exist on its surface.

Science Glossary

This glossary covers some concepts that come up frequently in the news, in biology, chemistry, geology, and physics.

Biology

Amino acid: one of about 20 similar small molecules that are the building blocks of proteins.

Antibiotic: a substance produced by or derived from a bacterium, fungus, or other organism that battles infections and diseases caused by microorganisms, especially bacteria; it works by killing the microorganism or halting its growth.

Archaeon (plural, archaea): one of a group of single-celled microorganisms; archaea are prokaryotes, like bacteria, but they share some similarities with eukaryotes.

Autoimmunity: a condition in which an individual's immune system reacts against his or her own tissues; leads to diseases such as lupus, some forms of diabetes, inflammatory bowel disease, and rheumatoid arthritis.

Bacterium (plural, bacteria): one of a large, varied class of microscopic and simple, single-celled organisms; bacteria live almost everywhere—some forms cause disease, while others are useful in digestion and other natural processes.

Biodiversity: richness of variety of life-forms—both plant and animal—in a given environment.

Cell: the smallest unit of life capable of living independently, or with other cells; usually bounded by a membrane. May include a nucleus and other specialized parts.

Cholesterol: a fatty substance in animal tissues. It is produced by the liver in humans; is found in foods such as butter, eggs, and meat; and is an essential body constituent.

Chromosome: one of the rod-like structures in cell nuclei that carry genetic material (DNA).

Cloning: the process of copying a particular piece of DNA to allow it to be sequenced, studied, or used in some other way; can also refer to producing a genetic copy of an organism.

DNA (deoxyribonucleic acid): the usually double-stranded molecule that carries genetic information, which determines the form and functioning of all living things.

Ecosystem: an interdependent community of living organisms and their climatic and geographical habitat.

Enzyme: a protein that promotes a particular chemical reaction in the body.

Estrogen: one of a group of hormones that promote development of female secondary sex characteristics and the growth and health of the female reproductive system; males also produce small amounts of estrogen.

Eukaryote: any of the group of single- or multi-celled organisms whose cells have distinct nuclei.

Evolution: the process of gradual change that can occur in a species as it adapts to its environment; natural selection is the process by which evolution occurs.

Gene: a portion of a DNA molecule that provides the blueprint for the assembly of a protein.

Gene pool: the collection and total diversity of genes in an interbreeding population.

Gene therapy: a treatment in which scientists try to implant functioning genes into a person's cells so the genes can produce proteins that the person lacks or that help the person fight disease.

Genetic sequencing: the process of finding the order of subunits in a gene or the order of all an organism's genes.

Genome: the complete set of an organism's genetic material.

Hormone: a substance secreted in one part of an organism that regulates the functioning of other tissues or organs.

Meiosis: the process of cell division that results in gametes (sperm or egg cells), all of which contain half the number of chromosomes as their precursor.

Metabolism: the sum total of the body's chemical processes providing energy for vital functions and enabling new material to be synthesized.

Mitosis: the process by which a cell divides its nucleus and other cell materials into two duplicate daughter cells with the same DNA.

Neuron or **nerve cell:** any of the cells in the nervous system that send electrical and chemical messages to other cells.

Nucleus (plural, nuclei): the center of an atom; or the portion of a eukaryotic cell that contains most of the cell's genetic material.

Organism: a living entity, capable of growth, metabolism, and usually reproduction.

Phenotype: the observable properties and characteristics of an organism arising at least in part from its genetic makeup.

Pheromone: a chemical secreted by an animal or plant to influence the behavior of other members of its species.

Placebo effect: a phenomenon in which patients show improvements even though they have taken a medically inactive substance, called a placebo.

Prokaryote: a single-celled organism that does not have a distinct nucleus, such as a bacterium or archaeon.

Protein: a complex molecule made up of one or more chains of amino acids; essential to the structure and function of all cells.

RNA (ribonucleic acid): a complex molecule similar to the genetic material DNA but usually single-stranded; several forms of RNA translate the genetic code of DNA and use that code to assemble proteins for structural and biological functions in the body. RNA also serves as the genetic material of some viruses.

Species: a population of organisms that breed with each other in nature and produce fertile offspring; other definitions of species exist to accommodate the diversity of life on Earth.

Stem cell: a cell that can develop into other types of cells; for instance, stem cells in bone marrow can differentiate into different types of blood cells.

Steroid: a type of chemical substance with a certain molecular structure. Some steroids are hormones that can suppress immune response or influence stress reaction, blood pressure, or sexual development.

Testosterone: a steroid hormone that stimulates the development and maintenance of male sexual characteristics and the production of sperm; women also produce small amounts of testosterone.

Virus: a microscopic, often disease-causing, agent made of genetic material surrounded by a protein shell; can only reproduce inside a living cell.

Chemistry

Acid: a class of compounds that contrasts with bases. Acids taste sour, turn litmus red/pink, and often produce hydrogen gas in contact with some metals. Acids donate protons (hydrogen atoms minus the electron) in chemical reactions.

Base: a substance that yields hydroxyl ions (OH-) when dissolved in water; any of a class of compounds whose aqueous solutions taste bitter, feel slippery, turn litmus blue, and react with acids to form salts; also known as **alkaline**.

Carbon fiber: an extremely strong, thin fiber made by pyrolyzing (decomposing by heat) synthetic fibers, such as rayon, until charred; used to make high-strength composites.

Chlorofluorocarbon (CFC): one of a group of industrial chemicals that contain chlorine, fluorine, and carbon and can damage Earth's ozone layer.

Element: a substance that cannot be chemically decomposed into simpler substances; all the atoms of an element have the same number of protons.

Isotope: an atom of a chemical element with the same number of protons in its nucleus as other atoms of that element, but with a different number of neutrons.

Molecule: the basic unit of a chemical compound, composed of two or more atoms bound together.

Noble gases or **inert gases:** a group of gases including helium, neon, argon, krypton, xenon, and radon that are not reactive except in rare and limited instances.

Osmosis: the transfer of a fluid across a semipermeable membrane, usually from an area of higher concentration to one of lower concentration.

Polymer: a huge molecule containing hundreds or thousands of smaller molecules arranged in repeating units.

Salt: a neutral compound produced by the reaction of an acid and a base.

Geology

Fault, tectonic: a crack or break in Earth's crust, often due to the slippage of tectonic plates past or over one another; usually geologically unstable.

Igneous: a type of rock formed by solidification from a molten state, especially from molten magma.

Magma: hot liquid rock material under Earth's surface, from which igneous rock is formed by cooling.

Metamorphic: in geology, the name given to rocks or minerals that have recrystallized under the influence of heat and pressure since their original formation.

Pangaea: a single supercontinent that scientists believe began to break apart at least 200 mil years ago to form the current continents.

Plate tectonics: theory that Earth's lithosphere—the uppermost layer that includes the crust—is made up of many separate rigid plates of rock that float on top of hot semi-liquid rock.

Sedimentary: a type of rock formed by the buildup of material at the bottoms of bodies of water.

Physics

Absolute zero: the theoretical temperature at which all motion within a molecule stops, corresponding to $-273.15°C$ $(-459.67°F)$.

Antimatter: matter that consists of antiparticles, such as antiprotons, that have an opposite charge from normal particles; when matter meets antimatter, both are destroyed, and their combined mass is converted to energy. Antimatter is created in certain radioactive decay processes but appears to be present in only small amounts in the universe.

Atom: the basic unit of a chemical element.

Atomic mass: the total mass of an atom of a given element; atoms of the same element with different atomic masses (different numbers of neutrons, not protons) are called **isotopes**.

Atomic number: the number of protons in an atom of a given element of the periodic table; the characteristic that sets atoms of different elements apart.

Axion: a hypothetical subatomic particle with low mass and energy that is thought to exist because of the properties of the strong nuclear force.

Bose-Einstein condensate (BEC): a "super-atom" comprising thousands of atoms super-cooled to within a few hundred millionths of a degree of absolute zero and thus condensed into the lowest energy state. Atoms bound in the BEC behave synchronously, giving the BEC wavelike properties.

Boson: one of the two primary categories of particles in the Standard Model; bosons include the Higgs boson and force-carrying particles such as photons, gluons, and the W and Z particles.

Dark energy: a mysterious, undefined energy leading to a repulsive force pervading all of space-time; proposed by cosmologists as counteracting gravity and accelerating the expansion of the universe; predicted to make up 68.3% of the universe's composition.

Dark matter: hypothetical, invisible matter that some scientists believe makes up 26.8% of the universe (dark matter and ordinary matter together make up 31.7% of the universe). Its existence was proposed to account for otherwise inexplicable gravitational forces observed in space.

Doppler effect: a change in the frequency of sound, light, or radio waves caused by the motion of the source emitting the waves or the motion of the person or instrument perceiving the waves.

Electron: negatively charged particle that is the least massive electrically charged fundamental particle.

Energy: capacity to perform work. Energy can take various forms, such as potential energy, kinetic energy, and chemical energy.

Entropy: a measure of disorder in a system.

Fermion: any one of a number of matter particles including electrons, protons, neutrons, neutrinos, and quarks; one of the two primary categories of particles in the Standard Model, the other being bosons.

Field: the existence of physical effects such as forces (gravitational, electric, etc.) is visualized and described mathematically by physicists in terms of fields, which show the strength and direction of a force at a given position.

Fission: a nuclear reaction that occurs when the nuclei of large, unstable atoms break apart, releasing large amounts of energy.

Fluorescence: luminescence that is caused by the absorption of radiation at one wavelength followed by an almost immediate re-radiation, usually at a different wavelength, that stops almost immediately when the causative radiation stops.

Force: in classical physics, something that causes acceleration in a body; can be thought of as a push or pull.

Fusion: a nuclear reaction occurring when atomic nuclei collide at high temperatures and combine to form one heavier atomic nucleus, releasing enormous energy in the process.

Gravity: an attractive force between any two objects or particles, proportional to the mass (or energy) of the objects; strength of the force decreases with greater distance; the only fundamental force still unaccounted for by the Standard Model.

Half-life: the time it takes for half of a given amount of a radioactive element to decay.

Hertz (Hz): a measure of frequency, or how many times a given event occurs per second; applied to sound waves, electrical current, and microchip clock speeds.

Higgs boson: a boson associated with a field accounting for the existence of mass in many particles.

Laser: light consisting of a cascade of photons all having the same wavelength; stands for Light Amplification by Stimulated Emission of Radiation.

Light-emitting diode (LED): a semiconductor that emits light when an electrical current is passed through it. The color of the light depends on the material used in making the diode.

Neutrino: a tiny fundamental particle with no electrical charge and very small mass that moves very quickly through the universe; comes in three varieties, or flavors, called electron, muon, and tau.

Neutron: a neutral particle found in the nuclei of atoms.

Particle accelerator: a large machine with a circular or long, straight tunnel in which charged particles are accelerated to extremely high speeds.

Phosphorescence: luminescence that is caused by the absorption of radiation at one wavelength followed by a delayed re-radiation, usually at a different wavelength, that continues for a time after the causative radiation stops.

Photon: the elementary unit, or quantum, of electromagnetic radiation, such as light. It has no mass or electrical charge and is one of the fundamental force-carrying particles described by the Standard Model.

Plasma: a high-energy state of matter different from solid, liquid, or gas in which atomic nuclei and the electrons orbiting them separate from each other.

Proton: a positively charged subatomic particle found in the nuclei of atoms.

Quantum: a natural unit of some physically measurable property, such as energy or electrical charge.

Quark: a fermion and a fundamental matter particle that makes up neutrons and protons, forming atomic nuclei; there are six different varieties, or flavors, of quarks grouped in pairs: up and down, charm and strange, top and bottom.

Radiation: energy emitted as rays or particles. Radiation includes heat, light, ultraviolet rays, gamma rays, X-rays, cosmic rays, alpha particles, and beta particles.

Relativity, general theory of: a theory of space-time proposed by Albert Einstein in 1915; it links gravity to the curvature of space-time.

Relativity, special theory of: Einstein's theory of space and time: all laws of physics are valid in all uniformly moving frames of reference, and the speed of light in a vacuum is always the same, so long as the source and the observer are moving uniformly (not accelerating).

Standard Model: prevailing theory of the interaction of subatomic particles. Particles are either fermions—such as electrons, neutrinos, and quarks—or bosons—such as Higgs bosons, gluons, W or Z bosons, and photons; successfully explains three of the four elementary forces acting on particles (strong, weak, electromagnetic) but thus far has not incorporated gravity.

String theory: a theory that seeks to unify quantum mechanics and general relativity, positing that the basic constituents of matter can best be understood not as point objects but as tiny oscillating "strings."

Subatomic particle: one of the small particles, such as electrons, neutrons, and protons, which make up an atom.

Superconductivity: the property of certain materials, usually metals and chemically complex ceramics, to conduct electricity without resistance, generally at very cold temperatures.

Thermodynamics: the branch of physics that describes how energy, heat, and temperature flow in physical systems.

Ultraviolet radiation: a form of light, invisible to the human eye, that has a shorter wavelength and greater energy than visible light but a longer wavelength and less energy than X-rays.

Virtual particle: subatomic particles that rapidly pop into and out of existence and can exert real forces; usually occur in particle-antiparticle pairs and are rapidly annihilated.

Mohs Scale of Hardness

Hardness is the ability of a solid substance to resist abrasion or deformation on its surface. Soft minerals scratch more easily than hard ones. For example, a diamond will scratch graphite because graphite is softer. In 1812, German mineralogist Frederick Mohs (1773-1839) created the arbitrary scale shown below to measure relative hardness using 10 minerals that were readily available at that time. The numbers in the Mohs scale are arranged in order of increasing hardness. An item's hardness is obtained by determining which mineral in the Mohs scale can scratch it.

Mohs scale		Selected items and their relative hardness	
1 . . . . . . Talc	6 . . . . . Orthoclase feldspar	2.5 . . . . . .Fingernail	5.5 . . . . .Knife blade
2 . . . . . . Gypsum	7 . . . . . Quartz	2.5-3 . . . . .Gold, silver	6-7 . . . . .Glass
3 . . . . . . Calcite	8 . . . . . Topaz	3 . . . . . . .Copper penny	6.5 . . . . .Iron pyrite
4 . . . . . . Fluorite	9 . . . . . Corundum	4-4.5 . . . .Platinum	7+. . . . . .Hardened steel file
5 . . . . . . Apatite	10 . . . . . Diamond	4-5 . . . . . .Iron	

Chemical Elements, Atomic Numbers, Year Discovered

See Periodic Table of the Elements on the following page for atomic weights.

Element	Symbol	Atomic number	Year discov.	Element	Symbol	Atomic number	Year discov.	Element	Symbol	Atomic number	Year discov.
Actinium	Ac	89	1899	Gold	Au	79	BCE	Potassium	K	19	1807
Aluminum	Al	13	1825	Hafnium	Hf	72	1923	Praseodymium	Pr	59	1885
Americium	Am	95	1944	Hassium	Hs	108	1984	Promethium	Pm	61	1945
Antimony	Sb	51	1450	Helium	He	2	1868	Protactinium	Pa	91	1917
Argon	Ar	18	1894	Holmium	Ho	67	1878	Radium	Ra	88	1898
Arsenic	As	33	13th cent.	Hydrogen	H	1	1766	Radon	Rn	86	1900
Astatine	At	85	1940	Indium	In	49	1863	Rhenium	Re	75	1925
Barium	Ba	56	1808	Iodine	I	53	1811	Rhodium	Rh	45	1803
Berkelium	Bk	97	1949	Iridium	Ir	77	1804	Roentgenium	Rg	111	1995
Beryllium	Be	4	1798	Iron	Fe	26	BCE	Rubidium	Rb	37	1861
Bismuth	Bi	83	15th cent.	Krypton	Kr	36	1898	Ruthenium	Ru	44	1845
Bohrium	Bh	107	1981	Lanthanum	La	57	1839	Rutherfordium	Rf	104	1969
Boron	B	5	1808	Lawrencium	Lr	103	1961	Samarium	Sm	62	1879
Bromine	Br	35	1826	Lead	Pb	82	BCE	Scandium	Sc	21	1879
Cadmium	Cd	48	1817	Lithium	Li	3	1817	Seaborgium	Sg	106	1974
Calcium	Ca	20	1808	Livermorium	Lv	116	2000	Selenium	Se	34	1817
Californium	Cf	98	1950	Lutetium	Lu	71	1907	Silicon	Si	14	1823
Carbon	C	6	BCE	Magnesium	Mg	12	1829	Silver	Ag	47	BCE
Cerium	Ce	58	1803	Manganese	Mn	25	1774	Sodium	Na	11	1807
Cesium	Cs	55	1860	Meitnerium	Mt	109	1982	Strontium	Sr	38	1790
Chlorine	Cl	17	1774	Mendelevium	Md	101	1955	Sulfur	S	16	BCE
Chromium	Cr	24	1797	Mercury	Hg	80	BCE	Tantalum	Ta	73	1802
Cobalt	Co	27	1735	Molybdenum	Mo	42	1782	Technetium	Tc	43	1937
Copernicium	Cn	112	1996	*Moscovium	Mc	115	2004	Tellurium	Te	52	1782
Copper	Cu	29	BCE	Neodymium	Nd	60	1885	*Tennessine	Ts	117	2010
Curium	Cm	96	1944	Neon	Ne	10	1898	Terbium	Tb	65	1843
Darmstadtium	Ds	110	1995	Neptunium	Np	93	1940	Thallium	Tl	81	1861
Dubnium (Hahnium)[1]	Db (Ha)	105	1970	Nickel	Ni	28	1751	Thorium	Th	90	1828
				*Nihonium	Nh	113	2004	Thulium	Tm	69	1879
Dysprosium	Dy	66	1886	Niobium[2]	Nb	41	1801	Tin	Sn	50	BCE
Einsteinium	Es	99	1952	Nitrogen	N	7	1772	Titanium	Ti	22	1791
Erbium	Er	68	1843	Nobelium	No	102	1958	Tungsten (Wolfram)	W	74	1783
Europium	Eu	63	1901	*Oganesson	Og	118	2006				
Fermium	Fm	100	1953	Osmium	Os	76	1804	Uranium	U	92	1789
Flerovium	Fl	114	1999	Oxygen	O	8	1774	Vanadium	V	23	1830
Fluorine	F	9	1771	Palladium	Pd	46	1803	Xenon	Xe	54	1898
Francium	Fr	87	1939	Phosphorus	P	15	1669	Ytterbium	Yb	70	1878
Gadolinium	Gd	64	1886	Platinum	Pt	78	1735	Yttrium	Y	39	1794
Gallium	Ga	31	1875	Plutonium	Pu	94	1941	Zinc	Zn	30	BCE
Germanium	Ge	32	1886	Polonium	Po	84	1898	Zirconium	Zr	40	1789

* = Element listed under name recommended by the Intl. Union of Pure and Applied Chemistry (IUPAC). Pending formal approval of the names (expected in Nov. 2016), these are shown in italics in the periodic table. (1) The name Dubnium (Db) was approved by IUPAC for element 105, but the name Hahnium (Ha) was used in most of the scientific literature before 1998 and is still sometimes used in the U.S. (2) Formerly Columbium.

Periodic Table of the Elements

Source: Los Alamos National Laboratory Chemistry Division; International Union of Pure and Applied Chemistry (IUPAC)

Shaded elements are commonly regarded as metals.

Element names in italics were awaiting formal IUPAC approval as of Oct. 2016.

Legend:
- atomic number: 14
- atomic weight[1]: 28.09
- symbol: Si
- name: Silicon

Note: Atomic weight shown is a weighted average of the atomic masses of normally found isotopes. * = Element has no stable nuclides. A value enclosed in brackets, e.g. [209], indicates the mass number of the longest-lived isotope of the element. However, four such elements (Bi, Th, Pa, and U) do have a characteristic terrestrial isotopic composition, and for these an atomic weight is tabulated. (1) For elements having two or more stable isotopes with a notable variation in atomic-weight values, a range is shown.

Basic Laws of Physics

Newton's Laws of Motion

1. An object in motion moves at a constant velocity in a straight line unless acted upon by a force. Likewise, an object at rest will stay at rest. These two properties are known as inertia.

2. The acceleration of an object is proportional to the force acting on it and inversely proportional to the mass of an object. Force (F) equals mass (m) times acceleration (a):

$$F = ma$$

3. For every action, there is an equal and opposite reaction. For example, if a force of one ton pushes down on an object, the object pushes up with an equal force. As per the second law, the amount of movement (acceleration) produced in the object will depend on the object's mass.

Law of Gravity

In common usage, gravity refers to the gravitational force between planets and objects on or near them. But in scientific parlance, gravitation represents one of four basic forces controlling the interactions of matter. (The others are the strong and weak nuclear forces and electromagnetic force.) The gravitational force (F) between objects is proportional to the product of their masses (m_1 and m_2) and inversely proportional to the square of the distance (d) between them. G represents the gravitational constant in Newton's law of gravity, a fixed ratio of approximately 6.67384×10^{-11} newton m²/kg². The basic law of gravity is:

$$F = G \frac{m_1 m_2}{d^2}$$

Near Earth's surface, Earth's gravitational force pulls objects downward at a constant acceleration of 9.8 m/s² (g). This allows calculation of the vertical velocity (v) of an object with an initial vertical velocity of v_0 in free fall at a given point in time (t) and calculation of the distance (d) of an object from Earth at any given time with a given initial velocity (v_0) and a known initial height (a) via the following equations (here, the effects of air resistance are ignored, and downward velocities and directions are negative):

$$v = v_0 - gt$$
$$d = -\tfrac{1}{2}g(t^2) + v_0 t + a$$

Assuming that height is measured in feet and speeds in feet per second, the maximum height (H) reached by an object with a positive (upward) initial velocity is expressed as:

$$H = a + \frac{v_0^2}{64}$$

For motion not near Earth's surface, more complicated equations are required. Also, if the object's upward velocity is very great, the object may escape Earth's gravity. Even near Earth's surface, there are slight complications. Gravity is lessened by the centrifugal force of the Earth's rotation. At the poles, where centrifugal force is absent, acceleration due to gravity is greater.

Gravity is weaker on a mountaintop than at sea level because the mountaintop is farther from Earth's center.

Conservation Laws

In physics, laws of conservation state that in a closed system, where neither mass nor energy is added or subtracted, certain measurable quantities remain constant.

Conservation of Mass: Mass is neither created nor destroyed within a closed system except when converted from or to energy.

Conservation of Momentum: All moving objects have momentum, and in a closed system, total momentum is always conserved. Linear momentum is the product of the mass of an object and its velocity. In the following equation, M and V represent the initial total mass and velocity of objects within a closed system. After a collision between those objects, the mass and velocity of individual objects may change (for example, one object breaks into smaller pieces, each traveling at a different velocity), but the product of the total mass and velocity in the system after the collision (mv) will remain the same.

$$MV = mv$$

Any object moving in a circle has another kind of momentum—angular momentum. This is because circular motion requires acceleration toward the center of the circle. The amount of acceleration depends on the speed of the object and the square of the radius of the circle. (Angular momentum is the product of this speed, the mass of the object, and the square of the radius.)

Conservation of Energy: The total amount of energy in a closed system will not change except when converted to mass.

Conservation of Mass-Energy: Although mass and energy can be converted into one another, the total amount of mass and energy together must be conserved. This is reflected in Einstein's famous equation, where m is mass, E is energy, and c is the speed of light in a vacuum (which is constant):

$$E = mc^2$$

Relativistic mass can describe how mass increases with velocity. The following equation—where m is the mass of a moving object, m_0 is the object's mass when not moving, v is the object's velocity in relation to a stationary observer, and c is the speed of light—shows the relationship:

$$m = \frac{m_0}{\sqrt{1 - \dfrac{v^2}{c^2}}}$$

The theory that no object can travel faster than the speed of light is based in this equation. As an object approaches c, so much energy is converted to mass that it no longer accelerates.

Laws of Thermodynamics

1. Heat is a form of energy. Within a closed system energy must be conserved except in nuclear reactions or other extreme conditions. It is neither created nor destroyed.

2. Within a self-sustaining system, heat can never go from an area of low temperature to an area of high temperature, for this would require added energy. Without added energy, disorder, or entropy, can only increase.

3. Absolute zero cannot be attained by any procedure in a finite number of steps. Although it can be approached asymptotically, it can never be reached.

Laws of Current Electricity

Electric current generally represents the flow of electrons through a conductor. The rate at which electrons flow can be measured in amperes, defined as the number of electrons (measured in a unit called the coulomb, equal to about 6.24 quintillion or 6.24×10^{18} electrons) moving past a particular point every second. One ampere is equal to 1 coulomb of charge passing each second. Like water, electrons tend to move from areas of high pressure to low pressure. The difference between these two pressures, known as potential difference, is measured in volts.

Certain substances, such as copper and carbon, allow electric currents to pass more readily than others—that is, they have greater conductivity. Resistance to conductivity is measured in ohms.

Ohm's Law: Electric current is directly proportional to the potential difference and inversely proportional to the total resistance of the circuit. I is electric current (measured in amperes), V is the potential difference (measured in volts), and R is resistance (measured in ohms):

$$I = \frac{V}{R}$$

Law of Electric Power: Electric power (P), measured in watts, represents the rate at which electricity is converted into some other form of energy (such as light, in the case of a lightbulb). For a direct-current circuit, P is the product of current and potential difference:

$$P = IV$$

Two Basic Laws of Quantum Physics

1. Heisenberg's uncertainty principle: Certain pairs of observable quantities like energy and time or position and momentum cannot be measured with complete accuracy simultaneously. Also known as the indeterminacy principle.

2. Pauli's exclusion principle: Two electrons in an atom cannot simultaneously occupy the same quantum or energy state. This has since been shown to be true for many subatomic particles.

Breaking the Sound Barrier; Speed of Sound

The prefix **Mach** is used to describe supersonic speed. It was named for Ernst Mach (1838-1916), a Czech-born Austrian physicist. Mach may be defined as the ratio of the velocity of an object to the velocity of sound in a particular medium. A plane moving at the speed of sound moves at Mach 1. At twice the speed of sound, it moves at Mach 2.

When a plane passes the sound barrier—that is, flies faster than the speed at which sound travels—people in the area, though not the people on the plane, hear what seem to be thunderclaps. These sounds are sometimes called sonic booms.

Sound is produced by vibrations of an object. It is transmitted by the alternating increase and decrease in pressure that radiates outward from a source through a material medium of molecules, like waves spreading out on a pond after a rock has been tossed in.

The **frequency of sound** is determined by the number of times the vibrating waves undulate per second. It is measured in cycles per second. The slower the cycle of waves, the lower the frequency. As the frequency increases, the sound becomes higher in pitch. The human ear is sensitive to frequencies between 20 and 20,000 vibrations per second, although this range varies among individuals.

Intensity, or loudness, is the strength of the pressure of these radiating waves and is measured in decibels.

The **speed of sound** varies depending on temperature and altitude. It moves faster in water than in air, for example. At sea level and a temperature of 59°F (15°C), the speed of sound is approximately 761 mph, or 1,100 ft per sec.

Light; Colors of the Spectrum

Light, a form of electromagnetic radiation similar to radiant heat, radio waves, and X-rays, is emitted from a source in straight lines and spreads in area as it travels. For emission from a point source, light per unit area diminishes in proportion to the square of the distance.

The English mathematician and physicist Isaac Newton (1642-1727) described light as an **emission of particles**; the Dutch astronomer, mathematician, and physicist Christiaan Huygens (1629-95) and others developed the theory that light travels in a **wave motion**. It is now believed that these two theories are essentially complementary. The development of quantum theory has led to results where light acts like a series of particles in some experiments and like a wave in others.

The first relatively accurate measurement of the **speed of light** was made by French physicist Armand Hippolyte Louis Fizeau (1819-96). Today the speed of light is known precisely as 299,792.458 km per sec (or 186,282.397 mi/sec) in a vacuum. In water the speed of light is about 25% less, and in glass, 33% less.

Color sensations are produced through the excitation of the retina of the eye by light vibrating at different frequencies. The different colors of the visible spectrum may be seen by viewing light refracted by passage through a prism, which separates light into its component wavelengths.

Customarily, the basic colors are taken to be the six monochromatic (single) colors that occupy relatively large areas of the spectrum: red, orange, yellow, green, blue, and violet. So-called primary colors can be combined to produce the sensation of other colors. However, scientists disagree about how many and what primary colors to recognize. The color sensation of **black** is due to complete lack of stimulation of the retina, that of **white** to complete stimulation.

Infrared and **ultraviolet rays**, which are below the red (long) end and above the violet (short) end of the visible spectrum, respectively, are invisible to the naked human eye. Heat is the principal effect of infrared rays, and chemical action that of ultraviolet rays. Some animals can see infrared or ultraviolet light.

Life Cycles of Selected Animals

Information reviewed by Ronald M. Nowak, author of *Walker's Mammals of the World* (6th ed., Johns Hopkins University Press, 1999). Average longevity figures supplied by Ronald T. Reuther. These apply to animals in captivity; the potential life span of animals is rarely attained in nature. Figures on gestation and incubation are averages based on estimates.

Animal	Gestation (days)	Average longevity (yrs.)	Maximum longevity (yrs.-mos.)	Animal	Gestation (days)	Average longevity (yrs.)	Maximum longevity (yrs.-mos.)
Ass	365	12	47	Leopard	98	12	23
Baboon	187	20	45	Lion	100	15	30
Bear (black)	219	18	36-10	Monkey (rhesus)	166	15	37
Bear (grizzly)	225	25	50	Moose	240	12	27
Bear (polar)	240	20	45	Mouse (domestic white)	19	3	6
Beaver	105	5	50	Mouse (meadow)	21	3	4
Bison	285	15	40	Opossum (American)	13	1	5
Camel	406	12	50	Pig (domestic)	112	10	27
Cat (domestic)	63	12	38	Puma	90	12	20
Chimpanzee	230	20	60	Rabbit (domestic)	31	5	18-10
Chipmunk	31	6	10	Rhinoceros (black)	450	15	45-10
Cow	284	15	30	Rhinoceros (white)	480	20	50
Deer (white-tailed)	201	8	20	Sea lion (California)	350	12	34
Dog (domestic)	61	12	21	Sheep (domestic)	154	12	23
Elephant (African)	660	35	70	Squirrel (gray)	44	10	23-6
Elephant (Asian)	645	40	77	Tiger	105	16	26-3
Elk	250	15	26-8	Wolf (maned)	63	5	15-8
Fox (red)	52	7	14	Zebra (Grant's)	365	15	50
Giraffe	457	10	36-2				
Goat (domestic)	151	8	18	**Animal**			**Incubation time (days)**
Gorilla	258	20	54	Chicken			21
Guinea pig	68	4	8	Duck			30
Hippopotamus	238	41	61	Goose			30
Horse	330	20	50	Pigeon			18
Kangaroo (gray)	36	7	24	Turkey			26

Geologic Time Scale

Our understanding of Earth's ancient history is largely a result of geoscientists' study of climate, rock strata, ice samples, mineral deposits, and fossils from around the world; clues to the planet's origin have also been found through the study of extraterrestrial bodies. Geologists divide Earth's history into the following units (MYA = million years ago):

PRECAMBRIAN TIME (4,600-541 MYA)

HADEAN EON (4,600-4,000 MYA) Earth has no continents, oceans, or life; surface conditions are defined by intense volcanic activity and widespread meteorite impact. Oldest known minerals and rocks, many of meteoric origin, date to this eon, which may also have seen the first appearance of life.

ARCHEAN EON (4,000-2,500 MYA) Earth's surface cools and water vapor in atmosphere condenses to form early oceans, which define small protocontinents; there is substantial evidence for the existence of single-celled organisms, bacteria and archaea, in these oceans.

PROTEROZOIC EON (2,500-541 MYA) Protocontinents merge into larger landmasses as Earth's crust continues to shift. Atmospheric oxygen levels increase, and first known multicellular life appears. Later, soft-bodied marine animals emerge.

PHANEROZOIC EON (541 MYA-present)

Paleozoic Era (541-252 MYA)

Cambrian Period (541-485 MYA). The supercontinent known as Gondwana, or Gondwanaland, dominates the Southern Hemisphere. Seas experience an explosion of invertebrate animal life, including thousands of species of trilobites; the first known vertebrates appear. There is no life on land.

Ordovician Period (485-444 MYA). Gondwanaland extends from South Pole to tropic regions; Northern Hemisphere is mostly open ocean. Average global temperatures are warmer than in the current era. First primitive land plants, early ancestors of starfish and mollusks, and first armored, jawless fishes appear. The period ends in mass extinction of a majority of species, possibly a result of a global drop in sea level due to glaciation.

Silurian Period (444-419 MYA). South Pole remains covered by supercontinent, but precursors of present-day N America, Europe, and Asia coalesce around the equator and middle latitudes. Appearance of first known vascular land plants, first freshwater fish, first jawed fish, first coral reefs, and first air-breathing animals (certain eurypterids, a scorpion-like creature).

Devonian Period (419-359 MYA). Collisions between Gondwanaland and ancestral landmasses of N America and Eurasia produce mountains visible today as northern Appalachians. Newly-formed ozone layer offers protection from sun's rays, allowing first air-breathing spiders and mites to appear on dry land. Fish with fins and scales and first amphibians emerge. Late Devonian mass extinction.

Carboniferous Period (359-299 MYA). Precursors of modern N America and Northern Europe lie in tropical latitudes N of the equator; warm and humid conditions there facilitate spread of lush forests and peat swamps that later form most of the world's coal and limestone. Later period sees emergence of first true conifers, Lepidodendrales ("scale trees") as tall as 100 ft, and first true reptiles.

Permian Period (299-252 MYA). All major landmasses collide to form the supercontinent Pangaea, surrounded by the world ocean Panthalassa. Gradual warming through much of the Permian allows for initial flourishing of species—including dinosaur precursors (up to 10 ft in length) and marine species in shallow inland seas. The period ended with a mass extinction—the largest of Earth's five mass extinctions. As much as 95% of all marine species and most land species went extinct.

Mesozoic Era (252-66 MYA)

Triassic Period (252-201 MYA). Pangaea separates into supercontinents of Laurasia and Gondwana; subtropical conditions extend as far N as present-day Wyoming and New England. Emergence of icthyosaurs and plesiosaurs (large marine reptiles), several species of dinosaurs (up to 15 ft long), first true mammals, and first insects to undergo metamorphosis from larva to pupa to adult. Triassic-Jurassic mass extinction.

Jurassic Period (201-145 MYA). N American continent drifts westward, opening Gulf of Mexico; rift forms between S America and Africa. Warm, moist climate contributes to flourishing of coral reefs and temperate and subtropical forests. Appearance of first angiosperms (flowering plants), pterosaurs (winged reptiles), the earliest known birds (offshoots of a dinosaur group), and huge dinosaurs such as the carnivorous *Allosaurus* and herbivorous *Apatosaurus*.

Cretaceous Period (145-66 MYA). African continental plate drifts N, creating roots of European Alps; gap between S America and Africa broadens; western movement of N America drives formation of Sierra Nevada and Rocky Mountains, turning the western interior of continent into a vast swamp. Later, sea levels rise and cover about one-third of Earth's present land area. The global climate is warm and mild. The period ends in a mass extinction of plant and animal species (including dinosaurs). Likely causes include an asteroid impact and increased volcanic activity.

Cenozoic Era (66 MYA-present)

Paleogene Period (66-23 MYA)
- Paleocene Epoch (66-56 MYA). Australia begins to separate from Antarctica; N America and Greenland begin to spread apart. Mammalian life predominates, including early marsupials, insectivores, creodonts (carnivorous relatives of cats and dogs), and primitive hoofed mammals.
- Eocene Epoch (56-33.9 MYA). Australia drifts farther from Antarctica; the Indian subcontinent becomes welded to Asia, and tectonic forces drive the upheaval of the Alpine-Himalayan system. Climate in N America and Europe is subtropical and moist, with temperate forests as far N as Greenland and Siberia. Ancestors of modern horses, elephants, rhinoceroses, camels, bats, primates, and squirrel-like rodents emerge; earliest known marine mammals appear in later Eocene.
- Oligocene Epoch (33.9-23 MYA). San Andreas fault develops between N American and Pacific plates. Mammalian species continue to diversify, producing modern horse and multiple rodent, camel, and rhinoceros-like species, as well as first known species of great ape. Long-term cooling trend begins that would later cause Pleistocene ice ages.

Neogene Period (23 MYA-2.6 MYA)
- Miocene Epoch (23-5.3 MYA). Crustal plate collisions continue to drive uplift of Alps, Himalayas, and Cordilleran Ranges in Americas; eroded sediment is deposited in shallow marine basins, forming reservoirs for oil fields of California, Romania, and Caspian Sea. Ocean currents prevent Antarctica from receiving warmer waters, fostering growth of Antarctic ice sheet. Northern forests become grassy prairies. Large apes related to the orangutan live in Asia and southern Europe. Oldest hominin fossils from Africa date to this epoch.
- Pliocene Epoch (5.3-2.6 MYA). Alps continue to rise in Europe, and subduction of the Pacific tectonic plate elevates the Sierra Nevada and volcanic Cascade Range. Climate becomes cooler and drier, driving formation of permanent Arctic ice cap. Rapid primate evolution produces *Ardipithecus* and *Australopithecus*, two of the earliest known direct ancestors of *Homo sapiens*.

Quaternary Period (2.6 MYA-present)
- Pleistocene Epoch (2.6 MYA-11,700 years ago). Glacier ice covers as much as 25% or more of Earth's land surface, carving numerous present-day features including the Great Lakes; increased rainfall in lower latitudes allows plant and animal life to flourish in northern and eastern Africa. Late Pleistocene brings worldwide extinction of many large mammals, including the mastodon, saber-toothed tiger, and ground sloth. Evidence of Neanderthals and Denisovans dates from the latter part of the Pleistocene.
- Holocene Epoch (11,700 years ago-present). Melting ice caused sea levels to rise 100 ft or more in early Holocene, covering large areas of land and extending continental shelf of N America. Humans proliferate, and civilization begins.

Biological Classification

In biology, classification is the identification, naming, and grouping of organisms into a formal system. The two fields that are most directly concerned with classification are taxonomy and systematics. Although they overlap, taxonomy is more concerned with nomenclature (naming) and with constructing hierarchical systems, and systematics with uncovering evolutionary relationships. Two kingdoms of living forms, Plantae and Animalia, have been recognized since Aristotle established the first taxonomy in the 4th century BCE. Plants and animals are examples of eukaryotes; their cells have nuclei bound by membranes. Two other kingdoms of eukaryotes that have been identified are Protista (one-celled organisms) and Fungi. The single-celled bacteria and archaea lack such nuclei. They are referred to as prokaryotes (or procaryotes) and are commonly placed in separate kingdoms. The seven basic categories of classification (from most general to most specific) are kingdom, phylum (or division), class, order, family, genus, and species. (In addition, many scientists group all eukaryotes in a single "domain." Bacteria and archaea are also often treated as separate domains.) Below are two examples of classification:

ZOOLOGICAL HIERARCHY

Kingdom	Phylum	Class	Order	Family	Genus	Species name	Common name
Animalia	Chordata	Mammalia	Primates	Hominidae	*Homo*	*Homo sapiens*	Human

BOTANICAL HIERARCHY

Kingdom	Division*	Class	Order	Family	Genus	Species name	Common name
Plantae	Magnoliophyta	Magnoliopsida	Magnoliales	Magnoliaceae	*Magnolia*	*M. virginiana*	Sweet bay

*In botany, the division is generally used in place of the phylum.

Major Venomous Animals

Snakes

Asian pit viper—2 ft to 5 ft long; throughout Asia; reactions and mortality vary, but most bites cause tissue damage; mortality generally low.

Australian brown snake—4 ft to 7 ft long; very slow onset of cardiac or respiratory distress; moderate mortality, but because death can be sudden and unexpected, it is the most dangerous of the Australian snakes; antivenom.

Barba amarilla or fer-de-lance—up to 7 ft long; from tropical Mexico to Brazil; severe tissue damage common; moderate mortality; antivenom.

Black mamba—up to 14 ft long; southern and central Africa; rapid onset of dizziness, difficulty breathing, erratic heartbeat; mortality high, nears 100% without antivenom.

Boomslang—less than 6 ft long; African savannahs; rapid onset of nausea and dizziness, often followed by slight recovery and then sudden death from internal hemorrhaging; bites rare, mortality high; antivenom.

Bushmaster—up to 12 ft long; tropical forests of Central and S America; few bites occur, but mortality high.

Common, or Asian, cobra—4 ft to 8 ft long; throughout S Asia; considerable tissue damage, sometimes paralysis; mortality probably not more than 10%; antivenom.

Copperhead—less than 4 ft long; New England to Texas; pain and swelling; very seldom fatal; antivenom seldom needed.

Coral snake—2 ft to 5 ft long; in Americas S of Canada; bite may be painless; slow onset of paralysis, impaired breathing; mortalities rare but high without antivenom and mechanical respiration.

Cottonmouth water moccasin—up to 5 ft long; wetlands of southern U.S. from Virginia to Texas; rapid onset of severe pain, swelling, tissue destruction can be extensive; mortality low; antivenom.

Death adder—less than 3 ft long; Australia; rapid onset of faintness, cardiac and respiratory distress; at least 50% mortality without antivenom.

Desert horned viper—up to 2 ft long; dry areas of Africa and western Asia; swelling and tissue damage; mortality low; antivenom.

European viper—1 ft to 3 ft long; throughout Europe; bleeding and tissue damage; mortality low; antivenom.

Gaboon viper—more than 6 ft long; S of the Sahara; massive tissue damage, internal bleeding; few recorded bites.

King cobra—up to 16 ft long; throughout S Asia; rapid swelling, dizziness, loss of consciousness, difficulty breathing, erratic heartbeat; mortality varies with amount of venom involved, but most bites involve nonfatal amounts; antivenom.

Krait—up to 5 ft long; SE Asia; rapid onset of sleepiness, numbness; up to 50% mortality even with use of antivenom.

Puff adder—up to 5 ft long, fat; S of the Sahara, throughout the Middle East; rapid large swelling, great pain, dizziness; moderate mortality, often from internal bleeding; antivenom.

Rattlesnake—2 ft to 6 ft long; throughout Western Hemisphere; rapid onset of severe pain, swelling; mortality low, but amputation of affected digits is sometimes necessary; antivenom. Mojave rattler may produce temporary paralysis.

Ringhals, or spitting, cobra—5 ft to 7 ft long; southern Africa; squirts venom through holes in front of fangs as a defense; venom severely irritating and can cause blindness.

Russell's viper or tic-polonga—more than 5 ft long; throughout Asia; internal bleeding; bite reports common; moderate mortality rate; antivenom.

Saw-scaled, or carpet, viper—up to 2 ft long; dry areas from India to Africa; severe bleeding, fever; high mortality, causes more human fatalities than any other snake; antivenom.

Sea snake—3 ft to 10 ft long; throughout Pacific, Indian Oceans except NE Pacific; almost painless bite; variety of muscle pain, paralysis; mortality low, many bites not envenomed; some antivenoms.

Sharp-nosed pit viper or hundred-pace snake—up to 5 ft long; S Vietnam, Taiwan, and China; the most toxic of Asian pit vipers; very rapid onset of swelling and tissue damage, internal bleeding; moderate mortality; antivenom.

Taipan—up to 11 ft long; Australia and New Guinea; rapid paralysis with severe breathing difficulty; mortality nears 100% without antivenom.

Tiger snake—2 ft to 6 ft long; southern Australia; pain, numbness, mental disturbances with rapid paralysis; may be deadliest of all land snakes, but antivenom is quite effective.

Yellow, or cape, cobra—7 ft long; southern Africa; most toxic venom of any cobra; rapid onset of swelling, breathing and cardiac difficulties; mortality is high without treatment; antivenom.

Note: Not all bites by venomous snakes are actually envenomed. Any animal bite, however, carries the danger of tetanus, and anyone suffering a venomous snake bite should seek medical attention. Antivenoms do not cure; they are only an aid in the treatment of bites. Mortality rates above are for envenomed bites: low mortality, c. 2% or less; moderate, 2%-5%; high, 5%-15%.

Lizards

Gila monster—up to 24 in. long, with heavy body and tail; high desert in SW U.S. and northern Mexico; immediate severe pain, transient low blood pressure; no recent mortality.

Mexican beaded lizard—similar to Gila monster; W coast of Mexico; reaction and mortality similar to Gila monster.

Insects

Ants, bees, hornets, wasps—global distribution; usual reaction is piercing pain in area of sting, though many people suffer allergic reactions (swelling, rashes); not directly fatal, except in cases of massive multiple stings, and a few may die within minutes from severe sensitivity to the venom (anaphylactic shock).

Spiders, scorpions

Black widow—small, round-bodied with red hourglass marking; the widow and its relatives are found in tropical and temperate zones; severe musculoskeletal pain, weakness, breathing difficulty, convulsions, which may be more serious in small children; low mortality; antivenom. The **redback** spider of Australia has the hourglass marking on its back, rather than on its front, but is otherwise identical to the black widow.

Brown recluse, or fiddleback, spider—small, oblong body; throughout U.S.; pain with later ulceration, which may last months, at place of bite; fever, nausea, and stomach cramps in severe cases; very low mortality.

Funnel web spider—several varieties, often large; Australia; slow onset of breathing, circulation difficulties; low mortality; antivenom.

Scorpion—crablike body with stinger in tail, various sizes; many varieties throughout tropical and subtropical areas; severe pain spreading from the wound, numbness, severe agitation, cramps, and even respiratory failure; low mortality, usually in children; antivenoms.

Tarantula—large, hairy spider; worldwide; the American tarantula, and probably all other tarantulas, are harmless to humans, though their bite may cause some pain and swelling.

Sea life

Cone-shell—mollusk in small shell; S Pacific and Indian Oceans; shoots barbs into victims; paralysis; low mortality.

Octopus—global distribution, usually in warm waters; rapid onset of paralysis with breathing difficulty; all varieties produce venom, but only a few can cause death.

Portuguese man-of-war—jellyfish-like siphonophore with tentacles up to 100 ft long; in most warm water areas; immediate severe pain; not directly fatal, though shock may cause death in rare cases.

Sea wasp—jellyfish, with tentacles up to 30 ft long; S Pacific; very rapid onset of circulatory problems; high mortality because of speed of toxic reaction; antivenom.

Stingray—several varieties of differing sizes; tropical and temperate seas and some freshwater; severe pain, rapid onset of nausea, vomiting, breathing difficulties; wound area may ulcerate, gangrene may occur; seldom fatal.

Stonefish—brownish fish that lies motionless on bottom of shallow waters; throughout S Pacific and Indian Oceans; extraordinary pain, rapid paralysis; low mortality; antivenom, warm water relieves pain.

Speeds of Selected Animals

Source: *Natural History* magazine. © American Museum of Natural History

Animal	Speed (mph)	Animal	Speed (mph)	Animal	Speed (mph)
Cheetah	70	Mongolian wild ass	40	Human	27.89
Pronghorn antelope	61	Greyhound	39.35	Elephant	25
Wildebeest	50	Whippet	35.50	Black mamba snake	20
Lion	50	Rabbit (domestic)	35	Six-lined race runner (lizard)	18
Thomson's gazelle	50	Mule deer	35	Wild turkey	15
Quarterhorse	47.5	Jackal	35	Squirrel	12
Elk	45	Reindeer	32	Pig (domestic)	11
Cape hunting dog	45	Giraffe	32	Chicken	9
Coyote	43	White-tailed deer	30	Spider (*Tegenaria atrica*)	1.17
Gray fox	42	Warthog	30	Giant tortoise	0.17
Hyena	40	Grizzly bear	30	Three-toed sloth	0.15
Zebra	40	Cat (domestic)	30	Garden snail	0.03

Note: Most of these measurements are for maximum speeds over approximate quarter-mile distances. Exceptions are the lion and elephant, whose speeds were clocked in the act of charging; the whippet, which was timed over a 200-yd course; the cheetah, timed over a 100-yd distance; a human, timed over a 15-yd segment of a 100-yd run; and the black mamba, six-lined race runner, spider, giant tortoise, three-toed sloth, and garden snail, which were measured over various small distances.

Most Popular Breeds of Cats, 2015

Source: The Cat Fanciers' Association
(ranked by total registrations)

Rank	Breed	Rank	Breed	Rank	Breed	Rank	Breed	Rank	Breed
1.	Exotic	10.	Oriental	18.	Siberian	27.	Balinese/	34.	European Burmese
2.	Persian	11.	Devon Rex	19.	Burmese		Javanese	35.	Havana Brown
3.	Maine Coon Cat	12.	Siamese	20.	Ocicat	28.	Chartreux	36.	American Bobtail
4.	Ragdoll	13.	Cornish Rex	21.	Egyptian Mau	29.	Bombay	37.	Korat
5.	British Shorthair	14.	Norwegian Forest	22.	Japanese Bobtail	30.	Colorpoint	38.	Burmilla
6.	American Shorthair		Cat	23.	Selkirk Rex		Shorthair	39.	American Wirehair
7.	Scottish Fold	15.	Birman	24.	Manx	31.	RagaMuffin	40.	Turkish Van
8.	Abyssinian	16.	Russian Blue	25.	Turkish Angora	32.	Singapura	41.	LaPerm
9.	Sphynx	17.	Tonkinese	26.	Somali	33.	American Curl	42.	Chinese Li Hua

Most Popular American Kennel Club Dog Breed Registrations, 2013-15

Source: American Kennel Club (AKC)

Breed	Rank 2015	2014	2013	Breed	Rank 2015	2014	2013
Labrador Retrievers	1	1	1	Miniature Schnauzers	16	16	17
German Shepherds	2	2	2	Australian Shepherds	17	18	20
Golden Retrievers	3	3	3	Cavalier King Charles Spaniels	18	19	18
Bulldogs	4	4	5	Shih Tzu	19	17	15
Beagles	5	5	4	Pembroke Welsh Corgis	20	22	24
French Bulldogs	6	9	11	Pomeranians	21	20	19
Yorkshire Terriers	7	6	6	Boston Terriers	22	23	23
Poodles	8	7	8	Shetland Sheepdogs	23	21	21
Rottweilers	9	10	9	Havanese	24	25	25
Boxers	10	8	7	Mastiffs	25	26	26
German Shorthaired Pointers	11	12	13	Brittanys	26	27	30
Siberian Huskies	12	13	14	English Springer Spaniels	27	28	28
Dachshunds	13	11	10	Chihuahuas	28	24	22
Doberman Pinschers	14	14	12	Bernese Mountain Dogs	29	32	32
Great Danes	15	15	16	Cocker Spaniels	30	30	29

Dog Breeds by Type

Source: American Kennel Club (AKC)

As of mid-2016, the AKC recognized 190 breeds and used the following seven groups to classify breeds, according to functions and other distinctive traits.

Herding Group: Australian Cattle Dog, Australian Shepherd, Bearded Collie, Beauceron, Belgian Malinois, Belgian Sheepdog, Belgian Tervuren, Bergamasco, Berger Picard, Border Collie, Bouvier des Flandres, Briard, Canaan Dog, Cardigan Welsh Corgi, Collie, Entlebucher Mountain Dog, Finnish Lapphund, German Shepherd Dog, Icelandic Sheepdog, Miniature American Shepherd, Norwegian Buhund, Old English Sheepdog, Pembroke Welsh Corgi, Polish Lowland Sheepdog, Puli, Pumi, Pyrenean Shepherd, Shetland Sheepdog, Spanish Water Dog, Swedish Vallhund.

Hound Group: Afghan Hound, American English Coonhound, American Foxhound, Basenji, Basset Hound, Beagle, Black and Tan Coonhound, Bloodhound, Bluetick Coonhound, Borzoi, Cirneco dell'Etna, Dachshund, English Foxhound, Greyhound, Harrier, Ibizan Hound, Irish Wolfhound, Norwegian Elkhound, Otterhound, Petit Basset Griffon Vendéen, Pharaoh Hound, Plott, Portuguese Podengo Pequeno, Redbone Coonhound, Rhodesian Ridgeback, Saluki, Scottish Deerhound, Sloughi, Treeing Walker Coonhound, Whippet.

Non-Sporting Group: American Eskimo Dog, Bichon Frise, Boston Terrier, Bulldog, Chinese Shar-Pei, Chow Chow, Coton de Tulear, Dalmatian, Finnish Spitz, French Bulldog, Keeshond, Lhasa Apso, Löwchen, Norwegian Lundehund, Poodle (standard and miniature), Schipperke, Shiba Inu, Tibetan Spaniel, Tibetan Terrier, Xoloitzcuintli.

Sporting Group: American Water Spaniel, Boykin Spaniel, Brittany, Chesapeake Bay Retriever, Clumber Spaniel, Cocker Spaniel, Curly-Coated Retriever, English Cocker Spaniel, English Setter, English Springer Spaniel, Field Spaniel, Flat-Coated Retriever, German Shorthaired Pointer, German Wirehaired Pointer, Golden Retriever, Gordon Setter, Irish Red and White Setter, Irish Setter, Irish Water Spaniel, Labrador Retriever, Lagotto Romagnolo, Nova Scotia Duck Tolling Retriever, Pointer, Spinone Italiano, Sussex Spaniel, Vizsla, Weimaraner, Welsh Springer Spaniel, Wirehaired Pointing Griffon, Wirehaired Vizsla.

Terrier Group: Airedale Terrier, American Hairless Terrier, American Staffordshire Terrier, Australian Terrier, Bedlington Terrier, Border Terrier, Bull Terrier, Cairn Terrier, Cesky Terrier, Dandie Dinmont Terrier, Glen of Imaal Terrier, Irish Terrier, Kerry Blue Terrier, Lakeland Terrier, Manchester Terrier (standard), Miniature Bull Terrier, Miniature Schnauzer, Norfolk Terrier, Norwich Terrier, Parson Russell Terrier, Rat Terrier, Russell Terrier, Scottish Terrier, Sealyham Terrier, Skye Terrier, Smooth Fox Terrier, Soft Coated Wheaten Terrier, Staffordshire Bull Terrier, Welsh Terrier, West Highland White Terrier, Wire Fox Terrier.

Toy Group: Affenpinscher, Brussels Griffon, Cavalier King Charles Spaniel, Chihuahua, Chinese Crested, English Toy Spaniel, Havanese, Italian Greyhound, Japanese Chin, Maltese, Manchester Terrier (toy), Miniature Pinscher, Papillon, Pekingese, Pomeranian, Poodle (toy), Pug, Shih Tzu, Silky Terrier, Toy Fox Terrier, Yorkshire Terrier.

Working Group: Akita, Alaskan Malamute, Anatolian Shepherd Dog, Bernese Mountain Dog, Black Russian Terrier, Boerboel, Boxer, Bullmastiff, Cane Corso, Chinook, Doberman Pinscher, Dogue de Bordeaux, German Pinscher, Giant Schnauzer, Great Dane, Great Pyrenees, Greater Swiss Mountain Dog, Komondor, Kuvasz, Leonberger, Mastiff, Neapolitan Mastiff, Newfoundland, Portuguese Water Dog, Rottweiler, Saint Bernard, Samoyed, Siberian Husky, Standard Schnauzer, Tibetan Mastiff.

Discoveries and Innovations: Biology, Chemistry, Medicine, Physics

Discovery	Date	Discoverer(s)	Nationality
Acetylene gas	1862	Berthelot	French
ACTH	1927	Evans, Long	U.S.
Adrenaline	1901	Takamine	Japanese
Aluminum, electrolytic process	1886	Hall	U.S.
Aluminum, isolated	1825	Oersted	Danish
Anesthesia, ether	1842	Long	U.S.
Anesthesia, local	1885	Koller	Austrian
Anesthesia, spinal	1898	Bier	German
Aniline dye	1856	Perkin	English
Anti-rabies	1885	Pasteur	French
Antiseptic surgery	1867	Lister	English
Antitoxin, diphtheria	1891	Von Behring	German
Argyrol	1897	Bayer	German
Arsphenamine	1910	Ehrlich	German
Aspirin	1853	Gerhardt	French
Atabrine	1932	Mietzsch, et al.	German
Atomic numbers	1913	Moseley	English
Atomic theory	1803	Dalton	English
Atomic time clock	1948	Lyons	U.S.
Atom-smashing theory	1919	Rutherford	English
Bacitracin	1943	Johnson, Meleneyl	U.S.
Bacteria, description	1676	Leeuwenhoek	Dutch
Bacterial genome, synthetic	2010	Venter	U.S.
Bleaching powder	1798	Tennant	English
Blood, circulation	1628	Harvey	English
Bordeaux mixture	1885	Millardet	French
Bromine from the sea	1826	Balard	French
Calcium carbide	1888	Wilson	U.S.
Calculus	1670	Newton	English
Camphor synthetic	1896	Haller	French
Canning (food)	1804	Appert	French
Carbon oxides	1925	Fisher	German
Chemotherapy	1909	Ehrlich	German
Chloamphenicol	1947	Burkholder	U.S.
Chlorine	1774	Scheele	Swedish
Chloroform	1831	Guthrie	U.S.
Chlortetracycline	1948	Duggen	U.S.
Classification of plants and animals	1735	Linnaeus	Swedish
Cloning, DNA	1973	Boyer, Cohen	U.S.
Cloning, mammal	1996	Wilmut, et al.	Scottish
Cocaine	1860	Niermann	German
Combustion explained	1777	Lavoisier	French
Conditioned reflex	1914	Pavlov	Russian
Cortisone	1936	Kendall	U.S.
Cortisone, synthesis	1946	Sarett	U.S.
Cosmic rays	1910	Gockel	Swiss
Cyclotron	1930	Lawrence	U.S.
DDT (not applied as insecticide until 1939)	1874	Zeidler	German
Denisovan humans (DNA analysis)	2010	Krause, et al. / Pääbo	German / Swedish
Deuterium	1932	Urey, Brickwedde, Murphy	U.S.
DNA (structure)	1953	Crick, Wilkins / Watson	English / U.S.
Electric resistance, law of	1827	Ohm	German
Electric waves	1888	Hertz	German
Electrolysis	1852	Faraday	English
Electromagnetism	1819	Oersted	Danish
Electron	1897	Thomson, J.	English
Electron diffraction	1936	Thomson, G. / Davisson	English / U.S.
Electroshock treatment	1938	Cerletti, Bini	Italian
Erythromycin	1952	McGuire	U.S.
Evolution, natural selection	1858	Darwin	English
Falling bodies, law of	1590	Galileo	Italian
Gases, law of combining volumes	1808	Gay-Lussac	French
Geometry, analytic	1619	Descartes	French
Gold, cyanide process for extraction	1887	MacArthur, R.Forrest, W. Forrest	Scottish
Gravitation, law	1687	Newton	English
Gravitational waves (detection)	2015	LIGO	U.S.-Intl.
Higgs boson	2012	CERN	International
HIV (human immunodeficiency virus)	1984	Montagnier / Gallo	French / U.S.
Holograph	1948	Gabor	Hung.-British
Homo floresiensis ("hobbit" humans)	2003	Morwood, et al.	New Zea.
Human genome sequence (first draft)	2001	Human Genome Project, Celera Genomics Corp.	U.S.-Intl.
Human heart transplant	1967	Barnard	S. African
In vitro fertilization	1978	Steptoe, Edwards	English
Indigo, synthesis of	1880	Baeyer	German
Induction, electric	1830	Henry	U.S.
Insulin	1922	Banting, Best / Macleod	Canadian / Scottish
Intelligence testing	1905	Binet, Simon	French
Isotopes, theory	1912	Soddy	English
Laser	1957	Gould	U.S.

Discovery	Date	Discoverer(s)	Nationality
Light, velocity	1675	Roemer	Danish
Light, wave theory	1690	Huygens	Dutch
Lithography	1796	Senefelder	Bohemian
Logarithms	1614	Napier	Scottish
LSD-25	1943	Hoffman	Swiss
Mendelian laws	1866	Mendel	Austrian
Mercator projection (map)	1568	Mercator (Kremer)	Flemish
Methanol	1661	Boyle	Irish
Milk condensation	1853	Borden	U.S.
Molecular hypothesis	1811	Avogadro	Italian
Motion, laws of	1687	Newton	English
Neomycin	1949	Waksman, Lechevalier	U.S.
Neutrino	1956	Reines, Cowan	U.S.
Neutron	1932	Chadwick	English
Nitric acid	1648	Glauber	German
Nitric oxide	1772	Priestley	English
Nitroglycerin	1846	Sobrero	Italian
Oil cracking process	1891	Dewar	U.S.
Oxygen	1774	Priestley	English
Oxytetracycline	1950	Finlay, et al.	U.S.
Ozone	1840	Schonbein	German
Paper, sulfite process	1867	Tilghman	U.S.
Paper, wood pulp, sulfate process	1884	Dahl	German
Penicillin	1928	Fleming	Scottish
Penicillin, practical use	1941	Florey, Chain	English
Periodic law and table of elements	1869	Mendeleyev	Russian
Physostigmine synthesis	1935	Julian	U.S.
Pill, birth-control	1954	Pincus, Rock	U.S.
Planetary motion, laws	1609	Kepler	German
Plutonium fission	1940	Kennedy, Wahl, Seaborg, Segre	U.S.
Polymyxin	1947	Ainsworth	English
Positron	1932	Anderson	U.S.
Proton	1919	Rutherford	New Zea.
Psychoanalysis	1900	Freud	Austrian
Pulsars	1967	Bell	English
Quantum theory	1900	Planck	German
Quasars	1963	Matthews, Sandage	U.S.
Quinine synthetic	1946	Woodward, Doering	U.S.
Radioactivity	1896	Becquerel	French
Radiocarbon dating	1947	Libby	U.S.
Radium	1898	Curie, Pierre	French
		Curie, Marie	Pol.-Fr.
Relativity theory	1905	Einstein	German
Reserpine	1949	Jal Vakil	Indian
Schick test	1913	Schick	U.S.
Silicon	1823	Berzelius	Swedish
Smallpox eradication	1979	World Health Org.	UN
Streptomycin	1944	Waksman, et al.	U.S.
Sulfanilamide	1935	Bovet, Trefouel	French
Sulfanilamide theory	1908	Gelmo	German
Sulfapyridine	1938	Ewins, Phelps	English
Sulfathiazole	1939	Fosbinder, Walter	U.S.
Sulfuric acid	1831	Phillips	English
Sulfuric acid, lead	1746	Roebuck	English
Superconductivity	1911	Onnes	Dutch
Superconductivity theory	1957	Bardeen, Cooper, Schreiffer	U.S.
Superconductors, high-temp.	1986	Bednorz, Muller	Ger., Swiss
Syphilis test	1906	Wassermann	German
Transplant, heart	1967	Barnard	S. African
Tuberculin	1890	Koch	German
Uranium fission, atomic reactor	1942	Fermi, Szilard	U.S.
Uranium fission theory	1939	Hahn, Meitner, Strassmann	German
		Bohr	Danish
		Fermi	Italian
		Einstein, Pegram, Wheeler	U.S.
Vaccine, measles	1963	Enders	U.S.
Vaccine, MMR	1971	Hilleman	U.S.
Vaccine, meningitis (first conjugate)	1987	Gordon, et al., Connaught Labs	U.S.
Vaccine, polio	1954	Salk	U.S.
Vaccine, polio, oral	1960	Sabin	U.S.
Vaccine, rabies	1885	Pasteur	French
Vaccine, smallpox	1796	Jenner	English
Vaccine, typhus	1909	Nicolle	French
Vaccine, varicella	1974	Takahashi	Japanese
Van Allen belts, radiation	1958	Van Allen	U.S.
Vitamin A	1913	McCollum, Davis	U.S.
Vitamin B	1916	McCollum	U.S.
Vitamin C	1928	Szent-Gyorgyi	Hungarian
		King	U.S.
Vitamin D	1922	McCollum	U.S.
Xerography	1938	Carlson	U.S.
X-ray	1895	Roentgen	German

Inventions

Invention	Date	Inventor(s)	Nationality
Adding machine	1642	Pascal	French
Adding machine	1885	Burroughs	U.S.
Aerosol spray	1926	Rotheim	Norwegian
Air brake	1868	Westinghouse	U.S.
Air conditioning	1902	Carrier	U.S.
Air pump	1654	Guericke	German
Airbag	1952	Hetrick	U.S.
Airplane, automatic pilot	1912	Sperry	U.S.
Airplane, experimental	1896	Langley	U.S.
Airplane, hydro	1911	Curtiss	U.S.
Airplane jet engine	1939	Ohain	German
Airplane with motor	1903	Wright Bros.	U.S.
Airship	1852	Giffard	French
Aqua-Lung	1943	Cousteau, Gagnan	French
Arc welder	1919	Thomson	U.S.
Aspartame	1965	Schlatter	U.S.
Autogyro	1920	de la Cierva	Spanish
Automobile, diff. gear	1885	Benz	German
Automobile, electric	1892	Morrison	U.S.
Automobile, exp'mtl	1864	Marcus	Austrian
Automobile, gasoline	1889	Daimler	German
Automobile, gasoline	1892	Duryea	U.S.
Automobile magneto	1897	Bosch	German
Automobile muffler	1904	Pope	U.S.
Automobile self-starter	1911	Kettering	U.S.
Bakelite	1907	Baekeland	Belg., U.S.
Bar code	1952	Woodland, Silver	U.S.
Barometer	1643	Torricelli	Italian
Bicycle, modern	1885	Starley	English
Bifocal lens	1780	Franklin	U.S.
Bottle machine	1895	Owens	U.S.
Braille printing	1829	Braille	French
Brassiere, modern	1913	Jacob	U.S.
Bubble gum	1928	Diemer	U.S.
Burner, gas	1855	Bunsen	German
Calculating machine	1833	Babbage	English
Calculator, electronic pocket	1972	Merryman, Van Tassel	U.S.
Camera, digital	1977	Lloyd, Sasson	U.S.
Camera, Kodak	1888	Eastman, Walker	U.S.
Camera, Polaroid Land	1948	Land	U.S.
Can, pop-top	1959	Fraze	U.S.
Car coupler	1873	Janney	U.S.
Carburetor, gasoline	1893	Maybach	German
Carding machine	1797	Whittemore	U.S.
Carpet sweeper	1876	Bissell	U.S.
Cash register	1879	Ritty	U.S.
Cassette, audio	1963	Philips Co.	Dutch
Cassette, videotape	1969	Sony	Japanese
CAT, or CT, scan	1973	Hounsfield	English
Cathode-ray tube	1897	Braun	German
Cellophane	1908	Brandenberger	Swiss
Celluloid	1870	Hyatt	U.S.
Cement, Portland	1824	Aspdin	English
Chronometer	1735	Harrison	English
Circuit breaker	1925	Hilliard	U.S.
Circuit, integrated	1959	Kilby, Noyce, Texas Instr.	U.S.
Clock, pendulum	1657	Huygens	Dutch
Coaxial cable system	1929	Affel, Espensched.	U.S.
Coca-Cola	1885	Pemberton	U.S.
Coffeemaker, auto. drip	1963	Bunn Corp.	U.S.
Compressed air rock drill	1871	Ingersoll	U.S.
Comptometer	1887	Felt	U.S.
Computer, automatic sequence	1944	Aiken, et al.	U.S.
Computer, electronic	1942	Atanasoff, Berry	U.S.
Computer, laptop	1987	Sinclair	English
Computer, mini	1960	Digital Corp.	U.S.
Condenser microphone (telephone)	1916	Wente	U.S.
Contact lens, corneal	1948	Tuohy	U.S.
Contraceptive, oral	1954	Pincus, Rock	U.S.
Corn, hybrid	1917	Jones	U.S.
Cotton gin	1793	Whitney	U.S.
Cream separator	1878	DeLaval	Swedish
Cultivator, disc	1878	Mallon	U.S.
Cyclotron	1931	Lawrence	U.S.
Cystoscope	1878	Nitze	German
Diapers, disposable	1950	Donovan	U.S.
Diesel engine	1895	Diesel	German
Disc, compact	1972	RCA	U.S.

Invention	Date	Inventor(s)	Nationality
Disc player, compact	1979	Sony, Philips Co.	Japanese, Dutch
Dishwasher	1893	Cochrane	U.S.
Disk, floppy	1970	IBM	U.S.
Disk, video	1972	Philips Co.	Dutch
Dynamite	1866	Nobel	Swedish
Dynamo, contin. current	1871	Gramme	Belgian
Electric battery	1800	Volta	Italian
Electric fan	1882	Wheeler	U.S.
Electrocardiograph	1903	Einthoven	Dutch
Electroencephalograph	1929	Berger	German
Electromagnet	1824	Sturgeon	English
Electron microscope	1931	Ruska, Knoll	German
Electron spectrometer	1944	Deutsch, Elliott, Evans	U.S.
Electron tube multigrid	1913	Langmuir	U.S.
Electronic paper (e-ink)	1974	Sheridon	U.S.
Electroplating	1805	Brugnatelli	Italian
Electrostatic generator	1929	Van de Graaff	U.S.
Elevator brake	1852	Otis	U.S.
Elevator, push button	1922	Larson	U.S.
Engine, automatic transmission	1910	Fottinger	German
Engine, coal-gas 4-cycle	1876	Otto	German
Engine, compression ignition	1883	Daimler	German
Engine, electric ignition	1883	Benz	German
Engine, gas, compound	1926	Eickemeyer	U.S.
Engine, gasoline	1872	Brayton	U.S.
Engine, gasoline	1889	Daimler	German
Engine, jet	1930	Whittle	English
Engine, steam, piston	1705	Newcomen	English
Engine, steam, piston	1769	Watt	Scottish
Engraving, half-tone	1852	Talbot	U.S.
Ferris wheel	1893	Ferris	U.S.
Fiber optic wire	1970	Keck, Maurer, Schultz	U.S.
Fiber optics	1955	Kapany	English
Fiberglass	1938	Owens-Corning	U.S.
Filament, tungsten	1913	Coolidge	U.S.
Flanged rail	1831	Stevens	U.S.
Flatiron, electric	1882	Seely	U.S.
Food, frozen	1923	Birdseye	U.S.
Freon	1930	Midgley, et al.	U.S.
Furnace (for steel)	1858	Siemens	German
Galvanometer	1820	Sweigger	German
Garbage bag, polyethylene	1950	Wasylyk	Canadian
Gas discharge tube	1922	Hull	U.S.
Gas lighting	1792	Murdoch	Scottish
Gas mantle	1885	Welsbach	Austrian
Gasoline, cracked	1913	Burton	U.S.
Gasoline, high octane	1930	Ipatieff	Russian
Gasoline (lead ethyl)	1922	Midgley	U.S.
Geiger counter	1913	Geiger	German
Geodesic dome	1948	Fuller	U.S.
Glass, laminated safety	1909	Benedictus	French
Glider	1853	Cayley	English
Google search software	1996	Brin, Page	U.S.
Gun, breechloader	1811	Thornton	U.S.
Gun, Browning	1897	Browning	U.S.
Gun, magazine	1875	Hotchkiss	U.S.
Gun, silencer	1908	Maxim, H. P.	U.S.
Guncotton	1847	Schoenbein	German
Gyrocompass	1911	Sperry	U.S.
Gyroscope	1852	Foucault	French
Hard drive, computer	1955	Johnson	U.S.
Harvester-thresher	1818	Lane	U.S.
Heart, artificial	1982	Jarvik	U.S.
Helicopter	1939	Sikorsky	U.S.
Hovercraft	1955	Cockerell	English
Hydrometer	1768	Baume	French
Ice resurfacing machine	1949	Zamboni	U.S.
Iron lung	1928	Drinker, Slaw	U.S.
Jet Ski	1973	Jacobsen	U.S.
Kaleidoscope	1817	Brewster	Scottish
Kevlar	1965	Kwolek, Blades	U.S.
Kidney dialysis machine	1941	Kolff	Dutch
Kinetoscope	1889	Edison	U.S.
Lamp, arc	1847	Staite	English
Lamp, fluorescent	1938	General Electric, Westinghouse	U.S.
Lamp, incandescent	1879	Edison	U.S.
Lamp, incand., gas	1913	Langmuir	U.S.
Lamp, klieg	1911	Kliegl, A. and J.	U.S.
Lamp, mercury vapor	1912	Hewitt	U.S.
Lamp, miner's safety	1816	Davy	English
Lamp, neon	1909	Claude	French
Lathe, turret	1845	Fitch	U.S.
Launderette	1934	Cantrell	U.S.
Lens, achromatic	1758	Dollond	English
Lens, fused bifocal	1908	Borsch	U.S.
Leyden jar (condenser)	1745	von Kleist	German
Lightning rod	1752	Franklin	U.S.
Linoleum	1860	Walton	English
Linotype	1884	Mergenthaler	U.S.
Linux	1991	Torvalds	Finnish
Liquid Paper	c.1951	Graham	U.S.
Lock, cylinder	1851	Yale	U.S.
Locomotive, electric	1851	Vail	U.S.
Locomotive, exp'mtl	1802	Trevithick	English
Locomotive, exp'mtl	1812	Fenton, et al.	English
Locomotive, exp'mtl	1814	Stephenson	English
Locomotive, 1st U.S.	1830	Cooper	U.S.
Locomotive, practical	1829	Stephenson	English
Loom, power	1785	Cartwright	English
Loudspeaker, dynamic	1924	Rice, Kellogg	U.S.
Machine gun	1862	Gatling	U.S.
Machine gun, improved	1872	Hotchkiss	U.S.
Machine gun (Maxim)	1883	Maxim, H. S.	U.S.-Eng.
Magnet, electro	1828	Henry	U.S.
Magnetic Resonance Imaging (MRI)	1971	Damadian	U.S.
Maser	1953	Townes	U.S.
Mason jar	1858	Mason	U.S.
Match, friction	1827	Walker	English
Mercerized textiles	1843	Mercer	English
Meter, induction	1888	Shallenberger	U.S.
Metronome	1816	Malezel	German
Microcomputer	1973	Truong, et al.	French
Micrometer	1636	Gascoigne	English
Microphone	1877	Berliner	U.S.
Microprocessor	1971	Intel Corp.	U.S.
Microscope, compound	1590	Janssen	Dutch
Microscope, electronic	1931	Knoll, Ruska	German
Microscope, field ion	1951	Mueller	German
Microwave oven	1947	Spencer	U.S.
Monitor, warship	1861	Ericsson	U.S.
Monotype	1887	Lanston	U.S.
Motor, AC	1892	Tesla	U.S.
Motor, DC	1837	Davenport	U.S.
Motor, induction	1887	Tesla	U.S.
Motorcycle	1885	Daimler	German
Mouse, computer	1968	Engelbart	U.S.
Movie machine	1894	Jenkins	U.S.
Movie, panoramic	1952	Waller	U.S.
Movie, talking	1927	Warner Bros.	U.S.
Mower, lawn	1831	Budding, Ferrabee	English
Mowing machine	1822	Bailey	U.S.
Neoprene	1930	Carothers	U.S.
Nylon	1937	Carothers, DuPont	U.S.
Oil cracking furnace	1891	Gavrilov	Russian
Oil filled power cable	1921	Emanueli	Italian
Oleomargarine	1869	Mege-Mouries	French
Ophthalmoscope	1851	Helmholtz	German
Pacemaker	1952	Zoll	U.S.
Pacemaker, implantable cardiac	1958	Greatbatch	U.S.
Paper	105	Ts'ai	Chinese
Paper clip	1900	Waaler	Norwegian
Paper machine	1809	Dickinson	U.S.
Parachute	1785	Blanchard	French
Pen, ballpoint	1888	Loud	U.S.
Pen, fountain	1884	Waterman	U.S.
Pen, steel	1780	Harrison	English
Pendulum	1583	Galileo	Italian
Percussion cap	1807	Forsythe	Scottish
Phonograph	1877	Edison	U.S.
Photo, color	1892	Ives	U.S.
Photo film, celluloid	1893	Reichenbach	U.S.
Photo film, transparent	1884	Eastman, Goodwin	U.S.
Photocopier	1938	Carlson	U.S.
Photoelectric cell	1895	Elster	German
Photographic paper	1835	Talbot	English
Photography	1816	Niepce	French
Photography	1835	Daguerre	French
Photography	1835	Talbot	English
Photophone	1880	Bell	U.S.-Scot.
Phototelegraphy	1925	Bell Labs	U.S.
Piano	1709	Cristofori	Italian
Piano, player	1863	Fourneaux	French

Invention	Date	Inventor(s)	Nationality
Pin, safety	1849	Hunt	U.S.
Pistol (revolver)	1836	Colt	U.S.
Plow, cast iron	1785	Ransome	English
Plow, disc	1896	Hardy	U.S.
Pneumatic hammer	1890	King	U.S.
Post-it note	1980	Fry, Silver	U.S.
Potato chip	1853	Crum	U.S.
Powder, smokeless	1884	Vieille	French
Printing press, rotary	1845	Hoe	U.S.
Printing press, web	1865	Bullock	U.S.
Propeller, screw	1804	Stevens	U.S.
Propeller, screw	1837	Ericsson	Swedish
Punch card accounting	1889	Hollerith	U.S.
Radar	1940	Watson-Watt	Scottish
Radio amplifier	1906	De Forest	U.S.
Radio beacon	1928	Donovan	U.S.
Radio crystal oscillator	1918	Nicolson	U.S.
Radio FM, 2-path	1933	Armstrong	U.S.
Radio, magnetic detector	1902	Marconi	Italian
Radio receiver, cascade tuning	1913	Alexanderson	U.S.
Radio receiver, heterodyne	1913	Fessenden	Canadian
Radio, signals	1895	Marconi	Italian
Radio transmitter triode modulation	1914	Alexanderson	U.S.
Radio tube diode	1904	Fleming	English
Radio tube oscillator	1915	De Forest	U.S.
Radio tube triode	1906	De Forest	U.S.
Rayon (acetate)	1895	Cross	English
Rayon (cuprammonium)	1890	Despeissis	French
Rayon (nitrocellulose)	1884	Chardonnet	French
Razor, electric	1928	Schick	U.S.
Razor, safety	1895	Gillette	U.S.
Reaper	1834	McCormick	U.S.
Record, cylinder	1887	Bell, Tainter	U.S.
Record, disc	1887	Berliner	U.S.
Record, long playing	1947	Goldmark	U.S.
Record, wax cylinder	1888	Edison	U.S.
Refrigerator car	1868	David	U.S.
Remote control	1898	Tesla	U.S.
Resin, synthetic	1931	Hill	English
Richter scale	1935	Richter	U.S.
Rifle, repeating	1860	Henry	U.S.
Rocket, liquid fuel	1926	Goddard	U.S.
Rollerblades	1980	Olson	U.S.
Rubber, vulcanized	1839	Goodyear	U.S.
Saccharin	1879	Remsen, Fahlberg	U.S.
Saw, circular	1777	Miller	English
Scotch tape	1930	Drew	U.S.
Seat belt	1959	Volvo	Swedish
Segway human transporter	2001	Kamen	U.S.
Seismograph	1880	Milne, Ewing, Gray	Eng.-Scot.
Sewing machine	1790	Saint	English
Shoe-lasting machine	1883	Matzeliger	U.S.
Shoe-sewing machine	1860	McKay	U.S.
Shrapnel shell	1784	Shrapnel	English
Shuttle, flying	1733	Kay	English
Skates, in-line	1759	Merlin	Belgian
Sleeping-car	1865	Pullman	U.S.
Slide rule	1620	Oughtred	English
Slinky	1943	James	U.S.
Smoke detector	1969	Smith, House	U.S.
Soap, hardwater	1928	Bertsch	German
Spectroscope	1859	Kirchoff, Bunsen	German
Spectroscope (mass)	1918	Dempster	U.S.
Spinning jenny	c.1764	Hargreaves	English
Spinning mule	1779	Crompton	English
Steam car	1770	Cugnot	French
Steam turbine	1884	Parsons	English
Steamboat, exp'mtl	1778	Jouffroy	French
Steamboat, exp'mtl	1785	Fitch	U.S.
Steamboat, exp'mtl	1787	Rumsey	U.S.
Steamboat, exp'mtl	1803	Fulton	U.S.
Steamboat, exp'mtl	1804	Stevens	U.S.
Steamboat, practical	1802	Symington	Scottish
Steamboat, practical	1807	Fulton	U.S.
Steel alloy, high-speed	1901	Taylor, White	U.S.
Steel (converter)	1856	Bessemer	English
Steel, manganese	1884	Hadfield	English
Steel, stainless	1916	Brearley	English

Invention	Date	Inventor(s)	Nationality
Stereoscope	1838	Wheatstone	English
Stethoscope	1819	Laennec	French
Stethoscope, binaural	1840	Cammann	U.S.
Stock ticker	1870	Edison	U.S.
Storage battery, rechargeable	1859	Plante	French
Stove, electric	1896	Hadaway	U.S.
Submarine	1891	Holland	U.S.
Submarine, even keel	1894	Lake	U.S.
Submarine, torpedo	1776	Bushnell	U.S.
Synthesizer	1964	Moog	U.S.
Tank, military	1914	Swinton	English
Tape recorder, magnetic	1899	Poulsen	Danish
Taser	1974	Cover	U.S.
Teflon	1938	Du Pont	U.S.
Telegraph, magnetic	1837	Morse	U.S.
Telegraph, quadruplex	1864	Edison	U.S.
Telegraph, railroad	1887	Woods	U.S.
Telegraph, wireless high frequency	1895	Marconi	Italian
Telephone[1]	1871	Meucci	U.S.-Italian
Telephone[1]	1876	Bell	U.S.-Scot.
Telephone amplifier	1912	De Forest	U.S.
Telephone answering machine (1st practical)	1954	Hashimoto	Japanese
Telephone, automatic	1891	Strowger	U.S.
Telephone, cellular	1947	Bell Labs	U.S.
Telephone, cordless[2]	1950	Gross	U.S.
Telephone, radio	1900	Poulsen	Danish
		Fessenden	Canadian
Telephone, radio	1906	De Forest	U.S.
Telephone, radio, long distance	1915	AT&T	U.S.
Telephone, recording	1898	Poulsen	Danish
Telescope	1608	Lippershey	Dutch
Telescope	1609	Galileo	Italian
Telescope, astronomical	1611	Kepler	German
Telescope, reflecting	1668	Newton	English
Teletype	1928	Morkrum, Kleinschmidt	U.S.
Television, color	1928	Baird	Scottish
Television, electronic	1927	Farnsworth	U.S.
Television, iconoscope	1923	Zworykin	U.S.
Television, mech. scanner	1923	Baird	Scottish
Tesla Coil	1891	Tesla	U.S.
Thermometer	1593	Galileo	Italian
Thermometer	1730	Reaumur	French
Thermometer, mercury	1714	Fahrenheit	German
3D printing (stereolithography)	1984	Hull	U.S.
Time recorder	1890	Bundy	U.S.
Tire, double-tube	1845	Thomson	Scottish
Tire, pneumatic	1888	Dunlop	Scottish
Toaster, automatic	1918	Strite	U.S.
Toilet, flush	1589	Harington	English
Torpedo, marine	1804	Fulton	U.S.
Tractor, crawler	1904	Holt	U.S.
Transformer, AC	1885	Stanley	U.S.
Transistor	1947	Shockley, Brattain, Bardeen	U.S.
Trolley car, electric	1884-87	Van DePoele, Sprague	U.S.
Tungsten, ductile	1912	Coolidge	U.S.
Tupperware®	1945	Tupper	U.S.
Turbine, gas	1849	Bourdin	French
Turbine, hydraulic	1849	Francis	U.S.
Turbine, steam	1884	Parsons	English
Type, movable	1447	Gutenberg	German
Typewriter	1867	Sholes, Soule, Glidden	U.S.
Universal Serial Bus (USB)	1994	Bhatt, et al.	U.S.
Vacuum cleaner, electric	1907	Spangler	U.S.
Vacuum evaporating pan	1846	Rillieux	U.S.
Velcro	1948	de Mestral	Swiss
Video game ("Pong")	1972	Bushnell	U.S.
Video home system (VHS)	1975	Matsushita, JVC	Japanese
Vinyl	1926	Semon	U.S.
Washer, electric	1901	Fisher	U.S.

Invention	Date	Inventor(s)	Nationality
Welding, atomic hydrogen	1924	Langmuir, Palmer	U.S.
Welding, electric	1877	Thomson	U.S.
Wheelchair, multiterrain	1986	Twitchell	U.S.
Wheelchair, stair-climbing	1962	Blanco	U.S.
Wiki software	1995	Cunningham	U.S.
Wind tunnel	1912	Eiffel	French
Windshield wiper	1903	Anderson	U.S.
Wire, barbed	1874	Glidden	U.S.
World Wide Web	1989	Berners-Lee	English
Wrench, double-acting	1913	Owen	U.S.
X-ray tube	1913	Coolidge	U.S.
Zeppelin	1900	Zeppelin	German
Zipper, early model	1893	Judson	U.S.
Zipper, improved	1913	Sundback	Canadian

(1) While Alexander Graham Bell has traditionally been credited with invention of the telephone, which he patented, Antonio Meucci developed a working model before Bell. (2) Al Gross held a number of important early patents in the field of wireless communication; other people were also involved in the development of practical cordless telephones.

Corporations Receiving U.S. Patents, 2015

Source: U.S. Patent and Trademark Office, U.S. Dept. of Commerce
(ranked by number of U.S. utility patents, or patents for inventions, granted)

Rank	Company	No. of patents
1.	International Business Machines Corp.	7,309
2.	Samsung Electronics Co., Ltd.	5,059
3.	Canon Kabushiki Kaisha	4,127
4.	Qualcomm, Inc.	2,900
5.	Google, Inc.	2,835
6.	Toshiba Corp.	2,582
7.	Sony Corp.	2,448
8.	LG Electronics Inc.	2,241
9.	Intel Corp.	2,046
10.	Microsoft Technology Licensing, LLC	1,955
11.	Apple, Inc.	1,937
12.	Samsung Display Co., Ltd.	1,825
13.	Taiwan Semiconductor Manufacturing Co., Ltd.	1,758
14.	General Electric Co.	1,756
15.	Ricoh Co., Ltd.	1,618
	Seiko Epson Corp.	1,618
17.	Panasonic Intellectual Property Management Co., Ltd.	1,474
18.	Toyota Jidosha K.K.	1,463
19.	Fujitsu Limited	1,455
20.	Telefonaktiebolaget LM Ericsson (Publ.)	1,406
21.	GM Global Technology Operations LLC	1,309
22.	Hewlett-Packard Development Co.	1,304
23.	Brother Kogyo Kabushiki Kaisha	1,187
24.	Ford Global Technologies, LLC	1,184
25.	Amazon Technologies, Inc.	1,136

Note: Reflects patent ownership at time of patent granting. Changes may occur after patent is granted. Where more than one assignee exists, patents are attributed to first-named assignee.

U.S. Patents by Country, 2015

Source: U.S. Patent and Trademark Office, U.S. Dept. of Commerce
(ranked by number of U.S. utility patents, or patents for inventions, granted)

Rank	Country	Patents	% change 2014-15	% share of total issued	Rank	Country	Patents	% change 2014-15	% share of total issued
1.	Japan	52,409	−2.7%	17.6%	7.	France	6,565	−1.9%	2.2%
2.	South Korea	17,924	8.8	6.0	8.	UK	6,417	−1.1	2.2
3.	Germany	16,549	0.0	5.5	9.	Israel	3,628	4.5	1.2
4.	Taiwan	11,690	3.2	3.9	10.	India	3,355	12.3	1.1
5.	China	8,116	12.2	2.7		United States	140,969	−2.5	47.2
6.	Canada	6,802	−3.4	2.3		All countries	298,407	−0.8	100.0

Note: Country of origin is determined by residence of first-named inventor in patent.

U.S. Patents by Category, 1977-2015

Source: U.S. Patent and Trademark Office, U.S. Dept. of Commerce
(ranked by number of utility patents, or patents for inventions, issued in 2015)

Rank	Category	1977-94	1995	2004	2014	2015	% change 1995-2015
1.	Active solid-state devices (e.g., transistors, solid-state diodes)	10,336	1,368	4,699	9,991	12,014	778.2%
2.	Multiplex communications	5,459	872	2,924	11,409	11,027	1,164.6
3.	Telecommunications	4,279	586	2,173	8,296	7,902	1,248.5
4.	Computer graphics processing and selective visual display systems	5,133	761	2,173	6,682	7,638	903.7
5.	Drug, bio-affecting and body treating compositions (class 514)	33,435	2,521	2,972	6,565	6,669	164.5
6.	Electrical computers and digital processing systems: multicomputer data transferring	683	163	1,605	7,040	6,358	3,800.6
7.	Television	10,605	940	1,280	5,191	6,062	544.9
8.	Drug, bio-affecting and body treating compositions (class 424)	12,657	1,368	2,203	5,549	6,043	341.7
9.	Data processing: database and file management or data structures	730	237	1,326	5,728	5,512	2,225.7
10.	Data processing: vehicles, navigation, and relative location	3,331	413	1,213	4,735	5,311	1,186.0
11.	Semiconductor device manufacturing: process	9,542	1,484	5,126	6,221	4,970	234.9
12.	Image analysis	3,722	407	1,794	4,980	4,675	1,048.6
13.	Pulse or digital communications	5,006	718	1,679	4,647	4,652	547.9
14.	Information security	114	20	224	4,004	4,365	21,725.0
15.	Chemistry: molecular biology and microbiology	12,478	1,498	2,672	4,335	4,066	171.4
16.	Surgery (class 606)	5,890	881	1,128	3,414	3,738	324.3
17.	Surgery (class 600)	9,711	1,091	1,581	3,764	3,605	230.4
18.	Electrical computers and digital processing systems: memory	2,372	409	1,337	2,838	3,171	675.3
19.	Electricity: electrical systems and devices	9,538	855	1,856	2,940	3,101	262.7
20.	Electrical computers and digital processing systems: support	938	241	831	3,355	3,045	1,163.5

TECHNOLOGY

Computer Milestones

1623: German mathematician Wilhelm Schickard developed the first mechanical calculator, capable of adding, subtracting, multiplying, and dividing.

1642: French mathematician Blaise Pascal built the first of more than four dozen copies of an adding and subtracting machine that he invented.

1801: French inventor Joseph Marie Jacquard demonstrated a new control system for looms. He "programmed" the loom, communicating desired weaving operations to the machine via patterns of holes in paper cards.

1833-71: British mathematician and scientist Charles Babbage used the Jacquard punch-card system in his design for a sophisticated, programmable "Analytical Engine" that foreshadowed basic features of today's computers. Babbage's concept was beyond the capabilities of the technology of his time, and the machine remained unfinished at his death in 1871.

1889: American engineer Herman Hollerith patented an electromechanical punch-card tabulating system that facilitated the handling of large amounts of statistical data and quickly found use in censuses in the U.S. and other countries.

1911: Hollerith's Tabulating Machine Company merged with two other enterprises to form the Computing-Tabulating-Recording Company, which was renamed the International Business Machines Corporation (IBM) in 1924.

1941: German engineer Konrad Züse completed the Z3, the first fully functional digital computer to be controlled by a program; the Z3 was not electronic—it was based on electrical switches called relays.

1942: Iowa State Coll. physicist John Vincent Atanasoff and assistant Clifford Berry completed a working model of the first fully electronic computer using vacuum tubes, which could operate much more quickly than relays; the rudimentary machine was not programmable.

1943: IBM and Harvard professor Howard Aiken completed the first large-scale automatic digital computer, the Mark I, a relay-based machine 55 ft long and 8 ft high. British scientists built the Colossus, an electronic computer for breaking German codes during World War II.

1946: ENIAC (Electronic Numerical Integrator and Computer), a 30-ton room-sized electronic computer with more than 18,000 vacuum tubes, was completed by physicist John Mauchly and engineer J. Presper Eckert at the Univ. of Pennsylvania for the U.S. Army. ENIAC could be programmed to do different tasks, but cables had to be plugged in, and switches had to be set by hand.

1951: Eckert and Mauchly's UNIVAC (Universal Automatic Computer) became the first commercially available computer in the U.S. The first customer was the Census Bureau. CBS-TV used a UNIVAC in 1952 to predict presidential election results.

1959: COBOL, a computer programming language designed for business use, first appeared, based on programming language innovations of American mathematician Grace Hopper.

1967: American computer pioneer Doug Engelbart applied for a patent on the mouse.

1969-71: The powerful Unix operating system was developed at Bell Laboratories; later versions became widely used on large computers and formed the basis for the Macintosh OS X operating system.

1971: Intel released the 4004, the first commercial microprocessor (an entire computer processing unit on a chip).

1973: The Alto computer, developed at Xerox's Palo Alto Research Center, became operational, implementing many features of modern commercial personal computers, including a graphical user interface (GUI) featuring windows, icons, and pointers that could be manipulated by a mouse.

1975: The first widely marketed personal computer (PC), the MITS Altair 8800, was introduced in kit form, with no keyboard, video display, or printer, for under $400. Microsoft was founded by Americans Bill Gates and Paul Allen.

1976: The first word-processing program for personal computers, Electric Pencil, was written. Apple Computer Company was founded by Americans Steven Jobs and Stephen Wozniak.

1977: Apple introduced the Apple II; capable of displaying text and graphics in color, the machine enjoyed phenomenal success.

1981: IBM unveiled its Personal Computer (IBM 5150), which used an operating system from Microsoft known as MS-DOS (Disk Operating System).

1984: Apple introduced the first Macintosh. The easy-to-use Macintosh came with a proprietary operating system and was the first popular computer to have a GUI and a mouse.

1990: Microsoft released Windows 3.0, the first workable version of its own GUI.

1991: The Unix-like Linux operating system was invented by Helsinki Univ. student Linus Torvalds and made available for free.

1996: The Palm Pilot, the first widely successful handheld computer and personal information manager, arrived.

1997: The IBM computer Deep Blue beat Russian world chess champion Garry Kasparov in a 6-game match, 2-1, with 3 draws.

2001: Apple introduced the Unix-based operating system OS X for the Macintosh.

2002: The total number of personal computers, including desktop and laptop machines of all types, shipped by manufacturers since 1975 reached 1 bil.

2006: Apple began using Intel microprocessors instead of the IBM PowerPC in its Macintosh computers.

2007: Amazon launched the Kindle, a hardware/software system for displaying books electronically; the product line later included tablet computers.

2008: Google released the Linux-based Android operating system for mobile devices.

2010: Apple released the iPad tablet computer and sold more than 3 mil devices in the first 80 days.

2012: Microsoft released Windows 8, featuring enhanced support for touchscreens and an interface with a grid of tiles displaying actively updated content and apps.

2015: Microsoft released Windows 10, promising faster startup and improved security, along with features like a personal digital assistant and a new web browser, Microsoft Edge.

2016: Univ. of Maryland scientists developed the first reprogrammable quantum computer; it used lasers to manipulate its five qubits, or bits of quantum information.

Nations With the Most Personal Computers in Use, 2015

Source: Computer Industry Almanac, year-end 2015

Rank	Nation	PCs in use (mil)	% of world total	Rank	Nation	PCs in use (mil)	% of world total
1.	U.S.	365.1	16.08%	10.	Italy	54.7	2.41%
2.	China	364.9	16.07	11.	South Korea	48.2	2.12
3.	India	117.9	5.19	12.	Mexico	42.3	1.86
4.	Japan	114.9	5.06	13.	Canada	36.0	1.58
5.	Russia	84.3	3.71	14.	Spain	32.9	1.45
6.	Germany	82.6	3.64	15.	Indonesia	23.7	1.04
7.	Brazil	67.7	2.98	**Top 15 countries**		**1,564.2**	**68.88**
8.	France	64.8	2.85	**World**		**2,271.0**	**100.00**
9.	United Kingdom	64.2	2.82				

World's Fastest Supercomputers, 2016
Source: Top500.org, as of midyear 2016

Rank	Name	Location	Manufacturer/ vendor	Processors (cores)	Top speed[1]
1.	Sunway TaihuLight	National Supercomputing Center, Wuxi, China.	NRCPC[2]	10,649,600	93.01
2.	Tianhe-2 (Milky Way-2)	National Supercomputing Center, Guangzhou, China.	NUDT[3]	3,120,000	33.86
3.	Titan	Oak Ridge National Laboratory, TN, U.S.	Cray	560,640	17.59
4.	Sequoia	Lawrence Livermore National Laboratory, CA, U.S.	IBM	1,572,864	17.17
5.	K Computer	RIKEN Advanced Institute for Computational Science, Japan	Fujitsu	705,024	10.51
6.	Mira.	Argonne National Laboratory, IL, U.S.	IBM	786,432	8.59
7.	Trinity	Los Alamos National Laboratory, NM, U.S.	Cray	301,056	8.10
8.	Piz Daint	Swiss National Supercomputing Centre, Switzerland.	Cray	115,984	6.27
9.	Hazel Hen.	Höchstleistungsrechenzentrum (HLRS), Germany	Cray	185,088	5.64
10.	Shaheen II	King Abdullah Univ. of Science and Technology, Saudi Arabia	Cray	196,608	5.54

Note: The 10 fastest supercomputers, and almost all of the 500 fastest supercomputers, use a version of the Linux operating system. (1) Top speed, in petaflops, achieved as measured according to the Linpack Benchmark. 1 petaflop = 1 quadrillion floating-point operations per sec. (2) NRCPC = National Research Center of Parallel Computer Engineering and Technology. (3) NUDT = National University of Defense Technology.

U.S. Sales of Selected Hardware, 2011-14
Source: Consumer Technology Association (fmr. Consumer Electronics Association)
(factory sales to dealers in thousands of units and millions of dollars)

Hardware	2011 Units	2011 Sales	2013 Units	2013 Sales	2014 Units	2014 Sales
Desktop computers[1]	10,655	$7,204	9,791	$6,539	9,705	$6,635
Notebooks and netbooks	27,383	15,417	24,619	15,202	25,573	16,403
Tablet PCs	31,900	15,937	77,405	26,476	76,457	24,551
E-readers	21,060	2,472	9,061	716	8,071	606
Smartphones	87,431	27,541	151,000	42,958	160,221	48,868
Electronic gaming hardware	NA	4,684	NA	3,091	NA	4,159
Digital video recorders (DVRs)	16,573	2,652	13,750	2,200	15,950	2,009
Digital cameras.	37,697	7,007	15,341	4,798	11,532	3,785
Digital camcorders	5,459	616	1,633	162	1,195	290
Portable media/MP3 players.	35,263	5,891	19,503	2,933	15,272	1,966
Smart watches	NA	NA	600	95	2,355	542
Wearable fitness technology[2]	3,200	240	10,267	921	16,800	1,508

NA = Not available. (1) Includes all-in-one computers. (2) Includes devices containing one or more of the following sensors: pedometer, accelerometer, altimeter/barometric pressure sensor, heart-rate monitor.

U.S. Household Penetration of Selected Technologies, 2009-15
Source: Consumer Technology Association (fmr. Consumer Electronics Association)
(% of all households for Jan. of year shown)

Product	2009	2010	2011	2012	2013	2014	2015
Smartphones	23%	33%	39%	46%	58%	64%	72%
Digital cameras.	77	80	79	74	73	66	64
Multifunction printers	62	66	66	68	65	63	63
Home network[1]	34	40	48	54	61	62	64
Home internet access.	78	78	78	78	78	78	78

Note: Based on sales data tracking and consumer surveys conducted by CEA/CTA. (1) Wired or wireless.

About the Internet

The internet is not owned or funded by any one institution, organization, or government. It has no CEO and is not a commercial service. Its development is guided by the Internet Society (ISOC), which is composed of volunteers. The ISOC appoints the Internet Architecture Board (IAB), which oversees issues of standards and network resources, among others.

Major Historical Highlights

1969: ARPANET, an experimental four-computer network, was established by the Advanced Research Projects Agency (ARPA) of the U.S. Defense Dept. Two years later, ARPANET linked about 23 computers ("hosts") at 15 sites, including MIT and Harvard.

1978: The first spam, or junk email, was sent over ARPANET.

1983: The set of communications rules (protocol) known as TCP/IP became the main networking protocol of ARPANET. Its adoption was tantamount to the birth of the internet. The military portion of ARPANET was moved onto MILNET.

1986: The U.S. National Science Foundation (NSF) launched NSFNET, the first large-scale network using internet technology.

1988: Internet Relay Chat (IRC) was developed by Finnish student Jarkko Oikarinen, enabling people to communicate via the internet in "real time."

1988: A "worm" crafted by Cornell Univ. computer science graduate student Robert Morris Jr. infected thousands of computers, shutting many down and causing millions of dollars of damage—the first known case of large-scale damage caused by a computer virus spread via the internet.

1989: Massachusetts-based The World—the first commercial internet service provider supplying dial-up access—debuted.

1989-90: English scientist Tim Berners-Lee invented the World Wide Web. Created as an environment in which scientists at the European Center for Nuclear Research in Switzerland could share information, it gradually evolved into a medium with text, graphics, audio, animation, and video.

1990: ARPANET was disbanded.

1991: NSFNET was opened to commercial traffic. Berners-Lee introduced the first browser, or software for accessing the web.

1993: The National Center for Supercomputing Applications (U.S.) released versions of Mosaic, the first web browser able to present both text and images on a single page.

1994: Netscape Communications released the Netscape Navigator browser.

1995: Microsoft released its Internet Explorer browser. It initially failed to make a dent in Netscape's dominance of the browser market, but Internet Explorer surpassed Netscape by 1999.

1996: A group of U.S. universities launched Internet2, an advanced, high-performance network for the research community and a test bed for development of new capabilities that might find use in the commercial internet.

1998: Under a contract with the U.S. Dept. of Commerce, the nonprofit Internet Corporation for Assigned Names and Numbers (ICANN) took over the management of assigning domain names and internet protocol (IP) addresses.

1999: Release of the free Napster file-sharing service enabled users to easily exchange files containing music or other content without regard to copyright restrictions.

2000: Estonia became the first country to pass a law declaring internet access a fundamental human right of its citizens.

2003: Niue, a self-governing Pacific island associated with New Zealand, became the first country to offer free nationwide wireless access to the internet, using Wi-Fi technology.

2004: The Mozilla Foundation released the first official version of the open-source browser Mozilla Firefox.

2008: Google introduced its Chrome browser. By 2012, Chrome ranked as the most widely used browser in the world, according to StatCounter.com.

2009: The U.S. relinquished direct control over ICANN.

2011: ICANN decided to allow the use of almost any characters in any language for the names of generic top-level domains.

2012: The number of Facebook users surpassed 1 bil.

2014: The number of internet hosts (websites) passed 1 bil.

2014: Estonia became the first country in the world to offer noncitizens "e-residency"—a government-issued transnational digital identity.

2016: The leak of more than 11.5 mil documents from Panamanian law firm Mossack Fonseca, which said it was the victim of a hack, exposed large-scale offshore tax evasion.

2016: A U.S. federal appeals court defined high-speed internet service as a utility, ruling that the Federal Communications Commission had the ability to require broadband providers to observe "net neutrality," under which all data is treated the same.

Internet Addresses

The fundamental part of an address on the internet is called the domain. The final part of a domain name, known as the **top-level domain (TLD)**, is its most basic part. For example, .com is the top-level domain of *The World Almanac*'s web address (www.worldalmanac.com). So-called generic top-level domains (gTLDs) consist of three or more letters. Domain names with two letters are generally for countries or regions. Country-code TLDs (ccTLDs) are usually managed by an organization within a certain country.

Safety and Security on the Internet

Common sense dictates some basic security rules:

- Pick passwords that are difficult to guess, preferably consisting of letters, numbers, and symbols, if permitted. Avoid using the same password for multiple websites. A password manager can generate passwords and then save them.

- Do not give out your phone number, address, credit card number, or other personal information unless needed for a transaction at a site you trust.

- If you feel someone is being threatening or dangerous, inform your internet service provider.

- Use protective firewall, antivirus, and antispyware software to guard your system against attacks by hackers.

- Be careful about opening email and file attachments from unknown correspondents.

- To avoid falling victim to the scam known as **phishing**—which uses a forged email message, purportedly from a respectable organization, to elicit personal data—do not click on hyperlinks in emails from companies with which you do business. Phishing emails typically contain a link leading to a fabricated website resembling the site of the ostensible sender. If you want to visit a company's website, open your browser and manually enter the site's address.

- Users of so-called **peer-to-peer** (P2P) file-sharing networks or protocols should open up only part of their computer system to sharing, not the entire hard drive.

- When manufacturers provide **patches** to solve security flaws or other problems with operating systems, web browsers, or other software, it is usually advisable to install these fixes. If a fix is not available for a serious security problem, consider switching to an alternative program.

Data Breaches and Information Exposure, 2011-15

Source: Symantec Global Intelligence Network

	2011	2012	2013	2014	2015
Total data breaches	211	156	253	312	305
Average number of identities exposed per breach (mil)	1.1	0.6	2.2	1.1	1.4
Total identities exposed (mil)	232	93	552	348	429

Percentage of breaches				**Percentage of breaches**			
Information type exposed in breach	2013	2014	2015	Information type exposed in breach	2013	2014	2015
Real names	72%	69%	78%	Financial information	18%	36%	33%
Home addresses	38	43	44	Email addresses	15	20	21
Birth dates	43	35	41	Phone numbers	19	21	19
Government ID numbers				Insurance	6	11	13
(e.g., Social Security)	40	45	38	User names and passwords	12	13	11
Medical records	34	34	36				

Note: Numbers are self-reported and are not necessarily inclusive of all data breaches.

Internet Crime Victims and Losses, 2015

Source: Internet Crime Complaint Center, Federal Bureau of Investigation

Rank	Type of crime	Victims	Rank	Type of crime	Loss amount
1.	Nonpayment/nondelivery	67,375	1.	Business email compromise	$246,226,016
2.	419/overpayment[1]	30,855	2.	Confidence fraud/romance	203,390,531
3.	Identity theft	21,949	3.	Nonpayment/nondelivery	121,329,122
4.	Auction	21,510	4.	Investment	119,177,899
5.	Other	19,963	5.	Identity theft	57,294,589
6.	Personal data breach	19,632	6.	Other	56,153,977
7.	Employment	18,758	7.	Advanced fee	50,721,226
8.	Extortion	17,804	8.	419/overpayment[1]	49,217,119
9.	Credit card fraud	17,172	9.	Personal data breach	43,477,526
10.	Phishing/vishing/smishing/pharming	16,594	10.	Credit card fraud	41,503,502

(1) In a "419," the perpetrator requests help transferring a substantial sum of money, offering a commission or share of the profits if the victim first sends money to pay for some transfer costs. In overpayment, the victim is sent a check to deposit and is instructed to wire a portion of the money to another party.

Nations With Highest Percentage of Population Using the Internet, 2000-15

Source: © International Telecommunication Union; ranked by 2015 figures

Rank	Nation	2000	2005	2009	2010	2011	2012	2013	2014	2015
1.	Iceland	44.47%	87.00%	93.00%	93.39%	94.82%	96.21%	96.55%	98.16%	98.20%
2.	Luxembourg	22.89	70.00	87.31	90.62	90.03	91.95	93.78	94.67	97.33
3.	Andorra	10.54	37.61	78.53	81.00	81.00	86.43	94.00	95.90	96.91
4.	Norway	52.00	81.99	92.08	93.39	93.49	94.65	95.05	96.30	96.81
5.	Liechtenstein	36.52	63.37	75.00	80.00	85.00	89.41	93.80	95.21	96.64
6.	Denmark	39.17	82.74	86.84	88.72	89.81	92.26	94.63	95.99	96.33
7.	Bahrain	6.15	21.30	53.00	55.00	77.00	88.00	90.00	90.50	93.48
8.	Monaco	42.18	55.46	70.10	75.00	80.30	87.00	90.70	92.40	93.36
9.	Japan	29.99	66.92	78.00	78.21	79.05	79.50	88.22	89.11	93.33
10.	Netherlands	43.98	81.00	89.63	90.72	91.42	92.86	93.96	93.17	93.10
11.	Qatar	4.86	24.73	53.10	69.00	69.00	69.30	85.30	91.49	92.88
12.	Finland	37.25	74.48	82.49	86.89	88.71	89.88	91.51	92.38	92.65
13.	United Kingdom	26.82	70.00	83.56	85.00	85.38	87.48	89.84	91.61	92.00
14.	United Arab Emirates	23.63	40.00	64.00	68.00	78.00	85.00	88.00	90.40	91.24
15.	Sweden	45.69	84.83	91.00	90.00	92.77	93.18	94.78	92.52	90.61
16.	South Korea	44.70	73.50	81.60	83.70	83.76	84.07	84.77	87.87	89.90
17.	Canada	51.30	71.66	80.30	80.30	83.00	83.00	85.80	87.12	88.47
18.	Estonia	28.58	61.45	72.50	74.10	76.50	78.39	79.40	84.24	88.41
19.	New Zealand	47.38	62.72	79.70	80.46	81.23	82.00	82.78	85.50	88.22
20.	Taiwan	28.10	58.01	69.90	71.50	72.00	75.99	80.00	83.99	87.98

Nations With the Most Internet Users, 2015

Source: Computer Industry Almanac, year-end 2015

Rank	Nation	Internet users (mil)	% of worldwide users	Rank	Nation	Internet users (mil)	% of worldwide users
1.	China	621.7	20.05%	10.	United Kingdom	54.4	1.75%
2.	India	285.9	9.22	11.	Italy	50.1	1.61
3.	United States	283.8	9.16	12.	Mexico	46.6	1.50
4.	Brazil	111.5	3.60	13.	South Korea	43.7	1.41
5.	Japan	111.2	3.59	14.	Turkey	39.2	1.26
6.	Russia	82.7	2.67	15.	Spain	37.0	1.19
7.	Indonesia	78.4	2.53		**Top 15 countries**	**1,971.9**	**63.61**
8.	Germany	70.4	2.27				
9.	France	55.3	1.78		**World total**	**3,100.0**	**100.00**

Most-Visited World Websites, 2016

Source: comScore Media Metrix

Some websites represent an aggregation of commonly owned domain names; examples of popular domains within a group added in parentheses by World Almanac editors.

Rank	Website	Visitors[1]	Rank	Website	Visitors[1]
1.	Google sites (YouTube, Blogger)	1,233,494	11.	Alibaba.com Corp.	308,058
2.	Microsoft sites (Bing, Xbox Live)	909,193	12.	Iqiyi sites	257,440
3.	Facebook (Instagram)	834,810	13.	SINA Corp.	254,218
4.	Yahoo! sites (Flickr, Tumblr)	557,106	14.	LE sites	251,163
5.	Baidu.com Inc.	456,405	15.	360buy Corp.	248,181
6.	Sohu.com Inc.	448,942	16.	Youku & Tudou	247,106
7.	Tencent Inc. (QQ)	426,826	17.	Apple Inc. (iTunes)	243,547
8.	Qihoo.com sites	382,244	18.	CBS Interactive (CNET, ZDNet)	240,452
9.	Amazon sites (Zappos, Audible, IMDb)	348,210	19.	BitTorrent Network	220,358
10.	Wikimedia Foundation sites (Wikipedia)	336,106	20.	NetEase.com Inc.	217,770

(1) Number of persons age 15 or older, in thousands, who visited a website from a desktop computer in any location at least once in June 2016.

Top Web Browsers Worldwide, 2009-16

Source: StatCounter Global Stats, gs.statcounter.com

Browser	% of browser market				
	2009	2012	2014	2015	2016
Chrome	3.01%	33.81%	45.28%	51.74%	58.26%
Firefox	30.50	23.73	17.52	15.68	13.97
Internet Explorer	60.11	32.04	21.38	17.19	9.77
Safari	3.02	7.12	10.60	9.79	9.74
Edge	—	—	—	0.05	2.79
Opera	2.64	1.72	1.39	1.83	1.77
Android	—	0.36	1.36	1.51	1.48

— = Not available. **Note:** Percent of users accessing the web via a particular browser, for July of year shown. Excludes mobile devices.

Top Operating Systems Worldwide, 2009-16

Source: StatCounter Global Stats, gs.statcounter.com

Operating system	% of OS market				
	2009	2012	2014	2015	2016
Android	0.02%	3.29%	16.38%	25.62%	32.48%
Windows 7	0.97	45.50	36.39	31.12	20.36
Apple iOS	0.36	5.16	11.62	11.37	12.25
Windows 10	—	—	—	0.20	11.78
Mac OS X	4.07	6.16	5.65	4.90	4.81
Windows 8.1	—	—	4.90	9.59	4.21

— = Not available. **Note:** Percent of users accessing the web with a particular operating system (OS), for July of year shown. Includes mobile devices' operating systems.

U.S. Internet Use by Selected Characteristics, 2013-15
Source: Pew Research Center

	% who are users 2013	2015	Race/ethnicity	% who are users 2013	2015	Annual household income	% who are users 2013	2015
All adults	84%	84%	White, non-Hispanic. . .	85%	85%	Less than $30,000 . . .	72%	74%
Gender			Black, non-Hispanic. . .	79	78	$30,000-$49,999	86	85
Male	84	85	Hispanic	81	81	$50,000-$74,999	93	95
Female	84	84				$75,000 or more	97	97
Age			**Education**					
18-29	97	96	No high school diploma	60	66	**Geography**		
30-49	92	93	High school graduate	76	76	Urban	86	85
50-64	81	81	Some college	92	90	Suburban	85	85
65+	56	58	College graduate.	96	95	Rural.	78	78

Note: Percent of U.S. adults, age 18 and over, who use the internet, email, or access the internet via a mobile device. Six surveys and 13,282 interviews were conducted in 2013; two surveys and 3,004 interviews in 2015.

Most-Visited U.S. Websites, 2016
Source: comScore Media Metrix; comScore qSearch

Some websites represent an aggregation of commonly owned domain names; examples of popular domains within a group as of June 2016 added in parentheses by World Almanac editors.

All U.S. Sites

Rank	Website	Visitors[1]
1.	Google sites (YouTube, Blogger)	241,883
2.	Facebook (Instagram).	208,800
3.	Yahoo! sites (Flickr, Rivals.com, Tumblr).	205,847
4.	Microsoft sites (Bing, Xbox Live).	197,490
5.	Amazon sites	181,761
6.	Comcast NBCUniversal	162,581
7.	AOL, Inc. (Moviefone, Huffington Post).	153,632
8.	Apple Inc. (iTunes)	151,703
9.	CBS Interactive (CNET, ZDNet)	147,113
10.	Turner Digital	143,618
11.	LinkedIn	125,098
12.	Mode Media	120,664
13.	The Weather Company.	119,988
14.	Wikimedia Foundation sites (Wikipedia).	116,507
15.	Twitter	114,740

Blog Sites

Rank	Website	Visitors[1]
1.	WordPress.com	81,743
2.	Blogger.	59,504
3.	WordPress	56,711
4.	Twentytwowords.com	19,989
5.	Eater sites.	14,293

Search and Navigation

Rank	Website	Searches (mil)	% of searches
1.	Google sites	10,492	64.4%
2.	Microsoft sites (Bing)	3,485	21.4
3.	Yahoo! sites	1,907	11.7
4.	Ask Network	246	1.5
5.	AOL Inc.	174	1.1

Email

Rank	Website	Visitors[1]
1.	Google Gmail	143,384
2.	Yahoo! Mail	64,337
3.	Outlook (Outlook.com)	34,449
4.	Outlook Web (primarily Outlook.office.com) . . .	15,212
5.	AOL Email	11,919

Social Networking Sites

Rank	Website	Visitors[1]
1.	Facebook and Messenger	207,350
2.	LinkedIn	125,098
3.	Instagram	114,948
4.	Twitter	114,740
5.	Pinterest	92,370
6.	Google+	80,164
7.	Tumblr.	55,745
8.	Snapchat	53,319
9.	Reddit	45,417
10.	Goodreads	20,170

Video Sites

Rank	Website[2]	Visitors[3]
1.	Google sites (YouTube).	161,189
2.	Facebook	83,945
3.	Yahoo! sites (Flickr)	59,987
4.	Vimeo	48,934
5.	Microsoft sites.	43,811
6.	Comcast NBCUniversal	41,328
7.	CBS Interactive	40,500
8.	BroadbandTV	36,846
9.	VEVO	35,470
10.	Turner Digital	34,539

Note: Search and navigation data are for desktop computer users only for searches from the properties' core search engines (as opposed to searches within, for example, YouTube or Gmail). (1) Number of persons age 2 and older, in thousands, who visited the media property (including website/apps) at least once from any U.S. location in June 2016. Mobile users under age 18 are not measured. (2) Excludes advertisement videos. (3) Number of persons age 2 and older, in thousands, who visited website from a desktop computer in any U.S. location at least once in Feb. 2016.

Fixed Broadband Penetration in Selected Countries, 2002-15
Source: Organisation for Economic Co-operation and Development (OECD)
(nonmobile broadband subscriptions per 100 inhabitants, for fourth quarter of given year; ranked by 2015 figures)

Country	2002	2005	2010	2011	2012	2013	2014	2015
France.	2.7	15.0	32.7	34.8	36.6	37.8	39.2	40.4
United States	6.7	16.3	31.3	28.3	34.3	35.6	36.7	37.9[1]
Germany.	3.9	13.0	32.6	33.3	34.7	35.5	36.5	37.6
Canada.	12.1	20.8	31.8	32.8	33.6	34.4	35.4	36.3
Japan	6.2	18.1	26.6	27.3	27.7	28.1	28.8	29.7
Italy.	1.7	11.8	21.8	22.5	22.7	22.9	23.6	24.5
United Kingdom	2.3	2.2	9.7	32.8	10.5	11.1	11.6	12.3

Note: Includes internet connections with speeds greater than 256 kilobits per second (256 kbps). (1) Estimate.

U.S. Fixed Broadband Internet Connections by Technology, 2011-15

Source: Federal Communications Commission
(residential internet connections in thousands, as of June of given year)

Connection type	2011	2012	2013	2014	2015
aDSL (asymmetric digital subscriber line) ..	8,909	12,875	14,233	17,246	19,319
sDSL (symmetric digital subscriber line) ...	16	30	34	33	24
Other wireline[1]	204	239	284	310	297
Cable modem	34,113	37,798	46,014	51,304	55,978
Fiber optic[2]	5,188	6,001	6,981	8,111	9,580
Satellite	—	87	791	1,424	1,690
Fixed wireless	145	214	337	553	669
Total	**48,577**	**57,243**	**68,673**	**78,981**	**87,556**

— = Less than 500 connections. **Note:** Numbers may not add up to totals due to rounding. Includes connections with transmission speeds of at least 3 megabits per second (3 mbps) downstream (internet to user) and 768 kilobits per second (768 kbps) upstream (user to internet). (1) Includes power line. (2) Fiber to the premises (FTTP).

Internet Use in the U.S., 2000-14

Source: The 2015 Digital Future Report, USC Annenberg School Center for the Digital Future

	2000	2002	2005	2006	2007	2008	2009	2010	2012	2013	2014
Weekly time online[1]	9.4	11.1	13.3	14.0	15.3	17.3	19.0	18.3	20.4	20.5	21.5
Weekly time online, at home[1]	3.3	6.8	7.8	8.9	10.0	10.1	10.6	12.3	14.1	14.1	16.1
Weekly time online, at work[2]	NA	5	6	8	7	8	9	9	9	10	10
% of internet users aged 18 and older who make purchases online...	45%	40%	46%	51%	67%	65%	65%	68%	76%	79%	78%
Average monthly spending by internet purchasers aged 18 and older	NA	NA	NA	NA	$66	$85	$88	$73	$91	$106	$115

NA = Not available. (1) Average number of active-use hours per week among internet users. (2) Average number of active-use hours per week among internet users who access the internet at work.

U.S. Internet Use by Race and Ethnicity, 2003-15

Source: U.S. Census Bureau survey for National Telecommunications and Information Administration, U.S. Dept. of Commerce
(number in thousands of civilian individuals, age 3 and older)

Survey date	Total U.S.[1] Number	% with internet use	White, non-Hispanic Number	% with internet use	African-American, non-Hispanic Number	% with internet use	Asian-American, non-Hispanic Number	% with internet use	American Indian or Alaska Native, non-Hispanic Number	% with internet use	Hispanic Number	% with internet use
Oct. 2003	161,636	58.7%	122,243	65.1%	14,898	45.2%	7,043	63.0%	676	48.1%	14,038	37.2%
Oct. 2007	177,987	62.4	130,432	68.9	17,223	50.1	8,686	68.4	793	47.1	17,760	41.6
Oct. 2009	197,941	68.4	141,213	74.3	20,848	59.5	9,243	72.3	1,017	54.9	22,186	49.3
Oct. 2010	209,472	71.7	145,989	76.7	22,389	63.7	9,949	74.2	1,094	62.5	26,246	56.6
July 2011	204,596	69.7	142,827	75	21,287	60.2	10,010	73.6	1,142	59.7	25,648	54.4
Oct. 2012	222,038	74.7	149,231	79.1	24,290	68.3	11,643	78.4	1,350	62.5	30,960	62.1
July 2013	213,708	71.4	142,313	75.4	22,996	64	11,739	75.3	1,424	61.5	30,771	61
July 2015	226,747	74.6	147,408	78	25,025	67.8	12,919	77.4	1,423	70.2	34,772	65.8

(1) Includes other race categories not shown.

Popular U.S. Online Purchases, 2002-14

Source: The 2015 Digital Future Report, USC Annenberg School Center for the Digital Future
(percent of internet users who buy item(s) online; ranked by 2014 figures)

Item	2002	2006	2008	2010	2012	2013	2014
Clothes	39%	42%	61%	59%	66%	68%	65%
Gifts	10	12	61	63	60	64	61
Electronic goods/appliances	14	11	47	50	51	54	55
Books	29	34	60	63	66	61	52
Travel	16	17	57	57	66	58	50
Software/games	12	11	43	44	37	43	36
Videos/DVDs	6	13	48	47	42	43	36
Computers/peripherals	10	11	43	44	40	38	36

Frequency of Selected Internet Activities in the U.S., 2014

Source: The 2015 Digital Future Report, USC Annenberg School Center for the Digital Future
(as % of all internet users age 12 and older)

Online activity	Several times a day	Daily	Weekly	Monthly	Less than monthly	Never
Check email	47%	35%	10%	3%	2%	3%
Browse the web	31	37	14	5	6	7
Visit social networking sites	27	30	13	4	6	20
Instant message	16	23	16	5	12	29
Look for news	12	36	22	9	12	9
Play games	12	22	16	5	14	33
Download or listen to music	11	20	22	12	13	22
Download or watch videos	10	18	25	11	11	25
Find or check a fact	9	22	30	16	14	9
Post on discussion boards	8	9	15	7	20	41
Look up a definition	6	14	28	19	21	12
Listen to online radio	6	14	19	9	15	36

Telecommunications Milestones

1753: Scottish surgeon Charles Morrison proposed using 26 electric lines, one for each letter of the alphabet, to make an electric telegraph. A letter would be indicated by charging the corresponding line, causing movement of a light object at the receiving end. Swiss scientist Georges-Louis Lesage built such a 26-line "electrostatic" system in 1774.

1837: In England, Charles Wheatstone and William Fothergill Cooke patented an electromagnetic telegraph. To indicate letters, their system used the magnetic field generated by a current to deflect compass needles. In 1839, they built the first commercial electric telegraph along a 13-mi (21-km) route.

1837: American inventor Samuel Morse filed a provisional patent application for a different type of electric telegraph that indicated letters by making marks of various lengths on paper. In 1844, he completed a 30-mi telegraph line from Washington, DC, to Baltimore, MD.

1866: The first successful transatlantic telegraph cable was laid.

1876: Alexander Graham Bell applied for a U.S. patent on the telephone. In his first successful experiment, on Mar. 10, he used the device to call his assistant.

1901: Italian inventor Guglielmo Marconi successfully transmitted the first transatlantic radio signal—from Cornwall, England, to Newfoundland, Canada.

1927: Commercial transatlantic telephone service (via radio) began between New York and London.

1946: The first commercial mobile phone service was launched, in St. Louis, MO.

1947: U.S. scientists invented the transistor, thereby giving birth to a revolution in telecommunications and electronics.

1948: U.S. mathematician/engineer Claude Shannon's epochal paper "A Mathematical Theory of Communication" laid the foundation for modern information theory. Its treatment of such crucial concepts as data compression and error detection and correction opened the way to digital communication.

1951: The mayors of Englewood, NJ, and Alameda, CA, made the first customer-dialed long-distance telephone call, facilitated by the introduction of area codes.

1956: The first transoceanic telephone cable went into service.

1962: NASA launched the world's first active communications satellite, AT&T's *Telstar 1.*

1978: Trials were conducted in Chicago and Newark, NJ, on a cellular approach to mobile telephony. This divided a region into a multitude of small overlapping areas, or cells, and made possible a significant increase in quality of calls and quantity of callers. Callers could be switched from one cell to another as they moved about.

1983: The first commercial cellular system in the U.S. went into operation in Chicago. A similar system was also launched in the Baltimore, MD-Washington, DC, area.

1984: As a result of a 1982 antitrust settlement with the U.S. government, AT&T, which handled most telephone service in the U.S., was broken up into several separate entities.

1994: The first smartphone, IBM's Simon Personal Communicator, went on the market. A bricklike touchscreen device, it combined a cellular phone with such features as an address book, calendar, calculator, email and faxing capability, and games.

2007: Apple released the iPhone, inaugurating a new era in multifunctional smartphones.

2012: By late in the year more than 1 bil smartphones of all types were in use worldwide.

2016: Users of Facebook's messaging app Messenger passed the 1 bil mark.

2016: Total sales of Apple's iPhone reached 1 bil units.

Global Communications Technology Developments, 2001-16

Source: ITU World Telecommunication/Information and Communication Technology (ICT) Indicators Database
(per 100 inhabitants; 2016 data is estimated)

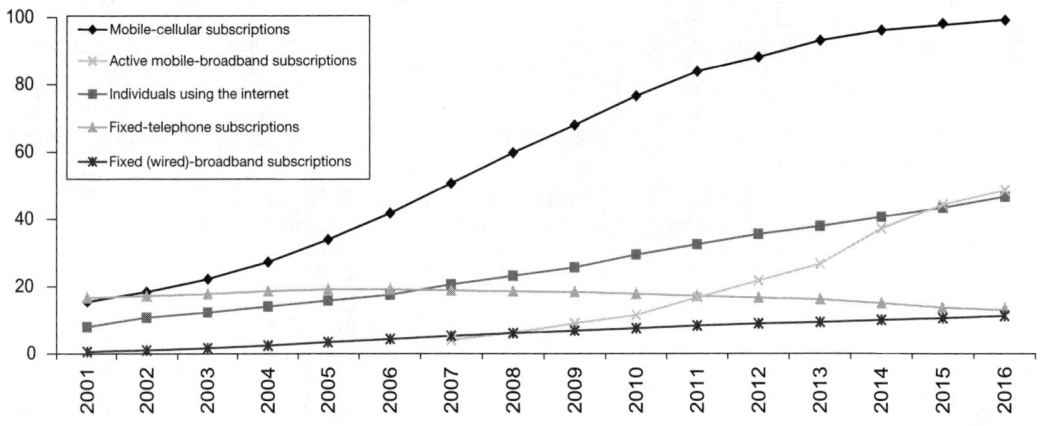

Nations With the Most Cellphone Use, 2015

Source: © International Telecommunication Union, estimated; ranked by countries with most cellphone subscriptions

Rank	Country	Subscriptions (thous.)	Per 100 pop.	Rank	Country	Subscriptions (thous.)	Per 100 pop.
1.	China	1,305,738	93.16	14.	Germany	96,360	116.71
2.	India	1,011,054	78.84	15.	Egypt	94,016	110.99
3.	United States	382,307	117.59	16.	Italy	92,520	151.32
4.	Indonesia	338,426	132.35	17.	South Africa	85,197	159.27
5.	Brazil	257,814	126.59	18.	Thailand	84,797	125.81
6.	Russia	227,289	159.95	19.	United Kingdom	80,284	125.75
7.	Japan	158,591	125.05	20.	Iran	74,219	93.38
8.	Nigeria	150,830	82.19	21.	Turkey	73,639	96.02
9.	Bangladesh	133,720	83.36	22.	France	66,681	102.61
10.	Pakistan	125,900	66.92	23.	Ukraine	60,720	144.02
11.	Vietnam	122,000	130.64	24.	Argentina	60,664	143.91
12.	Philippines	120,255	118.13	25.	South Korea	58,935	118.46
13.	Mexico	106,831	85.30		**World**	**7,215,563**	**98.61**

U.S. Wireless Industry, 1985-2015

Source: CTIA Semi-Annual Industry Survey, used with permission of CTIA. As of Dec. of year shown.

Year	Est. total subscribers	Total service revenues (thous.)	Cellphone antennas	Avg. monthly revenue per subscriber unit	Avg. local call length (min.)
1985	340,213	$482,428	913	NA	NA
1987	1,230,855	1,151,519	2,305	NA	2.33
1989	3,508,944	3,340,595	4,169	NA	2.48
1991	7,557,148	5,708,522	7,847	NA	2.38
1993	16,009,461	10,892,175	12,824	$76.55	2.41
1995	33,785,661	19,081,239	22,663	59.43	2.15
1997	55,312,293	27,485,633	51,600	49.39	2.31
1999	86,047,003	40,018,489	81,698	46.39	2.38
2000	109,478,031	52,466,020	104,288	48.55	2.56
2001	128,374,512	65,316,235	127,540	49.79	2.74
2002	140,766,842	76,508,187	139,338	51.00	2.73
2003	158,721,981	87,624,093	162,986	51.55	3.07
2004	182,140,362	102,121,210	175,725	52.54	3.05
2005	207,896,198	113,538,221	183,689	50.65	3.00
2006	233,040,781	125,456,825	195,613	49.07	3.03
2007	255,395,599	138,869,304	213,299	49.26	NA
2008	270,333,881	148,084,170	242,130	48.87	2.27
2009	285,646,191	152,551,854	247,081	47.97	1.81
2010	296,285,629	159,929,648	253,086	47.53	1.79
2011	315,963,848	169,767,314	283,385	46.11	1.78
2012	326,475,248	185,013,936	301,779	48.99	1.80
2013	335,652,171	189,192,812	304,360	48.79	NA
2014	355,445,472	187,848,447	298,055	46.64	NA
2015	377,921,241	191,949,025	307,626	44.65	NA

NA = Not available. **Note:** Survey conducted annually beginning 2013.

U.S. Use of Selected Mobile Phone Functions, 2007-14

Source: The 2015 Digital Future Report, USC Annenberg School Center for the Digital Future
(as % of mobile phone users age 12 and older)

Function	2007	2008	2009	2010	2012	2013	2014
Text message	31%	45%	54%	62%	82%	77%	83%
Take pictures	33	47	52	60	79	70	76
Access the internet	8	13	18	23	59	59	73
Play games	17	22	20	23	43	43	51

U.S. Use of Selected Mobile Phone Functions, 2014

Source: The 2015 Digital Future Report, USC Annenberg School Center for the Digital Future
(% of mobile phone users age 12 and older who used function)

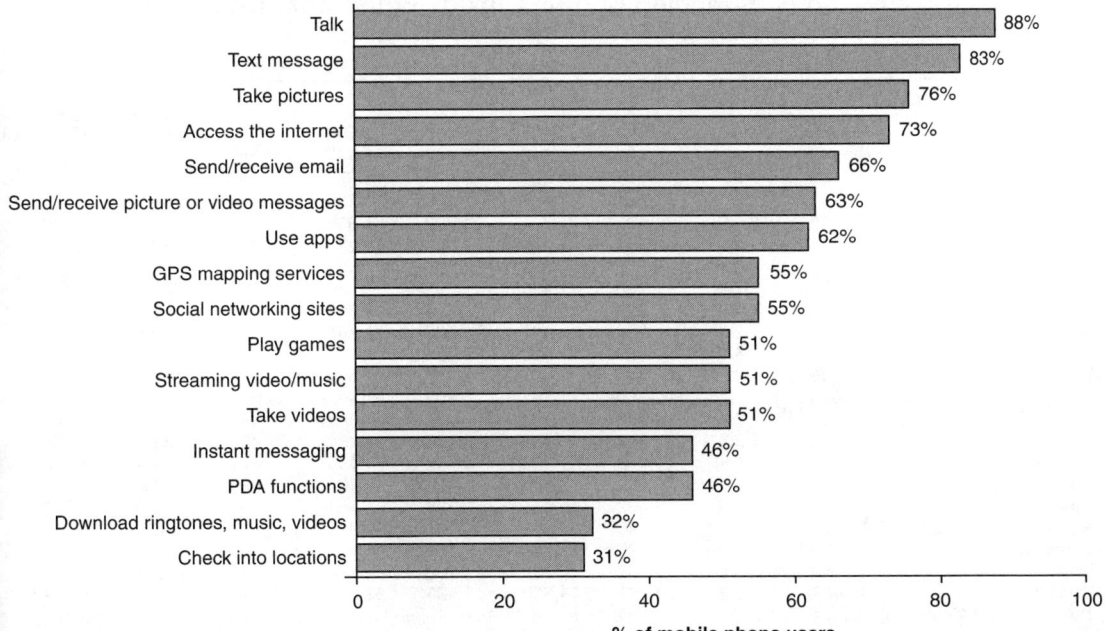

Function	%
Talk	88%
Text message	83%
Take pictures	76%
Access the internet	73%
Send/receive email	66%
Send/receive picture or video messages	63%
Use apps	62%
GPS mapping services	55%
Social networking sites	55%
Play games	51%
Streaming video/music	51%
Take videos	51%
Instant messaging	46%
PDA functions	46%
Download ringtones, music, videos	32%
Check into locations	31%

% of mobile phone users

ENVIRONMENT

U.S. Greenhouse Gas Emissions From Human Activities, 1990-2014

Source: U.S. Environmental Protection Agency

Gas and major source(s)	1990	2005	2010	2011	2012	2013	2014	% change, 1990-2014
Carbon dioxide (CO_2)	5,115.1	6,122.7	5,688.8	5,559.5	5,349.2	5,502.6	5,556.0	8.6%
Fossil fuel combustion	4,740.7	5,747.1	5,358.3	5,227.7	5,024.7	5,157.6	5,208.2	9.9
Methane (CH_4)	773.9	717.4	722.4	717.4	714.4	721.5	730.8	−5.6
Natural gas systems	206.8	177.3	166.2	170.1	172.6	175.6	176.1	−14.8
Enteric fermentation[1]	164.2	168.9	171.3	168.9	166.7	165.5	164.3	0.1
Landfills	179.6	154.0	142.1	144.4	142.3	144.3	148.0	−17.6
Petroleum systems	38.7	48.8	54.1	56.3	58.4	64.7	68.1	76.0
Nitrous oxide (N_2O)	406.2	397.6	410.3	416.5	409.3	403.4	403.5	−0.7
Agricultural soil management	303.3	297.2	320.7	323.1	323.1	318.6	318.4	5.0
Hydrofluorocarbons (HFCs), etc.[2]	102.0	141.1	164.0	172.0	170.1	172.5	180.1	76.6
Total U.S. emissions	6,397.1	7,378.8	6,985.5	6,865.4	6,643.0	6,800.0	6,870.5	7.4
Net U.S. emissions[3]	5,659.2	6,680.3	6,219.0	6,103.4	5,893.4	6,040.4	6,108.0	7.9

Note: Emissions given in terms of equivalent emissions of carbon dioxide (CO_2), using units of million metric tons of carbon dioxide equivalent (MMT CO_2 eq.). (1) Digestive process of ruminant animals, such as cattle and sheep, producing methane as a by-product. (2) Includes HFCs, PFCs (perfluorocarbons), SF_6 (sulfur hexafluoride), and NF_3 (nitrogen trifluoride). (3) Total emissions minus the net sum of all emissions (i.e., sources) of greenhouse gases to the atmosphere plus removals of CO_2 (i.e., sinks or negative emissions) from the atmosphere.

U.S. Greenhouse Gas Emissions, 2014

Source: Environmental Protection Agency

World Carbon Dioxide Emissions From the Use of Fossil Fuels, 2013

Source: U.S. Energy Information Administration

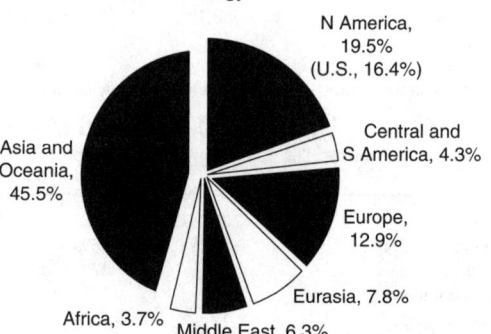

HFC = hydrofluorocarbon; PFC = perfluorocarbon; SF_6 = sulfur hexafluoride; NF_3 = nitrogen trifluoride. **Note:** Emissions sources are independently rounded; percentages may not add up to 100.

Top 20 Nations Producing Carbon Dioxide Emissions, 1980-2013

Source: Energy Information Administration, U.S. Dept. of Energy

(in million metric tons of carbon dioxide emitted from the consumption of energy; ranked by 2013 totals)

Country	1980	1990	2000	2005	2010	2012	2013	% change, 1980-2013	% change, 1990-2013
China	1,448	2,269	3,231	5,742	7,627	8,487	8,687	499.9%	282.9%
United States	4,776	5,041	5,864	5,999	5,578	5,270	5,402	13.1	7.2
India	291	579	991	1,181	1,776	1,780	1,887	548.5	225.9
Russia[1]	3,082	3,818	1,499	1,588	1,709	1,828	1,726	−44.0	−54.8
Japan	947	1,047	1,201	1,241	1,200	1,247	1,257	32.7	20.1
Germany[2]	761	698	855	834	798	793	805	5.8	15.3
Korea, South	132	242	439	494	597	639	651	393.2	169.0
Iran	117	202	321	451	563	602	612	423.1	203.0
Saudi Arabia	177	208	291	402	507	584	594	235.6	185.6
Canada	457	471	573	610	574	567	564	23.4	19.7
Brazil	186	237	344	371	459	504	535	187.6	125.7
United Kingdom	614	602	560	583	532	497	488	−20.5	−18.9
South Africa	235	298	386	432	471	508	482	105.1	61.7
Mexico	240	302	383	398	433	434	455	89.6	50.7
Indonesia	86	156	268	326	446	430	442	414.0	183.3
Australia	199	268	356	409	429	401	385	93.5	43.7
France	489	368	402	414	386	359	367	−24.9	−0.3
Italy	372	415	448	472	421	388	362	−2.7	−12.8
Poland	429	334	293	288	321	316	322	−24.9	−3.6
Turkey	69	129	202	231	268	323	339	362.3	147.3
World total[3]	18,487	21,640	24,147	28,559	31,583	32,659	33,010	78.6	52.5

(1) Numbers for 1980-90 are for the former Soviet Union. (2) Numbers for 1980-90 are for former West Germany. (3) Includes nations not listed.

Atmospheric Concentration of Carbon Dioxide, 1744-2015

Source: Carbon Dioxide Information Analysis Center, U.S. Dept. of Energy; Earth System Research Laboratory, Natl. Oceanic and Atmospheric Admin., U.S. Dept. of Commerce

Year[1]	CO$_2$ in ppm	Year[1]	CO$_2$ in ppm	Year[1]	CO$_2$ in ppm	Year[1]	CO$_2$ in ppm	Year[1]	CO$_2$ in ppm
1744	277	1903	295	1970	326	2006	382	2011	392
1791	280	1915	301	1980	339	2007	384	2012	394
1816	284	1927	306	1990	354	2008	386	2013	396
1843	287	1943	308	2000	370	2009	387	2014	399
1869	289	1960	317	2005	380	2010	390	2015	401
1878	290								

ppm = Parts per million. (1) Measurements for the years 1744-1943 were derived from a 200-m-deep ice core sample drilled near Siple Station in Antarctica in 1983-84. Measurements for 1960-2015 were taken directly from the atmosphere at Mauna Loa Observatory in Hawaii.

Emissions of Principal Air Pollutants in the U.S., 1970-2014

Source: Office of Air Quality Planning and Standards, U.S. Environmental Protection Agency; in million tons

Pollutant	1970	1975	1980	1985	1990	1995	2000	2005	2010	2014
Carbon monoxide	204.0	188.4	185.4	176.8	154.2	126.8	114.5	88.5	73.8	67.8
Nitrogen oxides[1]	26.9	26.4	27.1	25.8	25.5	25.0	22.6	20.4	14.8	12.4
Particulate matter[2]										
PM10	13.0	7.6	7.0	41.3	27.8	25.8	23.7	21.3	20.8	20.6
PM2.5	NA	NA	NA	NA	7.6	6.9	7.3	5.6	6.0	6.0
Sulfur dioxide	31.2	28.0	25.9	23.3	23.1	18.6	16.3	14.5	7.7	5.0
Volatile org. compounds[1]	34.7	30.8	31.1	27.4	24.1	22.0	17.5	17.8	17.8	17.1
Ammonia	NA	NA	NA	NA	4.3	4.7	4.9	3.9	4.3	4.2
Total[3]	309.8	281.2	276.5	294.6	266.6	229.8	206.8	172.0	145.2	133.1

NA = Not available. (1) Ozone, a major air pollutant and the primary constituent of smog, is not emitted directly to the air but is formed by sunlight acting on emissions of nitrogen oxides and volatile organic compounds. (2) PM10 = particulates 10 microns or smaller in diameter. PM2.5 = particulates 2.5 microns or smaller in diameter. (3) Totals are rounded, as are components of totals.

Sources of Air Pollutants in the U.S., 1970-2014

Source: Office of Air Quality Planning and Standards, U.S. Environmental Protection Agency; in thousand tons

Carbon monoxide sources	1970	1975	1980	1985	1990	1995	2000	2005	2010	2014
Fuel combustion, elec. util.	237	276	322	291	363	372	484	643	766	784
Industrial processes[1]	10,610	8,304	7,700	5,894	5,572	5,631	3,628	3,074	2,807	2,903
Transportation[2]	174,602	167,884	160,512	153,216	131,700	107,755	92,239	64,729	43,595	36,298
Total carbon monoxide[3]	**204,042**	**188,398**	**185,408**	**176,845**	**154,184**	**126,778**	**114,467**	**88,546**	**73,771**	**67,756**
Nitrogen oxide sources										
Fuel combustion, elec. util.	4,900	5,694	7,024	6,127	6,663	6,384	5,330	3,792	2,458	1,776
Industrial processes[1]	5,100	4,546	4,110	4,009	3,831	3,909	3,518	2,783	2,406	2,419
Transportation[2]	15,276	15,029	14,846	14,508	13,373	12,989	12,560	12,612	9,017	7,158
Total nitrogen oxide[3]	**26,882**	**26,378**	**27,080**	**25,757**	**25,527**	**24,955**	**22,598**	**20,355**	**14,846**	**12,412**
Sulfur dioxide sources										
Fuel combustion, elec. util.	17,398	18,268	17,469	16,272	15,909	12,080	11,396	10,404	5,696	3,195
Industrial processes[1]	11,661	7,993	6,725	5,597	5,402	4,945	3,516	2,721	1,447	1,254
Transportation[2]	551	635	717	809	874	741	697	682	158	100
Total sulfur dioxide[3]	**31,218**	**28,044**	**25,926**	**23,307**	**23,077**	**18,619**	**16,347**	**14,546**	**7,732**	**4,991**

(1) Industrial fuel combustion, chemical and allied manufacturing, metals processing, and petroleum and other industrial sectors. (2) Highway and off-highway vehicles. (3) Numbers may not add up to totals because not all categories are listed.

Average Global Temperature and Atmospheric Carbon Dioxide, 1880-2015

Source: Goddard Institute for Space Studies, National Aeronautics and Space Administration, via Earth Policy Institute

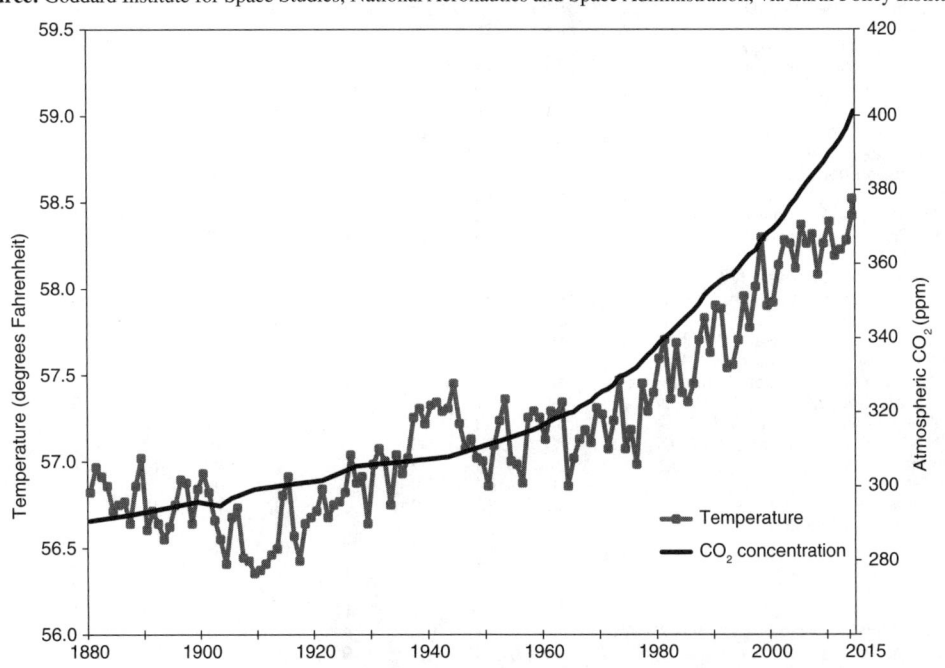

Air Pollution in Selected World Cities

Source: World Health Organization (WHO); *World Development Indicators 2015*, The World Bank

Particulate matter in the following table refers to smoke, soot, dust, and liquid droplets from combustion that are in the air—specifically, to particulates less than 10 microns in diameter (PM10) capable of reaching deep into the respiratory tract. The level of particulates, an important indicator of air quality, is significantly affected by the state of technology and pollution controls. WHO estimated that outdoor air pollution caused 3.7 mil premature deaths worldwide in 2012, due to exposure to PM10. **Sulfur dioxide** is a pollutant formed when fossil fuels containing sulfur are burned. **Nitrogen dioxide** is a poisonous, pungent gas formed when nitric oxide combines with hydrocarbons in sunlight, producing photochemical smog. Nitrogen oxides are emitted by bacteria, nitrogenous fertilizers, aerobic decomposition of organic matter, biomass combustion, and, especially, burning fuel for vehicles and industrial activities. Emissions of sulfur dioxide and nitrogen oxides lead to acid rain.

Data in the table represent the annual average of outdoor particulates, in micrograms per cubic meter (mpcm), that a resident of a city is exposed to. They are based on reports from urban monitoring sites. The figures give a general indication of air quality, but results should be interpreted with caution. World Health Organization standards for acceptable air quality are annual mean concentrations of 20 mpcm for particulate matter less than 10 microns in diameter and 40 mpcm for nitrogen dioxide and daily mean concentrations of 20 mpcm for sulfur dioxide.

City, country	Particulate matter[1]	Sulfur dioxide[2]	Nitrogen dioxide[2]	City, country	Particulate matter[1]	Sulfur dioxide[2]	Nitrogen dioxide[2]
Accra, Ghana	98[3]	NA	NA	Moscow, Russia	33	109	NA
Amsterdam, Netherlands	23	10	58	Mumbai, India	117	33	39
Bangkok, Thailand	42	11	23	New York, NY, U.S.	16	26	79
Barcelona, Spain	24	11	43	Oslo, Norway	22	8	43
Beijing, China	108	90	122	Paris, France	28	14	57
Berlin, Germany	24	18	26	Prague, Czech Republic	27	14	33
Cairo, Egypt	135[3]	69	NA	Quito, Ecuador	36	22	NA
Cape Town, South Africa	30[3]	21	72	Rio de Janeiro, Brazil	49	129	NA
Caracas, Venezuela	47	33	57	Rome, Italy	28	NA	NA
Chicago, IL, U.S.	22	14	57	São Paulo, Brazil	35	43	83
Delhi, India	229	24	41	Seoul, South Korea	46	44	60
Jakarta, Indonesia	48[3]	NA	NA	Shanghai, China	84	53	73
Kolkata, India	135	49	34	Sofia, Bulgaria	43	39	122
London, England, UK	22	25	77	Sydney, Australia	17	28	81
Los Angeles, CA, U.S.	20	9	74	Tehran, Iran	77	209	NA
Manila, Philippines	55	33	NA	Tokyo, Japan	28	18	68
Mexico City, Mexico	42	74	130	Toronto, ON, Canada	14	17	43
Milan, Italy	37	31	248	Warsaw, Poland	33	16	32
Montréal, QC, Canada	16	10	42				

NA = Not available. (1) WHO data is most recent available, as of 2009-14, unless noted. (2) World Bank data as of 2001. (3) As of 2008-12.

Air Quality of Selected U.S. Urban Areas, 1980-2015

Source: Office of Air Quality Planning and Standards, U.S. Environmental Protection Agency

Data indicate the number of days metropolitan statistical areas or corresponding core-based statistical areas failed to meet acceptable air-quality standards.

Urban area	1980	1990	2000	2005	2010	2011	2012	2013	2014	2015
Atlanta-Sandy Springs-Marietta, GA	19	33	28	6	2	0	3	1	1	0
Bakersfield, CA	47	59	68	39	17	18	17	22	25	14
Baltimore-Columbia-Towson, MD	51	14	8	6	6	5	2	0	0	0
Baton Rouge, LA	21	15	20	11	2	1	0	0	0	0
Boston-Cambridge-Newton, MA-NH	14	4	2	3	1	0	1	0	0	0
Chicago-Naperville-Elgin, IL-IN-WI	87	31	5	12	0	4	10	1	1	2
Cincinnati, OH-KY-IN	63	42	9	11	0	3	4	0	0	0
Cleveland-Elyria, OH	34	14	6	10	1	0	5	0	2	1
Dallas-Fort Worth-Arlington, TX	30	10	18	16	0	6	4	1	0	0
Denver-Aurora-Lakewood, CO	28	1	0	0	0	2	4	0	1	0
Detroit-Warren-Dearborn, MI	41	9	3	9	0	0	4	0	0	1
Fresno, CA	68	26	73	25	13	25	17	17	23	9
Houston-The Woodlands-Sugar Land, TX	68	48	31	19	1	7	4	1	0	5
Indianapolis-Carmel-Anderson, IN	43	6	18	4	1	0	2	0	1	1
Kansas City, MO-KS	43	5	6	6	0	2	4	1	0	0
Las Vegas-Henderson-Paradise, NV	24	8	1	3	0	0	2	1	1	0
Los Angeles-Long Beach-Anaheim, CA	189	124	46	34	5	14	11	4	13	16
Memphis, TN-MS-AR	58	8	6	6	0	0	1	0	0	0
Miami-Fort Lauderdale-West Palm Beach, FL	16	0	0	1	0	1	0	0	0	0
Minneapolis-St. Paul-Bloomington, MN-WI	64	14	1	3	0	0	1	0	0	0
Nashville-Davidson–Murfreesboro–Franklin, TN	42	52	6	2	0	0	1	0	0	0
New Orleans-Metairie, LA	4	1	5	1	17	29	7	3	0	0
New York-Newark-Jersey City, NY-NJ-PA	83	33	8	12	1	3	0	0	1	0
Philadelphia-Camden-Wilmington, PA-NJ-DE-MD	73	24	9	13	4	5	2	0	2	1
Phoenix-Mesa-Scottsdale, AZ	107	19	2	2	4	46	16	27	33	13
Pittsburgh, PA	119	92	29	29	16	5	4	1	1	2
Riverside-San Bernardino-Ontario, CA	160	132	76	56	33	35	42	37	34	28
Sacramento–Roseville–Arden-Arcade, CA	38	26	26	23	4	7	6	4	3	2
Salt Lake City, UT	70	46	13	3	6	3	0	9	2	2
San Francisco-Oakland-Hayward, CA	8	2	2	1	1	0	0	0	0	0
Seattle-Tacoma-Bellevue, WA	32	3	4	1	0	1	1	0	0	3
Tucson, AZ	49	0	0	1	0	0	0	3	0	0
Washington-Arlington-Alexandria, DC-VA-MD-WV	42	11	5	4	4	3	3	0	0	0
Winston-Salem, NC	0	3	4	0	0	0	0	0	0	0

Municipal Solid Waste, 2013

Source: U.S. Environmental Protection Agency

In 2013, Americans generated about 254 mil tons of refuse collected as municipal solid waste (MSW). Of that MSW, paper represented 27.0%; food 14.6%; yard trimmings 13.5%; plastics 12.8%; metals 9.1%; rubber, leather, and textiles 9.0%; wood 6.2%; glass 4.5%; and other material 3.3%. About 34.3%, or 87 mil tons, was recycled or composted; nearly half of recycled/composted materials consisted of paper and paperboard.

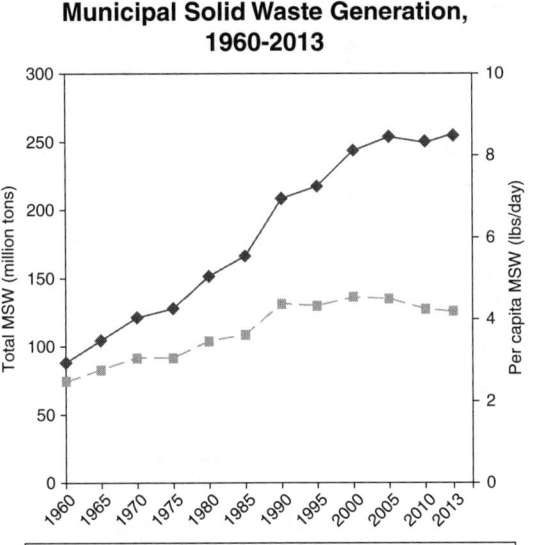

Municipal Solid Waste Generation, 1960-2013

- Total MSW (million tons)
- Per capita MSW (lbs/day)

Municipal Solid Waste Recycling, 1960-2013

- Percent of waste recycled
- Total recycling (million tons)

Hazardous Waste Sites in the U.S., 2016

Source: *National Priorities List*, U.S. Environmental Protection Agency; as of Apr. 2016

State/territory	Proposed Gen.	Proposed Fed.	Final Gen.	Final Fed.	Total	State/territory	Proposed Gen.	Proposed Fed.	Final Gen.	Final Fed.	Total
Alabama	2	0	10	3	15	Nebraska	0	0	15	1	16
Alaska	0	0	1	5	6	Nevada	0	0	1	0	1
Arizona	0	0	7	2	9	New Hampshire	1	0	19	1	21
Arkansas	0	0	9	0	9	New Jersey	1	0	108	6	115
California	2	0	73	24	99	New Mexico	0	0	15	1	16
Colorado	2	0	16	3	21	New York	2	0	81	4	87
Connecticut	1	0	13	1	15	North Carolina	0	0	37	2	39
Delaware	1	0	12	1	14	North Dakota	0	0	0	0	0
District of Columbia	0	0	0	1	1	Ohio	5	1	34	3	43
Florida	1	0	47	6	54	Oklahoma	1	0	6	1	8
Georgia	1	0	14	2	17	Oregon	1	0	11	2	14
Guam	0	0	1	1	2	Pennsylvania	2	0	89	6	97
Hawaii	0	0	1	2	3	Puerto Rico	1	0	15	1	17
Idaho	3	0	4	2	9	Rhode Island	0	0	10	2	12
Illinois	3	1	41	4	49	South Carolina	0	0	23	2	25
Indiana	2	0	38	0	40	South Dakota	0	0	1	1	2
Iowa	1	0	11	1	13	Tennessee	0	0	14	3	17
Kansas	1	0	11	1	13	Texas	2	0	47	4	53
Kentucky	0	0	12	1	13	Utah	3	0	10	5	18
Louisiana	4	0	10	1	15	Vermont	0	0	12	0	12
Maine	0	0	10	3	13	Virgin Islands	0	0	1	0	1
Maryland	1	0	10	10	21	Virginia	0	0	20	11	31
Massachusetts	1	0	26	6	33	Washington	0	0	38	13	51
Michigan	1	1	65	0	67	West Virginia	1	0	7	2	10
Minnesota	0	0	23	2	25	Wisconsin	1	0	37	0	38
Mississippi	1	0	8	0	9	Wyoming	0	0	1	1	2
Missouri	0	0	30	3	33	**Total**	**52**	**3**	**1,171**	**157**	**1,383**
Montana	3	0	16	0	19						

Note: Fed. = Hazardous waste produced by federal agency; Gen. = Non-fed. sites. Sites that have been proposed for federal Superfund financing are listed under Proposed; sites that have qualified for Superfund financing are under Final.

Renewable Water Resources, 2015
Source: Food and Agriculture Organization (FAO), United Nations

Globally, water supplies are abundant, but they are unevenly distributed among and within countries. In some areas, water withdrawals are so high, relative to supply, that surface water supplies are shrinking, and groundwater reserves are being depleted faster than they can be replenished by precipitation. According to the FAO, the U.S. (including Alaska and Hawaii) has 8,758 cubic meters per capita and 2,818 cubic kilometers of internal renewable water resources total.

The tables below take into account only countries for which data are available, draw upon studies done over a number of years, and use 2015 population data. Numbers represent each country's internal resources. Countries ranked by per capita figures.

Countries With Greatest Internal Water Resources

Country	Cubic m per capita	Total cubic km
Iceland	516,090	170.0
Guyana.	314,170	241.0
Suriname	182,320	99.0
Papua New Guinea	105,132	801.0
Bhutan	100,671	78.0
Gabon	95,072	164.0
Canada.	79,299	2,850.0
Solomon Islands.	76,594	44.7
Norway.	73,306	382.0
New Zealand	72,201	327.0

Countries With Lowest Internal Water Resources

Country	Cubic m per capita	Total cubic km
Kuwait.	0.0	0.0
Bahrain.	2.905	0.004
United Arab Emirates . . .	16.38	0.15
Egypt	19.67	1.8
Qatar	25.06	0.056
Saudi Arabia.	76.09	2.4
Yemen	78.26	2.1
Maldives	82.49	0.03
Jordan	89.8	0.682
Israel.	93.01	0.75

Top Countries by Forest Area, 1990-2013
Source: Food and Agriculture Organization, United Nations
(in square kilometers; ranked by 2013 area)

Country	Forest area, 1990	Forest area, 2013	% change, 1990-2013	% of land area covered by forest in 2013
Russia.	NA	8,150,125	NA	49.8%
Brazil.	5,467,050	4,955,060	−9.4%	59.3
Canada.	3,482,730	3,471,622	−0.3	38.2
United States	3,024,500	3,095,450	2.3	33.8
China	1,571,406	2,052,369	30.6	21.8
Congo, Dem. Rep. of.	1,603,630	1,532,008	−4.5	67.6
Australia	1,285,410	1,241,350	−3.4	16.2
Indonesia	1,185,450	923,788	−22.1	51.0
Peru	779,210	743,082	−4.6	58.1
India	639,390	703,252	10.0	23.7
Mexico	697,600	662,232	−5.1	34.1
Colombia	644,170	585,552	−9.1	52.8
Angola	609,760	581,056	−4.7	46.6
Bolivia.	627,950	553,420	−11.9	51.1
Zambia	528,000	489,682	−7.3	65.9
Venezuela.	520,260	470,118	−9.6	53.3
Tanzania	559,200	468,040	−16.3	52.8
Mozambique.	433,780	383,528	−11.6	48.8
Papua New Guinea	336,270	335,646	−0.2	74.1
Myanmar.	392,180	301,338	−23.2	46.1

Country	Forest area, 1990	Forest area, 2013	% change, 1990-2013	% of land area covered by forest in 2013
Sweden.	280,630	280,730	0.0%	68.9%
Argentina	347,930	277,056	−20.4	10.1
Japan	249,500	249,612	0.0	68.5
Gabon.	220,000	226,000	2.7	87.7
Congo Rep.	227,260	223,648	−1.6	65.5
Finland	218,750	222,180	1.6	73.1
Central African Republic	225,600	222,012	−1.6	35.6
Malaysia	223,760	221,666	−0.9	67.5
Sudan.	NA	195,588	NA	NA
Cameroon.	243,160	192,560	−20.8	40.7
Laos	176,449	183,831	4.2	79.6
Spain	138,095	183,496	32.9	36.7
Chile	152,630	171,334	12.3	23.0
France.	144,360	167,630	16.1	30.6
Guyana.	166,600	165,460	−0.7	84.1
Thailand	140,050	163,390	16.7	32.0
Paraguay	211,570	159,738	−24.5	40.2
Suriname	154,300	153,396	−0.6	98.3
Zimbabwe.	221,640	146,868	−33.7	38.0
Vietnam	93,630	145,150	55.0	46.8
World	**41,282,695**	**40,057,494**	**−3.0**	**30.8**

NA = Not available.

Largest Trees in the U.S.
Source: American Forests

More than 870 native and naturalized species of trees grow in the U.S. The trunk of the world's largest known living tree, the General Sherman giant sequoia in California, weighs almost 1,400 tons—about as much as 15 adult blue whales. To determine the country's largest trees (or "national champions"), American Forests uses a point system whereby trunk circumference, or girth (in inches) + height (in feet) + ¼ average crown spread (in feet) = total points. As of May 11, 2016.

Tree type	Girth at 4.5 ft (in.)	Height (ft)	Crown spread (ft)	Total points	Location
Giant sequoia (Gen. Sherman tree) . .	1,020	274	107	1,321	Sequoia National Park, CA
Coast redwood	950	321	75	1,290	Jedediah Smith Redwoods State Park, CA
Coast redwood	895	307	83	1,223	Jedediah Smith Redwoods State Park, CA
Coast redwood	845	349	89	1,216	Redwood National Park, CA
Coast redwood	867	299	101	1,191	Prairie Creek Redwoods State Park, CA
Western redcedar.	761	159	45	931	Olympic National Park, WA
Sitka spruce	668	191	96	883	Olympic National Park, WA
Coast Douglas-fir	599	200	37	808	Olympic National Park, WA
Coast Douglas-fir	505	281	71	804	Olympic National Forest, WA
Port-Orford-cedar	522	242	35	773	Coos, OR

Selected Endangered Animal Species

Source: Fish and Wildlife Service, U.S. Dept. of the Interior

Common name	Scientific name	Range
Albatross, Amsterdam	Diomedia amsterdamensis	Amsterdam Island, Indian Ocean
Antelope, giant sable	Hippotragus niger variani	Angola
Armadillo, giant	Priodontes maximus	Venezuela, Guyana, Argentina
Bandicoot, desert	Perameles eremiana	Australia
Bat, gray	Myotis grisescens	Central, southeastern U.S.
Bear, Mexican grizzly	Ursus arctos	Mexico
Bobcat, Mexican	Lynx rufus escuinapae	Mexico
Camel, Bactrian	Camelus bactrianus	Mongolia, China
Caribou, woodland	Rangifer tarandus caribou	Canada, U.S. (ID, WA)
Cheetah	Acinonyx jubatus	Africa, Asia Minor, India
Chimpanzee, pygmy	Pan paniscus	Dem. Rep. of the Congo
Condor, California	Gymnogyps californianus	U.S. (AZ, CA)
Crane, whooping	Grus americana	Canada, central U.S.
Crocodile, American	Crocodylus acutus	Caribbean (except for FL pop.), Central, S America
Deer, Columbian white-tailed	Odocoileus virginianus leucurus	U.S. (OR except pop. in Douglas Co., WA)
Dolphin, Chinese river	Lipotes vexillifer	China
Duck, Hawaiian	Anas wyvilliana	U.S. (HI)
Elephant, Asian	Elephas maximus	South-central and southeastern Asia
Fox, northern swift	Vulpes velox hebes	Canada
Frog, mountain yellow-legged	Rana muscosa	U.S. (CA, NV)
Gorilla	Gorilla gorilla	Central and western Africa
Hawk, Hawaiian	Buteo solitarius	U.S. (HI)
Hyena, brown	Parahyaena brunnea	Southern Africa
Impala, black-faced	Aepyceros melampus petersi	Angola, Namibia
Kangaroo, Tasmanian forester	Macropus giganteus tasmaniensis	Australia (Tasmania)
Leopard	Panthera pardus	Central Africa
Manatee, West Indian	Trichechus manatus	Southeastern U.S., Caribbean Sea, Mexico
Monkey, spider	Ateles geoffroyi frontatus	Costa Rica, Nicaragua
Ocelot	Leopardus pardalis	U.S. (AZ, TX), Mexico
Orangutan	Pongo pygmaeus	Borneo, Sumatra
Ostrich, West African	Struthio camelus spatzi	Western Sahara
Otter, marine	Lontra felina	Peru south to Straits of Magellan
Panda, giant	Ailuropoda melanoleuca	China
Panther, Florida	Puma concolor coryi	U.S. (FL)
Parakeet, golden	Aratinga guarouba	Brazil
Parrot, imperial	Amazona imperialis	Dominica
Penguin, Galapagos	Spheniscus mendiculus	Ecuador (Galapagos Islands)
Puma, eastern	Puma concolor couguar	Eastern N America (presumed extinct in wild)
Rhinoceros, black	Diceros bicornis	Sub-Saharan Africa
Salamander, Chinese giant	Andrias davidianus	China
Sea lion, Steller (Western pop.)	Eumetopias jubatus	U.S. (AK), Russia
Squirrel, Carolina northern flying	Glaucomys sabrinus coloratus	U.S. (NC, TN, VA)
Tiger	Panthera tigris	Asia
Tortoise, Galapagos	Geochelone nigra	Ecuador (Galapagos Islands)
Whale, gray (Western North Pacific pop.)	Eschrichtius robustus	NW Pacific Ocean
Whale, humpback	Megaptera novaeangliae	All major oceans
Wolf, red	Canis rufus	U.S. (FL, NC, SC)
Woodpecker, ivory-billed	Campephilus principalis	U.S. (AR)
Yak, wild	Bos mutus	China (Tibet), India
Zebra, mountain	Equus zebra zebra	South Africa

Status of Endangered and Threatened Species, 2016

Source: Fish and Wildlife Service, U.S. Dept. of the Interior; as of June 2016

Group	Endangered U.S.	Endangered Foreign	Threatened U.S.	Threatened Foreign	Total species[1]	U.S. species with recovery plans
Mammals	79	263	23	22	387	64
Birds	78	219	20	18	335	86
Fishes	92	19	70	3	184	104
Reptiles	16	70	27	24	137	34
Clams	75	2	13	0	90	71
Insects	64	4	11	0	79	42
Snails	38	1	12	0	51	29
Amphibians	20	8	15	1	44	22
Crustaceans	23	0	4	0	27	18
Corals	0	0	6	16	22	0
Arachnids	12	0	0	0	12	12
Animal subtotals	**497**	**586**	**201**	**84**	**1368**	**482**
Flowering Plants	700	1	161	0	862	645
Conifers and Cycads	1	0	3	2	6	3
Ferns and Allies	29	0	2	0	31	26
Lichens	2	0	0	0	2	2
Plant subtotals	**732**	**1**	**166**	**2**	**901**	**676**
Grand total	**1,229**	**587**	**367**	**86**	**2,269**	**1,158**

(1) 20 animal species are counted more than once in this table, primarily because these animals have distinct population segments, each with its own individual listing status. The U.S. dual-status species, all tallied as endangered, are Atlantic sturgeon, California tiger salamander, Chinook salmon, chum salmon, coho salmon, gray wolf, loggerhead sea turtle, mountain yellow-legged frog, roseate tern, piping plover, sockeye salmon, and steelhead. The foreign dual-status species are broad-snouted caiman, loggerhead sea turtle, scalloped hammerhead shark, and vicuña. Green sea turtles and humpback whales appear on both U.S. and foreign lists.

METEOROLOGY

National Weather Service Watches and Warnings

Source: National Weather Service, National Oceanic and Atmospheric Admin. (NOAA), U.S. Dept. of Commerce; *Glossary of Meteorology*, American Meteorological Society

The National Weather Service issues watches, warnings, and advisories for specific geographic areas to alert people to the possibility or imminent arrival of severe weather or of flooding. Often the weather hazard is a convective storm (a storm involving upward and downward movement of heat and moisture). A severe thunderstorm or tornado watch is issued when a severe convective storm, covering a relatively small geographic area or moving in a narrow path, is sufficiently intense to threaten life and property. Excessive localized convective rains are not classified as severe storms but are often the product of severe local storms. Such rainfall may result in phenomena, such as flash floods, that threaten life and property. Lightning occurs with all thunderstorms and, along with flash floods, is a leading cause of storm deaths and injuries.

Cyclone: Atmospheric circulation of winds rotating counterclockwise in the Northern Hemisphere and clockwise in the Southern Hemisphere. Tornadoes, hurricanes/typhoons, and the lows shown on weather maps are all examples of cyclones. Cyclones are usually accompanied by precipitation or stormy weather.

Severe thunderstorm: Thunderstorm (any local atmospheric disturbance) that produces a tornado, winds of at least 50 knots (58 mph), and/or hail at least 1 in. in diameter. A severe thunderstorm watch indicates conditions are favorable for the development of a severe thunderstorm within 4 to 8 hours. A severe thunderstorm warning indicates a severe thunderstorm has been sighted by radar or reported by a spotter.

Tornado: Violently rotating column of air that extends from the base of a thunderstorm to the ground. On a local scale, it is the most destructive of all atmospheric phenomena. Tornado paths range from a few feet to more than 100 mi long (avg. 5 mi) and from a few feet to more than 1 mi in diameter (avg. 220 yds). The average forward speed is 30 mph, and wind speeds can exceed 200 mph. A rotating column of air over water, whether or not linked to a thunderstorm, is called a **waterspout**.

Tropical storm: Cyclone that develops over tropical or subtropical waters with 1-min. sustained surface winds between 34 and 63 knots (39-73 mph). A tropical storm watch is issued when tropical storm conditions pose a threat to specified coastal areas within 48 hours. A tropical storm warning is issued when such conditions are expected in a specified coastal area within 36 hours.

Hurricane: Tropical cyclone having 1-min. sustained surface winds of 64 knots (74 mph) or more. (In the western North Pacific Ocean, west of the International Date Line, such storms are known as **typhoons**.) The hurricane-force winds form a circle or oval, sometimes as wide as 300 mi in diameter. In the lower latitudes, hurricanes usually move W or NW at 10-15 mph. When the center approaches 25° to 30° N, the direction of motion often changes to the NE, with increased forward speed. In the Atlantic, hurricane season is June 1-Nov. 30.

Hurricane season is May 15-Nov. 30 in the eastern Pacific. A hurricane warning is issued when a hurricane is forecast for an area within 36 hours.

Winter storm and **blizzard:** A winter storm watch is issued when there is a potential for heavy snow or significant ice accumulations, usually at least 24-36 hours in advance. A winter storm warning is issued when a winter storm is producing or is forecast to produce heavy snow or significant ice accumulations. A blizzard warning is issued for winter storm conditions where winds are 35 mph or more, there is sufficient falling and/or blowing snow to frequently reduce visibility to less than ¼ mi, and the conditions are expected to prevail for at least 3 hours.

River flooding: Occurs when rains, sometimes coupled with melting snow, quickly fill river basins with an excess of water. Torrential rains from decaying hurricanes or tropical systems are also a major cause. **Coastal flooding:** Tropical storm and hurricane winds or intense offshore low-pressure systems can drive ocean water inland. Coastal floods can also be produced by sea waves called **tsunamis**, produced by earthquakes or underwater volcanic eruptions or landslides. **Flash flooding:** Usually due to copious amounts of rain falling in a short time. Ice can also cause flash flooding. When ice accumulates at natural or artificial obstructions, it can stop the flow of water. The resulting buildup of water can lead to flooding upstream. If the jam suddenly gives way, a flash flood can happen downstream. Flash flooding typically occurs within 6 hours of the causative event.

Flash floods account for the majority of flood deaths in the U.S. and are the leading cause of deaths associated with thunderstorms. Urbanization significantly increases runoff because less rain is absorbed by the terrain, making flash flooding in urban areas extremely dangerous. Streets can become swift-moving rivers, and basements can fill with water.

A (flash) flood watch indicates flooding or flash flooding is possible within a designated area. A (flash) flood warning indicates flooding is in progress, imminent, or highly likely.

National Weather Service Marine Warnings and Advisories

Primary sources of dissemination are commercial radio, TV, U.S. Coast Guard radio stations, and NOAA VHF radio broadcasts. The NOAA Weather Radio All Hazards (NWR) network broadcasts on seven frequencies between 162.40 and 162.55 MHz. These broadcasts can usually be received within about 40 mi of the transmission site using a special radio receiver. The following are examples of the warnings and advisories that may be addressed to mariners.

Small craft advisory: Alerts mariners to sustained weather and/or sea conditions, present or forecast, potentially hazardous to small boats, including winds 20-33 knots (23-38 mph) and/or dangerous wave conditions. The advisory is also issued when sea or lake ice exists that could be hazardous to small boats. Criteria vary depending on region and type of marine environment.

Special marine warning: Indicates potentially hazardous weather conditions not covered by existing marine warnings.

The conditions are usually of short duration (2 hr. or less) and involve wind speeds of 34 knots (39 mph) or more, and/or hail at least ¾ in. in diameter or waterspouts.

Gale warning: Indicates winds of 34-47 knots (39-54 mph) not directly associated with a tropical storm are forecast for the area.

Storm warning: Indicates winds 48-63 knots (55-73 mph) not directly associated with a tropical storm are forecast for the area.

Hurricane and Tornado Classifications

Source: National Weather Service, NOAA, U.S. Dept. of Commerce

The Saffir-Simpson Hurricane Wind Scale, created by Herbert Saffir and expanded upon by Robert Simpson, rates a hurricane's intensity from 1 to 5. The scale, updated in 2012, provides examples of the type of damage and impacts associated with winds of the indicated intensity. The Fujita (or F) Scale was created by T. Theodore Fujita in 1971 to classify tornadoes. The Enhanced Fujita Scale, an update, was implemented in the U.S. in 2007. It uses 3-sec. gusts estimated at the point of damage based on a judgment of eight levels of damage to 28 indicators.

Saffir-Simpson Wind Scale (Hurricanes)			Enhanced Fujita Scale (Tornadoes)	
Category	Wind speed[1]	Summary of damage	Rank	3-sec. gust
1	74-95 mph	Very dangerous winds will produce some damage.	EF-0	65-85 mph
2	96-110 mph	Extremely dangerous winds will cause extensive damage.	EF-1	86-110 mph
3	111-129 mph	Devastating damage will occur.	EF-2	111-135 mph
4	130-156 mph	Catastrophic damage will occur.	EF-3	136-165 mph
5	Over 156 mph	Catastrophic damage will occur.	EF-4	166-200 mph
(1) 1-min. sustained winds.			EF-5	Over 200 mph

Monthly Normal Mean Temperatures, Precipitation in U.S. Cities

Source: National Climatic Data Center, NESDIS, NOAA, U.S. Dept. of Commerce

Normals are averages covering a 30-year period. The temperature and precipitation normals given here are based on records for 1981-2010. Temperatures listed below represent means of the normal daily maximum and normal daily minimum temperatures for each month. For stations that did not have continuous records from the same site for the entire 30 years, the means have been adjusted to the record at the present site. (*) = City station. Other figures are for airport stations. T = Temperature in Fahrenheit; P = Precipitation in inches.

	Jan.		Feb.		Mar.		Apr.		May		June		July		Aug.		Sept.		Oct.		Nov.		Dec.	
Station	T	P	T	P	T	P	T	P	T	P	T	P	T	P	T	P	T	P	T	P	T	P	T	P
Albany, NY	23	2.6	26	2.2	35	3.2	48	3.2	58	3.6	67	3.8	72	4.1	70	3.5	62	3.3	50	3.7	40	3.3	29	2.9
Albuquerque, NM	36	0.4	41	0.5	48	0.5	56	0.6	66	0.5	75	0.7	78	1.5	76	1.6	69	1.1	58	1.0	45	0.6	36	0.5
Anchorage, AK	17	0.7	20	0.7	27	0.6	37	0.5	48	0.7	55	1.0	59	1.8	57	3.3	49	3.0	35	2.0	22	1.2	19	1.1
Asheville, NC	37	3.7	40	3.8	47	3.8	55	3.3	63	3.7	71	4.7	74	4.3	73	4.4	66	3.8	56	2.9	47	3.7	39	3.6
Atlanta, GA	43	4.2	47	4.7	54	4.8	62	3.4	70	3.7	77	4.0	80	5.3	79	3.9	74	4.5	63	3.4	54	4.1	45	3.9
Atlantic City, NJ	33	3.2	35	2.9	42	4.2	52	3.6	61	3.4	71	3.1	76	3.7	74	4.1	67	3.2	56	3.4	47	3.3	37	3.7
Baltimore, MD	33	3.1	36	2.9	44	3.9	54	3.2	54	4.0	72	3.5	77	4.1	75	3.3	68	4.0	56	3.3	47	3.3	37	3.4
Barrow, AK	−13	0.1	−14	0.1	−13	0.1	2	0.2	21	0.2	36	0.3	41	1.0	39	1.1	32	0.1	17	0.4	−2	0.2	−8	0.1
Birmingham, AL	44	4.8	48	4.5	55	5.2	63	4.4	71	5.0	78	4.4	81	4.8	81	3.9	75	3.9	64	3.4	54	4.9	46	4.5
Bismarck, ND	13	0.4	18	0.5	30	0.9	44	1.3	56	2.4	65	3.2	71	2.9	70	2.3	59	1.6	45	1.3	29	0.7	16	0.5
Boise, ID	31	1.2	37	1.0	45	1.4	51	1.2	59	1.4	68	0.7	76	0.3	75	0.2	65	0.6	53	0.8	40	1.4	31	1.6
Boston, MA	29	3.4	32	3.3	38	4.3	48	3.7	58	3.5	68	3.7	73	3.4	72	3.4	65	3.4	54	3.9	45	4.0	35	3.8
Buffalo, NY	25	3.2	26	2.5	34	2.9	46	3.0	57	3.5	66	3.7	71	3.2	70	3.3	62	3.9	51	3.5	41	4.0	30	3.9
Burlington, VT	19	2.1	22	1.8	31	2.2	45	2.8	56	3.5	66	3.7	71	4.2	69	3.9	61	3.6	48	3.6	38	3.1	26	2.4
Caribou, ME	10	2.7	14	2.2	25	2.5	39	2.7	52	3.3	61	3.5	66	4.1	64	3.8	55	3.3	43	3.5	32	3.6	18	3.3
Charleston, SC	48	3.7	52	3.0	58	3.7	65	2.9	73	3.0	79	5.7	82	6.5	81	7.2	76	6.1	67	3.8	59	2.4	51	3.1
Charleston, WV	34	3.0	38	3.2	46	3.9	56	3.2	64	4.8	72	4.3	75	4.9	74	3.7	67	3.3	57	2.7	47	3.7	37	3.3
Chicago, IL	24	1.7	28	1.8	38	2.5	49	3.4	59	3.7	69	3.5	74	3.7	72	4.9	65	3.2	53	3.2	40	3.2	28	2.3
Cleveland, OH	28	2.7	31	2.3	38	2.9	50	3.5	60	3.7	69	3.4	74	3.5	72	3.5	65	3.8	54	3.1	44	3.6	32	3.1
Columbus, OH	30	2.7	33	2.3	42	3.0	53	3.4	63	4.2	72	4.0	75	4.8	74	3.3	67	2.8	55	2.6	44	3.2	34	3.0
Dallas-Ft. Worth, TX	46	2.1	50	2.7	58	3.5	66	3.1	74	4.9	81	3.8	85	2.2	86	1.9	78	2.6	68	4.2	57	2.7	47	2.6
Denver, CO	31	0.4	33	0.3	40	0.9	47	1.7	57	2.2	67	2.0	74	3.0	73	1.6	63	1.0	51	1.0	38	0.6	30	0.3
Des Moines, IA	23	1.0	27	1.3	39	2.3	52	3.9	62	4.7	72	4.9	76	4.5	74	4.1	66	3.1	53	2.6	39	2.2	26	1.4
Detroit, MI	26	2.0	28	2.0	37	2.3	49	2.9	60	3.4	69	3.5	74	3.4	72	3.0	64	3.3	52	2.5	42	2.8	30	2.4
Dodge City, KS	32	0.6	36	0.7	44	1.6	54	1.8	64	2.9	74	3.2	80	3.1	78	2.8	69	1.7	57	1.7	43	0.8	33	0.8
Duluth, MN	10	1.0	15	0.8	26	1.5	40	2.4	51	3.2	60	4.2	66	3.9	64	3.7	56	4.1	43	2.9	29	2.1	15	1.2
Fairbanks, AK	−8	0.6	−1	0.4	11	0.3	33	0.3	49	0.6	60	1.4	63	2.2	56	1.9	45	1.1	24	0.8	3	0.7	−4	0.6
Fresno, CA	47	2.2	52	2.0	57	2.0	62	1.0	70	0.4	77	0.2	83	0.0	82	0.0	76	0.2	66	0.6	54	1.1	47	1.8
Galveston, TX*	53	3.7	55	3.0	61	2.9	68	2.2	76	3.0	82	4.8	84	3.9	84	3.4	80	5.4	73	4.2	64	3.4	56	3.4
Grand Rapids, MI	24	2.1	27	1.8	36	2.4	48	3.4	59	4.0	68	3.8	73	3.8	71	3.6	63	4.3	51	3.3	40	3.5	29	2.5
Helena, MT	23	0.4	28	0.3	36	0.6	45	1.0	54	1.9	62	2.1	70	1.2	68	1.2	58	1.1	46	0.7	33	0.5	22	0.4
Honolulu, HI	73	2.3	73	2.0	75	2.0	76	0.6	78	0.6	80	0.3	81	0.5	82	0.6	82	0.7	80	1.8	78	2.4	75	3.2
Houston, TX	53	3.4	56	3.2	63	3.4	70	3.3	77	5.1	82	5.9	84	3.8	85	3.8	80	4.1	72	5.7	62	4.3	54	3.7
Huron, SD	17	0.5	22	0.6	33	1.5	47	2.3	58	3.1	68	3.9	74	2.9	72	2.4	62	2.5	48	1.8	33	0.9	19	0.5
Indianapolis, IN	28	2.7	32	2.3	42	3.6	53	3.8	63	5.1	72	4.3	75	4.6	74	3.1	67	3.1	55	3.1	44	3.7	32	3.2
Jackson, MS	46	5.0	50	4.8	57	5.0	64	5.0	72	4.4	79	4.1	82	4.8	81	4.2	76	3.0	65	3.9	56	4.8	48	5.2
Jacksonville, FL	53	3.3	56	3.2	62	4.0	67	2.6	74	2.5	80	6.5	82	6.6	82	6.8	78	8.2	70	3.9	62	2.1	55	2.8
Juneau, AK	28	5.4	30	4.1	34	3.8	41	2.9	49	3.4	55	3.2	57	4.6	56	5.7	50	8.6	42	8.6	33	6.0	30	5.8
Kansas City, MO	29	1.1	34	1.5	44	2.4	55	3.7	65	5.2	74	5.2	78	4.5	77	3.9	68	4.6	56	3.2	44	2.2	32	1.5
Knoxville, TN	38	4.3	42	4.3	50	4.3	59	4.0	67	4.5	75	3.8	78	5.1	78	3.3	71	3.2	60	2.5	50	4.0	41	4.5
Lander, WY	22	0.4	25	0.6	36	1.2	44	1.9	53	2.2	63	1.3	71	0.8	70	0.6	59	1.1	46	1.3	31	0.9	21	0.6
Lexington, KY	33	3.2	37	3.2	46	4.1	55	3.6	64	5.3	73	4.4	76	4.7	75	3.3	68	2.9	57	3.1	46	3.5	36	3.9
Little Rock, AR	41	3.6	45	3.7	53	4.7	62	5.1	71	4.9	79	3.7	83	3.3	83	2.6	75	3.2	64	4.9	53	5.3	43	5.0
Los Angeles, CA*	58	3.1	59	3.8	61	2.4	63	0.9	66	0.3	69	0.1	73	0.0	74	0.0	73	0.2	69	0.7	62	1.0	58	2.3
Louisville, KY	35	3.2	39	3.2	48	4.2	58	4.0	67	5.3	76	3.8	79	4.2	78	3.3	71	3.1	60	3.2	49	3.6	38	3.8
Marquette, MI*	19	1.8	21	1.3	29	2.0	40	2.5	51	2.5	60	2.7	67	2.8	67	2.6	59	3.2	47	3.1	35	2.6	24	2.0
Memphis, TN	41	4.0	46	4.4	54	5.2	63	5.5	72	5.3	80	3.6	83	4.6	82	2.9	75	3.1	64	4.0	53	5.5	44	5.7
Miami, FL	68	1.6	70	2.3	73	3.0	76	3.1	80	5.3	83	9.7	84	6.5	84	8.9	83	9.9	80	6.3	75	3.3	71	2.0
Milwaukee, WI	22	1.8	26	1.7	35	2.3	46	3.6	56	3.4	66	3.9	72	3.7	71	4.0	63	3.2	51	2.7	39	2.7	27	2.0
Minneapolis, MN	16	0.9	21	0.8	33	1.9	48	2.7	59	3.4	69	4.2	74	4.0	71	4.3	62	3.1	49	2.4	34	1.8	20	1.2
Mobile, AL	50	5.7	54	5.1	60	6.1	66	4.8	74	5.1	80	6.1	82	7.2	82	7.0	78	5.1	68	3.7	60	5.1	52	5.1
Moline, IL	23	1.5	27	1.6	39	2.9	51	3.6	62	4.3	72	4.5	75	4.3	74	4.5	65	3.1	53	3.0	40	2.6	27	2.2
Nashua, NH	24	3.7	27	3.2	35	4.3	46	4.0	57	2.9	66	4.3	71	3.7	70	4.5	62	3.4	50	4.7	40	4.1	30	3.7
Nashville, TN	38	3.8	42	3.9	50	4.1	59	4.0	68	5.5	76	4.1	79	3.6	79	3.2	72	3.4	60	3.0	50	4.3	40	4.2
New Orleans, LA	53	5.2	57	5.3	63	4.6	69	4.6	77	4.6	82	8.1	83	5.9	83	6.0	80	5.1	71	3.6	63	4.5	56	5.3
New York, NY*	33	3.7	35	3.1	43	4.4	53	4.5	62	4.2	71	4.4	77	4.6	75	4.4	68	4.3	57	4.4	48	4.0	38	4.0
Newark, NJ	32	3.5	35	2.9	42	4.2	53	4.2	63	4.1	72	4.0	77	4.8	76	3.7	68	3.8	57	3.6	47	3.7	37	3.8
Norfolk, VA	40	3.4	43	3.1	49	3.7	58	3.4	67	3.4	75	4.3	80	5.1	78	5.5	72	4.8	62	3.4	53	3.2	44	3.3
Oklahoma City, OK	39	1.4	44	1.6	52	3.1	61	3.1	70	4.7	78	4.9	83	2.9	82	3.3	74	4.1	63	3.7	51	2.0	41	1.9
Omaha, NE	24	0.7	28	0.9	40	2.0	52	3.0	62	4.8	72	4.2	77	3.8	75	3.8	66	2.7	53	2.2	39	1.6	26	1.0
Philadelphia, PA	33	3.0	36	2.7	44	3.8	54	3.6	64	3.7	73	3.4	78	4.4	77	3.5	69	3.8	58	3.2	48	3.0	38	3.6
Phoenix, AZ	56	0.9	60	0.9	65	1.0	73	0.3	82	0.1	91	0.0	95	1.1	94	1.0	88	0.6	77	0.6	64	0.7	55	0.9
Pittsburgh, PA	29	2.7	32	2.7	40	3.1	52	3.2	61	4.2	69	4.0	73	3.8	72	3.5	65	3.4	53	2.5	43	3.4	33	2.9
Portland, ME	22	3.4	26	3.3	34	4.2	44	4.3	54	4.0	63	3.8	69	3.6	68	3.1	60	3.7	49	4.9	39	4.9	29	4.0
Portland, OR	41	4.9	44	3.7	48	3.7	52	2.7	58	2.5	64	1.7	69	0.7	70	0.7	65	1.5	55	3.0	47	5.6	40	5.5
Providence, RI	29	3.9	32	3.3	39	5.0	49	4.4	59	3.6	68	3.6	74	3.3	72	3.6	65	3.9	54	3.9	45	4.5	34	4.2
Raleigh, NC	41	3.5	45	3.2	52	4.1	60	2.9	68	3.3	76	3.5	80	4.7	79	4.3	72	4.4	61	3.3	52	3.1	44	3.1
Rapid City, SD	25	0.3	27	0.4	35	0.9	45	1.8	55	3.2	65	2.5	73	1.9	72	1.6	61	1.3	48	1.4	35	0.5	25	0.4
Reno, NV	36	1.0	40	1.0	46	0.8	51	0.5	60	0.5	68	0.5	75	0.2	73	0.2	65	0.4	54	0.5	43	0.8	35	1.0
Richmond, VA	38	3.0	41	2.8	49	4.0	58	3.3	66	3.8	75	3.9	79	4.5	78	4.7	71	4.1	60	3.0	50	3.2	41	3.3
St. Louis, MO	32	2.4	36	2.2	46	3.3	57	3.7	67	4.7	76	4.3	80	4.1	79	3.0	70	3.1	59	3.3	47	3.9	35	2.8
Salt Lake City, UT	30	1.3	34	1.3	44	1.8	51	2.0	60	2.0	70	1.0	79	0.6	77	0.7	66	1.2	53	1.5	40	1.5	30	1.4
San Antonio, TX	52	1.8	56	1.8	62	2.3	69	2.1	77	4.0	82	4.1	85	2.7	85	2.1	80	3.0	71	4.1	61	2.3	53	1.9
San Diego, CA	57	2.0	58	2.3	59	1.8	62	0.8	64	0.1	66	0.1	70	0.0	72	0.0	71	0.2	67	0.6	61	1.0	57	1.5
San Francisco, CA	50	4.2	53	4.1	55	3.0	57	1.3	60	0.5	62	0.1	64	0.0	65	0.0	65	0.2	62	1.0	56	2.4	51	4.0
San Juan, PR	78	3.8	78	2.4	79	2.0	80	4.7	82	5.9	83	4.4	83	5.1	84	5.5	84	5.8	83	5.6	81	6.4	79	5.0
Santa Fe, NM	32	0.6	36	0.5	43	0.8	50	0.7	60	0.9	69	1.1	73	1.8	71	2.6	64	1.6	53	1.4	40	0.7	31	0.8
Savannah, GA	50	3.7	53	2.8	59	3.7	66	3.1	73	3.0	80	6.0	83	5.6	82	6.6	77	4.6	68	3.7	59	2.4	52	3.0
Seattle, WA	42	5.6	43	3.5	47	3.7	50	2.7	56	1.9	61	1.6	66	0.7	66	0.9	61	1.5	53	3.5	45	6.6	41	5.4
Spokane, WA	30	1.8	33	1.3	40	1.6	47	1.3	55	1.6	62	1.3	70	0.6	69	0.6	60	0.7	48	1.2	36	2.3	27	2.3
Springfield, MO	33	2.5	37	2.5	46	3.6	56	4.3	65	5.1	73	4.9	78	3.7	78	3.6	69	4.6	58	3.6	46	4.2	35	3.0
Tampa, FL	61	2.2	63	2.8	67	3.0	72	2.0	78	2.1	82	6.7	83	7.1	83	7.8	82	6.3	76	2.3	69	1.6	63	2.5
Washington, DC	36	2.8	39	2.6	47	3.5	57	3.1	66	4.0	75	3.8	80	3.7	78	2.9	71	3.7	60	3.4	50	3.2	40	3.1
Wilmington, DE	32	3.0	35	2.7	43	3.9	53	3.5	63	4.0	72	3.9	77	4.6	75	3.2	68	4.3	56	3.4	47	3.1	37	3.5
Windsor Locks, CT	26	3.2	30	2.9	38	3.6	49	3.7	60	4.4	69	4.4	74	4.2	72	3.9	64	3.9	52	4.4	42	3.9	32	3.4

Normal High and Low Temperatures, Precipitation in U.S. Cities

Source: National Climatic Data Center, NESDIS, NOAA, U.S. Dept. of Commerce

The normal temperatures and precipitation data given here are based on records for the period 1981-2010. The extreme temperatures are based on records from the time of each station's installation. (*) = City station. Other figures are for airport stations.

State	Station	NORMAL TEMPERATURE (°F) January Max.	Min.	July Max.	Min.	EXTREME TEMPERATURE (°F) Highest	Lowest	AVG. ANNUAL PRECIPITATION (in.)
Alabama	Mobile	61	40	91	73	105	3	66.15
Alaska	Anchorage	23	11	65	52	85	−34	16.58
Alaska	Barrow	−7	−20	47	35	79	−56	4.53
Alaska	Juneau	33	24	64	50	90	−22	62.27
Arizona	Phoenix	67	46	106	78	122	17	8.03
Arkansas	North Little Rock	50	33	92	73	111	−6	50.03
California	Los Angeles	65	49	74	64	110	23	12.82
California	San Francisco	56	44	72	55	106	20	20.65
Colorado	Denver	44	17	89	59	105	−19	14.92
Connecticut	Windsor Locks	35	18	85	63	102	−26	45.85
Delaware	Wilmington	40	25	86	68	103	11	43.08
District of Columbia	Washington–Reagan	43	29	88	71	105	−5	39.74
Florida	Jacksonville	65	41	92	73	105	7	52.39
Florida	Miami	76	60	91	77	98	30	61.90
Georgia	Atlanta	52	34	89	71	105	−8	49.71
Georgia	Savannah	60	39	92	73	105	3	47.96
Hawaii	Honolulu	80	66	88	75	95	53	17.10
Idaho	Boise	38	25	91	60	111	−25	11.73
Illinois	Chicago	31	17	84	64	104	−27	36.89
Indiana	Indianapolis	36	21	85	66	104	−27	42.44
Iowa	Des Moines	31	14	86	67	108	−26	36.01
Kansas	Dodge City	44	20	93	66	110	−21	21.60
Kentucky	Lexington	41	25	86	66	103	−21	45.17
Kentucky	Louisville	43	27	89	70	106	−22	44.91
Louisiana	New Orleans	62	45	91	75	102	11	62.66
Maine	Caribou	20	1	76	55	96	−41	38.49
Maine	Portland	31	13	79	59	103	−39	47.25
Maryland	Baltimore	41	24	87	67	105	−7	41.88
Massachusetts	Boston	36	22	81	65	102	−12	43.77
Michigan	Detroit	32	19	83	64	104	−21	33.47
Michigan	Grand Rapids	31	18	83	62	100	−22	38.27
Michigan	Sault Ste. Marie	23	8	76	54	98	−36	32.95
Minnesota	Duluth	19	2	76	55	97	−39	30.96
Minnesota	Minneapolis	24	8	83	64	105	−34	30.61
Mississippi	Jackson	56	35	92	72	107	2	54.14
Missouri	Kansas City	38	20	88	68	109	−23	38.86
Missouri	St. Louis	40	24	89	71	107	−18	40.96
Montana	Helena	33	13	86	54	105	−42	11.22
Nebraska	Omaha	33	14	87	66	114	−23	30.62
Nevada	Reno	46	25	92	58	108	−16	7.40
New Hampshire	Concord	31	10	82	58	102	−37	40.61
New Jersey	Atlantic City	42	25	86	67	106	−11	41.75
New Mexico	Albuquerque	47	26	90	66	107	−17	9.45
New York	Albany	31	15	82	61	100	−28	39.35
New York	Buffalo	31	19	80	62	99	−20	40.48
New York	New York–Central Park*	38	27	84	69	106	−15	49.94
North Carolina	Raleigh	51	31	90	70	105	−9	43.34
North Dakota	Bismarck	23	2	85	57	112	−44	17.85
Ohio	Cleveland	34	22	83	64	104	−20	39.14
Ohio	Columbus	37	23	85	66	102	−22	39.31
Oklahoma	Oklahoma City	50	29	94	72	110	−8	36.52
Oregon	Portland	47	36	81	58	107	−3	36.03
Pennsylvania	Philadelphia	40	26	87	69	104	−7	41.53
Pennsylvania	Pittsburgh	36	21	83	63	103	−22	38.19
Puerto Rico	San Juan	83	72	89	78	98	60	56.35
Rhode Island	Providence	37	21	83	64	104	−13	47.18
South Carolina	Charleston	59	38	91	73	105	6	51.03
South Dakota	Huron	27	7	86	61	112	−41	22.90
South Dakota	Rapid City	37	13	87	58	111	−31	16.29
Tennessee	Memphis	50	33	92	74	108	−13	53.68
Tennessee	Nashville	47	28	89	68	107	−17	47.25
Texas	Dallas-Fort Worth	56	36	96	75	113	−1	36.14
Texas	Houston	63	43	94	75	109	7	49.77
Utah	Salt Lake City	37	22	93	65	107	−30	16.10
Vermont	Burlington	27	10	81	60	101	−30	36.82
Virginia	Norfolk	48	33	87	72	105	−3	46.53
Virginia	Richmond	47	28	90	69	105	−12	43.60
Washington	Seattle-Tacoma	47	37	76	56	103	0	37.49
Washington	Spokane	34	25	83	56	108	−25	16.56
West Virginia	Charleston	43	26	85	66	104	−16	44.03
Wisconsin	Milwaukee	29	16	80	64	103	−26	34.76
Wyoming	Lander	33	10	87	56	101	−37	12.66

Mean annual snowfall (in.), selected cities: Based on climate normals 1981-2010: Albany, NY, 59.1; Anchorage, AK, 74.5; Boston, MA, 43.8; Burlington, VT, 81.2; Lander, WY, 91.4; Sault Ste. Marie, MI, 123.4.

Wettest spot: Mt. Waialeale in Kauai, HI, may be the rainiest place in the U.S. It has a recorded average annual rainfall of 460 in.

Temperature extremes: The highest temperature ever recorded under standard conditions in the U.S. was 134°F in Death Valley, CA, on July 10, 1913. The record low in the U.S. was −80°F at Prospect Creek, AK, Jan. 23, 1971.

Annual Climatological Data for U.S. Cities, 2015

Source: National Climatic Data Center, NESDIS, NOAA, U.S. Dept. of Commerce

Station	Elev. (ft)	TEMPERATURE (°F) Highest	Date	Lowest	Date	PRECIPITATION Total (in.)	Greatest in 24 hrs. (in.)	Date	Snowfall[1] Total snowfall (in.)	Greatest in 24 hrs. (in.)	Date	FASTEST WIND[2] MPH	Date	NO. OF DAYS Prec. 0.01 in. or more	Snow, sleet 1 in. or more
Albany, NY	281	95	7/29	−12	2/3	38.65	3.79	9/29-30	53.6	11.9	2/2	39	3/2	124	13
Albuquerque, NM	5,308	102	6/22	15	1/1	11.49	2.31	7/6-7	21.2	4.7	2/28	55	10/15	75	8
Anchorage, AK	222	83	6/16+	−8	11/18	18.95	1.58	9/28-29	33.9	4.8	11/20	43	2/6	120	11
Asheville, NC	2,174	92	8/4	3	2/19	54.35	3.13	6/21-22	10.1	4.3	2/25	40	2/15	149	4
Atlanta, GA	974	97	8/4	11	1/8	68.38	4.37	12/23-24	T	T	3/6	37	7/14	148	0
Atlantic City, NJ	117	95	9/3	−6	2/21	46.54	3.02	7/15	22.0	7.0	3/5	46	6/23	118	8
Baltimore, MD	196	97	7/19	1	2/20	51.16	3.11	6/27	28.2	6.3	2/21	41	8/4	126	10
Barrow, AK	38	67	6/19	−36	12/25	5.73	0.55	8/25	38.3	2.0	1/21	40	8/27	107	8
Birmingham, AL	630	99	8/4	8	1/8	60.92	4.43	12/24-25	0.8	0.7	2/25	43	1/25	131	0
Bismarck, ND	1,654	105	8/15	−21	1/12	17.73	2.46	5/16-17	28.4	4.0	12/11	61	6/19	95	9
Boise, ID	2,861	110	6/28	6	1/1	10.95	1.29	7/8-9	9.3	2.2	11/25	40	8/10	103	3
Boston, MA	180	96	9/8	−3	2/16	34.80	2.50	9/29-30	108.6	22.1	1/27	38	8/4	123	18
Buffalo, NY	717	91	7/29	−10	2/16+	36.79	2.86	8/14-15	82.1	8.2	2/2	43	10/29	161	26
Burlington, VT	348	94	9/7	−19	2/24	37.84	3.09	9/29-30	58.2	7.5	1/30	36	3/17	147	20
Caribou, ME	626	88	9/7	−22	2/24	36.17	1.61	9/29-30	118.1	8.6	3/15	41	8/3	163	30
Charleston, SC	48	99	7/23	18	2/20	74.89	11.85	10/3-4	T	T	1/7	40	11/2	118	0
Chicago, IL	658	92	9/6	−10	2/28	39.85	2.56	6/15	63.5	16.2	2/1	39	12/23	124	17
Cleveland, OH	805	93	7/29	−17	2/20	40.07	2.76	6/27	46.6	7.2	2/1	38	11/13	158	11
Columbus, OH	812	93	6/12	−11	2/24	45.00	2.25	7/12	29.3	6.8	2/21	45	5/11	142	10
Dallas-Ft. Worth, TX	562	106	8/10+	16	1/8	62.61	4.78	11/26-27	5.8	2.5	3/4	48	12/13	94	3
Denver, CO	5,382	98	8/15	−10	1/4	18.31	1.41	4/16-17	64.4	7.7	12/15	46	11/17	107	25
Des Moines, IA	971	97	7/13	−10	2/5	44.63	4.12	6/24-25	36.1	6.7	11/20	43	1/8	113	7
Detroit, MI	631	92	9/7	−13	2/20	30.32	2.25	5/30-31	50.9	13.7	2/1	40	11/12	133	14
Duluth, MN	1,429	93	8/15+	−19	2/23+	32.29	2.02	9/2	53.1	8.0	12/16	45	4/2	122	15
Fairbanks, AK	464	89	7/6	−43	2/7	14.38	1.08	8/25-26	70.0	11.2	9/29	38	4/19	107	21
Fresno, CA	375	108	8/17	28	1/2	8.98	1.25	12/21-22	T	T	5/7	29	4/14	41	0
Grand Rapids, MI	788	91	8/2	−13	2/20	33.11	2.44	4/9-10	52.1	8.8	2/1	45	12/24	138	18
Helena, MT	3,867	103	6/27	−6	11/27+	9.90	0.86	5/16	20.2	4.0	12/14	56	12/9	81	9
Honolulu, HI	18	93	8/12	57	1/5	21.04	4.42	8/23-24	—	—	—	38	1/2	122	—
Houston, TX	107	106	8/11	28	1/8	70.03	6.94	10/24-25	0.0	0.0	—	41	8/25	122	0
Huron, SD	1,284	96	6/9	−18	2/27+	25.58	3.14	8/18-19	29.4	5.4	11/30	51	6/27	85	9
Indianapolis, IN	797	94	9/4	−7	1/8	48.15	4.51	7/7-8	24.7	5.9	3/1	48	5/30	126	9
Jackson, MS	296	103	8/10+	13	1/8	59.28	4.56	11/6-7	—	—	—	36	2/1	110	—
Jacksonville, FL	34	98	7/12	24	2/20	44.54	3.41	11/8-9	—	—	—	49	6/22	118	—
Kansas City, MO	1,008	96	7/14	−3	1/8+	46.59	4.28	9/10	13.6	2.5	2/1	44	6/26	118	5
Knoxville, TN	982	96	6/26	3	2/20	51.66	2.34	11/29-30	9.3	4.3	2/25	46	6/28	134	2
Lander, WY	5,560	95	8/25+	−20	1/1	15.13	1.40	5/23-24	71.7	9.5	11/25	54	3/28	70	17
Lexington, KY	984	95	9/5	−18	2/20	59.89	5.22	4/2-3	38.4	10.2	2/16	36	4/2	137	6
Los Angeles, CA	326	99	10/10	36	1/1	5.96	1.80	9/15	—	—	—	37	12/11	29	—
Louisville, KY	484	95	9/5+	−6	2/20	62.41	6.02	4/2-3	23.9	8.3	3/4	45	7/17	126	5
Marquette, MI	1,415	91	7/27	−28	2/23	26.15	1.25	7/6	133.5	9.2	2/8	—	—	155	46
Memphis, TN	286	99	7/29+	9	1/8	52.66	3.41	7/2-3	5.9	3.1	3/5	36	7/14	114	2
Miami, FL	29	96	7/29	42	2/20	62.07	4.83	12/3-4	—	—	—	31	7/31	165	—
Milwaukee, WI	680	93	8/14+	−9	2/19	32.84	3.27	4/8-9	54.2	10.4	2/1	41	12/23	110	13
Minneapolis, MN	874	94	8/14	−11	2/23+	36.14	2.87	7/5-6	32.0	3.8	11/30	45	7/18	125	10
Mobile, AL	212	98	7/19	17	1/8	81.37	7.76	9/27-28	T	T	1/9+	40	7/17	123	0
Moline, IL	607	94	9/6	−18	2/28	44.54	4.01	2/1-2	47.9	13.8	2/1	41	4/21	111	11
Nashville, TN	574	97	8/4	4	1/8	50.80	2.59	7/1-2	5.9	2.9	3/5	46	7/28	128	1
New Orleans, LA	7	99	7/29	25	1/8	71.34	8.71	10/25-26	—	—	—	54	4/27	119	—
New York, NY	161	97	9/8	2	2/20	40.97	2.10	1/18	49.1	7.5	3/5	29	1/4	110	14
Newark, NJ	28	98	9/8	1	2/20	38.98	3.73	5/31	45.0	6.7	3/5	40	7/1	106	11
Norfolk, VA	69	99	6/23	9	2/20	50.19	3.08	7/18	12.7	5.5	2/26	36	10/5	129	4
North Little Rock, AR	565	102	7/29	8	12/8	51.14	3.25	5/10-11	10.0	6.4	3/4-5	—	—	104	3
Oklahoma City, OK	1,284	102	8/7	10	3/5	55.06	8.10	5/5-6	8.2	3.0	3/4	48	3/25	99	3
Philadelphia, PA	62	96	9/3	2	2/20	47.25	4.77	9/10-11	26.9	7.5	3/5	52	6/23	113	6
Phoenix, AZ	1,106	117	8/14	31	1/2	7.15	0.93	5/15	—	—	—	51	8/31	49	—
Pittsburgh, PA	1,175	92	7/28	−10	2/20	40.56	3.50	9/29-30	43.5	4.3	1/26	38	2/14	155	15
Portland, ME	72	92	9/7	−11	2/24	43.82	5.90	9/29-30	87.5	22.2	1/27	39	3/17	127	22
Portland, OR	223	103	7/30	24	11/30+	40.40	3.22	12/6-7	—	—	—	41	3/15	129	—
Providence, RI	53	97	9/8	−5	2/21	40.83	3.18	5/31	74.3	16.0	1/27	48	8/4	114	18
Raleigh-Durham, NC	430	100	6/16	7	2/20	57.10	2.76	10/2-3	7.9	3.2	2/26	36	6/20	129	3
Rapid City, SD	3,153	100	8/15+	−10	2/26	25.25	2.46	7/15	43.7	6.9	5/10	58	7/27	90	15
Reno, NV	4,407	102	7/2	9	1/1	8.52	1.08	11/1-2	11.9	3.7	12/24	54	7/7	56	4
Richmond, VA	167	100	6/23	4	2/21+	49.07	2.01	12/23-24	12.8	6.2	2/16	46	6/25	127	3
St. Louis, MO	710	100	7/28	1	2/19	61.24	5.37	12/26-27	12.8	3.9	2/28	46	7/20	122	4
Salt Lake City, UT	4,224	104	6/29	4	12/31	16.14	1.11	9/15-16	26.2	8.2	12/14	51	8/7	86	6
San Antonio, TX	821	104	8/11	28	1/8	44.22	4.21	10/23-24	T	T	2/17	43	9/25	89	0
San Diego, CA	81	99	10/9	41	12/27	9.89	1.84	5/14-15	—	—	—	28	11/16	45	—
San Francisco, CA	89	93	9/20	34	12/27	8.44	1.21	2/8	—	—	—	43	10/3	35	—
San Juan, PR	10	95	10/5+	71	3/31+	41.30	1.83	9/1-2	0.0	0.0	—	40	6/22	192	0
Sault Ste. Marie, MI	727	95	7/28	−24	2/20	32.88	2.35	12/13-14	86.6	6.4	12/29	44	12/24	153	30
Savannah, GA	143	99	7/11	20	1/8	47.60	2.94	4/25	T	T	6/19	51	4/25	126	0
Scottsbluff, NE	3,949	101	8/15	−12	1/8	23.56	3.04	5/9-10	37.7	6.5	12/15	47	7/27	98	11
Seattle, WA	434	95	7/19	25	11/30	44.83	2.36	12/8-9	T	T	12/27+	40	1/18	144	0
Spokane, WA	2,384	105	6/28	2	12/31	14.08	1.33	3/15	39.0	6.2	12/21	44	12/9	92	14
Springfield, MO	1,280	96	8/9	−5	2/19	59.74	6.96	12/26-27	13.6	4.8	2/16	40	7/5	118	4
Tampa, FL	40	97	7/11	34	2/20	63.50	4.39	8/3	0.0	0.0	—	32	2/26	129	0
Washington, DC	3	98	7/19	5	2/20	45.02	2.92	6/1-2	18.3	4.8	3/5	43	6/23	123	6
Wilmington, DE	77	96	9/3	2	2/20	48.74	3.84	6/1-2	22.9	7.0	3/5	53	6/23	119	7
Windsor Locks, CT	165	96	9/8	−9	2/21	39.21	2.34	9/29-30	59.0	10.8	2/2	44	3/18	118	16

(+) = Indicates value for extreme also occurred on an earlier date(s). (T) = Trace amount. — = Data not available or unreported. (1) Comprises all forms of frozen precipitation, including hail and sleet. (2) Sustained for at least 2 min., not peak gust.

Record Temperatures by State

Source: National Climatic Data Center, NESDIS, NOAA, U.S. Dept. of Commerce
(as of Apr. 28, 2016)

| State | LOWEST TEMPERATURE | | | | HIGHEST TEMPERATURE | | | |
	°F	Date	Station	Approx. elevation (ft)	°F	Date	Station	Approx. elevation (ft)
Alabama	−27	Jan. 30, 1966	New Market	732	112	Sept. 6, 1925	Centreville	220
Alaska	−80	Jan. 23, 1971	Prospect Creek Camp	955	100	June 27, 1915	Fort Yukon	445
Arizona	−40	Jan. 7, 1971	Hawley Lake	8,180	128	June 29, 1994	Lake Havasu City	449
Arkansas	−29	Feb. 13, 1905	Gravette	1,260	120	Aug. 10, 1936	Ozark	390
California	−45	Jan. 20, 1937	Boca	5,575	134	July 10, 1913	Greenland Ranch	−194
Colorado	−61	Feb. 1, 1985	Maybell	5,944	114	July 11, 1954[1]	Sedgwick	3,584
Connecticut	−32	Jan. 22, 1961[1]	Coventry	480	106	July 15, 1995[1]	Danbury	405
Delaware	−17	Jan. 17, 1893	Millsboro	20	110	July 21, 1930	Millsboro	20
Florida	−2	Feb. 13, 1899	Tallahassee	192	109	June 29, 1931	Monticello	98
Georgia	−17	Jan. 27, 1940	CCC Fire Camp F-16	1,000	112	Aug. 20, 1983[1]	Greenville	960
Hawaii	12	May 17, 1979	Mauna Kea Observ.	13,773	100	Apr. 27, 1931	Pahala	840
Idaho	−60	Jan. 18, 1943	Island Park	6,290	118	July 28, 1934	Orofino	1,320
Illinois	−36	Jan. 5, 1999	Congerville	640	117	July 14, 1954	East St. Louis	410
Indiana	−36	Jan. 19, 1994	New Whiteland	785	116	July 14, 1936	Collegeville	650
Iowa	−47	Feb. 3, 1996[1]	Elkader	788	118	July 20, 1934	Keokuk	651
Kansas	−40	Feb. 13, 1905	Lebanon	1,841	121	July 24, 1936[1]	Alton	1,685
Kentucky	−37	Jan. 19, 1994	Shelbyville	730	114	July 28, 1930	Greensburg	590
Louisiana	−16	Feb. 13, 1899	Minden	185	114	Aug. 10, 1936	Plain Dealing	251
Maine	−50	Jan. 16, 2009	Big Black River	885	105	July 10, 1911[1]	North Bridgton	449
Maryland	−40	Jan. 13, 1912	Oakland	2,420	109	July 10, 1936[1]	Cumberland Frederick	899 380
Massachusetts	−35	Jan. 12, 1981[1]	Chester	640	107	Aug. 2, 1975	Chester New Bedford	640 70
Michigan	−51	Feb. 9, 1934	Vanderbilt	905	112	July 13, 1936	Mio Stanwood	960 830
Minnesota	−60	Feb. 2, 1996	Tower	1,430	115	July 29, 1917	Beardsley	1,089
Mississippi	−19	Jan. 30, 1966	Corinth	385	115	July 29, 1930	Holly Springs	502
Missouri	−40	Feb. 13, 1905	Warsaw	705	118	July 14, 1954	Warsaw Union	705 540
Montana	−70	Jan. 20, 1954	Rogers Pass	5,545	117	July 5, 1937[1]	Medicine Lake	1,942
Nebraska	−47	Dec. 22, 1989[1]	Oshkosh	3,390	118	July 24, 1936[1]	Minden	2,160
Nevada	−50	Jan. 8, 1937	San Jacinto	5,203	125	June 29, 1994	Laughlin	605
New Hampshire	−50	Jan. 22, 1885	Mt. Washington	6,271	106	July 4, 1911	Nashua	135
New Jersey	−34	Jan. 5, 1904	River Vale	31	110	July 10, 1936	Runyon	20
New Mexico	−50	Feb. 1, 1951	Gavilan	7,425	122	June 27, 1994	Waste Isolat. Pilot Plant	3,411
New York	−52	Feb. 18, 1979	Old Forge	1,748	108	July 22, 1926	Troy	35
North Carolina	−34	Jan. 21, 1985	Mt. Mitchell	6,240	110	Aug. 21, 1983	Fayetteville	186
North Dakota	−60	Feb. 15, 1936	Parshall	1,950	121	July 6, 1936	Steele	1,853
Ohio	−39	Feb. 10, 1899	Milligan	875	113	July 21, 1934	Gallipolis	569
Oklahoma	−31	Feb. 10, 2011	Nowata	NA	120	Aug. 12, 1936[1]	Altus Irrigation Res. Sta.	1,380
Oregon	−54	Feb. 10, 1933[1]	Seneca	4,659	119	Aug. 10, 1898[1]	Pendleton	1,040
Pennsylvania	−42	Jan. 5, 1904	Smethport	1,469	111	July 10, 1936[1]	Phoenixville	105
Rhode Island	−28	Jan. 11, 1942	Wood River Junction	49	104	Aug. 2, 1975	Providence	60
South Carolina	−19	Jan. 21, 1985	Caesars Head	3,200	113	June 29, 2012	Columbia	242
South Dakota	−58	Feb. 17, 1936	McIntosh	2,179	120	July 15, 2006[1]	Fort Pierre	1,590
Tennessee	−32	Dec. 30, 1917	Mountain City	2,503	113	Aug. 9, 1930[1]	Perryville	371
Texas	−23	Feb. 8, 1933	Seminole	3,336	120	June 28, 1994[1]	Monahans	2,547
Utah	−50	Jan. 5, 1913	East Portal	7,615	117	July 5, 1985	Saint George	2,857
Vermont	−50	Dec. 30, 1933	Bloomfield	1,040	107	July 7, 1912	Vernon	226
Virginia	−30	Jan. 21, 1985	Mountain Lake Bio. Station	3,870	110	July 15, 1954[1]	Balcony Falls	732
Washington	−48	Dec. 30, 1968	Mazama Winthrop	2,141 1,749	118	Aug. 5, 1961[1]	Ice Harbor Dam	368
West Virginia	−37	Dec. 30, 1917	Lewisburg	2,300	112	July 10, 1936[1]	Martinsburg	534
Wisconsin	−55	Feb. 4, 1996[1]	Couderay	1,300	114	July 13, 1936	Wisconsin Dells	835
Wyoming	−66	Feb. 9, 1933	Riverside Ranger Sta.	6,500	115	July 15, 1988[1]	Diversion Dam	5,590

NA = Not available. (1) Also on earlier dates at the same or other places.

Tropical Cyclone Names in 2017

Source: National Weather Service, NOAA, U.S. Dept. of Commerce

If there are more than 21 named Atlantic storms in one season, remaining storms take names from the Greek alphabet, starting with Alpha. (This was only necessary in one year: 2005.)

Atlantic: Arlene, Bret, Cindy, Don, Emily, Franklin, Gert, Harvey, Irma, Jose, Katia, Lee, Maria, Nate, Ophelia, Philippe, Rina, Sean, Tammy, Vince, Whitney.

Eastern North Pacific: Adrian, Beatriz, Calvin, Dora, Eugene, Fernanda, Greg, Hilary, Irwin, Jova, Kenneth, Lidia, Max, Norma, Otis, Pilar, Ramon, Selma, Todd, Veronica, Wiley, Xina, York, Zelda.

World Temperature and Precipitation

Source: World Meteorological Organization (WMO)

Average daily maximum and minimum temperatures and annual precipitation based on records for the period 1961-90. Records of extreme temperatures include all available years of data for a given location and are usually for a longer period. Surface elevations are supplied by the WMO and may differ from figures in other sections of *The World Almanac.*

Station	Surface elevation (ft)	Temperature (°F) AVERAGE DAILY January Max.	January Min.	July Max.	July Min.	EXTREME Max.	EXTREME Min.	Avg. annual precipitation (in.)
Algiers, Algeria	82	61.7	42.6	87.1	65.3	NA	NA	27.0
Athens, Greece	49	56.1	44.6	88.9	73.0	NA	NA	14.6
Auckland, New Zealand	20	74.8	61.2	58.5	46.4	NA	NA	49.4
Bangkok, Thailand	66	89.6	69.8	90.9	77.0	104	51	59.0
Beijing, China	177	34.9	15.1	87.4	70.9	105	−17	22.7
Berlin, Germany	190	35.2	26.8	73.6	55.2	107	−4	23.3
Bogotá, Colombia	8,357	67.3	41.7	64.6	45.5	75	21	32.4
Bucharest, Romania	298	34.7	22.1	83.8	60.1	105	−18	23.4
Budapest, Hungary	456	34.2	24.8	79.7	59.7	103	−10	20.3
Buenos Aires, Argentina	82	85.8	67.3	59.7	45.7	104	22	45.2
Cairo, Egypt	243	65.8	48.2	93.9	71.1	118	34	1.0
Cape Town, South Africa	138	79.0	60.3	63.3	44.6	105	28	20.5
Caracas, Venezuela	2,739	79.9	60.8	81.3	66.0	96	45	36.1
Casablanca, Morocco	203	62.8	47.1	77.7	66.7	NA	NA	16.8
Copenhagen, Denmark	16	35.6	28.4	68.9	55.0	NA	NA	NA
Damascus, Syria	2,004	54.3	32.9	97.2	61.9	NA	NA	5.6
Dubai, United Arab Emirates[1]	16	75.2	56.7	105.1	84.0	117	45	3.7
Dublin, Ireland	279	45.7	36.5	66.0	52.5	86	8	28.8
Geneva, Switzerland	1,364	38.3	27.9	76.3	53.2	101	−3	35.6
Havana, Cuba	164	78.4	65.5	88.3	74.8	NA	NA	46.9
Hong Kong, China	203	65.5	56.5	88.7	79.9	97	32	87.2
Istanbul, Turkey	108	47.8	37.2	82.8	65.3	105	7	27.4
Jerusalem, Israel	2,483	53.4	39.4	83.8	63.0	107	26	23.2
Karachi, Pakistan	69	78.4	50.7	91.6	81.3	117	34	8.6
Lagos, Nigeria	125	90.0	72.3	82.8	72.1	NA	NA	59.3
Lima, Peru	43	79.0	66.9	66.4	59.4	NA	NA	0.2
London, England, UK	203	44.1	32.7	71.1	52.3	99	2	29.7
Manila, Philippines	79	85.8	74.8	89.1	76.8	NA	NA	49.6
Mexico City, Mexico	7,570	70.3	43.7	73.8	53.2	NA	NA	33.4
Montreal, Canada	118	21.6	5.2	79.2	59.7	100	−36	37.0
Mumbai (Bombay), India	36	85.3	66.7	86.2	77.5	110	46	85.4
Nairobi, Kenya	5,897	77.9	50.9	71.6	48.6	NA	NA	41.9
New Delhi, India[2]	709	69.8	45.7	94.5	80.2	113	34	31.3
Paris, France	213	42.8	33.6	75.2	55.2	105	−1	25.6
Prague, Czech Republic	1,197	32.7	22.5	73.9	53.2	98	−16	20.7
Reykjavik, Iceland	200	35.4	26.6	55.9	46.9	76	−3	31.5
Riyadh, Saudi Arabia	2,034	68.4	46.8	109.0	81.3	120	28	NA
Rome, Italy	79	53.8	35.4	88.2	62.1	NA	NA	33.0
San Salvador, El Salvador	2,037	86.5	61.3	86.2	66.4	105	45	68.3
São Paulo, Brazil	2,598	81.1	65.7	71.2	53.1	NA	NA	57.4
Seoul, South Korea	285	33.4	19.2	83.3	70.9	NA	NA	NA
Shanghai, China	23	45.9	32.9	88.9	76.6	104	10	43.8
Singapore	52	85.8	73.6	87.4	75.6	NA	NA	84.6
Stockholm, Sweden	171	30.7	23.0	71.4	56.1	97	−26	21.2
Sydney, Australia	10	79.5	65.5	62.4	43.9	114	32	46.4
Tehran, Iran	3,906	45.0	30.0	98.2	75.2	109	−5	9.1
Tokyo, Japan	118	49.1	34.2	83.8	72.1	NA	NA	55.4
Toronto, Canada	567	27.5	12.0	80.2	57.6	105	−26	30.8

NA = Not available. (1) Records are for 1974-91. (2) Records are for 1971-90.

Speed of Winds in the U.S.

Source: National Climatic Data Center, NESDIS, NOAA, U.S. Dept. of Commerce

Based on available records through 2015. Maximum speeds are highest 3-sec. wind speeds.

Station	Avg. mph	Max. mph	Station	Avg. mph	Max. mph	Station	Avg. mph	Max. mph
Albuquerque, NM	8.2	89	Helena, MT	6.9	68	Oklahoma City, OK	11.3	87
Anchorage, AK	7.0	71	Honolulu, HI	10.3	48	Omaha, NE	10.0	92
Atlanta, GA	8.3	71	Houston, TX	7.4	70	Philadelphia, PA	9.3	75
Baltimore, MD	7.3	72	Indianapolis, IN	9.5	85	Phoenix, AZ	6.1	77
Birmingham, AL	6.2	72	Jackson, MS	6.1	72	Pittsburgh, PA	7.9	62
Bismarck, ND	9.4	83	Jacksonville, FL	6.6	77	Portland, ME	8.0	72
Boise, ID	7.6	68	Little Rock, AR	7.0	87	Portland, OR	7.5	67
Boston, MA	11.5	76	Los Angeles, CA	7.4	53	Providence, RI	9.3	66
Buffalo, NY	10.3	75	Louisville, KY	7.8	75	Richmond, VA	7.7	72
Burlington, VT	8.3	63	Miami, FL	8.4	104	St. Louis, MO	9.1	70
Charleston, SC	7.9	67	Milwaukee, WI	10.2	70	Salt Lake City, UT	8.4	75
Chicago, IL	9.9	70	Minneapolis, MN	9.7	71	San Francisco, CA	10.6	71
Cleveland, OH	9.6	68	Mobile, AL	7.5	83	San Juan, PR	7.8	93
Dallas-Ft. Worth, TX	10.5	78	Mount Washington, NH	35.1	231	Seattle, WA	7.9	69
Denver, CO	9.9	72	Nashville, TN	7.1	67	Sioux Falls, SD	10.2	87
Des Moines, IA	9.8	77	New Orleans, LA	8.0	77	Washington, DC	9.0	74
Detroit, MI	9.5	78	New York, NY	6.6	62	Wichita, KS	11.5	101
Fairbanks, AK	4.4	59	Newark, NJ	9.8	78	Wilmington, DE	8.5	76

Wind Chill Temperature

Source: National Weather Service, NOAA, U.S. Dept. of Commerce

Temperature and wind combine to cause heat loss from body surfaces. For example, when the air temperature is 5°F, a 10-mph wind can cause body heat loss equal to that which could occur when the air temperature is –10°F with no wind. In other words, a 10-mph wind can make 5°F feel like –10°F. Wind speeds greater than 45 mph have little additional chilling effect. Direct sunlight can increase the wind chill temperature 10°F to 15°F. When the wind chill temperature falls within the shaded areas, frostbite can occur on exposed skin in the times indicated or less.

Wind speed (mph) \ Calm	Air temperature (°F)																	
	40	35	30	25	20	15	10	5	0	–5	–10	–15	–20	–25	–30	–35	–40	–45
	Wind chill temperature (°F)																	
5	36	31	25	19	13	7	1	–5	–11	–16	–22	–28	–34	–40	–46	–52	–57	–63
10	34	27	21	15	9	3	–4	–10	–16	–22	–28	–35	–41	–47	–53	–59	–66	–72
15	32	25	19	13	6	0	–7	–13	–19	–26	–32	–39	–45	–51	–58	–64	–71	–77
20	30	24	17	11	4	–2	–9	–15	–22	–29	–35	–42	–48	–55	–61	–68	–74	–81
25	29	23	16	9	3	–4	–11	–17	–24	–31	–37	–44	–51	–58	–64	–71	–78	–84
30	28	22	15	8	1	–5	–12	–19	–26	–33	–39	–46	–53	–60	–67	–73	–80	–87
35	28	21	14	7	0	–7	–14	–21	–27	–34	–41	–48	–55	–62	–69	–76	–82	–89
40	27	20	13	6	–1	–8	–15	–22	–29	–36	–43	–50	–57	–64	–71	–78	–84	–91
45	26	19	12	5	–2	–9	–16	–23	–30	–37	–44	–51	–58	–65	–72	–79	–86	–93

☐ 30 minutes   ☐ 10 minutes   ☐ 5 minutes

Heat Index

Source: National Weather Service, NOAA, U.S. Dept. of Commerce

The heat index, or apparent temperature, is a measure of how hot it feels when the relative humidity is factored in with the actual air temperature. For example, when air temperature is 100°F, and relative humidity is 50%, it feels as if it's 118°F with no humidity. Full sunlight can make one feel even hotter. On the chart, the shaded areas indicate the likelihood of heat disorders with prolonged exposure or strenuous activity.

Relative humidity (%)	Air temperature (°F)															
	80	82	84	86	88	90	92	94	96	98	100	102	104	106	108	110
	Apparent temperature (°F)															
40	80	81	83	85	88	91	94	97	101	105	109	114	119	124	130	136
45	80	82	84	87	89	93	96	100	104	109	114	119	124	130	137	
50	81	83	85	88	91	95	99	103	108	113	118	124	131	137		
55	81	84	86	89	93	97	101	106	112	117	124	130	137			
60	82	84	88	91	95	100	105	110	116	123	129	137				
65	82	85	89	93	98	103	108	114	121	128	136					
70	83	86	90	95	100	105	112	119	126	134						
75	84	88	92	97	103	109	116	124	132							
80	84	89	94	100	106	113	121	129								
85	85	90	96	102	110	117	126	135								
90	86	91	98	105	113	122	131									
95	86	93	100	108	117	127										
100	87	95	103	112	121	132										

☐ Caution   ☐ Extreme caution   ☐ Danger   ☐ Extreme danger

Ultraviolet (UV) Index Forecast

Source: National Weather Service (NWS), NOAA, U.S. Dept. of Commerce; U.S. Environmental Protection Agency (EPA); U.S. Food and Drug Administration, U.S. Dept. of Health and Human Services

The NWS and EPA developed and began offering a UV index in 1994 in response to increasing incidences of skin cancer, cataracts, and other effects from exposure to the sun's harmful rays. In 2004, they adapted their index to the Global Solar UV Index sponsored by the World Health Organization. The UV index is now a regular element of NWS atmospheric forecasts. For information on precautions to take after learning the UV index value, call the EPA's Stratospheric Ozone Protection Hotline at (800) 296-1996. For questions on scientific aspects, visit the NWS Climate Prediction Center online at www.cpc.ncep.noaa.gov.

The UV index, ranging from 0 to 11+, is an indication of the expected intensity of UV radiation reaching the Earth's surface during the solar noon hour (the time of day, dependent on location and time of year, when the sun appears to have reached its highest point in the sky). The lower the UV index value, the less the expected radiation. The UV index forecast is produced daily for 58 cities by the NWS Climate Prediction Center and uses the following scale.

UV index	Exposure	Minimum precautions
0-2	Low	Sunscreen with an SPF of at least 15
3-5	Moderate	Sunscreen, covering up
6-7	High	Sunscreen, hat, UV-blocking sunglasses, avoid sun 10 AM-4 PM
8-10	Very high	Same as above
11+	Extreme	Same as above

UV levels are influenced by:

Ozone. Ozone, a form of oxygen, the molecules of which consist of three atoms rather than two, absorbs UV radiation. The more ozone, the lower the UV radiation at the surface.

Sun height. The higher the sun is in the sky, the higher the UV radiation level.

Cloudiness. UV radiation levels are highest under cloudless skies. Even with cloud cover, UV radiation levels can be high due to the scattering of UV radiation by water molecules and fine particles in the atmosphere.

Reflectivity. Reflective surfaces intensify UV exposure. White sand reflects about 15% of UV radiation that reaches it; sea foam, 25%; snow, as much as 80%; water, up to 100% depending on reflection angle.

Altitude. At higher altitudes, UV radiation travels a shorter distance to reach Earth's surface so there is less atmosphere to absorb the rays. For every 1,000 m (3,281 ft) one travels above sea level, UV levels increase by 10%-12%. Snow and lack of pollutants intensify UV exposure at higher altitudes.

Latitude. The closer a location is to the equator, the higher the UV radiation level.

Lightning

Source: National Weather Service, NOAA, U.S. Dept. of Commerce

Lightning is a powerful electric discharge, or spark, that can occur in the atmosphere when an imbalance of positive and negative charges develops. It can travel within a cloud, between clouds, between a cloud and clear sky, or between a cloud and the ground. Lightning generally accompanies rainstorms but it can also be seen with snowstorms, volcano eruption clouds, and violent forest fires. In a common form of cloud-to-ground lightning, a negatively charged area in a thunderstorm sends charges down toward positively charged objects. Lightning can travel miles away from the area of a storm.

The transfer of charges in lightning generates a huge amount of heat, sending the temperature in the channel to 50,000°F or more and causing the air within it to expand rapidly. The sound of that expansion is thunder. Sound travels more slowly than light, so lightning is usually observed before thunder is heard.

An estimated 25 mil cloud-to-ground lightning bolts happen in the U.S. each year. They killed an annual average of 48 people in 1986-2015. This is a small number compared to U.S. deaths from fire (about 3,000 a year) and motor vehicle crashes (more than 30,000 annually in recent years), but it is still significant. In comparison, tornadoes caused an average of 70 deaths a year and hurricanes an average of 46 over the same 30-year time period. According to preliminary figures from the National Weather Service, 27 people were struck and killed by lightning in 2015; 130 more were injured.

Most lightning deaths and injuries occur in summer when people are outdoors. If outdoors, one should run to a safe building or vehicle when thunder is first heard, lightning is seen, or dark threatening clouds are observed developing overhead. Even while indoors, one is advised to stay away from windows and doors and to avoid contact with anything conducting electricity, including corded phones, computers and other electrical equipment, and tubs, showers, and other plumbing. One should stay inside until 30 min. after the last occurrence of lightning or thunder.

More information about lightning can be found online at www.lightningsafety.noaa.gov.

Global Temperature Extremes and Precipitation Records

Source: World Weather/Climate Extremes Archive, World Meteorological Organization (WMO) Commission for Climatology
(records in each category ranked from most to least extreme; as of Apr. 30, 2016)

Highest Temperature Extremes

Continent/area	Highest temp. (°F)	Place	Elevation (ft)	Date
North America	134	... Death Valley, CA, U.S. (Greenland Ranch/Furnace Creek)	−179	July 10, 1913
Africa	131[1]	... Kebili, Tunisia	125	July 7, 1931
Europe/Middle East/ Greenland	129	... Tirat Tsvi, Israel	−722	June 21, 1942
Southwest Pacific	123	... Oodnadatta, Australia	367	Jan. 2, 1960
South America	120	... Rivadavia, Argentina	2,192	Dec. 11, 1905
Continental Europe	118.4	... Athens, Greece (and Elefsina, Greece)	774	July 10, 1977
Antarctica	59	... Vanda Station (New Zealand), Wright Valley	49	May 1, 1974
Asia	NA[2]			

NA = Not available. (1) Previous record of 136.4°F set on Sept. 13, 1922, in El Azizia, Libya, was invalidated in Sept. 2012 after the WMO determined that an error had been made in recording the temperature. (2) Under investigation as of Apr. 2016.

Lowest Temperature Extremes

Continent/area	Lowest temp. (°F)	Place	Elevation (ft)	Date
Antarctica	−129	... Vostok Station (Soviet Union/Russia)	11,220	July 21, 1983
Asia	−90	... Verkhoyansk, Russia	350	Feb. 5 and 7, 1892
	−90	... Oimekon, Russia	2,625	Feb. 6, 1933
Europe/Middle East/ Greenland	−87	... Northice, Greenland	7,680	Jan. 9, 1954
North America	−81.4	... Snag, Yukon, Canada	2,120	Feb. 3, 1947
Continental Europe	−72.6	... Ust'-Shchugor, Russia	279	Dec. 31, 1978
South America	−27	... Sarmiento, Argentina	879	June 1, 1907
Southwest Pacific	−14	... Eweburn (now Ranfurly), New Zealand	1,388	July 17, 1903
Africa	−11	... Ifrane, Morocco	5,364	Feb. 11, 1935
Australia	−9.4	... Charlotte Pass, New South Wales	5,758	June 29, 1994

Highest Measured Average Annual Precipitation Extremes

Continent/area	Highest avg. (in.)[1]	Place	Elevation (ft)	Years in averaging period
Asia	467.4	... Mawsynram, India	4,695	38
Southwest Pacific	460	... Mt. Waialeale, Kauai, HI, U.S.	5,148	30
Africa	405	... Debundscha, Cameroon	30	32
South America	354	... Quibdo, Colombia	230	29
Australia	316.3	... Bellenden Ker, Queensland	5,102	34
North America	276	... Henderson Lake, British Columbia, Canada	12	15
Europe	180.8	... Crkvice, Montenegro	3,461	30
Antarctica	>31.5[2]	... Along coast of E and W and over the Antarctic Peninsula		3[3]

(1) Official greatest average annual precipitation. The frequently cited record of 523.6 in. in Lloro, Colombia (14 mi SE and at a higher elevation than Quibdo) is an estimate. (2) Water equivalent. (3) July 1996-June 1999.

Lowest Measured Average Annual Precipitation Extremes

Continent/area	Lowest avg. (in.)	Place	Elevation (ft)	Years in averaging period
South America	0.03	... Arica, Chile	213	59
Antarctica	0.08	... Amundsen-Scott South Pole Station (U.S.)	9,301	10
Africa	<0.1	... Wadi Halfa, Sudan	590	39
North America	1.2	... Batagues, Mexico	69	14
Asia	1.8	... Aden, Yemen	63	50
Southwest Pacific	4.05	... Troudaninna, Australia	46	42
Continental Europe	6.4	... Astrakhan, Russia	66	25

OCEANOGRAPHY
Tides and Their Causes
Source: National Ocean Service, NOAA, U.S. Dept. of Commerce

The tides are natural phenomena involving the movement of waves in the Earth's large fluid bodies as a result of the gravitational attraction of the sun and moon. These two variable influences combined produce the complex recurrent cycle of the tides. Tides may occur in both oceans and seas; to a limited extent in large lakes and in the atmosphere; and, to a very minute degree, in the Earth itself. The length of time between succeeding tides can vary.

The tide-generating force represents the difference between (1) the centrifugal force produced by Earth's revolution around the common center-of-gravity of the Earth-moon system and (2) the gravitational attraction of the moon acting upon the Earth's overlying waters. The moon is about 390 times closer to Earth than is the sun. So despite its smaller mass, the moon's tide-raising force is two times greater.

The tide-generating forces of the moon and sun acting tangentially to the Earth's surface tend to cause a maximum accumulation of waters at two diametrically opposite points on the Earth's surface and to withdraw compensating amounts of water from all points 90° removed from these tidal bulges. As the Earth rotates beneath the maxima and minima of these tide-generating forces, a sequence of two high tides, separated by two low tides, is produced each lunar day (24 hr. and 50 min., the time it takes for a specific site on the Earth to rotate from an exact point under the moon to the same point under the moon) in what is called a **semidiurnal tide**. Each ocean basin reacts differently to tidal forces.

Twice each month, when the sun, moon, and Earth are directly aligned—the moon between the Earth and sun (at new moon) or on the opposite side of Earth from the sun (at full moon)—the sun and moon exert gravitational forces in a mutual or additive fashion. The highest high tides and lowest low tides, called **spring tides**, are produced at these times. At two positions 90° in between, the moon and sun's gravitational forces—imposed at right angles—counteract each other to the greatest extent, and the range between high and low tides is reduced, resulting in **neap tides**.

The inclination of the moon's monthly orbit and of the sun to the equator during Earth's yearly passage through its orbit produce a difference in the height of succeeding high and low tides, known as the diurnal inequality. In most cases, this produces a so-called **mixed tide**. In extreme cases, these phenomena may result in a **diurnal tide**, with only one high tide and one low tide each day. There are other monthly and yearly variations in the tides because of the elliptical shape of the orbits.

The range of tides in the open ocean is generally less than in the coastal regions, where the incoming tide can be augmented by the continental shelves, as well as by bays and estuaries. The largest tidal ranges in the world occur in the Bay of Fundy, Canada, where the range of tide reaches 53.5 ft. The highest tides in the U.S. occur near Anchorage, AK, with tidal ranges up to 40 ft.

In every case, actual high or low tide can vary considerably from the average as a result of weather conditions such as strong winds, abrupt barometric pressure changes, or prolonged periods of extreme high or low pressure.

Mean Ranges of Tide

Place	Ft	In.	Place	Ft	In.	Place	Ft	In.
Baltimore, MD	1	2	Key West, FL	1	3	Provincetown, MA	9	3
Biloxi, MS	1	6	Los Angeles, CA	3	10	St. Petersburg, FL	1	7
Boston, MA	9	6	Miami Beach, FL	2	6	San Diego, CA	4	1
Charleston, SC	5	3	New London, CT	2	7	San Francisco, CA	4	1
Eastport, ME	18	4	New York, NY	4	6	San Juan, PR	1	1
Ft. Pulaski, GA	6	11	Newport, RI	3	6	Sandy Hook, NJ	4	8
Galveston, TX	1	0	Philadelphia, PA	6	1	Seattle, WA	7	8
Honolulu, HI	1	3	Portland, ME	9	1	Washington, DC	2	9

Note: Mean range is the difference in height between mean high water and mean low water.

El Niño and La Niña
Source: National Weather Service, NOAA, U.S. Dept. of Commerce

El Niño is a climatically significant disruption of the ocean-atmosphere system characterized by large-scale weakening of trade winds and warming of surface layer waters in the central and eastern equatorial Pacific. The term *El Niño*, Spanish for "the little boy" or "the Christ Child," was originally used by fishing crews to refer to a warm ocean current that appeared around Christmas off the west coast of Ecuador and Peru lasting several months. The term has come to be reserved for exceptionally strong, warm currents that bring heavy rains.

El Niño events generally occur at irregular intervals of two to seven years, at an average of once every three to four years. They typically last 12 to 18 months. The intensity of El Niño events varies depending on the area encompassed by the abnormally warm ocean temperatures. Some are strong, such as in 1982-83, 1997-98, and 2015-16. Others are considerably weaker, such as the 2009-10 event. The eastward extent of warmer-than-normal water varies from episode to episode.

El Niño influences weather around the globe, and its impacts are most clearly seen in the winter. During El Niño years, winter temperatures in the continental U.S. tend to be warmer than normal in the northern states and on the West Coast and cooler than normal in the Southeast. Conditions tend to be wetter than normal over central and southern California, the Southwest, and across much of the South, and drier than normal over the northern portions of the Rocky Mountains and in the Ohio Valley. Globally, El Niño brings wetter than normal conditions to Peru and Chile and dry conditions to Australia and Indonesia. It should be noted that El Niño is only one of a number of factors influencing seasonal variations of climate.

La Niña ("the little girl") is characterized by colder than normal sea surface temperatures in the equatorial Pacific. La Niña typically brings wetter, cooler conditions to the Pacific Northwest and drier, warmer conditions to much of the southern U.S. El Niño and La Niña are opposite phases of the El Niño-Southern Oscillation (ENSO) cycle, which involves a shift in tropical sea-level pressure between the Eastern and Western Hemispheres.

NOAA and other agencies monitor these events using satellites, weather balloons, and buoys in the Pacific Ocean. Numerical computer models of the ocean and atmosphere use these data to predict the onset and evolution of El Niño and La Niña. Following strong El Niño conditions in the Northern Hemisphere in late 2015 and early 2016, in Apr. 2016, NOAA predicted a weakening of El Niño, with a transition to a neutral ENSO cycle likely during late spring or early summer 2016, and an increasing chance of La Niña during the second half of the year.

DISASTERS

Some Notable Aircraft Disasters Since 1937

Source: National Transportation Safety Board; World Almanac research

Particularly notable disasters are in bold. Asterisk (*) indicates number of deaths includes people on ground. As of Aug. 2016.

Date	Aircraft	Site of accident	Deaths
1937, May 6	**German zeppelin Hindenburg**	**Burned at mooring, Lakehurst, NJ**	**36***
1944, Aug. 23	U.S. Air Force B-24 Liberator bomber	Hit school, Freckleton, England, UK.	61*
1945, July 28	U.S. Army B-25.	Hit Empire State Building after getting lost in fog, New York, NY.	14*
1952, Dec. 20	U.S. Air Force C-124	Crashed at Moses Lake, WA	87
1953, Mar. 3	**Canadian Pacific DH-106 Comet**	**Crashed on takeoff from Karachi, Pakistan; world's first fatal commercial passenger jet crash**	**11**
1953, June 18	U.S. Air Force C-124	Crashed, burned near Tokyo, Japan	129
1955, Oct. 6	United Airlines DC-4.	Crashed in Medicine Bow Peak, WY	66
1955, Nov. 1	United Airlines DC-6.	Bomb on board exploded near Longmont, CO.	44[1]
1956, June 20	Venezuelan Super Constellation	Crashed into Atlantic off Asbury Park, NJ	74
1956, June 30	TWA Super Const., United DC-7	Collided over Grand Canyon, AZ.	128
1960, Dec. 16	United DC-8, TWA Super Const.	Collided over New York, NY, killing all 128 on planes, 6 on ground.	134*
1962, Mar. 16	Flying Tiger Super Constellation	Vanished in W Pacific en route to Philippines from Guam	107
1962, June 3	Air France Boeing 707	Crashed on takeoff from Paris, France.	130
1962, June 22	Air France Boeing 707	Crashed in storm, Guadeloupe, French W Indies	113
1963, Feb. 1	Lebanese Middle East Airlines Vickers Viscount 754, Turkish Mil. Douglas C-47	Collided over Ankara, Turkey, killing all 17 on planes, 87 on ground	104*
1963, Nov. 29	Trans-Canada Air Lines DC-8	Crashed after takeoff from Montreal, QC, Canada.	118
1965, May 20	Pakistani Boeing 720	Crashed at airport in Cairo, Egypt	121
1966, Jan. 24	Air India Boeing 707	Crashed on Mont Blanc, France-Italy.	117
1966, Feb. 4	All-Nippon Boeing 727	Plunged into Tokyo Bay, Japan	133
1966, Mar. 5	BOAC (British Overseas Airways Corp.) Boeing 707	Crashed into Mt. Fuji, Japan, after encountering severe turbulence	124
1966, Dec. 24	U.S. military-chartered CL-44.	Crashed into village in S Vietnam.	129*
1967, Apr. 20	Globe Air Bristol Britannia	Crashed on approach to airport, Nicosia, Cyprus.	126
1967, July 19	Piedmont Boeing 727, Cessna 310	Collided over Hendersonville, NC.	82
1968, Apr. 20	S. African Airways Boeing 707	Crashed on takeoff from Windhoek, Namibia.	122
1968, May 3	Braniff International Electra	Crashed in storm near Dawson, TX.	85
1968, May 12	U.S. Air Force Lockheed C-130B	Hit by enemy mortar while evacuating Kham Duc Camp, S Vietnam	155
1969, Mar. 16	Venezuelan DC-9.	Crashed after takeoff from Maracaibo, Venezuela.	155[2]
1970, July 3	British-chartered DH-106 Comet	Crashed near Barcelona, Spain.	112
1970, July 5	Air Canada DC-8	Crashed near Toronto Intl. Airport, ON, Canada	108
1970, Nov. 14	Southern Airways DC-9	Crashed into mountains near Huntington, WV.	75[3]
1971, July 30	All-Nippon Boeing 727, Japan Air Force F-86 fighter.	Collided over Morioka, Japan.	162[4]
1971, Sept. 4	Alaska Airlines Boeing 727.	Crashed into mountain near Juneau, AK.	111
1972, May 18	Aeroflot Antonov 10A	Wings separated from fuselage; crashed on approach to Kharkov, USSR.	122
1972, June 18	British European Airways Trident-1C	Crashed near Staines after takeoff from London, Eng., UK.	118
1972, Aug. 14	East German Ilyushin 62	Crashed on takeoff from East Berlin, E Germany	156
1972, Aug. 31	Aeroflot Ilyushin 18V.	Crashed in field near Magnitogorsk, USSR.	101
1972, Oct. 1	Aeroflot Ilyushin 18V.	Crashed into Black Sea, USSR	109
1972, Oct. 13	Aeroflot Ilyushin 62.	Crashed near Moscow, USSR.	174
1972, Dec. 3	Spanish-chartered Convair CV-990	Crashed on takeoff from Canary Islands, Spain.	155
1972, Dec. 29	Eastern Airlines Lockheed Tristar.	Crashed on approach to Miami Intl. Airport, FL	99
1973, Jan. 22	Nigerian-chartered Boeing 707.	Burst into flames upon landing at Kano Airport, Nigeria	176
1973, Feb. 21	**Libyan Arab Boeing 727.**	**Flew off course, shot down by Israeli fighter planes over Sinai Desert.**	**108**
1973, Apr. 10	Invicta Airways Vickers Vanguard	Crashed during snowstorm on approach to Basel, Switzerland.	108
1973, June 3	Soviet Supersonic Tu-144	Crashed near Goussainville, France	14[5]
1973, July 11	Varig Airlines (Brazil) Boeing 707.	Crashed on approach to Orly Airport, Paris, France	123
1973, July 31	Delta Airlines DC-9.	Crashed while attempting landing in fog, Logan Airport, Boston, MA	89
1973, Sept. 30	Aeroflot Tupolev 104B.	Crashed after takeoff from Sverdlovsk, USSR.	108
1973, Oct. 13	Aeroflot Tupolev 104B.	Crashed on approach to Moscow, USSR.	122
1973, Dec. 22	Royal Air Maroc SE 210 Caravelle VIN	Flew into side of a mountain near Tangier, Morocco.	106
1974, Mar. 3	Turkish DC-10.	Crashed in Ermenonville, near Paris, France.	346
1974, Apr. 22	Pan American Boeing 707.	Crashed in Bali, Indonesia.	107
1974, Apr. 27	Aeroflot Ilyushin 18V.	Crashed after takeoff from Leningrad, USSR.	109
1974, Dec. 1	TWA Boeing 727	Crashed on approach in storm, Upperville, VA	92
1974, Dec. 4	Dutch-chartered DC-8	Crashed in storm near Colombo, Sri Lanka	191
1975, Apr. 4	U.S. Air Force Galaxy C-5A	Crashed on takeoff nr. Saigon, S Vietnam; carried orphans	155
1975, June 24	Eastern Airlines 727.	Crashed in storm, JFK Airport, New York, NY	113
1975, Aug. 3	Alia Royal Jordanian Boeing 707	Hit mountainside in heavy fog near Agadir, Morocco.	188
1975, Aug. 20	Czechoslovakian Air Ilyushin 62.	Crashed on approach to Damascus, Syria.	126
1976, Mar. 6	Aeroflot Ilyushin 18E.	Crashed between Moscow, USSR, and Yerevan, Armenia.	111
1976, Sept. 10	British Airways Trident, Yugoslavian DC-9	Collided near Zagreb, Yugoslavia	176
1976, Sept. 19	Turkish Boeing 727.	Hit mountain in southern Turkey.	154
1976, Oct. 13	Lloyd Aero Boliviano Boeing 707	Crashed into soccer field after takeoff from Santa Cruz, Bolivia	91[6]
1977, Mar. 27	**KLM 747, Pan American 747**	**Collided on foggy runway, Tenerife, Canary Islands, Spain; world's worst airline disaster**	**583**
1977, Nov. 19	TAP Portugal Boeing 727.	Crashed in Madeira, Portugal.	131
1977, Dec. 4	Malaysian Airlines Boeing 737	Hijacked and forced to fly to Singapore, crashed near Johor Strait	100
1978, Jan. 1	Air India 747	Crashed into sea after takeoff from Bombay, India	213
1978, Sept. 25	Pacific SW Air Boeing 727, Cessna 172	Collided over San Diego, CA.	144*
1978, Nov. 15	Indonesian-chartered DC-8	Crashed on approach to airport, Colombo, Sri Lanka	183
1979, May 25	**American Airlines DC-10**	**Crashed after takeoff from O'Hare Airport, Chicago, IL; highest death toll in U.S. aviation history**	**275***
1979, Aug. 11	Aeroflot/Moldova Tu-134, Aeroflot Tu-134	Collided over Ukraine.	178
1979, Nov. 23	Pakistani Boeing 707.	Crashed near Jidda, Saudi Arabia.	156
1979, Nov. 28	Air New Zealand DC-10.	Crashed into Mt. Erebus during Antarctica flyover.	257
1980, Mar. 14	PLL LOT Ilyushin 62.	Crashed making emergency landing, Warsaw, Poland.	87[7]
1980, Apr. 25	Dan-Air Services (UK) Boeing 727	Crashed into mountain, Tenerife, Canary Islands, Spain.	146

Date	Aircraft	Site of accident	Deaths
1980, July 8	Aeroflot Tupolev 154B	Crashed after takeoff from Alma-Ata, USSR	166
1980, Aug. 19	Saudi Arabian Tristar	Burned after emergency landing in Riyadh, Saudi Arabia	301
1981, Dec. 1	Inex Adria (Yugoslavia) DC-9	Crashed into mountain on island of Corsica, France	180
1982, Jan. 13	Air Florida Boeing 737	Crashed into Potomac R. after takeoff from Washington, DC	78
1982, June 8	VASP (Brazil) Boeing 727	Crashed into mountain near Fortaleza, Brazil	137
1982, June 28	Aeroflot Yokovlev 42	Crashed near Mozyr, USSR	132
1982, July 9	Pan Am Boeing 727	Crashed after takeoff from Kenner, LA, near New Orleans	153*
1983, July 11	Ecuadorean Boeing 737	Inexperienced pilot crashed into hill near Cuenca, Ecuador	119
1983, Sept. 1	**S. Korean Boeing 747**	**Shot down after violating Soviet airspace near Sakhalin; plane apparently misidentified**	**269**
1983, Sept. 23	Gulf Air Boeing 737	Bomb exploded in cargo hold over Mina Jebel Ali, UAE	112
1983, Nov. 27	Avianca Boeing 747	Crashed near Barajas Airport, Madrid, Spain	181
1984, Oct. 11	Aeroflot/East Siberia Tu-154	Crashed into vehicles on runway while landing in poor weather, Omsk, Russia	178*
1985, Feb. 19	Spanish Boeing 727	Crashed into Mt. Oiz, Spain	148
1985, June 23	Air India Boeing 747	Crashed into Atlantic off Ireland after bomb detonated on board	329
1985, July 10	Aeroflot Tupolev 154B	Crashed after takeoff from Uzbekistan, USSR	200
1985, Aug. 2	Delta Air Lines L-1011	Crashed at Dallas-Ft. Worth Airport, TX	135
1985, Aug. 12	**Japan Air Lines Boeing 747**	**Crashed into Mt. Ogura, Japan; world's worst single-plane disaster**	**520**
1985, Dec. 12	Arrow Air DC-8	Crashed after takeoff from Gander, NL, Canada	256[8]
1986, Mar. 31	Mexican Boeing 727	Crashed NW of Mexico City, Mexico	167
1986, Aug. 31	Aeromexico DC-9, Piper PA-28	Collided over Cerritos, CA	82*
1987, May 9	Polish IL-62M	Crashed after takeoff from Warsaw, Poland	183
1987, Aug. 16	Northwest Airlines MD-82	Crashed after takeoff from Romulus, MI	156
1987, Nov. 28	S. African Boeing 747	Crashed into Indian Ocean near Mauritius	159
1987, Nov. 29	Korean Air Boeing 707	Bomb planted by 2 N. Korean agents exploded while plane over Andaman Sea off Burma	115
1988, Mar. 17	Colombian Boeing 707	Crashed into mountainside near Venezuela border	143
1988, July 3	**Iran Air Airbus A300**	**Misidentified as hostile aircraft, shot down by U.S. Navy warship *Vincennes* over Persian Gulf**	**290**
1988, Oct. 19	Indian Airlines Boeing 737	Exploded after striking trees near runway, Ahmedabad, India	131
1988, Dec. 21	**Pan Am Boeing 747**	**Libyan agent planted bomb on board; exploded over Lockerbie, Scotland**	**270[9]**
1989, Feb. 8	U.S.-chartered Boeing 707	Crashed into mountain on Azores Isls., off Portugal	144
1989, June 7	Suriname DC-8	Crashed near Paramaribo Airport, Suriname	176
1989, July 19	United Airlines DC-10	Crashed on landing in Sioux City, IA	111
1989, Sept. 3	Cubana Aviacion Ilyushin 62M	Crashed on takeoff from Havana, Cuba	171*
1989, Sept. 19	**UTA DC-10**	**Bomb exploded on board flight from Chad to France while over desert in Niger**	**170**
1989, Oct. 21	Honduran Boeing 727	Crashed into mountain near Tegucigalpa, Honduras	131
1989, Nov. 27	Avianca (Colombia) Boeing 727	Bomb exploded on flight from Bogotá, Colombia	107
1990, Jan. 25	Avianca Boeing 707	Crashed on landing at JFK Airport, New York, NY	73
1990, Oct. 2	Xiamen Airlines Boeing 737	Hijacked after takeoff from Xiamen; collided with China Southern Airlines 757 on runway during emergency landing, Guangzhou, China	128
1991, May 26	Lauda-Air (Austria) Boeing 767-300	Exploded over rural Thailand	223
1991, July 11	Nigerian DC-8	Crashed on landing at Jidda, Saudi Arabia	261
1991, Oct. 5	U.S. Air Force Lockheed C-130 Hercules	Crashed after takeoff from Jakarta, Indonesia	135*
1992, July 31	Thai Airbus A300-310	Crashed into mountain N of Kathmandu, Nepal	113
1992, Sept. 26	Nigerian Air Force Lockheed C-130 Hercules	Transport full of military officers crashed near Lagos, Nigeria	158
1992, Sept. 28	Pakistan Intl. Air Airbus A300	Crashed into hillside near Kathmandu, Nepal	167
1992, Oct. 4	**El Al (Israel) Boeing 747-200F**	**Crashed into 2 apartment bldgs., Amsterdam, Netherlands**	**120***
1992, Nov. 24	China Southern Airlines Boeing 737	Crashed on approach to Giulin, China	141
1992, Dec. 22	Libyan Arab Air Boeing 727	Collided with Libyan Air Force MiG-23 on approach to Tripoli, Libya	159
1993, Feb. 8	Iran Air Tu-154, Iranian Air Force jet	Collided after military jet took off from Tehran, Iran	131
1993, May 19	SAM Colombia Boeing 727	Crashed into mountain near Medellin, Colombia	132
1993, Nov. 20	Macedonian Yakovlev 42D	Crashed into mountain near Skopje, Macedonia	116
1994, Jan. 3	Aeroflot Tu-154	Crashed and exploded after takeoff from Irkutsk, Russia	125*
1994, Apr. 26	China Airlines Airbus A300	Crashed on approach to Nagoya Airport, Japan	264
1994, June 6	China Northwest Airlines Tu-154	Crashed near Xian, China	160
1994, Sept. 8	USAir Boeing 737-300	Crashed near Pittsburgh Intl. Airport, Aliquippa, PA	132
1994, Oct. 31	American Eagle ATR-72-210	Crashed in field near Roselawn, IN	68
1995, Dec. 18	Zairean Lockheed L-188C Electra	Overloaded charter crashed in Lunda Norte, Angola	141
1995, Dec. 20	American Airlines Boeing 757	Crashed into mountain N of Cali, Colombia	159
1996, Jan. 8	African Air Antonov-32 cargo plane	Crashed into a market in Kinshasa, Zaire; all deaths on ground	237*
1996, Feb. 6	Dominican Boeing 757	Crashed into Atlantic off Dominican Republic	189
1996, Feb. 29	Peruvian Boeing 737	Crashed into hillside near Arequipa, Peru	123
1996, Apr. 3	U.S. Air Force Boeing T-43A	Crashed into mountain near Dubrovnik, Croatia	35[10]
1996, May 11	ValuJet DC-9	Crashed into Florida Everglades after improper cargo started fire	110
1996, July 17	Trans World Airlines Boeing 747	Exploded and crashed into Atlantic off Long Island, NY	230
1996, Aug. 29	Vnukovo Airlines (Russia) Tu-154	Crashed into mountain on Arctic island of Spitsbergen	141
1996, Nov. 7	Nigerian Boeing 727	Crashed into lagoon SE of Lagos, Nigeria	144
1996, Nov. 12	**Saudi Arabian Boeing 747, Kazakh Ilyushin 76 cargo plane**	**Collided near New Delhi, India; world's worst midair collision**	**349**
1996, Nov. 23	Ethiopian Airlines Boeing 767	Hijacked, then crashed into Indian Ocean off the Comoros	127
1997, Aug. 6	Korean Air Boeing 747-300	Crashed into jungle on Guam on approach to airport	228
1997, Sept. 26	Indonesian Airbus A300	Crashed near airport, Medan, Indonesia	234
1998, Feb. 16	China Airlines Airbus A300	Crashed on approach to airport in Taipei, Taiwan	203*
1998, Sept. 2	Swissair MD-11	Crashed into Atlantic off Nova Scotia, Canada	229
1999, Oct. 31	EgyptAir Boeing 767	Crashed off Nantucket, MA; result of deliberate actions by copilot, motives unknown	217
2000, Jan. 30	Kenya Airways Airbus A310	Crashed into Atlantic after takeoff from Abidjan, Côte d'Ivoire	169
2000, Jan. 31	Alaska Airlines MD-83	Crashed into Pacific off coast of Southern CA	88
2000, Apr. 19	Air Philippines Boeing 737-200	Crashed on approach to airport, Davao, Philippines	131

Date	Aircraft	Site of accident	Deaths
2000, July 25	**Air France Concorde**	**Crashed into hotel after takeoff from Paris; world's first Concorde crash**	**113***
2000, Aug. 23	Gulf Air Airbus A320.	Crashed into Persian Gulf on approach to airport in Bahrain.	143
2001, July 3	Vladivostokavia Tu-154	Crashed on approach to airport, Irkutsk, Russia	145
2001, Sept. 11	**2 Boeing 767s, 2 Boeing 757s**	**September 11 terrorist attacks**	**265[11]**
2001, Oct. 8	Cessna 525A Citation, Scandinavian Airlines System (SAS) MD-87	Collided in heavy fog on takeoff from Milan, Italy.	118*
2001, Nov. 12	**American Airlines Airbus A300**	**Crashed after takeoff from JFK Airport, New York, NY**	**265***
2002, Feb. 12	Iran Air Tours Tu-154	Crashed into mountain on approach to airport, Khorramabad, Iran . .	119
2002, Apr. 15	Air China Boeing 767	Crashed into mountainside in rain and fog on approach to airport, Pusan, S. Korea	129
2002, May 4	EAS Airlines BAC 1-11.	Crashed shortly after takeoff from Kano, Nigeria	149
2002, May 7	China Northern Airlines MD-82.	Plunged into sea, apparently after a passenger started fire in cabin, NE China	112
2002, May 25	China Airlines Boeing 747	Broke apart in midair, plunged into Taiwan Strait en route to Hong Kong airport	225
2002, July 27	**Ukraine Air Force Sukhoi Su-27**	**Crashed while performing, Lviv, Ukraine; world's worst air-show crash**	**77[12]**
2002, Aug. 19	Russian Mi-26 transport helicopter.	Hit by Chechen missile near Grozny, Chechnya	127
2003, Jan. 8	Turkish Airlines British Aerospace RJ-100	Crashed on approach to airport in Diyarbakir, Turkey	75
2003, Feb. 19	Iranian Revolutionary Guard Ilyushin 76 . .	Crashed into mountain near Kerman, Iran; passengers were Revolutionary Guard members.	275
2003, May 26	Ukrain.-Medit. Airlines Yak-42	Crashed into mountain in fog approaching Trabzon, Turkey; passengers incl. Spanish peacekeepers returning from Afghan. . . .	75
2003, July 8	Sudan Airways Boeing 737-200	Mechanical problems reported shortly after takeoff; crashed upon return to Port Sudan Airport.	115
2003, Dec. 25	Union Transp. Africains Boeing 727	Overloading caused crash on takeoff from Cotonou, Benin	141
2004, Jan. 3	Flash Airlines Boeing 737-300	Crashed into Red Sea after takeoff from Sharm el-Sheik, Egypt. . . .	148
2004, Aug. 24	Volga-Aviaexpress Tu-134, Sibir Airlines Tu-154.	2 planes that took off from Moscow crashed within minutes of each other; brought down by Chechen suicide bombers	90
2005, Aug. 14	Helios Airways Boeing 737-300	Crashed after air pressure failure on board, near Athens, Greece. . .	121
2005, Aug. 16	West Caribbean Airways MD-82	Crashed after engine failure, near Machiques, Venezuela.	160
2005, Sept. 5	Mandala Airlines Boeing 737-200.	Crashed shortly after takeoff from Medan, Sumatra, Indonesia.	145*
2005, Oct. 22	Bellview Airlines Boeing 737-200	Crashed during heavy electrical storm near Lagos, Nigeria.	117
2005, Dec. 6	Islamic Rep. of Iran Air Force Lockheed C-130.	Crashed into apartment building after reportedly attempting emergency landing back at airport, Tehran, Iran	116*
2005, Dec. 10	Sosoliso Airlines DC-9-30.	Crashed during storm on approach to Port Harcourt, Nigeria	107
2006, May 3	Armavia Airbus A320	Crashed into Black Sea on approach to airport, Sochi, Russia	113
2006, July 9	S7 Airlines Airbus A310	Skidded off runway, crashed into concrete barrier after landing, Irkutsk, Russia	125
2006, Aug. 22	Pulkovo Aviation Tu-154.	Crashed after encountering storm, near Donetsk, Ukraine	170
2006, Sept. 29	Gol Airlines Boeing 737	Crashed into Amazon jungle after midair collision with Embraer Legacy jet, Brazil	154
2007, May 5	Kenya Airways Boeing 737-800	Crashed shortly after takeoff from Douala, Cameroon.	114
2007, July 17	TAM Airlines Airbus 320.	Crashed into cargo depot, gas station after skidding off airport runway, São Paulo, Brazil	199*
2008, Aug. 20	Spanair Boeing-MD-82.	Swerved off runway, caught fire on takeoff attempt, Madrid, Spain. .	154
2009, Feb. 12	Colgan Air Bombardier Dash 8 Q400.	Crashed into house near airport, Buffalo, NY	50*
2009, June 1	**Air France Airbus A330**	**Plunged into Atlantic Ocean en route from Rio de Janeiro, Brazil, to Paris, France**.	**228**
2009, June 29	Yemenia Airbus A310-300	Fell into Indian Ocean on approach to Moroni, Comoros.	152
2009, July 15	Caspian Airlines Tupolev 154.	Crashed after takeoff from Tehran, Iran	168
2010, Apr. 10	Polish Air Force Tupolev 154M	Crashed on approach to Smolensk Air Base, killing Polish Pres. Lech Kaczynski, his wife, and several members of parliament. . . .	96
2010, May 12	Afriqiyah Airways Airbus A330-200	Crashed short of runway in Tripoli, Libya.	103
2010, May 22	Air India Express Boeing 737-800	Overran runway on landing at Mangalore, India.	158
2010, July 28	Airblue Airbus 321-231.	Crashed into Margalla Hills near Islamabad, Pakistan.	152
2012, Apr. 20	Bhoja Airlines Boeing 737-236.	Crashed on approach to airport in Islamabad, Pakistan.	127
2012, June 3	Dana Air MD-83	Crashed into residential area of Lagos, Nigeria	163*
2014, Mar. 8	Malaysia Airlines Boeing 777	All communication ceased shortly after takeoff from Kuala Lumpur. .	239
2014, July 17	Malaysia Airlines Boeing 777	Shot down in missile attack over Russian-occupied Donetsk, Ukraine. .	298
2014, July 24	Air Algérie Boeing-MD-83.	Crashed in desert near Gossi, Mali	116
2014, Dec. 28	Indonesia AirAsia Airbus A320-216	Disappeared over Java Sea between Surabaya and Singapore	162
2015, Mar. 24	Germanwings Airbus A320-211	Copilot deliberately crashed aircraft into French Alps.	150
2015, June 30	Indonesian Air Force Lockheed C-130B. . .	Transport plane crashed near Medan Soewondo Air Force Base . . .	139*
2015, Oct. 31	Metrojet Airbus A321-231.	Bomb on board detonated after takeoff from Sharm el Sheikh, Egypt	224

(1) Bomb was planted by Jack G. Graham in insurance plot to kill his mother, Daisie E. King, a passenger. (2) 84 on plane, 71 on ground killed. (3) Incl. 43 Marshall Univ. (WV) football players and coaches. (4) Fighter pilot parachuted to safety. (5) First supersonic plane crash; killed 8 on ground. (6) Crew of 3, 88 on ground killed. (7) Incl. 22 members of U.S. amateur boxing team. (8) Incl. 248 members of U.S. 101st Airborne Division. (9) Incl. 11 on ground. (10) Incl. U.S. Sec. of Commerce Ron Brown. (11) 4 planes were hijacked and crashed, with all on board killed (265, incl. 19 hijackers). American Airlines Flight 11, a Boeing 767-200, with 81 passengers, 11 crew, crashed into Tower 1 of World Trade Center (WTC); United Airlines Flight 175, a Boeing 767-200, with 56 passengers, 9 crew, crashed into Tower 2 of WTC; American Airlines Flight 77, a Boeing 757-200, with 58 passengers, 6 crew, crashed into Pentagon outside Washington, DC; United Airlines Flight 93, a Boeing 757-200, with 37 passengers, 7 crew, crashed near Shanksville, PA. The official death toll of 2,977 includes all those who perished on the ground at the Pentagon and the WTC, as well as those who died as many as 10 years later from pulmonary sarcoidosis, a lung disease caused by exposure to toxic dust created by the disaster. (12) The two pilots ejected to safety. All spectator deaths.

Egyptian Double Tragedy

Date: Oct. 31, 2015, and May 19, 2016. **Location:** Near Egypt. **Fatalities:** 224 and 66.

Over the span of seven months, two planes—one departing from Egypt, another bound for Cairo from France—never reached their destinations. On Oct. 31, 2015, a Metrojet Airbus A321 took off from the Red Sea resort town of Sharm el Sheikh, bound for St. Petersburg, Russia. Twenty minutes later, the aircraft exploded in midair, killing all 224 aboard, many of whom were Russian tourists. Russian investigators attributed the explosion to a homemade device with explosives equivalent to 1 kg of TNT. ISIS claimed credit, saying the bomb had been inside a soda can. On May 19, 2016, an EgyptAir A320 flying from Paris to Cairo plunged into the Mediterranean Sea just after entering Egyptian airspace. Investigators have not yet determined the cause of this second disaster.

Some Notable Shipwrecks Since 1854
Does not include most wartime disasters.

Date—vessel(s)	Incident	Est. deaths
1854, Mar. 1—City of Glasgow	British steamer left Liverpool for Philadelphia, never heard from again	480
1854, Sept. 27—Arctic and Vesta	U.S. Collins Line steamer sunk in collision with French steamer nr. Cape Race, Canada	285-351
1856, Jan. 23—Pacific	U.S. Collins Line steamer went missing in N Atlantic	186-286
1857, Sept. 12—Central America	U.S. mail steamship sank off Florida coast with $1.5 mil in gold	427
1858, Sept. 23—Austria	German steamer destroyed by fire in N Atlantic	471
1863, Apr. 27—Anglo-Saxon	British steamer wrecked at Cape Race, Canada	238
1865, Apr. 27—Sultana	Mississippi R. steamer carrying 2,300 released Civil War prisoners exploded nr. Memphis, TN. Worst maritime disaster in U.S. history	1,700+
1869, Feb. 20—Radetzky	Austrian steam frigate exploded in Adriatic Sea	345
1869, Oct. 27—Stonewall	U.S. steamer burned, Mississippi R. below Cairo, IL	200
1872, Nov. 7—Mary Celeste	U.S. half-brig sailing from New York to Genoa, Italy, found abandoned	Unknown
1873, Jan. 22—Northfleet	British steamer rammed by Spanish steamer *Murillo* off Dungeness, England, UK	300
1873, Apr. 1—Atlantic	British White Star steamer off Halifax, Nova Scotia, Canada	585
1873, Nov. 23—Ville du Havre and Loch Earn	French steamer sank after collision with British sailing ship	226
1874, Nov. 17—Cospatrick	Burned off Auckland, New Zealand	468
1875, May 7—Schiller	German steamer off Isles of Scilly, UK	312
1875, Nov. 4—Pacific	U.S. steamer sank after collision off Cape Flattery, WA	236
1878, Mar. 24—Eurydice	British frigate sank off Isle of Wight, England, UK	398
1878, Sept. 3—Princess Alice	British steamer sank after collision with *Bywell Castle* in Thames R.	700
1878, Dec. 18—Byzantin and Rinaldo	French and British steamers collided in Dardanelles, off Turkey	210
1883, Jan. 19—Cimbria and Sultan	German steamer sank in collision with British steamer in North Sea	389
1887, Nov. 15—Wah Yeung	Chinese steamer burned in Canton R., Hong Kong	400
1890, Feb. 17—Duburg	British steamer wrecked, China Sea	400
1890, Sept. 19—Ertogrul	Turkish frigate off Japan	540
1891, Mar. 17—Utopia and Anson	British steamer sank in collision with British ironclad off Gibraltar	562
1893, June 22—Victoria	British battleship sank after collision with warship *Camperdown*, off Syrian coast	358
1895, Jan. 30—Elbe and Craithie	German steamer sank in collision with British steamer in North Sea	332
1895, Mar. 11—Reina Regenta	Spanish cruiser foundered nr. Gibraltar	400
1898, Feb. 15—USS Maine	Explosion caused battleship to sink in Havana Harbor, Cuba	260
1898, July 4—La Bourgogne and Cromartyshire	French steamer sank in collision with British sailing ship off Nova Scotia, Canada	549
1904, May 15—Yoshino	Japanese cruiser sank after collision with cruiser *Kasuga* in fog off Liao-Tung Peninsula, China	329
1904, June 15—General Slocum	Excursion steamer burned off N. Brother Isl., New York, NY.	1,021
1904, June 28—Norge	Danish steamer wrecked on Rockall Isl., Scotland, UK	620
1906, Aug. 4—Sirio	Italian steamer wrecked off Cape Palos, Spain.	350
1907, Feb. 11—Larchmont	U.S. steamer sank after collision with U.S. schooner *Harry Knowlton* nr. Block Island, RI	131
1908, Mar. 23—Mutsu Maru	Japanese steamer sank in collision with another steamer nr. Hakodate, Japan	300
1909, Aug. 1—Waratah	British steamer vanished en route from Sydney to London	300
1911, Sept. 25—Liberté	French battleship exploded at Toulon	285
1912, Apr. 14-15—Titanic	British White Star steamer hit iceberg in N Atlantic.	1,503
1912, Sept. 28—Kichemaru	Japanese steamer sank off Japan coast	1,000
1914, May 29—Empress of Ireland	Canadian Pacific steamer collided with Norwegian coal transporter *Storstad* in St. Lawrence R., Canada	1,014
1914, Nov. 26—Bulwark	British battleship exploded in Sheerness Harbor, England, UK	788
1915, May 7—Lusitania	British Cunard Line steamer torpedoed and sunk by German submarine off Ireland	1,198
1915, July 24—Eastland	Steamer capsized, Chicago R., IL	844
1916, Feb. 26—Provence	French cruiser sank in Mediterranean; then-worst disaster in maritime history	3,100
1916, Mar. 5—Principe de Asturias	Spanish steamer wrecked nr. Santos, Brazil.	558
1917, Dec. 6—Mont Blanc and Imo	French ammunition ship and Belgian steamer collided in Halifax Harbor, Canada	1,900+
1918, Apr. 25—Kiang-Kwan	Chinese steamer sank after collision with Chinese gunboat *Chutai* off Hankow, China.	500
1918, July 12—Kawachi	Japanese battleship blew up in Tokayama Bay	500
1918, Oct. 25—Princess Sophia	Canadian-Pacific steamer sank off Vanderbilt Reef, Alaska	398
1919, Jan. 17—Chaonia	French steamer lost in Straits of Messina, Italy	460
1919, Sept. 9—Valbanera	Spanish steamer lost off FL coast	500
1920, Apr. 11—Afrique	French liner sank nr. La Rochelle, France.	553
1921, Mar. 18—Hong Kong	Chinese steamer wrecked, S China Sea	1,000
1922, Aug. 26—Niitaka	Japanese cruiser sank in storm off Kamchatka, USSR	300
1927, Sept. 20—Gentoku Maru	Japanese steamer capsized in Tsingtao Bay, China	278
1927, Oct. 25—Principessa Mafalda	Italian steamer blew up, sank off Porto Seguro, Brazil	314

Migrant Shipwrecks

Date: 2015-16. **Location:** Mediterranean Sea. **Fatalities:** 3,168 (Jan.-Aug. 2016).

The spectacle of rickety boats full of migrants—mostly refugees fleeing war-torn countries in Africa and Asia—became commonplace in 2015 and 2016, as multiple vessels capsized in the Mediterranean Sea. The number of deaths may be impossible to quantify, but according to the International Organization for Migration, in 2015, nearly 1 mil migrants arrived in Europe, primarily in Greece and Italy; 3,676 died during the crossing. In the first eight months of 2016, 3,168 perished, while 278,327 arrived safely in Europe.

Date—vessel(s)	Incident	Est. deaths
1934, Sept. 8—Morro Castle	U.S. steamer en route from Havana to New York, burned off Asbury Park, NJ	134
1940, June 17—Lancastria	Nazi forces sank Cunard liner evacuating British troops from France	2,500-6,000
1940, July 24—Meknes	French liner torpedoed by Nazis in English Channel	350
1942, Feb. 18—USS Truxtun and USS Pollux	Destroyer and cargo ship ran aground, sank off Newfoundland, Canada	204
1942, Oct. 2—Curacao and Queen Mary	British cruiser sank off Ireland after collision with liner carrying U.S. troops	338
1944, Dec. 17-18—Spence, Monaghan, Hull	3 U.S. destroyers sank during typhoon, Philippine Sea	790
1945, Jan. 30—Wilhelm Gustloff	Liner with German refugees, soldiers sunk by Soviet submarine in Baltic	5,000-9,000
1945, Apr. 16—Goya	Cargo ship carrying German refugees, soldiers sunk by Soviet submarine in Baltic	6,000-7,000
1945, May 3—Cap Arcona and Thielbeck	German ocean liner and freighter carrying concentration camp inmates sunk by British warplanes in Lubeck Bay, Germany	7,000-8,000
1947, Jan. 19—Himera	Greek steamer hit mine off Athens, Greece	392
1947, Apr. 16—Grandcamp	Ammonium nitrate explosion aboard French freighter caused fires throughout port, Texas City, TX	576+
1948, Dec. 3—Kiangya	Chinese refugee ship wrecked in explosion S of Shanghai	1,100+
1954, Sept. 26—Toya Maru	Japanese ferry sank, Tsugaru Strait, Japan	1,172
1956, July 26—Andrea Doria and Stockholm	Italian liner and Swedish liner collided off Nantucket Isl., MA	51
1957, July 14—Eshghabad	Soviet fishing boat ran aground in Caspian Sea	270
1961, Apr. 8—Dara	British liner exploded in Persian Gulf	236
1961, July 8—Save	Portuguese ship ran aground off Mozambique	259
1965, Nov. 13—Yarmouth Castle	Cruise ship burned and sank off Nassau, The Bahamas	89
1970, Dec. 15—Namyong-Ho	S. Korean ferry sank in Korea Strait	308
1975, Nov. 10—Edmund Fitzgerald	U.S. cargo ship sank during storm on Lake Superior	29
1980, Apr. 22—Don Juan	Sank off Mindoro Isl., Philippines, after colliding with barge	1,000+
1981, Jan. 27—Tamponas II	Indonesian car ferry caught fire and sank in Java Sea	580
1983, May 25—10th of Ramadan	Nile steamer caught fire and sank in Lake Nasser, Egypt	357
1986, May 25—Shamia	Ferry capsized in storm, Meghna R., Bangladesh	500+
1986, Sept. 1—Admiral Nakhimov and Pyotr Vasev	Soviet cruise ship collided with Soviet freighter in Black Sea	425
1987, Dec. 20—Doña Paz and Victor	Philippine ferry and oil tanker collided in Tablas Strait, Philippines	4,341
1988, Aug. 6	Indian ferry capsized on Ganges R.	400+
1988, Oct. 24—Doña Marilyn	Philippine ferry sank by typhoon near Leyte Isl.	350+
1991, Dec. 14—Salem Express	Ferry rammed coral reef nr. Safaga, Egypt	462
1993, Feb. 17—Neptune	Ferry capsized off Port-au-Prince, Haiti	500+
1993, Oct. 10—Seohae	S. Korean ferry capsized in Yellow Sea during storm	292
1994, Sept. 28—Estonia	Ferry sank in Baltic Sea off Finland	850+
1996, May 21—Bukoba	Overcrowded Tanzanian ferry sank in Lake Victoria	500+
1997, Sept. 8—Pride of la Gonâve	Haitian ferry sank off Montrouis, Haiti	200+
1999, Feb. 6—Harta Rimba	Cargo ship sank off Indonesia	280+
1999, May 1—Miss Majestic	"Duck" boat on tour sank, Lake Hamilton, AR	13
1999, Nov. 24—Dashun	Passenger ferry capsized nr. Yantai, China	280
2000, June 29—Cahaya Bahari	Overloaded ferry carrying refugees from religious strife capsized in storm off Sulawesi Isl., Indonesia	500+
2001, Oct. 19	Fishing boat overloaded with refugees, mainly from Middle East, sank off Indonesia	350+
2002, May 4—Salahuddin-2	Overloaded Bangladesh ferry sank in Meghna R.	300+
2002, Sept. 26—Joola	Overloaded Senegalese ferry capsized in ocean off The Gambia	1,863
2003, July 8—MV-Nasrin 1	Overcrowded ferry sank nr. Chandpur in Bangladesh R.	400
2003, Oct. 15—Andrew J. Barberi	NYC ferry crashed into dock on approach to Staten Island	11
2006, Feb. 3—Al-Salam Boccaccio 98	Ferry caught fire, sank in Red Sea off Egypt	1,000+
2006, Dec. 30—Senopati Nusantara	High waves capsized ferry en route to Java, Indonesia	400+
2007, Nov. 23—Explorer	Canadian cruise ship hit Antarctic iceberg; first commercial passenger ship to sink in region	0
2008, June 23—Princess of the Stars	Philippine ferry capsized during Typhoon *Fengshen* nr. Manila	800
2011, Sept. 10—MV Spice Islander	Overloaded ferry sank off coast of Tanzania	240+
2012, Jan 17—Costa Concordia	Cruise ship ran aground off Italian coast; captain abandoned ship before passengers	32
2013, Oct. 3	Boat carrying migrants fleeing Eritrea sank near Lampedusa Isl., Italy	366
2014, Apr. 16—Sewol	Ferry carrying 476 people sank off Korea's SW coast	304
2015, Feb. 8	Boat carrying migrants from N Africa sank in Mediterranean	329
2015, Apr. 19	Fishing boat overloaded with African migrants capsized off Libyan coast	800
2015, June 1	Chinese cruise ship sank in Yangtze R. during torrential rains	442
2015, Aug. 6	Vessel carrying migrants capsized in Mediterranean	200+
2016, Apr. 13	Small boat carrying migrants capsized in Mediterranean	450+
2016, May 24-28	Multiple boats overloaded with migrants sank in the Mediterranean	1,000+

Some Notable Railroad Disasters Since 1925

Date	Location	Deaths	Date	Location	Deaths
1925, June 16	Hackettstown, NJ	50	1952, July 9	Rzepin, Poland	160
1933, Dec. 23	Lagny-Pomponne, France	230	1952, Oct. 8	Harrow, England, UK	112
1937, July 16	Near Patna, India	107	1953, Dec. 24	Tangiwai, New Zealand	151
1938, Dec. 25	Near Kishinev, Romania	150	1953, Dec. 24	Sakvice, Czechoslovakia	103
1939, Dec. 22	Near Magdeburg, Germany	132	1955, Apr. 3	Guadalajara, Mexico	300
1943, Sept. 6	Frankford Junction, Philadelphia, PA	79	1957, Sept. 1	Kendal, Jamaica	178
1943, Dec. 16	Between Rennert and Buie, NC	72	1957, Sept. 29	Montgomery, W Pakistan	300
1944, Jan. 16	León Province, Spain	500	1957, Dec. 4	London, England, UK	90
1944, Mar. 2	Salerno, Italy	521	1958, May 8	Rio de Janeiro, Brazil	128
1944, Dec. 31	Bagley, UT	50	1960, Nov. 14	Pardubice, Czechoslovakia	117
1945, July 16	Munich, Germany	102	1962, May 3	Tokyo, Japan	163
1946, Mar. 20	Aracaju, Mexico	185	1963, Nov. 9	Yokohama, Japan	162
1949, Oct. 22	Near Dwor, Poland	200+	1965, Feb. 27	Near Port Sudan, Sudan	124
1950, Nov. 22	Richmond Hill, NY	79	1970, Feb. 1	Buenos Aires, Argentina	236
1952, Feb. 6	Woodbridge, NJ	84	1972, June 16	Near Soissons, France	108
1952, Mar. 4	Near Rio de Janeiro, Brazil	119	1972, Oct. 6	Near Saltillo, Mexico	204

Date	Location	Deaths	Date	Location	Deaths
1974, Aug. 30	Zagreb, Yugoslavia	153	1994, Dec. 30	Near Namkham, Myanmar	102
1981, June 6	Near Mansi, India	268	1995, Jan. 13	Dinajpur, Bangladesh	150
1982, Jan. 27	El Asnam, Algeria	120	1995, Aug. 20	Firozabad, India	350
1982, July 11	Tepic, Mexico	120	1995, Nov. 28	Baku, Azerbaijan	337
1983, Feb. 19	Empalme, Mexico	100	1997, Mar. 3	Punjab Province, Pakistan	128
1985, Jan. 13	Awash, Ethiopia	392	1997, May 4	Kisangani, Zaire	100+
1985, Sept. 12	Viseu, Portugal	118	1998, Feb. 19	Yaounde, Cameroon	120
1986, Aug. 6	Bihar, India	202	1998, June 3	Eschede, Germany	102
1987, July 2	Kasumbalesha Shaba, Zaire	125	1998, Nov. 26	Khanna, India	108
1987, Aug. 7	Between Moscow and Rostov, USSR	106	1999, Aug. 2	Gauhati, India	285
1987, Oct. 19	Jakarta, Indonesia	153	2002, Feb. 20	S of Cairo, Egypt	377
1988, June 4	Arzamas, USSR	100	2002, May 25	Muamba, Mozambique	195
1988, July 8	Kerala, India	108	2002, June 24	Igandu, Tanzania	281
1989, Jan. 15	Maizdi Khan, Bangladesh	135	2002, Sept. 10	Bihar, India	112
1989, June 4	Ufa, USSR	645	2004, Feb. 18	Neyshabur, NE Iran	300
1989, Aug. 11	Sinaloa, Mexico	112	2004, Apr. 22	Ryongchon, North Korea	161
1990, Jan. 4	Sindh Province, Pakistan	307	2005, Apr. 25	Near Amagasaki, Japan	107
1991, Mar. 5	Nacala, Mozambique	109	2005, July 13	Ghotki, Pakistan	132
1991, June 8	Ghotki, Pakistan	100	2005, Oct. 29	Andra Pradesh, India	110
1991, Sept. 5	Pointe-Noire, Congo Republic	110	2007, Aug. 2	Nr. Benaleka, Dem. Rep. of Congo	100
1993, Jan. 30	Rural Kenya	340	2010, May 28	W. Bengal, India	148
1993, Apr. 25	Near Karachi, Pakistan	150	2011, July 23	Wenzhou, China	140
1994, Sept. 22	Lubango, Angola	300			

Principal U.S. Mine Disasters Since 1867

Source: Bureau of Mines, U.S. Dept. of the Interior; Office of Mine Safety Health Research, Centers for Disease Control

All are bituminous coal mines unless otherwise noted.

Date	Location	Deaths	Date	Location	Deaths	Date	Location	Deaths
1867, Apr. 3	Winterpock, VA	69	1910, Jan. 31	Primero, CO	75	1923, Aug. 14	Kemmerer, WY	99
1869, Sept. 6	Plymouth, PA	110	1910, May 5	Palos, AL	84	1924, Mar. 8	Castle Gate, UT	172
1883, Feb. 16	Braidwood, IL	69	1910, Nov. 8	Delagua, CO	79	1924, Apr. 28	Benwood, WV	119
1884, Mar. 13	Pocahontas, VA	112	1911, Apr. 7	Troop, PA	73	1926, Jan. 13	Wilburton, OK	91
1891, Jan. 27	Mt. Pleasant, PA	109	1911, Apr. 8	Littleton, AL	128	1927, Apr. 30	Everettville, WV	97
1892, Jan. 7	Krebs, OK	100	1911, Dec. 9	Briceville, TN	84	1928, May 19	Mather, PA	195
1895, Mar. 20	Red Canyon, WY	62	1912, Mar. 20	McCurtain, OK	73	1929, Dec. 17	McAlester, OK	61
1900, May 1	Scofield, UT	200	1912, Mar. 26	Jed, WV	81	1930, Nov. 5	Millfield, OH	82
1902, May 19	Coal Creek, TN	184	1913, Apr. 23	Finleyville, PA	98	1940, Jan. 10	Bartley, WV	91
1902, July 10	Johnstown, PA	112	1913, Oct. 22	Dawson, NM	263	1940, Mar. 16	St. Clairsville, OH	72
1903, June 30	Hanna, WY	169	1914, Apr. 28	Eccles, WV	181	1940, July 15	Portage, PA	63
1904, Jan. 25	Cheswick, PA	179	1915, Mar. 2	Layland, WV	115	1943, Feb. 27	Washoe, MT	74
1905, Feb. 20	Virginia City, AL	112	1917, Apr. 27	Hastings, CO	121	1944, July 5	Powhatan Pt., OH	66
1907, Jan. 29	Stuart, WV	84	1917, June 8	Butte, MT[1]	163	1947, Mar. 25	Centralia, IL	111
1907, Dec. 6	Monongah, WV	362	1917, Aug. 4	Clay, KY	62	1951, Dec. 21	West Frankfort, IL	119
1907, Dec. 19	Van Meter, PA	239	1919, June 5	Wilkes-Barre, PA	92	1968, Nov. 20	Farmington, WV	78
1908, Nov. 28	Marianna, PA	154	1922, Nov. 6	Spangler, PA	79	1970, Dec. 30	Hyden, KY	38
1909, Jan. 12	Switchback, WV	67	1922, Nov. 22	Dolomite, AL	90	1972, Feb. 26	Saunders, WV	114
1909, Nov. 13	Cherry, IL	259	1923, Feb. 8	Dawson, NM	120	1972, May 2	Kellogg, ID[2]	91

Note: The world's worst mine disaster killed 1,549 workers in Manchuria, China, Apr. 25, 1942. (1) Copper mine. (2) Silver mine.

Some Notable U.S. Tornadoes Since 1925

Date	Location	Deaths	Date	Location	Deaths
1925, Mar. 18	MO, IL, IN	747	1973, May 26-27	South, Midwest	47
1927, Apr. 12	Rocksprings, TX	74	1974, Apr. 3-4	AL; GA; KY; Xenia, OH; other states	315
1927, May 9	AR; Poplar Bluff, MO	92	1977, Apr. 4	AL, MS, GA	22
1927, Sept. 29	St. Louis, MO	90	1979, Apr. 10	TX, OK	60
1930, May 6	Hill, Navarro, Ellis Cos., TX	41	1984, Mar. 28	NC, SC	57
1932, Mar. 21	Alabama	268	1985, May 31	NY; PA; OH; Ontario, Can.	75
1936, Apr. 5-6	Tupelo, MS; Gainesville, GA	454	1987, May 22	Saragosa, TX	30
1938, Sept. 29	Charleston, SC	32	1989, Nov. 15	Huntsville, AL	18
1942, Mar. 16	Central to NE Mississippi	75	1990, Aug. 28	Northern IL	25
1942, Apr. 27	Rogers and Mayes Cos., OK	52	1991, Apr. 26	KS, OK	23
1944, June 23	OH, PA, WV, MD	150	1992, Nov. 21-23	South, Midwest	26
1945, Apr. 12	OK, AR	102	1994, Mar. 27-28	AL, TN, GA, NC, SC	52
1947, Apr. 9	TX; Woodward, OK; KS	181	1995, May 6-7	Southern OK, northern TX	23
1948, Mar. 19	Bunker Hill and Gillespie, IL	33	1997, Mar. 1	Central AR	26
1949, Jan. 3	LA, AR	58	1997, May 27	Jarrell, TX	27
1952, Mar. 21-22	AR, MO, TN	208	1998, Feb. 22-23	Central FL	42
1953, May 11	Waco, TX	114	1998, Apr. 8	AL, GA, MS	39
1953, June 8	Flint-Beecher, MI; OH	142	1999, May 3	OK, KS	54
1953, June 9	Worcester and vicinity, MA	90	2000, Feb. 14	SW Georgia	22+
1953, Dec. 5	Vicksburg, MS	38	2002, Nov. 10-11	AL, MS, TN, IN, OH, PA	36
1955, May 25	Udall, KS; MO; Blackwell, OK; TX	115	2003, May 4-11	TN, MO, KS, IL, OK, WV, AL	48
1957, May 20	KS, MO	48	2005, Nov. 6	KY, IN	22
1958, June, 4	NW Wisconsin	30	2007, Mar. 1	AL, GA, MO, Midwest	20
1959, Feb. 10	St. Louis, MO	21	2008, Feb. 25	"Super Tuesday"—TN, AR, KY, AL, MO	57
1960, May 5-6	Southeastern OK, AR	30	2008, May 10	MS, OK, GA	23
1962, Mar. 31	Milton, FL	17	2011, Apr. 14-16	Southeast, Midwest, OK to VA	38
1965, Apr. 11	IA, IN, IL, OH, MI, WI	271	2011, Apr. 25-28	305 funnels from TX to NY	321
1966, Mar. 3	Jackson, MS; AL	57	2011, May 22	Joplin, MO	161
1967, Apr. 21	IL, MO, IA, MI	33	2012, Mar. 2-3	IL, IN, KY, OH, AL	42
1968, May 15	Midwest	71	2013, May 20	Moore, OK	24
1969, Jan. 23	Mississippi	32	2013, May 31	El Reno, OK	21
1970, May 11	Lubbock, TX	23			
1971, Feb. 21	Mississippi Delta: MS, LA, AR, TN	110			

Some Notable Hurricanes, Typhoons, Blizzards, Other Storms

C. = cyclone; H. = hurricane; TS. = tropical storm; T. = typhoon[1].

Date	Location	Est. deaths	Date	Location	Est. deaths
1881, Aug. 24-29	H., GA, SC	700	1991, Apr. 30	C., Bangladesh	139,000
1888, Mar. 11-14	Blizzard, Eastern U.S.	400	1991, Nov. 5	TS. Thelma, flash floods,	
1893, Aug. 15-Sept. 2	H., GA, SC	1,000+		central Philippines	7,000+
1893, Oct. 1	H., LA	1,100+	1992, Aug. 24-26	H. Andrew, Southern FL, LA.	65
1900, Sept. 8	H., Galveston, TX	8,000+	1993, Mar. 12-14	Blizzard, Eastern U.S.	270+
1906, Sept. 18	T., Hong Kong	10,000+	1993, June	Monsoon, Bangladesh	2,000
1906, Sept. 19-24	H., LA, MS	350	1994, Nov. 8-18	TS. Gordon, Caribbean, FL	830
1909, Sept. 20	H., LA	350+	1995, Oct. 2-4	H. Opal, S Mexico, FL, AL	59
1915, Aug. 16	H., Galveston, TX	275	1995, Nov. 2-3	T. Angela, Philippines	600+
1915, Sept. 29	H., LA	275	1996, Jan. 7-8	Blizzard, NE U.S.	100
1919, Sept. 6-14	H., Carib., FL Keys, Gulf, TX	600+[2]	1996, Aug. 22	Blizzard, Himalayas, N India.	239
1922, July 27	T., Swatow, China	100,000	1996, Aug. 29-Sept. 6	H. Fran, Carib., NC, VA, WV	30
1926, Sept. 11-22	H., FL, AL, MS	370+	1996, Sept. 9	T. Sally, S China	114
1926, Oct. 20	H., Cuba	600	1996, Nov. 6	C., Andhra Pradesh, India	1,000+
1928, Sept. 6-20	H., southern FL	2,500+	1996, Dec. 25	TS. Greg, eastern Malaysia	100+
1930, Sept. 3	H., Dominican Republic	2,000	1997, May 19	C., Bangladesh	108
1935, Aug. 29-	H., "Labor Day Hurricane,"		1997, Aug. 18-21	T. Winnie, Taiwan, E China	140+
Sept. 10	Caribbean, SE U.S.	400+	1997, Oct. 8-10	H. Pauline, SW Mexico	230
1937, Sept. 2	T., "The Great Typhoon,"		1998, June 9	C., Gujarat, India	1,320
	Hong Kong	10,000+	1998, Aug.	Monsoon, Bangladesh	326
1938, Sept. 21	H., "Long Isl. Express," NY,		1998, Sept. 21-23	H. Georges, Carib., FL, U.S. Gulf	600+
	New England	682	1998, Oct. 27-29	H. Mitch, Honduras, Nicaragua,	
1940, Nov. 11-12	"Armistice Day Blizzard,"			Guatemala, El Salvador	14,600
	NE, Midwest U.S.	154	1999, Sept. 4-17	H. Floyd, The Bahamas,	
1942, Oct.	T., W. Sundarbans, Bangladesh	61,000		E seaboard U.S.	56
1942, Oct. 15-16	H., Bengal, India	40,000	1999, Oct. 29	C., E India	9,392
1947, Dec. 26	Blizzard, NYC, N Atl. states	55	1999, Dec. 26-29	Gales, France, Switz., Germany	120
1952, Oct. 22	T., Philippines	440	2000, Dec. 27	Winter storm, TX, OK, AR	40+
1954, Aug. 30	H. Carol, NE U.S.	68	2001, July 30	T. Toraji, Taiwan	200
1954, Oct. 5-18	H. Hazel, E Canada, U.S., Haiti	347	2001, Nov. 6-12	T. Lingling, S Philip., Vietnam.	220+
1955, Aug. 7-21	H. Diane, Eastern U.S.	400	2002, Aug.-Sept.	T. Rusa, N. and S. Korea	115+
1955, Sept. 19	H. Hilda, Mexico	200	2003, Feb. 16-17	Blizzard, E seaboard U.S.	59
1956, Feb. 1-29	Blizzard, W Europe	1,000	2003, Sept. 7-19	H. Isabel, NC, VA, E seaboard	40+
1957, June 25-30	H. Audrey, TX to AL	390	2003, Sept. 12	T. Maemi, S. Korea	130
1958, Feb. 15-16	Blizzard, NE U.S.	171	2004, Mar. 7-19	C. Gafilo, Madagascar	198
1959, Sept. 17-19	T. Sarah, Japan, S. Korea	2,000	2004, May 19	C., Myanmar	220
1959, Sept. 26-27	T. Vera, Honshu, Japan	4,466	2004, Aug. 12-15	T. Rananim, eastern China	164
1960, Sept. 4-12	H. Donna, Caribbean, E U.S.	148	2004, Aug. 13-14	H. Charley, FL, SC	36
1961, Oct. 31	H. Hattie, Brit. Honduras	400	2004, Sept. 5-6	H. Frances, The Bahamas, FL	35
1962, Sept. 1	T. Wanda, Hong Kong	130-200	2004, Sept. 7-16	H. Ivan, Barbados, Grenada,	
1963, May 28-29	Windstorm, Bangladesh	22,000		U.S. Gulf Coast	115
1963, Oct. 4-8	H. Flora, Caribbean	6,000	2004, Sept. 16-26	H. Jeanne, Dom. Rep., Haiti, FL	1,500+
1964, June 30	T. Winnie, N Philippines	107	2005, July 7-11	H. Dennis, Jamaica, Haiti,	
1964, Sept. 5	T. Ruby, Hong Kong, China	735		Cuba, FL	50
1965, May 11-12	Windstorm, Bangladesh	17,000	2005, Aug. 25-29	H. Katrina, LA, MS, FL, AL, GA	1,833+[3]
1965, June 1-2	Windstorm, Bangladesh	30,000	2005, Aug. 31-Sept. 1	T. Talim, Taiwan, E China	129+
1965, Sept. 7-12	H. Betsy, FL, MS, LA	74	2005, Sept. 21-24	H. Rita, TX, LA	62[4]
1965, Dec. 15	Windstorm, Bangladesh	10,000	2005, Sept. 21-28	T. Damrey, SE Asia; Philippines;	
1966, June 4-10	H. Alma, Honduras, SE U.S.	51		Hainan, China	145
1966, Sept. 24-30	H. Inez, Carib., FL, Mexico	293	2005, Oct. 4	H. Stan, Central Amer., Mex.	1,000+[5]
1967, July 9	T. Billie, SW Japan	347	2006, Jul. 14	TS. Bilis, SE China	612
1967, Sept. 5-23	H. Beulah, Carib., Mex., TX	54	2006, Aug. 10	T. Saomai, SE China	295
1967, Dec. 12-20	Blizzard, SW U.S.	51	2006, Nov. 30	T. Durian, Philippines	450-1,000+
1969, Aug. 17-18	H. Camille, MS, LA	256	2007, June 6-7	C. Gonu, Oman, Iran	54[6]
1970, Sept. 15	T. Pitang (Georgia), Philippines	300	2007, Nov. 15	C. Sidr, southern Bangladesh	3,363
1970, Oct. 14	T. Sening (Joan), Philippines	583	2008, May 2-3	C. Nargis, southern Myanmar	138,366
1970, Oct. 15	T. Titang (Kate), Philippines	526	2008, June 20-25	T. Fengshen, Philippines, China	233
1970, Nov. 13	C., Bay of Bengal, Bangladesh	300,000	2008, Aug. 26-Sept. 1	H. Gustav, Haiti, Dom. Rep., U.S.	138
1971, Aug. 1	T. Rose, Hong Kong	130	2008, Sept. 1-4	TS. Hanna, Haiti	529
1972, June 19-29	H. Agnes, FL to NY	118	2008, Sept. 7-13	H. Ike, Haiti; Cuba; Galveston, TX	164
1972, Dec. 3	T. Theresa, Philippines	169	2009, May 23-26	C. Alia, India, Bangladesh	260
1973, June-Aug.	Monsoon rains, India	1,217	2009, July 6-9	T. Morakot, mudslides, Taiwan	700+
1974, July 11	T. Gilda, Japan, S. Korea	108	2009, Sept. 23-30	T. Ketsana, Philippines, Vietnam,	
1974, Sept. 19-20	H. Fifi, Honduras	2,000		Cambodia, Laos	498+
1975, Sept. 13-27	H. Eloise, Caribbean, NE U.S.	71	2009, Oct. 3-10	T. Parma, Philippines	375
1976, May 20	T. Olga, floods, Philippines	215	2009, Oct. 30-Nov. 3	T. Mirinae, Philippines, Vietnam	159+
1976, Sept. 25-Oct. 2	H. Liza, western Mexico	630	2010, May 29	TS. Agatha, Guatemala,	
1978, Oct. 27	T. Rita, Philippines	400		El Salvador, Honduras	184
1979, Aug. 30-Sept. 7	H. David, Caribbean, E U.S.	1,100	2010, July 13-17	T. Conson, Luzon Isl.,	
1980, Aug. 4-11	H. Allen, Caribbean, TX	272		Philippines	105+
1981, Nov. 25	T. Irma, Luzon Isl., Philippines	176	2011, Dec. 16	TS. Washi, Philippines	1,257
1983, June	Monsoon, India	900	2012, Jan. 24-Feb. 14	Blizzard/cold snap, E Europe	650+
1984, Sept. 2	T. Ike, southern Philippines	1,363	2012, Oct. 22-31	H. Sandy, Cuba, Haiti, Jamaica,	
1985, May 25	C., Bangladesh	15,000		Eastern U.S.	245[7]
1985, Oct. 26-Nov. 6	H. Juan, SE U.S.	97	2012, Dec. 4	T. Bopha, Philippines	1,146
1987, Nov. 25	T. Nina, Philippines	650	2013, Nov. 8	T. Haiyan, Philippines	7,986
1988, Sept. 10-17	H. Gilbert, Carib., Gulf of Mex.	260	2013, Nov. 10	C., Puntland, Somalia	162
1989, Sept. 16-22	H. Hugo, Bahamas, SE U.S.	86	2014, July 15	T. Rammasun, Philippines,	
1990, May 6-11	C. (mult.), SE India	450		China, Vietnam	173

(1) What hurricanes are called W of Intl. Date Line and N of equator. (2) Incl. about 500 lost on ships at sea. (3) Official toll as of Aug. 2006 was 1,577 in LA, 238 in MS, 14 in FL, and 2 each in AL and GA. (4) Incl. 55 indirect deaths, among them 20 people, mostly elderly evacuees from a nursing home, whose bus exploded and caught fire outside Dallas. (5) Incl. deaths from floods and landslides generated by heavy rainstorms. (6) First documented super cyclone in Arabian Sea. (7) Includes 87 indirect deaths in the U.S.

Some Notable Floods, Tidal Waves

Source: EM-DAT: The OFDA/CRED Intl. Disaster Database, Université catholique de Louvain, Brussels, Belgium, www.emdat.be; World Almanac research

Date	Location	Est. deaths	Date	Location	Est. deaths
1703	Awa, Japan	100,000+	1981, Apr.	N China	550
1889, May 31	Johnstown, PA	2,200+	1981, July	Sichuan, Hubei Prov., China	1,300
1903, June 15	Heppner, OR	325	1982, Jan. 23	Near Lima, Peru	600
1911	Chang Jiang R., China	100,000	1982, May 12	Guangdong, China	430
1913, Mar. 25-27	OH, IN	732	1982, Sept. 17-21	El Salvador, Guatemala	1,300+
1915, Aug. 17	Galveston, TX	275	1984, Aug.-Sept.	South Korea	200+
1927, Jan.-July	Mississippi Valley	246+	1987, July 22	Bangladesh	2,055
1927, Nov. 1	Mostagenem, Algeria	3,000	1987, Aug.-Sept.	Northern Bangladesh	1,000+
1928, Mar. 13	Dam collapse, Saugus, CA	450	1988, June-Sept.	Bangladesh	2,379
1928, Sept. 16	Lake Okeechobee, FL	1,770+	1988, Sept.	N India	1,000+
1931, Aug.	Huang He R., China	3,700,000	1989, July 14	China	2,000
1933	Shandong, China	18,000	1994, May-Oct.	Assam, India	2,001
1937, Jan. 22	OH, MS valleys	250	1995, July	NE China	1,200
1939, July	Hunan province, China	500,000	1995, Sept. 1-20	India	1,479
1946, Apr. 1	HI, AK	159	1996, June-July	Guizhou, Hebei, China	2,775
1947, Sept. 20	Honshu Isl., Japan	2,000	1997, Oct.-Nov.	Somalia	2,311
1949, July	China	57,000	1998, July 17	Papua New Guinea	3,000
1949, Oct.	Guatemala	40,000	1998, July-Aug.	Hunan, Sichuan, China	3,656
1950	Pakistan	2,900	1998, July-Sept.	Bangladesh	1,441
1951, Aug. 28	Manchuria	4,800	1998, Aug.	India	1,811
1953, Jan. 31	Storm surge, Zuiderzee, Netherlands	2,000	1999, Oct.-Dec.	Central Vietnam	700+
			1999, Dec. 15-20	NW Venezuela	30,000
1953, June 23	Japan	2,566	2000, Feb.-Mar.	Mozambique	700
1954, Aug.	China	30,000	2000, Sept. 19-30	India, Bangladesh	1,000+
1954, Aug. 17	Farahzad, Iran	2,000	2001, Aug. 1-6	Taiwan	100+
1955, Oct. 7-12	India, Pakistan	1,700	2001, Nov. 9-10	Northern Algeria	711+
1959, Nov. 1	Western Mexico	2,000	2002, Apr.-Aug.	China	800+
1959, Dec. 2	Frejus, France	412	2002, July-Aug.	India, Nepal, Bangladesh	1,100+
1959-61	China	2,000,000	2004, May 23-Jun. 1	Dom. Republic, Haiti	2,665
1960, Oct. 10	Bangladesh	6,000	2004, June-Sept.	Bangladesh, India, Myanmar, Nepal	2,000+
1960, Oct. 31	Bangladesh	4,000			
1961, July	N India	2,000	2004, June-Sept.	China	500
1962, Sept. 27	Barcelona, Spain	445	2004, Nov.-Dec.	Philippines	1,060+
1963, Oct. 9	Dam collapse, Vaiont, Italy	1,800	2004, Dec. 26	Indian Ocean nations	227,898
1967, Jan. 18-24	Eastern Brazil	894	2005, July 26-Aug. 5	Western Maharashtra state, India	1,200
1967, Mar. 19	Rio de Janeiro, Brazil	436			
1967, Nov. 26	Lisbon, Portugal	464	2006, Feb. 17	Leyte Isl., Philippines	1,000
1968, July	Rajasthan, Gujarat states, India	4,892	2006, July 17	S of Java, Indonesia	530+
			2007, July 21-Aug. 3	Bangladesh	1,110
1968, Oct. 7	NE India	780	2007, July-Sept.	India	1,103
1969, Jan. 18-26	Southern CA	100	2008, June-July	India	1,063
1969, Aug. 20-22	Western VA	189	2009, July-Sept.	India	992
1969, Oct. 1-8	Tunisia	500	2010, May-Aug.	China	1,691
1970, July 22	Himalayas, India	500	2010, June 13-24	Cenxi, China	377+
1972, Feb. 26	Buffalo Creek, WV	118	2010, July-Aug.	Pakistan	1,985
1972, June 9	Rapid City, SD	238	2010, Aug. 1-4	Zhouqu County, China	1,500+
1972, Aug. 7	Luzon Isl., Philippines	454	2011, Jan. 11-12	SE Brazil	900
1972, Aug. 19-31	Pakistan	1,500	2011, Mar. 11	NE Japan	20,896
1974, Mar. 29	Tubaro, Brazil	1,000	2011, Apr.-May	Northern Colombia	425+
1974, July	Bangladesh	28,700	2011, July-Dec.	Thailand	708+
1974, Aug. 12	Monty-Long, Bangladesh	2,500	2011, July-Dec.	Philippines, Cambodia, Myanmar	2,000+
1976, July 31	Big Thompson Canyon, CO	140			
1978, July	N, NE India	3,800	2012, July-Oct.	Nigeria	363
1979, July 17	Lomblem Isl., Indonesia	539	2012, Aug.-Oct.	Pakistan	480
1979, Aug. 11	Morvi, India	15,000	2012, Sept.-Oct.	Nigeria	431
1980, June	Sichuan, China	6,200	2013, June	Uttarakhand, India	6,054

Stampede in Mecca

Date: Sept. 24, 2015. **Location:** Mina, Saudi Arabia. **Fatalities:** 2,411+.

Two large groups of Muslim pilgrims attending the annual *hajj* to Mecca collided at a T-shaped intersection as they were preparing to re-enact the symbolic stoning of the devil. The Saudi health ministry officially listed 769 dead and 934 injured. The Associated Press, using information from governments whose citizens were killed in the crush of bodies, put the death toll at more than three times that number. (Other press agency estimates of fatalities also exceeded 2,000 killed.) That made it the deadliest stampede at Mecca ever, eclipsing 1,426 deaths in 1990 and 363 fatalities in 2006.

Some Major Earthquakes

Source: Global Volcanism Network, Smithsonian Institution; U.S. Geological Survey, U.S. Dept. of the Interior; World Almanac research
Magnitude of earthquakes (mag.) is a relative measurement of an earthquake's energy. Deaths include those in aftershocks or related events.

Date	Location	Deaths	Mag.	Date	Location	Deaths	Mag.
526, May 20	Antioch, Syria	250,000	NA	1949, July 10	Khait, Tajikistan	12,000	7.5
856	Corinth, Greece	45,000	NA	1949, Aug. 5	Pelileo, Ecuador	5,050	6.8
856, Dec. 22	Damghan, Iran	200,000	NA	1950, Aug. 15	Assam, India	1,526	8.6
893, Mar. 23	Ardabil, Iran	150,000	NA	1954, Sept. 9	Orleansville, Algeria	1,250	6.8
1057	Chihli, China	25,000	NA	1956, June 10-17	Northern Afghanistan	2,000	7.7
1138, Aug. 9	Aleppo, Syria	230,000	NA	1957, July 2	Northern Iran	1,200	7.1
1169, Feb. 11	Nr. Mt. Etna, Sicily	15,000	NA[1]	1960, Feb. 29	Agadir, Morocco	12,000	5.7
1268	Silicia, Asia Minor	60,000	NA	1960, May 21-30	Southern Chile	1,655	9.5[5]
1290, Sept. 27	Chihli, China	100,000	NA	1962, Sept. 1	NW Iran	12,255	7.1
1293, May 20	Kamakura, Japan	30,000	NA	1964, Mar. 27	Prince Wm. Sound, AK	131	9.2[6]
1531, Jan. 26	Lisbon, Portugal	30,000	NA	1966, Aug. 19	Eastern Turkey	2,529	6.8
1556, Jan. 24	Shaanxi, China	830,000	NA	1968, Aug. 31	NE Iran	12,000	7.3
1667, Nov.	Shemakha, Caucasia			1969, July 25	Guangdong, China	3,000	5.9
	(now Azerbaijan)	80,000	NA	1970, Jan. 5	Yunnan Prov., China	10,000	7.5
1693, Jan. 11	Catania, Italy	60,000	NA	1970, May 31	Chimbote, Peru	70,000	7.9
1737, Oct. 11	India, Calcutta	300,000	NA	1971, Feb. 9	San Fernando Valley, CA	65	6.6
1755, June 7	N Persia (current-day Iran)	40,000	NA	1972, Apr. 10	Southern Iran	5,054	7.1
1755, Nov. 1	Lisbon, Portugal	60,000	8.75[2]	1972, Dec. 23	Managua, Nicaragua	5,000	6.2
1783, Feb. 4	Calabria, Italy	30,000	NA	1974, May 10	China	20,000	6.8
1797, Feb. 4	Quito, Ecuador	41,000	NA	1974, Dec. 28	Northern Pakistan	5,300	6.2
1822, Sept. 5	Asia Minor, Aleppo	22,000	NA	1975, Feb. 4	Haicheng, China	2,000	7.0
1828, Dec. 28	Echigo, Japan	30,000	NA	1975, Sept. 6	Eastern Turkey	2,300	6.7
1868, Aug. 13-15	Peru, Ecuador	40,000	NA	1976, Feb. 4	Guatemala	23,000	7.5
1875, May 16	Venezuela, Colombia	16,000	NA	1976, May 6	NE Italy	1,000	6.5
1886, Aug. 31	Charleston, SC	60	6.6	1976, June 25	Irian Jaya, New Guinea	422	7.1
1896, June 15	Sanriku, Japan (tsunami)	27,120	8.5	1976, July 28	Tangshan, China	242,769	7.5
1902, Apr. 19	Quezaltenango and San			1976, Aug. 16	Mindanao, Philippines	8,000	7.9
	Marcos, Guatemala	2,000	7.5	1976, Nov. 24	NW Iran-Turkey border	5,000	7.3
1902, Dec. 16	Uzbekistan, Russia	4,700	6.4	1977, Mar. 4	Romania	1,500	7.2
1903, Apr. 28	Malazgirt, Turkey	3,500	7.0	1978, Sept. 16	NE Iran	15,000	7.8
1905, Apr. 4	Kangra, India	19,000	7.5	1980, Oct. 10	NW Algeria	5,000	7.7
1906, Jan. 31	Off coast of Esmeraldas,			1980, Nov. 23	Southern Italy	2,735	6.5
	Ecuador	1,000	8.8	1981, June 11	Southern Iran	3,000	6.9
1906, Mar. 16	Chia-i, Taiwan	1,250	6.8	1981, July 28	Southern Iran	1,500	7.3
1906, Apr. 18-19	San Francisco, CA	3,000+	7.7[3]	1982, Dec. 13	W Arabian Peninsula	2,800	6.0
1906, Aug. 17	Valparaiso, Chile	3,882	8.6	1983, Oct. 30	Eastern Turkey	1,342	6.9
1907, Oct. 21	Central Asia	12,000	8.1	1985, Sept. 19	Michoacan, Mexico	9,500	8.0
1908, Dec. 28	Messina, Italy	72,000	7.2	1986, Oct. 10	El Salvador	1,000+	5.5
1909, Jan. 23	Silakhor, Iran	5,000-		1987, Mar. 6	Colombia-Ecuador	1,000	7.0
		6,000	7.3	1988, Aug. 20	India-Nepal border	1,000	6.8
1912, Aug. 9	Murefte, Turkey	2,800	7.4	1988, Dec. 7	Spitak, Armenia	25,000	6.8
1914, Oct. 3	Burdur, Turkey	4,000	7.0	1989, Oct. 17	San Francisco Bay area, CA	63	6.9
1915, Jan. 13	Avezzano, Italy	32,610	7.0	1990, June 20	Western Iran	40,000+	7.4
1917, July 30	Yunnan prov., China	1,800	7.5	1990, July 16	Luzon, Philippines	1,621	7.7
1920, Dec. 16	Gansu, China	200,000	7.8[4]	1991, Feb. 1	Pakistan-Afgh. border	1,200	6.8
1923, Mar. 24	Sichuan, China	3,500	7.3	1991, Oct. 19	Northern India	2,000	7.0
1923, Mar. 25	Torbat-e Heydariyeh, Iran	2,200	5.7	1992, Dec. 12	Flores Isl., Indonesia	2,500	7.5
1923, Sept. 1	Yokohama, Japan	142,800	7.9	1993, Sept. 30	Maharashtra, S India	9,748	6.2
1925, Mar. 16	Yunnan prov., China	5,800	7.0	1994, Jan. 17	Northridge, CA	61	6.7
1927, Mar. 7	Tango, Japan	3,020	7.6	1994, June 6	Cauca, SW Colombia	1,000	6.8
1927, May 22	Gansu, China	40,900	7.6	1995, Jan. 16	Kobe, Japan	5,502	6.9
1929, May 1	Koppeh Dagh, Iran	3,800	7.2	1995, May 27	Sakhalin Isl., Russia	1,989	7.5
1930, May 6	Salmas, Iran	2,500	7.2	1997, Feb. 28	NW Iran	1,000+	6.1
1930, July 23	Irpinia, Italy	1,404	6.5	1997, May 10	Northern Iran	1,567	7.3
1931, Mar. 31	Managua, Nicaragua	2,500	6.0	1998, Feb. 4, 8	Hindu Kush, Afghanistan	2,323	5.9
1931, Apr. 27	Armenia-Azerbaijan border	2,800	5.7	1998, May 30	Afghanistan-Tajikistan		
1931, Aug. 10	Xinjiang, China	10,000	8.0		border	4,000+	6.6
1933, Mar. 2	Sanriku, Japan (tsunami)	2,990	8.4	1998, July 17	Papua New Guinea	2,183	7.0
1933, Mar. 10	Long Beach, CA	115	6.2	1999, Jan. 25	Armenia, Colombia	1,185+	6.1
1933, Aug. 25	Sichuan, China	9,300	7.5	1999, Aug. 17	Izmit, western Turkey	17,118+	7.6
1934, Jan. 15	Bihar, India-Nepal	10,700	8.1	1999, Sept. 20	Taichung, Taiwan	2,400	7.6
1935, Apr. 21	Miao-li, Taiwan	3,270	7.1	2001, Jan. 26	Gujarat, India	20,085	7.6
1935, May 30	Quetta, Pakistan	30,000	7.6	2002, Mar. 25-26	Hindu Kush, Afghanistan	1,000+	6.1
1939, Jan. 25	Chillan, Chile	28,000	7.8	2003, May 21	Northern Algeria	2,266	6.8
1939, Dec. 26	Erzincan, Turkey	32,700	7.8	2003, Dec. 26	Bam, SE Iran	31,000	6.6
1943, Sept. 10	Tottori, Japan	1,190	7.4	2004, Dec. 26	Sumatra-Andaman Isls.,		
1943, Nov. 26	Ladik, Turkey	4,000	7.6		Indonesia	227,898	9.1[7]
1944, Jan. 15	San Juan, Argentina	8,000	7.4	2005, Mar. 28	N Sumatra, Indonesia	1,313	8.6
1944, Feb. 1	Gerede, Turkey	2,790	7.4	2005, Oct. 8	Kashmir, Pakistan, India	86,000	7.6
1945, Jan. 12	Mikawa, Japan	1,961	7.1	2006, May 26	Java, Indonesia	5,749	6.3
1945, Nov. 27	Makran Coast, Pakistan	4,000	8.0	2008, May 12	E Sichuan Prov., China	87,857	7.9
1946, May 31	Ustukran, Turkey	1,300	5.9	2009, Sept. 30	Sumatra, Indonesia	1,117	7.5
1946, Nov. 10	Ancash, Peru	1,400	7.3	2010, Jan. 12	Haiti	316,000	7.0
1946, Dec. 20	Honshu, Japan	1,362	8.1	2010, Apr. 13	Southern Qinghai, China	2,698+	6.9
1948, June 28	Fukui, Japan	3,769	7.3	2011, Mar. 11	NE Japan	20,896	9.0[8]
1948, Oct. 5	Ashgabat, Turkmenistan	110,000	7.3	2015, Apr. 25	Nepal	8,669+	7.8

NA = Not available. (1) Once thought to have been a volcanic eruption; evidence indicates a destructive earthquake and tsunami occurred on this date. (2) This earthquake caused the most deadly tsunami to date in the Atlantic Ocean. (3) Incl. deaths from resulting fires; revised estimates of magnitude range from 7.7 to 7.9. (4) Commonly referred to as the Gansu quake; actually located within the Ningxia autonomous region. (5) The largest recorded earthquake; caused a deadly tsunami that spread across the Pacific Ocean as far as Japan. (6) The "Good Friday" earthquake sent a tsunami that hit British Columbia, Canada, and the U.S. Pacific coast. (7) This undersea earthquake triggered devastating Indian Ocean tsunamis. (8) The most powerful earthquake in Japan's history set off a tsunami that inundated much of the coast and caused a partial meltdown of the Fukushima nuclear power plant.

Some Notable Fires Since 1918

See also Some Notable Explosions Since 1920.

Date	Location	Deaths
1918, Oct. 12	Cloquet-Moose Lake, MN	453
1922, Oct. 4-5	Wind-blown fire, Haileybury, ON, Canada	43
1929, May 10	Forest fire, Xochilapa, Mexico	60
1930, Apr. 21	Penitentiary, Columbus, OH	320
1931, July 24	Home for aged, Pittsburgh, PA	48
1934, Dec. 11	Hotel Kerns, Lansing, MI	34
1938, May 16	Terminal Hotel, Atlanta, GA	35
1940, Apr. 23	Nightclub, Natchez, MS	198
1942, Nov. 28	Cocoanut Grove Nightclub, Boston, MA	492
1942, Dec. 12	Hostel, St. John's, NL, Canada	100
1943, Sept. 7	Gulf Hotel, Houston, TX	55
1944, July 6	Ringling Circus, Hartford, CT	168
1946, June 5	LaSalle Hotel, Chicago, IL	61
1946, Dec. 7	Winecoff Hotel, Atlanta, GA	119
1946, Dec. 12	Ice plant, tenement, New York, NY	37
1949, Apr. 5	Hospital, Effingham, IL	77
1949, Aug.	Forest fire, Landes, France	80
1950, Jan. 7	Mercy Hospital, Davenport, IA	41
1953, Mar. 29	Nursing home, Largo, FL	35
1953, Apr. 16	Metalworking plant, Chicago, IL	35
1957, Feb. 17	Home for aged, Warrenton, MO	72
1958, Mar. 19	Loft building, New York, NY	24
1958, Dec. 1	Parochial school, Chicago, IL	95
1958, Dec. 16	Store, Bogotá, Colombia	83
1960, Mar. 12	Chemical plant, Pusan, Korea	68
1960, July 14	Mental hospital, Guatemala City	225
1960, Nov. 13	Movie theater, Amude, Syria	152
1960, Dec. 19	USS Constellation, Brooklyn, NY	49
1961, Jan. 6	Thomas Hotel, San Francisco, CA	20
1961, Dec. 17	Circus, Niteroi, Brazil	323
1963, May 4	Theater, Diourbel, Senegal	64
1963, Nov. 18	Surfside Hotel, Atlantic City, NJ	25
1963, Nov. 23	Nursing home, Fitchville, OH	63
1963, Dec. 29	Roosevelt Hotel, Jacksonville, FL	22
1964, Dec. 18	Nursing home, Fountaintown, IN	20
1965, Aug. 11-16	Watts riot fires, Los Angeles, CA	30+
1966, Dec. 7	Barracks, Erzurum, Turkey	68
1967, Feb. 7	Restaurant, Montgomery, AL	25
1967, Feb. 7	Scrub fire, Hobart, Tasmania, Australia	62
1967, May 22	Dept. store, Brussels, Belgium	322
1967, July 16	State prison, Jay, FL	37
1967, July 29	USS Forrestal, off N Vietnam	134
1968, May 11	Wedding hall, Vijayawada, India	58
1969, Dec. 2	Nursing home, Notre Dame, QC, Canada	54
1970, Jan. 9	Nursing home, Marietta, OH	27
1970, Nov. 1	Dance hall, Grenoble, France	145
1970, Dec. 20	Hotel, Tucson, AZ	28
1971, Dec. 25	Hotel, Seoul, S. Korea	162
1972, May 13	Nightclub, Osaka, Japan	116
1972, July 5	Hospital, Sherborne, England, UK	30
1973, June 24	Bar, New Orleans, LA	32
1973, Aug. 3	Amusement park, Isle of Man, UK	51
1973, Nov. 29	Dept. store, Kumamoto, Japan	107
1973, Dec. 2	Theater, Seoul, S. Korea	50
1974, Feb. 1	Bank building, São Paulo, Brazil	189
1974, June 30	Discotheque, Port Chester, NY	24
1974, Nov. 3	Hotel, disco, Seoul, S. Korea	88
1975, Dec. 12	Tent city, Mina, Saudi Arabia	138
1976, Oct. 24	Social club, Bronx, NY	25
1977, Feb. 25	Rossiya Hotel, Moscow, Russia	45
1977, May 28	Nightclub, Southgate, KY	164
1977, June 9	Nightclub, Abidjan, Ivory Coast	41
1977, June 26	Jail, Columbia, TN	42
1977, Nov. 14	Hotel, Manila, Philippines	47
1978, Aug. 19	Movie theater, Abadan, Iran	425+
1979, July 14	Hotel, Saragossa, Spain	80
1979, Dec. 31	Social club, Chapais, QC, Can.	42
1980, May 20	Nursing home, Kingston, Jamaica	157
1980, Nov. 21	MGM Grand Hotel, Las Vegas, NV	84
1980, Dec. 4	Stouffer Inn, Harrison, NY	26
1981, Jan. 9	Boarding home, Keansburg, NJ	30
1981, Feb. 14	Discotheque, Dublin, Ireland	44
1982, Nov. 8	County jail, Biloxi, MS	29
1983, Feb. 13	Movie theater, Turin, Italy	64

Date	Location	Deaths
1983, Feb. 16	"Ash Wednesday" bushfires, S Australia and Victoria, Australia	75
1983, Dec. 17	Discotheque, Madrid, Spain	83
1984, May 11	Great Adventure Amusement Park, Jackson Twp., NJ	8
1985, Apr. 21	Movie theaters, Tabaco, Philippines	44
1985, Apr. 26	Hospital, Buenos Aires, Argentina	79
1985, May 11	Soccer stadium, Bradford, Eng., UK	53
1985, May 13	MOVE headquarters, row houses, Philadelphia, PA	11
1986, Dec. 31	Dupont Plaza Hotel, Puerto Rico	96
1987, May 6-June 2	Forest fire, Mohe, China	191
1987, Nov. 17	Subway, London, England	30
1988, Mar. 20	About 2,000 buildings, Lashio, Myan.	134
1990, Mar. 25	Social club, Bronx, NY	87
1991, Mar. 3	Munitions dump, Addis Ababa, Ethiopia	260+
1991, Aug-Oct.	Wildfires, Sumatra, Borneo, Indonesia	57
1991, Sept. 3	Processing plant, Hamlet, NC	25
1991, Oct. 20-21	Wildfire, Oakland, Berkeley, CA	24
1992, Mar.	Forest fire, Terai, Nepal	56
1993, Apr. 19	Cult compound, Waco, TX	72
1994, May 10	Toy factory, Bangkok, Thailand	213
1994, Nov. 2	Burning fuel flood, Durunka, Egypt	500
1994, Dec. 10	Theater, Karamay, China	300
1995, Oct. 28	Subway train, Baku, Azerbaijan	300
1995, Dec. 23	School, Mandi Dabwali, India	500+
1996, Mar. 19	Nightclub, Quezon City, Philippines	150+
1996, Mar. 28	Shopping mall, Bogor, Indonesia	78
1996, Nov. 20	Garley Building, Hong Kong	39
1997, Feb. 23	Worship site, Baripada, India	164
1997, Apr. 15	Encampment, Mina, Saudi Arabia	343
1997, June 7	Temple, Thanjavur, India	60+
1997, June 13	Movie theater, New Delhi, India	60
1997, July 11	Hotel, Pattaya, Thailand	90
1997, Sept.-Nov.	Drought-fueled fire, Sumatra, Indonesia	240
1998, Apr.-June	Wildfire, Oaxaca, Mexico	50
1998, Dec. 3	Orphanage, Manila, Philippines	28
1999, Mar. 24	Mt. Blanc Tunnel, France, Italy	40
1999, Oct. 30	Karaoke salon, Inchon, S. Korea	55+
2000, Mar. 17	Church, Kanungu, Uganda	530
2000, Nov. 11	Cable car, Kaprun, Austria	155
2000, Dec. 25	Shopping center, Luoyang, China	309
2001, Mar. 26	School, Machakos, Kenya	64
2001, Aug. 18	Hotel, Quezon City, Philippines	73
2001, Sept. 1	Nightclub, Tokyo, Japan	44
2001, Dec. 29	Fireworks accident, Lima, Peru	291
2003, Feb. 18	Subway train, Taegu, S. Korea	198
2003, Feb. 20	Pyrotechnics in nightclub, Warwick, RI	100
2003, Sept. 15	Prison, Riyadh, Saudi Arabia	94
2003, Nov. 24	Students' hostel, Moscow, Russia	36
2004, May 17	Prison, San Pedro Sula, Honduras	104
2004, July 16	Pvt. school, Kumbakonam, India	80+
2004, Aug. 1	Market, Asunción, Paraguay	400+
2004, Dec. 30	Club, Buenos Aires, Argentina	194
2005, Feb. 14	Mosque, Tehran, Iran	59
2005, Mar. 7	Prison, Higuey, Dom. Republic	159
2005, Sept. 5	Theater, Beni Suef, Egypt	32
2006, Dec. 9	Drug treatment center, Moscow, Russ.	45
2007, Mar. 20	Nursing home, Kamyshevatskaya, Russia	62
2007, Aug. 24-Sept. 2	Wildfires (arson), Greece	67
2008, Apr. 26	Factory fire, Casablanca, Morocco	55
2008, Sept.	Wildfires, Mozambique, S. Africa, Swaziland	89
2009, Jan. 1	Nightclub fire, Bangkok, Thailand	67
2009, Jan.-Feb.	Wildfires (arson), Victoria, Australia	173
2010, July	Bushfires, Nizhiny Novgorod, Russia	53
2010, Dec. 2-5	Grassland fire, Israel	44
2012, Feb. 14	Prison fire, Comayagua, Honduras	360+
2012, Nov. 24	Garment factory, Bagladesh	112
2013, Jan. 27	Pyrotechnics in nightclub, Santa Maria, Brazil	241
2014, May 2	Trade union building, Odessa, Ukraine	40+
2015, Apr. 12	Forest fires, Siberia, Russia	30
2016, Apr. 10	Fireworks at Hindu temple, Kerala, India	110+

Some Notable Explosions Since 1920

See also Principal U.S. Mine Disasters Since 1867. Some bombings related to political conflicts and terrorism are not included.

Date	Location	Deaths
1920, Sept. 16	Wall Street, New York, NY	30
1921, Sept. 21	Chem. storage facility, Oppau, Ger.	561
1924, Jan. 3	Food plant, Pekin, IL.	42
1927, May 18	School bombing, Bath, MI	45
1928, Apr. 13	Dance hall, West Plains, MO	40
1937, Mar. 18	School, New London, TX	311
1940, Sept. 12	Hercules Powder factory, Kenvil, NJ	55
1942, June 5	Ordnance plant, Elwood, IL	49
1944, Apr. 14	Harbor, Bombay, India	700
1944, July 17	Munitions ships, depot, Port Chicago, CA	322
1944, Oct. 20	Liquid natural gas tanks, Cleveland, OH	130
1947, Apr. 16	Freighter, chemical co. plant, Texas City, TX.	576
1948, July 28	Farben works, Ludwigshafen, Ger.	184
1950, May 19	Munitions barges, S. Amboy, NJ	30
1954, May 26	USS *Bennington*, off RI	103
1956, Aug. 7	Dynamite trucks, Cali, Colombia	1,100
1958, Apr. 18	Sunken munitions ship, Okinawa, Japan	40
1959, Apr. 10	WWII bomb, Philippines	38
1959, June 28	Rail tank cars, Meldrim, GA	25
1959, Aug. 7	Truck filled with explosives, Roseburg, OR	14
1959, Nov. 2	Explosives, Jamuri Bazar, India	46
1959, Dec. 13	2 apt. bldgs., Dortmund, Ger.	26
1960, Mar. 4	Belgian munitions ship, Havana, Cuba.	100
1962, Oct. 3	New York Telephone Co. office, New York, NY	23
1963, Jan. 2	Packing plant, Terre Haute, IN	17
1963, Mar. 9	Dynamite plant, S. Africa	45
1963, Aug. 13	Explosives dump, Gauhaiti, India	32
1963, Oct. 31	State Fair Coliseum, Indianapolis, IN	73
1964, July 23	Harbor munitions, Bone, Algeria	100
1965, Aug. 9	Missile silo, Searcy, AR	53
1965, Oct. 21	Bridge, Tila Bund, Pakistan	80
1965, Nov. 24	Armory, Keokuk, IA.	20
1967, Dec. 25	Apartment building, Moscow, USSR	20
1968, Apr. 6	Sports store, Richmond, IN	43
1969, Mar. 31	Coal mine, nr. Barroteran, Mexico	180
1970, Apr. 8	Subway construction, Osaka, Japan	73
1971, June 24	Tunnel under construction, Sylmar, CA	17
1973, Feb., 10	Liquid gas tank, Staten Island, NY	40
1975, Dec. 27	Coal mine, Chasnala, India	431
1976, Apr. 13	Munitions works, Lapua, Finland	40
1977, Nov. 11	Freight train, Iri, S. Korea	57
1977, Dec. 22	Grain elevator, Westwego, LA	35
1978, July 11	Propylene tank truck, Tarragona, Spain	150
1980, Oct. 23	School, Ortuella, Spain.	64
1982, Apr. 25	Antiques exhibition, Todi, Italy	33
1982, Nov. 2	Salang Tunnel, Afghanistan	1,000+
1984, Feb. 25	Oil pipeline, Cubatao, Brazil	508
1984, June 21	Naval supply depot, Severomorsk, USSR	200+
1984, Nov. 19	Gas storage area, NE Mexico City	334
1984, Dec. 3	Chemical plant, Bhopal, India.	3,849
1984, Dec. 5	Coal mine, Taipei, Taiwan	94
1985, June 25	Fireworks factory, Hallett, OK.	21
1988, Apr. 10	Army ammunitions dump nr. Rawalpindi and Islamabad, Pakistan	100
1988, July 6	Oil rig, North Sea off NE Scotland, UK.	167
1989, June 3	Gas pipeline, between Ufa, Asha, USSR	650+
1992, Mar. 3	Coal mine, Kozlu, Turkey	270+
1992, Apr. 22	Gas leak in sewers, Guadalajara, Mexico	200+
1992, May 9	Coal mine, Plymouth, Nova Scotia, Can.	26
1993, Feb. 26	World Trade Center, New York, NY	6
1994, July 18	Jewish community center, Buenos Aires, Argentina	100
1995, Apr. 19	Fed. office building, Oklahoma City, OK	168
1995, Apr. 29	Subway construction, S. Korea	110
1996, Jan. 31	Bank, Colombo, Sri Lanka	53
1996, Mar. 3-4	Jerusalem and Tel Aviv, Israel	33
1996, June 25	U.S. military housing complex, nr. Dhahran, Saudi Arabia	19
1996, July 24	Train, Colombo, Sri Lanka	86
1996, Nov. 16	Military apt., Dagestan region, Russia	68
1996, Nov. 21	Propane gas leak in building, San Juan, Puerto Rico	33
1996, Nov. 27	Coal mine, Shanxi Prov., China	91+
1996, Dec. 30	Train, Assam, India.	59+
1997, Dec. 2	Coal mine, Novokuznetsk, Russia	68

Date	Location	Deaths
1998, Feb. 14	2 oil tankers, Yaounde, Cameroon	120
1998, Feb. 14	17 bombs, Coimbatore, India	50
1998, Apr. 4	Coal mine, Donetsk, Ukraine	63
1998, Aug. 7	Bomb, U.S. emb., Nairobi, Kenya.	213
1998, Aug. 7	Bomb, U.S. emb., Dar-es-Salaam, Tanzania	11
1998, Sept. 8	2 buses, São Paulo, Brazil	59
1998, Oct. 17	Oil pipeline, Jesse, Nigeria	700+
1999, May 16	Fuel truck, Punjab Prov., Pakistan	75
1999, Sept. 9	Apartment building, Moscow, Russia	94
1999, Sept. 13	Apartment building, Moscow, Russia	118
1999, Sept. 16	Apartment building, Moscow, Russia	18
1999, Sept. 26	Fireworks factory, Celaya, Mexico	56
2000, Feb. 25	Bombs on 2 buses, Ozamis, Philippines	41
2000, Mar. 11	Coal mine, Krasnodon, Ukraine	80
2000, Apr. 16	Airport hangar, Dem. Rep. of Congo	100+
2000, July 16	Oil pipeline, Warri, Nigeria	30
2000, Sept. 9	Truck explosion, Urumqi, China	60
2000, Oct. 12	USS *Cole*, Yemen	17
2001, Mar. 6	School, Jianxi Prov., China.	41
2001, Apr. 21	Coal mine, Shaanxi, China.	51
2001, June 1	Dance club, Tel Aviv, Israel	21
2001, July 17	Coal mine, Guanxi, China.	76+
2001, Aug. 19	Coal mine, Donetsk region, Ukraine.	52
2001, Sept. 21	Chem. plant, Toulouse, France	29
2002, Jan. 21	Volcanic lava caused gas station blast, Goma, Dem. Rep. of Congo	50+
2002, Jan. 27	Munitions dump, Lagos, Nigeria	1,000+
2002, May 9	Land mine at parade, Kaspiisk, Russia	34+
2002, June 14	Car bomb outside U.S. consulate, Karachi, Pakistan	12
2002, June 18	Bomb on bus, Jerusalem, Israel	20
2002, July 5	Bomb in market, Larba, Algeria	35+
2002, Aug. 9	Explosion, Jalalabad, Afghanistan	25+
2002, Sept. 5	Car bomb, Kabul, Afghanistan	30
2002, Oct. 12	Nightclub bombings, Bali, Indonesia	202
2003, Aug. 25	Bombs in 2 taxis, Mumbai, India.	52
2003, Dec. 5	Bomb on train, Yessentuki, Russia.	45
2003, Dec. 23	Gas well explosion, Chongqing, China.	233
2004, Jan. 19	Natural gas facility, Skikda, Algeria	27
2004, Feb. 6	Bomb on subway car, Moscow, Russia	39
2004, Mar. 11	Bombs on commuter trains, Madrid, Spain.	191
2005, Feb. 14	Coal mine, NE China	214
2005, Mar. 23	Oil refinery, Texas City, TX.	15
2005, May 2	Arms cache, Baghlan Prov., Afghan.	34+
2005, July 7	Bombs in mass transit, London, Eng., UK	56
2005, Oct. 1	Bombings of restaurants, Bali, Indonesia	26
2005, Nov. 27	Coal mine, NE China	161+
2006, May 12	Oil pipeline, nr. Lagos, Nigeria	200
2006, July 1	Bombings of trains, station, Mumbai, India	207
2007, Mar. 19	Coal mine, Siberia, Russia	108
2007, Mar. 22	Natl. weapons depot, Maputo, Mozambique	117
2007, June 9	Oil pipeline, Pyongan Prov., N. Korea	110
2007, Nov. 18	Methane gas buildup in coal mine, E Ukraine	90
2008, May 15	Pipeline explosion in Lagos, Nigeria.	100+
2008, Sept. 20	Truck bomb outside hotel, Islamabad, Pakistan	40+
2009, Feb. 22	Coal mine, N China	74
2010, Apr. 5	Coal mine, Montcoal, WV	29
2010, May 8-9	Coal mine, Siberia, Russia	91
2010, June 17	Coal mine, Amaga, Colombia.	73
2010, Nov. 19	Coal mine, Ataru, New Zealand	29
2011, Mar. 28	Munitions factory, Abyan, Yemen.	150+
2011, July 13	Bombs in three locations in Mumbai, India	27
2012, Mar. 4	Arms depot, Brazzaville, Congo Rep.	250+
2013, Apr. 17	Fire at fertilizer plant, West, TX.	15
2013, June 3	Poultry plant, Mishzai, China	119+
2013, June 30	Fuel tanker, Kampala, Uganda	30+
2013, July 6	Derailed oil train, Lac-Megantic, QC, Canada	47
2013, Aug. 1	Weapons cache, Homs, Syria	40
2014, May 13	Coal mine, Soma, Turkey	301
2014, May 19	Bus fire near Barranquilla, Colombia	32
2015, Aug. 12	Chemical warehouse, Tianjin, China	173

Notable Nuclear Accidents

Oct. 7, 1957: Fire in the Windscale plutonium production reactor N of Liverpool, England, UK, released radioactive material; later blamed for 39 cancer deaths.

Jan. 3, 1961: Reactor explosion at a federal installation near Idaho Falls, ID, killed 3 workers. Radiation contained.

Oct. 5, 1966: Sodium cooling system malfunction caused a partial core meltdown at the Enrico Fermi demonstration breeder reactor, near Detroit, MI. Radiation contained.

Jan. 21, 1969: Coolant malfunction from an experimental underground reactor at Lucens Vad, Switzerland, released radiation into a cavern, which was then sealed.

Mar. 22, 1975: Fire at the Brown's Ferry reactor in Decatur, AL, caused dangerous lowering of cooling water levels.

Mar. 28, 1979: Worst commercial nuclear accident in the U.S. occurred as equipment failures and human mistakes led to a loss of coolant and a partial core meltdown at the Three Mile Island reactor in Middletown, PA.

Feb. 11, 1981: Eight workers were contaminated when 100,000 gallons of radioactive coolant leaked into the containment building of TVA's Sequoyah 1 plant near Chattanooga, TN.

Apr. 25, 1981: Some 100 workers were exposed to radiation during repairs of a nuclear plant at Tsuruga, Japan.

Jan. 6, 1986: Cylinder of nuclear material burst after being improperly heated at a Kerr-McGee plant in Gore, OK. One worker died; 100 were hospitalized.

Apr. 26, 1986: Fires and resulting explosions at the Chernobyl nuclear power plant near Kiev, USSR (now in Ukraine), left at least 31 dead in the immediate aftermath and spread radioactive material over much of Europe. An estimated 135,000 people were evacuated. Tens of thousands of excess cancer deaths (as well as increased birth defects) were expected.

Sept. 1987: Cesium chloride from an improperly discarded hospital irradiation machine contaminated more than 200 people and killed at least 4 in Goiânia, Brazil. The event focused international attention on improving security and safety standards for radioactive waste.

Mar. 11, 2011: A 9.0-magnitude earthquake caused a devastating tsunami that inundated the Fukushima Daiichi nuclear power plant on Japan's NE coast. Three of the plant's reactors suffered partial meltdowns, and more than 12,000 tons of radioactive water was released into the sea. More than two years later, the plant's owners reported that 300 tons of radioactive water was still leaking into the ocean every day.

Record Oil Spills

The exact number of barrels in a ton varies with the type of oil, but a good approximation is 7 barrels per ton. Each barrel contains 42 gallons.

Name, location	Date	Cause	Est. tons
BP *Deepwater Horizon* rig, Gulf of Mexico, U.S.	Apr. 20-July 15, 2010	Explosion	700,000[1]
Ixtoc I oil well, S Gulf of Mexico	June 3, 1979	Blowout	600,000
Nowruz oil field, Persian Gulf	Feb. 1983	Blowout	600,000
Atlantic Empress and *Aegean Captain*, off Trinidad and Tobago	July 19, 1979	Collision	300,000
ABT Summer, off Angola	May 28, 1991	Explosion	260,000
Castillo de Bellver, off Cape Town, South Africa	Aug. 6, 1983	Fire	250,000
Amoco Cadiz, near Portsall, France	Mar. 16, 1978	Grounding	223,000
Torrey Canyon, off Land's End, England, UK.	Mar. 18, 1967	Grounding	119,000
Sea Star, Gulf of Oman	Dec. 19, 1972	Collision	115,000
Urquiola, La Coruna, Spain	May 12, 1976	Grounding	100,000

(1) The Dept. of Energy estimated the spill at 4.9 mil barrels, or more than 200 mil gallons.

Other Notable Oil Spills

Name, location	Date	Cause	Gallons
Persian Gulf	Jan. 21, 1991	Intentional spillage by Iraq	130,000,000[1]
Braer, off Shetland Islands, UK	Jan. 5, 1993	Grounding	26,000,000
Prestige, off N Spain	Nov. 13-19, 2002	Ship broke in half	22,600,000
Aegean Sea, off N Spain	Dec. 3, 1992	Grounding	21,500,000
Sea Empress, off SW Wales, UK.	Feb. 15, 1996	Grounding	18,000,000
Newtown Creek, Greenpoint, Brooklyn, NY	Oct. 5, 1950-present	Industrial explosion[2]	17,000,000
World Glory, off South Africa	June 13, 1968	Hull failure	13,524,000
Exxon Valdez, Prince William Sound, AK.	Mar. 24, 1989	Grounding	10,080,000
Ashland Oil facility, Floreffe, PA; Monongahela R.	Jan. 2, 1988	Storage tank collapse	3,850,000

(1) Est. by Saudi Arabia. Some estimates as low as 25 mil gal. (2) Preceded by leaks in 1940s-50s.

Notable Droughts

Source: EM-DAT: The OFDA/CRED Intl. Disaster Database, Université catholique de Louvain, Brussels, Belgium, www.emdat.be; World Almanac research

Date	Location	Est. deaths	Date	Location	Est. deaths
1900	Bengal, India.	1,250,000	1974-76	Somalia.	19,000
1900	Cape Verde islands.	11,000	1981-85	Mozambique.	100,000
1910-14	Zinder Dept., Niger.	85,000	1981-85	Chad.	3,000
1920	China.	500,000	1983	Swaziland.	500
1920	Cape Verde islands.	24,000	1983-84	Eritrea, Ethiopia	300,000
1921	S Ukraine, Volga, USSR.	1,200,000	1983-85	N Sudan.	150,000
1928-30	Shaanxi, Henan, Gansu, China	3,000,000	1987	Somalia, Eritrea, Ethiopia.	967
1940-44	Cape Verde islands.	20,000	1987	NW India.	300
1942	Calcutta, Bengal, India	1,500,000	1988	Central China.	1,400
1943	Bangladesh.	1,900,000	1991	Jiangxi, Hunan Provinces, China	2,000
1946	Cape Verde islands.	30,000	1997	Irian Jaya, Indonesia.	672
1965	Ethiopia.	2,000	1999-2003	Pakistan	143
1965-67	India	1,500,000	2002	Malawi	500
1966	Lombok, Indonesia.	8,000	2006	SW China.	134
1973-78	Ethiopia.	100,000	2014	Tharparkar, Pakistan	166

Some Notable Miscellaneous Disasters Since 1950

Date	Event	Location	Details	Est. deaths
1952, Dec.	Pollution	London, England, UK	Heavy smog blanketed city; impeded breathing	4,000
1980, summer	Heat wave.	United States	June through Sept.	1,265
1984, Dec. 3	Industrial accident.	Bhopal, India.	Toxic gas leaked from a Union Carbide factory	16,000
1986, Aug. 21	Gas.	Nr. Lake Nyos, Cameroon	Volcanic lake released cloud of carbon dioxide gas	1,700
1990, July 2	Stampede.	Mecca, Saudi Arabia	Pilgrims panicked in tunnel leading to the holy city	1,426
2003, summer	Heat wave.	Europe	Abnormally high temperatures from Russia to Britain; France suffered most, with 14,800 dead	35,000
2013, Apr. 24	Building collapse.	Savar, Bangladesh	Garment factory found to have substandard foundation collapsed	1,100-
2015, Sept. 24	Stampede.	Mina, Saudi Arabia	Two groups of pilgrims collided during hajj to Mecca	2,411

AEROSPACE

Notable Human Spaceflight Missions

Source: National Aeronautics and Space Administration (NASA); Congressional Research Service; World Almanac research

The spaceflights listed are a selection of notable U.S. missions by NASA, unless otherwise noted, plus non-U.S. missions (shown with an asterisk). The non-U.S missions were sponsored by the USSR—later, the Commonwealth of Independent States (CIS) and, from 1997, Russia—or by China. Launch dates are Eastern standard time. **EVA** = extravehicular activity. **ASTP** = Apollo-Soyuz Test Project. **STS** = Space Transportation System, NASA's name for the overall shuttle program.

For shuttle flights, mission name is in parentheses following name of orbiter. Duration of flight is listed in hours:minutes for 1961-Apr. 1970; days (d.), hours (hr.), and minutes (min.) thereafter. Number of total flights taken by each crew member is given in parentheses when flight listed is not the person's first.

4/12/1961: *Vostok 1*; 1:48; Yuri A. Gagarin. **1st human orbital flight.**

5/5/1961: *Mercury-Redstone 3*; 0:15; Alan B. Shepard Jr. **1st American in space.**

7/21/1961: *Mercury-Redstone 4*; 0:15; Virgil I. Grissom. Flight successful but spacecraft sank shortly after splashdown; Grissom rescued.

8/6/1961: *Vostok 2*; 25:18; Gherman S. Titov. 1st spaceflight of more than 24 hours.

2/20/1962: *Mercury-Atlas 6*; 4:55; John H. Glenn Jr. **1st American in orbit**; three orbits.

5/24/1962: *Mercury-Atlas 7*; 4:56; M. Scott Carpenter. Manual retrofire error caused 250-mi landing overshoot.

8/11/1962: *Vostok 3*; 94:22; Andrian G. Nikolayev. *Vostok 3* and *4* made 1st group flight.

8/12/1962: *Vostok 4*; 70:57; Pavel R. Popovich. On 1st orbit, it came within 3 mi of *Vostok 3*.

10/3/1962: *Mercury-Atlas 8*; 9:13; Walter M. Schirra Jr. Landed 5 mi from target; six orbits.

5/15/1963: *Mercury-Atlas 9*; 34:19; L. Gordon Cooper. 1st U.S. evaluation of effects of one day in space on a person; 22 orbits.

6/14/1963: *Vostok 5*; 119:06; Valery F. Bykovsky. *Vostok 5* and *6* made 2nd group flight.

6/16/1963: *Vostok 6*; 70:50; Valentina V. Tereshkova. **1st woman in space**; passed within 3 mi of *Vostok 5*.

10/12/1964: *Voskhod 1*; 24:17; Vladimir M. Komarov, Konstantin P. Feoktistov, Boris B. Yegorov. 1st three-person orbital flight; 1st without space suits.

3/18/1965: *Voskhod 2*; 26:02; Pavel I. Belyayev, Aleksei A. Leonov. Leonov made **1st spacewalk** (10 min.).

3/23/1965: *Gemini-Titan 3*; 4:53; Virgil I. Grissom (2), John W. Young. 1st piloted spacecraft to change its orbital path.

6/3/1965: *Gemini-Titan 4*; 97:56; James A. McDivitt, Edward H. White II. White was **1st American to "walk in space"** (23 min.).

8/21/1965: *Gemini-Titan 5*; 190:55; L. Gordon Cooper (2), Charles Conrad Jr. Longest-duration human flight to date.

12/4/1965: *Gemini-Titan 7*; 330:35; Frank Borman, James A. Lovell Jr. Longest-duration *Gemini* flight.

12/15/1965: *Gemini-Titan 6A*; 25:51; Walter M. Schirra Jr. (2), Thomas P. Stafford. Completed 1st U.S. space rendezvous, with *Gemini 7*.

3/16/1966: *Gemini-Titan 8*; 10:41; Neil A. Armstrong, David R. Scott. **1st docking of one space vehicle with another**; mission aborted, control malfunction.

6/3/1966: *Gemini-Titan 9A*; 72:21; Thomas P. Stafford (2), Eugene A. Cernan. Performed simulation of lunar module rendezvous.

7/18/1966: *Gemini-Titan 10*; 70:47; John W. Young (2), Michael Collins. 1st use of Agena target vehicle's propulsion systems; 1st orbital docking.

9/12/1966: *Gemini-Titan 11*; 71:17; Charles Conrad Jr. (2), Richard F. Gordon Jr. 1st tethered flight; highest Earth-orbit altitude (850 mi).

11/11/1966: *Gemini-Titan 12*; 94:34; James A. Lovell Jr. (2), Edwin E. "Buzz" Aldrin Jr. Final *Gemini* mission; 5-hr. EVA.

1/27/1967: *Apollo 1*; Virgil I. Grissom, Edward H. White II, and Roger B. Chaffee died in a fire on the ground at Cape Canaveral, FL.

4/23/1967: *Soyuz 1*; 26:40; Vladimir M. Komarov (2). Crashed on reentry, killing Komarov; **1st space fatality**.

10/11/1968: *Apollo-Saturn 7*; 260:09; Walter M. Schirra Jr. (3), Donn F. Eisele, R. Walter Cunningham. **1st piloted flight** of *Apollo* spacecraft command-service module only; live TV footage of crew.

12/21/1968: *Apollo-Saturn 8*; 147:00; Frank Borman (2), James A. Lovell Jr. (3), William A. Anders. **1st lunar orbit** and piloted lunar return reentry (command-service module only); views of lunar surface televised to Earth.

1/14/1969: *Soyuz 4*; 71:21; Vladimir A. Shatalov. Docked with *Soyuz 5*.

1/15/1969: *Soyuz 5*; 72:54; Boris V. Volyanov, Aleksei S. Yeliseyev, Yevgeny V. Khrunov. Docked with *Soyuz 4*; Yeliseyev and Khrunov transferred to *Soyuz 4* via a spacewalk.

3/3/1969: *Apollo-Saturn 9*; 241:00; James A. McDivitt (2), David R. Scott (2), Russell L. Schweickart. 1st piloted flight of lunar module.

5/18/1969: *Apollo-Saturn 10*; 192:03; Thomas P. Stafford (3), John W. Young (3), Eugene A. Cernan (2). 1st lunar module orbit of Moon, 50,000 ft from Moon's surface.

7/16/1969: *Apollo-Saturn 11*; 195:18; Neil A. Armstrong (2), Michael Collins (2), Edwin E. "Buzz" Aldrin Jr. (2). **1st Moon landing** made by Armstrong and Aldrin (7/20); collected 47.5 lbs of soil, rock samples; lunar stay time 21:36.

10/11/1969: *Soyuz 6*; 118:43; Georgi S. Shonin, Valery N. Kubasov. 1st welding of metals in space.

10/12/1969: *Soyuz 7*; 118:40; Anatoly V. Flipchenko, Vladislav N. Volkov, Viktor V. Gorbatko. Space lab construction test made; *Soyuz 6*, *7*, and *8*: 1st time three spacecraft, seven crew members orbited the Earth at once.

10/13/1969: *Soyuz 8*; 118:51; Vladimir A. Shatalov (2), Aleksei S. Yeliseyev (2). Part of space lab construction team.

11/14/1969: *Apollo-Saturn 12*; 244:36; Charles Conrad Jr. (3), Richard F. Gordon Jr. (2), Alan L. Bean. Conrad and Bean made **2nd Moon landing** (11/18); collected 75 lbs of samples; lunar stay time 31:31.

4/11/1970: *Apollo-Saturn 13*; 142:54; James A. Lovell Jr. (4), Fred W. Haise Jr., John L. Swigert Jr. Aborted after service module oxygen tank ruptured; crew returned in lunar module.

6/1/1970: *Soyuz 9*; 17 d., 16 hr., 59 min.; Andrian G. Nikolayev (2), Vitaly I. Sevastyanov. Longest human spaceflight to date.

1/31/1971: *Apollo-Saturn 14*; 9 d., 2 min.; Alan B. Shepard Jr. (2), Stuart A. Roosa, Edgar D. Mitchell. Shepard and Mitchell made **3rd Moon landing** (2/5); collected 94 lbs of lunar samples; lunar stay 33:31.

4/19/1971: *Salyut 1*; launched without crew. **1st space station.**

4/22/1971: *Soyuz 10*; 1 d., 23 hr., 46 min.; Vladimir A. Shatalov (3), Aleksei S. Yeliseyev (3), Nikolay N. Rukavishnikov. **1st successful docking with a space station**; failed to enter space station.

6/6/1971: *Soyuz 11*; 23 d., 28 hr., 22 min.; Georgi T. Dobrovolskiy, Vladislav N. Volkov (2), Viktor I. Patsayev. Docked and entered *Salyut 1* space station; **crew died** during reentry from loss of pressurization.

7/26/1971: *Apollo-Saturn 15*; 12 d., 17 hr., 12 min.; David R. Scott (3), James B. Irwin, Alfred M. Worden. Scott and Irwin made **4th Moon landing** (7/30). 1st lunar rover use; 1st deep spacewalk; 170 lbs of samples; 66:55 stay.

12/7/1972: *Apollo-Saturn 17*; 12 d., 13 hr., 52 min.; Eugene A. Cernan (3), Ronald E. Evans, Harrison H. Schmitt. Cernan and Schmitt made 6th and **final crewed lunar landing** (12/11); collected 243 lbs of samples; record lunar stay over 75 hr.

5/14/1973: *Skylab 1*; launched without crew. **1st U.S. space station**; fell out of orbit 7/11/1979.

5/25/1973: *Skylab 2*; 28 d., 49 min.; Charles Conrad Jr. (4), Joseph P. Kerwin, Paul J. Weitz. 1st U.S.-piloted orbiting space station; crew repaired damage caused in boost.

11/16/1973: *Skylab 4*; 84 d., 1 hr., 16 min.; Gerald P. Carr, Edward G. Gibson, William R. Pogue. Final *Skylab* mission.

7/15/1975: *Soyuz 19 (ASTP)*; 6 d., 11 hr., 31 min.; Aleksei A. Leonov (2), Valery N. Kubasov (2). U.S.-USSR joint flight; crews linked up in space (7/17), conducted experiments, shared meals, held a joint news conference.

7/15/1975: *Apollo (ASTP)*; 9 d., 7 hr., 28 min.; Vance D. Brand, Thomas P. Stafford (4), Donald K. Slayton. Joint flight with *Soyuz 19*.

12/10/1977: *Soyuz 26*; 96 d., 10 hr.; Yuri V. Romanenko, Georgiy M. Grechko (2). 1st multiple docking at a space station (*Soyuz 26* and *27* docked at *Salyut 6*).

1/10/1978: *Soyuz 27*; 5 d., 22 hr., 59 min.; Vladimir A. Dzhanibekov. See *Soyuz 26*.

3/2/1978: *Soyuz 28*; 7 d., 22 hr., 16 min.; Aleksei A. Gubarev (2), Vladimir Remek. 1st international crew launch; Remek was 1st Czech in space.

4/12/1981: *Columbia (STS-1)*; 2 d., 6 hr., 21 min.; John W. Young (5), Robert L. Crippen. **1st reusable space shuttle** to fly into Earth's orbit.

11/12/1981: *Columbia (STS-2)*; 3 days; Joe H. Engle, Richard H. Truly. 1st scientific payload; 1st reuse of space shuttle.

11/11/1982: *Columbia (STS-5)*; 6 days; Vance D. Brand (2), Robert F. Overmyer, Joseph P. Allen, William B. Lenoir. 1st four-person crew.

6/18/1983: *Challenger (STS-7)*; 7 days; Robert L. Crippen (2), Frederick H. Hauck, John M. Fabian, Sally K. Ride, Norman E. Thagard. Ride was **1st U.S. woman in space**; 1st 5-person crew.

6/27/1983: *Soyuz T-9*; 150 days; Vladimir A. Lyakhov (2), Aleksandr Pavlovich. Docked at *Salyut 7*. 1st construction in space.

8/30/1983: *Challenger (STS-8)*; 7 days; Richard H. Truly (2), Daniel C. Brandenstein, Dale A. Gardner, Guion S. Bluford Jr., William E. Thornton. Bluford was **1st African-American in space**; **1st night launch**.

11/28/1983: *Columbia (STS-9)*; 11 days; John W. Young (6), Brewster H. Shaw Jr., Owen K. Garriott (2), Robert A.R. Parker, Byron K. Lichtenberg, Ulf Merbold. 1st six-person crew; 1st Spacelab mission.

2/3/1984: *Challenger (41-B)*; 8 days; Vance Brand (3), Robert L. Gibson, Ronald E. McNair, Bruce McCandless II, Robert L. Stewart. 1st untethered EVA.

2/8/1984: *Soyuz T-10B*; 63 days; Leonid Kizim, Vladimir Solovyov, Oleg Atkov. Docked with *Salyut 7*; crew set space duration record of 237 days (since eclipsed).

4/3/1984: *Soyuz T-11*; 182 days; Yury Malyshev (2), Gennady Strekalov (3), Rakesh Sharma. Docked with *Salyut 7*; Sharma was 1st Indian in space.

4/6/1984: *Challenger (41-C)*; 7 days; Robert L. Crippen (3), Francis R. Scobee, George D. Nelson, Terry J. Hart, James D. van Hoften. 1st in-orbit satellite repair.

8/30/1984: *Discovery (41-D)*; 7 days; Henry W. Hartsfield Jr. (2), Michael L. Coats, Richard M. Mullane, Steven A. Hawley, Judith A. Resnik, Charles D. Walker. 1st flight of non-astronaut (payload specialist Walker).

10/5/1984: *Challenger (41-G)*; 9 days; Robert L. Crippen (4), Jon A. McBride, Kathryn D. Sullivan, Sally K. Ride (2), David C. Leestma, Marc Garneau, Paul D. Scully-Power. 1st seven-person crew.

11/8/1984: *Discovery (51-A)*; 8 days; Frederick H. Hauck (2), David M. Walker, Anna L. Fisher, Dale A. Gardner (2), Joseph P. Allen (2). 1st satellite retrieval/repair.

4/12/1985: *Discovery (51-D)*; 7 days; Karol J. Bobko, Donald E. Williams, Charles D. Walker (2), M. Rhea Seddon, Jeffrey A. Hoffman, S. David Griggs, E. Jake Garn. Garn (R, UT) was **1st U.S. senator in space**.

6/17/1985: *Discovery (51-G)*; 8 days; Daniel C. Brandenstein (2), John O. Creighton, Shannon W. Lucid, John M. Fabian (2), Steven R. Nagel, Prince Sultan Salman al-Saud, Patrick Baudry. Launched three satellites; Salman al-Saud was 1st Arab in space; Baudry was 1st French person on U.S. mission.

10/3/1985: *Atlantis (51-J)*; 5 days; Karol J. Bobko (3), Ronald J. Grabe, David C. Hilmers, Robert L. Stewart (2), William A. Pailes. 1st *Atlantis* flight.

10/30/1985: *Challenger (61-A)*; 8 days; Henry W. Hartsfield Jr. (3), Steven R. Nagel (2), James F. Buchli (2), Guion S. Bluford (2), Bonnie J. Dunbar, Wubbo J. Ockels, Richard Furrer, Ernst Messerschmid. 1st eight-person crew; 1st German Spacelab mission.

1/12/1986: *Columbia (61-C)*; 7 days; Robert L. Gibson (2), Charles F. Bolden Jr., Franklin R. Chang Díaz, Steven A. Hawley (2), George D. Nelson (2), Robert J. Cenker, Bill Nelson. B. Nelson (D, FL) was **1st U.S. representative in space**.

1/28/1986: *Challenger (51-L)*; 73 seconds; Francis R. Scobee (2), Michael J. Smith, Judith A. Resnik (2), Ellison S. Onizuka (2), Ronald E. McNair, Gregory B. Jarvis, Christa McAuliffe. **Exploded 73 seconds after liftoff; all aboard were killed**, including McAuliffe, a New Hampshire schoolteacher who won competition to become 1st private citizen in space.

2/20/1986: *Mir[1]*; launched without crew. **Space station** with six docking ports launched.

3/13/1986: *Soyuz T-15*; 125 days; Leonid Kizim (3), Vladimir Solovyov (2). Ferry between stations; docked at *Mir*.

9/29/1988: *Discovery (STS-26)*; 4 days; Frederick H. Hauck (3), Richard O. Covey (2), George D. Nelson (3), John M. Lounge (2), David C. Hilmers (2). **1st shuttle flight since Challenger explosion** 1/28/1986.

5/4/1989: *Atlantis (STS-30)*; 4 days; David M. Walker (2), Ronald J. Grabe (2), Norman E. Thagard (3), Mary L. Cleave (2), Mark C. Lee. Launched Venus orbiter *Magellan*.

10/18/1989: *Atlantis (STS-34)*; 5 days; Donald E. Williams (2), Michael J. McCulley, Shannon W. Lucid (2), Franklin R. Chang Díaz (2), Ellen S. Baker. Launched Jupiter probe and orbiter *Galileo*.

4/24/1990: *Discovery (STS-31)*; 6 days; Loren J. Shriver (2), Charles F. Bolden Jr. (2), Steven A. Hawley (3), Bruce McCandless (2), Kathryn D. Sullivan (2). **Launched Hubble Space Telescope.**

10/6/1990: *Discovery (STS-41)*; 5 days; Richard N. Richards (2), Robert D. Cabana, Bruce E. Melnick, William M. Shepherd (2), Thomas D. Akers. Launched *Ulysses* spacecraft to investigate interstellar space and the Sun.

9/12/1992: *Endeavour (STS-47)*; 8 days; Robert L. Gibson (4), Curtis L. Brown Jr., Mark C. Lee (2), N. Jan Davis, Jay Apt (2), Mae Carol Jemison, Mamoru Mohri. Jemison was **1st black woman in space**; Lee and Davis were **1st married couple to travel together in space**; 1st Japanese Spacelab.

6/21/1993: *Endeavour (STS-57)*; 10 days; Ronald J. Grabe (4), Brian J. Duffy (2), G. David Low (3), Nancy J. Sherlock, Janice E. Voss, Peter J. K. Wisoff. Carried Spacelab commercial payload module.

12/2/1993: *Endeavour (STS-61)*; 11 days; Richard O. Covey (3), Kenneth D. Bowersox (2), F. Story Musgrave (5), Kathryn Thornton (3), Claude Nicollier (2), Jeffrey A. Hoffman (2), Thomas D. Akers (3). Hubble Space Telescope repaired; Akers set new U.S. EVA duration record (29 hr., 40 min.).

3/14/1995: *Soyuz TM-21*; 112 days; Norman E. Thagard (5), Vladimir Dezhurov, Gennady Strekalov (5). Docked with *Mir* 3/16. Thagard was 1st American onboard Russian spacecraft; Valery Polyakov returned to Earth, 3/22/1995, after record stay in space (439 days).

6/27/1995: *Atlantis (STS-71)*; 10 days; Robert L. Gibson (5), Charles J. Precourt (2), Ellen S. Baker (3), Bonnie J. Dunbar (4), Gregory J. Harbaugh (3), Anatoly Solovyev (4) (to *Mir*), Nikolai M. Budarin (to *Mir*), Norman E. Thagard (5) (from *Mir*), Gennady Strekalov (from *Mir*), Vladimir Dezhurov (from *Mir*). **1st shuttle-Mir docking**; exchanged crew members with *Mir*.

11/12/1995: *Atlantis (STS-74)*; 9 days; Kenneth D. Cameron (3), James D. Halsell Jr. (2), Jerry L. Ross (5), William S. McArthur Jr. (2), Chris A. Hadfield. 2nd shuttle-*Mir* docking (11/15-11/18); erected a 15-ft permanent docking tunnel to *Mir* for future use by U.S. orbiters.

9/16/1996: *Atlantis (STS-79)*; 11 days; William F. Readdy (3), Terry W. Wilcutt (2), Thomas D. Akers (4), John E. Blaha (5) (to *Mir*), Jay Apt (4), Carl E. Walz (3), Shannon W. Lucid (5) (from *Mir*). Docked with *Mir* 9/18; exchanged crew members;

Lucid set **U.S. and women's duration in space record** (188 days).

11/19/1996: *Columbia (STS-80)*; 18 days; Kenneth D. Cockrell (3), Kent V. Rominger (2), Tamara E. Jernigan (4), Thomas D. Jones (3), F. Story Musgrave (6). Longest-duration shuttle flight; Musgrave, 61, oldest thus far to fly in space; two science satellites deployed, retrieved.

8/5/1997: **Soyuz TM-26*; 198 days; Anatoly Solovyev (5), Pavel Vinogradov. Docked with *Mir* 8/7; repaired damaged space station.

8/7/1997: *Discovery (STS-85)*; 12 days; Curtis L. Brown Jr. (4), Kent V. Rominger (3), N. Jan Davis (3), Robert L. Curbeam Jr., Stephen K. Robinson, Bjarni V. Tryggvason. Deployed and retrieved satellite designed to study Earth's middle atmosphere; demonstrated robotic arm.

4/17/1998: *Columbia (STS-90)*; 16 days; Richard A. Searfoss (3), Scott D. Altman, Richard M. Linnehan (2), Dave R. Williams, Kathryn P. Hire, Jay C. Buckey, James A. Pawelczyk. Studied effects of microgravity on the nervous systems of the crew and more than 2,000 live animals; 1st surgery in space on animals meant to survive.

6/2/1998: *Discovery (STS-91)*; 10 days; Charles J. Precourt (4), Dominic L. Gorie, Wendy B. Lawrence (3), Franklin R. Chang Díaz (6), Janet L. Kavandi, Valery V. Ryumin (4), Andrew S. W. Thomas (2) (from *Mir*). Final docking mission with *Mir*; Thomas from *Mir*, 141 days in space.

10/29/1998: *Discovery (STS-95)*; 10 days; Curtis L. Brown Jr. (5), Steven W. Lindsey (2), Scott E. Parazynski (3), Stephen K. Robinson (2), Pedro Duque, Chiaki Mukai (2), John H. Glenn Jr. (2). The 77-year-old Glenn, one of the original *Mercury* astronauts, and at that point a senator (D, OH), became **oldest person to fly in space**; Duque was 1st Spaniard in space; experiments to study aging performed on Glenn.

12/4/1998: *Endeavour (STS-88)*; 12 days; Robert D. Cabana (4), Frederick W. Sturckow, Nancy J. Currie (3), Jerry L. Ross (6), James H. Newman (3), Sergei K. Krikalev (4). **1st assembly of International Space Station (ISS)**; attached U.S.-built *Unity* connecting module to Russian-built *Zarya* control module; 1st crew to enter ISS.

7/23/1999: *Columbia (STS-93)*; 5 days; Eileen M. Collins (3), Jeffrey S. Ashby, Steven A. Hawley (5), Catherine G. Coleman (2), Michel Tognini (2). Collins was **1st woman space shuttle commander**; deployed Chandra X-ray Observatory telescope.

2/11/2000: *Endeavour (STS-99)*; 12 days; Kevin R. Kregel (4), Dominic L. Gorie (2), Janet L. Kavandi (2), Janice E. Voss (5), Mamoru Mohri (2), Gerhard P.J. Thiele. Used radar to make most complete topographic map of Earth's surface ever produced.

10/31/2000: **Soyuz TM-31*; William M. Shepherd (4), Yuri Gidzenko (2), Sergei Krikalev (5). Established **1st permanent manning of ISS** with three-person crew for a 4-month stay.

7/12/2001: *Atlantis (STS-104)*; 13 days; Steven W. Lindsey (3), Charles O. Hobaugh, Michael L. Gernhardt (4), Janet L. Kavandi (3), James F. Reilly II (2). Installed the Joint Airlock, with nitrogen and oxygen tanks to permit future spacewalks from the ISS; three EVAs.

10/30/2002: **Soyuz TMA-1*[1]; Sergei Zalyotin (2), Frank De Winne, Yuri Lonchakov (2). 1st launch of *Soyuz TMA* (crew returned 11/10/2002 on *Soyuz TM-34* already docked at ISS).

1/16/2003: *Columbia (STS 107)*; 16 days; Rick D. Husband (2), William C. McCool, Michael P. Anderson (2), David M. Brown, Kalpana Chawla (2), Laurel B. Clark, Ilan Ramon. **Entire crew lost when *Columbia* broke apart** upon reentry, 2/1, due to heat shield damage; Ramon was 1st Israeli astronaut.

10/15/2003: **Shenzhou 5*; 21 hr.; Yang Liwei. **1st Chinese manned spacecraft.**

6/21/2004: *SpaceShipOne*[2]; 90 min.; Mike Melvill. **1st privately funded manned spaceflight.**

7/26/2005: *Discovery (STS-114)*; 14 days; Eileen M. Collins (4), James M. Kelly (2), Charles J. Camarda, Wendy B. Lawrence (4), Soichi Noguchi, Stephen K. Robinson (3), Andrew S.W. Thomas (3). **1st space shuttle flight since *Columbia* disaster**; tested new safety modifications to craft.

6/8/2007: *Atlantis (STS-117)*; 14 days; Frederick W. Sturckow (3), Lee J. Archambault, Patrick G. Forrester (2), John "Danny" Olivas, James F. Reilly (3), Steven R. Swanson, Clayton C. Anderson (to ISS), Sunita L. Williams (from ISS). Delivered truss segments and solar arrays to ISS; Williams set new record for **longest spaceflight by a woman (195 days)**.

8/8/2007: *Endeavour (STS-118)*; 13 days; Scott J. Kelly (2), Charles O. Hobaugh (2), Alvin B. Drew, Barbara R. Morgan, Tracy Caldwell Dyson, Rick A. Mastracchio (2), Dave R. Williams (2). Brought **Teacher in Space** project participant Morgan to ISS; attached new truss.

10/10/2007: **Soyuz TMA-11*[1]; Yuri I. Malenchenko (3), Sheikh Muszaphar Shukor (to ISS), Peggy A. Whitson (2) (from ISS), Yi So-yeon (from ISS). Delivered and installed components of ISS; malfunctioned on return to Earth, landing short of its touchdown area but causing no fatalities.

3/11/2008: *Endeavour (STS-123)*; 16 days; Dominic L. Gorie (4), Gregory H. Johnson, Richard M. Linnehan (4), Robert L. Behnken, Michael J. Foreman, Takao Doi (2), Garrett E. Reisman (to ISS), Léopold Eyharts (from ISS). Delivered and installed components of the Japanese Kibo science laboratory.

4/8/2008: **Soyuz TMA-12*[1]; Oleg Kononenko, Sergei Volkov, Yi So-yeon (to ISS), Richard Garriott (from ISS). Yi became 1st S. Korean in space.

9/25/2008: **Shenzhou 7*; 68 hr.; Jing Haipeng, Liu Boming, Zhai Zhigang. Zhai completed 1st Chinese spacewalk.

5/11/2009: *Atlantis (STS-125)*; 13 days; Scott D. Altman (4), Gregory C. Johnson, Andrew J. Feustel, Michael T. Good, John M. Grunsfeld (5), Michael J. Massimino (2), K. Megan McArthur. Final Hubble Space Telescope servicing mission.

6/15/2010: **Soyuz TMA-19*[1]; Fyodor Yurchikhin (3), Shannon Walker, Douglas H. Wheelock (2). 100th mission since launching of the International Space Station.

7/8/2011: *Atlantis (STS-135)*; 13 days; Christopher Ferguson (3), Doug Hurley (2), Sandy H. Magnus (3), Rex J. Walheim (3). **Final space shuttle mission.**

Note: Four Soviet cosmonauts have died during spaceflight: one person was killed on *Soyuz 1* (1967) when parachute lines tangled during descent; the three-person *Soyuz 11* crew (1971) was asphyxiated. Three Americans died in the *Apollo 1* (1967) fire on the ground at Cape Canaveral, FL; seven Americans died in the *Challenger* (1986) explosion; and six Americans and an Israeli astronaut died aboard *Columbia* (2003). (1) *Soyuz* crew often return from the ISS on spacecraft that launched and were docked at the station before their arrival. (2) Date of first successful flight; later, *SpaceShipOne* flew at least 100 km (62 mi) into space, 9/29/2004, piloted by Mike Melvill, and 10/4/2004, piloted by Brian Binnie, winning the $10-mil Ansari Prize for first private venture to accomplish this feat twice within two weeks.

U.S. Space Shuttles

Source: National Aeronautics and Space Administration (NASA)

After 135 launches, the United States ended its space shuttle program with the safe landing of the *Atlantis* shuttle on July 21, 2011, at Florida's Kennedy Space Center. Two shuttles—*Challenger* in 1986 and *Columbia* in 2003—were destroyed in flight, killing the entire 7-person crew carried on each. The surviving shuttles are now on display at museums around the country. *Enterprise* performed atmospheric test flights but never flew in space.

Atlantis: Kennedy Space Center, Titusville, FL; www.kennedyspacecenter.com

Discovery: Udvar-Hazy Center, Smithsonian National Air and Space Museum, Chantilly, VA; discovery.si.edu

Endeavour: California Science Center, Los Angeles, CA; www.californiasciencecenter.org

Enterprise: Intrepid Air, Sea, and Space Museum, New York, NY; www.intrepidmuseum.org/Space_Shuttle_Pavilion

The Future of U.S. Manned Space Exploration

Source: National Aeronautics and Space Administration (NASA); SpaceX

After the end of the U.S. space shuttle program, all U.S. astronauts visiting the International Space Station (ISS) had to rent space on Russian spacecraft. SpaceX, a private U.S. company based in Hawthorne, CA, aimed to add another option. On May 22, 2012, the company sent the first private spacecraft to the ISS, and returned it to Earth nine days later. In Oct. 2012, as part of a $1.6-bil deal with NASA, the company launched the first of 12 ISS cargo resupply missions. The seventh of those missions failed June 28, 2015, as a SpaceX Falcon 9 rocket burst into flames three minutes into flight.

One of SpaceX's stated goals was to make spaceflight cheaper by developing reusable rockets and spacecraft. On May 29, 2014, the company unveiled *Dragon 2*, a reusable spacecraft whose propulsive landing system enables it to touch down almost anywhere with the precision of a helicopter. On May 6, 2016, minutes after propelling a *Dragon* spacecraft to the International Space Station, SpaceX returned a Falcon 9 rocket to Earth, touching down vertically onto a drone ship 185 mi off the east coast of the U.S. So far, SpaceX's vehicles have carried cargo only, but the company expects to carry passengers into space before the end of the decade.

International Space Station

Source: National Aeronautics and Space Administration (NASA)

The International Space Station (ISS) is considered the largest cooperative scientific project in history. Construction began in 1998 and was completed in 2011. It has been inhabited continuously since 2000 and visited by more than 200 international crew members.

15 cooperating nations: Belgium, Canada, Denmark, France, Germany, Italy, Japan, Netherlands, Norway, Russia, Spain, Sweden, Switzerland, United Kingdom, and the U.S.

About the ISS
- It has a mass of 924,739 lbs and is about as long as a football field at 357.5 ft.
- It is entirely powered by an acre of solar panels.
- It requires three people to keep it running but has room for up to 10 people to live aboard.
- Astronauts typically spend 4-6 months aboard.

ISS Research
- Studying the effects of long-term exposure to reduced gravity on plants, crystals, plant and animal cells, and pathogens
- Studying the effects on humans of long-term exposure to reduced gravity
- Recording large-scale long-term changes in Earth's environment by observing the planet from orbit
- Testing recycling technologies for human life support

Summary of Worldwide Successful Launches, 1957-2015

Source: National Aeronautics and Space Administration (NASA); Space Launch Report

Year	1957-59	1960-69	1970-79	1980-89	1990-99	2000-09	2010-15	Total
Russia[1]	6	399	1,028	1,132	542	246	181	3,534
U.S.	18	614	247	191	300	206	102	1,678
China	—	—	8	16	33	52	101	210
ESA[2]	—	2	5	14	55	63	39	178
Ukraine	—	—	—	—	59	57	22	138
Japan	—	—	18	26	23	18	18	103
India	—	—	1	9	11	13	18	52
France	—	4	14	5	16	0	—	39
UK	—	1	6	4	7	0	—	18
Germany	—	—	3	7	6	0	—	16
Canada	—	—	4	5	4	0	0	13
Israel	—	—	—	—	—	3	2	5
Iran	—	—	—	—	—	1	3	4
S. Korea	—	—	—	—	—	1	0	1
N. Korea	—	—	—	—	—	—	1	1
Total	**24**	**1,020**	**1,334**	**1,409**	**1,056**	**660**	**487**	**5,990**

— = Not applicable. (1) Data for 1957-91 apply to the Soviet Union, for 1992-96 to the Commonwealth of Independent States, after 1996 to Russia. (2) European Space Agency. As of 2015, member states are Austria, Belgium, Czech Republic, Denmark, Estonia, Finland, France, Germany, Greece, Hungary, Ireland, Italy, Luxembourg, Netherlands, Norway, Poland, Portugal, Romania, Spain, Sweden, Switzerland, and United Kingdom. Canada and some EU states not listed participate in some projects under cooperation agreements.

Notable Lunar and Planetary Science Missions

Source: National Aeronautics and Space Administration (NASA)

Spacecraft	Launch date[1]	Mission	Remarks
Mariner 2	Aug. 27, 1962	Venus	Passed within 22,000 mi of Venus 12/14/1962; confirmed high surface temperature on planet; contact lost 1/3/1963 at 54 mil mi.
Ranger 7	July 28, 1964	Moon	Yielded over 4,000 photos of lunar surface.
Mariner 4	Nov. 28, 1964	Mars	1st probe to fly by Mars; passed behind planet 7/14/1965.
Ranger 8	Feb. 17, 1965	Moon	Yielded over 7,000 photos of lunar surface.
Venera 3	Nov. 16, 1965	Venus	Soviet probe; 1st artificial probe to impact on the surface of another planet, 3/1/1966; probe failed to send back data.
Surveyor 3	Apr. 17, 1967	Moon	Scooped and tested lunar soil.
Mariner 5	June 14, 1967	Venus	In solar orbit; closest Venus flyby 10/19/1967; allowed scientists to obtain accurate readings on the composition of the Venusian atmosphere.
Mariner 6	Feb. 24, 1969	Mars	Came within 2,000 mi of Mars 7/31/1969; collected data, photos.
Mariner 7	Mar. 27, 1969	Mars	Came within 2,000 mi of Mars 8/5/1969.
Venera 7	Aug. 17, 1970	Venus	Soviet probe; 1st probe to land safely on the surface of another planet.
Mariner 9	May 30, 1971	Mars	1st craft to orbit Mars 11/13/1971; sent back over 7,000 photos.
Pioneer 10	Mar. 2, 1972	Jupiter	Passed Jupiter 12/4/1973; took readings on Jupiter's composition. Exited planetary system 6/13/1983; last signal received 1/23/2003 from 7.6 bil mi.
Pioneer 11	Apr. 5, 1973	Jupiter, Saturn	Passed Jupiter 12/3/1974; Saturn 9/1/1979; discovered an additional ring and 2 moons around Saturn. Transmission ended 9/30/1995.
Mariner 10	Nov. 3, 1973	Venus, Mercury	Passed Venus 2/5/1974, arrived at Mercury 3/29/1974. 1st time gravity of a planet (Venus) used to whip spacecraft toward another (Mercury); 1st probe to visit 2 planets; took cloud and wind pattern readings in Venusian atmosphere.
Viking 1	Aug. 20, 1975	Mars	Landed on Mars 7/20/1976; 1st probe to land safely on Mars; performed chemical analysis of soil; functioned 6 years.
Viking 2	Sept. 9, 1975	Mars	Sister probe of *Viking 1*; landed on Mars 9/3/1976; functioned 3 years.
Voyager 2	Aug. 20, 1977	Jupiter, Saturn, Uranus, Neptune	Encountered Jupiter 7/9/1979, Saturn 8/25/1981, Uranus 1/24/1986, Neptune 8/25/1989. Confirmed existence of rings around Neptune. As of 8/2016 it was 10.3 bil mi from Sun and still returning data to Earth.

Spacecraft	Launch date[1]	Mission	Remarks
Voyager 1	Sept. 5, 1977	Jupiter, Saturn	Encountered Jupiter 3/5/1979; provided evidence of rings around Jupiter; passed near Saturn 11/12/1980; passed *Pioneer 10* to become most distant human-made object 2/17/1998. As of 8/2016 it was 12.6 bil mi from Sun and still returning data to Earth.
Pioneer Venus 1	May 20, 1978	Venus	Entered Venus orbit 12/4/1978; studied atmosphere, magnetic field, weather, and surface; fuel ran out; probe was destroyed in atmospheric entry, 8/1992.
Pioneer Venus 2 (multiprobe)	Aug. 8, 1978	Venus	Consisted of a "bus" carrying 1 large and 3 small atmospheric probes. All 4 probes entered the Venus atmosphere 12/9/1978, followed by the bus; took readings of atmosphere; probes impacted surface.
Magellan	May 4, 1989	Venus	Landed on Venus 8/10/1990; monitored geological activity; mapped more than 99% of planet surface, showed that about 85% is covered by volcanic flows; ceased operating 10/11/1994.
Galileo	Oct. 18, 1989	Jupiter	Used Earth's gravity to propel itself towards Jupiter; encountered Venus 2/10/1990, Jupiter 12/7/1995; encountered moons. Released probe into Jovian atmosphere; intentionally flown into Jupiter 9/21/2003 to prevent accidental contamination of Jupiter's moon Europa.
Mars Global Surveyor	Nov. 7, 1996	Mars	Began orbiting Mars 9/11/1997; began mapping entire surface 3/9/1999; discovered a weak magnetic field on planet; observed Martian moon Phobos; found evidence of liquid water in past 6/22/2000.
Mars Pathfinder	Dec. 4, 1996	Mars	Landed on Mars 7/4/1997; rover *Sojourner* made measurements of climate and soil composition, sending thousands of surface images; ceased operating 9/27/1997.
Cassini-Huygens	Oct. 15, 1997	Saturn	Began orbiting Saturn 6/30/2004; spotted evidence of a subterranean ocean and 300-mi-wide hot spots region on moon Titan; detected an atmosphere on moon Enceladus. *Huygens* probe landed on Titan 1/14/2005; found a muddy surface, possible water ice, channels carved by liquid methane springs.
Lunar Prospector	Jan. 6, 1998	Moon	Began orbiting Moon 1/11/1998; mapped abundance of 11 elements on Moon's surface; discovered evidence of water ice at both lunar poles; crashed into crater near Moon's south pole 7/31/1999 to end mission.
Deep Space 1	Oct. 24, 1998	Comet Borrelly	Flew within 1,500 mi of comet; sent back photos showing 6-mi-long nucleus.
Stardust	Feb. 7, 1999	Comet Wild 2	Reached comet 1/2/2004; gathered dust samples, capsule returned to Earth 1/15/2006. Spacecraft, on new mission Stardust-NExT (follow up for Deep Impact), reached comet Tempel 1, 2/14/2011.
2001 Mars Odyssey	Apr. 7, 2001	Mars	Reached Mars 10/24/2001; detected evidence of water ice near south pole; primary mission to study climate and geologic history completed 8/2004; began extended mission, aiming to identify minerals on Mars.
Genesis	Aug. 8, 2001	Sun	Orbited Sun, collected particles from solar wind; capsule containing specimens crashed to Earth 9/8/2004; some samples survived.
Mars Express/ Beagle 2 lander	June 3, 2003	Mars	1st European Space Agency probe to another planet; arrived at Mars 12/2003; performed remote sensing including photography in search of subsurface water; *Beagle 2* lander was deployed 12/19/2003, but contact was lost.
Mars Exploration Rovers	June 7 and July 10, 2003	Mars	Rovers *Spirit* and *Opportunity* landed on Mars 1/2004, found further evidence that water existed on surface; *Spirit* took 1st photo of a Martian meteor; survived severe dust storms in 2007. *Opportunity* explored massive Victoria Crater 2007-08, set record for most distance driven off-Earth (25 mi) 7/2014.
MESSENGER	Mar. 2, 2004	Mercury	Began returning images of Mercury during initial flyby 1/14/2008; entered orbit 3/17/2011; delivered 100,000th image 5/3/2012; impacted Mercury 4/30/2015.
Deep Impact	Jan. 12, 2005	Comet Tempel 1	Reached Tempel 1; deployed impact probe that slammed into comet 7/4/2005 with force roughly equivalent to 5 tons of TNT. Flyby spacecraft, on supplemental mission EPOXI, reached comet Hartley 2, 11/4/2010.
Mars Reconnaissance Orbiter	Aug. 12, 2005	Mars	Reached Mars 3/10/2006 and began taking detailed images of Martian surface; in 3/2008, found salt deposits suggesting ancient water supplies; in 6/2008, found largest known crater in solar system.
New Horizons (Pluto)	Jan. 19, 2006	Pluto, Charon	Flew past Jupiter 7/2007 on its way to Pluto and its largest moon, Charon. Returned first-ever photographs of Pluto 7/14/2015. Will examine other objects in the Kuiper Belt.
Phoenix Mars Lander	Aug. 4, 2007	Mars	Landed on Mars 5/25/2008; examined northern polar region, analyzed weather/minerals; water ice verified 7/31/2008; lost contact 11/2/2008.
Dawn	Sept. 27, 2007	Asteroid Belt (bet. Jupiter and Mars)	Will compare evolution of dwarf planet Ceres with Vesta, an asteroid, in an effort to shed light on formation of the solar system. Departed Vesta 8/2012; reached Ceres 3/6/2015.
Kepler	Mar. 9, 2009	Extrasolar planets	Detect potentially habitable Earth-size planets around other Milky Way stars. As of 9/30/2016, Kepler had discovered 2,000+ confirmed exoplanets, including Kepler-452b, considered extremely similar to Earth in composition and orbit.
Lunar Crater Observation and Sensing Satellite (LCROSS)	June 18, 2009	Moon	Impacted the Cabeus crater; detected presence of water ice in Moon's surface 10/9/2009. Lunar Reconnaissance Orbiter (LRO), launched with LCROSS, mapped Moon's surface.
Juno	Aug. 5, 2011	Jupiter	Entered Jupiter's orbit July 4, 2016, to return data for 20 months (37 orbits), incl. color images expected to improve understanding of the formation of the solar system.
Mars Science Laboratory	Nov. 26, 2011	Mars	*Curiosity* rover landed on Mars 8/6/2012 and began assessing Mars's past and present ability to support life.
Lunar Atmosphere and Dust Environment Explorer (LADEE)	Sept. 6, 2013	Moon	Studied the fragile lunar atmosphere from orbit for 100 days; impacted with lunar surface 4/17/2014.
Mars Atmosphere and Volatile Evolution (MAVEN)	Nov. 18, 2013	Mars	Entered orbit 9/21/2014; exploring Mars's upper atmosphere to determine how loss of atmospheric gas has changed its climate over time.
Osiris	Sept. 9, 2016	Bennu, an asteroid	Will attempt to bring back a small sample of the asteroid by 2023 to help scientists understand the source of Earth's organic materials and water and improve understanding of potential asteroid-Earth impacts.
Transiting Exoplanet Survey Satellite (TESS)	Dec. 2017	Solar neighborhood	Two-year survey will monitor more than 500,000 stars for temporary changes in brightness caused by planetary transits.
InSight	May 5, 2018	Mars	Landing craft will drill beneath surface of Mars to investigate how rocky planets form and develop.
Mars 2020	July/Aug. 2020	Mars	Rover to investigate potential for human habitation.
Europa	2020s	Europa	Spacecraft will perform multiple flybys of Jupiter's ocean-bearing moon, Europa, to determine if it is suitable for life.

Note: U.S./NASA missions unless otherwise noted. (1) In Coordinated Universal Time.

General Aviation and Air Taxi Active Aircraft, 2014

Source: Federal Aviation Administration; aircraft not associated with major airlines or the military

Aircraft type	Total active	Personal	Busi- ness	Instruc- tional	Aerial- apps.	Aerial obser- vation	Other work	Sight- seeing	Air medical	Other	On-demand operations
Fixed wing.......	161,321	105,368	25,958	10,586	3,082	3,752	919	841	499	3,651	6,664
Piston	139,182	102,546	15,001	10,398	1,227	3,127	632	834	473	2,699	2,245
Turboprop	9,777	1,410	3,380	121	1,836	591	231	6	24	454	1,722
Turbojet........	12,362	1,412	7,578	68	17	34	56	0	2	499	2,697
Rotorcraft.......	9,966	1,158	600	1,596	892	2,054	91	109	125	696	2,385
Piston	3,154	889	207	1,233	246	334	26	84	0	50	76
Turbine	6,812	269	393	364	646	1,719	65	25	125	646	2,310
Other aircraft.....	4,699	3,591	5	369	0	2	49	615	0	41	26
Gliders........	1,791	1,415	2	310	0	2	0	29	0	33	0
Lighter-than-air ..	2,908	2,176	3	60	0	0	49	586	0	8	26
Experimental.....	26,191	23,800	1,042	317	100	137	86	98	2	483	119
Amateur	18,873	17,752	591	108	58	72	8	2	0	247	35
Exhibition	1,893	1,609	23	24	0	9	40	96	0	93	0
Experimental light-sport	4,204	3,831	164	123	2	19	30	0	0	34	0
Other..........	1,221	608	265	62	40	38	7	0	2	109	83
Special light-sport	2,231	1,798	77	294	0	13	9	0	0	40	0
ALL AIRCRAFT ...	204,408	135,716	27,682	13,163	4,074	5,958	1,154	1,663	625	4,912	9,194

Note: Columns may not add to totals due to rounding. **Personal**—Flying for personal reasons; **Business**—Individual or group use for business transportation with or without a professional crew (includes fractional ownership); **Instructional**—Flying under the supervision of a flight instructor; **Aerial applications**—Includes agriculture and forestry, public health sprayings, fire fighting, etc.; **Aerial observation**—Includes aerial mapping/photography, patrol, search and rescue, hunting, traffic advisory, ranching, surveillance, oil and mineral exploration, etc.; **Other work**—Construction work, parachuting, aerial advertising, towing gliders, etc.; **Sightseeing**—Commercial sightseeing; **Air medical services**—Air ambulance services, rescue, human organ transportation, emergency medical services; **Other**—Positioning flights, proficiency flights, training, ferrying, sales demos, etc.; **On-demand operations**—On-demand air taxi, air tours, commuter, and air medical services.

Estimated Active Airmen Certificates Held, 2015

Source: Federal Aviation Administration, U.S. Dept. of Transportation

Category	Certificates	Category	Certificates	Category	Certificates
Pilot total..............	**590,039**	Rotorcraft (helicopters)		Repairmen	39,363
Student.............	122,729	(only).............	15,566	Parachute Rigger	8,846
Recreational (only)	190	Glider (only)	19,460	Ground Instructor	70,957
Sport (only).........	5,482	**Flight Instructor**		Dispatcher...........	23,754
Airplane[1]		**Certificates**	**102,628**	Flight Navigator.......	102
Private...........	170,718	**Instrument Ratings**....	**304,329**	Flight Attendant.......	200,319
Commercial........	101,164	**Nonpilot total**.......	**728,329**	Flight Engineer	42,460
Airline Transport....	154,730	Mechanic...........	342,528		

Note: The term airmen includes men and women certified as pilots, mechanics, or other aviation technicians. (1) Includes pilots with an airplane-only certificate as well as those with an airplane and a helicopter and/or glider certificate.

Aircraft Operating Statistics

Source: Airbus S.A.S.; The Boeing Company; Embraer S.A.; as of July 30, 2016

Manufacturer and model	Max. # of seats	Typical # of seats	Fuel capacity (gal)	Typical cruising speed (mph)[1]	Max. range (naut. mi)	Max. thrust (thous. lbs)	Manufacturer and model	Max. # of seats	Typical # of seats	Fuel capacity (gal)	Typical cruising speed (mph)[1]	Max. range (naut. mi)	Max. thrust (thous. lbs)
Airbus							757-300*....	280	243	11,466	614	3,395	43.5
A318......	132	107	6,400	630	3,200	24.0	767-200ER..	255	181	23,980	614	6,385	62.1
A319......	156	124	6,400	630	3,700	27.0	767-300ER..	350	218	23,980	614	5,990	63.3
A320......	180	150	6,400	630	3,300	27.0	767-400ER..	375	245	23,980	614	5,625	63.5
A321......	220	185	6,350	630	6,200	33.0	777-200	440	305	31,000	645	5,420	77.0
A330-200 ...	380	253	36,750	660	7,250	72.0	777-200ER..	440	301	45,220	645	7,725	93.7
A330-300 ...	440	295	26,765	660	5,850	72.0	777-200LR ..	314	301	47,890	645	9,395	115.3
A340-300 ...	440	295	37,150	660	7,400	34.0	777-300	550	368	45,220	645	6,005	98.0
A340-500 ...	375	313	56,870	660	9,000	56.0	777-300ER..	386	386	47,890	645	7,390	115.3
A340-600 ...	475	380	51,750	660	7,900	60.0	787-8						
A380......	853	525	84,600	684	8,300	70.0	Dreamliner	242	210	NA	652	8,200	NA
Boeing							787-9						
727-200*....	189	148	9,806	605	2,500	17.4	Dreamliner	280	250	NA	652	8,500	NA
737-600	132	110	6,875	602	3,225	22.7	**Embraer**						
737-700	149	126	6,875	602	3,440	26.3	190	114	100	4,267	599	2,450	20.0
737-700C ...	140	126	6,875	599	3,285	27.3	195	124	110	4,267	599	2,300	20.0
737-800	189	162	6,875	602	3,115	27.3	**McDonnell- Douglas**						
737-900	215	180	7,837	599	3,265	27.3	DC-10 series*	380	250	36,650	600	6,220	24.0
747-100*....	452	366	48,445	645	6,100	50.1	MD-11*.....	410	285	NA	NA	7,360	NA
747-200/300*	452	366	52,410	645	7,900	54.8	MD-80 series*	172	155	5,840	584	2,504	21.0
747-400	524	416	57,285	653	7,260	63.3	MD-90 series*	172	153	7,620	584	3,205	28.0
747-8	467	467	64,055	653	8,000	66.5							
757-200*....	228	200	11,489	614	3,900	43.5							

* = Aircraft no longer in production. NA = Not available. **Note:** Figures are for most commonly flown passenger models. When models within a series vary, maximums are shown. McDonnell-Douglas merged with Boeing in 1997. (1) Figures shown are converted from Mach speed (speed of sound), which varies depending on altitude and temperature. For comparison purposes, this table uses 768 mph as equivalent to Mach 1.

Milestones in Aviation History

Source: National Aeronautics and Space Administration (NASA); Smithsonian National Air and Space Museum; Air Transport Association of America; National Museum of the U.S. Air Force (USAF); National Park Service, U.S. Dept. of the Interior

1903, Dec. 17: Brothers Wilbur and Orville Wright (U.S.) made the first human-carrying, powered flight near Kitty Hawk, NC. Each brother made two flights; the longest, about 852 ft, lasted 59 sec.

1908, May 14: Charles Furnas (U.S.), worker for Wright brothers, became first American airplane passenger.

1911, Feb.: The Burgess Company and Curtiss, Inc. receive authorization to build Wright planes, becoming the first licensed airplane manufacturer in the U.S.

1911, Sept. 23: First transportation of mail by airplane officially approved by the U.S. Postal Service.

1914, Jan. 1: First scheduled passenger airline service began. A seaplane that landed on water operated between St. Petersburg and Tampa, FL.

1914, June 18: Lawrence Burst Sperry (U.S.) released the controls and stood in his airborne plane, successfully demonstrating his gyrostabilizer, the first autopilot system.

1918, Mar. 6: The Curtiss-Sperry "Flying Bomb" (U.S.) made its first successful flight. The first radio-controlled plane led to the development of cruise missiles.

1918, May 14: First scheduled airmail service began, between New York and Washington, DC, with intermediate stop in Philadelphia. In 1921, scheduled transcontinental airmail service began between New York City and San Francisco.

1919, June 14-15: Capt. John Alcock (UK) and Lt. Arthur W. Brown (U.S.) completed the first nonstop flight across the Atlantic Ocean. They traveled from Newfoundland, Canada, to Ireland in 16 hr., 12 min.

1923, Aug.: Rotating beacons enabled the first U.S. night flights.

1924, Apr. 6-Sept. 28: Two U.S. Army planes landed in Seattle, completing the first circumnavigation of the globe. They completed the 26,000-mi journey in 371 hours of flying time.

1926, May 12-13: Roald Amundsen (Norway), Umberto Nobile (Italy), Lincoln Ellsworth (U.S.), and Oscar Wisting (Norway) made the first flight over the North Pole, in a dirigible that flew between Spitsbergen, Norway, and Teller, AK. Two weeks earlier, Adm. Richard E. Byrd and Floyd Bennett (both U.S.) claimed to have made the first flight over the Pole (May 9, 1926) in a Fokker F-VII. But when Byrd's diary was released to the public in 1996, some historians began to question whether his plane had reached the Pole.

1927, May 20-21: Charles Lindbergh (U.S.) completed the first solo transatlantic flight in the *Spirit of St. Louis*. "Lucky Lindy" traveled 3,610 mi from New York to Paris in 33 hr., 29 min., 30 sec.

1929, Aug. 8-29: Hugo Eckener (Germany) piloted the *Graf Zeppelin* around the world in record time: 20,373 mi in 21 days, 5 hr., 31 min.

1929, Nov. 28: Adm. Richard E. Byrd (U.S.) and Bernt Balchen (Norway) became the first to fly to the South Pole and back, in 18 hr., 41 min.

1930, May 15: Ellen Church (U.S.) became first flight attendant.

1931, June 23-July 1: Wiley Post and Harold Gatty (both U.S.) broke the speed record for around-the-world flight, traveling 15,474 mi in 8 days, 15 hr., 51 min., in the monoplane *Winnie Mae.*

1931, Oct. 3-5: Clyde Pangborn and Hugh Herndon (both U.S.) completed the first nonstop transpacific flight. They traveled 4,558 mi from Misawa, Japan, to East Wenatchee, WA, in 41 hr., 34 min.

1932, May 20-21: Amelia Earhart (U.S.) completed first solo transoceanic flight by a woman, making the 2,026-mi journey from Newfoundland, Canada, to Ireland in 14 hr., 56 min.

1933, July 15-22: Wiley Post completed the first solo circumnavigation of the globe. His 15,596-mi trip took 7 days, 18 hr., 49 min.

1936, June 25: American Airlines began scheduled passenger service of the first Douglas DC-3 aircraft. The DC-3 was the first aircraft with a kitchen onboard and hence offered the first in-flight hot meal service.

1937, May 6: German *Hindenburg* zeppelin exploded in Lakehurst, NJ, killing 35 of the 97 people aboard (and one on the ground). The airship had made 34 transatlantic flights in 1936.

1938, July 10-13: Howard Hughes (U.S.) and four assistants established a new speed record for circumnavigating the globe: 14,824 mi in 3 days, 9 hr., 17 min.

1939, Aug. 27: The German-made Heinkel He 178 made the first successful flight powered by a jet engine.

1947, June 17-30: Pan American Airways began the first scheduled around-the-world passenger flights, from New York or San Francisco.

1947, Oct. 14: Chuck Yeager (U.S.) broke the sound barrier, reaching Mach 1 speed in a Bell X-1 rocket-powered aircraft.

1947, Nov. 2: Howard Hughes piloted the *Spruce Goose* on its maiden and only flight. The largest airplane ever built, it could carry 750 troops or two Sherman tanks.

1949, Mar. 2: James Gallagher (U.S.) piloted the first round-the-world flight to be refueled in midair. The *Lucky Lady* USAF B-50 covered 23,452 mi in 94 hr., 1 min. and was refueled four times.

1950, Sept. 22: Col. David Schilling (USAF) made the first nonstop transatlantic jet flight, covering 3,300 mi in 10 hr., 1 min.

1952, Aug. 26: The UK bomber Canberra made the first round-trip transatlantic crossing on the same day, from Northern Ireland to Newfoundland, Canada, and back in 7 hr., 59 min.

1953, May 18: Jacqueline Cochran (U.S.) became the first woman to fly faster than the speed of sound.

1956, Mar. 10: Britain's Fairey FD-2 aircraft set a world speed record of 1,132 mph.

1956, Nov. 11: Convair B-58 (USAF), the first supersonic bomber, was introduced.

1957, Jan. 15-18: Three USAF B-52 Stratofortresses made the first nonstop global flight by jet planes. They were refueled in flight by KC-97 aerial tankers.

1958, Oct. 24: A Mirage III-A achieved Mach 2 (twice the speed of sound) in level flight, first European plane to do so.

1962, Nov. 29: Britain and France signed an agreement to jointly develop the Concorde, a supersonic plane that could fly twice as fast as most U.S. jets.

1969, June 5: The Soviet Tupolev Tu-144 became the first passenger airliner to break the sound barrier.

1970, May 26: The Tupolev Tu-144 became first passenger airline to exceed Mach 2 with a top speed of about 1,335 mph at 53,475 ft.

1976, Aug. 23: The Concorde began the first scheduled supersonic commercial service.

1977, Aug. 23: The *Gossamer Condor*, built by aeronautical engineer Paul MacCready (U.S.), successfully demonstrated human-powered flight through pedalling, completing a figure-8 course of 1.15 mi.

1979, June 12: MacCready's human-powered *Gossamer Albatross* crossed the English Channel in 2 hr., 49 min.

1981, July 7: MacCready-developed *Solar Challenger* became first solar-powered airplane to cross the English Channel.

1995, Aug. 15-16: The Concorde set a new around-the-world speed record of 31 hr., 27 min., 49 sec.

1999, Mar. 1-21: Bertrand Piccard (Switz.) and Brian Jones (UK) completed the first around-the-world flight in a hot-air balloon. Their 29,055-mi journey began in Chateau-d'Oex, Switzerland, and ended 19 days, 21 hr., 55 min. later in the Egyptian desert.

2001, Aug. 13: Solar-powered, propeller-driven plane *Helios* (NASA) reached 96,863 ft, breaking altitude record for non-rocket-powered aircraft.

2002, June 19-July 4: Steve Fossett (U.S.) completed the first nonstop solo circumnavigation of globe in a balloon.

2003, Nov. 26: The Concorde flew its final flight.

2005, Mar. 1-3: Steve Fossett achieved the first nonstop solo circumnavigation in an airplane without refueling.

2006, Feb. 8-11: Steve Fossett flew the longest nonstop, non-refueled solo flight (25,766 mi).

2009, Dec. 15: Boeing's 787 Dreamliner, the company's most fuel-efficient plane and the first to be constructed primarily from composite materials, made its maiden voyage.

2011, Feb. 4: Northrop Grumman and the U.S. Navy reported the first successful flight for the unmanned X-47B fighter jet.

2012, May 22-31: SpaceX became the first private company to successfully launch (and later recover) a spacecraft to the International Space Station.

2015, July 3: *Solar Impulse 2* set record for longest nonstop solo flight and longest flight in a solar-powered plane (118 hr.), traveling from Japan to Hawaii.

2016, July 26: *Solar Impulse 2* became first fuel-free plane to circumnavigate the globe. The 17-leg journey began in Mar. 2015.

ASTRONOMY

Edited by Michael J. Kaufman, Dept. of Physics and Astronomy, San Jose State University

Celestial Events Summary, 2017

There are four eclipses in 2017: one total solar eclipse, one annular solar eclipse, a penumbral lunar eclipse, and a partial lunar eclipse. The total solar eclipse will be viewable by a large number of people across the U.S. as the path of totality extends from Oregon to South Carolina. The annular solar eclipse path extends from southern Chile and Argentina, and across the South Atlantic before making landfall again in Angola. The penumbral eclipse will result in a barely noticeable dimming of the Moon, and in the partial lunar eclipse the Earth's shadow will never extend more than a quarter of the way across the Moon.

The best meteor shower viewing will be the Quadrantids in Jan., the Eta Aquarids in May, the Perseids in Aug., and the Geminids in Dec. Other major meteor showers will be hampered by unfavorably bright Moon phases in 2017. At the start of the year, Jupiter, Saturn, and Mercury will be visible in the predawn sky. Venus is an "evening star" from Jan. through Mar. when it disappears into the glare of the Sun. Venus reemerges in the morning sky by early Apr. and remains visible in the morning for the rest of the year. Mars is in the evening sky into July, then becomes a prominent morning object from late Aug. through the end of the year. Jupiter is an evening object Apr. through Oct. before returning to the morning sky again in Nov. Saturn is

in the morning sky the first half of the year and an evening object from late June through late Dec. Mercury begins the year as a morning object, setting soon after the Sun, before moving to the morning sky by late Mar., back to the morning sky in May, the evening sky in July, morning in Sept., evening in Oct. and Nov., before returning to the morning sky to finish the year. The best opportunities for seeing Mercury in the morning sky occur in mid Jan. and mid May, while the best opportunity to see it in the evening sky occurs in late July.

The crescent Moon, with its subdued light, regularly pairs with the two brightest planets, Venus and Jupiter. Waxing crescent pairings are visible in the early evening soon after sunset, while waning crescent pairings are visible in the early morning before sunrise. The waxing crescent Moon pairs with Venus in each of the months from Jan. to Mar., while the waning crescent pairs with Venus in the early morning sky each month from Apr. through Nov. The waxing crescent Moon pairs with Jupiter in the evening in July-Sept., and the waning crescent pairs with Jupiter in Nov. and Dec. Jupiter and Venus will have an exceptionally close encounter on the evening of Nov. 13. The waxing crescent Moon joins Venus and Mars on Jan. 31.

Astronomical Positions and Constants

Two celestial bodies are in **conjunction** when they are due north and south of each other, either in **right ascension** (with respect to the north celestial pole) or in **celestial longitude** (with respect to the north ecliptic pole). Celestial bodies in conjunction will rise and set at nearly the same time. For the inner planets—Mercury and Venus—**inferior conjunction** occurs when either planet passes between Earth and the Sun, while **superior conjunction** occurs when either Mercury or Venus is on the far side of the Sun. Celestial bodies are in **opposition** when their right ascensions differ by exactly 12 hours, or when their celestial longitudes differ by 180°. In this case one of the two objects in opposition will rise while the other is setting. **Quadrature** refers to the arrangement where the coordinates of two bodies differ by exactly 90°. These terms may refer to the relative positions of any two bodies as seen from Earth, but one of the bodies is so frequently the Sun that mention of the Sun is omitted in that case.

When objects are in conjunction, the alignment is not perfect, and one usually passes above or below the other. The geocentric angular separation between the Sun and

an object is termed **elongation**. Elongation is limited only for Mercury and Venus; the greatest elongation for each of these bodies is approximately the time for longest observation. **Perihelion** is the point in an object's orbit when it is nearest to the Sun, and **aphelion** is the point when it is farthest from the Sun. **Perigee** is the point in an orbit where an object is nearest Earth, **apogee** the point when it is farthest from Earth. An **occultation** of a planet or a star is an eclipse of it by some other body, usually the Moon. A **transit** of the Sun occurs when Mercury or Venus passes directly between Earth and the Sun, appearing to cross the Sun's disk.

The following were adopted as part of the International Astronomical Union System of Astronomical Constants (1976/2009): **Speed of light**, 299,792.458 km per sec., or about 186,282 statute mi per sec.; **solar parallax**, 8".794143; **astronomical unit** (AU, mean distance between the Earth and Sun), 149,597,870 km, or 92,955,807 mi; **constant of nutation**, 9".2025; and **constant of aberration**, 20".49552.

Celestial Events Highlights, 2017

(In Coordinated Universal Time, or UTC, the standard time of the prime meridian.)

January

Mercury and **Saturn** are in the SE at sunrise all month.
Jupiter rises after midnight and is high in the SW at sunrise.
Venus, **Mars**, and **Neptune** are high in the SW at sunset.
Uranus is high in the SE at sunset early in the month and in the S at sunset late in the month.

Jan. 1: Neptune 0.02° N of Mars, Mercury in Sagittarius, Venus and Mars in Aquarius, Jupiter in Virgo, Saturn in Ophiuchus, Uranus in Pisces all year, Neptune in Aquarius all year
Jan. 2: Venus 1.90° S of Moon
Jan. 3: Neptune 0.40° S of Moon, Mars 0.24° S of Moon
Jan. 4: Earth at perihelion, Quadrantid meteor shower
Jan. 5: First Quarter Moon
Jan. 6: Uranus 3.27° N of Moon
Jan. 7: Mercury enters Capricorn
Jan. 9: Aldebaran 0.36° S of Moon

Jan. 10: Moon at perigee
Jan. 12: Full Moon, Venus at greatest elongation 47.1° E of Sun, Pollux 10.08° N of Moon
Jan. 13: Venus 0.41° N of Neptune
Jan. 15: Regulus 0.84° N of Moon
Jan. 19: Jupiter 2.69° S of Moon, Spica 6.37° S of Moon, Mercury at greatest elongation 24.1° W of Sun, Mars enters Pisces, Last Quarter Moon
Jan. 20: Spica 3.68° S of Jupiter
Jan. 22: Moon at apogee
Jan. 23: Antares 9.87° S of Moon, Venus enters Pisces
Jan. 24: Saturn 3.62° S of Moon
Jan. 26: Mercury 3.71° S of Moon
Jan. 28: New Moon
Jan. 30: Neptune 0.20° S of Moon
Jan. 31: Venus 4.06° N of Moon

February

Mercury is low in the SE at sunrise early in the month and disappears by the end of the month.
Saturn is high in the SE at sunrise all month.
Jupiter rises before midnight and is high in the SW at sunrise.
Venus, **Mars**, **Uranus**, and **Neptune** are all in the SW at sunset.

Feb. 1: Mars 2.33° N of Moon
Feb. 2: Uranus 3.48° N of Moon
Feb. 4: First Quarter Moon
Feb. 5: Aldebaran 0.24° S of Moon
Feb. 6: Moon at perigee, Mars enters Cetus
Feb. 7: Mercury enters Capricorn, Mars enters Pisces
Feb. 9: Pollux 10.10° N of Moon
Feb. 11: Full Moon, Penumbral Lunar Eclipse, Regulus 0.79° N of Moon
Feb. 15: Spica 6.47° S of Moon, Jupiter 2.70° S of Moon
Feb. 18: Last Quarter Moon, Moon at apogee
Feb. 19: Antares 9.95° S of Moon
Feb. 20: Saturn 3.58° S of Moon
Feb. 23: Spica 3.82° S of Jupiter, Saturn enters Sagittarius
Feb. 24: Mercury enters Aquarius
Feb. 26: Mercury 2.49° S of Moon, New Moon, Annular Solar Eclipse, Neptune 0.10° S of Moon
Feb. 27: Mars 0.62° N of Uranus
Feb. 28: Venus 10.26° N of Moon

March

Venus is low in the W at sunset early in the month and low in the E at sunrise at the end of the month.
Neptune is low in the SE at sunrise at the end of the month.
Saturn rises after midnight and is high in the S at sunrise.
Jupiter rises late evening and is low in the SW at sunrise.
Mercury is low in the W at sunset at the end of the month.
Mars and **Uranus** are in the W at sunset all month.

Mar. 1: Uranus 3.58° N of Moon, Mars 4.33° N of Moon
Mar. 2: Neptune 0.85° S of Sun
Mar. 3: Moon at perigee
Mar. 4: Mercury 1.13° S of Neptune
Mar. 5: Aldebaran 0.23° S of Moon, First Quarter Moon
Mar. 7: Mercury in superior conjunction 1.69° S of Sun
Mar. 8: Pollux 10.11° N of Moon, Mars enters Aries
Mar. 10: Regulus 0.80° N of Moon, Mercury enters Pisces
Mar. 12: Full Moon
Mar. 14: Jupiter 2.46° S of Moon, Spica 6.44° S of Moon
Mar. 16: Mercury 9.55° S of Venus
Mar. 18: Moon at apogee, Antares 9.89° S of Moon
Mar. 20: Equinox, Saturn 3.44° S of Moon, Last Quarter Moon
Mar. 25: Venus in inferior conjunction 8.29° N of Sun
Mar. 26: Neptune 0.00° N of Moon
Mar. 27: Mercury 2.41° N of Uranus, Venus 11.32° N of Moon
Mar. 28: New Moon
Mar. 29: Uranus 3.62° N of Moon, Mercury 6.59° N of Moon
Mar. 30: Moon at perigee, Mars 5.48° N of Moon
Mar. 31: Mercury enters Aries

April

Venus and **Neptune** are low in the E at sunrise all month.
Mercury is low in the E at sunrise late in the month.
Saturn rises middle of the night and is high in the SW at sunrise.
Mercury, **Uranus**, and **Neptune** are low in the W at sunset in the first half of the month.
Mars is in the W at sunset all month.
Jupiter is low in the E at sunset in the second half of the month.

Apr. 1: Aldebaran 0.34° S of Moon, Mercury at greatest elongation 19.0° E of Sun
Apr. 3: First Quarter Moon
Apr. 4: Pollux 9.99° N of Moon
Apr. 7: Regulus 0.72° N of Moon, Jupiter at opposition
Apr. 10: Jupiter 2.18° S of Moon
Apr. 11: Spica 6.39° S of Moon, Full Moon
Apr. 12: Mars enters Taurus
Apr. 14: Uranus 0.56° S of Sun
Apr. 15: Antares 9.74° S of Moon, Moon at apogee
Apr. 16: Saturn 3.23° S of Moon
Apr. 19: Last Quarter Moon
Apr. 20: Mercury in inferior conjunction 1.65° N of Sun, Mercury enters Pisces
Apr. 22: Neptune 0.20° N of Moon, Lyrid meteor shower
Apr. 23: Venus 5.18° N of Moon
Apr. 25: Uranus 3.71° N of Moon, Mercury 4.51° N of Moon
Apr. 26: New Moon
Apr. 27: Moon at perigee
Apr. 28: Mars 5.77° N of Moon, Aldebaran 0.49° S of Moon, Uranus 0.15° N of Mercury

May

Mercury, **Venus**, **Uranus**, and **Neptune** are in the ESE at sunrise all month.
Saturn rises late evening and is low in the SW at sunrise.
Mars is low in the W at sunset all month.
Jupiter is in the SE at sunset and up much of the night.

May 1: Pollux 9.77° N of Moon
May 3: First Quarter Moon
May 4: Regulus 0.52° N of Moon
May 6: Eta Aquarid meteor shower
May 7: Aldebaran 6.24° S of Mars, Jupiter 2.11° S of Moon, Mercury 2.23° S of Uranus
May 8: Spica 6.44° S of Moon
May 10: Full Moon
May 12: Antares 9.62° S of Moon, Moon at apogee
May 13: Saturn 3.07° S of Moon
May 17: Mercury at greatest elongation 25.8° W of Sun, Saturn enters Ophiuchus
May 18: Mercury enters Cetus
May 19: Last Quarter Moon
May 20: Neptune 0.47° N of Moon
May 22: Venus 2.39° N of Moon, Mercury enters Aries
May 23: Uranus 3.89° N of Moon
May 24: Mercury 1.61° N of Moon
May 25: New Moon
May 26: Moon at perigee, Aldebaran 0.57° S of Moon
May 27: Mars 5.35° N of Moon
May 29: Pollux 9.55° N of Moon
May 31: Regulus 0.25° N of Moon

June

Mercury is low in the E at sunrise early in the month and low in the W at sunset late in the month.
Saturn is up all night, setting around sunrise.
Venus, **Uranus**, and **Neptune** are in the E at sunrise all month.
Mars is low in the W at sunset all month.
Jupiter is high in the S at sunset, setting middle of the night.

June 1: First Quarter Moon
June 2: Uranus 1.78° N of Venus, Mercury enters Taurus, Venus 1.78° S of Uranus
June 3: Venus at greatest elongation 45.9° W of Sun

June 4: Jupiter 2.32° S of Moon, Spica 6.61° S of Moon, Mars enters Gemini
June 8: Antares 9.60° S of Moon, Moon at apogee
June 9: Full Moon, Venus enters Cetus
June 10: Saturn 3.08° S of Moon, Venus enters Aries
June 12: Aldebaran 5.07° S of Mercury
June 15: Saturn at opposition
June 16: Neptune 0.73° N of Moon
June 17: Last Quarter Moon
June 19: Uranus 4.14° N of Moon
June 20: Venus 2.37° N of Moon
June 21: Solstice, Mercury in superior conjunction 1.09° N of Sun, Mercury enters Gemini
June 22: Aldebaran 0.54° S of Moon
June 23: Moon at perigee
June 24: New Moon, Mercury 5.28° N of Moon, Mars 4.41° N of Moon
June 25: Pollux 9.41° N of Moon
June 28: Regulus 0.03° N of Moon, Mars 0.78° S of Mercury, Venus enters Taurus

July

Venus is low in the E at sunrise all month.
Uranus is high in the SE at sunrise.
Neptune is high in the S at sunrise.
Jupiter is high in the SE at sunset and sets middle of the night.
Mercury is low in the W at sunset all month.
Mars is low in the W at the beginning of the month, disappearing into sunlight later in the month.
Saturn rises before sunset and is up much of the night.

July 1: First Quarter Moon, Jupiter 2.71° S of Moon
July 2: Spica 6.83° S of Moon
July 3: Pollux 4.87° N of Mercury, Earth at aphelion
July 4: Mercury enters Cancer
July 5: Antares 9.69° S of Moon
July 6: Moon at apogee
July 7: Saturn 3.24° S of Moon
July 9: Full Moon
July 11: Pollux 5.72° N of Mars
July 13: Neptune 0.87° N of Moon
July 14: Aldebaran 3.16° S of Venus
July 16: Last Quarter Moon, Mercury enters Leo
July 17: Uranus 4.33° N of Moon, Mars enters Cancer
July 20: Aldebaran 0.44° S of Moon, Venus 2.73° N of Moon
July 21: Moon at perigee
July 23: Pollux 9.39° N of Moon, New Moon, Mars 3.11° N of Moon
July 25: Mercury 0.86° S of Moon, Regulus 0.07° S of Moon
July 26: Regulus 1.09° N of Mercury
July 27: Mars 1.10° N of Sun
July 28: Jupiter 3.14° S of Moon
July 29: Spica 6.98° S of Moon, Venus enters Orion
July 30: Mercury at greatest elongation 27.2° E of Sun, First Quarter Moon
July 31: Venus enters Gemini

August

Mars and **Venus** are low in the E at sunrise all month.
Uranus and **Neptune** rise late evening and are high in the SW at sunrise all month.
Mercury is low in the W at sunset the first half of the month, disappearing into sunlight later in the month.
Jupiter is in the SW at sunset and sets several hours later.
Saturn is high in the S at sunset and sets after midnight.

Aug. 2: Antares 9.79° S of Moon, Moon at apogee
Aug. 3: Saturn 3.45° S of Moon, Mercury enters Sextans
Aug. 7: Full Moon, Partial Lunar Eclipse

Aug. 9: Neptune 0.86° N of Moon
Aug. 12: Perseid meteor shower
Aug. 13: Uranus 4.40° N of Moon
Aug. 15: Last Quarter Moon
Aug. 16: Aldebaran 0.38° S of Moon
Aug. 17: Mars enters Leo
Aug. 18: Moon at perigee
Aug. 19: Venus 2.25° N of Moon, Pollux 9.41° N of Moon
Aug. 21: Mars 1.55° N of Moon, Pollux 7.26° N of Venus, New Moon, Total Solar Eclipse, Regulus 0.08° S of Moon
Aug. 22: Mercury 6.16° S of Moon
Aug. 24: Venus enters Cancer
Aug. 25: Jupiter 3.49° S of Moon, Spica 7.00° S of Moon
Aug. 26: Mercury in inferior conjunction 4.22° S of Sun
Aug. 28: Mercury enters Leo
Aug. 29: First Quarter Moon, Regulus 4.44° N of Mercury, Antares 9.80° S of Moon
Aug. 30: Moon at apogee, Saturn 3.56° S of Moon

September

Mercury, **Venus**, and **Mars** are all low in the E at sunrise all month.
Uranus is in the W at sunrise all month.
Saturn is in the S at sunset and sets around midnight.
Jupiter is low in the SW at sunset all month.

Sept. 2: Mercury 4.10° S of Mars
Sept. 5: Regulus 0.75° S of Mars, Neptune at opposition, Spica 3.38° S of Jupiter
Sept. 6: Neptune 0.77° N of Moon, Full Moon
Sept. 9: Uranus 4.33° N of Moon
Sept. 10: Regulus 0.59° N of Mercury, Venus enters Leo
Sept. 12: Mercury at greatest elongation 17.9° W of Sun, Aldebaran 0.44° S of Moon
Sept. 13: Last Quarter Moon, Moon at perigee
Sept. 15: Pollux 9.36° N of Moon
Sept. 16: Mercury 0.06° N of Mars
Sept. 18: Venus 0.55° N of Moon, Regulus 0.09° S of Moon, Mars 0.14° S of Moon, Mercury 0.03° N of Moon
Sept. 19: Regulus 0.49° S of Venus
Sept. 20: New Moon
Sept. 22: Spica 6.93° S of Moon, Jupiter 3.73° S of Moon, Equinox
Sept. 25: Antares 9.68° S of Moon
Sept. 26: Mercury enters Virgo
Sept. 27: Saturn 3.48° S of Moon, Moon at apogee
Sept. 28: First Quarter Moon

October

Mercury is low in the E at sunrise at the start of the month and low in the SW at sunset at the end of the month.
Venus and **Mars** are low in the SE at sunrise all month.
Jupiter is low in the SW at sunset early in the month.
Saturn is in the SW at sunset and sets several hours later.
Uranus rises before sunset and is up all night.
Neptune is low in the SE at sunset and sets before sunrise.

Oct. 3: Neptune 0.75° N of Moon
Oct. 5: Venus 0.22° N of Mars, Full Moon
Oct. 6: Uranus 4.21° N of Moon
Oct. 8: Mercury in superior conjunction 1.11° N of Sun, Venus enters Virgo
Oct. 9: Moon at perigee, Aldebaran 0.60° S of Moon
Oct. 12: Last Quarter Moon, Pollux 9.19° N of Moon, Mars enters Virgo
Oct. 13: Spica 2.94° S of Mercury
Oct. 15: Regulus 0.21° S of Moon
Oct. 17: Mars 1.78° S of Moon
Oct. 18: Venus 1.97° S of Moon, Jupiter 1.02° N of Mercury

Oct. 19: Spica 6.89° S of Moon, Uranus at opposition, New Moon

Oct. 20: Jupiter 3.92° S of Moon, Mercury 5.20° S of Moon

Oct. 21: Orionid meteor shower

Oct. 22: Mercury enters Libra

Oct. 23: Antares 9.50° S of Moon

Oct. 24: Saturn 3.25° S of Moon

Oct. 25: Moon at apogee

Oct. 26: Jupiter 1.02° N of Sun

Oct. 27: First Quarter Moon

Oct. 30: Neptune 0.88° N of Moon

November

Venus, **Mars**, and **Jupiter** are low in the SE at sunrise all month.

Mercury and **Saturn** are low in the SW at sunset all month.

Uranus and **Neptune** are in the SE at sunset and up most of the night.

Nov. 1: Spica 3.81° S of Venus

Nov. 3: Uranus 4.19° N of Moon

Nov. 4: Full Moon

Nov. 5: Mercury enters Scorpio

Nov. 6: Moon at perigee, Aldebaran 0.76° S of Moon

Nov. 9: Pollux 8.94° N of Moon

Nov. 10: Last Quarter Moon

Nov. 11: Regulus 0.45° S of Moon, Mercury enters Ophiuchus

Nov. 12: Antares 2.25° S of Mercury

Nov. 13: Jupiter 0.28° S of Venus, Venus enters Libra

Nov. 14: Jupiter enters Libra

Nov. 15: Mars 3.19° S of Moon, Spica 6.97° S of Moon, Mercury enters Scorpius

Nov. 16: Jupiter 4.09° S of Moon, Mercury enters Ophiuchus

Nov. 17: Venus 3.96° S of Moon, Leonid meteor shower

Nov. 18: New Moon, Saturn enters Sagittarius

Nov. 19: Antares 9.38° S of Moon

Nov. 20: Mercury 6.90° S of Moon

Nov. 21: Saturn 2.99° S of Moon, Moon at apogee

Nov. 24: Mercury at greatest elongation 22.0° E of Sun

Nov. 26: First Quarter Moon, Mercury enters Sagittarius

Nov. 27: Neptune 1.15° N of Moon

Nov. 28: Spica 3.36° S of Mars, Saturn 3.05° N of Mercury

Nov. 30: Uranus 4.32° N of Moon

December

Mercury is low in the SW at sunset early in the month and low in the SE at sunrise late in the month.

Saturn is low in the SW at sunset until late in the month.

Venus is low in the SE at sunrise all month.

Mercury and **Jupiter** are in the SE at sunrise all month.

Uranus is in the SE at sunset and up most of the night.

Neptune is high in the SE at sunset and sets around midnight.

Dec. 3: Aldebaran 0.82° S of Moon, Full Moon, Venus enters Scorpius

Dec. 4: Moon at perigee

Dec. 6: Mercury 1.35° S of Saturn, Pollux 8.72° N of Moon

Dec. 7: Venus enters Ophiuchus

Dec. 8: Antares 5.08° S of Venus, Regulus 0.73° S of Moon, Mercury enters Ophiuchus

Dec. 10: Last Quarter Moon

Dec. 12: Spica 7.18° S of Moon

Dec. 13: Mercury in inferior conjunction 1.72° N of Sun, Mars 4.16° S of Moon, Geminid meteor shower

Dec. 14: Jupiter 4.25° S of Moon

Dec. 15: Mercury 2.22° N of Venus

Dec. 16: Antares 9.40° S of Moon

Dec. 17: Mercury 1.76° S of Moon, Venus 4.14° S of Moon

Dec. 18: New Moon, Saturn 2.78° S of Moon

Dec. 19: Moon at apogee

Dec. 21: Solstice, Saturn 0.91° N of Sun, Mars enters Libra

Dec. 22: Venus enters Sagittarius

Dec. 24: Neptune 1.43° N of Moon

Dec. 25: Venus 1.13° S of Saturn

Dec. 26: First Quarter Moon

Dec. 27: Uranus 4.53° N of Moon

Dec. 31: Aldebaran 0.76° S of Moon

Meteorites and Meteor Showers

When a chunk of material, ice or rock, plunges into Earth's atmosphere and burns up in a fiery display, the event is a **meteor**. While the chunk of material is still in space, it is a **meteoroid**. If a portion of the material survives passage through the atmosphere and reaches the ground, the remnant on the ground is a **meteorite**.

Meteorites found on Earth are classified into types, depending on their composition: **irons**, those composed chiefly of iron, a small percentage of nickel, and traces of other metals such as cobalt; **stones**, stony meteors consisting of silicates; and **stony irons**, containing varying proportions of both iron and stone.

Serious study of meteorites as non-Earth objects began in the 20th century. Scientists use sophisticated chemical analysis, X-rays, and mass spectrography in determining their origin and composition. Although most meteorites are now believed to be fragments of asteroids or comets, geochemical studies have shown that a few Antarctic stones came from the Moon or from Mars, presumably ejected by the explosive impact of asteroids.

The largest known meteorite, estimated to weigh about 55 metric tons, is the Hoba meteorite near Grootfontein, Namibia. The Manicouagan impact crater in Quebec, Canada, with an estimated diameter of 60 mi, is one of the largest crater structures still visible on the surface of the Earth. Not obvious to the eye because of erosion, larger impact craters identified include the Vredefort crater in South Africa at 185 mi across and the Sudbury crater in Ontario, Canada, estimated at 125 mi across. The Bedout impact site off the NW coast of Australia gained attention in 2004 when scientists identified further evidence in support of the idea that it may be linked to the Permian extinction event 250 mil years ago.

Meteor showers vary in strength, but usually the three most visible meteor showers of the year are the **Perseids**, around Aug. 13, the **Orionids**, around Oct. 21, and the **Geminids**, around Dec. 14. These showers feature meteors at the rate of about 60 per hour. Best observing conditions occur in the absence of moonlight, usually when the Moon's phase is between waning crescent and waxing quarter. Bright moons can adversely affect viewing of some of the best showers of the year.

For most meteor showers the cometary debris is relatively uniformly scattered along the comet's orbit. However, in the case of the **Leonid** meteor shower, which occurs every year around Nov. 17-18, the debris from Comet Temple-Tuttle seems to be bunched up in one stretch. Hence, the meteor shower produced in most years is relatively weak. However, about every 33 years, Earth encounters the bunched-up debris when it crosses the comet's orbit. Sometimes the expected shower is a disappointment as in 1899 and 1933; at other times, the dense debris provides a spectacular show, as in 1833 and 1866. The Leonids stormed again more recently, producing rates of 1,000-3,000 meteors per hour in 2001.

Morning and Evening "Stars," 2017

(In Coordinated Universal Time, or UTC, the standard time of the prime meridian.)

	Morning	Evening		Morning	Evening
Jan.	Mercury Jupiter Saturn	Venus Mars Uranus Neptune	July	Venus Mars from July 25 Uranus Neptune	Mercury Mars to July 24 Jupiter Saturn
Feb.	Mercury Jupiter Saturn	Venus Mars Uranus Neptune	Aug.	Mercury from Aug. 27 Venus Mars Uranus Neptune	Mercury to Aug. 26 Jupiter Saturn
Mar.	Mercury to Mar. 7 Venus from Mar. 26 Jupiter Saturn Neptune from Mar. 2	Mercury from Mar. 8 Venus to Mar. 25 Mars Uranus Neptune to Mar. 1	Sept.	Mercury Venus Mars Neptune from Sept. 6	Jupiter Saturn Uranus Neptune to Sept. 5
Apr.	Mercury from Apr. 21 Venus Jupiter to Apr. 7 Saturn Uranus from Apr. 14 Neptune	Mercury to Apr. 20 Mars Jupiter from Apr. 8 Uranus to Apr. 13	Oct.	Mercury to Oct. 8 Venus Mars Jupiter from Oct. 27 Uranus from Oct. 20	Mercury from Oct. 9 Jupiter to Oct. 26 Saturn Uranus to Oct. 19 Neptune
May	Mercury Venus Saturn Uranus Neptune	Mars Jupiter	Nov.	Venus Mars Jupiter	Mercury Saturn Uranus Neptune
June	Mercury to June 21 Venus Saturn to June 15 Uranus Neptune	Mercury from June 22 Mars Jupiter Saturn from June 16	Dec.	Mercury from Dec. 14 Venus Mars Jupiter Saturn from Dec. 21	Mercury to Dec. 13 Saturn to Dec. 20 Uranus Neptune

Greenwich Sidereal Time for 0h UTC, 2017

UTC = Coordinated Universal Time. Add 12 hours to obtain right ascension of mean sun.

Date	Hr.	Min.	Date	Hr.	Min.	Date	Hr.	Min.	Date	Hr.	Min.
Jan. 1	6	43.4	Apr. 1	12	38.2	July 10	19	12.4	Oct. 8	1	7.3
Jan. 11	7	22.8	Apr. 11	13	17.6	July 20	19	51.9	Oct. 18	1	46.7
Jan. 21	8	2.2	Apr. 21	13	57.0	July 30	20	31.3	Oct. 28	2	26.1
Jan. 31	8	41.6									
			May 1	14	36.5	Aug. 9	21	10.7	Nov. 7	3	5.6
Feb. 10	9	21.1	May 11	15	15.9	Aug. 19	21	50.1	Nov. 17	3	45.0
Feb. 20	10	0.5	May 21	15	55.3	Aug. 29	22	29.6	Nov. 27	4	24.4
			May 31	16	34.7						
Mar. 2	10	39.9				Sept. 8	23	9.0	Dec. 7	5	3.8
Mar. 12	11	19.3	June 10	17	14.2	Sept. 18	23	48.4	Dec. 17	5	43.3
Mar. 22	11	58.8	June 20	17	53.6	Sept. 28	0	27.9	Dec. 27	6	22.7
			June 30	18	33.0						

Largest Telescopes

Astronomers indicate the size of telescopes not by length or magnification but by the diameter of the primary light-gathering component, such as the lens or mirror. The larger the diameter of the mirror or lens, the fainter the objects that can be detected. In principle, larger telescopes also have better resolving power—the ability to discern small details—than smaller telescopes. However, the Earth's atmosphere limits the details that can be seen using ground-based telescopes. That is why the Hubble Space Telescope, which orbits the Earth outside of its atmosphere, can achieve higher resolutions with its 2.4-m (7.9-ft) mirror than much larger telescopes on Earth. Adaptive optics systems can compensate for the blurring effects of the Earth's atmosphere, allowing ground-based telescopes to achieve higher levels of detail. Telescopes to detect ultraviolet, X-ray, and gamma radiation must be placed in space or high-altitude balloons because the atmosphere absorbs most of these types of radiation; as a result, such telescopes are generally much smaller than optical, infrared, and radio telescopes.

Refracting (lens) telescopes are currently not made with lens diameters of more than 40 in. Because **reflecting telescopes** can be made less expensively and with more precision than refracting telescopes, all modern large optical telescopes are made with mirrors. **Radio telescopes** are larger than optical telescopes because larger diameters are required to obtain equivalent resolution of radio's longer wavelengths. A technique called interferometry, originally developed for radio telescopes, uses arrays of telescopes to achieve better resolution.

Largest refracting (lens) optical telescope: Yerkes Observatory, 1 m (40 in.), at Williams Bay, WI

Largest reflecting (mirror) optical/infrared telescope: Gran Telescopio Canarias, 10.4 m (34 ft), on La Palma, Canary Islands (segmented mirror)

Largest infrared interferometer: Four 8.2-m (27-ft) telescopes of the Very Large Telescope Interferometer (VLTI) with a 200-m (656-ft) baseline on Cerro Paranal in Chile

Largest fully steerable radio dish: Robert Byrd Green Bank Telescope (GBT), 100 m (328 ft), in Green Bank, WV

Largest single radio dish: Five-hundred-meter Aperture Spherical Telescope (FAST), 500 m (1640 ft), in Guizhou, China

Largest baseline radio interferometer: 10 25-m (82-ft) diameter telescopes of the Very Long Baseline Array (VLBA), dispersed from Hawaii to the Virgin Islands with a resolution equal to a radio dish of 8,600 km (5,000 mi), making it the highest resolution telescope in the solar system

Largest submillimeter interferometer: 54 12-m (39-ft) and 12 7-m (23-ft) antennas of the Atacama Large Millimeter Array (ALMA), located at a site above 5,000 m (16,400 ft) in the Atacama Desert in Chile. The antennas can be spread out over a 16-km (10-mi) distance to increase the resolving power of the array.

Largest airborne telescope: Stratospheric Observatory for Infrared Astronomy (SOFIA), 2.5-m (8.2-ft) infrared telescope aboard a NASA 747

Constellations

Culturally, constellations are imagined patterns among the stars that, in some cases, have been recognized through millennia. Knowledge of constellations was once necessary in order to function as an astronomer. For today's astronomers, constellations are simply areas of the sky in which objects await observation and interpretation.

Because Western culture has dominated much of modern scientific discourse, constellations and celestial traditions of other cultures are not well known outside their regions of origin. Even the patterns with which we are most familiar today have undergone considerable change over the centuries.

Today, **88 constellations** are officially recognized. Although many have ancient origins, some are modern, devised out of unclaimed stars by astronomers a few centuries ago. Unclaimed stars were those too faint or inconveniently placed to be included in the more prominent constellations. Stars in a constellation are not necessarily near each other; they are just located in the same direction on the celestial sphere.

When Western astronomers began to travel to South Africa in the 16th and 17th centuries, they found an unfamiliar sky that showed numerous brilliant stars. Thus, constellations in the Southern Hemisphere are named after technological marvels of the time, as well as some arguably traditional forms, such as Musca, the fly.

Many of the commonly recognized constellations have their origins in ancient Asia Minor. These were adopted by the Greeks and Romans, who translated their names and stories into their own languages, modifying some details in the process. After the decline of those cultures, most such knowledge entered oral tradition or remained hidden in monastic libraries. In the 8th century, Muslims began to spread through the Mediterranean world. Wherever possible, everything was translated into Arabic to be taught in the universities the Muslims established throughout their newfound world.

In the 13th century, King Alfonso X of Castile, an avid student of astronomy, had Ptolemy's astronomical treatise *Almagest* translated into Latin. It thus became widely available to European scholars. In the process, the constellation names were translated, but the star names were retained in their Arabic forms. Thus the names of many stars—Altair, Alnitak, and Mirfak, among others—have Arabic roots, although linguistic adaptation and the inaccuracies of transliteration have wrought changes.

Until the 1920s, astronomers used curved boundaries for the constellation areas. As these were rather arbitrary, the International Astronomical Union adopted new constellation boundaries that run due N-S and E-W. These boundaries divide the sky into the 88 constellations, much as the contiguous U.S. is made up of the lower 48 states.

Common names of stars often referred to parts of the traditional figures they represented, such as Deneb, the tail of the swan, and Betelgeuse, the armpit of the giant. Astronomers may avoid traditional names by labeling stars with Greek letters, generally to denote order of brightness. Thus, the "alpha star" would typically be the brightest star in a constellation. The "of" implies possession, so the genitive (possessive) form of the constellation name is used as in Alpha Orionis, the first star of Orion (Betelgeuse). Astronomers usually use a three-letter abbreviation for the constellation name, as indicated below.

Asterisms are widely recognized patterns of stars. The so-called Big Dipper is a small part of the constellation Ursa Major, the big bear; the Sickle is the traditional head and mane of Leo, the lion; the three stars of the Summer Triangle are each in a different constellation, with Vega in Lyra the lyre, Deneb in Cygnus the swan, and Altair in Aquila the eagle. The northeast star of the asterism Great Square of Pegasus is Alpha Andromedae.

Name	Genitive case	Abbr.	Meaning
Andromeda	Andromedae	And	Chained Maiden
Antlia	Antliae	Ant	Air Pump
Apus	Apodis	Aps	Bird of Paradise
Aquarius	Aquarii	Aqr	Water Bearer
Aquila	Aquilae	Aql	Eagle
Ara	Arae	Ara	Altar
Aries	Arietis	Ari	Ram
Auriga	Aurigae	Aur	Charioteer
Boötes	Boötis	Boo	Herder
Caelum	Caeli	Cae	Chisel
Camelopardalis	Camelopardalis	Cam	Giraffe
Cancer	Cancri	Cnc	Crab
Canes Venatici	Canum Venaticorum	CVn	Hunting Dogs
Canis Major	Canis Majoris	CMa	Greater Dog
Canis Minor	Canis Minoris	CMi	Littler Dog
Capricornus	Capricorni	Cap	Sea-Goat
Carina	Carinae	Car	Keel
Cassiopeia	Cassiopeiae	Cas	Queen
Centaurus	Centauri	Cen	Centaur
Cepheus	Cephei	Cep	King
Cetus	Ceti	Cet	Whale
Chamaeleon	Chamaeleontis	Cha	Chameleon
Circinus	Circini	Cir	Compass (drawing)
Columba	Columbae	Col	Dove
Coma Berenices	Comae Berenices	Com	Berenice's Hair
Corona Australis	Coronae Australis	CrA	Southern Crown
Corona Borealis	Coronae Borealis	CrB	Northern Crown
Corvus	Corvi	Crv	Crow
Crater	Crateris	Crt	Cup
Crux	Crucis	Cru	Cross (southern)
Cygnus	Cygni	Cyg	Swan
Delphinus	Delphini	Del	Dolphin
Dorado	Doradus	Dor	Dolphinfish
Draco	Draconis	Dra	Dragon
Equuleus	Equulei	Equ	Little Horse
Eridanus	Eridani	Eri	River
Fornax	Fornacis	For	Furnace
Gemini	Geminorum	Gem	Twins
Grus	Gruis	Gru	Crane (bird)
Hercules	Herculis	Her	Hercules
Horologium	Horologii	Hor	Clock
Hydra	Hydrae	Hya	Water Snake (female)
Hydrus	Hydri	Hyi	Water Snake (male)
Indus	Indi	Ind	Indian

Name	Genitive case	Abbr.	Meaning
Lacerta	Lacertae	Lac	Lizard
Leo	Leonis	Leo	Lion
Leo Minor	Leonis Minoris	LMi	Littler Lion
Lepus	Leporis	Lep	Hare
Libra	Librae	Lib	Balance
Lupus	Lupi	Lup	Wolf
Lynx	Lyncis	Lyn	Lynx
Lyra	Lyrae	Lyr	Lyre
Mensa	Mensae	Men	Table Mountain
Microscopium	Microscopii	Mic	Microscope
Monoceros	Monocerotis	Mon	Unicorn
Musca	Muscae	Mus	Fly
Norma	Normae	Nor	Square (rule)
Octans	Octantis	Oct	Octant
Ophiuchus	Ophiuchi	Oph	Serpent Bearer
Orion	Orionis	Ori	Hunter
Pavo	Pavonis	Pav	Peacock
Pegasus	Pegasi	Peg	Flying Horse
Perseus	Persei	Per	Hero
Phoenix	Phoenicis	Phe	Phoenix
Pictor	Pictoris	Pic	Painter
Pisces	Piscium	Psc	Fishes
Piscis Austrinus	Piscis Austrini	PsA	Southern Fish
Puppis	Puppis	Pup	Stern (deck)
Pyxis	Pyxidis	Pyx	Compass (sea)
Reticulum	Reticuli	Ret	Reticle
Sagitta	Sagittae	Sge	Arrow
Sagittarius	Sagittarii	Sgr	Archer
Scorpius	Scorpii	Sco	Scorpion
Sculptor	Sculptoris	Scl	Sculptor
Scutum	Scuti	Sct	Shield
Serpens	Serpentis	Ser	Serpent
Sextans	Sextantis	Sex	Sextant
Taurus	Tauri	Tau	Bull
Telescopium	Telescopii	Tel	Telescope
Triangulum	Trianguli	Tri	Triangle
Triangulum Australe	Trianguli Australis	TrA	Southern Triangle
Tucana	Tucanae	Tuc	Toucan
Ursa Major	Ursae Majoris	UMa	Greater Bear
Ursa Minor	Ursae Minoris	UMi	Littler Bear
Vela	Velorum	Vel	Sail
Virgo	Virginis	Vir	Maiden
Volans	Volantis	Vol	Flying Fish
Vulpecula	Vulpeculae	Vul	Fox

Eclipses, 2017

(In Coordinated Universal Time, or UTC, the standard time of the prime meridian.)

There will be four eclipses in 2017: a total solar eclipse, an annular solar eclipse, a penumbral lunar eclipse, and a partial lunar eclipse. Penumbral lunar eclipses are unremarkable since no part of the Moon enters into the dark central shadow of the Earth.

During an annular eclipse of the Sun, the Moon's angular diameter is not large enough to block the entire disk of the Sun, and the Sun appears as a bright ring about the dark disk of the Moon. The tables below give the times in UTC of when the Moon or Sun will reach certain phases of eclipse. In the case of the lunar eclipses, the times are relevant for any observer who can see the Moon. In the case of solar eclipses, the tabulated times refer to when the given event begins or ends from specific points along the eclipse path; as the Moon's shadow sweeps quickly across the Earth, the observed duration and degree of eclipse depends on the observer's precise location.

I. Penumbral Eclipse of the Moon: Feb. 10-11

This eclipse is potentially visible to observers across Europe and Africa, as well as most of Asia and the Americas. However, penumbral eclipses are difficult to distinguish from a normal full moon, as the Moon never passes into the dark umbra of the Earth.

Event	Date	Hr.	Min.
Penumbral eclipse begins	Feb. 10	22	34.3
Greatest eclipse	11	0	45.0
Penumbral eclipse ends	11	2	53.4

II. Annular Eclipse of the Sun: Feb. 26

Observers along a roughly 20-mi-wide path extending from the S Pacific through southern Chile and Argentina, the S Atlantic, and Angola to the Dem. Rep. of the Congo-Zambia border, will be able to see the annular eclipse, where the Sun appears as a bright ring surrounding the Moon. Observers across much of South America, the Atlantic, and Western and Southern Africa will see a partial solar eclipse. The annular eclipse phase will last less than a minute.

Event	Date	Hr.	Min.
Penumbral eclipse begins	Feb. 26	12	10.8
Annular eclipse begins	26	13	15.3
Greatest eclipse	26	14	54.5
Annular eclipse ends	26	16	31.6
Penumbral eclipse ends	26	17	36.0

III. Partial Eclipse of the Moon: Aug. 7

This eclipse will be visible to observers across wide regions of Asia, Africa, and Europe. Only a small region of the Moon will enter the deepest part of the Earth's shadow.

Event	Date	Hr.	Min.
Penumbral eclipse begins	Aug. 7	15	50.0
Partial eclipse begins	7	17	22.9
Greatest eclipse	7	18	21.6
Partial eclipse ends	7	19	18.2
Penumbral eclipse ends	7	20	50.9

IV. Total Eclipse of the Sun: Aug. 21

This total solar eclipse will be remarkable for the path, which begins in the N Pacific, makes landfall in N Oregon, and proceeds SE across the U.S. before moving into the Atlantic off the South Carolina coast. The path of totality will be as much as 70 mi wide, and observers will be able to see the total phase for as long as 2 min., 40 sec. Observers from the Arctic Circle, across North and Central America, and in the northern half of South America will be able to see a partially eclipsed Sun.

Event	Date	Hr.	Min.
Partial eclipse begins	Aug. 21	15	46.8
Total eclipse begins	21	16	48.6
Greatest eclipse	21	18	26.7
Total eclipse ends	21	20	2.6
Partial eclipse ends	21	21	4.4

Total Solar Eclipses, 2017-35

Total solar eclipses actually take place nearly as often as total lunar eclipses. Total lunar eclipses are visible over at least half of the Earth, while total solar eclipses can be seen only along a very narrow path up to a few hundred miles wide and a few thousand miles long. Observing a total solar eclipse is thus a rarity for most people.

Solar eclipses can be dangerous to observe. This is not because the Sun emits more potent rays, but because the Sun is always dangerous to observe directly, and people are particularly likely to stare at it during a solar eclipse.

Date	Duration[1] min.	sec.	Width (mi)	Path of totality
2017, Aug. 21	2	40	71	Pacific Ocean, U.S., Atlantic Ocean
2019, July 2	4	33	125	S Pacific Ocean, S America
2020, Dec. 14	2	10	56	S Pacific Ocean, S America, S Atlantic Ocean
2021, Dec. 4	1	54	260	Antarctica
2024, Apr. 8	4	27	123	Mexico, midwestern U.S., E Canada
2026, Aug. 12	2	18	183	Greenland, Iceland, Spain
2027, Aug. 2	6	24	160	Spain, N Africa, Arabian peninsula
2028, July 22	5	10	140	Indian Ocean, Australia, New Zealand
2030, Nov. 25	3	45	105	Namibia, Botswana, South Africa, Indian Ocean, E Australia
2033, Mar. 30	2	37	485	Alaska, E Russia, Arctic
2034, Mar. 20	4	9	100	Central and NE Africa, Arabian Peninsula, Central and E Asia
2035, Sept. 2	2	54	72	China, Korea, Japan, Pacific Ocean

(1) Length of time at optimal viewing area.

Total Solar Eclipses in the U.S. in the 21st Century

During the 21st century there will be eight total solar eclipses visible somewhere in the continental U.S. The first comes after a long gap. The last total solar eclipse was on Feb. 26, 1979, in the northwestern U.S.

Date	Path of totality	Date	Path of totality
Aug. 21, 2017	Oregon to South Carolina	Mar. 30, 2052	Florida to Georgia
Apr. 8, 2024	Mexico to Texas and N through Maine	May 11, 2078	Louisiana to North Carolina
Aug. 23, 2044	Montana to North Dakota	May 1, 2079	New Jersey to the lower edge of New England
Aug. 12, 2045	Northern California to Florida	Sept. 14, 2099	North Dakota to Virginia

Beginnings of the Universe

One of the dominating astronomical discoveries of the 20th century was that the galaxies of the universe all seem to be moving away from Earth. Doppler redshifts were observed for spiral nebulae around 1920 even though they were not yet known to be galaxies. By the early 1930s, Edwin Hubble and M. L. Humason had established that the more distant a galaxy, the faster it was receding. It turned out that they were moving away not just from the Earth but from one another—that is, the **universe is expanding**. Scientists conclude that the universe must once, very long ago, have been extremely compact and dense, and a rapid expansion caused the energy and matter to rapidly expand. The beginning of this expansion is referred to as the **Big Bang**.

On the subatomic level, according to this theory, there were vast changes of energy and matter and the way physical laws operated during the first few minutes after the Big Bang. After those early minutes the percentages of the basic matter of the universe—hydrogen, helium, and lithium—were set. Everything was so compact and hot that radiation dominated the early universe and there were no stable, un-ionized atoms. The universe was opaque, in the sense that any energy emitted was quickly absorbed and then re-emitted. As the universe expanded, density and temperature continued to drop. A few hundred thousand years after the Big Bang, the temperature dropped far enough that electrons and nuclei could combine to form stable atoms as the universe became transparent. Once that occurred, the radiation that had been trapped was free to escape.

In the 1940s, George Gamov and others predicted that remnants of this escaped radiation should be observable. They had started to search for this background radiation when physicists

Arno Penzias and Robert Wilson, using a radio telescope, inadvertently found it.

In 2003, NASA's Wilkinson Microwave Anisotropy Probe made measurements of the temperature of this **cosmic microwave background radiation** to within millionths of a degree. From these measurements, scientists were able to deduce that our universe is 13.7 bil years old and that first-generation stars began to form a mere 200 mil years after the Big Bang.

In 2014, scientists operating a telescope in Antarctica claimed to have found direct evidence for cosmic inflation, the rapid expansion of the universe during the first 10-32 seconds after the Big Bang that helps explain why variations of the cosmic background radiation are so small. Follow-up observations have cast doubt on this result, and higher precision measurements are planned.

A related mystery is evidence suggesting hidden matter and hidden energy that cannot be directly observed. The presence of dark matter is indicated by the rotation curves of galaxies and the dynamics of clusters of galaxies. **Dark matter** may be composed of gas; large numbers of cool, compact objects like dead stars; even subatomic particles. Evidence for **dark energy** is derived from studies of distant Type Ia supernovae indicating that the expansion of the universe is accelerating rather than slowing. Dark energy seems to work on the very fabric of the universe, acting as a force that increases the rate at which space expands. Visible matter seems to constitute only about 4% of the total mass of the universe while the rest of the universe's mass is in the form of dark matter (27%) and dark energy (68%).

Galaxies

By the 20th century, more than 10,000 **nebulae**—cloud-like luminous objects in the sky—had been discovered. Some were correctly identified as star clusters and others as clouds of gas and dust. Those nebulae which were spiral or elliptical in shape were found in regions of the sky far from the glowing band that is our own Milky Way galaxy. Immanuel Kant had written in 1775 that some of these fuzzy objects might be **"island universes"** apart from our own. But the idea remained speculative until 1923-24, when Edwin Hubble discovered variable stars—stars whose varying brightness makes their distance from Earth calculable—in some of these nebulae. This provided conclusive evidence that these systems were far enough away to be outside our own island universe, the Milky Way galaxy.

Galaxies range in size from small dwarf elliptical ones, with perhaps 1 mil stars, to spiral galaxies containing 300 bil

stars, to giant elliptical galaxies that may be home to more than 10 tril stars. The diameters of galaxies range from 3,000 light-years in dwarf elliptical galaxies to over 500,000 light-years in giant elliptical galaxies. It is estimated that the Milky Way galaxy is about 100,000 light-years in diameter with about 400 bil stars.

Galaxies also congregate into **clusters**. The smallest are poor clusters of only a few dozen galaxies, while the largest rich clusters may contain thousands. The Milky Way is part of a poor cluster of about three dozen galaxies called the **Local Group**. The largest galaxy of the Local Group is Andromeda, a spiral galaxy visible to the unaided eye in the constellation of Andromeda on a very dark night. The Milky Way is the second largest galaxy in this group; most of the others are small.

The Solar System

The major planets of the solar system, in order of mean distance from the Sun, are **Mercury**, **Venus**, **Earth**, **Mars**, **Jupiter**, **Saturn**, **Uranus**, and **Neptune**. The dwarf planets in order of average distance from the Sun are **Ceres** (located between Mars and Jupiter), **Pluto**, **Haumea**, **Makemake**, and **Eris**. All planets orbit counterclockwise around the Sun as viewed from above the Earth's North Pole.

Because Mercury and Venus are nearer to the Sun than is Earth, their motions about the Sun appear from Earth as wide swings first to one side of the Sun then to the other, though both planets move around the Sun in almost circular orbits. When their passage takes them between Earth and the Sun or beyond the Sun in relation to Earth, they cannot be seen.

The planets that lie farther from the Sun than does Earth may be seen for longer periods. They are invisible only when so located in the sky that they rise and set at about

the same time as the Sun and are thus overwhelmed by the Sun's light.

Mercury and Venus, because they are between Earth and the Sun, show phases much as the Moon does. The planets farther from the Sun are always seen as full, although Mars does occasionally present a slightly gibbous phase, like the Moon when it is not quite full.

The planets appear to move rapidly among the stars because they are relatively closer to Earth. The stars are also in motion, some at tremendous speeds, but they are so far away that their motion does not change their apparent positions in the heavens enough to be perceived. The nearest star is about 9,000 times farther away than Neptune. The count for identified **moons** in the solar system orbiting planets and dwarf planets stood at 182 as of mid-2016. Several dwarf planet candidates are also known to have moons.

Planet Superlatives

Largest, most massive planet	Jupiter	Smallest, least massive planet	Mercury
Fastest orbiting planet	Mercury	Slowest orbiting planet	Neptune
Fastest sidereal rotation	Jupiter	Slowest sidereal rotation	Venus
Longest (synodic) day	Mercury	Shortest (synodic) day	Jupiter
Rotational pole closest to ecliptic	Uranus	Hottest planet	Venus
Most moons	Jupiter	No moons	Mercury, Venus
Planet with largest moon	Jupiter	Planet with moon with most eccentric orbit	Neptune
Greatest average density	Earth	Lowest average density	Saturn
Tallest mountain	Mars	Deepest oceans	Jupiter
Strongest magnetic fields	Jupiter	Greatest amount of liquid, surface water	Earth
Most circular orbit	Venus		

Selected Characteristics of the Sun and Planets

Object	at unit distance[1] "	Radius— at mean least distance[2] "	in mi mean radius	Volume[3]	Mass[3]	Density[3]	Sidereal period d.	hr.	min.	sec.	Gravity at surface[3]	Reflecting power[4]	Daytime surface temp. (°F)
Sun	959.50	976.0	432,500	1,304,000	333,000	0.26	25	9	7		28.00	—	9,941
Mercury	3.36	6.5	1,516	0.0562	0.0553	0.98	58	15	36		0.38	0.11	845
Venus	8.34	33.0	3,760	0.857	0.815	0.95	243		30[R]		0.91	0.65	867
Earth	8.78	—	3,959	1.000	1.000	1.00		23	56	4.2	1.00	0.37	59
Moon	2.40	986.2	1,079	0.0203	0.0123	0.61	27	7	43	40	0.16	0.12	260
Mars	4.67	12.8	2,106	0.151	0.107	0.71		24	37	22	0.38	0.15	−24
Jupiter	96.40	24.5	43,441	1,321.3	317.83	0.24		9	55	30	2.53	0.52	−162
Saturn	80.29	10.05	36,184	763.6	95.16	0.12		10	39	20	1.06	0.47	−218
Uranus	34.97	2.05	15,759	63.1	14.54	0.23		17	14	20[R]	0.90	0.51	−323
Neptune	33.95	1.2	15,301	57.7	17.15	0.30		16	6	40	1.14	0.41	−330

R = Retrograde rotation. (1) Angular radius, in seconds of arc, if object were seen at a distance of 1 astronomical unit. (2) Angular radius, in seconds of arc, when object is closest to Earth. (3) Earth = 1. (4) A value of 1 would indicate a perfect reflector.

Planets of the Solar System

The International Astronomical Union (IAU) on Aug. 24, 2006, at their General Assembly in Prague, Czech Republic, agreed on a new definition for planet, and in the process effectively removed Pluto's planet status. The ruling came after years of debate as to whether Pluto, discovered in 1930, should still be considered the ninth planet in our solar system because of its size, orbit, and other characteristics. New discoveries of other Pluto-like objects in the solar system, such as the 2003 discovery of Eris, a **Kuiper Belt object** (KBO) comparable in size to Pluto, also contributed to the debate.

Under the IAU's new definition, Mercury, Venus, Earth, Mars, Jupiter, Saturn, Uranus, and Neptune are regarded as "classical" planets. A **planet** is now defined as a celestial body that (a) is in orbit around the Sun, (b) has sufficient mass for its self-gravity to overcome rigid body forces so that it assumes a hydrostatic equilibrium (nearly round) shape, and (c) has cleared the neighborhood around its orbit.

Pluto, Eris, Ceres, Makemake, and Haumea are regarded as dwarf planets, with the status of Pluto's largest moon, Charon, still to be determined. A **dwarf planet** is a celestial body that (a) is in orbit around the Sun, (b) has sufficient mass for its self-gravity to overcome rigid body forces so that it assumes a hydrostatic equilibrium (nearly round) shape, (c) has not cleared the neighborhood around its orbit, and (d) is not a satellite.

The IAU also created a new category, **small solar system bodies**, for all other objects orbiting the Sun, including comets, asteroids, KBOs, and other small objects. It has not yet established a process by which other solar system objects will be classified.

Note: AU = astronomical unit (92.96 mil mi, mean distance of Earth from the Sun); **d.** = 1 Earth synodic (solar) day (24 hours); **synodic day** = rotation period of a planet measured with respect to the Sun (the "true" day, i.e., the time from midday to midday, or from sunrise to sunrise); **sidereal day** = rotation period of a planet with respect to the stars..

Mercury

```
Distance from the Sun
   Perihelion . . . . . . . . . . . . . . . . . . . .28.6 mil mi
   Semi-major axis (mean distance) . . 36 mil mi (0.387 AU)
   Aphelion. . . . . . . . . . . . . . . . . . . . . . . .43.4 mil mi
Period of revolution around Sun. . . . . . . . . . . . . . .87.97 d.
Orbital eccentricity . . . . . . . . . . . . . . . . . . . . . . . . 0.2056
Orbital inclination . . . . . . . . . . . . . . . . . . . . . . . . .7.00°
Synodic day (midday to midday) . . . . . . . . . . . . 175.94 d.
Sidereal day . . . . . . . . . . . . . . . . . . . . . . . . . . . 58.65 d.
Rotational inclination . . . . . . . . . . . . . . . . . . . . . .0.01°
Mass (Earth = 1). . . . . . . . . . . . . . . . . . . . . . . . . 0.0553
Mean radius . . . . . . . . . . . . . . . . . . . . . . . . . .1,516 mi
Mean density (Earth = 1) . . . . . . . . . . . . . . . . . . 0.984
Natural satellites. . . . . . . . . . . . . . . . . . . . . . . . . . . . 0
Average surface temperature. . . . . . . . . . . . . . . . . 333°F
```

Mercury, named for the Roman gods' messenger, is the closest planet to the Sun and the smallest planet in the solar system. Mercury orbits so close to the Sun that it can never be observed against a dark sky; it is always seen during morning or evening twilights. In 2008, the *Messenger* spacecraft made the first flybys of Mercury since the 1970s. *Messenger* went into orbit about Mercury in Mar. 2011 for a reconnaissance mission; the original one-year science program was extended in 2012. The goals of the mission included mapping, imaging, and measuring the surface composition of Mercury, as well as probing the planet's interior structure and interactions with the Sun. Among the discoveries were that at least part of Mercury's metallic core is liquid, that there may be water ice in shadowed craters near the poles, and that the planet's magnetic field is offset from the planet's center.

Orbit and rotation. Mercury moves with great speed around the Sun, averaging about 30 mi per second to complete its orbit, which takes about 88 Earth days. Mercury takes nearly 59 days to rotate on its axis. Because its orbital period is only about 50% longer than its sidereal rotation, the time from one sunrise to the next on Mercury is about 176 days—twice as long as a Mercurial year. Oddly, Mercury has a magnetic field, albeit a very weak one. It has been held that both a fluid core and rapid rotation—neither of which Mercury was believed to have—are necessary for the generation of a planetary magnetic field. Mercury may demonstrate the contrary.

Atmosphere. Mercury's atmosphere is almost nonexistent. What very little it has is composed of 42% oxygen, 29% sodium, 22% hydrogen, 6% helium, 0.5% potassium, and 0.5% other particles. Because of Mercury's lack of atmosphere, the surface during the day may reach a temperature of about 845°F, while the temperature at night may fall as low as −300°F. Earth-based observation has provided evidence of water ice near the poles.

Surface and composition. Mercury's surface is rocky and cratered similar to that of the Earth's moon. The most imposing feature on Mercury, the Caloris Basin, is a huge impact crater more than 800 mi in diameter. Mercury has a huge iron core that extends out to about 75% of the planet's radius; it has a higher percentage of iron than any other planet in the solar system.

Venus

```
Distance from the Sun
   Perihelion . . . . . . . . . . . . . . . . . . . . . . . .66.8 mil mi
   Semi-major axis (mean distance). . .67.2 mil mi (0.723 AU)
   Aphelion. . . . . . . . . . . . . . . . . . . . . . . . . . .67.7 mil mi
Period of revolution around Sun. . . . . . . . . . . . . . .224.7 d.
Orbital eccentricity . . . . . . . . . . . . . . . . . . . . . . . .0.0067
Orbital inclination . . . . . . . . . . . . . . . . . . . . . . . . . 3.39°
Synodic day (midday to midday) . . . . . 116.75 d. (retrograde)
Sidereal day . . . . . . . . . . . . . . . . . . . . 243.02 d. (retrograde)
Rotational inclination . . . . . . . . . . . . . . . . . . . . . 177.4°
Mass (Earth = 1) . . . . . . . . . . . . . . . . . . . . . . . . . .0.815
Mean radius . . . . . . . . . . . . . . . . . . . . . . . . . . .3,760 mi
Mean density (Earth = 1). . . . . . . . . . . . . . . . . . . .0.951
Natural satellites . . . . . . . . . . . . . . . . . . . . . . . . . . . . 0
Average surface temperature. . . . . . . . . . . . . . . . . 867°F
```

Venus, named for the Roman goddess of love, is the second planet out from the Sun. Because Venus is almost the same size as Earth, it is believed that the two planets were formed at the same time by the same general process and from the same mixture of chemical elements. Venus can easily be seen from Earth with the naked eye; it is the third-brightest object in the sky, exceeded only by the Sun and the Moon.

Orbit and rotation. It takes Venus 225 Earth days to complete its orbit around the Sun. Its synodic revolution—the amount of time it takes for Venus to return to the same position relative to Earth and the Sun, which is a result of the combination of its own motion with that of Earth—is 584 days. Because of this, every 19 months Venus is closer to Earth than to any other planet. The rotation period of Venus appears to be 243 days clockwise. In other words, its rotation is counter to the rotation of the other planets and counter to its own motion around the Sun. This rate and sense of rotation make for a solar day (sunrise to sunrise) on Venus of 116.8 Earth days. Night lasts 58 days, and day lasts 58 days. Venus has no detectable magnetic field.

Atmosphere. The Venusian atmosphere is very thick and toxic. It is composed primarily of 96.5% carbon dioxide, 3.5% nitrogen, and trace concentrations of sulfur dioxide, argon, water, carbon monoxide, helium, and neon. In addition, it exerts an atmospheric pressure at the surface more than 90 times Earth's normal sea-level pressure. The planet is covered with a dense, white, cloudy atmosphere that conceals whatever is below. These clouds are believed to contain sulfuric acid, meaning that it rains sulfuric acid on Venus. Due to the thickness of the atmosphere and resulting extreme greenhouse effect, the temperature is essentially the same day and night; the planet has an average surface temperature of about 867°F, making it the hottest planet in the solar system. Winds of about 200 mph in the clouds may account for the consistency in temperature despite the low rotation speed of the planet. However, at the surface, the winds are very slow.

Surface and composition. Radar-produced maps of the planet show large craters, continent-sized highlands, and extensive dry lowlands. No tectonic activity has been found similar to Earth's moving tectonic plates, but a system of global rift zones and numerous broad, low, dome-like structures, called coronae, may have been produced by the upwelling and subsidence of magma from the mantle. Volcanic surface features, such as vast lava plains, fields of small lava domes, and large shield volcanoes, are common. About 1,600 volcanoes and volcanic features appear on the Venusian surface; more than 85% of the surface is covered by volcanic flows. Theia Mons, a huge shield volcano, has a diameter of over 600 mi and a height of over 3.5 mi. (The largest Hawaiian volcano is only about 125 mi in diameter but rises nearly 5.5 mi from the ocean floor.) Aside from volcanoes, there are highly deformed mountain belts across Venus along with a few meteor-impact craters more than 20 mi wide. Erosion is a very slow process on Venus due to the lack of water. There are indications of some wind movement of dust and sand. The few impact craters on Venus suggest that the surface is generally geologically young—less than 800 mil years old. Despite the fact that probes have landed on Venus, there are very few pictures from the surface because the probes couldn't survive for more than a few hours in the high temperature and atmospheric pressure.

Mars

Distance from the Sun	
Perihelion	128.4 mil mi
Semi-major axis (mean distance)	141.6 mil mi (1.524 AU)
Aphelion	154.9 mil mi
Period of revolution around Sun	686.98 d. (1.88 yr.)
Orbital eccentricity	0.0935
Orbital inclination	1.85°
Synodic day (midday to midday)	24 hr., 39 min., 35 sec.
Sidereal day	24 hr., 37 min., 22 sec.
Rotational inclination	25.19°
Mass (Earth = 1)	0.107
Mean radius	2,106 mi
Mean density (Earth = 1)	0.713
Natural satellites	2
Average surface temperature	−81°F

Named for the Roman god of war, the Red Planet has some features much like Earth. Mars has climate, seasons, volcanoes, and possibly once had liquid water flowing across its surface. Mars can easily be seen with the naked eye on most clear nights, which is why it was one of the first planets to be studied by ancient astronomers. Later, when telescopes came into use, many observers claimed that canals made by Martians existed on the planet's surface, which led to speculation as to whether there was intelligent life there. Unmanned probes have since put all those theories to rest; the canals turned out to be topographic patterns and dust storms.

Mars is currently being explored by a number of robotic craft, both on the surface and in orbit. The *Curiosity*/Mars Science Laboratory, an SUV-sized robot, landed on the surface in Aug. 2012. Its mission was to understand the history of the Martian geology and climate, search for the presence of organic matter, and assess the planet's past suitability for life. An Indian orbiter is currently using remote sensing to study the Martian surface and atmosphere, while NASA's *MAVEN* spacecraft is studying the upper atmosphere of Mars and its interaction with the solar wind. The European Space Agency has an orbiter and lander scheduled to reach Mars in Oct. 2016.

Orbit and rotation. Although Mars's orbital path is nearly circular, it is somewhat more eccentric than that of most other planets. Mars is more than 26 mil mi farther from the Sun at its most distant point compared to its closest approach. Its orbit and speed in relation to Earth's bring it fairly close to Earth about every two years. Every 15-17 years the close approaches are especially favorable for observation.

Mars rotates in 24 hr. and 37 min., almost the same period of time as Earth. Mars's mean distance from the Sun is 142 mil mi. Because Mars's axis of rotation is inclined by about 25° from the vertical to the plane of its solar orbit about the Sun, the planet has seasons.

Unlike Earth's global magnetic field, the Martian magnetic field is small, weak, and localized and may be the remnant of a stronger field from the planet's past.

Atmosphere. The Martian atmosphere is composed primarily of 95.32% carbon dioxide, 2.7% nitrogen, 1.6% argon, 0.13% oxygen, 0.08% carbon monoxide, and in very minor quantities, water, hydrogen oxide, and neon. The atmosphere on Mars is very thin. It has an atmospheric pressure between 1% and 2% of Earth's (if Earth's atmosphere were that thin, there would not be enough oxygen to breathe). Because the Martian atmosphere is so thin and because of the planet's weak magnetic field, its surface is bombarded by cosmic radiation about 100 times as intense as on Earth.

Martian weather systems consist mainly of huge dust storms. On the poles, white caps (believed to be both water ice and carbon dioxide ice) grow in winter and shrink in summer. It is mainly the carbon dioxide that comes and goes with the seasons. The water ice is apparently in many layers with dust between them, indicating climatic cycles.

Surface and composition. Mars is an alien world with rust-red sand and pink skies. In the planet's beginning stages when it was much hotter, Mars's surface melted to a sufficient extent to separate into dense and lighter layers. Mars later cooled enough to allow liquid water to possibly flow across its surface. NASA scientists announced in Sept. 2015 the most convincing evidence to date that liquid water flows on the present-day Martian surface. Using imaging and spectroscopy instruments on the Mars Reconnaissance Orbiter, they showed that seasonal flows on Martian slopes contain hydrated minerals that can only form in the presence of liquid water.

Natural satellites. Mars has two small satellites called Phobos and Deimos, each discovered in 1877 by Asaph Hall. (Phobos measures about 11 by 17 mi and Deimos about 7 by 9 mi.) Deimos, the outer satellite, revolves around the planet in about 31 hours. Phobos, the inner satellite, whips around Mars in a little more than 7 hours, making three orbits each Martian day. Since it orbits Mars faster than the planet rotates, Phobos rises in the west and sets in the east, opposite to what other bodies appear to do in the Martian sky. Both moons are irregularly shaped and pitted with numerous craters. Their origins are not known; however, some astronomers consider them to be asteroid-like objects that were captured by Mars very early in its history.

Jupiter

Distance from the Sun	
Perihelion	460.1 mil mi
Semi-major axis (mean distance)	483.8 mil mi (5.204 AU)
Aphelion	507.4 mil mi
Period of revolution around Sun	11.862 yr.
Orbital eccentricity	0.0489
Orbital inclination	1.304°
Synodic day (midday to midday)	9 hr., 55 min., 33 sec.
Sidereal day	9 hr., 55 min., 30 sec.
Rotational inclination	3.13°
Mass (Earth = 1)	317.8
Mean radius	43,441 mi
Mean density (Earth = 1)	0.24
Natural satellites	67
Average temperature*	−162°F
*i.e., temperature where atmospheric pressure equals 1 Earth atmosphere.	

Jupiter, named for the Roman ruler of the gods, is the largest planet in the solar system (11 times the diameter of Earth). Its mass is more than twice the mass of all the other planets, moons, and asteroids put together. Visible to the naked eye and known to the ancients, it was a focus of the Italian scientist Galileo Galilei, who viewed the planet and its four largest moons through a homemade telescope.

Orbit and rotation. Jupiter is at an average distance of 484 mil mi from the Sun and takes almost 12 Earth years to make a complete revolution. The largest of the planets, Jupiter has an equatorial diameter of 88,846 mi; its polar diameter is more than 5,700 mi shorter. This noticeable oblateness is a result of the liquidity of the planet and its extremely rapid rotation rate—a Jupiter day is less than 10 Earth hours long. A point on Jupiter's equator moves at a speed of 22,000 mph, as compared with 1,000 mph for a point on Earth's equator. Jupiter's magnetic field is by far the strongest of any planet. Electrical activity caused by this field is so strong that it discharges trillions of watts into Jupiter's environment daily. In July 2016, NASA's *Juno* spacecraft entered orbit around the planet to begin a one-year study of Jupiter's composition, magnetic field, and auroras.

Atmosphere. Jupiter's atmosphere is primarily composed of 90% molecular hydrogen and 10% helium. Minor constituents include methane, ammonia, hydrogen deuteride, ethane, and water. Jupiter has a turbulent atmosphere characterized by thick clouds, high winds, and huge lightning storms many times larger than those on Earth. The atmospheric temperature varies, but the temperature at the tops of clouds may be about –280°F. The Great Red Spot seen prominently on Jupiter is a huge hurricane-like storm that is three times the diameter of Earth. In 2006, the Hubble Space Telescope detected the appearance of a second, smaller red spot.

Surface and composition. Gas giant planets like Jupiter, Saturn, and Neptune do not have a surface like Earth or any of the other rocky planets. The gases become denser with depth, until they may turn into a slush or slurry. Jupiter has a liquid hydrogen ocean more than 35,000 mi deep. It likely has a rocky core about the size of Earth, but 13 times more massive. There is no sharp interface between the gaseous atmosphere and the hydrogen ocean that accounts for most of Jupiter's volume. At lower depths, under enormous pressure, the liquid hydrogen takes on the properties of a metal. It is likely that this liquid metallic hydrogen is the source for both Jupiter's persistent radio noise and for its improbably strong magnetic field.

Natural satellites. Jupiter has 67 known satellites. Four of the moons (in order of distance from Jupiter), Io, Europa, Ganymede, and Callisto—all discovered by Galileo in 1610—are large and bright and are close in diameter to Earth's moon and Mercury. Because they move so rapidly around Jupiter, their change in position from night to night can be seen from Earth using binoculars.

Io is one of the most volcanically active bodies in the solar system. A gaseous, doughnut-shaped ring, or torus, enveloping Io's orbit around Jupiter may have been formed by material ejected from Io's active volcanoes. (This is not to be confused with Jupiter's rings.) These volcanoes, hotter than Earth's volcanoes, erupt mainly molten sulfur and result in a constantly changing surface appearance.

Europa may have a 30-mi-deep salty, liquid ocean beneath its icy crust, perhaps a small metallic core, and a very tenuous atmosphere. Ganymede is the biggest moon in the solar system. With a diameter of 3,120 mi, it is bigger than both Mercury and Pluto. Ganymede also has it own magnetic field produced by a molten core perhaps of iron sulfide. Callisto has the oldest, most heavily cratered surface in the solar system, a very thin atmosphere of carbon dioxide, and possibly a subsurface liquid ocean.

The other satellites are much smaller, with four closer to Jupiter than Io, five between Ganymede and Callisto, and the rest farther out. Most of Jupiter's moons orbit the planet at high inclinations from the equator, unlike the innermost satellites These moons may be captured asteroids.

Rings. Jupiter has a diffuse, dark set of rings that were discovered by the *Voyager 1* spacecraft and cannot be seen from Earth without powerful telescopes. They are composed of small dust grains blasted off the four innermost moons by meteoroid impacts.

Saturn

Saturn, named for the Roman ruler of the Titans, is the sixth planet from the Sun and most distant of the planets visible to the unaided eye. Saturn is second in size to Jupiter, but its mass is much smaller. Saturn is the only planet less dense than water, meaning that Saturn would float if there were a pool of water gigantic enough to hold it.

Orbit and rotation. Saturn's diameter is almost 74,900 mi at the equator, while its polar diameter is more than 7,300 mi shorter. Like Jupiter, its noticeable oblateness is a result of the liquidity of the planet and its extremely rapid rate of rotation; a day is little more than 10 Earth hours long.

Distance from the Sun	
Perihelion	840.44 mil mi
Semi-major axis (mean distance)	890.8 mil mi (9.582 AU)
Aphelion	941.07 mil mi
Period of revolution around Sun	29.458 yr.
Orbital eccentricity	0.0565
Orbital inclination	2.485°
Synodic day (midday to midday)	10 hr., 39 min., 23 sec.
Sidereal day	10 hr., 39 min., 22 sec.
Rotational inclination	26.73°
Mass (Earth = 1)	95.159
Mean radius	36,184 mi
Mean density (Earth = 1)	0.125
Natural satellites	62
Average temperature*	–218°F

*i.e., temperature where atmospheric pressure equals 1 Earth atmosphere.

Atmosphere. Saturn's atmosphere is composed primarily of 96.3% hydrogen, 3.3% helium, and traces of methane, ammonia, hydrogen deuteride, ethane, and water. Saturn's atmosphere is much like that of Jupiter, except that the temperature at the top of its cloud layer is at least 50°F colder.

Surface and composition. Saturn's atmosphere resembles Jupiter's; it likely has a small dense center surrounded by a deep ocean of hydrogen.

Natural satellites. Saturn has 62 known natural satellites, most of which were not discovered until space probes reached the planet. Saturn's moon Mimas has an impact crater 81 mi across (the moon itself is only 249 mi across). Enceladus has an atmosphere and shows evidence of geysers that spit water ice and vapor. Two tiny moons orbit within the rings, plowing through and making gaps in the rings along their orbits. Pan, the innermost satellite, creates the Encke Gap of Saturn's A-ring. Daphnis creates the Keeler Gap. The most intriguing Saturnian moon is Titan. The second-biggest moon in the solar system, Titan is bigger than Mercury. Its atmosphere is similar to Earth's atmosphere of long ago; it is made up of approximately 95% nitrogen with traces of methane. Titan's atmosphere extends about 360 mi into space whereas most of Earth's atmosphere lies within 37 mi of the surface. Photographs from Titan's surface, taken by the *Huygens* lander in 2005, show a muddy terrain, with possible deposits of water ice, channels carved by liquid methane springs, and an interesting boundary between light and dark material on the surface. In 2006, scientists found sand dunes on Titan's surface. The "sand" is believed to be tiny water ice crystals or organic compounds. Surface phenomena such as sand dunes are signs of erosion and wind. Unlike winds on Earth or Mars, Titan's winds are not the result of uneven solar heating on the moon's surface but rather Saturn's gravitational pull (similar to how the Moon acts on the Earth's oceans).

Rings. Saturn's ring system is the planet's most recognizable feature. It begins about 4,000 mi above the visible disk of Saturn lying above its equator and extends about 260,000 mi into space. The diameter of the ring system visible from Earth is about 170,000 mi; the rings are estimated to be about 700 ft thick. The rings are composed of rock and ice and range in size from tiny particles to large chunks of material the size of a bus. There are several divisions in the rings. The 2,920-mi Cassini division, the gap between the A and B rings, is the largest division.

Uranus

Uranus, discovered by Sir William Herschel in 1781, was the first planet discovered using a telescope. It was named for the father of the Titans in Roman mythology.

Orbit and rotation. Uranus has a diameter of over 31,000 mi and spins once in approximately 17.23 hours, according to magnetic data collected by *Voyager 2*. One of the most fascinating features of Uranus is how far over it is tipped. Its north pole lies 98° from its orbital plane. Thus, its seasons are extreme. Over its 84-year orbit, when the Sun rises at the north pole, it shines there for about 42 Earth years; then it sets, and the north pole is in darkness for 42 Earth years. In addition to its rotational tilt, Uranus's magnetic field axis is tipped 58.6° from its rotational axis and is displaced about 30% of its radius away from the planet's center.

Distance from the Sun	
Perihelion	1,703.4 mil mi
Semi-major axis (mean distance)	1,784.8 mil mi
	(19.201 AU)
Aphelion	1,866.4 mil mi
Period of revolution around Sun	84.01 yr.
Orbital eccentricity	0.0457
Orbital inclination	0.772°
Synodic day (midday to midday)	17 hr., 14 min., 23 sec.
	(retrograde)
Sidereal day	17 hr., 14 min., 24 sec. (retrograde)
Rotational inclination	97.77°
Mass (Earth = 1)	14.536
Mean radius	15,759 mi
Mean density (Earth = 1)	0.23
Natural satellites	27
Average temperature*	−323°F

*i.e., temperature where atmospheric pressure equals 1 Earth atmosphere.

Atmosphere. The atmosphere is composed primarily of 82.5% hydrogen, 15.2% helium, and 2.3% methane, with small amounts of hydrogen deuteride, ammonia ice, water ice, ammonia hydrosulfide, and methane ice.

Surface and composition. Uranus has no solid surface, and likely no rocky core but rather a mixture of rocks and assorted ices with about 15% hydrogen and some helium.

Natural satellites. Uranus has 27 known moons, which have orbits lying in the plane of the planet's equator. Five moons are relatively large, while 22 are very small and were only discovered with the *Voyager 2* mission or in later observations. Miranda has grooved markings, reminiscent of Jupiter's Ganymede, but often arranged in a chevron pattern. Rifts and channels on Ariel provide evidence of liquid flowing over its surface in the past. Umbriel is extremely dark, prompting some observers to regard its surface as among the oldest in the system. Titania has rifts and fractures, but not the evidence of flow found on Ariel. Oberon's main feature is its surface saturated with craters, unrelieved by other formations.

Rings. In the equatorial plane there is also a complex of 11 rings, 9 of which were discovered in 1978 by observers watching Uranus pass before a star.

Neptune

Distance from the Sun	
Perihelion	2,761.7 mil mi
Semi-major axis (mean distance)	2,793.1 mil mi (30.047 AU)
Aphelion	2,824.5 mil mi
Period of revolution around Sun	164.79 yr.
Orbital eccentricity	0.0113
Orbital inclination	1.769°
Synodic day (midday to midday)	16 hr., 6 min., 37 sec.
Sidereal day	16 hr., 6 min., 36 sec.
Rotational inclination	28.32°
Mass (Earth = 1)	17.147
Mean radius	15,301 mi
Mean density (Earth = 1)	0.297
Natural satellites	14
Average temperature*	−330°F

*i.e., temperature where atmospheric pressure equals 1 Earth atmosphere.

Named for the Roman god of the sea, Neptune was the first planet discovered through mathematical predictions before it was directly observed. Its approximate orbit and position were first calculated independently by British astronomer John Couch Adams and French astronomer Urbain Le Verrier in 1845. In 1846, German astronomer Johann Galle first observed Neptune through a telescope.

Orbit and rotation. Neptune orbits the Sun in 164.8 Earth years in a nearly circular orbit. Its magnetic field is considerably asymmetric to the planet's structure, similar to, but not so extreme as, Uranus's magnetic field. Neptune's magnetic field axis is tipped 46.9° from its rotational axis and is displaced more than 55% of its radius away from the planet's center.

Atmosphere. The Neptunian atmosphere is composed primarily of 80% hydrogen, 19% helium, 1.5% methane, and small amounts of hydrogen deuteride, ethane, ammonia ice, water ice, ammonia hydrosulfide, and methane ice. Neptune's atmosphere is quite blue, with quickly changing white clouds often suspended high above an apparent surface. A Great Dark Spot, reminiscent of Jupiter's Great Red Spot, was discovered in 1989 when *Voyager 2* visited the planet. Observations with the Hubble Space Telescope have shown that the Great Dark Spot originally seen by *Voyager* has apparently dissipated, but a new dark spot has since appeared. Lightning and auroras have been found on other giant planets, but only the aurora phenomenon has been seen on Neptune. As with the other giant planets, Neptune emits more energy than it receives from the Sun. The excess has been found to be 2.7 times the solar contribution.

Surface and composition. As with the other giant planets, Neptune may have no solid surface or exact diameter. However, a mean value of 30,600 mi may be assigned to a diameter between atmosphere levels where the pressure is about the same as sea level on Earth.

Natural satellites. The largest of Neptune's 14 satellites is Triton. It is the only large moon in a retrograde orbit, which suggests that it was captured rather than having formed along with the planet. Triton's large size, sufficient to raise significant tides on the planet, may one day, billions of years from now, bring Triton close enough to Neptune for Triton to be torn apart. Triton has a tenuous atmosphere of nitrogen with a trace of hydrocarbons and evidence of active geysers injecting material into it. Triton is the coldest object yet measured in the solar system with a surface temperature of −391°F. Only about half of Triton has been observed, but its terrain shows cratering and a strange regional feature described as resembling the skin of a cantaloupe. Nereid has the highest orbital eccentricity (0.75) of any moon. Its long looping orbit suggests that it was also captured. In 2003, two more moons, which orbit farther from their parent planet than any other moons in the solar system, were discovered. In July 2013, archival Hubble Space Telescope images were used to discover the existence of a 14th natural satellite of Neptune. At less than 20 km diameter, it is the smallest of Neptune's known moons. The *Voyager 2* probe in 1989 confirmed the existence of six rings around Neptune composed of very fine particles. There may be some clumps in the rings' structure. It is not known whether Neptune's satellites influence the formation or maintenance of the rings.

Dwarf Planets

Ceres

Distance from the Sun	
Perihelion	237 mil mi (2.55 AU)
Semi-major axis (mean distance)	257 mil mi (2.77 AU)
Period of revolution around Sun	4.6 yr.
Orbital eccentricity	0.0789
Orbital inclination	10.58°
Sidereal day	9.075 hr.
Mass (Earth = 1)	0.00015
Mean radius	294 mi

Ceres was the first asteroid discovered; Italian astronomer Guiseppe Piazzi first observed it on Jan. 1, 1801. In the 1800s, it was considered a planet but lost that designation. Ceres is the largest object in the asteroid belt, comprising nearly one third of all the mass of asteroids. In Aug. 2006, it was designated a dwarf planet by the Intl. Astronomical Union (IAU).

After a journey of over seven years, the *Dawn* spacecraft entered into orbit around Ceres in Mar. 2015, making *Dawn* the first spacecraft to visit a dwarf planet. Astronomers are particularly interested in asteroids since they are thought to be the rocky protoplanets, examples of the building blocks from which planets formed early in the history of the solar system.

Dawn's scientific instrumentation consists of cameras for surface imaging, a spectrometer for measuring surface mineralogy, and a neutron detector for measuring elemental composition of Ceres. *Dawn* has produced high-resolution maps of the entire surface and the most accurate measurements of Ceres's size and mass. The images show a heavily cratered surface with features such as extremely reflective spots within a crater—thought to be freshly exposed water ice—and at least one mountain several miles high.

Orbit and rotation. Ceres orbits the Sun in the asteroid belt region between Mars and Jupiter.

Surface and composition. Ceres's composition is similar to that of the stony meteorites known as carbonaceous chondrites. These are considered to be the oldest materials in the solar system, with a composition reflecting that of the primitive solar nebula. Extremely dark in color, probably because of their hydrocarbon content, they show evidence of having absorbed water. Thus, unlike the Earth and the Moon, they have never melted nor been reheated since they first formed. *Dawn* observations suggest that the surface of Ceres consists largely of water ice, though its interior is mostly rock. Up to 25% of Ceres's mass may be water ice. There is evidence for hydrothermal vents at the surface of Ceres, perhaps indicating that liquid water existed below the surface in the recent past. Further study using *Dawn* will try to confirm observations suggesting that water evaporates from the surface and produces a diffuse atmosphere.

Pluto

Distance from the Sun	
Perihelion	2,756.9 mil mi
Semi-major axis (mean distance)	3,670.1 mil mi
	(39.482 AU)
Aphelion	4,583.2 mil mi
Period of revolution around Sun	248.09 yr.
Orbital eccentricity	0.2488
Orbital inclination	17.14°
Synodic day (midday to midday)	.6 d., 9 hr., 17 min. (retrograde)
Sidereal day	6 d., 9 hr., 18 min. (retrograde)
Rotational inclination	119.59°
Mass (Earth = 1)	0.0022
Mean radius	736.5 mi
Mean density (Earth = 1)	0.339
Natural satellites	5
Average surface temperature	−369°F

Pluto, named for the Roman god of the underworld, is the largest Kuiper Belt object (KBO) by radius, and the second largest by mass. It was first discovered in 1930 by American astronomer Clyde Tombaugh and classified as a planet until 2006, when the IAU changed its designation to dwarf planet. In 2008, Pluto was designated by the IAU as the prototype for a class of objects called **plutoids**, bodies that (a) have an average distance from the Sun greater than Neptune's; (b) are large enough that gravity determines their shape; and (c) have not cleared their orbit of other objects. Haumea, Makemake, and Eris are also plutoids. Some 46 additional plutoid candidates have been identified through mid-2016. The *New Horizons* spacecraft, launched on a voyage to Pluto and beyond in 2006, made the first flyby of Pluto on July 14, 2015.

Orbit and rotation. Pluto's orbit is highly eccentric; although its average distance from the Sun is 3.7 bil mi, it may get as close as 2.76 bil mi. and as far as 4.58 bil mi. For about 20 years of its 248-year orbit, it is closer to the Sun than Neptune. Currently, it is beyond Neptune's orbit.

Atmosphere and surface. Before the *New Horizons* flyby, all observations of Pluto had been made with telescopes nearly 3 bil mi away, so the mission brought new data to light, some of which requires further analysis. The mass and density of Pluto suggests that it is composed of a rocky core with an overlying water-ice mantle. *New Horizons*'s close-up observations of Pluto revealed a mixed surface, with some ancient, heavily cratered terrain and other younger, smoother plains with no craters. The smooth terrain, estimated to be no more than 100 mil years old, is much younger than scientists expected and may indicate that geologic processes continue to modify Pluto. Nitrogen ice on the smooth plains appears to be flowing, like glaciers on Earth, onto the more heavily cratered surface. Compositional evidence shows that the smooth areas contain nitrogen, methane, and carbon monoxide ices. Scientists also found several mountain ranges rising more than 2 mi

above the smooth plains; they speculated that the mountains are made of water ice thrust up from below Pluto's nitrogen-rich icy surface.

New Horizons also provided the first close-up measurements of Pluto's atmosphere, confirming earlier measurements of methane, nitrogen, and carbon monoxide, the same molecules that form ice on Pluto's surface. Scientists speculate that the atmosphere forms from evaporation of surface ices when the dwarf planet is closer to the Sun. The new measurements also revealed hydrocarbon hazes as much as 50 mi above Pluto's surface. The hazes are thought to form when Pluto's tenuous atmosphere is exposed to the Sun's ultraviolet rays. Dark regions on Pluto's surface likely result from these hydrocarbons settling. Data from the flyby is being downloaded to Earth through the end of 2016; knowledge of Pluto will continue to improve as more data is downloaded and analyzed.

Natural satellites. Pluto has five known natural satellites. Charon, the biggest, has a diameter of 750 mi—about half of Pluto's diameter of 1,474 mi. No other planet or dwarf planet has a moon so close to its size. Discovered in 1978, Charon orbits Pluto at a distance of 12,200 mi and takes 6.39 days to move around the dwarf planet. In this same length of time, Pluto and Charon both rotate once on their axes, meaning that the Pluto-Charon system appears to rotate as virtually a rigid body. Both worlds are roughly spherical and have comparable densities. Because of these similarities and their peculiar relationship, there is debate as to whether Charon should one day be designated a dwarf planet. *New Horizons* provided the first detailed look at Charon, revealing a surface with less color and likely dominated by water ice. New evidence suggests Charon may have had a water ocean in the past. Much of Charon's surface is smoother than expected, with few craters, implying that Charon has an active geology capable of resurfacing. The images also reveal fractures extending hundreds of miles and a canyon around 5 mi deep.

Two other moons, discovered in 2005 and 2006, were officially named Nix and Hydra. Two additional moons, discovered in 2011 and 2012, were officially named Kerberos and Styx by the IAU in 2013. In late 2015, NASA released *New Horizons*-sourced images of Nix and Hydra, revealing irregularly shaped objects about 25 and 35 mi across, respectively. Astronomers examining *New Horizons* data have been surprised to find no additional moons.

Haumea

Distance from the Sun	
Semi-major axis (mean distance)	43.335 AU
Period of revolution around Sun	285 yr.
Orbital eccentricity	0.189
Orbital inclination	28.19°
Mass (Earth = 1)	0.0007
Mean radius	420 mi
Natural satellites	2

Haumea was discovered in 2004 and was accepted as a dwarf planet by the IAU in 2008.

Orbit and rotation. Haumea has a moderately eccentric orbit and takes about 285 years to go around the Sun.

Surface and composition. Spectra of Haumea indicate the presence of almost pure crystalline water ice. The surface reflects about 60% of the sunlight that reaches it. Haumea has a very oblong shape, twice as long as it is wide.

Natural satellites. Haumea has two natural satellites, Hi'iake and Namaka.

Makemake

Distance from the Sun	
Semi-major axis (mean distance)	45.791 AU
Period of revolution around Sun	310 yr.
Orbital eccentricity	0.159
Orbital inclination	28.96°
Mass (Earth = 1)	0.0007
Mean radius	450 mi
Natural satellites	1

Makemake was discovered in 2005 and was accepted as a dwarf planet by the IAU in 2008.

Orbit and rotation. Makemake has a moderately eccentric orbit and takes about 310 years to go around the Sun.

Surface and composition. Spectra of Makemake indicate the presence of frozen methane, as well as several organic compounds. The surface is highly reflective and appears similar to that of Pluto.

Natural satellites. Makemake has one natural satellite.

Eris

Distance from the Sun	
Semi-major axis (mean distance)........	67.6681 AU
Period of revolution around Sun...............	560 yr.
Orbital eccentricity........................	0.44177
Orbital inclination...........................	44.177°
Mass (Earth = 1)...........................	0.0027
Mean radius..............................	723 mi
Natural satellites................................	1

By mass, Eris is the largest known dwarf planet. Discovered in 2003 by astronomers at the California Institute of Technology, it is the most distant object ever seen in orbit around the Sun.

Orbit and rotation. Eris has a highly elliptical orbit and takes about 560 years to go around the Sun—more than twice the time it takes Pluto. Its inclination is steep, tilted at 44° to the planetary plane. It also has an extremely eccentric orbit. It will be at its closest to the Sun, actually coming inside part of Pluto's orbit, in about 280 years.

Surface and composition. Eris, with a surface covered in frozen methane, may be similar to Pluto and the Neptunian moon Triton. Observations made by the Hubble Space Telescope show that Eris's surface is almost white and uniform, reflecting 86% of the light that hits it. This makes it the most reflective body in the solar system. The dwarf planet's interior is likely a mixture of rock and ice.

Natural satellites. Eris has one moon, Dysnomia.

Small Solar System Bodies

Asteroids

Besides planets and moons, many smaller objects orbit the Sun. In 2006, the International Astronomical Union (IAU) officially designated these objects "small solar system bodies." Asteroids or minor planets are found mainly in a belt between the orbits of Mars and Jupiter. Within this belt there may be millions of asteroids of varying sizes. Most asteroids are very small. Ceres, which can be classified both as an asteroid and a dwarf planet, is 588 mi in diameter, about one-quarter the diameter of our Moon.

Some of these asteroids are gravitationally locked with Jupiter and the Sun so that they have roughly the same orbit as Jupiter but are either 60° ahead or behind the planet. These are the **Trojan asteroids.** Many of the smaller moons of the solar system, especially those in retrograde orbits, may be captured asteroids. Asteroids whose orbits either cross or come close to the Earth's orbit are labeled **Near Earth asteroids** or NEAs. A handful of asteroids have actually been imaged by the Arecibo and Goldstone radio telescopes and by the NEAR Shoemaker space probe. The *Galileo* spacecraft imaged the asteroids Gaspra and Ida (including Ida's moon Dactyl) on its way to Jupiter. As of July 2016, 12 asteroids had been visited by spacecraft.

Comets

Comets are small icy bodies that orbit the Sun. When one approaches the Sun, the energy from the Sun boils off material from the comet's icy nucleus, producing an enlarged head (or **coma**), and in many cases an extended tail. Because of that, comets are brighter when near the Sun. For large comets, the head may be 100,000 mi across and the tail more than a million mi long, though both are mainly empty space.

Comets have been known since ancient times. British astronomer Edmund Halley (1656-1742) ultimately realized that a group of historical reports were just repeated visits of the same object. Comets are the only astronomical objects named after their discoverers. In 1986, the European spacecraft *Giotto* took the first close-up images of a comet's nucleus, specifically of Comet Halley, showing it had a peanut-shaped nucleus with a longest dimension of about 10 mi.

In 1995, U.S. observers Alan Hale (1958-) and Thomas Bopp (1949-) independently discovered a comet that was then beyond the orbit of Jupiter. It is one of the brightest comets of all time. It also holds the record for length of time visible to the naked eye—19 months—and is the most photographed comet in history. In July 2009, an amateur astronomer discovered a large impact scar in the upper atmosphere of Jupiter, likely the result of another cometary impact. In 2014, the *Rosetta* spacecraft became the first spacecraft to orbit a comet, 67P/Churyumov-Gerasimenko. *Rosetta* also deployed a lander onto the comet surface. As of summer 2016, nine comets have been studied directly by spacecraft.

Kuiper Belt

The Kuiper Belt is a doughnut-shaped region that extends to about 50 AU (astronomical units) from the Sun and is thought to be the source of short-period comets such as Comets Halley or Swift-Tuttle. It is filled with icy bodies that are in solar orbit. The more than 1,000 objects found in this region in recent years are called Kuiper Belt objects (KBOs). It is estimated that there are more than 70,000 objects 60 mi in diameter or larger within the Kuiper Belt. Dwarf planets Pluto and Eris are considered KBO. There are at least six KBOs larger than 300 mi in diameter.

Oort Cloud

The Oort Cloud is a vast spherical region hypothesized to exist around the Sun and populated by comets. Dutch astronomer Jan Oort (1900-92) proposed its existence as the origin for long-period comets that enter the inner part of the solar system where the planets orbit. Current technology is not sufficient to detect any members of the Oort Cloud other than observed comets whose orbits may reach out as far as 50,000 AU. Recent examples of such long-period comets are Comets Hale-Bopp and Hyakutake.

The Sun

Distance from Earth, mean	92.96 mil mi (1 AU)
Sidereal day (rotation period).................	25.38 d.
Mass (Earth=1)...........................	332,900
Mean radius..............................	432,200 mi
Mean density (Earth=1)......................	0.255
Average surface temperature...................	9,941°F

The Sun is the Earth's primary source of light and heat and its closest star. The biggest object in the solar system, the Sun is 332,900 times more massive than Earth and contains 99.86% of the mass of the entire solar system. On the whole, the Sun is made up of about 92.1% hydrogen and 7.8% helium, with trace amounts of other elements. It has a mass and luminosity greater than that of 90% of the stars in the Milky Way galaxy. Although most of the stars that can be easily seen on a clear night are bigger and brighter than the Sun, its proximity to Earth makes it appear tremendously large and bright. The Sun is 400,000 times as bright as the full moon, and it gives Earth 6 mil times as much light as do all the other stars put together. Because of the great distance between the Sun and Earth, it takes about 499 sec., or slightly more than 8 min., for light from the Sun to reach Earth.

Composition. The Sun has six regions. The first three from the inside out are the core, the radiative zone, and the convective zone. Together they form the interior. The others, which comprise the visible surface, are the photosphere, the chromosphere, and the outermost region, the corona.

The Sun's heat and energy are produced in its core. Through a series of nuclear fusion reactions, hydrogen nuclei are converted to helium nuclei, releasing energy in the process. Temperatures in the core are theorized to be 28 mil °F. From the core, photons transport the energy outward through the radiative zone. It can take photons several million years to pass through this area. In the convective zone, gases move energy outward at a faster rate. Like a boiling pot, bubbles of gas bring energy to the surface.

The photosphere is the visible surface of the Sun, that is, the light that we see as sunlight. When sunlight is analyzed with a spectroscope, it is found to consist of a continuous spectrum composed of all the colors of the rainbow, crossed by many dark lines. The dark "absorption lines" are produced by gaseous materials in the outer layers of the Sun. More than 60 of the natural terrestrial elements have been identified in the Sun, all in gaseous form because of the Sun's intense heat.

Just above the photosphere is the chromosphere, which is visible to the naked eye only in total solar eclipses, during which it appears to be a pinkish-violet layer with occasional great prominences projecting above its general level. With proper instruments, the chromosphere can be seen or photographed whenever the Sun is visible. Above the chromosphere is the corona, also visible to the naked eye only at times of total eclipse or with instruments that permit the brighter portions of the corona to be seen. The corona surges millions of miles from the Sun; its atoms are all in a state of extreme excitation and high ionization that indicates temperatures nearly 2 mil °F.

Sunspots. These dark, irregularly shaped regions may reach diameters of thousands of miles. There is an intimate connection between sunspots and the corona. At times of low sunspot activity, the fine streamers of the corona are longer above the Sun's equator than over the polar regions of the Sun; during periods of high sunspot activity, the corona extends fairly evenly outward from all regions of the Sun but to a much greater distance in space. The average life of a sunspot group is two months, but some have lasted for more than a year. Sunspots reach a low point, on average, every 11.3 years, with a peak of activity occurring irregularly between two successive periods of minimal activity. The Sun experienced an unusually quiet period in 2008 and 2009; its latest period of maximum activity occurred in 2014, though this was among the weakest maximums ever recorded.

Solar wind and magnetic field. Magnetic arches, called prominences, may extend tens of thousands of miles into the corona and may release enormous amounts of energy heating the corona. Coronal mass ejections are enormous releases of solar energy. Coronal holes are regions where the corona appears dark in X-rays, and are associated with open magnetic field lines, where the magnetic field lines project out into space instead of back toward the Sun. It is in these regions where the high-speed solar wind originates.

The solar wind carries the Sun's magnetic field, which extends beyond the planets. This is called the interplanetary magnetic field (IMF). Far past Pluto and the Kuiper Belt, the solar wind and the IMF lose their influence. The boundary between them and interstellar space is called the heliopause. In 2013, NASA announced that the *Voyager 1* spacecraft, launched in 1977, seemed at last to have reached the heliopause, at a distance 18 bil km (11 bil mi) from the Sun.

Searching for Extrasolar Planets

The Sun is a typical star in many respects and—with over 400 bil stars in the Milky Way—it is plausible that many other stars might have planets. During the last 10 years of the 20th century, astronomers began to note evidence of planets orbiting stars other than the Sun. Astronomers have not directly observed most of these objects but merely inferred their existence from observations of their parent stars.

Astronomers have used two main techniques to detect planets. The first, called the radial-velocity method, uses the Doppler effect to detect periodic changes in the motion of a star caused by the gravitational tug of an unseen planet. The magnitude of the star's motion and the time it takes to repeat can be used to infer the planet's mass and distance from its host star. This technique is most sensitive to high-mass planets orbiting close to their stars because that situation produces more noticeable changes in a star's motion. The first planets discovered using this technique were as massive as the planet Jupiter and orbiting stars at distances closer than Mercury orbits the Sun.

The second technique, the transit method, relies on the dimming of a star's light as an unseen planet repeatedly passes in front of it. Astronomers are able to infer the diameter of the planet and the distance at which the planet orbits the star. When combined with the mass determined from the radial-velocity method, astronomers can determine the density of the unseen planet and begin to infer its similarity to planets in our solar system.

Astronomers have also used optical gravitational lensing to detect extrasolar planets. This technique, which detects the observed brightening of a distant background star as a planet passes in front of it, has allowed Southern Hemisphere astronomers to find the most distant planet yet detected, about halfway to the center of our own Milky Way galaxy.

In 2005, astronomers obtained the first direct image of an extrasolar planet around a normal star called GQ Lupi, which is like our Sun but younger. The planet is about 100 AU (astronomical units) away from the star and estimated to be about twice as massive as Jupiter.

In 2006, astronomers discovered what they call a "super Earth" orbiting a red dwarf 9,000 light-years away. The planet appears to have about 13 times Earth's mass and may be composed of rock and ice, but it is believed not to have liquid on its surface. In 2007, astronomers detected water in the atmosphere of an extrasolar planet for the first time.

In 2009, NASA launched Kepler, the first telescope sensitive enough to detect Earth-sized planets around other stars. Kepler's first-released data in 2010 indicated that small planets are more common than large planets. Kepler has now detected a large number of planets with diameters similar to that of Earth. Some of the planets are known to orbit within the host star's habitable zone, meaning that the conditions are such that liquid water could exist on the planetary surface. As of July 2016, astronomers had confirmed nearly 3,000 planets orbiting some 2,200 stars; 560 of those stars host at least three planets. More than 400 of the planets were at least as massive as Jupiter. Planets with masses less than Jupiter are now regularly discovered. Kepler 186f was the first Earth-sized planet to be confirmed in the habitable zone of a star. In July 2015, the Kepler team announced the discovery of Kepler-452b, an Earth-sized planet in the habitable zone of a star like the Sun, making this the most Earth-like of Kepler's discoveries to date. Another team of astronomers announced, Aug. 2016, the discovery of a possibly Earth-like planet, Proxima b, in orbit around Proxima Centauri, the star closest to the Sun. About 4.2 light years away, it is the closest known exoplanet to date.

NASA approved the Transiting Exoplanet Survey Satellite (TESS) mission in 2013. The mission, scheduled for launch in 2017, would conduct an all-sky survey of extrasolar planets.

Earth: Size, Computation of Time, Seasons

Distance from the Sun	
Perihelion	91.4 mil mi
Semi-major axis (mean distance)	93 mil mi (1.0000 AU)
Aphelion	94.5 mil mi
Period of revolution	365.256 d.
Orbital eccentricity	0.0167
Orbital inclination	0°
Synodic day (midday to midday)	24 hr., 0 min., 0 sec.
Sidereal day (rotation period)	23 hr., 56 min., 4.2 sec.
Rotational inclination	23.45°
Mass (Earth = 1)	1
Mean radius	3,958.8 mi
Mean density (Earth = 1)	1
Natural satellites	1
Average surface temperature	59°F

Earth is the fifth-largest planet and the third from the Sun. Its mass is 5.9736×10^{24} kg. Earth's equatorial diameter is 7,926 mi while its polar diameter is only 7,900 mi.

Size and dimensions. Earth is considered a solid mass, yet it has a large, liquid iron, **magnetic core** with a radius of about 2,160 mi. Surprisingly, it has a solid **inner core** that may be a large iron crystal, with a radius of 760 mi. Around the core is a thick shell, or **mantle**, of dense rock. This mantle is composed of materials rich in iron and magnesium. It is somewhat plastic-like, and under slow steady pressure, it can flow like a liquid. The mantle, in turn, is covered by a thin **crust** forming the solid granite and basalt base of the continents and ocean basins. Over broad areas of Earth's surface, the crust has a thin cover of sedimentary rock such as sandstone, shale, and limestone formed by weathering and by deposits of sands, clays, and plant and animal remains.

The temperature inside the Earth increases about 1°F with every 100 to 200 ft in depth, in the upper 100 km of Earth. It reaches nearly 8,000°F-9,000°F at the center. The heat is believed to come from radioactivity in rocks, pressures within Earth, and the original heat of formation.

Atmosphere. Earth's atmosphere is a blanket composed of 78% nitrogen, 21% oxygen, and 1% argon. Present in minute quantities are carbon dioxide, hydrogen, neon, helium, krypton, and xenon. Water vapor displaces other gases and varies from nearly zero to about 4% by volume. The atmosphere rests on Earth's surface with a weight equivalent to a layer of water 34 ft deep. For about 300,000 ft upward, the gases remain in the proportions stated. Gravity holds the gases to Earth. The weight of the air compresses it at the bottom so that the greatest density is at Earth's surface. Pressure and density decrease as height increases.

The lowest layer of the atmosphere extending up from the Earth's surface about 7.5 mi is the **troposphere**, which contains 90% of the air. This is also where most weather phenomena occur. The temperature drops with increasing height through this layer. The **stratosphere** extends about 23 mi above the troposphere; the temperature generally increases with height within this layer. The stratosphere contains **ozone**, which prevents ultraviolet rays from reaching Earth's surface. Since there is very little convection in the stratosphere, jets regularly cruise in the lower parts to provide a smoother ride for passengers.

Above the stratosphere is the **mesosphere**, where the temperature again decreases with height for another 19 mi. Extending above the mesosphere to the outer fringes of the atmosphere is the **thermosphere**, a region where temperature once more increases with height to a value measured in thousands of degrees Fahrenheit. The lower portion of this region, extending from 50 to about 400 mi in altitude, is characterized by high ion density and is thus called the **ionosphere**. Most meteors are in the lower thermosphere or the mesosphere at the time they are observed.

Longitude and latitude. Position on the globe is measured by meridians and parallels. Meridians, which are imaginary lines drawn around Earth through the poles, determine **longitude**. The meridian running through Greenwich, England, is the **prime meridian** of longitude; all others are either E or W. Parallels, which are imaginary circles parallel with the equator, determine **latitude**. The length of a degree of longitude varies as the cosine of the latitude. At the equator a degree of longitude is 69.171 statute mi; this is gradually reduced toward the poles. Value of a longitude degree at the poles is zero.

Latitude is reckoned by the number of degrees N or S of the **equator**, an imaginary circle on Earth's surface everywhere equidistant between the two poles. According to the International Astronomical Union, the length of a degree of latitude is 68.708 statute mi at the equator and varies slightly N and S because of the oblate form of the globe. At the poles, it is 69.403 statute mi.

Definitions of time. Earth rotates on its axis and follows an elliptical orbit around the Sun. The rotation makes the Sun appear to move across the sky from E to W. This rotation determines day and night, and the complete rotation, in relation to the Sun, is called the **apparent or true solar day**. A sundial thus measures **apparent solar time**. This length of time varies, but an average determines a mean solar day of 24 hours.

The mean solar day and **mean solar time** are in universal use for civil purposes. Mean solar time may be obtained from apparent solar time by correcting observations of the Sun for the **equation of time**. Mean solar time may be up to 16 min. different from apparent solar time.

Sidereal time is the measure of time defined by the diurnal motion of the vernal equinox and is determined from observation of the meridian transits of stars. One complete rotation of Earth relative to the equinox is called the **sidereal day**. The **mean sidereal day** is 23 hr., 56 min., 4.2 sec. of mean solar time.

The interval required for Earth to make one absolute revolution around the Sun is a **sidereal year**; it consisted of 365 days, 6 hr., 9 min., and 9.5 sec. of mean solar time (approximately 24 hr. per day) in 1900 and has been increasing at the rate of 0.0001 second annually.

The **tropical year**, upon which our calendar is based, is the interval between two consecutive returns of the Sun to the vernal equinox. The tropical year consisted of 365 days, 5 hr., 48 min., and 46 sec. in 1900. It has been decreasing at the rate of 0.53 sec. per century. The **calendar year** begins at midnight precisely, local clock time, on the night of Dec. 31-Jan. 1. The day and the calendar month also begin at midnight by the clock.

On Jan. 1, 1972, the Bureau International des Poids et Mesures in Paris introduced **International Atomic Time** (TAI) as the most precisely determined time scale for astronomical usage. The fundamental unit of TAI in the international system of units is the second, defined as the duration of 9,192,631,770 periods of the radiation corresponding to the transition between two hyperfine levels of the ground state of the cesium-133 atom. **Coordinated Universal Time** (UTC), which serves as the basis for civil timekeeping and is the standard time of the prime meridian, is officially defined by a formula which relates UTC to mean sidereal time in Greenwich, England. (UTC replaced Greenwich Mean Time as the basis for standard time for the world.)

Zones and seasons. The five zones of Earth's surface are the Torrid, lying between the Tropics of Cancer and Capricorn; the N Temperate, between Cancer and the Arctic Circle; the S Temperate, between Capricorn and the Antarctic Circle; and the two Frigid Zones, between the Polar Circles and the Poles.

The inclination, or tilt, of Earth's axis, 23°45′ away from a perpendicular to Earth's orbit of the Sun, determines the seasons. These are commonly marked in the N Temperate Zone, where spring begins at the vernal equinox, summer at the summer solstice, autumn at the autumnal equinox, and winter at the winter solstice. In the S Temperate Zone, the seasons are reversed. Spring begins at the autumnal equinox, summer at the winter solstice and so on.

The points at which the Sun crosses the equator are the **equinoxes**, when day and night are most nearly equal. The points at which the Sun is at a maximum distance from the equator are the **solstices**. Days and nights are then most unequal. However, at the equator, day and night are equal throughout the year.

In June, the North Pole is tilted 23°27′ toward the Sun, and the days in the Northern Hemisphere are longer than the nights, while the days in the Southern Hemisphere are shorter than the nights. In Dec., the North Pole is tilted 23°27′ away from the Sun, and the situation is reversed.

Seasons in 2017. In 2017, the four seasons begin in the Northern Hemisphere as shown. (Add 1 hour to Eastern Standard Time for Atlantic Time; subtract 1 hour for Central, 2 for Mountain, 3 for Pacific, 4 for Alaska, 5 for Hawaii-Aleutian. Also shown is Coordinated Universal Time.)

Season	Date	UTC	EST/EDT
Vernal Equinox (spring)	Mar. 20	10:29	6:29 EDT
Northern Solstice (summer)	June 21	4:24	0:24 EDT
Autumnal Equinox (fall)	Sept. 22	20:02	16:02 EDT
Southern Solstice (winter)	Dec. 21	16:28	11:28 EST

Poles. The geographic (rotation) poles, or points where Earth's axis of rotation cuts the surface, are not absolutely fixed in the body of Earth. The pole of rotation describes an irregular curve about its mean position.

Two periods have been detected in this motion: (1) an annual period due to seasonal changes in barometric pressure, to load of ice and snow on the surface, and to other seasonal phenomena; (2) a period of about 14 months due to the shape and constitution of Earth. In addition, there are small but as yet unpredictable irregularities. The whole motion is so small that the actual pole at any time remains within a circle of 30 or 40 ft in radius centered at the mean position of the pole.

The pole of rotation for the time being is, of course, the pole having a latitude of 90° and an indeterminate longitude.

Magnetic poles. Although Earth's magnetic field resembles that of an ordinary bar magnet, this magnetic field is probably produced by electric currents in the liquid currents of the Earth's outer core. The **north magnetic pole** of Earth is that region where the magnetic force is downward, and the **south magnetic pole** is that region where the magnetic force is upward. A compass placed at the magnetic poles experiences no directive force in azimuth (i.e., direction).

There are slow changes in the distribution of Earth's magnetic field. This slow temporal change is referred to as the secular change of the main magnetic field, and the magnetic poles shift due to this. The location of the N magnetic pole was first measured in 1831 at Cape Adelaide on the W coast of Boothia Peninsula in Canada's Northwest Territories (about latitude 70° N and longitude 96° W). Since then it has moved over 500 mi. It is now estimated to be at 82.7° N and 114.4° W, NW of Ellef Ringnes Island in northern Canada. Measurement for several decades by Canadian scientists indicates the motion of the pole has accelerated, now averaging about 25 mi per year.

The direction of the horizontal components of the magnetic field at any point is known as magnetic N at that point, and the angle by which it deviates E or W of true N is known as the magnetic declination.

A compass without error points in the direction of magnetic north. (In general, this is not the direction of the true rotational north pole.) If you follow the direction indicated by the N end of the compass, you will go along an irregular curve that eventually reaches the north magnetic pole (though not usually by a great-circle route). However, the action of the compass should not be thought of as due to any influence of the distant pole, but simply as an indication of the distribution of Earth's magnetism at the place of observation.

Rotation. The speed of Earth's rotation about its axis is slightly variable. The variations may be classified as:

(A) **Secular.** Tidal friction acts as a brake on the rotation and causes a slow secular increase in the length of the day, about 1 millisecond per century.

(B) **Irregular.** The speed of rotation may increase for a number of years (about 5 to 10) and then start decreasing. The maximum difference from the mean in the length of the day during a century is about 5 milliseconds. The accumulated difference in time has amounted to approximately 44 seconds since 1900. The cause is probably motion in the interior of Earth.

(C) **Periodic.** Seasonal variations exist with periods of 1 year and 6 months. The cumulative effect is such that each year, Earth is late about 30 milliseconds near June 1 and is ahead about 30 milliseconds near Oct. 1. The maximum seasonal variation in the length of the day is about 0.5 millisecond. It is believed that the principal cause of the annual variation is the seasonal change in the wind patterns of the Northern and Southern Hemispheres. The semiannual variation is due chiefly to tidal action of the Sun, which distorts the shape of Earth slightly.

The Moon

Distance from Earth	
Perigee	225,744 mi
Semi-major axis (mean distance)	238,855 mi
Apogee	251,966 mi
Period of revolution	27.322 d.
Orbital eccentricity	0.0549
Orbital inclination	5.145°
Synodic orbital period (period of phases)	29.53 d.
Sidereal day (rotation period)	27.322 d.
Rotational inclination	6.68°
Mass (Earth = 1)	0.0123
Mean radius	1,079 mi
Mean density (Earth = 1)	0.607
Average surface temperature	–100°F

The Moon is the second-brightest object in the sky (the Sun is the first). Earth's only natural satellite, the Moon is the force behind the rising and falling of tides, and it helps to regulate Earth's inclination as they orbit around the Sun. Many probes have been sent to the Moon, and between 1969 and 1972, 12 U.S. astronauts walked on its surface. The Moon is the subject of renewed international interest. In 2007, Japan and China orbited satellites around the Moon, India orbited a spacecraft in fall 2008, and the U.S. sent an orbiter and impactor in 2009. In Sept. 2009, American scientists announced the discovery of a thin layer of water ice near the lunar poles. The *LCROSS* mission impacted the lunar south polar region in Oct. 2009. The plume of material released in the impact contained water plus a variety of other chemical species, indicating that the lunar regolith harbors a rich and active chemistry. Since 2009, NASA has been mapping and measuring the surface composition and other properties of the Moon using the Lunar Reconnaissance Orbiter. In Sept. 2013, NASA launched *LADEE*, a mission to study the ephemeral lunar atmosphere and lunar dust from a low orbit. In Dec. 2013, China became the third nation to land a spacecraft on the Moon when *Chang'e 3* set down on Mare Imbrium. *Chang'e 3* released the *Yutu* rover to study the lunar surface.

Orbit and rotation. The Moon completes a circuit around Earth in a period that averages 27 days, 7 hr., 43.2 min. This is the Moon's sidereal period. Because of the motion of the Moon in common with Earth around the Sun, the mean duration of the lunar month—the period from one new moon to the next new moon—is 29 days, 12 hr., 44.05 min. This is the Moon's synodic period.

The mean distance of the Moon from Earth is 238,855 mi, but its orbit about Earth is elliptical, and thus the actual distance varies considerably. The maximum distance from Earth that the Moon may reach is 251,966 mi and the least distance is 225,744 mi.

The Moon rotates on its axis in a period of time that is exactly equal to its sidereal revolution about Earth—27.322 days. Thus the backside, or farside, of the Moon always faces away from Earth. But this does not mean that the backside is always dark. The farside of the Moon gets as much direct sunlight as the nearside; at new moon phase, the farside of the Moon is fully lit but not visible from Earth.

The Moon's revolution about Earth is irregular because of its elliptical orbit. The Moon's rotation, however, is regular, and this, together with the irregular revolution, produces what is called libration in longitude, which permits an observer on Earth to see first farther around the eastern side and then farther around the western side of the Moon. The Moon's variation north or south of the ecliptic permits one to see farther over first one pole of the Moon and then the other; this is called libration in latitude. These two libration effects permit observers on Earth to see a total of about 60% of the Moon's surface over a period of time.

Atmosphere and surface. The Moon, like the planet Mercury, has no real atmosphere to speak of. What little exists is variable and tenuous. With its long day and night, the daytime temperature can reach 260°F. The coldest nighttime temperature is –280°F. This day-to-night contrast is exceeded only by that on Mercury. The lunar surface has not changed much since humans began observing it. The side visible from Earth has large craters and vast dark areas called *maria* that were once lava. The farside has almost no maria but is pockmarked with craters; it was first photographed in 1959 by the Soviet space probe *Lunik III*.

Recent findings show that up to 300 mil metric tons of water ice may exist in craters at the lunar poles. In its interior, the Moon may have a small core, which supports the idea that most of the Moon's mass was ripped away from the early Earth when a Mars-sized object collided with Earth.

Harvest moon and hunter's moon. The harvest moon, the full moon nearest the autumnal equinox, ushers in a period of several days when the Moon rises soon after sunset. This phenomenon gives farmers in temperate latitudes extra hours of light in which to harvest their crops. The 2017 harvest moon falls on Sept. 6. Harvest moon in the Southern Hemisphere temperate latitudes falls on Mar. 12.

The next full moon after harvest moon is called the hunter's moon; it is accompanied by a similar but less marked phenomenon. In 2017, the hunter's moon occurs on Oct. 5 in the Northern Hemisphere and on Apr. 11 in the Southern Hemisphere.

Moon Phases, 2017
(In Coordinated Universal Time, or UTC, the standard time of the prime meridian.)

New Moon			Waxing Quarter			Full Moon			Waning Quarter		
Date	Hr.	Min.	Date	Hr.	Min.	Date	Hr.	Min.	Date	Hr.	Min.
Jan. 28	0	7	Jan. 5	19	47	Jan. 12	11	34	Jan. 19	22	13
Feb. 26	14	58	Feb. 4	4	19	Feb. 11	0	33	Feb. 18	19	33
Mar. 28	2	57	Mar. 5	11	32	Mar. 12	14	54	Mar. 20	15	58
Apr. 26	12	16	Apr. 3	18	39	Apr. 11	6	8	Apr. 19	9	57
May 25	19	44	May 3	2	47	May 10	21	42	May 19	0	33
June 24	2	31	June 1	12	42	June 9	13	10	June 17	11	33
July 23	9	46	July 1	0	51	July 9	4	7	July 16	19	26
Aug. 21	18	30	July 30	15	23	Aug. 7	18	11	Aug. 15	1	15
Sept. 20	5	30	Aug. 29	8	13	Sept. 6	7	3	Sept. 13	6	25
Oct. 19	19	12	Sept. 28	2	54	Oct. 5	18	40	Oct. 12	12	25
Nov. 18	11	42	Oct. 27	22	22	Nov. 4	5	23	Nov. 10	20	36
Dec. 18	6	30	Nov. 26	17	3	Dec. 3	15	47	Dec. 10	7	51
			Dec. 26	9	20						

CALENDAR

Western Calendars

The **Julian calendar**, under which all Western nations measured time until 1582 CE, was authorized by Julius Caesar in 46 BCE. It called for a year of 365¼ days, starting in Jan., with every fourth year being a **leap year** of 366 days. St. Bede, an Anglo-Saxon monk also known as the Venerable Bede, announced in 730 CE that the Julian year was 11 min., 14 sec. too long, a cumulative error of about a day every 128 years, but nothing was done about this for centuries.

By 1582 the accumulated error was estimated at 10 days. In that year, Pope Gregory XIII decreed that the day following Oct. 4, 1582, should be called Oct. 15, thus dropping 10 days and initiating the **Gregorian calendar**.

The Gregorian calendar perpetuated a chronological system devised by the monk Dionysius Exiguus (fl. 6th cent.). His chronology started with the first year following the birth of Jesus Christ, which he inaccurately took to be year 753 in the Roman calendar. Leap years were continued but, to prevent further displacements, centesimal years (years ending in 00) were made common years, not leap years, unless divisible by 400. Under this plan, 1600 and 2000 were leap years; 1700, 1800, and 1900 were not.

The Gregorian calendar was adopted at once by France, Italy, Spain, Portugal, and Luxembourg. Within two years, most German Catholic states, Belgium, and parts of Switzerland and the Netherlands were brought under the new calendar, and Hungary followed in 1587. The rest of the Netherlands, along with Denmark and the German Protestant states, made the change in 1699-1700.

The British government adopted the Gregorian calendar and imposed it on all its possessions, including the American colonies, in 1752, decreeing that the day following Sept. 2, 1752, should be called Sept. 14, a loss of 11 days. All dates preceding were marked OS, for Old Style. In addition, New Year's Day was moved to Jan. 1 from Mar. 25. (Under the old reckoning, for example, Mar. 24, 1700, was followed by Mar. 25, 1701.) Thus George Washington's birth date, which was Feb. 11, 1731, OS, became Feb. 22, 1732, NS (New Style). In 1753, Sweden also went Gregorian.

In 1793, the French revolutionary government adopted a calendar of 12 months of 30 days each with five extra days in Sept. of each common year and six extra days every fourth year. Napoleon reinstated the Gregorian calendar in 1806.

The Gregorian system later spread to non-European regions, replacing traditional calendars at least for official purposes. Japan in 1873, Egypt in 1875, China in 1912, and Turkey in 1925 made the change, usually in conjunction with political upheaval. In China, the republican government began reckoning years from its 1911 founding. After 1949, the People's Republic adopted the Common, or Christian Era, year count, even for the traditional lunar calendar, which it retained. In 1918, the Soviet Union decreed that the day after Jan. 31, 1918, OS, would be Feb. 14, 1918, NS. Greece changed over in 1923. For the first time in history, all major nations had one calendar. The Russian Orthodox church and some other Christian sects retained the Julian calendar.

To convert from the Julian to the Gregorian calendar, add 10 days to dates Oct. 5, 1582, through Feb. 28, 1700; after that date, add 11 days through Feb. 28, 1800; 12 days through Feb. 28, 1900; and 13 days through Feb. 28, 2100.

A **century** consists of 100 consecutive years. The 1st century CE may be said to have run from the years 1 through 100. The 20th century by this reckoning consisted of the years 1901 through 2000 and ended Dec. 31, 2000, as did the 2nd millennium CE. The 21st century thus technically began on Jan. 1, 2001.

For a **perpetual calendar**, see pages 386-87.

Gregorian Calendar

Choose the desired year from the table below or from the perpetual calendar (for years 1803 to 2080). The number after each year designates which calendar to use for that year, as shown in the perpetual calendar. (The Gregorian calendar was inaugurated Oct. 15, 1582. From that date through Dec. 31, 1582, use calendar 6.)

1583-1802

1583	7	1603	4	1623	1	1643	5	1663	2	1683	6	1703	2	1723	6	1743	3	1763	7	1783	4
1584	8	1604	12	1624	9	1644	13	1664	10	1684	14	1704	10	1724	14	1744	11	1764	8	1784	12
1585	3	1605	7	1625	4	1645	1	1665	5	1685	2	1705	5	1725	2	1745	6	1765	3	1785	7
1586	4	1606	1	1626	5	1646	2	1666	6	1686	3	1706	6	1726	3	1746	7	1766	4	1786	1
1587	5	1607	2	1627	6	1647	3	1667	7	1687	4	1707	7	1727	4	1747	1	1767	5	1787	2
1588	13	1608	10	1628	14	1648	11	1668	8	1688	12	1708	8	1728	12	1748	9	1768	13	1788	10
1589	1	1609	5	1629	2	1649	6	1669	3	1689	7	1709	3	1729	7	1749	4	1769	1	1789	5
1590	2	1610	6	1630	3	1650	7	1670	4	1690	1	1710	4	1730	1	1750	5	1770	2	1790	6
1591	3	1611	7	1631	4	1651	1	1671	5	1691	2	1711	5	1731	2	1751	6	1771	3	1791	7
1592	11	1612	8	1632	12	1652	9	1672	13	1692	10	1712	13	1732	10	1752	14	1772	11	1792	8
1593	6	1613	3	1633	7	1653	4	1673	1	1693	5	1713	1	1733	5	1753	2	1773	6	1793	3
1594	7	1614	4	1634	1	1654	5	1674	2	1694	6	1714	2	1734	6	1754	3	1774	7	1794	4
1595	1	1615	5	1635	2	1655	6	1675	3	1695	7	1715	3	1735	7	1755	4	1775	1	1795	5
1596	9	1616	13	1636	10	1656	14	1676	11	1696	8	1716	11	1736	8	1756	12	1776	9	1796	13
1597	4	1617	1	1637	5	1657	2	1677	6	1697	3	1717	6	1737	3	1757	7	1777	4	1797	1
1598	5	1618	2	1638	6	1658	3	1678	7	1698	4	1718	7	1738	4	1758	1	1778	5	1798	2
1599	6	1619	3	1639	7	1659	4	1679	1	1699	5	1719	1	1739	5	1759	2	1779	6	1799	3
1600	14	1620	11	1640	8	1660	12	1680	9	1700	6	1720	9	1740	13	1760	10	1780	14	1800	4
1601	2	1621	6	1641	3	1661	7	1681	4	1701	7	1721	4	1741	1	1761	5	1781	2	1801	5
1602	3	1622	7	1642	4	1662	1	1682	5	1702	1	1722	5	1742	2	1762	6	1782	3	1802	6

Julian Period

How many days have you lived? To determine this, multiply your age by 365, add the number of days since your last birthday, and account for all leap years. Chances are your calculations will go wrong somewhere. Astronomers, however, find it convenient to express dates and time intervals in days rather than in years, months, and days. This is done by placing events within the Julian period.

The Julian period was devised in 1582 by the French classical scholar Joseph Scaliger (1540-1609), who named it after his father, Julius Caesar Scaliger, not after the Julian calendar as might be supposed.

Scaliger began with a zero hour, or starting time, of noon on Jan. 1, 4713 BCE (on the Julian calendar). This was the most recent time that three major chronological cycles began on the same day: (1) the 28-year solar cycle, after which dates in the Julian calendar (e.g., Feb. 11) return to the same days of the week (e.g., Monday); (2) the 19-year lunar cycle, after which the phases of the moon return to the same dates of the year; and (3) the 15-year indiction cycle, used in ancient Rome to regulate taxes.

It will take 7,980 years to complete the period, the product of the numbers 28, 19, and 15.

Noon (Universal Time) of Jan. 1, 2017, will be Julian date (JD) 2,457,754; that many days will have passed since the start of the Julian period. The JD at noon of any date in 2017 may be found by adding to that number the day of the year for that date and subtracting one.

Julian Calendar

To find which of the 14 calendars of the perpetual calendar (pages 386-87) applies to any year under the Julian system, find the century for the desired year in the three leftmost columns below. Locate the desired year from among the four top rows. The number at the intersection of that row and column is the calendar designation for that year. For some years and countries, the Julian new year did not start Jan. 1; to find the correct perpetual calendar for Britain and its possessions, you can generally add one year for dates from Jan. 1 to Mar. 24. For example, to look up Feb. 2, 1705, Old Style, use the year 1706.

Year (last 2 digits of desired year)

		01	02	03	04	05	06	07	08	09	10	11	12	13	14	15	16	17	18	19	20	21	22	23	24	25	26	27	28
		29	30	31	32	33	34	35	36	37	38	39	40	41	42	43	44	45	46	47	48	49	50	51	52	53	54	55	56
		57	58	59	60	61	62	63	64	65	66	67	68	69	70	71	72	73	74	75	76	77	78	79	80	81	82	83	84
Century	00	85	86	87	88	89	90	91	92	93	94	95	96	97	98	99													
0 700 1400	12	7	1	2	10	5	6	7	8	3	4	5	13	1	2	3	11	6	7	1	9	4	5	6	14	2	3	4	12
100 800 1500	11	6	7	1	9	4	5	6	14	2	3	4	12	7	1	2	10	5	6	7	8	3	4	5	13	1	2	3	11
200 900 1600	10	5	6	7	8	3	4	5	13	1	2	3	11	6	7	1	9	4	5	6	14	2	3	4	12	7	1	2	10
300 1000 1700	9	4	5	6	14	2	3	4	12	7	1	2	10	5	6	7	8	3	4	5	13	1	2	3	11	6	7	1	9
400 1100 1800	8	3	4	5	13	1	2	3	11	6	7	1	9	4	5	6	14	2	3	4	12	7	1	2	10	5	6	7	8
500 1200 1900	14	2	3	4	12	7	1	2	10	5	6	7	8	3	4	5	13	1	2	3	11	6	7	1	9	4	5	6	14
600 1300 2000	13	1	2	3	11	6	7	1	9	4	5	6	14	2	3	4	12	7	1	2	10	5	6	7	8	3	4	5	13

Signs of the Zodiac

The zodiac is the apparent yearly path of the sun among the stars as viewed from Earth and was divided by the ancients into 12 equal sections or signs, each named for the constellation situated within its limits in ancient times. Astrologers claim that the temperament and destiny of each individual depend on the zodiac sign under which the person was born and the relationships between the planets at that time and throughout the person's life.

Below are the 12 traditional signs and the traditional range of dates pertaining to each:

♈ **Aries** (Ram), March 21-April 19

♉ **Taurus** (Bull), April 20-May 20

♊ **Gemini** (Twins), May 21-June 21

♋ **Cancer** (Crab), June 22-July 22

♌ **Leo** (Lion), July 23-August 22

♍ **Virgo** (Virgin), August 23-September 22

♎ **Libra** (Scales), September 23-October 23

♏ **Scorpio** (Scorpion), October 24-November 21

♐ **Sagittarius** (Archer), November 22-December 21

♑ **Capricorn** (Goat), December 22-January 19

♒ **Aquarius** (Water Bearer), January 20-February 18

♓ **Pisces** (Fishes), February 19-March 20

Chinese Calendar and Asian Festivals

The Chinese calendar, like the Jewish and Islamic calendars (see the Religion chapter), is a lunar calendar. It is divided into 12 months of 29 or 30 days (compensating for the lunar month's mean duration of 29 days, 12 hr., 44.05 min.). This calendar is synchronized with the solar year by the addition of extra months at fixed intervals.

The Chinese calendar runs on a 60-year cycle. The cycles 1876-1935 and 1936-95, along with the first 36 years of the current cycle, are shown below grouped by their association with 1 of 12 animals in the Chinese zodiac. This cycle began in 1996 and will last until 2055. Jan. 28, 2017, marks the beginning of the year 4715 in the Chinese calendar and is designated the Year of the Rooster. (Note: The first 3-7 weeks of each Western year belong to the previous Chinese year.)

Both the Western (Gregorian) and traditional lunar calendars are used publicly in China and in North and South Korea, and two New Year's celebrations are held. In Taiwan and Vietnam and in overseas Chinese communities, the lunar calendar is used only to set the dates for traditional festivals, with the Gregorian system in general use.

The 4-day Chinese New Year; the 3-day Vietnamese New Year festival, Tet; and the 3-to-4-day Korean festival, Suhl, begin at the second new moon after the winter solstice. The new moon in East Asia, which is west of the International Date Line, may be a day later than the new moon in the U.S. The festivals may start, therefore, anywhere between Jan. 21 and Feb. 19 of the Gregorian calendar.

Rat	Ox	Tiger	Hare (Rabbit)	Dragon	Snake	Horse	Sheep (Goat)	Monkey	Rooster	Dog	Pig (Boar)
1876	1877	1878	1879	1880	1881	1882	1883	1884	1885	1886	1887
1888	1889	1890	1891	1892	1893	1894	1895	1896	1897	1898	1899
1900	1901	1902	1903	1904	1905	1906	1907	1908	1909	1910	1911
1912	1913	1914	1915	1916	1917	1918	1919	1920	1921	1922	1923
1924	1925	1926	1927	1928	1929	1930	1931	1932	1933	1934	1935
1936	1937	1938	1939	1940	1941	1942	1943	1944	1945	1946	1947
1948	1949	1950	1951	1952	1953	1954	1955	1956	1957	1958	1959
1960	1961	1962	1963	1964	1965	1966	1967	1968	1969	1970	1971
1972	1973	1974	1975	1976	1977	1978	1979	1980	1981	1982	1983
1984	1985	1986	1987	1988	1989	1990	1991	1992	1993	1994	1995
1996	1997	1998	1999	2000	2001	2002	2003	2004	2005	2006	2007
2008	2009	2010	2011	2012	2013	2014	2015	2016	2017	2018	2019
2020	2021	2022	2023	2024	2025	2026	2027	2028	2029	2030	2031

Calendar for the Year 2017

January							February							March							April						
S	M	T	W	T	F	S	S	M	T	W	T	F	S	S	M	T	W	T	F	S	S	M	T	W	T	F	S
1	**2**	3	4	5	6	7				1	2	3	4				1	2	3	4							1
8	9	10	11	12	13	14	5	6	7	8	9	10	11	5	6	7	8	9	10	11	2	3	4	5	6	7	8
15	**16**	17	18	19	20	21	12	13	14	15	16	17	18	12	13	14	15	16	17	18	9	10	11	12	13	14	15
22	23	24	25	26	27	28	19	**20**	21	22	23	24	25	19	20	21	22	23	24	25	16	17	18	19	20	21	22
29	30	31					26	27	28					26	27	28	29	30	31		23	24	25	26	27	28	29
																					30						

May							June							July							August						
S	M	T	W	T	F	S	S	M	T	W	T	F	S	S	M	T	W	T	F	S	S	M	T	W	T	F	S
	1	2	3	4	5	6					1	2	3							1			1	2	3	4	5
7	8	9	10	11	12	13	4	5	6	7	8	9	10	2	3	**4**	5	6	7	8	6	7	8	9	10	11	12
14	15	16	17	18	19	20	11	12	13	14	15	16	17	9	10	11	12	13	14	15	13	14	15	16	17	18	19
21	22	23	24	25	26	27	18	19	20	21	22	23	24	16	17	18	19	20	21	22	20	21	22	23	24	25	26
28	**29**	30	31				25	26	27	28	29	30		23	24	25	26	27	28	29	27	28	29	30	31		
														30	31												

September							October							November							December						
S	M	T	W	T	F	S	S	M	T	W	T	F	S	S	M	T	W	T	F	S	S	M	T	W	T	F	S
					1	2	1	2	3	4	5	6	7				1	2	3	4						1	2
3	**4**	5	6	7	8	9	8	**9**	10	11	12	13	14	5	6	7	8	9	**10**	11	3	4	5	6	7	8	9
10	11	12	13	14	15	16	15	16	17	18	19	20	21	12	13	14	15	16	17	18	10	11	12	13	14	15	16
17	18	19	20	21	22	23	22	23	24	25	26	27	28	19	20	21	22	**23**	24	25	17	18	19	20	21	22	23
24	25	26	27	28	29	30	29	30	31					26	27	28	29	30			24	**25**	26	27	28	29	30
																					31						

Federal Holidays and Other Notable Dates, 2017

Some dates may be subject to change.

The dates in bold in the calendar above and named below in italics are U.S. federal holidays, designated by the president or Congress and applicable to federal employees and in the District of Columbia. Most U.S. states also observe these holidays, and many states observe others; practices vary by state. In most states the secretary of state's office can provide details.

January
1 New Year's Day
2 *New Year's Day* (federal holiday observed); Sugar Bowl; Rose Bowl; Cotton Bowl
9 College Football Playoff championship (Tampa, FL)
16 *Martin Luther King Jr. Day*
16-29 Australian Open tennis tournament
26 Australia Day
28 Chinese New Year
29 NFL Pro Bowl (Orlando, FL)

February
2 Groundhog Day
5 Super Bowl LI (Houston, TX)
12 Lincoln's Birthday
13-14 Westminster Dog Show
14 Valentine's Day
19 NBA All-Star Game (Charlotte, NC)
20 *Washington's Birthday* (observed), a.k.a. Presidents' Day or Washington-Lincoln Day
24-28 Carnival, Brazil
26 Academy Awards; Daytona 500
28 Mardi Gras

March
1 Ash Wednesday
4 Iditarod Trail Sled Dog Race begins
12 Daylight-saving time begins in U.S.; Purim (Feast of Lots) begins previous night
17 St. Patrick's Day
20 First day of spring (Northern Hemisphere)
21 Benito Juárez's Birthday, Mexico
31, Apr. 2 NCAA Women's Basketball Final Four (Dallas, TX)

April
1, 3 NCAA Men's Basketball Final Four (Glendale, AZ)
3-9 Master's golf tournament
11 Passover, 1st full day
14 Good Friday
16 Easter (Western and Orthodox)
17 Tax Day (IRS filing deadline); Patriots' Day; Boston Marathon
22 Earth Day
27 Take Our Daughters and Sons to Work Day
28 Arbor Day

May
1 May Day (International Workers' Day)
3 Buddha's Birthday, Hong Kong, Korea
5 Cinco de Mayo (Battle of Puebla Day), Mexico
6 Kentucky Derby
14 Mother's Day
20 Armed Forces Day; Preakness Stakes
28-June 11 French Open tennis tournament
22 Victoria Day, Canada
27 Ramadan (Islamic month of fasting), 1st full day
29 *Memorial Day*, or Decoration Day
30 Dragon Boat Festival, China

June
10 Belmont Stakes
14 Flag Day
15-18 U.S. Open golf tournament (Erin, WI)
18 Father's Day
21 First day of summer (Northern Hemisphere)

July
1 Canada Day
3-16 Wimbledon tennis tournament
4 *Independence Day*
6-14 Running of the Bulls (Pamplona, Spain)
13-16 U.S. Women's Open golf tournament (Bedminster, NJ)
14 Bastille Day, France
20-23 British Open golf tournament (Southport, Eng., UK)

August
7-13 PGA Championship (Charlotte, NC)

September
4 *Labor Day*, U.S., Canada
10 Grandparents' Day, U.S.
16 Independence Day, Mexico (celebration begins previous night)
17 Constitution Day and Citizenship Day, U.S.
21 Islamic New Year (Muharram 1) begins previous night; Rosh Hashanah (New Year), 1st full day
22 First day of autumn (Northern Hemisphere)
30 Yom Kippur (Day of Atonement) begins previous night

October
2 U.S. Supreme Court session begins
3 German Unity Day, Germany
9 *Columbus Day*; Thanksgiving Day, Canada
12 Día de la Raza, Spain, Mexico
31 Halloween

November
1 All Saints' Day
5 Daylight-saving time ends in U.S.; New York City Marathon
7 Election Day
10 *Veterans Day* (federal holiday observed)
11 Veterans Day; Remembrance Day, Canada
12 Remembrance Sunday, UK
23 *Thanksgiving Day*

December
10 Nobel Prizes awarded (winners announced in Oct.)
12 Día de la Virgen de Guadalupe, Mexico
13-20 Hanukkah (Festival of Lights) begins previous night
21 First day of winter (Northern Hemisphere)
25 *Christmas Day*
26 Boxing Day, Australia, Canada, New Zealand, UK
26-Jan. 1 Kwanzaa
30 Cotton Bowl; Fiesta Bowl; Orange Bowl

Perpetual Calendar

The number shown for each year indicates which Gregorian calendar to use. For 1583-1802, see “Gregorian Calendar” on page 383. For 1803-20, use numbers for 1983-2000, respectively. The years in the calendar labels are the last and next occurrences of each calendar.

1821 . . . 2	1847 . . . 6	1873 . . . 4	1899 . . . 1	1925 . . . 5	1951 . . . 2	1977 . . . 7	2003 . . . 4	2029 . . . 2	2055 . . . 6
1822 . . . 3	1848 . . 14	1874 . . . 5	1900 . . . 2	1926 . . . 6	1952 . . 10	1978 . . . 1	2004 . . 12	2030 . . . 3	2056 . . 14
1823 . . . 4	1849 . . . 2	1875 . . . 6	1901 . . . 3	1927 . . . 7	1953 . . . 5	1979 . . . 2	2005 . . . 7	2031 . . . 4	2057 . . . 2
1824 . . 12	1850 . . . 3	1876 . . 14	1902 . . . 4	1928 . . . 8	1954 . . . 6	1980 . . 10	2006 . . . 1	2032 . . 12	2058 . . . 3
1825 . . . 7	1851 . . . 4	1877 . . . 2	1903 . . . 5	1929 . . . 3	1955 . . . 7	1981 . . . 5	2007 . . . 2	2033 . . . 7	2059 . . . 4
1826 . . . 1	1852 . . 12	1878 . . . 3	1904 . . 13	1930 . . . 4	1956 . . . 8	1982 . . . 6	2008 . . 10	2034 . . . 1	2060 . . 12
1827 . . . 2	1853 . . . 7	1879 . . . 4	1905 . . . 1	1931 . . . 5	1957 . . . 3	1983 . . . 7	2009 . . . 5	2035 . . . 2	2061 . . . 7
1828 . . 10	1854 . . . 1	1880 . . 12	1906 . . . 2	1932 . . 13	1958 . . . 4	1984 . . . 8	2010 . . . 6	2036 . . 10	2062 . . . 1
1829 . . . 5	1855 . . . 2	1881 . . . 7	1907 . . . 3	1933 . . . 1	1959 . . . 5	1985 . . . 3	2011 . . . 7	2037 . . . 5	2063 . . . 2
1830 . . . 6	1856 . . 10	1882 . . . 1	1908 . . 11	1934 . . . 2	1960 . . 13	1986 . . . 4	2012 . . . 8	2038 . . . 6	2064 . . 10
1831 . . . 7	1857 . . . 5	1883 . . . 2	1909 . . . 6	1935 . . . 3	1961 . . . 1	1987 . . . 5	2013 . . . 3	2039 . . . 7	2065 . . . 5
1832 . . . 8	1858 . . . 6	1884 . . 10	1910 . . . 7	1936 . . 11	1962 . . . 2	1988 . . 13	2014 . . . 4	2040 . . . 8	2066 . . . 6
1833 . . . 3	1859 . . . 7	1885 . . . 5	1911 . . . 1	1937 . . . 6	1963 . . . 3	1989 . . . 1	2015 . . . 5	2041 . . . 3	2067 . . . 7
1834 . . . 4	1860 . . . 8	1886 . . . 6	1912 . . . 9	1938 . . . 7	1964 . . 11	1990 . . . 2	2016 . . 13	2042 . . . 4	2068 . . . 8
1835 . . . 5	1861 . . . 3	1887 . . . 7	1913 . . . 4	1939 . . . 1	1965 . . . 6	1991 . . . 3	2017 . . . 1	2043 . . . 5	2069 . . . 3
1836 . . 13	1862 . . . 4	1888 . . . 8	1914 . . . 5	1940 . . . 9	1966 . . . 7	1992 . . 11	2018 . . . 2	2044 . . 13	2070 . . . 4
1837 . . . 1	1863 . . . 5	1889 . . . 3	1915 . . . 6	1941 . . . 4	1967 . . . 1	1993 . . . 6	2019 . . . 3	2045 . . . 1	2071 . . . 5
1838 . . . 2	1864 . . 13	1890 . . . 4	1916 . . 14	1942 . . . 5	1968 . . . 9	1994 . . . 7	2020 . . 11	2046 . . . 2	2072 . . 13
1839 . . . 3	1865 . . . 1	1891 . . . 5	1917 . . . 2	1943 . . . 6	1969 . . . 4	1995 . . . 1	2021 . . . 6	2047 . . . 3	2073 . . . 1
1840 . . 11	1866 . . . 2	1892 . . 13	1918 . . . 3	1944 . . 14	1970 . . . 5	1996 . . . 9	2022 . . . 7	2048 . . 11	2074 . . . 2
1841 . . . 6	1867 . . . 3	1893 . . . 1	1919 . . . 4	1945 . . . 2	1971 . . . 6	1997 . . . 4	2023 . . . 1	2049 . . . 6	2075 . . . 3
1842 . . . 7	1868 . . 11	1894 . . . 2	1920 . . 12	1946 . . . 3	1972 . . 14	1998 . . . 5	2024 . . . 9	2050 . . . 7	2076 . . 11
1843 . . . 1	1869 . . . 6	1895 . . . 3	1921 . . . 7	1947 . . . 4	1973 . . . 2	1999 . . . 6	2025 . . . 4	2051 . . . 1	2077 . . . 6
1844 . . . 9	1870 . . . 7	1896 . . 11	1922 . . . 1	1948 . . 12	1974 . . . 3	2000 . . 14	2026 . . . 5	2052 . . . 9	2078 . . . 7
1845 . . . 4	1871 . . . 1	1897 . . . 6	1923 . . . 2	1949 . . . 7	1975 . . . 4	2001 . . . 2	2027 . . . 6	2053 . . . 4	2079 . . . 1
1846 . . . 5	1872 . . . 9	1898 . . . 7	1924 . . 10	1950 . . . 1	1976 . . 12	2002 . . . 3	2028 . . 14	2054 . . . 5	2080 . . . 9

1 — 2006/2017

JANUARY
S M T W T F S
1 2 3 4 5 6 7
8 9 10 11 12 13 14
15 16 17 18 19 20 21
22 23 24 25 26 27 28
29 30 31

FEBRUARY
S M T W T F S
1 2 3 4
5 6 7 8 9 10 11
12 13 14 15 16 17 18
19 20 21 22 23 24 25
26 27 28

MARCH
S M T W T F S
1 2 3 4
5 6 7 8 9 10 11
12 13 14 15 16 17 18
19 20 21 22 23 24 25
26 27 28 29 30 31

APRIL
S M T W T F S
1
2 3 4 5 6 7 8
9 10 11 12 13 14 15
16 17 18 19 20 21 22
23 24 25 26 27 28 29
30

MAY
S M T W T F S
1 2 3 4 5 6
7 8 9 10 11 12 13
14 15 16 17 18 19 20
21 22 23 24 25 26 27
28 29 30 31

JUNE
S M T W T F S
1 2 3
4 5 6 7 8 9 10
11 12 13 14 15 16 17
18 19 20 21 22 23 24
25 26 27 28 29 30

JULY
S M T W T F S
1
2 3 4 5 6 7 8
9 10 11 12 13 14 15
16 17 18 19 20 21 22
23 24 25 26 27 28 29
30 31

AUGUST
S M T W T F S
1 2 3 4 5
6 7 8 9 10 11 12
13 14 15 16 17 18 19
20 21 22 23 24 25 26
27 28 29 30 31

SEPTEMBER
S M T W T F S
1 2
3 4 5 6 7 8 9
10 11 12 13 14 15 16
17 18 19 20 21 22 23
24 25 26 27 28 29 30

OCTOBER
S M T W T F S
1 2 3 4 5 6 7
8 9 10 11 12 13 14
15 16 17 18 19 20 21
22 23 24 25 26 27 28
29 30 31

NOVEMBER
S M T W T F S
1 2 3 4
5 6 7 8 9 10 11
12 13 14 15 16 17 18
19 20 21 22 23 24 25
26 27 28 29 30

DECEMBER
S M T W T F S
1 2
3 4 5 6 7 8 9
10 11 12 13 14 15 16
17 18 19 20 21 22 23
24 25 26 27 28 29 30
31

2 — 2007/2018

JANUARY
S M T W T F S
1 2 3 4 5 6
7 8 9 10 11 12 13
14 15 16 17 18 19 20
21 22 23 24 25 26 27
28 29 30 31

FEBRUARY
S M T W T F S
1 2 3
4 5 6 7 8 9 10
11 12 13 14 15 16 17
18 19 20 21 22 23 24
25 26 27 28

MARCH
S M T W T F S
1 2 3
4 5 6 7 8 9 10
11 12 13 14 15 16 17
18 19 20 21 22 23 24
25 26 27 28 29 30 31

APRIL
S M T W T F S
1 2 3 4 5 6 7
8 9 10 11 12 13 14
15 16 17 18 19 20 21
22 23 24 25 26 27 28
29 30

MAY
S M T W T F S
1 2 3 4 5
6 7 8 9 10 11 12
13 14 15 16 17 18 19
20 21 22 23 24 25 26
27 28 29 30 31

JUNE
S M T W T F S
1 2
3 4 5 6 7 8 9
10 11 12 13 14 15 16
17 18 19 20 21 22 23
24 25 26 27 28 29 30

JULY
S M T W T F S
1 2 3 4 5 6 7
8 9 10 11 12 13 14
15 16 17 18 19 20 21
22 23 24 25 26 27 28
29 30 31

AUGUST
S M T W T F S
1 2 3 4
5 6 7 8 9 10 11
12 13 14 15 16 17 18
19 20 21 22 23 24 25
26 27 28 29 30 31

SEPTEMBER
S M T W T F S
1
2 3 4 5 6 7 8
9 10 11 12 13 14 15
16 17 18 19 20 21 22
23 24 25 26 27 28 29
30

OCTOBER
S M T W T F S
1 2 3 4 5 6
7 8 9 10 11 12 13
14 15 16 17 18 19 20
21 22 23 24 25 26 27
28 29 30 31

NOVEMBER
S M T W T F S
1 2 3
4 5 6 7 8 9 10
11 12 13 14 15 16 17
18 19 20 21 22 23 24
25 26 27 28 29 30

DECEMBER
S M T W T F S
1
2 3 4 5 6 7 8
9 10 11 12 13 14 15
16 17 18 19 20 21 22
23 24 25 26 27 28 29
30 31

3 — 2013/2019

JANUARY
S M T W T F S
1 2 3 4 5
6 7 8 9 10 11 12
13 14 15 16 17 18 19
20 21 22 23 24 25 26
27 28 29 30 31

FEBRUARY
S M T W T F S
1 2
3 4 5 6 7 8 9
10 11 12 13 14 15 16
17 18 19 20 21 22 23
24 25 26 27 28

MARCH
S M T W T F S
1 2
3 4 5 6 7 8 9
10 11 12 13 14 15 16
17 18 19 20 21 22 23
24 25 26 27 28 29 30
31

APRIL
S M T W T F S
1 2 3 4 5 6
7 8 9 10 11 12 13
14 15 16 17 18 19 20
21 22 23 24 25 26 27
28 29 30

MAY
S M T W T F S
1 2 3 4
5 6 7 8 9 10 11
12 13 14 15 16 17 18
19 20 21 22 23 24 25
26 27 28 29 30 31

JUNE
S M T W T F S
1
2 3 4 5 6 7 8
9 10 11 12 13 14 15
16 17 18 19 20 21 22
23 24 25 26 27 28 29
30

JULY
S M T W T F S
1 2 3 4 5 6
7 8 9 10 11 12 13
14 15 16 17 18 19 20
21 22 23 24 25 26 27
28 29 30 31

AUGUST
S M T W T F S
1 2 3
4 5 6 7 8 9 10
11 12 13 14 15 16 17
18 19 20 21 22 23 24
25 26 27 28 29 30 31

SEPTEMBER
S M T W T F S
1 2 3 4 5 6 7
8 9 10 11 12 13 14
15 16 17 18 19 20 21
22 23 24 25 26 27 28
29 30

OCTOBER
S M T W T F S
1 2 3 4 5
6 7 8 9 10 11 12
13 14 15 16 17 18 19
20 21 22 23 24 25 26
27 28 29 30 31

NOVEMBER
S M T W T F S
1 2
3 4 5 6 7 8 9
10 11 12 13 14 15 16
17 18 19 20 21 22 23
24 25 26 27 28 29 30

DECEMBER
S M T W T F S
1 2 3 4 5 6 7
8 9 10 11 12 13 14
15 16 17 18 19 20 21
22 23 24 25 26 27 28
29 30 31

4 — 2014/2025

JANUARY
S M T W T F S
1 2 3 4
5 6 7 8 9 10 11
12 13 14 15 16 17 18
19 20 21 22 23 24 25
26 27 28 29 30 31

FEBRUARY
S M T W T F S
1
2 3 4 5 6 7 8
9 10 11 12 13 14 15
16 17 18 19 20 21 22
23 24 25 26 27 28

MARCH
S M T W T F S
1
2 3 4 5 6 7 8
9 10 11 12 13 14 15
16 17 18 19 20 21 22
23 24 25 26 27 28 29
30 31

APRIL
S M T W T F S
1 2 3 4 5
6 7 8 9 10 11 12
13 14 15 16 17 18 19
20 21 22 23 24 25 26
27 28 29 30

MAY
S M T W T F S
1 2 3
4 5 6 7 8 9 10
11 12 13 14 15 16 17
18 19 20 21 22 23 24
25 26 27 28 29 30 31

JUNE
S M T W T F S
1 2 3 4 5 6 7
8 9 10 11 12 13 14
15 16 17 18 19 20 21
22 23 24 25 26 27 28
29 30

JULY
S M T W T F S
1 2 3 4 5
6 7 8 9 10 11 12
13 14 15 16 17 18 19
20 21 22 23 24 25 26
27 28 29 30 31

AUGUST
S M T W T F S
1 2
3 4 5 6 7 8 9
10 11 12 13 14 15 16
17 18 19 20 21 22 23
24 25 26 27 28 29 30
31

SEPTEMBER
S M T W T F S
1 2 3 4 5 6
7 8 9 10 11 12 13
14 15 16 17 18 19 20
21 22 23 24 25 26 27
28 29 30

OCTOBER
S M T W T F S
1 2 3 4
5 6 7 8 9 10 11
12 13 14 15 16 17 18
19 20 21 22 23 24 25
26 27 28 29 30 31

NOVEMBER
S M T W T F S
1
2 3 4 5 6 7 8
9 10 11 12 13 14 15
16 17 18 19 20 21 22
23 24 25 26 27 28 29
30

DECEMBER
S M T W T F S
1 2 3 4 5 6
7 8 9 10 11 12 13
14 15 16 17 18 19 20
21 22 23 24 25 26 27
28 29 30 31

5 — 2009/2015

JANUARY
S M T W T F S
1 2 3
4 5 6 7 8 9 10
11 12 13 14 15 16 17
18 19 20 21 22 23 24
25 26 27 28 29 30 31

FEBRUARY
S M T W T F S
1 2 3 4 5 6 7
8 9 10 11 12 13 14
15 16 17 18 19 20 21
22 23 24 25 26 27 28

MARCH
S M T W T F S
1 2 3 4 5 6 7
8 9 10 11 12 13 14
15 16 17 18 19 20 21
22 23 24 25 26 27 28
29 30 31

APRIL
S M T W T F S
1 2 3 4
5 6 7 8 9 10 11
12 13 14 15 16 17 18
19 20 21 22 23 24 25
26 27 28 29 30

MAY
S M T W T F S
1 2
3 4 5 6 7 8 9
10 11 12 13 14 15 16
17 18 19 20 21 22 23
24 25 26 27 28 29 30
31

JUNE
S M T W T F S
1 2 3 4 5 6
7 8 9 10 11 12 13
14 15 16 17 18 19 20
21 22 23 24 25 26 27
28 29 30

JULY
S M T W T F S
1 2 3 4
5 6 7 8 9 10 11
12 13 14 15 16 17 18
19 20 21 22 23 24 25
26 27 28 29 30 31

AUGUST
S M T W T F S
1
2 3 4 5 6 7 8
9 10 11 12 13 14 15
16 17 18 19 20 21 22
23 24 25 26 27 28 29
30 31

SEPTEMBER
S M T W T F S
1 2 3 4 5
6 7 8 9 10 11 12
13 14 15 16 17 18 19
20 21 22 23 24 25 26
27 28 29 30

OCTOBER
S M T W T F S
1 2 3
4 5 6 7 8 9 10
11 12 13 14 15 16 17
18 19 20 21 22 23 24
25 26 27 28 29 30 31

NOVEMBER
S M T W T F S
1 2 3 4 5 6 7
8 9 10 11 12 13 14
15 16 17 18 19 20 21
22 23 24 25 26 27 28
29 30

DECEMBER
S M T W T F S
1 2 3 4 5
6 7 8 9 10 11 12
13 14 15 16 17 18 19
20 21 22 23 24 25 26
27 28 29 30 31

6 — 2010/2021

JANUARY
S M T W T F S
1 2
3 4 5 6 7 8 9
10 11 12 13 14 15 16
17 18 19 20 21 22 23
24 25 26 27 28 29 30
31

FEBRUARY
S M T W T F S
1 2 3 4 5 6
7 8 9 10 11 12 13
14 15 16 17 18 19 20
21 22 23 24 25 26 27
28

MARCH
S M T W T F S
1 2 3 4 5 6
7 8 9 10 11 12 13
14 15 16 17 18 19 20
21 22 23 24 25 26 27
28 29 30 31

APRIL
S M T W T F S
1 2 3
4 5 6 7 8 9 10
11 12 13 14 15 16 17
18 19 20 21 22 23 24
25 26 27 28 29 30

MAY
S M T W T F S
1
2 3 4 5 6 7 8
9 10 11 12 13 14 15
16 17 18 19 20 21 22
23 24 25 26 27 28 29
30 31

JUNE
S M T W T F S
1 2 3 4 5
6 7 8 9 10 11 12
13 14 15 16 17 18 19
20 21 22 23 24 25 26
27 28 29 30

JULY
S M T W T F S
1 2 3
4 5 6 7 8 9 10
11 12 13 14 15 16 17
18 19 20 21 22 23 24
25 26 27 28 29 30 31

AUGUST
S M T W T F S
1 2 3 4 5 6 7
8 9 10 11 12 13 14
15 16 17 18 19 20 21
22 23 24 25 26 27 28
29 30 31

SEPTEMBER
S M T W T F S
1 2 3 4
5 6 7 8 9 10 11
12 13 14 15 16 17 18
19 20 21 22 23 24 25
26 27 28 29 30

OCTOBER
S M T W T F S
1 2
3 4 5 6 7 8 9
10 11 12 13 14 15 16
17 18 19 20 21 22 23
24 25 26 27 28 29 30
31

NOVEMBER
S M T W T F S
1 2 3 4 5 6
7 8 9 10 11 12 13
14 15 16 17 18 19 20
21 22 23 24 25 26 27
28 29 30

DECEMBER
S M T W T F S
1 2 3 4
5 6 7 8 9 10 11
12 13 14 15 16 17 18
19 20 21 22 23 24 25
26 27 28 29 30 31

7 2011/2022

JANUARY

S	M	T	W	T	F	S
						1
2	3	4	5	6	7	8
9	10	11	12	13	14	15
16	17	18	19	20	21	22
23	24	25	26	27	28	29
30	31					

FEBRUARY

S	M	T	W	T	F	S
		1	2	3	4	5
6	7	8	9	10	11	12
13	14	15	16	17	18	19
20	21	22	23	24	25	26
27	28					

MARCH

S	M	T	W	T	F	S
		1	2	3	4	5
6	7	8	9	10	11	12
13	14	15	16	17	18	19
20	21	22	23	24	25	26
27	28	29	30	31		

APRIL

S	M	T	W	T	F	S
					1	2
3	4	5	6	7	8	9
10	11	12	13	14	15	16
17	18	19	20	21	22	23
24	25	26	27	28	29	30

MAY

S	M	T	W	T	F	S
1	2	3	4	5	6	7
8	9	10	11	12	13	14
15	16	17	18	19	20	21
22	23	24	25	26	27	28
29	30	31				

JUNE

S	M	T	W	T	F	S
			1	2	3	4
5	6	7	8	9	10	11
12	13	14	15	16	17	18
19	20	21	22	23	24	25
26	27	28	29	30		

JULY

S	M	T	W	T	F	S
					1	2
3	4	5	6	7	8	9
10	11	12	13	14	15	16
17	18	19	20	21	22	23
24	25	26	27	28	29	30
31						

AUGUST

S	M	T	W	T	F	S
	1	2	3	4	5	6
7	8	9	10	11	12	13
14	15	16	17	18	19	20
21	22	23	24	25	26	27
28	29	30	31			

SEPTEMBER

S	M	T	W	T	F	S
				1	2	3
4	5	6	7	8	9	10
11	12	13	14	15	16	17
18	19	20	21	22	23	24
25	26	27	28	29	30	

OCTOBER

S	M	T	W	T	F	S
						1
2	3	4	5	6	7	8
9	10	11	12	13	14	15
16	17	18	19	20	21	22
23	24	25	26	27	28	29
30	31					

NOVEMBER

S	M	T	W	T	F	S
		1	2	3	4	5
6	7	8	9	10	11	12
13	14	15	16	17	18	19
20	21	22	23	24	25	26
27	28	29	30			

DECEMBER

S	M	T	W	T	F	S
				1	2	3
4	5	6	7	8	9	10
11	12	13	14	15	16	17
18	19	20	21	22	23	24
25	26	27	28	29	30	31

8 2012/2040

JANUARY

S	M	T	W	T	F	S
1	2	3	4	5	6	7
8	9	10	11	12	13	14
15	16	17	18	19	20	21
22	23	24	25	26	27	28
29	30	31				

FEBRUARY

S	M	T	W	T	F	S
			1	2	3	4
5	6	7	8	9	10	11
12	13	14	15	16	17	18
19	20	21	22	23	24	25
26	27	28	29			

MARCH

S	M	T	W	T	F	S
				1	2	3
4	5	6	7	8	9	10
11	12	13	14	15	16	17
18	19	20	21	22	23	24
25	26	27	28	29	30	31

APRIL

S	M	T	W	T	F	S
1	2	3	4	5	6	7
8	9	10	11	12	13	14
15	16	17	18	19	20	21
22	23	24	25	26	27	28
29	30					

MAY

S	M	T	W	T	F	S
		1	2	3	4	5
6	7	8	9	10	11	12
13	14	15	16	17	18	19
20	21	22	23	24	25	26
27	28	29	30	31		

JUNE

S	M	T	W	T	F	S
					1	2
3	4	5	6	7	8	9
10	11	12	13	14	15	16
17	18	19	20	21	22	23
24	25	26	27	28	29	30

JULY

S	M	T	W	T	F	S
1	2	3	4	5	6	7
8	9	10	11	12	13	14
15	16	17	18	19	20	21
22	23	24	25	26	27	28
29	30	31				

AUGUST

S	M	T	W	T	F	S
			1	2	3	4
5	6	7	8	9	10	11
12	13	14	15	16	17	18
19	20	21	22	23	24	25
26	27	28	29	30	31	

SEPTEMBER

S	M	T	W	T	F	S
						1
2	3	4	5	6	7	8
9	10	11	12	13	14	15
16	17	18	19	20	21	22
23	24	25	26	27	28	29
30						

OCTOBER

S	M	T	W	T	F	S
	1	2	3	4	5	6
7	8	9	10	11	12	13
14	15	16	17	18	19	20
21	22	23	24	25	26	27
28	29	30	31			

NOVEMBER

S	M	T	W	T	F	S
				1	2	3
4	5	6	7	8	9	10
11	12	13	14	15	16	17
18	19	20	21	22	23	24
25	26	27	28	29	30	

DECEMBER

S	M	T	W	T	F	S
						1
2	3	4	5	6	7	8
9	10	11	12	13	14	15
16	17	18	19	20	21	22
23	24	25	26	27	28	29
30	31					

9 1996/2024

JANUARY

S	M	T	W	T	F	S
	1	2	3	4	5	6
7	8	9	10	11	12	13
14	15	16	17	18	19	20
21	22	23	24	25	26	27
28	29	30	31			

FEBRUARY

S	M	T	W	T	F	S
				1	2	3
4	5	6	7	8	9	10
11	12	13	14	15	16	17
18	19	20	21	22	23	24
25	26	27	28	29		

MARCH

S	M	T	W	T	F	S
					1	2
3	4	5	6	7	8	9
10	11	12	13	14	15	16
17	18	19	20	21	22	23
24	25	26	27	28	29	30
31						

APRIL

S	M	T	W	T	F	S
	1	2	3	4	5	6
7	8	9	10	11	12	13
14	15	16	17	18	19	20
21	22	23	24	25	26	27
28	29	30				

MAY

S	M	T	W	T	F	S
			1	2	3	4
5	6	7	8	9	10	11
12	13	14	15	16	17	18
19	20	21	22	23	24	25
26	27	28	29	30	31	

JUNE

S	M	T	W	T	F	S
						1
2	3	4	5	6	7	8
9	10	11	12	13	14	15
16	17	18	19	20	21	22
23	24	25	26	27	28	29
30						

JULY

S	M	T	W	T	F	S
	1	2	3	4	5	6
7	8	9	10	11	12	13
14	15	16	17	18	19	20
21	22	23	24	25	26	27
28	29	30	31			

AUGUST

S	M	T	W	T	F	S
				1	2	3
4	5	6	7	8	9	10
11	12	13	14	15	16	17
18	19	20	21	22	23	24
25	26	27	28	29	30	31

SEPTEMBER

S	M	T	W	T	F	S
1	2	3	4	5	6	7
8	9	10	11	12	13	14
15	16	17	18	19	20	21
22	23	24	25	26	27	28
29	30					

OCTOBER

S	M	T	W	T	F	S
		1	2	3	4	5
6	7	8	9	10	11	12
13	14	15	16	17	18	19
20	21	22	23	24	25	26
27	28	29	30	31		

NOVEMBER

S	M	T	W	T	F	S
					1	2
3	4	5	6	7	8	9
10	11	12	13	14	15	16
17	18	19	20	21	22	23
24	25	26	27	28	29	30

DECEMBER

S	M	T	W	T	F	S
1	2	3	4	5	6	7
8	9	10	11	12	13	14
15	16	17	18	19	20	21
22	23	24	25	26	27	28
29	30	31				

10 2008/2036

JANUARY

S	M	T	W	T	F	S
		1	2	3	4	5
6	7	8	9	10	11	12
13	14	15	16	17	18	19
20	21	22	23	24	25	26
27	28	29	30	31		

FEBRUARY

S	M	T	W	T	F	S
					1	2
3	4	5	6	7	8	9
10	11	12	13	14	15	16
17	18	19	20	21	22	23
24	25	26	27	28	29	

MARCH

S	M	T	W	T	F	S
						1
2	3	4	5	6	7	8
9	10	11	12	13	14	15
16	17	18	19	20	21	22
23	24	25	26	27	28	29
30	31					

APRIL

S	M	T	W	T	F	S
		1	2	3	4	5
6	7	8	9	10	11	12
13	14	15	16	17	18	19
20	21	22	23	24	25	26
27	28	29	30			

MAY

S	M	T	W	T	F	S
				1	2	3
4	5	6	7	8	9	10
11	12	13	14	15	16	17
18	19	20	21	22	23	24
25	26	27	28	29	30	31

JUNE

S	M	T	W	T	F	S
1	2	3	4	5	6	7
8	9	10	11	12	13	14
15	16	17	18	19	20	21
22	23	24	25	26	27	28
29	30					

JULY

S	M	T	W	T	F	S
		1	2	3	4	5
6	7	8	9	10	11	12
13	14	15	16	17	18	19
20	21	22	23	24	25	26
27	28	29	30	31		

AUGUST

S	M	T	W	T	F	S
					1	2
3	4	5	6	7	8	9
10	11	12	13	14	15	16
17	18	19	20	21	22	23
24	25	26	27	28	29	30
31						

SEPTEMBER

S	M	T	W	T	F	S
	1	2	3	4	5	6
7	8	9	10	11	12	13
14	15	16	17	18	19	20
21	22	23	24	25	26	27
28	29	30				

OCTOBER

S	M	T	W	T	F	S
			1	2	3	4
5	6	7	8	9	10	11
12	13	14	15	16	17	18
19	20	21	22	23	24	25
26	27	28	29	30	31	

NOVEMBER

S	M	T	W	T	F	S
						1
2	3	4	5	6	7	8
9	10	11	12	13	14	15
16	17	18	19	20	21	22
23	24	25	26	27	28	29
30						

DECEMBER

S	M	T	W	T	F	S
	1	2	3	4	5	6
7	8	9	10	11	12	13
14	15	16	17	18	19	20
21	22	23	24	25	26	27
28	29	30	31			

11 1992/2020

JANUARY

S	M	T	W	T	F	S
			1	2	3	4
5	6	7	8	9	10	11
12	13	14	15	16	17	18
19	20	21	22	23	24	25
26	27	28	29	30	31	

FEBRUARY

S	M	T	W	T	F	S
						1
2	3	4	5	6	7	8
9	10	11	12	13	14	15
16	17	18	19	20	21	22
23	24	25	26	27	28	29

MARCH

S	M	T	W	T	F	S
1	2	3	4	5	6	7
8	9	10	11	12	13	14
15	16	17	18	19	20	21
22	23	24	25	26	27	28
29	30	31				

APRIL

S	M	T	W	T	F	S
			1	2	3	4
5	6	7	8	9	10	11
12	13	14	15	16	17	18
19	20	21	22	23	24	25
26	27	28	29	30		

MAY

S	M	T	W	T	F	S
					1	2
3	4	5	6	7	8	9
10	11	12	13	14	15	16
17	18	19	20	21	22	23
24	25	26	27	28	29	30
31						

JUNE

S	M	T	W	T	F	S
	1	2	3	4	5	6
7	8	9	10	11	12	13
14	15	16	17	18	19	20
21	22	23	24	25	26	27
28	29	30				

JULY

S	M	T	W	T	F	S
			1	2	3	4
5	6	7	8	9	10	11
12	13	14	15	16	17	18
19	20	21	22	23	24	25
26	27	28	29	30	31	

AUGUST

S	M	T	W	T	F	S
						1
2	3	4	5	6	7	8
9	10	11	12	13	14	15
16	17	18	19	20	21	22
23	24	25	26	27	28	29
30	31					

SEPTEMBER

S	M	T	W	T	F	S
		1	2	3	4	5
6	7	8	9	10	11	12
13	14	15	16	17	18	19
20	21	22	23	24	25	26
27	28	29	30			

OCTOBER

S	M	T	W	T	F	S
				1	2	3
4	5	6	7	8	9	10
11	12	13	14	15	16	17
18	19	20	21	22	23	24
25	26	27	28	29	30	31

NOVEMBER

S	M	T	W	T	F	S
1	2	3	4	5	6	7
8	9	10	11	12	13	14
15	16	17	18	19	20	21
22	23	24	25	26	27	28
29	30					

DECEMBER

S	M	T	W	T	F	S
		1	2	3	4	5
6	7	8	9	10	11	12
13	14	15	16	17	18	19
20	21	22	23	24	25	26
27	28	29	30	31		

12 2004/2032

JANUARY

S	M	T	W	T	F	S
				1	2	3
4	5	6	7	8	9	10
11	12	13	14	15	16	17
18	19	20	21	22	23	24
25	26	27	28	29	30	31

FEBRUARY

S	M	T	W	T	F	S
1	2	3	4	5	6	7
8	9	10	11	12	13	14
15	16	17	18	19	20	21
22	23	24	25	26	27	28
29						

MARCH

S	M	T	W	T	F	S
	1	2	3	4	5	6
7	8	9	10	11	12	13
14	15	16	17	18	19	20
21	22	23	24	25	26	27
28	29	30	31			

APRIL

S	M	T	W	T	F	S
				1	2	3
4	5	6	7	8	9	10
11	12	13	14	15	16	17
18	19	20	21	22	23	24
25	26	27	28	29	30	

MAY

S	M	T	W	T	F	S
						1
2	3	4	5	6	7	8
9	10	11	12	13	14	15
16	17	18	19	20	21	22
23	24	25	26	27	28	29
30	31					

JUNE

S	M	T	W	T	F	S
		1	2	3	4	5
6	7	8	9	10	11	12
13	14	15	16	17	18	19
20	21	22	23	24	25	26
27	28	29	30			

JULY

S	M	T	W	T	F	S
				1	2	3
4	5	6	7	8	9	10
11	12	13	14	15	16	17
18	19	20	21	22	23	24
25	26	27	28	29	30	31

AUGUST

S	M	T	W	T	F	S
1	2	3	4	5	6	7
8	9	10	11	12	13	14
15	16	17	18	19	20	21
22	23	24	25	26	27	28
29	30	31				

SEPTEMBER

S	M	T	W	T	F	S
			1	2	3	4
5	6	7	8	9	10	11
12	13	14	15	16	17	18
19	20	21	22	23	24	25
26	27	28	29	30		

OCTOBER

S	M	T	W	T	F	S
					1	2
3	4	5	6	7	8	9
10	11	12	13	14	15	16
17	18	19	20	21	22	23
24	25	26	27	28	29	30
31						

NOVEMBER

S	M	T	W	T	F	S
	1	2	3	4	5	6
7	8	9	10	11	12	13
14	15	16	17	18	19	20
21	22	23	24	25	26	27
28	29	30				

DECEMBER

S	M	T	W	T	F	S
			1	2	3	4
5	6	7	8	9	10	11
12	13	14	15	16	17	18
19	20	21	22	23	24	25
26	27	28	29	30	31	

13 2016/2044

JANUARY

S	M	T	W	T	F	S
					1	2
3	4	5	6	7	8	9
10	11	12	13	14	15	16
17	18	19	20	21	22	23
24	25	26	27	28	29	30
31						

FEBRUARY

S	M	T	W	T	F	S
	1	2	3	4	5	6
7	8	9	10	11	12	13
14	15	16	17	18	19	20
21	22	23	24	25	26	27
28	29					

MARCH

S	M	T	W	T	F	S
		1	2	3	4	5
6	7	8	9	10	11	12
13	14	15	16	17	18	19
20	21	22	23	24	25	26
27	28	29	30	31		

APRIL

S	M	T	W	T	F	S
					1	2
3	4	5	6	7	8	9
10	11	12	13	14	15	16
17	18	19	20	21	22	23
24	25	26	27	28	29	30

MAY

S	M	T	W	T	F	S
1	2	3	4	5	6	7
8	9	10	11	12	13	14
15	16	17	18	19	20	21
22	23	24	25	26	27	28
29	30	31				

JUNE

S	M	T	W	T	F	S
			1	2	3	4
5	6	7	8	9	10	11
12	13	14	15	16	17	18
19	20	21	22	23	24	25
26	27	28	29	30		

JULY

S	M	T	W	T	F	S
					1	2
3	4	5	6	7	8	9
10	11	12	13	14	15	16
17	18	19	20	21	22	23
24	25	26	27	28	29	30
31						

AUGUST

S	M	T	W	T	F	S
	1	2	3	4	5	6
7	8	9	10	11	12	13
14	15	16	17	18	19	20
21	22	23	24	25	26	27
28	29	30	31			

SEPTEMBER

S	M	T	W	T	F	S
				1	2	3
4	5	6	7	8	9	10
11	12	13	14	15	16	17
18	19	20	21	22	23	24
25	26	27	28	29	30	

OCTOBER

S	M	T	W	T	F	S
						1
2	3	4	5	6	7	8
9	10	11	12	13	14	15
16	17	18	19	20	21	22
23	24	25	26	27	28	29
30	31					

NOVEMBER

S	M	T	W	T	F	S
		1	2	3	4	5
6	7	8	9	10	11	12
13	14	15	16	17	18	19
20	21	22	23	24	25	26
27	28	29	30			

DECEMBER

S	M	T	W	T	F	S
				1	2	3
4	5	6	7	8	9	10
11	12	13	14	15	16	17
18	19	20	21	22	23	24
25	26	27	28	29	30	31

14 2000/2028

JANUARY

S	M	T	W	T	F	S
						1
2	3	4	5	6	7	8
9	10	11	12	13	14	15
16	17	18	19	20	21	22
23	24	25	26	27	28	29
30	31					

FEBRUARY

S	M	T	W	T	F	S
		1	2	3	4	5
6	7	8	9	10	11	12
13	14	15	16	17	18	19
20	21	22	23	24	25	26
27	28	29				

MARCH

S	M	T	W	T	F	S
			1	2	3	4
5	6	7	8	9	10	11
12	13	14	15	16	17	18
19	20	21	22	23	24	25
26	27	28	29	30	31	

APRIL

S	M	T	W	T	F	S
						1
2	3	4	5	6	7	8
9	10	11	12	13	14	15
16	17	18	19	20	21	22
23	24	25	26	27	28	29
30						

MAY

S	M	T	W	T	F	S
	1	2	3	4	5	6
7	8	9	10	11	12	13
14	15	16	17	18	19	20
21	22	23	24	25	26	27
28	29	30	31			

JUNE

S	M	T	W	T	F	S
				1	2	3
4	5	6	7	8	9	10
11	12	13	14	15	16	17
18	19	20	21	22	23	24
25	26	27	28	29	30	

JULY

S	M	T	W	T	F	S
						1
2	3	4	5	6	7	8
9	10	11	12	13	14	15
16	17	18	19	20	21	22
23	24	25	26	27	28	29
30	31					

AUGUST

S	M	T	W	T	F	S
		1	2	3	4	5
6	7	8	9	10	11	12
13	14	15	16	17	18	19
20	21	22	23	24	25	26
27	28	29	30	31		

SEPTEMBER

S	M	T	W	T	F	S
					1	2
3	4	5	6	7	8	9
10	11	12	13	14	15	16
17	18	19	20	21	22	23
24	25	26	27	28	29	30

OCTOBER

S	M	T	W	T	F	S
1	2	3	4	5	6	7
8	9	10	11	12	13	14
15	16	17	18	19	20	21
22	23	24	25	26	27	28
29	30	31				

NOVEMBER

S	M	T	W	T	F	S
			1	2	3	4
5	6	7	8	9	10	11
12	13	14	15	16	17	18
19	20	21	22	23	24	25
26	27	28	29	30		

DECEMBER

S	M	T	W	T	F	S
					1	2
3	4	5	6	7	8	9
10	11	12	13	14	15	16
17	18	19	20	21	22	23
24	25	26	27	28	29	30
31						

Other Calendars: Year and New Year's Day, 2017

Era	Year	Begins in 2017	Era	Year	Begins in 2017
Byzantine	7526	Sept. 14	Islamic/Muslim (Hijra)	1439	Sept. 21[1]
Chinese (Year of the Monkey)	4715	Jan. 28	Japanese[2]	29	Jan. 1
Diocletian	1734	Sept. 11	Jewish	5778	Sept. 21[1]
Grecian (Seleucidae)	2329	Sept. 14 or Oct. 14	Nabonassar (Babylonian)	2766	Apr. 19
Indian (Saka)	1939	Mar. 22	Roman (Ab Urbe Condita)	2770	Jan. 14

(1) Year begins the previous night. (2) Era starts at 0 with new emperor.

Chronological Cycles, 2017

Dominical Letter	A	Roman Indiction	10	Solar Cycle	10
Golden Number (lunar cycle)	IV	Epact	2	Julian Period (year of)	6730

Special Months

There are many thousands of special months, days, and weeks because of anniversaries, official proclamations, and promotional events, both trivial and serious. Here are a few of the special months:

January: Get Organized Month, National Mentoring Month, National Poverty in America Awareness Month

February: African American History Month, American Heart Month, Library Lovers' Month, Youth Leadership Month, Return Shopping Carts to the Supermarket Month

March: Irish-American Heritage Month, National Women's History Month, Red Cross Month, National Frozen Food Month, National Talk With Your Teen About Sex Month, National Colorectal Cancer Awareness Month

April: National Child Abuse Prevention Month, National Humor Month, Stress Awareness Month, Grange Month

May: Clean Air Month, Get Caught Reading Month, National Barbecue Month, Asian American and Pacific Islander Heritage Month, National Inventors Month, National Mental Health Awareness Month

June: National Candy Month; Great Outdoors Month; Lesbian, Gay, Bisexual, and Transgender Pride Month; National Safety Month

July: Cell Phone Courtesy Month, National Hot Dog Month, National Make a Difference to Children Month, Women's Motorcycle Month

August: National Black Business Month, Happiness Happens Month, National Immunization Awareness Month, National Toddler Month

September: Library Card Sign-Up Month, National Hispanic Heritage Month (Sept. 15-Oct. 15), National Biscuit Month

October: National Domestic Violence Awareness Month, National Breast Cancer Awareness Month, Diversity Awareness Month, National Popcorn Poppin' Month

November: National American Indian Heritage Month, National Adoption Month, American Diabetes Month, National Peanut Butter Lovers' Month

December: Safe Toys and Gifts Month, National Impaired Driving Prevention Month, National Tie Month

Standard Time Differences: World Cities

The time indicated in the table is fixed by law and is called the legal time or, more generally, standard time. Use of daylight-saving time varies widely. An asterisk (*) indicates morning of the following day. At 12:00 noon, Eastern Standard Time, the standard time (in 24-hour time) in selected cities is as shown.

City	Time		City	Time		City	Time		City	Time	
Abu Dhabi	21	00	Denver	10	00	Lisbon	17	00	St. Petersburg	20	00
Addis Ababa	20	00	Dhaka	23	00	London	17	00	Santiago	13	00
Amsterdam	18	00	Dublin	17	00	Los Angeles	9	00	São Paulo	14	00
Ankara	19	00	Edinburgh	17	00	Madrid	18	00	Sarajevo	18	00
Athens	19	00	Geneva	18	00	Manila	1	00*	Seoul	2	00*
Auckland	5	00*	Helsinki	19	00	Mecca	20	00	Shanghai	1	00*
Baghdad	20	00	Ho Chi Minh City	0	00*	Melbourne	3	00*	Singapore	1	00*
Bangkok	0	00*	Hong Kong	1	00*	Montevideo	14	00	Stockholm	18	00
Beijing	1	00*	Honolulu	7	00	Moscow	20	00	Sydney	3	00*
Belfast	17	00	Houston	11	00	Mumbai (Bombay)	22	30	Taipei	1	00*
Belgrade	18	00	Islamabad	22	00	Munich	18	00	Tashkent	22	00
Berlin	18	00	Istanbul	19	00	Nagasaki	2	00*	Tehran	20	30
Bogotá	12	00	Jakarta	0	00*	Nairobi	20	00	Tel Aviv	19	00
Brussels	18	00	Jerusalem	19	00	New Delhi	22	30	Tokyo	2	00*
Bucharest	19	00	Johannesburg	19	00	New York	12	00	Toronto	12	00
Budapest	18	00	Kabul	21	30	Oslo	18	00	Vancouver	9	00
Buenos Aires	14	00	Karachi	22	00	Paris	18	00	Vienna	18	00
Cairo	19	00	Kathmandu	22	45	Prague	18	00	Vladivostok	3	00*
Cape Town	19	00	Kiev	19	00	Pyongyang	1	30*	Warsaw	18	00
Caracas	1	00	Kinshasa	18	00	Quito	12	00	Wellington	5	00*
Casablanca	17	00	Kolkata (Calcutta)	22	30	Rio de Janeiro	14	00	Yangon (Rangoon)	23	30
Chicago	11	00	Lagos	18	00	Riyadh	20	00	Yokohama	2	00*
Copenhagen	18	00	Lima	12	00	Rome	18	00	Zurich	18	00

Wedding Anniversary Gifts

The traditional names for wedding anniversaries go back many years in social usage and have been used to suggest types of appropriate anniversary gifts. Traditional products for gifts are listed here in capital letters, with allowable revisions in parentheses, followed by common modern gifts for each anniversary.

Anniversary	Gift	Anniversary	Gift	Anniversary	Gift
1st	PAPER, clocks	9th	POTTERY (CHINA), leather goods	25th	SILVER, sterling silver
2nd	COTTON, china	10th	TIN, ALUMINUM, diamond	30th	PEARL, diamond
3rd	LEATHER, crystal, glass	11th	STEEL, fashion jewelry	35th	CORAL (JADE), jade
4th	LINEN (SILK), appliances	12th	SILK, pearls, colored gems	40th	RUBY, ruby
5th	WOOD, silverware	13th	LACE, textiles, furs	45th	SAPPHIRE, sapphire
6th	IRON, wood objects	14th	IVORY, gold jewelry	50th	GOLD, gold
7th	WOOL (COPPER), desk sets	15th	CRYSTAL, watches	55th	EMERALD, emerald
8th	BRONZE, linens, lace	20th	CHINA, platinum	60th	DIAMOND, diamond

Birthstones

Source: American Gem Society

Birth month	Ancient[1] birthstone	Modern birthstone	Birth month	Ancient[1] birthstone	Modern birthstone
January	Garnet	Garnet	July	Onyx	Ruby
February	Amethyst	Amethyst	August	Carnelian	Sardonyx or Peridot
March	Jasper	Bloodstone or Aquamarine	September	Chrysolite	Sapphire
April	Sapphire	Diamond	October	Aquamarine	Opal or Tourmaline
May	Chalcedony, Carnelian, or Agate	Emerald	November	Topaz	Topaz
June	Emerald	Pearl, Moonstone, or Alexandrite	December	Ruby	Turquoise, Tanzanite, or Zircon

(1) Varied by region and culture. Birthstones listed here are those of ancient Hebrew tradition.

Standard Time and Daylight-Saving Time

Source: National Institute of Standards and Technology, U.S. Dept. of Commerce

See also Time Zone map, page 476.

Standard Time

Standard time is reckoned from the prime meridian of longitude in Greenwich, England. The world is divided into 24 zones, each 15 deg of arc, or one hour in time apart. The Greenwich meridian (0 deg) extends through the center of the initial zone. Zones to the east are numbered from 1 to 12, with the prefix "minus" indicating the number of hours to be subtracted to obtain Greenwich Time. Each zone extends 7.5 deg on either side of its central meridian.

Westward zones are similarly numbered, but prefixed "plus," showing the number of hours that must be added to get Greenwich Time. Although these zones apply generally to ocean areas, the standard time maintained in many countries does not coincide with zone time.

The U.S. and possessions are divided into nine standard time zones. All places in each zone use, instead of their local time, the time counted from the transit of the mean sun across the standard time meridian that passes near the middle of that zone. These time zones are designated as Atlantic, Eastern, Central, Mountain, Pacific, Alaska, Hawaii-Aleutian, Samoa, and Chamorro (Guam and Northern Mariana Isls.); the time in these zones is reckoned from the 60th, 75th, 90th, 105th, 120th, 135th, 150th, and 165th meridians west of Greenwich and the 150th meridian east of Greenwich. The time zone line wanders to conform to local geography. The time in the various zones in the U.S. and U.S. territories west of Greenwich is earlier than Greenwich Time by 4, 5, 6, 7, 8, 9, 10, and 11 hours, respectively. However, Chamorro crosses the international date line and is 10 hours later than Greenwich Time.

24-Hour Time

With the 24-hour system, the day begins at midnight, and times are designated 00:00 through 23:59. Twenty-four-hour time is widely used in scientific work throughout the world. In the U.S., it is also used in operations of the armed forces. In Europe, it is frequently used by the transportation networks in preference to the 12-hour AM and PM system.

International Date Line

The date line, approximately coinciding with the 180th meridian, separates the calendar dates. The date must be advanced one day when crossing in a westerly direction and set back one day when crossing in an easterly direction. The date line frequently deviates from the 180th meridian because of decisions made by individual nations affected. The line is deflected eastward through the Bering Strait and westward of the Aleutians to prevent separating these areas by date. The line is deflected eastward of the Tonga and New Zealand islands in the South Pacific. In 1995, Kiribati announced that all of its islands east of the date line would observe the same date as islands to the west, though most maps and atlases do not depict this as a deviation in the date line. The line is established by international custom; there is no international authority prescribing its exact course.

Daylight-Saving Time

Daylight-saving time is achieved by advancing the clock one hour. Since 2007, daylight-saving time has begun at 2 AM on the second Sunday in Mar. and has ended at 2 AM on the first Sunday in Nov. **In 2017, daylight-saving time begins at 2 AM on Mar. 12 and ends at 2 AM on Nov. 5.** Prior to 2007, daylight-saving time traditionally ran from the first Sunday in Apr. to the last Sunday in Oct.

Daylight-saving time was first observed in the U.S. during World War I and again during World War II. In the intervening years, some states and communities observed daylight-saving time, using whatever beginning and ending dates they chose. In 1966, Congress passed the Uniform Time Act, which provided that any state or territory choosing to observe daylight-saving time must begin and end on the dates established by federal law. Any state could, by law, exempt itself; a 1972 amendment to the act authorized states in more than one time zone to exempt the entire state or one time zone only. Currently, most of Arizona, Hawaii, Puerto Rico, the U.S. Virgin Islands, Guam, American Samoa, and Northern Mariana Isls. do not observe daylight-saving time. All of Indiana, which is in two time zones, observed daylight-saving time for the first time in 2006.

Congress and the secretary of transportation both have authority to change time zone boundaries, which they have done on a number of occasions since 1966. In addition, efforts to conserve energy have prompted various changes in the times that daylight-saving time is observed.

Daylight-Saving Time: International Usage

Adjusting clock time so as to gain daylight on summer evenings is common throughout the world.

Canada, which extends over six time zones, generally observes daylight-saving time during the same period as the U.S. Most provincial governments observe the four-week extension to daylight-saving time that went into effect in 2007. Most of Saskatchewan remains on standard time year-round; communities elsewhere in Canada may also exempt themselves from daylight-saving time. Except for the state of Sonora, which shares a border with Arizona, most of Mexico observes daylight-saving time.

Member nations of the European Union observe a "summer-time period," a version of daylight-saving time, from the last Sunday of Mar. until the last Sunday in Oct.

Russia, which uses 11 time zones, moved to permanent standard time in Oct. 2014 after a three-year experiment to maintain year-round "summer hours" proved unpopular. From Oct. 2014 on, the country observed "winter hours" year-round.

China, which extends across five time zones, has decreed that the entire country be placed on Greenwich time plus 8 hours. Daylight-saving time is not observed. Japan, which lies within one time zone, also does not modify its legal time during the summer months.

Many countries in the Southern Hemisphere maintain daylight-saving time generally from Oct. to Mar. However, most countries near the equator do not deviate from standard time.

WEIGHTS AND MEASURES

Source: National Institute of Standards and Technology (NIST), U.S. Dept. of Commerce

International System of Units (SI)

Two systems of weights and measures coexist in the U.S. today: the **U.S. Customary System** and the **International System of Units** (SI, for Système International d'Unités). The SI is a more complete, coherent version of the **metric system**. Throughout U.S. history, the customary system—parts of which were inherited but are now different from the British Imperial System—has been generally used. Federal and state legislation gave it, through implication, standing as the primary weights and measures system. The metric system, however, is the only system that Congress has ever specifically sanctioned, dating back to an 1866 law. The U.S. was one of the original 17 countries to sign the International Metric Convention (or Treaty of the Meter) May 20, 1875, which established several intergovernmental organizations to oversee and refine the SI. The U.S. is represented at these organizations by the Natl. Institute of Standards and Technology (NIST).

Since that time, use of the metric system in the U.S. has slowly increased, particularly in the scientific community, the pharmaceutical industry, and the manufacturing sector—the last motivated by the predominant use of the metric system in international commerce.

On Dec. 23, 1975, Pres. Gerald R. Ford signed the Metric Conversion Act of 1975. It defined the "metric system of measurement" as the SI, as established in 1960 by the General Conference on Weights and Measures and interpreted in the U.S. by the secretary of commerce, who delegated that authority to the director of the NIST. The Trade and Competitiveness Act of 1988 declared the metric system the preferred system of weights and measures for U.S. trade and commerce, but explicitly permitted "the continued use of traditional systems of weights and measures in nonbusiness activities." The Code of Federal Regulations made the use of metric units mandatory for federal agencies in 1991. However, the metric system has still not become the system of choice for most Americans' daily use.

The following are the seven base SI units: **length**—meter; **mass**—kilogram; **time**—second; **electric current**—ampere; **thermodynamic temperature**—kelvin; **amount of substance**—mole; and **luminous intensity**—candela.

Frequently Used Conversions

Boldface indicates exact values. For greater accuracy, use the "multiply by" number in parentheses. For weights, avoirdupois (avdp) weight is the system applied to all goods except medicines, precious metals, and precious stones.

U.S. Customary to Metric

	If you have:	Multiply by:		To get:
Length	inches	**25.4**		millimeters
	inches	**2.54**		centimeters
	inches	**0.0254**		meters
	feet	0.3	**(0.3048)**	meters
	yards	0.9	**(0.9144)**	meters
	miles[1]	1.6	**(1.609344)**	kilometers
Area	sq inches	6.5	**(6.4516)**	sq cm
	sq feet	0.09	**(0.09290304)**	sq meters
	sq yards	0.84	**(0.83612736)**	sq meters
	acres	0.4	(0.4046873)	hectares
	sq miles[1]	2.6	(2.58998811)	sq kilometers
Weight	ounces (avdp)	28	(28.34952)	grams
	pounds (avdp)	454	**(453.59237)**	grams
	pounds (avdp)	0.45	**(0.45359237)**	kilograms
	short tons[2]	0.91	**(0.90718474)**	metric tons
	long tons[3]	1	(1.016047)	metric tons
Liquid	ounces	0.03	(0.02957353)	liters
	cups	0.24	(0.23658824)	liters
	pints	0.47	(0.473176473)	liters
	quarts	0.95	(0.946352946)	liters
	gallons	3.79	(3.785412)	liters

Metric to U.S. Customary

	If you have:	Multiply by:		To get:
Length	millimeters	0.04	(0.03937)	inches
	centimeters	0.4	(0.3937)	inches
	meters	39	(39.37)	inches
	meters	3.3	(3.280840)	feet
	meters	1.1	(1.093613)	yards
	kilometers	0.6	(0.621371)	miles[1]
Area	sq cm	0.16	(0.15500)	sq inches
	sq meters	10.8	(10.76391)	sq feet
	sq meters	1.2	(1.195990)	sq yards
	hectares	2.5	(2.471044)	acres
	sq kilometers	0.39	(0.386102)	sq miles[1]
Weight	grams	0.035	(0.03527396)	ounces (avdp)
	grams	0.002	(0.00220462)	pounds (avdp)
	kilograms	2.2	(2.204623)	pounds (avdp)
	metric tons	1.1	(1.102311)	short tons[2]
	metric tons	0.98	(0.9842065)	long tons[3]
Liquid	liters	33.8	(33.81402)	ounces
	liters	4.2	(4.226752)	cups
	liters	2.1	(2.113376)	pints
	liters	1.1	(1.056688)	quarts
	liters	0.26	(0.264172)	gallons

(1) Survey mile. (2) A short ton is 2,000 pounds. (3) A long ton is 2,240 pounds.

Temperature Conversions

The left-hand column below gives a temperature according to the **Celsius** scale, and the right-hand gives the same temperature according to the **Fahrenheit** scale. The lowest number on each scale is equivalent to absolute zero, the theoretical temperature at which all molecular motion would stop.

For temperatures not shown: To convert Fahrenheit to Celsius, subtract 32 degrees and divide by 1.8; to convert Celsius to Fahrenheit, multiply by 1.8 and add 32 degrees.

Celsius	Fahrenheit	Celsius	Fahrenheit	Celsius	Fahrenheit	Celsius	Fahrenheit	Celsius	Fahrenheit
−273.15	−459.67	−45.6	−50	−1.1	30	30	86	65.6	150
−250	−418	**−40**	**−40**	**0**	**32**	32.2	90	70	158
−200	−328	−34.4	−30	4.4	40	35	95	80	176
−184.4	−300	−30	−22	10	50	**37**	**98.6**	90	194
−156.7	−250	−28.9	−20	15.6	60	37.8	100	93.3	200
−150	−238	−23.3	−10	**20**	**68**	40	104	**100**	**212**
−128.9	−200	−20	−4	21.1	70	43.3	110	121.1	250
−101.1	−150	−17.8	0	23.9	75	48.9	120	148.9	300
−100	−148	−12.2	10	25	77	50	122	150	302
−73.3	−100	−10	14	26.7	80	54.4	130	200	392
−50	−58	−6.7	20	29.4	85	60	140	300	572

Note: Although the term *centigrade* is still frequently used, the International Committee on Weights and Measures and the National Institute of Standards and Technology have recommended since 1948 that this scale be called *Celsius*.

Boiling and Freezing Points

Water boils at 212°F (100°C) at sea level. For every 550 feet above sea level, the boiling point of water is lower by about 1°F. Methyl alcohol boils at 148.5°F. Average human oral temperature is 98.6°F. **Water freezes** at 32°F (0°C).

Mathematical Formulas

The value of π (the Greek letter pi) is approximately 3.14159265 (equal to the ratio of the circumference of a circle to its diameter). The equivalence is typically rounded further to 3.1416 or 3.14.

Calculating Circumference

Circle: Multiply the diameter by π.

Calculating Area

Circle: Multiply the square of the radius (equal to ½ the diameter) by π.
Rectangle: Multiply the length of the base by the height.
Sphere (surface): Multiply the square of the radius by π and multiply by 4.
Square: Square the length of one side.
Trapezoid: Add the length of the two parallel sides, multiply by the height, and divide by 2.
Triangle: Multiply the base by the height and divide by 2.

Calculating Volume

Cone: Multiply the square of the radius of the base by π, multiply by the height, and divide by 3.
Cube: Cube the length of one edge.
Cylinder: Multiply the square of the radius of the base by π and multiply by the height.
Pyramid: Multiply the area of the base by the height and divide by 3.
Rectangular prism: Multiply the length by the width by the height.
Sphere: Multiply the cube of the radius by π, multiply by 4, and divide by 3.

Playing Cards and Dice Chances

5-Card Poker Hands

Hand	Number possible	Odds against
Royal flush	4	649,739 to 1
Other straight flush	36	72,192 to 1
Four of a kind	624	4,164 to 1
Full house	3,744	693 to 1
Flush	5,108	508 to 1
Straight	10,200	254 to 1
Three of a kind	54,912	46 to 1
Two pairs	123,552	20 to 1
One pair	1,098,240	4 to 3 (1.37 to 1)
Nothing	1,302,540	1 to 1
Total	**2,598,960**	

Bridge

The odds—against suit distribution in a hand of 4-4-3-2 are about 4 to 1; against 5-4-2-2 about 8 to 1; against 6-4-2-1 about 20 to 1; against 7-4-1-1 about 254 to 1; against 8-4-1-0 about 2,211 to 1; and against 13-0-0-0 about 158,753,389,899 to 1.

Dice
(probabilities on 2 dice)

Total	Odds against (single toss)	Total	Odds against (single toss)
2	35 to 1	8	31 to 5
3	17 to 1	9	8 to 1
4	11 to 1	10	11 to 1
5	8 to 1	11	17 to 1
6	31 to 5	12	35 to 1
7	5 to 1		

Large Numbers

No. of zeros	U.S. term	British[1], French, German	No. of zeros	U.S. term	British[1], French, German
6	million	million	42	tredecillion	septillion
9	billion	milliard	45	quattuordecillion	1,000 septillion
12	trillion	billion	48	quindecillion	octillion
15	quadrillion	1,000 billion	51	sexdecillion	1,000 octillion
18	quintillion	trillion	54	septendecillion	nonillion
21	sextillion	1,000 trillion	57	octodecillion	1,000 nonillion
24	septillion	quadrillion	60	novemdecillion	decillion
27	octillion	1,000 quadrillion	63	vigintillion	1,000 decillion
30	nonillion	quintillion	100	googol	googol
33	decillion	1,000 quintillion	303	centillion	NA
36	undecillion	sextillion	600	NA	centillion
39	duodecillion	1,000 sextillion	googol	googolplex	googolplex

NA = Not available. (1) In recent years, it has become more common in Britain to use U.S. terminology for large numbers.

Prime Numbers to 1,009

A prime number is any positive integer greater than 1 that is divisible only by two positive integers—1 and itself.

	2	3	5	7	11	13	17	19	23
29	31	37	41	43	47	53	59	61	67
71	73	79	83	89	97	101	103	107	109
113	127	131	137	139	149	151	157	163	167
173	179	181	191	193	197	199	211	223	227
229	233	239	241	251	257	263	269	271	277
281	283	293	307	311	313	317	331	337	347
349	353	359	367	373	379	383	389	397	401
409	419	421	431	433	439	443	449	457	461
463	467	479	487	491	499	503	509	521	523
541	547	557	563	569	571	577	587	593	599
601	607	613	617	619	631	641	643	647	653
659	661	673	677	683	691	701	709	719	727
733	739	743	751	757	761	769	773	787	797
809	811	821	823	827	829	839	853	857	859
863	877	881	883	887	907	911	919	929	937
941	947	953	967	971	977	983	991	997	1,009

Common Fractions Converted to Decimals

8ths	16ths	32nds	64ths	Decimal
			1	= 0.015625
	1		2	= 0.03125
			3	= 0.046875
	1	2	4	= 0.0625
			5	= 0.078125
		3	6	= 0.09375
			7	= 0.109375
1	2	4	8	= 0.125
			9	= 0.140625
		5	10	= 0.15625
			11	= 0.171875
	3	6	12	= 0.1875
			13	= 0.203125
		7	14	= 0.21875
			15	= 0.234375
2	4	8	16	= 0.25

8ths	16ths	32nds	64ths	Decimal
			17	= 0.265625
	9		18	= 0.28125
			19	= 0.296875
5	10	20		= 0.3125
			21	= 0.328125
		11	22	= 0.34375
			23	= 0.359375
3	6	12	24	= 0.375
			25	= 0.390625
	13	26		= 0.40625
			27	= 0.421875
	7	14	28	= 0.4375
			29	= 0.453125
		15	30	= 0.46875
			31	= 0.484375
4	8	16	32	= 0.5

8ths	16ths	32nds	64ths	Decimal
			33	= 0.515625
	17		34	= 0.53125
			35	= 0.546875
9	18		36	= 0.5625
			37	= 0.578125
		19	38	= 0.59375
			39	= 0.609375
5	10	20	40	= 0.625
			41	= 0.640625
		21	42	= 0.65625
			43	= 0.671875
	11	22	44	= 0.6875
			45	= 0.703125
		23	46	= 0.71875
			47	= 0.734375
6	12	24	48	= 0.75

8ths	16ths	32nds	64ths	Decimal
			49	= 0.765625
	25		50	= 0.78125
			51	= 0.796875
13	26		52	= 0.8125
			53	= 0.828125
		27	54	= 0.84375
			55	= 0.859375
7	14	28	56	= 0.875
			57	= 0.890625
		29	58	= 0.90625
			59	= 0.921875
	15	30	60	= 0.9375
			61	= 0.953125
		31	62	= 0.96875
			63	= 0.984375
8	16	32	64	= 1.0

Roman Numerals

I — 1	IV — 4	VII — 7	X — 10	XX — 20	L — 50	C — 100	D — 500
II — 2	V — 5	VIII — 8	XI — 11	XXX — 30	LX — 60	CC — 200	CM — 900
III — 3	VI — 6	IX — 9	XIX — 19	XL — 40	XC — 90	CD — 400	M — 1,000

Note: The numerals V, X, L, C, D, or M shown with a horizontal line on top denote 1,000 times the original value.

Ancient Measures

Biblical		Greek		Roman	
Cubit	= 21.8 inches	Cubit	= 18.3 inches	Cubit	= 17.5 inches
Omer	= 0.45 peck	Stadion	= 607.2 or 622 feet	Stadium	= 202 yards
	= 3.964 liters	Obolos	= 715.38 milligrams	As, libra,	
Ephah	= 10 omers	Drachma	= 4.2923 grams	pondus	= 325.971 grams
Shekel	= 0.497 ounce	Mina	= 0.9463 pound		= 0.71864 pound
	= 14.1 grams	Talent	= 60 mina		

Metric System Prefixes

The following prefixes, in combination with the basic unit names, provide the multiples and submultiples in the metric system. For example, the unit name *meter*, with the prefix *kilo* added, produces *kilometer*, meaning "1,000 meters."

Prefix	Symbol	Multiples	Equivalent	Prefix	Symbol	Multiples	Equivalent
yotta	Y	10^{24}	septillionfold	deci	d	10^{-1}	tenth part
zetta	Z	10^{21}	sextillionfold	centi	c	10^{-2}	hundredth part
exa	E	10^{18}	quintillionfold	milli	m	10^{-3}	thousandth part
peta	P	10^{15}	quadrillionfold	micro	μ	10^{-6}	millionth part
tera	T	10^{12}	trillionfold	nano	n	10^{-9}	billionth part
giga	G	10^{9}	billionfold	pico	p	10^{-12}	trillionth part
mega	M	10^{6}	millionfold	femto	f	10^{-15}	quadrillionth part
kilo	k	10^{3}	thousandfold	atto	a	10^{-18}	quintillionth part
hecto	h	10^{2}	hundredfold	zepto	z	10^{-21}	sextillionth part
deka	da	10^{1}	tenfold	yocto	y	10^{-24}	septillionth part

Weight and Measurement Equivalents

In this table, there is a distinction between the international foot and the survey foot. The international foot, defined in 1959 as exactly equal to 0.3048 meter, is shorter than the survey foot by exactly 2 parts in 1 million. This means that an international mile is about ⅛ inch shorter than the survey mile. The survey foot is still used in the publication of some geodetic surveys within the U.S. In this table, the survey foot is indicated with capital letters, as FEET.

When the name of a unit is enclosed in brackets, e.g., [1 hand], either (1) the unit is not in general current use in the U.S. or (2) the unit is believed to be based on custom and usage rather than on formal definition.

Equivalents involving decimals are, in most instances, rounded to the third decimal place; exact equivalents are so designated.

Lengths

1 angstrom (Å)	= 0.1 nanometer (exactly)
	= 0.0001 micrometer (exactly)
	= 0.0000001 millimeter (exactly)
	= 0.000000004 inch
1 cable's length	= 120 fathoms (exactly)
	= 720 FEET (exactly)
	= 219 meters
1 centimeter (cm)	= 0.3937 inch
1 chain (ch) (engineer's)	= 30.48 meters (exactly)
	= 100 feet
1 chain (Gunter's or surveyor's)	= 66 FEET (exactly)
	= 20.1168 meters
1 decimeter (dm)	= 3.937 inches
1 degree (geographical)	= 364,566.929 feet
	= 69.047 miles (avg.)
	= 111.123 kilometers (avg.)
of latitude	= 68.708 miles at equator
	= 69.403 miles at poles
of longitude	= 69.171 miles at equator

1 dekameter (dam)	= 32.808 feet
1 fathom (fath)	= 6 FEET (exactly)
	= 1.8288 meters
1 foot (ft)	= 12 inches (exactly)
	= 0.3048 meters (exactly)
	= 0.015 chains (surveyor's)
1 furlong (fur)	= 660 FEET (exactly)
	= ⅛ survey mile (exactly)
	= 201.168 meters
[1 hand (height measure for horses, from ground to top of their shoulders)]	= 4 inches
1 inch (in.)	= 2.54 centimeters (exactly)
1 kilometer (km)	= 0.621371 mile
	= 3,280.8 feet
1 league (land)	= 3 survey miles (exactly)
	= 4.828 kilometers
1 link (engineer's)	= 1 foot
	= 0.305 meter
1 link (Gunter's or surveyor's)	= 7.92 inches (exactly)
	= 0.201 meter

1 meter (m)................= 39.37 inches
      = 1.09361 yards
1 micrometer (μm) ....= 0.001 millimeter (exactly)
      = 0.00003937 inch
1 mil ....= 0.001 inch (exactly)
      = 0.0254 millimeter (exactly)
1 mile (mi) (statute or land). . . .= 5,280 FEET (exactly)
      = 1.609344 kilometers (exactly)
1 mile (nmi) (international
   nautical) ....= 1.852 kilometers (exactly)
      = 1.151 miles
      = 6,076.1 feet
1 millimeter (mm) ....= 0.03937 inch
1 nanometer (nm)...........= 0.001 micrometer (exactly)
      = 0.00000003937 inch
1 pica (typography)..........= 12 points
1 point (pt) (typography)......= 0.013837 inch (exactly)
      = 0.351 millimeter
1 rod (rd), pole, or perch......= 16½ FEET (exactly)
      = 5.029 meters
1 yard (yd) ....= 3 feet (exactly)
      = 0.9144 meter (exactly)

Areas or Surfaces

1 acre (A) ....= 43,560 square FEET (exactly)
      = 4,840 square yards
      = 0.405 hectare
1 are (a) ....= 119.599 square yards
      = 0.025 acre
1 bolt (cloth measure):
   length ....= 100 yards
   width................= 45 or 60 inches
1 hectare (ha)..............= 2.471 acres
[1 square (building)] ....= 100 square feet
1 square centimeter (cm^2) ....= 0.155 square inch
1 square decimeter (dm^2).....= 15.500 square inches
1 square foot (ft^2) ....= 929.030 square centimeters
1 square inch (in.^{2}).........= 6.4516 square centimeters
      (exactly)
1 square kilometer (km^2) .....= 247.104 acres
      = 0.386102 square mile
1 square meter (m^2) ....= 1.196 square yards
      = 10.764 square feet
1 square mile (mi^2) ....= 640 acres (exactly)
      = 258.999 hectares
1 square millimeter (mm^2) ....= 0.002 square inch
1 square rod (rd^2), square
   pole, or square perch......= 25.293 square meters
1 square yard (yd^2).........= 0.836127 square meter

Capacities or Volumes

1 barrel (bbl), liquid..........= 31 to 42 gallons*

*There are a variety of "barrels" established by law or usage. For example, federal taxes on fermented liquors are based on a barrel of 31 gallons. Many state laws fix the "barrel for liquids" as 31½ gallons; one state fixes a 36-gallon barrel for cistern measurement. Federal law recognizes a 40-gallon barrel for "proof spirits." By custom, 42 gallons constitute a barrel of crude oil or petroleum products for statistical purposes, and this equivalent is recognized "for liquids" by some states.

1 barrel (bbl), standard for
   fruits, vegetables, and other
   dry commodities except dry
   cranberries ....= 7,056 cubic inches
      = 105 dry quarts
      = 3.281 bushels, struck measure
1 barrel, standard, cranberry . .= 86^{45}/$_{64}$ dry quarts
      = 2.709 bushels, struck measure
      = 5,826 cubic inches
1 board foot (lumber measure) = a foot-square board 1 inch
      thick
1 bushel (U.S.) (struck
   measure) ....= 2,150.42 cu in. (exactly)
      = 35.239 liters
[1 bushel, heaped (U.S.)] ....= 2,747.715 cubic inches
      = 1.278 bushels,
      struck measure**

**Frequently recognized as 1¼ bushels, struck measure.

[1 bushel (bu) (British Imperial)
   (struck measure)] ....= 1.032 U.S. bushels,
      struck measure
      = 2,219.36 cubic inches
1 cord (cd) (firewood) ....= 128 cubic feet (exactly)

1 cubic centimeter (cm^3) .....= 0.061 cubic inch
1 cubic decimeter (dm^3)......= 61.024 cubic inches
1 cubic foot (ft^3) ....= 7.481 gallons
      = 28.317 cubic decimeters
1 cubic inch (in^3) ....= 0.554 fluid ounce
      = 4.433 fluid drams
      = 16.387 cubic centimeters
1 cubic meter (m^3) ....= 1.308 cubic yards
1 cubic yard (yd^3)..........= 0.765 cubic meter
1 cup, measuring ....= 8 fluid ounces (exactly)
      = ½ liquid pint (exactly)
1 dekaliter (daL)...........= 2.642 gallons
      = 1.135 pecks
[1 dram, fluid (fl dr) (British)] . .= 0.961 U.S. fluid dram
      = 0.217 cubic inch
      = 3.552 milliliters
1 gallon (gal) (U.S.) ....= 4 quarts, liquid (exactly)
      = 231 cubic inches (exactly)
      = 3.785 liters
      = 0.833 British gallon
      = 128 U.S. fluid ounces (exactly)
[1 gallon (British Imperial)]....= 277.42 cubic inches
      = 1.201 U.S. gallons
      = 4.546 liters
      = 160 British fluid ounces
      (exactly)
1 gill (gi) ....= 7.219 cubic inches
      = 4 fluid ounces (exactly)
      = 0.118 liter
1 hectoliter (hL) ....= 26.418 gallons
      = 2.838 bushels
1 liter (L) (1 cubic decimeter
   exactly)................= 1.057 liquid quarts
      = 0.908 dry quart
      = 61.025 cubic inches
1 milliliter (mL) (1 cu cm
   exactly)................= 0.271 fluid dram
      = 16.231 minims
      = 0.061 cubic inch
1 ounce, liquid (U.S.) ....= 1.805 cubic inches
      = 29.573 milliliters
      = 1.041 British fluid ounces
[1 ounce, fluid (fl oz) (British)] = 0.961 U.S. fluid ounce
      = 1.734 cubic inches
      = 28.412 milliliters
1 peck (pk) ....= 8.810 liters
1 pint (pt), dry.............= 33.600 cubic inches
      = 0.551 liter
1 pint, liquid ....= 28.875 cubic inches (exactly)
      = 0.473 liter
1 quart (qt), dry (U.S.) ....= 67.201 cubic inches
      = 1.101 liters
      = 0.969 British quart
1 quart, liquid (U.S.).........= 2 pints, liquid (exactly)
      = 4 cups (exactly)
      = 57.75 cubic inches (exactly)
      = 0.946 liter
      = 0.833 British quart
[1 quart (British)] ....= 69.354 cubic inches
      = 1.032 U.S. dry quarts
      = 1.201 U.S. liquid quarts
1 tablespoon (T., Tbs, tbsp.) . .= 3 teaspoons (exactly)
      = 4 fluid drams
      = ½ fluid ounce (exactly)
1 teaspoon (t., tsp.) ....= ⅓ tablespoon (exactly)
      = 1⅓ fluid drams***

***The equivalent "1 teaspoon = 1⅓ fluid drams" has been found to correspond more closely with the actual capacities of teaspoons in use than the equivalent "1 teaspoon = 1 fluid dram" given by many dictionaries.

Weights or Masses

1 assay ton* (AT) ....= 29.167 grams

*Used in assaying. The assay ton bears the same relation to the milligram that a ton of 2,000 pounds avoirdupois bears to the ounce troy; hence, the weight in milligrams of precious metal obtained from one assay ton of ore gives directly the number of troy ounces to the net ton.

1 carat (c)................= 200 milligrams (exactly)
      = 3.086 grains
1 dram avoirdupois (dr avdp).. = 27^{11}/$_{32}$ (= 27.344) grains
      = 1.772 grams
1 gamma (γ)..............= 1 microgram (exactly)
1 grain (gr) ....= 64.79891 milligrams (exactly)

1 gram (g). . . . . = 15.432 grains
. . . . = 0.035 ounce, avoirdupois
1 hundredweight, gross or
    long** (gross cwt) . . . . = 112 pounds (exactly)
. . . . = 50.802 kilograms
**The gross, or long, ton and hundredweight are used commercially in the U.S. to only a limited extent, usually in restricted industrial fields. These units are the same as the British ton and hundredweight.

1 hundredweight, gross or
    short (cwt or net cwt) . . . . . . = 100 pounds (exactly)
. . . . = 45.359 kilograms
1 kilogram (kg) . . . . = 2.20462 pounds
1 microgram (μg) . . . . = 0.000001 gram (exactly)
1 milligram (mg) . . . . = 0.015 grain
1 ounce, avoirdupois (oz avdp) = 437.5 grains (exactly)
. . . . = 0.911 troy ounce
. . . . = 28.3495 grams
1 ounce, troy (oz t) . . . . = 480 grains (exactly)
. . . . = 1.097 avoirdupois ounces
. . . . = 31.103 grams

1 pennyweight (dwt) . . . . = 1.555 grams
1 pound, avoirdupois (lb avdp) = 7,000 grains (exactly)
. . . . = 1.215 troy pounds
. . . . = 453.59237 grams (exactly)
1 pound, troy (lb t) . . . . = 5,760 grains (exactly)
. . . . = 0.823 avoirdupois pound
. . . . = 373.242 grams
1 stone (st) . . . . = 14 pounds avdp (exactly)
. . . . = 6.350 kilograms
1 ton, gross or long. . . . . = 2,240 pounds (exactly)
. . . . = 1.12 net tons (exactly)
. . . . = 1.016 metric tons
1 ton, metric (t) . . . . = 2,204.623 pounds
. . . . = 0.984 gross ton
. . . . = 1.102 net tons
1 ton, net or short (tn). . . . . = 2,000 pounds (exactly)
. . . . = 0.893 gross ton
. . . . = 0.907 metric ton

Electrical Units

The **watt** (W) is the unit of power (electrical, mechanical, thermal). Electrical power is given by the product of the voltage and the current.

Energy is sold by the **joule** (J), but in common practice the billing of electrical energy is expressed in terms of the **kilowatt-hour** (kWh), which is 3,600,000 joules, or 3.6 megajoules.

The **horsepower** (hp) is a nonmetric unit sometimes used in mechanics. It is equal to 746 watts.

The **ohm** (Ω) is the unit of electrical resistance and represents the physical property of a conductor that offers a resistance to the flow of electricity, permitting just 1 ampere to flow at 1 volt of pressure.

Measures of Force and Pressure

Dyne (dyn) = force necessary to accelerate a 1-gram mass 1 centimeter per second squared = 0.000072 poundal

Poundal (pdl) = force necessary to accelerate a 1-pound mass 1 foot per second squared = 13,825.5 dynes = 0.138255 newton

Newton (N) = force needed to accelerate a 1-kilogram mass 1 meter per second squared = 100,000 dynes (exactly)

Pascal (pressure) (Pa) = 1 newton per square meter = 0.020885 pound per square foot

Atmosphere (air pressure at sea level) (atm) = 2,116.217 pounds per square foot = 14.6959 pounds per square inch = 1.0332 kilograms per square centimeter = 101,325 newtons per square meter

Measures of Alcohol

Pony . . . . = 1.0 fluid ounce
Shot . . . . = varies, usu. 1.0-
. . . . 1.5 fluid ounces
Jigger . . . . = 1.5 fluid ounces
Pint (pt) . . . . = 16 fluid ounces
. . . . = 0.625 fifth
Fifth. . . . . = 25.6 fluid ounces
. . . . = 1.6 pints
. . . . = 0.8 quart
. . . . = 0.757 liter

Quart (qt) . . . . = 32 fluid ounces
. . . . = 1.25 fifths
Wine bottle
    (standard) . . . . = 0.75 liter
. . . . = 25.4 fluid ounces
Magnum . . . . = 1.5 liters

For champagne and brandy:
Jeroboam . . . . = 2 magnums
. . . . = 3 liters
. . . . = 101 fluid ounces

For champagne:
Rehoboam . . . . = 3 magnums
Methuselah. . . . . = 4 magnums
Salmanazar . . . . = 6 magnums
Balthazar . . . . = 8 magnums
Nebuchadnezzar . . . = 10 magnums

Miscellaneous Measures

Caliber (cal)—the diameter of a gun bore. In the U.S., caliber is traditionally expressed in hundredths of inches, e.g., .22. In Britain, caliber is often expressed in thousandths of inches, e.g., .270. Now it is commonly expressed in millimeters, e.g., the 5.56 mm M16 rifle. The caliber of heavier weapons has long been expressed in millimeters, e.g., the 155 mm howitzer.

Naval guns' caliber refers to the barrel length as a multiple of the bore diameter. For example, a 5-inch, 50-caliber naval gun has a 5-inch bore and a barrel length of 250 inches.

Decibel (dB)—a measure of the relative intensity of sound. The threshold of hearing is given as 0 decibels. A 20-decibel sound is 10 times more intense than a 10-decibel sound; 30 decibels is 100 times more intense. (A 10-decibel increase corresponds generally to the perception of a sound being twice as loud.)

One decibel is the smallest difference between sounds detectable by the human ear. Long or repeated exposure to an 85-decibel-or-higher sound can damage hearing.

10 decibels . . . breathing
20 . . . . rustling leaves
30 . . . . whisper
40 . . . . refrigerator humming
50 . . . . quiet conversation
60 . . . . conversation, laughter
70 . . . . vacuum cleaner
80 . . . . city traffic
90 . . . . subway, lawn mower
100 . . . . chainsaw

Em—a printer's measure designating the width of any given type size. For example, an em of 10-point type is 10 points. An en is half an em.

Gauge (ga)—the diameter of a shotgun bore. Gauge numbers originally referred to the number of lead balls—of equal diameter as the gun barrel—required to make a pound. Thus, a 16-gauge shotgun's bore was smaller than a 12-gauge shotgun's. Today, an international agreement assigns millimeter measures to each gauge.

Gauge	Bore diameter (mm)	Gauge	Bore diameter (mm)
6	23.34	14	17.60
10	19.67	16	16.81
12	18.52	20	15.90

Horsepower (hp)—the power needed to lift 550 pounds 1 foot in 1 second or to lift 33,000 pounds 1 foot in 1 minute. Equivalent to 746 watts or 2,546 British thermal units per hour.

Karat or carat (k or c)—a measure of fineness for gold equal to $1/24$ part of pure gold in an alloy. Thus 24-karat gold is pure; 18-karat gold is ¼ alloy. The carat is also used as a unit of weight for precious stones; it is equal to 200 milligrams or 3.086 grains.

Knot (kn or kt)—a measure of the speed of ships. A knot equals 1 nautical mile (about 1.151 statute miles) per hour.

Quire (qr)—25 sheets of paper of the same size and quality.

Ream (rm)—500 sheets of paper of the same size and quality.

POSTAL INFORMATION

Administration of the U.S. Postal Service

The Postal Reorganization Act, creating a government-owned postal service under the executive branch and replacing the old executive Post Office Department, was signed into law Aug. 12, 1970. The service officially came into being on July 1, 1971. The U.S. Postal Service is governed by an 11-person board. Nine members are appointed by the president, with Senate approval. These nine choose a postmaster general. The board and the postmaster general choose the 11th member, who serves as deputy postmaster general.

Congress passed the Postal Accountability and Enhancement Act, which overhauled postal service operations for the first time since 1971, on Dec. 8, 2006. New operating provisions included the ability to adjust rates annually, negotiate for contracts, and invest profits in internal improvements. (The Postal Service last received a public service subsidy, i.e., taxpayer dollars, in 1982.)

Historical Postage Rates, 1851-2016

Postage cost for a prepaid, 1-oz. letter (the first-class standard after July 1, 1885).

Effective date	Rate	2016 dollars	Effective date	Rate	2016 dollars	Effective date	Rate	2016 dollars
July 1, 1851	$0.06[1]	$1.92	Mar. 2, 1974	$0.10	$0.49	Jan. 7, 2001	$0.34	$0.46
July 1, 1863	0.06	1.17	Dec. 31, 1975	0.13	0.58	June 30, 2002	0.37	0.49
Oct. 1, 1883	0.04	0.98	May 29, 1978	0.15	0.55	Jan. 8, 2006	0.39	0.46
July 1, 1885	0.02	0.51	Mar. 22, 1981	0.18	0.48	May 14, 2007	0.41	0.48
Nov. 2, 1917	0.03[2]	0.56	Nov. 1, 1981	0.20	0.53	May 12, 2008	0.42	0.47
July 1, 1919	0.02[2]	0.28	Feb. 17, 1985	0.22	0.49	May 11, 2009	0.44	0.49
July 6, 1932	0.03	0.53	Apr. 3, 1988	0.25	0.51	Jan. 22, 2012	0.45	0.47
Aug. 1, 1958	0.04	0.33	Feb. 3, 1991	0.29	0.51	Jan. 27, 2013	0.46	0.47
Jan. 7, 1963	0.05	0.39	Jan. 1, 1995	0.32	0.50	Jan. 26, 2014	0.49[3]	0.50
Jan. 7, 1968	0.06	0.41	Jan. 10, 1999	0.33	0.48	Apr. 10, 2016	0.47	0.47
May 16, 1971	0.08	0.47						

NA = Not available. (1) For prepaid domestic letters traveling under 3,000 miles. (2) The price increased one cent during World War I; Congress restored its prewar rate in 1919. (3) The Postal Regulatory Commission approved a 6% total price increase: a 1.7% increase for inflation and an additional 4.3% temporary increase to compensate for USPS losses during the 2008-09 recession.

Status of the U.S. Postal Service, 2001-15

Source: *Postal Facts 2016*, U.S. Postal Service

	2001	2005	2008	2009	2010	2011	2012	2013	2014	2015
Total mail items (bil)	207.5	211.7	202.7	176.7	170.9	168.3	159.9	158.4	155.4	154.2
First-class mail items (bil)	103.7	98.1	90.7	82.7	77.6	72.5	68.7	65.8	63.6	62.4
Stamped mail items (bil)	53.6	45.9	35.4	31.6	28.9	25.8	23.2	22.6	21.5	20.6
Advertising mail items (bil)	89.9	100.9	98.4	81.8	81.8	84.0	79.5	80.9	80.3	80.0
Annual revenue (bil)	$65.8	$69.9	$74.9	$68.0	$67.1	$65.7	$65.2	$67.3	$67.8	$68.8
Total retail revenue (bil).	$14.8	$17.3	$18.7	$17.7	$17.5	$16.9	$17.5	$18.3	$19.0	$19.2
Total customer visits (bil)	1.4	1.3	1.2	1.1	1.1	1.0	1.0	1.0	0.9	0.9
Delivery points (mil)	137.7	144.3	149.2	150.1	150.9	151.5	152.1	152.9	153.9	155.0
Total delivery routes	242,600	243,000	244,800	232,900	230,600	228,160	227,000	225,152	244,365	226,777
Total retail offices	38,123	37,142	36,723	36,496	36,222	35,756	35,369	35,434	35,649	35,520
Career employees	775,903	704,716	663,238	623,128	583,908	551,570	522,144	489,727	487,054	493,381

NA = Not available.

U.S. Domestic Mail Rates

Source: *Price List* (Notice 123), U.S. Postal Service. Effective Apr. 10, 2016; updated Aug. 28, 2016. Rates are for retail customers unless noted. Domestic rates apply to the U.S., its territories and possessions, APOs, FPOs, and Freely Associated States.

First-Class Mail

Includes written matter such as letters, postcards, bills, account statements, and any matter sealed or closed against inspection up to 13 oz. In most cases, delivery is within 2-3 business days.

Letters measuring up to 6⅛ by 11½ in. cost 47¢ for the first oz., 21¢ for each additional oz. or fraction thereof, up to 3.5 oz. Postcard postage is 34¢. Large envelopes up to 12 by 15 in. (or letters over 3.5 oz.) cost 94¢ for the first oz. and 21¢ for each additional oz. or fraction thereof. Presort- and automation-compatible mail can qualify for lower rates if certain piece minimums, mailing permits, and other requirements are met.

Forever Stamps. The USPS introduced the "Forever" stamp Apr. 12, 2007, at an initial cost of 41¢. The Forever stamp can be purchased at the current First-Class standard rate and will always be valid as First-Class postage on standard envelopes weighing 1 oz. or less, even after rates increase.

Priority Mail

Due to expeditious handling and transportation, Priority Mail is delivered within 1-3 business days in most cases. Can be any mailable article up to 70 lbs and not over 108 in. in length and girth combined.

Priority Mail Flat Rate: $6.45, or $6.80, regardless of weight, if matter fits into designated USPS flat-rate envelope. $6.80, $13.45, $16.75, or $18.75 if matter fits into flat-rate box.

Priority Mail Forever Prepaid Flat Rate packaging can be purchased online at the current priority mail flat rate and remains valid for use after future price increases.

Priority Mail Express

Provides guaranteed expedited service for any mailable article up to 70 lbs and not over 108 in. in combined length and girth. Offers next-day delivery to most destinations; $12.50 additional charge for Sunday or holiday delivery. Includes insurance up to $100, mailing receipt, proof of delivery signature record, and tracking.

Priority Mail Express Flat Rate: $22.95, regardless of weight, if matter fits into designated USPS flat-rate envelope.

Domestic Mail Services and Fees

Adult signature required: $5.70 per piece; person 21 years of age or older must sign for shipment.

Adult signature restricted delivery: $5.95 per piece; specific addressee or agent 21 years of age or older must sign for shipment.

Certificate of mailing: $1.30 per piece.

Certified mail: $3.30 per piece; provides proof of mailing and electronic verification of delivery or delivery attempt.

Collect on delivery (COD): $6.95 for amount to be collected/insurance desired up to $50; $8.70 for $50.01-$100; $1.75 for each additional $100.

Domestic money order: $1.20 for money orders $0.01 to $500; $1.60 for $500.01 to $1,000.

Pickup on demand: $20.00 per pickup; available for Priority Mail, Priority Mail Express, and USPS Retail Ground.

Restricted delivery: Starts at $4.95 per item when purchased in combination with certain services.

Return receipt: If requested at time of mailing, $2.70 for a receipt by mail, $1.35 for email receipt.

Signature confirmation: $2.35 online, $2.90 at post office.

Sunday/holiday delivery: Available for Priority Mail Express only. Fee: $12.50.

Tracking

Formerly known as Delivery Confirmation, tracking provides mailer with location and progress of item and date and time of delivery or attempted deliveries. Free of charge with most parcel services at time of mailing, except Standard Mail (fee: $0.35).

Change of Address

The USPS will forward mail to another address provided a Change of Address (COA) form has been filed in person (free) or online at www.usps.com ($1.00 authentication fee). The form, which can be picked up at any post office, printed off the Internet, or requested by phone at (800) ASK-USPS, can also be dropped in any mailbox for free filing.

Special Handling

Provides preferential handling, but not preferential delivery, to a practical extent. Available for First-Class Mail, Priority Mail, USPS Retail Ground, and Media Mail for $9.95 surcharge.

Registered Mail

The most secure service provided by the USPS. Full value of item must be declared at time of registration and mailing. Insurance is included in fee for articles with a declared value of $0.01 up to $50,000. Fee: $11.70 for a declared value of $0, up to $22.30 for articles with a declared value of $4,000.01 to $5,000. For each additional $1,000.00 or fraction thereof above $5,000.00, add $1.55.

International Mail Rates

Source: *Price List* (Notice 123), U.S. Postal Service. Effective Apr. 10, 2016; updated Aug. 28, 2016. Refer to www.usps.com for USPS price groups not shown here and weight limits by country.

First-Class Mail International

Letter-post items weighing up to 1 oz. and single postcards can be sent airmail for $1.15 to all countries.

Priority Mail International

Delivery is in 6-10 business days in many markets. Items must not be more than 108 in. in length and girth combined; max. weight is 70 lbs, though the limit varies by country.

Priority Mail International Flat Rate: $23.95 to Canada, $29.95-$32.95 to all other countries if matter fits into designated USPS flat-rate envelope (max. weight 4 lbs). Flat-rate boxes are $24.95-$59.95 to Canada, $33.95-$93.95 to all other countries.

Priority Mail Express International

Priority Mail Express International Flat Rate: $41.50 to Canada, $57.50 to Mexico, $59.50-$62.50 to all other countries if matter fits into flat-rate envelope (max. weight 4 lbs).

Global Express Guaranteed

Provides international expedited delivery, in partnership with FedEx, to certain countries. Item to be mailed must not weigh more than 70 lbs nor measure more than 108 in. in combined length and girth. Rate: Starts at $59.95 to countries in price group 1 up to $102.75 to countries in price group 8, for items not over 0.5 lb in weight.

International Mail Services and Fees

Business reply: Card: $1.30; envelope (up to 2 oz.): $1.80.

Customs clearance and delivery: $5.75-$6.00 per piece.

Insurance: Available to many countries for loss of or damage to items. Consult USPS for each country's indemnity limits.

Registered mail: Available for letter-post items only to most countries. Fee: $13.40-$13.95.

Return receipt: Shows to whom and when item is delivered. Fee: $3.70-$3.85 per piece (must be purchased at time of mailing).

Postal money order: $4.75 per money order; maximum amount for a single money order is $700. Only accepted in certain countries.

U.S. Postal Abbreviations

The abbreviations below are approved by the U.S. Postal Service for use in addresses.

Alabama	AL	Illinois	IL	Missouri	MO	Pennsylvania	PA
Alaska	AK	Indiana	IN	Montana	MT	Puerto Rico	PR
American Samoa	AS	Iowa	IA	Nebraska	NE	Rhode Island	RI
Arizona	AZ	Kansas	KS	Nevada	NV	South Carolina	SC
Arkansas	AR	Kentucky	KY	New Hampshire	NH	South Dakota	SD
California	CA	Louisiana	LA	New Jersey	NJ	Tennessee	TN
Colorado	CO	Maine	ME	New Mexico	NM	Texas	TX
Connecticut	CT	Marshall Islands[1]	MH	New York	NY	Utah	UT
Delaware	DE	Maryland	MD	North Carolina	NC	Vermont	VT
District of Columbia	DC	Massachusetts	MA	North Dakota	ND	Virgin Islands	VI
Florida	FL	Michigan	MI	Northern Mariana Isls.	MP	Virginia	VA
Georgia	GA	Micronesia,		Ohio	OH	Washington	WA
Guam	GU	Federated States of[1]	FM	Oklahoma	OK	West Virginia	WV
Hawaii	HI	Minnesota	MN	Oregon	OR	Wisconsin	WI
Idaho	ID	Mississippi	MS	Palau[1]	PW	Wyoming	WY

(1) Although an independent nation, this country is subject to domestic rates and fees.

Canadian Province and Territory Postal Abbreviations

Source: Canada Post

Alberta	AB	Newfoundland and		Nunavut	NU	Quebec	QC
British Columbia	BC	Labrador	NL	Ontario	ON	Saskatchewan	SK
Manitoba	MB	Northwest Territories	NT	Prince Edward Island	PE	Yukon	YT
New Brunswick	NB	Nova Scotia	NS				

SOCIAL SECURITY AND MEDICARE

Social Security Coverage

Source: Social Security Administration; World Almanac research; provisions shown are as under current law, Aug. 2016

Social Security Benefits

Social Security's **Old-Age, Survivors, and Disability Insurance (OASDI)** program benefits are based on a worker's **primary insurance amount (PIA)**, which is related by law to the average indexed monthly earnings (AIME) on which Social Security contributions have been paid. The full PIA is payable to a worker who retires at full retirement age (FRA), which is 65-67 depending on birth year, and to an entitled disabled worker at any age. Spouses and children of retired or disabled workers and survivors of deceased workers receive set proportions of the PIA subject to a family maximum amount. The PIA is calculated by applying varying percentages to succeeding parts of the AIME. The formula is adjusted annually to reflect changes in average annual wages.

Increases in Social Security benefits are initiated for December of each year, assuming the Consumer Price Index (CPI) for the third calendar quarter of the year increased relative to the base quarter, which is the third calendar quarter of the year in which an increase last took effect. The size of the benefit increase is determined by the percentage rise of the CPI between the quarters measured.

The **average monthly benefit** payable to all retired workers amounted to $1,342 in Dec. 2015. The average benefit for disabled workers in that month was $1,166.

Maximum Monthly Retired-Worker Benefits Payable to Individuals who Retired at Age 65[1]

Year attaining age 65	Maximum benefit— Payable at retirement	Payable effective Dec. 2015
1990	$975	$1,850
1995	1,199	1,917
1996	1,248	1,946
1997	1,326	2,009
1998	1,342	1,991
1999	1,373	2,010
2000	1,435	2,050
2001	1,538	2,123
2002	1,660	2,234
2003	1,721	2,284
2004	1,784	2,319
2005	1,874	2,372
2006	1,961	2,385
2007	1,998	2,352
2008	2,030	2,336
2009	2,172	2,362
2010	2,191	2,383
2011	2,249	2,446
2012	2,310	2,425
2013	2,414	2,492
2014	2,431	2,473
2015	2,452	2,452
2016	2,491	2,491

(1) Assumes retirement at beginning of year.

Amount of Work Required

To qualify for benefits, the worker generally must have worked a certain length of time in covered employment. Just how long depends on when the worker reaches age 62 or, if earlier, when he or she dies or becomes disabled. A person born after 1929 who dies, becomes disabled, or reaches 62 after 1991 must generally have had at least 10 years of work credit to qualify for benefits.

Contribution and Benefit Base

(annual limit on the amount of earnings subject to taxation under OASDI)

Calendar year	OASDI[1]	Calendar year	OASDI[1]	Calendar year	OASDI[1]
1994	$60,600	2002	$84,900	2010	$106,800
1995	61,200	2003	87,000	2011	106,800
1996	62,700	2004	87,900	2012	110,100
1997	65,400	2005	90,000	2013	113,700
1998	68,400	2006	94,200	2014	117,000
1999	72,600	2007	97,500	2015	118,500
2000	76,200	2008	102,000	2016	118,500
2001	80,400	2009	106,800		

(1) Old-Age, Survivors, and Disability Insurance.

A person is **fully insured** when he or she has one quarter of coverage for every year after age 21 is reached (or 1950, if later) up to but not including the year the worker reaches 62, dies, or becomes disabled. In 2016, a person earns one quarter of coverage for each $1,260 of annual earnings in covered employment, up to four quarters per year.

To receive **disability benefits**, the worker, in addition to being fully insured, must generally have credit for 20 quarters of coverage out of the 40 calendar quarters before he or she became disabled. A disabled blind worker need meet only the fully insured

requirement. Persons disabled before age 31 can qualify with a briefer period of coverage. Certain survivor benefits are payable if the deceased worker had 6 quarters of coverage in the 13 quarters preceding death.

Tax Rate Schedule

(percentage of covered earnings)

Year	Total (for employees and employers, each)	OASDI[1]	HI[2]
1979-80	6.13%	5.08%	1.05%
1981	6.65	5.35	1.30
1982-83	6.70	5.40	1.30
1984	7.00	5.70	1.30
1985	7.05	5.70	1.35
1986-87	7.15	5.70	1.45
1988-89	7.51	6.06	1.45
1990 and after[3]	7.65	6.20	1.45

Year	(for self-employed)		
1979-80	8.10%	7.05%	1.05%
1981	9.30	8.00	1.30
1982-83	9.35	8.05	1.30
1984	14.00	11.40	2.60
1985	14.10	11.40	2.70
1986-87	14.30	11.40	2.90
1988-89	15.02	12.12	2.90
1990 and after[3]	15.30	12.40	2.90

(1) Old-Age, Survivors, and Disability Ins. (2) Hospital Ins. (Medicare). (3) Public Law 111-147 exempted most employers from paying the employer share of OASDI payroll tax on wages paid Mar. 19-Dec. 31, 2010, to certain qualified individuals hired after Feb. 3, 2010. PL 111-312 reduced the OASDI payroll tax rate for 2011 by 2 percentage points for employees and for self-employed workers. PL 112-96 extended the 2011 rate reduction through 2012. The laws require that the general fund of the Treasury reimburses the OASI and DI Trust Funds for these temporary reductions.

What Aged Workers Receive

A person may receive monthly old-age benefits when he or she has enough work in covered employment and has reached retirement age—age 62 for reduced benefits or the age below for full benefits.

Full Retirement Age (FRA) by Birth Year

Year of birth	FRA	Year of birth	FRA
1937 or earlier	65	1955	66 and 2 mos.
1938	65 and 2 mos.	1956	66 and 4 mos.
1939	65 and 4 mos.	1957	66 and 6 mos.
1940	65 and 6 mos.	1958	66 and 8 mos.
1941	65 and 8 mos.	1959	66 and 10 mos.
1942	65 and 10 mos.	1960 or	
1943-54	66	later	67

Note: If born on Jan. 1, refer to the previous birth year.

In 2000, the retirement earnings test was eliminated beginning with the month when the beneficiary reaches **full retirement age (FRA)**. A person at or above FRA no longer receives reduced benefits because of earnings. However, a person's benefits are reduced $1 for every $3 of earnings above the limit allowed by law ($41,880 for 2016) if he or she retires in the same calendar year but months prior to FRA. For retirees who have not yet attained FRA, the reduction is $1 for every $2 of earnings over the exempt amount ($15,720 for 2016).

For workers who reached age 65 between 1982 and 1989, Social Security benefits are raised by 3% for each year in which the worker did not receive benefits between FRA and 70 (72 before 1984), whether because of earnings from work, because the worker did not apply for benefits, or because the worker declined benefits after entitlement. The **delayed retirement credit** is 1% per year for workers who reached age 65 before 1982. The rate for workers who reached age 65 in 1998-99 is 5.5%; 2000-01, 6.0%; 2002-03, 6.5%; 2004-05, 7.0%. For 2006-07, it is 7.5%. The delayed retirement credit rose to 8% per year for 2008 and years after.

For workers retiring early, benefits are permanently reduced 5/9 of 1% for each month before the FRA, up to 36 months. If the number of months exceeds 36, then the benefit is further reduced 5/12 of 1% per month.

For example, when FRA reaches 67, for workers who retire at exactly age 62, there are a total of 60 months of reduction. The reduction for the first 36 months is 5/9 of 36%, or 20%. The reduction for the remaining 24 months is 5/12 of 24%, or 10%. Thus, when the FRA reaches 67, the amount of reduction at age 62 will be 30%. The nearer to FRA a person is when he or she begins collecting a benefit, the larger the monthly benefit will be.

Benefits for Worker's Spouse

The spouse of a worker who is getting Social Security retirement or disability payments may become entitled to an insurance benefit of **one-half of the worker's PIA** if claiming benefits at full retirement age. Reduced spouse's benefits are available at age 62 and are permanently reduced 25/36 of 1% for each month before FRA, up to 36 months. If the number of months exceeds 36, then the benefit is further reduced 5/12 of 1% per month. Benefits are also payable to the aged divorced spouse of an insured worker if he or she was married to the worker for at least 10 years. To qualify for divorced spouse benefits, the insured worker does not have to be receiving benefits if the divorce occurred at least two years earlier. Benefits received as a spouse are reduced by the amount of one's PIA.

Benefits for Children of Workers

If a retired or disabled worker has a child under age 18, the **child** will usually get a benefit equal to **one-half of the worker's unreduced benefit**. So will the worker's spouse, regardless of age, if he or she is **caring for an entitled child** of the worker, and the child is under 16 or became disabled before age 22. However, total benefits paid on a worker's earnings record are subject to a family maximum. Total monthly benefits paid to the family of a worker who retired in 2015 at age 66 and always had the maximum earnings creditable under Social Security cannot exceed $4,673.

Entitled children generally stop receiving benefits at age 18, though they can continue receiving benefits until age 19 if they attend elementary or secondary school full-time. A child disabled before age 22 may get a benefit as long as the disability meets the definition in the law.

Benefits may also be paid to a grandchild or step-grandchild of a worker or of his or her spouse, in special circumstances.

OASDI Beneficiaries

Beneficiaries	May 2005	May 2010	May 2015	May 2016
Total (in thous.)[1]	48,068	53,349	59,530	60,535
Age 65 and over, total	33,811	36,914	42,536	43,779
Retired workers. . . .	27,413	30,734	36,419	37,615
Disabled workers. . .	112	339	465	486
Survivors/ dependents	6,286	5,841	5,652	5,678
Under age 65, total . . .	14,257	16,435	16,994	16,756
Retired workers. . . .	2,809	3,314	3,086	3,006
Disabled workers. . .	6,239	7,628	8,474	8,398
Survivors/ dependents	5,209	5,492	5,434	5,352
Total monthly benefits (in mil) . . .	$42,074	$56,966	$72,613	$74,651

OASDI = Old-Age, Survivors, and Disability Ins. (1) Numbers may not add up to totals due to rounding or incomplete enumeration.

What Disabled Workers Receive

A worker who becomes unable to work may be eligible for a monthly disability benefit. Benefits continue until it is determined that the individual is no longer disabled. When a disabled-worker beneficiary reaches FRA (66 years for workers born 1943-54), the disability benefit becomes a retired-worker benefit.

Benefits—like those for dependents of retired-worker beneficiaries generally—may be paid to dependents of disabled beneficiaries. However, the maximum family benefit in disability cases is generally lower than in retirement cases.

Survivor Benefits

If an insured worker should die, one or more types of benefits may be payable to survivors, again subject to a maximum family benefit described above.

1. If claiming benefits at FRA, the **surviving spouse** will receive a benefit equal to 100% of the deceased worker's benefit. Benefits claimed before FRA are reduced, with a maximum reduction of 28.5% at age 60. However, if the deceased worker claimed benefits before FRA, the surviving spouse's benefits are limited to the reduced amount the worker would be getting if alive, but not less than 82.5% of the worker's PIA. Remarriage after the worker's death ends the surviving spouse's benefit rights. However, if the widow(er) marries,

and the marriage later ends, he or she regains benefit rights. (A marriage after age 60, age 50 if disabled, is deemed not to have occurred for benefit purposes.) Survivor benefits may also be paid to a divorced spouse if the marriage lasted for at least 10 years.

Disabled widows and widowers may under certain circumstances qualify for benefits after attaining age 50 at the rate of 71.5% of the deceased worker's PIA. The widow or widower must have become totally disabled before or within seven years after the spouse's death or the last month in which he or she received mother's or father's insurance benefits.

2. There is a benefit for each **child under age 18**. The monthly benefit for a child of a deceased worker is 3/4 of the PIA, subject to the family maximum. A child who became disabled before age 22 may also receive benefits. Also, a child can receive benefits until age 19 if he or she is in full-time attendance at an elementary or secondary school.

3. There is a **mother's or father's benefit** for the widow(er) if children of the worker who are under age 16 are in his or her care. The benefit is 75% of the PIA (subject to the family maximum), and it continues until the youngest child reaches age 16, at which time payments stop even if the child's benefit continues. Benefits may continue if the widow(er) has a disabled child beneficiary age 16 or over in his or her care.

4. Dependent parents may be eligible for benefits if they have been receiving at least half their support from the worker before his or her death, have reached age 62, and (except in certain circumstances) have not remarried since the worker's death. Each parent gets 75% of the worker's PIA; if only one parent survives, the benefit is 82% (could be reduced for the family maximum).

5. A **lump sum** cash payment of **$255** is made if the worker was living with a spouse or has a child who is eligible for immediate monthly survivor benefits.

Self-Employed Workers

A self-employed person who has **net earnings of $400 or more** in a year must report such earnings for Social Security tax and credit purposes. Income from real estate, savings, dividends, loans, pensions, or insurance policies are not included unless it is part of a person's business.

A self-employed person receives one quarter of coverage for each $1,260 for 2016, up to a maximum of four quarters per year.

The nonfarm self-employed have the option of reporting their earnings as 2/3 of their gross income from self-employment. This option can be used only if actual net earnings from self-employment income are less than $1,600 and less than 2/3 of their gross income. The option may be used only five times. Also, the self-employed person must have actual net earnings of $400 or more in two of the three taxable years immediately preceding the year in which he or she uses the option.

When a person has both taxable wages and earnings from self-employment, wages are credited for Social Security purposes first; only as much self-employment income as brings total earnings up to the current taxable maximum becomes subject to the self-employment tax.

Farm Owners and Workers

Self-employed farmers whose gross annual earnings from farming are **$600-$2,400** may report 2/3 of their gross earnings instead of net earnings for Social Security purposes. (Farmers whose gross annual earnings are under $600 cannot use the optional method.) Farmers whose gross income is over $2,400 and whose net earnings are less than $1,600 can report $1,600. Cash or crop shares received from a tenant or share farmer count if the owner participated materially in production or management. The self-employed farmer pays contributions at the same rate as other self-employed persons.

Agricultural employees. A worker's earnings from farm work count toward benefits if (1) the employer pays the worker $150 or more in cash during the year or (2) the employer spends $2,500 or more in the year for agricultural labor. Under these rules, a person gets credit for one calendar quarter for each $1,260 in cash pay in 2016.

Foreign farm workers admitted to the U.S. on a temporary basis are not covered.

Household Workers

If an employer pays a household worker (e.g., maid, cook, laundry worker, nurse, babysitter, chauffeur, gardener) who is age 18 or older **$2,000 or more** in wages in 2016, the wages are covered under Social Security. This includes transportation costs paid for in cash. The job need not be regular or full-time.

The employee should get a Social Security card at the Social Security office and show it to the employer. The employer deducts the amount of the employee's Social Security tax from the worker's pay, adds an identical amount as the employer's Social Security tax, and sends the total amount to the federal government.

Medicare Coverage

Source: Centers for Medicare & Medicaid Services, U.S. Dept. of Health and Human Services

The Medicare health insurance program provides acute-care coverage for Social Security and Railroad Retirement beneficiaries age 65 and over; workers and spouses age 65 and over with sufficient Medicare-only coverage in federal, state, or local government employment; certain persons entitled to receive Social Security or Railroad Retirement disability benefits; certain disabled persons with Medicare-only coverage through government employment; certain persons with end-stage kidney disease; and certain persons in the vicinity of Libby, MT, with asbestos-related conditions. What follows is a basic description that may not cover all circumstances.

The **basic Medicare plan**, available nationwide, is a fee-for-service arrangement where the beneficiary may use any provider accepting Medicare. Some services are not covered, and there are some out-of-pocket costs.

Hospital insurance (Part A). The basic hospital insurance program pays covered services for hospital and post-hospital care, including:

- All necessary inpatient hospital care for the first 60 days of each benefit period, except for a deductible ($1,288 in 2016). For days 61-90, Medicare pays for services over and above the co-insurance ($322 per day in 2016). After 90 days, the beneficiary has 60 lifetime reserve days for which Medicare helps pay. The coinsurance amount for reserve days was $644 in 2016.
- Up to 100 days of care in a skilled-nursing facility in each benefit period. Hospital insurance pays for all covered services for the first 20 days; for days 21-100, the beneficiary pays coinsurance ($161 per day in 2016).
- Part-time home health care provided by nurses or other health workers.
- Limited coverage of hospice care for the terminally ill.

There is a premium for this insurance in certain—but not most—cases.

Medical insurance (Part B). Eligible elderly and disabled persons can receive benefits under this supplementary program only if they sign up and agree to a monthly premium. As of 2007, the monthly premium is tied to annual income. Individuals with an income of $85,000 or less and couples with an income of $170,000 or less pay $121.80 per person if they sign up upon becoming eligible in 2016. Part B covers certain medical services and supplies, including:

- Physicians' and surgeons' services, as well as some services furnished by other medical professionals.
- Services in an emergency room, outpatient clinic, or ambulatory surgical center.
- Home health care not covered under Part A.
- Laboratory tests, X-rays, and other diagnostic radiology services.
- Certain preventative care services and screening tests.
- Most physical and occupational therapy and speech pathology services.
- Comprehensive outpatient rehabilitation facility services and mental health care in a partial hospitalization psychiatric program, if inpatient care would otherwise be required.
- Radiation therapy, renal (kidney) dialysis and transplants, heart, lung, heart-lung, liver, pancreas, bone marrow, and intestinal transplants.
- Approved durable medical equipment for home use.
- Drugs that are not usually self-administered.
- Certain services for diabetes.
- Ambulance services when other transportation methods are contraindicated.
- Rural health clinic and health center services, including some telemedicine.

Part B services are generally subject to a deductible ($147 in 2016), coinsurance (generally 20% of the remaining allowed charges with certain exceptions), a deductible for blood, and amounts above the allowed charge if a doctor or supplier does not accept the Medicare-approved rate as payment in full. For outpatient hospital services, coinsurance varies by service, usually falling between 20% and 50% of allowed charges. There are no deductibles or coinsurance for certain services, such as lab tests paid under the clinical lab fee schedule, home health agency services (except some durable medical equipment, which is subject to 20% coinsurance), and some preventative care services. Payments for certain physical, speech, and occupational therapy services are subject to certain limits. Dental care, hearing aids, and routine eye care are generally not covered under the basic plan.

To get medical insurance (Part B), persons approaching age 65 may enroll during the seven-month initial enrollment period, which includes the month of their 65th birthday as well as the three months before and after. Persons desiring coverage to begin in the month they reach age 65 must enroll in the three months before their birthday. Persons who enroll after their initial enrollment period may be subject to late-enrollment premiums.

The monthly premium is deducted from the cash benefit for persons receiving Social Security, Railroad Retirement, or Civil Service Retirement benefits. Income from the medical premiums and the federal matching payments are put in a Supplementary Medical Insurance Trust Fund, from which benefits and administrative expenses are paid.

Medicare Advantage (Part C) (formerly Medicare+ Choice). Persons eligible for Medicare may have the option of getting services through a Medicare-certified local coordinated care plan, such as a health maintenance organization (HMO), local preferred provider organization (PPO), provider-sponsored organization (PSO), or other local Medicare-certified **managed care** plan; a regional preferred provider organization (RPPO); a private fee-for-service plan; or, in certain cases, a special-needs plan. Any such plan must provide at least the same benefits as Parts A and B, except for hospice services. They may provide added benefits (such as vision or hearing coverage) or reduce cost sharing or premiums. Enrollees may be required to use the plan's network of participating providers or pay higher out-of-pocket costs to go outside the network.

Prescription Drug Coverage (Part D). Effective Jan. 1, 2006, an optional Medicare prescription drug plan provides insurance coverage for prescription drugs. Medicare recipients pay a monthly premium (averaging about $32.50 in 2016, depending on the provider) and a portion of drug costs. The open enrollment period is Oct. 15-Dec. 7. Coverage varies depending on the drug plan selected.

Further details are available on the Internet at www.medicare.gov or by calling 1-800-MEDICARE (1-800-633-4227).

Medicare card. Persons qualifying for hospital insurance under Social Security receive a health insurance card. The card indicates whether the individual has taken out medical insurance protection. It is to be shown to the hospital, skilled-nursing facility, home health agency, doctor, or other provider of covered services.

Payments are generally made only in the 50 states, Puerto Rico, U.S. Virgin Isls., Guam, American Samoa, and Northern Mariana Isls.

Social Security Financing

Social Security is paid for by a tax on certain earnings (for 2016, on earnings up to $118,500) for **Old-Age, Survivors, and Disability Insurance (OASDI)** and on all earnings (no upper limit) for hospital insurance with the **Medicare** program; the taxable earnings base for OASDI is adjusted annually to reflect changes in average wages. The employed worker and his or her employer share Social Security taxes equally.

Employers remit amounts withheld from employee wages for Social Security and income taxes to the Internal Revenue Service; employer Social Security taxes are also payable at the same time. (Self-employed workers pay Social Security taxes when filing their regular income tax forms.) The Social Security taxes (along with revenues arising from partial taxation of the Social Security benefits of certain high-income people) are transferred to the Social Security Trust Funds; they can be used only to pay benefits, the cost of rehabilitation services, and administrative expenses. By law, money not immediately needed for those purposes is invested in obligations of the federal government, which must pay interest on the money borrowed and must repay the principal when the obligations are redeemed or mature.

On Jan. 1, 1974, the **Supplemental Security Income (SSI)** program, established by the Social Security Amendments of 1972, replaced federal grants to states for aid to the needy aged, blind, and disabled in the 50 states and the District of Columbia. The program provides for federal payments, based on uniform national standards and eligibility requirements, and for state supplementary payments, which vary by state. The Social Security Administration administers the federal payments— financed by general funds of the Treasury—as well as the state supplement for those states that choose to have it federally administered. States may supplement the federal payment of all recipients and must supplement it for persons otherwise adversely affected by the transition from the former public assistance programs. In May 2016, the number of persons receiving federally administered SSI payments was 8,333,558; the payments totaled about $4.8 bil.

The **maximum monthly federal SSI payment** for individuals without an eligible spouse and with no other countable income, living in their own household, was $733 in 2016. For couples where both members were eligible, the maximum payment was $1,100.

For further information, contact the Social Security Administration toll-free at 1-800-772-1213 or visit its website at www.ssa.gov.

Examples of Monthly Social Security Benefits Available, 2016

Benefit or beneficiary	For low earnings ($21,479)[1]	For med. earnings ($47,731)[1]	For max. earnings ($116,123)[1,2]
Primary insurance amount (worker retiring at 66 years, 0 months) . .	$992.80	$1,636.10	$2,639.40
Maximum family benefit (worker retiring at 66 years, 0 months).	1,489.30	2,987.30	4,619.70
Maximum family disability benefit (worker disabled at 55; in 2014) . .	1,504.50	2,633.40	4,210.20
Disabled worker (worker disabled at 55):			
Worker alone.	1,062.80	1,755.60	2,806.80
Worker, spouse, and 1 child	1,504.40	2,633.40	4,210.20
Retired worker claiming benefits at age 62:			
Worker alone[3]	790.40	1,301.60	2,090.80
Worker with spouse claiming benefits at—			
NRA or over.	1,317.30	2,169.30	3,484.60
Age 62[3]	1,159.20	1,909.00	3,066.50
Widow or widower claiming benefits at—			
Age 66 or over[4].	992.80	1,636.10	2,639.40
Age 60[4].	713.70	1,176.20	1,897.60
Disabled widow or widower claiming benefits at age 50-59[5]	709.80	1,169.80	1,887.10
1 surviving child[4].	744.60	1,227.00	1,979.50
Widow or widower NRA or over and 1 child[4]	1,489.30	2,863.10	4,618.90
Widowed mother or father and 1 child[4]	1,489.20	2,454.10	3,959.10
Widowed mother or father and 2 children[4].	1,489.20	2,987.10	4,619.70

NRA = Normal retirement age. **Note:** Effective Jan. 2016. (1) Career average earnings: an average of lifetime earnings indexed to the year prior to entitlement (2015 in this case). (2) Assumes work beginning at age 22. (3) Assumes maximum reduction. (4) Assumes worker lived and worked until NRA without receiving reduced benefits. (5) Effective Jan. 1984, disabled widow or widower claiming a benefit at age 50-59 receives a benefit equal to 71.5% of the primary insurance amount.

Social Security Recipients by Age, Sex, Race, and Hispanic Origin, 2015
Source: Social Security Administration

Characteristic/benefit	Total	White	Black	American Indian, Alaska Native	Asian	Native Hawaiian/ other Pacific Isl.	Hispanic
Social Security beneficiaries (thous.)[1]	49,744	42,439	5,388	787	1,607	91	3,771
Sex							
Male.	22,184	19,072	2,212	354	743	44	1,641
Female	27,559	23,367	3,176	432	864	47	2,131
Age							
15-54 years.	5,397	4,189	1,027	178	136	17	645
55-64 years.	6,590	5,344	1,045	130	159	17	565
65-74 years.	20,958	18,074	1,983	307	744	46	1,469
75 years or older	16,798	14,833	1,332	171	568	11	1,092
Supplemental Security Income recipients (thous.)[1] . .	6,847	4,614	1,869	196	325	25	1,103
Sex							
Male.	2,980	2,006	832	72	121	9	426
Female	3,867	2,608	1,036	124	205	16	676
Age							
15-54 years.	3,465	2,355	1,046	113	74	13	550
55-64 years.	1,856	1,261	512	50	55	4	242
65-74 years	839	567	184	17	82	4	172
75 years or older	687	430	127	17	115	3	139
Average annual benefit in 2014 (dollars)							
Social Security	$14,305	$14,531	$12,772	$13,399	$13,613	$14,318	$11,985
Supplemental Security Income.	7,927	7,989	7,778	8,338	7,453	NA	7,657

NA = Not available. **Note:** Race categories include people who reported being of that race, alone or in combination with another race. Persons of Hispanic origin may be of any race. The sum of the individual categories may not add up to totals because of rounding and because the totals include persons who reported being of more than one race. (1) Persons 15 or older receiving Social Security benefits or Supplemental Security Income in Mar. 2015.

Old-Age, Survivors, and Disability Insurance Beneficiaries, 2015

Source: Social Security Administration

State or area	Total benefits (thous.)	Total benefi- ciaries	Old-Age Retired workers	Old-Age Spouses	Old-Age Children	Survivors Widow(er)s and parents	Survivors Children	Disability Disabled workers	Disability Spouses	Disability Children
Alabama	$1,306,452	1,108,543	650,081	33,164	11,889	83,390	42,962	234,229	3,695	49,133
Alaska	107,985	91,960	62,053	2,799	1,830	5,336	4,589	12,620	183	2,550
Arizona	1,576,939	1,241,101	882,106	45,628	13,120	77,174	35,210	155,862	2,423	29,578
Arkansas	777,068	679,689	408,790	18,120	6,899	47,485	25,199	140,027	2,165	31,004
California	6,902,807	5,651,601	3,927,555	282,044	75,862	375,012	158,609	699,241	12,204	121,074
Colorado	1,012,557	813,266	570,807	33,280	7,538	51,954	23,246	105,960	1,281	19,200
Connecticut	901,648	659,238	474,950	21,364	7,173	39,075	18,457	81,784	746	15,689
Delaware	263,587	196,651	139,447	5,649	1,566	11,831	5,774	27,385	265	4,734
Dist. of Columbia	92,474	80,546	53,579	2,053	772	4,493	3,233	14,612	38	1,766
Florida	5,382,979	4,334,337	3,081,274	151,687	43,984	271,702	109,287	565,238	8,247	102,918
Georgia	2,072,624	1,714,145	1,117,129	48,164	18,864	115,341	66,005	285,889	4,244	58,509
Hawaii	320,859	256,912	195,436	8,805	3,846	15,073	6,153	22,800	402	4,397
Idaho	380,772	315,571	217,186	11,688	3,405	19,720	9,232	44,090	825	9,425
Illinois	2,758,249	2,174,883	1,490,706	82,551	23,896	157,732	71,420	288,827	4,369	55,382
Indiana	1,662,631	1,301,948	855,326	41,192	12,580	92,406	45,829	208,908	3,036	42,671
Iowa	775,036	622,906	439,571	21,217	5,953	44,761	17,980	78,222	945	14,257
Kansas	669,240	528,174	361,490	17,285	5,279	36,170	17,297	74,677	862	15,114
Kentucky	1,104,955	963,497	551,152	34,740	9,133	78,723	36,636	206,175	4,629	42,309
Louisiana	970,667	868,017	488,273	43,205	10,296	87,629	42,908	157,310	3,668	34,728
Maine	378,015	329,559	215,126	10,451	3,092	20,706	8,421	58,476	713	12,574
Maryland	1,239,738	952,251	664,164	31,528	9,133	60,300	31,833	131,074	999	23,220
Massachusetts	1,550,369	1,236,248	821,212	42,328	12,941	73,218	34,307	205,060	1,784	45,398
Michigan	2,787,250	2,141,824	1,393,156	76,816	22,993	149,534	69,255	350,684	6,020	73,366
Minnesota	1,255,533	979,776	698,101	33,096	9,438	60,464	25,744	126,390	1,194	25,349
Mississippi	730,844	647,420	381,880	16,381	8,343	48,181	30,465	131,143	2,187	28,840
Missouri	1,518,403	1,258,256	813,569	37,106	11,796	86,146	43,548	220,596	2,878	42,617
Montana	257,376	217,758	153,554	7,755	2,367	14,567	6,554	27,848	506	4,607
Nebraska	407,988	330,309	231,481	11,517	3,108	23,170	10,271	42,162	378	8,222
Nevada	613,347	492,121	353,170	14,924	5,190	28,159	13,593	65,211	813	11,061
New Hampshire	374,386	288,891	195,087	8,167	2,429	15,095	6,954	48,223	410	12,526
New Jersey	2,176,808	1,583,456	1,118,670	56,518	17,785	99,859	44,649	202,497	2,685	40,793
New Mexico	469,318	408,931	266,801	16,694	4,362	27,465	15,007	65,167	1,108	12,327
New York	4,498,413	3,513,125	2,388,547	137,484	43,701	222,704	98,122	510,196	7,813	104,558
North Carolina	2,448,986	1,984,962	1,339,587	47,839	18,420	120,100	63,068	330,353	4,275	61,320
North Dakota	148,605	125,786	87,569	5,362	1,054	10,965	4,304	13,917	150	2,465
Ohio	2,776,912	2,290,813	1,476,557	95,318	20,422	191,239	78,533	356,826	5,778	66,140
Oklahoma	899,398	758,912	484,224	24,852	7,817	57,711	29,429	127,565	2,147	25,167
Oregon	1,025,635	818,228	580,498	29,261	8,775	51,507	19,336	109,815	1,807	17,229
Pennsylvania	3,498,489	2,744,424	1,847,485	97,554	24,248	202,520	79,682	407,320	6,005	79,610
Rhode Island	272,007	217,881	147,006	5,247	2,372	12,101	5,701	37,476	288	7,690
South Carolina	1,319,979	1,066,150	709,839	26,976	10,117	68,153	35,996	178,822	2,508	33,739
South Dakota	198,746	168,626	120,981	5,770	1,428	12,154	5,306	19,212	176	3,599
Tennessee	1,676,300	1,392,164	884,653	42,274	13,587	98,135	49,885	251,021	4,050	48,559
Texas	4,661,488	3,928,648	2,516,258	195,753	44,920	317,793	147,871	569,586	11,330	125,137
Utah	468,330	375,685	253,880	18,459	4,770	23,117	15,597	47,923	727	11,212
Vermont	175,425	142,755	96,840	4,759	1,446	8,518	3,596	22,565	247	4,784
Virginia	1,817,456	1,443,127	979,680	51,046	14,066	96,719	44,160	212,711	3,095	41,650
Washington	1,630,544	1,260,474	873,750	50,425	13,472	77,930	31,733	179,674	2,442	31,048
West Virginia	554,566	468,120	265,919	23,321	4,882	44,224	17,222	91,995	3,132	17,425
Wisconsin	1,492,247	1,170,705	822,488	34,083	11,196	73,240	33,005	161,864	1,923	32,906
Wyoming	130,787	103,689	73,301	3,470	919	6,802	3,485	13,252	176	2,284
American Samoa	4,338	6,236	2,277	208	278	607	804	1,331	54	677
Guam	13,555	16,628	9,919	1,057	602	1,472	1,291	1,642	67	578
N. Mariana Isls.	1,742	2,750	1,489	116	186	311	315	249	10	74
Puerto Rico	700,656	842,927	445,673	61,662	11,674	76,865	28,412	173,131	7,075	38,435
Virgin Isls. (U.S.)	23,756	21,721	16,028	974	453	1,339	759	1,682	51	435
Foreign countries	402,455	627,230	390,368	104,546	10,851	92,364	14,608	10,773	529	3,191
Unknown	2,318	1,874	1,363	75	12	215	38	142	3	26
All areas	73,642,029	59,963,425	40,089,061	2,335,807	648,530	4,190,676	1,892,885	8,909,430	141,760	1,755,276

Outcomes of Applications for Disability Benefits, 1999-2013

Source: Social Security Administration

Year of application	Total	Pending final decision	Technical denial[1]	Medical denials Medical	Medical denials Subsequent nonmedical[2]	Medical allowances Awards	Medical allowances Subsequent denials[2]	Award rate[3]	Allowance rate[4]
1999	1,265,037	0	104,332	445,995	4,056	708,797	1,857	56.0%	61.3%
2000	1,364,323	0	136,054	456,467	3,817	766,047	1,938	56.1	62.6
2001	1,513,411	0	170,520	496,835	3,579	840,542	1,935	55.5	62.8
2002	1,715,710	0	231,067	580,430	4,067	898,047	2,099	52.3	60.7
2003	1,941,894	0	374,305	632,284	4,485	928,747	2,073	47.8	59.5
2004	2,262,119	0	615,672	677,811	5,634	961,376	1,626	42.5	58.5
2005	2,087,733	0	528,799	642,261	6,964	907,744	1,965	43.5	58.4
2006	2,164,393	0	611,238	653,612	7,276	890,350	1,917	41.1	57.5
2007	2,216,564	1,847	651,804	640,652	7,916	912,526	1,819	41.2	58.6
2008	2,358,630	3,940	717,216	658,133	9,028	968,529	1,784	41.1	59.3
2009	2,753,014	7,879	845,411	784,743	10,700	1,102,427	1,854	40.2	58.2
2010	2,981,613	17,204	978,922	851,373	19,181	1,112,846	2,087	37.5	56.2
2011	2,952,088	66,124	982,311	823,595	20,954	1,057,026	2,078	36.6	55.7
2012	2,885,480	251,069	964,712	730,700	23,846	912,350	2,173	34.6	54.9
2013	2,689,842	469,470	912,785	607,055	24,823	673,712	1,997	30.3	51.8

Note: Data as of mid-2014. Applications for more recent years may still be pending; award and allowance rates will change. Does not include Supplemental Security Income-only applications. (1) Application denied for non-medical reason. (2) Denied for non-medical reasons after medical criteria were adjudicated. (3) Percent of all applications, minus pending claims, in which benefits were awarded. (4) Percent of all medical decisions that resulted in an allowance.

OASDI Recipients and Monthly Payments, 1940-2015

Source: Social Security Administration

Year	Total recipients	Total (thous.)	Avg.[1]	Avg. (2015 dollars)[2]	Year	Total recipients	Total (thous.)	Avg.[1]	Avg. (2015 dollars)[2]
		Monthly benefits					Monthly benefits		
1940	222,488	$4,070	$18.29	$300.52	2000	45,414,794	$34,848,920	$767.35	$1,052.66
1945	1,288,107	23,801	18.48	236.67	2005	48,434,445	44,351,772	915.71	1,110.93
1950	3,477,243	126,857	36.48	349.38	2006	49,122,831	46,938,176	955.53	1,122.99
1955	7,960,616	411,613	51.71	444.56	2007	49,864,982	49,218,232	987.03	1,128.40
1960	14,844,589	936,321	63.07	491.17	2008	50,898,396	53,666,202	1,054.38	1,158.08
1965	20,866,767	1,516,802	72.69	531.14	2009	52,522,819	55,905,731	1,064.41	1,177.03
1970	26,228,629	2,628,326	100.21	594.94	2010	54,032,097	58,048,364	1,074.33	1,163.92
1975	32,085,372	5,727,903	178.52	764.05	2011	55,404,480	62,213,382	1,122.89	1,174.75
1980	35,618,840	10,694,022	300.23	838.81	2012	56,758,185	65,430,104	1,152.79	1,181.23
1985	37,058,353	15,901,643	429.10	929.87	2013	57,978,610	68,544,382	1,182.24	1,195.06
1990	39,832,125	21,686,763	544.45	977.53	2014	59,007,158	71,693,353	1,214.99	1,209.98
1995	43,387,259	28,148,078	648.76	1,003.68	2015	59,963,425	73,642,029	1,228.12	1,228.12

OASDI = Old-Age, Survivors, and Disability Insurance. **Note:** Disability insurance payments began in 1957. (1) Avg. monthly benefit does not necessarily reflect individual payments to OASDI recipients. (2) Adjusted for inflation.

Social Security Trust Funds

Source: Social Security Administration

Old-Age and Survivors Insurance (OASI) Trust Fund, 1940-2015

(in millions)

Fiscal year[1]	Total	Net payroll tax contribs.	Income from taxing benefits	General fund reimburse-ments[2]	Net interest[3]	Total	Benefit pymts.[4]	Admin. expenses	Transfers to Railroad Retirement program	Net increase in fund[5]	Year-end balance
			INCOME				DISBURSEMENTS				
1940	$592	$550	—	—	$42	$28	$16	$12	—	$564	$1,745
1950	2,367	2,106	—	$4	257	784	727	57	—	1,583	12,893
1960	10,360	9,843	—	—	517	11,073	10,270	202	$600	−713	20,829
1970	31,746	29,955	—	442	1,350	27,321	26,268	474	579	4,425	32,616
1980	100,051	97,608	—	557	1,886	103,228	100,626	1,160	1,442	−3,177	24,566
1990	278,607	260,069	$2,924	1,471	14,143	223,481	218,948	1,564	2,969	55,126	203,445
1995	326,067	289,525	5,114	11	31,417	294,456	288,607	1,797	4,052	31,611	447,946
2000	484,228	418,219	12,476	1	53,532	353,396	347,868	1,990	3,538	130,832	893,003
2005	599,992	502,998	15,332	—	81,662	436,919	430,439	2,900	3,579	163,073	1,615,623
2006	632,157	530,006	15,176	−350	87,324	455,560	449,191	2,911	3,458	176,597	1,792,220
2007	663,376	553,414	16,661	—	93,300	488,553	481,828	3,151	3,575	174,822	1,967,042
2008	692,873	573,750	16,396	—	102,727	509,864	502,973	3,259	3,632	183,009	2,150,052
2009	697,326	571,228	18,967	—	107,131	551,542	544,484	3,369	3,690	145,784	2,295,835
2010	682,448	552,037	21,068	737	108,606	579,907	572,515	3,462	3,930	102,541	2,398,377
2011	692,510	495,031	21,174	68,886	107,419	599,232	591,477	3,645	4,110	93,278	2,491,654
2012	728,981	500,661	27,150	95,927	105,243	634,700	627,208	3,352	4,139	94,281	2,585,936
2013	739,668	589,976	23,144	26,433	100,115	670,554	663,195	3,410	3,948	69,114	2,655,049
2014	763,295	642,256	24,641	126	96,271	705,645	698,235	3,153	4,257	57,650	2,712,699
2015	795,319	672,246	29,627	211	93,235	741,464	733,711	3,496	4,258	53,855	2,766,554

— = Not applicable. **Note:** Numbers may not add up to totals due to rounding. (1) Fiscal years 1977 and later consist of the 12 months ending on Sept. 30 of each year. Fiscal years prior to 1977 consisted of the 12 months ending on June 30 of each year. (2) Includes reimbursements from the general fund of the Treasury to the OASI Trust Fund for certain legislated measures since 1957. (3) Includes net profits or losses on marketable investments. Beginning in 1967, the trust fund paid administrative expenses on an estimated basis, with a final adjustment including interest made in the following fiscal year. Net interest includes these interest adjustments. Beginning in Oct. 1973, figures include relatively small gifts to the fund. (4) Beginning in 1967, includes payments for vocational rehabilitation services furnished to disabled persons receiving benefits because of their disabilities; beginning in 1983, includes reimbursements paid from the general fund to the trust fund for unnegotiated benefit checks. (5) Net change in assets during fiscal year, including amounts borrowed or repaid by other funds.

Disability Insurance (DI) Trust Fund, 1960-2015

(in millions)

Fiscal year[1]	Total	Net payroll tax contribs.	Income from taxing benefits	General fund reimburse-ments[2]	Net interest[3]	Total	Benefit pymts.[4]	Admin. expenses	Transfers to Railroad Retirement program	Net increase in fund[5]	Year-end balance
			INCOME				DISBURSEMENTS				
1960	$1,034	$987	—	—	$47	$533	$528	$32	−$27	$501	$2,167
1970	4,380	4,141	—	$16	223	2,954	2,795	149	10	1,426	5,104
1980	17,376	16,805	—	118	453	15,320	14,998	334	−12	2,056	7,680
1990	28,215	27,154	$158	138	766	25,124	24,327	717	80	3,091	11,455
1995	70,209	67,986	335	—	1,888	41,374	40,234	1,072	68	28,835	35,206
2000	77,023	70,001	756	—	6,266	56,008	54,244	1,608	159	21,014	113,752
2005	96,765	85,418	1,164	—	10,183	86,360	83,721	2,301	338	10,405	193,298
2006	101,571	90,001	1,174	—	10,396	92,932	90,064	2,480	388	8,640	201,938
2007	108,396	93,973	1,351	—	13,072	96,758	93,955	2,357	445	11,638	213,577
2008	109,816	97,432	1,373	8	11,003	107,153	104,222	2,513	418	2,663	216,239
2009	109,681	97,008	1,841	—	10,832	118,144	115,073	2,623	448	−8,462	207,777
2010	105,513	93,739	1,745	125	9,904	126,344	122,935	2,947	462	−20,831	186,946
2011	106,225	84,031	1,878	11,745	8,571	131,489	127,990	3,034	465	−25,264	161,682
2012	108,845	85,072	383	16,234	7,156	138,546	135,114	2,920	512	−29,701	131,981
2013	111,262	100,169	1,051	4,504	5,538	142,757	139,446	2,760	551	−31,494	100,486
2014	114,105	109,060	1,022	27	3,997	144,667	141,327	2,897	444	−30,562	69,925
2015	117,965	114,156	1,036	39	2,733	146,234	142,923	2,892	419	−28,269	41,656

— = Not applicable. **Note:** Numbers may not add up to totals due to rounding. (1) Fiscal years 1977 and later consist of the 12 months ending on Sept. 30 of each year. Fiscal years prior to 1977 consisted of the 12 months ending on June 30 of each year. (2) Includes reimbursements from the general fund of the Treasury to the DI Trust Fund for certain legislated measures since 1957. (3) Includes net profits or losses on marketable investments. Beginning in 1967, the trust fund paid administrative expenses on an estimated basis, with a final adjustment including interest made in the following fiscal year. Net interest includes these interest adjustments. The 1970 report describes the accounting for administrative expenses for years prior to 1967. Beginning in July 1974, figures include relatively small gifts to the fund. (4) Beginning in 1967, includes payments for vocational rehabilitation services furnished to persons receiving benefits because of a disability; beginning in 1983, includes reimbursements paid from the general fund to the trust fund for unnegotiated benefit checks. (5) Net change in assets during fiscal year, including amounts borrowed or repaid by other funds.

Supplementary Medical Insurance Trust Fund (Medicare SMI), 1975-2015

Source: Centers for Medicare & Medicaid Services, U.S. Dept. of Health and Human Services
(in millions)

Fiscal year[1]	Total	INCOME Premium from participants[2]	Govt. contribs.[3]	Transfers from states[4]	Interest and other income[5,6]	DISBURSEMENTS Total	Benefit pymts.[6,7,8]	Admin. expenses	Net change	Year-end balance[9]
1975	$4,322	$1,887	$2,330	—	$106	$4,170	$3,765	$404	$152	$1,424
1980	10,275	2,928	6,932	—	416	10,737	10,144	593	−462	4,532
1990	46,138[10]	11,494[10]	33,210	—	1,434[10]	43,022[10]	41,498	1,524[10]	3,115[10]	14,527[10]
2000	89,239	20,515	65,561	—	3,164	88,992	87,212[11]	1,780	247	45,896
2005	152,505	35,939	115,200	—	1,366	152,735	149,820[12]	2,914	−230	16,885
2006	211,951	44,241[13]	162,601	$3,630	1,478	195,557	192,083[12,13]	3,474	16,394	33,279
2007	237,890	49,666[13]	179,181	6,977	2,065	232,022	228,596[12,13]	3,426	5,867	39,146
2008	244,872	54,158[13]	180,434	7,042	3,238	224,869	221,445[13,14]	3,423	20,003	59,149
2009	262,573	57,709[13]	194,267	7,504	3,093	260,257	256,938[13]	3,318	2,317	61,466
2010	282,734	61,364[13]	213,709	4,493	3,168	272,224	268,710[13]	3,514	10,510	71,976
2011	301,523	64,502[13]	225,178	6,536	5,307	300,672	296,842[13]	3,830	851	72,827
2012	290,864	66,067[13]	210,508	8,324	5,965	291,907	287,777[13]	4,130	−1,043	71,783
2013	313,158	71,300[13]	227,208	8,666	5,985	315,123	311,367[13]	3,756	−1,965	69,818
2014	334,943	75,887[13]	244,351	8,727	5,978	333,438	329,141[13]	4,297	1,504	71,323
2015	357,530	79,398[13]	263,484	8,797	5,851	359,412	355,806[13]	3,606	−1,882	69,441

— = Not applicable. **Note:** Numbers may not add up to totals because of rounding. (1) Fiscal year 1975 consists of the 12 months ending on June 30, 1975; fiscal years 1980 and later consist of the 12 months ending on Sept. 30 of each year. (2) For Part D, premiums include both amounts withheld from Social Security benefit checks (and certain other federal benefit payments) and amounts paid directly to Part D plans (estimated). (3) For Part B, includes matching payments from the general fund, plus certain interest-adjustment items. For Part D, includes all federal govt. transfers. (4) As of 2006, Medicaid is no longer the primary payer for full-benefit dual eligibles; states pay 90% of estimated costs. (5) Other income includes recoveries of amounts reimbursed from the trust fund that are not trust fund obligations and other miscellaneous income. In 2008, includes an adjustment of $812 mil for interest inadvertently unearned as a result of Hospital Insurance (HI) hospice costs misallocated to, and paid from, the Part B account of the SMI trust fund May 2005-Sept. 2007. (6) Values after 2005 include additional premiums for Medicare Advantage (MA) plans that are deducted from beneficiaries' Social Security checks, transferred to HI and SMI trust funds, and then transferred to the plans. (7) Includes costs of Peer Review Organizations in 1983-2001 and costs of Quality Review Organizations beginning in 2002. (8) For Part D, includes payments to plans, subsidies to employer-sponsored retiree drug plans, payments to states for low-income eligibility determinations, and Part D drug premiums (the amount collected from beneficiaries and transferred to plans and an estimated amount for premiums paid directly to plans). Includes amounts for transitional assistance benefits in 2004-06. (9) The financial status of SMI depends on the trust fund's assets and liabilities. (10) Includes the impact of the Medicare Catastrophic Coverage Act of 1988. (11) Benefit payments less monies transferred from the HI trust fund for home health agency costs. (12) Certain HI hospice costs were misallocated to, and paid from, the Part B account of the SMI trust fund. See also footnote 14. (13) Includes an estimated $1.804 bil (2006), $2.295 bil (2007), $2.970 bil (2008), $3.699 bil (2009), $4.221 bil (2010), $4.843 bil (2011), $5.222 bil (2012), $6.306 bil (2013), $7.450 bil (2014), and $8.465 bil (2015) for premiums paid directly to Part D plans. (14) Benefit payments were $229.9 bil; amount shown does not include transfer of $8.5 bil from the general fund of the Treasury for HI hospice costs that were misallocated to, and paid from, the Part B account of the SMI trust fund from May 2005 to Sept. 2007. (The HI trust fund, in turn, transferred $8.5 bil to the general fund.)

Hospital Insurance Trust Fund (Medicare HI), 1975-2015

Source: Centers for Medicare & Medicaid Services, U.S. Dept. of Health and Human Services
(in millions)

Fiscal year[1]	Total	Payroll taxes	Taxation of benefits	INCOME Transfers from Railroad Retire-ment acct.	Reimb. for uninsured persons	Premiums from voluntary enrollees	Pymts. for military wage credits	Interest and other income[2,3]	DISBURSEMENTS Total	Benefit pymts.[3,4]	Admin. expenses[5]	Net change	Year-end balance
1975	$12,568	$11,291	—	$132	$481	$6	$48	$609	$10,612	$10,353	$259	$1,956	$9,870
1980	25,415	23,244	—	244	697	17	141	1,072	24,288	23,790	497	1,127	14,490
1990	79,563	70,655	—	367	413	113	107	7,908	66,687	65,912	774	12,876	95,631
2000	159,681	137,738	$8,787	465	470	1,392	2	10,827	130,284	127,934[6]	2,350	29,397	168,084
2005	196,921	168,954	8,765	445	286	2,303	0	16,168	184,142	181,292[7]	2,850	12,779	277,723
2006	210,309	180,392	10,319	471	408	2,632	0	16,086	184,901	181,815[7]	3,086	25,408	303,130
2007	219,207	187,992	10,593	483	468	2,761	0	16,910	202,827	200,191[7]	2,636	16,380	319,510
2008	229,729	197,195	11,733	526	506	2,913	0	16,856	230,240	227,008[8]	3,231	−511	319,000
2009	228,915	194,102	12,376	524	614	2,817	968[9]	17,514	238,001	234,659	3,343	−9,086	309,914
2010	218,004	183,603	13,760	535	−142	3,314	0	16,933	248,978	245,650	3,328	−30,975	278,939
2011	226,486	192,063	15,143	477	275	3,273	0	15,255	259,628	255,717	3,911	−33,142	245,797
2012	241,730	204,752	18,643	511	262	3,400	0	14,162	258,155	254,459	3,696	−16,425	229,372
2013	243,560	212,901	14,310	577	0	3,397	0	12,375	266,546	262,411	4,135	−22,986	206,386
2014	262,753	227,579	18,066	612	432	3,259	0	12,805	266,853	262,520	4,332	−4,100	202,286
2015	272,359	237,697	20,208	595	187	3,277	0	10,396	278,736	273,248	5,488	−6,377	195,909

— = Not applicable. **Note:** Numbers may not add up to totals because of rounding. (1) Fiscal year 1975 consists of the 12 months ending on June 30, 1975; fiscal years 1980 and later consist of the 12 months ending on Sept. 30 of each year. (2) Other income includes recoveries of amounts reimbursed from the trust fund that are not trust fund obligations, receipts from the fraud and abuse control program, and other small amounts of miscellaneous income. In 2008, includes an adjustment of −$853 mil for interest inadvertently earned as a result of HI hospice costs that were misallocated to, and paid from, the Part B account of the Supplementary Medical Insurance (SMI) trust fund from May 2005 to Sept. 2007. (3) Values after 2005 include additional premiums for Medicare Advantage (MA) plans that are deducted from beneficiaries' Social Security checks, transferred to the HI and SMI trust funds, and then transferred to the plans. (4) Includes costs of Peer Review Organizations from 1983 through 2001 (beginning with implementation of the Prospective Payment System on Oct. 1, 1983), and costs of Quality Improvement Organizations beginning in 2002. (5) Includes costs of experiments and demonstration projects. Beginning in 1997, includes fraud and abuse control expenses. (6) Includes monies transferred to the SMI trust fund for home health agency costs. (7) Certain HI hospice costs were misallocated to, and paid from, the Part B account of the SMI trust fund. (8) Benefit payments were $218.5 bil. Amount shown includes transfer of $8.484 bil to the general fund of the Treasury for HI hospice costs that were misallocated to, and paid from, the Part B account of the SMI trust fund from May 2005 to Sept. 2007. (The general fund, in turn, transferred $8.484 bil to the Part B account of the SMI trust fund.) (9) Includes the lump-sum general revenue adjustment of −$968 mil.

TAXES

Federal Personal Income Tax Return Facts, 2016

Source: George W. Smith III, CPA, Managing Partner, George W. Smith & Company, P.C.

Deadlines. The deadline for filing a 2016 U.S. individual income tax return (1040, 1040A, or 1040EZ) is Apr. 17, 2017. Maine and Massachusetts residents observe Patriots' Day Apr. 17, 2017, and receive an extension to Apr. 18.

Extensions. Taxpayers who cannot file a 2016 individual income tax return by the deadline can apply for a six-month extension to Oct. 16, 2017. To qualify for an extension, Form 4868 must be filed no later than Apr. 17, 2017. Approximately 9 mil extensions were filed in 2016.

E-Filing. On June 10, 2011, the IRS announced that 1 bil individual tax returns had been e-filed since the electronic filing program began as a pilot program in 1986. By May 13, 2016, 123.7 mil returns for income tax year 2015 had been e-filed, compared to 120.6 mil by mid-May in 2015.

Penalties. The IRS can levy two potential penalties after the filing due date when there is a balance owed. One penalty is for failing to file a timely tax return; the other is for failure to pay the tax when due. In addition, interest can be charged on any unpaid tax balance.

Refunds. The average refund was $2,732 for 2016 filing season returns, up from $2,698 in the previous tax year. The IRS refunded $279.9 bil through May 13, 2016. Of that sum, $244.8 bil was refunded with direct deposit.

Statute of limitations. Taxpayers who have not yet filed their 2013 federal tax return have until three years after the deadline to file and claim their refund. After that date, any refunds for 2013 income tax or withholding tax, including the earned income tax credit, will be lost.

Federal Income Tax Rates for Taxable-Income Brackets, 2016

Tax rate	Unmarried individuals	Married filing jointly or surviving spouses	Married filing separately	Head of household other than surviving spouses
10%	$1 to $9,275	$1 to $18,550	$1 to $9,275	$1 to $13,250
15%	$9,276 to $37,650	$18,551 to $75,300	$9,276 to $37,650	$13,251 to $50,400
25%	$37,651 to $91,150	$75,301 to $151,900	$37,651 to $75,950	$50,401 to $130,150
28%	$91,151 to $190,150	$151,901 to $231,450	$75,951 to $115,725	$130,151 to $210,800
33%	$190,151 to $413,350	$231,451 to $413,350	$115,726 to $206,675	$210,801 to $413,350
35%	$413,351 to $415,050	$413,351 to $466,950	$206,676 to $233,475	$413,351 to $441,000
39.6%	Over $415,050	Over $466,950	Over $233,475	Over $441,000

Standard Deduction, 2016

The standard deduction is a flat amount subtracted from the adjusted gross income of taxpayers who do not itemize deductions.

Single	$6,300
Married filing jointly or qualifying widow(er)	$12,600
Married filing separately	$6,300
Head of household	$9,300

Additional standard deduction. Elderly and blind, single: $1,550. Elderly and blind, married: $1,250.

Dependents. An individual reported as a dependent on another person's tax return generally may claim the greater of (1) $1,050 or (2) the sum of $350 plus the individual's earned income, not to exceed the standard deduction.

Personal exemption. Unless another person can claim the individual as a dependent in 2016 the personal exemption is $4,050 (phased out at higher income levels).

FICA and self-employment tax. For Social Security, wages are taxable up to $118,500. For Medicare, all wages are taxable.

Common Income Tax Errors

Periodically, the IRS issues a list of the most commonly made income tax errors.

1. Wrong or missing Social Security numbers.
2. Wrong names.
3. Filing status errors, such as Head of Household instead of Single.
4. Math mistakes, for example, when adding or subtracting items on a form or worksheet.
5. Errors in credits or deductions, like the Earned Income Tax Credit, Child and Dependent Care Credit, and standard deductions.
6. Wrong bank and/or account numbers for direct deposit of any tax refund.
7. Forms not signed or dated. An unsigned tax return is not valid. Both spouses must sign a joint return.
8. E-file PIN errors. E-filed returns can be signed electronically with a personal identification number (PIN). Usually, last year's PIN can be used, but if it is unknown, adjusted gross income information from last year's original return needs to be entered for verification.

Retirement Savings Plans and Income Tax

401(k) plan. The maximum amount that an individual can contribute to a 401(k) plan for 2016 is $18,000. Individuals born before 1967 can put away an additional $6,000, for a total of $24,000.

IRAs. 2016 contributions to IRAs and Roth IRAs are limited to $5,500. Anyone born before 1967 can contribute an extra $1,000. Funds may be deposited into a traditional IRA for 2016 until Apr. 17, 2017. Contributions after Apr. 17 will automatically be considered funds deposited for 2017.

Roth IRA. Contributions paid into a Roth IRA are not tax deductible. Distributions of funds including investment earnings held in the account for five years or longer and distributed after age 59½ are free of both income tax and the 10% early-withdrawal penalty. Withdrawals from the account in less than five years can be subject to tax and a 10% withdrawal penalty regardless of age. There are income limitations on contributions.

Distributions. There is a 10% penalty for IRA distributions before age 59½. Distributions paid to a beneficiary due to disability/death of the owner are not subject to this penalty, nor are payments used for certain unreimbursed medical expenses, higher-education expenses, or first-time homebuyer acquisition costs (up to $10,000).

The owner of a traditional IRA (or a SIMPLE plan, pension, or profit-sharing plan account) must begin receiving distributions by Apr. 1 of the calendar year following the year in which he or she reaches age 70½. Any employee who works beyond 70½ and is not a 5% or more owner of the business can continue to defer profit-sharing and pension plan distributions.

Tax Credits

A tax deduction reduces a taxpayer's taxable income whereas tax credits reduce the amount of tax owed.

Adoption credit. The adoption credit in 2016 for qualified expenses is $13,460. The credit limit is per person, not per year, and is adjusted annually for inflation. The credit is not refundable and phases out for taxpayers at higher income levels.

American Opportunity Tax Credit. This education credit provides up to $2,500 per student per year in the first four years of a student's postsecondary education.

Child and dependent care credit. This credit is for expenses for the care of taxpayers' qualifying children under age 13 or care of a disabled spouse or dependent, while the taxpayer works or looks for work.

Child tax credit. The maximum child tax credit is $1,000 for each qualifying child.

Earned Income Credit. Lower-income workers who maintain a household may be eligible for an Earned Income Credit. This credit is based on total earned income such as wages, commissions, and tips. Military personnel can include tax-free combat pay in income to compute the credit.

Energy credits. There are many energy-related credits— from the purchase of an alternative fuel vehicle and the installation of solar/fuel cell property in a residence, to the production of biodiesel or ethanol.

Alternative Minimum Tax

The Alternative Minimum Tax (AMT) was established in 1969 to prevent individuals with very high incomes from using special tax breaks to pay little or no tax. The AMT 2016 exemption for a single taxpayer is $53,900 and $83,800 for married filing jointly. For married taxpayers filing separate returns, the exemption is $41,900.

Estate and Gift Taxes

Estate tax. The Tax Relief Act of 2010 reinstated the estate tax with a 35% flat rate and increased the exemptions to $5 mil in 2011 and $5.12 mil in 2012. The rate was increased to 40% for 2013 and subsequent years. The 2016 exemption was set at $5.45 mil.

Gifting. U.S. citizens, residents, and nonresident aliens have an annual gift tax exclusion of up to $14,000 per individual to as many individuals as he or she chooses. For married couples the exclusion is $28,000, even if only one spouse does all the gifting.

International property. All property owned worldwide by American citizens is subject to U.S. estate tax rules and regulations.

Resident aliens. Aliens residing in the U.S. are subject to the same rules as American citizens.

Tax Rates for Estates and Trusts

If taxable income is—	The tax is—
Not over $2,550	15% of the taxable income
Over $2,550 but not over $5,950	$382.50 plus 25% of the excess over $2,550
Over $5,950 but not over $9,050	$1,232.50 plus 28% of the excess over $5,950
Over $9,050 but not over $12,400	$2,100.50 plus 33% of the excess over $9,050
Over $12,400	$3,206 plus 39.6% of the excess over $12,400

Taxable Social Security Benefits

Earnings limitations. Social Security recipients who have not reached the full retirement age of 66 in 2016 will lose $1 of their benefits for every $2 of earned income over $15,720. Recipients who reached full retirement age in 2016 will not lose any benefits if they earned $41,880 or less. Recipients will have to pay back some benefits if their income exceeded that amount.

Taxable benefits. Up to 50% of Social Security benefits may be taxable if the person's total income is more than $25,000 but

less than $34,000 for a single individual, head of household, qualifying widow(er), or a married person who is filing separately if spouses lived apart all year; or more than $32,000 but less than $44,000 for married individuals filing jointly. For higher incomes, 85% of Social Security benefits may become taxable.

If the only income received during the year was Social Security, these benefits are not taxable, and the recipient probably does not have to file a tax return.

Retention of Income Tax Records

Federal tax returns generally can be audited for up to three years after filing or six years if the IRS suspects underreported income, so it's wise to keep copies of an income tax return and records for at least seven years after filing a return.

Tax Audits

Audit odds. The IRS audit rate for individual income tax returns in fiscal year 2015 was 0.84%. The odds of an audit generally trend upward with higher taxpayer income, especially certain types of income. For taxpayers with incomes of $50,000-$75,000, the audit rate was 0.47%. For taxpayers with gross income of $1-$5 mil, the rate was 8.42%. The audit rate was below one in 100 for all incomes between $25,000 and $200,000 (more than 94% of all taxpayers). Most taxpayers have no reason to be concerned about being audited.

The audit selection process is not random. It is based on a set of formulas that are designed to spot questionable returns. If the IRS concludes that a person owes more tax, and he or she disagrees with the findings, the taxpayer can meet with a supervisor.

If the taxpayer still does not agree, he or she can appeal to a separate Appeals Office or take it to the U.S. Tax Court, Federal District Court, or the U.S. Court of Federal Claims.

Tax Court. The U.S. Tax Court is a federal court where taxpayers can dispute tax deficiencies as determined by the Commissioner of Internal Revenue before payment of the disputed amounts. The Tax Court is composed of presidentially appointed members. Many taxpayers choose the Tax Court because they are not required to pay the contested tax up front.

Appeals. For more information about audits, call the IRS at (800) TAX-FORM (829-3676) for its free Publication 556, *Examination of Returns, Appeal Rights, and Claims for Refund* or visit www.irs.gov.

IRS Contact Information

Website: www.irs.gov

Tax questions: (800) 829-1040

Forms/publications: (800) TAX-FORM (829-3676)

Spanish forms/publications: Taxpayers can view and download tax forms and publications in Spanish directly from www.irs.gov/Spanish/.

Hearing impaired: (800) 829-4059 (TTY/TDD)

Additional services: The Volunteer Income Tax Assistance (VITA) program offers free tax help to people who generally make $54,000 or less, persons with disabilities, and limited English speaking taxpayers who need assistance in preparing their own tax returns. www.irs.gov/help-resources or (800) 829-1040.

Report wrongdoing: Report misconduct, waste, fraud, or abuse by an IRS employee to the Treasury Inspector General for Tax Administration at (800) 366-4484 or complaints@ tigta.treas.gov.

Working With a Tax Preparer

The following are some suggestions when using a tax preparer:

- **Choose** wisely. Regulations require all paid tax return preparers including attorneys, certified public accountants, and IRS-enrolled agents to have a Preparer Tax Identification Number. Check the preparer's qualifications and history. Ask about service fees in advance.
- **Review** last year's tax return. Make note of any changes since then such as marriage, divorce, number of dependents, retirement, job changes, additional income, or new deductions.
- **Organize** your records with income items first, followed by itemized deductions (medical, taxes, interest, and charitable and other miscellaneous deductions), followed by gains, losses, rentals, or other items.

- **Time** spent with your preparer may affect your bill. If you provide disorganized records and deductions, there may be an additional cost to have your tax preparer organize your information.
- **Prepare** a list of questions in advance. Ask about any invoices or bills that you are not sure apply.
- **Alert** your preparer if you're waiting to receive additional information. He or she can begin preparing your tax return and include the missing data later to finalize your return. Amending a return after it is completed may incur additional fees.
- **Review** your tax return before signing it. Ask questions about any item you don't understand. Even though your preparer is required to sign the return, you are responsible for its contents.

Total U.S. Tax Collections by Type of Tax, 1960-2015

Source: *Internal Revenue Service Data Book, 2015*, Internal Revenue Service, U.S. Dept. of the Treasury
(as percent of total gross collection or total income taxes)

Fiscal year	Total IRS collections (bil)[1]	Income taxes				Employment taxes[4]	Estate taxes	Gift taxes	Excise taxes[5]
		Total	Business[2]	Individual[3]	Estate and trust[3]				
1960	$92	73.1%	33.0%	67.0%	—	12.2%	1.6%	0.20%	12.9%
1965	114	69.7	32.7	67.3	—	14.9	2.1	0.25	12.9
1970	196	70.9	25.3	74.7	—	19.1	1.7	0.22	8.1
1975	294	68.8	22.6	77.4	—	23.9	1.5	0.13	5.7
1980	519	69.3	20.1	79.9	—	24.7	1.2	0.04	4.7
1985	743	63.8	16.3	83.7	—	30.3	0.8	0.04	5.0
1990	1,056	61.6	16.9	83.1	—	34.8	0.9	0.20	2.6
1995	1,376	61.8	20.5	79.5	—	33.8	1.0	0.13	3.3
2000	2,097	65.5	17.2	82.8	—	30.5	1.2	0.20	2.6
2005	2,269	62.3	21.7	78.3	—	34.0	1.0	0.09	2.5
2010	2,345	62.0	19.1	80.0	0.8%	35.1	0.7	0.12	2.0
2011	2,415	65.8	15.3	83.8	0.9	31.8	0.1	0.27	2.0
2012	2,524	66.1	16.9	82.2	1.0	31.1	0.5	0.08	2.2
2013	2,855	65.7	16.6	82.1	1.3	31.4	0.5	0.20	2.1
2014	3,064	65.2	17.7	80.8	1.5	31.9	0.6	0.08	2.3
2015	3,303	66.1	17.9	80.6	1.5	31.0	0.5	0.06	2.3

— = Not available. **Note:** Numbers may not add up to totals because of rounding. (1) Credits to taxpayer accounts excluded beginning with fiscal year 2009. (2) Incl. taxes on corporation income and unrelated business income from tax-exempt organizations. (3) Income tax reported for estates and trusts is included in individual income tax in FY1960-2007. Estate and trust income tax is reported separately from FY2008 on. (4) Incl. taxes for Old-Age, Survivors, Disability, and Hospital Insurance; federal unemployment insurance; and Railroad Retirement. (5) Excl. excise taxes collected by the U.S. Customs and Border Protection and the Alcohol and Tobacco Tax and Trade Bureau. The IRS collected taxes on alcohol and tobacco until FY1988 and taxes on firearms until FY1991.

Taxes Collected by State Governments, 2015

Source: Annual Survey of State Government Tax Collections, U.S. Census Bureau, U.S. Dept. of Commerce
(as percent of total taxes collected or total sales and gross receipts taxes)

State	Total taxes collected in dollars (mil)[1]	Property taxes	Sales and gross receipts taxes			License taxes[3]	Individual income taxes	Corporation net income taxes	Other taxes[4]
			Total	General	Selective[2]				
Alabama	$9,755	3.5%	50.6%	49.9%	50.1%	5.1%	34.2%	5.5%	1.2%
Alaska	864	14.8	29.6	—	100.0	17.0		26.4	12.2
Arizona	14,082	6.3	58.6	78.4	21.6	3.3	26.7	4.9	0.3
Arkansas	9,190	11.8	48.0	72.2	27.8	4.2	29.0	5.2	1.8
California	151,173	1.5	34.6	73.5	26.5	6.2	51.6	6.0	0.1
Colorado	12,811	—	37.4	58.8	41.2	5.3	49.8	5.3	2.3
Connecticut	16,232	—	40.4	62.2	37.8	2.8	50.4	4.2	2.1
Delaware	3,514	—	14.2	—	100.0	39.6	32.4	11.4	2.4
Dist. of Columbia	7,087	31.8	24.7	75.0	25.0	2.3	26.4	6.3	8.6
Florida	37,218	<0.1	81.5	71.9	28.1	5.7	—	6.0	6.7
Georgia	19,724	4.4	38.3	69.6	30.4	3.2	49.1	5.1	<0.1
Hawaii	6,486	—	62.9	73.3	26.7	3.9	30.7	1.1	1.4
Idaho	3,975	—	48.8	75.4	24.6	8.4	37.2	5.5	0.2
Illinois	39,283	0.2	41.0	55.6	44.4	7.0	40.5	10.3	1.1
Indiana	17,400	0.1	60.9	68.7	31.3	3.8	30.1	5.2	<0.1
Iowa	9,189	<0.1	46.5	71.2	28.8	9.5	37.8	5.0	1.2
Kansas	7,884	8.4	50.5	76.8	23.2	4.8	28.7	5.8	1.9
Kentucky	11,598	4.9	47.0	59.9	40.1	4.2	35.1	6.5	2.4
Louisiana	9,719	0.6	54.6	55.1	44.9	4.0	30.7	2.6	7.5
Maine	4,064	0.9	49.2	64.0	36.0	6.6	37.7	4.2	1.4
Maryland	19,850	3.7	41.8	53.1	46.9	4.3	42.0	5.1	3.1
Massachusetts	27,012	<0.1	30.6	70.1	29.9	4.5	53.6	8.2	3.0
Michigan	26,957	7.3	48.7	70.2	29.8	5.8	32.7	4.4	1.1
Minnesota	24,439	3.4	40.7	55.1	44.9	5.7	42.4	6.0	1.7
Mississippi	7,907	0.3	61.6	70.2	29.8	7.7	22.6	6.8	1.0
Missouri	11,956	0.3	42.5	66.5	33.5	4.6	49.0	3.6	0.1
Montana	2,843	9.4	21.2	—	100.0	12.3	41.5	5.9	9.6
Nebraska	5,087	<0.1	45.5	77.2	22.8	3.4	44.0	6.8	0.3
Nevada	7,533	3.2	80.2	67.6	32.4	8.6	—	—	8.0
New Hampshire	2,488	16.3	39.0	—	100.0	13.0	3.9	23.2	4.7
New Jersey	31,568	<0.1	41.0	70.6	29.4	4.9	42.0	8.2	3.9
New Mexico	6,009	1.8	49.8	75.3	24.7	4.5	23.0	4.2	16.7
New York	78,243	—	30.6	54.7	45.3	2.3	55.9	6.5	4.7
North Carolina	25,062	—	42.7	64.1	35.9	7.0	44.7	5.3	0.3
North Dakota	5,740	0.1	33.8	71.6	28.4	3.9	9.3	3.2	49.6
Ohio	28,297	—	60.8	69.1	30.9	7.7	31.4	<0.1	0.1
Oklahoma	9,407	—	44.0	64.8	35.2	11.2	34.6	4.1	6.1
Oregon	10,575	0.2	14.2	—	100.0	9.3	69.1	5.9	1.3
Pennsylvania	36,110	0.1	50.9	53.7	46.3	6.2	31.8	7.0	4.1
Rhode Island	3,197	0.1	50.7	59.2	40.8	3.8	38.0	5.5	1.9
South Carolina	9,633	0.3	50.8	73.0	27.0	5.4	38.8	3.9	0.7
South Dakota	1,674	—	82.0	70.7	29.3	17.3	—	0.3	0.5
Tennessee	12,698	—	72.4	71.2	28.8	11.8	2.4	11.0	2.3
Texas	55,086	—	86.5	70.6	29.4	6.2	—	—	7.3
Utah	6,703	—	41.3	68.1	31.9	4.2	47.1	5.5	1.9
Vermont	3,043	34.0	33.7	35.7	64.3	3.7	23.3	3.7	1.6
Virginia	20,537	0.2	31.6	58.4	41.6	4.0	58.0	4.0	2.2
Washington	20,644	9.8	78.7	77.1	22.9	6.8	—	—	4.8
West Virginia	5,566	0.1	47.1	49.4	50.6	2.5	34.7	3.4	12.2
Wisconsin	17,019	1.0	44.9	64.0	36.0	6.0	41.5	6.1	0.5
Wyoming	2,356	13.5	42.2	81.5	18.5	6.5	—	—	37.7
U.S. total	**916,488**	**1.9**	**47.1**	**66.4**	**33.6**	**5.7**	**36.9**	**5.4**	**3.1**

— = Tax not collected by state. NA = Not available. **Note:** For fiscal year 2015 (July 1, 2014-June 30, 2015) for all states except AL and MI (ends Sept. 30), NY (Mar. 31), and TX (Aug. 31). (1) Incl. taxes not shown separately. (2) Incl. taxes on sale of alcoholic beverages, insurance premiums, motor fuels, public utilities, and tobacco products. (3) Incl. taxes on licenses for motor vehicles and corporations among others. (4) Incl. death and gift taxes and severance taxes (on extraction or harvest of natural resources).

State Government Personal Income Tax Rates, 2016

Source: Reproduced with permission from *CCH State Tax Guide*, published and copyrighted by CCH Inc., a Wolters Kluwer business
Alaska, Florida, Nevada, South Dakota, Texas, Washington, and Wyoming did not have state income taxes and are thus not listed. Tax rates apply in stages—for example, a single person in Connecticut making $60,000 in taxable income would pay 3% on the first $10,000 of income, 5% on the next $40,000, and so on. For further details on some states, see notes at end of table.

Alabama
Single, Head of household, or
Married filing separately
$0 to $500.	2%
$501 to $3,000	4%
$3,001 and over	5%

Married filing jointly
$0 to $1,000	2%
$1,001 to $6,000	4%
$6,001 and over	5%

Arizona[1,2,3]
Single or Married filing separately
$0 to $10,163.	2.59%
$10,164 to $25,406	2.88%
$25,407 to $50,812	3.36%
$50,813 to $152,434	4.24%
$152,435 and over	4.54%

Married filing jointly or
Head of household
$0 to $20,325.	2.59%
$20,326 to $50,812	2.88%
$50,813 to $101,623	3.36%
$101,624 to $304,868	4.24%
$304,869 and over	4.54%

Arkansas[2,3]
For net income less than $21,000:
$0 to $4,299	0.9%
$4,300 to $8,399.	2.4%
$8,400 to $12,599.	3.4%
$12,600 to $20,999.	4.4%

For net income from $21,000 to $75,000:
$0 to $4,299	0.9%
$4,300 to $8,399.	2.5%
$8,400 to $12,599.	3.5%
$12,600 to $20,999.	4.5%
$21,000 to $35,099.	5%
$35,100 to $75,000.	6%

For net income over $75,000:
$0 to $4,299	0.9%
$4,300 to $8,399.	2.5%
$8,400 to $12,599.	3.5%
$12,600 to $20,999.	4.5%
$21,000 to $35,099.	6%
$35,100 and over	6.9%

California[1,2]
Single or Married/registered
domestic partner filing separately
$0 to $8,015	1%
$8,016 to $19,001.	2%
$19,002 to $29,989.	4%
$29,990 to $41,629	6%
$41,630 to $52,612	8%
$52,613 to $268,750	9.3%
$268,751 to $322,499.	10.3%
$322,500 to $537,498.	11.3%
$537,499 and over	12.3%

Head of household
$0 to $16,040	1%
$16,041 to $38,003.	2%
$38,004 to $48,990.	4%
$48,991 to $60,630.	6%
$60,631 to $71,615.	8%
$71,616 to $365,499.	9.3%
$365,500 to $438,599.	10.3%
$438,600 to $730,997.	11.3%
$730,998 and over	12.3%

Married/registered domestic
partner filing jointly or Qualifying
widow(er)
$0 to $16,030	1%
$16,031 to $38,002.	2%
$38,003 to $59,978.	4%
$59,979 to $83,258.	6%
$83,259 to $105,224.	8%
$105,225 to $537,500.	9.3%
$537,501 to $644,998.	10.3%
$644,999 to $1,074,996	11.3%
$1,074,997 and over.	12.3%

Colorado
4.63% of federal taxable income

Connecticut
Single or Married filing separately
$0 to $10,000	3%
$10,001 to $50,000.	5%
$50,001 to $100,000.	5.5%
$100,001 to $200,000.	6%
$200,001 to $250,000.	6.5%
$250,001 to $500,000.	6.9%
$500,001 and over	6.99%

Head of household
$0 to $16,000	3%
$16,001 to $80,000.	5%
$80,001 to $160,000.	5.5%
$160,001 to $320,000.	6%
$320,001 to $400,000.	6.5%
$400,001 to $800,000.	6.9%
$800,001 and over	6.99%

Married filing jointly or
Qualifying widow(er)
$0 to $20,000	3%
$20,001 to $100,000.	5%
$100,001 to $200,000.	5.5%
$200,001 to $400,000.	6%
$400,001 to $500,000.	6.5%
$500,001 to $1,000,000	6.9%
$1,000,001 and over.	6.99%

Delaware
$0 to $2,000	0%
$2,001 to $5,000.	2.2%
$5,001 to $10,000.	3.9%
$10,001 to $20,000.	4.8%
$20,001 to $25,000.	5.2%
$25,001 to $60,000.	5.55%
$60,001 and over	6.6%

District of Columbia
$0 to $10,000	4%
$10,001 to $40,000.	6%
$40,001 to $60,000.	6.5%
$60,001 to $350,000.	8.5%
$350,001 to $1,000,000.	8.75%
$1,000,001 and over.	8.95%

Georgia
Single
$0 to $750.	1%
$751 to $2,250	2%
$2,251 to $3,750.	3%
$3,751 to $5,250.	4%
$5,251 to $7,000.	5%
$7,001 and over	6%

Head of household, Married
filing jointly, or Qualifying
widow(er)
$0 to $1,000	1%
$1,001 to $3,000.	2%
$3,001 to $5,000.	3%
$5,001 to $7,000.	4%
$7,001 to $10,000.	5%
$10,001 and over	6%

Married filing separately
$0 to $500.	1%
$501 to $1,500.	2%
$1,501 to $2,500.	3%
$2,501 to $3,500.	4%
$3,501 to $5,000.	5%
$5,001 and over	6%

Hawaii
Single or Married filing separately
$0 to $2,400	1.4%
$2,401 to $4,800.	3.2%
$4,801 to $9,600.	5.5%
$9,601 to $14,400.	6.4%
$14,401 to $19,200.	6.8%
$19,201 to $24,000.	7.2%
$24,001 to $36,000.	7.6%
$36,001 to $48,000.	7.9%
$48,001 and over	8.25%

Head of household
$0 to $3,600	1.4%
$3,601 to $7,200	3.2%
$7,201 to $14,400	5.5%
$14,401 to $21,600	6.4%

Connecticut (continued)
$21,601 to $28,800.	6.8%
$28,801 to $36,000.	7.2%
$36,001 to $54,000.	7.6%
$54,001 to $72,000.	7.9%
$72,001 and over	8.25%

Married filing jointly or
Surviving spouse
$0 to $4,800	1.4%
$4,801 to $9,600.	3.2%
$9,601 to $19,200.	5.5%
$19,201 to $28,800.	6.4%
$28,801 to $38,400.	6.8%
$38,401 to $48,000.	7.2%
$48,001 to $72,000.	7.6%
$72,001 to $96,000.	7.9%
$96,001 and over	8.25%

Idaho[1,2]
Single or Married filing
separately
$0 to $1,453	1.6%
$1,454 to $2,907.	3.6%
$2,908 to $4,361.	4.1%
$4,362 to $5,815.	5.1%
$5,816 to $7,269.	6.1%
$7,270 to $10,904.	7.1%
$10,905 and over	7.4%

Head of household, Married
filing jointly, or Surviving
spouse
$0 to $2,907	1.6%
$2,908 to $5,815.	3.6%
$5,816 to $8,723.	4.1%
$8,724 to $11,631.	5.1%
$11,632 to $14,539.	6.1%
$14,540 to $21,809.	7.1%
$21,810 and over	7.4%

Illinois
3.75% of federal AGI

Indiana
3.3% of AGI

Iowa[2]
$0 to $1,554	0.36%
$1,555 to $3,108	0.72%
$3,109 to $6,216.	2.43%
$6,217 to $13,986.	4.5%
$13,987 to $23,310.	6.12%
$23,311 to $31,080.	6.48%
$31,081 to $46,620.	6.8%
$46,621 to $69,930.	7.92%
$69,931 and over	8.98%

Kansas
Single, Head of household, or
Married filing separately
$0 to $15,000	2.7%
$15,001 and over	4.6%

Married filing jointly
$0 to $30,000	2.7%
$30,001 and over	4.6%

Kentucky
Single, Head of household,
Married filing jointly, or
Married filing separately
$0 to $3,000	2%
$3,001 to $4,000.	3%
$4,001 to $5,000.	4%
$5,001 to $8,000.	5%
$8,001 to $75,000.	5.8%
$75,001 and over	6%

Louisiana[1]
Single, Head of household, or
Married filing separately
$0 to $12,500	2%
$12,501 to $50,000.	4%
$50,001 and over	6%

Married filing jointly
$0 to $25,000	2%
$25,001 to $100,000.	4%
$100,001 and over	6%

Maine[2]
Single or Married filing separately
$0 to $21,049	5.8%
$21,050 to $37,499.	6.75%
$37,500 and over	7.15%

Head of household
$0 to $31,549	5.8%
$31,550 to $56,249.	6.75%
$56,250 and over	7.15%

Married filing jointly or
Qualifying widow(er)
$0 to $42,099	5.8%
$42,100 to $74,999.	6.75%
$75,000 and over	7.15%

Maryland
Single, Married filing separately,
or Dependent taxpayers
$0 to $1,000	2%
$1,001 to $2,000.	3%
$2,001 to $3,000.	4%
$3,001 to $100,000.	4.75%
$100,001 to $125,000.	5%
$125,001 to $150,000.	5.25%
$150,001 to $250,000.	5.5%
$250,001 and over	5.75%

Head of household, Married filing
jointly, or Qualifying widow(er)
$0 to $1,000	2%
$1,001 to $2,000.	3%
$2,001 to $3,000.	4%
$3,001 to $150,000.	4.75%
$150,001 to $175,000.	5%
$175,001 to $225,000.	5.25%
$225,001 to $300,000.	5.5%
$300,001 and over	5.75%

Massachusetts
Part A income (short-term capital gains)	12%
Part A income (interest and dividends)	5.10%
Part B income.	5.10%
Part C income.	5.10%

Michigan
4.25% of taxable income

Minnesota[2]
Single
$0 to $25,180	5.35%
$25,181 to $82,740.	7.05%
$82,741 to $155,650.	7.85%
$155,651 and over	9.85%

Head of household
$0 to $31,010	5.35%
$31,011 to $124,600.	7.05%
$124,601 to $207,540.	7.85%
$207,541 and over	9.85%

Married filing jointly
$0 to $36,820	5.35%
$36,821 to $146,270.	7.05%
$146,271 to $259,420.	7.85%
$259,421 and over	9.85%

Married filing separately
$0 to $18,410.	5.35%
$18,411 to $73,140.	7.05%
$73,141 to $129,710.	7.85%
$129,711 and over	9.85%

Mississippi
$0 to $5,000	3%
$5,001 to $10,000.	4%
$10,001 and over	5%

Missouri
$0 to $1,000	1.5%
$1,001 to $2,000.	2%
$2,001 to $3,000.	2.5%
$3,001 to $4,000.	3%
$4,001 to $5,000.	3.5%
$5,001 to $6,000.	4%
$6,001 to $7,000.	4.5%
$7,001 to $8,000.	5%
$8,001 to $9,000.	5.5%
$9,001 and over	6%

Montana[2]

$0 to $2,900	1%
$2,901 to $5,100	2%
$5,101 to $7,800	3%
$7,801 to $10,500	4%
$10,501 to $13,500	5%
$13,501 to $17,400	6%
$17,401 and over	6.9%

Nebraska[2]

Single or Married filing separately

$0 to $3,060	2.46%
$3,061 to $18,370	3.51%
$18,371 to $29,590	5.01%
$29,591 and over	6.84%

Head of household

$0 to $5,710	2.46%
$5,711 to $29,390	3.51%
$29,391 to $43,880	5.01%
$43,881 and over	6.84%

Married filing jointly or Surviving spouse

$0 to $6,120	2.46%
$6,121 to $36,730	3.51%
$36,731 to $59,180	5.01%
$59,181 and over	6.84%

New Hampshire

5% on interest and dividends only

New Jersey

Single or Married/civil-union partner filing separately

$0 to $20,000	1.4%
$20,001 to $35,000	1.75%
$35,001 to $40,000	3.5%
$40,001 to $75,000	5.525%
$75,001 to $500,000	6.37%
$500,001 and over	8.97%

Head of household, Married/ civil-union couple filing jointly, or Qualifying widow(er)/Surviving civil-union partner

$0 to $20,000	1.4%
$20,001 to $50,000	1.75%
$50,001 to $70,000	2.45%
$70,001 to $80,000	3.5%
$80,001 to $150,000	5.525%
$150,001 to $500,000	6.37%
$500,001 and over	8.97%

New Mexico[1]

Single

$0 to $5,500	1.7%
$5,501 to $11,000	3.2%
$11,001 to $16,000	4.7%
$16,001 and over	4.9%

Head of household, Married filing jointly, or Qualifying widow(er)

$0 to $8,000	1.7%
$8,001 to $16,000	3.2%
$16,001 to $24,000	4.7%
$24,001 and over	4.9%

Married filing separately

$0 to $4,000	1.7%
$4,001 to $8,000	3.2%
$8,001 to $12,000	4.7%
$12,001 and over	4.9%

New York[2]

Single or Married filing separately

$0 to $8,450	4%
$8,451 to $11,650	4.5%
$11,651 to $13,850	5.25%
$13,851 to $21,300	5.9%
$21,301 to $80,150	6.45%
$80,151 to $214,000	6.65%
$214,001 to $1,070,350	6.85%
$1,070,351 and over	8.82%

Head of household

$0 to $12,750	4%
$12,751 to $17,550	4.5%
$17,551 to $20,800	5.25%
$20,801 to $32,000	5.9%
$32,001 to $106,950	6.45%
$106,951 to $267,500	6.65%
$267,501 to $1,605,650	6.85%
$1,605,651 and over	8.82%

Married filing jointly or Qualifying widow(er)

$0 to $17,050	4%
$17,051 to $23,450	4.5%
$23,451 to $27,750	5.25%
$27,751 to $42,750	5.9%
$42,751 to $160,500	6.45%
$160,501 to $321,050	6.65%
$321,051 to $2,140,900	6.85%
$2,140,901 and over	8.82%

North Carolina

5.75% on state taxable income

North Dakota[2]

Single

$0 to $37,650	1.1%
$37,651 to $91,150	2.04%
$91,151 to $190,150	2.27%
$190,151 to $413,350	2.64%
$413,351 and over	2.9%

Head of household

$0 to $50,400	1.1%
$50,401 to $130,150	2.04%
$130,151 to $210,800	2.27%
$210,801 to $413,350	2.64%
$413,351 and over	2.9%

Married filing jointly or Surviving spouse

$0 to $62,900	1.1%
$62,901 to $151,900	2.04%
$151,901 to $231,450	2.27%
$231,451 to $413,350	2.64%
$413,351 and over	2.9%

Married filing separately

$0 to $31,450	1.1%
$31,451 to $75,950	2.04%
$75,951 to $115,725	2.27%
$115,726 to $206,675	2.64%
$206,676 and over	2.9%

Ohio[2,3]

$0 to $5,200	0.495%
$5,201 to $10,400	0.99%
$10,401 to $15,650	1.98%
$15,651 to $20,900	2.476%
$20,901 to $41,700	2.969%
$41,701 to $83,350	3.465%
$83,351 to $104,250	3.96%
$104,251 to $208,500	4.597%
$208,501 and over	4.997%

Oklahoma

Single or Married filing separately

$0 to $1,000	0.5%
$1,001 to $2,500	1%
$2,501 to $3,750	2%
$3,751 to $4,900	3%
$4,901 to $7,200	4%
$7,201 and over	5%

Head of household, Married filing jointly, or Qualifying widow(er)

$0 to $2,000	0.5%
$2,001 to $5,000	1%
$5,001 to $7,500	2%
$7,501 to $9,800	3%
$9,801 to $12,200	4%
$12,201 and over	5%

Oregon[2]

Single or Married filing separately

$0 to $3,350	5%
$3,351 to $8,450	7%
$8,451 to $125,000	9%
$125,001 and over	9.9%

Married filing jointly, Head of household, or Qualifying widow(er)

$0 to $6,700	5%
$6,701 to $16,900	7%
$16,901 to $250,000	9%
$250,001 and over	9.9%

Pennsylvania

3.07% of taxable compensation, net profits, net gains from the sale of property, rent, royalties, patents or copyrights, income from estates or trusts, dividends, interest, and winnings

Rhode Island[2]

$0 to $60,850	3.75%
$60,851 to $138,300	4.75%
$138,301 and over	5.99%

South Carolina[2]

$0 to $2,920	0%
$2,921 to $5,840	3%
$5,841 to $8,760	4%
$8,761 to $11,680	5%
$11,681 to $14,600	6%
$14,601 and over	7%

Tennessee

5% on interest and dividends

Utah

5% on state taxable income

Vermont[2]

Single

$0 to $37,650	3.55%
$37,651 to $91,150	6.8%
$91,151 to $190,150	7.8%
$190,151 to $413,350	8.8%
$413,351 and over	8.95%

Head of household

$0 to $50,400	3.55%
$50,401 to $130,150	6.8%
$130,151 to $210,800	7.8%
$210,801 to $413,350	8.8%
$413,351 and over	8.95%

Married or Civil union filing jointly

$0 to $62,850	3.55%
$62,851 to $151,900	6.8%
$151,901 to $231,450	7.8%
$231,451 to $413,350	8.8%
$413,351 and over	8.95%

Married or Civil union filing separately

$0 to $31,425	3.55%
$31,426 to $75,950	6.8%
$75,951 to $115,725	7.8%
$115,726 to $206,675	8.8%
$206,676 and over	8.95%

Virginia

$0 to $3,000	2%
$3,001 to $5,000	3%
$5,001 to $17,000	5%
$17,001 and over	5.75%

West Virginia

Single, Head of household, Married filing jointly, or Widow(er) with dependent child

$0 to $10,000	3%
$10,001 to $25,000	4%
$25,001 to $40,000	4.5%
$40,001 to $60,000	6%
$60,001 and over	6.5%

Married filing separately

$0 to $5,000	3%
$5,001 to $12,500	4%
$12,501 to $20,000	4.5%
$20,001 to $30,000	6%
$30,001 and over	6.5%

Wisconsin[1,2]

Single or Head of household

$0 to $11,120	4%
$11,121 to $22,230	5.84%
$22,231 to $244,750	6.27%
$244,751 and over	7.65%

Married filing jointly

$0 to $14,820	4%
$14,821 to $29,640	5.84%
$29,641 to $326,330	6.27%
$326,331 and over	7.65%

Married filing separately

$0 to $7,410	4%
$7,411 to $14,820	5.84%
$14,821 to $163,170	6.27%
$163,171 and over	7.65%

AGI = Adjusted gross income; AMT = Alternative minimum tax. (1) Community property state in which, in general, one-half of the community income is taxable to each spouse. (2) Brackets indexed for inflation annually. (3) 2016 adjusted brackets were not available. Bracketed rates listed are for 2015. Other notes, by state: **Arkansas:** For net income from $75,001 to $80,000, reduce amount of tax due by bracket adjustment amount as follows: $75,001 to $76,000: deduct $440; $76,001 to $77,000: deduct $340; $77,001 to $78,000: deduct $240; $78,001 to $79,000: deduct $140; $79,001 to $80,000: deduct $40; $80,001 and over: deduct $0. **California:** An additional 1% tax is imposed on taxable income in excess of $1 mil. **Colorado:** Individual taxpayers are subject to an AMT equal to the amount by which 3.47% of their Colorado alternative minimum taxable income exceeds their Colorado normal tax. **Connecticut:** Resident estates and trusts are subject to a 6.9% rate on all income. **District of Columbia:** Subject to availability of funding; otherwise 2015 rates remain in effect. **Illinois:** Surcharge is imposed on certain types of sales income. **Indiana:** Counties may impose an AGI tax on residents or on nonresidents, or a county option income tax. **Iowa:** An AMT of 6.7% of alternative minimum income is imposed if the minimum tax exceeds the taxpayer's regular income tax liability. **Kansas:** Married filing jointly with taxable income of $12,500 or less, and all other individuals with taxable income of $5,000 or less, have a tax liability of zero. **Massachusetts:** Part A income represents either interest and dividends or short-term capital gains, long-term capital gains from collectibles, and long-term capital gains from pre-1996 installment sales. Part B income represents wages, salaries, tips, pensions, business income, rents, etc. Part C income represents gains from the sale of capital assets held for more than one year. 5.85% optional rate may be elected for Part A interest and dividend income, Part B income after exemptions, and Part C income. **Minnesota:** A 6.75% AMT is imposed. **Montana:** Minimum tax, $1. **Nebraska:** There is an additional tax on taxpayers with federal AGI of more than a certain amount, which is $311,300 for married filing jointly ($155,650 for married filing separately) in 2016. **New Mexico:** Qualified nonresident taxpayers may pay an alternative tax of 0.75% of gross receipts from sales in New Mexico. **New York:** A supplemental tax is imposed to recapture the tax table benefit. **Vermont:** The tax amount is increased by 24% for certain items.

EDUCATION

U.S. Public Schools: Students, Staff, Spending, 1899-2014

Source: National Center for Education Statistics, U.S. Dept. of Education

	1899-1900	1919-20	1939-40	1959-60	1969-70	1979-80	1989-90	1999-2000	2013-14[1]
Population (thous.)									
Total U.S. population[2]	75,995	104,514	131,028	177,830	201,385	225,055	246,819	279,040	316,498
Population 5-17 years of age	21,573	27,571	30,151	43,881	52,386	48,043	44,947	52,811	53,743
Percentage 5-17 years of age	28.4%	26.4%	23.0%	24.7%	26.0%	21.3%	18.2%	18.9%	17.0%
Enrollment (thous.)									
Elementary and secondary[3]	15,503	21,578	25,434	36,087	45,550	41,651	40,543	46,857	50,045
Pre-kindergarten and grades 1-8	14,984	19,378	18,833	27,602	32,513	28,034	29,152	33,486	35,251
Grades 9-12	519	2,200	6,601	8,485	13,037	13,616	11,390	13,371	14,794
Percent of pop. ages 5-17 enrolled	71.9%	78.3%	84.4%	82.2%	87.0%	86.7%	90.2%	88.7%	93.1%
High school as percent of all enrolled	3.3%	10.2%	26.0%	23.5%	28.6%	32.7%	28.1%	28.5%	29.6%
High school graduates	62	231	1,143	1,627	2,589	2,748	2,320	2,554	3,169
Instructional staff (thous.)									
Total instructional staff	*	678	912	1,457	2,286	2,406	2,986	3,819	4,167
Teachers, librarians, and other nonsupervisory instructional staff	423	657	875	1,393	2,195	2,300	2,860	3,682	3,999
Revenue and expenditures (mil)									
Total revenue	$220	$970	$2,261	$14,747	$40,267	$96,881	$208,548	$372,944	$603,687
Total expenditures	215	1,036	2,344	15,613	40,683	95,962	212,770	381,838	606,490
Current expenditures[4,5]	180	861	1,942	12,329	34,218	86,984	188,229	323,889	535,665
Capital outlay	35	154	258	2,662	4,659	6,506	17,781	43,357	45,474
Interest on school debt	*	18	131	490	1,171	1,874	3,776	9,135	17,247
Others	*	3	13	133	636	598	2,983	5,457	8,103
Salaries and pupil cost									
Avg. annual salary of instruct. staff[6]	$325	$871	$1,441	$4,995	$8,626	$15,970	$31,367	$41,807	$56,610
Expenditure per capita total pop.	3	10	18	88	202	426	862	1,368	1,916
Current expenditure per pupil ADA[5,7]	17	53	88	375	816	2,272	4,980	7,394	11,352

* = Data not collected. **Note:** Because of rounding, details may not add up to totals. Prior to 1959-60, data do not include Alaska and Hawaii. (1) Revenues and expenditures are fiscal year 2013 (2012-13 school year) provisional data; high school graduates and expenditure per pupil ADA are projected. (2) Data for 1899-1900 are based on total population from the decennial census. From 1919-20 to 1959-60, total population figures include armed forces overseas, as of July 1 preceding the school year. Data for later years are for resident population excluding armed forces overseas. (3) Data for 1899-1960 are school year enrollment; data for later years are fall enrollment. (4) In 1899-1900, includes interest on school debt. (5) Because of changes in the definition of "current expenditures," data for 1959-60 and later years are not entirely comparable with prior years. (6) Data prior to 1959-60 include supervisors, principals, teachers, and nonsupervisory instructional staff. (7) ADA = average daily attendance.

U.S. Public High School Graduation Rates, 2013-14

Source: National Center for Education Statistics, U.S. Dept. of Education

State	Rate	Rank	State	Rate	Rank	State	Rate	Rank	State	Rate	Rank
Alabama	86.3%	15	Illinois	86.0%	17	Montana	85.4%	19	Rhode Island	80.8%	27
Alaska	71.1	39	Indiana	87.9	6	Nebraska	89.7	2	South Carolina	80.1	28
Arizona	75.7	35	Iowa	90.5	1	Nevada	70.0	40	South Dakota	82.7	23
Arkansas	86.9	12	Kansas	85.7	18	New Hampshire	88.1	5	Tennessee	87.2	10
California	81.0	26	Kentucky	87.5	8	New Jersey	88.6	3	Texas	88.3	4
Colorado	77.3	33	Louisiana	74.6	36	New Mexico	68.5	41	Utah	83.9	22
Connecticut	87.0	11	Maine	86.5	13	New York	77.8	31	Vermont	87.8	7
Delaware	87.0	11	Maryland	86.4	14	North Carolina	83.9	22	Virginia	85.3	20
District of Columbia	61.4	42	Massachusetts	86.1	16	North Dakota	87.2	10	Washington	78.2	30
Florida	76.1	34	Michigan	78.6	29	Ohio	81.8	24	West Virginia	84.5	21
Georgia	72.5	37	Minnesota	81.2	25	Oklahoma	82.7	23	Wisconsin	88.6	3
Hawaii	81.8	24	Mississippi	77.6	32	Oregon	72.0	38	Wyoming	78.6	29
Idaho	77.3	33	Missouri	87.3	9	Pennsylvania	85.3	20	**Total U.S.**	**82.3**	

Note: The 4-year adjusted cohort graduation rate (ACGR) is the number of students who graduate in 4 years with a regular high school diploma divided by the number of students who form the adjusted cohort for the graduating class. From the beginning of 9th grade (or the earliest high school grade), students who are entering that grade for the first time form a cohort that is "adjusted" by adding any students who subsequently transfer into the cohort and subtracting any students who subsequently transfer out, emigrate to another country, or die.

High School Dropouts by Sex, Race, and Ethnicity, 1960-2014

Source: Current Population Survey, U.S. Census Bureau, U.S. Dept. of Commerce

(data for Oct. of year shown unless otherwise noted)

Year[1]	Total dropout rate				Male dropout rate				Female dropout rate			
	All races[2]	White	Black	Hispanic	All races[2]	White	Black	Hispanic	All races[2]	White	Black	Hispanic
1960[3]	27.2%	NA	NA	NA	27.8%	NA	NA	NA	26.7%	NA	NA	NA
1970[4]	15.0	13.2%	27.9%	NA	14.2	12.2%	29.4%	NA	15.7	14.1%	26.6%	NA
1980	14.1	11.4	19.1	35.2%	15.1	12.3	20.8	37.2%	13.1	10.5	17.7	33.2%
1990	12.1	9.0	13.2	32.4	12.3	9.3	11.9	34.3	11.8	8.7	14.4	30.3
2000	10.9	6.9	13.1	27.8	12.0	7.0	15.3	31.8	9.9	6.9	11.1	23.5
2005[5]	9.4	6.0	10.4	22.4	10.8	6.6	12.0	26.4	8.0	5.3	9.0	18.1
2006[5]	9.3	5.8	10.7	22.1	10.3	6.4	9.7	25.7	8.3	5.3	11.7	18.1
2007[5]	8.7	5.3	8.4	21.4	9.8	6.0	8.0	24.7	7.7	4.5	8.8	18.0
2008[5]	8.0	4.8	9.9	18.3	8.5	5.4	8.7	19.9	7.5	4.2	11.1	16.7
2009[5]	8.1	5.2	9.3	17.6	9.1	6.3	10.6	19.0	7.0	4.1	8.1	16.1
2010[5]	7.4	5.1	8.0	15.1	8.5	5.9	9.5	17.3	6.3	4.2	6.7	12.8
2011[5]	7.1	5.0	7.3	13.6	7.7	5.4	8.3	14.6	6.5	4.6	6.4	12.4
2012[5]	6.6	4.3	7.5	12.7	7.3	4.8	8.1	13.9	5.9	3.8	7.0	11.3
2013[5]	6.8	5.1	7.3	11.7	7.2	5.5	8.2	12.6	6.3	4.7	6.6	10.8
2014[5]	6.5	5.2	7.4	10.6	7.1	5.7	7.1	11.8	5.9	4.8	7.7	9.3

NA = Not available. **Note:** Table shows "status" dropouts, defined as 16- to 24-year-olds who are not enrolled in school and who have not completed a high school program, regardless of when they left school. People who have received GED credentials are not shown. Excludes persons in prison or in the military, and other persons not living in households. Race categories exclude persons of Hispanic ethnicity unless otherwise noted. (1) Because of changes in data collection procedures, data for years prior to 1992 may not be comparable to later years. (2) Includes other racial/ethnic categories not separately shown. (3) Based on the Apr. 1960 decennial census. (4) White and black data include persons of Hispanic ethnicity. (5) White and black data exclude persons identifying themselves as being of two or more races.

Overview of U.S. Public Schools, 2014-15

Source: National Center for Education Statistics, U.S. Dept. of Education; National Education Association (NEA)

State	Local school districts	Elementary schools[1,2]	Secondary schools[2,3]	Classroom teachers	Total enrollment	Pupils per teacher	Teachers' avg. pay	Expend. per pupil
Alabama	136	990	434	46,408*	733,089	15.8*	$48,611	$9,185
Alaska	54	199	83	7,759	127,001	16.4	66,755	20,117*
Arizona	627*	1,335	734	59,884*	1,068,192*	17.8*	45,406*	7,461*
Arkansas	254	718	368	31,229*	475,778*	15.2*	47,823	9,649*
California	1,028*	6,954	2,606	276,518*	6,230,033*	22.5*	72,535*	11,145*
Colorado	178	1,300	389	54,551*	888,767	16.3*	49,828*	9,842
Connecticut	196*	815	286	41,089*	538,634*	13.1*	71,709*	17,759*
Delaware	37*	159	36	9,062	134,074*	14.8*	59,195	15,858*
Dist. of Columbia	41*	166	39	6,328*	76,829*	12.1*	75,490*	14,779*
Florida	67	2,829	695	170,285	2,721,459*	16.0*	48,992	9,223*
Georgia	201	1,776	457	110,799	1,744,240	15.7	53,382	9,172*
Hawaii	1	208	52	10,956*	178,246	16.3*	57,189	12,014*
Idaho	137*	449	197	15,373	303,148*	19.7*	45,218	8,928*
Illinois	865*	3,107	937	126,770*	2,067,564*	16.3*	61,083*	13,870*
Indiana	402	1,370	460	60,538*	1,028,654	17.0*	50,877*	8,034
Iowa	338	969	371	35,422*	506,336	14.3*	53,408	10,622
Kansas	286*	943	352	34,666*	490,291*	14.1*	48,990*	9,822*
Kentucky	173*	983	422	40,777	685,176	16.8	51,155	11,465
Louisiana	136	930	281	45,322	723,805	16.0	47,886	11,084
Maine	198*	453	149	14,660*	181,897*	12.4*	50,017*	8,957*
Maryland	24	1,130	246	59,891*	874,514	14.6*	65,477	14,496*
Massachusetts	405	1,430	382	71,806	955,844	13.3	75,398	16,594
Michigan	841	2,213	939	85,597*	1,499,041	17.5*	63,856	14,873
Minnesota	519	1,280	836	55,518	857,039*	15.4*	56,670	11,510*
Mississippi	151*	626	325	32,012*	492,279*	15.4*	42,564*	8,779*
Missouri	557	1,591	642	73,303	886,473	12.1	47,409	10,566*
Montana	410*	485	339	10,364*	144,129	13.9*	50,670	10,788*
Nebraska	245	730	307	24,207	312,281	12.9	50,525	10,012
Nevada	17*	480	132	27,962*	496,480*	17.8*	56,703*	8,956*
New Hampshire	161*	376	106	15,699*	183,981*	11.7*	58,554*	17,115*
New Jersey	590*	1,956	494	112,969*	1,347,166*	11.9*	69,038*	20,925*
New Mexico	89	611	238	21,860*	333,810	15.3*	46,625	10,356
New York	695*	3,307	1,130	199,758*	2,538,915*	12.7*	77,628*	21,366*
North Carolina	115	1,899	536	94,566	1,446,230	15.3	47,819	8,917
North Dakota	177*	297	183	8,334*	101,408*	12.2*	50,025*	8,518*
Ohio	1,016*	2,488	1,013	107,385*	1,842,822*	17.2*	56,172*	11,530*
Oklahoma	516	1,222	561	42,195	688,300	16.3	45,317	8,043
Oregon	196	882	277	27,463	567,383	20.7	59,811	11,127
Pennsylvania	499*	2,165	805	118,397*	1,711,467*	14.5*	64,447	15,691*
Rhode Island	49*	224	73	9,797*	127,503*	13.0*	65,918*	19,676*
South Carolina	86	914	288	49,167*	756,866	15.4*	48,486	9,678
South Dakota	151	437	239	9,430*	129,772	13.8*	40,934	8,991*
Tennessee	141	1,387	384	64,093*	971,803*	15.2*	47,979*	8,809*
Texas	1,219	5,983	2,097	342,284	5,215,342	15.2	50,713	8,826
Utah	141	649	261	27,337*	622,153	22.8*	45,848*	7,711*
Vermont	286*	232	68	7,865*	76,102*	9.7*	57,642*	23,149*
Virginia	132	1,495	406	101,393*	1,279,546*	12.6*	50,620	10,979*
Washington	299	1,504	617	56,166*	1,074,057	19.1*	52,502	9,963*
West Virginia	55*	568	124	23,124*	279,899	12.1*	45,783	12,930*
Wisconsin	424	1,576	560	55,625*	873,767*	15.7*	54,535*	11,424*
Wyoming	48	244	97	7,504	93,303	12.4	57,414	16,318
Total U.S.	**15,609***	**67,034**	**24,053**	**3,141,487***	**49,682,888***	**15.8***	**57,420**	**11,709***

* = NEA estimate. (1) Includes primary and middle schools (schools with no grade higher than 8th). (2) 2013-14 estimates. (3) Includes schools with no grade lower than 7th.

Programs for Students With Disabilities, 1990-2014

Source: Office of Special Education and Rehabilitative Services, U.S. Dept. of Education

Federally funded educational programs for disabled students serve children and young adults 3-21 years old.
(numbers served in thousands)

Type of disability	1990 -91	2000 -01	2004 -05	2005 -06	2006 -07	2007 -08[1]	2008 -09[1]	2009 -10	2010 -11	2011 -12	2012 -13	2013 -14
Learning disabilities	2,129	2,860	2,798	2,740	2,665	2,569	2,476	2,431	2,361	2,303	2,277	2,264
Speech impairments	985	1,388	1,463	1,468	1,475	1,454	1,426	1,416	1,396	1,373	1,356	1,334
Intellectual disabilities[2]	534	624	578	556	534	500	478	463	448	435	430	425
Emotional disturbance	389	480	489	477	464	442	420	407	390	373	362	354
Multiple disabilities	96	131	140	141	142	138	130	131	130	132	133	132
Hearing impairments	58	77	79	79	80	79	78	79	78	78	77	77
Orthopedic impairments	49	82	73	71	69	67	70	65	63	61	59	56
Other health impairments[3]	55	303	521	570	610	641	659	689	716	743	779	817
Visual impairments	23	29	29	29	29	29	29	29	28	28	28	28
Autism	—	93	191	223	258	296	336	378	417	455	498	538
Deaf-blindness	1	1	2	2	2	2	2	2	2	2	1	1
Traumatic brain injury	—	16	24	24	25	25	26	25	26	26	26	26
Developmental delay	—	213	332	339	333	357	354	368	382	393	402	410
All disabilities	**4,710**	**6,296**	**6,720**	**6,718**	**6,687**	**6,597**	**6,483**	**6,481**	**6,436**	**6,401**	**6,429**	**6,464**

— = Not available or not reliable data. **Note:** Counts based on reports from states and District of Columbia. Details may not add up to totals because of rounding and/or incomplete enumeration. (1) Vermont not included. In 2006-07, the total number of 3- to 21-year-olds served in Vermont was 14,010. (2) Referred to in some prior years as "mental retardation." (3) Includes limited strength, vitality, or alertness due to chronic or acute health problems such as a heart condition, tuberculosis, rheumatic fever, nephritis, asthma, sickle cell anemia, hemophilia, epilepsy, lead poisoning, leukemia, or diabetes.

Revenues for Public Elementary and Secondary Schools by State, 2012-13

Source: National Center for Education Statistics, U.S. Dept. of Education; amounts in thousands

State/territory	Total	Federal Amount	Federal % of tot. rev.	State Amount	State % of tot. rev.	Local and intermediate Amount	Local and intermediate % of tot. rev.
Alabama	$7,188,210	$850,523	11.8%	$3,936,486	54.8%	$2,401,201	33.4%
Alaska	2,670,758	324,045	12.1	1,830,051	68.5	516,661	19.3
American Samoa	64,420	54,272	84.2	9,890[1]	10.6	258	0.4
Arizona	9,385,733	1,278,835	13.6	3,965,426	42.2	4,141,471	44.1
Arkansas	5,051,804	612,256	12.1	2,624,126	51.9	1,815,421	35.9
California	66,026,445	7,388,302	11.2	35,878,654	54.3	22,759,489	34.5
Colorado	8,905,156	702,772	7.9	3,765,335	42.3	4,437,048	49.8
Connecticut	10,549,973	461,506	4.4	4,163,960	39.5	5,924,506	56.2
Delaware	1,909,503	192,422	10.1	1,123,567	58.8	593,514	31.1
District of Columbia	2,094,445	200,097	9.6	NA	NA	1,894,347	90.4
Florida	24,506,837	3,087,261	12.6	9,455,551	38.6	11,964,026	48.8
Georgia	17,492,816	1,864,121	10.7	7,620,092	43.6	8,008,603	45.8
Guam	290,408	69,078	23.8	NA	NA	221,330	76.2
Hawaii	2,331,839	310,777	13.3	1,962,993	84.2	58,069	2.5
Idaho	2,103,804	251,215	11.9	1,347,311	64.0	505,278	24.0
Illinois	26,879,107	2,313,498	8.6	7,003,524	26.1	17,562,085	65.3
Indiana	11,887,836	1,036,984	8.7	6,654,115	56.0	4,196,737	35.3
Iowa	6,033,012	472,925	7.8	3,118,397	51.7	2,441,689	40.6
Kansas	5,866,415	502,059	8.6	3,229,626	55.1	2,134,730	36.4
Kentucky	7,120,960	875,760	12.3	3,878,756	54.5	2,366,445	33.2
Louisiana	8,439,545	1,280,583	15.2	3,651,777	43.3	3,507,185	41.6
Maine	2,584,962	196,780	7.6	1,032,121	39.9	1,356,060	52.5
Maryland	13,800,320	831,092	6.0	6,093,647	44.2	6,875,581	49.8
Massachusetts	16,436,188	936,545	5.7	6,479,966	39.4	9,019,677	54.9
Michigan	18,632,336	1,819,662	9.8	10,938,995	58.7	5,873,659	31.5
Minnesota	11,215,788	709,817	6.3	7,233,164	64.5	3,272,807	29.2
Mississippi	4,394,942	707,620	16.1	2,213,480	50.4	1,473,842	33.5
Missouri	10,311,473	927,013	9.0	3,382,862	32.8	6,001,597	58.2
Montana	1,657,908	213,213	12.9	797,417	48.1	647,279	39.0
Nebraska	3,800,737	358,790	9.4	1,217,700	32.0	2,224,247	58.5
Nevada	4,140,625	401,968	9.7	1,397,295	33.7	2,341,362	56.5
New Hampshire	2,875,406	164,398	5.7	1,020,239	35.5	1,690,769	58.8
New Jersey	27,087,144	1,184,706	4.4	11,052,695	40.8	14,849,743	54.8
New Mexico	3,695,203	561,650	15.2	2,535,796	68.6	597,756	16.2
New York	59,007,178	3,234,775	5.5	23,665,880	40.1	32,106,522	54.4
North Carolina	13,107,879	1,652,625	12.6	8,150,584	62.2	3,304,670	25.2
North Dakota	1,354,505	159,520	11.8	690,150	51.0	504,835	37.3
Northern Mariana Islands	61,275	28,024	45.7	33,251[1]	48.9	NA	NA
Ohio	22,609,388	1,944,765	8.6	9,830,868	43.5	10,833,755	47.9
Oklahoma	5,912,975	732,453	12.4	2,906,491	49.2	2,274,031	38.5
Oregon	6,160,158	569,756	9.2	3,041,818	49.4	2,548,584	41.4
Pennsylvania	27,446,614	2,186,130	8.0	9,841,441	35.9	15,419,043	56.2
Puerto Rico	3,577,365	1,234,613	34.5	2,342,270[1]	65.8	481	0.0
Rhode Island	2,336,776	202,770	8.7	909,689	38.9	1,224,317	52.4
South Carolina	8,414,913	845,279	10.0	3,904,090	46.4	3,665,545	43.6
South Dakota	1,323,242	198,333	15.0	413,443	31.2	711,466	53.8
Tennessee	9,084,504	1,182,985	13.0	4,151,138	45.7	3,750,381	41.3
Texas	50,053,709	5,872,123	11.7	20,134,113	40.2	24,047,473	48.0
Utah	4,860,217	449,443	9.2	2,527,828	52.0	1,882,946	38.7
Vermont	1,641,315	116,847	7.1	1,459,459	88.9	65,009	4.0
Virgin Islands (U.S.)	206,300	35,112	17.0	NA	NA	171,188	83.0
Virginia	15,106,627	1,108,890	7.3	5,880,122	38.9	8,117,614	53.7
Washington	12,142,892	1,042,169	8.6	7,160,382	59.0	3,940,341	32.4
West Virginia	3,543,326	380,192	10.7	2,089,304	59.0	1,073,830	30.3
Wisconsin	10,809,097	850,329	7.9	4,858,710	45.0	5,100,059	47.2
Wyoming	1,694,441	113,949	6.7	881,087	52.0	699,405	41.3

NA = Not applicable. (1) Reported state revenue data are revenues received from the central government of the jurisdiction.

Fighting, Bullying, and Safety Concerns of High School Students, 2015

Source: *Youth Risk Behavior Surveillance–United States, 2015*, Centers for Disease Control and Prevention

	In a physical fight on school property[1] Female	Male	Total	Bullied on school property[2] Female	Male	Total	Electronically bullied[2,3] Female	Male	Total	Did not go to school because of safety concerns[4] Female	Male	Total
Race/ethnicity[5]												
White......	3.2%	8.0%	5.6%	29.1%	18.1%	23.5%	26.0%	10.8%	18.4%	5.4%	2.9%	4.2%
Black......	9.4	15.4	12.6	15.1	11.2	13.2	11.9	5.6	8.6	6.4	6.9	6.8
Hispanic ...	7.1	10.7	8.9	19.3	13.7	16.5	16.7	8.1	12.4	7.4	7.6	7.6
Grade												
9	8.2	14.7	11.6	29.0	18.3	23.4	22.7	11.0	16.5	7.7	4.9	6.4
10	4.6	10.0	7.3	25.5	16.1	20.8	23.2	9.9	16.6	6.3	4.4	5.4
11	4.1	8.3	6.5	24.2	16.4	20.3	21.4	8.4	14.7	5.3	3.7	4.6
12	2.5	6.4	4.5	19.8	12.1	15.9	19.5	9.2	14.3	4.3	6.9	5.7
Total	5.0	10.3	7.8	24.8	15.8	20.2	21.7	9.7	15.5	6.0	5.0	5.6

(1) One or more times during the 12 months before the survey. (2) During the 12 months before the survey. (3) Including being bullied through email, chat rooms, instant messaging, websites, or texting. (4) On at least one day during the 30 days before the survey. (5) Race categories include non-Hispanics only. Hispanics may be of any race.

Program for International Student Assessment (PISA) Scores, 2003-12

Source: National Center for Education Statistics, U.S. Dept. of Education

Scores are reported on a scale from 0 to 1,000. The PISA test is administered to 15-year-old students.

Education system	Mathematics 2003	Mathematics 2012	Mathematics % change, 2003-12	Science 2006	Science 2012	Science % change, 2006-12
Albania	—	394	—	—	397	—
Argentina	—	388	—	391	406	3.68%
Australia*	524	504	-3.84%	527	521	-1.02
Austria*	506	506	-0.01	511	506	-0.99
Belgium*	529	515	-2.75	510	505	-0.96
Brazil	356	391	9.96	390	405	3.68
Bulgaria	—	439	—	434	446	2.85
Canada*	532	518	-2.71	534	525	-1.69
Chile*	—	423	—	438	445	1.54
Colombia	—	376	—	388	399	2.74
Costa Rica	—	407	—	—	429	—
Croatia	—	471	—	493	491	-0.37
Cyprus	—	440	—	—	438	—
Czech Rep.*	516	499	-3.39	513	508	-0.89
Denmark*	514	500	-2.77	496	498	0.52
Estonia*	—	521	—	531	541	1.88
Finland*	544	519	-4.69	563	545	-3.17
France*	511	495	-3.10	495	499	0.76
Germany*	503	514	2.10	516	524	1.64
Greece*	445	453	1.81	473	467	-1.41
Hong Kong	550	561	1.97	542	555	2.35
Hungary*	490	477	-2.65	504	494	-1.91
Iceland*	515	493	-4.33	491	478	-2.58
Indonesia	360	375	4.15	393	382	-2.94
Ireland*	503	501	-0.27	508	522	2.69
Israel*	—	466	—	454	470	3.56
Italy*	466	485	4.22	475	494	3.82
Japan*	534	536	0.43	531	547	2.89
Jordan	—	386	—	422	409	-2.99
Kazakhstan	—	432	—	—	425	—
Korea, South*	542	554	2.13	522	538	3.00
Latvia	483	491	1.49	490	502	2.58
Liechtenstein	536	535	-0.15	522	525	0.49
Lithuania	—	479	—	488	496	1.59
Luxembourg*	493	490	-0.68	486	491	1.01
Macao	527	538	2.06%	511	521	1.90%
Malaysia	—	421	—	—	420	—
Mexico*	385	413	7.28	410	415	1.29
Montenegro[1]	—	410	—	412	410	-0.41
Netherlands*	538	523	-2.76	525	522	-0.53
New Zealand*	523	500	-4.53	530	516	-2.78
Norway*	495	489	-1.17	487	495	1.64
Peru	—	368	—	—	373	—
Poland*	490	518	5.56	498	526	5.63
Portugal*	466	487	4.52	474	489	3.16
Qatar	—	376	—	349	384	9.83
Romania	—	445	—	418	439	4.87
Russia	468	482	2.94	479	486	1.42
Serbia[1]	—	449	—	436	445	2.10
Shanghai, China	—	613	—	—	580	—
Singapore	—	573	—	—	551	—
Slovakia*	498	482	-3.32	488	471	-3.53
Slovenia*	—	501	—	519	514	-0.90
Spain*	485	484	-0.16	488	496	1.64
Sweden*	509	478	-6.05	503	485	-3.68
Switzerland*	527	531	0.83	512	515	0.74
Taiwan	—	560	—	532	523	-1.72
Thailand	417	427	2.34	421	444	5.46
Tunisia	359	388	8.11	386	398	3.25
Turkey*	423	448	5.80	424	463	9.34
United Arab Emirates	—	434	—	—	448	—
UK*	—	494	—	515	514	-0.13
U.S.*	483	481	-0.31	489	497	1.74
Uruguay	422	409	-3.06	428	416	-2.87
Vietnam	—	511	—	—	528	—
OECD trend score[2]	500	496	-0.68	498	501	0.57

— = Not available. * = Organization for Economic Cooperation and Development (OECD) nation. (1) Montenegro and Serbia were a united country under the 2003 assessment. (2) The OECD trend scores are based on the averages of OECD countries with each country weighted equally.

Mathematics, Reading, and Science Achievement of U.S. Students, 1998-2015

Source: National Assessment of Educational Progress, National Center for Education Statistics, U.S. Dept. of Education

Percent of public school students in a grade who scored at or above basic levels in national tests. Basic level denotes a partial mastery of prerequisite knowledge and skills fundamental for proficient work at each grade.

State	4th grade Math 2000	4th grade Math 2015	4th grade Reading 1998	4th grade Reading 2015	8th grade Math 2000	8th grade Math 2015	8th grade Reading 1998	8th grade Reading 2015	8th grade Science 2000	8th grade Science 2011
AL	55	75	56	65	53	56	67	71	53	54
AK	NA	78	NA	61	NA	71	NA	71	NA	68
AZ	57	79	51	62	60	72	72	74	55	57
AR	55	79	54	65	49	66	68	70	53	62
CA	50	72	48	59	50	64	63	70	38	52
CO	NA	82	67	71	NA	73	77	78	NA	74
CT	76	81	76	74	70	72	81	82	64	69
DE	NA	82	53	70	NA	69	64	73	NA	63
DC	24	69	27	56	23	51	44	56	NA	24
FL	NA	85	53	75	NA	64	67	75	NA	62
GA	57	78	54	68	54	67	68	73	52	63
HI	55	79	45	61	51	70	59	68	40	55
ID	68	83	NA	69	70	75	NA	81	71	75
IL	63	77	NA	68	67	72	NA	77	59	60
IN	77	89	NA	75	74	77	NA	80	66	68
IA	75	84	67	71	NA	76	NA	81	NA	73
KS	76	83	70	68	76	76	81	79	NA	70
KY	59	84	62	75	60	68	74	78	60	71
LA	57	78	44	63	47	57	63	66	44	56
ME	73	85	72	71	73	76	83	81	72	78
MD	60	79	58	68	62	71	70	76	57	64
MA	77	90	70	82	70	81	79	83	70	76
MI	71	77	62	63	68	68	NA	76	68	72
MN	76	87	67	71	80	82	78	81	72	76
MS	45	78	47	60	42	60	62	63	41	47
MO	71	82	61	70	64	71	75	77	66	72
MT	72	84	72	72	79	79	83	82	79	80
NE	65	86	NA	74	73	77	NA	81	52	72
NV	60	76	51	61	55	65	70	71	NA	58
NH	NA	91	74	79	NA	84	NA	85	NA	79
NJ	NA	86	NA	75	NA	79	NA	80	NA	69
NM	50	73	51	54	48	61	71	65	48	58
NY	66	79	62	68	63	69	76	73	NA	62
NC	73	85	58	73	67	69	74	72	54	61
ND	73	88	NA	73	76	80	NA	80	72	82
OH	73	85	NA	72	73	75	NA	76	72	73
OK	67	84	66	71	62	67	80	76	60	63
OR	65	79	58	67	71	73	78	79	68	71
PA	NA	83	NA	74	NA	72	NA	78	NA	66
RI	65	80	64	72	59	72	76	76	58	63
SC	59	79	53	65	53	65	66	71	48	61
SD	NA	83	NA	68	NA	77	NA	80	NA	79
TN	59	82	57	66	52	68	71	76	55	64
TX	76	86	59	64	67	75	74	72	52	67
UT	69	84	62	74	66	76	77	81	67	77
VT	73	85	NA	76	73	79	NA	83	71	80
VA	71	87	62	74	65	76	78	77	61	73
WA	NA	83	64	71	NA	74	76	77	NA	72
WV	65	78	60	64	58	62	75	72	57	64
WI	NA	83	69	71	NA	78	78	79	NA	75
WY	71	88	64	75	69	78	76	81	69	77
U.S.	**64**	**81**	**58**	**68**	**62**	**70**	**71**	**75**	**57**	**65**

NA = Not administered.

Enrollment in U.S. Public and Private Schools, 1889-2026

Source: National Center for Education Statistics, U.S. Dept. of Education

Of all students enrolled in private schools in fall 2013, 68% attended religious schools and 32% attended nonsectarian schools.

School year[1]	Public school[2]	Private school[2]	% private[3]	School year[1]	Public school[2]	Private school[2]	% private[3]
1889-90	12,723	1,611	11.2%	1979-80	41,651	5,000[4]	10.7%
1899-1900	15,503	1,352	8.0	1989-90	40,543	5,599	12.1
1909-10	17,814	1,558	8.0	1999-2000	46,857	6,018	11.4
1919-20	21,578	1,699	7.3	2009-10	49,361	5,488	10.0
1929-30	25,678	2,651	9.4	2011-12	49,522	5,268	9.6
1939-40	25,434	2,611	9.3	2012-13	49,771	5,333[4]	9.7
1949-50	25,111	3,380	11.9	2013-14	50,045	5,396	9.7
1959-60	35,182	5,675	13.9	2025-26[5]	51,420	5,090	9.0
1969-70	45,550	5,500[4]	10.8				

Note: "Private" includes all nonpublic schools. (1) Fall enrollment. (2) In thousands. Data from fall 1980 onward covers an expanded universe of private schools; comparisons with earlier years should be avoided. (3) Percent of U.S. students enrolled in private schools. (4) Estimated. (5) Projected.

Characteristics of Public Charter Schools and Students, 1999-2014

Source: National Center for Education Statistics, U.S. Dept. of Education

	1999-2000	2001-02	2003-04	2005-06	2007-08	2009-10	2011-12	2013-14
Number of charter school students	339,678	571,029	789,479	1,012,906	1,276,731	1,610,285	2,057,599	2,519,065
Sex	Percentage of charter school students who were—							
Male	51.0%	50.8%	50.3%	49.9%	49.5%	49.5%	49.6%	49.6%
Female	49.0	49.2	49.7	50.1	50.5	50.5	50.4	50.4
Race/ethnicity								
White	42.5	42.6	41.8	40.5	38.8	37.3	35.6	34.9
Black	33.5	32.5	31.9	32.1	31.8	30.3	28.7	27.1
Asian/Pacific Islander	2.8	3.1	3.2	3.6	3.8	3.9	4.0	4.1
Amer. Ind./AK Native	1.5	1.7	1.5	1.4	1.2	1.0	0.9	0.8
Two or more races	NA	NA	NA	NA	NA	1.4	2.8	3.0
Hispanic	19.6	20.1	21.5	22.4	24.5	26.0	28.0	30.0
Number of charter schools	1,524	2,348	2,977	3,780	4,388	4,952	5,696	6,465
School level	Percentage of charter schools that were—							
Elementary	54.6%	50.6%	52.0%	52.1%	53.3%	54.1%	54.9%	56.2%
Secondary	25.9	24.2	26.2	28.0	27.8	26.8	24.9	23.5
Combined	18.6	21.6	21.0	18.6	18.3	18.8	19.5	19.6
Enrollment size								
Under 300	77.1	73.6	71.1	69.6	65.6	61.5	55.8	51.7
300-499	12.0	13.6	15.6	16.5	19.3	20.8	23.1	24.3
500-999	8.6	9.9	10.1	10.9	12.0	14.0	17.0	19.0
1,000 or more	2.4	2.8	3.2	3.0	3.1	3.7	4.2	4.9
Locale								
City	NA	NA	52.7	52.5	54.3	54.8	55.4	56.5
Suburban	NA	NA	22.0	22.2	22.0	21.1	21.2	26.1
Town	NA	NA	9.6	9.4	8.5	8.0	7.4	7.0
Rural	NA	NA	15.8	16.0	15.2	16.1	16.0	10.4

NA = Not available. **Note:** Race categories exclude persons of Hispanic ethnicity, who may be of any race.

Homeschooled Students, 2011-12

Source: National Center for Education Statistics, U.S. Dept. of Education

A total of 1,770,000 U.S. students in grades K-12 were homeschooled in 2011-12, up from 1.5 mil in 2007 and 850,000 in 1999. In a 2012 U.S. Dept. of Education survey of parents who homeschool their children, the reasons they gave as most important in their decision to homeschool included concern over the school environment, with such factors as safety, drugs, or negative peer pressure (25%); dissatisfaction with academic instruction in schools (19%); desire to provide religious instruction (16%); desire to provide moral instruction (5%); desire to provide a nontraditional approach to education (5%); and the child having a physical or mental health problem (5%). In all, 91% cited concern over school environment as one of their reasons, 77% cited moral instruction, 74% cited dissatisfaction with academic instruction, and 64% cited religious instruction.

Characteristic	No. of students (thous.)	% distrib.	Home-schooling rate[1]	Characteristic	No. of students (thous.)	% distrib.	Home-schooling rate[1]
Total	1,770	NA	3.4%	**Grade equivalent**			
Household locale				Kindergarten-2nd grade	415	23%	3.1%
City	489	28%	3.2	3rd-5th grade	416	23	3.4
Suburban	601	34	3.1	6th-8th grade	425	24	3.5
Town	132	7	2.7	9th-12th grade	514	29	3.7
Rural	548	31	4.5				
Race/ethnicity[2]				**Parents' education**			
White	1,201	68	4.5	Less than high school	203	11	3.4
Black	139	8	1.9	High school	355	20	3.4
Asian/Pacific Islander	73	4	2.6	Vocational/technical or some college	525	30	3.4
Other race(s)	90	5	3.2	Bachelor's degree	436	25	3.7
Hispanic	267	15	2.3	Graduate/professional school	252	14	3.3
Poverty status							
Poor	348	20	3.5				
Not poor	1,422	80	3.4				

NA = Not applicable. **Note:** Numbers may not add up to totals because of rounding. Homeschooled students are school-age children in a grade equivalent to K-12 who receive instruction at home all or most of the time. Excludes students enrolled in public or private school more than 25 hours per week or homeschooled because of temporary illness only. (1) Percentage of total subgroup (e.g., all "City" students) that is homeschooled. (2) Race categories exclude persons of Hispanic ethnicity, who may be of any race.

Common Core State Standards
Source: Common Core State Standards Initiative

In 2009, members of the Council of Chief State School Officers and the National Governors Association Center for Best Practices met to develop the Common Core State Standards, a set of college- and career-readiness standards for kindergarten through 12th grade in English language arts/literacy and mathematics. The Common Core State Standards were released in June 2010. As of Aug. 2016, 42 states; Washington, DC; American Samoa; Guam; Northern Mariana Islands; and the U.S. Virgin Islands had adopted and were working to implement the standards, which are designed to ensure that students graduating from high school are prepared to take credit-bearing introductory courses in two- or four-year college programs or to enter the workforce.

Assessment took place starting in the 2014-15 school year. Most states used tests developed by the Partnership for Assessment of Readiness for College and Careers (PARCC) or the Smarter Balanced Assessment Consortium.

The Common Core standards have received both support and criticism. Proponents claimed that the Common Core standards would better prepare students for college or work and make them more competitive in the world. Critics claimed that teachers and parents did not have enough input in developing the standards, that the federal government would be too involved in education (in spite of the state-level adoption of Common Core), and that implementing the standards would be too costly.

Population With Upper Secondary Education in Selected Countries, 2014
Source: Organization for Economic Cooperation and Development
Ranked by percentage of the population ages 25-64 that have received at least an upper secondary (senior high school) education.

Country	%	Country	%	Country	%	Country	%	Country	%
Russian Federation[1]	95%	Switzerland	88%	Norway	82%	New Zealand	74%	Saudi Arabia[1]	51%
Czech Republic	93	Finland	87	Sweden	82	Iceland	73	Brazil[1]	46
Estonia	91	Germany	87	Denmark	80	Greece	68	Portugal	43
Poland	91	Slovenia	86	Ireland	79	South Africa[2]	65	Costa Rica	40
Slovak Republic	91	Israel	85	United Kingdom	79	Chile[1]	61	Turkey	36
Lithuania	91	Korea	85	Australia	77	Italy	59	Mexico	34
Canada	90	Austria	84	Netherlands	76	Spain	57	Indonesia[3]	31
United States	90	Hungary	83	France[1]	75	Colombia	52	China[4]	24
Latvia	90	Luxembourg	82	Belgium	74				

(1) 2013. (2) 2012. (3) 2011. (4) 2010.

Financial Aid to U.S. Undergraduate Students, 2000-14
Source: National Center for Education Statistics, U.S. Dept. of Education

Control and level of institution/ year	Number enrolled	Number receiving financial aid	Percent receiving aid	Percent of enrolled students in student aid programs				Average award[1]			
				Federal grants	State/ local grants	Institutional grants	Student loans[2]	Federal grants	State/ local grants	Institutional grants	Student loans[2]
All institutions											
2000-01	1,976,600	1,390,527	70.3%	31.6%	31.2%	31.1%	40.1%	$3,361	$2,756	$6,407	$5,088
2013-14	2,504,847	2,076,901	82.9	45.3	32.2	41.3	47.4	4,564	3,125	9,676	7,063
Public											
2000-01	1,333,236	872,109	65.4	30.0	33.5	22.7	30.7	3,255	2,307	3,075	4,123
2013-14	1,751,924	1,409,393	80.4	44.9	37.3	32.4	39.9	4,550	2,983	4,987	6,251
4-year											
2000-01	804,793	573,430	71.3	26.6	36.5	29.6	40.7	3,473	2,795	3,536	4,341
2013-14	1,076,346	892,158	82.9	38.0	37.4	45.3	49.6	4,629	3,752	5,476	6,701
2-year											
2000-01	528,443	298,679	56.5	35.2	28.8	12.1	15.3	3,004	1,364	1,357	3,238
2013-14	675,578	517,235	76.6	56.0	37.2	11.8	24.4	4,464	1,749	1,991	4,798
Private nonprofit											
2000-01	439,369	363,044	82.6	28.4	31.8	68.1	57.7	3,891	4,052	9,959	5,433
2013-14	513,574	458,513	89.3	33.7	26.1	81.1	61.1	4,768	3,789	16,952	8,123
4-year											
2000-01	419,499	347,638	82.9	27.4	32.2	70.1	58.1	3,961	4,057	10,081	5,407
2013-14	504,584	450,215	89.2	33.1	26.1	81.6	61.0	4,788	3,792	17,088	8,128
2-year											
2000-01	19,870	15,406	77.5	49.2	23.9	25.7	49.5	3,068	3,909	2,930	6,095
2013-14	8,990	8,298	92.3	70.6	27.3	49.5	65.5	4,246	3,644	4,378	7,875
Private for-profit											
2000-01	203,995	155,374	76.2	49.3	15.2	6.2	63.5	3,125	3,371	2,081	7,458
2013-14	239,349	208,995	87.3	72.8	8.1	21.5	73.2	4,427	3,301	2,517	8,397
4-year											
2000-01	81,075	51,739	63.8	36.1	11.9	8.3	57.7	3,103	3,905	2,184	7,771
2013-14	90,408	80,758	89.3	72.4	10.5	34.4	78.0	4,661	3,045	3,104	8,648
2-year											
2000-01	122,920	103,635	84.3	58.0	17.3	4.8	67.3	3,135	3,128	1,963	7,281
2013-14	148,941	128,237	86.1	73.0	6.7	13.6	70.3	4,285	3,543	1,614	8,228

Note: Data for full-time, first-time, degree-seeking undergraduate students. (1) Average amounts for students participating in indicated programs, in constant 2014-15 dollars. (2) Includes only loans made directly to students. Does not include Parent Loans for Undergraduate Students (PLUS) and other loans made directly to parents.

Charges at U.S. Institutions of Higher Education, 1969-2015

Source: National Center for Education Statistics, U.S. Dept. of Education

Data are for the entire academic year and are average charges for full-time students at degree-granting postsecondary institutions.
Room and board based on full-time students. For 1989-90 on, board is based on 20 meals per week.

	Tuition and fees			Board rates			Dormitory charges		
Public (in-state)	All institutions	2-yr	4-yr	All institutions	2-yr	4-yr	All institutions	2-yr	4-yr
1969-70	$323	$178	$358	$508	$465	$510	$366	$308	$369
1979-80	583	355	738	867	893	865	715	574	725
1989-90	1,356	756	1,780	1,635	1,581	1,638	1,513	962	1,557
1999-2000	2,504	1,348	3,349	2,364	1,834	2,406	2,440	1,549	2,519
2001-02	2,700	1,380	3,735	2,598	2,036	2,645	2,723	1,722	2,816
2002-03	2,903	1,483	4,046	2,669	2,164	2,712	2,930	1,954	3,029
2003-04	3,319	1,702	4,587	2,822	2,221	2,876	3,106	2,089	3,212
2004-05	3,629	1,849	5,027	2,931	2,353	2,981	3,304	2,174	3,418
2005-06	3,874	1,935	5,351	3,035	2,306	3,093	3,545	2,251	3,664
2006-07	4,102	2,018	5,666	3,191	2,390	3,253	3,757	2,407	3,878
2007-08	4,291	2,061	5,943	3,331	2,409	3,404	3,952	2,506	4,082
2008-09	4,512	2,136	6,312	3,554	2,769	3,619	4,190	2,664	4,331
2009-10	4,763	2,283	6,717	3,655	2,571	3,755	4,401	2,854	4,564
2010-11	5,075	2,441	7,132	3,845	2,683	3,956	4,646	2,955	4,832
2011-12	5,563	2,651	7,713	3,946	2,866	4,042	4,849	3,100	5,031
2012-13	5,899	2,792	8,070	4,061	2,888	4,163	5,062	3,247	5,241
2013-14	6,122	2,882	8,312	4,205	2,953	4,308	5,304	3,447	5,479
2014-15	6,371	2,955	8,543	4,313	3,072	4,412	5,504	3,559	5,677
Private (nonprofit and for-profit)									
1969-70	$1,533	$1,034	$1,562	$560	$546	$561	$434	$413	$436
1979-80	3,130	2,062	3,225	955	923	957	827	766	831
1989-90	8,147	5,196	8,396	1,948	1,811	1,953	1,923	1,663	1,935
1999-2000	14,100	8,225	14,616	2,877	2,753	2,879	3,236	3,067	3,242
2001-02	15,742	10,076	16,211	3,104	2,633	3,109	3,567	3,116	3,576
2002-03	16,383	10,651	16,826	3,206	3,870	3,197	3,752	3,232	3,764
2003-04	17,315	11,545	17,763	3,364	4,432	3,354	3,945	3,581	3,952
2004-05	18,154	12,122	18,604	3,485	3,700	3,483	4,178	4,475	4,173
2005-06	18,862	12,450	19,292	3,645	4,781	3,637	4,400	4,173	4,404
2006-07	20,048	12,708	20,517	3,785	3,429	3,788	4,606	4,147	4,613
2007-08	20,972	13,126	21,427	3,992	4,074	3,991	4,804	4,484	4,808
2008-09	21,570	13,562	22,036	4,209	4,627	4,206	5,025	4,537	5,032
2009-10	21,764	14,862	22,269	4,329	4,390	4,329	5,248	5,211	5,248
2010-11	22,042	13,687	22,677	4,430	4,475	4,430	5,403	4,939	5,410
2011-12	22,850	13,961	23,464	4,586	4,475	4,586	5,622	5,169	5,627
2012-13	23,943	14,149	24,523	4,709	3,977	4,712	5,831	5,228	5,837
2013-14	25,101	14,168	25,696	4,863	4,198	4,865	6,021	5,493	6,026
2014-15	26,184	14,254	26,740	5,019	4,560	5,021	6,221	5,504	6,229

U.S. Student Loan Balances by Age, 2004-14

Source: *Student Loan Borrowing and Repayment Trends, 2015*, Federal Reserve Bank of New York; Equifax

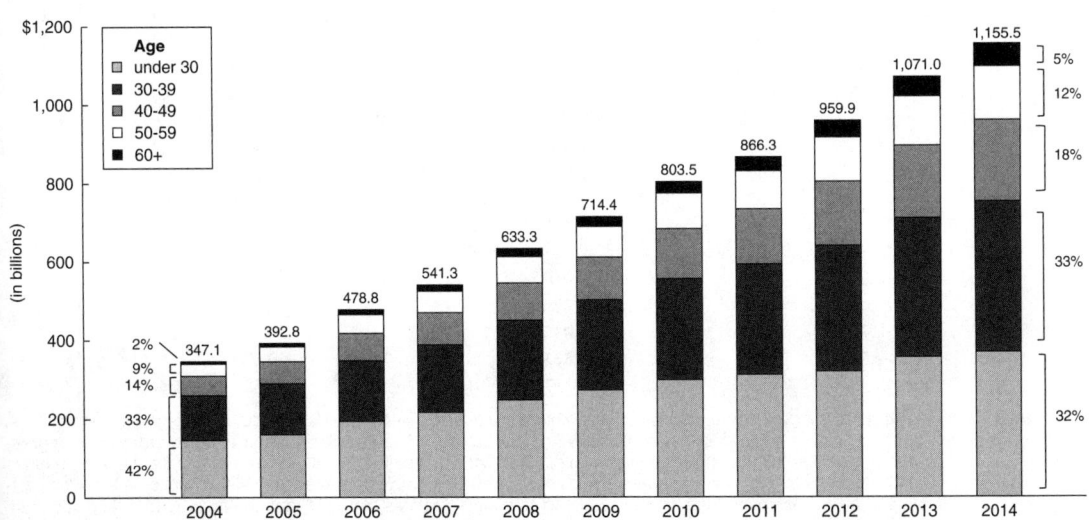

Note: Total annual balances include loans held by persons of unknown ages.

Student Loan Debt by State, 2004-14

Source: *Student Debt and the Class of 2014*, Project on Student Debt, Institute for College Access

State	Average debt 2004	Average debt 2014	% change, 2004-14	% with debt 2004	% with debt 2014	State	Average debt 2004	Average debt 2014	% change, 2004-14	% with debt 2004	% with debt 2014
Alabama	$18,042	$29,425	63%	57%	54%	Nebraska	$17,384	$26,278	51%	62%	63%
Alaska	15,648	26,742	71	48	50	Nevada	14,144	20,211	43	46	46
Arizona	18,147	22,609	25	48	57	New Hampshire	21,441	33,410	56	65	76
Arkansas	16,210	25,344	56	59	55	New Jersey	16,223	28,318	75	58	68
California	16,071	21,382	33	49	55	New Mexico	—	18,969	—	—	48
Colorado	16,352	25,064	53	53	56	New York	18,857	27,822	48	62	61
Connecticut	18,906	29,750	57	57	62	North Carolina	16,863	25,218	50	51	61
Delaware	14,780	33,808	129	45	62	North Dakota	22,409	—	—	73	—
Florida	18,857	24,947	32	51	54	Ohio	19,182	29,353	53	62	67
Georgia	15,354	26,518	73	53	62	Oklahoma	16,942	23,430	38	55	55
Hawaii	13,509	24,554	82	29	47	Oregon	17,267	26,106	51	63	62
Idaho	22,273	26,091	17	68	72	Pennsylvania	19,556	33,264	70	69	70
Illinois	15,650	28,984	85	56	67	Rhode Island	19,328	31,841	65	68	65
Indiana	19,425	29,222	50	54	61	South Carolina	16,775	29,163	74	55	59
Iowa	24,204	29,732	23	76	68	South Dakota	19,023	26,023	37	82	69
Kansas	16,266	25,521	57	57	65	Tennessee	16,905	25,510	51	41	60
Kentucky	14,250	25,939	82	52	64	Texas	17,170	26,250	53	51	59
Louisiana	18,993	23,025	21	61	47	Utah	12,362	18,921	53	43	54
Maine	19,410	30,908	59	64	68	Vermont	20,706	29,060	40	56	65
Maryland	12,597	27,457	118	52	58	Virginia	15,831	26,432	67	57	60
Massachusetts	17,021	29,391	73	60	65	Washington	17,415	24,804	42	56	58
Michigan	18,754	29,450	57	58	62	West Virginia	18,246	26,854	47	69	69
Minnesota	19,580	31,579	61	72	70	Wisconsin	16,560	28,810	74	60	70
Mississippi	15,503	26,177	69	60	60	Wyoming	15,352	23,708	54	44	46
Missouri	15,511	25,844	67	59	59	Wash., DC	19,357	—	—	58	—
Montana	18,019	26,946	50	68	67	**U.S.**	**18,550**	**28,950**	**56**	**65**	**69**

— = Not calculated; usable cases covered less than 30% of bachelor's degree recipients, or underlying data showed a state-level change of 30% or more in average debt from previous year.

College Enrollment by Selected Characteristics, 1947-2014

Source: National Center for Education Statistics, U.S. Dept. of Education
(numbers in thousands)

Year	Total enrollment[1]	Attendance status Full-time	Attendance status Part-time	Attendance status % part-time	Sex of student Male	Sex of student Female	Control of institution Public	Control of institution Private Total	Control of institution Private Nonprofit	Control of institution For-profit
1947[2]	2,338	NA	NA	NA	1,659	679	1,152	1,186	NA	NA
1950[2]	2,281	NA	NA	NA	1,560	721	1,140	1,142	NA	NA
1955[2]	2,653	NA	NA	NA	1,733	920	1,476	1,177	NA	NA
1965	5,921	4,096	1,825[3]	30.8%	3,630	2,291	3,970	1,951	NA	NA
1970	8,581	5,816	2,765	32.2	5,044	3,537	6,428	2,153	2,134	18
1975	11,185	6,841	4,344	38.8	6,149	5,036	8,835	2,350	2,311	39
1980	12,097	7,098	4,999	41.3	5,874	6,223	9,457	2,640	2,528	112[4]
1985	12,247	7,075	5,172	42.2	5,819	6,429	9,479	2,768	2,572	196
1990	13,819	7,821	5,998	43.4	6,284	7,535	10,845	2,974	2,760	214
1995	14,262	8,129	6,133	43.0	6,343	7,919	11,092	3,169	2,929	240
2000	15,312	9,010	6,303	41.2	6,722	8,591	11,753	3,560	3,109	450
2001	15,928	9,448	6,481	40.7	6,961	8,967	12,233	3,695	3,167	528
2002	16,612	9,946	6,665	40.1	7,202	9,410	12,752	3,860	3,266	594
2003	16,912	10,326	6,585	38.9	7,260	9,651	12,859	4,053	3,341	712
2004	17,272	10,610	6,662	38.6	7,387	9,885	12,980	4,292	3,412	880
2005	17,488	10,797	6,691	38.3	7,456	10,032	13,022	4,466	3,455	1,011
2006	17,759	10,957	6,802	38.3	7,575	10,184	13,180	4,579	3,513	1,066
2007	18,248	11,270	6,978	38.2	7,816	10,432	13,491	4,757	3,571	1,186
2008	19,103	11,748	7,355	38.5	8,189	10,914	13,972	5,131	3,662	1,469
2009	20,314	12,605	7,708	37.9	8,733	11,581	14,811	5,503	3,768	1,735
2010	21,019	13,087	7,932	37.7	9,046	11,974	15,142	5,877	3,855	2,023
2011	21,011	13,003	8,008	38.1	9,034	11,976	15,116	5,894	3,927	1,968
2012	20,645	12,734	7,910	38.3	8,919	11,726	14,885	5,760	3,951	1,808
2013	20,376	12,597	7,779	38.2	8,861	11,515	14,746	5,630	3,974	1,656
2014	20,207	12,454	7,753	38.2	8,797	11,410	14,655	5,552	3,996	1,556

NA = Not available. **Note:** Data for 1947-95 are for institutions of higher education, while later data are for degree-granting institutions. Degree-granting institutions grant associate's or higher degrees and participate in Title IV federal financial aid programs. The degree-granting classification is very similar to the earlier higher education classification, but it includes more two-year colleges and excludes a few higher education institutions that do not grant degrees. (1) Fall enrollment. (2) Degree-credit enrollment only. (3) Includes part-time resident students and all extension students (students attending courses at sites separate from the primary reporting campus). In later years, part-time student enrollment was collected as a distinct category. (4) Large increases are due to the addition of schools accredited by the Accrediting Commission of Career Schools and Colleges of Technology.

U.S. Bachelor's Degrees Conferred, 1899-2026

Source: National Center for Education Statistics, U.S. Dept. of Education
(*) figures are projected.

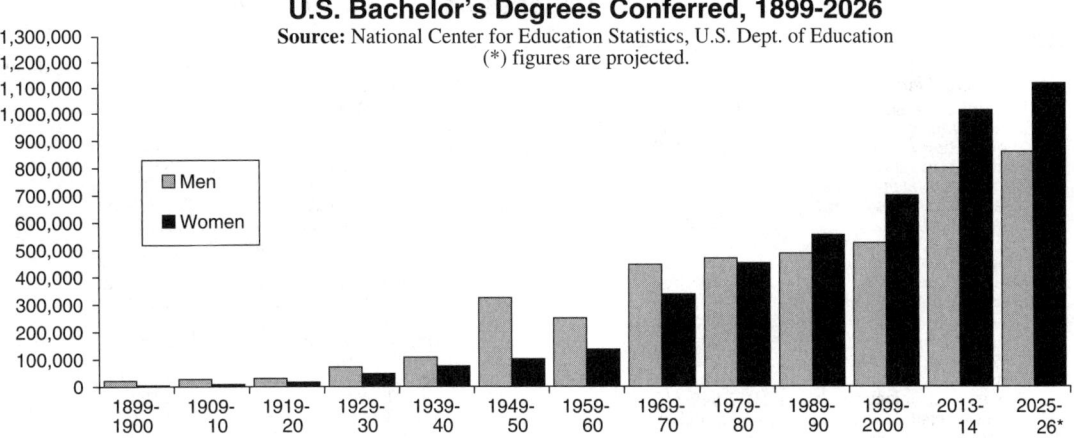

Financial Aid for College and Other Postsecondary Education

Reviewed by National Association of Student Financial Aid Administrators; as of Aug. 2016

The cost of postsecondary education in the U.S. continues to increase, but financial aid—in the form of **grants** (no repayment needed), **loans**, and/or **work-study** programs—is widely available to help families meet these expenses. Most federal aid is limited to families that demonstrate financial need as determined by standard formulas and is designed to help students attend the college of their choice regardless of their ability to pay. Financial aid personnel at each school can provide information about all aid programs (federal, state, institutional, and private) available to students, how to apply, and deadlines.

All applicants for federal aid must file a Free Application for Federal Student Aid (**FAFSA**), generally as soon as possible after Oct. 1 for the academic year starting the following Aug. or Sept. This change from Jan. in prior years allows students to apply for aid earlier. Figures provided should match federal income tax forms filed for the previous year. (The use of tax data that has already been filed ensures timely processing.) This is made easier by the availability of the IRS Data Retrieval Tool, which allows online applicants to access and transfer IRS tax return information directly into their FAFSA. Many other sources of aid—state governments, employers and unions, civic organizations, and the institutions themselves—also use the FAFSA to determine eligibility for aid. Some federal programs pay for postsecondary education in return for service: AmeriCorps (1-800-942-2677), Reserve Officers' Training Corps (1-800-USA-ROTC [Army], 1-800-USA-NAVY [Navy], and 1-800-522-0033 [Air Force]), the G.I. Bill (1-888-442-4551), and the National Health Service Corps (1-800-221-9393). A student must reapply for aid annually.

A **federal formula**, based on information provided on the FAFSA, takes into account such factors as family income in the preceding calendar year, parental and student assets (excluding the parents' home, farm, or certain small businesses), and length of time to parents' retirement. Financial aid personnel have the authority to consider unusual expenses, such as very high medical expenses, which are not reported on the FAFSA. Outside scholarships are also taken into account in determining eligibility for federal, institutional, and state financial aid programs.

The formula determines a family's **expected family contribution** (EFC), which is divided among the number of family members—excluding parents—in college. The EFC is subtracted from the total cost of attending college for each person. The difference determines financial need and the maximum federal aid for which the family may be eligible.

(Some institutions use a separate formula for need-based institutional aid.) Some schools guarantee to meet the full financial need of each admitted student. Schools might try to cover a student's financial need using various forms of financial aid but be unable to because of a lack of funds.

The **aid package** offered by each school may include one or more of the following resources: Federal Pell Grants, for those who demonstrate sufficient financial need; Federal Supplemental Educational Opportunity Grants, for those who still have significant need after receiving Federal Pell Grants; grants from the school; Federal Work-Study or other work programs; and federal Direct Subsidized and Unsubsidized Loans (often referred to as Direct loans). Parents of undergraduates and students in graduate or professional school may apply for a PLUS loan. Direct Unsubsidized Loans and Direct PLUS loans are available regardless of financial need, but students and parents must still complete the FAFSA to get these loans.

Loans have varying interest rates and other requirements. Repayment of Direct Subsidized Loans, and Direct Unsubsidized Loans generally does not begin until after graduation; deferments, income-based repayment plans, and loan forgiveness are available on federal loans for students who meet certain requirements. For PLUS loans, parents and graduate-level students must pass a credit check and may need to begin repayment of both principal and interest while the student is still in school.

Terms may vary, but federal student loans must be repaid, even if financial circumstances change, education is incomplete or not as expected, or post-graduation income is less than expected. The loan servicer or lender is required to provide a loan repayment schedule that states the first payment due date, the number and frequency of payments, and the amount due. Some loans have a grace period, a set period of time (in most cases six months) after graduation before repayment begins. Direct loans have a number of repayment plan options—including graduated repayments, extended repayment, income-based repayment—or offer loan consolidation.

Certain federal income **tax credits and refunds** are available to families who meet requirements.

Rules for financial aid are complex and changeable. Comprehensive resources on financial aid from the U.S. Dept. of Education, including fact-sheets, videos, worksheets, and other tools, are available online at studentaid.ed.gov/sa/resources/.

Further information and FAFSA forms are available from schools or from the Federal Student Aid Information Center: 1-800-4-FED-AID, Mon.-Fri., 8 AM-10 PM ET; www.fafsa.ed.gov.

Endowment Assets of Colleges and Universities, 2015

Source: 2015 NACUBO-Commonfund Study of Endowments, National Association of College and University Business Officers (NACUBO)

Rank	College/university	Endowment assets[1]	% change, 2014-15	Rank	College/university	Endowment assets[1]	% change, 2014-15
1.	Harvard University	$36,448,817	1.6%	22.	Dartmouth College	$4,663,491	4.4%
2.	Yale University	25,572,100	7.0	23.	Vanderbilt University	4,133,542	1.2
3.	The University of Texas System	24,083,150	−5.3	24.	Pennsylvania State University	3,635,730	5.5
4.	Princeton University	22,723,473	8.2	25.	Ohio State University	3,633,887	2.4
5.	Stanford University	22,222,957	3.6	26.	University of Pittsburgh	3,588,775	2.7
6.	Massachusetts Institute of Technology	13,474,743	8.4	27.	New York University	3,576,180	4.5
				28.	Johns Hopkins University	3,412,617	−1.1
7.	The Texas A&M University System and Foundations	10,477,102	−5.6	29.	University of Minnesota and Foundations	3,297,460	3.8
8.	Northwestern University	10,193,037	4.2	30.	University of Washington	3,076,226	8.6
9.	University of Pennsylvania	10,133,569	5.8	31.	Brown University	3,073,349	2.5
10.	University of Michigan	9,952,113	2.3	32.	University of North Carolina at Chapel Hill and Foundations	2,988,806	10.9
11.	Columbia University	9,639,065	4.5				
12.	University of Notre Dame	8,566,952	6.6	33.	University of Wisconsin Foundation	2,465,051	5.7
13.	University of California	7,997,099	8.3				
14.	University of Chicago	7,549,710	0.1	34.	Purdue University	2,397,902	−1.9
15.	Duke University	7,296,545	3.7	35.	Williams College	2,395,100	6.3
16.	Washington University in St. Louis	6,818,748	2.6	36.	University of Illinois and Foundation	2,388,469	4.9
17.	Emory University	6,684,305	0.0	37.	University of Richmond	2,371,810	2.5
18.	University of Virginia	6,180,515	3.9	38.	Michigan State University	2,274,813	6.0
19.	Cornell University	6,037,546	2.5	39.	Boston College	2,219,600	4.1
20.	Rice University	5,557,479	0.5	40.	California Institute of Technology	2,198,887	5.0
21.	University of Southern California	4,709,511	2.5				

Note: Market value of endowment assets in the fiscal year. (1) In thousands.

Average ACT Scores and Characteristics of College-Bound Students, 1990-2016

Source: ACT, Inc. (formerly American College Testing)

SCORES	Unit	1990	1995	2000	2005	2009	2010	2011	2012	2013	2014	2015	2016
Composite score	Points	20.6	20.8	21.0	20.9	21.1	21.0	21.1	21.1	20.9	21.0	21.0	20.8
Male	Points	21.0	21.0	21.2	21.1	21.3	21.2	21.2	21.2	20.9	21.1	21.1	20.9
Female	Points	20.3	20.7	20.9	20.9	20.9	20.9	21.0	21.0	20.9	20.9	21.0	20.9
English score	Points	20.5	20.2	20.5	20.4	20.6	20.5	20.6	20.5	20.2	20.3	20.4	20.1
Male	Points	20.1	19.8	20.0	20.0	20.2	20.1	20.2	20.0	19.8	20.0	20.0	19.8
Female	Points	20.9	20.6	20.9	20.8	20.9	20.8	20.9	20.9	20.6	20.7	20.8	20.6
Math score	Points	19.9	20.2	20.7	20.7	21.0	21.0	21.1	21.1	20.9	20.9	20.8	20.6
Male	Points	20.7	20.9	21.4	21.3	21.6	21.6	21.6	21.7	21.4	21.4	21.3	21.0
Female	Points	19.3	19.7	20.2	20.2	20.4	20.5	20.6	20.6	20.5	20.5	20.4	20.3
PARTICIPANTS													
Total number	(Thous.)	817	945	1,065	1,186	1,480	1,569	1,623	1,666	1,799	1,846	1,924	2,090
Male	Percent	46%	44%	43%	44%	45%	45%	46%	46%	46%	46%	47%	46%
White	Percent	79	80	72	66	64	62	60	59	58	56	55	54
Black	Percent	9	9	10	12	13	14	14	13	13	13	13	13
Hispanic[1]	Percent	4	5	5	7	9	10	12	14	14	15	16	16
Composite score													
27 or above	Percent	12	13	14	14	12	16	17	17	13	17	18	17
18 or below	Percent	35	34	32	34	34	35	34	34	36	36	37	39

Note: Minimum score, 1; maximum score, 36. Test scores and characteristics of college-bound students are based on the performance of all ACT-tested students who graduated in the spring of a given school year and took the ACT assessment during junior or senior year of high school. (1) Persons of Hispanic origin may be of any race.

Average ACT Composite Scores by State, 2016

Source: ACT, Inc. (formerly American College Testing)

State	Avg. comp. score	% grads taking ACT	State	Avg. comp. score	% grads taking ACT	State	Avg. comp. score	% grads taking ACT
Alabama	19.1	100%	Kentucky	20.0	100%	North Dakota	20.3	100%
Alaska	20.0	53	Louisiana	19.5	100	Ohio	22.0	73
Arizona	20.1	58	Maine	23.6	10	Oklahoma	20.4	82
Arkansas	20.2	96	Maryland	23.0	27	Oregon	21.7	39
California	22.6	33	Massachusetts	24.8	28	Pennsylvania	23.1	23
Colorado	20.6	100	Michigan	20.3	100	Rhode Island	23.3	20
Connecticut	24.5	34	Minnesota	21.1	100	South Carolina	18.5	100
Delaware	23.6	21	Mississippi	18.4	100	South Dakota	21.9	76
District of Columbia	22.2	44	Missouri	20.2	100	Tennessee	19.9	100
Florida	19.9	81	Montana	20.3	100	Texas	20.6	46
Georgia	21.1	60	Nebraska	21.4	88	Utah	20.2	100
Hawaii	18.7	94	Nevada	17.7	100	Vermont	23.4	29
Idaho	22.7	39	New Hampshire	24.5	23	Virginia	23.3	31
Illinois	20.8	100	New Jersey	23.1	32	Washington	23.1	25
Indiana	22.3	41	New Mexico	19.9	70	West Virginia	20.7	67
Iowa	22.1	68	New York	23.9	29	Wisconsin	20.5	100
Kansas	21.9	74	North Carolina	19.1	100	Wyoming	20.0	100

Mean SAT Scores of College-Bound Seniors, 1975-2016

Source: The College Board
(recentered scale; for school year ending in year shown)

	1975	1980	1985	1990	1995	2000	2005	2008	2009	2010	2011	2012	2013	2014	2015	2016[2]
Critical reading score[1]	512	502	509	500	504	505	508	500	499	500	497	496	496	497	495	494
Male	515	506	514	505	505	507	513	502	502	502	500	498	499	499	497	495
Female	509	498	503	496	502	504	505	499	497	498	495	493	494	495	493	493
Math score.	498	492	500	501	506	514	520	514	514	515	514	514	514	513	511	508
Male	518	515	522	521	525	533	538	532	533	533	531	532	531	530	527	524
Female	479	473	480	483	490	498	504	499	498	499	500	499	499	499	496	494
Writing score.	NA	NA	NA	NA	NA	NA	NA	493	492	491	489	488	488	487	484	482
Male	NA	NA	NA	NA	NA	NA	NA	486	485	485	482	481	482	481	478	475
Female	NA	NA	NA	NA	NA	NA	NA	499	498	497	496	494	493	492	490	487

NA = Not applicable. **Note:** In 1995, the College Board recentered the scoring scale for the SAT. Earlier scores have been adjusted to account for this recentering. (1) Pre-2006 scores are for the Verbal section. (2) Through Jan. 2016; beginning in Mar. 2016, students took a redesigned SAT test. The College Board advised against comparing 2016 SAT results with previous year's data.

Mean SAT Scores by State, 1990-2016

Source: The College Board; National Center for Education Statistics, U.S. Dept. of Education
(for school year ending in year shown; V = Verbal, M = Math, CR = Critical reading, W = Writing)

	1990		2000		2010			2015			2016[1]			% grads
State	V	M	V	M	CR	M	W	CR	M	W	CR	M	W	taking SAT[2]
Alabama	545	534	559	555	556	550	544	545	538	533	557	551	543	6.1%
Alaska	514	501	519	515	518	515	491	509	503	482	485	479	460	51.9
Arizona	521	520	521	523	519	525	500	523	527	502	528	532	505	34.3
Arkansas	545	532	563	554	566	566	552	568	569	551	570	569	553	4.1
California	494	508	497	518	501	516	500	495	506	491	491	500	485	60.4
Colorado	533	534	534	537	568	572	555	582	587	567	587	589	571	12.3
Connecticut	506	496	508	509	509	514	513	504	506	504	500	500	497	89.3
Delaware	510	496	502	496	493	495	481	462	461	445	458	453	440	100.0
District of Columbia	483	467	494	486	474	464	466	441	440	432	433	433	419	100.0
Florida	495	493	498	500	496	498	479	486	480	468	481	475	462	74.3
Georgia	478	473	488	486	488	490	475	490	485	475	493	490	476	76.9
Hawaii	480	505	488	519	483	505	470	487	508	477	491	511	476	61.4
Idaho	542	524	540	541	543	541	517	467	463	442	465	453	446	99.9
Illinois	542	547	568	586	585	600	577	599	616	587	605	622	592	4.0
Indiana	486	486	498	501	494	505	477	496	499	478	496	499	477	70.9
Iowa	584	588	589	600	603	613	582	589	600	566	602	611	572	2.9
Kansas	566	563	574	580	590	595	567	588	592	568	594	604	571	4.8
Kentucky	548	541	548	550	575	575	563	588	587	574	604	599	586	4.0
Louisiana	551	537	562	558	555	550	547	563	559	553	584	577	571	4.6
Maine	501	490	504	500	468	467	454	468	473	451	486	485	472	95.9
Maryland	506	502	507	509	501	506	495	491	493	478	490	490	476	78.7
Massachusetts	503	498	511	513	512	526	509	516	529	507	517	530	506	86.2
Michigan	529	534	557	569	585	605	576	594	609	585	594	608	581	3.5
Minnesota	552	558	581	594	594	607	580	595	607	576	607	620	588	5.4
Mississippi	552	538	562	549	566	548	552	580	563	570	595	584	585	3.1
Missouri	548	541	572	577	593	595	580	596	599	582	605	608	589	3.7
Montana	540	542	543	546	538	538	517	561	556	538	565	557	539	15.0
Nebraska	559	562	560	571	585	593	568	589	590	576	590	595	573	3.5
Nevada	511	511	510	517	496	501	473	494	494	470	511	509	488	49.8
New Hampshire	518	510	520	519	520	524	510	525	530	511	527	531	510	69.8
New Jersey	495	498	498	513	495	514	497	500	521	499	495	514	492	81.4
New Mexico	554	546	549	543	553	549	534	551	544	528	553	545	525	12.1
New York	489	496	494	506	484	499	478	489	502	478	489	501	477	74.9
North Carolina	478	470	492	496	497	511	477	498	504	476	502	508	475	63.2
North Dakota	579	578	588	609	580	594	559	597	608	586	585	594	560	1.9
Ohio	526	522	533	539	538	548	522	557	563	537	556	563	534	13.7
Oklahoma	553	542	563	560	569	568	547	576	569	548	582	573	553	4.4
Oregon	515	509	527	527	523	524	499	523	521	502	525	520	500	46.6
Pennsylvania	497	490	498	497	492	501	480	499	504	482	500	506	481	70.6
Rhode Island	498	488	505	500	494	495	488	494	494	484	490	491	480	76.8
South Carolina	475	467	484	482	484	495	468	488	487	467	494	493	471	65.4
South Dakota	580	570	587	588	592	603	571	592	597	564	586	581	558	2.8
Tennessee	558	544	563	553	576	571	565	581	574	568	586	582	571	7.0
Texas	490	489	493	500	484	505	473	470	486	454	466	478	449	64.3
Utah	566	555	570	569	568	559	547	579	575	554	579	579	558	4.5
Vermont	507	493	513	508	519	521	506	523	524	507	520	520	501	61.3
Virginia	501	496	509	500	512	512	497	518	516	499	520	517	498	72.2
Washington	513	511	526	528	524	532	508	502	510	484	501	506	481	66.2
West Virginia	520	514	526	511	515	507	500	509	497	495	525	511	502	14.7
Wisconsin	552	559	584	597	595	604	579	591	605	575	605	618	588	3.6
Wyoming	534	538	545	545	570	567	546	589	586	562	603	600	587	3.3
National average	500	501	505	514	501	516	492	495	511	484	494	508	482	48.8

Note: In 1995, the College Board recentered the scoring scale for the SAT. In 2005, the Verbal portion became Critical reading, and a writing test was added. The 2006 graduating class was the first to take the new test. (1) Through Jan. 2016; beginning in Mar. 2016, students took a redesigned SAT test. (2) Percentage of students from the class of 2015 who took the SAT in each state.

Four-Year Colleges and Universities

Note: These listings **include only accredited degree-granting institutions** in the U.S. and U.S. territories with a total enrollment of 1,200 or more. Only four-year colleges and universities that award a bachelor's degree as their highest undergraduate degree are included. Data reported **only for institutions that provided updated information** on Peterson's Annual Survey of Undergraduate Institutions for the 2015-16 academic year, with some exceptions.

All institutions are coeducational except those where the ZIP code is followed directly by a number in parentheses: (1) = men only; (2) = primarily men; (3) = women only; (4) = primarily women; (5) undergraduate: men only, graduate: coed; (6) undergraduate: women only, graduate: coed.

The **Tuition & fees** column shows the annual tuition and required fees for full-time students or, where indicated, the tuition and standard fees per unit for part-time students. Where tuition varies according to residence, the figure is given for the most local resident and is coded as follows: (A) = area residents, (S) = state residents; all other figures apply to all students regardless of residence. Where annual expenses are expressed as a lump sum (including full-time tuition, mandatory fees, and room and board), the figure is entered under Tuition & fees and coded (C) = comprehensive fee. **Room & board** is the typical cost for one academic year.

Control: 1 = independent (nonprofit), 2 = independent-religious, 3 = proprietary (profit-making), 4 = federal, 5 = state, 6 = commonwealth (Puerto Rico), 7 = territory (U.S. territories), 8 = county, 9 = district, 10 = city, 11 = state and local, 12 = state-related, 13 = private (unspecified). **Degree** means the highest degree offered: B = bachelor's, M = master's, D = doctorate.

Enrollment is the total number of matriculated undergraduate and (if applicable) graduate students.

Faculty is the total number of full-time and part-time faculty members teaching courses.

Grad. rate is the percentage of full-time, first-time bachelor's (or equivalent) degree-seeking undergraduate students entering school in 2009 (or most recent available year prior) who obtained their degrees within six years.

NA indicates category is inapplicable, or data is not available from a consistent source.

Name, address	Year founded	Tuition & fees	Room & board	Control, degree	Enrollment	Faculty	Grad. rate
Abilene Christian Univ., Abilene, TX 79699-9100	1906	$30,830	$9,310	2-D	4,544	404	61%
Abraham Baldwin Agr. Coll., Tifton, GA 31793	1933	$4,066(S)	$9,105	5-B	3,327	162	NA
Acad. of Art Univ., San Francisco, CA 94105-3410	1929	$26,490	$15,250	3-M	13,800	1,434	31
Adams State Univ., Alamosa, CO 81101	1921	$8,574(S)	$8,500	5-D	3,560	239	29
Adelphi Univ., Garden City, NY 11530-0701	1896	$34,025	$13,510	1-D	7,256	1,014	67
Adrian Coll., Adrian, MI 49221-2575	1859	$32,660	$9,740	2-M	1,656	195	54
Adventist Univ. of Health Sciences, Orlando, FL 32803	1913	$13,480	$4,200	1-D	1,984	266	NA
Alabama Agr. & Mech. Univ., Huntsville, AL 35811	1875	$9,366(S)	$8,140	5-D	5,814	290	100
Alabama State Univ., Montgomery, AL 36101-0271	1867	$8,720(S)	$5,422	5-D	5,383	409	32
Albany Coll. of Pharm & Health Sciences, Albany, NY 12208	1881	$31,550	$10,410	1-D	1,559	132	77
Albany State Univ., Albany, GA 31705-2717	1903	$5,488(S)	$7,788	5-M	3,910	220	40
Albertus Magnus Coll., New Haven, CT 06511-1189	1925	$28,930	$12,960	2-M	1,550	134	44
Albion Coll., Albion, MI 49224-1831	1835	$39,128	$11,066	2-B	1,376	144	65
Albright Coll., Reading, PA 19612-5234	1856	$39,850	$10,770	2-M	1,759	171	58
Alcorn State Univ., Lorman, MS 39096-7500	1871	$6,384(S)	$8,996	5-M	3,518	216	34
Alfred Univ., Alfred, NY 14802-1205	1836	$31,070	$12,196	1-D	2,286	187	60
Allegheny Coll., Meadville, PA 16335	1815	$44,250	$11,170	1-B	1,931	197	75
Alliant Intl. Univ.–San Diego, San Diego, CA 92131-1799	1952	$15,812	$11,268	1-D	3,523	626	NA
Alma Coll., Alma, MI 48801-1599	1886	$35,806	$9,822	2-B	1,385	167	59
Alvernia Univ., Reading, PA 19607-1799	1958	$32,270	$11,430	2-D	2,856	328	51
Alverno Coll., Milwaukee, WI 53234-3922 (6)	1887	$25,660	$7,634	2-M	2,209	238	42
Amberton Univ., Garland, TX 75041-5595	1971	$7,500	NA	2-M	1,379	40	NA
American InterContinental Univ. Online, Schaumburg, IL 60173	1970	NA	NA	3-M	22,424	396	NA
American Intl. Coll., Springfield, MA 01109-3189	1885	$33,200	$13,420	1-D	3,542	440	38
American Public Univ. System, Charles Town, WV 25414	1991	$6,880	NA	3-M	52,513	2,270	NA
American Univ., Washington, DC 20016-8001	1893	$44,593	$14,526	2-D	13,200	1,409	81
American Univ. of Puerto Rico, Bayamon, PR 00960-2037	1963	NA	NA	1-M	2,468	162	NA
Amherst Coll., Amherst, MA 01002-5000	1821	$50,562	$13,210	1-B	1,795	285	95
Anderson Univ., Anderson, IN 46012-3495	1917	$28,650	$9,550	2-D	2,325	277	54
Anderson Univ., Anderson, SC 29621-4035	1911	$25,880	$9,174	2-D	3,212	315	48
Andrews Univ., Berrien Springs, MI 49104	1874	$27,000	$8,532	2-D	3,366	300	54
Angelo State Univ., San Angelo, TX 76909	1928	$7,864(S)	$7,702	5-D	8,483	325	37
Anna Maria Coll., Paxton, MA 01612	1946	$35,074	$13,112	2-D	1,468	NA	34
Appalachian State Univ., Boone, NC 28608	1899	$6,852(S)	$7,845	5-D	17,932	1,327	71
Aquinas Coll., Grand Rapids, MI 49506-1799	1886	$30,062	$8,814	2-M	1,802	223	58
Arcadia Univ., Glenside, PA 19038-3295	1853	$39,560	$13,200	2-D	3,984	493	58
Arizona State Univ. at the Downtown Phoenix campus, Phoenix, AZ 85004	2006	$10,158(S)	$13,000	5-D	10,952	551	64
Arizona State Univ. at the Polytechnic campus, Mesa, AZ 85212	1995	$7,864(S)	$11,760	5-D	4,078	209	58
Arizona State Univ. at the Tempe campus, Tempe, AZ 85287	1885	$10,158(S)	$11,061	5-D	51,984	2,229	66
Arizona State Univ. at the West campus, Glendale, AZ 85306	1984	$9,684(S)	$10,474	5-D	3,619	290	71
Arkansas State Univ., State University, AR 72467	1909	$8,050(S)	$8,140	5-D	13,410	711	39
Arkansas Tech Univ., Russellville, AR 72801	1909	$7,740(S)	$6,918	5-M	12,054	579	47
Armstrong State Univ., Savannah, GA 31419-1997	1935	$6,332(S)	$10,498	5-D	7,103	444	33
Art Ctr. Coll. of Design, Pasadena, CA 91103	1930	$40,596	NA	1-M	2,133	NA	68
Asbury Univ., Wilmore, KY 40390-1198	1890	$28,829	$6,748	2-M	1,895	240	63
Ashford Univ., San Diego, CA 92123	1918	NA	NA	3-M	10,568	748	NA
Ashland Univ., Ashland, OH 44805-3702	1878	$20,872	$9,602	2-D	5,428	627	NA
Ashworth Coll., Norcross, GA 30092	1987	NA	NA	3-M	57,650	NA	NA
Aspen Univ., Denver, CO 80246-1930	1987	$4,650	NA	1-D	2,000	NA	NA
Assumption Coll., Worcester, MA 01609-1296	1904	$36,160	$11,264	2-M	2,433	224	73
Athens State Univ., Athens, AL 35611	1822	$6,270(S)	NA	5-B	3,042	191	NA
Atlantic Univ. Coll., Guaynabo, PR 00970	1983	NA	NA	1-M	1,236	NA	NA
Auburn Univ., Auburn University, AL 36849	1856	$10,424(S)	$12,584	5-D	27,287	1,399	73
Auburn Univ. at Montgomery, Montgomery, AL 36124-4023	1967	$9,350(S)	$5,520	5-D	4,919	346	22
Augsburg Coll., Minneapolis, MN 55454-1351	1869	$36,415	$9,660	2-D	3,522	383	56
Augustana Coll., Rock Island, IL 61201-2296	1860	$39,621	$10,037	2-B	2,478	NA	76
Augustana Univ., Sioux Falls, SD 57197	1860	$30,944	$7,480	2-M	1,837	161	75
Augusta Univ., Augusta, GA 30912	1828	$8,282(S)	$13,200	5-D	7,957	1,482	NA
Aurora Univ., Aurora, IL 60506-4892	1893	$22,830	$10,000	1-D	5,423	501	56
Austin Coll., Sherman, TX 75090-4400	1849	$36,230	$11,793	2-M	1,272	120	73
Austin Peay State Univ., Clarksville, TN 37044	1927	$7,501(S)	$8,350	5-M	10,099	597	38
Avila Univ., Kansas City, MO 64145-1698	1916	$26,450	$7,500	2-M	1,866	238	53
Azusa Pacific Univ., Azusa, CA 91702-7000	1899	$34,754	$5,438	2-D	9,975	1,181	67

Name, address	Year founded	Tuition & fees	Room & board	Control, degree	Enroll-ment	Faculty	Grad. rate
Babson Coll., Babson Park, MA 02457-0310	1919	$46,784	$14,928	1-M	3,057	260	91%
Baker Coll., Flint, MI 48507-5508	1911	$9,000	$3,000	1-D	24,677	NA	NA
Baldwin Wallace Univ., Berea, OH 44017-2088	1845	$29,908	$8,370	2-M	4,009	454	67
Ball State Univ., Muncie, IN 47306	1918	$9,498(S)	$9,656	5-D	21,196	1,245	61
Bard Coll., Annandale-on-Hudson, NY 12504	1860	$49,906	$14,118	1-D	2,290	273	78
Barnard Coll., New York, NY 10027-6598 (3)	1889	$47,631	$15,110	1-B	2,548	349	89
Barry Univ., Miami Shores, FL 33161-6695	1940	$28,822	$10,400	2-D	7,971	NA	33
Baruch Coll. of the City Univ. of New York, New York, NY 10010-5585	1919	$6,861(S)	NA	11-M	18,433	1,224	70
Bastyr Univ., Kenmore, WA 98028-4966	1978	$23,355	NA	1-D	1,266	299	NA
Bates Coll., Lewiston, ME 04240-6028	1855	$48,435	$14,105	1-B	1,792	184	88
Bayamón Central Univ., Bayamón, PR 00960-1725	1970	NA	NA	2-M	1,202	153	NA
Baylor Univ., Waco, TX 76798	1845	$42,006	$11,754	2-D	16,787	1,250	70
Bay Path Univ., Longmeadow, MA 01106-2292 (6)	1897	$32,739	$12,610	1-M	3,107	393	57
Becker Coll., Worcester, MA 01609	1784	$32,810	$12,400	1-M	2,153	230	28
Belhaven Univ., Jackson, MS 39202-1789	1883	$21,816	$8,000	2-M	4,452	406	53
Bellarmine Univ., Louisville, KY 40205-0671	1950	$37,650	$11,360	2-D	3,846	448	67
Bellevue Univ., Bellevue, NE 68005-3098	1965	NA	NA	1-D	10,304	411	37
Belmont Abbey Coll., Belmont, NC 28012-1802	1876	$18,500	$10,094	2-B	1,495	135	43
Belmont Univ., Nashville, TN 37212-3757	1951	$30,000	$10,970	2-D	7,350	779	69
Beloit Coll., Beloit, WI 53511-5596	1846	$47,060	$8,146	1-B	1,358	148	81
Bemidji State Univ., Bemidji, MN 56601-2699	1919	$8,366(S)	$7,690	5-M	5,013	267	45
Benedict Coll., Columbia, SC 29204	1870	$18,286	$8,104	2-B	2,641	NA	NA
Benedictine Coll., Atchison, KS 66002-1499	1859	$26,690	$9,165	2-M	2,189	165	68
Benedictine Univ., Lisle, IL 60532	1887	$32,170	$9,200	2-D	5,954	663	53
Bentley Univ., Waltham, MA 02452-4705	1917	$44,085	$14,520	1-D	5,552	484	89
Berea Coll., Berea, KY 40404	1855	$570	$6,410	1-B	1,621	185	62
Berkeley Coll.–New York City campus, New York, NY 10017-4604	1936	$24,750	NA	3-B	3,968	NA	28
Berkeley Coll.–Woodland Park campus, Woodland Park, NJ 07424-3353	1931	$24,750	NA	3-M	3,854	412	26
Berklee Coll. of Mus, Boston, MA 02215-3693	1945	$41,398	$18,000	1-M	5,272	692	49
Berry Coll., Mount Berry, GA 30149-0159	1902	$31,996	$11,190	2-M	2,245	227	64
Bethel Coll., Mishawaka, IN 46545-5591	1947	$27,390	$8,470	2-M	1,719	205	64
Bethel Univ., St. Paul, MN 55112-6999	1871	$34,140	$9,770	2-D	4,791	288	73
Bethel Univ., McKenzie, TN 38201	1842	$32,990	$9,440	2-M	5,553	420	34
Beth Medrash Govoha, Lakewood, NJ 08701-2797 (1)	1943	$19,240	NA	2-M	5,788	NA	NA
Bethune-Cookman Univ., Daytona Beach, FL 32114-3099	1904	$14,410	$8,710	2-M	3,831	292	32
Binghamton Univ., State Univ. of New York, Vestal, NY 13850	1946	$270/cr. hr.(S)	NA	5-D	16,913	978	81
Biola Univ., La Mirada, CA 90639-0001	1908	$36,696	$9,704	1-D	6,222	555	71
Birmingham-Southern Coll., Birmingham, AL 35254	1856	$33,128	$11,350	2-B	1,231	114	65
Black Hills State Univ., Spearfish, SD 57799	1883	$8,004(S)	$6,458	5-M	4,489	235	30
Bloomfield Coll., Bloomfield, NJ 07003-9981	1868	$28,600	$11,500	2-M	1,980	219	31
Bloomsburg Univ. of Pennsylvania, Bloomsburg, PA 17815-1301	1839	$9,326(S)	$8,480	5-D	9,777	494	62
Bluefield State Coll., Bluefield, WV 24701-2198	1895	$6,120(S)	NA	5-B	1,486	129	23
Bob Jones Univ., Greenville, SC 29614	1927	$14,900	$6,280	2-D	3,108	220	64
Boise State Univ., Boise, ID 83725-0399	1932	$6,876(S)	$6,429	5-D	22,113	1,302	38
Boston Coll., Chestnut Hill, MA 02467-3800	1863	$49,324	$13,496	2-D	13,705	1,530	92
Boston Univ., Boston, MA 02215	1839	$48,436	$14,520	1-D	32,158	2,656	85
Bowdoin Coll., Brunswick, ME 04011	1794	$48,212	$13,142	1-B	1,799	240	93
Bowie State Univ., Bowie, MD 20715-9465	1865	$7,658(S)	$10,850	5-D	5,430	408	39
Bowling Green State Univ., Bowling Green, OH 43403	1910	$10,726(S)	$8,496	5-D	16,908	1,007	56
Bradley Univ., Peoria, IL 61625-0002	1897	$31,480	$9,700	1-D	5,338	553	74
Brandeis Univ., Waltham, MA 02454-9110	1948	$49,598	$13,706	1-D	5,752	520	87
Brandman Univ., Irvine, CA 92618	2009	NA	NA	1-D	8,004	776	NA
Brenau Univ., Gainesville, GA 30501 (3)	1878	$25,878	$11,998	1-M	2,789	326	49
Bridgewater Coll., Bridgewater, VA 22812-1599	1880	$32,590	$11,920	2-B	1,834	154	53
Bridgewater State Univ., Bridgewater, MA 02325-0001	1840	$8,903(S)	$11,700	5-M	11,089	810	58
Brigham Young Univ., Provo, UT 84602-1001	1875	$5,150	$7,330	2-D	33,469	1,766	80
Brigham Young Univ.–Hawaii, Laie, HI 96762-1294	1955	$4,940	$5,746	2-B	2,555	228	52
Brigham Young Univ.–Idaho, Rexburg, ID 83460	1888	NA	NA	2-B	14,944	NA	NA
Brookline Coll., Phoenix, AZ 85021	1979	NA	NA	3-B	1,468	43	NA
Brooklyn Coll. of the City Univ. of New York, Brooklyn, NY 11210-2889	1930	$3,670(S)	$4,210	11-D	17,410	1,248	54
Brooks Inst., Ventura, CA 93001	1945	NA	NA	3-M	1,240	NA	NA
Brown Univ., Providence, RI 02912	1764	$51,366	$13,200	1-D	9,458	885	96
Bryan Coll., Dayton, TN 37321	1930	$23,300	$6,690	2-M	1,550	124	56
Bryant & Stratton Coll.–Wauwatosa campus, Wauwatosa, WI 53226		NA	NA	3-B	1,264	NA	NA
Bryant Univ., Smithfield, RI 02917	1863	$40,962	$14,975	1-M	3,670	281	80
Bryn Mawr Coll., Bryn Mawr, PA 19010-2899 (6)	1885	$48,790	$15,370	1-D	1,692	213	85
Bucknell Univ., Lewisburg, PA 17837	1846	$51,960	$12,656	1-M	3,625	425	90
Buffalo State Coll., State Univ. of New York, Buffalo, NY 14222-1095	1867	$7,669(S)	$12,332	5-M	10,330	847	49
Butler Univ., Indianapolis, IN 46208-3485	1855	$37,010	$12,055	1-D	4,798	562	75
Cabrini Univ., Radnor, PA 19087	1957	$29,842	$12,026	2-M	2,428	285	50
Caldwell Univ., Caldwell, NJ 07006-6195	1939	$31,200	$10,965	2-D	2,138	267	52
California Baptist Univ., Riverside, CA 92504-3206	1950	$31,372	$10,680	2-D	8,541	672	60
California Coll. of the Arts, San Francisco, CA 94107	1907	$43,708	$12,220	1-M	1,988	499	59
California Coll. San Diego, San Diego, CA 92111	1978	NA	NA	3-B	1,299	NA	NA
California Inst. of Integral Studies, San Francisco, CA 94103	1968	$28,692	NA	1-D	1,495	231	NA
California Inst. of Tech, Pasadena, CA 91125-0001	1891	$45,390	$13,371	1-D	2,255	357	91
California Inst. of the Arts, Valencia, CA 91355-2340	1961	$45,030	NA	1-D	1,448	340	56
California Lutheran Univ., Thousand Oaks, CA 91360-2787	1959	$39,760	$13,060	2-D	4,126	437	66
California Polytechnic State Univ., San Luis Obispo, San Luis Obispo, CA 93407	1901	$9,000(S)	$12,009	5-M	20,944	1,411	79
California State Polytechnic Univ., Pomona, Pomona, CA 91768-2557	1938	$6,976(S)	$15,238	5-D	23,717	1,225	63
California State Univ., Bakersfield, Bakersfield, CA 93311	1970	$6,811(S)	$12,561	5-M	9,225	473	41
California State Univ. Channel Islands, Camarillo, CA 93012	2002	NA	NA	5-D	3,599	294	NA
California State Univ., Chico, Chico, CA 95929-0722	1887	$12,498(S)	$12,234	5-M	17,462	982	59
California State Univ., Dominguez Hills, Carson, CA 90747-0001	1960	$6,274(S)	NA	5-M	14,635	966	35
California State Univ., East Bay, Hayward, CA 94542-3000	1957	$6,564(S)	$14,183	5-D	15,528	839	45
California State Univ., Fresno, Fresno, CA 93740-8027	1911	NA	$10,604	5-D	24,136	1,307	58
California State Univ., Fullerton, Fullerton, CA 92834-9480	1957	$6,441(S)	$14,574	5-D	38,128	2,044	56
California State Univ., Long Beach, Long Beach, CA 90840	1949	$6,452(S)	$12,382	5-D	37,446	2,250	65

Name, address	Year founded	Tuition & fees	Room & board	Control, degree	Enroll-ment	Faculty	Grad. rate
California State Univ., Los Angeles, Los Angeles, CA 90032-8530	1947	$6,353(S)	$12,833	5-D	24,488	1,120	41%
California State Univ., Monterey Bay, Seaside, CA 93955-8001	1994	$5,963(S)	$10,112	5-M	7,102	497	53
California State Univ., Northridge, Northridge, CA 91330	1958	$6,569(S)	$10,996	5-D	41,548	2,088	50
California State Univ., Sacramento, Sacramento, CA 95819	1947	$6,602(S)	$13,460	5-D	29,349	1,491	44
California State Univ., San Bernardino, San Bernardino, CA 92407	1965	$6,577(S)	$9,372	5-D	20,024	986	51
California State Univ., San Marcos, San Marcos, CA 92096-0001	1990	$1,792(S)	$13,240	5-M	12,793	757	53
California State Univ., Stanislaus, Turlock, CA 95382	1957	$6,708(S)	$9,508	5-D	9,282	549	55
California Univ. of Pennsylvania, California, PA 15419-1394	1852	$9,936(S)	$10,086	5-M	7,854	400	52
Calvin Coll., Grand Rapids, MI 49546-4388	1876	$30,660	$9,690	2-M	3,990	358	73
Cambridge Coll., Cambridge, MA 02138-5304	1971	NA	NA	1-D	3,757	453	NA
Cameron Univ., Lawton, OK 73505-6377	1908	$5,580(S)	$4,888	5-M	5,178	310	24
Campbellsville Univ., Campbellsville, KY 42718-2799	1906	$23,828	$7,770	2-M	3,128	265	37
Campbell Univ., Buies Creek, NC 27506	1887	$28,820	$10,250	2-D	4,743	305	51.7
Canisius Coll., Buffalo, NY 14208-1098	1870	$34,690	$12,766	2-M	3,904	431	70
Capella Univ., Minneapolis, MN 55402	1993	NA	NA	3-D	36,375	NA	NA
Capital Univ., Columbus, OH 43209-2394	1830	$32,830	$9,422	2-D	3,465	422	63
Cardinal Stritch Univ., Milwaukee, WI 53217-3985	1937	$27,540	$7,700	2-D	3,177	281	44
Caribbean Univ., Bayamón, PR 00960-0493	1969	$6,180	NA	1-D	4,175	404	27
Carleton Coll., Northfield, MN 55057-4001	1866	$49,263	$12,783	1-B	2,014	245	95
Carlow Univ., Pittsburgh, PA 15213-3165 (4)	1929	$26,832	$10,572	2-D	2,272	266	50
Carnegie Mellon Univ., Pittsburgh, PA 15213-3891	1900	$52,310	$13,270	1-M	13,648	1,013	88
Carroll Coll., Helena, MT 59625-0002	1909	$30,754	$9,218	2-B	1,430	165	63
Carroll Univ., Waukesha, WI 53186-5593	1846	$29,535	$9,032	2-D	3,385	330	57
Carson-Newman Univ., Jefferson City, TN 37760	1851	$26,360	$8,430	2-D	2,528	215	45
Carthage Coll., Kenosha, WI 53140	1847	$36,570	$9,970	2-M	2,778	NA	54
Case Western Reserve Univ., Cleveland, OH 44106	1826	$44,560	$13,850	1-D	11,340	989	81
Castleton Univ., Castleton, VT 05735	1787	$10,772(S)	$9,414	5-M	2,184	228	50
Catawba Coll., Salisbury, NC 28144-2488	1851	$29,333	$10,487	2-M	1,275	179	47
The Catholic Univ. of America, Washington, DC 20064	1887	$40,932	$13,356	2-D	6,521	766	69
Cedar Crest Coll., Allentown, PA 18104-6196 (4)	1867	$35,600	$10,765	2-M	1,591	188	58
Cedarville Univ., Cedarville, OH 45314-0601	1887	$28,110	$6,880	2-D	3,654	380	72
Centenary Coll., Hackettstown, NJ 07840-2100	1867	$30,942	$10,420	2-M	2,400	226	57
Central Coll., Pella, IA 50219	1853	$34,612	$9,980	2-B	1,274	105	67
Central Connecticut State Univ., New Britain, CT 06050-4010	1849	$9,300(S)	$11,134	5-D	12,086	949	57
Central Michigan Univ., Mount Pleasant, MI 48859	1892	$11,850(S)	$9,088	5-D	26,968	1,136	59
Central Penn Coll., Summerdale, PA 17093-0309	1881	$17,151	$7,170	3-M	1,330	141	45
Central State Univ., Wilberforce, OH 45384	1887	$6,246(S)	$9,644	5-B	1,804	200	19
Central Washington Univ., Ellensburg, WA 98926	1891	$8,688(S)	$10,175	5-M	11,996	725	51
Centre Coll., Danville, KY 40422-1394	1819	$38,200	$9,620	2-B	1,367	144	86
Chadron State Coll., Chadron, NE 69337	1911	NA	NA	5-M	2,649	NA	NA
Chamberlain Coll. of Nursing, Addison, IL 60101	2005	$18,160	NA	3-B	17,374	388	NA
Chaminade Univ. of Honolulu, Honolulu, HI 96816-1578	1955	$21,780	$12,290	2-M	1,865	149	46
Champlain Coll., Burlington, VT 05402-0670	1878	$37,536	$14,050	1-M	4,006	483	58
Chapman Univ., Orange, CA 92866	1861	$48,710	$14,368	2-D	8,305	951	79
Charleston Southern Univ., Charleston, SC 29423-8087	1964	$23,440	$9,270	2-M	3,621	292	39
Charter Oak State Coll., New Britain, CT 06053-2142	1973	$9,015(S)	NA	5-B	1,735	173	NA
Chatham Univ., Pittsburgh, PA 15232-2826 (4)	1869	$35,475	$11,042	1-D	2,224	316	56
Chestnut Hill Coll., Philadelphia, PA 19118-2693	1924	$34,140	$10,300	2-D	1,951	324	49
Chicago State Univ., Chicago, IL 60628	1867	$9,846(S)	$8,724	5-D	5,211	366	19
Chowan Univ., Murfreesboro, NC 27855	1848	$23,400	$8,680	2-M	1,532	95	24
Christian Brothers Univ., Memphis, TN 38104-5581	1871	$30,106	$7,000	2-M	1,842	179	52
Christopher Newport Univ., Newport News, VA 23606-3072	1960	$12,526(S)	$10,614	5-M	5,172	455	70
The Citadel, The Military Coll. of South Carolina, Charleston, SC 29409 (2)	1842	$13,024(S)	$6,381	5-M	3,506	288	69
City Coll. of the City Univ. of New York, New York, NY 10031-9198	1847	$6,740(S)	NA	11-D	16,027	1,625	42
City Univ. of Seattle, Seattle, WA 98121	1973	$16,020	NA	1-D	2,065	332	29
Claflin Univ., Orangeburg, SC 29115	1869	$15,010	$8,420	2-M	1,886	NA	44
Claremont McKenna Coll., Claremont, CA 91711	1946	$49,545	$15,280	1-M	1,349	165	92
Clarion Univ. of Pennsylvania, Clarion, PA 16214	1867	$9,788(S)	$8,152	5-D	5,712	294	49
Clark Atlanta Univ., Atlanta, GA 30314	1865	$21,945	$10,478	2-D	3,661	292	38
Clarkson Univ., Potsdam, NY 13699	1896	$46,132	$14,260	1-D	3,910	309	73
Clark Univ., Worcester, MA 01610-1477	1887	$43,150	$8,450	1-D	3,485	312	83
Clayton State Univ., Morrow, GA 30260-0285	1969	$6,194(S)	$9,926	5-M	7,012	395	32
Clemson Univ., Clemson, SC 29634	1889	$13,882(S)	$8,718	5-D	22,698	1,263	82
Cleveland State Univ., Cleveland, OH 44115	1964	$9,696(S)	$12,500	5-D	17,260	1,119	39
Coastal Carolina Univ., Conway, SC 29528-6054	1954	$10,530(S)	$8,690	5-D	10,263	714	43
Coe Coll., Cedar Rapids, IA 52402-5092	1851	$39,080	$8,510	2-B	1,416	177	67
Coker Coll., Hartsville, SC 29550	1908	$26,568	$8,242	1-M	1,219	105	49
Colby Coll., Waterville, ME 04901-8840	1813	$49,120	$12,610	1-B	1,857	211	94
Colby-Sawyer Coll., New London, NH 03257	1837	$38,860	$13,000	1-B	1,369	137	53
Colegio Universitario de San Juan, San Juan, PR 00918	1971	NA	NA	10-B	1,785	NA	NA
Colgate Univ., Hamilton, NY 13346-1386	1819	$49,970	$12,570	1-M	2,861	352	90
The Coll. at Brockport, State Univ. of New York, Brockport, NY 14420-2997	1867	$7,904(S)	$11,540	5-M	8,161	619	69
Coll. for Creative Studies, Detroit, MI 48202-4034	1926	$38,950	$8,450	1-M	1,459	289	62
Coll. of Charleston, Charleston, SC 29424-0001	1770	$11,360(S)	$11,629	5-M	11,531	988	68
Coll. of Coastal Georgia, Brunswick, GA 31520	1961	$4,434(S)	$8,458	5-B	3,131	190	NA
Coll. of Mount St. Vincent, Riverdale, NY 10471-1093	1911	$35,050	$8,720	1-M	1,918	NA	52
The Coll. of New Jersey, Ewing, NJ 08628	1855	$15,466(S)	$12,498	5-M	7,406	853	85
The Coll. of New Rochelle, New Rochelle, NY 10805-2308 (4)	1904	$33,600	$12,700	1-M	1,551	184	42
Coll. of St. Benedict, Saint Joseph, MN 56374 (3)	1887	$40,846	$10,229	2-B	1,943	167	85
Coll. of St. Elizabeth, Morristown, NJ 07960-6989 (4)	1899	$31,688	$12,744	2-D	1,247	158	49
The Coll. of St. Rose, Albany, NY 12203-1419	1920	$29,826	$11,878	1-M	4,411	354	61
The Coll. of St. Scholastica, Duluth, MN 55811-4199	1912	$33,994	$8,932	2-D	4,360	387	70
Coll. of Staten Island of the City Univ. of New York, Staten Island, NY 10314-6600	1955	$6,809(S)	$13,332	11-D	13,775	1,230	42
Coll. of the Holy Cross, Worcester, MA 01610-2395	1843	$48,940	$13,225	2-B	2,916	334	92
Coll. of the Ozarks, Point Lookout, MO 65726	1906	$430	$6,500	2-B	1,452	143	73
The Coll. of William & Mary, Williamsburg, VA 23187-8795	1693	$19,372(S)	$10,978	5-D	8,484	NA	90
The Coll. of Wooster, Wooster, OH 44691-2363	1866	$44,950	$10,650	2-B	2,058	215	82
Colorado Christian Univ., Lakewood, CO 80226	1914	$29,360	$10,316	2-M	1,218	NA	NA

Name, address	Year founded	Tuition & fees	Room & board	Control, degree	Enroll-ment	Faculty	Grad. rate
The Colorado Coll., Colorado Springs, CO 80903-3294	1874	$50,892	$11,668	1-M	2,131	212	87%
Colorado Mesa Univ., Grand Junction, CO 81501-3122	1925	$8,008(S)	$10,176	5-D	9,448	542	37
Colorado Mountain Coll., Glenwood Springs, CO 81601	1965	$62/cr. hr.(A)	NA	9-B	5,847	544	NA
Colorado Mountain Coll., Leadville, CO 80461	1965	NA	NA	9-B	1,209	NA	NA
Colorado Mountain Coll., Steamboat Springs, CO 80487	1965	$62/credit(A)	$8,572	9-B	2,606	NA	NA
Colorado School of Mines, Golden, CO 80401-1887	1874	$17,353(S)	$11,008	5-D	5,924	516	77
Colorado State Univ., Fort Collins, CO 80523-0015	1870	$10,558(S)	$10,794	5-D	31,943	1,028	68
Colorado State Univ.–Pueblo, Pueblo, CO 81001-4901	1933	$8,282(S)	$9,230	5-M	7,563	372	32
Colorado Tech Univ. Colorado Springs, Colorado Springs, CO 80907	1965	NA	NA	3-D	2,359	343	NA
Colorado Tech Univ. Online, Colorado Springs, CO 80907	NA	NA	NA	3-M	25,797	613	NA
Columbia Centro Universitario, Caguas, PR 00726	1966	$9,730	NA	3-M	1,864	145	32
Columbia Coll., Columbia, SC 29203-5998 (4)	1854	$28,100	$7,400	2-D	1,650	175	50
Columbia Coll. Chicago, Chicago, IL 60605-1996	1890	$25,798	$13,298	1-M	8,961	1,133	42
Columbia Southern Univ., Orange Beach, AL 36561	1993	$210/credit	NA	3-M	19,793	499	NA
Columbia Univ., New York, NY 10027	1754	$53,000	$12,860	1-D	6,102	NA	96
Columbia Univ., School of General Studies, New York, NY 10027-6939	1754	$51,114	$10,356	1-B	2,005	NA	NA
Columbus State Univ., Columbus, GA 31907-5645	1958	$7,056(S)	$8,780	5-D	8,440	525	31
Concordia Coll., Moorhead, MN 56562	1891	$36,878	$7,810	2-M	2,177	248	73
Concordia Univ., Portland, OR 97211-6099	1905	$28,420	$8,010	2-M	3,111	259	45
Concordia Univ. Chicago, River Forest, IL 60305-1499	1864	$30,640	$9,172	2-D	5,238	429	51
Concordia Univ. Irvine, Irvine, CA 92612-3299	1972	$32,780	$10,240	2-D	4,505	420	61
Concordia Univ., Nebraska, Seward, NE 68434-1556	1894	$28,480	$7,800	2-M	2,457	240	59
Concordia Univ., St. Paul, St. Paul, MN 55104-5494	1893	$21,250	$8,500	2-D	4,380	428	46
Concordia Univ. Texas, Austin, TX 78726	1926	$28,160	$9,284	2-M	2,504	302	35
Concordia Univ. Wisconsin, Mequon, WI 53097-2402	1881	$26,740	$9,970	2-D	8,268	582	58
Concord Univ., Athens, WV 24712-1000	1872	$7,080(S)	$8,350	5-M	2,507	172	38
Connecticut Coll., New London, CT 06320	1911	$49,350	$13,615	1-M	1,922	261	83
Coppin State Univ., Baltimore, MD 21216-3698	1900	$4,889(S)	$9,236	5-M	3,800	312	NA
Corban Univ., Salem, OR 97301-9392	1935	$29,640	$9,240	2-D	1,232	115	57
Cornell Univ., Ithaca, NY 14853-0001	1865	$49,116	$13,678	1-D	21,904	2,139	93
Cornerstone Univ., Grand Rapids, MI 49525-5897	1941	$26,100	$8,560	2-M	2,572	406	61
Creighton Univ., Omaha, NE 68178-0001	1878	$36,422	$10,294	2-D	8,435	845	79
Crown Coll., St. Bonifacius, MN 55375-9001	1916	NA	NA	2-M	1,269	160	50
The Culinary Inst. of America, Hyde Park, NY 12538-1499	1946	$29,250	$10,365	1-B	2,859	189	NA
Cumberland Univ., Lebanon, TN 37087	1842	$21,210	$7,550	1-M	1,481	159	37
Curry Coll., Milton, MA 02186-9984	1879	$37,505	$14,970	1-M	2,950	490	47
Daemen Coll., Amherst, NY 14226-3592	1947	$25,995	$12,050	1-D	2,769	297	49
Dakota State Univ., Madison, SD 57042-1799	1881	$8,754(S)	$6,060	5-D	3,145	141	39
Dallas Baptist Univ., Dallas, TX 75211-9299	1965	$24,890	$7,326	2-D	5,319	629	58
Dalton State Coll., Dalton, GA 30720	1963	$4,238(S)	$8,446	5-B	5,040	244	21
Dartmouth Coll., Hanover, NH 03755	1769	$49,506	$14,242	1-D	6,350	734	94
Davenport Univ., Grand Rapids, MI 49512	1866	$17,218	$9,132	1-M	8,423	855	39
Davidson Coll., Davidson, NC 28035	1837	$46,966	$13,153	2-B	1,784	185	93
Delaware State Univ., Dover, DE 19901-2277	1891	$7,523(S)	$10,820	5-D	4,288	350	42
Delaware Valley Univ., Doylestown, PA 18901-2697	1896	$35,256	$12,618	1-D	2,266	207	57
Delta State Univ., Cleveland, MS 38733-0001	1924	$6,112(S)	$7,064	5-D	3,614	256	35
Denison Univ., Granville, OH 43023	1831	$47,290	$11,570	1-B	2,282	246	80
DePaul Univ., Chicago, IL 60604-2287	1898	$36,361	$12,873	2-D	23,539	1,885	73
DePauw Univ., Greencastle, IN 46135	1837	$44,678	$11,700	2-B	2,265	266	82
DeSales Univ., Center Valley, PA 18034-9568	1964	$33,550	$12,050	2-D	3,136	366	70
DeVry Coll. of New York, New York, NY 10016-5267	1998	$17,512	NA	3-M	1,495	87	NA
DeVry Univ., Pomona, CA 91768-2642	1983	$17,132	NA	3-M	1,729	96	NA
DeVry Univ., Orlando, FL 32839	2000	$17,132	NA	3-M	1,205	48	NA
DeVry Univ., Decatur, GA 30030-2556	1969	$17,132	NA	3-M	1,921	148	NA
DeVry Univ., Chicago, IL 60618-5994	1931	$17,132	NA	3-M	1,294	164	NA
DeVry Univ., Columbus, OH 43209-2705	1952	$17,132	NA	3-M	1,971	65	NA
DeVry Univ. Online, Addison, IL 60101-6106	2000	$17,132	NA	3-M	20,432	2,500	NA
Dickinson Coll., Carlisle, PA 17013-2896	1773	$49,464	$12,362	1-B	2,420	272	85
Dickinson State Univ., Dickinson, ND 58601-4896	1918	$6,173(S)	$6,200	5-B	1,317	138	33
Dixie State Univ., St. George, UT 84770-3876	1911	$4,620(S)	$5,615	5-B	8,503	582	19
Dominican Coll., Orangeburg, NY 10962-1210	1952	$27,438	$12,420	1-D	2,061	208	45
Dominican Univ., River Forest, IL 60305-1099	1901	$30,670	$9,380	2-D	3,696	462	59
Dominican Univ. of California, San Rafael, CA 94901-2298	1890	$42,550	$13,380	2-M	1,863	285	66
Dordt Univ., Sioux Center, IA 51250-1697	1955	NA	NA	2-M	1,405	105	62
Drake Univ., Des Moines, IA 50311-4516	1881	$35,206	$9,850	1-D	4,991	456	75
Drew Univ., Madison, NJ 07940-1493	1867	$46,384	$12,672	2-D	2,082	253	67
Drexel Univ., Philadelphia, PA 19104-2875	1891	$48,791	$14,367	1-D	26,359	2,168	67
Drury Univ., Springfield, MO 65802	1873	$25,905	$8,000	1-M	1,571	158	67
Duke Univ., Durham, NC 27708-0586	1838	$49,498	$14,690	2-D	15,386	1,335	94
Duquesne Univ., Pittsburgh, PA 15282-0001	1878	$33,778	$11,418	2-D	9,404	1,009	72
D'Youville Coll., Buffalo, NY 14201-1084	1908	$24,270	$11,180	1-D	2,909	298	44
East Carolina Univ., Greenville, NC 27858-4353	1907	$6,580(S)	$8,984	5-D	28,289	1,461	61
East Central Univ., Ada, OK 74820	1909	$5,874(S)	$5,350	5-M	4,447	271	37
East Stroudsburg Univ. of Pennsylvania, East Stroudsburg, PA 18301-2999	1893	$9,397(S)	$8,058	5-M	6,828	340	55
East Tennessee State Univ., Johnson City, TN 37614	1911	$8,477(S)	$7,952	5-D	14,334	917	43
East Texas Baptist Univ., Marshall, TX 75670-1498	1912	$24,218	$8,629	2-M	1,308	119	46
Eastern Connecticut State Univ., Willimantic, CT 06226-2295	1889	$10,016(S)	$12,108	5-M	5,261	499	56
Eastern Illinois Univ., Charleston, IL 61920	1895	$11,312(S)	$9,546	5-M	8,520	597	58
Eastern Kentucky Univ., Richmond, KY 40475-3102	1906	$8,520(S)	$8,360	5-D	16,844	1,144	45
Eastern Mennonite Univ., Harrisonburg, VA 22802-2462	1917	$30,800	$9,860	2-M	1,640	204	63
Eastern Michigan Univ., Ypsilanti, MI 48197	1849	$10,417(S)	$9,398	5-D	21,634	1,384	40
Eastern New Mexico Univ., Portales, NM 88130	1934	$5,170(S)	$6,568	5-M	5,887	330	27
Eastern Oregon Univ., La Grande, OR 97850-2899	1929	$7,757(S)	$9,642	5-M	3,488	215	26
Eastern Univ., St. Davids, PA 19087-3696	1952	$30,590	$10,190	2-D	3,762	564	62
Eastern Washington Univ., Cheney, WA 99004-2431	1882	$235/cr. hr.(S)	NA	5-D	12,361	666	46
Eckerd Coll., St. Petersburg, FL 33711	1958	$40,020	$10,920	2-B	1,789	168	64
ECPI Univ., Virginia Beach, VA 23462	1966	NA	NA	3-B	13,717	1,371	NA
Edgewood Coll., Madison, WI 53711-1997	1927	$26,550	$9,400	2-D	2,678	309	60
Edinboro Univ. of Pennsylvania, Edinboro, PA 16444	1857	$9,535(S)	$10,166	5-D	6,837	371	49

Name, address	Year founded	Tuition & fees	Room & board	Control, degree	Enroll- ment	Faculty	Grad. rate
EDP Univ. of Puerto Rico, Hato Rey, PR 00918	1968	$5,940	NA	1-M	1,716	176	30%
Elizabeth City State Univ., Elizabeth City, NC 27909-7806	1891	$4,657(S)	$7,642	5-M	1,585	113	39
Elizabethtown Coll., Elizabethtown, PA 17022-2298	1899	$41,710	$10,140	2-M	1,820	179	78
Elmhurst Coll., Elmhurst, IL 60126-3296	1871	$35,500	$10,078	2-M	3,298	351	67
Elmira Coll., Elmira, NY 14901	1855	$41,900	$12,000	1-M	1,376	170	55
Elms Coll., Chicopee, MA 01013-2839.	1928	$32,280	$11,708	2-D	1,712	177	67
Elon Univ., Elon, NC 27244-2010.	1889	$32,172	$10,998	2-D	6,631	585	83
Embry-Riddle Aeron Univ.–Daytona, Daytona Beach, FL 32114-3900	1926	$33,886	$10,826	1-D	5,806	NA	55
Embry-Riddle Aeron Univ.–Prescott, Prescott, AZ 86301-3720.	1978	$33,826	$10,228	1-M	2,265	NA	59
Embry-Riddle Aeron Univ.–Worldwide, Daytona Beach, FL 32114-3900	1970	$8,836	NA	1-D	14,701	NA	NA
Emerson Coll., Boston, MA 02116-4624	1880	$41,052	$15,700	1-D	4,467	479	80
Emmanuel Coll., Boston, MA 02115.	1919	$36,504	$13,920	2-M	2,201	201	64
Emory Univ., Atlanta, GA 30322-1100.	1836	$47,954	$13,486	2-D	13,788	1,177	89
Emporia State Univ., Emporia, KS 66801-5415	1863	$5,936(S)	$7,968	5-D	6,094	276	42
Endicott Coll., Beverly, MA 01915-2096.	1939	$30,492	$14,112	1-D	4,879	469	71
Eugene Lang Coll. of Liberal Arts, New York, NY 10011-8601	1978	$42,080	$17,295	1-B	1,550	200	53
Evangel Univ., Springfield, MO 65802	1955	$21,436	$7,582	2-D	1,958	NA	47
Everest Univ., Tampa, FL 33614	1890	NA	NA	1-M	3,430	61	NA
Everglades Univ., Boca Raton, FL 33431	1989	$16,648	NA	1-M	1,451	229	51
Everglades Univ., Maitland, FL 32751	NA	$16,648	NA	1-M	1,451	229	51
Everglades Univ., Sarasota, FL 34240.	2003	$16,648	NA	1-M	1,451	229	51
The Evergreen State Coll., Olympia, WA 98505	1967	$8,205(S)	$9,492	5-M	4,190	224	57
Excelsior Coll., Albany, NY 12203-5159.	1970	$490/credit	NA	1-M	40,103	NA	NA
Fairfield Univ., Fairfield, CT 06824.	1942	$46,000	$13,860	2-D	5,138	578	82
Fairleigh Dickinson Univ., Coll. at Florham, Madison, NJ 07940-1099	1942	$39,092	$12,632	1-D	3,233	NA	56
Fairleigh Dickinson Univ., Metropolitan campus, Teaneck, NJ 07666-1914	1942	$36,910	$12,918	1-D	8,774	NA	49
Fairmont State Univ., Fairmont, WV 26554	1865	$6,620(S)	$8,766	5-M	4,041	325	29
Farmingdale State Coll., Farmingdale, NY 11735	1912	$7,808(S)	$12,500	5-B	8,648	701	49
Fashion Inst. of Tech, New York, NY 10001-5992 (4)	1944	$7,200(S)	$13,291	11-M	9,571	970	NA
Faulkner Univ., Montgomery, AL 36109-3398	1942	$19,280	$7,130	2-D	3,262	300	21
Fayetteville State Univ., Fayetteville, NC 28301-4298	1867	$2,833(S)	$6,987	5-D	6,104	342	32
Felician Univ., Lodi, NJ 07644-2117.	1942	$32,990	$12,380	2-D	1,957	212	39
Ferris State Univ., Big Rapids, MI 49307	1884	$11,460(S)	$9,434	5-D	14,715	NA	51
Ferrum Coll., Ferrum, VA 24088	1913	$29,795	$9,970	2-B	1,451	116	25
FIDM/Fashion Inst. of Design & Merchandising, Los Angeles campus, Los Angeles, CA 90015-1421.	1969	$29,930	NA	3-B	2,814	252	80
Fisher Coll., Boston, MA 02116-1500.	1903	$29,640	$15,459	1-M	1,959	190	46
Fitchburg State Univ., Fitchburg, MA 01420-2697	1894	$9,260(S)	$8,840	5-M	6,818	304	50
Flagler Coll., St. Augustine, FL 32085-1027.	1968	$17,600	$10,015	1-B	2,702	237	61
Florida Agr. & Mech. Univ., Tallahassee, FL 32307-3200	1887	$5,785(S)	$10,100	5-D	9,928	728	40
Florida Atlantic Univ., Boca Raton, FL 33431-0991	1961	$6,039(S)	$11,748	5-D	30,364	1,248	46
Florida Gulf Coast Univ., Fort Myers, FL 33965-6565	1991	NA	$8,359	5-D	14,860	799	49
Florida Inst. of Tech., Melbourne, FL 32901-6975	1958	$40,446	$13,610	1-D	6,631	562	57
Florida Intl. Univ., Miami, FL 33199	1965	$6,556(S)	$10,870	5-D	49,892	2,347	58
Florida Memorial Univ., Miami-Dade, FL 33054.	1879	$15,280	$6,422	2-M	1,750	173	33
Florida National Univ., Hialeah, FL 33012	1982	$13,250	NA	3-M	2,492	123	88
Florida Southern Coll., Lakeland, FL 33801-5698	1885	$31,460	$10,210	2-D	2,629	256	57
Florida State Univ., Tallahassee, FL 32306	1851	$6,507(S)	$10,208	5-D	40,920	1,758	79
Fontbonne Univ., St. Louis, MO 63105-3098	1917	$24,610	$9,107	2-M	1,713	201	54
Fordham Univ., New York, NY 10458	1841	$47,317	$16,350	2-D	15,286	1,598	81
Fort Hays State Univ., Hays, KS 67601-4099	1902	NA	NA	5-M	14,210	544	42
Fort Lewis Coll., Durango, CO 81301-3999	1911	$7,601(S)	$9,130	5-M	3,692	252	40
Fort Valley State Univ., Fort Valley, GA 31030	1895	$6,448(S)	$7,920	5-M	2,594	142	31
Framingham State Univ., Framingham, MA 01701-9101	1839	$8,700(S)	$10,840	5-M	6,398	337	56
Franciscan Univ. of Steubenville, Steubenville, OH 43952-1763	1946	$25,680	$8,300	2-M	2,716	242	79
Francis Marion Univ., Florence, SC 29502-0547	1970	$10,100(S)	$7,472	5-M	3,947	291	42
Franklin & Marshall Coll., Lancaster, PA 17604-3003	1787	$50,400	$12,770	1-B	2,249	282	87
Franklin Pierce Univ., Rindge, NH 03461-0060	1962	$33,320	$12,546	1-D	2,239	286	43
Franklin Univ., Columbus, OH 43215-5399	1902	$14,520	NA	1-M	5,734	814	13
Freed-Hardeman Univ., Henderson, TN 38340-2399	1869	$20,468	$7,390	2-D	1,828	150	58
Fresno Pacific Univ., Fresno, CA 93702-4709	1944	$26,638	$7,360	2-M	3,483	427	54
Friends Univ., Wichita, KS 67213.	1898	$25,830	$7,320	2-M	1,882	231	38
Frostburg State Univ., Frostburg, MD 21532-1099	1898	$8,488(S)	$8,574	5-D	5,645	386	49
Full Sail Univ., Winter Park, FL 32792-7437 (2).	1979	NA	NA	3-M	8,921	702	NA
Furman Univ., Greenville, SC 29613	1826	$46,012	$11,522	1-M	2,884	257	83
Gallaudet Univ., Washington, DC 20002-3625.	1864	$16,078	NA	1-D	1,477	298	46
Gannon Univ., Erie, PA 16541-0001	1925	$29,258	$11,710	2-D	4,416	395	66
Gardner-Webb Univ., Boiling Springs, NC 28017	1905	$29,610	$9,780	2-D	4,305	300	52
Geneva Coll., Beaver Falls, PA 15010-3599	1848	$25,450	$9,630	2-M	1,512	193	67
George Fox Univ., Newberg, OR 97132-2697	1891	$31,866	$9,864	2-D	3,899	604	71
George Mason Univ., Fairfax, VA 22030	1957	$10,952(S)	$10,510	5-D	33,925	2,557	69
The George Washington Univ., Washington, DC 20052	1821	$49,837	$15,205	1-D	26,212	2,487	83
Georgetown Coll., Georgetown, KY 40324-1696.	1829	$34,280	$8,710	2-M	1,364	149	56
Georgetown Univ., Washington, DC 20057	1789	$50,547	$15,568	2-D	18,459	2,041	94
Georgia Coll. & State Univ., Milledgeville, GA 31061.	1889	$9,170(S)	$11,612	5-D	6,889	436	60
Georgia Gwinnett Coll., Lawrenceville, GA 30043	2006	$5,648(S)	$12,300	5-B	11,468	650	20
Georgia Inst. of Tech, Atlanta, GA 30332-0001	1885	$12,204(S)	$13,194	5-D	24,268	1,175	85
Georgian Court Univ., Lakewood, NJ 08701-2697.	1908	$31,618	$10,808	2-M	2,122	247	52
Georgia Southern Univ., Statesboro, GA 30458	1906	$7,318(S)	$9,800	5-D	20,459	884	50
Georgia Southwestern State Univ., Americus, GA 31709-4693.	1906	$6,198(S)	$8,640	5-M	2,755	153	33
Georgia State Univ., Atlanta, GA 30302-3083	1913	$10,686(S)	$13,646	5-D	32,080	1,707	54
Gettysburg Coll., Gettysburg, PA 17325-1483	1832	$49,140	$11,730	2-B	2,454	308	83
Glenville State Coll., Glenville, WV 26351-1200	1872	$8,784(S)	$10,994	5-B	1,732	130	30
Global Univ., Springfield, MO 65804	1948	NA	NA	2-D	4,551	633	NA
Golden Gate Univ., San Francisco, CA 94105-2968	1901	$15,120	NA	1-D	2,735	489	NA
Goldey-Beacom Coll., Wilmington, DE 19808-1999.	1886	NA	NA	1-M	1,352	56	49
Gonzaga Univ., Spokane, WA 99258.	1887	$39,730	$11,158	2-D	7,491	713	83

Name, address	Year founded	Tuition & fees	Room & board	Control, degree	Enroll-ment	Faculty	Grad. rate
Gordon Coll., Wenham, MA 01984-1899	1889	$36,060	$10,412	2-M	2,045	194	69%
Goucher Coll., Baltimore, MD 21204-2794.	1885	$42,180	$11,942	1-M	2,148	186	69
Governors State Univ., University Park, IL 60484	1969	$12,332(S)	$9,638	5-D	5,938	487	NA
Grace Coll., Winona Lake, IN 46590-1294.	1948	$24,670	$7,930	2-D	2,303	199	60
Graceland Univ., Lamoni, IA 50140	1895	$27,010	$8,280	2-D	2,292	165	52
Grambling State Univ., Grambling, LA 71245	1901	$5,140(S)	$8,638	5-D	4,553	199	39
Grand Valley State Univ., Allendale, MI 49401-9403	1960	$11,078(S)	$8,360	5-D	25,325	1,749	65
Grand View Univ., Des Moines, IA 50316-1599	1896	$25,474	$8,172	2-M	1,988	216	47
Granite State Coll., Concord, NH 03301	1972	$7,257(S)	NA	11-M	2,180	190	54
Grantham Univ., Lenexa, KS 66219.	1951	NA	NA	3-M	9,463	10	NA
Greensboro Coll., Greensboro, NC 27401-1875	1838	$26,900	$10,100	2-M	1,264	96	43
Greenville Coll., Greenville, IL 62246-0159	1892	$25,088	$8,288	2-M	1,321	180	48
Grinnell Coll., Grinnell, IA 50112-1690.	1846	$48,758	$11,980	1-B	1,705	209	86
Grove City Coll., Grove City, PA 16127-2104	1876	$16,154	$8,802	2-B	2,444	233	85
Guilford Coll., Greensboro, NC 27410-4173	1837	$34,090	$9,560	2-B	1,917	152	59
Gustavus Adolphus Coll., St. Peter, MN 56082-1498	1862	$41,332	$9,176	2-B	2,386	240	83
Gwynedd Mercy Univ., Gwynedd Valley, PA 19437-0901	1948	$32,380	$11,300	2-D	2,582	299	56
Hamilton Coll., Clinton, NY 13323-1296.	1812	$49,500	$12,570	1-B	1,872	232	92
Hamline Univ., St. Paul, MN 55104-1284.	1854	$37,886	$9,736	2-D	4,258	389	63
Hampshire Coll., Amherst, MA 01002	1965	$48,810	$13,274	1-B	1,410	165	68
Hampton Univ., Hampton, VA 23668	1868	$23,112	$10,176	1-D	4,269	399	60
Hannibal-LaGrange Univ., Hannibal, MO 63401-1999.	1858	$21,010	$7,610	2-M	1,252	138	48
Harding Univ., Searcy, AR 72149-0001	1924	$17,805	$6,628	2-D	6,009	489	64
Hardin-Simmons Univ., Abilene, TX 79698-0001.	1891	$25,230	$8,288	2-D	2,112	204	53
Harrisburg Univ. of Sci. & Tech, Harrisburg, PA 17101	2005	$23,900	$7,000	1-M	2,099	NA	NA
Harrison Coll., Indianapolis, IN 46204	1902	NA	NA	3-B	3,756	290	33
Harris-Stowe State Univ., St. Louis, MO 63103-2136	1857	$5,220(S)	$9,250	5-B	1,390	174	7
Hartwick Coll., Oneonta, NY 13820-4020.	1797	$41,440	$11,120	1-B	1,392	189	56
Harvard Univ., Cambridge, MA 02138	1636	$45,278	$15,381	1-D	10,857	1,152	98
Hastings Coll., Hastings, NE 68901	1882	$28,490	$8,080	2-M	1,212	119	58
Haverford Coll., Haverford, PA 19041-1392.	1833	$49,098	$14,888	1-B	1,233	164	90
Hawai`i Pacific Univ., Honolulu, HI 96813	1965	$23,460	$13,899	1-M	4,781	510	49
Heidelberg Univ., Tiffin, OH 44883-2462	1850	$29,200	$10,000	2-M	1,217	152	39
Henderson State Univ., Arkadelphia, AR 71999-0001	1890	$7,808(S)	$6,862	5-M	3,527	244	34
Hendrix Coll., Conway, AR 72032-3080.	1876	$42,440	$11,580	2-M	1,338	140	68
Heritage Univ., Toppenish, WA 98948-9599	1982	$18,566	NA	1-M	1,241	185	16
High Point Univ., High Point, NC 27268.	1924	$33,405	$12,572	2-D	4,573	421	65
Hillsdale Coll., Hillsdale, MI 49242-1298	1844	$24,592	$9,760	1-D	1,526	184	77
Hobart & William Smith Colleges, Geneva, NY 14456-3397	1822	$51,523	$13,050	1-M	2,351	230	81
Hodges Univ., Naples, FL 34119	1990	$13,220	NA	1-M	1,724	119	NA
Hofstra Univ., Hempstead, NY 11549	1935	$40,460	$13,950	1-D	10,814	1,161	60
Holy Family Univ., Philadelphia, PA 19114	1954	$29,168	$13,576	2-D	2,712	281	57
Hood Coll., Frederick, MD 21701-8575	1893	$35,150	$11,840	1-D	2,288	264	63
Hope Coll., Holland, MI 49422-9000	1866	$31,560	$9,690	2-B	3,376	383	77
Hope Intl. Univ., Fullerton, CA 92831-3138	1928	$28,550	$9,050	2-M	1,303	252	42
Houston Baptist Univ., Houston, TX 77074-3298.	1960	$30,800	$7,858	2-M	3,160	244	33
Howard Univ., Washington, DC 20059-0002	1867	$23,970	$13,646	1-D	10,002	1,520	60
Humboldt State Univ., Arcata, CA 95521-8299	1913	NA	$12,114	5-M	8,790	566	46
Hunter Coll. of the City Univ. of New York, New York, NY 10065-5085.	1870	$275/credit (S)	NA	11-D	22,920	2,288	54
Husson Univ., Bangor, ME 04401-2999.	1898	$16,060	$8,922	1-D	3,418	349	44
Idaho State Univ., Pocatello, ID 83209.	1901	$6,784(S)	$6,338	5-D	13,133	734	31
Illinois Inst. of Tech, Chicago, IL 60616-3793	1890	$44,884	$12,818	1-D	7,792	800	73
Illinois State Univ., Normal, IL 61790-2200	1857	$13,666(S)	$9,850	5-D	20,760	1,264	73
Illinois Wesleyan Univ., Bloomington, IL 61702-2900	1850	$42,490	$9,796	1-B	1,842	213	83
Immaculata Univ., Immaculata, PA 19345	1920	$33,280	$13,210	2-D	2,961	368	70
Indiana State Univ., Terre Haute, IN 47809	1865	$8,580(S)	$9,028	5-D	13,584	693	35
Indiana Tech, Fort Wayne, IN 46803-1297	1930	$24,860	$9,521	1-D	6,355	510	35
Indiana Univ. Bloomington, Bloomington, IN 47405-7000	1820	$10,388(S)	$10,040	5-D	48,514	2,379	77
Indiana Univ. East, Richmond, IN 47374-1289	1971	$7,072(S)	NA	5-M	4,716	296	28
Indiana Univ. Kokomo, Kokomo, IN 46904-9003	1945	$7,072(S)	NA	5-M	4,090	233	29
Indiana Univ. Northwest, Gary, IN 46408-1197	1959	$7,072(S)	NA	5-M	5,848	364	24
Indiana Univ. of Pennsylvania, Indiana, PA 15705-1087	1875	$9,936(S)	$11,880	5-D	13,775	716	53
Indiana Univ.–Purdue Univ. Fort Wayne, Fort Wayne, IN 46805-1499	1917	$8,079(S)	$6,844	5-M	13,214	801	25
Indiana Univ.–Purdue Univ. Indianapolis, Indianapolis, IN 46202	1969	$9,205(S)	$9,430	5-D	30,105	3,327	45
Indiana Univ. South Bend, South Bend, IN 46634-7111	1922	$7,072(S)	NA	5-M	7,574	476	24
Indiana Univ. Southeast, New Albany, IN 47150-6405	1941	$7,072(S)	NA	5-M	6,173	483	28
Indiana Wesleyan Univ., Marion, IN 46953-4974.	1920	$24,728	$7,988	2-D	3,186	267	65
Indian River State Coll., Fort Pierce, FL 34981-5596.	1960	$2,492(S)	$5,700	5-B	17,665	859	NA
Inter Amer. Univ. of Puerto Rico, Aguadilla campus, Aguadilla, PR 00605	1957	$5,044	NA	1-M	4,581	257	24
Inter Amer. Univ. of Puerto Rico, Arecibo campus, Arecibo, PR 00614-4050	1957	$4,962	NA	1-M	4,878	298	NA
Inter Amer. Univ. of Puerto Rico, Barranquitas campus, Barranquitas, PR 00794	1957	$5,791	NA	1-M	2,116	143	44
Inter Amer. Univ. of Puerto Rico, Bayamón campus, Bayamón, PR 00957	1912	$6,180	NA	1-M	4,630	286	27
Inter Amer. Univ. of Puerto Rico, Fajardo campus, Fajardo, PR 00738-7003	1965	$4,272	NA	1-M	2,071	108	22
Inter Amer. Univ. of Puerto Rico, Guayama campus, Guayama, PR 00785	1958	$6,167	NA	1-M	2,127	181	26
Inter Amer. Univ. of Puerto Rico, Metropolitan campus, San Juan, PR 00919-1293.	1960	$7,122	NA	1-D	9,094	594	29
Inter Amer. Univ. of Puerto Rico, Ponce campus, Mercedita, PR 00715-1602	1962	$4,962	NA	1-D	5,734	295	25
Inter American Univ. of Puerto Rico, San Germán campus, San Germán, PR 00683-5008.	1912	$6,180	$2,700	1-D	4,999	291	34
Iona Coll., New Rochelle, NY 10801-1890.	1940	$35,324	$13,980	2-M	3,977	341	66
Iowa State Univ. of Sci. & Tech, Ames, IA 50011	1858	$7,969(S)	$8,070	5-D	35,714	1,884	71
Ithaca Coll., Ithaca, NY 14850	1892	$40,658	$14,674	1-D	6,769	790	76
Jackson State Univ., Jackson, MS 39217	1877	$6,886(S)	$8,226	5-D	9,802	606	43
Jacksonville State Univ., Jacksonville, AL 36265-1602	1883	$9,300(S)	$7,128	5-D	8,314	456	31
Jacksonville Univ., Jacksonville, FL 32211	1934	$32,620	$13,320	1-D	4,048	340	41
James Madison Univ., Harrisonburg, VA 22807.	1908	$10,018(S)	$9,396	5-D	21,227	1,459	83
John Brown Univ., Siloam Springs, AR 72761-2121	1919	$24,468	$8,664	2-M	2,400	200	61
John Carroll Univ., University Heights, OH 44118-4581	1886	$37,180	$10,920	2-M	3,700	423	71

Name, address	Year founded	Tuition & fees	Room & board	Control, degree	Enroll-ment	Faculty	Grad. rate
John F. Kennedy Univ., Pleasant Hill, CA 94523-4817 (4)	1964	$11,472	NA	1-D	1,580	237	NA
John Jay Coll. of Criminal Justice of the City Univ. of New York, New York, NY 10019-1093	1964	$6,059(S)	NA	11-M	14,732	NA	41%
Johns Hopkins Univ., Baltimore, MD 21218	1876	$50,410	$14,976	1-D	7,374	751	94.4
Johnson & Wales Univ., Denver, CO 80220	1993	$30,746	$8,268	1-M	1,388	127	53
Johnson & Wales Univ., North Miami, FL 33181	1992	$30,746	$8,268	1-B	1,752	79	41
Johnson & Wales Univ., Charlotte, NC 28202	2004	$29,576	NA	1-B	2,255	120	49
Johnson & Wales Univ., Providence, RI 02903-3703	1914	$30,746	$8,268	1-D	9,454	617	55
Johnson C. Smith Univ., Charlotte, NC 28216-5398	1867	$18,236	$7,100	1-M	1,438	160	46
Johnson State Coll., Johnson, VT 05656	1828	$10,224(S)	$9,696	5-M	1,662	179	35
Judson Univ., Elgin, IL 60123-1498	1963	$28,700	$9,650	2-D	1,274	159	52
Juniata Coll., Huntingdon, PA 16652-2119	1876	$42,170	$11,590	2-M	1,583	149	73
Kalamazoo Coll., Kalamazoo, MI 49006-3295	1833	$42,846	$8,886	2-B	1,443	126	83
Kansas State Univ., Manhattan, KS 66506	1863	$9,350(S)	$8,430	5-D	24,146	1,277	62
Kean Univ., Union, NJ 07083	1855	$11,581(S)	$12,565	5-D	14,112	1,362	50
Keene State Coll., Keene, NH 03435	1909	$13,613(S)	$10,390	5-M	4,383	420	63
Keiser Univ., Fort Lauderdale, FL 33309	1977	$17,596	NA	1-D	17,129	1,597	68
Kendall Coll., Chicago, IL 60201-2899	1934	$19,459	$10,350	3-B	1,275	209	20
Kennesaw State Univ., Kennesaw, GA 30144	1963	$7,326(S)	$9,497	5-D	33,252	1,755	42
Kent State Univ., Kent, OH 44242-0001	1910	$10,012(S)	$9,908	5-D	29,762	1,762	56
Kent State Univ. at Geauga, Burton, OH 44021-9500	1964	$5,664(S)	NA	5-B	2,530	145	24
Kent State Univ. at Stark, Canton, OH 44720-7599	1967	$5,664(S)	NA	5-M	4,757	270	27
Kentucky State Univ., Frankfort, KY 40601	1886	$307/cr. hr. (S)	NA	12-D	1,586	129	22
Kenyon Coll., Gambier, OH 43022-9623	1824	$49,140	$11,890	1-B	1,698	200	89
Kettering Univ., Flint, MI 48504	1919	$36,980	$7,240	1-M	2,089	134	57
Keuka Coll., Keuka Park, NY 14478-0098	1890	$29,281	$11,070	2-M	1,933	445	53
Keystone Coll., La Plume, PA 18440	1868	$24,300	$10,050	1-M	1,484	249	36
King's Coll., Wilkes-Barre, PA 18711-0801	1946	$33,090	$11,958	2-M	2,310	216	66
King Univ., Bristol, TN 37620-2699	1867	$27,276	$8,180	2-D	2,920	304	45
Knox Coll., Galesburg, IL 61401	1837	$41,847	$9,012	1-B	1,397	142	77
Kutztown Univ. of Pennsylvania, Kutztown, PA 19530-0730	1866	$9,145(S)	$9,070	5-D	9,000	450	54
La Roche Coll., Pittsburgh, PA 15237-5898	1963	$26,250	$10,630	2-M	1,523	201	45
La Salle Univ., Philadelphia, PA 19141-1199	1863	$41,100	$14,500	2-D	5,675	439	63
La Sierra Univ., Riverside, CA 92515	1922	$30,470	$7,800	2-D	2,476	116	49
Lafayette Coll., Easton, PA 18042-1798	1826	$47,010	$13,920	2-B	2,533	279	90
Lake Erie Coll., Painesville, OH 44077-3389	1856	$29,960	$9,178	1-M	1,244	113	52
Lake Forest Coll., Lake Forest, IL 60045	1857	$44,840	$9,810	1-M	1,572	196	73
Lake Superior State Univ., Sault Sainte Marie, MI 49783	1946	$10,637(S)	$9,290	5-M	2,438	178	40
Lakeland Coll., Sheboygan, WI 53082-0359	1862	NA	NA	2-M	3,749	71	42
Lamar Univ., Beaumont, TX 77710	1923	$9,251(S)	$8,302	5-D	14,965	517	32
Lander Univ., Greenwood, SC 29649-2099	1872	$11,632(S)	$8,246	5-M	3,049	249	40
Lane Coll., Jackson, TN 38301-4598	1882	$9,930	$6,620	2-B	1,376	73	32
Langston Univ., Langston, OK 73050	1897	$5,042(S)	$9,272	5-D	2,495	191	50
Lasell Coll., Newton, MA 02466-2709	1851	$33,600	$13,900	1-M	2,209	263	52
Lawrence Tech Univ., Southfield, MI 48075-1058	1932	$30,300	$9,470	1-D	4,161	416	45
Lawrence Univ., Appleton, WI 54911	1847	$43,740	$9,210	1-B	1,561	197	76
Le Moyne Coll., Syracuse, NY 13214	1946	$33,030	$12,970	2-M	3,478	346	67
Lebanon Valley Coll., Annville, PA 17003-1400	1866	$39,030	$10,510	2-D	1,918	243	74
Lee Univ., Cleveland, TN 37320-3450	1918	$15,770	$7,880	2-M	5,041	419	52
Lehigh Univ., Bethlehem, PA 18015-3094	1865	$46,230	$12,280	1-D	7,054	681	88
Lehman Coll. of the City Univ. of New York, Bronx, NY 10468-1589	1931	$6,729(S)	NA	11-M	12,220	912	36
Lenoir-Rhyne Univ., Hickory, NC 28601	1891	$33,730	$11,600	2-M	2,303	269	48
Lesley Univ., Cambridge, MA 02138-2790 (4)	1909	$26,250	$15,300	1-D	4,606	243	54
LeTourneau Univ., Longview, TX 75607-7001	1946	$27,900	$9,580	2-M	2,796	216	51
Lewis & Clark Coll., Portland, OR 97219-7899	1867	$45,104	$11,218	1-D	3,526	410	72
Lewis-Clark State Coll., Lewiston, ID 83501-2698	1893	$5,900(S)	$6,194	5-B	3,633	253	21
Lewis Univ., Romeoville, IL 60446	1932	$30,050	$10,320	2-D	6,679	675	66
Liberty Univ., Lynchburg, VA 24515	1971	$23,020	$9,306	2-D	14,420	NA	54
Life Univ., Marietta, GA 30060-2903	1974	$10,860	$12,450	1-D	2,708	184	18
LIM Coll., New York, NY 10022-5268 (4)	1939	$25,725	$20,350	3-M	1,700	196	50
Limestone Coll., Gaffney, SC 29340-3799	1845	$23,900	$8,550	1-M	1,280	117	37
Lincoln Memorial Univ., Harrogate, TN 37752-1901	1897	$20,546	$7,300	1-D	3,735	290	40
Lincoln Univ., Jefferson City, MO 65101	1866	$7,042(S)	$6,070	5-M	2,944	184	20
Lincoln Univ., Lincoln University, PA 19352	1854	$10,718(S)	$9,268	12-M	1,832	163	66
Lindenwood Univ., St. Charles, MO 63301-1695	1827	$16,022	$7,934	2-D	11,620	1,678	49
Lindsey Wilson Coll., Columbia, KY 42728	1903	$23,762	$9,120	2-D	2,651	247	26
Linfield Coll., McMinnville, OR 97128-6894	1849	$38,654	$10,850	2-B	1,700	204	63
Lipscomb Univ., Nashville, TN 37204-3951	1891	$28,624	$11,032	2-D	4,680	574	55
Lock Haven Univ. of Pennsylvania, Lock Haven, PA 17745-2390	1870	$9,665(S)	$9,344	5-M	4,607	234	50
Loma Linda Univ., Loma Linda, CA 92350	1905	NA	NA	2-D	4,270	840	NA
Long Island Univ.–LIU Brooklyn, Brooklyn, NY 11201-8423	1926	$35,546	$12,600	1-D	8,170	866	28
Long Island Univ.–LIU Post, Brookville, NY 11548-1300	1954	$35,546	$13,138	1-D	8,623	930	49
Longwood Univ., Farmville, VA 23909	1839	$11,910(S)	$10,272	5-M	5,087	329	66
Loras Coll., Dubuque, IA 52004-0178	1839	$31,545	$7,700	2-M	1,528	155	70
Los Angeles Film Sch., Hollywood, CA 90028	1999	$71,166/ deg. prog.	NA	3-B	1,358	116	NA
Louisiana State Univ. & Agr. & Mech. Coll., Baton Rouge, LA 70803	1860	$9,842(S)	$11,200	5-D	31,524	1,450	67
Louisiana State Univ. at Alexandria, Alexandria, LA 71302-9121	1960	$5,583(S)	$9,750	5-B	3,104	170	27
Louisiana State Univ. Health Sciences Ctr., New Orleans, LA 70112-2223	1931	$6,093(S)	$4,797	5-D	1,727	893	NA
Louisiana State Univ. in Shreveport, Shreveport, LA 71115-2399	1965	$6,903(S)	NA	5-D	4,428	178	37
Louisiana Tech Univ., Ruston, LA 71272	1894	$8,854(S)	$5,670	5-D	12,371	437	53
Lourdes Univ., Sylvania, OH 43560-2898	1958	$20,270	$9,400	2-M	1,530	186	26
Loyola Marymount Univ., Los Angeles, CA 90045-2659	1911	$42,569	$14,470	2-D	9,392	NA	79
Loyola Univ. Chicago, Chicago, IL 60660	1870	$41,384	$13,770	2-D	16,437	1,632	73
Loyola Univ. Maryland, Baltimore, MD 21210-2699	1852	$45,365	$13,310	2-D	5,977	577	84
Loyola Univ. New Orleans, New Orleans, LA 70118-6195	1912	$38,504	$12,964	2-D	4,087	430	66
Lubbock Christian Univ., Lubbock, TX 79407-2099	1957	$20,360	$6,070	2-M	1,958	179	42
Luther Coll., Decorah, IA 52101	1861	$40,040	$8,500	2-B	2,337	234	77
Luther Rice Coll. & Sem., Lithonia, GA 30038-2454	1962	NA	NA	2-M	1,650	NA	NA

Name, address	Year founded	Tuition & fees	Room & board	Control, degree	Enroll- ment	Faculty	Grad. rate
Lycoming Coll., Williamsport, PA 17701-5192	1812	$35,900	$10,884	2-B	1,289	122	64%
Lynchburg Coll., Lynchburg, VA 24501-3199	1903	$35,555	$9,590	2-D	2,794	282	56
Lyndon State Coll., Lyndonville, VT 05851-0919	1911	$10,246(S)	$9,696	5-M	1,436	160	39
Lynn Univ., Boca Raton, FL 33431-5598	1962	$36,150	$11,640	1-D	2,693	NA	44
Macalester Coll., St. Paul, MN 55105-1899	1874	$50,639	$11,266	1-B	2,172	257	90
Madonna Univ., Livonia, MI 48150-1173	1947	$18,740	$9,230	2-D	3,710	307	49
Maharishi Univ. of Mgmt, Fairfield, IA 52557	1971	$26,530	$7,400	1-D	1,530	NA	39
Malone Univ., Canton, OH 44709	1892	$27,960	$8,948	2-M	1,726	170	57
Manchester Univ., North Manchester, IN 46962-1225	1889	$30,802	$9,620	2-D	1,536	98	54
Manhattan Coll., Riverdale, NY 10471	1853	$38,930	$14,430	2-M	4,071	438	72
Manhattanville Coll., Purchase, NY 10577-2132	1841	$36,920	$14,520	1-D	2,921	315	57
Mansfield Univ. of Pennsylvania, Mansfield, PA 16933	1857	$9,806(S)	$10,976	5-M	2,316	157	50
Marian Univ., Indianapolis, IN 46222-1997	1851	$30,500	$9,436	2-D	2,900	283	56
Marian Univ., Fond du Lac, WI 54935-4699	1936	$28,280	$7,000	2-D	2,099	237	41
Marietta Coll., Marietta, OH 45750-4000	1835	$35,330	$11,100	1-M	1,331	160	66
Marist Coll., Poughkeepsie, NY 12601-1387	1929	$33,800	$14,850	1-M	6,474	619	78
Marquette Univ., Milwaukee, WI 53201-1881	1881	$38,470	$11,440	2-D	11,491	1,152	80
Marshall Univ., Huntington, WV 25755	1837	$6,814(S)	$9,832	5-D	13,621	716	45
Mars Hill Univ., Mars Hill, NC 28754	1856	$29,382	$8,924	2-M	1,410	147	34
Martin Univ., Indianapolis, IN 46218-3867	1977	NA	NA	1-M	1,236	43	NA
Mary Baldwin Coll., Staunton, VA 24401-3610 (4)	1842	$30,635	$9,230	1-D	1,666	213	37
Marygrove Coll., Detroit, MI 48221-2599 (4)	1905	NA	NA	2-M	2,953	64	34
Maryland Inst. Coll. of Art, Baltimore, MD 21217	1826	$43,870	$12,030	1-M	2,155	342	73
Marymount Manhattan Coll., New York, NY 10021-4597	1936	$28,700	$15,500	1-B	1,928	306	42
Marymount Univ., Arlington, VA 22207-4299	1950	$28,310	$12,220	2-D	3,363	354	50
Maryville Coll., Maryville, TN 37804-5907	1819	$32,866	$10,442	2-B	1,213	119	53
Maryville Univ. of St. Louis, St. Louis, MO 63141-7299	1872	$26,958	$10,240	1-D	6,414	594	71
Marywood Univ., Scranton, PA 18509-1598	1915	$32,692	$13,900	2-D	3,010	404	70
Massachusetts Coll. of Art & Design, Boston, MA 02115-5882	1873	$11,725(S)	$13,175	5-M	1,990	267	72
Massachusetts Coll. of Lib. Arts, North Adams, MA 01247-4100	1894	$9,475(S)	$9,828	5-M	1,641	168	52
Massachusetts Inst. of Tech, Cambridge, MA 02139-4307	1861	$46,704	$13,730	1-D	11,331	1,544	92
Massachusetts Maritime Acad, Buzzards Bay, MA 02532-1803 (2)	1891	$7,614(S)	$11,474	5-M	1,674	119	72
The Master's Coll. & Sem., Santa Clarita, CA 91321-1200	1927	$31,970	$10,000	2-D	1,719	238	67
McDaniel Coll., Westminster, MD 21157-4390	1867	$40,580	$10,800	1-M	3,126	586	70
McKendree Univ., Lebanon, IL 62254-1299	1828	$28,740	$9,200	2-D	3,001	266	56
McNeese State Univ., Lake Charles, LA 70609	1939	$7,290(S)	$6,814	5-M	8,162	403	41
MCPHS Univ., Boston, MA 02115-5896	1823	$30,530	$15,174	1-D	7,074	686	72
Medaille Coll., Buffalo, NY 14214-2695	1875	$26,252	$11,240	1-D	2,383	294	50
Medgar Evers Coll. of the City Univ. of New York, Brooklyn, NY 11225-2298	1969	$6,650(S)	NA	11-B	6,701	490	NA
Medical Univ. of South Carolina, Charleston, SC 29425	1824	NA	NA	5-D	2,775	223	NA
Mercer Univ., Macon, GA 31207	1833	$34,450	$11,460	2-D	6,832	715	62
Mercy Univ., Dobbs Ferry, NY 10522-1189	1951	$18,076	$13,700	1-D	11,295	1,055	37
Mercy Coll. of Ohio, Toledo, OH 43604 (4)	1993	$12,530	$5,460	2-B	1,243	215	44
Mercyhurst Univ., Erie, PA 16546	1926	$33,314	$11,232	2-M	2,806	261	65
Meredith Coll., Raleigh, NC 27607-5298 (6)	1891	$33,730	$10,040	1-M	1,949	213	62
Merrimack Coll., North Andover, MA 01845-5800	1947	$37,670	$13,500	2-M	3,644	392	71
Messiah Coll., Mechanicsburg, PA 17055	1909	$33,180	$9,920	2-D	3,302	341	80
Methodist Univ., Fayetteville, NC 28311-1498	1956	$30,740	$11,344	2-M	2,416	213	44
Metropolitan State Univ., St. Paul, MN 55106-5000	1971	$7,566(S)	NA	5-D	8,354	NA	NA
Metropolitan State Univ. of Denver, Denver, CO 80204	1963	$6,929(S)	NA	5-M	20,676	1,418	25
Miami Univ., Oxford, OH 45056	1809	$14,287(S)	$11,644	12-D	19,076	1,192	80
Miami Univ. Hamilton, Hamilton, OH 45011-3399	1968	NA	NA	5-M	4,194	224	NA
Michigan State Univ., East Lansing, MI 48824	1855	$13,560(S)	$9,474	5-D	50,543	2,839	77
Michigan Tech Univ., Houghton, MI 49931	1885	$14,286(S)	$9,857	5-D	7,242	451	65
MidAmerica Nazarene Univ., Olathe, KS 66062-1899	1966	$27,650	$7,900	2-M	2,015	221	54
Middle Georgia State Univ., Macon, GA 31206	2015	$4,542(S)	$7,870	5-M	7,676	360	24
Middle Tennessee State Univ., Murfreesboro, TN 37132	1911	$8,404(S)	$8,550	5-D	22,511	1,247	46
Middlebury Coll., Middlebury, VT 05753-6002	1800	$47,828	$13,628	1-D	2,558	347	94
Midland Coll., Midland, TX 79705-6329	1969	$1,968(A)	$4,906	11-B	4,618	255	NA
Midway Univ., Midway, KY 40347-1120	1847	$22,000	$8,000	2-D	1,600	118	38
Midwestern State Univ., Wichita Falls, TX 76308	1922	$8,005(S)	$7,070	5-M	6,043	345	44
Miles Coll., Fairfield, AL 35064	1905	NA	NA	2-B	1,738	147	NA
Millersville Univ. of Pennsylvania, Millersville, PA 17551-0302	1855	$10,918(S)	$12,188	5-D	7,988	449	62
Millikin Univ., Decatur, IL 62522-2084	1901	$30,630	$9,916	2-D	2,154	272	60
Mills Coll., Oakland, CA 94613-1000 (6)	1852	$45,635	$13,528	1-D	1,397	202	67
Milwaukee School of Engineering, Milwaukee, WI 53202-3109 (2)	1903	$37,980	$8,835	1-M	2,939	265	64
Minnesota State Univ. Mankato, Mankato, MN 56001	1868	$7,836(S)	$8,430	5-D	15,407	754	49
Minnesota State Univ. Moorhead, Moorhead, MN 56563	1885	$8,096(S)	$7,798	5-M	5,836	367	41
Minot State Univ., Minot, ND 58707-0002	1913	$6,390(S)	$6,222	5-M	3,348	279	42
Misericordia Univ., Dallas, PA 18612-1098	1924	$30,740	$13,150	2-D	3,065	317	72
Mississippi Coll., Clinton, MS 39058	1826	$16,740	$9,190	2-D	5,036	433	54
Mississippi State Univ., Mississippi State, MS 39762	1878	$7,502(S)	$9,068	5-D	20,873	1,053	60
Mississippi Univ. for Women, Columbus, MS 39701-9998	1884	$6,065(S)	$6,808	5-D	2,673	201	49
Mississippi Valley State Univ., Itta Bena, MS 38941-1400	1946	$5,936(S)	$7,177	5-M	2,309	150	22
Missouri Baptist Univ., St. Louis, MO 63141-8660	1964	$23,886	$9,510	2-D	5,276	290	36
Missouri Southern State Univ., Joplin, MO 64801-1595	1937	$5,877(S)	$6,622	5-M	5,783	350	36
Missouri State Univ., Springfield, MO 65897	1905	$7,970(S)	$8,130	5-D	22,273	1,142	52
Missouri Univ. of Sci. & Tech, Rolla, MO 65409	1870	$9,784(S)	$9,464	5-D	8,889	486	65
Missouri Valley Coll., Marshall, MO 65340-3197	1889	$19,750	$8,400	2-M	1,699	171	29
Missouri Western State Univ., St. Joseph, MO 64507-2294	1915	$6,652(S)	$7,590	5-M	5,513	385	29
Molloy Coll., Rockville Centre, NY 11571-5002	1955	$28,030	$13,940	1-D	4,894	704	71
Monmouth Univ., West Long Branch, NJ 07764-1898	1933	$33,728	$12,506	1-D	6,394	638	67
Monroe Coll., Bronx, NY 10468-5407	1933	$14,148	$9,400	3-M	6,862	471	68
Montana State Univ., Bozeman, MT 59717	1893	$6,968(S)	$8,650	5-D	15,688	984	52
Montana State Univ., Billings, Billings, MT 59101	1927	$5,808(S)	$7,510	5-M	4,429	325	27
Montana State Univ.–Northern, Havre, MT 59501-7751	1929	NA	NA	5-M	1,273	96	30
Montana Tech of The Univ. of Montana, Butte, MT 59701-8997	1895	$6,797(S)	$8,562	5-D	2,980	228	42
Montclair State Univ., Montclair, NJ 07043-1624	1908	$11,773(S)	$13,884	5-D	20,465	1,814	66
Moody Bible Inst., Chicago, IL 60610-3284	1886	NA	NA	2-M	3,349	211	68
Moravian Coll., Bethlehem, PA 18018-6650	1742	$38,832	$11,636	2-M	2,261	197	69

Name, address	Year founded	Tuition & fees	Room & board	Control, degree	Enroll- ment	Faculty	Grad. rate
Morehead State Univ., Morehead, KY 40351.	1922	$8,098(S)	$8,420	5-D	10,875	438	40%
Morehouse Coll., Atlanta, GA 30314 (1).	1867	$26,742	$13,322	1-B	2,167	212	51
Morgan State Univ., Baltimore, MD 21251.	1867	$7,378(S)	$9,232	5-D	7,005	558	100
Morningside Coll., Sioux City, IA 51106.	1894	$28,155	$8,710	2-M	2,830	247	55
Morrisville State Coll., Morrisville, NY 13408-0901	1908	$8,040(S)	$13,488	5-B	2,911	261	NA
Mount Aloysius Coll., Cresson, PA 16630-1999.	1939	$21,850	$9,940	2-M	1,877	203	NA
Mount Holyoke Coll., South Hadley, MA 01075 (3)	1837	$43,886	$12,860	1-M	2,215	234	85
Mount Ida Coll., Newton, MA 02459-3310	1899	$33,820	$13,000	1-M	1,345	169	40
Mount Mary Univ., Milwaukee, WI 53222-4597 (6)	1913	$26,760	$7,970	2-D	1,313	194	42
Mount Mercy Univ., Cedar Rapids, IA 52402-4797	1928	$28,226	$8,600	2-M	1,877	151	65
Mount St. Joseph Univ., Cincinnati, OH 45233-1670.	1920	$27,500	$8,810	2-D	1,983	250	71
Mount St. Mary Coll., Newburgh, NY 12550-3494.	1960	$28,233	$13,828	1-M	2,508	276	59
Mount St. Mary's Univ., Los Angeles, CA 90049 (4)	1925	$37,722	$11,451	2-D	3,474	499	66
Mount St. Mary's Univ., Emmitsburg, MD 21727-7799.	1808	$37,500	$12,400	2-M	2,257	220	69
Mount Vernon Nazarene Univ., Mount Vernon, OH 43050-9500.	1964	$26,950	$7,550	2-M	2,131	242	58
Muhlenberg Coll., Allentown, PA 18104-5586	1848	$45,875	$10,770	2-B	2,397	285	85
Murray State Univ., Murray, KY 42071.	1922	$7,608(S)	$8,206	5-D	10,998	708	48
Musians Inst., Hollywood, CA 90028	1976	NA	NA	3-B	1,337	204	NA
Muskingum Univ., New Concord, OH 43762	1837	NA	NA	2-M	2,099	NA	NA
National Louis Univ., Chicago, IL 60603	1886	NA	NA	1-D	4,384	437	NA
National Univ., La Jolla, CA 92037-1011	1971	$12,744	NA	1-M	17,488	NA	30
Nazareth Coll. of Rochester, Rochester, NY 14618-3790.	1924	$31,520	$12,918	1-D	2,871	486	73
Nebraska Wesleyan Univ., Lincoln, NE 68504-2796	1887	$29,800	$8,340	2-M	2,083	233	69
Neumann Univ., Aston, PA 19014-1298.	1965	$26,918	$11,754	2-D	2,901	303	50
Nevada State Coll., Henderson, NV 89015	2002	$4,568(A)	NA	5-B	3,534	253	20
New England Coll., Henniker, NH 03242-3293	1946	$35,290	$13,268	1-D	2,393	237	31
New England Inst. of Tech, East Greenwich, RI 02818	1940	$24,651	NA	1-M	2,919	345	NA
New Jersey City Univ., Jersey City, NJ 07305-1597	1927	$11,179(S)	$10,604	5-D	8,237	809	29
New Jersey Inst. of Tech, Newark, NJ 07102	1881	$16,108(S)	$13,300	5-D	11,325	801	61
New Mexico Highlands Univ., Las Vegas, NM 87701	1893	$4,800(S)	$7,164	5-M	3,563	282	18
New Mexico Inst. of Mining & Tech, Socorro, NM 87801.	1889	$6,613(S)	$7,586	5-D	2,150	172	49
New Mexico State Univ., Las Cruces, NM 88003-8001	1888	$6,094(S)	$8,064	5-D	15,490	1,049	42
New Orleans Baptist Theol. Sem., New Orleans, LA 70126-4858 (2)	1917	NA	NA	2-D	2,036	NA	NA
The New School for Public Engagement, New York, NY 10011-8603.	1919	$1,150/cr. hr.	$18,930	1-D	1,763	415	NA
New York City Coll. of Tech of the City Univ. of New York, Brooklyn, NY 11201-2983.	1946	$6,650(S)	NA	11-B	17,424	1,427	30
New York Inst. of Tech, Old Westbury, NY 11568-8000	1955	$33,480	$13,090	1-D	8,048	901	46
New York Univ., New York, NY 10012-1019	1831	$47,750	$17,580	1-D	49,274	6,843	82
Newman Univ., Wichita, KS 67213-2097	1933	$25,828	$7,340	2-M	3,595	244	50
Niagara Univ., Niagara University, NY 14109	1856	$29,900	$12,300	2-D	4,128	368	63
Nicholls State Univ., Thibodaux, LA 70310	1948	$7,349(S)	$9,676	5-M	6,298	311	37
Nichols Coll., Dudley, MA 01571-5000.	1815	$33,400	$13,500	1-M	1,454	81	47
Norfolk State Univ., Norfolk, VA 23504	1935	$9,060(S)	$8,624	5-D	6,027	NA	34
North Carolina Agr. & Tech State Univ., Greensboro, NC 27411.	1891	$5,535(S)	$6,755	5-D	10,725	710	47
North Carolina Central Univ., Durham, NC 27707-3129	1910	$5,755(S)	$8,165	5-D	8,011	553	42
North Carolina State Univ., Raleigh, NC 27695.	1887	$8,880(S)	$10,635	5-D	34,015	2,034	76
North Carolina Wesleyan Coll., Rocky Mount, NC 27804-8677.	1956	$28,150	$9,524	2-B	2,119	249	23
North Central Coll., Naperville, IL 60566-7063.	1861	$35,421	$10,089	2-M	2,962	274	67
North Dakota State Univ., Fargo, ND 58102	1890	$7,978(S)	$7,502	5-D	14,516	853	54
North Greenville Univ., Tigerville, SC 29688-1892.	1892	$17,594	$9,892	2-D	2,691	209	55
North Park Univ., Chicago, IL 60625-4895.	1891	$25,860	$8,460	2-D	3,138	305	56
Northcentral Univ., Scottsdale, AZ 85255	1996	$10,368	NA	3-D	11,029	470	NA
Northeastern Illinois Univ., Chicago, IL 60625-4699	1961	$11,050(S)	$11,100	5-M	9,891	625	22
Northeastern State Univ., Tahlequah, OK 74464-2399	1846	$5,547(S)	$6,490	5-D	8,276	511	26
Northeastern Univ., Boston, MA 02115-5096.	1898	$45,530	$15,000	1-D	24,944	1,660	84
Northern Arizona Univ., Flagstaff, AZ 86011	1899	$10,358(S)	$9,132	5-D	29,031	1,621	52
Northern Illinois Univ., De Kalb, IL 60115-2854	1895	$12,200(S)	$9,670	5-D	20,130	1,099	50
Northern Kentucky Univ., Highland Heights, KY 41099	1968	$9,120(S)	$6,358	5-D	14,699	1,006	40
Northern Michigan Univ., Marquette, MI 49855-5301.	1899	$9,620(S)	$9,286	5-D	8,781	456	51
Northern New Mexico Coll., Española, NM 87532.	1909	NA	NA	5-B	2,272	253	NA
Northern State Univ., Aberdeen, SD 57401-7198	1901	$8,043(S)	$6,942	5-M	3,531	169	54
Northwest Missouri State Univ., Maryville, MO 64468-6001	1905	$8,459(S)	$9,538	5-M	6,593	314	49
Northwest Nazarene Univ., Nampa, ID 83686-5897	1913	$28,150	$7,000	2-D	2,229	NA	49
Northwest Univ., Kirkland, WA 98033	1934	$28,086	$7,790	2-D	1,238	252	54
Northwestern Oklahoma State Univ., Alva, OK 73717-2799	1897	$6,113(S)	$4,400	5-M	2,136	170	18
Northwestern State Univ. of Louisiana, Natchitoches, LA 71497.	1884	$7,006(S)	$8,584	5-D	8,944	492	42
Northwestern Univ., Evanston, IL 60208	1851	$49,047	$14,936	1-D	21,642	1,693	93
Northwood Univ., Michigan campus, Midland, MI 48640-2398	1959	$24,170	$9,590	1-M	1,669	143	56
Norwich Univ., Northfield, VT 05663	1819	$32,812	$11,984	1-M	3,672	332	57
Notre Dame Coll., South Euclid, OH 44121-4293	1922	$27,520	$9,180	2-M	1,393	118	NA
Notre Dame de Namur Univ., Belmont, CA 94002-1908	1851	$32,208	$12,872	2-D	2,030	248	48
Notre Dame of Maryland Univ., Baltimore, MD 21210-2476 (4).	1873	$33,670	$10,930	2-D	2,764	136	56
Nova Southeastern Univ., Fort Lauderdale, FL 33314-7796	1964	$26,910	$10,874	1-D	23,236	1,699	44
Nyack Coll., Nyack, NY 10960.	1882	$24,850	$9,200	2-D	2,664	284	46
Oakland City Univ., Oakland City, IN 47660-1099.	1885	$23,400	$9,180	2-D	1,450	97	59
Oakland Univ., Rochester, MI 48309-4401	1957	$11,513(S)	$9,250	5-D	20,261	1,169	44
Oakwood Univ., Huntsville, AL 35896	1896	$16,720	$9,312	2-M	1,824	171	46
Oberlin Coll., Oberlin, OH 44074	1833	$50,594	$13,630	1-M	2,929	372	88
Occidental Coll., Los Angeles, CA 90041-3314	1887	$49,248	$14,236	1-M	2,114	260	88
Ohio Christian Univ., Circleville, OH 43113-9487.	1948	$20,415	$3,949	2-M	4,058	349	NA
Ohio Dominican Univ., Columbus, OH 43219-2099.	1911	$30,270	$10,530	2-M	2,534	243	45
Ohio Northern Univ., Ada, OH 45810-1599	1871	$28,810	$10,890	2-D	3,238	288	66
The Ohio State Univ., Columbus, OH 43210	1870	$10,037(S)	$11,666	5-D	58,663	5,297	83
The Ohio State Univ.–Newark campus, Newark, OH 43055-1797.	1957	$7,140(S)	$8,290	5-M	2,476	150	33
Ohio Univ., Athens, OH 45701-2979	1804	$11,548(S)	$10,864	5-D	29,157	1,323	67
Ohio Univ.–Chillicothe, Chillicothe, OH 45601	1946	$2,590(S)	NA	5-M	2,200	NA	NA
Ohio Univ.–Lancaster, Lancaster, OH 43130-1097	1968	$2,530(S)	NA	5-M	1,728	NA	NA
Ohio Univ.–Southern campus, Ironton, OH 45638-2214	1956	NA	NA	5-M	1,836	NA	NA
Ohio Univ.–Zanesville, Zanesville, OH 43701-2695.	1946	NA	NA	5-B	2,042	130	NA
Ohio Wesleyan Univ., Delaware, OH 43015	1842	$43,230	$6,230	2-B	1,675	216	71

Name, address	Year founded	Tuition & fees	Room & board	Control, degree	Enrollment	Faculty	Grad. rate
Oklahoma Baptist Univ., Shawnee, OK 74804	1910	$25,310	$7,010	2-M	1,940	187	52%
Oklahoma Christian Univ., Oklahoma City, OK 73136-1100	1950	$19,890	$7,030	2-M	2,581	233	49
Oklahoma City Univ., Oklahoma City, OK 73106-1402	1904	$30,726	$8,624	2-D	2,987	353	60
Oklahoma Panhandle State Univ., Goodwell, OK 73939-0430	1909	$7,391(S)	$5,344	5-B	1,387	91	38
Oklahoma State Univ., Stillwater, OK 74078	1890	$7,778(S)	$8,190	5-D	25,806	1,354	62
Oklahoma Wesleyan Univ., Bartlesville, OK 74006-6299	1909	$23,180	$7,488	2-M	1,527	111	45
Old Dominion Univ., Norfolk, VA 23529	1930	$9,768(S)	$10,404	5-D	24,672	1,355	53
Olivet Nazarene Univ., Bourbonnais, IL 60914	1907	$32,790	$7,900	2-D	4,892	442	61
Oral Roberts Univ., Tulsa, OK 74171	1963	$25,676	$8,640	2-D	3,614	274	55
Oregon Health & Sci. Univ., Portland, OR 97239-3098	1974	$16,035(S)	NA	12-D	2,895	110	NA
Oregon Inst. of Tech, Klamath Falls, OR 97601-8801	1947	NA	NA	5-M	3,911	257	45
Oregon State Univ., Corvallis, OR 97331	1868	$10,107(S)	$11,691	5-D	29,576	1,621	64
Otterbein Univ., Westerville, OH 43081	1847	$31,624	$12,080	2-D	2,808	317	61
Ouachita Baptist Univ., Arkadelphia, AR 71998-0001	1886	$24,940	$7,380	2-B	1,538	159	65
Our Lady of the Lake Coll., Baton Rouge, LA 70808	1990	$11,439	NA	2-D	1,641	NA	33
Our Lady of the Lake Univ. of San Antonio, San Antonio, TX 78207-4689	1895	$26,148	$7,556	2-D	3,334	335	38
Pace Univ., New York, NY 10038	1906	$41,275	$17,938	1-D	8,724	808	49
Pace Univ., Pleasantville campus, Pleasantville, NY 10570	NA	$41,325	$15,010	1-D	4,119	437	61
Pacific Lutheran Univ., Tacoma, WA 98447	1890	$37,950	$10,330	2-D	3,275	353	68
Pacific Union Coll., Angwin, CA 94508-9707	1882	$28,131	$7,485	2-M	1,555	143	44
Pacific Univ., ForeSt. Grove, OR 97116-1797	1849	$41,054	$11,822	1-D	3,810	NA	71
Palm Beach Atlantic Univ., West Palm Beach, FL 33416-4708	1968	$27,150	$8,854	2-D	3,918	365	44
Palm Beach State Coll., Lake Worth, FL 33461-4796	1933	$2,444(S)	NA	5-B	29,174	1,185	NA
Palmer Coll. of Chiropractic, Davenport, IA 52803-5287	1897	NA	NA	1-D	2,310	15	NA
Park Univ., Parkville, MO 64152-3795	1875	$10,600	$7,980	1-M	9,800	174	42
Parsons School of Design, New York, NY 10011	1896	NA	NA	1-M	5,176	1,117	62
Peirce Coll., Philadelphia, PA 19102-4699 (4)	1865	$14,184	NA	1-M	1,708	121	NA
Penn State Abington, Abington, PA 19001	1950	$13,954(S)	NA	12-B	3,966	304	48
Penn State Altoona, Altoona, PA 16601-3760	1939	$14,610(S)	$10,920	12-B	3,839	302	69
Penn State Berks, Reading, PA 19610-6009	1924	$14,610(S)	$11,950	12-B	2,906	220	63
Penn State Brandywine, Media, PA 19063-5596	1966	$13,964(S)	NA	12-B	1,457	135	41
Penn State Erie, The Behrend Coll., Erie, PA 16563-0001	1948	$14,610(S)	$10,920	12-M	4,327	330	69
Penn State Harrisburg, Middletown, PA 17057-4898	1966	$14,610(S)	$12,450	12-D	4,678	371	64
Penn State Univ. Park, University Park, PA 16802	1855	$17,514(S)	$10,920	12-D	47,307	3,099	86
Pennsylvania Coll. of Health Sciences, Lancaster, PA 17602 (4)	1903	$24,453	NA	1-M	1,377	220	68
Pennsylvania Coll. of Tech, Williamsport, PA 17701-5778	1965	$15,810(S)	$11,108	12-B	5,514	472	NA
Pepperdine Univ., Malibu, CA 90263	1937	$48,342	$13,810	2-D	7,632	705	84
Peru State Coll., Peru, NE 68421	1867	$6,397(S)	$6,998	5-M	2,358	109	NA
Pfeiffer Univ., Misenheimer, NC 28109-0960	1885	$27,125	$10,135	2-M	2,019	150	59
Philadelphia Univ., Philadelphia, PA 19144	1884	$36,520	$12,140	1-D	3,757	NA	65
Piedmont Coll., Demorest, GA 30535	1897	$21,990	$9,050	2-D	2,264	238	45
Pittsburg State Univ., Pittsburg, KS 66762	1903	$6,230(S)	$6,936	5-D	7,244	408	48
Plymouth State Univ., Plymouth, NH 03264-1595	1871	$13,128(S)	$10,868	5-D	5,156	426	58
Point Loma Nazarene Univ., San Diego, CA 92106-2899	1902	$32,400	$9,800	2-M	3,663	372	75
Point Park Univ., Pittsburgh, PA 15222-1984	1960	$28,250	$10,620	1-M	3,841	454	50
Point Univ., West Point, GA 31833	1937	$18,500	$6,600	2-B	1,582	152	48
Polk State Coll., Winter Haven, FL 33881-4299	1964	$3,367(S)	NA	5-B	10,657	367	NA
Polytechnic Univ. of Puerto Rico, Hato Rey, PR 00919	1966	$8,040	NA	1-D	4,291	226	16
Pomona Coll., Claremont, CA 91711	1887	$47,620	$15,150	1-B	1,663	235	93
Pontifical Catholic Univ. of Puerto Rico, Ponce, PR 00717-0777	1948	$5,130	$4,558	2-D	7,682	385	39
Portland State Univ., Portland, OR 97207-0751	1946	$6,684(S)	$10,260	5-D	27,488	1,540	41
Prairie View A&M Univ., Prairie View, TX 77446-0519	1878	$9,745(S)	$8,419	5-D	8,268	488	34
Pratt Inst., Brooklyn, NY 11205-3899	1887	$48,154	$12,026	1-M	4,617	1,113	65
Presbyterian Coll., Clinton, SC 29325	1880	$36,130	$9,750	2-D	1,379	113	70
Princeton Univ., Princeton, NJ 08544-1019	1746	$43,450	$14,160	1-D	8,138	1,172	97
Providence Coll., Providence, RI 02918	1917	$45,400	$13,390	2-M	4,735	530	85
Purchase Coll., State Univ. of New York, Purchase, NY 10577-1400	1967	$8,267(S)	$12,576	5-M	4,207	438	59
Purdue Univ., West Lafayette, IN 47907	1869	$10,002(S)	$10,030	5-D	39,409	2,593	76
Purdue Univ. Northwest, Hammond, IN 46323-2094	1951	$6,758(S)	$5,485	5-D	9,301	506	31
Purdue Univ. Northwest, Westville, IN 46391-9542	1967	NA	NA	5-M	6,177	289	21
Queens Coll. of the City Univ. of New York, Flushing, NY 11367-1597	1937	$6,938(S)	NA	11-M	19,520	1,534	58
Queens Univ. of Charlotte, Charlotte, NC 28274-0002	1857	$32,560	$11,486	2-M	2,286	314	53
Quincy Univ., Quincy, IL 62301-2699	1860	$27,128	$10,000	2-M	1,293	114	52
Quinnipiac Univ., Hamden, CT 06518-1940	1929	$43,640	$15,170	1-D	9,654	971	76
Radford Univ., Radford, VA 24142	1910	$9,809(S)	$8,677	5-D	9,743	728	59
Ramapo Coll. of New Jersey, Mahwah, NJ 07430-1680	1969	$13,698(S)	$11,640	5-M	6,026	495	74
Randolph-Macon Coll., Ashland, VA 23005-5505	1830	$37,600	$10,880	2-B	1,418	156	58
Rasmussen Coll. Lake Elmo/Woodbury, Lake Elmo, MN 55042	NA	$15,255	NA	3-B	1,855	23	NA
Reed Coll., Portland, OR 97202-8199	1908	$49,940	$12,590	1-M	1,453	150	79
Regent Univ., Virginia Beach, VA 23464-9800	1977	$16,700	$8,480	2-D	7,429	652	48
Regis Coll., Weston, MA 02493	1927	$37,540	$14,380	2-D	1,954	210	47
Regis Univ., Denver, CO 80221-1099	1877	$33,710	$10,040	2-D	8,725	803	73
Reinhardt Univ., Waleska, GA 30183-2981	1883	$20,266	$7,568	2-M	1,422	172	36
Rensselaer Polytechnic Inst., Troy, NY 12180-3590	1824	$50,797	$14,630	1-D	7,113	478	81
Rhode Island Coll., Providence, RI 02908-1991	1854	$8,197(S)	$10,394	5-D	8,512	772	44
Rhode Island School of Design, Providence, RI 02903-2784	1877	$45,840	$12,600	1-M	2,481	470	89
Rhodes Coll., Memphis, TN 38112-1690	1848	$44,942	$11,068	1-M	2,063	224	83
Rice Univ., Houston, TX 77251-1892	1912	$42,253	$13,650	1-D	6,719	862	93
Rider Univ., Lawrenceville, NJ 08648-3001	1865	$39,830	$14,230	1-M	5,075	590	64
Ringling Coll. of Art & Design, Sarasota, FL 34234-5895	1931	$42,020	$13,850	1-B	1,262	154	70
Rivier Univ., Nashua, NH 03060	1933	NA	NA	2-D	2,441	193	49
Roanoke Coll., Salem, VA 24153-3794	1842	$41,304	$12,810	2-B	2,005	219	66
Robert Morris Univ., Moon Township, PA 15108-1189	1921	$27,194	$12,130	1-D	5,377	488	58
Robert Morris Univ. Illinois, Chicago, IL 60605	1913	$25,950	$12,600	1-M	3,056	222	73
Roberts Wesleyan Coll., Rochester, NY 14624-1997	1866	$29,540	$10,212	2-M	1,712	267	62
Rochester Inst. of Tech, Rochester, NY 14623-5603	1829	$37,124	$11,918	1-D	16,640	1,483	70
Rockford Univ., Rockford, IL 61108-2393	1847	$29,180	$8,140	1-M	1,281	165	42
Rockhurst Univ., Kansas City, MO 64110-2561	1910	$34,790	$9,465	2-D	2,825	250	72
Rogers State Univ., Claremore, OK 74017-3252	1909	$6,430(S)	$8,961	5-M	4,031	266	21
Roger Williams Univ., Bristol, RI 02809	1956	$31,800	$14,846	1-D	4,808	505	64
Rollins Coll., Winter Park, FL 32789-4499	1885	$44,760	$13,910	1-D	2,521	233	71

Name, address	Year founded	Tuition & fees	Room & board	Control, degree	Enroll-ment	Faculty	Grad. rate
Roosevelt Univ., Chicago, IL 60605	1945	$28,119	$12,800	1-D	5,352	636	37%
Rose-Hulman Inst. of Tech, Terre Haute, IN 47803-3999 (2)	1874	$42,741	$12,660	1-M	2,356	193	77
Rowan Univ., Glassboro, NJ 08028-1701	1923	$12,864(S)	$11,627	5-D	16,155	1,433	66
Rush Univ., Chicago, IL 60612-3832	1969	NA	NA	1-D	1,566	796	NA
Rutgers Univ.–Camden, Camden, NJ 08102-1401	1927	$14,000(S)	$11,710	5-D	6,408	634	57
Rutgers Univ.–Newark, Newark, NJ 07102	1892	$13,597(S)	$12,841	5-D	11,720	868	68
Rutgers Univ.–New Brunswick, Piscataway, NJ 08854-8097	1766	$14,131(S)	$12,054	5-D	49,428	4,060	80
Sacred Heart Univ., Fairfield, CT 06825	1963	$37,170	$14,140	2-D	8,235	762	63
The Sage Colleges, Troy, NY 12180	1916	$28,400	$12,220	1-D	2,897	305	60
Saginaw Valley State Univ., University Center, MI 48710	1963	$8,969(S)	$8,600	5-D	9,766	755	40
St. Ambrose Univ., Davenport, IA 52803-2898	1882	$29,150	$9,869	2-D	3,311	294	63
St. Anselm Coll., Manchester, NH 03102-1310	1889	$37,904	$13,334	2-B	1,927	215	73
St. Augustine Coll., Chicago, IL 60640-3501	1980	$9,840	NA	1-B	1,430	154	NA
St. Bonaventure Univ., St. Bonaventure, NY 14778-2284	1858	$31,389	$11,128	2-M	2,011	222	64
St. Catherine Univ., St. Paul, MN 55105 (6)	1905	$37,842	$8,750	2-D	4,961	525	64
St. Cloud State Univ., St. Cloud, MN 56301-4498	1869	$7,816(S)	$7,930	5-D	16,245	880	47
St. Edward's Univ., Austin, TX 78704	1885	$40,828	$12,172	2-M	4,620	468	63
St. Francis Coll., Brooklyn Heights, NY 11201-4398	1884	$22,300	$12,000	2-M	2,672	300	52
St. Francis Univ., Loretto, PA 15940-0600	1847	$33,344	$11,524	2-D	2,336	236	71
St. John Fisher Coll., Rochester, NY 14618-3597	1948	$30,690	$11,460	2-D	3,823	447	70
St. John's Univ., Collegeville, MN 56321 (5)	1857	$40,226	$9,604	2-M	1,869	159	77
St. John's Univ., Queens, NY 11439	1870	$39,460	$16,390	2-D	20,881	1,432	59
St. Joseph's Coll., Long Island campus, Patchogue, NY 11772-2399	1916	$24,123	NA	1-M	3,537	393	68
St. Joseph's Coll., New York, Brooklyn, NY 11205-3688	1916	$24,113	NA	1-M	1,212	189	66
St. Joseph's Coll. of Maine, Standish, ME 04084	1912	NA	NA	2-M	3,355	126	50
St. Joseph's Univ., Philadelphia, PA 19131-1395	1851	$42,180	$14,928	2-D	8,629	728	79
St. Lawrence Univ., Canton, NY 13617-1455	1856	$49,410	$12,730	1-M	2,534	207	87
St. Leo Univ., Saint Leo, FL 33574-6665	1889	$21,130	$10,210	2-D	6,138	212	42
St. Louis Coll. of Pharm, St. Louis, MO 63110-1088	1864	$28,955	$10,045	1-D	1,389	147	NA
St. Louis Univ., St. Louis, MO 63103	1818	$39,226	$10,640	2-D	12,914	1,169	74
St. Martin's Univ., Lacey, WA 98503	1895	$33,194	$10,340	2-M	1,689	217	49
St. Mary's Coll., Notre Dame, IN 46556 (3)	1844	$37,400	$11,320	2-D	1,657	206	79
St. Mary's Coll. of California, Moraga, CA 94575	1863	$42,930	$14,490	2-D	4,257	525	60
St. Mary's Coll. of Maryland, St. Mary's City, MD 20686-3001	1840	$13,895(S)	$12,080	5-M	1,773	190	78
St. Mary's Univ., San Antonio, TX 78228-8507	1852	$27,840	$8,908	2-D	3,625	367	60
St. Mary's Univ. of Minnesota, Winona, MN 55987-1399	1912	$32,575	$8,635	2-D	5,931	560	61
St. Michael's Coll., Colchester, VT 05439	1904	$40,750	$10,975	2-M	2,367	250	76
St. Norbert Coll., De Pere, WI 54115-2099	1898	$34,237	$8,794	2-M	2,180	199	73
St. Olaf Coll., Northfield, MN 55057-1098	1874	$42,940	$9,790	2-B	3,046	333	89
St. Petersburg Coll., St. Petersburg, FL 33733-3489	1927	$2,754(S)	NA	11-B	31,767	1,780	NA
St. Peter's Univ., Jersey City, NJ 07306-5997	1872	NA	NA	2-D	3,406	314	55
St. Thomas Aquinas Coll., Sparkill, NY 10976	1952	$29,240	$12,000	1-M	1,836	162	55
St. Thomas Univ., Miami Gardens, FL 33054-6459	1961	$27,960	$11,320	2-D	4,935	283	39
St. Vincent Coll., Latrobe, PA 15650-2690	1846	$32,770	$10,793	2-D	1,857	222	69
St. Xavier Univ., Chicago, IL 60655-3105	1847	NA	NA	2-M	4,709	431	52
Salisbury Univ., Salisbury, MD 21801-6837	1925	$9,086(S)	$11,010	5-D	8,671	656	67
Salve Regina Univ., Newport, RI 02840-4192	1934	$36,740	$13,250	2-D	2,758	304	72
Samford Univ., Birmingham, AL 35229	1841	$29,402	$9,830	2-D	5,206	515	74
Sam Houston State Univ., Huntsville, TX 77341	1879	$9,337(S)	$8,676	5-D	20,031	905	50
Samuel Merritt Univ., Oakland, CA 94609-3108 (4)	1909	$45,493	NA	1-D	1,603	NA	NA
San Diego State Univ., San Diego, CA 92182	1897	$6,976(S)	$15,826	5-D	34,254	1,702	69
San Francisco State Univ., San Francisco, CA 94132-1722	1899	$6,476(S)	$12,234	5-D	30,256	NA	51
San Jose State Univ., San Jose, CA 95192-0001	1857	$7,323(S)	$14,217	5-M	32,773	1,755	57
Santa Clara Univ., Santa Clara, CA 95053	1851	$45,300	$13,425	2-D	8,680	934	84
Santa Fe Coll., Gainesville, FL 32606	1966	NA	NA	11-B	15,745	829	NA
Sarah Lawrence Coll., Bronxville, NY 10708-5999	1926	$51,034	$14,596	1-M	1,643	295	77
Savannah Coll. of Art & Design, Savannah, GA 31402-3146	1978	$34,295	$13,710	1-M	12,455	695	67
Savannah State Univ., Savannah, GA 31404	1890	$6,616(S)	$7,520	5-M	4,800	220	27
School of the Art Inst. of Chicago, Chicago, IL 60603-3103	1866	$43,960	$12,850	1-M	3,591	764	63
School of Visual Arts, New York, NY 10010-3994	1947	$36,500	$18,300	3-M	4,407	1,168	69
Schreiner Univ., Kerrville, TX 78028-5697	1923	$25,750	$9,806	2-M	1,230	109	40
Seattle Pacific Univ., Seattle, WA 98119-1997	1891	$37,086	$10,353	2-D	4,175	385	71
Seattle Univ., Seattle, WA 98122-1090	1891	$39,690	$11,122	2-D	7,273	748	78
Seton Hall Univ., South Orange, NJ 07079-2697	1856	$36,926	$13,692	2-D	9,903	952	64
Seton Hill Univ., Greensburg, PA 15601	1883	$32,420	$10,612	2-M	2,016	196	61
Sewanee: The Univ. of the South, Sewanee, TN 37383-1000	1857	$42,400	$12,100	2-D	1,797	223	78
Shawnee State Univ., Portsmouth, OH 45662-4344	1986	$7,364(S)	$9,766	5-M	3,898	334	24
Shaw Univ., Raleigh, NC 27601-2399	1865	$16,480	$8,158	2-M	1,646	171	29
Shenandoah Univ., Winchester, VA 22601-5195	1875	$31,322	$9,990	2-D	3,820	439	55
Shepherd Univ., Shepherdstown, WV 25443	1871	$6,830(S)	$9,682	5-M	3,861	367	48
Shippensburg Univ. of Pennsylvania, Shippensburg, PA 17257-2299	1871	$10,052(S)	$11,428	5-D	7,058	365	57
Shorter Univ., Rome, GA 30165	1873	$20,846	$9,400	2-M	1,472	145	46
Siena Coll., Loudonville, NY 12211-1462	1937	$34,611	$14,105	2-M	3,179	347	75
Siena Heights Univ., Adrian, MI 49221-1796	1919	$23,750	$9,710	2-M	2,642	268	51
Simmons Coll., Boston, MA 02115 (6)	1899	$37,380	$14,040	1-D	5,660	844	74
Simpson Coll., Indianola, IA 50125-1297	1860	$35,876	$7,963	2-M	1,690	198	68
Skidmore Coll., Saratoga Springs, NY 12866	1903	$48,970	$13,072	1-B	2,642	358	86
Slippery Rock Univ. of Pennsylvania, Slippery Rock, PA 16057-1383	1889	$9,645(S)	$10,022	5-D	8,628	403	68
Smith Coll., Northampton, MA 01063 (6)	1871	$46,288	$15,470	1-D	2,874	NA	87
Sonoma State Univ., Rohnert Park, CA 94928-3609	1960	$7,330(S)	$12,814	5-M	9,408	606	59
South Carolina State Univ., Orangeburg, SC 29117-0001	1896	$10,088(S)	$9,402	5-D	3,054	203	36
South Dakota School of Mines & Tech, Rapid City, SD 57701-3995	1885	$11,170(S)	$7,300	5-D	2,843	175	51
South Dakota State Univ., Brookings, SD 57007	1881	$8,172(S)	$7,462	5-D	12,589	690	58
SouthEast Missouri State Univ., Cape Girardeau, MO 63701-4799	1873	$6,990(S)	$8,285	5-M	11,987	576	48
Southeastern Baptist Theol. Sem., Wake Forest, NC 27588-1889	1950	NA	NA	2-D	2,262	138	25
Southeastern Louisiana Univ., Hammond, LA 70402	1925	$7,280(S)	$7,370	5-D	14,594	595	37
Southeastern Oklahoma State Univ., Durant, OK 74701-0609	1909	$6,215(S)	$6,487	5-M	3,751	270	29
Southeastern Univ., Lakeland, FL 33801-6099	1935	$22,840	$9,148	2-D	4,538	341	39
Southern Adventist Univ., Collegedale, TN 37315-0370	1892	$21,150	$6,450	2-D	3,125	174	48
Southern Arkansas Univ.–Magnolia, Magnolia, AR 71753	1909	$7,881(S)	$5,704	5-M	4,095	280	31

Name, address	Year founded	Tuition & fees	Room & board	Control, degree	Enrollment	Faculty	Grad. rate
The Southern Baptist Theol. Sem., Louisville, KY 40280-0004	1858	NA	NA	2-D	3,190	NA	NA
Southern Connecticut State Univ., New Haven, CT 06515-1355	1893	$9,600(S)	$11,614	5-D	10,473	960	52%
Southern Illinois Univ. Carbondale, Carbondale, IL 62901-4701	1869	$13,137(S)	$9,996	5-D	17,292	900	45
Southern Illinois Univ. Edwardsville, Edwardsville, IL 62026-0001	1957	$10,855(S)	$9,211	5-D	14,265	845	49
Southern Methodist Univ., Dallas, TX 75275	1911	$50,358	$16,125	2-D	11,643	1,116	79
Southern Nazarene Univ., Bethany, OK 73008	1899	$22,680	$7,970	2-M	3,906	NA	60
Southern New Hampshire Univ., Manchester, NH 03106-1045	1932	$31,136	$12,062	1-D	3,147	371	60
Southern Oregon Univ., Ashland, OR 97520	1926	$8,145(S)	$11,295	5-M	6,052	307	39
Southern Tech Coll., Fort Myers, FL 33907	1940	$13,860	NA	1-B	1,259	160	20
Southern Univ. & Agr. & Mech. Coll., Baton Rouge, LA 70813	1880	$6,534(S)	$7,501	5-D	7,699	546	29
Southern Univ. at New Orleans, New Orleans, LA 70126-1009 (4)	1959	NA	NA	5-M	3,141	102	NA
Southern Utah Univ., Cedar City, UT 84720-2498	1897	$6,530(S)	$7,067	5-M	8,881	502	39
Southern Wesleyan Univ., Central, SC 29630-1020	1906	$22,800	$7,950	2-M	1,883	193	39
Southwest Baptist Univ., Bolivar, MO 65613-2597	1878	$21,840	$7,160	2-D	3,615	301	51
Southwest Minnesota State Univ., Marshall, MN 56258	1963	$8,062(S)	$7,352	5-M	6,896	194	43
Southwestern Assemblies of God Univ., Waxahachie, TX 75165-5735	1927	$20,530	$6,936	2-M	1,984	161	38
Southwestern Coll., Winfield, KS 67156-2499	1885	$27,250	$7,050	2-D	1,471	174	44
Southwestern Oklahoma State Univ., Weatherford, OK 73096-3098	1901	$6,090(S)	$5,220	5-D	5,113	273	33
Southwestern Univ., Georgetown, TX 78626	1840	$39,060	$12,288	2-B	1,515	164	75
Spalding Univ., Louisville, KY 40203-2188	1814	$24,337	$7,600	2-D	2,202	NA	43
Spelman Coll., Atlanta, GA 30314-4399 (3)	1881	$26,638	$12,363	1-B	2,144	250	76
Spring Arbor Univ., Spring Arbor, MI 49283-9799	1873	$25,515	$8,870	2-M	3,404	138	52
Springfield Coll., Springfield, MA 01109-3797	1885	$33,455	$11,210	1-D	3,254	211	72
Spring Hill Coll., Mobile, AL 36608-1791	1830	$34,092	$12,226	2-M	1,496	135	53
Stanford Univ., Stanford, CA 94305-9991	1891	$47,331	$14,601	1-D	16,770	1,615	93
State Coll. of Florida Manatee-Sarasota, Bradenton, FL 34206-7046	1957	$3,074(S)	NA	5-B	10,314	442	NA
State Univ. of New York at Fredonia, Fredonia, NY 14063-1136	1826	$8,074(S)	$12,500	5-M	4,845	488	65
State Univ. of New York at New Paltz, New Paltz, NY 12561	1828	$7,737(S)	$11,480	5-M	7,752	664	73
State Univ. of New York at Oswego, Oswego, NY 13126	1861	$7,934(S)	$12,990	5-M	7,937	600	63
State Univ. of New York at Plattsburgh, Plattsburgh, NY 12901-2681	1889	$7,854(S)	$11,370	5-M	5,718	455	65
State Univ. of New York Coll. at Cortland, Cortland, NY 13045	1868	$8,050(S)	$12,200	5-M	6,926	623	73
State Univ. of New York Coll. at Geneseo, Geneseo, NY 14454-1401	1871	$8,113(S)	$11,980	5-M	5,699	353	82
State Univ. of New York Coll. at Old Westbury, Old Westbury, NY 11568-0210	1965	$7,643(S)	$10,390	5-M	4,353	351	40
State Univ. of New York Coll. at Oneonta, Oneonta, NY 13820-4015	1889	$7,548(S)	$11,530	5-M	6,023	483	67
State Univ. of New York Coll. at Potsdam, Potsdam, NY 13676	1816	$7,923(S)	$11,870	5-M	3,904	359	55
State Univ. of New York Coll. of Agr. & Tech at Cobleskill, Cobleskill, NY 12043	1916	$7,719(S)	$12,728	5-B	2,446	175	55
State Univ. of New York Coll. of Environmental Sci. & Forestry, Syracuse, NY 13210-2779	1911	$7,470(S)	$14,490	5-D	2,384	174	75
State Univ. of New York Coll. of Tech at Canton, Canton, NY 13617	1906	$7,938(S)	$11,800	5-B	3,183	242	34
State Univ. of New York Coll. of Tech at Delhi, Delhi, NY 13753	1913	$8,075(S)	$11,330	5-M	3,450	241	52
State Univ. of New York Downstate Med. Ctr., Brooklyn, NY 11203-2098	1858	$6,755(S)	$8,944	5-D	1,694	981	NA
State Univ. of New York Empire State Coll., Saratoga Springs, NY 12866-4391	1971	$6,985(S)	NA	5-M	11,882	1,064	NA
State Univ. of New York Maritime Coll., Throggs Neck, NY 10465-4198	1874	$7,809(S)	$11,516	5-M	1,860	148	56
State Univ. of New York Polytechnic Inst., Utica, NY 13504-3050	1966	$7,759(S)	$11,714	5-D	2,792	244	49
State Univ. of New York Upstate Med. Univ., Syracuse, NY 13210-2334	1950	NA	NA	5-D	1,787	54	NA
Stephen F. Austin State Univ., Nacogdoches, TX 75962	1923	$9,342(S)	$8,868	5-D	12,606	704	41
Stetson Univ., DeLand, FL 32723	1883	$43,240	$12,326	1-D	4,330	425	64
Stevens Inst. of Tech, Hoboken, NJ 07030	1870	$48,838	$13,500	1-D	6,359	404	82
Stevenson Univ., Stevenson, MD 21153	1952	$30,998	$12,490	1-M	4,185	474	56
Stockton Univ., Galloway, NJ 08205-9441	1969	$12,820(S)	$11,707	5-D	8,674	676	73
Stonehill Coll., Easton, MA 02357	1948	$38,550	$14,720	2-B	2,494	284	87
Stony Brook Univ., State Univ. of New York, Stony Brook, NY 11794	1957	$8,855(S)	$12,032	5-D	25,272	1,704	68
Stratford Univ., Falls Church, VA 22043	1976	$14,985	NA	3-D	1,241	164	NA
Suffolk Univ., Boston, MA 02108-2770	1906	$33,934	$14,648	1-D	8,046	705	56
Sullivan Univ., Louisville, KY 40205	1864	NA	NA	3-D	3,792	308	NA
Sul Ross State Univ., Alpine, TX 79832	1920	$7,210(S)	$7,810	5-M	1,973	148	19
Susquehanna Univ., Selinsgrove, PA 17870	1858	$44,340	$11,620	2-B	2,203	260	71
Swarthmore Coll., Swarthmore, PA 19081-1397	1864	$47,442	$13,958	1-B	1,581	212	94
Syracuse Univ., Syracuse, NY 13244	1870	$43,318	$14,880	1-D	21,789	1,628	81
Tarleton State Univ., Stephenville, TX 76402	1899	$8,393(S)	$9,045	5-D	12,333	666	44
Taylor Univ., Upland, IN 46989-1001	1846	$30,270	$8,497	2-M	2,168	215	77
Temple Univ., Philadelphia, PA 19122-6096	1884	$15,688(S)	$11,146	12-D	38,027	2,866	71
Tennessee State Univ., Nashville, TN 37209-1561	1912	$6,930(S)	$6,240	5-D	9,167	538	39
Tennessee Tech Univ., Cookeville, TN 38505	1915	$8,011(S)	$8,700	5-D	11,118	680	51
Texas A&M Intl. Univ., Laredo, TX 78041-1900	1969	$8,446(S)	$7,882	5-D	7,192	NA	41
Texas A&M Univ., College Station, TX 77843	1876	$9,428(S)	$10,338	5-D	63,429	3,599	79
Texas A&M Univ.–Central Texas, Killeen, TX 76549	2009	$20,879(S)	NA	5-M	2,466	178	NA
Texas A&M Univ.–Commerce, Commerce, TX 75429-3011	1889	$7,432(S)	$8,326	5-D	12,302	705	52
Texas A&M Univ.–Corpus Christi, Corpus Christi, TX 78412-5503	1947	$8,621(S)	$9,195	5-D	11,661	594	37
Texas A&M Univ.–Kingsville, Kingsville, TX 78363	1925	$7,700(S)	$8,407	5-D	9,207	NA	33
Texas A&M Univ.–Texarkana, Texarkana, TX 75505-5518	1971	NA	NA	5-M	1,653	NA	NA
Texas Christian Univ., Fort Worth, TX 76129-0002	1873	$40,720	$11,800	2-D	10,323	972	76
Texas Lutheran Univ., Seguin, TX 78155-5999	1891	$27,900	$9,390	2-M	1,376	126	47
Texas Southern Univ., Houston, TX 77004-4584	1947	$8,126(S)	$9,438	5-D	9,233	605	16
Texas State Univ., San Marcos, TX 78666	1899	$9,944(S)	$7,840	5-D	37,979	1,860	53
Texas Tech Univ., Lubbock, TX 79409	1923	$9,781(S)	$8,505	5-D	35,859	1,631	60
Texas Wesleyan Univ., Fort Worth, TX 76105-1536	1890	$24,454	$8,651	2-D	2,647	233	36
Texas Woman's Univ., Denton, TX 76201 (4)	1901	$8,566(S)	$7,443	5-D	15,286	881	41
Thomas Coll., Waterville, ME 04901-5097	1894	$25,722	$10,228	1-M	1,367	87	45
Thomas Edison State Univ., Trenton, NJ 08608-1176	1972	$6,135(S)	NA	5-M	20,606	NA	NA
Thomas Jefferson Univ., Philadelphia, PA 19107	1824	NA	NA	1-D	3,326	NA	NA
Thomas More Coll., Crestview Hills, KY 41017-3495	1921	$29,450	$7,304	2-M	1,909	139	47
Tiffin Univ., Tiffin, OH 44883-2161	1888	$22,850	$10,200	1-M	3,511	365	43
Touro Coll., New York, NY 10010	1971	$16,980	$11,970	1-D	12,021	1,335	59
Towson Univ., Towson, MD 21252-0001	1866	$9,182(S)	$11,638	5-D	22,284	1,678	70
Trevecca Nazarene Univ., Nashville, TN 37210-2877	1901	$23,748	$8,300	2-D	2,640	209	51
Trine Univ., Angola, IN 46703-1764	1884	$30,960	NA	1-D	3,420	212	56
Trinity Christian Coll., Palos Heights, IL 60463-0929	1959	$26,440	$9,390	2-M	1,320	146	62

Name, address	Year founded	Tuition & fees	Room & board	Control, degree	Enroll-ment	Faculty	Grad. rate
Trinity Coll., Hartford, CT 06106-3100	1823	$50,776	$13,144	1-M	2,397	295	86%
Trinity Intl. Univ., Deerfield, IL 60015-1284	1897	NA	NA	2-D	2,671	82	52
Trinity Univ., San Antonio, TX 78212-7200	1869	$37,856	$12,362	2-M	2,479	311	83
Trinity Washington Univ., Washington, DC 20017-1094 (3)	1897	NA	NA	2-M	1,630	NA	NA
Troy Univ., Troy, AL 36082	1887	$9,646(S)	$6,525	5-D	18,430	1,123	36
Truett-McConnell Coll., Cleveland, GA 30528	1946	$17,900	$7,420	2-M	2,017	115	32
Truman State Univ., Kirksville, MO 63501-4221	1867	$7,456(S)	$8,480	5-M	6,208	397	73
Tufts Univ., Medford, MA 02155	1852	$50,604	$13,094	1-D	11,137	995	92
Tulane Univ., New Orleans, LA 70118-5669	1834	$49,638	$13,758	1-D	13,449	1,204	83
Tusculum Coll., Greeneville, TN 37743-9997	1794	$23,125	$8,500	2-M	1,809	152	36
Tuskegee Univ., Tuskegee, AL 36088	1881	$20,320	$9,140	1-D	2,995	207	46
Union Coll., Schenectady, NY 12308-2311	1795	$50,013	$12,261	1-B	2,269	234	88
Union Inst. & Univ., Cincinnati, OH 45206-1925	1969	$12,144	NA	1-D	1,391	289	NA
Union Univ., Jackson, TN 38305-3697	1823	$29,190	$9,440	2-D	3,573	242	66
United States Air Force Acad., USAF Academy, CO 80840-5025	1954	$0(C)	NA	4-B	4,111	506	81
United States Military Acad., West Point, NY 10996 (2)	1802	$0(C)	NA	4-B	4,348	641	83
United States Naval Acad., Annapolis, MD 21402-5000	1845	$0(C)	NA	4-B	4,525	592	86
United Talmudical Sem., Brooklyn, NY 11211 (1)	1949	NA	NA	2-M	1,500	NA	NA
Universidad Adventista de las Antillas, Mayagüez, PR 00681-0118	1957	$6,850	$5,200	2-M	1,418	84	33
Universidad del Este, Carolina, PR 00984	1949	$5,820	NA	1-M	13,058	NA	25
Universidad del Turabo, Gurabo, PR 00778-3030	1972	$5,820	NA	1-D	17,509	1,171	19
Universidad Metropolitana, San Juan, PR 00928-1150	1980	$5,820	NA	1-D	13,919	1,250	26
Univ. at Albany, State Univ. of New York, Albany, NY 12222-0001	1844	$8,996(S)	$12,422	5-D	17,178	1,169	68
Univ. at Buffalo, the State Univ. of New York, Buffalo, NY 14260	1846	$9,381(S)	$13,061	5-D	29,806	1,847	74
The Univ. of Akron, Akron, OH 44325	1870	$10,509(S)	$11,322	5-D	23,046	1,505	40
The Univ. of Alabama, Tuscaloosa, AL 35487	1831	$10,197(S)	$9,030	5-D	37,098	1,799	67
The Univ. of Alabama at Birmingham, Birmingham, AL 35294	1969	$9,596(S)	$5,900	5-D	18,542	765	55
The Univ. of Alabama in Huntsville, Huntsville, AL 35899	1950	$9,128(S)	$9,205	5-D	7,866	553	49
Univ. of Alaska Anchorage, Anchorage, AK 99508	1954	$6,074(S)	$11,179	5-D	17,321	1,406	NA
Univ. of Alaska Fairbanks, Fairbanks, AK 99775-7520	1917	$7,374(S)	$8,380	5-D	8,700	993	43
Univ. of Alaska Southeast, Juneau, AK 99801	1972	NA	NA	5-M	3,458	229	31
The Univ. of Arizona, Tucson, AZ 85721	1885	$10,877(S)	$9,840	5-D	43,088	1,903	61
Univ. of Arkansas, Fayetteville, AR 72701-1201	1871	$8,522(S)	$9,880	5-D	26,754	1,320	62
Univ. of Arkansas at Little Rock, Little Rock, AR 72204-1099	1927	$8,108(S)	$5,708	5-D	11,645	740	24
Univ. of Arkansas at Monticello, Monticello, AR 71656	1909	NA	NA	5-M	3,920	240	24
Univ. of Arkansas at Pine Bluff, Pine Bluff, AR 71601-2799	1873	$6,271(S)	$7,270	5-D	2,658	199	26
Univ. of Arkansas for Med. Sciences, Little Rock, AR 72205-7199	1879	$8,497(S)	$6,300	5-D	3,021	516	NA
Univ. of Arkansas–Fort Smith, Fort Smith, AR 72913-3649	1928	$5,891(S)	$8,077	11-B	6,823	412	27
Univ. of Baltimore, Baltimore, MD 21201-5779	1925	$8,018(S)	NA	5-D	3,526	405	NA
Univ. of Bridgeport, Bridgeport, CT 06604	1927	$30,850	$12,990	1-D	5,433	534	33
Univ. of California, Berkeley, Berkeley, CA 94720-1500	1868	$13,431(S)	$15,422	5-D	38,204	2,258	91
Univ. of California, Davis, Davis, CA 95616	1905	$13,951(S)	$14,517	5-D	35,186	1,830	85
Univ. of California, Irvine, Irvine, CA 92697	1965	$14,750(S)	$12,947	5-D	30,836	1,510	88
Univ. of California, Los Angeles, Los Angeles, CA 90095	1919	$13,251(S)	$13,452	5-D	43,301	2,542	91
Univ. of California, Merced, Merced, CA 95343	2005	$13,772(S)	$15,646	5-D	6,685	373	66
Univ. of California, Riverside, Riverside, CA 92521-0102	1954	$13,527(S)	$15,700	5-D	18,608	NA	73
Univ. of California, San Diego, La Jolla, CA 92093	1959	$13,557(S)	$12,071	5-D	28,294	1,213	86
Univ. of California, Santa Barbara, Santa Barbara, CA 93106-2014	1909	$13,968(S)	$14,192	5-D	23,497	1,079	81
Univ. of California, Santa Cruz, Santa Cruz, CA 95064	1965	$13,481(S)	$15,123	5-D	17,868	NA	78
Univ. of Central Arkansas, Conway, AR 72035-0001	1907	$7,889(S)	$5,982	5-D	11,754	735	45
Univ. of Central Florida, Orlando, FL 32816	1963	$6,368(S)	$9,300	5-D	63,002	1,938	71
Univ. of Central Missouri, Warrensburg, MO 64093	1871	$7,322(S)	$8,102	5-M	14,395	714	52
Univ. of Central Oklahoma, Edmond, OK 73034-5209	1890	$6,096(S)	$7,130	5-M	16,910	1,111	39
Univ. of Charleston, Charleston, WV 25304-1099	1888	$30,100	$9,100	1-D	2,327	203	47
Univ. of Chicago, Chicago, IL 60637-1513	1891	$50,193	$14,772	1-D	12,962	1,750	92
Univ. of Cincinnati, Cincinnati, OH 45221	1819	$11,000(S)	$10,750	5-D	36,087	2,283	66
Univ. of Colorado Boulder, Boulder, CO 80309	1876	$11,091(S)	$13,194	5-D	32,775	2,053	71
Univ. of Colorado Colorado Springs, Colorado Springs, CO 80918	1965	$9,428(S)	$9,500	5-D	11,696	733	44
Univ. of Colorado Denver, Denver, CO 80217-3364	1912	$10,378(S)	NA	5-D	23,670	4,108	46
Univ. of Connecticut, Storrs, CT 06269	1881	$13,366(S)	$12,436	5-D	26,541	1,589	81
Univ. of Dallas, Irving, TX 75062-4736	1955	$37,230	$11,540	2-D	2,387	227	70
Univ. of Dayton, Dayton, OH 45469	1850	$39,090	$12,190	2-D	11,250	1,017	79
Univ. of Delaware, Newark, DE 19716	1743	$12,520(S)	$11,830	12-D	22,074	1,655	81
Univ. of Denver, Denver, CO 80208	1864	$44,178	$11,498	1-D	11,797	1,279	77
Univ. of Detroit Mercy, Detroit, MI 48221	1877	$39,882	$9,224	2-D	4,920	724	63
Univ. of Dubuque, Dubuque, IA 52001-5099	1852	$27,895	$9,070	2-M	2,118	216	48
Univ. of Evansville, Evansville, IN 47722	1854	$32,946	$11,240	2-D	2,398	234	69
The Univ. of Findlay, Findlay, OH 45840-3653	1882	$32,402	$9,538	2-D	5,029	330	55
Univ. of Florida, Gainesville, FL 32611	1853	$6,389(S)	$9,910	5-D	52,286	3,915	87
Univ. of Georgia, Athens, GA 30602	1785	$11,622(S)	$9,450	5-D	36,130	NA	84
Univ. of Guam, Mangilao, GU 96923	1952	$5,338(S)	$1,910	7-M	3,958	NA	29
Univ. of Hartford, West Hartford, CT 06117-1599	1877	$37,790	$11,986	1-D	6,912	852	60
Univ. of Hawaii at Hilo, Hilo, HI 96720-4091	1970	$7,548(S)	$9,970	5-D	3,924	338	38
Univ. of Hawaii at Manoa, Honolulu, HI 96822	1907	$11,692(S)	$11,529	5-D	18,865	1,459	57
Univ. of Hawaii–West Oahu, Kapolei, HI 96707	1976	$7,452(S)	NA	5-B	2,692	77	29
Univ. of Holy Cross, New Orleans, LA 70131-7399	1916	$10,912	NA	2-M	1,298	NA	NA
Univ. of Houston, Houston, TX 77204	1927	$10,710(S)	$9,849	5-D	42,704	2,266	51
Univ. of Houston–Clear Lake, Houston, TX 77058-1002	1971	$7,278(S)	$9,588	5-D	8,906	561	NA
Univ. of Houston–Downtown, Houston, TX 77002	1974	$6,938(S)	NA	5-M	14,262	717	13
Univ. of Houston–Victoria, Victoria, TX 77901-4450	1973	$7,086(S)	$7,664	5-M	4,407	239	NA
Univ. of Idaho, Moscow, ID 83844-2282	1889	$7,020(S)	$8,328	5-D	11,372	703	57
Univ. of Illinois at Chicago, Chicago, IL 60607-7128	1946	$13,664(S)	$10,882	5-D	29,048	1,572	60
Univ. of Illinois at Springfield, Springfield, IL 62703-5407	1969	$12,403(S)	$11,600	5-D	5,402	380	48
Univ. of Illinois at Urbana-Champaign, Champaign, IL 61820	1867	$15,626(S)	$11,000	5-D	44,942	NA	84
Univ. of Indianapolis, Indianapolis, IN 46227-3697	1902	$26,170	$9,324	2-D	5,442	542	56
The Univ. of Iowa, Iowa City, IA 52242-1316	1847	$8,104(S)	$9,728	5-D	31,387	1,616	70
The Univ. of Kansas, Lawrence, KS 66045	1866	$10,057(S)	$9,324	5-D	27,259	1,803	61
Univ. of Kentucky, Lexington, KY 40506-0032	1865	$10,936(S)	$11,434	5-D	22,705	1,966	61
Univ. of La Verne, La Verne, CA 91750-4443	1891	$38,560	$12,510	1-D	4,883	478	64
Univ. of Louisiana at Lafayette, Lafayette, LA 70504	1898	$8,256(S)	$8,952	5-D	17,508	793	46
Univ. of Louisiana at Monroe, Monroe, LA 71209-0001	1931	$7,658(S)	$7,048	5-D	8,645	415	39

Name, address	Year founded	Tuition & fees	Room & board	Control, degree	Enroll-ment	Faculty	Grad. rate
Univ. of Louisville, Louisville, KY 40292-0001	1798	$10,542(S)	$7,942	5-D	21,295	1,263	53%
Univ. of Maine, Orono, ME 04469	1865	$10,610(S)	$9,576	5-D	10,922	845	55
Univ. of Maine at Augusta, Augusta, ME 04330-9410	1965	$7,448(S)	NA	5-B	4,683	260	12
Univ. of Maine at Farmington, Farmington, ME 04938-1990	1863	$9,217(S)	$8,970	5-M	2,016	173	59
Univ. of Maine at Fort Kent, Fort Kent, ME 04743-1292	1878	$7,575(S)	$7,590	5-B	1,559	87	39
Univ. of Maine at Presque Isle, Presque Isle, ME 04769-2888	1903	$7,300(S)	$8,044	5-B	1,289	102	45
Univ. of Mgmt. & Tech., Arlington, VA 22209	1998	NA	NA	3-M	1,260	NA	NA
Univ. of Mary, Bismarck, ND 58504-9652	1959	$17,380	$6,378	2-D	2,872	272	70
Univ. of Mary Hardin-Baylor, Belton, TX 76513	1845	$24,880	$7,300	2-D	3,898	278	43
Univ. of Maryland, Baltimore Cty, Baltimore, MD 21250	1963	$11,006(S)	$10,868	5-D	13,839	825	61
Univ. of Maryland, Coll. Park, College Park, MD 20742	1856	$9,996(S)	$10,972	5-D	37,610	2,488	86
Univ. of Maryland Eastern Shore, Princess Anne, MD 21853-1299	1886	$9,807(S)	$8,994	5-D	4,454	345	32
Univ. of Maryland Univ. Coll., Adelphi, MD 20783	1947	$7,056(S)	NA	5-D	50,247	2,811	NA
Univ. of Mary Washington, Fredericksburg, VA 22401-5358	1908	$11,070(S)	$9,856	5-M	4,647	383	70
Univ. of Massachusetts Amherst, Amherst, MA 01003	1863	$13,443(S)	$11,457	5-D	29,269	1,473	78
Univ. of Massachusetts Boston, Boston, MA 02125-3393	1964	$12,682(S)	NA	5-D	17,030	1,271	42
Univ. of Massachusetts Dartmouth, North Dartmouth, MA 02747-2300	1895	$12,588(S)	$11,622	5-D	8,916	599	46
Univ. of Massachusetts Lowell, Lowell, MA 01854	1894	$13,427(S)	$11,670	5-D	17,450	1,112	56
Univ. of Memphis, Memphis, TN 38152	1912	$9,269(S)	$9,061	5-D	20,585	1,435	45
Univ. of Miami, Coral Gables, FL 33124	1925	$47,004	$13,310	1-D	16,848	1,549	82
Univ. of Michigan, Ann Arbor, MI 48109	1817	$13,856(S)	$10,554	5-D	43,651	3,328	90
Univ. of Michigan–Dearborn, Dearborn, MI 48128	1959	$11,704(S)	NA	5-D	9,066	555	53
Univ. of Michigan–Flint, Flint, MI 48502-1950	1956	$10,458(S)	$8,178	5-D	8,470	584	38
Univ. of Minnesota, Crookston, Crookston, MN 56716-5001	1966	$11,646(S)	$7,506	5-B	2,823	116	45
Univ. of Minnesota, Duluth, Duluth, MN 55812-2496	1947	$13,082(S)	$7,210	5-D	10,878	611	60
Univ. of Minnesota, Morris, Morris, MN 56267-2134	1959	$12,846(S)	$7,804	5-B	1,856	168	65
Univ. of Minnesota, Twin Cities campus, Minneapolis, MN 55455-0213	1851	$13,790(S)	$9,314	5-D	50,678	3,691	77
Univ. of Mississippi, University, MS 38677	1844	$7,444(S)	$10,128	5-D	23,212	1,295	61
Univ. of Mississippi Med. Ctr., Jackson, MS 39216-4505	1955	NA	NA	5-D	2,092	836	NA
Univ. of Missouri, Columbia, MO 65211	1839	$9,509(S)	$9,808	5-D	35,448	1,377	69
Univ. of Missouri–Kansas City, Kansas City, MO 64110-2499	1929	$9,582(S)	$9,815	5-D	16,699	1,172	51
Univ. of Missouri–St. Louis, St. Louis, MO 63121	1963	$10,065(S)	$9,052	5-D	16,763	959	41
Univ. of Mobile, Mobile, AL 36613	1961	$20,470	$9,160	2-M	1,566	170	42
Univ. of Montana, Missoula, MT 59812-0002	1893	$6,446(S)	$8,826	5-D	13,044	834	46
The Univ. of Montana Western, Dillon, MT 59725-3598	1893	$4,893(S)	$7,482	5-B	1,469	96	41
Univ. of Montevallo, Montevallo, AL 35115	1896	$11,410(S)	$6,900	5-M	3,033	224	45
Univ. of Mount Olive, Mount Olive, NC 28365	1951	$18,400	$7,400	2-B	3,855	183	44
Univ. of Mount Union, Alliance, OH 44601-3993	1846	$28,550	$9,540	2-M	2,191	248	61
Univ. of Nebraska at Kearney, Kearney, NE 68849-0001	1903	$6,724(S)	$9,230	5-M	6,747	453	57
Univ. of Nebraska at Omaha, Omaha, NE 68182	1908	$6,750(S)	$8,408	5-D	15,227	1,044	42
Univ. of Nebraska–Lincoln, Lincoln, NE 68588	1869	$8,279(S)	$10,310	5-D	25,260	1,064	67
Univ. of Nebraska Med. Ctr., Omaha, NE 68198	1869	NA	NA	5-D	3,625	1,232	NA
Univ. of Nevada, Las Vegas, Las Vegas, NV 89154	1957	$6,823(S)	$10,730	5-D	28,605	NA	41
Univ. of Nevada, Reno, Reno, NV 89557	1874	$7,142(S)	$10,868	5-D	20,898	1,166	59
Univ. of New England, Biddeford, ME 04005-9526	1831	$34,760	$12,920	1-D	7,795	545	65
Univ. of New Hampshire, Durham, NH 03824	1866	$16,986(S)	$10,618	5-D	15,398	1,034	79
Univ. of New Haven, West Haven, CT 06516-1916	1920	$35,650	$14,720	1-D	6,786	635	54
Univ. of New Mexico, Albuquerque, NM 87131-2039	1889	$7,954(S)	$8,690	5-D	27,353	1,601	47
Univ. of New Orleans, New Orleans, LA 70148	1958	$8,094(S)	$9,515	5-D	8,423	402	35
Univ. of North Alabama, Florence, AL 35632-0001	1830	$9,508(S)	$6,516	5-M	7,078	361	38
Univ. of North Carolina at Asheville, Asheville, NC 28804-3299	1927	$6,977(S)	$8,746	5-M	3,891	316	60
The Univ. of North Carolina at Chapel Hill, Chapel Hill, NC 27599	1789	$8,591(S)	$10,902	5-D	29,084	1,661	90
The Univ. of North Carolina at Charlotte, Charlotte, NC 28223-0001	1946	$6,532(S)	$10,220	5-D	27,983	1,551	53
The Univ. of North Carolina at Greensboro, Greensboro, NC 27412-5001	1891	$6,704(S)	$8,252	5-D	19,393	988	56
The Univ. of North Carolina at Pembroke, Pembroke, NC 28372-1510	1887	$5,564(S)	$7,377	5-M	6,441	391	38
The Univ. of North Carolina Wilmington, Wilmington, NC 28403-3297	1947	$6,691(S)	$9,466	5-D	14,918	1,016	71
Univ. of North Dakota, Grand Forks, ND 58202	1883	$7,965(S)	$7,236	5-D	14,951	753	54
Univ. of Northern Colorado, Greeley, CO 80639	1890	$8,166(S)	$10,360	5-D	11,936	712	48
Univ. of Northern Iowa, Cedar Falls, IA 50614	1876	$7,817(S)	$8,320	5-D	11,981	740	68
Univ. of North Florida, Jacksonville, FL 32224	1965	$6,394(S)	$9,664	5-D	15,675	900	55
Univ. of North Georgia, Dahlonega, GA 30597	1873	$7,178(S)	$9,494	5-D	17,289	779	54
Univ. of North Texas, Denton, TX 76203	1890	$7,589(S)	$8,199	5-D	37,175	1,489	52
Univ. of North Texas at Dallas, Dallas, TX 75241	2001	$7,848(S)	NA	5-D	2,488	167	NA
Univ. of Northwestern Ohio, Lima, OH 45805-1498	1920	$9,640	$2,700	1-B	3,848	127	NA
Univ. of Northwestern–St. Paul, St. Paul, MN 55113-1598	1902	$28,870	$8,954	2-M	3,427	208	63
Univ. of Notre Dame, Notre Dame, IN 46556	1842	$47,929	$13,846	2-D	12,179	1,309	95
Univ. of Oklahoma, Norman, OK 73019-0390	1890	$8,065(S)	$9,742	5-D	27,428	1,447	66
Univ. of Oklahoma Health Sciences Ctr., Oklahoma City, OK 73190	1890	$6,318(S)	NA	5-D	3,326	444	NA
Univ. of Oregon, Eugene, OR 97403	1876	$10,289(S)	$11,785	5-D	24,032	1,675	72
Univ. of Pennsylvania, Philadelphia, PA 19104	1740	$49,536	$13,990	1-D	21,395	2,085	95
Univ. of Phoenix–Online campus, Phoenix, AZ 85034-7209	1989	NA	NA	3-D	292,797	11,477	NA
Univ. of Pikeville, Pikeville, KY 41501	1889	$19,600	$8,376	2-D	2,533	151	36
Univ. of Pittsburgh, Pittsburgh, PA 15260	1787	$18,192(S)	$10,900	12-D	28,649	NA	82
Univ. of Pittsburgh at Bradford, Bradford, PA 16701-2812	1963	$13,372(S)	$8,592	12-B	1,461	163	44
Univ. of Pittsburgh at Greensburg, Greensburg, PA 15601-5860	1963	$13,382(S)	$9,750	12-B	1,562	158	56
Univ. of Pittsburgh at Johnstown, Johnstown, PA 15904-2990	1927	$13,374(S)	$9,080	12-B	2,957	NA	61
Univ. of Portland, Portland, OR 97203-5798	1901	$40,250	$11,902	2-D	4,338	363	78
Univ. of Puerto Rico in Aguadilla, Aguadilla, PR 00604	1972	$2,019(S)	NA	6-B	3,076	NA	NA
Univ. of Puerto Rico in Arecibo, Arecibo, PR 00614	1967	$1,870(S)	NA	6-B	4,352	NA	NA
Univ. of Puerto Rico in Bayamón, Bayamón, PR 00959	1971	$2,014(S)	NA	6-B	4,965	254	33
Univ. of Puerto Rico in Carolina, Carolina, PR 00984-4800	1974	$3,056(S)	NA	6-B	4,321	NA	NA
Univ. of Puerto Rico in Cayey, Cayey, PR 00736	1967	NA	NA	6-B	3,830	164	42
Univ. of Puerto Rico in Humacao, Humacao, PR 00791	1962	$2,049(S)	$8,751	6-B	3,774	257	45
Univ. of Puerto Rico in Ponce, Ponce, PR 00732-7186	1970	$2,019(S)	$8,280	6-B	3,229	188	38
Univ. of Puerto Rico in Utuado, Utuado, PR 00641-2500	1979	$2,014(S)	NA	6-B	1,623	107	NA
Univ. of Puerto Rico, Mayagüez campus, Mayagüez, PR 00681-9000	1911	NA	NA	6-D	13,852	NA	NA
Univ. of Puerto Rico, Med. Sciences campus, San Juan, PR 00936-5067 (4)	1950	NA	NA	6-D	2,381	NA	NA
Univ. of Puerto Rico, Río Piedras campus, San Juan, PR 00931-3300	1903	NA	NA	6-D	18,966	1,084	47
Univ. of Puget Sound, Tacoma, WA 98416	1888	$44,976	$11,480	1-D	2,774	281	78
Univ. of Redlands, Redlands, CA 92373-0999	1907	$44,900	$13,090	1-D	5,215	NA	72
Univ. of Rhode Island, Kingston, RI 02881	1892	$12,862(S)	$7,400	5-D	16,613	1,106	63
Univ. of Richmond, University of Richmond, VA 23173	1830	$49,420	$11,460	1-D	3,552	411	88

Name, address	Year founded	Tuition & fees	Room & board	Control, degree	Enroll- ment	Faculty	Grad. rate
Univ. of Rio Grande, Rio Grande, OH 45674	1876	$23,860	$9,920	1-M	2,161	175	39%
Univ. of Rochester, Rochester, NY 14627	1850	$48,290	$14,364	1-D	11,105	840	88
Univ. of St. Francis, Joliet, IL 60435-6169	1920	$29,950	$9,084	2-D	2,555	304	65
Univ. of St. Francis, Fort Wayne, IN 46808-3994	1890	$28,310	$9,090	2-M	2,240	270	56
Univ. of St. Joseph, West Hartford, CT 06117-2700 (4)	1932	$36,140	$14,850	2-D	2,553	292	55
Univ. of St. Mary, Leavenworth, KS 66048-5082	1923	$26,650	$8,978	2-D	1,427	293	41
Univ. of St. Thomas, St. Paul, MN 55105-1096	1885	$38,105	$9,750	2-D	10,243	NA	76
Univ. of St. Thomas, Houston, TX 77006-4696	1947	$31,520	$8,500	2-D	3,411	356	57
Univ. of San Diego, San Diego, CA 92110-2492	1949	$44,586	$12,042	2-D	8,251	863	79
Univ. of San Francisco, San Francisco, CA 94117-1080	1855	$44,494	$13,990	2-D	10,828	1,245	71
The Univ. of Scranton, Scranton, PA 18510	1888	$41,044	$13,918	2-D	5,422	548	80
Univ. of Sioux Falls, Sioux Falls, SD 57105-1699	1883	$25,480	$6,700	2-M	1,564	140	49.2
Univ. of South Alabama, Mobile, AL 36688-0002	1963	$8,790(S)	$7,250	5-D	16,211	1,041	35
Univ. of South Carolina, Columbia, SC 29208	1801	$11,482(S)	$9,872	5-D	32,971	2,373	NA
Univ. of South Carolina Aiken, Aiken, SC 29801	1961	$9,878(S)	$7,290	5-M	3,448	266	43
Univ. of South Carolina Beaufort, Bluffton, SC 29909	1959	$9,848(S)	$7,400	5-B	1,980	NA	23
Univ. of South Carolina Upstate, Spartanburg, SC 29303-4999	1967	$10,518(S)	$7,682	5-M	5,509	429	38
The Univ. of South Dakota, Vermillion, SD 57069-2390	1862	$8,022(S)	$7,089	5-D	10,061	595	57
Univ. of South Florida, Tampa, FL 33620-9951	1956	$6,410(S)	$9,400	5-D	42,067	1,734	68
Univ. of South Florida, St. Petersburg, St. Petersburg, FL 33701	1965	$5,830(S)	$9,250	5-M	4,750	278	38
Univ. of South Florida Sarasota-Manatee, Sarasota, FL 34243	1956	$5,587(S)	NA	5-M	2,041	139	NA
Univ. of Southern California, Los Angeles, CA 90089	1880	$50,210	$13,855	1-D	43,401	3,346	92
Univ. of Southern Indiana, Evansville, IN 47712-3590	1965	$7,385(S)	$8,532	5-D	9,029	677	41
Univ. of Southern Maine, Portland, ME 04104-9300	1878	$8,920(S)	$9,400	5-D	7,739	541	33
Univ. of Southern Mississippi, Hattiesburg, MS 39406-0001	1910	$7,334(S)	$8,610	5-D	14,551	907	50
The Univ. of Tampa, Tampa, FL 33606-1490	1931	$27,044	$9,900	1-M	7,959	655	55
The Univ. of Tennessee, Knoxville, TN 37996	1794	$12,436(S)	$9,926	5-D	27,845	1,731	70
The Univ. of Tennessee at Chattanooga, Chattanooga, TN 37403-2598	1886	$8,356(S)	$8,388	5-D	11,388	691	44
The Univ. of Tennessee at Martin, Martin, TN 38238	1900	$8,326(S)	$5,896	5-M	6,827	510	46
The Univ. of Texas at Arlington, Arlington, TX 76019	1895	$8,878(S)	$8,398	5-D	39,740	NA	42
The Univ. of Texas at Austin, Austin, TX 78712-1111	1883	$9,810(S)	$11,456	5-D	50,950	3,044	80
The Univ. of Texas at Dallas, Richardson, TX 75080	1969	$11,806(S)	$9,944	5-D	24,554	1,198	67
The Univ. of Texas at El Paso, El Paso, TX 79968-0001	1913	$7,259(S)	NA	5-D	23,397	1,260	NA
The Univ. of Texas at San Antonio, San Antonio, TX 78249-0617	1969	$8,737(S)	$7,564	5-D	28,787	1,355	31
The Univ. of Texas at Tyler, Tyler, TX 75799-0001	1971	$7,312(S)	$7,312	5-D	8,785	NA	41
The Univ. of Texas Health Sci. Ctr. at Houston, Houston, TX 77225-0036	1972	$7,434(S)	NA	5-D	4,811	128	95
The Univ. of Texas Health Sci. Ctr. at San Antonio, San Antonio, TX 78229-3900	1976	NA	NA	5-D	3,093	NA	NA
The Univ. of Texas Med. Branch, Galveston, TX 77555	1891	NA	NA	5-D	2,430	NA	NA
The Univ. of Texas of the Permian Basin, Odessa, TX 79762-0001	1969	$6,458(S)	$8,904	5-M	5,937	251	40
The Univ. of Texas Rio Grande Valley, Edinburg, TX 78539	1927	$7,292(S)	$7,632	5-D	28,584	1,258	NA
The Univ. of the Arts, Philadelphia, PA 19102-4944	1870	$39,908	$14,552	1-M	1,876	511	63
Univ. of the Cumberlands, Williamsburg, KY 40769-1372	1889	$23,360	$9,000	2-D	6,276	417	37
Univ. of the District of Columbia, Washington, DC 20008-1175	1976	$7,421(S)	$15,027	9-D	4,803	576	14
Univ. of the Incarnate Word, San Antonio, TX 78209-6397	1881	$27,798	$11,800	2-D	8,666	600	54
Univ. of the Pacific, Stockton, CA 95211-0197	1851	$42,934	$12,858	1-D	6,281	768	70
Univ. of the Sacred Heart, San Juan, PR 00914-0383	1935	NA	NA	2-M	5,666	367	35.3
Univ. of the Sciences, Philadelphia, PA 19104-4495	1821	$38,850	$15,188	1-D	2,664	419	72
Univ. of the Virgin Islands, Saint Thomas, VI 00802-9990	1962	$5,235(S)	$9,900	7-M	2,321	257	24
The Univ. of Toledo, Toledo, OH 43606-3390	1872	$9,560(S)	$11,494	5-D	20,377	1,068	41
The Univ. of Tulsa, Tulsa, OK 74104-3189	1894	$41,024	$11,116	1-D	4,671	443	69
Univ. of Utah, Salt Lake City, UT 84112-1107	1850	$8,197(S)	$9,000	5-D	31,551	2,111	64
Univ. of Vermont, Burlington, VT 05405	1791	$16,738(S)	$11,150	5-D	12,815	797	76
Univ. of Virginia, Charlottesville, VA 22903	1819	$14,468(S)	$10,400	5-D	23,883	1,465	93
The Univ. of Virginia's Coll. at Wise, Wise, VA 24293	1954	$9,355(S)	$10,256	5-B	2,028	192	41
Univ. of Washington, Seattle, WA 98195	1861	$11,839(S)	$11,310	5-D	45,408	2,664	84
Univ. of Washington, Bothell, Bothell, WA 98011-8246	1990	$11,758(S)	$10,833	5-M	5,277	294	70
Univ. of Washington, Tacoma, Tacoma, WA 98402-3100	1990	$11,905(S)	$10,833	5-D	4,599	290	63
The Univ. of West Alabama, Livingston, AL 35470	1835	$8,734(S)	$6,460	5-M	4,032	250	28
Univ. of West Florida, Pensacola, FL 32514-5750	1963	$8,401(S)	$9,912	5-D	12,798	606	47
Univ. of West Georgia, Carrollton, GA 30118	1933	$7,188(S)	$8,998	5-D	12,834	694	39
Univ. of Wisconsin–Eau Claire, Eau Claire, WI 54702-4004	1916	$8,822(S)	$7,322	5-D	10,460	525	67
Univ. of Wisconsin–Green Bay, Green Bay, WI 54311-7001	1968	$7,824(S)	$7,270	5-M	6,779	321	47
Univ. of Wisconsin–La Crosse, La Crosse, WI 54601-3742	1909	$8,832(S)	$5,850	5-D	10,387	616	69
Univ. of Wisconsin–Madison, Madison, WI 53706-1380	1848	$10,416(S)	$8,804	5-D	43,389	2,896	85
Univ. of Wisconsin–Milwaukee, Milwaukee, WI 53201-0413	1956	$9,428(S)	$10,030	5-D	27,109	1,538	44
Univ. of Wisconsin–Oshkosh, Oshkosh, WI 54901	1871	$7,437(S)	$7,386	5-D	14,411	628	54
Univ. of Wisconsin–Parkside, Kenosha, WI 53141-2000	1968	$7,481(S)	$7,712	5-M	4,442	222	33
Univ. of Wisconsin–Platteville, Platteville, WI 53818-3099	1866	$7,488(S)	$7,160	5-M	8,945	426	52
Univ. of Wisconsin–River Falls, River Falls, WI 54022	1874	$7,937(S)	$7,674	5-M	5,958	293	NA
Univ. of Wisconsin–Stevens Point, Stevens Point, WI 54481-3897	1894	$7,674(S)	$6,828	5-D	9,231	NA	65
Univ. of Wisconsin–Stout, Menomonie, WI 54751	1891	$9,203(S)	$6,504	5-D	9,535	485	NA
Univ. of Wisconsin–Superior, Superior, WI 54880-4500	1893	$8,036(S)	$6,410	5-M	2,489	201	40
Univ. of Wisconsin–Whitewater, Whitewater, WI 53190-1790	1868	$7,600(S)	$7,082	5-M	12,351	591	60
Univ. of Wyoming, Laramie, WY 82071	1886	$4,892(S)	$10,037	5-D	12,648	819	55
Upper Iowa Univ., Fayette, IA 52142-1857	1857	$28,073	$7,910	1-M	5,162	659	38
Urbana Univ., Urbana, OH 43078-2091	1850	NA	NA	1-M	1,551	120	NA
Ursinus Coll., Collegeville, PA 19426	1869	$47,700	$11,900	1-B	1,643	179	78
Ursuline Coll., Pepper Pike, OH 44124-4398 (4)	1871	$28,520	$9,490	2-D	1,236	194	44
Utah State Univ., Logan, UT 84322	1888	$6,664(S)	$5,790	5-D	28,622	1,156	49
Utah Valley Univ., Orem, UT 84058-5999	1941	$5,386(S)	NA	5-M	33,211	1,846	30
Utica Coll., Utica, NY 13502-4892	1946	$19,996	$10,434	1-D	4,463	433	42
Valdosta State Univ., Valdosta, GA 31698	1906	$6,298(S)	$7,912	5-D	11,302	606	36
Valencia Coll., Orlando, FL 32802-3028	1967	$2,474(S)	NA	5-B	44,050	1,717	44
Valley City State Univ., Valley City, ND 58072	1890	$6,800(S)	$5,900	5-M	1,422	NA	41
Valparaiso Univ., Valparaiso, IN 46383	1859	$36,160	$10,520	2-D	4,540	414	67
Vanderbilt Univ., Nashville, TN 37240-1001	1873	$44,712	$14,670	1-D	12,567	1,179	92
Vanguard Univ. of Southern California, Costa Mesa, CA 92626-9601	1920	$30,050	$9,750	2-M	2,184	243	56
Vassar Coll., Poughkeepsie, NY 12604	1861	$53,090	$12,400	1-B	2,435	338	91
Vaughn Coll. of Aeronautics & Tech, Flushing, NY 11369 (2)	1932	$23,775	$13,575	1-M	1,537	204	56
Vermont Tech Coll., Randolph Center, VT 05061-0500	1866	$13,850(S)	$9,696	5-B	1,546	158	NA
Villanova Univ., Villanova, PA 19085-1699	1842	$47,616	$12,707	2-D	10,925	1,032	90
Virginia Coll. in Birmingham, Birmingham, AL 35209	1989	NA	NA	3-M	3,826	NA	NA

Name, address	Year founded	Tuition & fees	Room & board	Control, degree	Enroll- ment	Faculty	Grad. rate
Virginia Commonwealth Univ., Richmond, VA 23284-9005	1838	$12,772(S)	$9,586	5-D	31,242	3,279	62%
Virginia Military Inst., Lexington, VA 24450 (2)	1839	$16,536(S)	$8,666	5-B	1,717	197	74
Virginia Polytechnic Inst. & State Univ., Blacksburg, VA 24061	1872	$12,485(S)	$8,266	5-D	32,663	1,966	83
Virginia State Univ., Petersburg, VA 23806-0001	1882	$8,226(S)	$10,252	5-D	4,696	480	49
Virginia Union Univ., Richmond, VA 23220-1170	1865	$16,533	$8,413	2-D	1,922	138	32
Virginia Wesleyan Coll., Norfolk, VA 23502-5599	1961	$34,428	$8,680	2-B	1,441	130	47
Viterbo Univ., La Crosse, WI 54601-4797	1890	$26,150	$8,510	2-D	2,756	320	51
Wagner Coll., Staten Island, NY 10301-4495	1883	$42,480	$13,000	1-D	2,202	251	64
Wake Forest Univ., Winston-Salem, NC 27109	1834	$49,308	$14,748	1-D	7,837	812	88
Walden Univ., Minneapolis, MN 55401	1970	$15,330	NA	3-D	52,799	2,754	NA
Waldorf Univ., Forest City, IA 50436-1713	1903	$20,884	$6,994	2-M	1,457	46	31
Walla Walla Univ., College Place, WA 99324-1198	1892	$25,866	$6,855	2-M	1,887	NA	56
Walsh Coll. of Accountancy & Bus. Admin, Troy, MI 48007-7006	1922	$15,459	NA	1-M	2,549	182	NA
Walsh Univ., North Canton, OH 44720-3396	1958	$27,710	$9,920	2-D	2,859	282	55
Wartburg Coll., Waverly, IA 50677-0903	1852	$38,380	$9,460	2-B	1,537	177	69
Washburn Univ., Topeka, KS 66621	1865	$7,910(S)	$6,830	10-D	6,615	554	36
Washington Adventist Univ., Takoma Park, MD 20912	1904	$21,395	$8,300	2-M	1,493	134	26
Washington & Jefferson Coll., Washington, PA 15301	1781	$43,226	$11,406	1-M	1,350	154	76
Washington & Lee Univ., Lexington, VA 24450-0303	1749	$46,417	$10,985	1-D	2,172	331	91
Washington Coll., Chestertown, MD 21620-1197	1782	$43,850	$10,612	1-B	1,427	171	75
Washington State Univ., Pullman, WA 99164	1890	$11,967(S)	$11,356	5-D	20,195	1,886	64
Washington State Univ.–Spokane, Spokane, WA 99210-1495	1989	$11,089(S)	NA	5-D	1,480	NA	93
Washington State Univ.–Tri-Cities, Richland, WA 99354	1989	$10,868(S)	NA	5-D	1,593	NA	57
Washington State Univ.–Vancouver, Vancouver, WA 98686	1989	$10,883(S)	NA	5-D	3,305	NA	60
Washington Univ. in St. Louis, St. Louis, MO 63130-4899	1853	$49,770	$15,596	1-D	14,688	1,277	93
Wayland Baptist Univ., Plainview, TX 79072-6998	1908	$16,830	$6,690	2-M	5,223	577	33
Waynesburg Univ., Waynesburg, PA 15370-1222	1849	$22,030	$9,170	2-D	1,869	230	62
Wayne State Coll., Wayne, NE 68787	1910	$6,042(S)	$6,760	5-M	3,431	217	49
Wayne State Univ., Detroit, MI 48202	1868	$12,745(S)	$10,061	5-D	27,222	1,799	35
Weber State Univ., Ogden, UT 84408-1001	1889	$5,339(S)	$4,219	5-M	25,955	1,298	38
Webster Univ., St. Louis, MO 63119-3194	1915	$25,500	$10,860	1-D	4,474	607	62
Wellesley Coll., Wellesley, MA 02481 (3)	1870	$48,802	$15,114	1-B	2,356	356	93
Wentworth Inst. of Tech, Boston, MA 02115-5998	1904	$32,500	$13,390	1-M	4,576	371	66
Wesleyan Univ., Middletown, CT 06459	1831	$50,612	$13,950	1-D	3,138	445	94
Wesley Coll., Dover, DE 19901-3875	1873	$24,100	$10,670	2-M	1,770	170	22
West Chester Univ. of Pennsylvania, West Chester, PA 19383	1871	$9,462(S)	$8,427	5-D	16,606	NA	71
West Coast Univ., North Hollywood, CA 91606	1909	$16,625	NA	3-M	1,792	NA	NA
West Liberty Univ., West Liberty, WV 26074	1837	$6,702(S)	$8,810	5-M	2,340	NA	48
West Texas A&M Univ., Canyon, TX 79016-0001	1909	$7,681(S)	$7,196	5-D	9,491	424	43
West Virginia State Univ., Institute, WV 25112-1000	1891	$6,662(S)	$10,806	5-M	3,166	201	28
West Virginia Univ., Morgantown, WV 26506	1867	$7,632(S)	$9,872	5-D	29,175	1,478	57
West Virginia Univ. Inst. of Tech, Montgomery, WV 25136	1895	$6,336(S)	$9,348	5-B	1,263	114	19
West Virginia Wesleyan Coll., Buckhannon, WV 26201	1890	$29,952	$4,080	2-M	1,518	152	50
Western Carolina Univ., Cullowhee, NC 28723	1889	$6,903(S)	$8,131	5-D	10,382	676	58
Western Connecticut State Univ., Danbury, CT 06810-6885	1903	$9,516(S)	$11,738	5-D	5,826	614	49
Western Governors Univ., Salt Lake City, UT 84107	1998	$6,070	NA	1-M	57,821	1,654	NA
Western Illinois Univ., Macomb, IL 61455-1390	1899	$11,509(S)	$9,580	5-D	11,094	679	53
Western Intl. Univ., Phoenix, AZ 85021-2914	1978	NA	NA	3-M	2,993	NA	NA
Western Kentucky Univ., Bowling Green, KY 42101	1906	$9,482(S)	$7,368	5-D	20,063	1,185	50
Western Michigan Univ., Kalamazoo, MI 49008	1903	$11,029(S)	$9,238	5-D	23,556	1,440	54
Western New England Univ., Springfield, MA 01119	1919	$34,030	$12,894	1-D	3,954	377	57
Western New Mexico Univ., Silver City, NM 88062-0680	1893	NA	NA	5-M	2,697	259	NA
Western Oregon Univ., Monmouth, OR 97361-1394	1856	$8,796(S)	$9,638	5-M	5,445	375	45
Western State Colorado Univ., Gunnison, CO 81231	1901	$8,451(S)	$9,307	5-M	2,726	164	42
Western Washington Univ., Bellingham, WA 98225-5996	1893	$8,611(S)	$10,342	5-M	15,060	898	72
Westfield State Univ., Westfield, MA 01086	1838	$8,815(S)	$10,691	5-M	6,496	519	63
Westminster Coll., New Wilmington, PA 16172-0001	1852	$35,210	$10,690	2-M	1,310	148	71
Westminster Coll., Salt Lake City, UT 84105-3697	1875	$31,228	$9,338	1-M	2,821	388	62
Westmont Coll., Santa Barbara, CA 93108-1099	1937	$42,900	$13,510	2-B	1,304	147	77
Wheaton Coll., Wheaton, IL 60187-5593	1860	$32,950	$9,200	2-D	2,929	305	89
Wheaton Coll., Norton, MA 02766	1834	$47,700	$12,165	1-B	1,598	189	79
Wheeling Jesuit Univ., Wheeling, WV 26003-6295	1954	$28,030	$7,070	2-D	1,385	166	64
Whitman Coll., Walla Walla, WA 99362-2083	1859	$46,138	$11,564	1-B	1,470	234	87
Whittier Coll., Whittier, CA 90608-0634	1887	$41,636	$12,245	1-D	2,189	188	66
Whitworth Univ., Spokane, WA 99251-0001	1890	$40,562	$11,170	2-M	2,650	329	75
Wichita State Univ., Wichita, KS 67260	1895	$7,528(S)	$10,626	5-D	14,495	828	43
Widener Univ., Chester, PA 19013-5792	1821	$1,346/credit	NA	1-D	6,218	632	57
Wilkes Univ., Wilkes-Barre, PA 18766-0002	1933	$32,356	$13,266	1-D	5,053	343	59
Willamette Univ., Salem, OR 97301-3931	1842	$45,617	$11,200	2-D	3,076	280	79
William Carey Univ., Hattiesburg, MS 39401-5499	1906	$11,700	$5,870	2-M	3,248	NA	NA
William Paterson Univ. of New Jersey, Wayne, NJ 07470-8420	1855	$12,365(S)	$10,885	5-D	10,862	1,064	48
William Peace Univ., Raleigh, NC 27604-1194	1857	$27,080	$10,350	2-B	1,038	129	43
William Penn Univ., Oskaloosa, IA 52577-1799	1873	$24,510	$3,738	2-M	1,635	215	30
William Woods Univ., Fulton, MO 65251-1098	1870	$22,160	$8,960	2-D	2,171	257	51
Williams Coll., Williamstown, MA 01267	1793	$50,070	$13,220	1-M	2,153	350	96
Wilmington Coll., Wilmington, OH 45177	1870	$24,500	$9,500	2-M	1,458	119	52
Wilmington Univ., New Castle, DE 19720-6491	1967	$8,354	NA	1-D	15,828	2,171	23
Wingate Univ., Wingate, NC 28174	1896	$29,170	$10,780	2-D	3,149	288	54
Winona State Univ., Winona, MN 55987	1858	$9,047(S)	$8,120	5-D	8,472	512	59
Winston-Salem State Univ., Winston-Salem, NC 27110-0003	1892	$7,187(S)	$8,528	5-M	6,427	336	37
Winthrop Univ., Rock Hill, SC 29733	1886	$14,456(S)	$8,320	5-M	6,031	555	55
Wittenberg Univ., Springfield, OH 45501-0720	1845	$38,090	$10,126	2-M	1,876	179	64
Wofford Coll., Spartanburg, SC 29303-3663	1854	$38,705	$11,180	2-B	1,613	155	82
Woodbury Univ., Burbank, CA 91504-1099	1884	$36,408	$10,668	1-M	1,489	298	46
Worcester Polytechnic Inst., Worcester, MA 01609-2280	1865	$45,599	$13,410	1-D	6,573	514	85
Worcester State Univ., Worcester, MA 01602-2597	1874	$8,857(S)	$11,560	5-M	6,306	417	51
Wright State Univ., Dayton, OH 45435	1964	$8,730(S)	$9,304	5-D	16,842	660	40
Xavier Univ., Cincinnati, OH 45207	1831	$35,080	$11,380	2-D	6,538	699	71
Xavier Univ. of Louisiana, New Orleans, LA 70125-1098	1925	$22,349	$8,800	2-D	2,969	248	38
Yale Univ., New Haven, CT 06520	1701	$49,480	$15,170	1-D	12,385	1,635	96
Yeshiva Univ., New York, NY 10033-3201	1886	$41,530	$11,250	1-D	6,203	1,028	92
York Coll. of Pennsylvania, York, PA 17405-7199	1787	$18,780	$10,460	1-D	4,739	469	57
York Coll. of the City Univ. of New York, Jamaica, NY 11451-0001	1967	$6,748(S)	NA	11-M	8,511	NA	27
Youngstown State Univ., Youngstown, OH 44555-0001	1908	$8,317(S)	$8,990	5-D	12,468	1,047	30

DIRECTORY

Associations and Organizations

Source: World Almanac research

Selected list, generally by category and first distinctive key word in each title. Listed by acronym when that is the official name. Year established is in parentheses. Entries for religious organizations include addresses and leadership information for 2016.

Academic and Educational

Academies, Natl. (1863): (202) 334-2000; www.nationalacademies.org

African American Life and History, Assn. for the Study of (1915): (202) 238-5910; www.asalh.org

Alpha Delta Kappa (1947): (816) 363-5525; www.alphadeltakappa.org

AMIDEAST (America-Mideast Educational and Training Services, Inc.) (1951): (202) 776-9600; www.amideast.org

Anthropological Assn., American (1902): (703) 528-1902; www.aaanet.org

Archaeological Institute of America (1879): (617) 353-9361; www.archaeological.org

Arts, Americans for the (1960): (202) 371-2830; www.artsusa.org

Arts and Sciences, American Academy of (1780): (617) 576-5000; www.amacad.org

Beta Gamma Sigma Inc. (1913): (314) 432-5650; www.betagammasigma.org

Beta Sigma Phi Intl. (1931): (816) 444-6800; www.betasigmaphi.org

Biological Sciences, American Institute of (1947): (703) 674-2500; www.aibs.org

Classical Studies, Society for (fmr. American Philological Assn.) (1869): (215) 898-4975; www.apaclassics.org

College Board (1900): (212) 713-8000; www.collegeboard.org

Colleges and Universities, Assn. of American (1915): (202) 387-3760; www.aacu.org

Community Colleges, American Assn. of (1920): (202) 728-0200; www.aacc.nche.edu

Consumer Interests, American Council on (1953): (727) 493-2131; www.consumerinterests.org

Delta Kappa Gamma Society Intl. (1929): (512) 478-5748; www.dkg.org

Education, American Council on (1918): (202) 939-9300; www.acenet.edu

Education, Council for Advancement and Support of (1974): (202) 328-2273; www.case.org

Education of Young Children, Natl. Assn. for the (1926): (202) 232-8777; www.naeyc.org

Educators for World Peace, Intl. Assn. of (1973): (256) 534-5501; www.iaewpeace.org

English-Speaking Union of the U.S. (1920): (212) 818-1200; www.esuus.org

Entomological Society of America (1889): (301) 731-4535; www.entsoc.org

Family Relations, Natl. Council on (1938): (888) 781-9331; www.ncfr.org

Foreign Study, American Institute for (1964): (866) 906-2437; www.aifs.com

Freedom of Information Coalition, Natl. (1958): (573) 882-4856; www.nfoic.org

French Institute/Alliance Française (1971): (212) 355-6100; www.fiaf.org

Genealogical Society, Natl. (1903): (703) 525-0050; www.ngsgenealogy.org

Genetic Assn., American (1914): (541) 264-5612; www.theaga.org

Geological Society of America (1888): (303) 357-1000; www.geosociety.org

Hemispheric Affairs, Council on (1975): (202) 223-4975; www.coha.org

Industrial and Applied Mathematics, Society for (1952): (215) 382-9800; www.siam.org

Intl. Education, Institute of (1919): (212) 883-8200; www.iie.org

Intl. Educational Exchange, Council on (1947): (207) 553-4000; www.ciee.org

Intl. Law, American Society of (1906): (202) 939-6000; www.asil.org

Irish American Cultural Inst. (1962): (973) 605-1991; www.iaci-usa.org

IRTS Foundation (fmr. Intl. Radio and TV Society Foundation) (1939): (212) 867-6650; www.irts.org

Law Libraries, American Assn. of (1906): (312) 939-4764; www.aallnet.org

Learned Societies, American Council of (1919): (212) 697-1505; www.acls.org

Libraries Assn., Special (1909): (703) 647-4900; www.sla.org

Linguistic Society of America (1924): (202) 835-1714; www.lsadc.org

Literacy Assn., Intl. (fmr. Intl. Reading Assn.) (1956): (302) 731-1600; www.reading.org

Mathematical Society, American (1888): (401) 455-4000; www.ams.org

Mensa, Ltd., American (1960): (817) 607-0060; www.us.mensa.org

Meteorological Society, American (1919): (617) 227-2425; www.ametsoc.org

Metric Assn., Inc., U.S. (1916): www.us-metric.org

Microbiology, American Society for (1899): (202) 737-3600; www.asm.org

Modern Language Assn. of America (1883): (646) 576-5000; www.mla.org

Museums, American Alliance of (1906): (202) 289-1818; www.aam-us.org

Music Education, Natl. Assn. for (fmr. Music Educators Natl. Conference) (1907): (703) 860-4000; www.nafme.org

Musicological Society, American (1934): (877) 679-7648; www.ams-net.org

Negro College Fund, United (1944): (800) 331-2244; www.uncf.org

Oriental Society, American (1842): (734) 647-4760; www.americanorientalsociety.org

ORT America (1922): (212) 505-7700; www.ortamerica.org

PEN American Center (1922): (212) 334-1660; www.pen.org

Phi Beta Kappa Society (1776): (202) 265-3808; www.pbk.org

Phi Theta Kappa Honor Society (1918): (800) 946-9995; www.ptk.org

Philosophical Assn., American (1900): (302) 831-1112; www.apaonline.org

Physics, American Inst. of (1931): (301) 209-3100; www.aip.org

Physiological Society, American (1887): (301) 634-7164; www.the-aps.org

Poetry Society of America (1910): (212) 254-9628; www.poetrysociety.org

Poets, Academy of American (1934): (212) 274-0343; www.poets.org

Political Science, Academy of (1880): (212) 870-2500; www.psqonline.org

Religion, American Academy of (1909): (404) 727-3049; www.aarweb.org

Science, American Assn. for the Advancement of (1848): (202) 326-6400; www.aaas.org

Science Fiction Society, World (1939): www.wsfs.org

Sciences, Natl. Academy of (1863): (202) 334-2000; www.nasonline.org

Sigma Beta Delta (1994): (314) 516-4723; www.sigmabetadelta.org

Sociological Assn., American (1905): (202) 383-9005; www.asanet.org

Tau Beta Pi Assn. (1885): (865) 546-4578; www.tbp.org

Teach For America (1990): (212) 279-2080; www.teachforamerica.org

Theological Schools in the U.S. and Canada, Assn. of (1918): (412) 788-6505; www.ats.edu

Theosophical Society in America (1875): (630) 668-1571; www.theosophical.org

Universities, Assn. of American (1900): (202) 408-7500; www.aau.edu

World Learning (1932): (802) 257-7751; www.worldlearning.org

Animal Welfare and Environment

Animal Welfare Institute (1951): (202) 337-2332; www.awionline.org

Animals, American Society for the Prevention of Cruelty to (ASPCA) (1866): (212) 876-7700; www.aspca.org

Animals, People for the Ethical Treatment of (PETA) (1980): (757) 622-7382; www.peta.org

Appalachian Trail Conservancy (1925): (304) 535-6331; www.appalachiantrail.org

Audubon Society, Natl. (1905): (212) 979-3000; www.audubon.org

Cat Fanciers' Assn., Inc., The (1906): (330) 680-4070; www.cfa.org

Conservation Intl. (1987): (703) 341-2400; www.conservation.org

Defenders of Wildlife (1947): (800) 385-9712; www.defenders.org

Ducks Unlimited (1937): (901) 758-3825; www.ducks.org

Forest History Society (1946): (919) 682-9319; www.foresthistory.org

Foresters, Society of American (1900): (301) 897-8720; www.safnet.org

Friends of the Earth (1969): (202) 783-7400; www.foe.org

Garden Club of America (1913): (212) 753-8287; www.gcamerica.org

Garden Clubs, Inc., Natl. (1929): (314) 776-7574; www.gardenclub.org

Geographic Society, Natl. (1888): (813) 979-6845; www.nationalgeographic.com

Green Mountain Club (1910): (802) 244-7037; www.greenmountainclub.org

Greenpeace (1971): (202) 462-1177; www.greenpeaceusa.org

Hiking Society, American (1976): (301) 565-6704; www.americanhiking.org

Horse Council, American (1969): (202) 296-4031; www.horsecouncil.org

Humane Society of the U.S., The (1954): (202) 452-1100; www.humanesociety.org

Natural Resources Defense Council (1970): (212) 727-2700; www.nrdc.org

Nature Conservancy, The (1951): (703) 841-5300; www.nature.org

Ocean Conservancy (1972): (202) 429-5609; www.oceanconservancy.org

Ornithologists' Union, American (1883): www.aou.org

Recreation and Park Assn., Natl. (1965): (800) 626-6772; www.nrpa.org

Recycling Coalition, Inc., Natl. (1978): (202) 618-2107; www.nrcrecycles.org

Rose Society, American (1892): (318) 938-5402; www.ars.org

Save the Redwoods League (1918): (415) 362-2352; www.saveredwoods.org

Sierra Club (1892): (415) 977-5500; www.sierraclub.org

Water Environment Federation (1928): (800) 666-0206; www.wef.org

Wildflower Center, Lady Bird Johnson (1982): (512) 232-0100; www.wildflower.org

Wildlife Federation, Natl. (1936): (800) 822-9919; www.nwf.org

World Wildlife Fund (1961): (202) 293-4800; www.worldwildlife.org

Children and Social Services

Big Brothers Big Sisters of America (1904): (813) 720-8778; www.bbbs.org

Boy Scouts of America (1910): (972) 580-2000; www.scouting.org

Boys & Girls Clubs of America (1906): (404) 487-5700; www.bgca.org

Camp Fire (fmr. Camp Fire Boys & Girls) (1910): (816) 285-2010; www.campfire.org

Child Welfare League of America (1920): (202) 688-4200; www.cwla.org

Children's Aid Society (1913): (205) 251-7148; www.childrensaid.org

Children's Book Council, The (1945): (212) 966-1990; www.cbcbooks.org

Feeding America (fmr. America's Second Harvest) (1976): (800) 771-2303; www.feedingamerica.org

4-H Council, Natl. (1914): (301) 961-2800; www.4-h.org

Future Business Leaders of America-Phi Beta Lambda, Inc. (1942): (800) 325-2946; www.fbla-pbl.org

Future Farmers of America Org., Natl. (1928): (317) 802-6060; www.ffa.org

Gifted Children, Natl. Assn. for (1954): (202) 785-4268; www.nagc.org

Girl Scouts of the USA (1912): (212) 852-8000; www.girlscouts.org

Honor Society, Natl. (1921): (703) 860-0200; www.nhs.us

Junior Achievement USA® (1919): (719) 540-8000; www.ja.org

Junior Auxiliaries, Inc., Natl. Assn. of (1941): (662) 332-3000; www.najanet.org

Junior Chamber Intl. USA (1914): (636) 778-3010; www.usjaycees.org
Junior Honor Society, Natl. (1929): (703) 860-0200; www.njhs.us
Missing and Exploited Children, Natl. Center for (1984): (703) 224-2150; www.missingkids.com
Pilot Intl. (1921): (478) 477-1208; www.pilotinternational.org
Student Councils, Natl. Assn. of (1931): (703) 860-0200; www.nasc.us

Fraternal

Eagles, Fraternal Order of (1898): (614) 883-2200; www.foe.com
Eastern Star, General Grand Chapter, Order of the (1876): (202) 667-4737; www.easternstar.org
Elks of the USA, Benevolent and Protective Order of (1868): (773) 755-4700; www.elks.org
Freemasonry, Scottish Rite of, Supreme Council, 33°, Northern Masonic Jurisdiction (1813): (781) 862-4410; www.scottishritenmj.org
Freemasonry, Scottish Rite of, Supreme Council, 33°, Southern Jurisdiction (1802): (202) 232-3579; www.srmason-sj.org
Kiwanis Intl. (1915): (317) 875-8755; www.kiwanis.org
Knights of Columbus (1882): (203) 752-4000; www.kofc.org
Knights of Pythias, Order of (1864): (781) 436-5966; www.pythias.org
Lions Clubs Intl. (1917): (630) 571-5466; www.lionsclubs.org
Men, Natl. Coalition for (1977): (888) 223-1280; www.ncfm.org
Moose Intl., Inc. (1888): (630) 859-2000; www.mooseintl.org
Odd Fellows, Independent Order of (1819): (336) 725-5955; www.ioof.org
Rotary Intl. (1905): (847) 866-3000; www.rotary.org
Shriners Intl. (1872): (813) 281-0300; www.shrinersinternational.org
Sons of Italy in America, Order (1905): (202) 547-2900; www.osia.org
Sons of Norway (1895): (612) 827-3611; www.sofn.com
Woodmen of America, Modern (1883): (800) 447-9811; www.modern-woodmen.org

Historical

Civil War Trust (1987): (202) 367-1861; www.civilwar.org
Colonial Dames XVII Century, Natl. Soc. (1915): (202) 293-1700; www.colonialdames17c.org
Daughters of the American Revolution (1890): (202) 628-1776; www.dar.org
Daughters of the Confederacy, United (1894): (804) 355-1636; www.hqudc.org
Historic Preservation, Natl. Trust for (1949): (202) 588-6000; www.preservationnation.org
Historical Assn., American (1884): (202) 544-2422; www.historians.org
Lewis and Clark Trail Heritage Foundation (1969): (406) 454-1234; lewisandclark.org
Mayflower Descendants, General Soc. of (1897): (508) 746-3188; www.themayflowersociety.org
Pilgrims, Natl. Soc. Sons and Daughters of the (1908): www.nssdp.org
Railway Historical Society, Natl. (1935): (215) 557-6606; www.nrhs.com
Sons of the American Revolution, Natl. Soc. (1889): (502) 589-1776; www.sar.org
Sons of Confederate Veterans (1896): (800) 380-1896; www.scv.org
State and Local History, American Assn. for (1940): (615) 320-3203; www.aaslh.org
Supreme Court Historical Society (1974): (202) 543-0400; www.supremecourthistory.org
Theodore Roosevelt Assn. (1920): (516) 921-6319; www.theodoreroosevelt.org
Thoreau Society (1941): (978) 369-5310; www.thoreausociety.org
Titanic Historical Society, Inc. (1963): (413) 543-4770; www.titanichistoricalsociety.org
Victorian Society in America (1966): (215) 636-9872; www.victoriansociety.org

Industrial and Trade

Aerospace Industries Assn. (1919): (703) 358-1000; www.aia-aerospace.org
Better Business Bureaus, Council of (1912): (703) 276-0100; www.bbb.org
Chamber of Commerce, U.S. (1912): (202) 659-6000; www.uschamber.com
Chemistry Council, American (1872): (202) 249-7000; www.americanchemistry.com
Construction Specifications Institute (1948): (800) 689-2900; www.csinet.org
CropLife America (1933): (202) 296-1585; www.croplifeamerica.org
Electrical Manufacturers Assn., Natl. (1926): (703) 841-3200; www.nema.org
Fire Protection Assn., Natl. (NFPA) (1896): (617) 770-3000; www.nfpa.org
Fisheries Soc., American (1870): (301) 897-8616; www.fisheries.org
Foreign Trade Council, Natl. (1914): (202) 887-0278; www.nftc.org
Funeral Consumers Alliance (1963): (802) 865-8300; www.funerals.org
Hotel & Lodging Assn., American (1910): (202) 289-3100; www.ahla.com
Insurance Assn., American (1866): (202) 828-7100; www.aiadc.org
Magazine Media, Assn. of (1919): (212) 872-3700; www.magazine.org
Manufacturers, Natl. Assn. of (1895): (202) 637-3000; www.nam.org
Newspaper Assn. of America (1992): (571) 366-1000; www.naa.org
Nuclear Society, American (1954): (708) 352-6611; www.ans.org
Orchestras, League of American (1942): (212) 262-5161; www.symphony.org
Petroleum Institute, American (1919): (202) 682-8000; www.api.org
Printing Industries of America, Inc. (1887): (412) 741-6860; www.printing.org
Publishers, Assn. of American (1970): (212) 255-1041; www.publishers.org
Retail Federation, Natl. (1908): (202) 783-7971; www.nrf.com
Safety Council, Natl. (1913): (630) 285-1121; www.nsc.org
Shipbuilders Council of America (1920): (202) 737-3234; www.shipbuilders.org
Small Business Assn., Natl. (1937): (800) 345-6728; www.nsba.biz
Software & Information Industry Assn. (1999): (202) 289-7442; www.siia.net
Tall Buildings and Urban Habitat, Council on (1969): (312) 567-3487; www.ctbuh.org
Toy Industry Assn., Inc. (1916): (212) 675-1141; www.toyassociation.org
Water Works Assn., American (1881): (303) 794-7711; www.awwa.org
Zoos & Aquariums, Assn. of (1924): (301) 562-0777; www.aza.org

Lifestyle and Travel

AAA (American Automobile Assn.) (1902): (407) 444-7000; www.aaa.com
AARP (fmr. American Assn. of Retired Persons) (1958): (888) 687-2277; www.aarp.org
AFS Intercultural Programs USA (1947): (800) 237-4636; www.afsusa.org
Aircraft Owners and Pilots Assn. (1939): (800) 872-2672; www.aopa.org
Appalachian Mountain Club (1876): (617) 523-0636; www.outdoors.org
Boat Owners Assn. of the U.S. (1966): (800) 395-2628; www.boatus.com
Camp Assn., American (1910): (765) 342-8456; www.acacamps.org
Consumer Federation of America (1968): (202) 387-6121; www.consumerfed.org
Consumers Union (1936): (914) 378-2000; www.consumersunion.org
Green America (fmr. Co-op America) (1982): (800) 584-7336; www.greenamerica.org
Helicopter Society Intl., American (1943): (703) 684-6777; www.vtol.org
Hostelling Intl. USA (1934): (240) 650-2100; www.hiusa.org
Jewish Community Centers Assn. of North America (1917): (212) 532-4949; www.jcca.org
Motorcyclist Assn., American (1924): (614) 856-1900; www.americanmotorcyclist.com
Parents Without Partners, Inc. (1957): (800) 637-7974; www.parentswithoutpartners.org

Planetary Society (1980): (626) 793-5100; www.planetary.org
SCRABBLE® Players Assn., N. American (2009): www.scrabbleplayers.com
Sports Car Club of America (1944): (785) 357-7222; www.scca.org
Toastmasters Intl. (1924): (949) 858-8255; www.toastmasters.org
YMCA (Young Men's Christian Assn.) of the USA (1851): (800) 872-9622; www.ymca.net
YWCA (Young Women's Christian Assn.) USA (1858): (202) 467-0801; www.ywca.org

Military and Veterans

Air Force Assn. (1946): (703) 247-5800; www.afa.org
American Legion (1919): (317) 630-1200; www.legion.org
American Legion Auxiliary (1919): (317) 569-4500; www.alaforveterans.org
AMVETS (American Veterans) (1944): (877) 726-8387; www.amvets.org
Army, Assn. of the United States (1950): (703) 841-4300; www.ausa.org
Blinded Veterans Assn. (1958): (800) 669-7079; www.bva.org
Civil Air Patrol (1941): (877) 227-9142; www.gocivilairpatrol.com
Coast Guard Combat Veterans Assn. (1985): (610) 539-1000; www.coastguardcombatvets.com
Disabled American Veterans (1920): (859) 441-7300; www.dav.org
82nd Airborne Division Assn., Inc. (1944): (910) 223-1182; www.82ndairborneassociation.org
Ex-Prisoners of War, American (1942): (817) 649-2979; www.axpow.org
Fleet Reserve Assn. (1924): (703) 683-1400; www.fra.org
Iraq and Afghanistan Veterans of America (2004): (212) 982-9699; www.iava.org
Jewish War Veterans of the U.S.A. (1896): (202) 265-6280; www.jwv.org
Legion of Valor Museum (1991): (559) 498-0510; www.fresnovetsmuseum.com
Marine Corps League (1937): (703) 207-9588; www.mclnational.org
Military Officers Assn. of America (1929): (703) 549-2311; www.moaa.org
Military Order of the World Wars (1919): (703) 683-4911; www.moww.org
National Guard Assn. of the U.S. (1878): (202) 789-0031; www.ngaus.org
Naval Institute, U.S. (1873): (410) 268-6110; www.usni.org
Navy League of the United States (1902): (703) 528-1775; www.navyleague.org
Ninety-Nines, Inc. (Intl. Org. of Women Pilots) (1929): (405) 685-7969; www.ninety-nines.org
Non-Commissioned Officers Assn. (1960): (210) 653-6161; www.ncoausa.org
Paralyzed Veterans of America (1946): (800) 424-8200; www.pva.org
POW/MIA Families, Natl. League of (1970): (703) 465-7432; www.pow-miafamilies.org
Purple Heart, Military Order of the (1932): (703) 642-5360; www.purpleheart.org
Reserve Officers Assn. of the U.S. (1922): (202) 479-2200; www.roa.org
Sons of the American Legion (1932): (317) 630-1200; www.legion.org/sons
Tin Can Sailors (Natl. Assn. of Destroyer Veterans) (1976): (800) 223-5535; www.destroyers.org
Uniformed Services, Natl. Assn. for (1968): (800) 842-3451; www.naus.org
USO, Inc. (United Service Org.) (1941): (888) 484-3876; www.uso.org
USS Los Angeles CA-135 Assn. (1977): www.uss-la-ca135.org/2la-assoc.htm
USS Missouri Memorial Assn., Inc. (1998): (808) 455-1600; www.ussmissouri.com
Veterans of Foreign Wars (1899): (816) 756-3390; www.vfw.org
Veterans of Foreign Wars, Ladies Auxiliary to the (1914): (816) 561-8655; www.ladiesauxvfw.org
Vietnam Veterans of America (1978): (301) 585-4000; www.vva.org
Women's Army Corps Veterans' Assn. (1946): (256) 820-6824; www.armywomen.org
Wounded Warrior Project (2002): (877) 832-6997; www.woundedwarriorproject.org

Political

Abortion Federation, Natl. (1977): (202) 667-5881; www.prochoice.org

Action Network, American (2010): (202) 559-6420; americanactionnetwork.org

Advancement and Support of Education, Council for (1974): (202) 328-2273; www.case.org

American Indians, Natl. Congress of (1944): (202) 466-7767; www.ncai.org

American-Islamic Relations, Council on (1994): (202) 488-8787; www.cair.org

Black Lives Matter (2012): www.blacklivesmatter.com

Brady Campaign to Prevent Gun Violence (1974): (202) 370-8100; www.bradycampaign.org

Center for Responsive Politics (1983): (202) 857-0044; www.opensecrets.org

Cities, Natl. League of (1924): (202) 626-3100; www.nlc.org

Civil Liberties Union, American (ACLU) (1920): (212) 549-2500; www.aclu.org

Coalition to Stop Gun Violence (1974): (202) 408-0061; www.csgv.org

Coffee Party USA (2010): (301) 259-1869; www.coffeepartyusa.com

Common Cause (1970): (202) 833-1200; www.commoncause.org

Concerned Women for America (1979): (202) 488-7000; www.cwfa.org

Congress of Racial Equality (CORE) (1942): (212) 598-4000; www.core-online.org

Conservation Voters, League of (1969): (202) 785-8683; www.lcv.org

Constitution Party (1992): (717) 390-1993; www.constitutionparty.com

Crime and Delinquency, Natl. Council on (1907): (800) 306-6223; www.nccdglobal.org

Crossroads GPS (Grassroots Political Strategies) (2010): (202) 706-7051; www.crossroadsgps.org

Democratic Natl. Committee (1848): (202) 863-8000; www.democrats.org

Everytown for Gun Safety (2013): (646) 324-8250; www.everytown.org

Feminists for Life of America (1972): (703) 836-3354; www.feministsforlife.org

Future Fund, Amer. (2007): (515) 661-4233; www.americanfuturefund.com

Gay & Lesbian Alliance Against Defamation (GLAAD) (1985): (212) 629-3322; www.glaad.org

Governors Assn., Natl. (1908): (202) 624-5300; www.nga.org

Grange of the Order of Patrons of Husbandry, Natl. (1867): (202) 628-3507; www.nationalgrange.org

Gray Panthers (1970): (202) 737-6637

Greens/Green Party of the USA (1984): (202) 319-7191; www.gp.org

Homeless, Natl. Coalition for the (1984): (202) 462-4822; www.nationalhomeless.org

Human Rights Campaign (1980): (202) 628-4160; www.hrc.org

Immigration Equality (1994): (212) 714-2904; immigrationequality.org

Immigration Reform, Federation for American (FAIR) (1979): (202) 328-7004; www.fairus.org

Japanese American Citizens League (1929): (415) 921-5225; www.jacl.org

Jewish Committee, American (1906): (212) 751-4000; www.ajc.org

John Birch Society (1958): (920) 749-3780; www.jbs.org

LGBTQ Task Force, Natl. (fmr. Natl. Gay and Lesbian Task Force) (1973): (202) 393-5177; www.thetaskforce.org

Libertarian Party (1971): (202) 333-0008; www.lp.org

Marriage, Natl. Org. for (2007): (888) 894-3604; www.nationformarriage.org

Marry, Freedom to (2003): (212) 851-8418; www.freedomtomarry.org

Mayors, U.S. Conference of (1932): (202) 293-7330; www.usmayors.org

NAACP (Natl. Assn. for the Advancement of Colored People) (1909): (410) 580-5777; www.naacp.org

NRA (National Rifle Assn.) (1871): (800) 672-3888; www.nra.org

Parliamentarians, Natl. Assn. of (1930): (816) 833-3892; www.parliamentarians.org

Patriot Majority (2005): www.patriot majority.org

Progress, Center for American (2003): (202) 682-1611; www.americanprogress.org

Reform Party Natl. Committee (1995): (972) 275-9297; www.reformparty.org

Republican Natl. Committee (1856): (202) 863-8500; www.gop.com

Southern Christian Leadership Conference (1957): (404) 522-1420; sclcnational.org

Southern Poverty Law Center (1971): (334) 956-8200; www.splcenter.org

State Governments, Council of (1933): (859) 244-8000; www.csg.org

Tax Foundation (1937): (202) 464-6200; www.taxfoundation.org

Tax Reform, Americans for (1985): (202) 785-0266; www.atr.org

Taxpayers Union, Natl. (1969): (703) 683-5700; www.ntu.org

Tea Party Federation, Natl. (2010): www.thenationalteapartyfederation.com

Tea Party Patriots (2009): www.teaparty patriots.org

Term Limits, U.S. (1992): (202) 261-3532; www.termlimits.org

Urban League, Natl. (1910): (212) 558-5300; www.nul.org

Women, Natl. Organization for (NOW) (1966): (202) 628-8669; www.now.org

Women and Families, Natl. Partnership for (1971): (202) 986-2600; www.national partnership.org

Women Voters, League of (1920): (202) 429-1965; www.lwv.org

Women's Christian Temperance Union (1874): (847) 864-1397; www.wctu.org

Zionist Organization of America (1897): (212) 481-1500; www.zoa.org

Religious

African Methodist Episcopal Church (1787): 500 8th Ave. S., Nashville, TN 37203; (615) 254-0911; www.ame-church. com; Gen. Sec., Dr. Jeffery Cooper

African Methodist Episcopal Zion Church (1796): 3225 West Sugar Creek Rd., Charlotte, NC 28269; (704) 599-4630; www.amez.org; Senior Bishop, George E. Battle Jr.

American Baptist Churches USA (1907): P.O. Box 851, Valley Forge, PA 19482; (610) 768-2000; www.abc-usa.org; Gen. Sec., A. Roy Medley

Antiochian Orthodox Christian Archdiocese of North America (1895): P.O. Box 5238, Englewood, NJ 07631; (201) 871-1355; www.antiochian.org; Primate, Archbishop Metropolitan Joseph

Armenian Apostolic Church of America: *Eastern Prelacy* (1958): 138 E. 39th St., New York, NY 10016; (212) 689-7810; www.armenianprelacy.org; Prelate, Archbishop Oshagan Choloyan; *Western Prelacy* (1973): 6252 Honolulu Ave., La Crescenta, CA 91214; (818) 248-7737; www.westernprelacy.org; Prelate, Archbishop Moushegh Mardirossian

Assemblies of God USA (1914): 1445 N. Boonville Ave., Springfield, MO 65802; (417) 862-2781; www.ag.org; Gen. Supt., Dr. George O. Wood

Atheists, American (1963): P.O. Box 158, Cranford, NJ 07016; (908) 276-7300; www. atheists.org; Pres., David P. Silverman

Bahá'ís of the U.S., Natl. Spiritual Assembly of the (1909): 1233 Central St., Evanston, IL 60201; (847) 733-3400; www.bahai.us; Sec., Kenneth E. Bowers

Baptist Bible Fellowship Intl. (1950): 720 E. Kearney St., Springfield, MO 65803; (417) 862-5001; www.bbfi.org; Pres., Eddie Lyons

Baptist Convention, Southern (1845): 901 Commerce St., Nashville, TN 37203; (615) 244-2355; www.sbc.net; Pres., Dr. Ronnie Floyd

Baptist Convention, USA, Inc., Natl. (1886): 1700 Baptist World Center Dr., Nashville, TN 37207; (615) 228-6292; www.nationalbaptist.com; Pres., Dr. Jerry Young

Baptist Convention of America Intl., Inc., Natl. (1880): 777 S.R.L. Thornton Fwy., Ste. 210, Dallas, TX 75203; (214) 942-3311; www.nbcainc.com; Pres., Rev. Samuel C. Tolbert Jr.

Baptist Conventional of America, Natl. Missionary (1988): 6925 Wofford Dr., Dallas, TX 75227; (877) 886-6222; www.nmbca.com; Pres., Dr. Nehemiah Davis

Bible Society, American (1816): 101 N. Independence Mall East FL8, Philadelphia, PA 19106; (215) 309-0900; www.american bible.org; Pres., Dr. Roy L. Peterson

Biblical Literature, Society of (1880): 825 Houston Mill Rd., Atlanta, GA 30329; (404) 727-3100; www.sbl-site.org; Exec. Dir., Dr. John F. Kutsko

B'nai B'rith Intl. (1843): 1120 20th St. NW, Ste. 300 N, Washington, DC 20036; (202) 857-6600; www.bnaibrith.org; Pres., Gary P. Saltzman

Brethren in Christ Church (c. 1778): 431 Grantham Rd., Mechanicsburg, PA 17055; (717) 697-2634; www.bic-church.org; Natl. Dir., Dr. Alan Robinson

Buddhist Churches of America (1899): 1710 Octavia St., San Francisco, CA 94109; (415) 776-5600; www.buddhist churchesofamerica.org; Pres., Kent Matsuda

Catholic Bishops, U.S. Conference of (2001): 3211 4th St. NE, Washington, DC 20017; (202) 541-3000; www.usccb.org; Gen. Sec., Msgr. J. Brian Bransfield

Christian Church (Disciples of Christ) (1832): Disciples Center, P.O. Box 1986, Indianapolis, IN 46206; (317) 635-3100; www.disciples.org; Gen. Min. and Pres., Rev. Dr. Sharon E. Watkins

Christian Methodist Episcopal Church (1870): 4466 Elvis Presley Blvd., Memphis, TN 38116; (901) 345-0580; www.thecmechurch.org; Senior Bishop, Lawrence Reddick

Church of the Brethren (1708): General Offices, 1451 Dundee Ave., Elgin, IL 60120; (847) 742-5100; www.brethren.org; Interim Gen. Sec., Dale Minnich

Church of Christ (1830): P.O. Box 472, Independence, MO 64051; (816) 206-0147; www.churchofchrist-tl.org; Sec., Council of Apostles, Duane L. Ely

Church of God (Anderson, IN) (1881): Box 2420, Anderson, IN 46018; (765) 642-0256; www.jesusisthesubject.org; Gen. Dir., Jim Lyon

Church of God (Cleveland, TN) (1886): 2490 Keith St. NW, Cleveland, TN 37311; (423) 472-3361; www.churchofgod.org; Gen. Overseer, Dr. Mark Williams

Church of God in Christ (1897): Mason Temple, 930 Mason St., Memphis, TN 38126; (901) 947-9300; www.cogic.org; Presiding Bishop, Bishop Charles E. Blake Sr.

Church of Jesus Christ (1862): World Operations Ctr., 110 Walton Tea Room Rd., Greensburg, PA 15601; (724) 837-4425; www.thechurchofjesuschrist.org

Church of Jesus Christ of Latter-day Saints, The (Mormons) (1830): 50 W. North Temple St., Salt Lake City, UT 84150; (801) 240-2640; www.lds.org; Pres., Thomas S. Monson

Church of the Nazarene (1908): Global Ministry Center, 17001 Prairie Star Pkwy., Lenexa, KS 66220; (913) 577-0500; www.nazarene.org; Gen. Sec., David P. Wilson

Community of Christ (reorganized Church of Jesus Christ of Latter-Day Saints) (1830): Intl. Headquarters, 1001 W. Walnut, Independence, MO 64050; (816) 833-1000; www.cofchrist.org; Pres., Stephen M. Veazey

Community Churches, International Council of (1950): 21116 Washington Pkwy., Frankfort, IL 60423; (815) 464-5690; www.icccusa.org; Interim Exec. Dir., Don Ashmall

Conservative Judaism, United Synagogue of (1913): 120 Broadway, Ste. 1540, New York, NY 10271; (212) 533-7800; www.uscj.org; Pres., Margo Gold

Converge Worldwide (fmr. Baptist General Conference) (1852): 2002 S. Arlington Heights Rd., Arlington Heights, IL 60005; (800) 323-4215; www.converge.org; Pres., Scott Ridout

Cumberland Presbyterian Church (1810): 8207 Traditional Pl., Cordova, TN 38016; (901) 276-4572; www.cumberland.org

Episcopal Church (1789): 815 Second Ave., New York, NY 10017; (212) 716-6000; www.episcopalchurch.org; Presiding Bishop and Primate, Most Rev. Michael B. Curry

Evangelical Lutheran Church in America (1988): 8765 W. Higgins Rd., Chicago, IL 60631; (773) 380-2700; www.elca.org; Presiding Bishop, Rev. Elizabeth A. Eaton

First Church of Christ, Scientist, The (1879): 210 Massachusetts Ave., Boston, MA 02115; (617) 450-2000; www.christianscience.com; Pres., Annu Matthai

Free Methodist Church USA (1860): 770 N. High School Rd., Indianapolis, IN 46214; (317) 244-3660; www.fmcusa.org; Chief Operating Officer, Larry Roberts

Freedom From Religion Foundation (1978): P.O. Box 750, Madison, WI 53701; (608) 256-8900; www.ffrf.org

Friends General Conference (1900): 1216 Arch St., #2B, Philadelphia, PA 19107; (215) 561-1700; www.fgcquaker.org; Gen. Sec., Barry Crossno

Gideons Intl., The (1899): P.O. Box 140800, Nashville, TN 37214; (615) 564-5000; www.gideons.org

Greek Orthodox Archdiocese of America (1922): 8 E. 79th St., New York, NY 10075; (212) 570-3500; www.goarch.org; Primate, Archbishop Demetrios

Hadassah, the Women's Zionist Organization of America, Inc. (1912): 40 Wall St., New York, NY 10005; (800) 664-5646; www.hadassah.org; Exec. Dir. and CEO, Janice Weinman

Interfaith Alliance (1994): 2101 L St. NW, Ste. 400, Washington, DC 20037; (202) 466-0567; www.interfaithalliance.org; Exec. Dir., Rabbi Jack Moline

Islamic Society of North America: 6555 S. County Rd. 750 East, Plainfield, IN 46168; (317) 839-8157; www.isna.net; Pres., Azhar Azeez

Jehovah's Witnesses (1931): 25 Columbia Heights, Brooklyn, NY 11201; (718) 560-5000; www.jw.org

Jewish Congress, American (1918): 260 Madison Ave., 2nd Fl., New York, NY 10016; (212) 879-4500; www.ajcongress. org; Pres., Jack Rosen

Jewish Reconstructionist Communities (2012): 1299 Church Rd., Wyncote, PA 19095; (215) 576-0800; www.jewishrecon. org; Pres., Rabbi Deborah Waxman

Jewish Women, Natl. Council of (1893): 475 Riverside Dr., Ste. 1901, New York, NY 10115; (212) 645-4048; www.ncjw.org; Pres., Debbie Hoffmann

Lutheran Church—Missouri Synod (1847): 1333 S. Kirkwood Rd., St. Louis, MO 63122; (800) 248-1930; www.lcms.org; Pres., Rev. Dr. Matthew C. Harrison

Mennonite Church USA (2001): 718 N. Main St., Newton, KS 67114; (316) 283-5100; www.mennoniteusa.org; Exec. Dir., Ervin Stutzman

Moravian Church in North America (1735): www.moravian.org; *Northern Prov.*: 1021 Center St., P.O. Box 1245, Bethlehem, PA 18016; (610) 867-7566; Pres., Rev. Dr. Betsy Miller; *Southern Prov.*: 459 S. Church St., Winston-Salem, NC 27101; (336) 725-5811; Pres., Rev. David Guthrie

North American Shia Ithnasheri Muslim Communities, Org. of (1986): P.O. Box 29691, Minneapolis, MN 55429; (905) 763-7512; www.nasimco.org; Pres., Mohamed A. Dewji

Orthodox Union (1898): 11 Broadway, New York, NY 10004; (212) 563-4000; www. ou.org; Exec. Vice Pres., Allen Fagin

Pentecostal Assemblies of the World, Inc. (1906): 3939 N. Meadows Dr., Indianapolis, IN 46205; (317) 547-9541; www.pawinc.org; Presiding Bishop, Charles H. Ellis, III

Presbyterian Church (U.S.A.) (1983): 100 Witherspoon St., Louisville, KY 40202;

(800) 728-7228; www.pcusa.org; Interim Exec. Dir., Luis Antonio De La Rosa

Progressive Natl. Baptist Convention, Inc. (1961): 601 50th St. NE, Washington, DC 20019; (202) 396-0558; www.pnbc.org; Pres., Dr. James C. Perkins

Rabbis, Central Conference of American (1889): 355 Lexington Ave., New York, NY 10017; (212) 972-3636; www.ccarnet.org; Pres., Richard A. Block

Reform Judaism, Union for (1873): 633 3rd Ave., New York, NY 10017; (212) 650-4000; www.urj.org; Pres., Rabbi Rick Jacobs

Secular Humanism, Council for (1980): P.O. Box 664, Amherst, NY 14226; (716) 636-7571; www.secularhumanism.org; Pres. and CEO, Ronald A. Lindsay

Separation of Church and State, Americans United for (1947): 1901 L St. NW, Ste. 400, Washington, DC 20036; (202) 466-3234; www.au.org; Exec. Dir., Rev. Barry W. Lynn

Seventh-day Adventist Church (1863): 12501 Old Columbia Pike, Silver Spring, MD 20904; (301) 680-6000; www.adventist. org; Pres., Ted N. C. Wilson

Seventh Day Baptist (1802): P.O. Box 1678, Janesville, WI 53547; (608) 752-5055; www.seventhdaybaptist.org; Pres., Rev. Dale Thorngate

Unitarian Universalist Assn. of Congregations (1961): 24 Farnsworth St., Boston, MA 02210; (617) 742-2100; www.uua.org; Pres., Rev. Peter Morales

United Church of Christ (1957): 700 Prospect Ave., Cleveland, OH 44115; (216) 736-2100; www.ucc.org; Pres., Rev. John C. Dorhauer

United Methodist Church (1968): 100 Maryland Ave. NE, Washington, DC 20002; (202) 488-5600; www.umc.org

United Pentecostal Church Intl. (1945): 8855 Dunn Rd., Hazelwood, MO 63042; (314) 837-7300; www.upci.org; Gen. Supt., David K. Bernard

Wesleyan Church (1843): 13300 Olio Rd., Fishers, IN 46037; (317) 774-7900; www. wesleyan.org; Gen. Supt., Rev. Dr. Wayne Schmidt

Businesses and Corporations

Source: World Almanac research

Listed below are major corporations offering products and services to U.S. consumers, as of July 2016. Alphabetization is by first key word or founder last name. Listings generally include examples of products offered.

Company name (NYSE/Nasdaq symbol, if traded on those markets): Address; Telephone number; Website; Top executive; Business, products, or services.

Abbott Laboratories (ABT): 100 Abbott Park Rd., Abbott Park, IL 60064; (224) 667-6100; www.abbott.com; Miles D. White; develops, mfr. pharmaceutical, nutritional, diagnostic prods. Acquired CFR Pharmaceuticals, 9/26/2014; agreed to acquire medical device company St. Jude Medical, 4/28/2016.

AbbVie (ABBV): 1 N. Waukegan Rd., N. Chicago, IL 60064; (847) 932-7900; www.abbvie.com; Richard A. Gonzalez; pharmaceuticals; spun off from Abbott Laboratories, 1/1/2013. Acquired Pharmacyclics, 5/26/2015.

ABC: see Walt Disney Co.

Accenture Inc. (ACN): 161 N. Clark St., Chicago, IL 60601; (312) 737-8842; www.accenture.com; Pierre Nanterme; management consulting. Acquired Dutch digital serv. co. MOBGEN, 7/19/2016.

Activision Blizzard Inc. (ATVI): 3100 Ocean Park Blvd., Santa Monica, CA 90405; (310) 255-2000; www.activision blizzard.com; Bobby Kotick; video game publisher (*World of Warcraft, Call of Duty, Candy Crush Saga*).

adidas Group: Adi-Dassler-Strasse 1, D-91074 Herzogenaurach, Germany; +49 (0) 9132-84-0; www.adidas-group.com; Herbert Hainer; apparel and accessories mfr. (Reebok, TaylorMade Golf).

Advance Publications, Inc.: 950 W. Fingerboard Rd., Staten Island, NY, 10305; (718) 981-1234; www.advance.net;

Steven Newhouse; communications, newspaper and magazine publisher (*Parade*; Condé Nast subsids.: *New Yorker, Vanity Fair, Vogue*).

Aetna, Inc. (AET): 151 Farmington Ave., Hartford, CT 06156; (860) 273-0123; www. aetna.com; Mark T. Bertolini; health care, employee benefits. Announced plans to acquire Humana, 7/3/2015.

Aflac, Inc. (AFL): 1932 Wynnton Rd., Columbus, GA 31999; (706) 596-3493; www.aflac.com; Daniel P. Amos; supplemental health and life insurance.

Alaska Air Group, Inc. (ALK): 19300 International Blvd., Seattle, WA 98188; (206) 433-3200; www.alaskaair.com; Bradley D. Tilden; airline carriers (Alaska Airlines, Horizon Air). Announced plans to acquire Virgin America airline, 4/4/2016.

Alcoa Inc. (AA): 201 Isabella St., Pittsburgh, PA 15212; (412) 553-4545; www. alcoa.com; Klaus Kleinfeld; prod., mfr. of aluminum, aluminum prods. (aerospace, automotive, industrial materials and components). Acquired RTI Intl. Metals, 7/23/2015.

Alibaba Group (BABA): 969 West Wen Yi Road, Yu Hang District, Hangzhou 311121, China; +86 571-8502-2088; www. alibaba.com; Jack Yun; online shopping, logistics, marketing; data mgmt.; financial serv. Record-high U.S. IPO, 9/19/2014.

Allstate Corp. (ALL): 2775 Sanders Rd., Northbrook, IL 60062; (847) 402-5000;

www.allstate.com; Thomas J. Wilson; personal property and casualty insurance; financial services.

Alphabet Inc. (GOOG): 1600 Amphitheatre Pkwy., Mountain View, CA 94043; (650) 253-0000; www.abc.xyz; Larry Page; Google and other internet-related prods. and services (leading search engine, ad sales; YouTube). Acquired Nest Labs, Inc., 2/7/2014. Sold Motorola Mobility to Lenovo, 10/30/2014. Reorganized corp. as Alphabet, 10/2/2015.

Altice USA: 1111 Stewart Ave., Bethpage, NY 11714; (516) 803-2300; www.altice. net; Dexter Goei; telecom., internet, cable provider. Formed 6/21/2016 through Dutch parent co. buyout of Cablevision Systems Corp. and acquisition of Suddenlink, 12/21/2015.

Altria Group, Inc. (MO): 6601 W. Broad St., Richmond, VA 23230; (804) 484-8897; www.altria.com; Martin J. Barrington; tobacco co. (Marlboro, Merit, Parliament, Virginia Slims). (Altria spun off Philip Morris's intl. operations in 2008 but owns Philip Morris brands in U.S.)

Amazon.com, Inc. (AMZN): 440 Terry Ave. N., Seattle, WA 98109; (206) 266-1000; www.amazon.com; Jeffrey P. Bezos; online retailer of books, music, other consumer and household prods. Acquired game platform Twitch, 9/25/2014; video firm Elemental Technologies, 10/19/2015.

American Airlines Group, Inc. (AAL): 4333 Amon Carter Blvd., Ft. Worth, TX 76155; (817) 963-1234; www.aa.com; Doug Parker; airlines (American Airlines, American Eagle). Formed from merger of American Airlines and US Airways, 12/9/2013.

American Electric Power Co., Inc. (AEP): 1 Riverside Plz., Columbus, OH 43215; (614) 716-1000; www.aep.com; Nicholas K. Akins; public utilities.

American Express Co. (AXP): World Financial Ctr., 200 Vesey St., 50th Fl., NY, NY 10285; (212) 640-2000; www.american express.com; Kenneth I. Chenault; charge and credit cards, travel-related services.

American Greetings Corp.: 1 American Rd., Cleveland, OH 44144; (216) 252-7300; www.americangreetings.com; Morry Weiss; greeting cards, stationery, party goods, gift items. Acquired by Weiss Family, 8/7/2013.

American Intl. Group, Inc. (AIG): 180 Maiden Ln., NY, NY 10038; (212) 770-7000; www.aigcorporate.com; Peter D. Hancock; insurance, financial services. AIG received $182 bil in govt. bailouts, 2008.

AmerisourceBergen (ABC): 1300 Morris Dr., Chesterbrook, PA, 19087; (610) 727-7000; www.amerisourcebergen.com; Steven H. Collis; distrib. of generic and brand-name pharmaceuticals.

Amgen, Inc. (AMGN): 1 Amgen Center Dr., Thousand Oaks, CA 91320; (805) 447-1000; www.amgen.com; Robert A. Bradway; biopharmaceuticals.

Anheuser-Busch InBev (BUD): Brouwerij-plein 1, 3000 Leuven, Belgium; +32 (16) 276111; www.ab-inbev.com; Carlos Brito; brewer (Budweiser, Bud Light, Michelob, Corona, Stella Artois), soft drinks. Acquired Oriental Brewery, 3/31/2014. Agreed on terms to acquire brewing competitor SAB-Miller, 11/15/2015.

Anthem, Inc. (ANTM): 120 Monument Cir., Indianapolis, IN 46204; (317) 488-6000; www.anthem.com; Joseph R. Swedish; health insurance co. Fmr. WellPoint, Inc.; renamed 12/3/2014. Agreed to acquire Cigna, 7/24/2015.

Apple Inc. (AAPL): 1 Infinite Loop, Cupertino, CA 95014; (408) 996-1010; www.apple.com; Tim Cook; mfr. of computers (Mac), digital media devices (iPod, iPhone, iPad) and distrib. (iTunes store, Apple Music). Acquired Beats Music, Beats Electronics, 8/1/2014; Faceshift, 11/2015.

ARAMARK Corp. (ARMK): 1101 Market St., Philadelphia, PA 19107; (215) 238-3000; www.aramark.com; Eric J. Foss; food/support services to institutions and facilities, uniforms and career apparel. IPO, 12/12/2013.

ArcelorMittal USA, Inc.: 1 South Dearborn, Chicago, IL 60603; (312) 899-3440; www.usaarcelormittal.com; John L. Brett; steel; U.S. subsidiary of Arcelor Mittal, based in Luxembourg.

Archer Daniels Midland Co. (ADM): 77 W. Wacker Dr., Ste. 4600, Chicago, IL 60601; (312) 634-8100; www.adm.com; Juan R. Luciano; agricultural commodities and prods. Agreed to acquire Eatem Foods Co., 10/1/2015. Sold global cocoa business to Olam International Ltd., 10/16/2015.

Armstrong World Industries, Inc. (AWI): 2500 Columbia Ave., P.O. Box 3001, Lancaster, PA 17604; (717) 397-0611; www.armstrong.com; Victor D. Grizzle; mfr. of flooring, ceiling prods., cabinets.

AT&T Inc. (T): 208 S. Akard St., Dallas, TX 75202; (210) 821-4105; www.att.com; Randall L. Stephenson; telecommunications, global information management. Acquired Mexican wireless provider Iusacell, 1/16/2015; DirecTV, 7/24/2015; Quickplay Media, 6/28/2016.

Automatic Data Processing, Inc. (ADP): 1 ADP Blvd., Roseland, NJ 07068; (973) 974-5000; www.adp.com; Carlos A. Rodriguez; payroll and tax processing serv.

AutoNation, Inc. (AN): 200 SW 1st Ave., Ste. 1600, Ft. Lauderdale, FL 33301; (954) 769-6000; www.autonation.com; Mike Jackson; auto retailer; new and used vehicles; auto parts, maintenance, and repair; auto finance and insurance.

Avon Products, Inc. (AVP): 777 Third Ave., NY, NY 10017; (212) 282-7000; www.avon.com; Sheri S. McCoy; cosmetics, fragrances, skin and personal care items; fashion.

Bank of America Corp. (BAC): 100 N. Tryon St., Charlotte, NC 28255; (704) 386-5681; www.bankofamerica.com; Brian T. Moynihan; banking and financial services.

Barnes & Noble, Inc. (BKS): 122 Fifth Ave., NY, NY 10011; (212) 633-3300; www.barnesandnobleinc.com; Leonard S. Riggio; leading U.S. bookseller (retail and college), publisher (Sterling Pub. Co.). Spun off college bookstores business Barnes & Noble Education, 8/3/2015.

Baxter International Inc. (BAX): 1 Baxter Pkwy., Deerfield, IL 60015; (224) 948-2000; www.baxter.com; José Almeida; mfr. of health care prods. Spun off pharmaceutical business into Baxalta, 7/1/2015.

Bear Stearns Cos. Inc.: see JPMorgan Chase & Co.

Becton, Dickinson & Co. (BDX): 1 Becton Dr., Franklin Lakes, NJ 07417; (201) 847-6800; www.bd.com; Vincent A. Forlenza; medical, laboratory, diagnostic prods. Acquired med. tech. firm Alverix, Inc., 1/7/2014.

Berkshire Hathaway Inc. (BRK.A): 3555 Farnam St., Ste. 1440, Omaha, NE 68131; (402) 346-1400; www.berkshirehathaway.com; Warren E. Buffett; diversified holdings incl. insurance (GEICO), building materials (Benjamin Moore & Co., Shaw), apparel (Fruit of the Loom), food (Dairy Queen). Aquired Duracell from Procter & Gamble, 2/29/2016; Bought Precision Castparts, 1/29/2016.

Bertelsmann AG: Carl-Bertelsmann-Str. 270, 33311 Gütersloh, Germany; +49 (0) 5241-80-62321; www.bertelsmann.de; Thomas Rabe; intl. media corp., trade book publisher (Penguin Random House: Knopf, Doubleday).

Best Buy Co., Inc. (BBY): 7601 Penn Ave. S., Richfield, MN 55423; (612) 291-1000; www.bestbuy.com; Hubert Joly; retailer of software, appliances, cellular phones, consumer electronics.

Blackstone Group LP, The (BX): 345 Park Ave., NY, NY 10154; (212) 583-5000; www.blackstone.com; Stephen A. Schwarzman; asset mgmt., financial services.

Boeing Co. (BA): 100 N. Riverside, Chicago, IL 60606; (312) 544-2000; Dennis A. Muilenburg; world's leading aerospace co., mfr. of commercial jet and military aircraft; one of the largest U.S. defense contractors.

Brink's Co., The (BCO): 1801 Bayberry Ct., P.O. Box 18100, Richmond, VA 23226; (804) 289-9600; www.brinkscompany.com; Doug A. Pertz; security (armored transport, money processing, trans. of valuables).

Bristol-Myers Squibb Co. (BMY): 345 Park Ave., NY, NY 10154; (212) 546-4000; www.bms.com; Giovanni Caforio; development, mfr., and sale of pharmaceuticals (Plavix, Eliquis, Atripla). Acquired Cormorant Pharmaceuticals, 7/5/2016.

Brown-Forman Corp. (BF.B): 850 Dixie Hwy., Louisville, KY 40210; (502) 585-1100; www.brown-forman.com; Paul C. Varga; distilled spirits (Jack Daniel's, Finlandia), wine and champagne (Sonoma-Cutrer, Korbel). Sold Southern Comfort and Tuaca brands to Sazerac, 3/1/2016.

Brunswick Corp. (BC): 1 N. Field Ct., Lake Forest, IL 60045; (847) 735-4700; www.brunswick.com; Mark D. Schwabero; leisure and recreation prods., incl. marine engines and boats; billiards, bowling, and fitness equip. bowling centers.

Burger King: see Restaurant Brands Intl.

Caesars Entertainment Corp. (CZR): One Caesars Palace Dr., Las Vegas, NV 89109; (702) 407-6000; www.caesars.com; Mark Frissora; casinos; gambling services (Caesars, Harrah's, Horseshoe, World Series of Poker). Operating unit filed for Ch. 11 reorganization, 1/15/2015.

Campbell Soup Co. (CPB): One Campbell Pl., Camden, NJ 08103; (856) 342-4800; www.campbellsoupcompany.com; Denise Morrison; soup mfr.; sauces (Pace, Prego), V8 juice, Pepperidge Farm prods. Acquired Garden Fresh Gourmet, 6/29/2015.

Capital One Financial Corporation (COF): 1680 Capital One Dr., McLean, VA 22102; (703) 720-1000; www.capitalone.com; Richard D. Fairbank; financial services.

Cardinal Health, Inc. (CAH): 7000 Cardinal Pl., Dublin, OH 43017; (614) 757-5000; www.cardinalhealth.com; George S. Barrett; pharmaceutical and med. equip. dist. co. Acquired med. device mfr. AccessClosure, 5/12/2014.

Carlyle Group, The (CG): 1001 Pennsylvania Ave. NW, Washington, DC 20004; (202) 729-5399; www.carlyle.com; William E. Conway Jr.; private equity group.

Caterpillar Inc. (CAT): 501 SW Jefferson Ave., Peoria, IL 61630; (309) 675-2337; www.caterpillar.com; Douglas R. Oberhelman; mfr. of construction and mining equip.

CBRE Group, Inc. (CBG): 400 S. Hope St., 25th Fl., Los Angeles, CA 90071; (213) 613-3333; www.cbre.com; Bob Sulentic; commercial real estate.

CBS Corp. (CBS): 51 W. 52nd St., NY, NY 10019; (212) 975-4321; www.cbs corporation.com; Leslie Moonves; TV networks (CBS, Showtime); TV distribution; radio stations; book publishing (Simon & Schuster).

CenturyLink, Inc. (CTL): 100 CenturyLink Dr., Monroe, LA 71203; (318) 388-9000; www.centurylink.com; Glen F. Post III; telecommunications provider.

Charter Communications, Inc. (CHTR): 400 Atlantic St., Stamford, CT 06901; (203) 905-7801; www.charter.com; Tom Rutledge; cable TV provider. Acquired Time Warner Cable and Bright House Networks, 5/18/2016.

Chevron Corp. (CVX): 6001 Bollinger Canyon Rd., San Ramon, CA 94583; (925) 842-1000; www.chevron.com; John S. Watson; integrated energy co.

Chiquita Brands Intl., Inc.: 550 S. Caldwell St., Charlotte, NC 28202; (980) 636-5000; www.chiquita.com; Brian W. Kocher; fruits and vegetables. Acquired by Cutrale-Safra, 1/6/2015.

CHS, Inc. (CHSCP): 5500 Cenex Dr., Inver Grove Heights, MN 55077; (651) 355-6000; www.chsinc.com; Carl Casale; grain marketing, oil refining, and pipeline operations.

Chubb Ltd. (CB): 15 Mountain View Rd., Warren, NJ 07059; (908) 903-2000; www.chubb.com; Evan Greenberg; property/casualty insurance. ACE Limited acquired The Chubb Corporation, 1/14/16.

Church & Dwight Co., Inc. (CHD): Princeton South Corporate Center, 500 Charles Ewing Blvd., Ewing, NJ 08628; (800) 524-1328; www.churchdwight.com; Matthew T. Farrell; top world producer of sodium bicarbonate (ARM & HAMMER baking soda); household (OxiClean) and personal care prods. (Arrid, Trojan, First Response).

Cigna Corp. (CI): 900 Cottage Grove Rd., Bloomfield, CT 06002; (860) 226-6000; www.cigna.com; David M. Cordani; insurance provider. Acquisition by Anthem announced, 7/24/2015 .

Cintas Corp. (CTAS): 6800 Cintas Blvd., Cincinnati, OH 45262; (513) 459-1200; www.cintas.com; Scott D. Farmer; uniform supplier.

Cisco Systems, Inc. (CSCO): 170 W. Tasman Dr., San Jose, CA 95134; (408) 526-4000; www.cisco.com; Chuck Robbins; networking and communication prods.

Citigroup, Inc. (C): 388 Greenwich St. Park Ave., NY, NY 10013; (212) 559-1000; www.citigroup.com; Michael L. Corbat; diversified financial services.

Clorox Co. (CLX): 1221 Broadway, Oakland, CA 94612; (510) 271-7000; www.clorox. com; Benno Dorer; consumer prods. (Clorox, Formula 409, Pine-Sol, S.O.S., Tilex; Scoop Away, Fresh Step cat litters; Kingsford charcoal; Hidden Valley dressing; Glad plastic bags; Brita water systems; Burt's Bees personal care prods.). Acquired Renew Life probiotics, 5/3/2016.

Coca-Cola Co. (KO): 1 Coca-Cola Plz., Atlanta, GA 30313; (404) 676-2121; www. coca-cola.com; Muhtar Kent; beverages (Coca-Cola, Sprite, DASANI water), juice prods. (Minute Maid).

Colgate-Palmolive Co. (CL): 300 Park Ave., NY, NY 10022; (212) 310-2000; www. colgate.com; Ian M. Cook; soap (Irish Spring), detergent (Palmolive), household cleansers (Ajax), toothpaste (Colgate, Tom's of Maine), pet food (Hill's Science Diet).

Comcast Corp. (CMCSA): 1701 JFK Blvd., Philadelphia, PA 19103; (215) 286-1700; www.comcast.com; Brian L. Roberts; cable provider; broadband media services; programming (E!, NBC, Bravo, USA, Telemundo). Acquired DreamWorks Animation, 8/22/2016.

Computer Sciences Corp. (CSC): 3170 Fairview Park Dr., Falls Church, VA 22042; (703) 876-1000; www.csc.com; Mike Lawrie; technology services.

ConAgra Foods, Inc. (CAG): 222 W. Merchandise Mart Plaza, Ste. 1300, Chicago, IL 60654; (312) 549-5000; www.conagrafoods.com; Sean Connolly; food processor (Chef Boyardee, Healthy Choice frozen dinners, Egg Beaters, Reddi-wip); food service supplier.

ConocoPhillips Co. (COP): 600 N. Dairy Ashford, P.O. Box 2197, Houston, TX 77252; (281) 293-1000; www.conoco phillips.com; Ryan M. Lance; oil and gas exploration and prod. co. Spun off refining and marketing segment, 5/1/2012, as Phillips 66.

Consolidated Edison, Inc. (ED): 100 Summit Lake Dr., Valhalla, NY 10595; (914) 286-7000; www.conedison.com; John McAvoy; electric, natural gas utilities.

Continental Airlines, Inc.: see United Continental Holdings, Inc.

Corning Inc. (GLW): 1 Riverfront Plz., Corning, NY 14831; (607) 974-9000; www. corning.com; Wendell P. Weeks; mfr. of telecommunications, specialty equip., fiber optics. Acquired Samsung's fiber-optics business, 3/31/2015.

Costco Wholesale Corp. (COST): 999 Lake Dr., Issaquah, WA 98027; (425) 313-8100; www.costco.com; W. Craig Jelinek; wholesale warehouse stores.

Countrywide Financial: see Bank of America Corp.

Crown Holdings, Inc. (CCK): 1 Crown Way, Philadelphia, PA 19154; (215) 698-5100; www.crowncork.com; Timothy J. Donahue; leading producer of packaging prods. Acquired Mivisa Envases, 4/23/2014; Empaque, 2/18/2015.

CSX Corp. (CSX): 500 Water St., 15th Fl., Jacksonville, FL 32202; (904) 359-3200; www.csx.com; Michael J. Ward; rail freight transport.

CVS Health (CVS): 1 CVS Dr., Woonsocket, RI 02895; (401) 765-1500; www.cvs.com; Larry J. Merlo; retail drugstores. Fmr. CVS Caremark Corp.; ended tobacco sales and renamed co., 9/3/2014. Acquired Target's pharmacy/clinic businesses, 12/16/2015.

Dana Holding Corp. (DAN): 3939 Technology Dr., Maumee, OH 43537; (419) 887-3000; www.dana.com; James Kamsickas; truck and auto parts, supplies.

Darden Restaurants, Inc. (DRI): 1000 Darden Center Dr., Orlando, FL 32837; (407) 245-4000; www.darden.com; Eugene Lee Jr.; casual-dining restaurants (Olive Garden, LongHorn Steakhouse). Sold Red Lobster, 7/28/2014.

Dean Foods Co. (DF): 2711 N. Haskell Ave., Ste. 3400, Dallas, TX 75204; (214) 303-3400; www.deanfoods.com; Greg A. Tanner; milk and specialty dairy prods.

(Land O' Lakes, Meadow Land). Acquired Friendly's ice cream prods., 6/20/2016.

Deere & Co. (DE): One John Deere Pl., Moline, IL 61265; (309) 765-8000; www.deere.com; Samuel R. Allen; mfr. of farm equip., industrial equip., lawn and garden tractors.

Dell Inc.: 1 Dell Way, Round Rock, TX 78682; (512) 338-4400; www.dell.com; Michael S. Dell; laptop and desktop computers, network accessories, peripherals, tablets, smartphones. Acquired by founder Michael Dell and Silver Lake Partners, 10/29/2013. Bought data mining co. StatSoft, 3/24/2014. Announced plans to acquire EMC Corp for $67 bil, 10/12/2015; agreed to sell IT services subsidiary Perot Systems to NTT Data, 3/28/2016.

Delta Air Lines, Inc. (DAL): 1030 Delta Blvd., Atlanta, GA 30354; (404) 715-2600; www.delta.com; Ed Bastian; air transportation.

Dillard's, Inc. (DDS): 1600 Cantrell Rd., Little Rock, AR 72201; (501) 376-5200; www.dillards.com; William Dillard II; dept. store chain.

Dish Network Corp. (DISH): 9601 S. Meridian Blvd., Englewood, CO 80112; (303) 723-1000; www.dish.com; Charlie Ergen; satellite media services.

Walt Disney Co., The (DIS): 500 S. Buena Vista St., Burbank, CA 91521; (818) 560-1000; disney.go.com; Robert A. Iger; motion pictures (Lucasfilm, Touchstone, Pixar); TV (ABC, ESPN) and radio; publishing; theme parks (Walt Disney World, Disneyland) and resorts. Acquired Maker Studios, 3/24/2014.

Doctor's Associates Inc.: 325 Bic Dr., Milford, CT 06461; (203) 877-4281; www. subway.com; Suzanne Greco; restaurants (Subway).

Dole Food Co., Inc.: One Dole Dr., Westlake Village, CA 91362; (818) 879-6600; www.dole.com; David Murdock; food prods., fresh fruits, vegetables.

Dollar Tree (DLTR): 500 Volvo Pkwy., Chesapeake, VA 23320; (757) 321-5000; www.dollartree.com; Bob Sasser; discount retailer. Acquired Family Dollar, 7/6/2015.

R. R. Donnelley & Sons Co. (RRD): 35 W. Wacker Dr., Chicago, IL 60601; (312) 326-8000; www.rrdonnelley.com; Thomas J. Quinlan III; commercial printing; photos/graphics, translation; printer of *The World Almanac*. Acquired Courier Corp., 6/8/2015.

Dow Chemical Co. (DOW): 2030 Dow Ctr., Midland, MI 48674; (989) 636-1000; www. dow.com; Andrew N. Liveris; chemicals, plastics. Sold most of chlorine assets to Olin Corp., 10/5/2015. Agreed to $130-bil merger with DuPont, 12/11/2015.

Dow Jones & Co., Inc.: see News Corp.

Dr Pepper Snapple Group, Inc. (DPS): 5301 Legacy Dr., Plano, TX 75024; (972) 673-7000; www.drpeppersnapplegroup. com; Larry D. Young; bottler and distrib. of nonalcoholic beverages (Dr Pepper, Hawaiian Punch, 7UP, Snapple, Mott's).

Duke Energy Corp. (DUK): 550 S. Tryon St., Charlotte, NC 28202; (980) 373-8649; www.duke-energy.com; Lynn J. Good; utilities, fiber optic networks.

Dun & Bradstreet Corp. (DNB): 103 JFK Pkwy., Short Hills, NJ 07078; (973) 921-5500; www.dnb.com; Bob Carrigan; business information, research.

Dupont (E. I. du Pont de Nemours & Co.) (DD): 1007 Market St., Wilmington, DE 19898; (302) 774-1000; www.dupont.com; Edward D. Breen; petroleum, consumer prods. Spun off Chemours, 7/1/2015. Agreed to $130-bil merger with Dow Chemical Co., 12/11/2015.

Eastman Kodak Co. (KODK): 343 State St., Rochester, NY 14650; (585) 724-4000; www.kodak.com; Jeffrey J. Clarke; imaging technology and services. Emerged from Chap. 11 reorganization, 9/3/2013; relisted on NYSE, 11/1/2013.

Eaton Corp. (ETN): Eaton Ctr., 1111 Superior Ave., Cleveland, OH 44114; (216) 523-5000; www.eaton.com; Craig Arnold; mfr. vehicle components, controls.

eBay Inc. (EBAY): 2065 Hamilton Ave., San Jose, CA 95125; (408) 376-7400; www. ebay.com; Devin N. Wenig; e-commerce (StubHub). Spun off PayPal, 7/17/2015.

Edison Intl. (EIX): 2244 Walnut Grove Ave., Rosemead, CA 91770; (626) 302-2222; www.edison.com; Pedro Pizarro.; electric utilities.

Electronic Arts Inc. (EA): 209 Redwood Shores Pkwy., Redwood City, CA 94065; (650) 628-1500; www.ea.com; Andrew Wilson; leading U.S. video game publisher (Madden NFL, Battlefield, The Sims, UFC).

Electronic Data Systems: see Hewlett-Packard Co.

Eli Lilly and Co. (LLY): Lilly Corporate Center, Indianapolis, IN 46285; (317) 276-2000; www.lilly.com; John C. Lechleiter; pharmaceutical research, development, and manufacturing (Prozac, Strattera, Cialis). Acquired Novartis Animal Health, 1/1/2015.

EMC Corp. (EMC): 176 South St., Hopkinton, MA 01748; (508) 435-1000; www.emc. com; Joseph M. Tucci; data storage/protection. Announced plans to merge with Dell, 10/12/2015.

Emerson Electric Co. (EMR): 8000 W. Florissant Ave., St. Louis, MO 63136; (314) 553-2000; www.emerson.com; David N. Farr; electrical, electronics prods. and systems.

Energizer Holdings, Inc. (ENR): 533 Maryville Univ. Dr., St. Louis, MO 63141; (314) 985-2000; www.energizer.com; Alan Hoskins; batteries, flashlights, personal care prods.

Enterprise Products Partners L.P. (EPD): 1100 Louisiana St., 10th Fl., Houston, TX 77002; (713) 381-6500; www.enterprise products.com; A.J. Teague; oil processing/transport and waterborne freight.

Estée Lauder Cos. Inc. (EL): 767 Fifth Ave., NY, NY 10153; (212) 572-4200; www. elcompanies.com; Fabrizio Freda; cosmetics (Clinique, Bobbi Brown), fragrance, skin care prods. Acquired GLAMGLOW, 1/16/2015.

Exelon Corp. (EXC): 10 S. Dearborn St., 48th Fl., Chicago, IL 60680; (800) 483-3220; www.exeloncorp.com; Christopher M. Crane; electricity generation/distrib.; natural gas. Acquired Pepco Holdings, 3/23/2016.

Express Scripts Holding Co. (ESRX): 1 Express Way, St. Louis, MO 63121; (314) 996-0900; www.express-scripts.com; Tim Wentworth; U.S. pharmacy benefits mgmt. co.

ExxonMobil Corp. (XOM): 5959 Las Colinas Blvd., Irving, TX 75039; (972) 444-1000; www.exxonmobil.com; Rex W. Tillerson; integrated energy, oil co.

Facebook, Inc. (FB): 1 Hacker Way, Menlo Park, CA 94025; (650) 308-7300; www. facebook.com; Mark Zuckerberg; social networking platforms, services. Acquired Little Eye Labs, 1/7/2014; WhatsApp, 2/19/2014; Oculus VR, 7/21/2014.

Federal Home Loan Mortgage Corp. (Freddie Mac): 8200 Jones Branch Dr., McLean, VA 22102; (703) 903-2000; www.freddiemac.com; Donald H. Layton; residential mortgage provider. Under U.S. govt. mgmt. since 9/7/2008.

Federal Natl. Mortgage Assn. (Fannie Mae): 3900 Wisconsin Ave. NW, Washington, DC 20016; (202) 752-7000; www. fanniemae.com; Timothy J. Mayopoulos; provider of residential mortgage funds. Under U.S. govt. mgmt. since 9/7/2008.

FedEx Corp. (FDX): 942 S. Shady Grove Rd., Memphis, TN 38120; (901) 818-7500; www.fedex.com; Frederick W. Smith; delivery services. Acquired TNT Express, 5/25/2016.

First Data Corp.: 5565 Glenridge Connector NE, Ste. 2000, Atlanta, GA 30342; (404) 890-2000; www.firstdata.com; Frank Bisignano; financial transaction processing.

FirstEnergy Corp. (FE): 76 S. Main St., Akron, OH 44308; (800) 736-3402; www.firstenergycorp.com; Charles E. Jones; public electricity supplier.

Fluor Corp. (FLR): 6700 Las Colinas Blvd., Irving, TX 75039; (469) 398-7000; www.fluor.com; David T. Seaton; international engineering and construction co.

Foot Locker, Inc. (FL): 330 W. 34th St., NY, NY 10001; (212) 720-3700; www.foot locker-inc.com; Richard A. Johnson; retail athletic stores (Footaction, Foot Locker, Champs Sports).

Ford Motor Co. (F): 1 American Rd., Dearborn, MI 48126; (313) 322-3000; www.ford.com; William C. Ford Jr.; auto mfr.; motor vehicle sales (Ford, Lincoln); auto financing (Ford Motor Credit).

Fox: see News Corp. or 21st Century Fox.

Gannett Co., Inc. (GCI): 7950 Jones Branch Dr., McLean, VA 22107; (703) 854-6000; www.gannett.com; Robert Dickey; newspaper publisher (*USA Today*). Original Gannett Co., spun off network and cable TV and digital media divisions as TEGNA, Inc., 6/29/2015, newspapers as new entity retaining name.

Gap Inc. (GPS): 2 Folsom St., San Francisco, CA 94105; (650) 952-4400; www.gapinc.com; Art Peck; casual apparel retailer (Gap, Banana Republic, Old Navy).

General Dynamics Corp. (GD): 2941 Fairview Park Dr., Ste. 100, Falls Church, VA 22042; (703) 876-3000; www.general dynamics.com; Phebe N. Novakovic; defense contractor: aerospace, combat systems, marine systems, computing devices.

General Electric Co. (GE): 3135 Easton Tpke., Fairfield, CT 06828; (203) 373-2211; www.ge.com; Jeffrey Immelt; electrical, electronic equip., financial services, radio and TV broadcasting, aircraft engines, power generation. Acquired power businesses of France's Alstom, 11/2/2015. Sold appliances business to China's Haier Group, 6/6/2016.

General Mills, Inc. (GIS): One General Mills Blvd., Minneapolis, MN 55426; (763) 764-7600; www.generalmills.com; Kendall J. Powell; food mfr. (Betty Crocker, Bisquick, Cheerios, Chex, Häagen-Dazs, Pillsbury, Progresso, Total, Wheaties, Yoplait). Acquired Annie's Homegrown, 10/21/2014. Sold vegetable brands Green Giant and LeSeur to B&G Foods, 11/2/2015.

General Motors Co. (GM): 300 Renaissance Ctr., Detroit, MI 48265; (313) 556-5000; www.gm.com; Mary T. Barra; auto mfr. (Chevrolet, Cadillac, Buick, GMC); auto financing (GM Financial); vehicle security (OnStar). General Motors Corp. filed for Chap. 11 reorganization, 6/1/2009; sold profitable components to a new, smaller co. called General Motors Co., 7/10/2009.

Genuine Parts Co. (GPC): 2999 Circle 75 Pkwy., Atlanta, GA 30339; (678) 934-5000; www.genpt.com; Thomas C. Gallagher; distrib. of auto (NAPA), industrial replacement parts.

Gilead Sciences, Inc., (GILD): 333 Lakeside Dr., Foster City, CA 94404; (650) 574-3000; www.gilead.com; John F. Milligan, PhD; biopharmaceuticals.

Goldman Sachs Group, Inc. (GS): 200 West St., 29th Fl., NY, NY 10282; (212) 902-1000; www.goldmansachs.com; Lloyd Blankfein; investment banking, asset mgmt., securities services.

Goodyear Tire & Rubber Co. (GT): 200 Innovation Way, Akron, OH 44316; (330) 796-2121; www.goodyear.com; Richard J. Kramer; tires and other auto prods.

Google, Inc.: see Alphabet Inc.

Graham Holdings Co. (GHC): 1300 N. 17th St. NW, Arlington, VA 22209; (703) 345-6300; www.ghco.com; Timothy O'Shaughnessy; media (newspapers, Slate.com, TV), education (Kaplan), home health care. Fmr. Washington Post. Co.; renamed after 2013 sale of newspaper.

Great Atlantic & Pacific Tea Co., Inc.: 2 Paragon Dr., Montvale, NJ 07645; (201) 573-9700; www.aptea.com; Paul Hertz; supermarkets (A&P, Food Basics, Food Emporium, Super Fresh, Waldbaum's, Pathmark).

Halliburton Co. (HAL): 3000 N. Sam Houston Pkwy. E., Houston, TX 77032; (281) 871-4000; www.halliburton.com; David J. Lesar; oil field mgmt., energy services.

Hanesbrands Inc. (HBI): 1000 E. Hanes Mill Rd., Winston-Salem, NC 27105; (336) 519-8080; www.hanesbrands.com; Richard A. Noll; apparel mfr. (Hanes, Barely There, Bali, Champion, Gear for Sports, Just My Size, L'eggs, Maidenform, Playtex, Wonderbra). Acquired DB Apparel, 9/3/2014; Knights Apparel, 4/8/2015; Pacific Brands Ltd., 7/15/2016.

Harley-Davidson, Inc. (HOG): 3700 W. Juneau Ave., Milwaukee, WI 53208; (414) 342-4680; www.harley-davidson.com; Matt Levatich; mfr. motorcycles, parts, accessories.

Hartford Financial Services Group, Inc. (HIG): One Hartford Plz., Hartford, CT 06155; (860) 547-5000; www.thehartford.com; Christopher J. Swift; insurance, financial services.

Hasbro, Inc. (HAS): 1027 Newport Ave., Pawtucket, RI 02862; (401) 431-8697; www.hasbro.com; Brian Goldner; toy and game mfr. (Milton Bradley, Playskool, G.I. Joe, Parker Bros., Nerf, Play-Doh). Acquired Boulder Media, 7/13/2016.

HCA Holdings, Inc. (HCA): 1 Park Plz., Nashville, TN 37203; (615) 344-9551; www.hcahealthcare.com; R. Milton Johnson; owns and operates hospitals; other diagnostic, surgical, health treatment centers. Agreed to acquire CareNow, 10/28/2014.

H. J. Heinz Co.: see Kraft Heinz Co.

Henkel Corp.: 19001 N. Scottsdale Rd., Scottsdale, AZ 85255; (480) 754-3425; www.henkelna.com; Jeffrey C. Piccolomini; consumer prods. (Dial soap, Purex detergent, Right Guard antiperspirant, Renuzit air fresheners); U.S. subsidiary of Germany's Henkel co.

Hershey Co., The (HSY): 100 Crystal A Dr., Hershey, PA 17033; (717) 534-4200; www.thehersheycompany.com; John P. Bilbrey; chocolate prods. mfr. (Reese's, Kit Kat, Mounds, Almond Joy, Jolly Rancher, Twizzlers, Milk Duds, York, Brookside). Acquired Allan Candy Co., 12/4/2014.

Hertz Global Holdings, Inc. (HTZ): 225 Brae Blvd., Park Ridge, NJ 07656; (201) 307-2000; www.hertz.com; John P. Tague; car rentals.

Hess Corp. (HES): 1185 Ave. of the Americas, 40th Fl., NY, NY 10036; (212) 997-8500; www.hess.com; John B. Hess; integrated oil and gas co.

Hewlett-Packard Co. (HPQ): 1501 Page Mill Rd., Palo Alto, CA 94304; (650) 857-1501; www.hp.com; Dion Weisler; computers, electronic prods. and systems. Agreed to sell Snapfish to District Photo, 4/21/2015. Bought Wi-Fi equip. mfr. Aruba Networks, 5/19/2015.

Hillshire Brands Co.: see Tyson Foods, Inc.

Hilton Worldwide (HLT): 7930 Jones Branch Dr., Ste. 1100, McLean, VA 22102; (703) 883-1000; www.hiltonworldwide.com; Christopher J. Nassetta; hotels and resorts (Doubletree, Embassy, Hampton). Sold landmark Waldorf Astoria, 2/11/2015.

Home Depot, Inc. (HD): 2455 Paces Ferry Rd. NW, Atlanta, GA 30339; (770) 433-8211; www.homedepot.com; Craig Menear; home improvement warehouse stores. Acquired Blinds.com, 1/23/2014.

Honeywell Intl. Inc. (HON): 115 Tabor Rd., Morris Plains, NJ 07962; (973) 455-2000; www.honeywell.com; David Cote; industrial and home control systems, aerospace guidance systems. Acquired Datamax-O'Neil, 3/2/2015.

Hormel Foods Corp. (HRL): 1 Hormel Pl., Austin, MN 55912; (507) 437-5611; www.hormelfoods.com; Jeffrey M. Ettinger; food processor, primarily meat (SPAM, Dinty Moore, Jennie-O, Skippy). Acquired Muscle Milk, 8/12/2014; Applegate Farms, 7/13/2015. Agreed to sell Diamond Crystal Brands, 4/26/2016.

Hostess Brands LLC: 1 E Armour Blvd., Kansas City, MO 64111; (816) 701-4600; www.hostessbrands.com; William Toler; baked goods wholesaler, distrib. Agreed

to acquisition by Gores Holdings Inc., 7/5/2016.

Houghton Mifflin Harcourt Co. (HMHC): 222 Berkeley St., Boston, MA 02116; (617) 351-5000; www.hmhco.com; Linda K. Zecher; publisher of textbooks and other educational prods. (Holt McDougal, Clarion), trade and reference books. Acquired SchoolChapters, Inc., 7/1/2014; Scholastic's educational tech. business, 5/29/2015.

H&R Block, Inc. (HRB): 1 H&R Block Way, Kansas City, MO 64105; (816) 854-3000; www.hrblock.com; William C. Cobb; tax return preparation; business and consulting services.

Humana Inc. (HUM): 500 W. Main St., Louisville, KY 40202; (502) 580-1000; www.humana.com; Bruce D. Broussard; managed health care service provider, related specialty prods. Announced plans to merge with Aetna, 7/3/2015.

IAC/InterActiveCorp (IAC): 555 W. 18th St., NY, NY 10011; (212) 314-7300; www.iac.com; Barry Diller; Internet conglomerate (Ask.com, Match.com, Citysearch, The Daily Beast, Vimeo).

iHeartMedia, Inc.: 200 E. Basse Rd., San Antonio, TX 78209; (210) 822-2828; www.iheartmedia.com; Robert Pittman; radio stations; outdoor advertising. Fmr. Clear Channel Communications; renamed 9/16/2014.

Illinois Tool Works Inc. (ITW): 155 Harlem Ave., Glenview, IL 60025; (847) 724-7500; www.itw.com; E. Scott Santi; consumer, industrial tools; food equip. (Hobart), packaging (Zip-Pak).

Ingersoll-Rand plc (IR): 170/175 Lakeview Dr., Airside Business Park, Swords, Dublin, Ireland; 353-1-870-7400; company.ingersollrand.com; Michael W. Lamach; low-speed vehicles (Club Car); refrigeration equip. (Thermo King); industrial equip.; air conditioning systems (Trane, American Standard).

Ingram Micro Inc. (IM): 3351 Michelson Dr., Ste. 100, Irvine, CA 92612; (714) 566-1000; www.ingrammicro.com; Alain Monié; IT equip. wholesaler and distrib. in over 160 countries.

Intel Corp. (INTC): 2200 Mission College Blvd., Santa Clara, CA 95054; (408) 765-8080; www.intel.com; Andy D. Bryant; mfr. semiconductors, microprocessors (Core, Centrino). Acquired Altera Corp., 12/28/2015.

International Business Machines Corp. (IBM): One New Orchard Rd., Armonk, NY 10504; (914) 499-1900; www.ibm.com; Virginia M. Rometty; advanced information processing technology equip., services. Sold chip-mfr. unit to GlobalFoundries, 7/1/2015.

International Paper Co. (IP): 6400 Poplar Ave., Memphis, TN 38197; (901) 419-7000; www.internationalpaper.com; Mark Sutton; paper/forest prods. Spun off distr. business xpedx, which merged with Unisource to form Veritiv Corp., 7/1/2014.

INTL FCStone Inc. (INTL): 708 Third Ave., 15th Fl., NY, NY 10017; (212) 485-3500; www.intlfcstone.com; Sean O'Connor; securities and commodities advising.

J.C. Penney Co., Inc. (JCP): 6501 Legacy Dr., Plano, TX 75024; (972) 431-1000; www.jcpenney.com; Marvin Ellison; dept. store retailer, general merchandise catalog sales.

J.Crew Group, Inc.: 770 Broadway, NY, NY 10003; (212) 209-2500; www.jcrew.com; Millard S. Drexler; retail and mail order apparel and accessories.

JetBlue Airways Corp. (JBLU): 27-01 Queens Plz. N., Long Island City, NY 11101; (718) 286-7900; www.jetblue.com; Robin Hayes; air transportation.

Jo-Ann Stores, Inc.: 5555 Darrow Rd., Hudson, OH 44236; (330) 656-2600; www.joann.com; Jill Soltau; specialty fabric and craft stores.

Johnson Controls, Inc. (JCI): 5757 N. Green Bay Ave., Milwaukee, WI 53209; (414) 524-1200; www.johnsoncontrols.com; Alex A. Molinaroli; equip. and controls for heating, ventilating, AC, refrigeration, and building security; auto interiors, batteries. Agreed to spin off auto interiors unit, 5/18/2014. Acquired Air Distribution Technologies, 6/16/2014. Agreed to acquire security/fire co. Tyco, 1/25/2016.

Johnson & Johnson (JNJ): 1 Johnson & Johnson Plz., New Brunswick, NJ 08933; (732) 524-0400; www.jnj.com; Alex Gorsky; health care prods. (Band-Aid, Neosporin), pharmaceuticals (Tylenol, Motrin, Sudafed), toiletries (Neutrogena, Aveeno). Sold Ortho-Clinical Diagnostics to The Carlyle Group, 6/30/2014. Acquired hair care co. Vogue Intl., 7/18/2016.

S. C. Johnson & Son, Inc.: 1525 Howe St., Racine, WI 53403; (262) 260-2000; www.scjohnson.com; H. Fisk Johnson; cleaning and other household prods. (Johnson's Wax, Windex, Pledge, Fantastik, Raid, OFF!, Shout, Glade, Scrubbing Bubbles, Ziploc bags). Acquired UK-based Deb Group, 3/26/2015; HomeBrands A.S., 3/2/2015.

JPMorgan Chase & Co. (JPM): 270 Park Ave., Fl. 12, NY, NY 10017; (212) 270-6000; www.jpmorganchase.com; James Dimon; financial services.

Kate Spade & Co. (KATE): 2 Park Ave., NY, NY 10016; (212) 354-4900; www.katespadeandco.com; Craig. A. Leavitt; women's apparel. Fmr. known as Fifth & Pacific Cos., renamed 2/26/2014.

KBR, Inc. (KBR): 601 Jefferson St., Ste. 3400, Houston, TX 77002; (713) 753-2000; www.kbr.com; Stuart Bradie; engineering; construction mgmt. services.

Kellogg Co. (K): One Kellogg Sq., Battle Creek, MI 49016; (269) 961-2000; www.kelloggcompany.com; John A. Bryant; mfr. of ready-to-eat cereals, other food prods. (Frosted Flakes, Rice Krispies, Pop-Tarts, Nutri-Grain, Keebler, Eggo, Pringles, Gardenburger).

Kelly Services, Inc. (KELYA): 999 W. Big Beaver Rd., Troy, MI 48084; (248) 362-4444; www.kellyservices.com; Carl T. Camden; temporary staffing services.

Kimberly-Clark Corp. (KMB): 351 Phelps Dr., Irving, TX 75038; (972) 281-1200; www.kimberly-clark.com; Thomas J. Falk; personal care prods. (Kleenex, Scott, Cottonelle, Huggies, Kotex).

Kinder Morgan, Inc. (KMI): 1001 Louisiana St., Ste. 1000, Houston, TX 77002; (713) 369-9000; www.kindermorgan.com; Richard D. Kinder; energy trans. and storage. Acquired Kinder Morgan Energy Partners, Kinder Morgan Management, and El Paso Pipeline Partners, 11/26/2014; Hiland Partners, 2/13/2015.

Kmart Corp.: see Sears Holdings Corp.

Koch Industries, Inc.: P.O. Box 2256, Wichita, KS 67201; (316) 828-5500; www.kochind.com; Charles G. Koch; forest prod. mfr.; oil refineries/pipeline; chemicals; pollution-control equip.; ranching.

Kraft Heinz Co. (KHC): 1 PPG Pl., Ste. 3100, Pittsburgh, PA 15222; (412) 456-5700; www.kraftheinzcompany.com; Bernardo Hees; food and beverage mfr. (Ore-Ida, 57 Varieties ketchup, Velveeta, Crystal Light, Maxwell House, Kool-Aid, Lunchables, Jell-O, Oscar Mayer). Formed from merger of Kraft Foods Group with H.J. Heinz Co., 7/2/2015.

Kroger Co. (KR): 1014 Vine St., Cincinnati, OH 45202; (513) 762-4000; www.thekrogerco.com; W. Rodney McMullen; grocery, convenience, and mall jewelry stores.

L Brands, Inc. (fmr. Limited Brands) (LB): 3 Limited Pkwy., Columbus, OH 43230; (614) 415-7000; www.lb.com; Leslie H. Wexner; apparel stores (La Senza, Victoria's Secret, PINK, Henri Bendel), home decor, personal care (Bath & Body Works).

Las Vegas Sands Corp. (LVS): 3355 Las Vegas Blvd. S., Las Vegas, NV 89109; (702) 414-1000; www.lasvegassands.com; Sheldon G. Adelson; casino-resort operator (Venetian, Palazzo, Sands Macao).

La-Z-Boy Inc. (LZB): 1284 N. Telegraph Rd., Monroe, MI 48162; (734) 242-1444; www.la-z-boy.com; Kurt L. Darrow; reclining chairs, other furniture.

Levi Strauss & Co.: 1155 Battery St., San Francisco, CA 94111; (415) 501-6000; www.levistrauss.com; Charles Bergh; blue jeans, casual sportswear (Dockers).

Liberty Mutual Holding Co. Inc.: 175 Berkeley St., Boston, MA 02116; (617) 357-9500; www.libertymutual.com; David H. Long; insurance prods. and services.

LinkedIn Corp. (LNKD): 2029 Stierlin Ct., Ste. 200, Mountain View, CA, 94043; (650) 687-3600; www.linkedin.com; Jeff Weiner; social networking services. Acquired lynda.com, 5/14/2015. Agreed to acquisition by Microsoft, 6/13/2016.

Liz Claiborne, Inc.: see J.C. Penney Co., Inc.

L.L.Bean, Inc.: 15 Casco St., Freeport, ME 04033; (207) 552-2000; www.llbean.com; Stephen Smith; catalog and retail outdoor apparel, footwear, gear.

Lockheed Martin Corp. (LMT): 6801 Rockledge Dr., Bethesda, MD 20817; (301) 897-6000; www.lockheedmartin.com; Marillyn A. Hewson; leading U.S. defense contractor; aircraft, electronics, missiles, information tech., and communications. Acquired Zeta Associates, 8/18/2014; Bought Sikorsky Aircraft from United Technologies, 11/6/2015.

Loews Corp. (L): 667 Madison Ave., NY, NY 10065; (212) 521-2000; www.loews.com; James S. Tisch; hotels, insurance (CNA Financial), offshore drilling (Diamond).

Lorillard, Inc.: see Reynolds American, Inc.

Lowe's Cos., Inc. (LOW): 1000 Lowe's Blvd., Mooresville, NC 28117; (704) 758-1000; www.lowes.com; Robert A. Niblock; building material and home improvement superstores.

Macy's, Inc. (M): 7 W. 7th St., Cincinnati, OH 45202; (513) 579-7000; www.macysinc.com; Terry J. Lundgren; dept. stores (Macy's, Bloomingdale's). Acquired cosmetics retailer Bluemercury, Inc., 3/9/2015.

ManpowerGroup (MAN): 100 Manpower Pl., Milwaukee, WI 53212; (414) 961-1000; www.manpowergroup.com; Jonas Prising; employment services.

Marathon Oil Corp. (MRO): 5555 San Felipe St., Houston, TX 77056; (713) 629-6600; www.marathonoil.com; Lee M. Tillman; integrated oil co.

Marriott International, Inc. (MAR): 10400 Fernwood Rd., Bethesda, MD 20817; (301) 380-3000; www.marriott.com; Arne M. Sorenson; hotels (Renaissance, Courtyard, Fairfield Inn, Ritz-Carlton). Acquired Protea Hospitality Group, 4/1/2014; Delta Hotels and Resorts, 4/1/2015. Agreed to acquire Starwood Hotels & Resorts to create world's largest hotel co., 11/16/2015.

Mars, Inc.: 6885 Elm St., McLean, VA 22101; (703) 821-4900; www.mars.com; Grant F. Reid; food mfr., including of chocolate (M&M's, Snickers, Dove), food (Uncle Ben's), pet food (Pedigree, Whiskas, Iams, Eukanuba, Sheba).

Massachusetts Mutual Life Insurance Co. (MassMutual Financial Group): 1295 State St., Springfield, MA 01111; (413) 744-1000; www.massmutual.com; Roger W. Crandall; financial planning and investment, life insurance.

MasterCard Inc. (MA): 2000 Purchase St., Purchase, NY 10577; (914) 249-2000; www.mastercard.com; Ajay Banga; financial services.

Mattel, Inc. (MAT): 333 Continental Blvd., El Segundo, CA 90245; (310) 252-2000; www.mattel.com; Christopher A. Sinclair; toymaker (Barbie, Fisher-Price, Hot Wheels, Matchbox, American Girls). Acquired MEGA Brands, 4/30/2014.

McClatchy Co. (MNI): 2100 Q St., Sacramento, CA 95816; (916) 321-1855; www.mcclatchy.com; Patrick J. Talamantes; newspaper publisher.

McDonald's Corp. (MCD): 2111 McDonald's Dr., Oak Brook, IL 60523; (630) 623-3000; www.mcdonalds.com; Steve Easterbrook; fast food.

McGraw-Hill Financial: see S&P Global, Inc.

McKesson Corp. (MCK): 1 Post St., San Francisco, CA 94104; (415) 983-8300; www.mckesson.com; John H. Hammergren; distrib. of drugs and toiletries; provides mgmt. software and services.

Medco Health Solutions, Inc.: see Express Scripts Holding Co.

Merck & Co., Inc. (MRK): 2000 Galloping Hill Rd., Kenilworth, NJ 07033; (908) 740-4000; www.merck.com; Kenneth C. Frazier; pharmaceuticals (Gardasil, Propecia, Singulair, Vytorin, Zocor). Acquired Idenix Pharmaceuticals, 8/5/2014; Cubist Pharmaceuticals, 1/21/2015. Sold consumer care business to Bayer, 10/1/2014.

Meredith Corp. (MDP): 1716 Locust St., Des Moines, IA 50309; (515) 284-3000; www.meredith.com; Stephen M. Lacy; magazine publishing (*Better Homes and Gardens*, *Eating Well*, *Parents*, *Family Circle*, *Every Day With Rachael Ray*, *FamilyFun*), book publishing, broadcasting, online media (allrecipes.com).

Merrill Lynch & Co., Inc.: see Bank of America Corp.

MetLife, Inc. (MET): 200 Park Ave., NY, NY 10166; (212) 578-2211; www.metlife.com; Steven A. Kandarian; insurance, financial services.

MGM Resorts Intl. (MGM): 3600 Las Vegas Blvd. S., Las Vegas, NV 89109; (702) 693-7120; www.mgmresorts.com; James J. Murren; hotel-casino operator (Mirage, New York-New York, Luxor, Bellagio, Circus Circus, Monte Carlo). Announced formation of joint venture hotel co. MGM Hakkasan Hospitality, 4/15/2014.

Microsoft Corp. (MSFT): One Microsoft Way, Redmond, WA 98052; (425) 882-8080; www.microsoft.com; Satya Nadella; software (Windows, Word, Excel); video game consoles (Xbox). Acquired Nokia's devices and services businesses, 4/25/2014; Minecraft developer Mojang, 11/6/2014. Agreed to acquire networking site LinkedIn, 6/13/2016.

Miller Brewing Co.: see SABMiller plc.

Molson Coors Brewing Co. (TAP): 1801 California St., Ste. 4600, Denver, CO 80202; (303) 927-2337; www.molsoncoors.com; Mark Hunter; brewer. Agreed to acquire SABMiller's global Miller brands and majority stake in joint venture, MillerCoors (pending closing of Anheuser-Busch InBev's SABMiller acquisition), 11/11/2015.

Mondelēz International, Inc. (MDLZ): 3 Pkwy N., Ste. 300, Deerfield, IL 60015; (847) 646-2000; www.mondelezinternational.com; Irene B. Rosenfeld; global food mfr., including Nabisco (Oreo), Cadbury, Tang, Trident.

Monsanto Co. (MON): 800 N. Lindbergh Blvd., Saint Louis, MO 63167; (314) 694-1000; www.monsanto.com; Hugh Grant; agricultural biotechnology.

Morgan Stanley (MS): 1585 Broadway, NY, NY 10036; (212) 761-4000; www.morganstanley.com; James P. Gorman; diversified financial services.

Motorola Solutions, Inc. (MSI): 1303 E. Algonquin Rd., Schaumburg, IL 60196; (847) 576-5000; www.motorolasolutions.com; Gregory Q. Brown; electronic equip. and components; communication devices. Sold enterprise business to Zebra Tech. Corp., 10/27/2014.

Nationwide Mutual Insurance Co.: One Nationwide Plz., Columbus, OH 43215; (614) 249-7111; www.nationwide.com; Stephen S. Rasmussen; property/casualty, life insurance; financial services.

Navistar Intl. Corp. (NAV): 2701 Navistar Dr., Lisle, IL 60532; (331) 332-5000; www.navistar.com; Troy Clarke; mfr. heavy-duty trucks, parts, school buses.

NBC Universal: 30 Rockefeller Plz., NY, NY 10112; (212) 664-4444; www.nbcuni.com; Stephen B. Burke; news/entertainment producer; TV and CATV stations (NBC, Bravo, USA, Telemundo); film production. Owned by Comcast and General Electric.

NCR Corp. (NCR): 3097 Satellite Blvd., Duluth, GA 30096; (937) 445-1936; www.ncr.com; William R. Nuti; mfr. ATMs, retail technology, hardware and software; computer services and supplies.

Nestlé USA, Inc.: 800 N. Brand Blvd., Glendale, CA 91203; (818) 549-6000; www.nestleusa.com; Paul Grimwood; candy (Baby Ruth, Raisinets), beverages (Nestea, Ovaltine), food (Buitoni, Coffee-Mate), frozen foods (Stouffer's, Häagen-Dazs, Lean Cuisine), pet foods (Purina, Alpo, Friskies). Subsidiary of Nestlé SA in Switzerland.

Netflix, Inc. (NFLX): 100 Winchester Cir., Los Gatos, CA 95032; (408) 540-3700; www.netflix.com; Reed Hastings; online DVD rentals; streaming video. Announced it had gained exclusive streaming rights to Disney films beginning Sept., 5/23/2016.

New York Life Insurance Co.: 51 Madison Ave., NY, NY 10010; (212) 576-7000; www.newyorklife.com; Theodore A. Mathas; life insurance, annuities, mutual funds.

New York Times Co. (NYT): 620 8th Ave., NY, NY 10018; (212) 556-1234; www.nytco.com; Arthur O. Sulzberger Jr.; newspapers.

Newell Brands (NWL): 6655 Peachtree Dunwoody Rd., Atlanta, GA 30328; (770) 418-7000; www.newellbrands.com; Michael B. Polk; housewares (Rubbermaid, Calphalon); hair accessories (Goody); writing utensils (Parker, Sharpie, Paper Mate); hardware and tools (Irwin, Lenox); juvenile prods. (Graco).

News Corp. (NWS): 1211 Ave. of the Americas, NY, NY 10036; (212) 416-3400; www.newscorp.com; K. Rupert Murdoch; publisher (HarperCollins; *Wall Street Journal*, *Barron's*); websites (MarketWatch). Spun off TV, entertainment cos. as 21st Century Fox, Inc., 6/28/2013.

NextEra Energy, Inc. (NEE): 700 Universe Blvd., Juno Beach, FL 33408; (561) 694-4000; www.nexteraenergy.com; James L. Robo; electricity generation/distrib.

NIKE, Inc. (NKE): 1 Bowerman Dr., Beaverton, OR 97005; (503) 671-6453; nike.com; Mark G. Parker; athletic footwear and apparel mfr.

Nokia (NOK): Karaportti 3, Espoo 02610, Finland +358 (0) 10 44 88 000, www.nokia.com; Rajeev Suri; telecom. equip., computer software. Acquired Alcatel-Lucent, 1/4/2016.

Nordstrom, Inc. (JWN): 1600 7th Ave., Seattle, WA 98101; (206) 628-2111; www.nordstrom.com; Blake W. Nordstrom; upscale dept. store chain.

Norfolk Southern Corp. (NSC): Three Commercial Pl., Norfolk, VA 23510; (855) 667-3655; www.nscorp.com; James A. Squires; railway operator; freight carrier.

Northrop Grumman Corp. (NOC): 2980 Fairview Park Dr., Falls Church, VA 22042; (703) 280-2900; www.northropgrumman.com; Wes Bush; defense contractor: aircraft, electronics, data systems, information systems, missiles.

Northwest Airlines Corp.: see Delta Air Lines, Inc.

Northwestern Mutual Life Insurance Co.: 720 E. Wisconsin Ave., Milwaukee, WI 53202; (414) 271-1444; www.northwesternmutual.com; John E. Schlifske; life insurance, investment prods. and services, annuities. Sold Russell Investments to London Stock Exchange Group, 12/3/2014.

Occidental Petroleum Corp. (OXY): Five Greenway Plz., Ste. 110, Houston, TX 77046; (713) 215-7000; www.oxy.com; Vicki A. Holub; oil, natural gas, chemicals, plastics. Spun off California assets into separate co., 12/1/2014.

Office Depot, Inc. (ODP): 6600 N. Military Trl., Boca Raton, FL 33496; (561) 438-4800; www.officedepot.com; Roland C. Smith; office supply retail stores. Terminated merger with Staples, Inc. following federal injunction, 5/16/2016.

Omnicom Group Inc. (OMC): 437 Madison Ave., NY, NY 10022; (212) 415-3600; www.omnicomgroup.com; John D. Wren; advertising, marketing, interactive/digital media.

Oracle Corp. (ORCL): 500 Oracle Pkwy., Redwood Shores, CA 94065; (650) 506-7000; www.oracle.com; Lawrence J. Ellison; database and file mgmt. software. Acquired MICROS Systems, 9/8/2014. Acquired Datalogix, 1/23/2015, CloudMonkey, 8/6/2015.

Payless ShoeSource, Inc.: 3231 SE 6th Ave., Topeka, KS 66607; (785) 233-5171; www.collectivebrands.com; W. Paul Jones; shoe mfr./retailer.

PepsiCo, Inc. (PEP): 700 Anderson Hill Rd., Purchase, NY 10577; (914) 253-2000; www.pepsico.com; Indra K. Nooyi; soft drinks and other beverages (Pepsi-Cola, Mountain Dew, Gatorade, Tropicana), snacks and cereals (Fritos, Lay's, Ruffles, Quaker).

Pfizer, Inc. (PFE): 235 E. 42nd St., NY, NY 10017; (212) 733-2323; www.pfizer.com; Ian Read; biopharmaceuticals (Celebrex, Lipitor, Viagra, Zoloft); human and animal health care prods. Announced plans to acquire Hospira, 2/5/2015. Terminated $160-bil merger with Allergan following new anti-inversion rules, 4/6/2016. Agreed to acquire Anacor Pharmaceuticals, 5/16/2016.

PG&E Corp. (PCG): 77 Beale St., 24th Fl., San Francisco, CA 94105; (415) 973-8200; www.pgecorp.com; Anthony F. Earley Jr.; operates Pacific Gas and Electric public utility.

Philip Morris Intl. Inc. (PM): 120 Park Ave., Fl. 7, NY, NY 10017; (917) 663-2000; www.pmi.com; André Calantzopoulos; intl. mfr. and distrib. of tobacco. (Altria spun off intl. Philip Morris operations in 2008 but owns Philip Morris brands in U.S.) Acquired Nicocigs, Ltd., 6/26/2014.

Phillips 66 Co. (PSX): P.O. Box 4428, Houston, TX 77210; (281) 293-6600; www.phillips66.com; Greg C. Garland; oil, gas refining and marketing. Spun off from ConocoPhillips, 5/1/2012.

Pitney Bowes Inc. (PBI): 3001 Summer St., Stamford, CT 06926; (203) 356-5000; www.pb.com; Marc B. Lautenbach; postage meters and mailing equip.

Post Holdings, Inc. (POST): 2503 S. Hanley Rd., St. Louis, MO 63144; (314) 644-7600; www.postfoods.com; Robert V. Vitale; ready-to-eat cereals. Acquired MOM Brands Co., 5/4/2015.

PPG Industries, Inc. (PPG): 1 PPG Pl., Pittsburgh, PA 15272; (412) 434-3131; www.ppg.com; Charles E. Bunch; glass prods., silicas, fiberglass, chemicals, sealants. Acquired Masterwork Paint Co., 7/1/2014; Comex, 11/5/2014.

Priceline Group Inc. (PCLN): 800 Connecticut Ave., Norwalk, CT 06854; (203) 299-8000; www.pricelinegroup.com; Jefferey H. Boyd; online travel services (booking.com, Kayak, Open Table).

Procter & Gamble Co. (PG): 1 Procter & Gamble Plz., Cincinnati, OH 45202; (513) 983-1100; www.pg.com; David S. Taylor; soaps and detergents (Ivory, Cheer, Tide, Mr. Clean); toiletries (Crest, Scope, Head & Shoulders, Old Spice); pharmaceuticals (Pepto-Bismol, Vicks cough medicines); paper prods. (Charmin toilet tissues, Bounty towels), Tampax tampons; disposable diapers (Pampers, Luvs); Gillette razors. Agreed to sell Duracell to Berkshire Hathaway, 2/29/2016.

Prudential Financial, Inc. (PRU): 751 Broad St., Newark, NJ 07102; (973) 802-6000; www.prudential.com; John R. Strangfeld Jr.; insurance, financial services.

Publix Super Markets Inc.: 3300 Publix Corporate Pkwy., Lakeland, FL 33811; (863) 688-1188; www.publix.com; Todd Jones; supermarket chain.

PVH Corp. (PVH): 200 Madison Ave., NY, NY 10016; (212) 381-3500; www.pvh.com; Emanuel Chirico; apparel mfr., including licensed brands (Calvin Klein, IZOD, Tommy Hilfiger).

Qualcomm Inc. (QCOM): 5775 Morehouse Dr., San Diego, CA 92121; (858) 587-1121; www.qualcomm.com; Paul E. Jacobs; telecommunications.

Quest Diagnostics Inc. (DGX): 3 Giralda Farms, Madison, NJ 07940; (800) 222-0446; www.questdiagnostics.com; Stephen Rusckowski; leading clinical laboratory. Acquired Summit Health, 4/21/2014.

RadioShack Corp.: 300 RadioShack Cir., Fort Worth, TX 76102; (817) 415-3011; www.radioshack.com; Dene Rogers; consumer electronics retailer. Filed for Ch. 11 reorganization, 2/5/2015. General Wireless, Inc. acquired 1,743 remaining Radio Shack stores, 3/31/2015.

Ralcorp Holdings, Inc.: see ConAgra Foods, Inc.

Ralph Lauren Corp. (RL): 650 Madison Ave., NY, NY 10022; (212) 318-7000; www.ralphlauren.com; Stefan Larsson; men's and women's apparel, home furnishings, fragrances.

Raytheon Co. (RTN): 870 Winter St., Waltham, MA 02451; (781) 522-3000; www.raytheon.com; Thomas A. Kennedy; defense, communications systems. Acquired cybersecurity co. Websense, 5/29/2015.

Reader's Digest Assn., Inc.: see Trusted Media Brands, Inc.

Republic Services, Inc. (RSG): 18500 N. Allied Way, Phoenix, AZ 85054; (480) 627-2700; www.republicservices.com; Donald W. Slager; waste mgmt. co.

Restaurant Brands Intl. (QSR): 226 Wyecroft Rd., Oakville, ON L6K 3X7, Canada; (905) 845-6511; www.rbi.com; Daniel Schwartz; fast food restaurants (Burger King, Tim Hortons). Co. formed through acquisition of Tim Hortons, Inc. by former co. Burger King Worldwide, 12/12/2014.

Revlon, Inc. (REV): One New York Plaza, NY, NY 10004; (212) 527-4000; www.revlon.com; Fabian Garcia; cosmetics, skin care. Acquired CBBeauty, 4/30/2015.

Reynolds American Inc. (RAI): 401 N. Main St., Winston-Salem, NC 27101; (336) 741-2000; www.reynoldsamerican.com; Susan Cameron; cigarettes (Camel, Pall Mall, Doral, Newport), smokeless tobacco (Grizzly, Kodiak), e-cigarettes (VUSE). Acquired Lorillard, 6/12/2015.

Rite Aid Corp. (RAD): 30 Hunter Ln., Camp Hill, PA 17011; (717) 761-2633; www.riteaid.com; John T. Standley; retail drugstores. Agreed to buy pharmacy-benefit manager EnvisionRx, 2/11/2015. Agreed to acquisition by Walgreens Boots Alliance, 10/27/2015.

Rockwell Automation, Inc. (ROK): 1201 S. 2nd St., Milwaukee, WI 53204; (414) 382-2000; www.rockwellautomation.com; Blake Moret; industrial automation co. Agreed to acquire conveying system mfr. MagneMotion, 2/10/2016.

Rohm and Haas Co.: see Dow Chemical Co.

Ryder System, Inc. (R): 11690 NW 105th St., Miami, FL 33178; (305) 500-3726; www.ryder.com; Robert E. Sanchez; truck-leasing service.

SABMiller plc: 1 Stanhope Gate, London, W1K 1AF, United Kingdom; + 44 1483 264000; www.sabmiller.com; Alan Clark; brewer (Peroni, Grolsch). Agreed to merge with Anheuser-Busch InBev, 11/11/2015.

Safeway Inc.: 5918 Stoneridge Mall Rd., Pleasanton, CA 94588; (925) 467-3000; www.safeway.com; Bob Miller; supermarkets. Acquired by Albertson Holdings LLC, 1/30/2015.

S&P Global, Inc. (SPGI): 55 Water St., NY, NY 10041; (212) 438-1000; www.spglobal.com; Douglas L. Peterson; financial information, services (Standard & Poor's). Formerly McGraw-Hill Financial; renamed 4/27/16. Agreed to sell J.D. Power & Associates to XIO Group, 4/15/16.

Schering-Plough Corp.: see Merck & Co., Inc.

Schlumberger Limited Co. (SLB): 300 Schlumberger Dr., Sugarland, TX 77478; (713) 375-3400; www.slb.com; Paal Kibsgaard; oil equip. and services.

Sears Holdings Corp. (SHLD): 3333 Beverly Rd., Hoffman Estates, IL 60179; (847) 286-2500; www.searsholdings.com; Edward S. Lampert; U.S. retailer. Spun off Land's End, Inc., 4/4/2014.

Shell Oil Co.: 910 Louisiana St., Houston, TX 77002; (713) 241-6161; www.shell.us; Ben van Beurden; integrated oil co.; subsidiary of Royal Dutch Shell.

Sherwin-Williams Co. (SHW): 101 W. Prospect Ave., Cleveland, OH 44115; (216) 566-2000; www.sherwin-williams.com; John G. Morikis; paint and varnish producer (Dutch Boy, Krylon, Minwax). Agreed to acquire Valspar Corp., 3/20/2016.

Simon Property Group, Inc. (SPG): 225 W. Washington St., Indianapolis, IN 46204; (317) 636-1600; www.simon.com; David E. Simon; global real estate.

Sirius XM Holdings Inc. (SIRI): 1221 Avenue of the Americas, Fl. 36, NY, NY 10020; (212) 584-5100; www.siriusxm.com; James E. Meyer; satellite radio.

Smithfield Foods, Inc.: 200 Commerce St., Smithfield, VA 23430; (757) 365-3000; www.smithfieldfoods.com; Kenneth M. Sullivan; pork producer and processor. Subsidiary of China-based WH Group since 9/26/2013.

J. M. Smucker Co. (SJM): One Strawberry Ln., Orrville, OH 44667; (330) 682-3000; www.smuckers.com; Mark T. Smucker; leading producer of fruit spreads, peanut butter (Jif), oils (Crisco), coffee (Folgers), baking prods. (Pillsbury), pet foods (Milk-Bone, Kibbles'n Bits).

Sony Corp. of America: 25 Madison Ave., NY, NY 10016; (212) 833-6800; www.sony.com; Michael Lynton; U.S. subsidiary of Japan-based Sony Corp.; electronics, movies, music.

Southwest Airlines Co. (LUV): 2702 Love Field Dr., Dallas, TX 75235; (214) 792-4000; www.southwest.com; Gary C. Kelly; air transportation.

Sprint Nextel Corp. (S): 6200 Sprint Pkwy., Overland Park, KS 66251; (703) 433-4000; www.sprint.com; Marcelo Claure; wireless and long-distance telecommunications. Sold 72% of co. shares to SoftBank Corp., 7/5/2013.

Stanley Black & Decker, Inc. (SWK): 1000 Stanley Dr., New Britain, CT 06053; (860) 225-5111; www.stanleyblackanddecker.com; John F. Lundgren; hand and power tools (DeWalt, Bostitch), fastening prods. (Gripco, Masterfix).

Staples, Inc. (SPLS): 500 Staples Dr., Framingham, MA 01702; (508) 253-5000; www.staples.com; Shira Goodman; office-supply retailer. Acquired PNI Digital Media, 7/11/2014. Terminated Office Depot acquisition following federal injunction, 5/16/2016.

Starbucks Corp. (SBUX): 2401 Utah Ave. S., Seattle, WA 98134; (206) 447-1575; www.starbucks.com; Howard S. Schultz; coffee producer; world's leading specialty coffee retailer.

Starwood Hotels & Resorts Worldwide, Inc. (HOT): 1 StarPoint, Stamford, CT 06902; (203) 964-6000; www.starwoodhotels.com; Thomas B. Mangas; hotel and resort co. (Westin, Sheraton, W Hotels). Agreed to acquisition by Marriott Intl., 11/16/2015.

State Farm Mutual Automobile Ins. Co.: 1 State Farm Plz., Bloomington, IL 61710; (309) 766-2311; www.statefarm.com; Michael L. Tipsord; auto/homeowners insurance. Sold Canadian operations to Desjardins Group, 1/1/2015.

Sun Microsystems, Inc.: see Oracle Corp.

SUPERVALU Inc. (SVU): East View Innovation Ctr., 7075 Flying Cloud Dr., Eden Prairie, MN 55344; (952) 828-4000; www.supervalu.com; Sam Duncan; food retailer, wholesale distrib. (Save-A-Lot, Cub Foods, Shoppers).

SYSCO Corp. (SYY): 1390 Enclave Pkwy., Houston, TX 77077; (281) 584-1390; www.sysco.com; William J. DeLaney; food-service distrib. Acquired European food distributor Brakes Group, 7/5/2016.

Target Corp. (TGT): 1000 Nicollet Mall, Minneapolis, MN 55403; (612) 304-6073; www.target.com; Brian Cornell; discount retailer.

TEGNA Inc. (TGNA): 7950 Jones Branch Dr., McLean, VA 22107; (703) 854-7000; www.tegna.com; Gracia C. Martore; network and cable TV, websites (careerbuilder.com, cars.com). Spun off from Gannett Co., 6/29/2015.

Tenneco Inc. (TEN): 500 N. Field Dr., Lake Forest, IL 60045; (847) 482-5000; www.tenneco.com; Gregg M. Sherrill; automotive parts (Monroe, Walker).

Tesla Motors, Inc. (TSLA): 3500 Deer Creek Rd., Palo Alto, CA 94304; (650) 681-5000; www.teslamotors.com; Elon Musk; electric vehicles and batteries.

Texas Instruments Inc. (TXN): 12500 TI Blvd., Dallas, TX 75266; (972) 995-2011; www.ti.com; Richard K. Templeton; processors, semiconductors, software, handheld calculators.

Textron Inc. (TXT): 40 Westminster St., Providence, RI 02903; (401) 421-2800; www.textron.com; Scott C. Donnelly; aircraft (Cessna, Bell, Beechcraft); pilot training; industrial, auto prods.; financial services.

3M Co. (MMM): 3M Center, St. Paul, MN 55144; (651) 733-1110; www.3m.com; Inge G. Thulin; abrasives, adhesives, electrical, health care, cleaning (Scotch-Brite, O-Cel-O sponges, Scotchgard), printing, consumer prods. (Scotch Tape, Post-it).

TIAA-CREF: 730 Third Ave., NY, NY 10017; (401) 490-9000; www.tiaa-cref.org; Roger W. Ferguson Jr.; financial services provider. Bought Nuveen Investments, 10/1/2014.

Time Inc. (TIME): 225 Liberty St., NY, NY, 10281; (212) 522-1212; www.timeinc.com; Joseph A. Ripp; magazine publishing (*Time*, *Sports Illustrated*, *People*, *Fortune*). Spun off from Time Warner, 6/9/2014.

Time Warner Inc. (TWX): One Time Warner Ctr., NY, NY 10019; (212) 484-8000; www.timewarner.com; Jeffrey L. Bewkes; TV and CATV (Cartoon Network, HBO, CNN, TBS, TNT), motion pictures (Warner Bros.), recordings. AOL and Time Warner completed the largest corporate merger in history in 2001; Time Warner spun off AOL, 12/9/2009. Spun off magazine holdings as Time Inc., 6/9/2014.

TJX Cos., Inc. (TJX): 770 Cochituate Rd., Framingham, MA 01701; (508) 390-1000; www.tjx.com; Carol Meyrowitz; off-price apparel retailer (T.J. Maxx, Marshalls); home furnishing retailer (HomeGoods).

T-Mobile US, Inc. (TMUS): 12920 SE 38th St., Bellevue, WA 98006; (425) 378-4000; www.t-mobile.com; John J. Legere; wireless telecommunications.

Toro Co. (TTC): 8111 Lyndale Ave. S, Bloomington, MN 55420; (952) 888-8801; www.thetorocompany.com; Michael J. Hoffman; lawn and turf maintenance prods. (Lawn-Boy), snow removal equip.; irrigation systems.

Toys "R" Us, Inc.: 1 Geoffrey Way, Wayne, NJ 07470; (973) 617-3500; www.toysrus.com; David A. Brandon; children's specialty retailer.

The Travelers Companies, Inc. (TRV): 485 Lexington Ave., New York, NY 10017; (917) 778-6000; www.travelers.com; Alan D. Schnitzer; insurance.

Tribune Media Co. (TRCO): 435 N. Michigan Ave., Chicago, IL 60611; (312) 222-9100; www.tribunemedia.com; Peter Liguori; broadcasting (incl. WGN and 41 other owned/operated television stations, radio), Tribune Studios. Fmr. known as Tribune Co., renamed 8/4/2014. See Tronc, Inc.

Tronc, Inc. (TRNC): 435 N. Michigan Ave., Chicago, IL 60611; (312) 222-9100; www.tronc.com; Justin Dearborn; newspaper publishers (*L.A. Times*, *Chicago Tribune*). Formerly Tribune Publishing Co., spun off from Tribune Media, 8/4/2014.

Trusted Media Brands, Inc: 750 Third Ave., 3rd Fl., NY, NY 10017; (914) 238-1000; www.tmbi.com; Bonnie Kintzer; publisher (*Taste of Home*, *Reader's Digest*, *Birds & Blooms*); marketer of books, music, video prods. Emerged from second Ch. 11 reorganization since 2010, 7/31/2013. Formerly Reader's Digest Assn., Inc., renamed 9/28/2015.

21st Century Fox, Inc. (FOXA): 1211 Avenue of the Americas, New York, NY 10036; (212) 852-7000; www.21cf.com; James Murdoch; TV and film production; broadcast and CATV channels (Fox, FX, Fox Sports, National Geographic); media streaming service (hulu). Spun off from News Corp., 6/28/2013.

Twitter, Inc. (TWTR): 1355 Market St., Ste. 900, San Francisco, CA, 94103; (415) 222-9670; twitter.com; Jack Dorsey; microblogging/social networking services. Acquired video-streaming startup Periscope, 3/9/2015. Acquired employee/management feedback startup Peer, 4/7/2016.

Tyco Intl. Ltd. (TYC): 9 Roszel Rd., Princeton, NJ 08540; (609) 720-4200; www.tyco.com; George R. Oliver; security and fire safety prods. Agreed to acquisition by Johnson Controls, 1/25/2016.

Tyson Foods, Inc. (TSN): 2200 W. Don Tyson Pkwy., Springdale, AR 72762; (479) 290-4000; www.tysonfoods.com; Donnie Smith; fresh and processed poultry; beef and pork prods. (Ball Park, Sara Lee, Hillshire Farm, Jimmy Dean). Acquired Hillshire Brands Co., 8/28/2014.

UBS Financial Services Inc.: 1285 Ave. of the Americas, NY, NY 10019; (212) 713-2000; www.ubs.com; Sergio P. Ermotti; financial services; subsidiary of Switzerland's UBS AG.

Unilever USA (UN/UL): 800 Sylvan Ave., Englewood Cliffs, NJ 07632; (201) 894-4000; www.unileverusa.com; Paul Polman; food (Hellmann's, Knorr, Lipton, Klondike), hygiene prods. (Dove, Q-tips, Vaseline). Subsidiary of Unilever NV (Neth.) and Unilever plc (UK). Acquired Dermalogica skincare, 8/3/2015; Murad Skincare, 9/1/2015.

Union Pacific Corp. (UNP): 1400 Douglas St., Omaha, NE, 68179; (402) 544-5000; www.up.com; Lance M. Fritz; one of the largest railroad freight cos. in U.S.

Unisys Corp. (UIS): 801 Lakeview Dr., Ste. 100, Blue Bell, PA 19422; (215) 986-4011; www.unisys.com; Peter A. Altabef; designs, manuf. IT systems; IT consulting.

United Continental Holdings, Inc. (UAL): 233 S. Wacker Dr., Chicago IL 60606; (312) 997-8000; www.united.com; Oscar Munoz; air transportation (United Airlines).

United Parcel Service, Inc. (UPS): 55 Glenlake Pkwy. NE, Atlanta, GA 30328; (404) 828-6000; www.ups.com; David Abney; shipping, logistics. Acquired UK-based Polar Speed, 2/11/2014.

United States Steel Corp. (X): 600 Grant St., Pittsburgh, PA 15219; (412) 433-1121; www.ussteel.com; Mario Longhi; steel, tin prods., resource mgmt.

United Technologies Corp. (UTX): 10 Farm Springs Rd., Farmington, CT 06032; (860) 728-7000; www.utc.com; Gregory J. Hayes; aerospace, industrial prods. and services (Carrier, Otis, Pratt & Whitney). Sold Sikorsky Aircraft to Lockheed Martin, 11/6/2015.

UnitedHealth Group Inc. (UNH): UHG Center, 9900 Bren Rd. E., Minnetonka, MN 55343; (952) 936-1300; www.unitedhealthgroup.com; Stephen J. Hemsley; health insurance. Acquired benefit mgmt. co. Catamaran Corp., 7/23/2015.

U.S. Bancorp (USB): 800 Nicollet Mall, Minneapolis, MN, 55402; (651) 466-3000; www.usbank.com; Richard K. Davis; financial services.

Valero Energy Corp. (VLO): One Valero Way, San Antonio, TX 78249; (210) 345-2000; www.valero.com; Joe Gorder; fuel mfg. and marketing. Spun off CST Brands, 5/1/2013.

Verizon Communications Inc. (VZ): 1 Verizon Way, Basking Ridge, NJ 07920; (908) 559-5490; www.verizon.com; Lowell McAdam; telecom. services. Acquired Vodafone's 45% stake in Verizon Wireless, giving it full ownership, 2/21/2014. Acquired AOL, 6/23/2015. Sold CA, FL, TX wireline operations to Frontier Communications, 4/1/2016. Agreed to acquire Yahoo's core internet business, 7/25/2016.

VF Corp. (VFC): 105 Corporate Center Blvd., Greensboro, NC 27408; (336) 424-6000; www.vfc.com; Eric C. Wiseman; apparel (Lee, Wrangler, North Face, Timberland).

Viacom Inc. (VIA): 1515 Broadway, NY, NY 10036; (212) 258-6000; www.viacom.com; Philippe P. Dauman; media networks (BET, Comedy Central, MTV, VH1, Nickelodeon); movies (Paramount).

Visa Inc. (V): 900 Metro Center Blvd., Foster City, CA 94404; (650) 432-3200; www.visa.com; Charles W. Scharf; financial services. Acquired Visa Europe Ltd., 6/21/2016.

Visteon Corp. (VC): One Village Center Dr., Van Buren Twp., MI 48111; (734) 710-5000; www.visteon.com; Sachin Lawande; automotive parts mfr. Acquired Johnson Controls' automotive electronics business, 7/1/2014.

Walgreens Boots Alliance, Inc. (WBA): 108 Wilmot Rd., Deerfield, IL 60015; (847) 914-2500; www.walgreensbootsalliance.com; Stefano Pessina; retail drugstores, pharmaceutical wholesale/distrib. (Alliance Healthcare). Formed through merger of Swiss-based Boots Alliance with Walgreens Co., 12/31/2014. Agreed to acquire RiteAid, 10/27/2015.

Wal-Mart Stores, Inc. (WMT): 702 SW 8th St., Bentonville, AR 72716; (479) 273-4000; www.walmartstores.com; Doug McMillon; discount stores, discount warehouse clubs (Sam's Club).

Washington Post Co.: see Graham Holdings Co.

Waste Management, Inc. (WM): 1001 Fannin St., Ste. 4000, Houston, TX 77002; (713) 512-6200; www.wm.com; David P. Steiner; waste, recycling. Acquired Deffenbaugh Disposal, 3/26/2015.

WellPoint, Inc.: see Anthem, Inc.

Wells Fargo & Co. (WFC): 420 Montgomery St., San Francisco, CA 94104; (866) 249-3302; www.wellsfargo.com; John G. Stumpf; financial services.

Wendy's Co. (WEN): 1 Dave Thomas Blvd., Dublin, OH 43017; (614) 764-3100; www.aboutwendys.com; Emil J. Brolick; fast food restaurants.

Western Union Co. (WU): 12500 E. Belford Ave., Englewood, CO 80112; (720) 332-1000; www.westernunion.com; Hikmet Ersek; money transfers, payment services.

WestRock Co. (WRK): 501 S. 5th St., Richmond, VA 23219; (804) 444-1000; www.westrock.com; Steven C. Vorhees; packaging, shipping containers; chemicals. Formed through merger of Rock-Tenn Co. and MeadWestvaco Corp., 7/1/2015.

Weyerhaeuser Co. (WY): 33663 Weyerhaeuser Way S., Federal Way, WA 98003; (253) 924-2345; www.weyerhaeuser.com; Doyle R. Simons; produces, distributes wood prods.; real estate development. Acquired rival Plumb Creek Timber Co., 2/19/2016.

Whirlpool Corp. (WHR): 2000 N. M-63, Benton Harbor, MI 49022; (269) 923-5000; www.whirlpoolcorp.com; Jeff M. Fettig; mfr. of major home appliances (KitchenAid, Amana, Maytag). Acquired American Dryer Corp., 7/3/2015.

Whole Foods Market, Inc. (WFM): 550 Bowie St., Austin, TX 78703; (512) 477-4455; www.wholefoodsmarket.com; John P. Mackey/Walter Robb; grocery stores specializing in natural/organic foods.

Winnebago Industries, Inc. (WGO): 605 W. Crystal Lake Rd., Forest City, IA 50436; (641) 585-3535; www.winnebagoind.com; Michael J. Happe; mfr. of motor homes, or recreational vehicles (RVs).

Wm. Wrigley Jr. Co.: see Mars, Inc.

World Fuel Services Corp. (INT): 9800 NW 41st St., Ste. 400, Miami, FL 33178; (305) 428-8000; www.wfscorp.com; Michael J. Kasbar; marketer and financer of fuel to large-scale aviation and marine-related firms. Acquired Watson Petroleum Ltd., 3/10/2014.

Xerox Corp. (XRX): 45 Glover Ave., P.O. Box 4505, Norwalk, CT 06856; (203) 968-3000; www.xerox.com; Ursula M. Burns; printers, multifunction devices, document publishing technology and support. Acquired Consilience Software, Inc., 10/3/2014. Acquired RSA Medical, 9/10/2015.

Yahoo! Inc. (YHOO): 701 First Ave., Sunnyvale, CA 94089; (408) 349-3300; www.yahoo.com; Marissa Mayer; Internet media co. Acquired blogging platform and social networking site Tumblr, 6/20/2013; video advertising platform BrightRoll, 12/15/2014. Announced planned buyout of core internet business by Verizon Communications, Inc., 7/25/2016.

Yum! Brands, Inc. (YUM): 1441 Gardiner Ln., Louisville, KY 40213; (502) 874-8300; www.yum.com; Greg Creed; fast food restaurants (Pizza Hut, KFC, Taco Bell).

Labor Unions and Professional Organizations

Source: Bureau of Labor Statistics, U.S. Dept. of Labor; AFL-CIO; World Almanac research

= Member of Change to Win Federation, formed in 2005 by unions disaffiliated from AFL-CIO. * = Independent union or one not otherwise affiliated with Change to Win or AFL-CIO. All other unions listed are affiliated with AFL-CIO as of 2016. Year established is in parentheses.

Labor Unions

Air Line Pilots Assn. (ALPA) (1931): 51,902 members, 31 U.S. and Canadian airlines; (703) 689-2270; www.alpa.org

American Federation of Labor and Congress of Industrial Organizations (AFL-CIO) (1955): federation of 56 unions, 12,475,220 members; (202) 637-5000; www.aflcio.org

Automobile, Aerospace & Agricultural Implement Workers of America, International Union, United (UAW) (1935): 408,639 members, 600+ locals; (313) 926-5000; www.uaw.org

Bakery, Confectionary, Tobacco Workers, and Grain Millers International Union (BCTGM) (1886): 70,861 members, 143 locals; (301) 933-8600; www.bctgm.org

Bricklayers and Allied Craftworkers, International Union of (BAC) (1865): 72,963 members, 40+ locals; (202) 783-3788; www.bacweb.org

***Carpenters and Joiners of America, United Brotherhood of** (UBC) (1881): nearly 447,743 members, 600+ locals; (202) 546-6206; www.carpenters.org

#Change to Win Federation (2005): 4 unions, ex-affiliates of AFL-CIO, 3,718,648 members; (202) 721-0660; www.changetowin.org

Communications Workers of America (CWA) (1938): 628,413 members, 1,200 locals; (202) 434-1100; www.cwa-union.org

***Education Assn., Natl.** (NEA) (1857): 2,952,972 members, 14,000+ affiliates; (202) 833-4000; www.nea.org

Electrical Workers, International Brotherhood of (IBEW) (1891): 662,175 members, 900 locals; (202) 833-7000; www.ibew.org

Engineers, International Union of Operating (IUOE) (1896): 377,304 members, 123 locals; (202) 429-9100; www.iuoe.org

#Farm Workers of America, United (UFW) (1962): 8,274 members; (661) 823-6151; www.ufw.org

***Federal Employees, Natl. Federation of** (NFFE; affiliated with IAM) (1917): 110,000 members, about 200 locals; (202) 216-4420; www.nffe.org

Fire Fighters, International Assn. of (IAFF) (1918): 298,765 members, 3,100+ locals; (202) 737-8484; www.iaff.org

Flight Attendants, Assn. of (AFA-CWA) (1945): 35,660 members, 18 airlines; merged with Communications Workers of America in 2004; (202) 434-1300; www.afanet.org

#Food and Commercial Workers International Union, United (UFCW) (1979): 1,271,150 members, 1,000+ locals; (202) 223-3111; www.ufcw.org

Glass, Molders, Pottery, Plastics and Allied Workers Intl. Union (GMP) (1842): 25,710 members, 250+ locals; (610) 565-5051; www.gmpiu.org

Government Employees, American Federation of (AFGE) (1932): 319,230 members, 1,100 locals; (202) 737-8700; www.afge.org

#Graphic Communications Conference (GCC/IBT) (1983): 66,441 members; merged with Teamsters in 2005; (202) 462-1400; www.gciu.org

Iron Workers, Intl. Assn. of Bridge, Structural, Ornamental, and Reinforcing (1896): 128,314 members, 800+ locals; (202) 383-4800; www.ironworkers.org

Laborers' International Union of North America (LiUNA) (1903): 536,787 members, 400 locals; (202) 737-8320; www.liuna.org

Letter Carriers, Natl. Assn. of (NALC) (1889): 278,297 members, 2,000+ locals; (202) 393-4695; www.nalc.org

#Locomotive Engineers and Trainmen, Brotherhood of (BLET) (1863): 56,326 members, 500+ locals; (216) 241-2630; www.ble-t.org

Longshoremen's Assn., Intl. (ILA) (1892): 37,826 members, approx. 200 locals; (212) 425-1200; www.ilaunion.org

Machinists and Aerospace Workers, International Assn. of (IAM) (1888): 568,814 members; affiliated with TCU in 2005; (301) 967-4500; www.goiam.org

#Maintenance of Way Employes, Division of the Intl. Brotherhood of Teamsters; Brotherhood of (BMWED) (1887): 36,597 members, 770 locals; merged with Teamsters in 2004; (248) 662-2660; www.bmwed.org (Note: In honor of tradition, the union maintains the variant spelling of "employes" in its logo.)

Mine Workers of America, United (UMWA) (1890): 71,341 members, 600 locals; (703) 291-2400; www.umwa.org

Musicians of the United States and Canada, American Federation of (AFM) (1896): 76,290 members, 240+ locals; (212) 869-1330; www.afm.org

Newspaper Guild—Communications Workers of America, The (TNG) (CWA) (1933): 34,000+ members, 90 locals; (202) 434-7177; www.newsguild.org

***Nurses Assn., American** (ANA) (1911): 146,000 members, 54 constituent state and territorial assns.; (301) 628-5000; www.nursingworld.org

Office and Professional Employees Intl. Union (OPEIU) (1945): 104,975 members, 200 locals; (800) 346-7348; www.opeiu.org

Painters and Allied Trades, International Union of (IUPAT) (1887): 107,067 members, 425 locals; (410) 564-5900; www.iupat.org

Plumbing and Pipe Fitting Industry of the U.S. and Canada, United Assn. of Journeymen and Apprentices of the (UA) (1889): 340,000 members, 300+ locals; (410) 269-2000; www.ua.org

***Police, Fraternal Order of** (1915): 330,000+ members, 2,200+ affiliates; (615) 399-0900; www.fop.net

Police Assns., International Union of (IUPA) (1979): 100,000+ members; (941) 487-2560; www.iupa.org

Postal Workers Union, American (APWU) (1971): 247,467 members, 900+ locals; (202) 842-4200; www.apwu.org

Roofers, Waterproofers and Allied Workers, United Union of (1906): 20,934 members; (202) 463-7663; www.unionroofers.com

***Rural Letter Carriers' Assn., Natl.** (1903): 105,620 members, 50 state org.; (703) 684-5545; www.nrlca.org

***Security, Police, Fire Professionals of America, Intl. Union,** (SPFPA) (1948): 16,577 members, 200 locals; (586) 772-7250; www.spfpa.org

#Service Employees International Union (SEIU) (1921): 1,887,941 members, 150+ locals; (202) 730-7000; www.seiu.org

Sheet Metal, Air, Rail, and Transportation Workers, Int. Assn. of (SMART) (2008, from merger of Sheet Metal Workers' Intl. Assn. and United Transportation Union): 206,482 members, 700 locals; (202) 662-0800; www.smart-union.org

State, County, and Municipal Employees, American Federation of (AFSCME) (1932): 1,305,128 members, 3,400 locals; (202) 429-1000; www.afscme.org

Steel, Paper and Forestry, Rubber, Manufacturing, Energy, Allied Industrial and Service Workers International Union, United (USW) (2005): 591,318 members, 1,800+ locals; formed from merger of the unions United Steelworkers of America (USWA) (1936) and Paper,

Allied-Industrial, Chemical and Energy Workers (PACE) (1999); (412) 562-2400; www.usw.org

Teachers, American Federation of (AFT) (1916): 1,613,448 members, 3,000+ locals; (202) 879-4400; www.aft.org

#Teamsters, International Brotherhood of (IBT) (1903): 1,279,064 members, 475 locals; (202) 624-6800; www.teamster.org

Theatrical Stage Employees, Moving Picture Technicians, Artists and Allied Crafts of the U.S., Its Territories, and Canada, Intl. Alliance of (IATSE) (1893): 122,109 members, 375+ locals; (212) 730-1770; www.iatse-intl.org

Transit Union, Amalgamated (ATU) (1892): 192,601 members, 270 locals; (301) 431-7100; www.atu.org

Transport Workers Union of America (TWU) (1934): 116,691 members, 100 locals; (202) 719-3900; www.twu.org

Transportation Communications Intl. Union (TCU) (1899): affiliated with IAM in 2005; see Machinists and Aerospace Workers.

*Treasury Employees Union, Natl. (NTEU) (1938): 77,540 members, 200+ chapters; (202) 572-5500; www.nteu.org

UNITE HERE (UNITE, 1900; HERE, 1891; merged 2004): 264,104+ members, 131 locals; (212) 265-7000; www.unitehere.org

#Workers United (affiliated with SEIU) (2009): 90,071 members

*Writers Guild of America, West (1933): 22,159 members; (323) 951-4000; www.wga.org

Professional Organizations and Societies

Accountants, American Institute of Certified Public (1887): 412,000+ members; (888) 777-7077; www.aicpa.org

ACMP—The Chamber Music Network (1947): 5,400 members; (212) 645-7424; www.acmp.net

Actuaries, Soc. of (1949): 24,000 members; (847) 706-3500; www.soa.org

Administrative Professionals, Intl. Assn. of (1942): 24,000 members; (816) 891-6600; www.iaap-hq.org

Agricultural and Biological Engineers, American Soc. of (1907): 8,000+ members; (269) 429-0300; www.asabe.org

AIGA (fmr. American Institute of Graphic Arts) (1914): 25,000+ members; (212) 807-1990; www.aiga.org

Air & Waste Management Assn. (1907): 5,000+ members; (412) 232-3444; www.awma.org

AMSUS—The Society of the Federal Health Professionals (1891): nearly 8,000 members; (301) 897-8800; www.amsus.org

APICS—The Assn. for Operations Management (1957): 45,000+ members; (773) 867-1777; www.apics.org

Architects, American Institute of (1857): nearly 88,000 members; (202) 626-7300; www.aia.org

ASIS Intl. (fmr. Amer. Soc. for Industrial Security) (1955): 38,000 members; (703) 519-6200; www.asisonline.org

Astrologers, Inc., American Federation of (1938): 4,000 members; (480) 838-1751; www.astrologers.com

Astronomical Society, American (1899): 7,000 members; (202) 328-2010; www.aas.org

Authors Guild, The (1912): 9,000+ members; (212) 563-5904; www.authorsguild.org

Bankers of America, Independent Community (1930): 6,000+ members; (202) 659-8111; www.icba.org

Bar Assn., American (1878): nearly 400,000 members; (312) 988-5000; www.abanet.org

Bar Assn., Federal (1920): 18,000+ members; (571) 481-9100; www.fedbar.org

Biochemistry and Molecular Biology, American Society for (1906): 12,000+ members; (240) 283-6600; www.asbmb.org

Broadcasters, Natl. Assn. of (1923): 8,300 members; (202) 429-5300; www.nab.org

Business Women's Assn., American (1949): 40,000 members; (800) 228-0007; www.abwa.org

Cartoonists Society, Natl. (1946): 500+ members; (407) 994-6703; www.reuben.org

Ceramic Society, American (1898): 9,500+ members; (240) 646-7054; www.ceramics.org

Chemical Society, American (1876): 157,000+ members; (202) 872-4600; www.chemistry.org

Chiefs of Police, Intl. Assn. of (1893): 20,000+ members; (703) 836-6767; www.theiacp.org

Chiropractic Assn., American (1963): 15,000+ members; (703) 276-8800; www.acatoday.org

Civil Engineers, American Soc. of (1852): 150,000+ members; (703) 295-6300; www.asce.org

College Admission Counseling, Natl. Assn. for (1937): 15,000+ members; (703) 836-2222; www.nacacnet.org

Communication Assn., Natl. (1914): 8,000+ members; (202) 464-4622; www.natcom.org

Composers, Authors & Publishers, American Soc. of (ASCAP) (1914): 575,000+ members; (212) 621-6000; www.ascap.com

Computing Machinery, Assn. for (1947): 100,000+ members; (212) 626-0500; www.acm.org

Computing Professionals, Institute for the Certification of (1973): nearly 55,000 members; (847) 299-4227; www.iccp.org

Counseling Assn., American (1952): 50,000+ members; (800) 347-6647; www.counseling.org

Country Music Assn. (1958): 7,100+ members; (615) 244-2840; www.cmaworld.com

Dental Assn., American (1859): 158,000+ members; (312) 440-2500; www.ada.org

Directors Guild of America (1936): 16,000+ members; (310) 289-2000; www.dga.org

Electrical and Electronics Engineers, Institute of (1963): 425,000+ members; (732) 562-5501; www.ieee.org

Electronics Technicians, Intl. Soc. of Certified (1980): 50,000+ members; (817) 921-9101; www.iscet.org

Energy Engineers, Assn. of (1977): 17,500+ members; (770) 447-5083; www.aeecenter.org

Engineers, Natl. Society of Professional (1934): 31,000+ members; (703) 684-2800; www.nspe.org

Environmental Assessment Assn. (1972): 3,500 members; (877) 743-6806; www.eaa-assoc.org

Environmental Health Assn., Natl. (1937): 5,000 members; (303) 756-9090; www.neha.org

Family Physicians, American Academy of (1947): 120,900 members; (913) 906-6000; www.aafp.org

Farm Bureau Federation, American (1919): 6.2 mil+ members; (202) 406-3600; www.fb.org

Farmers Union, Natl. (1902): 200,000 families; (202) 554-1600; www.nfu.org

Financial Professionals, Assn. for (1979): 16,000+ members; (301) 907-2862; www.afponline.org

Financial Service Professionals, Soc. of (1928): 11,000 members; (610) 526-2500; www.financialpro.org

Fire Chiefs, Intl. Assn. of (1873): nearly 12,000 members; (703) 273-0911; www.iafc.org

Fire Protection Engineers, Soc. of (1950): 4,200+ members; (301) 718-2910; www.sfpe.org

Food Technologists, Institute of (1939): 17,600 members; (312) 782-8424; www.ift.org

Forensic Sciences, American Academy of (1948): 7,000+ members; (719) 636-1100; www.aafs.org

Funeral Directors Assn., Natl. (1882): 19,700 members; (262) 789-1880; www.nfda.org

General Contractors of America, Associated (1918): 26,000+ cos.; (703) 548-3118; www.agc.org

Geographers, Assn. of American (1904): 10,000 members; (202) 234-1450; www.aag.org

Ground Water Assn., Natl. (1948): 12,000+ members; (614) 898-7791; www.ngwa.org

Heating, Refrigerating and Air-Conditioning Engineers, Inc., American Soc. of (1894): 55,000+ members; (404) 636-8400; www.ashrae.org

Home Builders, Natl. Assn. of (1942): 140,000+ members; (202) 266-8200; www.nahb.org

Human Resource Management, Soc. for (SHRM) (1948): 285,000 members; (703) 548-3440; www.shrm.org

Illustrators, Society of (1901): 1,000 members; (212) 838-2560; www.societyillustrators.org

Industrial Designers Society of America (1965): 3,200+ members; (703) 707-6000; www.idsa.org

Intelligence Officers, Assn. of Former (1975): 24 chap., 5,000+ members; (703) 790-0320; www.afio.com

Interior Designers, American Soc. of (1975): 25,000+ members; (202) 546-3480; www.asid.org

Jail Assn., American (1981): 4,000+ members; (301) 790-3930; www.aja.org

Journalists, Society of Professional (1909): about 9,000 members; (317) 927-8000; www.spj.org

Landscape Architects, American Society of (1899): 15,000+ members; (202) 898-2444; www.asla.org

Legal Administrators, Assn. of (1971): nearly 10,000 members; (847) 267-1252; www.alanet.org

Library Assn., American (1876): 55,000+ members; (800) 545-2433; www.ala.org

Lifesaving Assn., U.S. (1964): 12,600+ members; (866) 367-8752; www.usla.org

Logistics, Intl. Society of (SOLE) (1966): 3,000+ members; (301) 459-8446; www.sole.org

Magicians, Intl. Brotherhood of (1922): nearly 11,000 members; (636) 724-2400; www.magician.org

Management Accountants, Inst. of (1919): 80,000+ members; (201) 573-9000; www.imanet.org

Management Assn., American (1923): 4,100 cos., 38,000 ind.; (877) 566-9441; www.amanet.org

Marketing Assn., American (1937): 30,000+ members; (312) 542-9000; www.ama.org

Master Brewers Assn. of the Americas (1887): 3,000+ members; (651) 454-7250; www.mbaa.com

Material and Process Engineering, Soc. for the Advancement of (1944): 5,000+ members; (626) 331-0616; www.sampe.org

Mechanical Engineers, American Soc. of (1880): 130,000+ members; (973) 882-1170; www.asme.org

Medical Assn., American (1847): 250,000 members; (800) 621-8335; www.ama-assn.org

Medical Library Assn. (1898): 4,000+ members; (312) 419-9094; www.mlanet.org

Motion Picture Arts & Sciences, Academy of (1927): 7,000+ members; (310) 247-3000; www.oscars.org

Motion Picture and Television Engineers, Soc. of (1916): 6,000+ members; (914) 761-1100; www.smpte.org

Mystery Writers of America (1945): 3,000+ members; (212) 888-8171; www.mysterywriters.org

NALS...the association for legal professionals (fmr. Natl. Assn. of Legal Secretaries) (1929): 6,000 members; (918) 582-5188; www.nals.org

Notaries, American Society of (1965): approx. 20,000 members; (850) 671-5164; www.notaries.org

Nursing, Natl. League for (1893): 40,000 members, 1,200 institutions; (800) 669-1656; www.nln.org

Operations Management, Assn. for (APICS) (1957): 45,000+ members, 300+ intl. partners; (773) 867-1777; www.apics.org

Optometric Assn., American (1898): 39,000 members; (800) 365-2219; www.aoa.org

Organists, American Guild of (1896): 17,000 members; (212) 870-2310; www.agohq.org

Pharmacists Assn., American (1852): 62,000+ members; (202) 628-4410; www.pharmacist.com

Physical Therapy Assn., American (1921): 90,000+ members; (703) 684-2782; www.apta.org

Plastics Engineers, Society of (1942): nearly 20,000 members; (203) 775-0471; www.4spe.org

Police Assn.—United States Section, Intl. (1962): 10,000 members; (855) 241-9998; www.ipa-usa.org

Population Assn. of America (1930): 3,000 members; (301) 565-6710; www.populationassociation.org

Postmasters of the U.S., Natl. Assn. of (1898): 42,000+ members, 95 clubs; (703) 683-9027; www.napus.org

Press Club, Natl. (1908): 3,500+ members; (202) 662-7500; www.press.org

Professional Ball Players of America, Assn. of (1924): 11,000 members; (714) 528-2012; www.apbpa.org

Professional Beauty Assn. (1904): 12,000+ members; (480) 281-0424; www.probeauty.org

Psychiatric Assn., American (1844): 36,500+ members; (703) 907-7300; www.psychiatry.org

Psychological Assn., American (1892): nearly 117,500 members; (202) 336-5500; www.apa.org

Public Administration, American Soc. for (1939): 8,000 members; (202) 393-7878; www.aspanet.org

Public Health Assn., American (1872): 25,000+ members; (202) 777-2742; www.apha.org

Public Relations Soc. of America (1947): 22,000+ members; (212) 460-1400; www.prsa.org

Range Management, Society for (1948): 4,000+ members; (303) 986-3309; www.rangelands.org

Real Estate Appraisers, Natl. Assn. of (1966): 10,000+ members; (877) 743-6806; www.narea-assoc.org

Rehabilitation Assn., Natl. (1923): 5,600 members; (703) 836-0850; www.national rehab.org

Road & Transportation Builders Assn., American (1902): 6,000+ members; (202) 289-4434; www.artba.org

Safety Engineers, American Soc. of (1911): 36,000+ members; (847) 699-2929; www.asse.org

School Administrators, American Assn. of (1865): 13,000+ members; (703) 528-0700; www.aasa.org

Science Teachers Assn., Natl. (1944): 55,000 members; (703) 243-7100; www.nsta.org

Screen Actors Guild—American Federation of Television and Radio Artists (2012): 160,000 members; (855) 724-2387; www.sagaftra.org

Songwriters Guild of America (1931): 5,000+ members; (615) 742-9945; www.songwritersguild.com

Sportscasters Assn., American (1979): 500+ members; (212) 227-8080; www.americansportscastersonline.com

Surgeons, American College of (1913): 80,000+ members; (312) 202-5000; www.facs.org

Tax Administrators, Federation of (1937): (202) 624-5890; www.taxadmin.org

Teachers of English, Natl. Council of (1911): 35,000+ members; (217) 328-3870; www.ncte.org

Teachers of English to Speakers of Other Languages, Inc. (1966): 11,387 members; (703) 836-0774; www.tesol.org

Teachers of French, American Assn. of (1927): nearly 10,000 members; (815) 310-0490; www.frenchteachers.org

Teachers of German, American Assn. of (1926): 4,000+ members; (856) 795-5553; www.aatg.org

Teachers of Mathematics, Natl. Council of (1920): 80,000 members; (703) 620-9840; www.nctm.org

Teachers of Spanish and Portuguese, American Assn. of (1917): 11,000+ members; (248) 960-2180; www.aatsp.org

Television Arts and Sciences, Natl. Academy of (1955): (212) 586-8424; www.emmyonline.org

Theological Library Assn., American (1946): 800+ members; (312) 454-5100; www.atla.com

Transportation Engineers, Inst. of (1930): nearly 13,000 members; (202) 785-0060; www.ite.org

Travel Agents, American Soc. of (1931): 12,000 members; (703) 739-2782; www.asta.org

Underwriters, Soc. of Chartered Property and Casualty (1944): 22,000+ members; (800) 932-2728; www.cpcusociety.org

University Women, American Assn. of (1881): 100,000+ members; (202) 785-7700; www.aauw.org

Veterinary Medical Assn., American (1863): 88,000+ members; (800) 248-2862; www.avma.org

Women in Communications, The Assn. for (1909): 2,000+ members; (417) 886-8606; www.womcom.org

Women Engineers, Society of (1950): 27,000 members; (877) 793-4636; societyofwomenengineers.swe.org

Women in Media, Alliance for (1951): nearly 10,000 members; (202) 750-3664; www.allwomeninmedia.org

Professional Sports Organizations

Source: World Almanac research

Major League Baseball

Office of the Commissioner, 245 Park Ave., 31st Fl., New York, NY 10167; (212) 931-7800; www.mlb.com

American League

Baltimore Orioles (1953): 333 W. Camden St., Baltimore, MD 21201; (410) 685-9800; www.orioles.com

Boston Red Sox (1901): 4 Yawkey Way, Boston, MA 02215; (617) 267-9440; www.redsox.com

Chicago White Sox (1900, as Chicago White Stockings): 333 W. 35th St., Chicago, IL 60616; (312) 674-1000; www.whitesox.com

Cleveland Indians (1901, as Cleveland Blues): 2401 Ontario St., Cleveland, OH 44115; (216) 420-4200; www.indians.com

Detroit Tigers (1901): 2100 Woodward Ave., Detroit, MI 48201; (313) 471-2000; www.tigers.com

Houston Astros (1962, as Houston Colt 45s): 501 Crawford St., Houston, TX 77002; (713) 259-8000; www.astros.com. (The Astros were a National League team, 1962-2012; the franchise joined the AL West beginning with the 2013 season.)

Kansas City Royals (1969): One Royal Way, Kansas City, MO 64129; (816) 921-8000; www.royals.com

Los Angeles Angels of Anaheim (1961): 2000 Gene Autry Way, Anaheim, CA 92806; (714) 940-2000; www.angels.com

Minnesota Twins (1960): 1 Twins Way, Minneapolis, MN 55403; (612) 659-3400; www.twinsbaseball.com

New York Yankees (1903): One E. 161st St., Bronx, NY 10451; (718) 293-4300; www.yankees.com

Oakland Athletics (1901, as Philadelphia Athletics): 7000 Coliseum Way, Oakland, CA 94621; (510) 638-4900; athletics.com

Seattle Mariners (1977): P.O. Box 4100, Seattle, WA 98104; (206) 346-4000; www.mariners.com

Tampa Bay Rays (1995, as Tampa Bay Devil Rays): One Tropicana Dr., St. Petersburg, FL 33705; (727) 825-3137; www.raysbaseball.com

Texas Rangers (1960, as Washington Senators): 1000 Ballpark Way, Arlington, TX 76011; (817) 273-5222; www.texas rangers.com

Toronto Blue Jays (1976): One Blue Jays Way, Ste. 3200, Toronto, ON M5V 1J1, Canada; (416) 341-1000; www.bluejays.com

National League

Arizona Diamondbacks (1998): 401 E. Jefferson St., Phoenix, AZ 85004; (602) 462-6500; www.dbacks.com

Atlanta Braves (1876, as Boston Red Stockings): 755 Hank Aaron Dr., Atlanta, GA 30315; (404) 522-7630; www.braves.com

Chicago Cubs (1876, as Chicago White Stockings): 1060 W. Addison, Chicago, IL 60613; (773) 404-2827; www.cubs.com

Cincinnati Reds (1869, as Cincinnati Red Stockings): 100 Main St., Cincinnati, OH 45202; (513) 765-7000; www.reds.com

Colorado Rockies (1991): 2001 Blake St., Denver, CO 80205; (303) 292-0200; www.rockies.com

Los Angeles Dodgers (1890): 1000 Elysian Park Ave., Los Angeles, CA 90012; (323) 224-1500; www.dodgers.com

Miami Marlins (1991, as Florida Marlins): 501 Marlins Way, Miami, FL 33125; (305) 480-1300; www.marlins.com

Milwaukee Brewers (1970): One Brewers Way, Milwaukee, WI 53214; (414) 902-4400; www.brewers.com

New York Mets (1961): Citi Field, 120-01 Roosevelt Ave., Corona, NY 11368; (718) 507-6387; www.mets.com

Philadelphia Phillies (1883): One Citizens Bank Way, Philadelphia, PA 19148; (215) 463-6000; www.phillies.com

Pittsburgh Pirates (1887, as Pittsburgh Alleghenies): 115 Federal St., Pittsburgh, PA 15212; (412) 323-5000; www.pirates.com

St. Louis Cardinals (1892, as St. Louis Browns): 700 Clark St., St. Louis, MO 63102; (314) 345-9600; www.cardinals.com

San Diego Padres (1969): 100 Park Blvd., San Diego, CA 92101; (619) 795-5000; www.padres.com

San Francisco Giants (1883, as New York Gothams): 24 Willie Mays Plz., San Francisco, CA 94107; (415) 972-2000; www.sfgiants.com

Washington Nationals (1969, as Montréal Expos): 1500 South Capitol St., SE, Washington, DC 20003; (202) 675-6287; www.nationals.com

National Basketball Association

League Office, 645 Fifth Ave., New York, NY 10022; (212) 407-8000; www.nba.com

Atlanta Hawks (1949, as Tri-Cities Blackhawks): 101 Marietta St. NW, Ste. 1900, Atlanta, GA 30303; (866) 715-1500; www.nba.com/hawks/

Boston Celtics (1946): 226 Causeway St., 4th Fl., Boston, MA 02114; (866) 423-5849; www.nba.com/celtics/

Brooklyn Nets (1967, as New Jersey Americans): 15 MetroTech Ctr., 11th Fl., Brooklyn, NY 11201; (718) 933-3000; www.nba.com/nets/

Charlotte Hornets (2004, as Charlotte Bobcats): 333 E. Trade St., Charlotte, NC 28202; (704) 688-8600; www.nba.com/hornets/

Chicago Bulls (1966): 1901 W. Madison St., Chicago, IL 60612; (312) 455-4000; www.nba.com/bulls/

Cleveland Cavaliers (1970): One Center Ct., Cleveland, OH 44115; (216) 420-2000; www.nba.com/cavaliers/

Dallas Mavericks (1980): 2909 Taylor St., Dallas, TX 75226; (214) 747-6287; www.nba.com/mavericks/

Denver Nuggets (1967, as Denver Rockets): 1000 Chopper Cir., Denver, CO 80204; (303) 405-1100; www.nba.com/nuggets/

Detroit Pistons (1957): Six Championship Dr., Auburn Hills, MI 48326; (248) 377-0100; www.nba.com/pistons/

Golden State Warriors (1946, as Philadelphia Warriors): 1011 Broadway, Oakland, CA 94607; (510) 986-2200; www.nba.com/warriors/

Houston Rockets (1967, as San Diego Rockets): 1510 Polk St., Houston, TX 77002; (713) 627-3865; www.nba.com/rockets/

Indiana Pacers (1967): 125 S. Pennsylvania St., Indianapolis, IN 46204; (317) 917-2500; www.nba.com/pacers/

Los Angeles Clippers (1970, as Buffalo Braves): 1111 S. Figueroa St., Ste. 1100, Los Angeles, CA 90015; (213) 742-7500; www.nba.com/clippers/

Los Angeles Lakers (1947, as Minneapolis Lakers): 555 N. Nash St., El Segundo, CA 90245; (310) 426-6000; www.nba.com/lakers/

Memphis Grizzlies (1995, as Vancouver Grizzlies): 191 Beale St., Memphis, TN 38103; (901) 888-4667; www.nba.com/grizzlies/

Miami Heat (1988): 601 Biscayne Blvd., Miami, FL 33132; (786) 777-1000; www.nba.com/heat/

Milwaukee Bucks (1968): 1001 N. 4th St., Milwaukee, WI 53203; (414) 227-0500; www.nba.com/bucks/

Minnesota Timberwolves (1989): 600 Hennepin Ave., Ste. 300, Minneapolis, MN 55403; (612) 673-1600; www.nba.com/timberwolves/

New Orleans Pelicans (1988, as Charlotte Hornets): 5800 Airline Dr., Metairie, LA 70003; (504) 593-4700; www.nba.com/pelicans/

New York Knickerbockers (1946): Two Pennsylvania Plz., New York, NY 10121; (212) 465-6471; www.nba.com/knicks/

Oklahoma City Thunder (1967, as Seattle SuperSonics): 208 Thunder Dr., Oklahoma City, OK 73102; (405) 208-4800; www.nba.com/thunder/

Orlando Magic (1989): 8701 Maitland Summit Blvd., Orlando, FL 32810; (407) 916-2400; www.nba.com/magic/

Philadelphia 76ers (1937, as Syracuse Nationals): 3601 S. Broad St., Philadelphia, PA 19148; (215) 339-7676; www.nba.com/sixers/

Phoenix Suns (1968): 201 E. Jefferson St., Phoenix, AZ 85004; (602) 379-7900; www.nba.com/suns/

Portland Trail Blazers (1970): One Center Ct., Ste. 200, Portland, OR 97227; (503) 234-9291; www.nba.com/blazers/

Sacramento Kings (1945, as Rochester Royals): One Sports Pkwy., Sacramento, CA 95834; (916) 928-0000; www.nba.com/kings/

San Antonio Spurs (1967, as Dallas Chaparrals): One AT&T Center, San Antonio, TX 78219; (210) 444-5000; www.nba.com/spurs/

Toronto Raptors (1995): 40 Bay St., Toronto, ON M5J 2X2, Canada; (416) 366-3865; www.nba.com/raptors/

Utah Jazz (1974, as New Orleans Jazz): 301 W. South Temple, Salt Lake City, UT 84101; (801) 325-2500; www.nba.com/jazz/

Washington Wizards (1961, as Chicago Packers): 601 F St. NW, Washington, DC 20004; (202) 661-5000; www.nba.com/wizards/

National Hockey League

NHL Headquarters, 1185 Ave. of the Americas, 15th Fl., New York, NY 10036; (212) 789-2000; www.nhl.com

Anaheim Ducks (1993): 2695 E. Katella Ave., Anaheim, CA 92806; (877) 945-3946; ducks.nhl.com

Arizona Coyotes (1979, as Winnipeg Jets): 9400 W. Maryland Ave., Glendale, AZ 85305; (623) 772-3200; coyotes.nhl.com

Boston Bruins (1924): 100 Legends Way, Boston, MA 02114; (617) 624-1900; bruins.nhl.com

Buffalo Sabres (1970): One Seymour H. Knox III Plz., Buffalo, NY 14203; (716) 855-4100; sabres.nhl.com

Calgary Flames (1980): P.O. Box 1540, Station M, Calgary, AB T2P 3B9, Canada; (403) 777-2177; flames.nhl.com

Carolina Hurricanes (1972, as New England Whalers): 1400 Edwards Mill Rd., Raleigh, NC 27607; (919) 467-7825; hurricanes.nhl.com

Chicago Blackhawks (1926): 1901 W. Madison St., Chicago, IL 60612; (312) 455-7000; blackhawks.nhl.com

Colorado Avalanche (1972, as Quebec Nordiques): 1000 Chopper Cir., Denver, CO 80204; (303) 405-1100; avalanche.nhl.com

Columbus Blue Jackets (2000): 200 W. Nationwide Blvd., Suite Level, Columbus, OH 43215; (614) 246-4625; bluejackets.nhl.com

Dallas Stars (1967, as Minnesota North Stars): 2601 Ave. of the Stars, Frisco, TX 75034; (214) 387-5500; stars.nhl.com

Detroit Red Wings (1926, as Detroit Cougars): 600 Civic Center Dr., Detroit, MI 48226; (313) 471-7444; redwings.nhl.com

Edmonton Oilers (1972, as Alberta Oilers): 11230 - 110 St., Edmonton, AB T5G 3H7, Canada; (780) 414-4000; oilers.nhl.com

Florida Panthers (1993): One Panther Pkwy., Sunrise, FL 33323; (954) 835-7000; panthers.nhl.com

Los Angeles Kings (1967): 1111 S. Figueroa St., Ste. 3100, Los Angeles, CA 90015; (213) 742-7100; kings.nhl.com

Minnesota Wild (2000): 317 Washington St., St. Paul, MN 55102; (651) 602-6000; wild.nhl.com

Montréal Canadiens (1917): 1909, avenue des Canadiens-de-Montréal, Montréal, QC H4B 5G0, Canada; (514) 932-2582; canadiens.nhl.com

Nashville Predators (1998): 501 Broadway, Nashville, TN 37203; (615) 770-2355; predators.nhl.com

New Jersey Devils (1974, as Kansas City Scouts): Prudential Center, 25 Lafayette St., Newark, NJ 07102; (973) 757-6100; devils.nhl.com

New York Islanders (1972): 620 Atlantic Ave., Brooklyn, NY 11217; (917) 618-6700; islanders.nhl.com

New York Rangers (1926): Two Pennsylvania Plz., New York, NY 10121; (212) 465-6000; rangers.nhl.com

Ottawa Senators (1992): 1000 Palladium Dr., Ottawa, ON K2V 1A5, Canada; (613) 599-0250; senators.nhl.com

Philadelphia Flyers (1967): 3601 S. Broad St., Philadelphia, PA 19148; (215) 336-3600; flyers.nhl.com

Pittsburgh Penguins (1967): 1001 5th Ave., Pittsburgh, PA 15219; (412) 642-1800; penguins.nhl.com

St. Louis Blues (1967): 1401 Clark Ave. at Brett Hull Way, St. Louis, MO 63103; (314) 622-2500; blues.nhl.com

San Jose Sharks (1991): 525 W. Santa Clara St., San Jose, CA 95113; (408) 287-7070; sharks.nhl.com

Tampa Bay Lightning (1992): 401 Channelside Dr., Tampa, FL 33602; (813) 301-6500; lightning.nhl.com

Toronto Maple Leafs (1919, as Toronto St. Pats): 40 Bay St., Ste. 400, Toronto, ON M5J 2X2, Canada; (416) 815-5700; mapleleafs.nhl.com

Vancouver Canucks (1946, joined NHL in 1970): 800 Griffiths Way, Vancouver, BC V6B 6G1, Canada; (604) 899-7400; canucks.nhl.com

Washington Capitals (1974): 627 N. Glebe Rd., Ste. 850, Arlington, VA 22203; (202) 266-2200; capitals.nhl.com

Winnipeg Jets (1999, as Atlanta Thrashers): 345 Graham Ave., Winnipeg, MB R3C 5S6, Canada; (204) 987-7825; jets.nhl.com

National Football League

League Office, 345 Park Ave., New York, NY 10154; (212) 450-2000; www.nfl.com

Arizona Cardinals (1898, as Morgan Athletic Club): P.O. Box 888, Phoenix, AZ 85001; (602) 379-0101; www.azcardinals.com

Atlanta Falcons (1966): 4400 Falcon Pkwy., Flowery Branch, GA 30542; (770) 965-3115; www.atlantafalcons.com

Baltimore Ravens (1996): 1101 Russell St., Baltimore, MD 21230; (410) 261-7283; www.baltimoreravens.com

Buffalo Bills (1960): One Bills Dr., Orchard Park, NY 14127; (716) 648-1800; www.buffalobills.com

Carolina Panthers (1995): 800 S. Mint St., Charlotte, NC 28202; (704) 358-7000; www.panthers.com

Chicago Bears (1920, as Decatur Staleys): 1920 Football Dr., Lake Forest, IL 60045; (847) 615-2327; www.chicagobears.com

Cincinnati Bengals (1968): One Paul Brown Stadium, Cincinnati, OH 45202; (513) 621-3550; www.bengals.com

Cleveland Browns (1946): 76 Lou Groza Blvd., Berea, OH 44017; (440) 824-3434; www.clevelandbrowns.com

Dallas Cowboys (1960): One AT&T Way, Arlington, TX 76011; (817) 892-4000; www.dallascowboys.com

Denver Broncos (1960): 13655 Broncos Pkwy., Englewood, CO 80112; (303) 649-9000; www.denverbroncos.com

Detroit Lions (1930, as Portsmouth Spartans): 222 Republic Dr., Allen Park, MI 48101; (313) 262-2000; www.detroitlions.com

Green Bay Packers (1919): 1265 Lombardi Ave., Green Bay, WI 54304; (920) 569-7500; www.packers.com

Houston Texans (2002): Two NRG Park, Houston, TX 77054; (832) 667-2002; www.houstontexans.com

Indianapolis Colts (1953, as Baltimore Colts): 7001 W. 56th St., Indianapolis, IN 46254; (317) 297-2658; www.colts.com

Jacksonville Jaguars (1995): One EverBank Field Dr., Jacksonville, FL 32202; (904) 633-2000; www.jaguars.com

Kansas City Chiefs (1960, as Dallas Texans): One Arrowhead Dr., Kansas City, MO 64129; (816) 920-9300; www.kcchiefs.com

Los Angeles Rams (1937, as Cleveland Rams): 29899 Agoura Rd., Agoura Hills, CA 91301; (310) 277-4700; www.therams.com

Miami Dolphins (1966): 347 Don Shula Dr., Miami Gardens, FL 33056; (305) 943-8000; www.miamidolphins.com

Minnesota Vikings (1961): 9520 Viking Dr., Eden Prairie, MN 55344; (952) 828-6500; www.vikings.com

New England Patriots (1960): One Patriot Pl., Foxboro, MA 02035; (508) 543-8200; www.patriots.com

New Orleans Saints (1967): 5800 Airline Dr., Metairie, LA 70003; (504) 733-0255; www.neworleanssaints.com

New York Giants (1925): 1925 Giants Dr., E. Rutherford, NJ 07073; (201) 935-8111; www.giants.com

New York Jets (1960, as New York Titans): One Jets Dr., Florham Park, NJ 07932; (800) 469-5387; www.newyorkjets.com

Oakland Raiders (1960): 1220 Harbor Bay Pkwy., Alameda, CA 94502; (510) 864-5000; www.raiders.com

Philadelphia Eagles (1933): One NovaCare Way, Philadelphia, PA 19145; (215) 463-2500; www.philadelphiaeagles.com

Pittsburgh Steelers (1933): 3400 S. Water St., Pittsburgh, PA 15203; (412) 432-7800; www.steelers.com

San Diego Chargers (1960, as Los Angeles Chargers): P.O. Box 609609, San Diego, CA 92160; (858) 874-4500; www.chargers.com

San Francisco 49ers (1946): 4949 Centennial Blvd., Santa Clara, CA 95054; (408) 562-4949; www.49ers.com

Seattle Seahawks (1976): 12 Seahawks Way, Renton, WA 98056; (888) 635-4295; www.seahawks.com

Tampa Bay Buccaneers (1976): One Buccaneer Pl., Tampa, FL 33607; (813) 870-2700; www.buccaneers.com

Tennessee Titans (1960, as Houston Oilers): 460 Great Circle Rd., Nashville, TN 37228; (615) 565-4000; www.titansonline.com

Washington Redskins (1932, as Boston Braves): 21300 Redskin Park Dr., Ashburn, VA 20147; (703) 726-7000; www.redskins.com

Health Organizations

Source: World Almanac research

Entries are roughly alphabetized by the basic condition addressed or organization name. Year established is in parentheses. Always check with a physician before embarking on any new health-related undertaking.

Al-Anon Family Groups (1951): (757) 563-1600; www.al-anon.alateen.org

Alcoholics Anonymous (1935): (212) 870-3400; www.aa.org

Alcoholism and Drug Dependence, Inc., Natl. Council on (1944): (212) 269-7797; www.ncadd.org

Aging, Natl. Institute on (1974): (800) 222-2225; www.nia.nih.gov

Aging's Eldercare Locator, Admin. on (1991): (800) 677-1116; www.eldercare.gov

AIDSinfo: (800) 448-0440; www.aidsinfo.nih.gov

Allergy, Asthma and Immunology, American Academy of (1943): (414) 272-6071; www.aaaai.org

ALS Assn. [Lou Gehrig's disease] (1985): (202) 407-8580; www.alsa.org

Alzheimer's Assn. (1979): (800) 272-3900; www.alz.org

Anorexia Nervosa and Associated Disorders, Natl. Assn. of (1976): (630) 577-1333; www.anad.org

Arc of the United States, The (1950): (800) 433-5255; www.thearc.org

Arthritis Foundation (1948): (800) 283-7800; www.arthritis.org

Arthritis and Musculoskeletal and Skin Diseases, Natl. Institute of (1986): (877) 226-4267; www.niams.nih.gov

Asthma and Allergy Foundation of America (1953): (800) 727-8462; www.aafa.org

Autism Society (1965): (800) 328-8476; www.autism-society.org

Blind, American Council of the (1961): (202) 467-5081; (800) 424-8666; www.acb.org

Blind, Natl. Federation of the (1940): (410) 659-9314; www.nfb.org

Blindness, Foundation Fighting (1971): (800) 683-5555; www.blindness.org

Blindness, Prevent (1908): (800) 331-2020; www.preventblindness.org

Brain Tumor Society, Natl. (2008): (617) 924-9997; www.braintumor.org

Breast Cancer Diagnosis, After (ABCD) (1999): (414) 977-1780; (800) 977-4121; www.abcdbreastcancersupport.org

Cancer Institute's Cancer Information Service, Natl. (1975): (800) 422-6237; www.cancer.gov/aboutnci/cis/

Cancer Society, American (1913): (800) 227-2345; www.cancer.org

Centers for Disease Control and Prevention (CDC) (1946): (800) 232-4636; www.cdc.gov

Cerebral Palsy, United (1949): (202) 776-0406; (800) 872-5827; www.ucp.org

Child Abuse and Family Violence, Natl. Council on (1984): (202) 429-6695; www.nccafv.org

Childhelp Natl. Child Abuse Hotline (1959): (800) 422-4453; www.childhelp.org

Children, Natl. Center for Missing and Exploited (1984): (703) 224-2150; (800) 843-5678; www.missingkids.com

Children's Tumor Foundation (1978): (212) 344-6633; (800) 323-7938; www.ctf.org

Chronic Pain Assn., American (1980): (800) 533-3231; www.theacpa.org

Continence, Natl. Assn. for (1982): (843) 419-5307; (800) 252-3337; www.nafc.org

Cooley's Anemia Foundation (1954): (800) 522-7222; www.thalassemia.org

Crohn's and Colitis Foundation of America (1967): (800) 932-2423; www.ccfa.org

Cystic Fibrosis Foundation (1955): (800) 344-4823 or (301) 951-4422; www.cff.org

Deaf, Natl. Assn. of the (1880): (301) 587-1788, TTY (301) 587-1789; www.nad.org

Depression and Bipolar Support Alliance (1985): (800) 826-3632; www.dbsalliance.org

Diabetes Assn., American (1940): (800) 342-2383; www.diabetes.org

Diabetes and Digestive and Kidney Diseases, Natl. Institute of (1950): (301) 496-3583; www.kidney.niddk.nih.gov

Dial-A-Hearing Screening Test: (800) 222-EARS (222-3277)

Domestic Violence Hotline, Natl. (1996): (800) 799-7233; TTY (800) 787-3224; www.thehotline.org

Down Syndrome Congress, Natl. (1973): (800) 232-6372; www.ndsccenter.org

Down Syndrome Society, Natl. (1979): (800) 221-4602; www.ndss.org

Dyslexia Assn., Intl. (1949): (410) 296-0232; www.interdys.org

Easterseals [special needs] (1919): (800) 221-6827; www.easterseals.com

Endometriosis Assn. (1980): (414) 355-2200; www.endometriosisassn.org

Epilepsy Foundation (1967): (800) 332-1000; www.epilepsyfoundation.org

Fat Acceptance, Natl. Assn. to Advance (1969): (916) 558-6880; www.naafa.org

First Candle [sudden infant death syndrome] (1987): (800) 221-7437; www.sidsalliance.org

FoodSafety.gov—Gateway to Federal Food Safety Information: Food: (888) 723-3366; Meat, poultry, eggs: (888) 674-6854; Illness or food poisoning: (800) 232-4636 (CDC)

Gamblers Anonymous (1957): (626) 960-3500; www.gamblersanonymous.org

Geriatrics Society, American (1942): (212) 308-1414; www.americangeriatrics.org

Headache Foundation, Natl. (1970): (888) 643-5552; www.headaches.org

HealthyWomen (1988): (877) 986-9472; www.healthywomen.org

Hearing Society, Intl. (1951): (734) 522-7200; www.ihsinfo.org

Heart Assn., American (1924): (800) 242-8721; www.heart.org

Hearts, Inc., Mended (1951): (888) 432-7899; www.mendedhearts.org

Hospice Education Institute (1985): (800) 331-1620; www.hospiceworld.org

Hospice Intl., Children's (1983): (703) 684-0330; www.chionline.org

Hospital Assn., American (1899): (312) 422-3000; (800) 424-4301; www.aha.org

Huntington's Disease Society of America (1967): (800) 345-4372; www.hdsa.org

JDRF (fmr. Juvenile Diabetes Research Foundation) (1970): (800) 533-2873; www.jdrf.org

Kidney Foundation, Natl. (1950): (800) 622-9010; www.kidney.org

Kidney Fund, American (1971): (866) 300-2900; www.kidneyfund.org

La Leche League Intl. [breastfeeding] (1957): (800) 525-3243; www.llli.org

Leukemia and Lymphoma Society (1949): (800) 955-4572; www.lls.org

Liver Foundation, American (1976): (800) 465-4837; www.liverfoundation.org

Living Bank [organ donation] (1968): (713) 961-9431; (800) 528-2971; www.livingbank.org

Lung Assn., American (1904): (800) 586-4872; www.lung.org

Lung Line (1983): (800) 222-5864; www.nationaljewish.org/about/contact/lung-line/

Lupus Foundation of America, Inc. (1977): (202) 349-1155; (800) 558-0121; www.lupus.org

March of Dimes [babies' health] (1938): (914) 997-4488; www.marchofdimes.org

Marfan Foundation. (1981): (800) 8-MARFAN (862-7326); www.marfan.org

Mayo Clinic (1889): (507) 284-2511; www.mayoclinic.org

ME/CFS Initiative, Solve [myalgic encephalomyelitis/chronic fatigue syndrome] (1987): (704) 364-0016; solvecfs.org

Mental Health, Natl. Institute of (1946): (866) 615-6464; www.nimh.nih.gov

Mental Health America (1909): (703) 684-7722; (800) 969-6642; www.nmha.org

Mental Illness, Natl. Alliance on (1979): (800) 950-6264; www.nami.org

Multiple Sclerosis Society, Natl. (1946): (800) 344-4867; www.nationalmssociety.org

Muscular Dystrophy Assn. (1950): (800) 572-1717; www.mda.org

Myeloma Foundation, Intl. (1990): (800) 452-2873; www.myeloma.org

Narcotics Anonymous (1953): (818) 773-9999; www.na.org

Natl. Health Council (1920): (202) 785-3910; www.nationalhealthcouncil.org

Natl. Health Information Center (1979): (240) 453-8280; www.health.gov/NHIC/

Natl. Institutes of Health (NIH) (1887): (301) 496-4000; www.nih.gov

Neurological Disorders and Stroke, Natl. Institute of (1950): (301) 496-5751; (800) 352-9424; www.ninds.nih.gov

Organ Sharing, United Network for (1984): (804) 782-4800; (888) 894-6361; www.unos.org

Osteoporosis Foundation, Natl. (1984): (800) 231-4222; www.nof.org

Overeaters Anonymous (1960): (505) 891-2664; www.oa.org

Parkinson Foundation, Natl. (1957): (800) 473-4636; www.parkinson.org

Parkinson's Disease Foundation (1957): (800) 457-6676; www.pdf.org

Pediatrics, American Academy of (1930): (800) 433-9016; www.aap.org

Phoenix House [substance abuse] (1967): (888) 671-9392; www.phoenixhouse.org

Planned Parenthood Federation of America, Inc. (1916): (800) 230-7526; www.plannedparenthood.org

Plastic Surgeons, American Society of (1931): (800) 514-5058; www.plastic-surgery.org

Post-Polio Health Intl. (1960): (314) 534-0475; www.post-polio.org

Psoriasis Foundation, Natl. (1966): (800) 723-9166; www.psoriasis.org

Rare Disorders, Natl. Org. for (1983): (203) 744-0100; www.rarediseases.org

Rehabilitation Information Center, Natl. (1977): (800) 346-2742; TTY (301) 459-5984; www.naric.com

Reye's Syndrome Foundation, Natl. (1974): (800) 233-7393; www.reyessyndrome.org

Runaway Safeline, Natl. (1971): (800) 786-2929; www.1800runaway.org

Scleroderma Foundation (1989): (978) 463-5843; (800) 722-4673; www.scleroderma.org

Sexual Health Assn., American (1914): (919) 361-8400; www.ashastd.org

Sickle Cell Disease Assn. of America (1971): (410) 528-1555; (800) 421-8453; www.sicklecelldisease.org

Sjögren's Syndrome Foundation (1983): (800) 475-6473; www.sjogrens.org

Speech-Language-Hearing Assn., American (1925): (800) 638-8255, TTY (301) 296-5650; www.asha.org

Spinal Assn., United (1946): (718) 803-3782; www.spinalcord.org

Stroke Assn., Natl. (1984): (800) 787-6537; www.stroke.org

Stuttering Assn., Natl. (1977): (212) 944-4050; (800) 937-8888; www.nsastutter.org

Stuttering Foundation of America (1947): (800) 992-9392; www.stutteringhelp.org

Substance Abuse and Mental Health Services Admin.: (877) 726-4727; www.samhsa.gov

Sudden Infant Death Syndrome Institute, Amer. (1983): (239) 431-5425; www.sids.org

Suicide Prevention Lifeline, Natl. (2004): (800) 273-TALK (8255); www.suicidepreventionlifeline.org

Therapy Dogs Intl. (1976): (973) 252-9800; www.tdi-dog.org

Tourette Assn. of America (fmr. Tourette Syndrome Assn.) (1972): (718) 224-2999; www.tsa-usa.org

Tuberous Sclerosis Alliance (1974): (301) 562-9890; (800) 225-6872; www.tsalliance.org

Urological Assn., American (1902): (866) 746-4282; www.auanet.org

Visual Impairments, Natl. Assn. of Parents of Children with (1980): (800) 284-4422; www.napvi.org

Women's Health Network, Natl. (1975): (202) 682-2640; www.nwhn.org

UNITED STATES FACTS

Superlative U.S. Statistics

Source: U.S. Geological Survey, U.S. Dept. of the Interior; U.S. Census Bureau, U.S. Dept. of Commerce; World Almanac research

Superlative Statistics for the 50 States

Total area for 50 states and Washington, DC		3,796,742 sq mi
Land area for 50 states and Washington, DC		3,531,905 sq mi
Water area for 50 states and Washington, DC		264,837 sq mi
Largest state	Alaska	665,384 sq mi
Smallest state	Rhode Island	1,545 sq mi
Largest county (excluding Alaska)	San Bernardino County, CA	20,105 sq mi
Smallest county	Arlington County, VA[1]	26 sq mi
Largest incorporated city (by area, pop. 1,000+)	Sitka, AK	4,811 sq mi
Northernmost city	Barrow, AK	71°17′ N
Northernmost point	Point Barrow, AK	71°23′ N
Southernmost city	Hilo, HI	19°43′ N
Southernmost settlement	Naalehu, HI	19°03′ N
Southernmost point	Ka Lae (South Cape), island of Hawaii	18°55′ N (155°41′ W)
Easternmost city	Eastport, ME	66°59′24″ W
Easternmost settlement[2]	Attu Station, AK	173°11′ E
Easternmost point[2]	Pochnoi Point, Semisopochnoi Island, AK	179°52′ E
Westernmost city	Adak (formerly Adak Station), AK	173°11′ E
Westernmost settlement	Adak (formerly Adak Station), AK	173°11′ E
Westernmost point	Amatignak Island, AK	179°09′ W
Highest incorporated city	Leadville, CO	10,158 ft
Lowest settlement	Bombay Beach, CA	−208 ft
Highest point on Atlantic coast	Cadillac Mountain, Mount Desert Island, ME	1,530 ft
Oldest national park	Yellowstone National Park (1872), WY-MT-ID	2,219,791 acres
Largest national park	Wrangell-St. Elias, AK	8,323,146 acres
Longest river system	Mississippi-Missouri-Red Rock	3,710 mi
Highest mountain	Denali (fmr. Mt. McKinley), AK	20,310 ft
Lowest point	Death Valley, CA	−282 ft
Deepest lake	Crater Lake, OR	1,949 ft
Rainiest spot	Mount Waialeale, Kauai, HI	annual avg. rainfall 422 in.
Largest gorge	Grand Canyon, Colorado River, AZ	277 mi long, 600 ft to 18 mi wide, 1 mi deep
Deepest gorge	Hells Canyon, Snake River, OR-ID	7,900 ft
Largest dam	New Cornelia Tailings, Ten Mile Wash, AZ[3]	274,026,000 cu yds material used
Tallest building	One World Trade Center, New York, NY	1,776 ft
Largest building	Boeing Everett Production Facility, Everett, WA	472,000,000 cu ft; covers 98 acres
Largest office building	Pentagon, Arlington, VA	77,015,000 cu ft; covers 29 acres
Tallest supported structure	KVLY-TV Tower, Blanchard, ND	2,063 ft
Tallest freestanding tower	Stratosphere Tower, Las Vegas, NV	1,149 ft
Longest bridge span	Verrazano-Narrows Bridge, New York, NY	4,260 ft
Highest bridge	Royal Gorge Bridge, Cañon City, CO	1,053 ft above water
Deepest well (onshore)	Bertha Rogers No. 1 (inactive gas well), Washita County, OK	31,441 ft

Superlative Statistics for the 48 Contiguous States

Total area for 48 states and Washington, DC		3,129,611 sq mi
Land area for 48 states and Washington, DC		2,958,868 sq mi
Water area for 48 states and Washington, DC		170,743 sq mi
Largest state	Texas	268,596 sq mi
Northernmost city	Bellingham, WA	48°46′ N
Northernmost settlement	Angle Inlet, MN	49°20′ N
Northernmost point	Northwest Angle, MN	49°21′ N
Southernmost city	Key West, FL	24°33′ N
Southernmost mainland city	Florida City, FL	25°27′ N
Southernmost point	Ballast Key, FL	24°31′ N
Easternmost settlement	Lubec, ME	66°58′49″ W
Easternmost point	West Quoddy Head, ME	66°57′ W
Westernmost town	La Push, WA	124°38′ W
Westernmost point	Bodelteh Islands, WA	124°46′ W
Highest mountain	Mount Whitney, CA	14,505 ft

(1) Smallest county by land area is Kalawao County, Hawaii, at 12 sq mi; its total area (including water) is 53 sq mi. Superlative shown is for smallest total area. (2) As measured if the prime meridian and 180° longitude are considered east-west boundaries. (3) Privately owned industrial dam composed of tailings, remnants of a mining process.

Highest and Lowest Elevations in U.S. States and Territories

Source: U.S. Geological Survey, U.S. Dept. of the Interior
(negative sign indicates below sea level)

State/territory	Highest point Name	County	Elev. (ft)	Lowest point Name	County	Elev. (ft)
Alabama	Cheaha Mountain	Cleburne	2,413	Gulf of Mexico		Sea level
Alaska	Denali (fmr. Mt. McKinley)	Denali	20,310	Pacific Ocean		Sea level
American Samoa	Lata Mountain	Tau Island	3,160	Pacific Ocean		Sea level
Arizona	Humphreys Peak	Coconino	12,637	Colorado R.	Yuma	70
Arkansas	Magazine Mountain	Logan	2,753	Ouachita R.	Ashley-Union	55
California	Mount Whitney	Inyo-Tulare	14,505	Death Valley	Inyo	−282
Colorado	Mount Elbert	Lake	14,440	Arikaree R.	Yuma	3,315
Connecticut	S. slope of Mt. Frissell (peak in MA)	Litchfield	2,380	Long Island Sound		Sea level
Delaware	Nr. Ebright Azimuth	New Castle	450	Atlantic Ocean		Sea level
Dist. of Columbia	Fort Reno Park	NW quadrant	409	Potomac R.		1
Florida	Britton Hill	Walton	345	Atlantic Ocean		Sea level
Georgia	Brasstown Bald	Towns-Union	4,840	Atlantic Ocean		Sea level
Guam	Mount Lamlam	Agat District	1,332	Pacific Ocean		Sea level
Hawaii	Pu'u Wekiu, Mauna Kea	Hawaii	13,796	Pacific Ocean		Sea level
Idaho	Borah Peak	Custer	12,668	Snake R.	Nez Perce	710
Illinois	Charles Mound	Jo Daviess	1,235	Mississippi R.	Alexander	279
Indiana	Hoosier Hill	Wayne	1,257	Ohio R.	Posey	320
Iowa	Hawkeye Point	Osceola	1,670	Mississippi R.	Lee	480
Kansas	Mount Sunflower	Wallace	4,039	Verdigris R.	Montgomery	679
Kentucky	Black Mountain	Harlan	4,139	Mississippi R.	Fulton	257
Louisiana	Driskill Mountain	Bienville	535	New Orleans	Orleans	−8
Maine	Mount Katahdin	Piscataquis	5,269	Atlantic Ocean		Sea level
Maryland	Hoye Crest	Garrett	3,360	Atlantic Ocean		Sea level
Massachusetts	Mount Greylock	Berkshire	3,491	Atlantic Ocean		Sea level
Michigan	Mount Arvon	Baraga	1,979	Lake Erie		571
Minnesota	Eagle Mountain	Cook	2,301	Lake Superior		601
Mississippi	Woodall Mountain	Tishomingo	806	Gulf of Mexico		Sea level
Missouri	Taum Sauk Mountain	Iron	1,772	St. Francis R.	Dunklin	230
Montana	Granite Peak	Park	12,807	Kootenai R.	Lincoln	1,800
Nebraska	Panorama Point	Kimball	5,424	Missouri R.	Richardson	840
Nevada	Boundary Peak	Esmeralda	13,146	Colorado R.	Clark	479
New Hampshire	Mount Washington	Coos	6,289	Atlantic Ocean		Sea level
New Jersey	High Point	Sussex	1,803	Atlantic Ocean		Sea level
New Mexico	Wheeler Peak	Taos	13,167	Red Bluff Reservoir	Eddy	2,842
New York	Mount Marcy	Essex	5,343	Atlantic Ocean		Sea level
North Carolina	Mount Mitchell	Yancey	6,683	Atlantic Ocean		Sea level
North Dakota	White Butte	Slope	3,506	Red R. of the North	Pembina	750
Northern Mariana Isls.	Mount Agrihan	Agrihan Island	3,166	Pacific Ocean		Sea level
Ohio	Campbell Hill	Logan	1,550	Ohio R.	Hamilton	455
Oklahoma	Black Mesa	Cimarron	4,973	Little R.	McCurtain	289
Oregon	Mount Hood	Clackamas-Hood R.	11,247	Pacific Ocean		Sea level
Pennsylvania	Mount Davis	Somerset	3,213	Delaware R.	Delaware	Sea level
Puerto Rico	Cerro de Punta	Ponce District	4,390	Atlantic Ocean		Sea level
Rhode Island	Jerimoth Hill	Providence	812	Atlantic Ocean		Sea level
South Carolina	Sassafras Mountain	Pickens	3,560	Atlantic Ocean		Sea level
South Dakota	Harney Peak	Pennington	7,244	Big Stone Lake	Roberts	966
Tennessee	Clingmans Dome	Sevier	6,644	Mississippi R.	Shelby	178
Texas	Guadalupe Peak	Culberson	8,751	Gulf of Mexico		Sea level
Utah	Kings Peak	Duchesne	13,518	Beaver Dam Wash	Washington	2,000
Vermont	Mount Mansfield	Chittenden	4,395	Lake Champlain		95
Virgin Islands	Crown Mountain	St. Thomas Island	1,556	Atlantic Ocean		Sea level
Virginia	Mount Rogers	Grayson-Smyth	5,729	Atlantic Ocean		Sea level
Washington	Mount Rainier	Pierce	14,410	Pacific Ocean		Sea level
West Virginia	Spruce Knob	Pendleton	4,863	Potomac R.	Jefferson	240
Wisconsin	Timms Hill	Price	1,951	Lake Michigan		579
Wyoming	Gannett Peak	Fremont	13,810	Belle Fourche R.	Crook	3,099

U.S. Coastline by State

Source: National Oceanic and Atmospheric Administration, U.S. Dept. of Commerce
(in statute miles; only states with coastline or shoreline are shown)

	Coastline[1]	Shoreline[2]		Coastline[1]	Shoreline[2]
Atlantic Coast	**2,069**	**28,673**	**Gulf Coast**	**1,631**	**17,141**
Connecticut	0	618	Alabama	53	607
Delaware	28	381	Florida	770	5,095
Florida	580	3,331	Louisiana	397	7,721
Georgia	100	2,344	Mississippi	44	359
Maine	228	3,478	Texas	367	3,359
Maryland	31	3,190			
Massachusetts	192	1,519	**Pacific Coast**	**7,623**	**40,298**
New Hampshire	13	131	Alaska	5,580	31,383
New Jersey	130	1,792	California	840	3,427
New York	127	1,850	Hawaii	750	1,052
North Carolina	301	3,375	Oregon	296	1,410
Pennsylvania	0	89	Washington	157	3,026
Rhode Island	40	384			
South Carolina	187	2,876	**Arctic Coast**	**1,060**	**2,521**
Virginia	112	3,315	**United States**	**12,383**	**88,633**

(1) Length of general outline of seacoast. Measurements were made in 1948 with a unit measure of 30 minutes of latitude on charts as near the scale of 1:1,200,000 as possible. Includes coastlines of large sounds and bays. (2) Shoreline of outer coast, offshore islands, sounds, bays, rivers, and creeks to the head of tidewater or to a point where tidal waters narrow to a width of 100 ft. Figures obtained in 1939-40 with a recording instrument on the largest-scale charts and maps then available.

States: Capitals, Key Dates, Geographic Data

Source: *Statistical Abstract of the United States*, U.S. Census Bureau, U.S. Dept. of Commerce

The 13 colonies that declared independence from Great Britain and fought the War of Independence (American Revolution) became the 13 original states. They were, in the order in which they ratified the Constitution: Delaware, Pennsylvania, New Jersey, Georgia, Connecticut, Massachusetts, Maryland, South Carolina, New Hampshire, Virginia, New York, North Carolina, and Rhode Island.

State	Settled[1]	Capital	Entered Union Date	Entered Union Order	Extent (mi) Length (approx.	Extent (mi) Width mean)	Area (sq mi) Land	Area (sq mi) Water	Area (sq mi) Total	Rank by tot. area
AL	1702	Montgomery	Dec. 14, 1819	22	330	190	50,645	1,775	52,420	30
AK	1784	Juneau	Jan. 3, 1959	49	1,480[2]	810	570,641	94,743	665,384	1
AZ	1776	Phoenix	Feb. 14, 1912	48	400	310	113,594	396	113,990	6
AR	1686	Little Rock	June 15, 1836	25	260	240	52,035	1,143	53,179	29
CA	1769	Sacramento	Sept. 9, 1850	31	770	250	155,779	7,916	163,695	3
CO	1858	Denver	Aug. 1, 1876	38	380	280	103,642	452	104,094	8
CT	1634	Hartford	Jan. 9, 1788	5	110	70	4,842	701	5,543	48
DE	1638	Dover	Dec. 7, 1787	1	96	30	1,949	540	2,489	49
DC	NA	NA	NA	NA	NA	NA	61	7	68	51
FL	1565	Tallahassee	Mar. 3, 1845	27	447	361	53,625	12,133	65,758	22
GA	1733	Atlanta	Jan. 2, 1788	4	300	230	57,513	1,912	59,425	24
HI	1820	Honolulu	Aug. 21, 1959	50	NA	NA	6,423	4,509	10,932	43
ID	1842	Boise	July 3, 1890	43	479	305	82,643	926	83,569	14
IL	1720	Springfield	Dec. 3, 1818	21	390	210	55,519	2,395	57,914	25
IN	1733	Indianapolis	Dec. 11, 1816	19	270	140	35,826	593	36,420	38
IA	1788	Des Moines	Dec. 28, 1846	29	310	200	55,857	416	56,273	26
KS	1727	Topeka	Jan. 29, 1861	34	400	210	81,759	520	82,278	15
KY	1774	Frankfort	June 1, 1792	15	380	140	39,486	921	40,408	37
LA	1699	Baton Rouge	Apr. 30, 1812	18	380	130	43,204	9,174	52,378	31
ME	1624	Augusta	Mar. 15, 1820	23	320	190	30,843	4,537	35,380	39
MD	1634	Annapolis	Apr. 28, 1788	7	250	90	9,707	2,699	12,406	42
MA	1620	Boston	Feb. 6, 1788	6	190	50	7,800	2,754	10,554	44
MI	1668	Lansing	Jan. 26, 1837	26	490	240	56,539	40,175	96,714	11
MN	1805	St. Paul	May 11, 1858	32	400	250	79,627	7,309	86,936	12
MS	1699	Jackson	Dec. 10, 1817	20	340	170	46,923	1,509	48,432	32
MO	1735	Jefferson City	Aug. 10, 1821	24	300	240	68,742	965	69,707	21
MT	1809	Helena	Nov. 8, 1889	41	630	280	145,546	1,494	147,040	4
NE	1823	Lincoln	Mar. 1, 1867	37	430	210	76,824	524	77,348	16
NV	1849	Carson City	Oct. 31, 1864	36	490	320	109,781	791	110,572	7
NH	1623	Concord	June 21, 1788	9	190	70	8,953	397	9,349	46
NJ	1660	Trenton	Dec. 18, 1787	3	150	70	7,354	1,368	8,723	47
NM	1610	Santa Fe	Jan. 6, 1912	47	370	343	121,298	292	121,590	5
NY	1614	Albany	July 26, 1788	11	330	283	47,126	7,429	54,555	27
NC	1660	Raleigh	Nov. 21, 1789	12	500	150	48,618	5,201	53,819	28
ND	1812	Bismarck	Nov. 2, 1889	39	340	211	69,001	1,698	70,698	19
OH	1788	Columbus	Mar. 1, 1803	17	220	220	40,861	3,965	44,826	34
OK	1889	Oklahoma City	Nov. 16, 1907	46	400	220	68,595	1,304	69,899	20
OR	1811	Salem	Feb. 14, 1859	33	360	261	95,988	2,391	98,379	9
PA	1682	Harrisburg	Dec. 12, 1787	2	283	160	44,743	1,312	46,054	33
RI	1636	Providence	May 29, 1790	13	40	30	1,034	511	1,545	50
SC	1670	Columbia	May 23, 1788	8	260	200	30,061	1,960	32,020	40
SD	1859	Pierre	Nov. 2, 1889	40	370	210	75,811	1,305	77,116	17
TN	1769	Nashville	June 1, 1796	16	491	115	41,235	909	42,144	36
TX	1682	Austin	Dec. 29, 1845	28	790	660	261,232	7,365	268,596	2
UT	1847	Salt Lake City	Jan. 4, 1896	45	350	270	82,170	2,727	84,897	13
VT	1724	Montpelier	Mar. 4, 1791	14	160	80	9,217	400	9,616	45
VA	1607	Richmond	June 25, 1788	10	430	200	39,490	3,285	42,775	35
WA	1811	Olympia	Nov. 11, 1889	42	360	240	66,456	4,842	71,298	18
WV	1727	Charleston	June 20, 1863	35	240	130	24,038	192	24,230	41
WI	1766	Madison	May 29, 1848	30	310	260	54,158	11,339	65,496	23
WY	1834	Cheyenne	July 10, 1890	44	360	280	97,093	720	97,813	10

NA = Not applicable. **Note:** Land and water areas may not add up to totals because of rounding. (1) First permanent settlement by Europeans. (2) Does not include Aleutian Islands or Alexander Archipelago.

Continental Divide of the U.S.

The Continental Divide of the U.S., also known as the Great Divide, is located at the watershed created by the mountain ranges, or tablelands, of the Rocky Mountains. This watershed separates the waters that ultimately drain into the Atlantic Ocean and its marginal seas from those waters that drain into the Pacific Ocean. The majority of water flowing E in the U.S. drains into the Gulf of Mexico and then the Atlantic. The majority of water flowing W drains through the Columbia River or Colorado River, which flows into the Gulf of California before reaching the Pacific.

The location and route of the Continental Divide across the U.S. can be described as follows:

Beginning at the U.S.-Mexico border, near longitude 108°45′ W, the Divide, in a northerly direction, crosses New Mexico along the western edge of the Rio Grande drainage basin, entering Colorado near longitude 106°41′ W. From there by an irregular route N across Colorado along the western summits of the Rio Grande and Arkansas, South Platte,

and North Platte river basins, and across Rocky Mountain National Park, entering Wyoming near longitude 106°52′ W.

From there in a northwesterly direction, forming the western rims of the North Platte, Big Horn, and Yellowstone river basins, crossing the SW portion of Yellowstone National Park. From there in a westerly and then northerly direction forming the boundary between Idaho and Montana, to a point on the boundary near longitude 114°00′ W. From there northeasterly and northwesterly through Montana and Glacier National Park, entering Canada near longitude 114°04′ W.

Depending on how a "divide" is defined, the U.S. can also be characterized as having a Northern (or Laurentian) Divide, Eastern Divide, and St. Lawrence Seaway Divide. Some of the waters at the Northern Divide drain into Hudson Bay and the Arctic Ocean. The Appalachian Mountains mark the Eastern Divide, with waters joining the Atlantic or Gulf of Mexico. The waters at the St. Lawrence Seaway Divide, near Chicago, flow into the Gulf of St. Lawrence or Gulf of Mexico.

Chronological List of Territories, With State Admissions to Union

Source: U.S. National Archives and Records Administration

Territory	Date of act creating territory	When act took effect	Date of admission as state	Years as terr.
Northwest Territory[1]	July 13, 1787	No fixed date	Mar. 1, 1803[2]	16
Territory South of Ohio River (Southwest Territory)	May 26, 1790	No fixed date	June 1, 1796[3]	6
Mississippi	Apr. 7, 1798	When president acted	Dec. 10, 1817	19
Indiana	May 7, 1800	July 4, 1800	Dec. 11, 1816	16
Orleans	Mar. 26, 1804	Oct. 1, 1804	Apr. 30, 1812[4]	7
Michigan	Jan. 11, 1805	June 30, 1805	Jan. 26, 1837	31
Louisiana-Missouri[5]	Mar. 3, 1805	July 4, 1805	Aug. 10, 1821	16
Illinois	Feb. 3, 1809	Mar. 1, 1809	Dec. 3, 1818	9
Alabama	Mar. 3, 1817	When MS formed state govt.	Dec. 14, 1819	2
Arkansas	Mar. 2, 1819	July 4, 1819	June 15, 1836	17
Florida	Mar. 30, 1822	No fixed date	Mar. 3, 1845	23
Wisconsin	Apr. 20, 1836	July 3, 1836	May 29, 1848	12
Iowa	June 12, 1838	July 3, 1838	Dec. 28, 1846	8
Oregon	Aug. 14, 1848	Date of act	Feb. 14, 1859	10
Minnesota	Mar. 3, 1849	Date of act	May 11, 1858	9
New Mexico	Sept. 9, 1850	On president's proclamation	Jan. 6, 1912	61
Utah	Sept. 9, 1850	Date of act	Jan. 4, 1896	46
Washington	Mar. 2, 1853	Date of act	Nov. 11, 1889	36
Kansas	May 30, 1854	Date of act	Jan. 29, 1861	6
Nebraska	May 30, 1854	Date of act	Mar. 1, 1867	12
Colorado	Feb. 28, 1861	Date of act	Aug. 1, 1876	15
Dakota	Mar. 2, 1861	Date of act	Nov. 2, 1889	28
Nevada	Mar. 2, 1861	Date of act	Oct. 31, 1864	3
Arizona	Feb. 24, 1863	Date of act	Feb. 14, 1912	49
Idaho	Mar. 3, 1863	Date of act	July 3, 1890	27
Montana	May 26, 1864	Date of act	Nov. 8, 1889	25
Wyoming	July 25, 1868	When officers were qualified	July 10, 1890	22
Alaska	May 17, 1884[6]	No fixed date	Jan. 3, 1959	75
Oklahoma	May 2, 1890	Date of act	Nov. 16, 1907	17
Hawaii	Apr. 30, 1900	June 14, 1900	Aug. 21, 1959	59

(1) Included what is now Ohio, Indiana, Illinois, Michigan, Wisconsin, and E Minnesota. (2) Date of admission for Ohio, the first state created out of territory, based on the date its General Assembly first met. Congress approved Ohio's entry into the Union on Feb. 19, 1803. (3) Admitted as the state of Tennessee. (4) Admitted as the state of Louisiana. (5) The act renaming Louisiana Territory as Missouri Territory (June 4, 1812) became effective Dec. 7, 1812. (6) Act constituted Alaska as a district, though it was often referred to and administered as a territory. The Territory of Alaska was formally organized by an act of Aug. 24, 1912.

U.S. Geographic Centers

Source: U.S. Geological Survey, U.S. Dept. of the Interior

There is no generally accepted definition of a geographic center and no uniform method for determining it. Geographic center is defined here as the center of gravity of the surface of an area, or that point on which an area would balance if it were a plane of uniform thickness.

No government agency has officially established any points marking the geographic center of the U.S., the conterminous U.S. (48 states), or the North American continent. In 1941, private citizens erected a monument in Lebanon, KS, marking it as the geographic center of the then U.S. (conterminous). A cairn in Rugby, ND, was completed in 1932 designating that location as the center of the North American continent. The geographic centers in the following list are approximate. They are indicated by county then city unless otherwise noted.

U.S. (50 states): W of Castle Rock, Butte County, South Dakota; 44°58′ N, 103°46′ W
Conterminous U.S. (48 states): nr. Lebanon, Smith County, Kansas; 39°50′ N, 98°35′ W
North American continent: 6 mi W of Balta, Pierce County, North Dakota; 48°10′ N, 100°10′ W
Alabama: Chilton, 12 mi SW of Clanton
Alaska: approx. 60 mi NW of Denali; 63°50′ N, 152° W
Arizona: Yavapai, 55 mi E-SE of Prescott
Arkansas: Pulaski, 12 mi NW of Little Rock
California: Madera, 38 mi E of Madera
Colorado: Park, 30 mi NW of Pikes Peak
Connecticut: Hartford, at East Berlin
Delaware: Kent, 11 mi S of Dover
District of Columbia: near 4th and L Sts. NW
Florida: Hernando, 12 mi N-NW of Brooksville
Georgia: Twiggs, 18 mi SE of Macon
Hawaii: off Maui; 20°15′ N, 156°20′ W
Idaho: Custer, SW of Challis
Illinois: Logan, 28 mi NE of Springfield
Indiana: Boone, 14 mi N-NW of Indianapolis
Iowa: Story, 5 mi NE of Ames
Kansas: Barton, 15 mi NE of Great Bend
Kentucky: Marion, 3 mi N-NW of Lebanon
Louisiana: Avoyelles, 3 mi SE of Marksville
Maine: Piscataquis, 18 mi N of Dover
Maryland: Prince George's, 4.5 mi NW of Davidsonville
Massachusetts: Worcester, N part of city of Worcester
Michigan: Wexford, 5 mi N-NW of Cadillac

Minnesota: Crow Wing, 10 mi SW of Brainerd
Mississippi: Leake, 9 mi W-NW of Carthage
Missouri: Miller, 20 mi SW of Jefferson City
Montana: Fergus, 11 mi W of Lewistown
Nebraska: Custer, 10 mi NW of Broken Bow
Nevada: Lander, 26 mi SE of Austin
New Hampshire: Belknap, 3 mi E of Ashland
New Jersey: Mercer, 5 mi SE of Trenton
New Mexico: Torrance, 12 mi S-SW of Willard
New York: Madison, 12 mi S of Oneida and 26 mi SW of Utica
North Carolina: Chatham, 10 mi NW of Sanford
North Dakota: Sheridan, 5 mi SW of McClusky
Ohio: Delaware, 25 mi N-NE of Columbus
Oklahoma: Oklahoma, 8 mi N of Oklahoma City
Oregon: Crook, 25 mi S-SE of Prineville
Pennsylvania: Centre, 2.5 mi SW of Bellefonte
Rhode Island: Kent, 1 mi S-SW of Crompton
South Carolina: Richland, 13 mi SE of Columbia
South Dakota: Hughes, 8 mi NE of Pierre
Tennessee: Rutherford, 5 mi NE of Murfreesboro
Texas: McCulloch, 15 mi NE of Brady
Utah: Sanpete, 3 mi N of Manti
Vermont: Washington, 3 mi E of Roxbury
Virginia: Buckingham, 5 mi SW of Buckingham
Washington: Chelan, 10 mi W-SW of Wenatchee
West Virginia: Braxton, 4 mi E of Sutton
Wisconsin: Wood, 9 mi SE of Marshfield
Wyoming: Fremont, 58 mi E-NE of Lander

Lengths of U.S. Boundaries

The length of the boundary between the U.S. and Canada is 5,525 mi—3,987 mi between the conterminous U.S. and Canada and 1,538 mi between Alaska and Canada. A 1925 treaty established a permanent International Boundary Commission to maintain the boundary. The U.S.-Mexican border, first established by treaty in 1848, is 1,954-miles long. It largely follows the Rio Grande and Colorado River, from the Gulf of Mexico to the Pacific Ocean. It is overseen by the International Boundary and Water Commission.

Origins of the Names of U.S. States and Territories

Source: State officials; Smithsonian Institution; Topographic Division, U.S. Geological Survey, U.S. Dept. of the Interior

Alabama: Choctaw word for a Chickasaw tribe. First noted in accounts of Hernando de Soto expedition.

Alaska: Russian version of Aleutian (Eskimo) word *alakshak* for "peninsula," "great lands," or "land that is not an island."

American Samoa: Etymology varies.

Arizona: Spanish version of Pima Indian word for "little spring place" or Aztec *arizuma*, meaning "silver-bearing."

Arkansas: Algonquin name for Quapaw Indians, meaning "south wind."

California: Bestowed by Spanish conquistadors (possibly Hernán Cortés). It was the name of an imaginary island in the 1510 Spanish novel *Las Sergas de Esplandián*, by Garci Rodríguez de Montalvo. The Spanish first visited *Baja* (Lower) *California* in 1533. The present-day U.S. state was called *Alta* (Upper) *California*.

Colorado: From Spanish for "red," first applied to Colorado River.

Connecticut: From Mohican and other Algonquin words meaning "long river place."

Delaware: Named for Lord De La Warr, early governor of Virginia; first applied to river, then to Indian tribe (Lenni-Lenape).

District of Columbia: For Christopher Columbus, 1791.

Florida: Named by Juan Ponce de León *Pascua Florida*, "Flowery Easter," on Easter Sunday, 1513.

Georgia: Named by colonial administrator James Oglethorpe for King George II of England in 1732.

Guam: From Chamorro name, *Guahan*, meaning "we have."

Hawaii: Possibly derived from *Hawaiki* or *Owhyhee*, Polynesian word for "homeland."

Idaho: Said to be a coined name with the invented meaning "gem of the mountains"; suggested for the Pikes Peak mining territory (Colorado), then applied to the new mining territory of the Pacific Northwest. Another theory suggests *Idaho* may be Kiowa Apache term for the Comanche.

Illinois: French for *Illini* or "land of *Illini*," Algonquin word meaning "men" or "warriors."

Indiana: Means "land of the Indians."

Iowa: Indian word variously translated as "here I rest" or "beautiful land." Named for the Iowa River, which was named for the Iowa Indians.

Kansas: Sioux word for "south wind people."

Kentucky: Indian word variously translated as "dark and bloody ground," "meadowland," and "land of tomorrow."

Louisiana: Part of territory called Louisiana by René-Robert Cavelier Sieur de La Salle for French King Louis XIV.

Maine: From Maine, ancient French province. Also descriptive, referring to the mainland as distinct from coastal islands.

Maryland: For Queen Henrietta Maria, wife of Charles I of England.

Massachusetts: From Indian tribe whose name meant "at or about the Great Hill" in Blue Hills region south of Boston.

Michigan: From Chippewa *mici gama*, meaning "great water," after lake of the same name.

Minnesota: From Dakota Sioux word meaning "cloudy water" or "sky-tinted water" of the Minnesota River.

Mississippi: Probably Chippewa *mici zibi*, meaning "great river" or "gathering-in of all the waters." Also Algonquin word *messipi*.

Missouri: Algonquin Indian term meaning "river of the big canoes."

Montana: Latin or Spanish for "mountainous."

Nebraska: From Omaha or Otos Indian word meaning "broad water" or "flat river," describing the Platte River.

Nevada: Spanish, meaning "snow-clad."

New Hampshire: Named by Capt. John Mason of Plymouth Council, in 1629, for his home county in England.

New Jersey: The Duke of York, in 1664, gave a patent to Lord John Berkeley and Sir George Carteret for *Nova Caesaria*, or New Jersey, after England's Isle of Jersey.

New Mexico: Spaniards in Mexico applied term to land north and west of Rio Grande in the 16th century.

New York: For James, Duke of York and Albany, who received patent for New Netherland from his brother Charles II and sent an expedition to capture it, 1664.

North Carolina: In 1619, Charles I gave patent to Sir Robert Heath for Province of Carolana, from *Carolus*, Latin name for Charles. Charles II granted a new patent to Earl of Clarendon and others. Divided into North and South Carolina, 1710.

North Dakota: Sioux word *Dakota*, meaning "friend" or "ally."

Northern Mariana Isls.: For Mariana of Austria, queen regent of Spain.

Ohio: Iroquois word for "fine or good river."

Oklahoma: Choctaw word meaning "red man," proposed by Rev. Allen Wright, Choctaw-speaking Indian.

Oregon: Origin unknown. One theory is that the name derives from *wauregan*, meaning "beautiful," term used by Indians in New England.

Pennsylvania: William Penn, Quaker who was made full proprietor of area by King Charles II in 1681, suggested "Sylvania," or "woodland," for his tract. The king's government owed 16,000 pounds to Penn's father, Adm. William Penn, and the land was granted as partial settlement. Charles II added "Penn" to "Sylvania," against the modest proprietor's desires, in honor of the admiral.

Puerto Rico: Spanish for "rich port."

Rhode Island: Origin unknown. One theory notes that Giovanni de Verrazzano recorded observing an island about the size of the Greek island of Rhodes in 1524. Another theory is that Dutch explorer Adriaen Block named the state *Roode Eylandt* for its red clay.

South Carolina: See North Carolina.

South Dakota: See North Dakota.

Tennessee: *Tanasi* was the name of Cherokee villages on the Little Tennessee River. From 1784 to 1788, this was the State of Franklin, or Frankland.

Texas: Variant of word used by Caddo and other Indians meaning "friends" or "allies" and applied to them by the Spanish in eastern Texas. Also written *Texias*, *Tejas*, *Teysas*.

Utah: From a Navajo word meaning "upper," or "higher up," as applied to Shoshone tribe called Ute. Proposed name *Deseret*, "land of honeybees," from Book of Mormon, was rejected by Congress.

Vermont: From French words *vert* (green) and *mont* (mountain). The Green Mountains were said to have been named by Samuel de Champlain. When the state was formed in 1777, Dr. Thomas Young suggested combining *vert* and *mont*.

Virgin Islands, U.S.: From Spanish name *Las Once Mil Virgenes* (11,000 Virgins), which Christopher Columbus gave to island group.

Virginia: Named by Sir Walter Raleigh, who outfitted an expedition in 1584, in honor of England's Queen Elizabeth, the Virgin Queen.

Washington: Named after George Washington. When the bill creating the Territory of Columbia was introduced in the 32nd Congress, its name was changed to Washington because of the existence of the District of Columbia.

West Virginia: So named when western counties of Virginia refused to secede from the U.S. in 1863.

Wisconsin: Indian name, spelled *Ouisconsin* or *Mesconsing* by early chroniclers, believed to mean "grassy place" in Chippewa. Congress made it *Wisconsin*.

Wyoming: From Algonquin words for "large prairie place," "at the big plains," or "on the great plain."

Territorial Sea of the U.S.

According to a Dec. 27, 1988, proclamation by Pres. Ronald Reagan, "The territorial sea of the United States henceforth extends to 12 nautical miles from the baselines of the United States determined in accordance with international law. In accordance with international law, as reflected in the applicable provisions of the 1982 United Nations Convention on the Law of the Sea, within the territorial sea of the United States, the ships of all countries enjoy the right of innocent passage and the ships and aircraft of all countries enjoy the right of transit passage through international straits."

Major Accessions of Territory by the U.S.

Source: U.S. Dept. of the Interior; U.S. Census Bureau, U.S. Dept. of Commerce

Not including territories such as the Panama Canal Zone and the Philippines, which are no longer under U.S. jurisdiction.

Accession	Date	Area (sq mi)	Accession	Date	Area (sq mi)	Accession	Date	Area (sq mi)
Territory in 1790[1]	NA	888,685	Mexican Cession	1848	529,017	Guam[3]	1899	212
Louisiana Purchase	1803	827,192	Gadsden Purchase	1853	29,640	American Samoa[4]	1900	76
Treaty of Florida	1819	72,003	Alaska	1867	586,412	U.S. Virgin Islands	1917	133
Texas	1845	390,143	Hawaii	1898	6,450	Northern Marianas[5]	1986	179
Oregon Territory	1846	285,680	Puerto Rico[2]	1899	3,435			

NA = Not applicable. (1) Includes that part of a drainage basin of Red River of the North, south of 49th parallel, sometimes considered part of Louisiana Purchase. (2) Ceded by Spain in 1898, ratified in 1899, and became the Commonwealth of Puerto Rico by Act of Congress on July 25, 1952. (3) Acquired in 1898; ratified 1899. (4) Acquired in 1899; ratified 1900. (5) Part of the UN Trust Territory of the Pacific Islands, which U.S. began administering in 1947; became U.S. commonwealth Nov. 3, 1986.

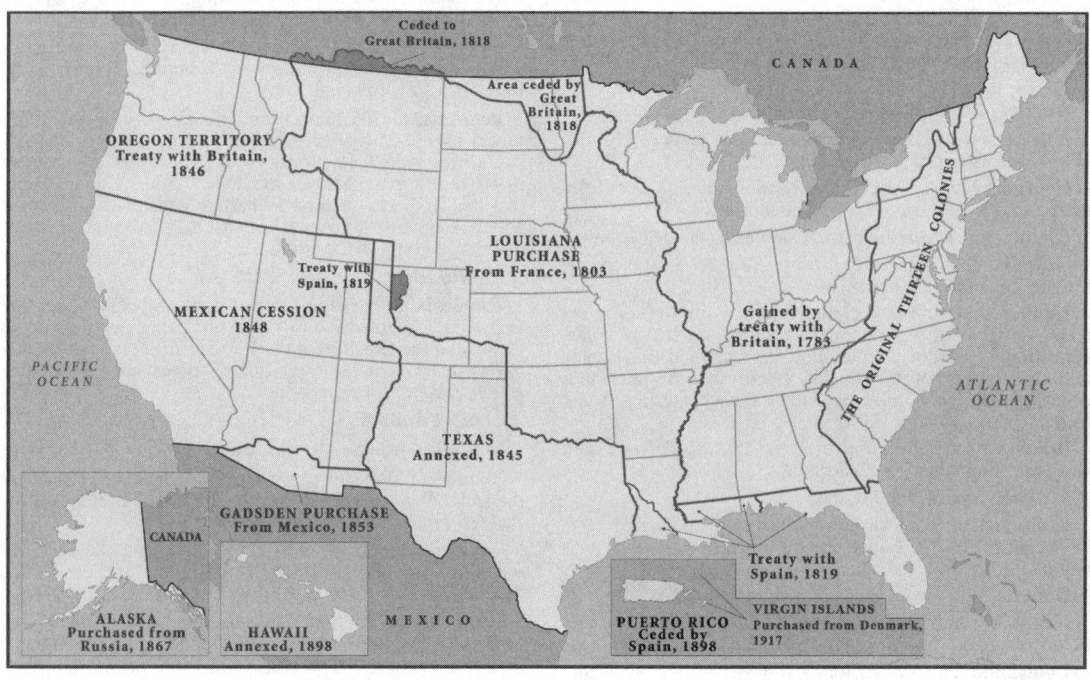

National Park System Recreation Visits, 1905-2015

Source: National Park Service (NPS), U.S. Dept. of the Interior

An NPS site, regardless of its designation (as a park, monument, or preserve, etc.), is generally referred to as a unit. Not all units report public use statistics.

Year	Units reporting visits	Recreation visits	Year	Units reporting visits	Recreation visits
1905	6	140,954	1995	328	269,564,307
1910	9	173,416	2000	344	285,891,275
1915	12	314,299	2001	345	279,873,926
1920	26	1,022,091	2002	349	277,299,880
1925	39	1,900,499	2003	353	266,230,290
1930	45	3,038,935	2004	356	276,908,337
1935	85	7,435,659	2005	356	273,488,751
1940	113	16,410,148	2006	359	272,623,980
1945	143	10,855,548	2007	360	275,581,547
1950	139	32,706,172	2008	360	274,852,949
1955	150	48,891,000	2009	360	285,579,941
1960	166	71,586,000	2010	363	281,303,769
1965	182	118,662,500	2011	367	278,939,216
1970	217	168,135,100	2012	367	282,765,682
1975	251	188,085,700	2013	370	273,630,895
1980	275	220,463,211	2014	376	292,800,082
1985	303	263,441,808	2015	378	307,247,252
1990	316	255,581,467			

Most-Visited Sites in the National Park System, 2015

Source: National Park Service (NPS), U.S. Dept. of the Interior

Attendance at 378 of 409 NPS sites totaled 307,247,252 recreation visits in 2015. (Not all units report public use statistics.)

Rank	Site (location)	Rec. visits
1.	Blue Ridge Parkway (NC-VA)	15,054,603
2.	Golden Gate Natl. Recreation Area (CA)	14,888,537
3.	Great Smoky Mountains Natl. Park (NC-TN)	10,712,674
4.	Lincoln Memorial (DC)	7,941,771
5.	Lake Mead Natl. Recreation Area (AZ-NV)	7,298,465
6.	George Washington Memorial Parkway (DC-MD-VA)	7,286,463
7.	Gateway Natl. Recreation Area (NJ-NY)	6,392,565
8.	Natchez Trace Parkway (MS-AL-TN)	5,785,812
9.	Vietnam Veterans Memorial (DC)	5,597,077
10.	Grand Canyon Natl. Park (AZ)	5,520,736
11.	World War II Memorial (DC)	5,068,224
12.	Chesapeake & Ohio Canal Natl. Historical Park (DC-MD-WV)	4,798,312
13.	Castle Clinton Natl. Monument (NY)	4,597,029
14.	Cape Cod Natl. Seashore (MA)	4,503,220
15.	Independence Natl. Historical Park (PA)	4,311,582
16.	Statue of Liberty Natl. Monument (NY)	4,279,020
17.	San Francisco Maritime Natl. Historical Park (CA)	4,173,014
18.	Rocky Mountain Natl. Park (CO)	4,155,916
19.	Yosemite Natl. Park (CA)	4,150,217
20.	Yellowstone Natl. Park (ID-MT-WY)	4,097,710
21.	Korean War Veterans Memorial (DC)	4,077,835
22.	Gulf Islands Natl. Seashore (FL-MS)	3,976,883
23.	Delaware Water Gap Natl. Recreation Area (NJ-PA)	3,735,134
24.	Zion Natl. Park (UT)	3,648,846
25.	Martin Luther King Jr. Memorial (DC)	3,530,401
26.	Colonial Natl. Historical Park (VA)	3,343,909
27.	Franklin Delano Roosevelt Memorial (DC)	3,290,080
28.	Olympic Natl. Park (WA)	3,263,761
29.	Chattahoochee River Natl. Recreation Area (GA)	3,173,204
30.	Grand Teton Natl. Park (WY)	3,149,921
31.	Thomas Jefferson Memorial (DC)	3,102,442
32.	Acadia Natl. Park (ME)	2,811,184
33.	Point Reyes Natl. Seashore (CA)	2,501,106
34.	Glen Canyon Natl. Recreation Area (AZ-UT)	2,495,093
35.	Rock Creek Park (DC)	2,443,772
36.	Mount Rushmore Natl. Memorial (SD)	2,434,297
37.	Glacier Natl. Park (MT)	2,366,056
38.	Cuyahoga Valley Natl. Park (OH)	2,284,612
39.	Assateague Island Natl. Seashore (MD-VA)	2,275,606
40.	Cape Hatteras Natl. Seashore (NC)	2,274,635
41.	Boston Natl. Historical Park (MA)	2,262,841
42.	Kennesaw Mountain Natl. Battlefield Park (GA)	2,174,870
43.	Valley Forge Natl. Historical Park (PA)	2,143,965
44.	Joshua Tree Natl. Park (CA)	2,025,756
45.	National Capital Parks Central[1] (DC)	1,833,085
46.	Hawaii Volcanoes Natl. Park (HI)	1,832,660
47.	Bryce Canyon Natl. Park (UT)	1,745,804
48.	Jefferson Natl. Expansion Memorial (MO)	1,698,656
49.	Canaveral Natl. Seashore (FL)	1,689,754
50.	Indiana Dunes Natl. Lakeshore (IN)	1,640,195

(1) Incl. recreation visits to Constitution Gardens.

National Parks and Other Areas Administered by National Park Service

As of Dec. 31, 2015, the National Park Service (NPS) administered about 84,617,508 acres of federal and non-federal land across 405 sites. Date when area was authorized or established by Congress or by presidential proclamation is given in parentheses; any date that follows indicates when a site received its current designation or was transferred to the NPS. Figure after the date is gross area acres as of Dec. 31, 2015. Table does not include parks administered by other agencies, such as the Forest Service or Bureau of Land Management. NA = Not available.

The table also omits national monuments designated after 2015: Belmont-Paul Women's Equality (DC), Castle Mountains (CA), Katahdin Woods and Waters (ME), and Stonewall (NY). The federal government has not yet purchased the property of the planned Ronald Reagan Boyhood Home Natl. Historic Site, designated by public law in 2002.

National Parks

Acadia, ME (1916/1929): 49,055. Incl. Mount Desert Isl., half of Isle au Haut, Schoodic Peninsula on mainland. Highest elevation on Eastern seaboard.

American Samoa, AS (1988): 8,257. Paleotropical rain forest, coral reef.

Arches, UT (1929/1971): 76,679. Contains giant red sandstone arches and other products of erosion.

Badlands, SD (1929/1978): 242,756. Reformations and native prairie; animal fossils 23-37 mil years old.

Big Bend, TX (1935): 801,163. Rio Grande, Chisos Mtns.

Biscayne, FL (1968/1980): 172,971. Aquatic park encompassing chain of islands south of Miami.

Black Canyon of the Gunnison, CO (1933/1999): 30,750. Has canyon 2,900 ft deep and 40 ft wide at narrowest part.

Bryce Canyon, UT (1923/1928): 35,835. Colorful display of erosion effects.

Canyonlands, UT (1964): 337,598. At junction of Colorado and Green Rivers; extensive evidence of prehistoric peoples.

Capitol Reef, UT (1937/1971): 241,904. 70-mi uplift of sandstone cliffs dissected by high-walled gorges.

Carlsbad Caverns, NM (1923/1930): 46,766. More than 110 limestone caves, incl. Carlsbad Cavern; Chihuahuan Desert.

Channel Islands, CA (1938/1980): 249,561. Sea lion breeding place, nesting seabirds, unique plants.

Congaree, SC (1976/2003): 26,276. Largest intact tract of old-growth bottomland hardwood forest in U.S.

Crater Lake, OR (1902): 183,224. Deepest U.S. lake, in crater of Mt. Mazama, volcano that erupted about 7,700 years ago.

Cuyahoga Valley, OH (1974/2000): 32,571. Along Ohio and Erie Canal system between Akron and Cleveland.

Death Valley, CA-NV (1933/1994): 3,373,063. Large desert. Incl. lowest point in Western Hemisphere and Scotty's Castle.

Denali, AK (1917/1980): 4,740,911. Formerly known as Mt. McKinley; highest mountain in U.S.

Dry Tortugas, FL (1935/1992): 64,701. Ft. Jefferson and seven coral reef and sand islands near Key West.

Everglades, FL (1934): 1,508,976. Largest remaining subtropical wilderness in continental U.S; incl. East Everglades Expansion Area acreage added in 1989.

Gates of the Arctic, AK (1978/1984): 7,523,897. Vast wilderness in north central region. Limited federal facilities.

Glacier, MT (1910): 1,013,324. Rocky Mt. scenery, numerous glaciers and glacial lakes. Part of Waterton-Glacier Intl. Peace Park established by U.S. and Canada in 1932.

Glacier Bay, AK (1925/1986): 3,223,383. Tidewater glaciers that move down mountainsides and break up into sea.

Grand Canyon, AZ (1893/1919): 1,201,647. Carved by Colorado River.

Grand Teton, WY (1929): 310,044. Incl. highest peaks of Teton Mtns.; summer feeding ground of largest American elk herd.

Great Basin, NV (1922/1986): 77,180. Incl. Wheeler Peak, Lexington Arch, Lehman Caves.

Great Sand Dunes, CO (1932/2000): 107,302. North America's tallest dunes.

Great Smoky Mountains, NC-TN (1926/1934): 522,427. Largest Eastern U.S. mountain range; magnificent forests.

Guadalupe Mountains, TX (1966): 86,367. Extensive Permian limestone fossil reef; tremendous earth fault.

Haleakalā, HI (1916/1960): 33,265. Dormant volcano on island of Maui with large craters.

Hawai'i Volcanoes, HI (1916/1961): 323,431. Contains Kilauea and Mauna Loa, active volcanoes.

Hot Springs, AR (1832/1921): 5,549. Waters from park's 47 hot springs used for bathing and drinking.

Isle Royale, MI (1931): 571,790. Largest island in Lake Superior.

Joshua Tree, CA (1936/1994): 790,636. Desert region incl. Joshua trees, other plant and animal life.

Katmai, AK (1918/1980): 3,674,368. "Valley of Ten Thousand Smokes," scene of 1912 volcanic eruption.

Kenai Fjords, AK (1978/1980): 669,650. Marine mammals, birdlife; Harding Icefield, one of four major icecaps in U.S.

Kings Canyon, CA (1890/1940): 461,901. Mountain wilderness, dominated by Kings River Canyons and High Sierra; giant sequoias.

Kobuk Valley, AK (1978/1980): 1,750,716. Contains geological and recreational sites. Limited federal facilities.

Lake Clark, AK (1978/1980): 2,619,836. Across Cook Inlet from Anchorage; scenic wilderness, fish and wildlife. Limited federal facilities.

Lassen Volcanic, CA (1907/1916): 106,589. Contains Lassen Peak, recently active volcano; other volcanic phenomena.

Mammoth Cave, KY (1926/1941): 52,830. Longest known cave system in world (more than 390 mi currently surveyed), river 300 ft below surface.

Mesa Verde, CO (1906): 52,485. Most notable and best preserved prehistoric cliff dwellings in U.S.

Mount Rainier, WA (1899): 236,382. Most glaciated peak in contiguous U.S.

North Cascades, WA (1968): 504,781. Mountainous region with many glaciers, lakes.

Olympic, WA (1909/1938): 922,650. Mountain wilderness containing remnant of Pacific Northwest rain forest, active glaciers, shoreline, rare elk.

Petrified Forest, AZ (1906/1962): 221,416. Extensive petrified wood and Indian artifacts. Contains part of Painted Desert.

Pinnacles, CA (1908/2013): 26,686. A release site for captive-bred California condors; talus caves.

Redwood, CA (1968): 138,999. 40 mi of Pacific coastline, groves of ancient redwoods and world's tallest trees.

Rocky Mountain, CO (1915): 265,795. On Continental Divide; incl. peaks over 14,000 ft.

Saguaro, AZ (1933/1994): 91,442. Part of Sonoran Desert; incl. giant saguaro cacti, unique to region.

Sequoia, CA (1890): 404,063. Giant sequoia groves; world's largest tree (by volume). Mt. Whitney, highest mountain in conterminous U.S.

Shenandoah, VA (1926): 199,173. Portion of Blue Ridge Mtns.; overlooks Shenandoah Valley; Skyline Drive.

Theodore Roosevelt, ND (1947/1978): 70,447. Contains part of Roosevelt's ranch and scenic badlands.

Virgin Islands, VI (1956): 14,948. Covers 75% of St. John Isl. and Hassel Isl.; beaches, Carib Indian petroglyphs, evidence of colonial Danes.

Voyageurs, MN (1971): 218,200. Abundant lakes, forests, wildlife.

Wind Cave, SD (1903): 33,931. Limestone caverns in Black Hills; extensive wildlife incl. bison herd.

Wrangell-St. Elias, AK (1978/1980): 8,323,146. Largest area in park system; most peaks over 16,000 ft. No federal facilities.

Yellowstone, ID-MT-WY (1872): 2,219,791. World's first national park. World's greatest geyser area with about 10,000 geysers, hot springs; falls and canyons of Yellowstone River; grizzly bear, moose, largest bison herd on U.S. public land.

Yosemite, CA (1890): 761,348. Yosemite Valley, country's highest waterfall, grove of sequoias, mountains.

Zion, UT (1909/1919): 147,237. Unusual shapes, landscapes resulting from erosion and faulting; evidence of past volcanic activity; contains 2,394-ft monolith "Great White Throne."

National Historical Parks

Abraham Lincoln Birthplace, Hodgenville, KY (1916/1959): 345. Memorial building, sinking spring.

Adams, Quincy, MA (1946/1998): 24. Home of Pres. John Adams, John Quincy Adams, and descendants.

Appomattox Court House, VA (1930/1954): 1,774. Where Confederate Gen. Lee surrendered to Gen. Grant, signaling Civil War's end.

Blackstone River Valley, MA-RI (2014): 1,489. Preserves the valley's industrial heritage.

Boston, MA (1974): 44. Incl. Faneuil Hall, Old North Church, Bunker Hill, Paul Revere House.

Cane River Creole, LA (1994): 206. Preserves Creole culture as it developed along the Cane River.

Cedar Creek and Belle Grove, VA (2002): 3,706. Civil War battle site and an antebellum plantation in Shenandoah Valley.

Chaco Culture, NM (1907/1980): 33,960. Ruins of pueblos built by prehistoric peoples incl. Pueblo, Hopi, and Navajo.

Chesapeake & Ohio Canal, MD-DC-WV (1938/1971): 19,612. 184-mi historic canal; DC to Cumberland, MD.

Colonial, VA (1930/1936): 8,677. Incl. most of Jamestown Isl., site of first successful English colony; Yorktown, site of Cornwallis's surrender to George Washington; Colonial Parkway.

Cumberland Gap, KY-TN-VA (1940): 24,547. Mountain pass of Wilderness Road, which carried first great migration of pioneers into America's interior.

Dayton Aviation Heritage, OH (1992): 111. Commemorates area's involvement in aviation.

First State, DE-PA (2013/2014): 1,155. Locations date from colonial past of DE, first state to ratify Constitution.

George Rogers Clark, Vincennes, IN (1966): 26. Commemorates American defeat of British in West during Revolution.

Harpers Ferry, MD-VA-WV (1944/1963): 3,669. At confluence of Shenandoah and Potomac Rivers, the site of John Brown's 1859 raid on the Army arsenal.

Harriet Tubman Underground Railroad, MD (2013/2014): 480. Protects landscapes on the Eastern Shore, where Tubman was born and guided other slaves to freedom.

Hopewell Culture, OH (1923/1992): 1,766. Remains of ceremonial mounds built in the Ohio River Valley, 200 BCE-500 CE.

Independence, Philadelphia, PA (1948): 45. Several properties associated with American Revolution and founding of U.S., incl. Independence Hall, Liberty Bell Center.

Jean Lafitte (and Preserve), LA (1907/1978): 22,421. Incl. Chalmette, site of 1815 Battle of New Orleans; French Quarter.

Kalaupapa, HI (1980): 10,779. Former colony on Molokai Isl. for those with Hansen's disease (leprosy).

Kaloko-Honokohau, HI (1978): 1,163. Preserves native culture of Hawaii.

Keweenaw, MI (1992): 1,869. Site of first significant copper mine in U.S.

Klondike Gold Rush, AK-WA (1976): 12,996. Preserves Chilkoot Trail used in 1898 Gold Rush. Museum in Seattle.

Lewis and Clark, OR-WA (1958/2004): 3,410. Lewis and Clark encampment, 1805-06. Incorporates former Fort Clatsop Natl. Mem. Park and OR-WA state parks.

Lowell, MA (1978): 141. Textile mills, canal, 19th-cent. structures; park shows planned city of Industrial Revolution.

Lyndon B. Johnson, TX (1969/1980): 1,570. President's birthplace, boyhood home, ranch.

Marsh-Billings-Rockefeller, VT (1992): 643. Boyhood home of conservationist George Perkins Marsh.

Minute Man, MA (1959): 1,027. Where Minute Men battled British, Apr. 19, 1775. Also contains Nathaniel Hawthorne's home.

Morristown, NJ (1933): 1,711. Site of important military encampments during the American Revolution; Washington's headquarters, 1779-80.

Natchez, MS (1988): 108. Mansions, townhouses, and villas related to history of Natchez.

New Bedford Whaling, MA (1996): 34. Preserves structures and relics associated with the city's 19th-cent. whaling industry.

New Orleans Jazz, LA (1994): 5. Preserves, educates, and interprets jazz as it has evolved in New Orleans.

Nez Perce, ID-MT-OR-WA (1965): 4,565. Illustrates history and culture of Nez Perce, or Nimiipuu, homeland (38 separate sites).

Palo Alto Battlefield, TX (1978): 3,442. Scene of first battle of the Mexican War.

Paterson Great Falls, NJ (2011): 51. Falls helped make city one of U.S.'s earliest industrial centers.

Pecos, NM (1965/1990): 6,694. Ruins of ancient Pueblo of Pecos, archaeological sites, and two associated Spanish colonial missions from 17th and 18th centuries.

Puʻuhonua o Hōnaunau, HI (1955/1978): 420. Until 1819, a sanctuary for Hawaiians vanquished in battle and for those guilty of crimes or breaking taboos.

Rosie the Riveter/WWII Home Front, Richmond, CA (2000): 145. Site of shipyard that employed thousands of women during WWII; commemorates women who worked in wartime industries.

Salt River Bay (and Ecological Preserve), St. Croix, VI (1992): 989. Only known site where, in 1493, members of a Columbus party landed on what is now U.S. territory.

San Antonio Missions, TX (1978): 948. Four Spanish missions, 18th-cent. irrigation system.

San Francisco Maritime, CA (1988): 50. Artifacts, photographs, and historic vessels related to development of the Pacific Coast.

San Juan Island, WA (1966): 2,146. Commemorates peaceful relations between U.S., Canada, and Great Britain since the 1872 boundary disputes.

Saratoga, NY (1938): 3,410. Scene of a major 1777 battle that became a turning point in the American Revolution.

Sitka, AK (1910/1972): 116. Scene of last major resistance of Tlingit to the Russians, 1804.

Thomas Edison, West Orange, NJ (1955/1962): 21. Inventor's home and laboratory.

Tumacacori, AZ (1908/1990): 360. Historic Spanish mission building near site first visited by Father Kino in 1691.

Valley Forge, PA (1976): 3,468. Continental Army campsite in 1777-78 winter.

War in the Pacific, GU (1978): 2,031. Seven distinct units illustrating the Pacific theater of WWII. Limited federal facilities.

Women's Rights, NY (1980): 7. Seneca Falls site where Lucretia Mott, Elizabeth Cady Stanton organized movement in 1848.

National Battlefields/Parks/Sites

Antietam, MD (1890/1978): 3,230. Battle here ended first Confederate invasion of North, Sept. 17, 1862.

Big Hole, MT (1910/1963): 976. Site of major battle with Nez Perce Indians, Aug. 9-10, 1877.

Brices Cross Roads, Baldwyn, MS (1929): 1. Site of Confederate victory, June 10, 1864.

Cowpens, SC (1929/1972): 842. American Revolution battlefield, Jan. 17, 1781.

Fort Donelson, TN-KY (1928/1985): 1,309. Site of first major Union victory, Feb. 14-16, 1862.

Fort Necessity, PA (1931/1961): 903. Site of first battle of French and Indian War, July 3, 1754.

Kennesaw Mountain, GA (1917/1935): 2,894. Site of major battle of Atlanta campaign in Civil War.

Manassas, VA (1940): 5,073. Scene of two Civil War battles.

Monocacy, MD (1934/1976): 1,647. Civil War battle in defense of Washington, DC, fought here, July 9, 1864.

Moores Creek, Currie, NC (1926/1980): 88. Commemorates Feb. 27, 1776, battle between Patriots and Loyalists.

Petersburg, VA (1926/1962): 2,740. Scene of Union campaigns, 1864-65.

Richmond, VA (1936): 8,004. Site of battles defending Confederate capital.

River Raisin, Monroe, MI (2010): 42. Site of major battles of War of 1812.

Stones River, TN (1927/1960): 709. Scene of battle that began federal offensive to trisect Confederacy, Dec. 31, 1862-Jan. 2, 1863.

Tupelo, MS (1929/1961): 1. Site of crucial battle over Union Gen. Sherman's supply line, July 14-15, 1865.

Wilson's Creek, MO (1960/1970): 2,368. Site of second major Civil War battle, Aug. 10, 1861, for control of Missouri.

National Military Parks

Chickamauga and Chattanooga, GA-TN (1890): 9,078. Where Gen. Sherman and Union armies gained control of TN, 1863.

Fredericksburg and Spotsylvania, VA (1927/1933): 8,380. Sites of several major Civil War battles and campaigns.

Gettysburg, PA (1895/1933): 6,033. Site of decisive Confederate defeat in North, July 1863, and of Gettysburg Address.

Guilford Courthouse, NC (1917/1933): 251. American Revolution battle site.

Horseshoe Bend, AL (1956): 2,040. On Tallapoosa River, where Gen. Andrew Jackson broke power of Upper Creek Indian Confederacy on Mar. 27, 1814.

Kings Mountain, SC (1931/1933): 3,945. Site of American Revolution battle, fought on Oct. 7, 1780.

Pea Ridge, AR (1956): 4,300. Civil War battle, Mar. 7-8, 1862.

Shiloh, TN-MS (1894/1933): 7,926. Major Civil War battle site; incl. Indian burial mounds.

Vicksburg, MS-LA (1899/1933): 1,802. Union victory gave North control of Mississippi and split Confederate forces.

National Memorials

Arkansas Post, AR (1960): 758. First permanent French settlement in lower Mississippi River valley.

Arlington House, The Robert E. Lee Memorial, VA (1925/1972): 28. Lee's home overlooking the Potomac River.

Chamizal, El Paso, TX (1966/1974): 55. Commemorates 1963 settlement of 99-year border dispute with Mexico.

Coronado, AZ (1941/1952): 4,830. Commemorates first European exploration of the Southwest.

De Soto, Bradenton, FL (1948): 30. Commemorates 16th-cent. Spanish explorations.

Federal Hall, New York, NY (1939/1955): 0.45. First seat of U.S. government under the Constitution.

Flight 93, Shanksville, PA (2002): 2,320. Commemorates passengers and crew of Flight 93, who died thwarting an attack on Sept. 11, 2001. First features of memorial completed and dedicated in 2011.

Fort Caroline, Jacksonville, FL (1950): 138. On St. Johns River, site of first attempt by France, in 16th cent., at permanent North American settlement.

Franklin Delano Roosevelt Memorial, DC (1982): 8. Statues of Pres. Roosevelt and Eleanor Roosevelt; waterfalls and gardens.

General Grant, New York, NY (1958): 0.76. Tomb of Ulysses Grant and wife; largest mausoleum in U.S.

Hamilton Grange, New York, NY (1962): 1.04. Home of Alexander Hamilton.

Jefferson National Expansion, St. Louis, MO (1935): 193. Commemorates 19th cent. westward expansion; incl. Gateway Arch.

Johnstown Flood, PA (1964): 178. Commemorates 1889 flood.

Korean War Veterans Memorial, DC (1986): 1.56. Honors those who served in the Korean War.

Lincoln Boyhood, Lincoln City, IN (1962): 200. Site of Abraham Lincoln's boyhood home and grave site of his mother.

Lincoln Memorial, DC (1911/1933): 7. Marble statue of 16th president.

Lyndon Baines Johnson Memorial Grove on the Potomac, DC (1973): 17. Overlooks Potomac River; vista of the Capitol.

Martin Luther King Jr., DC (1996): 3. Granite statue of Dr. King close to where he delivered "I Have a Dream" speech.

Mount Rushmore, SD (1925): 1,278. World-famous sculpture of presidents Washington, Jefferson, Lincoln, T. Roosevelt.

Perry's Victory and International Peace Memorial, Put-in-Bay, OH (1936/1972): 25. World's most massive Doric column promotes pursuit of peace through arbitration and disarmament.

Port Chicago Naval Magazine, Danville, CA (2009): 5. Where 1944 munitions ship explosion killed 320 men.

Roger Williams, Providence, RI (1965): 5. Memorial to founder of Rhode Island.

Thaddeus Kosciuszko, Philadelphia, PA (1972): 0.02. Memorial to Polish hero of American Revolution.

Theodore Roosevelt Island, DC (1932/1933): 89. Statue of Roosevelt in wooded island sanctuary.

Thomas Jefferson Memorial, DC (1934): 18. Statue of Jefferson in an inscribed circular, colonnaded structure.

Vietnam Veterans Memorial, DC (1980): 2. Black granite wall with names of those missing or killed in action in Vietnam War.

Washington Monument, DC (1876/1933): 106. Obelisk honoring the first U.S. president. Construction began in 1848 with private funding.

World War I Memorial, DC (1981/2014): 1.39. Formerly Pershing Park, dedicated to Gen. John J. Pershing.

World War II Memorial, DC (1994/2004): 8. Oval plaza with central pool commemorating those who fought and died.

Wright Brothers, Kill Devil Hills, NC (1927/1953): 428. Site of first powered flight.

National Historic Sites

Allegheny Portage Railroad, PA (1964): 1,284. Linked Pennsylvania Canal system and the West.

Andersonville, GA (1970): 516. Civil War POW camp.

Andrew Johnson, Greeneville, TN (1935/1963): 17. Two homes and the tailor shop of 17th U.S. president.

Bent's Old Fort, CO (1960): 799. Replica of fort on Sante Fe Trail.

Boston African-American, MA (1980): 0.59. Pre-Civil War black-owned structures.

Brown v. Board of Education, Topeka, KS (1992): 1.85. Commemorates landmark 1954 U.S. Supreme Court decision, which ended legal segregation in schools.

Carl Sandburg Home, Flat Rock, NC (1968): 264. Home of Pulitzer Prize-winning poet and biographer.

Carter G. Woodson Home, DC (1976/2006): 0.15. Home of "Father of Black History."

Charles Pinckney, Mt. Pleasant, SC (1988): 28. Farm of a principal author and signer of the Constitution.

Christiansted, St. Croix, VI (1952/1961): 27. Commemorates Danish colony.

Clara Barton, Glen Echo, MD (1974): 9. Home of American Red Cross founder.

Edgar Allan Poe, Philadelphia, PA (1978/1980): 0.52. Writer's home.

Eisenhower, Gettysburg, PA (1967): 690. Home of 34th president.

Eleanor Roosevelt, Hyde Park, NY (1977): 181. Former first lady's personal retreat.

Eugene O'Neill, Danville, CA (1976): 13. Home where playwright wrote his final plays, incl. *The Iceman Cometh.*

First Ladies, Canton, OH (2000): 0.46. Home of first lady Ida Sexton McKinley. Library now devoted to America's first ladies.

Ford's Theatre, DC (1866/1970): 0.3. Incl. theater where Lincoln was assassinated, house where he died, and Lincoln Museum.

Fort Bowie, AZ (1964): 999. Focal point of operations against Geronimo and Apaches.

Fort Davis, TX (1961): 523. Frontier outpost in West Texas; established to guard the San Antonio-El Paso Road.

Fort Laramie, WY (1938/1960): 867. Military post on Oregon Trail.

Fort Larned, KS (1964/1966): 718. Military post on Santa Fe Trail.

Fort Point, CA (1970): 29. West Coast fortification; protected San Francisco during and after Civil War.

Fort Raleigh, NC (1941): 513. First attempted English settlement in North America.

Fort Scott, KS (1965/1978): 17. Commemorates U.S. frontier. Focal point of black troop activity, training during Civil War.

Fort Smith, AR-OK (1961): 75. One of the earliest U.S. posts in Missouri Territory, active 1817-90.

Fort Union Trading Post, MT-ND (1966): 440. Principal fur-trading post on upper Missouri, 1829-67.

Fort Vancouver, WA-OR (1948/1961): 207. Headquarters for Hudson's Bay Company.

Frederick Douglass, DC (1962/1988): 9. Home of black abolitionist, writer, orator.

Frederick Law Olmsted, Brookline, MA (1979): 7. Home of city planner, famous for designing Central Park in NYC.

Friendship Hill, PA (1978): 675. Home of Albert Gallatin, Jefferson's and Madison's secretary of treasury.

Golden Spike, UT (1957): 2,735. Commemorates completion of first transcontinental railroad in 1869.

Grant-Kohrs Ranch, MT (1972): 1,618. Ranch house owned by John Grant, 19th-cent. range-cattle industry pioneer.

Hampton, Towson, MD (1948): 62. 18th-cent. Georgian mansion, which in 1790 was largest house in U.S.

Harry S. Truman, MO (1983): 13. House of 33rd president from 1919 on and farm where he worked as young man.

Herbert Hoover, West Branch, IA (1965): 187. Birthplace and boyhood home of 31st president.

Home of Franklin D. Roosevelt, Hyde Park, NY (1944): 850. FDR's birthplace, home, and "summer White House."

Hopewell Furnace, PA (1938/1985): 848. 19th-cent. iron-making village.

Hubbell Trading Post, AZ (1965): 160. Oldest continuously operating trading post in SW; founded in 1878 on Navajo Nation.

James A. Garfield, Mentor, OH (1980): 8. Home of 20th president; site of his front-porch campaign.

Jimmy Carter, Plains, GA (1987): 72. Birthplace and home of 39th president.

John Fitzgerald Kennedy, Brookline, MA (1967): 0.09. Birthplace and childhood home of 35th president.

John Muir, Martinez, CA (1964): 344. Home of Sierra Club co-founder and "Father of the National Park Service."

Knife River Indian Villages, ND (1974): 1,749. Remnants of villages last occupied by Hidatsa and Mandan Indians.

Lincoln Home, Springfield, IL (1971): 12. Lincoln's residence when he was elected 16th president, 1860.

Little Rock Central High School, AR (1998): 27. Commemorates 1957 desegregation during which federal troops were called in to protect nine black students.

Longfellow House—Washington's Headquarters, Cambridge, MA (1972): 2. Poet's home, 1837-82; Washington's headquarters during Boston siege, 1775-76.

Maggie L. Walker, Richmond, VA (1978): 1.29. Home of black leader and first female bank president, daughter of former slave.

Manzanar, Lone Pine, CA (1992): 814. Manzanar War Relocation Ctr., a WWII Japanese-American internment camp.

Martin Luther King Jr., Atlanta, GA (1980): 39. Birthplace, grave, church of the civil rights leader.

Martin Van Buren, Kinderhook, NY (1974): 285. Lindenwald, home of 8th president.

Mary McLeod Bethune Council House, DC (1982/1991): 0.07. Commemorates Bethune's leadership in the black women's movement.

Minidoka, ID (2008): 396. WWII Japanese internment center.

Minuteman Missile, SD (1999): 44. Missile launch facilities dating back to Cold War era.

Nicodemus, KS (1996): 5. Only remaining Western town established by African Americans during Reconstruction.

Ninety Six, SC (1976): 1,022. Colonial trading village and site of Gen. Nathanael Greene's siege on Loyalist-held fort in 1781.

Pennsylvania Avenue, DC (1965/1996): 18. Incl. area between Capitol and White House, encompassing U.S. Navy Memorial, Freedom Plaza, Old Post Office Pavilion, and other sites.

President William Jefferson Clinton Birthplace Home, Hope, AR (2010): 0.68. Birthplace and early home of 42nd president.

Puʻukoholā Heiau, Kawaihae, HI (1972): 86. Ruins of temple built by King Kamehameha, first king of united Hawaiian islands.

Sagamore Hill, Oyster Bay, NY (1962): 83. Home of Pres. Theodore Roosevelt from 1885 until his death in 1919.

Saint-Gaudens, Cornish, NH (1964): 191. Home, studio, and gardens of American sculptor Augustus Saint-Gaudens.

Saint Paul's Church, New York, NY (1943): 6. Site associated with John Peter Zenger's "freedom of the press" trial.

Salem Maritime, MA (1938): 9. Major fishing and whaling port famous for 1692 witchcraft trials.

Sand Creek Massacre, CO (2000): 12,583. Site where more than 160 Cheyenne and Arapaho Indians were killed by U.S. soldiers in 1864.

San Juan, PR (1949): 75. 16th-cent. Spanish fortifications.

Saugus Iron Works, MA (1974): 9. Reconstructed 17th-cent. colonial ironworks.

Springfield Armory, MA (1974): 55. Small-arms manufacturing center for nearly 200 years.

Steamtown, Scranton, PA (1986): 62. Rail yard, roadhouse, repair shops of former Delaware, Lackawanna & Western Railroad.

Theodore Roosevelt Birthplace, New York, NY (1962): 0.11. Reconstructed brownstone where 26th president was born.

Theodore Roosevelt Inaugural, Buffalo, NY (1966): 1.18. Wilcox House, where 26th president took office of office, 1901.

Thomas Stone, Port Tobacco, MD (1978): 328. Home of signer of Declaration of Independence.

Tuskegee Airmen, AL (1998): 90. Airfield where pilots of all-black WWII air corps unit received flight training.

Tuskegee Institute, AL (1974): 58. College founded by Booker T. Washington in 1881 for blacks.

Ulysses S. Grant, St. Louis, MO (1989): 10. Home of Grant during pre-Civil War years.

Vanderbilt Mansion, Hyde Park, NY (1940): 212. Mansion of 19th-cent. financier.

Washita Battlefield, OK (1996): 315. Scene of Nov. 27, 1868, battle between Plains tribes and U.S. army.

Weir Farm, Wilton, CT (1990): 74. Home and studio of American impressionist painter J. Alden Weir.

Whitman Mission, Walla Walla, WA (1936/1963): 139. Site of Protestant missionaries to Cayuse Indians beginning in 1830s.

William Howard Taft, Cincinnati, OH (1969): 4. Birthplace and early home of 27th president.

Name	Location	Year[1]	Acreage
National Lakeshores			
Apostle Islands	WI	1970	69,377
Indiana Dunes	IN	1966	15,347
Pictured Rocks	MI	1966	73,236
Sleeping Bear Dunes	MI	1970	71,210
National Monuments			
African Burial Ground	NY	2006	0.35
Agate Fossil Beds	NE	1965	3,058
Alibates Flint Quarries	TX	1965	1,371
Aniakchak[2]	AK	1978	137,176
Aztec Ruins	NM	1923	318
Bandelier	NM	1916	33,677
Booker T. Washington	VA	1956	239
Buck Island Reef	VI	1961	19,015
Cabrillo	CA	1913	160
Canyon de Chelly	AZ	1931	83,840
Cape Krusenstern	AK	1978	649,096
Capulin Volcano	NM	1916	793
Casa Grande Ruins	AZ	1918	473
Castillo de San Marcos	FL	1924	19
Castle Clinton	NY	1946	1
Cedar Breaks	UT	1933	6,155
César E. Chávez	CA	2012	117
Charles Young Buffalo Soldiers	OH	2013	60
Chiricahua	AZ	1924	12,025
Colorado	CO	1911	20,536
Craters of the Moon	ID	1924	53,571
Devils Postpile	CA	1911	800
Devils Tower	WY	1906	1,347
Dinosaur	CO-UT	1915	210,282
Effigy Mounds	IA	1949	2,526
El Malpais	NM	1987	114,314
El Morro	NM	1906	1,279
Florissant Fossil Beds	CO	1969	5,998
Fort Frederica	GA	1936	284
Fort Matanzas	FL	1924	300
Fort McHenry (and Historic Shrine)	MD	1925	43
Fort Monroe	VA	2011	328
Fort Pulaski	GA	1924	5,623
Fort Stanwix	NY	1935	16
Fort Sumter	SC	1948	235
Fort Union	NM	1954	721
Fossil Butte	WY	1972	8,198
George Washington Birthplace	VA	1930	662
George Washington Carver	MO	1943	210
Gila Cliff Dwellings	NM	1907	533
Governors Island	NY	2001	23
Grand Portage	MN	1951	710
Hagerman Fossil Beds	ID	1988	4,351
Hohokam Pima[3]	AZ	1972	1,690
Homestead NM of America	NE	1936	211
Honouliuli	HI	2015	154
Hovenweep	CO-UT	1923	785
Jewel Cave	SD	1908	1,274
John Day Fossil Beds	OR	1974	14,062
Lava Beds	CA	1925	46,692
Little Bighorn Battlefield	MT	1946	765
Montezuma Castle	AZ	1906	1,016
Muir Woods	CA	1908	554
Natural Bridges	UT	1908	7,636
Navajo	AZ	1909	360
Ocmulgee	GA	1934	704
Oregon Caves (and Preserve)	OR	1909	4,554
Organ Pipe Cactus	AZ	1937	330,689
Petroglyph	NM	1990	7,209
Pipe Spring	AZ	1923	40
Pipestone	MN	1937	282
Poverty Point[2]	LA	1988	911
Pullman	IL	2015	0.40
Rainbow Bridge	UT	1910	160
Russell Cave	AL	1961	310
Salinas Pueblo Missions	NM	1909	1,071

Name	Location	Year[1]	Acreage
Scotts Bluff	NE	1919	3,005
Statue of Liberty	NJ-NY	1924	61
Sunset Crater Volcano	AZ	1930	3,040
Timpanogos Cave	UT	1922	250
Tonto	AZ	1907	1,120
Tule Springs Fossil Beds	NV	2014	22,650
Tuzigoot	AZ	1939	812
Virgin Islands Coral Reef	VI	2001	12,708
Waco Mammoth	TX	2015	107
Walnut Canyon	AZ	1915	3,529
White Sands	NM	1933	143,733
World War II Valor in the Pacific	HI-CA	2008	59
Wupatki	AZ	1924	35,422
Yucca House[2]	CO	1919	34

National Parkways

Name	Location	Year[1]	Acreage
Blue Ridge	NC-VA	1933	95,974
George Washington Memorial	MD-DC-VA	1930	7,035
John D. Rockefeller Jr. Memorial	WY	1972	23,777
Natchez Trace	MS-TN-AL	1938	52,302

National Preserves

Name	Location	Year[1]	Acreage
Aniakchak[2]	AK	1980	464,118
Bering Land Bridge	AK	1980	2,697,391
Big Cypress[4]	FL	1974	720,564
Big Thicket	TX	1974	109,092
Craters of the Moon	ID	2002	410,733
Denali	AK	1917	1,334,118
Gates of the Arctic	AK	1978	948,608
Glacier Bay	AK	1925	58,406
Great Sand Dunes	CO	2000	41,686
Katmai	AK	1918	418,699
Lake Clark	AK	1978	1,410,294
Little River Canyon	AL	1992	15,288
Mojave	CA	1994	1,542,782
Noatak	AK	1978	6,587,071
Tallgrass Prairie	KS	1996	10,893
Timucuan Ecological and Historic	FL	1988	46,263
Valles Caldera	NM	2014	89,000
Wrangell-St. Elias	AK	1978	4,852,645
Yukon-Charley Rivers	AK	1978	2,526,512

National Recreation Areas

Name	Location	Year[1]	Acreage
Amistad	TX	1965	58,500
Bighorn Canyon	MT-WY	1966	120,296
Boston Harbor Islands	MA	1996	1,482
Chattahoochee River	GA	1978	9,779
Chickasaw	OK	1902	9,899
Curecanti	CO	1965	43,095
Delaware Water Gap	NJ-PA	1965	67,581
Gateway	NJ-NY	1972	26,607
Gauley River	WV	1988	11,606
Glen Canyon	AZ-UT	1958	1,254,117
Golden Gate	CA	1972	82,027
Lake Chelan	WA	1968	61,949
Lake Mead	AZ-NV	1936	1,495,806
Lake Meredith	TX	1965	44,978
Lake Roosevelt (fmr. Coulee Dam)	WA	1946	100,390
Ross Lake	WA	1968	117,575
Santa Monica Mountains	CA	1978	156,670
Whiskeytown-Shasta-Trinity[5]	CA	1965	42,503

National Reserves

Name	Location	Year[1]	Acreage
City of Rocks	ID	1988	14,407
Ebey's Landing Historical	WA	1978	19,333

National Rivers

Name	Location	Year[1]	Acreage
Big South Fork (and Rec. Area)	KY-TN	1976	123,710
Buffalo	AR	1972	94,293
Mississippi (and Rec. Area)	MN	1988	53,775
New River Gorge	WV	1978	72,186
Ozark Scenic Riverways	MO	1964	80,785

National Seashores

Name	Location	Year[1]	Acreage
Assateague Island[6]	MD-VA	1965	41,347
Canaveral	FL	1975	57,662
Cape Cod	MA	1961	43,607
Cape Hatteras	NC	1937	30,351
Cape Lookout	NC	1966	28,243
Cumberland Island	GA	1972	36,347
Fire Island	NY	1964	19,580
Gulf Islands	FL-MS	1971	138,306
Padre Island	TX	1962	130,434
Point Reyes	CA	1962	71,055

International Historic Site

Name	Location	Year[1]	Acreage
Saint Croix Island	ME	1949	7

Other Designations

Name	Location	Year[1]	Acreage
Catoctin Mountain Park	MD	1954	5,891
Constitution Gardens	DC	1974	39
Fort Washington Park	MD	1930	341
Greenbelt Park	MD	1950	1,175
National Capital Parks	DC-MD	1933	8,693
National Mall	DC	1933	156
Piscataway Park	MD	1961	4,626
Prince William Forest Park	VA	1948	16,081
Rock Creek Park	DC	1890	1,755
White House	DC	1933	18
Wolf Trap National Park for the Performing Arts	VA	1966	130

National Wild and Scenic Rivers

Rivers in this system are designated by Congress or the Secretary of the Interior. As of Dec. 2014 (the last designation), the system included 12,709 miles of 208 rivers in 40 states and Puerto Rico. Not all of the rivers that the NPS administers are official units of the park system. Only official NPS units are listed here.

Name	Location	Year[1]	Acreage
Alagnak Wild[2]	AK	1980	30,665
Bluestone Scenic	WV	1978	4,310
Delaware Scenic	NJ-PA	1978	1,973
Great Egg Harbor Scenic and Rec.	NJ	1992	43,311
Missouri Recreational	NE-SD	1991	48,457
Niobrara Scenic	NE	1991	29,101
Obed	TN	1976	5,073
Rio Grande	TX	1978	9,600
Saint Croix Scenic Riverway[7]	MN-WI	1968	92,746
Upper Delaware Scenic and Rec.	NY-PA	1978	75,000

Affiliated Areas

Affiliated areas are administered in connection with the NPS but are not owned by that agency.

Name	Location	Year[1]	Acreage
Aleutian World War II Natl. Historic Site (NHS)	AK	1996	135
American Memorial Park	MP	1978	133
Benjamin Franklin Natl. Memorial (NMEM)	PA	1972	NA
Chicago Portage NHS	IL	1952	91
Chimney Rock NHS	NE	1956	83
Fallen Timbers Battlefield and Fort Miamis NHS	OH	1999	185
Father Marquette NMEM	MI	1975	52
Gloria Dei (Old Swedes') Church NHS	PA	1942	4
Green Springs Natl. Historic Landmark District	VA	1974	15,645
Historic Camden Revolutionary War Site	SC	1982	107
Ice Age Natl. Scientific Reserve	WI	1964	32,500
International Peace Garden	ND-MB	1949	2,330
Iñupiat Heritage Center	AK	1999	0
Jamestown NHS	VA	1940	22
Kate Mullany NHS	NY	2004	0.06
Lower East Side Tenement NHS	NY	1998	1.2
New Jersey Coastal Heritage Trail Route	NJ	1988	NA
Oklahoma City NMEM	OK	2004	6
Pinelands Natl. Reserve	NJ	1978	1,164,025
Red Hill Patrick Henry NMEM	VA	1986	NA
Roosevelt Campobello Intl. Park	NB	1964	2,722
Sewall-Belmont House NHS	DC	1974	0.35
Thomas Cole NHS	NY	1999	3
Touro Synagogue NHS	RI	1946	0.23
Wing Luke Museum of the Asian Pacific American Experience	WA	2013	NA

NA = Not available. (1) Year current designation received. (2) No federal facilities; state services may be available at certain sites. (3) Located on Gila River Indian Reservation; not open to the public. (4) Total incl. acreage added in 1988 expansion. (5) Shasta and Trinity units are administered by the Forest Service. Figure given is NPS acreage only. (6) Figure given includes acreage administered by U.S. Fish and Wildlife Service. (7) Total incl. Lower Saint Croix acreage added in 1972.

National Trails System

Source: National Park Service and Bureau of Land Management, U.S. Dept. of the Interior; U.S. Forest Service, USDA

As of mid-2016, the National Trails System included 11 national scenic trails, 19 national historic trails, more than 1,250 national recreation trails, and 6 connecting and side trails. National scenic trails and national historic trails are established by Congress and administered by the NPS, Forest Service, or BLM. Official NPS units are indicated by an asterisk.

Name	Location	Year[1]	Length (mi)[2]	Name	Location	Year[1]	Length (mi)[2]
National Scenic Trails				El Camino Real de los Tejas....	TX-LA	2004	2,600
*Appalachian	ME to GA	1968	2,175	El Camino Real de Tierra Adentro	NM-TX	2000	404
Arizona.....................	AZ	2009	800	Iditarod	AK	1978	2,350
Continental Divide	MT, ID, WY,			Juan Bautista de Anza	AZ-CA	1990	1,200
	CO, NM	1978	3,200	Lewis and Clark	IL to Pacific	1978	3,700
Florida	FL	1983	1,300	Mormon Pioneer..............	IL to UT	1978	1,300
Ice Age	WI	1980	1,000	Nez Perce (Nee-Me-Poo)	OR to MT	1986	1,170
*Natchez Trace..............	MS-AL-TN	1983	64	Old Spanish	NM to CA	2002	2,700
New England	MA-CT	2009	215	Oregon	MO to OR	1978	2,170
North Country...............	NY to ND	1980	4,600	Overmountain Victory.........	NC, SC,		
Pacific Crest...............	CA-OR-WA	1968	2,638		TN, VA	1980	330
Pacific Northwest	MT-ID-WA	2009	1,200	Pony Express	MO to CA	1992	2,000
*Potomac Heritage	VA to PA	1983	710	Santa Fe....................	MO, KS, OK,		
National Historic Trails[3]					CO, NM	1987	1,203
Ala Kahakai	HI	2000	175	Selma to Montgomery	AL	1996	54
California	MO, NE to			Star-Spangled Banner	VA-DC-MD	2008	290
	CA, OR	1992	5,600	Trail of Tears	GA, NC, KY		
Capt. John Smith Chesapeake...	VA, DC,				to OK	1987	5,045
	MD, DE	2006	3,000	Washington-Rochambeau			
				Revolutionary Route	MA to VA	2009	1,000+

(1) Year designation was received. (2) Authorized or currently completed length. (3) Trails may include both overland and water routes.

U.S. Forest Service Special Designated Areas

Source: U.S. Forest Service, U.S. Dept. of Agriculture; as of Sept. 30, 2015

These areas within the National Forest System have been specially designated by presidential proclamation or act of Congress. Size does not include acreage within National Forest boundaries not federally owned or administered by the Forest Service. Not shown is Sand to Snow National Monument (CA), designated in 2016.

NM = Natl. Monument; NRA = Natl. Recreation Area; NS(A) = Natl. Scenic (Area); NVM = Natl. Volcanic Monument; SMA = Special Management Area.

Area	Location	Estab.	Acreage	Area	Location	Estab.	Acreage
Admiralty Island NM..............	AK	1980	985,567	Jewel Cave NM	SD	1908	2,531
Allegheny NRA..................	PA	1984	23,790	Kelly Butte SMA	WA	1998	5,669
Ancient Bristlecone Pine Forest.....	CA	2009	31,825	Kings River SMA	CA	1987	50,886
Arapaho NRA...................	CO	1978	31,046	Land Between the Lakes NRA......	KY-TN	1998	171,251
Barkshead (Ozark #2) Natl. Game				Livingston (Ozark #1) Natl. Game			
Refuge......................	AR	1926	5,851	Refuge	AR	1926	8,755
Bear Creek NSA.................	VA	2009	5,122	Misty Fiords NM................	AK	1980	2,295,939
Beech Creek NSA & Botanical Area..				Moccasin (Ozark #3) Natl. Game			
Beech Creek NSA..............	OK	1988	8,042	Refuge	AR	1926	4,048
Beech Creek Natl. Botanical Area	OK	1988	538	Mono Basin NSA	CA	1984	51,353
Berryessa Snow Mountain NM......	CA	2015	197,394	Moosalamoo NRA	VT	2006	15,913
Big Levels Game Refuge	VA	1935	12,147	Mount Baker NRA...............	WA	1984	8,789
Black Mountain (Ozark #5)				Mount Hood NRA	OR	2009	34,465
Natl. Game Refuge...........	AR	1926	18,929	Mount Pleasant NSA	VA	1994	6,864
Bowen Gulch Protection Area	CO	1993	10,768	Mount Rogers NRA	VA	1966	114,236
Bridgeport Winter Recreation Area...	CA	2009	7,251	Mount St. Helens NVM............	WA	1989	112,864
Browns Canyon NM	CO	2015	11,819	Newberry NVM.................	OR	1990	56,483
Caney Creek (Ouachita #4)				Noontootly Natl. Game Refuge.....	GA	1938	24,670
Natl. Game Refuge...........	AR	1935	8,038	Norbeck Wildlife Preserve	SD	1920	27,630
Cascade Head NS Research Area...	OR	1974	7,188	North Cascades NSA	WA	1984	88,178
Catahoula Wildlife Mgmt. Preserve ..	LA	1941	37,586	Oak Mountain (Ouachita #2)			
Cherokee Natl. Game Refuge #1....	TN	1924	9,862	Natl. Game Refuge.............	AR	1935	8,551
Chimney Rock NM...............	CO	2012	4,724	Ocala Natl. Game Refuge	FL	1930	68,241
Columbia River Gorge NSA	OR-WA	1986	82,911	Opal Creek Scenic Recreation Area..	OR	1996	13,011
Burdoin Mountain SMA..........	WA	1986	7,253	Oregon Dunes NRA	OR	1972	30,290
Gates of the Columbia R. Gorge SMA	OR-WA	1986	53,431	Ouachita Natl. Wildlife Preserve.....	AR	1935	138,039
Rowena SMA.................	OR-WA	1986	3,608	Quinault SMA	WA	1988	5,415
Wind Mountain SMA............	WA	1986	14,801	Piedra SMA	CO	1993	60,498
Coosa Bald NSA.................	GA	1991	7,043	Pigeon Creek (Ouachita #1)			
Cradle of Forestry in America				Natl. Game Refuge.............	AR	1935	8,107
Natl. Historic Area..............	NC	1968	7,793	Pine Ridge NRA	NE	1986	6,636
Crystal Springs Watershed.........	OR	2009	2,094	Pisgah Natl. Game Preserve	NC	1916	71,895
Cultus Creek...................	OR	2009	278	Rattlesnake NRA	MT	1980	60,081
Ed Jenkins NRA.................	GA	1991	23,541	Red Dirt Natl. Wildlife Mgmt. Pres. ..	LA	1941	40,213
Flaming Gorge NRA..............	UT-WY	1968	187,397	Robert S. Kerr Botanical Area	OK	1988	7,971
Fossil Ridge Rec. Mgmt. Area	CO	1993	43,363	Robert T. Stafford White Rocks NRA	VT	1984	36,563
Francis Marion Natl. Wildlife Pres...	SC	1948	54,430	Roubideau SMA.................	CO	1993	18,696
Frank Church-River of No Return				San Gabriel Mountains NM	CA	2014	336,578
Special Mining Mgmt. Zone-Clear				Santa Rosa & San Jacinto Mtns. NM	CA	2000	69,384
Creek	ID	1980	13,879	Sawtooth NRA	ID	1972	730,867
Giant Sequoia NM	CA	2000	328,374	Seng Mountain NSA.............	VA	2009	5,195
Grand Canyon Natl. Game Preserve	AZ	1906	622,273	Sheep Mountain Game Refuge	WY	1924	21,526
Grand Island NRA	MI	1990	13,334	Smith River NRA	CA	1990	322,151
Grey Towers Natl. Historic Site	PA	2004	95	Spring Mountains NRA...........	NV	1993	315,668
Haw Creek (Ozark #4) Natl. Game				Spruce Knob-Seneca Rocks NRA ...	WV	1965	57,499
Refuge......................	AR	1926	3,783	Tabeguache SMA...............	CO	1993	9,029
Hells Canyon NRA	OR-ID	1975	634,410	Tahquitz Natl. Game Preserve	CA	1926	18,813
Hermosa Creek SMA.............	CO	2014	69,938	Upper Big Bottom..............	OR	2009	1,581
Indian Nations Scenic Wildlife Area ..	OK	1988	44,518	Whiskeytown-Shasta-Trinity NRA ...	CA	1965	173,065
James Peak Protection Area	CO	2002	17,509	Winding Stair Mountain NRA	OK	1988	26,617
Jemez NRA	NM	1993	48,841				

National Heritage Areas

Source: National Park Service (NPS), U.S. Dept. of the Interior; Alliance of National Heritage Areas

National Heritage Areas (NHAs) are designated by Congress for their national importance. NHAs are not units of the National Park system, though the NPS advises and provides limited financial assistance. NHC = Natl. Heritage Corridor.

Name	Location	Year[1]	Size (sq mi)	Name	Location	Year[1]	Size (sq mi)
Abraham Lincoln.	IL	2008	25,975	The Last Green Valley NHC . . .	CT-MA	1994	1,086
Arabia Mountain	GA	2006	64	Mississippi Delta.	MS	2009	10,976
Atchafalaya.	LA	2006	10,400	Mississippi Gulf Coast	MS	2004	4,289
Augusta Canal	GA	1996	3+	Mississippi Hills	MS	2009	NA[4]
Baltimore	MD	2009	18	Mormon Pioneer.	UT	2006	16,070
Blue Ridge	NC	2003	10,515	MotorCities	MI	1998	10,000+
Cache La Poudre River[2]	CO	2009	45	Muscle Shoals	AL	2009	3,913
Cane River	LA	1994	181	National Aviation Heritage Area	OH	2004	NA[5]
Champlain Valley Natl. Heritage Partnership.	NY-VT	2006	NA[3]	National Coal Heritage Area . . .	WV	1996	5,300
Crossroads of the American Revolution	NJ	2006	2,155	Niagara Falls[2]	NY	2008	13
Delaware & Lehigh NHC[2]	PA	1988	165	Northern Plains.	ND	2009	800
Erie Canalway NHC	NY	2000	4,834	Northern Rio Grande	NM	2006	10,000
Essex	MA	1996	500	Ohio & Erie Canalway[2]	OH	1996	110
Freedom's Frontier	KS-MO	2006	31,021	Oil Region.	PA	2004	708
Freedom's Way	MA-NH	2009	994	Path of Progress Natl. Heritage Tour Route[2]	PA	1988	500
Great Basin Natl. Heritage Route	NV-UT	2006	15,704	Rivers of Steel	PA	1996	5,000+
Gullah Geechee Cultural Heritage Corridor	NC, SC, GA, FL	2006	12,818	Sangre de Cristo.	CO	2009	3,000+
Hudson River Valley[2]	NY	1996	154	Schuylkill River Valley.	PA	2000	1,750
Illinois & Michigan Canal NHC	IL	1984	862	Shenandoah Valley Battlefields Natl. Historic District	VA	1996	3,939
John H. Chafee Blackstone River Valley NHC.	MA-RI	1986	720+	Silos & Smokestacks	IA	1996	20,000+
Journey Through Hallowed Ground[2].	PA, MD, WV, VA	2008	180	South Carolina NHC.	SC	1996	NA[6]
Kenai Mountains-Turnagain Arm	AK	2009	650	South Park	CO	2009	1,800
Lackawanna Heritage Valley . . .	PA	2000	350	Tennessee Civil War[7]	TN	1996	42,144
				Upper Housatonic Valley.	MA-CT	2006	964
				Wheeling.	WV	2000	12
				Yuma Crossing	AZ	2000	21

NA = Not available. (1) Year designation was received. (2) Figure given is length of area. (3) Covers 11 counties in both states. (4) Parts of 30 counties. (5) 8 counties. (6) 17 counties. (7) Spans entire state of Tennessee.

Attractions in and Around Washington, DC

Most attractions are free. Hours are subject to change, especially on holidays, when some attractions may be closed. For a free official visitors guide and map, visit washington.org or call Destination DC at 1-800-422-8644.

Arlington National Cemetery

Arlington National Cemetery, on the former Custis-Lee estate in Arlington, VA, was first used as a burial site during the Civil War. It is the final resting place of Pres. William Howard Taft and Pres. John F. Kennedy and his wife, Jacqueline Bouvier Kennedy Onassis. More than 400,000 U.S. military personnel from every major war are buried at Arlington. The **Tomb of the Unknown Soldier**, dedicated in 1921, is guarded by soldiers 24 hrs. a day.

A number of monuments and memorials are located throughout the 624-acre cemetery. They include the **Women in Military Service for America Memorial** (dedicated 1997), which honors the 2.5 mil women who have served in the U.S. military.

Open daily 8 AM-5 PM (8 AM-7 PM, Apr.-Sept.). Arlington, VA; (877) 907-8585. **Website:** www.arlingtoncemetery.mil

The **U.S. Marine Corps War Memorial** stands north of Arlington National Cemetery. A bronze statue depicts the raising of the U.S. flag on Mt. Suribachi, Feb. 23, 1945, during the World War II battle of Iwo Jima. The memorial grounds are open daily 6 AM-midnight. (703) 289-2500. **Website:** www.nps.gov/gwmp/

Bureau of Engraving and Printing

The Bureau of Engraving and Printing of the U.S. Treasury Dept. is the headquarters for the making of U.S. paper money. Free public tours are offered Mon.-Fri., 9 AM-2 PM (6 PM in spring and summer, when tickets are required). 14th and C Sts. SW; (866) 874-2330. **Website:** www.moneyfactory.gov

The Capitol

The United States Capitol was originally designed by Dr. William Thornton, an amateur architect, whose submission in 1793 won him $500 and a city lot. Three other architects designed or supervised construction of the Capitol before its completion.

The present cast-iron dome at its greatest exterior height measures 135 ft, 5 in. and is topped by the bronze Statue of Freedom, which stands 19½ ft and weighs 14,985 lbs. On its base are the words *E Pluribus Unum* (out of many, one). Restoration work on the dome began in 2014; it was expected to be complete before the presidential inauguration in Jan. 2017.

The Capitol Visitor Center is open to the public Mon.-Sat., 8:30 AM-4:30 PM. Free guided tours are available by pass 8:40 AM to 3:20 PM. The Senate and House galleries are not part of the tour. To enter either gallery or to observe Congress in session, those living in the U.S. may obtain tickets from their U.S. representative or senators. Visitors from other countries may inquire about passes at the Visitor Center. Between Constitution and Independence Aves., bounded by First St.; (202) 226-8000. **Website:** www.visitthecapitol.gov

Federal Bureau of Investigation

The Federal Bureau of Investigation discontinued tours of its headquarters following the Sept. 11, 2001, terrorist attacks. In 2014, the agency opened up the FBI Education Center to the public. Visits must be arranged in advance through the office of one's congressional delegate. J. Edgar Hoover Bldg., Pennsylvania Ave., between 9th and 10th Sts. NW; (202) 324-3000. **Website:** www.fbi.gov

Folger Shakespeare Library

The Folger Shakespeare Library, on Capitol Hill, is a research institution with the world's largest collection of Shakespearean materials and other rare books and manuscripts of the Renaissance period. Open to the public Mon.-Sat., 10 AM-5 PM, and Sun., 12 PM-5 PM. Building and garden tours are available. 201 E. Capitol St. SE; (202) 544-4600. **Website:** www.folger.edu

Holocaust Memorial Museum

The U.S. Holocaust Memorial Museum (opened 1993) documents the Holocaust through displays, interactive videos, and lectures. The permanent exhibition is recommended for visitors age 11 and up.

The museum is open daily, 10 AM-5:20 PM. Entry into the permanent exhibition is timed, Mar. through Aug. Timed passes are available at the door each day on a first-come, first-served basis; advance passes can be ordered online for a fee. 100 Raoul Wallenberg Pl. SW; (202) 488-0400. **Website:** www.ushmm.org

Jefferson Memorial

Dedicated Apr. 13, 1943, the Thomas Jefferson Memorial stands on the south shore of the Tidal Basin in West Potomac Park. The circular stone structure combines architectural elements of the dome of the Pantheon in Rome and the rotunda designed by Jefferson for the Univ. of Virginia.

The memorial is open 24 hrs. a day and staffed 9:30 AM-10 PM. Ohio and E. Basin Drs. SW; (202) 426-6841. **Website:** www.nps.gov/thje/

Kennedy Center

The John F. Kennedy Center for the Performing Arts opened in 1971. Designed by Edward Durell Stone, it includes an opera house, concert hall, theaters, restaurants, and a library. Free tours available Mon.-Fri., 10 AM-5 PM, and Sat.-Sun., 10 AM-1 PM. 2700 F St. NW; (800) 444-1324. **Website:** www.kennedy-center.org

Martin Luther King Jr. Memorial

The MLK Jr. Memorial (dedicated 2011) features a 30-ft figure of Dr. King emerging from a block of granite. The memorial, designed by sculptor Lei Yixin, is located on the Tidal Basin between the Lincoln and Jefferson Memorials.

The memorial is open 24 hrs. a day and staffed 9:30 AM-10 PM. Independence Ave. SW and West Basin Dr. SW; (202) 426-6841. **Website:** www.nps.gov/mlkm/

Korean War Veterans Memorial

The Korean War Veterans Memorial, dedicated 1995 at the Mall's west end, features a multiservice formation of 19 combat-ready soldiers in ponchos. A granite wall, with images of service members, juts into the Pool of Remembrance.

The memorial is open 24 hrs. a day and staffed 9:30 AM-10 PM. Independence Ave. SW and French Dr. SW; (202) 426-6841. **Website:** www.nps.gov/kowa/

Library of Congress

Established by and for Congress in 1800, the Library of Congress extends its services to other government agencies and libraries, scholars, and the public. It contains more than 162 mil items in some 470 languages, making it the world's largest library.

The Thomas Jefferson Building (Main Reading Room and exhibition galleries) is open Mon.-Sat., 8:30 AM-4:30 PM. The James Madison Memorial and John Adams Buildings have longer hours. 101 Independence Ave. SE; (202) 707-8000. **Website:** www.loc.gov

Lincoln Memorial

Designed by Henry Bacon and dedicated in 1922, the Lincoln Memorial in West Potomac Park is a large marble hall enclosing a statue, designed by Daniel Chester French, of Abraham Lincoln seated in an armchair. The text of the Gettysburg Address is engraved in the south chamber, that of Lincoln's second inaugural speech in the north chamber.

The memorial is open 24 hrs. a day and staffed 9:30 AM-10 PM. Independence Ave. and French Dr. SW; (202) 426-6841. **Website:** www.nps.gov/linc/

Mount Vernon

Mount Vernon, George Washington's estate, is about 15 mi from Washington, DC, in northern Virginia. The house is believed to be an enlargement of one built by Augustine Washington in 1735. His son Lawrence renamed the estate after British Adm. Edward Vernon. George Washington, Lawrence's half brother, inherited it in 1761. The estate has been restored to its 18th-cent. appearance. Washington and his wife, Martha, are buried on the grounds.

Open all year; hours vary seasonally. Mount Vernon, VA; (703) 780-2000. Admission (in-person price; discounted online): adults $20, seniors (62+) $19, youth (6-11) $10, ages 5 and under free. **Website:** www.mountvernon.org

National Archives and Records

Original copies of the Declaration of Independence, the Constitution, and the Bill of Rights are on display at the National Archives Museum. The National Archives also holds other U.S. government records, historic maps, photographs, and manuscripts.

The museum is open daily 10 AM-5:30 PM. Constitution Ave. bet. 7th and 9th Sts. NW; (866) 272-6272. **Website:** www.archives.gov

National Gallery of Art

The National Gallery of Art, established by Congress, opened in 1941. The original West Building was designed by John Russell Pope. The East Building, opened in 1978, was designed by I. M. Pei. Galleries are open Mon.-Sat., 10 AM-5 PM, and Sun., 11 AM-6 PM. The Sculpture Garden has extended hours in summer. 4th St. and Constitution Ave NW; (202) 737-4215. **Website:** www.nga.gov

The Pentagon

The Pentagon, headquarters of the Dept. of Defense, is the largest low-rise office building in the U.S. It houses some 23,000 employees in offices occupying 3,705,793 sq ft. The building was severely damaged when struck by a plane on Sept. 11, 2001.

Tours are available by reservation only, which must be made online 14-90 days in advance. Non-U.S. citizens must present a foreign passport or permanent resident card to enter. Arlington, VA; (703) 697-1776. **Website:** pentagontours.osd.mil

Franklin Delano Roosevelt Memorial

Opened in 1997, the FDR Memorial features four spaces with bronze statues and panels depicting FDR through his four terms in office. The 8.14-acre memorial is on the Tidal Basin.

Open daily with staff on grounds 9:30 AM-10 PM. Ohio and W. Basin Drs. SW; (202) 426-6841. **Website:** www.nps.gov/frde/

Smithsonian Institution

The Smithsonian Institution, established in 1846, is the world's largest museum and research complex. It holds some 138.1 mil artifacts and specimens in its trust. Seventeen of its 19 museums and the National Zoo are in the DC area. The **Smithsonian Institution Building** (or The Castle) houses the Smithsonian Information Center. Also on the National Mall are the **National Museum of African American History and Culture**, **National Museum of American History**, the **National Museum of Natural History**, the **National Air and Space Museum**, the **National Museum of the American Indian**, the **Hirshhorn Museum and Sculpture Garden**, the **Arthur M. Sackler Gallery**, the **Freer Gallery of Art**, the **National Museum of African Art**, and the **Arts and Industries Building** (a special-events space). Located nearby are the **National Postal Museum**, the **National Museum of American Art**, the **National Portrait Gallery**, and the **Renwick Gallery**. The **Anacostia Community Museum** is in SE DC. The Air and Space Museum's **Udvar-Hazy Center** is near Dulles Airport in Virginia.

Most museums are open daily, 10 AM-5:30 PM (later in summer); (202) 633-1000. **Website:** www.si.edu

Vietnam Veterans Memorial

Originally dedicated in 1982, the Vietnam Veterans Memorial recognizes those who served in the Vietnam War. The names of more than 58,000 Americans who lost their lives or remain missing are inscribed on polished black-granite walls arranged to form a V, designed by Maya Ying Lin.

Two additions have been made to Lin's design, the Frederick Hart sculpture *Three Servicemen* (1984), and the Vietnam Women's Memorial (1993), designed by Glenna Goodacre, honoring the more than 11,500 women who served in Vietnam.

The memorial is open 24 hrs. a day and staffed 9:30 AM-10 PM. Constitution Ave. and Bacon Dr. NW; (202) 426-6841. **Website:** www.nps.gov/vive/

Washington Monument

The Washington Monument, dedicated in 1885, is a tapering shaft, or obelisk, of white marble, 554 ft, $7^{11}\!/_{32}$ in. in height and 55 ft, 1½ in. square at the base. Eight small windows, two on each side, are located on the observation deck at the 500-ft level.

Open daily, 9 AM-5 PM (10 PM in summer). Same-day timed passes are available first-come, first-served; advance passes can be obtained for a fee. In late Sept. 2016, the Park Service announced the monument's indefinite closure until its elevator could be modernized, a project that might last up to nine months. 15th St. and Constitution Ave. NW; (202) 426-6841. **Website:** www.nps.gov/wamo/

White House

The White House, the president's residence, stands on 18 acres on the south side of Pennsylvania Ave., between the Treasury and the old Executive Office Building. The sandstone walls, quarried at Aquia Creek, VA, were first made white with lime-based whitewash in 1798, though the name did not become official until 1901.

Free self-guided tours of the residence's public areas are available Tues.-Thurs., 7:30-11:30 AM, and Fri. and Sat., 7:30 AM-1:30 PM. Tour requests must be made at least 21 days in advance through one's member of Congress. Foreign visitors may make requests through their embassy. Tours are scheduled on a first-come, first-served basis. 1600 Pennsylvania Ave. NW; (202) 456-7041. **Website:** www.whitehouse.gov

The White House Visitor Center at 1450 Pennsylvania Ave. NW is open daily 7:30 AM-4 PM; (202) 208-1631. **Website:** www. nps.gov/whho/

National World War II Memorial

The National WWII Memorial, opened in 2004, is dedicated to the approx. 16 mil veterans who served and the more than 400,000 who died in the war. The 8.25-acre site is at the east end of the Lincoln Memorial Reflecting Pool.

The 43-ft archways at the north and south entrances represent the Atlantic and Pacific theaters. A wall of 4,048 gold stars, each representing 100 American deaths, stands in an oval plaza surrounded by 56 pillars standing for the states, territories, and the Dist. of Columbia.

The memorial is open 24 hrs. a day and staffed 9:30 AM-10 PM. 17th St. and Independence Ave. SW; (202) 426-6841. **Website:** www.nps.gov/wwii/

UNITED STATES HISTORY

This chapter includes the following sections:

Chronology of Events

1492 Christopher Columbus and crew sighted land Oct. 12 in what is now the Bahamas.

1513 Juan Ponce de León explored Florida coast.

1524 Giovanni da Verrazzano led French expedition along coast from Carolina north to Nova Scotia; entered New York Harbor.

1526 San Miguel de Guadalupe, **first European settlement** in what became U.S. territory, was established in the summer off South Carolina coast; abandoned in Oct.

1539 Hernando de Soto landed in Florida May 28; crossed Mississippi River, 1541.

1540 Francisco Vásquez de Coronado explored Southwest north of Rio Grande. **Hernando de Alarcón** reached Colorado River; **García López de Cárdenas** reached Grand Canyon. Others explored California coast.

1562 First French colony in what became U.S. territory founded on Parris Island off South Carolina coast; abandoned, 1564.

1565 St. Augustine, FL, oldest continuously occupied European settlement in U.S., founded Sept. 8 by Pedro Menéndez de Avilés. Spain ceded settlement to U.S. in 1821.

1579 Sir Francis Drake entered San Francisco Bay and claimed region for Britain.

1585 First English colony in America, sponsored by Sir Walter Raleigh, founded on **Roanoke Island**, off North Carolina coast; colony failed.

1587 Second colony attempted on Roanoke Island. Virginia Dare of colony became **first English infant born** in the New World. Settlers of second colony found to have vanished, 1590.

1607 Capt. **John Smith** and 105 cavaliers in three ships landed on Virginia coast and started Jamestown, **first permanent English settlement** in New World.

1609 Henry Hudson, English explorer of Northwest Passage, employed by Dutch, sailed into New York Harbor in Sept. and up Hudson to Albany. **Samuel de Champlain** explored Lake Champlain, to the north. Spaniards settled **Santa Fe, NM**.

1619 House of Burgesses, **first representative assembly** in New World, elected July 30 at Jamestown, VA. **First black laborers**—indentured servants—in English North American colonies, brought by Dutch to Jamestown in Aug. Chattel slavery legally recognized, 1650.

1620 Pilgrims, Puritan separatists, left Plymouth, England, Sept. 16 on *Mayflower*; reached Cape Cod Nov. 19; 103 passengers landed at Plymouth, Dec. 26. **Mayflower Compact**, signed Nov. 11, was agreement to form a self-government. Half of colony died during harsh winter.

1624 Dutch settled in Albany and along Hudson River, establishing the colony of **New Netherland** in May.

1626 Peter Minuit bought **Manhattan** for Dutch West India Co. from Manahatta Indians during summer for goods valued at $24; named island **New Amsterdam**.

1630 Settlement of **Boston** established by Massachusetts colonists led by John Winthrop; Winthrop began *The History of New England*. **William Bradford**, a governor of Plymouth Colony, began his chronicle *History of Plymouth Plantation (1620-1647)*, first published in entirety in 1856.

1634 Maryland founded as Catholic colony under charter to Lord Baltimore. Act of Toleration passed 1649 provided for religious tolerance.

1635 Boston Latin School, **oldest public school** in continuous existence in U.S., founded Apr. 23.

1636 Roger Williams founded **Providence, RI**, in June, as a democratically ruled colony with separation of church and state. Charter granted, 1644. **Harvard College** founded; oldest institution of higher learning in U.S.

1640 First book printed in America, the so-called *Bay Psalm Book*.

1647 Liberal constitution drafted in Rhode Island. First law in America providing for **free compulsory basic education** enacted in Massachusetts.

1660 British Parliament passed first **Navigation Act** Dec. 1, regulating colonial commerce to suit English needs.

1661 Missionary John Eliot's translation of the New Testament into Algonquian became the **first Bible printed** in North America.

1664 British troops Sept. 8 seized New Netherland from Dutch. Charles II granted New Netherland and city of New Amsterdam to brother, Duke of York; both renamed **New York**. Dutch recaptured colony 1673 but ceded it to Britain Nov. 10, 1674.

1670 Charles Town, SC, founded by English colonists in Apr.

1673 Regular mail service on horseback instituted Jan. 1 between New York and Boston. **Jacques Marquette** and **Louis Jolliet** reached the upper Mississippi and traveled down it.

1674 Future **Salem witch trial** judge Samuel Sewall began renowned diary covering events through 1729.

1676 Bloody **Indian war** in New England ended Aug. 12. King Philip, Wampanoag chief, and Narragansett Indians killed. **Nathaniel Bacon** led planters against autocratic British Gov. Sir William Berkeley, burned Jamestown, VA, Sept. 19. Rebellion collapsed when Bacon died; 23 followers executed.

1678 A book of poetry by **Anne Bradstreet** (first published in Britain) revised and expanded for posthumous publication in Massachusetts. Considered first female poet in American colonies.

1679 Fire destroyed 150 houses in Boston. City imported **first fire engines** from England.

1681 John Bunyan's *The Pilgrim's Progress* published in America; became best seller.

1682 René-Robert Cavelier, Sieur de La Salle, claimed lower Mississippi River country for France and called it Louisiana Apr. 9. Had French outposts built in Illinois and Texas, 1684. Killed during mutiny, 1687. Spanish colonists became the **first Europeans to settle Texas**, at site of present-day El Paso.

1683 William Penn signed treaty with Delaware Indians Apr. 23 and made payment for **Pennsylvania** lands. The **first German colonists** in America settled near Philadelphia.

1689 New York's English colonial governor, **Sir Edmund Andros**, resigned after armed uprising in Boston on Apr. 18.

1690 First colonial newspaper, *Publick Occurrences*, published by Benjamin Harris but shut down after one issue for lack of official permission. Harris also published *New England Primer* for use as elementary school textbook. Large-scale **whaling** operations began in Nantucket, MA.

1620: Pilgrims and other colonists sign the Mayflower Compact to form a "civil body politic."

1692 Hysteria over **witchcraft** began in Salem Village (now Danvers), MA; 14 women and 6 men were executed by special court.

1697 *The Essays* of **Sir Francis Bacon**, first published in England in 1597, was published in America; it became a best seller.

1699 Former privateer Capt. **William Kidd** arrested and sent to England; hanged for piracy, 1701. French settlements made in Mississippi, Louisiana.

1702 Legislation enacted making **Church of England** the established church in Maryland.

1704 Indians and French allies attacked **Deerfield**, MA, Feb. 29; killed 40, captured and marched off 100. *Boston News Letter*, **first regular newspaper**, started by postmaster John Campbell.

1710 British-colonial troops captured French fort, Port Royal, Nova Scotia, in **Queen Anne's War**, 1702-13. France yielded Nova Scotia by treaty, 1713.

1712 Slaves revolted in New York City Apr. 6; 21 were executed. Second uprising, 1741; 13 slaves hanged, 13 burned, 71 deported.

1716 First theater in colonies opened in Williamsburg, VA.

1726 Great Awakening, general revival of evangelical religion, began in colonies.

1731 America's **first subscription library** (paying members could freely borrow books) cofounded in Philadelphia by Benjamin Franklin.

1732 Benjamin Franklin published the **first *Poor Richard's Almanack***; published annually until 1757. Georgia, last of 13 colonies, chartered.

1733 Influenza epidemic swept through New York City and Philadelphia.

1735 Editor **John Peter Zenger** was acquitted of libel Aug. 5 in New York City after criticizing the British governor's conduct in office.

1739 A series of **slave uprisings** put down in South Carolina.

1741 Famous sermon "Sinners in the Hands of an Angry God," delivered July 8 at Enfield, MA, by Jonathan Edwards, one of the most important preachers in the **Great Awakening** religious revival. Danish navigator **Vitus Bering**, commanding Russian expedition, reached Alaska.

1744 King George's War pitted British and colonials versus French. Colonials captured Louisbourg, Cape Breton Isl., Nova Scotia, June 17, 1745. Returned to France 1748 by Treaty of Aix-la-Chapelle.

1752 According to legend, **Benjamin Franklin**, flying kite in thunderstorm, proved lightning is electricity, June 15; invented lightning rod. **Liberty Bell**, cast in England, was delivered to Pennsylvania.

1754 French and Indian War began with Ft. Necessity campaign in Pennsylvania. Skirmish May 28, battle at fort July 3-4. British moved Acadian French from Nova Scotia to Louisiana Oct. 8, 1755. British captured Québec Sept. 18, 1759, in battles in which French Gen. Joseph de Montcalm and British Gen. James Wolfe were killed. Peace pact signed Feb. 10, 1763. French lost Canada and Midwest. Delegates from seven colonies to New York for **Albany Congress**, July 19, approved plan of union by Benjamin Franklin; plan rejected by the colonies.

1757 First streetlights appeared in Philadelphia.

1764 Sugar Act, Apr. 5, placed duties on lumber, foodstuffs in colonies. First law passed by Parliament to specifically raise revenue from colonies, alleviate French and Indian War debts. British enforced this act, unlike with **Molasses Act** of 1733.

1765 Stamp Act, enacted by Parliament Mar. 22, required revenue stamps to help fund royal troops. Nine colonies, at Stamp Act Congress in New York Oct. 7-25, adopted Declaration of Rights. Stamp Act repealed Mar. 17, 1766. **Quartering Act**, requiring colonists to house British troops, went into effect Mar. 24.

1767 Townshend Acts levied taxes on glass, lead, paper, paint, and tea. In 1770 all duties except on tea were repealed.

1770 British troops fired Mar. 5 into Boston mob, killed five including **Crispus Attucks**, a black man, reportedly leader of group; later called **Boston Massacre**.

1773 East India Co. tea ships turned back at Boston, New York, and Philadelphia in May. Cargo ship burned at Annapolis, Oct. 14; cargo thrown overboard at **Boston Tea Party**, Dec. 16, to protest the tea tax. **First museum** in the colonies was officially established in Charleston, SC; later named the Charleston Museum.

1776: Thomas Jefferson's final draft of the Declaration of Independence eliminated a phrase in an early draft that called slavery "an execrable commerce."

1774 "Intolerable Acts" of Parliament curtailed Massachusetts self-rule; barred use of Boston Harbor until dumped tea was paid for. **First Continental Congress** held in Philadelphia Sept. 5-Oct. 26; called for civil disobedience against British. Rhode Island **abolished slavery**.

1775 Patrick Henry addressed Virginia convention, Mar. 23, said, "Give me liberty, or give me death!" **Paul Revere, William Dawes**, and Dr. **Samuel Prescott**, Apr. 18, rode to alert patriots that British were on their way to Concord, MA, to destroy arms. At **Lexington**, MA, Apr. 19, Minutemen lost eight. On return from **Concord**, British suffered 273 casualties. Col. Ethan Allen (joined by Col. Benedict Arnold) captured **Ft. Ticonderoga** in New York, May 10, also Crown Point. Colonials headed for **Bunker Hill** and fortified nearby Breed's Hill, Charlestown, MA. Repulsed British under Gen. William Howe twice before retreating, June 17. Continental Congress June 15 named **George Washington** commander in chief; established a postal system, July 26. Benjamin Franklin became the **first postmaster general**.

1776 Thomas Paine's *Common Sense*, famous pro-independence pamphlet, published Jan. 10; quickly sold some 100,000 copies. France and Spain agreed May 2 to provide arms to U.S. In Continental Congress June 7, Richard Henry Lee (VA) moved "that these United Colonies are, and of right ought to be, free and independent states." Resolution adopted July 2. **Declaration of Independence** approved July 4, signed Aug. 2. Col. William Moultrie's batteries at **Charleston, SC**, repulsed British sea attack June 28. Washington lost **Battle of Long Island** Aug. 27; evacuated New York. **Nathan Hale** executed as spy by British Sept. 22. Brig. Gen. Arnold's Lake Champlain fleet was defeated in **Battle of Valcour Island** Oct. 11, but British returned to Canada. Howe failed to destroy Washington's army at White Plains, NY, Oct. 28. Hessians captured Ft. Washington, Manhattan, and 3,000 men, Nov. 16; captured Ft. Lee, NJ, Nov. 20. Washington, in Pennsylvania, recrossed **Delaware River** Dec. 25-26, defeated Hessians at **Battle of Trenton**, NJ, Dec. 26.

1777 Washington defeated Lord Charles Cornwallis at **Princeton**, NJ, Jan. 3. Continental Congress, June 14, authorized an **American flag**, the Stars and Stripes. Maj. Gen. John Burgoyne's force of 8,000 from Canada captured **Ft. Ticonderoga**, NY, July 6. Americans beat back Burgoyne at Bemis Heights, Oct. 7, cut off British escape route. Burgoyne surrendered 5,000 men at Saratoga, NY, Oct. 17. **Articles of Confederation** adopted by Continental Congress, Nov. 15; took effect Mar. 1, 1781.

1778 France signed treaty of aid with U.S. Feb. 6; sent fleet. British evacuated Philadelphia, June 18.

1779 George Rogers Clark took Ft. Vincennes in what is now Indiana in Feb. **John Paul Jones** on the *Bonhomme Richard* defeated *Serapis* in British North Sea waters, Sept. 23.

1780 Charleston, SC, fell to the British May 12, but Loyalists were defeated in battle of **Kings Mountain**, NC, Oct. 7 in what Thomas Jefferson called "the turn of the tide of success." **Benedict Arnold** found to be a traitor Sept. 23. Arnold escaped, made brigadier general in British army.

1781 Bank of North America, **first commercial bank**, incorporated May 26. Cornwallis retired to **Yorktown, VA**. Adm. Francois Joseph de Grasse landed 3,000 French and stopped British fleet in **Hampton Roads**, VA. Washington and Jean Baptiste de Rochambeau joined forces, arrived near Williamsburg, Sept. 26. Siege of Cornwallis began, Oct. 6; **Cornwallis surrendered** Oct. 19.

1782 New British cabinet agreed in Mar. to **recognize U.S. independence**. Preliminary agreement signed in Paris, Nov. 30. Use of **scarlet letter A**, sewn on clothing or branded on skin of adulterers, discontinued in New England.

1783 Massachusetts Supreme Court decision in final Quock Walker trial **declared slavery illegal**. Newspapers typically published weekly; **first regular daily newspaper**, *Pennsylvania Evening Post*, went on sale in Philadelphia, May 30. Britain, U.S. signed **Paris peace treaty**, Sept. 3, recognizing American independence; Congress ratified it Jan. 14, 1784. Washington ordered army disbanded Nov. 3, bade farewell to his officers at Fraunces Tavern, New York City, Dec. 4.

1784 Thomas Jefferson's proposal to **ban slavery in new territories** after 1802 was narrowly defeated, Mar. 1.

1785 Regular **stagecoach routes** established between Albany, NY; New York City; and Philadelphia.

1786 Delegates from five states at Annapolis, MD, Sept. 11-14 asked Congress to call a **constitutional convention**.

1787 **Shays's Rebellion** of debt-ridden farmers in Massachusetts failed, Jan. 25. **Constitutional convention** opened in Philadelphia, May 25, with Washington presiding. Constitution accepted by delegates, Sept. 17. Delaware was first state to ratify it, Dec. 7; Pennsylvania and New Jersey followed. **Northwest Ordinance** adopted July 13 by Continental Congress for Northwest Territory, north of Ohio River, west of New York; made rules for statehood and guaranteed freedom of religion, support for schools, no slavery. *Federalist Papers* first appeared in *NY Independent Journal*.

1788 A large fire in **New Orleans**, then a Spanish territory, destroyed much of the city, Mar. 21. **Constitution adopted** June 21 after being ratified by the requisite ninth state (New Hampshire); also ratified by Georgia, Connecticut, Massachusetts, Maryland, South Carolina, Virginia, and New York throughout the year. **First U.S. senators elected** Sept. 30, from Pennsylvania.

1789 **George Washington** chosen president by all electors voting (73 eligible, 69 voting, 4 absent); **John Adams**, vice president, got 34 votes. **First Congress** met at Federal Hall, New York City, and declared Constitution in effect, Mar. 4; Washington inaugurated there Apr. 30; **first inaugural ball** held May 7. U.S. **State Dept.** established by Congress July 27. (Thomas Jefferson installed as first secretary of state Feb. 1790.) **War Dept.** created Aug. 7, with Henry Knox as secretary; **Treasury Dept.** created Sept. 2, with Alexander Hamilton to be secretary. **Supreme Court** created by Federal Judiciary Act, Sept. 24; **John Jay** confirmed by Congress as first Supreme Court chief justice, Sept. 26.

1790 **First Supreme Court session** held Feb. 2 in New York City. Congress, Mar. 1, authorized decennial **U.S. census**. Collection of data took 18 months. **Naturalization Act** (two-year residency) passed Mar. 26. John Carroll consecrated as **first American Catholic bishop**, Aug. 15. Congress met in **Philadelphia**, new temporary capital, Dec. 6.

1791 **Bill of Rights**, submitted to states, Sept. 25, 1789, went into effect Dec. 15. First Bank of the United States, **first bank chartered by federal government**, established in Philadelphia.

1792 Coinage Act established **U.S. Mint** in Philadelphia, Apr. 2. Gen. **"Mad" Anthony Wayne** made commander in Ohio-Indiana area, trained American Legion, established string of forts. Routed Indians at Fallen Timbers on Maumee River, Aug. 20, 1794; checked British at Fort Miami, OH, same year. **White House** cornerstone laid Oct. 13.

1793 Washington inaugurated for second term, Mar. 4, having received 132 electoral votes; **John Adams** again became vice president, having received second highest total, 77. Washington declared **U.S. neutrality**, Apr. 22, in war between Britain and France. Eli Whitney invented **cotton gin** (patented 1794), reviving Southern slavery.

1794 **Whiskey Rebellion**, western Pennsylvania farmers protesting liquor tax of 1791, suppressed by federal militia in Sept. **Jay's Treaty**, controversial treaty with Britain negotiated by John Jay, signed Nov. 19, ratified June 24, 1795. This treaty intended to settle long-standing differences between U.S. and Britain.

1795 U.S. bought peace from **Algerian pirates** by paying $1 mil ransom for 115 seamen Sept. 5, followed by annual

1804-06: Meriwether Lewis, William Clark, and the rest of Corps of Discovery—including Sacagawea—explored the Missouri and Columbia Rivers from St. Louis to the Pacific Ocean and back.

tributes. Gen. Wayne signed **Treaty of Greenville** with Indians, opening Northwest Territory to settlers. Univ. of North Carolina became **first operating state university**.

1796 **Washington's farewell address** as president delivered Sept. 17. Warned against permanent alliances with foreign powers, big public debt, large military establishment, and devices of "small, artful, enterprising minority."

1797 **John Adams** inaugurated as second president Mar. 4, having received 71 electoral votes; **Thomas Jefferson** became vice president, having received 68. U.S. frigate *United States* launched at Philadelphia, May 10; *Constellation* at Baltimore, Sept. 7; *Constitution* (Old Ironsides) at Boston, Oct. 21.

1798 **Alien and Sedition Acts** passed by Federalists June-July; intended to silence political opposition. **War with France threatened** over French raids on U.S. shipping and rejection of U.S. diplomats. Navy (45 ships) and 365 privateers captured 84 French ships. USS *Constellation* took French warship *Insurgente*, 1799. Napoleon stopped French raids after becoming first consul.

1800 Federal government moved to **Washington, DC**.

1801 **John Marshall** named Supreme Court chief justice, Jan. 20. **Thomas Jefferson**, who had received same number of electoral votes as Aaron Burr in 1800 election, won out over Burr in House vote Feb. 17; Burr named vice president. **Tripoli declared war** June 10 against U.S., which refused added tribute to commerce-raiding Arab corsairs. Land and naval campaigns forced Tripoli to negotiate peace, June 4, 1805. **Oldest U.S. art institution**, Pennsylvania Academy of Fine Arts, founded in Philadelphia.

1802 Congress established U.S. Military Academy at **West Point**, NY.

1803 Supreme Court, in *Marbury v. Madison*, overturned U.S. law for first time, Feb. 24. Napoleon sold all of Louisiana, stretching to Canadian border, to U.S. for $11.25 mil in bonds, plus $3.75 mil indemnities to American citizens with claims against France. U.S. took title Dec. 20. **Louisiana Purchase** doubled U.S. area.

1804 **Meriwether Lewis** and **William Clark** expedition ordered by Pres. Thomas Jefferson to explore what is now Northwest U.S. Started from St. Louis May 14; ended Sept. 23, 1806, back in St. Louis. Vice Pres. **Aaron Burr** shot Alexander Hamilton in duel July 11 in Weehawken, NJ; Hamilton died next day.

1805 U.S. Marines aided by Arab mercenaries, Apr. 27, captured Tripolitan port of Derna. Major victory in war against

1808: Laws outlawing slave importation go into effect, but an estimated 250,000 enslaved persons are illegally brought to the U.S., 1808-60.

Barbary pirates; inspiration for "to the shores of Tripoli" in Marines Corps hymn.
1807 Robert Fulton made **first practical steamboat trip**; left New York City Aug. 17 and reached Albany, NY, 150 mi away, in 32 hr. **Embargo Act** banned all trade with foreign countries, forbidding ships to set sail for foreign ports Dec. 22.
1808 Legislation outlawing slave imports goes into effect. Some 250,000 slaves were illegally imported 1808-60.
1810 Third U.S. Census found population of 7,239,881. The slave population was put at 1,191,364 and the population of all other non-white free persons at 186,446.
1811 Indiana Territory governor William Henry Harrison defeated Indians led by Tenskwatawa, called the Prophet, in **Battle of Tippecanoe**, Nov. 7. Construction began on **Cumberland Road** in Cumberland, MD; road became important route to West. About 400 **slaves revolted** in Louisiana and marched on New Orleans. The insurrection was suppressed; two whites, some 75 slaves killed.
1812 War of 1812 had three main causes: Britain seized U.S. ships trading with France; Britain had seized 4,000 naturalized U.S. sailors by 1810; Britain armed Indians, who raided Western border. U.S. stopped trade with Europe 1807 and 1809. Trade with Britain only was stopped 1810. Unaware that Britain had raised blockade against France two days before, **Congress declared war** June 18. British took **Detroit** Aug. 16.
1813 Oliver H. Perry defeated British fleet at **Battle of Lake Erie**, Sept. 10. U.S. won **Battle of the Thames**, Ontario, Oct. 5, but failed in Canadian invasion attempts. York (Toronto) and Buffalo, NY, were burned.
1814 Troops under Andrew Jackson defeated Creek Indians led by Chief Weatherford at Battle of Horseshoe Bend in Alabama, Mar. 29, ending **Creek Indian War**, begun a year earlier. British landed in Maryland in Aug., defeated U.S. force Aug. 24, **burned Capitol and White House**. Maryland militia stopped British advance, Sept. 12. British bombardment of Ft. McHenry, Baltimore, for 25 hr., Sept. 13-14, failed, inspiring **Francis Scott Key** to write the words to **"The Star-Spangled Banner."** U.S. won naval **Battle of Lake Champlain** Sept. 11. Peace treaty with Great Britain signed at Ghent, Belgium, Dec. 24.
1815 Some 5,300 British, unaware of peace treaty, attacked U.S. entrenchments near **New Orleans**, Jan. 8. British had more than 2,000 casualties; Americans lost 71. U.S. flotilla finally ended attacks by **pirates** from Ottoman states of Algiers, Tunis, Tripoli.
1816 Second Bank of the U.S. chartered Apr. 10. The **American Colonization Society**, which sought to address slavery issue by transporting freed blacks to Africa, formed in Washington, DC, Dec. 1816-Jan. 1817.
1817 Thomas Hopkins Gallaudet established the **first free public school for the deaf** in Hartford, CT.
1818 Connecticut expanded **suffrage** among white male voters. Massachusetts followed suit in 1820, and New York in 1821, reducing or eliminating property qualifications.
1819 Spain ceded **Florida** to U.S. Feb. 22. American steamship *Savannah* made first part-steam-powered, part-sail-powered **crossing of Atlantic**, traveling from Savannah, GA, to Liverpool, England, in 29 days. **Washington Irving**'s *Sketch Book* became best seller.

1820 First organized immigration of blacks to Africa from U.S. began with 86 free blacks sailing to Sierra Leone in Feb. Henry Clay's **Missouri Compromise** bill passed by Congress, Mar. 3. Slavery was allowed in Missouri but not west of the Mississippi River, north of 36° 30´ (the southern line of Missouri). Compromise repealed 1854.
1821 Emma Willard founded Troy Female Seminary, **first U.S. women's college**. Stephen Austin established **first American community in Texas**, San Felipe de Austin. James Fenimore Cooper's *The Spy*, novel set during American Revolution, published and became a best seller.
1822 Tension between sports and academics surfaced when Yale College Pres. Timothy Dwight banned a **primitive form of football**, setting fines for violators.
1823 Monroe Doctrine, opposing European intervention in the Americas, enunciated by Pres. James Monroe Dec. 2. The **Hudson River School**, painters who focused on the beauties of nature, began to receive public attention.
1824 Pawtucket, RI, **weavers strike**, is first organized factory strike in U.S. and one of earliest known involving women workers. **Slavery abolished** in state of Illinois Aug. 2.
1825 After a deadlocked election, **John Quincy Adams** was elected president by the House, Feb. 9. **Erie Canal** opened; first boat left Buffalo, NY, Oct. 26, reached New York City Nov. 4. John Stevens, of Hoboken, NJ, built and operated **first experimental steam locomotive** in U.S.
1826 Thomas Jefferson and **John Adams** both died July 4. **James Fenimore Cooper**'s *The Last of the Mohicans* published.
1827 Massachusetts became first state to pass a law providing for tax-supported **public high schools**.
1828 Baltimore & Ohio, the **first U.S. passenger railroad**, began operations July 4. South Carolina Dec. 19 declared right of **state nullification of federal laws**, opposing the "Tariff of Abominations." **Noah Webster** published his *American Dictionary of the English Language*.
1829 Andrew Jackson inaugurated as president, Mar. 4.
1830 Famous **debate** culminating Jan. 27 between Sen. **Daniel Webster** (MA) and Robert Hayne (SC), on state right to nullify federal law. **Mormon church** organized by Joseph Smith in Fayette, NY, Apr. 6. Pres. Jackson, May 28, signed **Indian Removal Act**, granting president authority to negotiate treaties whereby Indians living east of Mississippi R. give up lands in exchange for lands in West.
1831 William Lloyd Garrison began **abolitionist newspaper** *The Liberator* Jan. 1. **Nat Turner**, black slave in Virginia, led local slave rebellion, starting Aug. 21; 57 whites killed. Troops called in, 100 slaves killed. Turner captured, tried, and hanged Nov. 11.
1832 Black Hawk War in Illinois and Wisconsin Apr.-Sept. pushed Sauk and Fox Indians west across Mississippi.
1833 American Anti-Slavery Society founded in Philadelphia, Dec. 4. **Oberlin College** became first to adopt coeducation in U.S.
1835 According to tradition, the **Liberty Bell** cracked July 8 while tolling death of Chief Justice John Marshall. **Seminole Indians** in Florida under Osceola began attacks Nov. 1, protesting forced removal. The unpopular war ended Aug. 14, 1842; most of the Indians sent to Oklahoma. **Texas** proclaimed right to secede from Mexico; **Sam Houston** put in

1838: Cherokee Indians are marched from their homes in southeast U.S. to present-day Oklahoma on the "Trail of Tears."

command of Texas army, Nov. 2-4. **Gold** discovered on Cherokee land in Georgia. Indians forced to cede lands, Dec. 20, and to cross Mississippi.

1836 Texans besieged at **Alamo** in San Antonio by Mexicans under Antonio López de Santa Anna, Feb. 23-Mar. 6; entire garrison killed. Texas independence had been declared, Mar. 2. At San Jacinto Apr. 21, Sam Houston and Texans defeated Mexicans. Ralph Waldo Emerson published his first work, *Nature*, espousing his philosophy of **transcendentalism**. Marcus Whitman, H. H. Spaulding, and wives reached Fort Walla Walla on Columbia River, OR, **first white women to cross the Continental Divide**, in the Rocky Mountains.

1838 Cherokee Indians forced to walk **"Trail of Tears"** from southeast U.S. to area in present-day Oklahoma. At least 4,000—nearly one-fifth of Cherokee population—are estimated to have died.

1841 **First emigrant wagon train bound for California**, 47 people, left Independence, MO, May 1; reached California Nov. 4. Edgar Allan Poe published one of the **first American detective stories**, *The Murders in the Rue Morgue*.

1842 **Webster-Ashburton Treaty** signed Aug. 9, fixing U.S.-Canada border in Maine and Minnesota. **First use of anesthetic** (sulfuric ether gas) in an operation performed by Georgia doctor Crawford Long.

1843 More than 1,000 settlers left Independence, MO, for Oregon May 22, arriving in Oct. via **Oregon Trail**.

1844 **First message over first telegraph line** sent May 24 by inventor Samuel F. B. Morse from Washington to Baltimore: "What hath God wrought?"

1845 Congress **overrode a presidential veto for the first time**, Mar. 3, after Pres. John Tyler vetoed a tariff bill. Congress of **Texas** voted for annexation by U.S., July 4; Texas admitted to Union, Dec. 29. **Edgar Allan Poe**'s poem "The Raven" published.

1846 **Mexican War** began after Pres. James K. Polk ordered Gen. Zachary Taylor to seize disputed Texan land settled by Mexicans. After border clash, U.S. declared war May 13; Mexico declared war May 23. About 12,000 U.S. troops took Vera Cruz Mar. 27, 1847, and Mexico City Sept. 14, 1847. Treaty signed Feb. 2, 1848, ended war, and Mexico ceded claims to Texas, California, and other territory. Bear flag of **Republic of California** raised by American settlers at Sonoma, June 14. Treaty with Britain June 15 set **Oregon territory** boundary at 49th parallel (extension of existing line). Expansionists had used slogan "54°40′ or fight." The term **"manifest destiny,"** coined by journalist in 1845, also came into play. **Mormons**, after violent clashes with settlers over polygamy, left Nauvoo, IL, for West under Brigham Young. They settled July 1847 at Salt Lake City, UT. Elias Howe invented **sewing machine**.

1847 **First adhesive U.S. postage stamps**—Benjamin Franklin 5¢, Washington 10¢—sold July 1. **Henry Wadsworth Longfellow**'s *Evangeline* published.

1848 Gold discovered Jan. 24 in California; 80,000 prospectors emigrated in 1849. Lucretia Mott and Elizabeth Cady Stanton led Seneca Falls, NY, **Women's Rights Convention** July 19-20.

1850 Sen. Henry Clay's **Compromise of 1850** admitted California as 31st state Sept. 9, with slavery forbidden; made Utah and New Mexico territories; made **Fugitive Slave Law** harsher; and ended District of Columbia slave trade. **Nathaniel Hawthorne**'s *The Scarlet Letter* published.

1851 **Herman Melville**'s *Moby-Dick* published.

1852 **Harriet Beecher Stowe**'s *Uncle Tom's Cabin* published.

1853 Japan receives Comm. Matthew C. Perry, July 14. He negotiated treaty to **open Japan** to U.S. ships. New York City hosted **first World's Fair** in the U.S., beginning July 14. **Stephen Foster** published "My Old Kentucky Home."

1854 **Republican Party** formed at Ripon, WI, Feb. 28. Opposed Kansas-Nebraska Act, which left issue of slavery to vote of settlers. Act became law May 30. Treaty ratified with Mexico Apr. 25, providing for **Gadsden Purchase** of a strip of land. **Henry David Thoreau**'s *Walden* published.

1855 **First railroad train crossed Mississippi River** on river's first bridge, between Rock Island, IL, and Davenport, IA, Apr. 21. **Walt Whitman**'s *Leaves of Grass* published.

1856 Proslavery group sacked **Lawrence, KS**, May 21; abolitionist John Brown led antislavery contingent against Missourians at Osawatomie, KS, Aug. 30. Antislavery Republican

Party's **first presidential nominee**, John C. Frémont, defeated by James Buchanan. Abraham Lincoln made 50 speeches for Frémont. **First U.S. kindergarten** opened in Watertown, WI.

1857 In **Dred Scott** case, which involved determination of constitutionality of already-repealed Missouri Compromise, Supreme Court decided Mar. 6 that slaves did not become free in a free state, and blacks were not and could not be citizens. **Currier & Ives**, firm of American lithographers, issued their first print.

1858 **First Atlantic cable** completed by Cyrus W. Field Aug. 5. **Lincoln-Douglas debates** in Illinois, Aug. 21-Oct. 15.

1859 Edwin L. Drake drilled the **first commercially productive oil well** near Titusville, PA, Aug. 27. Abolitionist John Brown, with 21 men, seized U.S. armory at **Harpers Ferry**, WV, Oct. 16. U.S. Marines captured raiders, killing several. Brown was hanged for treason Dec. 2.

1860 Shoeworkers in Lynn, MA, went on strike Feb. 22. Within a week, strike spread to include 20,000 shoeworkers throughout New England in country's **largest strike to date**. **First Pony Express** between Sacramento, CA, and St. Joseph, MO, started Apr. 3. Republican **Abraham Lincoln** elected president Nov. 6 in four-way race.

1861 Seven southern states set up **Confederate States of America** Feb. 8, with **Jefferson Davis** as president. **Civil War** began as Confederates fired on **Ft. Sumter** in Charleston, SC, Apr. 12; they captured it Apr. 14. Pres. Lincoln called for 75,000 volunteers Apr. 15. Lincoln blockaded Southern ports Apr. 19, cutting off vital exports and aid. By May, 11 states had seceded. Confederates repelled Union forces at first **Battle of Bull Run**, July 21. **First transcontinental telegraph line** put in operation.

1862 Union forces were victorious in Western campaigns, took New Orleans May 1. Battles in East were largely inconclusive despite heavy casualties. The **Battle of Antietam**, in western Maryland Sept. 17, was bloodiest one-day battle of war; each side lost more than 2,000 men. **Homestead Act**, which granted free farms to settlers, approved May 20. **Land Grant Act**, which provided for public land sale to benefit

1863: Pres. Abraham Lincoln's Gettysburg Address commemorates the deaths of thousands in fewer than 300 words.

agricultural education, approved July 7. It eventually led to establishment of state university systems.

1863 Pres. Lincoln issued **Emancipation Proclamation** Jan. 1, freeing "all slaves in areas still in rebellion." Union forces won major victory at Gettysburg, PA, July 1-3. Confederate forces under siege surrendered **Vicksburg, MS**, to Union forces under Gen. Ulysses S. Grant, July 4; control of Mississippi River in Union hands. About 1,000 were killed or wounded in **draft riots** in New York City; some blacks were hanged by mobs July 13-16. Pres. Lincoln gave his **Gettysburg Address** Nov. 19. Lincoln declared **Thanksgiving** a national holiday.

1864 Gen. **William Tecumseh Sherman** marched through Georgia, taking Atlanta Sept. 1 and Savannah Dec. 22. **Sand Creek massacre** of Cheyenne and Arapaho Indians Nov. 29. Soldiers drove Indians out of village; about 150 killed.

1865 Gen. **Robert E. Lee surrendered** 27,800 Confederate troops to Gen. Grant at Appomattox Court House in VA, Apr. 9. J. E. Johnston surrendered 31,200 to Sherman at Durham Station, NC, Apr. 18. Last rebel troops surrendered May 26. Pres. Lincoln shot Apr. 14 by **John Wilkes Booth** in Ford's Theater, Washington, DC; died the following morning. Vice Pres. **Andrew Johnson** was sworn in as president. Booth was hunted down and fatally wounded, perhaps by his own hand, Apr. 26. Four co-conspirators were hanged July 7. **13th Amendment**, abolishing slavery, ratified Dec. 6.

1866 Congress took control of Southern **Reconstruction**, backed freedmen's rights in legislation vetoed by Pres. Andrew Johnson; veto overridden by Congress, Apr. 9. **Ku Klux Klan** formed secretly in South to terrorize blacks who voted. Disbanded 1869-71.

1867 **Alaska** sold to U.S. by Russia for $7.2 mil Mar. 30, through efforts of Sec. of State William H. Seward. Fraternal society the **Grange** was organized Dec. 4 to protect farmer interests. **Horatio Alger**'s *Ragged Dick* published.

1868 Pres. Andrew Johnson dismissed Sec. of War Edwin M. Stanton without Senate approval. **Johnson impeached** by the House Feb. 24 for violation of Tenure of Office Act, though charges were actually made in response to his opposition to congressional Reconstruction. He was acquitted by the Senate Mar.-May. **14th Amendment**, providing for citizenship of all persons born or naturalized in U.S. and subject to the jurisdiction thereof, ratified July 9. **Louisa May Alcott**'s *Little Women* published. *The World Almanac*, a publication of the *New York World* newspaper, appeared for first time.

1869 **Transcontinental railroad** completed; golden spike driven at Promontory Summit, UT, May 10, marking junction of Central Pacific and Union Pacific lines. Attempt to "corner" gold led to financial **"Black Friday"** in New York Sept. 24. **Woman suffrage law** passed in Wyoming Territory Dec. 10. **Knights of Labor** labor union formed in Philadelphia. By 1886, it had 700,000 members nationally.

1870 **15th Amendment**, making race no bar to voting rights, ratified Feb. 8. **First U.S. boardwalk** completed, in Atlantic City, NJ. **U.S. Weather Bureau** founded.

1871 **Great Chicago fire** destroyed city Oct. 8-11. **National Rifle Association (NRA)** founded.

1872 **Amnesty Act** May 22 restored civil rights to citizens of the South, except for 500 Confederate leaders. Congress established Yellowstone, **first national park**. James McNeill Whistler painted famous portrait known informally as **"Whistler's Mother."**

1873 **First U.S. postal card** issued May 1. **Jesse James** and his gang robbed their first passenger train July 21. Banks failed, panic began in Sept. **Depression** lasted five years. **"Boss" William Tweed** of New York City was convicted Nov. 19 of stealing public funds; he died in jail in 1878. New York's Bellevue Hospital started **first nursing school.**

1874 **Women's Christian Temperance Union** established in Cleveland. **First public zoo** in U.S. established in Philadelphia.

1875 Congress passed **Civil Rights Act** Mar. 1, giving equal rights to blacks in public accommodations and jury duty. Supreme Court invalidated act in 1883. First **Kentucky Derby** held May 17. First **Jim Crow segregation law** enacted, in Tennessee.

1876 **Alexander Graham Bell** patented the telephone Mar. 7. Col. **George A. Custer** and 264 soldiers of the 7th Cavalry were killed June 25 in "last stand," **Battle of the Little Bighorn**, MT, in Sioux Indian War. Democrat **Samuel J. Tilden** received majority of popular votes for president over Republican **Rutherford B. Hayes**, Nov. 7, but 22 electoral votes were in dispute. Congress agreed to certify Hayes as winner in Feb. 1877 after Republicans agreed to end federal Reconstruction of South.

1877 **Molly Maguires**—Irish terrorist society in mining areas of Scranton, PA—was broken up by hanging, June 21, of 11 leaders for murders of mine officials and police. Pres. Rutherford B. Hayes sent federal troops to control violent national **railroad strike**, which began in July.

1878 **First commercial telephone exchange** opened, New Haven, CT, Jan. 28. **Thomas A. Edison** founded Edison Electric Light Co. on Oct. 15.

1879 **F. W. Woolworth** opened his first five-and-ten store, in Utica, NY, Feb. 22. French actress **Sarah Bernhardt** made her U.S. debut Nov. 8 at New York City's Booth Theater. Economist and social philosopher **Henry George** published *Progress & Poverty*, advocating single tax on land.

1881 **Clara Barton** founded **American Red Cross** May 21. Pres. **James A. Garfield** shot in Washington, DC, July 2, by mentally disturbed office seeker; died Sept. 19. Famous gun battle between the Earp brothers and outlaw rustlers Oct. 26 near the **OK Corral**, Tombstone, AZ. **Booker T. Washington** founded Tuskegee Institute for black students. **Helen Hunt Jackson**'s *A Century of Dishonor*, about mistreatment of Indians, published.

1882 **Chinese Exclusion Act**, barring immigration of Chinese laborers for 10 years, later made permanent, passed by Congress May 6; prohibited naturalization of Chinese resident aliens.

1883 Civil Service Act, or **Pendleton Act**, passed Jan. 16, created foundations of American civil service system. The **Brooklyn Bridge** opened May 24 as world's longest suspension bridge. Transcontinental **Northern Pacific Railroad** was completed Sept. 8. **Buffalo Bill Cody**'s Wild West Show began its 30-year touring run.

1884 Switchback Railway—**first U.S. roller coaster** built as amusement park ride—opened at Coney Island in New York City. **Mark Twain**'s *The Adventures of Huckleberry Finn* published.

1885 **Washington Monument** dedicated Feb. 21.

1886 **Haymarket riot** and bombing, May 4, followed labor battles for 8-hr. work day in Chicago; seven police and four workers died. Eight anarchists found guilty Aug. 20; four hanged Nov. 11. **Coca-Cola** first sold, May 8, at Jacob's Pharmacy in Atlanta. Apache Indian **Geronimo** surrendered Sept. 4, ending last major Indian war. **Statue of Liberty** dedicated Oct. 28. **American Federation of Labor** (AFL) formed Dec. 8 by 25 craft unions.

1887 **Interstate Commerce Act** enacted Feb. 4, created Interstate Commerce Commission.

1888 **Great blizzard** struck Eastern U.S. Mar. 11-14, causing about 400 deaths. Ernest Thayer's poem **"Casey at the Bat"** recited for first time in public at New York City theater in May.

1889 U.S. opened 2-mil acre **Oklahoma District** to settlement Apr. 22, initiating land run; "sooner" settlers illegally entered the territory before that date to stake favorable claims. More than 2,200 lives lost in **Johnstown flood** (PA) May 31. **Electric lights** installed at White House.

1890: Jacob Riis's *How the Other Half Lives* **documents urban slums and tenements, instigating reform.**

1890 **Sherman Antitrust Act** passed July 2, began federal effort to curb monopolies. Massacre at **Wounded Knee**, SD, Dec. 29, the last major conflict between Indians and U.S. troops; about 200 Indian men, women, and children and 29 soldiers were killed. **Jacob Riis**'s *How the Other Half Lives*, about city slums, published, instigating reform legislation in New York City. **Emily Dickinson**'s poems published, four years after her death.

1891 **Forest Reserve Act**, Mar. 3, let president close public forest land to settlement for establishment of national parks. **Carnegie Hall**, in New York City, opened May 5.

1892 **Ellis Island**, in New York Bay, opened Jan. 1 to receive immigrants; closed 1954. **Homestead strike** (PA) at Carnegie steel mills; 7 guards and 11 strikers and spectators shot to death July 6. James J. Corbett defeated John L. Sullivan Sept. 7 to become **first world heavyweight champion** under Marquess of Queensbury rules.

1893 **Columbian Exposition** world's fair held May-Oct. in Chicago. Financial panic led to four-year **depression**. **Mormon Temple** dedicated in Salt Lake City, UT.

1894 Thomas A. Edison's **kinetoscope**, for motion pictures (invented 1887), given first public showing Apr. 14. **Jacob S. Coxey** led army of unemployed from the Midwest, reaching Washington, DC, Apr. 30. Coxey arrested May 1 for trespassing on Capitol grounds; his army disbanded. **Pullman strike** began May 11 at railroad car plant in Chicago. Milton Hershey started **Hershey Chocolate Company**.

1895 **"America, the Beautiful"** appeared for first time, in church publication, July 4. **Stephen Crane**'s *The Red Badge of Courage* published.

1896 Supreme Court, in *Plessy v. Ferguson*, May 18, approved racial segregation under the **"separate but equal"** doctrine. **William Jennings Bryan** delivered "Cross of Gold" speech July 9; won Democratic Party nomination. **John Philip Sousa** composed "Stars and Stripes Forever" on Dec. 25.

1897 **Olney-Pauncefote Treaty** with Britain, Jan. 11, gave wide scope to arbitration in settling disputes; never ratified by U.S. John J. McDermott won **first Boston Marathon** Apr. 19. First Klondike gold arrived in San Francisco July 14, helping set off **Klondike gold rush**. **First subway service** in country opens to public in Boston, Sept. 1.

1898 U.S. battleship *Maine* exploded Feb. 15 in Havana, Cuba; 260 killed. U.S. blockaded Cuba Apr. 22 in aid of independence forces. U.S. declared **war on Spain** Apr. 24; destroyed Spanish fleet in Philippines May 1; took Guam June 20. U.S. took **Puerto Rico** July 25-Aug. 12. Spain agreed Dec. 10 to cede Philippines, Puerto Rico, and Guam, and approved independence for Cuba. Annexation of **Hawaii** signed by Pres. William McKinley, July 7.

1899 Filipino insurgents, unable to get recognition of independence from U.S., started guerrilla war Feb. 4. Their leader, Emilio Aguinaldo, captured May 23, 1901. **Philippine insurrection** ended 1902. Some 200,000 civilians and 20,000 Filipino troops died, mostly from disease and starvation. Pres. McKinley signed treaty officially ending **Spanish-American War**, Feb. 10. U.S. declared **Open Door Policy** Sept. 6, to make China an open international market. Philosopher **John Dewey**'s *School and Society*, advocating progressive education ("learn by doing"), published. Pianist Scott Joplin's "Maple Leaf Rag" published, popularizing **ragtime music**.

1900 **International Ladies' Garment Workers Union** founded in New York City June 3. Fought sweatshop working conditions. **Carry Nation**, Kansas temperance leader, began raiding saloons with a hatchet. U.S. helped suppress **Boxer Rebellion** in Beijing, China. Eastman Kodak Co. introduced the **Brownie camera**, popularizing picture-taking.

1901 Texas had first significant oil strike at **Spindletop** well near Beaumont, Jan. 10. U.S. withdrew troops from **Cuba** May 20, and Cuba became independent. Pres. **McKinley** shot Sept. 6 in Buffalo, NY, by anarchist Leon Czolgosz; died Sept. 14. Vice Pres. **Theodore Roosevelt** sworn in as youngest-ever president, at age 42 years, 11 months. **Booker T. Washington**'s *Up From Slavery* published.

1902 Permanent **Bureau of the Census** established Mar. 6. **Helen Keller** autobiography appeared in serial form.

1903 Treaty between U.S. and Colombia to have U.S. dig **Panama Canal** signed Jan. 22, but rejected by Colombia's Congress. Panama declared independence from Colombia with U.S. support Nov. 3; recognized by Pres. Roosevelt

Nov. 6. U.S., Panama signed canal treaty Nov. 18. Wisconsin set first **direct primary voting system**, May 23. **Henry Ford** founded Ford Motor Co., June 16. Boston defeated Pittsburgh, 5 games to 3, Oct. 13 in **first modern World Series**. **First successful flight** in heavier-than-air mechanically propelled airplane by **Orville Wright** Dec. 17 near Kitty Hawk, NC, 120 ft in 12 sec. Later flight same day by **Wilbur Wright**, 852 ft in 59 sec. Improved plane patented, 1906. **Iroquois Theater fire** in Chicago killed about 600 out of 1,900 in audience, Dec. 30. Pioneering film *Great Train Robbery* produced.

1904 St. Louis hosted **first Olympics in U.S.**, July 1-Nov. 23. First section of **New York City subway** system opened, Oct. 27. **Ida Tarbell** published muckraking *The History of the Standard Oil Company*. **Henry James**'s last major novel, *The Golden Bowl*, published.

1905 **Industrial Workers of the World**, which advocated Marxian theory of class struggle between workers and capitalists, founded in Chicago, June 27. **Rotary**, oldest service club organization in U.S., founded in Chicago.

1906 **San Francisco earthquake** and fire, Apr. 18-19, caused more than 3,000 deaths and $400 mil in damages. **Upton Sinclair**'s *The Jungle*, which exposed working conditions in meat-packing industry, published. Helped spur passage of the **Pure Food and Drug Act** and **Meat Inspection Act** June 30.

1907 Financial panic and **depression** started Mar. 13. Pres. Roosevelt sent **"Great White Fleet"** of 16 U.S. battleships around the world in show of power.

1908 Springfield, IL, torn by **anti-black rioting**, Aug. 14-15. Henry Ford introduced **Model T** car, priced at $850, Oct. 1.

1909 Adm. Robert E. Peary claimed to have reached **North Pole** Apr. 6 on sixth attempt, accompanied by black explorer Matthew Henson and four Inuit; may have fallen short. National Conference on the Negro convened May 30, leading to founding of **National Association for the Advancement of Colored People** (NAACP).

1910 **Boy Scouts** of America founded Feb. 8. Former Pres. Roosevelt called for **"new nationalism"** in famous speech in Kansas, Aug. 10.

1911 Building with New York City's **Triangle Shirtwaist Co.** factory caught fire Mar. 25; 146 died. Supreme Court ruled May 15 that **Standard Oil Co.** must be dissolved because it unreasonably restrained trade. **First transcontinental airplane flight** (with numerous stops) by C. P. Rodgers, from New York to Pasadena, CA, Sept. 17-Nov. 5; time in air 82 hr., 4 min.

1906: Damages caused by the San Francisco earthquake and subsequent fires leave 225,000 (more than half the area population) homeless.

1917: The first U.S. troops join the stalemated fight in Europe; by the end of the war, an estimated 4 mil Americans served in the conflict known today as World War I.

1912 American Girl Guides founded Mar. 12; name changed in 1913 to **Girl Scouts**. U.S. Marines, Aug. 14, sent to **Nicaragua**, which was in default of loans to U.S. and Europe.

1913 **16th Amendment**, authorizing federal income tax, ratified Feb. 3. The **Armory Show** in New York City brought modern art to U.S. for first time, Feb. 17. **17th Amendment**, providing for direct popular election of U.S. senators, ratified Apr. 8. **Federal Reserve System** authorized Dec. 23, in major reform of U.S. banking and finance.

1914 **Ford Motor Co.** raised basic wage rates from $2.40 for 9-hr. day to $5 for 8-hr. day, Jan. 5, increasing stability in labor force. When U.S. sailors were arrested in Tampico, Mexico, Apr. 9, Atlantic fleet was sent to **Veracruz**, occupied city. Pres. Woodrow Wilson proclaimed **U.S. neutrality** in the European war, Aug. 4. The **Panama Canal** officially opened Aug. 15. The **Clayton Antitrust Act** passed Oct. 15, strengthening federal antimonopoly powers.

1915 **First transcontinental telephone call**, New York to San Francisco, completed Jan. 25 by Alexander Graham Bell and Thomas A. Watson. British ship *Lusitania* sunk May 7 by German submarine; 1,198 passengers died, including 128 Americans. (In notice in morning newspapers the day *Lusitania* set sail, Germany had warned Americans against taking passage on British vessels.) As result of U.S. campaign, Germany issued apology and promise of payments, Oct. 5. U.S. troops landed in **Haiti**, July 28. Haiti became virtual U.S. protectorate under Sept. 16 treaty. Pres. Wilson asked for a military fund increase, Dec. 7. D. W. Griffith's film *The Birth of a Nation* released. William J. Simmons partly inspired by film to revive **Ku Klux Klan**, which peaks in 1920s.

1916 Gen. **John J. Pershing** entered Mexico in Mar. to pursue **Francisco (Pancho) Villa**, who had raided U.S. border areas. Forces withdrew Feb. 5, 1917. **Rural Credits Acts** passed July 17, followed by **Warehouse Act** Aug. 11; both provided financial aid to farmers. Bomb exploded during **San Francisco Preparedness Day parade** July 22, killed 10. Thomas J. Mooney, labor organizer, and Warren K. Billings, shoeworker, convicted 1917; both later pardoned. U.S. bought **Virgin Islands** from Denmark Aug. 4. U.S. established military government in the **Dominican Republic** Nov. 29.

Jeannette Rankin (R, MT) elected to House of Representatives, **first female member of Congress**.

1917 Germany, suffering from British blockade, declared almost unrestricted **submarine warfare** Jan. 31. U.S. cut diplomatic ties with Germany Feb. 3 and formally **declared war** Apr. 6. Jones Act, passed Mar. 2, made **Puerto Rico** a U.S. territory, its inhabitants U.S. citizens. **Conscription law** passed May 18. First U.S. troops arrived in Europe June 26.

1918 Pres. Wilson set out his **14 Points** as basis for peace, Jan. 8. More than 1 mil American troops were in Europe by July. Allied counteroffensive launched at Château-Thierry July 18. War ended with signing of **armistice** Nov. 11. **Influenza pandemic** killed an estimated 20 mil worldwide, 548,000 in U.S.

1919 **18th Amendment**, providing for prohibition of manufacture, sale, or transportation of alcoholic beverages, ratified Jan. 16, to take effect on Jan. 16, 1920. **First transatlantic flight**, by U.S. Navy seaplane, left Rockaway, NY, May 8; stopped at Newfoundland, Azores, Lisbon May 27. **Boston police strike** Sept. 9, earliest strike conducted by government employees. About 250 **foreign-born radicals** deported Dec. 21 to Soviet Union.

1920 In national **Red Scare**, some 2,700 Communists, anarchists, and other radicals were arrested Jan.-May. **League of Women Voters** founded Feb. 14. Senate refused Mar. 19 to ratify **League of Nations Covenant**. Nicola Sacco and **Bartolomeo Vanzetti** accused of killing two men in Massachusetts payroll holdup Apr. 15; found guilty 1921. A seven-year campaign for their release failed; both executed Aug. 23, 1927. Verdict repudiated 1977 by proclamation of Massachusetts Gov. Michael Dukakis. **19th Amendment** ratified Aug. 18, giving women the vote. **First regular licensed radio broadcasting** began Aug. 20. **Wall St. bombing** in New York City killed 30, injured 100, did $2 mil damage, Sept. 16. **Sinclair Lewis**'s *Main Street* published.

1921 Congress sharply curbed immigration, set **national quota system** May 19. Joint congressional resolution declaring **peace with Germany, Austria, and Hungary** signed July 2 by Pres. Warren G. Harding; treaties were signed in Aug. In so-called **Black Sox scandal**, eight Chicago White Sox players were banned from baseball Aug. 4 for conspiring with gamblers to throw the 1919 World Series. Limitation of Armaments Conference met in Washington, DC, Nov. 12-Feb. 6, 1922. Major powers agreed to curtail naval construction, outlaw poison gas, restrict submarine attacks on merchant vessels, and respect China's integrity.

1922 During nationwide coal strike, union miners killed some 21 strikebreakers at Herrin, IL, June 21-22, in incident referred to as the **Herrin Massacre**. T. S. Eliot's *The Waste Land* published.

1923 **First sound-on-film motion picture**, *Phonofilm*, shown at Rivoli Theater, New York City, beginning in Apr. Pres. Calvin Coolidge addressed Congress, Dec. 6; **first radio broadcast of president's annual speech**.

1924 Law approved by Congress June 15 made all **Native Americans U.S. citizens**. Nellie Tayloe Ross elected governor of Wyoming, and **Miriam (Ma) Ferguson** elected governor of Texas Nov. 9. Ross inaugurated as nation's **first female governor** Jan. 5, 1925. Ferguson installed Jan. 20, 1925. **George Gershwin** wrote "Rhapsody in Blue."

1925 In so-called "Monkey Trial," John T. Scopes found guilty of having taught **evolution** in Dayton, TN, high school and fined, July 24. **F. Scott Fitzgerald**'s *The Great Gatsby* published.

1926 Dr. Robert H. Goddard, Mar. 16, demonstrated **first liquid-fuel rocket**. Congress established **Army Air Corps** July 2. **Air Commerce Act** passed Nov. 2, established government agencies for development of airports, radio navigation, and other services. **Ernest Hemingway**'s *The Sun Also Rises* published.

1927 Capt. **Charles A. Lindbergh** left Roosevelt Field, NY, May 20 alone in *Spirit of St. Louis* on first New York-Paris nonstop flight. Reached Le Bourget airfield May 21, 3,610 mi in 33½ hr. *The Jazz Singer*, **first feature-length film** in which **spoken dialogue was part of narrative action**, released Oct. 6. The musical *Show Boat* opened in New York City Dec. 27.

1928 **Amelia Earhart** became first woman to fly across the Atlantic, June 17. **Herbert Hoover** elected president Nov. 6, defeating New York Gov. Alfred E. Smith, a Catholic.

AFGHANISTAN	ALBANIA	ALGERIA	ANDORRA	ANGOLA
ANTIGUA AND BARBUDA	ARGENTINA	ARMENIA	AUSTRALIA	AUSTRIA
AZERBAIJAN	THE BAHAMAS	BAHRAIN	BANGLADESH	BARBADOS
BELARUS	BELGIUM	BELIZE	BENIN	BHUTAN
BOLIVIA	BOSNIA AND HERZEGOVINA	BOTSWANA	BRAZIL	BRUNEI
BULGARIA	BURKINA FASO	BURUNDI	CABO VERDE	CAMBODIA
CAMEROON	CANADA	CENTRAL AFRICAN REPUBLIC	CHAD	CHILE
CHINA	COLOMBIA	COMOROS	CONGO, DEM. REP. OF THE	CONGO REPUBLIC
COSTA RICA	CÔTE D'IVOIRE	CROATIA	CUBA	CYPRUS
CZECH REPUBLIC	DENMARK	DJIBOUTI	DOMINICA	DOMINICAN REPUBLIC
ECUADOR	EGYPT	EL SALVADOR	EQUATORIAL GUINEA	ERITREA

Note: Flag proportions have been standardized to fit page.

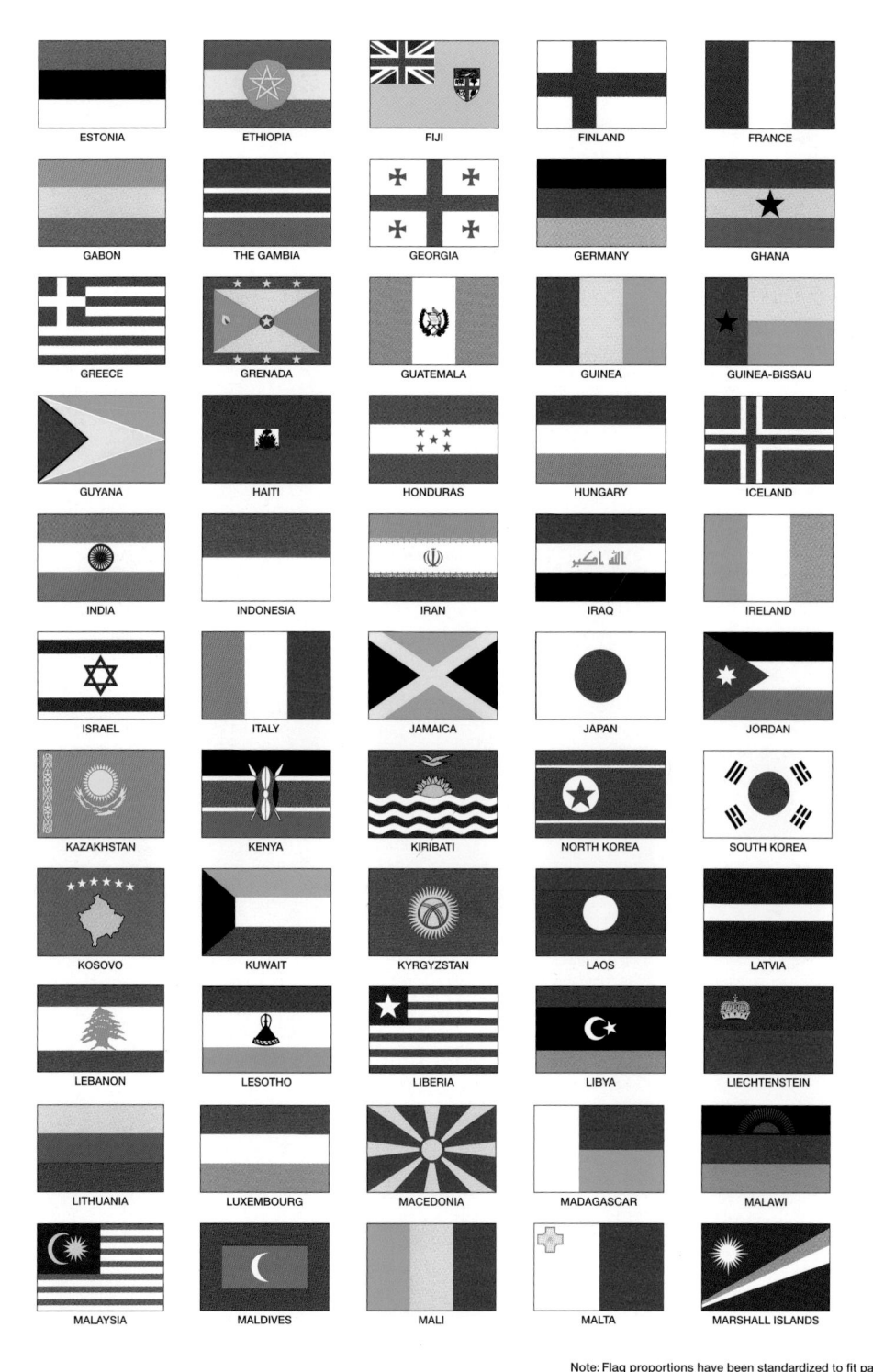

Note: Flag proportions have been standardized to fit page.

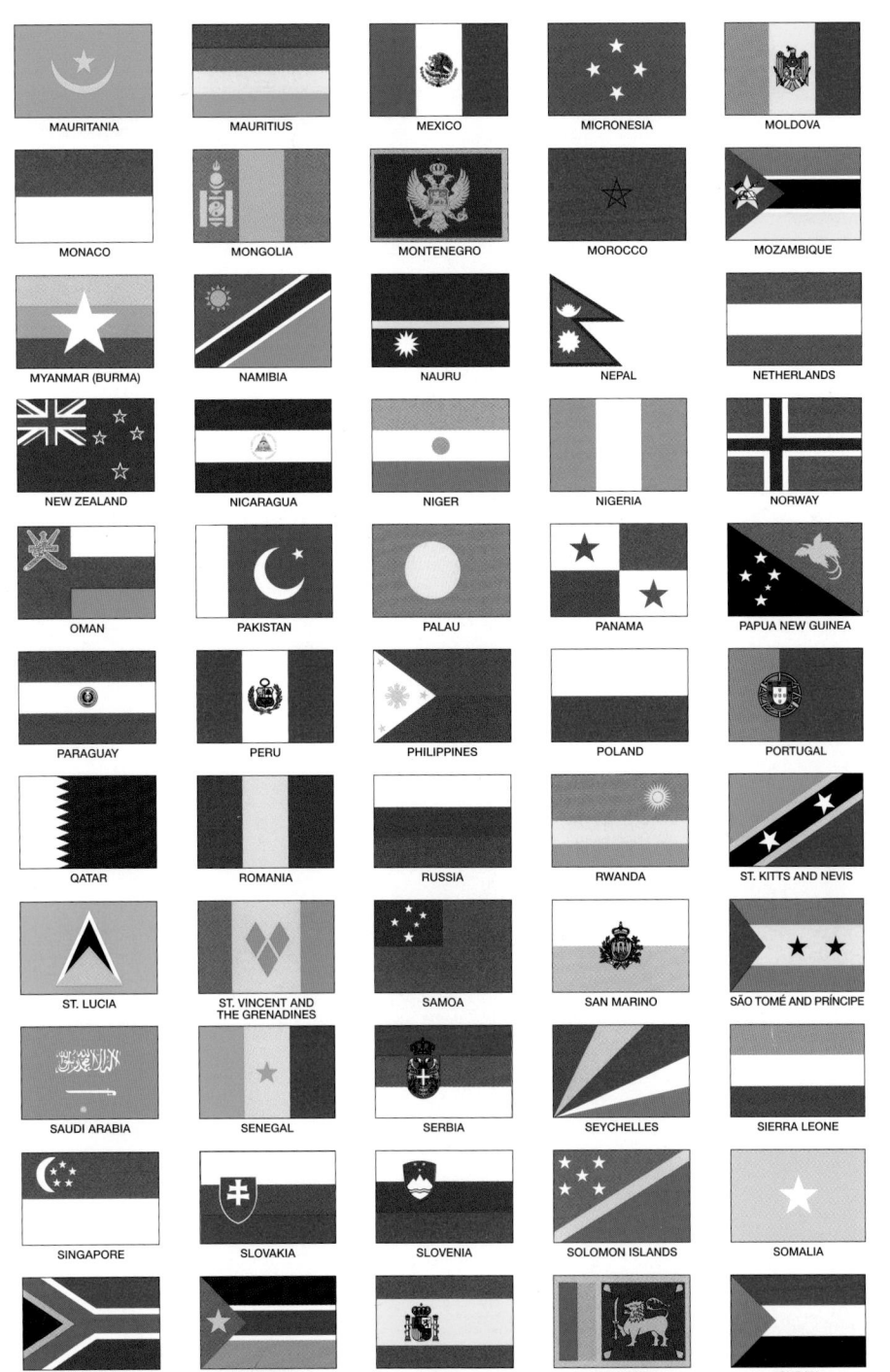

MAURITANIA

MAURITIUS

MEXICO

MICRONESIA

MOLDOVA

MONACO

MONGOLIA

MONTENEGRO

MOROCCO

MOZAMBIQUE

MYANMAR (BURMA)

NAMIBIA

NAURU

NEPAL

NETHERLANDS

NEW ZEALAND

NICARAGUA

NIGER

NIGERIA

NORWAY

OMAN

PAKISTAN

PALAU

PANAMA

PAPUA NEW GUINEA

PARAGUAY

PERU

PHILIPPINES

POLAND

PORTUGAL

QATAR

ROMANIA

RUSSIA

RWANDA

ST. KITTS AND NEVIS

ST. LUCIA

ST. VINCENT AND
THE GRENADINES

SAMOA

SAN MARINO

SÃO TOMÉ AND PRÍNCIPE

SAUDI ARABIA

SENEGAL

SERBIA

SEYCHELLES

SIERRA LEONE

SINGAPORE

SLOVAKIA

SLOVENIA

SOLOMON ISLANDS

SOMALIA

SOUTH AFRICA

SOUTH SUDAN

SPAIN

SRI LANKA

SUDAN

Note: Flag proportions have been standardized to fit page.

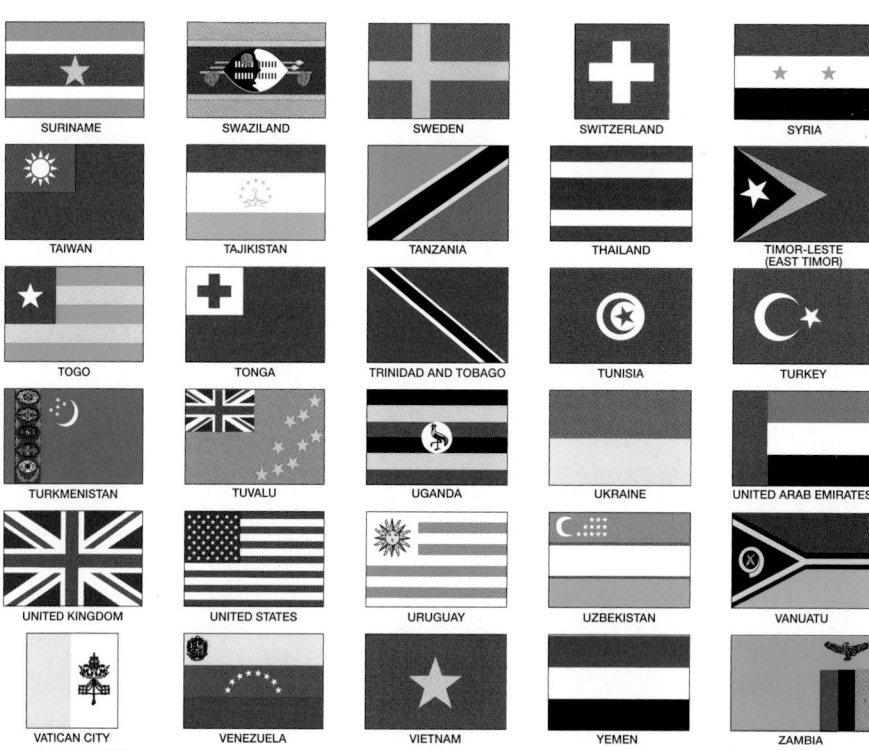

SURINAME · SWAZILAND · SWEDEN · SWITZERLAND · SYRIA

TAIWAN · TAJIKISTAN · TANZANIA · THAILAND · TIMOR-LESTE (EAST TIMOR)

TOGO · TONGA · TRINIDAD AND TOBAGO · TUNISIA · TURKEY

TURKMENISTAN · TUVALU · UGANDA · UKRAINE · UNITED ARAB EMIRATES

UNITED KINGDOM · UNITED STATES · URUGUAY · UZBEKISTAN · VANUATU

VATICAN CITY · VENEZUELA · VIETNAM · YEMEN · ZAMBIA

ZIMBABWE

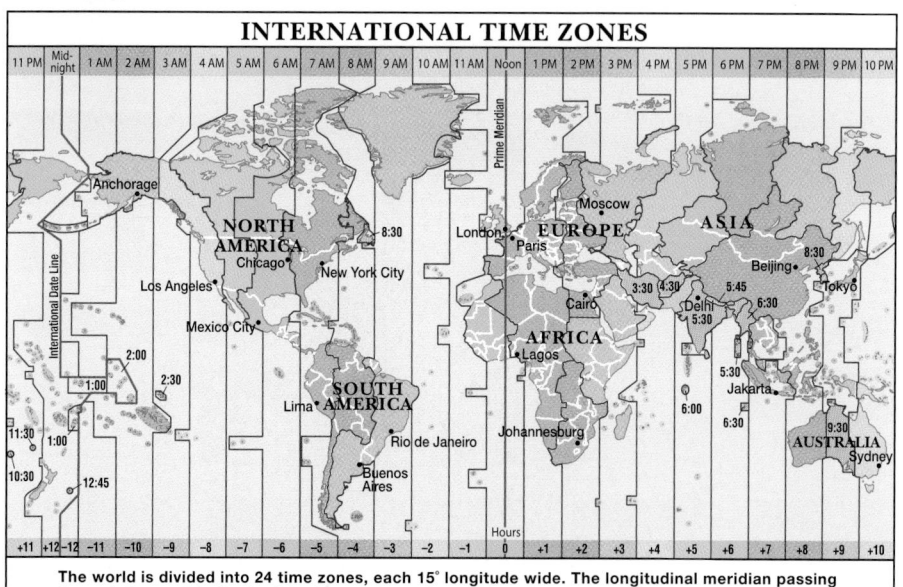

INTERNATIONAL TIME ZONES

The world is divided into 24 time zones, each 15° longitude wide. The longitudinal meridian passing through Greenwich, England, is the starting point, and is called the *prime meridian*. The 12th zone is divided by the 180th meridian (International Date Line). When the line is crossed going west, the date is advanced one day; when crossed going east, the date becomes a day earlier.

Note: Flag proportions have been standardized to fit page.

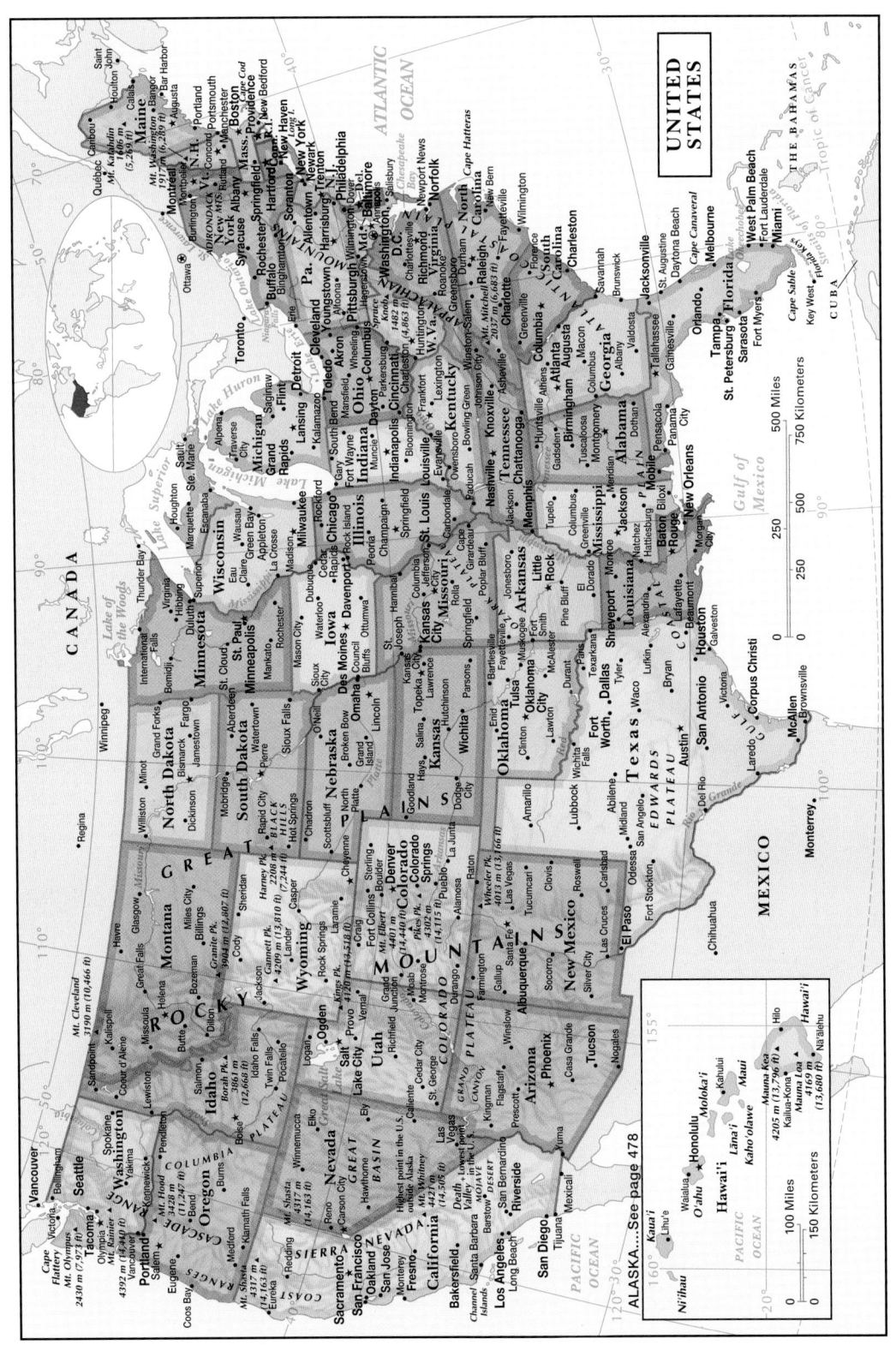

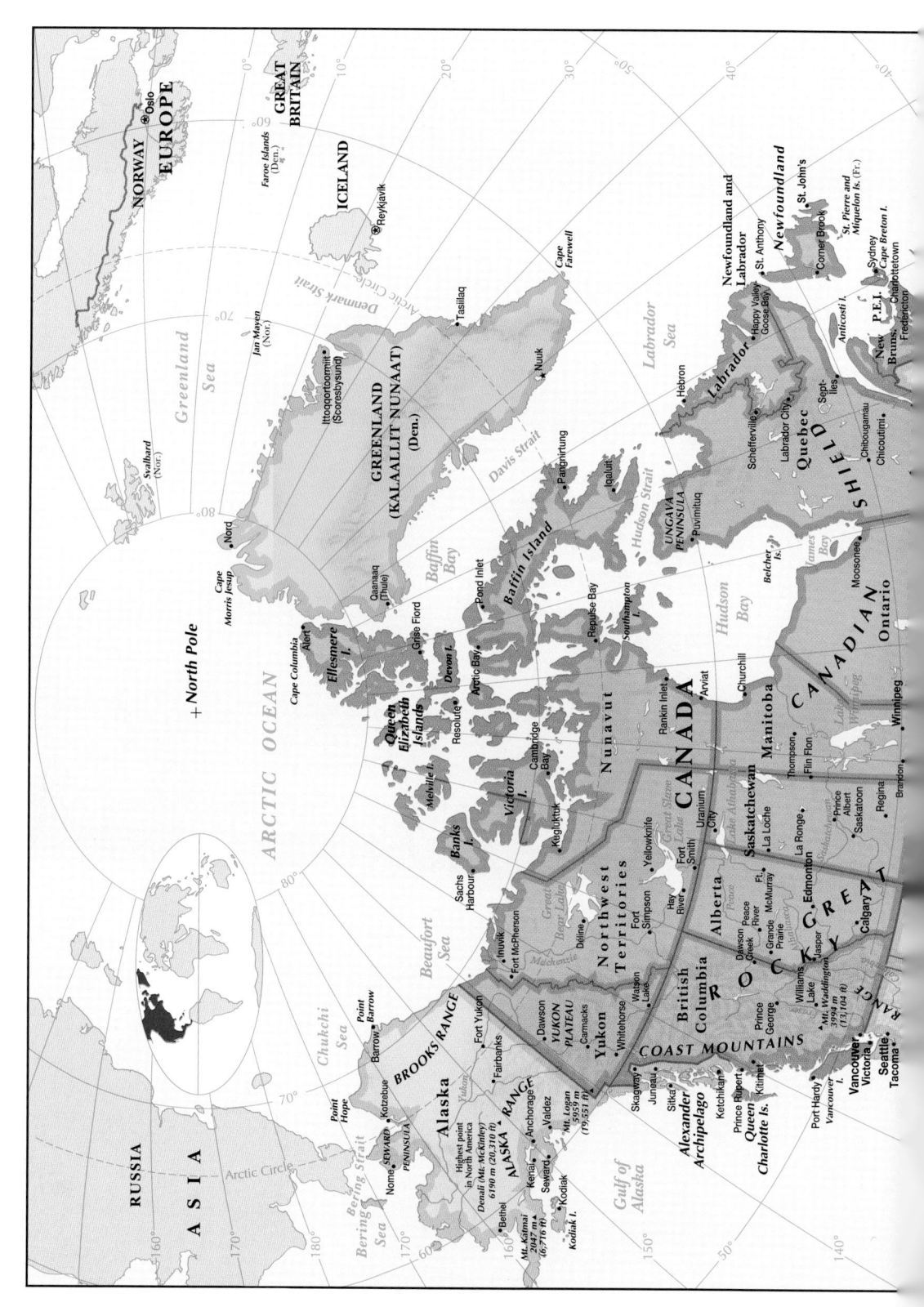

NORWAY
Oslo
EUROPE
GREAT BRITAIN

Faroe Islands (Den.)

ICELAND
Reykjavík

Cape Farewell

Denmark Strait
Arctic Circle

Greenland Sea

Jan Mayen (Nor.)

Svalbard (Nor.)

Tasiilaq

Ittoqqortoormiit (Scoresbysund)

GREENLAND (KALAALLIT NUNAAT) (Den.)

Nuuk

Baffin Bay

Davis Strait

Labrador Sea

Newfoundland and Labrador
St. Anthony
Happy Valley Goose Bay
Corner Brook
St. John's
Newfoundland
St. Pierre and Miquelon Is. (Fr.)
Sydney
Cape Breton I.
Anticosti I.
New P.E.I.
Bruns. Charlottetown
Fredericton

Labrador

Hebron

Schefferville
Labrador City
Sept-Îles
Quebec

Chibougamau
Chicoutimi

CANADIAN SHIELD

Cape Morris Jesup

Cape Columbia
Alert
Ellesmere I.

Qaanaaq (Thule)
Grise Fiord

Qaasuaq

Pangnirtung
Iqaluit

Baffin Island

UNGAVA PENINSULA
Puvirnituq

Ontario

North Pole

ARCTIC OCEAN

Queen Elizabeth Islands

Devon I.
Resolute
Melville I.

Arctic Bay

Pond Inlet

Repulse Bay

Southampton I.

Rankin Inlet
Arviat

Churchill

Belcher Is.
James Bay

Hudson Bay

Moosonee

Hudson Strait

Cambridge Bay

Victoria I.

Banks I.
Sachs Harbour

Kugluktuk

Nunavut

CANADA

Great Slave Lake
Yellowknife
Fort Smith
Uranium City

Manitoba

Thompson
Flin Flon

Lake Winnipeg
Winnipeg
Brandon

Chukchi Sea

Point Barrow

Great Bear Lake

Inuvik
Fort McPherson

Déline

Northwest Territories

Hay River
Fort Simpson

Saskatchewan
La Loche
La Ronge
Prince Albert
Saskatoon
Regina

Alberta
Pt.
Grande
Prairie
Edmonton

Peace River

Dawson Creek

GREAT

Beaufort Sea

BROOKS RANGE

Fort Yukon
Dawson
YUKON PLATEAU
Carmacks

Yukon
Whitehorse
Watson Lake

Mackenzie

British Columbia

Williams Lake
Mt. Waddington 3994 m (13,104 ft)
Jasper
Calgary

ROCKY

RANGE

Chukchi Sea

Point Hope
Kotzebue
Nome
SEWARD PENINSULA
Bethel

Arctic Circle

Barrow

Fairbanks

Highest point in North America
Denali (Mt. McKinley) 6190 m (20,310 ft)

Anchorage
Valdez
Mt. Logan 5959 m (19,551 ft)

Alaska

ALASKA RANGE

Kenai
Seward
Kodiak I.

Mt. Katmai 2047 m (6,716 ft)

Gulf of Alaska

Skagway
Juneau
Sitka
Ketchikan

Alexander Archipelago

Prince Rupert
Kitimat
Queen Charlotte Is.

Prince George

Port Hardy
Vancouver
Victoria
Vancouver I.

COAST MOUNTAINS

Seattle
Tacoma

RUSSIA
ASIA

ASIA

Bering Strait
Bering Sea

RANGE

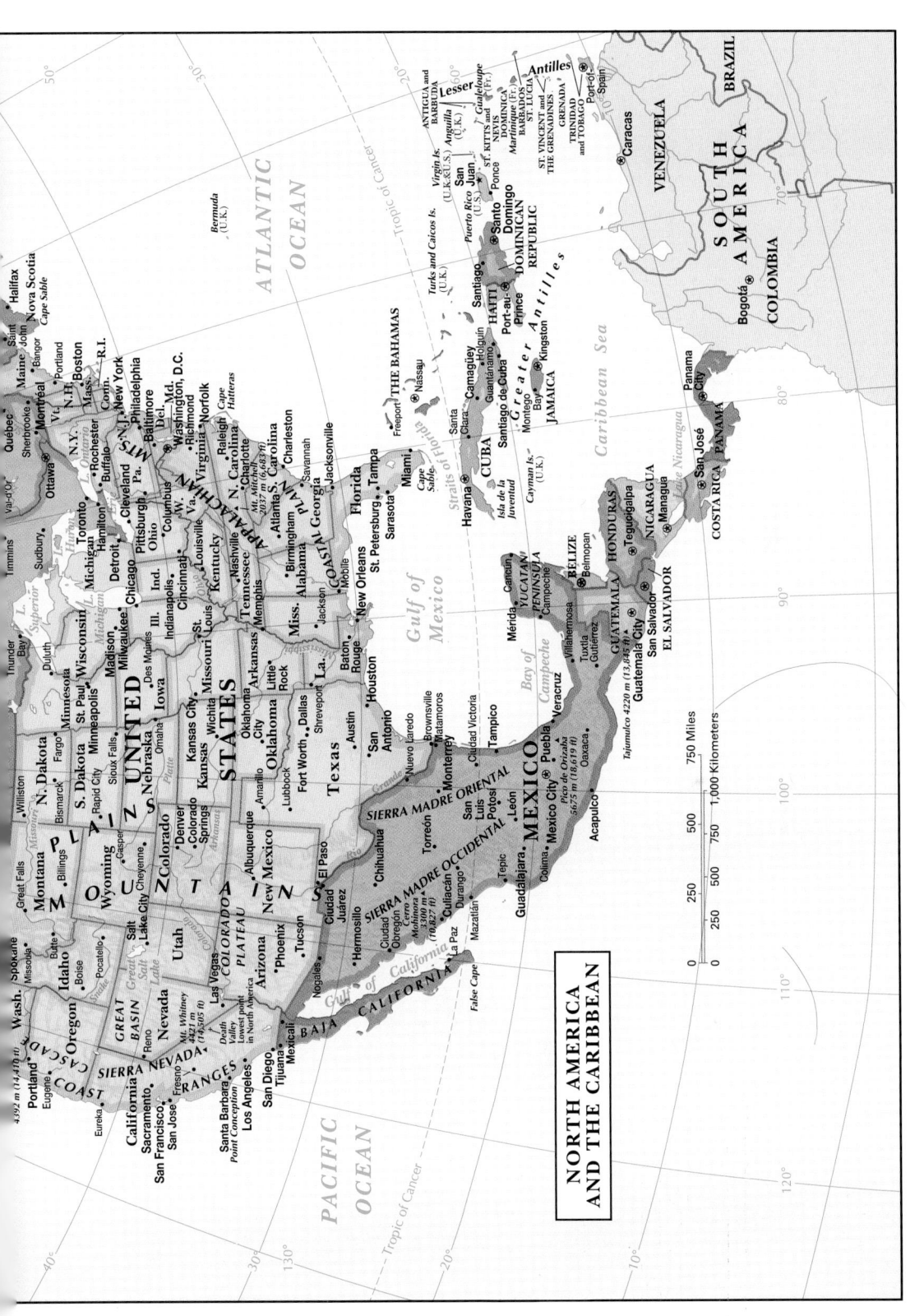

NORTH AMERICA AND THE CARIBBEAN

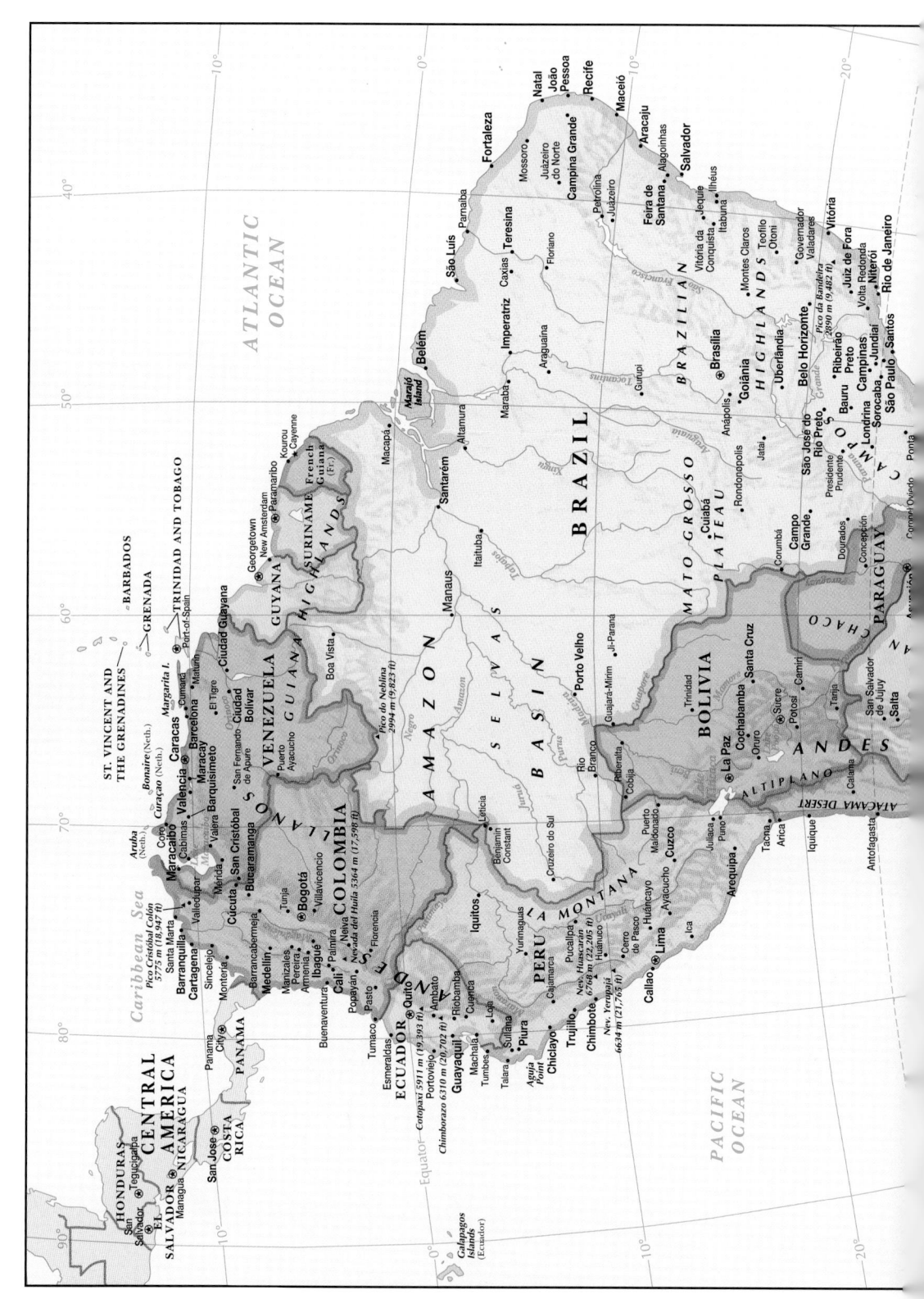

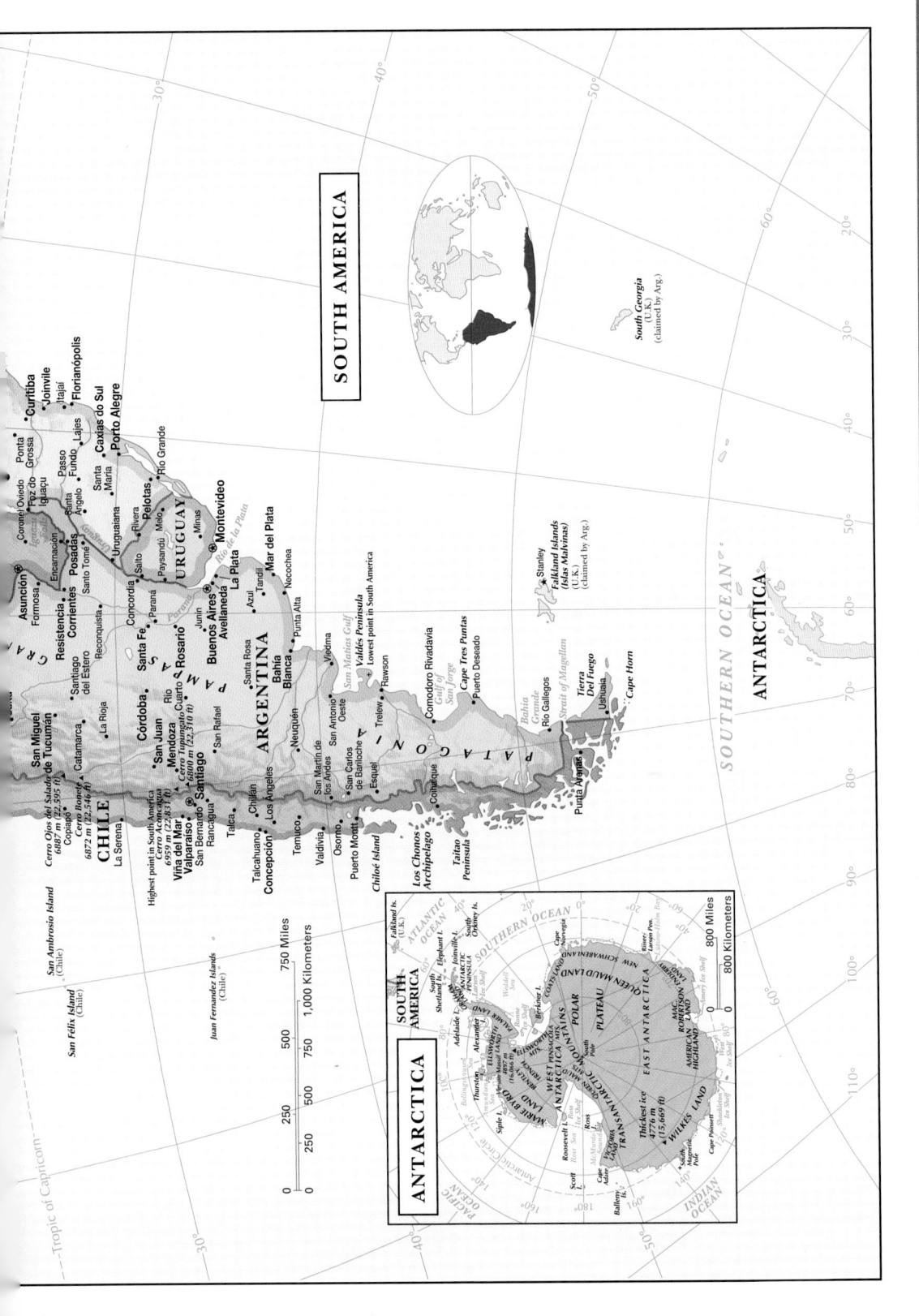

SOUTH AMERICA

South Georgia
(U.K.)
(claimed by Arg.)

SOUTHERN OCEAN

ANTARCTICA

Curitiba
Joinville
Itajaí
Florianópolis
Ponta
Grossa
Coronel Oviedo
Lajes
Caxias do Sul
Porto Alegre
Passo Fundo
Santa
Ângelo
Rio Grande
Santa
Maria
Pelotas
Encarnación
Santo Tomé
Uruguaiana
Salto
Rivera
Melo
Montevideo
Asunción
Formosa
Posadas
Paysandú
Minas
Mar del Plata
Resistencia
Corrientes
La Plata
Santiago
del Estero
Reconquista
Concordia
Avellaneda
Buenos Aires
Necochea
Santa Fe
Paraná
Tandil
Reconquista
Rosario
Junín
Azul
Punta Alta
Catamarca
Córdoba
Santa Rosa
Bahía
Blanca
Viedma
La Rioja
Río Cuarto
San Juan
Mendoza
Neuquén
San Antonio
Oeste
Valdés Peninsula
Lowest point in South America
San Rafael
San Martín de
los Andes
Rawson
Comodoro Rivadavia
Cape Tres Puntas
San Bernardo
Santiago
San Carlos
de Bariloche
Esquel
Trelew
Puerto Deseado
Rancagua
Los Angeles
Coihaique
Río Gallegos
Talca
Chillán
Ushuaia
Cape Horn
Talcahuano
Concepción
Temuco
Valdivia
Osorno
Puerto Montt
Chiloé Island
Los Chonos
Archipelago
Taitao
Peninsula
Punta Arenas
Stanley
Falkland Islands
(Islas Malvinas)
(U.K.)
(claimed by Arg.)

Highest point in South America
Cerro Aconcagua
6959 m (22,831 ft)

San Miguel
de Tucumán

Cerro Ojos del Salado
6887 m (22,595 ft)
Copiapó
Cerro Bonete
6872 m (22,546 ft)
La Serena

Cerro Tupungato
6800 m (22,310 ft)

CHILE
ARGENTINA
URUGUAY
PAMPAS
PATAGONIA
GRAN CHACO

San Ambrosio Island
(Chile)

San Félix Island
(Chile)

Juan Fernández Islands
(Chile)

Tropic of Capricorn

0   250   500   750 Miles
0   250   500   750   1,000 Kilometers

ANTARCTICA

SOUTH
AMERICA

SOUTH
AMERICA

ATLANTIC
OCEAN

Falkland Is.
(U.K.)

South
Shetland Is.
Elephant I.
South
Orkney Is.
Joinville I.

Adelaide I.
ANTARCTIC
PENINSULA

Alexander I.

Weddell
Sea

Berkner I.

Cape
Norvegia

QUEEN MAUD LAND
NEW SCHWABENLAND

Riiser-
Larsen Pen.

COATS LAND

SOUTHERN OCEAN

Bellingshausen
Sea

ELLSWORTH
LAND

Thurston I.

Siple I.

MARIE BYRD
LAND

Roosevelt I.

Ross
Sea

Ross
Ice Shelf

Scott

Cape
Colbeck

Cape
Adare

Balleny
Is.

PACIFIC
OCEAN

ANTARCTIC CIRCLE

INDIAN
OCEAN

TRANSANTARCTIC MTS.

WEST
ANTARCTICA

POLAR
PLATEAU

EAST ANTARCTICA

Thickest Ice
4776 m
(15,669 ft)

South
Pole

South
Magnetic
Pole

MAC
ROBERTSON
LAND

AMERICAN
HIGHLAND

WILKES LAND

McMurdo

0   800 Miles
0   800 Kilometers

EUROPE

GREENLAND
(KALAALLIT NUNAAT)
(Denmark)

Ísafjördur

ICELAND
Keflavík · Reykjavík · Akureyri
Seydhisfjördur

Arctic Circle

Norwegian Sea

Narvik

Bodø

Namsos

Faroe
Torshavn · *Islands*
(Den.)

Trondheim
Molde · Östersund
Ålesund
Sundsvall

Shetland
Islands
(U.K.)

NORWAY **SWEDEN**

Bergen · Borlänge
Uppsala

Orkney
Islands
Thurso

Haugesund
Stavanger · Drammen · **Oslo** · Karlstad · Örebro
Skien · **Stockholm**

Inverness · Kristiansand

Scotland · Aberdeen
Norrköping · Linköping

Vänern
Vättern

**ATLANTIC
OCEAN**

Glasgow · Dundee
North
Göteborg · Jönköping · Växjö · Öland

Londonderry · Edinburgh · Ayr
Ålborg
Halmstad
Helsingborg

Northern
Ireland · **Belfast** · **UNITED**
KINGDOM · **Newcastle**
Sea
Jutland · Århus · Copenhagen
Esbjerg · **DENMARK** Odense · Malmö

Galway · **IRELAND** · Dublin
Bornholm
(Den.)

Limerick · Liverpool · **Leeds** · Kingston upon Hull
Kiel
Lübeck · Rostock · Gdańsk

Cork · Waterford · **Manchester**
Sheffield
NORTHERN

Birmingham · Coventry
Groningen · **Hamburg** · Szczecin

Wales · Swansea · **England** · Norwich
NETHERLANDS · Bremen
Madgeburg · Bydgoszcz

Cardiff · **Bristol** · **London** · Amsterdam
Berlin · **Hannover**
Oder · Poznań

Plymouth · The Hague · **Rotterdam** · Bielefeld
Leipzig
POLAND

Land's End · Portsmouth · Dover · Antwerp · Essen · **GERMANY**
Kassel · Dresden · Wrocław

Channel Is. · Le Havre · **Brussels** · Lille · Cologne · Bonn
Erfurt · Chemnitz · Liberec · Walbrzych
(U.K.)
BELGIUM · Liège · Wiesbaden
Prague
Ostrava

Brest · Caen · Rouen · LUXEMBOURG · **Frankfurt**
Plzeň · **CZECH REP.** · Brno

Rennes · Le Mans · **Paris** · Luxembourg · Mannheim
Nürnberg
Regensburg

Nantes · Orleans · Nancy · Saarbrücken
Stuttgart
Bratislava

Tours · Strasbourg
Augsburg · **Munich** · Linz

Dijon · Basel · Zürich · Salzburg · **Vienna**
Innsbruck · **AUSTRIA** · Győr · **HUN**

FRANCE · Limoges
SWITZERLAND **LIECHTENSTEIN**
Graz

Bay
Bern
Klagenfurt

of
Clermont-Ferrand · **Lyon**
Mt. Blanc · Matterhorn · **SLOVENIA**
Biscay
4810 m (15,781 ft) · 4478 m (14,692 ft) · Udine · Zagreb

A Coruña · Saint-Etienne · Grenoble
Bergamo · Trieste · Ljubljana · Rijeka · **CROATIA**

Gijón
Donostia– · **Torino** · Milan · Verona · Venice
Banja Luka

Vigo · Santander · Bilbao · San Sebastián · Genoa · Parma · Bologna
BOS. &
HERZ.

Porto · Braga · Pamplona · **Toulouse** · Nice
SAN
MARINO · Ancona · Split · Sarajevo

Leon · Vitoria-Gasteiz · Montpellier · **Marseille** · Pisa · **Florence**
Dubrovnik

Coimbra · Pico de Aneto · Avignon · Toulon · **MONACO**
Perugia

IBERIAN · Valladolid · Salamanca · **PYRENEES**
Corsica · Elba
Adriatic

PORTUGAL · Zaragoza · **ANDORRA**
(Fr.) · **VATICAN CITY** · **Rome**
Sea

Lisbon · **Madrid** · **Barcelona**
Ajaccio · **ITALY**

Setubal · Badajoz · Toledo · Tarragona
Foggia

Cape · **SPAIN** · Castellon de la Plana
Sassari · **Naples** · Bari

St. Vincent · Cordoba · *PENINSULA* · Valencia
Sardinia · Vesuvius
Taranto

Seville · Majorca · Minorca
(It.) · 1277 m (4,190 ft) · Salerno

Cádiz · Málaga · Alicante · Palma de · *Balearic* Is.
Cagliari

Strait of · Granada · Murcia · Mallorca · (Sp.)
Tyrrhenian
Ionian

Gibraltar · **GIBRALTAR** · Cartagena
Sea
Sea

(U.K.) · Almería
Palermo · Messina

Rabat · Algiers
Etna · Reggio di

Mediterranean
3369 m (11,053 ft) · Calabria

AFRICA
Sicily · Catania
(It.)

Tunis
Sea

MOROCCO · **ALGERIA** · **TUNISIA** · MALTA · Valletta

| 0 | 250 | 500 Miles |
| 0 | 250 | 500 | 750 Kilometers |

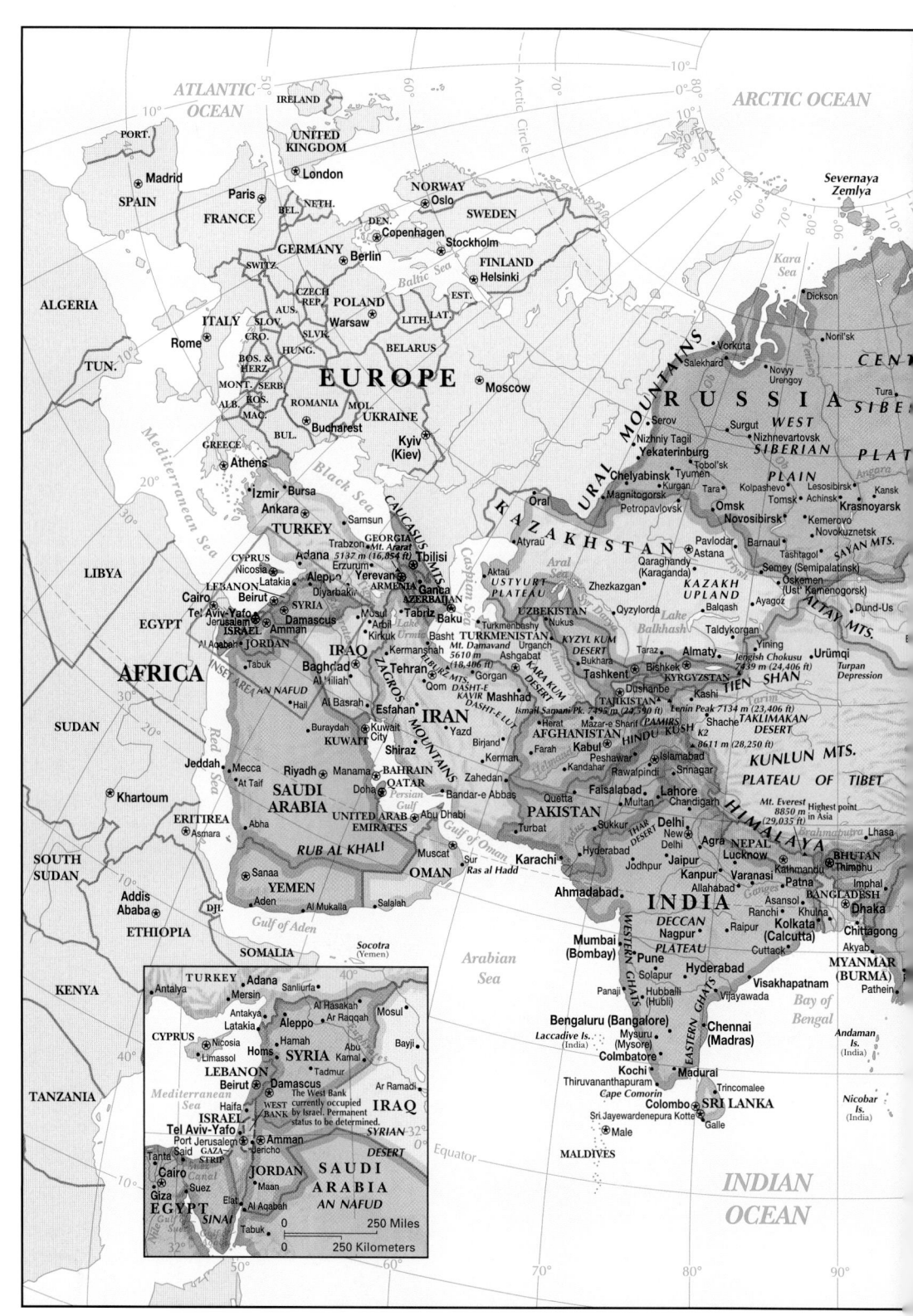

ATLANTIC
OCEAN

ARCTIC OCEAN

IRELAND

UNITED
KINGDOM

London

NORWAY
Oslo

Severnaya
Zemlya

PORT.

Madrid

Paris

NETH.

SPAIN

FRANCE

BEL.

DEN.
Copenhagen

SWEDEN

Stockholm

Kara
Sea

Dickson

CEN

ALGERIA

GERMANY
Berlin

SWITZ.

CZECH
REP.
AUS.

POLAND
Warsaw

FINLAND
Helsinki

Baltic Sea

EST.
LITH.
LAT.

Vorkuta

Salekhard

Novyy
Urengoy

RUSSIA

SIBE

ITALY

Rome

SLOV.
CRO.

HUNG.

BELARUS

Serov

Surgut

Nizhnevartovsk

WEST

PLAT

TUN.

BOS. &
HERZ.
MONT. SERB.

EUROPE

Moscow

Nizhniy Tagil

Yekaterinburg

Tobol'sk

SIBERIAN

Tura

PLAIN

ALB.
MAC.

ROMANIA

MOL.
UKRAINE

URAL

Oral

Chelyabinsk
Magnitogorsk

Tyumen
Kurgan
Tara

Omsk

Kolpashevo

Lesosibirsk

Kansk

LIBYA

GREECE

BUL.

Bucharest

Kyiv
(Kiev)

Black Sea

Izmir
Bursa

Samsun

KAZAKHSTAN

Atyrau

Petropavlovsk

Novosibirsk

Tomsk

Kemerovo

Achinsk

Krasnoyarsk

Novokuznetsk

TURKEY

Ankara

Trabzon

CAUCASUS MTS.
Mt. Ararat
5137 m (16,854 ft)

Tbilisi

Aral
Sea

Pavlodar

Astana

Barnaul

Tashtagol

SAYAN MTS.

CYPRUS
Nicosia

Adana

Latakia
Aleppo

Erzurum

GEORGIA

ARMENIA
Yerevan

AZERBAIJAN
Ganca

Baku

USTYURT
PLATEAU

Zhezkazgan

QaraghandyKOS.
(Karaganda)

KAZAKH
UPLAND

Semey (Semipalatinsk)

Öskemen
(Ust' Kamenogorsk)

ALTAY
MTS.

Dund-Us

LEBANON
Beirut

Cairo

Diyarbakı

SYRIA

Mosul

Arbil

Tabriz

Caspian Sea

Turkmenbashy

Nukus

Qyzylorda

Lake
Balkhash

Taldykorgan

Ayagoz

EGYPT

Tel Aviv-Yafo

Jerusalem
ISRAEL
Al Aqabah

Damascus

JORDAN

Amman

Kirkuk
Basht

Urmia

Urganch

KYZYL KUM
DESERT

Bukhara

Taraz

Almaty

Bishkek

Yining

Jengish Chokusu
7439 m (24,406 ft)

Urümqi

Turpan
Depression

IRAQ

Baghdad

Al Hillah

Tehran

Mt. Damavand
5610 m
(18,406 ft)

Ashgabat

KARA KUM DESERT

TURKMENISTAN

DASHT-E
KAVIR

Mashhad

Gorgan

UZBEKISTAN

TAJIKISTAN

Dushanbe

Kashi

TIEN SHAN

KYRGYZSTAN

AFRICA

Tabuk

AN NAFUD

Hail

Al Basrah

Buraydah

Esfahan

IRAN

Qom

Yazd

DASHT-E LUT

Birjand

Ismail Samani Pk. 7495 m (24,590 ft)

Herat

Lenin Peak 7134 m (23,406 ft)

Shache

TAKLIMAKAN
DESERT

SUDAN

Jeddah

Mecca
At Taif

Kuwait
City

Shiraz

KUWAIT

Kerman

AFGHANISTAN

Farah

HINDU KUSH

Kabul

Peshawar

Mazar-e Sharif

Islamabad

Rawalpindi

Srinagar

8611 m (28,250 ft)

K2

KUNLUN MTS.

PLATEAU OF TIBET

Khartoum

SAUDI
ARABIA

Riyadh

Manama

BAHRAIN
QATAR

Doha

Zahedan

UNITED ARAB
EMIRATES

Abu Dhabi

Bandar-e Abbas

Quetta

Kandahar

Faisalabad

Multan

Chandigarh

Lahore

PAKISTAN

HIMALAYA

Mt. Everest
8850 m
(29,035 ft)

Highest point
in Asia

Lhasa

ERITREA

Asmara

Abha

RUB AL KHALI

Persian
Gulf

Muscat

Gulf of Oman

Sur
Ras al Hadd

OMAN

Turbat

Sukkur

THAR
DESERT

Hyderabad

Karachi

Delhi
New
Delhi

Jodhpur

Jaipur

Agra

Kanpur

Lucknow

Kathmandu

NEPAL

Varanasi

Patna

BHUTAN

Thimphu

Imphal

SOUTH
SUDAN

Addis
Ababa

ETHIOPIA

DJI.

Sanaa

Aden

YEMEN

Al Mukalla

Salalah

Gulf of Aden

Ahmadabad

INDIA

Allahabad

Asansol

Ranchi

BANGLADESH

Dhaka

Chittagong

KENYA

Socotra
(Yemen)

Arabian
Sea

Mumbai
(Bombay)

Pune

DECCAN
PLATEAU

Nagpur

Raipur

Kolkata
(Calcutta)

Khulna

Akyab

MYANMAR
(BURMA)

Pathein

SOMALIA

Hyderabad

Solapur

WESTERN GHATS

Visakhapatnam

Bay of
Bengal

Andaman
Is.
(India)

Panaji

Hubballi
(Hubli)

Vijayawada

TANZANIA

Laccadive Is.
(India)

Bengaluru (Bangalore)

Mysuru
(Mysore)

Chennai
(Madras)

EASTERN GHATS

Coimbatore

Kochi

Madurai

Trincomalee

Nicobar
Is.
(India)

Thiruvananthapuram

Cape Comorin

Colombo

Sri Jayewardenepura Kotte

SRI LANKA

Galle

Male

MALDIVES

Equator

INDIAN
OCEAN

TURKEY

Adana

Antalya

Mersin

Sanliurfa

Al Hasakah

Mosul

Antakya

Latakia

Aleppo

Ar Raqqah

CYPRUS

Nicosia

Limassol

Homs

Hamah

SYRIA

Abu
Kamal

Bayji

LEBANON

Beirut

Tadmur

Damascus

The West Bank
currently occupied
by Israel. Permanent
status to be determined.

Ar Ramadi

IRAQ

Mediterranean
Sea

Haifa

WEST
BANK

ISRAEL

Tel Aviv-Yafo

Jerusalem

Jericho

SYRIAN
DESERT

Port
Said

GAZA
STRIP

Amman

Tanta

Cairo

JORDAN

Maan

SAUDI
ARABIA

AN NAFUD

Giza

Suez

Elat

Al Aqabah

EGYPT

SINAI

Tabuk

0   250 Miles

0   250 Kilometers

484

ASIA

Chukchi
Sea
Bering Strait
Provideniya
180°
80°
170°
170°
70°
60°
50°
40°
Anadyr
Wrangel I.
East
Siberian
Sea
160°
150°
New Siberian
Islands
Cherskiy
170°
Laptev
Sea
130°
120°
Tiksi
Nordvik
Zyryanka
KOLYMA MOUNTAINS
Susuman
Verkhoyansk
180°
Shiveluch
3283 m (10,771 ft)
Kluchevskaya
4835 m (15,863 ft)
Karymsky
1536 m (5,039 ft)
Petropavlovsk-Kamchatskiy
30°
Magadan
KAMCHATKA PEN.
VERKHOYANSK RA.
Aldan
Vilyuysk
Yakutsk
Okhotsk
Sea of
Okhotsk
Alaid
2339 m
(7,674 ft)
TRAL
ERIAN
TEAU
Lensk
Bodaybo
Ust'-Kut
Bratsk
Tulun
Irkutsk
Lake
Baykal
Ulan-
Ude
Berkakit
STANOVOY
RANGE
Tynda
Komsomol'sk-
na-Amure
Svobodnyy
Blagoveshchensk
Okha
Sakhalin
Sarycheva
1496 m
(4,908 ft)
Kuril
Is.
(Russia)
Yuzhno-
Sakhalinsk
Tiatia
1819 m
(5,968 ft)
170°
Khabarovsk
Tatar Strait
Darhan
Moron
Choybalsan
Ulaanbaatar
GREATER KHINGAN RANGE
YABLONOVYY RANGE
Chita
Hailar
Qiqihar
Yichun
Jixi
Harbin
Jilin
Ussuriysk
Vladivostok
Chongjin
Hokkaido
Sapporo
Hakodate
Akita
Sendai
Sea of Japan
(East Sea)
Niigata
Honshu
Tokyo
Yokohama
160°
MONGOLIA
MONGOLIAN
PLATEAU
Bayanhongor
Changchun
Fushun
Shenyang
Anshan
N. KOREA
Hamhung
Pyongyang
JAPAN
Kyoto
Kobe
Nagoya
Osaka
Mt. Fuji 3776 m (12,388 ft)
20°
Hohhot
GOBI DESERT
Beijing
Dalian
Incheon
Seoul
Sejong
City
Daegu
Busan
Hiroshima
Shikoku
Kitakyushu
Fukuoka
Kyushu
Baotou
Tianjin
Shijiazhuang
Taiyuan
S. KOREA
Nagasaki
Kagoshima
Yumen
Yinchuan
Handan
Jinan
Qingdao
Ryukyu Is.
(Japan)
Okinawa
Naha
Tropic of Cancer
PACIFIC
OCEAN
Qinghai
Lake
Xining
Lanzhou
Xi'an
Luoyang
Xuzhou
Zhengzhou
Huainan
Nanjing
Hefei
Shanghai
Hangzhou
Yellow
Sea
Huang
Grand
CHINA
Wuhan
Jingdezhen
East China
Sea
10°
Chengdu
Chongqing
Zigong
Nanchang
Changsha
Shaoyang
Ganzhou
Wenzhou
Fuzhou
Gulyang
Guilin
Liuzhou
Xiamen
Taipei
Kunming
Myitkyina
Nanning
Guangzhou
Macao
Hong Kong
TAIWAN
Kaohsiung
Northern
Mariana
Islands
(U.S.)
Phongsali
Haiphong
Mandalay
Taunggyi
Nay Pyi Taw
LAOS
Hanoi
Louangphabang
Vientiane
Vinh
Hue
Zhanjiang
Haikou
Hainan
(China)
Laoag
Baguio
Luzon
PHILIPPINES
Quezon City
Manila
Naga
Samar
Philippine
Sea
0
500
1,000 Miles
0
500
1,000
1,500 Kilometers
Chiang Mai
Pyay
Yangon
(Rangoon)
THAILAND
Nakhon
Ratchasima
VIETNAM
Da Nang
Mindoro
Panay
Leyte
Tacloban
Cebu
Butuan
PALAU
Equator 0°
150°
Mawlamyine
Dawei
Nakhon
Sawan
CAMBODIA
Bangkok
Batdambang
Phnom Penh
Nha Trang
Ho Chi Minh City
South
China
Sea
Puerto
Princesa
Iloilo
Negros
Palawan
Mindanao
Davao
Zamboanga
Sulu
Sea
Jayapura
PAPUA
NEW GUINEA
Port Moresby
Isthmus
of Kra
Phuket
Kompong Som
Can Tho
Gulf of
Thailand
Kota Kinabalu
Sandakan
Celebes
Sea
Ternate
Halmahera
Manado
New
Guinea
Hat Yai
Bandar Seri Begawan
BRUNEI
Tarakan
Gorontalo
Ceram
Ambon
MALAYSIA
Natuna Is.
Kuching
Samainda
Celebes
Banda
Sea
Arafura
Sea
Banda Aceh
George
Town
Kuala
Lumpur
Kelang
Medan
Putrajaya
SINGAPORE
Singapore
Pontianak
Borneo
Balikpapan
Palopo
Moluccas
Sibolga
Pekanbaru
Sampit
Banjarmasin
Parepare
Baubau
Makassar
Padang
Jambi
Sumatra
Palembang
Java
Sea
INDONESIA
TIMOR-LESTE
AUSTRALIA
Bandar Lampung
Jakarta
Semarang
Surabaya
Ende
Dili
Timor
Bengkulu
Bandung
Yogyakarta
Java
Malang
Bali
Mataram
Sumba
Kupang
Timor
Sea
140°
130°
100°
110°
120°

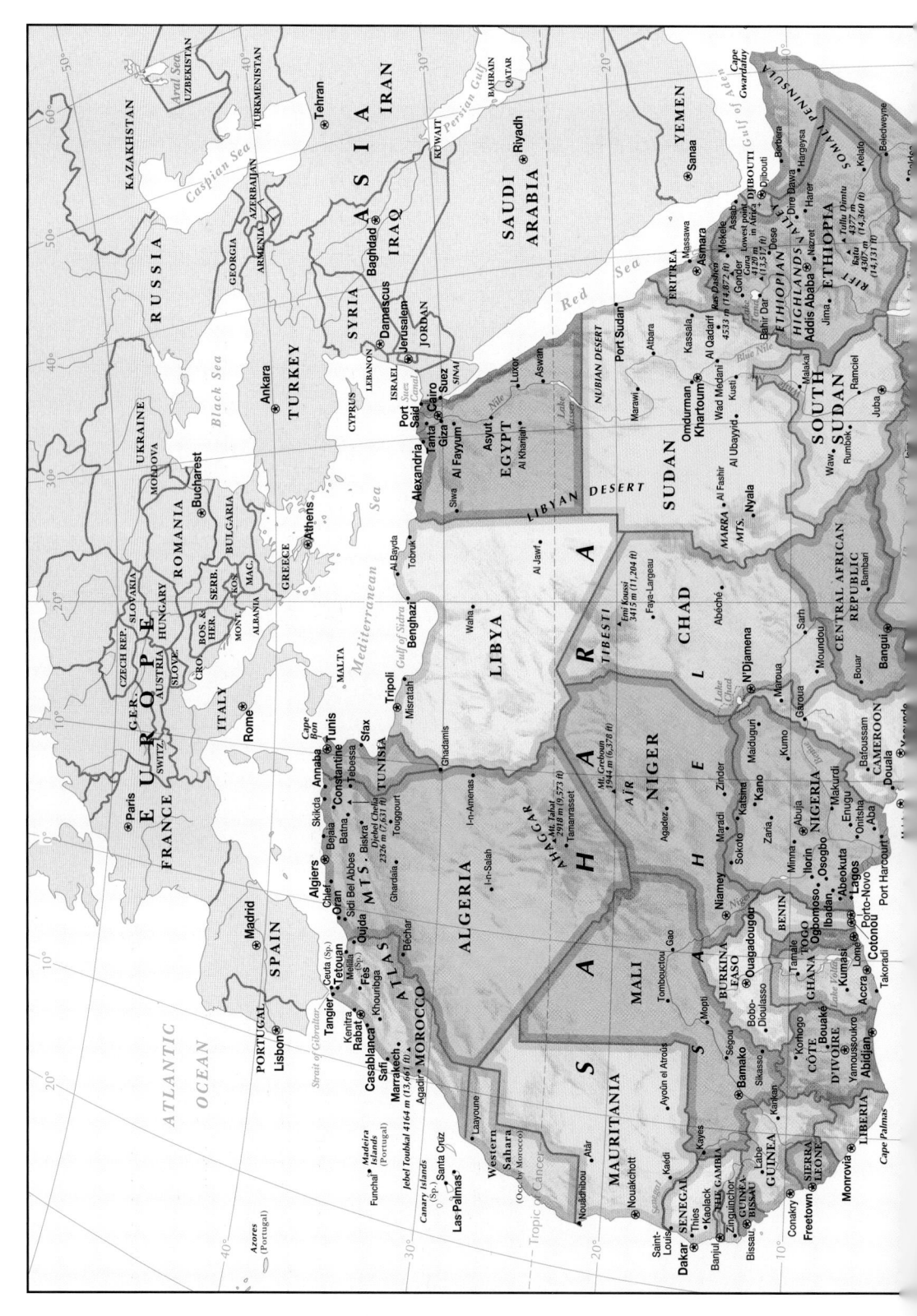

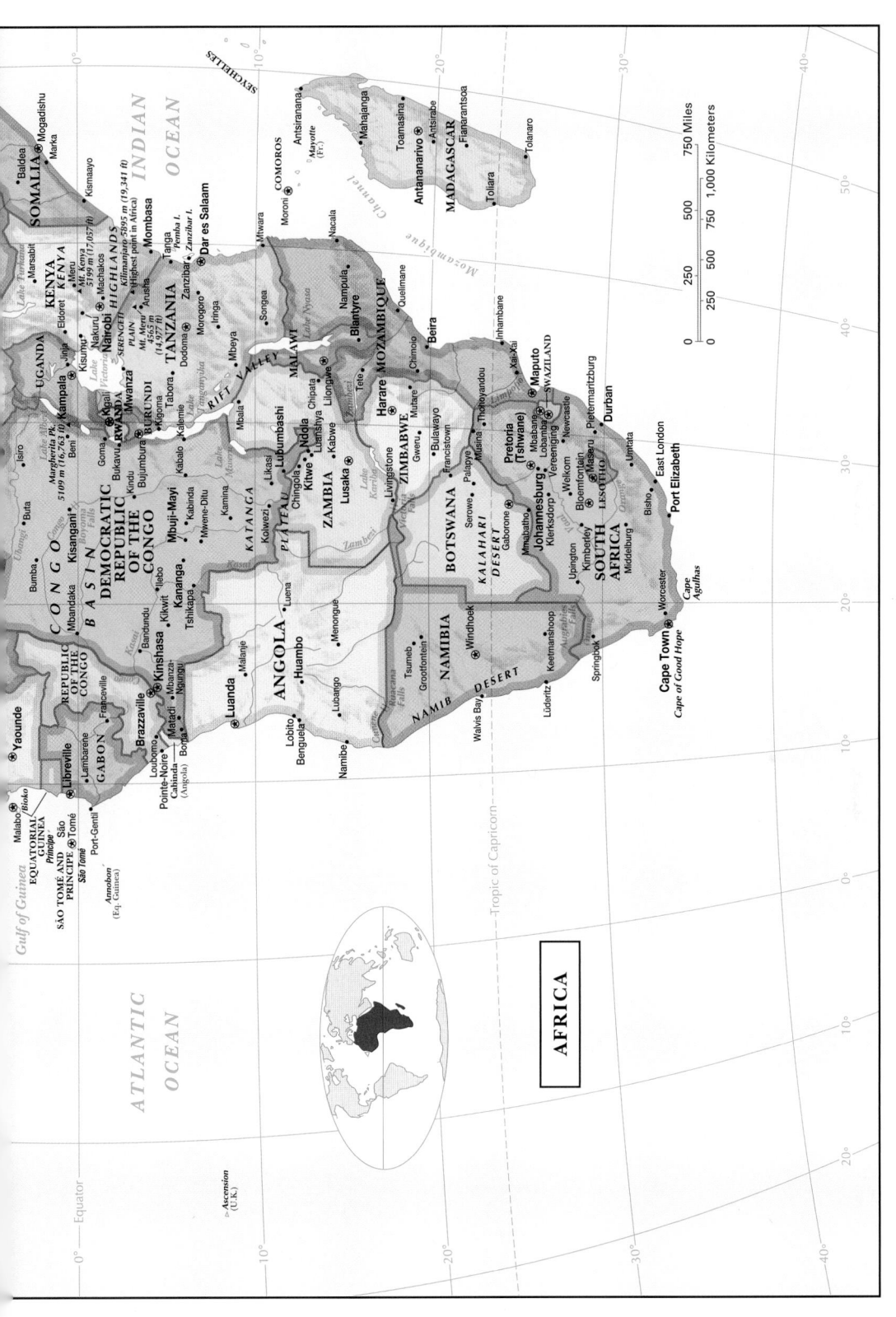

AFRICA

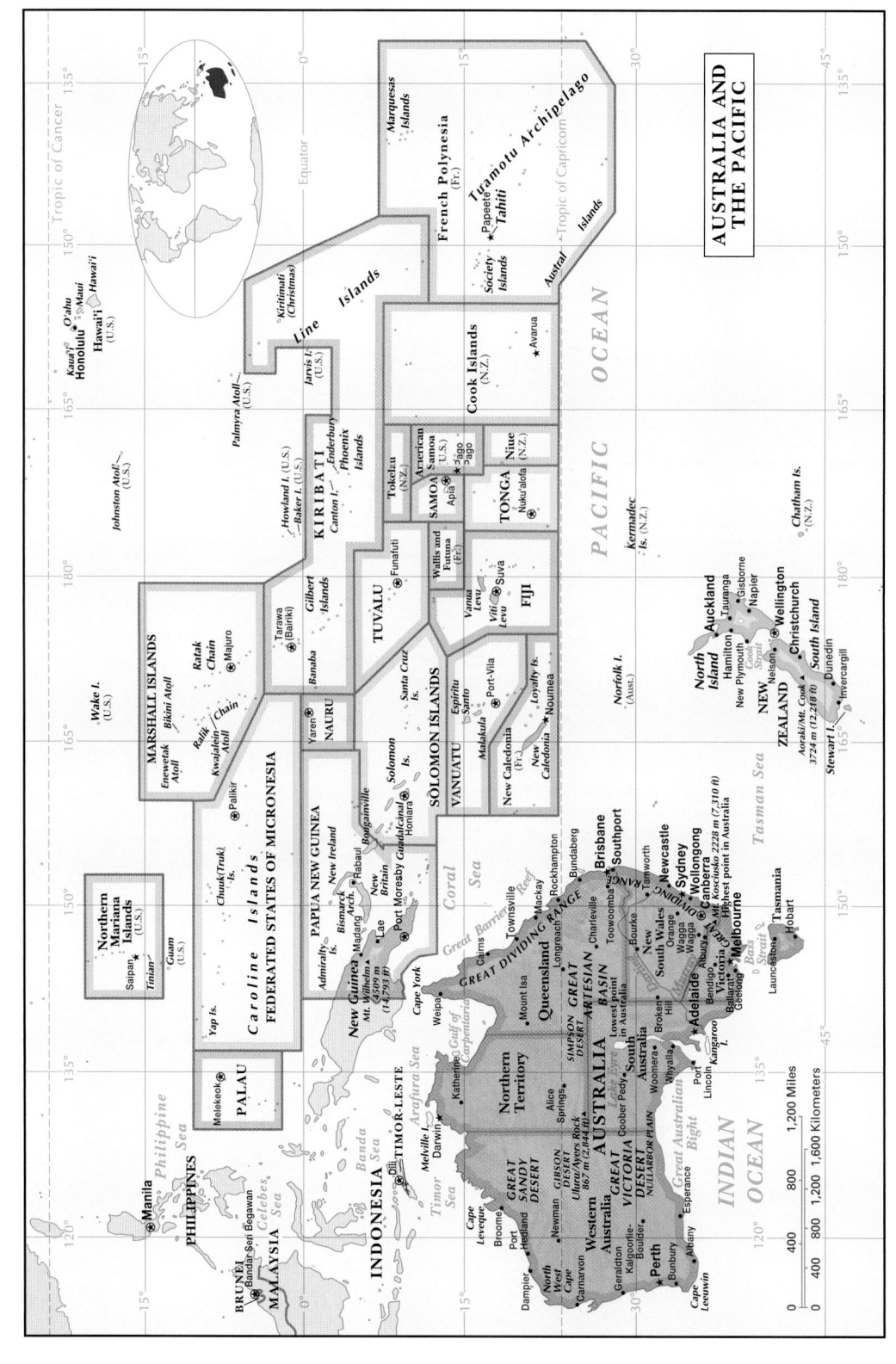

AUSTRALIA AND THE PACIFIC

1929 Gangsters killed seven rivals in Chicago **St. Valentine's Day massacre** Feb. 14, which won Al Capone control of Chicago's underworld. Stock market crash Oct. 29 marked end of past prosperity as stock prices plummeted. Stock losses for 1929-31 estimated at $50 bil; beginning of **Great Depression**. Albert B. Fall, former interior sec., was convicted of accepting $10,000 bribe in leasing of the **Elk Hills (Teapot Dome)** naval oil reserve; sentenced Nov. 1 to a year in prison and fined. **William Faulkner**'s *The Sound and the Fury* published.

1930 London **Naval Reduction Treaty** signed by U.S., Britain, Italy, France, and Japan Apr. 22; in effect Jan. 1, 1931; expired Dec. 31, 1936. **Hawley-Smoot Tariff** signed; rate hikes slash world trade. **Sinclair Lewis** became first American to win a Nobel Prize in literature. **Dashiell Hammett**'s *The Maltese Falcon* published.

1931 Empire State Building opened in New York City May 1, displacing NYC's Chrysler Building as world's tallest. **Al Capone** convicted of tax evasion Oct. 17. **Charlie Chaplin** film *City Lights* released.

1932 Reconstruction Finance Corp. established Jan. 22 to stimulate banking and business. Unemployment at 12 mil. Twenty-month-old **Charles Lindbergh Jr.** kidnapped Mar. 1; found dead May 12. Bruno Hauptmann found guilty Feb. 1935; executed Apr. 3, 1936. Unemployed World War I veterans demanding Congress pay promised bonus early launched **Bonus March** on Washington, DC, May 29. **Franklin D. Roosevelt** elected president for first time in Democratic landslide, Nov. 8. Chicago Bears won **first NFL title game** Dec. 18, defeating the Portsmouth (OH) Spartans, 9-0.

1933 Pres. Roosevelt named **Frances Perkins** U.S. sec. of labor; **first woman in U.S. cabinet.** Pres. Roosevelt ordered **all U.S. banks closed** Mar. 6. In a "100 days" special session, Mar. 9-June 16, Congress passed **New Deal**, including measures to regulate banks, distribute funds to the jobless, create jobs, raise agricultural prices, and set wage and production standards for industry. **Gold standard** dropped by U.S. in favor of "modified gold bullion standard"; announced by Pres. Roosevelt Apr. 19, ratified by Congress June 5. **Tennessee Valley Authority (TVA)** created by act of Congress, May 18. **Prohibition** ended in the U.S. as 36th state ratified **21st Amendment** Dec. 5. Pres. Roosevelt foreswore armed intervention in **Western Hemisphere** nations, Dec. 26.

1934 Pres. Roosevelt signed law creating **Securities and Exchange Commission**, June 6. U.S. troops pulled out of **Haiti**, Aug. 6.

1935 Works Progress Administration (WPA) instituted May 6. Rural Electrification Administration created May 11. National Industrial Recovery Act struck down by Supreme Court May 27. **Boulder Dam** (later renamed **Hoover Dam**) completed, May 29. **Social Security Act** passed by Congress Aug. 8-9. Comedian **Will Rogers** and aviator Wiley Post killed Aug. 15 in Alaska plane crash. Sen. **Huey Long**, former Louisiana governor, shot Sept. 8 by a political rival's son-in-law; died Sept. 10. George Gershwin's jazz opera *Porgy and Bess* opened Oct. 10 in New York. **Committee for Industrial Organization** (later Congress of Industrial Organizations) formed to expand industrial unionism Nov. 9.

1936 Jesse Owens won four gold medals at the **Berlin Olympics** in Aug. **Baseball Hall of Fame** founded in Cooperstown, NY. **Margaret Mitchell**'s *Gone With the Wind* published.

1937 Airship *Hindenburg* caught fire May 6 as it was landing in Lakehurst, NJ; 36 killed. **Golden Gate Bridge** in San Francisco opened May 27. **Joe Louis** knocked out James J. Braddock to become world heavyweight champ June 22. Aviator **Amelia Earhart** and copilot Fred Noonan disappeared July 2 near Howland Isl., in the Pacific. Pres. Roosevelt proposed judicial reforms that would allow him to appoint additional Supreme Court justices; his **"court-packing"** plan defeated. **Auto, steel labor unions** won first big contracts.

1938 National minimum wage enacted June 25. Orson Welles's radio dramatization of H. G. Wells's *War of the Worlds*, Oct. 30, caused Martian invasion scare among some who had missed the introduction. **Seabiscuit** beat War Admiral in match race of the century, at Pimlico track, MD, Nov. 1. Artist Anna Mary Robertson, **"Grandma Moses,"** discovered. **Thornton Wilder**'s *Our Town* produced on Broadway.

1939 Opera singer **Marian Anderson** performed for integrated crowd of 75,000 at Lincoln Memorial Apr. 9 after Daughters of the American Revolution refused to let Anderson sing in DC's Constitution Hall. **New York World's Fair**—theme: "The World of Tomorrow"—opened Apr. 30, closed Oct. 31. Reopened for second season May 11-Oct. 27, 1940. **Lou Gehrig**, seriously ill with disease that would come to bear his name, said farewell to fans at Yankee Stadium, July 4. Albert Einstein alerted Pres. Roosevelt to **A-bomb possibilities** in Aug. 2 letter. **U.S. declared its neutrality** in European war Sept. 5. Pres. Roosevelt proclaimed limited **national emergency** Sept. 8, unlimited emergency May 27, 1941. Both ended by Pres. Harry Truman, Apr. 28, 1952.

Pocket Books, **first paperback publisher** in U.S., established. **John Steinbeck**'s *The Grapes of Wrath* published. *The Wizard of Oz* and *Gone With the Wind* released, the latter to become highest-grossing film of all time (inflation-adjusted).

1940 U.S. OK'd sale of **surplus war material** to Britain June 3; announced transfer of 50 overaged destroyers Sept. 3. **First peacetime military draft** in U.S. history approved, Sept. 14. **Forty-hour work week** went into effect, Oct. 24. Pres. **Roosevelt** elected Nov. 5 to third presidential term. **Richard Wright**'s *Native Son* published.

1941 Four Freedoms—freedom of speech and religion, freedom from want and fear—termed essential by Pres. Roosevelt in speech to Congress Jan. 6. **Lend-Lease Act** signed Mar. 11 provided $7 bil in military credits for Britain. Lend-lease for USSR approved in Nov. Pres. Roosevelt signed executive order June 25 barring federal government and war contractors from **racial discrimination**. Order also established Fair Employment Practice Committee. The **Atlantic Charter**, 8-point declaration of principles, issued by Pres. Roosevelt and British Prime Min. Winston Churchill, Aug. 14. Japan attacked **Pearl Harbor**, Hawaii, 7:55 AM Hawaiian time, Dec. 7; 19 ships sunk or damaged, 2,403 dead. Pres. Roosevelt called it "a date which will live in infamy." U.S. declared war on Japan Dec. 8. Germany and Italy declared war on U.S. Dec. 11. U.S. responded with declaration of war later on same day. Japanese invaded **Philippines**, Dec. 22; Wake Island fell, Dec. 23. *Citizen Kane*, directed by Orson Welles, released.

1942 Pres. Roosevelt issued executive order Feb. 19 authorizing relocation of Japanese-Americans. Federal government began forcibly moving 110,000 Japanese-Americans from West Coast to **detention camps**; exclusion lasted three years. Japanese troops took **Bataan** peninsula Apr. 8 and **Corregidor** May 6. **Battle of Midway** June 4-7 was Japan's first major defeat. Marines landed on **Guadalcanal** Aug. 7; last Japanese not expelled until Feb. 9, 1943. U.S., Britain invaded **North Africa** Nov. 8. **First nuclear chain reaction** (fission of uranium isotope U-235) produced at Univ. of Chicago under physicists Arthur Compton, Enrico Fermi, others, Dec. 2. The movie *Casablanca*, starring Humphrey Bogart and Ingrid Bergman, released.

1943 *Oklahoma!* opened Mar. 31 on Broadway. Pres. Roosevelt signed June 10 pay-as-you-go income tax bill. Starting July 1, wage and salary earners were subject to **paycheck withholding tax**. **Detroit race riot** June 21 left 34 dead, 700 injured. Six killed in riot in New York City's **Harlem** section Aug. 2. U.S., Britain invaded **Sicily** July 9, Italian **mainland**

1942: Pres. Franklin D. Roosevelt orders the relocation of 110,000 Japanese-Americans to detention camps for the duration of the war.

Sept. 3. Marines in Nov. recaptured the **Gilbert Islands**, captured by Japan in 1941 and 1942.

1944 U.S., Allied forces invaded Europe at Normandy, France, on **"D Day,"** June 6, in massive amphibious operation. **GI Bill of Rights**, providing benefits to veterans, signed by Pres. Roosevelt June 22. Representatives of the U.S. and other major powers met at **Dumbarton Oaks**, Washington, DC, Aug. 21-Oct. 7, to work out formation of postwar world organization that would become the **United Nations**. U.S. forces landed on **Leyte**, Philippines, Oct. 20. Pres. **Roosevelt** elected to fourth term as president Nov. 7. **Battle of the Bulge**, failed Nazi counteroffensive, waged Dec. 16 to Jan. 28, 1945.

1945 Yalta Conference met in the Crimea, USSR, Feb. 4-11. Pres. Roosevelt, Prime Min. Churchill, and Soviet leader Joseph Stalin agreed that their countries, plus France, would occupy Germany and that the Soviet Union would enter war against Japan. Marines landed on **Iwo Jima** Feb. 19, won control Mar. 16 after heavy casualties. U.S. forces invaded **Okinawa** Apr. 1, captured it June 21. Pres. **Roosevelt** died in Warm Springs, GA, Apr. 12; Vice Pres. **Harry S. Truman** became president. Germany surrendered May 7; May 8 proclaimed **V-E Day**. **First atomic bomb**, produced at Los Alamos, NM, exploded at Alamogordo, NM, July 16. Bomb dropped on **Hiroshima**, Japan, Aug. 6, killing about 75,000; bomb dropped on **Nagasaki**, Japan, Aug. 9, killing about 40,000. Japan agreed to surrender Aug. 14; formally surrendered Sept. 2. At **Potsdam Conference**, July 17-Aug. 2, leaders of U.S., USSR, and Britain agreed on disarmament of Germany, occupation zones, war crimes trials. **Empire State Building** struck accidentally by Army B-25 bomber, July 28, killing 14. U.S. forces entered **Korea** south of 38th parallel to displace Japanese Sept. 8. Gen. **Douglas MacArthur** took over supervision of Japan Sept. 9.

1946 Steel strike by 750,000 started Jan. 21, settled in four weeks. Strike by 400,000 **mine workers** began Apr. 1 (settled May 29); other industries (including rail, maritime) followed. Former Prime Min. Winston Churchill employed the phrase **"Iron Curtain"** in Mar. 5 speech at Westminster College in Fulton, MO. Atomic bomb tested off **Bikini Atoll** in Pacific, July 1. In all, U.S. conducted 23 nuclear tests between 1946 and 1958. **Philippines** given independence by U.S. July 4. Mother Frances Xavier Cabrini **first American to be canonized**, July 7. Dr. Benjamin Spock's *Baby and Child Care* published as **baby boom** began.

1947 Pres. Truman asked Congress for financial and military aid for Greece and Turkey to help combat Communist subversion, Mar. 12; **Truman Doctrine** approved May 15. UN Security Council voted Apr. 2 to place under U.S. trusteeship the **Pacific islands** formerly mandated to Japan. **Jackie Robinson** joined Brooklyn Dodgers Apr. 11, breaking color barrier in major league baseball. The **Marshall Plan** for U.S. aid to European countries proposed by Sec. of State George C. Marshall June 5. Congress authorized some $12 bil in next four years. **Taft-Hartley Labor Act** restricting labor union power vetoed by Pres. Truman June 20; Congress overrode veto. Air Force Capt. **Chuck Yeager** broke sound barrier, Oct. 14, in X-1 rocket plane.

1948 Organization of American States (OAS) founded Apr. 30 by 21 countries. USSR halted all surface traffic into **West Berlin** June 24; in response, U.S. and British troops launched an **airlift**. Soviet blockade halted May 12, 1949; airlift ended Sept. 30. Pres. **Truman** elected Nov. 2, defeating NY Gov. Thomas E. Dewey in historic upset. Former State Dept. official **Alger Hiss** indicted Dec. 15 for perjury, after denying he had passed secret documents to Whittaker Chambers to go to a Communist spy ring; convicted Jan. 21, 1950. **Kinsey Report** on sexuality in the human male published.

1949 North Atlantic Treaty Organization (**NATO**) established Aug. 24 by U.S., Canada, and 10 Western European nations, agreeing that an armed attack against one would be considered an attack against all. Eleven leaders of U.S. **Communist Party** convicted Oct. 14 of advocating violent overthrow of U.S. government; sentenced to prison. Supreme Court upheld convictions, 1951. Pres. Truman, Oct. 26, signed legislation raising **federal minimum wage** from 40¢ an hour to 75¢. **Arthur Miller**'s *Death of a Salesman* opened on Broadway.

1950 Masked bandits robbed **Brink's, Inc.**, Boston express office, Jan. 17, of $2.8 mil. Case solved 1956; eight sentenced to life. Pres. Truman authorized production of **H-bomb** Jan. 31. Special Senate committee to investigate organized crime established May 3, chaired by Sen. **Estes Kefauver** (D, TN).

North Korean forces **invaded South Korea** June 25. UN asked for troops to restore peace. Pres. Truman ordered Air Force and Navy to Korea June 27. Truman approved ground forces, airstrikes against North Korea June 30. U.S. sent 35 military advisers to **South Vietnam** June 27 and agreed to aid anti-Communist government. U.S. forces landed at **Inchon**, South Korea, Sept. 15. UN forces took Pyongyang Oct. 20, reached China border Nov. 20. China sent troops across border Nov. 26. U.S. banned shipments Dec. 8 to **Communist China** and to Asiatic ports trading with it.

Army **seized all U.S. railroads** Aug. 27 on Truman's order to prevent general strike; returned to owners in 1952. Two members of **Puerto Rican nationalist movement** tried to kill Pres. Truman Nov. 1.

Peanuts comic strip appeared in newspapers. Variety show *Your Show of Shows* debuted on TV. David Riesman's *The Lonely Crowd* published.

1951 22nd Amendment, limiting presidential term of office, ratified Feb. 27. **Julius Rosenberg**; his wife, **Ethel Rosenberg**; and **Morton Sobell** found guilty Mar. 29 of conspiracy to commit wartime espionage. Rosenbergs received death penalty. Sobell sentenced to 30 years; released 1969. Pres. Truman removed Gen. **Douglas MacArthur** from Korea command Apr. 11 for unauthorized policy statements. **Korea cease-fire** talks began in July; lasted two years. Fighting ended July 27, 1953. **Transcontinental TV** began Sept. 4 with Pres. Truman's address at Japanese Peace Treaty Conference in San Francisco. **Japanese peace treaty** signed in San Francisco Sept. 8 by U.S., Japan, and 47 other nations. **J. D. Salinger**'s *Catcher in the Rye* published. *I Love Lucy* sitcom premiered on TV.

1952 Pres. Truman ordered seizure of nation's **steel mills** Apr. 8 to avert strike; ruled illegal by Supreme Court June 2. **Peace contract** between West Germany, U.S., Great Britain, and France signed May 26. Last racial and ethnic barriers to naturalization removed, June 26-27, with passage of **Immigration and Naturalization Act** of 1952. **Puerto Rico** proclaimed commonwealth July 25, after referendum Mar. 3. Richard Nixon, as vice-pres. candidate, gave **"Checkers" speech**, so called because of sentimental reference to his dog Checkers, Sept. 23. **First hydrogen device explosion** Nov. 1 in Pacific. **Ralph Ellison**'s *Invisible Man* published.

1953 Federal jury in New York convicted 13 **Communist** leaders on conspiracy charges, Jan. 20. **Julius and Ethel Rosenberg** executed in electric chair, June 19, for relaying nuclear secrets to Soviet Union. **Korean War armistice** signed July 27. California Gov. **Earl Warren** sworn in Oct. 5 as 14th chief justice of U.S. Supreme Court.

1954 *Nautilus*, **first atomic-powered submarine**, launched at Groton, CT, Jan. 21. Five members of Congress were wounded in the House Mar. 1 by four **Puerto Rican independence supporters** who fired at random from a spectators' gallery. At televised hearings, Apr. 22-June 17, before a Senate subcommittee, Army officials accused Sen. **Joseph McCarthy** (R, WI) of seeking preferential treatment for a draftee and McCarthy accused Army of hindering probe of Communist infiltration. McCarthy was cleared in the hearings, but the Senate later voted to condemn him, 67-22, for abuse of the Senate during hearings and debates. Supreme Court ruled unanimously May 17 that racial segregation in public schools was unconstitutional, in *Brown v. Board of Education* of Topeka. **Ernest Hemingway** won Nobel Prize in literature for *The Old Man and the Sea*.

1955 U.S. agreed Feb. 12 to help train **South Vietnamese army**. Supreme Court ordered "all deliberate speed" in **integration** of public schools, May 31. A summit meeting of leaders of **Big 4**—U.S., Britain, France, and USSR—took place July 18-23 in Geneva, Switzerland. **Rosa Parks** refused Dec. 1 to give her seat to white man on bus in Montgomery, AL. Her arrest, detention, and conviction sparked boycott of bus system, organized by Rev. **Martin Luther King Jr.**, by Montgomery's black community Dec. 5. Bus segregation ordinance declared unconstitutional by federal court in 1956. Boycott ended Dec. 23 of that year. America's two largest labor organizations merged Dec. 5, creating **AFL-CIO**. Russian-born U.S. citizen **Vladimir Nabokov**'s *Lolita* published.

1956 Massive resistance to Supreme Court **desegregation rulings** was called for Mar. 12 by 101 Southern congressmen. U.S. Supreme Court, Apr. 23, unanimously ruled against **racial segregation** on intrastate buses.

1955: Rosa Parks's arrest for refusing to give up her seat on a bus in Montgomery, AL, sparks a boycott that would desegregate public transportation.

Federal-Aid Highway Act signed June 29, creating **interstate highway system**. **First transatlantic telephone cable** activated Sept. 25. In Game 5, Oct. 8, Yankee right-hander Don Larsen pitched **only perfect World Series game**. **Eugene O'Neill**'s *Long Day's Journey Into Night* opened Nov. 7 on Broadway.

1957 Congress approved **Civil Rights Act of 1957**, Apr. 29, first such bill since Reconstruction to protect voting rights. Pres. Eisenhower signed act into law Sept. 9; provided for creation of Civil Rights Commission. The U.S. surgeon general July 12 said studies showed "direct link" between cigarette **smoking and lung cancer**.

Arkansas Gov. Orval Faubus (D) called National Guardsmen Sept. 4 to bar nine black students from entering all-white high school in **Little Rock**. Faubus complied Sept. 21 with federal court order to remove Guardsmen, but local authorities ordered black students to withdraw. Pres. Eisenhower sent troops Sept. 24 to enforce court order.

Jack Kerouac's *On the Road* published.

1958 Army launched **first U.S. Earth-orbiting satellite**, *Explorer I*, Jan. 31 from Cape Canaveral, FL; discovered Van Allen radiation belt. U.S. Marines sent to **Lebanon** to protect elected government from threatened overthrow July-Oct. Nuclear sub *Nautilus* made **first undersea crossing of North Pole** Aug. 5. Presidential aide **Sherman Adams** resigned Sept. 22 over scandal involving alleged improper gifts. **First domestic jet airline passenger service** in U.S. opened by National Airlines Dec. 10 between New York and Miami.

1959 Alaska admitted as 49th state, Jan. 3; **Hawaii** admitted as 50th, Aug. 21. **St. Lawrence Seaway** linking Atlantic Ocean and Great Lakes opened to traffic, Apr. 25.

Vice Pres. Richard Nixon, on tour of USSR, held **"kitchen debate,"** July 24, with Soviet Prem. Nikita Khrushchev at U.S. exhibit in Moscow. Prem. **Khrushchev** paid unprecedented visit to U.S. Sept. 15-27; made transcontinental tour.

Pres. Eisenhower issued injunction Oct. 12, upheld and made effective by Supreme Court Nov. 7, ending record **116-day steel strike**. In **quiz show scandal**, Columbia Univ. Prof. Charles Van Doren admitted to U.S. House subcommittee Nov. 2 that he had been coached before appearances on NBC-TV's *21* in 1956; he had won $129,000. William Wyler's *Ben-Hur* released; the movie won a record 11 Academy Awards the following year.

1960 Sit-ins began Feb. 1 when four black college students in Greensboro, NC, refused to move from a Woolworth lunch counter after being denied service. By Sept. 1961, more than 70,000 students, whites and blacks, had participated in sit-ins. Pres. Eisenhower signed **Civil Rights Act** May 6.

A U.S. **U-2 reconnaissance plane** was shot down in the Soviet Union May 1; pilot Gary Powers captured. The incident led to cancellation of Paris summit conference; Powers traded for Soviet spy, 1962. A **birth control pill** approved as safe for first time by Food and Drug Administration May 9. Vice Pres. **Richard Nixon** and Sen. **John F. Kennedy** faced each other Sept. 26 in first in series of televised debates. Kennedy defeated Nixon to win presidency, Nov. 8. U.S. announced Dec. 15 its backing of rightist group in **Laos**, which took power the next day.

Alfred Hitchcock film *Psycho* released.

1961 U.S. severed diplomatic and consular relations with Cuba Jan. 3, after disputes over nationalizations of U.S. firms, U.S. military presence at Guantánamo base. U.S.-directed invasion of Cuba's **Bay of Pigs** Apr. 17 by Cuban exiles unsuccessfully attempted to overthrow the regime of Prem. Fidel Castro.

Peace Corps created by executive order, Mar. 1. **23rd Amendment**, giving DC citizens the right to vote in presidential elections, ratified Mar. 29. Alan B. Shepard Jr. rocketed from Cape Canaveral, FL, in a Mercury capsule May 5, in **first U.S.-crewed suborbital space flight**.

"Freedom Rides" from Washington, DC, across Deep South were launched May 20 to protest segregation in interstate transportation.

Joseph Heller's *Catch-22* published.

1962 Pres. Kennedy said Feb. 14 that U.S. military advisers in **Vietnam** would fire if fired upon. Lt. Col. John H. Glenn Jr. became **first American in orbit** Feb. 20 when he circled the Earth three times in the Mercury capsule *Friendship 7*.

In *Baker v. Carr*, Mar. 26, U.S. Supreme Court ruled that constitutional challenges to unequal distribution of voters among legislative districts could be resolved by federal courts. **James Meredith** became first black student at Univ. of Mississippi Oct. 1 after 3,000 federal troops put down riots.

A Soviet **offensive missile buildup** in Cuba was revealed Oct. 22 by Pres. Kennedy, who ordered naval and air quarantine on shipment of offensive military equipment to the island. He and Soviet Prem. Khrushchev agreed Oct. 28 on formula to end crisis. Kennedy announced Nov. 2 that missile bases in Cuba were being dismantled. **Rachel Carson**'s *Silent Spring* launched environmentalist movement.

1963 In *Gideon v. Wainwright*, Mar. 18, Supreme Court ruled that all criminal defendants have a right to counsel.

March for civil rights began May 2 in Birmingham, AL; led to desegregation accord, which in turn sparked rioting and violence. Univ. of Alabama **desegregated** after Gov. George Wallace stepped aside when confronted by federally deployed National Guard troops June 11. Civil rights leader **Medgar Evers** assassinated June 12. On Aug. 28, 200,000 joined in **March on Washington** in support of black demands for equal rights led by **Rev. Martin Luther King Jr.**; highlight was King's **"I Have a Dream" speech**.

Supreme Court ruled June 17 that laws requiring **recitation of Lord's Prayer or Bible verses** in public schools were unconstitutional. Pres. Kennedy, on Europe trip, addressed huge crowd in **West Berlin**, June 23. **Limited nuclear test-ban treaty** agreed upon July 25 by the U.S., the Soviet Union, and Britain. Four black girls killed in bombing of **16th St. Baptist Church** in Birmingham, AL, Sept. 15.

South Vietnam Pres. **Ngo Dinh Diem** assassinated Nov. 2; U.S. had earlier withdrawn support. Pres. **Kennedy** shot and fatally wounded Nov. 22 as he rode in motorcade through downtown Dallas, TX. Vice Pres. **Lyndon B. Johnson** sworn in as president. **Lee Harvey Oswald** arrested and charged with murder but was himself shot and fatally wounded Nov. 24. Nightclub owner **Jack Ruby** convicted of Oswald's murder; Ruby died in 1967 while awaiting retrial following reversal of his conviction. **Betty Friedan**'s feminist work *The Feminine Mystique* published.

1964 Panama suspended relations with U.S. Jan. 9 after riots. U.S. offered Dec. 18 to negotiate new canal treaty. **The Beatles** appeared Feb. 9 on *The Ed Sullivan Show*. Supreme Court ruled Feb. 17 that **congressional districts** as near as practicable be equal in population. U.S. reported May 27 it was sending military planes to **Laos**.

Three **civil rights workers** reported missing in Mississippi June 22; bodies found Aug. 4. Eighteen white men tried. On Oct. 20, 1967, an all-white federal jury convicted seven of conspiracy in the slayings. Omnibus **civil rights bill** signed by Pres. Johnson July 2, banning discrimination in voting, jobs, public accommodations.

Congress Aug. 7 passed **Tonkin Gulf Resolution**, authorizing presidential action in Vietnam, after North Vietnamese boats reportedly attacked U.S. destroyers Aug. 2. (Resolution repealed, 1971.) Congress approved War on Poverty bill Aug. 11, providing for a domestic Peace Corps (**VISTA**), **Job Corps**, and antipoverty funding. The **Warren Commission** released a report Sept. 27 concluding that Lee Harvey Oswald was solely responsible for the Kennedy assassination. Pres. **Johnson** elected to full term, Nov. 3, defeating Sen. **Barry Goldwater** (R, AZ) in landslide. **Verrazano-Narrows Bridge** opened in New York City, Nov. 21, with world's then-longest suspension span.

1965 In State of the Union address Jan. 4, Pres. Johnson outlined plans for **"Great Society,"** program of civil rights, antipoverty, and health-care legislation. Johnson in Feb. ordered continuous bombing of **North Vietnam** below 20th parallel.

Malcolm X assassinated by Nation of Islam members Feb. 21 at New York City rally. March from **Selma to Montgomery**, AL, Mar. 21-25, by Rev. Martin Luther King Jr. to demand federal protection of blacks' voting rights. Some 14,000 U.S. troops sent to **Dominican Republic** during civil war Apr. 28. All troops withdrawn by next year. Bill establishing **Medicare**, government health insurance program for elderly, signed by Pres. Johnson July 30.

New **Voting Rights Act**, which banned literacy tests and other voter qualification tests, signed Aug. 6. Arrest of black motorist by white police officers precipitated **Watts riot** in predominantly-black Los Angeles neighborhood Aug. 11-16. Riots resulted in 34 deaths and $200 mil in property damage.

National **immigration quota system** abolished Oct. 3. **Electric power failure** blacked out most of northeastern U.S., parts of two Canadian provinces the night of Nov. 9-10.

1966 U.S. forces began firing into **Cambodia** May 1. Bombing of **Hanoi** area of North Vietnam by U.S. planes began June 29. By Dec. 31, 385,300 U.S. troops were stationed in South Vietnam, plus 60,000 offshore and 33,000 in Thailand.

Supreme Court ruled June 13, in *Miranda v. Arizona*, that suspects must be read their rights before police questioning. **Medicare** began July 1. In **Univ. of Texas shooting** rampage, 25-year-old student Charles Whitman killed 15 and wounded 31 from tower observation deck on Austin campus, Aug. 1; shot dead by police.

Dept. of Transportation created, Oct. 15. Edward Brooke (R, MA) elected Nov. 8 as first black U.S. senator in 85 years. Robert C. Weaver named secretary of newly created Dept. of Housing and Urban Development, becoming **first black cabinet member.**

1967 Green Bay Packers beat Kansas City Chiefs, 35-10, in **first Super Bowl**, Jan. 15, in Los Angeles. Three astronauts died Jan. 27 in *Apollo 1* fire on ground at Cape Canaveral, FL. **25th Amendment**, providing for presidential succession,

1967: A major anti-Vietnam War demonstration, a march on the Pentagon, draws more than 70,000 protesters.

ratified Feb. 10. Pres. Johnson and Soviet Prem. **Aleksei Kosygin** met June 23 and 25 at Glassboro State College in New Jersey; agreed not to let any crisis push them into war.

Riots erupted among residents of predominantly black Newark, NJ, July 12-17; 26 killed, 1,500 injured, more than 1,000 arrested. In **Detroit**, MI, July 23-30, 43 died, 2,000 injured; 5,000 left homeless by rioting, looting, and burning in city's black neighborhoods. **Thurgood Marshall** sworn in Oct. 2 as first black U.S. Supreme Court justice. **Antiwar march** on Washington, Oct. 21-22, drew at least 70,000 participants. Carl B. Stokes (D, Cleveland) and Richard G. Hatcher (D, Gary, IN) elected **first black mayors** of major U.S. cities Nov. 7.

1968 In **"Tet offensive,"** Communist troops attacked several provincial capitals and other major cities, including Saigon, Jan. 30, but suffered heavy casualties. Pres. Johnson **curbed bombing** of North Vietnam Mar. 31. Peace talks began in Paris May 10. All bombing of North halted Oct. 31.

Rev. **Martin Luther King Jr.** assassinated Apr. 4 in Memphis, TN. **James Earl Ray**, an escaped convict, pleaded guilty to slaying, was sentenced to 99 years. Students at **Columbia Univ.**, Apr. 23-24, seized school buildings in protest against school's involvement in military research, among other issues. Sen. **Robert F. Kennedy** (D, NY) shot June 5 in Los Angeles after celebrating presidential primary victories, died June 6. **Sirhan Sirhan** convicted of murder, 1969; death sentence commuted to life in prison, 1972.

Vice Pres. Hubert Humphrey nominated for president at **Democratic National Convention** in Chicago, marked by clash between police and antiwar protesters, Aug. 26-29. Republican nominee **Richard Nixon** won presidency, defeating Humphrey in close race Nov. 5.

Apollo 8 **orbited moon** in five-day mission, Dec. 21-27. North Korea released 82-man crew of the **USS *Pueblo*** Dec. 22, 11 months after seizing the ship in Sea of Japan; one crew member had been killed in battle.

1969 Expanded four-party **Vietnam peace talks** began Jan. 18. U.S. force peaked at 543,400 in Apr.; withdrawal started July 8. Pres. Nixon set Vietnamization policy of expanding role of South Vietnamese forces Nov. 3. Earl Warren retired upon swearing in **Warren Burger**, June 23, as Supreme Court chief justice. In incident that marked birth of **gay rights** movement, police clashed with patrons of gay bar, the **Stonewall Inn**, in New York City June 27.

U.S. astronaut **Neil Armstrong**, commander of the *Apollo 11* mission, became the **first person to set foot on the moon**, July 20, followed by astronaut **Edwin "Buzz" Aldrin**. Astronaut **Michael Collins** remained aboard command module.

Woodstock rock music festival near Bethel, NY, drew 300,000-500,000 people, Aug. 15-18. **Anti-Vietnam War demonstrations** held in cities across the U.S., marking Vietnam Moratorium day, Oct. 15; on Nov. 15, some 250,000 marched in Washington, DC. Massacre of hundreds of civilians by U.S. troops at **My Lai**, South Vietnam, in 1968 reported Nov. 16. **Kurt Vonnegut**'s *Slaughterhouse Five* published. *Sesame Street* launched on public TV.

1970 A federal jury Feb. 18 found the **"Chicago 7"** antiwar activists not guilty of conspiring to incite riots during 1968 Democratic National Convention. However, five were convicted of crossing state lines with intent to incite riots.

Three astronauts safely returned to Earth Apr. 17 after oxygen tank on *Apollo 13* ruptured. Lunar landing had been canceled. Millions of Americans participated in antipollution demonstrations Apr. 22 to mark **first Earth Day**.

U.S. and South Vietnamese forces crossed **Cambodian** borders Apr. 30 to get at enemy bases. Four students killed May 4 at **Kent State Univ.** in Ohio by National Guardsmen during war protest. In protest at **Jackson State Univ.** in Mississippi, two killed when police fired on protesters.

First female U.S. generals appointed June 11. **Postal reform** measure signed Aug. 12 created an independent U.S. Postal Service. Pres. Nixon, Dec. 31, signed **clean air bill** calling for development of cleaner auto engine and national air quality standards for 10 major pollutants. Garry Trudeau's *Doonesbury* comic strip launched in 30 papers.

1971 **Charles Manson** and three of his cult followers found guilty Jan. 25 of first-degree murder in 1969 slaying of actress Sharon Tate and six others. A court-martial jury

Mar. 29 convicted Lt. **William Calley** in murder of 22 South Vietnamese at **My Lai** on Mar. 16, 1968. He was sentenced to life in prison Mar. 31, later reduced to 20 years.

Pres. Nixon, Apr. 14, relaxed 20-year **trade embargo with China**. *New York Times* began publishing June 13 classified **Pentagon Papers**, secret Pentagon study on U.S. involvement in Vietnam leaked by Daniel Ellsberg, military analyst consulting for government. Supreme Court June 30 upheld, 6-3, right to publish the documents. **26th Amendment**, lowering the minimum voting age to 18, ratified June 30. Pres. Nixon, Aug. 15, instituted 90-day **wage and price freeze**.

U.S. bombers initiated massive five-day strike Dec. 26 in North Vietnam in retaliation for alleged violations of agreements reached prior to 1968 bombing halt.

1972 Pres. Nixon arrived in **Beijing** Feb. 21 for eight-day visit to China, in "journey for peace." Joint communiqué released Feb. 27 called for increased Sino-U.S. contacts. Senate, Mar. 22, approved **Equal Rights Amendment** banning discrimination on basis of sex; sent measure to states for ratification.

North Vietnamese forces launched biggest attacks in four years across the demilitarized zone Mar. 30. The U.S. responded Apr. 15 with **resumption of bombing** of Hanoi and Haiphong. Pres. Nixon announced May 8 the mining of North Vietnam ports.

Gov. **George C. Wallace** (D, AL), campaigning for president at Laurel, MD, shopping center May 15, shot and seriously wounded. **Arthur Bremer** convicted Aug. 4, sentenced to 63 years for shooting Wallace and three others. In **first visit of U.S. president to Moscow**, Pres. Nixon arrived May 22 for summit talks with Kremlin leaders that culminated in landmark strategic arms pact (**SALT I**). Five men arrested June 17 for breaking into Democratic National Committee offices in **Watergate** office complex in Washington, DC. U.S. Supreme Court in *Furman v. Georgia* June 29 ruled **capital punishment** as practiced was unconstitutional.

Mark Spitz won seven gold medals in world record times at the Munich Olympics in Aug.-Sept.

Last U.S. combat troops left Vietnam Aug. 11. Pres. **Nixon** reelected Nov. 7 in landslide, carrying 49 states to defeat Sen. George McGovern (D, SD). Three astronauts, part of *Apollo 17*, made 6th and last lunar landing on Dec. 11. Full-scale **bombing of North Vietnam** resumed after Paris peace negotiations reached impasse Dec. 18.

The Godfather, directed by Francis Ford Coppola, is released.

1973 In *Roe v. Wade*, Supreme Court ruled, 7-2, Jan. 22, fetus not a person with constitutional rights and that right to privacy protected woman's decision to have abortion; states may not ban abortions during first three months of pregnancy but may regulate, not ban, abortions during second trimester.

Four-party **Vietnam peace pacts** signed in Paris Jan. 27. **End of military draft** announced on same day. Last U.S. troops left Vietnam Mar. 29. North Vietnam released some 590 U.S. prisoners by Apr. 1. Pres. Nixon announced, Apr. 30, resignation of top Nixon aides H. R. Haldeman and John Ehrlichman and firing of White House Counsel **John Dean** as a consequence of the widening **Watergate** scandal. Dean told Senate hearings June 25 that Nixon, his aides, and Justice Dept. had conspired to cover up Watergate facts. The U.S. officially ceased bombing in **Cambodia** at midnight Aug. 14 in accord with June congressional action.

Vice Pres. **Spiro Agnew**, Oct. 10, resigned and pleaded no contest to charge of tax evasion while Maryland governor. **Gerald R. Ford**, Oct. 12, became **first appointed vice president** under 25th Amendment; sworn in Dec. 6. The **"Saturday Night Massacre"** occurred Oct. 20, when Pres. Nixon ordered Atty. Gen. Elliot Richardson to fire Watergate special prosecutor **Archibald Cox**, who had sought handover of Nixon's subpoenaed **White House tapes**. Richardson refused to comply and resigned; Dep. Atty. Gen. William Ruckelshaus refused and was fired. Solicitor Gen. Robert Bork, as acting atty. gen., then fired Cox. Nixon administration named **Leon Jaworski**, Nov. 1, to succeed Cox.

Skylab, **first U.S. space station**, launched May 14. **Secretariat** became first Triple Crown winner since **Citation** in

1974: Pres. Richard Nixon resigns from office and departs the White House.

1948 by winning Belmont Stakes June 9 in record time. **Billie Jean King** defeated Bobby Riggs in three straight sets in tennis's nationally televised "Battle of the Sexes," Sept. 20. Total **ban on oil exports** to U.S. imposed by Arab oil-producing nations Oct. 19-21 after outbreak of an Arab-Israeli war; lifted Mar. 1974. Congress overrode Nov. 7 Pres. Nixon's veto of **war powers bill** curbing president's power to commit forces to hostilities abroad without congressional approval.

1974 On Apr. 8, **Hank Aaron** of the Atlanta Braves hit his 715th career home run to break Babe Ruth's record.

House Judiciary Committee opened **impeachment** hearings May 9 against Pres. Nixon. John Ehrlichman and three **White House "plumbers"** found guilty July 12 of conspiring to violate the civil rights of the psychiatrist of **Pentagon Papers** leaker Daniel Ellsberg by breaking into psychiatrist's office. Supreme Court ruled, 8-0, July 24 that Pres. Nixon had to turn over 64 **audio tapes of White House conversations**. House Judiciary Committee, in televised hearings July 24-30, recommended **articles of impeachment** against Pres. Nixon, involving conspiracy to obstruct justice in Watergate cover-up, abuses of power, and defiance of committee subpoenas.

Pres. **Nixon** announced his **resignation**, Aug. 8, and stepped down the next day. His support in Congress had begun to collapse Aug. 5 after release of tapes appearing to implicate him in Watergate cover-up. Vice Pres. **Ford** sworn in Aug. 9 as 38th U.S. president. Pres. Ford, Aug. 20, nominated **Nelson Rockefeller** to be vice president; Rockefeller sworn in Dec. 10. Citing need to move on, Pres. Ford, Sept. 8, issued **pardon to Nixon** for any federal crimes he committed while president.

New York Times published article Dec. 22 on CIA engagement in illegal domestic surveillance. Reports of other apparently illegal CIA activities, recorded in **"family jewels"** file kept by the CIA, leaked out over the years.

1975 Former Atty. Gen. John Mitchell and ex-presidential advisers H. R. Haldeman and John Ehrlichman found guilty Jan. 1 of **Watergate cover-up** charges. Mitchell released 1979, last of 25 jailed over scandal to leave prison.

Bill Gates and Paul Allen founded Microsoft, Apr. 4. U.S. launched **evacuation from Saigon** of Americans and some South Vietnamese Apr. 29 as Communist forces completed takeover of South Vietnam; **South Vietnamese** government officially surrendered Apr. 30. U.S. merchant ship *Mayaguez* and its crew of 39 seized by Cambodian forces in Gulf of Siam May 12. In rescue operation, U.S. Marines attacked

Koh Tang Island, recovered ship and crew but inadvertently left three Marines behind. Congress voted $405 mil for **South Vietnam refugees** May 16; 140,000 flown to U.S.

Publishing heiress **Patricia (Patty) Hearst**, kidnapped Feb. 5, 1974, by Symbionese Liberation Army (SLA), captured in San Francisco Sept. 18 with other militants. She was convicted Mar. 20, 1976, of bank robbery.

1976 In **right-to-die** case, New Jersey Supreme Court, Mar. 31, allowed comatose Karen Ann Quinlan to be removed from respirator; she survived until 1985. U.S. Supreme Court reinstated **death penalty**, July 2, subject to conditions.

U.S. celebrated **200th anniversary of independence** July 4 with festivals, parades, and New York City's Operation Sail, gathering of tall ships from around the world. **"Legionnaire's disease"** killed 29 people who attended American Legion convention July 21-24 in Philadelphia.

Viking I made successful landing on Mars, July 20. Two U.S. officers on routine mission near DMZ slain by **North Korean soldiers** Aug. 18; North Korea stated "regret."

1977 Convicted murderer Gary Gilmore executed by Utah firing squad Jan. 17; **first use of capital punishment** in U.S. since 1967. Pres. Jimmy Carter Jan. 21 pardoned most Vietnam War **draft evaders**.

Natural gas shortage caused by severe winter weather led Congress Feb. 2 to approve emergency gas bill temporarily authorizing reallocation from surplus areas. Pres. Carter signed act Aug. 4 creating new cabinet-level **Energy Dept.** FBI Dec. 7 released 40,000 pages of previously secret files relating to **Kennedy assassination**.

George Lucas's first *Star Wars* film released.

1978 Senate voted Apr. 18 to turn over **Panama Canal** to Panama on Dec. 31, 1999; Mar. 16 vote had given approval to treaty guaranteeing area's neutrality after the year 2000. Californians, June 6, approved **Proposition 13**, state constitutional amendment slashing property taxes.

Supreme Court, June 28, ruled that while race could be a factor in admission to institutions of higher education, **numerical quotas** could not be used.

Egyptian Pres. **Anwar al-Sadat** and Israeli Prem. **Menachem Begin** reached accord on "framework for peace," Sept. 17, after Pres. Carter-mediated talks at **Camp David**. New York's Chemical Bank Dec. 20 initiated industry-wide move to raise **lending rate** to near-record 11.75%.

1979 Partial meltdown released radioactive material Mar. 28 at nuclear reactor on **Three Mile Island** near Middletown, PA. American Airlines DC-10 **jetliner crashed** May 25 after losing an engine following takeoff from Chicago, killing 275 people.

In speech July 15, Pres. Carter spoke of national "crisis of confidence" and outlined proposed 10-year, $140-bil program to reduce **dependence on foreign oil**. Militant followers of **Ayatollah Khomeini** took hostage some 90 people, including 66 Americans, Nov. 4 at **American embassy in Tehran**, Iran. Khomeini demanded return of ailing former Shah Muhammad Reza Pahlavi to stand trial.

1980 Pres. Carter announced, Jan. 4, economic sanctions against USSR in retaliation for Soviet invasion of Afghanistan. At Carter's request, U.S. Olympic Committee voted, Apr. 12, against U.S. participation in **Moscow Summer Olympics**. At **Winter Olympics** in Lake Placid, NY, U.S. hockey team defeated Russian team Feb. 22 en route to gold medal in "miracle on ice."

Eight Americans were killed, Apr. 24, in ill-fated attempt to rescue hostages held by Iranian militants. **Mt. St. Helens**, in Washington state, erupted May 18. The blast, with others May 25 and June 12, left 57 dead. In sweeping victory, Nov. 4, **Ronald Reagan** (R) was elected 40th president, defeating incumbent Pres. Carter. Republicans gained control of Senate. Former Beatle **John Lennon** was shot and killed by Mark David Chapman, Dec. 8, in New York City.

1981 Minutes after Reagan's inauguration Jan. 20, 52 **American hostages in Iran** were freed after being held for 444 days. Pres. **Reagan** was shot and seriously wounded, Mar. 30, in Washington, DC; also seriously wounded were a Secret Service agent, a police officer, and Press Sec. **James Brady**. **John W. Hinckley Jr.** arrested, found not guilty by reason of insanity in 1982, and committed to mental institution.

World's **first reusable spacecraft**, space shuttle *Columbia*, sent into space, Apr. 12. U.S. Centers for Disease Control, June 5, reported first cases of what became known as **AIDS**.

1983: Sally Ride is the first American woman to travel in space.

Air controllers went on **strike** Aug. 3; most were fired by Pres. Reagan after defying back-to-work order. Reagan signed into law Aug. 13 **tax-cut legislation**, expected to save taxpayers $750 bil over five years, largest tax cut to date. The Senate confirmed, Sept. 21, appointment of **Sandra Day O'Connor** as **first female Supreme Court justice**.

1982 The 13-year-old Justice Dept. lawsuit against **AT&T** was settled Jan. 8. AT&T agreed to give up 22 Bell System companies and was allowed to expand. **Equal Rights Amendment**, sent to states in 1972, defeated when deadline for ratification passed June 30 with support from only 35 of the 38 states needed. The economy showed signs of recovery from a **recession** that began in mid-1981, as Dow Jones industrial average hit 1,016.93 Oct. 13, its highest level in 18 months.

NFL strike ended Nov. 16 after 57 days when players and team owners settled with $1.6-bil pact. Singer **Michael Jackson**'s album *Thriller*, released Nov. 30, became monumental best-seller. Retired dentist Dr. Barney B. Clark became **first permanent artificial heart recipient**, Dec. 2; he died Mar. 23, 1983. The House, Dec. 16, cited EPA administrator Anne Gorsuch for contempt after she refused to release records relating to enforcement of **Superfund** law.

1983 Pres. Reagan, Jan. 3, declared Times Beach, MO, a federal disaster area because of toxic **dioxin** in soil, prompting evacuations and town's closure. Harold Washington (D) elected Apr. 12 as **first black mayor of Chicago**. On Apr. 20, Pres. Reagan signed compromise bipartisan bill designed to save **Social Security** from bankruptcy.

Sally Ride became **first American woman to travel in space**, June 18, when space shuttle *Challenger* launched from Cape Canaveral, FL. On Sept. 1, **South Korean passenger jet** in Soviet air space was apparently misidentified and shot down; 269 people, including 61 Americans, killed.

On Oct. 23, 241 U.S. Marines and sailors were killed when TNT-laden **suicide truck bomb** blew up Marine barracks at Beirut International Airport in **Lebanon**. U.S. troops, with small force from six Caribbean nations, invaded **Grenada** Oct. 25; deposed Marxist regime.

1984 Seven regional companies took over **local telephone service** from AT&T, Jan. 1. On space shuttle *Challenger*'s fourth trip, launched Feb. 3, two astronauts became **first humans to fly free of a spacecraft**. On May 7, Vietnam War veterans reached settlement with chemical companies in class-action suit over the herbicide **Agent Orange**.

Former Vice Pres. **Walter Mondale** won Democratic presidential nomination, June 6. He chose Rep. **Geraldine Ferraro** (D, NY) as vice presidential candidate, first woman to be nominated for position by major political party. Pres. Reagan signed bill July 17 cutting federal transportation aid to states that keep their **drinking age** under 21. Pres. **Reagan** reelected Nov. 6 in Republican landslide, carrying 49 states for record 525 electoral votes. **Bernhard Goetz** shot and wounded four allegedly menacing teenage boys on NYC subway train, Dec. 22; acquitted of major charges but successfully sued.

1985 First international **AIDS conference** met in Atlanta, GA Apr. 15-17. Visiting Germany, Pres. Reagan, May 5, laid wreath at Bergen-Belsen Nazi concentration camp site and at

1985: Pres. Ronald Reagan is inaugurated for a second term after winning reelection over Walter Mondale in a landslide with 49 states and 525 electoral votes.

military cemetery at **Bitburg**, where some Nazis were buried. Philadelphia police bombed a rowhouse occupied by **MOVE radical group**, May 13; 11 killed, and fire damaged two blocks of houses. On June 14, **terrorists seized TWA jet** after takeoff from Athens, Greece, with 153 passengers and crew. Thirty-nine Americans held hostage for 17 days; one U.S. service member killed.

Reversing an Apr. 23 decision, the **Coca-Cola Co.** said, July 10, it would resume marketing soda made under its original "Classic" formula. **Live Aid** rock concert broadcast around the world July 13, raised $70 mil for famine relief in Ethiopia.

On Oct. 7, four **Palestinian hijackers** seized Italian cruise ship *Achille Lauro* in the Mediterranean for two days. One American, Leon Klinghoffer, killed. For first time in six years U.S. and Soviet leaders met at **summit in Geneva**, Nov. 19-20. **General Electric** agreed Dec. 11 to buy RCA Corp.

1986 The U.S. officially observed **Martin Luther King Jr. Day** for first time Jan. 20. Space shuttle *Challenger* exploded 73 seconds after liftoff, Jan. 28, killing six astronauts and Teacher in Space Project participant Christa McAuliffe. In four-day extravaganza in July, the U.S. celebrated 100th birthday of the **Statue of Liberty**.

The Senate confirmed, Sept. 17, Reagan's nomination of **William Rehnquist** as chief justice and **Antonin Scalia** as associate justice of U.S. Supreme Court. Congress completed action Oct. 2 overriding a veto to place economic sanctions on **South Africa**. Lebanese newspaper first broke news of **Iran-Contra scandal** Nov. 3, involving secret U.S. sale of arms to Iran and diversion of some of the proceeds to support the Contras, a right-wing, anti-Communist insurgent movement in Nicaragua.

Financier **Ivan Boesky** agreed Nov. 14 to pay $100 mil in fines and illicit profits for **insider trading**. Robert Penn Warren named America's **first poet laureate**.

1987 Pres. Reagan produced nation's **first trillion-dollar budget**, Jan. 5. FDA approved, Mar. 20, AZT—first drug shown to be effective in fight against **AIDS**. Nearly 1.4 mil so-called **illegal aliens** met May 4 deadline for applying for amnesty under immigration measure passed in 1986.

Joint public hearings by Senate and House committees investigating **Iran-Contra affair** opened May 5. Lt. Col. **Oliver North**, former National Security Council staff member, said he had believed all his activities were authorized by his superiors. Hearings ended Aug. 3. Pres. Reagan in speech to nation, Aug. 12, denied knowing of diversion of funds to Contras.

An **Iraqi missile** killed 37 sailors on the USS *Stark* in the Persian Gulf, May 17. Iraq called it an accident. The 200th anniversary of **U.S. Constitution** signing was observed, Sept. 17, in Philadelphia and around the U.S. **Stock market crashed**, Oct. 19, with the Dow Jones industrial average plummeting a then-record 508 points to 1,738, ending bull market that began mid-1982. Pres. Reagan and Soviet leader Mikhail Gorbachev Dec. 8, signed **pact to dismantle** all 1,752 U.S. and 859 Soviet intermediate- and shorter-range (300-3,400 mi) missiles.

1988 *Phantom of the Opera* opened Jan. 26; it would go on to be longest-running Broadway show ever. In report issued May 16, Surgeon Gen. C. Everett Koop declared **cigarettes addictive**.

A missile, fired from U.S. Navy warship *Vincennes* in the Persian Gulf, mistakenly struck a commercial **Iranian airliner**, July 3, killing all 290 aboard. **George H. W. Bush** (R) elected 41st U.S. president, Nov. 8, decisively defeating Massachusetts Gov. **Michael Dukakis** (D). **Pan Am Flight 103** exploded and crashed, due to terrorist bomb, into town of Lockerbie, Scotland, Dec. 21, killing all 259 people aboard and 11 on the ground. Investment firm **Drexel Burnham Lambert** agreed, Dec. 21, to plead guilty to insider trading and other violations, and pay penalties of $650 mil. U.S. suffered widespread **drought** conditions, the worst in over 50 years.

1989 Major oil spill occurred when *Exxon Valdez* struck Bligh Reef in Alaska's Prince William Sound, Mar. 24. Oliver North convicted, May 4, on charges related to **Iran-Contra scandal**. Conviction thrown out on appeal in 1991 because of his immunized testimony. TV comedy series *Seinfeld* premiered July 5 on NBC.

A measure to rescue **savings and loan industry** signed into law, Aug. 9, by Pres. Bush, launching largest federal rescue to date. Army Gen. **Colin Powell** became **first black chairman of Joint Chiefs of Staff** after being nominated Aug. 10 by Pres. Bush.

Baseball legend **Pete Rose** banned from game for life Aug. 24 for involvement with gamblers. **Hurricane Hugo** swept through the Carolinas Sept. 22, causing at least 86 deaths and $7 bil damage. An **earthquake** struck the San Francisco Bay area just before a World Series game, Oct. 17, causing 63 deaths.

L. Douglas Wilder (D) declared governor of Virginia Nov. 27, **first elected black governor** in U.S. history. U.S. troops invaded Panama, Dec. 20, overthrowing the government of **Manuel Noriega**. Noriega, wanted by U.S. authorities on drug charges, surrendered Jan. 3, 1990.

1990 Junk bond financier **Michael Milken** pleaded guilty to fraud-related charges, Apr. 14; agreed to pay $500 mil in restitution and sentenced Nov. 21 to 10 years in prison. Pres. Bush signed **Americans With Disabilities Act** barring discrimination against and requiring accommodations for the disabled, July 26.

Operation Desert Shield forces left for Saudi Arabia Aug. 7 to defend that country following invasion of **Kuwait** by Iraq, Aug. 2. David Souter confirmed Sept. 27 to serve on Supreme Court, replacing retiring Justice **William Brennan**. Pres. Bush Nov. 15 signed new **Clean Air Act**, focused on urban pollution, cancer-causing emissions from industrial sources.

1991 The U.S. and its allies defeated Iraq in **Persian Gulf War** and liberated Kuwait, which Iraq had invaded. They launched air attacks, Jan. 16, followed by ground war, starting Feb. 24; Bush declared cease-fire, Feb. 27.

An 8-month **recession** showed signs of having ended in Mar. The **Dow Jones** industrial average closed above 3,000 for first time, Apr. 17. Supreme Court Justice **Thurgood Marshall** announced, June 17, plans to retire. Senate, voting 52-48 on Oct. 15, confirmed nomination of **Clarence Thomas** to replace Marshall, after contentious hearings marked by allegations that Thomas had sexually harassed former aide Anita Hill. House Speaker Tom Foley announced Oct. 3 closure of **House Bank** by end of year after revelations that House members had written numerous bad checks.

1992 Major U.S. carrier Trans World Airlines (**TWA**) filed for bankruptcy, Jan. 31. **Riots** swept South Central Los Angeles Apr. 29 after jury acquitted four white police officers on all but one count in 1991 videotaped beating of black motorist **Rodney King**. Death toll in L.A. violence was put at 53. **27th Amendment**, regarding congressional pay raises, ratified May 7.

Hurricane Andrew ravaged South Florida and Louisiana Aug. 24-26, causing 65 deaths. White supremacist and fugitive Randall Weaver surrendered Aug. 31 after 11-day **FBI siege** at his **Ruby Ridge**, ID, cabin, during which his wife, son, and a deputy sheriff were killed.

Bill Clinton (D) elected 42nd president, Nov. 3, defeating Pres. Bush (R) and independent Ross Perot. A UN-sanctioned military force, led by U.S. troops, arrived in **Somalia** Dec. 9. Presidents of U.S., Canada, and Mexico Dec. 17 signed North American Free Trade Agreement (**NAFTA**), which took effect Jan. 1, 1994.

1993 A bomb exploded in a parking garage beneath the **World Trade Center** in New York City, Feb. 26, killing six. Four

1991: U.S. and allies force the Iraqi army to retreat from Kuwait in Operation Desert Storm.

men found guilty, Mar. 4, 1994. Four federal agents killed, Feb. 28, during unsuccessful raid on **Branch Davidian** compound near **Waco**, TX. A 51-day siege by agents ended Apr. 19 when the compound burned down, leaving more than 70 cult members dead. Eleven cult members acquitted Feb. 26, 1994, of deaths of federal agents.

Janet Reno became **first female attorney general** Mar. 12. Federal jury, Apr. 17, found two Los Angeles police officers guilty and two not guilty of violating civil rights of motorist **Rodney King** in 1991 videotaped beating.

In a May 14 plebiscite, voters in **Puerto Rico** supported continuing commonwealth status with U.S. **"Motor-voter" bill** signed by Pres. Clinton, May 20, easing voting procedures. **"Great Flood of 1993"** inundated parts of nine Midwestern states in summer, leaving about 50 dead and $15 bil in damages.

Pres. Clinton, July 2, approved recommendations that 33 major U.S. military bases be closed. On July 19 he announced **"don't ask, don't tell, don't pursue"** policy for homosexuals in the military. **Ruth Bader Ginsburg** sworn in, Aug. 10, as 107th Supreme Court justice, replacing retiring Justice **Byron White**. Pres. Clinton, Aug. 10, signed measure designed to **cut federal budget deficits** by $496 bil over five years, through spending cuts and new taxes. **Brady Bill**, a major gun-control measure, signed into law by Pres. Clinton Nov. 30.

1994 A predawn **earthquake** in the Los Angeles area, Jan. 17, claimed 61 lives. Pres. Clinton Feb. 3 lifted 19-year ban on U.S. trade with **Vietnam**. Byron De La Beckwith convicted Feb. 5 of 1963 murder of civil rights leader **Medgar Evers**. Longtime CIA officer **Aldrich Ames** and his wife charged, Feb. 21, with spying for Russians. Under plea bargain, he received life in prison, while she drew 63 months.

U.S. troops, Mar. 25, officially ended peacekeeping and humanitarian aid mission in **Somalia**, begun in 1992. Congressional committees, late July, began **Whitewater hearings**. Kenneth Starr named Aug. 5 as independent counsel to probe Whitewater affair. Major league **baseball players** went on strike following Aug. 11 games. World Series canceled; strike ended Apr. 25, 1995. Senate Majority Leader George Mitchell (D, ME), Sept. 26, dropped efforts to pass Pres. Clinton's **health-care reform** package.

Republicans gained control of both House and Senate in Nov. 8 elections after many years of Democratic control. House speaker **Tom Foley** (MA) was among the defeated Democrats.

1995 **Newt Gingrich** (R, GA) elected U.S. House speaker. A bill to end Congress's exemption from federal labor laws, first in series of measures in Republicans' **"Contract With America,"** cleared Congress Jan. 17; signed into law Jan. 23. Pres. Clinton, Jan. 31, authorized $20-bil loan to **Mexico**. Last UN peacekeeping troops withdrew from **Somalia** Feb. 28-Mar. 3, with aid of U.S. Marines. In **Haiti**, peacekeeping responsibilities were transferred from U.S. to UN forces Mar. 31, with U.S. providing 2,400 soldiers.

Truck **bomb exploded outside Oklahoma City federal office building** Apr. 19, killing 168 people; antigovernment extremist Timothy McVeigh arrested as key suspect, Apr. 21. U.S. space shuttle *Atlantis* made first in series of dockings with Russian space station *Mir*, June 29-July 4. The U.S. announced July 11 it was reestablishing **relations with Vietnam**.

Ten Muslim militants convicted, Oct. 1, in failed plot to blow up **UN Headquarters**, other buildings and assassinate political leaders. Former football star **O. J. Simpson** found not guilty Oct. 3 of June 1994 murders of former wife, Nicole Brown Simpson, and a friend of hers. Hundreds of thousands of black men participated in **Million Man March** and rally in Washington, DC, Oct. 16, organized by Rev. Louis Farrakhan.

Cumulative number of **AIDS** cases reported in the U.S. since 1981 passed 500,000 by Oct. 31, with more than 310,000 deaths. Five Americans among seven killed, Nov. 13, in **bombing** of U.S. military post in **Riyadh, Saudi Arabia**. Budget impasse between Congress and Pres. Clinton led to partial **government shutdown** Nov. 14; operations resumed Nov. 20 under continuing resolutions. After talks outside Dayton, OH, warring parties in **Bosnia and Herzegovina** reached agreement Nov. 21 to end their conflict; treaty signed Dec. 14, and U.S. peacekeeping troops arrived. A 1973 federal law imposing **55-mph speed limit** repealed Nov. 28.

1996 Senate, Jan. 26, approved, 87-4, Second Strategic Arms Reduction Treaty (**START II**) with Russia. Congress, Mar. 27-28, approved **line item veto**; struck down by Supreme Court, June 1998.

James and Susan McDougal convicted May 28 of fraud and conspiracy in **Whitewater** case; Arkansas Gov. Jim Guy Tucker (D) convicted on similar charges. The antitax **Freemen** surrendered to federal authorities June 13 after 81-day standoff near Jordan, MT; four were convicted, July 1998, of conspiring to defraud banks.

Bomb exploded at **Khobar Towers** military complex near Dhahran, Saudi Arabia, June 25, killing 19 American service personnel. Homemade pipe bomb exploded July 27 in **Atlanta**, GA, park during **Summer Olympics**; one person killed. Extremist Eric Robert Rudolph, arrested in May 2003, pleaded guilty to this and other bombings.

Major **welfare reform bill** signed into law, Aug. 22. Federal Defense of Marriage Act (**DOMA**), passed by wide margins and signed Sept. 21, barred federal recognition of same-sex marriages and permitted states to disregard same-sex marriages from other states. U.S. signed **Comprehensive Test Ban Treaty**, Sept. 24, which banned all nuclear weapons tests and explosions; Senate failed to ratify treaty. Pres. **Clinton reelected**, Nov. 5.

1997 **Madeleine Albright** sworn in as sec. of state Jan. 23, becoming first female State Dept. head. Former CIA official Harold Nicholson pleaded guilty, Mar. 3, to **spying for Russia**. Thirty-nine members of **Heaven's Gate** religious cult found dead in Rancho Santa Fe, CA, house Mar. 26, in apparent mass suicide.

Timothy McVeigh convicted of conspiracy and murder, June 2, in 1995 **Oklahoma City** bombing; executed June 2001. Co-conspirator Terry Nichols convicted Dec. 23 on related charges; later sentenced to life in prison. Two Islamic militants convicted, Nov. 12, of key roles in 1993 bombing of **World Trade Center**. The film *Titanic*, released Dec. 14, went on to win 11 Oscars and gross over $600 mil.

1998 Media outlets reported Jan. 21 on evidence of sexual relationship between Pres. Clinton and former White House intern **Monica Lewinsky**. Clinton initially denied affair, but in grand jury testimony and address to the nation, Aug. 17, acknowledged relationship that was "not appropriate." On Sept. 9, independent counsel **Kenneth Starr** sent findings to House; the Judiciary Committee, Oct. 5, voted 21-16 to recommend full inquiry. House, Dec. 19, approved two articles of **impeachment** charging Clinton with grand jury perjury and obstruction of justice in cover-up.

"Unabomber" Theodore Kaczynski, arrested in Montana in 1993, pleaded guilty Jan. 22 to California and New Jersey bombings that killed three people; sentenced in May to four life terms plus 30 years. **Karla Faye Tucker** executed Feb. 3; first woman executed in Texas in 135 years.

Bombs at U.S. embassies in Nairobi, Kenya, and Dar es Salaam, Tanzania, killed at least 257, Aug. 7; U.S. launched retaliatory strikes, Aug. 20, against targets in Afghanistan and Sudan. On Sept. 30, Pres. Clinton announced federal **budget surplus** of $70 bil for fiscal 1998, first since 1969.

Pres. Clinton, Nov. 13, settled suit by agreeing to pay $850,000 to **Paula Jones**, who alleged he had made an unwanted sexual advance in 1991. Biggest U.S. **tobacco companies**, in settlement Nov. 23, agreed to pay states and territories $206 bil over 25 years to cover public health costs.

1999 *The Sopranos* TV drama debuted, Jan. 10. Pres. **Clinton** was acquitted, Feb. 12, at end of Senate impeachment trial. Perjury article failed with 45 votes; obstruction of justice article drew 50-50 vote, short of the needed two-thirds.

Dr. **Jack Kevorkian** convicted of second-degree murder Mar. 26 in death of terminally ill man. One man pleaded guilty Apr. 5, another convicted Nov. 4, in 1998 kidnapping and beating death of **Matthew Shepard**, an openly gay student at the Univ. of Wyoming.

Eric Harris, 18, and Dylan Klebold, 17, killed 12 fellow students and a teacher Apr. 20 at **Columbine High School** in Littleton, CO, then fatally shot themselves. **John F. Kennedy Jr.** killed in crash of private plane July 16.

2000 Across U.S., midnight celebrations marked changeover to year 2000 on Jan. 1; feared **Y2K** computer glitch caused few problems. Vermont Gov. Howard Dean (D) on Apr. 26 signed first state law recognizing same-sex **civil unions**. Scientists from U.S. and Britain announced jointly, June 26, that they had determined structure of the **human genome**.

Six-year-old **Elián González** was returned to father in Cuba June 28, seven months after rescue from boat wreck in which his mother and other refugees drowned. **Tiger Woods** became youngest player, at age 24, to win all four of golf's majors, with record score in British Open, July 23.

Food and Drug Administration announced, Sept. 28, approval of **RU-486**, a pill that induces abortions. Seventeen U.S. sailors died Oct. 12 in terrorist bombing of USS *Cole*, which was refueling in Aden, Yemen.

On election night, Nov. 7, the winner of **Florida's electoral votes** remained uncertain, leaving national result in doubt. Florida Supreme Court, Dec. 8, ordered manual recount of certain ballots; on Dec. 12, U.S. Supreme Court reversed that decision, and Vice Pres. **Al Gore** (D), next day, conceded to Texas Gov. **George W. Bush** (R).

2001 **AOL-Time Warner merger** completed Jan. 11. FBI agent **Robert Hanssen** arrested Feb. 20, charged with spying for Soviet Union and Russia over 20-year period; under plea bargain, sentenced in 2002 to life in prison. **U.S. Navy spy plane** collided with Chinese fighter plane over South China Sea Apr. 1, killing fighter pilot; 24 U.S. crew members detained in Hainan until U.S. apology, Apr. 12.

Sen. **James Jeffords** (R, VT) May 24 left his party, giving Democrats control of Senate. Pres. George W. Bush signed, June 7, $1.35-tril tax-cut package. Bush announced Aug. 9 he would allow federal funding of limited research on existing **stem-cell** lines from human embryos.

On morning of **Sept. 11**, two hijacked commercial airliners struck **World Trade Center twin towers** in New York City in **worst-ever terrorist attack** on American soil. A third hijacked plane destroyed a portion of the **Pentagon**; a fourth crashed in a field near Shanksville, PA. Some 3,000 people were killed, including about 2,750 at World Trade Center. Five people died and 14 became ill from exposure to **anthrax** through U.S. postal system, Oct. 4-Nov. 21.

U.S. and Britain, Oct. 7, launched airstrike campaign against Afghan-based terrorist organization **al-Qaeda** and Afghanistan's ruling **Taliban** militia. Pres. Bush created **Office of Homeland Security**, Oct. 8, and on Oct. 26 signed USA **Patriot Act**, with wide-ranging provisions aimed at preventing terrorism. **Taliban** surrendered Kabul, Nov. 13, and fled from Kandahar, their stronghold, Dec. 7. U.S. government, Dec. 11, indicted al-Qaeda member **Zacarias Moussaoui** as Sept. 11 co-conspirator; he pleaded guilty, sentenced in May 2006 to life in prison. Operation in Afghanistan's **Tora Bora** cave complex, Dec. 12-17, failed to capture al-Qaeda leader **Osama bin Laden**.

2001: The attacks of Sept. 11, 2001, kill more than 2,750 people in New York, including 343 firefighters.

Leading energy-trading company **Enron** filed for bankruptcy, Dec. 2. Pres. Bush announced, Dec. 13, U.S. withdrawal from **1972 Antiballistic Missile Treaty** with Russians.

2002 Taliban and al-Qaeda fighters captured in Afghanistan flown to U.S. naval base at **Guantánamo Bay** in Cuba, starting Jan. 11.

In State of the Union address, Jan. 29, Pres. Bush called Iran, Iraq, and North Korea part of **"axis of evil."** By Mar. 6, 1,200 U.S. troops were involved in **Operation Anaconda** against al-Qaeda and Taliban forces in Afghanistan. Independent prosecutor's report, Mar. 20, found insufficient evidence that Pres. Clinton or Hillary Clinton committed any crime in connection with **Whitewater**. Pres. Bush, Mar. 27, signed into law McCain-Feingold **campaign-finance reform bill** banning unregulated, unrestricted "soft money" donations; part of bill struck down by Supreme Court, June 2007.

Ceremonial last girder removed May 30 from **World Trade Center** site, signaling end of massive clean-up and recovery operation. **WorldCom** filed for bankruptcy, July 21.

"Shoe-Bomber" Richard Reid pleaded guilty Oct. 4 to all charges stemming from incident aboard plane in Dec. 2001; sentenced Jan. 2003 to life in prison. On Oct. 10-11 the House, 296-133, and Senate, 77-23, gave Bush backing to use military force against **Iraq**. Bush administration revealed Oct. 16 that **North Korea** had acknowledged developing nuclear arms. Bush signed measure, Nov. 25, creating cabinet **Dept. of Homeland Security**.

U.S. Catholic bishops, Nov. 13, approved revised policies dealing with priests who sexually abuse minors. Cardinal **Bernard Law**, accused of covering up sexual abuse by priests, resigned as archbishop of Boston Dec. 13. **Trent Lott** (R, MS) bowed out as new Senate majority leader Dec. 20 after remarks apparently supporting segregation.

2003 On Jan. 10-11, Gov. George Ryan (R) pardoned or **commuted death sentences** of all 171 on Illinois death row.

Space shuttle *Columbia* broke apart Feb. 1 during descent toward planned landing; all seven crew members killed. Report issued Aug. 26 blamed damage sustained during liftoff; also cited "broken safety culture" at NASA. Senate, Mar. 6, approved the **Strategic Offensive Reductions Treaty** (SORT, or Moscow Treaty) for reducing nuclear stockpiles signed in 2002 by U.S. and Russian leaders.

U.S.-led military offensive aimed at ousting **Saddam Hussein** got underway Mar. 19, when 40 Tomahawk cruise missiles hit targets in Baghdad. U.S. forces Mar. 21 seized oil fields near Basra. By Apr. 9, U.S. forces reported control over much of Baghdad. Pres. Bush, speaking from aircraft carrier May 1, declared **end of major combat operations in Iraq**; insurgents continued to mount attacks.

Pres. Bush signed bill May 28 providing $330 bil in **tax cuts** over several years. A power failure caused **blackouts** affecting some 50 mil people, mostly in northeastern U.S. and Canada, on Aug. 14.

The Roman Catholic archdiocese of Boston agreed to pay up to $85 mil in **sex abuse settlement** announced Sept. 9. Californians, Oct. 7, voted to recall Gov. Gray Davis (D) and replace him with actor-turned-politician **Arnold Schwarzenegger** (R). Rev. V. Gene Robinson consecrated Nov. 2 as Episcopal Church's **first openly gay bishop**.

Senate, Nov. 3, approved $87.5 bil for **U.S. military forces in Iraq** and help rebuilding the country. Virginia jury, Nov. 17, found **John Muhammad** guilty in 2002 Washington, DC, area **sniper attacks** that killed 10; sentenced to death. Another Virginia jury found accomplice **Lee Malvo** guilty, Dec. 18; sentenced to life without parole.

Pres. Bush signed bill Dec. 8 to overhaul **Medicare**, adding prescription drug benefit and expanding role of private insurance companies. **Saddam Hussein captured** by U.S. forces Dec. 13, in underground hideout southeast of Tikrit.

2004 *The Lord of the Rings: The Return of the King* won 11 Oscars, Feb. 29.

Photos showing abuse of **Abu Ghraib prison** inmates in Iraq by American soldiers emerged Apr. 3. On May 17, as a result of a Nov. 2003 court decision, Massachusetts became the first state in which **same-sex marriage** was legal.

U.S.-led coalition transferred power to interim Iraqi government, June 28. **9/11 Commission Report**, released July 22, called for restructuring U.S. intelligence operations.

Boston Red Sox won World Series Oct. 27, for first time since 1918.

Pres. **Bush reelected** Nov. 2, with 286 electoral votes, defeating Sen. John Kerry (D, MA), with 251. Republicans increased majorities in Senate and House. Pres. Bush signed intelligence reform bill Dec. 17, creating a director of national intelligence.

2005 Two U.S. soldiers found guilty, Jan. 14, in **Abu Ghraib** prisoner abuses in Iraq and sentenced to prison terms.

Condoleezza Rice became first black woman sec. of state, Jan. 26. **Alberto Gonzales** became first Hispanic U.S. atty. gen., Feb. 3. **Terri Schiavo**, in a persistent vegetative state since 1990, died Mar. 31, 13 days after feeding tube was removed following legal battle.

Vanity Fair article revealed May 31 that former FBI official W. Mark Felt was **"Deep Throat"**—key source for *Washington Post* reporters Bob Woodward and Carl Bernstein probing 1972 Watergate break-in.

Hurricane Katrina hit Gulf coast, Aug. 29, causing devastation in Louisiana, Mississippi, and Alabama. Breaches in levees on Lake Pontchartrain, Aug. 30, flooded New Orleans. Relief efforts widely criticized as insufficient.

Chief Justice **William H. Rehnquist** died Sept. 3. Bush Sept. 5 nominated as successor **John G. Roberts Jr.**; on Sept. 29 he was confirmed by Senate, 78-22, and sworn in as 17th chief justice. On Oct. 31 Bush nominated **Samuel A. Alito Jr.** to replace retiring Justice Sandra Day O'Connor; confirmed Jan. 31, 2006.

House Majority Leader **Tom DeLay** (R, TX) indicted in Texas Sept. 28 on money laundering charges; later convicted.

New York Times, Dec. 16, reported that Pres. Bush in 2002 had secretly authorized National Security Agency to **eavesdrop without court warrant** on people in U.S. suspected of terrorist activities. Congress passed and Bush, Dec. 30, signed **anti-torture legislation**.

2006 Former top Republican lobbyist **Jack Abramoff** pleaded guilty Jan. 3 to bribery and other charges; in plea agreement, promised to cooperate with investigation into his dealings with members of Congress.

U.S. Supreme Court ruled June 29 that Pres. Bush's system for trying terrorism detainees at **Guantánamo Bay** was unauthorized under federal law and Geneva Conventions. Bush, July 19, issued his **first veto**, on bill to end funding constraints on human embryonic **stem cell research**.

British authorities announced Aug. 10 they had foiled terrorist plot to use **liquid explosives** on flights between Britain and U.S. Pres. Bush Sept. 6 confirmed existence of **secret overseas prisons** for terrorism suspects run by CIA. Bush signed bill Oct. 26 authorizing 700-mi fence along **U.S.-Mexico border**.

Democrats won control of House and Senate in **midterm congressional elections** Nov. 7. Pres. Bush announced Nov. 8 that Defense Sec. **Donald Rumsfeld**, a focus of criticism over Iraq war, had resigned.

2007 Rep. Nancy Pelosi (D, CA) chosen Jan. 4 as **first woman Speaker of the House**. On Jan. 10, Pres. Bush announced troop **"surge"** in Iraq, backed by Lt. Gen. **David Petraeus**, new top U.S. commander there.

2007: Rep. Nancy Pelosi (D, CA) is chosen as first woman Speaker of the U.S. House of Representatives; she passed the gavel to John Boehner (R, OH) four years later.

Reports of substandard conditions at **Walter Reed Army Medical Center** in Washington, DC, led to ousters of military officials, Mar. 1-2. I. Lewis **"Scooter" Libby**, former chief of staff for Vice Pres. Cheney, found guilty Mar. 6 of perjury and obstructing justice in investigation into a leak exposing undercover CIA agent; Bush commuted sentence.

A senior at **Virginia Tech** killed 27 students and five faculty members on Apr. 16 before killing himself. On Apr. 18, Supreme Court upheld, 5-4, a 2003 federal law that banned so-called **partial birth abortions**.

U.S. Senate and House May 24 approved Iraq and Afghanistan war funding, with benchmarks for withdrawal of troops from Iraq; Congress also raised federal hourly **minimum wage** from $5.15 to $7.25 over two years.

Dow Jones industrial average closed over 14,000 July 19, just 59 trading days after passing 13,000. Pres. Bush issued an executive order July 20 banning any "cruel, inhuman, or degrading" treatment of **imprisoned terror suspects**. *Harry Potter and the Deathly Hallows*, final novel in J. K. Rowling's series, released July 21, earning record U.S. sales.

A **Minneapolis highway bridge** collapsed Aug. 1, causing 13 deaths. Congress, Aug. 4, cleared bill allowing **National Security Agency** to monitor communications without court warrants if believed related to terrorism. Barry Bonds tied Hank Aaron's all-time career **home-run record** at 755 on Aug. 4 in San Diego; hit No. 756 on Aug. 7.

José Padilla convicted of conspiracy in terrorism case, Aug. 16; sentenced to 17 years, 4 months. Atty. Gen. **Alberto Gonzales**, blamed for alleged politically motivated firings of U.S. attorneys, announced resignation Aug. 27.

Report by former U.S. Sen. George J. Mitchell, released Dec. 13, presented evidence of **performance-enhancing drug use** by 86 Major League Baseball players.

Under law signed Dec. 17, New Jersey became the first state to **repeal the death penalty** since U.S. Supreme Court reinstated it in 1976. An energy bill mandating an increase in automobile **fuel-economy standards** to 35 mi per gallon by 2030 signed by Pres. Bush Dec. 19.

2008 Sen. **John McCain** (AZ) won New Hampshire primary, Jan. 8; clinched 2008 Republican presidential nomination by early Mar. Among Democrats, Sen. **Barack Obama** (IL) moved ahead of closest rival Sen. **Hillary Clinton** (NY) to clinch nomination in early June.

The Federal Reserve cut key interest rates, Jan. 22 and 30, to aid U.S. economy; $168-bil **economic stimulus** package, signed Feb. 13 by Pres. Bush, provided tax rebates.

In Mar. 18 speech, Sen. Obama discussed America's racial divide and condemned inflammatory rhetoric used by Rev. **Jeremiah Wright**, his former pastor.

U.S. Supreme Court ruled June 12 that foreign prisoners at **Guantánamo Bay** could legally challenge detention. **Oil prices spiked** above $140 per barrel in June; national average price for gallon of regular gas topped $4.

Sec. of State Condoleezza Rice signed agreements in Czech Republic, July 8, and Poland, Aug. 20, to place components of a U.S. **missile defense system** there (agreements rescinded by Obama administration, 2009). Measure signed July 10 by Pres. Bush expanded government power to spy on suspected terrorists. U.S., Sept. 1, gave Iraqi forces security responsibilities in Anbar province, formerly center of a Sunni insurgency. U.S. airstrike in **Afghanistan** village, Aug. 22, killed up to 90 civilians.

Meeting Aug. 25-28, Democrats nominated **Obama** for president and Sen. **Joe Biden** (DE) for vice president. Meeting Sept. 1-4, Republicans nominated **McCain** for president and Alaska Gov. **Sarah Palin** for vice president.

With financial system in crisis, federal government Sept. 7 took control of mortgage finance companies **Fannie Mae** and **Freddie Mac**. A week later, investment titan **Merrill Lynch** agreed to sell itself to Bank of America for $50 bil, and **Lehman Brothers** declared bankruptcy after finding no buyer. The Fed Sept. 16 took control of insurance giant **AIG**, giving it a credit line that expanded to $144 bil by Oct. 31.

On Sept. 20, a Treasury Dept. plan was introduced to purchase up to $700 bil of **"toxic" mortgage-backed securities** to restore confidence. Legislation to implement Troubled Assets Relief Program (**TARP**) failed in the House, Sept. 29, sending Dow Jones industrial average down 778 points. Revised **bailout plan** passed Senate Oct. 1, 74-25, and House

Oct. 3, 263-171; gave Treasury immediate access to half of $700 bil in TARP funds. On Oct. 21 Fed pledged $540 bil as a backup to protect money market funds.

Barack Obama elected, Nov. 4, as **first African-American president** in U.S. history, earning 53% of popular vote and 365 of 538 electoral votes. Democrats also increased majorities in House and Senate. California voters approved **Proposition 8**, banning same-sex marriages in the state.

U.S. government Nov. 23 announced plan to provide $20 bil in cash and up to $306 bil more as backup to protect ailing **Citigroup** from potential mortgage losses. Pres.-elect Obama Nov. 24 named **Timothy Geithner** to be treasury sec.; he was confirmed Jan. 26, 2009. The Dow dropped 7.7% Dec. 1 after reports that manufacturing had hit 26-year low and that U.S. economy fell into **recession** in Dec. 2007.

Pres.-elect Obama named former rival **Hillary Clinton**, Dec. 1, to be sec. of state (confirmed Jan. 2009). Illinois Gov. **Rod Blagojevich** (D) arrested Dec. 9, accused of seeking to sell Senate seat being vacated by Obama. Convicted in a state senate trial, he was removed from office, Jan. 2009. Financier **Bernard Madoff** arrested Dec. 11 for **Ponzi scheme**; sentenced to 150 years in jail in guilty plea, June 2009. Fed, Dec. 16, cut benchmark interest rate to near zero. On Dec. 19, Pres. Bush announced that $17 bil in **TARP funds** would be used to help keep **General Motors** and **Chrysler** afloat.

2009 Inaugurated Jan. 20 as president, **Barack Obama** issued executive orders Jan. 22 restricting CIA interrogation practices and calling for U.S. military prison at **Guantánamo Bay**, Cuba, to close (closing blocked by Congress).

Treasury Sec. Geithner, Feb. 10, outlined $2-tril program to stabilize banking and ease credit markets with **stress tests** for banks. Pres. Obama signed **stimulus** bill Feb. 17, with $212 bil in tax cuts and $575 bil in new spending; introduced $275-bil program Feb. 18 to aid homeowners. Geithner, Mar. 23, introduced Public-Private Investment Program (PPIP), offering incentives to encourage purchases of **"toxic assets."**

Vermont, Apr. 7, became first state with law allowing **same-sex marriage** without prior judicial mandate. Justice Dept. Apr. 16 released G.W. Bush-administration memos offering legal rationale for harsh CIA interrogation methods, including **waterboarding**. After outbreak of **swine flu**, in Mexico and then in U.S., officials declared public health emergency Apr. 26.

Chrysler LLC filed for bankruptcy protection Apr. 30; union given stake in reorganized company. Obama, May 19, tightened vehicle **fuel efficiency** standards. **General Motors** filed for bankruptcy June 1, under plan providing new federal funds. On June 9, 10 financial firms received go-ahead from U.S. Treasury to return some $68 bil in **TARP funds**.

George Tiller, Kansas doctor who performed **late-term abortions**, murdered May 31; anti-abortion activist was convicted Jan. 2010 and sentenced to life in prison.

Speaking June 4 in Egypt, Pres. Obama called for "new beginning" in relations with **Muslim world**. U.S. military completed **withdrawal from Iraq's cities** and towns June 30. **Sonia Sotomayor** confirmed Aug. 6 for U.S. Supreme Court vacancy left by retirement of **David Souter**; sworn in Aug. 8, she became first Hispanic to join the Court.

Government reported Oct. 29 that real GDP grew at 3.5% annual rate in July-Sept., signaling technical **end of recession**. However, **unemployment** in Oct. topped 10%. Obama Nov. 6 signed measure extending unemployment benefits and $8,000 tax credit for first-time **homebuyers**.

Pres. Obama announced Oct. 30 an end to travel and immigration restrictions on people with **AIDS**. On Nov. 5, 12 soldiers and a civilian were killed in shooting at **Ft. Hood**, TX; Army Maj. Nidal Malik Hasan, shot and captured, later sentenced to death. Obama Dec. 1 announced a **surge** of 30,000 troops to **Afghanistan**. He received **Nobel Peace Prize**, Dec. 10, and brokered multination **greenhouse-gas accord**, reached Dec. 18 in Copenhagen.

Detroit-bound air passengers, Dec. 25, thwarted attempt by Nigerian man to ignite **explosives** in his underwear.

2010 On Jan. 19, **Scott Brown** (R) elected to U.S. Senate seat vacated by Sen. **Edward Kennedy** (D, MA), ending Democrats' filibuster-proof majority. In **Citizens United** v. FEC, U.S. Supreme Court Jan. 21 held that corporations and unions could spend unlimited funds on advertising to influence election outcomes.

U.S. and other coalition troops launched offensive against **Taliban** in Helmand Province, Afghanistan, Feb. 13. Pres. Obama, Mar. 18, signed $18-bil **job-stimulus** measure. On Mar. 21, the House voted, 219-212, with no GOP support, to approve **"Obamacare"** health-care reform bill as passed by Senate in Dec. 2009. The measure, signed by Obama on Mar. 23, aimed in part at extending health insurance to millions of uninsured.

Meeting Apr. 8 in Prague, Obama and Russian Pres. **Dmitri Medvedev** signed New Strategic Arms Reduction Treaty, or **New START** (ratified by Senate Dec. 2010). On Apr. 15, Obama outlined plans for **NASA** to send manned missions to an asteroid by 2025 and to Mars by the mid-2030s.

On Apr. 20, a gas explosion and fire engulfed *Deepwater Horizon* drilling platform in the Gulf of Mexico, killing 11 people and creating a huge oil spill; record settlement of about $20 bil in penalties and claims against energy giant BP approved in 2016 by a federal court.

Arizona Gov. **Jan Brewer** (R), Apr. 23, signed controversial **immigration** measure (key provisions struck down by U.S. Supreme Court, June 2012). Pres. Obama May 10 nominated **Elena Kagan** to replace retiring Supreme Court Justice **John Paul Stevens**; confirmed by Senate, Aug. 5. Obama June 23 named Gen. **David Petraeus** commander in Afghanistan, replacing Gen. Stanley McChrystal, who was forced to resign after remarks criticizing the administration. Ten **Russian agents** were arrested June 27 on spy charges; later exchanged for four Russians convicted of spying for the UK and U.S.

Obama signed major **financial reform** bill, July 21, and measure to aid small business, Sept. 27.

More than 75,000 Afghanistan documents, many of them classified, were published July 25 on website run by **Wiki-Leaks** and in some news outlets. Last U.S. combat unit left Iraq Aug. 19 and Obama, Aug. 31, declared **U.S. combat mission in Iraq ended**; however, 50,000 troops remained in noncombat units.

In Nov. 2 elections **Republicans gained control** of the U.S. House but not the Senate. The **Fed** Nov. 3 announced plan to buy $600 bil worth of Treasury securities in effort to stimulate economy.

Bipartisan **Simpson-Bowles** commission released report Dec. 1 calling for deep cuts in government spending and entitlements and for lowering taxes while closing loopholes, to stabilize national debt. Obama, Dec. 17, signed $858-bil compromise measure that temporarily extended both **Bush-era tax cuts** and unemployment insurance benefits while reducing Social Security payroll tax for one year. **"Don't ask, don't tell"** policy for gays in the military repealed Dec. 22.

2011 **John Boehner** (R, OH) elected House Speaker, Jan. 5. Gunman in Tucson, AZ, Jan. 8, killed six people and injured 13 others, including Rep. **Gabrielle Giffords** (D, AZ); shooter **Jared Loughner** sentenced, Nov. 2012, to seven life terms plus 140 years. A measure to limit **collective bargaining** by most public sector employees, championed by Wisconsin Gov. **Scott Walker** (R), passed state legislature Mar. 9-10.

Former MLB slugger **Barry Bonds** was convicted Apr. 13 of obstructing justice for evasive answers to a grand jury investigating banned **performance-enhancing drugs** (conviction overturned in 2015). Pres. Obama Apr. 27 denounced rumors by so-called **birthers** and released his birth certificate.

On May 2, in Abbottabad, Pakistan, a CIA-led squadron of U.S. Navy SEALs killed al-Qaeda leader **Osama bin Laden**.

The single **deadliest U.S. tornado** in more than a half-century hit Joplin, MO, May 22, claiming about 160 lives. Congress passed and Obama, May 26, signed measure extending key provisions of USA **Patriot Act**.

House rejected measure to raise federal **debt ceiling** without compensating deficit reductions, May 31. **Budget control act** shaped by Vice Pres. Joe Biden and Senate minority leader **Mitch McConnell** (R, KY) passed by bipartisan votes, Aug. 1-2. It called for raising the debt ceiling and cutting some $900 bil in spending, with another $1.5 tril in cuts to be worked out by supercommittee. Standard & Poor's, Aug. 5, downgraded nation's **credit rating**.

U.S. stepped up **drone attacks** against jihadists in **Yemen** after Pres. **Ali Abdullah Saleh** and others were wounded June 3 in a rocket attack. Former Illinois Gov. **Rod Blagojevich** (D) was convicted in a retrial on corruption charges June 27 and sentenced to 14 years in prison. Gen.

2011: As administration officials monitored the operation from Washington, U.S. forces kill Osama bin Laden, mastermind of the Sept. 11, 2001, terrorist attacks.

David Petraeus confirmed June 30 to replace **Leon Panetta** as CIA director; Panetta confirmed July 1 to replace retiring Defense Sec. **Robert Gates**. NASA's **space shuttle** program ended with landing of the *Atlantis*, July 21.

A left-wing movement that began Sept. 17 in New York City as **Occupy Wall Street** expanded to demonstrations across the U.S. and overseas.

Anwar al-Awlaki, a U.S. citizen and Muslim cleric linked to terrorist attacks in U.S., was killed Sept. 30 in U.S. drone attack in Yemen. Formalities Dec. 12-15 marked what was said to be the end of the **U.S. military mission in Iraq**. Last U.S. troop convoy left Dec. 18. Since 2003 U.S.-led invasion, nearly 4,500 U.S. service members had been killed and 32,000 wounded.

2012 Pres. Obama Feb. 10 announced compromise **health insurance** mandate that avoided requiring religiously affiliated employers to directly provide contraceptive coverage. Congress voted Feb. 17 to extend **payroll tax cut** through 2012.

Obama May 9 became first sitting president to endorse **same-sex marriage**. Social networking giant **Facebook**'s initial public offering raised $16 bil May 18. Wisconsin Gov. **Scott Walker** (R) easily survived June 5 recall election. Obama June 15 announced executive action ending deportation of qualified young **undocumented immigrants**. **Jerry Sandusky**, former assistant football coach at **Penn State**, was convicted June 22 in sexual abuse of 10 boys.

U.S. Supreme Court, June 28, upheld **Obamacare** penalties for those who do not obtain health insurance. Twelve people were killed and 70 injured, July 20, in **movie-theater shooting** in Aurora, CO; James Holmes was convicted in July 2015 and sentenced to multiple life terms. A gunman opened fire Aug. 5 at a **Sikh temple** in Oak Creek, WI, leaving six dead, before killing himself. NASA rover *Curiosity* landed on Mars Aug. 6.

Former Massachusetts Gov. **Mitt Romney** and running mate Rep. **Paul Ryan** (WI) were nominated at GOP convention Aug. 27-30. Meeting Sept. 4-6, Democrats nominated the **Obama-Biden** ticket. *Mother Jones* magazine, Sept. 17, posted a video, covertly recorded at a May 2012 fundraiser, in which Romney appeared to write off 47% of Americans as dependent on government handouts.

U.S. facility in **Benghazi**, Libya, was attacked by terrorists Sept. 11-12 and ambassador **Chris Stevens** and three other Americans died; report released Dec. 18 blamed State Dept. for "grossly inadequate" security. An inspector general's report, Sept. 19, cited serious flaws in Justice Dept. gun-buying **Operation Fast and Furious**.

On Oct. 22, **Lance Armstrong**, accused in doping scandal, was banned from cycling. **Hurricane Sandy** made landfall in the U.S. Oct. 29, devastating mid-Atlantic coastal areas, and leaving over 200 dead.

Pres. **Obama reelected** Nov. 6, with 51% of popular vote. Voters in Maine, Maryland, and Washington approved ballot measures to legalize **same-sex marriage**, becoming the first states to do so by popular vote. Colorado and Washington became the first to vote to allow recreational use of **marijuana**.

Retired Army Gen. **David Petraeus** resigned as CIA director Nov. 9 after FBI cybercrime investigation uncovered his extramarital affair and related security breaches. Adam Lanza fatally shot 20 children and six adults before killing himself, Dec. 14, at **Sandy Hook** Elementary School in Newtown, CT.

With **"fiscal cliff"** of automatic budget cuts (sequestration) and expiring tax breaks looming, Vice Pres. Biden and Senate Minority Leader **McConnell** negotiated compromise, Dec. 30-31, to make Bush-era tax cuts permanent up to certain ceilings, while deferring possible sequestration.

2013 Pres. Barack Obama was officially sworn in for second term, Jan. 20. Sen. **John Kerry** (D, MA) confirmed as secretary of state, Jan. 29; former Sen. **Chuck Hagel** (R, NE) confirmed Feb. 26 as defense secretary. **Sequestration** took effect Mar. 1, triggering $1.2 tril in spending cuts to defense and domestic programs over 10 years.

Two bombs at the **Boston Marathon**, Apr. 15, killed three spectators and injured 264. Bombers were identified as Chechen immigrant brothers **Dzhokhar** and **Tamerlan Tsarnaev**. In shootout Apr. 18 with police, Tamerlan was shot, run over by vehicle driven by his brother, and died. Dzhokhar was captured Apr. 19; convicted and sentenced to death in 2015.

IRS executive **Lois Lerner**, May 10, apologized for the agency's singling out of groups with conservative-leaning names but denied any political motivation and disclaimed personal wrongdoing. She was put on leave after invoking the Fifth Amendment before a House committee, May 22. **Boy Scouts** of America leadership voted May 23 to let openly **gay youths** be members.

The *Guardian* newspaper, June 5, disclosed details of a classified **Natl. Security Agency surveillance** program that monitored phone records and tracked emails and internet activity. **Edward Snowden**, a contractor for the CIA, claimed responsibility for leaks after having left the U.S. The **Supreme Court**, June 25, struck down a key provision of the 1965 **Voting Rights Act** and, June 26, struck down provision in the 1996 Defense of Marriage Act (**DOMA**) that denied federal benefits to **same-sex couples**.

A jury found **George Zimmerman** not guilty July 13 in the 2012 killing of **Trayvon Martin**, an unarmed black teenager, in Sanford, FL. Zimmerman, a neighborhood watch volunteer, claimed self-defense. **Detroit** filed for bankruptcy protection, July 18. Once-fugitive mobster **James "Whitey" Bulger** was found guilty of murder and other charges Aug. 12 and sentenced to life in prison.

A military judge Aug. 21 sentenced Army Pfc. **Chelsea Manning** (formerly Bradley Manning) to 30 years in prison for releasing over 700,000 U.S. military and diplomatic documents to the **WikiLeaks** website. Army Staff Sgt. **Robert Bales**, who pleaded guilty to having killed 16 Afghan civilians, was sentenced to life Aug. 23. A gunman killed 12 people at the **Navy Yard** in Washington, DC, Sept. 16; he was killed by responding police.

After Congress failed to produce a budget agreement, the U.S. **government partially shut** down Oct. 1. With public widely opposed to the shutdown, the Senate, Oct. 16, approved a compromise measure, agreed to by House. Federal and state **health insurance exchanges** opened Oct. 1 in rollout of a signature Obamacare feature, but the federal exchange website was plagued by design flaws and technical glitches. **JPMorgan Chase** agreed, Nov. 19, to $13-bil settlement on charges of deceptive practices in sales of troubled mortgages.

White House panel, Dec. 18, issued sweeping recommendations aimed at limiting **NSA surveillance** and increasing oversight. **Dow Jones** industrial average closed 2013 up 26.5%, its biggest yearly gain since 1995.

2014 Janet Yellen confirmed Jan. 6 as first woman to chair the **Federal Reserve. General Motors**, Feb. 7, began a recall of vehicles with defects ultimately linked to more than 120 deaths. **Toyota** agreed Mar. 19 to a $1.2-bil criminal fine on charges that it had concealed information about defective parts.

Pres. Obama reported Apr. 1 that 7.1 mil people had signed up for coverage via state and federal health insurance marketplaces under **Obamacare**, despite federal website glitches and other issues.

A heavily armed man killed 6 people and injured 13 others near the Univ. of California-**Santa Barbara**, May 23.

U.S. Army Sgt. **Bowe Bergdahl**, captured by the Taliban in 2009, was freed in a prisoner exchange May 31; the U.S. released five Taliban members from Guantánamo Bay. Veterans Affairs Sec. **Eric Shinseki** resigned May 30 after revelations that VA hospitals had manipulated schedules to disguise long waiting times. Congress July 30-31 passed a bill allowing veterans to be treated at non-VA hospitals under certain conditions.

The EPA, June 2, proposed new regulations requiring states to reduce power plants' **carbon dioxide emissions** by 2030. House Majority Leader **Eric Cantor** (R, VA) lost primary June 10 to **Dave Brat**, a Tea Party-backed political novice.

The militant group known as the Islamic State of Iraq and Syria (ISIS) expanded territory in Iraq and Syria, declaring a **"caliphate"** June 29. Obama announced June 19 that the U.S. would send up to 300 military advisers to Iraq; he authorized **airstrikes**, Aug. 7, to disrupt ISIS operations there.

U.S. Supreme Court ruled June 30 that "closely held corporations" could not be required to offer **contraceptive** coverage under Obamacare provisions against owners' religious beliefs. A white police officer shot and killed unarmed black 18-year-old **Michael Brown**, Aug. 9, in a confrontation in **Ferguson**, MO, precipitating sometimes violent protests; a grand jury declined to indict the officer Nov. 24.

ISIS released video Aug. 19 showing beheading of kidnapped American journalist **James Foley**; later videos showed beheading of American journalist **Steven Sotloff** (released Sept. 2) and U.S. aid worker **Peter Kassig** (Nov. 16).

Bank of America agreed Aug. 21 to settlement on charges it had misled investors into buying toxic mortgage-backed securities. Former Virginia Gov. **Bob McDonnell** (R) convicted Sept. 4 on corruption charges (conviction overturned by U.S. Supreme Court ruling, June 2016).

U.S. announced Sept. 16 it would send 3,000 military personnel to West Africa in response to **Ebola** epidemic. A man armed with a knife broke into the White House, Sept. 19, sparking congressional inquiry into security lapses; **Secret Service** Dir. Julia Pierson resigned Oct. 1.

Congress authorized $500 mil to arm and train **Syrian rebels**; bill signed Sept. 19 by Obama. Afghan and U.S. officials signed agreement Sept. 30 providing for 9,800 American and at least 2,000 NATO **troops to remain** beyond formal end of combat mission in Dec. 2014. U.S. federal jury Oct. 22 convicted four former guards employed by **Blackwater** security firm (now known as Academi) in 2007 shootings that killed 17 Iraqi civilians. New York City's **One World Trade Center**, tallest building in the Western Hemisphere, welcomed first tenants Nov. 3.

GOP gained control of Senate and strengthened hold on House in **midterm elections** Nov. 4. Obama Nov. 7 approved an approximate doubling of U.S. noncombat military personnel in Iraq, to about 3,000. Labor Dept. announced Nov. 7 that the Oct. **unemployment rate** had dipped to 5.8%, lowest since July 2008.

Obama and Chinese Pres. **Xi Jinping** announced agreement Nov. 12 to reduce carbon outputs in effort to fight **climate change**. Obama Nov. 20 announced **executive actions on**

2014: The fatal police shooting of unarmed black 18-year-old Michael Brown sparks large-scale protests in Ferguson, MO, and draws attention to racial disparities in law enforcement.

immigration that could affect an estimated 4-5 mil undocumented immigrants. (Implementation was blocked pending resolution of a legal challenge.)

House Intelligence Committee report, released Nov. 21, found no intelligence failure prior to 2012 **Benghazi** attack but concluded there was inadequate protection at the facility in Libya.

Tamir Rice, a black 12-year-old boy, was fatally shot by a white police officer, Nov. 22, in **Cleveland**, OH; he had been carrying a pellet gun. A grand jury in Dec. 2015 decided against indicting the officer. A grand jury decided Dec. 3 not to indict a New York City police officer for using a non-regulation chokehold while trying to detain **Eric Garner**, a black man who had died July 17 in custody; protests broke out in **New York City** and other cities, turning violent in some. A black man shot and killed two New York City police officers in their patrol car, Dec. 20, then killed himself.

A Senate Intelligence Committee report released Dec. 9 condemned CIA use of **enhanced interrogation techniques** as both ineffective and more brutal than acknowledged. Hackers accessed Sony Pictures Entertainment data and, Dec. 16, threatened violence against U.S. theaters that showed *The Interview*, a comedy about plot to assassinate North Korean dictator **Kim Jong Un**.

Pres. Obama and Cuban Pres. **Raúl Castro** Dec. 17 announced that their countries would work to reestablish diplomatic relations, broken since 1959 Communist takeover. A U.S.-led operation and multinational NATO alliance formally ended combat missions in **Afghanistan** Dec. 28 after over 13 years; 2,215 Americans had been killed and more than 20,000 wounded there since Oct. 2001.

The **Dow Jones** industrial average closed up 7.5% for the year, in sixth straight year of growth. The Centers for Disease Control confirmed 667 **measles** cases for 2014, a record high since health officials declared the disease eliminated from the U.S. in 2000.

2015 **Standard & Poor's** agreed Feb. 3 to pay $1.4 bil to settle suits charging it had issued inflated ratings for subprime mortgage bonds. **Morgan Stanley**, Feb. 15, agreed to pay $2.6 bil to resolve Justice Dept. claims it had misrepresented the quality of mortgage-backed securities. Oregon Gov. **John Kitzhaber** (D) resigned effective Feb. 18 over influence peddling scandal; his replacement, **Kate Brown** (D), became the country's first openly bisexual governor.

The FCC, voting 3-2, Feb. 26, approved **net neutrality** regulations. Former CIA Dir. **David Petraeus** reached a plea deal Mar. 3 with the Justice Dept. over charges he had shared highly classified information with his biographer and lover; sentenced to probation and fined. Justice Dept. Mar. 4 released a review exposing widespread **mistreatment of African Americans** by the Ferguson, MO, police department, and mandated sweeping policy changes.

A New York court Mar. 5 approved an $8.5-bil settlement between **Bank of America** and investors in mortgage securities issued by the former **Countrywide Financial Corp.**, which it had bought in 2008. Shareholders of insurance giant **AIG**, Mar. 20, won approval to receive $970.5-mil., settling claims that they had been misled about exposure to high-risk subprime mortgage loans.

The race for the 2016 **Republican presidential nomination** opened with the Mar. 23 candidacy announcement of Sen. **Ted Cruz** (TX). Billionaire real estate mogul **Donald Trump** announced his outsider candidacy June 14, pledging to "make America great again" and denouncing past trade deals and illegal immigrants from Mexico. Former Florida Gov. **Jeb Bush** entered June 15. Among the 14 other major candidates to announce were Sen. **Marco Rubio** (FL), Apr. 13; retired neurosurgeon **Ben Carson** and former Hewlett-Packard CEO **Carly Fiorina**, May 4; Wisconsin Gov. **Scott Walker**, July 13; and Ohio Gov. **John Kasich**, July 21.

In the **Democratic presidential race**, former first lady, senator (NY), and Sec. of State **Hillary Clinton** launched her campaign Apr. 12, in a video in which she promised to be a champion of "everyday Americans." She was the presumed frontrunner despite a developing controversy over her use of a private email account and server for official State Dept. business. Self-described democratic socialist Sen. **Bernie Sanders** (I, VT), announced his candidacy for the Democratic nomination, May 26. Others announcing included former Maryland Gov. **Martin O'Malley**, May 30.

Facing a fourth year of severe drought, California Gov. **Jerry Brown** (D) issued the state's first-ever **mandatory water restrictions** Apr. 1. GOP governors in Indiana and Arkansas, Apr. 2, signed so-called **religious freedom laws**, revised after objections that they could authorize denial of services based on sexual orientation or gender identification.

On Apr. 11, Pres. Obama met in Panama with **Cuban Pres. Raúl Castro** in the first formal talks between leaders of the two countries in over 50 years. The U.S. dropped Cuba from its list of state sponsors of terrorism May 29.

A 25-year-old black man, **Freddie Gray**, died Apr. 19 from a spinal cord injury sustained while being transported in a **Baltimore** police van. The incident spurred riots; six police officers were indicted but none were convicted (all pending charges dropped as of July 2016). The U.S. Senate Apr. 23 confirmed **Loretta Lynch** as attorney general, 56-43.

ISIS forces completed capture of key Iraqi city of **Ramadi**, May 17. Pres. Obama June 2 signed a bill to end the National Security Agency's **bulk collection of phone data**; after six months, responsibility for the collected data would shift to telecom companies, with NSA access requiring a warrant.

American Pharoah became first horse in 37 years to claim thoroughbred racing's **Triple Crown**, after winning the 147th Belmont Stakes, June 6 in Elmont, NY. Los Angeles June 13 enacted a phased-in $15 **minimum hourly wage**.

A 21-year-old white gunman fatally shot nine African Americans, June 17, at Emanuel African Methodist Episcopal Church, in **Charleston**, SC. A website linked to the alleged shooter, Dylann Roof, showed him with the **Confederate flag**, leading several states, including South Carolina, to remove that flag from state grounds.

The **Supreme Court** June 25 ruled 6-3, in *King v. Burwell*, that federal subsidies for health-care coverage under **Obamacare** were legal in all states. In *Obergefell v. Hodges*, June 26, the Court ruled, 5-4, that a constitutional right to marry existed for **same-sex couples** in any state. In the aftermath, county clerk **Kim Davis** of Rowan County, KY, was jailed Sept. 3 for ignoring a federal judge's orders to issue marriage licenses to same-sex couples; she was released Sept. 8.

Defense Sec. **Ashton Carter** July 7 told a Senate committee that a three-year, $500-mil program to train some 15,000 Syrian moderate opposition fighters against ISIS had ended up with just 60 recruits in training. The federal Office of Personnel Management July 9 announced hackers had stolen personal information of about 22 mil people in 2014 **data breaches**.

Iran and six world powers led by the U.S. formally agreed July 14 on a deal to limit **Iranian nuclear capability** for the next 15 years, in return for a lifting of economic sanctions. Israeli Prime Min. **Benjamin Netanyahu**, Mar. 3, had addressed a joint session of Congress to express opposition; opponents in the U.S. Senate failed, Sept. 10, to muster the 60 votes needed to block passage. After a nine-year journey, NASA's *New Horizons* spacecraft, July 14, carried out the first-ever flyby of **Pluto**.

U.S. and **Cuba** reopened embassies in their respective countries July 20, reestablishing relations. Pres. Obama Aug. 3 unveiled the EPA's final plan for imposing nationwide limits on **carbon dioxide** output from the electric power sector.

Shaken by China's apparent economic slowdown, the Dow plunged 1,089 points when trading opened Aug. 24, and fell 588 points for the day. **General Motors** agreed Sept. 17 to pay $900 mil to settle a Justice Dept. criminal investigation into its failure to recall an ignition switch defect that had led to more than 120 deaths.

A federal judge Sept. 3 nullified a four-game suspension imposed on New England Patriots quarterback **Tom Brady** by NFL Commissioner **Roger Goodell** for supposed misconduct in **"Deflategate,"** the Patriots' alleged intentional underinflation of footballs for the AFC championship game in Jan. 2015.

During first U.S. visit, Sept. 22-27, Roman Catholic leader **Pope Francis** spoke before a joint session of Congress, calling on lawmakers to end the death penalty and take action on immigration reform and climate change. Following protracted conflict with party conservatives, House Speaker **John Boehner** (R, OH) Sept. 25 announced he would resign both his speakership and his congressional seat at the end of

2015: A Supreme Court decision effectively legalizes same-sex marriage nationwide.

Oct. Narrowly avoiding a government shutdown, the House Sept. 30 followed the Senate in passing a stopgap measure funding federal agencies and Planned Parenthood through Dec. 11.

Russia, Sept. 30, began **airstrikes in Syria** that it claimed targeted ISIS; Western sources said the strikes were mostly aimed at U.S.-backed rebels. A U.S. plane bombed an **Afghanistan hospital** operated by **Doctors Without Borders**, Oct. 3, killing more than 40; Pres. Obama apologized for the incident, which U.S. officials attributed to a belief that the facility had been used by the Taliban. In the face of escalating conflict, Obama Oct. 15 said he would keep 5,500 U.S. troops in Afghanistan into 2017.

A 26-year-old student opened fire Oct. 1 at a community college in **Roseburg, OR**, killing an instructor and eight students; he killed himself after being injured by responding police.

Officials from the U.S. and 11 other nations completed negotiations, Oct. 5, on terms of the **Trans-Pacific Partnership** (TPP), intended to eliminate thousands of tariffs between member countries. Obama in June had gained "fast-track" trade promotion authority (TPA), allowing him to eventually submit the TPP to Congress for a vote without amendments.

The House passed a **budget bill**, Oct. 28, that increased spending by $80 bil through 2017 and raised the federal debt ceiling ahead of a Nov. 3 debt-default deadline. The Senate followed on Oct. 30. Rep. **Paul Ryan** (R, WI) was elected speaker of the House, Oct. 29.

An Oct. 22 joint mission by U.S. and Iraqi forces freed about 70 hostages held by **ISIS** in the Iraqi province of Kirkuk; one U.S. soldier was fatally wounded. On Oct. 30, Obama announced he would deploy dozens of special operations forces to help fight ISIS in **Syria**.

After years of delay, and a veto action in Feb., Pres. Obama, Nov. 6 announced a final decision against building the **Keystone XL oil pipeline**. Two civilians and a police officer were killed and nine wounded Nov. 27 at a **Planned Parenthood** clinic in Colorado Springs, CO; the alleged shooter was arrested after a five-hour standoff.

A married man and woman fatally shot 14 people and injured 21 at a Dec. 2 holiday party for the man's employer, the **San Bernardino** (CA) County Dept. of Public Health; the couple were killed in a shootout with police. Defense Sec. **Ash Carter** Dec. 3 announced that all combat positions would be open to women, starting in 2016. The U.S. Justice Dept. announced Dec. 7 a civil rights investigation into the **Chicago Police Department**, two weeks after release of a police video that showed a white officer fatally shooting black teenager Laquan McDonald without apparent cause.

Pres. Obama Dec. 10 signed into law a revision of the **No Child Left Behind** education law that gave more discretion to states and localities. Officials representing the U.S. and 195 other parties reached agreement in Paris, Dec. 12, on a plan to reduce greenhouse gases linked to **climate change**. The Federal Reserve, Dec. 16, raised its key **interest rates** a fraction of a percent from near-zero levels of the past seven years. Pres. Obama signed a combined $1.8-tril spending and tax relief package Dec. 18, for which newly installed House Speaker **Paul Ryan** had helped gain GOP support.

Patrick Henry's Speech to the Virginia Convention

The following is an excerpt from Patrick Henry's speech to the Virginia Convention, which met at St. John's Church in Richmond, on Mar. 23, 1775, to react to British oppression.

Gentlemen may cry, peace, peace—but there is no peace. The war is actually begun! The next gale that sweeps from the north will bring to our ears the clash of resounding arms! Our brethren are already in the field! Why stand we here idle? What is it that gentlemen wish? What would they have? Is life so dear, or peace so sweet, as to be purchased at the price of chains and slavery? Forbid it, Almighty God! I know not what course others may take; but as for me, give me liberty, or give me death!

Adoption of the Declaration of Independence

On June 7, 1776, Richard Henry Lee, who had issued the first call for a congress of the colonies, introduced in the Continental Congress at Philadelphia a resolution declaring "that these United Colonies are, and of right ought to be, free and independent states, that they are absolved from all allegiance to the British Crown, and that all political connection between them and the state of Great Britain is, and ought to be, totally dissolved."

The resolution, seconded by John Adams on behalf of the Massachusetts delegation, came up again June 11 when a committee of five chaired by Thomas Jefferson (VA) was appointed to express the purpose of the resolution in a declaration of independence. The other four were John Adams, Benjamin Franklin (PA), Robert R. Livingston (NY), and Roger Sherman (CT).

Drafting the Declaration was assigned to Jefferson, who worked on a portable desk of his own construction in a room at Market and 7th St. The committee reported the result on June 28, 1776. The members of the Congress suggested a number of changes, which Jefferson called "deplorable." They did not approve Jefferson's arraignment of the British people and King George III for encouraging and fostering the slave trade, which Jefferson called "an execrable commerce." They eliminated 630 words and added 146, leaving 1,322 words in the final draft. In its final form, capitalization was erratic. Jefferson had written that men were endowed with "inalienable" rights; in the final copy it came out as "unalienable."

The Lee-Adams resolution of independence was adopted by 12 yeas on July 2—the actual date of the act of independence. The Declaration, which explains the act, was adopted July 4.

After the Declaration was adopted, July 4, 1776, it was turned over to printer John Dunlap to be printed on broadsides. The original copy was lost and one of his broadsides was attached to a page in the journal of the Congress. It was read aloud July 8 in Philadelphia; Easton, PA; and Trenton, NJ. On July 9, it was read by order of Gen. George Washington to the troops assembled on the Common in New York City (now City Hall Park).

The Continental Congress of July 19, 1776, adopted the following resolution:

"Resolved, That the Declaration passed on the 4th, be fairly engrossed on parchment with the title and stile of 'The Unanimous Declaration of the thirteen United States of America' and that the same, when engrossed, be signed by every member of Congress." (Engrossing meant clearly writing out an official document.)

Not all delegates who signed the engrossed Declaration had been present on July 4. Among them were Robert Morris (PA), William Williams (CT), and Samuel Chase (MD), who signed on Aug. 2. Oliver Wolcott (CT), George Wythe (VA), Richard Henry Lee (VA), and Elbridge Gerry (MA) signed in Aug. and Sept.; Matthew Thornton (NH) joined the Congress Nov. 4 and signed later. Thomas McKean (DE) rejoined Washington's army before signing and said later that he signed in 1781.

Charles Carroll of Carrollton was appointed a delegate by Maryland on July 4, 1776, presented his credentials July 18, and signed the engrossed Declaration on Aug. 2. Born Sept. 19, 1737, he was 95 years old and the last surviving signer when he died Nov. 14, 1832.

Two Pennsylvania delegates who did not support the Declaration July 4, 1776, were replaced. The four New York delegates did not have authority from their state to vote on July 4. On July 9, the New York state convention authorized its delegates to approve the Declaration, and the Congress was so notified on July 15, 1776. The four signed the Declaration on Aug. 2.

Declaration of Independence

The Declaration of Independence was adopted by the Continental Congress in Philadelphia on July 4, 1776. John Hancock was president of the Congress, and Charles Thomson was secretary. A copy of the Declaration, engrossed (i.e., written in a clear hand) on parchment, was signed by members of Congress on and after Aug. 2, 1776. On Jan. 18, 1777, Congress ordered that "an authenticated copy, with the names of the members of Congress subscribing the same, be sent to each of the United States, and that they be desired to have the same put on record." Authenticated copies were printed in broadside form in Baltimore, where the Continental Congress was then in session. The following text is that of the original printed by John Dunlap in Philadelphia for the Continental Congress. The original is on display at the National Archives in Washington, DC.

In CONGRESS, July 4, 1776.
A DECLARATION
By the REPRESENTATIVES of the
UNITED STATES OF AMERICA,
In GENERAL CONGRESS assembled.

When in the Course of human Events, it becomes necessary for one People to dissolve the Political Bands which have connected them with another, and to assume among the Powers of the Earth, the separate and equal Station to which the Laws of Nature and of Nature's God entitle them, a decent Respect to the Opinions of Mankind requires that they should declare the causes which impel them to the Separation.

We hold these Truths to be self-evident, that all Men are created equal, that they are endowed by their Creator with certain unalienable Rights, that among these are Life, Liberty, and the Pursuit of Happiness—That to secure these Rights, Governments are instituted among Men, deriving their just Powers from the Consent of the Governed, that whenever any Form of Government becomes destructive of these Ends, it is the Right of the People to alter or to abolish it, and to institute new Government, laying its Foundation on such Principles, and organizing its Powers in such Form, as to them shall seem most likely to effect their Safety and Happiness. Prudence, indeed, will dictate that Governments long established should not be changed for light and transient Causes; and accordingly all Experience hath shewn, that Mankind are more disposed to suffer, while Evils are sufferable, than to right themselves by abolishing the Forms to which they are accustomed. But when a long Train of Abuses and Usurpations, pursuing invariably the same Object, evinces a Design to reduce them under absolute Despotism, it is their Right, it is their Duty, to throw off such Government, and to provide new Guards for their future Security. Such has been the patient Sufferance of these Colonies; and such is now the Necessity which constrains them to alter their former Systems of Government. The History of the present King of Great Britain is a History of repeated Injuries and Usurpations, all having in direct Object the Establishment of an absolute Tyranny over these States. To prove this, let Facts be submitted to a candid World.

He has refused his Assent to Laws, the most wholesome and necessary for the public Good.

He has forbidden his Governors to pass Laws of immediate and pressing Importance, unless suspended in their Operation till his Assent should be obtained; and when so suspended, he has utterly neglected to attend to them.

He has refused to pass other Laws for the Accommodation of large Districts of People, unless those People would relinquish the Right of Representation in the Legislature, a Right inestimable to them, and formidable to Tyrants only.

He has called together Legislative Bodies at Places unusual, uncomfortable, and distant from the Depository of their Public Records, for the sole Purpose of fatiguing them into Compliance with his Measures.

He has dissolved Representative Houses repeatedly, for opposing with manly Firmness his Invasions on the Rights of the People.

He has refused for a long Time, after such Dissolutions, to cause others to be elected; whereby the Legislative Powers, incapable of Annihilation, have returned to the People at large for their exercise; the State remaining in the mean time exposed to all the Dangers of Invasion from without, and Convulsions within.

He has endeavoured to prevent the Population of these States; for that Purpose obstructing the Laws for Naturalization of Foreigners; refusing to pass others to encourage their Migrations hither, and raising the Conditions of new Appropriations of Lands.

He has obstructed the Administration of Justice, by refusing his Assent to Laws for establishing Judiciary Powers.

He has made Judges dependent on his Will alone, for the Tenure of their Offices, and the Amount and payment of their Salaries.

He has erected a Multitude of new Offices, and sent hither Swarms of Officers to harrass our People, and eat out their Substance.

He has kept among us, in Times of Peace, Standing Armies, without the consent of our Legislatures.

He has affected to render the Military independent of, and superior to the Civil Power.

He has combined with others to subject us to a Jurisdiction foreign to our Constitution, and unacknowledged by our Laws; giving his Assent to their Acts of pretended Legislation:

For Quartering large bodies of armed troops among us:

For protecting them, by a mock Trial, from Punishment for any Murders which they should commit on the Inhabitants of these States:

For cutting off our Trade with all Parts of the World:

For imposing Taxes on us without our Consent:

For depriving us, in many Cases, of the Benefits of Trial by Jury:

For transporting us beyond Seas to be tried for pretended Offences:

For abolishing the free System of English Laws in a neighbouring Province, establishing therein an arbitrary Government, and enlarging its Boundaries, so as to render it at once an Example and fit Instrument for introducing the same absolute Rule into these Colonies:

For taking away our Charters, abolishing our most valuable Laws, and altering fundamentally the Forms of our Governments:

For suspending our own Legislatures, and declaring themselves invested with Power to legislate for us in all Cases whatsoever.

He has abdicated Government here, by declaring us out of his Protection and waging War against us.

He has plundered our Seas, ravaged our Coasts, burnt our towns, and destroyed the Lives of our People.

He is, at this Time, transporting large Armies of foreign Mercenaries to complete the works of Death, Desolation, and Tyranny, already begun with circumstances of Cruelty

and Perfidy, scarcely paralleled in the most barbarous Ages, and totally unworthy the Head of a civilized Nation.

He has constrained our fellow Citizens taken Captive on the high Seas to bear Arms against their Country, to become the Executioners of their Friends and Brethren, or to fall themselves by their Hands.

He has excited domestic Insurrections amongst us, and has endeavoured to bring on the Inhabitants of our Frontiers, the merciless Indian Savages, whose known Rule of Warfare, is an undistinguished Destruction, of all Ages, Sexes and Conditions.

In every stage of these Oppressions we have Petitioned for Redress in the most humble Terms: Our repeated Petitions have been answered only by repeated Injury. A Prince, whose Character is thus marked by every act which may define a Tyrant, is unfit to be the Ruler of a free People.

Nor have we been wanting in Attentions to our British Brethren. We have warned them from Time to Time of Attempts by their Legislature to extend an unwarrantable Jurisdiction over us. We have reminded them of the Circumstances of our Emigration and Settlement here. We have appealed to their native Justice and Magnanimity, and we have conjured them by the Ties of our common Kindred to disavow these Usurpations, which, would inevitably interrupt our Connections and Correspondence. They too have been deaf to the Voice of Justice and of Consanguinity. We must, therefore, acquiesce in the Necessity, which denounces our Separation, and hold them, as we hold the rest of Mankind, Enemies in War, in Peace, Friends.

We, therefore, the Representatives of the UNITED STATES OF AMERICA, in General Congress, Assembled, appealing to the Supreme Judge of the World for the Rectitude of our Intentions, do, in the Name, and by Authority of the good People of these Colonies, solemnly Publish and Declare, That these United Colonies are, and of Right ought to be, Free and Independent States; that they are absolved from all Allegiance to the British Crown, and that all political Connection between them and the State of Great Britain, is and ought to be totally dissolved; and that as Free and Independent States, they have full Power to levy War, conclude Peace, contract Alliances, establish Commerce, and to do all other Acts and Things which Independent States may of right do. And for the support of this declaration, with a firm Reliance on the Protection of Divine Providence, we mutually pledge to each other our Lives, our Fortunes, and our sacred Honor.

JOHN HANCOCK, President.

Attest.

CHARLES THOMSON, Secretary.

Signers of the Declaration of Independence

Delegate (state)	Occupation	Birthplace	Born	Died
Adams, John (MA)	Lawyer	Braintree (Quincy), MA	Oct. 30, 1735	July 4, 1826
Adams, Samuel (MA)	Political leader	Boston, MA	Sept. 27, 1722	Oct. 2, 1803
Bartlett, Josiah (NH)	Physician, judge	Amesbury, MA	Nov. 21, 1729	May 19, 1795
Braxton, Carter (VA)	Farmer	Newington Plantation, VA	Sept. 10, 1736	Oct. 10, 1797
Carroll, Charles, of Carrollton (MD)	Merchant	Annapolis, MD	Sept. 19, 1737	Nov. 14, 1832
Chase, Samuel (MD)	Judge	Princess Anne, MD	Apr. 17, 1741	June 19, 1811
Clark, Abraham (NJ)	Surveyor	Elizabethtown, NJ	Feb. 15, 1726	Sept. 15, 1794
Clymer, George (PA)	Merchant	Philadelphia, PA	Mar. 16, 1739	Jan. 23, 1813
Ellery, William (RI)	Lawyer	Newport, RI	Dec. 22, 1727	Feb. 15, 1820
Floyd, William (NY)	Soldier	Brookhaven, NY	Dec. 17, 1734	Aug. 4, 1821
Franklin, Benjamin (PA)	Printer, publisher	Boston, MA	Jan. 17, 1706	Apr. 17, 1790
Gerry, Elbridge (MA)	Merchant	Marblehead, MA	July 17, 1744	Nov. 23, 1814
Gwinnett, Button (GA)	Merchant	Gloucester, England	c. 1735	May 19, 1777
Hall, Lyman (GA)	Physician	Wallingford, CT	Apr. 12, 1724	Oct. 19, 1790
Hancock, John (MA)	Merchant	Braintree (Quincy), MA	Jan. 12, 1737	Oct. 8, 1793
Harrison, Benjamin (VA)	Farmer	Charles City County, VA	Apr. 5, 1726	Apr. 24, 1791
Hart, John (NJ)	Farmer	Stonington, CT	c. 1711	May 11, 1779
Hewes, Joseph (NC)	Merchant	Kingston, NJ	Jan. 23, 1730	Nov. 10, 1779
Heyward, Thomas, Jr. (SC)	Lawyer, farmer	St. Luke's Parish, SC	July 28, 1746	Mar. 6, 1809
Hooper, William (NC)	Lawyer	Boston, MA	June 17, 1742	Oct. 14, 1790
Hopkins, Stephen (RI)	Judge, educator	Providence, RI	Mar. 7, 1707	July 13, 1785
Hopkinson, Francis (NJ)	Judge, author	Philadelphia, PA	Oct. 2, 1737	May 9, 1791
Huntington, Samuel (CT)	Judge	Windham, CT	July 3, 1731	Jan. 5, 1796
Jefferson, Thomas (VA)	Lawyer	Shadwell, VA	Apr. 13, 1743	July 4, 1826
Lee, Francis Lightfoot (VA)	Farmer	Westmoreland County, VA	Oct. 14, 1734	Jan. 11, 1797
Lee, Richard Henry (VA)	Farmer	Westmoreland County, VA	Jan. 20, 1732	June 19, 1794
Lewis, Francis (NY)	Merchant	Llandaff, Wales	Mar. 21, 1713	Dec. 31, 1802
Livingston, Philip (NY)	Merchant	Albany, NY	Jan. 15, 1716	June 12, 1778
Lynch, Thomas, Jr. (SC)	Farmer	Winyah, SC	Aug. 5, 1749	(at sea) 1779
McKean, Thomas (DE)	Lawyer	New London, PA	Mar. 19, 1734	June 24, 1817
Middleton, Arthur (SC)	Farmer	Charleston, SC	June 26, 1742	Jan. 1, 1787
Morris, Lewis (NY)	Farmer	Morrisania (Bronx County), NY	Apr. 8, 1726	Jan. 22, 1798
Morris, Robert (PA)	Merchant	Liverpool, England	Jan. 31, 1734	May 8, 1806
Morton, John (PA)	Judge	Ridley, PA	c. 1724	Apr. 1777
Nelson, Thomas, Jr. (VA)	Farmer	Yorktown, VA	Dec. 26, 1738	Jan. 4, 1789
Paca, William (MD)	Judge	Abingdon, MD	Oct. 31, 1740	Oct. 23, 1799
Paine, Robert Treat (MA)	Judge	Boston, MA	Mar. 11, 1731	May 12, 1814
Penn, John (NC)	Lawyer	Caroline County, VA	May 17, 1741	Sept. 14, 1788
Read, George (DE)	Judge	Cecil County, MD	Sept. 18, 1733	Sept. 21, 1798
Rodney, Caesar (DE)	Judge	Dover, DE	Oct. 7, 1728	June 29, 1784
Ross, George (PA)	Judge	New Castle, DE	May 10, 1730	July 14, 1779
Rush, Benjamin (PA)	Physician	Byberry Twp. (Philadelphia), PA	Jan. 4, 1746	Apr. 19, 1813
Rutledge, Edward (SC)	Lawyer	Charleston, SC	Nov. 23, 1749	Jan. 23, 1800
Sherman, Roger (CT)	Lawyer	Newton, MA	Apr. 19, 1721	July 23, 1793
Smith, James (PA)	Lawyer	Ireland	c. 1719	July 11, 1806
Stockton, Richard (NJ)	Lawyer	Princeton, NJ	Oct. 1, 1730	Feb. 28, 1781
Stone, Thomas (MD)	Lawyer	Charles County, MD	c. 1743	Oct. 5, 1787
Taylor, George (PA)	Ironmaster	Ireland	c. 1716	Feb. 23, 1781
Thornton, Matthew (NH)	Physician	Ireland	c. 1714	June 24, 1803
Walton, George (GA)	Judge	Cumberland County, VA	c. 1741	Feb. 2, 1804
Whipple, William (NH)	Merchant, judge	Kittery, ME	Jan. 14, 1730	Nov. 28, 1785
Williams, William (CT)	Merchant	Lebanon, CT	Apr. 8, 1731	Aug. 2, 1811
Wilson, James (PA)	Judge	Carskerdo, Scotland	Sept. 14, 1742	Aug. 21, 1798
Witherspoon, John (NJ)	Clergyman, educator	Gifford, Scotland	Feb. 5, 1723	Nov. 15, 1794
Wolcott, Oliver (CT)	Judge	Windsor, CT	Nov. 20, 1726	Dec. 1, 1797
Wythe, George (VA)	Lawyer	Elizabeth City County, VA	c. 1726	June 8, 1806

Origin of the Constitution

The War of Independence was conducted by delegates from the original 13 states, who composed the Congress of the United States of America, known as the Continental Congress. In 1777 the Congress submitted to the legislatures of the states the Articles of Confederation and Perpetual Union, which were ratified by New Hampshire, Massachusetts, Rhode Island, Connecticut, New York, New Jersey, Pennsylvania, Delaware, Virginia, North Carolina, South Carolina, Georgia, and finally, in 1781, Maryland.

The first article read: "The stile of this confederacy shall be the United States of America." This did not signify a sovereign nation, because the states delegated only those powers they could not handle individually, such as to wage war, make treaties, and contract debts for general expenses (e.g., paying the army). Taxes for payment of such debts were levied by the individual states. The president signed himself "President of the United States in Congress assembled," but here the United States were considered in the plural, a cooperating group.

When the war was over, it became evident that a stronger federal union was needed. The Congress left the initiative to the legislatures. Virginia in Jan. 1786 appointed commissioners to meet with representatives of other states; delegates from Virginia, Delaware, New York, New Jersey, and Pennsylvania met at Annapolis. Alexander Hamilton prepared their call asking delegates from all states to meet in Philadelphia in May 1787 "to render the Constitution of the federal government adequate to the exigencies of the union." Congress endorsed the plan on Feb. 21, 1787. Delegates were appointed by all states except Rhode Island.

The convention was called for May 14, 1787, but a quorum was not present until May 25. George Washington was chosen president (presiding officer). The states certified 65 delegates, but 10 did not attend. The work was done by 55, not all of whom were present at all sessions. Of the 55 attending delegates, 39 signed Sept. 17, 1787, some with reservations, and 16 failed to sign. Some historians have said 74 delegates (nine more than the 65 actually certified) were named, and 19 failed to attend. These additional persons refused the appointment, were never delegates, and were never counted as absentees. Washington sent the Constitution to Congress, and that body, Sept. 28, 1787, ordered it sent to the legislatures, "in order to be submitted to a convention of delegates chosen in each state by the people thereof."

The Constitution was ratified by votes of state conventions as follows: Delaware, Dec. 7, 1787, unanimous; Pennsylvania, Dec. 12, 1787, 46 to 23; New Jersey, Dec. 18, 1787, unanimous; Georgia, Jan. 2, 1788, unanimous; Connecticut, Jan. 9, 1788, 128 to 40; Massachusetts, Feb. 6, 1788, 187 to 168; Maryland, Apr. 28, 1788, 63 to 11; South Carolina, May 23, 1788, 149 to 73; New Hampshire, June 21, 1788, 57 to 46; Virginia, June 25, 1788, 89 to 79; New York, July 26, 1788, 30 to 27. Nine states were needed to establish the operation of the Constitution "between the states so ratifying the same," and New Hampshire was the ninth state. The government did not declare the Constitution in effect until the first Wednesday in Mar. 1789, which was Mar. 4. After that, North Carolina ratified it on Nov. 21, 1789, 194 to 77; and Rhode Island, May 29, 1790, 34 to 32. Vermont in convention ratified it on Jan. 10, 1791, and by act of Congress approved on Feb. 18, 1791, was admitted into the Union as the 14th state, Mar. 4, 1791.

Constitution of the United States

The text of the Constitution given here is from the centennial edition of *The Constitution of the United States of America: Analysis and Interpretation*, prepared by the Library of Congress and issued by the U.S. Government Printing Office July 1, 2014. Text in brackets indicates that an item has been superseded or amended, or provides background information. **Boldface text** preceding an article, section, or amendment is a brief summary, added by *The World Almanac*.

The Original Seven Articles

PREAMBLE

We the People of the United States, in Order to form a more perfect Union, establish Justice, insure domestic Tranquility, provide for the common defence, promote the general Welfare, and secure the Blessings of Liberty to ourselves and our Posterity, do ordain and establish this Constitution for the United States of America.

ARTICLE I.

Section 1—Legislative powers, in whom vested.

All legislative Powers herein granted shall be vested in a Congress of the United States, which shall consist of a Senate and House of Representatives.

Section 2—House of Representatives, how and by whom chosen. Qualifications of a Representative. Representatives and direct taxes, how apportioned and enumerated. Vacancies to be filled. Choosing of officers and power of impeachment.

The House of Representatives shall be composed of Members chosen every second Year by the People of the several States, and the Electors in each State shall have the Qualifications requisite for Electors of the most numerous Branch of the State Legislature.

No Person shall be a Representative who shall not have attained to the Age of twenty five Years, and been seven Years a Citizen of the United States, and who shall not, when elected, be an Inhabitant of that State in which he shall be chosen.

[Representatives and direct Taxes shall be apportioned among the several States which may be included within this Union, according to their respective Numbers, which shall be determined by adding to the whole Number of free Persons, including those bound to Service for a Term of Years, and excluding Indians not taxed, three fifths of all other Persons.] *[The previous sentence was superseded by Amendment XIV, section 2.]* The actual Enumeration shall be made within three Years after the first Meeting of the Congress of the United States, and within every subsequent Term of ten Years, in such Manner as they shall by Law direct. The Number of Representatives shall not exceed one for every thirty Thousand, but each State shall have at Least one Representative; and until such enumeration shall be made, the State of New Hampshire shall be entitled to chuse three, Massachusetts eight, Rhode-Island and Providence Plantations one, Connecticut five, New York six, New Jersey four, Pennsylvania eight, Delaware one, Maryland six, Virginia ten, North Carolina five, South Carolina five, and Georgia three.

When vacancies happen in the Representation from any State, the Executive Authority thereof shall issue Writs of Election to fill such Vacancies.

The House of Representatives shall chuse their Speaker and other Officers; and shall have the sole Power of Impeachment.

Section 3—Senators, how and by whom chosen. How assembled. Qualifications of a Senator. President of the Senate. President pro tempore and other officers of the Senate, how chosen. Power to try impeachments. Judgment in cases of impeachment.

The Senate of the United States shall be composed of two Senators from each State, [chosen by the Legislature] *[The preceding words were superseded by Amendment XVII.]* thereof, for six Years; and each Senator shall have one Vote.

Immediately after they shall be assembled in Consequence of the first Election, they shall be divided as equally as may be into three Classes. The Seats of the Senators of the first Class shall be vacated at the Expiration of the second Year, of the second Class at the Expiration of the fourth Year, and of the third Class at the Expiration of the sixth Year, so that one third may be chosen every second Year; [and if Vacancies happen by Resignation, or otherwise, during the Recess of the Legislature of any State, the Executive thereof may make temporary Appointments until the next Meeting of the Legislature, which shall then fill such Vacancies.] *[The words in brackets were superseded by Amendment XVII.]*

No Person shall be a Senator who shall not have attained to the Age of thirty Years, and been nine Years a Citizen of the United States, and who shall not, when elected, be an Inhabitant of that State for which he shall be chosen.

The Vice President of the United States shall be President of the Senate, but shall have no Vote, unless they be equally divided.

The Senate shall chuse their other Officers, and also a President pro tempore, in the Absence of the Vice President, or when he shall exercise the Office of President of the United States.

The Senate shall have the sole Power to try all Impeachments. When sitting for that Purpose, they shall be on Oath or Affirmation. When the President of the United States is tried, the Chief Justice shall preside: And no Person shall be convicted without the Concurrence of two thirds of the Members present.

Judgment in Cases of Impeachment shall not extend further than to removal from Office, and disqualification to hold and enjoy any Office of honor, Trust or Profit under the United States: but the Party convicted shall nevertheless be liable and subject to Indictment, Trial, Judgment and Punishment, according to Law.

Section 4—Times, places, manner of elections. Time of assembly.

The Times, Places and Manner of holding Elections for Senators and Representatives, shall be prescribed in each State by the Legislature thereof; but the Congress may at any time by Law make or alter such Regulations, except as to the Places of chusing Senators.

The Congress shall assemble at least once in every Year, and such Meeting shall be [on the first Monday in December], *[The words in brackets were superseded by Amendment XX, section 2.]* unless they shall by Law appoint a different Day.

Section 5—Membership, quorums, adjournments. Rules of proceedings. Journal of proceedings. Time of adjournments.

Each House shall be the Judge of the Elections, Returns and Qualifications of its own Members, and a Majority of each shall constitute a Quorum to do Business; but a smaller Number may adjourn from day to day, and may be authorized to compel the Attendance of absent Members, in such Manner, and under such Penalties as each House may provide.

Each House may determine the Rules of its Proceedings, punish its Members for disorderly Behaviour, and, with the Concurrence of two thirds, expel a Member.

Each House shall keep a Journal of its Proceedings, and from time to time publish the same, excepting such Parts as may in their Judgment require Secrecy; and the Yeas and Nays of the Members of either House on any question shall, at the Desire of one fifth of those Present, be entered on the Journal.

Neither House, during the Session of Congress, shall, without the Consent of the other, adjourn for more than three days, nor to any other Place than that in which the two Houses shall be sitting.

Section 6—Compensation, privileges. Incompatible offices.

The Senators and Representatives shall receive a Compensation for their Services, to be ascertained by Law, and paid out of the Treasury of the United States. They shall in all Cases, except Treason, Felony and Breach of the Peace, be privileged from Arrest during their Attendance at the Session of their respective Houses, and in going to and returning from the same; and for any Speech or Debate in either House, they shall not be questioned in any other Place.

No Senator or Representative shall, during the Time for which he was elected, be appointed to any civil Office under the Authority of the United States, which shall have been created, or the Emoluments whereof shall have been encreased during such time; and no Person holding any Office under the United States, shall be a Member of either House during his Continuance in Office.

Section 7—House to originate revenue bills. Legislative process; bill presented to the President before becoming law. Passing of bill over objections of President, veto.

All Bills for raising Revenue shall originate in the House of Representatives; but the Senate may propose or concur with Amendments as on other Bills.

Every Bill which shall have passed the House of Representatives and the Senate, shall, before it become a Law, be presented to the President of the United States; If he approve he shall sign it, but if not he shall return it, with his Objections to that House in which it shall have originated, who shall enter the Objections at large on their Journal, and proceed to reconsider it. If after such Reconsideration two thirds of that House shall agree to pass the Bill, it shall be sent, together with the Objections, to the other House, by which it shall likewise be reconsidered, and if approved by two thirds of that House, it shall become a Law. But in all such Cases the Votes of both Houses shall be determined by Yeas and Nays, and the Names of the Persons voting for and against the Bill shall be entered on the Journal of each House respectively. If any Bill shall not be returned by the President within ten Days (Sundays excepted) after it shall have been presented to him, the Same shall be a Law, in like Manner as if he had signed it, unless the Congress by their Adjournment prevent its Return, in which Case it shall not be a Law.

Every Order, Resolution, or Vote to which the Concurrence of the Senate and House of Representatives may be necessary (except on a question of Adjournment) shall be presented to the President of the United States; and before the Same shall take Effect, shall be approved by him, or being disapproved by him, shall be repassed by two thirds of the Senate and House of Representatives, according to the Rules and Limitations prescribed in the Case of a Bill.

Section 8—Powers of Congress.

The Congress shall have Power To lay and collect Taxes, Duties, Imposts and Excises, to pay the Debts and provide for the common Defence and general Welfare of the United States; but all Duties, Imposts and Excises shall be uniform throughout the United States;

To borrow Money on the credit of the United States;

To regulate Commerce with foreign Nations, and among the several States, and with the Indian Tribes;

To establish an uniform Rule of Naturalization, and uniform Laws on the subject of Bankruptcies throughout the United States;

To coin Money, regulate the Value thereof, and of foreign Coin, and fix the Standard of Weights and Measures;

To provide for the Punishment of counterfeiting the Securities and current Coin of the United States;

To establish Post Offices and post Roads;

To promote the Progress of Science and useful Arts, by securing for limited Times to Authors and Inventors the exclusive Right to their respective Writings and Discoveries;

To constitute Tribunals inferior to the supreme Court;

To define and punish Piracies and Felonies committed on the high Seas, and Offences against the Law of Nations;

To declare War, grant Letters of Marque and Reprisal, and make Rules concerning Captures on Land and Water;

To raise and support Armies, but no Appropriation of Money to that Use shall be for a longer Term than two Years;

To provide and maintain a Navy;

To make Rules for the Government and Regulation of the land and naval Forces;

To provide for calling forth the Militia to execute the Laws of the Union, suppress Insurrections and repel Invasions;

To provide for organizing, arming, and disciplining, the Militia, and for governing such Part of them as may be employed in the Service of the United States, reserving to the States respectively, the Appointment of the Officers, and the Authority of training the Militia according to the discipline prescribed by Congress;

To exercise exclusive Legislation in all Cases whatsoever, over such District (not exceeding ten Miles square) as may, by Cession of particular States, and the Acceptance of Congress, become the Seat of the Government of the United States, and to exercise like Authority over all Places purchased by the Consent of the Legislature of the State in which the Same shall be, for the Erection of Forts, Magazines, Arsenals, dock-Yards, and other needful Buildings;—And

To make all Laws which shall be necessary and proper for carrying into Execution the foregoing Powers, and all other Powers vested by this Constitution in the Government of the United States, or in any Department or Officer thereof.

Section 9—Powers denied to Congress: Importation of slaves. Habeas corpus. Bills of attainder. Taxes, how apportioned. Export duty. Preference to ports. Money, how drawn from Treasury. Titles of nobility.

The Migration or Importation of such Persons as any of the States now existing shall think proper to admit, shall not be prohibited by the Congress prior to the Year one thousand eight hundred and eight, but a Tax or duty may be imposed on such Importation, not exceeding ten dollars for each Person.

The Privilege of the Writ of Habeas Corpus shall not be suspended, unless when in Cases of Rebellion or Invasion the public Safety may require it.

No Bill of Attainder or ex post facto Law shall be passed.

No Capitation, or other direct, Tax shall be laid, [unless in Proportion to the Census or Enumeration herein before directed to be taken]. *[Words in brackets modified by Amendment XVI.]*

No Tax or Duty shall be laid on Articles exported from any State.

No Preference shall be given by any Regulation of Commerce or Revenue to the Ports of one State over those of another: nor shall Vessels bound to, or from, one State, be obliged to enter, clear, or pay Duties in another.

No Money shall be drawn from the Treasury, but in Consequence of Appropriations made by Law; and a regular Statement and Account of the Receipts and Expenditures of all public Money shall be published from time to time.

No Title of Nobility shall be granted by the United States: And no Person holding any Office of Profit or Trust under them, shall, without the Consent of the Congress, accept of any present, Emolument, Office, or Title, of any kind whatever, from any King, Prince, or foreign State.

Section 10—States prohibited from the exercise of certain powers.

No State shall enter into any Treaty, Alliance, or Confederation; grant Letters of Marque and Reprisal; coin Money; emit Bills of Credit; make any Thing but gold and silver Coin a Tender in Payment of Debts; pass any Bill of Attainder, ex post facto Law, or Law impairing the Obligation of Contracts, or grant any Title of Nobility.

No State shall, without the Consent of the Congress, lay any Imposts or Duties on Imports or Exports, except what may be absolutely necessary for executing it's inspection Laws: and the net Produce of all Duties and Imposts, laid by any State on Imports or Exports, shall be for the Use of the Treasury of the United States; and all such Laws shall be subject to the Revision and Controul of the Congress.

No State shall, without the Consent of Congress, lay any Duty of Tonnage, keep Troops, or Ships of War in time of Peace, enter into any Agreement or Compact with another State, or with a foreign Power, or engage in War, unless actually invaded, or in such imminent Danger as will not admit of delay.

ARTICLE II.

Section 1—President, powers and term of office. Electors, number and how appointed. Electors to vote for President. Qualifications of President. On whom duties devolve in case of removal, death, etc., of President. President's compensation. Oath of office.

The executive Power shall be vested in a President of the United States of America. He shall hold his Office during the Term of four Years, and, together with the Vice President, chosen for the same Term, be elected, as follows:

Each State shall appoint, in such Manner as the Legislature thereof may direct, a Number of Electors, equal to the whole Number of Senators and Representatives to which the State may be entitled in the Congress: but no Senator or Representative, or Person holding an Office of Trust or Profit under the United States, shall be appointed an Elector.

[The Electors shall meet in their respective States, and vote by Ballot for two Persons, of whom one at least shall not be an Inhabitant of the same State with themselves. And they shall make a List of all the Persons voted for, and of the Number of Votes for each; which List they shall sign and certify, and transmit sealed to the Seat of the Government of the United States, directed to the President of the Senate. The President of the Senate shall, in the Presence of the Senate and House of Representatives, open all the Certificates, and the Votes shall then be counted. The Person having the greatest Number of Votes shall be the President, if such Number be a Majority of the whole Number of Electors appointed; and if there be more than one who have such Majority, and have an equal Number of Votes, then the House of Representatives shall immediately chuse by Ballot one of them for President; and if no Person have a Majority, then from the five highest on the List the said House shall in like Manner chuse the President. But in chusing the President, the Votes shall be taken by States, the Representation from each State having one Vote; A quorum for this Purpose shall consist of a Member or Members from two thirds of the States, and a Majority of all the States shall be necessary to a Choice. In every Case, after the Choice of the President, the Person having the greatest Number of Votes of the Electors shall be the Vice President. But if there should remain two or more who have equal Votes, the Senate shall chuse from them by Ballot the Vice President.] *[This clause was superseded by Amendment XII.]*

The Congress may determine the Time of chusing the Electors, and the Day on which they shall give their Votes; which Day shall be the same throughout the United States.

No Person except a natural born Citizen, or a Citizen of the United States, at the time of the Adoption of this Constitution, shall be eligible to the Office of President; neither shall any Person be eligible to that Office who shall not have attained to the Age of thirty five Years, and been fourteen Years a Resident within the United States. *[For qualification of the Vice President, see Amendment XII.]*

[In Case of the Removal of the President from Office, or of his Death, Resignation, or Inability to discharge the Powers and Duties of the said Office, the Same shall devolve on the Vice President, and the Congress may by Law provide for the Case of Removal, Death, Resignation or Inability, both of the President and Vice President, declaring what Officer shall then act as President, and such Officer shall act accordingly, until the Disability be removed, or a President shall be elected.] *[This clause was superseded by Amendment XXV.]*

The President shall, at stated Times, receive for his Services, a Compensation, which shall neither be encreased nor diminished during the Period for which he shall have been elected, and he shall not receive within that Period any other Emolument from the United States, or any of them.

Before he enter on the Execution of his Office, he shall take the following Oath or Affirmation:—

"I do solemnly swear (or affirm) that I will faithfully execute the Office of President of the United States, and will to the best of my Ability, preserve, protect and defend the Constitution of the United States."

Section 2—President to be Commander in Chief. Power to make treaties; nominations for, appointments to certain offices. Power to fill vacancies during Senate recess.

The President shall be Commander in Chief of the Army and Navy of the United States, and of the Militia of the several States, when called into the actual Service of the United States; he may require the Opinion, in writing, of the principal Officer in each of the executive Departments, upon any Subject relating to the Duties of their respective Offices, and he shall have Power to Grant Reprieves and Pardons for Offences against the United States, except in Cases of Impeachment.

He shall have Power, by and with the Advice and Consent of the Senate, to make Treaties, provided two thirds of the Senators present concur; and he shall nominate, and by and with the Advice and Consent of the Senate, shall appoint Ambassadors, other public Ministers and Consuls, Judges of the supreme Court, and all other Officers of the United States, whose Appointments are not herein otherwise provided for, and which shall be established by Law: but the Congress may by Law vest the Appointment of such inferior Officers, as they think proper, in the President alone, in the Courts of Law, or in the Heads of Departments.

The President shall have Power to fill up all Vacancies that may happen during the Recess of the Senate, by granting Commissions which shall expire at the End of their next Session.

Section 3—President shall communicate to, may convene and adjourn Congress; shall receive ambassadors, execute laws, and commission officers.

He shall from time to time give to the Congress Information on the State of the Union, and recommend to their Consideration such Measures as he shall judge necessary and expedient; he may, on extraordinary Occasions, convene both Houses, or either of them, and in Case of Disagreement between them, with Respect to the Time of Adjournment, he may adjourn them to such Time as he shall think proper; he shall receive Ambassadors and other public Ministers; he shall take Care that the Laws be faithfully executed, and shall Commission all the Officers of the United States.

Section 4—All civil offices forfeited for certain crimes.

The President, Vice President and all civil Officers of the United States, shall be removed from Office on Impeachment for, and Conviction of, Treason, Bribery, or other high Crimes and Misdemeanors.

ARTICLE III.

Section 1—Judicial powers, tenure, compensation.

The judicial Power of the United States, shall be vested in one supreme Court, and in such inferior Courts as the Congress may from time to time ordain and establish. The Judges, both of the supreme and inferior Courts, shall hold their Offices during good Behaviour, and shall, at stated Times, receive for their Services, a Compensation, which shall not be diminished during their Continuance in Office.

Section 2—Judicial power, cases to which it extends. Jurisdiction of Supreme Court. Trial by jury; where held.

The judicial Power shall extend to all Cases, in Law and Equity, arising under this Constitution, the Laws of the United States, and Treaties made, or which shall be made, under their Authority;—to all Cases affecting Ambassadors, other public Ministers and Consuls;—to all Cases of admiralty and maritime Jurisdiction;—to Controversies to which the United States shall be a Party;—to Controversies between two or more States;—[between a State and Citizens of another State;]—between Citizens of different States;—between Citizens of the same State claiming Lands under Grants of different States, [and between a State, or the Citizens thereof, and foreign States, Citizens or Subjects.] *[This section was modified by Amendment XI.]*

In all Cases affecting Ambassadors, other public Ministers and Consuls, and those in which a State shall be Party, the supreme Court shall have original Jurisdiction. In all the other Cases before mentioned, the supreme Court shall have appellate Jurisdiction, both as to Law and Fact, with such Exceptions, and under such Regulations as the Congress shall make.

The Trial of all Crimes, except in Cases of Impeachment, shall be by Jury; and such Trial shall be held in the State where the said Crimes shall have been committed; but when not committed within any State, the Trial shall be at such Place or Places as the Congress may by Law have directed.

Section 3—Treason defined. Punishment of.

Treason against the United States, shall consist only in levying War against them, or in adhering to their Enemies, giving them Aid and Comfort. No Person shall be convicted of Treason unless on the Testimony of two Witnesses to the same overt Act, or on Confession in open Court.

The Congress shall have Power to declare the Punishment of Treason, but no Attainder of Treason shall work Corruption of Blood, or Forfeiture except during the Life of the Person attainted.

ARTICLE IV.

Section 1—Each State to give credit to the public acts, etc., of every other State.

Full Faith and Credit shall be given in each State to the public Acts, Records, and judicial Proceedings of every other State. And the Congress may by general Laws prescribe the Manner in which such Acts, Records and Proceedings shall be proved, and the Effect thereof.

Section 2—Privileges of citizens of each State. Fugitives from justice to be delivered up. Fugitives from service or labor, to be delivered up.

The Citizens of each State shall be entitled to all Privileges and Immunities of Citizens in the several States.

A Person charged in any State with Treason, Felony, or other Crime, who shall flee from Justice, and be found in another State, shall on Demand of the executive Authority of the State from which he fled, be delivered up, to be removed to the State having Jurisdiction of the Crime.

[No Person held to Service or Labour in one State, under the Laws thereof, escaping into another, shall, in Consequence of any Law or Regulation therein, be discharged from such Service or Labour, but shall be delivered up on Claim of the Party to whom such Service or Labour may be due.] *[This clause was superseded by Amendment XIII.]*

Section 3—Admission of new States. Power of Congress over territory and other property.

New States may be admitted by the Congress into this Union; but no new State shall be formed or erected within the Jurisdiction of any other State; nor any State be formed by the Junction of two or more States, or Parts of States, without the Consent of the Legislatures of the States concerned as well as of the Congress.

The Congress shall have Power to dispose of and make all needful Rules and Regulations respecting the Territory or other Property belonging to the United States; and nothing in this Constitution shall be so construed as to Prejudice any Claims of the United States, or of any particular State.

Section 4—Republican form of government guaranteed; each State to be protected.

The United States shall guarantee to every State in this Union a Republican Form of Government, and shall protect each of them against Invasion; and on Application of the Legislature, or of the Executive (when the Legislature cannot be convened) against domestic Violence.

ARTICLE V.

Constitution, how amended; proviso.

The Congress, whenever two thirds of both Houses shall deem it necessary, shall propose Amendments to this Constitution, or, on the Application of the Legislatures of two thirds of the several States, shall call a Convention for proposing Amendments, which, in either Case, shall be valid to all Intents and Purposes, as Part of this Constitution, when ratified by the Legislatures of three fourths of the several States, or by Conventions in three fourths thereof, as the one or the other Mode of Ratification may be proposed by the Congress; Provided that no Amendment which may be made prior to the Year One thousand eight hundred and eight shall in any Manner affect the first and fourth Clauses in the Ninth Section of the first Article; and that no State, without its Consent, shall be deprived of its equal Suffrage in the Senate.

ARTICLE VI.

Certain debts and engagements shall be valid. Constitution, laws and treaties made, shall be supreme law of the United States. Oath to support Constitution, by whom taken; no religious test shall be required.

All Debts contracted and Engagements entered into, before the Adoption of this Constitution, shall be as valid against the United States under this Constitution, as under the Confederation.

This Constitution, and the Laws of the United States which shall be made in Pursuance thereof; and all Treaties made, or which shall be made, under the Authority of the United States, shall be the supreme Law of the Land; and the Judges in every State shall be bound thereby, any Thing in the Constitution or Laws of any State to the Contrary notwithstanding.

The Senators and Representatives before mentioned, and the Members of the several State Legislatures, and all executive and judicial Officers, both of the United States and of the several States, shall be bound by Oath or Affirmation, to support this Constitution; but no religious Test shall ever be required as a Qualification to any Office or public Trust under the United States.

ARTICLE VII.

Ratification to establish the Constitution.

The Ratification of the Conventions of nine States, shall be sufficient for the Establishment of this Constitution between the States so ratifying the Same.

The Word, "the," being interlined between the seventh and eighth Lines of the first Page, The Word "Thirty" being partly written on an Erazure in the fifteenth Line of the first Page, The Words "is tried" being interlined between the thirty second and thirty third Lines of the first Page and the Word "the" being interlined between the forty third and forty fourth Lines of the second Page.

Attest William Jackson Secretary

done in Convention by the Unanimous Consent of the States present the Seventeenth Day of September in the Year of our Lord one thousand seven hundred and Eighty seven and of the Independance of the United States of America the Twelfth. In witness whereof We have hereunto subscribed our Names,

G^o. Washington, Presid^t. and deputy from Virginia

New Hampshire—John Langdon, Nicholas Gilman

Massachusetts—Nathaniel Gorham, Rufus King

Connecticut—W^m. Saml. Johnson, Roger Sherman

New York—Alexander Hamilton

New Jersey—Wil: Livingston, David Brearley, W^m. Paterson, Jona: Dayton

Pennsylvania—B Franklin, Thomas Mifflin, Robt. Morris, Geo. Clymer, Thos. FitzSimons, Jared Ingersoll, James Wilson, Gouv Morris

Delaware—Geo: Read, Gunning Bedford jun, John Dickinson, Richard Bassett, Jaco: Broom

Maryland—James McHenry, Dan of St Thos. Jenifer, Danl Carroll

Virginia—John Blair, James Madison Jr.

North Carolina—W^m. Blount, Rich^d. Dobbs Spaight, Hu Williamson

South Carolina—J. Rutledge, Charles Cotesworth Pinckney, Charles Pinckney, Pierce Butler

Georgia—William Few, Abr Baldwin

Origin of the Bill of Rights

Congress, at its first session in New York, NY, submitted to the states 12 amendments Sept. 25, 1789, to clarify certain individual and state rights not named in the Constitution. They are generally called the Bill of Rights.

Influential in framing these amendments was the Declaration of Rights of Virginia, written by George Mason (1725-92) in 1776. Mason, a Virginia delegate to the Constitutional Convention, did not sign the Constitution and opposed its ratification on the ground that it did not sufficiently oppose slavery or safeguard individual rights.

In the preamble to the resolution offering the proposed amendments, Congress said: "The Conventions of a number of the States, having at the time of their adopting the Constitution, expressed a desire, in order to prevent misconstruction or abuse of its powers, that further declaratory and restrictive clauses should be added: And as extending the ground of public confidence in the Government, will best insure the beneficent ends of its institution."

Ten of these amendments, originally three to 12 inclusive, were ratified by the states as follows: New Jersey, Nov. 20, 1789; Maryland, Dec. 19, 1789; North Carolina, Dec. 22, 1789; South Carolina, Jan. 19, 1790; New Hampshire, Jan. 25, 1790; Delaware, Jan. 28, 1790; New York, Feb. 27, 1790; Pennsylvania, Mar. 10, 1790; Rhode Island, June 7, 1790; Vermont, Nov. 3, 1791; Virginia, Dec. 15, 1791; Massachusetts, Mar. 2, 1939; Georgia, Mar. 18, 1939; Connecticut, Apr. 19, 1939. These original 10 ratified amendments follow as Amendments I to X inclusive.

Of the two original proposed amendments that were not ratified promptly by the necessary number of states, the first related to apportionment of Representatives; the second, relating to compensation of members of Congress, was ratified in 1992 and became Amendment XXVII.

The Bill of Rights
In force Dec. 15, 1791

AMENDMENT I.

Religious establishment prohibited. Freedom of speech and of press; right to assemble and to petition.

Congress shall make no law respecting an establishment of religion, or prohibiting the free exercise thereof; or abridging the freedom of speech, or of the press; or the right of the people peaceably to assemble, and to petition the Government for a redress of grievances.

AMENDMENT II.

Right to keep and bear arms.

A well regulated Militia, being necessary to the security of a free State, the right of the people to keep and bear Arms shall not be infringed.

AMENDMENT III.

Conditions for quartering of soldiers.

No Soldier shall, in time of peace be quartered in any house, without the consent of the Owner, nor in time of war, but in a manner to be prescribed by law.

AMENDMENT IV.

Protection from unreasonable search and seizure.

The right of the people to be secure in their persons, houses, papers, and effects, against unreasonable searches and seizures, shall not be violated, and no Warrants shall issue but upon probable cause, supported by Oath or affirmation, and particularly describing the place to be searched, and the persons or things to be seized.

AMENDMENT V.

Provisions concerning prosecution and due process of law. Compensation of private property taken for public use.

No person shall be held to answer for a capital, or otherwise infamous crime, unless on a presentment or indictment of a Grand Jury, except in cases arising in the land or naval forces, or in the Militia, when in actual service in time of War or public danger; nor shall any person be subject for the same offence to be twice put in jeopardy of life or limb; nor shall be compelled in any criminal case to be a witness against himself, nor be deprived of life, liberty, or property, without due process of law; nor shall private property be taken for public use, without just compensation.

AMENDMENT VI.

Rights of accused in criminal prosecutions.

In all criminal prosecutions, the accused shall enjoy the right to a speedy and public trial, by an impartial jury of the State and district wherein the crime shall have been committed, which district shall have been previously ascertained by law, and to be informed of the nature and cause of the accusation; to be confronted with the witnesses against him; to have compulsory process for obtaining witnesses in his favor, and to have the Assistance of Counsel for his defense.

AMENDMENT VII.

Right of trial by jury in civil cases.

In Suits at common law, where the value in controversy shall exceed twenty dollars, the right of trial by jury shall be preserved, and no fact tried by a jury, shall be otherwise reexamined in any Court of the United States, than according to the rules of the common law.

AMENDMENT VIII.

Excessive bail or fines; cruel and unusual punishment.

Excessive bail shall not be required, nor excessive fines imposed, nor cruel and unusual punishments inflicted.

AMENDMENT IX.

Unenumerated rights.

The enumeration in the Constitution, of certain rights, shall not be construed to deny or disparage others retained by the people.

AMENDMENT X.

Rights reserved to States.

The powers not delegated to the United States by the Constitution, nor prohibited by it to the States, are reserved to the States respectively, or to the people.

Amendments Since the Bill of Rights

AMENDMENT XI.

Judicial powers construed.

[Proposed by Congress Mar. 4, 1794. Ratification complete Feb. 7, 1795, though official announcement of ratification not made until Jan. 8, 1798.]

The Judicial power of the United States shall not be construed to extend to any suit in law or equity, commenced or prosecuted against one of the United States by Citizens of another State, or by Citizens or Subjects of any Foreign State.

AMENDMENT XII.

Election of President and Vice-President.

[Proposed by Congress Dec. 9, 1803; ratified June 15, 1804.]

The Electors shall meet in their respective states and vote by ballot for President and Vice-President, one of whom, at least, shall not be an inhabitant of the same state with themselves; they shall name in their ballots the person voted for as President, and in distinct ballots the person voted for as Vice-President, and they shall make distinct lists of all persons voted for as President, and of all persons voted for as Vice-President, and of the number of votes for each, which lists they shall sign and certify, and transmit sealed to the seat of the government of the United States, directed to the President of the Senate;—The President of the Senate shall, in the presence of the Senate and House of Representatives, open all the certificates and the votes shall then be counted;—The person having the greatest number of votes for President, shall be the President, if such number be a majority of the whole number of Electors appointed; and if no person have such majority, then from the persons having the highest numbers not exceeding three on the list of those voted for as President, the House of Representatives shall choose immediately, by ballot, the President. But in choosing the President, the votes shall be taken by states, the representation from each state having one vote; a quorum for this purpose shall consist of a member or members from two-thirds of the states, and a majority of all the states shall be necessary to a choice. [And if the House of Representatives shall not choose a President whenever the right of choice shall devolve upon them, before the fourth day of March next following, then the Vice-President shall act as President, as in the case of the death or other constitutional disability of the President.] *[The words in brackets were superseded by Amendment XX, section 3.]* The person having the greatest number of votes as Vice-President, shall be the Vice-President, if such number be a majority of the whole number of Electors appointed, and if no person have a majority, then from the two highest numbers on the list, the Senate shall choose the Vice-President; a quorum for the purpose shall consist of two-thirds of the whole number of Senators, and a majority of the whole number shall be necessary to a choice. But no person constitutionally ineligible to the office of President shall be eligible to that of Vice-President of the United States.

THE RECONSTRUCTION AMENDMENTS

[Amendments XIII, XIV, and XV are commonly known as the Reconstruction Amendments inasmuch as they followed the Civil War and were drafted by Republicans who wanted to impose their own policy of reconstruction on the South. Southern postbellum legislatures in states including Mississippi, South Carolina, and Georgia had set up laws that effectively perpetuated slavery under other names.]

AMENDMENT XIII.

Slavery abolished.

[Proposed by Congress Jan. 31, 1865; ratified Dec. 6, 1865.]

Section 1. Neither slavery nor involuntary servitude, except as a punishment for crime whereof the party shall have been duly convicted, shall exist within the United States, or any place subject to their jurisdiction.

Section 2. Congress shall have power to enforce this article by appropriate legislation.

AMENDMENT XIV.

Citizenship rights not to be abridged.

[Proposed by Congress June 13, 1866, ratified July 9, 1868, and declared to have been ratified in a proclamation by the Secretary of State, July 28, 1868.]

Section 1. All persons born or naturalized in the United States, and subject to the jurisdiction thereof, are citizens of the United States and of the State wherein they reside. No State shall make or enforce any law which shall abridge the privileges or immunities of citizens of the United States; nor shall any State deprive any person of life, liberty, or property, without due process of law; nor deny to any person within its jurisdiction the equal protection of the laws.

Section 2. Representatives shall be apportioned among the several States according to their respective numbers, counting the whole number of persons in each State, excluding Indians not taxed. But when the right to vote at any election for the choice of electors for President and Vice-President of the United States, Representatives in Congress, the Executive and Judicial officers of a State, or the members of the Legislature thereof, is denied to any of the male inhabitants of such State, being [twenty-one] *[The words in brackets were changed by Amendment XXVI.]* years of age, and citizens of the United States, or in any way abridged, except for participation in rebellion, or other crime, the basis of representation therein shall be reduced in the proportion which the number of such male citizens shall bear to the whole number of male citizens twenty-one years of age in such State.

Section 3. No person shall be a Senator or Representative in Congress, or elector of President and Vice-President, or hold any office, civil or military, under the United States, or under any State, who, having previously taken an oath, as a member of Congress, or as an officer of the United States, or as a member of any State legislature, or as an executive or judicial officer of any State, to support the Constitution of the United States, shall have engaged in insurrection or rebellion against the same, or given aid or comfort to the enemies thereof. But Congress may by a vote of two-thirds of each House, remove such disability.

Section 4. The validity of the public debt of the United States, authorized by law, including debts incurred for payment of pensions and bounties for services in suppressing insurrection or rebellion, shall not be questioned. But neither the United States nor any State shall assume or pay any debt or obligation incurred in aid of insurrection or rebellion against the United States, or any claim for the loss or emancipation of any slave; but all such debts, obligations and claims shall be held illegal and void.

Section 5. The Congress shall have power to enforce, by appropriate legislation, the provisions of this article.

AMENDMENT XV.

Race no bar to voting rights.

[Proposed by Congress Feb. 26, 1869; ratified Feb. 3, 1870.]

Section 1. The right of citizens of the United States to vote shall not be denied or abridged by the United States or by any State on account of race, color, or previous condition of servitude.

Section 2. The Congress shall have power to enforce this article by appropriate legislation.

AMENDMENT XVI.

Income taxes authorized.

[Proposed by Congress July 12, 1909; ratified Feb. 3, 1913.]

The Congress shall have power to lay and collect taxes on incomes, from whatever source derived, without apportionment among the several States, and without regard to any census or enumeration.

AMENDMENT XVII.

Popular election of Senators.

[Proposed by Congress May 13, 1912; ratified Apr. 8, 1913.]

The Senate of the United States shall be composed of two Senators from each State, elected by the people thereof, for six years; and each Senator shall have one vote. The electors in each State shall have the qualifications requisite for electors of the most numerous branch of the State legislatures.

When vacancies happen in the representation of any State in the Senate, the executive authority of such State shall issue writs of election to fill such vacancies: Provided, That the legislature of any State may empower the executive thereof to make temporary appointments until the people fill the vacancies by election as the legislature may direct.

This amendment shall not be so construed as to affect the election or term of any Senator chosen before it becomes valid as part of the Constitution.

AMENDMENT XVIII.

Liquor prohibition amendment.

[Proposed by Congress Dec. 18, 1917; ratified Jan. 16, 1919. Repealed by Amendment XXI, effective Dec. 5, 1933.]
Section 1. After one year from the ratification of this article the manufacture, sale, or transportation of intoxicating liquors within, the importation thereof into, or the exportation thereof from the United States and all territory subject to the jurisdiction thereof for beverage purposes is hereby prohibited.

Section 2. The Congress and the several States shall have concurrent power to enforce this article by appropriate legislation.

Section 3. This article shall be inoperative unless it shall have been ratified as an amendment to the Constitution by the legislatures of the several States, as provided in the Constitution, within seven years from the date of the submission hereof to the States by the Congress.

AMENDMENT XIX.

Nationwide suffrage to women.

[Proposed by Congress June 4, 1919; ratified Aug. 18, 1920.]
The right of citizens of the United States to vote shall not be denied or abridged by the United States or by any State on account of sex.

Congress shall have power to enforce this article by appropriate legislation.

AMENDMENT XX.

Commencement of terms of office

[Proposed by Congress Mar. 2, 1932; ratified Jan. 23, 1933.]
Section 1. The terms of the President and Vice President shall end at noon on the 20th day of January, and the terms of Senators and Representatives at noon on the 3d day of January, of the years in which such terms would have ended if this article had not been ratified; and the terms of their successors shall then begin.

Section 2. The Congress shall assemble at least once in every year, and such meeting shall begin at noon on the 3d day of January, unless they shall by law appoint a different day.

Section 3. If, at the time fixed for the beginning of the term of the President, the President elect shall have died, the Vice President elect shall become President. If a President shall not have been chosen before the time fixed for the beginning of his term, or if the President elect shall have failed to qualify, then the Vice President elect shall act as President until a President shall have qualified; and the Congress may by law provide for the case wherein neither a President elect nor a Vice President elect shall have qualified, declaring who shall then act as President, or the manner in which one who is to act shall be selected, and such person shall act accordingly until a President or Vice President shall have qualified.

Section 4. The Congress may by law provide for the case of the death of any of the persons from whom the House of Representatives may choose a President whenever the right of choice shall have devolved upon them, and for the case of the death of any of the persons from whom the Senate may choose a Vice President whenever the right of choice shall have devolved upon them.

Section 5. Sections 1 and 2 shall take effect on the 15th day of October following the ratification of this article.

Section 6. This article shall be inoperative unless it shall have been ratified as an amendment to the Constitution by the legislatures of three-fourths of the several States within seven years from the date of its submission.

AMENDMENT XXI.

Repeal of Amendment XVIII.

[Proposed by Congress Feb. 20, 1933; ratified Dec. 5, 1933.]
Section 1. The eighteenth article of amendment to the Constitution of the United States is hereby repealed.

Section 2. The transportation or importation into any State, Territory, or possession of the United States for delivery or use therein of intoxicating liquors, in violation of the laws thereof, is hereby prohibited.

Section 3. This article shall be inoperative unless it shall have been ratified as an amendment to the Constitution by conventions in the several States, as provided in the Constitution, within seven years from the date of the submission hereof to the States by the Congress.

AMENDMENT XXII.

Limit on presidential terms of office.

[Proposed by Congress Mar. 24, 1947; ratified Feb. 27, 1951.]
Section 1. No person shall be elected to the office of the President more than twice, and no person who has held the office of President, or acted as President, for more than two years of a term to which some other person was elected President shall be elected to the office of the President more than once. But this Article shall not apply to any person holding the office of President when this Article was proposed by Congress, and shall not prevent any person who may be holding the office of President, or acting as President, during the term within which this Article becomes operative from holding the office of President or acting as President during the remainder of such term.

Section 2. This Article shall be inoperative unless it shall have been ratified as an amendment to the Constitution by the legislatures of three-fourths of the several States within seven years from the date of its submission to the States by the Congress.

AMENDMENT XXIII.

Presidential vote for District of Columbia.

[Proposed by Congress June 16, 1960; ratified Mar. 29, 1961.]
Section 1. The District constituting the seat of Government of the United States shall appoint in such manner as the Congress may direct:

A number of electors of President and Vice President equal to the whole number of Senators and Representatives in Congress to which the District would be entitled if it were a State, but in no event more than the least populous State; they shall be in addition to those appointed by the States, but they shall be considered, for the purposes of the election of President and Vice President, to be electors appointed by a State; and they shall meet in the District and perform such duties as provided by the twelfth article of amendment.

Section 2. The Congress shall have power to enforce this article by appropriate legislation.

AMENDMENT XXIV.

Poll tax barred in federal elections.

[Proposed by Congress Sept. 14, 1962; ratified Jan. 23, 1964.]
Section 1. The right of citizens of the United States to vote in any primary or other election for President or Vice President, for electors for President or Vice President, or for

Senator or Representative in Congress, shall not be denied or abridged by the United States or any State by reason of failure to pay any poll tax or other tax.

Section 2. The Congress shall have power to enforce this article by appropriate legislation.

AMENDMENT XXV.

Presidential vacancy, inability, and succession.

[Proposed by Congress July 6, 1965; ratified Feb. 10, 1967.]

Section 1. In case of the removal of the President from office or of his death or resignation, the Vice President shall become President.

Section 2. Whenever there is a vacancy in the office of the Vice President, the President shall nominate a Vice President who shall take office upon confirmation by a majority vote of both Houses of Congress.

Section 3. Whenever the President transmits to the President pro tempore of the Senate and the Speaker of the House of Representatives his written declaration that he is unable to discharge the powers and duties of his office, and until he transmits to them a written declaration to the contrary, such powers and duties shall be discharged by the Vice President as Acting President.

Section 4. Whenever the Vice President and a majority of either the principal officers of the executive departments or of such other body as Congress may by law provide, transmit to the President pro tempore of the Senate and the Speaker of the House of Representatives their written declaration that the President is unable to discharge the powers and duties of his office, the Vice President shall immediately assume the powers and duties of the office as Acting President.

Thereafter, when the President transmits to the President pro tempore of the Senate and the Speaker of the House of Representatives his written declaration that no inability exists, he shall resume the powers and duties of his office unless the Vice President and a majority of either the principal officers of the executive department or of such other body as Congress may by law provide, transmit within four days to the President pro tempore of the Senate and the Speaker of the House of Representatives their written declaration that the President is unable to discharge the powers and duties of his office. Thereupon Congress shall decide the issue, assembling within forty-eight hours for that purpose if not in session. If the Congress, within twenty-one days after receipt of the latter written declaration, or, if Congress is not in session, within twenty-one days after Congress is required to assemble, determines by two-thirds vote of both Houses that the President is unable to discharge the powers and duties of his office, the Vice President shall continue to discharge the same as Acting President; otherwise, the President shall resume the powers and duties of his office.

AMENDMENT XXVI.

Voting age lowered to 18 years.

[Proposed by Congress Mar. 23, 1971; ratified July 1, 1971.]

Section 1. The right of citizens of the United States, who are eighteen years of age or older, to vote shall not be denied or abridged by the United States or by any State on account of age.

Section 2. The Congress shall have power to enforce this article by appropriate legislation.

AMENDMENT XXVII.

Congressional pay.

[Proposed by Congress Sept. 25, 1789; ratified May 7, 1992.]

No law, varying the compensation for the services of the Senators and Representatives, shall take effect, until an election of Representatives shall have intervened.

How a Bill Becomes a Law

A senator or representative introduces a bill in Congress by sending it to the clerk of the Senate or the House, who assigns it a number and title. This procedure is termed the first reading. The clerk then refers the bill to the appropriate committee of the Senate or House.

If the committee does not wish to consider the bill, it will table it. Otherwise, the committee holds hearings to listen to opinions and facts offered by members and other interested parties. The committee then debates the bill and may offer amendments. A vote is taken, and if favorable, the bill is sent back to the clerk of the Senate or House.

The clerk reads the bill to the house—the second reading. Members may then debate the bill and suggest amendments.

After debate and any amendments, the bill is given a third reading, simply of the title, and put to a voice or roll-call vote.

If the bill passes, it goes to the other house, where it may be defeated or passed, with or without amendments. If defeated, the bill dies. If passed with amendments, a conference committee made up of members of both houses works out the differences between the two bills and arrives at a compromise.

After passage of the final version by both houses, the bill is sent to the president. If the president signs it, the bill becomes a law. The president may instead veto the bill by refusing to sign it and sending it back to the house where it originated, with reasons for the veto.

The president's objections are then read and debated, and a roll-call vote is taken. If the bill receives less than a two-thirds majority, it is defeated. If it receives at least two-thirds, it is sent to the other house. If that house also passes it by at least a two-thirds majority, the president's veto is overridden, and the bill becomes a law.

If the president neither signs nor vetoes the bill within 10 days—not including Sundays—it automatically becomes a law even without the president's signature. However, if Congress adjourns within those 10 days, the bill is automatically killed; this indirect rejection is termed a pocket veto.

Under the Line Item Veto Act, effective Jan. 1, 1997, the president was authorized, under certain circumstances, to veto a bill in part. The legislation was found unconstitutional by the Supreme Court, June 25, 1998.

Presidential Oath of Office

The Constitution (Article II) directs that the president-elect shall take the following oath to be inaugurated: "I do solemnly swear [affirm] that I will faithfully execute the office of President of the United States, and will, to the best of my ability, preserve, protect, and defend the Constitution of the United States."

Custom decrees the addition of the words "So help me God" at the end of the oath when taken by the president-elect, with the left hand on the Bible for the duration of the oath, and the right hand slightly raised.

Presidential Succession

If, by reason of death, resignation, removal from office, inability, or failure to qualify, there is neither a president nor vice president to discharge the powers and duties of the office of president, then the speaker of the House of Representatives shall upon his resignation as speaker and as representative, act as president. The same rule shall apply in the case of the death, resignation, removal from office, or inability of an individual acting as president.

If, at the time when a speaker is to begin the discharge of the powers and duties of the office of president, there is no speaker, or the speaker fails to qualify as acting president, then the president pro tempore of the Senate, upon his resignation as president pro tempore and as senator, shall act as president.

An individual acting as president shall continue to act until the expiration of the then current presidential term, except that (1) if his discharge of the powers and duties of the office is founded in whole or in part in the failure of both the president-elect and the vice president-elect to qualify, then he shall act only until a president or vice president qualifies, and (2) if his discharge of the powers and duties of the office is founded in whole or in part on the inability of the president or vice president, then he shall act only until the removal of the disability of one of such individuals.

If, by reason of death, resignation, removal from office, or failure to qualify, there is no president pro tempore to act as president, then the officer of the United States who is highest on the following list, and who is not under any disability to discharge the powers and duties of president shall act as president: the secretaries of state, treasury, and defense; the attorney general; the secretaries of interior, agriculture, commerce, labor, health and human services, housing and urban development, transportation, energy, education, veterans affairs, and homeland security.

Legislation approved July 18, 1947; amended Sept. 9, 1965, Oct. 15, 1966, Aug. 4, 1977, Sept. 27, 1979, and Mar. 9, 2006. See also Constitutional Amendment XXV.

Confederate States: Secession and Government

The American Civil War (1861-65) grew out of sectional disputes over the continued existence of slavery in the South. Southern legislators contended that the states retained many rights, including the right to own slaves and the right to secede.

The war was not fought by state against state but by one federal regime against another. A Confederate government in Richmond, VA, assumed control over the economic, political, and military life of the seceding states, under protest from Georgia and South Carolina.

South Carolina voted unanimously in convention to secede from the Union, repealing its 1788 ratification of the U.S. Constitution on Dec. 20, 1860, to take effect on Dec. 24. Other states seceded in 1861. Their votes in conventions were: Mississippi, Jan. 9, 84-15; Florida, Jan. 10, 62-7; Alabama, Jan. 11, 61-39; Georgia, Jan. 19, 208-89; Louisiana, Jan. 26, 113-17; Texas, Feb. 1, 166-7, ratified by popular vote (34,794 to 11,325) Feb. 23; Virginia, Apr. 17, 88-55, ratified by popular vote (128,884 to 32,134) May 23; Arkansas, May 6, 69-1; Tennessee, May 7, ratified by popular vote (104,019 to 47,238) June 8; North Carolina, unanimous, May 20.

Missouri Unionists stopped secession in conventions Feb. 28 and Mar. 9, 1861. Under the protection of Confederate troops, secessionist members of the legislature adopted a resolution of secession at Neosho, Oct. 31. The Confederate Congress seated the secessionists' representatives.

Kentucky did not secede, and its government remained Unionist. In a part of the state occupied by Confederate troops, Kentuckians approved secession, and the Confederate Congress admitted their representatives.

The Maryland legislature voted against secession Apr. 27, 1861, 53-13. Delaware did not secede. Pro-Union residents of western Virginia held conventions at Wheeling and, on June 17, 1861, formed the Restored Government of Virginia. It was admitted to the Union as West Virginia on June 20, 1863. Its constitution provided for gradual abolition of slavery.

Forty-two delegates from South Carolina, Georgia, Alabama, Mississippi, Louisiana, and Florida met in convention in Montgomery, AL, on Feb. 4, 1861. They adopted a provisional constitution of the Confederate States of America and elected Jefferson Davis (MS) as provisional president and Alexander H. Stephens (GA) as provisional vice president.

A permanent constitution was adopted Mar. 11. It banned the African slave trade but did not bar interstate commerce in slaves. On July 20 the Congress moved to Richmond. Davis was elected president in Nov. 1861 and was inaugurated Feb. 22, 1862.

The Confederate Congress adopted a flag ("The Stars and Bars") consisting of one white stripe and two red stripes and a blue canton with a circle of white stars. The Confederate battle flag, carried by the Army of Northern Virginia, was more popularly known. It has blue diagonal crossbars with 13 white stars, for the 11 states in the Confederacy plus Kentucky and Missouri, against a red field.

The Gettysburg Address

Delivered by Pres. Abraham Lincoln at the dedication of the Soldiers' National Cemetery in Gettysburg, PA, on Nov. 19, 1863. Five handwritten copies of the Gettysburg Address as made by Lincoln are known to exist. The text differs slightly between copies. The Bliss copy, made for Alexander Bliss, is shown here. The copy is kept on display in the White House.

Four score and seven years ago our fathers brought forth on this continent, a new nation, conceived in Liberty, and dedicated to the proposition that all men are created equal.

Now we are engaged in a great civil war, testing whether that nation, or any nation so conceived and so dedicated, can long endure. We are met on a great battle-field of that war. We have come to dedicate a portion of that field, as a final resting place for those who here gave their lives that that nation might live. It is altogether fitting and proper that we should do this.

But, in a larger sense, we can not dedicate—we can not consecrate—we can not hallow—this ground. The brave men, living and dead, who struggled here, have consecrated it, far above our poor power to add or detract. The world will little note, nor long remember what we say here, but it can never forget what they did here.

It is for us the living, rather, to be dedicated here to the unfinished work which they who fought here have thus far so nobly advanced. It is rather for us to be here dedicated to the great task remaining before us—that from these honored dead we take increased devotion to that cause for which they gave the last full measure of devotion—that we here highly resolve that these dead shall not have died in vain—that this nation, under God, shall have a new birth of freedom—and that government of the people, by the people, for the people, shall not perish from the earth.

Origin of the United States National Motto

In God We Trust, designated as the U.S. National Motto by Congress in 1956, originated during the Civil War as an inscription for U.S. coins. On Nov. 13, 1861, the Rev. M. R. Watkinson, of Ridleyville, PA, wrote to Treasury Sec. Salmon P. Chase requesting "recognition of the Almighty God in some form on our coins." Chase ordered designs prepared with the inscription *In God We Trust* and backed coinage legislation that authorized use of this slogan. The motto first appeared on some U.S. coins in 1864 and sporadically thereafter until 1938, after which all U.S. coins bear the inscription. A joint resolution passed by the 84th Congress and signed by Pres. Dwight D. Eisenhower July 30, 1956, declared *In God We Trust* the national motto of the United States.

Great Seal of the U.S.

On July 4, 1776, the Continental Congress appointed a committee consisting of Benjamin Franklin, John Adams, and Thomas Jefferson "to bring in a device for a seal of the United States of America." The designs submitted by this and a subsequent committee were considered unacceptable. After many delays, a third committee, appointed early in 1782, presented a design prepared by lawyer William Barton. Charles Thomson, the secretary of Congress, suggested certain changes, and Congress finally approved the design on June 20, 1782. The obverse side of the seal shows an American bald eagle. In its mouth is a ribbon bearing the motto *E Pluribus Unum* (out of many, one). In the eagle's talons are 13 arrows of war and an olive branch of peace. The reverse side shows an unfinished pyramid with an eye (Eye of Providence) above it.

The Flag of the U.S.—The Stars and Stripes

The 50-star flag of the United States was raised for the first time officially at 12:01 AM on July 4, 1960, at Ft. McHenry National Monument in Baltimore, MD. The 50th star had been added for Hawaii; a year earlier the 49th, for Alaska.

There are so many myths and legends surrounding the history of the Stars and Stripes that the facts are difficult, and in some cases impossible, to establish. For example, it is not certain who designed the Stars and Stripes, who made the first such flag, or even whether it ever flew during any battle of the American Revolution.

Historians agree, however, that the Stars and Stripes originated as the result of a resolution offered by the Marine Committee of the Second Continental Congress at Philadelphia and adopted on June 14, 1777. It read:

"Resolved: that the flag of the United States be thirteen stripes, alternate red and white; that the union be thirteen stars, white in a blue field, representing a new constellation."

Congress gave no hint as to the designer of the flag, no instructions as to the arrangement of the stars, and no information on its appropriate uses.

The resolution establishing the flag was not published until Sept. 2, 1777. Despite repeated requests, George Washington did not get the flags until 1783, after the war was over. And there is no certainty that they were the Stars and Stripes.

Early Flags

Many historians consider the first flag of the U.S. to have been the Grand Union (sometimes called Great Union) flag, although the Continental Congress never officially adopted it. This flag was a modification of the British Meteor flag, which had the red cross of St. George and the white cross of St. Andrew combined in the blue canton. For the Grand Union flag, six horizontal stripes were imposed on the red field, dividing it into 13 alternating red and white stripes. On Jan. 1, 1776, when the Continental Army came into formal existence, this flag was unfurled on Prospect Hill, Somerville, MA. Washington wrote that "we hoisted the Union Flag in compliment to the United Colonies."

One of several flags about which controversy has raged is in Easton, PA. Containing the devices of the national flag in reversed order, this flag has been in the public library in Easton for more than 150 years. Some contend that this flag was actually the first Stars and Stripes, first displayed on July 8, 1776. This flag has 13 red and white stripes in the canton and 13 white stars centered in a blue field.

A flag was hastily improvised from garments by the defenders of Ft. Schuyler at Rome, NY, Aug. 3-22, 1777. Historians believe it was the Grand Union Flag.

The Sons of Liberty had a flag of nine red and white stripes, to signify nine colonies, when they met in New York in 1765 to oppose the Stamp Tax. By 1775, the flag had grown to 13 red and white stripes, with a rattlesnake on it.

At Concord, MA, Apr. 19, 1775, the minutemen from Bedford, MA, are said to have carried a flag having a silver arm with sword on a red field. At Cambridge, MA, the Sons of Liberty used a plain red flag with a green pine tree on it.

In June 1775, Washington went from Philadelphia to Boston to take command of the army. He was escorted to New York by the Philadelphia Light Horse Troop, which carried a yellow flag that had an elaborate coat of arms—the shield charged with 13 knots, the motto "For These We Strive"—and a canton of 13 blue and silver stripes.

In Feb. 1776, Col. Christopher Gadsden, a member of the Continental Congress, gave the South Carolina Provincial Congress a flag "such as is to be used by the commander-in-chief of the American Navy." It had a yellow field, with a rattlesnake about to strike and the words "Don't Tread on Me."

At the Battle of Bennington, Aug. 16, 1777, patriots used a flag of seven white and six red stripes with a blue canton extending down nine stripes and showing an arch of 11 white stars over the figure 76 and a star in each of the upper corners. The stars are seven-pointed. This flag is preserved in a museum in Bennington, VT.

At the Battle of Cowpens, Jan. 17, 1781, the 3rd Maryland Regiment is said to have carried a flag of 13 red and white stripes, with a blue canton containing 12 stars in a circle around one star.

Who Designed the Flag? No one knows for certain. Francis Hopkinson, designer of a naval flag, declared he had designed the flag and in 1781 asked Congress to reimburse him for his services. Congress did not do so.

Who Called the Flag "Old Glory"? The flag is said to have been named Old Glory by William Driver, a sea captain of Salem, MA. One legend has it that he did so when he raised the flag on his brig in 1824. But his daughter said he named it at his 21st birthday celebration on Mar. 17, 1824, when his mother presented the homemade flag to him.

The Betsy Ross Legend. The widely publicized legend that Betsy Ross made the first Stars and Stripes in June 1776, at the request of a committee composed of George Washington, Robert Morris, and George Ross, an uncle, was first made public in 1870, by a grandson of Ross. Historians have been unable to find a historical record of such a meeting or committee.

Adding New Stars

On the admission of Vermont and Kentucky to the Union, Congress designated that after May 1, 1795, the flag should have 15 stripes, alternating red and white, and 15 white stars on a blue field.

When more new states were admitted, it became evident that the flag would become burdened with stripes. Congress ordered that after July 4, 1818, the flag should have 13 stripes, symbolizing 13 original states; that the union have 20 stars, and that whenever a new state was admitted a new star should be added on the July 4 following admission.

No law designates the permanent arrangement of the stars. However, since 1912, when a new state has been admitted, the new design has been announced by executive order. No star is specifically identified with any state.

Pledge of Allegiance to the Flag

I pledge allegiance to the flag of the United States of America, and to the republic for which it stands, one nation under God, indivisible, with liberty and justice for all.

This, the current official version of the Pledge of Allegiance, developed from a pledge first published in the Sept. 8, 1892, issue of *Youth's Companion*, a weekly magazine. The original pledge contained the phrase "my flag," which was changed more than 30 years later to "flag of the United States of America." A 1954 act of Congress added the words "under God." (In 2002, the 9th Circuit U.S. Court of Appeals ruled that recitation of the pledge in public schools could not include that phrase. In 2004, however, the U.S. Supreme Court voted to decline to decide the case on a technicality. The lower court's decision was thus overturned.)

The authorship of the pledge was in dispute for many years. *Youth's Companion* stated in 1917 that the original draft was written by James B. Upham, an executive of the magazine who died in 1910. A leaflet circulated by the magazine later named Upham as the originator of the first draft.

Francis Bellamy, a former member of the *Youth's Companion* editorial staff, publicly claimed authorship of the pledge in 1923. In 1939, the United States Flag Association, acting on the advice of a committee named to study the controversy, upheld the claim by Bellamy, who had died eight years earlier. In 1957 the Library of Congress issued a report attributing the authorship to Bellamy.

According to the federal Flag Code, the pledge should be given while standing at attention facing the flag with the right hand over the heart. Those not in military uniform should remove any non-religious head coverings with their right hand and hold it at the left shoulder, the hand being over the heart. Those in uniform should remain silent, face the flag, and render a military salute.

History of the U.S. National Anthem

"The Star-Spangled Banner" was ordered played by the military and naval services by Pres. Woodrow Wilson in 1916. It was designated the national anthem by Act of Congress, Mar. 3, 1931. The words were written by Francis Scott Key, of Georgetown, MD, during the bombardment of Ft. McHenry in Baltimore, MD, Sept. 13-14, 1814. Key was a lawyer, a graduate of St. John's College, Annapolis, MD, and a volunteer in a light artillery company. When a friend, Dr. Beanes, a Maryland physician, was taken aboard Adm. Cockburn's British squadron for interfering with ground troops, Key and U.S. Col. J. S. Skinner, carrying a note from Pres. Madison, went to the fleet under a flag of truce on a cartel ship to ask for Beanes's release. Cockburn consented, but as the fleet was about to sail up the Patapsco to bombard Ft. McHenry, he detained them, first on HMS *Surprise* and then on a supply ship.

Key witnessed the bombardment from his own vessel. It began at 7 AM, Sept. 13, and lasted 25 hours. The British fired more than 1,500 shells, each weighing as much as 220 lbs. They were unable to approach closely because the U.S. had

sunk 22 vessels to form a barrier. Only four Americans were killed and 24 wounded. A British bomb ship was disabled.

During the shelling, Key wrote a stanza on the back of an envelope. The next day at Indian Queen Inn in Baltimore, he wrote out the poem and gave it to his brother-in-law, Judge J. H. Nicholson. Nicholson suggested use of the tune "Anacreon in Heaven" (attributed to British composer John Stafford Smith) and had the poem printed on broadsides, of which two copies survive. On Sept. 20 it appeared in the *Baltimore American*. Later Key made three copies; one is in the Library of Congress and one in the Pennsylvania Historical Society.

The flag that Key saw during the bombardment is preserved in the Smithsonian Institution, Washington, DC. It measures 30 by 42 ft and has 15 alternating red and white stripes and 15 stars, for the original 13 states plus Kentucky and Vermont. It was sewn by flag maker Mary Pickersgill. Her house in Baltimore was restored in 1953 and is preserved as part of the Star-Spangled Banner Flag House museum.

The Star-Spangled Banner

I

Oh, say can you see by the dawn's early light
What so proudly we hailed at the twilight's last gleaming?
Whose broad stripes and bright stars thru the perilous fight,
O'er the ramparts we watched were so gallantly streaming?
And the rockets' red glare, the bombs bursting in air,
Gave proof through the night that our flag was still there.
Oh, say does that star-spangled banner yet wave
O'er the land of the free and the home of the brave?

II

On the shore, dimly seen through the mists of the deep,
Where the foe's haughty host in dread silence reposes,
What is that which the breeze, o'er the towering steep,
As it fitfully blows, half conceals, half discloses?
Now it catches the gleam of the morning's first beam,
In full glory reflected now shines in the stream:
'Tis the star-spangled banner! Oh long may it wave
O'er the land of the free and the home of the brave!

III

And where is that band who so vauntingly swore
That the havoc of war and the battle's confusion,
A home and a country should leave us no more!
Their blood has washed out their foul footsteps' pollution.
No refuge could save the hireling and slave
From the terror of flight, or the gloom of the grave:
And the star-spangled banner in triumph doth wave
O'er the land of the free and the home of the brave!

IV

Oh! thus be it ever, when freemen shall stand
Between their loved home and the war's desolation!
Blest with victory and peace, may the heav'n rescued land
Praise the Power that hath made and preserved us a nation.
Then conquer we must, when our cause it is just,
And this be our motto: "In God is our trust."
And the star-spangled banner in triumph shall wave
O'er the land of the free and the home of the brave!

Statue of Liberty National Monument

Since 1886, the Statue of Liberty, formally known as "Liberty Enlightening the World," has stood as a symbol of freedom in New York Harbor. As a gift from the people of France to the people of the U.S., it also commemorates French-American friendship. It was designed by French sculptor Frédéric Auguste Bartholdi (1834-1904).

On Washington's Birthday, Feb. 22, 1877, Congress approved the use of a site on Bedloe's Island suggested by Bartholdi. This island of 12 acres had been owned in the 17th cent. by a Walloon colonist named Isaac Bedloe. On Aug. 3, 1956, Pres. Dwight Eisenhower approved a measure changing the name to Liberty Island.

The statue was finished on May 21, 1884, and presented to the U.S. minister to France, Levi Parsons Morton, July 4, 1884, by Ferdinand de Lesseps, who was head of the Franco-American Union, promoter of the Panama Canal, and builder of the Suez Canal.

On Aug. 5, 1884, the cornerstone for the pedestal was laid on the foundations of Fort Wood, erected by the government in 1811. The American Committee for the Statue of Liberty had raised an inadequate $125,000, and *New York World* newspaper owner Joseph Pulitzer appealed Mar. 16, 1885, for general donations. By Aug. 11, 1885, he had raised $100,000. The statue itself arrived dismantled, in 214 packing cases, from Rouen, France, in June 1885. The last rivet of the statue was driven on Oct. 28, 1886, when Pres. Grover Cleveland dedicated the monument.

The Statue of Liberty National Monument was designated as such in 1924. It is administered by the National Park Service. A $2.5-mil building housing the American Museum of Immigration was opened by Pres. Richard Nixon on Sept. 26, 1972, at the base of the statue. It houses a permanent exhibition tracing the history of American immigration.

Four years of restoration work funded and led by the Statue of Liberty-Ellis Island Foundation were completed before the statue's 1986 centennial. The $87-mil project included the replacement of the 1,600 wrought iron bands that hold the statue's copper skin to its frame, replacement of the torch, and installation of an elevator. A four-day Liberty Weekend extravaganza of concerts, tall ships, ethnic festivals, and fireworks, July 3-6, 1986, celebrated the 100th anniversary. U.S. Supreme Court Chief Justice Warren E. Burger swore in 5,000 new citizens on Ellis Island, while 20,000 others across the country were sworn in through a satellite telecast. Other ceremonies followed on Oct. 28, 1986, the statue's exact 100th birthday.

After the Sept. 11, 2001, terrorist attacks, Liberty Island was closed to visitors. On Dec. 20, 2001, the secretary of the interior reopened the island after installing airport-type screening facilities at passenger embarkation areas at Battery Park in Manhattan and Liberty State Park in New Jersey.

The federal government increased security throughout the park before reopening the statue. In addition to federally funded security upgrades, significant safety improvements were made to meet building codes. Access to the statue was restored on Aug. 3, 2004.

Following the 125th anniversary celebration Oct. 28, 2011, the statue was closed. A $30-mil renovation brought the statue up to contemporary safety standards and allowed for increased visitor access. The island remained open to visitors, and views of the statue were largely unobstructed, but visitors could not go inside. The statue interior reopened Oct. 28, 2012, but damages caused by Hurricane Sandy the next week forced all of Liberty Island to close again.

The island and the statue officially reopened to visitors July 4, 2013. Advance reservations are recommended for visiting the museum and statue pedestal and are required for the crown. Reservations can be made at www.statuecruises.com or by calling 1-877-LADY-TIX. Fees start at $18 for adults ($9 child/$14 senior). Visitors to the statue's interior must follow a number of guidelines including age and height restrictions. Park rangers conduct English-language tours throughout the day. Standard self-guided audio tours are available in nine languages; a children's version of the audio tour is available in five languages. For more information, visit www.nps.gov/stli and www.libertyellisfoundation.org.

Statue Statistics

The statue weighs 450,000 lbs, or 225 tons. The copper sheeting weighs 200,000 lbs. There are 377 steps from the main lobby to the crown platform. There are 146 steps from the top of the pedestal (the statue's feet) to the crown platform.

Statue feature	Measurement	
	Ft	In.
Height from base to torch tip...............	151	1
Foundation of pedestal to torch tip..........	305	1
Heel to top of head	111	1
Hand, length	16	5
Index finger, length	8	0
Fingernail size.........................		13x10
Head from chin to cranium................	17	3
Head thickness, ear to ear................	10	0
Nose, length	4	6
Right arm, length	42	0
Right arm, max. thickness	12	0
Waist, thickness........................	35	0
Mouth, width	3	0
Tablet, length.........................	23	7
Tablet, width..........................	13	7

Ellis Island

Ellis Island was the gateway to America for over 12 mil immigrants between 1892 and 1924. In the late 18th cent., Samuel Ellis, a New York City merchant, purchased the island. From Ellis, it passed to New York state before the U.S. government bought it in 1808. On Jan. 1, 1892, the government opened the first federal immigration center in the U.S. there. The 27.5-acre site eventually supported more than 35 buildings, including the Main Building with its Great Hall, which was designed to process 5,000 people a day. In Ellis Island's peak year, 1907, it received 1,004,756 immigrants; on its peak day (Apr. 17, 1907), 11,747 immigrants were processed.

Closed as an immigration station in 1954, Ellis Island was proclaimed part of the Statue of Liberty National Monument in 1965 by Pres. Lyndon B. Johnson. After a six-year, $170-mil restoration project funded by the Statue of Liberty-Ellis Island Foundation, Ellis Island was reopened as a museum in 1990, now called the Ellis Island National Museum of Immigration. Artifacts, historic photographs and documents, oral histories, and ethnic music depicting 400 years of American immigration are housed in the museum.

In 1998, the U.S. Supreme Court ruled that nearly 90% of the island (the 24.2 acres that are landfill) lies in New Jersey while the original 3.3 acres, on which the museum is located, are in New York. (The decision settled the issue of jurisdiction over potential development.)

The American Family Immigration History Center opened in Apr. 2001. Visitors there can access immigrant arrival records on more than 51 million individuals who entered the U.S. through the Port of New York and Ellis Island from 1892 to 1957. The searchable digitized archives include ships' images and manifests and passenger information such as age, ethnicity, and port of departure. **Website:** www.libertyellisfoundation.org

Damage caused by storm surges from Hurricane Sandy in late Oct. 2012 forced Ellis Island to close for repairs. New galleries opened May 20, 2015, focusing on post-Ellis Island era immigration.

PRESIDENTS OF THE UNITED STATES

U.S. Presidents

	Name	Politics	Born	Birthplace	Inaug.	Age at inaug.	Died	Age at death
1.	George Washington	Fed.	1732, Feb. 22	VA	1789	57	1799, Dec. 14	67
2.	John Adams	Fed.	1735, Oct. 30	MA	1797	61	1826, July 4	90
3.	Thomas Jefferson	Dem.-Rep.	1743, Apr. 13	VA	1801	57	1826, July 4	83
4.	James Madison	Dem.-Rep.	1751, Mar. 16	VA	1809	57	1836, June 28	85
5.	James Monroe	Dem.-Rep.	1758, Apr. 28	VA	1817	58	1831, July 4	73
6.	John Quincy Adams	Dem.-Rep.	1767, July 11	MA	1825	57	1848, Feb. 23	80
7.	Andrew Jackson	Dem.	1767, Mar. 15	SC	1829	61	1845, June 8	78
8.	Martin Van Buren	Dem.	1782, Dec. 5	NY	1837	54	1862, July 24	79
9.	William Henry Harrison	Whig	1773, Feb. 9	VA	1841	68	1841, Apr. 4	68
10.	John Tyler	Whig	1790, Mar. 29	VA	1841	51	1862, Jan. 18	71
11.	James Knox Polk	Dem.	1795, Nov. 2	NC	1845	49	1849, June 15	53
12.	Zachary Taylor	Whig	1784, Nov. 24	VA	1849	64	1850, July 9	65
13.	Millard Fillmore	Whig	1800, Jan. 7	NY	1850	50	1874, Mar. 8	74
14.	Franklin Pierce	Dem.	1804, Nov. 23	NH	1853	48	1869, Oct. 8	64
15.	James Buchanan	Dem.	1791, Apr. 23	PA	1857	65	1868, June 1	77
16.	Abraham Lincoln	Rep.	1809, Feb. 12	KY	1861	52	1865, Apr. 15	56
17.	Andrew Johnson	Dem.[1]	1808, Dec. 29	NC	1865	56	1875, July 31	66
18.	Ulysses S. Grant	Rep.	1822, Apr. 27	OH	1869	46	1885, July 23	63
19.	Rutherford Birchard Hayes	Rep.	1822, Oct. 4	OH	1877	54	1893, Jan. 17	70
20.	James Abram Garfield	Rep.	1831, Nov. 19	OH	1881	49	1881, Sept. 19	49
21.	Chester Alan Arthur	Rep.	1829, Oct. 5	VT	1881	51	1886, Nov. 18	57
22.	Grover Cleveland	Dem.	1837, Mar. 18	NJ	1885	47	1908, June 24	71
23.	Benjamin Harrison	Rep.	1833, Aug. 20	OH	1889	55	1901, Mar. 13	67
24.	Grover Cleveland	Dem.	1837, Mar. 18	NJ	1893	55	1908, June 24	71
25.	William McKinley	Rep.	1843, Jan. 29	OH	1897	54	1901, Sept. 14	58
26.	Theodore Roosevelt	Rep.	1858, Oct. 27	NY	1901	42	1919, Jan. 6	60
27.	William Howard Taft	Rep.	1857, Sept. 15	OH	1909	51	1930, Mar. 8	72
28.	(Thomas) Woodrow Wilson	Dem.	1856, Dec. 28	VA	1913	56	1924, Feb. 3	67
29.	Warren Gamaliel Harding	Rep.	1865, Nov. 2	OH	1921	55	1923, Aug. 2	57
30.	(John) Calvin Coolidge	Rep.	1872, July 4	VT	1923	51	1933, Jan. 5	60
31.	Herbert Clark Hoover	Rep.	1874, Aug. 10	IA	1929	54	1964, Oct. 20	90
32.	Franklin Delano Roosevelt	Dem.	1882, Jan. 30	NY	1933	51	1945, Apr. 12	63
33.	Harry S. Truman	Dem.	1884, May 8	MO	1945	60	1972, Dec. 26	88
34.	Dwight David Eisenhower	Rep.	1890, Oct. 14	TX	1953	62	1969, Mar. 28	78
35.	John Fitzgerald Kennedy	Dem.	1917, May 29	MA	1961	43	1963, Nov. 22	46
36.	Lyndon Baines Johnson	Dem.	1908, Aug. 27	TX	1963	55	1973, Jan. 22	64
37.	Richard Milhous Nixon[2]	Rep.	1913, Jan. 9	CA	1969	56	1994, Apr. 22	81
38.	Gerald Rudolph Ford	Rep.	1913, July 14	NE	1974	61	2006, Dec. 26	93
39.	James Earl (Jimmy) Carter	Dem.	1924, Oct. 1	GA	1977	52		
40.	Ronald Wilson Reagan	Rep.	1911, Feb. 6	IL	1981	69	2004, June 5	93
41.	George Herbert Walker Bush	Rep.	1924, June 12	MA	1989	64		
42.	Wm. Jefferson (Bill) Clinton	Dem.	1946, Aug. 19	AR	1993	46		
43.	George Walker Bush	Rep.	1946, July 6	CT	2001	54		
44.	Barack Hussein Obama	Dem.	1961, Aug. 4	HI	2009	47		

(1) Andrew Johnson, a Democrat, had been nominated vice president by Republicans and elected with Lincoln on National Union ticket. (2) Resigned Aug. 9, 1974.

U.S. Presidents, Vice Presidents, Congresses

	President	Service		Vice President	Congresses
1.	George Washington	Apr. 30, 1789-Mar. 3, 1797	1.	John Adams	1, 2, 3, 4
2.	John Adams	Mar. 4, 1797-Mar. 3, 1801	2.	Thomas Jefferson	5, 6
3.	Thomas Jefferson	Mar. 4, 1801-Mar. 3, 1805	3.	Aaron Burr	7, 8
		Mar. 4, 1805-Mar. 3, 1809	4.	George Clinton	9, 10
4.	James Madison	Mar. 4, 1809-Mar. 3, 1813		George Clinton[1]	11, 12
		Mar. 4, 1813-Mar. 3, 1817	5.	Elbridge Gerry[2]	13, 14
5.	James Monroe	Mar. 4, 1817-Mar. 3, 1825	6.	Daniel D. Tompkins	15, 16, 17, 18
6.	John Quincy Adams	Mar. 4, 1825-Mar. 3, 1829	7.	John C. Calhoun	19, 20
7.	Andrew Jackson	Mar. 4, 1829-Mar. 3, 1833		John C. Calhoun[3]	21, 22
		Mar. 4, 1833-Mar. 3, 1837	8.	Martin Van Buren	23, 24
8.	Martin Van Buren	Mar. 4, 1837-Mar. 3, 1841	9.	Richard M. Johnson	25, 26
9.	William Henry Harrison[4]	Mar. 4, 1841-Apr. 4, 1841	10.	John Tyler	27
10.	John Tyler	Apr. 6, 1841-Mar. 3, 1845		(None)	27, 28
11.	James K. Polk	Mar. 4, 1845-Mar. 3, 1849	11.	George M. Dallas	29, 30
12.	Zachary Taylor[4]	Mar. 5, 1849-July 9, 1850	12.	Millard Fillmore	31
13.	Millard Fillmore	July 10, 1850-Mar. 3, 1853		(None)	31, 32
14.	Franklin Pierce	Mar. 4, 1853-Mar. 3, 1857	13.	William R. King[5]	33, 34
15.	James Buchanan	Mar. 4, 1857-Mar. 3, 1861	14.	John C. Breckinridge	35, 36
16.	Abraham Lincoln[4]	Mar. 4, 1861-Mar. 3, 1865	15.	Hannibal Hamlin	37, 38
		Mar. 4, 1865-Apr. 15, 1865	16.	Andrew Johnson	39
17.	Andrew Johnson	Apr. 15, 1865-Mar. 3, 1869		(None)	39, 40
18.	Ulysses S. Grant	Mar. 4, 1869-Mar. 3, 1873	17.	Schuyler Colfax	41, 42
		Mar. 4, 1873-Mar. 3, 1877	18.	Henry Wilson[6]	43, 44
19.	Rutherford B. Hayes	Mar. 4, 1877-Mar. 3, 1881	19.	William A. Wheeler	45, 46
20.	James A. Garfield[4]	Mar. 4, 1881-Sept. 19, 1881	20.	Chester A. Arthur	47
21.	Chester A. Arthur	Sept. 20, 1881-Mar. 3, 1885		(None)	47, 48
22.	Grover Cleveland[7]	Mar. 4, 1885-Mar. 3, 1889	21.	Thomas A. Hendricks[8]	49, 50
23.	Benjamin Harrison	Mar. 4, 1889-Mar. 3, 1893	22.	Levi P. Morton	51, 52
24.	Grover Cleveland[7]	Mar. 4, 1893-Mar. 3, 1897	23.	Adlai E. Stevenson	53, 54
25.	William McKinley[4]	Mar. 4, 1897-Mar. 3, 1901	24.	Garret A. Hobart[9]	55, 56
		Mar. 4, 1901-Sept. 14, 1901	25.	Theodore Roosevelt	57
26.	Theodore Roosevelt	Sept. 14, 1901-Mar. 3, 1905		(None)	57, 58
		Mar. 4, 1905-Mar. 3, 1909	26.	Charles W. Fairbanks	59, 60
27.	William H. Taft	Mar. 4, 1909-Mar. 3, 1913	27.	James S. Sherman[10]	61, 62

President	Service	Vice President	Congresses
28. Woodrow Wilson	Mar. 4, 1913-Mar. 3, 1921	28. Thomas R. Marshall	63, 64, 65, 66
29. Warren G. Harding[4]	Mar. 4, 1921-Aug. 2, 1923	29. Calvin Coolidge	67
30. Calvin Coolidge	Aug. 3, 1923-Mar. 3, 1925	(None)	68
	Mar. 4, 1925-Mar. 3, 1929	30. Charles G. Dawes	69, 70
31. Herbert C. Hoover	Mar. 4, 1929-Mar. 3, 1933	31. Charles Curtis	71, 72
32. Franklin D. Roosevelt[4,11]	Mar. 4, 1933-Jan. 20, 1941	32. John N. Garner	73, 74, 75, 76, 77
	Jan. 20, 1941-Jan. 20, 1945	33. Henry A. Wallace	77, 78, 79
	Jan. 20, 1945-Apr. 12, 1945	34. Harry S. Truman	79
33. Harry S. Truman	Apr. 12, 1945-Jan. 20, 1949	(None)	79, 80, 81
	Jan. 20, 1949-Jan. 20, 1953	35. Alben W. Barkley	81, 82, 83
34. Dwight D. Eisenhower	Jan. 20, 1953-Jan. 20, 1961	36. Richard M. Nixon	83, 84, 85, 86, 87
35. John F. Kennedy[4]	Jan. 20, 1961-Nov. 22, 1963	37. Lyndon B. Johnson	87, 88
36. Lyndon B. Johnson	Nov. 22, 1963-Jan. 20, 1965	(None)	88, 89
	Jan. 20, 1965-Jan. 20, 1969	38. Hubert H. Humphrey	89, 90, 91
37. Richard M. Nixon[13]	Jan. 20, 1969-Jan. 20, 1973	39. Spiro T. Agnew[12]	91, 92, 93
	Jan. 20, 1973-Aug. 9, 1974	40. Gerald R. Ford[14]	93
38. Gerald R. Ford[15]	Aug. 9, 1974-Jan. 20, 1977	41. Nelson A. Rockefeller[16]	93, 94, 95
39. Jimmy Carter	Jan. 20, 1977-Jan. 20, 1981	42. Walter F. Mondale	95, 96, 97
40. Ronald W. Reagan	Jan. 20, 1981-Jan. 20, 1989	43. George H. W. Bush	97, 98, 99, 100, 101
41. George H. W. Bush	Jan. 20, 1989-Jan. 20, 1993	44. Dan Quayle	101, 102, 103
42. Bill Clinton	Jan. 20, 1993-Jan. 20, 2001	45. Al Gore	103, 104, 105, 106, 107
43. George W. Bush	Jan. 20, 2001-Jan. 20, 2009	46. Dick Cheney	107, 108, 109, 110, 111
44. Barack H. Obama	Jan. 20, 2009-	47. Joe Biden	111, 112, 113, 114

(1) Died Apr. 20, 1812. (2) Died Nov. 23, 1814. (3) Resigned Dec. 28, 1832, to become U.S. senator. (4) Died in office. (5) Died Apr. 18, 1853. (6) Died Nov. 22, 1875. (7) Terms not consecutive. (8) Died Nov. 25, 1885. (9) Died Nov. 21, 1899. (10) Died Oct. 30, 1912. (11) First president to be inaugurated under 20th Amendment, Jan. 20, 1937. (12) Resigned Oct. 10, 1973, after pleading no contest to a charge of tax evasion. (13) Resigned Aug. 9, 1974. (14) First nonelected vice president, chosen under 25th Amendment procedure. (15) First president never elected president or vice president. (16) Second nonelected vice president, chosen under 25th Amendment. Confirmed Dec. 19, 1974.

Vice Presidents of the U.S.

The numerals given vice presidents do not coincide with those given presidents because some presidents (Tyler, Fillmore, A. Johnson, Arthur) had none, and some had more than one.

Name	Birthplace	Born	Home	Inaug.	Politics/ party	Place of death	Died	Age at death
1. John Adams	Quincy, MA	1735	MA	1789	Fed.	Quincy, MA	1826	90
2. Thomas Jefferson	Shadwell, VA	1743	VA	1797	Dem.-Rep.	Monticello, VA	1826	83
3. Aaron Burr	Newark, NJ	1756	NY	1801	Dem.-Rep.	Staten Island, NY	1836	80
4. George Clinton	Little Britain, NY	1739	NY	1805	Dem.-Rep.	Washington, DC	1812	73
5. Elbridge Gerry	Marblehead, MA	1744	MA	1813	Dem.-Rep.	Washington, DC	1814	70
6. Daniel D. Tompkins	Scarsdale, NY	1774	NY	1817	Dem.-Rep.	Staten Island, NY	1825	51
7. John C. Calhoun[1]	Abbeville, SC	1782	SC	1825	Dem.-Rep.	Washington, DC	1850	68
8. Martin Van Buren	Kinderhook, NY	1782	NY	1833	Dem.	Kinderhook, NY	1862	79
9. Richard M. Johnson[2]	Louisville, KY	1780	KY	1837	Dem.	Frankfort, KY	1850	70
10. John Tyler	Greenway, VA	1790	VA	1841	Whig	Richmond, VA	1862	71
11. George M. Dallas	Philadelphia, PA	1792	PA	1845	Dem.	Philadelphia, PA	1864	72
12. Millard Fillmore	Cayuga Co., NY	1800	NY	1849	Whig	Buffalo, NY	1874	74
13. William R. King	Sampson Co., NC	1786	AL	1853	Dem.	Cahaba, AL	1853	67
14. John C. Breckinridge	Lexington, KY	1821	KY	1857	Dem.	Lexington, KY	1875	54
15. Hannibal Hamlin	Paris, ME	1809	ME	1861	Rep.	Bangor, ME	1891	81
16. Andrew Johnson	Raleigh, NC	1808	TN	1865	Dem.[3]	Carter Co., TN	1875	66
17. Schuyler Colfax	New York, NY	1823	IN	1869	Rep.	Mankato, MN	1885	62
18. Henry Wilson	Farmington, NH	1812	MA	1873	Rep.	Washington, DC	1875	63
19. William A. Wheeler	Malone, NY	1819	NY	1877	Rep.	Malone, NY	1887	68
20. Chester A. Arthur	Fairfield, VT	1829	NY	1881	Rep.	New York, NY	1886	57
21. Thomas A. Hendricks	Zanesville, OH	1819	IN	1885	Dem.	Indianapolis, IN	1885	66
22. Levi P. Morton	Shoreham, VT	1824	NY	1889	Rep.	Rhinebeck, NY	1920	96
23. Adlai E. Stevenson[4]	Christian Co., KY	1835	IL	1893	Dem.	Chicago, IL	1914	78
24. Garret A. Hobart	Long Branch, NJ	1844	NJ	1897	Rep.	Paterson, NJ	1899	55
25. Theodore Roosevelt	New York, NY	1858	NY	1901	Rep.	Oyster Bay, NY	1919	60
26. Charles W. Fairbanks	Unionville Centre, OH	1852	IN	1905	Rep.	Indianapolis, IN	1918	66
27. James S. Sherman	Utica, NY	1855	NY	1909	Rep.	Utica, NY	1912	57
28. Thomas R. Marshall	N. Manchester, IN	1854	IN	1913	Dem.	Washington, DC	1925	71
29. Calvin Coolidge	Plymouth Notch, VT	1872	MA	1921	Rep.	Northampton, MA	1933	60
30. Charles G. Dawes	Marietta, OH	1865	IL	1925	Rep.	Evanston, IL	1951	85
31. Charles Curtis	Topeka, KS	1860	KS	1929	Rep.	Washington, DC	1936	76
32. John Nance Garner	Red River Co., TX	1868	TX	1933	Dem.	Uvalde, TX	1967	98
33. Henry A. Wallace	Adair County, IA	1888	IA	1941	Dem.	Danbury, CT	1965	77
34. Harry S. Truman	Lamar, MO	1884	MO	1945	Dem.	Kansas City, MO	1972	88
35. Alben W. Barkley	Graves Co., KY	1877	KY	1949	Dem.	Lexington, VA	1956	78
36. Richard M. Nixon	Yorba Linda, CA	1913	CA	1953	Rep.	New York, NY	1994	81
37. Lyndon B. Johnson	Stonewall, TX	1908	TX	1961	Dem.	San Antonio, TX	1973	64
38. Hubert H. Humphrey	Wallace, SD	1911	MN	1965	Dem.	Waverly, MN	1978	66
39. Spiro T. Agnew[5]	Baltimore, MD	1918	MD	1969	Rep.	Berlin, MD	1996	77
40. Gerald R. Ford[6]	Omaha, NE	1913	MI	1973	Rep.	Rancho Mirage, CA	2006	93
41. Nelson A. Rockefeller[7]	Bar Harbor, ME	1908	NY	1974	Rep.	New York, NY	1979	70
42. Walter F. Mondale	Ceylon, MN	1928	MN	1977	Dem.			
43. George H. W. Bush	Milton, MA	1924	TX	1981	Rep.			
44. James Danforth (Dan) Quayle Jr.	Indianapolis, IN	1947	IN	1989	Rep.			
45. Albert A. Gore	Washington, DC	1948	TN	1993	Dem.			
46. Richard B. Cheney	Lincoln, NE	1941	WY	2001	Rep.			
47. Joseph R. Biden Jr.	Scranton, PA	1942	DE	2009	Dem.			

(1) Resigned Dec. 28, 1832, having been elected to the Senate to fill a vacancy. (2) Richard M. Johnson was the only vice president to be chosen by the Senate because of a tied vote in the Electoral College. (3) Democrat Andrew Johnson was nominated vice president by Republicans and elected with Lincoln on the National Union ticket. (4) Grandfather of Democratic candidate for president in 1952 and 1956. (5) Resigned Oct. 10, 1973, after pleading no contest to a charge of tax evasion. (6) First nonelected vice president, chosen under 25th Amendment procedure. (7) Second nonelected vice president, chosen under 25th Amendment.

Biographies of the Presidents

George Washington (1789-97), first president, Federalist, was born on Feb. 22, 1732, in Wakefield on Pope's Creek, Westmoreland Co., VA, the son of Augustine and Mary Ball Washington. He spent his early childhood on a farm near Fredericksburg. His father died when Washington was 11. He studied mathematics and surveying, and at 16, he went to live with his elder half brother, Lawrence, who built and named Mount Vernon in Virginia. Washington surveyed the lands of Thomas Fairfax in the Shenandoah Valley. He accompanied Lawrence to Barbados, West Indies, where he contracted smallpox and was deeply scarred. Lawrence died in 1752, and Washington inherited his property. He valued land, and when he died, he owned 70,000 acres in Virginia and 40,000 acres in what is now West Virginia.

Washington's military service began in 1753, when Lt. Gov. Robert Dinwiddie of Virginia sent him on missions deep into Ohio country. He clashed with the French and had to surrender Fort Necessity on July 3, 1754. He was an aide to the British general Edward Braddock and was at his side when the army was ambushed and defeated (July 9, 1755) on a march to Fort Duquesne. He helped take Fort Duquesne from the French in 1758.

After Washington's marriage to Martha Dandridge Custis, a widow, in 1759, he managed his family estate at Mount Vernon. Although not in favor of independence initially, he opposed the repressive measures of the British crown and took charge of the Virginia troops before war broke out. He was made commander of the newly created Continental Army by the Continental Congress on June 15, 1775.

The American victory was due largely to Washington's leadership. He was resourceful, a disciplinarian, and a dependable force for unity. Washington favored a federal government. He became chairman of the Constitutional Convention of 1787 and helped get the Constitution ratified. Unanimously elected president by the Electoral College, he was inaugurated Apr. 30, 1789, on the balcony of New York's Federal Hall. He was reelected in 1792. Washington made an effort to avoid partisan politics as president.

Refusing to consider a third term, Washington retired to Mount Vernon in Mar. 1797. A ride in snow and rain around his estate led to what present-day doctors believe to have been an attack of acute epiglottitis. Doctors were unsuccessful in treating the inflammation in his throat, and Washington died Dec. 14, 1799.

John Adams (1797-1801), second president, Federalist, was born on Oct. 30, 1735, in Braintree (now Quincy), MA, the son of John and Susanna Boylston Adams. He was a great-grandson of Henry Adams, who came from England in 1636. He graduated from Harvard in 1755, then taught school and studied law. He married Abigail Smith in 1764. In 1770, he successfully defended in court the British soldiers who fired on civilians in the Boston Massacre. He was a delegate to the Continental Congress and a signer of the Declaration of Independence. In 1778, Congress sent Adams and John Jay to join Benjamin Franklin as diplomatic representatives in Europe. Because he ran second to Washington in Electoral College balloting in Feb. 1789, Adams became the nation's first vice president, a post he characterized as highly insignificant; he was reelected in 1792.

In 1796 Adams was chosen president by the electors. His administration was marked by growing conflict with fellow Federalist Alexander Hamilton and with others in his own cabinet who supported Hamilton's strongly anti-French position. Adams avoided full-scale war with France but became unpopular, especially after securing passage of the Alien and Sedition Acts in 1798. His foreign policy contributed significantly to the election of Thomas Jefferson in 1800.

Adams lived for a quarter century after he left office, during which time he wrote extensively. He died July 4, 1826, on the same day as his rival Thomas Jefferson (the 50th anniversary of the Declaration of Independence).

Thomas Jefferson (1801-09), third president, Democratic-Republican, was born on Apr. 13, 1743, in Shadwell in Goochland (now Albemarle) Co., VA, the son of Peter and Jane Randolph Jefferson. His father died when Jefferson was 14, leaving him 2,750 acres and his slaves. Jefferson attended (1760-62) the College of William and Mary, read Greek and Latin classics, and played the violin. In 1769 he was elected to the Virginia House of Burgesses. In 1770 he began building his home, Monticello, and in 1772 he married Martha Wayles Skelton, a wealthy widow. Jefferson helped establish the Virginia Committee of Correspondence. As a member of the Second Continental Congress he drafted the Declaration of Independence. He also was a member of the Virginia House of Delegates (1776-79) and was elected governor of Virginia in 1779. He was reelected in 1780 but resigned the next year after British troops invaded Virginia. During his term he wrote the statute on religious freedom. After his wife's death in 1782, Jefferson again became a delegate to the Congress, and in 1784 he drafted the report that was the basis for the Ordinances of 1784, 1785, and 1787. He was minister to France from 1785 to 1789, when George Washington appointed him secretary of state.

Jefferson's strong faith in the consent of the governed conflicted with the emphasis on executive control, favored by Sec. of the Treasury Alexander Hamilton, and Jefferson resigned as secretary of state on Dec. 31, 1793. In the 1796 election Jefferson was the Democratic-Republican candidate for president; John Adams won the election, and Jefferson became vice president. In 1800, Jefferson and Aaron Burr received equal numbers of Electoral College votes; the House of Representatives elected Jefferson president. Jefferson was a strong advocate of westward expansion; major events of his first term were the Louisiana Purchase (1803) and the Lewis and Clark expedition. An important development during his second term was passage of the Embargo Act, barring U.S. ships from setting sail to foreign ports. Jefferson established the Univ. of Virginia and designed its buildings. He died July 4, 1826, on the same day as John Adams (the 50th anniversary of the Declaration of Independence).

Based on contemporary accounts, plantation records, and DNA taken from descendants of Jefferson and of Sally Hemings, one of his slaves, many historians conclude that Jefferson fathered one or more of her six children.

James Madison (1809-17), fourth president, Democratic-Republican, was born on Mar. 16, 1751, in Port Conway, King George Co., VA, the son of James and Eleanor Rose Conway Madison. Madison graduated from the College of New Jersey in 1771. He served in the Virginia Constitutional Convention (1776), and, in 1780, became a delegate to the Second Continental Congress. He was chief recorder at the Constitutional Convention in 1787 and supported ratification in the *Federalist Papers*, written with Alexander Hamilton and John Jay. In 1789 Madison was elected to the House of Representatives, where he helped frame the Bill of Rights and fought against passage of the Alien and Sedition Acts. In the 1790s, he helped found the Democratic-Republican Party, which ultimately became the Democratic Party. He became Jefferson's secretary of state in 1801.

Madison was elected president in 1808. His first term was marked by tensions with Great Britain, and his conduct of foreign policy was criticized by the Federalists and by his own party. Nevertheless, he was reelected in 1812, the year war was declared on Great Britain. The war that many considered a second American revolution ended with a treaty that did not settle any of the issues. Madison's most important action after the war was demilitarizing the U.S.-Canadian border.

In 1817, Madison retired to his estate, Montpelier, where he served as an elder statesman. He edited his famous papers on the Constitutional Convention and helped found the Univ. of Virginia, of which he became rector in 1826. He died June 28, 1836.

James Monroe (1817-25), fifth president, Democratic-Republican, was born on Apr. 28, 1758, in Westmoreland Co., VA, the son of Spence and Elizabeth Jones Monroe. He entered the College of William and Mary in 1774 but left to serve in the Third Virginia Regiment during the American Revolution. After the war, he studied law with Thomas Jefferson. In 1782 he was elected to the Virginia House of Delegates, and he served (1783-86) as a delegate to the Continental Congress. He opposed ratification of the Constitution because it lacked a bill of rights. Monroe was elected to the U.S. Senate in 1790. In 1794, Pres. Washington appointed Monroe minister to France. He was again minister to France (1803) under Pres. Jefferson as well as minister to Great Britain (1803-07). He served twice as governor of Virginia (1799-1802, 1811).

In 1816 Monroe was elected president; he was reelected in 1820 with all but one Electoral College vote. His administration became known as the Era of Good Feeling. He obtained Florida from Spain, settled boundary disputes with Britain over Canada, and eliminated border forts. He supported the antislavery position that led to the Missouri Compromise. His most significant contribution was the Monroe Doctrine, which opposed European intervention in the Western Hemisphere and became a cornerstone of U.S. foreign policy.

Although Monroe retired to Oak Hill, VA, financial problems forced him to sell his property and move to New York City. He died there on July 4, 1831.

John Quincy Adams (1825-29), sixth president, independent Federalist, later Democratic Republican, was born on July 11, 1767, in Braintree (now Quincy), MA, the son of John and Abigail Adams. His father was the second president. He studied abroad and at Harvard College, from which he graduated in 1787. In 1803, he was elected to the U.S. Senate. President Monroe chose him as his secretary of state in 1817. In this capacity he negotiated the cession of Florida from Spain, supported exclusion of slavery in the Missouri Compromise, and helped formulate the Monroe Doctrine.

After no candidate won an Electoral College majority in 1824, the presidential election was decided by the House of Representatives. Adams won with support from rival Henry Clay, whom he named secretary of state, fueling accusations of a "corrupt bargain." His expansion of executive powers was strongly opposed, and in the 1828 election he lost to Andrew Jackson. In 1831 he entered the House of Representatives and served 17 years. He opposed slavery, the annexation of Texas, and the Mexican War. He helped establish the Smithsonian Institution.

Adams suffered a stroke in the House and died in the Speaker's Room on Feb. 23, 1848.

Andrew Jackson (1829-37), seventh president, Democratic-Republican, later a Democrat, was born on Mar. 15, 1767, in the Waxhaw district, on the border of North and South Carolina, the son of Andrew and Elizabeth Hutchinson Jackson. At the age of 13, he joined the militia to fight in the American Revolution and was captured. Orphaned at age 14, Jackson was raised by an uncle. By age 20, he was practicing law, and he later served as prosecuting attorney in Nashville, TN. In 1796 he helped draft the constitution of Tennessee, and for a year he occupied its one seat in the House of Representatives. The next year he served in the U.S. Senate.

In the War of 1812, Jackson crushed the Creek Indians at Horseshoe Bend, AL (1814), and, with a greatly outnumbered army consisting chiefly of backwoods militia members and volunteers, defeated Gen. Edward Pakenham's British troops at the Battle of New Orleans (1815). Nicknamed "Old Hickory" for his toughness, he emerged a national hero.

In 1818 Jackson briefly invaded Spanish Florida to quell Seminoles and outlaws who harassed frontier settlements. He ran for president against John Quincy Adams in 1824, but did not achieve a majority despite winning the most popular and electoral votes. The House of Representatives decided the election and chose Adams. In the 1828 election, however, Jackson defeated Adams, carrying the West and the South.

As president, Jackson introduced what became known as the spoils system—rewarding party members with government posts. A self-professed champion of the common man, he also

viewed the Second Bank of the U.S. as a bastion of privilege and made it a major issue in the election of 1832, the first where candidates were chosen at national conventions rather than in congressional caucuses. Defeating Henry Clay, Jackson increasingly diverted funds from the national bank into so-called pet banks run by members of his own party. When South Carolina refused to collect imports under a federal tariff, which it declared null and void, Jackson won passage of legislation confirming his right to use military force to obtain compliance; eventually the tariff rate was reduced and the nullifiers backed down. After leaving office in 1837, he retired to the Hermitage, his estate outside Nashville, where he died on June 8, 1845.

Martin Van Buren (1837-41), eighth president, Democrat, was born on Dec. 5, 1782, in Kinderhook, NY, the son of Abraham and Maria Hoes Van Buren. After attending local schools, he studied law and became a lawyer at the age of 20. A consummate politician, Van Buren began his career in the New York state senate and then served as state attorney general (1816-19). He was elected to the U.S. Senate in 1821. He helped swing Eastern support to Andrew Jackson in the 1828 election and served as Jackson's secretary of state from 1829 to 1831. In 1832 he was elected vice president. Known as the "Little Magician," Van Buren was extremely influential in Jackson's administration.

In 1836, Van Buren defeated William Henry Harrison for president and took office as the financial panic of 1837 initiated a nationwide depression. Although he instituted the independent treasury system, his refusal to spend land revenues led to his defeat by William Henry Harrison in 1840. In 1844 he lost the Democratic nomination to James K. Polk. In 1848 he again ran for president on the Free Soil ticket but lost. He died in Kinderhook on July 24, 1862.

William Henry Harrison (1841), ninth president, Whig, who served only 31 days, was born on Feb. 9, 1773, in Berkeley, Charles City Co., VA, the son of Benjamin Harrison—a signer of the Declaration of Independence—and of Elizabeth Bassett Harrison. He attended Hampden-Sydney College. Harrison served as secretary of the Northwest Territory in 1798 and was its delegate to the House of Representatives in 1799. He was the first governor of Indiana Territory and served as superintendent of Indian affairs. With 900 men he put down a Shawnee uprising at Tippecanoe, IN, on Nov. 7, 1811. A generation later, in 1840, he waged a rousing presidential campaign using the slogan "Tippecanoe and Tyler Too." The Tyler of the slogan was his running mate, John Tyler.

Although born to one of the wealthiest, most prestigious, and most influential families in Virginia, Harrison also campaigned with the slogan "Log Cabin and Hard Cider." He caught pneumonia during his inauguration and died Apr. 4, 1841, after only one month in office.

John Tyler (1841-45), 10th president, independent Whig, was born on Mar. 29, 1790, in Greenway, Charles City Co., VA, the son of John and Mary Armistead Tyler. His father was governor of Virginia (1808-11). Tyler graduated from the College of William and Mary in 1807 and in 1811 was elected to the Virginia legislature. In 1816 he was chosen for the U.S. House of Representatives. He served in the Virginia legislature again from 1823 to 1825, when he was elected governor of Virginia. After a stint in the U.S. Senate (1827-36), he was elected vice president (1840).

When William Henry Harrison died only a month after taking office, Tyler succeeded him. Because he was the first person to occupy the presidency without having been elected to that office, he was referred to as "His Accidency." He gained passage of the Preemption Act of 1841, which gave squatters on government land the right to buy 160 acres at the minimum auction price. His last act as president was to sign a resolution annexing Texas. Tyler accepted renomination in 1844 from some Democrats but withdrew in favor of the official party candidate, James K. Polk. A strong advocate of states' rights, he served briefly in the Confederate House of Representatives before he died in Richmond, VA, on Jan. 18, 1862.

James Knox Polk (1845-49), 11th president, Democrat, was born on Nov. 2, 1795, in Mecklenburg Co., NC, the son of Samuel and Jane Knox Polk. He graduated from the Univ. of North Carolina in 1818 and served in the Tennessee state legislature from 1823 to 1825. He served in the U.S. House of Representatives from 1825 to 1839, the last four years as Speaker. He was governor of Tennessee from 1839 to 1841. In 1844, after the Democratic National Convention became deadlocked, it nominated Polk, who became the first "dark horse" candidate for president. He was nominated primarily because he favored annexation of Texas.

As president, Polk reestablished the independent treasury system originated by Van Buren. He was so intent on acquiring California from Mexico that he sent troops to the Mexican border and, when Mexicans attacked, declared that a state of war existed. The Mexican War ended with the annexation of California and much of the Southwest as part of America's "manifest destiny." Polk compromised on the Oregon boundary ("54-40 or fight!") by accepting the 49th parallel and yielding Vancouver Island to the British. Polk died in Nashville, TN, on June 15, 1849, a few months after leaving office.

Zachary Taylor (1849-50), 12th president, Whig, who served only 16 months, was born on Nov. 24, 1784, in Orange Co., VA, the son of Richard and Sarah Strother Taylor. He grew up on his father's plantation near Louisville, KY, where he was educated by private tutors. In 1808 Taylor joined the regular army and was commissioned first lieutenant. He fought in the War of 1812, the Black Hawk War (1832), and the second Seminole War (beginning in 1837). He was called "Old Rough and Ready." In 1846 Pres. Polk sent him with an army to the Rio Grande. When the Mexicans attacked him, Polk declared war. Outnumbered four to one, Taylor defeated Antonio López de Santa Anna at Buena Vista (1847).

A national hero, Taylor received the Whig nomination in 1848 and was elected president, even though he had never bothered to vote. He resumed the spoils system and, though a slaveholder, worked to admit California as a free state. He fell ill, likely from a case of acute gastroenteritis, and died in office on July 9, 1850.

Millard Fillmore (1850-53), 13th president, Whig, was born on Jan. 7, 1800, in Cayuga Co., NY, the son of Nathaniel and Phoebe Millard Fillmore. Although he had little schooling, he became a law clerk at the age of 22 and was admitted to the bar a year later. He was elected to the New York state assembly in 1828 and served until 1831. From 1833 until 1835 and again from 1837 to 1843, he represented his district in the U.S. House of Representatives. He opposed the entrance of Texas as a slave state and voted for a protective tariff. In 1844 he was defeated for governor of New York.

In 1848, he was elected vice president; he became president after Taylor's death. Fillmore favored the Compromise of 1850 and signed the Fugitive Slave Law. His policies pleased neither expansionists nor slaveholders, and he was not renominated in 1852. In 1856 he was nominated by the American (Know-Nothing) Party, but despite the support of the Whigs, he was defeated by James Buchanan. He died in Buffalo, NY, on Mar. 8, 1874.

Franklin Pierce (1853-57), 14th president, Democrat, was born on Nov. 23, 1804, in Hillsboro, NH, the son of Benjamin Pierce, Revolutionary War general and governor of New Hampshire, and Anna Kendrick. He graduated from Bowdoin College in 1824 and was admitted to the bar in 1827. He was elected to the New Hampshire state legislature in 1829 and was chosen Speaker in 1831. He went to the U.S. House in 1833 and was elected a U.S. senator in 1837. He enlisted in the Mexican War and became brigadier general under Gen. Winfield Scott.

In 1852 Pierce was nominated as the Democratic presidential candidate on the 49th ballot. He decisively defeated Gen. Scott, his Whig opponent, in the election. Although he was against slavery, Pierce was influenced by proslavery Southerners. He supported the controversial Kansas-Nebraska Act, which left the question of slavery in the new territories of Kansas and Nebraska to popular vote. Pierce signed a reciprocity treaty with Canada and approved the Gadsden Purchase, from Mexico, of a border area on a proposed railroad route. Denied renomination, he spent most of his remaining years in Concord, NH, where he died on Oct. 8, 1869.

James Buchanan (1857-61), 15th president, Federalist, later Democrat, was born on Apr. 23, 1791, near Mercersburg, PA, the son of James and Elizabeth Speer Buchanan. He graduated from Dickinson College in 1809 and was admitted to the bar in 1812. He fought in the War of 1812 as a volunteer. He was twice elected to the Pennsylvania general assembly, and in 1821 he entered the U.S. House of Representatives. After briefly serving (1832-33) as minister to Russia, he was elected U.S. senator from Pennsylvania. As Polk's secretary of state (1845-49), he ended the Oregon dispute with Britain and supported the Mexican War and annexation of Texas. As minister to Great Britain, he signed the Ostend Manifesto (1854), declaring a U.S. right to take Cuba by force should efforts to purchase it fail.

Nominated by Democrats, Buchanan was elected president in 1856. On slavery he favored popular sovereignty and choice by state constitutions but did not consistently uphold this position. He denied the right of states to secede but opposed coercion and attempted to keep peace by not provoking secessionists. Buchanan left office having failed to deal decisively with the situation. He died at Wheatland, his estate, near Lancaster, PA, on June 1, 1868.

Abraham Lincoln (1861-65), 16th president, Whig, then Republican, was born on Feb. 12, 1809, in a log cabin on a farm in Hardin (now Larue) Co., KY, the son of Thomas and Nancy Hanks Lincoln. The Lincolns moved to Spencer Co., IN, near Gentryville, when Lincoln was 7. After Lincoln's mother died, his father married Mrs. Sarah Bush Johnston in 1819. In 1830 the family moved to Macon Co., IL.

Defeated in 1832 in a race for the state legislature, Lincoln was elected on the Whig ticket two years later and served in the lower house from 1834 to 1842. In 1837 Lincoln was admitted to the bar and became partner in a Springfield, IL, law office. In 1846, he was elected to Congress, where he attracted attention during a single term for his opposition to the Mexican War and his position on slavery. In 1856 he campaigned for the newly founded Republican Party, and in 1858 he became its senatorial candidate against Stephen A. Douglas. Although he lost the election, Lincoln gained national recognition from his debates with Douglas.

In 1860, Lincoln was nominated for president by the Republican Party on a platform of restricting slavery. He ran against Douglas, a northern Democrat; John C. Breckinridge, a Southern proslavery Democrat; and John Bell, of the Constitutional Union Party. In response to Lincoln's victory, South Carolina seceded from the Union on Dec. 20, 1860, soon followed by six other Southern states.

The Civil War erupted when South Carolina's Fort Sumter, which Lincoln decided to resupply, was attacked by Confederate forces on Apr. 12, 1861. Lincoln called for recruits from the North, and four more Southern states seceded. Hundreds of thousands of Union and Confederate soldiers were killed or wounded in four years of battle that followed. On Sept. 22, 1862, five days after the Battle of Antietam, Lincoln announced that slaves in territory then in rebellion would be free Jan. 1, 1863, under his Emancipation Proclamation. His speeches, including his Gettysburg and inaugural addresses, are remembered for their eloquence.

Lincoln was reelected, in 1864, over Gen. George B. McClellan, a Democrat. Confederate Gen. Robert E. Lee surrendered on Apr. 9, 1865. On Apr. 14, Lincoln was shot by actor

John Wilkes Booth in Ford's Theater, in Washington, DC. He died the next day.

Andrew Johnson (1865-69), 17th president, Democrat, was born on Dec. 29, 1808, in Raleigh, NC, the son of Jacob and Mary McDonough Johnson. He was apprenticed to a tailor as a youth but ran away after two years and eventually settled in Greeneville, TN, where he was elected councilman and later mayor. In 1835 he was sent to the state general assembly. In 1843 he was elected to the U.S. House of Representatives, where he served for 10 years. Johnson was also governor of Tennessee from 1853 to 1857, when he was elected to the U.S. Senate. Although Johnson had held slaves, he opposed secession and tried to prevent Tennessee from seceding. In Mar. 1862, Lincoln appointed him military governor of occupied Tennessee.

In 1864, in order to balance Lincoln's ticket with a Southern Democrat, the Republicans nominated Johnson for vice president. He was elected vice president with Lincoln and succeeded to the presidency upon Lincoln's death. Soon afterward, in conflict with Congress over the president's power over the South, he proclaimed an amnesty to all Confederates, except certain leaders, if they would ratify the 13th Amendment abolishing slavery. States doing so added anti-Negro provisions that enraged Congress, which restored military control over the South. When Johnson removed Sec. of War Edwin M. Stanton without notifying the Senate, the House impeached him in Feb. 1868 on the charge of violating the Tenure of Office Act. In reality, the House was responding to his opposition to harsh congressional Reconstruction, expressed in repeated vetoes. He was acquitted in the Senate by one-vote margins on each of two counts.

Johnson was denied renomination but remained politically active. He was reelected to the Senate in 1874. Johnson died July 31, 1875, at Carter Station, TN.

Ulysses S. Grant (1869-77), 18th president, Republican, was born on Apr. 27, 1822, in Point Pleasant, OH, the son of Jesse R. and Hannah Simpson Grant. The next year the family moved to Georgetown, OH. Grant was named Hiram Ulysses. Upon entering West Point in 1839, he found his name had been put down as Ulysses S. Grant, with his middle name first and his mother's maiden name as his middle name. He eventually adopted it as his true name but maintained the "S" did not stand for anything. Grant graduated in 1843. During the Mexican War, Grant served under both Gen. Zachary Taylor and Gen. Winfield Scott. In 1854, he resigned his commission because of loneliness and drinking problems, and in the following years he engaged in generally unsuccessful farming and business ventures. With the start of the Civil War, he was named colonel and then brigadier general of the Illinois Volunteers. He took Forts Henry and Donelson and fought at Shiloh. His brilliant campaign against Vicksburg and his victory at Chattanooga made him so prominent that Lincoln placed him in command of all Union armies. Grant accepted Confederate Gen. Robert E. Lee's surrender at Appomattox Court House on Apr. 9, 1865.

Grant was nominated for president by the Republicans in 1868 and elected over Democrat Horatio Seymour. The 15th Amendment, the amnesty bill, and peaceful settlement of disputes with Great Britain were events of his administration. The Liberal Republicans and Democrats opposed him with Horace Greeley in the 1872 election, but Grant was reelected. His second administration was marked by scandals, including the Crédit Mobilier affair, the Whiskey Ring, in which high-ranked officials conspired to defraud the government of taxes, and the impeachment of his secretary of war. An attempt by the Stalwarts (Old Guard Republicans) to nominate him in 1880 failed. Left penniless by the 1884 collapse of an investment firm in which he was a partner, he wrote his well-regarded memoirs while suffering from cancer to provide income for his family. He died at Mt. McGregor, NY, on July 23, 1885.

Rutherford Birchard Hayes (1877-81), 19th president, Republican, was born on Oct. 4, 1822, in Delaware, OH, the son of Rutherford and Sophia Birchard Hayes. He was reared by his uncle, Sardis Birchard. Hayes graduated from Kenyon College in 1842 and from Harvard Law School in 1845. He practiced law in Lower Sandusky (now Fremont), OH, and was city solicitor of Cincinnati from 1858 to 1861. During the Civil War, he was major of the 23rd Ohio Volunteers. He was wounded several times, and by the end of the war he had risen to the rank of brevet major general. While serving (1865-67) in the U.S. House of Representatives, Hayes supported Reconstruction and Johnson's impeachment. He was twice elected governor of Ohio (1867, 1869). After losing a race for the U.S. House in 1872, he was reelected governor of Ohio in 1875.

In 1876, Hayes was nominated for president. He believed he had lost the election to Democrat Samuel J. Tilden. But a few Southern states submitted two sets of electoral votes, and the result was in dispute. An electoral commission, consisting of 8 Republicans and 7 Democrats, awarded all disputed votes to Hayes, allowing him to become president by one electoral vote. Hayes, keeping a promise to Southerners, withdrew troops from areas still occupied in the South, ending the era of Reconstruction. He proposed civil service reforms, alienating those favoring the spoils system, and advocated repeal of the Tenure of Office Act restricting presidential power to dismiss officials. He supported sound money and specie payments.

Hayes died in Fremont, OH, on Jan. 17, 1893.

James Abram Garfield (1881), 20th president, Republican, was born on Nov. 19, 1831, in Orange, Cuyahoga Co., OH, the son of Abram and Eliza Ballou Garfield. His father died in 1833, and he was reared in poverty by his mother. He worked as a canal bargeman, a farmer, and a carpenter. He attended Western Reserve Eclectic Institute and graduated from Williams College in 1856. He returned to Western Reserve to teach and in 1857, at age 25, he became the school's president. In 1859 he was elected to the Ohio legislature. Antislavery and antisecession, he volunteered for military service in the Civil War, becoming colonel of the 42nd Ohio Infantry and brigadier in 1862. He fought at Shiloh, TN, was chief of staff for Gen. William Starke Rosecrans, and was made major general for gallantry at Chickamauga, GA. He entered Congress as a radical Republican in 1863, calling for execution or exile of Confederate leaders, but he moderated his views after the Civil War. On the electoral commission in 1877 he voted for Hayes against Tilden on strict party lines.

Garfield was a senator-elect in 1880 when he became the Republican nominee for president. He was chosen as a compromise over Gen. Grant, James G. Blaine, and John Sherman, and won election despite some bitterness among Grant's supporters. For much of his brief tenure as president, Garfield was concerned with a fight with New York Sen. Roscoe Conkling, who opposed two major appointments made by Garfield. On July 2, 1881, Garfield was shot and seriously wounded by a mentally disturbed office seeker, Charles J. Guiteau, while entering a railroad station in Washington, DC. He died on Sept. 19, 1881, in Elberon, NJ.

Chester Alan Arthur (1881-85), 21st president, Republican, was born on Oct. 5, 1829, in Fairfield, VT, to William and Malvina Stone Arthur. He graduated from Union College in 1848, taught school in Vermont, then studied law and practiced in New York City. In 1853, he argued in a fugitive slave case that slaves transported through New York State were thereby freed. In 1871, he was appointed collector of the Port of New York. Pres. Hayes, an opponent of the spoils system, forced him to resign in 1878. This made the New York machine enemies of Hayes. Arthur and the Stalwarts (Old Guard Republicans) tried to nominate Grant for a third term as president in 1880. When Garfield was nominated, Arthur was nominated for vice president in the interests of harmony.

Upon Garfield's assassination, Arthur became president. Despite his past connections, he signed major civil service reform legislation. Arthur tried to dissuade Congress from enacting the high protective tariff of 1883. He was defeated for renomination in 1884 by James G. Blaine. He died in New York City on Nov. 18, 1886.

Grover Cleveland (1885-89; 1893-97) *(According to a State Dept. ruling, Grover Cleveland should be counted as both the 22nd and the 24th president because his two terms were not consecutive)*, Democrat, was born Stephen Grover Cleveland on Mar. 18, 1837, in Caldwell, NJ, the son of Richard F. and Ann Neal Cleveland. When he was a small boy, his family moved to New York. Prevented by his father's death from attending college, he studied on his own and was admitted to the bar in Buffalo, NY, in 1859. In succession he became assistant district attorney (1863), sheriff (1871), mayor (1881), and governor of New York (1882). He was an independent, honest administrator who hated corruption. Cleveland was nominated for president over opposition from New York City's Tammany Hall in 1884 and defeated Republican James G. Blaine.

As president, he enlarged the civil service and vetoed many pension raids on the Treasury. In the 1888 election he was defeated by Benjamin Harrison, although his popular vote was larger. Reelected over Harrison in 1892, he faced a money crisis brought about by a lowered gold reserve, circulation of paper, and exorbitant silver purchases under the Sherman Silver Purchase Act. He obtained a repeal of the Sherman Act but was unable to secure effective tariff reform. A severe economic depression and labor troubles racked his administration, but he refused to interfere in business matters and rejected Jacob Coxey's demand for unemployment relief. In 1894, he broke the Pullman strike. Cleveland was not renominated in 1896. He died in Princeton, NJ, on June 24, 1908.

Benjamin Harrison (1889-93), 23rd president, Republican, was born on Aug. 20, 1833, in North Bend, OH, the son of John Scott and Elizabeth Irwin Harrison. His great-grandfather, Benjamin Harrison, was a signer of the Declaration of Independence; his grandfather, William Henry Harrison, was the ninth president; his father was a member of Congress. He attended school on his father's farm and graduated from Miami Univ. in Oxford, OH, in 1852. He was admitted to the bar in 1854 and practiced in Indianapolis, IN. During the Civil War, he rose to the rank of brevet brigadier general and fought at Kennesaw Mountain, Peachtree Creek, Nashville, and in the Atlanta campaign. He lost the 1876 gubernatorial election in Indiana but succeeded in becoming a U.S. senator in 1881.

In 1888 he defeated Cleveland for president despite receiving fewer popular votes. As president, he expanded the pension list and signed the McKinley high tariff bill, the Sherman Antitrust Act, and the Sherman Silver Purchase Act. During his administration, six states were admitted to the Union. He was defeated for reelection in 1892. He died in Indianapolis, IN, on Mar. 13, 1901.

William McKinley (1897-1901), 25th president, Republican, was born on Jan. 29, 1843, in Niles, OH, the son of William and Nancy Allison McKinley. McKinley briefly attended Allegheny College. When the Civil War broke out in 1861, he enlisted and served for the duration. He rose to captain and in 1865 was made brevet major. After studying law in Albany, NY, he opened a law office in Canton, OH (1867). He served twice in the U.S. House (1877-83; 1885-91) and led the fight there for the McKinley Tariff, passed in 1890; he was not reelected to the House as a result. He served two terms (1892-96) as governor of Ohio.

In 1896 he was elected president as a proponent of a protective tariff and sound money (gold standard) over William Jennings Bryan, the Democrat and a proponent of free silver. McKinley was reluctant to intervene in Cuba, but the loss of the battleship *Maine* at Havana crystallized opinion. He demanded Spain's withdrawal from Cuba; Spain made some concessions, but Congress announced a state of war as of Apr. 21, 1898. He was reelected in the 1900 campaign, defeating Bryan's anti-imperialist arguments with the promise of a "full dinner pail." He was known for a conservative stance on business issues. On Sept. 6, 1901, at the Pan-American Exposition, in Buffalo, NY, he was shot by Leon Czolgosz, an anarchist. He died Sept. 14.

Theodore Roosevelt (1901-09), 26th president, Republican, was born on Oct. 27, 1858, in New York City, the son of Theodore and Martha Bulloch Roosevelt. He was a fifth cousin of Franklin D. Roosevelt and an uncle of Eleanor Roosevelt. Roosevelt graduated from Harvard Univ. in 1880. He attended Columbia Law School briefly but abandoned law to enter politics. He was elected to the New York State Assembly in 1881 and served until 1884. He spent the next two years ranching and hunting in the Dakota Territory. In 1886, he ran unsuccessfully for mayor of New York City. He was civil service commissioner in Washington, DC, from 1889 to 1895. From 1895 to 1897, he served as New York City's police commissioner. He was assistant secretary of the Navy under McKinley. The Spanish-American War made him nationally known. He organized the First U.S. Volunteer Cavalry (Rough Riders) and, as lieutenant colonel, led the charge up Kettle Hill in San Juan, Cuba. Elected New York governor in 1898, he fought the spoils system and achieved taxation of corporation franchises.

Nominated for vice president in 1900, Roosevelt became the nation's youngest president when McKinley was assassinated. He was reelected in 1904. As president he fought corruption of politics by big business, dissolved the Northern Securities Co. and others for violating antitrust laws, intervened in the 1902 coal strike on behalf of the public, obtained the Elkins Law (1903) forbidding rebates to favored corporations, and helped pass the Hepburn Railway Rate Act of 1906 (extending jurisdiction of the Interstate Commerce Commission). He helped obtain passage of the Pure Food and Drug Act (1906) and of employers' liability laws. Roosevelt vigorously organized conservation efforts. He mediated the peace between Japan and Russia in 1905, for which he won the Nobel Peace Prize. He abetted the 1903 revolution in Panama that led to U.S. acquisition of territory for the Panama Canal.

In 1908 Roosevelt obtained the nomination of William H. Taft, who was elected. Feeling that Taft had abandoned his policies, he unsuccessfully sought the nomination in 1912. He then ran on the Progressive "Bull Moose" ticket against Taft and Woodrow Wilson, splitting the Republicans and ensuring Wilson's election. During the campaign he was shot by a mentally deranged man but was not seriously wounded. In 1916, after unsuccessfully seeking the presidential nomination, he supported the Republican candidate, Charles E. Hughes. He strongly promoted U.S. intervention in World War I.

Roosevelt was a voracious reader and wrote some 40 books, including *The Winning of the West*. He died Jan. 6, 1919, at Sagamore Hill, his home in Oyster Bay, NY.

William Howard Taft (1909-13), 27th president, Republican, and 10th chief justice of the U.S., was born on Sept. 15, 1857, in Cincinnati, OH, the son of Alphonso and Louisa Maria Torrey Taft. His father was secretary of war and attorney general in Grant's cabinet and minister to Austria and Russia under Arthur. Taft graduated from Yale in 1878 and from Cincinnati Law School in 1880. After working as a law reporter for Cincinnati newspapers, he served as assistant prosecuting attorney (1881-82), assistant county solicitor (1885), superior court judge (1887), U.S. solicitor-general (1890), and federal circuit judge (1892). In 1900 he became head of the U.S. Philippines Commission and was the first civil governor of the Philippines (1901-04). In 1904 he served as secretary of war, and in 1906 he was sent to Cuba to help avert a threatened revolution.

Taft was groomed for the presidency by Theodore Roosevelt and elected over William Jennings Bryan in 1908. Taft vigorously continued Roosevelt's trust-busting, instituted the Dept. of Labor, and drafted amendments calling for direct election of senators and an income tax. However, his tariff and conservation policies angered progressives. Although renominated in 1912, he was opposed by Roosevelt, who ran on the Progressive Party ticket; the result was Wilson's election.

Taft, with reservations, supported the League of Nations. After leaving office, he was professor of constitutional law at Yale (1913-21) and chief justice of the U.S. (1921-30). Taft was the only person to have been both president and chief justice. He died in Washington, DC, on Mar. 8, 1930.

(Thomas) Woodrow Wilson (1913-21), 28th president, Democrat, was born on Dec. 28, 1856, in Staunton, VA, the son of Joseph Ruggles and Janet (Jessie) Woodrow Wilson. He grew up in Georgia and South Carolina. He attended Davidson College in North Carolina before graduating from Princeton Univ. in 1879. He studied law at the Univ. of Virginia and political science at Johns Hopkins Univ., where he received his PhD in 1886. He taught at Bryn Mawr (1885-88) and at Wesleyan (1888-90) before joining the faculty at Princeton. He was president of Princeton from 1902 until 1910, when he was elected governor of New Jersey. In 1912 he was nominated for president with the aid of William Jennings Bryan, who sought to block James "Champ" Clark and New York City's Tammany Hall. Wilson won because Theodore Roosevelt, running as a "Bull Moose" Progressive, siphoned votes away from Republican candidate Taft.

As president, Wilson protected American interests in revolutionary Mexico and fought for American rights on the high seas. He oversaw the creation of the Federal Reserve system, cut the tariff, and developed a reputation as a reformer. His sharp warnings to Germany led to the resignation of his secretary of state, Bryan, a pacifist. In 1916 he was reelected by a slim margin with the slogan "He kept us out of war," although his attempts to mediate in the war failed. After several American ships were sunk by the Germans, he secured a declaration of war against Germany on Apr. 6, 1917.

Wilson outlined his peace program on Jan. 8, 1918, in the Fourteen Points, a state paper that enunciated a doctrine of self-determination for the settlement of territorial disputes. The Germans accepted his terms and an armistice on Nov. 11, 1918. Wilson went to Paris to help negotiate the peace treaty, the crux of which he considered the League of Nations. The Senate demanded reservations that would not make the U.S. subordinate to the votes of other nations in case of war. Wilson refused and toured the country to get support. After he suffered a severe stroke in Oct. 1919, his wife, Edith Wilson, concealed the extent of his infirmity, controlled access to him, and in effect largely acted in his place.

Wilson was awarded the 1919 Nobel Peace Prize, but the treaty embodying the League of Nations was ultimately rejected by the Senate in 1920. He left the White House in Mar. 1921. He died in Washington, DC, on Feb. 3, 1924.

Warren Gamaliel Harding (1921-23), 29th president, Republican, was born on Nov. 2, 1865, near Corsica (now Blooming Grove), OH, the son of George Tyron and Phoebe Elizabeth Dickerson Harding. He attended Ohio Central College, studied law, and became editor and publisher of a county newspaper. He entered the political arena as state senator (1901-04) and then served as lieutenant governor (1904-06). In 1910 he ran unsuccessfully for governor of Ohio; in 1914 he was elected to the U.S. Senate. In the Senate he voted for antistrike legislation, women's suffrage, and the Volstead Prohibition Enforcement Act over Pres. Wilson's veto. He opposed the League of Nations.

In 1920 he was nominated for president and defeated James M. Cox in the election. The Republicans capitalized on war weariness and fear that Wilson's League of Nations would curtail U.S. sovereignty. Harding stressed a return to "normalcy" and worked for tariff revision and the repeal of excess profits law and high income taxes. In the so-called Teapot Dome scandal, his secretary of the interior, Albert B. Fall, resigned and was later convicted of accepting bribes in the leasing of government-owned oil reserves to private companies.

As rumors began to circulate about the corruption in his administration, Harding fell ill after a trip to Alaska, and he died

suddenly in San Francisco on Aug. 2, 1923. Harding's letters to a longtime mistress were made public by the Library of Congress in 2014, and DNA evidence in 2015 confirmed another mistress's claim that he had fathered her daughter.

(John) Calvin Coolidge (1923-29), 30th president, Republican, was born on July 4, 1872, in Plymouth Notch, VT, the son of John Calvin and Victoria J. Moor Coolidge. Coolidge graduated from Amherst College in 1895. He entered Republican state politics and served as mayor of Northampton, MA, as state senator, as lieutenant governor, and in 1919, as governor. In Sept. 1919, Coolidge attained national prominence by calling out the state guard in the Boston police strike. He declared, "There is no right to strike against the public safety by anybody, anywhere, anytime." This brought his name before the Republican convention of 1920, where he was nominated for vice president.

Coolidge succeeded to the presidency on Harding's death. As president, he opposed the League of Nations and the soldiers' bonus bill, which was passed over his veto. In 1924 he was elected to the presidency by a huge majority. He substantially reduced the national debt. He twice vetoed legislation to aid financially hard-pressed farmers.

With Republicans eager to renominate him, Coolidge simply announced on Aug. 2, 1927, "I do not choose to run for president in 1928." He died in Northampton, MA, on Jan. 5, 1933.

Herbert Clark Hoover (1929-33), 31st president, Republican, was born on Aug. 10, 1874, in West Branch, IA, the son of Jesse Clark and Hulda Randall Minthorn Hoover. Hoover grew up in Indian Territory (now Oklahoma) and Oregon and graduated from Stanford Univ. with a degree in geology in 1895. He worked briefly with the U.S. Geological Survey and then managed mines in Australia, Asia, Europe, and Africa. While chief engineer of imperial mines in China, he directed food relief for victims of the Boxer Rebellion. He gained a reputation not only as an engineer but as a humanitarian as he directed the American Relief Committee, London (1914-15) and the U.S. Commission for Relief in Belgium (1915-19). He was U.S. Food Administrator (1917-19), American Relief Administrator (1918-23), and in charge of Russian Relief (1918-23). He served as secretary of commerce under both Harding and Coolidge.

In 1928 Hoover was elected president over Alfred E. Smith. In 1929 the stock market crashed, and the economy collapsed. During the Great Depression, Hoover inaugurated some government assistance programs, but he was opposed to administration of aid through a federal bureaucracy. As the effects of the Depression continued, he was defeated in the 1932 election by Franklin D. Roosevelt. Hoover remained active after leaving office. Pres. Truman named him coordinator of the European Food Program (1946) and chairman of the Commission on Organization of the Executive Branch (1947-49); he was later appointed by Pres. Eisenhower to serve in the same role (1953-55).

Hoover died in New York City on Oct. 20, 1964.

Franklin Delano Roosevelt (1933-45), 32nd president, Democrat, was born on Jan. 30, 1882, in Hyde Park, NY, the son of James and Sara Delano Roosevelt, and a fifth cousin of former Pres. Theodore Roosevelt. He graduated from Harvard Univ. in 1903. He attended Columbia University Law School without taking a degree and was admitted to the New York State bar in 1907. His political career began when he was elected to the New York State senate in 1910. In 1913 Pres. Wilson appointed him assistant secretary of the navy, a post he held during World War I.

In 1920 Roosevelt ran for vice president with James Cox and was defeated. From 1921 to 1928 he worked in his New York law office and was also vice president of a bank. In Aug. 1921, he was stricken with poliomyelitis, which left his legs paralyzed. As a result of therapy, he was able to stand and walk a few steps with the aid of leg braces.

Roosevelt served two terms as governor of New York (1929-33). In 1932, Democratic convention delegate W. G. McAdoo, pledged to nominee John N. Garner, threw his votes to Roosevelt, who was nominated for president. The Depression and the promise to repeal Prohibition ensured his election. He asked for emergency powers, proclaimed the New Deal, and put into effect a vast number of administrative changes. Foremost was the use of public funds for relief and public works, resulting in deficit financing. He greatly expanded the federal government's regulation of business and by an excess profits tax and progressive income taxes produced a redistribution of earnings on an unprecedented scale. He also promoted legislation establishing the Social Security system. He was the last president inaugurated on Mar. 4 (1933) and the first inaugurated on Jan. 20 (1937).

Roosevelt was the first president to use radio for "fireside chats." When the Supreme Court nullified some New Deal laws, he sought power to "pack" the Court with additional justices, but Congress refused to give him the authority. He was the first president to break the no-third-term tradition (1940) and was elected to a fourth term in 1944 despite failing health.

Roosevelt was openly hostile to fascist governments before World War II and launched a lend-lease program on behalf of the Allies. With British Prime Min. Winston Churchill he wrote a declaration of principles to be followed after Nazi defeat (the Atlantic Charter of Aug. 14, 1941) and urged the Four Freedoms (freedom of speech, of worship, from want, from fear) Jan. 6, 1941. After Japan attacked Pearl Harbor on Dec. 7, 1941, the U.S. entered the war. Roosevelt guided the nation through the war and conferred with allied heads of state but did not live to see the end of the war. He died of a cerebral hemorrhage in Warm Springs, GA, on Apr. 12, 1945.

Harry S. Truman (1945-53), 33rd president, Democrat, was born on May 8, 1884, in Lamar, MO, the son of John Anderson and Martha Ellen Young Truman. A family disagreement over whether his middle name should be Shipp or Solomon, after his two grandfathers, resulted in his using only the middle initial S. After graduating from high school (1901) in Independence, MO, he worked in the mailroom of the *Kansas City Star*, as a railroad timekeeper, and as a clerk in Kansas City banks until about 1905. He ran his family's farm from 1906 to 1917, then served in France during World War I. After the war he opened a haberdashery, was a judge on the Jackson Co. Court (1922-24), and attended Kansas City School of Law (1923-25).

Truman was elected to the U.S. Senate in 1934 and reelected in 1940. In 1944, with Roosevelt's backing, he was nominated for vice president and elected. On Roosevelt's death in 1945, Truman became president. In 1948, in a famous upset victory, he defeated Republican Thomas E. Dewey to win a new term.

Truman authorized the first uses of the atomic bomb (Hiroshima and Nagasaki, Aug. 6 and 9, 1945), bringing World War II to a rapid end. He was responsible for what came to be called the Truman Doctrine to aid nations such as Greece and Turkey threatened by Communist takeover, and his strong commitment to NATO and to the Marshall Plan helped bring the two about. In 1948-49, he broke a Soviet blockade of West Berlin with a massive airlift. When Communist North Korea invaded South Korea (June 1950), he won UN approval for a "police action" and, without prior congressional consent, sent in forces under Gen. Douglas MacArthur. When MacArthur opposed his policy of limited objectives, Truman removed him.

He died in Kansas City, MO, on Dec. 26, 1972.

Dwight David Eisenhower (1953-61), 34th president, Republican, was born on Oct. 14, 1890, in Denison, TX, the son of David Jacob and Ida Elizabeth Stover Eisenhower, as David Dwight Eisenhower. He grew up on a small farm in Abilene, KS, and graduated from West Point in 1915. He was on the staff of Gen. Douglas MacArthur in the Philippines from 1935 to 1939. In 1942, he was made commander of Allied forces landing in North Africa; the next year he was made full general. He became supreme Allied commander in Europe that same year and led the Normandy invasion (June 6, 1944). He was subsequently given the rank of general of the Army.

On May 7, 1945, Eisenhower received the surrender of Germany at Rheims, France. He returned to the U.S. to serve as chief of staff (1945-48). His memoir, *Crusade in Europe* (1948), was a best-seller. In 1948 he became president of Columbia Univ.; in 1950 he became commander of NATO forces.

Eisenhower was nominated for president by the Republicans in 1952. He defeated Illinois Gov. Adlai E. Stevenson in the 1952 election and defeated Stevenson in 1956 to win reelection. Eisenhower called himself a moderate, favored the "free market system" versus government price and wage controls, kept government out of labor disputes, reorganized the defense establishment, and promoted missile programs. He continued foreign aid, helped negotiate a cease-fire truce in the Korean War, endorsed Taiwan and SE Asia defense treaties, backed the UN in condemning the Anglo-French raid on Egypt, and advocated the "open skies" policy of mutual inspection with the USSR. He sent U.S. troops into Little Rock, AR, in Sept. 1957, to enforce school integration.

Eisenhower died on Mar. 28, 1969, in Washington, DC.

John Fitzgerald Kennedy (1961-63), 35th president, Democrat, was born on May 29, 1917, in Brookline, MA, the son of Joseph P. and Rose Fitzgerald Kennedy. He graduated from Harvard Univ. in 1940. While serving in the Navy (1941-45), he commanded a PT (patrol torpedo) boat in the Solomons and won the Navy and Marine Corps Medal. In 1956, while recovering from spinal surgery, he wrote *Profiles in Courage*, which won a Pulitzer Prize in 1957. He served in the U.S. House of Representatives from 1947 to 1953 and was elected to the Senate in 1952 and 1958. In 1960, he won the Democratic nomination for president and narrowly defeated Republican Vice Pres. Richard M. Nixon. Kennedy was the youngest president ever elected to the office and the first Catholic.

Despite the image of youth and vigor he conveyed to the public, Kennedy suffered from serious medical problems, including Addison's disease and severe chronic back pain that required him to wear a back brace. The public was not aware of the extent of these problems or of his frequent sexual liaisons.

In Apr. 1961, the new Kennedy administration suffered a severe setback when an invasion force of anti-Castro Cubans, trained and directed by the CIA, failed to establish a beachhead at the Bay of Pigs in Cuba. But he weathered a major foreign crisis with his successful demand on Oct. 22, 1962, that the Soviet Union dismantle its missile bases in Cuba. Kennedy also defied Soviet attempts to force the Allies out of Berlin. He established the Peace Corps, spurred space exploration, and won passage of other "New Frontier" legislation. But Congress balked at initiatives such as medical coverage for the elderly and aid to education. After some delay he introduced major civil rights legislation, but died before it could be passed.

On Nov. 22, 1963, Kennedy was assassinated while riding in a motorcade in Dallas, TX. A commission chaired by Chief Justice Earl Warren concluded in Sept. 1964 that the sole assassin had been Lee Harvey Oswald, a former U.S. Marine and an ardent Marxist. Oswald was captured shortly after the assassination and charged but was shot dead by nightclub owner Jack Ruby while being moved to a county jail.

Lyndon Baines Johnson (1963-69), 36th president, Democrat, was born on Aug. 27, 1908, near Stonewall, TX, the son of Sam Ealy and Rebekah Baines Johnson. He graduated from Southwest Texas State Teachers College in 1930 and attended Georgetown University Law School. He taught public speaking in Houston (1930-31) and then served as secretary to Rep. R. M. Kleberg (1931-35). In 1937 Johnson won an election to fill the vacancy left by the death of a U.S. representative. In 1938 he was elected to the first of five full terms. During 1941 and 1942 he also served in the Navy in the Pacific, earning a Silver Star for bravery. He was elected U.S. senator in 1948 and reelected in 1954. He became Democratic leader of the Senate in 1953. At the 1960 party convention he was elected vice president on the ticket led by the successful Democratic nominee, John F. Kennedy.

Johnson became president when Kennedy was assassinated. He was elected to a full term in 1964. Johnson's domestic program was of considerable importance. He won passage of major civil rights, anti-poverty, aid to education, and healthcare (Medicare, Medicaid) legislation—the "Great Society" program. However, his escalation of the war in Vietnam came to overshadow the achievements of his administration. In the face of increasing division in the nation and in his own party over his handling of the war, Johnson declined to seek another term.

Johnson died on Jan. 22, 1973, in San Antonio, TX.

Richard Milhous Nixon (1969-74), 37th president, Republican, was born on Jan. 9, 1913, in Yorba Linda, CA, the son of Francis Anthony and Hannah Milhous Nixon. He graduated from Whittier College in 1934 and from Duke University Law School in 1937. After practicing law in Whittier, CA, and serving briefly in the Office of Price Administration in 1942, he entered the Navy and served in the South Pacific. Nixon was elected to the U.S. House of Representatives in 1946 and 1948. He achieved prominence as the House Un-American Activities Committee member who forced the showdown leading to the Alger Hiss perjury conviction. In 1950 he was elected to the Senate.

Nixon was elected vice president in the Eisenhower landslides of 1952 and 1956. He won the Republican nomination for president in 1960 but was narrowly defeated by John F. Kennedy. He ran unsuccessfully for governor of California in 1962. In 1968 he again won the GOP presidential nomination, then defeated Hubert Humphrey for the presidency.

As president, Nixon appointed four Supreme Court justices, including the chief justice, moving the court to the right. As a New Federalist, he sought to shift greater responsibility to state and local governments. At the same time, he championed important federal initiatives, including creation of the Office of Management and Budget and the Environmental Protection Agency. The economy suffered periods of high unemployment and inflation, and he imposed wage and price controls in 1971.

In foreign affairs, Nixon dramatically altered relations with China, which he visited in 1972—the first U.S. president to do so. With adviser Henry Kissinger, he pursued détente with the Soviet Union, signing major arms limitation and other treaties and increasing trade. He began a gradual withdrawal from Vietnam, but U.S. troops remained there through his first term. He ordered an incursion into Cambodia (1970) and the bombing of Hanoi and mining of Haiphong Harbor (1972). Reelected by a large majority in Nov. 1972, he secured a Vietnam cease-fire in Jan. 1973.

Nixon's second term was cut short by scandal, after disclosures relating to a June 1972 burglary of Democratic Party headquarters in the Watergate office complex in DC. The courts and Congress sought tapes of Nixon's office conversations; Nixon claimed executive privilege, but the Supreme Court ruled against him. In July 1974, the House Judiciary Committee recommended adoption of three impeachment articles charging him with obstruction of justice, abuse of power, and contempt of Congress. On Aug. 5, he released transcripts of conversations that linked him to cover-up activities. He resigned on Aug. 9, becoming the first president ever to do so.

In later years, Nixon emerged as an elder statesman. He died Apr. 22, 1994, in New York City.

Gerald Rudolph Ford (1974-77), 38th president, Republican, was born on July 14, 1913, in Omaha, NE, the son of Leslie and Dorothy Gardner King, and was named Leslie Lynch King Jr. When he was two, his parents divorced, and he and his mother moved to Grand Rapids, MI. There she married Gerald R. Ford, who formally adopted him and gave him his name. Ford graduated from the Univ. of Michigan in 1935 and from Yale Law School in 1941. He began practicing law in Grand Rapids, but in 1942, he joined the Navy and served in the Pacific, leaving the service in 1946 as a lieutenant commander. He entered the U.S. House of Representatives in 1949 and spent 25 years in the House, eight of them as Republican leader.

On Oct. 12, 1973, after Vice Pres. Spiro T. Agnew resigned, Pres. Nixon nominated Ford to replace him. It was the first use of the procedures set out in the 25th Amendment. When Nixon resigned, Aug. 9, 1974, because of the Watergate scandal, Ford became president; he was the only president who was never elected either to the presidency or to the vice presidency.

Ford was widely credited with having contributed to rebuilding morale after the Nixon presidency, though he was criticized when he pardoned Nixon for any federal crimes he might have committed as president. Ford vetoed 48 bills in his first 21 months in office, mostly in the interest of fighting high inflation; he was less successful in curbing high unemployment. In foreign policy, Ford continued to pursue détente.

Ford was narrowly defeated in the 1976 election. He died Dec. 26, 2006, at home in Rancho Mirage, CA.

James Earl (Jimmy) Carter (1977-81), 39th president, Democrat, was the first president from the Deep South since before the Civil War. He was born on Oct. 1, 1924, in Plains, GA, the son of James and Lillian Gordy Carter. Carter graduated from the U.S. Naval Academy in 1946 and in 1952 entered the Navy's nuclear submarine program as an aide to Capt. (later Adm.) Hyman Rickover. He studied nuclear physics at Union College. Carter's father died in 1953, and he left the Navy to take over the family peanut farming businesses. He served in the Georgia state senate (1963-67) and as governor of Georgia (1971-75). In 1976, Carter won the Democratic nomination and defeated Pres. Gerald R. Ford.

On his first full day in office, Carter pardoned all Vietnam draft evaders. He played a major role in the negotiations leading to the 1979 peace treaty between Israel and Egypt, and he won passage of new treaties with Panama providing for U.S. control of the Panama Canal to end in 2000. Carter was widely criticized, however, for the poor state of the economy and was viewed by some as weak in his handling of foreign policy. In Nov. 1979, Iranian student militants attacked the U.S. embassy in Tehran and held members of the embassy staff hostage. Efforts to obtain release of the hostages were a major preoccupation during the rest of his term. He reacted to the Soviet invasion of Afghanistan by imposing a grain embargo and boycotting the Moscow Olympic Games.

Carter was defeated by Ronald Reagan in the 1980 election. The 52 American hostages in Iran were finally released on inauguration day, 1981, just after Reagan officially became president. After leaving office, Carter played an active role in diplomatic and humanitarian efforts around the world, especially through the Carter Center, which he founded with his wife, Rosalynn, in 1982. He was awarded the Nobel Peace Prize in 2002.

Ronald Wilson Reagan (1981-89), 40th president, Republican, was born on Feb. 6, 1911, in Tampico, IL, the son of John Edward and Nellie Wilson Reagan. Reagan graduated from Eureka College in 1932, after which he worked as a sports announcer in Des Moines, IA. He began a successful career as a movie actor in 1937. During World War II Reagan served in the Army Air Force, making training films. He was president of the Screen Actors Guild in 1947-52 and in 1959-60. Reagan was elected governor of California in 1966 and reelected in 1970.

In 1980, Reagan gained the Republican presidential nomination and won a landslide victory over Jimmy Carter. He was easily reelected in 1984. Reagan forged a bipartisan coalition in Congress, which led to enactment of his program of large-scale tax cuts, cutbacks in many government programs, and a major defense buildup. He signed a Social Security reform bill designed to provide for the long-term solvency of the system. In 1986, he signed into law a major tax-reform bill. He was shot and seriously wounded in 1981 by John Hinckley, who was tried and found not guilty by reason of insanity.

In 1982, the U.S. joined France and Italy in maintaining a peacekeeping force in Beirut, Lebanon; the next year Reagan sent a task force to invade Grenada after two Marxist coups on the island. Reagan's opposition to international terrorism led to the U.S. bombing of Libyan military installations in 1986. He strongly supported El Salvador, the Nicaraguan contras, and other anticommunist governments and forces throughout the world. He also held four summit meetings with Soviet leader Mikhail Gorbachev and signed a treaty in 1987 eliminating short- and medium-range missiles from Europe.

In 1986, it was revealed that the U.S. had sold weapons through Israeli brokers to Iran in exchange for the release of U.S. hostages being held in Lebanon and that subsequently some of the money had been illegally diverted to the Nicaraguan contras. The scandal led to the resignation of leading White House aides, but no proof of Reagan's involvement was discovered. As Reagan left office in Jan. 1989, the nation was experiencing its sixth consecutive year of economic prosperity, while also piling up large budget deficits.

In 1994, Reagan revealed that he was suffering from Alzheimer's disease. He died on June 5, 2004, in Los Angeles, CA.

George Herbert Walker Bush (1989-93), 41st president, Republican, was born on June 12, 1924, in Milton, MA, the son of Prescott and Dorothy Walker Bush. He served as a U.S. Navy pilot in World War II. After graduating from Yale Univ. in 1948, he settled in Texas, where, in 1953, he helped found an oil company. After losing a bid for a U.S. Senate seat in 1964, he was elected to the House of Representatives in 1966 and 1968. He lost a second U.S. Senate race in 1970. Subsequently he served as U.S. ambassador to the United Nations (1971-73), headed the U.S. Liaison Office in Beijing (1974-75), and was director of the CIA (1976-77). Following an unsuccessful bid for the 1980 Republican presidential nomination, Bush became Ronald Reagan's running mate, and served as vice president from 1981 to 1989.

In 1988, Bush gained the GOP presidential nomination and defeated Gov. Michael Dukakis (D, MA) to win the presidency. Bush took office faced with U.S. budget and trade deficits, and insolvent U.S. savings and loan institutions. He faced a severe budget deficit annually, struggled with military cutbacks, and vetoed abortion-rights legislation. In 1990 he agreed to a budget deficit-reduction plan that included tax hikes, despite a campaign promise to the contrary, angering many conservatives.

Bush supported Soviet reforms, Eastern Europe democratization, and good relations with Beijing. In Dec. 1989, he sent troops to Panama; they overthrew the government and captured military dictator Gen. Manuel Noriega. Bush reacted to Iraq's Aug. 1990 invasion of Kuwait by sending U.S. forces to the Persian Gulf area and assembling a UN-backed coalition, including NATO and Arab League members. After a month-long air war, in Feb. 1991, Allied forces retook Kuwait in a four-day ground assault. The quick victory, with extremely light casualties on the U.S. side, gave Bush at that time one of the highest presidential approval ratings in history. His popularity plummeted by the end of 1991, however, as the economy slipped into recession. He was defeated by Bill Clinton in the 1992 election.

Bush saw his son George W. inaugurated as the 43rd president in 2001. In 2005 the elder Bush teamed with former Pres. Clinton to raise money for natural disaster victims.

William Jefferson (Bill) Clinton (1993-2001), 42nd president, Democrat, was born Aug. 19, 1946, in Hope, AR, son of William Blythe and Virginia Cassidy Blythe, and was named William Jefferson Blythe IV. Blythe died in an auto accident before his son was born. His widow married Roger Clinton, whose last name Bill Clinton then took. Clinton earned his undergraduate degree from Georgetown Univ. in 1968. While attending Oxford Univ. as a Rhodes scholar, he legally avoided the draft and possible service in Vietnam, according to some critics by misleading his draft board. Clinton worked on George McGovern's 1972 presidential campaign and earned a degree from Yale Law School in 1973. He taught at the Univ. of Arkansas law school until 1976, when he was elected state attorney general. In 1978 he was elected governor, becoming the nation's youngest at the time. Though defeated for reelection in 1980, he was returned to office several times thereafter. He married law school classmate Hillary Rodham in 1975.

Clinton won most of the 1992 presidential primaries, moving his party toward the center as he tried to broaden his appeal; as the Democratic nominee he defeated Pres. George H. W. Bush and independent candidate H. Ross Perot in the Nov. election. In 1993, Clinton won passage of a deficit reduction measure and congressional approval of the North American Free Trade Agreement. However, his administration's plan for major health care reform legislation died in Congress. After 1994 midterm elections, Clinton faced Republican majorities in both houses of Congress. He followed a centrist course at home, sent troops to Bosnia to help implement a peace settlement, and cultivated relations with Russia and China.

Though accused of improprieties in his involvement in the Whitewater Development Corp., an Arkansas land-development venture, Clinton won reelection with 49% of the vote in 1996. Independent prosecutor Kenneth Starr did not find wrongdoing related to Whitewater, but did report evidence of an affair between Clinton and White House intern Monica Lewinsky. In 1998, Clinton became only the second U.S. president to be impeached by the House of Representatives. He was charged with perjury and obstruction of justice in an attempted cover-up of the affair but was acquitted by the Senate.

In 1999 the United States joined other NATO nations in an aerial bombing campaign that induced Serbia to withdraw troops from Kosovo, where they had been terrorizing ethnic Albanians. On Clinton's last full day in office, the Whitewater investigation ended in a deal; Clinton admitted having given false testimony and agreed to penalties. After leaving office he actively supported the political career of his wife, Hillary Clinton. He took a leadership role in various humanitarian programs and founded what became the Bill, Hillary and Chelsea Clinton Foundation.

George Walker Bush (2001-09), 43rd president, Republican, was born on July 6, 1946, in New Haven, CT. He was the oldest of six children born to the 41st president, George Herbert Walker Bush, and the former Barbara Pierce. He became the first son of a former president to occupy the White House since John Quincy Adams took office in 1825.

Bush grew up in Midland and Houston, TX. He attended Phillips Academy in Andover, MA, and then Yale Univ., graduating in 1968. Eligible for the draft, he fulfilled his military service requirement with the Texas Air National Guard. After earning a master's degree from Harvard Business School, he returned to Midland in 1975 and went into the oil business. Two years later he married Laura Welch, a librarian; they had twin daughters, Barbara and Jenna, in 1981. After aiding his father's winning 1988 presidential campaign, he became managing partner of the Texas Rangers baseball team. He was elected governor of Texas in 1994 and reelected in 1998.

In 2000, Bush won the Republican presidential nomination and, with running mate Dick Cheney, defeated the Democratic ticket led by Vice Pres. Al Gore, in one of the closest-ever U.S. presidential elections. The result was not settled until a mid-Dec. ruling by the U.S. Supreme Court left Florida's crucial electoral votes in Bush's column.

In May 2001, Bush won passage of a tax cut package projected at $1.35 tril over 10 years. After the Sept. 11, 2001, terrorist attacks on the U.S., he rallied support for a "war against terrorism." By Dec. 2001, the U.S. military, aided by forces from other nations, had deposed Afghanistan's Taliban regime, which was sheltering al-Qaeda terrorists. In Mar. 2003, the U.S., aided mainly by UK forces, launched an air and ground war against Iraq and deposed its autocratic leader, Saddam Hussein. No evidence was found that his regime had developed weapons of mass destruction, the key rationale for the war. A sovereign government was formed in June 2004, but insurgent violence and U.S. troop casualties continued.

Bush was reelected in Nov. 2004 with 51% of the popular vote, but his push for Social Security and immigration reforms in his second term failed in Congress, and his administration drew criticism for its response to Hurricane Katrina in Aug.-Sept. 2005. In 2006, Bush exercised his first veto to maintain restrictions on federal funding for stem cell research.

After Democrats won majorities in House and Senate 2006 midterm elections, Bush accepted the resignation of Defense Sec. Donald Rumsfeld, a target of widespread criticism over the Iraq war. Two months later, he announced a "surge" in U.S. troop strength in Iraq. A sharp drop in casualties ensued, aided also by a shift in alliances, and in late 2008 the administration reached an agreement with Iraq allowing U.S. troops to remain there through but not beyond 2011. But the Taliban was gaining strength in Afghanistan and Pakistan, and the Bush administration was damaged by revelations of prisoner abuse and extreme interrogation methods.

The U.S. economy fell into recession in Dec. 2007; Bush and congressional leaders responded with a $168-bil stimulus plan. Problems in home finance and credit markets triggered a deep economic crisis in Sept. and the Treasury Dept. announced a bailout of mortgage finance firms Fannie Mae and Freddie Mac. Lehman Bros. filed for bankruptcy, and the Federal Reserve rescued insurance giant AIG with a line of credit reaching $144 bil. A Bush administration-backed plan to buy up to $700 bil in devalued mortgage-related assets cleared Congress Oct. 3, after a severe stock market plunge bolstered support. The crisis added to Bush's unpopularity and contributed to the GOP loss of the 2008 presidential election.

In early 2010 Bush and former Pres. Clinton established a nonprofit organization to raise funds for earthquake relief in Haiti. Bush published a memoir entitled *Decision Points* (2010) and a biography of his father, *41* (2014).

Barack Hussein Obama, 44th president, Democrat, was born Aug. 4, 1961, in Honolulu, HI. His father, Barack Obama Sr., was a black Kenyan, and his mother, Stanley Ann Dunham, a white American. They divorced and, after his mother remarried, the family moved to Indonesia. Obama lived with his maternal grandparents in Hawaii while attending high school. He graduated from Columbia Univ. (1983) and, after working as a community organizer in Chicago, earned a law degree from Harvard Univ. (1991), where he was president of the law review. Obama practiced civil rights law in Chicago and taught at the Univ. of Chicago Law School. In 1992, he married attorney Michelle Robinson. They have two daughters, Malia and Natasha (Sasha).

Obama served eight years (1997-2004) in the Illinois state senate. Nominated to a U.S. Senate seat in a Mar. 2004 primary, he was already known for his memoir *Dreams From My Father* (1995) and gained wider attention with his keynote address at the 2004 Democratic National Convention. He was easily elected to the seat. Another book, *The Audacity of Hope* (2006), was an immediate best-seller.

Stressing his opposition to the Iraq war and a message of "hope and change," Obama won the 2008 Democratic presidential nomination, defeating expected front-runner Sen. Hillary Clinton (NY). As a major recession deepened, Obama, with running mate Sen. Joe Biden (DE), outpolled the Republican ticket, headed by Sen. John McCain (AZ), and became the nation's first African-American president.

Pres. Obama was awarded the 2009 Nobel Peace Prize for "efforts to strengthen international diplomacy and cooperation between peoples." He gradually pulled U.S. troops from Iraq, with no residual force left after 2011, but as sectarian strife heightened they were reintroduced, in what were called non-combat roles. In Afghanistan, after implementing a temporary troop surge, he began force reductions. He stepped up drone strikes against Islamist militants in Afghanistan and Pakistan and authorized a 2011 raid that killed al-Qaeda leader Osama bin Laden. He also authorized U.S. participation in NATO airstrikes leading to the overthrow of Libyan dictator Muammar al-Qaddafi. Rival militias in Libya refused to disarm, however, and the U.S. ambassador and three other Americans were killed in an attack (Sept. 2012) by Islamist radicals on the U.S. consulate in Benghazi, Libya.

On the domestic front, the administration, early in 2009, won passage of a $787-bil economic stimulus package, and the U.S. pulled out of recession, though growth was slow. In 2010, Obama won passage of a top policy priority in a controversial health care reform bill aimed in part at extending coverage to uninsured Americans. After Democrats lost their House majority in Nov. 2010 elections, a battle over raising the federal debt limit led to agreement on spending cuts to be worked out by a bipartisan congressional committee; since no deal could be reached, large automatic cuts ("sequester") in both defense and other domestic spending were slated for 2013. Obama, in 2012, became the first sitting president to publicly support same-sex marriage, and signed an executive order ending deportations for most young undocumented immigrants who came to the U.S. as children. In Aug. 2012 his administration finalized regulations greatly tightening fuel emission standards for motor vehicles.

Obama and Biden were reelected in Nov. 2012, defeating a GOP ticket headed by former Massachusetts Gov. Mitt Romney. A compromise in Congress averted a year-end "fiscal cliff" by making expiring Bush tax cuts permanent for most people, while postponing the sequester. Further negotiations failed, and the sequester took effect in Mar. 2013. In Oct. 2013, the government partially shut down for lack of funding authorization, with Republicans balking over the Affordable Care Act, or Obamacare; they yielded after 16 days. Over succeeding years spending battles continued, pitting the White House and congressional Democrats against Republicans. In 2013 the administration was embattled over reports that the Internal Revenue Service had singled out Tea Party organizations for special scrutiny and was embarrassed by a botched rollout of Obamacare and by leaks of classified information indicating extensive U.S. surveillance by the Natl. Security Agency (NSA). The Boston Marathon bombing in Apr. 2013 was a reminder that the U.S. homeland remained vulnerable to terrorism. In 2014, revelations of mismanagement at the Dept. of Veterans Affairs led to resignation of the VA secretary.

Abroad, Russian forces annexed the Crimean region of Ukraine (Mar. 2014) and pro-Russian separatists, reportedly bolstered by Russian forces, expanded their control in areas of eastern Ukraine; Obama joined Europe in imposing limited economic sanctions. In the Middle East, the administration revived Arab-Israeli peace talks, but they broke down, and Israel (July 2014) launched a major operation in Gaza, with heavy civilian casualties, following rocket attacks by the Palestinian militant Islamic group Hamas. Obama called for an end to the repressive regime of Syria's Bashar al-Assad, pitted against rebel factions in a bloody civil war since 2011. But when Assad forces appeared to have launched a chemical weapons attack on civilians in 2013, crossing what Obama had called a "red line," the president held back from punitive action and agreed to a Russian-brokered disarmament pact with the regime. Meanwhile, the Sunni extremist group Islamic State in Iraq and Syria (ISIS), aided by foreign recruits, took over large areas of both countries, proclaiming a caliphate (June 2014) and driving out, persecuting, or killing non-Sunnis. Obama authorized sending U.S. military advisers to Iraq. After ISIS released videos showing executions of abducted Americans and others, he announced (Sept. 2014) extended U.S. airstrikes against ISIS in both Iraq and Syria along with previously withheld arms to aid moderate Syrian rebels.

After Nov. 2014 midterm elections the Obama administration faced Republican majorities in both houses of Congress, with relations between the parties highly polarized. Citing congressional failure to enact immigration reform measures, Obama in late Nov. 2014 issued an executive order to protect from possible deportation the millions of undocumented immigrants who are parents of U.S. citizens and permanent legal residents (actions challenged by a coalition of states in the courts). In 2015, his administration issued regulations (later temporarily stayed by the Court) to drastically cut back carbon emissions from coal-fired power plants, and Obama made a long delayed decision to kill plans for the Keystone XL oil pipeline.

In Dec. 2014, Obama began a process of normalizing relations with Cuba, and he made a historic visit there in Mar. 2016. He also spearheaded a controversial multination accord with Iran (July 2015) intended to curb Iranian nuclear weapons development in return for ending economic sanctions. Obama supported the 12-nation Trans-Pacific Partnership (signed Feb. 2016), but ratification by Congress faced resistance, especially from many members of his own party. In May 2016, on a trip to Asia, he visited Vietnam, where he ended a long-standing U.S. arms embargo, and became the first sitting U.S. president to visit Hiroshima.

Responding to incidents such as the mass shooting of children at Sandy Hook Elementary School (Dec. 2012), Obama repeatedly and unsuccessfully called on Congress to enact gun control measures; he also took executive action, with limited results. Obama confronted incidents involving deaths of black people—including children—in encounters with police (as in Ferguson, MO, Aug. 2014) and revenge killings of police (as in Dallas and Baton Rouge, July 2016), as well as terrorist attacks in San Bernardino, CA, and Orlando, FL.

Obama strongly supported 2016 Democratic presidential nominee Hillary Clinton, his former secretary of state, and denounced GOP nominee Donald Trump as unfit for the office. He nominated U.S. Appeals Court Judge Merrick Garland to the seat left vacant by the death (Feb. 2016) of conservative Supreme Court Justice Antonin Scalia, but the Republican-controlled Senate refused to move on the nomination with the presidential election approaching.

Presidential Facts

Oldest president: Ronald Reagan, who was 77 when he left office

Youngest president: Theodore Roosevelt, who was 42 when sworn in after McKinley's death

Youngest person elected president: John F. Kennedy, who was 43 when elected in 1960

Tallest president: Abraham Lincoln, who was 6 feet, 4 inches

Shortest president: James Madison, who was 5 feet, 4 inches

Heaviest president: William Howard Taft, who was 332 pounds in 1911

First president to live in the White House: John Adams, who moved there in 1800

First president inaugurated in Washington, DC: Thomas Jefferson, in 1801

First president whose parents were immigrants: Andrew Jackson; his parents emigrated from Ireland in 1765

First president born a U.S. citizen: Martin Van Buren, in Kinderhook, NY, 1782

First president born outside the original colonies: Abraham Lincoln, in Kentucky, 1809

First president born west of the Mississippi: Herbert Hoover, in West Branch, IA, 1874

Most common presidential home state: Virginia, with 8 presidents

First president born in a hospital: Jimmy Carter, in Plains, GA, 1924

First president to have a telephone in the White House: Rutherford B. Hayes, in 1879

First president to travel outside U.S. while in office: Theodore Roosevelt visited Panama Canal site, 1906

First president to address the nation on radio: Warren G. Harding, in 1922

First president to appear on TV: Franklin D. Roosevelt, at opening ceremonies for the 1939 World's Fair

First president to give a live, televised news conference: John F. Kennedy, in 1961

First president to hold an Internet chat: Bill Clinton, in 1999

Presidents who lost the popular vote while winning election: John Quincy Adams, in 1824 (elected by the House after general election failed to produce a majority); Rutherford B. Hayes, in 1876; Benjamin Harrison, in 1888; George W. Bush, in 2000 (Popular vote totals before 1824 are unknown.)

Only presidents chosen by the House of Representatives: Thomas Jefferson (1st term) and John Quincy Adams

Only president never elected either president or vice president: Gerald Ford; named vice president when Spiro Agnew resigned (1973), became president when Nixon resigned (1974)

Left-handed presidents: James Garfield, Herbert Hoover, Harry Truman, Gerald Ford, Ronald Reagan, George H. W. Bush, Bill Clinton, and Barack Obama

Only Catholic president: John F. Kennedy; the most common religious affiliations have been Episcopalian (11) and Presbyterian (7)

Only bachelor presidents: James Buchanan, who never married, and Grover Cleveland, who married Frances Folsom in the White House in 1886

Only divorced president: Ronald Reagan; divorced from Jane Wyman in 1948, married Nancy Davis in 1952

Presidents who died on July 4: John Adams and Thomas Jefferson (both 1826) and James Monroe (1831)

Only president buried in Washington, DC: Woodrow Wilson, interred at Washington National Cathedral

Presidential Libraries

Presidential libraries are coordinated by the National Archives and Records Administration (www.archives.gov/presidential-libraries/). Materials for presidents before Herbert Hoover are held by private institutions. The Barack Obama Foundation announced in July 2016 that his presidential library would be in Jackson Park, on Chicago's South Side. Under the Presidential Records Act, material is available to the public through Freedom of Information Act requests starting five years after a president has left office.

Herbert Hoover Library and Museum
210 Parkside Dr.
West Branch, IA 52358
Phone: (319) 643-5301
Email: hoover.library@nara.gov
Website: hoover.archives.gov

Franklin D. Roosevelt Library and Museum
4079 Albany Post Rd.
Hyde Park, NY 12538-1990
Phone: (800) FDR-VISIT
Email: roosevelt.library@nara.gov
Website: www.fdrlibrary.marist.edu

Harry S. Truman Library and Museum
500 West U.S. Hwy. 24
Independence, MO 64050-2481
Phone: (800) 833-1225
Email: truman.library@nara.gov
Website: www.trumanlibrary.org

Dwight D. Eisenhower Library
200 SE 4th St.
Abilene, KS 67410-2900
Phone: (877) RING-IKE
Email: eisenhower.library@nara.gov
Website: eisenhower.archives.gov

John F. Kennedy Library and Museum
Columbia Pt.
Boston, MA 02125-3312

Phone: (866) JFK-1960
Email: kennedy.library@nara.gov
Website: www.jfklibrary.org

Lyndon Baines Johnson Library and Museum
2313 Red River St.
Austin, TX 78705-5737
Phone: (512) 721-0200
Email: johnson.library@nara.gov
Website: www.lbjlibrary.org

Richard Nixon Library and Museum
18001 Yorba Linda Blvd.
Yorba Linda, CA 92886-3903
Phone: (714) 983-9120
Email: nixon@nara.gov
Website: www.nixonlibrary.gov

Gerald R. Ford Library and Museum
Library: 1000 Beal Ave.
Ann Arbor, MI 48109-2109
Phone: (734) 205-0555
Museum: 303 Pearl St. NW
Grand Rapids, MI 49504-5353
Phone: (616) 254-0400
Email: ford.library@nara.gov
Website: www.fordlibrarymuseum.gov

Jimmy Carter Library and Museum
441 Freedom Pkwy.
Atlanta, GA 30307-1498
Phone: (404) 865-7100

Email: carter.library@nara.gov
Website: www.jimmycarterlibrary.gov

Ronald Reagan Library and Museum
40 Presidential Dr.
Simi Valley, CA 93065-0600
Phone: (800) 410-8354
Email: reagan.library@nara.gov
Website: www.reagan.utexas.edu

George Bush Library and Museum
1000 George Bush Dr. West
College Station, TX 77845
Phone: (979) 691-4000
Email: library.bush@nara.gov
Website: bushlibrary.tamu.edu

William J. Clinton Library and Museum
1200 President Clinton Ave.
Little Rock, AR 72201
Phone: (501) 374-4242
Email: clinton.library@nara.gov
Website: www.clintonlibrary.gov

George W. Bush Library and Museum
2943 SMU Blvd.
Dallas, TX 75205
Phone: (214) 346-1650
Email: gwbush.library@nara.gov
Website: www.georgewbushlibrary.smu.edu

Presidential Impeachment in U.S. History

The U.S. Constitution provides for impeachment and removal from office of federal officials on grounds of "Treason, Bribery, or other high Crimes and Misdemeanors" (Article II, Sect. 4). Impeachment is the bringing of charges by the House of Representatives. It is followed by a Senate trial; a two-thirds majority vote of Senators present is needed for conviction and removal from office.

In 1868, **Andrew Johnson** became the first president impeached by the House, for his removal of Sec. of War Edwin M. Stanton without first notifying the Senate. He was tried but not convicted. In 1974, impeachment articles against Pres. **Richard Nixon**, in connection with the Watergate scandal, were adopted by the House Judiciary Committee. He resigned Aug. 9, and the House accepted the committee report without taking further action. In 1998, Pres. **Bill Clinton** was impeached by the House in connection with his cover-up of a sexual relationship with former White House intern Monica Lewinsky. He was tried in the Senate in 1999 and acquitted.

Wives and Children of the Presidents

Name (born-died; married)	State	Sons/ daughters	Name (born-died; married)	State	Sons/ daughters
Martha Dandridge Custis Washington (1731-1802; 1759)	VA	None	Mary Scott Lord Dimmick Harrison (1858-1948; 1896)	PA	0/1
Abigail Smith Adams (1744-1818; 1764)	MA	3/2	Ida Saxton McKinley (1847-1907; 1871)	OH	0/2
Martha Wayles Skelton Jefferson (1748-82; 1772)	VA	1/5	Alice Hathaway Lee Roosevelt (1861-84; 1880)	MA	0/1
Dolley Payne Todd Madison (1768-1849; 1794)	NC	None	Edith Kermit Carow Roosevelt (1861-1948; 1886)	CT	4/1
Elizabeth Kortright Monroe (1768-1830; 1786)	NY	1/2	Helen Herron Taft (1861-1943; 1886)	OH	2/1
Louisa Catherine Johnson Adams (1775-1852; 1797)	MD[1]	3/1	Ellen Louise Axson Wilson (1860-1914; 1885)	GA	0/3
Rachel Donelson Robards Jackson (1767-1828; 1791)	VA	1/0[2]	Edith Bolling Galt Wilson (1872-1961; 1915)	VA	None
Hannah Hoes Van Buren (1783-1819; 1807)	NY	4/0	Florence Kling De Wolfe Harding (1860-1924; 1891)	OH	None
Anna Tuthill Symmes Harrison (1775-1864; 1795)	NJ	6/4	Grace Anna Goodhue Coolidge (1879-1957; 1905)	VT	2/0
Letitia Christian Tyler (1790-1842; 1813)	VA	3/5	Lou Henry Hoover (1875-1944; 1899)	IA	2/0
Julia Gardiner Tyler (1820-89; 1844)	NY	5/2	Anna Eleanor Roosevelt (1884-1962; 1905)	NY	5/1
Sarah Childress Polk (1803-91; 1824)	TN	None	Elizabeth Virginia (Bess) Wallace Truman (1885-1982; 1919)	MO	0/1
Margaret (Peggy) Mackall Smith Taylor (1788-1852; 1810)	MD	1/5	Mamie Geneva Doud Eisenhower (1896-1979; 1916)	IA	2/0
Abigail Powers Fillmore (1798-1853; 1826)	NY	1/1	Jacqueline Lee Bouvier Kennedy (1929-94; 1953)	NY	2/1
Caroline Carmichael McIntosh Fillmore (1813-81; 1858)	NJ	None	Claudia (Lady Bird) Alta Taylor Johnson (1912-2007; 1934)	TX	0/2
Jane Means Appleton Pierce (1806-63; 1834)	NH	3/0	Thelma Catherine Patricia Ryan Nixon (1912-93; 1940)	NV	0/2
Mary Todd Lincoln (1818-82; 1842)	KY	4/0	Elizabeth (Betty) Bloomer Warren Ford (1918-2011; 1948)	IL	3/1
Eliza McCardle Johnson (1810-76; 1827)	TN	3/2	Eleanor Rosalynn Smith Carter (1927- ; 1946)	GA	3/1
Julia Boggs Dent Grant (1826-1902; 1848)	MO	3/1	Anne Frances (Nancy) Robbins Davis Reagan (1921-2016; 1952)	NY	1/1[3]
Lucy Ware Webb Hayes (1831-89; 1852)	OH	7/1	Barbara Pierce Bush (1925- ; 1945)	NY	4/2
Lucretia Rudolph Garfield (1832-1918; 1858)	OH	5/2	Hillary Diane Rodham Clinton (1947- ; 1975)	IL	0/1
Ellen Lewis Herndon Arthur (1837-80; 1859)	VA	2/1	Laura Lane Welch Bush (1946- ; 1977)	TX	0/2
Frances Folsom Cleveland (1864-1947; 1886)	NY	2/3	Michelle LaVaughn Robinson Obama (1964- ; 1992)	IL	0/2
Caroline Lavinia Scott Harrison (1832-92; 1853)	OH	1/1			

Note: Pres. Buchanan was unmarried. Children not born to the marriages shown are not listed unless otherwise noted. (1) Born in London, father a MD citizen. (2) Adopted son. (3) Pres. Reagan's first wife, whom he later divorced, was Jane Wyman. They had a daughter who died in infancy, a daughter who lived past infancy, and an adopted son.

First Lady Michelle Obama

Michelle Robinson Obama was born in Chicago, IL, Jan. 17, 1964. She graduated from Princeton Univ., 1985, earned a law degree from Harvard Univ., 1988, and joined Chicago law firm Sidley & Austin. She served as assistant commissioner of planning and development for the city of Chicago, then as founding executive director of the Chicago chapter of Public Allies, an AmeriCorps program. She began working for the Univ. of Chicago in 1996, first as associate dean of student services, then as the Univ. of Chicago Medical Center's vice president of community and external affairs. Michelle and Barack Obama were married in 1992; in 1998, their daughter Malia was born, followed by Natasha (Sasha) in 2001.

As First Lady, Michelle Obama has focused on supporting military families, helping women balance career and family, encouraging national service, advocating the arts and arts education, and promoting access to education for girls worldwide. She also launched a major campaign to address childhood obesity in the U.S.

Burial Places of the Presidents

President	Burial place	President	Burial place	President	Burial place
Washington	Mt. Vernon, VA	Pierce	Concord, NH	Wilson	Wash. Natl. Cathedral, DC
J. Adams	Quincy, MA	Buchanan	Lancaster, PA	Harding	Marion, OH
Jefferson	Charlottesville, VA	Lincoln	Springfield, IL	Coolidge	Plymouth Notch, VT
Madison	Montpelier Station, VA	A. Johnson	Greeneville, TN	Hoover	West Branch, IA
Monroe	Richmond, VA	Grant	New York, NY	F. Roosevelt	Hyde Park, NY
J. Q. Adams	Quincy, MA	Hayes	Fremont, OH	Truman	Independence, MO
Jackson	Nashville, TN	Garfield	Cleveland, OH	Eisenhower	Abilene, KS
Van Buren	Kinderhook, NY	Arthur	Albany, NY	Kennedy	Arlington Natl. Cem., VA
W. H. Harrison	North Bend, OH	Cleveland	Princeton, NJ	L. B. Johnson	Stonewall, TX
Tyler	Richmond, VA	B. Harrison	Indianapolis, IN	Nixon	Yorba Linda, CA
Polk	Nashville, TN	McKinley	Canton, OH	Ford	Grand Rapids, MI
Taylor	Louisville, KY	T. Roosevelt	Oyster Bay, NY	Reagan	Simi Valley, CA
Fillmore	Buffalo, NY	Taft	Arlington Natl. Cem., VA		

PRESIDENTIAL ELECTIONS

Note: Historical election statistics as of Sept. 2016. For information about the 2016 election, see pp. 8-44.

Popular and Electoral Vote for President, 1789-2012

(D) Democrat; (DR) Democratic Republican; (F) Federalist; (LB) Libertarian; (LR) Liberal Republican; (NR) National Republican; (P) People's; (PR) Progressive; (R) Republican; (W) Whig; * = See notes below table.

Year	President elected	Popular	Elec.	Major losing candidate(s)	Popular	Elec.
1789	George Washington	Unknown	69	No major opposition	—	—
1792	George Washington	Unknown	132	No major opposition	—	—
1796	John Adams (F)	Unknown	71	Thomas Jefferson (DR)	Unknown	68
1800*	Thomas Jefferson (DR)	Unknown	73	Aaron Burr (DR)	Unknown	73
1804	Thomas Jefferson (DR)	Unknown	162	Charles Pinckney (F)	Unknown	14
1808	James Madison (DR)	Unknown	122	Charles Pinckney (F)	Unknown	47
1812	James Madison (DR)	Unknown	128	DeWitt Clinton (F)	Unknown	89
1816	James Monroe (DR)	Unknown	183	Rufus King (F)	Unknown	34
1820	James Monroe (DR)	Unknown	231	John Quincy Adams (DR)	Unknown	1
1824*	John Quincy Adams (DR)	113,122	84	Andrew Jackson (DR)	151,271	99
				Henry Clay (DR)	46,587	37
				William H. Crawford (DR)	44,282	41
1828	Andrew Jackson (D)	642,553	178	John Quincy Adams (NR)	500,897	83
1832	Andrew Jackson (D)	701,780	219	Henry Clay (NR)	484,205	49
1836	Martin Van Buren (D)	764,176	170	William H. Harrison (W)	550,816	73
1840	William H. Harrison (W)	1,275,390	234	Martin Van Buren (D)	1,128,854	60
1844	James K. Polk (D)	1,339,494	170	Henry Clay (W)	1,300,004	105
1848	Zachary Taylor (W)	1,361,393	163	Lewis Cass (D)	1,223,460	127
				Martin Van Buren (Free Soil)	291,501	—
1852	Franklin Pierce (D)	1,607,510	254	Winfield Scott (W)	1,386,942	42
1856	James Buchanan (D)	1,836,072	174	John C. Fremont (R)	1,342,345	114
				Millard Fillmore (W-American)	873,053	8
1860	Abraham Lincoln (R)	1,865,908	180	Stephen A. Douglas (D)	848,019	12
				John C. Breckinridge (D)	845,763	72
				John Bell (Constitutional Union)	589,581	39
1864	Abraham Lincoln (R)	2,218,388	212	George McClellan (D)	1,812,807	21
1868	Ulysses S. Grant (R)	3,013,650	214	Horatio Seymour (D)	2,708,744	80
1872*	Ulysses S. Grant (R)	3,598,235	286	Horace Greeley (D-LR)	2,834,671	—
1876*	Rutherford B. Hayes (R)	4,034,311	185	Samuel J. Tilden (D)	4,288,546	184
1880	James A. Garfield (R)	4,446,158	214	Winfield S. Hancock (D)	4,444,260	155
1884	Grover Cleveland (D)	4,874,621	219	James G. Blaine (R)	4,848,936	182
1888	Benjamin Harrison (R)	5,443,892	233	Grover Cleveland (D)	5,534,488	168
1892	Grover Cleveland (D)	5,551,883	277	Benjamin Harrison (R)	5,179,244	145
				James Weaver (P)	1,027,329	22
1896	William McKinley (R)	7,108,480	271	William J. Bryan (D-P)	6,511,495	176
1900	William McKinley (R)	7,218,039	292	William J. Bryan (D)	6,358,345	155
1904	Theodore Roosevelt (R)	7,626,593	336	Alton B. Parker (D)	5,082,898	140
1908	William H. Taft (R)	7,676,258	321	William J. Bryan (D)	6,406,801	162
1912	Woodrow Wilson (D)	6,293,152	435	Theodore Roosevelt (PR)	4,119,207	88
				William H. Taft (R)	3,483,922	8
1916	Woodrow Wilson (D)	9,126,300	277	Charles E. Hughes (R)	8,546,789	254
1920	Warren G. Harding (R)	16,153,115	404	James M. Cox (D)	9,133,092	127
1924	Calvin Coolidge (R)	15,719,921	382	John W. Davis (D)	8,386,704	136
				Robert M. La Follette (PR)	4,822,856	13
1928	Herbert Hoover (R)	21,437,277	444	Alfred E. Smith (D)	15,007,698	87
1932	Franklin D. Roosevelt (D)	22,829,501	472	Herbert Hoover (R)	15,760,684	59
1936	Franklin D. Roosevelt (D)	27,757,333	523	Alfred Landon (R)	16,684,231	8
1940	Franklin D. Roosevelt (D)	27,313,041	449	Wendell Willkie (R)	22,348,480	82
1944	Franklin D. Roosevelt (D)	25,612,610	432	Thomas E. Dewey (R)	22,117,617	99
1948	Harry S. Truman (D)	24,179,345	303	Thomas E. Dewey (R)	21,991,291	189
				Strom Thurmond (States' Rights)	1,169,021	39
				Henry A. Wallace (PR)	1,157,172	—
1952	Dwight D. Eisenhower (R)	33,936,234	442	Adlai E. Stevenson (D)	27,314,992	89
1956*	Dwight D. Eisenhower (R)	35,590,472	457	Adlai E. Stevenson (D)	26,022,752	73
1960*	John F. Kennedy (D)	34,226,731	303	Richard M. Nixon (R)	34,108,157	219
1964	Lyndon B. Johnson (D)	43,129,566	486	Barry M. Goldwater (R)	27,178,188	52
1968	Richard M. Nixon (R)	31,785,480	301	Hubert H. Humphrey (D)	31,275,166	191
				George C. Wallace (Amer. Indep.)	9,906,473	46
1972*	Richard M. Nixon (R)	47,169,911	520	George S. McGovern (D)	29,170,383	17
1976*	Jimmy Carter (D)	40,830,763	297	Gerald R. Ford (R)	39,147,793	240
1980	Ronald Reagan (R)	43,904,153	489	Jimmy Carter (D)	35,483,883	49
				John B. Anderson (independent)	5,719,437	—
1984	Ronald Reagan (R)	54,455,075	525	Walter F. Mondale (D)	37,577,185	13
1988*	George H. W. Bush (R)	48,886,097	426	Michael S. Dukakis (D)	41,809,074	111
1992	Bill Clinton (D)	44,909,889	370	George H. W. Bush (R)	39,104,545	168
				H. Ross Perot (independent)	19,742,267	—
1996	Bill Clinton (D)	47,402,357	379	Bob Dole (R)	39,198,755	159
				H. Ross Perot (Reform)	8,085,402	—
2000*	George W. Bush (R)	50,456,002	271	Al Gore (D)	50,999,897	266
				Ralph Nader (Green)	2,882,955	—
2004*	George W. Bush (R)	62,040,610	286	John Kerry (D)	59,028,444	251
2008	Barack H. Obama (D)	69,498,516	365	John McCain (R)	59,948,283	173
2012	Barack H. Obama (D)	65,915,795	332	Mitt Romney (R)	60,933,504	206

***1800**—Elected by House of Representatives because of tied electoral vote. **1824**—Elected by House of Representatives because no candidate polled a majority. By 1824, the Democratic Republicans had become a loose coalition of competing political groups. By 1828, Andrew Jackson supporters were known as Democrats and John Q. Adams and Henry Clay supporters as National Republicans. **1872**—Greeley died Nov. 29, 1872. His electoral votes were split among four individuals. **1876**—FL, LA, OR, and SC election returns were disputed. Congress in joint session (Mar. 2, 1877) declared Hayes and Wheeler elected president and vice president. **1956**—Democrats elected 74 electors, but one from AL refused to vote for Stevenson. **1960**—Sen. Harry F. Byrd (D, VA) received 15 electoral votes. **1972**—John Hospers of CA received a vote from an elector of VA. **1976**—Ronald Reagan of CA received a vote from an elector of WA. **1988**—Sen. Lloyd Bentsen (D, TX) received a vote from an elector of WV. **2000**—One Gore elector from Washington, DC, abstained. Nader was listed as "independent" on the ballot in some states; he was not on the ballot in all states. **2004**—One MN elector voted for VP candidate John Edwards for both president and vice president.

Presidential Popular Vote, 2012

Candidate (party)	Vote total	Percent of vote	Candidate (party)	Vote total	Percent of vote
Barack Obama (Democrat)	65,915,795	51.06%	Thomas Robert Stevens (Objectivist)	4,091	<0.01%
Mitt Romney (Republican)	60,933,504	47.20	Jim Carlson (Grassroots)	3,149	<0.01
Gary Johnson (Libertarian)	1,275,971	0.99	Jill Reed (Unaffiliated)	2,877	<0.01
Jill Stein (Green)	469,627	0.36	Merlin Miller (American Third Position)	2,701	<0.01
Virgil Goode (Constitution/U.S. Taxpayers)	122,389	0.09	Sheila "Samm" Tittle (We the People)	2,572	<0.01
Roseanne Barr (Peace and Freedom)	67,326	0.05	Gloria La Riva (Socialism and Liberation)	1,608	<0.01
Ross C. "Rocky" Anderson (Justice/ Natural Law)	43,018	0.03	Jerry White (Socialist Equality)	1,279	<0.01
			Dean Morstad (Constitutional Govt.)	1,094	<0.01
Tom Hoefling (American Independent, America's Party)	40,628	0.03	Jerry Litzel (nominated by petition)	1,027	<0.01
			Barbara Dale Washer (Reform)	1,016	<0.01
Randall Terry (Independent/no party affiliation)	13,107	0.01	Jeff Boss (NSA Did 911)	1,007	<0.01
			Andre Barnett (Reform)	956	<0.01
Richard Duncan (Independent)	12,557	0.01	Jack Fellure (Prohibition)	518	<0.01
Peta Lindsay (Socialism and Liberation)	7,791	0.01	Write-in votes (other/miscellaneous)	136,040	0.11
Chuck Baldwin (Reform)	5,017	<0.01	None of these candidates (Nevada)	5,770	<0.01
Will Christensen (Constitution)	4,453	<0.01	**Total**	**129,085,410**	
Stewart Alexander (Socialist)	4,405	<0.01	Voting age population, Nov. 2012	235,248,000	
James Harris (Socialist Workers)	4,117	<0.01	Percentage casting vote for president	54.87%	

Note: Party designations vary from one state to another; party label listed may not necessarily represent a political party organization. Vote totals for the candidates listed above include any write-in votes they received.

The Electoral College

The president and the vice president are the only elective federal officials not chosen by direct vote of the people. They are elected by the members of the Electoral College, an institution provided for in the U.S. Constitution.

On presidential election day, the first Tuesday after the first Monday in Nov. of every fourth year, each state chooses as many electors as it has senators and representatives in Congress. In 1964, for the first time, as provided by the 23rd Amendment to the Constitution, the District of Columbia voted for three electors. Thus, with 100 senators and 435 representatives, there are 538 members of the Electoral College, with a majority of 270 electoral votes needed to elect the president and vice president.

Political parties were not part of the Founding Fathers' original plan. But today, each political party chooses its electors, by nomination at a state convention or by vote of the party central committee in each state. An elector cannot be a member of Congress or federal office holder. In some states, electors' names may be printed below the names of the presidential and vice presidential candidates on the Nov. ballot. In any case, the electors of the party receiving the highest vote are elected. Two states, Maine and Nebraska, allow for proportional allocation.

The electors meet on the first Monday after the second Wednesday in Dec. in their respective state capitals or in some other place prescribed by state legislatures. By long-established custom, they vote for their party nominees, although this is not required by federal law. They may be bound to do so by state law or party pledge.

The Constitution requires electors to cast a ballot for at least one person who is not an inhabitant of that elector's home state. This ensures that presidential and vice presidential candidates from the same party will not be from the same state. (In 2000, Republican vice presidential nominee Dick Cheney changed his voter registration to Wyoming, where he grew up and which he'd once represented in Congress, from George W. Bush's home state of Texas.)

Certified and sealed lists of the votes of the electors in each state are sent to the president of the U.S. Senate. He or she then opens them in the presence of members of the Senate and House of Representatives in a joint session held in early Jan. The electoral votes of all the states are then officially counted.

If no candidate for president has a majority, the House of Representatives chooses a president from the top three candidates, with all representatives from each state combining to cast one vote for that state. The House decided the outcomes of the 1800 and 1824 presidential elections. If no candidate for vice president has a majority, the Senate chooses from the top two, with the senators voting as individuals. The Senate chose the vice president following the 1836 election.

Under the electoral college system, a candidate who fails to be the top vote getter in the popular vote still may win a majority of electoral votes. This happened in the elections of 1876, 1888, and 2000.

Voter Turnout in Presidential Elections, 1932-2012

Source: U.S. Census Bureau, U.S. Dept. of Commerce; Office of the Clerk, U.S. House of Representatives

Year	Candidates	Voter participation (% of voting-age population)	Year	Candidates	Voter participation (% of voting-age population)
1932	F. D. Roosevelt-Hoover	52.6%	1976	Carter-Ford	53.6%
1936	F. D. Roosevelt-Landon	56.9	1980	Reagan-Carter	52.8
1940	F. D. Roosevelt-Willkie	58.8	1984	Reagan-Mondale	53.3
1944	F. D. Roosevelt-Dewey	56.1	1988	G. H. W. Bush-Dukakis	50.3
1948	Truman-Dewey	51.1	1992	Clinton-G. H. W. Bush-Perot	55.2
1952	Eisenhower-Stevenson	61.6	1996	Clinton-Dole-Perot	49.0
1956	Eisenhower-Stevenson	59.3	2000	G. W. Bush-Gore	50.3
1960	Kennedy-Nixon	62.8	2004	G. W. Bush-Kerry	55.7
1964	L. B. Johnson-Goldwater	61.4	2008	Obama-McCain	57.1
1968	Nixon-Humphrey	60.7	2012	Obama-Romney	54.9
1972	Nixon-McGovern	55.1[1]			

(1) The drop in voter participation followed the expansion of eligibility with the enfranchisement of 18- to 20-year-olds.

Major-Party Nominees for President and Vice President, 1856-2012

Asterisk (*) denotes winning ticket.

	Democratic			Republican	
Year	President	Vice President	Year	President	Vice President
1856	James Buchanan*	John Breckinridge	1856	John Frémont	William Dayton
1860	Stephen A. Douglas[1]	Herschel V. Johnson	1860	Abraham Lincoln*	Hannibal Hamlin
1864	George McClellan	G. H. Pendleton	1864	Abraham Lincoln*	Andrew Johnson
1868	Horatio Seymour	Francis Blair	1868	Ulysses S. Grant*	Schuyler Colfax
1872	Horace Greeley	B. Gratz Brown	1872	Ulysses S. Grant*	Henry Wilson
1876	Samuel J. Tilden	Thomas Hendricks	1876	Rutherford B. Hayes*	William Wheeler
1880	Winfield Hancock	William English	1880	James A. Garfield*	Chester A. Arthur
1884	Grover Cleveland*	Thomas Hendricks	1884	James G. Blaine	John Logan
1888	Grover Cleveland	A. G. Thurman	1888	Benjamin Harrison*	Levi Morton
1892	Grover Cleveland*	Adlai Stevenson	1892	Benjamin Harrison	Whitelaw Reid
1896	William J. Bryan	Arthur Sewall	1896	William McKinley*	Garret Hobart
1900	William J. Bryan	Adlai Stevenson	1900	William McKinley*	Theodore Roosevelt
1904	Alton Parker	Henry Davis	1904	Theodore Roosevelt*	Charles Fairbanks
1908	William J. Bryan	John Kern	1908	William H. Taft*	James Sherman
1912	Woodrow Wilson*	Thomas Marshall	1912	William H. Taft	James Sherman[2]
1916	Woodrow Wilson*	Thomas Marshall	1916	Charles E. Hughes	Charles Fairbanks
1920	James M. Cox	Franklin D. Roosevelt	1920	Warren G. Harding*	Calvin Coolidge
1924	John W. Davis	Charles W. Bryan	1924	Calvin Coolidge*	Charles G. Dawes
1928	Alfred E. Smith	Joseph T. Robinson	1928	Herbert Hoover*	Charles Curtis
1932	Franklin D. Roosevelt*	John N. Garner	1932	Herbert Hoover	Charles Curtis
1936	Franklin D. Roosevelt*	John N. Garner	1936	Alfred M. Landon	Frank Knox
1940	Franklin D. Roosevelt*	Henry A. Wallace	1940	Wendell L. Willkie	Charles McNary
1944	Franklin D. Roosevelt*	Harry S. Truman	1944	Thomas E. Dewey	John W. Bricker
1948	Harry S. Truman*	Alben W. Barkley	1948	Thomas E. Dewey	Earl Warren
1952	Adlai E. Stevenson	John J. Sparkman	1952	Dwight D. Eisenhower*	Richard M. Nixon
1956	Adlai E. Stevenson	Estes Kefauver	1956	Dwight D. Eisenhower*	Richard M. Nixon
1960	John F. Kennedy*	Lyndon B. Johnson	1960	Richard M. Nixon	Henry Cabot Lodge
1964	Lyndon B. Johnson*	Hubert H. Humphrey	1964	Barry M. Goldwater	William E. Miller
1968	Hubert H. Humphrey	Edmund S. Muskie	1968	Richard M. Nixon*	Spiro T. Agnew
1972	George S. McGovern	R. Sargent Shriver Jr.[3]	1972	Richard M. Nixon*	Spiro T. Agnew
1976	Jimmy Carter*	Walter F. Mondale	1976	Gerald R. Ford	Bob Dole
1980	Jimmy Carter	Walter F. Mondale	1980	Ronald Reagan*	George H. W. Bush
1984	Walter F. Mondale	Geraldine Ferraro	1984	Ronald Reagan*	George H. W. Bush
1988	Michael S. Dukakis	Lloyd Bentsen	1988	George H. W. Bush*	Dan Quayle
1992	Bill Clinton*	Al Gore	1992	George H. W. Bush	Dan Quayle
1996	Bill Clinton*	Al Gore	1996	Bob Dole	Jack Kemp
2000	Al Gore	Joseph Lieberman	2000	George W. Bush*	Richard Cheney
2004	John Kerry	John Edwards	2004	George W. Bush*	Richard Cheney
2008	Barack Obama*	Joe Biden	2008	John McCain	Sarah Palin
2012	Barack Obama*	Joe Biden	2012	Mitt Romney	Paul Ryan

(1) Douglas and Johnson were nominated at the Baltimore convention. An earlier convention in Charleston, SC, failed to reach a consensus and resulted in a split in the party. The Southern faction of the Democrats nominated John Breckinridge for president and Joseph Lane for vice president. (2) Died Oct. 30; replaced on ballot by Nicholas Butler. (3) Chosen by Democratic National Committee after Thomas Eagleton withdrew because of controversy over past treatments for depression.

Third-Party and Independent Presidential Candidates

In most elections since 1860, fewer than one vote in 20 has been cast for a third-party candidate. Still, independent and third-party candidates often bring attention to prominent issues and can affect the outcome between major-party candidates.

Major vote getters among third-party and independent candidates include James B. Weaver (People's Party), 1892; former Pres. Theodore Roosevelt (Progressive Party), 1912; Robert M. La Follette (Progressive Party), 1924; George C. Wallace (American Independent Party), 1968; and H. Ross Perot, as an independent in 1992 and with the Reform Party in 1996. In these six elections, non-major-party candidates combined polled at least 10% of the vote.

Roosevelt outpolled the Republican candidate, William Howard Taft, in 1912, capturing 28% of the popular vote and 88 electoral votes. In 1948, Strom Thurmond (States' Rights [Dixiecrat]) won 39 electoral votes from five Southern states; however, third-party candidates received only 5.75% of the popular vote. George Wallace's popularity in the same region in 1968 allowed him to get 46 electoral votes and 13.5% of the popular vote.

In 1992, Ross Perot captured 19% of the popular vote but failed to win a single electoral vote. In 1996, Perot won 8% of the popular vote; all third-party candidates combined won just over 10%. In 2000, Ralph Nader (Green, independent) won about 3% of the vote.

Notable Third-Party and Independent Campaigns by Year

Party	Presidential nominee	Year	Issues	Strength in
Anti-Masonic	William Wirt	1832	Against secret societies and oaths	PA, VT
Liberty	James G. Birney	1844	Anti-slavery	North
Free Soil	Martin Van Buren	1848	Anti-slavery	NY, OH
American (Know-Nothing)	Millard Fillmore	1856	Anti-immigrant	Northeast, South
Greenback	Peter Cooper	1876	For "cheap money," labor rights	National
Greenback	James B. Weaver	1880	For "cheap money," labor rights	National
Prohibition	John P. St. John	1884	Anti-liquor	National
People's (Populist)	James B. Weaver	1892	For "cheap money," end of national banks	South, West
Socialist	Eugene V. Debs	1900-12; 1920	For public ownership	National
Progressive (Bull Moose)	Theodore Roosevelt	1912	Against high tariffs	Midwest, West
Progressive	Robert M. La Follette	1924	For farmer and labor rights	Midwest, West
Socialist	Norman Thomas	1928-48	For liberal reforms	National
Union	William Lemke	1936	Anti-New Deal	National
States' Rights (Dixiecrat)	Strom Thurmond	1948	For states' rights	South
Progressive	Henry A. Wallace	1948	Anti-Cold War	NY, CA
American Independent	George C. Wallace	1968	For states' rights	South
American	John G. Schmitz	1972	For "law and order"	West, OH, LA
None (independent)	John B. Anderson	1980	A third party	National
None (independent)	H. Ross Perot	1992	Federal budget deficit	National
Reform	H. Ross Perot	1996	Deficit, campaign finance	National
Green, independent	Ralph Nader	2000-08	Corporate power, domestic priorities	National
Libertarian	Gary Johnson	2012	Public debt, civil liberties	National

Presidential Election Results by State, 1960-2012

Source: Federal Election Commission; local secretaries of state; state elections offices. State election results may vary slightly from those provided by the FEC.

Alabama Vote Since 1960

2012: Romney, R, 1,255,925; Obama, D, 795,696; Johnson, Ind., 12,328; Stein, Ind., 3,397; Goode, Ind., 2,981.

2008: McCain, R, 1,266,546; Obama, D, 813,479; Nader, Ind., 6,788; Barr, Ind., 4,991; Baldwin, Ind., 4,310.

2004: Bush, R, 1,176,394; Kerry, D, 693,933; Nader, Ind., 6,701; Badnarik, Ind., 3,529; Peroutka, Ind., 1,994.

2000: Bush, R, 941,173; Gore, D, 692,611; Nader, Ind., 18,323; Buchanan, Ind., 6,351; Browne, LB, 5,893; Phillips, Ind., 775; Hagelin, Ind., 447.

1996: Dole, R, 769,044; Clinton, D, 662,165; Perot, RF, 92,149; Browne, LB, 5,290; Phillips, Ind., 2,365; Hagelin, Natural Law, 1,697; Harris, Ind., 516.

1992: Bush, R, 804,283; Clinton, D, 690,080; Perot, Ind., 183,109; Marrou, LB, 5,737; Fulani, New Alliance, 2,161.

1988: Bush, R, 815,576; Dukakis, D, 549,506; Paul, LB, 8,460; Fulani, Ind., 3,311.

1984: Reagan, R, 872,849; Mondale, D, 551,899; Bergland, LB, 9,504.

1980: Reagan, R, 654,192; Carter, D, 636,730; Anderson, Ind., 16,481; Rarick, Amer. Ind., 15,010; Clark, LB, 13,318; Bubar, Statesman, 1,743; Hall, Comm., 1,629; DeBerry, Soc. Workers, 1,303; McReynolds, Soc., 1,006; Commoner, Citizens, 517.

1976: Carter, D, 659,170; Ford, R, 504,070; Maddox, Amer. Ind., 9,198; Bubar, Prohib., 6,669; Hall, Comm., 1,954; MacBride, LB, 1,481.

1972: Nixon, R, 728,701; McGovern, D, 219,108 plus Natl. Dem. Party of AL, 37,815; Schmitz, Conservative, 11,918; Munn, Prohib., 8,551.

1968: Wallace, 3rd party, 691,425; Humphrey, D, 196,579; Nixon, R, 146,923; Munn, Prohib., 4,022.

1964: Goldwater, R, 479,085; D (electors unpledged), 209,848; scattered, 105.

1960: Kennedy, D, 324,050; Nixon, R, 237,981; Faubus, States' Rights, 4,367; Decker, Prohib., 2,106; King, Afro-Americans, 1,485; scattered, 236.

Alaska Vote Since 1960

2012: Romney, R, 164,676; Obama, D, 122,640; Johnson, LB, 7,392; Stein, Green, 2,917.

2008: McCain, R, 193,841; Obama, D, 123,594; Nader, Ind., 3,783; Baldwin, AK Ind., 1,660; Barr, LB, 1,589.

2004: Bush, R, 190,889; Kerry, D, 111,025; Nader, Populist, 5,069; Peroutka, AK Ind., 2,092; Badnarik, LB, 1,675; Cobb, Green, 1,058.

2000: Bush, R, 167,398; Gore, D, 79,004; Nader, Green, 28,747; Buchanan, RF, 5,192; Browne, LB, 2,636; Hagelin, Natural Law, 919; Phillips, Const., 596.

1996: Dole, R, 122,746; Clinton, D, 80,380; Perot, RF, 26,333; Nader, Green, 7,597; Browne, LB, 2,276; Phillips, U.S. Taxpayers, 925; Hagelin, Natural Law, 729.

1992: Bush, R, 102,000; Clinton, D, 78,294; Perot, Ind., 73,481; Gritz, Populist/America First, 1,379; Marrou, LB, 1,378.

1988: Bush, R, 119,251; Dukakis, D, 72,584; Paul, LB, 5,484; Fulani, New Alliance, 1,024.

1984: Reagan, R, 138,377; Mondale, D, 62,007; Bergland, LB, 6,378.

1980: Reagan, R, 86,112; Carter, D, 41,842; Clark, LB, 18,479; Anderson, Ind., 11,155; write-in, 857.

1976: Ford, R, 71,555; Carter, D, 44,058; MacBride, LB, 6,785.

1972: Nixon, R, 55,349; McGovern, D, 32,967; Schmitz, Amer., 6,903.

1968: Nixon, R, 37,600; Humphrey, D, 35,411; Wallace, 3rd party, 10,024.

1964: Johnson, D, 44,329; Goldwater, R, 22,930.

1960: Nixon, R, 30,953; Kennedy, D, 29,809.

Arizona Vote Since 1960

2012: Romney, R, 1,233,654; Obama, D, 1,025,232; Johnson, LB, 32,100; Stein, Green, 7,816.

2008: McCain, R, 1,230,111; Obama, D, 1,034,707; Barr, LB, 12,555; Nader, New Prog., 11,301; McKinney, Green, 3,406.

2004: Bush, R, 1,104,294; Kerry, D, 893,524; Badnarik, LB, 11,856.

2000: Bush, R, 781,652; Gore, D, 685,341; Nader, Green, 45,645; Buchanan, RF, 12,373; Smith, LB, 5,775; Hagelin, Natural Law, 1,120.

1996: Clinton, D, 653,288; Dole, R, 622,073; Perot, RF, 112,072; Browne, LB, 14,358.

1992: Bush, R, 572,086; Clinton, D, 543,050; Perot, Ind., 353,741; Gritz, Populist/America First, 8,141; Marrou, LB, 6,759; Hagelin, Natural Law, 2,267.

1988: Bush, R, 702,541; Dukakis, D, 454,029; Paul, LB, 13,351; Fulani, New Alliance, 1,662.

1984: Reagan, R, 681,416; Mondale, D, 333,854; Bergland, LB, 10,585.

1980: Reagan, R, 529,688; Carter, D, 246,843; Anderson, Ind., 76,952; Clark, LB, 18,784; DeBerry, Soc. Workers, 1,100; Commoner, Citizens, 551; Hall, Comm., 25; Griswold, Workers World, 2.

1976: Ford, R, 418,642; Carter, D, 295,602; McCarthy, Ind., 19,229; MacBride, LB, 7,647; Camejo, Soc. Workers, 928; Anderson, Amer., 564; Maddox, Amer. Ind., 85.

1972: Nixon, R, 402,812; McGovern, D, 198,540; Jenness, Soc. Workers, 30,945; Schmitz, Amer. Ind., 21,208.

1968: Nixon, R, 266,721; Humphrey, D, 170,514; Wallace, 3rd party, 46,573; McCarthy, New Party, 2,751; Cleaver, Peace/ Freedom, 217; Halstead, Soc. Workers, 85; Blomen, Soc. Labor, 75.

1964: Goldwater, R, 242,535; Johnson, D, 237,753; Hass, Soc. Labor, 482.

1960: Nixon, R, 221,241; Kennedy, D, 176,781; Hass, Soc. Labor, 469.

Arkansas Vote Since 1960

2012: Romney, R, 647,744; Obama, D, 394,409; Johnson, LB, 16,276; Stein, Green, 9,305; Lindsay, Socialism/Liberation, 1,734.

2008: McCain, R, 638,017; Obama, D, 422,310; Nader, Ind., 12,882; Barr, LB, 4,776; Baldwin, Const., 4,023; McKinney, Green, 3,470; La Riva, Socialism/Liberation, 1,139.

2004: Bush, R, 572,898; Kerry, D, 469,953; Nader, Populist, 6,171; Badnarik, LB, 2,352; Peroutka, Const., 2,083; Cobb, Green, 1,488.

2000: Bush, R, 472,940; Gore, D, 422,768; Nader, Green, 13,421; Buchanan, RF, 7,358; Browne, LB, 2,781; Phillips, Const., 1,415; Hagelin, Natural Law, 1,098.

1996: Clinton, D, 475,171; Dole, R, 325,416; Perot, RF, 69,884; Nader, Ind., 3,649; Browne, Ind., 3,076; Phillips, Ind., 2,065; Forbes, Ind., 932; Collins, Ind., 823; Masters, Ind., 749; Moorehead, Ind., 747; Hagelin, Ind., 729; Hollis, Ind., 538; Dodge, Ind., 483.

1992: Clinton, D, 505,823; Bush, R, 337,324; Perot, Ind., 99,132; Phillips, U.S. Taxpayers, 1,437; Marrou, LB, 1,261; Fulani, New Alliance, 1,022.

1988: Bush, R, 466,578; Dukakis, D, 349,237; Duke, Populist, 5,146; Paul, LB, 3,297.

1984: Reagan, R, 534,774; Mondale, D, 338,646; Bergland, LB, 2,220.

1980: Reagan, R, 403,164; Carter, D, 398,041; Anderson, Ind., 22,468; Clark, LB, 8,970; Commoner, Citizens, 2,345; Bubar, Statesman, 1,350; Hall, Comm., 1,244.

1976: Carter, D, 498,604; Ford, R, 267,903; McCarthy, Ind., 639; Anderson, Amer. Ind., 389.

1972: Nixon, R, 445,751; McGovern, D, 198,899; Schmitz, Amer. Ind., 3,016.

1968: Wallace, 3rd party, 235,627; Nixon, R, 189,062; Humphrey, D, 184,901.

1964: Johnson, D, 314,197; Goldwater, R, 243,264; Kasper, Natl. States' Rights, 2,965.

1960: Kennedy, D, 215,049; Nixon, R, 184,508; Faubus, Natl. States' Rights, 28,952.

California Vote Since 1960

2012: Obama, D, 7,854,285; Romney, R, 4,839,958; Johnson, LB, 143,221; Stein, Green, 85,638; Barr, Peace/Freedom, 53,824; Hoefling, Amer. Ind., 38,372.

2008: Obama, D, 8,274,473; McCain, R, 5,011,781; Nader, Peace/Freedom, 108,381; Barr, LB, 67,582; Alan Keyes, Amer. Ind., 40,673; McKinney, Green, 38,774.

2004: Kerry, D, 6,745,485; Bush, R, 5,509,826; Badnarik, LB, 50,165; Cobb, Green, 40,771; Peltier, Peace/Freedom, 27,607; Peroutka, Amer. Ind., 26,645.

2000: Gore, D, 5,861,203; Bush, R, 4,567,429; Nader, Green, 418,707; Browne, LB, 45,520; Buchanan, RF, 44,987; Phillips, Amer. Ind., 17,042; Hagelin, Natural Law, 10,934.

1996: Clinton, D, 5,119,835; Dole, R, 3,828,380; Perot, RF, 697,847; Nader, Green, 237,016; Browne, LB, 73,600; Feinland, Peace/Freedom, 25,332; Phillips, Amer. Ind., 21,202; Hagelin, Natural Law, 15,403.

1992: Clinton, D, 5,121,325; Bush, R, 3,630,575; Perot, Ind., 2,296,006; Marrou, LB, 48,139; Daniels, Ind., 18,597; Phillips, U.S. Taxpayers, 12,711.

1988: Bush, R, 5,054,917; Dukakis, D, 4,702,233; Paul, LB, 70,105; Fulani, Ind., 31,181.

1984: Reagan, R, 5,305,410; Mondale, D, 3,815,947; Bergland, LB, 48,400.

1980: Reagan, R, 4,524,858; Carter, D, 3,083,661; Anderson, Ind., 739,833; Clark, LB, 148,434; Commoner, Ind., 61,063; Smith, Peace/Freedom, 18,116; Rarick, Amer. Ind., 9,856.

1976: Ford, R, 3,882,244; Carter, D, 3,742,284; McCarthy, write-in, 58,412; MacBride, LB, 56,388; Maddox, Amer. Ind., 51,098; Wright, People's, 41,731; Camejo, Soc. Workers, 17,259; Hall, Comm., 12,766; write-in, 4,935.

1972: Nixon, R, 4,602,096; McGovern, D, 3,475,847; Schmitz, Amer. Ind., 232,554; Spock, Peace/Freedom, 55,167; Hospers, LB, 980; Jenness, Soc. Workers, 574; Hall, Comm., 373; Fisher, Soc. Labor, 197; Munn, Prohib., 53; Green, Universal, 21.

1968: Nixon, R, 3,467,664; Humphrey, D, 3,244,318; Wallace, 3rd party, 487,270; Peace/Freedom, 27,707; McCarthy, Alternative, 20,721; Gregory, write-in, 3,230; Blomen, Soc. Labor, 341; Mitchell, Comm., 260; Munn, Prohib., 59; Soeters, Defense, 17.

1964: Johnson, D, 4,171,877; Goldwater, R, 2,879,108; Hass, Soc. Labor, 489; DeBerry, Soc. Workers, 378; Munn, Prohib., 305; Hensley, Universal, 19.

1960: Nixon, R, 3,259,722; Kennedy, D, 3,224,099; Decker, Prohib., 21,706; Hass, Soc. Labor, 1,051.

Colorado Vote Since 1960

2012: Obama, D, 1,323,102; Romney, R, 1,185,243; Johnson, LB, 35,545; Stein, Green, 7,508; Goode, Const., 6,234; Barr, Peace/Freedom, 5,059; Reed, unaff., 2,589; Anderson, Justice, 1,260; Tittle, We the People, 792; Hoefling, Amer. Ind., 679; La Riva, Socialism/Liberation, 317; Alexander, Soc. USA, 308; Miller, A3P, 266; Stevens, Objectivist, 235; Harris, Soc. Workers, 192; White, Soc. Equality, 189.

2008: Obama, D, 1,288,633; McCain, R, 1,073,629; Nader, unaff., 13,352; Barr, LB, 10,898; Baldwin, Const., 6,233; Alan Keyes, Amer. Ind., 3,051; McKinney, Green, 2,822; McEnulty, unaff., 829; Jay, Boston Tea, 598; Allen, HeartQuake '08, 348; Stevens, Objectivist, 336; Moore, Soc. USA, 226; La Riva, Socialism/Liberation, 158; Harris, Soc. Workers, 154; Lyttle, U.S. Pacifist, 110; Amondson, Prohib., 85.

2004: Bush, R, 1,101,255; Kerry, D, 1,001,732; Nader, RF, 12,718; Badnarik, LB, 7,664; Peroutka, Amer. Const., 2,562; Cobb, Green, 1,591; Andress, Ind., 804; Amondson, Concerns of People, 378; Van Auken, Soc. Equal., 329; Harris, Soc. Workers, 241; Brown, Soc., 216; Dodge, Prohib., 140.

2000: Bush, R, 883,748; Gore, D, 738,227; Nader, Green, 91,434; Browne, LB, 12,799; Buchanan, RF, 10,465; Hagelin, RF, 2,240; Phillips, Amer. Const., 1,319; McReynolds, Soc., 712; Harris, Soc. Workers, 216; Dodge, Prohib., 208.

1996: Dole, R, 691,848; Clinton, D, 671,152; Perot, RF, 99,629; Nader, Green, 25,070; Browne, LB, 12,392; Phillips, Amer. Const., 2,813; Collins, Ind., 2,809; Hagelin, Natural Law, 2,547; Hollis, Soc., 669; Moorehead, Workers World, 599; Templin, Amer., 557; Dodge, Prohib., 375; Harris, Soc. Workers, 244.

1992: Clinton, D, 629,681; Bush, R, 562,850; Perot, Ind., 366,010; Marrou, LB, 8,669; Fulani, New Alliance, 1,608.

1988: Bush, R, 728,177; Dukakis, D, 621,453; Paul, LB, 15,482; Dodge, Prohib., 4,604.

1984: Reagan, R, 821,817; Mondale, D, 454,975; Bergland, LB, 11,257.

1980: Reagan, R, 652,264; Carter, D, 367,973; Anderson, Ind., 130,633; Clark, LB, 25,744; Commoner, Citizens, 5,614; Bubar, Statesman, 1,180; Pulley, Soc., 520; Hall, Comm., 487.

1976: Ford, R, 584,367; Carter, D, 460,353; McCarthy, Ind., 26,107; MacBride, LB, 5,330; Bubar, Prohib., 2,882.

1972: Nixon, R, 597,189; McGovern, D, 329,980; Schmitz, Amer., 17,269; Fisher, Soc. Labor, 4,361; Spock, People's, 2,403; Hospers, LB, 1,111; Jenness, Soc. Workers, 555; Munn, Prohib., 467; Hall, Comm., 432.

1968: Nixon, R, 409,345; Humphrey, D, 335,174; Wallace, 3rd party, 60,813; Blomen, Soc. Labor, 3,016; Gregory, New Party, 1,393; Munn, Prohib., 275; Halstead, Soc. Workers, 235.

1964: Johnson, D, 476,024; Goldwater, R, 296,767; DeBerry, Soc. Workers, 2,537; Munn, Prohib., 1,356; Hass, Soc. Labor, 302.

1960: Nixon, R, 402,242; Kennedy, D, 330,629; Hass, Soc. Labor, 2,803; Dobbs, Soc. Workers, 572.

Connecticut Vote Since 1960

2012: Obama, D, 905,083; Romney, R, 634,892; Johnson, LB, 12,580; Anderson, Ind., 5,487.

2008: Obama, D, 997,772; McCain, R, 629,428; Nader, Ind., 19,162.

2004: Kerry, D, 857,488; Bush, R, 693,826; Nader, petitioning cand., 12,969; Cobb, Green, 9,564; Badnarik, LB, 3,367; Peroutka, Concerned Citizens, 1,543.

2000: Gore, D, 816,015; Bush, R, 561,094; Nader, Green, 64,452; Phillips, Concerned Citizens, 9,695; Buchanan, RF, 4,731; Browne, LB, 3,484.

1996: Clinton, D, 735,740; Dole, R, 483,109; Perot, RF, 139,523; Nader, Green, 24,321; Browne, LB, 5,788; Phillips, Concerned Citizens, 2,425; Hagelin, Natural Law, 1,703.

1992: Clinton, D, 682,318; Bush, R, 578,313; Perot, Ind., 348,771; Marrou, LB, 5,391; Fulani, New Alliance, 1,363.

1988: Bush, R, 750,241; Dukakis, D, 676,584; Paul, LB, 14,071; Fulani, New Alliance, 2,491.

1984: Reagan, R, 890,877; Mondale, D, 569,597.

1980: Reagan, R, 677,210; Carter, D, 541,732; Anderson, Ind., 171,807; Clark, LB, 8,570; Commoner, Citizens, 6,130; scattered, 836.

1976: Ford, R, 719,261; Carter, D, 647,895; Maddox, George Wallace Party, 7,101; LaRouche, U.S. Labor, 1,789.

1972: Nixon, R, 810,763; McGovern, D, 555,498; Schmitz, Amer., 17,239; scattered, 777.

1968: Humphrey, D, 621,561; Nixon, R, 556,721; Wallace, 3rd party, 76,650; scattered, 1,300.

1964: Johnson, D, 826,269; Goldwater, R, 390,996; scattered, 1,313.

1960: Kennedy, D, 657,055; Nixon, R, 565,813.

Delaware Vote Since 1960

2012: Obama, D, 242,584; Romney, R, 165,484; Johnson, LB, 3,882; Stein, Green, 1,940.

2008: Obama, D, 255,459; McCain, R, 152,374; Nader, Ind. (DE), 2,401; Barr, LB, 1,109; Baldwin, Const., 626; McKinney, Green, 385; Calero, Soc. Workers, 58.

2004: Kerry, D, 200,152; Bush, R, 171,660; Nader, Ind., 2,153; Badnarik, LB, 586; Peroutka, Const., 289; Cobb, Green, 250; Brown, Natural Law, 100.

2000: Gore, D, 180,068; Bush, R, 137,288; Nader, Green, 8,307; Buchanan, RF, 777; Browne, LB, 774; Phillips, Const., 208; Hagelin, Natural Law, 107.

1996: Clinton, D, 140,355; Dole, R, 99,062; Perot, RF, 28,719; Browne, LB, 2,052; Phillips, U.S. Taxpayers, 348; Hagelin, Natural Law, 274.

1992: Clinton, D, 126,054; Bush, R, 102,313; Perot, Ind., 59,213; Fulani, New Alliance, 1,105.

1988: Bush, R, 139,639; Dukakis, D, 108,647; Paul, LB, 1,162; Fulani, New Alliance, 443.

1984: Reagan, R, 152,190; Mondale, D, 101,656; Bergland, LB, 268.

1980: Reagan, R, 111,252; Carter, D, 105,754; Anderson, Ind., 16,288; Clark, LB, 1,974; Greaves, Amer., 400.

1976: Carter, D, 122,596; Ford, R, 109,831; McCarthy, nonpartisan, 2,437; Anderson, Amer., 645; LaRouche, U.S. Labor, 136; Bubar, Prohib., 103; Levin, Soc. Labor, 86.

1972: Nixon, R, 140,357; McGovern, D, 92,283; Schmitz, Amer., 2,638; Munn, Prohib., 238.

1968: Nixon, R, 96,714; Humphrey, D, 89,194; Wallace, 3rd party, 28,459.

1964: Johnson, D, 122,704; Goldwater, R, 78,078; Munn, Prohib., 425; Hass, Soc. Labor, 113.

1960: Kennedy, D, 99,590; Nixon, R, 96,373; Faubus, States' Rights, 354; Decker, Prohib., 284; Hass, Soc. Labor, 82.

District of Columbia Vote Since 1964

2012: Obama, D, 267,070; Romney, R, 21,381; Stein, DC Statehood Green, 2,458; Johnson, LB, 2,083.

2008: Obama, D, 245,800; McCain, R, 17,367; Nader, Ind., 958; McKinney, Green, 590.

2004: Kerry, D, 202,970; Bush, R, 21,256; Nader, Ind., 1,485; Cobb, DC Statehood Green, 737; Badnarik, LB, 502; Harris, Soc. Workers, 130.

2000: Gore, D, 171,923; Bush, R, 18,073; Nader, Green, 10,576; Browne, LB, 669; Harris, Soc. Workers, 114.

1996: Clinton, D, 158,220; Dole, R, 17,339; Nader, Green, 4,780; Perot, RF, 3,611; Browne, LB, 588; Hagelin, Natural Law, 283; Harris, Soc. Workers, 257.

1992: Clinton, D, 192,619; Bush, R, 20,698; Perot, Ind., 9,681; Fulani, New Alliance, 1,459; Daniels, Ind., 1,186.

1988: Dukakis, D, 159,407; Bush, R, 27,590; Fulani, New Alliance, 2,901; Paul, LB, 554.

1984: Mondale, D, 180,408; Reagan, R, 29,009; Bergland, LB, 279.

1980: Carter, D, 130,231; Reagan, R, 23,313; Anderson, Ind., 16,131; Commoner, Citizens, 1,826; Clark, LB, 1,104; Hall, Comm., 369; DeBerry, Soc. Workers, 173; Griswold, Workers World, 92; write-in, 690.

1976: Carter, D, 137,818; Ford, R, 27,873; Camejo, Soc. Workers, 545; MacBride, LB, 274; Hall, Comm., 219; LaRouche, U.S. Labor, 157.

1972: McGovern, D, 127,627; Nixon, R, 35,226; Reed, Soc. Workers, 316; Hall, Comm., 252.

1968: Humphrey, D, 139, 566; Nixon, R, 31,012.

1964: Johnson, D, 169,796; Goldwater, R, 28,801.

Florida Vote Since 1960

2012: Obama, D, 4,237,756; Romney, R, 4,163,447; Johnson, LB, 44,726; Stein, Green, 8,947; Barr, Peace/Freedom, 8,154; Stevens, Objectivist, 3,856; Goode, Const., 2,607; Anderson, Justice, 1,754; Hoefling, Amer. Ind., 946; Barnett, RF, 820; Alexander, Soc., 799; Lindsay, Socialism/Liberation, 322.

2008: Obama, D, 4,282,074; McCain, R, 4,045,624; Nader, Ecology (FL), 28,124; Barr, LB, 17,218; Baldwin, Const., 7,915; McKinney, Green, 2,887; Keyes, Amer. Ind., 2,550; La Riva, Socialism/Liberation, 1,516; Jay, Boston Tea, 795; Harris, Soc. Workers, 533; Stevens, Objectivist, 419; Moore, Soc. USA, 405; Amondson, Prohib., 293.

2004: Bush, R, 3,964,522; Kerry, D, 3,583,544; Nader, RF, 32,971; Badnarik, LB, 11,996; Peroutka, Const., 6,626; Cobb, Green, 3,917; Brown, Soc., 3,502; Harris, Soc. Workers, 2,732.

2000: Bush, R, 2,912,790; Gore, D, 2,912,253; Nader, Green, 97,488; Buchanan, RF, 17,484; Browne, LB, 16,415; Hagelin, Natural Law, 2,281; Moorehead, Workers World, 1,804; Phillips, Const., 1,371; McReynolds, Soc., 622; Harris, Soc. Workers, 562.

1996: Clinton, D, 2,545,968; Dole, R, 2,243,324; Perot, RF, 483,776; Browne, LB, 23,312.

1992: Bush, R, 2,171,781; Clinton, D, 2,071,651; Perot, Ind., 1,052,481; Marrou, LB, 15,068.

1988: Bush, R, 2,616,597; Dukakis, D, 1,655,851; Paul, LB, 19,796, Fulani, New Alliance, 6,655.

1984: Reagan, R, 2,728,775; Mondale, D, 1,448,344.

1980: Reagan, R, 2,046,951; Carter, D, 1,419,475; Anderson, Ind., 189,692; Clark, LB, 30,524; write-in, 285.

1976: Carter, D, 1,636,000; Ford, R, 1,469,531; McCarthy, Ind., 23,643; Anderson, Amer., 21,325.

1972: Nixon, R, 1,857,759; McGovern, D, 718,117; scattered, 7,407.

1968: Nixon, R, 886,804; Humphrey, D, 676,794; Wallace, 3rd party, 624,207.

1964: Johnson, D, 948,540; Goldwater, R, 905,941.

1960: Nixon, R, 795,476; Kennedy, D, 748,700.

Georgia Vote Since 1960

2012: Romney, R, 2,078,688; Obama, D, 1,773,827; Johnson, LB, 45,324.

2008: McCain, R, 2,048,759; Obama, D, 1,844,123; Barr, LB, 28,731.

2004: Bush, R, 1,914,254; Kerry, D, 1,366,149; Badnarik, LB, 18,387.

2000: Bush, R, 1,419,720; Gore, D, 1,116,230; Browne, LB, 36,332; Buchanan, Ind., 10,926.

1996: Dole, R, 1,080,843; Clinton, D, 1,053,849; Perot, RF, 146,337; Browne, LB, 17,870.

1992: Clinton, D, 1,008,966; Bush, R, 995,252; Perot, Ind., 309,657; Marrou, LB, 7,110.

1988: Bush, R, 1,081,331; Dukakis, D, 714,792; Paul, LB, 8,435; Fulani, New Alliance, 5,099.

1984: Reagan, R, 1,068,722; Mondale, D, 706,628.

1980: Carter, D, 890,955; Reagan, R, 654,168; Anderson, Ind., 36,055; Clark, LB, 15,627.

1976: Carter, D, 979,409; Ford, R, 483,743; write-in, 4,306.

1972: Nixon, R, 881,496; McGovern, D, 289,529; Schmitz, Amer., 812; scattered, 2,935.

1968: Wallace, 3rd party, 535,550; Nixon, R, 380,111; Humphrey, D, 334,440; write-in, 162.

1964: Goldwater, R, 616,600; Johnson, D, 522,557.

1960: Kennedy, D, 458,638; Nixon, R, 274,472; write-in, 239.

Hawaii Vote Since 1960

2012: Obama, D, 306,658; Romney, R, 121,015; Johnson, LB, 3,840; Stein, Green, 3,184.

2008: Obama, D, 325,871; McCain, R, 120,566; Nader, Ind. (HI), 3,825; Barr, LB, 1,314; Baldwin, Const., 1,013; McKinney, Green, 979.

2004: Kerry, D, 231,708; Bush, R, 194,191; Cobb, Green, 1,737; Badnarik, LB, 1,377.

2000: Gore, D, 205,286; Bush, R, 137,845; Nader, Green, 21,623; Browne, LB, 1,477; Buchanan, RF, 1,071; Phillips, Const., 343; Hagelin, Natural Law, 306.

1996: Clinton, D, 205,012; Dole, R, 113,943; Perot, RF, 27,358; Nader, Green, 10,386; Browne, LB, 2,493; Hagelin, Natural Law, 570; Phillips, Taxpayers, 358.

1992: Clinton, D, 179,310; Bush, R, 136,822; Perot, Ind., 53,003; Gritz, Populist/America First, 1,452; Marrou, LB, 1,119.

1988: Dukakis, D, 192,364; Bush, R, 158,625; Paul, LB, 1,999; Fulani, New Alliance, 1,003.

1984: Reagan, R, 184,934; Mondale, D, 147,098; Bergland, LB, 2,167.

1980: Carter, D, 135,879; Reagan, R, 130,112; Anderson, Ind., 32,021; Clark, LB, 3,269; Commoner, Citizens, 1,548; Hall, Comm., 458.

1976: Carter, D, 147,375; Ford, R, 140,003; MacBride, LB, 3,923.

1972: Nixon, R, 168,865; McGovern, D, 101,409.

1968: Humphrey, D, 141,324; Nixon, R, 91,425; Wallace, 3rd party, 3,469.

1964: Johnson, D, 163,249; Goldwater, R, 44,022.

1960: Kennedy, D, 92,410; Nixon, R, 92,295.

Idaho Vote Since 1960

2012: Romney, R, 420,911; Obama, D, 212,787; Johnson, LB, 9,453; Stein, Ind., 4,402; Anderson, Ind., 2,499; Goode, Const., 2,222.

2008: McCain, R, 403,012; Obama, D, 236,440; Nader, Ind., 7,175; Baldwin, Const., 4,747; Barr, LB, 3,658.

2004: Bush, R, 409,235; Kerry, D, 181,098; Badnarik, LB, 3,844; Peroutka, Const., 3,084.

2000: Bush, R, 336,937; Gore, D, 138,637; Buchanan, RF, 7,615; Browne, LB, 3,488; Phillips, Const., 1,469; Hagelin, Natural Law, 1,177.

1996: Dole, R, 256,595; Clinton, D, 165,443; Perot, RF, 62,518; Browne, LB, 3,325; Phillips, U.S. Taxpayers, 2,230; Hagelin, Natural Law, 1,600.

1992: Bush, R, 202,645; Clinton, D, 137,013; Perot, Ind., 130,395; Gritz, Populist/America First, 10,281; Marrou, LB, 1,167.

1988: Bush, R, 253,881; Dukakis, D, 147,272; Paul, LB, 5,313; Fulani, Ind., 2,502.

1984: Reagan, R, 297,523; Mondale, D, 108,510; Bergland, LB, 2,823.

1980: Reagan, R, 290,699; Carter, D, 110,192; Anderson, Ind., 27,058; Clark, LB, 8,425; Rarick, Amer., 1,057.

1976: Ford, R, 204,151; Carter, D, 126,549; Maddox, Amer., 5,935; MacBride, R, 3,558; LaRouche, U.S. Labor, 739.

1972: Nixon, R, 199,384; McGovern, D, 80,826; Schmitz, Amer., 28,869; Spock, People's, 903.

1968: Nixon, R, 165,369; Humphrey, D, 89,273; Wallace, 3rd party, 36,541.

1964: Johnson, D, 148,920; Goldwater, R, 143,557.

1960: Nixon, R, 161,597; Kennedy, D, 138,853.

Illinois Vote Since 1960

2012: Obama, D, 3,019,512; Romney, R, 2,135,216; Johnson, LB, 56,229; Stein, Green, 30,222.

2008: Obama, D, 3,419,348; McCain, R, 2,031,179; Nader, Ind., 30,948; Barr, LB, 19,642; McKinney, Green, 11,838; Baldwin, Const., 8,256; Polachek, New Party, 1,149.

2004: Kerry, D, 2,891,550; Bush, R, 2,345,946; Badnarik, LB, 32,442.

2000: Gore, D, 2,589,026; Bush, R, 2,019,421; Nader, Green, 103,759; Buchanan, Ind., 16,106; Browne, LB, 11,623; Hagelin, RF, 2,127.

1996: Clinton, D, 2,341,744; Dole, R, 1,587,021; Perot, RF, 346,408; Browne, LB, 22,548; Phillips, U.S. Taxpayers, 7,606; Hagelin, Natural Law, 4,606.

1992: Clinton, D, 2,453,350; Bush, R, 1,734,096; Perot, Ind., 840,515; Marrou, LB, 9,218; Fulani, New Alliance, 5,267; Gritz, Populist/America First, 3,577; Hagelin, Natural Law, 2,751; Warren, Soc. Workers, 1,361.

1988: Bush, R, 2,310,939; Dukakis, D, 2,215,940; Paul, LB, 14,944; Fulani, Solidarity, 10,276.

1984: Reagan, R, 2,707,103; Mondale, D, 2,086,499; Bergland, LB, 10,086.

1980: Reagan, R, 2,358,049; Carter, D, 1,981,413; Anderson, Ind., 346,754; Clark, LB, 38,939; Commoner, Citizens, 10,692; Hall, Comm., 9,711; Griswold, Workers World, 2,257; DeBerry, Soc. Workers, 1,302; write-in, 604.

1976: Ford, R, 2,364,269; Carter, D, 2,271,295; McCarthy, Ind., 55,939; Hall, Comm., 9,250; MacBride, LB, 8,057; Camejo, Soc. Workers, 3,615; Levin, Soc. Labor, 2,422; LaRouche, U.S. Labor, 2,018; write-in, 1,968.

1972: Nixon, R. 2,788,179; McGovern, D, 1,913,472; Fisher, Soc. Labor, 12,344; Hall, Comm., 4,541; Schmitz, Amer., 2,471; others, 2,229.

1968: Nixon, R, 2,174,774; Humphrey, D, 2,039,814; Wallace, 3rd party, 390,958; Blomen, Soc. Labor, 13,878; write-in, 325.

1964: Johnson, D, 2,796,833; Goldwater, R, 1,905,946; write-in, 62.

1960: Kennedy, D, 2,377,846; Nixon, R, 2,368,988; Hass, Soc. Labor, 10,560; write-in, 15.

Indiana Vote Since 1960

2012: Romney, R, 1,420,543; Obama, D, 1,152,887; Johnson, LB, 50,111.

2008: Obama, D, 1,374,039; McCain, R, 1,345,648; Barr, LB, 29,257.

2004: Bush, R, 1,479,438; Kerry, D, 969,011; Badnarik, LB, 18,058.

2000: Bush, R, 1,245,836; Gore, D, 901,980; Buchanan, Ind., 16,959; Browne, LB, 15,530.

1996: Dole, R, 1,006,693; Clinton, D, 887,424; Perot, RF, 224,299; Browne, LB, 15,632.

1992: Bush, R, 989,375; Clinton, D, 848,420; Perot, Ind., 455,934; Marrou, LB, 7,936; Fulani, New Alliance, 2,583.

1988: Bush, R, 1,297,763; Dukakis, D, 860,643; Fulani, New Alliance, 10,215.

1984: Reagan, R, 1,377,230; Mondale, D, 841,481; Bergland, LB, 6,741.

1980: Reagan, R, 1,255,656; Carter, D, 844,197; Anderson, Ind., 111,639; Clark, LB, 19,627; Commoner, Citizens, 4,852; Greaves, Amer., 4,750; Hall, Comm., 702; DeBerry, Soc., 610.

1976: Ford, R, 1,185,958; Carter, D, 1,014,714; Anderson, Amer., 14,048; Camejo, Soc. Workers, 5,695; LaRouche, U.S. Labor, 1,947.

1972: Nixon, R, 1,405,154; McGovern, D, 708,568; Reed, Soc. Workers, 5,575; Spock, Peace/Freedom, 4,544; Fisher, Soc. Labor, 1,688.

1968: Nixon, R, 1,067,885; Humphrey, D, 806,659; Wallace, 3rd party, 243,108; Munn, Prohib., 4,616; Halstead, Soc. Workers, 1,293; Gregory, write-in, 36.

1964: Johnson, D, 1,170,848; Goldwater, R, 911,118; Munn, Prohib., 8,266; Hass, Soc. Labor, 1,374.

1960: Nixon, R, 1,175,120; Kennedy, D, 952,358; Decker, Prohib., 6,746; Hass, Soc. Labor, 1,136.

Iowa Vote Since 1960

2012: Obama, D, 822,544; Romney, R, 730,617; Johnson, LB, 12,926; Stein, Green, 3,769; Goode, Const., 3,038; Litzel, Ind., 1,027; Harris, Soc. Workers, 445; La Riva, Socialism/Liberation, 372.

2008: Obama, D, 828,940; McCain, R, 682,379; Nader, Peace/Freedom, 8,014; Barr, LB, 4,590; Baldwin, Const., 4,445; McKinney, Green, 1,423; Harris, Soc. Workers, 292; Moore, Soc. USA, 182; La Riva, Socialism/Liberation, 121.

2004: Bush, R, 751,957; Kerry, D, 741,898; Nader, petitioning cand., 5,973; Badnarik, LB, 2,992; Peroutka, Const., 1,304; Cobb, Green, 1,141; Harris, Soc. Workers, 373; Van Auken, petitioning cand., 176.

2000: Gore, D, 638,517; Bush, R, 634,373; Nader, Green, 29,374; Buchanan, RF, 5,731; Browne, LB, 3,209; Hagelin, Ind., 2,281; Phillips, Const., 613; Harris, Soc. Workers, 190; McReynolds, Soc., 107.

1996: Clinton, D, 620,258; Dole, R, 492,644; Perot, RF, 105,159; Nader, Green, 6,550; Hagelin, Natural Law, 3,349; Browne, LB, 2,315; Phillips, Taxpayers, 2,229; Harris, Soc. Workers, 331.

1992: Clinton, D, 586,353; Bush, R, 504,891; Perot, Ind., 253,468; Hagelin, Natural Law, 3,079; Gritz, Populist/America First, 1,177; Marrou, LB, 1,076.

1988: Dukakis, D, 670,557; Bush, R, 545,355; LaRouche, Ind., 3,526; Paul, LB, 2,494.

1984: Reagan, R, 703,088; Mondale, D, 605,620; Bergland, LB, 1,844.

1980: Reagan, R, 676,026; Carter, D, 508,672; Anderson, Ind., 115,633; Clark, LB, 13,123; Commoner, Citizens, 2,273; McReynolds, Soc., 534; Hall, Comm., 298; DeBerry, Soc. Workers, 244; Greaves, Amer., 189; Bubar, Statesman, 150; scattered, 519.

1976: Ford, R, 632,863; Carter, D, 619,931; McCarthy, Ind., 20,051; Anderson, Amer., 3,040; MacBride, LB, 1,452.

1972: Nixon, R, 706,207; McGovern, D, 496,206; Schmitz, Amer., 22,056; Jenness, Soc. Workers, 488; Hall, Comm., 272; Green, Universal, 199; Fisher, Soc. Labor, 195; scattered, 321.

1968: Nixon, R, 619,106; Humphrey, D, 476,699; Wallace, 3rd party, 66,422; Halstead, Soc. Workers, 3,377; Cleaver, Peace/Freedom, 1,332; Munn, Prohib., 362; Blomen, Soc. Labor, 241.

1964: Johnson, D, 733,030; Goldwater, R, 449,148; Munn, Prohib., 1,902; Hass, Soc. Labor, 182; DeBerry, Soc. Workers, 159.

1960: Nixon, R, 722,381; Kennedy, D, 550,565; Hass, Soc. Labor, 230; write-in, 634.

Kansas Vote Since 1960

2012: Romney, R, 692,634; Obama, D, 440,726; Johnson, LB, 20,456; Baldwin, RF, 5,017.

2008: McCain, R, 699,655; Obama, D, 514,765; Nader, Ind., 10,527; Barr, LB, 6,706; Baldwin, RF, 4,148.

2004: Bush, R, 736,456; Kerry, D, 434,993; Nader, RF, 9,348; Badnarik, LB, 4,013; Peroutka, Ind., 2,899.

2000: Bush, R, 622,332; Gore, D, 399,276; Nader, Ind., 36,086; Buchanan, RF, 7,370; Browne, LB, 4,525; Hagelin, Ind., 1,373; Phillips, Const., 1,254.

1996: Dole, R, 583,245; Clinton, D, 387,659; Perot, RF, 92,639; Browne, LB, 4,557; Phillips, Ind., 3,519; Hagelin, Ind., 1,655.

1992: Bush, R, 449,951; Clinton, D, 390,434; Perot, Ind., 312,358; Marrou, LB, 4,314.

1988: Bush, R, 554,049; Dukakis, D, 422,636; Paul, Ind., 12,553; Fulani, Ind., 3,806.

1984: Reagan, R, 674,646; Mondale, D, 332,471; Bergland, LB, 3,585.

1980: Reagan, R, 566,812; Carter, D, 326,150; Anderson, Ind., 68,231; Clark, LB, 14,470; Shelton, Amer., 1,555; Hall, Comm., 967; Bubar, Statesman, 821; Rarick, Conservative, 789.

1976: Ford, R, 502,752; Carter, D, 430,421; McCarthy, Ind., 13,185; Anderson, Amer., 4,724; MacBride, LB, 3,242; Maddox, Conservative, 2,118; Bubar, Prohib., 1,403.

1972: Nixon, R, 619,812; McGovern, D, 270,287; Schmitz, Conservative, 21,808; Munn, Prohib., 4,188.

1968: Nixon, R, 478,674; Humphrey, D, 302,996; Wallace, 3rd party, 88,921; Munn, Prohib., 2,192.

1964: Johnson, D, 464,028; Goldwater, R, 386,579; Munn, Prohib., 5,393; Hass, Soc. Labor, 1,901.

1960: Nixon, R, 561,474; Kennedy, D, 363,213; Decker, Prohib., 4,138.

Kentucky Vote Since 1960

2012: Romney, R, 1,087,190; Obama, D, 679,370; Johnson, LB, 17,063; Terry, Ind., 6,872; Stein, Green, 6,337.

2008: McCain, R, 1,048,462; Obama, D, 751,985; Nader, Ind., 15,378; Barr, LB, 5,989; Baldwin, Const., 4,694.

2004: Bush, R, 1,069,439; Kerry, D, 712,733; Nader, Ind., 8,856; Badnarik, LB, 2,619; Peroutka, Const., 2,213.

2000: Bush, R, 872,520; Gore, D, 638,923; Nader, Green, 23,118; Buchanan, RF, 4,152; Browne, LB, 2,885; Hagelin, Natural Law, 1,513; Phillips, Const., 915.

1996: Clinton, D, 636,614; Dole, R, 623,283; Perot, RF, 120,396; Browne, LB, 4,009; Phillips, U.S. Taxpayers, 2,204; Hagelin, Natural Law, 1,493.

1992: Clinton, D, 665,104; Bush, R, 617,178; Perot, Ind., 203,944; Marrou, LB, 4,513.

1988: Bush, R, 734,281; Dukakis, D, 580,368; Duke, Populist, 4,494; Paul, LB, 2,118.
1984: Reagan, R, 815,345; Mondale, D, 536,756.
1980: Reagan, R, 635,274; Carter, D, 616,417; Anderson, Ind., 31,127; Clark, LB, 5,531; McCormack, Respect for Life, 4,233; Commoner, Citizens, 1,304; Pulley, Soc., 393; Hall, Comm., 348.
1976: Carter, D, 615,717; Ford, R, 531,852; Anderson, Amer., 8,308; McCarthy, Ind., 6,837; Maddox, Amer. Ind., 2,328; MacBride, LB, 814.
1972: Nixon, R, 676,446; McGovern, D, 371,159; Schmitz, Amer., 17,627; Spock, People's, 1,118; Jenness, Soc. Workers, 685; Hall, Comm., 464.
1968: Nixon, R, 462,411; Humphrey, D, 397,547; Wallace, 3rd party, 193,098; Halstead, Soc. Workers, 2,843.
1964: Johnson, D, 669,659; Goldwater, R, 372,977; Kasper, Natl. States' Rights, 3,469.
1960: Nixon, R, 602,607; Kennedy, D, 521,855.

Louisiana Vote Since 1960

2012: Romney, R, 1,152,262; Obama, D, 809,141; Johnson, LB, 18,157; Stein, Green, 6,978; Goode, Const., 2,508; Tittle, We the People, 1,767; Anderson, Justice, 1,368; Lindsay, Socialism/Liberation, 622; Fellure, Prohib., 518; Harris, Soc. Workers, 389; White, Soc. Equality, 355.
2008: McCain, R, 1,148,275; Obama, D, 782,989; Paul, LA Taxpayers, 9,368; McKinney, Green, 9,187; Nader, Ind., 6,997; Baldwin, Const., 2,581; Harris, Soc. Workers, 735; La Riva, Socialism/Liberation, 354; Amondson, Prohib., 275.
2004: Bush, R, 1,102,169; Kerry, D, 820,299; Nader, Better Life, 7,032; Peroutka, Const., 5,203; Badnarik, LB, 2,781; Brown, Protect Working Families, 1,795; Amondson, Prohib., 1,566; Cobb, Green, 1,276; Harris, Soc. Workers, 985.
2000: Bush, R, 927,871; Gore, D, 792,344; Nader, Green, 20,473; Buchanan, RF, 14,356; Phillips, Const., 5,483; Browne, LB, 2,951; Harris, Soc. Workers, 1,103; Hagelin, Natural Law, 1,075.
1996: Clinton, D, 927,837; Dole, R, 712,586; Perot, RF, 123,293; Browne, LB, 7,499; Nader, Liberty, Ecology, Community, 4,719; Phillips, U.S. Taxpayers, 3,366; Hagelin, Natural Law, 2,981; Moorehead, Workers World, 1,678.
1992: Clinton, D, 815,971; Bush, R, 733,386; Perot, Ind., 211,478; Gritz, Populist/America First, 18,545; Marrou, LB, 3,155; Daniels, Ind., 1,663; Phillips, U.S. Taxpayers, 1,552; Fulani, New Alliance, 1,434; LaRouche, Ind., 1,136.
1988: Bush, R, 883,702; Dukakis, D, 717,460; Duke, Populist, 18,612; Paul, LB, 4,115.
1984: Reagan, R, 1,037,299; Mondale, D, 651,586; Bergland, LB, 1,876.
1980: Reagan, R, 792,853; Carter, D, 708,453; Anderson, Ind., 26,345; Rarick, Amer. Ind., 10,333; Clark, LB, 8,240; Commoner, Citizens, 1,584; DeBerry, Soc. Workers, 783.
1976: Carter, D, 661,365; Ford, R, 587,446; Maddox, Amer., 10,058; Hall, Comm., 7,417; McCarthy, Ind., 6,588; MacBride, LB, 3,325.
1972: Nixon, R, 686,852; McGovern, D, 298,142; Schmitz, Amer., 52,099; Jenness, Soc. Workers, 14,398.
1968: Wallace, 3rd party, 530,300; Humphrey, D, 309,615; Nixon, R, 257,535.
1964: Goldwater, R, 509,225; Johnson, D, 387,068.
1960: Kennedy, D, 407,339; Nixon, R, 230,890; States' Rights (unpledged), 169,572.

Maine Vote Since 1960

2012: Obama, D, 401,306; Romney, R, 292,276; Johnson, LB, 9,352; Stein, Green, 8,119.
2008: Obama, D, 421,923; McCain, R, 295,273; Nader, Ind., 10,636; McKinney, Green, 2,900.
2004: Kerry, D, 396,842; Bush, R, 330,201; Nader, Better Life, 8,069; Cobb, Green, 2,936; Badnarik, LB, 1,965; Peroutka, Const., 735.
2000: Gore, D, 319,951; Bush, R, 286,616; Nader, Green, 37,127; Buchanan, RF, 4,443; Browne, LB, 3,074; Phillips, Const., 579.
1996: Clinton, D, 312,788; Dole, R, 186,378; Perot, RF, 85,970; Nader, Green, 15,279; Browne, LB, 2,996; Phillips, Taxpayers, 1,517; Hagelin, Natural Law, 825.
1992: Clinton, D, 263,420; Perot, Ind., 206,820; Bush, R, 206,504; Marrou, LB, 1,681.
1988: Bush, R, 307,131; Dukakis, D, 243,569; Paul, LB, 2,700; Fulani, New Alliance, 1,405.

1984: Reagan, R, 336,500; Mondale, D, 214,515.
1980: Reagan, R, 238,522; Carter, D, 220,974; Anderson, Ind., 53,327; Clark, LB, 5,119; Commoner, Citizens, 4,394; Hall, Comm., 591; write-in, 84.
1976: Ford, R, 236,320; Carter, D, 232,279; McCarthy, Ind., 10,874; Bubar, Prohib., 3,495.
1972: Nixon, R, 256,458; McGovern, D, 160,584; scattered, 229.
1968: Humphrey, D, 217,312; Nixon, R, 169,254; Wallace, 3rd party, 6,370.
1964: Johnson, D, 262,264; Goldwater, R, 118,701.
1960: Nixon, R, 240,608; Kennedy, D, 181,159.

Maryland Vote Since 1960

2012: Obama, D, 1,677,844; Romney, R, 971,869; Johnson, LB, 30,195; Stein, Green, 17,110.
2008: Obama, D, 1,629,467; McCain, R, 959,862; Nader, MD Ind., 14,713; Barr, LB, 9,842; McKinney, Green, 4,747; Baldwin, RF, 3,760.
2004: Kerry, D, 1,334,493; Bush, R, 1,024,703; Nader, Populist, 11,854; Badnarik, LB, 6,094; Cobb, Green, 3,632; Peroutka, Const., 3,421.
2000: Gore, D, 1,144,008; Bush, R, 813,827; Nader, Green, 53,768; Browne, LB, 5,310; Buchanan, RF, 4,248; Phillips, Const., 918.
1996: Clinton, D, 966,207; Dole, R, 681,530; Perot, RF, 115,812; Browne, LB, 8,765; Phillips, Taxpayers, 3,402; Hagelin, Natural Law, 2,517.
1992: Clinton, D, 988,571; Bush, R, 707,094; Perot, Ind., 281,414; Marrou, LB, 4,715; Fulani, New Alliance, 2,786.
1988: Bush, R, 876,167; Dukakis, D, 826,304; Paul, LB, 6,748; Fulani, New Alliance, 5,115.
1984: Reagan, R, 879,918; Mondale, D, 787,935; Bergland, LB, 5,721.
1980: Carter, D, 726,161; Reagan, R, 680,606; Anderson, Ind., 119,537; Clark, LB, 14,192.
1976: Carter, D, 759,612; Ford, R, 672,661.
1972: Nixon, R, 829,305; McGovern, D, 505,781; Schmitz, Amer., 18,726.
1968: Humphrey, D, 538,310; Nixon, R, 517,995; Wallace, 3rd party, 178,734.
1964: Johnson, D, 730,912; Goldwater, R, 385,495; write-in, 50.
1960: Kennedy, D, 565,800; Nixon, R, 489,538.

Massachusetts Vote Since 1960

2012: Obama, D, 1,921,290; Romney, R, 1,188,314; Johnson, LB, 30,920; Stein, Green, 20,691.
2008: Obama, D, 1,904,097; McCain, R, 1,108,854; Nader, Ind., 28,841; Barr, LB, 13,189; McKinney, Green, 6,550; Baldwin, RF, 4,971.
2004: Kerry, D, 1,803,800; Bush, R, 1,071,109; Badnarik, LB, 15,022; Cobb, Green, 10,623.
2000: Gore, D, 1,616,487; Bush, R, 878,502; Nader, Green, 173,564; Browne, LB, 16,366; Buchanan, RF, 11,149; Hagelin, Natural Law, 2,884.
1996: Clinton, D, 1,571,509; Dole, R, 718,058; Perot, RF, 227,206; Browne, LB, 20,424; Hagelin, Natural Law, 5,183; Moorehead, Workers World, 3,276.
1992: Clinton, D, 1,318,639; Bush, R, 805,039; Perot, Ind., 630,731; Marrou, LB, 9,021; Fulani, New Alliance, 3,172; Phillips, U.S. Taxpayers, 2,218; Hagelin, Natural Law, 1,812; LaRouche, Ind., 1,027.
1988: Dukakis, D, 1,401,415; Bush, R, 1,194,635; Paul, LB, 24,251; Fulani, New Alliance, 9,561.
1984: Reagan, R, 1,310,936; Mondale, D, 1,239,606.
1980: Reagan, R, 1,057,631; Carter, D, 1,053,802; Anderson, Ind., 382,539; Clark, LB, 22,038; DeBerry, Soc. Workers, 3,735; Commoner, Citizens, 2,056; McReynolds, Soc., 62; Bubar, Statesman, 34; Griswold, Workers World, 19; scattered, 2,382.
1976: Carter, D, 1,429,475; Ford, R, 1,030,276; McCarthy, Ind., 65,637; Camejo, Soc. Workers, 8,138; Anderson, Amer., 7,555; LaRouche, U.S. Labor, 4,922; MacBride, LB, 135.
1972: McGovern, D, 1,332,540; Nixon, R, 1,112,078; Jenness, Soc. Workers, 10,600; Schmitz, Amer., 2,877; Fisher, Soc. Labor, 129; Spock, People's, 101; Hall, Comm., 46; Hospers, LB, 43; scattered, 342.
1968: Humphrey, D, 1,469,218; Nixon, R, 766,844; Wallace, 3rd party, 87,088; Blomen, Soc. Labor, 6,180; Munn, Prohib., 2,369; scattered, 53; blank, 25,394.

1964: Johnson, D, 1,786,422; Goldwater, R, 549,727; Hass, Soc. Labor, 4,755; Munn, Prohib., 3,735; scattered, 159; blank, 48,104.

1960: Kennedy, D, 1,487,174; Nixon, R, 976,750; Hass, Soc. Labor, 3,892; Decker, Prohib., 1,633; others, 31; blank and void, 26,024.

Michigan Vote Since 1960

2012: Obama, D, 2,564,569; Romney, R, 2,115,256; Stein, Green, 21,897; Goode, U.S. Taxpayers, 16,119; Johnson, Ind., 7,774, Anderson, Natural Law, 5,147;

2008: Obama, D, 2,872,579; McCain, R, 2,048,639; Nader, Natural Law, 33,085; Barr, LB, 23,716; Baldwin, U.S. Taxpayers, 14,685; McKinney, Green, 8,892.

2004: Kerry, D, 2,479,183; Bush, R, 2,313,746; Nader, Ind., 24,035; Badnarik, LB, 10,552; Cobb, Green, 5,325; Peroutka, U.S. Taxpayers, 4,980; Brown, Natural Law, 1,431.

2000: Gore, D, 2,170,418; Bush, R, 1,953,139; Nader, Green, 84,165; Browne, LB, 16,711; Phillips, U.S. Taxpayers, 3,791; Hagelin, Natural Law, 2,426.

1996: Clinton, D, 1,989,653; Dole, R, 1,481,212; Perot, RF, 336,670; Browne, LB, 27,670; Hagelin, Natural Law, 4,254; Moorehead, Workers World, 3,153; White, Soc. Equality, 1,554.

1992: Clinton, D, 1,871,182; Bush, R, 1,554,940; Perot, Ind., 824,813; Marrou, LB, 10,175; Phillips, U.S. Taxpayers, 8,263; Hagelin, Natural Law, 2,954.

1988: Bush, R, 1,965,486; Dukakis, D, 1,675,783; Paul, LB, 18,336; Fulani, Ind., 2,513.

1984: Reagan, R, 2,251,571; Mondale, D, 1,529,638; Bergland, LB, 10,055.

1980: Reagan, R, 1,915,225; Carter, D, 1,661,532; Anderson, Ind., 275,223; Clark, LB, 41,597; Commoner, Citizens, 11,930; Hall, Comm., 3,262; Griswold, Workers World, 30; Greaves, Amer., 21; Bubar, Statesman, 9.

1976: Ford, R, 1,893,742; Carter, D, 1,696,714; McCarthy, Ind., 47,905; MacBride, LB, 5,406; Wright, People's, 3,504; Camejo, Soc. Workers, 1,804; LaRouche, U.S. Labor, 1,366; Levin, Soc. Labor, 1,148; scattered, 2,160.

1972: Nixon, R, 1,961,721; McGovern, D, 1,459,435; Schmitz, Amer., 63,321; Fisher, Soc. Labor, 2,437; Jenness, Soc. Workers, 1,603; Hall, Comm., 1,210.

1968: Humphrey, D, 1,593,082; Nixon, R, 1,370,665; Wallace, 3rd party, 331,968; Halstead, Soc. Workers, 4,099; Blomen, Soc. Labor, 1,762; Cleaver, New Politics, 4,585; Munn, Prohib., 60; scattered, 29.

1964: Johnson, D, 2,136,615; Goldwater, R, 1,060,152; DeBerry, Soc. Workers, 3,817; Hass, Soc. Labor, 1,704; Prohib. (no candidate listed), 699; scattered, 145.

1960: Kennedy, D, 1,687,269; Nixon, R, 1,620,428; Dobbs, Soc. Workers, 4,347; Decker, Prohib., 2,029; Daly, Tax Cut, 1,767; Hass, Soc. Labor, 1,718; Ind. Amer. (unpledged), 539.

Minnesota Vote Since 1960

2012: Obama, D, 1,546,167; Romney, R, 1,320,225; Johnson, LB, 35,098; Stein, Green, 13,023; Goode, Const., 3,722; Carlson, Grassroots, 3,149; Anderson, Justice, 1,996; Morstad, Constitutional, 1,092; Harris, Soc. Workers, 1,051; Lindsay, Socialism/Liberation, 397.

2008: Obama, D, 1,573,354; McCain, R, 1,275,409; Nader, Ind., 30,152; Barr, LB, 9,174; Baldwin, Const., 6,787; McKinney, Green, 5,174; Calero, Soc. Workers, 790.

2004: Kerry, D, 1,445,014; Bush, R, 1,346,695; Nader, Better Life, 18,683; Badnarik, LB, 4,639; Cobb, Green, 4,408; Peroutka, Const., 3,074; Harens, other, 2,387; Van Auken, Soc. Equal., 539; Calero, Soc. Workers, 416.

2000: Gore, D, 1,168,266; Bush, R, 1,109,659; Nader, Green, 126,696; Buchanan, RF MN, 22,166; Browne, LB, 5,282; Phillips, Const., 3,272; Hagelin, RF, 2,294; Harris, Soc. Workers, 1,022.

1996: Clinton, D, 1,120,438; Dole, R, 766,476; Perot, RF, 257,704; Nader, Green, 24,908; Browne, LB, 8,271; Peron, Grass Roots, 4,898; Phillips, U.S. Taxpayers, 3,416; Hagelin, Natural Law, 1,808; Birrenbach, Ind. Grass Roots, 787; Harris, Soc. Workers, 684; White, Soc. Equality, 347.

1992: Clinton, D, 1,020,997; Bush, R, 747,841; Perot, Ind., 562,506; Marrou, LB, 3,373; Gritz, Populist/America First, 3,363; Hagelin, Natural Law, 1,406.

1988: Dukakis, D, 1,109,471; Bush, R, 962,337; McCarthy, MN Prog., 5,403; Paul, LB, 5,109.

1984: Mondale, D, 1,036,364; Reagan, R, 1,032,603; Bergland, LB, 2,996.

1980: Carter, D, 954,173; Reagan, R, 873,268; Anderson, Ind., 174,997; Clark, LB, 31,593; Commoner, Citizens, 8,406; Hall, Comm., 1,117; DeBerry, Soc. Workers, 711; Griswold, Workers World, 698; McReynolds, Soc., 536; write-in, 281.

1976: Carter, D, 1,070,440; Ford, R, 819,395; McCarthy, Ind., 35,490; Anderson, Amer., 13,592; Camejo, Soc. Workers, 4,149; MacBride, LB, 3,529; Hall, Comm., 1,092.

1972: Nixon, R, 898,269; McGovern, D, 802,346; Schmitz, Amer., 31,407; Fisher, Soc. Labor, 4,261; Spock, People's, 2,805; Jenness, Soc. Workers, 940; Hall, Comm., 662; scattered, 962.

1968: Humphrey, D, 857,738; Nixon, R, 658,643; Wallace, 3rd party, 68,931; Cleaver, Peace/Freedom, 935; Halstead, Soc. Workers, 808; McCarthy, write-in, 585; Mitchell, Comm., 415; Blomen, Industrial Govt., 285; scattered, 2,613.

1964: Johnson, D, 991,117; Goldwater, R, 559,624; Hass, Industrial Govt., 2,544; DeBerry, Soc. Workers, 1,177.

1960: Kennedy, D, 779,933; Nixon, R, 757,915; Dobbs, Soc. Workers, 3,077; Hass, Industrial Govt., 962.

Mississippi Vote Since 1960

2012: Romney, R, 710,746; Obama, D, 562,949; Johnson, LB, 6,676; Goode, Const., 2,609; Stein, Green, 1,588; Washer, RF, 1,016.

2008: McCain, R, 724,597; Obama, D, 554,662; Nader, Ind., 4,011; Baldwin, Const., 2,551; Barr, LB, 2,529; McKinney, Green, 1,034; Weill, RF, 481.

2004: Bush, R, 684,981; Kerry, D, 458,094; Nader, RF, 3,177; Badnarik, LB, 1,793; Peroutka, Const., 1,759; Harris, Ind., 1,268; Cobb, Green, 1,073.

2000: Bush, R, 572,844; Gore, D, 404,614; Nader, Ind., 8,122; Phillips, Const., 3,267; Buchanan, RF, 2,265; Browne, LB, 2,009; Harris, Ind., 613; Hagelin, Natural Law, 450.

1996: Dole, R, 439,838; Clinton, D, 394,022; Perot, RF, 52,222; Browne, LB, 2,809; Phillips, U.S. Taxpayers, 2,314; Hagelin, Natural Law, 1,447; Collins, Ind., 1,205.

1992: Bush, R, 487,793; Clinton, D, 400,258; Perot, Ind., 85,626; Fulani, New Alliance, 2,625; Marrou, LB, 2,154; Phillips, U.S. Taxpayers, 1,652; Hagelin, Natural Law, 1,140.

1988: Bush, R, 557,890; Dukakis, D, 363,921; Duke, Ind., 4,232; Paul, LB, 3,329.

1984: Reagan, R, 582,377; Mondale, D, 352,192; Bergland, LB, 2,336.

1980: Reagan, R, 441,089; Carter, D, 429,281; Anderson, Ind., 12,036; Clark, LB, 5,465; Griswold, Workers World, 2,402; Pulley, Soc. Workers, 2,347.

1976: Carter, D, 381,309; Ford, R, 366,846; Anderson, Amer., 6,678; McCarthy, Ind., 4,074; Maddox, Ind., 4,049; Camejo, Soc. Workers, 2,805; MacBride, LB, 2,609.

1972: Nixon, R, 505,125; McGovern, D, 126,782; Schmitz, Amer., 11,598; Jenness, Soc. Workers, 2,458.

1968: Wallace, 3rd party, 415,349; Humphrey, D, 150,644; Nixon, R, 88,516.

1964: Goldwater, R, 356,528; Johnson, D, 52,618.

1960: D. (electors unpledged), 116,248; Kennedy, D, 108,362; Nixon, R, 73,561. *Mississippi's victorious slate of 8 unpledged Dem. electors cast their votes for Sen. Harry F. Byrd (D, VA).

Missouri Vote Since 1960

2012: Romney, R, 1,482,440; Obama, D, 1,223,796; Johnson, LB, 43,151; Goode, Const., 7,936.

2008: McCain, R, 1,445,814; Obama, D, 1,441,911; Nader, Ind., 17,813; Barr, LB, 11,386; Baldwin, Const., 8,201.

2004: Bush, R, 1,455,713; Kerry, D, 1,259,171; Badnarik, LB, 9,831; Peroutka, Const., 5,355.

2000: Bush, R, 1,189,924; Gore, D, 1,111,138; Nader, Green, 38,515; Buchanan, RF, 9,818; Browne, LB, 7,436; Phillips, Const., 1,957; Hagelin, Natural Law, 1,104.

1996: Clinton, D, 1,025,935; Dole, R, 890,016; Perot, RF, 217,188; Phillips, U.S. Taxpayers, 11,521; Browne, LB, 10,522; Hagelin, Natural Law, 2,287.

1992: Clinton, D, 1,053,873; Bush, R, 811,159; Perot, Ind., 518,741; Marrou, LB, 7,497.

1988: Bush, R, 1,084,953; Dukakis, D, 1,001,619; Fulani, New Alliance, 6,656; Paul, write-in, 434.

1984: Reagan, R, 1,274,188; Mondale, D, 848,583.

1980: Reagan, R, 1,074,181; Carter, D, 931,182; Anderson, Ind., 77,920; Clark, LB, 14,422; DeBerry, Soc. Workers, 1,515; Commoner, Citizens, 573; write-in, 31.
1976: Carter, D, 999,163; Ford, R, 928,808; McCarthy, Ind., 24,329.
1972: Nixon, R, 1,154,058; McGovern, D, 698,531.
1968: Nixon, R, 811,932; Humphrey, D, 791,444; Wallace, 3rd party, 206,126.
1964: Johnson, D, 1,164,344; Goldwater, R, 653,535.
1960: Kennedy, D, 972,201; Nixon, R, 962,221.

Montana Vote Since 1960

2012: Romney, R, 267,928; Obama, D, 201,839; Johnson, LB, 14,165.
2008: McCain, R, 242,763; Obama, D, 231,667; Paul, Const., 10,638; Nader, Ind., 3,686; Barr, LB, 1,355.
2004: Bush, R, 266,063; Kerry, D, 173,710; Nader, Ind., 6,168; Peroutka, Const., 1,764; Badnarik, LB, 1,733; Cobb, Green, 996.
2000: Bush, R, 240,178; Gore, D, 137,126; Nader, Green, 24,437; Buchanan, RF, 5,697; Browne, LB, 1,718; Phillips, Const., 1,155; Hagelin, Natural Law, 675.
1996: Dole, R, 179,652; Clinton, D, 167,922; Perot, RF, 55,229; Browne, LB, 2,526; Hagelin, Natural Law, 1,754.
1992: Clinton, D, 154,507; Bush, R, 144,207; Perot, Ind., 107,225; Gritz, Populist/America First, 3,658.
1988: Bush, R, 190,412; Dukakis, D, 168,936; Paul, LB, 5,047; Fulani, New Alliance, 1,279.
1984: Reagan, R, 232,450; Mondale, D, 146,742; Bergland, LB, 5,185.
1980: Reagan, R, 206,814; Carter, D, 118,032; Anderson, Ind., 29,281; Clark, LB, 9,825.
1976: Ford, R, 173,703; Carter, D, 149,259; Anderson, Amer., 5,772.
1972: Nixon, R, 183,976; McGovern, D, 120,197; Schmitz, Amer., 13,430.
1968: Nixon, R, 138,835; Humphrey, D, 114,117; Wallace, 3rd party, 20,015; Munn, Prohib., 510; Caton, New RF, 470; Halstead, Soc. Workers, 457.
1964: Johnson, D, 164,246; Goldwater, R, 113,032; Kasper, Natl. States' Rights, 519; Munn, Prohib., 499; DeBerry, Soc. Workers, 332.
1960: Nixon, R, 141,841; Kennedy, D, 134,891; Decker, Prohib., 456; Dobbs, Soc. Workers, 391.

Nebraska Vote Since 1960

2012: Romney, R, 475,064; Obama, D, 302,081; Johnson, LB, 11,109; Terry, petitioning cand., 2,408.
2008: McCain, R, 452,979; Obama, D, 333,319; Nader, petitioning cand., 5,406; Baldwin, Nebraska, 2,972; Barr, LB, 2,740; McKinney, Green, 1,028.
2004: Bush, R, 512,814; Kerry, D, 254,328; Nader, petitioning cand., 5,698; Badnarik, LB, 2,041; Peroutka, Nebraska, 1,314; Cobb, Green, 978; Calero, petitioning cand., 82.
2000: Bush, R, 433,862; Gore, D, 231,780; Nader, Green, 24,540; Buchanan, Ind., 3,646; Browne, LB, 2,245; Hagelin, Natural Law, 478; Phillips, Ind., 468.
1996: Dole, R, 363,467; Clinton, D, 236,761; Perot, RF, 71,278; Browne, LB, 2,792; Phillips, Ind., 1,928; Hagelin, Natural Law, 1,189.
1992: Bush, R, 343,678; Clinton, D, 216,864; Perot, Ind., 174,104; Marrou, LB, 1,340.
1988: Bush, R, 397,956; Dukakis, D, 259,235; Paul, LB, 2,534; Fulani, New Alliance, 1,740.
1984: Reagan, R, 459,135; Mondale, D, 187,475; Bergland, LB, 2,075.
1980: Reagan, R, 419,214; Carter, D, 166,424; Anderson, Ind., 44,854; Clark, LB, 9,041.
1976: Ford, R, 359,219; Carter, D, 233,287; McCarthy, Ind., 9,383; Maddox, Amer. Ind., 3,378; MacBride, LB, 1,476.
1972: Nixon, R, 406,298; McGovern, D, 169,991; scattered, 817.
1968: Nixon, R, 321,163; Humphrey, D, 170,784; Wallace, 3rd party, 44,904.
1964: Johnson, D, 307,307; Goldwater, R, 276,847.
1960: Nixon, R, 380,553; Kennedy, D, 232,542.

Nevada Vote Since 1960

2012: Obama, D, 531,373; Romney, R, 463,567; Johnson, LB, 10,968; None of These Candidates, 5,770; Goode, Ind. Amer., 3,240.

2008: Obama, D, 533,736; McCain, R, 412,827; None of These Candidates, 6,267; Nader, Ind., 6,150; Barr, LB, 4,263; Baldwin, Const., 3,194; McKinney, Green, 1,411.
2004: Bush, R, 418,690; Kerry, D, 397,190; Nader, Ind., 4,838; None of These Candidates, 3,688; Badnarik, LB, 3,176; Peroutka, Ind. Amer., 1,152; Cobb, Green, 853.
2000: Bush, R, 301,575; Gore, D, 279,978; Nader, Green, 15,008; Buchanan, Citizens First, 4,747; None of These Candidates, 3,315; Browne, LB, 3,311; Phillips, Ind. Amer., 621; Hagelin, Natural Law, 415.
1996: Clinton, D, 203,974; Dole, R, 199,244; Perot, RF, 43,986; None of These Candidates, 5,608; Nader, Green, 4,730; Browne, LB, 4,460; Phillips, Ind. Amer., 1,732; Hagelin, Natural Law, 545.
1992: Clinton, D, 189,148; Bush, R, 175,828; Perot, Ind., 132,580; Gritz, Populist/America First, 2,892; Marrou, LB, 1,835.
1988: Bush, R, 206,040; Dukakis, D, 132,738; Paul, LB, 3,520; Fulani, New Alliance, 835.
1984: Reagan, R, 188,770; Mondale, D, 91,655; Bergland, LB, 2,292.
1980: Reagan, R, 155,017; Carter, D, 66,666; Anderson, Ind., 17,651; Clark, LB, 4,358.
1976: Ford, R, 101,273; Carter, D, 92,479; MacBride, LB, 1,519; Maddox, Amer. Ind., 1,497; scattered, 5,108.
1972: Nixon, R, 115,750; McGovern, D, 66,016.
1968: Nixon, R, 73,188; Humphrey, D, 60,598; Wallace, 3rd party, 20,432.
1964: Johnson, D, 79,339; Goldwater, R, 56,094.
1960: Kennedy, D, 54,880; Nixon, R, 52,387.

New Hampshire Vote Since 1960

2012: Obama, D, 369,561; Romney, R, 329,918; Johnson, LB, 8,212; Goode, Const., 708.
2008: Obama, D, 384,826; McCain, R, 316,534; Nader, Ind., 3,503; Barr, LB, 2,217; Phillies, LB, 531.
2004: Kerry, D, 340,511; Bush, R, 331,237; Nader, Ind., 4,479.
2000: Bush, R, 273,559; Gore, D, 266,348; Nader, Green, 22,198; Browne, LB, 2,757; Buchanan, Independence, 2,615; Phillips, Const., 328.
1996: Clinton, D, 246,166; Dole, R, 196,486; Perot, RF, 48,387; Browne, LB, 4,214; Phillips, Taxpayers, 1,344.
1992: Clinton, D, 209,040; Bush, R, 202,484; Perot, Ind., 121,337; Marrou, LB, 3,548.
1988: Bush, R, 281,537; Dukakis, D, 163,696; Paul, LB, 4,502; Fulani, New Alliance, 790.
1984: Reagan, R, 267,051; Mondale, D, 120,377; Bergland, LB, 735.
1980: Reagan, R, 221,705; Carter, D, 108,864; Anderson, Ind., 49,693; Clark, LB, 2,067; Commoner, Citizens, 1,325; Hall, Comm., 129; Griswold, Workers World, 76; DeBerry, Soc. Workers, 72; scattered, 68.
1976: Ford, R, 185,935; Carter, D, 147,645; McCarthy, Ind., 4,095; MacBride, LB, 936; Reagan, write-in, 388; LaRouche, U.S. Labor, 186; Camejo, Soc. Workers, 161; Levin, Soc. Labor, 66; scattered, 215.
1972: Nixon, R, 213,724; McGovern, D, 116,435; Schmitz, Amer., 3,386; Jenness, Soc. Workers, 368; scattered, 142.
1968: Nixon, R, 154,903; Humphrey, D, 130,589; Wallace, 3rd party, 11,173; New Party, 421; Halstead, Soc. Workers, 104.
1964: Johnson, D, 182,065; Goldwater, R, 104,029.
1960: Nixon, R, 157,989; Kennedy, D, 137,772.

New Jersey Vote Since 1960

2012: Obama, D, 2,125,101; Romney, R, 1,477,568; Johnson, LB, 21,045; Stein, Green, 9,888; Goode, Const., 2,064; Anderson, Justice, 1,724; Boss, Ind., 1,007; Harris, Soc. Workers, 710; Miller, A3P, 664; Lindsay, Socialism/Liberation, 521.
2008: Obama, D, 2,215,422; McCain, R, 1,613,207; Nader, Ind., 21,298; Barr, Ind., 8,441; Baldwin, Ind., 3,956; McKinney, Ind., 3,636; Moore, Ind., 699; Boss, Ind., 639; Calero, Ind., 523; La Riva, Ind., 416.
2004: Kerry, D, 1,911,430; Bush, R, 1,670,003; Nader, Ind., 19,418; Badnarik, Ind., 4,514; Peroutka, Ind., 2,750; Cobb, Ind., 1,807; Brown, Ind., 664; Van Auken, Ind., 575; Calero, Ind., 530.
2000: Gore, D, 1,788,850; Bush, R, 1,284,173; Nader, Ind., 94,554; Buchanan, Ind., 6,989; Browne, Ind., 6,312; Hagelin, Ind., 2,215; McReynolds, Ind., 1,880; Phillips, Ind., 1,409; Harris, Ind., 844.

1996: Clinton, D, 1,652,361; Dole, R, 1,103,099; Perot, RF, 262,134; Nader, Green, 32,465; Browne, LB, 14,763; Hagelin, Natural Law, 3,887; Phillips, U.S. Taxpayers, 3,440; Harris, Soc. Workers, 1,837; Moorehead, Workers World, 1,337; White, Soc. Equality, 537.

1992: Clinton, D, 1,436,206; Bush, R, 1,356,865; Perot, Ind., 521,829; Marrou, LB, 6,822; Fulani, New Alliance, 3,513; Phillips, U.S. Taxpayers, 2,670; LaRouche, Ind., 2,095; Warren, Soc. Workers, 2,011; Daniels, Ind., 1,996; Gritz, Populist/America First, 1,867; Hagelin, Natural Law, 1,353.

1988: Bush, R, 1,740,604; Dukakis, D, 1,317,541; Lewin, Peace/Freedom, 9,953; Paul, LB, 8,421.

1984: Reagan, R, 1,933,630; Mondale, D, 1,261,323; Bergland, LB, 6,416.

1980: Reagan, R, 1,546,557; Carter, D, 1,147,364; Anderson, Ind., 234,632; Clark, LB, 20,652; Commoner, Citizens, 8,203; McCormack, Right to Life, 3,927; Lynen, Middle Class, 3,694; Hall, Comm., 2,555; Pulley, Soc. Workers, 2,198; McReynolds, Soc., 1,973; Gahres, Down With Lawyers, 1,718; Griswold, Workers World, 1,288; Wendelken, Ind., 923.

1976: Ford, R, 1,509,688; Carter, D, 1,444,653; McCarthy, Ind., 32,717; MacBride, LB, 9,449; Maddox, Amer., 7,716; Levin, Soc. Labor, 3,686; Hall, Comm., 1,662; LaRouche, U.S. Labor, 1,650; Camejo, Soc. Workers, 1,184; Wright, People's, 1,044; Bubar, Prohib., 554; Zeidler, Soc., 469.

1972: Nixon, R, 1,845,502; McGovern, D, 1,102,211; Schmitz, Amer., 34,378; Spock, People's, 5,355; Fisher, Soc. Labor, 4,544; Jenness, Soc. Workers, 2,233; Mahalchik, America First, 1,743; Hall, Comm., 1,263.

1968: Nixon, R, 1,325,467; Humphrey, D, 1,264,206; Wallace, 3rd party, 262,187; Halstead, Soc. Workers, 8,667; Gregory, Peace/Freedom, 8,084; Blomen, Soc. Labor, 6,784.

1964: Johnson, D, 1,867,671; Goldwater, R, 963,843; DeBerry, Soc. Workers, 8,181; Hass, Soc. Labor, 7,075.

1960: Kennedy, D, 1,385,415; Nixon, R, 1,363,324; Dobbs, Soc. Workers, 11,402; Lee, Conservative, 8,708; Hass, Soc. Labor, 4,262.

New Mexico Vote Since 1960

2012: Obama, D, 415,335; Romney, R, 335,788; Johnson, LB, 27,788; Stein, Green, 2,691; Anderson, Ind., 1,174; Goode, Const., 982.

2008: Obama, D, 472,422; McCain, R, 346,832; Nader, Ind., 5,327; Barr, LB, 2,428; Baldwin, Const., 1,597; McKinney, Green, 1,552.

2004: Bush, R, 376,930; Kerry, D, 370,942; Nader, Ind., 4,053; Badnarik, LB, 2,382; Cobb, Green, 1,226; Peroutka, Const., 771.

2000: Gore, D, 286,783; Bush, R, 286,417; Nader, Green, 21,251; Browne, LB, 2,058; Buchanan, RF, 1,392; Hagelin, Natural Law, 361; Phillips, Const., 343.

1996: Clinton, D, 273,495; Dole, R, 232,751; Perot, RF, 32,257; Nader, Green, 13,218; Browne, LB, 2,996; Phillips, Taxpayers, 713; Hagelin, Natural Law, 644.

1992: Clinton, D, 261,617; Bush, R, 212,824; Perot, Ind., 91,895; Marrou, LB, 1,615.

1988: Bush, R, 270,341; Dukakis, D, 244,497; Paul, LB, 3,268; Fulani, New Alliance, 2,237.

1984: Reagan, R, 307,101; Mondale, D, 201,769; Bergland, LB, 4,459.

1980: Reagan, R, 250,779; Carter, D, 167,826; Anderson, Ind., 29,459; Clark, LB, 4,365; Commoner, Citizens, 2,202; Bubar, Statesman, 1,281; Pulley, Soc. Workers, 325.

1976: Ford, R, 211,419; Carter, D, 201,148; Camejo, Soc. Workers, 2,462; MacBride, LB, 1,110; Zeidler, Soc., 240; Bubar, Prohib., 211.

1972: Nixon, R, 235,606; McGovern, D, 141,084; Schmitz, Amer., 8,767; Jenness, Soc. Workers, 474.

1968: Nixon, R, 169,692; Humphrey, D, 130,081; Wallace, 3rd party, 25,737; Chavez, 1,519; Halstead, Soc. Workers, 252.

1964: Johnson, D, 194,017; Goldwater, R, 131,838; Hass, Soc. Labor, 1,217; Munn, Prohib., 543.

1960: Kennedy, D, 156,027; Nixon, R, 153,733; Decker, Prohib., 777; Hass, Soc. Labor, 570.

New York Vote Since 1960

2012: Obama, D, 4,485,741; Romney, R, 2,490,431; Johnson, LB, 47,256; Stein, Green, 39,982; Goode, Const., 6,274; Lindsay, Socialism/Liberation, 2,050.

2008: Obama, D, 4,804,945; McCain, R, 2,752,771; Nader, Populist, 41,249; Barr, LB, 19,596; McKinney, Green, 12,801; Calero, Soc. Workers, 3,615; La Riva, Socialism/Liberation, 1,639.

2004: Kerry, D, 4,314,280; Bush, R, 2,962,567; Nader, Ind., 99,873; Badnarik, LB, 11,607; Calero, Soc. Workers, 2,405.

2000: Gore, D, 4,112,965; Bush, R, 2,405,570; Nader, Green, 244,360; Buchanan, RF, 31,554; Hagelin, Independence, 24,369; Browne, LB, 7,664; Harris, Soc. Workers, 1,790; Phillips, Const., 1,503.

1996: Clinton, D, 3,756,177; Dole, R, 1,933,492; Perot, RF, 503,458; Nader, Green, 75,956; Phillips, Right to Life, 23,580; Browne, LB, 12,220; Hagelin, Natural Law, 5,011; Moorehead, Workers World, 3,473; Harris, Soc. Workers, 2,762.

1992: Clinton, D, 3,444,450; Bush, R, 2,346,649; Perot, Ind., 1,090,721; Warren, Soc. Workers, 15,472; Marrou, LB, 13,451; Fulani, New Alliance, 11,318; Hagelin, Natural Law, 4,420.

1988: Dukakis, D, 3,347,882; Bush, R, 3,081,871; Marra, Right to Life, 20,497; Fulani, New Alliance, 15,845.

1984: Reagan, R, 3,664,763; Mondale, D, 3,119,609; Bergland, LB, 11,949.

1980: Reagan, R, 2,893,831; Carter, D, 2,728,372; Anderson, Liberal, 467,801; Clark, LB, 52,648; McCormack, Right to Life, 24,159; Commoner, Citizens, 23,186; Hall, Comm., 7,414; DeBerry, Soc. Workers, 2,068; Griswold, Workers World, 1,416; scattered, 1,064.

1976: Carter, D, 3,389,558; Ford, R, 3,100,791; MacBride, LB, 12,197; Hall, Comm., 10,270; Camejo, Soc. Workers, 6,996; LaRouche, U.S. Labor, 5,413; blank, void, and scattered, 143,037.

1972: Nixon, R, 3,824,642; McGovern, D, 2,767,956 and Liberal, 183,128 (total, 2,951,084); Reed, Soc. Workers, 7,797; Fisher, Soc. Labor, 4,530; Hall, Comm., 5,641; blank, void, and scattered, 161,641.

1968: Humphrey, D, 3,378,470; Nixon, R, 3,007,932; Wallace, 3rd party, 358,864; Gregory, Peace/Freedom, 24,517; Halstead, Soc. Workers, 11,851; Blomen, Soc. Labor, 8,432; blank, void, and scattered, 171,624.

1964: Johnson, D, 4,913,156; Goldwater, R, 2,243,559; Hass, Soc. Labor, 6,085; DeBerry, Soc. Workers, 3,215; scattered, 188; blank and void, 151,383.

1960: Kennedy, D, 3,423,909 and Liberal, 406,176 (total, 3,830,085); Nixon, R, 3,446,419; Dobbs, Soc. Workers, 14,319; scattered, 256; blank and void, 88,896.

North Carolina Vote Since 1960

2012: Romney, R, 2,270,395; Obama, D, 2,178,391; Johnson, LB, 44,515.

2008: Obama, D, 2,142,651; McCain, R, 2,128,474; Barr, LB, 25,722.

2004: Bush, R, 1,961,166; Kerry, D, 1,525,849; Badnarik, LB, 11,731.

2000: Bush, R, 1,631,163; Gore, D, 1,257,692; Browne, LB, 13,891; Buchanan, RF, 8,874.

1996: Dole, R, 1,225,938; Clinton, D, 1,107,849; Perot, RF, 168,059; Browne, LB, 8,740; Hagelin, Natural Law, 2,771.

1992: Bush, R, 1,134,661; Clinton, D, 1,114,042; Perot, Ind., 357,864; Marrou, LB, 5,171.

1988: Bush, R, 1,237,258; Dukakis, D, 890,167; Fulani, New Alliance, 5,682; Paul, write-in, 1,263.

1984: Reagan, R, 1,346,481; Mondale, D, 824,287; Bergland, LB, 3,794.

1980: Reagan, R, 915,018; Carter, D, 875,635; Anderson, Ind., 52,800; Clark, LB, 9,677; Commoner, Citizens, 2,287; DeBerry, Soc. Workers, 416.

1976: Carter, D, 927,365; Ford, R, 741,960; Anderson, Amer., 5,607; MacBride, LB, 2,219; LaRouche, U.S. Labor, 755.

1972: Nixon, R, 1,054,889; McGovern, D, 438,705; Schmitz, Amer., 25,018.

1968: Nixon, R, 627,192; Wallace, 3rd party, 496,188; Humphrey, D, 464,113.

1964: Johnson, D, 800,139; Goldwater, R, 624,844.

1960: Kennedy, D, 713,136; Nixon, R, 655,420.

North Dakota Vote Since 1960

2012: Romney, R, 188,163; Obama, D, 124,827; Johnson, LB, 5,231; Stein, Green, 1,361; Goode, Const., 1,185.

2008: McCain, R, 168,601; Obama, D, 141,278; Nader, Ind., 4,189; Barr, LB, 1,354; Baldwin, Const., 1,199.

2004: Bush, R, 196,651; Kerry, D, 111,052; Nader, Ind., 3,756; Badnarik, LB, 851; Peroutka, Const., 514.

2000: Bush, R, 174,852; Gore, D, 95,284; Nader, Ind., 9,486; Buchanan, RF, 7,288; Browne, Ind., 660; Phillips, Const., 373; Hagelin, Ind., 313.

1996: Dole, R, 125,050; Clinton, D, 106,905; Perot, RF, 32,515; Browne, LB, 847; Phillips, Ind., 745; Hagelin, Natural Law, 349.

1992: Bush, R, 136,244; Clinton, D, 99,168; Perot, Ind., 71,084.

1988: Bush, R, 166,559; Dukakis, D, 127,739; Paul, LB, 1,315; LaRouche, Natl. Econ. Recovery, 905.

1984: Reagan, R, 200,336; Mondale, D, 104,429; Bergland, LB, 703.

1980: Reagan, R, 193,695; Carter, D, 79,189; Anderson, Ind., 23,640; Clark, LB, 3,743; Commoner, LB, 429; McLain, Natl. People's League, 296; Greaves, Amer., 235; Hall, Comm., 93; DeBerry, Soc. Workers, 89; McReynolds, Soc., 82; Bubar, Statesman, 54.

1976: Ford, R, 153,470; Carter, D, 136,078; Anderson, Amer., 3,698; McCarthy, Ind., 2,952; Maddox, Amer. Ind., 269; Mac-Bride, LB, 256; scattered, 371.

1972: Nixon, R, 174,109; McGovern, D, 100,384; Schmitz, Amer., 5,646; Jenness, Soc. Workers, 288; Hall, Comm., 87.

1968: Nixon, R, 138,669; Humphrey, D, 94,769; Wallace, 3rd party, 14,244; Halstead, Soc. Workers, 128; Munn, Prohib., 38; Troxell, Ind., 34.

1964: Johnson, D, 149,784; Goldwater, R, 108,207; DeBerry, Soc. Workers, 224; Munn, Prohib., 174.

1960: Nixon, R, 154,310; Kennedy, D, 123,963; Dobbs, Soc. Workers, 158.

Ohio Vote Since 1960

2012: Obama, D, 2,827,709; Romney, R, 2,661,437; Johnson, LB, 49,493; Stein, Green, 18,573; Duncan, Ind., 12,502; Goode, Const., 8,152; Alexander, Soc., 2,944.

2008: Obama, D, 2,940,044; McCain, R, 2,677,820; Nader, Ind., 42,337; Barr, LB, 19,917; Baldwin, Const., 12,565; McKinney, Green, 8,518; Duncan, Ind., 3,905; Moore, Soc., 2,735.

2004: Bush, R, 2,859,768; Kerry, D, 2,741,167; Badnarik, non-partisan, 14,676; Peroutka, nonpartisan, 939.

2000: Bush, R, 2,351,209; Gore, D, 2,186,190; Nader, Ind., 117,857; Buchanan, Ind., 26,724; Browne, LB, 13,475; Hagelin, Natural Law, 6,169; Phillips, Ind., 3,823.

1996: Clinton, D, 2,148,222; Dole, R, 1,859,883; Perot, RF, 483,207; Browne, Ind., 12,851; Moorehead, Ind., 10,813; Hagelin, Natural Law, 9,120; Phillips, Ind., 7,361.

1992: Clinton, D, 1,984,942; Bush, R, 1,894,310; Perot, Ind., 1,036,426; Marrou, LB, 7,252; Fulani, New Alliance, 6,413; Gritz, Populist/America First, 4,699; Hagelin, Natural Law, 3,437; LaRouche, Ind., 2,446.

1988: Bush, R, 2,416,549; Dukakis, D, 1,939,629; Fulani, Ind., 12,017; Paul, Ind., 11,926.

1984: Reagan, R, 2,678,559; Mondale, D, 1,825,440; Bergland, LB, 5,886.

1980: Reagan, R, 2,206,545; Carter, D, 1,752,414; Anderson, Ind., 254,472; Clark, LB, 49,033; Commoner, Citizens, 8,564; Hall, Comm., 4,729; Congress, Ind., 4,029; Griswold, Workers World, 3,790; Bubar, Statesman, 27.

1976: Carter, D, 2,011,621; Ford, R, 2,000,505; McCarthy, Ind., 58,258; Maddox, Amer. Ind., 15,529; MacBride, LB, 8,961; Hall, Comm., 7,817; Camejo, Soc. Workers, 4,717; LaRouche, U.S. Labor, 4,335; scattered, 130.

1972: Nixon, R, 2,441,827; McGovern, D, 1,558,889; Schmitz, Amer., 80,067; Fisher, Soc. Labor, 7,107; Hall, Comm., 6,437; Wallace, Ind., 460.

1968: Nixon, R, 1,791,014; Humphrey, D, 1,700,586; Wallace, 3rd party, 467,495; Gregory, 372; Blomen, Soc. Labor, 120; Halstead, Soc. Workers, 69; Mitchell, Comm., 23; Munn, Prohib., 19.

1964: Johnson, D, 2,498,331; Goldwater, R, 1,470,865.

1960: Nixon, R, 2,217,611; Kennedy, D, 1,944,248.

Oklahoma Vote Since 1960

2012: Romney, R, 891,325; Obama, D, 443,547.

2008: McCain, R, 960,165; Obama, D, 502,496.

2004: Bush, R, 959,792; Kerry, D, 503,966.

2000: Bush, R, 744,337; Gore, D, 474,276; Buchanan, RF, 9,014; Browne, LB, 6,602.

1996: Dole, R, 582,315; Clinton, D, 488,105; Perot, RF, 130,788; Browne, LB, 5,505.

1992: Bush, R, 592,929; Clinton, D, 473,066; Perot, Ind., 319,878; Marrou, LB, 4,486.

1988: Bush, R, 678,367; Dukakis, D, 483,423; Paul, LB, 6,261; Fulani, New Alliance, 2,985.

1984: Reagan, R, 861,530; Mondale, D, 385,080; Bergland, LB, 9,066.

1980: Reagan, R, 695,570; Carter, D, 402,026; Anderson, Ind., 38,284; Clark, LB, 13,828.

1976: Ford, R, 545,708; Carter, D, 532,442; McCarthy, Ind., 14,101.

1972: Nixon, R, 759,025; McGovern, D, 247,147; Schmitz, Amer., 23,728.

1968: Nixon, R, 449,697; Humphrey, D, 301,658; Wallace, 3rd party, 191,731.

1964: Johnson, D, 519,834; Goldwater, R, 412,665.

1960: Nixon, R, 533,039; Kennedy, D, 370,111.

Oregon Vote Since 1960

2012: Obama, D, 970,488; Romney, R, 754,175; Johnson, LB, 24,089; Stein, Pacific Green, 19,427; Christensen, Const., 4,432; Anderson, OR Prog., 3,384.

2008: Obama, D, 1,037,291; McCain, R, 738,475; Nader, Peace Party of OR, 18,614; Baldwin, Const., 7,693; Barr, LB, 7,635; McKinney, Pacific Green, 4,543.

2004: Kerry, D, 943,163; Bush, R, 866,831; Badnarik, LB, 7,260; Cobb, Pacific Green, 5,315; Peroutka, Const., 5,257.

2000: Gore, D, 720,342; Bush, R, 713,577; Nader, Green, 77,357; Browne, LB, 7,447; Buchanan, Ind., 7,063; Hagelin, RF, 2,574; Phillips, Const., 2,189.

1996: Clinton, D, 649,641; Dole, R, 538,152; Perot, RF, 121,221; Nader, Pacific, 49,415; Browne, LB, 8,903; Phillips, Taxpayers, 3,379; Hagelin, Natural Law, 2,798; Hollis, Soc., 1,922.

1992: Clinton, D, 621,314; Bush, R, 475,757; Perot, Ind., 354,091; Marrou, LB, 4,277; Fulani, New Alliance, 3,030.

1988: Dukakis, D, 616,206; Bush, R, 560,126; Paul, LB, 14,811; Fulani, Ind., 6,487.

1984: Reagan, R, 658,700; Mondale, D, 536,479.

1980: Reagan, R, 571,044; Carter, D, 456,890; Anderson, Ind., 112,389; Clark, LB, 25,838; Commoner, Citizens, 13,642; scattered, 1,713.

1976: Ford, R, 492,120; Carter, D, 490,407; McCarthy, Ind., 40,207; write-in, 7,142.

1972: Nixon, R, 486,686; McGovern, D, 392,760; Schmitz, Amer., 46,211; write-in, 2,289.

1968: Nixon, R, 408,433; Humphrey, D, 358,866; Wallace, 3rd party, 49,683; write-ins: McCarthy, 1,496; N. Rockefeller, 69; others, 1,075.

1964: Johnson, D, 501,017; Goldwater, R, 282,779; write-in, 2,509.

1960: Nixon, R, 408,060; Kennedy, D, 367,402.

Pennsylvania Vote Since 1960

2012: Obama, D, 2,990,274; Romney, R, 2,680,434; Johnson, LB, 49,991; Stein, Green, 21,341.

2008: Obama, D, 3,276,363; McCain, R, 2,655,885; Nader, Ind., 42,977; Barr, LB, 19,912.

2004: Kerry, D, 2,938,095; Bush, R, 2,793,847; Badnarik, LB, 21,185; Cobb, Green, 6,319; Peroutka, Const., 6,318.

2000: Gore, D, 2,485,967; Bush, R, 2,281,127; Nader, Green, 103,392; Buchanan, RF, 16,023; Phillips, Const., 14,428; Browne, LB, 11,248.

1996: Clinton, D, 2,215,819; Dole, R, 1,801,169; Perot, RF, 430,984; Browne, LB, 28,000; Phillips, Const., 19,552; Hagelin, Natural Law, 5,783.

1992: Clinton, D, 2,239,164; Bush, R, 1,791,841; Perot, Ind., 902,667; Marrou, LB, 21,477; Fulani, New Alliance, 4,661.

1988: Bush, R, 2,300,087; Dukakis, D, 2,194,944; McCarthy, Consumer, 19,158; Paul, LB, 12,051.

1984: Reagan, R, 2,584,323; Mondale, D, 2,228,131; Bergland, LB, 6,982.
1980: Reagan, R, 2,261,872; Carter, D, 1,937,540; Anderson, Ind., 292,921; Clark, LB, 33,263; DeBerry, Soc. Workers, 20,291; Commoner, Consumer, 10,430; Hall, Comm., 5,184.
1976: Carter, D, 2,328,677; Ford, R, 2,205,604; McCarthy, Ind., 50,584; Maddox, Const., 25,344; Camejo, Soc. Workers, 3,009; LaRouche, U.S. Labor, 2,744; Hall, Comm., 1,891; others, 2,934.
1972: Nixon, R, 2,714,521; McGovern, D, 1,796,951; Schmitz, Amer., 70,593; Jenness, Soc. Workers, 4,639; Hall, Comm., 2,686; others, 2,715.
1968: Humphrey, D, 2,259,405; Nixon, R, 2,090,017; Wallace, 3rd party, 378,582; Gregory, Peace/Freedom, 7,821; Blomen, Soc. Labor, 4,977; Halstead, Soc. Workers, 4,862; others, 2,264.
1964: Johnson, D, 3,130,954; Goldwater, R, 1,673,657; DeBerry, Soc. Workers, 10,456; Hass, Soc. Labor, 5,092; scattered, 2,531.
1960: Kennedy, D, 2,556,282; Nixon, R, 2,439,956; Hass, Soc. Labor, 7,185; Dobbs, Soc. Workers, 2,678; scattered, 440.

Rhode Island Vote Since 1960

2012: Obama, D, 279,677; Romney, R, 157,204; Johnson, LB, 4,388; Stein, Green, 2,421; Goode, Const., 430; Anderson, Justice, 416; Lindsay, Socialism/Liberation, 132.
2008: Obama, D, 296,571; McCain, R, 165,391; Nader, Ind., 4,829; Barr, LB, 1,382; McKinney, Green, 797; Baldwin, Const., 675; La Riva, Socialism/Liberation, 122.
2004: Kerry, D, 259,765; Bush, R, 169,046; Nader, RF, 4,651; Cobb, Green, 1,333; Badnarik, LB, 907; Peroutka, Const., 339; Parker, Workers World, 253.
2000: Gore, D, 249,508; Bush, R, 130,555; Nader, Ind., 25,052; Buchanan, RF, 2,273; Browne, Ind., 742; Hagelin, Ind., 271; Moorehead, Ind., 199; Phillips, Ind., 97; McReynolds, Ind., 52; Harris, Ind., 34.
1996: Clinton, D, 233,050; Dole, R, 104,683; Perot, RF, 43,723; Nader, Green, 6,040; Browne, LB, 1,109; Phillips, U.S. Taxpayers, 1,021; Hagelin, Natural Law, 435; Moorehead, Workers World, 186.
1992: Clinton, D, 213,299; Bush, R, 131,601; Perot, Ind., 105,045; Fulani, New Alliance, 1,878.
1988: Dukakis, D, 225,123; Bush, R, 177,761; Paul, LB, 825; Fulani, New Alliance, 280.
1984: Reagan, R, 212,080; Mondale, D, 197,106; Bergland, LB, 277.
1980: Carter, D, 198,342; Reagan, R, 154,793; Anderson, Ind., 59,819; Clark, LB, 2,458; Hall, Comm., 218; McReynolds, Soc., 170; DeBerry, Soc. Workers, 90; Griswold, Workers World, 77.
1976: Carter, D, 227,636; Ford, R, 181,249; MacBride, LB, 715; Camejo, Soc. Workers, 462; Hall, Comm., 334; Levin, Soc. Labor, 188.
1972: Nixon, R, 220,383; McGovern, D, 194,645; Jenness, Soc. Workers, 729.
1968: Humphrey, D, 246,518; Nixon, R, 122,359; Wallace, 3rd party, 15,678; Halstead, Soc. Workers, 383.
1964: Johnson, D, 315,463; Goldwater, R, 74,615.
1960: Kennedy, D, 258,032; Nixon, R, 147,502.

South Carolina Vote Since 1960

2012: Romney, R, 1,071,645; Obama, D, 865,941; Johnson, LB, 16,321; Stein, Green, 5,446; Goode, Const., 4,765.
2008: McCain, R, 1,034,896; Obama, D, 862,449; Barr, LB, 7,283; Baldwin, Const., 6,827; Nader, petitioning cand., 5,053; McKinney, Green, 4,461.
2004: Bush, R, 937,974; Kerry, D, 661,699; Nader, Ind., 5,520; Peroutka, Const., 5,317; Badnarik, LB, 3,608; Brown, United Citizens, 2,124; Cobb, Green, 1,488.
2000: Bush, R, 786,892; Gore, D, 566,039; Nader, United Citizens, 20,279; Browne, LB, 4,898; Buchanan, RF, 3,309; Phillips, Const., 1,682; Hagelin, Natural Law, 943.
1996: Dole, R, 573,458; Clinton, D, 506,283; Perot, RF/Patriot, 64,386; Browne, LB, 4,271; Phillips, U.S. Taxpayers, 2,043; Hagelin, Natural Law, 1,248.

1992: Bush, R, 577,507; Clinton, D, 479,514; Perot, Ind., 138,872; Marrou, LB, 2,719; Phillips, U.S. Taxpayers, 2,680; Fulani, New Alliance, 1,235.
1988: Bush, R, 606,443; Dukakis, D, 370,554; Paul, LB, 4,935; Fulani, United Citizens, 4,077.
1984: Reagan, R, 615,539; Mondale, D, 344,459; Bergland, LB, 4,359.
1980: Reagan, R, 439,277; Carter, D, 428,220; Anderson, Ind., 13,868; Clark, LB, 4,807; Rarick, Amer. Ind., 2,086.
1976: Carter, D, 450,807; Ford, R, 346,149; Anderson, Amer., 2,996; Maddox, Amer. Ind., 1,950; write-in, 681.
1972: Nixon, R, 477,044; McGovern, D, 184,559, and United Citizens, 2,265 (total, 186,824); Schmitz, Amer., 10,075; write-in, 17.
1968: Nixon, R, 254,062; Wallace, 3rd party, 215,430; Humphrey, D, 197,486.
1964: Goldwater, R, 309,048; Johnson, D, 215,700; write-ins: Wallace, 5; Nixon, 1; Powell, 1; Thurmond, 1.
1960: Kennedy, D, 198,129; Nixon, R, 188,558; write-in, 1.

South Dakota Vote Since 1960

2012: Romney, R, 210,610; Obama, D, 145,039; Johnson, LB, 5,795; Goode, Const., 2,371.
2008: McCain, R, 203,054; Obama, D, 170,924; Nader, Ind., 4,267; Baldwin, Const., 1,895; Barr, Ind., 1,835.
2004: Bush, R, 232,584; Kerry, D, 149,244; Nader, Ind., 4,320; Peroutka, Const., 1,103; Badnarik, LB, 964.
2000: Bush, R, 190,700; Gore, D, 118,804; Buchanan, RF, 3,322; Phillips, Ind., 1,781; Browne, LB, 1,662.
1996: Dole, R, 150,543; Clinton, D, 139,333; Perot, RF, 31,250; Browne, LB, 1,472; Phillips, Taxpayers, 912; Hagelin, Natural Law, 316.
1992: Bush, R, 136,718; Clinton, D, 124,888; Perot, Ind., 73,295.
1988: Bush, R, 165,415; Dukakis, D, 145,560; Paul, LB, 1,060; Fulani, New Alliance, 730.
1984: Reagan, R, 200,267; Mondale, D, 116,113.
1980: Reagan, R, 198,343; Carter, D, 103,855; Anderson, Ind., 21,431; Clark, LB, 3,824; Pulley, Soc. Workers, 250.
1976: Ford, R, 151,505; Carter, D, 147,068; MacBride, LB, 1,619; Hall, Comm., 318; Camejo, Soc. Workers, 168.
1972: Nixon, R, 166,476; McGovern, D, 139,945; Jenness, Soc. Workers, 994.
1968: Nixon, R, 149,841; Humphrey, D, 118,023; Wallace, 3rd party, 13,400.
1964: Johnson, D, 163,010; Goldwater, R, 130,108.
1960: Nixon, R, 178,417; Kennedy, D, 128,070.

Tennessee Vote Since 1960

2012: Romney, R, 1,462,330; Obama, D, 960,709; Johnson, Ind., 18,623; Stein, Green, 6,515; Goode, Const., 6,022; Anderson, Ind., 2,639; Miller, Ind., 1,739.
2008: McCain, R, 1,479,178; Obama, D, 1,087,437; Nader, Ind., 11,560; Barr, Ind., 8,547; Baldwin, Ind., 8,191; McKinney, Ind., 2,499; Moore, Ind., 1,326; Jay, Ind., 1,011.
2004: Bush, R, 1,384,375; Kerry, D, 1,036,477; Nader, Ind., 8,992; Badnarik, Ind., 4,866; Peroutka, Ind., 2,570.
2000: Bush, R, 1,061,949; Gore, D, 981,720; Nader, Green, 19,781; Browne, LB, 4,284; Buchanan, RF, 4,250; Brown, Ind., 1,606; Phillips, Ind., 1,015; Hagelin, RF, 613; Venson, Ind., 535.
1996: Clinton, D, 909,146; Dole, R, 863,530; Perot, RF, 105,918; Nader, Ind., 6,427; Browne, Ind., 5,020; Phillips, Ind., 1,818; Collins, Ind., 688; Hagelin, Ind., 636; Michael, Ind., 408; Dodge, Ind., 324.
1992: Clinton, D, 933,521; Bush, R, 841,300; Perot, Ind., 199,968; Marrou, LB, 1,847.
1988: Bush, R, 947,233; Dukakis, D, 679,794; Paul, Ind., 2,041; Duke, Ind., 1,807.
1984: Reagan, R, 990,212; Mondale, D, 711,714; Bergland, LB, 3,072.
1980: Reagan, R, 787,761; Carter, D, 783,051; Anderson, Ind., 35,991; Clark, LB, 7,116; Commoner, Citizens, 1,112; Bubar, Statesman, 521; McReynolds, Soc., 519; Hall, Comm., 503; DeBerry, Soc. Workers, 490; Griswold, Workers World, 400; write-in, 152.

1976: Carter, D, 825,879; Ford, R, 633,969; Anderson, Amer., 5,769; McCarthy, Ind., 5,004; Maddox, Amer. Ind., 2,303; MacBride, LB, 1,375; Hall, Comm., 547; LaRouche, U.S. Labor, 512; Bubar, Prohib., 442; Miller, Ind., 316; write-in, 230.
1972: Nixon, R, 813,147; McGovern, D, 357,293; Schmitz, Amer., 30,373; write-in, 369.
1968: Nixon, R, 472,592; Wallace, 3rd party, 424,792; Humphrey, D, 351,233.
1964: Johnson, D, 635,047; Goldwater, R, 508,965; write-in, 34.
1960: Nixon, R, 556,577; Kennedy, D, 481,453; Faubus, States' Rights, 11,304; Decker, Prohib., 2,458.

Texas Vote Since 1960

2012: Romney, R, 4,569,843; Obama, D, 3,308,124; Johnson, LB, 88,580; Stein, Green, 24,657.
2008: McCain, R, 4,479,328; Obama, D, 3,528,633 Barr, LB, 56,116.
2004: Bush, R, 4,526,917; Kerry, D, 2,832,704; Badnarik, LB, 38,787.
2000: Bush, R, 3,799,639; Gore, D, 2,433,746; Nader, Green, 137,994; Browne, LB, 23,160; Buchanan, Ind., 12,394.
1996: Dole, R, 2,736,167; Clinton, D, 2,459,683; Perot, RF, 378,537; Browne, LB, 20,256; Phillips, U.S. Taxpayers, 7,472; Hagelin, Natural Law, 4,422.
1992: Bush, R, 2,496,071; Clinton, D, 2,281,815; Perot, Ind., 1,354,781; Marrou, LB, 19,699.
1988: Bush, R, 3,036,829; Dukakis, D, 2,352,748; Paul, LB, 30,355; Fulani, New Alliance, 7,208.
1984: Reagan, R, 3,433,428; Mondale, D, 1,949,276.
1980: Reagan, R, 2,510,705; Carter, D, 1,881,147; Anderson, Ind., 111,613; Clark, LB, 37,643; write-in, 528.
1976: Carter, D, 2,082,319; Ford, R, 1,953,300; McCarthy, Ind., 20,118; Anderson, Amer., 11,442; Camejo, Soc. Workers, 1,723; write-in, 2,982.
1972: Nixon, R, 2,298,896; McGovern, D, 1,154,289; Jenness, Soc. Workers, 8,664; Schmitz, Amer., 6,039; others, 3,393.
1968: Humphrey, D, 1,266,804; Nixon, R, 1,227,844; Wallace, 3rd party, 584,269; write-in, 489.
1964: Johnson, D, 1,663,185; Goldwater, R, 958,566; Lightburn, Const., 5,060.
1960: Kennedy, D, 1,167,932; Nixon, R, 1,121,699; Sullivan, Const., 18,169; Decker, Prohib., 3,870; write-in, 15.

Utah Vote Since 1960

2012: Romney, R, 740,600; Obama, D, 251,813; Johnson, LB, 12,572; Anderson, Justice, 5,335; Stein, Green, 3,817; Goode, Const., 2,871; La Riva, unaff., 393.
2008: McCain, R, 596,030; Obama, D, 327,670; Baldwin, Const., 12,012; Nader, unaff., 8,416; Barr, LB, 6,966; McKinney, unaff., 982; La Riva, unaff., 262.
2004: Bush, R, 663,742; Kerry, D, 241,199; Nader, Ind., 11,305; Peroutka, Const., 6,841; Badnarik, LB, 3,375; Jay, Personal Choice, 946; Harris, Soc. Workers, 393.
2000: Bush, R, 515,096; Gore, D, 203,053; Nader, Green, 35,850; Buchanan, RF, 9,319; Browne, LB, 3,616; Phillips, Ind. American, 2,709; Hagelin, Natural Law, 763; Harris, Soc. Workers, 186; Youngkeit, Ind., 161.
1996: Dole, R, 361,911; Clinton, D, 221,633; Perot, RF, 66,461; Nader, Green, 4,615; Browne, LB, 4,129; Phillips, Taxpayers, 2,601; Templin, Ind. American, 1,290; Crane, Ind., 1,101; Hagelin, Natural Law, 1,085; Moorehead, Workers World, 298; Harris, Soc. Workers, 235; Dodge, Prohib., 111.
1992: Bush, R, 322,632; Perot, Ind., 203,400; Clinton, D, 183,429; Gritz, Populist/America First, 28,602; Marrou, LB, 1,900; Hagelin, Natural Law, 1,319; LaRouche, Ind., 1,089.
1988: Bush, R, 428,442; Dukakis, D, 207,352; Paul, LB, 7,473; Dennis, Amer., 2,158.
1984: Reagan, R, 469,105; Mondale, D, 155,369; Bergland, LB, 2,447.
1980: Reagan, R, 439,687; Carter, D, 124,266; Anderson, Ind., 30,284; Clark, LB, 7,226; Commoner, Citizens, 1,009; Greaves, Amer., 965; Rarick, Amer. Ind., 522; Hall, Comm., 139; DeBerry, Soc. Workers, 124.
1976: Ford, R, 337,908; Carter, D, 182,110; Anderson, Amer., 13,304; McCarthy, Ind., 3,907; MacBride, LB, 2,438; Maddox, Amer. Ind., 1,162; Camejo, Soc. Workers, 268; Hall, Comm., 121.
1972: Nixon, R, 323,643; McGovern, D, 126,284; Schmitz, Amer., 28,549.

1968: Nixon, R, 238,728; Humphrey, D, 156,665; Wallace, 3rd party, 26,906; Peace/Freedom, 180; Halstead, Soc. Workers, 89.
1964: Johnson, D, 219,628; Goldwater, R, 181,785.
1960: Nixon, R, 205,361; Kennedy, D, 169,248; Dobbs, Soc. Workers, 100.

Vermont Vote Since 1960

2012: Obama, D, 199,239; Romney, R, 92,698; Johnson, LB, 3,487; Anderson, Justice, 1,128; Lindsay, Socialism/Liberation, 695.
2008: Obama, D, 219,262; McCain, R, 98,974; Nader, Ind., 3,339; Barr, LB, 1,067; Baldwin, Const., 500; Calero, Soc. Workers, 150; La Riva, Socialism/Liberation, 149; Moore, Liberty Union, 141.
2004: Kerry, D, 184,067; Bush, R, 121,180; Nader, Ind., 4,494; Badnarik, LB, 1,102; Parker, Liberty Union, 265; Calero, Soc. Workers, 244.
2000: Gore, D, 149,022; Bush, R, 119,775; Nader, Green, 20,374; Buchanan, RF, 2,192; Lane, Grass Roots, 1,044; Browne, LB, 784; Hagelin, Natural Law, 219; McReynolds, Liberty Union, 161; Phillips, Const., 153; Harris, Soc. Workers, 70.
1996: Clinton, D, 137,894; Dole, R, 80,352; Perot, RF, 31,024; Nader, Green, 5,585; Browne, LB, 1,183; Hagelin, Natural Law, 498; Peron, Grass Roots, 480; Phillips, Taxpayers, 382; Hollis, Liberty Union, 292; Harris, Soc. Workers, 199.
1992: Clinton, D, 133,590; Bush, R, 88,122; Perot, Ind., 65,985.
1988: Bush, R, 124,331; Dukakis, D, 115,775; Paul, LB, 1,000; LaRouche, Ind., 275.
1984: Reagan, R, 135,865; Mondale, D, 95,730; Bergland, LB, 1,002.
1980: Reagan, R, 94,598; Carter, D, 81,891; Anderson, Ind., 31,760; Commoner, Citizens, 2,316; Clark, LB, 1,900; McReynolds, Liberty Union, 136; Hall, Comm., 118; DeBerry, Soc. Workers, 75; scattered, 413.
1976: Ford, R, 100,387; Carter, D, 77,798 and Ind. Vermonters, 991 (total, 79,789); McCarthy, Ind., 4,001; Camejo, Soc. Workers, 430; LaRouche, U.S. Labor, 196; scattered, 99.
1972: Nixon, R, 117,149; McGovern, D, 68,174; Spock, Liberty Union, 1,010; Jenness, Soc. Workers, 296; scattered, 318.
1968: Nixon, R, 85,142; Humphrey, D, 70,255; Wallace, 3rd party, 5,104; Gregory, New Party, 579; Halstead, Soc. Workers, 295.
1964: Johnson, D, 107,674; Goldwater, R, 54,868.
1960: Nixon, R, 98,131; Kennedy, D, 69,186.

Virginia Vote Since 1960

2012: Obama, D, 1,971,820; Romney, R, 1,822,522; Johnson, LB, 31,216; Goode, Const., 13,058; Stein, Green, 8,627.
2008: Obama, D, 1,959,532; McCain, R, 1,725,005; Nader, Ind., 11,483; Barr, LB, 11,067; Baldwin, Ind. Green, 7,474; McKinney, Green, 2,344.
2004: Bush, R, 1,716,959; Kerry, D, 1,454,742; Badnarik, LB, 11,032; Peroutka, Const., 10,161.
2000: Bush, R, 1,437,490; Gore, D, 1,217,290; Nader, Green, 59,398; Browne, LB, 15,198; Buchanan, RF, 5,455; Phillips, Const., 1,809.
1996: Dole, R, 1,138,350; Clinton, D, 1,091,060; Perot, RF, 159,861; Phillips, Taxpayers, 13,687; Browne, LB, 9,174; Hagelin, Natural Law, 4,510.
1992: Bush, R, 1,150,517; Clinton, D, 1,038,650; Perot, Ind., 348,639; LaRouche, Ind., 11,937; Marrou, LB, 5,730; Fulani, New Alliance, 3,192.
1988: Bush, R, 1,309,162; Dukakis, D, 859,799; Fulani, Ind., 14,312; Paul, LB, 8,336.
1984: Reagan, R, 1,337,078; Mondale, D, 796,250.
1980: Reagan, R, 989,609; Carter, D, 752,174; Anderson, Ind., 95,418; Commoner, Citizens, 14,024; Clark, LB, 12,821; DeBerry, Soc. Workers, 1,986.
1976: Ford, R, 836,554; Carter, D, 813,896; Camejo, Soc. Workers, 17,802; Anderson, Amer., 16,686; LaRouche, U.S. Labor, 7,508; MacBride, LB, 4,648.
1972: Nixon, R, 988,493; McGovern, D, 438,887; Schmitz, Amer., 19,721; Fisher, Soc. Labor, 9,918.
1968: Nixon, R, 590,319; Humphrey, D, 442,387; Wallace, 3rd party, 320,272; Blomen, Soc. Labor, 4,671; Gregory, Peace/Freedom, 1,680; Munn, Prohib., 601. *10,561 votes for Wallace were omitted in the count.
1964: Johnson, D, 558,038; Goldwater, R, 481,334; Hass, Soc. Labor, 2,895.
1960: Nixon, R, 404,521; Kennedy, D, 362,327; Coiner, Conservative, 4,204; Hass, Soc. Labor, 397.

Washington Vote Since 1960

2012: Obama, D, 1,755,396; Romney, R, 1,290,670; Johnson, LB, 42,202; Stein, Green, 20,928; Goode, Const., 8,851; Anderson, Justice, 4,946; Lindsay, Socialism/Liberation, 1,318; Harris, Soc. Workers, 1,205.

2008: Obama, D, 1,750,848; McCain, R, 1,229,216; Nader, Ind., 29,489; Barr, LB, 12,728; Baldwin, Const., 9,432; McKinney, Green, 3,819; La Riva, Socialism/Liberation, 705; Harris, Soc. Workers, 641.

2004: Kerry, D, 1,510,201; Bush, R, 1,304,894; Nader, Ind., 23,283; Badnarik, LB, 11,955; Peroutka, Const., 3,922; Cobb, Green, 2,974; Parker, Workers World, 1,077; Harris, Soc. Workers, 547; Van Auken, Soc. Equality, 231.

2000: Gore, D, 1,247,652; Bush, R, 1,108,864; Nader, Green, 103,002; Browne, LB, 13,135; Buchanan, Freedom, 7,171; Hagelin, Natural Law, 2,927; Phillips, Const., 1,989; Moorehead, Workers World, 1,729; McReynolds, Soc., 660; Harris, Soc. Workers, 304.

1996: Clinton, D, 1,123,323; Dole, R, 840,712; Perot, RF, 201,003; Nader, Ind., 60,322; Browne, LB, 12,522; Hagelin, Natural Law, 6,076; Phillips, U.S. Taxpayers, 4,578; Collins, Ind., 2,374; Moorehead, Workers World, 2,189; Harris, Soc. Workers, 738.

1992: Clinton, D, 993,037; Bush, R, 731,234; Perot, Ind., 541,780; Marrou, LB, 7,533; Gritz, Populist/America First, 4,854; Hagelin, Natural Law, 2,456; Phillips, U.S. Taxpayers, 2,354; Fulani, New Alliance, 1,776; Daniels, Ind., 1,171.

1988: Dukakis, D, 933,516; Bush, R, 903,835; Paul, LB, 17,240; LaRouche, Ind., 4,412.

1984: Reagan, R, 1,051,670; Mondale, D, 798,352; Bergland, LB, 8,844.

1980: Reagan, R, 865,244; Carter, D, 650,193; Anderson, Ind., 185,073; Clark, LB, 29,213; Commoner, Citizens, 9,403; DeBerry, Soc. Workers, 1,137; McReynolds, Soc., 956; Hall, Comm., 834; Griswold, Workers World, 341.

1976: Ford, R, 777,732; Carter, D, 717,323; McCarthy, Ind., 36,986; Maddox, Amer. Ind., 8,585; Anderson, Amer., 5,046; MacBride, LB, 5,042; Wright, People's, 1,124; Camejo, Soc. Workers, 905; LaRouche, U.S. Labor, 903; Hall, Comm., 817; Levin, Soc. Labor, 713; Zeidler, Soc., 358.

1972: Nixon, R, 837,135; McGovern, D, 568,334; Schmitz, Amer., 58,906; Spock, Ind., 2,644; Hospers, LB, 1,537; Fisher, Soc. Labor, 1,102; Jenness, Soc. Workers, 623; Hall, Comm., 566.

1968: Humphrey, D, 616,037; Nixon, R, 588,510; Wallace, 3rd party, 96,990; Cleaver, Peace/Freedom, 1,609; Blomen, Soc. Labor, 488; Mitchell, Free Ballot, 377; Halstead, Soc. Workers, 270.

1964: Johnson, D, 779,699; Goldwater, R, 470,366; Hass, Soc. Labor, 7,772; DeBerry, Freedom Soc., 537.

1960: Nixon, R, 629,273; Kennedy, D, 599,298; Hass, Soc. Labor, 10,895; Curtis, Const., 1,401; Dobbs, Soc. Workers, 705.

West Virginia Vote Since 1960

2012: Romney, R, 417,655; Obama, D, 238,269; Johnson, LB, 6,302; Stein, Mountain, 4,406; Terry, NPA, 3,806.

2008: McCain, R, 397,466; Obama, D, 303,857; Nader, unaff., 7,219; Baldwin, Const., 2,465; McKinney, Mountain, 2,355.

2004: Bush, R, 423,778; Kerry, D, 326,541; Nader, Ind., 4,063; Badnarik, LB, 1,405.

2000: Bush, R, 336,475; Gore, D, 295,497; Nader, Green, 10,680; Buchanan, RF, 3,169; Browne, LB, 1,912; Hagelin, Natural Law, 367.

1996: Clinton, D, 327,812; Dole, R, 233,946; Perot, RF, 71,639; Browne, LB, 3,062.

1992: Clinton, D, 331,001; Bush, R, 241,974; Perot, Ind., 108,829; Marrou, LB, 1,873.

1988: Dukakis, D, 341,016; Bush, R, 310,065; Fulani, New Alliance, 2,230.

1984: Reagan, R, 405,483; Mondale, D, 328,125.

1980: Carter, D, 367,462; Reagan, R, 334,206; Anderson, Ind., 31,691; Clark, LB, 4,356.

1976: Carter, D, 435,864; Ford, R, 314,726.

1972: Nixon, R, 484,964; McGovern, D, 277,435.

1968: Humphrey, D, 374,091; Nixon, R, 307,555; Wallace, 3rd party, 72,560.

1964: Johnson, D, 538,087; Goldwater, R, 253,953.

1960: Kennedy, D, 441,786; Nixon, R, 395,995.

Wisconsin Vote Since 1960

2012: Obama, D, 1,620,985; Romney, R, 1,407,966; Johnson, LB, 20,439; Stein, Green, 7,665; White, Soc. Equality, 553; La Riva, Socialism/Liberation, 526.

2008: Obama, D, 1,677,211; McCain, R, 1,262,393; Nader, Ind., 17,605; Barr, LB, 8,858; Baldwin, Ind., 5,072; McKinney, Green, 4,216; Wamboldt, Ind., 764; Moore, Ind., 540; La Riva, Ind., 237.

2004: Kerry, D, 1,489,504; Bush, R, 1,478,120; Nader, Ind., 16,390; Badnarik, LB, 6,464; Cobb, Green, 2,661; Brown, Ind., 471; Harris, Ind., 411.

2000: Gore, D, 1,242,987; Bush, R, 1,237,279; Nader, Green, 94,070; Buchanan, RF, 11,446; Browne, LB, 6,640; Phillips, Const., 2,042; Moorehead, Workers World, 1,063; Hagelin, RF, 878; Harris, Soc. Workers, 306.

1996: Clinton, D, 1,071,971; Dole, R, 845,029; Perot, RF, 227,339; Nader, Green, 28,723; Phillips, U.S. Taxpayers, 8,811; Browne, LB, 7,929; Hagelin, Natural Law, 1,379; Moorehead, Workers World, 1,333; Hollis, Soc., 848; Harris, Soc. Workers, 483.

1992: Clinton, D, 1,041,066; Bush, R, 930,855; Perot, Ind., 544,479; Marrou, LB, 2,877; Gritz, Populist/America First, 2,311; Daniels, Ind., 1,883; Phillips, U.S. Taxpayers, 1,772; Hagelin, Natural Law, 1,070.

1988: Dukakis, D, 1,126,794; Bush, R, 1,047,499; Paul, LB, 5,157; Duke, Populist, 3,056.

1984: Reagan, R, 1,198,584; Mondale, D, 995,740; Bergland, LB, 4,883.

1980: Reagan, R, 1,088,845; Carter, D, 981,584; Anderson, Ind., 160,657; Clark, LB, 29,135; Commoner, Citizens, 7,767; Rarick, Const., 1,519; McReynolds, Soc., 808; Hall, Comm., 772; Griswold, Workers World, 414; DeBerry, Soc. Workers, 383; scattered, 1,337.

1976: Carter, D, 1,040,232; Ford, R, 1,004,987; McCarthy, Ind., 34,943; Maddox, Amer. Ind., 8,552; Zeidler, Soc., 4,298; MacBride, LB, 3,814; Camejo, Soc. Workers, 1,691; Wright, People's, 943; Hall, Comm., 749; LaRouche, U.S. Labor, 738; Levin, Soc. Labor, 389; scattered, 2,839.

1972: Nixon, R, 989,430; McGovern, D, 810,174; Schmitz, Amer., 47,525; Spock, Ind., 2,701; Fisher, Soc. Labor, 998; Hall, Comm., 663; Reed, Ind., 506; scattered, 893.

1968: Nixon, R, 809,997; Humphrey, D, 748,804; Wallace, 3rd party, 127,835; Blomen, Soc. Labor, 1,338; Halstead, Soc. Workers, 1,222; scattered, 2,342.

1964: Johnson, D, 1,050,424; Goldwater, R, 638,495; DeBerry, Soc. Workers, 1,692; Hass, Soc. Labor, 1,204.

1960: Nixon, R, 895,175; Kennedy, D, 830,805; Dobbs, Soc. Workers, 1,792; Hass, Soc. Labor, 1,310.

Wyoming Vote Since 1960

2012: Romney, R, 170,962; Obama, D, 69,286; Johnson, LB, 5,326; Goode, Const., 1,452.

2008: McCain, R, 164,958; Obama, D, 82,868; Nader, Ind., 2,525; Barr, LB, 1,594; Baldwin, Ind., 1,192.

2004: Bush, R, 167,629; Kerry, D, 70,776; Nader, Ind., 2,741; Badnarik, LB, 1,171; Peroutka, Ind., 631.

2000: Bush, R, 147,947; Gore, D, 60,481; Buchanan, RF, 2,724; Browne, LB, 1,443; Phillips, Ind., 720; Hagelin, Natural Law, 411.

1996: Dole, R, 105,388; Clinton, D, 77,934; Perot, RF, 25,928; Browne, LB, 1,739; Hagelin, Natural Law, 582.

1992: Bush, R, 79,347; Clinton, D, 68,160; Perot, Ind., 51,263.

1988: Bush, R, 106,867; Dukakis, D, 67,113; Paul, LB, 2,026; Fulani, New Alliance, 545.

1984: Reagan, R, 133,241; Mondale, D, 53,370; Bergland, LB, 2,357.

1980: Reagan, R, 110,700; Carter, D, 49,427; Anderson, Ind., 12,072; Clark, LB, 4,514.

1976: Ford, R, 92,717; Carter, D, 62,239; McCarthy, Ind., 624; Reagan, Ind., 307; Anderson, Amer., 290; MacBride, LB, 89; Brown, Ind., 47; Maddox, Amer. Ind., 30.

1972: Nixon, R, 100,464; McGovern, D, 44,358; Schmitz, Amer., 748.

1968: Nixon, R, 70,927; Humphrey, D, 45,173; Wallace, 3rd party, 11,105.

1964: Johnson, D, 80,718; Goldwater, R, 61,998.

1960: Nixon, R, 77,451; Kennedy, D, 63,331.

UNITED STATES GOVERNMENT

EXECUTIVE BRANCH	LEGISLATIVE BRANCH	JUDICIAL BRANCH
President	**CONGRESS**	**Supreme Court of the United States**
Vice President	**Senate/House of Representatives**	Courts of Appeals
Executive Office of the President	Architect of the Capitol	District Courts
Council of Economic Advisers	Congressional Budget Office	Territorial Courts
Council on Environmental Quality	Government Accountability Office	Court of International Trade
Executive Residence	Government Publishing Office	Court of Federal Claims
National Security Council	Library of Congress	Bankruptcy Courts
Office of Administration	Medicare Payment Advisory Commission	Tax Court
Office of Management and Budget	Stennis Center for Public Service	Court of Appeals for the Armed Forces
Office of National Drug Control Policy	U.S. Botanic Garden	Court of Appeals for Veterans Claims
Office of Science and Technology Policy		Administrative Office of the Courts
Office of the U.S. Trade Representative		Federal Judicial Center
Office of the Vice President		Sentencing Commission
White House Office*		Judicial Panel on Multidistrict Litigation

*Includes Domestic Policy Council, National Security Advisor, National Economic Council, Office of Cabinet Affairs, Office of the Chief of Staff, Office of Communications, Office of Digital Strategy, Office of the First Lady, Office of Legislative Affairs, Office of Management and Administration, Oval Office Operations, Office of Presidential Personnel, Office of Public Engagement and Intergovernmental Affairs, Office of Scheduling and Advance, Office of the Staff Secretary, and Office of the White House Counsel.

The Obama Administration

As of Aug. 2016; mailing addresses are for Washington, DC, except where otherwise noted.
Terms of office of the president and vice president: Jan. 20, 2013, to Jan. 20, 2017.

President: By law, Pres. Barack H. Obama received an annual salary of $400,000 (taxable) and an annual expense allowance of $50,000 (nontaxable) for costs resulting from official duties. This does not include amounts available for expenditures within the Executive Office of the President, including $3,850,000 for necessary expenses for the White House, up to $100,000 a year for travel expenses, and up to $19,000 for official entertainment.
Website: www.whitehouse.gov/administration/president-obama
Vice President: By law, Vice Pres. Joseph R. Biden received an annual salary of $237,700 (taxable) and an annual expense allowance of $20,000 for costs resulting from official duties, plus $90,000 for official entertainment expenses (nontaxable).
Website: www.whitehouse.gov/administration/vice-president-biden

Cabinet Department Heads

(Salary: $205,700 per year)

Secretary of State: John Kerry
Secretary of the Treasury: Jack Lew
Secretary of Defense: Ashton Carter
Attorney General (Dept. of Justice): Loretta E. Lynch
Secretary of the Interior: Sally Jewell
Secretary of Agriculture: Thomas J. Vilsack
Secretary of Commerce: Penny Pritzker
Secretary of Labor: Thomas E. Perez
Secretary of Health and Human Services: Sylvia Mathews Burwell
Secretary of Housing and Urban Development: Julián Castro
Secretary of Transportation: Anthony Foxx
Secretary of Energy: Ernest Moniz
Secretary of Education: John King
Secretary of Veterans Affairs: Robert A. McDonald
Secretary of Homeland Security: Jeh Johnson

Executive Agencies

Council of Economic Advisers: Jason Furman, chair; www.whitehouse.gov/administration/eop/cea/
Council on Environmental Quality: Christy Goldfuss, managing dir.; www.whitehouse.gov/administration/eop/ceq/
Office of Administration: Catherine G. Solomon, dir.; www.whitehouse.gov/administration/eop/oa/
Office of Management and Budget: Shaun L. S. Donovan, dir.; www.whitehouse.gov/omb/
Office of Natl. Drug Control Policy: Michael Botticelli, dir.; www.whitehouse.gov/ondcp/
Office of Science and Technology Policy: John Holdren, dir.; www.whitehouse.gov/administration/eop/ostp/
Office of the U.S. Trade Representative: Amb. Michael Froman; www.ustr.gov

White House Staff

1600 Pennsylvania Ave. NW, 20500; www.whitehouse.gov

Director, National Intelligence: James R. Clapper
Assistants to the President:
  Chief of Staff: Denis McDonough
  Deputy Chief of Staff for Implementation: Kristie Canegallo
  Deputy Chief of Staff for Operations: Anita Breckenridge
  Cabinet Secretary: Broderick D. Johnson
  Counsel to the President: Warren N. Eggleston
  White House Press Secretary: Joshua R. Earnest
  National Security Advisor: Susan Rice
  Deputy National Security Advisors: Avril D. Haines, Benjamin J. Rhodes
  Director of Communications: Jennifer R. Psaki
  Director of the Domestic Policy Council: Cecilia Muñoz
  Economic Policy and Director of the National Economic Council: Jeffrey D. Zients
  Homeland Security and Counterterrorism: Lisa O. Monaco
  Director of Legislative Affairs: Amy D. Rosenbaum
  Director of Political Strategy and Outreach: David M. Simas
  Director of Presidential Personnel: Rodin A. Mehrbani
  Director of Speechwriting: Cody S. Keenan
  Director of Scheduling and Advance: Chase M. Cushman
  Management and Administration: Maju S. Varghese
Senior Advisors: Brian C. Deese, Valerie B. Jarrett, Shailagh J. Murray
Physician to the President: Ronny L. Jackson
Chief of Staff to the Vice President: Steve Ricchetti
White House Social Secretary: Deesha Dyer
Chief of Staff to the First Lady: Christina M. Tchen
Senior Advisor to the First Lady: Melissa E. Winter

The U.S. Cabinet

The heads of major executive departments of the federal government constitute the Cabinet. This institution, not provided for in the U.S. Constitution, developed as an advisory body out of the desire of presidents to consult on policy matters. Aside from its advisory role, the Cabinet as a body has no formal function and wields no executive authority. Individual members exercise authority as heads of their departments, reporting to the president. The Cabinet meets at times set by the president. In addition, the Cabinet commonly includes other officials designated by the president as being of Cabinet rank.

The officials so designated by Pres. Barack Obama include Vice Pres. Joseph R. Biden, White House Chief of Staff Denis McDonough, Environmental Protection Agency Administrator Gina McCarthy, Office of Management and Budget Director Shaun L. S. Donovan, U.S. Trade Representative Ambassador Michael Froman, U.S. Ambassador to the United Nations Samantha Power, Council of Economic Advisers Chair Jason Furman, and Small Business Administration Administrator Maria Contreras-Sweet.

Department of State

2201 C St. NW, 20520; www.state.gov

The Dept. of Foreign Affairs was created by act of Congress on July 27, 1789, and the name changed to Dept. of State on Sept. 15, 1789. Conducts U.S. foreign policy. The Foreign Service protects American citizens and interests through embassies in some 180 countries under eight geographic bureaus. Maintains contact with foreign governments, negotiates agreements and treaties, and supports U.S. foreign trade. Promotes democracy, international security, human rights—including issues related to AIDS, human trafficking, war crimes, and migration—and arms and narcotics control. Represents the nation in international organizations. Issues passports to U.S. citizens and visas to foreigners. **Budget:** $27.5 bil (2014); $26.5 bil (2015); $30.9 bil (est. 2016). Budget for other intl. programs: $18.7 bil (2014); $21.0 bil (2015); $16.0 bil (est. 2016).

- Intl. Boundary and Water Commission (4171 North Mesa, Ste. C-100, El Paso, TX 79902); www.ibwc.gov
- Intl. Information Programs (2201 C St. NW, SA-5, Rm. 5B17, 20520); www.state.gov/r/iip/
- Intl. Narcotics and Law Enforcement Affairs (2201 C St. NW, Rm. 7826 HST, 20520); www.state.gov/j/inl/
- Intl. Organization Affairs (2201 C St. NW, Rm. 6323, 20520); www.state.gov/p/io/
- Population, Refugees, and Migration (2201 C St. NW, Rm. 6825 HST, 20520); www.state.gov/j/prm/
- U.S. Global AIDS Coordinator (2201 C St. NW, Ste. 10300, SA-22, 20520); www.state.gov/s/gac/

Secretaries of State

President	Secretary	Home	Sworn in
Washington	Thomas Jefferson	VA	1789
	Edmund J. Randolph	VA	1794
	Timothy Pickering	PA	1795
Adams, J.	Timothy Pickering	PA	1797
	John Marshall	VA	1800
Jefferson	James Madison	VA	1801
Madison	Robert Smith	MD	1809
	James Monroe	VA	1811
Monroe	John Quincy Adams	MA	1817
Adams, J. Q.	Henry Clay	KY	1825
Jackson	Martin Van Buren	NY	1829
	Edward Livingston	LA	1831
	Louis McLane	DE	1833
	John Forsyth	GA	1834
Van Buren	John Forsyth	GA	1837
Harrison, W. H.	Daniel Webster	MA	1841
Tyler	Daniel Webster	MA	1841
	Abel P. Upshur	VA	1843
	John C. Calhoun	SC	1844
Polk	John C. Calhoun	SC	1845
	James Buchanan	PA	1845
Taylor	James Buchanan	PA	1849
	John M. Clayton	DE	1849
Fillmore	John M. Clayton	DE	1850
	Daniel Webster	MA	1850
	Edward Everett	MA	1852
Pierce	William L. Marcy	NY	1853
Buchanan	William L. Marcy	NY	1857
	Lewis Cass	MI	1857
	Jeremiah S. Black	PA	1860
Lincoln	Jeremiah S. Black	PA	1861
	William H. Seward	NY	1861
Johnson, A.	William H. Seward	NY	1865
Grant	Elihu B. Washburne	IL	1869
	Hamilton Fish	NY	1869
Hayes	Hamilton Fish	NY	1877
	William M. Evarts	NY	1877
Garfield	William M. Evarts	NY	1881
	James G. Blaine	ME	1881
Arthur	James G. Blaine	ME	1881
	F. T. Frelinghuysen	NJ	1881
Cleveland	F. T. Frelinghuysen	NJ	1885
	Thomas F. Bayard	DE	1885
Harrison, B.	Thomas F. Bayard	DE	1889
	James G. Blaine	ME	1889
	John W. Foster	IN	1892
Cleveland	Walter Q. Gresham	IN	1893
	Richard Olney	MA	1895
McKinley	Richard Olney	MA	1897
	John Sherman	OH	1897
	William R. Day	OH	1898
	John M. Hay	DC	1898

President	Secretary	Home	Sworn in
Roosevelt, T.	John M. Hay	DC	1901
	Elihu Root	NY	1905
	Robert Bacon	NY	1909
Taft	Robert Bacon	NY	1909
	Philander C. Knox	PA	1909
Wilson	Philander C. Knox	PA	1913
	William J. Bryan	NE	1913
	Robert Lansing	NY	1915
	Bainbridge Colby	NY	1920
Harding	Charles E. Hughes	NY	1921
Coolidge	Charles E. Hughes	NY	1923
	Frank B. Kellogg	MN	1925
Hoover	Frank B. Kellogg	MN	1929
	Henry L. Stimson	NY	1929
Roosevelt, F. D.	Cordell Hull	TN	1933
	Edward R. Stettinius Jr.	VA	1944
Truman	Edward R. Stettinius Jr.	VA	1945
	James F. Byrnes	SC	1945
	George C. Marshall	PA	1947
	Dean G. Acheson	CT	1949
Eisenhower	John Foster Dulles	NY	1953
	Christian A. Herter	MA	1959
Kennedy	D. Dean Rusk	NY	1961
Johnson, L. B.	D. Dean Rusk	NY	1963
Nixon	William P. Rogers	NY	1969
	Henry A. Kissinger	DC	1973
Ford	Henry A. Kissinger	DC	1974
Carter	Cyrus R. Vance	NY	1977
	Edmund S. Muskie	ME	1980
Reagan	Alexander M. Haig Jr.	CT	1981
	George P. Shultz	CA	1982
Bush, G. H. W.	James A. Baker III	TX	1989
	Lawrence S. Eagleburger	MI	1992
Clinton	Warren M. Christopher	CA	1993
	Madeleine K. Albright	DC	1997
Bush, G. W.	Colin L. Powell	NY	2001
	Condoleezza Rice	AL	2005
Obama	Hillary Rodham Clinton	NY	2009
	John Kerry	MA	2013

Department of the Treasury

1500 Pennsylvania Ave. NW, 20220; www.treasury.gov

Organized by act of Congress on Sept. 2, 1789. Responsible for the fiscal affairs of the U.S. Serves as the government's financial agent; collects, borrows, and disburses funds for the federal government. Monitors the nation's financial infrastructure and economic development; recommends domestic and international financial, monetary, economic, trade, and tax policies. Manufactures currency and coins. Carries out monetary and tax law enforcement activities, sanctions, embargoes, and fights illicit finance—counterfeiting, money laundering, narcotics trafficking, terrorist financing. **Budget** (including interest on the public debt): $446.9 bil (2014); $485.6 bil (2015); $540.4 bil (est. 2016).

- Alcohol and Tobacco Tax and Trade Bureau (1310 G St. NW, Box 12, 20005); www.ttb.gov
- Bureau of Engraving and Printing (14th and C Sts. SW, 20228); www.moneyfactory.gov
- Bureau of the Fiscal Service (401 14th St. SW, 20227); www.fiscal.treasury.gov
- Financial Crimes Enforcement Network (P.O. Box 39, Vienna, VA 22183); www.fincen.gov
- Internal Revenue Service (1111 Constitution Ave. NW, 20224); www.irs.gov
- U.S. Mint (801 9th St. NW, 20220); www.usmint.gov

Secretaries of the Treasury

President	Secretary	Home	Sworn in
Washington	Alexander Hamilton	NY	1789
	Oliver Wolcott Jr.	CT	1795
Adams, J.	Oliver Wolcott Jr.	CT	1797
	Samuel Dexter	MA	1801
Jefferson	Samuel Dexter	MA	1801
	Albert Gallatin	PA	1801
Madison	Albert Gallatin	PA	1809
	George W. Campbell	TN	1814
	Alexander J. Dallas	PA	1814
	William H. Crawford	GA	1816
Monroe	William H. Crawford	GA	1817
Adams, J. Q.	Richard Rush	PA	1825

President	Secretary	Home	Sworn in
Jackson	Samuel D. Ingham	PA	1829
	Louis McLane	DE	1831
	William J. Duane	PA	1833
	Roger B. Taney	MD	1833
	Levi Woodbury	NH	1834
Van Buren	Levi Woodbury	NH	1837
Harrison, W. H.	Thomas Ewing	OH	1841
Tyler	Thomas Ewing	OH	1841
	Walter Forward	PA	1841
	John C. Spencer	NY	1843
	George M. Bibb	KY	1844
Polk	Robert J. Walker	MS	1845
Taylor	William M. Meredith	PA	1849
Fillmore	Thomas Corwin	OH	1850
Pierce	James Guthrie	KY	1853
Buchanan	Howell Cobb	GA	1857
	Phillip F. Thomas	MD	1860
	John A. Dix	NY	1861
Lincoln	Salmon P. Chase	OH	1861
	William P. Fessenden	ME	1864
	Hugh McCulloch	IN	1865
Johnson, A.	Hugh McCulloch	IN	1865
Grant	George S. Boutwell	MA	1869
	William A. Richardson	MA	1873
	Benjamin H. Bristow	KY	1874
	Lot M. Morrill	ME	1876
Hayes	John Sherman	OH	1877
Garfield	William Windom	MN	1881
Arthur	Charles J. Folger	NY	1881
	Walter Q. Gresham	IN	1884
	Hugh McCulloch	IN	1884
Cleveland	Daniel Manning	NY	1885
	Charles S. Fairchild	NY	1887
Harrison, B.	William Windom	MN	1889
	Charles Foster	OH	1891
Cleveland	John G. Carlisle	KY	1893
McKinley	Lyman J. Gage	IL	1897
Roosevelt, T.	Lyman J. Gage	IL	1901
	Leslie M. Shaw	IA	1902
	George B. Cortelyou	NY	1907
Taft	Franklin MacVeagh	IL	1909
Wilson	William G. McAdoo	NY	1913
	Carter Glass	VA	1918
	David F. Houston	MO	1920
Harding	Andrew W. Mellon	PA	1921
Coolidge	Andrew W. Mellon	PA	1923
Hoover	Andrew W. Mellon	PA	1929
	Ogden L. Mills	NY	1932
Roosevelt, F. D.	William H. Woodin	NY	1933
	Henry Morgenthau Jr.	NY	1934
Truman	Fred M. Vinson	KY	1945
	John W. Snyder	MO	1946
Eisenhower	George M. Humphrey	OH	1953
	Robert B. Anderson	CT	1957
Kennedy	C. Douglas Dillon	NJ	1961
Johnson, L. B.	C. Douglas Dillon	NJ	1963
	Henry H. Fowler	VA	1965
	Joseph W. Barr	IN	1968
Nixon	David M. Kennedy	IL	1969
	John B. Connally	TX	1971
	George P. Shultz	IL	1972
	William E. Simon	NJ	1974
Ford	William E. Simon	NJ	1974
Carter	W. Michael Blumenthal	MI	1977
	G. William Miller	RI	1979
Reagan	Donald T. Regan	NY	1981
	James A. Baker III	TX	1985
	Nicholas F. Brady	NJ	1988
Bush, G. H. W.	Nicholas F. Brady	NJ	1989
Clinton	Lloyd M. Bentsen	TX	1993
	Robert E. Rubin	NY	1995
	Lawrence H. Summers	CT	1999
Bush, G. W.	Paul H. O'Neill	MO	2001
	John W. Snow	OH	2003
	Henry M. Paulson Jr.	FL	2006
Obama	Timothy F. Geithner	NY	2009
	Jack Lew	NY	2013

Department of Defense

1400 Defense Pentagon, 20301; www.defense.gov

The Dept. of Defense, originally designated the National Military Establishment, was created on Sept. 18, 1947. Directs and controls the armed forces and assists the president in protecting the nation's security. Military departments of the Army, Navy, and Air Force are each separately organized under its own secretary but all function under the command of the secretary of defense. They conduct military operations as unified commands. The chairman of the Joint Chiefs of Staff is the principal military adviser to the president. Undersecretaries supervise acquisition, technology, and logistics; intelligence; personnel and readiness; and policy. **Budget** for military programs: $577.9 bil (2014); $562.5 bil (2015); $576.3 bil (est. 2016). **Budget** for civil programs: $63.9 bil (2014); $69.7 bil (2015); $70.4 bil (est. 2016).

- Def. Advanced Research Projects Agency (675 N. Randolph St., Arlington, VA 22203); www.darpa.mil
- Def. Intelligence Agency (200 MacDill Blvd., 20340); www.dia.mil
- Def. Security Cooperation Agency (2800 Defense Pentagon, 20301); www.dsca.mil
- Missile Def. Agency (5700 18th St., Bldg. 245, Fort Belvoir, VA 22060-5573); www.mda.mil
- Natl. Geospatial-Intelligence Agency (7500 GEOINT Dr., Springfield, VA 22150); www.nga.mil
- Natl. Security Agency/Central Security Service (9800 Savage Rd., Ste. 6272, Ft. Meade, MD 20755); www.nsa.gov

Secretaries of Defense

President	Secretary	Home	Sworn in
Truman	James V. Forrestal	NY	1947
	Louis A. Johnson	WV	1949
	George C. Marshall	PA	1950
	Robert A. Lovett	NY	1951
Eisenhower	Charles E. Wilson	MI	1953
	Neil H. McElroy	OH	1957
	Thomas S. Gates Jr.	PA	1959
Kennedy	Robert S. McNamara	MI	1961
Johnson, L. B.	Robert S. McNamara	MI	1963
	Clark M. Clifford	MD	1968
Nixon	Melvin R. Laird	WI	1969
	Elliot L. Richardson	MA	1973
	James R. Schlesinger	VA	1973
Ford	James R. Schlesinger	VA	1974
	Donald H. Rumsfeld	IL	1975
Carter	Harold Brown	CA	1977
Reagan	Caspar W. Weinberger	CA	1981
	Frank C. Carlucci	PA	1987
Bush, G. H. W.	Richard B. Cheney	WY	1989
Clinton	Les Aspin	WI	1993
	William J. Perry	CA	1994
	William S. Cohen	ME	1997
Bush, G. W.	Donald H. Rumsfeld	IL	2001
	Robert M. Gates	TX	2006
Obama	Robert M. Gates	TX	2009
	Leon E. Panetta	CA	2011
	Chuck Hagel	NE	2013
	Ashton Carter	PA	2015

Secretaries of War

The War Dept. (which included jurisdiction over the Navy until 1798) was created by act of Congress on Aug. 7, 1789.

President	Secretary	Home	Sworn in
Washington	Henry Knox	MA	1789
	Timothy Pickering	PA	1795
	James McHenry	MD	1796
Adams, J.	James McHenry	MD	1797
	Samuel Dexter	MA	1800
Jefferson	Henry Dearborn	MA	1801
Madison	William Eustis	MA	1809
	John Armstrong	NY	1813
	James Monroe	VA	1814
	William H. Crawford	GA	1815
Monroe	John C. Calhoun	SC	1817
Adams, J. Q.	James Barbour	VA	1825
	Peter B. Porter	NY	1828
Jackson	John H. Eaton	TN	1829
	Lewis Cass	MI	1831
	Benjamin F. Butler	NY	1837
Van Buren	Joel R. Poinsett	SC	1837
Harrison, W. H.	John Bell	TN	1841
Tyler	John Bell	TN	1841
	John C. Spencer	NY	1841
	James M. Porter	PA	1843
	William Wilkins	PA	1844
Polk	William L. Marcy	NY	1845
Taylor	George W. Crawford	GA	1849
Fillmore	Charles M. Conrad	LA	1850
Pierce	Jefferson Davis	MS	1853

President	Secretary	Home	Sworn in
Buchanan	John B. Floyd	VA	1857
	Joseph Holt	KY	1861
Lincoln	Simon Cameron	PA	1861
	Edwin M. Stanton	PA	1862
Johnson, A.	Edwin M. Stanton	PA	1865
	John M. Schofield	IL	1868
Grant	John A. Rawlins	IL	1869
	William T. Sherman	OH	1869
	William W. Belknap	IA	1869
	Alphonso Taft	OH	1876
	James D. Cameron	PA	1876
Hayes	George W. McCrary	IA	1877
	Alexander Ramsey	MN	1879
Garfield	Robert T. Lincoln	IL	1881
Arthur	Robert T. Lincoln	IL	1881
Cleveland	William C. Endicott	MA	1885
Harrison, B.	Redfield Proctor	VT	1889
	Stephen B. Elkins	WV	1891
Cleveland	Daniel S. Lamont	NY	1893
McKinley	Russell A. Alger	MI	1897
	Elihu Root	NY	1899
Roosevelt, T.	Elihu Root	NY	1901
	William H. Taft	OH	1904
	Luke E. Wright	TN	1908
Taft	Jacob M. Dickinson	TN	1909
	Henry L. Stimson	NY	1911
Wilson	Lindley M. Garrison	NJ	1913
	Newton D. Baker	OH	1916
Harding	John W. Weeks	MA	1921
Coolidge	John W. Weeks	MA	1923
	Dwight F. Davis	MO	1925
Hoover	James W. Good	IL	1929
	Patrick J. Hurley	OK	1929
Roosevelt, F. D.	George H. Dern	UT	1933
	Harry H. Woodring	KS	1937
	Henry L. Stimson	NY	1940
Truman	Robert P. Patterson	NY	1945
	Kenneth C. Royall[1]	NC	1947

(1) Last member of Cabinet with this title. The War Dept. became the Dept. of the Army with the creation of the Defense Dept. in 1947, though the Army secretary maintained Cabinet-level status until 1949.

Secretaries of the Navy

The Navy Dept. was created by act of Congress on Apr. 30, 1798. The Marine Corps is part of this department.

President	Secretary	Home	Sworn in
Adams, J.	Benjamin Stoddert	MD	1798
Jefferson	Benjamin Stoddert	MD	1801
	Robert Smith	MD	1801
Madison	Paul Hamilton	SC	1809
	William Jones	PA	1813
	Benjamin W. Crowninshield	MA	1814
Monroe	Benjamin W. Crowninshield	MA	1817
	Smith Thompson	NY	1818
	Samuel L. Southard	NJ	1823
Adams, J. Q.	Samuel L. Southard	NJ	1825
Jackson	John Branch	NC	1829
	Levi Woodbury	NH	1831
	Mahlon Dickerson	NJ	1834
Van Buren	Mahlon Dickerson	NJ	1837
	James K. Paulding	NY	1838
Harrison, W. H.	George E. Badger	NC	1841
Tyler	George E. Badger	NC	1841
	Abel P. Upshur	VA	1841
	David Henshaw	MA	1843
	Thomas W. Gilmer	VA	1844
	John Y. Mason	VA	1844
Polk	George Bancroft	MA	1845
	John Y. Mason	VA	1846
Taylor	William B. Preston	VA	1849
Fillmore	William A. Graham	NC	1850
	John P. Kennedy	MD	1852
Pierce	James C. Dobbin	NC	1853
Buchanan	Isaac Toucey	CT	1857
Lincoln	Gideon Welles	CT	1861
Johnson, A.	Gideon Welles	CT	1865
Grant	Adolph E. Borie	PA	1869
	George M. Robeson	NJ	1869

President	Secretary	Home	Sworn in
Hayes	Richard W. Thompson	IN	1877
	Nathan Goff Jr.	WV	1881
Garfield	William H. Hunt	LA	1881
Arthur	William E. Chandler	NH	1882
Cleveland	William C. Whitney	NY	1885
Harrison, B.	Benjamin F. Tracy	NY	1889
Cleveland	Hilary A. Herbert	AL	1893
McKinley	John D. Long	MA	1897
Roosevelt, T.	John D. Long	MA	1901
	William H. Moody	MA	1902
	Paul Morton	IL	1904
	Charles J. Bonaparte	MD	1905
	Victor H. Metcalf	CA	1906
	Truman H. Newberry	MI	1908
Taft	George von L. Meyer	MA	1909
Wilson	Josephus Daniels	NC	1913
Harding	Edwin Denby	MI	1921
Coolidge	Edwin Denby	MI	1923
	Curtis D. Wilbur	CA	1924
Hoover	Charles Francis Adams	MA	1929
Roosevelt, F. D.	Claude A. Swanson	VA	1933
	Charles Edison	NJ	1940
	Frank Knox	IL	1940
	James V. Forrestal	NY	1944
Truman	James V. Forrestal[1]	NY	1945

(1) Last member of Cabinet with this title. The Navy Dept. became a branch of the Dept. of Defense when the latter was created in 1947, though the Navy secretary maintained Cabinet-level status until 1949.

Department of Justice

950 Pennsylvania Ave. NW, 20530; www.justice.gov

The Office of Attorney General was established by act of Congress on Sept. 24, 1789. It officially reached Cabinet rank in Mar. 1792, when the first attorney general, Edmund Randolph, attended his initial Cabinet meeting. The Dept. of Justice, headed by the attorney general, was created June 22, 1870. Provides for the enforcement of federal laws and investigation of violations; furnishes legal counsel in cases involving the federal government and interprets laws relating to the activities of other federal departments; supervises federal penal institutions. The attorney general and Office of Legal Counsel render legal advice, upon request, to the president and department heads. The solicitor general conducts all suits brought before the U.S. Supreme Court in which the federal government is concerned. The Civil Division represents the U.S. government in many civil or criminal matters. The 93 U.S. attorneys (for 94 federal districts) are the principal litigators in the U.S. and its territories. **Budget:** $28.6 bil (2014); $26.9 bil (2015); $39.1 bil (est. 2016).

- Bureau of Alcohol, Tobacco, Firearms and Explosives (99 New York Ave. NE, 20226); www.atf.gov
- Drug Enforcement Admin. (8701 Morrissette Dr., Springfield, VA 22152); www.dea.gov
- Executive Office for Immigration Review (5107 Leesburg Pike, Falls Church, VA 22041); www.justice.gov/eoir/
- Federal Bureau of Investigation (935 Pennsylvania Ave. NW, 20535); www.fbi.gov
- Federal Bureau of Prisons (320 First St. NW, 20534); www.bop.gov
- INTERPOL Washington (U.S. Natl. Central Bureau) (20530); www.justice.gov/interpol-washington/
- U.S. Marshals Service (20530-1000); www.usmarshals.gov
- U.S. Parole Commission (90 K St. NE, 3rd Fl., 20530); www.justice.gov/uspc/

Attorneys General

President	Attorney General	Home	Sworn in
Washington	Edmund J. Randolph	VA	1789
	William Bradford	PA	1794
	Charles Lee	VA	1795
Adams, J.	Charles Lee	VA	1797
Jefferson	Levi Lincoln	MA	1801
	John Breckenridge	KY	1805
	Caesar A. Rodney	DE	1807
Madison	Caesar A. Rodney	DE	1807
	William Pinkney	MD	1811
	Richard Rush	PA	1814
Monroe	Richard Rush	PA	1817
	William Wirt	VA	1817

President	Attorney General	Home	Sworn in
Adams, J. Q.	William Wirt	VA	1825
Jackson	John M. Berrien	GA	1829
	Roger B. Taney	MD	1831
	Benjamin F. Butler	NY	1833
Van Buren	Benjamin F. Butler	NY	1837
	Felix Grundy	TN	1838
	Henry D. Gilpin	PA	1840
Harrison, W. H.	John J. Crittenden	KY	1841
Tyler	John J. Crittenden	KY	1841
	Hugh S. Legaré	SC	1841
	John Nelson	MD	1843
Polk	John Y. Mason	VA	1845
	Nathan Clifford	ME	1846
	Isaac Toucey	CT	1848
Taylor	Reverdy Johnson	MD	1849
Fillmore	John J. Crittenden	KY	1850
Pierce	Caleb Cushing	MA	1853
Buchanan	Jeremiah S. Black	PA	1857
	Edwin M. Stanton	PA	1860
Lincoln	Edward Bates	MO	1861
	James Speed	KY	1864
Johnson, A.	James Speed	KY	1865
	Henry Stanbery	OH	1866
	William M. Evarts	NY	1868
Grant	Ebenezer R. Hoar	MA	1869
	Amos T. Akerman	GA	1870
	George H. Williams	OR	1871
	Edwards Pierrepont	NY	1875
	Alphonso Taft	OH	1876
Hayes	Charles Devens	MA	1877
Garfield	I. Wayne MacVeagh	PA	1881
Arthur	Benjamin H. Brewster	PA	1882
Cleveland	Augustus H. Garland	AR	1885
Harrison, B.	William H. H. Miller	IN	1889
Cleveland	Richard Olney	MA	1893
	Judson Harmon	OH	1895
McKinley	Joseph McKenna	CA	1897
	John W. Griggs	NJ	1898
	Philander C. Knox	PA	1901
Roosevelt, T.	Philander C. Knox	PA	1901
	William H. Moody	MA	1904
	Charles J. Bonaparte	MD	1906
Taft	George W. Wickersham	NY	1909
Wilson	James C. McReynolds	TN	1913
	Thomas W. Gregory	TX	1914
	A. Mitchell Palmer	PA	1919
Harding	Harry M. Daugherty	OH	1921
Coolidge	Harry M. Daugherty	OH	1923
	Harlan F. Stone	NY	1924
	John G. Sargent	VT	1925
Hoover	William D. Mitchell	MN	1929
Roosevelt, F. D.	Homer S. Cummings	CT	1933
	Frank Murphy	MI	1939
	Robert H. Jackson	NY	1940
	Francis Biddle	PA	1941
Truman	Thomas C. Clark	TX	1945
	J. Howard McGrath	RI	1949
	James P. McGranery	PA	1952
Eisenhower	Herbert Brownell Jr.	NY	1953
	William P. Rogers	MD	1957
Kennedy	Robert F. Kennedy	MA	1961
Johnson, L. B.	Robert F. Kennedy	MA	1963
	Nicholas Katzenbach	IL	1964
	W. Ramsey Clark	TX	1967
Nixon	John N. Mitchell	NY	1969
	Richard G. Kleindienst	AZ	1972
	Elliot L. Richardson	MA	1973
	William B. Saxbe	OH	1974
Ford	William B. Saxbe	OH	1974
	Edward H. Levi	IL	1975
Carter	Griffin B. Bell	GA	1977
	Benjamin R. Civiletti	MD	1979
Reagan	William French Smith	CA	1981
	Edwin Meese III	CA	1985
	Richard L. Thornburgh	PA	1988
Bush, G. H. W.	Richard L. Thornburgh	PA	1989
	William P. Barr	NY	1991
Clinton	Janet Reno	FL	1993
Bush, G. W.	John Ashcroft	MO	2001
	Alberto R. Gonzales	TX	2005
	Michael B. Mukasey	NY	2007
Obama	Eric H. Holder Jr.	DC	2009
	Loretta E. Lynch	NY	2015

Department of the Interior

1849 C St. NW, 20240; www.doi.gov

Created by act of Congress on Mar. 3, 1849. Custodian of natural resources. Has the responsibility of protecting and conserving the country's land, water, minerals, fish, and wildlife; of promoting the wise use of all these natural resources; of maintaining national parks and recreation areas; and of preserving historic places. It also provides for the welfare of American Indian reservation communities and of inhabitants of island territories under U.S. administration. **Budget:** $11.3 bil (2014); $12.3 bil (2015); $14.0 bil (est. 2016).

- Bureau of Indian Affairs (MS-3658-MIB, 1849 C St. NW, 20240); www.indianaffairs.gov
- Bureau of Land Management (1849 C St. NW, 20240); www.blm.gov
- Bureau of Ocean Energy Management (1849 C St. NW, 20240); www.boem.gov
- Bureau of Reclamation (1849 C St. NW, 20240); www.usbr.gov
- Bureau of Safety and Environmental Enforcement (1849 C St. NW, 20240); www.bsee.gov
- National Park Service (1849 C St. NW, 20240); www.nps.gov
- Office of Surface Mining Reclamation and Enforcement (1951 Constitution Ave. NW, 20240); www.osmre.gov
- U.S. Fish and Wildlife Service (1849 C St. NW, 20240); www.fws.gov
- U.S. Geological Survey (12201 Sunrise Valley Dr., Reston, VA 20192; www.usgs.gov

Secretaries of the Interior

President	Secretary	Home	Sworn in
Taylor	Thomas Ewing	OH	1849
Fillmore	Thomas M. T. McKennan	PA	1850
	Alex H. H. Stuart	VA	1850
Pierce	Robert McClelland	MI	1853
Buchanan	Jacob Thompson	MS	1857
Lincoln	Caleb B. Smith	IN	1861
	John P. Usher	IN	1863
Johnson, A.	John P. Usher	IN	1865
	James Harlan	IA	1865
	Orville H. Browning	IL	1866
Grant	Jacob D. Cox	OH	1869
	Columbus Delano	OH	1870
	Zachariah Chandler	MI	1875
Hayes	Carl Schurz	MO	1877
Garfield	Samuel J. Kirkwood	IA	1881
Arthur	Henry M. Teller	CO	1882
Cleveland	Lucius Q. C. Lamar	MS	1885
	William F. Vilas	WI	1888
Harrison, B.	John W. Noble	MO	1889
Cleveland	M. Hoke Smith	GA	1893
	David R. Francis	MO	1896
McKinley	Cornelius N. Bliss	NY	1897
	Ethan A. Hitchcock	MO	1898
Roosevelt, T.	Ethan A. Hitchcock	MO	1901
	James R. Garfield	OH	1907
Taft	Richard A. Ballinger	WA	1909
	Walter L. Fisher	IL	1911
Wilson	Franklin K. Lane	CA	1913
	John B. Payne	IL	1920
Harding	Albert B. Fall	NM	1921
	Hubert Work	CO	1923
Coolidge	Hubert Work	CO	1923
	Roy O. West	IL	1929
Hoover	Ray Lyman Wilbur	CA	1929
Roosevelt, F. D.	Harold L. Ickes	IL	1933
Truman	Harold L. Ickes	IL	1945
	Julius A. Krug	WI	1946
	Oscar L. Chapman	CO	1949
Eisenhower	Douglas McKay	OR	1953
	Fred A. Seaton	NE	1956
Kennedy	Stewart L. Udall	AZ	1961
Johnson, L. B.	Stewart L. Udall	AZ	1963
Nixon	Walter J. Hickel	AK	1969
	Rogers C. B. Morton	MD	1971
Ford	Rogers C. B. Morton	MD	1971
	Stanley K. Hathaway	WY	1975
	Thomas S. Kleppe	ND	1975
Carter	Cecil D. Andrus	ID	1977
Reagan	James G. Watt	CO	1981
	William P. Clark	CA	1983
	Donald P. Hodel	OR	1985
Bush, G. H. W.	Manuel Lujan	NM	1989
Clinton	Bruce Babbitt	AZ	1993
Bush, G. W.	Gale Norton	CO	2001
	Dirk Kempthorne	ID	2006
Obama	Kenneth L. Salazar	CO	2009
	Sally Jewell	WA	2013

Department of Agriculture

1400 Independence Ave. SW, 20250; www.usda.gov

Created by act of Congress on May 15, 1862. On Feb. 8, 1889, its commissioner was renamed secretary of agriculture and became a member of the Cabinet. Provides leadership on food, agriculture, and natural resources; supports scientific research and education for agriculture, nutrition, and food safety. Develops nutrition assistance programs, promotes healthy eating, supplies food stamps, grades and inspects the commercial supply of food. Responsible for the health of the land through sustainable management and conservation, manages public lands in national forests and grasslands; safeguards against invasive pests and diseases; ensures the health and care of animals and plants. Oversees assistance and conservation programs for farmers and ranchers and programs to improve the rural economy and quality of life. Facilitates domestic and international marketing of U.S. agricultural products. **Budget:** $141.8 bil (2014); $139.1 bil (2015); $153.8 bil (est. 2016).

- Agricultural Research Service (1400 Independence Ave. SW, 20250); www.ars.usda.gov
- Economic Research Service (1400 Independence Ave. SW, Mail Stop 1800, 20250); www.ers.usda.gov
- Food and Nutrition Service (3101 Park Center Dr., Alexandria, VA 22302); www.fns.usda.gov
- Food Safety and Inspection Service (1400 Independence Ave. SW, 20250); www.fsis.usda.gov
- Foreign Agricultural Service (1400 Independence Ave. SW, Mail Stop 1001, 20250); www.fas.usda.gov
- Forest Service (1400 Independence Ave. SW, 20250); www.fs.fed.us
- Natl. Agricultural Statistics Service (1400 Independence Ave. SW, 20250); www.nass.usda.gov
- Natural Resources Conservation Service (1400 Independence Ave. SW, 20250); www.nrcs.usda.gov

Secretaries of Agriculture

President	Secretary	Home	Sworn in
Cleveland	Norman J. Colman	MO	1889
Harrison, B.	Jeremiah M. Rusk	WI	1889
Cleveland	J. Sterling Morton	NE	1893
McKinley	James Wilson	IA	1897
Roosevelt, T.	James Wilson	IA	1901
Taft	James Wilson	IA	1909
Wilson	David F. Houston	MO	1913
	Edwin T. Meredith	IA	1920
Harding	Henry C. Wallace	IA	1921
Coolidge	Henry C. Wallace	IA	1923
	Howard M. Gore	WV	1924
	William M. Jardine	KS	1925
Hoover	Arthur M. Hyde	MO	1929
Roosevelt, F. D.	Henry A. Wallace	IA	1933
	Claude R. Wickard	IN	1940
Truman	Clinton P. Anderson	NM	1945
	Charles F. Brannan	CO	1948
Eisenhower	Ezra Taft Benson	UT	1953
Kennedy	Orville L. Freeman	MN	1961
Johnson, L. B.	Orville L. Freeman	MN	1963
Nixon	Clifford M. Hardin	IN	1969
	Earl L. Butz	IN	1971
Ford	Earl L. Butz	IN	1974
	John A. Knebel	VA	1976
Carter	Bob Bergland	MN	1977
Reagan	John R. Block	IL	1981
	Richard E. Lyng	CA	1986
Bush, G. H. W.	Clayton K. Yeutter	NE	1989
	Edward Madigan	IL	1991
Clinton	Mike Espy	MS	1993
	Dan Glickman	KS	1995
Bush, G. W.	Ann M. Veneman	CA	2001
	Mike Johanns	NE	2005
	Ed Schafer	ND	2008
Obama	Thomas J. Vilsack	IA	2009

Department of Commerce

1401 Constitution Ave. NW, 20230; www.commerce.gov

The Dept. of Commerce was formed by Congress Mar. 4, 1913, when it divided the Dept. of Commerce and Labor into two departments. Fosters, serves, and promotes the nation's economic development and technological advancement; supports the comprehension and use of the environment and its oceanic life; assists states, communities, and individuals with economic progress; promotes trade abroad and ensures an effective export control and treaty compliance system. Issues trademarks and patents, maintains measurement standards, and manages the federal telecommunications spectrum. Collects, analyzes, and distributes statistics regarding the nation and the economy through the Bureaus of the Census and of Economic Analysis. NOAA explores, monitors, and conserves oceans and coasts, tracks weather and other environmental data. **Budget:** $7.9 bil (2014); $9.0 bil (2015); $10.5 bil (est. 2016).

- Bureau of the Census (4600 Silver Hill Rd., 20233); www.census.gov
- Bureau of Economic Analysis (4600 Silver Hill Rd., 20233); www.bea.gov
- Minority Business Development Agency (1401 Constitution Ave. NW, 20230); www.mbda.gov
- Natl. Institute of Standards and Technology (100 Bureau Dr., Stop 1070, Gaithersburg, MD 20899); www.nist.gov
- Natl. Oceanic and Atmospheric Admin. (1401 Constitution Ave. NW, Rm. 5128, 20230); www.noaa.gov
- Natl. Technical Information Service (5301 Shawnee Rd., Alexandria, VA 22312); www.ntis.gov
- Natl. Telecommunications and Information Admin. (1401 Constitution Ave. NW, 20230); www.ntia.doc.gov

Secretaries of Commerce

President	Secretary	Home	Sworn in
Wilson	William C. Redfield	NY	1913
	Joshua W. Alexander	MO	1919
Harding	Herbert C. Hoover	CA	1921
Coolidge	Herbert C. Hoover	CA	1923
	William F. Whiting	MA	1928
Hoover	Robert P. Lamont	IL	1929
	Roy D. Chapin	MI	1932
Roosevelt, F. D.	Daniel C. Roper	SC	1933
	Harry L. Hopkins	NY	1939
	Jesse H. Jones	TX	1940
	Henry A. Wallace	IA	1945
Truman	Henry A. Wallace	IA	1945
	W. Averell Harriman	NY	1947
	Charles W. Sawyer	OH	1948
Eisenhower	Sinclair Weeks	MA	1953
	Lewis L. Strauss	NY	1958
	Frederick H. Mueller	MI	1959
Kennedy	Luther H. Hodges	NC	1961
Johnson, L. B.	Luther H. Hodges	NC	1963
	John T. Connor	NJ	1965
	Alex B. Trowbridge	NJ	1967
	Cyrus R. Smith	NY	1968
Nixon	Maurice H. Stans	MN	1969
	Peter G. Peterson	IL	1972
	Frederick B. Dent	SC	1973
Ford	Frederick B. Dent	SC	1974
	Rogers C. B. Morton	MD	1975
	Elliot L. Richardson	MA	1975
Carter	Juanita M. Kreps	NC	1977
	Philip M. Klutznick	IL	1979
Reagan	Malcolm Baldrige	CT	1981
	C. William Verity Jr.	OH	1987
Bush, G. H. W.	Robert A. Mosbacher	TX	1989
	Barbara H. Franklin	PA	1992
Clinton	Ronald H. Brown	DC	1993
	Mickey Kantor	CA	1996
	William M. Daley	IL	1997
	Norman Y. Mineta	CA	2000
Bush, G. W.	Donald L. Evans	TX	2001
	Carlos M. Gutierrez	MI	2005
Obama	Gary F. Locke	WA	2009
	John Bryson	CA	2011
	Penny Pritzker	IL	2013

Secretaries of Commerce and Labor

The Dept. of Commerce and Labor was created by Congress on Feb. 14, 1903.

President	Secretary	Home	Sworn in
Roosevelt, T.	George B. Cortelyou	NY	1903
	Victor H. Metcalf	CA	1904
	Oscar S. Straus	NY	1906
Taft	Charles Nagel	MO	1909

Department of Labor

200 Constitution Ave. NW, 20210; www.dol.gov

The Dept. of Labor was formed by Congress Mar. 4, 1913, when it divided the Dept. of Commerce and Labor into two departments. Administers federal labor laws to foster, promote, and develop the welfare of job seekers, wage earners, and retirees of the U.S.; to improve working conditions; and to advance opportunities for profitable employment. Administers standards for wages and overtime pay, safety and health conditions, workers' compensation. Tracks changes in employment, prices, and other national economic measurements. Regulates pension and welfare benefit plans, the hiring and employment of migrant and seasonal workers, and requirements pertaining to the mining, construction, and transportation industries. Monitors labor unions and their funds. **Budget:** $56.8 bil (2014); $45.2 bil (2015); $43.5 bil (est. 2016).

- Bureau of Labor Statistics (2 Massachusetts Ave. NE, 20212); www.bls.gov
- Employment and Training Admin. (200 Constitution Ave. NW, 20210); www.doleta.gov
- Mine Safety and Health Admin. (201 12th St. S, Ste. 401, Arlington, VA 22202); www.msha.gov
- Occupational Safety and Health Admin. (200 Constitution Ave. NW, 20210); www.osha.gov
- Office of Federal Contract Compliance Programs (200 Constitution Ave. NW, 20210); www.dol.gov/ofccp/
- Office of Labor-Management Standards (200 Constitution Ave. NW, 20210); www.dol.gov/olms/
- Office of Workers' Compensation Programs (200 Constitution Ave. NW, 20210); www.dol.gov/owcp/
- Wage and Hour Div. (200 Constitution Ave. NW, 20210); www.dol.gov/whd/

Secretaries of Labor

President	Secretary	Home	Sworn in
Wilson	William B. Wilson	PA	1913
Harding	James J. Davis	PA	1921
Coolidge	James J. Davis	PA	1923
Hoover	James J. Davis	PA	1929
	William N. Doak	VA	1930
Roosevelt, F. D.	Frances Perkins	NY	1933
Truman	L. B. Schwellenbach	WA	1945
	Maurice J. Tobin	MA	1949
Eisenhower	Martin P. Durkin	IL	1953
	James P. Mitchell	NJ	1953
Kennedy	Arthur J. Goldberg	IL	1961
	W. Willard Wirtz	IL	1962
Johnson, L. B.	W. Willard Wirtz	IL	1963
Nixon	George P. Shultz	IL	1969
	James D. Hodgson	CA	1970
	Peter J. Brennan	NY	1973
Ford	Peter J. Brennan	NY	1974
	John T. Dunlop	CA	1975
	W. J. Usery Jr.	GA	1976
Carter	F. Ray Marshall	TX	1977
Reagan	Raymond J. Donovan	NJ	1981
	William E. Brock	TN	1985
	Ann D. McLaughlin	DC	1987
Bush, G. H. W.	Elizabeth H. Dole	NC	1989
	Lynn Martin	IL	1991
Clinton	Robert B. Reich	MA	1993
	Alexis M. Herman	AL	1997
Bush, G. W.	Elaine L. Chao	KY	2001
Obama	Hilda L. Solis	CA	2009
	Thomas E. Perez	MD	2013

Department of Housing and Urban Development

451 7th St. SW, 20410; www.hud.gov

Created by act of Congress on Sept. 9, 1965. Responsible for housing needs and the improvement and development of urban areas. Supports affordable housing, provides grants for community development and redevelopment. Enforces fair and safe housing standards. Provides funds to assist homeless individuals and families with emergency and transitional shelters. The Federal Housing Administration provides mortgage insurance on loans made by approved lenders. **Budget:** $38.5 bil (2014); $35.5 bil (2015); $28.7 bil (est. 2016).

- Fannie Mae (Federal Natl. Mortgage Association) (3900 Wisconsin Ave. NW, 20016); www.fanniemae.com
- Federal Housing Admin. (451 7th St. SW, 20410); www.fha.gov
- Freddie Mac (Federal Home Loan Mortgage Corporation) (8200 Jones Branch Dr., McLean, VA 22102); www.freddiemac.com
- Ginnie Mae (Government Natl. Mortgage Association) (451 7th St. SW, Rm. B-133, 20410); www.ginniemae.gov

Note: Fannie Mae and Freddie Mac are government-sponsored enterprises (GSEs).

Secretaries of Housing and Urban Development

President	Secretary	Home	Sworn in
Johnson, L. B.	Robert C. Weaver	WA	1966
	Robert C. Wood	MA	1969
Nixon	George W. Romney	MI	1969
	James T. Lynn	OH	1973
Ford	James T. Lynn	OH	1974
	Carla Anderson Hills	CA	1975
Carter	Patricia Roberts Harris	DC	1977
	Moon Landrieu	LA	1979
Reagan	Samuel R. Pierce Jr.	NY	1981
Bush, G. H. W.	Jack F. Kemp	NY	1989
Clinton	Henry G. Cisneros	TX	1993
	Andrew M. Cuomo	NY	1997
Bush, G. W.	Mel Martinez	FL	2001
	Alphonso Jackson	TX	2004
	Steve Preston	VA	2008
Obama	Shaun L. S. Donovan	NY	2009
	Julián Castro	TX	2014

Department of Transportation

1200 New Jersey Ave. SE, 20590; www.transportation.gov

Created by act of Congress on Oct. 15, 1966. Promotes and develops rapid, safe, efficient, and convenient transportation in the U.S.; monitors and administers assistance to transportation industries; negotiates and implements international transportation agreements. Manages airspace, commercial space transportation, and the movement of hazardous materials. Resolves railroad rate and service disputes and reviews proposed railroad mergers. Analyzes and shares research and statistics to develop and improve transportation. Develops and enforces regulations on the nation's pipeline transportation system. The Maritime Administration maintains a fleet of cargo ships in reserve for war or national emergencies and commissions officers of the Merchant Marine. Operates the U.S. portion of the St. Lawrence Seaway between Montréal and Lake Erie. **Budget:** $76.2 bil (2014); $75.4 bil (2015); $77.8 bil (est. 2016).

- Federal Aviation Admin. (800 Independence Ave. SW, 20591); www.faa.gov
- Federal Highway Admin. (1200 New Jersey Ave. SE, 20590); www.fhwa.dot.gov
- Federal Railroad Admin. (1200 New Jersey Ave. SE, 20590); www.fra.dot.gov
- Federal Transit Admin. (1200 New Jersey Ave. SE, 20590); www.fta.dot.gov
- Maritime Admin. (1200 New Jersey Ave. SE, 20590); www.marad.dot.gov
- Natl. Highway Traffic Safety Admin. (1200 New Jersey Ave. SE, 20590); www.nhtsa.gov
- Office of the Asst. Sec. for Research and Technology (1200 New Jersey Ave. SE, 20590); www.rita.dot.gov

Secretaries of Transportation

President	Secretary	Home	Sworn in
Johnson, L. B.	Alan S. Boyd	FL	1966
Nixon	John A. Volpe	MA	1969
	Claude S. Brinegar	CA	1973
Ford	Claude S. Brinegar	CA	1974
	William T. Coleman Jr.	PA	1975
Carter	Brock Adams	WA	1977
	Neil E. Goldschmidt	OR	1979
Reagan	Andrew L. Lewis Jr.	PA	1981
	Elizabeth H. Dole	NC	1983
	James H. Burnley	NC	1987
Bush, G. H. W.	Samuel K. Skinner	IL	1989
	Andrew H. Card Jr.	MA	1992
Clinton	Federico F. Peña	CO	1993
	Rodney E. Slater	AR	1997
Bush, G. W.	Norman Y. Mineta	CA	2001
	Mary E. Peters	AZ	2006
Obama	Raymond L. LaHood	IL	2009
	Anthony Foxx	NC	2013

Department of Energy

1000 Independence Ave. SW, 20585; energy.gov

Created by federal law on Aug. 4, 1977. Secures the nation's energy and promotes scientific and technological innovation. Oversees the national energy supply and electric grid. Investigates and promotes clean and reliable energy. Manages and cleans up nuclear and other radioactive material, including nuclear weapons. The Office of Scientific and Technical Information supports much of America's scientific research through program offices, education initiatives, national laboratories, and technology centers. Four power marketing administrations sell power from federal hydroelectric projects across the West and Southeast. **Budget:** $23.6 bil (2014); $25.4 bil (2015); $27.4 bil (est. 2016).

- Energy Information Admin. (1000 Independence Ave. SW, 20585); www.eia.gov
- Federal Energy Regulatory Commission (independent regulatory agency) (888 1st St. NE, 20426); www.ferc.gov
- Natl. Nuclear Security Admin. (1000 Independence Ave. SW, 20585); www.nnsa.energy.gov
- Office of Scientific and Technical Information (P.O. Box 62, Oak Ridge, TN 37831); www.osti.gov

Secretaries of Energy

President	Secretary	Home	Sworn in
Carter	James R. Schlesinger	VA	1977
	Charles W. Duncan Jr.	WY	1979
Reagan	James B. Edwards	SC	1981
	Donald P. Hodel	OR	1982
	John S. Herrington	CA	1985
Bush, G. H. W.	James D. Watkins	CA	1989
Clinton	Hazel R. O'Leary	MN	1993
	Federico F. Peña	CO	1997
	Bill Richardson	NM	1998
Bush, G. W.	Spencer Abraham	MI	2001
	Samuel W. Bodman	MA	2005
Obama	Steven Chu	CA	2009
	Ernest Moniz	MA	2013

Department of Health and Human Services

200 Independence Ave. SW, 20201; www.hhs.gov

The Dept. of Health, Education, and Welfare was created by Congress on Apr. 11, 1953. On Sept. 27, 1979, Congress approved creation of a separate Dept. of Education. The existing department was renamed the Dept. of Health and Human Services. Administers a wide range of programs in the fields of health care and social services that affect nearly all Americans. Medicare and Medicaid provide health care insurance for one in four Americans. The HRSA improves health care services for people who are uninsured, isolated, or medically vulnerable; oversees organ, tissue, and blood cell donations. The FDA assures the safety of food, drugs, cosmetics, biological products, and medical devices. The CDC monitors and safeguards against disease outbreaks. The NIH supports research projects nationwide and 27 health institutes and centers. The surgeon general is the nation's chief health educator and leads the U.S. Public Health Service Commissioned Corps. **Budget:** $936.0 bil (2014); $1.0 tril (2015); $1.1 tril (est. 2016).

- Agency for Healthcare Research and Quality (5600 Fishers Ln., 7th Fl., Rockville, MD 20857); www.ahrq.gov
- Centers for Disease Control and Prevention (1600 Clifton Rd., Atlanta, GA 30329); www.cdc.gov
- Centers for Medicare and Medicaid Services (7500 Security Blvd., Baltimore, MD 21244); www.cms.gov
- Food and Drug Admin. (10903 New Hampshire Ave., Silver Spring, MD 20993); www.fda.gov
- Health Resources and Services Admin. (5600 Fishers Ln., Rockville, MD 20857); www.hrsa.gov
- Natl. Institutes of Health (9000 Rockville Pike, Bethesda, MD 20892); www.nih.gov
- Office of the Surgeon General (Tower Bldg., Plaza Level 1, Rm. 100, 1101 Wootton Pkwy., Rockville, MD 20852); www.surgeongeneral.gov

Secretaries of Health and Human Services

President	Secretary	Home	Sworn in
Carter	Patricia Roberts Harris	DC	1979
Reagan	Richard S. Schweiker	PA	1981
	Margaret M. Heckler	MA	1983
Reagan	Otis R. Bowen	IN	1985
Bush, G. H. W.	Louis W. Sullivan	GA	1989
Clinton	Donna E. Shalala	WI	1993
Bush, G. W.	Tommy Thompson	WI	2001
	Michael O. Leavitt	UT	2005
Obama	Kathleen Sebelius	KS	2009
	Sylvia Mathews Burwell	WV	2014

Secretaries of Health, Education, and Welfare

President	Secretary	Home	Sworn in
Eisenhower	Oveta Culp Hobby	TX	1953
	Marion B. Folsom	NY	1955
	Arthur S. Flemming	OH	1958
Kennedy	Abraham A. Ribicoff	CT	1961
	Anthony J. Celebrezze	OH	1962
Johnson, L. B.	Anthony J. Celebrezze	OH	1963
	John W. Gardner	NY	1965
	Wilbur J. Cohen	MI	1968
Nixon	Robert H. Finch	CA	1969
	Elliot L. Richardson	MA	1970
	Caspar W. Weinberger	CA	1973
Ford	Caspar W. Weinberger	CA	1974
	Forrest D. Mathews	AL	1975
Carter	Joseph A. Califano Jr.	DC	1977
	Patricia Roberts Harris	DC	1979

Department of Education

400 Maryland Ave. SW, 20202; www.ed.gov

The Dept. of Health, Education, and Welfare was created by Congress on Apr. 11, 1953. On Sept. 27, 1979, Congress approved creation of a separate Dept. of Education. Works with state agencies and local systems to ensure equal access to all levels of education and seeks to improve the quality of that education through federal support, research programs, and information sharing. Oversees a variety of financial aid distributed through competition, need-based requests, or a set formula. Sets policy goals and initiatives like No Child Left Behind. Conducts research and gathers educational information to disseminate to educators and the general public. **Budget:** $59.6 bil (2014); $90.0 bil (2015); $79.1 bil (est. 2016).

Secretaries of Education

President	Secretary	Home	Sworn in
Carter	Shirley Hufstedler	CA	1979
Reagan	Terrel H. Bell	UT	1981
	William J. Bennett	NY	1985
	Lauro F. Cavazos	TX	1988
Bush, G. H. W.	Lauro F. Cavazos	TX	1989
	Lamar Alexander	TN	1991
Clinton	Richard W. Riley	SC	1993
Bush, G. W.	Roderick R. Paige	TX	2001
	Margaret Spellings	TX	2005
Obama	Arne Duncan	IL	2009
	John King	NY	2016

Department of Veterans Affairs

810 Vermont Ave. NW, 20420; www.va.gov

Pres. Ronald Reagan signed a bill in 1988 granting Cabinet-level status to the Veterans Administration. The agency became the Dept. of Veterans Affairs on Mar. 15, 1989. Supports veterans and their families with nationwide programs for health care, financial assistance, and burial benefits. Compensates for disabilities incurred during wartime. Provides pensions for veterans with low incomes, education assistance, loan guaranty, and life insurance. Manages America's largest medical education and health professions training program, which includes hospitals, clinics, nursing homes, veterans centers, rehabilitation treatment, readjustment counseling, and home-care programs. Also funds medical research pertaining to veterans issues. Manages 131 national cemeteries; provides headstones and markers. **Budget:** $149.1 bil (2014); $159.2 bil (2015); $177.6 bil (est. 2016).

Secretaries of Veterans Affairs

President	Secretary	Home	Sworn in
Bush, G. H. W.	Edward J. Derwinski	IL	1989
Clinton	Jesse Brown	IL	1993
	Togo D. West Jr.	NC	1998
Bush, G. W.	Anthony J. Principi	CA	2001
	R. James Nicholson	CO	2005
	James B. Peake	MO	2007
Obama	Eric K. Shinseki	VA	2009
	Robert A. McDonald	OH	2014

Department of Homeland Security

20528 (requires no street address); www.dhs.gov

Created by act of Congress on Nov. 25, 2002. Provides a unified core for the national network of organizations and institutions involved in efforts to secure the U.S., its borders, infrastructure, and major events. Provides funding, intelligence, and training for law enforcement and disaster relief. Leads and coordinates response teams to natural and manmade emergencies. Identifies threats, administers the Natl. Terrorism Advisory System. **Budget:** $43.3 bil (2014); $42.6 bil (2015); $51.8 bil (est. 2016).

- Fed. Emergency Management Agency (500 C St. SW, 20472); www.fema.gov
- Immigration and Customs Enforcement (500 12th St. SW, 20536); www.ice.gov
- Transportation Security Admin. (601 S. 12th St., Arlington, VA 20598); www.tsa.gov
- U.S. Citizenship and Immigration Services (20 Massachusetts Ave. NW, 20529); www.uscis.gov
- U.S. Coast Guard (2703 Martin Luther King Jr. Ave. SE, 20593); www.uscg.mil

- U.S. Customs and Border Protection (1300 Pennsylvania Ave. NW, 20229); www.cbp.gov
- U.S. Fire Admin. (16825 S. Seton Ave., Emmitsburg, MD 21727); www.usfa.fema.gov
- U.S. Secret Service (245 Murray Ln., 20223); www.secretservice.gov

Secretaries of Homeland Security

President	Secretary	Home	Sworn in
Bush, G. W.	Thomas Ridge	PA	2003
	Michael Chertoff	NJ	2005
Obama	Janet A. Napolitano	AZ	2009
	Jeh Johnson	NY	2014

Other Notable U.S. Government Agencies

Source: *The U.S. Government Manual*; National Archives and Records Administration; World Almanac research
All addresses are for Washington, DC, unless otherwise noted; as of Aug. 2016.

Administrative Conference of the U.S.: chair vacant (1120 20th St. NW, Ste. 706S, 20036); www.acus.gov
African Development Foundation: C. D. Glin, pres. and CEO (1400 I St. NW, 20005); www.usadf.gov
AMTRAK: Joseph H. Boardman, pres. and CEO (60 Massachusetts Ave. NE, 20002); www.amtrak.com
Broadcasting Board of Governors: Jeff Shell, chair (330 Independence Ave. SW, 20237); www.bbg.gov
Central Intelligence Agency: John O. Brennan, dir. (20505); www.cia.gov
Commodity Futures Trading Commission: Timothy G. Massad, chair (3 Lafayette Centre, 1155 21st St. NW, 20581); www.cftc.gov
Consumer Financial Protection Bureau: Rich Cordray, dir. (P.O. Box 4503, Iowa City, IA 52244); www.consumerfinance.gov
Consumer Product Safety Commission: Elliot F. Kaye, chair (4330 East-West Hwy., Bethesda, MD 20814); www.cpsc.gov
Corp. for Natl. and Community Service: Wendy Spencer, CEO (250 E St. SW, 20525); www.nationalservice.gov
Court Services and Offender Supervision Agency for DC: Nancy M. Ware, dir. (633 Indiana Ave. NW, 20004); www.csosa.gov
Defense Nuclear Facilities Safety Board: Joyce L. Connery, chair (625 Indiana Ave. NW, Ste. 700, 20004); www.dnfsb.gov
Election Assistance Commission: Thomas Hicks, chair (1335 East-West Hwy., Ste. 4300, Silver Spring, MD 20910); www.eac.gov
Environmental Protection Agency: Gina McCarthy, admin. (Cabinet rank) (1200 Pennsylvania Ave. NW, 20460); www.epa.gov
Equal Employment Opportunity Commission: Jenny R. Yang, chair (131 M St. NE, 20507); www.eeoc.gov
Export-Import Bank of the U.S.: Fred P. Hochberg, pres. and chair (811 Vermont Ave. NW, 20571); www.exim.gov
Farm Credit Admin.: Kenneth A. Spearman, chair and CEO (1501 Farm Credit Dr., McLean, VA 22102); www.fca.gov
Federal Communications Commission: Tom Wheeler, chair (445 12th St. SW, 20554); www.fcc.gov
Federal Deposit Insurance Corp.: Martin J. Gruenberg, chair (550 17th St. NW, 20429); www.fdic.gov
Federal Election Commission: Matthew S. Petersen, chair (999 E St. NW, 20463); www.fec.gov
Federal Housing Finance Agency: Melvin L. Watt, dir. (400 7th St. SW, 20219); www.fhfa.gov
Federal Labor Relations Authority: Carol Waller Pope, chair (1400 K St. NW, 20424); www.flra.gov
Federal Maritime Commission: Mario Cordero, chair (800 N. Capitol St. NW, 20573); www.fmc.gov
Federal Mediation and Conciliation Service: Allison Beck, dir. (2100 K St. NW, 20427); www.fmcs.gov
Federal Mine Safety and Health Review Commission: Mary Lu Jordan, chair (1331 Pennsylvania Ave. NW, Ste. 520N, 20004); www.fmshrc.gov
Federal Reserve System: Janet L. Yellen, chair (20th St. and Constitution Ave. NW, 20551); www.federalreserve.gov
Federal Retirement Thrift Investment Board: Michael Kennedy, chair (77 K St. NE, 20002); www.frtib.gov
Federal Trade Commission: Edith Ramirez, chair (600 Pennsylvania Ave. NW, 20580); www.ftc.gov
General Services Admin.: Denise Turner Roth, admin. (1800 F St. NW, 20405); www.gsa.gov
Institute of Museum and Library Services: Kathryn K. Matthew, dir. (955 L'Enfant Plaza North SW, Ste. 4000, 20024); www.imls.gov
Inter-American Foundation: Robert N. Kaplan, pres. and CEO (1331 Pennsylvania Ave. NW, Ste. 1200N, 20004); www.iaf.gov
Merit Systems Protection Board: Susan Tsui Grundmann, chair (1615 M St. NW, 20419); www.mspb.gov
Natl. Aeronautics and Space Admin.: Charles F. Bolden Jr., admin. (300 E Street SW, Ste. 5R30, 20546); www.nasa.gov

Natl. Archives and Records Admin.: David S. Ferriero, archivist (8601 Adelphi Rd., College Park, MD 20740); www.archives.gov
Natl. Capital Planning Commission: L. Preston Bryant Jr., chair (401 9th St. NW, N. Lobby, Ste. 500, 20004); www.ncpc.gov
Natl. Council on Disability: Clyde E. Terry, chair (1331 F St. NW, Ste. 850, 20004); www.ncd.gov
Natl. Credit Union Admin.: Rick Metsger, chair (1775 Duke St., Alexandria, VA 22314); www.ncua.gov
Natl. Endowment for the Arts: Jane Chu, chair (400 7th St. SW, 20506); www.arts.gov
Natl. Endowment for the Humanities: William Adams, chair (400 7th St. SW, 20506); www.neh.gov
Natl. Indian Gaming Commission: Jonodev Osceola Chaudhuri, chair (1849 C St. NW, Mail Stop #1621, 20240); www.nigc.gov
Natl. Labor Relations Board: Mark G. Pearce, chair (1015 Half St. SE, 20570); www.nlrb.gov
Natl. Mediation Board: Linda Puchala, chair (1301 K St. NW, Ste. 250 East, 20005); www.nmb.gov
Natl. Science Foundation: France A. Córdova, dir. (4201 Wilson Blvd., Arlington, VA 22230); www.nsf.gov
Natl. Transportation Safety Board: Christopher A. Hart, chair (490 L'Enfant Plaza SW, 20594); www.ntsb.gov
Nuclear Regulatory Commission: Stephen G. Burns, chair (20555); www.nrc.gov
Nuclear Waste Technical Review Board: Rodney C. Ewing, chair (2300 Clarendon Blvd., Ste. 1300, Arlington, VA 22201); www.nwtrb.gov
Occupational Safety and Health Review Commission: Cynthia L. Attwood, acting chair (1120 20th St. NW, 9th Fl., 20036); www.oshrc.gov
Office of the Dir. of Natl. Intelligence: James R. Clapper, dir. (20511); www.dni.gov
Office of Government Ethics: Walter M. Shaub Jr., dir. (1201 New York Ave. NW, Ste. 500, 20005); www.oge.gov
Office of Personnel Management: Beth F. Cobert, acting dir. (1900 E St. NW, 20415); www.opm.gov
Office of Special Counsel: Carolyn Lerner, spec. counsel (1730 M St. NW, Ste. 218, 20036); osc.gov
Overseas Private Investment Corp.: Elizabeth L. Littlefield, pres. and CEO (1100 New York Ave. NW, 20527); www.opic.gov
Peace Corps: Carrie Hessler-Radelet, dir. (1111 20th St. NW, 20526); www.peacecorps.gov
Pension Benefit Guaranty Corp.: W. Thomas Reeder Jr., dir. (1200 K St. NW, 20005); www.pbgc.gov
Postal Regulatory Commission: Robert G. Taub, acting chair (901 New York Ave. NW, Ste. 200, 20268); www.prc.gov
Railroad Retirement Board: chair vacant (844 N. Rush St., Chicago, IL 60611); www.rrb.gov
Securities and Exchange Commission: Mary Jo White, chair (100 F St. NE, 20549); www.sec.gov
Selective Service System: Lawrence G. Romo, dir. (Natl. Headquarters, Arlington, 20419); www.sss.gov
Small Business Admin.: Maria Contreras-Sweet, admin. (Cabinet rank) (409 3rd St. SW, 20416); www.sba.gov
Social Security Admin.: Carolyn W. Colvin, acting comm. (1100 West High Rise, 6401 Security Blvd., Baltimore, MD 21235); www.ssa.gov
Tennessee Valley Authority: Bill Johnson, CEO and pres. (400 W. Summit Hill Dr., Knoxville, TN 37902); www.tva.gov
U.S. Agency for Intl. Development: Gayle E. Smith, admin. (Ronald Reagan Bldg., 20523); www.usaid.gov
U.S. Commission on Civil Rights: Martin R. Castro, chair (1331 Pennsylvania Ave. NW, Ste. 1150, 20425); www.usccr.gov
U.S. Intl. Trade Commission: Meredith M. Broadbent, chair (500 E St. SW, 20436); www.usitc.gov
U.S. Postal Service: Megan J. Brennan, postmaster general and CEO (475 L'Enfant Plaza SW, 20260); www.usps.com
U.S. Trade and Development Agency: Leocadia I. Zak, dir. (1000 Wilson Blvd., Ste. 1600, Arlington, VA 22209); www.ustda.gov

CONGRESS

Floor Leaders in the U.S. Senate, 1920-2016

Majority leaders				Minority leaders			
Name	Party	State	Tenure	Name	Party	State	Tenure
Charles Curtis[1]	Rep.	KS	1925-1929	Oscar W. Underwood[2]	Dem.	AL	1920-1923
James E. Watson	Rep.	IN	1929-1933	Joseph T. Robinson	Dem.	AR	1923-1933
Joseph T. Robinson	Dem.	AR	1933-1937	Charles L. McNary	Rep.	OR	1933-1944
Alben W. Barkley	Dem.	KY	1937-1947	Wallace H. White	Rep.	ME	1944-1947
Wallace H. White	Rep.	ME	1947-1949	Alben W. Barkley	Dem.	KY	1947-1949
Scott W. Lucas	Dem.	IL	1949-1951	Kenneth S. Wherry	Rep.	NE	1949-1951
Ernest W. McFarland	Dem.	AZ	1951-1953	Henry Styles Bridges	Rep.	NH	1952-1953
Robert A. Taft	Rep.	OH	1953	Lyndon B. Johnson	Dem.	TX	1953-1955
William F. Knowland	Rep.	CA	1953-1955	William F. Knowland	Rep.	CA	1955-1959
Lyndon B. Johnson	Dem.	TX	1955-1961	Everett M. Dirksen	Rep.	IL	1959-1969
Mike Mansfield	Dem.	MT	1961-1977	Hugh D. Scott	Rep.	PA	1969-1977
Robert C. Byrd	Dem.	WV	1977-1981	Howard H. Baker Jr.	Rep.	TN	1977-1981
Howard H. Baker Jr.	Rep.	TN	1981-1985	Robert C. Byrd	Dem.	WV	1981-1987
Robert J. Dole	Rep.	KS	1985-1987	Robert J. Dole	Rep.	KS	1987-1995
Robert C. Byrd	Dem.	WV	1987-1989	Thomas A. Daschle	Dem.	SD	1995-2001[3]
George J. Mitchell	Dem.	ME	1989-1995	Trent Lott	Rep.	MS	2001-2002[3,4]
Robert J. Dole	Rep.	KS	1995-1996	Thomas A. Daschle	Dem.	SD	2003-2005
Trent Lott	Rep.	MS	1996-2001[3]	Harry M. Reid	Dem.	NV	2005-2007
Thomas A. Daschle	Dem.	SD	2001-2003[3]	Mitch McConnell	Rep.	KY	2007-2015
William Frist	Rep.	TN	2003-2007[4]	Harry M. Reid	Dem.	NV	2015-
Harry M. Reid	Dem.	NV	2007-2015				
Mitch McConnell	Rep.	KY	2015-				

Note: The offices of party (majority and minority) leaders in the Senate did not evolve until the 20th century. (1) First Republican to be formally designated floor leader. Henry Cabot Lodge (MA) served as unofficial party leader prior to Curtis's election. (2) First Democrat to be designated floor leader. (3) Democrats held the majority Jan. 3, 2001, until Dick Cheney (R) was installed as vice pres., Jan. 20. Republicans subsequently lost the majority when Jim Jeffords (VT) switched his affiliation from Republican to Independent, June 6, 2001. (4) Trent Lott resigned from Republican leadership Dec. 20, 2002. William Frist was elected Republican leader Dec. 23, 2002, and began service Jan. 7, 2003, as majority leader.

Speakers of the U.S. House of Representatives, 1789-2016

Name	Party	State	Tenure	Name	Party	State	Tenure
Frederick A. C. Muhlenberg	Federalist	PA	1789-1791	Michael C. Kerr	Dem.	IN	1875-1876
Jonathan Trumbull	Federalist	CT	1791-1793	Samuel J. Randall	Dem.	PA	1876-1881
Frederick A. C. Muhlenberg	Federalist	PA	1793-1795	J. Warren Keifer	Rep.	OH	1881-1883
Jonathan Dayton	Federalist	NJ	1795-1799	John G. Carlisle	Dem.	KY	1883-1889
Theodore Sedgwick	Federalist	MA	1799-1801	Thomas B. Reed	Rep.	ME	1889-1891
Nathaniel Macon	Dem.-Rep.	NC	1801-1807	Charles F. Crisp	Dem.	GA	1891-1895
Joseph B. Varnum	Dem.-Rep.	MA	1807-1811	Thomas B. Reed	Rep.	ME	1895-1899
Henry Clay	Dem.-Rep.	KY	1811-1814	David B. Henderson	Rep.	IA	1899-1903
Langdon Cheves	Dem.-Rep.	SC	1814-1815	Joseph G. Cannon	Rep.	IL	1903-1911
Henry Clay	Dem.-Rep.	KY	1815-1820	Champ Clark	Dem.	MO	1911-1919
John W. Taylor	Dem.-Rep.	NY	1820-1821	Frederick H. Gillett	Rep.	MA	1919-1925
Philip P. Barbour	Dem.-Rep.	VA	1821-1823	Nicholas Longworth	Rep.	OH	1925-1931
Henry Clay	Dem.-Rep.	KY	1823-1825	John N. Garner	Dem.	TX	1931-1933
John W. Taylor	Dem.	NY	1825-1827	Henry T. Rainey	Dem.	IL	1933-1934
Andrew Stevenson	Dem.	VA	1827-1834	Joseph W. Byrns	Dem.	TN	1935-1936
John Bell	Dem.	TN	1834-1835	William B. Bankhead	Dem.	AL	1936-1940
James K. Polk	Dem.	TN	1835-1839	Sam Rayburn	Dem.	TX	1940-1947
Robert M. T. Hunter	Dem.	VA	1839-1841	Joseph W. Martin Jr.	Rep.	MA	1947-1949
John White	Whig	KY	1841-1843	Sam Rayburn	Dem.	TX	1949-1953
John W. Jones	Dem.	VA	1843-1845	Joseph W. Martin Jr.	Rep.	MA	1953-1955
John W. Davis	Dem.	IN	1845-1847	Sam Rayburn	Dem.	TX	1955-1961
Robert C. Winthrop	Whig	MA	1847-1849	John W. McCormack	Dem.	MA	1962-1971
Howell Cobb	Dem.	GA	1849-1851	Carl B. Albert	Dem.	OK	1971-1977
Linn Boyd	Dem.	KY	1851-1855	Thomas P. O'Neill Jr.	Dem.	MA	1977-1987
Nathaniel P. Banks	American	MA	1856-1857	James C. Wright Jr.	Dem.	TX	1987-1989
James L. Orr	Dem.	SC	1857-1859	Thomas S. Foley	Dem.	WA	1989-1995
William Pennington	Rep.	NJ	1860-1861	Newt Gingrich	Rep.	GA	1995-1999
Galusha A. Grow	Rep.	PA	1861-1863	J. Dennis Hastert	Rep.	IL	1999-2007
Schuyler Colfax	Rep.	IN	1863-1869	Nancy Pelosi	Dem.	CA	2007-2011
Theodore M. Pomeroy	Rep.	NY	1869	John Boehner	Rep.	OH	2011-2015
James G. Blaine	Rep.	ME	1869-1875	Paul Ryan	Rep.	WI	2015-

Political Divisions of Congress, 1901-2016

Source: Office of the Clerk, U.S. House of Representatives; Congressional Research Service, Library of Congress

All figures reflect post-election party breakdown except where noted; **boldface** denotes party in majority immediately after election.

		SENATE					HOUSE OF REPRESENTATIVES				
Congress	Years	Total members	Dem.	Rep.	Other parties	Vacant	Total members	Dem.	Rep.	Other parties	Vacant
57th	1901-1903	90	32	**56**	2		357	151	**200**	6	
58th	1903-1905	90	33	**57**			386	176	**207**	3	
59th	1905-1907	90	32	**58**			386	135	**251**		
60th	1907-1909	92	31	**61**			391	167	**223**	1	
61st	1909-1911	92	32	**60**			391	172	**219**		
62nd	1911-1913	96	44	**52**			394	**230**	162	2	
63rd	1913-1915	96	**51**	44	1		435	**291**	134	10	
64th	1915-1917	96	**56**	40			435	**230**	196	9	
65th	1917-1919	96	**54**	42			435	214[1]	**215**	6	
66th	1919-1921	96	47	**49**			435	192	**240**	2	1
67th	1921-1923	96	37	**59**			435	131	**302**	2	
68th	1923-1925	96	42	**53**	1		435	207	**225**	3	

Congress	Years	SENATE Total members	Dem.	Rep.	Other parties	Vacant	HOUSE OF REPRESENTATIVES Total members	Dem.	Rep.	Other parties	Vacant
69th	1925-1927	96	41	**54**	1		435	183	**247**	5	
70th	1927-1929	96	46	**48**	1	1	435	194	**238**	3	
71st	1929-1931	96	39	**56**	1		435	164	**270**	1	
72nd	1931-1933	96	47	**48**	1		435	216[2]	**218**	1	
73rd	1933-1935	96	**59**	36	1		435	**313**	117	5	
74th	1935-1937	96	**69**	25	2		435	**322**	103	10	
75th	1937-1939	96	**76**	16	4		435	**334**	88	13	
76th	1939-1941	96	**69**	23	4		435	**262**	169	4	
77th	1941-1943	96	**66**	28	2		435	**267**	162	6	
78th	1943-1945	96	**57**	38	1		435	**222**	209	4	
79th	1945-1947	96	**57**	38	1		435	**242**	191	2	
80th	1947-1949	96	45	**51**			435	188	**246**	1	
81st	1949-1951	96	**54**	42			435	**263**	171	1	
82nd	1951-1953	96	**49**	47			435	**235**	199	1	
83rd	1953-1955	96	47	**48**	1		435	213	**221**	1	
84th	1955-1957	96	**48**	47	1		435	**232**	203		
85th	1957-1959	96	**49**	47			435	**234**	201		
86th	1959-1961	100	**65**	35			437[3]	**283**	153	1	
87th	1961-1963	100	**64**	36			437[3]	**263**	174		
88th	1963-1965	100	**66**	34			435	**259**	176		
89th	1965-1967	100	**68**	32			435	**295**	140		
90th	1967-1969	100	**64**	36			435	**247**	187		1
91st	1969-1971	100	**57**	43			435	**243**	192		
92nd	1971-1973	100	**54**	44	2		435	**255**	180		
93rd	1973-1975	100	**56**	42	2		435	**242**	192	1	
94th	1975-1977	100	**60**	38	2		435	**291**	144		
95th	1977-1979	100	**61**	38	1		435	**292**	143		
96th	1979-1981	100	**58**	41	1		435	**277**	158		
97th	1981-1983	100	46	**53**	1		435	**242**	192	1	
98th	1983-1985	100	46	**54**			435	**269**	166		
99th	1985-1987	100	47	**53**			435	**253**	182		
100th	1987-1989	100	**55**	45			435	**258**	177		
101st	1989-1991	100	**55**	45			435	**260**	175		
102nd	1991-1993	100	**56**	44			435	**267**	167	1	
103rd	1993-1995	100	**57**	43			435	**258**	176	1	
104th	1995-1997	100	48	**52**			435	204	**230**	1	
105th	1997-1999	100	45	**55**			435	206	**228**	1	
106th	1999-2001	100	45	**55**			435	211	**223**	1	
107th	2001-2003	100	50	**50**[4]			435	212	**221**	2	
108th	2003-2005	100	48	**51**	1		435	204	**229**	1	1
109th	2005-2007	100	44	**55**	1		435	202	**232**	1	
110th	2007-2009	100	**49**	49	2[5]		435	**233**	202		
111th	2009-2011	100	**57**	41	2[5]		435	**257**	178		
112th	2011-2013	100	**51**	47	2[5]		435	193	**242**		
113th	2013-2015	100	**53**	45	2[5]		435	201	**234**		
114th	2015-	100	44	**54**	2[5]		435	188	**246**		1

(1) Democrats organized the House with help of other parties. (2) Democrats organized the House because of Republican deaths. (3) Number of House seats was increased temporarily when proclamations were issued declaring Alaska (Jan. 3, 1959) and Hawaii (Aug. 21, 1959) new states. (4) While the Senate was split 50-50, control was held by whichever party had an incumbent vice president. Republican Sen. Jim Jeffords (VT) changed his party designation to Independent on June 6, 2001, switching control of the Senate to Democrats. (5) Both Independent senators chose to caucus with the Democrats.

Congressional Bills Vetoed, 1789-2016

Source: Virtual Reference Desk, U.S. Senate; as of Sept. 30, 2016

The president has 10 days (excluding Sundays) to consider a bill or joint resolution passed by Congress. The president can sign it into law or exercise a veto. Only a two-thirds vote in both the Senate and the House can override a regular veto. (A pocket veto cannot be overridden as it takes effect when Congress is adjourned.)

President	Regular vetoes	Pocket vetoes	Total vetoes	Vetoes overridden	President	Regular vetoes	Pocket vetoes	Total vetoes	Vetoes overridden
Washington	2	—	2	—	B. Harrison	19	25	44	1
J. Adams	—	—	—	—	Cleveland[2]	42	128	170	5
Jefferson	—	—	—	—	McKinley	6	36	42	—
Madison	5	2	7	—	T. Roosevelt	42	40	82	1
Monroe	1	—	1	—	Taft	30	9	39	1
J. Q. Adams	—	—	—	—	Wilson	33	11	44	6
Jackson	5	7	12	—	Harding	5	1	6	—
Van Buren	—	1	1	—	Coolidge	20	30	50	4
W. H. Harrison	—	—	—	—	Hoover	21	16	37	3
Tyler	6	4	10	1	F. D. Roosevelt	372	263	635	9
Polk	2	1	3	—	Truman	180	70	250	12
Taylor	—	—	—	—	Eisenhower	73	108	181	2
Fillmore	—	—	—	—	Kennedy	12	9	21	—
Pierce	9	—	9	5	L. Johnson	16	14	30	—
Buchanan	4	3	7	—	Nixon	26	17	43	7
Lincoln	2	5	7	—	Ford	48	18	66	12
A. Johnson	21	8	29	15	Carter	13	18	31	2
Grant	45	48	93	4	Reagan	39	39	78	9
Hayes	12	1	13	1	G. H. W. Bush[3]	29	15	44	1
Garfield	—	—	—	—	Clinton[4]	36	1	37	2
Arthur	4	8	12	1	G. W. Bush	12	—	12	4
Cleveland[1]	304	110	414	2	Obama	12	—	12	1
					Total[3,4]	**1,508**	**1,066**	**2,574**	**111**

— = 0. (1) First term only. (2) Second term only. (3) Excluded from the figures are two bills that Pres. George H. W. Bush claimed to be pocket vetoed but which Congress considered to be enacted because the president had failed to return them during a Congressional recess. (4) Does not include line-item vetoes, which were ruled unconstitutional by the U.S. Supreme Court on June 25, 1998.

Congressional Firsts and Milestones

Cities where Congress has convened: New York City (1789-90); Philadelphia (1790-1800); Washington, DC (1800-).

First meeting of Congress in the Capitol Building: Nov. 17, 1800.

First Congressional override of a presidential veto: Pres. John Tyler's veto of an appropriation bill, Mar. 3, 1845.

House of Representatives

First House meeting: Mar. 4, 1789, at Federal Hall in New York, NY. A quorum of 30 representatives was not reached until Apr. 1, 1789.

First House meeting in its current Capitol Building chamber: Dec. 16, 1857.

First former president to serve as representative: John Quincy Adams (MA, 1831-48); president, 1825-29.

First woman representative: Jeannette Rankin (R, MT, 1917-19, 1941-43).

First woman House speaker: Nancy Pelosi (D, CA), on Jan. 4, 2007.

First black representative: Joseph Rainey (R, SC, 1870-79).

First black woman representative: Shirley Chisholm (D, NY, 1969-83).

First elected Hispanic-American representative: Romualdo Pacheco (R, CA, 1877-83); Pacheco was born in California when it was Mexican territory.

First Asian-Pacific American representative: India-born Dalip Saund (D, CA, 1957-63).

Longest-serving representative: John Dingell Jr. (D, MI, 1955-2015), with more than 59 years of service.

Longest-serving House speaker: Sam Rayburn (D, TX, 1913-61) served as House speaker for 17 years, 2 months, and 2 days (non-consecutive).

Longest consecutive service by a single family: A member of the Dingell family has represented one of Michigan's districts since 1933: John Dingell (D, 1933-55), John Dingell Jr. (D, 1955-2015), and Debbie Dingell (D, 2015-).

Oldest representative: Ralph Hall (D-R, TX, 1981-2015); retired at age 91.

Oldest-known freshman representative: James B. Bowler (D, IL), who won a special election July 7, 1953, aged 78.

Youngest representative: William Charles Cole Claiborne (TN), who was elected at 22 years of age and began service Nov. 23, 1797. The House chose to seat him then and two years later when he was reelected despite the Constitutional requirement that U.S. representatives be at least 25 years of age.

First live-TV broadcast of House proceedings: Mar. 19, 1979, by public television and C-SPAN. Al Gore Jr. (D, TN) was the first representative to give a speech before cameras that day.

First declaration of war made by the House: June 4, 1812, against Great Britain and Ireland.

Senate

First Senate meeting: Mar. 4, 1789, at Federal Hall in New York, NY. A quorum of senators was not reached until Apr. 6, 1789.

First Senate meeting in its current chamber in the Capitol Building: Jan. 4, 1859.

First woman senator: Rebecca Felton (D, GA, 1922). Appointed to a seat left vacant by a death, 87-year-old Felton served only 24 hours after being sworn in Nov. 21. (Felton was also the oldest freshman senator and the last senator to have been a slave owner.)

First elected woman senator: Hattie Caraway (D, AR, 1931-45). Appointed in 1931 to fill the vacancy left by the death of her husband, Thaddeus H. Caraway, she was elected in 1932.

First black senator: Hiram R. Revels (R, MS, 1870-71).

First black woman senator: Carol Moseley-Braun (D, IL, 1993-99).

First American Indian senators: Charles Curtis (R, KS, 1907-13, 1915-29) and Robert Owen (D, OK, 1907-25).

First Hispanic-American senator: Mexico-born Octaviano Larrazolo (R, NM, 1928-29).

First Asian-American senator: Hiram L. Fong (R, HI, 1959-77).

First Jewish senator: David Levy Yulee (D, FL, 1845-51, 1855-61).

Longest-serving senator: Robert C. Byrd (D, WV, 1959-2010) died while in office, having served 51 years, 5 months, and 26 days.

Oldest senator: Strom Thurmond (R, SC), who turned 100 years of age on Dec. 5, 2002, one month before he retired from office.

Youngest senator: John H. Eaton (TN), who was 28 years, 5 months old when he was sworn in Nov. 16, 1818, despite the Constitutional requirement that U.S. senators be at least 30 years old.

Longest speech by a senator (since 1900): 24 hours, 18 minutes, by Strom Thurmond (D, SC) in his filibuster against the 1957 Civil Rights Act, Aug. 28-29, 1957.

First Senate impeachment trial of a president: Pres. Andrew Johnson, on Mar. 5, 1868; he was acquitted by a one-vote margin.

Number of Senate impeachment trials: 19, resulting in 7 acquittals, 8 convictions, 3 dismissals, and 1 resignation with no further action.

First regular live-TV broadcast from the Senate chamber: June 2, 1986, by the C-SPAN network.

Number of senators who have received the Nobel Peace Prize: 5 (Elihu Root, Frank Kellogg, Cordell Hull, Al Gore, Barack Obama). Root is the only one of the five to receive the award while serving as senator.

Number of senators who have changed party affiliation during their Senate service (since 1890): 21.

Congressional Activity, 1947-2016

Source: *Congressional Record*, U.S. Govt. Publishing Office; Library of Congress

Congress in recent years has been widely perceived as being less productive than in previous sessions. The data below shows the number of public laws and measures passed in every session of Congress since 1947.

Congress (years)	Public laws passed	Measures passed	Congress (years)	Public laws passed	Measures passed
80th (1947-48)	906	4,132	98th (1983-84)	623	2,670
81st (1949-50)	921	5,764	99th (1985-86)	664	2,698
82nd (1951-52)	594	4,593	100th (1987-88)	713	2,932
83rd (1953-54)	781	5,201	101st (1989-90)	650	2,691
84th (1955-56)	1,028	5,713	102nd (1991-92)	590	2,615
85th (1957-58)	936	5,126	103rd (1993-94)	465	2,054
86th (1959-60)	800	4,165	104th (1995-96)	333	1,834
87th (1961-62)	885	4,769	105th (1997-98)	394	2,077
88th (1963-64)	666	3,425	106th (1999-2000)	580	2,779
89th (1965-66)	810	4,116	107th (2001-02)	377	2,163
90th (1967-68)	640	3,390	108th (2003-04)	498	2,674
91st (1969-70)	695	3,318	109th (2005-06)	482	2,684
92nd (1971-72)	607	2,840	110th (2007-08)	460	3,336
93rd (1973-74)	649	3,088	111th (2009-10)	383	2,939
94th (1975-76)	588	3,176	112th (2011-12)	283	1,744
95th (1977-78)	633	3,211	113th (2013-14)	296	1,788
96th (1979-80)	613	2,960	114th (2015-16)	188*	1,536*
97th (1981-82)	473	2,267			

* = As of June 30, 2016. Incomplete congressional session; should not be compared to earlier years. **Note:** Measures passed refers to bills, joint resolutions, concurrent resolutions, or simple resolutions approved by the House or Senate. Public laws are bills or joint resolutions that have been enacted.

U.S. SUPREME COURT

Justices of the U.S. Supreme Court

The Supreme Court comprises the chief justice of the U.S. and eight associate justices, all appointed for life by the president with advice and consent of the U.S. Senate. Names of chief justices are in **boldface**. Terms of service begin with the year each justice took the judicial oath. Service years are the number of complete years served by a justice. 2016 salaries: chief justice, $260,700; associate justice, $249,300. The U.S. Supreme Court Building is at 1 First St. NE, Washington, DC 20543.

Website: www.supremecourt.gov

Current membership. Chief justice: John G. Roberts Jr.; associate justices in seniority order: Anthony M. Kennedy, Clarence Thomas, Ruth Bader Ginsburg, Stephen G. Breyer, Samuel A. Alito Jr., Sonia Sotomayor, Elena Kagan.

Name, appointed from	Term	Yrs.	Born	Died
John Jay, NY	1789-1795	5	1745	1829
John Rutledge, SC[1]	1790-1791	1	1739	1800
William Cushing, MA	1790-1810*	20	1732	1810
James Wilson, PA	1789-1798	8	1742	1798
John Blair, VA	1790-1795*	5	1732	1800
James Iredell, NC	1790-1799	9	1751	1799
Thomas Johnson, MD	1792-1793	<1	1732	1819
William Paterson, NJ	1793-1806	13	1745	1806
John Rutledge, SC[2,3]	1795	<1	1739	1800
Samuel Chase, MD	1796-1811	15	1741	1811
Oliver Ellsworth, CT	1796-1800	4	1745	1807
Bushrod Washington, VA	1799-1829*	30	1762	1829
Alfred Moore, NC	1800-1804	3	1755	1810
John Marshall, VA	1801-1835	34	1755	1835
William Johnson, SC	1804-1834	30	1771	1834
Henry B. Livingston, NY	1807-1823	16	1757	1823
Thomas Todd, KY	1807-1826	18	1765	1826
Gabriel Duvall, MD	1811-1835	23	1752	1844
Joseph Story, MA	1812-1845*	33	1779	1845
Smith Thompson, NY	1823-1843	20	1768	1843
Robert Trimble, KY	1826-1828	2	1777	1828
John McLean, OH	1830-1861*	31	1785	1861
Henry Baldwin, PA	1830-1844	14	1780	1844
James M. Wayne, GA	1835-1867	32	1790	1867
Roger B. Taney, MD	1836-1864	28	1777	1864
Philip P. Barbour, VA	1836-1841	4	1783	1841
John Catron, TN	1837-1865	28	1786	1865
John McKinley, AL	1838-1852*	14	1780	1852
Peter V. Daniel, VA	1842-1860*	18	1784	1860
Samuel Nelson, NY	1845-1872	27	1792	1873
Levi Woodbury, NH	1845-1851	5	1789	1851
Robert C. Grier, PA	1846-1870	23	1794	1870
Benjamin R. Curtis, MA	1851-1857	5	1809	1874
John A. Campbell, AL	1853-1861*	8	1811	1889
Nathan Clifford, ME	1858-1881	23	1803	1881
Noah H. Swayne, OH	1862-1881	18	1804	1884
Samuel F. Miller, IA	1862-1890	28	1816	1890
David Davis, IL	1862-1877	14	1815	1886
Stephen J. Field, CA	1863-1897	33	1816	1899
Salmon P. Chase, OH	1864-1873	8	1808	1873
William Strong, PA	1870-1880	10	1808	1895
Joseph P. Bradley, NJ	1870-1892	21	1813	1892
Ward Hunt, NY	1873-1882	9	1810	1886
Morrison R. Waite, OH	1874-1888	14	1816	1888
John M. Harlan, KY	1877-1911	33	1833	1911
William B. Woods, GA	1881-1887	6	1824	1887
Stanley Matthews, OH	1881-1889	7	1824	1889
Horace Gray, MA	1882-1902	20	1828	1902
Samuel Blatchford, NY	1882-1893	11	1820	1893
Lucius Q. C. Lamar, MS	1888-1893	5	1825	1893
Melville W. Fuller, IL	1888-1910	21	1833	1910
David J. Brewer, KS	1890-1910	20	1837	1910
Henry B. Brown, MI	1891-1906	15	1836	1913
George Shiras Jr., PA	1892-1903	10	1832	1924
Howell E. Jackson, TN	1893-1895	2	1832	1895
Edward D. White, LA[1]	1894-1910	16	1845	1921
Rufus W. Peckham, NY	1896-1909	13	1838	1909
Joseph McKenna, CA	1898-1925	26	1843	1926
Oliver W. Holmes, MA	1902-1932	29	1841	1935
William R. Day, OH	1903-1922	19	1849	1923
William H. Moody, MA	1906-1910	3	1853	1917
Horace H. Lurton, TN	1910-1914	4	1844	1914
Charles E. Hughes, NY[1]	1910-1916	5	1862	1948
Willis Van Devanter, WY	1911-1937	26	1859	1941
Joseph R. Lamar, GA	1911-1916	5	1857	1916
Edward D. White, LA[2]	1910-1921	10	1845	1921
Mahlon Pitney, NJ	1912-1922	10	1858	1924
James C. McReynolds, TN	1914-1941	26	1862	1946
Louis D. Brandeis, MA	1916-1939	22	1856	1941
John H. Clarke, OH	1916-1922	5	1857	1945
William H. Taft, CT	1921-1930	8	1857	1930
George Sutherland, UT	1922-1938	15	1862	1942
Pierce Butler, MN	1923-1939	16	1866	1939
Edward T. Sanford, TN	1923-1930	7	1865	1930
Harlan F. Stone, NY[1]	1925-1941	16	1872	1946
Charles E. Hughes, NY[2]	1930-1941	11	1862	1948
Owen J. Roberts, PA	1930-1945	15	1875	1955
Benjamin N. Cardozo, NY	1932-1938	6	1870	1938
Hugo L. Black, AL	1937-1971	34	1886	1971
Stanley F. Reed, KY	1938-1957	19	1884	1980
Felix Frankfurter, MA	1939-1962	23	1882	1965
William O. Douglas, CT	1939-1975	36[4]	1898	1980
Frank Murphy, MI	1940-1949	9	1890	1949
Harlan F. Stone, NY[2]	1941-1946	4	1872	1946
James F. Byrnes, SC	1941-1942	1	1879	1972
Robert H. Jackson, NY	1941-1954	13	1892	1954
Wiley B. Rutledge, IA	1943-1949	6	1894	1949
Harold H. Burton, OH	1945-1958	13	1888	1964
Fred M. Vinson, KY	1946-1953	7	1890	1953
Tom C. Clark, TX	1949-1967	17	1899	1977
Sherman Minton, IN	1949-1956	7	1890	1965
Earl Warren, CA	1953-1969	15	1891	1974
John Marshall Harlan, NY	1955-1971	16	1899	1971
William J. Brennan Jr., NJ	1956-1990	33	1906	1997
Charles E. Whittaker, MO	1957-1962	5	1901	1973
Potter Stewart, OH	1958-1981	22	1915	1985
Byron R. White, CO	1962-1993	31	1917	2002
Arthur J. Goldberg, IL	1962-1965	2	1908	1990
Abe Fortas, TN	1965-1969	3	1910	1982
Thurgood Marshall, NY	1967-1991	24	1908	1993
Warren E. Burger, VA	1969-1986	17	1907	1995
Harry A. Blackmun, MN	1970-1994	24	1908	1999
Lewis F. Powell Jr., VA	1972-1987	15	1907	1998
William H. Rehnquist, AZ[1]	1972-1986	14	1924	2005
John Paul Stevens, IL	1975-2010	34	1920	
Sandra Day O'Connor, AZ	1981-2006	24	1930	
William H. Rehnquist, VA[2]	1986-2005	18	1924	2005
Antonin Scalia, VA	1986-2016	29	1936	2016
Anthony M. Kennedy, CA	1988-		1936	
David H. Souter, NH	1990-2009	18	1939	
Clarence Thomas, GA	1991-		1948	
Ruth Bader Ginsburg, NY	1993-		1933	
Stephen G. Breyer, MA	1994-		1938	
John G. Roberts Jr., MD	2005-		1955	
Samuel A. Alito Jr., NJ	2006-		1950	
Sonia Sotomayor, NY	2009-		1954	
Elena Kagan, MA	2010-		1960	

* = Because of inadequate government record keeping, date of oath is estimated. (1) Later, chief justice, as listed. (2) Formerly associate justice. (3) Named acting chief justice; confirmation rejected by the Senate. (4) Longest term of service.

Supreme Court History and Notable Firsts

The U.S. Supreme Court first convened Feb. 1, 1790, in New York, NY. Acting on the authority of Congress as outlined in the Judiciary Act of 1789, the court consisted of Chief Justice John Jay and five associate justices who held sessions for a few weeks in Feb. and Aug. The justices also served twice a year in each of the nation's then-13 judicial districts, a requirement known as riding circuit. Since it was established, 112 justices have served on the court for an average of 16 years.

The court's first major legal decision, *Chisholm v. Georgia* (1793), ruled that federal courts held jurisdiction over disputes between individual states and citizens of other states. (The 11th Amendment, which the states ratified in 1795, removed that jurisdiction.) The court over time has expanded its impact on the nation's affairs. Since 1803 it has declared unconstitutional 170 acts of Congress and more than 1,070 state and territorial laws and municipal statutes. The court receives approximately 10,000 petitions annually and hears oral arguments in about 75-80 cases per term.

Of 160 nominations to the court (including chief justice nominations), just 12 have been rejected by the Senate, most recently Robert Bork in 1987. (George W. Bush-nominee Harriet Miers withdrew her nomination before the Senate considered it, in 2005.) On Mar. 16, 2016, Pres. Barack Obama nominated appellate court judge Merrick Garland to fill the seat vacated by the death of Associate Justice Antonin Scalia. The Senate had not held hearings on his nomination as of Aug. 2016; on July 20, the delay surpassed the previous record of 125 days between nomination and confirmation, held by Louis D. Brandeis since 1916.

Justices may be removed from the court by impeachment. In 1804, the House of Representatives, in the control of Jeffersonian Republicans, impeached Samuel Chase, a Federalist; he was acquitted by the Senate in 1805.

First fully vested justice: James Wilson took the Constitutional Oath of the Court Oct. 5, 1789
First Jewish justice: Louis D. Brandeis (1916-39)
First and only person to serve as both U.S. president and chief justice: William Howard Taft (president, 1909-13; chief justice, 1921-30)

First justice to take an oath at the White House: Frank Murphy, Jan. 18, 1940
First African-American justice: Thurgood Marshall (1967-91)
First woman justice: Sandra Day O'Connor (1981-2006)
First Hispanic justice: Sonia Sotomayor (2009-)

U.S. Supreme Court Decisions by Issue and Leadership Era, 1946-2016

Source: Supreme Court Database, supremecourtdatabase.org

Decisions through the end of the 2015-16 term. Figures are the number of cases decided in each issue category (number of 5-4 decisions in parentheses). The Court begins its term the first Monday in Oct. and typically recesses in late June.

| Issue | Number of decisions under Chief Justice— | | | | |
	Vinson (1946-53)	Warren (1953-69)	Burger (1969-86)	Rehnquist (1986-2005)	Roberts (2005-)
Attorneys[1]	2 (0)	12 (1)	37 (5)	31 (7)	18 (2)
Civil rights	74 (7)	316 (27)	555 (78)	326 (69)	144 (30)
Criminal procedure	123 (29)	462 (70)	627 (109)	509 (136)	253 (58)
Due process	47 (6)	40 (5)	144 (18)	86 (23)	21 (5)
Economic activity	224 (37)	493 (48)	452 (52)	346 (40)	181 (18)
Federal taxation	49 (2)	118 (5)	75 (7)	56 (3)	12 (2)
Federalism	33 (1)	94 (3)	107 (6)	124 (26)	42 (8)
First amendment	44 (8)	206 (44)	236 (56)	140 (36)	44 (14)
Interstate relations	12 (2)	14 (0)	40 (0)	23 (1)	7 (1)
Judicial power	135 (18)	299 (20)	366 (33)	286 (28)	106 (22)
Miscellaneous[2]	24 (0)	18 (0)	11 (0)	16 (0)	6 (1)
Privacy	4 (0)	2 (0)	48 (9)	42 (6)	17 (1)
Private action[3]	0 (0)	0 (0)	0 (0)	0 (0)	2 (1)
Unions	41 (4)	131 (8)	109 (24)	55 (11)	20 (4)
Total	**812 (114)**	**2,205 (231)**	**2,807 (397)**	**2,040 (386)**	**873 (167)**

Note: Decision types include orally argued judgments, per curiams, and opinions; per curiams without oral arguments; equally divided votes; and decrees. (1) Includes cases on commercial fees, attorneys' fees, admission to state or federal bar, attorney discipline, and disbarment. (2) Includes cases that could not be classified. (3) Includes cases on civil procedures, commercial transactions, contracts, evidence, personal and real property, torts, and wills and trusts.

Selected Landmark Decisions of the U.S. Supreme Court, 1803-2015

1803: *Marbury v. Madison*. The Court ruled that Congress exceeded its power in the Judiciary Act of 1789. The Court thus established its power to review acts of Congress and to declare invalid those it found to be in conflict with the Constitution.

1819: *Trustees of Dartmouth College v. Woodward*. The Court ruled that a state could not arbitrarily alter the terms of a college's contract. The Court later used a similar principle to limit the states' ability to interfere with business contracts.

1819: *McCulloch v. Maryland*. The Court ruled that Congress had the authority to charter a national bank, under the Constitution's granting of power to enact all laws "necessary and proper" to responsibilities of government.

1824: *Gibbons v. Ogden*. The Court ruled that New York state had overstepped its authority in granting a monopoly to two steamboat operators. According to the ruling, Congress's power to regulate interstate commerce included transportation.

1857: *Dred Scott v. Sandford*. The Court declared unconstitutional the already-repealed Missouri Compromise of 1820 because it deprived a person of property—a slave—without due process of law. The Court also ruled that slaves were not citizens of any state nor of the U.S. The latter part of the decision was overturned by ratification of the 14th Amendment in 1868.

1880: *Strauder v. West Virginia*. The Court struck down a state law mandating that jurors must be white, ruling it a violation of the right to equal protection under the 14th Amendment.

1896: *Plessy v. Ferguson*. The Court ruled that a state law requiring federal railroad trains to provide separate but equal facilities for black and white passengers neither infringed upon federal authority to regulate interstate commerce nor violated the 13th and 14th Amendments. The "separate but equal" doctrine remained in effect until the 1954 ***Brown v. Board of Education*** decision.

1904: *Northern Securities Co. v. U.S.* The Court ruled that a holding company formed solely to eliminate competition between two railroad lines was a combination in restraint of trade, violating the 1890 federal Sherman Antitrust Act.

1908: *Muller v. Oregon*. The Court upheld a state law limiting the working hours of women. (Louis D. Brandeis, counsel for the state, cited evidence from social workers, physicians, and factory inspectors that long work hours were harmful to women.)

1911: *Standard Oil Co. of New Jersey v. U.S.* The Court ruled that the Standard Oil Trust must be dissolved because of its unreasonable restraint of trade.

1919: *Schenck v. U.S.* The Court sustained the Espionage Act of 1917, maintaining that freedom of speech and press could be constrained if "the words used … create a clear and present danger."

1925: *Gitlow v. New York*. The Court ruled that the 1st Amendment prohibition against government abridgment of the freedom of speech applied to the states as well as to the federal government. The decision was the first of a number of rulings holding that the 14th Amendment extended the guarantees of the Bill of Rights to state action.

1935: Schechter Poultry Corp. v. U.S. The Court ruled that Congress exceeded its authority to delegate legislative powers and to regulate interstate commerce when it enacted the National Industrial Recovery Act (1933), which afforded the U.S. president too much discretionary power.

1944: Korematsu v. U.S. The Court upheld the constitutionality of an order barring all persons of Japanese ancestry, including U.S. citizens, from much of the West Coast, forcing them into internment camps, ruling that the need to prevent espionage outweighed the petitioner's civil rights. The ruling, never officially overturned, followed **Hirabayashi v. U.S.** (1943), in which the Court upheld the imposition of curfews on minority populations perceived to be a potential wartime threat.

1951: Dennis v. U.S. The Court upheld convictions under the Smith Act of 1940 for invoking Communist theory advocating the forcible overthrow of the government. In **Yates v. U.S.** (1957), the Court moderated this ruling by allowing such advocacy in the abstract, if not connected to action to achieve the goal.

1952: Youngstown Sheet & Tube Co. v. Sawyer. The Court ruled that the president had exceeded his wartime power in ordering the seizure of private steel mills during a nationwide steelworkers' strike. The Court held that neither the Constitution nor his role as commander-in-chief gave the president the authority to interfere in labor issues.

1954: Brown v. Board of Education of Topeka. The Court ruled that separate public schools for black and white students were inherently unequal, so state-sanctioned segregation in public schools violated the equal protection guarantee of the 14th Amendment. The Court decided **Bolling v. Sharpe** the same year, ruling that the congressionally mandated segregated public school system in the District of Columbia violated the 5th Amendment's due process guarantee of personal liberty. In **Brown II** (1955), the Court ordered the integration of schools with "all deliberate speed." The Brown rulings also led to abolition of state-sponsored segregation in other public facilities.

1957: Roth v. U.S.; Alberts v. California. The Court ruled obscene material—defined as appealing primarily to "prurient interest" in the view of "the average person, applying contemporary community standards"—was not protected by 1st Amendment guarantees of freedom of speech and press, being "utterly without redeeming social importance." This definition was modified in later decisions, including **Miller v. California** (1973).

1958: Cooper v. Aaron. The Court held that Arkansas could not nullify **Brown v. Board of Education** (1954) through the passage of legislation or constitutional amendments barring integration. The opinion of the Court affirmed its reading of the Constitution as the "supreme law of the land."

1961: Mapp v. Ohio. The Court ruled that indigent evidence obtained in violation of the 4th Amendment guarantee against unreasonable search and seizure must be excluded from use in state as well as federal cases.

1962: Baker v. Carr. The Court held that constitutional challenges to the unequal distribution of voters among legislative districts could be resolved by federal courts.

1962: Engel v. Vitale. The Court held that government bodies could not encourage the recitation of a state-composed prayer in public schools, even if nondenominational, because that would be an unconstitutional attempt to establish religion.

1963: Gideon v. Wainwright. The Court ruled that indigent defendants, even in state cases, have a right to legal counsel as guaranteed by the 6th Amendment.

1964: New York Times Co. v. Sullivan. The Court ruled that the 1st Amendment protected the press from libel suits for defamatory reports about public officials unless an injured party could prove that a defamatory report was made out of "actual malice," with "reckless disregard" for the truth.

1964: Heart of Atlanta Motel v. U.S. The Court upheld the constitutionality of Title II of the 1964 Civil Rights Act banning racial discrimination in motels/hotels engaged in interstate commerce (by accommodating travelers from other states). The Court in **Katzenbach v. McClung** (1964) held that Title II also applied to restaurants and businesses that purchased a substantial percentage of food or goods from other states.

1965: Griswold v. Connecticut. The Court ruled that a state unconstitutionally interfered with privacy in a marriage when it prohibited all persons, including married couples, from using contraceptives.

1966: Miranda v. Arizona. The Court ruled that, under the guarantee of due process, suspects in custody, before being questioned, must be informed that they have the right to remain silent, that anything they say may be used against them, and that they have the right to counsel.

1968: Terry v. Ohio. The Court ruled that a "stop and frisk" performed without a warrant or probable cause was not a violation of 4th Amendment rights, provided that the law enforcement officer had a reasonable suspicion that the subject was armed and dangerous, or had committed or was about to commit a crime.

1973: Roe v. Wade; Doe v. Bolton. The Court ruled that the fetus was not a "person" with constitutional rights and that a right to privacy inherent in the 14th Amendment's due process guarantee of personal liberty protected a woman's decision to have an abortion. During the first trimester of pregnancy, the Court maintained, the decision should be left entirely to a woman and her physician. Some regulation of abortion procedures was allowed in the second trimester and some restriction of abortion in the third.

1974: U.S. v. Nixon. The Court ruled that neither the separation of powers nor the need to preserve the confidentiality of presidential communications could alone justify an absolute executive privilege of immunity from judicial demands for evidence to be used in a criminal trial.

1976: Gregg v. Georgia; Proffitt v. Florida; Jurek v. Texas. The Court ruled that death, as a punishment for persons convicted of first-degree murder, was not in and of itself cruel and unusual punishment in violation of the 8th Amendment. But the Court ruled that the sentencing judge and jury must consider the character of the offender and the circumstances of the particular crime.

1978: Regents of the Univ. of Calif. v. Bakke. The Court ruled that an admissions program for a state medical school, under which a set number of places were reserved for minorities, violated the 1964 Civil Rights Act, which forbids the exclusion of anyone from a federally funded program based on race. However, the Court ruled that race could be considered as one of a complex of factors.

1985: New Jersey v. T.L.O. The Court ruled that officials who carry out searches on school grounds do not violate students' 4th Amendment rights because students' privacy rights may be outweighed by schools' need to maintain learning environments. The ruling put in place less stringent standards of required "reasonableness" for such searches.

1986: Bowers v. Hardwick. The Court refused to extend any right of privacy to homosexual activity, upholding a Georgia antisodomy law that in effect made such activity a crime. Georgia's supreme court struck down the law in 1998, and in **Lawrence v. Texas** (2003), the U.S. Supreme Court struck down all state antisodomy laws as violations of liberty prohibited in the 14th Amendment's due process clause. In **Romer v. Evans** (1996), the Court struck down a Colorado constitutional provision that barred homosexuals from recognition as a protected class, ruling that it violated the 14th Amendment's Equal Protection clause.

1989: Texas v. Johnson. The Court held the actions of a political activist who burned an American flag outside of the 1984 Republican National Convention were expressive and therefore protected by the 1st Amendment. The ruling invalidated laws in 48 states prohibiting flag desecration.

1990: Cruzan v. Missouri. The Court ruled that while a person had the right to refuse life-sustaining medical treatment, a state could require evidence that a comatose patient would not have wanted to live before withholding treatment. In two 1997 rulings, **Washington v. Glucksberg** and **Vacco v. Quill**, the Court ruled that states could ban doctor-assisted suicide.

1995: U.S. Term Limits, Inc. v. Thornton. The Court ruled that neither states nor Congress could limit terms of members of Congress because the Constitution reserves to the people the right to choose federal lawmakers.

1995: Adarand Constructors, Inc. v. Peña. The Court held that federal programs that classify people by race, unless "narrowly tailored" to further a "compelling governmental interest," may violate the right to equal protection and are thus subject to strict scrutiny.

1997: Clinton v. Jones. Rejecting an appeal by Pres. Clinton in a sexual harassment suit, the Court ruled that a sitting president did not have temporary immunity from a lawsuit for actions outside the realm of official duties.

1997: City of Boerne v. Flores. The Court overturned the portion of a 1993 law banning enforcement of state laws that "substantially burden" religious practice unless there is a "compelling governmental interest" to do so. The Court held that the act was an unwarranted intrusion by Congress on states' prerogatives and an infringement of the judiciary's role.

1997: *Reno v. ACLU*. Citing the right to free expression, the Court overturned a provision making it a crime to display or distribute "obscene or indecent" or "patently offensive" material on the Internet. The Court ruled, however, in *NEA v. Finley* (1998) that "general standards of decency" may be used as a criterion in federal arts funding.

1998: *Clinton v. City of New York*. The Court struck down the Line-Item Veto Act (1996), holding that it unconstitutionally gave the president "the unilateral power to change the text of duly enacted statutes."

1998: *Faragher v. City of Boca Raton*; *Burlington Industries, Inc. v. Ellerth*. The Court issued new guidelines for workplace sexual harassment suits, holding employers responsible for misconduct by supervisory employees. And in *Oncale v. Sundowner Offshore Services, Inc.* the same year, the Court ruled that the law against discrimination based on sex applies even if the harasser and harassed are the same sex.

1999: *Dept. of Commerce v. U.S. House of Representatives*. Upholding a challenge to plans for the 2000 census, the Court prohibited statistical sampling, favored by Democrats, in apportioning seats in the U.S. House. The Court maintained that an actual head count was required.

1999: *Alden v. Maine*; *Florida Prepaid v. College Savings Bank*; *College Savings Bank v. Florida Prepaid*. In a series of rulings, the Court applied the principle of sovereign immunity to shield states in large part from being sued under federal law.

2000: *Boy Scouts of America v. Dale*. The Court ruled that the Boy Scouts could dismiss a troop leader after learning he was gay, holding that the right to freedom of association outweighed a New Jersey antidiscrimination statute.

2000: *Bush v. Gore*. The Court ruled that manual recounts in Florida of ballots cast in the 2000 presidential election could not proceed because inconsistent evaluation standards violated the equal protection clause. In effect, the ruling meant the existing official results would stand, making George W. Bush the narrow winner of the election.

2001: *Good News Club v. Milford Central School*. The justices found that a private religious organization could not be denied equal access to a public school facility for after-school meetings because that would be a violation of the group's free speech rights.

2002: *Federal Maritime Commission v. South Carolina State Ports Authority*. The Court ruled that the 11th Amendment gave states immunity from private lawsuits involving federal agencies.

2002: *Atkins v. Virginia*. The Court ruled that the execution of mentally retarded criminals violated the 8th Amendment ban on cruel and unusual punishment. The Court ruled in *Roper v. Simmons* (2005) that executions of convicts who committed their crimes before age 18 were also prohibited on the same grounds.

2002: *Zelman v. Simmons-Harris*. The Court ruled that publicly funded tuition vouchers could be used at religious schools without violating the separation of church and state.

2003: *Grutter v. Bollinger*; *Gratz v. Bollinger*. The Court upheld the use of race as a factor in the Univ. of Michigan Law School's admissions policies because of the school's interest in a diverse student body. In a second decision, however, the Court ruled against a strict point system based on racial and ethnic backgrounds as used in the university's undergraduate admissions process.

2004: *Tennessee v. Lane*. The Court ruled that disabled individuals could sue states under the Americans With Disabilities Act (1990) for failing to provide adequate access to state courthouses, despite states' usual immunity from private lawsuits in federal court under the 11th Amendment, which the Court ruled on in *Federal Maritime Commission v. South Carolina State Ports Authority* (2002).

2004: *Locke v. Davey*. The justices decided that a scholarship program provided by the state of Washington did not violate the right to free exercise of religion in denying aid to students preparing for the clergy.

2004: *Ashcroft v. ACLU*. The Court struck down federal legislation passed in 1998 to restrict online access to pornography by minors, on the basis that the law violated the 1st Amendment right of free speech.

2005: *Kelo v. City of New London*. The Court ruled that local governments could force property owners to sell their land in order to facilitate private development projects deemed to be economically beneficial to the community.

2006: *Garcetti v. Ceballos*. The Court ruled that the 1st Amendment guarantee of free speech did not protect statements made by public employees in the course of their official duties.

2006: *Hamdan v. Rumsfeld*. The Court ruled that Pres. George W. Bush's system for trying terrorism detainees at the U.S. military base in Guantánamo Bay, Cuba, was unauthorized under federal law and the international Geneva Conventions. The Court furthermore ruled in *Boumediene v. Bush* (2008) that detainees had a right to challenge their detention in federal court by applying for a writ of habeas corpus.

2007: *Gonzales v. Carhart*; *Gonzales v. Planned Parenthood Federation of America*. The Court upheld a 2003 federal law prohibiting the abortion procedure known as intact dilation and extraction, or "partial-birth" abortion.

2007: *Parents Involved in Community Schools v. Seattle School District No. 1*; *Meredith v. Jefferson County Board of Education*. The Court ruled that two school districts could not, to encourage diversity, use "racial classifications in making school assignments."

2008: *Crawford v. Marion County Election Board*. The Court upheld the constitutionality of an Indiana law requiring in-person voters to present valid government photo identification.

2008: *District of Columbia v. Heller*. The Court overturned DC's handgun ban, ruling that the 2nd Amendment protected an individual's right to own guns for personal use.

2010: *Citizens United v. Federal Election Commission*. The Court ruled that a federal law barring corporations from using general funds to finance campaign advertisements was unconstitutional. The decision cast doubt on many laws restricting political spending by corporations and unions.

2011: *Snyder v. Phelps*. The justices found that an antigay church whose members protested at the funeral of a Marine could not be held liable for intrusion or the emotional distress of the father of the deceased because the protests were protected by the 1st Amendment.

2012: *U.S. v. Jones*. The Court ruled that attaching a GPS tracking device to a suspect's car and monitoring its movements requires a search warrant, as the 4th Amendment prohibition against unreasonable search and seizure applies.

2012: *Miller v. Alabama*. The Court ruled that mandatory life sentences without the possibility of parole violate juvenile offenders' 8th Amendment right to freedom from cruel and unusual punishment. The decision extended *Graham v. Florida*, a 2010 case in which the Court held that juveniles may not receive life sentences for crimes that do not result in homicides.

2012: *Natl. Federation of Independent Business v. Sebelius*. The Court ruled Congress acted within its powers of taxation in enacting the individual-mandate provision of the Patient Protection and Affordable Care Act (ACA), which required Americans without government- or employer-provided health insurance to purchase it or pay a fine. The Court ruled unconstitutional the provision of the act's Medicaid expansion that threatened non-compliant states with loss of funding.

2013: *Shelby County v. Holder*. The justices ruled that a key provision of the 1965 Voting Rights Act, meant to prevent discriminatory voting regulations from being enacted, was unconstitutional because it relied on outdated information to identify jurisdictions for additional scrutiny.

2013: *U.S. v. Windsor*. The Court struck down the central provision of the 1996 federal Defense of Marriage Act (DOMA), which prohibited federal recognition of same-sex marriages. A separate decision the same year, in *Hollingsworth v. Perry*, had the effect of legalizing same-sex marriage in California.

2014: *Riley v. California*; *U.S. v. Wurie*. The Court unanimously decided that police generally could not search the mobile telephones of arrested individuals without first obtaining a search warrant.

2014: *Burwell v. Hobby Lobby Stores*; *Conestoga Wood Specialties Corp. v. Burwell*. The justices ruled that some closely held corporations could claim an exemption—based on their owners' religious beliefs and the 1993 Religious Freedom Restoration Act—from a 2010 ACA mandate requiring many businesses to provide health insurance that covers contraception.

2015: *Obergefell v. Hodges*. The court ruled that state bans on same-sex marriage violated same-sex couples' rights under the due process and equal protection clauses of the 14th Amendment.

See also Year in Review: Notable Supreme Court Decisions.

STATES AND OTHER AREAS OF THE U.S.

Sources: Population: Decennial Censuses and Population Estimates Program, U.S. Census Bureau, U.S. Dept. of Commerce; population as of July 1, 2015, unless otherwise noted. Pop. density is for land area only. **Racial distribution** categories are abbreviated; their full forms are white, black or African American, Asian, American Indian and Alaska Native, Native Hawaiian and other Pacific Islander, two or more races. Categories may not add up to 100% due to rounding. **Hispanic** or Latino persons may be of any race. **Area:** Geography Division, U.S. Census Bureau, U.S. Dept. of Commerce. **Acres forested:** U.S. Forest Service, U.S. Dept. of Agriculture; source year may vary. **Chief airports:** Federal Aviation Admin., U.S. Dept. of Transportation. Chief airports had 500,000+ boardings in 2015; not all states had airports meeting this threshold. All **Economy** data as of 2015 unless otherwise noted. **Chief manuf. goods:** Manufacturing and Construction Division, U.S. Census Bureau, U.S. Dept. of Commerce. **Chief crops:** Natl. Agricultural Statistics Service, U.S. Dept. of Agriculture. **Farm income:** Economic Research Service, U.S. Dept. of Agriculture; 2014 cash receipts. **Nonfuel minerals:** Office of Mineral Information, U.S. Dept. of Interior; preliminary data. Some states exclude small amounts to avoid disclosing proprietary data. **Commercial fishing:** Natl. Marine Fisheries Service, U.S. Dept. of Commerce. **Gross state product** and **Per cap. pers. income:** Bureau of Economic Analysis, U.S. Dept. of Commerce; as of Dec. 2015. **Sales tax:** Federation of Tax Administrators; as of Jan. 1, 2016. **Gasoline tax:** American Petroleum Institute; as of July 1, 2016; incl. state excise tax, federal excise tax (18.4 cents per gallon), and other state fees. **Employment distrib.** and **Unemployment:** Bureau of Labor Statistics, U.S. Dept. of Labor; distribution is for non-farm jobs as of May 2015. **Min. wage:** U.S. Dept. of Labor; as of July 1, 2016. If a state has no minimum wage, or the state minimum wage is lower than the federal minimum wage, the federal rate of $7.25 applies. Small businesses may have lower minimum wages. Some municipalities may have different minimum wages. **New private housing:** Manufacturing and Construction Division, U.S. Census Bureau, U.S. Dept. of Commerce. Figures are building permits issued and est. value of the construction. **Broadband internet:** Industry Analysis and Tech. Division, Fed. Communications Commission. Broadband connections have minimum speeds of at least 3 megabits per second (Mbps) downstream and 200 kilobits per second (kbps) upstream as of Dec. 2014; figure given is broadband as a percentage of total internet connections. **Commercial banks** and **Savings institutions:** Federal Deposit Insurance Corp., as of June 30, 2015; FDIC-insured institutions only. **Lottery:** North American Assn. of State and Provincial Lotteries, FY 2015. Data may be unaudited and in some cases were gathered by third party. Some states report round sums; others report exact figures. **Fed. civ. employees:** Office of Personnel Mgmt., U.S. Dept. of Labor; as of Mar. 2016. **Education:** Natl. Ctr. for Education Statistics; high school graduation rates as of 2013-14 school year; number of colleges/univ. as of 2014-15. Data for 4-yr. private institutions does not include for-profit colleges/universities. **Energy:** Energy Information Admin., U.S. Dept. of Energy; average per capita monthly electricity consumption and cost for residential customers in 2014. **Tourism:** U.S. Travel Assn.; tourist spending in 2014. Other information from sources in individual states. NA = Not available; AFB = air force base; JRB = joint reserve base; NAS = naval air station.

Famous persons lists may include non-natives associated with the state as well as persons born there. **Websites** are subject to change and are not endorsed by *The World Almanac*.

Alabama (AL)

Heart of Dixie, Camellia State

People. Population: 4,858,979; rank: 24. **Pop. change** (2010-15): 1.6%. **Pop. density:** 95.9 per sq mi. **Racial distribution:** 69.5% white; 26.8% black; 1.4% Asian; 0.7% Amer. Ind.; 0.1% Hawaiian/Pacific Islander; 2 or more races, 1.6%. **Hispanic pop.:** 4.2%.

Geography. Total area: 52,420 sq mi; rank: 30. **Land area:** 50,645 sq mi; rank: 28. **Acres forested:** 23.1 mil. **Location:** East South Central state extending N-S from Tennessee to the Gulf of Mexico; E of the Mississippi R. **Climate:** long, hot summers; mild winters; generally abundant rain. **Topography:** coastal plains, including Prairie Black Belt, give way to hills, broken terrain; highest elevation 2,413 ft. **Capital:** Montgomery. **Chief airports:** Birmingham, Huntsville.

Economy. Chief industries: chemicals, electronics, apparel, primary metals, lumber and wood products, food processing, fabricated metals, automotive tires, oil and gas exploration. **Chief manuf. goods:** poultry processing, paper and paperboard, iron and steel, petroleum, automotive tires, aerospace, aluminum, auto body and parts. **Chief crops:** cotton, greenhouse and nursery, hay, peanuts, corn, soybeans. **Farm income:** crops, $1.27 bil; livestock/animal prods., $5.16 bil. **Nonfuel minerals:** $1.3 bil; cement (portland), stone (crushed), lime, sand and gravel (construction), sand and gravel (industrial). **Commercial fishing:** $70.1 mil. **Chief port:** Mobile. **Gross state product:** $204.2 bil. **Sales tax:** 4.0%. **Gasoline tax:** 39.31 cents/gal. **Employment distrib.:** 19.2% govt.; 19.4% trade/trans./util.; 13.2% mfg.; 11.7% ed./health; 11.8% prof./bus. serv.; 9.9% leisure/hosp.; 5.0% finance; 4.6% constr./mining/log.; 1.1% info.; 4.2% other serv. **Unemployment:** 6.1%. **Min. wage/hr.:** none ($7.25). **Per cap. pers. income:** $38,965. **New private housing:** 14,054 units/$2.4 bil. **Broadband internet:** 88.0%. **Commercial banks:** 159; deposits: $90.6 bil. **Savings institutions:** 10; deposits: $865 mil.

Federal govt. Fed. civ. employees: 37,878; **avg. salary:** $82,243. **Notable fed. facilities:** Redstone Arsenal; Ft. Rucker; Marshall Space Flight Ctr.; Anniston Army Depot; Maxwell AFB and Gunter Annex; Army Corps of Engineers, Mobile District.

Education. High school grad. rate: 86.3%. **4-year public coll./univ.:** 14; **2-yr. public:** 25; **4-yr. private:** 20.

Energy. Electricity use/cost: 1,265 kWh, $145.25.

State data. Motto: Audemus Jura Nostra Defendere (We dare defend our rights). **Flower:** Camellia. **Bird:** Northern flicker (yellowhammer is local nickname). **Tree:** Southern longleaf pine. **Song:** "Alabama." **Entered union:** Dec. 14, 1819; rank: 22nd.

Tourism. Tourist spending: $8.9 bil. **Attractions:** First White House of the Confederacy, Civil Rights Memorial, Alabama Shakespeare Festival, in Montgomery; Ivy Green (Helen Keller birthplace), Tuscumbia; Barber Vintage Motorsports Museum, Civil Rights Institute, Vulcan Park and Museum (world's largest cast iron statue), in Birmingham; G. W. Carver Interpretive Museum, Tuskegee; W. C. Handy Home, Museum, and Library, Frank Lloyd Wright's Rosenbaum House, in Florence; U.S. Space & Rocket Ctr., Huntsville; Moundville Archaeological Park; USS *Alabama* Memorial Park, Mobile; Gulf State Park, Gulf Shores. **Information:** Alabama Tourism Dept., 401 Adams Ave., Ste. 126, P.O. Box 4927, Montgomery, AL 36103; 1-800-ALABAMA, (334) 242-4169; www.alabama.travel

History. Alabama was inhabited by the Creek, Cherokee, Chickasaw, Alabama, and Choctaw peoples when Spanish explorers arrived in the early 1500s. The French made the first permanent settlement at Ft. Louis, 1702, and founded Mobile, 1711. France later gave up the entire region to England under the Treaty of Paris, 1763. Spanish forces took control of the Mobile Bay area, 1780, and it remained under Spanish control until seized by U.S. troops, 1813. Most of present-day Alabama was held by the Creeks until Gen. Andrew Jackson broke their power, 1814. When Alabama became a state, 1819, black slaves made up about one-third of the population. The Indian Removal Act of 1830 forced most remaining Creeks west. The state seceded, 1861, and the Confederate states were organized Feb. 4, at Montgomery, the first capital. The state was readmitted, 1868. Birmingham, founded 1871, became a center for iron- and steelmaking. The Montgomery bus boycott, 1955, sparked by Rosa Parks, helped launch the civil rights movement. Other confrontations occurred at Birmingham, 1963, and Selma, 1965. The leading political figure from the 1960s through the '80s, four-term gov. George Wallace, started as a segregationist but later won with black support. Growth in the auto industry boosted the state economy as the 21st cent. began. A string of tornadoes in western Alabama in Apr. 2011 killed at least 248. Jefferson County, which includes the city of Birmingham, filed for the then-most expensive municipal bankruptcy in history in Nov. 2011.

Famous Alabamians. Hank Aaron, Tallulah Bankhead, Charles Barkley, Hugo L. Black, Paul "Bear" Bryant, George Washington Carver, Nat King Cole, Courteney Cox, William Christopher "W. C." Handy, Polly Holliday, Bo Jackson, Helen Keller, Coretta Scott King, Harper Lee, Joe Louis, Willie Mays, Jim Nabors, Jesse Owens, Terrell Owens, Rosa Parks, Condoleezza Rice, Lionel Richie, Octavia Spencer, Channing Tatum, George C. Wallace, Booker T. Washington, Hank Williams.

Website. www.alabama.gov

Alaska (AK)

The Last Frontier (unofficial)

People. Population: 738,432; rank: 48. **Pop. change** (2010-15): 4.0%. **Pop. density:** 1.3 per sq mi. **Racial distribution:** 66.5% white; 3.9% black; 6.3% Asian; 14.8% Amer. Ind.; 1.3% Hawaiian/Pacific Islander; 2 or more races, 7.2%. **Hispanic pop.:** 7.0%.

Geography. Total area: 665,384 sq mi; rank: 1. **Land area:** 570,641 sq mi; rank: 1. **Acres forested:** 15.4 mil. **Location:**

NW corner of North America, bordered on E by Canada. **Climate:** SE, SW, and central regions, moist and mild; far N extremely dry. Extended summer days, winter nights throughout. **Topography:** includes Pacific and Arctic mountain systems, central plateau, and Arctic slope. Denali, formerly Mt. McKinley, 20,310 ft, is the highest point in N. America. **Capital:** Juneau. **Chief airport:** Anchorage.

Economy. Chief industries: petroleum, tourism, fishing, mining, forestry, transportation, aerospace. **Chief manuf. goods:** petroleum, seafood. **Chief crops:** greenhouse products, barley, oats, hay, potatoes, carrots. **Farm income:** crops, $26.10 mil; livestock/animal prods., $5.78 mil. **Nonfuel minerals:** $3.1 bil; zinc, gold, lead, silver, sand and gravel (construction). **Commercial fishing:** $1.7 bil. **Chief ports:** Anchorage, Dutch Harbor, Kodiak, Juneau, Sitka, Valdez. **Gross state product:** $52.8 bil. **Sales tax:** none. **Gasoline tax:** 30.65 cents/gal. **Employment distrib.:** 24.7% govt.; 20.2% trade/trans./util.; 3.3% mfg.; 14.4% ed./health; 8.3% prof./bus. serv.; 10.8% leisure/hosp.; 3.6% finance; 9.5% constr./mining/log.; 1.8% info.; 3.4% other serv. **Unemployment:** 6.5%. **Min. wage/hr.:** $9.75. **Per cap. pers. income:** $55,940. **New private housing:** 1,298 units/$324.6 mil. **Broadband internet:** 78.4%. **Commercial banks:** 6; deposits: $11.2 bil. **Savings institutions:** 1; deposits: $285 mil.

Federal govt. Fed. civ. employees: 10,870; **avg. salary:** $79,083. **Notable fed. facilities:** Joint Base Elmendorf-Richardson; Ft. Wainwright; Eielson AFB; Ft. Greely.

Education. High school grad. rate: 71.1%. **4-year public coll./univ.:** 3; **2-yr. public:** 2; **4-yr. private:** 2.

Energy. Electricity use/cost: 605 kWh, $115.79.

State data. Motto: North to the future. **Flower:** Forget-me-not. **Bird:** Willow ptarmigan. **Tree:** Sitka spruce. **Song:** "Alaska's Flag." **Entered union:** Jan. 3, 1959; rank: 49th.

Tourism. Tourist spending: $2.5 bil. **Attractions:** Portage Glacier, in Chugach Natl. Forest; Mendenhall Glacier, in Tongass Natl. Forest; Totem Heritage Ctr., Ketchikan; Glacier Bay Natl. Park and Preserve; Denali (formerly Mt. McKinley, N. America's highest peak), in Denali Natl. Park and Preserve; Mt. Roberts Tramway, Juneau; Alaska Maritime Natl. Wildlife Refuge; St. Michael's Cathedral, Alaska Raptor Ctr., in Sitka; White Pass & Yukon Route railroad, Skagway; Katmai Natl. Park and Preserve; Univ. of Alaska Museum of the North, Fairbanks. **Information:** Alaska Travel Industry Association, 2600 Cordova St., Ste. 201, Anchorage, AK 99503; 1-800-327-9372; www.travelalaska.com

History. Early inhabitants included the Tlingit-Haida and Athabascan peoples. Ancestors of the Aleut and Inuit (Eskimo) probably arrived from Siberia between 10,000 and 6,000 years ago. Vitus Bering, a Dane sailing for Russia, was the first European to land in Alaska, 1741. Russians, pursuing the fur trade, established a permanent settlement on Kodiak Island, 1784. Sec. of State William H. Seward bought Alaska from Russia for $7.2 mil in 1867, a deal some called "Seward's Folly." Discovery of gold in the Klondike region of Canada's Yukon Territory, 1896, triggered an Alaskan gold rush. Alaska became a territory, 1912, and a state, 1959. A huge oil find at Prudhoe Bay, 1968, led to construction of the Trans-Alaska Pipeline, 1974-77. The *Exxon Valdez* supertanker ran aground, 1989, spilling about 11 mil gallons of crude oil; the cleanup cost more than $2.2 bil. Repeated attempts by Congress members to pass a bill permitting oil and gas drilling in the Arctic National Wildlife Refuge have failed.

Famous Alaskans. Tom Bodett, Susan Butcher, Ernest Gruening, Jewel (Kilcher), Tony Knowles, Sydney Laurence, Sarah Palin, Libby Riddles, Curt Schilling, Jefferson "Soapy" Smith.

Website. www.alaska.gov

Arizona (AZ)

Grand Canyon State

People. Population: 6,828,065; rank: 14. **Pop. change** (2010-15): 6.8%. **Pop. density:** 60.1 per sq mi. **Racial distribution:** 83.5% white; 4.8% black; 3.4% Asian; 5.3% Amer. Ind.; 0.3% Hawaiian/Pacific Islander; 2 or more races, 2.7%. **Hispanic pop.:** 30.7%.

Geography. Total area: 113,990 sq mi; rank: 6. **Land area:** 113,594 sq mi; rank: 6. **Acres forested:** 18.5 mil. **Location:** southwestern U.S. **Climate:** clear and dry in southern regions and northern plateau; high central areas have heavy winter snows. **Topography:** Colorado Plateau in the N, containing the Grand Canyon; Mexican Highlands run NW to SE; Sonoran Desert in the SW. **Capital:** Phoenix. **Chief airports:** Mesa, Phoenix, Tucson.

Economy. Chief industries: manufacturing, construction, tourism, mining, agriculture. **Chief manuf. goods:** aerospace,

semiconductors, navigational instruments, cement, plastics, structural metals, dairy, printing, furniture. **Chief crops:** cotton, grapes, apples, lettuce, hay, potatoes, sorghum, barley, corn, wheat. **Farm income:** crops, $2.11 bil; livestock/animal prods., $2.38 bil. **Nonfuel minerals:** $6.8 bil; copper, molybdenum concentrates, sand and gravel (construction), cement (portland), stone (crushed). **Gross state product:** $290.6 bil. **Sales tax:** 5.6%. **Gasoline tax:** 37.40 cents/gal. **Employment distrib.:** 15.2% govt.; 19.0% trade/trans./util.; 5.9% mfg.; 15.3% ed./health; 15.0% prof./bus. serv.; 11.5% leisure/hosp.; 7.6% finance; 5.4% constr./mining/log.; 1.8% info.; 3.3% other serv. **Unemployment:** 6.1%. **Min. wage/hr.:** $8.05. **Per cap. pers. income:** $39,060. **New private housing:** 28,910 units/$7.0 bil. **Broadband internet:** 90.1%. **Commercial banks:** 59; deposits: $102.4 bil. **Savings institutions:** 7; deposits: $3.2 bil. **Lottery:** total sales: $750.0 mil; profit: $176.0 mil.

Federal govt. Fed. civ. employees: 31,166; **avg. salary:** $69,898. **Notable fed. facilities:** Luke AFB; Davis-Monthan AFB; Ft. Huachuca; Yuma Proving Ground.

Education. High school grad. rate: 75.7%. **4-year public coll./univ.:** 8; **2-yr. public:** 20; **4-yr. private:** 14.

Energy. Electricity use/cost: 1,013 kWh, $120.51.

State data. Motto: Ditat Deus (God enriches). **Flower:** Blossom of the saguaro cactus. **Bird:** Cactus wren. **Tree:** Paloverde. **Song:** "Arizona." **Entered union:** Feb. 14, 1912; rank: 48th.

Tourism. Tourist spending: $17.6 bil. **Attractions:** Grand Canyon; Painted Desert, in Grand Canyon and Petrified Forest Natl. Parks; Glen Canyon Natl. Recreation Area; Canyon de Chelly Natl. Monument; Meteor Crater, near Winslow; London Bridge, Lake Havasu City; Biosphere 2, Oracle; Navajo Natl. Monument; Tombstone historic mining town; Tempe Town Lake. **Information:** Arizona Office of Tourism, 1110 W. Washington St., Ste. 155, Phoenix, AZ 85007; 1-866-275-5816; www.visitarizona.com

History. Paleo-Indians hunted large game in the area at least 12,000 years ago. Anasazi, Mogollon, and Hohokam civilizations lived there c. 300 BCE-1300 CE; Navajo and Apache came c. 15th cent. Marcos de Niza, a Spanish Franciscan, and Estevanico, a black former slave, explored, 1539; explorer Francisco Vásquez de Coronado visited, 1540. Eusebio Francisco Kino, a Jesuit missionary, taught Indians, 1692-1711, and left missions. Tubac, a Spanish fort, became the first European settlement, 1752. Spain ceded Arizona to Mexico, 1821. The U.S. took over, 1848, after the Mexican War. The area below the Gila R. came from Mexico in the Gadsden Purchase, 1853. Arizona became a territory, 1863. Apache wars ended with Geronimo's surrender, 1886. Arizona became a state, 1912, and grew rapidly after 1960 with a fourfold rise in population over the next four decades. Barry Goldwater was a leading conservative voice in the U.S. Senate (1953-65, 1969-87). The border with Mexico is a major gateway for illegal immigration to the U.S. In 2012, the U.S. Supreme Court struck down most provisions of a 2010 state immigration law that allowed police to make warrantless arrests of those reasonably suspected of having immigrated illegally, but left a provision requiring police to check the immigration status of those stopped or arrested for any other reason.

Famous Arizonans. Bruce Babbitt, Cochise, Alice Cooper, Geronimo, Gabrielle Giffords, Barry Goldwater, Zane Grey, Carl Hayden, George W. P. Hunt, Helen Hull Jacobs, Bil Keane, Percival Lowell, John McCain, John J. Rhodes, Linda Ronstadt, Emma Stone, Morris K. Udall, Stewart L. Udall, Frank Lloyd Wright.

Website. www.az.gov

Arkansas (AR)

Natural State, Razorback State

People. Population: 2,978,204; rank: 33. **Pop. change** (2010-15): 2.1%. **Pop. density:** 57.2 per sq mi. **Racial distribution:** 79.5% white; 15.7% black; 1.6% Asian; 1.0% Amer. Ind.; 0.3% Hawaiian/Pacific Islander; 2 or more races, 2.0%. **Hispanic pop.:** 7.2%.

Geography. Total area: 53,179 sq mi; rank: 29. **Land area:** 52,035 sq mi; rank: 27. **Acres forested:** 19.0 mil. **Location:** West South Central state. **Climate:** long, hot summers, mild winters; generally abundant rainfall. **Topography:** eastern delta and prairie, southern lowland forests, and the northwestern highlands, which include the Ozark Plateaus. **Capital:** Little Rock. **Chief airports:** Bentonville, Little Rock.

Economy. Chief industries: manufacturing, agriculture, tourism, forestry. **Chief manuf. goods:** poultry processing, motor vehicles and parts, iron and steel, paper and paperboard, plastics, preserved fruits and vegetables, aerospace, rubber. **Chief crops:** rice, soybeans, cotton, hay, wheat, corn, sorghum, tomatoes, peaches, watermelons, pecans, blueberries, grapes. **Farm income:** crops, $4.53 bil; livestock/animal prods., $5.75 bil. **Nonfuel minerals:** $991 mil; bromine, sand and gravel (industrial), stone (crushed), cement (portland), sand and gravel (construction). **Chief port:** Helena. **Gross state product:** $123.2 bil. **Sales tax:** 6.5%. **Gasoline tax:** 40.20 cents/gal. **Employment distrib.:** 17.5% govt.; 20.9% trade/trans./util.; 12.5% mfg.; 14.7% ed./health; 11.6% prof./bus. serv.; 9.5% leisure/hosp.; 4.0% finance; 4.5% constr./mining/log.; 1.1% info.; 3.6% other serv. **Unemployment:** 5.2%. **Min. wage/hr.:** $8.00. **Per cap. pers. income:** $39,107. **New private housing:** 8,500 units/$1.4 bil. **Broadband internet:** 85.2%. **Commercial banks:** 125; deposits: $56.1 bil. **Savings institutions:** 4; deposits: $412 mil. **Lottery:** total sales: $409.1 mil; profit: $72.8 mil.

Federal govt. Fed. civ. employees: 13,150; **avg. salary:** $68,594. **Notable fed. facilities:** Little Rock AFB; Pine Bluff Arsenal; Natl. Ctr. for Toxicological Research, Jefferson.

Education. High school grad. rate: 86.9%. **4-year public coll./univ.:** 11; **2-yr. public:** 22; **4-yr. private:** 12.

Energy. Electricity use/cost: 1,143 kWh, $108.63.

State data. Motto: Regnat Populus (The people rule). **Flower:** Apple blossom. **Bird:** Northern mockingbird. **Tree:** Pine. **Song:** "Arkansas." **Entered union:** June 15, 1836; rank: 25th.

Tourism. Tourist spending: $6.6 bil. **Attractions:** Eureka Springs; Ozark Folk Ctr. State Park, Mountain View; Blanchard Springs Caverns, in Ozark Natl. Forest; Crater of Diamonds State Park, Murfreesboro; Toltec Mounds Archeological State Park, Scott; Buffalo Natl. River; Hot Springs Natl. Park; Pea Ridge Natl. Military Park; William J. Clinton Presidential Library and Museum, Little Rock Central High School Natl. Historic Site, in Little Rock; Crystal Bridges Museum of American Art, Bentonville. **Information:** Arkansas Dept. of Parks & Tourism, 1 Capitol Mall, Little Rock, AR 72201; 1-800-NATU-RAL; www.arkansas.com

History. Quapaw, Caddo, Osage, Cherokee, and Choctaw peoples lived in the area at the time of European contact. The first European explorers were Hernando de Soto, 1541; Jacques Marquette and Louis Jolliet, 1673; and René-Robert Cavelier, sieur de La Salle, 1682. French fur trader Henri de Tonty founded the first settlement, 1686, at Arkansas Post. In 1762, the area was ceded by France to Spain, then given back, 1800, and was part of the Louisiana Purchase, 1803. It was made a territory, 1819, and entered the Union as a slave state, 1836. Arkansas seceded in 1861, after the Civil War began; it was readmitted, 1868. Pres. Eisenhower sent federal troops, 1957, to keep Gov. Orval Faubus from blocking racial integration at Central High School in Little Rock. Wal-Mart, now the world's leading retailer, opened its first store in Rogers, 1962. Elected five times as governor, Bill Clinton later served two terms as president (1993-2001). His presidential library opened, 2004, in Little Rock.

Famous Arkansans. Daisy Bates, Dee Brown, Paul "Bear" Bryant, Glen Campbell, Hattie Wyatt Caraway, Johnny Cash, Wesley Clark, Bill Clinton, Jay Hanna "Dizzy" Dean, Orval Faubus, James William Fulbright, Al Green, John Grisham, Levon Helm, John H. Johnson, Douglas MacArthur, John Little McClellan, James S. McDonnell, Scottie Pippen, Dick Powell, Brooks Robinson, Winthrop Rockefeller, Mary Steenburgen, Edward Durell Stone, Billy Bob Thornton, Sam Walton, Archibald Yell.

Website. www.arkansas.gov

California (CA)
Golden State

People. Population: 39,144,818; rank: 1. **Pop. change** (2010-15): 5.1%. **Pop. density:** 251.3 per sq mi. **Racial distribution:** 72.9% white; 6.5% black; 14.7% Asian; 1.7% Amer. Ind.; 0.5% Hawaiian/Pacific Islander; 2 or more races, 3.8%. **Hispanic pop.:** 38.8%.

Geography. Total area: 163,695 sq mi; rank: 3. **Land area:** 155,779 sq mi; rank: 3. **Acres forested:** 31.9 mil. **Location:** western coast of U.S. **Climate:** moderate temperatures and rainfall along the coast; extremes in the interior. **Topography:** long mountainous coastline; central valley; Sierra Nevada on the E; desert basins in southern interior; rugged mountains in N. **Capital:** Sacramento. **Chief airports:** Burbank, Fresno, Long Beach, Los Angeles, Oakland, Ontario, Palm Springs, Sacramento, San Diego, San Francisco, San Jose, Santa Ana.

Economy. Chief industries: agriculture, tourism, apparel, electronics, telecommunications, entertainment. **Chief manuf. goods:** petroleum, aerospace, precision instruments, semiconductors, telecom and broadcasting equip., pharmaceutical, wineries, plastics, medical equip., preserved fruits and vegetables, printing, dairy, cut and sew apparel, motor vehicles. **Chief crops:** grapes, nursery products, almonds, lettuce, hay, strawberries, floriculture, tomatoes, cotton, oranges, pistachios, walnuts, broccoli, carrots, rice, peaches, lemons. **Farm income:** crops, $38.70 bil; livestock/animal prods., $15.32 bil. **Nonfuel minerals:** $3.3 bil; sand and gravel (construction), cement (portland), boron minerals, stone (crushed), gold. **Commercial fishing:** $253.8 mil. **Chief ports:** Long Beach, Los Angeles, San Diego, Port Hueneme, Richmond, Oakland, San Francisco, Stockton. **Gross state product:** $2.5 tril. **Sales tax:** 7.5%. **Gasoline tax:** 56.97 cents/gal. **Employment distrib.:** 15.6% govt.; 18.0% trade/trans./util.; 7.8% mfg.; 15.5% ed./health; 15.5% prof./bus. serv.; 11.6% leisure/hosp.; 4.9% finance; 4.8% constr./mining/log.; 3.0% info.; 3.4% other serv. **Unemployment:** 6.2%. **Min. wage/ hr.:** $10.00. **Per cap. pers. income:** $52,651. **New private housing:** 98,188 units/$22.6 bil. **Broadband internet:** 93.7%. **Commercial banks:** 223; deposits: $1.1 tril. **Savings institutions:** 18; deposits: $17.4 bil. **Lottery:** total sales: $5.5 bil; profit: $1.4 bil.

Federal govt. Fed. civ. employees: 140,330; **avg. salary:** $83,475. **Notable fed. facilities:** USMC Camp Pendleton; Naval Base Coronado; Marine Corps Air Ground Combat Ctr., 29 Palms; Marine Corps Air Station Miramar; Travis AFB; Naval Research Lab, Monterey; Lawrence Livermore Natl. Lab; Lawrence Berkeley Natl. Lab; NASA Jet Propulsion Lab; Edwards AFB (NASA Dryden Flight Research Ctr., AF Test Ctr.); San Francisco Mint.

Education. High school grad. rate: 81.0%. **4-year public coll./univ.:** 34; **2-yr. public:** 115; **4-yr. private:** 138.

Energy. Electricity use/cost: 562 kWh, $91.26.

State data. Motto: Eureka (I have found it). **Flower:** Golden poppy. **Bird:** California valley quail. **Tree:** California redwood. **Song:** "I Love You, California." **Entered union:** Sept. 9, 1850; rank: 31st.

Tourism. Tourist spending: $124.2 bil. **Attractions:** *Queen Mary*, Aquarium of the Pacific, in Long Beach; Palomar Observatory, Palomar Mountain; Disneyland Resort, Anaheim; Getty Center, Universal Studios Hollywood, Griffith Observatory, in Los Angeles; Tournament of Roses and Rose Bowl, Pasadena; The California Museum, California State Railroad Museum, in Sacramento; San Diego Zoo, USS *Midway* Museum, in San Diego; Yosemite Valley; Lassen Volcanic, Sequoia, and Kings Canyon Natl. Parks; Mojave and Sonoran Deserts; Death Valley; Golden Gate Park, Alcatraz Island, in San Francisco; Napa Valley wine region; Monterey Bay Aquarium, Monterey Peninsula; Ancient Bristlecone Pine Forest (oldest known living trees on Earth), in Inyo Natl. Forest; Redwood Natl. and State Parks; Muir Woods Natl. Monument, Mill Valley. **Information:** California Tourism, P.O. Box 1499, Sacramento, CA 95812-1499; 1-877-225-4367; www.visitcalifornia.com

History. Early inhabitants included more than 100 different Native American tribes with multiple dialects. The first European explorers were Juan Rodríguez Cabrillo, 1542, and Sir Francis Drake, 1579. The first settlement was the Spanish Alta California mission at San Diego, 1769, first in a string founded by Franciscan Father Junípero Serra. California became a province of independent Mexico, 1821. U.S. traders and settlers arrived in the 19th cent. and staged the Bear Flag revolt, 1846, in protest against Mexican rule; later that year U.S. forces occupied California. At the end of the Mexican War, Mexico ceded the territory to the U.S., 1848; that same year gold was discovered, and the famed gold rush began. California became a state, 1850. An economic downturn in the 1870s spurred riots against Chinese immigrants, who had come as laborers in the boom years. An earthquake and related fires devastated San Francisco, 1906. During World War II, Japanese Americans, many of them U.S. citizens, were held in detention camps, 1942-45. Ronald Reagan, a former movie actor, became state governor (1967-75) and U.S. president (1981-89). A budget crisis, 2003, resulted in the recall of Gov. Gray Davis and the election of another actor, Arnold Schwarzenegger. Led by Hollywood in entertainment and Silicon Valley in technology, the state's economy dwarfs that of most nations. Still, billion-dollar budget deficits have been a perennial problem. As much of the state entered the fourth year of a devastating drought, Gov. Jerry Brown Apr. 1,

2015, ordered a mandatory statewide reduction in water use for residents and businesses. A married couple in early Dec. 2015 fatally shot 14 people at a workplace in San Bernardino after pledging allegiance to ISIS on social media; both died in a shootout with police.

Famous Californians. Tom Brady, Edmund G. (Pat) Brown, Jerry Brown, Luther Burbank, Julia Child, Ted Danson, Cameron Diaz, Leonardo DiCaprio, Joe DiMaggio, Landon Donovan, Clint Eastwood, Dianne Feinstein, John C. Fremont, Tom Hanks, William Randolph Hearst, Helen Hunt, Steve Jobs, Jimmie Johnson, Angelina Jolie, Jack Kemp, Jason Kidd, Brie Larson, Lisa Leslie, Monica Lewinsky, Jack London, George Lucas, Phil Mickelson, Marilyn Monroe, John Muir, Richard M. Nixon, Gwyneth Paltrow, George S. Patton Jr., Gregory Peck, Nancy Pelosi, Ronald Reagan, Sally K. Ride, William Saroyan, Arnold Schwarzenegger, Junípero Serra, O. J. Simpson, Kevin Spacey, Leland Stanford, Gwen Stefani, John Steinbeck, Shirley Temple, Earl Warren, Serena Williams, Ted Williams, Venus Williams, Tiger Woods.

Website. www.ca.gov

Colorado (CO)
Centennial State

People. Population: 5,456,574; rank: 22. **Pop. change** (2010-15): 8.5%. **Pop. density:** 52.6 per sq mi. **Racial distribution:** 87.5% white; 4.5% black; 3.2% Asian; 1.6% Amer. Ind.; 0.2% Hawaiian/Pacific Islander; 2 or more races, 2.9%. **Hispanic pop.:** 21.3%.

Geography. Total area: 104,094 sq mi; rank: 8. **Land area:** 103,642 sq mi; rank: 8. **Acres forested:** 22.9 mil. **Location:** W central U.S. **Climate:** low relative humidity, abundant sun, wide daily/seasonal temperature ranges; alpine conditions in the high mountains. **Topography:** eastern dry high plains; hilly to mountainous central plateau; western Rocky Mts. of high ranges with broad valleys, deep, narrow canyons. **Capital:** Denver. **Chief airports:** Colorado Springs, Denver.

Economy. Chief industries: manufacturing, construction, government, tourism, agriculture, aerospace, electronics equip. **Chief manuf. goods:** animal slaughtering, beer, petroleum, pharmaceuticals, aerospace, medical equip., precision instruments, printing, semiconductors. **Chief crops:** hay, corn, potatoes, wheat, onions, dry edible beans, sunflowers, sugar beets, barley, proso millet, cabbage, peaches, lettuce, apples, cantaloupes. **Farm income:** crops, $2.30 bil; livestock/animal prods., $5.24 bil. **Nonfuel minerals:** $2.4 bil; molybdenum concentrates, sand and gravel (construction), cement (portland), gold, stone (crushed). **Gross state product:** $314.9 bil. **Sales tax:** 2.9%. **Gasoline tax:** 40.40 cents/gal. **Employment distrib.:** 16.8% govt.; 17.2% trade/trans./util.; 5.5% mfg.; 12.5% ed./health; 15.7% prof./bus. serv.; 12.1% leisure/hosp.; 6.2% finance; 7.1% constr./mining/log.; 2.8% info.; 4.0% other serv. **Unemployment:** 3.9%. **Min. wage/hr.:** $8.31. **Per cap. pers. income:** $50,410. **New private housing:** 31,871 units/$7.5 bil. **Broadband internet:** 91.3%. **Commercial banks:** 132; deposits: $114.0 bil. **Savings institutions:** 13; deposits: $2.7 bil. **Lottery:** total sales: $538.0 mil; profit: $128.0 mil.

Federal govt. Fed. civ. employees: 36,383; **avg. salary:** $81,915. **Notable fed. facilities:** U.S. Air Force Academy; Peterson AFB; Denver Mint; Ft. Carson; Natl. Renewable Energy Lab; Transportation Tech. Ctr.; NORAD and USNORTHCOM Alt. Command Ctr., Cheyenne Mtn. Complex; Denver Fed. Ctr.; Natl. Ctr. for Atmospheric Research; Natl. Inst. of Standards & Technology, Boulder; Natl. Wildlife Research Ctr.; NOAA Earth System Environmental Lab.

Education. High school grad. rate: 77.3%. **4-year public coll./univ.:** 14; **2-yr. public:** 14; **4-yr. private:** 14.

Energy. Electricity use/cost: 687 kWh, $83.73.

State data. Motto: Nil Sine Numine (Nothing without Providence). **Flower:** Rocky Mountain columbine. **Bird:** Lark bunting. **Tree:** Colorado blue spruce. **Songs:** "Where the Columbines Grow"; "Rocky Mountain High." **Entered union:** Aug. 1, 1876; rank: 38th.

Tourism. Tourist spending: $18.0 bil. **Attractions:** Denver Museum of Nature & Science, Denver Botanic Gardens, Denver Zoo; Red Rocks Park and Amphitheatre, Morrison; Natl. Ctr. for Atmospheric Research, Boulder; Rocky Mountain, Black Canyon of the Gunnison, and Mesa Verde (Anasazi cliff dwellings) Natl. Parks; Aspen, Breckenridge, Steamboat, and Vail ski resorts; Garden of the Gods, Colorado Springs; Great Sand Dunes Natl. Park and Preserve; Dinosaur and Colorado Natl. Monuments; Pikes Peak and Mount Evans; Grand Mesa Natl. Forest; historic mining towns of Central

City, Silverton, Cripple Creek; Bent's Old Fort Natl. Historic Site, near La Junta; Georgetown Loop Historic Mining and Railroad Park; Durango & Silverton Narrow Gauge Railroad Museum, Durango; Cumbres & Toltec Scenic Railroad, Antonito; gambling in Black Hawk, Central City, Cripple Creek and on tribal land in Ignacio and Towaoc. **Information:** Colorado Tourism Office, 1625 Broadway, Ste. 1700, Denver, CO 80202; 1-800-COLORADO; www.colorado.com

History. Paleo-Indians hunted big game in the area at least 11,000 years ago. Anasazi cliff dwellers flourished around Mesa Verde until about 1300 CE; other Native Americans were the Ute, Pueblo, Cheyenne, and Arapaho. The region was claimed by Spain but passed to France, 1800. The U.S. acquired eastern Colorado in the Louisiana Purchase, 1803. Lt. Zebulon M. Pike explored the area, 1806, sighting the peak that bears his name. After the Mexican War, 1846-48, U.S. immigrants settled in the east, former Mexicans in the south. Gold was discovered in 1858, causing a population boom. Congress created Colorado Territory, 1861. Conflict between newcomers and displaced Native Americans led to the Sand Creek Massacre, 1864, in which U.S. soldiers and settlers killed some 150 Cheyenne and Arapaho. U.S. Army troops forced the removal to reservations (mostly in present-day Oklahoma) of most Native Americans in the state, 1867. The 1870s brought statehood, 1876, and rich silver finds that turned Leadville into a boomtown. Federal military and civilian employment in Colorado surged in the 1940s and '50s; since then, tourism and technology have fueled the economy. The state's Hispanic population grew from 5.8% in 1980 to 20.7% in 2010. Colorado became the first state in the U.S. to legalize the sale of recreational marijuana in Jan. 2014. The state raised $63 mil in tax revenue from combined medical and recreational marijuana sales in 2014.

Famous Coloradans. Tim Allen, Chauncey Billups, Frederick Bonfils, Molly Brown, William N. Byers, M. Scott Carpenter, Lon Chaney, Jack Dempsey, Mamie Eisenhower, Douglas Fairbanks, Barney Ford, Roy Halladay, Chief Ourey, Trey Parker, "Baby Doe" Tabor, Lowell Thomas, Byron R. White, Paul Whiteman.

Website. www.colorado.gov

Connecticut (CT)
Constitution State, Nutmeg State

People. Population: 3,590,886; rank: 29. **Pop. change** (2010-15): 0.5%. **Pop. density:** 741.6 per sq mi. **Racial distribution:** 80.8% white; 11.6% black; 4.6% Asian; 0.5% Amer. Ind.; 0.1% Hawaiian/Pacific Islander; 2 or more races, 2.2%. **Hispanic pop.:** 15.4%.

Geography. Total area: 5,543 sq mi; rank: 48. **Land area:** 4,842 sq mi; rank: 48. **Acres forested:** 1.8 mil. **Location:** New England state in NE corner of U.S. **Climate:** moderate; winters avg. slightly below freezing; warm, humid summers. **Topography:** western upland, the Berkshires, in the NW, highest elevations; narrow central lowland N-S; hilly eastern upland drained by rivers. **Capital:** Hartford. **Chief airport:** Windsor Locks.

Economy. Chief industries: manufacturing, retail trade, government, services, finances, insurance, real estate. **Chief manuf. goods:** aerospace, chemicals, fabricated metals, precision instruments, toiletries, medical equip., printing, plastics. **Chief crops:** nursery stock, Christmas trees, mushrooms, sweet corn, apples, tobacco, hay. **Farm income:** crops, $382.16 mil; livestock/animal prods., $247.67 mil. **Nonfuel minerals:** $232 mil; stone (crushed), sand and gravel (construction), clays (common), stone (dimension), gemstones (natural). **Commercial fishing:** $14.1 mil. **Chief ports:** New Haven, Bridgeport, New London. **Gross state product:** $258.5 bil. **Sales tax:** 6.35%. **Gasoline tax:** 56.70 cents/gal. **Employment distrib.:** 14.3% govt.; 17.6% trade/trans./util.; 9.4% mfg.; 19.4% ed./health; 12.9% prof./bus. serv.; 9.2% leisure/hosp.; 7.8% finance; 3.6% constr./mining/log.; 2.0% info.; 3.8% other serv. **Unemployment:** 5.6%. **Min. wage/hr.:** $9.60. **Per cap. pers. income:** $66,972. **New private housing:** 6,077 units/$1.3 bil. **Broadband internet:** 96.9%. **Commercial banks:** 31; deposits: $98.0 bil. **Savings institutions:** 32; deposits: $22.4 bil. **Lottery:** total sales: $1.1 bil; profit: $319.7 mil.

Federal govt. Fed. civ. employees: 8,040; **avg. salary:** $84,066. **Notable fed. facilities:** U.S. Coast Guard Academy; Naval Sub Base New London.

Education. High school grad. rate: 87.0%. **4-year public coll./univ.:** 9; **2-yr. public:** 12; **4-yr. private:** 19.

Energy. Electricity use/cost: 730 kWh, $144.10.

State data. Motto: Qui Transtulit Sustinet (He who transplanted still sustains). **Flower:** Mountain laurel. **Bird:**

American robin. **Tree:** White oak. **Song:** "Yankee Doodle." **Fifth** of the 13 original states to ratify the Constitution, Jan. 9, 1788.

Tourism. Tourist spending: $10.6 bil. **Attractions:** Mark Twain House and Museum, Hartford; Yale Univ. Art Gallery, Peabody Museum of Natural History, in New Haven; Mystic Seaport, Mystic Aquarium; Barnum Museum, Bridgeport; Gillette Castle State Park, East Haddam; USS *Nautilus* (1st nuclear-powered submarine) at Submarine Force Library and Museum, Groton; Mashantucket Pequot Museum and Research Ctr.; Foxwoods Resort Casino, Ledyard; Mohegan Sun, Uncasville; Lake Compounce (est. 1846; oldest continuously operating amusement park in U.S.), Bristol; Philip Johnson Glass House, New Canaan. **Information:** Connecticut Commission on Culture and Tourism, One Constitution Plz., 2nd Fl., Hartford, CT 06103; 1-888-CTVISIT, (860) 256-2800; www.ctvisit.com

History. At the time of European contact, inhabitants of the area were Algonquian peoples, including the Mohegan and Pequot. Dutch explorer Adriaen Block was the first European visitor, 1614. By 1634, English settlers from Plymouth had started colonies along the Connecticut R.; in 1637 they defeated the Pequots. The Colony of Connecticut was chartered by England, 1662; New Haven colony was added, 1665. A Patriot stronghold in the American Revolution, the state actively supported the antislavery movement and the Union cause in the Civil War. The state economy prospered in the 20th cent. from insurance- and defense-related industries. *Nautilus*, the first nuclear-powered submarine, was launched at Groton, 1954. Connecticut Sen. Joseph Lieberman was the Democratic nominee for vice president in 2000. American Indian casinos, starting with Foxwoods in 1992, were an economic boon to the state, but tourism revenues declined sharply with the recession that began in late 2007. Twenty children and six staff members were killed in a mass shooting at Sandy Hook Elementary School in Newtown, Dec. 14, 2012.

Famous "Nutmeggers." Ethan Allen, P. T. Barnum, Michael Bolton, Glenn Close, Samuel Colt, Ann Coulter, Jonathan Edwards, Nathan Hale, Katharine Hepburn, Isaac Hull, Norman Lear, Seth MacFarlane, John Mayer, Robert Mitchum, J. P. Morgan, Ralph Nader, Israel Putnam, Wallace Stevens, Harriet Beecher Stowe, Mark Twain, Noah Webster, Eli Whitney.

Website. www.ct.gov

Delaware (DE)
First State, Diamond State

People. Population: 945,934; rank: 45. **Pop. change** (2010-15): 5.3%. **Pop. density:** 485.3 per sq mi. **Racial distribution:** 70.4% white; 22.4% black; 3.9% Asian; 0.7% Amer. Ind.; 0.1% Hawaiian/Pacific Islander; 2 or more races, 2.5%. **Hispanic pop.:** 9.0%.

Geography. Total area: 2,489 sq mi; rank: 49. **Land area:** 1,949 sq mi; rank: 49. **Acres forested:** 0.4 mil. **Location:** Delmarva Peninsula on the Atlantic coastal plain. **Climate:** moderate. **Topography:** Piedmont Plateau to the N, sloping to a near sea-level plain. **Capital:** Dover.

Economy. Chief industries: chemicals, agriculture, finance, poultry, shellfish, tourism, auto assembly, food processing, transportation equip. **Chief manuf. goods:** pharmaceuticals, poultry processing, soap and cleaning compounds, precision instruments, basic chemicals, plastics. **Chief crops:** soybeans, corn, greenhouse and nursery, wheat, potatoes, barley, hay, watermelons, lima beans, green peas, pumpkins, mushrooms, cabbage. **Farm income:** crops, $316.98 mil; livestock/animal prods., $1.16 bil. **Nonfuel minerals:** $15 mil; stone (crushed), sand and gravel (construction), magnesium compounds, gemstones (natural). **Commercial fishing:** $6.6 mil. **Chief port:** Wilmington. **Gross state product:** $68.1 bil. **Sales tax:** none. **Gasoline tax:** 41.40 cents/gal. **Employment distrib.:** 14.4% govt.; 17.9% trade/trans./util.; 6.0% mfg.; 16.9% ed./health; 13.7% prof./bus. serv.; 11.5% leisure/hosp.; 10.1% finance; 4.5% constr./mining/log.; 1.0% info.; 4.0% other serv. **Unemployment:** 4.9%. **Min. wage/hr.:** $8.25. **Per cap. pers. income:** $47,662. **New private housing:** 5,221 units/$641.7 mil. **Broadband internet:** 96.4%. **Commercial banks:** 35; deposits: $340.7 bil. **Savings institutions:** 5; deposits: $3.9 bil. **Lottery:** total sales: $598.4 mil; profit: $203.3 mil.

Federal govt. Fed. civ. employees: 2,981; **avg. salary:** $72,837. **Notable fed. facilities:** Dover AFB; Bombay Hook Natl. Wildlife Refuge.

Education. High school grad. rate: 87.0%. **4-year public coll./univ.:** 2; **2-yr. public:** 3; **4-yr. private:** 4.

Energy. Electricity use/cost: 950 kWh, $126.26.

State data. Motto: Liberty and independence. **Flower:** Peach blossom. **Bird:** Blue hen chicken. **Tree:** American holly. **Song:** "Our Delaware." **First** of original 13 states to ratify the Constitution, Dec. 7, 1787.

Tourism. Tourist spending: $1.9 bil. **Attractions:** Fort Christina (site of founding of colony of New Sweden), Holy Trinity (Old Swedes) Church (erected 1698, oldest church in U.S. still standing as built and in use), Hagley Museum and Library, Nemours Mansion and Gardens, in Wilmington; Winterthur Museum, Garden, and Library, near Wilmington; New Castle Historic District; John Dickinson "Penman of the Revolution" Plantation, First State Heritage Park, Dover Intl. Speedway, in Dover; Rehoboth Beach. **Information:** Delaware Tourism Office, 99 Kings Hwy., Dover, DE 19901; 1-866-2VISITDE; www.visitdelaware.com

History. The Lenni Lenape (Delaware) people lived in the region at the time of European contact. Henry Hudson located the Delaware R., 1609. In 1610, English explorer Samuel Argall entered Delaware Bay and named the area after Virginia's governor, Lord De La Warr. Dutch, Swedish, and Finnish settlers were followed by the British, who took control in 1664. After 1682, Delaware became part of Pennsylvania, and in 1704 it was granted its own assembly. It adopted a constitution as the state of Delaware, 1776, and was the first state to ratify the federal Constitution, 1787. Although it remained in the Union during the Civil War, Delaware retained slavery until the 13th Amendment abolished it in 1865. The DuPont company, founded as a gunpowder mill in 1802, became an industrial giant in the 20th cent. making nylon, Teflon, and other synthetics. Pro-business laws drew many out-of-state firms to incorporate in Delaware. In 2000, Ruth Ann Minner was elected Delaware's first woman governor.

Famous Delawareans. Thomas F. Bayard, Joseph Biden, Henry Seidel Canby, E. I. du Pont, John P. Marquand, Howard Pyle, Caesar Rodney, Susan Stroman.

Website. www.delaware.gov

Florida (FL)
Sunshine State

People. Population: 20,271,272; rank: 3. **Pop. change** (2010-15): 7.8%. **Pop. density:** 378.0 per sq mi. **Racial distribution:** 77.7% white; 16.8% black; 2.8% Asian; 0.5% Amer. Ind.; 0.1% Hawaiian/Pacific Islander; 2 or more races, 2.0%. **Hispanic pop.:** 24.5%.

Geography. Total area: 65,758 sq mi; rank: 22. **Land area:** 53,625 sq mi; rank: 26. **Acres forested:** 17.3 mil. **Location:** peninsula jutting southward 500 mi between the Atlantic and Gulf of Mexico. **Climate:** subtropical N of Bradenton-Lake Okeechobee-Vero Beach line; tropical S of line. **Topography:** land is flat or rolling; highest point is 345 ft in the NW. **Capital:** Tallahassee. **Chief airports:** Clearwater, Fort Lauderdale, Fort Myers, Jacksonville, Miami, Orlando, Pensacola, Sanford, Sarasota, Tampa, West Palm Beach.

Economy. Chief industries: tourism, agriculture, manufacturing, construction, services, international trade. **Chief manuf. goods:** navigational instruments, medical equip., cement, broadcasting equip., beverages, phosphatic fertilizer, preserved fruits and vegetables, structural metal, printing. **Chief crops:** greenhouse and nursery, oranges, sugarcane, tomatoes, green peppers, grapefruit, strawberries, snap beans, sweet corn, potatoes, cucumbers, tangerines. **Farm income:** crops, $6.08 bil; livestock/animal prods., $2.38 bil. **Nonfuel minerals:** $2.8 bil; phosphate rock, stone (crushed), cement (portland), sand and gravel (construction), cement (masonry). **Commercial fishing:** $257.7 mil. **Chief ports:** Pensacola, Tampa, Port Manatee, Miami, Port Everglades, Jacksonville, Canaveral. **Gross state product:** $882.8 bil. **Sales tax:** 6.0%. **Gasoline tax:** 54.98 cents/gal. **Employment distrib.:** 13.3% govt.; 20.5% trade/trans./util.; 4.2% mfg.; 14.9% ed./health; 15.1% prof./bus. serv.; 14.2% leisure/hosp.; 6.6% finance; 5.5% constr./mining/log.; 1.6% info.; 4.1% other serv. **Unemployment:** 5.4%. **Min. wage/hr.:** $8.05. **Per cap. pers. income:** $44,101. **New private housing:** 109,924 units/$23.4 bil. **Broadband internet:** 93.7%. **Commercial banks:** 229; deposits: $474.6 bil. **Savings institutions:** 25; deposits: $28.3 bil. **Lottery:** total sales: $5.6 bil; profit: $1.5 bil.

Federal govt. Fed. civ. employees: 77,547; **avg. salary:** $77,120. **Notable fed. facilities:** John F. Kennedy Space Ctr.; Eglin AFB; MacDill AFB; Hurlburt Field; Pensacola NAS; Jacksonville NAS; Mayport Naval Sta.

Education. High school grad. rate: 76.1%. **4-year public coll./univ.:** 38; **2-yr. public:** 4; **4-yr. private:** 62.

Energy. Electricity use/cost: 1,092 kWh, $129.86.

State data. Motto: In God we trust. **Flower:** Orange blossom. **Bird:** Northern mockingbird. **Tree:** Sabal palmetto palm. **Song:** "Old Folks at Home." **Entered union:** Mar. 3, 1845; rank: 27th.

Tourism. Tourist spending: $85.3 bil. **Attractions:** Miami Beach; Castillo de San Marcos Natl. Monument, St. Augustine Lighthouse & Museum, Lightner Museum, in St. Augustine (oldest permanent European settlement in U.S.); Walt Disney World Resort, SeaWorld Orlando, Universal Studios, Discovery Cove, in Orlando; Kennedy Space Ctr., U.S. Astronaut Hall of Fame; Everglades Natl. Park; Ringling Museum of Art, Ringling Circus Museum, in Sarasota; Cypress Gardens at Legoland Florida, Winter Haven; Busch Gardens, Big Cat Rescue, in Tampa; Florida Caverns State Park, Marianna; Key West. **Information:** Visit Florida, 2540 W. Executive Center Cir., Ste. 200, Tallahassee, FL 32301; 1-888-7FLA-USA; www.visitflorida.com

History. Florida has been inhabited for at least 12,000 years. Timucua, Apalachee, and Calusa peoples were living in the region when the earliest Europeans came; later the Seminole migrated from Georgia to Florida, becoming dominant there in the early 18th cent. The first European to see Florida was Spain's Ponce de León, 1513. France established a colony, Ft. Caroline, on the St. Johns R., 1564. Spain settled St. Augustine, 1565, and Spanish troops massacred most of the French. Britain's Sir Francis Drake burned St. Augustine, 1586. In 1763, Spain ceded Florida to Great Britain, which held the area 20 years before returning it to Spain. Florida was ceded to the U.S. in the Adams-Onís Treaty, 1819. The Seminole War, 1835-42, resulted in the removal of most Native Americans to Indian Territory. Florida joined the Union in 1845, seceded in 1861, and was readmitted in 1868. In the late 19th cent., hotel and railroad builder Henry M. Flagler laid the foundations of the tourism industry. The state experienced phenomenal population growth in the 20th cent., especially after 1950. The first U.S. astronaut was launched into space from Cape Canaveral, 1961. Walt Disney World opened near Orlando, 1971. Hurricane Andrew slammed Florida, 1992, causing at least $25 bil in property damage. A dispute over Florida's presidential vote in 2000 was decided by the U.S. Supreme Court and resulted in George W. Bush's Electoral College victory. Four hurricanes hit the state in 2004, causing more than $40 bil in damages. In June 2016, a gunman carried out the deadliest mass shooting in modern U.S. history when he killed 49 people at a gay nightclub in Orlando; he was killed by responding police.

Famous Floridians. Edna Buchanan, Jeb Bush, Marjory Stoneman Douglas, Henry Morrison Flagler, Carl Hiaasen, Perez Hilton, Zora Neale Hurston, James Weldon Johnson, Deacon Jones, MacKinlay Kantor, Osceola, Claude Pepper, Tom Petty, Henry B. Plant, A. Philip Randolph, Marjorie Kinnan Rawlings, Janet Reno, Marco Rubio, Deion Sanders, Emmitt Smith, Joseph W. Stilwell, Amar'e Stoudemire, Charles P. Summerall.

Website. www.myflorida.com

Georgia (GA)

Empire State of the South, Peach State

People. Population: 10,214,860; rank: 8. **Pop. change** (2010-15): 5.4%. **Pop. density:** 177.6 per sq mi. **Racial distribution:** 61.6% white; 31.7% black; 4.0% Asian; 0.5% Amer. Ind.; 0.1% Hawaiian/Pacific Islander; 2 or more races, 2.0%. **Hispanic pop.:** 9.4%.

Geography. Total area: 59,425 sq mi; rank: 24. **Land area:** 57,513 sq mi; rank: 21. **Acres forested:** 24.7 mil. **Location:** South Atlantic state. **Climate:** maritime tropical air masses dominate in summer; polar air masses in winter; E central area drier. **Topography:** most southerly of the Blue Ridge Mts. cover NE and N central; central Piedmont extends to the fall line of rivers; coastal plain levels to the coast flatlands. **Capital:** Atlanta. **Chief airports:** Atlanta, Savannah.

Economy. Chief industries: services, manufacturing, retail trade. **Chief manuf. goods:** carpet and rugs, animal slaughtering and processing, motor vehicles and parts, plastics, aircrafts, paper, chemicals, food. **Chief crops:** cotton, greenhouse and nursery, peanuts, pecans, corn, tomatoes, cucumbers, onions, watermelons, tobacco, squash, blueberries, hay, cabbage, soybeans, peaches, snap beans, wheat. **Farm income:** crops, $3.29 bil; livestock/animal prods., $6.67 bil. **Nonfuel minerals:** $1.7 bil; clays (kaolin), stone (crushed), cement (portland), clays (fuller's earth), cement (masonry). **Commercial fishing:** $16.2 mil. **Chief ports:** Savannah, Brunswick. **Gross state product:** $495.7 bil.

Sales tax: 4.0%. **Gasoline tax:** 49.57 cents/gal. **Employment distrib.:** 15.6% govt.; 21.1% trade/trans./util.; 8.8% mfg.; 12.5% ed./health; 15.3% prof./bus. serv.; 10.9% leisure/hosp.; 5.4% finance; 4.2% constr./mining/log.; 2.4% info.; 3.6% other serv. **Unemployment:** 5.9%. **Min. wage/hr.:** $5.15 ($7.25). **Per cap. pers. income:** $40,551. **New private housing:** 45,549 units/$8.0 bil. **Broadband internet:** 91.1%. **Commercial banks:** 232; deposits: $209.8 bil. **Savings institutions:** 16; deposits: $3.5 bil. **Lottery:** total sales: $4.2 bil; profit: $980.5 mil.

Federal govt. Fed. civ. employees: 71,106; **avg. salary:** $76,673. **Notable fed. facilities:** Ft. Benning; Ft. Stewart; Fed. Law Enforcement Training Ctr.; Robins AFB; Ft. Gordon; Naval Sub Base Kings Bay; Moody AFB; Centers for Disease Control; Marine Corps Logistics Base Albany.

Education. High school grad. rate: 72.5%. **4-year public coll./univ.:** 29; **2-yr. public:** 26; **4-yr. private:** 33.

Energy. Electricity use/cost: 1,152 kWh, $134.14.

State data. Motto: Wisdom, justice, and moderation. **Flower:** Cherokee rose. **Bird:** Brown thrasher. **Tree:** Southern live oak. **Song:** "Georgia on My Mind." **Fourth** of the 13 original states to ratify the Constitution, Jan. 2, 1788.

Tourism. Tourist spending: $26.7 bil. **Attractions:** Georgia State Capitol, Stone Mountain, Centennial Olympic Park, Six Flags Over Georgia, Martin Luther King Jr. Natl. Historic Site, Jimmy Carter Library and Museum, Atlanta Botanical Garden, Georgia Aquarium (largest in Western Hemisphere), in Atlanta; Kennesaw Mountain Natl. Battlefield Park; Chickamauga and Chattanooga Natl. Military Park; Chattahoochee-Oconee Natl. Forest; Dahlonega, site of earliest U.S. gold rush; Brasstown Bald (highest mtn. in state); Franklin D. Roosevelt's Little White House Historic Site, Warm Springs; Callaway Gardens, Pine Mountain; Andersonville Natl. Historic Site (Confederate military prison); Okefenokee Natl. Wildlife Refuge; Jekyll, St. Simons, and Cumberland barrier islands; Savannah Historic District. **Information:** Dept. of Economic Development, 75 Fifth St., NW, Ste. 1200, Atlanta, GA 30308; 1-800-VISITGA; www.exploregeorgia.org

History. Creek and Cherokee peoples were living in the region when Spaniards founded Santa Catalina mission, 1566, on Saint Catherines Island. Gen. James Oglethorpe established a colony at Savannah, 1733, for the poor and religiously persecuted. Oglethorpe defeated a Spanish army from Florida at Bloody Marsh, 1742. Georgia was a battleground in the American Revolution, with the British finally evacuating Savannah in 1782. When Georgia entered the Union, 1788, its plantation economy relied on slaves for rice and cotton growing. The Cherokee were removed to Indian Territory, 1838-39, and thousands died on the long march, known as the Trail of Tears. By 1860 the number of slaves exceeded 462,000 (nearly 44% of the total population). Georgia seceded from the Union, 1861, and was invaded by Union forces, 1864, under Gen. William T. Sherman, who took Atlanta, Sept. 2, and proceeded on his famous "march to the sea," ending in Savannah in Dec. Georgia was readmitted, 1870. Born 1929 in Atlanta, Martin Luther King Jr. made the city his base during the civil rights struggles of the 1960s. Atlanta became the leading city of the "New South," world headquarters of Coca-Cola and CNN, and host of the 1996 Summer Olympic Games. Hispanics are a rapidly growing economic and political force in the state. Eight Atlanta educators received prison sentences in Apr. 2015 for conspiring to elevate students' scores on standardized tests.

Famous Georgians. Kim Basinger, Griffin Bell, James Brown, Erskine Caldwell, Jimmy Carter, Ray Charles, Ty Cobb, James Dickey, Walt Frazier, John C. Fremont, Newt Gingrich, Nancy Grace, Joel Chandler Harris, "Doc" Holliday, Larry Holmes, Holly Hunter, Alan Jackson, Martin Luther King Jr., Gladys Knight, Sidney Lanier, Little Richard, Juliette Gordon Low, Margaret Mitchell, Jessye Norman, Sam Nunn, Flannery O'Connor, Otis Redding, Burt Reynolds, Julia Roberts, Jackie Robinson, Ryan Seacrest, Clarence Thomas, Travis Tritt, Ted Turner, Carl Vinson, Alice Walker, Herschel Walker, Joanne Woodward, Trisha Yearwood, Andrew Young.

Website. www.georgia.gov

Hawai'i (HI)

Aloha State

People. Population: 1,431,603; rank: 40. **Pop. change** (2010-15): 5.2%. **Pop. density:** 222.9 per sq mi. **Racial distribution:** 26.7% white; 2.6% black; 37.3% Asian; 0.5% Amer. Ind.; 9.9% Hawaiian/Pacific Islander; 2 or more races, 23.0%. **Hispanic pop.:** 10.4%.

Geography. Total area: 10,932 sq mi; **rank:** 43. **Land area:** 6,423 sq mi; **rank:** 47. **Acres forested:** 1.7 mil. **Location:** Pacific archipelago of about 132 islands 2,100 mi SW of U.S. mainland. **Climate:** subtropical, with wide variations in rainfall; Mt. Waialeale, on Kaua'i, wettest spot in U.S. (annual avg. rainfall 422 in.). **Topography:** islands are tops of a chain of submerged volcanic mountains; Mauna Loa, Kilauea are active volcanoes. **Capital:** Honolulu. **Chief airports:** Hilo, Honolulu, Kahului, Kailua Kona, Lihue.

Economy. Chief industries: tourism, defense, sugar, pineapples. **Chief manuf. goods:** concrete, printing, baked goods, sugar, preserved fruits and vegetables, apparel. **Chief crops:** flowers and nursery, pineapples, seed crops, sugarcane, macadamia nuts, coffee, algae, papayas, tomatoes, bananas, basil, ginger. **Farm income:** crops, $567.84 mil; livestock/animal prods., $150.21 mil. **Nonfuel minerals:** $129 mil; stone (crushed), sand and gravel (construction), gemstones (natural). **Commercial fishing:** $101.2 mil. **Chief ports:** Honolulu, Hilo, Barbers Point, Kahului. **Gross state product:** $79.7 bil. **Sales tax:** 4.0%. **Gasoline tax:** 61.40 cents/gal. **Employment distrib.:** 19.9% govt.; 18.2% trade/trans./util.; 2.1% mfg.; 13.0% ed./health; 12.8% prof./bus. serv.; 17.8% leisure/hosp.; 4.4% finance; 6.2% constr./mining/log.; 1.3% info.; 4.2% other serv. **Unemployment:** 3.6%. **Min. wage/hr.:** $8.50. **Per cap. pers. income:** $47,753. **New private housing:** 5,422 units/$1.6 bil. **Broadband internet:** 97.2%. **Commercial banks:** 8; deposits: $31.8 bil. **Savings institutions:** 5; deposits: $6.6 bil.

Federal govt. Fed. civ. employees: 22,003; **avg. salary:** $75,598. **Notable fed. facilities:** Joint Base Pearl Harbor-Hickam; Schofield Barracks; Marine Corps Base Hawaii, Kaneohe Bay; Tripler Army Med. Ctr.; Ft. Shafter; Wheeler Army Airfield; Prince Kuhio Federal Bldg.

Education. High school grad. rate: 81.8%. **4-year public coll./univ.:** 4; **2-yr. public:** 6; **4-yr. private:** 6.

Energy. Electricity use/cost: 506 kWh, $187.59.

State data. Motto: Ua mau ke ea o ka aina i ka pono (The life of the land is perpetuated in righteousness). **Flower:** Yellow hibiscus. **Bird:** Hawaiian goose. **Tree:** Kukui (candlenut). **Song:** "Hawai'i Pono'i" (Hawai'i's Own). **Entered union:** Aug. 21, 1959; **rank:** 50th.

Tourism. Tourist spending: $20.8 bil. **Attractions:** Oahu Isl.: Natl. Memorial Cemetery of the Pacific, Waikiki Beach, Diamond Head, in Honolulu; USS *Arizona* Memorial, Pearl Harbor; Polynesian Cultural Ctr., Laie; Hanauma Bay; Nu'uanu Pali. Kaua'i Isl.: Waimea Canyon. Maui Isl.: Haleakala Natl. Park. Hawai'i Isl.: Hawaii Volcanoes Natl. Park, Wailoa and Wailuku River State Parks. **Information:** Hawaii Visitors and Conventions Bureau, 2270 Kalakaua Ave., Ste. 801, Honolulu, HI 96815; 1-800-GOHAWAII; www.gohawaii.com

History. Polynesians from islands 2,000 mi to the S settled the Hawaiian Islands, probably 300-600 CE. The first European visitor was British captain James Cook, 1778. King Kamehameha I united the islands by 1810. Christian missionaries arrived, 1819, bringing Western culture. Under the reign, 1825-54, of King Kamehameha III, a constitution, legislature, and public school system were instituted. Sugar production began, 1835, and it became the dominant industry. Queen Liliuokalani was deposed, 1893, and a republic was established, 1894, headed by Sanford B. Dole, born in Hawaii to American missionaries. Annexation by the U.S. came in 1898. The Japanese attack on Pearl Harbor, Dec. 7, 1941, brought the U.S. into World War II. Hawai'i attained statehood, 1959. Hurricane Iniki pounded Kaua'i, 1992, causing about $1 bil in damage. In 2006, Pres. George W. Bush designated the Northwestern Hawaiian Islands Natl. Monument, a marine area of 140,000 sq mi. Gov. David Ige in 2015 declared a state of emergency over a crisis of homelessness in the state, the highest per capita in the country.

Famous Islanders. Bernice Pauahi Bishop, Tia Carrere, Alexander Cartwright, St. Damien de Veuster, Don Ho, Daniel K. Inouye, Duke Kahanamoku, King Kamehameha, Nicole Kidman, Brook Mahealani Lee, Jason Scott Lee, Queen Liliuokalani, Bruno Mars, Bette Midler, Barack Obama, Ellison S. Onizuka, Michelle Wie.

Website. www.ehawaii.gov

Idaho (ID)
Gem State

People. Population: 1,654,930; **rank:** 39. **Pop. change** (2010-15): 5.6%. **Pop. density:** 20.0 per sq mi. **Racial distribution:** 93.4% white; 0.8% black; 1.5% Asian; 1.7% Amer. Ind.; 0.2% Hawaiian/Pacific Islander; 2 or more races, 2.3%. **Hispanic pop.:** 12.2%.

Geography. Total area: 83,569 sq mi; **rank:** 14. **Land area:** 82,643 sq mi; **rank:** 11. **Acres forested:** 21.6 mil. **Location:** northwestern Mountain state bordering British Columbia, Canada. **Climate:** tempered by Pacific westerly winds; drier, colder, continental climate in SE; altitude an important factor. **Topography:** Snake R. plains in the S; central region of mountains, canyons, gorges (Hells Canyon, 7,900 ft, deepest in N. America); subalpine northern region. **Capital:** Boise. **Chief airport:** Boise.

Economy. Chief industries: manufacturing, agriculture, tourism, lumber, mining, electronics. **Chief manuf. goods:** computers and electronics, preserved fruits and vegetables, cheese, lumber. **Chief crops:** potatoes, wheat, hay, sugar beets, barley, greenhouse and nursery, onions, dry beans, corn, mint, apples, hops, peaches, lentils, peas, cherries, plums and prunes, oats. **Farm income:** crops, $3.27 bil; livestock/animal prods., $5.47 bil. **Nonfuel minerals:** $713 mil; phosphate rock, sand and gravel (construction), silver, lead, stone (crushed). **Chief port:** Lewiston. **Gross state product:** $65.2 bil. **Sales tax:** 6.0%. **Gasoline tax:** 51.40 cents/gal. **Employment distrib.:** 18.0% govt.; 19.9% trade/trans./util.; 9.0% mfg.; 14.4% ed./health; 12.2% prof./bus. serv.; 10.2% leisure/hosp.; 4.9% finance; 6.5% constr./mining/log.; 1.4% info.; 3.5% other serv. **Unemployment:** 4.1%. **Min. wage/hr.:** $7.25. **Per cap. pers. income:** $37,509. **New private housing:** 9,954 units/$1.9 bil. **Broadband internet:** 87.9%. **Commercial banks:** 32; deposits: $21.1 bil. **Savings institutions:** 1; deposits: $502 mil. **Lottery:** total sales: $210.2 mil; profit: $45.0 mil.

Federal govt. Fed. civ. employees: 8,183; **avg. salary:** $68,373. **Notable fed. facilities:** Idaho Natl. Lab; Mountain Home AFB.

Education. High school grad. rate: 77.3%. **4-year public coll./univ.:** 4; **2-yr. public:** 4; **4-yr. private:** 6.

Energy. Electricity use/cost: 982 kWh, $95.50.

State data. Motto: Esto Perpetua (It is perpetual). **Flower:** Syringa. **Bird:** Mountain bluebird. **Tree:** White pine. **Song:** "Here We Have Idaho." **Entered union:** July 3, 1890; **rank:** 43rd.

Tourism. Tourist spending: $4.4 bil. **Attractions:** Hells Canyon (deepest river gorge in N. America); World Ctr. for Birds of Prey, Boise Art Museum, in Boise; Craters of the Moon Natl. Monument and Preserve; Sun Valley; Shoshone Falls, near Twin Falls; Lava Hot Springs; Lake Coeur d'Alene; Sawtooth Natl. Recreation Area; Frank Church-River of No Return Wilderness Area; Nez Perce Natl. Historical Park. **Information:** Idaho Division of Tourism Development, 700 W. State St., P.O. Box 83720, Boise, ID 83720; 1-800-VISITID; www.visitid.org

History. Paleo-Indian hunters roamed the land over 13,000 years ago; later inhabitants included Shoshone, Northern Paiute, Bannock, and Nez Percé peoples. The Meriwether Lewis and William Clark Expedition took place 1804-06. Next came fur traders, 1809-34, and missionaries, 1830s-50s. Mormons made their first permanent settlement at Franklin, 1860. Idaho's gold rush began the same year and brought thousands of permanent settlers. A series of Indian wars followed, including a campaign by Chief Joseph and the Nez Percé that ended with his surrender in Montana, 1877. Idaho became a territory, 1863, and a state, 1890. In the 20th cent., it emerged as a leader in potato, lumber, and silver output. The Sun Valley ski resort opened in 1936, boosting tourism. Startup of Lewiston's river port, 1975, opened Idaho to oceangoing trade. Fueled by technology job growth, the state's population jumped 21.2% in 2000-10.

Famous Idahoans. William Borah, Frank Church, Lou Dobbs, Fred Dubois, W. Mark Felt, Chief Joseph, Harmon Killebrew, Ezra Pound, Marilynne Robinson, Sacagawea, Picabo Street, Lana Turner.

Website. www.idaho.gov

Illinois (IL)
Prairie State

People. Population: 12,859,995; **rank:** 5. **Pop. change** (2010-15): 0.2%. **Pop. density:** 231.6 per sq mi. **Racial distribution:** 77.3% white; 14.7% black; 5.5% Asian; 0.6% Amer. Ind.; 0.1% Hawaiian/Pacific Islander; 2 or more races, 1.9%. **Hispanic pop.:** 16.9%.

Geography. Total area: 57,914 sq mi; **rank:** 25. **Land area:** 55,519 sq mi; **rank:** 24. **Acres forested:** 5.0 mil. **Location:** East North Central state; western, southern, and eastern boundaries formed by Mississippi, Ohio, and Wabash Rivers, respectively. **Climate:** temperate; typically cold, snowy winters, hot summers. **Topography:** prairie and fertile plains throughout; open hills in the southern region. **Capital:** Springfield. **Chief airports:** Chicago (2).

Economy. Chief industries: services, manufacturing, travel, wholesale and retail trade, finance, insurance, real estate, construction, health care, agriculture. **Chief manuf. goods:** food, petroleum, plastics, chemicals, agricultural machinery, pharmaceuticals, motor vehicles, printing. **Chief crops:** corn, soybeans, hay, wheat, greenhouse and nursery, apples, peaches, sorghum. **Farm income:** crops, $16.38 bil; livestock/animal prods., $3.20 bil. **Nonfuel minerals:** $2.2 bil; sand and gravel (industrial), stone (crushed), sand and gravel (construction), cement (portland), tripoli. **Chief port:** Chicago. **Gross state product:** $775.0 bil. **Sales tax:** 6.25%. **Gasoline tax:** 51.85 cents/gal. **Employment distrib.:** 13.9% govt.; 20.0% trade/trans./util.; 9.5% mfg.; 15.1% ed./health; 15.5% prof./bus. serv.; 10.1% leisure/hosp.; 6.3% finance; 3.8% constr./mining/log.; 1.6% info.; 4.2% other serv. **Unemployment:** 5.9%. **Min. wage/hr.:** $8.25. **Per cap. pers. income:** $49,471. **New private housing:** 19,571 units/$4.1 bil. **Broadband internet:** 93.4%. **Commercial banks:** 491; deposits: $443.1 bil. **Savings institutions:** 72; deposits: $21.3 bil. **Lottery:** total sales: $2.8 bil; profit: $690.3 mil.

Federal govt. Fed. civ. employees: 41,252; **avg. salary:** $83,164. **Notable fed. facilities:** Great Lakes Naval Station; Fermi Natl. Accelerator Lab; Argonne Natl. Lab; Scott AFB; Rock Island Arsenal.

Education. High school grad. rate: 86.0%. **4-year public coll./univ.:** 12; **2-yr. public:** 48; **4-yr. private:** 80.

Energy. Electricity use/cost: 745 kWh, $88.78.

State data. Motto: State sovereignty, national union. **Flower:** Native violet. **Bird:** Northern cardinal. **Tree:** White oak. **Song:** "Illinois." **Entered union:** Dec. 3, 1818; rank: 21st.

Tourism. Tourist spending: $36.3 bil. **Attractions:** Art Institute of Chicago, Field Museum of Natural History, Shedd Aquarium, Millennium Park, Navy Pier, in Chicago; Illinois State Museum, Abraham Lincoln Presidential Library and Museum, in Springfield; Cahokia Mounds State Historic Site, Collinsville; Starved Rock State Park; Crab Orchard Natl. Wildlife Refuge; Forts Kaskaskia, de Chartres, Massac; Shawnee Natl. Forest; Dickson Mounds Museum, Lewistown. **Information:** Illinois Bureau of Tourism, 100 W. Randolph St., Ste. 3-400, Chicago, IL 60601; 1-800-2CONNECT; www.enjoyillinois.com

History. The region has been inhabited for at least 10,000 years; seminomadic Algonquian peoples, including the Peoria, Illinois, Kaskaskia, and Tamaroa, lived there at the time of European contact. Fur traders were the first Europeans in Illinois, followed shortly by Louis Jolliet and Jacques Marquette, 1673, and René-Robert Cavelier, sieur de La Salle, 1680, who built a fort near present-day Peoria. French priests established the first permanent settlements at Cahokia, near present-day St. Louis, 1699, and Kaskaskia, 1703. France ceded the area to Britain, 1763, and in 1778, American Gen. George Rogers Clark took Kaskaskia from the British without a shot. Illinois became a separate territory, 1809, and a state, 1818. Defeat of Native American tribes in the Black Hawk War, 1832, and canal, rail, and road construction brought rapid change. Mormon settlers at Nauvoo, 1839, met with hostility, and a Carthage mob killed Mormon leader Joseph Smith and his brother, 1844. The Great Chicago Fire, 1871, destroyed the city's downtown. Illinois became a center for the labor movement, leading to bitter conflicts such as the Haymarket riot, 1886, and Pullman strike, 1894. Social reformer Jane Addams founded Hull House, 1889, to aid immigrants and the poor. The expansion of manufacturing, 1900-70, drew African Americans from the South in the Great Migration. Chicago police violently suppressed antiwar protests at the 1968 Democratic National Convention. Dennis Hastert was the longest serving Republican Speaker of the House, 1999-2007. Barack Obama, elected in 2004, was only the fifth African American to serve in the U.S. Senate; he became the 44th U.S. president in 2009. Political corruption and criminality have plagued the state for decades; since 1960, five former governors have been charged with criminal offenses. The U.S. Justice Dept. in early Dec. 2015 launched an investigation of the Chicago Police Dept. after a video of a white officer fatally shooting a black teen in Oct. 2014 sparked protests.

Famous Illinoisans. Jane Addams, Saul Bellow, John Belushi, Jack Benny, Ray Bradbury, Gwendolyn Brooks, St. Frances Xavier Cabrini, Al Capone, Hillary Rodham Clinton, Clarence Darrow, John Deere, Stephen A. Douglas, Katherine Dunham, Wyatt Earp, Roger Ebert, James T. Farrell, Marshall Field, Harrison Ford, Betty Friedan, Benny Goodman, Ulysses S. Grant, Dennis Hastert, Hugh Hefner, Ernest Hemingway, Charlton Heston, Jennifer Hudson, Henry J. Hyde, Abraham Lincoln, Vachel Lindsay, David Mamet, Edgar Lee Masters, Oscar Mayer, Cyrus McCormick, Eliot Ness, Bob Newhart, Michelle Obama, Ronald Reagan, Shonda Rhimes, Donald Rumsfeld, Carl Sandburg, Shel Silverstein, Adlai E. Stevenson, James Watson, Frank Lloyd Wright, Philip K. Wrigley. **Website.** www.illinois.gov

Indiana (IN)
Hoosier State

People. Population: 6,619,680; rank: 16. **Pop. change** (2010-15): 2.1%. **Pop. density:** 184.8 per sq mi. **Racial distribution:** 85.8% white; 9.6% black; 2.1% Asian; 0.4% Amer. Ind.; 0.1% Hawaiian/Pacific Islander; 2 or more races, 1.9%. **Hispanic pop.:** 6.7%.

Geography. Total area: 36,420 sq mi; rank: 38. **Land area:** 35,826 sq mi; rank: 38. **Acres forested:** 4.9 mil. **Location:** East North Central state; Lake Michigan on N border. **Climate:** four distinct seasons with temperate climate. **Topography:** hilly southern region; fertile rolling plains of central region; flat, heavily glaciated N; dunes along Lake Michigan shore. **Capital:** Indianapolis. **Chief airport:** Indianapolis.

Economy. Chief industries: manufacturing, services, agriculture, government, wholesale and retail trade, transportation, public utilities. **Chief manuf. goods:** motor vehicles and parts, iron and steel mills, pharmaceuticals, petroleum, plastics, medical equip., printing. **Chief crops:** corn, soybeans, greenhouse and nursery, wheat, hay, tomatoes, watermelons, apples. **Farm income:** crops, $8.72 bil; livestock/animal prods., $4.29 bil. **Nonfuel minerals:** $916 mil; stone (crushed), cement (portland), lime, sand and gravel (construction), stone (dimension). **Chief ports:** Burns Harbor-Portage, Mt. Vernon, Jeffersonville. **Gross state product:** $336.4 bil. **Sales tax:** 7.0%. **Gasoline tax:** 50.47 cents/gal. **Employment distrib.:** 14.1% govt.; 19.5% trade/trans./util.; 16.7% mfg.; 15.2% ed./health; 10.4% prof./bus. serv.; 10.2% leisure/hosp.; 4.3% finance; 4.5% constr./mining/log.; 1.0% info.; 4.1% other serv. **Unemployment:** 4.8%. **Min. wage/hr.:** $7.25. **Per cap. pers. income:** $40,998. **New private housing:** 18,483 units/$3.7 bil. **Broadband internet:** 90.8%. **Commercial banks:** 129; deposits: $107.8 bil. **Savings institutions:** 32; deposits: $5.3 bil. **Lottery:** total sales: $1.0 bil; profit: $242.7 mil.

Federal govt. Fed. civ. employees: 22,771; **avg. salary:** $72,469. **Notable fed. facilities:** Naval Surface Warfare Ctr., Crane Div.; Grissom Air Reserve Base.

Education. High school grad. rate: 87.9%. **4-year public coll./univ.:** 15; **2-yr. public:** 1; **4-yr. private:** 39.

Energy. Electricity use/cost: 1,009 kWh, $115.56.

State data. Motto: Crossroads of America. **Flower:** Peony. **Bird:** Cardinal. **Tree:** Tulip poplar. **Song:** "On the Banks of the Wabash, Far Away." **Entered union:** Dec. 11, 1816; rank: 19th.

Tourism. Tourist spending: $10.5 bil. **Attractions:** Lincoln Boyhood Natl. Memorial, Lincoln City; George Rogers Clark Natl. Historical Park, Vincennes; Tippecanoe Battlefield Museum and Park, Battle Ground; Benjamin Harrison Presidential Site, Indianapolis Motor Speedway and Hall of Fame Museum, Indianapolis Museum of Art, in Indianapolis; Indiana Dunes Natl. Lakeshore, Chesterton; College Football Hall of Fame, Studebaker Natl. Museum, in South Bend; Hoosier Natl. Forest. **Information:** Indiana Office of Tourism Development, 1 North Capital, Ste. 600, Indianapolis, IN 46204; 1-800-677-9800; www.visitindiana.com

History. When the Europeans arrived, Miami, Potawatomi, Kickapoo, Piankashaw, Wea, and Shawnee peoples inhabited the region. René-Robert Cavelier, sieur de La Salle, visited the present South Bend area, 1679 and 1681. The first French fort was built near present-day Lafayette, 1717. A French trading post was established, 1731-32, at Vincennes. France ceded the area to Britain, 1763. During the American Revolution, American Gen. George Rogers Clark captured Vincennes, 1778, and defeated British forces, 1779. Indiana became a territory, 1800, and a state, 1816. The Miami were beaten, 1794, at Fallen Timbers, and Gen. William H. Harrison defeated Tecumseh's Indian confederation, 1811, at Tippecanoe. Manufacturing grew rapidly after the Civil War. U.S. Steel founded Gary, 1906. An automotive test track was the site of the first Indianapolis 500 race, 1911. The auto industry remains key to the state economy; in 2008, Honda opened a $550-mil plant near Greensburg. Heavy rain in June 2008 flooded southwest and central Indiana. Some rights groups and businesses criticized the state's Religious Freedom Restoration Act as discriminatory to LGBT individuals; the legislature passed an amended version of the bill in response.

Famous "Hoosiers." Larry Bird, Ambrose Burnside, Meg Cabot, Hoagy Carmichael, Jim Davis, James Dean, Eugene

V. Debs, John Dillinger, Theodore Dreiser, Paul Dresser, Jeff Gordon, Benjamin Harrison, Gil Hodges, Michael Jackson, David Letterman, Carole Lombard, Marjorie Main, John Mellencamp, Jane Pauley, Cole Porter, Gene Stratton Porter, Ernie Pyle, Dan Quayle, James Whitcomb Riley, Oscar Robertson, Red Skelton, Tony Stewart, Booth Tarkington, Kurt Vonnegut, Lew Wallace, Ryan White, Wendell L. Willkie, Wilbur Wright.

Website. www.in.gov

Iowa (IA)

Hawkeye State

People. Population: 3,123,899; rank: 30. **Pop. change** (2010-15): 2.5%. **Pop. density:** 55.9 per sq mi. **Racial distribution:** 91.8% white; 3.5% black; 2.4% Asian; 0.5% Amer. Ind.; 0.1% Hawaiian/Pacific Islander; 2 or more races, 1.8%. **Hispanic pop.:** 5.7%.

Geography. Total area: 56,273 sq mi; rank: 26. **Land area:** 55,857 sq mi; rank: 23. **Acres forested:** 2.9 mil. **Location:** West North Central state bordered by Mississippi R. on the E, Missouri R. on the W. **Climate:** humid, continental. **Topography:** watershed from NW to SE; soil especially rich and land level in the N central counties. **Capital:** Des Moines. **Chief airports:** Cedar Rapids, Des Moines.

Economy. Chief industries: agriculture, communications, construction, finance, insurance, trade, services, manufacturing. **Chief manuf. goods:** machinery, vegetable oils, animal slaughtering and processing, laundry equip., plastics, motor vehicles and parts. **Chief crops:** corn, soybeans, hay, greenhouse and nursery, oats. **Farm income:** crops, $13.77 bil; livestock/animal prods., $16.88 bil. **Nonfuel minerals:** $817 mil; stone (crushed), cement (portland), sand and gravel (industrial), sand and gravel (construction), lime. **Gross state product:** $174.1 bil. **Sales tax:** 6.0%. **Gasoline tax:** 50.10 cents/gal. **Employment distrib.:** 16.5% govt.; 19.9% trade/trans./util.; 13.2% mfg.; 14.5% ed./health; 8.6% prof./bus. serv.; 9.3% leisure/hosp.; 6.8% finance; 5.8% constr./mining/log.; 1.5% info.; 3.9% other serv. **Unemployment:** 3.7%. **Min. wage/hr.:** $7.25. **Per cap. pers. income:** $44,971. **New private housing:** 12,097 units/$2.2 bil. **Broadband internet:** 85.7%. **Commercial banks:** 331; deposits: $75.7 bil. **Savings institutions:** 8; deposits: $2.6 bil. **Lottery:** total sales: $324.8 mil; profit: $74.5 mil.

Federal govt. Fed. civ. employees: 8,546; **avg. salary:** $69,828. **Notable fed. facilities:** Ames Lab; Natl. Animal Disease Ctr.

Education. High school grad. rate: 90.5%. **4-year public coll./univ.:** 3; **2-yr. public:** 16; **4-yr. private:** 34.

Energy. Electricity use/cost: 891 kWh, $99.49.

State data. Motto: Our liberties we prize, and our rights we will maintain. **Flower:** Wild rose. **Bird:** Eastern goldfinch. **Tree:** Oak. **Song:** "The Song of Iowa." **Entered union:** Dec. 28, 1846; rank: 29th.

Tourism. Tourist spending: $8.3 bil. **Attractions:** Des Moines Art Ctr., Iowa State Fairgrounds, Iowa State Capitol, in Des Moines; Natl. Czech & Slovak Museum & Library, Cedar Rapids; Herbert Hoover Natl. Historic Site, Presidential Library and Museum, in West Branch; Effigy Mounds Natl. Monument, Marquette; Amana Colonies; Figge Art Museum, Davenport; Living History Farms, Urbandale; Adventureland, Altoona; Boone & Scenic Valley Railroad and Museum; riverboat cruises and casino gambling, Mississippi and Missouri Rivers; Iowa Great Lakes, Okoboji; American Gothic House, Eldon; *Field of Dreams* movie site, Dyersville; Natl. Mississippi River Museum & Aquarium, Dubuque. **Information:** Iowa Tourism Office, Iowa Dept. of Economic Development, 200 E. Grand Ave., Des Moines, IA 50309; 1-888-472-6035; www.traveliowa.com

History. Early inhabitants were Mound Builders who dwelt on Iowa's fertile plains. Later, Iowa and Yankton Sioux lived in the area. The first Europeans, Jacques Marquette and Louis Jolliet, gave France its claim to the area, 1673. In 1762, France ceded the region to Spain, but Napoleon took it back, 1800. It became part of the U.S. through the Louisiana Purchase, 1803. Native American Sauk and Fox tribes moved into the area but relinquished their land in defeat after the 1832 uprising led by Sauk chieftain Black Hawk. Iowa became a territory in 1838 and a free state in 1846, strongly supporting the Union. Fertile land lured farmers from eastern states, 1850-1900, and the population rose rapidly. Growth slowed in the 20th cent., as farming became mechanized. Surging demand for ethanol fuel from Iowa corn contributed more than $2.6 bil to the state economy in 2005. Severe flooding in eastern Iowa

in June 2008 caused billions of dollars in damages and forced the evacuation of thousands of residents.

Famous Iowans. Tom Arnold, Johnny Carson, William F. "Buffalo Bill" Cody, Mamie Dowd Eisenhower, Michael Emerson, Bob Feller, George Gallup, Susan Glaspell, James Norman Hall, Herbert Hoover, Shawn Johnson, Ashton Kutcher, Ann Landers, Cloris Leachman, Glenn Miller, Lillian Russell, Billy Sunday, James A. Van Allen, Abigail Van Buren, Carl Van Vechten, Henry Wallace, Kurt Warner, John Wayne, Meredith Willson, Elijah Wood, Grant Wood.

Website. www.iowa.gov

Kansas (KS)

Sunflower State

People. Population: 2,911,641; rank: 34. **Pop. change** (2010-15): 2.1%. **Pop. density:** 35.6 per sq mi. **Racial distribution:** 86.7% white; 6.3% black; 2.9% Asian; 1.2% Amer. Ind.; 0.1% Hawaiian/Pacific Islander; 2 or more races, 2.9%. **Hispanic pop.:** 11.6%.

Geography. Total area: 82,278 sq mi; rank: 15. **Land area:** 81,759 sq mi; rank: 13. **Acres forested:** 2.5 mil. **Location:** West North Central state with Missouri R. on E. **Climate:** temperate but continental, with great extremes between summer and winter. **Topography:** hilly Osage Plains in the E; central region level prairie and hills; high plains in the W. **Capital:** Topeka. **Chief airport:** Wichita.

Economy. Chief industries: manufacturing, finance, insurance, real estate, services. **Chief manuf. goods:** animal slaughtering, aerospace, petroleum, plastics, machinery, navigational instruments, printing. **Chief crops:** wheat, corn, soybeans, hay, sorghum, sunflowers, cotton, potatoes. **Farm income:** crops, $6.10 bil; livestock/animal prods., $10.47 bil. **Nonfuel minerals:** $1.1 bil; helium (Grade-A), cement (portland), salt, stone (crushed), helium (crude). **Chief port:** Kansas City. **Gross state product:** $147.8 bil. **Sales tax:** 6.5%. **Gasoline tax:** 42.43 cents/gal. **Employment distrib.:** 18.6% govt.; 18.8% trade/trans./util.; 11.4% mfg.; 13.9% ed./health; 12.8% prof./bus. serv.; 9.2% leisure/hosp.; 5.7% finance; 4.6% constr./mining/log.; 1.4% info.; 3.4% other serv. **Unemployment:** 4.2%. **Min. wage/hr.:** $7.25. **Per cap. pers. income:** $45,876. **New private housing:** 8,644 units/$1.6 bil. **Broadband internet:** 87.7%. **Commercial banks:** 305; deposits: $61.3 bil. **Savings institutions:** 15; deposits: $6.9 bil. **Lottery:** total sales: $250.0 mil; profit: $75.0 mil.

Federal govt. Fed. civ. employees: 15,886; **avg. salary:** $70,008. **Notable fed. facilities:** Ft. Riley; Leavenworth Fed. Penitentiary; McConnell AFB; Colmery-O'Neil VA Medical Ctr.; Dwight D. Eisenhower VA Medical Ctr.

Education. High school grad. rate: 85.7%. **4-year public coll./univ.:** 8; **2-yr. public:** 25; **4-yr. private:** 25.

Energy. Electricity use/cost: 928 kWh, $112.95.

State data. Motto: Ad Astra per Aspera (To the stars through difficulties). **Flower:** Native sunflower. **Bird:** Western meadowlark. **Tree:** Cottonwood. **Song:** "Home on the Range." **Entered union:** Jan. 29, 1861; rank: 34th.

Tourism. Tourist spending: $7.4 bil. **Attractions:** Eisenhower Presidential Library and Museum, Abilene; Natl. Agricultural Ctr. and Hall of Fame, Bonner Springs; Boot Hill Museum, Dodge City; Old Cowtown Museum, Wichita; Ft. Scott and Ft. Larned Natl. Historic Sites; Kansas Cosmosphere and Space Ctr., Hutchinson; U.S. Cavalry Museum, Ft. Riley; Tallgrass Prairie Natl. Preserve, Strong City; Kansas Speedway, Kansas City. **Information:** Kansas Dept. of Commerce, Travel and Tourism Div., 1000 SW Jackson St., Ste. 100, Topeka, KS 66612; (785) 296-2009; www.travelks.com

History. Wichita, Pawnee, Kansa, and Osage peoples lived in the area when Spain's Francisco de Coronado explored it in 1541. These Native Americans—hunters who also farmed—were joined on the Plains by the nomadic Cheyenne, Arapaho, Comanche, and Kiowa about 1800. France claimed the region, 1682, ceded its claim to Spain, 1762, then regained control, 1800, before selling it to the U.S. in the Louisiana Purchase, 1803. After 1830, thousands of Native Americans were removed from more eastern states to Kansas. Organized as a territory, 1854, the area witnessed violent clashes between pro- and antislavery settlers and became known as "Bleeding Kansas." It entered the Union as a free state, 1861. After the Civil War, rail construction and huge cattle drives from Texas turned Abilene and Dodge City into cowboy capitals. Russian Mennonite immigrants brought a new strain of winter wheat, 1874, transforming Kansas agriculture. Carry Nation launched her anti-saloon crusade in the

1890s. Part of the Dust Bowl, the state experienced drought and depression in the 1930s. Topeka was the focus of the famous *Brown v. Board of Education* decision, 1954, that led to desegregation of U.S. public schools. Bob Dole represented Kansas in the U.S. Senate (1969-96) but failed in several efforts to win higher office.

Famous Kansans. Kirstie Alley, Roscoe "Fatty" Arbuckle, Ed Asner, John Brown, Walter P. Chrysler, Glenn Cunningham, John Steuart Curry, Robert Joseph "Bob" Dole, Amelia Earhart, Dwight D. Eisenhower, Melissa Etheridge, Ron Evans, Georgia Neese Clark Gray, Maurice Greene, James Butler "Wild Bill" Hickok, Cyrus K. Holliday, Dennis Hopper, William Inge, Don Johnson, Walter Johnson, Nancy Landon Kassebaum, Buster Keaton, Emmett Kelly, Alfred M. "Alf" Landon, Hattie McDaniel, Oscar Micheaux, Carry Nation, Charlie Parker, Gordon Parks, Jim Ryun, Barry Sanders, Vivian Vance, William Allen White, Jess Willard.

Website. www.kansas.gov

Kentucky (KY)
Bluegrass State

People. Population: 4,425,092; rank: 26. **Pop. change** (2010-15): 2.0%. **Pop. density:** 112.1 per sq mi. **Racial distribution:** 88.1% white; 8.3% black; 1.4% Asian; 0.3% Amer. Ind.; 0.1% Hawaiian/Pacific Islander; 2 or more races, 1.8%. **Hispanic pop.:** 3.4%.

Geography. Total area: 40,408 sq mi; rank: 37. **Land area:** 39,486 sq mi; rank: 37. **Acres forested:** 12.5 mil. **Location:** East South Central state bordered on N by Illinois, Indiana, Ohio; on E by West Virginia and Virginia; on S by Tennessee; on W by Missouri. **Climate:** moderate, with plentiful rainfall. **Topography:** mountainous in E; rounded hills of the Knobs region in the N; Bluegrass region in heart of state; wooded rocky hillsides of the Pennyroyal Plateau; Western Coal Field; the fertile Jackson Purchase region in the SW. **Capital:** Frankfort. **Chief airports:** Cincinnati, Lexington, Louisville.

Economy. Chief industries: manufacturing, services, finance, insurance and real estate, retail trade, public utilities. **Chief manuf. goods:** motor vehicles and parts, aluminum, basic chemicals, plastics, iron and steel, rubber, printing. **Chief crops:** hay, corn, soybeans, tobacco, wheat. **Farm income:** crops, $2.84 bil.; livestock/animal prods., $3.66 bil. **Nonfuel minerals:** $571 mil; stone (crushed), lime, cement (portland), sand and gravel (construction), sand and gravel (industrial). **Chief ports:** Louisville, Hickman-Fulton County. **Gross state product:** $194.6 bil. **Sales tax:** 6.0%. **Gasoline tax:** 44.40 cents/gal. **Employment distrib.:** 16.7% govt.; 20.8% trade/trans./util.; 12.7% mfg.; 14.2% ed./health; 11.3% prof./bus. serv.; 10.3% leisure/hosp.; 4.9% finance; 4.5% constr./mining/log.; 1.2% info.; 3.3% other serv. **Unemployment:** 5.4%. **Min. wage/hr.:** $7.25. **Per cap. pers. income:** $38,989. **New private housing:** 10,566 units/$1.5 bil. **Broadband internet:** 85.5%. **Commercial banks:** 182; deposits: $73.3 bil. **Savings institutions:** 14; deposits: $1.4 bil. **Lottery:** total sales: $899.1 mil; profit: $236.1 mil.

Federal govt. Fed. civ. employees: 23,096; **avg. salary:** $65,115. **Notable fed. facilities:** U.S. Bullion Depository, Ft. Knox; Ft. Campbell; Fed. Medical Ctr., Lexington; Army Corps of Engineers, Louisville District.

Education. High school grad. rate: 87.5%. **4-year public coll./univ.:** 8; **2-yr. public:** 16; **4-yr. private:** 26.

Energy. Electricity use/cost: 1,177 kWh, $119.66.

State data. Motto: United we stand, divided we fall. **Flower:** Goldenrod. **Bird:** Northern cardinal. **Tree:** Tulip poplar. **Song:** "My Old Kentucky Home." **Entered union:** June 1, 1792; rank: 15th.

Tourism. Tourist spending: $8.7 bil. **Attractions:** Churchill Downs (Kentucky Derby), Louisville Slugger Museum and Factory, in Louisville; Land Between the Lakes Natl. Recreation Area (Kentucky and Barkley Lakes); Mammoth Cave Natl. Park (world's longest known cave system); Abraham Lincoln Birthplace Natl. Historical Park, Hodgenville; My Old Kentucky Home State Park, Bardstown; Cumberland Gap Natl. Historical Park, Middlesboro; Kentucky Horse Park, Lexington; Shaker Village of Pleasant Hill, Harrodsburg; Natl. Corvette Museum, Bowling Green. **Information:** Kentucky Dept. of Travel, Capital Plaza Tower, 22nd Fl., 500 Mero St., Frankfort, KY 40601; 1-800-225-8747; www.kentuckytourism.com

History. Paleo-Indians first arrived about 14,000 years ago. Much later, Shawnee, Wyandot, Delaware, and Cherokee peoples used the area mostly for hunting. Explored by Thomas Walker and Christopher Gist, 1750-51, Kentucky was the first area W of the Alleghenies settled by American pioneers. The first permanent settlement was Harrodsburg, 1774. Daniel Boone blazed the Wilderness Trail through the Cumberland Gap and founded Ft. Boonesborough, 1775. Clashes with Native Americans were frequent, 1774-94. Virginia dropped its claims to the region, and Kentucky became a state, 1792. Tobacco growing, horse breeding, coal mining, and bourbon whiskey making were major industries in the 19th cent. A slave state, Kentucky tried to stay neutral in the Civil War, but then opted for the Union; many Kentuckians sided with the Confederacy. The U.S. gold depository at Ft. Knox opened, 1937. Prior to the 2008 economic downturn, auto manufacturing had grown in recent decades. A Rowan County clerk attracted national attention after being jailed in Sept. 2015 for refusing to issue marriage licenses to same-sex couples.

Famous Kentuckians. Muhammad Ali, Alben W. Barkley, Ned Beatty, Louis D. Brandeis, John C. Breckinridge, Kit Carson, Albert B. "Happy" Chandler, Henry Clay, George Clooney, Rosemary Clooney, Jefferson Davis, D. W. Griffith, "Casey" Jones, Jennifer Lawrence, Abraham Lincoln, Mary Todd Lincoln, Thomas Hunt Morgan, Carry Nation, Colonel Harland Sanders, Diane Sawyer, Jesse Stuart, Zachary Taylor, Hunter S. Thompson, Robert Penn Warren, Whitney M. Young Jr.

Website. www.kentucky.gov

Louisiana (LA)
Pelican State

People. Population: 4,670,724; rank: 25. **Pop. change** (2010-15): 3.0%. **Pop. density:** 108.1 per sq mi. **Racial distribution:** 63.2% white; 32.5% black; 1.8% Asian; 0.8% Amer. Ind.; 0.1% Hawaiian/Pacific Islander; 2 or more races, 1.6%. **Hispanic pop.:** 5.0%.

Geography. Total area: 52,378 sq mi; rank: 31. **Land area:** 43,204 sq mi; rank: 33. **Acres forested:** 15.0 mil. **Location:** West South Central state on the Gulf Coast. **Climate:** subtropical, affected by continental weather patterns. **Topography:** lowlands of marshes and Mississippi R. floodplain; Red R. Valley lowlands; upland hills in the Florida Parishes; avg. elevation, 100 ft. **Capital:** Baton Rouge. **Chief airport:** Metairie.

Economy. Chief industries: wholesale and retail trade, tourism, manufacturing, construction, transportation, communication, public utilities, finance, insurance, real estate, mining. **Chief manuf. goods:** petroleum, chemicals, plastics material and resin, pesticides and fertilizers, cleaning prods., paper and paperboard, ships, structural metals. **Chief crops:** sugarcane, cotton, rice, soybeans, corn, sweet potatoes. **Farm income:** crops, $2.61 bil; livestock/animal prods., $1.34 bil. **Nonfuel minerals:** $689 mil; salt, sand and gravel (construction), sand and gravel (industrial), stone (crushed), lime. **Commercial fishing:** $487.4 mil. **Chief ports:** New Orleans, Baton Rouge, Lake Charles, Port of S. Louisiana (La Place), Shreveport, Plaquemine, St. Bernard, Alexandria. **Gross state product:** $243.3 bil. **Sales tax:** 4.0%. **Gasoline tax:** 38.41 cents/gal. **Employment distrib.:** 16.5% govt.; 19.8% trade/trans./util.; 6.9% mfg.; 15.7% ed./health; 10.6% prof./bus. serv.; 11.8% leisure/hosp.; 4.5% finance; 9.2% constr./mining/log.; 1.3% info.; 3.8% other serv. **Unemployment:** 6.3%. **Min. wage/hr.:** none ($7.25). **Per cap. pers. income:** $43,252. **New private housing:** 13,830 units/$2.8 bil. **Broadband internet:** 87.2%. **Commercial banks:** 126; deposits: $94.3 bil. **Savings institutions:** 21; deposits: $3.5 bil. **Lottery:** total sales: $452.5 mil; profit: $184.8 mil.

Federal govt. Fed. civ. employees: 17,827; **avg. salary:** $72,432. **Notable federal facilities:** Ft. Polk (Joint Readiness Training Ctr.); Barksdale AFB; Strategic Petroleum Reserve; Michoud Assembly Facility, USDA Southern Regional Research Ctr., New Orleans NAS JRB.

Education. High school grad. rate: 74.6%. **4-year public coll./univ.:** 17; **2-yr. public:** 16; **4-yr. private:** 11.

Energy. Electricity use/cost: 1,291 kWh, $123.61.

State data. Motto: Union, justice, and confidence. **Flower:** Magnolia. **Bird:** Eastern brown pelican. **Tree:** Bald cypress. **Song:** "Give Me Louisiana." **Entered union:** Apr. 30, 1812; rank: 18th.

Tourism. Tourist spending: $11.1 bil. **Attractions:** Mardi Gras, French Quarter, Bourbon Street, in New Orleans; Jean Lafitte Natl. Historical Park and Preserve; Longfellow-Evangeline State Historic Site, St. Martinville; Kent Plantation House, Alexandria; Oak Alley Plantation, Vacherie; Hodges Gardens State Park, Florien; USS *Kidd* Veterans Memorial, Baton Rouge. **Information:** Louisiana Office of Tourism, P.O. Box 94291, Baton Rouge, LA 70804-9291; 1-800-677-4082; www.louisianatravel.com

History. Caddo, Tunica, Choctaw, Chitimacha, and Cha- wash peoples lived in the region at the time of European contact. Spanish explorers in the early 16th cent. reached the mouth of the Mississippi. René-Robert Cavelier, sieur de La Salle, 1682, claimed the region for France. Early French and Spanish settlers were the ancestors of Louisiana Creoles. Cajuns descended from the Acadians, French settlers expelled by the British from Nova Scotia, Canada, in 1755. France ceded the Louisiana region to Spain, 1762, took it back, 1800, and sold it to the U.S., 1803, in the Louisiana Purchase. Admit- ted as a state in 1812, Louisiana witnessed the Battle of New Orleans, 1815. Cotton and sugar plantations relied on black slaves, who made up close to 47% of the population in 1860, on the eve of the Civil War. Louisiana seceded, 1861, and was readmitted, 1868. Jazz was born in New Orleans in the early 20th cent. As governor (1928-32), Huey Long pushed populist programs. Many tropical storms and floods have battered Lou- isiana, including Hurricane Katrina and subsequent flooding, 2005, which devastated New Orleans. The offshore oil and gas industry developed after World War II. An oil rig explo- sion off the state's Gulf coast spilled millions of barrels of oil, damaging coastal wetlands and many of the state's marine- dependent industries in 2010. Rain caused severe flooding in and around Baton Rouge and Lafayette, Aug. 2016, killing 13 people and damaging thousands of homes.

Famous Louisianans. Louis Armstrong, Pierre Beaure- gard, Judah P. Benjamin, Braxton Bragg, Kate Chopin, Harry Connick Jr., Ellen DeGeneres, Fats Domino, George "Buddy" Guy, Lillian Hellman, Grace King, Jerry Lee Lewis, Bob Liv- ingston, Huey Long, Eli Manning, Peyton Manning, Wynton Marsalis, Tim McGraw, Leonidas K. Polk, Anne Rice, Bill Rus- sell, Henry Miller Shreve, Britney Spears, Madam C. J. Walker (Sarah Breedlove), Edward Douglass White Jr. **Website.** www.louisiana.gov

Maine (ME)
Pine Tree State

People. Population: 1,329,328; rank: 42. **Pop. change** (2010-15): 0.1%. **Pop. density:** 43.1 per sq mi. **Racial dis- tribution:** 94.9% white; 1.4% black; 1.2% Asian; 0.7% Amer. Ind.; <0.05% Hawaiian/Pacific Islander; 2 or more races, 1.7%. **Hispanic pop.:** 1.6%.

Geography. Total area: 35,380 sq mi; rank: 39. **Land area:** 30,843 sq mi; rank: 39. **Acres forested:** 17.6 mil. **Location:** New England state at northeastern tip of U.S. **Climate:** south- ern interior and coast influenced by air masses from the S and W; northern clime harsher, avg. over 100 in. snow in winter. **Topography:** Appalachian Mts. extend through state; western borders have rugged terrain; long sand beaches on southern coast; northern coast mainly rocky promontories, peninsulas, fjords. **Capital:** Augusta. **Chief airport:** Portland.

Economy. Chief industries: manufacturing, agriculture, fishing, services, trade, government, finance, insurance, real estate, construction. **Chief manuf. goods:** paper, ships and boats, cardboard, frozen/canned fruits and vegeta- bles, plastics, baked goods. **Chief crops:** potatoes, green- house and nursery, wild blueberries, apples, hay, maple syrup. **Farm income:** crops, $426.55 mil; livestock/animal prods., $404.79 mil. **Nonfuel minerals:** $96 mil; sand and gravel (construction), cement (portland), stone (crushed), stone (dimension), cement (masonry). **Commercial fish- ing:** $548.9 mil. **Chief ports:** Searsport, Portland, Eastport. **Gross state product:** $56.6 bil. **Sales tax:** 5.5%. **Gasoline tax:** 48.41 cents/gal. **Employment distrib.:** 16.4% govt.; 19.3% trade/trans./util.; 8.4% mfg.; 20.5% ed./health; 10.7% prof./bus. serv.; 10.4% leisure/hosp.; 5.1% finance; 4.6% con- str./mining/log.; 1.2% info.; 3.5% other serv. **Unemployment:** 4.4%. **Min. wage/hr.:** $7.50. **Per cap. pers. income:** $42,077. **New private housing:** 3,699 units/$683.0 mil. **Broadband internet:** 88.0%. **Commercial banks:** 11; deposits: $14.3 bil. **Savings institutions:** 21; deposits: $10.6 bil. **Lottery:** total sales: $253.1 mil; profit: $54.6 mil.

Federal govt. Fed. civ. employees: 10,231; **avg. salary:** $68,197. **Notable fed. facilities:** Portsmouth Naval Shipyard.

Education. High school grad. rate: 86.5%. **4-year public coll./univ.:** 8; **2-yr. public:** 7; **4-yr. private:** 12.

Energy. Electricity use/cost: 549 kWh, $83.91.

State data. Motto: Dirigo (I direct). **Flower:** White pine cone and tassel. **Bird:** Black-capped chickadee. **Tree:** East- ern white pine. **Song:** "State of Maine Song." **Entered union:** Mar. 15, 1820; rank: 23rd.

Tourism. Tourist spending: $3.6 bil. **Attractions:** Acadia Natl. Park, Bar Harbor, on Mt. Desert Island; Old Orchard Beach; Old Port historic waterfront, Victoria Mansion, Port- land; Portland Head Light, Cape Elizabeth; Maine Maritime Museum, Bath; Baxter State Park; L.L. Bean flagship store and outlet shopping, Freeport. **Information:** Maine Office of Tourism, 59 State House Station, Augusta, ME 04333; 1-888- 624-6345; www.visitmaine.com

History. Paleo-Indians arrived about 11,500 years ago. Maine was inhabited by Algonquian peoples including the Abnaki, Penobscot, and Passamaquoddy at the time of Euro- pean contact. French settled, 1604, at the St. Croix R., the English, c. 1607, on the Kennebec; both settlements failed. A royal charter, 1691, made Maine part of Massachusetts. Maine broke off, 1819, and became a separate state, 1820. Drawing on vast forest resources, the pulp and paper industry developed after the Civil War. Bath Iron Works began building U.S. Navy vessels and other ships in the 1890s. Mail-order and retail giant L.L. Bean was founded, 1912. Women have fared well in state politics: Margaret Chase Smith became the first woman to serve in both houses of Congress (House, 1940-49; Senate, 1949-73), and Olympia Snowe and Susan Collins represented Maine in the Senate since the mid-1990s (Snowe retired in Jan. 2013).

Famous "Down Easters." Leon Leonwood (L. L.) Bean, James G. Blaine, Patrick Dempsey, Hannibal Hamlin, Sarah Orne Jewett, Stephen King, Henry Wadsworth Longfellow, Sir Hiram and Hudson Maxim, Edna St. Vincent Millay, George J. Mitchell, Edmund Muskie, Judd Nelson, Edwin Arlington Robinson, Joan Benoit Samuelson, Liv Tyler, Kate Douglas Wiggin, Ben Ames Williams. **Website.** www.maine.gov

Maryland (MD)
Old Line State, Free State

People. Population: 6,006,401; rank: 19. **Pop. change** (2010-15): 4.0%. **Pop. density:** 618.8 per sq mi. **Racial dis- tribution:** 59.6% white; 30.5% black; 6.5% Asian; 0.6% Amer. Ind.; 0.1% Hawaiian/Pacific Islander; 2 or more races, 2.7%. **Hispanic pop.:** 9.5%.

Geography. Total area: 12,406 sq mi; rank: 42. **Land area:** 9,707 sq mi; rank: 42. **Acres forested:** 2.5 mil. **Location:** South Atlantic state stretching from the ocean to the Alle- gheny Mts. **Climate:** continental in the W; humid subtropical in the E. **Topography:** coastal plain on Eastern Shore sepa- rated by Chesapeake Bay from coastal plain, Piedmont Pla- teau, and the Blue Ridge. **Capital:** Annapolis. **Chief airport:** Glen Burnie (Baltimore).

Economy. Chief industries: manufacturing, biotechnology and information technology, services, tourism. **Chief manuf. goods:** navigational instruments, pharmaceutical and medi- cine, broadcasting equip., plastics, printing, milk and ice cream. **Chief crops:** greenhouse and nursery, corn, soybeans, wheat, hay, tomatoes, watermelons, barley, potatoes, apples. **Farm income:** crops, $959.05 mil; livestock/animal prods., $1.47 bil. **Nonfuel minerals:** $306 mil; cement (portland), stone (crushed), sand and gravel (construction), cement (masonry), stone (dimension). **Commercial fishing:** $90.2 mil. **Chief port:** Baltimore. **Gross state product:** $363.8 bil. **Sales tax:** 6.0%. **Gasoline tax:** 51.90 cents/gal. **Employment distrib.:** 18.8% govt.; 17.1% trade/trans./util.; 3.9% mfg.; 16.5% ed./ health; 16.1% prof./bus. serv.; 10.5% leisure/hosp.; 5.4% finance; 6.0% constr./mining/log.; 1.3% info.; 4.3% other serv. **Unemployment:** 5.2%. **Min. wage/hr.:** $8.75. **Per cap. pers. income:** $56,127. **New private housing:** 17,057 units/$3.1 bil. **Broadband internet:** 95.4%. **Commercial banks:** 85; depos- its: $126.2 bil. **Savings institutions:** 27; deposits: $5.0 bil. **Lottery:** total sales: $2.8 bil; profit: $964.7 mil.

Federal govt. Fed. civ. employees: 128,725; **avg. sal- ary:** $102,672. **Notable fed. facilities:** U.S. Naval Academy; Beltsville Agriculture Res. Ctr.; Ft. Meade; Aberdeen Prov- ing Ground; Joint Base Andrews; Naval Air Sys. Command; Goddard Space Flight Ctr.; Natl. Inst. of Health; Natl. Inst. of Standards & Technology; Food & Drug Admin.; Bureau of the Census; Walter Reed Natl. Military Med. Ctr., Bethesda; Natl. Marine Fisheries Serv.; Natl. Oceanic and Atmospheric Admin.

Education. High school grad. rate: 86.4%. **4-year public coll./univ.:** 13; **2-yr. public:** 16; **4-yr. private:** 20.

Energy. Electricity use/cost: 1,025 kWh, $139.68.

State data. Motto: Fatti Maschii, Parole Femine (Manly deeds, womanly words). **Flower:** Black-eyed Susan. **Bird:** Baltimore oriole. **Tree:** White oak. **Song:** "Maryland, My Maryland." **Seventh** of original 13 states to ratify the Consti- tution, Apr. 28, 1788.

Tourism. Tourist spending: $15.9 bil. **Attractions:** Ocean City; Ft. McHenry—the defense of which inspired Francis Scott Key to write "The Star-Spangled Banner," Pimlico Race Course (Preakness Stakes), Edgar Allan Poe House and Museum, Oriole Park at Camden Yards, Natl. Aquarium, Inner Harbor, in Baltimore; Antietam Natl. Battlefield, Sharpsburg; South Mountain State Battlefield, Middletown; U.S. Naval Academy, Maryland State House (oldest in continuous legislative use in U.S.), in Annapolis; Natl. Cryptologic Museum, Ft. Meade. **Information:** Maryland Office of Tourism Development, 401 E. Pratt St., 14th Fl., Baltimore, MD 21202; 1-866-639-3526; www.visitmaryland.org

History. Europeans encountered Algonquian-speaking Nanticoke and Piscataway and Iroquois-speaking Susquehannock when they first visited the area. Italian navigator Giovanni da Verrazzano reached the Chesapeake region in the early 16th cent. English Capt. John Smith explored and mapped the area, 1608. William Claiborne set up a trading post on Kent Island in Chesapeake Bay, 1631. King Charles I granted land to Cecilius Calvert, Lord Baltimore, 1632; Calvert's brother Leonard, with about 200 settlers, founded St. Mary's, 1634. During the Revolutionary War, Baltimore (1776-77) and Annapolis (1783-84) served as temporary capitals of the U.S. When a British fleet tried to take Ft. McHenry in the War of 1812, Marylander Francis Scott Key wrote "The Star-Spangled Banner," 1814. Born into slavery at Tuckahoe in 1818, Frederick Douglass became a leading abolitionist. Although a slaveholding state, Maryland stayed in the Union during the Civil War and was the site of the battle of Antietam, 1862. Gov. Spiro Agnew, elected U.S. vice pres., 1968 and 1972, pleaded no contest to tax evasion and resigned, 1973. Israeli and Egyptian leaders reached a historic peace accord at the Camp David presidential retreat, 1978. A major effort is under way to clean up pollution in the Chesapeake Bay watershed. The death of Freddie Gray, a young black man in police custody, touched off a week of sometimes violent protests in Baltimore in Apr. 2015. Six law enforcement officers were charged in his death; after three were acquitted, the charges against the others were dropped in July 2016.

Famous Marylanders. John Astin, Benjamin Banneker, Tom Clancy, Frederick Douglass, Matthew Henson, Francis Scott Key, Thurgood Marshall, H. L. Mencken, Kweisi Mfume, Ogden Nash, Charles Willson Peale, Michael Phelps, William Pinkney, Edgar Allan Poe, Cal Ripken Jr., Babe Ruth, Upton Sinclair, Roger B. Taney, Harriet Tubman, John Waters, Montel Williams.

Website. www.maryland.gov

Massachusetts (MA)

Bay State, Old Colony

People. Population: 6,794,422; rank: 15. **Pop. change** (2010-15): 3.8%. **Pop. density:** 871.1 per sq mi. **Racial distribution:** 82.1% white; 8.4% black; 6.6% Asian; 0.5% Amer. Ind.; 0.1% Hawaiian/Pacific Islander; 2 or more races, 2.3%. **Hispanic pop.:** 11.2%.

Geography. Total area: 10,554 sq mi; rank: 44. **Land area:** 7,800 sq mi; rank: 45. **Acres forested:** 3.0 mil. **Location:** New England state on Atlantic seaboard. **Climate:** temperate, with colder, drier clime in western region. **Topography:** jagged indented coast from Rhode Island around Cape Cod; flat land yields to stony upland pastures near central region and gentle hilly country in W; except in W, land is rocky, sandy, and not fertile. **Capital:** Boston. **Chief airport:** Boston.

Economy. Chief industries: services, trade, manufacturing. **Chief manuf. goods:** electronics and instruments, pharmaceuticals, telecom and broadcasting equip., plastics, medical equip., printing. **Chief crops:** greenhouse and nursery, cranberries, tomatoes, sweet corn, apples, hay, tobacco. **Farm income:** crops, $314.28 mil; livestock/animal prods., $144.03 mil. **Nonfuel minerals:** $305 mil; stone (crushed), sand and gravel (construction), stone (dimension), lime, clays (common). **Commercial fishing:** $525.1 mil. **Chief ports:** Boston, Fall River. **Gross state product:** $476.7 bil. **Sales tax:** 6.25%. **Gasoline tax:** 44.94 cents/gal. **Employment distrib.:** 13.1% govt.; 16.0% trade/trans./util.; 7.0% mfg.; 21.7% ed./health; 15.4% prof./bus. serv.; 10.2% leisure/hosp.; 6.2% finance; 4.3% constr./mining/util.; 2.4% info.; 3.8% other serv. **Unemployment:** 5.0%. **Min. wage/hr.:** $10.00. **Per cap. pers. income:** $61,032. **New private housing:** 17,424 units/$4.0 bil. **Broadband internet:** 96.1%. **Commercial banks:** 48; deposits: $304.3 bil. **Savings institutions:** 124; deposits: $67.2 bil. **Lottery:** total sales $5.0 bil; profit: $985.9 mil.

Federal govt. Fed. civ. employees: 24,768; **avg. salary:** $84,784. **Notable fed. facilities:** Thomas P. O'Neill Jr. Fed.

Bldg.; J.W. McCormack Bldg.; JFK Fed. Bldg.; Hanscom AFB; Army Natick Soldier Systems Ctr.

Education. High school grad. rate: 86.1%. **4-year public coll./univ.:** 14; **2-yr. public:** 16; **4-yr. private:** 82.

Energy. Electricity use/cost: 615 kWh, $106.94.

State data. Motto: Ense Petit Placidam Sub Libertate Quietem (By the sword we seek peace, but peace only under liberty). **Flower:** Mayflower. **Bird:** Black-capped chickadee. **Tree:** American elm. **Song:** "All Hail to Massachusetts." **Sixth** of original 13 states to ratify the Constitution, Feb. 6, 1788.

Tourism. Tourist spending: $19.5 bil. **Attractions:** Provincetown art colony; Cape Cod; Plymouth Rock, Plimoth Plantation, Mayflower II, in Plymouth; Freedom Trail, Museum of Fine Arts, New England Aquarium, Faneuil Hall, Boston Harbor Isls. Natl. Recreation Area, Boston Public Garden, in Boston; Tanglewood, Hancock Shaker Village, Berkshire Scenic Railway Museum, Norman Rockwell Museum, in the Berkshires region; Peabody Essex Museum, House of the Seven Gables, in Salem; Old Sturbridge Village; Historic Deerfield; Walden Pond, Louisa May Alcott's Orchard House, in Concord; Naismith Memorial Basketball Hall of Fame, Springfield. **Information:** Massachusetts Office of Travel & Tourism, 10 Park Plz., Ste. 4510, Boston, MA 02116; 1-800-227-MASS; www.massvacation.com

History. Early inhabitants were Algonquian peoples: Nauset, Wampanoag, Massachuset, Pennacook, Nipmuc, and Pocumtuc. Pilgrims settled in Plymouth, 1620, giving thanks for their survival with a Thanksgiving feast alongside Wampanoag living there, 1621. About 20,000 new settlers arrived, 1630-40. Colonist-Native American relations deteriorated, leading to King Philip's War, 1675-76, which the colonists won. Witch trials at Salem, 1692, led to the execution of 20 people. Demonstrations against British restrictions set off the Boston Massacre, 1770, and the Boston Tea Party, 1773. The first bloodshed of American Revolution was at Lexington, 1775. After statehood, Massachusetts prospered from shipbuilding, seafaring, and the making of textiles, shoes, and metal goods, while artists, writers, and social reformers flourished. The controversial Sacco-Vanzetti case, 1920-27, ended with the execution of two Italian immigrants on murder and robbery charges. After World War II, old industries declined, knowledge-intensive enterprises thrived, and the Kennedys became a dominant political family. The state's highest court ruled, 2003, that same-sex couples could legally marry. Two bombs exploded Apr. 15, 2013, near the finish line of the Boston Marathon, killing three and injuring more than 250. The surviving of two brothers believed to have planted the bombs was convicted on multiple charges in Apr. 2015 and sentenced to death.

Famous "Bay Staters." John Adams, John Quincy Adams, Samuel Adams, Louisa May Alcott, Horatio Alger, Susan B. Anthony, Crispus Attucks, Clara Barton, Michael Bloomberg, George H. W. Bush, Steve Carell, John Cheever, E. E. Cummings, Bette Davis, Emily Dickinson, Charles Eliot, Ralph Waldo Emerson, William Lloyd Garrison, Edward Everett Hale, John Hancock, Nathaniel Hawthorne, Oliver Wendell Holmes Jr., Winslow Homer, Elias Howe, John F. Kennedy, Jack Kerouac, John Kerry, Emeril Lagasse, Jack Lemmon, James Russell Lowell, Cotton Mather, Maria Mitchell, Samuel F. B. Morse, Conan O'Brien, Paul Revere, Norman Rockwell, Dr. Seuss (Theodor Seuss Geisel), Henry David Thoreau, Barbara Walters, James Abbott McNeil Whistler, John Greenleaf Whittier.

Website. www.mass.gov

Michigan (MI)

Great Lakes State, Wolverine State

People. Population: 9,922,576; rank: 10. **Pop. change** (2010-15): 0.4%. **Pop. density:** 175.5 per sq mi. **Racial distribution:** 79.7% white; 14.2% black; 3.0% Asian; 0.7% Amer. Ind.; <0.05% Hawaiian/Pacific Islander; 2 or more races, 2.3%. **Hispanic pop.:** 4.9%.

Geography. Total area: 96,714 sq mi; rank: 11. **Land area:** 56,539 sq mi; rank: 22. **Acres forested:** 20.3 mil. **Location:** East North Central state bordering four of the Great Lakes, divided into an Upper and Lower Peninsula by the Straits of Mackinac, which link Lakes Michigan and Huron. **Climate:** well-defined seasons tempered by the Great Lakes. **Topography:** low rolling hills give way to northern tableland of hilly belts in Lower Peninsula; Upper Peninsula is level in the E with swampy areas; western region is higher and more rugged. **Capital:** Lansing. **Chief airports:** Detroit, Grand Rapids.

Economy. Chief industries: manufacturing, services, tourism, agriculture, forestry/lumber. **Chief manuf. goods:** motor vehicles and parts, plastics, metalworking machinery, non-wood office furniture, fabricated metals. **Chief crops:** greenhouse and nursery, soybeans, corn, wheat, sugar beets, apples, blueberries, potatoes, dry beans, cherries, hay, cucumbers, tomatoes, grapes. **Farm income:** crops, $4.59 bil; livestock/animal prods., $3.95 bil. **Nonfuel minerals:** $2.8 bil; iron ore (usable shipped), cement (portland), nickel concentrates, stone (crushed), sand and gravel (construction). **Commercial fishing:** $11.5 mil. **Chief ports:** Detroit, Escanaba, Calcite, Port Inland, Muskegon, Port Huron. **Gross state product:** $466.5 bil. **Sales tax:** 6.0%. **Gasoline tax:** 51.66 cents/gal. **Employment distrib.:** 13.8% govt.; 17.8% trade/trans./util.; 13.7% mfg.; 15.3% ed./health; 15.4% prof./bus. serv.; 10.0% leisure/hosp.; 4.9% finance; 3.8% constr./mining/log.; 1.3% info.; 3.9% other serv. **Unemployment:** 5.4%. **Min. wage/hr.:** $8.50. **Per cap. pers. income:** $42,427. **New private housing:** 18,226 units/$3.9 bil. **Broadband internet:** 91.4%. **Commercial banks:** 128; deposits: $180.6 bil. **Savings institutions:** 14; deposits: $9.9 bil. **Lottery:** total sales: $2.8 bil; profit: $796.5 mil.

Federal govt. Fed. civ. employees: 25,394; **avg. salary:** $81,535. **Notable fed. facilities:** Army TACOM Life Cycle Mgmt., Detroit Arsenal; DLA Logistics Info. Service; Selfridge Air Natl. Guard Base; Hart-Dole-Inouye Fed. Ctr.

Education. High school grad. rate: 78.6%. **4-year public coll./univ.:** 18; **2-yr. public:** 28; **4-yr. private:** 50.

Energy. Electricity use/cost: 654 kWh, $94.52.

State data. Motto: Si Quaeris Peninsulam Amoenam, Circumspice (If you seek a pleasant peninsula, look about you). **Flower:** Apple blossom. **Bird:** American robin. **Tree:** White pine. **Song:** "Michigan, My Michigan." **Entered union:** Jan. 26, 1837; **rank:** 26th.

Tourism. Tourist spending: $18.1 bil. **Attractions:** Henry Ford Museum and Greenfield Village, Dearborn; Frederik Meijer Gardens and Sculpture Park, Grand Rapids; Tahquamenon Falls (of Longfellow's poem *Song of Hiawatha*); De Zwaan windmill, Tulip Time Festival, in Holland; Soo Locks (bet. Lakes Superior and Huron), Sault Ste. Marie; Air Zoo, Portage; Mackinac Island; Belle Isle Park, Detroit Institute of Arts, Charles H. Wright Museum of African-American History, Motown Historical Museum, in Detroit. **Information:** Michigan Economic Development Corp., 300 N. Washington Sq., Lansing, MI 48913; 1-888-784-7328; www.michigan.org

History. Hunting and fishing peoples lived in the region as early as 11,000 years ago. Ojibwa, Ottawa, Miami, Potawatomi, and Huron inhabited the area at the time of European contact. French fur traders and missionaries arrived in the 17th cent. and established a settlement at Sault Ste. Marie, 1668. British took over, 1763, and crushed a Native American uprising led by Ottawa chieftain Pontiac. The area was ceded to the U.S. by the Treaty of Paris, 1783, but the British remained until 1796. Michigan was organized as a territory, 1805. The British seized Ft. Mackinac and Detroit, 1812, but the U.S. regained control, 1814. The opening of the Erie Canal, 1825, and new land laws and Native American cessions led the way for a flood of settlers. Strongly antislavery, Michigan became a state, 1837, and supplied 90,000 soldiers to the Union army in the Civil War. In the 20th cent., automobile manufacturing was the backbone of the economy. Henry Ford launched the Model T car, 1908; the United Auto Workers union was founded, 1935. Motown music flourished in Detroit in the 1960s, but riots in 1967 dealt the city a heavy blow. As the auto industry faltered, Michigan lost more than 20% of its automotive-related jobs in 2002-07. In 2009, the federal government loaned billions of dollars to GM and Chrysler to keep them solvent. Detroit formally emerged from a 17-month bankruptcy process—the largest in municipal history—in Dec. 2014, having shed nearly $7 bil in debts. As of July 2016, nine state and local officials had been criminally charged for their alleged roles in the lead-contamination crisis in Flint's municipal water supply system.

Famous Michiganders. Ralph Bunche, Paul de Kruif, Thomas Edison, Eminem (Marshall Mathers), Edna Ferber, Gerald R. Ford, Henry Ford, Aretha Franklin, Edgar Guest, Lee Iacocca, Magic Johnson, Casey Kasem, Will Kellogg, Ring Lardner, Elmore Leonard, Charles Lindbergh, Joe Louis, Madonna, Malcolm X, Terry McMillan, Michael Moore, Larry Page, Pontiac, Gilda Radner, Mitt Romney, Diana Ross, Tom Selleck, Sinbad (David Adkins), John Smoltz, Lily Tomlin, Serena Williams.

Website. www.michigan.gov

Minnesota (MN)

North Star State, Gopher State

People. Population: 5,489,594; **rank:** 21. **Pop. change** (2010-15): 3.5%. **Pop. density:** 68.9 per sq mi. **Racial**

distribution: 85.4% white; 6.0% black; 4.9% Asian; 1.3% Amer. Ind.; 0.1% Hawaiian/Pacific Islander; 2 or more races, 2.4%. **Hispanic pop.:** 5.2%.

Geography. Total area: 86,936 sq mi; **rank:** 12. **Land area:** 79,627 sq mi; **rank:** 14. **Acres forested:** 17.4 mil. **Location:** West North Central state bounded on the E by Wisconsin and Lake Superior, on the N by Canada, on the W by the Dakotas, and on the S by Iowa. **Climate:** northern part of state lies in the moist Great Lakes storm belt; the western border lies at the edge of the semiarid Great Plains. **Topography:** central hill and lake region covers approx. half the state; to the NE, rocky ridges and deep lakes; to the NW, flat plain; to the S, rolling plains and deep river valleys. **Capital:** St. Paul. **Chief airport:** Minneapolis.

Economy. Chief industries: agribusiness, forest products, mining, manufacturing, tourism. **Chief manuf. goods:** petroleum and asphalt, computers and electronics, milk and cheese, printing, animal slaughtering, paper and prod., medical equip. **Chief crops:** corn, soybeans, hay, sugar beets, wheat, potatoes, greenhouse and nursery, dry edible beans, green peas, sunflowers. **Farm income:** crops, $9.95 bil; livestock/animal prods., $8.85 bil. **Nonfuel minerals:** $959 mil; iron ore (usable shipped), sand and gravel (industrial), sand and gravel (construction), stone (crushed), stone (dimension). **Commercial fishing:** $0.2 mil. **Chief ports:** Two Harbors, Silver Bay, Duluth, St. Paul. **Gross state product:** $333.3 bil. **Sales tax:** 6.875%. **Gasoline tax:** 47.00 cents/gal. **Employment distrib.:** 14.8% govt.; 18.2% trade/trans./util.; 10.9% mfg.; 18.2% ed./health; 12.3% prof./bus. serv.; 9.2% leisure/hosp.; 6.3% finance; 4.4% constr./mining/log.; 1.7% info.; 3.9% other serv. **Unemployment:** 3.7%. **Min. wage/hr.:** $9.00. **Per cap. pers. income:** $50,541. **New private housing:** 19,545 units/$4.1 bil. **Broadband internet:** 90.2%. **Commercial banks:** 360; deposits: $209.4 bil. **Savings institutions:** 20; deposits: $3.7 bil. **Lottery:** total sales: $546.9 mil; profit: $135.8 mil.

Federal govt. Fed. civ. employees: 16,088; **avg. salary:** $77,927. **Notable fed. facilities:** Bishop Henry Whipple Fed. Bldg.; Minneapolis-St. Paul Air Reserve Station.

Education. High school grad. rate: 81.2%. **4-year public coll./univ.:** 12; **2-yr. public:** 31; **4-yr. private:** 34.

Energy. Electricity use/cost: 810 kWh, $97.26.

State data. Motto: L'Etoile du Nord (The star of the north). **Flower:** Pink and white lady's-slipper. **Bird:** Common loon. **Tree:** Red pine. **Song:** "Hail! Minnesota." **Entered union:** May 11, 1858; **rank:** 32nd.

Tourism. Tourist spending: $13.2 bil. **Attractions:** Minneapolis Institute of Arts, Walker Art Center, Minneapolis Sculpture Garden, Minnehaha Falls (in Longfellow's poem *Song of Hiawatha*), Guthrie Theater, in Minneapolis; Mall of America, Bloomington; Ordway Ctr. for the Performing Arts, Science Museum of Minnesota, in St. Paul; Voyageurs Natl. Park; Mayo Clinic, Rochester; North Shore (Lake Superior); Lake Minnetonka; Boundary Waters Canoe Area Wilderness; Superior Natl. Forest; Aerial Lift Bridge, Duluth. **Information:** Explore Minnesota Tourism, Metro Square, 121 7th Pl. E., Ste. 100, St. Paul, MN 55101; 1-888-TOURISM; www.explore minnesota.com

History. Inhabited for at least 10,000 years, the region was home to Dakota Sioux when Europeans arrived. French fur traders Pierre Esprit Radisson and Médard Chouart, sieur des Groseilliers, explored in the mid-17th cent. In 1679, Daniel Greysolon, sieur Duluth, claimed the entire region for France. Ojibwa arrived in the 18th cent. and warred with the Sioux for over 100 years. Britain took the area east of the Mississippi, 1763. The U.S. took over that portion after the American Revolution and gained the western area, 1803, in the Louisiana Purchase. The U.S. built Ft. St. Anthony (now Ft. Snelling), 1819, and bought Native American lands, 1837, spurring an influx of settlers from the east. Minnesota became a territory, 1849, and a state, 1858. The Sioux staged a bloody uprising, the Battle of Wood Lake, 1862, and were driven from the state. Railroad construction after the Civil War spurred the growth of the grain, timber, and iron mining industries. The opening of the St. Lawrence Seaway, 1959, aided the port of Duluth. Elected as a reformer, former pro wrestler Jesse Ventura served as governor, 1999-2003. Two-term Sen. Paul Wellstone, one of a long line of liberal Minnesota Democrats, died when his campaign plane crashed, 2002. The I-35W Mississippi River Bridge in Minneapolis collapsed in 2007, killing 13.

Famous Minnesotans. Andrews Sisters, Warren E. Burger, Ethan and Joel Coen, Bob Dylan, F. Scott Fitzgerald, Al Franken, Judy Garland, Cass Gilbert, Hubert H. Humphrey, Garrison Keillor, Sister Elizabeth Kenny, Jessica Lange, Sinclair

Lewis, Paul Manship, E. G. Marshall, William J. and Charles H. Mayo, Eugene McCarthy, Walter F. Mondale, Prince (Prince Rogers Nelson), Charles M. Schulz, Ann Sothern, Harold Stassen, Thorstein Veblen, Jesse Ventura, Lindsey Vonn, Paul Wellstone.

Website. www.minnesota.gov

Mississippi (MS)
Magnolia State

People. Population: 2,992,333; rank: 32. **Pop. change** (2010-15): 0.8%. **Pop. density:** 63.8 per sq mi. **Racial distribution:** 59.5% white; 37.6% black; 1.1% Asian; 0.6% Amer. Ind.; 0.1% Hawaiian/Pacific Islander; 2 or more races, 1.2%. **Hispanic pop.:** 3.1%.

Geography. Total area: 48,432 sq mi; rank: 32. **Land area:** 46,923 sq mi; rank: 31. **Acres forested:** 19.4 mil. **Location:** East South Central state bordered on the W by the Mississippi R., on the S by the Gulf of Mexico. **Climate:** semitropical, with abundant rainfall and long growing season. **Topography:** low, fertile delta between the Yazoo and Mississippi Rivers; loess bluffs stretch around delta border; sandy gulf coastal terraces followed by piney woods and prairie; rugged, high sandy hills in extreme NE followed by Prairie Black Belt, Pontotoc Ridge, and flatwoods into the N central highlands. **Capital:** Jackson.

Economy. Chief industries: warehousing and distribution, services, manufacturing, government, wholesale and retail trade. **Chief manuf. goods:** petroleum, upholstered furniture, poultry processing, motor vehicle parts, plastics, ships and boats, chemicals. **Chief crops:** cotton, soybeans, rice, hay, corn, sweet potatoes. **Farm income:** crops, $2.79 bil; livestock/animal prods., $3.79 bil. **Nonfuel minerals:** $192 mil; sand and gravel (construction), stone (crushed), clays (fuller's earth), clays (ball), sand and gravel (industrial). **Commercial fishing:** $26.0 mil. **Chief ports:** Pascagoula, Vicksburg, Gulfport, Biloxi, Greenville. **Gross state product:** $107.1 bil. **Sales tax:** 7.0%. **Gasoline tax:** 37.19 cents/gal. **Employment distrib.:** 21.6% govt.; 19.9% trade/trans./util.; 12.5% mfg.; 12.3% ed./health; 8.8% prof./bus. serv.; 11.8% leisure/hosp.; 3.7% finance; 4.8% constr./mining/log.; 1.2% info.; 3.5% other serv. **Unemployment:** 6.5%. **Min. wage/hr.:** none ($7.25). **Per cap. pers. income:** $35,444. **New private housing:** 6,845 units/$1.1 bil. **Broadband internet:** 85.7%. **Commercial banks:** 96; deposits: $49.2 bil. **Savings institutions:** 4; deposits: $363 mil.

Federal govt. Fed. civ. employees: 17,635; **avg. salary:** $69,368. **Notable fed. facilities:** Keesler AFB; Meridian NAS; Columbus AFB; NASA Stennis Space Ctr.; Army Corps of Eng. Waterways Experiment Sta.; Naval Constr. Battalion Ctr., Gulfport.

Education. High school grad. rate: 77.6%. **4-year public coll./univ.:** 8; **2-yr. public:** 15; **4-yr. private:** 9.

Energy. Electricity use/cost: 1,248 kWh, $141.22.

State data. Motto: Virtute et Armis (By valor and arms). **Flower:** Magnolia. **Bird:** Northern mockingbird. **Tree:** Magnolia. **Song:** "Go, Mississippi!" **Entered union:** Dec. 10, 1817; rank: 20th.

Tourism. Tourist spending: $6.1 bil. **Attractions:** Vicksburg Natl. Military Park and Cemetery; Natchez Trace Parkway; antebellum home tours in Natchez and other cities; Tupelo Natl. Battlefield, Elvis Presley Birthplace, in Tupelo; Smith Robertson Museum and Cultural Ctr., Mynelle Gardens, Eudora Welty House, in Jackson; Mardi Gras parades on Gulf Coast; Beauvoir (Jefferson Davis Home and Presidential Library), Biloxi; Gulf Islands Natl. Seashore; Delta Blues Museum, Clarksdale. **Information:** Mississippi Division of Tourism, P.O. Box 849, Jackson, MS 39205; 1-866-SEE-MISS; www.visitmississippi.org

History. Choctaw, Chickasaw, and Natchez peoples were living in the region at the time of European contact. The Spaniard Hernando de Soto explored the area, 1540-41. René-Robert Cavelier, sieur de La Salle, traced the Mississippi R. from Illinois to its mouth and claimed the entire Mississippi Valley for France, 1682. The first settlement was the French Ft. Maurepas, 1699, on Biloxi Bay. The region was ceded to Britain, 1763, and claimed by Spain, 1779-98, then became a U.S. territory, 1798, and a state, 1817. Slavery spread along with cotton plantations; slaves made up 55% of the population, 1860. Mississippi seceded, 1861. In the Civil War, Union forces captured Vicksburg, 1863, and caused extensive damage elsewhere. Mississippi reentered the Union, 1870. For the next 100 years, resistance to desegregation and violence against blacks made the state a battleground for the civil rights

movement. Hurricanes Camille, 1969, and Katrina, 2005, caused substantial damage to the Gulf Coast. Since the early 1990s, casino gambling has boosted the economy, but the state's poverty rate remained the highest in the nation in 2010.

Famous Mississippians. Margaret Walker Alexander, Dana Andrews, Jimmy Buffett, Bo Diddley, Medgar Evers, William Faulkner, Brett Favre, Shelby Foote, Morgan Freeman, John Grisham, Fannie Lou Hamer, Jim Henson, Faith Hill, John Lee Hooker, Robert Johnson, James Earl Jones, B. B. King, L. Q. C. Lamar, Trent Lott, Gerald McRaney, Willie Morris, Walter Payton, Elvis Presley, Leontyne Price, Charley Pride, LeAnn Rimes, Robin Roberts, Muddy Waters, Eudora Welty, Tennessee Williams, Oprah Winfrey, Johnny Winter, Richard Wright, Tammy Wynette.

Website. www.ms.gov

Missouri (MO)
Show Me State

People. Population: 6,083,672; rank: 18. **Pop. change** (2010-15): 1.6%. **Pop. density:** 88.5 per sq mi. **Racial distribution:** 83.3% white; 11.8% black; 2.0% Asian; 0.6% Amer. Ind.; 0.1% Hawaiian/Pacific Islander; 2 or more races, 2.2%. **Hispanic pop.:** 4.1%.

Geography. Total area: 69,707 sq mi; rank: 21. **Land area:** 68,742 sq mi; rank: 18. **Acres forested:** 15.4 mil. **Location:** West North Central state near the geographic center of the conterminous U.S.; bordered on the E by Mississippi R., on the NW by Missouri R. **Climate:** continental, susceptible to cold Canadian air; moist, warm Gulf air; and drier SW air. **Topography:** rolling hills, open, fertile plains, and well-watered prairie N of the Missouri R.; S of the river, land is rough and hilly with deep, narrow valleys; alluvial plain in the SE; low elevation in the W. **Capital:** Jefferson City. **Chief airports:** Kansas City, St. Louis.

Economy. Chief industries: agriculture, manufacturing, aerospace, tourism. **Chief manuf. goods:** motor vehicles and parts, aerospace, pharmaceuticals, plastics, soap, animal slaughtering and processing, printing. **Chief crops:** soybeans, corn, hay, cotton and cottonseed, wheat, rice, sorghum. **Farm income:** crops, $5.73 bil; livestock/animal prods., $5.26 bil. **Nonfuel minerals:** $2.6 bil; cement (portland), stone (crushed), lead, lime, sand and gravel (industrial). **Gross state product:** $293.4 bil. **Sales tax:** 4.225%. **Gasoline tax:** 35.70 cents/gal. **Employment distrib.:** 15.6% govt.; 18.8% trade/trans./util.; 9.1% mfg.; 15.9% ed./health; 13.5% prof./bus. serv.; 10.8% leisure/hosp.; 6.1% finance; 4.3% constr./mining/log.; 1.9% info.; 4.1% other serv. **Unemployment:** 5.0%. **Min. wage/hr.:** $7.65. **Per cap. pers. income:** $42,752. **New private housing:** 18,344 units/$3.1 bil. **Broadband internet:** 88.6%. **Commercial banks:** 320; deposits: $136.7 bil. **Savings institutions:** 24; deposits: $20.4 bil. **Lottery:** total sales: $1.1 bil; profit: $270.7 mil.

Federal govt. Fed. civ. employees: 35,542; **avg. salary:** $67,778. **Notable fed. facilities:** Federal Reserve banks; Ft. Leonard Wood; Jefferson Barracks Natl. Cemetery; Natl. Personnel Records Ctr.; Whiteman AFB.

Education. High school grad. rate: 87.3%. **4-year public coll./univ.:** 13; **2-yr. public:** 14; **4-yr. private:** 51.

Energy. Electricity use/cost: 1,095 kWh, $116.47.

State data. Motto: Salus Populi Suprema Lex Esto (Let the welfare of the people be the supreme law). **Flower:** Hawthorn. **Bird:** Eastern bluebird. **Tree:** Flowering dogwood. **Song:** "Missouri Waltz." **Entered union:** Aug. 10, 1821; rank: 24th.

Tourism. Tourist spending: $13.5 bil. **Attractions:** Silver Dollar City, Branson; Mark Twain Boyhood Home and Museum, Hannibal; Pony Express Natl. Museum, St. Joseph; Harry S. Truman Library and Museum, Independence; Gateway Arch (part of Jefferson Natl. Expansion Memorial), Ulysses S. Grant Natl. Historic Site, St. Louis Zoo, in St. Louis; Worlds of Fun amusement park, Kansas City; Lake of the Ozarks; Ozark Natl. Scenic Riverways; Natl. Churchill Museum, Fulton; State Capitol, Jefferson City; Wilson's Creek Natl. Battlefield; George Washington Carver Natl. Monument, Diamond; Bass Pro Shops Outdoor World, Springfield. **Information:** Missouri Division of Tourism, P.O. Box 1055, Jefferson City, MO 65102; 1-800-519-2100; www.visitmo.com

History. In the 17th cent., when French explorers arrived, Algonquian-speaking Sauk, Fox, and Illinois as well as Siouan-speaking Osage, Missouri, Iowa, and Kansa peoples were living in the region; few remained by the 1830s. French miners and lead miners made the first settlement, c. 1735, at Ste. Genevieve. The territory was ceded to Spain by the French,

1762, then returned to France, 1800, and acquired by the U.S. in the Louisiana Purchase, 1803. Powerful earthquakes rocked New Madrid, 1811-12. Missouri became a territory, 1812, and entered the Union as a slave state, 1821. St. Louis became the gateway for pioneers heading west. Though Missouri stayed with the Union, pro- and antislavery forces battled there during the Civil War. In the late 19th cent. railroad building and the cattle trade made Kansas City a boomtown. The most notable Missourian of the 20th cent., Harry S. Truman, was U.S. president, 1945-53. The state, a political bellwether, voted for the winner in every presidential election from 1960 to 2004. In May 2011, a tornado in Joplin killed about 162. The police-shooting death of Michael Brown in Ferguson in Aug. 2014 touched off major protests that spread nationwide and revived debate over the relationship between law enforcement officers and the communities they serve. The Univ. of Missouri system's president resigned, Nov. 2015, after protesters asserted administrators failed to address racial incidents against African-American students.

Famous Missourians. Maya Angelou, Robert Altman, John Ashcroft, Burt Bacharach, Josephine Baker, Scott Bakula, Thomas Hart Benton, Yogi Berra, Chuck Berry, George Caleb Bingham, Daniel Boone, Omar Bradley, William S. Burroughs, Kate Capshaw, Dale Carnegie, George Washington Carver, Bob Costas, Walter Cronkite, Sheryl Crow, Walt Disney, T. S. Eliot, Richard "Dick" Gephardt, John Goodman, Betty Grable, Jon Hamm, Edwin Hubble, Jesse James, Rush Limbaugh, Marianne Moore, Reinhold Niebuhr, J. C. Penney, John J. Pershing, Brad Pitt, Joseph Pulitzer, Ginger Rogers, Bess Truman, Harry S. Truman, Kathleen Turner, Tina Turner, Mark Twain, Dick Van Dyke, Tennessee Williams, Lanford Wilson, Shelley Winters, Jane Wyman.

Website. www.mo.gov

Montana (MT)
Treasure State

People. Population: 1,032,949; rank: 44. **Pop. change** (2010-15): 4.4%. **Pop. density:** 7.1 per sq mi. **Racial distribution:** 89.2% white; 0.6% black; 0.8% Asian; 6.6% Amer. Ind.; 0.1% Hawaiian/Pacific Islander; 2 or more races, 2.7%. **Hispanic pop.:** 3.6%.

Geography. Total area: 147,040 sq mi; rank: 4. **Land area:** 145,546 sq mi; rank: 4. **Acres forested:** 25.9 mil. **Location:** Mountain state bounded on the E by the Dakotas, on the S by Wyoming, on the SSW by Idaho, on the N by Canada. **Climate:** colder, continental climate with low humidity. **Topography:** Rocky Mts. in western third of state; eastern two-thirds gently rolling northern Great Plains. **Capital:** Helena. **Chief airport:** Bozeman.

Economy. Chief industries: agriculture, timber, mining, tourism, oil and gas. **Chief manuf. goods:** sawmills, softwood veneer and plywood, petroleum. **Chief crops:** wheat, barley, hay, sugar beets, potatoes, dry beans, flaxseed, cherries, corn, oats. **Farm income:** crops, $2.36 bil; livestock/animal prods., $2.27 bil. **Nonfuel minerals:** $1.3 bil; palladium, molybdenum concentrates, copper, platinum, gold. **Gross state product:** $45.9 bil. **Sales tax:** none. **Gasoline tax:** 46.15 cents/gal. **Employment distrib.:** 19.9% govt.; 20.6% trade/trans./util.; 4.2% mfg.; 16.1% ed./health; 8.7% prof./bus. serv.; 13.1% leisure/hosp.; 5.1% finance; 7.2% constr./mining/log.; 1.3% info.; 3.8% other serv. **Unemployment:** 4.1%. **Min. wage/hr.:** $8.05. **Per cap. pers. income:** $41,280. **New private housing:** 4,826 units/$827.4 mil. **Broadband internet:** 80.1%. **Commercial banks:** 63; deposits: $21.3 bil. **Savings institutions:** 2; deposits: $81 mil. **Lottery:** total sales: $52.5 mil; profit: $11.7 mil.

Federal govt. Fed. civ. employees: 9,217; **avg. salary:** $66,535. **Notable fed. facilities:** Malmstrom AFB and missile silos; Ft. Peck, Hungry Horse, Libby, Yellowtail, and other dams.

Education. High school grad. rate: 85.4%. **4-year public coll./univ.:** 6; **2-yr. public:** 11; **4-yr. private:** 4.

Energy. Electricity use/cost: 854 kWh, $86.93.

State data. Motto: Oro y Plata (Gold and silver). **Flower:** Bitterroot. **Bird:** Western meadowlark. **Tree:** Ponderosa pine. **Song:** "Montana." **Entered union:** Nov. 8, 1889; rank: 41st.

Tourism. Tourist spending: $4.3 bil. **Attractions:** Glacier and Yellowstone Natl. Parks; Museum of the Rockies, Bozeman; Museum of the Plains Indian, Blackfeet Reservation, in Browning; Custer Natl. Cemetery at Little Bighorn Battlefield Natl. Monument; Lewis and Clark Caverns State Park, Whitehall; Lewis and Clark Natl. Historic Trail Interpretive Ctr., Great Falls. **Information:** Travel Montana, Dept. of Commerce, 301

S. Park Ave., P.O. Box 200533, Helena, MT 59601; 1-800-VIS-ITMT; www.visitmt.com

History. Paleo-Indian hunters reached the area over 12,000 years ago. Cheyenne, Blackfoot, Crow, Assiniboin, Salish (Flatheads), Kootenai, and Kalispel peoples lived in the region before Europeans arrived. French explorers visited the region, 1742. The U.S. acquired the area partly through the Louisiana Purchase, 1803, partly through the Lewis and Clark Expedition, 1804-06. Fur traders and missionaries established posts in the early 19th cent. Gold was discovered on Grasshopper Creek, 1862, and Montana Territory was established, 1864. Indian uprisings reached their peak with the defeat of Gen. George Custer at the Battle of Little Bighorn, 1876. Chief Joseph and the Nez Percé tribe surrendered in Montana, 1877, after being driven from their lands in Oregon. Mining activity and the coming of the Northern Pacific Railway, 1883, brought population growth. Montana became a state, 1889. Copper wealth from the Butte pits resulted in the turn of the century "War of Copper Kings" as feuding factions contended for "the richest hill on earth." During the first half of the 20th cent., the Anaconda Copper firm wielded enormous political influence. Jeannette Rankin, a suffragist and pacifist, was the first woman elected to Congress, 1916. Mike Mansfield served 34 years in Congress and was Senate Democratic leader, 1961-77. An 18-year hunt for notorious "Unabomber" Theodore Kaczynski ended with his arrest, 1996, at his cabin near Lincoln.

Famous Montanans. Dana Carvey, Gary Cooper, Marcus Daly, Chet Huntley, Phil Jackson, Will James, Myrna Loy, David Lynch, Mike Mansfield, Brent Musburger, Jeannette Rankin, Charles M. Russell, Lester Thurow.

Website. www.mt.gov

Nebraska (NE)
Cornhusker State

People. Population: 1,896,190; rank: 37. **Pop. change** (2010-15): 3.8%. **Pop. density:** 24.7 per sq mi. **Racial distribution:** 89.1% white; 5.0% black; 2.3% Asian; 1.4% Amer. Ind.; 0.1% Hawaiian/Pacific Islander; 2 or more races, 2.1%. **Hispanic pop.:** 10.4%.

Geography. Total area: 77,348 sq mi; rank: 16. **Land area:** 76,824 sq mi; rank: 15. **Acres forested:** 1.5 mil. **Location:** West North Central state with the Missouri R. for a border on NE and E. **Climate:** continental semiarid. **Topography:** till plains of the central lowland in the eastern third rises to the Great Plains and hill country of the N central and NW. **Capital:** Lincoln. **Chief airport:** Omaha.

Economy. Chief industries: agriculture, manufacturing. **Chief manuf. goods:** animal slaughtering, grain and oilseed, farm machinery, medical equip., motor vehicle parts, printing, structural metals. **Chief crops:** corn, sorghum, soybeans, hay, wheat, dry beans, oats, potatoes, sugar beets. **Farm income:** crops, $10.12 bil; livestock/animal prods., $14.53 bil. **Nonfuel minerals:** $382 mil; cement (portland), sand and gravel (industrial), stone (crushed), sand and gravel (construction), lime. **Gross state product:** $114.0 bil. **Sales tax:** 5.5%. **Gasoline tax:** 45.10 cents/gal. **Employment distrib.:** 17.2% govt.; 20.2% trade/trans./util.; 9.5% mfg.; 15.0% ed./health; 11.6% prof./bus. serv.; 9.3% leisure/hosp.; 7.1% finance; 5.0% constr./mining/log.; 1.7% info.; 3.6% other serv. **Unemployment:** 3.0%. **Min. wage/hr.:** $9.00. **Per cap. pers. income:** $48,006. **New private housing:** 8,096 units/$1.3 bil. **Broadband internet:** 88.8%. **Commercial banks:** 201; deposits: $55.3 bil. **Savings institutions:** 10; deposits: $5.1 bil. **Lottery:** total sales: $160.0 mil; profit: $37.1 mil.

Federal govt. Fed. civ. employees: 9,696; **avg. salary:** $72,376. **Notable fed. facilities:** Offutt AFB.

Education. High school grad. rate: 89.7%. **4-year public coll./univ.:** 7; **2-yr. public:** 8; **4-yr. private:** 16.

Energy. Electricity use/cost: 1,022 kWh, $106.33.

State data. Motto: Equality before the law. **Flower:** Goldenrod. **Bird:** Western meadowlark. **Tree:** Cottonwood. **Song:** "Beautiful Nebraska." **Entered union:** Mar. 1, 1867; rank: 37th.

Tourism. Tourist spending: $4.8 bil. **Attractions:** Univ. of Nebraska State Museum at Morrill Hall, Nebraska State Capitol, in Lincoln; Stuhr Museum of the Prairie Pioneer, Grand Island; Boys Town; Omaha's Henry Doorly Zoo and Aquarium, Joslyn Art Museum, The Durham Museum, in Omaha; Ashfall Fossil Beds State Hist. Park, near Royal; Strategic Air and Space Museum, Ashland; Arbor Lodge State Historical Park, Nebraska City; Buffalo Bill Ranch State Historical Park, North

Platte; Pioneer Village, Minden; Oregon Trail landmarks, incl. at Scotts Bluff Natl. Monument and Chimney Rock Natl. Historic Site; Great Platte River Road Archway, Museum of Nebraska Art, in Kearney. **Information:** Nebraska Division of Travel and Tourism, 301 Centennial Mall S., Lincoln, NE 68508; 1-888-444-1867; www.visitnebraska.com

History. When Europeans arrived, Pawnee, Ponca, Omaha, and Oto peoples lived in the region. Spanish and French explorers and fur traders visited the area prior to its acquisition in the Louisiana Purchase, 1803. Meriwether Lewis and William Clark passed through, 1804-06. The first permanent settlement was Bellevue, near Omaha, 1823. The 1834 Indian Intercourse Act declared Nebraska Indian country and excluded white settlement, but conflicts with settlers eventually forced Native Americans to move to reservations. Nebraska became a territory, 1854, and a state, 1867. Many Civil War veterans settled under free land terms of the 1862 Homestead Act; as agriculture grew, struggles followed between homesteaders and ranchers. Since the mid-1930s, Nebraska has been the only state with a unicameral legislature. A leader in agribusiness, Nebraska has also become a major telemarketing center. The "Oracle of Omaha," investor Warren Buffett, one of the world's wealthiest men, announced in 2006 he would give most of his $44-bil fortune to charity.

Famous Nebraskans. Grover Cleveland Alexander, Fred Astaire, Marlon Brando, Charles W. Bryan, William Jennings Bryan, Warren Buffett, Johnny Carson, Willa Cather, Dick Cavett, Dick Cheney, Loren Eiseley, Father Edward J. Flanagan, Henry Fonda, Bob Gibson, Rollin Kirby, Harold Lloyd, Malcolm X, J. Sterling Morton, John G. Neihardt, Nick Nolte, George W. Norris, Tom Osborne, Roscoe Pound, Red Cloud, Mari Sandoz, Robert Taylor, Darryl F. Zanuck.

Website. www.nebraska.gov

Nevada (NV)
Sagebrush State, Battle Born State, Silver State

People. Population: 2,890,845; rank: 35. **Pop. change** (2010-15): 7.0%. **Pop. density:** 26.3 per sq mi. **Racial distribution:** 75.7% white; 9.3% black; 8.5% Asian; 1.6% Amer. Ind.; 0.8% Hawaiian/Pacific Islander; 2 or more races, 4.1%. **Hispanic pop.:** 28.1%.

Geography. Total area: 110,572 sq mi; rank: 7. **Land area:** 109,781 sq mi; rank: 7. **Acres forested:** 10.6 mil. **Location:** Mountain state bordered on N by Oregon and Idaho, on E by Utah, on SE by Arizona, and on SW and W by California. **Climate:** semiarid and arid. **Topography:** rugged N-S mountain ranges; highest elevation, Boundary Peak, 13,146 ft; southern area is within the Mojave Desert; lowest elevation, Colorado R., at southern tip of state, 479 ft. **Capital:** Carson City. **Chief airports:** Las Vegas, Reno.

Economy. Chief industries: gaming, tourism, mining, manufacturing, government, retailing, warehousing, trucking. **Chief manuf. goods:** gaming machines, cement and concrete, plastics, printing, architectural and structural metals, electricity instruments. **Chief crops:** hay, onions, potatoes, alfalfa, wheat, garlic, mint, barley. **Farm income:** crops, $264.93 mil; livestock/animal prods., $602.81 mil. **Nonfuel minerals:** $6.9 bil; gold, copper, silver, lime, diatomite. **Gross state product:** $141.3 bil. **Sales tax:** 6.85%. **Gasoline tax:** 52.26 cents/gal. **Employment distrib.:** 12.4% govt.; 19.0% trade/trans./util.; 3.3% mfg.; 9.8% ed./health; 12.9% prof./bus. serv.; 27.1% leisure/hosp.; 4.7% finance; 6.9% constr./mining/log.; 1.0% info.; 2.8% other serv. **Unemployment:** 6.7%. **Min. wage/hr.:** $8.25. **Per cap. pers. income:** $42,185. **New private housing:** 14,083 units/$2.1 bil. **Broadband internet:** 92.4%. **Commercial banks:** 37; deposits: $57.4 bil. **Savings institutions:** 8; deposits: $111.9 bil.

Federal govt. Fed. civ. employees: 10,648; **avg. salary:** $73,477. **Notable fed. facilities:** Nevada Natl. Security Site; Hawthorne Army Depot; Creech AFB; Nellis AFB; Fallon NAS; Natl. Wild Horse & Burro Ctr. at Palomino Valley.

Education. High school grad. rate: 70.0%. **4-year public coll./univ.:** 6; **2-yr. public:** 1; **4-yr. private:** 3.

Energy. Electricity use/cost: 894 kWh, $115.64.

State data. Motto: All for our country. **Flower:** Sagebrush. **Bird:** Mountain bluebird. **Trees:** Single-leaf piñon and bristlecone pine. **Song:** "Home Means Nevada." **Entered union:** Oct. 31, 1864; rank: 36th.

Tourism. Tourist spending: $33.5 bil. **Attractions:** Legalized gambling, incl. at Lake Tahoe, Reno, Las Vegas, Laughlin, and Elko; Hoover Dam, Lake Mead Natl. Recreation Area, near Boulder City; Great Basin Natl. Park; Valley of Fire State

Park; Red Rock Canyon Natl. Conservation Area; Las Vegas Strip, Fremont St., Natl. Atomic Testing Museum, Pinball Hall of Fame, Las Vegas Motor Speedway, in Las Vegas; Natl. Automobile Museum, Reno. **Information:** Commission on Tourism, 401 N. Carson St., Carson City, NV 89701; 1-800-NEVADA-8; www.travelnevada.com

History. Shoshone, Paiute, Bannock, and Washoe peoples lived in the area at the time of European contact. Nevada was first explored by Spaniards, 1776. In the 1820s, fur traders Peter Skene Ogden, a Canadian, and Jedediah Smith separately explored the area. It was acquired by the U.S., 1848, at the end of the Mexican War. A trading post at Mormon Station, now Genoa, was established, 1850. Discovery of the Comstock Lode, rich in gold and silver, 1859, spurred a population boom. Nevada became a territory, 1861, and a state, 1864. Hoover Dam was built, 1931-36. With gambling legal since 1931, a surge in resort casino construction after World War II turned Las Vegas into one of the nation's most popular tourist destinations. An influx of both native and foreign-born Hispanics and Asians, attracted by the thriving service and construction industries, helped make Nevada the fastest-growing state in the U.S. in 1990-2005. The recession in recent years has had an equally powerful effect. Nevada had the highest state unemployment and home foreclosure rates in 2011.

Famous Nevadans. Andre Agassi, Kyle Busch, Walter Van Tilburg Clark, George W. G. Ferris, Sarah Winnemucca Hopkins, Paul Laxalt, Dat So La Lee, John William Mackay, Anne Henrietta Martin, Pat McCarran, Key Pittman, William Morris Stewart.

Website. www.nv.gov

New Hampshire (NH)
Granite State

People. Population: 1,330,608; rank: 41. **Pop. change** (2010-15): 1.1%. **Pop. density:** 148.6 per sq mi. **Racial distribution:** 93.9% white; 1.5% black; 2.6% Asian; 0.3% Amer. Ind.; <0.05% Hawaiian/Pacific Islander; 2 or more races, 1.6%. **Hispanic pop.:** 3.4%.

Geography. Total area: 9,349 sq mi; rank: 46. **Land area:** 8,953 sq mi; rank: 44. **Acres forested:** 4.8 mil. **Location:** New England state bounded on S by Massachusetts, on W by Vermont, on N by Canada, on E by Maine and the Atlantic Ocean. **Climate:** highly varied, due to its nearness to high mountains and ocean. **Topography:** low, rolling coast followed by countless hills and mountains rising out of a central plateau. **Capital:** Concord. **Chief airport:** Manchester.

Economy. Chief industries: tourism, manufacturing, agriculture, trade, mining. **Chief manuf. goods:** navigational instruments, circuit boards, electrical equip., fabricated metal, machinery, medical equip., plastics. **Chief crops:** greenhouse and nursery, apples, sweet corn, hay, Christmas trees, berries, maple syrup. **Farm income:** crops, $106.13 mil; livestock/animal prods., $143.83 mil. **Nonfuel minerals:** $111 mil; sand and gravel (construction), stone (crushed), stone (dimension), gemstones (natural). **Commercial fishing:** $26.8 mil. **Chief port:** Portsmouth. **Gross state product:** $72.6 bil. **Sales tax:** none. **Gasoline tax:** 42.23 cents/gal. **Employment distrib.:** 13.7% govt.; 21.2% trade/trans./util.; 9.9% mfg.; 17.9% ed./health; 11.6% prof./bus. serv.; 10.3% leisure/hosp.; 5.5% finance; 3.9% constr./mining/log.; 1.9% info.; 4.0% other serv. **Unemployment:** 3.4%. **Min. wage/hr.:** $7.25. **Per cap. pers. income:** $54,817. **New private housing:** 3,763 units/$736.9 mil. **Broadband internet:** 93.6%. **Commercial banks:** 16; deposits: $24.6 bil. **Savings institutions:** 26; deposits: $6.7 bil. **Lottery:** total sales: $281.4 mil; profit: $74.3 mil.

Federal govt. Fed. civ. employees: 4,268; **avg. salary:** $85,376. **Notable fed. facilities:** Army Cold Regions Res. and Engineering Lab.

Education. High school grad. rate: 88.1%. **4-year public coll./univ.:** 6; **2-yr. public:** 7; **4-yr. private:** 11.

Energy. Electricity use/cost: 619 kWh, $108.57.

State data. Motto: Live free or die. **Flower:** Purple lilac. **Bird:** Purple finch. **Tree:** White birch. **Song:** "Old New Hampshire." **Ninth** of original 13 states to ratify the Constitution, June 21, 1788.

Tourism. Tourist spending: $3.8 bil. **Attractions:** Mt. Washington Cog Railway, Mt. Washington (highest peak in Northeast); Lake Winnipesaukee; Crawford, Franconia, Pinkham Notches (mountain passes), Flume Gorge, Cannon Mountain Aerial Tramway, in White Mountains region; Strawbery Banke Museum, Portsmouth; Canterbury Shaker Village;

Saint-Gaudens Natl. Historic Site, Cornish; Mt. Monadnock; Santa's Village, Jefferson. **Information:** Division of Travel & Tourism Development, 172 Pembroke Rd., P.O. Box 1856; Concord, NH 03302; 1-800-FUN-IN-NH; www.visitnh.gov

History. The area has been inhabited for about 10,000 years. Algonquian-speaking peoples, including the Pennacook, lived in the region when the Europeans arrived. The first explorers to visit the area were England's Martin Pring, 1603, and France's Samuel de Champlain, 1605. The first settlement was Odiorne's Point (now port of Rye), 1623. Before the American Revolution, New Hampshire residents raided a British fort at Portsmouth, 1774, and drove the royal governor out, 1775. New Hampshire became the first colony to adopt its own constitution, 1776. After statehood, 1788, New Hampshire became a textile manufacturing center. The mill towns declined in the first half of the 20th cent., but tourism and technology industries, lured by low taxes, have revived the economy since the 1960s. A state law requires it to hold the first primary of the presidential campaign season.

Famous New Hampshirites. Dan Brown, Salmon P. Chase, Ralph Adams Cram, Mary Baker Eddy, Daniel Chester French, Robert Frost, Horace Greeley, Sarah Josepha Buell Hale, John Irving, Seth Meyers, Bode Miller, Franklin Pierce, Augustus Saint-Gaudens, Adam Sandler, Alan B. Shepard Jr., Sarah Silverman, David H. Souter, Daniel Webster.

Website. www.nh.gov

New Jersey (NJ)
Garden State

People. Population: 8,958,013; rank: 11. **Pop. change** (2010-15): 1.9%. **Pop. density:** 1,218.1 per sq mi. **Racial distribution:** 72.6% white; 14.8% black; 9.7% Asian; 0.6% Amer. Ind.; 0.1% Hawaiian/Pacific Islander; 2 or more races, 2.1%. **Hispanic pop.:** 19.7%.

Geography. Total area: 8,723 sq mi; rank: 47. **Land area:** 7,354 sq mi; rank: 46. **Acres forested:** 2.0 mil. **Location:** Middle Atlantic state bounded on N and E by New York and Atlantic Ocean, on S and W by Delaware and Pennsylvania. **Climate:** moderate, with marked difference between NW and SE extremities. **Topography:** Appalachian Valley in NW also has highest elevation, High Pt., 1,803 ft; Appalachian Highlands, flat-topped NE-SW mountain ranges; Piedmont Plateau, low plains broken by high ridges (Palisades) rising 400-500 ft; Coastal Plain, covering three-fifths of state in SE, rises from sea level to gentle slopes. **Capital:** Trenton. **Chief airports:** Atlantic City, Newark.

Economy. Chief industries: pharmaceuticals, telecommunications, biotechnology, printing and publishing. **Chief manuf. goods:** petroleum, pharmaceuticals, toiletries, chemicals, plastics, printing, navigational instruments, medical equip., paper prod. **Chief crops:** greenhouse and nursery, blueberries, peaches, corn, hay, tomatoes, bell peppers, cranberries, soybeans, apples. **Farm income:** crops, $890.51 mil; livestock/animal prods., $132.77 mil. **Nonfuel minerals:** $309 mil; stone (crushed), sand and gravel (construction), sand and gravel (industrial), greensand marl, peat. **Commercial fishing:** $151.9 mil. **Chief ports:** Newark-Elizabeth, Camden. **Gross state product:** $568.2 bil. **Sales tax:** 7.0%. **Gasoline tax:** 32.90 cents/gal. **Employment distrib.:** 15.3% govt.; 21.3% trade/trans./util.; 5.8% mfg.; 16.5% ed./health; 16.1% prof./bus. serv.; 9.1% leisure/hosp.; 6.2% finance; 3.8% constr./mining/log.; 1.7% info.; 4.2% other serv. **Unemployment:** 5.6%. **Min. wage/hr.:** $8.38. **Per cap. pers. income:** $59,782. **New private housing:** 30,560 units/$4.1 bil. **Broadband internet:** 96.4%. **Commercial banks:** 91; deposits: $232.2 bil. **Savings institutions:** 55; deposits: $70.3 bil. **Lottery:** total sales: $3.0 bil; profit: $960.0 mil.

Federal govt. Fed. civ. employees: 20,498; **avg. salary:** $90,976. **Notable fed. facilities:** Joint Base McGuire-Dix-Lakehurst; Picatinny Arsenal; FAA William J. Hughes Technical Ctr.

Education. High school grad. rate: 88.6%. **4-year public coll./univ.:** 13; **2-yr. public:** 19; **4-yr. private:** 28.

Energy. Electricity use/cost: 670 kWh, $105.65.

State data. Motto: Liberty and prosperity. **Flower:** Purple violet. **Bird:** Eastern goldfinch. **Tree:** Red oak. **Third** of the original 13 states to ratify the Constitution, Dec. 18, 1787.

Tourism. Tourist spending: $20.4 bil. **Attractions:** 130 mi of beaches, boardwalks on the Jersey Shore at Atlantic City (with gambling), Seaside Heights, Ocean City, Wildwood; Grover Cleveland Birthplace, Caldwell; Cape May Historic District; Thomas Edison Natl. Historical Park, West Orange; Six Flags Great Adventure, Jackson; Liberty State Park,

Liberty Science Ctr., in Jersey City; Pine Barrens wilderness; Princeton Univ., Princeton Battlefield State Park, in Princeton; Morristown Natl. Historical Park; Adventure Aquarium, Battleship *New Jersey*, Walt Whitman House, in Camden. **Information:** Dept. of State, Division of Travel and Tourism, P.O. Box 460, Trenton, NJ 08625; 1-800-VISITNJ; www.visitnj.org

History. The Lenni Lenape (Delaware) peoples lived in the region and had mostly peaceful relations with European colonists, who arrived after the explorers Giovanni da Verrazzano, 1524, and Henry Hudson, 1609. The first permanent European settlement was Dutch, at Bergen (now Jersey City), 1660. When the British took New Netherland, 1664, the area between the Delaware and Hudson Rivers was given to Lord John Berkeley and Sir George Carteret. During the American Revolution, New Jersey was the scene of many major battles, including Trenton, 1776; Princeton, 1777; and Monmouth, 1778. New Jersey was the third state to ratify the Constitution, 1787, and the first to approve the Bill of Rights, 1789. In a duel at Weehawken, 1804, Vice Pres. Aaron Burr fatally shot former Treasury Sec. Alexander Hamilton. Canal and railroad building stimulated the growth of cities and industries in the 19th cent. The 20th-cent. arrival of large numbers of African Americans, Italians, Irish, European Jews, Puerto Ricans, South Asians, and other groups made New Jersey one of the most diverse states in the U.S. Construction of resort casinos in Atlantic City from the late 1970s revitalized tourism. Gov. James McGreevey resigned, 2004, after acknowledging an extramarital affair with a man identified as his former homeland security adviser. An estimated 37 people in New Jersey were killed when Hurricane Sandy (by then downgraded to a tropical storm) made landfall in 2012. Former members of Gov. Chris Christie's administration faced federal charges in 2014-16 over allegations that officials had created traffic jams on a toll bridge to punish a political opponent.

Famous New Jerseyans. Buzz Aldrin, Jason Alexander, Samuel Alito, Count Basie, Judy Blume, Jon Bon Jovi, Bill Bradley, Aaron Burr, Grover Cleveland, Stephen Crane, Danny DeVito, Thomas Edison, Albert Einstein, James Gandolfini, Allen Ginsberg, Alexander Hamilton, Ed Harris, Whitney Houston, Joyce Kilmer, Jack Nicholson, Shaquille O'Neal, Thomas Paine, Bill Parcells, Dorothy Parker, Joe Pesci, Molly Pitcher, Paul Robeson, Philip Roth, Antonin Scalia, Wally Schirra, H. Norman Schwarzkopf, Frank Sinatra, Bruce Springsteen, Martha Stewart, Meryl Streep, Dave Thomas, John Travolta, Walt Whitman, William Carlos Williams, Woodrow Wilson.

Website. www.nj.gov

New Mexico (NM)
Land of Enchantment

People. Population: 2,085,109; rank: 36. **Pop. change** (2010-15): 1.3%. **Pop. density:** 17.2 per sq mi. **Racial distribution:** 82.5% white; 2.6% black; 1.7% Asian; 10.5% Amer. Ind.; 0.2% Hawaiian/Pacific Islander; 2 or more races, 2.5%. **Hispanic pop.:** 48.0%.

Geography. Total area: 121,590 sq mi; rank: 5. **Land area:** 121,298 sq mi; rank: 5. **Acres forested:** 24.7 mil. **Location:** southwestern state bounded by Colorado on the N; Oklahoma, Texas, and Mexico on the E and S; Arizona on the W. **Climate:** dry, with temperatures rising or falling 5°F with every 1,000 ft elevation. **Topography:** eastern third, Great Plains; central third, Rocky Mts. (85% of the state is over 4,000-ft elevation); western third, high plateau. **Capital:** Santa Fe. **Chief airport:** Albuquerque.

Economy. Chief industries: government, services, trade. **Chief manuf. goods:** semiconductors, medical equip., navigational/measuring/medical/control instruments, aircraft, chemicals, jewelry. **Chief crops:** hay, pecans, corn, greenhouse and nursery, chiles, onions, cotton, wheat, peanuts. **Farm income:** crops, $700.54 mil; livestock/animal prods., $2.96 bil. **Nonfuel minerals:** $1.8 bil; copper, potash, sand and gravel (construction), cement (portland), salt. **Gross state product:** $92.2 bil. **Sales tax:** 5.125%. **Gasoline tax:** 37.28 cents/gal. **Employment distrib.:** 23.3% govt.; 16.5% trade/trans./util.; 3.2% mfg.; 16.6% ed./health; 12.1% prof./bus. serv.; 11.7% leisure/hosp.; 4.0% finance; 7.6% constr./mining/log.; 1.5% info.; 3.4% other serv. **Unemployment:** 6.6%. **Min. wage/hr.:** $7.50. **Per cap. pers. income:** $38,457. **New private housing:** 4,599 units/$872.1 mil. **Broadband internet:** 85.3%. **Commercial banks:** 53; deposits: $29.3 bil. **Savings institutions:** 6; deposits: $831 mil. **Lottery:** total sales: $137.0 mil; profit: $41.1 mil.

Federal govt. Fed. civ. employees: 21,816; **avg. salary:** $71,923. **Notable fed. facilities:** Kirtland, Cannon, Holloman AF Bases; Los Alamos Natl. Lab; White Sands Missile Range; Natl. Solar Observatory; Natl. Radio Astronomy Observatory (Very Large Array); Sandia Natl. Labs.

Education. High school grad. rate: 68.5%. **4-year public coll./univ.:** 9; **2-yr. public:** 19; **4-yr. private:** 3.

Energy. Electricity use/cost: 633 kWh, $77.79.

State data. Motto: Crescit Eundo (It grows as it goes). **Flower:** Yucca. **Bird:** Roadrunner. **Tree:** Piñon. **Songs:** "O, Fair New Mexico"; "Asi Es Nuevo Mexico." **Entered union:** Jan. 6, 1912; rank: 47th.

Tourism. Tourist spending: $6.9 bil. **Attractions:** Carlsbad Caverns Natl. Park (with Lechuguilla Cave, among world's longest caves); Petroglyph Natl. Monument, Sandia Peak Tramway, in Albuquerque; New Mexico History Museum, Museum of Intl. Folk Art, in Santa Fe (oldest U.S. capital); White Sands Natl. Monument (world's largest gypsum dune field); Chaco Culture Natl. Historical Park; Acoma Pueblo, or Sky City, built atop a 367-ft mesa; Taos Art Colony, Taos Ski Valley; Elephant Butte Lake State Park; Shiprock volcanic remnant; Intl. UFO Museum and Research Ctr., Roswell. **Information:** New Mexico Dept. of Tourism, 491 Old Santa Fe Trl., Santa Fe, NM 87501; 1-800-733-6396; www.newmexico.org

History. Inhabited for more than 10,000 years, the region was home to Sandia, Clovis, Folsom, Mogollon, and Anasazi cultures, followed by the Pueblo people, Anasazi descendants; later, nomadic Navajo and Apache came. Spanish Franciscan Marcos de Niza and a former black slave, Estevanico, explored the area, 1539, seeking gold; Coronado followed, 1540. First settlements were near San Juan Pueblo, 1598, and at Santa Fe, 1610. Settlers alternately traded and fought with the Apache, Comanche, and Navajo. Trade on the Santa Fe Trail to Missouri started, 1821. After the Mexican War began, 1846, Gen. Stephen Kearny took Santa Fe without firing a shot, and declared New Mexico part of the U.S. All Hispanic New Mexicans and Pueblo became U.S. citizens by terms of the 1848 treaty ending the war. New Mexico became a territory, 1850, but did not attain statehood until 1912. Mexican revolutionary leader Pancho Villa raided Columbus, 1916, and U.S. troops were sent to the area. The world's first atomic bomb was exploded at a test site near Alamogordo, 1945. An underground nuclear waste depository opened near Carlsbad, 1999. Spaceport America, a state-owned commercial spaceport, hosted its first test launch in 2006.

Famous New Mexicans. Ben Abruzzo, Maxie Anderson, Jeff Bezos, William Bonney (Billy the Kid), Kit Carson, Bob Foster, Neil Patrick Harris, Tony Hillerman, Peter Hurd, Jean Baptiste Lamy, Nancy Lopez, Bill Mauldin, Georgia O'Keeffe, Bill Richardson, Kim Stanley, Al Unser, Bobby Unser.

Website. www.newmexico.gov

New York (NY)
Empire State

People. Population: 19,795,791; rank: 4. **Pop. change** (2010-15): 2.2%. **Pop. density:** 420.1 per sq mi. **Racial distribution:** 70.1% white; 17.6% black; 8.8% Asian; 1.0% Amer. Ind.; 0.1% Hawaiian/Pacific Islander; 2 or more races, 2.4%. **Hispanic pop.:** 18.8%.

Geography. Total area: 54,555 sq mi; rank: 27. **Land area:** 47,126 sq mi; rank: 30. **Acres forested:** 18.9 mil. **Location:** Middle Atlantic state bordered by the New England states, Atlantic Ocean on E; New Jersey and Pennsylvania on S; Lakes Ontario and Erie on W; Canada on N. **Climate:** variable; the SE region moderated by the ocean. **Topography:** highest and most rugged mountains in the NE Adirondack upland; St. Lawrence-Champlain lowlands extend from Lake Ontario NE along the Canadian border; Hudson-Mohawk lowland follows rivers N and W, 10-30 mi wide; Atlantic coastal plain in the SE; Appalachian Highlands, covering half the state westward from the Hudson Valley, include the Catskill Mts., Finger Lakes; plateau of Erie-Ontario lowlands. **Capital:** Albany. **Chief airports:** Albany, Buffalo, Islip, New York (2), Rochester, Syracuse, White Plains.

Economy. Chief industries: manufacturing, finance, communications, tourism, transportation, services. **Chief manuf. goods:** pharmaceuticals, photographic chemicals, electronics, automotive parts, toiletries, printing, plastics, apparel. **Chief crops:** greenhouse and nursery, apples, corn, hay, cabbage, onions, soybeans, potatoes, snap beans, grapes, squash, pumpkins, tomatoes, wheat, cucumbers, green peas. **Farm income:** crops, $2.11 bil; livestock/animal prods., $4.26 bil. **Nonfuel minerals:** $1.5 bil; salt, stone (crushed),

sand and gravel (construction), cement (portland), wollastonite. **Commercial fishing:** $53.9 mil. **Chief ports:** New York, Buffalo, Albany. **Gross state product:** $1.4 tril. **Sales tax:** 4.0%. **Gasoline tax:** 61.80 cents/gal. **Employment distrib.:** 15.6% govt.; 16.7% trade/trans./util.; 4.8% mfg.; 20.7% ed./health; 13.6% prof./bus. serv.; 9.8% leisure/hosp.; 7.5% finance; 4.1% constr./mining/log.; 2.8% info.; 4.4% other serv. **Unemployment:** 5.3%. **Min. wage/hr.:** $9.00. **Per cap. pers. income:** $57,705. **New private housing:** 74,611 units/$10.8 bil. **Broadband internet:** 95.1%. **Commercial banks:** 154; deposits: $1.3 tril. **Savings institutions:** 55; deposits: $66.7 bil. **Lottery:** total sales: $9.2 bil; profit: $3.1 bil.

Federal govt. Fed. civ. employees: 52,223; **avg. salary:** $80,592. **Notable fed. facilities:** Ft. Drum; West Point Military Academy; Merchant Marine Academy; NY Fed. Reserve; U.S. Army Watervliet Arsenal; Brookhaven Natl. Lab; U.S. Mission to the United Nations.

Education. High school grad. rate: 77.8%. **4-year public coll./univ.:** 43; **2-yr. public:** 36; **4-yr. private:** 165.

Energy. Electricity use/cost: 591 kWh, $118.63.

State data. Motto: Excelsior (Ever upward). **Flower:** Rose. **Bird:** Eastern bluebird. **Tree:** Sugar maple. **Song:** "I Love New York." **Eleventh** of original 13 states to ratify the Constitution, July 26, 1788.

Tourism. Tourist spending: $65.3 bil. **Attractions:** New York City; Adirondack and Catskill Mountains; Watkins Glen State Park; Thousand Islands region; Niagara Falls; Saratoga Race Course, Saratoga Springs; Philipsburg Manor, Old Dutch Church of Sleepy Hollow, in Sleepy Hollow; Washington Irving's Sunnyside, Tarrytown; Corning Museum of Glass; Fenimore Art Museum, Natl. Baseball Hall of Fame and Museum, in Cooperstown; Ft. Ticonderoga; New York State Capitol, Albany; Home of Franklin D. Roosevelt Natl. Historic Site, Hyde Park; Long Island beaches; Sagamore Hill (Theodore Roosevelt's "Summer White House"), Oyster Bay. **Information:** Empire State Development, Travel Information Center, 30 South Pearl St., Albany, NY 12245; 1-800-CALL-NYS; www.iloveny.com

History. When Europeans arrived, Algonquians including the Mahican, Wappinger, and Lenni Lenape inhabited the region, as did the Iroquoian Mohawk, Oneida, Onondaga, Cayuga, and Seneca tribes, who established the League of the Five Nations. Italian Giovanni da Verrazzano entered New York harbor, 1524. In 1609, England's Henry Hudson visited the river later named for him, and France's Samuel de Champlain explored the lake that now bears his name. The first permanent settlement was Dutch, near present-day Albany, 1624. New Amsterdam was settled, 1626, at the southern tip of Manhattan island. A British fleet seized New Netherland, 1664. Key battles of the American Revolution included Saratoga, 1777. In the 19th cent., New York City emerged as one of the world's great metropolitan areas, a center for trade, finance, and arts, and a haven for millions of immigrants. Completion of the Erie Canal, 1825, established the state as a gateway to the West. The first women's rights convention was held in Seneca Falls, 1848. Although the state backed the Union in the Civil War, an 1863 military draft triggered three days of riots in New York City. Industry declined in the 20th cent., and California and Texas passed New York in population. Attica was the scene of a bloody prison revolt, 1971. Two jet aircraft hijacked by terrorists on Sept. 11, 2001, destroyed the World Trade Center in lower Manhattan. An estimated 65 people in New York state were killed when Hurricane Sandy (by then downgraded to a tropical storm) made landfall in Oct. 2012. Citing concerns over health risks, Gov. Andrew Cuomo in Dec. 2014 announced a statewide ban on hydraulic fracturing (or "fracking") as a method to access the state's natural gas resources.

Famous New Yorkers. Woody Allen, Susan B. Anthony, James Baldwin, Lucille Ball, Ann Bancroft, L. Frank Baum, Milton Berle, Humphrey Bogart, Barbara Boxer, Mel Brooks, Benjamin Cardozo, De Witt Clinton, James Fenimore Cooper, Peter Cooper, Aaron Copland, Francis Ford Coppola, Tom Cruise, Robert De Niro, George Eastman, Jimmy Fallon, Millard Fillmore, Lou Gehrig, George and Ira Gershwin, Ruth Bader Ginsburg, Rudolph Giuliani, Jackie Gleason, Stephen Jay Gould, Julia Ward Howe, Charles Evans Hughes, Washington Irving, Henry and William James, John Jay, Edward Koch, Fiorello LaGuardia, Herman Melville, Arthur Miller, J. Pierpont Morgan Jr., Eddie Murphy, Joyce Carol Oates, Carroll O'Connor, Rosie O'Donnell, Eugene O'Neill, Jerry Orbach, George Pataki, Colin Powell, Nancy Reagan, John Roberts, John D. Rockefeller, Nelson Rockefeller, Richard Rodgers, Ray Romano, Eleanor Roosevelt, Franklin D.

Roosevelt, Theodore Roosevelt, Tim Russert, J. D. Salinger, Caroline Kennedy Schlossberg, Jerry Seinfeld, Al Sharpton, Paul Simon, Alfred E. Smith, Elizabeth Cady Stanton, Barbra Streisand, Donald Trump, William (Boss) Tweed, Martin Van Buren, Luther Vandross, Gore Vidal, Denzel Washington, Edith Wharton, Walt Whitman, Mark Zuckerberg. **Website.** www.ny.gov

North Carolina (NC)
Tar Heel State, Old North State

People. Population: 10,042,802; rank: 9. **Pop. change** (2010-15): 5.3%. **Pop. density:** 206.6 per sq mi. **Racial distribution:** 71.2% white; 22.1% black; 2.8% Asian; 1.6% Amer. Ind.; 0.1% Hawaiian/Pacific Islander; 2 or more races, 2.1%. **Hispanic pop.:** 9.1%.

Geography. Total area: 53,819 sq mi; rank: 28. **Land area:** 48,618 sq mi; rank: 29. **Acres forested:** 18.8 mil. **Location:** South Atlantic state bounded on N by Virginia, on S by South Carolina, on SW by Georgia, on W by Tennessee, and on E by Atlantic. **Climate:** subtropical in SE, medium-continental in mountain region; tempered by the Gulf Stream and mountains in W. **Topography:** coastal plain and tidewater in two-fifths of state, extending to the fall line of the rivers; Piedmont Plateau in another two-fifths has gentle to rugged hills; southern Appalachian Mts. contain the Blue Ridge and Great Smoky Mts. **Capital:** Raleigh. **Chief airports:** Charlotte, Greensboro, Raleigh.

Economy. Chief industries: manufacturing, agriculture, tourism. **Chief manuf. goods:** transportation, tobacco, pharmaceuticals, toiletries, plastics, animal slaughtering and processing, household furniture, fabric and apparel. **Chief crops:** greenhouse and nursery, tobacco, cotton, soybeans, corn, Christmas trees, sweet potatoes, wheat, peanuts, blueberries, cucumbers, tomatoes, hay, potatoes. **Farm income:** crops, $4.14 bil; livestock/animal prods., $8.85 bil. **Nonfuel minerals:** $943 mil; stone (crushed), phosphate rock, sand and gravel (construction), sand and gravel (industrial), stone (dimension). **Commercial fishing:** $94.1 mil. **Chief ports:** Morehead City, Wilmington. **Gross state product:** $499.4 bil. **Sales tax:** 4.75%. **Gasoline tax:** 52.65 cents/gal. **Employment distrib.:** 17.2% govt.; 18.8% trade/trans./util.; 10.5% mfg.; 13.4% ed./health; 14.1% prof./bus. serv.; 11.0% leisure/hosp.; 5.0% finance; 4.6% constr./mining/log.; 1.7% info.; 3.6% other serv. **Unemployment:** 5.7%. **Min. wage/hr.:** $7.25. **Per cap. pers. income:** $40,656. **New private housing:** 54,757 units/$9.7 bil. **Broadband internet:** 89.1%. **Commercial banks:** 78; deposits: $349.5 bil. **Savings institutions:** 21; deposits: $3.9 bil. **Lottery:** total sales: $2.0 bil; profit: $520.6 mil.

Federal govt. Fed. civ. employees: 43,007; **avg. salary:** $73,014. **Notable fed. facilities:** Ft. Bragg; Camp Lejeune Marine Base, Marine Corps Air Station Cherry Point; NOAA Natl. Centers for Environmental Information.; Natl. Inst. of Environmental Health Sciences, EPA Research and Dev. Labs, all in Research Triangle Park.

Education. High school grad. rate: 83.9%. **4-year public coll./univ.:** 16; **2-yr. public:** 59; **4-yr. private:** 49.

Energy. Electricity use/cost: 1,136 kWh, $126.09.

State data. Motto: Esse Quam Videri (To be rather than to seem). **Flower:** Dogwood. **Bird:** Cardinal. **Tree:** Pine. **Song:** "The Old North State." **Twelfth** of the original 13 states to ratify the Constitution, Nov. 21, 1789.

Tourism. Tourist spending: $22.1 bil. **Attractions:** Cape Hatteras and Cape Lookout Natl. Seashores; Great Smoky Mountains Natl. Park; Guilford Courthouse Natl. Military Park; Moore's Creek Natl. Battlefield (1776 victory ended British rule in colony); Bennett Place (site of largest troop surrender of Civil War), Durham; Ft. Raleigh Natl. Historic Site, North Carolina Aquarium, on Roanoke Island; Wright Brothers Natl. Mem., Kill Devil Hills; USS *North Carolina*, Wilmington; North Carolina Zoo, Asheboro; North Carolina Symphony, Marbles Kids Museum, North Carolina Museum of Art, North Carolina Museum of Natural Sciences, in Raleigh; Carl Sandburg Home, Flat Rock; Biltmore House and Gardens, North Carolina Arboretum, in Asheville; U.S. Natl. Whitewater Ctr., Discovery Place, in Charlotte; Fort Macon State Park, Atlantic Beach. **Information:** North Carolina Division of Tourism, Film and Sports Development, 4324 Mail Service Ctr., Raleigh, NC 27699; 1-800-VISIT-NC, (919) 733-8372; www.visitnc.com

History. Algonquian, Siouan, and Iroquoian peoples lived in the region at the time of European contact. Sir Walter Raleigh tried to found a colony, 1584-87; the "Lost Colony" on Roanoke Island, 1587, seemingly disappeared. Permanent settlers came from Virginia in the mid-17th cent. The province's congress was the first to vote for independence, 1776. In the Revolutionary War, Gen. Charles Cornwallis's forces were defeated at Kings Mountain, 1780, and forced out after Guilford Courthouse, 1781. The state ratified the Constitution, 1789, only after Congress passed the Bill of Rights. North Carolina, where one-third of the population was slaves, seceded from the Union, 1861, and provided more troops to the Confederacy than any other state; it was readmitted, 1868. The Wright brothers made the first powered airplane flight at Kitty Hawk, 1903. Sit-ins at segregated Greensboro lunch counters, 1960, drew national attention to the civil rights movement. Long reliant on tobacco, textiles, and wood products, North Carolina has prospered since the 1960s from advanced technologies in the Raleigh-Durham-Chapel Hill area and banking in Charlotte. The hurricane-prone state was hit hard by Hazel, 1954, Fran, 1996, and Floyd, 1999. The state drew immediate backlash in Mar. 2016 after passing a "bathroom bill" requiring people to use public facilities that correspond with the sex listed on their birth certificate, a problem for transgender individuals.

Famous North Carolinians. David Brinkley, Shirley Caesar, John Coltrane, Rick Dees, Elizabeth Hanford Dole, Dale Earnhardt Sr., John Edwards, Ava Gardner, Richard Jordan Gatling, Billy Graham, Andy Griffith, O. Henry, Andrew Jackson, Andrew Johnson, Michael Jordan, William Rufus King, Charles Kuralt, Meadowlark Lemon, Dolley Madison, Thelonious Monk, Edward R. Murrow, Richard Petty, James K. Polk, Charlie Rose, Carl Sandburg, Enos Slaughter, Dean Smith, James Taylor, Thomas Wolfe. **Website.** www.nc.gov

North Dakota (ND)
Peace Garden State

People. Population: 756,927; rank: 47. **Pop. change** (2010-15): 12.5%. **Pop. density:** 11.0 per sq mi. **Racial distribution:** 88.6% white; 2.4% black; 1.4% Asian; 5.5% Amer. Ind.; 0.1% Hawaiian/Pacific Islander; 2 or more races, 2.1%. **Hispanic pop.:** 3.5%.

Geography. Total area: 70,698 sq mi; rank: 19. **Land area:** 69,001 sq mi; rank: 17. **Acres forested:** 0.8 mil. **Location:** West North Central state situated exactly in the middle of North America, bounded on the N by Canada, on the E by Minnesota, on the S by South Dakota, on the W by Montana. **Climate:** continental, with a wide range of temperatures and moderate rainfall. **Topography:** Central Lowland in the E comprises the flat Red R. Valley and the Rolling Drift Prairie; Missouri Plateau of the Great Plains on the W. **Capital:** Bismarck.

Economy. Chief industries: agriculture, mining, tourism, manufacturing, telecommunications, energy, food processing. **Chief manuf. goods:** machinery, wood prods., motor vehicles and parts, furniture, processed foods. **Chief crops:** wheat, soybeans, corn, sugar beets, barley, dry beans, sunflowers, canola, potatoes, flaxseed, hay, dry peas, lentils, oats. **Farm income:** crops, $7.02 bil; livestock/animal prods., $1.61 bil. **Nonfuel minerals:** $243 mil; sand and gravel (construction), stone (crushed), lime, clays (common), sand and gravel (industrial). **Gross state product:** $54.8 bil. **Sales tax:** 5.0%. **Gasoline tax:** 41.40 cents/gal. **Employment distrib.:** 19.5% govt.; 22.0% trade/trans./util.; 5.5% mfg.; 14.1% ed./health; 8.0% prof./bus. serv.; 9.3% leisure/hosp.; 5.3% finance; 11.0% constr./mining/log.; 1.5% info.; 4.0% other serv. **Unemployment:** 2.7%. **Min. wage/hr.:** $7.25. **Per cap. pers. income:** $54,376. **New private housing:** 6,256 units/$953.0 mil. **Broadband internet:** 93.7%. **Commercial banks:** 86; deposits: $24.2 bil. **Savings institutions:** 2; deposits: $1.6 bil. **Lottery:** total sales: $27.0 mil; profit $6.7 mil.

Federal govt. Fed. civ. employees: 5,445; **avg. salary:** $67,482. **Notable fed. facilities:** Minot AFB, Grand Forks AFB; Northern Prairie Wildlife Res. Ctr.; Garrison Dam Natl. Fish Hatchery; Grand Forks Human Nutrition Res. Ctr.

Education. High school grad. rate: 87.2%. **4-year public coll./univ.:** 9; **2-yr. public:** 5; **4-yr. private:** 6.

Energy. Electricity use/cost: 1,240 kWh, $113.39.

State data. Motto: Liberty and union, now and forever one and inseparable. **Flower:** Wild prairie rose. **Bird:** Western meadowlark. **Tree:** American elm. **Song:** "North Dakota Hymn." **Entered union:** Nov. 2, 1889; rank: 39th.

Tourism. Tourist spending: $3.4 bil. **Attractions:** North Dakota Heritage Ctr., North Dakota State Capitol, in Bismarck; Bonanzaville, West Fargo; Ft. Union Trading Post Natl. Historic Site; Intl. Peace Garden, Dunseith; Elkhorn Ranch site, in Theodore Roosevelt Natl. Park; Ft. Abraham

Lincoln State Park and Museum, Mandan; Dakota Dinosaur Museum, Dickinson; Knife River Indian Villages Natl. Historic Site; Scandinavian Heritage Park, Minden. **Information:** North Dakota Tourism Division, Century Center, 1600 E. Century Ave., Ste. 2, P.O. Box 2057, Bismarck, ND 58502; 1-800-435-5663; www.ndtourism.com

History. Paleo-Indian peoples hunted in the area at least 11,000 years ago. At the time of European contact, the Ojibwa, Yanktonai and Teton Sioux, Mandan, Arikara, and Hidatsa peoples lived in the region. Pierre de Varennes, sieur de La Vérendrye, was the first French fur trader in the area, 1738, followed by the English at the end of the 18th cent. Lewis and Clark built Ft. Mandan, near present-day Washburn, 1804-05, and wintered there. The first permanent settlement was at Pembina, 1812. Missouri River steamboats reached the area, 1832. Dakota Territory was organized, 1861. The first railroad arrived, 1872. The "bonanza farm" craze of the 1870s-80s led to statehood, 1889. The Nonpartisan League, a farmers' group favoring state ownership of industries, helped elect Lynn Frazier as governor, 1916, but he and others were ousted in a recall vote, 1921. The predominantly agricultural state has one of the nation's lowest unemployment rates, mostly due to increased oil production since late 2008 in the state's Bakken Formation.

Famous North Dakotans. Maxwell Anderson, Angie Dickinson, Josh Duhamel, John Bernard Flannagan, Phil Jackson, Louis L'Amour, Peggy Lee, Roger Maris, Eric Sevareid, Vilhjalmur Stefansson, Lawrence Welk.

Website. www.nd.gov

Ohio (OH)
Buckeye State

People. Population: 11,613,423; rank: 7. **Pop. change** (2010-15): 0.7%. **Pop. density:** 284.2 per sq mi. **Racial distribution:** 82.7% white; 12.7% black; 2.1% Asian; 0.3% Amer. Ind.; 0.1% Hawaiian/Pacific Islander; 2 or more races, 2.1%. **Hispanic pop.:** 3.6%.

Geography. Total area: 44,826 sq mi; rank: 34. **Land area:** 40,861 sq mi; rank: 35. **Acres forested:** 8.1 mil. **Location:** East North Central state bounded on the N by Michigan and Lake Erie; on the E and S by Pennsylvania, West Virginia, and Kentucky; on the W by Indiana. **Climate:** temperate but variable; weather subject to much precipitation. **Topography:** generally rolling plain; Allegheny Plateau in E; Lake Erie Plains extend southward; central plains in the W. **Capital:** Columbus. **Chief airports:** Akron, Cleveland, Columbus, Dayton.

Economy. Chief industries: manufacturing, trade, services. **Chief manuf. goods:** motor vehicles and parts, petroleum, plastics and rubber, iron and steel, aircraft, machinery, fabricated metal, printing. **Chief crops:** corn, soybeans, hay, wheat, grapes, potatoes, tomatoes, apples, strawberries, tobacco. **Farm income:** crops, $5.89 bil; livestock/animal prods., $4.11 bil. **Nonfuel minerals:** $1.3 bil; stone (crushed), salt, sand and gravel (construction), lime, sand and gravel (industrial). **Commercial fishing:** $4.1 mil. **Chief ports:** Cincinnati, Toledo, Conneaut, Cleveland, Ashtabula. **Gross state product:** $608.1 bil. **Sales tax:** 5.75%. **Gasoline tax:** 46.40 cents/gal. **Employment distrib.:** 14.2% govt.; 18.5% trade/trans./util.; 12.4% mfg.; 16.9% ed./health; 12.9% prof./bus. serv.; 10.4% leisure/hosp.; 5.4% finance; 4.0% constr./mining/log.; 1.3% info.; 4.0% other serv. **Unemployment:** 4.9%. **Min. wage/hr.:** $8.10. **Per cap. pers. income:** $43,478. **New private housing:** 20,047 units/$4.0 bil. **Broadband internet:** 88.4%. **Commercial banks:** 152; deposits: $268.8 bil. **Savings institutions:** 83; deposits: $30.3 bil. **Lottery:** total sales: $3.7 bil; profit: $1.1 bil.

Federal govt. Fed. civ. employees: 48,536; **avg. salary:** $80,302. **Notable fed. facilities:** Wright-Patterson AFB; Defense Supply Ctr., Columbus; NASA Glenn Research Ctr.; Joint Systems Manufacturing Ctr.

Education. High school grad. rate: 81.8%. **4-year public coll./univ.:** 35; **2-yr. public:** 25; **4-yr. private:** 68.

Energy. Electricity use/cost: 901 kWh, $112.62.

State data. Motto: With God, all things are possible. **Flower:** Scarlet carnation. **Bird:** Northern cardinal. **Tree:** Ohio buckeye. **Song:** "Beautiful Ohio." **Entered union:** Mar. 1, 1803; rank: 17th.

Tourism. Tourist spending: $18.5 bil. **Attractions:** Hopewell Culture Natl. Historical Park, Chillicothe; Cuyahoga Valley Natl. Park; Armstrong Air and Space Museum, Wapakoneta; Natl. Museum of the U.S. Air Force, near Dayton; Pro Football Hall of Fame, First Ladies Natl. Historic Site, in Canton; Kings Island amusement park, Mason; Lake Erie Islands, Cedar Point amusement park, in Sandusky; birthplaces, homes of, and memorials to presidents W. H. Harrison, Grant, Hayes,

Garfield, B. Harrison, McKinley, Taft, and Harding; Amish Country, particularly in Holmes County; German Village historic neighborhood, Franklin Park Conservatory and Botanical Gardens, in Columbus; Rock and Roll Hall of Fame and Museum, West Side Market, Cleveland Metroparks Zoo, in Cleveland; Cincinnati Museum Center at Union Terminal; Toledo Zoo. **Information:** Division of Travel and Tourism, P.O. Box 1001, Columbus, OH 43216; 1-800-BUCKEYE; www.discoverohio.com

History. Paleo-Indians hunted in the area about 11,000 years ago; the Adena and Hopewell cultures followed. Wyandot, Delaware, Miami, and Shawnee peoples sparsely occupied the area when the first Europeans arrived. René-Robert Cavelier, sieur de La Salle, visited the region, 1669. France claimed it, 1682, but ceded it to Britain, 1763. After the American Revolution, Ohio became part of the Northwest Territory, 1787. The first permanent settlement was at Marietta, 1788. Cincinnati was also founded, 1788; Cleveland, 1796. Indian warfare abated with the Treaty of Greenville, 1795. Ohio became a state, 1803. In the War of 1812, Oliver Hazard Perry's victory on Lake Erie and William Henry Harrison's invasion of Canada, 1813, ended British incursions. Columbus, founded 1812, became the state capital, 1816. Before the Civil War, Ohioans aided the Underground Railroad, helping runaway slaves. Agricultural for much of the 19th cent., the state became an industrial powerhouse in the 20th cent. but struggled to replace well-paying manufacturing jobs that began disappearing even before the 2007-09 recession. No Republican has ever won the presidency without winning Ohio's electoral votes.

Famous Ohioans. Berenice Abbott, Sherwood Anderson, Neil Armstrong, George Bellows, Halle Berry, Ambrose Bierce, Erma Bombeck, Drew Carey, Hart Crane, George Custer, Clarence Darrow, Paul Laurence Dunbar, Thomas Edison, Clark Gable, John Glenn, Zane Grey, Bob Hope, William Dean Howells, LeBron James, Maya Lin, Toni Morrison, Paul Newman, Jack Nicklaus, Annie Oakley, Jesse Owens, Jack Paar, Pontiac, Eddie Rickenbacker, John D. Rockefeller Sr. and Jr., Roy Rogers, Pete Rose, Arthur Schlesinger Jr., Gen. William Sherman, Steven Spielberg, Gloria Steinem, Harriet Beecher Stowe, Robert A. Taft, William H. Taft, Tecumseh, James Thurber, Ted Turner, Orville and Wilbur Wright.

Website. www.ohio.gov

Oklahoma (OK)
Sooner State

People. Population: 3,911,338; rank: 28. **Pop. change** (2010-15): 4.3%. **Pop. density:** 57.0 per sq mi. **Racial distribution:** 74.8% white; 7.8% black; 2.2% Asian; 9.1% Amer. Ind.; 0.2% Hawaiian/Pacific Islander; 2 or more races, 6.0%. **Hispanic pop.:** 10.1%.

Geography. Total area: 69,899 sq mi; rank: 20. **Land area:** 68,595 sq mi; rank: 19. **Acres forested:** 12.3 mil. **Location:** West South Central state bounded on the N by Colorado and Kansas, on the E by Missouri and Arkansas, on the S and W by Texas and New Mexico. **Climate:** temperate; southern humid belt merging with colder northern continental; humid eastern and dry western zones. **Topography:** high plains predominate in the W, hills and small mountains in the E; the E central region is dominated by the Arkansas R. Basin, and the S by the Red R. Plains. **Capital:** Oklahoma City. **Chief airports:** Oklahoma City, Tulsa.

Economy. Chief industries: manufacturing, mineral and energy exploration and production, agriculture, services. **Chief manuf. goods:** animal slaughtering and processing, petroleum, plastics and rubber, fabricated metals, machinery, motor vehicles and parts. **Chief crops:** wheat, greenhouse and nursery, hay, cotton, corn, soybeans, pecans, sorghum, peanuts. **Farm income:** crops, $1.29 bil; livestock/animal prods., $6.23 bil. **Nonfuel minerals:** $744 mil; stone (crushed), cement (portland), sand and gravel (industrial), sand and gravel (construction), helium (Grade-A). **Chief port:** Catoosa. **Gross state product:** $180.4 bil. **Sales tax:** 4.5%. **Gasoline tax:** 35.40 cents/gal. **Employment distrib.:** 21.5% govt.; 18.3% trade/trans./util.; 7.6% mfg.; 14.1% ed./health; 10.8% prof./bus. serv.; 10.3% leisure/hosp.; 4.8% finance; 7.6% constr./mining/log.; 1.3% info.; 3.7% other serv. **Unemployment:** 4.2%. **Min. wage/hr.:** $7.25. **Per cap. pers. income:** $44,272. **New private housing:** 11,545 units/$2.2 bil. **Broadband internet:** 89.7%. **Commercial banks:** 229; deposits: $78.1 bil. **Savings institutions:** 4; deposits: $5.0 bil. **Lottery:** total sales: $171.6 mil; profit: $60.9 mil.

Federal govt. Fed. civ. employees: 37,285; **avg. salary:** $68,280. **Notable fed. facilities:** Tinker AFB; FAA Mike

Monroney Aeronautical Ctr.; Ft. Sill; Altus AFB; McAlester Army Ammunition Plant; Vance AFB; Natl. Severe Storms Lab.

Education. High school grad. rate: 82.7%. **4-year public coll./univ.:** 17; **2-yr. public:** 13; **4-yr. private:** 14.

Energy. Electricity use/cost: 1,138 kWh, $114.17.

State data. Motto: Labor Omnia Vincit (Labor conquers all things). **Flower:** Oklahoma rose. **Bird:** Scissor-tailed flycatcher. **Tree:** Redbud. **Song:** "Oklahoma!" **Entered union:** Nov. 16, 1907; rank: 46th.

Tourism. Tourist spending: $7.8 bil. **Attractions:** Cherokee Heritage Ctr., Tahlequah; Oklahoma City Natl. Memorial and Museum, Natl. Cowboy and Western Heritage Museum, White Water Bay and Frontier City amusement parks, Museum of Osteology, Bricktown neighborhood, in Oklahoma City; Will Rogers Memorial Museums, Claremore and Oologah; Philbrook Museum of Art, Gilcrease Museum, in Tulsa; Wichita Mountains Wildlife Refuge; Woolaroc Museum and Wildlife Preserve, Price Tower Arts Center, in Bartlesville; Sequoyah's Cabin, Sallisaw; Sam Noble Museum of Natural History, Norman. **Information:** Travel and Tourism Division, 120 N. Robinson, 6th Fl., P.O. Box 52002, Oklahoma City, OK 73152-2002; 1-800-652-6552; www.travelok.com

History. Few Native Americans inhabited the region when Spanish explorer Coronado arrived, 1541, in the 16th and 17th cent., French traders visited. Part of the Louisiana Purchase, 1803, Oklahoma was known as Indian Country and, from 1834, Indian Territory. It became home to the "Five Civilized Tribes"—Cherokee, Choctaw, Chickasaw, Creek, and Seminole—after the forced removal of Indians from the eastern U.S., 1828-46. The land was also used by Comanche, Osage, and other Plains Indians. As white settlers pressed west, land was opened for homesteading by "runs" and lottery. The first run was in 1889; the most famous run, 1893, was to the Cherokee Outlet. Oklahoma became a state, 1907. In the early 20th cent., oil finds brought wealth to the Tulsa area; Tulsa's Greenwood section, then known as the "Negro Wall Street," was looted and destroyed by a white mob, 1921. Depression and drought drove many "Okies" from the Dust Bowl to California in the 1930s. A truck bomb in Oklahoma City, 1995, destroyed a federal office building, killing 168 people; an anti-government extremist was executed for the crime, 2001. A tornado in Moore killed 23 people May 20, 2013; the widest tornado on record touched down in El Reno May 31, 2013, killing 10 people. Since 2010, Oklahoma has experienced thousands of earthquakes (more than 900 greater than 3 magnitude in 2015 alone) believed to be connected with the use of disposal wells for waste from oil and gas operations.

Famous Oklahomans. Troy Aikman, Carl Albert, Gene Autry, Johnny Bench, William Boyd (Hopalong Cassidy), Garth Brooks, Lon Chaney, Gordon Cooper, Ralph Ellison, John Hope Franklin, James Garner, Vince Gill, Woody Guthrie, Paul Harvey, Ron Howard, Patrick J. Hurley, Ben Johnson, Jeane Kirkpatrick, Louis L'Amour, Shannon Lucid, Wilma Mankiller, Mickey Mantle, Reba McEntire, Wiley Post, Tony Randall, Oral Roberts, Will Rogers, Barry Switzer, Maria Tallchief, Jim Thorpe, Carrie Underwood, J. C. Watts Jr.

Website. www.ok.gov

Oregon (OR)
Beaver State

People. Population: 4,028,977; rank: 27. **Pop. change** (2010-15): 5.2%. **Pop. density:** 42.0 per sq mi. **Racial distribution:** 87.6% white; 2.1% black; 4.4% Asian; 1.8% Amer. Ind.; 0.4% Hawaiian/Pacific Islander; 2 or more races, 3.7%. **Hispanic pop.:** 12.7%.

Geography. Total area: 98,379 sq mi; rank: 9. **Land area:** 95,988 sq mi; rank: 10. **Acres forested:** 29.7 mil. **Location:** Pacific state bounded on N by Washington, on E by Idaho, on S by Nevada and California, on W by the Pacific. **Climate:** mild and humid on coast; continental dryness and extreme temperatures in the interior. **Topography:** Coast Range of rugged mountains; fertile Willamette R. Valley to E and S; Cascade Mt. Range of volcanic peaks E of the valley; plateau E of Cascades, remaining two-thirds of state. **Capital:** Salem. **Chief airport:** Portland.

Economy. Chief industries: manufacturing, services, trade, finance, insurance, real estate, government, construction. **Chief manuf. goods:** wood prods., frozen produce, printing, computers and electronics, transportation equip., industrial machinery. **Chief crops:** greenhouse and nursery, grass seed, hay, wheat, potatoes, Christmas trees, onions, pears, hazelnuts, corn, grapes, cherries, blackberries,

blueberries, peppermint, snap beans, apples, hops. **Farm income:** crops, $3.33 bil; livestock/animal prods., $1.90 bil.

Nonfuel minerals: $398 mil; stone (crushed), sand and gravel (construction), cement (portland), diatomite, perlite (crude). **Commercial fishing:** $158.1 mil. **Chief ports:** Portland, Coos Bay. **Gross state product:** $215.3 bil. **Sales tax:** none. **Gasoline tax:** 49.52 cents/gal. **Employment distrib.:** 17.2% govt.; 18.4% trade/trans./util.; 10.1% mfg.; 14.6% ed./health; 13.1% prof./bus. serv.; 10.8% leisure/hosp.; 5.3% finance; 5.1% constr./mining/log.; 1.9% info.; 3.4% other serv. **Unemployment:** 5.7%. **Min. wage/hr.:** $9.75. **Per cap. pers. income:** $42,974. **New private housing:** 17,510 units/$3.6 bil. **Broadband internet:** 90.5%. **Commercial banks:** 45; deposits: $64.8 bil. **Savings institutions:** 6; deposits: $905 mil. **Lottery:** total sales: $1.1 bil; profit: $544.5 mil.

Federal govt. Fed. civ. employees: 18,723; **avg. salary:** $75,176. **Notable fed. facilities:** Bonneville Power Admin.

Education. High school grad. rate: 72.0%. **4-year public coll./univ.:** 9; **2-yr. public:** 17; **4-yr. private:** 24.

Energy. Electricity use/cost: 930 kWh, $97.29.

State data. Motto: She flies with her own wings. **Flower:** Oregon grape. **Bird:** Western meadowlark. **Tree:** Douglas fir. **Song:** "Oregon, My Oregon." **Entered union:** Feb. 14, 1859; rank: 33rd.

Tourism. Tourist spending: $10.4 bil. **Attractions:** John Day Fossil Beds Natl. Monument; Multnomah Falls, Columbia River Gorge; Timberline Lodge, Mount Hood Natl. Forest; Crater Lake Natl. Park; Oregon Dunes Natl. Recreation Area; Ft. Clatsop (Lewis and Clark Natl. Historical Park), Astoria Column, in Astoria; Oregon Caves Natl. Monument; Intl. Rose Test Garden, Lan Su Chinese Garden, Pittock Mansion, Oregon Museum of Science and Industry, in Portland; Oregon Shakespeare Festival, Ashland; High Desert Museum, Bend; "Spruce Goose" (largest aircraft ever built), Evergreen Aviation and Space Museum, McMinnville; Yaquina Head Outstanding Natural Area, Oregon Coast Aquarium, in Newport. **Information:** Travel Oregon, 670 Hawthorne SE, Ste. 240, Salem, OR 97301; 1-800-547-7842; www.traveloregon.com

History. More than 100 Native American tribes inhabited the area at the time of European contact, including the Chinook, Yakima, Cayuse, Modoc, and Nez Percé. Capt. Robert Gray sighted and sailed into the Columbia R., 1792. Lewis and Clark, traveling overland, wintered at its mouth, 1805-06. Fur traders sent by John Jacob Astor established the Astoria trading post in the Columbia River region, 1811. Settlers arrived in the Willamette Valley, 1834. In 1843, the first large wave of settlers arrived via the Oregon Trail. Oregon became a territory, 1848, and a state, 1859. Early in the 20th cent., the "Oregon System"—political reforms that included initiative, referendum, recall, direct primary, and woman suffrage—was adopted. Originally dominated by forest products, the economy diversified after World War II, with technology firms clustering in the "Silicon Forest" area around Portland. Oregonians were the first in the U.S. to pass measures allowing physician-assisted suicide for terminally ill patients, 1994, and establishing an all-mail voting system, 1998. Gov. John Kitzhaber resigned a month into his unprecedented fourth term in 2015, amidst an ethics scandal. A 41-day armed occupation of Malheur Natl. Wildlife Refuge ended in Feb. 2016.

Famous Oregonians. Ernest Bloch, Bill Bowerman, Ty Burrell, Beverly Cleary, Matt Groening, Ernest Haycox, Chief Joseph, Ken Kesey, Phil Knight, Ursula K. Le Guin, Edwin Markham, Tom McCall, John McLoughlin, Joaquin Miller, Bob Packwood, Linus Pauling, Steve Prefontaine, John "Jack" Reed, Alberto Salazar, Mary Decker Slaney, William Simon U'Ren.

Website. www.oregon.gov

Pennsylvania (PA)
Keystone State

People. Population: 12,802,503; rank: 6. **Pop. change** (2010-15): 0.8%. **Pop. density:** 286.1 per sq mi. **Racial distribution:** 82.6% white; 11.7% black; 3.4% Asian; 0.4% Amer. Ind.; 0.1% Hawaiian/Pacific Islander; 2 or more races, 1.9%. **Hispanic pop.:** 6.8%.

Geography. Total area: 46,054 sq mi; rank: 33. **Land area:** 44,743 sq mi; rank: 32. **Acres forested:** 16.9 mil. **Location:** Middle Atlantic state bordered on the E by the Delaware R., on the S by the Mason-Dixon Line, on the W by West Virginia and Ohio, on the N/NE by Lake Erie and New York. **Climate:** continental with wide fluctuations in seasonal temperatures. **Topography:** Allegheny Mts. run SW-NE, with Piedmont and

Coast Plain in the SE triangle; Allegheny Front a diagonal spine across the state's center; N and W rugged plateau falls to Lake Erie Lowland. **Capital:** Harrisburg. **Chief airports:** Harrisburg, Philadelphia, Pittsburgh.

Economy. Chief industries: agribusiness, advanced manufacturing, health care, travel and tourism, depository institutions, biotechnology, printing and publishing, research and consulting, trucking and warehousing, transportation by air, engineering and management, legal services. **Chief manuf. goods:** petroleum, pharmaceuticals, plastics, iron and steel, printing, paper and paperboard, confectionery and snacks, animal slaughtering and processing. **Chief crops:** greenhouse and nursery, mushrooms, corn, hay, soybeans, apples, tomatoes, wheat, grapes, peaches, potatoes, strawberries, tobacco. **Farm income:** crops, $2.58 bil; livestock/animal prods., $5.69 bil. **Nonfuel minerals:** $1.7 bil; stone (crushed), cement (portland), lime, sand and gravel (construction), cement (masonry). **Commercial fishing:** $0.1 mil. **Chief ports:** Philadelphia, Pittsburgh. **Gross state product:** $689.2 bil. **Sales tax:** 6.0%. **Gasoline tax:** 69.80 cents/gal. **Employment distrib.:** 12.1% govt.; 19.2% trade/trans./util.; 9.6% mfg.; 20.5% ed./health; 13.4% prof./bus. serv.; 9.7% leisure/hosp.; 5.3% finance; 4.4% constr./mining/log.; 1.4% info.; 4.3% other serv. **Unemployment:** 5.1%. **Min. wage/hr.:** $7.25. **Per cap. pers. income:** $49,180. **New private housing:** 22,854 units/$4.4 bil. **Broadband internet:** 92.2%. **Commercial banks:** 151; deposits: $299.7 bil. **Savings institutions:** 71; deposits: $56.6 bil. **Lottery:** total sales: $3.8 bil; profit: $1.1 bil.

Federal govt. Fed. civ. employees: 59,258; **avg. salary:** $74,532. **Notable fed. facilities:** Army War College, Carlisle Barracks; Naval Supply Systems Command (NAVSUP), Mechanicsburg; Philadelphia Mint, Defense Supply Ctr., Naval Surface Warfare Ctr., in Phila.; DLA Distribution Ctr. Susquehanna, New Cumberland, Mechanicsburg; Tobyhanna Army Depot; Letterkenny Army Depot.

Education. High school grad. rate: 85.3%. **4-year public coll./univ.:** 45; **2-yr. public:** 17; **4-yr. private:** 104.

Energy. Electricity use/cost: 854 kWh, $113.72.

State data. Motto: Virtue, liberty, and independence. **Flower:** Mountain laurel. **Bird:** Ruffed grouse. **Tree:** Eastern hemlock. **Song:** "Pennsylvania." **Second** of the original 13 states to ratify the Constitution, Dec. 12, 1787.

Tourism. Tourist spending: $24.4 bil. **Attractions:** Liberty Bell Ctr. at Independence Natl. Historical Park, Franklin Institute, Philadelphia Museum of Art, in Philadelphia; Valley Forge Natl. Historical Park, King of Prussia; Gettysburg Natl. Military Park; Pennsylvania Dutch Country, Lancaster County; Hersheypark, Hershey; Duquesne Incline, Carnegie Museums of Pittsburgh, Heinz Hall for the Performing Arts, in Pittsburgh; Pocono Mountains; Pine Creek Gorge (Pennsylvania Grand Canyon), Allegheny Natl. Forest; Fallingwater (house designed by Frank Lloyd Wright), Mill Run; Johnstown Flood Natl. Memorial; Steamtown Natl. Historic Site, Scranton; U.S. Brig *Niagara*, Erie Maritime Museum, Presque Isle State Park, in Erie; Oil Region Natl. Heritage Area; Longwood Gardens, Kennett Square. **Information:** Pennsylvania Tourism Office, Dept. of Community and Economic Development, Commonwealth Keystone Building, 4th Fl., 400 North St., Harrisburg, PA 17120-0225; 1-800-VISITPA; www.visitpa.com

History. When Europeans came, Algonquian-speaking Lenni Lenape (Delaware) and Shawnee and the Iroquoian Susquehannocks, Erie, and Seneca occupied the region. Swedish explorers made the first permanent settlement, 1643, on Tinicum Island. The Dutch seized the settlement, 1655, but lost it to the British, 1664. The region was given by Charles II to William Penn, 1681. Philadelphia ("brotherly love") was the capital of the colonies during most of the American Revolution and of the U.S., 1790-1800; the Declaration of Independence, 1776, and Constitution, 1787, were signed here. Philadelphia was taken by the British, 1777. George Washington's troops encamped at Valley Forge in the bitter winter of 1777-78. Slavery was abolished, 1780. Union victory at the Battle of Gettysburg, July 1-3, 1863, marked a turning point in the Civil War. A dam collapse at Johnstown, 1889, killed at least 2,200 people. From the late 19th to the mid-20th cent., Pittsburgh prospered from coal and steel; later, heavy industry declined, but the city revived as a hub of finance, health care, and research. The Three Mile Island nuclear plant near Harrisburg had a near-meltdown, 1979. One of four hijacked planes on Sept. 11, 2001, crashed near Shanksville; the Flight 93 national memorial was officially dedicated on the site in 2011.

Famous Pennsylvanians. Marian Anderson, Maxwell Anderson, George Blanda, Kobe Bryant, James Buchanan, Andrew Carnegie, Rachel Carson, Wilt Chamberlain, Noam Chomsky, Perry Como, Bill Cosby, Cyrus H. K. Curtis, Thomas Eakins, Tina Fey, Stephen Foster, Benjamin Franklin, Robert Fulton, Martha Graham, Milton Hershey, Gene Kelly, Grace Kelly (Princess Grace of Monaco), Dan Marino, George C. Marshall, Chris Matthews, John J. McCloy, Margaret Mead, Andrew W. Mellon, Joe Montana, Stan Musial, Joe Namath, John O'Hara, Arnold Palmer, Robert E. Peary, Mike Piazza, Pink (Alecia Beth Moore), Mary Roberts Rinehart, Fred Rogers, Betsy Ross, Will Smith, Jimmy Stewart, Taylor Swift, Jim Thorpe, Johnny Unitas, John Updike, Honus Wagner, Andy Warhol, Benjamin West.

Website. www.pa.gov

Rhode Island (RI)
Little Rhody, Ocean State

People. Population: 1,056,298; rank: 43. **Pop. change** (2010-15): 0.3%. **Pop. density:** 1,021.6 per sq mi. **Racial distribution:** 84.8% white; 7.9% black; 3.6% Asian; 1.0% Amer. Ind.; 0.2% Hawaiian/Pacific Islander; 2 or more races, 2.6%. **Hispanic pop.:** 14.4%.

Geography. Total area: 1,545 sq mi; rank: 50. **Land area:** 1,034 sq mi; rank: 50. **Acres forested:** 0.4 mil. **Location:** New England state. **Climate:** invigorating and changeable. **Topography:** eastern lowlands of Narragansett Basin; western uplands of flat and rolling hills. **Capital:** Providence. **Chief airport:** Warwick.

Economy. Chief industries: services, manufacturing. **Chief manuf. goods:** plastics, fabricated metals, electrical equip., jewelry. **Chief crops:** greenhouse and nursery, sweet corn, berries, potatoes, apples, hay. **Farm income:** crops, $49.22 mil; livestock/animal prods., $26.01 mil. **Nonfuel minerals:** $70 mil; sand and gravel (construction), stone (crushed), sand and gravel (industrial), gemstones (natural). **Commercial fishing:** $86.2 mil. **Chief ports:** Providence, Davisville, Newport. **Gross state product:** $57.0 bil. **Sales tax:** 7.0%. **Gasoline tax:** 52.40 cents/gal. **Employment distrib.:** 12.5% govt.; 15.3% trade/trans./util.; 8.5% mfg.; 21.7% ed./health; 13.4% prof./bus. serv.; 11.9% leisure/hosp.; 6.7% finance; 3.6% constr./mining/log.; 1.6% info.; 4.7% other serv. **Unemployment:** 6.0%. **Min. wage/hr.:** $9.60. **Per cap. pers. income:** $50,080. **New private housing:** 998 units/$211.6 mil. **Broadband internet:** 96.1%. **Commercial banks:** 12; deposits: $25.1 bil. **Savings institutions:** 11; deposits: $2.9 bil. **Lottery:** total sales: $866.0 mil; profit: $381.9 mil.

Federal govt. Fed. civ. employees: 7,152; **avg. salary:** $89,684. **Notable fed. facilities:** Naval War College; Naval Undersea Warfare Ctr.; EPA Atlantic Ecology Div. Lab.

Education. High school grad. rate: 80.8%. **4-year public coll./univ.:** 2; **2-yr. public:** 1; **4-yr. private:** 10.

Energy. Electricity use/cost: 583 kWh, $100.09.

State data. Motto: Hope. **Flower:** Violet. **Bird:** Rhode Island red chicken. **Tree:** Red maple. **Song:** "Rhode Island." **Thirteenth** of original 13 states to ratify the Constitution, May 29, 1790.

Tourism. Tourist spending: $1.9 bil. **Attractions:** Block Island; mansions (The Breakers, The Elms, others), Cliff Walk, Intl. Tennis Hall of Fame and Museum, Touro Synagogue (completed 1763, oldest in U.S.), in Newport; First Baptist Church in America, Rhode Island School of Design Museum of Art, WaterFire art installation, in Providence; Slater Mill Historic Site, Pawtucket; Gilbert Stuart Birthplace and Museum, Saunderstown. **Information:** Rhode Island Tourism Division, 315 Iron Horse Way, Ste. 101, Providence, RI 02908; 1-800-556-2484; www.visitrhodeisland.com

History. When Europeans arrived, Narragansett, Niantic, Nipmuc, and Wampanoag peoples lived in the region. Italian Giovanni da Verrazzano visited the area, 1524. The first permanent settlement was founded at Providence, 1636, by Roger Williams, who was exiled from the Massachusetts Bay Colony. Anne Hutchinson, also exiled, settled Portsmouth, 1638. Quaker and Jewish immigrants seeking freedom of worship began arriving, 1650s-60s. The colonists broke the power of the Narragansett in the Great Swamp Fight, 1675, the decisive battle in King Philip's War. The colony was the first to formally renounce all allegiance to King George III, May 4, 1776. Initially opposed to joining the Union, Rhode Island was the last of the 13 colonies to ratify the Constitution, 1790. Trade, textiles, and metal goods dominated the economy in the 19th cent., and Newport became a fashionable resort after the Civil War. The U.S. Navy was the state's largest civilian employer, 1945-73, until the destroyer force was relocated from Newport. A nightclub fire in West Warwick killed 100 people in 2003.

Famous Rhode Islanders. Ambrose Burnside, George M. Cohan, Viola Davis, Nelson Eddy, Jabez Gorham, Nathanael Greene, Elisabeth Hasselbeck, Christopher and Oliver La Farge, Cormac McCarthy, John McLaughlin, Matthew C. and Oliver Hazard Perry, Gilbert Stuart, Meredith Vieira.

Website. www.ri.gov

South Carolina (SC)
Palmetto State

People. Population: 4,896,146; rank: 23. **Pop. change** (2010-15): 5.9%. **Pop. density:** 162.9 per sq mi. **Racial distribution:** 68.4% white; 27.6% black; 1.6% Asian; 0.5% Amer. Ind.; 0.1% Hawaiian/Pacific Islander; 2 or more races, 1.8%. **Hispanic pop.:** 5.5%.

Geography. Total area: 32,020 sq mi; rank: 40. **Land area:** 30,061 sq mi; rank: 40. **Acres forested:** 12.9 mil. **Location:** South Atlantic state bordered by North Carolina on the N; Georgia on the SW and W; the Atlantic Ocean on the E, SE, and S. **Climate:** humid subtropical. **Topography:** Blue Ridge province in NW has highest peaks; piedmont lies between the mountains and the fall line; coastal plain covers two-thirds of state. **Capital:** Columbia. **Chief airports:** Charleston, Columbia, Greer, Myrtle Beach.

Economy. Chief industries: tourism, agriculture, manufacturing. **Chief manuf. goods:** chemicals and synthetics, motor vehicles and parts, plastics, paper and paper prods., turbines, rubber, textiles. **Chief crops:** greenhouse and nursery, tobacco, soybeans, cotton, corn, peaches, wheat, tomatoes, peanuts. **Farm income:** crops, $1.08 bil; livestock/animal prods., $1.59 bil. **Nonfuel minerals:** $679 mil; cement (portland), stone (crushed), sand and gravel (construction), sand and gravel (industrial), cement (masonry). **Commercial fishing:** $23.0 mil. **Chief ports:** Charleston, Georgetown. **Gross state product:** $198.7 bil. **Sales tax:** 6.0%. **Gasoline tax:** 35.15 cents/gal. **Employment distrib.:** 17.8% govt.; 18.9% trade/trans./util.; 11.6% mfg.; 11.8% ed./health; 13.3% prof./bus. serv.; 12.1% leisure/hosp.; 4.8% finance; 4.7% constr./mining/log.; 1.3% info.; 3.6% other serv. **Unemployment:** 6.0%. **Min. wage/hr.:** none ($7.25). **Per cap. pers. income:** $38,041. **New private housing:** 31,030 units/$6.2 bil. **Broadband internet:** 89.5%. **Commercial banks:** 78; deposits: $74.1 bil. **Savings institutions:** 12; deposits: $1.0 bil. **Lottery:** total sales: $1.4 bil; profit: $343.5 mil.

Federal govt. Fed. civ. employees: 20,737; **avg. salary:** $72,238. **Notable fed. facilities:** Ft. Jackson; Joint Base Charleston; Marine Corps Recruit Depot Parris Island; Shaw AFB; USMC Air Station Beaufort; Savannah River Site.

Education. High school grad. rate: 80.1%. **4-year public coll./univ.:** 13; **2-yr. public:** 20; **4-yr. private:** 22.

Energy. Electricity use/cost: 1,187 kWh, $147.74.

State data. Motto: Dum Spiro Spero (While I breathe, I hope). **Flower:** Yellow jessamine. **Bird:** Carolina wren. **Tree:** Palmetto. **Song:** "Carolina." **Eighth** of the original 13 states to ratify the Constitution, May 23, 1788.

Tourism. Tourist spending: $12.9 bil. **Attractions:** Historic Charleston, Waterfront Park, Charleston Museum (est. 1773, oldest in U.S.), Middleton Place, Magnolia Plantation and Gardens, Drayton Hall, in Charleston; Ft. Sumter Natl. Monument (where first shots of Civil War were fired), in Charleston Harbor; Cypress Gardens, Moncks Corner; Boone Hall Plantation and Gardens, Mt. Pleasant; Brookgreen Gardens, Murrells Inlet; Myrtle Beach; Hilton Head Island; Andrew Jackson State Park, Lancaster; South Carolina State Museum, Riverbanks Zoo, in Columbia. **Information:** SC Dept. of Parks, Recreation, and Tourism, 1205 Pendleton St., Columbia, SC 29201; 1-866-224-9339, (803) 734-1700; www.discoversouthcarolina.com

History. When Europeans arrived, Cherokee, Catawba, and Muskogean peoples lived in the area. Spanish and French came in the 16th cent. The first English colonists settled near the Ashley R., 1670, and moved to the site of present-day Charleston, 1680. The colonists seized the government, 1775, and the royal governor fled. The British took Charleston, 1780, but were defeated at Kings Mountain that same year and at Cowpens, 1781. In the 1830s, South Carolinians, angered by federal protective tariffs, adopted the Nullification Doctrine, holding that a state can void an act of Congress. Plantation agriculture relied on slave labor to cultivate rice and cotton; slaves made up 57% of the population in 1860, when South Carolina was the first state to secede from the Union. Confederate troops fired on and forced the surrender of U.S. troops at Ft. Sumter, in Charleston Harbor, 1861, launching the Civil War. The state was readmitted to the Union, 1868. Strom Thurmond, who ran for president as a segregationist in 1948, later served 48 years in the U.S. Senate (1955-2003). Formerly dependent on textiles, the state has attracted new industries by courting foreign investment. The state removed the Confederate flag from its capitol grounds in July 2015 after an alleged white supremacist shot and killed nine black parishioners at a Charleston church the previous month.

Famous South Carolinians. Aziz Ansari, Charles F. Bolden Jr., James F. Byrnes, John C. Calhoun, Stephen Colbert, Marian Wright Edelman, Joe Frazier, DuBose Heyward, Ernest F. Hollings, Andrew Jackson, Jesse Jackson, "Shoeless" Joe Jackson, Jasper Johns, Andie MacDowell, Francis Marion, Ronald E. McNair, Charles Pinckney, John Rutledge, Thomas Sumter, Strom Thurmond, John B. Watson.

Website. www.sc.gov

South Dakota (SD)
Coyote State, Mount Rushmore State

People. Population: 858,469; rank: 46. **Pop. change** (2010-15): 5.4%. **Pop. density:** 11.3 per sq mi. **Racial distribution:** 85.5% white; 1.8% black; 1.4% Asian; 8.9% Amer. Ind.; 0.1% Hawaiian/Pacific Islander; 2 or more races, 2.2%. **Hispanic pop.:** 3.6%.

Geography. Total area: 77,116 sq mi; rank: 17. **Land area:** 75,811 sq mi; rank: 16. **Acres forested:** 1.9 mil. **Location:** West North Central state bounded on the N by North Dakota, on the E by Minnesota and Iowa, on the S by Nebraska, on the W by Wyoming and Montana. **Climate:** characterized by extremes of temperature, persistent winds, low precipitation and humidity. **Topography:** Prairie Plains in the E; rolling hills of the Great Plains in the W; the Black Hills, rising 3,500 ft, in the SW corner. **Capital:** Pierre.

Economy. Chief industries: agriculture, services, manufacturing. **Chief manuf. goods:** animal slaughtering, machinery, semiconductors, surgical appliances. **Chief crops:** corn, soybeans, wheat, hay, sunflowers, sorghum, oats, barley. **Farm income:** crops, $6.23 bil; livestock/animal prods., $4.65 bil. **Nonfuel minerals:** $293 mil; gold, cement (portland), sand and gravel (construction), stone (crushed), lime. **Gross state product:** $46.7 bil. **Sales tax:** 4.0%. **Gasoline tax:** 48.40 cents/gal. **Employment distrib.:** 18.2% govt.; 20.5% trade/trans./util.; 9.6% mfg.; 16.2% ed./health; 7.1% prof./bus. serv.; 10.9% leisure/hosp.; 7.0% finance; 5.7% constr./mining/log.; 1.4% info.; 3.5% other serv. **Unemployment:** 3.1%. **Min. wage/hr.:** $8.55. **Per cap. pers. income:** $45,002. **New private housing:** 4,482 units/$740.7 mil. **Broadband internet:** 92.6%. **Commercial banks:** 81; deposits: $448.8 bil. **Savings institutions:** 4; deposits: $1.7 bil. **Lottery:** total sales: $250.3 mil; profit: $112.1 mil.

Federal govt. Fed. civ. employees: 8,168; **avg. salary:** $64,350. **Notable fed. facilities:** Ellsworth AFB.

Education. High school grad. rate: 82.7%. **4-year public coll./univ.:** 7; **2-yr. public:** 5; **4-yr. private:** 7.

Energy. Electricity use/cost: 1,046 kWh, $109.45.

State data. Motto: Under God, the people rule. **Flower:** Pasqueflower. **Bird:** Chinese ring-necked pheasant. **Tree:** Black Hills spruce. **Song:** "Hail, South Dakota." **Entered union:** Nov. 2, 1889; rank: 40th.

Tourism. Tourist spending: $2.8 bil. **Attractions:** Mt. Rushmore Natl. Memorial, Keystone; Harney Peak (tallest E of Rockies); Custer State Park; Crazy Horse Memorial (mtn. carving in progress); Wind Cave Natl. Park, near Hot Springs; Black Hills Natl. Forest; Needles Hwy., part of Peter Norbeck Natl. Scenic Byway; Minuteman Missile Natl. Historic Site; Deadwood (1876 gold rush town); Jewel Cave Natl. Monument, near Custer; Badlands Natl. Park; Great Lakes of South Dakota; Great Plains Zoo and Delbridge Museum of Natural History, Sioux Falls; Corn Palace, Mitchell; Reptile Gardens, Chapel in the Hills, Bear Country USA, in Rapid City. **Information:** Dept. of Tourism and State Development, Capitol Lake Plaza, 711 E. Wells Ave., c/o 500 E. Capitol Ave., Pierre, SD 57501; 1-800-SDAKOTA; www.travelsd.com

History. Paleo-Indians hunted in the region at least 11,500 years ago. At the time of first European contact, Mandan, Hidatsa, Arikara, and Sioux lived in the area. The French Vérendrye brothers explored the region, 1742-43. The U.S. acquired the territory in the Louisiana Purchase, 1803, and Meriwether Lewis and William Clark passed through, 1804-06. In 1817 a trading post opened at what would become

Ft. Pierre. Dakota Territory was established, 1861. Gold was discovered, 1874, in the Black Hills on Lakota Sioux land; the "Great Dakota Boom" began in 1879. South Dakota became a state, 1889. The massacre of more than 200 Native American men, women, and children at Wounded Knee, 1890, ended Sioux resistance. Armed supporters of the American Indian Movement, a Native American rights group, occupied the area, leading to a 70-day standoff, 1973. Major economic activities include agribusiness and, since the 1980s, credit card services. Republicans scored a key election victory, 2004, with the defeat of three-term U.S. Sen. Tom Daschle, a national Democratic leader.

Famous South Dakotans. Sparky Anderson, Bob Barker, Black Elk, Tom Brokaw, Crazy Horse, Tom Daschle, Myron Floren, Mary Hart, Cheryl Ladd, Ernest O. Lawrence, George McGovern, Russell Means, Billy Mills, Allen H. Neuharth, Pat O'Brien, Sitting Bull.

Website. www.sd.gov

Tennessee (TN)
Volunteer State

People. Population: 6,600,299; rank: 17. **Pop. change** (2010-15): 4.0%. **Pop. density:** 160.1 per sq mi. **Racial distribution:** 78.8% white; 17.1% black; 1.8% Asian; 0.4% Amer. Ind.; 0.1% Hawaiian/Pacific Islander; 2 or more races, 1.8%. **Hispanic pop.:** 5.2%.

Geography. Total area: 42,144 sq mi; rank: 36. **Land area:** 41,235 sq mi; rank: 34. **Acres forested:** 14.0 mil. **Location:** East South Central state bounded on the N by Kentucky and Virginia; on the E by North Carolina; on the S by Georgia, Alabama, and Mississippi; on the W by Arkansas and Missouri. **Climate:** humid continental to the N; humid subtropical to the S. **Topography:** rugged country in the E; the Great Smoky Mts. of the Unakas; low ridges of the Appalachian Valley; flat Cumberland Plateau; slightly rolling terrain and knobs of the Interior Low Plateau, the largest region; Eastern Gulf Coastal Plain to the W, laced with streams; Mississippi Alluvial Plain, a narrow strip of swamp and floodplain in the extreme W. **Capital:** Nashville. **Chief airports:** Alcoa, Memphis, Nashville.

Economy. Chief industries: manufacturing, trade, services, tourism, finance, insurance, real estate. **Chief manuf. goods:** motor vehicles and parts, computers and electronics, food, chemicals, plastics, printing, appliances, aluminum. **Chief crops:** greenhouse and nursery, soybeans, cotton, corn, tobacco, hay, tomatoes, wheat. **Farm income:** crops, $2.45 bil; livestock/animal prods., $1.82 bil. **Nonfuel minerals:** $1.1 bil; stone (crushed), zinc, cement (portland), sand and gravel (construction), sand and gravel (industrial). **Chief ports:** Memphis, Nashville, Chattanooga. **Gross state product:** $314.2 bil. **Sales tax:** 7.0%. **Gasoline tax:** 39.80 cents/gal. **Employment distrib.:** 14.4% govt.; 20.8% trade/trans./util.; 11.6% mfg.; 14.5% ed./health; 13.5% prof./bus. serv.; 10.8% leisure/hosp.; 5.1% finance; 4.1% constr./mining/log.; 1.5% info.; 3.7% other serv. **Unemployment:** 5.8%. **Min. wage/hr.:** none ($7.25). **Per cap. pers. income:** $42,069. **New private housing:** 32,219 units/$5.6 bil. **Broadband internet:** 91.2%. **Commercial banks:** 203; deposits: $128.3 bil. **Savings institutions:** 11; deposits: $3.1 bil. **Lottery:** total sales: $1.5 bil; profit: $347.8 mil.

Federal govt. Fed. civ. employees: 26,289; **avg. salary:** $71,588. **Notable fed. facilities:** Tennessee Valley Authority; Oak Ridge Natl. Lab; Arnold Engineering Development Ctr.; Ft. Campbell; NSA Mid-South, Millington.

Education. High school grad. rate: 87.2%. **4-year public coll./univ.:** 9; **2-yr. public:** 13; **4-yr. private:** 47.

Energy. Electricity use/cost: 1,286 kWh, $132.76.

State data. Motto: Agriculture and commerce. **Flower:** (cultivated) iris; (wildflower) passion flower, Tennessee coneflower. **Bird:** Northern mockingbird. **Tree:** Tulip poplar. **Songs:** "My Homeland, Tennessee"; "When It's Iris Time in Tennessee"; "My Tennessee"; "Tennessee Waltz"; "Rocky Top"; "Smoky Mountain Rain." **Entered union:** June 1, 1796; rank: 16th.

Tourism. Tourist spending: $17.8 bil. **Attractions:** Lookout Mountain, Tennessee Aquarium, Ruby Falls, in Chattanooga; Great Smoky Mountains Natl. Park; Lost Sea (largest underground lake in U.S.), Sweetwater; Cherokee Natl. Forest; Cumberland Gap Natl. Historical Park; James K. Polk Ancestral Home, Columbia; American Museum of Science and Energy, Oak Ridge; The Hermitage (home of Pres. Andrew Jackson), Country Music Hall of Fame and Museum, Ryman Auditorium, Belle Meade Plantation, Parthenon replica, Grand Ole Opry, in Nashville; Dollywood theme park,

Pigeon Forge; Graceland (home of Elvis Presley), Sun Studio, in Memphis; Alex Haley Museum and Interpretive Ctr., Henning; Casey Jones Village, Jackson; Bristol Motor Speedway. **Information:** Dept. of Tourist Development, Wm. Snodgrass/Tennessee Tower, 312 Rosa L. Parks Ave., 25th Fl., Nashville, TN 37243; 1-800-462-8366; www.tnvacation.com

History. Inhabited for at least 20,000 years, the region was home to Creek and Yuchi peoples when the first Europeans arrived; the Cherokee moved into the region in the early 18th cent. Spanish explorers visited the area, 1540. English traders crossed the Great Smoky Mtns. from the east, while France's Jacques Marquette and Louis Jolliet sailed down the Mississippi on the west, 1673. The first permanent settlement was of Virginians on the Watauga R., 1769. After the American Revolution, in which Tennesseans fought in eastern campaigns, the region became a territory, 1790, and a state, 1796. Slavery was widespread in western Tennessee, where cotton was the main crop, but much less common in the east. The state seceded, 1861, and saw many Civil War engagements; some 187,000 Tennesseans fought for the Confederacy and 51,000 for the Union. Tennessee was readmitted in 1866, the only former Confederate state not to have a postwar military government. The famous Scopes trial, 1925, questioned the teaching of evolution in public schools. In the 1930s, the Tennessee Valley Authority, a federal program, brought electric power to rural areas. Nashville became the capital of country music while Memphis fostered the blues and, with Elvis Presley in the 1950s, rock 'n' roll. Martin Luther King Jr. was assassinated in Memphis, 1968. Since the 1970s, auto plants have become major employers, as has Federal Express. Al Gore Jr., U.S. vice pres. (1993-2001), lost his 2000 presidential bid partly because he failed to carry his home state of Tennessee. Record amounts of rainfall flooded parts of Tennessee, including Nashville, in May 2010.

Famous Tennesseans. Roy Acuff, Kenny Chesney, Davy Crockett, David Farragut, Ernie Ford, Aretha Franklin, Bill Frist, Al Gore Jr., Alex Haley, William C. Handy, Sam Houston, Cordell Hull, Andrew Jackson, Andrew Johnson, Casey Jones, Estes Kefauver, Grace Moore, Dolly Parton, Minnie Pearl, James Polk, Elvis Presley, Wilma Rudolph, Dinah Shore, Bessie Smith, Fred Thompson, Justin Timberlake, Tina Turner, Hank Williams Jr., Alvin York.

Website. www.tn.gov

Texas (TX)
Lone Star State

People. Population: 27,469,114; rank: 2. **Pop. change** (2010-15): 9.2%. **Pop. density:** 105.2 per sq mi. **Racial distribution:** 79.7% white; 12.5% black; 4.7% Asian; 1.0% Amer. Ind.; 0.1% Hawaiian/Pacific Islander; 2 or more races, 1.9%. **Hispanic pop.:** 38.8%.

Geography. Total area: 268,596 sq mi; rank: 2. **Land area:** 261,232 sq mi; rank: 2. **Acres forested:** 63.1 mil. **Location:** southwestern state bounded on the SE by the Gulf of Mexico; on the SW by Mexico, separated by the Rio Grande; surrounding states are Louisiana, Arkansas, Oklahoma, New Mexico. **Climate:** extremely varied; driest region is the Trans-Pecos; wettest is the NE. **Topography:** Gulf Coast Plain in the S and SE; North Central Plains slope upward with some hills; the Great Plains extend over the Panhandle, are broken by low mountains; the Trans-Pecos is the southern extension of the Rockies. **Capital:** Austin. **Chief airports:** Austin, Dallas, El Paso, Fort Worth, Houston (2), Midland, San Antonio.

Economy. Chief industries: manufacturing, trade, oil and gas extraction, services. **Chief manuf. goods:** petroleum, chemicals and resins, computers and electronics, animal slaughtering and processing, plastics, aerospace. **Chief crops:** cotton, greenhouse and nursery, corn, wheat, sorghum, hay, peanuts, onions, rice, pecans, grapefruit. **Farm income:** crops, $7.73 bil; livestock/animal prods., $17.03 bil. **Nonfuel minerals:** $5.3 bil; stone (crushed), sand and gravel (industrial), cement (portland), sand and gravel (construction), salt. **Commercial fishing:** $262.6 mil. **Chief ports:** Houston, Galveston, Brownsville, Beaumont, Port Arthur, Corpus Christi, Texas City, Freeport. **Gross state product:** $1.6 tril. **Sales tax:** 6.25%. **Gasoline tax:** 38.40 cents/gal. **Employment distrib.:** 15.9% govt.; 20.2% trade/trans./util.; 7.0% mfg.; 13.7% ed./health; 13.4% prof./bus. serv.; 10.9% leisure/hosp.; 6.1% finance; 7.6% constr./mining/log.; 1.7% info.; 3.6% other serv. **Unemployment:** 4.5%. **Min. wage/hr.:** $7.25. **Per cap. pers. income:** $46,745. **New private housing:** 175,443 units/$29.1 bil. **Broadband internet:** 92.6%. **Commercial banks:** 515; deposits: $656.1 bil. **Savings**

institutions: 41; **deposits:** $74.0 bil. **Lottery:** total sales: $4.5 bil; profit: $1.2 bil.

Federal govt. Fed. civ. employees: 113,810; **avg. salary:** $74,660. **Notable fed. facilities:** Ft. Hood; Ft. Bliss; Sheppard, Dyess, Goodfellow AF Bases; Joint Base San Antonio; NASA Johnson Space Ctr.; Naval Air Training School, Corpus Christi NAS; Red River Army Depot; Western Currency Facility, Ft. Worth.

Education. High school grad. rate: 88.3%. **4-year public coll./univ.:** 44; **2-yr. public:** 63; **4-yr. private:** 59.

Energy. Electricity use/cost: 1,158 kWh, $137.39.

State data. Motto: Friendship. **Flower:** Bluebonnet. **Bird:** Northern mockingbird. **Tree:** Pecan. **Song:** "Texas, Our Texas." **Entered union:** Dec. 29, 1845; rank: 28th.

Tourism. Tourist spending: $66.0 bil. **Attractions:** Big Bend and Guadalupe Mountains Natl. Parks; Fort Davis Natl. Historic Site; Six Flags Over Texas, Arlington; SeaWorld San Antonio, Six Flags Fiesta Texas, The Alamo, San Antonio Missions Natl. Historical Park, San Antonio River Walk, in San Antonio; Natl. Cowgirl Museum and Hall of Fame, Kimbell Art Museum, Ft. Worth Zoo, Bureau of Engraving and Printing, in Ft. Worth; Lyndon B. Johnson Natl. Historical Park, Johnson City; LBJ Presidential Library and Museum, Bullock Texas State History Museum, Austin; George Bush Presidential Library and Museum, College Station; Dallas Arboretum and Botanical Garden, Sixth Floor Museum at Dealey Plaza, George W. Bush Presidential Library and Museum, in Dallas; USS *Lexington*, Texas State Aquarium, Padre Island Natl. Seashore, in Corpus Christi. **Information:** Texas Tourism, P.O. Box 141009, Austin, TX 78714; 1-800-452-9292, (512) 486-5876; www.traveltexas.com

History. Humans have lived in the region for at least 12,000 years. Coahuiltecan, Karankawa, Caddo, Jumano, and Tonkawa peoples were in the area when the first Europeans came; later, Apache, Comanche, Cherokee, and Wichita arrived. Early Spanish explorers included Alonso Alvarez de Pineda, who sailed along the Texas coast, 1519; Cabeza de Vaca, shipwrecked near Galveston along with the former slave Estevanico, 1528; and Coronado, who crossed the Panhandle, 1541. Spaniards made the first settlement at Ysleta, near El Paso, 1682. Americans moved into the land early in the 19th cent. Mexico, of which Texas was a part, won independence from Spain, 1821. Texans rebelled, 1836, losing to Mexican Gen. Santa Anna at the Alamo but winning decisively under Sam Houston at San Jacinto. With Houston as president, 1836-38 and 1841-44, the Republic of Texas functioned as a nation until admitted to the Union. With a slave population of 30%, Texas seceded, 1861; mostly unscathed by the Civil War, it was readmitted, 1870. In 1900 a powerful hurricane lashed Galveston, killing at least 8,000. Cotton and cattle were dominant until 1901, when the Spindletop gusher, near Beaumont, launched the petroleum and petrochemical industries. By 2000, the state population ranked second in the U.S. With wealth and population came political power, notably in the presidencies of Lyndon B. Johnson (1963-69), George H. W. Bush (1989-93), and George W. Bush (2001-09). Record rains triggered floods that killed at least 15 people in late May/early June 2016. Amid nationwide backlash over police killings of black men, a black military veteran in July 2016 fatally shot five police officers in Dallas.

Famous Texans. Lance Armstrong, Stephen F. Austin, Lloyd Bentsen, James Bowie, Drew Brees, Carol Burnett, George H. W. Bush, George W. Bush, Earl Campbell, Joan Crawford, Dwight D. Eisenhower, Morgan Fairchild, Farrah Fawcett, George Foreman, Sam Houston, Howard Hughes, Molly Ivins, Lyndon B. Johnson, Tommy Lee Jones, Janis Joplin, Barbara Jordan, Beyoncé Knowles, Mary Martin, Matthew McConaughey, Chester Nimitz, Sandra Day O'Connor, H. Ross Perot, Katherine Anne Porter, Dan Rather, Sam Rayburn, Ann Richards, Michael Strahan, George Strait, Babe Didrikson Zaharias.

Website. www.texas.gov

Utah (UT)
Beehive State

People. Population: 2,995,919; rank: 31. **Pop. change** (2010-15): 8.4%. **Pop. density:** 36.5 per sq mi. **Racial distribution:** 91.2% white; 1.3% black; 2.5% Asian; 1.5% Amer. Ind.; 1.0% Hawaiian/Pacific Islander; 2 or more races, 2.4%. **Hispanic pop.:** 13.7%.

Geography. Total area: 84,897 sq mi; rank: 13. **Land area:** 82,170 sq mi; rank: 12. **Acres forested:** 18.3 mil. **Location:** middle Rocky Mountain state; its SE corner touches Colorado, New Mexico, and Arizona and is the only spot in the

U.S. where four states join. **Climate:** arid; ranges from warm desert in SW to alpine in NE. **Topography:** high Colorado Plateau is cut by brilliantly colored canyons of the SE; broad, flat, desertlike Great Basin of the W; the Great Salt Lake and Bonneville Salt Flats to the NW; Middle Rockies in the NE run E-W; valleys and plateaus of the Wasatch Front. **Capital:** Salt Lake City. **Chief airport:** Salt Lake City.

Economy. Chief industries: services, trade, manufacturing, government, transportation, utilities. **Chief manuf. goods:** food, petroleum, nonferrous metal, motor vehicles and parts, aerospace, sporting goods, fabricated metal, computers and electronics. **Chief crops:** hay, greenhouse and nursery, wheat, cherries, onions, apples, barley, peaches, corn. **Farm income:** crops, $534.56 mil; livestock/animal prods., $1.84 bil. **Nonfuel minerals:** $2.9 bil; molybdenum concentrates, copper, magnesium metal, potash, salt. **Gross state product:** $147.1 bil. **Sales tax:** 5.95%. **Gasoline tax:** 47.81 cents/gal. **Employment distrib.:** 17.2% govt.; 19.0% trade/trans./util.; 8.9% mfg.; 13.2% ed./health; 13.9% prof./bus. serv.; 9.9% leisure/hosp.; 5.8% finance; 7.0% constr./mining/log.; 2.5% info.; 2.7% other serv. **Unemployment:** 3.5%. **Min. wage/hr.:** $7.25. **Per cap. pers. income:** $39,045. **New private housing:** 18,297 units/$3.9 bil. **Broadband internet:** 92.9%. **Commercial banks:** 58; deposits: $441.8 bil. **Savings institutions:** 5; deposits: $73.7 bil.

Federal govt. Fed. civ. employees: 27,816; **avg. salary:** $68,550. **Notable fed. facilities:** Hill AFB; Tooele Army Depot; Army Dugway Proving Ground; NSA Utah Data Ctr.

Education. High school grad. rate: 83.9%. **4-year public coll./univ.:** 7; **2-yr. public:** 1; **4-yr. private:** 10.

Energy. Electricity use/cost: 747 kWh, $79.49.

State data. Motto: Industry. **Flower:** Sego lily. **Bird:** (California) sea gull. **Tree:** Blue spruce. **Song:** "Utah, This Is the Place." **Entered union:** Jan. 4, 1896; rank: 45th.

Tourism. Tourist spending: $8.0 bil. **Attractions:** Temple Square (site of Mormon Church headquarters), Salt Lake City; Great Salt Lake; Zion, Canyonlands, Bryce Canyon, Arches, and Capitol Reef Natl. Parks; Dinosaur, Rainbow Bridge, Timpanogos Cave, and Natural Bridges Natl. Monuments; Lake Powell; Flaming Gorge Natl. Recreation Area; Utah Olympic Park, Sundance Film Festival, in Park City. **Information:** Utah Office of Tourism, Council Hall/Capitol Hill, 300 N. State St., Salt Lake City, UT 84114; 1-800-200-1160; www.utah.com

History. Ute, Gosiute, Southern Paiute, and Navajo peoples lived in the region at the time of European contact. Spanish Franciscans visited the area, 1776; American fur traders followed. Permanent settlement began with the arrival of the Latter-day Saints, or Mormons, 1847, who created a prosperous economy. Organized in 1849, the State of Deseret asked admission to the Union; instead, Congress established Utah Territory, 1850, and appointed Brigham Young governor. The Union Pacific and Central Pacific railroads met near Promontory Point, May 10, 1869, creating the first transcontinental railroad. Statehood was not achieved until 1896, after a long controversy over the Mormon practices of economic isolationism and polygamy (the church renounced the latter in 1890). The 20th cent. brought expansion in mining, defense-related industries, and, more recently, information technologies. More than two-thirds of Utahans are Mormons; the church has its world headquarters in Salt Lake City. Utah experienced 60% population growth, 1990-2010, and has the highest birthrate and lowest median age of any state in the U.S.

Famous Utahans. Maude Adams, Roseanne Barr, Ezra Taft Benson, John Moses Browning, Butch Cassidy, Marriner S. Eccles, Philo T. Farnsworth, David M. Kennedy, J. Willard Marriott, Merlin Olsen, the Osmonds, Ivy Baker Priest, George W. Romney, Wallace Stegner, Brigham Young, Loretta Young.

Website. www.utah.gov

Vermont (VT)
Green Mountain State

People. Population: 626,042; rank: 50. **Pop. change** (2010-15): <0.05%. **Pop. density:** 67.9 per sq mi. **Racial distribution:** 94.8% white; 1.3% black; 1.6% Asian; 0.4% Amer. Ind.; <0.05% Hawaiian/Pacific Islander; 2 or more races, 1.9%. **Hispanic pop.:** 1.8%.

Geography. Total area: 9,616 sq mi; rank: 45. **Land area:** 9,217 sq mi; rank: 43. **Acres forested:** 4.5 mil. **Location:** northern New England state. **Climate:** temperate, with considerable temperature extremes; heavy snowfall in mountains. **Topography:** Green Mts. N-S backbone 20-36 mi wide; avg. altitude 1,000 ft. **Capital:** Montpelier. **Chief airport:** Burlington.

Economy. Chief industries: manufacturing, tourism, agriculture, trade, finance, insurance, real estate, government. **Chief manuf. goods:** dairy, plastics, printing, wood furniture, sporting goods, metalworking machinery. **Chief crops:** greenhouse and nursery, hay, maple syrup, apples, berries, sweet corn. **Farm income:** crops, $178.62 mil; livestock/animal prods., $813.60 mil. **Nonfuel minerals:** $118 mil; stone (crushed), sand and gravel (construction), stone (dimension), talc (crude), gemstones (natural). **Gross state product:** $30.4 bil. **Sales tax:** 6.0%. **Gasoline tax:** 48.86 cents/gal. **Employment distrib.:** 18.5% govt.; 17.6% trade/trans./util.; 9.7% mfg.; 20.7% ed./health; 8.9% prof./bus. serv.; 10.7% leisure/hosp.; 3.9% finance; 5.3% constr./mining/log.; 1.4% info.; 3.4% other serv. **Unemployment:** 3.7%. **Min. wage/hr.:** $9.60. **Per cap. pers. income:** $47,864. **New private housing:** 1,998 units/$334.0 mil. **Broadband internet:** 89.6%. **Commercial banks:** 14; deposits: $10.0 bil. **Savings institutions:** 9; deposits: $2.1 bil. **Lottery:** total sales: $111.8 mil; profit: $22.8 mil.

Federal govt. Fed. civ. employees: 3,316; **avg. salary:** $75,679. **Notable fed. facilities:** Law Enforcement Support Ctr.

Education. High school grad. rate: 87.8%. **4-year public coll./univ.:** 5; **2-yr. public:** 1; **4-yr. private:** 17.

Energy. Electricity use/cost: 569 kWh, $99.34.

State data. Motto: Freedom and unity. **Flower:** Red clover. **Bird:** Hermit thrush. **Tree:** Sugar maple. **Song:** "These Green Mountains." **Entered union:** Mar. 4, 1791; rank: 14th.

Tourism. Tourist spending: $2.3 bil. **Attractions:** Shelburne Museum; Shelburne Farms; Vermont Marble Museum, Proctor; Bennington Battle Monument; Pres. Calvin Coolidge Homestead, Plymouth; Ben & Jerry's Factory, Waterbury; Stowe, Killington, and Burke ski resorts; Hildene (Robert Todd Lincoln home), Manchester; Marsh-Billings-Rockefeller Natl. Historical Park, Woodstock. **Information:** Vermont Dept. of Tourism and Marketing, Natl. Life Building, 6th Fl., Montpelier, VT 05620; 1-800-VERMONT, (802) 828-3237; www.vermontvacation.com

History. Inhabited for 10,000 years or more, the region attracted Abenaki and Mahican peoples before Europeans arrived. France's Champlain explored the lake that now bears his name, 1609. The first European settlement was on Isle la Motte in Lake Champlain, 1666. During the American Revolution, Ethan Allen and the Green Mountain Boys captured Ft. Ticonderoga (NY), 1775. Under a constitution that provided for public schools and abolished slavery, settlers declared a republic, 1777. Vermont joined the Union, 1791. Agriculture dominated in the 19th cent. Still mainly rural, the state expanded tourism and manufacturing after World War II, and IBM became the largest private employer. Vermont was the first state to recognize same-sex civil unions (2000) and to enact equal same-sex marriage rights via legislation (2009).

Famous Vermonters. Ethan Allen, Chester A. Arthur, Calvin Coolidge, Howard Dean, John Deere, George Dewey, John Dewey, Stephen A. Douglas, Dorothy Canfield Fisher, James Fisk, James "Jim" Jeffords, Jody Williams.

Website. www.vermont.gov

Virginia (VA)
Old Dominion

People. Population: 8,382,993; rank: 12. **Pop. change** (2010-15): 4.8%. **Pop. density:** 212.3 per sq mi. **Racial distribution:** 70.2% white; 19.7% black; 6.5% Asian; 0.5% Amer. Ind.; 0.1% Hawaiian/Pacific Islander; 2 or more races, 2.9%. **Hispanic pop.:** 9.0%.

Geography. Total area: 42,775 sq mi; rank: 35. **Land area:** 39,490 sq mi; rank: 36. **Acres forested:** 16.0 mil. **Location:** South Atlantic state bounded by the Atlantic Ocean on the E and surrounded by North Carolina, Tennessee, Kentucky, West Virginia, and Maryland. **Climate:** mild and equable. **Topography:** mountain and valley region in the W, including the Blue Ridge Mts.; rolling Piedmont Plateau; tidewater, or coastal plain, including the Eastern Shore. **Capital:** Richmond. **Chief airports:** Arlington, Dulles, Highland Springs, Norfolk.

Economy. Chief industries: services, trade, government, manufacturing, tourism, agriculture. **Chief manuf. goods:** beverages and tobacco, transportation equip., animal slaughtering and processing, plastics, textiles, paper and paper prods., printing, pharmaceuticals, furniture, chemicals. **Chief crops:** greenhouse and nursery, soybeans, tomatoes, corn, tobacco, hay, cotton, apples, wheat, peanuts, potatoes. **Farm income:** crops, $1.35 bil; livestock/animal prods., $2.83 bil. **Nonfuel minerals:** $1.2 bil; stone (crushed), cement (portland), sand and gravel (construction), lime, zirconium concentrates. **Commercial fishing:** $168.2 mil. **Chief ports:** Norfolk

Harbor, Newport News, Richmond, Hopewell. **Gross state product:** $479.8 bil. **Sales tax:** 5.3%. **Gasoline tax:** 40.79 cents/gal. **Employment distrib.:** 18.3% govt.; 17.0% trade/trans./util.; 5.8% mfg.; 13.2% ed./health; 18.3% prof./bus. serv.; 10.3% leisure/hosp.; 5.1% finance; 5.0% constr./mining/log.; 1.7% info.; 5.2% other serv. **Unemployment:** 4.4%. **Min. wage/hr.:** $7.25. **Per cap. pers. income:** $52,136. **New private housing:** 28,469 units/$4.7 bil. **Broadband internet:** 92.7%. **Commercial banks:** 134; deposits: $239.2 bil. **Savings institutions:** 6; deposits: $36.4 bil. **Lottery:** total sales: $1.8 bil; profit: $533.8 mil.

Federal govt. Fed. civ. employees: 134,141; **avg. salary:** $91,418. **Notable fed. facilities:** Pentagon; Norfolk Naval Sta., Shipyard, and other Hampton Roads military bases; Ft. Belvoir; Joint Base Langley-Eustis; NASA Langley Res. Ctr.; CIA George Bush Ctr. for Intelligence, Langley; FBI Academy, Quantico USMC Base; Dahlgren Nav. Surface Warfare Ctr. and Lab; USDA Food and Nutrition Serv.; U.S. Geological Survey Natl. Ctr.

Education. High school grad. rate: 85.3%. **4-year public coll./univ.:** 16; **2-yr. public:** 24; **4-yr. private:** 38.

Energy. Electricity use/cost: 1,172 kWh, $130.04.

State data. Motto: Sic Semper Tyrannis (Thus always to tyrants). **Flower:** American dogwood. **Bird:** Northern cardinal. **Tree:** American dogwood. **Song emeritus:** "Carry Me Back to Old Virginia." **Tenth** of original 13 states to ratify the Constitution, June 25, 1788.

Tourism. Tourist spending: $22.9 bil. **Attractions:** Colonial Williamsburg, Busch Gardens Williamsburg, Jamestown Settlement, in Williamsburg; Yorktown Victory Ctr.; Wolf Trap Natl. Park for the Performing Arts, near Vienna; Arlington Natl. Cemetery; George Washington's Mount Vernon; Thomas Jefferson's Monticello, Charlottesville; Stratford Hall (Robert E. Lee birthplace); Appomattox Court House Natl. Historical Park; Shenandoah Natl. Park; Blue Ridge Natl. Parkway; Virginia Beach; Kings Dominion amusement park, Doswell. **Information:** Virginia Tourism Corp., 901 E. Byrd St., Richmond, VA 23219; 1-800-VISITVA; www.virginia.org

History. Cherokee and Susquehanna peoples and the Algonquians of the Powhatan Confederacy were in the region when Europeans arrived. English settlers founded Jamestown, 1607. Four of the first five U.S. presidents—Washington, Jefferson, Madison, and Monroe—came from Virginia. The conclusive battle of the American Revolution took place at Yorktown, 1781. The state profited from tobacco, cotton, and the slave trade; in 1860, slaves made up nearly one-third of the population. Virginia seceded from the Union, 1861, and Richmond became the capital of the Confederacy. Western counties, loyal to the Union, split off to become West Virginia, 1863. The war ended with Robert E. Lee's surrender to Ulysses S. Grant at Appomattox, 1865; Virginia was readmitted to the Union, 1870. In the 20th cent., expansion of federal civilian jobs and military facilities transformed the economy. State officials pledged "massive resistance" to racial integration in the mid-1950s but eventually accommodated it. In 1989, L. Douglas Wilder became the first elected black governor in U.S. history. On Sept. 11, 2001, terrorist hijackers crashed a jet into U.S. defense headquarters at the Pentagon, in Arlington. Seven-term Rep. Eric Cantor became the first House majority leader ever to lose a primary in 2014.

Famous Virginians. Arthur Ashe, Sandra Bullock, Richard E. Byrd, James B. Cabell, Henry Clay, Katie Couric, Gabby Douglas, Jubal Early, Jerry Falwell, William Henry Harrison, Patrick Henry, A. P. Hill, Thomas Jefferson, Joseph E. Johnston, Robert E. Lee, Meriwether Lewis and William Clark, James Madison, John Marshall, George Mason, James Monroe, Sean Parker, George Pickett, Pocahontas, Edgar Allan Poe, John Randolph, Walter Reed, Rev. Pat Robertson, John Smith, J. E. B. Stuart, William Styron, Zachary Taylor, John Tyler, Maggie Walker, Booker T. Washington, George Washington, L. Douglas Wilder, Woodrow Wilson.

Website. www.virginia.gov

Washington (WA)
Evergreen State

People. Population: 7,170,351; rank: 13. **Pop. change** (2010-15): 6.6%. **Pop. density:** 107.9 per sq mi. **Racial distribution:** 80.3% white; 4.1% black; 8.4% Asian; 1.9% Amer. Ind.; 0.7% Hawaiian/Pacific Islander; 2 or more races, 4.6%. **Hispanic pop.:** 12.4%.

Geography. Total area: 71,298 sq mi; rank: 18. **Land area:** 66,456 sq mi; rank: 20. **Acres forested:** 22.2 mil. **Location:** Pacific state bordered by Canada on the N, Idaho on the E, Oregon on the S, the Pacific Ocean on the W. **Climate:** mild, dominated by the Pacific Ocean and protected by the

Cascades. **Topography:** Olympic Mts. on NW peninsula; open land along coast to Columbia R.; flat terrain of Puget Sound Lowland; high peaks of Cascade Mts. to the E; Columbia Basin in central portion; highlands to the NE; mountains to the SE. **Capital:** Olympia. **Chief airports:** Seattle, Spokane.

Economy. Chief industries: advanced technology, aerospace, biotechnology, intl. trade, forestry, tourism, recycling, agriculture and food processing. **Chief manuf. goods:** aerospace, petroleum, food, paper, milled lumber, plastics, structural metals, computers and electronics. **Chief crops:** apples, potatoes, wheat, hay, cherries, greenhouse and nursery, forest products, pears, grapes, onions, hops, sweet corn, Christmas trees, mint, raspberries. **Farm income:** crops, $6.95 bil; livestock/animal prods., $3.16 bil. **Nonfuel minerals:** $936 mil; sand and gravel (construction), stone (crushed), gold, cement (portland), zinc. **Commercial fishing:** $329.1 mil. **Chief ports:** Seattle, Tacoma, Vancouver, Kelso-Longview, Anacortes. **Gross state product:** $443.7 bil. **Sales tax:** 6.5%. **Gasoline tax:** 67.80 cents/gal. **Employment distrib.:** 18.0% govt.; 18.7% trade/trans./util.; 8.8% mfg.; 14.4% ed./health; 12.4% prof./bus. serv.; 9.8% leisure/hosp.; 4.7% finance; 5.9% constr./mining/log.; 3.7% info.; 3.7% other serv. **Unemployment:** 5.7%. **Min. wage/hr.:** $9.47. **Per cap. pers. income:** $51,146. **New private housing:** 40,374 units/$8.5 bil. **Broadband internet:** 92.4%. **Commercial banks:** 76; deposits: $126.7 bil. **Savings institutions:** 14; deposits: $7.8 bil. **Lottery:** total sales: $600.3 mil; profit: $141.3 mil.

Federal govt. Fed. civ. employees: 53,406; **avg. salary:** $75,511. **Notable fed. facilities:** Bonneville Power Admin.; Lewis-McChord Joint Base; Fairchild AFB; Hanford Site (fmr. nuclear weapons production facility); Naval Base Kitsap (Bremerton and Bangor); Whidbey Island NAS; Pacific Northwest Natl. Lab.

Education. High school grad. rate: 78.2%. **4-year public coll./univ.:** 23; **2-yr. public:** 20; **4-yr. private:** 23.

Energy. Electricity use/cost: 1,005 kWh, $87.14.

State data. Motto: Alki (By and by). **Flower:** Western rhododendron. **Bird:** Willow goldfinch. **Tree:** Western hemlock. **Song:** "Washington, My Home." **Entered union:** Nov. 11, 1889; rank: 42nd.

Tourism. Tourist spending: $15.7 bil. **Attractions:** Seattle Center, Space Needle, EMP Museum, Museum of Flight, Pike Place Market, Underground Tour, in Seattle; Mount Rainier, Olympic, and North Cascades Natl. Parks; Mount St. Helens Natl. Volcanic Monument; Puget Sound; San Juan Islands; Grand Coulee Dam; Columbia R. Gorge Natl. Scenic Area; Riverfront Park, Spokane; Snoqualmie Falls. **Information:** WA State Tourism Office, 128 10th Ave. SW, P.O. Box 42525, Olympia, WA 98504; 1-866-964-8913; www.experiencewa.com

History. People of the Clovis culture lived in the region 11,000 years ago. At the time of European contact, Native Americans in the area included Nez Percé, Spokane, Yakima, Cayuse, Okanogan, Walla Walla, and Colville peoples in the interior, and Nooksak, Chinook, Nisqually, Clallam, Makah, Quinault, and Puyallup peoples along the coast. Spain's Bruno de Heceta sailed the coast, 1775. In 1792, British naval officer George Vancouver mapped the Puget Sound area, and American Capt. Robert Gray sailed up the Columbia R. Fur traders and missionaries arrived in the first half of the 19th cent. Final agreement on the border of Washington and Canada was made with Britain, 1846. Completion in 1883 of a transcontinental rail link between Puget Sound and the eastern U.S. aided immigration, and Washington became a state in 1889. In the 20th cent., cheap hydroelectric power spurred growth in the aluminum and aircraft industries. Founded in 1975, Microsoft became a computer software giant. Mount St. Helens erupted, 1980. With grunge music, Starbucks coffee, and Amazon.com, Seattle became a national trendsetter in the 1990s. Violent street protests disrupted a World Trade Organization meeting there in 1999. Gary Locke, in office 1997-2005, was the first U.S. governor of Chinese ancestry. A mudslide in Mar. 2014 killed 43 people in a rural area north of Seattle.

Famous Washingtonians. Paul Allen, Glenn Beck, Raymond Carver, Kurt Cobain, Bing Crosby, William O. Douglas, Bill Gates, Jimi Hendrix, Henry M. Jackson, Gary Larson, Mary McCarthy, Robert Motherwell, Edward R. Murrow, Apolo Ohno, Chris Pratt, Theodore Roethke, Ann Rule, Hope Solo, Hilary Swank, Julia Sweeney, Adam West, Marcus Whitman, Minoru Yamasaki. **Website.** access.wa.gov

West Virginia (WV)

Mountain State

People. Population: 1,844,128; rank: 38. **Pop. change** (2010-15): –0.5%. **Pop. density:** 76.7 per sq mi. **Racial**

distribution: 93.6% white; 3.6% black; 0.8% Asian; 0.2% Amer. Ind.; <0.05% Hawaiian/Pacific Islander; 2 or more races, 1.6%. **Hispanic pop.:** 1.5%.

Geography. Total area: 24,230 sq mi; rank: 41. **Land area:** 24,038 sq mi; rank: 41. **Acres forested:** 12.1 mil. **Location:** South Atlantic state bounded on the N by Pennsylvania, Maryland; on the S, W, and NW by Virginia, Kentucky, Ohio; on the E by Maryland and Virginia. **Climate:** humid continental climate except for marine modification in the lower panhandle. **Topography:** hilly to mountainous; Allegheny Plateau in the W covers two-thirds of state; mountains here are the highest in the state, over 4,000 ft. **Capital:** Charleston.

Economy. Chief industries: manufacturing, services, mining, tourism. **Chief manuf. goods:** chemicals, aluminum, motor vehicle parts, lumber and plywood, primary and fabricated metals. **Chief crops:** hay, apples, corn, peaches, soybeans, tobacco, wheat. **Farm income:** crops, $150.18 mil; livestock/animal prods., $682.67 mil. **Nonfuel minerals:** $395 mil; stone (crushed), cement (portland), lime, sand and gravel (industrial), cement (masonry). **Chief port:** Huntington. **Gross state product:** $73.7 bil. **Sales tax:** 6.0%. **Gasoline tax:** 51.60 cents/gal. **Employment distrib.:** 21.5% govt.; 17.3% trade/trans./util.; 6.1% mfg.; 16.8% ed./health; 8.6% prof./bus. serv.; 9.9% leisure/hosp.; 4.7% finance; 6.8% constr./mining/log.; 1.2% info.; 7.1% other serv. **Unemployment:** 6.7%. **Min. wage/hr.:** $8.75. **Per cap. pers. income:** $37,047. **New private housing:** 2,814 units/$417.2 mil. **Broadband internet:** 88.6%. **Commercial banks:** 74; deposits: $30.9 bil. **Savings institutions:** 4; deposits: $808 mil. **Lottery:** total sales: $1.2 bil; profit: $508.3 mil.

Federal govt. Fed. civ. employees: 15,036; **avg. salary:** $74,482. **Notable fed. facilities:** Natl. Radio Astronomy Observatory, Green Bank; Bureau of the Fiscal Service Bldg.; Alderson Fed. Prison Camp; FBI Criminal Justice Information Services.

Education. High school grad. rate: 84.5%. **4-year public coll./univ.:** 13; **2-yr. public:** 9; **4-yr. private:** 9.

Energy. Electricity use/cost: 1,158 kWh, $108.14.

State data. Motto: Montani Semper Liberi (Mountaineers are always free). **Flower:** Big rhododendron. **Bird:** Cardinal. **Tree:** Sugar maple. **Songs:** "The West Virginia Hills"; "This Is My West Virginia"; "West Virginia, My Home, Sweet Home." **Entered union:** June 20, 1863; rank: 35th.

Tourism. Tourist spending: $3.0 bil. **Attractions:** Harpers Ferry Natl. Historical Park, Appalachian Trail Conservancy and Visitor Ctr., in Harpers Ferry; Clay Center for the Arts and Sciences and Avampato Discovery Museum, Charleston; The Greenbrier resort, White Sulphur Springs; Berkeley Springs State Park; Seneca Rocks State Park; New River Gorge Natl. River; Beckley Exhibition Coal Mine; Monongahela Natl. Forest; Fenton Art Glass Company, Williamstown; Mountain State Forest Festival, Elkins; Mountain State Art & Craft Fair, Ripley; Natl. Radio Astronomy Observatory in Green Bank (with world's largest fully steerable radio telescope); Cass Scenic Railroad State Park. **Information:** West Virginia Division of Tourism, Capitol Complex, Bldg. 6, Rm. 525, Charleston, WV 25305; 1-800-CALLWVA; gotowv.com

History. Sparsely inhabited at the time of European contact, the area was primarily Native American hunting grounds. British explorers Thomas Batts and Robert Fallam reached the New R., 1671. Coal, discovered in 1742, was mined extensively by the mid-19th cent. White settlement led to conflicts with Native Americans, including a major battle in which settlers defeated an Indian confederacy at Point Pleasant, 1774. The region joined the Union as part of Virginia, 1788. Longstanding tensions between the E and W parts of the state came to a head in 1861, when Virginia seceded. Delegates of western counties, meeting at Wheeling, repudiated the act and created a new state, Kanawha, later renamed West Virginia, which was admitted to the Union in 1863. Poverty has been a problem for much of the state's subsequent history. It continued to rank low in per capita personal income, despite billions of dollars in federal contracts brought to the state by nine-term U.S. Sen. Robert Byrd, who passed away in 2010. Coal mining, though dangerous, continues to be a major industry; nearly 30 miners were killed in a mine explosion in 2010. In Jan. 2014, Gov. Earl Ray Tomblin banned water use for some 300,000 people for up to 10 days after coal processing chemicals leaked into a waterway. Flash flooding across the state killed at least 23 people in late June 2016.

Famous West Virginians. George Brett, Pearl S. Buck, Robert C. Byrd, Henry Louis Gates Jr., Stonewall Jackson, Don Knotts, Michael Joseph Owens, Brad Paisley, Mary Lou Retton, Walter Reuther, Cyrus Vance, Jerry West, Charles "Chuck" Yeager. **Website.** www.wv.gov

Wisconsin (WI)
Badger State

People. Population: 5,771,337; rank: 20. **Pop. change** (2010-15): 1.5%. **Pop. density:** 106.6 per sq mi. **Racial distribution:** 87.6% white; 6.6% black; 2.8% Asian; 1.1% Amer. Ind.; 0.1% Hawaiian/Pacific Islander; 2 or more races, 1.8%. **Hispanic pop.:** 6.6%.
Geography. Total area: 65,496 sq mi; rank: 23. **Land area:** 54,158 sq mi; rank: 25. **Acres forested:** 17.1 mil. **Location:** East North Central state bounded on the N by Lake Superior and Upper Michigan, on the E by Lake Michigan, on the S by Illinois, on the W by the St. Croix and Mississippi Rivers. **Climate:** long, cold winters and short, warm summers tempered by the Great Lakes. **Topography:** narrow Lake Superior Lowland plain met by Northern Highland, which slopes gently to the sandy crescent Central Plain; Western Upland in the SW; three broad parallel limestone ridges running N-S are separated by wide and shallow lowlands in the SE. **Capital:** Madison. **Chief airports:** Madison, Milwaukee.
Economy. Chief industries: services, manufacturing, trade, government, agriculture, tourism. **Chief manuf. goods:** transportation, dairy, animal slaughtering and processing, paper, printing, plastics, computers and electronics. **Chief crops:** corn, greenhouse and nursery, soybeans, potatoes, cranberries, hay, wheat, snap beans, apples, peas. **Farm income:** crops, $3.36 bil; livestock/animal prods., $9.41 bil. **Nonfuel minerals:** $3.6 bil; sand and gravel (industrial), sand and gravel (construction), stone (crushed), lime, stone (dimension). **Commercial fishing:** $5.1 mil. **Chief ports:** Superior, Milwaukee, Green Bay. **Gross state product:** $305.8 bil. **Sales tax:** 5.0%. **Gasoline tax:** 51.30 cents/gal. **Employment distrib.:** 14.3% govt.; 18.4% trade/trans./util.; 16.0% mfg.; 15.0% ed./health; 10.6% prof./bus. serv.; 9.5% leisure/hosp.; 5.2% finance; 4.1% constr./mining/log.; 1.6% info.; 5.1% other serv. **Unemployment:** 4.6%. **Min. wage/hr.:** $7.25. **Per cap. pers. income:** $45,617. **New private housing:** 16,793 units/$3.1 bil. **Broadband internet:** 88.2%. **Commercial banks:** 239; deposits: $128.8 bil. **Savings institutions:** 30; deposits: $11.5 bil. **Lottery:** total sales: $574.6 mil; profit: $166.8 mil.
Federal govt. Fed. civ. employees: 15,159; **avg. salary:** $71,941. **Notable fed. facilities:** Ft. McCoy; USDA Forest Products Lab.
Education. High school grad. rate: 88.6%. **4-year public coll./univ.:** 14; **2-yr. public:** 17; **4-yr. private:** 30.
Energy. Electricity use/cost: 694 kWh, $94.88.
State data. Motto: Forward. **Flower:** Wood violet. **Bird:** American robin. **Tree:** Sugar maple. **Song:** "On, Wisconsin!" **Entered union:** May 29, 1848; rank: 30th.
Tourism. Tourist spending: $10.6 bil. **Attractions:** Wade House, Greenbush; Villa Louis, Prairie du Chien; Circus World Museum, Baraboo; Wisconsin Dells; Old World Wisconsin, Eagle; shoreline and state parks of Door County; Chequamegon-Nicolet Natl. Forest; House on the Rock, Taliesin, in Spring Green; Monona Terrace Community and Convention Ctr., Madison; Milwaukee Art Museum, Pabst Mansion, in Milwaukee. **Information:** Wisconsin Dept. of Tourism, 201 W. Washington Ave., P.O. Box 8690, Madison, WI 53708; 1-800-432-TRIP; www.travelwisconsin.com
History. At the time of European contact, Ojibwa, Menominee, Winnebago, Kickapoo, Sauk, Fox, and Potawatomi peoples inhabited the area. French explorer Jean Nicolet reached Green Bay, 1634; French missionaries and fur traders followed. The British took over, 1763. The U.S. won the land after the American Revolution but did not wield control until forts were established at Green Bay and Prairie du Chien, 1816. Native Americans rebelled against the seizure of tribal lands in the Black Hawk War, 1832, but were defeated and relocated to reservations. Wisconsin became a territory, 1836, and a state, 1848. Some 96,000 soldiers served the Union cause during the Civil War. Many immigrants arrived from Germany, Poland, and Scandinavia. Wisconsin agriculture focused on dairy; Milwaukee became a manufacturing center. As governor, 1901-06, Robert La Follette pushed Progressive reforms such as direct primary voting and consumer protection laws. The era of McCarthyism ended when anti-Communist crusader U.S. Sen. Joseph McCarthy of Wisconsin was censured by the Senate, 1954. The state legislature passed controversial measures in 2011 to restrict collective bargaining by some 170,000 public-sector employees and in 2014 became the 25th state to pass a "right-to-work" law allowing private-sector workers to choose not to join unions and pay dues even if they benefit from union contracts.

Famous Wisconsinites. Don Ameche, Carrie Chapman Catt, Willem Dafoe, Edna Ferber, Hamlin Garland, King Camp Gillette, Harry Houdini, Robert La Follette, (Vladzio Valentino) Liberace, Alfred Lunt, Pat O'Brien, Georgia O'Keeffe, Danica Patrick, Les Paul, William H. Rehnquist, John Ringling, Donald K. "Deke" Slayton, Spencer Tracy, Orson Welles, Laura Ingalls Wilder, Thornton Wilder, Frank Lloyd Wright.
Website. www.wisconsin.gov

Wyoming (WY)
Equality State, Cowboy State

People. Population: 586,107; rank: 51. **Pop. change** (2010-15): 4.0%. **Pop. density:** 6.0 per sq mi. **Racial distribution:** 92.7% white; 1.4% black; 1.0% Asian; 2.7% Amer. Ind.; 0.1% Hawaiian/Pacific Islander; 2 or more races, 2.1%. **Hispanic pop.:** 9.9%.
Geography. Total area: 97,813 sq mi; rank: 10. **Land area:** 97,093 sq mi; rank: 9. **Acres forested:** 10.5 mil. **Location:** Mountain state in the high western plateaus of the Great Plains. **Climate:** semidesert conditions throughout; true desert in the Bighorn and Great Divide Basins. **Topography:** eastern Great Plains rise to the foothills of the Rocky Mts.; the Continental Divide crosses the state from the NW to the SE. **Capital:** Cheyenne.
Economy. Chief industries: mineral extraction, oil, natural gas, tourism and recreation, agriculture. **Chief manuf. goods:** petroleum, chemicals, fabricated metal, beet sugar, lumber. **Chief crops:** hay, sugar beets, barley, dry beans, wheat, corn, greenhouse and nursery, oats. **Farm income:** crops, $401.47 mil; livestock/animal prods., $1.43 bil. **Livestock:** $1.18 bil. **Nonfuel minerals:** $2.4 bil; soda ash, helium (Grade-A), clays (bentonite), sand and gravel (construction), cement (portland). **Gross state product:** $38.6 bil. **Sales tax:** 4.0%. **Gasoline tax:** 42.40 cents/gal. **Employment distrib.:** 26.0% govt.; 18.9% trade/trans./util.; 3.4% mfg.; 9.8% ed./health; 6.6% prof./bus. serv.; 12.1% leisure/hosp.; 3.7% finance; 14.5% constr./mining/log.; 1.3% info.; 3.6% other serv. **Unemployment:** 4.2%. **Min. wage/hr.:** $5.15 ($7.25). **Per cap. pers. income:** $55,303. **New private housing:** 1,903 units/$607.7 mil. **Broadband internet:** 84.1%. **Commercial banks:** 44; deposits: $14.4 bil. **Savings institutions:** 2; deposits: $393 mil. **Lottery:** total sales: $17.5 mil.
Federal govt. Fed. civ. employees: 5,548; **avg. salary:** $64,408. **Notable fed. facilities:** Warren AFB.
Education. High school grad. rate: 78.6%. **4-year public coll./univ.:** 1; **2-yr. public:** 7; **4-yr. private:** 1.
Energy. Electricity use/cost: 863 kWh, $90.60.
State data. Motto: Equal rights. **Flower:** Indian paintbrush. **Bird:** Western meadowlark. **Tree:** Plains cottonwood. **Song:** "Wyoming." **Entered union:** July 10, 1890; rank: 44th.
Tourism. Tourist spending: $3.2 bil. **Attractions:** Yellowstone Natl. Park (est. 1872, first U.S. national park); Grand Teton Natl. Park; Natl. Elk Refuge, Jackson; Devils Tower Natl. Monument; Ft. Laramie Natl. Historic Site; Oregon Trail ruts, Guernsey; Buffalo Bill Historical Ctr., Cody; Cheyenne Frontier Days. **Information:** Wyoming Travel and Tourism, 1520 Etchepare Cir., Cheyenne, WY 82007; 1-800-225-5996; www.wyomingtourism.org
History. Inhabited for at least 12,000 years, the region supported Shoshone, Crow, Cheyenne, Oglala Sioux, and Arapaho peoples when Europeans arrived. France's Vérendrye brothers were the first Europeans to see the region, 1742-43. John Colter, an American, traversed the Yellowstone area, 1807-08. Trappers and fur traders followed in the 1820s. Forts Laramie and Bridger became important stops on trails to the West Coast. Population grew after the Union Pacific railroad crossed the state, 1867-68. Wyoming became a territory, 1868, and the first to extend full voting rights to women, 1869. Statehood was attained, 1890. Disputes between large landowners and small ranchers culminated in the Johnson County Cattle War, 1892; federal troops were called in to restore order. Nellie Tayloe Ross was the first woman governor to take office in the U.S., 1925. Wyoming, the least populous state, has relied on the energy, tourism, and ranching industries in recent decades. Dick Cheney, Wyoming's representative in the U.S. House, 1979-89, served as U.S. vice pres. (2001-09).
Famous Wyomingites. James Bridger, Dick Cheney, William F. "Buffalo Bill" Cody, Curt Gowdy, Esther Hobart Morris, Nellie Tayloe Ross.
Website. www.wyoming.gov

District of Columbia (DC)

People. Population: 672,228; rank: 49. **Pop. change** (2010-15): 11.7%. **Pop. density:** 11,020.1 per sq mi. **Racial distribution:** 44.1% white; 48.3% black; 4.2% Asian; 0.6% Amer. Ind.; 0.2% Hawaiian/Pacific Islander; 2 or more races, 2.7%. **Hispanic pop.:** 10.6%.

Geography. Total area: 68 sq mi; rank: 51. **Land area:** 61 sq mi; rank: 51. **Acres forested:** NA. **Location:** at the confluence of the Potomac and Anacostia Rivers, flanked by Maryland on the N, E, and SE and by Virginia on the SW. **Climate:** hot humid summers, mild winters. **Topography:** low hills rise toward the N away from the Potomac R. and slope to the S; highest elevation, 409 ft; lowest on Potomac R., 1 ft.

Economy. Chief industries: government, legal, publishing, medical, service, tourism. **Gross state product:** $122.5 bil. **Sales tax:** 5.75%. **Gasoline tax:** 41.90 cents/gal. **Employment distrib.:** 30.9% govt.; 4.4% trade/trans./util.; 0.2% mfg.; 16.6% ed./health; 21.3% prof./bus. serv.; 9.8% leisure/hosp.; 3.9% finance; 1.8% constr./mining/log.; 2.1% info.; 9.0% other serv. **Unemployment:** 6.9%. **Min. wage/hr.:** $11.50. **Per cap. pers. income:** $71,496. **New private housing:** 4,956 units/$495.0 mil. **Broadband internet:** 93.7%. **Commercial banks:** 32; deposits: $45.0 bil. **Savings institutions:** 3; deposits: $166 mil. **Lottery:** total sales: $212.3 mil; profit: $54.3 mil.

Federal govt. Fed. civ. employees: 171,082; **avg. salary:** $111,561.

Education. High school grad. rate: 61.4%. **4-year public coll./univ.:** 2; **2-yr. public:** 0; **4-yr. private:** 13.

Energy. Electricity use/cost: 721 kWh, $91.90.

District data. Motto: Justitia omnibus (Justice for all). **Flower:** American beauty rose. **Bird:** Wood thrush. **Tree:** Scarlet oak.

Tourism. Tourist spending: $10.1 bil. **Attractions:** See Attractions in and Around Washington, DC, pp. 463-64. **Information:** Destination DC, 901 7th St. NW, 4th Fl., Washington, DC, 20001-3719; 1-800-422-8644; www.washington.org

History. The District of Columbia, coextensive with the city of Washington, is the seat of the U.S. federal government. It lies on the west central edge of Maryland on the Potomac R., opposite Virginia. The Piscataway, an Algonquian-speaking people, were living in the region when Europeans arrived in the 17th cent. Proposals for a "federal town" for the deliberations of the Continental Congress were made in 1783. Authorized by Congress, 1790, Pres. George Washington chose the Potomac site and persuaded landowners to sell their holdings to the government. Its area was originally 100 sq mi taken from the sovereignty of Maryland and Virginia. Virginia's portion south of the Potomac was given back to that state in 1846.

Pres. Washington chose Pierre Charles L'Enfant, a Frenchman, to plan the capital. Surveyor Andrew Ellicott finished the official map and design of the city, assisted by Benjamin Banneker, a black architect and astronomer. Washington laid the cornerstone of the north wing of the Capitol building, 1793, and Pres. John Adams moved to the new national capital, 1800. The City of Washington was incorporated, 1802. British troops invaded, 1814, setting fire to the Capitol, the President's House (as the White House was then called), and other buildings. Pres. Abraham Lincoln ended slavery in the district, 1862. Many African Americans arrived after the Civil War, but racial segregation remained legal until the mid-20th cent. After federal government expansion spurred population growth, 1930-50, an exodus to the suburbs shrank the city's population, 1950-2005.

The 23rd Amendment (1961) granted residents the right to vote for president and vice president. Congress, which has legislative authority over the District under the Constitution, approved legislation in 1970 giving the District one delegate to the House of Representatives, who could vote in committee but not on the floor. Voters approved, 1974, a congressionally drafted charter giving them the right to elect their own mayor and city council. The district won the right to levy taxes, but Congress retained power to veto council actions and approve the city budget. Security measures were dramatically increased after terrorists attacked the U.S. on Sept. 11, 2001. After a 34-year absence, major league baseball returned to the city in 2005.

Famous Washingtonians. Edward Albee, Michael Chabon, Frederick Douglass, John Foster Dulles, Kevin Durant, Edward Kennedy "Duke" Ellington, Marvin Gaye, Katharine Graham, Goldie Hawn, Taraji P. Henson, J. Edgar Hoover, Bill Nye, Pete Sampras, John Philip Sousa.

Website. www.dc.gov

OUTLYING U.S. AREAS

American Samoa (AS)

People. Population (2015 est.): 54,343. **Pop. change** (2010-15): –2.1%. **Pop. density:** 715.0 per sq mi. **Racial distribution** (2010): 92.6% Hawaiian/Pacific Islander; 3.6% Asian; 1.2% other; 2 or more races 2.7%. **Languages:** Samoan, English, Tongan.

Geography. Total area: 581 sq mi. **Land area:** 76 sq mi. **Acres forested:** 43,631. **Location:** most southerly of all lands under U.S. sovereignty, about 2,300 mi SW of Honolulu. It is an unincorporated territory consisting of seven islands: Samoan group: **Tutuila** (52.59 sq mi), **Aunu'u** (0.59 sq mi); Manu'a group: **Ta'u** (17.57 sq mi), **Olosega** (2.03 sq mi), **Ofu** (2.83 sq mi); and the atolls **Rose** (0.03 sq mi) and **Swains** (1.38 sq mi). **Climate:** marine tropical, avg. temp 82°F with little seasonal variation; avg. annual rainfall about 36 in. **Topography:** volcanic islands, rugged peaks, and limited coastal plains. About 70% of the land is bush and mountains. **Capital:** Pago Pago, on Tutuila. **Airport:** Pago Pago.

Economy. Chief industries: tuna fishing and processing, trade, services, tourism. **Chief crops:** giant taro, taro, yams, coconuts, breadfruits, bananas, papayas. **Livestock** (2008): 35,709 chickens, 16,904 hogs/pigs. **Nonfuel minerals:** crushed stone, traprock. **Commercial fishing** (2008): $9.7 mil. **Unemployment** (2007): 29.8%. **Gross domestic product** (2014): $645 mil. **Broadband internet:** NA. **Commercial banks:** 2; deposits: $174 mil.

Education. 4-year coll./univ.: 1; **2-yr. public:** 0; **4-yr. private:** 0.

Energy. Total electricity production (2013 est.): 156.4 mil kWh.

Fed. civ. employees (Mar. 2016): 84; **avg. salary:** $66,323.

Misc. data. Motto: Samoa Muamua le Atua (In Samoa, God is first). **Flower:** Paogo (Ula-fala). **Plant:** Ava. **Song:** "Amerika Samoa."

Tourism. Attractions: Natl. Park of American Samoa; Natl. Marine Sanctuary of American Samoa; Jean P. Haydon Museum. **Information:** Office of Tourism, Dept. of Commerce, American Samoa Govt., P.O. Box 1147, Pago Pago, AS 96799; (684) 699-9411; www.amsamoatourism.com

History. A tripartite agreement between Great Britain, Germany, and the U.S. in 1899 gave the U.S. sovereignty over the eastern islands of the Samoan group; these islands became American Samoa. Local chiefs ceded Tutuila and Aunu'u to the U.S. in 1900 and the Manu'a group and Rose Island in 1904; Swains Island was annexed in 1925. Samoa (Western), comprising the larger islands of the Samoan group, was a New Zealand mandate and UN Trusteeship until it became independent Jan. 1, 1962 (now called Samoa).

From 1900 to 1951, American Samoa was under the jurisdiction of the U.S. Navy. Since 1951, it has been under the Interior Dept. On Jan. 3, 1978, the first popularly elected Samoan governor and lieutenant governor were inaugurated. Previously, the governor was appointed by the Sec. of the Interior. American Samoa has a bicameral legislature and elects a delegate to the U.S. House of Representatives who has a voice but no vote, except in committees.

Five of the seven islands are volcanoes. Scientists discovered a rapidly growing volcano, Vailulu'u, between Ta'u and Rose in 1975.

The tuna canning industry has been the backbone of the economy since the 1950s, but one of the two canneries closed in 2009. An 8.1-magnitude earthquake in Sept. 2009 triggered a tsunami that severely damaged Tutuila.

American Samoans are of Polynesian origin. They are nationals of the U.S. As of 2010, 109,637 lived in the U.S., including 18,287 in Hawaii and 40,100 in California.

Website. www.americansamoa.gov

Guam (GU)

People. Population (2015 est.): 161,785. **Pop change** (2010-15): 1.5%. **Pop. density:** 770.4 per sq mi. **Racial/ethnic distribution** (2010 est.): 37.3% Chamorro; 26.3% Filipino; 12.0% other Pac. Isl.; 7.1% white. **Languages:** English, Chamorro, Philippine/other Pacific Island languages.

Geography. Total area: 571 sq mi. **Land area:** 210 sq mi. **Acres forested:** 63,830. **Location:** largest and southernmost of the Mariana Islands in the West Pacific, 3,700 mi W of Hawaii. **Climate:** tropical, with temperatures from 70° to 90°F; rainy July to Nov., avg. annual rainfall about 80-100 in. **Topography:** coralline limestone plateau in the N; southern chain of low volcanic mountains slope gently to the W, more steeply to coastal cliffs on the E; general elevation, 500 ft; highest point, Mt. Lamlam, 1,332 ft. **Capital:** Hagåtña. **Chief airport:** Tumuning.

Economy. Chief industries: U.S. military, tourism, construction, shipping, concrete products, printing and publishing. **Chief manuf. goods:** textiles, foods. **Chief crops:** watermelons, cucumbers, eggplant, long beans, bananas, corn. **Livestock** (2007): 533 chickens, 112 cattle, 635 hogs/pigs, 124 goats. **Nonfuel minerals** (2008): $3.8 mil; crushed stone. **Commercial fishing** (2008): $499,095. **Chief port:** Apra Harbor. **Gross domestic product** (2014): $5.5 bil. **Employment distrib.** (Dec. 2012): 30.2% trade/trans; 26.7% serv.; 25.5% govt.; 10.6% constr.; 2.7% mfg.; 0.2% agric. **Unemployment** (Mar. 2015): 6.9%. **Per capita income** (2010): $12,864. **Broadband internet:** 97.6%. **Commercial banks:** 5; deposits $2.3 bil. **Savings institutions:** 1; deposits: $91 mil.

Education. 4-year public coll./univ.: 1; **2-yr. public:** 1; **4-yr. private:** 1.

Energy. Total electricity production (2013 est.): 1.6 bil kWh.

Federal govt. Fed. employees (Mar. 2016): 2,387; **avg. salary:** $63,759. **Notable fed. facilities:** Andersen AFB.

Misc. data. Motto: Where America's day begins. **Flower:** Puti Tai Nobio (Bougainvillea). **Bird:** Ko'ko (Guam rail). **Tree:** Ifit (Intsia bijuga). **Song:** "Stand Ye Guamanians."

Tourism. Attractions: Ritidian Point, Guam Natl. Wildlife Refuge; War in the Pacific Natl. Historical Park; Chamorro Village; Two Lovers Point. **Information:** Guam Visitors Bureau, 401 Pale San Vitores Rd., Tumon, Guam 96913; (671) 646-5278; www.visitguam.org

History. Guam was probably settled by voyagers from the Indonesian-Philippine archipelago by 3rd cent. BCE. Pottery, rice cultivation, and megalithic technology show strong East Asian cultural influence. Centralized, village clan-based communities engaged in agriculture and offshore fishing. The estimated population by the early 16th cent. was 50,000-75,000. Portuguese explorer Ferdinand Magellan, sailing for Spain, arrived in the Marianas Mar. 6, 1521. They were colonized in 1668 by Spanish missionaries, who named them the Mariana Islands in honor of Maria Anna, queen of Spain. When Spain ceded Guam to the U.S., it sold the other Marianas to Germany. Japan obtained a League of Nations mandate over the German islands in 1919; in Dec. 1941 it seized Guam, which was retaken by the U.S. in July-Aug. 1944.

Guam is a self-governing organized unincorporated U.S. territory. The Organic Act of 1950 provided for a governor, elected to a four-year term, and a 21-member unicameral legislature, elected biennially by the residents, who are American citizens. In 1970, the first governor was elected. In 1972, a U.S. law gave Guam one U.S. House delegate, who has a voice but no vote except in committees.

Guam's quest to change its status to a U.S. commonwealth began in the late 1970s. The Guam Commission on Self-Determination, created in 1984, developed a draft Commonwealth Act. In 1993, legislation proposing a change of status was submitted to the U.S. Congress. In 1994, the U.S. Congress passed legislation transferring 3,200 acres of land on Guam from federal to local control. The Navy approved in 2015 a plan to move 5,000 Marines stationed in Okinawa, Japan, to Guam.

Website. www.guam.gov

Commonwealth of the Northern Mariana Islands (MP)

People. Population (2015 est.): 52,344. **Pop. change** (2010-15): –2.9%. **Pop. density:** 287.6 per sq mi. **Racial/ethnic distribution** (2010 est.): 50.0% Asian; 34.9% Hawaiian/Pacific Islander; 2.5% other; 2 or more races/ethnicities, 12.7%. **Languages:** Philippine languages, Chinese, Chamorro (official), English (official), other Pacific Island languages.

Geography. Total area: 1,976 sq mi. **Land area:** 182 sq mi. **Acres forested:** 50,218. **Location:** between Guam and the Tropic of Cancer, the 14 islands of the Northern Marianas form a 300-mi-long archipelago. The indigenous population is concentrated on the three largest of the six inhabited islands: **Saipan,** the seat of government and commerce, **Rota,** and **Tinian. Climate:** tropical, with avg. temperature around 82°F, moderated by NE trade winds; avg. annual rainfall 80-100 in. **Topography:** limestone southern islands with even terraces, coral reefs; volcanic northern isles. **Capital:** Saipan. **Airport:** Saipan.

Economy. Chief industries: banking, construction, fishing, mining, tourism, apparel manufacturing, retail. **Chief manuf. goods:** apparel, stone, clay and glass prods. **Chief crops:** bananas, cucumbers, sweet potatoes, taro, watermelons. **Livestock** (2007): 9,700 chickens, 1,395 cattle, 1,483 hogs/pigs. **Commercial fishing** (2010 est.): $608,971. **Chief port:** Saipan. **Gross domestic product** (2014): $839 mil.

Employment distrib.: 1.9% agriculture; 10.0% industry; 88.1% services. **Unemployment** (2010): 11.2%. **Broadband internet:** NA. **Commercial banks:** 3; deposits: $647 mil.

Education. 4-year public coll./univ.: 1; **2-yr. public:** 0; **4-yr. private:** 0.

Energy. Total electricity production (2009): 60,600 kWh.

Federal govt. Fed. civ. employees (Mar. 2016): 63; **avg. salary:** $61,896.

Misc. data. Flower: Plumeria. **Bird:** Mariana fruit-dove. **Tree:** Flame tree. **Song:** "Gi Talo Gi Halom Tasi" (In the Middle of the Sea).

Tourism. Attractions: House of Taga; American Memorial Park; Banzai Cliff. **Information:** Marianas Visitors Authority, P.O. Box 500861, Saipan, MP 96950; (670) 664-3200; www.mymarianas.com

History. The people of the Northern Marianas are predominantly of Chamorro cultural extraction, although Carolinians and immigrants from other areas of E. Asia and Micronesia have also settled in the islands. English is among the several languages commonly spoken.

The German-controlled Northern Marianas were placed under Japanese control by a League of Nations mandate after World War I. The U.S. captured the islands during World War II. From July 18, 1947, the U.S. administered the Northern Marianas under a trusteeship agreement with the UN Security Council. In 1975, the residents voted to become a U.S. commonwealth.

The Northern Mariana Islands has been self-governing since 1978, when a constitution drafted and adopted by the people became effective and a popularly elected bicameral legislature (two-year term), with offices of governor (four-year term) and lieut. governor, was inaugurated. Pres. Ronald Reagan proclaimed the Northern Marianas a commonwealth, 1986, and the UN formally ended its trusteeship, 1990. In 2008, U.S. law gave the islands one delegate to the U.S. House of Representatives who has a voice but no vote, except in committees.

Under the 1976 Commonwealth Covenant with the U.S., the islands are exempt from federal immigration and import laws, and minimum wage is lower than on the mainland. The garment-making industry, which has since boomed, has drawn accusations of sweatshop conditions from some critics. Legislation passed in 2007 was intended to raise the minimum wage to the federal rate by 2015, but it stood at $6.05 in 2015 with another 50-cent increase scheduled for Sept. 2016.

Website. gov.mp

Commonwealth of Puerto Rico (PR)
Estado Libre Asociado de Puerto Rico

People. Population: 3,474,182 (about 4.6 mil additional Puerto Ricans reside in mainland U.S.). **Pop. change** (2010-15): –6.8%. **Pop. density:** 1,014.7 per sq mi. **Racial distribution:** 75.8% white; 12.4% black; 0.2% Asian; 0.5% Amer. Ind.; <0.05% Hawaiian/Pacific Islander; 2 or more races, 3.3%. **Hispanic pop.:** 99.0%. **Languages:** Spanish and English are joint official languages.

Geography. Total area: 5,325 sq mi. **Land area:** 3,424 sq mi. **Acres forested:** 1.2 mil. **Location:** island between the Atlantic to the N and the Caribbean to the S; it is easternmost of the West Indies group called the Greater Antilles, of which Cuba, Hispaniola, and Jamaica are the larger islands. **Climate:** mild, with a mean temperature of 77°F. **Topography:** mountainous throughout three-fourths of its rectangular area, surrounded by a broken coastal plain; highest peak, Cerro de Punto, 4,390 ft. **Capital:** San Juan. **Chief airport:** San Juan.

Economy. Chief industries: manufacturing, service, tourism. **Chief manuf. goods:** pharmaceuticals, medical equip., electronics, apparel, food products. **Chief crops:** pumpkins, coffee, watermelons, plantains, yams, oranges, pineapples, sugarcane, bananas. **Livestock** (2007): 1.4 mil chickens, 5.1 mil broilers, 490,817 cattle, 11,137 sheep, 69,892 hogs/pigs. **Nonfuel minerals** (2008): $164 mil; crushed stone, lime, salt, cement (portland), clays (common). **Commercial fishing** (2008): $3.8 mil. **Chief ports:** San Juan, Ponce, Mayaguez. **Gross domestic product** (2015): $102.9 bil. **Employment distrib.:** 25.7% govt.; 19.5% trade/trans./util.; 8.0% mfg.; 13.9% ed./health; 12.4% prof./bus. serv.; 9.3% leisure/hosp.; 4.6% finance; 2.5% constr./mining/log.; 2.3% info.; 2.0% other serv. **Unemployment** (Dec. 2014 est.): 13.7%. **Per capita income** (2015): $18,347. **Broadband internet:** 64.3%. **Commercial banks:** 7; deposits: $67.9 bil. **Lottery** (2009): total sales: $421.2 mil; profit: $146.9 mil.

Federal govt. Fed. civ. employees (Mar. 2016): 9,402; **avg. salary:** $65,906. **Notable fed. facilities:** PR Natl. Guard Training Area at Camp Santiago; Ft. Buchanan; Intl. Inst. of Tropical Forestry; Vieques Natl. Wildlife Refuge; USGS Caribbean Water Science Ctr.

Education. 4-year public coll./univ.: 14; **2-yr. public:** 4; **4-yr. private:** 45.

Energy. Total electricity production (2012 est.): 20.0 bil kWh.

Misc. data. Motto: Joannes Est Nomen Eius (John is his name). **Flower:** Maga. **Bird:** Reinita. **Tree:** Ceiba. **Anthem:** "La Borinqueña."

Tourism. Attractions: Museo de Arte de Ponce; San Felipe del Morro and San Cristóbal forts, San Juan Natl. Historic Site, Walled City of Old San Juan, Casa Blanca in San Juan; Arecibo Observatory; Cordillera Central mtn. range; El Yunque Natl. Forest (only tropical rain forest in Natl. Forest system); Cathedral of San Juan Bautista; Porta Coeli (Doorway to Heaven) Church and Religious Art Museum, San Germán; Rio Camuy Cave Park, Camuy; Mosquito Bay. **Information:** The Puerto Rico Tourism Company, La Princesa Bldg. #2, Paseo La Princesa, Old San Juan, PR 00902; (800) 866-7827; www.seepuertorico.com

History. Puerto Rico (or Borinquen, after the original Arawak Indian name, Boriquen) was visited by Christopher Columbus on his second voyage, Nov. 19, 1493. In 1508, the Spanish arrived.

Sugarcane was introduced, 1515, and slaves were imported three years later. Gold mining petered out, 1570. Spaniards fought off a series of British and Dutch attacks; slavery was abolished, 1873. Under the Treaty of Paris, Puerto Rico was ceded to the U.S. after the Spanish-American War, 1898. In 1952 the people voted in favor of commonwealth status.

The Commonwealth of Puerto Rico is a self-governing part of the U.S. with a primarily Hispanic culture. The island's citizens have virtually the same control over their internal affairs as do the 50 states of the U.S. However, they do not vote in national general elections, only in national primaries.

Puerto Rico is represented in the U.S. House of Representatives by a Resident Commissioner who has a voice but no vote, except in committees.

No federal income tax is collected from residents on income earned from local sources in Puerto Rico. Nevertheless, as part of the U.S. legal system, Puerto Rico is subject to the provisions of the U.S. Constitution; most federal laws apply as they do in the 50 states.

Puerto Rico's famous "Operation Bootstrap," begun in the late 1940s, succeeded in changing the island from the "Poorhouse of the Caribbean" to an area with the highest per capita income in Latin America. This program encouraged manufacturing and development of the tourist trade by selective tax exemptions, low-interest loans, and other incentives. Despite the marked success of Puerto Rico's development efforts over an extended period of time, per capita income in Puerto Rico is low in comparison to that of the 50 states.

In plebiscites held in 1967, 1993, and 1998, voters chose to retain commonwealth status. Protests mounted in the late-1990s over the U.S. Navy's use of Vieques Island for live ammunition training; official military exercises there were terminated, 2003. Puerto Rico went into default for the first time in its history Aug. 2015 after it missed a bond payment. Pres. Barack Obama signed contentious debt-relief legislation June 30, 2016, one day before Puerto Rico failed to make a fourth, much larger payment. The island had a total debt load of more than $70 bil.

Cultural facilities and events. Festival Casals classical music concerts, mid-June; Puerto Rico Symphony Orchestra at Music Conservatory; Botanical Garden and Museum of Anthropology, Art, and History at the Univ. of Puerto Rico; Institute of Puerto Rican Culture, at the Dominican Convent.

Famous Puerto Ricans. Julia de Burgos, Marta Casals Istomin, Pablo Casals, José Celso Barbosa, Orlando Cepeda, Roberto Clemente, José de Diego, José Feliciano, Doña Felisa Rincón de Gautier, Luis A. Ferré, José Ferrer, Commodore Diégo E. Hernández, Miguel Hernández Agosto, Rafael Hernández (El Jíbarito), Rafael Hernández Colón, Raúl Juliá, René Marqués, Ricky Martin, Concha Meléndez, Rita Moreno, Luis Muñoz Marín, Luis Palés Matos, Joaquin Phoenix, Adm. Horacio Rivero.

Website. www.pr.gov (in Spanish)

Virgin Islands (VI)

St. John, St. Croix, St. Thomas

People. Population (2015 est.): 103,574. **Pop. change** (2010-15): –2.7%. **Pop. density:** 772.9 per sq mi. **Racial distribution** (2010): 76.0% black; 15.6% white; 6.2% other race; 2 or more races, 2.1%. **Languages:** English (official), Spanish, Creole.

Geography. Total area: 733 sq mi. **Land area:** 134 sq mi. **Acres forested:** 45,163. **Location:** 3 larger and 50 smaller islands and cays in the S and W of the V.I. group (British V.I. colony to the N and E), which is situated 70 mi E of Puerto Rico;

W of Anegada Passage, a major channel connecting the Atlantic Ocean and Caribbean Sea. **Climate:** subtropical; sun tempered by gentle trade winds; humidity is low; avg. temperature 78°F. **Topography:** St. Thomas is mainly a ridge of hills running E-W and has little tillable land; St. Croix rises abruptly in the N, slopes to flatlands and lagoons in the S; St. John has steep, lofty hills and valleys with little level tillable land. **Capital:** Charlotte Amalie on St. Thomas. **Chief airport:** Charlotte Amalie.

Economy. Chief industries: retail, petroleum, tourism, prof. consulting. **Chief manuf. goods:** rum, stone, glass and clay products, electronics, textiles. **Chief crops:** cucumbers, coconuts, mangoes, tomatoes, bananas. **Livestock** (2007): 699 chickens, 776 cattle, 2,981 sheep, 1,125 hogs/pigs, 2,331 goats. **Nonfuel minerals:** crushed stone, limestone, traprock. **Commercial fishing** (2011): $7.1 mil. **Chief port:** Charlotte Amalie. **Gross domestic product** (2014): $3.7 bil. **Employment distrib.:** 28.7% govt.; 21.3% trade/trans./util.; 1.6% mfg.; 6.3% ed./health; 8.9% prof./bus. serv.; 19.5% leisure/hosp.; 5.5% finance; 3.9% constr./mining/log.; 1.6% info.; 2.6% other serv. **Unemployment** (2014): 13.0%. **Per capita income** (2012): $19,982. **Broadband internet:** 48.1%. **Commercial banks:** 4; deposits: $1.8 bil.

Education. 4-year public coll./univ.: 1; **2-yr. public:** 0; **4-yr. private:** 0.

Energy. Total electricity production (2012 est.): 777.9 mil kWh.

Federal govt. Fed. civ. employees (Mar. 2016): 349; **avg. salary:** $67,088.

Misc. data. Motto: United in pride and hope. **Flower:** Yellow cedar. **Bird:** Yellow breast. **Song:** "Virgin Islands March."

Tourism. Attractions: St. Croix Isl.: Salt River Bay Natl. Historic Park and Ecological Preserve, Christiansted Natl. Historic Site. St. John and Hassel Isls.: Virgin Islands Natl. Park. St. Thomas Isl.: Blackbeard's Castle, Coral World Ocean Park, Magens Bay, 99 Steps. **Information:** USVI Division of Tourism, P.O. Box 6400, St. Thomas 00804; 1-800-372-USVI; www.visitusvi.com

History. The islands were visited by Columbus in 1493. Spanish forces, 1555, defeated the Caribes and claimed the territory; by 1596 the native population was annihilated. The first permanent settlement in the U.S. territory, 1672, was by the Danes; U.S. purchased the islands, 1917, for defense purposes.

The Virgin Islands has a republican form of government, headed by a governor and lieut. governor elected, since 1970, by popular vote for four-year terms. There is a 15-member unicameral legislature, elected by popular vote for a two-year term. Residents of the V.I. have been U.S. citizens since 1927. Since 1973 they have elected a U.S. House delegate, who has a voice but no vote except in committees.

Website. www.vi.gov

Other Islands

Navassa lies between Haiti and Jamaica, 100 mi S of Guantánamo Bay, Cuba, in the Caribbean. It covers 1,147 acres and is uninhabited. Claimed 1857, a Coast Guard lighthouse was built 1917, now inoperative. Natl. Wildlife Refuge since 1999. Administered by the Dept. of Interior.

The three coral islands of **Wake Atoll**—**Wake, Wilkes,** and **Peale**—lie in the Pacific Ocean on a direct route from Hawaii to Hong Kong, about 2,300 mi W of Honolulu and 1,500 mi NE of Guam. The group is 4.5 mi long, 1.5 mi wide. Land area totals 2.5 sq mi. The U.S. annexed Wake Atoll Jan. 17, 1899. Japan occupied Wake 1941-45. Designated a National Historic Landmark in 1985. Wake is owned by the U.S. Air Force, administered by the Dept. of Interior, and used by the Army as a missile launch facility. The population consists of military personnel and contractors. Most infrastructure was damaged by super typhoon Ioke in 2006.

The following mostly uninhabited islands are part of the **Pacific/Remote Islands National Wildlife Refuge Complex**, which along with Wake Atoll are administered by the Dept. of Interior: **Midway Atoll**, acquired in 1867, has three main islands—Sand, Spit, and Eastern—1,250 mi WNW of Honolulu, with an area of about 1,500 acres. Naval activity ended in 1997. Has the world's largest colony of Laysan albatross. **Johnston Atoll**, 800 mi WSW of Honolulu, is two natural and two artificial islands across 107 sq mi administered by the Navy. Johnston was a nuclear test site in 1958, 1962; the Army disposed of chemical weapons 1990-2000. Cleanup ended in 2005. **Kingman Reef** is a barren, coral atoll 932 mi S of Hawaii, annexed 1922. **Palmyra Atoll** is 54 islets over 753 sq mi, 1,052 mi S of Hawaii; annexed with Hawaii in 1898. Part privately owned by the Nature Conservancy. **Jarvis Island** covers 1,086 acres, 1,300 mi S of Honolulu near the equator. West of Jarvis are **Howland and Baker Islands**, 36 mi apart and about 1,600 mi SW of Honolulu.

Sources: Population: Decennial Census and Population Estimates Program, U.S. Census Bureau, U.S. Dept. of Commerce. Population is as of July 1, 2015; population rank is indicated within parentheses. **Pop. density** specifies the number of persons per square mile (sq mi) of land **area**. Unless otherwise noted, **all other figures** are estimates for 2010-14 from the American Community Survey, U.S. Census Bureau. **Racial distribution** categories are abbreviated; their full forms are white, black or African American, Asian, American Indian and Alaska Native, Native Hawaiian and other Pacific Islander, some other race, two or more races. **Hispanic** or Latino persons may be of any race. **Language** is what is spoken at home; languages and Census-defined language groups other than Spanish spoken by less than 5% of the population over age 5 are generally omitted. **Employment:** Bureau of Labor Statistics, U.S. Dept. of Labor, for 2015. **Per capita income:** Bureau of Economic Analysis, U.S. Dept. of Commerce; figures apply to MSAs for 2014. **Educational attainment** is the percentage of persons ages 25 and up who have graduated high school (HS) and who have a bachelor's degree or higher. **Avg. commute** is the time it takes for workers 16 years and over to travel from home to work. "Drive" includes only those who drive to work alone. Forms of transport used by less than 10% are omitted. **Avg. home:** National Association of Realtors®. Figures represent median 2015 sales price of existing single-family homes in the metropolitan area; data not available for all cities. **Avg. rent** is the median gross rent (rent asked plus est. avg. cost of utilities) per month. **Mayor** (or other city leader) and **website:** World Almanac research as of mid-2016; subject to change. A nonpartisan mayor is one whose party affiliation was not indicated on the ballot.

Included here are the 100 most populous U.S. cities, according to U.S. Census Bureau estimates released in May 2016. Most data are for the city proper; some, where noted, apply to the Metropolitan Statistical Area (MSA). Inc. = incorporated; est. = established.

Albuquerque, New Mexico

Population: 559,121 (32). **Pop. density:** 2,972. **Pop. change (2010-15):** 2.2%. **Area:** 188.1 sq mi. **Racial distribution:** 71.7% white; 3.3% black; 2.6% Asian; 4.2% Amer. Ind.; 0.1% Pac. Isl.; 13.9% other; 2+ races 4.2%. **Hispanic pop.:** 47.3%. **Foreign born:** 10.7%. **U.S. citizens:** 93.2%. **Language:** 70.1% English only; 24.6% Spanish.
Employment: 251,968 employed; 5.7% unemployed. **Per capita income:** $37,345; change (2013-14): 4.1%. **Below poverty level:** 18.5%; 14.8% of families. **Educational attainment:** 88.9% HS; 33.2% bachelor's. **Avg. commute:** 21.2 min. 79.8% drive. **Housing units:** 240,961; 92.5% occupied. **Home ownership:** 59.3%. **Avg. home:** $180,800; change (2013-15): 3.7%. **Avg. rent:** $798.
Mayor: Richard J. Berry, nonpartisan
History: Founded 1706 by the Spanish; inc. 1890.
Website: www.cabq.gov

Anaheim, California

Population: 350,742 (56). **Pop. density:** 7,018. **Pop. change (2010-15):** 4.0%. **Area:** 50.0 sq mi. **Racial distribution:** 65.7% white; 2.4% black; 15.7% Asian; 0.3% Amer. Ind.; 0.3% Pac. Isl.; 12.2% other; 2+ races 3.3%. **Hispanic pop.:** 52.8%. **Foreign born:** 37.0%. **U.S. citizens:** 79.5%. **Language:** 39.1% English only; 44.0% Spanish.
Employment: 161,008 employed; 5.7% unemployed. **Per capita income:** $50,751; change (2013-14): 3.8%. **Below poverty level:** 16.9%; 14.0% of families. **Educational attainment:** 75.5% HS; 24.8% bachelor's. **Avg. commute:** 27.6 min. 75.5% drive; 13.4% carpool. **Housing units:** 104,764; 94.7% occupied. **Home ownership:** 47.4%. **Avg. home:** $707,500; change (2013-15): 8.6%. **Avg. rent:** $1,362.
Mayor: Tom Tait, nonpartisan
History: Founded 1857; inc. 1870. Home of Disneyland, the Anaheim Ducks, and the Los Angeles Angels.
Website: www.anaheim.net

Anchorage, Alaska

Population: 298,695 (65). **Pop. density:** 175. **Pop. change (2010-15):** 1.8%. **Area:** 1,706.7 sq mi. **Racial distribution:** 65.6% white; 5.9% black; 8.5% Asian; 6.9% Amer. Ind.; 2.2% Pac. Isl.; 1.6% other; 2+ races 9.4%. **Hispanic pop.:** 8.3%. **Foreign born:** 9.7%. **U.S. citizens:** 95.7%. **Language:** 82.3% English only; 4.7% Spanish.
Employment: 150,301 employed; 5.0% unemployed. **Per capita income:** $57,131; change (2013-14): 5.2%. **Below poverty level:** 8.3%; 5.6% of families. **Educational attainment:** 92.5% HS; 32.9% bachelor's. **Avg. commute:** 19.4 min. 75.2% drive; 12.1% carpool. **Housing units:** 113,715; 92.5% occupied. **Home ownership:** 59.8%. **Avg. rent:** $1,172.
Mayor: Ethan Berkowitz, nonpartisan
History: Founded 1914 as a construction camp for railroad; HQ of Alaska Defense Command, WWII. Severely damaged in earthquake, 1964. Current population center of Alaska.
Website: www.muni.org

Arlington, Texas

Population: 388,125 (50). **Pop. density:** 4,047. **Pop. change (2010-15):** 6.0%. **Area:** 95.9 sq mi. **Racial distribution:** 66.0% white; 19.8% black; 7.0% Asian; 0.4% Amer. Ind.; 0.1% Pac. Isl.; 4.0% other; 2+ races 2.6%. **Hispanic pop.:** 28.7%. **Foreign born:** 19.7%. **U.S. citizens:** 87.8%. **Language:** 67.5% English only; 22.3% Spanish.
Employment: 193,972 employed; 4.0% unemployed. **Per capita income:** $49,506; change (2013-14): 3.9%. **Below poverty level:** 16.9%; 13.5% of families. **Educational attainment:** 84.6% HS; 28.9% bachelor's. **Avg. commute:** 26.1 min. 81.8% drive; 11.6% carpool. **Housing units:** 146,698; 91.1% occupied. **Home ownership:** 56.7%. **Avg. home:** $207,200; change (2013-15): 18.0%. **Avg. rent:** $861.
Mayor: Jeff Williams, nonpartisan
History: Settled in 1840s; inc. 1884.
Website: www.arlington-tx.gov

Atlanta, Georgia

Population: 463,878 (39). **Pop. density:** 3,485. **Pop. change (2010-15):** 9.7%. **Area:** 133.1 sq mi. **Racial distribution:** 39.7% white; 52.9% black; 3.8% Asian; 0.2% Amer. Ind.; <0.05% Pac. Isl.; 1.4% other; 2+ races 2.0%. **Hispanic pop.:** 5.6%. **Foreign born:** 7.6%. **U.S. citizens:** 94.7%. **Language:** 89.2% English only; 5.1% Spanish.
Employment: 218,702 employed; 6.3% unemployed. **Per capita income:** $43,472; change (2013-14): 3.9%. **Below poverty level:** 25.2%; 19.9% of families. **Educational attainment:** 88.4% HS; 47.1% bachelor's. **Avg. commute:** 25.4 min. 68.5% drive; 10.0% public trans. **Housing units:** 226,741; 80.1% occupied. **Home ownership:** 44.1%. **Avg. home:** $173,600; change (2013-15): 24.4%. **Avg. rent:** $969.
Mayor: Kasim Reed, nonpartisan
History: Founded as Terminus 1837; renamed Atlanta 1845; inc. 1847. Played major role in Civil War; became permanent state capital 1877. Birthplace of civil rights movement; host to 1996 Olympic Games.
Website: www.atlantaga.gov

Aurora, Colorado

Population: 359,407 (54). **Pop. density:** 2,341. **Pop. change (2010-15):** 10.2%. **Area:** 153.5 sq mi. **Racial distribution:** 63.9% white; 16.0% black; 5.0% Asian; 1.0% Amer. Ind.; 0.3% Pac. Isl.; 8.1% other; 2+ races 5.7%. **Hispanic pop.:** 28.9%. **Foreign born:** 20.2%. **U.S. citizens:** 86.6%. **Language:** 68.2% English only; 21.1% Spanish.
Employment: 173,902 employed; 4.2% unemployed. **Per capita income:** $53,983; change (2013-14): 4.6%. **Below poverty level:** 16.2%; 12.3% of families. **Educational attainment:** 86.5% HS; 27.1% bachelor's. **Avg. commute:** 28.8 min. 76.4% drive; 11.5% carpool. **Housing units:** 130,835; 94.3% occupied. **Home ownership:** 57.3%. **Avg. home:** $353,600; change (2013-15): 26.0%. **Avg. rent:** $983.
Mayor: Steve Hogan, nonpartisan
History: Founded 1891; originally called Fletcher; renamed Aurora 1907; inc. 1929. Early growth stimulated by presence of military bases; fast-growing trade, technology, and med. science center.
Website: www.auroragov.org

Austin, Texas

Population: 931,830 (11). **Pop. density:** 2,980. **Pop. change (2010-15):** 14.2%. **Area:** 312.7 sq mi. **Racial distribution:** 74.6% white; 7.8% black; 6.6% Asian; 0.5% Amer. Ind.; 0.1% Pac. Isl.; 7.4% other; 2+ races 3.1%. **Hispanic pop.:** 34.8%. **Foreign born:** 18.4%. **U.S. citizens:** 86.4%. **Language:** 67.4% English only; 25.0% Spanish.
Employment: 523,592 employed; 3.0% unemployed. **Per capita income:** $47,026; change (2013-14): 3.6%. **Below poverty level:** 19.0%; 13.3% of families. **Educational attainment:** 87.0% HS; 46.0% bachelor's. **Avg. commute:** 23.2 min. 73.0% drive; 10.3% carpool. **Housing units:** 373,473; 92.2% occupied. **Home ownership:** 44.8%. **Avg. home:** $263,300; change (2013-15): 18.1%. **Avg. rent:** $1,012.
Mayor: Steve Adler, nonpartisan
History: First permanent settlement 1835; capital of Rep. of Texas 1839; named after Stephen Austin; inc. 1840.
Website: www.austintexas.gov

Bakersfield, California

Population: 373,640 (52). **Pop. density:** 2,513. **Pop. change (2010-15):** 7.1%. **Area:** 148.7 sq mi. **Racial distribution:** 67.4% white; 8.2% black; 6.6% Asian; 1.3% Amer. Ind.; 0.1% Pac. Isl.; 12.2% other; 2+ races 4.2%. **Hispanic pop.:** 46.9%. **Foreign born:** 18.5%. **U.S. citizens:** 88.9%. **Language:** 61.8% English only; 31.4% Spanish.
Employment: 163,744 employed; 9.1% unemployed. **Per capita income:** $36,165; change (2013-14): 2.8%. **Below poverty level:** 20.2%; 16.5% of families. **Educational attainment:** 79.7% HS; 20.7% bachelor's. **Avg. commute:** 22.6 min.

79.9% drive; 12.7% carpool. **Housing units:** 120,028; 93.3% occupied. **Home ownership:** 56.9%. **Avg. rent:** $985.
Mayor: Harvey L. Hall, nonpartisan
History: Named after Col. Thomas Baker, an early settler; inc. 1898.
Website: www.bakersfieldcity.us

Baltimore, Maryland

Population: 621,849 (29). **Pop. density:** 7,682. **Pop. change (2010-15):** 0.1%. **Area:** 80.9 sq mi. **Racial distribution:** 30.3% white; 63.0% black; 2.5% Asian; 0.3% Amer. Ind.; <0.05% Pac. Isl.; 1.5% other; 2+ races 2.3%. **Hispanic pop.:** 4.5%. **Foreign born:** 7.5%. **U.S. citizens:** 95.3%. **Language:** 91.2% English only; 3.8% Spanish.
Employment: 272,756 employed; 7.7% unemployed. **Per capita income:** $53,690; change (2013-14): 3.2%. **Below poverty level:** 24.2%; 19.5% of families. **Educational attainment:** 80.9% HS; 27.7% bachelor's. **Avg. commute:** 30.1 min. 60.4% drive; 18.2% public trans. **Housing units:** 296,631; 81.7% occupied. **Home ownership:** 47.2%. **Avg. home:** $242,800; change (2013-15): -3.6%. **Avg. rent:** $944.
Mayor: Stephanie C. Rawlings-Blake, Democrat
History: Founded by Maryland legislature 1729; inc. 1797; War of 1812 British artillery barrage of Ft. McHenry (1814) inspired Francis Scott Key to write "Star-Spangled Banner." Birthplace of America's railroads 1828; rebuilt after fire 1904. Site of National Aquarium.
Website: www.baltimorecity.gov

Baton Rouge, Louisiana

Population: 228,590 (97). **Pop. density:** 2,661. **Pop. change (2010-15):** -0.4%. **Area:** 85.9 sq mi. **Racial distribution:** 38.7% white; 55.0% black; 3.5% Asian; 0.2% Amer. Ind.; <0.05% Pac. Isl.; 0.8% other; 2+ races 1.8%. **Hispanic pop.:** 3.3%. **Foreign born:** 5.3%. **U.S. citizens:** 96.6%. **Language:** 91.9% English only; 2.6% Spanish.
Employment: 110,718 employed; 6.0% unemployed. **Per capita income:** $42,249; change (2013-14): 3.0%. **Below poverty level:** 25.5%; 16.9% of families. **Educational attainment:** 85.9% HS; 32.7% bachelor's. **Avg. commute:** 21 min. 77.9% drive; 11.6% carpool. **Housing units:** 101,274; 87.5% occupied. **Home ownership:** 50.1%. **Avg. home:** $181,500; change (2013-15): 6.8%. **Avg. rent:** $787.
Mayor-President: Melvin "Kip" Holden, Democrat
History: Claimed by Spain at time of Louisiana Purchase 1803; est. independence by rebellion 1810; inc. as town 1817. Became state capital 1849; Union-held most of Civil War.
Website: www.brgov.com

Boise, Idaho

Population: 218,281 (99). **Pop. density:** 2,712. **Pop. change (2010-15):** 5.8%. **Area:** 80.5 sq mi. **Racial distribution:** 89.5% white; 1.5% black; 3.6% Asian; 0.8% Amer. Ind.; 0.2% Pac. Isl.; 1.3% other; 2+ races 3.0%. **Hispanic pop.:** 7.7%. **Foreign born:** 7.3%. **U.S. citizens:** 95.7%. **Language:** 90.0% English only; 4.3% Spanish.
Employment: 113,747 employed; 3.6% unemployed. **Per capita income:** $37,991; change (2013-14): 3.2%. **Below poverty level:** 15.2%; 9.6% of families. **Educational attainment:** 93.8% HS; 39.1% bachelor's. **Avg. commute:** 18.1 min. 79.3% drive. **Housing units:** 92,158; 94.0% occupied. **Home ownership:** 59.6%. **Avg. home:** $188,800; change (2013-15): 15.3%. **Avg. rent:** $793.
Mayor: David H. Bieter, nonpartisan
History: Gold discovered in area, 1862; inc., proclaimed capital of Idaho Terr., 1964; on Oregon Trail.
Website: www.cityofboise.org

Boston, Massachusetts

Population: 667,137 (23). **Pop. density:** 13,794. **Pop. change (2010-15):** 7.5%. **Area:** 48.4 sq mi. **Racial distribution:** 53.3% white; 25.1% black; 9.2% Asian; 0.4% Amer. Ind.; <0.05% Pac. Isl.; 7.4% other; 2+ races 4.7%. **Hispanic pop.:** 18.4%. **Foreign born:** 27.0%. **U.S. citizens:** 85.5%. **Language:** 63.4% English only; 16.1% Spanish.
Employment: 342,272 employed; 4.6% unemployed. **Per capita income:** $64,311; change (2013-14): 3.9%. **Below poverty level:** 21.9%; 17.1% of families. **Educational attainment:** 85.0% HS; 44.6% bachelor's. **Avg. commute:** 29.4 min. 39.1% drive; 33.3% public trans.; 14.7% walk. **Housing units:** 273,665; 91.8% occupied. **Home ownership:** 34.2%. **Avg. home:** $403,900; change (2013-15): 7.4%. **Avg. rent:** $1,298.
Mayor: Martin J. Walsh, nonpartisan
History: Settled 1630 by John Winthrop; capital of Mass. Bay Colony; figured strongly in American Revolution, earning distinction as the "Cradle of Liberty"; inc. 1822.
Website: www.boston.gov

Buffalo, New York

Population: 258,071 (78). **Pop. density:** 6,390. **Pop. change (2010-15):** -1.2%. **Area:** 40.4 sq mi. **Racial distribution:** 49.3%

white; 37.6% black; 4.2% Asian; 0.5% Amer. Ind.; <0.05% Pac. Isl.; 4.9% other; 2+ races 3.6%. **Hispanic pop.:** 10.0%. **Foreign born:** 8.6%. **U.S. citizens:** 94.6%. **Language:** 84.1% English only; 7.3% Spanish.
Employment: 103,518 employed; 7.1% unemployed. **Per capita income:** $43,676; change (2013-14): 3.0%. **Below poverty level:** 30.9%; 26.2% of families. **Educational attainment:** 82.5% HS; 24.7% bachelor's. **Avg. commute:** 20.4 min. 67.2% drive; 11.7% public trans.; 10.2% carpool. **Housing units:** 133,538; 83.5% occupied. **Home ownership:** 41.6%. **Avg. home:** $129,800; change (2013-15): -0.9%. **Avg. rent:** $696.
Mayor: Byron W. Brown, Democrat
History: Settled 1780 by Seneca Indians; raided twice by British in War of 1812. Served as western terminus for Erie Canal; became a center for trade and manufacturing; inc. 1832. A last stop on the Underground Railroad. Key point for Canada-U.S. political, trade, and social relations.
Website: www.city-buffalo.com

Chandler, Arizona

Population: 260,828 (76). **Pop. density:** 4,026. **Pop. change (2010-15):** 10.1%. **Area:** 64.8 sq mi. **Racial distribution:** 77.3% white; 5.1% black; 8.9% Asian; 1.3% Amer. Ind.; 0.2% Pac. Isl.; 3.1% other; 2+ races 4.1%. **Hispanic pop.:** 23.6%. **Foreign born:** 14.5%. **U.S. citizens:** 92.6%. **Language:** 76.9% English only; 13.4% Spanish.
Employment: 135,664 employed; 4.5% unemployed. **Per capita income:** $39,846; change (2013-14): 3.1%. **Below poverty level:** 9.7%; 6.9% of families. **Educational attainment:** 91.4% HS; 39.7% bachelor's. **Avg. commute:** 23.6 min. 77.5% drive; 12.3% carpool. **Housing units:** 94,598; 91.8% occupied. **Home ownership:** 62.4%. **Avg. home:** $216,400; change (2013-15): 17.9%. **Avg. rent:** $1,103.
Mayor: Jay Tibshraeny, nonpartisan
History: Formed 1912; population doubled in 1990s as the self-proclaimed high-tech oasis in the Silicon Desert.
Website: www.chandleraz.gov

Charlotte, North Carolina

Population: 827,097 (17). **Pop. density:** 2,711. **Pop. change (2010-15):** 12.0%. **Area:** 305.1 sq mi. **Racial distribution:** 51.9% white; 35.0% black; 5.6% Asian; 0.4% Amer. Ind.; 0.1% Pac. Isl.; 4.5% other; 2+ races 2.7%. **Hispanic pop.:** 13.4%. **Foreign born:** 15.3%. **U.S. citizens:** 89.7%. **Language:** 79.8% English only; 11.8% Spanish.
Employment: 424,507 employed; 4.9% unemployed. **Per capita income:** $42,425; change (2013-14): 4.2%. **Below poverty level:** 17.3%; 13.7% of families. **Educational attainment:** 88.1% HS; 40.7% bachelor's. **Avg. commute:** 24.5 min. 76.4% drive; 10.5% carpool. **Housing units:** 328,282; 91.0% occupied. **Home ownership:** 55.4%. **Avg. home:** $198,100; change (2013-15): 13.7%. **Avg. rent:** $902.
Mayor: Jennifer W. Roberts, Democrat
History: Settled by Scotch-Irish immigrants 1740s; inc. 1768 and named after Queen Charlotte, British King George III's wife. Scene of first major U.S. gold discovery 1799.
Website: charmeck.org

Chesapeake, Virginia

Population: 235,429 (94). **Pop. density:** 691. **Pop. change (2010-15):** 5.3%. **Area:** 340.8 sq mi. **Racial distribution:** 62.5% white; 29.8% black; 3.2% Asian; 0.3% Amer. Ind.; 0.1% Pac. Isl.; 1.1% other; 2+ races 2.9%. **Hispanic pop.:** 4.9%. **Foreign born:** 4.7%. **U.S. citizens:** 98.1%. **Language:** 92.9% English only; 3.2% Spanish.
Employment: 111,295 employed; 4.5% unemployed. **Per capita income:** $45,276; change (2013-14): 2.7%. **Below poverty level:** 9.1%; 7.6% of families. **Educational attainment:** 91.0% HS; 29.4% bachelor's. **Avg. commute:** 24.7 min. 86.6% drive. **Housing units:** 85,540; 94.0% occupied. **Home ownership:** 71.7%. **Avg. home:** $209,000; change (2013-15): 8.3%. **Avg. rent:** $1,163.
Mayor: Alan P. Krasnoff, Independent
History: Region settled in 1620s with first English colonies on banks of Elizabeth River; home to Great Dismal Swamp Canal, first envisioned by George Washington in 1763. Battle of Great Bridge fought here Dec. 1775; inc. 1963.
Website: www.cityofchesapeake.net

Chicago, Illinois

Population: 2,720,546 (3). **Pop. density:** 11,944. **Pop. change (2010-15):** 0.8%. **Area:** 227.8 sq mi. **Racial distribution:** 48.4% white; 31.9% black; 5.7% Asian; 0.3% Amer. Ind.; <0.05% Pac. Isl.; 11.5% other; 2+ races 2.2%. **Hispanic pop.:** 28.9%. **Foreign born:** 20.9%. **U.S. citizens:** 87.8%. **Language:** 64.1% English only; 24.5% Spanish.
Employment: 1,273,727 employed; 6.4% unemployed. **Per capita income:** $50,960; change (2013-14): 3.2%. **Below poverty level:** 22.7%; 18.7% of families. **Educational attainment:** 81.6% HS; 34.9% bachelor's. **Avg. commute:** 33.7 min. 49.9%

drive; 27.2% public trans. **Housing units:** 1,190,998; 86.4% occupied. **Home ownership:** 44.7%. **Avg. home:** $218,900; change (2013-15): 14.4%. **Avg. rent:** $963.
Mayor: Rahm Emanuel, nonpartisan
History: Site acquired from Indians 1795; significant white settlement began with completion of Erie Canal 1825; chartered as city 1837. Boomed with arrival of railroads and canal to Mississippi R.; one-third of city destroyed by fire 1871. Major grain and livestock market.
Website: www.cityofchicago.org

Chula Vista, California

Population: 265,757 (74). **Pop. density:** 5,355. **Pop. change (2010-15):** 8.6%. **Area:** 49.6 sq mi. **Racial distribution:** 67.7% white; 4.5% black; 14.3% Asian; 0.4% Amer. Ind.; 0.4% Pac. Isl.; 7.2% other; 2+ races 5.4%. **Hispanic pop.:** 58.4%. **Foreign born:** 30.5%. **U.S. citizens:** 85.4%. **Language:** 42.9% English only; 45.8% Spanish; 6.5% Tagalog.
Employment: 113,064 employed; 6.5% unemployed. **Per capita income:** $51,459; change (2013-14): 3.1%. **Below poverty level:** 12.1%; 10.1% of families. **Educational attainment:** 81.3% HS; 27.4% bachelor's. **Avg. commute:** 27.1 min. 79.1% drive; 11.0% carpool. **Housing units:** 84,682; 91.0% occupied. **Home ownership:** 58.2%. **Avg. home:** $542,600; change (2013-15): 16.9%. **Avg. rent:** $1,302.
Mayor: Mary Casillas Salas, nonpartisan
History: Visited by Spanish in 1542; became part of Spanish land grant in 1795; came into the U.S. during the Mexican War in 1847; inc. 1911. WWII brought aircraft industry and growth.
Website: www.chulavistaca.gov

Cincinnati, Ohio

Population: 298,550 (66). **Pop. density:** 3,830. **Pop. change (2010-15):** 0.6%. **Area:** 77.9 sq mi. **Racial distribution:** 50.4% white; 43.5% black; 1.9% Asian; 0.3% Amer. Ind.; <0.05% Pac. Isl.; 1.1% other; 2+ races 2.8%. **Hispanic pop.:** 3.0%. **Foreign born:** 5.1%. **U.S. citizens:** 96.6%. **Language:** 92.6% English only; 2.9% Spanish.
Employment: 135,237 employed; 5.0% unemployed. **Per capita income:** $45,878; change (2013-14): 3.9%. **Below poverty level:** 30.9%; 25.1% of families. **Educational attainment:** 85.1% HS; 32.3% bachelor's. **Avg. commute:** 22.4 min. 72.0% drive. **Housing units:** 162,183; 80.9% occupied. **Home ownership:** 39.4%. **Avg. home:** $145,400; change (2013-15): 7.3%. **Avg. rent:** $653.
Mayor: John Cranley, nonpartisan
History: Founded 1788; named after the Society of Cincinnati, an organization of Revolutionary War officers; chartered as village 1802; inc. 1819.
Website: www.cincinnati-oh.gov

Cleveland, Ohio

Population: 388,072 (51). **Pop. density:** 4,994. **Pop. change (2010-15):** -2.0%. **Area:** 77.7 sq mi. **Racial distribution:** 40.1% white; 52.1% black; 1.7% Asian; 0.4% Amer. Ind.; <0.05% Pac. Isl.; 2.3% other; 2+ races 3.3%. **Hispanic pop.:** 10.0%. **Foreign born:** 4.7%. **U.S. citizens:** 97.4%. **Language:** 88.0% English only; 7.4% Spanish.
Employment: 148,890 employed; 6.3% unemployed. **Per capita income:** $46,960; change (2013-14): 3.8%. **Below poverty level:** 35.9%; 31.1% of families. **Educational attainment:** 77.4% HS; 15.2% bachelor's. **Avg. commute:** 24.2 min. 70.6% drive; 10.6% public trans. **Housing units:** 212,269; 78.5% occupied. **Home ownership:** 43.5%. **Avg. home:** $125,100; change (2013-15): 6.3%. **Avg. rent:** $661.
Mayor: Frank G. Jackson, nonpartisan
History: Surveyed in 1796; given recognition as village 1815; inc. 1836; annexed Ohio City 1854.
Website: www.city.cleveland.oh.us

Colorado Springs, Colorado

Population: 456,568 (40). **Pop. density:** 2,339. **Pop. change (2010-15):** 8.5%. **Area:** 195.2 sq mi. **Racial distribution:** 79.6% white; 6.2% black; 3.0% Asian; 0.6% Amer. Ind.; 0.2% Pac. Isl.; 5.3% other; 2+ races 5.1%. **Hispanic pop.:** 17.0%. **Foreign born:** 8.2%. **U.S. citizens:** 95.6%. **Language:** 86.8% English only; 8.2% Spanish.
Employment: 207,004 employed; 4.5% unemployed. **Per capita income:** $41,971; change (2013-14): 3.5%. **Below poverty level:** 13.9%; 9.9% of families. **Educational attainment:** 92.8% HS; 36.3% bachelor's. **Avg. commute:** 20.9 min. 79.5% drive; 10.4% carpool. **Housing units:** 181,832; 93.6% occupied. **Home ownership:** 58.8%. **Avg. home:** $238,600; change (2013-15): 10.1%. **Avg. rent:** $888.
Mayor: John Suthers, nonpartisan
History: Founded 1871 at the foot of Pike's Peak; inc. 1872.
Website: coloradosprings.gov

Columbus, Ohio

Population: 850,106 (15). **Pop. density:** 3,898. **Pop. change (2010-15):** 7.5%. **Area:** 218.1 sq mi. **Racial distribution:** 61.7% white; 27.8% black; 4.5% Asian; 0.2% Amer. Ind.; <0.05% Pac. Isl.; 2.0% other; 2+ races 3.8%. **Hispanic pop.:** 5.7%. **Foreign born:** 11.3%. **U.S. citizens:** 93.0%. **Language:** 85.7% English only; 4.4% Spanish.
Employment: 426,088 employed; 4.1% unemployed. **Per capita income:** $44,902; change (2013-14): 2.9%. **Below poverty level:** 22.3%; 17.4% of families. **Educational attainment:** 88.3% HS; 33.4% bachelor's. **Avg. commute:** 21.3 min. 80.4% drive. **Housing units:** 377,593; 87.4% occupied. **Home ownership:** 45.9%. **Avg. home:** $164,700; change (2013-15): 15.3%. **Avg. rent:** $822.
Mayor: Andrew J. Ginther, nonpartisan
History: First settlement 1797; laid out as new state capital 1812 with current name; inc. 1834.
Website: www.columbus.gov

Corpus Christi, Texas

Population: 324,074 (58). **Pop. density:** 1,857. **Pop. change (2010-15):** 6.1%. **Area:** 174.5 sq mi. **Racial distribution:** 85.2% white; 4.5% black; 1.9% Asian; 0.5% Amer. Ind.; <0.05% Pac. Isl.; 5.7% other; 2+ races 2.1%. **Hispanic pop.:** 60.8%. **Foreign born:** 8.1%. **U.S. citizens:** 95.3%. **Language:** 61.4% English only; 36.0% Spanish.
Employment: 144,139 employed; 4.7% unemployed. **Per capita income:** $41,961; change (2013-14): 3.8%. **Below poverty level:** 17.6%; 13.7% of families. **Educational attainment:** 81.2% HS; 21.2% bachelor's. **Avg. commute:** 19.3 min. 80.0% drive; 11.5% carpool. **Housing units:** 126,615; 89.5% occupied. **Home ownership:** 56.7%. **Avg. home:** $181,500; change (2013-15): 18.9%. **Avg. rent:** $872.
Mayor: Nelda Martinez, nonpartisan
History: Settled 1839; inc. 1852. One of the largest U.S. ports.
Website: www.cctexas.com

Dallas, Texas

Population: 1,300,092 (9). **Pop. density:** 3,808. **Pop. change (2010-15):** 8.3%. **Area:** 341.4 sq mi. **Racial distribution:** 58.2% white; 24.6% black; 3.0% Asian; 0.3% Amer. Ind.; <0.05% Pac. Isl.; 11.8% other; 2+ races 2.2%. **Hispanic pop.:** 41.7%. **Foreign born:** 24.2%. **U.S. citizens:** 81.2%. **Language:** 57.3% English only; 37.7% Spanish.
Employment: 617,065 employed; 4.1% unemployed. **Per capita income:** $49,506; change (2013-14): 3.9%. **Below poverty level:** 24.1%; 20.6% of families. **Educational attainment:** 74.3% HS; 29.7% bachelor's. **Avg. commute:** 25.6 min. 77.0% drive; 11.0% carpool. **Housing units:** 526,185; 88.8% occupied. **Home ownership:** 43.0%. **Avg. home:** $207,200; change (2013-15): 18.0%. **Avg. rent:** $852.
Mayor: Mike Rawlings, nonpartisan
History: First settled 1841; platted 1846; inc. 1871. Developed as financial and commercial center of Southwest; headquarters of regional Federal Reserve Bank; major center for distribution and high-tech manufacturing.
Website: www.dallascityhall.com

Denver, Colorado

Population: 682,545 (19). **Pop. density:** 4,451. **Pop. change (2010-15):** 13.1%. **Area:** 153.3 sq mi. **Racial distribution:** 74.7% white; 9.8% black; 3.5% Asian; 1.1% Amer. Ind.; 0.1% Pac. Isl.; 7.4% other; 2+ races 3.4%. **Hispanic pop.:** 31.2%. **Foreign born:** 16.0%. **U.S. citizens:** 89.2%. **Language:** 72.5% English only; 20.8% Spanish.
Employment: 359,291 employed; 3.7% unemployed. **Per capita income:** $53,983; change (2013-14): 4.6%. **Below poverty level:** 18.3%; 13.7% of families. **Educational attainment:** 85.6% HS; 43.7% bachelor's. **Avg. commute:** 24.5 min. 69.7% drive. **Housing units:** 290,624; 93.3% occupied. **Home ownership:** 49.7%. **Avg. home:** $353,600; change (2013-15): 26.0%. **Avg. rent:** $913.
Mayor: Michael B. Hancock, nonpartisan
History: Settled 1858 by gold prospectors and miners; inc. 1861; became territorial capital 1867; growth spurred by gold and silver boom. Became financial, industrial, cultural center of Rocky Mt. region.
Website: www.denvergov.org

Detroit, Michigan

Population: 677,116 (21). **Pop. density:** 4,880. **Pop. change (2010-15):** -4.8%. **Area:** 138.8 sq mi. **Racial distribution:** 12.6% white; 80.9% black; 1.2% Asian; 0.3% Amer. Ind.; <0.05% Pac. Isl.; 2.8% other; 2+ races 2.1%. **Hispanic pop.:** 7.3%. **Foreign born:** 5.2%. **U.S. citizens:** 96.5%. **Language:** 90.2% English only; 6.2% Spanish.
Employment: 210,242 employed; 12.4% unemployed. **Per capita income:** $44,500; change (2013-14): 4.1%. **Below poverty level:** 39.8%; 34.8% of families. **Educational attainment:** 77.8% HS; 13.1% bachelor's. **Avg. commute:** 26.8 min. 69.3% drive; 12.8% carpool. **Housing units:** 363,280; 70.0% occupied. **Home ownership:** 50.7%. **Avg. home:** $63,400 (2012). **Avg. rent:** $756.
Mayor: Mike Duggan, nonpartisan

History: Founded by French 1701; controlled by British 1760; acquired by U.S. 1796; destroyed by fire 1805; fought over during War of 1812; inc. 1815; capital of state 1837-47. Auto manufacturing began 1890.
Website: www.detroitmi.gov

Durham, North Carolina

Population: 257,636 (79). **Pop. density:** 2,357. **Pop. change (2010-15):** 12.4%. **Area:** 109.3 sq mi. **Racial distribution:** 46.8% white; 40.2% black; 4.7% Asian; 0.4% Amer. Ind.; <0.05% Pac. Isl.; 4.8% other; 2+ races 3.0%. **Hispanic pop.:** 13.9%. **Foreign born:** 14.5%. **U.S. citizens:** 89.2%. **Language:** 79.9% English only; 12.7% Spanish.
Employment: 128,180 employed; 4.6% unemployed. **Per capita income:** $45,867; change (2013-14): 2.8%. **Below poverty level:** 19.6%; 13.8% of families. **Educational attainment:** 87.2% HS; 47.3% bachelor's. **Avg. commute:** 21.3 min. 74.6% drive; 11.6% carpool. **Housing units:** 107,319; 91.6% occupied. **Home ownership:** 49.9%. **Avg. home:** $222,900; change (2013-15): 15.7%. **Avg. rent:** $871.
Mayor: William V. Bell, nonpartisan
History: Inc. 1869. Trinity College moved to Durham in 1892, renamed Duke Univ. in 1924.
Website: durhamnc.gov

El Paso, Texas

Population: 681,124 (20). **Pop. density:** 2,653. **Pop. change (2010-15):** 4.5%. **Area:** 256.7 sq mi. **Racial distribution:** 82.7% white; 3.6% black; 1.2% Asian; 0.5% Amer. Ind.; 0.2% Pac. Isl.; 9.6% other; 2+ races 2.2%. **Hispanic pop.:** 79.7%. **Foreign born:** 24.9%. **U.S. citizens:** 86.2%. **Language:** 29.4% English only; 68.4% Spanish.
Employment: 273,172 employed; 4.8% unemployed. **Per capita income:** $31,799; change (2013-14): 3.3%. **Below poverty level:** 21.5%; 18.5% of families. **Educational attainment:** 77.2% HS; 22.7% bachelor's. **Avg. commute:** 22.4 min. 79.9% drive; 11.2% carpool. **Housing units:** 236,626; 92.3% occupied. **Home ownership:** 59.3%. **Avg. home:** $142,100; change (2013-15): 0.6%. **Avg. rent:** $747.
Mayor: Oscar Leeser, nonpartisan
History: First settled 1598; inc. 1873; arrival of railroad, 1881, boosted city's population and industries.
Website: www.elpasotexas.gov

Fort Wayne, Indiana

Population: 260,326 (77). **Pop. density:** 2,353. **Pop. change (2010-15):** 2.6%. **Area:** 110.6 sq mi. **Racial distribution:** 73.9% white; 15.6% black; 3.6% Asian; 0.3% Amer. Ind.; 0.1% Pac. Isl.; 2.9% other; 2+ races 3.6%. **Hispanic pop.:** 8.1%. **Foreign born:** 7.5%. **U.S. citizens:** 95.4%. **Language:** 88.9% English only; 6.0% Spanish.
Employment: 117,289 employed; 4.8% unemployed. **Per capita income:** $39,477; change (2013-14): 4.0%. **Below poverty level:** 18.9%; 14.8% of families. **Educational attainment:** 88.2% HS; 25.8% bachelor's. **Avg. commute:** 20 min. 84.6% drive. **Housing units:** 113,559; 89.4% occupied. **Home ownership:** 63.2%. **Avg. home:** $115,900; change (2013-15): 8.7%. **Avg. rent:** $661.
Mayor: Tom Henry, Democrat
History: French fort 1680; U.S. fort 1794; settled by 1832; inc. 1840 prior to Wabash-Erie Canal completion in 1843.
Website: www.cityoffortwayne.org

Fort Worth, Texas

Population: 833,319 (16). **Pop. density:** 2,447. **Pop. change (2010-15):** 11.6%. **Area:** 340.5 sq mi. **Racial distribution:** 65.4% white; 18.9% black; 3.7% Asian; 0.6% Amer. Ind.; 0.1% Pac. Isl.; 8.4% other; 2+ races 2.9%. **Hispanic pop.:** 34.2%. **Foreign born:** 17.5%. **U.S. citizens:** 87.8%. **Language:** 67.2% English only; 27.2% Spanish.
Employment: 375,355 employed; 4.2% unemployed. **Per capita income:** $49,506; change (2013-14): 3.9%. **Below poverty level:** 19.3%; 15.2% of families. **Educational attainment:** 80.4% HS; 26.7% bachelor's. **Avg. commute:** 26.1 min. 81.8% drive; 10.9% carpool. **Housing units:** 297,134; 90.5% occupied. **Home ownership:** 57.7%. **Avg. home:** $207,200; change (2013-15): 18.0%. **Avg. rent:** $878.
Mayor: Betsy Price, nonpartisan
History: Established as military post 1849; inc. 1873; oil discovered 1917.
Website: fortworthtexas.gov

Fremont, California

Population: 232,206 (96). **Pop. density:** 2,998. **Pop. change (2010-15):** 8.2%. **Area:** 77.5 sq mi. **Racial distribution:** 29.3% white; 3.7% black; 52.2% Asian; 0.6% Amer. Ind.; 0.6% Pac. Isl.; 7.4% other; 2+ races 6.3%. **Hispanic pop.:** 14.1%. **Foreign born:** 44.0%. **U.S. citizens:** 80.6%. **Language:** 42.0% English only; 9.0% Spanish; 16.1% Chinese, 6.7% Hindi, 6.5% other Asian languages.

Employment: 112,253 employed; 3.7% unemployed. **Per capita income:** $72,364; change (2013-14): 4.6%. **Below poverty level:** 6.3%; 4.1% of families. **Educational attainment:** 91.5% HS; 51.7% bachelor's. **Avg. commute:** 30.5 min. 74.0% drive; 10.8% carpool. **Housing units:** 74,649; 95.9% occupied. **Home ownership:** 63.2%. **Avg. home:** $782,300; change (2013-15): 21.5%. **Avg. rent:** $1,663.
Mayor: Bill Harrison, nonpartisan
History: Area first settled by Spanish 1769; inc. 1956 with consolidation of five communities.
Website: www.fremont.gov

Fresno, California

Population: 520,052 (34). **Pop. density:** 4,579. **Pop. change (2010-15):** 4.6%. **Area:** 113.6 sq mi. **Racial distribution:** 51.2% white; 7.9% black; 12.9% Asian; 1.0% Amer. Ind.; 0.2% Pac. Isl.; 21.8% other; 2+ races 5.0%. **Hispanic pop.:** 48.0%. **Foreign born:** 21.1%. **U.S. citizens:** 87.2%. **Language:** 57.6% English only; 28.7% Spanish.
Employment: 211,497 employed; 11.1% unemployed. **Per capita income:** $35,785; change (2013-14): 2.6%. **Below poverty level:** 30.6%; 24.9% of families. **Educational attainment:** 74.8% HS; 20.1% bachelor's. **Avg. commute:** 21.5 min. 77.3% drive; 12.1% carpool. **Housing units:** 174,104; 92.0% occupied. **Home ownership:** 47.4%. **Avg. rent:** $890.
Mayor: Ashley Swearengin, nonpartisan
History: Founded by railroad company 1872; inc. 1885.
Website: www.fresno.gov

Garland, Texas

Population: 236,897 (91). **Pop. density:** 4,153. **Pop. change (2010-15):** 4.2%. **Area:** 57.0 sq mi. **Racial distribution:** 47.4% white; 13.1% black; 10.7% Asian; 0.4% Amer. Ind.; 0.1% Pac. Isl.; 22.3% other; 2+ races 5.9%. **Hispanic pop.:** 40.1%. **Foreign born:** 27.4%. **U.S. citizens:** 82.6%. **Language:** 53.0% English only; 34.6% Spanish; 5.3% Vietnamese.
Employment: 115,765 employed; 4.2% unemployed. **Per capita income:** $49,506; change (2013-14): 3.9%. **Below poverty level:** 16.8%; 13.6% of families. **Educational attainment:** 76.5% HS; 21.6% bachelor's. **Avg. commute:** 27.6 min. 79.1% drive; 13.4% carpool. **Housing units:** 80,168; 93.5% occupied. **Home ownership:** 63.9%. **Avg. home:** $207,200; change (2013-15): 18.0%. **Avg. rent:** $941.
Mayor: Douglas Athas, nonpartisan
History: Settled 1850s; inc. 1891.
Website: www.garlandtx.gov

Gilbert, Arizona

Population: 247,542 (85). **Pop. density:** 3,641. **Pop. change (2010-15):** 18.0%. **Area:** 68.0 sq mi. **Racial distribution:** 83.9% white; 3.3% black; 6.2% Asian; 0.9% Amer. Ind.; 0.2% Pac. Isl.; 2.0% other; 2+ races 3.5%. **Hispanic pop.:** 15.6%. **Foreign born:** 9.3%. **U.S. citizens:** 96.3%. **Language:** 85.3% English only; 7.4% Spanish.
Employment: 123,692 employed; 4.2% unemployed. **Per capita income:** $39,846; change (2013-14): 3.1%. **Below poverty level:** 6.8%; 5.3% of families. **Educational attainment:** 95.5% HS; 40.3% bachelor's. **Avg. commute:** 26.9 min. 78.5% drive; 11.2% carpool. **Housing units:** 77,238; 92.7% occupied. **Home ownership:** 71.3%. **Avg. home:** $216,400; change (2013-15): 17.9%. **Avg. rent:** $1,263.
Mayor: John Lewis, nonpartisan
History: Est. 1891; inc. 1920.
Website: www.gilbertaz.gov

Glendale, Arizona

Population: 240,126 (89). **Pop. density:** 4,057. **Pop. change (2010-15):** 6.0%. **Area:** 59.2 sq mi. **Racial distribution:** 76.3% white; 6.2% black; 3.7% Asian; 1.7% Amer. Ind.; 0.1% Pac. Isl.; 8.4% other; 2+ races 3.6%. **Hispanic pop.:** 36.9%. **Foreign born:** 16.8%. **U.S. citizens:** 89.4%. **Language:** 69.2% English only; 24.3% Spanish.
Employment: 108,044 employed; 5.5% unemployed. **Per capita income:** $39,846; change (2013-14): 3.1%. **Below poverty level:** 21.7%; 17.0% of families. **Educational attainment:** 83.3% HS; 21.6% bachelor's. **Avg. commute:** 26.9 min. 73.4% drive; 15.3% carpool. **Housing units:** 89,492; 87.7% occupied. **Home ownership:** 55.8%. **Avg. home:** $216,400; change (2013-15): 17.9%. **Avg. rent:** $863.
Mayor: Jerry Weiers, nonpartisan
History: Est. 1892; inc. 1910.
Website: www.glendaleaz.com

Greensboro, North Carolina

Population: 285,342 (68). **Pop. density:** 2,252. **Pop. change (2010-15):** 5.9%. **Area:** 126.7 sq mi. **Racial distribution:** 49.5% white; 41.1% black; 4.0% Asian; 0.4% Amer. Ind.; 0.1% Pac. Isl.; 2.7% other; 2+ races 2.3%. **Hispanic pop.:** 7.4%. **Foreign born:** 10.8%. **U.S. citizens:** 92.7%. **Language:** 86.3% English only; 6.5% Spanish.

Employment: 133,882 employed; 5.7% unemployed. **Per capita income:** $37,782; change (2013-14): 3.9%. **Below poverty level:** 19.8%; 14.6% of families. **Educational attainment:** 88.4% HS; 36.3% bachelor's. **Avg. commute:** 20.5 min. 81.1% drive. **Housing units:** 126,557; 89.5% occupied. **Home ownership:** 51.8%. **Avg. home:** $151,500; change (2013-15): 15.6%. **Avg. rent:** $751.
Mayor: Nancy Vaughan, nonpartisan
History: Settled 1749; site of Revolutionary War conflict, 1781, between Generals Nathanael Greene and Cornwallis; inc. 1807. Origin of civil rights sit-in movement.
Website: www.greensboro-nc.gov

Henderson, Nevada

Population: 285,667 (67). **Pop. density:** 2,730. **Pop. change (2010-15):** 10.8%. **Area:** 104.7 sq mi. **Racial distribution:** 78.4% white; 5.9% black; 7.9% Asian; 0.4% Amer. Ind.; 0.4% Pac. Isl.; 3.2% other; 2+ races 3.8%. **Hispanic pop.:** 14.9%. **Foreign born:** 12.1%. **U.S. citizens:** 95.9%. **Language:** 82.1% English only; 8.8% Spanish.
Employment: 136,216 employed; 6.7% unemployed. **Per capita income:** $39,533; change (2013-14): 3.8%. **Below poverty level:** 10.2%; 7.2% of families. **Educational attainment:** 92.6% HS; 30.7% bachelor's. **Avg. commute:** 23.5 min. 81.8% drive. **Housing units:** 115,316; 88.5% occupied. **Home ownership:** 62.0%. **Avg. home:** $216,800; change (2013-15): 24.7%. **Avg. rent:** $1,155.
Mayor: Andy A. Hafen, nonpartisan
History: Early growth spurred by WWII magnesium mining; inc. 1953.
Website: www.cityofhenderson.com

Hialeah, Florida

Population: 237,069 (90). **Pop. density:** 11,039. **Pop. change (2010-15):** 5.1%. **Area:** 21.5 sq mi. **Racial distribution:** 94.4% white; 2.3% black; 0.3% Asian; 0.1% Amer. Ind.; <0.05% Pac. Isl.; 2.2% other; 2+ races 0.7%. **Hispanic pop.:** 95.6%. **Foreign born:** 73.0%. **U.S. citizens:** 62.7%. **Language:** 7.3% English only; 92.2% Spanish.
Employment: 105,484 employed; 6.7% unemployed. **Per capita income:** $48,224; change (2013-14): 3.9%. **Below poverty level:** 25.8%; 23.1% of families. **Educational attainment:** 70.9% HS; 13.2% bachelor's. **Avg. commute:** 24 min. 79.5% drive. **Housing units:** 72,353; 95.2% occupied. **Home ownership:** 48.5%. **Avg. home:** $280,000; change (2013-15): 13.6%. **Avg. rent:** $1,002.
Mayor: Carlos Hernandez, nonpartisan
History: Founded 1917; inc. 1925. Industrial and residential city NW of Miami; site of Hialeah Park Race Track.
Website: www.hialeahfl.gov

Honolulu, Hawaii

Population: 352,769 (55). **Pop. density:** 5,829. **Pop. change (2010-15):** 4.2%. **Area:** 60.5 sq mi. **Racial distribution:** 18.0% white; 1.9% black; 54.1% Asian; 0.1% Amer. Ind.; 8.3% Pac. Isl.; 0.8% other; 2+ races 16.8%. **Hispanic pop.:** 5.9%. **Foreign born:** 27.5%. **U.S. citizens:** 87.1%. **Language:** 63.5% English only; 1.3% Spanish; 7.0% Chinese, 6.8% Japanese, 4.8% Tagalog, 8.6% other Pac. Isl. languages.
Employment: 452,965 employed; 3.4% unemployed. **Per capita income:** $49,722; change (2013-14): 3.9%. **Below poverty level:** 12.0%; 7.7% of families. **Educational attainment:** 88.3% HS; 35.2% bachelor's. **Avg. commute:** 22.6 min. 57.1% drive; 12.8% carpool; 12.5% public trans. **Housing units:** 144,570; 88.5% occupied. **Home ownership:** 43.1%. **Avg. home:** $707,700; change (2013-15): 7.0%. **Avg. rent:** $1,297.
Mayor: Kirk Caldwell, nonpartisan
History: Europeans entered harbor 1778; declared capital of kingdom of Hawaii by King Kamehameha III 1850. Pearl Harbor naval base attacked by Japanese Dec. 7, 1941.
Website: www.honolulu.gov

Houston, Texas

Population: 2,296,224 (4). **Pop. density:** 3,647. **Pop. change (2010-15):** 8.6%. **Area:** 629.6 sq mi. **Racial distribution:** 57.8% white; 23.3% black; 6.3% Asian; 0.4% Amer. Ind.; <0.05% Pac. Isl.; 10.3% other; 2+ races 1.9%. **Hispanic pop.:** 43.9%. **Foreign born:** 28.4%. **U.S. citizens:** 79.5%. **Language:** 53.1% English only; 37.9% Spanish.
Employment: 1,088,772 employed; 4.3% unemployed. **Per capita income:** $54,820; change (2013-14): 4.1%. **Below poverty level:** 22.9%; 19.6% of families. **Educational attainment:** 75.9% HS; 29.8% bachelor's. **Avg. commute:** 26.1 min. 79.9% drive; 12.2% carpool. **Housing units:** 913,006; 86.8% occupied. **Home ownership:** 44.5%. **Avg. home:** $213,400; change (2013-15): 17.7%. **Avg. rent:** $862.
Mayor: Sylvester Turner, Democrat
History: Founded 1836; inc. 1837; capital of Rep. of Texas 1837-39; developed rapidly after completion of channel to Gulf of Mexico 1914. World center of oil, natural gas technology.
Website: www.houstontx.gov

Indianapolis, Indiana

Population: 853,173 (14). **Pop. density:** 2,360. **Pop. change (2010-15):** 3.8%. **Area:** 361.5 sq mi. **Racial distribution:** 62.0% white; 27.9% black; 2.4% Asian; 0.2% Amer. Ind.; <0.05% Pac. Isl.; 4.7% other; 2+ races 2.7%. **Hispanic pop.:** 9.6%. **Foreign born:** 8.7%. **U.S. citizens:** 93.7%. **Language:** 87.4% English only; 8.4% Spanish.
Employment: 407,013 employed; 5.0% unemployed. **Per capita income:** $44,017; change (2013-14): 3.0%. **Below poverty level:** 21.4%; 17.0% of families. **Educational attainment:** 84.6% HS; 27.6% bachelor's. **Avg. commute:** 22.7 min. 81.8% drive. **Housing units:** 381,610; 86.1% occupied. **Home ownership:** 54.6%. **Avg. home:** $153,200; change (2013-15): 12.1%. **Avg. rent:** $784.
Mayor: Joe Hogsett, Democrat
History: Settled 1820; became capital 1825.
Website: www.indy.gov

Irvine, California

Population: 256,927 (81). **Pop. density:** 3,918. **Pop. change (2010-15):** 20.4%. **Area:** 65.6 sq mi. **Racial distribution:** 50.8% white; 2.1% black; 38.8% Asian; 0.3% Amer. Ind.; 0.1% Pac. Isl.; 2.7% other; 2+ races 5.2%. **Hispanic pop.:** 9.9%. **Foreign born:** 36.6%. **U.S. citizens:** 84.4%. **Language:** 54.2% English only; 6.0% Spanish; 9.6% Chinese, 6.7% Korean.
Employment: 124,377 employed; 3.3% unemployed. **Per capita income:** $50,751; change (2013-14): 3.8%. **Below poverty level:** 12.4%; 6.8% of families. **Educational attainment:** 96.1% HS; 65.6% bachelor's. **Avg. commute:** 23.9 min. 79.0% drive. **Housing units:** 87,934; 94.8% occupied. **Home ownership:** 49.2%. **Avg. home:** $707,500; change (2013-15): 8.6%. **Avg. rent:** $1,863.
Mayor: Steven S. Choi, nonpartisan
History: Univ. of CA–Irvine campus announced 1959; planned city developed around campus 1960s; inc. 1971.
Website: www.cityofirvine.org

Irving, Texas

Population: 236,607 (93). **Pop. density:** 3,530. **Pop. change (2010-15):** 9.1%. **Area:** 67.0 sq mi. **Racial distribution:** 57.7% white; 12.8% black; 15.3% Asian; 0.4% Amer. Ind.; <0.05% Pac. Isl.; 11.1% other; 2+ races 2.7%. **Hispanic pop.:** 41.7%. **Foreign born:** 34.2%. **U.S. citizens:** 74.8%. **Language:** 45.7% English only; 37.2% Spanish.
Employment: 120,344 employed; 3.8% unemployed. **Per capita income:** $49,506; change (2013-14): 3.9%. **Below poverty level:** 16.0%; 13.9% of families. **Educational attainment:** 80.0% HS; 33.8% bachelor's. **Avg. commute:** 23 min. 78.4% drive; 12.4% carpool. **Housing units:** 90,577; 91.4% occupied. **Home ownership:** 38.7%. **Avg. home:** $207,200; change (2013-15): 18.0%. **Avg. rent:** $906.
Mayor: Beth Van Duyne, nonpartisan
History: Founded 1903; inc. 1914; remained small until 1950s.
Website: www.cityofirving.org

Jacksonville, Florida

Population: 868,031 (12). **Pop. density:** 1,161. **Pop. change (2010-15):** 5.4%. **Area:** 747.4 sq mi. **Racial distribution:** 60.2% white; 30.6% black; 4.4% Asian; 0.3% Amer. Ind.; 0.1% Pac. Isl.; 1.2% other; 2+ races 3.2%. **Hispanic pop.:** 8.2%. **Foreign born:** 9.7%. **U.S. citizens:** 95.4%. **Language:** 86.2% English only; 6.2% Spanish.
Employment: 414,152 employed; 5.6% unemployed. **Per capita income:** $43,413; change (2013-14): 3.2%. **Below poverty level:** 17.8%; 13.7% of families. **Educational attainment:** 88.1% HS; 25.5% bachelor's. **Avg. commute:** 23.5 min. 80.4% drive; 10.0% carpool. **Housing units:** 369,318; 85.5% occupied. **Home ownership:** 60.3%. **Avg. home:** $195,000; change (2013-15): 11.4%. **Avg. rent:** $932.
Mayor: Lenny Curry, Republican
History: Settled 1816 as Cowford; renamed after Andrew Jackson 1822; inc. 1832; rechartered 1851; scene of conflicts in Seminole and Civil Wars.
Website: www.coj.net

Jersey City, New Jersey

Population: 264,290 (75). **Pop. density:** 17,867. **Pop. change (2010-15):** 6.3%. **Area:** 14.8 sq mi. **Racial distribution:** 35.2% white; 25.5% black; 24.8% Asian; 0.3% Amer. Ind.; <0.05% Pac. Isl.; 11.2% other; 2+ races 3.0%. **Hispanic pop.:** 27.4%. **Foreign born:** 39.8%. **U.S. citizens:** 78.1%. **Language:** 47.5% English only; 22.8% Spanish; 5.3% Tagalog.
Employment: 133,184 employed; 5.3% unemployed. **Per capita income:** $61,440; change (2013-14): 4.1%. **Below poverty level:** 19.0%; 16.2% of families. **Educational attainment:** 85.0% HS; 42.5% bachelor's. **Avg. commute:** 35.6 min. 47.5% public trans.; 32.6% drive. **Housing units:** 110,140; 87.7% occupied. **Home ownership:** 29.9%. **Avg. home:** $397,900; change (2013-15): 1.6%. **Avg. rent:** $1,187.
Mayor: Steven M. Fulop, nonpartisan

History: Site bought from American Indians, 1630; chartered as town by British 1668; scene of Revolutionary War conflict 1779; chartered under present name 1838. Important station on Underground Railroad.
Website: www.cityofjerseycity.com

Kansas City, Missouri

Population: 475,378 (36). **Pop. density:** 1,509. **Pop. change (2010-15):** 3.2%. **Area:** 315.0 sq mi. **Racial distribution:** 59.5% white; 29.2% black; 2.5% Asian; 0.5% Amer. Ind.; 0.3% Pac. Isl.; 4.5% other; 2+ races 3.6%. **Hispanic pop.:** 10.1%. **Foreign born:** 7.6%. **U.S. citizens:** 95.5%. **Language:** 88.0% English only; 7.0% Spanish.
Employment: 243,342 employed; 5.5% unemployed. **Per capita income:** $46,319; change (2013-14): 3.0%. **Below poverty level:** 19.4%; 14.8% of families. **Educational attainment:** 88.0% HS; 31.6% bachelor's. **Avg. commute:** 21.4 min. 80.0% drive. **Housing units:** 225,464; 85.5% occupied. **Home ownership:** 55.4%. **Avg. home:** $170,400; change (2013-15): 10.1%. **Avg. rent:** $796.
Mayor: Sly James, nonpartisan
History: Settled by 1838 at confluence of Missouri and Kansas Rivers; inc. 1850.
Website: kcmo.gov

Laredo, Texas

Population: 255,473 (82). **Pop. density:** 2,612. **Pop. change (2010-15):** 7.8%. **Area:** 97.8 sq mi. **Racial distribution:** 93.8% white; 0.4% black; 0.6% Asian; 0.4% Amer. Ind.; <0.05% Pac. Isl.; 4.2% other; 2+ races 0.6%. **Hispanic pop.:** 95.3%. **Foreign born:** 27.2%. **U.S. citizens:** 80.5%. **Language:** 8.9% English only; 90.4% Spanish.
Employment: 102,375 employed; 4.3% unemployed. **Per capita income:** $28,355; change (2013-14): 3.2%. **Below poverty level:** 31.2%; 26.9% of families. **Educational attainment:** 65.4% HS; 17.6% bachelor's. **Avg. commute:** 21.2 min. 78.6% drive; 14.6% carpool. **Housing units:** 70,439; 92.3% occupied. **Home ownership:** 61.8%. **Avg. rent:** $750.
Mayor: Pete Saenz, nonpartisan
History: Founded by Spanish colonists in 1755; part of U.S. from 1848. Fast growth fueled by immigration; principal port of entry into Mexico.
Website: www.cityoflaredo.com

Las Vegas, Nevada

Population: 623,747 (28). **Pop. density:** 4,669. **Pop. change (2010-15):** 6.7%. **Area:** 133.6 sq mi. **Racial distribution:** 65.7% white; 11.4% black; 6.3% Asian; 0.7% Amer. Ind.; 0.6% Pac. Isl.; 10.8% other; 2+ races 4.5%. **Hispanic pop.:** 32.2%. **Foreign born:** 21.3%. **U.S. citizens:** 87.2%. **Language:** 66.5% English only; 25.4% Spanish.
Employment: 278,680 employed; 7.0% unemployed. **Per capita income:** $39,533; change (2013-14): 3.8%. **Below poverty level:** 17.7%; 13.2% of families. **Educational attainment:** 83.0% HS; 21.6% bachelor's. **Avg. commute:** 25.2 min. 77.4% drive; 11.5% carpool. **Housing units:** 248,663; 85.7% occupied. **Home ownership:** 52.5%. **Avg. home:** $216,800; change (2013-15): 24.7%. **Avg. rent:** $983.
Mayor: Caroline G. Goodman, nonpartisan
History: Occupied by Mormons 1855-57; bought by railroad 1903; inc. 1911; gambling legalized 1931.
Website: www.lasvegasnevada.gov

Lexington, Kentucky

Population: 314,488 (61). **Pop. density:** 1,109. **Pop. change (2010-15):** 6.0%. **Area:** 283.7 sq mi. **Racial distribution:** 76.0% white; 14.4% black; 3.5% Asian; 0.3% Amer. Ind.; <0.05% Pac. Isl.; 2.9% other; 2+ races 2.8%. **Hispanic pop.:** 6.8%. **Foreign born:** 9.1%. **U.S. citizens:** 93.4%. **Language:** 88.2% English only; 6.1% Spanish.
Employment: 157,688 employed; 3.9% unemployed. **Per capita income:** $42,231; change (2013-14): 3.6%. **Below poverty level:** 19.3%; 12.2% of families. **Educational attainment:** 89.2% HS; 40.2% bachelor's. **Avg. commute:** 19.8 min. 79.1% drive. **Housing units:** 136,989; 90.6% occupied. **Home ownership:** 54.9%. **Avg. home:** $148,100; change (2013-15): 3.0%. **Avg. rent:** $766.
Mayor: Jim Gray, nonpartisan
History: Site founded and named in 1775 after site of the Revolutionary War's opening battle at Lexington, MA; settled 1779; chartered 1782; inc. 1832.
Website: www.lexingtonky.gov

Lincoln, Nebraska

Population: 277,348 (72). **Pop. density:** 3,033. **Pop. change (2010-15):** 7.0%. **Area:** 91.5 sq mi. **Racial distribution:** 86.8% white; 4.3% black; 4.3% Asian; 0.6% Amer. Ind.; 0.1% Pac. Isl.; 1.1% other; 2+ races 2.8%. **Hispanic pop.:** 6.7%. **Foreign born:** 7.9%. **U.S. citizens:** 95.3%. **Language:** 88.1% English only; 4.4% Spanish.

Employment: 147,734 employed; 2.5% unemployed. **Per capita income:** $43,399; change (2013-14): 2.4%. **Below poverty level:** 16.2%; 10.3% of families. **Educational attainment:** 93.1% HS; 36.2% bachelor's. **Avg. commute:** 18.1 min. 80.8% drive. **Housing units:** 112,122; 95.0% occupied. **Home ownership:** 56.8%. **Avg. home:** $156,800; change (2013-15): 9.4%. **Avg. rent:** $727.
Mayor: Chris Beutler, nonpartisan
History: Originally called Lancaster; chosen state capital 1867, renamed after Abraham Lincoln; inc. 1869.
Website: lincoln.ne.gov

Long Beach, California

Population: 474,140 (37). **Pop. density:** 9,423. **Pop. change (2010-15):** 2.5%. **Area:** 50.3 sq mi. **Racial distribution:** 53.6% white; 13.0% black; 13.1% Asian; 1.0% Amer. Ind.; 1.0% Pac. Isl.; 12.1% other; 2+ races 6.3%. **Hispanic pop.:** 41.7%. **Foreign born:** 26.1%. **U.S. citizens:** 85.8%. **Language:** 54.6% English only; 32.7% Spanish.
Employment: 221,277 employed; 7.4% unemployed. **Per capita income:** $50,751; change (2013-14): 3.8%. **Below poverty level:** 20.7%; 16.5% of families. **Educational attainment:** 79.3% HS; 29.0% bachelor's. **Avg. commute:** 29 min. 73.4% drive. **Housing units:** 174,603; 93.5% occupied. **Home ownership:** 40.2%. **Avg. home:** $476,800; change (2013-15): 17.5%. **Avg. rent:** $1,118.
Mayor: Robert Garcia, nonpartisan
History: Settled as early as 1784 by Spanish; by 1884, present site developed on harbor; inc. 1888; oil discovered 1921.
Website: www.longbeach.gov

Los Angeles, California

Population: 3,971,883 (2). **Pop. density:** 8,475. **Pop. change (2010-15):** 4.6%. **Area:** 468.7 sq mi. **Racial distribution:** 52.6% white; 9.2% black; 11.5% Asian; 0.6% Amer. Ind.; 0.2% Pac. Isl.; 22.4% other; 2+ races 3.5%. **Hispanic pop.:** 48.6%. **Foreign born:** 38.6%. **U.S. citizens:** 77.9%. **Language:** 39.9% English only; 42.9% Spanish.
Employment: 1,867,915 employed; 7.1% unemployed. **Per capita income:** $50,751; change (2013-14): 3.8%. **Below poverty level:** 22.4%; 18.2% of families. **Educational attainment:** 74.9% HS; 31.5% bachelor's. **Avg. commute:** 29.6 min. 67.3% drive; 10.9% public trans. **Housing units:** 1,427,355; 93.1% occupied. **Home ownership:** 37.2%. **Avg. home:** $476,800; change (2013-15): 17.5%. **Avg. rent:** $1,194.
Mayor: Eric Garcetti, nonpartisan
History: Founded by Spanish 1781; captured by U.S. 1846; inc. 1850; grew rapidly after coming of railroads, 1876 and 1885. Hollywood is a district of L.A.
Website: www.lacity.org

Louisville, Kentucky

Population: 615,366 (30). **Pop. density:** 2,334. **Pop. change (2010-15):** 2.9%. **Area:** 263.6 sq mi. **Racial distribution:** 71.3% white; 22.6% black; 2.2% Asian; 0.1% Amer. Ind.; <0.05% Pac. Isl.; 0.7% other; 2+ races 3.0%. **Hispanic pop.:** 4.6%. **Foreign born:** 6.7%. **U.S. citizens:** 95.7%. **Language:** 91.6% English only; 3.8% Spanish.
Employment: 352,193 employed; 4.9% unemployed. **Per capita income:** $42,996; change (2013-14): 4.1%. **Below poverty level:** 18.4%; 13.8% of families. **Educational attainment:** 86.9% HS; 27.4% bachelor's. **Avg. commute:** 22.3 min. 81.8% drive. **Housing units:** 273,381; 89.5% occupied. **Home ownership:** 60.8%. **Avg. home:** $154,500; change (2013-15): 10.8%. **Avg. rent:** $713.
Mayor: Greg Fischer, Democrat
History: Settled 1778; named for Louis XVI of France; inc. 1828; base for Union forces in Civil War.
Website: www.louisvilleky.gov

Lubbock, Texas

Population: 249,042 (83). **Pop. density:** 2,030. **Pop. change (2010-15):** 8.0%. **Area:** 122.7 sq mi. **Racial distribution:** 77.7% white; 8.0% black; 2.4% Asian; 0.5% Amer. Ind.; <0.05% Pac. Isl.; 8.2% other; 2+ races 3.1%. **Hispanic pop.:** 33.2%. **Foreign born:** 5.9%. **U.S. citizens:** 96.6%. **Language:** 77.9% English only; 18.8% Spanish.
Employment: 120,135 employed; 3.3% unemployed. **Per capita income:** $37,434; change (2013-14): 2.4%. **Below poverty level:** 21.5%; 14.0% of families. **Educational attainment:** 86.0% HS; 29.5% bachelor's. **Avg. commute:** 15.4 min. 82.0% drive; 11.1% carpool. **Housing units:** 99,545; 90.8% occupied. **Home ownership:** 53.6%. **Avg. rent:** $816.
Mayor: Dan Pope, nonpartisan
History: Settled 1879; laid out 1891; inc. 1909 through merger of two towns.
Website: www.mylubbock.us

Madison, Wisconsin

Population: 248,951 (84). **Pop. density:** 3,239. **Pop. change (2010-15):** 6.6%. **Area:** 76.9 sq mi. **Racial distribution:** 79.2%

white; 7.2% black; 8.1% Asian; 0.3% Amer. Ind.; <0.05% Pac. Isl.; 1.7% other; 2+ races 3.5%. **Hispanic pop.:** 6.6%. **Foreign born:** 10.7%. **U.S. citizens:** 92.9%. **Language:** 84.8% English only; 5.4% Spanish.
Employment: 146,474 employed; 3.1% unemployed. **Per capita income:** $49,969; change (2013-14): 1.9%. **Below poverty level:** 19.6%; 9.8% of families. **Educational attainment:** 95.0% HS; 55.0% bachelor's. **Avg. commute:** 19.4 min. 63.0% drive. **Housing units:** 108,191; 95.4% occupied. **Home ownership:** 48.7%. **Avg. home:** $238,000; change (2013-15): 7.4%. **Avg. rent:** $922.
Mayor: Paul R. Soglin, nonpartisan
History: Settled 1832; selected as site for state capital, named after James Madison, 1836; chartered 1856.
Website: www.cityofmadison.com

Memphis, Tennessee

Population: 655,770 (24). **Pop. density:** 2,066. **Pop. change (2010-15):** 0.5%. **Area:** 317.4 sq mi. **Racial distribution:** 30.3% white; 62.8% black; 1.7% Asian; 0.2% Amer. Ind.; <0.05% Pac. Isl.; 3.1% other; 2+ races 1.8%. **Hispanic pop.:** 6.5%. **Foreign born:** 6.2%. **U.S. citizens:** 95.5%. **Language:** 90.6% English only; 6.1% Spanish.
Employment: 266,480 employed; 7.3% unemployed. **Per capita income:** $41,935; change (2013-14): 2.3%. **Below poverty level:** 27.4%; 22.6% of families. **Educational attainment:** 83.5% HS; 24.7% bachelor's. **Avg. commute:** 21.6 min. 79.7% drive; 12.5% carpool. **Housing units:** 296,857; 83.6% occupied. **Home ownership:** 49.9%. **Avg. home:** $147,000; change (2013-15): 13.6%. **Avg. rent:** $831.
Mayor: Jim Strickland, nonpartisan
History: French, Spanish, and U.S. forts by 1797; settled by 1819; inc. as town 1826, as city 1840; surrendered charter to state 1879 after yellow fever epidemics; rechartered as city 1893.
Website: www.cityofmemphis.org

Mesa, Arizona

Population: 471,825 (38). **Pop. density:** 3,422. **Pop. change (2010-15):** 7.0%. **Area:** 137.9 sq mi. **Racial distribution:** 84.5% white; 3.5% black; 2.0% Asian; 2.2% Amer. Ind.; 0.3% Pac. Isl.; 4.9% other; 2+ races 2.6%. **Hispanic pop.:** 26.8%. **Foreign born:** 12.4%. **U.S. citizens:** 91.4%. **Language:** 78.4% English only; 17.8% Spanish.
Employment: 212,831 employed; 5.2% unemployed. **Per capita income:** $39,846; change (2013-14): 3.1%. **Below poverty level:** 16.3%; 12.5% of families. **Educational attainment:** 87.4% HS; 24.3% bachelor's. **Avg. commute:** 24.8 min. 77.4% drive; 11.7% carpool. **Housing units:** 200,158; 83.7% occupied. **Home ownership:** 60.5%. **Avg. home:** $216,400; change (2013-15): 17.9%. **Avg. rent:** $875.
Mayor: John Giles, nonpartisan
History: Founded by Mormons 1878; inc. 1883. Population boomed fivefold 1960-80.
Website: www.mesaaz.gov

Miami, Florida

Population: 441,003 (44). **Pop. density:** 12,256. **Pop. change (2010-15):** 10.0%. **Area:** 36.0 sq mi. **Racial distribution:** 74.9% white; 19.6% black; 0.9% Asian; 0.2% Amer. Ind.; <0.05% Pac. Isl.; 3.2% other; 2+ races 1.2%. **Hispanic pop.:** 70.7%. **Foreign born:** 57.6%. **U.S. citizens:** 67.9%. **Language:** 22.7% English only; 70.0% Spanish.
Employment: 200,420 employed; 6.1% unemployed. **Per capita income:** $48,224; change (2013-14): 3.9%. **Below poverty level:** 29.9%; 25.0% of families. **Educational attainment:** 72.0% HS; 23.5% bachelor's. **Avg. commute:** 26.6 min. 69.2% drive; 11.4% public trans. **Housing units:** 188,603; 80.8% occupied. **Home ownership:** 31.6%. **Avg. home:** $280,000; change (2013-15): 13.6%. **Avg. rent:** $958.
Mayor: Tomás Regalado, nonpartisan
History: Site of fort 1836; settlement began 1870; inc. 1896. Modern city developed into financial and recreation center; land speculation in 1920s added to city's growth, as did Cuban, Central and South American, and Haitian immigration since 1960.
Website: www.miamigov.com

Milwaukee, Wisconsin

Population: 600,155 (31). **Pop. density:** 6,240. **Pop. change (2010-15):** 0.8%. **Area:** 96.2 sq mi. **Racial distribution:** 47.0% white; 39.3% black; 3.7% Asian; 1.4% Amer. Ind.; <0.05% Pac. Isl.; 5.8% other; 2+ races 3.7%. **Hispanic pop.:** 17.7%. **Foreign born:** 9.8%. **U.S. citizens:** 93.4%. **Language:** 80.6% English only; 13.6% Spanish.
Employment: 263,728 employed; 6.7% unemployed. **Per capita income:** $48,638; change (2013-14): 3.2%. **Below poverty level:** 29.4%; 25.3% of families. **Educational attainment:** 81.8% HS; 22.8% bachelor's. **Avg. commute:** 22.1 min. 70.9% drive; 11.1% carpool. **Housing units:** 257,965; 89.2% occupied. **Home ownership:** 43.0%. **Avg. home:** $220,400; change (2013-15): 9.8%. **Avg. rent:** $784.
Mayor: Tom Barrett, Democrat

History: Indian trading post by 1674; settlement began 1835; inc. 1848. Famous beer industry.
Website: city.milwaukee.gov

Minneapolis, Minnesota

Population: 410,939 (46). **Pop. density:** 7,608. **Pop. change (2010-15):** 7.3%. **Area:** 54.0 sq mi. **Racial distribution:** 66.4% white; 17.9% black; 5.9% Asian; 1.4% Amer. Ind.; <0.05% Pac. Isl.; 3.6% other; 2+ races 4.8%. **Hispanic pop.:** 9.8%. **Foreign born:** 15.1%. **U.S. citizens:** 91.1%. **Language:** 79.6% English only; 8.0% Spanish.
Employment: 224,547 employed; 3.3% unemployed. **Per capita income:** $53,166; change (2013-14): 3.9%. **Below poverty level:** 22.6%; 16.1% of families. **Educational attainment:** 89.0% HS; 47.0% bachelor's. **Avg. commute:** 22.6 min. 61.6% drive; 13.5% public trans. **Housing units:** 180,737; 92.3% occupied. **Home ownership:** 48.6%. **Avg. home:** $225,100; change (2013-15): 14.7%. **Avg. rent:** $854.
Mayor: Betsy Hodges, Democrat (DFL)
History: Site visited by French missionary Louis Hennepin 1680; located on military-reservation land 1819; inc. 1867.
Website: minneapolismn.gov

Nashville, Tennessee

Population: 654,610 (25). **Pop. density:** 1,375. **Pop. change (2010-15):** 8.2%. **Area:** 475.9 sq mi. **Racial distribution:** 61.3% white; 28.3% black; 3.2% Asian; 0.3% Amer. Ind.; 0.1% Pac. Isl.; 4.6% other; 2+ races 2.4%. **Hispanic pop.:** 10.1%. **Foreign born:** 12.1%. **U.S. citizens:** 91.9%. **Language:** 83.8% English only; 8.9% Spanish.
Employment: 347,995 employed; 4.5% unemployed. **Per capita income:** $47,392; change (2013-14): 3.4%. **Below poverty level:** 19.2%; 14.6% of families. **Educational attainment:** 86.2% HS; 35.8% bachelor's. **Avg. commute:** 23.4 min. 79.5% drive; 10.3% carpool. **Housing units:** 277,528; 90.2% occupied. **Home ownership:** 53.5%. **Avg. home:** $204,200; change (2013-15): 15.8%. **Avg. rent:** $858.
Mayor: Megan Barry, nonpartisan
History: Settled 1779; first chartered 1806; became permanent state capital 1843. Home of Grand Ole Opry.
Website: www.nashville.gov

New Orleans, Louisiana

Population: 389,617 (49). **Pop. density:** 2,300. **Pop. change (2010-15):** 12.0%. **Area:** 169.4 sq mi. **Racial distribution:** 34.0% white; 59.6% black; 3.0% Asian; 0.3% Amer. Ind.; <0.05% Pac. Isl.; 1.5% other; 2+ races 1.7%. **Hispanic pop.:** 5.4%. **Foreign born:** 6.0%. **U.S. citizens:** 96.6%. **Language:** 90.6% English only; 4.5% Spanish.
Employment: 169,098 employed; 6.5% unemployed. **Per capita income:** $46,282; change (2013-14): 3.2%. **Below poverty level:** 27.7%; 22.7% of families. **Educational attainment:** 84.8% HS; 34.4% bachelor's. **Avg. commute:** 23.1 min. 69.9% drive. **Housing units:** 191,310; 78.6% occupied. **Home ownership:** 46.9%. **Avg. home:** $169,700; change (2013-15): 3.0%. **Avg. rent:** $927.
Mayor: Mitchell J. Landrieu, Democrat
History: Founded by French 1718; became major seaport on Mississippi R.; acquired by U.S. as part of Louisiana Purchase 1803; inc. 1805. Americans defeated British forces at Battle of New Orleans in 1815.
Website: www.nola.gov

New York, New York

Population: 8,550,405 (1). **Pop. density:** 28,363. **Pop. change (2010-15):** 4.4%. **Area:** 301.5 sq mi. **Racial distribution:** 43.6% white; 24.7% black; 13.2% Asian; 0.4% Amer. Ind.; <0.05% Pac. Isl.; 14.7% other; 2+ races 3.2%. **Hispanic pop.:** 28.8%. **Foreign born:** 37.1%. **U.S. citizens:** 82.4%. **Language:** 51.0% English only; 24.6% Spanish; 5.8% Chinese.
Employment: 3,959,898 employed; 5.7% unemployed. **Per capita income:** $61,440; change (2013-14): 4.1%. **Below poverty level:** 20.6%; 17.5% of families. **Educational attainment:** 80.1% HS; 35.0% bachelor's. **Avg. commute:** 39.4 min. 56.2% public trans.; 22.2% drive; 10.1% walk. **Housing units:** 3,407,932; 90.8% occupied. **Home ownership:** 31.9%. **Avg. home:** $397,900; change (2013-15): 1.6%. **Avg. rent:** $1,234.
Mayor: Bill de Blasio, Democrat
History: Trading post est. 1624; British took control from Dutch 1664, named city New York; briefly U.S. capital; under new charter, 1898, city expanded to include five boroughs: Bronx, Brooklyn, Queens, and Staten Island, as well as Manhattan. Sept. 11, 2001, terrorist attacks destroyed World Trade Center, killed more than 2,750.
Website: www.nyc.gov

Newark, New Jersey

Population: 281,944 (70). **Pop. density:** 11,654. **Pop. change (2010-15):** 1.7%. **Area:** 24.2 sq mi. **Racial distribution:** 24.5% white; 50.8% black; 1.8% Asian; 0.6% Amer. Ind.; 0.1%

Pac. Isl.; 17.5% other; 2+ races 4.7%. **Hispanic pop.:** 34.8%. **Foreign born:** 27.9%. **U.S. citizens:** 81.7%. **Language:** 53.9% English only; 31.7% Spanish; 7.9% Portuguese.
Employment: 108,039 employed; 8.8% unemployed. **Per capita income:** $61,440; change (2013-14): 4.1%. **Below poverty level:** 29.9%; 26.9% of families. **Educational attainment:** 71.4% HS; 13.3% bachelor's. **Avg. commute:** 33.9 min. 48.0% drive; 26.8% public trans.; 13.3% carpool. **Housing units:** 108,936; 84.2% occupied. **Home ownership:** 22.3%. **Avg. home:** $376,900; change (2013-15): –1.2%. **Avg. rent:** $978.
Mayor: Ras J. Baraka, nonpartisan
History: Settled by Puritans 1666; used as supply base by George Washington 1776; inc. as town 1833, as city 1836.
Website: www.ci.newark.nj.us

Norfolk, Virginia

Population: 246,393 (86). **Pop. density:** 4,556. **Pop. change (2010-15):** 1.4%. **Area:** 54.1 sq mi. **Racial distribution:** 47.8% white; 42.6% black; 3.4% Asian; 0.4% Amer. Ind.; 0.2% Pac. Isl.; 1.9% other; 2+ races 3.7%. **Hispanic pop.:** 7.1%. **Foreign born:** 6.8%. **U.S. citizens:** 96.5%. **Language:** 89.9% English only; 5.0% Spanish.
Employment: 105,107 employed; 5.6% unemployed. **Per capita income:** $45,276; change (2013-14): 2.7%. **Below poverty level:** 20.5%; 15.8% of families. **Educational attainment:** 86.6% HS; 25.6% bachelor's. **Avg. commute:** 21.6 min. 71.6% drive. **Housing units:** 95,699; 90.3% occupied. **Home ownership:** 43.7%. **Avg. home:** $209,000; change (2013-15): 8.3%. **Avg. rent:** $965.
Mayor: Kenneth Cooper Alexander, nonpartisan
History: Founded 1682; burned by colonists to prevent capture by British during Revolutionary War; rebuilt and inc. as town 1805, as city 1845. Site of world's largest naval base; major East Coast commercial port and cruise terminal.
Website: www.norfolk.gov

North Las Vegas, Nevada

Population: 234,807 (95). **Pop. density:** 2,396. **Pop. change (2010-15):** 8.2%. **Area:** 98.0 sq mi. **Racial distribution:** 52.3% white; 20.1% black; 6.0% Asian; 0.5% Amer. Ind.; 1.0% Pac. Isl.; 15.2% other; 2+ races 4.9%. **Hispanic pop.:** 38.9%. **Foreign born:** 21.7%. **U.S. citizens:** 86.7%. **Language:** 60.4% English only; 32.6% Spanish.
Employment: 100,088 employed; 7.5% unemployed. **Per capita income:** $39,533; change (2013-14): 3.8%. **Below poverty level:** 16.9%; 13.7% of families. **Educational attainment:** 77.7% HS; 15.2% bachelor's. **Avg. commute:** 26.5 min. 81.7% drive; 10.8% carpool. **Housing units:** 77,334; 87.9% occupied. **Home ownership:** 55.2%. **Avg. home:** $216,800; change (2013-15): 24.7%. **Avg. rent:** $1,116.
Mayor: John J. Lee, nonpartisan
History: Inc. 1946.
Website: www.cityofnorthlasvegas.com

Oakland, California

Population: 419,267 (45). **Pop. density:** 7,501. **Pop. change (2010-15):** 7.0%. **Area:** 55.9 sq mi. **Racial distribution:** 39.7% white; 26.1% black; 16.5% Asian; 0.8% Amer. Ind.; 0.6% Pac. Isl.; 10.3% other; 2+ races 6.0%. **Hispanic pop.:** 25.9%. **Foreign born:** 27.1%. **U.S. citizens:** 85.0%. **Language:** 59.7% English only; 21.8% Spanish; 7.7% Chinese.
Employment: 198,693 employed; 5.9% unemployed. **Per capita income:** $72,364; change (2013-14): 4.6%. **Below poverty level:** 21.0%; 16.8% of families. **Educational attainment:** 80.6% HS; 38.6% bachelor's. **Avg. commute:** 29.2 min. 54.0% drive; 19.1% public trans.; 11.2% carpool. **Housing units:** 171,156; 91.1% occupied. **Home ownership:** 39.8%. **Avg. home:** $782,300; change (2013-15): 21.5%. **Avg. rent:** $1,114.
Mayor: Libby Schaaf, nonpartisan
History: Area settled by Spanish 1820; inc. 1854.
Website: www.oaklandnet.com

Oklahoma City, Oklahoma

Population: 631,346 (27). **Pop. density:** 1,041. **Pop. change (2010-15):** 8.5%. **Area:** 606.7 sq mi. **Racial distribution:** 67.3% white; 14.6% black; 4.2% Asian; 3.0% Amer. Ind.; 0.1% Pac. Isl.; 4.1% other; 2+ races 6.8%. **Hispanic pop.:** 18.0%. **Foreign born:** 12.4%. **U.S. citizens:** 91.4%. **Language:** 80.4% English only; 14.3% Spanish.
Employment: 300,624 employed; 3.5% unemployed. **Per capita income:** $46,675; change (2013-14): 3.6%. **Below poverty level:** 18.2%; 14.1% of families. **Educational attainment:** 85.0% HS; 28.5% bachelor's. **Avg. commute:** 20.5 min. 82.0% drive; 11.4% carpool. **Housing units:** 259,863; 88.7% occupied. **Home ownership:** 58.8%. **Avg. home:** $149,600; change (2013-15): –2.3%. **Avg. rent:** $763.
Mayor: Mick Cornett, nonpartisan
History: Settled during land rush in Midwest 1889; inc. 1890; became capital 1910; oil discovered 1928. Bomb in 1995 destroyed federal office bldg., killed 168 people.
Website: www.okc.gov

Omaha, Nebraska

Population: 443,885 (43). **Pop. density:** 3,332. **Pop. change (2010-15):** 2.6%. **Area:** 133.2 sq mi. **Racial distribution:** 77.0% white; 12.8% black; 2.8% Asian; 0.7% Amer. Ind.; <0.05% Pac. Isl.; 3.6% other; 2+ races 3.1%. **Hispanic pop.:** 13.3%. **Foreign born:** 9.8%. **U.S. citizens:** 93.1%. **Language:** 84.6% English only; 10.3% Spanish.
Employment: 225,426 employed; 3.1% unemployed. **Per capita income:** $48,821; change (2013-14): 2.8%. **Below poverty level:** 16.8%; 12.2% of families. **Educational attainment:** 87.8% HS; 33.8% bachelor's. **Avg. commute:** 18.5 min. 82.2% drive. **Housing units:** 186,826; 92.1% occupied. **Home ownership:** 58.1%. **Avg. home:** $159,100; change (2013-15): 9.2%. **Avg. rent:** $797.
Mayor: Jean Stothert, nonpartisan
History: Founded 1854; inc. 1857. Large food-processing, telecommunications, information-processing center.
Website: www.cityofomaha.org

Orlando, Florida

Population: 270,934 (73). **Pop. density:** 2,638. **Pop. change (2010-15):** 13.2%. **Area:** 102.7 sq mi. **Racial distribution:** 59.1% white; 28.5% black; 3.6% Asian; 0.4% Amer. Ind.; 0.1% Pac. Isl.; 5.8% other; 2+ races 2.6%. **Hispanic pop.:** 26.8%. **Foreign born:** 18.3%. **U.S. citizens:** 89.7%. **Language:** 66.8% English only; 22.9% Spanish.
Employment: 147,007 employed; 4.6% unemployed. **Per capita income:** $37,104; change (2013-14): 3.6%. **Below poverty level:** 19.8%; 15.6% of families. **Educational attainment:** 88.9% HS; 33.4% bachelor's. **Avg. commute:** 24.5 min. 78.7% drive. **Housing units:** 122,286; 83.9% occupied. **Home ownership:** 37.4%. **Avg. home:** $198,000; change (2013-15): 20.0%. **Avg. rent:** $999.
Mayor: Buddy Dyer, nonpartisan
History: Ft. Gatlin built just south of present-day Orlando in 1838; name changed from Jernigan to Orlando 1856; inc. 1875. Walt Disney World opened in 1971.
Website: www.cityoforlando.net

Philadelphia, Pennsylvania

Population: 1,567,442 (5). **Pop. density:** 11,682. **Pop. change (2010-15):** 2.6%. **Area:** 134.2 sq mi. **Racial distribution:** 41.6% white; 43.0% black; 6.7% Asian; 0.3% Amer. Ind.; 0.1% Pac. Isl.; 5.6% other; 2+ races 2.6%. **Hispanic pop.:** 13.0%. **Foreign born:** 12.5%. **U.S. citizens:** 93.7%. **Language:** 78.1% English only; 10.1% Spanish.
Employment: 648,280 employed; 6.9% unemployed. **Per capita income:** $54,936; change (2013-14): 3.7%. **Below poverty level:** 26.7%; 21.2% of families. **Educational attainment:** 81.4% HS; 24.5% bachelor's. **Avg. commute:** 32.2 min. 50.2% drive; 26.5% public trans. **Housing units:** 669,642; 86.7% occupied. **Home ownership:** 52.9%. **Avg. home:** $223,700; change (2013-15): 1.5%. **Avg. rent:** $915.
Mayor: Jim F. Kenney, Democrat
History: First settled by Swedes 1638; Swedes surrendered to Dutch 1654; settled by English and Scottish Quakers 1678; named Philadelphia 1682; chartered 1701. Continental Congresses convened 1774, 1775; Declaration of Independence signed here 1776; natl. capital 1790-1800; state capital 1683-1799.
Website: www.phila.gov

Phoenix, Arizona

Population: 1,563,025 (6). **Pop. density:** 3,020. **Pop. change (2010-15):** 7.8%. **Area:** 517.6 sq mi. **Racial distribution:** 75.7% white; 6.8% black; 3.3% Asian; 2.0% Amer. Ind.; 0.2% Pac. Isl.; 8.9% other; 2+ races 3.0%. **Hispanic pop.:** 40.5%. **Foreign born:** 20.2%. **U.S. citizens:** 85.7%. **Language:** 63.4% English only; 30.4% Spanish.
Employment: 714,068 employed; 5.4% unemployed. **Per capita income:** $39,846; change (2013-14): 3.1%. **Below poverty level:** 23.2%; 18.5% of families. **Educational attainment:** 80.8% HS; 26.5% bachelor's. **Avg. commute:** 24.5 min. 75.0% drive; 12.0% carpool. **Housing units:** 598,176; 87.1% occupied. **Home ownership:** 54.0%. **Avg. home:** $216,400; change (2013-15): 17.9%. **Avg. rent:** $876.
Mayor: Greg Stanton, nonpartisan
History: Founded 1867; inc. 1881; became territorial capital 1889.
Website: www.phoenix.gov

Pittsburgh, Pennsylvania

Population: 304,391 (63). **Pop. density:** 5,497. **Pop. change (2010-15):** –0.4%. **Area:** 55.4 sq mi. **Racial distribution:** 66.8% white; 24.6% black; 4.8% Asian; 0.2% Amer. Ind.; <0.05% Pac. Isl.; 0.5% other; 2+ races 3.1%. **Hispanic pop.:** 2.7%. **Foreign born:** 7.5%. **U.S. citizens:** 95.1%. **Language:** 90.0% English only; 2.1% Spanish.
Employment: 149,820 employed; 5.1% unemployed. **Per capita income:** $49,349; change (2013-14): 3.2%. **Below**

poverty level: 22.8%; 16.2% of families. Educational attainment: 91.0% HS; 37.2% bachelor's. Avg. commute: 23.2 min. 55.5% drive; 16.9% public trans.; 10.9% walk. Housing units: 154,942; 85.4% occupied. Home ownership: 48.8%. Avg. rent: $794.

Mayor: William "Bill" Peduto, Democrat
History: Settled around Ft. Pitt 1758; inc. 1816; became an inland port; by Civil War, already a center for iron production.
Website: pittsburghpa.gov

Plano, Texas

Population: 283,558 (69). Pop. density: 3,957. Pop. change (2010-15): 8.5%. Area: 71.7 sq mi. Racial distribution: 68.9% white; 7.5% black; 18.2% Asian; 0.4% Amer. Ind.; 0.1% Pac. Isl.; 2.0% other; 2+ races 3.1%. Hispanic pop.: 14.7%. Foreign born: 24.1%. U.S. citizens: 87.1%. Language: 68.0% English only; 11.9% Spanish.
Employment: 149,036 employed; 3.7% unemployed. Per capita income: $49,506; change (2013-14): 3.9%. Below poverty level: 7.6%; 5.4% of families. Educational attainment: 93.4% HS; 54.6% bachelor's. Avg. commute: 25.7 min. 81.5% drive. Housing units: 107,326; 95.2% occupied. Home ownership: 63.1%. Avg. home: $207,200; change (2013-15): 18.0%. Avg. rent: $1,115.
Mayor: Harry LaRosiliere, nonpartisan
History: Settled 1846; inc. 1873.
Website: www.plano.gov

Portland, Oregon

Population: 632,309 (26). Pop. density: 4,738. Pop. change (2010-15): 8.0%. Area: 133.5 sq mi. Racial distribution: 77.3% white; 6.1% black; 7.5% Asian; 0.8% Amer. Ind.; 0.5% Pac. Isl.; 3.1% other; 2+ races 4.6%. Hispanic pop.: 9.6%. Foreign born: 14.0%. U.S. citizens: 92.3%. Language: 80.6% English only; 7.1% Spanish.
Employment: 332,868 employed; 4.8% unemployed. Per capita income: $45,794; change (2013-14): 4.0%. Below poverty level: 18.3%; 12.1% of families. Educational attainment: 90.9% HS; 44.4% bachelor's. Avg. commute: 24.7 min. 58.0% drive; 11.8% public trans. Housing units: 267,514; 94.3% occupied. Home ownership: 52.8%. Avg. home: $312,100; change (2013-15): 17.6%. Avg. rent: $945.
Mayor: Charlie Hales, nonpartisan
History: Settled by pioneers 1845; developed as trading center, aided by California Gold Rush 1849; chartered 1851.
Website: www.portlandoregon.gov

Raleigh, North Carolina

Population: 451,066 (42). Pop. density: 3,121. Pop. change (2010-15): 11.0%. Area: 144.5 sq mi. Racial distribution: 60.9% white; 28.9% black; 4.3% Asian; 0.3% Amer. Ind.; 0.1% Pac. Isl.; 3.3% other; 2+ races 2.1%. Hispanic pop.: 10.9%. Foreign born: 13.3%. U.S. citizens: 90.9%. Language: 82.6% English only; 9.6% Spanish.
Employment: 228,433 employed; 4.6% unemployed. Per capita income: $46,636; change (2013-14): 2.8%. Below poverty level: 16.3%; 11.8% of families. Educational attainment: 90.7% HS; 47.6% bachelor's. Avg. commute: 21.9 min. 79.8% drive. Housing units: 182,734; 91.0% occupied. Home ownership: 53.2%. Avg. home: $238,200; change (2013-15): 21.0%. Avg. rent: $914.
Mayor: Nancy McFarlane, nonpartisan
History: Named after Sir Walter Raleigh; site chosen for state capital 1788; laid out 1792; inc. 1795; occupied by Union Gen. William Sherman 1865.
Website: www.raleighnc.gov

Reno, Nevada

Population: 241,445 (87). Pop. density: 2,251. Pop. change (2010-15): 6.6%. Area: 107.3 sq mi. Racial distribution: 79.5% white; 3.0% black; 6.4% Asian; 1.0% Amer. Ind.; 0.7% Pac. Isl.; 5.5% other; 2+ races 3.8%. Hispanic pop.: 24.7%. Foreign born: 16.4%. U.S. citizens: 90.3%. Language: 74.4% English only; 17.9% Spanish.
Employment: 115,324 employed; 6.2% unemployed. Per capita income: $46,120; change (2013-14): 4.2%. Below poverty level: 19.1%; 13.1% of families. Educational attainment: 85.8% HS; 29.4% bachelor's. Avg. commute: 19.3 min. 76.5% drive; 10.9% carpool. Housing units: 102,408; 89.0% occupied. Home ownership: 46.6%. Avg. home: $283,600; change (2013-15): 29.9%. Avg. rent: $862.
Mayor: Hillary Schieve, nonpartisan
History: Founded 1857; originally named Lakes Crossing; name changed to Reno, after a Union Civil War general, 1868, with arrival of transcontinental railroad.
Website: www.reno.gov

Richmond, Virginia

Population: 220,289 (98). Pop. density: 3,682. Pop. change (2010-15): 7.9%. Area: 59.8 sq mi. Racial distribution: 43.8% white; 48.9% black; 2.2% Asian; 0.3% Amer. Ind.; <0.05% Pac. Isl.; 1.3% other; 2+ races 3.5%. Hispanic pop.: 6.4%. Foreign born: 7.0%. U.S. citizens: 95.1%. Language: 90.0% English only; 5.7% Spanish.
Employment: 107,496 employed; 5.2% unemployed. Per capita income: $47,083; change (2013-14): 2.6%. Below poverty level: 25.5%; 20.0% of families. Educational attainment: 82.4% HS; 35.4% bachelor's. Avg. commute: 21.7 min. 70.7% drive; 11.2% carpool. Housing units: 99,123; 86.7% occupied. Home ownership: 42.7%. Avg. home: $227,300; change (2013-15): 9.5%. Avg. rent: $893.
Mayor: Dwight C. Jones, nonpartisan
History: First settled 1607; became capital of Commonwealth of Virginia 1779; attacked by British under Benedict Arnold 1781; inc. 1782; capital of Confederate States of America 1861-65.
Website: www.richmondgov.com

Riverside, California

Population: 322,424 (59). Pop. density: 3,972. Pop. change (2010-15): 5.5%. Area: 81.2 sq mi. Racial distribution: 67.0% white; 6.2% black; 7.2% Asian; 1.1% Amer. Ind.; 0.2% Pac. Isl.; 13.5% other; 2+ races 4.9%. Hispanic pop.: 51.5%. Foreign born: 22.9%. U.S. citizens: 86.5%. Language: 58.3% English only; 34.0% Spanish.
Employment: 138,842 employed; 6.4% unemployed. Per capita income: $33,258; change (2013-14): 3.6%. Below poverty level: 19.7%; 14.4% of families. Educational attainment: 78.1% HS; 22.1% bachelor's. Avg. commute: 29.2 min. 75.7% drive; 13.2% carpool. Housing units: 98,247; 92.3% occupied. Home ownership: 55.4%. Avg. home: $290,700; change (2013-15): 20.4%. Avg. rent: $1,158.
Mayor: William "Rusty" Bailey, nonpartisan
History: Founded 1870; inc. 1886. Known for its citrus industry, home of the parent navel orange tree; historic Mission Inn resort.
Website: www.riversideca.gov

Sacramento, California

Population: 490,712 (35). Pop. density: 5,011. Pop. change (2010-15): 4.9%. Area: 97.9 sq mi. Racial distribution: 50.0% white; 13.6% black; 18.7% Asian; 0.8% Amer. Ind.; 1.5% Pac. Isl.; 8.5% other; 2+ races 6.9%. Hispanic pop.: 27.6%. Foreign born: 22.1%. U.S. citizens: 89.5%. Language: 63.1% English only; 17.4% Spanish.
Employment: 213,736 employed; 6.4% unemployed. Per capita income: $46,852; change (2013-14): 2.9%. Below poverty level: 22.3%; 17.7% of families. Educational attainment: 82.9% HS; 29.3% bachelor's. Avg. commute: 24.2 min. 72.3% drive; 12.6% carpool. Housing units: 193,173; 91.9% occupied. Home ownership: 47.6%. Avg. home: $289,300; change (2013-15): 20.8%. Avg. rent: $1,008.
Mayor: Kevin Johnson, nonpartisan
History: Settled 1839; important trading center during California Gold Rush 1840s; became state capital 1854.
Website: www.cityofsacramento.org

St. Louis, Missouri

Population: 315,685 (60). Pop. density: 5,096. Pop. change (2010-15): -1.1%. Area: 62.0 sq mi. Racial distribution: 45.5% white; 48.1% black; 2.8% Asian; 0.2% Amer. Ind.; <0.05% Pac. Isl.; 0.8% other; 2+ races 2.6%. Hispanic pop.: 3.7%. Foreign born: 6.8%. U.S. citizens: 95.7%. Language: 90.4% English only; 3.1% Spanish.
Employment: 153,139 employed; 6.1% unemployed. Per capita income: $47,391; change (2013-14): 3.3%. Below poverty level: 27.8%; 22.0% of families. Educational attainment: 83.2% HS; 30.4% bachelor's. Avg. commute: 23.8 min. 71.1% drive. Housing units: 175,656; 79.5% occupied. Home ownership: 44.2%. Avg. home: $150,600; change (2013-15): 12.1%. Avg. rent: $742.
Mayor: Francis Slay, Democrat
History: Founded 1764 as fur trading post by French; acquired by U.S. 1803; chartered 1822; became independent city 1876. Lies on Mississippi R. near confluence with Missouri R.
Website: www.stlouis-mo.gov

St. Paul, Minnesota

Population: 300,851 (64). Pop. density: 5,788. Pop. change (2010-15): 5.4%. Area: 52.0 sq mi. Racial distribution: 60.2% white; 15.5% black; 16.0% Asian; 0.9% Amer. Ind.; <0.05% Pac. Isl.; 2.7% other; 2+ races 4.7%. Hispanic pop.: 9.5%. Foreign born: 18.2%. U.S. citizens: 90.2%. Language: 72.7% English only; 7.1% Spanish; 9.4% Hmong.
Employment: 148,121 employed; 3.7% unemployed. Per capita income: $53,166; change (2013-14): 3.9%. Below poverty level: 22.9%; 17.5% of families. Educational attainment: 86.4% HS; 38.6% bachelor's. Avg. commute: 22.8 min. 69.5% drive; 10.4% carpool. Housing units: 120,058; 93.6% occupied. Home ownership: 49.4%. Avg. home: $225,100; change (2013-15): 14.7%. Avg. rent: $823.

Mayor: Chris Coleman, nonpartisan
History: Founded in early 1840s as Pig's Eye Landing; became capital of Minnesota territory 1849; chartered as St. Paul 1854.
Website: www.stpaul.gov

St. Petersburg, Florida

Population: 257,083 (80). **Pop. density:** 4,163. **Pop. change (2010-15):** 4.8%. **Area:** 61.8 sq mi. **Racial distribution:** 69.0% white; 23.9% black; 3.3% Asian; 0.3% Amer. Ind.; 0.1% Pac. Isl.; 0.8% other; 2+ races 2.6%. **Hispanic pop.:** 6.9%. **Foreign born:** 10.5%. **U.S. citizens:** 95.6%. **Language:** 88.6% English only; 4.8% Spanish.
Employment: 129,477 employed; 4.6% unemployed. **Per capita income:** $41,296; change (2013-14): 3.4%. **Below poverty level:** 17.2%; 11.9% of families. **Educational attainment:** 88.6% HS; 30.0% bachelor's. **Avg. commute:** 22.1 min. 80.2% drive. **Housing units:** 127,814; 82.2% occupied. **Home ownership:** 58.7%. **Avg. home:** $173,000; change (2013-15): 15.3%. **Avg. rent:** $927.
Mayor: Rick Kriseman, nonpartisan
History: Founded 1888; inc. 1903. Site of Salvador Dali Museum.
Website: www.stpete.org

San Antonio, Texas

Population: 1,469,845 (7). **Pop. density:** 3,188. **Pop. change (2010-15):** 10.2%. **Area:** 461.0 sq mi. **Racial distribution:** 77.1% white; 6.8% black; 2.4% Asian; 0.7% Amer. Ind.; 0.1% Pac. Isl.; 10.2% other; 2+ races 2.7%. **Hispanic pop.:** 63.3%. **Foreign born:** 14.2%. **U.S. citizens:** 91.1%. **Language:** 55.1% English only; 41.3% Spanish.
Employment: 651,496 employed; 3.7% unemployed. **Per capita income:** $41,372; change (2013-14): 3.7%. **Below poverty level:** 20.1%; 16.0% of families. **Educational attainment:** 81.1% HS; 24.9% bachelor's. **Avg. commute:** 23.3 min. 79.0% drive; 11.3% carpool. **Housing units:** 532,241; 91.0% occupied. **Home ownership:** 55.0%. **Avg. home:** $195,000; change (2013-15): 14.0%. **Avg. rent:** $840.
Mayor: Ivy R. Taylor, nonpartisan
History: First Spanish garrison 1718; Battle of the Alamo 1836; city subsequently captured by Texans; inc. 1837; first town meeting in Texas took place here, 1845.
Website: www.sanantonio.gov

San Bernardino, California

Population: 216,108 (100). **Pop. density:** 3,513. **Pop. change (2010-15):** 2.8%. **Area:** 61.5 sq mi. **Racial distribution:** 54.5% white; 13.9% black; 4.8% Asian; 0.9% Amer. Ind.; 0.3% Pac. Isl.; 20.7% other; 2+ races 5.0%. **Hispanic pop.:** 61.2%. **Foreign born:** 23.0%. **U.S. citizens:** 85.1%. **Language:** 52.3% English only; 42.2% Spanish.
Employment: 76,884 employed; 8.2% unemployed. **Per capita income:** $33,258; change (2013-14): 3.6%. **Below poverty level:** 33.0%; 28.2% of families. **Educational attainment:** 67.7% HS; 11.7% bachelor's. **Avg. commute:** 27.1 min. 73.5% drive; 16.0% carpool. **Housing units:** 63,450; 90.7% occupied. **Home ownership:** 48.9%. **Avg. home:** $290,700; change (2013-15): 20.4%. **Avg. rent:** $944.
Mayor: R. Carey Davis, nonpartisan
History: Named by Spanish Franciscan missionaries 1810; major Mormon settlement in the 1850s, later recalled to Utah; inc. 1854. Population grew in 1860s when gold was discovered nearby; later became a transportation hub.
Website: www.sbcity.org

San Diego, California

Population: 1,394,928 (8). **Pop. density:** 4,290. **Pop. change (2010-15):** 6.8%. **Area:** 325.2 sq mi. **Racial distribution:** 64.1% white; 6.7% black; 16.6% Asian; 0.6% Amer. Ind.; 0.4% Pac. Isl.; 6.8% other; 2+ races 4.8%. **Hispanic pop.:** 29.5%. **Foreign born:** 26.3%. **U.S. citizens:** 87.2%. **Language:** 59.8% English only; 22.7% Spanish.
Employment: 667,796 employed; 4.9% unemployed. **Per capita income:** $51,459; change (2013-14): 3.1%. **Below poverty level:** 15.8%; 11.2% of families. **Educational attainment:** 87.3% HS; 42.3% bachelor's. **Avg. commute:** 22.9 min. 74.9% drive. **Housing units:** 518,300; 92.4% occupied. **Home ownership:** 47.5%. **Avg. home:** $542,600; change (2013-15): 16.9%. **Avg. rent:** $1,359.
Mayor: Kevin L. Faulconer, nonpartisan
History: Claimed by Spanish 1542; first mission est. 1769; scene of conflict during Mexican-American War 1846; inc. 1850.
Website: www.sandiego.gov

San Francisco, California

Population: 864,816 (13). **Pop. density:** 18,442. **Pop. change (2010-15):** 7.3%. **Area:** 46.9 sq mi. **Racial distribution:** 49.5% white; 5.7% black; 33.6% Asian; 0.4% Amer. Ind.; 0.4% Pac. Isl.; 6.0% other; 2+ races 4.4%. **Hispanic pop.:** 15.3%.

Foreign born: 35.5%. **U.S. citizens:** 86.1%. **Language:** 55.4% English only; 11.3% Spanish; 18.5% Chinese.
Employment: 528,074 employed; 3.6% unemployed. **Per capita income:** $72,364; change (2013-14): 4.6%. **Below poverty level:** 13.3%; 7.8% of families. **Educational attainment:** 86.7% HS; 52.9% bachelor's. **Avg. commute:** 31 min. 36.2% drive; 32.9% public trans.; 10.3% walk. **Housing units:** 380,518; 91.7% occupied. **Home ownership:** 36.6%. **Avg. home:** $782,300; change (2013-15): 21.5%. **Avg. rent:** $1,533.
Mayor: Edwin M. Lee, nonpartisan
History: Nearby Farallon Islands sighted by Spanish 1542; city settled by 1776; claimed by U.S. 1846; became major city during California Gold Rush 1849; inc. 1850. Devastated by earthquake 1906.
Website: www.sfgov.org

San Jose, California

Population: 1,026,908 (10). **Pop. density:** 5,816. **Pop. change (2010-15):** 7.5%. **Area:** 176.6 sq mi. **Racial distribution:** 45.3% white; 3.2% black; 33.2% Asian; 0.6% Amer. Ind.; 0.3% Pac. Isl.; 12.5% other; 2+ races 4.8%. **Hispanic pop.:** 33.1%. **Foreign born:** 38.7%. **U.S. citizens:** 82.6%. **Language:** 43.8% English only; 23.7% Spanish; 10.3% Vietnamese, 6.4% Chinese.
Employment: 518,215 employed; 4.6% unemployed. **Per capita income:** $73,887; change (2013-14): 4.8%. **Below poverty level:** 11.8%; 8.3% of families. **Educational attainment:** 82.5% HS; 38.2% bachelor's. **Avg. commute:** 26.6 min. 77.7% drive; 11.1% carpool. **Housing units:** 322,187; 96.4% occupied. **Home ownership:** 57.4%. **Avg. home:** $950,400; change (2013-15): 21.8%. **Avg. rent:** $1,528.
Mayor: Sam Liccardo, nonpartisan
History: Founded by Spanish, 1777, between San Francisco and Monterey; state capital 1849-51; inc. 1850.
Website: www.sanjoseca.gov

Santa Ana, California

Population: 335,400 (57). **Pop. density:** 12,355. **Pop. change (2010-15):** 3.0%. **Area:** 27.1 sq mi. **Racial distribution:** 47.3% white; 1.2% black; 10.4% Asian; 0.5% Amer. Ind.; 0.2% Pac. Isl.; 38.8% other; 2+ races 1.6%. **Hispanic pop.:** 78.6%. **Foreign born:** 47.3%. **U.S. citizens:** 68.2%. **Language:** 17.2% English only; 72.3% Spanish; 7.2% Vietnamese.
Employment: 151,591 employed; 5.2% unemployed. **Per capita income:** $50,751; change (2013-14): 3.8%. **Below poverty level:** 22.1%; 19.5% of families. **Educational attainment:** 54.1% HS; 11.8% bachelor's. **Avg. commute:** 24.7 min. 71.9% drive; 14.9% carpool. **Housing units:** 77,149; 96.5% occupied. **Home ownership:** 45.4%. **Avg. home:** $707,500; change (2013-15): 8.6%. **Avg. rent:** $1,307.
Mayor: Miguel Pulido, nonpartisan
History: Founded 1769; inc. 1869.
Website: www.santa-ana.org

Scottsdale, Arizona

Population: 236,839 (92). **Pop. density:** 1,288. **Pop. change (2010-15):** 8.8%. **Area:** 183.9 sq mi. **Racial distribution:** 89.3% white; 1.8% black; 4.0% Asian; 1.1% Amer. Ind.; <0.05% Pac. Isl.; 1.6% other; 2+ races 2.0%. **Hispanic pop.:** 9.7%. **Foreign born:** 10.7%. **U.S. citizens:** 95.1%. **Language:** 87.0% English only; 5.9% Spanish.
Employment: 121,861 employed; 4.3% unemployed. **Per capita income:** $39,846; change (2013-14): 3.1%. **Below poverty level:** 8.8%; 5.7% of families. **Educational attainment:** 96.2% HS; 53.2% bachelor's. **Avg. commute:** 21.8 min. 77.9% drive; 10.6% work at home. **Housing units:** 126,210; 79.9% occupied. **Home ownership:** 66.8%. **Avg. home:** $216,400; change (2013-15): 17.9%. **Avg. rent:** $1,132.
Mayor: W. J. "Jim" Lane, nonpartisan
History: Founded 1888 by Army Chaplain Winfield Scott; inc. 1951; slogan "West's Most Western Town" adopted same year.
Website: www.scottsdaleaz.gov

Seattle, Washington

Population: 684,451 (18). **Pop. density:** 8,164. **Pop. change (2010-15):** 12.1%. **Area:** 83.8 sq mi. **Racial distribution:** 69.9% white; 7.3% black; 14.2% Asian; 0.7% Amer. Ind.; 0.5% Pac. Isl.; 1.7% other; 2+ races 5.7%. **Hispanic pop.:** 6.4%. **Foreign born:** 18.0%. **U.S. citizens:** 91.4%. **Language:** 77.4% English only; 4.5% Spanish.
Employment: 401,056 employed; 4.1% unemployed. **Per capita income:** $58,205; change (2013-14): 4.5%. **Below poverty level:** 14.0%; 7.6% of families. **Educational attainment:** 93.1% HS; 57.9% bachelor's. **Avg. commute:** 26 min. 51.0% drive; 19.6% public trans. **Housing units:** 311,286; 93.4% occupied. **Home ownership:** 46.2%. **Avg. home:** $379,700; change (2013-15): 12.9%. **Avg. rent:** $1,131.
Mayor: Ed Murray, nonpartisan
History: Settled 1851; inc. 1869. Suffered severe fire 1889; played prominent role during Alaska Gold Rush 1897; growth

followed opening of Panama Canal 1914. Center of aircraft industry during WWII.
Website: www.seattle.gov

Stockton, California

Population: 305,658 (62). **Pop. density:** 4,957. **Pop. change (2010-15):** 4.5%. **Area:** 61.7 sq mi. **Racial distribution:** 44.8% white; 11.6% black; 21.7% Asian; 0.9% Amer. Ind.; 0.8% Pac. Isl.; 13.3% other; 2+ races 6.9%. **Hispanic pop.:** 41.3%. **Foreign born:** 26.2%. **U.S. citizens:** 85.8%. **Language:** 54.4% English only; 27.0% Spanish. **Employment:** 116,692 employed; 9.6% unemployed. **Per capita income:** $36,136; change (2013-14): 4.1%. **Below poverty level:** 25.8%; 21.4% of families. **Educational attainment:** 74.9% HS; 17.4% bachelor's. **Avg. commute:** 26.8 min. 75.7% drive; 16.5% carpool. **Housing units:** 100,577; 90.8% occupied. **Home ownership:** 49.6%. **Avg. rent:** $958.
Mayor: Anthony Silva, nonpartisan
History: Site purchased 1842; settled 1849; inc. 1850. Chief distribution point for agric. products of San Joaquin Valley.
Website: www.stocktongov.com

Tampa, Florida

Population: 369,075 (53). **Pop. density:** 3,254. **Pop. change (2010-15):** 9.6%. **Area:** 113.4 sq mi. **Racial distribution:** 63.6% white; 25.9% black; 3.7% Asian; 0.8% Amer. Ind.; 0.1% Pac. Isl.; 2.8% other; 2+ races 3.0%. **Hispanic pop.:** 23.3%. **Foreign born:** 15.4%. **U.S. citizens:** 91.9%. **Language:** 74.3% English only; 18.2% Spanish. **Employment:** 177,174 employed; 5.2% unemployed. **Per capita income:** $41,296; change (2013-14): 3.4%. **Below poverty level:** 22.0%; 17.0% of families. **Educational attainment:** 86.2% HS; 33.7% bachelor's. **Avg. commute:** 23.3 min. 77.9% drive. **Housing units:** 160,170; 87.0% occupied. **Home ownership:** 49.6%. **Avg. home:** $173,000; change (2013-15): 15.3%. **Avg. rent:** $956.
Mayor: Bob Buckhorn, nonpartisan
History: U.S. army fort on site 1824; inc. 1851. Ybor City, Tampa's Latin Quarter, a Natl. Historical Landmark District.
Website: www.tampagov.net

Toledo, Ohio

Population: 279,789 (71). **Pop. density:** 3,466. **Pop. change (2010-15):** −2.5%. **Area:** 80.7 sq mi. **Racial distribution:** 64.6% white; 26.6% black; 1.2% Asian; 0.3% Amer. Ind.; <0.05% Pac. Isl.; 2.5% other; 2+ races 4.7%. **Hispanic pop.:** 7.6%. **Foreign born:** 3.4%. **U.S. citizens:** 98.2%. **Language:** 93.6% English only; 3.2% Spanish. **Employment:** 121,193 employed; 5.8% unemployed. **Per capita income:** $40,635; change (2013-14): 4.2%. **Below poverty level:** 27.7%; 22.7% of families. **Educational attainment:** 85.5% HS; 17.7% bachelor's. **Avg. commute:** 19.2 min. 82.8% drive. **Housing units:** 138,358; 85.1% occupied. **Home ownership:** 54.6%. **Avg. home:** $107,300; change (2013-15): 31.3%. **Avg. rent:** $638.
Mayor: Paula Hicks-Hudson, nonpartisan
History: Site of Ft. Industry 1794; Battle of Ft. Meigs 1812; figured in Toledo War 1835-36 between OH and MI over borders; inc. 1837.
Website: toledo.oh.gov

Tucson, Arizona

Population: 531,641 (33). **Pop. density:** 2,303. **Pop. change (2010-15):** 1.9%. **Area:** 230.8 sq mi. **Racial distribution:** 75.0% white; 5.0% black; 2.8% Asian; 2.7% Amer. Ind.; 0.2% Pac. Isl.; 10.5% other; 2+ races 3.9%. **Hispanic pop.:** 42.2%. **Foreign born:** 14.9%. **U.S. citizens:** 91.1%. **Language:** 66.4% English only; 28.7% Spanish. **Employment:** 235,245 employed; 5.9% unemployed. **Per capita income:** $37,031; change (2013-14): 3.3%. **Below poverty level:** 25.1%; 18.6% of families. **Educational attainment:** 84.2% HS; 25.0% bachelor's. **Avg. commute:** 22.1 min. 73.9% drive; 10.2% carpool. **Housing units:** 232,207; 88.0% occupied. **Home ownership:** 49.6%. **Avg. home:** $182,900; change (2013-15): 7.8%. **Avg. rent:** $750.
Mayor: Jonathan Rothschild, Democrat
History: Settled 1775 by Spanish as a presidio; acquired by U.S. in Gadsden Purchase 1853; inc. 1877.
Website: www.tucsonaz.gov

Tulsa, Oklahoma

Population: 403,505 (47). **Pop. density:** 2,050. **Pop. change (2010-15):** 2.8%. **Area:** 196.8 sq mi. **Racial distribution:** 66.0% white; 15.2% black; 2.6% Asian; 4.2% Amer. Ind.; 0.1% Pac. Isl.; 4.6% other; 2+ races 7.2%. **Hispanic pop.:** 14.8%. **Foreign born:** 10.1%. **U.S. citizens:** 92.6%. **Language:** 84.3% English only; 11.7% Spanish. **Employment:** 190,230 employed; 3.9% unemployed. **Per capita income:** $49,807; change (2013-14): 4.1%. **Below poverty level:** 20.0%; 16.1% of families. **Educational attainment:**

86.8% HS; 30.1% bachelor's. **Avg. commute:** 18.4 min. 81.1% drive; 10.8% carpool. **Housing units:** 186,726; 87.6% occupied. **Home ownership:** 52.9%. **Avg. home:** $150,200; change (2013-15): 5.0%. **Avg. rent:** $738.
Mayor: Dewey F. Bartlett Jr., Republican
History: Settled in 1836 by Creek Indians; modern town founded 1882; inc. 1898; oil discovered early 20th century. Emerging telecommunications hub.
Website: www.cityoftulsa.org

Virginia Beach, Virginia

Population: 452,745 (41). **Pop. density:** 1,813. **Pop. change (2010-15):** 3.1%. **Area:** 249.7 sq mi. **Racial distribution:** 68.1% white; 19.2% black; 6.5% Asian; 0.3% Amer. Ind.; 0.1% Pac. Isl.; 1.3% other; 2+ races 4.4%. **Hispanic pop.:** 7.2%. **Foreign born:** 8.9%. **U.S. citizens:** 96.4%. **Language:** 88.1% English only; 4.4% Spanish. **Employment:** 220,565 employed; 4.3% unemployed. **Per capita income:** $45,276; change (2013-14): 2.7%. **Below poverty level:** 8.3%; 6.6% of families. **Educational attainment:** 93.4% HS; 33.5% bachelor's. **Avg. commute:** 23.1 min. 81.8% drive. **Housing units:** 179,842; 91.9% occupied. **Home ownership:** 64.1%. **Avg. home:** $209,000; change (2013-15): 8.3%. **Avg. rent:** $1,239.
Mayor: William D. Sessoms Jr., nonpartisan
History: Area founded by Capt. John Smith 1607; formed by merger with Princess Anne Co. 1963.
Website: www.vbgov.com

Washington, District of Columbia

Population: 672,228 (22). **Pop. density:** 10,994. **Pop. change (2010-15):** 11.1%. **Area:** 61.1 sq mi. **Racial distribution:** 40.2% white; 49.6% black; 3.6% Asian; 0.3% Amer. Ind.; <0.05% Pac. Isl.; 3.8% other; 2+ races 2.5%. **Hispanic pop.:** 9.9%. **Foreign born:** 14.0%. **U.S. citizens:** 91.5%. **Language:** 83.5% English only; 8.0% Spanish. **Employment:** 361,544 employed; 6.9% unemployed. **Per capita income:** $62,975; change (2013-14): 2.6%. **Below poverty level:** 18.2%; 14.3% of families. **Educational attainment:** 88.9% HS; 53.4% bachelor's. **Avg. commute:** 29.8 min. 38.0% public trans.; 34.0% drive; 12.4% walk. **Housing units:** 300,798; 88.9% occupied. **Home ownership:** 41.6%. **Avg. home:** $385,200; change (2013-15): 0.9%. **Avg. rent:** $1,302.
Mayor: Muriel Bowser, Democrat
History: U.S. capital; site on Potomac R. chosen by George Washington 1790 on land ceded from VA and MD (portion S of Potomac returned to VA 1846); Congress first met 1800; inc. 1802; sacked by British, War of 1812. Sept. 11, 2001, terrorist attack on the Pentagon killed 125.
Website: dc.gov

Wichita, Kansas

Population: 389,965 (48). **Pop. density:** 2,441. **Pop. change (2010-15):** 1.9%. **Area:** 159.7 sq mi. **Racial distribution:** 75.2% white; 11.4% black; 4.8% Asian; 1.0% Amer. Ind.; <0.05% Pac. Isl.; 3.1% other; 2+ races 4.5%. **Hispanic pop.:** 15.7%. **Foreign born:** 10.2%. **U.S. citizens:** 93.9%. **Language:** 83.4% English only; 10.9% Spanish. **Employment:** 179,279 employed; 5.0% unemployed. **Per capita income:** $45,297; change (2013-14): 1.8%. **Below poverty level:** 17.3%; 13.0% of families. **Educational attainment:** 87.1% HS; 28.8% bachelor's. **Avg. commute:** 17.8 min. 84.8% drive. **Housing units:** 167,926; 89.5% occupied. **Home ownership:** 60.6%. **Avg. home:** $132,900; change (2013-15): 8.8%. **Avg. rent:** $708.
Mayor: Jeff Longwell, nonpartisan
History: Founded 1864; inc. 1871. Established itself as aircraft manufacturing hub between WWI and WWII.
Website: www.wichita.gov

Winston-Salem, North Carolina

Population: 241,218 (88). **Pop. density:** 1,821. **Pop. change (2010-15):** 4.8%. **Area:** 132.5 sq mi. **Racial distribution:** 57.3% white; 34.8% black; 2.0% Asian; 0.2% Amer. Ind.; <0.05% Pac. Isl.; 3.7% other; 2+ races 2.0%. **Hispanic pop.:** 15.3%. **Foreign born:** 10.8%. **U.S. citizens:** 91.8%. **Language:** 83.1% English only; 13.8% Spanish. **Employment:** 107,708 employed; 5.5% unemployed. **Per capita income:** $38,443; change (2013-14): 4.0%. **Below poverty level:** 24.0%; 17.9% of families. **Educational attainment:** 84.6% HS; 32.7% bachelor's. **Avg. commute:** 19.6 min. 82.4% drive. **Housing units:** 104,959; 88.2% occupied. **Home ownership:** 55.7%. **Avg. home:** $147,700; change (2013-15): 14.8%. **Avg. rent:** $722.
Mayor: Allen Joines, Democrat
History: Salem founded 1766; Winston founded 1849; became Winston-Salem 1913. The Reynolds Building, completed 1929, used as model for Empire State Building (designed by same architects).
Website: www.cityofws.org

Census Origins and Methods

A census is conducted in the U.S. every 10 years. The primary purpose is to apportion seats in the House of Representatives. Census data is also used to determine the boundaries of state legislative districts and the distribution of federal funds to local, state, and tribal governments.

The first U.S. census, mandated by Article 1, Section 2 of the Constitution, was conducted in 1790, a little more than a year after George Washington became president. It counted the numbers of free white males ages 16 and over (as a measure of available workers and military personnel), free white males under 16, free white females, all other free persons, and slaves. The data was collected over 18 months, at a cost of about $44,000, or $1.2 million in current dollars. The 1790 census counted a total of 3.9 million people, resulting in an increase from 65 to 105 seats in the U.S. House of Representatives.

As the nation grew, so did the scope of the census. The first inquiries on manufacturing were made in 1810. Questions on "the pursuits, industry, education, and resources of the country" were added to the 1840 census. It took a full 10 years to publish the results of the 1880 and 1890 censuses due to the number of questions asked. Because of those delays, Congress limited the 1900 census to questions on population, mortality, agriculture, and manufacturing.

Today, the secretary of commerce and the Census Bureau are directed by law to collect data on population, housing, employment, agriculture, manufacturing, trade, construction, transportation, and governments, among other things, at stated intervals. They also conduct smaller-scale surveys on behalf of other federal agencies.

U.S. marshals administered the earliest decennial censuses by visiting each household and reporting to the president (1790), to the secretary of state (1800-40), or to the secretary of the interior (1850-70). Trained census-takers were hired for the 1880 census and thereafter. In 1902, Congress authorized a permanent Census Office within the Interior Department. In 1903, the agency was transferred to the new Department of Commerce and Labor and remained with the Commerce Department when a separate labor department was created in 1913.

The 1790 through 1820 decennial censuses were officially enumerated the first Monday in Aug. The 1830-1900 censuses were as of June 1, though the 1890 census was not started until June 2 (June 1 was a Sunday). The 1910 census was as of Apr. 15, the 1920 census as of Jan. 1, and every census since 1930 has been for Apr. 1.

The Census Bureau began using statistical sampling techniques in the 1940s, the first modern computer in the 1950s, and enumeration by mail in the 1960s. These innovations allowed the Bureau to publish data more quickly, at a lower cost and with less burden on the public. Any personally identifiable information gathered is withheld from the public for 72 years, after which records are made available through the National Archives. The 1940 census records, the most recent set to be released, can be accessed at 1940census.archives.gov.

Prior to 2010, about five in six households responded to the short-form census while one in six households answered a long-form questionnaire, which asked about details such as ancestry, marital status, and occupation. The 2005 implementation of the American Community Survey (ACS) made the long-form questionnaire no longer necessary. Conducted yearly on a random sample of the population, the ACS gathers demographic, economic, and housing information on communities across the country.

U.S. Population by State and Region, 2000, 2015

Source: Population Estimates Program and Decennial Census, U.S. Census Bureau, U.S. Dept. of Commerce
(ranked by 2015 resident population)

Rank	State	2015[1]	2000[2]	% change, 2000-15	Rank	State	2015[1]	2000[2]	% change, 2000-15
1.	California	39,144,818	33,871,653	15.6%	29.	Connecticut	3,590,886	3,405,602	5.4%
2.	Texas	27,469,114	20,851,790	31.7	30.	Iowa	3,123,899	2,926,382	6.7
3.	Florida	20,271,272	15,982,824	26.8	31.	Utah	2,995,919	2,233,198	34.2
4.	New York	19,795,791	18,976,821	4.3	32.	Mississippi	2,992,333	2,844,656	5.2
5.	Illinois	12,859,995	12,419,647	3.5	33.	Arkansas	2,978,204	2,673,400	11.4
6.	Pennsylvania	12,802,503	12,281,054	4.2	34.	Kansas	2,911,641	2,688,824	8.3
7.	Ohio	11,613,423	11,353,145	2.3	35.	Nevada	2,890,845	1,998,257	44.7
8.	Georgia	10,214,860	8,186,816	24.8	36.	New Mexico	2,085,109	1,819,046	14.6
9.	North Carolina	10,042,802	8,046,485	24.8	37.	Nebraska	1,896,190	1,711,265	10.8
10.	Michigan	9,922,576	9,938,480	−0.2	38.	West Virginia	1,844,128	1,808,350	2.0
11.	New Jersey	8,958,013	8,414,347	6.5	39.	Idaho	1,654,930	1,293,956	27.9
12.	Virginia	8,382,993	7,079,030	18.4	40.	Hawaii	1,431,603	1,211,537	18.2
13.	Washington	7,170,351	5,894,141	21.7	41.	New Hampshire	1,330,608	1,235,786	7.7
14.	Arizona	6,828,065	5,130,632	33.1	42.	Maine	1,329,328	1,274,923	4.3
15.	Massachusetts	6,794,422	6,349,105	7.0	43.	Rhode Island	1,056,298	1,048,319	0.8
16.	Indiana	6,619,680	6,080,517	8.9	44.	Montana	1,032,949	902,195	14.5
17.	Tennessee	6,600,299	5,689,267	16.0	45.	Delaware	945,934	783,600	20.7
18.	Missouri	6,083,672	5,596,683	8.7	46.	South Dakota	858,469	754,844	13.7
19.	Maryland	6,006,401	5,296,507	13.4	47.	North Dakota	756,927	642,200	17.9
20.	Wisconsin	5,771,337	5,363,715	7.6	48.	Alaska	738,432	626,931	17.8
21.	Minnesota	5,489,594	4,919,492	11.6	49.	Dist. of Columbia	672,228	572,059	17.5
22.	Colorado	5,456,574	4,302,015	26.8	50.	Vermont	626,042	608,827	2.8
23.	South Carolina	4,896,146	4,011,816	22.0	51.	Wyoming	586,107	493,782	18.7
24.	Alabama	4,858,979	4,447,351	9.3		**United States**	**321,418,820**	**281,424,603**	**14.2**
25.	Louisiana	4,670,724	4,468,958	4.5		Northeast[3]	56,283,891	53,594,784	5.0
26.	Kentucky	4,425,092	4,042,285	9.5		Midwest[4]	67,907,403	64,395,194	5.5
27.	Oregon	4,028,977	3,421,436	17.8		South[5]	121,182,847	100,235,846	20.9
28.	Oklahoma	3,911,338	3,450,652	13.4		West[6]	76,044,679	63,198,779	20.3

Note: The U.S. resident population consists of individuals whose usual residence, or where they live and sleep most of the time, is in one of the 50 states or DC. It excludes overseas U.S. military personnel and civilian U.S. citizens living abroad. (1) Estimates are as of July 1. (2) Figures are for Apr. 1 of decennial census year. Population figures may reflect revisions/corrections to initial tabulated census counts. (3) Incl. the states of the New England (Connecticut, Maine, Massachusetts, New Hampshire, Rhode Island, Vermont) and Middle Atlantic (New Jersey, New York, Pennsylvania) divisions. (4) Incl. the states of the East North Central (Illinois, Indiana, Michigan, Ohio, Wisconsin) and West North Central (Iowa, Kansas, Minnesota, Missouri, Nebraska, North Dakota, South Dakota) divisions. (5) Incl. the states of the South Atlantic (Delaware, DC, Florida, Georgia, Maryland, North Carolina, South Carolina, Virginia, West Virginia), East South Central (Alabama, Kentucky, Mississippi, Tennessee), and West South Central (Arkansas, Louisiana, Oklahoma, Texas) divisions. (6) Incl. the states of the Mountain (Arizona, Colorado, Idaho, Montana, Nevada, New Mexico, Utah, Wyoming) and Pacific (Alaska, California, Hawaii, Oregon, Washington) divisions.

Density of U.S. Population by State, 1930-2010

Source: Decennial Censuses, U.S. Census Bureau, U.S. Dept. of Commerce

(per square mile of land area, as measured for the 2010 census)

State	1930	1950	1970	1990	2010	State	1930	1950	1970	1990	2010
AL......	52.3	60.5	68.0	79.8	94.4	MT	3.7	4.1	4.8	5.5	6.8
AK......	0.1	0.2	0.5	1.0	1.2	NE......	17.9	17.3	19.3	20.5	23.8
AZ......	3.8	6.6	15.6	32.3	56.3	NV......	0.8	1.5	4.5	10.9	24.6
AR......	35.6	36.7	37.0	45.2	56.0	NH	52.0	59.6	82.4	123.9	147.0
CA......	36.4	68.0	128.1	191.0	239.1	NJ......	549.5	657.5	974.7	1,051.1	1,195.5
CO	10.0	12.8	21.3	31.8	48.5	NM	3.5	5.6	8.4	12.5	17.0
CT......	331.8	414.5	626.1	678.8	738.1	NY......	267.1	314.7	387.0	381.7	411.2
DE......	122.3	163.2	281.3	341.9	460.8	NC	65.2	83.5	104.5	136.3	196.1
DC 7,975.1		13,140.0	12,392.0	9,941.3	9,856.5	ND	9.9	9.0	9.0	9.3	9.7
FL......	27.4	51.7	126.6	241.3	350.6	OH	162.7	194.5	260.7	265.5	282.3
GA	50.6	59.9	79.8	112.6	168.4	OK	34.9	32.6	37.3	45.9	54.7
HI	57.3	77.8	119.7	172.6	211.8	OR	9.9	15.8	21.8	29.6	39.9
ID	5.4	7.1	8.6	12.2	19.0	PA......	215.3	234.6	263.6	265.6	283.9
IL.......	137.4	156.9	200.2	205.9	231.1	RI	665.0	766.0	915.8	970.6	1,018.1
IN	90.4	109.8	145.0	154.8	181.0	SC......	57.8	70.4	86.2	116.0	153.9
IA	44.2	46.9	50.6	49.7	54.5	SD......	9.1	8.6	8.8	9.2	10.7
KS......	23.0	23.3	27.5	30.3	34.9	TN......	63.5	79.8	95.2	118.3	153.9
KY......	66.2	74.6	81.5	93.3	109.9	TX......	22.3	29.5	42.9	65.0	96.3
LA......	48.6	62.1	84.3	97.7	104.9	UT......	6.2	8.4	12.9	21.0	33.6
ME	25.9	29.6	32.2	39.8	43.1	VT......	39.0	41.0	48.2	61.1	67.9
MD	168.1	241.4	404.1	492.6	594.8	VA......	61.3	84.0	117.7	156.7	202.6
MA	544.8	601.3	729.4	771.3	839.4	WA	23.5	35.8	51.3	73.2	101.2
MI	85.6	112.7	157.0	164.4	174.8	WV	71.9	83.4	72.6	74.6	77.1
MN	32.2	37.5	47.8	54.9	66.6	WI......	54.3	63.4	81.6	90.3	105.0
MS	42.8	46.4	47.2	54.8	63.2	WY	2.3	3.0	3.4	4.7	5.8
MO	52.8	57.5	68.0	74.4	87.1	**U.S.**	**34.7**	**42.6**	**57.5**	**70.4**	**87.4**

Note: For the sake of comparison, the densities of Alaska and Hawaii in 1930 and 1950 are included though they were not yet states.

U.S. Area and Population, 1790-2010

Source: Decennial Censuses, U.S. Census Bureau, U.S. Dept. of Commerce

Census date	AREA (square miles)			RESIDENT POPULATION			
						Increase over preceding census	
	Total area[1]	Land area	Water area[1]	Number	Per sq mi of land	Number	%
1790 (Aug. 2)	891,364	864,746	24,065	3,929,214	4.5	—	—
1800 (Aug. 4)	891,364	864,746	24,065	5,308,483	6.1	1,379,269	35.1%
1810 (Aug. 6)	1,722,685	1,681,828	34,175	7,239,881	4.3	1,931,398	36.4
1820 (Aug. 7)	1,792,552	1,749,462	38,544	9,638,453	5.5	2,398,572	33.1
1830 (June 1)	1,792,552	1,749,462	38,544	12,860,702	7.4	3,222,249	33.4
1840 (June 1)	1,792,552	1,749,462	38,544	17,063,453	9.8	4,203,751	32.7
1850 (June 1)	2,991,655	2,940,042	52,705	23,191,876	7.9	6,128,423	35.9
1860 (June 1)	3,021,295	2,969,640	52,747	31,443,321	10.6	8,251,445	35.6
1870 (June 1)	3,612,299	3,540,705	68,082	38,558,371	10.9	7,115,050	22.6
1880 (June 1)	3,612,299	3,540,705	68,082	50,189,209	14.2	11,630,838	30.2
1890 (June 1)	3,612,299	3,540,705	68,082	62,979,766	17.8	12,790,557	25.5
1900 (June 1)	3,618,770	3,547,314	67,901	76,212,168	21.5	13,232,402	21.0
1910 (Apr. 15)	3,618,770	3,547,045	68,170	92,228,496	26.0	16,016,328	21.0
1920 (Jan. 1)	3,618,770	3,546,931	68,284	106,021,537	29.9	13,793,041	15.0
1930 (Apr. 1)	3,618,770	3,554,608	60,607	123,202,624	34.7	17,181,087	16.2
1940 (Apr. 1)	3,618,770	3,554,608	60,607	132,164,569	37.2	8,961,945	7.3
1950 (Apr. 1)	3,618,770	3,552,206	63,005	151,325,798	42.6	19,161,229	14.5
1960 (Apr. 1)	3,618,770	3,540,911	74,212	179,323,175	50.6	27,997,377	18.5
1970 (Apr. 1)	3,618,770	3,536,855	78,444	203,302,031	57.5	23,978,856	13.4
1980 (Apr. 1)	3,618,770	3,539,289	79,481	226,542,199	64.0	23,240,168	11.4
1990 (Apr. 1)	3,717,796	3,536,278	181,518	248,718,302	70.3	22,176,103	9.8
2000 (Apr. 1)	3,794,083	3,537,438	256,645	281,424,603	79.6	32,706,301	13.1
2010 (Apr. 1)	3,796,742	3,531,905	264,837	308,746,065	87.4	27,321,462	9.7

Note: Area and population density figures represent the area within the boundaries of the U.S. under its jurisdiction on the date in question including, in some cases, considerable areas not organized or settled and not covered by the census. Beginning in 1870, area data include Alaska; from 1900 on, data include Hawaii. Population figures may reflect revisions/corrections to initial tabulated census counts. (1) Figures for 1790-1980 cover inland water only. Figures for 1990 include inland, coastal, and Great Lakes water. Figures for 2000-10 include additional territorial water.

U.S. Population by Official

Source: Decennial Censuses, U.S. Census Bureau,
(population figures for 1790-1860

State	1790	1800	1810	1820	1830	1840	1850	1860	1870	1880	1890	1900	1910	1920
AL	—	1	9	128	310	591	772	964	996,992	1,262,505	1,513,401	1,828,697	2,138,093	2,348,174
AK	—	—	—	—	—	—	—	—	—	—	33,426	32,052	63,592	64,356	55,036
AZ	—	—	—	—	—	—	—	—	9,658	40,440	88,243	122,931	204,354	334,162
AR	—	—	1	14	30	98	210	435	484,471	802,525	1,128,211	1,311,564	1,574,449	1,752,204
CA	—	—	—	—	—	—	93	380	560,247	864,694	1,213,398	1,485,053	2,377,549	3,426,861
CO	—	—	—	—	—	—	—	34	39,864	194,327	413,249	539,700	799,024	939,629
CT	238	251	262	275	298	310	371	460	537,454	622,700	746,258	908,420	1,114,756	1,380,631
DE	59	64	73	73	77	78	92	112	125,015	146,608	168,493	184,735	202,322	223,003
DC[1]	—	8	15	23	30	34	52	75	131,700	177,624	230,392	278,718	331,069	437,571
FL	—	—	—	—	35	54	87	140	187,748	269,493	391,422	528,542	752,619	968,470
GA	83	163	251	341	517	691	906	1,057	1,184,109	1,542,180	1,837,353	2,216,331	2,609,121	2,895,832
HI	—	—	—	—	—	—	—	—	—	—	—	154,001	191,874	255,881
ID	—	—	—	—	—	—	—	—	14,999	32,610	88,548	161,772	325,594	431,866
IL	—	—	12	55	157	476	851	1,712	2,539,891	3,077,871	3,826,352	4,821,550	5,638,591	6,485,280
IN	—	6	25	147	343	686	988	1,350	1,680,637	1,978,301	2,192,404	2,516,462	2,700,876	2,930,390
IA	—	—	—	—	—	43	192	675	1,194,020	1,624,615	1,912,297	2,231,853	2,224,771	2,404,021
KS	—	—	—	—	—	—	—	107	364,399	996,096	1,428,108	1,470,495	1,690,949	1,769,257
KY[1]	74	221	407	564	688	780	982	1,156	1,321,011	1,648,690	1,858,635	2,147,174	2,289,905	2,416,630
LA	—	—	77	153	216	352	518	708	726,915	939,946	1,118,588	1,381,625	1,656,388	1,798,509
ME[2]	97	152	229	298	399	502	583	628	626,915	648,936	661,086	694,466	742,371	768,014
MD	320	342	381	407	447	470	583	687	780,894	934,943	1,042,390	1,188,044	1,295,346	1,449,661
MA[2]	379	423	472	523	610	738	995	1,231	1,457,351	1,783,085	2,238,947	2,805,346	3,366,416	3,852,356
MI	—	—	5	7	28	212	398	749	1,184,059	1,636,937	2,093,890	2,420,982	2,810,173	3,668,412
MN	—	—	—	—	—	—	6	172	439,706	780,773	1,310,283	1,751,394	2,075,708	2,387,125
MS	—	8	31	75	137	376	607	791	827,922	1,131,597	1,289,600	1,551,270	1,797,114	1,790,618
MO	—	—	20	67	140	384	682	1,182	1,721,295	2,168,380	2,679,185	3,106,665	3,293,335	3,404,055
MT	—	—	—	—	—	—	—	—	20,595	39,159	142,924	243,329	376,053	548,889
NE	—	—	—	—	—	—	—	29	122,993	452,402	1,062,656	1,066,300	1,192,214	1,296,372
NV	—	—	—	—	—	—	—	7	42,491	62,266	47,355	42,335	81,875	77,407
NH	142	184	214	244	269	285	318	326	318,300	346,991	376,530	411,588	430,572	443,083
NJ	184	211	246	278	321	373	490	672	906,096	1,131,116	1,444,933	1,883,669	2,537,167	3,155,900
NM	—	—	—	—	—	—	62	94	91,874	119,565	160,282	195,310	327,301	360,350
NY	340	589	959	1,373	1,919	2,429	3,097	3,881	4,382,759	5,082,871	6,003,174	7,268,894	9,113,614	10,385,227
NC	394	478	557	639	738	753	869	993	1,071,361	1,399,750	1,617,949	1,893,810	2,206,287	2,559,123
ND[3]	—	—	—	—	—	—	—	—	2,405	36,909	190,983	319,146	577,056	646,872
OH	—	42	231	581	938	1,519	1,980	2,340	2,665,260	3,198,062	3,672,329	4,157,545	4,767,121	5,759,394
OK[4]	—	—	—	—	—	—	—	—	—	—	258,657	790,391	1,657,155	2,028,283
OR	—	—	—	—	—	—	12	52	90,923	174,768	317,704	413,536	672,765	783,389
PA	434	602	810	1,049	1,348	1,724	2,312	2,906	3,521,951	4,282,891	5,258,113	6,302,115	7,665,111	8,720,017
RI	69	69	77	83	97	109	148	175	217,353	276,531	345,506	428,556	542,610	604,397
SC	249	346	415	503	581	594	669	704	705,606	995,577	1,151,149	1,340,316	1,515,400	1,683,724
SD[3]	—	—	—	—	—	—	—	5	11,776	98,268	348,600	401,570	583,888	636,547
TN	36	106	262	423	682	829	1,003	1,110	1,258,520	1,542,359	1,767,518	2,020,616	2,184,789	2,337,885
TX	—	—	—	—	—	—	213	604	818,579	1,591,749	2,235,527	3,048,710	3,896,542	4,663,228
UT	—	—	—	—	—	—	11	40	86,336	143,963	210,779	276,749	373,351	449,396
VT	85	154	218	236	281	292	314	315	330,551	332,286	332,422	343,641	355,956	352,428
VA[1]	692	808	878	938	1,044	1,025	1,119	1,220	1,225,163	1,512,565	1,655,980	1,854,184	2,061,612	2,309,187
WA	—	—	—	—	—	—	1	12	23,955	75,116	357,232	518,103	1,141,990	1,356,621
WV[1]	56	79	105	137	177	225	302	377	442,014	618,457	762,794	958,800	1,221,119	1,463,701
WI	—	—	—	—	—	31	305	776	1,054,670	1,315,497	1,693,330	2,069,042	2,333,860	2,632,067
WY	—	—	—	—	—	—	—	—	9,118	20,789	62,555	92,531	145,965	194,402
U.S.[5]	3,929	5,308	7,240	9,638	12,861	17,063	23,192	31,443	38,558,371	50,189,209	62,979,766	76,212,168	92,228,496	106,021,537

Note: With some exceptions, pop. shown is number of residents in a state (or territory of the same name) at the time of each decennial census. Figures may differ from originally published census data because of revisions. Excl. overseas U.S. military personnel and civilian U.S. citizens living abroad. (1) 1790-1860 VA figures are for present-day boundaries. That is, they incl. pop. in areas then part of DC (1800-40) and excl. pop. of areas that went to KY (1790) and WV (1790-1860). (2) 1790-1810 figures for MA do not incl. district taken to form state of ME in 1820. (3) 1860 SD figure is for area reported as "unorganized Dakota"; 1870-80 figures are for present-day ND and SD. (4) 1890-1900 figures incl. pop. for Indian Terr. (5) 1830-40 totals excl. persons (5,318 in 1830; 6,100 in 1840) on public ships in service of the U.S. not credited to any state. 1890 total incl. Indian Terr. and Indian Reservations pop. (325,464) specially enumerated.

Estimated Population of American Colonies, 1630-1780

Source: U.S. Census Bureau, U.S. Dept. of Commerce
(numbers in thousands)

Colony	1630	1650	1670	1690	1700	1720	1740	1750	1760	1770	1780
Total	4.6	50.4	111.9	210.4	250.9	466.2	905.6	1,170.8	1,593.6	2,148.1	2,780.4
Connecticut	—	4.1	12.6	21.6	26.0	58.8	89.6	111.3	142.5	183.9	206.7
Delaware	—	0.2	0.7	1.5	2.5	5.4	19.9	28.7	33.3	35.5	45.4
Georgia	—	—	—	—	—	—	2.0	5.2	9.6	23.4	56.1
Kentucky[1]	—	—	—	—	—	—	—	—	—	15.7	45.0
Maine (counties)[2]	0.4	1.0	—	—	—	—	—	—	20.0	31.3	49.1
Maryland	—	4.5	13.2	24.0	29.6	66.1	116.1	141.1	162.3	202.6	245.5
Massachusetts and Plymouth[2,3]	0.9	15.6	35.3	56.9	55.9	91.0	151.6	188.0	202.6	235.3	268.6
New Hampshire	0.5	1.3	1.8	4.2	5.0	9.4	23.3	27.5	39.1	62.4	87.8
New Jersey	—	—	1.0	8.0	14.0	29.8	51.4	71.4	93.8	117.4	139.6
New York	0.4	4.1	5.8	13.9	19.1	36.9	63.7	76.7	117.1	162.9	210.5
North Carolina	—	—	3.9	7.6	10.7	21.3	51.8	73.0	110.4	197.2	270.1
Pennsylvania	—	—	—	11.4	18.0	31.0	85.6	119.7	183.7	240.1	327.3
Rhode Island	—	0.8	2.2	4.2	5.9	11.7	25.3	33.2	45.5	58.2	52.9
South Carolina	—	—	0.2	3.9	5.7	17.0	45.0	64.0	94.1	124.2	180.0
Tennessee[4]	—	—	—	—	—	—	—	—	—	1.0	10.0
Vermont[5]	—	—	—	—	—	—	—	—	—	10.0	47.6
Virginia	2.5	18.7	35.3	53.0	58.6	87.8	180.4	231.0	339.7	447.0	538.0

Note: With the exception of KY, ME, Plymouth, TN, and VT, colonies shown are the original 13 states (ratified the Constitution 1787-90). (1) Admitted as state 1792. (2) For 1660-1750, the pop. of ME counties are included with MA. ME was annexed by MA in the 1650s but became a separate state in 1820. (3) Plymouth became part of Prov. of Massachusetts in 1691. (4) Admitted as state 1796. (5) Admitted as state 1791.

Census, 1790-2010

U.S. Dept. of Commerce
only are in thousands)

1930	1940	1950	1960	1970	1980	1990	2000	2010	State
2,646,248	2,832,961	3,061,743	3,266,740	3,444,354	3,894,025	4,040,389	4,447,351	4,779,753	AL
59,278	72,524	128,643	226,167	302,583	401,851	550,043	626,931	710,235	AK
435,573	499,261	749,587	1,302,161	1,775,399	2,716,546	3,665,339	5,130,632	6,392,017	AZ
1,854,482	1,949,387	1,909,511	1,786,272	1,923,322	2,286,357	2,350,624	2,673,400	2,915,919	AR
5,677,251	6,907,387	10,586,223	15,717,204	19,971,069	23,667,764	29,758,213	33,871,653	37,253,956	CA
1,035,791	1,123,296	1,325,089	1,753,947	2,209,596	2,889,735	3,294,473	4,302,015	5,029,196	CO
1,606,903	1,709,242	2,007,280	2,535,234	3,032,217	3,107,564	3,287,116	3,405,602	3,574,097	CT
238,380	266,505	318,085	446,292	548,104	594,338	666,168	783,600	897,934	DE
486,869	663,091	802,178	763,956	756,668	638,432	606,900	572,059	601,767	DC
1,468,211	1,897,414	2,771,305	4,951,560	6,791,418	9,746,961	12,938,071	15,982,824	18,801,332	FL
2,908,506	3,123,723	3,444,578	3,943,116	4,587,930	5,462,982	6,478,149	8,186,816	9,687,850	GA
368,300	422,770	499,794	632,772	769,913	964,691	1,108,229	1,211,537	1,360,301	HI
445,032	524,873	588,637	667,191	713,015	944,127	1,006,734	1,293,956	1,567,652	ID
7,630,654	7,897,241	8,712,176	10,081,158	11,110,285	11,427,409	11,430,602	12,419,647	12,830,632	IL
3,238,503	3,427,796	3,934,224	4,662,498	5,195,392	5,490,210	5,544,156	6,080,517	6,483,802	IN
2,470,939	2,538,268	2,621,073	2,757,537	2,825,368	2,913,808	2,776,831	2,926,382	3,046,355	IA
1,880,999	1,801,028	1,905,299	2,178,611	2,249,071	2,364,236	2,477,588	2,688,824	2,853,118	KS
2,614,589	2,845,627	2,944,806	3,038,156	3,220,711	3,660,324	3,686,892	4,042,285	4,339,367	KY
2,101,593	2,363,880	2,683,516	3,257,022	3,644,637	4,206,116	4,220,164	4,468,958	4,533,372	LA
797,423	847,226	913,774	969,265	993,722	1,125,043	1,227,928	1,274,923	1,328,361	ME
1,631,526	1,821,244	2,343,001	3,100,689	3,923,897	4,216,933	4,780,753	5,296,507	5,773,626	MD
4,249,614	4,316,721	4,690,514	5,148,578	5,689,170	5,737,093	6,016,425	6,349,105	6,547,629	MA
4,842,325	5,256,106	6,371,766	7,823,194	8,881,826	9,262,044	9,295,287	9,938,480	9,883,706	MI
2,563,953	2,792,300	2,982,483	3,413,864	3,806,103	4,075,970	4,375,665	4,919,492	5,303,925	MN
2,009,821	2,183,796	2,178,914	2,178,141	2,216,994	2,520,770	2,575,475	2,844,656	2,967,297	MS
3,629,367	3,784,664	3,954,653	4,319,813	4,677,623	4,916,766	5,116,901	5,596,683	5,988,927	MO
537,606	559,456	591,024	674,767	694,409	786,690	799,065	902,195	989,415	MT
1,377,963	1,315,834	1,325,510	1,411,330	1,485,333	1,569,825	1,578,417	1,711,265	1,826,341	NE
91,058	110,247	160,083	285,278	488,738	800,508	1,201,675	1,998,257	2,700,551	NV
465,293	491,524	533,242	606,921	737,681	920,610	1,109,252	1,235,786	1,316,470	NH
4,041,334	4,160,165	4,835,329	6,066,782	7,171,112	7,365,011	7,730,188	8,414,347	8,791,909	NJ
423,317	531,818	681,187	951,023	1,017,055	1,303,302	1,515,069	1,819,046	2,059,181	NM
12,588,066	13,479,142	14,830,192	16,782,304	18,241,391	17,558,165	17,990,778	18,976,821	19,378,102	NY
3,170,276	3,571,623	4,061,929	4,556,155	5,084,411	5,880,095	6,632,448	8,046,485	9,535,483	NC
680,845	641,935	619,636	632,446	617,792	652,717	638,800	642,200	672,591	ND
6,646,697	6,907,612	7,946,627	9,706,397	10,657,423	10,797,603	10,847,115	11,353,145	11,536,504	OH
2,396,040	2,336,434	2,233,351	2,328,284	2,559,463	3,025,487	3,145,576	3,450,652	3,751,351	OK
953,786	1,089,684	1,521,341	1,768,687	2,091,533	2,633,156	2,842,337	3,421,436	3,831,074	OR
9,631,350	9,900,180	10,498,012	11,319,366	11,800,766	11,864,720	11,882,842	12,281,054	12,702,379	PA
687,497	713,346	791,896	859,488	949,723	947,154	1,003,464	1,048,319	1,052,567	RI
1,738,765	1,899,804	2,117,027	2,382,594	2,590,713	3,120,729	3,486,310	4,011,816	4,625,364	SC
692,849	642,961	652,740	680,514	666,257	690,768	696,004	754,844	814,191	SD
2,616,556	2,915,841	3,291,718	3,567,089	3,926,018	4,591,023	4,877,203	5,689,267	6,346,105	TN
5,824,715	6,414,824	7,711,194	9,579,677	11,198,655	14,225,513	16,986,335	20,851,790	25,145,565	TX
507,847	550,310	688,862	890,627	1,059,273	1,461,037	1,722,850	2,233,198	2,763,885	UT
359,611	359,231	377,747	389,881	444,732	511,456	562,758	608,827	625,741	VT
2,421,851	2,677,773	3,318,680	3,966,949	4,651,448	5,346,797	6,189,197	7,079,030	8,001,024	VA
1,563,396	1,736,191	2,378,963	2,853,214	3,413,244	4,132,353	4,866,669	5,894,141	6,724,540	WA
1,729,205	1,901,974	2,005,552	1,860,421	1,744,237	1,950,186	1,793,477	1,808,350	1,852,994	WV
2,939,006	3,137,587	3,434,575	3,951,777	4,417,821	4,705,642	4,891,769	5,363,715	5,686,986	WI
225,565	250,742	290,529	330,066	332,416	469,557	453,589	493,782	563,626	WY
123,202,624	132,164,569	151,325,798	179,323,175	203,302,031	226,542,199	248,718,302	281,424,603	308,746,065	U.S.

U.S. Center of Population, 1790-2010

Source: Decennial Censuses, Geography Division, U.S. Census Bureau, U.S. Dept. of Commerce

The country's **(mean) center of population** is the center of population gravity. In other words, it is the point upon which the U.S. would balance if the country were a rigid, weightless plane and its population was distributed thereon, with each individual assuming an equal weight.

Census year	N Latitude °	′	″	W Longitude °	′	″	Approximate location
1790	39	16	30	76	11	12	Kent Co., MD, 23 miles east of Baltimore
1800	39	16	6	76	56	30	Howard Co., MD, 18 miles west of Baltimore
1810	39	11	30	77	37	12	Loudoun Co., VA, 40 miles northwest by west of Washington, DC
1820	39	5	42	78	33	0	Hardy Co., WV[1], 16 miles east of Moorefield
1830	38	57	54	79	16	54	Grant Co., WV[1], 19 miles west-southwest of Moorefield
1840	39	2	0	80	18	0	Upshur Co., WV[1], 16 miles south of Clarksburg
1850	38	59	0	81	19	0	Wirt Co., WV[1], 23 miles southeast of Parkersburg
1860	39	0	24	82	48	48	Pike Co., OH, 20 miles south by east of Chillicothe
1870	39	12	0	83	35	42	Highland Co., OH, 48 miles east by north of Cincinnati
1880	39	4	8	84	39	40	Boone Co., KY, 8 miles west by south of Cincinnati, OH
1890	39	11	56	85	32	53	Decatur Co., IN, 20 miles east of Columbus
1900	39	9	36	85	48	54	Bartholomew Co., IN, 6 miles southeast of Columbus
1910	39	10	12	86	32	20	Monroe Co., IN, in the city of Bloomington
1920	39	10	21	86	43	15	Owen Co., IN, 8 miles south-southeast of Spencer
1930	39	3	45	87	8	6	Greene Co., IN, 3 miles northeast of Linton
1940	38	56	54	87	22	35	Sullivan Co., IN, 2 miles southeast by east of Carlisle
1950	38	50	21	88	9	33	Richland Co., IL, 8 miles north-northwest of Olney
1950[2]	38	48	15	88	22	8	Clay Co., IL, 3 miles northeast of Louisville
1960[2]	38	35	58	89	12	35	Clinton Co., IL, 6.5 miles northwest of Centralia
1970[2]	38	27	47	89	42	22	St. Clair Co., IL, 5 miles east-southeast of Mascoutah
1980[2]	38	8	13	90	34	26	Jefferson Co., MO, 0.25 mile west of DeSoto
1990[2]	37	52	20	91	12	55	Crawford Co., MO, 9.7 miles southeast of Steelville
2000[2]	37	41	49	91	48	34	Phelps Co., MO, 2.8 miles east of Edgar Springs
2010[2]	37	31	3	92	10	23	Texas Co., MO, 2.7 miles northeast of Plato

(1) Pres. Lincoln signed a bill Dec. 31, 1862, approving statehood for West Virginia (made up of former Virginia counties). It was admitted to the Union June 20, 1863. (2) Incl. Alaska and Hawaii.

U.S. Congressional Apportionment by Census Year, 1850-2010

Source: Decennial Censuses, U.S. Census Bureau, U.S. Dept. of Commerce

The U.S. Constitution, in Article 1, Section 2, mandates that the population be counted every 10 years so that the number of U.S. representatives can be apportioned among the states. Every state is entitled to at least one House seat. The size of a state's resident population, both citizens and noncitizens, determines if it may send additional representatives to Congress. A congressional apportionment has been made after every decennial census except for that of 1920. Prior to 1870, slaves were counted as being only three-fifths of a person in the apportionment population. Since the 1970 census (excluding 1980), overseas military personnel and federal civilian employees as well as their dependents have been allocated to a home state for apportionment purposes. Residents of the District of Columbia, Puerto Rico, and U.S. island areas are not included in the apportionment population as they lack voting seats in the U.S. House.

Under a law approved in 1941, House seats are allocated using the Huntington-Hill, or equal proportions, method. It allows for the least possible variation in the average number of people each House member represents.

The first House of Representatives, in 1789, had 65 members as provided by the Constitution. Virginia (10), Massachusetts (8), and Pennsylvania (8) had the most representatives. As the nation's population grew, the number of representatives was increased. A 1911 act fixed the total House membership at 435. (Alaska and Hawaii each gained one House seat when they became states, temporarily raising the total to 437 representatives until after the 1960 census was conducted.)

State	2010	2000	1990	1970	1950	1900	1850	State	2010	2000	1990	1970	1950	1900	1850
AL.....	7	7	7	7	9	9	7	NE.....	3	3	3	3	4	6	NA
AK.....	1	1	1	1	1	NA	NA	NV.....	4	3	2	1	1	1	NA
AZ.....	9	8	6	4	2	NA	NA	NH	2	2	2	2	2	2	3
AR.....	4	4	4	4	6	7	2	NJ.....	12	13	13	15	14	10	5
CA.....	53	53	52	43	30	8	2	NM	3	3	3	2	2	NA	NA
CO	7	7	6	5	4	3	NA	NY.....	27	29	31	39	43	37	33
CT.....	5	5	6	6	6	5	4	NC	13	13	12	11	12	10	8
DE.....	1	1	1	1	1	1	1	ND	1	1	1	1	2	2	NA
FL.....	27	25	23	15	8	3	1	OH	16	18	19	23	23	21	21
GA	14	13	11	10	10	11	8	OK	5	5	6	6	6	5	NA
HI	2	2	2	2	1	NA	NA	OR	5	5	5	4	4	2	1
ID	2	2	2	2	2	1	NA	PA.....	18	19	21	25	30	32	25
IL......	18	19	20	24	25	25	9	RI	2	2	2	2	2	2	2
IN	9	9	10	11	11	13	11	SC.....	7	6	6	6	6	7	6
IA	4	5	5	6	8	11	2	SD.....	1	1	1	2	2	2	NA
KS.....	4	4	4	5	6	8	NA	TN.....	9	9	9	8	9	10	10
KY.....	6	6	6	7	8	11	10	TX.....	36	32	30	24	22	16	2
LA.....	6	7	7	8	8	7	4	UT.....	4	3	3	2	2	1	NA
ME	2	2	2	2	3	4	6	VT.....	1	1	1	1	1	2	3
MD	8	8	8	8	7	6	6	VA.....	11	11	11	10	10	10	13
MA	9	10	10	12	14	14	11	WA	10	9	9	7	7	3	NA
MI	14	15	16	19	18	12	4	WV	3	3	3	4	6	5	NA
MN	8	8	8	8	9	9	2	WI.....	8	8	9	9	10	11	3
MS	4	4	5	5	6	8	5	WY	1	1	1	1	1	1	NA
MO	8	9	9	10	11	16	7								
MT	1	1	1	2	2	1	NA	**Total...**	**435**	**435**	**435**	**435**	**437**	**391**	**237**

NA = Not applicable.

U.S. Slave and "Free Colored" Population, 1790, 1820, 1860

Source: Decennial Censuses, U.S. Census Bureau, U.S. Dept. of Commerce

	1790			1820			1860		
	Slaves	% slaves[1]	Free colored	Slaves	% slaves[1]	Free colored	Slaves	% slaves[1]	Free colored
Northern states[2]	40,354	2.1%	27,070	19,108	0.4%	99,307	18	0.0%	225,224
Connecticut	2,764	1.2	2,808	97	0.0	7,870	0	0.0	8,627
New Jersey............	11,423	6.2	2,762	7,557	2.7	12,460	18	0.0	25,318
New York	21,324	6.3	4,654	10,088	0.7	29,279	0	0.0	49,005
Pennsylvania	3,737	0.9	6,537	211	0.0	30,202	0	0.0	56,949
Border/disputed states ..	124,353	27.5	12,056	248,860	22.4	55,794	429,403	13.2	118,652
Delaware	8,887	15.0	3,899	4,509	6.2	12,958	1,798	1.6	19,829
Kansas...............	—	—	—	—	—	—	2	0.0	625
Kentucky.............	12,430	16.9	114	126,732	22.5	2,759	225,483	19.5	10,684
Maryland.............	103,036	32.2	8,043	107,397	26.4	39,730	87,189	12.7	83,942
Missouri	—	—	—	10,222	15.4	347	114,931	9.7	3,572
Southern states	532,974	35.3	20,401	1,265,534	37.8	75,775	3,521,110	38.7	132,760
Alabama..............	—	—	—	41,879	32.7	571	435,080	45.1	2,690
Arkansas	—	—	—	1,617	11.3	59	111,115	25.5	144
Florida	—	—	—	—	—	—	61,745	44.0	932
Georgia..............	29,264	35.5	398	149,656	43.9	1,763	462,198	43.7	3,500
Louisiana	—	—	—	69,064	45.0	10,476	331,726	46.9	18,647
Mississippi	—	—	—	32,814	43.5	458	436,631	55.2	773
North Carolina	100,572	25.5	4,975	204,917	32.1	14,712	331,059	33.4	30,463
South Carolina	107,094	43.0	1,801	258,475	51.4	6,826	402,406	57.2	9,914
Tennessee	3,417	9.6	361	80,107	18.9	2,737	275,719	24.8	7,300
Texas	—	—	—	—	—	—	182,566	30.2	355
Virginia	292,627	39.1	12,866	427,005	39.7	38,173	490,865	30.7	58,042
Total territories[3]	—	—	—	4,520	19.4	2,758	3,229	1.1	11,434
Total states and territories	697,681	17.8	59,527	1,538,022	16.0	233,634	3,953,760	12.6	488,070

Note: "Free colored" was an official Census Bureau designation in these decades. States are grouped roughly by allegiance in the Civil War. (1) Percentage of total pop., all races. (2) The following states are not listed separately but are included in totals for Northern states (relevant census years in parentheses): CA (1860), IL (1820, 1860), IN (1820, 1860), IA (1860), ME (1790, 1820, 1860), MA (1790, 1820, 1860), MI (1820, 1860), MN (1860), NH (1790, 1820, 1860), OH (1820, 1860), OR (1860), RI (1790, 1820, 1860), VT (1790, 1820, 1860), WI (1820, 1860). (3) Incl. AZ (1860), CO (1860), Dakota (1860), DC (1820, 1860), NE (1860), NV (1860), NM (1860), UT (1860), WA (1860).

U.S. Population by Sex, Race, Residence, and Median Age, 1790-2010

Source: Decennial Censuses, U.S. Census Bureau, U.S. Dept. of Commerce

(numbers in thousands, unless otherwise noted)

| | SEX | | RACE[2] | | | | RESIDENCE | | MEDIAN AGE (years) | | |
| | | | | Black | | | | | | | |
Census date	Male	Female	White	Number	% tot. pop.	Other	Urban[3]	Rural	All races	White[2]	Black[2]
Conterminous U.S.[1]											
1790 (Aug. 2)	NA	NA	3,172	757	19.3%	NA	202	3,728	NA	NA	NA
1800 (Aug. 4)	NA	NA	4,306	1,002	18.9	NA	322	4,986	NA	NA	NA
1810 (Aug. 6)	NA	NA	5,862	1,378	19.0	NA	525	6,714	NA	16.0	NA
1820 (Aug. 7)	4,897	4,742	7,867	1,772	18.4	NA	693	8,945	16.7	16.6	17.2
1830 (June 1)	6,532	6,334	10,537	2,329	18.1	NA	1,127	11,733	17.2	17.3	17.2
1840 (June 1)	8,689	8,381	14,196	2,874	16.8	NA	1,845	15,218	17.8	17.9	17.6
1850 (June 1)	11,838	11,354	19,553	3,639	15.7	NA	3,574	19,617	18.9	19.2	17.4
1860 (June 1)	16,085	15,358	26,923	4,442	14.1	79	6,217	25,227	19.4	19.7	17.5
1870 (June 1)	19,494	19,065	33,589	4,880	12.7	89	9,902	28,656	20.2	20.4	18.5
1880 (June 1)	25,519	24,637	43,403	6,581	13.1	172	14,130	36,059	20.9	21.4	18.0
1890 (June 1)	32,237	30,711	55,101	7,489	11.9	358	22,106	40,874	22.0	22.5	17.8
1900 (June 1)	38,816	37,178	66,809	8,834	11.6	351	30,215	45,997	22.9	23.4	19.4
1910 (Apr. 15).	47,332	44,640	81,732	9,828	10.7	413	42,064	50,164	24.1	24.5	20.8
1920 (Jan. 1)	53,900	51,810	94,821	10,463	9.9	427	54,253	51,768	25.3	25.5	22.3
1930 (Apr. 1).	62,137	60,638	110,287	11,891	9.7	597	69,161	54,042	26.5	26.9	23.5
1940 (Apr. 1).	66,062	65,608	118,215	12,866	9.8	589	74,705	57,459	29.0	29.5	25.3
United States											
1950 (Apr. 1).	74,833	75,864	135,150	15,045	10.0	713	96,847	54,479	30.2	30.8	26.1
1960 (Apr. 1).	88,331	90,992	158,832	18,872	10.5	1,620	125,269	54,054	29.5	30.3	23.5
1970 (Apr. 1).	98,926	104,309	178,098	22,581	11.1	2,557	149,647	53,565	28.1	28.9	22.4
1980 (Apr. 1).	110,053	116,493	194,713	26,683	11.8	5,150	167,051	59,495	30.0	30.9	24.9
1990 (Apr. 1).	121,284	127,507	208,741	30,517	12.3	9,533	187,053	61,656	32.8	33.7	27.9
2000 (Apr. 1).	138,054	143,368	194,553	34,658	12.3	13,118	222,361	59,061	35.3	38.6	30.2
2010 (Apr. 1).	151,781	156,964	196,818	38,929	12.6	18,147	249,253	59,492	37.2	42.0	32.4

NA = Not available. **Note:** Population figures may reflect revisions/corrections to initial tabulated census counts. (1) Excludes Alaska and Hawaii. (2) New race categories were introduced in the 2000 census. Race data for 2000 and on are for people who reported being of one race alone. "White" does not include people who reported being of Hispanic or Latino origin. "Other" comprises Asians, Native Hawaiians and other Pacific Islanders, American Indians and Alaska Natives. Because of these changes, race data from 2000 on are not comparable to figures from previous years. (3) The Census Bureau's definition of "urban" has changed over time. Figures for 2000 and 2010 include residents of urbanized areas (50,000 or more inhabitants) and urban clusters (at least 2,500 but fewer than 50,000 inhabitants).

U.S. Population by Race and Hispanic Origin, 2000-10

Source: Decennial Censuses, U.S. Census Bureau, U.S. Dept. of Commerce

| | 2010 | | 2000 | | % change, 2000-10[2] | |
	One race alone	One or more races[1]	One race alone	One or more races[1]	One race alone	One or more races
Total population	299,736,465	308,746,065	274,595,678	281,421,906	9.2%	9.7%
Race						
White.	223,553,265	231,040,398	211,460,626	216,930,975	5.7	6.5
Black or African American.	38,929,319	42,020,743	34,658,190	36,419,434	12.3	15.4
Asian	14,674,252	17,320,856	10,242,998	11,898,828	43.3	45.6
American Indian and Alaska Native . . .	2,932,248	5,220,579	2,475,956	4,119,301	18.4	26.7
Native Hawaiian and other Pac. Isl. . . .	540,013	1,225,195	398,835	874,414	35.4	40.1
Some other race	19,107,368	21,748,084	15,359,073	18,521,486	24.4	17.4
Hispanic origin and race						
Hispanic or Latino, any race	47,435,002	50,477,594	33,081,736	35,305,818	43.4	43.0
Not Hispanic or Latino.	252,301,463	258,267,944	241,513,942	246,116,088	4.5	4.9
White	196,817,552	201,856,108	194,552,774	198,177,900	1.2	1.9
Black or African American	37,685,848	40,123,525	33,947,837	35,383,751	11.0	13.4
Asian	14,465,124	16,722,710	10,123,169	11,579,494	42.9	44.4
American Indian and Alaska Native. .	2,247,098	4,029,675	2,068,883	3,444,700	8.6	17.0
Native Hawaiian and other Pac. Isl.	481,576	1,014,888	353,509	748,149	36.2	35.7
Some other race	604,265	1,033,866	467,770	1,770,645	29.2	−41.6

Note: Population figures may reflect revisions/corrections to initial tabulated census counts. (1) Alone or in combination with one or more of the other races listed. Numbers do not add up to totals because of individuals reporting more than one race. (2) An error in data processing resulted in the overstatement in the 2000 census of the number of people reporting more than one race, in particular race combinations involving some other race. Percent change in multiple-race populations between 2000 and 2010 should ideally be calculated with specific race combinations (e.g., White and Black or White and Asian).

U.S. Population Growth by Race and Hispanic Origin, 1970-2030

Source: Decennial Censuses and Population Projections Program, U.S. Census Bureau, U.S. Dept. of Commerce
(numbers in millions)

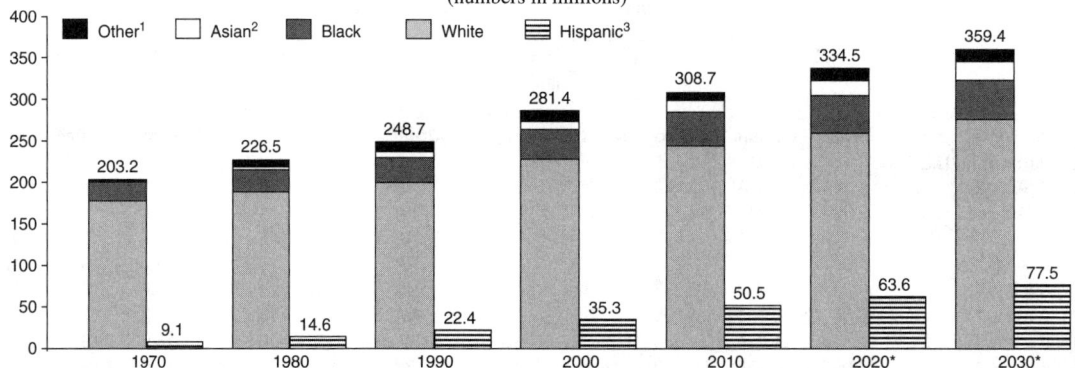

*Projected. **Note:** Because of changes in census questions and methods, data on race and Hispanic origin are not wholly comparable over time. Population figures may reflect revisions/corrections to initial tabulated census counts. (1) Includes American Indians and Alaska Natives as well as other races not shown. For 2000 and on, this category also includes Native Hawaiians and other Pacific Islanders along with persons reporting two or more races. (2) Figures for 1970-90 include Pacific Islanders. (3) May be of any race. 1970 figure is based on sample of households.

State Population by Race and Hispanic Origin, 2010

Source: Decennial Census, U.S. Census Bureau, U.S. Dept. of Commerce
(percentage of state or country's total population)

| State | One race alone[1] | | | | | | Two or more races[1] | Hispanic or Latino, any race |
	White	Black or African American	Asian	American Indian and Alaska Native	Native Hawaiian and other Pacific Islander	Some other race		
Alabama	67.0%	26.0%	1.1%	0.5%	0.04%	0.08%	1.3%	3.9%
Alaska	64.1	3.1	5.3	14.4	1.02	0.16	6.4	5.5
Arizona	57.8	3.7	2.7	4.0	0.17	0.13	1.8	29.6
Arkansas	74.5	15.3	1.2	0.7	0.19	0.07	1.6	6.4
California	40.1	5.8	12.8	0.4	0.35	0.23	2.6	37.6
Colorado	70.0	3.8	2.7	0.6	0.11	0.15	2.0	20.7
Connecticut	71.2	9.4	3.8	0.2	0.03	0.34	1.7	13.4
Delaware	65.3	20.8	3.2	0.3	0.03	0.17	2.0	8.2
District of Columbia	34.8	50.0	3.5	0.2	0.04	0.24	2.1	9.1
Florida	57.9	15.2	2.4	0.3	0.05	0.26	1.5	22.5
Georgia	55.9	30.0	3.2	0.2	0.05	0.20	1.6	8.8
Hawaii	22.7	1.5	37.7	0.2	9.43	0.14	19.4	8.9
Idaho	84.0	0.6	1.2	1.1	0.14	0.10	1.7	11.2
Illinois	63.7	14.3	4.5	0.1	0.02	0.12	1.4	15.8
Indiana	81.5	9.0	1.6	0.2	0.03	0.13	1.5	6.0
Iowa	88.7	2.9	1.7	0.3	0.06	0.07	1.4	5.0
Kansas	78.2	5.7	2.3	0.8	0.07	0.10	2.3	10.5
Kentucky	86.3	7.7	1.1	0.2	0.05	0.11	1.5	3.1
Louisiana	60.3	31.8	1.5	0.6	0.03	0.15	1.3	4.2
Maine	94.4	1.1	1.0	0.6	0.02	0.08	1.4	1.3
Maryland	54.7	29.0	5.5	0.2	0.04	0.21	2.2	8.2
Massachusetts	76.1	6.0	5.3	0.2	0.02	0.94	1.9	9.6
Michigan	76.6	14.0	2.4	0.6	0.02	0.10	1.9	4.4
Minnesota	83.1	5.1	4.0	1.0	0.04	0.11	1.9	4.7
Mississippi	58.0	36.9	0.9	0.5	0.03	0.06	0.9	2.7
Missouri	81.0	11.5	1.6	0.4	0.10	0.09	1.8	3.5
Montana	87.8	0.4	0.6	6.1	0.06	0.05	2.2	2.9
Nebraska	82.1	4.4	1.7	0.8	0.05	0.12	1.6	9.2
Nevada	54.1	7.7	7.1	0.9	0.57	0.18	2.9	26.5
New Hampshire	92.3	1.0	2.1	0.2	0.02	0.14	1.4	2.8
New Jersey	59.3	12.8	8.2	0.1	0.02	0.31	1.5	17.7
New Mexico	40.5	1.7	1.3	8.5	0.06	0.18	1.4	46.3
New York	58.3	14.4	7.3	0.3	0.03	0.42	1.7	17.6
North Carolina	65.3	21.2	2.2	1.1	0.06	0.16	1.6	8.4
North Dakota	88.9	1.1	1.0	5.3	0.04	0.05	1.5	2.0
Ohio	81.1	12.0	1.7	0.2	0.03	0.13	1.8	3.1
Oklahoma	68.7	7.3	1.7	8.2	0.11	0.08	5.1	8.9
Oregon	78.5	1.7	3.6	1.1	0.33	0.14	2.9	11.7
Pennsylvania	79.5	10.4	2.7	0.1	0.02	0.13	1.4	5.7
Rhode Island	76.4	4.9	2.8	0.4	0.03	0.84	2.2	12.4
South Carolina	64.1	27.7	1.3	0.4	0.05	0.12	1.4	5.1
South Dakota	84.7	1.2	0.9	8.5	0.04	0.06	1.8	2.7
Tennessee	75.6	16.5	1.4	0.3	0.04	0.10	1.4	4.6
Texas	45.3	11.5	3.8	0.3	0.07	0.14	1.3	37.6
Utah	80.4	0.9	2.0	1.0	0.87	0.13	1.8	13.0
Vermont	94.3	0.9	1.3	0.3	0.02	0.09	1.6	1.5
Virginia	64.8	19.0	5.5	0.3	0.06	0.19	2.3	7.9
Washington	72.5	3.4	7.1	1.3	0.58	0.18	3.7	11.2
West Virginia	93.2	3.4	0.7	0.2	0.02	0.06	1.3	1.2
Wisconsin	83.3	6.2	2.3	0.9	0.03	0.07	1.4	5.9
Wyoming	85.9	0.8	0.8	2.1	0.06	0.08	1.5	8.9
United States	**63.7**	**12.2**	**4.7**	**0.7**	**0.16**	**0.20**	**1.9**	**16.3**

Note: Population figures may reflect revisions/corrections to initial tabulated census counts. (1) Not Hispanic or Latino.

American Indian and Alaska Native Population by State, 2010

Source: Decennial Census, U.S. Census Bureau, U.S. Dept. of Commerce
(ranked by one race alone)

Rank	State	One race alone[1]	More than one race[2]	Rank	State	One race alone[1]	More than one race[2]
1.	California	362,801	360,424	27.	Kansas	28,150	30,980
2.	Oklahoma	321,687	161,073	28.	Missouri	27,376	45,000
3.	Arizona	296,529	56,857	29.	Pennsylvania	26,843	54,249
4.	New Mexico	193,222	26,290	30.	Ohio	25,292	64,832
5.	Texas	170,972	144,292	31.	Arkansas	22,248	25,340
6.	North Carolina	122,110	61,972	32.	Idaho	21,441	14,944
7.	New York	106,906	114,152	33.	Maryland	20,420	38,237
8.	Alaska	104,871	33,441	34.	Tennessee	19,994	34,880
9.	Washington	103,869	95,129	35.	South Carolina	19,524	22,647
10.	South Dakota	71,817	10,256	36.	Massachusetts	18,850	31,855
11.	Florida	71,458	91,104	37.	Indiana	18,462	31,276
12.	Montana	62,555	16,046	38.	Nebraska	18,427	11,389
13.	Michigan	62,007	77,088	39.	Mississippi	15,030	10,880
14.	Minnesota	60,916	40,984	40.	Wyoming	13,336	5,260
15.	Colorado	56,010	51,822	41.	Connecticut	11,256	19,884
16.	Wisconsin	54,526	31,702	42.	Iowa	11,084	13,427
17.	Oregon	53,203	56,020	43.	Kentucky	10,120	21,235
18.	Illinois	43,963	57,488	44.	Maine	8,568	9,914
19.	North Dakota	36,591	6,405	45.	Rhode Island	6,058	8,336
20.	Utah	32,927	17,137	46.	Delaware	4,181	5,718
21.	Georgia	32,151	51,873	47.	Hawaii	4,164	29,306
22.	Nevada	32,062	23,883	48.	West Virginia	3,787	9,527
23.	Louisiana	30,579	24,500	49.	New Hampshire	3,150	7,374
24.	Virginia	29,225	51,699	50.	Vermont	2,207	5,172
25.	New Jersey	29,026	41,690	51.	District of Columbia	2,079	4,442
26.	Alabama	28,218	28,900		**United States**	**2,932,248**	**2,288,331**

(1) Respondents who self-identified as American Indian and Alaska Native (AIAN) alone. (2) Respondents who self-identified as AIAN in combination with one or more other races.

American Indian and Alaska Native Population by Selected Tribal Groupings, 2010

Source: Decennial Census, U.S. Census Bureau, U.S. Dept. of Commerce
(ranked by American Indian and Alaska Native [AIAN] alone, one tribal grouping alone)

Tribal grouping	AIAN alone — One tribal grouping alone[1]	AIAN alone — One or more tribal groupings[2]	AIAN alone or in combination — One or more tribal groupings[3]	Tribal grouping	AIAN alone — One tribal grouping alone[1]	AIAN alone — One or more tribal groupings[2]	AIAN alone or in combination — One or more tribal groupings[3]
Total	2,879,638	2,932,248	5,220,579	Crow	10,332	10,860	15,203
AIAN tribes, not specified	693,709	693,709	1,545,963	Kiowa	9,437	10,355	13,787
Amer. Ind. tribes, specified	1,935,363	2,032,133	3,397,251	Paiute	9,340	10,205	13,767
Navajo	286,731	295,016	332,129	Osage	8,938	10,063	18,576
Cherokee	284,247	300,463	819,105	Yakama	8,786	9,096	11,527
Mexican Amer. Ind.	121,221	123,550	175,494	Menominee	8,374	8,627	11,133
Chippewa	112,757	115,402	170,742	Houma	8,169	8,240	10,768
Sioux	112,176	116,477	170,110	Colville	8,114	8,314	10,549
Choctaw	103,910	110,308	195,764	Arapaho	8,014	8,402	10,861
Apache	63,193	69,694	111,810	Shoshone	7,852	8,462	13,002
Lumbee	62,306	62,957	73,691	Delaware	7,843	8,215	18,264
Pueblo	49,695	52,026	62,540	Yuman	7,727	8,278	10,089
Creek	48,352	52,948	88,332	Ute	7,435	8,220	11,491
Iroquois	40,570	42,461	81,002	Ottawa	7,272	8,048	13,033
Chickasaw	27,973	30,206	52,278	Canadian/French Amer. Ind.	6,433	7,051	14,822
Blackfeet	27,279	31,798	105,304	Cree	2,211	2,950	7,983
Pima	22,040	23,205	26,655	All other Amer. Ind. tribes	270,141	282,747	429,629
Yaqui	21,679	23,195	32,595	Amer. Ind. tribes, not specified	131,943	132,060	234,320
S. Amer. Ind.	20,901	21,380	47,233	AK Native tribes, specified	98,892	103,086	138,850
Potawatomi	20,412	20,874	33,771	Yup'ik	28,927	29,618	33,889
Tohono O'Odham	19,522	20,247	23,478	Inupiat[4]	24,859	25,736	33,360
Central Amer. Ind.	15,882	16,454	27,844	Alaskan Athabascan	15,623	16,427	22,484
Puget Sound Salish	14,320	14,535	20,260	Tlingit-Haida	15,256	16,115	26,080
Seminole	14,080	16,448	31,971	Aleut	11,920	12,643	19,282
Spanish Amer. Ind.	13,460	13,758	19,951	Tsimshian	2,307	2,547	3,755
Hopi	12,580	14,634	18,327	AK Native tribes, not specified	19,731	19,904	29,933
Comanche	12,284	13,471	23,330				
Cheyenne	11,375	12,493	19,051				

Note: This table measures the number of responses, not respondents. Respondents who self-identified with multiple tribal groupings are counted more than once. A tribal grouping refers to combined individual tribes (e.g., Fort Sill Apache and San Carlos Apache as Apache or King Salmon Tribe and Native Village of Kanatak as Aleut). (1) For example, Navajo or Alaskan Athabascan. (2) As in footnote 1 or in combination with other tribal groupings (e.g., Yakama and Aleut). (3) As in footnotes 1 or 2 or in combination with another race (e.g., Apache, Navajo, and white; or Inupiat, white, and black). (4) Eskimo in previous censuses.

Largest U.S. Cities by Population, 1850-2015

Source: Population Estimates Program and Decennial Censuses, U.S. Census Bureau, U.S. Dept. of Commerce
(ranked by 2015 population)

Rank	City	2015	2000	1990	1980	1970	1950	1900	1850
1.	New York, NY	8,550,405	8,008,654	7,322,564	7,071,639	7,895,563	7,891,957	3,437,202	515,547
2.	Los Angeles, CA	3,971,883	3,694,742	3,485,557	2,968,528	2,811,801	1,970,358	102,479	1,610
3.	Chicago, IL	2,720,546	2,896,016	2,783,726	3,005,072	3,369,357	3,620,962	1,698,575	29,963
4.	Houston, TX	2,296,224	1,953,631	1,630,864	1,595,138	1,233,535	596,163	44,633	2,396
5.	Philadelphia, PA	1,567,442	1,517,550	1,585,577	1,688,210	1,949,996	2,071,605	1,293,697	121,376
6.	Phoenix, AZ	1,563,025	1,321,045	983,392	789,704	584,303	106,818	5,544	—
7.	San Antonio, TX	1,469,845	1,144,646	935,393	785,940	654,153	408,442	53,321	3,488
8.	San Diego, CA	1,394,928	1,223,400	1,110,623	875,538	697,471	334,387	17,700	—
9.	Dallas, TX	1,300,092	1,188,580	1,007,618	904,599	844,401	434,462	42,638	—
10.	San Jose, CA	1,026,908	894,943	782,224	629,400	459,913	95,280	21,500	—
11.	Austin, TX	931,830	656,562	465,648	345,890	253,539	132,459	22,258	629
12.	Jacksonville, FL[1]	868,031	735,617	635,230	540,920	504,265	204,517	28,429	1,045
13.	San Francisco, CA[2]	864,816	776,733	723,959	678,974	715,674	775,357	342,782	34,776
14.	Indianapolis, IN[1]	853,173	791,926	741,915	710,868	746,992	427,173	169,164	8,091
15.	Columbus, OH	850,106	711,470	632,945	565,021	540,025	375,901	125,560	17,882
16.	Fort Worth, TX	833,319	534,694	447,619	385,164	393,455	278,778	26,688	—
17.	Charlotte, NC	827,097	540,167	395,934	315,474	241,420	134,042	18,091	1,065
18.	Seattle, WA	684,451	951,270	1,027,974	1,203,368	1,514,063	1,849,568	285,704	21,019
19.	Denver, CO	682,545	563,662	515,342	425,259	322,261	130,485	15,906	—
20.	El Paso, TX	681,124	563,376	516,259	493,846	530,831	467,591	80,671	—
21.	Detroit, MI	677,116	553,693	467,610	492,686	514,678	415,786	133,859	—
22.	Washington, DC	672,228	572,059	606,900	638,432	756,668	802,178	278,718	40,001
23.	Boston, MA	667,137	650,100	610,337	646,174	623,988	396,000	102,320	8,841
24.	Memphis, TN	655,770	589,141	574,283	562,994	641,071	801,444	560,892	136,881
25.	Nashville-Davidson, TN[1]	654,610	569,892	510,786	477,811	447,877	174,307	80,865	10,165
26.	Portland, OR	632,309	651,154	736,014	786,741	905,787	949,708	508,957	169,054
27.	Oklahoma City, OK	631,346	506,132	444,724	404,014	368,164	243,504	10,037	—
28.	Las Vegas, NV	623,747	529,121	438,802	368,148	379,967	373,628	90,426	—
29.	Baltimore, MD	621,849	479,137	258,204	164,674	125,787	24,624	—	—
30.	Louisville/Jefferson Co., KY[1]	615,366	256,231	269,555	298,694	361,706	369,129	204,731	43,194
31.	Milwaukee, WI	600,155	596,974	628,088	636,297	717,372	637,392	285,315	20,061
32.	Albuquerque, NM	559,121	448,607	384,619	332,619	244,920	96,815	6,238	—
33.	Tucson, AZ	531,641	486,699	405,371	330,537	262,933	45,454	7,531	—
34.	Fresno, CA	520,052	427,652	354,091	217,491	165,655	91,669	12,470	—
35.	Sacramento, CA	490,712	407,018	369,365	275,741	257,105	137,572	29,282	6,820
36.	Kansas City, MO	475,378	461,522	429,321	361,498	358,879	250,767	2,252	—
37.	Long Beach, CA	474,140	441,545	434,829	448,028	507,330	456,622	163,752	—
38.	Mesa, AZ	471,825	396,375	288,104	152,404	63,049	16,790	722	—
39.	Atlanta, GA	463,878	416,267	393,929	425,022	495,039	331,314	89,872	2,572
40.	Colorado Springs, CO	456,568	425,257	393,089	262,199	172,106	5,390	—	—
41.	Virginia Beach, VA	452,745	390,007	335,719	313,939	346,929	251,117	102,555	—
42.	Raleigh, NC	451,066	360,890	280,430	215,105	135,517	45,472	21,085	—
43.	Omaha, NE	443,885	276,094	212,092	150,255	122,830	65,679	13,643	4,518
44.	Miami, FL	441,003	362,470	358,648	346,681	334,859	249,276	1,681	—
45.	Oakland, CA	419,267	399,484	372,242	339,337	361,561	384,575	66,960	—
46.	Minneapolis, MN	410,939	382,747	368,383	370,951	434,400	521,718	202,718	—
47.	Tulsa, OK	403,505	393,049	367,302	360,919	330,350	182,740	1,390	—
48.	Wichita, KS	389,965	477,459	505,616	573,822	750,879	914,808	381,768	17,034
49.	New Orleans, LA	389,617	346,753	304,017	279,838	276,554	168,279	24,671	—
50.	Arlington, TX	388,125	484,674	496,938	557,927	593,471	570,445	287,104	116,375
51.	Cleveland, OH	388,072	332,969	261,717	160,113	90,229	7,692	1,079	—
52.	Bakersfield, CA	373,640	246,889	174,978	105,611	69,515	34,784	4,836	—
53.	Tampa, FL	369,075	303,447	280,015	271,577	277,714	124,681	15,839	—
54.	Aurora, CO	359,407	275,921	222,103	158,588	74,974	11,421	202	—
55.	Urban Honolulu, HI[3]	352,769	371,657	365,272	365,048	324,871	248,034	39,306	—
56.	Anaheim, CA	350,742	328,014	266,406	219,494	166,408	14,556	1,456	—
57.	Santa Ana, CA	335,400	337,977	293,827	204,023	155,710	45,533	4,933	—
58.	Corpus Christi, TX	324,074	277,454	257,453	232,134	204,525	108,287	4,703	—
59.	Riverside, CA	322,424	255,166	226,546	170,591	140,089	46,764	7,973	—
60.	St. Louis, MO	315,685	348,189	396,685	452,801	622,236	856,796	575,238	77,860
61.	Lexington-Fayette Urban Co., KY[1]	314,488	260,512	225,366	204,165	108,137	55,534	26,369	8,159
62.	Stockton, CA	305,658	334,563	369,879	423,959	520,089	676,806	321,616	46,601
63.	Pittsburgh, PA	304,391	243,771	210,943	148,283	109,963	70,853	17,506	—
64.	St. Paul, MN	300,851	260,283	226,338	174,431	48,081	11,254	—	—
65.	Anchorage, AK	298,695	331,285	364,040	385,409	453,514	503,998	325,902	115,435
66.	Cincinnati, OH	298,550	286,840	272,235	270,230	309,866	311,349	163,065	1,112
67.	Henderson, NV	285,667	223,891	183,894	155,642	144,076	74,389	10,035	—
68.	Greensboro, NC	285,342	313,782	332,943	354,635	383,062	303,616	131,822	3,829
69.	Plano, TX	283,558	272,537	275,221	329,248	381,930	438,776	246,070	38,894
70.	Newark, NJ	281,944	222,030	127,885	72,331	17,872	2,126	1,304	—
71.	Toledo, OH	279,789	175,381	64,948	24,363	16,395	—	—	—
72.	Lincoln, NE	277,348	225,581	191,972	171,932	149,518	98,884	40,169	—
73.	Orlando, FL	270,934	185,951	164,674	128,291	99,006	52,367	2,481	—
74.	Chula Vista, CA	265,757	240,055	228,517	223,532	260,350	299,017	206,433	6,856
75.	Jersey City, NJ	264,290	173,556	135,160	83,927	67,901	15,927	—	—
76.	Chandler, AZ	260,828	292,648	328,175	357,870	462,768	580,132	352,387	42,261
77.	Fort Wayne, IN	260,326	205,727	172,971	172,391	178,269	133,607	45,115	4,282
78.	Buffalo, NY	258,071	176,581	89,862	29,673	13,763	3,799	—	—
79.	Durham, NC	257,636	248,232	240,318	238,647	216,159	96,738	1,575	—
80.	St. Petersburg, FL	257,083	176,576	122,899	91,449	69,024	51,910	13,429	—

Rank City	2015	2000	1990	1980	1970	1950	1900	1850
81. Irvine, CA	256,927	187,035	136,612	101,149	95,438	71,311	6,679	—
82. Laredo, TX	255,473	143,072	110,330	62,134	—	—	—	—
83. Lubbock, TX	249,042	208,054	190,766	170,616	171,809	96,056	19,164	1,525
84. Madison, WI	248,951	234,403	261,250	266,979	307,951	213,513	46,624	14,326
85. Gilbert, AZ	247,542	199,564	186,206	174,361	149,101	71,747	—	—
86. Norfolk, VA	246,393	109,697	29,122	5,717	1,971	1,114	—	—
87. Reno, NV	241,445	185,776	143,485	131,885	133,683	87,811	13,650	—
88. Winston-Salem, NC	241,218	218,812	147,864	97,172	36,228	8,179	—	—
89. Glendale, AZ	240,126	180,480	133,850	100,756	72,863	32,497	4,500	—
90. Hialeah, FL	237,069	226,419	188,008	145,254	102,452	19,676	—	—
91. Garland, TX	236,897	215,768	180,635	138,857	81,437	10,571	819	—
92. Scottsdale, AZ	236,839	199,184	151,982	114,486	89,580	—	—	—
93. Irving, TX	236,607	191,615	155,037	109,943	97,260	2,621	—	—
94. Chesapeake, VA	235,429	115,488	47,849	42,739	46,067	3,875	—	—
95. North Las Vegas, NV	234,807	202,705	130,075	88,622	67,823	—	—	—
96. Fremont, CA	232,206	227,818	219,531	220,394	165,291	125,629	11,269	3,905
97. Baton Rouge, LA	228,590	203,413	173,339	131,945	100,869	—	—	—
98. Richmond, VA	220,289	197,790	202,798	219,214	249,332	230,310	85,050	27,570
99. Boise City, ID	218,281	185,787	125,551	102,249	74,990	34,393	5,957	—
100. San Bernardino, CA	216,108	185,401	164,676	117,389	108,794	63,058	6,150	—

— = Not available. **Note:** 2015 population estimates are as of July 1. Decennial census figures for 1950-2000 are for Apr. 1; 1850 and 1900 are for June 1. Figures may reflect revisions/corrections to initial tabulated census counts. Cities are incorporated places unless otherwise noted. (1) Consolidated city-county government. For years predating consolidation, city population figures are shown. (2) 1850 figure is for 1852, from state census. 1850 census results were destroyed by fire. (3) Census designated place (CDP). Figures for years prior to 2015 are for Honolulu CDP and are not directly comparable.

Population Change in Largest U.S. Cities, 2010-15

Source: Population Estimates Program and Decennial Census, U.S. Census Bureau, U.S. Dept. of Commerce

(ranked by % change, 2010-15; 2015 estimates are as of July 1; 2010 decennial census figures are for Apr. 1)

	Cities With Most Growth				Cities With Least Growth		
		Population	% change,			Population	% change,
Rank	City	2015	2010	2010-15	Rank City	2015	2010	2010-15

Rank	City	2015	2010	% change 2010-15	Rank	City	2015	2010	% change 2010-15
1.	Irvine, CA	256,927	212,375	21.0%	1.	Detroit, MI	677,116	713,777	−5.1%
2.	Gilbert, AZ	247,542	208,453	18.8	2.	Toledo, OH	279,789	287,208	−2.6
3.	Austin, TX	931,830	790,390	17.9	3.	Cleveland, OH	388,072	396,815	−2.2
4.	Denver, CO	682,545	600,158	13.7	4.	Buffalo, NY	258,071	261,310	−1.2
5.	Orlando, FL	270,934	238,300	13.7	5.	St. Louis, MO	315,685	319,294	−1.1
6.	New Orleans, LA	389,617	343,829	13.3	6.	Pittsburgh, PA	304,391	305,704	−0.4
7.	Charlotte, NC	827,097	731,424	13.1	7.	Baton Rouge, LA	228,590	229,493	−0.4
8.	Durham, NC	257,636	228,330	12.8	8.	Baltimore, MD	621,849	620,961	0.1
9.	Seattle, WA	684,451	608,660	12.5	9.	Cincinnati, OH	298,550	296,943	0.5
10.	Fort Worth, TX	833,319	741,206	12.4	10.	Milwaukee, WI	600,155	594,833	0.9
11.	Washington, DC	672,228	601,723	11.7	11.	Chicago, IL	2,720,546	2,695,598	0.9
12.	Raleigh, NC	451,066	403,892	11.7	12.	Memphis, TN	655,770	646,889	1.4
13.	Henderson, NV	285,667	257,729	10.8	13.	Norfolk, VA	246,393	242,803	1.5
14.	San Antonio, TX	1,469,845	1,327,407	10.7	14.	Newark, NJ	281,944	277,140	1.7
15.	Aurora, CO	359,407	325,078	10.6	15.	Wichita, KS	389,965	382,368	2.0
16.	Chandler, AZ	260,828	236,123	10.5	16.	Tucson, AZ	531,641	520,116	2.2
17.	Atlanta, GA	463,878	420,003	10.4	17.	Anchorage, AK	298,695	291,826	2.4
18.	Miami, FL	441,003	399,457	10.4	18.	Albuquerque, NM	559,121	545,852	2.4
19.	Tampa, FL	369,075	335,709	9.9	19.	Long Beach, CA	474,140	462,257	2.6
20.	Colorado Springs, CO	456,568	416,427	9.6	20.	Fort Wayne, IN	260,326	253,691	2.6

Note: This table shows which of the 100 largest U.S. cities by 2015 population size experienced the most and least population growth since 2010. Figures may reflect revisions/corrections to initial tabulated census counts. Cities are typically incorporated places.

Largest U.S. Counties by Population, 2000, 2015

Source: Population Estimates Program and Decennial Census, U.S. Census Bureau, U.S. Dept. of Commerce

(ranked by 2015 population, estimated as of July 1; 2000 decennial census figures are for Apr. 1)

Rank	County	2015	2000	% change, 2000-15	Rank	County	2015	2000	% change, 2000-15
1.	Los Angeles Co., CA	10,170,292	9,519,338	6.8%	16.	Santa Clara Co., CA	1,918,044	1,682,585	14.0%
2.	Cook Co., IL	5,238,216	5,376,815	−2.6	17.	Bexar Co., TX	1,897,753	1,392,931	36.2
3.	Harris Co., TX	4,538,028	3,400,578	33.4	18.	Broward Co., FL	1,896,425	1,623,018	16.8
4.	Maricopa Co., AZ	4,167,947	3,072,149	35.7	19.	Wayne Co., MI	1,759,335	2,061,162	−14.6
5.	San Diego Co., CA	3,299,521	2,813,833	17.3	20.	New York Co., NY	1,644,518	1,537,372	7.0
6.	Orange Co., CA	3,169,776	2,846,289	11.4	21.	Alameda Co., CA	1,638,215	1,443,741	13.5
7.	Miami-Dade Co., FL	2,693,117	2,253,779	19.5	22.	Middlesex Co., MA	1,585,139	1,466,394	8.1
8.	Kings Co., NY	2,636,735	2,465,525	6.9	23.	Philadelphia Co., PA	1,567,442	1,517,550	3.3
9.	Dallas Co., TX	2,553,385	2,218,774	15.1	24.	Suffolk Co., NY	1,501,587	1,419,369	5.8
10.	Riverside Co., CA	2,361,026	1,545,387	52.8	25.	Sacramento Co., CA	1,501,335	1,223,499	22.7
11.	Queens Co., NY	2,339,150	2,229,379	4.9	26.	Bronx Co., NY	1,455,444	1,332,650	9.2
12.	San Bernardino Co., CA	2,128,133	1,709,434	24.5	27.	Palm Beach Co., FL	1,422,789	1,131,191	25.8
13.	King Co., WA	2,117,125	1,737,044	21.9	28.	Nassau Co., NY	1,361,350	1,334,544	2.0
14.	Clark Co., NV	2,114,801	1,375,765	53.7	29.	Hillsborough Co., FL	1,349,050	998,948	35.0
15.	Tarrant Co., TX	1,982,498	1,446,219	37.1	30.	Orange Co., FL	1,288,126	896,344	43.7

Note: Decennial pop. figures may reflect revisions/corrections to initial tabulated census counts. The 10 smallest counties or county equivalents by estimated 2015 population: (1) Kalawao Co., HI (pop. 89); (2) Loving Co., TX (112); (3) King Co., TX (282); (4) Kenedy Co., TX (407); (5) Arthur Co., NE (456); (6) Petroleum Co., MT (475) and McPherson Co., NE (475); (8) Blaine Co., NE (487); (9) Loup Co., NE (585); and (10) Yakutat City and Borough, AK (613).

Largest U.S. Metropolitan Areas by Population, 2000-15

Source: Population Estimates Program and Decennial Censuses, U.S. Census Bureau, U.S. Dept. of Commerce

(ranked by 2015 population, estimated as of July 1; 2000 and 2010 decennial census figures are for Apr. 1)

Metropolitan Statistical Areas (MSAs) are defined, or delineated geographically, for federal statistical use by the Office of Management and Budget (OMB) with technical assistance from the Census Bureau. An MSA consists of at least one urbanized area of 50,000 or more inhabitants, plus adjacent territory closely integrated socially and economically with the core as measured by commuting ties. The Census Bureau's 2015 population estimates are for delineations issued by the OMB in Feb. 2013, which designated 381 MSAs in the U.S. About 85.6% of the resident population lived in an MSA in 2015.

Rank	Metropolitan Statistical Area	Population 2015	Population 2010	Population 2000	Percent change 2010-15	Percent change 2000-15
1.	New York-Newark-Jersey City, NY-NJ-PA	20,182,305	19,567,410	18,944,519	3.1%	6.5%
2.	Los Angeles-Long Beach-Anaheim, CA	13,340,068	12,828,837	12,365,627	4.0	7.9
3.	Chicago-Naperville-Elgin, IL-IN-WI	9,551,031	9,461,105	9,098,316	1.0	5.0
4.	Dallas-Fort Worth-Arlington, TX	7,102,796	6,426,214	5,204,126	10.5	36.5
5.	Houston-The Woodlands-Sugar Land, TX	6,656,947	5,920,416	4,693,161	12.4	41.8
6.	Washington-Arlington-Alexandria, DC-VA-MD-WV	6,097,684	5,636,232	4,837,428	8.2	26.1
7.	Philadelphia-Camden-Wilmington, PA-NJ-DE-MD	6,069,875	5,965,343	5,687,147	1.8	6.7
8.	Miami-Fort Lauderdale-West Palm Beach, FL	6,012,331	5,564,635	5,007,564	8.0	20.1
9.	Atlanta-Sandy Springs-Roswell, GA	5,710,795	5,286,728	4,263,438	8.0	33.9
10.	Boston-Cambridge-Newton, MA-NH	4,774,321	4,552,402	4,391,344	4.9	8.7
11.	San Francisco-Oakland-Hayward, CA	4,656,132	4,335,391	4,123,740	7.4	12.9
12.	Phoenix-Mesa-Scottsdale, AZ	4,574,531	4,192,887	3,251,876	9.1	40.7
13.	Riverside-San Bernardino-Ontario, CA	4,489,159	4,224,851	3,254,821	6.3	37.9
14.	Detroit-Warren-Dearborn, MI	4,302,043	4,296,250	4,452,557	0.1	-3.4
15.	Seattle-Tacoma-Bellevue, WA	3,733,580	3,439,809	3,043,878	8.5	22.7
16.	Minneapolis-St. Paul-Bloomington, MN-WI	3,524,583	3,348,859	3,031,918	5.2	16.2
17.	San Diego-Carlsbad, CA	3,299,521	3,095,313	2,813,833	6.6	17.3
18.	Tampa-St. Petersburg-Clearwater, FL	2,975,225	2,783,243	2,395,997	6.9	24.2
19.	Denver-Aurora-Lakewood, CO	2,814,330	2,543,482	2,179,240	10.6	29.1
20.	St. Louis, MO-IL	2,811,588	2,787,701	2,675,343	0.9	5.1
21.	Baltimore-Columbia-Towson, MD	2,797,407	2,710,489	2,552,994	3.2	9.6
22.	Charlotte-Concord-Gastonia, NC-SC	2,426,363	2,217,012	1,717,372	9.4	41.3
23.	Portland-Vancouver-Hillsboro, OR-WA	2,389,228	2,226,009	1,927,881	7.3	23.9
24.	Orlando-Kissimmee-Sanford, FL	2,387,138	2,134,411	1,644,561	11.8	45.2
25.	San Antonio-New Braunfels, TX	2,384,075	2,142,508	1,711,703	11.3	39.3
26.	Pittsburgh, PA	2,353,045	2,356,285	2,431,087	-0.1	-3.2
27.	Sacramento—Roseville—Arden-Arcade, CA	2,274,194	2,149,127	1,796,857	5.8	26.6
28.	Cincinnati, OH-KY-IN	2,157,719	2,114,580	1,994,830	2.0	8.2
29.	Las Vegas-Henderson-Paradise, NV	2,114,801	1,951,269	1,375,765	8.4	53.7
30.	Kansas City, MO-KS	2,087,471	2,009,342	1,811,254	3.9	15.3
31.	Cleveland-Elyria, OH	2,060,810	2,077,240	2,148,143	-0.8	-4.1
32.	Columbus, OH	2,021,632	1,901,974	1,675,013	6.3	20.7
33.	Austin-Round Rock, TX	2,000,860	1,716,289	1,249,763	16.6	60.1
34.	Indianapolis-Carmel-Anderson, IN	1,988,817	1,887,877	1,658,462	5.3	19.9
35.	San Jose-Sunnyvale-Santa Clara, CA	1,976,836	1,836,911	1,735,819	7.6	13.9
36.	Nashville-Davidson—Murfreesboro—Franklin, TN	1,830,345	1,670,890	1,381,287	9.5	32.5
37.	Virginia Beach-Norfolk-Newport News, VA-NC	1,724,876	1,676.822	1,580.057	2.9	9.2
38.	Providence-Warwick, RI-MA	1,613,070	1,600,852	1,582,997	0.8	1.9
39.	Milwaukee-Waukesha-West Allis, WI	1,575,747	1,555,908	1,500,741	1.3	5.0
40.	Jacksonville, FL	1,449,481	1,345,596	1,122,750	7.7	29.1
41.	Oklahoma City, OK	1,358,452	1,252,987	1,095,421	8.4	24.0
42.	Memphis, TN-MS-AR	1,344,127	1,324,829	1,213,230	1.5	10.8
43.	Louisville-Jefferson County, KY-IN	1,278,413	1,235,708	1,121,109	3.5	14.0
44.	Raleigh, NC	1,273,568	1,130,490	797,071	12.7	59.8
45.	Richmond, VA	1,271,334	1,208,101	1,055,683	5.2	20.4
46.	New Orleans-Metairie, LA	1,262,888	1,189,866	1,337,726	6.1	-5.6
47.	Hartford-West Hartford-East Hartford, CT	1,211,324	1,212,381	1,148,618	-0.1	5.5
48.	Salt Lake City, UT	1,170,266	1,087,873	939,122	7.6	24.6
49.	Birmingham-Hoover, AL	1,145,647	1,128,047	1,052,238	1.6	8.9
50.	Buffalo-Cheektowaga-Niagara Falls, NY	1,135,230	1,135,509	1,170,111	0.0	-3.0
51.	Rochester, NY	1,081,954	1,079,671	1,062,452	0.2	1.8
52.	Grand Rapids-Wyoming, MI	1,038,583	988,938	930,670	5.0	11.6
53.	Tucson, AZ	1,010,025	980,263	843,746	3.0	19.7

Population by Urban and Rural, 1790-2010

Source: Decennial Censuses, U.S. Census Bureau, U.S. Dept. of Commerce

The Census Bureau currently defines an area as urban if it has at least 2,500 people (at least 1,500 of which are not in institutional group quarters, such as a correctional facility). All other areas are rural. Prior to 1950, the definition of urban was limited to incorporated places and other areas meeting certain criteria.

Year	Total pop.	No. of places of 2,500 or more	% of total pop. Urban	% of total pop. Rural
Pre-1950 urban definition				
1790	3,929,214	24	5.1%	94.9%
1800	5,308,483	33	6.1	93.9
1810	7,239,881	46	7.3	92.7
1820	9,638,453	61	7.2	92.8
1830	12,860,702	90	8.8	91.2
1840	17,063,353	131	10.8	89.2
1850	23,191,876	237	15.4	84.6
1860	31,443,321	392	19.8	80.2
1870	38,558,371	663	25.7	74.3
1880	50,189,209	939	28.2	71.8
1890	62,979,766	1,348	35.1	64.9
1900	76,212,168	1,740	39.6	60.4
1910	92,228,496	2,266	45.6	54.4
1920	106,021,537	2,725	51.2	48.8

Year	Total pop.	No. of places of 2,500 or more	% of total pop. Urban	% of total pop. Rural
1930	123,202,624	3,183	56.1%	43.9%
1940	132,164,569	3,485	56.5	43.5
1950	151,325,798	4,077	59.6	40.4
1960	179,323,175	5,023	63.1	36.9
1950-90 urban definition				
1950	151,325,798	4,307	64.0	36.0
1960	179,323,175	5,445	69.9	30.1
1970	203,302,031	6,433	73.6	26.3
1980	226,542,199	7,749	73.7	26.3
1990	248,718,302	8,510	75.2	24.8
Current urban definition				
1990	248,718,302	8,510	78.0	22.0
2000	281,424,603	9,063	79.0	21.0
2010	308,746,065	9,644	80.7	19.3

Note: Figures may not add up to 100 due to rounding.

Mobility of U.S. Population by Selected Characteristics, 2014-15

Source: Annual Social and Economic Supplement, Current Population Survey (CPS), U.S. Census Bureau, U.S. Dept. of Commerce
(numbers in thousands)

	Total movers	Location of new residence					Total movers	Location of new residence			
		Same county	Diff. county, same state	Diff. state	Abroad			Same county	Diff. county, same state	Diff. state	Abroad
Age						**Marital status[1]**					
1 to 14 years.........	7,820	5,104	1,331	1,014	371	Married, spouse present	9,900	5,860	1,868	1,616	556
15 years and older	28,504	17,800	5,322	4,079	1,302	Married, spouse absent	610	307	94	101	108
25 years and older	21,085	13,033	3,944	3,153	952	Widowed.............	803	514	168	107	15
65 years and older	1,865	1,110	386	356	11	Divorced............	3,187	2,076	568	467	76
85 years and older	228	143	36	46	1	Separated...........	1,005	682	182	113	30
Income[1]						Never married........	12,999	8,362	2,443	1,676	518
Without income.......	3,983	2,418	668	504	393	**Educational attainment[2]**					
Under $5,000 or loss ..	2,604	1,563	485	375	181	Not a H.S. graduate ...	2,425	1,697	386	225	117
$5,000-$9,999	2,225	1,376	414	343	92	High school graduate ..	5,667	3,735	1,047	710	175
$10,000-$19,999	4,812	3,112	899	647	155	Some college or					
$20,000-$29,999	4,059	2,681	738	523	116	associate's degree ..	5,937	3,723	1,168	874	171
$30,000-$39,999	3,029	1,971	565	384	109	Bachelor's degree.....	4,462	2,573	870	725	294
$40,000-$59,999	3,567	2,279	694	523	71	Prof. or grad. degree ...	2,593	1,306	472	620	196
$60,000-$74,999	1,501	905	282	246	68	**Tenure**					
$75,000-$99,999	1,195	664	235	247	50	In owner-occupied unit	10,451	6,478	2,086	1,593	294
$100,000 and over	1,529	832	344	286	68	In renter-occupied unit[3]	25,872	16,426	4,567	3,499	1,379
						Total movers	**36,324**	**22,905**	**6,653**	**5,093**	**1,673**

Note: Total movers consists of persons ages 1 and older who moved to a new residence in the 12 months preceding the survey. Figures may not add up to totals due to rounding. (1) Ages 15 and older. (2) Ages 25 and older. (3) Includes units occupied without payment of cash rent.

Mobility of U.S. Population, 1948-2015

Source: Annual Social and Economic Supplement, Current Population Survey (CPS), U.S. Census Bureau, U.S. Dept. of Commerce
(numbers in thousands unless otherwise noted)

Mobility period	Total movers	Location of new residence							
		Same county		Diff. county, same state		Diff. state		Abroad	
		No.	(%)	No.	(%)	No.	(%)	No.	(%)
1947-48	28,672	19,202	67.0%	4,638	16.2%	4,370	15.2%	462	1.6%
1950-51	31,464	20,694	65.8	5,276	16.8	5,188	16.5	306	1.0
1955-56	34,040	22,186	65.2	5,859	17.2	5,053	14.8	942	2.8
1960-61	36,533	24,289	66.5	5,493	15.0	5,753	15.7	998	2.7
1965-66	37,586	24,165	64.3	6,275	16.7	6,263	16.7	883	2.3
1970-71	37,705	23,018	61.0	6,197	16.4	6,946	18.4	1,544	4.1
1975-76	36,793	22,399	60.9	7,106	19.3	6,140	16.7	1,148	3.1
1980-81	38,200	23,097	60.5	7,614	19.9	6,175	16.2	1,313	3.4
1985-86	43,237	26,401	61.1	8,665	20.0	6,971	16.1	1,200	2.8
1990-91	41,539	25,151	60.5	7,881	19.0	7,122	17.1	1,385	3.3
1995-96	42,537	26,696	62.8	8,009	18.8	6,471	15.2	1,361	3.2
2000-01	39,007	21,918	56.2	7,550	19.4	7,783	20.0	1,756	4.5
2005-06	39,837	24,851	62.4	8,010	20.1	5,679	14.3	1,296	3.3
2010-11	35,038	23,330	66.6	5,868	16.7	4,756	13.6	1,084	3.1
2014-15	36,324	22,905	63.1	6,653	18.3	5,093	14.0	1,673	4.6

Note: Total movers consists of persons ages 1 and older who moved to a new residence in the 12 months preceding the survey. Figures may not add up to totals due to rounding. Because of changes in survey processing, numbers may not be comparable over time.

U.S. Households by Size, 1900-2010

Source: Decennial Censuses, U.S. Census Bureau, U.S. Dept. of Commerce

The household population does not include those living in group quarters (either institutionalized like a correctional facility or noninstitutionalized like a college dormitory). Data not available for 1930; 1950 figures are based on a sample of the population. Average household size is shown above each bar.

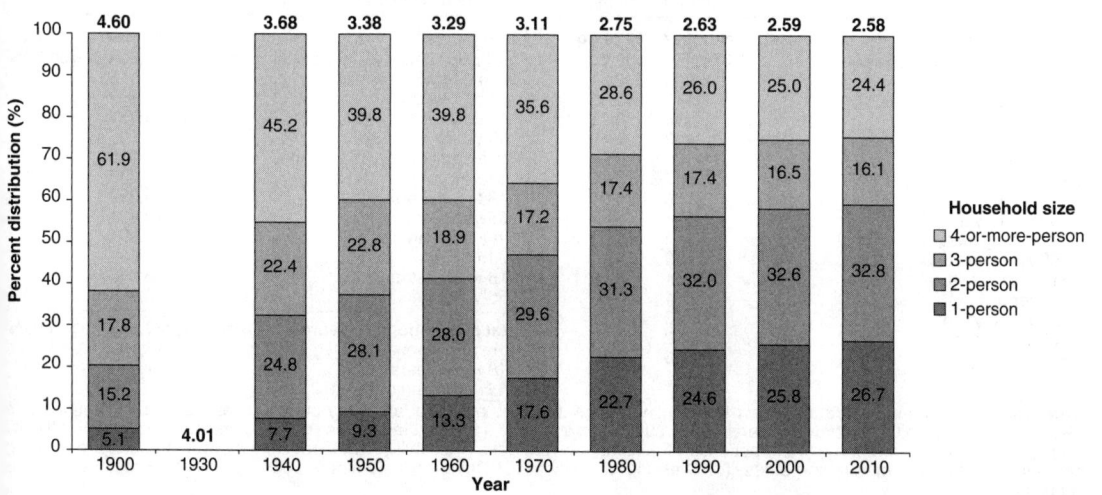

U.S. Population by Age, Sex, and Household, 2015

Source: American Community Survey (ACS), U.S. Census Bureau, U.S. Dept. of Commerce

	Number	% of tot.		Number	% of tot.
Total population[1]	321,418,821	100.0%	Sex		
Age			Male	158,167,834	49.2%
Under 5 years	19,793,807	6.2	Female	163,250,987	50.8
5 to 14 years	41,209,862	12.8	Total households[2]	118,208,250	100.0%
15 to 17 years	12,626,041	3.9	Family households	77,530,756	65.6
18 years and over	247,789,111	77.1	2-person household	33,807,959	28.6
Male	120,542,426	37.5	3-person household	17,463,608	14.8
Female	127,246,685	39.6	4-person household	14,818,778	12.5
18 to 24 years	31,341,948	9.8	5-or-more-person household	11,440,411	9.7
25 to 34 years	43,897,832	13.7	Married-couple family household	56,715,795	48.0
35 to 44 years	40,804,130	12.7	Male HH, no wife present	5,730,981	4.8
45 to 54 years	43,135,580	13.4	Female HH, no husband present	15,083,980	12.8
55 to 64 years	40,877,141	12.7	Nonfamily households	40,677,494	34.4
65 years and over	47,732,480	14.9	1-person household, or HH living alone	32,962,990	27.9
75 years and over	20,145,213	6.3	HH 65 years and over	12,414,334	10.5
85 years and over	6,161,167	1.9	2-person household	6,247,586	5.3
Median age (years)	37.8	NA	3-or-more-person household	1,466,918	1.2
			Average household size	2.65	NA

NA = Not applicable. HH = Householder, or person in whose name a home is owned or rented. **Note:** Data based on sample and subject to sampling variability. (1) Includes population living in group quarters (institutional and noninstitutional, e.g., correctional facilities, university housing). (2) Number of occupied housing units, not household members. Group quarters are not considered households.

Elderly U.S. Population, 1900-2060

Source: Decennial Censuses and Population Projections Program, U.S. Census Bureau, U.S. Dept. of Commerce
(numbers of resident population in thousands)

Year	65 and over Number	65 and over % tot. pop.	85 and over Number	85 and over % tot. pop.	Year	65 and over Number	65 and over % tot. pop.	85 and over Number	85 and over % tot. pop.
1900[1]	3,080	4.1%	122	0.2%	2010	40,268	13.0%	5,493	1.8%
1920[1]	4,933	4.7	210	0.2	2020	56,441	16.9	6,727	2.0
1940[1]	9,019	6.8	365	0.3	2030	74,107	20.6	9,132	2.5
1960	16,560	9.2	929	0.5	2040	82,344	21.7	14,634	3.9
1980	25,549	11.3	2,240	1.0	2050	87,996	22.1	18,972	4.8
2000	34,992	12.4	4,240	1.5	2060	98,164	23.6	19,724	4.7

Note: 1900 figures are for June 1; 1920 figures are for Jan. 1; and 1940-2010 figures are for Apr. 1. 2020-60 projections are as of July 1. (1) Excludes Alaska and Hawaii.

U.S. Population Projections by Age, 2020-60

Source: Population Projections Program, U.S. Census Bureau, U.S. Dept. of Commerce
(numbers of resident population in thousands)

Age	2020 No.	2020 % distrib.	2030 No.	2030 % distrib.	2040 No.	2040 % distrib.	2050 No.	2050 % distrib.	2060 No.	2060 % distrib.
Total	334,503	100.0%	359,402	100.0%	380,219	100.0%	398,328	100.0%	416,795	100.0%
Under 5 years	20,568	6.2	21,178	5.9	21,471	5.7	22,147	5.6	22,778	5.5
5 to 13 years	36,824	11.0	38,322	10.7	39,087	10.3	39,887	10.0	41,193	9.9
14 to 17 years	16,737	5.0	16,773	4.7	17,627	4.6	17,854	4.5	18,338	4.4
18 to 24 years	30,555	9.1	30,794	8.6	31,815	8.4	32,717	8.2	33,300	8.0
25 to 44 years	89,518	26.8	95,795	26.7	96,854	25.5	99,653	25.0	103,010	24.7
45 to 64 years	83,861	25.1	82,434	22.9	91,021	23.9	98,074	24.6	100,013	24.0
65 years and over	56,441	16.9	74,107	20.6	82,344	21.7	87,996	22.1	98,164	23.6
85 years and over	6,727	2.0	9,132	2.5	14,634	3.9	18,972	4.8	19,724	4.7
100 years and over	89	0.0	138	0.0	193	0.1	387	0.1	604	0.1

Note: Projections are as of July 1 of given year. They are based on assumptions about future births, deaths, and net international migration.

Disability Status of U.S. Population by Age, 2015

Source: American Community Survey (ACS), U.S. Census Bureau, U.S. Dept. of Commerce
(numbers in thousands, by difficulty type)

Characteristic	Number	% of pop.	Characteristic	Number	% of pop.
Total population (all ages)	316,451	100.00%	Total population (5 years and over)	296,658	100.00%
With a disability[1]	39,906	12.61	With a cognitive difficulty[2]	15,115	5.10
Under 5 years	149	0.05	5 to 17 years	2,199	0.74
Under 18 years	3,034	0.96	18 to 64 years	8,751	2.95
18 to 64 years	20,412	6.45	65 years and over	4,165	1.40
65 years and over	16,461	5.20	With an ambulatory difficulty[3]	20,920	7.05
With a hearing difficulty	11,267	3.56	5 to 17 years	336	0.11
Under 5 years	106	0.03	18 to 64 years	10,092	3.40
Under 18 years	436	0.14	65 years and over	10,491	3.54
18 to 64 years	3,970	1.25	With a self-care difficulty[4]	7,974	2.69
65 years and over	6,862	2.17	5 to 17 years	505	0.17
With a vision difficulty	7,334	2.32	18 to 64 years	3,650	1.23
Under 5 years	84	0.03	65 years and over	3,818	1.29
Under 18 years	540	0.17			
18 to 64 years	3,789	1.20	Total population (18 years and over)	242,959	100.00%
65 years and over	3,005	0.95	With an independent living difficulty[5]	14,185	5.84
			18 to 64 years	7,274	2.99
			65 years and over	6,910	2.84

Note: Data based on sample and subject to sampling variability. Does not include military personnel and civilian institutionalized population (i.e., those under formal supervision or custody in a facility). (1) Identified by the ACS as persons "who exhibit difficulty with specific functions and may, in the absence of accommodation, have a disability." (2) Concentrating, remembering, or making decisions. (3) Walking or climbing stairs. (4) Dressing or bathing. (5) Doing errands alone, such as visiting a doctor's office or shopping.

Marital Status of the U.S. Population, 1960-2015

Source: Annual Social and Economic Supplements, Current Population Surveys (CPS), U.S. Census Bureau, U.S. Dept. of Commerce
(numbers in millions)

Marital status	Both sexes				Male				Female			
	2015	2000	1980	1960	2015	2000	1980	1960	2015	2000	1980	1960
Total..................	255.0	213.8	171.9	124.9	123.6	103.1	81.9	60.3	131.4	110.7	89.9	64.6
Married[1]	133.6	120.2	104.8	84.4	66.3	59.7	51.8	41.8	67.2	60.5	53.0	42.6
Never married	81.0	60.0	44.5	27.5	43.1	32.3	24.2	15.3	38.0	27.8	20.2	12.3
Divorced	25.8	19.9	9.9	2.8	11.0	8.6	3.9	1.1	14.9	11.3	6.0	1.7
Widowed	14.6	13.7	12.7	10.2	3.3	2.6	2.0	2.1	11.3	11.1	10.8	8.1
% of total or subset pops.												
Married[1]	52.4%	56.2%	61.0%	67.6%	53.7%	57.9%	63.2%	69.3%	51.2%	54.7%	58.9%	65.9%
Never married	31.8	28.1	25.9	22.0	34.8	31.3	29.6	25.3	28.9	25.1	22.5	19.0
Divorced	10.1	9.3	5.8	2.3	8.9	8.3	4.8	1.8	11.3	10.2	6.6	2.6
Widowed	5.7	6.4	7.4	8.1	2.6	2.5	2.4	3.5	8.6	10.0	12.0	12.5

Note: Total population for 1980, 2000, and 2015 is persons ages 15 and older and for 1960, persons ages 14 and older. Data is based on sample of occupied households in the civilian noninstitutional population. Figures may not add up to totals due to rounding. (1) Comprises subcategories Married, spouse present; Married, spouse absent; and Separated.

Living Arrangements of Children in the U.S. by Parental Presence, 1970-2015

Source: Annual Social and Economic Supplements, Current Population Surveys (CPS), U.S. Census Bureau, U.S. Dept. of Commerce

Race and Hispanic origin/year	No. of children (thous.)	Both parents[4]	Total[5]	Mother only—				Father only	Neither parent
				Married spouse absent	Divorced	Widowed	Never married		
All children									
2015	73,623	69%	23%	1%	7%	1%	11%	4%	4%
White alone[1]									
1970	58,791	90	8	3	3	2	Z	1	2
1980	52,242	83	14	4	7	2	1	2	2
1990	51,390	79	16	4	8	1	3	3	2
2000	56,455	75	17	NA	NA	NA	NA	4	3
2015	53,621	75	18	1	7	1	7	4	3
Black alone[1]									
1970	9,422	58	30	16	5	4	4	2	10
1980	9,375	42	44	16	11	4	13	2	12
1990	10,018	38	51	12	10	2	27	4	8
2000	11,412	38	49	NA	NA	NA	NA	4	9
2015	11,091	39	49	2	8	1	34	4	8
Hispanic[2]									
1970[3]	4,006	78	NA	NA	NA	NA	NA	NA	NA
1980	5,459	75	20	8	6	2	4	2	3
1990	7,174	67	27	10	7	2	8	3	3
2000	11,613	65	25	NA	NA	NA	NA	4	5
2015	17,981	67	26	2	5	1	13	3	4

NA = Not available. Z = Less than 1%. **Note:** Children are defined as all persons under 18 years of age excluding those who are a family reference person or spouse. Data based on sample of occupied households in the civilian noninstitutional population. (1) One race only, not in combination with another race. (2) May be of any race. (3) Data based on 1970 decennial census. (4) Includes married and unmarried couples. (5) Includes children whose mothers are separated, a subcategory not shown in detail here.

Children in the U.S. by Selected Characteristics, 2015

Source: Annual Social and Economic Supplement, Current Population Survey (CPS), U.S. Census Bureau, U.S. Dept. of Commerce
(numbers in thousands)

Characteristic	Number	% of tot.	Characteristic	Number	% of tot.
All children	73,623	100.0%	Presence of siblings in living arrangement		
Age of child			None...........................	15,052	20.4%
Under 1 year.......................	3,873	5.3	One sibling	28,474	38.7
1-2 years...........................	7,979	10.8	Two siblings	17,928	24.4
3-5 years...........................	12,038	16.4	Three siblings	7,676	10.4
6-8 years...........................	12,339	16.8	Four siblings	2,672	3.6
9-11 years..........................	12,358	16.8	Five or more siblings.............	1,821	2.5
12-14 years.........................	12,385	16.8	Presence of grandparents in living		
15-17 years.........................	12,652	17.2	arrangement		
Race of child			Grandparent is householder		
White alone, not Hispanic.............	38,084	51.7	Grandmother and grandfather	2,474	3.4
Black alone.........................	11,091	15.1	Grandmother only	2,088	2.8
Asian alone.........................	3,736	5.1	Grandfather only	323	0.4
Hispanic (any race)...................	17,981	24.4	No grandparents present	65,911	89.5

Note: Children are defined as all persons under 18 years of age excluding those who are a family reference person or spouse. Data based on sample of occupied households in the civilian noninstitutional population.

Unmarried-Partner Households in the U.S. by Sex of Partners, 2015

Source: American Community Survey (ACS), U.S. Census Bureau, U.S. Dept. of Commerce

Type of household	Number	% of total	% of cat.	Type of household	Number	% of total	% of cat.
Total households	118,208,250	100.0%	—	Female HH, female partner	223,317	0.2%	3.0%
Unmarried-partner households...	7,347,757	6.2	100.0%	Male HH, male partner	210,222	0.2	2.9
Male HH, female partner	3,505,774	3.0	47.7	All other households..........	110,860,493	93.8	100.0
Female HH, male partner	3,408,444	2.9	46.4				

HH = Householder, or person in whose name a home is owned or rented. **Note:** Data based on sample and subject to sampling variability. A household includes all people occupying a housing unit; the household population does not include people living in group quarters (e.g., correctional facilities, university housing).

Persons Granted Lawful Permanent Resident Status by State, 2014

Source: Office of Immigration Statistics, U.S. Dept. of Homeland Security
(ranked by fiscal year 2014 number)

State/territory	Number	State/territory	Number	State/territory	Number	State/territory	Number
Total	1,016,518	North Carolina	17,152	Kentucky	5,634	New Hampshire	2,103
California	198,379	Arizona	16,908	Kansas	4,861	Delaware	2,085
New York	141,406	Ohio	14,641	Nebraska	4,442	Mississippi	1,587
Florida	109,310	Minnesota	13,764	Oklahoma	4,441	Alaska	1,505
Texas	95,295	Connecticut	11,252	Louisiana	4,382	Maine	1,382
New Jersey	51,609	Colorado	10,872	South Carolina	4,233	North Dakota	1,351
Illinois	36,535	Nevada	10,089	Iowa	4,225	South Dakota	1,108
Massachusetts	29,776	Tennessee	8,507	Alabama	3,685	Guam	1,089
Virginia	28,477	Indiana	8,008	New Mexico	3,359	Vermont	791
Maryland	24,787	Oregon	7,379	Rhode Island	3,297	West Virginia	783
Pennsylvania	23,944	Missouri	6,419	District of Columbia	3,169	Montana	451
Georgia	23,792	Utah	6,166	Arkansas	2,793	Wyoming	414
Washington	22,710	Wisconsin	5,997	Puerto Rico	2,709	Other[1]	1,336
Michigan	18,185	Hawaii	5,741	Idaho	2,202	Unknown	1

Note: Applicants for lawful permanent resident (LPR) status, or "green cards," may already live in the U.S. They include refugees and asylees, temp. workers, foreign students, family members of U.S. citizens, and unauthorized immigrants. Applicants from outside the U.S. are granted LPR status upon entry with a visa. (1) Incl. Amer. Samoa, Northern Mariana Isls., U.S. Virgin Isls., and armed forces posts.

Persons Granted Lawful Permanent Resident Status by Top Areas of Residence, 2014

Source: Office of Immigration Statistics, U.S. Dept. of Homeland Security
(ranked by fiscal year 2014 number)

Core Based Statistical Area (CBSA)[1]	Number	% of total	Core Based Statistical Area (CBSA)[1]	Number	% of total
Total	1,016,518	100.0%	Charlotte-Concord-Gastonia, NC-SC	5,421	0.5%
New York-Newark-Jersey City, NY-NJ-PA	174,714	17.2	San Antonio-New Braunfels, TX	5,404	0.5
Los Angeles-Long Beach-Anaheim, CA	80,527	7.9	Columbus, OH	5,287	0.5
Miami-Fort Lauderdale-West Palm Beach, FL	72,038	7.1	Nashville-Davidson–Murfreesboro–Franklin, TN	4,584	0.5
Washington-Arlington-Alexandria, DC-VA-MD-WV	39,531	3.9	Bridgeport-Stamford-Norwalk, CT	4,414	0.4
Houston-The Woodlands-Sugar Land, TX	33,856	3.3	El Paso, TX	4,403	0.4
Chicago-Naperville-Elgin, IL-IN-WI	33,042	3.3	Urban Honolulu, HI	4,358	0.4
San Francisco-Oakland-Hayward, CA	32,904	3.2	Indianapolis-Carmel-Anderson, IN	4,251	0.4
Dallas-Fort Worth-Arlington, TX	28,780	2.8	Providence-Warwick, RI-MA	4,193	0.4
Boston-Cambridge-Newton, MA-NH	24,026	2.4	Raleigh, NC	4,028	0.4
Atlanta-Sandy Springs-Roswell, GA	19,626	1.9	Salt Lake City, UT	3,967	0.4
San Jose-Sunnyvale-Santa Clara, CA	18,590	1.8	Kansas City, MO-KS	3,654	0.4
San Diego-Carlsbad, CA	17,670	1.7	Hartford-West Hartford-East Hartford, CT	3,439	0.3
Philadelphia-Camden-Wilmington, PA-NJ-DE-MD	17,665	1.7	St. Louis, MO-IL	3,279	0.3
Seattle-Tacoma-Bellevue, WA	17,529	1.7	Jacksonville, FL	3,266	0.3
Riverside-San Bernardino-Ontario, CA	13,362	1.3	Louisville-Jefferson County, KY-IN	3,209	0.3
Detroit-Warren-Dearborn, MI	12,814	1.3	Cleveland-Elyria, OH	3,074	0.3
Phoenix-Mesa-Scottsdale, AZ	11,956	1.2	McAllen-Edinburg-Mission, TX	3,045	0.3
Minneapolis-St. Paul-Bloomington, MN-WI	11,202	1.1	Cincinnati, OH-KY-IN	2,999	0.3
Orlando-Kissimmee-Sanford, FL	10,217	1.0	Worcester, MA-CT	2,983	0.3
Tampa-St. Petersburg-Clearwater, FL	9,647	0.9	Stockton-Lodi, CA	2,982	0.3
Sacramento–Roseville–Arden-Arcade, CA	8,724	0.9	Fresno, CA	2,878	0.3
Las Vegas-Henderson-Paradise, NV	8,652	0.9	Virginia Beach-Norfolk-Newport News, VA-NC	2,755	0.3
Baltimore-Columbia-Towson, MD	8,437	0.8	Milwaukee-Waukesha-West Allis, WI	2,685	0.3
Denver-Aurora-Lakewood, CO	7,375	0.7	Other CBSAs	187,227	18.4
Portland-Vancouver-Hillsboro, OR-WA	6,228	0.6	Non-CBSA or unknown	13,487	1.3
Austin-Round Rock, TX	6,134	0.6			

Note: Applicants for lawful permanent resident (LPR) status, or "green cards," may already live in the U.S. They include refugees and asylees, temp. workers, foreign students, family members of U.S. citizens, and unauthorized immigrants. Applicants from outside the U.S. are granted LPR status upon entry with a visa. (1) CBSAs refer collectively to metropolitan and micropolitan statistical areas. These areas are defined for federal statistical use by the Office of Management and Budget with Census Bureau assistance.

Unauthorized Immigrant Population in the U.S., 2000, 2014

Source: Pew Research Center
(ranked by 2014 est. population; numbers in thousands)

Country of Birth				State of Residence			
	Est. population		% change,		Est. population		% change,
Country	2014	2000	2000-14	State	2014	2000	2000-14
All countries	11,100	8,600	29.1%	All states	11,100	8,600	29.1%
Mexico	5,850	4,450	31.5	California	2,350	2,250	4.4
El Salvador	700	500	40.0	Texas	1,650	1,050	57.1
Guatemala	525	200	162.5	Florida	850	900	−5.6
India	500	240	108.3	New York	775	750	3.3
Honduras	350	140	150.0	New Jersey	500	325	53.8
China[1]	325	325	0.0	Illinois	450	375	20.0
Philippines	180	120	50.0	Georgia	375	170	120.6
Dominican Republic	170	180	−5.6	North Carolina	350	220	59.1
Korea[2]	160	110	45.5	Arizona	325	350	−7.1
Ecuador	130	90	44.4	Virginia	300	200	50.0
Colombia	130	150	−13.3	Washington	250	150	66.7
Peru	100	100	0.0	Maryland	250	160	56.3
Haiti	100	130	−23.1	Massachusetts	210	170	23.5
Brazil	100	90	11.1	Nevada	210	170	23.5
Canada	100	55	81.8	Colorado	200	130	53.8

Note: Unauthorized immigrant population estimates are made using the residual method. The estimated number of immigrants residing legally in the country is subtracted from the total foreign-born pop. Numbers are rounded independently and may not add up to totals. (1) Incl. Hong Kong and Taiwan. (2) Incl. North and South Korea.

U.S. Foreign-Born Population

Source: Annual Social and Economic Supplements, Current Population Surveys (CPS), U.S. Census Bureau, U.S. Dept. of Commerce

Percentage of Population That Is Foreign-Born, 1900-2015

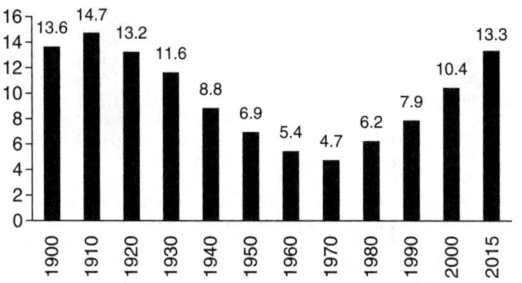

Foreign-Born Population by Region of Birth, 1995-2013

(numbers in thousands)

Region	2013[1] No.	2013[1] %	2000	1995
Asia............	11,763	29.3%	7,916	6,121
Under 18......	801	33.2	696	767
Europe	4,441	11.1	4,382	3,937
Under 18......	244	10.1	247	232
Latin America	21,047	52.5	15,323	11,777
Under 18......	1,098	45.5	1,786	1,451
Other[2].........	2,856	7.1	2,364	2,658
Under 18......	269	11.2	249	275
All regions......	40,107	100.0	29,985	24,493
Under 18	2,412	100.0	2,977	2,726

(1) Figures are percentage of total foreign-born population or of all foreign-born under 18 years of age. (2) Including those born at sea.

U.S. Foreign-Born Population: Top Countries of Origin, 1880-2015

Source: American Community Survey (ACS), Decennial Censuses, U.S. Census Bureau, U.S. Dept. of Commerce

(numbers in thousands; percentage is of all foreign-born excluding population born at sea)

1880 Country	No.	%	1920 Country	No.	%	1960 Country	No.	%	2000 Country	No.	%	2015[4] Country	No.	%
Germany	1,967	29.4	Germany	1,686	12.1	Italy	1,257	12.9	Mexico	9,177	29.5	Mexico	11,643	26.9
Ireland	1,855	27.8	Italy	1,610	11.6	Germany	990	10.2	China[2]	1,519	4.9	China[2]	2,677	6.2
UK	918	13.7	U.S.S.R.	1,400	10.1	Canada	953	9.8	Philippines	1,369	4.4	India	2,390	5.5
Canada	717	10.7	Poland	1,140	8.2	UK	765	7.9	India	1,023	3.3	Philippines	1,982	4.6
Sweden	194	2.9	Canada	1,138	8.2	Poland	748	7.7	Vietnam	988	3.2	El Salvador	1,352	3.1
Norway	182	2.7	UK	1,135	8.2	U.S.S.R.	691	7.1	Cuba	873	2.8	Vietnam	1,301	3.0
France	107	1.6	Ireland	1,037	7.5	Mexico	576	5.9	Korea[3]	864	2.8	Cuba	1,211	2.8
China[1]	104	1.6	Sweden	626	4.5	Ireland	339	3.5	Canada	821	2.6	Dominican Republic	1,063	2.5
Switzerland	89	1.3	Austria	576	4.1	Austria	305	3.1	El Salvador	817	2.6	Korea[3]	1,060	2.4
Czech.	85	1.3	Mexico	486	3.5	Hungary	245	2.5	Germany	707	2.3	Guatemala	928	2.1
Total	**6,680**	**100.0**	**Total**	**13,921**	**100.0**	**Total**	**9,738**	**100.0**	**Total**	**31,108**	**100.0**	**Total**	**43,290**	**100.0**

(1) Incl. Taiwan. (2) Incl. Hong Kong and Taiwan. (3) North and South Korea. (4) Data based on sample and subject to sampling variability. The Census Bureau collects data from residents regardless of immigration status, so the foreign-born population implicitly includes unauthorized migrants.

Language Spoken at Home by the U.S. Population, 2015

Source: American Community Survey (ACS), U.S. Census Bureau, U.S. Dept. of Commerce

(number of speakers 5 years of age and over by language or language group most often used)

Language	Number (thous.)	% of tot. pop.	% English inability[1]	Language	Number (thous.)	% of tot. pop.	% English inability[1]
Total population	301,625.0	100.00	10.9%	Other Slavic languages	317.4	0.11%	37.7%
Speak only English........	236,908.9	78.54	NA	Other West Germanic langs. ..	336.6	0.11	25.6
Speak another language	64,716.1	21.46	40.0	Other Indo-European langs....	463.9	0.15	34.2
Spanish				Asian and Pacific Island languages			
Spanish or Spanish Creole....	40,045.8	13.28	41.0	Chinese	3,333.6	1.11	55.7
Other Indo-European languages				Hmong	228.7	0.08	40.9
Armenian	235.5	0.08	44.0	Japanese	446.1	0.15	41.7
French (incl. Patois, Cajun)....	1,266.4	0.42	20.1	Korean	1,108.8	0.37	53.2
French Creole..............	863.4	0.29	41.2	Laotian	152.1	0.05	49.5
German	933.4	0.31	14.9	Mon-Khmer, Cambodian......	219.8	0.07	51.4
Greek	289.3	0.10	26.8	Tagalog.................	1,737.2	0.58	32.4
Gujarati..................	404.8	0.13	34.5	Thai....................	159.2	0.05	51.8
Hindi....................	812.8	0.27	21.2	Vietnamese..............	1,468.3	0.49	58.9
Italian	605.7	0.20	27.7	Other Asian languages.......	1,201.4	0.40	31.0
Persian	429.5	0.14	38.3	Other Pacific Island langs.	445.9	0.15	37.5
Polish	541.9	0.18	39.2	All other languages			
Portuguese or				African languages...........	1,104.6	0.37	31.8
Portuguese Creole	717.6	0.24	35.1	Arabic...................	1,156.9	0.38	37.2
Russian..................	905.1	0.30	44.0	Hebrew..................	200.6	0.07	14.6
Scandinavian languages	116.7	0.04	9.1	Hungarian................	78.9	0.03	25.0
Serbo-Croatian.............	253.6	0.08	35.3	Navajo..................	160.0	0.05	20.7
Urdu	481.4	0.16	29.4	Other Native North American			
Yiddish	169.8	0.06	35.7	languages	182.7	0.06	16.5
Other Indic languages	992.2	0.33	40.9	Other and unspecified langs. ..	148.1	0.05	40.6

NA = Not applicable. **Note:** Data based on sample and subject to sampling variability. (1) Percent of respondents who speak the language at left who indicated that they spoke English less than "very well." For example, 44.0% of respondents who use Armenian at home do not speak English very well.

U.S. Population by Ancestry Reported, 2015

Source: American Community Survey (ACS), U.S. Census Bureau, U.S. Dept. of Commerce
(numbers in thousands; ranked by number)

Ancestry	Number	% of total	Ancestry	Number	% of total	Ancestry	Number	% of total
Total population	321,419	100.0%	Norwegian	4,433	1.4%	French Canadian	2,072	0.6%
German	45,526	14.2	Dutch	4,141	1.3	Arab[4].............	1,963	0.6
Irish..............	32,713	10.2	European	3,931	1.2	Welsh	1,777	0.6
English	23,959	7.5	Swedish	3,829	1.2	Hungarian..........	1,411	0.4
American	21,845	6.8	Sub-Saharan African[1]..	3,482	1.1	British	1,398	0.4
Italian	17,070	5.3	Scotch-Irish[2]........	2,982	0.9	Czech	1,391	0.4
Polish	9,231	2.9	West Indian (excl.			Other ancestry not		
French (excl. Basque)..	7,970	2.5	Hispanic groups)[3] ...	2,950	0.9	shown here........	138,943	43.2
Scottish............	5,511	1.7	Russian............	2,723	0.8	Unclassified or not		
						reported	50,826	15.8

Note: Data based on sample and subject to sampling variability. Because respondents could self-identify with more than one ancestry, numbers do not add up to total. (1) Incl. Cabo Verdean, Ethiopian, Ghanian, Kenyan, Liberian, Nigerian, Senegalese, Sierra Leonean, Somali, South African, Sudanese, Ugandan, Zimbabwean, African, and other sub-Saharan African. (2) Excl. persons reporting Irish-Scotch ancestry. (3) Incl. Bahamian, Barbadian, Belizean, Bermudan, British or Dutch West Indian, Haitian, Jamaican, Trinidadian and Tobagonian, U.S. Virgin Islander, West Indian, and other West Indian. (4) Incl. Egyptian, Iraqi, Jordanian, Lebanese, Moroccan, Palestinian, Syrian, Arab, and other Arab.

U.S. Population by Race, Hispanic Origin, and Age, 2015

Source: American Community Survey (ACS), U.S. Census Bureau, U.S. Dept. of Commerce

Race and origin/age	Number	% of group	Race and origin/age	Number	% of group
White (not Hispanic or Latino)	197,534,496	100.0%	Native Hawaiian and other		
Under 5 years................	9,842,514	5.0	Pacific Islander	554,946	100.0%
Under 18 years................	37,787,644	19.1	Under 5 years................	43,798	7.9
18 to 64 years................	122,643,021	62.1	Under 18 years................	145,729	26.3
65 years and over.............	37,103,831	18.8	18 to 64 years................	365,288	65.8
85 years and over.............	5,052,302	2.6	65 years and over.............	43,929	7.9
Black or African American........	40,695,277	100.0	85 years and over.............	3,352	0.6
Under 5 years................	2,774,029	6.8	Some other race	15,375,942	100.0
Under 18 years................	10,400,604	25.6	Under 5 years................	1,256,089	8.2
18 to 64 years................	26,029,197	64.0	Under 18 years................	4,567,391	29.7
65 years and over.............	4,265,476	10.5	18 to 64 years................	9,988,515	65.0
85 years and over.............	449,528	1.1	65 years and over.............	820,036	5.3
Asian	17,273,777	100.0	85 years and over.............	76,019	0.5
Under 5 years................	923,038	5.3	Two or more races	9,981,530	100.0
Under 18 years................	3,497,579	20.2	Under 5 years................	1,469,499	14.7
18 to 64 years................	11,766,507	68.1	Under 18 years................	4,615,158	46.2
65 years and over.............	2,009,691	11.6	18 to 64 years................	4,883,991	48.9
85 years and over.............	207,501	1.2	65 years and over.............	482,381	4.8
American Indian and Alaska Native	2,597,249	100.0	85 years and over.............	44,409	0.4
Under 5 years................	181,033	7.0	Hispanic or Latino (any race)	56,496,122	100.0
Under 18 years................	711,353	27.4	Under 5 years................	5,094,864	9.0
18 to 64 years................	1,638,312	63.1	Under 18 years................	18,113,195	32.1
65 years and over.............	247,584	9.5	18 to 64 years................	34,627,599	61.3
85 years and over.............	20,303	0.8	65 years and over.............	3,755,328	6.6
			85 years and over.............	402,761	0.7

Note: Data based on sample and subject to sampling variability. Categories are for one race alone, not in combination with any other race, unless otherwise noted.

Educational Attainment of the U.S. Population, 2015

Source: American Community Survey (ACS), U.S. Census Bureau, U.S. Dept. of Commerce
(numbers in thousands; population 25 years of age and over)

Race and origin/highest ed. completed	Number	% of group	Race and origin/highest ed. completed	Number	% of group
White (not Hispanic or Latino)	142,711	100.0%	Native Hawaiian and other		
Less than H.S. diploma	11,044	7.7	Pacific Islander....................	335	100.0%
H.S. diploma or equiv. credential	39,858	27.9	Less than H.S. diploma	42	12.4
Some college or associate's degree.....	42,986	30.1	H.S. diploma or equiv. credential	117	35.0
Bachelor's degree or higher...........	48,823	34.2	Some college or associate's degree.....	124	36.9
Black or African American.............	25,578	100.0	Bachelor's degree or higher...........	53	15.7
Less than H.S. diploma	3,904	15.3	Some other race	8,911	100.0
H.S. diploma or equiv. credential	8,062	31.5	Less than H.S. diploma	3,502	39.3
Some college or associate's degree.....	8,437	33.0	H.S. diploma or equiv. credential	2,545	28.6
Bachelor's degree or higher...........	5,175	20.2	Some college or associate's degree.....	1,880	21.1
Asian	12,076	100.0	Bachelor's degree or higher...........	984	11.0
Less than H.S. diploma	1,627	13.5	Two or more races	4,099	100.0
H.S. diploma or equiv. credential	1,869	15.5	Less than H.S. diploma	520	12.7
Some college or associate's degree.....	2,262	18.7	H.S. diploma or equiv. credential	928	22.6
Bachelor's degree or higher...........	6,318	52.3	Some college or associate's degree.....	1,415	34.5
American Indian and Alaska Native	1,584	100.0	Bachelor's degree or higher...........	1,236	30.2
Less than H.S. diploma	331	20.9	Hispanic or Latino (any race)	31,653	100.0
H.S. diploma or equiv. credential	503	31.8	Less than H.S. diploma	10,763	34.0
Some college or associate's degree.....	526	33.2	H.S. diploma or equiv. credential	8,738	27.6
Bachelor's degree or higher...........	223	14.1	Some college or associate's degree.....	7,475	23.6
			Bachelor's degree or higher...........	4,677	14.8

H.S. = High school. **Note:** Data based on sample and subject to sampling variability. Categories are for one race alone, not in combination with any other race, unless otherwise noted.

Populations, ZIP, and Area Codes for U.S. Places of 10,000 or More

Source: Decennial Census and Population Estimates Program, U.S. Census Bureau, U.S. Dept. of Commerce; NeuStar Inc.; www.usps.com

The following is a list of places of 10,000 or more residents according to the U.S. Census Bureau's population estimates for 2015 and the results of the 2010 census.

This list includes **places incorporated** under state law as cities, towns, villages, or boroughs, and **Census designated places (CDPs)**, marked with a (c). This list also includes, in italics, **minor civil divisions (MCDs)** in Connecticut, Maine, Massachusetts, New Hampshire, Rhode Island, and Vermont. **Townships are not included.** Neither CDPs nor MCDs are incorporated areas. The Census Bureau delineates CDPs as statistical counterparts to incorporated places but does not typically include CDPs in its estimates program. MCDs are often the primary political or administrative divisions of a county. (Balance) indicates that the population given is for a consolidated area minus the residents of any separately incorporated places within its boundaries.

An asterisk (*) denotes that the **ZIP code** given is for general delivery; mail routes and/or P.O. boxes within the place may use a different one. Telephone **area codes** are given in parentheses. New phone numbers may be assigned a different area code from that of existing phone numbers in an area. These areas of overlay are noted. When two or more area codes are listed for one place, consult local operators for assistance. Area codes based on latest information as of Sept. 2016. — = Not available.

Alabama

Area code 938 overlays area code 256.

ZIP	Place	Area code	2010 population	2015 estimate
*35007	Alabaster	(205)	30,352	32,707
*35950	Albertville	(256)	21,160	21,462
*35010	Alexander City	(256)	14,875	14,718
*36201	Anniston	(256)	23,106	22,347
*35611	Athens	(256)	21,897	24,966
*36502	Atmore	(251)	10,194	10,049
*36830	Auburn	(334)	53,380	62,059
*35020	Bessemer	(205)	27,456	26,730
*35203	Birmingham	(205)	212,237	212,461
35040	Calera	(205)	11,620	13,213
*35215	Center Point	(205)	16,921	16,655
35043	Chelsea	(205)	10,183	12,059
*35055	Cullman	(256)	14,775	15,350
36526	Daphne	(251)	21,570	24,896
*35601	Decatur	(256)	55,683	55,437
*36301	Dothan	(334)	65,496	68,567
*36330	Enterprise	(334)	26,562	27,978
*36027	Eufaula	(334)	13,137	12,596
35064	Fairfield	(205)	11,117	10,907
*36532	Fairhope	(251)	15,326	18,730
*35630	Florence	(256)	39,319	40,026
*36535	Foley	(251)	14,618	17,218
35214	Forestdale (c)	(205)	10,162	—
*35967	Fort Payne	(256)	14,012	14,150
*35901	Gadsden	(256)	36,856	36,084
35071	Gardendale	(205)	13,893	13,711
36542	Gulf Shores	(251)	9,741	11,131
35640	Hartselle	(256)	14,255	14,493
*35080	Helena	(205)	16,793	18,264
*35209	Homewood	(205)	25,167	25,708
*35216	Hoover	(205)	81,619	84,848
*35023	Hueytown	(205)	16,105	15,710
*35801	Huntsville	(256)	180,105	190,582
35210	Irondale	(205)	12,349	12,423
36265	Jacksonville	(256)	12,548	12,222
*35501	Jasper	(205)	14,352	14,071
35094	Leeds	(205)	11,773	11,936
*35758	Madison	(256)	42,938	46,962
36054	Millbrook	(334)	14,640	15,314
*36602	Mobile	(251)	195,111	194,288
*36104	Montgomery	(334)	205,764	200,602
35004	Moody	(205)	11,726	12,593
*35223	Mountain Brook	(205)	20,413	20,691
*35661	Muscle Shoals	(256)	13,146	13,706
*35476	Northport	(205)	23,330	24,772
*36801	Opelika	(334)	26,477	29,527
36203	Oxford	(256)	21,348	21,249
*36360	Ozark	(334)	14,907	14,719
35124	Pelham	(205)	21,352	22,885
*35125	Pell City	(205)	12,695	13,646
*36867	Phenix City	(334)	32,822	37,570
35127	Pleasant Grove	(205)	10,110	10,260
*36066	Prattville	(334)	33,960	35,420
36610	Prichard	(251)	22,659	22,351
36206	Saks (c)	(256)	10,744	—
36571	Saraland	(251)	13,405	13,906
*35768	Scottsboro	(256)	14,770	14,722
*36701	Selma	(334)	20,756	19,519
*35150	Sylacauga	(256)	12,749	12,657
*35160	Talladega	(256)	15,676	15,709
36619	Tillman's Corner (c)	(251)	17,398	—
*36081	Troy	(334)	18,033	18,853
35173	Trussville	(205)	19,933	21,023
*35401	Tuscaloosa	(205)	90,468	98,332
*35216	Vestavia Hills	(205)	34,033	34,174

Alaska

Area code 907 applies to the entire state.

ZIP	Place	2010 population	2015 estimate
*99501	Anchorage	291,826	298,695
99711	Badger (c)	19,482	—
*99708	College (c)	12,964	—
*99701	Fairbanks	31,535	32,325
99801	Juneau	31,275	32,756
99654	Knik-Fairview (c)	14,923	—

Arizona

ZIP	Place	Area code	2010 population	2015 estimate
85086	Anthem (c)	(623)	21,700	—
*85119	Apache Junction	(480)	35,840	38,074
85123	Arizona City (c)	(520)	10,475	—
*85323	Avondale	(623)	76,238	80,684
*85326	Buckeye	(623)	50,876	62,138
*86442	Bullhead City	(928)	39,540	39,445
86322	Camp Verde	(928)	10,873	11,155
*85122	Casa Grande	(520)	48,571	51,460
85740	Casas Adobes (c)	(520)	66,795	—
85718	Catalina Foothills (c)	(520)	50,796	—
*85225	Chandler	(480)	236,123	260,828
86323	Chino Valley	(928)	10,817	11,137
85128	Coolidge	(520)	11,825	12,297
86326	Cottonwood	(928)	11,265	11,818
*85607	Douglas	(520)	17,378	16,592
*85746	Drexel Heights (c)	(520)	27,749	—
85335	El Mirage	(623)	31,797	33,935
85131	Eloy	(520)	16,631	17,059
*86001	Flagstaff	(928)	65,870	70,320
85132	Florence	(520)	25,536	31,110
85705	Flowing Wells (c)	(520)	16,419	—
*86427	Fort Mohave (c)	(928)	14,364	—
85367	Fortuna Foothills (c)	(928)	26,265	—
*85268	Fountain Hills	(480)	22,489	23,899
*85234	Gilbert	(480)	208,453	247,542
*85301	Glendale	(623)	226,721	240,126
85118	Gold Canyon (c)	(480)	10,159	—
*85338	Goodyear	(623)	65,275	79,003
*85622	Green Valley (c)	(520)	21,391	—
*86401	Kingman	(928)	28,068	28,912
*86403	Lake Havasu City	(928)	52,527	53,553
*85653	Marana	(520)	34,961	41,315
*85138	Maricopa	(520)	43,482	48,602
*85201	Mesa	(480)	439,041	471,825
86401	New Kingman-Butler (c)	(928)	12,134	—
*85087	New River (c)	(623)	14,952	—
*85621	Nogales	(520)	20,837	20,252
*85737	Oro Valley	(520)	41,011	43,565
85253	Paradise Valley	(480)	12,820	13,922
*85541	Payson	(928)	15,301	15,345
*85345	Peoria	(623)	154,065	171,237
*85003	Phoenix	(480)/(602)/(623)	1,445,632	1,563,025
*86301	Prescott	(928)	39,843	41,899
*86314	Prescott Valley	(928)	38,822	42,197
*85142	Queen Creek	(480)	26,361	34,614
85648	Rio Rico (c)	(520)	18,962	—
85629	Sahuarita	(520)	25,259	25,707
85349	San Luis	(928)	25,505	31,520
*85142	San Tan Valley (c)	(480)	81,321	—
*85251	Scottsdale	(480)	217,385	236,839
*86336	Sedona	(928)	10,031	10,388
*85901	Show Low	(928)	10,660	10,860
*85635	Sierra Vista	(520)	43,888	43,355
85650	Sierra Vista Southeast (c)	(520)	14,797	—
85350	Somerton	(928)	14,287	15,048
*85351	Sun City (c)	(623)	37,499	—
*85375	Sun City West (c)	(623)	24,535	—
85248	Sun Lakes (c)	(480)	13,975	—
*85374	Surprise	(623)	117,517	128,422
85749	Tanque Verde (c)	(520)	16,901	—
*85281	Tempe	(480)	161,719	175,826
*85701	Tucson	(520)	520,116	531,641
85735	Tucson Estates (c)	(520)	12,192	—
85641	Vail (c)	(520)	10,208	—
86326	Verde Village (c)	(928)	11,605	—
*85364	Yuma	(928)	93,064	94,139

Arkansas

ZIP	Place	Area code	2010 population	2015 estimate
*71923	Arkadelphia	(870)	10,714	10,745
*72501	Batesville	(870)	10,248	10,668
*72714	Bella Vista	(479)	26,461	27,999
*72015	Benton	(501)	30,681	34,177
*72712	Bentonville	(479)	35,301	44,499

ZIP	Place	Area code	2010 population	2015 estimate
*72315	Blytheville	(870)	15,620	14,694
*72022	Bryant	(501)	16,688	19,986
72023	Cabot	(501)	23,776	25,587
*71701	Camden	(870)	12,183	11,347
*72719	Centerton	(479)	9,515	12,023
*72032	Conway	(501)	58,908	64,980
*71730	El Dorado	(870)	18,884	18,386
*72701	Fayetteville	(479)	73,580	82,830
*72335	Forrest City	(870)	15,371	14,672
*72901	Fort Smith	(479)	86,209	88,194
*72601	Harrison	(870)	12,943	13,138
72342	Helena-West Helena	(870)	12,282	11,109
*71901	Hot Springs	(501)	35,193	35,635
*71909	Hot Springs Village (c)	(501)	12,807	—
*72076	Jacksonville	(501)	28,364	28,643
*72401	Jonesboro	(870)	67,263	73,907
*72201	Little Rock	(501)	193,524	197,992
*71753	Magnolia	(870)	11,577	11,669
*72104	Malvern	(501)	10,318	10,928
72364	Marion	(870)	12,345	12,292
72113	Maumelle	(501)	17,163	17,931
*72653	Mountain Home	(870)	12,448	12,330
*72114	North Little Rock	(501)	62,304	66,504
*72450	Paragould	(870)	26,113	27,900
*71601	Pine Bluff	(870)	49,083	44,772
*72756	Rogers	(479)	55,964	63,159
*72801	Russellville	(479)	27,920	29,166
*72143	Searcy	(501)	22,858	24,196
*72120	Sherwood	(501)	29,523	30,517
72761	Siloam Springs	(479)	15,039	16,081
*72764	Springdale	(479)	69,797	77,859
71854	Texarkana	(870)	29,919	30,353
*72956	Van Buren	(479)	22,791	23,081
*72301	West Memphis	(870)	26,245	25,052

California

Area code 424 overlays area code 310. Area code 442 overlays 760. Area code 628 overlays 415. Area code 657 overlays 714. Area code 669 overlays 408. Area code 747 overlays 818.

ZIP	Place	Area code	2010 population	2015 estimate
92301	Adelanto	(760)	31,765	33,166
*91301	Agoura Hills	(818)	20,330	20,915
*94501	Alameda	(510)	73,812	78,630
94507	Alamo (c)	(925)	14,570	—
94706	Albany	(510)	18,539	19,735
*91801	Alhambra	(626)	83,089	85,551
*92656	Aliso Viejo	(949)	47,823	50,195
*91901	Alpine (c)	(619)	14,236	—
*91001	Altadena (c)	(626)	42,777	—
95127	Alum Rock (c)	(408)	15,536	—
*94503	American Canyon	(707)	19,454	20,554
*92805	Anaheim	(714)	336,265	350,742
96007	Anderson	(530)	9,932	10,217
95843	Antelope (c)	(916)	45,770	—
*94509	Antioch	(925)	102,372	110,542
*92307	Apple Valley	(760)	69,135	72,174
*91006	Arcadia	(626)	56,364	58,408
*95521	Arcata	(707)	17,231	17,843
*95825	Arden-Arcade (c)	(916)	92,186	—
*93420	Arroyo Grande	(805)	17,252	18,108
*90701	Artesia	(562)	16,522	16,961
93203	Arvin	(661)	19,304	20,876
94577	Ashland (c)	(510)	21,925	—
*93422	Atascadero	(805)	28,310	29,819
95301	Atwater	(209)	28,168	29,237
*95603	Auburn	(530)	13,330	13,953
93204	Avenal	(559)	15,505	13,301
91746	Avocado Heights (c)	(626)	15,411	—
91702	Azusa	(626)	46,361	49,690
*93301	Bakersfield	(661)	347,483	373,640
91706	Baldwin Park	(626)	75,390	77,071
92220	Banning	(951)	29,603	30,945
*92310	Barstow	(760)	22,639	23,692
94565	Bay Point (c)	(925)	21,349	—
92223	Beaumont	(951)	36,877	43,811
*90201	Bell	(323)	35,477	36,205
*90201	Bell Gardens	(213)/(323)/(562)	42,072	43,106
*90706	Bellflower	(562)	76,616	78,441
94002	Belmont	(650)	25,835	27,218
94510	Benicia	(707)	26,997	28,167
*94704	Berkeley	(510)	112,580	120,972
*90210	Beverly Hills	(213)/(310)/(323)	34,109	34,869
*92314	Big Bear City (c)	(909)	12,304	—
92316	Bloomington (c)	(951)	23,851	—
*92225	Blythe	(760)	20,817	19,208
*91902	Bonita (c)	(619)	12,538	—
92221	Bostonia (c)	(619)	15,379	—
92227	Brawley	(760)	24,953	25,897
*92821	Brea	(562)/(714)	39,282	41,944
94513	Brentwood	(925)	51,481	58,968
*90620	Buena Park	(714)	80,530	83,270
*91502	Burbank	(818)	103,340	105,319
*94010	Burlingame	(650)	28,806	30,459
91301	Calabasas	(818)	23,058	24,319
*92231	Calexico	(760)	38,572	40,053
*93505	California City	(760)	14,120	13,277
*93010	Camarillo	(805)	65,201	67,608
95682	Cameron Park (c)	(530)	18,228	—
92058	Camp Pendleton South (c)	(760)	10,616	—
*95008	Campbell	(408)	39,349	41,117
92587	Canyon Lake	(951)	10,561	11,080
95010	Capitola	(831)	9,918	10,189
*92008	Carlsbad	(760)	105,328	113,453
*95608	Carmichael (c)	(916)	61,762	—
*93013	Carpinteria	(805)	13,040	13,727
*90745	Carson	(310)	91,714	93,281
92077	Casa de Oro-Mt. Helix (c)	(619)	18,762	—
*91384	Castaic (c)	(661)	19,015	—
*94546	Castro Valley (c)	(510)	61,388	—
*92234	Cathedral City	(760)	51,200	53,826
95307	Ceres	(209)	45,417	47,963
90703	Cerritos	(562)	49,041	49,975
*94541	Cherryland (c)	(510)	14,728	—
*95926	Chico	(530)	86,187	90,316
*91708	Chino	(909)	77,983	85,595
91709	Chino Hills	(909)	74,799	78,309
93610	Chowchilla	(559)	18,720	18,510
*91910	Chula Vista	(619)	243,916	265,757
91702	Citrus (c)	(626)	10,866	—
*95610	Citrus Heights	(916)	83,301	87,056
91711	Claremont	(909)	34,926	36,283
94517	Clayton	(925)	10,897	11,867
95422	Clearlake	(707)	15,250	15,182
*93612	Clovis	(559)	95,631	104,180
92236	Coachella	(760)	40,704	44,635
93210	Coalinga	(559)	13,380	16,564
92324	Colton	(909)	52,154	54,621
*90040	Commerce	(323)	12,823	13,081
*90220	Compton	(310)	96,455	98,462
*94520	Concord	(925)	122,067	128,667
*93212	Corcoran	(559)	24,813	22,477
*92882	Corona	(951)	152,374	164,226
*92118	Coronado	(619)	18,912	24,812
*92626	Costa Mesa	(714)/(949)	109,960	113,204
92679	Coto de Caza (c)	(949)	14,866	—
*91722	Covina	(626)	47,796	48,984
92325	Crestline (c)	(909)	10,770	—
90201	Cudahy	(323)	23,805	24,311
*90230	Culver City	(310)	38,883	39,717
*95014	Cupertino	(408)	58,302	60,572
90630	Cypress	(714)	47,802	49,290
*94015	Daly City	(415)/(650)	101,123	106,562
*92629	Dana Point	(949)	33,351	34,181
*94526	Danville	(925)	42,039	44,400
*95616	Davis	(530)	65,622	67,666
90250	Del Aire (c)	(310)/(323)	10,001	—
*93215	Delano	(661)	53,041	52,733
95315	Delhi (c)	(209)	10,755	—
*92240	Desert Hot Springs	(760)	25,938	28,335
91765	Diamond Bar	(909)	55,544	56,897
95619	Diamond Springs (c)	(530)	11,037	—
93618	Dinuba	(559)	21,453	23,702
*94514	Discovery Bay (c)	(925)	13,352	—
95620	Dixon	(707)	18,351	19,390
*90240	Downey	(562)	111,772	114,219
*91008	Duarte	(626)	21,321	21,990
94568	Dublin	(925)	46,036	57,721
92544	East Hemet (c)	(951)	17,418	—
90022	East Los Angeles (c)	(323)	126,496	—
94303	East Palo Alto	(650)	28,155	29,662
90221	East Rancho Dominguez (c)	(310)/(323)	15,135	—
91775	East San Gabriel (c)	(626)	14,874	—
*91752	Eastvale[1]	(909)/(951)	53,668	59,039
*92020	El Cajon	(619)	99,478	103,569
*92243	El Centro	(760)	42,598	43,956
94530	El Cerrito	(510)	23,549	24,954
95762	El Dorado Hills (c)	(916)	42,108	—
*91731	El Monte	(626)	113,475	116,732
*93446	El Paso de Robles (Paso Robles)	(805)	29,793	31,580
90245	El Segundo	(310)	16,654	17,037
*94803	El Sobrante (c) (Contra Costa Co.)	(510)	12,669	—
92503	El Sobrante (c) (Riverside Co.)	(714)/(909)	12,723	—
*95624	Elk Grove	(916)	153,015	166,913
*94608	Emeryville	(510)	10,080	11,694
*92024	Encinitas	(760)	59,518	62,930
*92025	Escondido	(760)	143,911	151,451
*95501	Eureka	(707)	27,191	27,017
93221	Exeter	(559)	10,334	10,548
95628	Fair Oaks (c)	(916)	30,912	—
*94533	Fairfield	(707)	105,321	112,970
94541	Fairview (c)	(510)	10,003	—
*92028	Fallbrook (c)	(760)	30,534	—

ZIP	Place	Area code	2010 population	2015 estimate
93223	Farmersville	(559)	10,588	10,774
*93015	Fillmore	(805)	15,002	15,548
90001	Florence-Graham (c)	(323)	63,387	—
95828	Florin (c)	(916)	47,513	—
*95630	Folsom	(916)	72,203	76,375
*92335	Fontana	(909)	196,069	207,460
95841	Foothill Farms (c)	(916)	33,121	—
95540	Fortuna	(707)	11,926	12,000
94404	Foster City	(650)	30,567	33,477
*92704	Fountain Valley	(714)	55,313	56,987
*94538	Fremont	(510)	214,089	232,206
92596	French Valley (c)	(951)	23,067	—
*93706	Fresno	(559)	494,665	520,052
*92831	Fullerton	(714)	135,161	140,847
95632	Galt	(209)	23,647	25,303
95215	Garden Acres (c)	(209)	10,648	—
*92843	Garden Grove	(714)	170,883	175,393
*90247	Gardena	(310)	58,829	60,447
*95020	Gilroy	(408)	48,821	53,231
92509	Glen Avon (c)	(951)	20,199	—
*91201	Glendale	(818)	191,719	201,020
*91741	Glendora	(626)	50,073	52,009
*93117	Goleta	(805)	29,888	30,944
*92313	Grand Terrace	(951)	12,040	12,464
95746	Granite Bay (c)	(916)	20,402	—
*95945	Grass Valley	(530)	12,860	12,944
93927	Greenfield	(831)	16,330	17,184
*93433	Grover Beach	(805)	13,156	13,600
91745	Hacienda Heights (c)	(626)	54,038	—
94019	Half Moon Bay	(650)	11,324	12,657
*93230	Hanford	(559)	53,967	55,659
90716	Hawaiian Gardens	(562)	14,254	14,592
*90250	Hawthorne	(310)/(323)	84,293	88,451
*94541	Hayward	(510)	144,186	158,289
95448	Healdsburg	(707)	11,254	11,742
*92543	Hemet	(951)	78,657	83,861
94547	Hercules	(510)	24,060	25,314
90254	Hermosa Beach	(310)	19,506	19,860
*92344	Hesperia	(760)	90,173	93,295
92346	Highland	(909)	53,104	54,854
94010	Hillsborough	(650)	10,825	11,451
*95023	Hollister	(831)	34,928	37,462
92879	Home Gardens (c)	(909)	11,570	—
*92647	Huntington Beach	(714)	189,992	201,899
90255	Huntington Park	(323)	58,114	59,430
92251	Imperial	(760)	14,758	17,095
*91932	Imperial Beach	(619)	26,324	27,408
*92201	Indio	(760)	76,036	87,533
*90301	Inglewood	(310)/(323)	109,673	111,666
*92602	Irvine	(949)	212,375	256,927
93117	Isla Vista (c)	(805)	23,096	—
*91752	Jurupa Valley[2]	(951)	95,004	100,314
93630	Kerman	(559)	13,544	14,475
93930	King City	(831)	12,874	13,902
93631	Kingsburg	(559)	11,382	11,824
*91011	La Cañada Flintridge	(818)	20,246	20,590
*91214	La Crescenta-Montrose (c)	(818)	19,653	—
*90631	La Habra	(562)/(949)	60,239	62,131
*91941	La Mesa	(619)	57,065	60,089
*90638	La Mirada	(562)/(714)	48,527	49,520
90623	La Palma	(562)/(714)	15,568	15,904
91977	La Presa (c)	(619)	34,169	—
*91744	La Puente	(626)	39,816	40,745
*92253	La Quinta	(760)	37,467	40,476
95401	La Riviera (c)	(916)	10,802	—
91750	La Verne	(909)	31,063	32,681
92694	Ladera Ranch (c)	(949)	22,980	—
94549	Lafayette	(925)	23,893	25,843
*92652	Laguna Beach	(949)	22,723	23,365
*92653	Laguna Hills	(949)	30,344	31,748
*92677	Laguna Niguel	(949)	62,979	65,806
*92637	Laguna Woods	(949)	16,192	16,406
92352	Lake Arrowhead (c)	(909)	12,424	—
*92530	Lake Elsinore	(951)	51,821	61,981
*92630	Lake Forest	(949)	77,264	82,492
*93535	Lake Los Angeles (c)	(661)	12,328	—
92530	Lakeland Village (c)	(909)/(951)	11,541	—
92040	Lakeside (c)	(619)	20,648	—
*90714	Lakewood	(562)	80,048	81,611
93241	Lamont (c)	(661)	15,120	—
*93534	Lancaster	(661)	156,633	161,103
*94939	Larkspur	(415)	11,926	12,417
95330	Lathrop	(209)	18,023	20,866
*90260	Lawndale	(310)	32,769	33,430
*91945	Lemon Grove	(619)	25,320	26,709
95824	Lemon Hill (c)	(916)	13,729	—
93245	Lemoore	(559)	24,531	25,647
90304	Lennox (c)	(310)	22,753	—
95648	Lincoln	(916)	42,819	46,474
95901	Linda (c)	(530)	17,773	—
93247	Lindsay	(559)	11,768	13,217
95062	Live Oak (c)	(831)	17,158	—
*94550	Livermore	(925)	80,968	88,126
95334	Livingston	(209)	13,058	13,902
*95240	Lodi	(209)	62,134	64,596
92354	Loma Linda	(951)	23,261	24,045
90717	Lomita	(310)	20,256	20,785
*93436	Lompoc	(805)	42,434	44,164
*90802	Long Beach	(562)	462,257	474,140
*90720	Los Alamitos	(562)/(949)	11,449	11,716
*94022	Los Altos	(650)	28,976	30,671
*90012	Los Angeles	(213)/(310)/(323)	3,792,621	3,971,883
93635	Los Banos	(209)	35,972	37,457
*95030	Los Gatos	(408)	29,413	30,705
*93402	Los Osos (c)	(805)	14,276	—
90262	Lynwood	(213)/(310)/(323)	69,772	71,989
*93638	Madera	(559)	61,416	64,208
95954	Magalia (c)	(530)	11,310	—
*90265	Malibu	(310)	12,645	12,965
*90266	Manhattan Beach	(310)	35,135	35,818
*95336	Manteca	(209)	67,096	75,448
93933	Marina	(831)	19,718	21,229
94553	Martinez	(925)	35,824	38,137
95901	Marysville	(530)	12,072	12,216
90270	Maywood	(323)	27,395	27,888
93250	McFarland	(661)	12,707	13,985
*95521	McKinleyville (c)	(707)	15,177	—
92570	Mead Valley (c)	(951)	18,510	—
93640	Mendota	(559)	11,014	11,430
*92586	Menifee	(951)	77,519	87,174
*94025	Menlo Park	(650)	32,026	33,449
*95340	Merced	(209)	78,958	82,436
*94941	Mill Valley	(415)	13,903	14,394
94030	Millbrae	(650)	21,532	22,795
*95035	Milpitas	(408)	66,790	77,604
91752	Mira Loma (c)	(951)	21,930	—
*92691	Mission Viejo	(949)	93,305	97,156
*95350	Modesto	(209)	201,165	211,266
*91016	Monrovia	(626)	36,590	37,463
91763	Montclair	(909)	36,664	38,690
90640	Montebello	(323)	62,500	63,921
*93940	Monterey	(831)	27,810	28,338
*91754	Monterey Park	(323)/(626)/(818)	60,269	61,468
*93021	Moorpark	(805)	34,421	36,104
*94556	Moraga	(925)	16,016	17,256
*92551	Moreno Valley	(951)	193,365	204,198
*95037	Morgan Hill	(408)	37,882	42,948
*93442	Morro Bay	(805)	10,234	10,639
*94041	Mountain View	(650)	74,066	80,435
*92562	Murrieta	(951)	103,466	109,830
92407	Muscoy (c)	(909)	10,644	—
*94558	Napa	(707)	76,915	80,434
*91950	National City	(619)	58,582	61,060
94560	Newark	(510)	42,573	45,336
95360	Newman	(209)	10,224	10,899
*92657	Newport Beach	(949)	85,186	87,127
93444	Nipomo (c)	(805)	16,714	—
92860	Norco	(951)	27,063	26,289
95603	North Auburn (c)	(530)	13,022	—
94025	North Fair Oaks (c)	(650)	14,687	—
95660	North Highlands (c)	(916)	42,694	—
92705	North Tustin (c)	(714)/(949)	24,917	—
*90650	Norwalk	(562)	105,549	107,140
*94947	Novato	(415)	51,904	55,530
*91377	Oak Park (c)	(805)/(818)	13,811	—
95361	Oakdale	(209)	20,675	22,259
*94601	Oakland	(510)	390,724	419,267
94561	Oakley	(925)	35,432	39,813
*92054	Oceanside	(760)	167,086	175,691
93308	Oildale (c)	(661)	32,684	—
95961	Olivehurst (c)	(530)	13,656	—
*91761	Ontario	(909)	163,924	171,214
*92868	Orange	(714)	136,416	140,992
95662	Orangevale (c)	(916)	33,960	—
*93455	Orcutt (c)	(805)	28,905	—
94563	Orinda	(925)	17,643	19,279
*95965	Oroville	(530)	15,546	16,260
*93030	Oxnard	(805)	197,899	207,254
93950	Pacific Grove	(831)	15,041	15,674
94044	Pacifica	(650)	37,234	39,260
*92260	Palm Desert	(760)	48,445	51,869
*92262	Palm Springs	(760)	44,552	47,371
*93550	Palmdale	(661)	152,750	158,351
*94303	Palo Alto	(650)	64,403	66,853
*90274	Palos Verdes Estates	(310)	13,438	13,682
*95969	Paradise	(530)	26,218	26,476
90723	Paramount	(562)	54,098	55,412
95823	Parkway (c)	(916)	14,670	—
93648	Parlier	(559)	14,494	15,138
*91101	Pasadena	(323)/(626)/(818)	137,122	142,250
	Paso Robles. *See* El Paso de Robles			
95363	Patterson	(209)	20,413	21,498
92509	Pedley (c)	(951)	12,672	—
*92570	Perris	(951)	68,386	74,971
*94952	Petaluma	(707)	57,941	60,438
*92371	Phelan (c)	(760)	14,304	—
*90660	Pico Rivera	(562)	62,942	64,218
*94611	Piedmont	(510)	10,667	11,376

ZIP	Place	Area code	2010 population	2015 estimate
94564	Pinole	(510)	18,390	19,269
94565	Pittsburg	(925)	63,264	69,424
*92870	Placentia	(714)	50,533	52,495
95667	Placerville	(530)	10,389	10,650
94523	Pleasant Hill	(925)	33,152	34,810
*94566	Pleasanton	(925)	70,285	79,510
*91765	Pomona	(909)	149,058	153,266
*93041	Port Hueneme	(805)	21,723	22,423
*93257	Porterville	(559)	54,165	56,058
*92064	Poway	(858)	47,811	50,157
93907	Prunedale (c)	(831)	17,560	—
*93536	Quartz Hill (c)	(661)	10,912	—
92065	Ramona (c)	(760)	20,292	—
*95670	Rancho Cordova	(916)	64,776	71,017
*91730	Rancho Cucamonga	(909)	165,269	175,236
92270	Rancho Mirage	(760)	17,218	18,083
90275	Rancho Palos Verdes	(310)	41,643	42,732
*92019	Rancho San Diego (c)	(619)	21,208	—
92688	Rancho Santa Margarita	(949)	47,853	49,324
96080	Red Bluff	(530)	14,076	14,131
*96001	Redding	(530)	89,861	91,582
*92373	Redlands	(909)	68,747	71,035
*90277	Redondo Beach	(310)	66,748	68,166
*94063	Redwood City	(650)	76,815	85,288
93654	Reedley	(559)	24,194	25,569
*92376	Rialto	(909)	99,171	103,132
*94801	Richmond	(510)	103,701	109,708
*93555	Ridgecrest	(760)	27,616	28,780
95673	Rio Linda (c)	(916)	15,106	—
95366	Ripon	(209)	14,297	15,151
95367	Riverbank	(209)	22,678	24,122
*92501	Riverside	(951)	303,871	322,424
*95677	Rocklin	(916)	56,974	61,213
*94928	Rohnert Park	(707)	40,911	42,407
93560	Rosamond (c)	(661)	18,150	—
93314	Rosedale (c)	(661)	14,058	—
*91770	Rosemead	(626)	53,764	54,908
95826	Rosemont (c)	(916)	22,681	—
*95678	Roseville	(916)	118,788	130,269
90720	Rossmoor (c)	(714)	10,244	—
91748	Rowland Heights (c)	(626)	48,993	—
*92519	Rubidoux (c)	(951)	34,280	—
*95814	Sacramento	(916)	466,488	490,712
95368	Salida (c)	(209)	13,722	—
*93907	Salinas	(831)	150,441	157,380
*94960	San Anselmo	(415)	12,336	12,653
*92401	San Bernardino	(909)	209,924	216,108
94066	San Bruno	(650)	41,114	43,185
*93001	San Buenaventura (Ventura)	(805)	106,433	109,708
94070	San Carlos	(650)	28,406	29,931
*92672	San Clemente	(949)	63,522	65,526
*92101	San Diego	(619)/(858)	1,307,402	1,394,928
92065	San Diego Country Estates (c)	(760)	10,109	—
91773	San Dimas	(909)	33,371	34,630
*91340	San Fernando	(818)	23,645	24,931
*94102	San Francisco	(415)	805,235	864,816
*91775	San Gabriel	(626)	39,718	40,424
*92582	San Jacinto	(951)	44,199	46,951
*95113	San Jose	(408)	945,942	1,026,908
*92675	San Juan Capistrano	(949)	34,593	36,454
*94577	San Leandro	(510)	84,950	90,712
94580	San Lorenzo (c)	(510)	23,452	—
*93401	San Luis Obispo	(805)	45,119	47,339
*92069	San Marcos	(760)	83,781	92,931
*91108	San Marino	(626)	13,147	13,464
*94402	San Mateo	(650)	97,207	103,536
*94806	San Pablo	(510)	29,139	30,407
*94901	San Rafael	(415)	57,713	59,162
*94583	San Ramon	(925)	72,148	76,134
93657	Sanger	(559)	24,270	24,950
*92701	Santa Ana	(714)/(949)	324,528	335,400
*93101	Santa Barbara	(805)	88,410	91,842
*95050	Santa Clara	(408)	116,468	126,215
*91350	Santa Clarita	(661)	176,320	182,371
*95060	Santa Cruz	(831)	59,946	64,220
90670	Santa Fe Springs	(562)	16,223	18,026
*93454	Santa Maria	(805)	99,553	105,093
*90401	Santa Monica	(310)	89,736	93,220
*93060	Santa Paula	(805)	29,321	30,546
*95401	Santa Rosa	(707)	167,815	174,972
*92071	Santee	(619)	53,413	57,787
*95070	Saratoga	(408)	29,926	30,968
*95066	Scotts Valley	(831)	11,580	11,945
90740	Seal Beach	(562)	24,168	24,619
93955	Seaside	(831)	33,025	34,533
93662	Selma	(559)	23,219	24,414
93263	Shafter	(661)	16,988	18,336
*96019	Shasta Lake	(916)	10,164	10,159
*91024	Sierra Madre	(626)	10,917	11,163
*90755	Signal Hill	(562)	11,016	11,565
*93065	Simi Valley	(805)	124,237	126,788
92075	Solana Beach	(858)	12,867	13,449
93960	Soledad	(831)	25,738	25,003

ZIP	Place	Area code	2010 population	2015 estimate
95476	Sonoma	(707)	10,648	11,037
91733	South El Monte	(626)	20,116	20,878
90280	South Gate	(323)/(562)	94,396	96,401
*96150	South Lake Tahoe	(530)	21,403	21,706
*91030	South Pasadena	(213)/(323)/(626)/(818)	25,619	26,151
*94080	South San Francisco	(650)	63,632	67,271
91744	South San Jose Hills (c)	(626)	20,551	—
90605	South Whittier (c)	(562)	57,156	—
*91977	Spring Valley (c) (San Diego Co.)	(619)	28,205	—
*94305	Stanford (c)	(650)	13,809	—
90680	Stanton	(714)	38,186	38,872
91381	Stevenson Ranch (c)	(661)	17,557	—
*95202	Stockton	(209)	291,707	305,658
*94585	Suisun City	(707)	28,111	29,492
93543	Sun Village (c)	(661)	11,565	—
*94086	Sunnyvale	(408)	140,081	151,754
*96130	Susanville	(530)	17,947	15,247
94941	Tamalpais-Homestead Valley (c)	(415)	10,735	—
*93561	Tehachapi	(661)	14,414	13,021
*92590	Temecula	(951)	100,097	112,011
92883	Temescal Valley (c)	(951)	22,535	—
91780	Temple City	(626)	35,558	36,365
*91360	Thousand Oaks	(805)	126,683	129,339
*90503	Torrance	(310)	145,438	148,475
*95376	Tracy	(209)	82,922	87,075
*96161	Truckee	(916)	16,180	16,299
*93274	Tulare	(559)	59,278	62,315
*95380	Turlock	(209)	68,549	72,292
*92780	Tustin	(714)/(949)	75,540	80,583
*92277	Twentynine Palms	(760)	25,048	26,025
*95482	Ukiah	(707)	16,075	15,917
94587	Union City	(510)	69,516	74,494
*91784	Upland	(909)	73,732	76,443
*95687	Vacaville	(707)	92,428	96,803
91744	Valinda (c)	(626)	22,822	—
92343	Valle Vista (c)	(951)	14,578	—
*94590	Vallejo	(707)	115,942	121,253
	Ventura. See San Buenaventura			
*92392	Victorville	(760)	115,903	122,225
90043	View Park-Windsor Hills (c)	(310)	11,075	—
91722	Vincent (c)	(925)	15,922	—
95829	Vineyard (c)	(916)	24,836	—
*93277	Visalia	(559)	124,442	130,104
*92084	Vista	(760)	93,834	100,890
*91789	Walnut	(626)	29,172	30,237
*94596	Walnut Creek	(925)	64,173	68,910
90255	Walnut Park (c)	(213)	15,966	—
93280	Wasco	(661)	25,545	26,279
*95076	Watsonville	(831)	51,199	53,628
90502	West Carson (c)	(310)	21,699	—
*91790	West Covina	(626)	106,098	108,484
*90069	West Hollywood	(310)/(323)	34,399	36,222
91746	West Puente Valley (c)	(626)	22,636	—
*95691	West Sacramento	(916)	48,744	52,721
*90606	West Whittier-Los Nietos (c)	(562)	25,540	—
*92683	Westminster	(714)	89,701	92,114
*90047	Westmont (c)	(323)	31,853	—
*90602	Whittier	(562)	85,331	87,438
92595	Wildomar	(951)	32,176	35,632
*90222	Willowbrook (c)	(323)	35,983	—
95492	Windsor	(707)	26,801	27,464
92040	Winter Gardens (c)	(619)	20,631	—
95388	Winton (c)	(209)	10,613	—
92504	Woodcrest (c)	(909)/(951)	14,347	—
*95695	Woodland	(530)	55,468	58,567
*92886	Yorba Linda	(714)	64,234	67,973
*95991	Yuba City	(530)	64,925	66,941
92399	Yucaipa	(909)	51,367	53,328
*92284	Yucca Valley	(760)	20,700	21,600

(1) Place was incorporated after the 2010 Census was conducted. Data in 2010 column is for Eastvale CDP. (2) Place was incorporated after the 2010 Census was conducted. Data in 2010 column is Census Bureau estimate.

Colorado

Area code 720 overlays area code 303.

ZIP	Place	Area code	2010 population	2015 estimate
*80004	Arvada	(303)	106,433	115,368
*80010	Aurora	(303)	325,078	359,407
80221	Berkley (c)	(970)	11,207	—
*80908	Black Forest (c)	(719)	13,116	—
*80302	Boulder	(303)	97,385	107,349
*80601	Brighton	(303)	33,352	37,585
*80020	Broomfield	(303)	55,889	65,065
*81212	Cañon City	(719)	16,400	16,395
80108	Castle Pines[1]	(303)	10,360	10,347
*80104	Castle Rock	(303)	48,231	55,591
*80015	Centennial	(303)	100,377	109,741

ZIP	Place	Area code	2010 population	2015 estimate
80111	Cherry Creek (c)	(303)	11,120	—
81222	Cimarron Hills (c)	(719)	16,161	—
81520	Clifton (c)	(970)	19,889	—
*80903	Colorado Springs	(719)	416,427	456,568
*80128	Columbine (c)	(303)	24,280	—
*80022	Commerce City	(303)	45,913	53,696
80304	Dakota Ridge (c)	(303)	32,005	—
*80202	Denver	(303)	600,158	682,545
*81301	Durango	(970)	16,887	18,006
81632	Edwards (c)	(970)	10,266	—
*80110	Englewood	(303)	30,255	33,082
*80516	Erie	(303)	18,135	21,420
*80620	Evans	(970)	18,537	21,383
80221	Federal Heights	(303)	11,467	12,381
*80520	Firestone	(303)	10,147	11,999
80913	Fort Carson (c)	(719)	13,813	—
*80525	Fort Collins	(970)	143,986	161,175
*80701	Fort Morgan	(970)	11,315	11,319
80817	Fountain	(719)	25,846	27,767
*80530	Frederick	(303)	8,679	11,413
*81521	Fruita	(970)	12,646	12,795
*80401	Golden	(303)	18,867	20,330
*81501	Grand Junction	(970)	58,566	60,358
*80631	Greeley	(970)	92,889	100,883
*80111	Greenwood Village	(303)	13,925	15,663
*80126	Highlands Ranch (c)	(303)	96,713	—
80534	Johnstown	(970)	9,887	14,896
*80127	Ken Caryl (c)	(303)	32,438	—
80026	Lafayette	(303)	24,453	27,729
*80226	Lakewood	(303)	142,980	152,597
*80120	Littleton	(303)	41,737	46,368
*80124	Lone Tree	(303)	10,218	13,175
*80501	Longmont	(303)	86,270	92,088
80027	Louisville	(303)	18,376	20,396
*80537	Loveland	(970)	66,859	75,182
*81401	Montrose	(970)	19,132	19,062
*80233	Northglenn	(303)	35,789	39,197
*80134	Parker	(303)	45,297	49,550
*81003	Pueblo	(719)	106,595	109,412
81007	Pueblo West (c)	(719)	29,637	—
80911	Security-Widefield (c)	(719)	32,882	—
*80221	Sherrelwood (c)	(303)	18,287	—
*80487	Steamboat Springs	(970)	12,088	12,435
80751	Sterling	(970)	14,777	14,104
80027	Superior	(303)	12,483	12,980
80134	The Pinery (c)	(303)	10,517	—
*80229	Thornton	(303)	118,772	133,451
80229	Welby (c)	(303)	14,846	—
*80031	Westminster	(303)	106,114	113,130
*80033	Wheat Ridge	(303)	30,166	31,192
*80550	Windsor	(970)	18,644	21,751

(1) Place was incorporated after the 2010 Census was conducted. Data in 2010 column is Census Bureau estimate.

Connecticut

Area code 475 overlays area code 203. Area code 959 overlays 860. See introductory note.

ZIP	Place	Area code	2010 population	2015 estimate
06401	Ansonia	(203)	19,249	18,854
06001	Avon	(860)	18,098	18,414
06037	Berlin	(860)	19,866	20,560
06801	Bethel	(203)	18,584	19,529
06002	Bloomfield	(860)	20,486	20,749
06405	Branford	(203)	28,026	28,145
*06604	Bridgeport	(203)	144,229	147,629
*06010	Bristol	(860)	60,477	60,452
06804	Brookfield	(203)	16,452	17,143
06019	Canton	(860)	10,292	10,330
*06410	Cheshire	(203)	29,261	29,262
06413	Clinton	(860)	13,260	13,047
*06415	Colchester	(860)	16,068	16,130
06238	Coventry	(860)	12,435	12,438
06416	Cromwell	(860)	14,005	14,034
*06810	Danbury	(203)	80,893	84,657
*06820	Darien	(203)	20,732	21,787
06418	Derby	(203)	12,902	12,700
*06424	East Hampton	(860)	12,959	12,858
*06108	East Hartford	(860)	51,252	50,821
*06512	East Haven	(203)	29,257	28,935
06333	East Lyme	(860)	19,159	19,343
*06088	East Windsor	(860)	11,162	11,400
06029	Ellington	(860)	15,602	15,916
*06082	Enfield	(860)	44,654	44,323
*06825	Fairfield	(203)	59,404	61,523
*06032	Farmington	(860)	25,340	25,629
06033	Glastonbury	(860)	34,427	34,678
*06035	Granby	(860)	11,282	11,298
*06830	Greenwich	(203)	61,171	62,695
*06830	Greenwich (c)	(203)	12,942	—
06351	Griswold	(860)	11,951	11,830
06340	Groton	(860)	40,115	39,692
06437	Guilford	(203)	22,375	22,350

ZIP	Place	Area code	2010 population	2015 estimate
*06514	Hamden	(203)	60,960	61,218
*06101	Hartford	(860)	124,775	124,006
*06239	Killingly	(860)	17,370	17,131
06339	Ledyard	(860)	15,051	15,025
06443	Madison	(203)	18,269	18,223
*06040	Manchester	(860)	58,241	58,007
*06040	Manchester (c)	(860)	30,577	—
*06250	Mansfield	(860)	26,543	26,043
*06450	Meriden	(203)	60,868	59,988
06457	Middletown	(860)	47,648	46,756
*06460	Milford (balance)	(203)	51,271	52,087
*06460	Milford	(203)	52,759	53,592
06468	Monroe	(203)	19,479	19,833
06353	Montville	(860)	19,571	19,396
06770	Naugatuck	(203)	31,862	31,538
*06051	New Britain	(860)	73,206	72,808
06840	New Canaan	(203)	19,738	20,387
06812	New Fairfield	(203)	13,881	14,126
*06511	New Haven	(203)	129,779	130,322
06320	New London	(860)	27,620	27,179
06776	New Milford	(860)	28,142	27,276
*06111	Newington	(860)	30,562	30,604
06470	Newtown	(203)	27,560	28,022
06471	North Branford	(203)	14,407	14,263
06473	North Haven	(203)	24,093	23,828
*06850	Norwalk	(203)	85,603	88,485
06360	Norwich	(860)	40,493	39,899
06475	Old Saybrook	(860)	10,242	10,160
06477	Orange	(203)	13,956	13,944
06478	Oxford	(203)	12,683	13,013
06374	Plainfield	(860)	15,405	15,077
06062	Plainville	(860)	17,716	17,773
06782	Plymouth	(860)	12,243	11,813
*06877	Ridgefield	(203)	24,638	25,244
06067	Rocky Hill	(860)	19,709	20,021
*06483	Seymour	(203)	16,540	16,475
06484	Shelton	(203)	39,559	41,296
06070	Simsbury	(860)	23,511	24,348
06071	Somers	(860)	11,444	11,432
06074	South Windsor	(860)	25,709	25,789
06488	Southbury	(203)	19,904	19,675
06489	Southington	(860)	43,069	43,817
*06075	Stafford	(860)	12,087	11,837
*06901	Stamford	(203)	122,643	128,874
06378	Stonington	(860)	18,545	18,370
*06268	Storrs (c)	(860)	15,344	—
*06614	Stratford	(203)	51,384	52,609
*06078	Suffield	(860)	15,735	15,662
06084	Tolland	(860)	15,052	14,849
*06790	Torrington	(860)	36,383	34,906
06611	Trumbull	(203)	36,018	36,628
06066	Vernon	(860)	29,179	28,959
*06492	Wallingford	(203)	45,135	44,893
06492	Wallingford Center (c)	(203)	18,209	—
*06702	Waterbury	(203)	110,366	108,802
*06385	Waterford	(860)	19,517	19,281
*06795	Watertown	(860)	22,514	21,911
*06105	West Hartford	(860)	63,268	63,053
06516	West Haven	(203)	55,564	54,927
06883	Weston	(203)	10,179	10,387
*06880	Westport	(203)	26,391	27,899
*06109	Wethersfield	(860)	26,668	26,367
06226	Willimantic (c)	(860)	17,737	—
06897	Wilton	(203)	18,062	18,714
*06094	Winchester	(860)	11,242	10,829
*06280	Windham	(860)	25,268	24,799
*06095	Windsor	(860)	29,044	29,016
06096	Windsor Locks	(860)	12,498	12,537
*06716	Wolcott	(203)	16,680	16,673

Delaware

Area code 302 applies to the entire state.

ZIP	Place	2010 population	2015 estimate
19701	Bear (c)	19,371	—
19713	Brookside (c)	14,353	—
*19901	Dover	36,047	37,522
19702	Glasgow (c)	14,303	—
19707	Hockessin (c)	13,527	—
19709	Middletown	18,871	20,372
19963	Milford	9,559	10,252
*19711	Newark	31,454	33,817
19808	Pike Creek Valley (c)	11,217	—
19977	Smyrna	10,023	11,319
*19801	Wilmington	70,851	71,948

District of Columbia

Area code 202 applies to the entire district.

ZIP	Place	2010 population	2015 estimate
*20001	Washington	601,723	672,228

Florida

Part of area code 321 overlays area code 407. Area code 754 overlays 954. Area code 786 overlays 305.

ZIP	Place	Area code	2010 population	2015 estimate
*32828	Alafaya (c)	(407)	78,113	—
*32701	Altamonte Springs	(407)	41,496	43,159
33572	Apollo Beach (c)	(813)	14,055	—
*32712	Apopka	(407)	41,542	48,382
*32233	Atlantic Beach	(904)	12,655	13,193
33823	Auburndale	(863)	13,507	15,035
*33160	Aventura	(305)	35,762	37,649
*33825	Avon Park	(863)	8,836	10,086
32807	Azalea Park (c)	(407)	12,556	—
*33830	Bartow	(863)	17,298	18,972
34667	Bayonet Point (c)	(727)	23,467	—
33507	Bayshore Gardens (c)	(941)	16,323	—
*33756	Bellair-Meadowbrook Terrace (c)	(904)	13,343	—
33430	Belle Glade	(561)	17,467	18,251
*34420	Belleview (c)	(352)	23,355	—
*33509	Bloomingdale (c)	(813)	22,711	—
*33431	Boca Raton	(561)	84,392	93,235
*34135	Bonita Springs	(239)	43,914	51,704
*33436	Boynton Beach	(561)	68,217	73,966
*34201	Bradenton	(941)	49,546	54,437
*33510	Brandon (c)	(813)	103,483	—
32503	Brent (c)	(850)	21,804	—
33142	Brownsville (c)	(305)	15,313	—
34743	Buenaventura Lakes (c)	(407)	26,079	—
32404	Callaway	(850)	14,405	15,161
32920	Cape Canaveral	(321)	9,912	10,206
*33914	Cape Coral	(239)	154,305	175,229
*33618	Carrollwood (c)	(813)	33,365	—
*32707	Casselberry	(407)	26,241	27,056
33558	Cheval (c)	(813)	10,702	—
33625	Citrus Park (c)	(813)	24,252	—
*33755	Clearwater	(727)	107,685	113,003
*34711	Clermont	(352)	28,742	32,390
*32922	Cocoa	(321)	17,140	17,711
*32931	Cocoa Beach	(321)	11,231	11,595
*33063	Coconut Creek	(954)	52,909	59,302
32809	Conway (c)	(407)	13,467	—
*33328	Cooper City	(954)	28,547	35,364
*33134	Coral Gables	(305)	46,780	51,117
*33065	Coral Springs	(954)	121,096	129,485
33157	Coral Terrace (c)	(305)	24,376	—
33015	Country Club (c)	(305)	47,105	—
33196	Country Walk (c)	(305)	15,997	—
*32536	Crestview	(850)	20,978	23,270
*33189	Cutler Bay	(305)	40,286	44,865
33919	Cypress Lake (c)	(239)	11,846	—
*33004	Dania Beach	(954)	29,639	31,446
*33314	Davie	(954)	91,992	100,882
*32114	Daytona Beach	(386)	61,005	64,736
*32713	DeBary	(386)	19,320	19,998
*33441	Deerfield Beach	(954)	75,018	79,768
*32720	DeLand	(386)	27,031	30,195
*33444	Delray Beach	(561)	60,522	66,255
*32738	Deltona	(386)	85,182	88,474
*32541	Destin	(850)	12,305	13,523
32836	Doctor Phillips (c)	(407)	10,981	—
*33166	Doral	(305)	45,704	56,035
*34698	Dunedin	(727)	35,321	36,164
33610	East Lake (c)	(813)	30,962	—
33619	East Lake-Orient Park (c)	(813)	22,753	—
32583	East Milton (c)	(850)	11,074	—
*32132	Edgewater	(386)	20,750	21,566
33614	Egypt Lake-Leto (c)	(813)	35,282	—
34680	Elfers (c)	(727)	13,986	—
*34223	Englewood (c)	(941)	14,863	—
32534	Ensley (c)	(850)	20,602	—
*33928	Estero[1]	(239)	22,612	30,799
*32726	Eustis	(352)	18,558	19,986
32804	Fairview Shores (c)	(305)	10,239	—
*32034	Fernandina Beach	(904)	11,487	12,339
32514	Ferry Pass (c)	(850)	28,921	—
33547	Fish Hawk (c)	(813)	14,087	—
32003	Fleming Island (c)	(904)	27,126	—
*33034	Florida City	(305)	11,245	12,122
32960	Florida Ridge (c)	(772)	18,164	—
32714	Forest City (c)	(407)	13,854	—
*33301	Fort Lauderdale	(954)	165,521	178,590
*33901	Fort Myers	(239)	62,298	74,013
*34981	Fort Pierce	(772)	41,590	44,484
*32548	Fort Walton Beach	(850)	19,507	21,817
33172	Fountainbleau (c)	(305)	59,764	—
34747	Four Corners (c)	(863)	26,116	—
32259	Fruit Cove (c)	(904)	29,362	—
34432	Fruitville (c)	(941)	13,224	—
*32601	Gainesville	(352)	124,354	130,128
33534	Gibsonton (c)	(813)	14,234	—
33138	Gladeview (c)	(954)	11,535	—
33143	Glenvar Heights (c)	(305)	16,898	—
34116	Golden Gate (c)	(239)	23,961	—
33055	Golden Glades (c)	(305)	33,145	—
32733	Goldenrod (c)	(407)	12,039	—
32560	Gonzalez (c)	(850)	13,273	—
33170	Goulds (c)	(305)	10,103	—
*33463	Greenacres	(561)	37,573	39,676
*34736	Groveland	(352)	8,729	—
33581	Gulf Gate Estates (c)	(941)	10,911	11,528
*33707	Gulfport	(727)	12,029	12,322
*33844	Haines City	(863)	20,535	22,807
*33009	Hallandale Beach	(954)	37,113	39,488
*33010	Hialeah	(305)	224,669	237,069
*33016	Hialeah Gardens	(305)	21,744	23,926
33846	Highland City (c)	(863)	10,834	—
*33455	Hobe Sound (c)	(772)	11,521	—
*34690	Holiday (c)	(727)	22,403	—
*32125	Holly Hill	(386)	11,659	11,943
*33019	Hollywood	(954)	140,768	149,728
*33030	Homestead	(305)	60,512	66,498
34447	Homosassa Springs (c)	(352)	13,791	—
34787	Horizon West (c)	(352)	14,000	—
*34667	Hudson (c)	(727)	12,158	—
32837	Hunters Creek (c)	(407)	14,321	—
*34142	Immokalee (c)	(239)	24,154	—
33908	Iona (c)	(239)	15,369	—
33162	Ives Estates (c)	(305)	19,525	—
*32202	Jacksonville	(904)	821,784	868,031
*32250	Jacksonville Beach	(904)	21,362	23,064
33568	Jasmine Estates (c)	(727)	18,989	—
*34957	Jensen Beach (c)	(772)	11,707	—
*33458	Jupiter	(561)	55,156	62,707
33478	Jupiter Farms (c)	(561)	11,994	—
33183	Kendale Lakes (c)	(305)	56,148	—
*33156	Kendall (c)	(305)	75,371	—
33193	Kendall West (c)	(305)	36,154	—
33149	Key Biscayne	(305)	12,344	12,990
33037	Key Largo (c)	(305)	10,433	—
*33040	Key West	(305)	24,649	25,755
33556	Keystone (c)	(813)	24,039	—
*34744	Kissimmee	(407)	59,682	69,152
*32159	Lady Lake	(352)	13,926	14,717
32054	Lake Butler (c)	(386)	15,400	—
*32055	Lake City	(386)	12,046	12,161
33612	Lake Magdalene (c)	(813)	28,509	—
*32746	Lake Mary	(407)	13,822	16,021
*33853	Lake Wales	(863)	14,225	15,541
*33460	Lake Worth	(561)	34,910	37,498
*33801	Lakeland	(863)	97,422	104,401
33801	Lakeland Highlands (c)	(863)	11,056	—
32073	Lakeside (c)	(904)	30,943	—
34951	Lakewood Park (c)	(772)	11,323	—
*34639	Land O' Lakes (c)	(813)	31,996	—
*33465	Lantana	(561)	10,423	11,136
*33770	Largo	(727)	77,648	81,000
*33319	Lauderdale Lakes	(954)	32,593	34,796
*33313	Lauderhill	(954)	66,887	71,579
33714	Lealman (c)	(727)	19,879	—
*34748	Leesburg	(352)	20,117	21,993
*33936	Lehigh Acres (c)	(239)	86,784	—
*33033	Leisure City (c)	(305)	22,655	—
*33074	Lighthouse Point	(954)	10,344	11,104
32810	Lockhart (c)	(407)	13,060	—
*32750	Longwood	(407)	13,657	14,085
*33549	Lutz (c)	(813)	19,344	—
32444	Lynn Haven	(850)	18,493	20,156
*32751	Maitland	(407)	15,751	17,463
33550	Mango (c)	(813)	11,313	—
*34145	Marco Island	(239)	16,413	17,690
*33063	Margate	(954)	53,284	57,234
32824	Meadow Woods (c)	(407)	25,558	—
*32901	Melbourne	(321)	76,068	80,127
*32953	Merritt Island (c)	(321)	34,743	—
*33125	Miami	(305)	399,457	441,003
*33140	Miami Beach	(305)	87,779	92,312
*33014	Miami Gardens	(305)	107,167	113,187
*33014	Miami Lakes	(305)	29,361	30,972
33138	Miami Shores	(305)	10,493	10,831
*33166	Miami Springs	(305)	13,809	14,490
*32068	Middleburg (c)	(904)	13,008	—
32563	Midway (c) (Santa Rosa Co.)	(850)	16,115	—
34715	Minneola	(352)	9,403	10,735
*33023	Miramar	(305)	122,041	137,132
*32757	Mount Dora	(352)	12,370	13,519
32526	Myrtle Grove (c)	(850)	15,870	—
*34102	Naples	(239)	19,537	21,512
32566	Navarre (c)	(850)	31,378	—
*34653	New Port Richey	(727)	14,911	15,842
34653	New Port Richey East (c)	(727)	10,036	—
*32168	New Smyrna Beach	(386)	22,464	24,298
*32578	Niceville	(850)	12,749	14,714
*33917	North Fort Myers (c)	(239)	39,407	—
*33068	North Lauderdale	(954)	41,023	43,703
*33161	North Miami	(305)	58,786	62,435
*33160	North Miami Beach	(305)	41,523	43,971
*33408	North Palm Beach	(561)	12,015	12,853

ZIP	Place	Area code	2010 population	2015 estimate
*34286	North Port	(941)	57,357	62,345
33624	Northdale (c)	(813)	22,079	—
33860	Oak Ridge (c)	(407)	22,685	—
*33334	Oakland Park	(954)	41,363	44,319
32065	Oakleaf Plantation (c)	(904)	20,315	—
*34470	Ocala	(352)	56,315	58,218
34761	Ocoee	(407)	35,579	43,608
*33163	Ojus (c)	(305)	18,036	—
34677	Oldsmar	(813)	13,591	14,170
*33265	Olympia Heights (c)	(305)	13,488	—
*33054	Opa-locka	(305)	15,219	16,565
*32763	Orange City	(386)	10,599	11,210
*32801	Orlando	(407)	238,300	270,934
*32174	Ormond Beach	(386)	38,137	40,970
*32765	Oviedo	(407)	33,342	38,551
32571	Pace (c)	(850)	20,039	—
*32177	Palatka	(386)	10,558	10,390
*32905	Palm Bay	(321)	103,190	107,888
*33410	Palm Beach Gardens	(561)	48,452	52,923
*34990	Palm City (c)	(772)	23,120	—
*32137	Palm Coast	(386)	75,180	82,893
*34683	Palm Harbor (c)	(727)	57,439	—
*33601	Palm River-Clair Mel (c)	(813)	21,024	—
*33406	Palm Springs	(561)	18,928	22,341
32082	Palm Valley (c)	(904)	20,019	—
*34221	Palmetto	(941)	12,606	13,249
*33157	Palmetto Bay	(305)	23,410	24,642
33157	Palmetto Estates (c)	(305)	13,535	—
*32401	Panama City	(850)	36,484	38,286
*32417	Panama City Beach	(850)	12,018	12,624
*33067	Parkland	(954)	23,962	30,177
*33026	Pembroke Pines	(954)	154,750	166,611
*33502	Pensacola	(850)	51,923	53,193
*32809	Pine Castle (c)	(407)	10,805	—
*32808	Pine Hills (c)	(407)	60,076	—
33156	Pinecrest	(305)	18,223	19,452
*33781	Pinellas Park	(727)	49,079	51,617
33168	Pinewood (c)	(305)	16,520	—
*33566	Plant City	(813)	34,721	37,406
*33311	Plantation	(954)	84,955	92,560
*34758	Poinciana (c)	(407)	53,193	—
*33060	Pompano Beach	(954)	99,845	107,762
*33952	Port Charlotte (c)	(941)	54,392	—
*32129	Port Orange	(386)	56,048	59,866
32927	Port St. John (c)	(321)	12,267	—
*34953	Port St. Lucie	(772)	164,603	179,413
34992	Port Salerno (c)	(772)	10,091	—
*33032	Princeton (c)	(305)	22,038	—
*33950	Punta Gorda	(941)	16,641	18,150
33177	Richmond West (c)	(305)	31,973	—
*33569	Riverview (c)	(813)	71,050	—
*33404	Riviera Beach	(561)	32,488	34,005
*32955	Rockledge	(321)	24,926	26,626
*33411	Royal Palm Beach	(561)	34,140	37,633
*33570	Ruskin (c)	(813)	17,208	—
34695	Safety Harbor	(727)	16,884	17,454
*32084	Saint Augustine	(904)	12,975	14,128
*34769	Saint Cloud	(407)	35,183	45,298
*33701	Saint Petersburg	(727)	244,769	257,083
33912	San Carlos Park (c)	(239)	16,824	—
*32771	Sanford	(407)	53,570	58,111
*34231	Sarasota	(941)	51,917	55,118
33577	Sarasota Springs (c)	(941)	14,395	—
32937	Satellite Beach	(321)	10,109	10,633
*32958	Sebastian	(772)	21,929	24,007
*33870	Sebring	(863)	10,491	10,497
*33770	Seminole	(813)	17,233	18,153
34610	Shady Hills (c)	(727)	11,523	—
33505	South Bradenton (c)	(941)	22,178	—
32121	South Daytona	(386)	12,252	12,584
*33243	South Miami	(305)	11,657	12,242
33157	South Miami Heights (c)	(305)	35,696	—
33595	South Venice (c)	(941)	13,949	—
32824	Southchase (c)	(407)	15,921	—
*34604	Spring Hill (c)	(352)	98,621	—
*34994	Stuart	(772)	15,593	16,462
*33553	Sun City Center (c)	(813)	19,258	—
33160	Sunny Isles Beach	(305)	20,832	22,123
*33325	Sunrise	(954)	84,439	92,700
*33283	Sunset (c)	(305)	16,389	—
33144	Sweetwater	(305)	13,499	20,840
*32301	Tallahassee	(850)	181,376	189,907
*33321	Tamarac	(954)	60,427	64,681
*33184	Tamiami (c)	(305)	55,271	—
*33602	Tampa	(813)	335,709	369,075
*34689	Tarpon Springs	(727)	23,484	24,605
32778	Tavares	(352)	13,951	15,430
*33617	Temple Terrace	(813)	24,541	25,731
33412	The Acreage (c)	(561)	38,704	—
33186	The Crossings (c)	(305)	22,758	—
33196	The Hammocks (c)	(305)	51,003	—
*32162	The Villages (c)	(352)	51,442	—
33592	Thonotosassa (c)	(813)	13,014	—
33186	Three Lakes (c)	(305)	15,047	—
*32780	Titusville	(321)	43,761	45,393

ZIP	Place	Area code	2010 population	2015 estimate
33615	Town 'n' Country (c)	(813)	78,442	—
34655	Trinity (c)	(813)	10,907	—
33613	University (c) (Hillsborough Co.)	(813)	41,163	—
32826	University (c) (Orange Co.)	(407)	31,084	—
33165	University Park (c)	(305)	26,995	—
32401	Upper Grand Lagoon (c)	(850)	13,963	—
*33594	Valrico (c)	(813)	35,545	—
*34285	Venice	(941)	20,748	22,211
*32960	Vero Beach	(772)	15,220	16,358
32960	Vero Beach South (c)	(772)	23,092	—
32955	Viera East (c)	(321)	10,757	—
33901	Villas (c)	(239)	11,569	—
32507	Warrington (c)	(850)	14,531	—
32779	Wekiwa Springs (c)	(407)	21,998	—
*33414	Wellington	(561)	56,508	62,560
*33544	Wesley Chapel (c)	(813)	44,092	—
33714	West Lealman (c)	(727)	15,651	—
33138	West Little River (c)	(305)	34,699	—
*32912	West Melbourne	(321)	18,355	20,679
*33401	West Palm Beach	(561)	99,919	106,779
33023	West Park	(954)	14,156	15,097
32505	West Pensacola (c)	(850)	21,339	—
33626	Westchase (c)	(813)	21,747	—
33165	Westchester (c)	(305)	29,862	—
*33326	Weston	(954)	65,333	69,959
33165	Westwood Lakes (c)	(305)	11,838	—
*33005	Wilton Manors	(954)	11,632	12,385
*34787	Winter Garden	(407)	34,568	40,356
*33880	Winter Haven	(863)	33,874	37,689
*32789	Winter Park	(407)	27,852	29,943
*32708	Winter Springs	(407)	33,282	34,789
32092	World Golf Village (c)	(904)	12,310	—
32547	Wright (c)	(850)	23,127	—
*32097	Yulee (c)	(904)	11,491	—
*33540	Zephyrhills	(813)	13,288	14,611

(1) Place was incorporated after the 2010 Census was conducted. Data in 2010 column is for Estero CDP.

Georgia

Area codes 404/470/678 overlay area code 770. Area code 762 overlays 706.

ZIP	Place	Area code	2010 population	2015 estimate
*30101	Acworth	(770)	20,425	22,131
*31701	Albany	(229)	77,434	74,843
*30004	Alpharetta	(770)	57,551	63,693
*31709	Americus	(229)	17,041	16,028
*30601	Athens-Clarke Co. (balance)	(706)	115,452	122,604
*30301	Atlanta	(404)	420,003	463,878
*30901	Augusta-Richmond Co. (balance)	(706)	195,844	197,182
*39817	Bainbridge	(229)	12,697	12,507
30032	Belvedere Park (c)	(404)	15,152	—
30326	Brookhaven[1]	(404)	49,217	51,910
*31520	Brunswick	(912)	15,383	16,157
*30518	Buford	(404)	12,225	13,748
*30701	Calhoun	(706)	15,650	16,309
30032	Candler-McAfee (c)	(404)	23,025	—
*30114	Canton	(770)	22,958	25,469
*30117	Carrollton	(770)	24,388	26,203
*30120	Cartersville	(770)	19,731	20,319
*30341	Chamblee	(770)	9,892	28,244
30021	Clarkston	(770)	7,554	12,215
*30337	College Park	(404)	13,942	14,601
*31901	Columbus	(706)	189,885	200,579
*30013	Conyers	(404)	15,195	15,875
*31015	Cordele	(229)	11,147	10,943
*30014	Covington	(770)	13,118	13,916
31805	Cusseta-Chattahoochee Co.	(706)	11,267	11,368
*30132	Dallas	(770)	11,544	12,870
*30720	Dalton	(706)	33,128	33,853
*30030	Decatur	(404)	19,335	21,957
*30340	Doraville	(770)	8,330	10,896
*31533	Douglas	(912)	11,589	11,718
*30134	Douglasville	(770)	30,961	32,897
30333	Druid Hills (c)	(404)	14,568	—
*31021	Dublin	(478)	16,201	16,197
*30096	Duluth	(770)	26,600	29,193
*30338	Dunwoody	(770)	46,267	48,733
*30344	East Point	(404)	33,712	35,467
30809	Evans (c)	(706)	29,011	—
*30213	Fairburn	(770)	12,950	13,967
*30214	Fayetteville	(770)	15,945	16,990
*30297	Forest Park	(770)	18,468	19,383
*30501	Gainesville	(770)	33,804	38,712
39854	Georgetown (c)	(912)	11,823	—
*30223	Griffin	(770)	23,643	23,211
30813	Grovetown	(706)	11,216	13,093
*31313	Hinesville	(912)	33,437	33,398
*30114	Holly Springs	(770)	9,189	10,719

ZIP	Place	Area code	2010 population	2015 estimate
30549	Jefferson	(706)	9,432	10,195
30022	Johns Creek	(770)	76,728	83,335
*30144	Kennesaw	(770)	29,783	33,584
31548	Kingsland	(912)	15,946	16,487
*30240	LaGrange	(706)	29,588	30,695
*30045	Lawrenceville	(770)	28,546	30,493
*30047	Lilburn	(404)	11,596	12,655
30122	Lithia Springs (c)	(770)	15,491	—
30052	Loganville	(770)	10,458	11,248
30126	Mableton (c)	(770)	37,115	—
*31201	Macon-Bibb Co.[1]	(478)	155,292	153,515
*30060	Marietta	(404)	56,579	59,067
*30907	Martinez (c)	(706)	35,795	—
*30253	McDonough	(770)	22,084	23,417
*31061	Milledgeville	(478)	17,715	18,931
*30004	Milton	(770)	32,661	37,547
*30655	Monroe	(770)	13,234	13,641
*31768	Moultrie	(229)	14,268	14,377
30087	Mountain Park (c)	(404)	11,554	—
*30263	Newnan	(770)	33,039	37,291
*30071	Norcross	(770)	9,116	16,634
30319	North Atlanta (c)	(770)	40,456	—
30033	North Decatur (c)	(404)	16,698	—
30033	North Druid Hills (c)	(404)	18,947	—
*30269	Peachtree City	(770)	34,364	35,240
*30092	Peachtree Corners[1]	(770)	38,011	40,978
31069	Perry	(478)	13,839	15,457
31322	Pooler	(912)	19,140	23,133
30127	Powder Springs	(404)	13,940	14,826
30074	Redan (c)	(770)	33,015	—
31324	Richmond Hill	(912)	9,281	11,935
*30274	Riverdale	(404)	15,134	15,989
*30161	Rome	(706)	36,303	36,323
*30077	Roswell	(404)	88,346	94,501
31558	Saint Marys	(912)	17,121	17,968
31522	Saint Simons (c)	(912)	12,743	—
*30350	Sandy Springs	(770)	93,853	105,330
*31401	Savannah	(912)	136,286	145,674
30079	Scottdale (c)	(404)	10,631	—
*30080	Smyrna	(770)	51,271	56,146
*30078	Snellville	(404)	18,242	19,733
*30458	Statesboro	(912)	28,422	30,721
30281	Stockbridge	(770)	25,636	28,202
30518	Sugar Hill	(404)	18,522	21,747
30024	Suwanee	(770)	15,355	18,694
*31792	Thomasville	(229)	18,413	18,742
*31794	Tifton	(229)	16,350	16,725
*30084	Tucker (c)	(770)	27,581	—
30291	Union City	(404)	19,456	20,805
*31601	Valdosta	(229)	54,518	55,724
*30474	Vidalia	(912)	10,473	10,679
30180	Villa Rica	(770)	13,956	14,904
*31088	Warner Robins	(478)	66,588	73,490
*31501	Waycross	(912)	14,649	14,053
31410	Wilmington Island (c)	(912)	15,138	—
30680	Winder	(770)	14,099	15,447
*30188	Woodstock	(770)	23,896	29,898

(1) Place was incorporated after the 2010 Census was conducted. Data in 2010 column is Census Bureau estimate.

Hawaii

Area code 808 applies to the entire state.

ZIP	Place	2000 population	2010 population
96821	East Honolulu (c)	—	49,914
96706	Ewa Beach (c)	14,650	14,955
96706	Ewa Gentry (c)	4,939	22,690
96701	Halawa (c)	13,891	14,014
96749	Hawaiian Paradise Park (c)	7,051	11,404
*96720	Hilo (c)	40,759	43,263
*96813	Honolulu, urban (c)	371,657	337,256[1]
*96732	Kahului (c)	20,146	26,337
96740	Kailua (c) (Hawaii Co.)	9,870	11,975
96734	Kailua (c) (Honolulu Co.)	36,513	38,635
96744	Kaneohe (c)	34,970	34,597
96746	Kapaa (c)	9,472	10,699
*96707	Kapolei (c)	—	15,186
96753	Kihei (c)	16,749	20,881
*96761	Lahaina (c)	9,118	11,704
96707	Makakilo (c)	13,156	18,248
96789	Mililani Mauka (c)	—	21,039
96789	Mililani Town (c)	28,608	27,629
96792	Nanakuli (c)	10,814	12,666
96782	Pearl City (c)	30,976	47,698
96797	Royal Kunia (c)	—	14,525
96857	Schofield Barracks (c)	14,428	16,370
96786	Wahiawa (c)	16,151	17,821
96792	Waianae (c)	10,506	13,177
96793	Wailuku (c)	12,296	15,313
96701	Waimalu (c)	29,371	13,730
96797	Waipahu (c)	33,108	38,216
96797	Waipio (c)	11,672	11,674

(1) 2015 est. pop. was 352,769.

Idaho

Area code 208 applies to the entire state. Area code 986 overlays 208 effective Sept. 5, 2017.

ZIP	Place	2010 population	2015 estimate
*83401	Ammon	13,816	14,960
83221	Blackfoot	11,899	11,740
*83702	Boise	205,671	218,281
83318	Burley	10,345	10,436
*83605	Caldwell	46,237	51,686
83202	Chubbuck	13,922	14,428
*83814	Coeur d'Alene	44,137	49,122
83616	Eagle	19,908	23,612
*83714	Garden City	10,972	11,550
83835	Hayden	13,294	14,133
*83402	Idaho Falls	56,813	59,184
83338	Jerome	10,890	11,184
83634	Kuna	15,210	17,226
83501	Lewiston	31,894	32,544
*83642	Meridian	75,092	90,739
*83843	Moscow	23,800	25,060
83647	Mountain Home	14,206	13,730
*83651	Nampa	81,557	89,839
*83201	Pocatello	54,255	54,441
*83854	Post Falls	27,574	30,453
*83440	Rexburg	25,484	27,663
*83301	Twin Falls	44,125	47,468

Illinois

Area code 224 overlays area code 847. Area code 331 overlays 630. Area code 779 overlays 815. Area code 872 overlays 312/773.

ZIP	Place	Area code	2010 population	2015 estimate
60101	Addison	(630)	36,942	37,208
*60102	Algonquin	(847)	30,046	30,571
60803	Alsip	(708)	19,277	19,346
62002	Alton	(618)	27,865	27,003
60002	Antioch	(847)	14,430	14,329
*60005	Arlington Heights	(847)	75,101	75,926
*60505	Aurora	(630)	197,899	200,661
*60010	Barrington	(847)	10,327	10,353
*60103	Bartlett	(630)	41,208	41,545
*60510	Batavia	(630)	26,045	26,495
*60083	Beach Park	(847)	13,638	13,976
*62220	Belleville	(618)	44,478	42,034
60104	Bellwood	(708)	19,071	19,308
61008	Belvidere	(815)	25,585	25,132
*60106	Bensenville	(630)	18,352	18,440
60402	Berwyn	(708)	56,657	56,368
*60108	Bloomingdale	(630)	22,018	22,254
*61701	Bloomington	(309)	76,610	78,292
60406	Blue Island	(708)	23,706	23,652
*60440	Bolingbrook	(630)	73,366	74,306
60914	Bourbonnais	(815)	18,631	18,569
60915	Bradley	(815)	15,895	15,617
60455	Bridgeview	(708)	16,446	16,407
60513	Brookfield	(708)	18,978	18,944
*60089	Buffalo Grove	(847)	41,496	41,503
60459	Burbank	(708)	28,925	29,128
60527	Burr Ridge	(630)	10,559	10,818
62206	Cahokia	(618)	15,241	14,402
60409	Calumet City	(708)	37,042	37,031
*60119	Campton Hills	(630)/(847)	11,131	11,345
61520	Canton	(309)	14,704	14,211
*62901	Carbondale	(618)	25,902	26,399
*60188	Carol Stream	(630)	39,711	40,356
60110	Carpentersville	(847)	37,691	38,512
60013	Cary	(847)	18,271	17,965
62801	Centralia	(618)	13,032	12,655
*61821	Champaign	(217)	81,055	86,096
60410	Channahon	(815)	12,560	12,594
61920	Charleston	(217)	21,838	21,196
62629	Chatham	(217)	11,500	12,351
*60602	Chicago	(312)/(773)	2,695,598	2,720,546
*60411	Chicago Heights	(708)	30,276	30,284
60415	Chicago Ridge	(708)	14,305	14,373
60804	Cicero	(708)	83,891	83,886
62234	Collinsville	(618)	25,579	24,754
62236	Columbia	(618)	9,707	10,191
60478	Country Club Hills	(708)	16,541	16,795
60435	Crest Hill	(815)	20,837	21,153
60445	Crestwood	(708)	10,950	10,984
*60014	Crystal Lake	(815)	40,743	40,448
*61832	Danville	(217)	33,027	32,108
60561	Darien	(630)	22,086	22,256
*62521	Decatur	(217)	76,122	73,254
60015	Deerfield	(847)	18,225	19,019
60115	DeKalb	(815)	43,862	43,211
*60018	Des Plaines	(847)	58,364	58,677
61021	Dixon	(815)	15,733	15,319
60419	Dolton	(708)	23,153	23,197
*60515	Downers Grove	(630)	47,833	49,732
61244	East Moline	(309)	21,302	21,350
*61611	East Peoria	(309)	23,402	23,080

ZIP	Place	Area code	2010 population	2015 estimate
*62201	East St. Louis	(618)	27,006	26,790
*62025	Edwardsville	(618)	24,293	24,992
62401	Effingham	(217)	12,328	12,604
*60120	Elgin	(847)	108,188	112,111
*60007	Elk Grove Village	(847)	33,127	33,238
60126	Elmhurst	(630)	44,121	45,957
60707	Elmwood Park	(708)	24,883	24,840
*60201	Evanston	(847)	74,486	75,527
60805	Evergreen Park	(708)	19,852	19,841
*62208	Fairview Heights	(618)	17,078	16,827
*60130	Forest Park	(708)	14,167	14,123
60020	Fox Lake	(847)	10,579	10,518
60423	Frankfort	(815)	17,782	18,653
*60131	Franklin Park	(847)	18,333	18,312
61032	Freeport	(815)	25,638	24,476
60030	Gages Lake (c)	(847)	10,198	—
*61401	Galesburg	(309)	32,195	31,273
60134	Geneva	(630)	21,495	21,806
62034	Glen Carbon	(618)	12,934	12,966
*60137	Glen Ellyn	(630)	27,450	28,201
*60139	Glendale Heights	(630)	34,208	34,435
*60025	Glenview	(847)	44,692	47,446
62035	Godfrey	(618)	17,982	17,759
62040	Granite City	(618)	29,849	29,054
60030	Grayslake	(847)	20,957	20,915
60031	Gurnee	(847)	31,295	31,056
60133	Hanover Park	(630)	37,973	38,333
*60426	Harvey	(708)	25,282	25,194
60429	Hazel Crest	(708)	14,100	14,118
62948	Herrin	(618)	12,501	12,910
*60457	Hickory Hills	(708)	14,049	14,122
*60035	Highland Park	(847)	29,763	29,743
*60521	Hinsdale	(630)	16,816	17,628
*60195	Hoffman Estates	(847)	51,895	52,138
*60491	Homer Glen	(708)	24,220	24,395
*60430	Homewood	(708)	19,323	19,373
60142	Huntley	(847)	24,291	26,005
*62650	Jacksonville	(217)	19,446	19,103
*60436	Joliet	(815)	147,433	147,861
60458	Justice	(708)	12,926	12,968
60901	Kankakee	(815)	27,537	26,676
61443	Kewanee	(309)	12,916	12,533
60525	La Grange	(708)	15,550	15,723
60526	La Grange Park	(708)	13,579	13,608
60045	Lake Forest	(847)	19,375	19,408
*60102	Lake in the Hills	(847)	28,965	29,024
*60047	Lake Zurich	(847)	19,631	19,993
60438	Lansing	(708)	28,331	28,349
*60439	Lemont	(630)	16,000	16,788
*60048	Libertyville	(847)	20,315	20,436
62656	Lincoln	(217)	14,504	13,966
*60645	Lincolnwood	(847)	12,590	12,646
60046	Lindenhurst	(847)	14,462	14,408
60532	Lisle	(630)	22,390	22,964
*60441	Lockport	(815)	24,839	25,175
60148	Lombard	(630)	43,165	43,797
*61111	Loves Park	(815)	23,996	23,455
60534	Lyons	(708)	10,729	10,722
*61115	Machesney Park	(815)	23,499	22,927
61455	Macomb	(309)	19,288	18,547
62959	Marion	(618)	17,193	17,803
*60426	Markham	(708)	12,508	12,682
*60443	Matteson	(708)	19,009	19,195
61938	Mattoon	(217)	18,555	18,113
*60153	Maywood	(708)	24,090	24,012
*60050	McHenry	(815)	26,992	26,657
*60160	Melrose Park	(708)	25,411	25,379
60445	Midlothian	(708)	14,819	14,847
60447	Minooka	(815)	10,924	11,243
60448	Mokena	(708)	18,740	19,923
*61265	Moline	(309)	43,483	42,681
60538	Montgomery	(630)	18,438	19,489
60450	Morris	(815)	13,636	14,363
61550	Morton	(309)	16,267	16,306
60053	Morton Grove	(847)	23,270	23,448
62864	Mount Vernon	(618)	15,277	15,087
60060	Mundelein	(847)	31,064	31,582
*60540	Naperville	(630)	141,853	147,100
60451	New Lenox	(815)	24,394	25,800
60714	Niles	(847)	29,803	29,876
*61761	Normal	(309)	52,497	54,373
*60634	Norridge	(708)	14,572	14,621
60542	North Aurora	(630)	16,760	17,456
*60064	North Chicago	(847)	32,574	29,491
*60062	Northbrook	(847)	33,170	33,663
60164	Northlake	(708)	12,323	12,312
60452	Oak Forest	(708)	27,962	28,074
*60453	Oak Lawn	(708)	56,690	56,781
*60301	Oak Park	(708)	51,878	52,287
62269	O'Fallon	(618)	28,281	29,002
*60462	Orland Park	(708)	56,767	58,619
60543	Oswego	(630)	30,355	33,955
61350	Ottawa	(815)	18,768	18,342
*60067	Palatine	(847)	68,557	69,308

ZIP	Place	Area code	2010 population	2015 estimate
60463	Palos Heights	(708)	12,515	12,545
60465	Palos Hills	(708)	17,484	17,565
*60466	Park Forest	(708)	21,975	21,954
60068	Park Ridge	(847)	37,480	37,757
*61554	Pekin	(309)	34,094	33,223
*61602	Peoria	(309)	115,007	115,070
*60544	Plainfield	(815)	39,581	42,527
60545	Plano	(630)	10,856	11,282
61764	Pontiac	(815)	11,931	11,794
60070	Prospect Heights	(847)	16,256	16,386
*62301	Quincy	(217)	40,633	40,780
61866	Rantoul	(217)	12,941	13,008
60471	Richton Park	(708)	13,646	13,695
60305	River Forest	(708)	11,172	11,199
60171	River Grove	(708)	10,227	10,219
60827	Riverdale	(708)	13,549	13,536
*61201	Rock Island	(309)	39,018	38,620
*61101	Rockford	(815)	152,871	148,278
60008	Rolling Meadows	(847)	24,099	24,190
60446	Romeoville	(815)	39,680	39,719
61073	Roscoe	(815)	10,785	10,565
60172	Roselle	(630)	22,763	22,994
60073	Round Lake	(847)	18,289	18,461
60073	Round Lake Beach	(847)	28,175	27,852
*60174	Saint Charles	(630)	32,974	33,460
60411	Sauk Village	(708)	10,506	10,493
*60193	Schaumburg	(847)	74,227	74,693
*60176	Schiller Park	(847)	11,793	11,806
*62269	Shiloh	(618)	12,651	12,961
*60436	Shorewood	(815)	15,615	16,747
*60077	Skokie	(847)	64,784	64,821
60177	South Elgin	(847)	21,985	22,365
60473	South Holland	(708)	22,030	22,043
*62701	Springfield	(217)	116,250	116,565
61081	Sterling	(815)	15,370	15,057
60107	Streamwood	(630)	39,858	40,554
61364	Streator	(815)	13,710	13,182
60501	Summit	(708)	11,054	11,389
*62221	Swansea	(618)	13,430	13,543
60178	Sycamore	(815)	17,519	17,712
62568	Taylorville	(217)	11,246	10,873
*60477	Tinley Park	(708)	56,703	57,143
62294	Troy	(618)	9,888	10,036
*61801	Urbana	(217)	41,250	42,311
60061	Vernon Hills	(847)	25,113	26,314
60181	Villa Park	(630)	21,904	21,969
60555	Warrenville	(630)	13,140	13,317
61571	Washington	(309)	15,134	16,664
62298	Waterloo	(618)	9,811	10,236
60084	Wauconda	(847)	13,603	13,814
*60085	Waukegan	(847)	89,078	88,475
*60185	West Chicago	(630)	27,086	27,447
60154	Westchester	(708)	16,718	16,729
60558	Western Springs	(708)	12,975	13,369
60559	Westmont	(630)	24,685	24,941
*60187	Wheaton	(630)	52,894	53,715
60090	Wheeling	(847)	37,648	38,079
60091	Wilmette	(847)	27,087	27,413
60093	Winnetka	(847)	12,187	12,472
*60191	Wood Dale	(630)	13,770	13,917
62095	Wood River	(618)	10,657	10,294
60517	Woodridge	(630)	32,971	33,370
60098	Woodstock	(815)	24,770	25,189
60482	Worth	(708)	10,789	10,784
60560	Yorkville	(630)	16,921	18,451
60099	Zion	(847)	24,413	24,117

Indiana

Area code 463 overlays area code 317. Area code 930 overlays 812.

ZIP	Place	Area code	2010 population	2015 estimate
*46011	Anderson	(765)	56,129	55,305
46706	Auburn	(260)	12,731	12,979
46123	Avon	(317)	12,446	16,451
47421	Bedford	(812)	13,413	13,347
46107	Beech Grove	(317)	14,192	14,548
*47408	Bloomington	(812)	80,405	84,067
46714	Bluffton	(260)	9,897	10,005
46112	Brownsburg	(317)	21,285	24,996
*46032	Carmel	(317)	79,191	88,713
46303	Cedar Lake	(219)	11,560	12,000
46304	Chesterton	(219)	13,068	13,433
*47129	Clarksville	(812)	21,724	21,866
*47201	Columbus	(812)	44,061	46,690
47331	Connersville	(765)	13,481	13,010
47933	Crawfordsville	(765)	15,915	16,024
*46307	Crown Point	(219)	27,317	28,879
*46311	Dyer	(219)	16,390	16,051
46312	East Chicago	(219)	29,698	28,699
*46514	Elkhart	(574)	50,949	52,348
*47708	Evansville	(812)	117,429	119,943
*46038	Fishers	(317)	76,794	88,658
*46802	Fort Wayne	(260)	253,691	260,326
*46041	Frankfort	(765)	16,422	16,060

ZIP	Place	Area code	2010 population	2015 estimate
46131	Franklin	(317)	23,712	24,598
*46402	Gary	(219)	80,294	77,156
*46526	Goshen	(574)	31,719	32,983
46530	Granger (c)	(574)	30,465	—
46135	Greencastle	(765)	10,326	10,401
46140	Greenfield	(317)	20,602	21,497
47240	Greensburg	(812)	11,492	11,819
*46142	Greenwood	(317)	49,791	55,586
46319	Griffith	(219)	16,893	16,378
*46320	Hammond	(219)	80,830	77,614
*46322	Highland	(219)	23,727	22,936
46342	Hobart	(219)	29,059	28,404
46750	Huntington	(260)	17,391	17,095
*46201	Indianapolis (balance)	(317)	820,445	853,173
*47546	Jasper	(812)	15,038	15,451
*47130	Jeffersonville	(812)	44,953	46,960
*46902	Kokomo	(765)	45,468	57,995
*46350	La Porte	(219)	22,053	21,916
*47901	Lafayette	(765)	67,140	71,111
46405	Lake Station	(219)	12,572	12,054
46226	Lawrence	(317)	46,001	47,809
46052	Lebanon	(765)	15,792	15,892
46947	Logansport	(574)	18,396	17,793
47250	Madison	(812)	11,967	12,040
*46952	Marion	(765)	29,948	29,081
46151	Martinsville	(765)	11,828	11,690
*46410	Merrillville	(219)	35,246	35,224
*46360	Michigan City	(219)	31,479	31,459
*46544	Mishawaka	(574)	48,252	48,261
*47302	Muncie	(765)	70,085	70,087
46321	Munster	(219)	23,603	22,984
*47150	New Albany	(812)	36,372	36,732
47362	New Castle	(765)	18,114	17,621
46774	New Haven	(260)	14,794	15,709
*46060	Noblesville	(317)	51,969	59,093
*46970	Peru	(765)	11,417	11,060
*46168	Plainfield	(317)	27,631	30,590
46563	Plymouth	(574)	10,033	10,035
46368	Portage	(219)	36,828	36,738
47907	Purdue University (c)	(765)	12,183	—
*47374	Richmond	(765)	36,812	35,854
46373	Saint John	(219)	14,850	16,495
46375	Schererville	(219)	29,243	28,791
47274	Seymour	(812)	17,503	19,478
46176	Shelbyville	(765)	19,191	19,133
*46601	South Bend	(574)	101,168	101,516
46224	Speedway	(317)	11,812	12,127
*47802	Terre Haute	(812)	60,785	60,825
*46383	Valparaiso	(219)	31,730	32,626
47591	Vincennes	(812)	18,423	18,012
46992	Wabash	(260)	10,666	10,381
*46580	Warsaw	(574)	13,559	14,472
47501	Washington	(812)	11,509	12,078
*47906	West Lafayette	(765)	29,596	45,550
*46074	Westfield	(317)	30,068	36,738
47396	Yorktown	(765)	9,405	11,231
46077	Zionsville	(317)	14,160	26,296

Iowa

ZIP	Place	Area code	2010 population	2015 estimate
50009	Altoona	(515)	14,541	16,984
*50010	Ames	(515)	58,965	65,060
*50021	Ankeny	(515)	45,582	56,764
52722	Bettendorf	(563)	33,217	35,505
*50036	Boone	(515)	12,661	12,692
52601	Burlington	(319)	25,663	25,410
*50613	Cedar Falls	(319)	39,260	41,255
*52401	Cedar Rapids	(319)	126,326	130,405
*52732	Clinton	(563)	26,885	26,064
50325	Clive	(515)	15,447	17,419
52241	Coralville	(319)	18,907	20,608
*51501	Council Bluffs	(712)	62,230	62,597
*52801	Davenport	(563)	99,685	102,582
*50309	Des Moines	(515)	203,433	210,330
*52001	Dubuque	(563)	57,637	58,799
50501	Fort Dodge	(515)	25,206	24,649
52627	Fort Madison	(319)	11,051	10,717
50111	Grimes	(515)	8,246	10,676
50125	Indianola	(515)	14,782	15,467
*52240	Iowa City	(319)	67,862	74,220
50131	Johnston	(515)	17,278	20,871
52632	Keokuk	(319)	10,780	10,609
52302	Marion	(319)	34,768	37,330
50158	Marshalltown	(641)	27,552	27,620
*50401	Mason City	(641)	28,079	27,366
52761	Muscatine	(563)	22,886	23,968
50208	Newton	(641)	15,254	15,125
52317	North Liberty	(319)	13,374	15,931
50211	Norwalk	(515)	8,945	10,135
52577	Oskaloosa	(641)	11,463	11,607
52501	Ottumwa	(641)	25,023	24,624
50219	Pella	(641)	10,352	10,363
*51101	Sioux City	(712)	82,684	82,821

ZIP	Place	Area code	2010 population	2015 estimate
51301	Spencer	(712)	11,233	11,212
50588	Storm Lake	(712)	10,600	10,910
*50322	Urbandale	(515)	39,463	44,062
*50701	Waterloo	(319)	68,406	68,460
50263	Waukee	(515)	13,790	18,990
50677	Waverly	(319)	9,874	10,066
*50265	West Des Moines	(515)	56,609	64,113

Kansas

ZIP	Place	Area code	2010 population	2015 estimate
67002	Andover	(316)	11,791	12,745
67005	Arkansas City	(620)	12,415	12,136
66002	Atchison	(913)	11,021	10,712
67037	Derby	(316)	22,158	23,509
*67801	Dodge City	(620)	27,340	27,912
67042	El Dorado	(316)	13,021	12,931
66801	Emporia	(620)	24,916	24,649
*67846	Garden City	(620)	26,658	27,005
*66030	Gardner	(913)	19,123	20,868
67530	Great Bend	(620)	15,995	15,717
*67601	Hays	(785)	20,510	21,092
67060	Haysville	(316)	10,826	11,212
*67501	Hutchinson	(620)	42,080	41,569
*66441	Junction City	(785)	23,353	24,621
*66101	Kansas City	(913)	145,786	151,306
66043	Lansing	(913)	11,265	11,767
*66044	Lawrence	(785)	87,643	93,917
*66048	Leavenworth	(913)	35,251	35,980
*66211	Leawood	(913)	31,867	34,579
*66215	Lenexa	(913)	48,190	52,490
*67901	Liberal	(620)	20,525	20,746
*66502	Manhattan	(785)	52,281	56,308
67460	McPherson	(620)	13,155	13,144
*66202	Merriam	(913)	11,003	11,288
*67114	Newton	(316)	19,132	19,216
*66061	Olathe	(913)	125,872	134,305
66067	Ottawa	(785)	12,649	12,387
*66204	Overland Park	(913)	173,372	186,515
67357	Parsons	(620)	10,500	10,090
*66762	Pittsburg	(620)	20,233	20,409
*66208	Prairie Village	(913)	21,447	21,877
*67401	Salina	(785)	47,707	47,813
*66203	Shawnee	(913)	62,209	65,046
*66603	Topeka	(785)	127,473	127,265
*67202	Wichita	(316)	382,368	389,965
67156	Winfield	(620)	12,301	12,204

Kentucky
Area code 364 overlays area code 270.

ZIP	Place	Area code	2010 population	2015 estimate
*41101	Ashland	(606)	21,684	21,108
40004	Bardstown	(502)	11,700	13,091
*40403	Berea	(859)	13,561	14,882
*42101	Bowling Green	(270)	58,067	63,616
41005	Burlington (c)	(859)	15,926	—
*42718	Campbellsville	(270)	9,108	11,237
*41011	Covington	(859)	40,640	40,997
*40422	Danville	(859)	16,218	16,690
*42701	Elizabethtown	(270)	28,531	29,678
*41018	Erlanger	(859)	18,082	18,797
*41042	Florence	(859)	29,951	32,227
42223	Fort Campbell North (c)	(270)	13,685	—
40121	Fort Knox (c)	(270)	10,124	—
41075	Fort Thomas	(859)	16,325	16,398
*40601	Frankfort	(502)	25,527	27,830
40324	Georgetown	(502)	29,098	32,356
*42141	Glasgow	(270)	14,028	14,470
*42420	Henderson	(270)	28,757	28,890
*42240	Hopkinsville	(270)	31,577	32,205
41051	Independence	(859)	24,757	26,819
*40269	Jeffersontown	(502)	26,595	26,946
40342	Lawrenceburg	(502)	10,505	11,103
*40507	Lexington-Fayette	(859)	295,803	314,488
*40202	Louisville-Jefferson Co. (balance)	(502)	597,337	615,366
*40222	Lyndon	(502)	11,002	11,372
42431	Madisonville	(270)	19,591	19,539
42066	Mayfield	(270)	10,024	10,080
40047	Mount Washington	(502)	9,117	14,028
42071	Murray	(270)	17,741	18,954
*41071	Newport	(859)	15,273	15,354
*40356	Nicholasville	(859)	28,015	29,754
*42301	Owensboro	(270)	57,265	59,042
*42003	Paducah	(270)	25,024	24,864
*40160	Radcliff	(502)	21,688	22,387
*40475	Richmond	(859)	31,364	33,533
*40207	Saint Matthews	(502)	17,472	18,025
*40066	Shelbyville	(502)	14,045	15,253
40165	Shepherdsville	(502)	11,222	11,967
*40216	Shively	(502)	15,264	15,713
*42501	Somerset	(606)	11,196	11,439
*40391	Winchester	(859)	18,368	18,446

Louisiana

ZIP	Place	Area code	2010 population	2015 estimate
*70510	Abbeville	(337)	12,257	12,434
*71301	Alexandria	(318)	47,723	47,889
70714	Baker	(225)	13,895	13,695
71220	Bastrop	(318)	11,365	10,713
*70801	Baton Rouge	(225)	229,493	228,590
70360	Bayou Blue (c)	(985)	12,352	—
*70364	Bayou Cane (c)	(985)	19,355	—
*70037	Belle Chasse (c)	(504)	12,679	—
*70427	Bogalusa	(985)	12,232	11,933
*71111	Bossier City	(318)	61,315	68,094
70518	Broussard	(337)	8,197	11,303
70837	Central	(225)	26,864	28,295
*70043	Chalmette (c)	(504)	16,751	—
70433	Claiborne (c)	(985)	11,507	—
*70526	Crowley	(337)	13,265	13,144
*70726	Denham Springs	(225)	10,215	10,125
70634	DeRidder	(337)	10,578	10,890
70047	Destrehan (c)	(985)	11,535	—
70072	Estelle (c)	(504)	16,377	—
70535	Eunice	(337)	10,398	10,310
70810	Gardere (c)	(225)	10,580	—
*70737	Gonzales	(225)	9,781	10,678
*70053	Gretna	(504)	17,736	17,880
*70401	Hammond	(985)	20,019	20,480
*70058	Harvey (c)	(504)	20,348	—
*70360	Houma	(985)	33,727	34,287
70121	Jefferson (c)	(504)	11,193	—
70546	Jennings	(337)	10,383	10,180
*70062	Kenner	(504)	66,702	67,091
*70501	Lafayette	(337)	120,623	127,657
*70601	Lake Charles	(337)	71,993	76,070
*70068	LaPlace (c)	(985)	29,872	—
70070	Luling (c)	(985)	12,119	—
*70471	Mandeville	(985)	11,560	12,345
*70072	Marrero (c)	(504)	33,141	—
*70001	Metairie (c)	(504)	138,481	—
*71055	Minden	(318)	13,082	12,690
*71201	Monroe	(318)	48,815	49,598
*70380	Morgan City	(985)	12,404	11,835
70611	Moss Bluff (c)	(337)	11,557	—
*71457	Natchitoches	(318)	18,323	18,365
*70560	New Iberia	(337)	30,617	30,754
*70112	New Orleans	(504)	343,829	389,617
*70570	Opelousas	(337)	16,634	16,591
*71360	Pineville	(318)	14,555	14,403
70769	Prairieville (c)	(225)	26,895	—
70394	Raceland (c)	(985)	10,193	—
70123	River Ridge (c)	(504)	13,494	—
*71270	Ruston	(318)	21,859	22,340
70817	Shenandoah (c)	(318)	18,399	—
*71102	Shreveport	(318)	199,311	197,204
*70458	Slidell	(985)	27,068	27,942
*70663	Sulphur	(337)	20,410	20,189
70056	Terrytown (c)	(504)	23,319	—
*70301	Thibodaux	(985)	14,566	14,584
70056	Timberlane (c)	(504)	10,243	—
70094	Waggaman (c)	(504)	10,015	—
*71291	West Monroe	(318)	13,065	12,966
70058	Woodmere (c)	(504)	12,080	—
*70592	Youngsville	(337)	8,105	11,961
70791	Zachary	(225)	14,960	16,448

Maine

Area code 207 applies to the entire state. See introductory note.

ZIP	Place	2010 population	2015 estimate
*04210	Auburn	23,055	22,871
*04330	Augusta	19,136	18,471
*04401	Bangor	33,039	32,391
*04005	Biddeford	21,277	21,282
04011	Brunswick	20,278	20,495
04011	Brunswick (c)	15,175	—
04105	Falmouth	11,185	11,988
04038	Gorham	16,381	17,181
04043	Kennebunk	10,798	11,209
*04240	Lewiston	36,592	36,202
*04473	Orono	10,362	10,700
*04101	Portland	66,194	66,881
04072	Saco	18,482	19,078
04073	Sanford[1]	20,798	20,893
*04074	Scarborough	18,919	19,691
*04106	South Portland	25,002	25,556
04084	Standish	9,874	10,139
*04901	Waterville	15,722	16,261
04090	Wells	9,589	10,073
*04092	Westbrook	17,494	17,978
*04062	Windham	17,001	17,816
03909	York	12,529	12,862

(1) Place was incorporated after the 2010 Census was conducted. Data in 2010 column is Census Bureau estimate for Sanford MCD.

Maryland

Area code 240 overlays area code 301. Area codes 443/667 overlay 410.

ZIP	Place	Area code	2010 population	2015 estimate
21001	Aberdeen	(410)	14,959	15,580
20607	Accokeek (c)	(301)	10,573	—
*20783	Adelphi (c)	(301)	15,086	—
*21401	Annapolis	(410)	38,394	39,474
21403	Annapolis Neck (c)	(410)	10,950	—
21227	Arbutus (c)	(410)	20,483	—
21012	Arnold (c)	(410)	23,106	—
*20906	Aspen Hill (c)	(301)	48,759	—
21220	Ballenger Creek (c)	(410)	18,274	—
*21201	Baltimore	(410)	620,961	621,849
*21014	Bel Air	(410)	10,120	10,190
21050	Bel Air North (c)	(410)	30,568	—
21014	Bel Air South (c)	(410)	47,709	—
*20705	Beltsville (c)	(301)	16,772	—
20603	Bensville (c)	(301)	11,923	—
*20814	Bethesda (c)	(301)	60,858	—
*20715	Bowie	(301)	54,727	58,025
21225	Brooklyn Park (c)	(410)	14,373	—
20619	California (c)	(301)	11,857	—
20705	Calverton (c)	(301)	17,724	—
21613	Cambridge	(410)	12,326	12,507
*20748	Camp Springs (c)	(301)	19,096	—
21234	Carney (c)	(410)	29,941	—
*21228	Catonsville (c)	(410)	41,567	—
20657	Chesapeake Ranch Estates (c)	(301)	10,519	—
20782	Chillum (c)	(301)	33,513	—
20871	Clarksburg (c)	(301)	13,766	—
20735	Clinton (c)	(301)	35,970	—
20904	Cloverly (c)	(301)	15,126	—
21030	Cockeysville (c)	(410)	20,776	—
*20904	Colesville (c)	(301)	14,647	—
*20740	College Park	(301)	30,413	32,301
*21044	Columbia (c)	(410)	99,615	—
21114	Crofton (c)	(410)	27,348	—
*21502	Cumberland	(301)	20,859	20,130
20872	Damascus (c)	(301)	15,257	—
21222	Dundalk (c)	(410)	63,597	—
20737	East Riverdale (c)	(301)	15,509	—
*21601	Easton	(410)	15,945	16,617
21040	Edgewood (c)	(410)	25,562	—
21784	Eldersburg (c)	(410)	30,531	—
21075	Elkridge (c)	(410)	15,593	—
*21921	Elkton	(410)	15,443	15,782
*21043	Ellicott City (c)	(410)	65,834	—
21221	Essex (c)	(410)	39,262	—
20904	Fairland (c)	(301)	23,681	—
21061	Ferndale (c)	(410)	16,746	—
*20747	Forestville (c)	(301)	12,353	—
*20744	Fort Washington (c)	(301)	23,717	—
*21701	Frederick	(301)	65,239	69,479
*20877	Gaithersburg	(301)	59,933	67,456
*20874	Germantown (c)	(301)	86,395	—
20745	Glassmanor (c)	(301)	17,295	—
*21061	Glen Burnie (c)	(410)	67,639	—
20906	Glenmont (c)	(301)	13,529	—
20769	Glenn Dale (c)	(301)	13,466	—
*20770	Greenbelt	(301)	23,068	24,272
*21740	Hagerstown	(301)	39,662	40,432
21740	Halfway (c)	(301)	10,701	—
21078	Havre de Grace	(410)	12,952	13,504
20748	Hillcrest Heights (c)	(301)	16,469	—
*20781	Hyattsville	(301)	17,557	18,501
21043	Ilchester (c)	(410)	23,476	—
21085	Joppatowne (c)	(410)	12,616	—
20902	Kemp Mill (c)	(301)	12,564	—
*20774	Kettering (c)	(301)	12,790	—
*21122	Lake Shore (c)	(410)	19,477	—
20785	Landover (c)	(301)	23,078	—
*20787	Langley Park (c)	(301)	18,755	—
*20706	Lanham (c)	(301)	10,157	—
*20774	Largo (c)	(301)	10,709	—
*20707	Laurel	(301)	25,115	26,215
20653	Lexington Park (c)	(410)	11,626	—
21090	Linthicum (c)	(410)	10,324	—
21207	Lochearn (c)	(410)	25,333	—
20724	Maryland City (c)	(301)	16,093	—
21093	Mays Chapel (c)	(410)	11,420	—
21220	Middle River (c)	(410)	25,191	—
21207	Milford Mill (c)	(410)	29,042	—
*20716	Mitchellville (c)	(301)	10,967	—
*20886	Montgomery Village (c)	(301)	32,032	—
20784	New Carrollton	(301)	12,135	12,786
*20852	North Bethesda (c)	(301)	43,828	—
20878	North Potomac (c)	(301)	24,410	—
21811	Ocean Pines (c)	(410)	11,710	—
21113	Odenton (c)	(301)	37,132	—
*20832	Olney (c)	(301)	33,844	—
21236	Overlea (c)	(410)	12,275	—

ZIP	Place	Area code	2010 population	2015 estimate
21117	Owings Mills (c)	(410)	30,622	—
*20745	Oxon Hill (c)	(301)	17,722	—
21234	Parkville (c)	(410)	30,734	—
21401	Parole (c)	(410)	15,922	—
*21122	Pasadena (c)	(410)	24,287	—
21128	Perry Hall (c)	(410)	28,474	—
*21207	Pikesville (c)	(410)	30,764	—
*20850	Potomac (c)	(301)	44,965	—
21133	Randallstown (c)	(410)	32,430	—
20855	Redland (c)	(301)	17,242	—
*21136	Reisterstown (c)	(410)	25,968	—
*21122	Riviera Beach (c)	(410)	12,677	—
*20850	Rockville	(301)	61,209	66,980
20772	Rosaryville (c)	(301)	10,697	—
21237	Rosedale (c)	(410)	19,257	—
21221	Rossville (c)	(410)	15,147	—
*21801	Salisbury	(410)	30,343	32,899
20723	Scaggsville (c)	(301)	24,333	—
*20706	Seabrook (c)	(301)	17,287	—
21144	Severn (c)	(410)	44,231	—
21146	Severna Park (c)	(410)	37,634	—
*20901	Silver Spring (c)	(301)	71,452	—
20707	South Laurel (c)	(301)	26,112	—
*20746	Suitland (c)	(301)	25,825	—
21842	Summerfield (c)	(410)	10,898	—
*20912	Takoma Park	(301)	16,715	17,713
*21204	Towson (c)	(410)	55,197	—
20854	Travilah (c)	(301)	12,159	—
*20602	Waldorf (c)	(301)	67,752	—
20743	Walker Mill (c)	(301)	11,302	—
*21157	Westminster	(410)	18,590	18,670
*20902	Wheaton (c)	(301)	48,284	—
20904	White Oak (c)	(301)	17,403	—
21207	Woodlawn (c) (Baltimore Co.)	(410)	37,879	—

Massachusetts

Area code 339 overlays area code 781. Area code 351 overlays 978. Area code 774 overlays 508. Area code 857 overlays 617. See introductory note.

ZIP	Place	Area code	2010 population	2015 estimate
02351	Abington	(781)	15,985	16,227
*01720	Acton	(978)	21,924	23,549
*02743	Acushnet	(508)	10,303	10,477
01001	Agawam	(413)	28,438	28,839
01913	Amesbury	(978)	16,283	17,414
*01002	Amherst	(413)	37,819	39,833
*01002	Amherst Center (c)	(413)	19,065	—
*01810	Andover	(978)	33,201	35,299
*02476	Arlington	(781)	42,844	44,815
01721	Ashland	(508)	16,593	17,573
*01331	Athol	(978)	11,584	11,654
02703	Attleboro	(508)	43,593	44,284
01501	Auburn	(508)	16,188	16,516
02630	Barnstable	(508)	45,193	44,331
*01730	Bedford	(781)	13,320	14,171
01007	Belchertown	(413)	14,649	14,929
02019	Bellingham	(508)	16,332	16,891
02478	Belmont	(617)	24,729	25,584
01915	Beverly	(978)	39,502	41,186
*01821	Billerica	(978)	40,243	42,683
*02108	Boston	(617)	617,594	667,137
*02532	Bourne	(508)	19,754	19,681
*02184	Braintree	(781)	35,744	37,497
*02324	Bridgewater	(508)	26,563	27,628
*02301	Brockton	(508)	93,810	95,314
*02446	Brookline	(617)	58,732	59,195
*01803	Burlington	(781)	24,498	25,920
*02139	Cambridge	(617)	105,162	110,402
02021	Canton	(781)	21,561	22,817
*02330	Carver	(508)	11,509	11,629
01507	Charlton	(508)	12,981	13,406
01824	Chelmsford	(978)	33,802	35,149
02150	Chelsea	(617)	35,177	39,398
*01020	Chicopee	(413)	55,298	56,741
01510	Clinton	(978)	13,606	13,805
01742	Concord	(978)	17,668	19,830
01923	Danvers	(978)	26,493	27,849
*02747	Dartmouth	(508)	34,032	34,715
*02026	Dedham	(781)	24,729	25,397
02638	Dennis	(508)	14,207	14,005
01826	Dracut	(978)	29,457	31,352
01571	Dudley	(508)	11,390	11,587
*02332	Duxbury	(781)	15,059	15,483
02333	East Bridgewater	(508)	13,794	14,343
*01028	East Longmeadow	(413)	15,720	16,213
01027	Easthampton	(413)	16,053	16,030
*02334	Easton	(508)	23,112	23,908
02149	Everett	(617)	41,667	46,050
02719	Fairhaven	(508)	15,873	16,140
*02720	Fall River	(508)	88,857	88,777
*02540	Falmouth	(508)	31,531	31,524
01420	Fitchburg	(978)	40,318	40,545
02035	Foxborough	(508)	16,865	17,456
*01701	Framingham	(508)	68,318	71,209
02038	Franklin	(508)	31,635	33,147
*01440	Gardner	(978)	20,228	20,333
*01930	Gloucester	(978)	28,789	29,781
01519	Grafton	(508)	17,765	18,540
*01301	Greenfield	(413)	17,456	17,450
*01450	Groton	(978)	10,646	11,296
*02339	Hanover	(781)	13,879	14,424
*02341	Hanson	(781)	10,209	10,630
02645	Harwich	(508)	12,243	12,180
*01830	Haverhill	(978)	60,879	62,765
*02043	Hingham	(781)	22,157	23,120
02343	Holbrook	(781)	10,791	11,050
01520	Holden	(508)	17,346	18,645
01746	Holliston	(508)	13,547	14,525
*01040	Holyoke	(413)	39,880	40,684
01748	Hopkinton	(508)	14,925	16,674
01749	Hudson	(978)	19,063	19,864
01749	Hudson (c)	(978)	14,907	—
02045	Hull	(781)	10,293	10,491
01938	Ipswich	(978)	13,175	13,804
02364	Kingston	(781)	12,629	13,301
02347	Lakeville	(508)	10,602	11,338
*01840	Lawrence	(978)	76,377	80,231
01524	Leicester	(508)	10,970	11,334
01453	Leominster	(978)	40,759	41,569
*02420	Lexington	(781)	31,394	33,394
*01028	Longmeadow	(413)	15,784	15,898
*01850	Lowell	(978)	106,519	110,699
01056	Ludlow	(413)	21,103	21,472
*01462	Lunenburg	(978)	10,086	11,241
*01901	Lynn	(781)	90,329	92,457
01940	Lynnfield	(781)	11,596	12,761
02148	Malden	(781)	59,450	61,068
*02048	Mansfield	(508)	23,184	23,687
01945	Marblehead	(781)	19,808	20,517
01752	Marlborough	(508)	38,499	39,818
*02050	Marshfield	(781)	25,132	25,709
02649	Mashpee	(508)	14,006	14,154
01754	Maynard	(978)	10,106	10,676
02052	Medfield	(508)	12,024	12,718
*02155	Medford	(781)	56,173	57,403
02053	Medway	(508)	12,752	13,253
02176	Melrose	(781)	26,983	27,997
01844	Methuen	(978)	47,255	49,660
*02346	Middleborough	(508)	23,116	24,350
01757	Milford	(508)	27,999	28,614
01757	Milford (c)	(508)	25,055	—
*01527	Millbury	(508)	13,261	13,537
02186	Milton	(617)	27,003	27,374
*02584	Nantucket	(508)	10,172	10,925
01760	Natick	(508)	33,006	36,262
*02494	Needham	(781)	28,886	30,564
*02740	New Bedford	(508)	95,072	94,958
01950	Newburyport	(978)	17,416	17,982
*02456	Newton	(617)	85,146	88,817
02056	Norfolk	(508)	11,227	11,908
01247	North Adams	(413)	13,708	13,263
01845	North Andover	(978)	28,352	29,721
*02760	North Attleborough	(508)	28,712	29,071
*01864	North Reading	(978)	14,892	15,626
*01060	Northampton	(413)	28,549	28,540
01532	Northborough	(508)	14,155	15,042
01534	Northbridge	(508)	15,707	16,544
*02766	Norton	(508)	19,031	19,468
02061	Norwell	(781)	10,506	10,984
02062	Norwood	(781)	28,602	29,095
01540	Oxford	(508)	13,709	13,916
01069	Palmer	(413)	12,140	12,191
*01960	Peabody	(978)	51,251	52,504
*02359	Pembroke	(781)	17,837	18,273
01463	Pepperell	(978)	11,497	12,165
*01201	Pittsfield	(413)	44,737	43,303
*02360	Plymouth	(508)	56,468	58,890
*02169	Quincy	(617)	92,271	93,618
02368	Randolph	(781)	32,112	33,699
*02767	Raynham	(508)	13,383	13,797
01867	Reading	(781)	24,747	25,704
02769	Rehoboth	(508)	11,608	12,008
02151	Revere	(781)	51,755	53,422
02370	Rockland	(781)	17,489	17,832
*01970	Salem	(978)	41,340	42,869
*02563	Sandwich	(508)	20,675	20,445
01906	Saugus	(781)	26,628	27,994
*02066	Scituate	(781)	18,133	18,478
02771	Seekonk	(508)	13,722	14,968
02067	Sharon	(781)	17,612	18,173
*01545	Shrewsbury	(508)	35,608	36,805
*02725	Somerset	(508)	18,165	18,288
*02143	Somerville	(617)	75,754	80,318
01075	South Hadley	(413)	17,514	17,743

ZIP	Place	Area code	2010 population	2015 estimate
02664	South Yarmouth (c)	(508)	11,092	—
*01745	Southborough	(508)	9,767	10,038
01550	Southbridge	(508)	16,719	16,865
01562	Spencer	(508)	11,688	11,810
*01103	Springfield	(413)	153,060	154,341
02180	Stoneham	(781)	21,437	22,002
02072	Stoughton	(781)	26,962	28,431
01776	Sudbury	(978)	17,659	18,874
01907	Swampscott	(781)	13,787	14,477
02777	Swansea	(508)	15,865	16,387
*02780	Taunton	(508)	55,874	56,789
01876	Tewksbury	(978)	28,961	30,915
01879	Tyngsborough	(978)	11,292	12,267
01569	Uxbridge	(508)	13,457	13,892
01880	Wakefield	(781)	24,932	26,847
02081	Walpole	(508)	24,070	25,102
*02451	Waltham	(781)	60,632	63,378
02571	Wareham	(508)	21,822	22,408
*02742	Watertown	(617)	31,915	34,319
01778	Wayland	(508)	12,994	13,684
01570	Webster	(508)	16,767	16,893
01570	Webster (c)	(508)	11,412	—
*02457	Wellesley	(781)	27,982	29,000
*01089	West Springfield	(413)	28,391	28,693
*01581	Westborough	(508)	18,272	18,934
*01085	Westfield	(413)	41,094	41,690
01886	Westford	(978)	21,951	23,831
02493	Weston	(781)	11,261	12,057
02790	Westport	(508)	15,532	15,814
02090	Westwood	(781)	14,618	16,055
*02188	Weymouth	(781)	53,743	55,957
02382	Whitman	(781)	14,489	14,849
01095	Wilbraham	(413)	14,219	14,638
01887	Wilmington	(978)	22,325	23,534
01475	Winchendon	(978)	10,300	10,698
01890	Winchester	(781)	21,374	22,417
02152	Winthrop	(617)	17,497	18,164
*01801	Woburn	(781)	38,120	39,555
*01602	Worcester	(508)	181,045	184,815
*02093	Wrentham	(508)	10,955	11,548
*02664	Yarmouth	(508)	23,793	23,467

Michigan
Area code 947 overlays area code 248.

ZIP	Place	Area code	2010 population	2015 estimate
49221	Adrian	(517)	21,133	20,691
48101	Allen Park	(313)	28,210	27,425
49401	Allendale (c)	(616)	17,579	—
49707	Alpena	(989)	10,483	10,175
*48103	Ann Arbor	(734)	113,934	117,070
*48326	Auburn Hills	(248)	21,412	22,672
*49014	Battle Creek	(269)	52,347	51,589
*48708	Bay City	(989)	34,932	33,917
48505	Beecher (c)	(810)	10,232	—
48072	Berkley	(248)	14,970	15,268
48025	Beverly Hills	(248)	10,267	10,424
49307	Big Rapids	(231)	10,601	10,397
*48012	Birmingham	(248)	20,103	20,857
*48509	Burton	(810)	29,999	28,788
49601	Cadillac	(231)	10,355	10,373
*48017	Clawson	(248)	11,825	12,015
49036	Coldwater	(517)	10,945	10,844
49321	Comstock Park (c)	(616)	10,088	—
49508	Cutlerville (c)	(616)	14,370	—
*48120	Dearborn	(313)	98,153	95,171
*48127	Dearborn Heights	(313)	57,774	56,145
*48201	Detroit	(313)	713,777	677,116
*49506	East Grand Rapids	(616)	10,694	11,311
*48823	East Lansing	(517)	48,579	48,471
48021	Eastpointe	(586)	32,442	32,657
49829	Escanaba	(906)	12,616	12,334
*48333	Farmington	(248)	10,372	10,523
*48331	Farmington Hills	(248)	79,740	81,330
48430	Fenton	(810)	11,756	11,442
48220	Ferndale	(248)	19,900	20,177
*48502	Flint	(810)	102,434	98,310
49506	Forest Hills (c)	(616)	25,867	—
48026	Fraser	(586)	14,480	14,636
*48135	Garden City	(734)	27,692	26,920
49417	Grand Haven	(616)	10,412	11,062
*49503	Grand Rapids	(616)	188,040	195,097
*49418	Grandville	(616)	15,378	15,953
48230	Grosse Pointe Park	(313)	11,555	11,220
48230	Grosse Pointe Woods	(313)	16,135	15,762
*48212	Hamtramck	(313)	22,423	22,002
48225	Harper Woods	(313)	14,236	13,836
48840	Haslett (c)	(517)	19,220	—
48030	Hazel Park	(248)	16,422	16,597
48203	Highland Park	(313)	11,776	10,949
*49423	Holland	(616)	33,051	33,742
48842	Holt (c)	(517)	23,973	—

ZIP	Place	Area code	2010 population	2015 estimate
48141	Inkster	(313)/(734)	25,369	24,672
48846	Ionia	(616)	11,394	11,372
*49201	Jackson	(517)	33,534	33,133
*49428	Jenison (c)	(616)	16,538	—
*49001	Kalamazoo	(269)	74,262	76,041
*49508	Kentwood	(616)	48,707	51,357
*48915	Lansing	(517)	114,297	115,056
48146	Lincoln Park	(313)	38,144	37,012
*48150	Livonia	(734)	96,942	94,635
48071	Madison Heights	(248)	29,694	30,198
49855	Marquette	(906)	21,355	21,297
48122	Melvindale	(313)	10,715	10,404
*48640	Midland	(989)	41,863	42,200
*48161	Monroe	(734)	20,733	20,092
*48046	Mount Clemens	(586)	16,314	16,400
*48858	Mount Pleasant	(989)	26,016	26,060
*49440	Muskegon	(231)	38,401	38,401
49444	Muskegon Heights	(231)	10,856	10,796
*48047	New Baltimore	(586)	12,084	12,354
*49120	Niles	(269)	11,600	11,333
49505	Northview (c)	(616)	14,541	—
*49441	Norton Shores	(231)	23,994	24,208
*48374	Novi	(248)	55,224	58,723
48237	Oak Park	(248)	29,319	29,752
*48864	Okemos (c)	(517)	21,369	—
*48867	Owosso	(906)	15,194	14,699
*48340	Pontiac	(248)	59,515	59,917
*48060	Port Huron	(810)	30,184	29,330
*49024	Portage	(269)	46,292	48,177
*48192	Riverview	(734)	12,486	12,181
*48308	Rochester	(248)	12,711	12,993
*48306	Rochester Hills	(248)	70,995	73,424
48174	Romulus	(313)/(734)	23,989	23,417
48066	Roseville	(586)	47,299	47,637
*48067	Royal Oak	(248)	57,236	59,008
*48601	Saginaw	(989)	51,508	49,347
*48080	Saint Clair Shores	(586)	59,715	59,903
*49783	Sault Ste. Marie	(906)	14,144	13,827
48178	South Lyon	(248)	11,327	11,722
*48033	Southfield	(248)	71,739	73,156
48195	Southgate	(734)	30,047	29,293
*48310	Sterling Heights	(586)	129,699	132,052
49091	Sturgis	(269)	10,994	10,896
48180	Taylor	(313)/(734)	63,131	61,568
*49684	Traverse City	(231)	14,674	15,218
48183	Trenton	(734)	18,853	18,380
*48083	Troy	(248)	80,980	83,280
*49534	Walker	(616)	23,537	24,647
*48088	Warren	(586)	134,056	135,358
48917	Waverly (c)	(517)	23,925	—
48184	Wayne	(734)	17,593	17,081
*48185	Westland	(734)	84,094	82,000
48393	Wixom	(248)	13,498	13,746
48183	Woodhaven	(734)	12,875	12,539
*48192	Wyandotte	(734)	25,883	25,156
*49509	Wyoming	(616)	72,125	75,275
*48197	Ypsilanti	(734)	19,435	19,945

Minnesota

ZIP	Place	Area code	2010 population	2015 estimate
56007	Albert Lea	(507)	18,016	17,674
56308	Alexandria	(320)	11,070	11,843
*55304	Andover	(763)	30,598	32,213
*55303	Anoka	(612)	17,142	17,350
55124	Apple Valley	(952)	49,084	51,221
55912	Austin	(507)	24,718	24,563
*56601	Bemidji	(218)	13,431	14,594
55309	Big Lake	(763)	10,060	10,368
*55014	Blaine	(763)	57,186	62,124
*55420	Bloomington	(952)	82,893	86,435
*56401	Brainerd	(218)	13,590	13,371
*55430	Brooklyn Center	(763)	30,104	30,770
*55443	Brooklyn Park	(763)	75,781	79,149
55313	Buffalo	(763)	15,453	16,026
*55337	Burnsville	(952)	60,306	61,481
55316	Champlin	(763)	23,089	23,884
55317	Chanhassen	(952)	22,952	25,332
55318	Chaska	(952)	23,770	25,199
55720	Cloquet	(218)	12,124	12,075
55421	Columbia Heights	(612)	19,496	19,715
*55433	Coon Rapids	(763)	61,476	62,240
55016	Cottage Grove	(651)	34,589	35,918
*55422	Crystal	(763)	22,151	22,943
*55802	Duluth	(218)	86,265	86,110
*55121	Eagan	(651)	64,206	66,286
*55005	East Bethel	(763)	11,626	11,692
*55344	Eden Prairie	(952)	60,797	63,496
*55424	Edina	(952)	47,941	50,138
55330	Elk River	(763)	22,974	23,963
*56031	Fairmont	(507)	10,666	10,221
55021	Faribault	(507)	23,352	23,650
55024	Farmington	(651)	21,086	22,731

ZIP	Place	Area code	2010 population	2015 estimate
*56537	Fergus Falls	(218)	13,138	13,281
55025	Forest Lake	(651)	18,375	19,618
*55432	Fridley	(763)	27,208	27,713
*55427	Golden Valley	(763)	20,371	21,270
*55744	Grand Rapids	(218)	10,869	11,127
*55304	Ham Lake	(763)	15,296	16,062
55033	Hastings	(651)	22,172	22,554
*55746	Hibbing	(218)	16,361	16,204
*55343	Hopkins	(952)	17,591	18,076
55038	Hugo	(651)	13,332	14,388
55350	Hutchinson	(320)	14,178	13,913
*55076	Inver Grove Heights	(651)	33,880	34,857
55044	Lakeville	(952)	55,954	60,633
*55014	Lino Lakes	(651)	20,216	21,050
*55109	Little Canada	(651)	9,773	10,319
*56001	Mankato	(507)	39,309	41,044
*55311	Maple Grove	(763)	61,567	68,385
*55109	Maplewood	(651)	38,018	40,567
56258	Marshall	(507)	13,680	13,652
*55118	Mendota Heights	(651)	11,071	11,223
*55401	Minneapolis	(612)	382,578	410,939
*55345	Minnetonka	(952)	49,734	51,669
*55362	Monticello	(763)	12,759	13,299
*56560	Moorhead	(218)	38,065	42,005
55112	Mounds View	(763)	12,155	12,914
55112	New Brighton	(651)	21,456	22,351
*54427	New Hope	(763)	20,339	21,032
56073	New Ulm	(507)	13,522	13,327
55056	North Branch	(651)	10,125	10,215
*56002	North Mankato	(507)	13,394	13,529
55109	North St. Paul	(651)	11,460	12,322
55057	Northfield	(507)	20,007	20,380
*55128	Oakdale	(651)	27,378	28,080
*55330	Otsego	(763)	13,571	15,551
55060	Owatonna	(507)	25,599	25,725
*55446	Plymouth	(763)	70,576	75,907
*55372	Prior Lake	(952)	22,796	25,282
*55303	Ramsey	(763)	23,668	25,828
55066	Red Wing	(651)	16,459	16,445
55423	Richfield	(612)	35,228	36,216
55422	Robbinsdale	(763)	13,953	14,418
*55901	Rochester	(507)	106,769	112,225
55374	Rogers	(763)	8,597	12,562
55068	Rosemount	(651)	21,874	23,413
*55113	Roseville	(651)	33,660	35,580
*56301	Saint Cloud	(320)	65,842	67,109
*55416	Saint Louis Park	(952)	45,250	48,171
55376	Saint Michael	(763)	16,399	17,196
*55101	Saint Paul	(651)	285,068	300,851
56082	Saint Peter	(507)	11,196	11,666
56377	Sartell	(320)	15,876	16,788
56379	Sauk Rapids	(320)	12,773	13,424
55378	Savage	(952)	26,911	30,391
*55379	Shakopee	(952)	37,076	39,981
55126	Shoreview	(651)	25,043	26,477
*55075	South St. Paul	(651)	20,160	20,405
*55082	Stillwater	(651)	18,225	18,924
*55127	Vadnais Heights	(651)	12,302	13,266
*55387	Waconia	(952)	10,697	11,968
*55118	West St. Paul	(651)	19,540	19,727
*55110	White Bear Lake	(651)	23,797	25,205
56201	Willmar	(320)	19,610	19,638
55987	Winona	(507)	27,592	27,094
*55125	Woodbury	(651)	61,961	67,855
56187	Worthington	(507)	12,764	13,090

Mississippi

Area code 769 overlays area code 601.

ZIP	Place	Area code	2010 population	2015 estimate
39520	Bay St. Louis	(228)	9,260	12,030
*39530	Biloxi	(228)	44,054	45,637
39042	Brandon	(601)	21,705	23,529
*39601	Brookhaven	(601)	12,513	12,414
39272	Byram	(601)	11,489	11,509
39046	Canton	(601)	13,189	13,676
*38614	Clarksdale	(662)	17,962	16,847
*38732	Cleveland	(662)	12,334	12,327
*39056	Clinton	(601)	25,216	25,254
*39701	Columbus	(662)	23,640	23,168
*38834	Corinth	(662)	14,573	14,866
39540	D'Iberville	(228)	9,486	11,400
39553	Gautier	(228)	18,572	18,570
*38701	Greenville	(662)	34,400	32,054
*38930	Greenwood	(662)	15,205	15,431
*38901	Grenada	(662)	13,092	12,900
*39501	Gulfport	(228)	67,793	71,856
*39401	Hattiesburg	(601)	45,989	46,805
38632	Hernando	(662)	14,090	15,503
38637	Horn Lake	(662)	26,066	26,915
*39201	Jackson	(601)	173,514	170,674
*39440	Laurel	(601)	18,540	18,837
39560	Long Beach	(228)	14,792	15,555

ZIP	Place	Area code	2010 population	2015 estimate
*39110	Madison	(601)	24,149	25,799
*39648	McComb	(601)	12,790	12,661
*39301	Meridian	(601)	41,148	39,661
*39563	Moss Point	(228)	13,704	13,654
*39120	Natchez	(601)	15,792	15,128
*39564	Ocean Springs	(228)	17,442	17,636
38654	Olive Branch	(662)	33,484	36,010
*38655	Oxford	(662)	18,916	22,314
*39567	Pascagoula	(228)	22,392	22,126
*39208	Pearl	(601)	25,092	26,462
39465	Petal	(601)	10,454	10,701
39466	Picayune	(601)	10,878	10,675
*39157	Ridgeland	(601)	24,047	24,351
*38671	Southaven	(662)	48,982	52,589
*39759	Starkville	(662)	23,888	25,366
*38801	Tupelo	(662)	34,546	35,680
*39180	Vicksburg	(601)	23,856	23,131
39773	West Point	(662)	11,307	10,990
39194	Yazoo City	(662)	11,403	11,245

Missouri

ZIP	Place	Area code	2010 population	2015 estimate
63123	Affton (c)	(314)	20,307	—
63010	Arnold	(636)	20,808	21,357
*63011	Ballwin	(636)	30,404	30,577
63137	Bellefontaine Neighbors	(314)	10,860	10,798
64012	Belton	(816)	23,116	23,168
*64015	Blue Springs	(816)	52,575	54,148
*65613	Bolivar	(417)	10,325	10,714
*65616	Branson	(417)	10,520	11,431
63044	Bridgeton	(314)	11,550	11,786
*63701	Cape Girardeau	(573)	37,941	39,462
64836	Carthage	(417)	14,378	14,319
*63017	Chesterfield	(636)	47,484	47,864
*63105	Clayton	(314)	15,939	15,884
*65201	Columbia	(573)	108,500	119,108
*63128	Concord (c)	(314)	16,421	—
63126	Crestwood	(314)	11,912	11,966
63141	Creve Coeur	(314)	17,833	18,276
*63366	Dardenne Prairie	(636)	11,494	12,890
63025	Eureka	(636)	10,189	10,602
64024	Excelsior Springs	(816)	11,084	11,486
63640	Farmington	(573)	16,240	18,181
63135	Ferguson	(314)	21,203	21,059
63028	Festus	(636)	11,602	12,065
*63031	Florissant	(314)	52,158	52,268
65473	Fort Leonard Wood (c)	(573)	15,061	—
65251	Fulton	(573)	12,790	12,939
*64118	Gladstone	(816)	25,410	26,861
64029	Grain Valley	(816)	12,854	13,379
64030	Grandview	(816)	24,475	25,256
63401	Hannibal	(573)	17,916	17,839
*63042	Hazelwood	(314)	25,703	25,661
*64050	Independence	(816)	116,830	117,255
63755	Jackson	(573)	13,758	14,869
*65101	Jefferson City	(573)	43,079	43,169
63136	Jennings	(314)	14,712	14,819
*64801	Joplin	(417)	50,150	51,818
*64106	Kansas City	(816)	459,787	475,295
63857	Kennett	(573)	10,932	10,662
63501	Kirksville	(660)	17,505	17,520
63122	Kirkwood	(314)	27,540	27,750
*63367	Lake St. Louis	(636)	14,545	15,375
65536	Lebanon	(417)	14,474	14,688
*64063	Lee's Summit	(816)	91,364	95,094
63125	Lemay (c)	(314)	16,645	—
*64068	Liberty	(816)	29,149	30,450
*63011	Manchester	(636)	18,094	18,229
65340	Marshall	(660)	13,065	13,039
63043	Maryland Heights	(314)	27,472	27,389
64468	Maryville	(660)	11,972	11,879
63129	Mehlville (c)	(314)	28,380	—
65265	Mexico	(573)	11,543	11,660
65270	Moberly	(660)	13,974	13,919
*64850	Neosho	(417)	11,835	12,156
65714	Nixa	(417)	19,022	20,984
63129	Oakville (c)	(314)	36,143	—
*63366	O'Fallon	(636)	79,329	85,040
63034	Old Jamestown (c)	(314)	19,184	—
63114	Overland	(314)	16,062	15,959
65721	Ozark	(417)	17,820	19,120
*63901	Poplar Bluff	(573)	17,023	17,266
64083	Raymore	(816)	19,206	20,374
*64133	Raytown	(816)	29,526	29,401
65738	Republic	(417)	14,751	16,005
*65401	Rolla	(573)	19,559	20,019
63074	Saint Ann	(314)	13,020	12,940
*63301	Saint Charles	(636)	65,794	68,796
*64501	Saint Joseph	(816)	76,780	76,596
*63101	Saint Louis	(314)	319,294	315,685
*63376	Saint Peters	(636)	52,575	56,971
*65301	Sedalia	(660)	21,387	21,516
63801	Sikeston	(573)	16,318	16,436

ZIP	Place	Area code	2010 population	2015 estimate
63138	Spanish Lake (c).	(314)	19,650	—
*65802	Springfield.	(417)	159,498	166,810
63017	Town and Country.	(314)	10,815	11,106
63379	Troy.	(314)	10,540	11,542
63084	Union	(636)	10,204	10,957
63130	University City.	(314)	35,371	35,058
64093	Warrensburg.	(660)	18,838	19,927
63090	Washington.	(636)	13,982	14,050
64870	Webb City.	(417)	10,996	11,165
63119	Webster Groves	(314)	22,995	23,177
63385	Wentzville.	(636)	29,070	35,603
*65775	West Plains.	(417)	11,986	12,285
*63040	Wildwood	(636)	35,517	35,899

Montana
Area code 406 applies to the entire state.

ZIP	Place	2010 population	2015 estimate
*59101	Billings	104,170	110,263
*59715	Bozeman	37,280	43,405
*59701	Butte-Silver Bow (balance)	33,525	33,922
*59401	Great Falls	58,505	59,638
*59601	Helena	28,190	30,581
*59901	Kalispell	19,927	22,052
*59801	Missoula	66,788	71,022

Nebraska
Area code 531 overlays area code 402.

ZIP	Place	Area code	2010 population	2015 estimate
68310	Beatrice	(402)	12,459	12,388
*68005	Bellevue	(402)	50,137	55,510
68138	Chalco (c)	(402)	10,994	—
*68601	Columbus	(402)	22,111	22,797
*68025	Fremont	(402)	26,397	26,474
*68801	Grand Island	(308)	48,520	51,440
*68901	Hastings	(402)	24,907	24,924
*68847	Kearney	(308)	30,787	33,021
*68128	La Vista	(402)	15,758	16,921
68850	Lexington	(308)	10,230	10,075
*68502	Lincoln	(402)	258,379	277,348
*68701	Norfolk	(402)	24,210	24,366
*69101	North Platte	(308)	24,733	24,194
*68104	Omaha	(402)	408,958	443,885
*68046	Papillion	(402)	18,894	19,510
*69361	Scottsbluff	(308)	15,039	14,802
68776	South Sioux City	(402)	13,353	13,319

Nevada
Area code 725 overlays area code 702.

ZIP	Place	Area code	2010 population	2015 estimate
*89005	Boulder City	(702)	15,023	15,551
*89701	Carson City	(775)	55,274	54,521
*89801	Elko	(775)	18,297	20,279
89124	Enterprise (c)	(702)	108,481	—
89408	Fernley	(775)	19,368	19,418
*89410	Gardnerville Ranchos (c)	(775)	11,312	—
*89015	Henderson	(702)	257,729	285,667
*89101	Las Vegas	(702)	583,756	623,747
*89027	Mesquite	(702)	15,276	17,496
*89030	North Las Vegas	(702)	216,961	234,807
*89048	Pahrump (c)	(775)	36,441	—
*89121	Paradise (c)	(702)	223,167	—
*89501	Reno	(775)	225,221	241,445
*89441	Spanish Springs (c)	(775)	15,064	—
*89431	Sparks	(775)	90,264	96,094
89815	Spring Creek (c)	(702)	12,361	—
89147	Spring Valley (c)	(702)	178,395	—
89135	Summerlin South (c).	(702)	24,085	—
*89433	Sun Valley (c)	(775)	189,372	—
89110	Sunrise Manor (c).	(702)	19,299	—
89122	Whitney (c)	(702)	38,585	—
*89121	Winchester (c).	(702)	27,978	—

New Hampshire
Area code 603 applies to the entire state. See introductory note.

ZIP	Place	2010 population	2015 estimate
03031	Amherst	11,201	11,261
03110	Bedford	21,203	22,204
03743	Claremont.	13,355	12,984
*03301	Concord	42,695	42,620
03038	Derry	33,109	33,199
03038	Derry (c).	22,015	—
*03820	Dover	29,987	30,880
03824	Durham.	14,638	16,645
03824	Durham (c).	10,345	—
03833	Exeter	14,306	14,567
03045	Goffstown.	17,651	17,945
*03842	Hampton.	15,430	15,281
03755	Hanover	11,260	11,401
03106	Hooksett.	13,451	14,098
03051	Hudson.	24,467	24,911
*03431	Keene.	23,409	23,265
*03246	Laconia.	15,951	16,227
*03766	Lebanon	13,151	13,579
03053	Londonderry.	24,129	25,196
03053	Londonderry (c)	11,037	—
*03101	Manchester.	109,565	110,229
03054	Merrimack	25,494	25,648
03055	Milford	15,115	15,284
*03060	Nashua.	86,494	87,970
03076	Pelham.	12,897	13,303
*03801	Portsmouth	20,779	21,530
03077	Raymond	10,138	10,285
*03867	Rochester.	29,752	30,038
03079	Salem.	28,776	28,898
03878	Somersworth	11,766	11,759
03087	Windham	13,592	14,439

New Jersey
Area code 551 overlays area code 201. Area code 848 overlays 732. Area code 862 overlays 973.

ZIP	Place	Area code	2010 population	2015 estimate
07712	Asbury Park	(732)	16,116	15,818
*08401	Atlantic City	(609)	39,558	39,260
07001	Avenel (c)	(732)	17,011	—
07002	Bayonne	(201)	63,024	66,311
08722	Beachwood.	(732)	11,045	11,214
*08031	Bellmawr.	(856)	11,583	11,462
07621	Bergenfield	(201)	26,764	27,621
08805	Bound Brook.	(732)	10,402	10,497
08807	Bradley Gardens (c)	(908)	14,206	—
08302	Bridgeton	(856)	25,349	25,031
08015	Browns Mills (c)	(609)	11,223	—
*08102	Camden	(856)	77,344	76,119
07008	Carteret.	(732)	22,844	24,170
08002	Cherry Hill Mall (c)	(856)	14,171	—
07010	Cliffside Park.	(201)	23,594	24,857
*07013	Clifton.	(973)	84,136	86,334
*08108	Collingswood	(856)	13,926	14,000
07067	Colonia (c)	(732)	17,795	—
*07801	Dover	(973)	18,157	18,346
07628	Dumont.	(201)	17,479	18,001
*07018	East Orange	(973)	64,270	64,949
*07724	Eatontown.	(732)	12,709	12,301
08043	Echelon (c)	(856)	10,743	—
07020	Edgewater.	(201)	11,513	12,034
*07201	Elizabeth.	(908)	124,969	129,007
07407	Elmwood Park	(201)	19,403	20,279
*07631	Englewood	(201)	27,147	28,539
07410	Fair Lawn	(201)	32,457	33,597
07022	Fairview	(201)	13,835	14,451
07932	Florham Park	(973)	11,696	11,835
08863	Fords (c)	(732)	15,187	—
07024	Fort Lee	(201)	35,345	36,672
07417	Franklin Lakes	(201)	10,590	10,899
08823	Franklin Park (c)	(732)	13,295	—
07728	Freehold	(732)	12,052	11,959
07026	Garfield.	(973)	30,487	31,802
08028	Glassboro	(856)	18,579	19,216
07452	Glen Rock	(201)	11,601	11,999
08030	Gloucester City.	(856)	11,456	11,329
*08053	Greentree (c)	(856)	11,367	—
07093	Guttenberg	(201)	11,176	11,665
*07601	Hackensack	(201)	43,010	44,834
08033	Haddonfield	(856)	11,593	11,414
08690	Hamilton Square (c)	(609)	12,784	—
08037	Hammonton	(609)	14,791	14,618
07029	Harrison	(973)	13,620	15,474
07604	Hasbrouck Heights	(201)	11,842	12,227
*07506	Hawthorne	(973)	18,791	19,074
08904	Highland Park.	(732)	13,982	14,347
07642	Hillsdale	(201)	10,219	10,559
07030	Hoboken.	(201)	50,005	53,635
*08753	Holiday City-Berkeley (c)	(732)	12,831	—
07843	Hopatcong	(973)	15,147	14,510
08830	Iselin (c)	(732)	18,695	—
*07302	Jersey City	(201)	247,597	264,290
*07032	Kearny	(201)/(973)	40,684	42,137
07405	Kinnelon	(973)	10,248	10,392
08701	Lakewood (c)	(732)	53,805	—
07035	Lincoln Park	(973)	10,521	10,405
07036	Linden.	(732)/(908)	40,499	42,021
08021	Lindenwold	(856)	17,613	17,458
07643	Little Ferry	(201)	10,626	10,963
07644	Lodi.	(201)/(973)	24,136	24,835
07740	Long Branch	(732)	30,719	30,941
07940	Madison	(973)	15,845	16,126
08835	Manville	(908)	10,344	10,429

ZIP	Place	Area code	2010 population	2015 estimate
08053	Marlton (c)	(856)	10,133	—
08836	Martinsville (c)	(908)	11,980	—
08619	Mercerville (c)	(609)	13,230	—
08840	Metuchen	(732)	13,574	13,886
08846	Middlesex	(732)	13,635	13,934
08332	Millville	(856)	28,400	28,230
08057	Moorestown-Lenola (c)	(856)	14,217	—
*07960	Morristown	(973)	18,411	18,594
*08901	New Brunswick	(732)	55,181	57,035
07646	New Milford	(201)	16,341	16,801
07974	New Providence	(908)	12,171	12,469
*07102	Newark	(973)	277,140	281,944
07031	North Arlington	(201)	15,392	15,904
*07060	North Plainfield	(908)	21,936	22,140
07436	Oakland	(201)	12,754	13,165
*08050	Ocean Acres (c)	(609)	16,142	—
08226	Ocean City	(609)	11,701	11,355
08857	Old Bridge (c)	(732)	23,753	—
07650	Palisades Park	(201)	19,622	20,743
*07652	Paramus	(201)	26,342	26,974
07055	Passaic	(973)	69,781	71,085
*07505	Paterson	(973)	146,199	147,754
08070	Pennsville (c)	(856)	11,888	—
*08861	Perth Amboy	(732)	50,814	52,682
08865	Phillipsburg	(908)	14,950	14,515
08021	Pine Hill	(856)	10,233	10,510
*07060	Plainfield	(908)	49,808	51,217
*08232	Pleasantville	(609)	20,249	20,755
08742	Point Pleasant	(732)	18,392	18,523
07442	Pompton Lakes	(973)	11,097	11,202
*08540	Princeton	(609)	12,307	29,603
08536	Princeton Meadows (c)	(609)	13,834	—
07065	Rahway	(732)	27,346	29,508
07446	Ramsey	(201)	14,473	15,102
*07701	Red Bank	(732)	12,206	12,204
07657	Ridgefield	(201)	11,032	11,373
07660	Ridgefield Park	(201)	12,729	13,102
*07451	Ridgewood	(201)/(973)	24,958	25,621
07456	Ringwood	(973)	12,228	12,448
07661	River Edge	(201)	11,340	11,668
07751	Robertsville (c)	(732)	11,297	—
07203	Roselle	(908)	21,085	21,670
07204	Roselle Park	(908)	13,297	13,670
07070	Rutherford	(201)	18,061	18,690
*08872	Sayreville	(732)	42,704	44,920
*07094	Secaucus	(201)	16,264	19,104
07078	Short Hills (c)	(973)	13,165	—
08244	Somers Point	(609)	10,795	10,688
*08873	Somerset (c)	(732)	22,083	—
08876	Somerville	(908)	12,098	12,200
07080	South Plainfield	(732)/(908)	23,385	24,290
*08882	South River	(732)	16,008	16,399
08003	Springdale (c)	(856)	14,518	—
*07901	Summit	(908)	21,457	22,074
07670	Tenafly	(201)	14,488	14,880
*07724	Tinton Falls	(732)	17,892	17,772
*08753	Toms River (c)	(732)	88,791	—
*07512	Totowa	(973)	10,804	10,973
*08608	Trenton	(609)	84,913	84,225
07087	Union City	(201)	66,455	69,156
07043	Upper Montclair (c)	(973)	11,565	—
08406	Ventnor City	(609)	10,650	10,486
*08360	Vineland	(856)	60,724	60,818
07463	Waldwick	(201)	9,625	10,095
07057	Wallington	(201)/(973)	11,335	11,716
07465	Wanaque	(201)/(973)	11,116	11,848
07728	West Freehold (c)	(908)	13,613	—
07093	West New York	(201)	49,708	53,366
*07090	Westfield	(908)	30,316	30,548
*07675	Westwood	(201)	10,908	11,247
08094	Williamstown (c)	(609)/(856)	15,567	—
07095	Woodbridge (c)	(732)/(908)	19,265	—
*08096	Woodbury	(856)	10,174	10,020
07424	Woodland Park	(973)	11,819	12,518

New Mexico

ZIP	Place	Area code	2010 population	2015 estimate
*88310	Alamogordo	(575)	30,403	30,753
*87101	Albuquerque	(505)	545,852	559,121
*88210	Artesia	(575)	11,301	12,036
*88220	Carlsbad	(575)	26,138	28,957
*88021	Chaparral (c)	(505)	14,631	—
*88101	Clovis	(575)	37,775	39,480
*88030	Deming	(575)	14,855	14,522
*87532	Española	(505)	10,224	10,066
*87401	Farmington	(505)	45,877	42,871
*87301	Gallup	(505)	21,678	23,240
*88240	Hobbs	(575)	34,122	38,416
*88001	Las Cruces	(575)	97,618	101,643
*87701	Las Vegas	(505)	13,753	13,386
*87544	Los Alamos (c)	(505)	12,019	—
87031	Los Lunas	(505)	14,835	15,336
*88260	Lovington	(575)	11,009	11,800
87107	North Valley (c)	(505)	11,333	—
*88130	Portales	(575)	12,280	11,995
*87124	Rio Rancho	(505)	87,521	94,171
*88201	Roswell	(575)	48,366	48,544
*87501	Santa Fe	(505)	67,947	84,099
*88061	Silver City	(575)	10,315	10,004
87105	South Valley (c)	(505)	40,976	—
*88063	Sunland Park	(575)	14,106	15,940

New York

Area codes 347/929 overlay area code 718. Area codes 332 (effective June 10, 2017)/ 646/917 overlay 212. Area code 680 overlays 315 effective Mar. 11, 2017. Area code 934 overlays 631.

ZIP	Place	Area code	2010 population	2015 estimate
*12202	Albany	(518)	97,856	98,469
12010	Amsterdam	(518)	18,620	18,008
*13021	Auburn	(315)	27,687	26,985
*11702	Babylon	(631)	12,166	12,161
11510	Baldwin (c)	(516)	24,033	—
*14020	Batavia	(585)	15,465	15,010
11706	Bay Shore (c)	(631)	26,337	—
12508	Beacon	(845)	15,541	14,347
11710	Bellmore (c)	(516)	16,218	—
11714	Bethpage (c)	(516)	16,429	—
*13901	Binghamton	(607)	47,376	46,032
11716	Bohemia (c)	(631)	10,180	—
11717	Brentwood (c)	(631)	60,664	—
*14610	Brighton (c)	(585)	36,609	—
*14201	Buffalo	(716)	261,310	258,071
*14424	Canandaigua	(585)	10,545	10,431
11720	Centereach (c)	(631)	31,578	—
*11722	Central Islip (c)	(631)	34,450	—
*14227	Cheektowaga (c)	(716)	75,178	—
12047	Cohoes	(518)	16,168	16,538
11725	Commack (c)	(631)	36,124	—
11726	Copiague (c)	(631)	22,993	—
11727	Coram (c)	(631)	39,113	—
*14830	Corning	(607)	11,183	10,897
13045	Cortland	(607)	19,204	18,907
11729	Deer Park (c)	(631)	27,745	—
14043	Depew	(716)	15,303	15,146
*11746	Dix Hills (c)	(631)	26,892	—
10522	Dobbs Ferry	(914)	10,875	11,131
*14048	Dunkirk	(716)	12,563	12,081
11730	East Islip (c)	(631)	14,475	—
11758	East Massapequa (c)	(516)	19,069	—
11554	East Meadow (c)	(516)	38,132	—
11731	East Northport (c)	(631)	20,217	—
11772	East Patchogue (c)	(631)	22,469	—
10709	Eastchester (c)	(914)	19,554	—
14226	Eggertsville (c)	(716)	15,019	—
*14901	Elmira	(607)	29,200	28,213
11003	Elmont (c)	(516)	33,198	—
11731	Elwood (c)	(631)	11,177	—
*13760	Endicott	(607)	13,392	13,014
13762	Endwell (c)	(607)	11,446	—
13219	Fairmount (c)	(315)	10,224	—
11738	Farmingville (c)	(631)	15,481	—
*11001	Floral Park	(516)	15,863	15,969
*13602	Fort Drum (c)	(315)	12,955	—
11768	Fort Salonga (c)	(631)	10,008	—
11010	Franklin Square (c)	(516)	29,320	—
14063	Fredonia	(716)	11,230	10,705
11520	Freeport	(516)	42,860	43,334
13069	Fulton	(315)	11,896	11,552
*11530	Garden City	(516)	22,371	22,612
14456	Geneva	(315)	13,261	13,062
11542	Glen Cove	(516)	26,964	27,400
12801	Glens Falls	(518)	14,700	14,291
12078	Gloversville	(518)	15,665	15,023
*11023	Great Neck	(516)	9,989	10,143
14616	Greece (c)	(585)	14,519	—
11740	Greenlawn (c)	(631)	13,742	—
11946	Hampton Bays (c)	(631)	13,603	—
10528	Harrison	(914)	27,472	28,348
*11788	Hauppauge (c)	(631)	20,882	—
10927	Haverstraw	(845)	11,910	12,187
*11550	Hempstead	(516)	53,891	55,547
*11801	Hicksville (c)	(516)	41,547	—
11741	Holbrook (c)	(631)	27,195	—
11742	Holtsville (c)	(631)	19,714	—
11743	Huntington (c)	(631)	18,046	—
*11746	Huntington Station (c)	(631)	33,029	—
*14617	Irondequoit (c)	(585)	51,692	—
11751	Islip (c)	(631)	18,689	—
*14850	Ithaca	(607)	30,014	30,788
*14701	Jamestown	(716)	31,146	30,075
*10535	Jefferson Valley-Yorktown (c)	(914)	14,142	—
11753	Jericho (c)	(516)	13,567	—
13790	Johnson City	(607)	15,174	14,773
*14217	Kenmore	(716)	15,423	15,160

ZIP	Place	Area code	2010 population	2015 estimate
11754	Kings Park (c)	(631)	17,282	—
*12401	Kingston	(845)	23,893	23,436
10950	Kiryas Joel	(845)	20,175	22,851
14218	Lackawanna	(716)	18,141	17,965
11755	Lake Grove	(631)	11,163	11,235
11779	Lake Ronkonkoma (c)	(631)	20,155	—
*14086	Lancaster	(716)	10,352	10,258
11756	Levittown (c)	(516)	51,881	—
11757	Lindenhurst	(631)	27,253	27,277
*14094	Lockport	(716)	21,165	20,624
11561	Long Beach	(516)	33,275	33,550
11563	Lynbrook	(516)	19,427	19,558
10543	Mamaroneck	(914)	18,929	19,375
11949	Manorville (c)	(631)	14,314	—
11758	Massapequa (c)	(516)	21,685	—
11762	Massapequa Park	(516)	17,008	17,232
13662	Massena	(315)	10,936	10,629
11950	Mastic (c)	(631)	15,481	—
11951	Mastic Beach[1]	(631)	12,930	14,841
11763	Medford (c)	(631)	24,142	—
11747	Melville (c)	(631)	18,985	—
11566	Merrick (c)	(516)	22,097	—
11953	Middle Island (c)	(631)	10,483	—
*10940	Middletown	(845)	28,086	27,812
11764	Miller Place (c)	(631)	12,339	—
11501	Mineola	(516)	18,799	19,139
10952	Monsey (c)	(845)	18,412	—
10549	Mount Kisco	(914)	10,877	11,145
11766	Mount Sinai (c)	(631)	12,118	—
*10550	Mount Vernon	(914)	67,292	68,628
10954	Nanuet (c)	(845)	17,882	—
11767	Nesconset (c)	(631)	13,387	—
11590	New Cassel (c)	(516)	14,059	—
10956	New City (c)	(845)	33,559	—
*10801	New Rochelle	(914)	77,062	79,846
*10001	New York	(212)/(718)	8,175,133	8,550,405
*12550	Newburgh	(845)	28,866	28,290
*14301	Niagara Falls	(716)	50,193	48,916
11701	North Amityville (c)	(631)	17,862	—
11703	North Babylon (c)	(631)	17,509	—
11706	North Bay Shore (c)	(631)	18,944	—
11710	North Bellmore (c)	(516)	19,941	—
11713	North Bellport (c)	(631)	11,545	—
11757	North Lindenhurst (c)	(631)	11,652	—
11758	North Massapequa (c)	(516)	17,886	—
11566	North Merrick (c)	(516)	12,272	—
11040	North New Hyde Park (c)	(516)	14,899	—
14120	North Tonawanda	(716)	31,568	30,785
11580	North Valley Stream (c)	(516)	16,628	—
11793	North Wantagh (c)	(516)	11,960	—
11572	Oceanside (c)	(516)	32,109	—
13669	Ogdensburg	(315)	11,128	10,883
14760	Olean	(585)/(716)	14,452	13,870
13421	Oneida	(315)	11,393	11,134
13820	Oneonta	(607)	13,901	13,862
10562	Ossining	(914)	25,060	25,441
13126	Oswego	(315)	18,142	17,787
11772	Patchogue	(631)	11,798	12,463
10965	Pearl River (c)	(845)	15,876	—
10566	Peekskill	(914)	23,583	24,043
11803	Plainview (c)	(516)	26,217	—
*12901	Plattsburgh	(518)	19,989	19,806
*10573	Port Chester	(914)	28,967	29,620
*11050	Port Washington (c)	(516)	15,846	—
12601	Poughkeepsie	(845)	32,736	30,371
11961	Ridge (c)	(631)	13,336	—
11901	Riverhead (c)	(631)	13,299	—
*14604	Rochester	(585)	210,565	209,802
*11570	Rockville Centre	(516)	24,023	24,201
11778	Rocky Point (c)	(631)	14,014	—
*13440	Rome	(315)	33,725	32,573
*11779	Ronkonkoma (c)	(631)	19,082	—
11575	Roosevelt (c)	(516)	16,258	—
12306	Rotterdam (c)	(518)	20,652	—
10580	Rye	(914)	15,720	16,046
11780	Saint James (c)	(631)	13,338	—
13454	Salisbury	(315)	12,093	—
12866	Saratoga Springs	(518)	26,586	27,765
11782	Sayville (c)	(631)	16,853	—
*10583	Scarsdale	(914)	17,166	17,885
*12305	Schenectady	(518)	66,135	65,305
11783	Seaford (c)	(516)	15,294	—
11784	Selden (c)	(631)	19,851	—
11733	Setauket-East Setauket (c)	(631)	15,477	—
11967	Shirley (c)	(631)	27,854	—
10591	Sleepy Hollow	(914)	9,870	10,242
*11787	Smithtown (c)	(631)	26,470	—
11735	South Farmingdale (c)	(516)	14,486	—
10977	Spring Valley	(845)	31,347	32,598
*11790	Stony Brook (c)	(631)	13,740	—
10980	Stony Point (c)	(845)	12,147	—
10901	Suffern	(845)	10,723	11,001
*11791	Syosset (c)	(516)	18,829	—
*13202	Syracuse	(315)	145,170	144,142
10591	Tarrytown	(914)	11,277	11,560

ZIP	Place	Area code	2010 population	2015 estimate
11776	Terryville (c)	(631)	11,849	—
*14150	Tonawanda	(716)	15,130	14,907
*14150	Tonawanda (c)	(716)	58,144	—
*12180	Troy	(518)	50,129	49,906
11553	Uniondale (c)	(516)	24,759	—
*13501	Utica	(315)	62,235	61,100
*11580	Valley Stream	(516)	37,511	37,962
11793	Wantagh (c)	(516)	18,871	—
*13601	Watertown	(315)	27,023	26,780
12189	Watervliet	(518)	10,254	10,214
*11704	West Babylon (c)	(631)	43,213	—
10993	West Haverstraw	(845)	10,165	10,421
11552	West Hempstead (c)	(516)	18,862	—
11795	West Islip (c)	(631)	28,335	—
*14224	West Seneca (c)	(716)	44,711	—
*11590	Westbury	(516)	15,146	15,379
*10601	White Plains	(914)	56,853	58,459
11797	Woodbury (c)	(516)	10,686	10,879
11598	Woodmere (c)	(516)	17,121	—
11798	Wyandanch (c)	(631)	11,647	—
*10701	Yonkers	(914)	195,976	201,116

(1) Place was incorporated after the 2010 Census was conducted. Data in 2010 column is for Mastic Beach CDP.

North Carolina

Area code 743 overlays area code 336. Area code 980 overlays 704. Area code 984 overlays 919.

ZIP	Place	Area code	2010 population	2015 estimate
*28001	Albemarle	(704)	15,903	16,003
*27502	Apex	(919)	37,476	45,585
27263	Archdale	(336)	11,415	11,564
*27203	Asheboro	(336)	25,012	26,103
*28801	Asheville	(828)	83,393	88,512
28012	Belmont	(704)	10,076	10,533
*28607	Boone	(828)	17,122	18,156
*27215	Burlington	(336)	49,963	52,472
27510	Carrboro	(919)	19,582	21,156
*27511	Cary	(919)	135,234	159,769
*27514	Chapel Hill	(919)	57,233	59,568
*28204	Charlotte	(704)	731,424	827,097
*27520	Clayton	(919)	16,116	19,304
27012	Clemmons	(336)	18,627	19,844
*28025	Concord	(704)	79,066	87,696
28031	Cornelius	(704)	24,866	28,092
*28036	Davidson	(704)	10,944	12,207
*27701	Durham	(919)	228,330	257,636
*27288	Eden	(336)	15,527	15,403
*27909	Elizabeth City	(252)	18,683	17,988
27244	Elon	(336)	9,419	10,024
*28301	Fayetteville	(910)	200,564	201,963
27526	Fuquay-Varina	(919)	17,937	23,907
27529	Garner	(919)	25,745	28,053
*28052	Gastonia	(704)	71,741	74,543
*27530	Goldsboro	(919)	36,437	35,826
27253	Graham	(336)	14,153	14,647
*27401	Greensboro	(336)	269,666	285,342
*27834	Greenville	(252)	84,554	90,597
28075	Harrisburg	(704)	11,526	14,539
*28532	Havelock	(252)	20,735	20,364
*27536	Henderson	(252)	15,368	15,271
*28739	Hendersonville	(828)	13,137	13,814
*28601	Hickory	(828)	40,010	40,374
*27260	High Point	(336)	104,371	110,268
27540	Holly Springs	(919)	24,661	31,377
28348	Hope Mills	(910)	15,176	16,163
*28078	Huntersville	(704)	46,773	52,704
28079	Indian Trail	(704)	33,518	37,073
*28540	Jacksonville	(910)	70,145	67,357
*28081	Kannapolis	(704)	42,625	46,144
*27284	Kernersville	(336)	23,123	23,811
28086	Kings Mountain	(704)	10,296	10,760
*28501	Kinston	(252)	21,677	21,337
*27545	Knightdale	(919)	11,401	14,256
*28352	Laurinburg	(910)	15,962	15,507
28451	Leland	(910)	13,527	17,924
*28645	Lenoir	(828)	18,228	17,888
27023	Lewisville	(336)	12,639	13,567
*27292	Lexington	(336)	18,931	19,326
*28092	Lincolnton	(704)	10,486	10,900
*28358	Lumberton	(910)	21,542	21,667
*28105	Matthews	(704)	27,198	30,678
27302	Mebane	(919)	11,393	13,698
28227	Mint Hill	(704)	22,722	25,627
*28110	Monroe	(704)	32,797	34,623
*28115	Mooresville	(704)	32,711	36,009
*28655	Morganton	(828)	16,918	16,692
27560	Morrisville	(919)	18,576	23,820
*27030	Mount Airy	(336)	10,388	10,354
28120	Mount Holly	(704)	13,656	14,176
28411	Murraysville (c)	(910)	14,215	—
*28560	New Bern	(252)	29,524	30,070
28658	Newton	(828)	12,968	13,035
*28374	Pinehurst	(910)	13,124	15,752

ZIP	Place	Area code	2010 population	2015 estimate
28399	Piney Green (c)	(910)	13,293	—
*27601	Raleigh	(919)	403,892	451,066
*27320	Reidsville	(336)	14,520	14,067
27870	Roanoke Rapids	(252)	15,754	15,345
*27801	Rocky Mount	(252)	57,477	55,806
*28144	Salisbury	(704)	33,662	34,017
*27330	Sanford	(919)	28,094	29,144
*28150	Shelby	(704)	20,323	20,189
27577	Smithfield	(919)	10,966	12,022
*28387	Southern Pines	(910)	12,334	13,539
*28390	Spring Lake	(910)	11,964	13,234
28104	Stallings	(704)	13,831	15,270
*28677	Statesville	(704)	24,532	26,221
27358	Summerfield	(336)	10,232	10,861
27886	Tarboro	(252)	11,415	11,164
*27360	Thomasville	(336)	26,757	27,061
*27587	Wake Forest	(919)	30,117	38,199
28173	Waxhaw	(704)	9,859	13,495
28104	Weddington	(704)	9,459	10,531
*28401	Wilmington	(910)	106,476	115,933
*27893	Wilson	(252)	49,167	49,643
*27101	Winston-Salem	(336)	229,617	241,218

North Dakota
Area code 701 applies to the entire state.

ZIP	Place	2010 population	2015 estimate
*58501	Bismarck	61,272	71,167
*58601	Dickinson	17,787	23,765
*58102	Fargo	105,549	118,523
*58201	Grand Forks	52,838	57,011
*58401	Jamestown	15,427	15,422
58554	Mandan	18,331	21,382
*58701	Minot	40,888	49,450
58078	West Fargo	25,830	33,597
*58801	Williston	14,716	26,977

Ohio
Area code 220 overlays area code 740. Area code 234 overlays 330. Area code 380 overlays 614. Area code 567 overlays 419.

ZIP	Place	Area code	2010 population	2015 estimate
*44301	Akron	(330)	199,110	197,542
44601	Alliance	(330)	22,322	22,055
44001	Amherst	(440)	12,021	12,135
44805	Ashland	(419)	20,362	20,317
*44004	Ashtabula	(440)	19,124	18,371
45701	Athens	(740)	23,832	25,044
44202	Aurora	(330)	15,548	15,838
44515	Austintown (c)	(330)	29,677	—
44011	Avon	(440)	21,193	22,544
44012	Avon Lake	(440)	22,581	23,453
44203	Barberton	(330)	26,550	26,234
44140	Bay Village	(440)	15,651	15,402
44122	Beachwood	(216)	11,953	11,762
*45432	Beavercreek	(937)	45,193	46,277
44146	Bedford	(216)/(440)	13,074	12,747
*44146	Bedford Heights	(216)/(440)	10,751	10,625
43311	Bellefontaine	(937)	13,370	13,117
44017	Berea	(440)	19,093	18,874
43209	Bexley	(614)	13,057	13,654
*45242	Blue Ash	(513)	12,114	12,159
*44512	Boardman (c)	(330)	35,376	—
*43402	Bowling Green	(419)	30,028	31,246
44141	Brecksville	(440)	13,656	13,440
45211	Bridgetown (c)	(513)	14,407	—
44147	Broadview Heights	(440)	19,400	19,229
44142	Brook Park	(216)/(440)	19,212	18,809
44144	Brooklyn	(216)	11,169	10,899
44212	Brunswick	(330)	34,255	34,689
44820	Bucyrus	(419)	12,362	11,916
*43725	Cambridge	(740)	10,635	10,402
*44703	Canton	(330)	73,007	71,885
*45822	Celina	(419)	10,400	10,387
*45458	Centerville	(937)	23,999	23,882
45601	Chillicothe	(740)	21,901	21,727
*45202	Cincinnati	(513)	296,943	298,550
43113	Circleville	(740)	13,314	13,857
45315	Clayton	(937)	13,209	13,146
*44102	Cleveland	(216)	396,815	388,072
*44118	Cleveland Heights	(216)	46,121	44,962
*43201	Columbus	(614)	787,033	850,106
44030	Conneaut	(440)	12,841	12,712
43812	Coshocton	(740)	11,216	11,121
*44221	Cuyahoga Falls	(330)	49,652	49,146
*45402	Dayton	(937)	141,527	140,599
43512	Defiance	(419)	16,494	16,776
43015	Delaware	(740)	34,753	37,995
*45247	Dent (c)	(513)	10,497	—
44622	Dover	(330)	12,826	12,899
*43016	Dublin	(614)	41,751	45,098
*44112	East Cleveland	(216)	17,843	17,344
43920	East Liverpool	(330)	11,195	10,846
*44095	Eastlake	(440)	18,577	18,232
*44035	Elyria	(440)	54,533	53,775
45322	Englewood	(937)	13,465	13,460
*44117	Euclid	(216)	48,920	47,676
45324	Fairborn	(937)	32,352	33,452
*45011	Fairfield	(513)	42,510	42,767
44126	Fairview Park	(440)	16,826	16,407
*45840	Findlay	(419)	41,202	41,149
*45224	Finneytown (c)	(513)	12,741	—
45240	Forest Park	(513)	18,720	18,676
45230	Forestville (c)	(513)	10,532	—
44830	Fostoria	(419)	13,441	13,167
45005	Franklin	(513)	11,771	11,783
43420	Fremont	(419)	16,734	16,297
43230	Gahanna	(614)	33,248	34,590
44833	Galion	(419)	10,512	10,127
*44125	Garfield Heights	(216)	28,849	28,097
44232	Green	(330)	25,699	25,898
45331	Greenville	(937)	13,227	13,006
43123	Grove City	(614)	35,575	39,388
*45011	Hamilton	(513)	62,477	62,407
45030	Harrison	(513)	9,897	10,666
43056	Heath	(740)	10,310	10,489
43026	Hilliard	(614)	28,435	33,649
45424	Huber Heights	(937)	38,101	38,176
*44236	Hudson	(330)	22,262	22,437
45638	Ironton	(740)	11,129	10,900
*44240	Kent	(330)	28,904	29,810
*45429	Kettering	(937)	56,163	55,525
44107	Lakewood	(216)	52,131	50,656
43130	Lancaster	(740)	38,780	39,766
45036	Lebanon	(513)	20,033	20,623
*45801	Lima	(419)	38,771	37,873
43140	London	(740)	9,904	10,060
*44052	Lorain	(440)	64,097	63,647
*45140	Loveland	(513)	12,081	12,585
44124	Lyndhurst	(216)/(440)	14,001	13,691
*44056	Macedonia	(330)	11,188	11,686
*45248	Mack (c)	(513)	11,585	—
*44901	Mansfield	(419)	47,821	46,830
44137	Maple Heights	(216)	23,138	22,631
45750	Marietta	(740)	14,085	13,900
*43302	Marion	(740)	36,837	36,363
*43040	Marysville	(937)	22,094	22,817
45040	Mason	(513)	30,712	32,662
*44646	Massillon	(330)	32,149	32,252
43537	Maumee	(419)	14,286	13,940
44124	Mayfield Heights	(440)	19,155	18,840
*44256	Medina	(330)	26,678	26,339
*44060	Mentor	(440)	47,159	46,901
*45343	Miamisburg	(937)	20,181	20,034
44130	Middleburg Heights	(216)/(440)	15,946	15,696
*45042	Middletown	(513)	48,694	48,760
45211	Monfort Heights (c)	(513)	11,948	—
*45050	Monroe	(513)	12,442	13,393
45242	Montgomery	(513)	10,251	10,506
43050	Mount Vernon	(740)	16,990	16,742
*44216	New Franklin	(330)	14,227	14,275
44663	New Philadelphia	(330)	17,288	17,484
*43055	Newark	(740)	47,573	47,986
44446	Niles	(330)	19,266	18,651
*44720	North Canton	(330)	17,488	17,441
44070	North Olmsted	(440)	32,718	32,004
*44039	North Ridgeville	(440)	29,465	32,483
44133	North Royalton	(440)	30,444	30,311
45239	Northbrook (c)	(513)	10,668	—
44203	Norton	(330)	12,085	12,036
44857	Norwalk	(419)	17,012	16,827
*45212	Norwood	(513)	19,207	19,915
*43616	Oregon	(419)	20,291	20,102
45056	Oxford	(513)	21,371	22,104
44077	Painesville	(440)	19,563	19,776
*44129	Parma	(216)/(440)	81,601	79,937
44130	Parma Heights	(216)/(440)	20,718	20,246
43062	Pataskala	(740)	14,962	15,245
*43551	Perrysburg	(419)	20,623	21,423
43147	Pickerington	(614)/(740)	18,291	19,745
45356	Piqua	(937)	20,522	20,790
*45662	Portsmouth	(740)	20,226	20,226
43065	Powell	(614)	11,500	12,972
44266	Ravenna	(330)	11,724	11,619
*45215	Reading	(513)	10,385	10,324
*43068	Reynoldsburg	(614)	35,893	37,158
44143	Richmond Heights	(216)/(440)	10,546	10,469
45431	Riverside	(937)	25,201	24,972
44116	Rocky River	(440)	20,213	20,376
44460	Salem	(330)	12,303	12,003
*44870	Sandusky	(419)	25,793	25,212
44131	Seven Hills	(216)/(440)	11,804	11,690
*44122	Shaker Heights	(216)	28,448	27,646
45241	Sharonville	(513)	13,560	13,774

ZIP	Place	Area code	2010 population	2015 estimate
*45365	Sidney	(937)	21,229	20,858
44139	Solon	(440)	23,348	23,043
*44121	South Euclid	(216)	22,295	21,794
45066	Springboro	(513)	17,409	18,213
45246	Springdale	(513)	11,223	11,182
*45501	Springfield	(937)	60,608	59,680
*43952	Steubenville	(740)	18,659	18,219
44224	Stow	(330)	34,837	34,797
44241	Streetsboro	(330)	16,028	16,312
*44136	Strongsville	(440)	44,750	44,668
44471	Struthers	(330)	10,713	10,375
43560	Sylvania	(419)	18,965	18,965
44278	Tallmadge	(330)	17,537	17,512
44883	Tiffin	(419)	17,963	17,687
*43604	Toledo	(419)	287,208	279,789
45067	Trenton	(513)	11,869	12,281
*45426	Trotwood	(937)	24,431	24,096
*45373	Troy	(937)	25,058	25,659
44087	Twinsburg	(330)	18,795	18,872
*44122	University Heights	(216)	13,539	13,202
*43221	Upper Arlington	(614)	33,771	34,907
43078	Urbana	(937)	11,793	11,547
45891	Van Wert	(419)	10,846	10,798
45377	Vandalia	(937)	15,246	15,106
*44089	Vermilion	(440)	10,594	10,434
*44281	Wadsworth	(330)	21,567	21,860
*44481	Warren	(330)	41,557	40,245
*44122	Warrensville Heights	(216)	13,542	13,238
43160	Washington Court House	(740)	14,192	14,019
*45449	West Carrollton	(937)	13,143	12,980
*43081	Westerville	(614)	36,120	38,384
44145	Westlake	(440)	32,729	32,428
*45239	White Oak (c)	(513)	19,167	—
43213	Whitehall	(614)	18,062	18,694
44092	Wickliffe	(440)	12,750	12,545
*44094	Willoughby	(440)	22,268	22,631
44095	Willowick	(440)	14,171	13,957
45177	Wilmington	(937)	12,520	12,449
44691	Wooster	(330)	26,119	26,749
43085	Worthington	(614)	13,575	14,498
45385	Xenia	(937)	25,719	25,976
*44503	Youngstown	(330)	66,982	64,628
*43701	Zanesville	(740)	25,487	25,498

Oklahoma

Area code 539 overlays area code 918.

ZIP	Place	Area code	2010 population	2015 estimate
*74820	Ada	(580)	16,810	17,303
*73521	Altus	(580)	19,813	19,214
*73401	Ardmore	(580)	24,283	25,176
*74003	Bartlesville	(918)	35,750	36,595
73008	Bethany	(405)	19,051	19,589
74008	Bixby	(918)	20,884	24,657
*74012	Broken Arrow	(918)	98,850	106,563
*73018	Chickasha	(405)	16,036	16,488
73020	Choctaw	(405)	11,146	12,179
*74017	Claremore	(918)	18,581	18,997
*73115	Del City	(405)	21,332	22,022
*73533	Duncan	(580)	23,431	23,231
*74701	Durant	(580)	15,856	17,286
*73034	Edmond	(405)	81,405	90,092
73036	El Reno	(405)	16,749	18,516
*73644	Elk City	(580)	11,693	12,717
*73701	Enid	(580)	49,379	51,776
*74033	Glenpool	(918)	10,808	13,225
73044	Guthrie	(405)	10,191	11,270
73942	Guymon	(580)	11,442	11,921
74037	Jenks	(918)	16,924	20,740
*73501	Lawton	(580)	96,867	96,655
*74501	McAlester	(918)	18,383	18,310
*74354	Miami	(918)	13,570	13,611
*73110	Midwest City	(405)	54,371	57,249
*73160	Moore	(405)	55,081	60,451
*74401	Muskogee	(918)	39,223	38,456
73064	Mustang	(405)	17,395	20,226
*73069	Norman	(405)	110,925	120,284
*73102	Oklahoma City	(405)	579,999	631,346
74447	Okmulgee	(918)	12,321	12,244
74055	Owasso	(918)	28,915	34,542
*74601	Ponca City	(580)	25,387	24,758
74063	Sand Springs	(918)	18,906	19,783
*74066	Sapulpa	(918)	20,544	20,579
*74801	Shawnee	(405)	29,857	31,286
*74074	Stillwater	(405)	45,688	48,967
*74464	Tahlequah	(918)	15,753	16,598
*74103	Tulsa	(918)	391,906	403,505
*73112	Warr Acres	(405)	10,043	10,431
73096	Weatherford	(580)	10,833	12,126
*73801	Woodward	(580)	12,051	12,993
*73099	Yukon	(405)	22,709	25,892

Oregon

Area code 458 overlays area code 541. Area code 971 overlays 503.

ZIP	Place	Area code	2010 population	2015 estimate
*97321	Albany	(541)	50,158	52,175
*97006	Aloha (c)	(503)	49,425	—
97601	Altamont (c)	(541)	19,257	—
97520	Ashland	(541)	20,078	20,861
*97005	Beaverton	(503)	89,803	96,577
*97701	Bend	(541)	76,639	87,014
97229	Bethany (c)	(503)	20,646	—
97013	Canby	(503)	15,829	17,271
97291	Cedar Mill (c)	(503)	14,546	—
97502	Central Point	(541)	17,169	17,995
97420	Coos Bay	(541)	15,967	16,182
97113	Cornelius	(503)	11,869	12,317
*97330	Corvallis	(541)	54,462	55,780
97338	Dallas	(503)	14,583	15,277
*97009	Damascus	(503)	10,539	10,952
*97401	Eugene	(541)	156,185	163,460
97116	Forest Grove	(503)	21,083	23,897
97301	Four Corners (c)	(503)	15,947	—
97027	Gladstone	(503)	11,497	11,986
*97526	Grants Pass	(541)	34,533	37,088
*97030	Gresham	(503)	105,594	110,553
*97015	Happy Valley	(503)	13,903	18,493
97303	Hayesville (c)	(503)	19,936	—
97838	Hermiston	(541)	16,745	17,201
*97123	Hillsboro	(503)	91,611	102,347
*97303	Keizer	(503)	36,478	37,895
*97601	Klamath Falls	(541)	20,840	21,399
97850	La Grande	(541)	13,082	13,074
*97034	Lake Oswego	(503)	36,619	38,496
97355	Lebanon	(541)	15,518	16,324
97128	McMinnville	(503)	32,187	33,892
*97501	Medford	(541)	74,907	79,805
*97222	Milwaukie	(503)	20,291	20,830
97361	Monmouth	(503)	9,534	10,032
97132	Newberg	(503)	22,068	22,780
97365	Newport	(541)	9,989	10,268
97268	Oak Grove (c)	(503)	16,629	—
97006	Oak Hills (c)	(503)	11,333	—
97267	Oatfield (c)	(503)	13,415	—
97914	Ontario	(541)	11,366	10,999
97045	Oregon City	(503)	31,859	35,831
97801	Pendleton	(541)	16,612	16,881
*97201	Portland	(503)	583,776	632,309
97756	Redmond	(541)	26,215	28,654
*97470	Roseburg	(541)	21,181	22,114
97051	Saint Helens	(503)	12,883	13,158
*97301	Salem	(503)	154,637	164,549
97055	Sandy	(503)	9,570	10,644
97140	Sherwood	(503)	18,194	19,283
*97477	Springfield	(541)	59,403	60,870
97058	The Dalles	(541)	13,620	15,340
*97223	Tigard	(503)	48,035	51,253
97060	Troutdale	(503)	15,962	16,631
97062	Tualatin	(503)	26,054	27,154
97068	West Linn	(503)	25,109	26,593
97070	Wilsonville	(503)	19,509	22,729
97071	Woodburn	(503)	24,080	25,173

Pennsylvania

Area code 267 overlays area code 215. Area code 272 overlays 570. Area code 484 overlays 610. Area code 878 overlays 412/724.

ZIP	Place	Area code	2010 population	2015 estimate
*18101	Allentown	(610)	118,032	120,207
15101	Allison Park (c)	(412)/(724)	21,552	—
*16601	Altoona	(814)	46,320	45,344
19003	Ardmore (c)	(610)	12,455	—
15234	Baldwin	(412)	19,767	19,819
18603	Berwick	(570)	10,477	10,223
15102	Bethel Park	(412)	32,313	32,118
*18016	Bethlehem	(610)	74,982	74,892
*17815	Bloomsburg	(570)	14,855	14,585
19008	Broomall (c)	(610)	10,789	—
*16001	Butler	(724)	13,757	13,289
*17013	Carlisle	(717)	18,682	19,143
15108	Carnot-Moon (c)	(412)	11,372	—
*17201	Chambersburg	(717)	20,268	20,691
*19013	Chester	(610)	33,972	34,092
19320	Coatesville	(610)	13,100	13,148
17109	Colonial Park (c)	(717)	13,229	—
17512	Columbia	(717)	10,400	10,388
19023	Darby	(610)	10,687	10,687
19026	Drexel Hill (c)	(610)	28,043	—
*18512	Dunmore	(570)	14,057	13,379
*18301	East Stroudsburg	(570)	9,840	10,140
*18042	Easton	(610)	26,800	26,915
17022	Elizabethtown	(717)	11,545	11,586
*18049	Emmaus	(610)	11,211	11,368
17522	Ephrata	(717)	13,394	13,861
*16501	Erie	(814)	101,786	99,475

ZIP	Place	Area code	2010 population	2015 estimate
16063	Fernway (c)	(724)	12,414	—
15237	Franklin Park	(412)	13,470	14,415
18052	Fullerton (c)	(610)	14,925	—
*15601	Greensburg	(724)	14,892	14,495
*17331	Hanover	(717)	15,289	15,496
*17101	Harrisburg	(717)	49,528	49,081
*18201	Hazleton	(570)	25,340	24,825
16148	Hermitage	(724)	16,220	16,028
17033	Hershey (c)	(717)	14,257	—
19044	Horsham (c)	(215)	14,842	—
*15701	Indiana	(724)	13,975	14,100
15025	Jefferson Hills	(412)	10,619	11,360
*15901	Johnstown	(814)	20,978	19,966
*19406	King of Prussia (c)	(610)	19,936	—
18704	Kingston	(570)	13,182	12,941
*17601	Lancaster	(717)	59,322	59,339
19446	Lansdale	(215)	16,269	16,512
19050	Lansdowne	(610)	10,620	10,639
*17042	Lebanon	(717)	25,477	25,534
*19055	Levittown (c)	(215)	52,983	—
15068	Lower Burrell	(724)	11,761	11,466
*15132	McKeesport	(412)	19,731	19,453
*16335	Meadville	(814)	13,388	13,061
*15146	Monroeville	(412)/(724)	28,386	28,176
18936	Montgomeryville (c)	(215)	12,624	—
18707	Mountain Top (c)	(570)	10,982	—
15120	Munhall	(412)	11,406	11,247
*15668	Murrysville	(412)/(724)	20,079	20,134
18634	Nanticoke	(570)	10,465	10,258
*16108	New Castle	(724)	23,273	22,375
*15068	New Kensington	(724)	13,116	12,713
*19401	Norristown	(610)	34,324	34,412
16301	Oil City	(814)	10,557	10,137
*19107	Philadelphia	(215)	1,526,006	1,567,442
*19460	Phoenixville	(610)	16,440	16,658
*15201	Pittsburgh	(412)	305,704	304,391
15239	Plum	(412)	27,126	27,505
*19464	Pottstown	(610)	22,377	22,664
17901	Pottsville	(570)	14,324	13,802
*19601	Reading	(610)	88,082	87,879
15857	Saint Marys	(814)	13,070	12,652
*18503	Scranton	(570)	76,089	77,118
*16146	Sharon	(724)	14,038	13,562
17404	Shiloh (c)	(717)	11,218	—
15129	South Park Twp. (c)	(814)	13,416	—
*16801	State College	(814)	42,034	42,161
15401	Uniontown	(724)	10,372	9,990
15241	Upper St. Clair (c)	(412)	19,229	—
15301	Washington	(724)	13,663	13,497
*17268	Waynesboro	(717)	10,568	10,848
17315	Weigelstown (c)	(717)	12,875	—
*19380	West Chester	(610)	18,461	19,842
*15122	West Mifflin	(412)	20,313	20,075
18052	Whitehall	(412)	13,944	13,834
*18701	Wilkes-Barre	(570)	41,498	40,780
15221	Wilkinsburg	(412)	15,930	15,731
*17701	Williamsport	(570)	29,381	29,201
19090	Willow Grove (c)	(215)	15,726	—
19610	Wyomissing	(610)	10,461	10,469
19050	Yeadon	(610)	11,443	11,523
*17401	York	(717)	43,718	43,992

Rhode Island
Area code 401 applies to the entire state. See introductory note.

ZIP	Place	2010 population	2015 estimate
02806	Barrington	16,310	16,240
02809	Bristol	22,954	22,357
*02830	Burrillville	15,955	16,303
02863	Central Falls	19,376	19,303
*02816	Coventry	35,014	34,988
*02905	Cranston	80,387	81,073
02864	Cumberland	33,506	34,529
02818	East Greenwich	13,146	13,128
02914	East Providence	47,037	47,408
02919	Johnston	28,769	29,247
*02865	Lincoln	21,105	21,670
02842	Middletown	16,150	16,051
*02882	Narragansett	15,868	15,650
*02840	Newport	24,672	24,232
02842	Newport East (c)	11,769	—
*02852	North Kingstown	26,486	26,197
*02908	North Providence	32,078	32,480
02896	North Smithfield	11,967	12,314
*02860	Pawtucket	71,148	71,591
02871	Portsmouth	17,389	17,373
*02903	Providence	178,042	179,207
*02857	Scituate	10,329	10,549
*02917	Smithfield	21,430	21,632
*02879	South Kingstown	30,639	30,826
02878	Tiverton	15,780	15,780
02864	Valley Falls (c)	11,547	—
*02885	Warren	10,611	10,487
*02886	Warwick	82,672	81,699

ZIP	Place	2010 population	2015 estimate
02893	West Warwick	29,191	28,852
02891	Westerly	22,787	22,693
02891	Westerly (c)	17,936	—
02895	Woonsocket	41,186	41,475

South Carolina
Area code 854 overlays area code 843.

ZIP	Place	Area code	2010 population	2015 estimate
*29801	Aiken	(803)	29,524	30,604
*29621	Anderson	(864)	26,686	27,335
*29902	Beaufort	(843)	12,361	13,306
29611	Berea (c)	(864)	14,295	—
*29910	Bluffton	(843)	12,530	16,728
29033	Cayce	(803)	12,528	13,619
*29401	Charleston	(843)	120,083	132,609
*29631	Clemson	(864)	13,905	15,446
*29201	Columbia	(803)	129,272	133,803
*29526	Conway	(843)	17,103	21,053
29204	Dentsville (c)	(803)	14,062	—
*29640	Easley	(864)	19,993	20,765
29681	Five Forks (c)	(864)	14,140	—
*29501	Florence	(843)	37,056	38,228
29206	Forest Acres	(803)	10,361	10,615
*29715	Fort Mill	(803)	10,811	13,662
*29341	Gaffney	(864)	12,414	12,566
29605	Gantt (c)	(864)	14,229	—
29445	Goose Creek	(843)	35,938	40,633
*29601	Greenville	(864)	58,409	64,579
*29646	Greenwood	(864)	23,222	23,260
*29650	Greer	(864)	25,515	28,365
29410	Hanahan	(843)	17,997	21,575
*29928	Hilton Head Island	(843)	37,099	40,512
29063	Irmo	(803)	11,097	12,056
29412	James Island[1]	(843)	11,187	11,789
29456	Ladson (c)	(843)	13,790	—
*29072	Lexington	(803)	17,870	20,138
29662	Mauldin	(864)	22,889	25,135
*29464	Mount Pleasant	(843)	67,843	81,317
*29575	Myrtle Beach	(843)	27,109	31,035
29108	Newberry	(803)	10,277	10,331
*29841	North Augusta	(803)	21,348	22,522
*29410	North Charleston	(843)	97,471	108,304
*29582	North Myrtle Beach	(843)	13,752	15,579
29073	Oak Grove (c)	(803)	10,291	—
*29115	Orangeburg	(803)	13,964	13,460
29611	Parker (c)	(864)	11,431	—
29935	Port Royal	(843)	10,678	12,122
29020	Red Hill (c)	(843)	13,223	—
*29730	Rock Hill	(803)	66,154	71,548
29407	Saint Andrews (c)	(843)	20,493	—
29210	Seven Oaks (c)	(803)	15,144	—
*29681	Simpsonville	(864)	18,238	20,736
29577	Socastee (c)	(843)	19,952	—
*29306	Spartanburg	(864)	37,013	37,867
*29483	Summerville	(843)	43,392	48,848
*29150	Sumter	(803)	40,524	40,816
29687	Taylors (c)	(864)	21,617	—
*29607	Wade Hampton (c)	(864)	20,622	—
*29169	West Columbia	(803)	14,988	16,060

(1) Place was incorporated after the 2010 Census was conducted. Data in 2010 column is Census Bureau estimate.

South Dakota
Area code 605 applies to the entire state.

ZIP	Place	2010 population	2015 estimate
*57401	Aberdeen	26,091	28,102
*57006	Brookings	22,056	23,657
*57350	Huron	12,592	13,313
57301	Mitchell	15,254	15,669
57501	Pierre	13,646	14,002
*57701	Rapid City	67,956	73,569
*57103	Sioux Falls	153,888	171,544
*57783	Spearfish	10,494	11,283
57069	Vermillion	10,571	10,738
57201	Watertown	21,482	22,073
57078	Yankton	14,454	14,557

Tennessee
Area code 629 overlays area code 615.

ZIP	Place	Area code	2010 population	2015 estimate
38002	Arlington	(901)	11,517	11,625
*37303	Athens	(423)	13,458	13,688
*38133	Bartlett	(901)	54,613	58,579
*37027	Brentwood	(615)	37,060	41,763
*37620	Bristol	(423)	26,702	26,666
*37402	Chattanooga	(423)	167,674	176,588
*37040	Clarksville	(931)	132,929	149,176
*37311	Cleveland	(423)	41,285	43,898

ZIP	Place	Area code	2010 population	2015 estimate
*37716	Clinton	(865)	9,841	10,049
37315	Collegedale	(423)	8,282	10,743
*38017	Collierville	(901)	43,965	48,863
*38401	Columbia	(931)	34,681	36,800
*38501	Cookeville	(931)	30,435	32,113
*38555	Crossville	(931)	10,795	11,411
*37055	Dickson	(615)	14,538	15,359
*38024	Dyersburg	(731)	17,145	16,781
37412	East Ridge	(423)	20,979	21,260
*37643	Elizabethton	(423)	14,176	13,772
*37922	Farragut	(865)	20,676	21,919
*37064	Franklin	(615)	62,487	72,639
37066	Gallatin	(615)	30,278	34,334
*38138	Germantown	(901)	38,844	39,240
*37072	Goodlettsville	(615)	15,921	16,994
*37743	Greeneville	(423)	15,062	15,094
*37075	Hendersonville	(615)	51,372	56,018
*38301	Jackson	(731)	65,211	66,975
*37601	Johnson City	(423)	63,152	66,027
*37660	Kingsport	(423)	48,205	53,014
*37902	Knoxville	(865)	178,874	185,291
*37086	La Vergne	(615)	32,588	34,794
38002	Lakeland	(901)	12,430	12,553
38464	Lawrenceburg	(931)	10,428	10,569
*37087	Lebanon	(615)	26,190	30,262
37091	Lewisburg	(931)	11,100	11,480
37355	Manchester	(931)	10,102	10,517
38237	Martin	(731)	11,473	10,959
*37801	Maryville	(865)	27,465	28,464
*37110	McMinnville	(931)	13,605	13,759
*38103	Memphis	(901)	646,889	655,770
37343	Middle Valley (c)	(423)	12,684	—
*38053	Millington	(901)	10,176	11,027
*37813	Morristown	(423)	29,137	29,478
*37122	Mount Juliet	(615)	23,671	31,540
*37130	Murfreesboro	(615)	108,755	126,118
*37201	Nashville-Davidson (balance)	(615)	601,222	654,610
*37830	Oak Ridge	(865)	29,330	29,302
38242	Paris	(731)	10,156	10,150
37148	Portland	(615)	11,480	12,323
37415	Red Bank	(423)	11,651	11,769
*37862	Sevierville	(865)	14,807	16,490
37865	Seymour (c)	(865)	10,919	—
*37160	Shelbyville	(931)	20,335	21,317
37167	Smyrna	(615)	39,974	46,607
*37379	Soddy-Daisy	(423)	12,714	13,171
37174	Spring Hill	(931)	29,036	36,055
37172	Springfield	(615)	16,440	16,808
*37388	Tullahoma	(931)	18,655	19,128
*38261	Union City	(731)	10,895	10,573
37188	White House	(615)	10,255	11,226

Texas

Area code 346 overlays area codes 281/713/832. Area code 430 overlays 903. Area codes 469/972 overlay 214. Area code 682 overlays 817. Area code 737 overlays 512.

ZIP	Place	Area code	2010 population	2015 estimate
*79601	Abilene	(325)	117,063	121,721
75001	Addison	(214)	13,056	15,518
78516	Alamo	(956)	18,353	19,246
77039	Aldine (c)	(713)	15,869	—
*78332	Alice	(361)	19,104	19,408
*75002	Allen	(214)	84,246	98,143
78573	Alton	(956)	12,341	15,760
*77511	Alvin	(713)	24,236	25,791
*79109	Amarillo	(806)	190,695	198,645
79714	Andrews	(432)	11,088	13,816
*77515	Angleton	(979)	18,862	19,429
75409	Anna	(972)	8,249	11,463
*76001	Arlington	(817)	365,438	388,125
77346	Atascocita (c)	(281)	65,844	—
*75751	Athens	(903)	12,710	12,788
*78712	Austin	(512)	790,390	931,830
*76020	Azle	(817)	10,947	11,693
*75180	Balch Springs	(214)	23,728	25,210
*77414	Bay City	(979)	17,614	17,598
*77520	Baytown	(713)	71,802	76,335
*77701	Beaumont	(409)	118,296	118,129
*76021	Bedford	(817)	46,979	49,337
*78102	Beeville	(361)	12,863	13,277
*77401	Bellaire	(713)	16,855	18,518
*76704	Bellmead	(254)	9,901	10,164
76513	Belton	(254)	18,216	20,547
*76126	Benbrook	(817)	21,234	22,629
*79720	Big Spring	(432)	27,282	28,862
*78006	Boerne	(830)	10,471	13,674
75418	Bonham	(903)	10,127	10,079
*79007	Borger	(806)	13,251	12,964
*77833	Brenham	(979)	15,716	16,579
*78520	Brownsville	(956)	175,023	183,887
*76801	Brownwood	(325)	19,288	19,031
78717	Brushy Creek (c)	(512)	21,764	—
*77801	Bryan	(979)	76,201	82,118

ZIP	Place	Area code	2010 population	2015 estimate
78610	Buda	(512)	7,295	13,705
76354	Burkburnett	(940)	10,811	11,043
*76028	Burleson	(817)	36,690	43,625
*79015	Canyon	(806)	13,303	14,887
*78130	Canyon Lake (c)	(830)	21,262	—
*75006	Carrollton	(214)	119,097	133,168
*75104	Cedar Hill	(214)	45,028	48,507
*78613	Cedar Park	(512)	48,937	65,945
77530	Channelview (c)	(713)	38,289	—
78108	Cibolo	(210)	15,349	26,637
77450	Cinco Ranch (c)	(281)	18,274	—
*76031	Cleburne	(817)	29,337	30,020
77015	Cloverleaf (c)	(713)	22,942	—
77531	Clute	(979)	11,211	11,444
*77840	College Station	(979)	93,857	107,889
76034	Colleyville	(817)	22,807	25,487
*77301	Conroe	(936)	56,207	68,602
78109	Converse	(210)	18,198	21,987
*75019	Coppell	(214)	38,659	41,159
76522	Copperas Cove	(254)	32,032	33,081
*76208	Corinth	(940)	19,935	20,998
*78401	Corpus Christi	(361)	305,215	324,074
*75110	Corsicana	(903)	23,770	23,952
76036	Crowley	(817)	12,838	14,853
*75201	Dallas	(214)	1,197,816	1,300,092
77536	Deer Park	(281)	32,010	33,806
*78840	Del Rio	(830)	35,591	36,153
*75020	Denison	(903)	22,682	23,150
*76201	Denton	(940)	113,383	131,044
*75115	DeSoto	(214)	49,047	52,486
*77539	Dickinson	(281)	18,680	19,895
78537	Donna	(956)	15,798	16,523
79029	Dumas	(806)	14,691	15,001
*75116	Duncanville	(214)	38,524	39,826
*78852	Eagle Pass	(830)	26,248	28,765
*78539	Edinburg	(956)	77,100	84,497
77437	El Campo	(979)	11,602	11,604
*79910	El Paso	(915)	649,121	681,124
*75119	Ennis	(214)	18,513	19,007
*76039	Euless	(817)	51,277	54,219
*75234	Farmers Branch	(214)	28,616	32,689
*75022	Flower Mound	(214)	64,669	71,253
76119	Forest Hill	(817)	12,355	12,881
75126	Forney	(214)	14,661	18,418
76544	Fort Hood (c)	(254)	29,589	—
*76133	Fort Worth	(817)	741,206	833,319
77498	Four Corners (c)	(281)	12,382	—
78624	Fredericksburg	(830)	10,530	11,094
*77541	Freeport	(979)	12,049	12,154
77545	Fresno (c)	(281)	19,069	—
*77546	Friendswood	(281)	35,805	38,800
*75034	Frisco	(214)	116,989	154,407
*76240	Gainesville	(940)	16,002	16,292
77547	Galena Park	(713)	10,887	11,162
*77550	Galveston	(409)	47,743	50,180
*75040	Garland	(214)	226,876	236,897
*76528	Gatesville	(254)	15,751	15,724
*78626	Georgetown	(512)	47,400	63,716
75154	Glenn Heights	(214)	11,278	12,042
*75051	Grand Prairie	(214)	175,396	187,809
*76051	Grapevine	(817)	46,334	51,404
77449	Greatwood (c)	(281)	11,538	—
*75401	Greenville	(903)	25,557	26,515
77619	Groves	(409)	16,144	15,750
*76117	Haltom City	(817)	42,409	44,206
76548	Harker Heights	(254)	26,700	29,142
*78550	Harlingen	(956)	64,849	65,774
*75652	Henderson	(903)	13,712	13,529
79045	Hereford	(806)	15,370	15,021
76643	Hewitt	(254)	13,549	14,252
78557	Hidalgo	(956)	11,198	13,709
75067	Highland Village	(214)	15,056	16,149
*79927	Horizon City	(915)	16,735	19,288
*77002	Houston	(281)/(713)/(832)	2,099,451	2,296,224
*77338	Humble	(713)	15,133	15,665
*77340	Huntsville	(936)	38,548	40,938
*76053	Hurst	(817)	37,337	39,016
78634	Hutto	(512)	14,698	22,722
*75062	Irving	(214)	216,290	236,607
77029	Jacinto City	(281)	10,553	10,782
75766	Jacksonville	(903)	14,544	14,884
78729	Jollyville (c)	(512)	16,151	—
*77449	Katy	(713)	14,102	16,158
*76248	Keller	(817)	39,627	45,758
*78028	Kerrville	(830)	22,347	23,136
*75662	Kilgore	(903)	12,975	14,947
*76541	Killeen	(254)	127,921	140,806
*78363	Kingsville	(361)	26,213	26,225
78640	Kyle	(512)	28,016	35,733
78572	La Homa (c)	(956)	11,985	—
77568	La Marque	(409)	14,509	15,908
*77571	La Porte	(281)	33,800	35,148
77566	Lake Jackson	(979)	26,849	27,533
*78734	Lakeway	(512)	11,391	14,217
*75146	Lancaster	(214)	36,361	38,801
*78041	Laredo	(956)	236,091	255,473

ZIP	Place	Area code	2010 population	2015 estimate
*77573	League City	(281)	83,560	98,312
*78641	Leander	(512)	26,521	37,889
*78268	Leon Valley	(210)	10,151	11,174
*79336	Levelland	(806)	13,542	13,914
*75067	Lewisville	(214)	95,290	104,039
75068	Little Elm	(214)	25,898	38,341
*78233	Live Oak	(210)	13,131	15,346
78644	Lockhart	(512)	12,698	13,446
*75601	Longview	(903)	80,455	82,287
*79401	Lubbock	(806)	229,573	249,042
*75901	Lufkin	(936)	35,067	36,333
77657	Lumberton	(409)	11,943	12,421
76063	Mansfield	(817)	56,368	64,274
*75670	Marshall	(903)	23,523	23,820
*78501	McAllen	(956)	129,877	140,269
*75070	McKinney	(214)	131,117	162,898
78570	Mercedes	(956)	15,570	16,657
*75149	Mesquite	(214)	139,824	144,788
*79701	Midland	(432)	111,147	132,950
76065	Midlothian	(214)	18,037	22,318
*76067	Mineral Wells	(940)	16,788	14,754
*78572	Mission	(956)	77,058	83,298
*77083	Mission Bend (c)	(281)	36,501	—
*77489	Missouri City	(713)	67,358	74,139
*75455	Mount Pleasant	(903)	15,564	16,051
*75094	Murphy	(214)	17,708	20,610
*75961	Nacogdoches	(936)	32,996	33,894
77627	Nederland	(409)	17,547	17,196
*78130	New Braunfels	(830)	57,740	70,543
77479	New Territory (c)	(281)	15,186	—
*76117	North Richland Hills	(817)	63,343	69,204
*79761	Odessa	(432)	99,940	118,968
*77630	Orange	(409)	18,595	19,347
*75801	Palestine	(903)	18,712	18,288
*79065	Pampa	(806)	17,994	18,177
*75460	Paris	(903)	25,171	24,782
*77502	Pasadena	(281)/(713)/(832)	149,043	153,784
*77581	Pearland	(281)/(713)/(832)	91,252	108,821
78721	Pecan Grove (c)	(254)	15,963	—
*78660	Pflugerville	(512)	46,936	57,122
78577	Pharr	(956)	70,400	76,538
*79072	Plainview	(806)	22,194	20,919
*75074	Plano	(214)	259,841	283,558
*77640	Port Arthur	(409)	53,818	55,340
77979	Port Lavaca	(361)	12,248	12,416
77651	Port Neches	(409)	13,040	12,786
78374	Portland	(361)	15,099	16,116
75078	Prosper	(214)	9,423	15,967
*78580	Raymondville	(965)	11,284	11,139
*75154	Red Oak	(214)	10,769	12,022
76140	Rendon (c)	(817)	12,552	—
*75080	Richardson	(214)	99,223	110,815
*77469	Richmond	(281)/(713)/(832)	11,679	12,138
78582	Rio Grande City	(956)	13,834	14,404
76701	Robinson	(254)	10,509	11,484
78380	Robstown	(361)	11,487	11,576
*78382	Rockport	(361)	8,766	10,490
*75087	Rockwall	(214)	37,490	42,566
78584	Roma	(956)	9,765	10,223
*77471	Rosenberg	(832)	30,618	35,510
*78681	Round Rock	(512)	99,887	115,997
*75088	Rowlett	(214)	56,199	60,236
75189	Royse City	(214)	9,349	11,465
75048	Sachse	(214)	20,329	24,554
*76179	Saginaw	(817)	19,806	22,079
*76901	San Angelo	(325)	93,200	100,450
*78201	San Antonio	(210)	1,327,401	1,469,845
78586	San Benito	(956)	24,250	24,496
79849	San Elizario (c)	(915)	13,603	—
78589	San Juan	(956)	33,856	36,556
*78666	San Marcos	(512)	44,894	60,684
*77510	Santa Fe	(409)	12,222	13,007
*78154	Schertz	(210)	31,465	37,938
77586	Seabrook	(281)	11,952	13,716
75159	Seagoville	(214)	14,835	15,894
*78155	Seguin	(830)	25,175	27,864
*75090	Sherman	(903)	38,521	40,667
77459	Sienna Plantation (c)	(281)	13,721	—
*79549	Snyder	(325)	11,202	11,768
*79927	Socorro	(915)	32,013	33,222
77587	South Houston	(713)	16,983	17,544
76092	Southlake	(817)	26,575	29,941
*77373	Spring (c)	(281)/(713)/(832)	54,298	—
*77477	Stafford	(281)	17,693	18,459
*76401	Stephenville	(254)	17,123	20,120
*77478	Sugar Land	(281)/(713)/(832)	78,817	88,156
*75482	Sulphur Springs	(903)	15,449	16,098
79556	Sweetwater	(325)	10,906	10,809
76574	Taylor	(512)	15,191	16,702
*76501	Temple	(254)	66,102	72,277
*75160	Terrell	(214)	15,816	16,981
*75501	Texarkana	(903)	36,411	37,280
*77590	Texas City	(409)	45,099	47,618
75056	The Colony	(214)	36,328	41,779
*77381	The Woodlands (c)	(281)	93,847	—
78260	Timberwood Park (c)	(830)	13,447	—

ZIP	Place	Area code	2010 population	2015 estimate
*77375	Tomball	(281)	10,753	11,540
76262	Trophy Club	(817)	8,024	11,759
*75702	Tyler	(903)	96,900	103,700
*78148	Universal City	(210)	18,530	19,986
75205	University Park	(214)	23,068	24,759
*78801	Uvalde	(830)	15,751	16,476
*76384	Vernon	(940)	11,002	10,573
*77901	Victoria	(361)	62,592	67,574
*77662	Vidor	(409)	10,579	10,945
*76704	Waco	(254)	124,805	132,356
*76148	Watauga	(817)	23,497	24,525
*75165	Waxahachie	(214)	29,621	33,384
*76086	Weatherford	(817)	25,250	28,742
77598	Webster	(281)	10,400	11,116
78728	Wells Branch (c)	(512)	12,120	—
*78596	Weslaco	(956)	35,670	39,474
79764	West Odessa (c)	(432)	22,707	—
77005	West University Place	(713)	14,787	15,741
76108	White Settlement	(817)	16,116	17,077
*76301	Wichita Falls	(940)	104,553	104,710
75098	Wylie	(214)	41,427	46,708

Utah

Area code 385 overlays area code 801.

ZIP	Place	Area code	2010 population	2015 estimate
84004	Alpine	(801)	9,555	10,235
84003	American Fork	(801)	26,263	28,326
84065	Bluffdale	(801)	7,598	10,931
*84010	Bountiful	(801)	42,552	43,784
84302	Brigham City	(435)	17,899	18,752
*84720	Cedar City	(435)	28,857	30,184
84062	Cedar Hills	(801)	9,796	10,265
84014	Centerville	(801)	15,335	16,877
*84015	Clearfield	(801)	30,112	30,653
84015	Clinton	(801)	20,426	21,399
*84047	Cottonwood Heights	(801)	33,433	34,343
84020	Draper	(801)	42,274	46,774
*84005	Eagle Mountain	(801)	21,415	27,332
84025	Farmington	(801)	18,275	22,566
*84029	Grantsville	(435)	8,893	10,027
*84032	Heber City	(435)	11,362	14,302
*84096	Herriman	(801)	21,785	30,835
84003	Highland	(801)	15,523	17,989
*84117	Holladay	(801)	26,472	30,864
84737	Hurricane	(435)	13,748	15,501
84037	Kaysville	(801)	27,300	30,472
84118	Kearns (c)	(801)	35,731	—
*84041	Layton	(801)	67,311	74,143
*84043	Lehi	(801)	47,407	58,486
84042	Lindon	(801)	10,070	10,810
*84321	Logan	(435)	48,174	50,371
84044	Magna (c)	(801)	26,505	—
*84047	Midvale	(801)	27,964	32,613
*84106	Millcreek (c)	(801)	62,139	—
*84107	Murray	(801)	46,746	49,250
84341	North Logan	(435)	8,269	10,181
*84404	North Ogden	(801)	17,357	18,446
84054	North Salt Lake	(801)	16,322	19,796
*84401	Ogden	(801)	82,825	85,444
*84057	Orem	(801)	88,328	94,457
84651	Payson	(801)	18,294	19,548
84062	Pleasant Grove	(801)	33,509	38,052
*84601	Provo	(801)	112,488	115,264
*84065	Riverton	(801)	38,753	41,900
*84067	Roy	(801)	36,884	37,964
*84770	Saint George	(435)	72,897	80,202
*84101	Salt Lake City	(801)	186,440	192,672
*84070	Sandy	(801)	87,461	93,613
84655	Santaquin	(801)	9,128	10,572
*84043	Saratoga Springs	(801)	17,781	25,407
84335	Smithfield	(435)	9,495	10,782
*84095	South Jordan	(801)	50,418	66,648
84403	South Ogden	(801)	16,532	16,955
*84115	South Salt Lake	(801)	23,617	24,788
84660	Spanish Fork	(801)	34,691	37,935
*84663	Springville	(801)	29,466	32,286
84075	Syracuse	(801)	24,331	27,395
*84118	Taylorsville	(801)	58,652	60,514
84074	Tooele	(435)	31,605	33,157
*84078	Vernal	(435)	9,089	11,200
84780	Washington	(435)	18,761	24,299
84401	West Haven	(801)	10,272	11,921
*84084	West Jordan	(801)	103,712	111,946
*84015	West Point	(801)	9,511	10,345
*84119	West Valley City	(801)	129,480	136,208
*84010	Woods Cross	(801)	9,761	11,284

Vermont

Area code 802 applies to the entire state. See introductory note.

ZIP	Place	2010 population	2015 estimate
05201	Bennington	15,764	15,345
*05301	Brattleboro	12,046	11,679

ZIP	Place	2010 population	2015 estimate
*05401	Burlington	42,417	42,452
*05446	Colchester	17,067	17,383
*05452	Essex	19,587	20,946
*05452	Essex Junction	9,271	10,111
05468	Milton	10,352	10,827
*05701	Rutland	16,495	15,824
*05403	South Burlington	17,904	18,791

Virginia
Area code 571 overlays area code 703.

ZIP	Place	Area code	2010 population	2015 estimate
*22314	Alexandria	(703)	139,966	153,511
22003	Annandale (c)	(703)	41,008	—
*22201	Arlington (c)	(703)	207,627	—
*20146	Ashburn (c)	(703)	43,511	—
22041	Bailey's Crossroads (c)	(703)	23,643	—
*24060	Blacksburg	(540)	42,620	44,215
23235	Bon Air (c)	(804)	16,366	—
23112	Brandermill (c)	(804)	13,173	—
*24201	Bristol	(276)	17,835	17,141
20148	Broadlands (c)	(703)	12,313	—
20111	Buckhall (c)	(703)	16,293	—
20109	Bull Run (c)	(703)	14,983	—
*22015	Burke (c)	(703)	41,055	—
22015	Burke Centre (c)	(703)	17,326	—
*20165	Cascades (c)	(434)	11,912	—
24018	Cave Spring (c)	(540)	24,922	—
*20120	Centreville (c)	(703)	71,135	—
*20151	Chantilly (c)	(703)	23,039	—
*22901	Charlottesville	(434)	43,475	46,597
22026	Cherry Hill (c)	(703)	16,000	—
*23320	Chesapeake	(757)	222,209	235,429
*23831	Chester (c)	(804)	20,987	—
*24073	Christiansburg	(540)	21,041	21,943
23834	Colonial Heights	(804)	17,411	17,820
20165	Countryside (c)	(703)	10,072	—
22701	Culpeper	(540)	16,379	17,557
22193	Dale City (c)	(703)	65,969	—
*24541	Danville	(434)	43,055	42,082
20170	Dranesville (c)	(703)	11,921	—
23222	East Highland Park (c)	(804)	14,796	—
22033	Fair Oaks (c)	(703)	30,223	—
*22030	Fairfax	(703)	22,565	24,013
22039	Fairfax Station (c)	(703)	12,030	—
*22046	Falls Church	(703)	12,332	13,892
22308	Fort Hunt (c)	(703)	16,045	—
*22310	Franconia (c)	(703)	18,245	—
20171	Franklin Farm (c)	(703)	19,288	—
*22401	Fredericksburg	(540)	24,286	28,118
22630	Front Royal	(540)	14,440	15,070
*20155	Gainesville (c)	(703)	11,481	—
*23060	Glen Allen (c)	(804)	14,774	—
22066	Great Falls (c)	(703)	15,427	—
22306	Groveton (c)	(703)	14,598	—
*23669	Hampton	(757)	137,436	136,454
*22801	Harrisonburg	(540)	48,914	52,538
*20170	Herndon	(703)	23,292	24,568
23075	Highland Springs (c)	(804)	15,711	—
24019	Hollins (c)	(540)	14,673	—
23860	Hopewell	(804)	22,591	22,378
22303	Huntington (c)	(703)	11,267	—
22306	Hybla Valley (c)	(703)	15,801	—
22043	Idylwood (c)	(703)	17,288	—
22038	Kings Park West (c)	(703)	13,390	—
22315	Kingstowne (c)	(703)	15,556	—
22192	Lake Ridge (c)	(703)	41,058	—
23228	Lakeside (c)	(804)	11,849	—
20176	Lansdowne (c)	(703)	11,253	—
23060	Laurel (c)	(804)	16,713	—
*20175	Leesburg	(703)	42,616	51,209
22312	Lincolnia (c)	(703)	22,855	—
20136	Linton Hall (c)	(703)	35,725	—
*22079	Lorton (c)	(703)	18,610	—
20165	Lowes Island (c)	(703)	10,756	—
*24501	Lynchburg	(434)	75,568	79,812
24572	Madison Heights (c)	(434)	11,285	—
*20110	Manassas	(703)	37,821	41,764
*20111	Manassas Park	(703)	14,273	15,726
23235	Manchester (c)	(804)	10,804	—
*24112	Martinsville	(276)	13,821	13,645
22191	Marumsco (c)	(703)	35,036	—
*22101	McLean (c)	(703)	48,115	—
20171	McNair (c)	(703)	17,513	—
23234	Meadowbrook (c)	(804)	18,312	—
*23111	Mechanicsville (c)	(804)	36,348	—
*22081	Merrifield (c)	(703)	15,212	—
22025	Montclair (c)	(703)	19,570	—
22121	Mount Vernon (c)	(703)	12,416	—
22191	Neabsco (c)	(703)	12,068	—
22122	Newington (c)	(703)	12,943	—
22153	Newington Forest (c)	(703)	12,442	—
*23607	Newport News	(757)	180,719	182,385

ZIP	Place	Area code	2010 population	2015 estimate
*23502	Norfolk	(757)	242,803	246,393
*22124	Oakton (c)	(703)	34,166	—
*23704	Petersburg	(804)	32,420	32,477
23662	Poquoson	(757)	12,150	12,059
*23704	Portsmouth	(757)	95,535	96,201
*24141	Radford	(540)	16,408	17,403
*20190	Reston (c)	(703)	58,404	—
*23219	Richmond	(276)/(804)	204,214	220,289
*24011	Roanoke	(540)	97,032	99,897
24281	Rose Hill (c) (Fairfax Co.)	(276)	20,226	—
24153	Salem	(540)	24,802	25,432
23233	Short Pump (c)	(804)	24,729	—
20152	South Riding (c)	(703)	24,256	—
*22150	Springfield (c)	(703)	30,484	—
*24401	Staunton	(540)	23,746	24,416
*20164	Sterling (c)	(703)	27,822	—
20109	Sudley (c)	(703)	16,203	—
*23434	Suffolk	(757)	84,585	88,161
20164	Sugarland Run (c)	(703)	11,799	—
24502	Timberlake (c)	(434)	12,183	—
23229	Tuckahoe (c)	(804)	44,990	—
*22102	Tysons Corner (c)	(703)	19,627	—
*22180	Vienna	(703)	15,687	16,522
*23451	Virginia Beach	(757)	437,994	452,745
23888	Wakefield (c)	(757)	11,275	—
22980	Waynesboro	(540)	21,006	21,491
*22042	West Falls Church (c)	(703)	29,207	—
22152	West Springfield (c)	(703)	22,460	—
*23185	Williamsburg	(757)	14,068	15,052
*22601	Winchester	(540)	26,203	27,284
*22182	Wolf Trap (c)	(703)	16,131	—
24381	Woodlawn (c) (Fairfax Co.)	(276)	20,804	—

Washington

ZIP	Place	Area code	2010 population	2015 estimate
98520	Aberdeen	(360)	16,896	16,276
*98221	Anacortes	(360)	15,778	16,403
*98223	Arlington	(360)	17,926	18,949
98335	Artondale (c)	(253)	12,653	—
*98001	Auburn	(253)	70,180	77,006
98110	Bainbridge Island	(206)	23,025	23,840
98604	Battle Ground	(360)	17,571	19,407
*98004	Bellevue	(425)	122,363	139,820
*98225	Bellingham	(360)	80,885	85,146
*98390	Bonney Lake	(360)	17,374	19,903
*98011	Bothell	(425)	33,505	42,939
98036	Bothell West (c)	(425)	16,607	—
*98337	Bremerton	(360)	37,729	39,520
98178	Bryn Mawr-Skyway (c)	(206)	15,645	—
*98166	Burien	(206)	33,313	50,467
98607	Camas	(360)	19,355	21,846
98531	Centralia	(360)	16,336	16,753
99004	Cheney	(509)	10,590	11,534
98072	Cottage Lake (c)	(425)	22,494	—
98042	Covington	(253)	17,575	19,197
*98198	Des Moines	(206)	29,673	31,221
*98031	East Hill-Meridian (c)	(253)	29,878	—
98056	East Renton Highlands (c)	(425)	11,140	—
98802	East Wenatchee	(509)	13,190	13,659
98204	Eastmont (c)	(425)	20,101	—
*98020	Edmonds	(425)	39,709	41,375
98387	Elk Plain (c)	(253)	14,205	—
*98926	Ellensburg	(509)	18,174	19,001
98022	Enumclaw	(360)	10,669	11,609
*98201	Everett	(425)	103,019	108,010
98058	Fairwood (c) (King Co.)	(425)	19,102	—
*98001	Federal Way	(253)	89,306	95,171
98248	Ferndale	(360)	11,415	13,010
98597	Five Corners (c)	(360)	18,159	—
98433	Fort Lewis (c)	(253)	11,046	—
98375	Frederickson (c)	(253)	18,719	—
98338	Graham (c)	(253)	23,491	—
98930	Grandview	(509)	10,862	11,176
98665	Hazel Dell (c)	(360)	19,435	—
98011	Inglewood-Finn Hill (c)	(425)	22,707	—
*98027	Issaquah	(425)	30,434	36,081
98626	Kelso	(360)	11,925	11,901
98028	Kenmore	(425)	20,460	22,030
*99336	Kennewick	(509)	73,917	78,896
*98031	Kent	(253)/(425)	92,411	126,952
98033	Kingsgate (c)	(425)	13,065	—
*98033	Kirkland	(425)	48,787	87,281
98029	Klahanie (c)	(425)	10,674	—
*98503	Lacey	(360)	42,393	46,409
98155	Lake Forest Park	(206)	12,598	13,243
98042	Lake Morton-Berrydale (c)	(253)/(425)	10,160	—
98258	Lake Stevens	(425)	28,069	30,886
98391	Lake Tapps (c)	(253)	11,859	—
98002	Lakeland North (c)	(253)	12,942	—
98002	Lakeland South (c)	(253)	11,574	—
*98498	Lakewood	(253)	58,163	59,829

ZIP	Place	Area code	2010 population	2015 estimate
98632	Longview	(360)	36,648	36,848
98264	Lynden	(360)	11,951	13,517
*98036	Lynnwood	(425)	35,836	36,997
98290	Maltby (c)	(360)/(425)	10,830	—
98038	Maple Valley	(425)	22,684	25,686
98012	Martha Lake (c)	(425)	15,473	—
*98270	Marysville	(360)	60,020	66,773
98040	Mercer Island	(206)	22,699	25,042
*98082	Mill Creek	(425)	18,244	20,043
98012	Mill Creek East (c)	(425)	15,709	—
98272	Monroe	(360)	17,304	18,090
98837	Moses Lake	(509)	20,366	22,082
*98273	Mount Vernon	(360)	31,743	34,053
98043	Mountlake Terrace	(425)	19,909	20,989
98275	Mukilteo	(425)	20,254	21,226
*98059	Newcastle	(425)	10,380	11,370
98037	North Lynnwood (c)	(425)	16,574	—
*98277	Oak Harbor	(360)	22,075	22,693
*98501	Olympia	(360)	46,478	50,302
98662	Orchards (c)	(360)	19,556	—
*98444	Parkland (c)	(253)	35,803	—
*99301	Pasco	(509)	59,781	69,451
*98362	Port Angeles	(360)	19,038	19,448
*98366	Port Orchard	(360)	11,144	13,607
98370	Poulsbo	(360)	9,200	10,041
98390	Prairie Ridge (c)	(360)	11,464	—
*99163	Pullman	(509)	29,799	32,816
*98371	Puyallup	(253)	37,022	39,659
*98052	Redmond	(425)	54,144	60,598
*98057	Renton	(425)	90,927	100,242
*99352	Richland	(509)	48,058	54,248
98686	Salmon Creek (c)	(360)	19,686	—
*98074	Sammamish	(425)	45,780	52,253
*98148	SeaTac	(206)	26,909	28,215
*98101	Seattle	(206)/(425)	608,660	684,451
*98284	Sedro-Woolley	(360)	10,540	10,815
*98133	Shoreline	(206)	53,007	55,439
98208	Silver Firs (c)	(206)/(425)	20,891	—
*98315	Silverdale (c)	(360)	19,204	—
*98065	Snoqualmie	(425)	10,670	13,169
*98373	South Hill (c)	(253)	52,431	—
98387	Spanaway (c)	(253)	27,227	—
*99201	Spokane	(509)	208,916	213,272
*99206	Spokane Valley	(509)	89,755	94,919
98944	Sunnyside	(509)	15,858	16,325
*98402	Tacoma	(253)	198,397	207,948
*98188	Tukwila	(206)	19,107	20,018
*98501	Tumwater	(360)	17,371	19,190
98053	Union Hill-Novelty Hill (c)	(425)	18,805	—
*98466	University Place	(253)	31,144	32,842
*98661	Vancouver	(360)	161,791	172,860
*98070	Vashon (c)	(206)	10,624	—
99362	Walla Walla	(509)	31,731	32,237
98671	Washougal	(360)	14,095	15,288
*98801	Wenatchee	(509)	31,925	33,636
*99353	West Richland	(509)	11,811	13,746
98166	White Center (c)	(206)	13,495	—
*98072	Woodinville	(425)	10,938	11,782
*98903	Yakima	(509)	91,067	93,701

West Virginia
Area code 681 overlays area code 304; both apply to the entire state.

ZIP	Place	2010 population	2015 estimate
*25801	Beckley	17,614	17,056
24701	Bluefield	10,447	10,323
*25301	Charleston	51,400	49,736
*26301	Clarksburg	16,578	16,152
*26554	Fairmont	18,704	18,733
*25701	Huntington	49,138	48,638
*25401	Martinsburg	17,227	17,700
*26505	Morgantown	29,660	30,708
*26101	Parkersburg	31,492	30,991
25177	Saint Albans	11,044	10,700
*25303	South Charleston	13,450	13,045
*25526	Teays Valley (c)	13,175	—
*26105	Vienna	10,749	10,573
26062	Weirton	19,746	19,175
26003	Wheeling	28,486	27,648

Wisconsin
Area code 534 overlays area code 715.

ZIP	Place	Area code	2010 population	2015 estimate
54301	Allouez	(920)	13,975	13,930
*54911	Appleton	(920)	72,623	74,139
*54304	Ashwaubenon	(920)	16,963	17,176
53913	Baraboo	(608)	12,048	12,155
53916	Beaver Dam	(920)	16,214	16,564
54311	Bellevue	(920)	14,570	15,317
*53511	Beloit	(608)	36,966	36,891
*53045	Brookfield	(262)	37,920	38,025

ZIP	Place	Area code	2010 population	2015 estimate
*53209	Brown Deer	(414)	11,999	12,102
53105	Burlington	(262)	10,464	10,650
53108	Caledonia	(262)	24,705	24,684
53012	Cedarburg	(262)	11,412	11,482
*54729	Chippewa Falls	(715)	13,661	14,047
53110	Cudahy	(414)	18,267	18,353
54115	De Pere	(920)	23,800	24,724
*54703	Eau Claire	(715)	65,883	67,778
*53711	Fitchburg	(608)	25,260	27,996
*54935	Fond du Lac	(920)	43,021	42,933
53538	Fort Atkinson	(920)	12,368	12,426
53132	Franklin	(414)	35,451	36,222
53022	Germantown	(262)	19,749	19,993
*53209	Glendale	(414)	12,872	12,870
53024	Grafton	(262)	11,459	11,527
*54303	Green Bay	(920)	104,057	105,207
53129	Greendale	(414)	14,046	14,333
*53220	Greenfield	(414)	36,720	37,349
53027	Hartford	(262)	14,223	14,355
*54303	Howard	(920)	17,399	19,250
*54016	Hudson	(715)	12,719	13,566
*53545	Janesville	(608)	63,575	64,123
54130	Kaukauna	(920)	15,462	15,854
*53140	Kenosha	(262)	99,218	99,858
*54601	La Crosse	(608)	51,320	52,306
54140	Little Chute	(920)	10,449	11,026
*53714	Madison	(608)	233,209	248,951
*54220	Manitowoc	(920)	33,736	33,010
54143	Marinette	(715)	10,968	10,799
*54449	Marshfield	(715)	19,118	18,620
54952	Menasha	(920)	17,353	17,572
*53051	Menomonee Falls	(262)	35,626	36,119
54751	Menomonie	(715)	16,264	16,305
*53092	Mequon	(262)	23,132	23,946
53562	Middleton	(608)	17,442	18,979
*53202	Milwaukee	(414)	594,833	600,155
53566	Monroe	(608)	10,827	10,796
*53406	Mount Pleasant	(262)	26,197	26,272
53150	Muskego	(262)	24,135	24,755
*54956	Neenah	(920)	25,501	25,792
*53151	New Berlin	(262)	39,584	39,825
53154	Oak Creek	(414)	34,451	35,243
53066	Oconomowoc	(262)	15,759	16,360
54650	Onalaska	(608)	17,736	18,468
53575	Oregon	(608)	9,231	10,043
*54901	Oshkosh	(920)	66,083	66,555
53072	Pewaukee	(262)	13,195	14,138
53818	Platteville	(608)	11,224	12,572
53158	Pleasant Prairie	(262)	19,719	20,726
54467	Plover	(715)	12,123	12,319
53074	Port Washington	(262)	11,250	11,576
53901	Portage	(608)	10,324	10,382
*53402	Racine	(262)	78,860	77,742
*53076	Richfield	(262)	11,300	11,530
54022	River Falls	(715)	15,000	15,269
*53081	Sheboygan	(920)	49,288	48,797
53211	Shorewood	(414)	13,162	13,311
53172	South Milwaukee	(414)	21,156	21,233
*54481	Stevens Point	(715)	26,717	26,604
53589	Stoughton	(608)	12,611	13,067
*54173	Suamico	(920)	11,346	12,187
*53590	Sun Prairie	(608)	29,364	32,365
54880	Superior	(715)	27,244	26,579
53089	Sussex	(262)	10,518	10,753
*54241	Two Rivers	(920)	11,712	11,331
53593	Verona	(608)	10,619	12,540
*53094	Watertown	(920)	23,861	23,819
*53186	Waukesha	(262)	70,718	71,970
53597	Waunakee	(608)	12,097	13,311
53963	Waupun	(920)	11,340	11,343
*54403	Wausau	(715)	39,106	39,094
*53213	Wauwatosa	(414)	46,396	47,614
*53214	West Allis	(414)	60,411	60,620
*53095	West Bend	(262)	31,078	31,695
*54476	Weston	(715)	14,868	15,069
*53217	Whitefish Bay	(414)	14,110	14,110
53190	Whitewater	(262)	14,390	14,692
*54494	Wisconsin Rapids	(715)	18,367	17,897

Wyoming
Area code 307 applies to the entire state.

ZIP	Place	2010 population	2015 estimate
*82601	Casper	55,316	60,285
*82001	Cheyenne	59,466	63,335
*82930	Evanston	12,359	12,133
*82716	Gillette	29,087	32,649
*82935	Green River	12,515	12,465
*83001	Jackson	9,577	10,523
*82070	Laramie	30,816	32,158
82501	Riverton	10,615	10,873
*82901	Rock Springs	23,036	23,962
82801	Sheridan	17,444	17,873

Chronology of World History

Note: In this section, the notation BCE (before the common era) is applied to years dating to the traditional BC (before Christ) era, and CE (common era) is applied to AD (anno domini) dates. This notation is now preferred in scientific and academic publications. The traditional Gregorian calendar system and its dates and years are unaltered except by these labels.

Other abbreviations used in this chapter include the following: KYA = thousand years ago, MYA = million years ago, c. = circa, fl. = flourished, r. = ruled, b. = born, d. = died.

Prehistory: Our Ancestors Emerge

Reviewed by Marc Kissel, Ph.D., Univ. of Notre Dame, July 2016

Evidence of the origins of *Homo sapiens*, the genus and species to which all living humans belong, comes from an ever increasing number of fossils and DNA studies, and from the archaeological record. Put together, the latest evidence suggests that humans evolved from an ape-like ancestor that lived in eastern and central Africa 8 to 5 million years ago.

Current theories trace the first hominin[1] (primates more closely related to humans than to any other living primate) to Africa, where several distinct genera appear in the fossil record 6-4 MYA. Skeletally, hominins are defined by signs of bipedalism (walking on two legs). They lived in a variety of environments, including swampy forest margins, woodlands, and open savannas (usually near lakes or springs).

Claims of the earliest hominin are inherently controversial. The earliest currently proposed species are *Sahelanthropus tchadensis* (c. 7 MYA, Chad) and *Orrorin tugenensis* (c. 6 MYA, Kenya). The recently described species *Ardipithecus ramidus* (4.4 MYA, Ethiopia) had a chimp-sized brain and a fairly primitive body plan but was bipedal.

Although all humans living today are members of a single species, the fossil record confirms that our ancestors coexisted with a number of similar species throughout our evolutionary history. Starting around 4 MYA one of these earliest hominins gave rise to the australopithecines, a genus of early hominins referred to as "bipedal apes." Scientists divided these into two groups, "gracile" and "robust," each containing a number of species.

The robust australopithecines were characterized by larger molar and premolar teeth; they probably went extinct around 1 MYA. Members of this species adapted a new dietary niche of eating hard foods such as nuts and tubers and have been found in both E and S Africa.

The gracile lineage most likely led to modern humans. *Australopithecus sediba* (2 MYA, South Africa) shows a mosaic of both Australopithecus and early *Homo* traits, leading some to suggest that this is the predecessor to our genus; the morphology of its hand is very suggestive of tool-use. However, while originally believed to arise solely within the genus *Homo*, recent work at the sites of Dikika (3.3 MYA, Ethopia) and Lomekwi (3.3 MYA, Kenya) suggest that earlier hominins were making stone tools.

Our genus, *Homo*, arose 3-2 MYA, with fossils showing early members of our genus being fully bipedal, having larger brains, and hands well-adapted to tool use. The Oldowan tools first appear 2.6 MYA and were used to cut and scrape meat. It is not known whether these early hominins had the ability to speak, but they were social primates, had campsites, and subsisted by gathering plants and small animals and by scavenging other kills, as well as perhaps hunting.

Homo ergaster appeared in E Africa around 1.9 MYA and was the first to leave the continent, spreading throughout Eurasia by c. 1.8 MYA. *H. ergaster* is sometimes grouped with *H. erectus*,

a species first identified on the Indonesian island of Java. It was capable of hunting large and medium-sized animals, such as antelopes and horses, learned to make and control fire, and produced bifacially-flaked tools (sharpened on both sides).

The ability to control fire enormously expanded the human food niche as well as creating new opportunities in the social world. Fire-making possibly began as early as 1 MYA in Africa and is clearly documented throughout Eurasia after c. 500 KYA. Hearths were found in northern Israel by c. 750 KYA, and by 465 KYA in southwestern France.

After about 800 KYA, Europe provides a particularly rich set of fossil evidence usually assigned to *H. erectus*, *H. antecessor*, or *H. heidelbergensis*. This population gave rise to the Neanderthals, who appeared c. 350 KYA. While originally portrayed as savage and unhuman-like, recent research suggests they could probably speak, were proficient hunters of large game, had sophisticated tools and weapons, had ornamentation and other forms of symbolic expression, and a well-developed social organization. On the island of Flores, Indonesia, remains of a species known as *Homo floresiensis*, a 1.1-m (3.5-ft) tall hominin, date from c. 100-60 KYA. Its small stature may be due to limited food and few predators on the small island.

While currently undated, the remains of *Homo naledi* revolutionized the study of human origins. It has a human-like foot and lower limbs, but other aspects of the skeleton, such as the pelvis and shoulder, are more primitive looking. They seem to have been deliberately deposited into a cave system, suggesting an early form of burial.

The oldest modern human fossils (*Homo sapiens*) date to c. 160 KYA and were found at the Herto site in Ethiopia's Middle Awash Valley. The species quickly spread out of Africa, reaching Israel by c. 100 KYA, and Romania by c. 35 KYA. Migration from Asia to Australia took place as early as 60 KYA. What happened when they met other hominins is a subject of intense research. Genetic evidence in the form of ancient DNA suggests that Neanderthals interbred with modern humans. Genetic data also tells us about the Denisovans, a population of early humans dated to c. 50 KYA. Some modern populations retain Denisovan DNA, suggesting a complex web of interactions between these populations.

First confirmation for the crossing from Asia to the Americas by the Bering land bridge dates to the end of the last Ice Age, at 14 KYA. Their arrival was rapidly followed by the extinction of the indigenous Pleistocene megafauna (e.g., mammoths, mastodons) due either to overexploitation by humans, climate change, or a combination of both.

Wooden throwing spears about 3 m (10 ft) long were fashioned by big-game hunters 300 KYA at Schöningen, Germany. Scraping tools, dated after 750 KYA in Europe, N Africa, the Middle East, and Central Asia, suggest the preparation of hides for clothing. Some of the oldest evidence of personal adornment date to around 300 KYA in the form of ochre, while various sites around 100 KYA from South Africa, Morocco, and Israel show the use of perforated shell beads, suggestive of symbolic expression. Although they were probably invented much earlier, impressions in burnt clay from the Czech Republic document the ability to weave cloth baskets and nets by 28 KYA.

Some of the earliest well-dated cave paintings come from the island of Sulawesi, Indonesia, where they date to around the same time as the earliest cave paintings in Europe. The painted caves of Cosquer and Chauvet in southern France have (contested) radiocarbon dates of c. 32 KYA. Painting, engraving, and bodily decoration flourished in Europe 15 KYA, along with stone and ivory sculpture. More than 200 western European caves show remarkable examples of naturalistic wall painting. A few musical instruments—bone flutes with precisely bored holes—have been found in sites dated after 40 KYA.

Skeletal data suggests that after 60-30 KYA the number of people who survived to become grandparents increased. With more adults available to provide child care, humans began to develop more complex, multigenerational social systems. In general, as human cognitive capacities slowly expanded over the Pleistocene, a variety of behavioral modes—in toolmaking, diet, shelter, social arrangements, and spiritual expression—arose as humans adapted to different geographic and climatic zones. By about 13,000 years ago, sites from all over the world

The 18,000-year-old "hobbit" skull (left) found on Flores in Indonesia in 2004 appears to show that the species coexisted with modern humans (skull on right).

show seasonal migration patterns and efficient exploitation of a wide range of plant and animal foods, some of which were eventually domesticated.

Shortly after 12 KYA, among widely separated foraging communities in both hemispheres, a series of dramatic technological and social changes occurred, marking the Neolithic, or New Stone Age. As the world climate became drier and warmer, population/resource imbalances ensued, creating the conditions that allowed for increased human interference in the life cycles of certain plants and animals. This interference ultimately resulted in the appearance of domestication, initially in the northern Middle East.

Domesticated plants and animals encouraged population growth and the appearance of permanent settlements. Agricultural economies increasingly replaced or assimilated hunting and gathering. Reliance upon domesticated plants and animals, coupled with technological advances like pottery-making, precipitated a dramatic increase in world population and social complexity. Genetic research suggests that mutations related to traits currently found in some human populations, such as Europeans' ability to process lactose, arose after this time.

Sites in the Americas, SE Europe, and the Middle East show roughly contemporaneous (12-6 KYA) evidence of Neolithic

domestication economies; similar evidence of E and S Asian, W European, and sub-Saharan African Neolithic adaptations dates to 10-7 KYA. From W Asian sources, farming and the herding of sheep and goats spread rapidly throughout the Mediterranean Basin, perhaps in as short a time interval as 100-200 years. The variety of crops—wheat, barley, rice, maize, squash, beans, and tubers—and a mix of other characteristics suggest that this adaptation occurred independently in as many as 12 or 13 places in both hemispheres.

Evidence for fermented beverages likewise coincides with the early Neolithic settled farming lifestyle. Northern Chinese farmers concocted a wine-like drink from rice, honey, and fruit between 9 and 8 KYA. In highland W Asia, in what is today Iran, vintners were fermenting grapes and making wine by c. 7.4 KYA. The plants and animals associated with the Neolithic Revolution provided the basis for all subsequent social and cultural evolution worldwide.

---

(1) Although "hominid" was standard usage several decades ago, "hominin" is now more commonly used in reference to human ancestors because of developments in the interpretation of primate evolution.

Earliest Civilizations: 4000-1000 BCE

Mesopotamia. Recorded history began with writing in Mesopotamia in the Tigris-Euphrates river valley. The Sumerians used clay tablets with pictographs to keep records after 4000 BCE. A **cuneiform** (wedge-shaped) script, evolved by 3000 BCE as a full syllabic alphabet. Neighboring peoples adapted the script for their own use.

Sumerian life centered, from 4000 BCE, on large cities (Eridu, Ur, Uruk, Nippur, Kish, and Lagash) organized around temples and priestly bureaucracies, with surrounding plains watered by vast irrigation works and worked with traction plows. Sailboats, wheeled vehicles, potter's wheels, and kilns were used. Copper was smelted and tempered from c. 4000 BCE; bronze was produced not long after. Ores, as well as precious stones and metals, were obtained through long-distance ship and caravan trade. Iron was used from c. 2000 BCE. Improved ironworking, developed partly by the Hittites, became widespread by 1200 BCE.

Sumerian political primacy passed among cities and their kingly dynasties. Semitic-speaking peoples, with cultures derived from the Sumerian, founded a succession of dynasties that ruled in Mesopotamia and neighboring areas for most of 1,800 years. Among them were the **Akkadians** (first under Sargon I, c. 2350 BCE), the Amorites (whose laws, codified by **Hammurabi**, c. 1792-1750 BCE, have biblical parallels), and the Assyrians, with interludes of rule by the Hittites, Kassites, and Mitanni.

Mesopotamian learning, preserved in vast libraries such as Elba, was practically oriented. Scribes maintained lists of astronomical phenomena, plants, animals, and stones. Medical texts listed ailments and herbal cures. The Sumerians worshipped anthropomorphic gods representing natural forces. Sacrifices were made at **ziggurats**, or huge stepped temples.

The Syria-Palestine area, site of some of the earliest urban remains (Jericho, 7000 BCE) and of the **Ebla** civilization (fl. 2500 BCE), experienced Egyptian cultural and political influence along with Mesopotamian. The **Phoenician** coast was an active commercial center. A phonetic alphabet was invented here before 1600 BCE. It became the ancestor of many other alphabets.

Egypt. Agricultural villages along the Nile R. were united by around 3300 BCE into two kingdoms, Upper and Lower Egypt. They were unified (c. 3100 BCE) under the pharaoh Menes, as detailed on the Narmer Palate. A bureaucracy supervised construction of canals and monuments (**pyramids** starting 2700 BCE). Control over Nubia to the S was asserted from 2600 BCE.

Brilliant **Old Kingdom** period achievements in architecture, sculpture, and painting reached their height during the 3rd and 4th dynasties. **Hieroglyphic writing** appeared by 3200 BCE, recording a sophisticated literature that included religious writings, philosophy, history, and science. An ordered hierarchy of gods, including totemistic animal elements, was served by a powerful priesthood in Memphis. The pharaoh was identified with the falcon god Horus. Other trends included belief in an afterlife and short-lived quasi-monotheistic reforms introduced by the pharaoh **Akhenaton** (c. 1379-1362 BCE), who was married to Nefertiti.

After a period of dominance by Semitic Hyksos from Asia (c. 1700-1550 BCE), the **New Kingdom** established an empire in Syria. Egypt became increasingly embroiled in Asiatic wars and diplomacy. Conquered by Persia in 525 BCE, it eventually faded away as an independent culture.

South Asia. The bronze age Indus Civilization spanned more than a million square kilometers in Pakistan and the Northwestern India with many sites that expanded beyond the fertile core area of the Indus river system. The civilization independently grew out of local traditions developing complex trade networks and technologies during the Regionalization Era (5500-2600 BCE). The fully urban Harappan 2600-1900 BCE phase featured a standardized system of weights, uniform bricks, stamp seals featuring animals and unicorns, well laid out streets, and water management systems. Long distance trade with Mesopotamia and complex technologies were important. The writing system is one of the last to not be fully deciphered.

The major urban centers such as Dholavira, Harappa, and **Mohenjo-daro** were independent states. The civilization gradually changed due to environmental and cultural changes during the Localization Era (1900-1300 BCE). Post-Indus cultural complexes include the Gandara Grave culture (Swat, c. 1500-500 BCE) and the Painted Grey Ware (1200-800 BCE) culture, which some have associated with Vedic chiefdoms of the **Rig Veda**.

Europe. On Crete, the Bronze Age **Minoan civilization** emerged c. 2500 BCE. A prosperous economy and richly decorative art was supported by seaborne commerce. Mycenae and other cities in mainland Greece and Asia Minor (e.g., **Troy**) preserved elements of the culture until c. 1200 BCE. Cretan Linear A script (c. 2000-1700 BCE) remains undeciphered; Linear B script (c. 1300-1200 BCE) records an early Greek dialect. The possible connection between Mycenaean monumental stonework and the megalithic monuments of Western Europe, Iberia, and Malta (c. 4000-1500 BCE) is unclear.

China. Proto-Chinese Neolithic cultures had long covered N and SE China when the first large political state was organized in the

The Pyramids of Giza, including the Great Pyramid, were built during Egypt's 4th dynasty (c. 2575-2465 BCE).

N by the **Shang dynasty** (c. 1523 BCE). Shang kings called themselves Sons of Heaven, and they presided over a cult of human and animal sacrifice to ancestors and nature gods. The Chou dynasty, starting c. 1027 BCE, expanded the area of the Sons of Heaven's dominion, but feudal states exercised most temporal power.

A writing system with 2,000 characters was already in use under the Shang, with **pictographs** later supplemented by phonetic characters. Many of its principles and symbols, despite changes in spoken Chinese, were preserved in later writing systems. Technical advances allowed urban specialists to create fine ceramic and jade products, and bronze casting after 1500 BCE was the most advanced in the world. Bronze artifacts discovered in northern Thailand date from 3600 BCE, hundreds of years before similar Middle Eastern finds.

Americas. Olmecs settled (1500 BCE) on the Gulf coast of Mexico and developed the first known civilization in the Western Hemisphere. Temple cities and huge stone sculptures date from 1200 BCE. A rudimentary calendar and writing system existed. Olmec religion—centered on a jaguar god—and art forms influenced later Mesoamerican cultures.

Formation of Classical Societies: 1000-400 BCE

Greece. After a period of decline during the Dorian Greek invasions (1200-1000 BCE), the Aegean area developed a unique civilization. Drawing on Mycenaean traditions, Mesopotamian learning (weights and measures, lunisolar calendar, astronomy, musical scales), the Phoenician alphabet (modified for Greek), and Egyptian art, **Greek city-states** saw a rich elaboration of intellectual life. The two great epic poems attributed to **Homer**, the *Iliad* and the *Odyssey*, were probably composed around the 8th cent. BCE. Long-range commerce was aided by metal coinage (introduced by the Lydians in Asia Minor before 700 BCE). Colonies were founded around the Mediterranean (Cumae in Italy in 760 BCE; Massalia in France c. 600 BCE) and Black Sea shores.

Philosophy, starting with Ionian speculation on the nature of matter (Thales, c. 634-546 BCE), continued by other "Pre-Socratics" (e.g., Heraclitus, c. 535-415 BCE; Parmenides, b. c. 515 BCE), reached a high point in Athens in the rationalist idealism of **Plato** (c. 428-347 BCE), a disciple of **Socrates** (c. 469-399 BCE; executed for alleged impiety), and in **Aristotle** (384-322 BCE), a pioneer in many fields, from natural sciences to logic, ethics, and metaphysics. The arts were highly valued. Architecture culminated in the **Parthenon** (438 BCE) by Phidias (fl. 490-430 BCE). Poetry (Sappho, c. 610-580 BCE; Pindar, c. 518-438 BCE) and drama (Aeschylus, 525-456 BCE; Sophocles, c. 496-406 BCE; Euripides, c. 484-406 BCE) thrived. Male beauty and strength, a chief artistic theme, were celebrated at the national games at Olympia.

Ruled by local tyrants or **oligarchies**, the Greeks were not politically united but managed to resist inclusion in the Persian Empire. Persian king Darius was defeated at Marathon (490 BCE), his son Xerxes at Salamis (480 BCE), and the Persian army at Plataea (479 BCE). Democracy sprouted in Athens as statesman Pericles (495-429 BCE) sought participation in government from all citizens. Local warfare was common; the **Peloponnesian Wars** (431-404 BCE) ended in Sparta's victory over Athens. Greek political power subsequently waned, but Greek cultural forms spread far and wide.

Hebrews. Nomadic Hebrew tribes entered Canaan before 1200 BCE, settling among other Semitic peoples speaking the same language. They brought from the desert a **monotheistic** faith said to have been revealed to Abraham in Canaan c. 1800 BCE and Moses at Mt. Sinai c. 1250 BCE, after the Hebrews' escape from bondage in Egypt. David (r. 1000-961 BCE) and Solomon (r. 961-922 BCE) united them in a kingdom that briefly dominated the area. **Phoenicians** to the N founded Mediterranean colonies (Carthage, c. 814 BCE) and sailed into the Atlantic.

A temple in Jerusalem became the national religious center, with sacrifices performed by a hereditary priesthood. Polytheistic influences, especially of the fertility cult of Baal, were opposed by **prophets** (Elijah, Amos, Isaiah).

Divided into **two kingdoms** after Solomon, the Hebrews were unable to resist the revived Assyrian empire, which conquered **Israel**, the northern kingdom, in 722 BCE. **Judah**, the southern kingdom, was conquered in 586 BCE by the Babylonians under Nebuchadnezzar II. With the fixing of most of the biblical canon by the mid-4th cent. BCE and the emergence of rabbis, Judaism successfully survived the loss of Hebrew autonomy. A Jewish kingdom was revived under the Hasmoneans (168-42 BCE).

China. During the **Eastern Zhou** dynasty (770-256 BCE), Chinese culture spread E to the sea and S to the Yangtze R. Large feudal states on the periphery of the empire contended for preeminence but continued to recognize the Son of Heaven (king), who retained a purely ritual role enriched with courtly music and dance. In the Age of Warring States (403-221 BCE), when the first sections of the **Great Wall** were built, the Qin state in the W gained supremacy and finally united all of China.

Iron tools entered China c. 500 BCE. Casting techniques were advanced, aiding agriculture. Peasants owned their land and owed civil and military service to nobles. China's cities grew in number and size; barter remained the chief trade medium.

Intellectual ferment among noble scribes and officials produced a classical age of Chinese literature and philosophy. **Confucius** (551-479 BCE) urged a restoration of a supposedly harmonious social order of the past through proper conduct in accordance with one's station and through filial and ceremonial piety. The *Analects* attributed to him are revered throughout E Asia.

Among other thinkers, **Mencius** (d. 289 BCE) added the view that the Mandate of Heaven can be removed from an unjust dynasty. The Legalists sought to curb the supposed natural wickedness of people through new institutions and harsh laws. The Naturalists emphasized the balance of opposites—yin, yang—in the world. **Daoists** sought mystical knowledge through meditation and disengagement.

India. The political and cultural center of India shifted from the Indus to the Ganges River Valley. Buddhism, Jainism, and mystical revisions of orthodox Vedism all developed c. 500-300 BCE. The *Upanishads*, last part of the *Veda*, urged escape from the cycle of rebirth into the physical world. Vedism remained the preserve of the Brahman caste.

In contrast, **Buddhism**, founded by Siddhartha Gautama (c. 563-c. 483 BCE)—Buddha ("Enlightened One")—appealed to merchants in the urban centers and took hold at first (and most lastingly) on the geographic fringes of Indian civilization. The classic Indian epics were composed in this era: the *Ramayana* perhaps c. 300 BCE, the *Mahabharata* over a period starting around 400 BCE.

Northern India was divided into a large number of monarchies and aristocratic republics, probably derived from tribal groupings, when the Magadha kingdom was formed in Bihar c. 542 BCE. It soon became the dominant power. The **Maurya** dynasty, founded by Chandragupta c. 321 BCE, expanded the kingdom, uniting most of Northern India in a centralized bureaucratic empire. The third Mauryan king, **Asoka** (r. c. 274-236 BCE), conquered most of the subcontinent. He converted to Buddhism, inscribed its tenets on pillars throughout India, and downplayed the caste system.

Before its final decline in India, Buddhism developed into a popular worship of heavenly Bodhisattvas ("enlightened beings"), and it produced a refined architecture (the Great Stupa [shrine] at Sanchi, 100 CE) and sculpture (Gandhara reliefs, 1-400 CE).

Persia. Aryan peoples (Persians, Medes) dominated the area of present Iran by the beginning of the 1st millennium BCE. The prophet **Zoroaster** (b. c. 628 BCE) introduced a dualistic religion in which the forces of good (Ahura Mazda, "Lord of Wisdom") and evil (Ahriman) battle for dominance; individuals are judged by their actions and earn damnation or salvation. Zoroaster's hymns (*Gathas*) are included in the *Avesta*, the Zoroastrian scriptures. A version of this faith became the established religion of the Persian Empire.

Africa. Nubia, periodically occupied by Egypt since about 2600 BCE, ruled Egypt c. 750-661 BCE and survived as an independent Egyptianized kingdom (**Kush**; capital Meroe) for 1,000 years. The Iron Age Nok culture flourished c. 500 BCE-200 CE on the Benue Plateau of **Nigeria**.

Americas. The Chavin culture controlled Northern Peru c. 900 BCE to 200 BCE. Its ceremonial centers, featuring the jaguar god, survived long after. Its architecture, ceramics, and textiles had influenced other Peruvian cultures. **Mayan civilization** began to develop in Central America as early as 1500 BCE.

Great Empires Unite the Classical World: 400 BCE-400 CE

Persia and the Mediterranean. Cyrus, ruler of a small kingdom in Persia from 559 BCE, united the Persians and Medes within 10 years and conquered Asia Minor and Babylonia in another 10. His son Cambyses, followed by **Darius** (r. 522-486 BCE), added vast lands to the E and N as far as the Indus Valley and Central Asia, as well as Egypt and Thrace. The whole empire was ruled by an international bureaucracy and army, with Persians holding the chief positions. The resources and styles of all the subject civilizations were exploited to create a rich syncretic art.

The kingdom of Macedon, which under Philip II dominated the Greek world and Egypt, was passed on to Philip's son **Alexander** in 336 BCE. Within 13 years, Alexander had conquered all the Persian dominions. Imbued by his tutor Aristotle with Greek ideals, Alexander encouraged colonization, and Greek-style cities were founded. After his death in 323 BCE, wars of succession divided the empire into three significant dynasties—the **Antigonids** in Asia Minor and Macedon, the **Ptolemies** in Egypt, and the **Seleucids** in Mesopotamia. In the ensuing 300 years (the **Hellenistic Era**), a cosmopolitan Greek-oriented culture permeated the ancient world from Western Europe to the borders of India, absorbing native elites everywhere.

Hellenistic philosophy stressed the private individual's search for happiness. The Cynics followed Diogenes (c. 372-287 BCE), who stressed self-sufficiency and restriction of desires and expressed contempt for luxury and social convention. Zeno (c. 335-c. 263 BCE) and the **Stoics** exalted reason, identified it with virtue, and counseled an ascetic disregard for misfortune. The **Epicureans** tried to build lives of moderate pleasure without political or emotional involvement. Hellenistic arts imitated life realistically, especially in sculpture and literature (comedies of Menander, 342-292 BCE).

The sciences thrived, especially at Alexandria, where the Ptolemies financed a great library and museum. Fields of study included mathematics (**Euclid**'s geometry, c. 300 BCE); astronomy (heliocentric theory of Aristarchus, 310-230 BCE; Julian calendar, 45 BCE; **Ptolemy**'s *Almagest*, c. 150 CE); geography (world map of Eratosthenes, 276-194 BCE); hydraulics (**Archimedes**, 287-212 BCE); medicine (Galen, 130-200 CE); and chemistry. Inventors refined uses for siphons, valves, gears, springs, screws, levers, cams, and pulleys.

A restored Persian empire under the **Parthians** (northern Iranian tribespeople) controlled the eastern Hellenistic world from 250 BCE to 229 CE. The Parthians and the succeeding **Sassanian dynasty** (c. 224-651 CE) fought with Rome periodically. The Sassanians revived Zoroastrianism as a state religion and patronized a nationalist artistic and scholarly renaissance.

Rome. The city of Rome was founded, according to legend, by Romulus in 753 BCE. Through military expansion and colonization, and by granting citizenship to leading members of conquered tribes, the city annexed all of Italy S of the Po R. in the 100-year period before 268 BCE. The Latin and other Italic tribes were annexed first, followed by the **Etruscans** (founders of a great civilization N of Rome) and Greek colonies in the S. With a large standing army and reserve forces of several hundred thousand, Rome was able to defeat **Carthage** in the three

Punic Wars (264-241 BCE, 218-201 BCE, 149-146 BCE), despite the invasion of Italy by **Hannibal** (218 BCE), thus gaining Sicily and territory in Spain and N Africa.

Rome exploited local disputes to conquer Greece and Asia Minor in the 2nd cent. BCE and Egypt in the 1st (after the defeat and suicide of **Antony and Cleopatra**, 30 BCE). The Mediterranean civilized world, up to the disputed Parthian border, was now Roman and remained so for 500 years. Less civilized regions were added to the Empire: Gaul (conquered by **Julius Caesar**, 58-51 BCE), Britain (43 CE), and Dacia NE of the Danube (107 CE).

The original aristocratic republican government, with democratic features added in the 5th and 4th cent. BCE, deteriorated under the pressures of empire and class conflict (**Gracchus** brothers, social reformers, murdered in 133 BCE and 121 BCE; slave revolts in 135 BCE and 73 BCE). After a series of civil wars (Marius vs. Sulla, 88-82 BCE; Caesar vs. **Pompey**, 49-45 BCE; triumvirate vs. Caesar's assassins, 44-43 BCE; Antony vs. Octavian, 32-30 BCE), the empire came under the rule of a deified monarch (first emperor, **Augustus**, 27 BCE-14 CE).

Provincials (nearly all granted citizenship by Caracalla, 212 CE) came to dominate the army and civil service. Traditional **Roman law**, systematized and interpreted by independent jurists, and local self-rule in provincial cities were supplanted by a vast tax-collecting bureaucracy in the 3rd and 4th cent. The legal rights of women, children, and slaves were strengthened.

Roman innovations in **civil engineering** included water mills, windmills, and rotary mills and the use of cement that hardened under water. Monumental architecture (baths, theaters, temples) relied on the arch and the dome. A network of roads (some still standing) stretched 53,000 mi, passing through mountain tunnels as long as 3.5 mi. Aqueducts brought water to cities; underground sewers removed waste.

Roman art and literature were derivative of Greek models. Innovations were made in sculpture (naturalistic busts, equestrian statues), decorative wall painting (as at Pompeii), satire (**Juvenal**, 60-127 CE), history (**Tacitus**, 56-120 CE), and prose romance (**Petronius**, d. 66 CE). Gladiatorial contests dominated public amusements, which were supported by the state.

India. The **Gupta** monarchs reunited Northern India c. 320 CE. Their peaceful and prosperous reign saw a revival of Hindu religious thought and Brahman power. The old Vedic traditions were combined with devotion to many indigenous deities (who were seen as manifestations of Vedic gods). Caste lines were reinforced, and Buddhist practices gradually disappeared or were integrated with **Hindu** traditions. The art (often erotic), architecture, and literature of the period, patronized by the Gupta court, are considered among India's finest achievements (Kalidasa, poet and dramatist, fl. c. 400 CE). Mathematical innovations included the use of zero and decimal numbers. Invasions by White Huns from the NW led to the empire's destruction c. 550 CE. Rich cultures also developed in Southern India during this period. Emotional Tamil religious poetry contributed to the Hindu revival. The Pallava kingdom controlled much of Southern India c. 350-880 CE and helped to spread Indian civilization to SE Asia.

China. The Qin ruler Shih Huang Ti (r. 221-210 BCE), known as the First Emperor, centralized political authority; standardized the written language, laws, weights, measures, and coinage; and conducted a census. But he tried to destroy most philosophical texts. The **Han** dynasty (202 BCE-220 CE) instituted the Mandarin bureaucracy, which lasted 2,000 years. Local officials were selected by examination in Confucian classics and trained at the imperial university and provincial schools.

The invention of **paper** facilitated this bureaucratic system. Agriculture was promoted, but peasants bore most of the tax burden. Irrigation was improved, water clocks and sundials were used, astronomy and mathematics thrived, and landscape painting was perfected.

With the expansion S and W (to nearly the present borders of today's China), trade was opened with India, SE Asia, and the Middle East over sea and caravan routes. Indian missionaries brought Mahayana Buddhism to China by the 1st cent. CE and spawned a variety of sects. Daoism was revived and merged with popular superstitions. **Daoist and Buddhist monasteries** and convents multiplied in the turbulent centuries after the collapse of the Han dynasty in 220 CE.

China's Great Wall, first built during the Age of Warring States (403-221 BCE), was rebuilt, extended, and modified over thousands of years to protect China from invaders.

Monotheism Spreads: 1-750 CE

Roman Empire. Polytheism was practiced in the Roman Empire, and religions indigenous to particular Middle Eastern nations became international. Roman citizens worshiped **Isis** of Egypt, **Mithras** of Persia, **Demeter** of Greece, and the great mother **Cybele** of Phrygia. Their cults centered on mysteries (secret ceremonies) and the promise of an afterlife, symbolized by the death and rebirth of the god. The Jews of the empire preserved their monotheistic religion, Judaism, the world's oldest (c. 1300 BCE) continuous religion. Its teachings are contained in the Bible (the Old Testament). 1st-cent. CE Judaism embraced several sects, including the **Sadducees**, mostly drawn from the Temple priesthood, who were culturally Hellenized; the **Pharisees**, who upheld the full range of traditional customs and practices as of equal weight to literal scriptural law and elaborated synagogue worship; and the **Essenes**, an ascetic, millenarian sect. Messianic fervor led to repeated, unsuccessful rebellions against Rome (66-70, 135 CE). As a result, the Temple in Jerusalem was destroyed and the population decimated; this event marked the beginning of the Diaspora (living in exile). To preserve the faith, codification of law was begun at the academy of Yavneh. The work continued for some 500 years in Palestine and in Babylonia, ending in the final redaction (c. 600) of the **Talmud**, a huge collection of legal and moral debates, rulings, liturgy, biblical exegesis, and legendary materials.

Christianity. Emerging as a distinct sect by the second half of the 1st cent. CE, Christianity is based on the teachings of **Jesus**, whom believers considered the Savior (Messiah or Christ) and son of God. Missionary activities of the Apostles and such early leaders as **Paul of Tarsus** spread the faith. Intermittent persecution, as in Rome under Nero in 64 CE, on grounds of suspected disloyalty, failed to disrupt Christian communities. Each congregation, generally urban and of plebeian character, was tightly organized under a leader (bishop), elders (presbyters or priests), and assistants (deacons). The four **Gospels** (accounts of the life and teachings of Jesus) and the Acts of the Apostles were written down in the late 1st and early 2nd cent. and circulated along with letters of Paul and other Christian leaders. An authoritative canon of these writings was not fixed until the 4th cent.

A school for priests was established at Alexandria in the 2nd cent. Its teachers (**Origen**, c. 182-251) helped define doctrine and promote the faith in Greek-style philosophical works. Neoplatonism underwent Christian coloration in the writings of Church Fathers such as **Augustine** (354-430). Christian hermits began to associate in monasteries, first in Egypt (St. Pachomius, c. 290-345), then in other eastern lands, then in the W (**St. Benedict's rule**, 529). Devotion to saints, especially Mary, mother of Jesus, spread. Under **Constantine** (r. 306-37), Christianity became in effect the established religion of the Empire. Pagan temples were expropriated, state funds were used to build churches and support the hierarchy, and laws were adjusted in accordance with Christian ideas. Pagan worship was banned by the end of the 4th cent., and severe restrictions were placed on Judaism.

The newly established church was rocked by doctrinal disputes, often exacerbated by regional rivalries. Chief heresies (as defined by church councils, backed by imperial authority) were **Arianism**, which denied the divinity of Jesus; **Monophysitism**, denying the human nature of Christ; **Donatism**, which regarded as invalid any sacraments administered by sinful clergy; and **Pelagianism**, which denied the necessity of unmerited divine aid (grace) for salvation.

Islam. The earliest Arab civilization emerged by the end of the 2nd millennium BCE in the watered highlands of Yemen. Seaborne and caravan trade in frankincense and myrrh connected the area with the Nile and Fertile Crescent. The Minaean, Sabean (Sheba), and Himyarite states successively held sway. By Muhammad's time (7th cent. CE), the region was a province of Sassanian Persia. In the N, the Nabataean kingdom at Petra and the kingdom of Palmyra were Aramaicized, Romanized, and finally absorbed, as neighboring Judea had been, into the Roman Empire. Nomads shared the central region with a few trading towns and oases. Wars between tribes and raids on communities were common and were celebrated in a poetic tradition that by the 6th cent. helped establish a classic literary Arabic.

About 610, **Muhammad**, a 40-year-old Arab man of Mecca, emerged as a prophet. He proclaimed a revelation from the one true God, calling on contemporaries to abandon idolatry and restore the faith of Abraham. He introduced his religion as **Islam**, meaning "submission" to the one God, Allah, as a continuation of the biblical faith of Abraham, Moses, and Jesus, all respected as prophets in this system. His teachings, recorded in the Quran, in many ways were inclusive of Abrahamic monotheistic ideas known to the Jews and Christians in Arabia. A key aspect of the Abrahamic connection was insistence on justice in society, which led to severe opposition among the aristocrats in Mecca. As conditions worsened for Muhammad and his followers, he decided in 622 to make a *hegira* (flight) to Medina, 200 mi to the N. This event marks the beginning of the Muslim lunar calendar. Hostilities between Mecca and Medina increased, and in 629 Muhammad conquered Mecca. By the time he died in 632, nearly all the Arabian peninsula accepted his political and religious leadership.

After his death the majority of Muslims (later known as **Sunni** Muslims) recognized the leadership of the **caliph** (successor) Abu Bakr (632-34), followed by Umar (634-44), Uthman (644-56), and Ali (656-60). A minority, the **Shiites**, insisted instead on the leadership of Ali, Muhammad's cousin and son-in-law. By 644, **Muslim rule** over Arabia was confirmed. Muslim armies had threatened the Byzantine and Persian empires, which were weakened by wars and disaffection among subject peoples (including Coptic and Syriac Christians opposed to the Byzantine Orthodox establishment). Syria, Palestine, Egypt, Iraq, and Persia fell to Muslim armies. The new administration assimilated existing systems in the region; hence the conquered peoples participated in running the empire. The Quran recognized the so-called Peoples of the Book, i.e., Christians, Jews, and Zoroastrians, as tolerated monotheists, and Muslim policy was relatively tolerant to minorities living as "protected" peoples. An expanded tax system, based on conquests of the Persian and Byzantine empires, provided revenue to organize campaigns against neighboring non-Muslim regions.

Under the **Umayyads** (661-750) and **Abbasids** (750-1256), territorial expansion led Muslim armies across N Africa and into Spain (711). Muslim armies in the W were stopped at Tours, France, in 732 by the Frankish ruler **Charles Martel**. Asia Minor, the Indus Valley, and Transoxiana were conquered in the E. The conversion of conquered peoples to Islam was gradual. In many places the official Arabic language supplanted the local tongues. But in the eastern regions the Arab rulers and their armies adopted Persian cultures and language as part of their Muslim identity.

Disputes over succession and pious opposition to injustices in society led to a number of oppositional movements, which led to the factionalization of Muslim community. The **Shiites** supported leadership candidates descended from Muhammad, believing them to be carriers of some kind of divine authority. The **Kharijites** supported an egalitarian system derived from the Quran, opposing and even engaging in battle against those who did not agree with them.

Islam's primary religious text, the Quran, dates to c. 632 CE and contains 114 chapters known as *sura*.

New Peoples Enter World History: 400-900 CE

Barbarian invasions and fall of Rome. Germanic tribes infiltrated S and E from their Baltic homeland during the 1st millennium BCE, reaching southern Germany by 100 BCE and the Black Sea by 214 CE. Organized into large federated tribes under elected kings, most resisted Roman domination and raided the empire in times of civil war (Goths took Dacia in 214, raided Thrace in 251-69). Germanic troops and commanders dominated the Roman armies by the end of the 4th cent. **Huns**, invaders from Asia, entered Europe in 372, driving more Germans into the empire. Emperor Valens allowed Visigoths to cross the Danube in 376. Huns under Attila (d. 453) raided Gaul, Italy, and the Balkans.

The western empire, weakened by overtaxation and social stagnation, was overrun in the 5th cent. Gaul was effectively lost in 406-07, Spain in 409, Britain in 410, and Africa in 429-39. Rome was sacked in 410 by Visigoths under Alaric and in 455 by Vandals. The **last western emperor**, Romulus Augustulus, was deposed in 476 by the Germanic chief Odoacer.

Celts. Celtic cultures, which in pre-Roman times covered most of W Europe, were confined almost entirely to the British Isles after the Germanic invasions. **St. Patrick** completed (c. 457-92) the conversion of Ireland and a strong monastic tradition took hold. Irish monastic missionaries in Scotland, England, and on the continent (Columba, c. 521-97; Columbanus, c. 543-615) helped restore Christianity after the Germanic invasions. **Monasteries** became centers of classic and Christian learning and presided over the recording of a Christianized Celtic mythology, elaborated by secular writers and bards. An intricate decorative art style developed, especially in book illumination (Lindisfarne Gospels, c. 700; Book of Kells, 8th cent.).

Successor states. The Visigothic kingdom in Spain (from 419) and much of France (to 507) saw continuation of Roman administration, language, and law (Breviary of Alaric, 506) until its destruction by the Muslims (711). The Vandal kingdom in Africa (from 429) was conquered by the Byzantines in 533. Italy was ruled successively by an Ostrogothic kingdom under Byzantine suzerainty (489-554), direct Byzantine government, and German Lombards (568-774). The Lombards divided the peninsula between the Byzantines and papacy under the dynamic reformer **Pope Gregory the Great** (590-604) and successors.

King Clovis (r. 481-511) united the Franks on both sides of the Rhine and, after his conversion to Christianity, defeated the Arian heretics, Burgundians (after 500), and Visigoths (507) with the support of native clergy and the papacy. Under the **Merovingian** kings, a feudal system emerged: power was fragmented among hierarchies of military landowners. Social stratification, which in late Roman times had acquired legal, hereditary sanction, was reinforced.

The Carolingians (747-987) expanded the kingdom and restored central power. **Charlemagne** (r. 768-814) conquered nearly all the Germanic lands, including Lombard Italy. He was crowned emperor by Pope Leo III in Rome in 800. A centuries-long decline in commerce and arts was reversed under Charlemagne's patronage. He welcomed Jews to his kingdom, which became a center of Jewish learning (Rashi, 1040-1105). He sponsored the Carolingian Renaissance of learning under the Anglo-Latin scholar Alcuin (c. 732-804), who reformed church liturgy.

Byzantine Empire. Under **Diocletian** (r. 284-305) the Roman empire had been divided into two parts to facilitate administration and defense. **Constantine** founded (330) **Constantinople** (at old Byzantium) as a fully Christian city. Commerce and taxation financed a sumptuous, orientalized court, a class of hereditary bureaucratic families, and magnificent urban construction (Hagia Sophia, 532-37). The city's fortifications and naval innovations repelled assaults by Goths, Huns, Slavs, Bulgars, Avars, Arabs, and Scandinavians. Greek replaced Latin as the official language by c. 700. **Byzantine art**, a solemn, sacral, and stylized variation of late classical styles (mosaics at the Church of San Vitale, Ravenna, Italy, 526-48), was a starting point for medieval art in Eastern and Western Europe.

Justinian (r. 527-65) briefly reconquered parts of Spain, N Africa, and Italy, codified **Roman law** (Codex Justinianus [529] was medieval Europe's chief legal text), closed the Platonic Academy at Athens, and ordered all pagans to convert. Lombards in Italy and Arabs in Africa retook most of his conquests. The Isaurian dynasty from Anatolia (from 717) and the Macedonian

dynasty (867-1054) restored military and commercial power. The Iconoclast controversy (726-843) over the permissibility of images helped alienate the Eastern Church from the papacy.

Abbasid Empire. Baghdad (established 762) became seat of the **Abbasid dynasty** (established 750), while Umayyads continued to rule in Spain. A brilliant cosmopolitan civilization emerged, inaugurating a Muslim-Arab golden age. Arabic was the lingua franca of the empire; intellectual sources from Persian, Sanskrit, Greek, and Syriac were rendered into Arabic. Christians and Jews equally participated in this translation movement, which also involved interaction between Jewish legal thought and Islamic law, as much as between Christian theology and Muslim scholasticism. Persian-style court life, with art and music, flourished at the court of **Harun al-Rashid** (786-809), celebrated in the masterpiece known to English readers as *The Arabian Nights*. The sciences, medicine, and mathematics were pursued at Baghdad, Cordova, and Cairo (c. 969). The culmination of this intellectual synthesis in Islamic civilization came with the scientific and philosophical works of **Avicenna** (Ibn Sina, 980-1037), **Averroes** (Ibn Rushd, 1126-98), and **Maimonides** (1135-1204), a Jew who wrote in Arabic. This intellectual tradition was translated into Latin and opened a new period in Christian thought.

The decentralization of the Abbasid empire, from 874, led to the establishment of various Muslim dynasties under different ethnic groups. Persians, Berbers, and Turks ruled different regions, retaining connection with the Abbasid caliph at the religious level. The Abbasid period also saw various religious movements against the orthodox position held by governing authorities. This situation in Muslim religion led to the establishment of different legal, theological, and mystical schools of thought. The most influential mass movement was **Sufism**, which aimed at the reaching out of the average individual in quest of a spiritual path. Al-Ghazali (1058-1111) is credited with reconciling personal Sufism with orthodox Sunni tradition.

Africa. Immigrants from Saba in S Arabia helped set up the **Axum** kingdom in Ethiopia in the 1st cent. (their language, Ge'ez, is preserved by the Ethiopian Church). In the 3rd cent., when the kingdom became Christianized, it defeated Kushite Meroe and expanded its influence into Yemen. Axum was the center of a vast ivory trade and controlled the Red Sea coast until c. 1100. Arab conquest in Egypt cut Axum's political and economic ties with Byzantium.

The Iron Age entered W Africa by the end of the 1st millennium BCE. **Ghana**, the first known sub-Saharan state, ruled in the upper Senegal-Niger region c. 400-1240, controlling the trade of gold from mines in the S to trans-Sahara caravan routes to the N. The **Bantu** peoples, probably of W African origin, began to spread E and S perhaps 2,000 years ago, displacing the Pygmies and Bushmen of central and southern Africa during a 1,500-year period.

Japan. The advanced Neolithic Yayoi period, when irrigation, rice farming, and iron and bronze casting techniques were introduced from China or Korea, persisted to c. 400 CE. The myriad Japanese states were then united by the **Yamato** clan, under an emperor who acted as chief priest of the animistic Shinto cult. Japanese political and military intervention by the 6th cent. in Korea, then under strong Chinese influence, quickened a Chinese cultural invasion of Japan, bringing Buddhism, the Chinese language (which long remained a literary and governmental medium), Chinese ideographs, and Buddhist styles in painting, sculpture, literature, and architecture (7th cent., Horyuji temple at Nara). The Taika Reforms (646) tried unsuccessfully to centralize Japan according to Chinese bureaucratic and Buddhist philosophical values.

A nativist reaction against the Buddhist **Nara** period (710-94) ushered in the **Heian** period (794-1185) centered at the new capital, Kyoto. Japanese elegance and simplicity modified Chinese styles in architecture, scroll painting, and literature; the writing system was also simplified. The courtly novel *Tale of Genji* (1010-20) testifies to the enhanced role of women in medieval Japanese literature and culture.

Southeast Asia. The historic peoples of SE Asia began arriving some 2,500 years ago from China and Tibet, displacing scattered aborigines. Their agriculture relied on rice and yams. Indian cultural influences were strongest; literacy and Hindu and Buddhist ideas followed the S India-China trade route. From the

The Khmer empire (fl. 800-1300) erected the Angkor complex—including dozens of temples, reservoirs, and canals—over a period of hundreds of years.

southern tip of Indochina, the kingdom of **Funan** (1st-7th cent.) traded as far W as Persia. It was absorbed by Chenla, itself conquered by the **Khmer** empire (800-1300). The Khmers, under Hindu god-kings (Suryavarman II, 1113-c. 1150), built the monumental Angkor Wat temple center for the royal phallic cult. The **Nam-Viet** kingdom in Annam, dominated by China and Chinese culture for 1,000 years, emerged in the 10th cent., growing at the expense of the Khmers, who also lost ground in the NW to the new, highly organized **Thai** kingdom. On Sumatra, the **Srivijaya** empire controlled vital sea lanes (7th-10th

cent.). A Buddhist dynasty, the Sailendras, ruled central **Java** (8th-9th cent.), building at Borobudur one of the largest stupas (dome-shaped Buddhist shrines) in the world.

China. The Sui dynasty (581-618) ushered in a period of commercial, artistic, and scientific achievement in China, which continued under the **Tang** dynasty (618-906). Inventions like the magnetic compass, gunpowder, the abacus, and printing were introduced or perfected. Medical innovations included cataract surgery. The state, from its cosmopolitan capital, Chang-an, supervised foreign trade, which exchanged Chinese silks, porcelains, and art for spices and ivory over Central Asian caravan routes and sea routes reaching Africa. A golden age of poetry bequeathed valuable works to later generations (Tu Fu, 712-70; Li Po, 701-62). Landscape painting flourished.

Commercial and industrial expansion continued under the **Northern Sung** dynasty (960-1126), facilitated by paper money and credit notes. But commerce never achieved full respectability; government monopolies expropriated successful merchants. The population, long stable at 50 million, doubled in 200 years with the introduction of early-ripening rice and the double harvest. In art, native Chinese styles were revived.

Americas. From 300 to 600, a Native American empire stretched from the Valley of Mexico to Guatemala, centering on the huge city **Teotihuacán** (founded 100 BCE). To the S, in Guatemala, a high **Mayan** civilization developed (150-900) around hundreds of rural ceremonial centers. The Mayans improved on Olmec writing and the calendar and pursued astronomy and mathematics. In South America, a widespread pre-Inca culture grew from **Tiahuanacu**, Bolivia, near Lake Titicaca (Gateway of the Sun doorway, c. 700).

Christian Europe Regroups and Expands: 900-1300

Scandinavia. Pagan Danish and Norse (Viking) adventurers, traders, and pirates raided the coasts of the British Isles (Dublin, c. 831), France, and even the Mediterranean for over 200 years beginning in the late 8th cent. Inland settlement in the W was limited to Great Britain (King Canute, 994-1035) and Normandy, settled (911) under Rollo, as a fief of France. Vikings also reached Iceland (874), Greenland (c. 986), and North America (**Leif Ericson** and others, c. 1000). Norse traders (**Varangians**) developed Russian river commerce from the 8th to the 11th cent. and helped set up a state at Kiev in the late 9th cent. Conversion to Christianity occurred in the 10th cent., reaching Sweden 100 years later. In the 11th cent. Norman bands conquered Southern Italy and Sicily, and Duke **William of Normandy** conquered (1066) England, bringing feudal government and the French language, essential elements in later English civilization.

Central and East Europe. Slavs began to expand from about 150 CE in all directions in Europe. By the 7th cent. they reached as far S as the Adriatic and Aegean seas. In the Balkan Peninsula they dislocated Romanized local populations or assimilated newcomers (Bulgarians, a Turkic people). The first **Slavic states** were Moravia (628) in Central Europe and the Bulgarian state (680) in the Balkans. Byzantine missions of St. Methodius and Cyril (whose Greek-based cyrillic alphabet is still used by some Southern and Eastern Slavs) converted (863) Moravia.

The Eastern Slavs, part-civilized under the overlordship of the Turkish-Jewish **Khazar** trading empire (7th-10th cent.), gravitated toward Constantinople by the 9th cent. The **Kievan** state adopted (989) Eastern Christianity under Prince Vladimir. King Boleslav I (992-1025) began **Poland**'s long history of conquest. The Magyars (**Hungarians**), in present-day Hungary since 896, accepted (1001) Latin Christianity.

Germany. The German kingdom that emerged after the breakup of Charlemagne's Western Empire remained a confederation of largely autonomous states. Otto I, a Saxon who was king from 936, established the **Holy Roman Empire**—a union of Germany and Northern Italy—in alliance with Pope John XII, who crowned (962) him emperor; he defeated (955) the Magyars. Imperial power was greatest under the **Hohenstaufens** (1138-1254), despite the growing opposition of the papacy, which ruled central Italy and the Lombard League cities. Frederick II (1194-1250) improved administration and patronized the arts. After his death, German influence was removed from Italy.

Christian Spain. From its northern mountain redoubts, Christian rule slowly migrated S through the 11th cent., when Muslim unity collapsed. After the capture (1085) of **Toledo**, the kingdoms of Portugal, Castile, and Aragon undertook repeated crusades of reconquest, finally completed in 1492. Elements of Islamic civilization persisted in recaptured areas, influencing all Western Europe.

Crusades. Pope Urban II called for a crusade (1095) to restore Asia Minor to Byzantium and the Holy Land to Christendom. This first crusade captured Jerusalem and led to the foundation of four Frankish states in the Levant. The defeat inflicted upon crusaders at the Battle of Hattin (1187) by **Saladin** (c. 1137-93), the Kurdish ruler of Egypt and Syria, effectively negated territorial gains. Many crusades followed until 1291. The 4th crusade sacked Constantinople (1204). Other crusades were launched against Christian heretics (Albigensian Crusade, 1229), pagans, and enemies of the papacy.

Economy. The agricultural base of European life benefited from improvements in **plow design** (c. 1000) and by the draining of lowlands and clearing of forests, leading to a rural population increase. Towns grew in Northern Italy, Flanders, and Northern Germany (Hanseatic League). Improvements in **loom design** permitted factory textile production. **Guilds** dominated urban trades from the 12th cent. Banking (centered in Italy, 12th-15th cent.) facilitated long-distance trade.

Christianity. The split between the Eastern and Western churches was formalized in 1054. Western and Central Europe was divided into 500 bishoprics under one united hierarchy, but conflicts between secular and church authorities were frequent (German **Investiture Controversy**, 1075-1122). Clerical power was first strengthened through the international monastic reform begun at Cluny in 910. Popular religious enthusiasm often expressed itself in heretical movements (Waldensians from 1173), but was channeled by the **Dominican** (1215) and **Franciscan** (1223) friars into the religious mainstream.

Arts. Romanesque architecture (9th to mid-12th cent.) expanded on late Roman models, using the rounded arch and massed stone to support enlarged basilicas. Painting and sculpture followed Byzantine models. The literature of **chivalry** was exemplified by the epic (*Chanson de Roland*, c. 1100) and by courtly love poems of the troubadours of Provence and minnesingers of Germany. **Gothic** architecture emerged in France (choir of St. Denis, c. 1140) and spread along with French cultural influence. Rib vaulting and pointed arches were used to combine soaring heights with delicacy, and they freed walls for display of stained glass. Exteriors were covered with painted relief sculpture and embellished with elaborate architectural detail.

Learning. Law, medicine, and philosophy were advanced at independent **universities** (Bologna, Paris, 12th cent.), originally corporations of students and masters. Twelfth-cent. translations of Greek classics, especially by Aristotle, encouraged an analytic approach. Scholastic philosophy, from Anselm (1033-1109) to **Aquinas** (1225-74), attempted to understand revelation through reason.

Apogee of Central Asian Power and the Spread of Islam: 1250-1500

Turks. Turkic peoples, of Central Asian ancestry, were a military threat to the Byzantine and Persian Empires from the 6th cent. After several waves of invasions, during which most of the Turks adopted Islam, the **Seljuk Turks** took (1055) Baghdad. They ruled Persia, Iraq, and, after 1071, Asia Minor, where massive numbers of Turks settled. The empire was divided in the 12th cent. into smaller states ruled by Seljuks, Kurds, and Mamluks (a military caste of former Turk, Kurd, and Circassian slaves), which governed Egypt and the Middle East until the Ottoman era (c. 1290-1922).

Osman I (r. c. 1290-1326) and succeeding sultans united Anatolian Turkish warriors in a militaristic state that waged holy war against Byzantium and Balkan Christians. Most of the Balkans had been subdued and Anatolia united when Constantinople fell (1453). By the mid-16th cent., Hungary, the Middle East, and N Africa had been conquered. The Turkish advance was stopped at Vienna (1529) and at the naval battle of Lepanto (1571) by Spain, Venice, and the papacy.

The **Ottoman state** was governed in accordance with orthodox Muslim law. Greek, Armenian, and Jewish communities were segregated and were ruled by religious leaders responsible for taxation; they dominated trade. Many state offices and most army ranks were filled by slaves, in part through a system of child conscription among Christians.

India. Mahmud of Ghazni (971-1030) led repeated Turkish raids into N India. Turkish power was consolidated in 1206 with the start of the **Sultanate at Delhi**. Centralization of state power under the early Delhi sultans went far beyond traditional Indian practice. Muslim rule of much of the subcontinent lasted until the British conquest 600 years later, though Hinduism remained the majority religion.

Mongols. Genghis Khan (c. 1167-1227) first united the feuding Mongol tribes and built their armies into an effective offensive force around a core of highly mobile cavalry. He and his immediate successors created the largest land empire in history; by 1279 it stretched from the E coast of Asia to the Danube and from the Siberian steppes to the Arabian Sea. East-West trade and contacts were facilitated (Marco Polo, c. 1254-1324). The western Mongols were Islamized by 1295; successor states soon lost their Mongol character by assimilation. They were briefly reunited under the Turk Tamerlane (1336-1405).

Kublai Khan ruled China from his new capital Beijing (established c. 1264). Naval campaigns against Japan (1274, 1281) and Java (1293) were defeated, the latter by the Hindu-Buddhist maritime kingdom of Majapahit. The **Yuan** dynasty used Mongols and other foreigners (including Europeans) in official posts and tolerated the return of Nestorian Christianity (suppressed 841-45) and the spread of Islam in the S and W. A native reaction expelled the Mongols in 1367-68.

Russia. The Kievan state in Russia, weakened by the decline of Byzantium and the rise of the Catholic Polish-Lithuanian state, was overrun (1238-40) by the Mongols. Only the northern trading republic of Novgorod remained independent. The grand dukes of Moscow emerged as leaders of a coalition of princes that eventually (by 1481) defeated the Mongols. After the fall of Constantinople in 1453, the **Tsars** (Caesars) at Moscow (from Ivan III, r. 1462-1505) set up an independent Russian Orthodox Church. Commerce failed to revive. The isolated Russian state remained agrarian with the peasant class falling into serfdom.

Persia. A revival of Persian literature, making use of the Arab alphabet and literary forms, began in the 10th cent. (epic of Firdausi, 935-1020). An art revival, influenced by Chinese styles introduced after the Mongols came to power in Iran, began in the 13th cent. Persian cultural and political forms, and often the Persian language, were used for centuries by Turkish and Mongol elites from the Balkans to India. Persian mystics from Rumi (1207-73) to Jami (1414-92) promoted **Sufism** in their poetry.

Africa. Two militant Islamic Berber dynasties emerged from the Sahara to carve out empires from the Sahel to central Spain—the **Almoravids** (c. 1050-1140) and the fanatical **Almohads** (c. 1125-1269). The Ghanaian empire was replaced in the upper Niger by Mali (c. 1230-1340), whose Muslim rulers imported Egyptians to help make **Timbuktu** a center of commerce (in gold, leather, and slaves) and learning. The Songhay empire (to 1590) replaced Mali. To the S, forest kingdoms produced refined artworks (Ife terra cotta, **Benin** bronzes).

Other **Muslim states** in Nigeria (Hausas) and Chad originated in the 11th cent. and continued in some form until the 19th-cent. European conquest. Less-developed Bantu kingdoms existed across central Africa.

Some 40 Muslim Arab-Persian trading colonies and city-states were established all along the E African coast from the 10th cent. (Kilwa, Mogadishu). The interchange with Bantu peoples produced the **Swahili** language and culture. Gold, palm oil, and slaves were brought from the interior, stimulating the growth of the Monamatapa kingdom of the Zambezi (15th cent.). The Christian Ethiopian empire (from 13th cent.) continued the traditions of Axum.

Southeast Asia. Islam was introduced into Malaya and the Indonesian islands by Arab, Persian, and Indian traders. Coastal Muslim cities and states (starting before 1300) soon dominated the interior. Chief among these was the **Malacca** state (c. 1400-1511), on the Malay peninsula.

Arts and Statecraft Thrive in Europe; New Asian Empires Rise: 1350-1600

Italy. Distinctive Italian achievements in literature and fine arts during the late Middle Ages (**Dante**, 1265-1321; Giotto, 1276-1337) led to the vigorous new styles of the Renaissance (14th-16th cent.). Patronized by the rulers of the quarreling petty states of Italy (**Medicis** in Florence and the papacy, c. 1400-1737), the plastic arts perfected realistic techniques, including **perspective** (Masaccio, 1401-28; Leonardo **da Vinci**, 1452-1519). Classical motifs were used in architecture, and increased talent and expense were put into secular buildings. The Florentine dialect was refined as a national literary language (**Petrarch**, 1304-74). Greek refugees from the E strengthened the respect of humanist scholars for the classic sources. Soon an international movement aided by the spread of **printing** (Gutenberg, c. 1397-1468), **humanism** was optimistic about the power of human reason (Erasmus of Rotterdam, 1466-1536, **More's** *Utopia*, 1516) and valued individual effort in the arts and in politics (**Machiavelli**, 1469-1527).

France. The French monarchy, strengthened in its repeated struggles with powerful nobles (Burgundy, Flanders, Aquitaine) by alliances with the growing commercial towns, consolidated bureaucratic control under Philip IV (r. 1285-1314) and extended French influence into Germany and Italy (popes at Avignon, France, 1309-1417). The **Hundred Years War** (1337-1453) ended English dynastic claims in France (battles of Crécy, 1346, and Poitiers, 1356; Joan of Arc executed, 1431). A French Renaissance, dating from royal invasions (1494, 1499) of Italy, was encouraged at the court of Francis I (r. 1515-47), who centralized taxation and law. French vernacular literature consciously asserted its independence (La Pléiade, 1549).

England. The evolution of England's political institutions began with the **Magna Carta** (1215), by which King John guaranteed the privileges of nobles and church and assured jury trial. After the **Wars of the Roses** (1455-85), the **Tudor** dynasty reasserted royal prerogatives (Henry VIII, r. 1509-47), but the trend toward independent departments and ministerial government also continued. English trade (wool exports from c. 1340) was protected by the nation's growing maritime power (**Spanish Armada** destroyed, 1588).

English replaced French and Latin in the late 14th cent. in law and literature (**Chaucer**, c. 1340-1400), and English translation of the Bible began (Wycliffe, 1380s). **Elizabeth I** (r. 1558-1603) presided over the development of poetry (Spenser, 1552-99), drama (**Shakespeare**, 1564-1616), and music.

German Empire. From among a welter of minor feudal states, church lands, and independent cities, the **Habsburgs** assembled a far-flung territorial domain, based in Austria from 1276. Family members held the title of Holy Roman Emperor from 1438 to the Empire's dissolution in 1806 but failed to centralize its domains, leaving Germany disunited for centuries. Resistance to Turkish expansion brought Hungary under Austrian control from the 16th cent. The Netherlands, Luxembourg, and Burgundy were added in 1477, curbing French expansion.

The Flemish painting tradition of naturalism, technical proficiency, and bourgeois subject matter began in the 15th cent. (Jan **van Eyck**, c. 1390-1441), the earliest northern manifestation of the Renaissance. Albrecht **Dürer** (1471-1528) typified the merging of late Gothic and Italian trends in 16th-cent. German art. Imposing civic architecture flourished in the prosperous commercial cities.

Black Death. The bubonic plague reached Europe from the E in 1348, killing up to half the population by 1350 (and recurring periodically in most areas until the early 18th cent.). Labor scarcity forced wages to rise and brought greater freedom to the peasantry, making possible **peasant uprisings** (Jacquerie in France, 1358; Wat Tyler's rebellion in England, 1381).

Spain. Despite the unification of Castile and Aragon in 1479, the two countries retained separate governments, and the nobility, especially in Aragon and Catalonia, retained many privileges. Spanish lands in Italy (Naples, Sicily) and the Netherlands entangled the country in European wars through the mid-17th cent., while explorers, traders, and conquerors built up a Spanish empire in the Americas and the Philippines.

From the late 15th cent., a **golden age** of literature and art produced works of social satire (plays of Lope de Vega, 1562-1635; **Cervantes**, 1547-1616), as well as spiritual intensity (**El Greco**, 1541-1614; **Velázquez**, 1599-1660).

Explorations. Organized European maritime exploration began, seeking to evade the Venice-Ottoman monopoly of eastern trade and to promote Christianity. A key goal was to satisfy a growing taste for Asian goods. Beginning in 1418, expeditions from Portugal explored the W coast of Africa, until Vasco da Gama rounded the Cape of Good Hope in 1497 and reached India. A Portuguese trading empire was consolidated by the seizure of Goa (1510) and Malacca (1551). Japan was reached in 1542. The voyages of Christopher **Columbus** (1492-1504) uncovered a world new to Europeans, which Spain hastened to subdue. Navigation schools in Spain and Portugal, the development of large sailing ships (carracks) mounted with cannons, and the invention (c. 1475) of the rifle aided European penetration.

Mughals and Safavids. E of the Ottoman Empire, two Muslim dynasties ruled unchallenged in the 16th and 17th cent. The Mughal dynasty of India, founded by Persianized Turkish invaders from the NW under Babur, dates from their 1526 conquest of the Delhi Sultanate. The dynasty ruled most of India for more than 200 years, surviving nominally until 1857. **Akbar** (r. 1556-1605) consolidated administration at his glorious court, where the Urdu language (Persian-influenced Hindi) developed. Trade relations with Europe increased. Under Shah Jahan (1629-58), a secularized art fusing Hindu and Muslim elements flourished in miniature painting and in architecture (**Taj Mahal**). **Sikhism** (founded late 15th cent.) combined elements of both faiths. Suppression of Hindus and Shiite Muslims in S India in the late 17th cent. weakened the empire.

Intense devotion to the Shiite sect characterized the Safavids (1502-1736) of Persia and led to hostilities with the Sunni Ottomans for more than a century. The prosperity and the strength of the empire are evidenced by the mosques at its capital city, **Isfahan**. The Safavids enhanced Iranian national consciousness.

China. The **Ming** emperors (1368-1644), the last native dynasty in China, wielded strong personal power. European trade (Portuguese monopoly through **Macao** from 1557) was strictly controlled. Jesuit scholars and scientists (Matteo Ricci, 1552-1610) introduced some Western science; their writings familiarized the West with China. The arts thrived, especially in the areas of painting and ceramics. Chinese manufacturing boomed, bringing in new profits from world trade.

Japan. After the decline of the first hereditary *shogunate* (chief generalship) at **Kamakura** (1185-1333), fragmentation of power accelerated, as did the consequent social mobility. Under Kamakura and the Ashikaga shogunate (1338-1573), the *daimyos* (lords) and *samurai* (warriors) grew more powerful and promoted a martial ideology. Japanese pirates and traders plied the China coast. Popular Buddhist movements included the nationalist Nichiren sect (from c. 1250) and **Zen** (brought from China, 1191), which stressed meditation and a disciplined aesthetic (tea ceremony, gardening, martial arts, *No* drama).

Change and Expansion in Europe: 1500-1700

Reformation. Theological debate and protests against real and perceived clerical corruption existed in the medieval Christian world, expressed by such dissenters as John **Wycliffe** (c. 1320-84) and his followers (the Lollards) in England, and **Huss** (burned as a heretic, 1415) in Bohemia.

Martin Luther, one of the primary catalysts of Protestantism, was excommunicated by Pope Leo X in 1521 over his 95 Theses (1517).

Martin **Luther** (1483-1546) preached that faith alone, without the mediation of clergy or good works, leads to salvation. He attacked the authority of the pope, rejected priestly celibacy, and recommended individual study of the Bible (which he translated into German c. 1525). His 95 Theses (1517) led to his excommunication (1521). John **Calvin** (1509-64) said that God's elect were predestined for salvation and all others for damnation; good conduct and success were signs of election. Calvin in Geneva and John **Knox** (1505-72) in Scotland established theocratic states.

Henry VIII asserted English national authority and secular power by breaking away (1534) from the Catholic Church, creating what would become the Anglican Church. Monastic property was confiscated, and some Protestant doctrines given official sanction.

Religious wars. A century and a half of religious wars began with a southern German peasant uprising (1524), repressed with Luther's support. Radical sects—democratic, pacifist, millenarian—arose (Anabaptists ruled Münster, 1534-35) and were suppressed violently. Civil war in France from 1562 between **Huguenots** (Protestant nobles and merchants) and Catholics ended with the 1598 **Edict of Nantes**, tolerating Protestants (revoked 1685). Habsburg attempts to restore Catholicism in Germany were resisted in 25 years of fighting. The 1555 Peace of Augsburg guarantee of religious independence to local princes and cities was confirmed only after the **Thirty Years' War** (1618-48), when much of Germany was devastated by local and foreign armies (Sweden, France).

A Catholic Reformation, or **Counter-Reformation**, met the Protestant challenge, defining an official theology at the Council of Trent (1545-63). The **Jesuit** order (Society of Jesus), founded in 1534 by Ignatius Loyola (1491-1556), helped reconvert large areas of Poland, Hungary, and S Germany and sent missionaries to the New World, India, and China. The **Inquisition** suppressed heresy in Catholic countries. A revival of religious fervor appeared in devotional literature (Teresa of Avila, 1515-82) and in grandiose **Baroque** art (Bernini, 1598-1680).

Scientific Revolution. The late nominalist thinkers (Ockham, c. 1300-49) of Paris and Oxford challenged Aristotelian orthodoxy, allowing for a freer scientific approach. At the same time, metaphysical values, such as the Neoplatonic faith in an orderly, mathematical cosmos, still motivated and directed inquiry. Nicolaus **Copernicus** (1473-1543) promoted the heliocentric theory, which was confirmed when Johannes **Kepler** (1571-1630) discovered the mathematical laws describing the elliptical orbits of the planets. The traditional Christian-Aristotelian belief that the heavens and the Earth were fundamentally different collapsed when **Galileo Galilei** (1564-1642) discovered moving sunspots, irregular moon topography, and moons around Jupiter, but he faced religious opposition (Galileo's retraction, 1633). He and Sir Isaac **Newton** (1642-1727) developed a mechanics that unified cosmic and earthly phenomena. Newton and Gottfried von **Leibniz** (1646-1716) invented calculus. René **Descartes** (1596-1650), best known for his influential philosophy, also invented analytic geometry.

An explosion of **observational science** included the discovery of blood circulation (Harvey, 1578-1657) and microscopic life (Leeuwenhoek, 1632-1723) and advances in anatomy (Vesalius, 1514-64, dissected corpses) and chemistry (Boyle, 1627-91). Scientific research institutes were founded in Florence (1657), London (**Royal Society**, 1660), and Paris (1666). Inventions proliferated (Savery's steam engine, 1698).

Arts. Mannerist trends of the High Renaissance (**Michelangelo**, 1475-1564) exploited virtuosity, grace, novelty, and exotic subjects and poses. The notion of artistic genius was promoted. Private connoisseurs entered the art market. These trends were elaborated in the 17th cent. **Baroque** era on a grander scale. Dynamic movement in painting and sculpture was emphasized by sharp lighting effects, rich materials (colored marble, gilt), and realistic details. Curved facades, broken lines, rich detail, and ceiling decoration characterized Baroque architecture. Monarchs, princes, and prelates, usually Catholic, used Baroque art to enhance and embellish their authority, as in royal portraits (Velázquez, 1599-1660; Van Dyck, 1599-1641).

National styles emerged. In France, a taste for rectilinear order and serenity (Poussin, 1594-1665), linked to the new rational philosophy, was expressed in classical forms. The influence of **classical values** in French literature (tragedies of **Racine**, 1639-99) gave rise to the "battle of the Ancients and Moderns." New forms included the essay (**Montaigne**, 1533-92) and novel (*Princesse de Clèves*, La Fayette, 1678).

Dutch painting of the 17th cent. was unique in its wide social distribution. The Flemish tradition of undemonstrative realism reached its peak in **Rembrandt** (1606-69) and Jan Vermeer (1632-75).

Economy. European economic expansion, known as the **commercial revolution**, was stimulated by new trade with the East, by New World gold and silver, and by a doubling of population (50 million in 1450, 100 million in 1600). **New business and financial techniques** were developed and refined, such as joint-stock companies, insurance, and letters of credit and exchange. The Bank of Amsterdam (1609) and the Bank of England (1694) broke the old monopoly of private banking families. The rise of a business mentality was typified by the spread of clock towers in cities in the 14th cent. By the mid-15th cent., portable clocks were available; the first watch was invented in 1502.

By 1650, most governments had adopted the **mercantile system**, in which they sought to amass metallic wealth by protecting merchants' foreign and colonial trade monopolies. The rise in prices and the new coin-based economy undermined craft guild and feudal manorial systems. Expanding industries

The exact purpose of the Incan city of Machu Picchu, built in the 15th century and abandoned less than 150 years later, is unknown; one theory is that it served as a royal retreat.

(clothweaving, mining) benefited from technical advances. Coal began to replace wood as the chief fuel; it was used to fuel new 16th-cent. blast furnaces making cast iron.

New World. The **Aztecs** united much of the Mesoamerican area in a militarist empire by 1519 from their capital, Tenochtitlán (pop. 300,000), which was the center of a cult requiring ritual human sacrifice. Most of the civilized areas of South America were ruled by the centralized Inca Empire (1476-1534), stretching 2,000 mi from Ecuador to NW Argentina. Lavish and sophisticated traditions in pottery, weaving, sculpture, and architecture were maintained in both regions.

These empires, beset by revolts, fell in two short campaigns to gold-seeking Spanish forces based in the Antilles and Panama. Hernán **Cortés** took Mexico (1519-21); Francisco **Pizarro**, Peru (1532-35). From these centers, land and sea expeditions claimed most of North and South America for Spain. The indigenous high cultures did not survive the impact of **Christian missionaries** and the new upper class of whites. Although the Spanish administration intermittently concerned itself with their welfare, the population was devastated by European diseases and remained impoverished at most levels. New World silver and such native products as potatoes, tobacco, corn, peanuts, chocolate, and rubber exercised a major economic influence on Europe.

Brazil, which the Portuguese reached in 1500 and settled after 1530, and the Caribbean colonies of several European nations developed a plantation economy where sugarcane, tobacco, cotton, coffee, rice, indigo, and lumber were grown by slaves. From the early 16th to late 19th cent., 10 million Africans were transported to **slavery** in the Americas and Caribbean islands.

Netherlands. The urban, Calvinist northern provinces of the Netherlands rebelled (1568) against Habsburg Spain and founded an oligarchic mercantile republic. Their control of the Baltic grain market enabled them to exploit Mediterranean food shortages. Religious refugees—French and Belgian Protestants, Iberian Jews—added to the commercial talent pool. After Spain absorbed Portugal (1580), the Dutch seized Portuguese possessions and created a vast commercial empire ultimately centered in parts of the Caribbean and in Indonesia. The Dutch also challenged or supplanted Portuguese traders in China and Japan. Revolution in 1640 restored Portuguese independence.

England. Anglicanism became firmly established under **Elizabeth I** after a brief Catholic interlude under "Bloody" Mary I (1553-58). But religious and political conflicts led to a rebellion (1642) by Parliament. Forces of the Roundheads (Puritans) defeated the Cavaliers (Royalists); Charles I was beheaded (1649). The new Commonwealth was ruled as a military dictatorship by Oliver **Cromwell**, who also brutally crushed (1649-51) an Irish rebellion. Conflicts within the Puritan camp (democratic Levelers defeated, 1649) aided the Stuart restoration (1660), but Parliament was strengthened and the peaceful **"Glorious Revolution"** (1688) advanced political and religious liberties (writings of **Locke**, 1632-1704). British privateers (Drake, 1540-96) challenged Spanish control of the New World and penetrated Asian trade routes (Madras taken, 1639). North American colonies (Jamestown, 1607; Plymouth, 1620) provided an outlet for private enterprise and religious dissenters from Europe. The British East India company gained growing sway in 18th-cent. India, as Mughal power declined.

France. Emerging from the religious civil wars in 1628, France regained military and commercial great power status (under the ministries of **Richelieu**, Mazarin, and Colbert). Under **Louis XIV** (r. 1643-1715), royal absolutism triumphed over nobles and local *parlements* (defeat of Fronde, 1648-53). Durable colonies were founded in Canada (1608), the Caribbean (1626), and India (1674).

Sweden. Sweden seceded from the Scandinavian Union in 1523. The thinly populated agrarian state (with copper, iron, and timber exports) was united by the Vasa kings, whose conquests by the mid-17th cent. made Sweden the dominant Baltic power. The empire collapsed in the Great Northern War (1700-21).

Poland. After the union with Lithuania in 1447, Poland ruled vast territories from the Baltic to the Black Sea, resisting German and Turkish incursions. Catholic nobles failed to gain the loyalty of their Orthodox Christian subjects in the E; commerce and trades were practiced by German and Jewish immigrants. The bloody 1648-49 Cossack uprising began the kingdom's dismemberment.

Russia. Growing authority of the tsars continued with advancing serfdom. Around 1700, **Peter the Great** imported new Western styles and technologies. Steady territorial expansion created a vast territory touching China, the Ottoman Empire, and east-central Europe.

China. A new dynasty, the **Manchus**, invaded from the NE, seized power in 1644, and expanded Chinese control to its greatest extent in Central and SE Asia. Trade and diplomatic contact with Europe grew, carefully controlled by China. New crops (sweet potato, maize, peanut) allowed economic and population growth (pop. 300 million, in 1800). Traditional arts and literature were pursued with increased sophistication (*Dream of the Red Chamber*, novel, mid-18th cent.).

Japan. Tokugawa Ieyasu, shogun from 1603, finally unified and pacified feudal Japan. Hereditary nobles (daimyos and samurai) monopolized government office and the professions. An urban merchant class grew, literacy spread, and a cultural renaissance occurred (**haiku**, a verse innovation of the poet Basho, 1644-94). Fear of European domination led to persecution of Christian converts from 1597 and to substantial isolation from outside contact from 1640.

Philosophy, Industry, and Revolution: 1700-1800

Science and reason. Greater faith in reason and empirical observation, instead of tradition and religious beliefs, espoused since the Renaissance (Francis Bacon, 1561-1626), was bolstered by scientific discoveries. René **Descartes** (1596-1650) used a rationalistic approach modeled on geometry and introspection to discover "self-evident" truths as a foundation of knowledge. Sir Isaac **Newton** emphasized induction from experimental observation. Baruch de **Spinoza** (1632-77), who called for political and intellectual freedom, developed a systematic rationalistic philosophy in his classic work *Ethics*.

French philosophers assumed leadership of the **Enlightenment** in the 18th cent. Montesquieu (1689-1755) used British history to support his notions of limited government. **Voltaire**'s (1694-1778) diaries and novels of exotic travel illustrated the intellectual trends toward secular ethics and relativism. Jean-Jacques **Rousseau**'s (1712-78) radical concepts of the **social contract** and of the inherent goodness of the common man gave impetus to antimonarchical republicanism. The *Encyclopedia* (1751-72, edited by Diderot and d'Alembert), designed as a monument to reason, was largely devoted to practical technology.

In England, ideals of liberty were connected with empiricist philosophy and science in the followers of John **Locke**. But British empiricism, especially as developed by the skeptical David **Hume** (1711-76), radically reduced the role of reason in philosophy, as did the evolutionary approach to law and politics of Edmund Burke (1729-97) and the utilitarian ethics of Jeremy Bentham (1748-1832). Adam Smith (1723-90) and other economists called for a rationalization of economic activity by removing artificial barriers to a supposedly natural free exchange of goods known as **laissez-faire**.

German writers participated in the new philosophical trends popularized by Christian von Wolff (1679-1754). Immanuel **Kant**'s (1724-1804) transcendental idealism, unifying an empirical epistemology with a priori moral and logical concepts, directed German thought away from skepticism. Italian contributions included work on electricity (Galvani, 1737-98; Volta, 1745-1827), the pioneer historiography of Vico (1668-1744), and writings on penal reform (Beccaria, 1738-94). Benjamin Franklin (1706-90) was celebrated in Europe for his varied achievements.

The growth of the **press** (*Spectator*, 1711-12) and the wide distribution of sentimental **novels** attested to the increase of a large bourgeois public.

Arts. Rococo art, characterized by extravagant decorative effects, asymmetries copied from organic models, and artificial pastoral subjects, was favored by the continental aristocracy for most of the century (Watteau, 1684-1721) and had musical analogies in the ornamentalized polyphony of late Baroque. The **Neoclassical** art after 1750, associated with the new scientific archaeology, was more streamlined and was infused with the supposed moral and geometric rectitude of the Roman Republic (David, 1748-1825). In England, **town planning** on a grand scale began.

Industrial Revolution in England. Agricultural improvements, such as the sowing drill (1701) and livestock breeding, were implemented on the large fields provided by enclosure of common lands by private owners. Profits from agriculture and from colonial and foreign trade (1800 volume, £54 mil) were channeled through hundreds of banks and the **Stock Exchange** (est. 1773) into new industrial processes.

The Newcomen steam pump (1712) aided coal mining. Coal fueled the new efficient steam engines patented by James Watt in 1769, and coke-smelting produced cheap, sturdy iron for machinery by the 1730s. The **flying shuttle** (1733) and **spinning jenny** (c. 1764) were used in the large new cotton textile factories, where women and children were much of the workforce. Goods were transported cheaply over **canals** (2,000 mi; built 1760-1800). By the early 19th cent., industrialization spread in Western Europe and North America.

American Revolution. The British colonies in North America attracted a mass immigration of religious dissenters and poor people throughout the 17th and 18th cent., coming from the British Isles, Germany, the Netherlands, and other countries including imported African slaves. The population reached 3 million non-natives by the 1770s. The indigenous population was greatly reduced by European diseases and by wars with the various colonies. British attempts to control colonial trade and to tax the colonists to pay for the costs of colonial administration and defense clashed with local self-government and eventually provoked the colonies to a successful rebellion.

New technological developments, including mechanized manufacturing processes and innovations in power sources, enabled the industrial revolution from about 1760 on.

Central and East Europe. The monarchs of the three states that dominated E Europe—Austria, Prussia, and Russia—expanded royal power and centralized institutions in their kingdoms, which were enlarged by the division (1772-95) of Poland.

Under **Frederick II** (the Great) (r. 1740-86), Prussia, with its efficient modern army, doubled in size. State monopolies and tariff protection fostered industry, and some legal reforms were introduced. Austria's heterogeneous realms were unified under **Maria Theresa** (r. 1740-80) and **Joseph II** (r. 1765-90). Reforms in education, law, and religion were enacted, and the Austrian serfs were freed (1781). With its defeat in the Seven Years' War in 1763, Austria failed to regain Silesia, which had been seized by Prussia, but it was compensated by expansion to the E and S (Hungary, Slavonia, 1699; Galicia, 1772).

Russia, whose borders continued to expand, adopted some Western bureaucratic and economic policies under **Peter I** (r. 1682-1725) and **Catherine II** (r. 1762-96). Trade and cultural contacts with the West multiplied from the new Baltic Sea capital, **St. Petersburg** (est. 1703).

French Revolution. The growing French middle class lacked political power and resented aristocratic tax privileges, especially in light of the successful American Revolution. Peasants lacked adequate land and were burdened with feudal obligations to nobles. War with Britain led to the loss of French Canada and drained the treasury, finally forcing the king to call the **Estates-General** in 1789 for the first time since 1614, in an atmosphere of food riots (poor crop in 1788).

Aristocratic resistance to absolutism was soon overshadowed by the reformist Third Estate (middle class), which proclaimed itself the **National Constituent Assembly** June 17 and took the "Tennis Court Oath" on June 20 to secure a constitution. The storming of the **Bastille** fortress/prison on July 14, 1789, by Parisian artisans was followed by looting and the seizure of aristocratic property throughout France. Assembly reforms included abolition of class and regional privileges, a Declaration of Rights, suffrage by taxpayers (75% of male population), and the **Civil Constitution of the Clergy** providing for election and loyalty oaths for priests. A republic was declared Sept. 22, 1792, in spite of royalist pressure from Austria and Prussia, which had declared war in Apr. (joined by Britain the next year). Louis XVI was beheaded Jan. 21, 1793, and Queen Marie Antoinette was beheaded Oct. 16, 1793.

Royalist uprisings in La Vendée and military reverses led to institution of a **reign of terror** in which tens of thousands of opponents of the Revolution and criminals were executed. Radical reforms in the **Convention** period (Sept. 1793-Oct. 1795) included the abolition of colonial slavery, economic measures to aid the poor, support of public education, and a short-lived de-Christianization.

Division among radicals (execution of Hebert, Danton, and Robespierre, 1794) aided the ascendancy of a moderate **Directory**, which consolidated military victories. **Napoleon Bonaparte** (1769-1821), a popular young general, exploited political divisions and participated in a coup Nov. 9, 1799, making himself first consul (dictator).

India. Sikh and Hindu rebels (Rajputs, Marathas) and Afghans destroyed the power of the Mughals during the 18th cent. After France's defeat (1763) in the Seven Years' War, Britain was the primary European trade power in India. Its control of inland **Bengal** and **Bihar** was recognized (1765) by the Mughal shah, who granted the **British East India Co.** (under Clive, 1725-74) the right to collect land revenue there. Despite objections from Parliament (1784 India Act), the company's involvement in local wars and politics led to repeated acquisitions of new territory. The company exported Indian textiles, sugar, and indigo, but industry was discouraged to promote British imports.

Nationalism Gathers Momentum: 1800-40

French ideals and empire spread. Inspired by the ideals of the French Revolution, and supported by the expanding French armies, new republican regimes arose near France: the **Batavian** Republic in the Netherlands (1795-1806), the **Helvetic** Republic in Switzerland (1798-1803), the **Cisalpine** Republic in Northern Italy (1797-1805), the **Ligurian** Republic in Genoa (1797-1805), and the **Parthenopean** Republic in Southern Italy (1799). A Roman Republic existed briefly in 1798 after Pope Pius VI was arrested by French troops. In Italy and Germany, new nationalist sentiments were stimulated both in imitation of and in reaction to developments in France (anti-French and anti-Jacobin peasant uprisings in Italy, 1796-99).

From 1804, when Napoleon declared himself emperor, to 1812, a succession of military victories (Austerlitz, 1805; Jena, 1806) extended his control over most of Europe through puppet states (**Confederation of the Rhine** united W German states for the first time and **Grand Duchy of Warsaw** revived Polish national hopes), expansion of the empire, and alliances.

Among the lasting reforms initiated under Napoleon's absolutist reign were establishment of the Bank of France, centralization of tax collection, codification of law along Roman models (Code Napoléon), and reform and extension of secondary and university education. In an 1801 concordat, the papacy recognized the effective autonomy of the French Catholic Church.

Napoleon's continental successes were offset by a British victory under Adm. Horatio Nelson in the **Battle of Trafalgar** (1805). Some 400,000 French soldiers were killed in the Napoleonic Wars, along with about 600,000 foreign troops.

Last gasp of old regimes. The disastrous 1812 invasion of Russia exposed Napoleon's overextension. After Napoleon's 1814 exile to Elba, his armies were defeated (1815) at **Waterloo** by British and Prussian troops.

At the **Congress of Vienna**, the monarchs and princes of Europe redrew their boundaries, to the advantage of Prussia (in Saxony and the Ruhr), Austria (in Illyria and Venetia), and Russia (in Poland and Finland). British conquest of Dutch and French colonies (S Africa, Ceylon, Mauritius) was recognized. France, under the restored Bourbons, retained its expanded 1792 borders. The settlement brought 50 years of international peace to Europe.

But the Congress was unable to check the advance of liberal ideals and of nationalism among the smaller European nations. The 1825 **Decembrist uprising** by liberal officers in Russia was easily suppressed. But an independence movement in **Greece**, stirred by commercial prosperity and a cultural revival, succeeded in expelling Ottoman rule by 1831, with the aid of Britain, France, and Russia.

A constitutional monarchy was secured in France by the **1830 Revolution**; Louis Philippe became king. The revolutionary contagion spread to **Belgium**, which gained its independence (1830) from the Dutch monarchy, to **Poland**, whose rebellion was defeated (1830-31) by Russia, and to Germany.

Haiti's Toussaint L'Ouverture was a leader of the revolution that led to Haiti's establishment as a free, self-governing state in 1804.

Romanticism. A new style in intellectual and artistic life replaced Neoclassicism and Rococo after the mid-18th cent. By the early 19th cent., Romanticism prevailed in Europe.

Rousseau had begun the reaction against rationalism; in education (*Émile*, 1762) he stressed subjective spontaneity over regularized instruction. German writers (Lessing, 1729-81; Herder, 1744-1803) favorably compared the German folk song to classical forms and began a cult of Shakespeare, whose passion and "natural" wisdom was a model for the romantic *Sturm und Drang* (Storm and Stress) movement. **Goethe**'s *Sorrows of Young Werther* (1774) set the model for the tragic, passionate genius.

A new interest in **Gothic architecture** in England after 1760 (Walpole, 1717-97) spread through Europe, associated with an aesthetic Christian and mystic revival (**Blake**, 1757-1827). Celtic, Norse, and German mythology and folk tales were revived or imitated (Grimm's *Fairy Tales*, 1812-22). The medieval revival (Scott's *Ivanhoe*, 1819) led to a new interest in history, stressing national differences and organic growth (**Carlyle**, 1795-1881; Michelet, 1798-1874), corresponding to theories of natural evolution (Lamarck's *Philosophie Zoologique*, 1809; Lyell's *Geology*, 1830-33). A reaction against classicism characterized the English **romantic poets** (beginning with **Wordsworth**, 1770-1850). Revolution and war fed an emphasis on freedom and conflict, expressed by both poets (**Byron**, 1788-1824; **Hugo**, 1802-85) and philosophers (**Hegel**, 1770-1831).

Wild gardens replaced the formal French variety, and painters favored rural, stormy, and mountainous landscapes (**Turner**, 1775-1851; **Constable**, 1776-1837). Clothing became freer, with wigs, hoops, and ruffles discarded. Originality and genius were expected in the life and work of inspired artists (Murger's *Scenes From Bohemian Life*, 1847-49). Exotic locales and themes (as in Gothic horror stories) were used in art and literature (Delacroix, 1798-1863; **Poe**, 1809-49). Music exhibited the new dramatic style and a breakdown of classical forms (**Beethoven**, 1770-1827). The use of folk melodies and modes aided the growth of distinct national traditions (Glinka in Russia, 1804-57).

Latin America. François **Toussaint L'Ouverture** led a successful slave revolt in Haiti, which subsequently became the first Caribbean state to achieve independence (1804). The mainland Spanish colonies won their independence (1810-24) under such leaders as Simón **Bolívar** (1783-1830). Brazil became an independent empire (1822) under the Portuguese prince regent. A new class of military officers divided power with large landholders and the church.

United States. Territory under U.S. control nearly doubled in size with the **Louisiana Purchase** (1803). Heavy immigration and exploitation of ample natural resources fueled rapid economic growth. The spread of the franchise, public education, and antislavery sentiment were signs of a widespread democratic ethic.

China. Failure to keep pace with Western arms technology exposed China to greater European influence and hampered efforts to bar imports of opium, which had damaged Chinese society and drained wealth overseas. In the **Opium War** (1839-42), Britain forced China to expand trade opportunities and to cede Hong Kong.

New Complexities: Reforms and Imperialism: 1840-80

Idea of progress. As a result of the cumulative scientific, economic, and political changes of the preceding eras, the idea took hold among literate people in the West that continuing growth and improvement constituted the usual state of human and natural life.

Charles **Darwin**'s statement of the **theory of evolution** and survival of the fittest (*On the Origin of Species*, 1859), defended by intellectuals and scientists against theological objections, was taken as confirmation that progress was the natural direction of life. The controversy helped define popular ideas of the dedicated scientist and of science's increasing control over the world (Foucault's demonstration of Earth's rotation, 1851; **Pasteur**'s germ theory, 1861).

Charles Darwin's *On the Origin of Species* (1859) was based on his travels more than 20 years earlier on the British survey ship HMS *Beagle*.

Liberals following Ricardo (1772-1823) in their faith that unrestrained competition would bring continuous economic expansion sought to adjust political life to new social realities and believed that unregulated competition of ideas would yield truth (**Mill**, 1806-73). In England, successive reform bills (1832, 1867, 1884) gave representation to the new industrial towns and extended the franchise to the middle and lower classes and to Catholics, Dissenters, and Jews. On both sides of the Atlantic, reformists tried to improve conditions for the mentally ill (**Dix**, 1802-87), women (Anthony, 1820-1906), and prisoners. Slavery was barred in the British Empire (1833), the U.S. (1865), and Brazil (1888).

Socialist theories based on ideas of human perfectibility or progress were widely disseminated. Utopian socialists such as Saint-Simon (1760-1825) envisaged an orderly, just society directed by a technocratic elite. A model factory town, New Lanark, Scotland, was set up by utopian Robert Owen (1771-1858), and communal experiments were tried in the U.S. (Brook Farm, MA, 1841-47). Bakunin's (1814-76) anarchism represented the opposite extreme of total freedom. Karl **Marx** (1818-83) posited the inevitable triumph of socialism in industrial countries through a dialectical process of class conflict. Effective development of oceanic steamship lines (Cunard Lines, 1840s) and the opening of the **Suez Canal** accelerated shipping and commerce. Telegraph lines (Australia-Europe, 1871) sped communication. International organizations included the General (later Universal) Postal Union (1874) and conferences to limit epidemics like cholera. The initial **Geneva Convention** (1864) regulated treatment of prisoners of war.

Spread of industry. The technical processes and managerial innovations of the English industrial revolution spread to Europe (especially Germany) and the U.S., causing an explosion of industrial production, demand for raw materials, and competition for markets. Inventors, both trained and self-taught, provided means for larger-scale production (Bessemer steel, 1856; sewing machine, 1846). Many inventions were shown at the universal prosperity-themed 1851 London Great Exhibition at the **Crystal Palace**.

Local specialization and long-distance trade were aided by a revolution in transportation and communication. Railroads were first introduced in the 1820s in England and the U.S. Over 150,000 mi of track had been laid worldwide by 1880, with another 100,000 mi laid in the next decade. Steamships were improved (*Savannah* crossed Atlantic, 1819). The **telegraph**, perfected by 1844 (Morse), connected the Old and New Worlds by cable in 1866 and quickened the pace of international commerce and politics. The first commercial **telephone** exchange went into operation in the U.S. in 1878.

The new class of industrial workers, uprooted from their rural homes, lacked job security and suffered from dangerous overcrowding at work and at home. Many responded by organizing **trade unions** (legalized in England, 1824; France, 1884). The U.S. Knights of Labor had 700,000 members by 1886. The First International (1864-76) tried to unite workers worldwide around a Marxist program. The quasi-Socialist Paris Commune uprising (1871) was violently suppressed. Acts to reduce child labor and regulate conditions were passed (1833-50 in England). Social security measures were introduced by the Bismarck regime (1883-89) in Germany.

Revolutions of 1848. Among the causes of the continent-wide revolutions were an international collapse of credit and resulting unemployment, bad harvests in 1845-47, and a cholera epidemic. The new urban proletariat and expanding bourgeoisie demanded greater political roles. Republics were proclaimed in France, Rome, and Venice. Nationalist feelings reached fever pitch in the Habsburg empire, as Hungary declared independence under Kossuth, a Slav Congress demanded equality, and Piedmont tried to drive Austria from Lombardy. A national liberal assembly at Frankfurt called for German unification.

But riots fueled bourgeois fear of socialism (**Marx** and **Engels**, *Communist Manifesto*, 1848), and peasants remained conservative. The old establishment—the Papacy, the Habsburgs with the help of the Tsarist Russian army—was able to rout the revolutionaries by 1849. The French Republic succumbed to a renewed monarchy by 1852 (Emperor Napoleon III).

Great nations unified. Using the "blood and iron" tactics of Bismarck from 1862, Prussia controlled N Germany by 1867 (war with Denmark, 1864; Austria, 1866). After defeating France in 1870 (annexation of Alsace-Lorraine), it won the allegiance of S German states. A new **German Empire** was proclaimed (1871). **Italy**, inspired by Giuseppe Mazzini (1805-72) and Giuseppe Garibaldi (1807-82), was unified by the reformed Piedmont kingdom through uprisings, plebiscites, and war.

The **United States** expanded its area after the 1846-48 Mexican War and defeated (1861-65) a secession attempt by Southern states in the **Civil War.** Canadian provinces were united in an autonomous **Dominion of Canada** (1867). Control in **India** was removed from the East India Co. and centralized under British administration after the 1857-58 Sepoy rebellion, laying the groundwork for the modern Indian state. Queen Victoria was named Empress of India (1876).

Europe dominates Asia. The Ottoman Empire began to weaken in the face of Balkan nationalisms and European imperial incursions in N Africa (**Suez Canal**, 1869). The Ottomans had lost control of most of both regions by 1882. Russia completed its expansion S by 1884 (despite the temporary setback of the **Crimean War** with Turkey, Britain, and France, 1853-56), taking Turkestan, all the Caucasus, and Chinese areas in the E and sponsoring Balkan Slavs against the Turks. A succession of reformist and reactionary regimes presided over a slow modernization (serfs freed, 1861). Persian independence suffered as Russia and British India competed for influence.

China was forced to sign a series of unequal treaties with European powers and Japan. Overpopulation and an inefficient dynasty brought misery and caused rebellions (Taiping, Muslims) leaving tens of millions dead. **Japan** was forced by the U.S. (Commodore Perry's visits, 1853-54) and Europe to end its isolation. The Meiji restoration (1868) gave power to a Westernizing oligarchy, abolishing feudalism and expanding education. Intensified empire-building gave Burma to Britain (1824-85) and Indochina to France (1862-95). Christian missionary activity followed imperial and trade expansion in Asia.

Arts. The official **Beaux Arts** school in Paris set an international style of imposing public buildings (Paris Opera, 1861-74; Vienna Opera, 1861-69) and uplifting statues (Bartholdi's Statue of Liberty, 1884). Realist painting, influenced by photography (Daguerre, 1837), appealed to a new mass audience with social or historical narrative (Wilkie, 1785-1841; Poynter, 1836-1919) or with serious religious, moral, or social messages (pre-Raphaelites, Millet's *Angelus*, 1858), often drawn from ordinary life. The **Impressionists** (Monet, 1840-1926; Pissarro, 1830-1903; Renoir, 1841-1919) rejected the formalism, sentimentality, and precise techniques of academic art in favor of a spontaneous, undetailed rendering of the world through careful representation of the effect of natural light on objects. They were strongly influenced by Asian and African styles.

Realistic **novelists** presented the full panorama of social classes and personalities but retained sentimentality and moral judgment (**Dickens**, 1812-70; **Eliot**, 1819-80; **Tolstoy**, 1828-1910; **Balzac**, 1799-1850).

Veneer of Stability: 1880-1900

Imperialism triumphant. The vast **African** interior, visited by European explorers (Barth, 1821-65; Livingstone, 1813-73), was conquered by the European powers in rapid, competitive thrusts from their coastal bases after 1880, mostly for domestic political and international strategic reasons. W African Muslim kingdoms (Fulani), Arab slave traders (Zanzibar), and Bantu military confederations (Zulu) were alike subdued. Only Christian Ethiopia (defeat of Italy, 1896) and Liberia resisted successfully. France (W Africa) and Britain ("Cape to Cairo," **Boer War**, 1899-1902) were the major beneficiaries. The ideology of "the white man's burden" (Kipling, *Barrack Room Ballads*, 1892) justified the conquests, which in fact reflected Europe's weapons superiority.

W European foreign capital investment soared to nearly $40 bil by 1914, but most was in E Europe (France, Germany), the Americas (Britain), and Europe's colonies. The foundation of the modern interdependent world economy was laid, with cartels dominating raw material trade. Global developments included a new agreement on international patents (1883), the modern Olympics (1896), and the global spread of department stores.

An industrious world. Industrial and technological proficiency characterized the two new great powers—Germany and the U.S. Coal and iron deposits enabled Germany to reach second- or third-place status in iron, steel, and shipbuilding by the 1900s. German electrical and chemical industries were world leaders. The U.S. post-Civil War boom (interrupted by financial panics—1884, 1893, 1896) was shaped by massive immigration from S and E Europe from 1880, government subsidy of railroads, and huge private monopolies (Standard Oil, 1870; U.S. Steel, 1901). The **Spanish-American War**, 1898 (Philippine Insurrection, 1899-1902), and the **Open Door policy** in China (1899) made the U.S. a world power.

England led in **urbanization**, with London the world capital of finance, insurance, and shipping. Sewer systems (Paris, 1850s), electric subways (London, 1890), parks, and bargain department stores helped improve living standards for most of the urban population of the industrial world. Birthrates declined in the West while infant mortality rates plunged (demographic transition, 1880-1920).

Upheavals in Asia. Asian reaction to European economic, military, and religious incursions took the form of imitation of Western techniques and adoption of Western ideas of progress and freedom. The Chinese "self-strengthening" movement of the 1860s and 1870s included rail, port, and arsenal improvements and metal and textile mills. Reformers such as **K'ang** Yu-wei (1858-1927) won liberalizing reforms in 1898, right after the European and Japanese "scramble for concessions."

A universal education system in Japan and importation of foreign industrial, scientific, and military experts aided Japan's rapid modernization after 1868 under the authoritarian Meiji regime. Japan's victory in the **Sino-Japanese War** (1894-95) put Formosa and Korea in its power. Industrialization began in earnest by 1890.

In India, the British alliance with the remaining princely states masked reform sentiment among the Westernized urban elite; higher education had been conducted largely in English for 50 years. The **Indian National Congress**, founded in 1885, demanded a larger government role for Indians.

Fin-de-siècle **sophistication.** **Naturalist** writers pushed realism to its extreme limits, adopting a quasi-scientific attitude and writing about formerly taboo subjects such as sex, crime, extreme poverty, and corruption (Flaubert, 1821-80; Zola, 1840-1902; Hardy, 1840-1928). Unseen or repressed psychological motivations were explored in the clinical and theoretical works of Sigmund **Freud** (1856-1939) and in works of fiction (**Dostoyevsky**, 1821-81; Henry James, 1843-1916; Schnitzler, 1862-1931).

A contempt for bourgeois life or a desire to shock a complacent audience was shared by the French **symbolist** poets (Verlaine, 1844-96; Rimbaud, 1854-91), by neopagan English writers (Swinburne, 1837-1909), by continental dramatists (**Ibsen**, 1828-1906), and by satirists (**Wilde**, 1854-1900). The German philosopher Friedrich **Nietzsche** (1844-1900) was influential in his elitism and pessimism.

Postimpressionist art neglected long-cherished conventions of representation (**Cézanne**, 1839-1906) and showed a willingness to learn from primitive and non-European art (**Gauguin**, 1848-1903; Japanese prints).

Racism. Gobineau (1816-82) gave a pseudobiological foundation to modern racist theories, which spread in Europe in the latter 19th cent., along with **Social Darwinism**, the belief that societies are and should be organized as a struggle for survival of the fittest. The medieval period was interpreted as an era of natural Germanic rule (Chamberlain, 1855-1927), and notions of racial superiority were associated with German national aspirations (Treitschke, 1834-96). **Anti-Semitism**, with a new racist rationale, became a significant political force in Germany (Anti-Semitic Petition, 1880), Austria (Lueger, 1844-1910), and France (**Dreyfus affair**, 1894-1906).

Imperialism's High Point: 1900-09

Alliances. While the peace of Europe (and its dependencies) continued to hold (1907 **Hague Conference** extended the rules of war and international arbitration procedures), imperial rivalries, protectionist trade practices (in Germany and France), and the escalating arms race (British *Dreadnought* battleship launched; Germany widens Kiel canal, 1906) exacerbated minor disputes (German-French Moroccan "crises," 1905, 1911).

Security was sought through balance-of-power alliances: **Triple Alliance** (Germany, Austria-Hungary, Italy; renewed in 1902 and 1907); Anglo-Japanese Alliance (1902), Franco-Russian Alliance (1899), **Entente Cordiale** (Britain, France, 1904), Anglo-Russian Treaty (1907), German-Ottoman friendship. Global developments included the establishment of an international court in The Hague, the first transatlantic radio transmission (1901), and the creation of the first international association for European football (1904).

Ottomans decline. The Ottoman government was unable to resist further loss of territory, and earlier reform efforts gave way to greater authoritarianism. Nearly all European lands were lost in 1912 to Serbia, Greece, Montenegro, and Bulgaria. Italy took Libya and the Dodecanese islands the same year. Britain took Kuwait (1899) and the Sinai (1906). The **Young Turk** revolution in 1908 forced the sultan to restore a constitution, and it introduced some social reform and secularization.

British Empire. British trade and cultural influence remained dominant in the empire, but constitutional reforms presaged its eventual dissolution. The colonies of **Australia** were united in 1901 under a self-governing commonwealth. **New Zealand** acquired dominion status in 1907. The old Boer republics joined Cape Colony and Natal in the self-governing Union of **South Africa** in 1910.

The 1909 Indian Councils Act enhanced the role of elected province legislatures in **India**. The Muslim League (founded 1906) sought separate communal representation.

East Asia. Japan exploited its growing industrial power to expand its empire. Victory in the 1904-05 war against Russia (naval battle of Tsushima, 1905) assured Japan's domination of **Korea** (annexed 1910) and Manchuria (Port Arthur taken, 1905).

In China, central authority began to crumble (empress died, 1908). Reforms (Confucian exam system ended 1905, modernization of the army, building of railroads) were inadequate, and secret societies of reformers and nationalists, inspired by the Westernized **Sun** Yat-sen (1866-1925), fomented periodic uprisings in the S.

Siam, whose independence had been guaranteed by Britain and France in 1896, was split into spheres of influence by those countries in 1907.

Russia. The population of the Russian Empire approached 150 million in 1900. Reforms in education, in law, and in local institutions (*zemstvos*) and an industrial boom starting in the 1880s (oil, railroads) created the beginnings of a modern society, despite the autocratic tsarist regime. Liberals (1903 Union of Liberation), Socialists (Social Democrats founded 1898, Bolsheviks split off 1903), and populists (Social Revolutionaries founded 1901) were periodically repressed, and national minorities were persecuted (anti-Jewish pogroms, 1903, 1905-06).

An industrial crisis after 1900 and harvest failures aggravated poverty among urban workers, and the 1904-05 defeat by Japan (which checked Russia's Asian expansion) sparked the **Revolution of 1905-06**. A **Duma** (parliament) was created under Tsar Nicholas II. Agricultural reform (under Stolypin, prime minister, 1906-11) created a large class of land-owning peasants (*kulaks*).

The world shrinks. Developments in transportation and communication and mass population movements helped create an awareness of an interdependent world. Early **automobiles** (Daimler, Benz, 1885) were experimental or were designed as luxuries. Assembly-line mass production (Ford Motor Co., 1903) made the invention practical, and by 1910 nearly 500,000 motor vehicles were registered in the U.S. alone. **Heavier-than-air flights** began in 1903 in the U.S. (Wright brothers' *Flyer*), preceded by glider, balloon, and model plane advances in several countries. Trade was advanced by improvements in **ship design** (gyrocompass, 1910), speed (*Lusitania* crossed Atlantic in five days, 1907), and reach (Panama Canal begun, 1904).

The first transatlantic **radio** telegraphic transmission occurred in 1901, six years after Marconi discovered radio. Radio transmission of human speech had been made in 1900. Telegraphic transmission of photos was achieved in 1904, lending immediacy to news reports. **Phonographs**, popularized by Caruso's recordings (starting 1902), made for quick international spread of musical styles (ragtime). **Motion pictures**, perfected in the 1890s (Dickson, Lumière brothers), became a popular and artistic medium after 1900; newsreels appeared in 1909.

Emigration from crowded European centers soared in the decade: 9 million migrated to the U.S., and millions more went to Siberia, Canada, Argentina, Australia, South Africa, and Algeria. Some 70 million Europeans emigrated in the century before 1914. Several million Chinese, Indians, and Japanese migrated to SE Asia, where their urban skills often enabled them to take a predominant economic role.

Social reform. The social and economic problems of the poor were kept in the public eye by realist fiction writers (Dreiser's *Sister Carrie*, 1900; Gorky's *Lower Depths*, 1902; Sinclair's *The Jungle*, 1906), journalists (U.S. **muckrakers**—Steffens, Tarbell), and artists (Ashcan school). Frequent labor strikes and occasional assassinations by anarchists or radicals (Empress Elizabeth of Austria, 1898; King Umberto I of Italy, 1900; U.S. Pres. McKinley, 1901; Russian Interior Min. Plehve, 1904; Portugal's King Carlos, 1908) added to social tension and fear of revolution. Feminist agitators for the vote surfaced in several countries.

But democratic reformism responded in part. In Germany, Bernstein's (1850-1932) **revisionist Marxism**, downgrading revolution, was accepted by the powerful Social Democrats and trade unions. The British Fabian Society (the Webbs, Shaw) and the Labour Party (founded 1906) worked for reforms such as social security and union rights (1906), while woman suffragists grew more militant. U.S. **progressives** fought big business (Pure Food and Drug Act, 1906). In France, the 10-hour workday (1904) and separation of church and state (1905) were reform victories, as was universal suffrage in Austria (1907).

Arts. An unprecedented period of experimentation, centered in France, produced several new **painting styles**: Fauvism exploited bold color areas (Matisse, *Woman With Hat*, 1905); expressionism reflected powerful inner emotions (Brücke group, 1905); Cubism combined several views of an object on one flat surface (Picasso, *Demoiselles*, 1906-07); futurism tried to depict speed and motion (Italian Futurist Manifesto, 1910). **Architects** explored new uses of steel structures, with facades either neoclassical (Adler and Sullivan in U.S.), curvilinear Art Nouveau (Gaudi's Casa Mila, 1905-10), or functionally streamlined (Wright's Robie House, 1909).

Music and dance shared the experimental spirit. Ruth St. Denis (1877-1968) and Isadora Duncan (1878-1927) pioneered modern dance, while Sergei Diaghilev in Paris revitalized classic ballet from 1909. Composers explored atonal music (Debussy, 1862-1918) and dissonance (Schoenberg, 1874-1951) or revolutionized classical forms (Stravinsky, 1882-1971), often showing jazz or folk music influences.

Emigration from densely populated European countries to the Americas soared in the early 20th century; many landed on Ellis Island, in New York Harbor, en route to U.S. cities.

War and Revolution: 1910-19

War threatens. Germany under Wilhelm II sought a political and imperial role consonant with its industrial strength, challenging Britain's world supremacy and threatening France, which was still resenting the loss (1871) of Alsace-Lorraine. Austria wanted to curb an expanded Serbia (after 1912) and the threat it posed to its own Slav lands. Russia feared Austrian and German political and economic aims in the Balkans and Turkey.

An accelerated arms race resulted from these circumstances. The German standing army rose to more than 2 million men by 1914. Russia and France had more than a million each, and Austria and the British Empire nearly a million each. Dozens of enormous battleships were built by the powers after 1906.

The **assassination of Austrian Archduke Franz Ferdinand** by a Serbian nationalist, June 28, 1914, was the trigger for war. The system of alliances made the conflict Europe-wide; Germany's invasion of Belgium to outflank France forced Britain to enter the war. Patriotic fervor was nearly unanimous among all classes in most countries.

World War I. German forces were stopped in France in one month. The rival armies dug **trench networks**. Artillery and improved machine guns prevented either side from any lasting advance despite repeated assaults (600,000 dead at **Verdun**, Feb.-July 1916). German deployment of poisonous chlorine gas (Ypres, 1915) was first major use of lethal **chemical weapons**. The entrance of more than 1 million U.S. troops tipped the balance after mid-1917, forcing Germany to sue for peace the next year. The formal armistice was signed on Nov. 11, 1918, and the German emperor abdicated.

In the E, the Russian armies were thrown back (battle of **Tannenberg**, Aug. 20, 1914), and the war grew unpopular in Russia. An allied attempt to relieve Russia through Turkey failed (**Gallipoli**, 1915). The **Russian Revolution** (1917) abolished the monarchy. The new Bolshevik regime signed the capitulatory Brest-Litovsk peace in Mar. 1918. Italy entered the war on the allied side in May 1915 but was pushed back by Oct. 1917. A renewed offensive with Allied aid in Oct.-Nov. 1918 forced Austria to surrender.

The British Navy successfully blockaded Germany, which responded with submarine U-boat attacks; **unrestricted submarine warfare** against neutrals after Jan. 1917 helped bring the U.S. into the war. Other battlefields included Palestine and Mesopotamia, both of which Britain wrested from the Turks in 1917, and the African and Pacific colonies of Germany, most of which fell to Britain, France, Australia, Japan, and South Africa.

Settlement. At the **Paris Peace Conference** (Jan.-June 1919), concluded by the **Treaty of Versailles**, and in subsequent negotiations and local wars (Russian-Polish War, 1920), the **map of Europe** was redrawn with a nod to U.S. Pres. Woodrow Wilson's principle of self-determination. Austria and Hungary were separated, and much of their land was given to Yugoslavia (formerly Serbia), Romania, Italy, and the newly independent Poland and Czechoslovakia. Germany lost territory in the W, N, and E, while Finland and the Baltic states were detached from Russia. The Ottoman Empire ended (1922) and most of its Arab lands went to British-sponsored Arab states or to direct French and British rule. Belgium's sovereignty was recognized.

From 1916, the civilian populations and economies of both sides were mobilized to an unprecedented degree. Hardships intensified among fighting nations in 1917 (French mutiny crushed in May). More than 10 million soldiers died in the war.

A huge **reparations** burden and partial demilitarization were imposed on Germany. Pres. Wilson obtained approval for a League of Nations, but the U.S. Senate refused to allow the U.S. to join.

Russian revolution. Military defeats and high casualties caused a contagious lack of confidence in Tsar Nicholas, who was forced to abdicate Mar. 1917. A liberal provisional government failed to end the war, and massive desertions, riots, and fighting between factions followed. A moderate socialist government under Aleksandr Kerensky was overthrown (Nov. 1917) in a violent coup by the **Bolsheviks** in Petrograd under **Lenin**, who later disbanded the elected Constituent Assembly.

The Bolsheviks brutally suppressed all opposition and ended the war with Germany in Mar. 1918. **Civil war** broke out in the summer between the Red Army (the Bolsheviks and their supporters), and monarchists, anarchists, minority nationalities (Ukrainians, Georgians, Poles), and others. Small U.S., British, French, and Japanese units also opposed the Bolsheviks (1918-19; Japan in Vladivostok to 1922). The civil war, anarchy, and pogroms devastated the country until the 1920 Red Army victory. The **Communist Party** leadership retained absolute power.

Other European revolutions. An unpopular monarchy in **Portugal** was overthrown in 1910. The new republic took severe anticlerical measures in 1911.

After a century of Home Rule agitation, during which **Ireland** was devastated by famine (1 million dead, 1846-47) and emigration, republican militants staged an unsuccessful uprising in Dublin during **Easter 1916**. The execution of the leaders and mass arrests by the British won popular support for the rebels. The **Irish Free State**, comprising all but the six northern counties, achieved dominion status in 1922.

In the aftermath of the world war, radical revolutions were attempted in Germany (**Spartacist** uprising, Jan. 1919), **Hungary** (Kun regime, 1919), and elsewhere. All were suppressed or failed for lack of support.

Chinese revolution. The Manchu Dynasty was overthrown and a republic proclaimed in Oct. 1911. First Pres. Sun Yat-sen resigned in favor of strongman Yuan Shih-k'ai. Sun organized the parliamentarian **Kuomintang** party.

Students launched protests on May 4, 1919, against League of Nations concessions in China to Japan. Nationalist, liberal, and socialist ideas and political groups spread. The **Communist Party** was founded in 1921. A Communist regime took power in Mongolia with Soviet support in 1921.

India restive. Indian objections to British rule erupted in nationalist riots as well as in the nonviolent tactics of Mahatma **Gandhi** (1869-1948). Nearly 400 unarmed demonstrators were shot at **Amritsar** in Apr. 1919. Britain approved limited self-rule that year.

Mexican revolution. Under the long Diaz dictatorship (1877-1911) the economy advanced, but Indian and mestizo lands were confiscated, and concessions to foreigners (mostly U.S.) damaged the middle class. A revolution in 1910 led to civil wars and U.S. intervention (1914, 1916-17). Land reform and a more democratic constitution (1917) were achieved.

Sciences. Scientific specialization prevailed by the 20th cent. Advances in knowledge and technological aptitude increased with the geometric rise in the number of practitioners. Physicists challenged common-sense views of causality, observation, and a mechanistic universe, putting science further beyond popular grasp (**Einstein**'s general theory of relativity, 1915-16; Bohr's quantum mechanics, 1913; Heisenberg's uncertainty principle, 1927).

Revolution in Russia proceeded fitfully and was sometimes violent, as the government was forced to reorganize four times between the overthrow of the tsar in Mar. 1917 and the final Bolshevik coup in Nov.

Aftermath of War: 1920-29

U.S. Easy credit, technological ingenuity, and war-related industrial decline in Europe caused a long economic boom, in which ownership of new products—**autos, phones, radios**—became more democratized. **Prosperity**, an increase in women workers, women's suffrage (19th Amendment ratified, 1920), and drastic change in fashion (**flappers**, mannish bob for women, clean-shaven men) created a wide perception of social change despite prohibition of alcoholic beverages (1919-33). Union membership and strikes increased. Fear of radicals led to Palmer raids (1919-20) and the Sacco-Vanzetti case (1921-27).

Europe sorts itself out. Germany's liberal **Weimar constitution** (1919) could not guarantee a stable government in the face of rightist violence (Rathenau assassinated, 1922) and Communist refusal to cooperate with Socialists. Reparations and Allied occupation of the Rhineland caused staggering inflation that destroyed middle-class savings, but economic expansion resumed after mid-decade, aided by U.S. loans. A sophisticated, **innovative culture** developed in architecture and design (Bauhaus, 1919-28), film (Lang, *M*, 1931), painting (Grosz), music (Weill, *Threepenny Opera*, 1928), theater (Brecht, *A Man's a Man*, 1926), criticism (Benjamin), philosophy (Jung), and fashion. This culture was considered decadent and socially disruptive by rightists.

England elected its first Labour governments (Jan. 1924, June 1929). A 10-day general strike in support of coal miners failed in May 1926. In **Italy**, strikes, political chaos, and violence by small Fascist bands culminated in the Oct. 1922 Fascist March on Rome, which established **Mussolini**'s dictatorship. Strikes were outlawed (1926), and Italian influence was pressed in the Balkans (Albania made a protectorate, 1926). A conservative dictatorship was also established in **Portugal** in a 1926 military coup.

Czechoslovakia, the only stable democracy to emerge from the war in Central or E Europe, faced opposition from Germans (in the Sudetenland), Ruthenians, and some Slovaks. As the industrial heartland of the old Habsburg empire, it remained fairly prosperous. With French backing, it formed the Little Entente with Yugoslavia (1920) and **Romania** (1921) to block Austrian or Hungarian irredentism. Croats and Slovenes in **Yugoslavia** demanded a federal state until King Alexander I proclaimed (1929) a royal dictatorship. Poland faced internal nationality problems as well (Germans, Ukrainians, Jews); Pilsudski ruled as dictator from 1926. The Baltic states were threatened by traditionally dominant ethnic Germans and by Soviet-supported Communists.

An economic collapse and famine in **Russia** (1921-22) claimed 5 million lives. The New Economic Policy (1921) allowed land ownership by peasants and some private commerce and industry. **Stalin** was absolute ruler within four years of Lenin's death (1924). He inaugurated a brutal collectivization program (1929-32) and used foreign Communist parties for Soviet state advantage. Industrialization advanced rapidly.

Internationalism. Revulsion against World War I led to pacifist agitation, to the Kellogg-Briand Pact renouncing aggressive war (1928), and to **naval disarmament** pacts (Washington, 1922; London, 1930). But the League of Nations was able to arbitrate only minor disputes (Greece-Bulgaria, 1925). A number of countries pulled back from global contacts, as with American isolationism and Russia's separation from international capitalism.

Middle East. Mustafa Kemal (**Ataturk**) led **Turkish** nationalists in resisting Italian, French, and Greek military advances (1919-23). The sultanate was abolished (1922), and

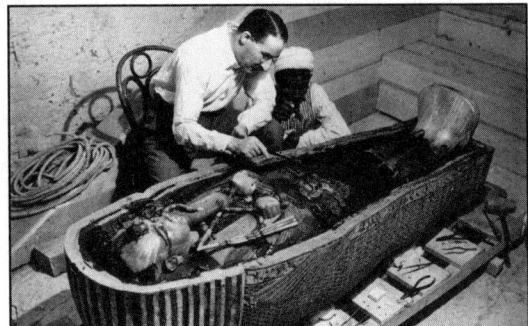

Howard Carter's 1922 discovery of the tomb of Tutankhamun, who ruled as pharaoh in the 14th century BCE, is considered the archaeological find of the century.

elaborate reforms were passed, including secularization of law and adoption of the Latin alphabet. Ethnic conflict led to persecution of **Armenians** (more than 1 million dead in 1915, 1 million expelled), Greeks (forced Greek-Turk population exchange, 1923), and Kurds (1925 uprising).

With evacuation of the Turks from **Arab** lands, the puritanical Wahabi dynasty of E Arabia conquered (1919-25) what is now Saudi Arabia. British, French, and Arab dynastic and nationalist maneuvering resulted in the creation of two more Arab monarchies in 1921—Iraq and Transjordan (both under British control)—and two French mandates—Syria and Lebanon. Jewish immigration into British-mandated **Palestine**, inspired by the Zionist movement, was resisted by Arabs, at times violently (1921, 1929 massacres).

Reza Khan ruled **Persia** after his 1921 coup (shah from 1925), centralized control, and created the trappings of a modern secular state.

In 1922, English archaeologist Howard Carter discovered the tomb of the boy pharaoh **Tutankhamun** in the Valley of the Kings in Egypt.

China. The Kuomintang under **Chiang Kai-shek** (1887-1975) subdued the warlords by 1928. The Communists were brutally suppressed after their alliance with the Kuomintang was broken in 1927. Relative peace thereafter allowed for industrial and financial improvements, with some Russian, British, and U.S. cooperation.

Arts. Nearly all bounds of subject matter, style, and attitude were broken in the arts of the period. **Abstract** art first took inspiration from natural forms or narrative themes (Kandinsky from 1911) and then worked free of any representational aims (Malevich's suprematism, 1915-19; Mondrian's geometric style from 1917). The **Dada** movement (from 1916) mocked artistic pretension with absurd collages and constructions. Paradox, illusion, and psychological taboos were exploited by **surrealists** by the late 1920s (Dali, Magritte). Architectural schools celebrated industrial values, whether vigorous abstract constructivism (Tatlin, *Monument to the Third International*, 1919) or the machined, streamlined **Bauhaus** style, which was extended to many design fields (Helvetica typeface).

Prose writers explored revolutionary narrative modes related to dreams (Kafka's *Trial*, 1925), internal monologue (Joyce's *Ulysses*, 1922), and word play (Stein's *Making of Americans*, 1925). Poets and novelists wrote of modern alienation (Eliot's *Waste Land*, 1922) and aimlessness ("The Lost Generation").

Rise of Totalitarians: 1930-39

Depression. A worldwide financial panic and economic depression began with the Oct. 1929 U.S. stock market crash and the May 1931 failure of the Austrian Credit-Anstalt. A credit crunch caused international bankruptcies and **unemployment**: 12 million jobless by 1932 in the U.S., 5.6 million in Germany, 2.7 million in England. Governments responded with **tariff restrictions** (Smoot-Hawley Act, 1930; Ottawa Imperial Conference, 1932), which dried up world trade. Government public works programs were vitiated by deflationary budget balancing.

Germany. Years of agitation by violent extremists were brought to a head by the Depression. Nazi leader Adolf Hitler was named chancellor in Jan. 1933 and given dictatorial power by

the Reichstag in Mar. Opposition parties were disbanded, strikes banned, and all aspects of economic, cultural, and religious life were brought under central government and Nazi party control and manipulated by sophisticated propaganda. Severe persecution of Jews began (**Nuremberg Laws**, Sept. 1935). Many Jews, political opponents, and others were sent to concentration camps (Dachau, 1933), where thousands died or were killed. Public works, renewed conscription (1935), arms production, and a four-year plan (1936) all but ended unemployment.

Hitler's expansionism started with reincorporation of the Saar (1935), occupation of the **Rhineland** (Mar. 1936), and annexation of Austria (Mar. 1938). At **Munich** (Sept. 1938)

Britain and France attempted to appease Hitler and avoid war by successfully encouraging Czechoslovakia's surrender of the Sudetenland territory.

Russia. Rapid industrialization was achieved through successive **five-year plans** starting in 1928, using severe labor discipline and mass forced labor. Industry was financed by exploitation of agriculture, which was almost totally collectivized by the early 1930s (*kolkhoz* [collective farm]; *sovkhoz* [state farm], often in newly worked lands). Millions perished in a series of manufactured disasters: extermination (1929-34) of kulaks (peasant landowners), severe famine (1932-33), party purges and show trials (Great Purge, 1936-38), suppression of nationalities, and poor conditions in labor camps. Purges also increased Stalin's power in the Communist party.

Spain. An industrial revolution during World War I created an urban proletariat, which was attracted to socialism and anarchism; Catalan nationalists challenged central authority. The five years after King Alfonso left Spain in Apr. 1931 were dominated by tension between intermittent leftist and anticlerical governments and clericals, monarchists, and other rightists. Anarchist and Communist rebellions were crushed, but a July 1936 extreme right rebellion led by Gen. Francisco **Franco** and aided by Nazi Germany and Fascist Italy succeeded after a three-year **civil war** (more than 1 million dead in battles and atrocities). The war polarized international public opinion.

Italy. Despite propaganda for the ideal of the Corporate State, few domestic reforms were attempted. An entente with Hungary and Austria (Mar. 1934), a pact with Germany and Japan (Nov. 1937), and intervention by 50,000-75,000 troops in Spain (1936-39) sealed Italy's identification with the fascist bloc (anti-Semitic laws after Mar. 1938). Ethiopia was conquered (1935-36) and Albania annexed (Jan. 1939) in conscious imitation of ancient Rome.

Eastern Europe. Repressive regimes fought for power against an active opposition (liberals, socialists, Communists, peasants, Nazis). Minority groups and Jews were restricted within national boundaries that did not coincide with ethnic population patterns. In the destruction of **Czechoslovakia**, Hungary occupied S Slovakia (Nov. 1938) and Ruthenia (Mar. 1939), and a pro-Nazi regime took power in the rest of Slovakia. Other boundary disputes (e.g., Poland-Lithuania, Yugoslavia-Bulgaria, and Romania-Hungary) doomed attempts to build joint fronts against Germany or Russia. Economic depression was severe.

East Asia. After a period of liberalism in **Japan**, nativist militarists dominated the government with peasant support. Manchuria was seized (Sept. 1931-Feb. 1932), and a puppet state was set up (Manchukuo). Adjacent Jehol (Inner Mongolia) was occupied in 1933. **China** proper was invaded in July 1937; large areas were conquered by Oct. 1938. Hundreds of thousands of rapes, murders, and other atrocities were attributed to the Japanese.

Communist forces left Kuomintang-besieged strongholds in the S of China in a Long March (1934-35) to the N. The Kuomintang-Communist civil war was suspended in Jan. 1937 in the face of threatening Japan.

Democracies. The Roosevelt Administration, in office Mar. 1933, embarked on an extensive program of **New Deal**

Italy's Benito Mussolini and Germany's Adolf Hitler affirmed their total political and military alliance with 1939's Pact of Steel.

social reform and economic stimulation, including protection for labor unions (heavy industries organized), Social Security, public works, wage-and-hour laws, and assistance to farmers. Isolationist sentiment (1937 Neutrality Act) prevented U.S. intervention in Europe, but military expenditures were increased in 1939.

French political instability and polarization prevented resolution of economic and international security questions. The **Popular Front** government under Leon Blum (June 1936-Apr. 1938) passed social reforms (40-hour work week) and raised arms spending. National coalition governments, which ruled Britain from Aug. 1931, brought economic recovery but failed to define a consistent international policy until Chamberlain's government (from May 1937), which practiced **appeasement** of Germany and Italy.

India. Twenty years of agitation for autonomy and then for independence (Gandhi's **salt march**, 1930) achieved some constitutional reform (extended provincial powers, 1935) despite Muslim-Hindu strife. Social issues assumed prominence with peasant uprisings (1921), strikes (1928), Gandhi's efforts for untouchables (1932 "fast unto death"), and social and agrarian reform by the provinces after 1937.

Arts. The streamlined, geometric design motifs of Art Deco (from 1925) prevailed through the 1930s. **Abstract art** flourished (Moore sculptures from 1931) alongside a new **realism** related to social and political concerns (Socialist Realism, the official Soviet style from 1934; Mexican muralist Rivera, 1886-1957; Orozco, 1883-1949), which were also expressed in fiction and poetry (Steinbeck's *Grapes of Wrath*, 1939; Sandburg's *The People, Yes*, 1936). Modern architecture (International Style, 1932) was unchallenged in its use of artificial materials (concrete, glass), lack of decoration, and monumentality (Rockefeller Center, 1929-40). Larger-than-life U.S.-made films captured a worldwide audience (*Gone With the Wind, The Wizard of Oz*, both 1939).

War, Hot and Cold: 1940-49

War in Asia-Pacific. Japan occupied Indochina in Sept. 1940, dominated Thailand in Dec. 1941, and attacked Hawaii (**Pearl Harbor**), the Philippines, Hong Kong, and Malaya on Dec. 7, 1941 (precipitating U.S. entrance into the war). Indonesia was attacked in Jan. 1942, and Burma was conquered in Mar. 1942. The Battle of **Midway** (June 1942) turned back the Japanese advance. "Island-hopping" battles (**Guadalcanal**, Aug. 1942-Jan. 1943; **Leyte Gulf**, Oct. 1944; **Iwo Jima**, Feb.-Mar. 1945; **Okinawa**, Apr. 1945) and massive bombing raids on Japan from June 1944 wore out Japanese defenses. U.S. atom bombs, dropped Aug. 6 and 9 on **Hiroshima** and **Nagasaki**, forced Japan to agree, on Aug. 14, to surrender; formal surrender was on Sept. 2, 1945.

War in Europe. The Nazi-Soviet nonaggression pact (Aug. 1939) freed Germany to attack Poland (Sept. 1939). Britain and France, which had guaranteed Polish independence, declared war on Germany. Russia seized E Poland (Sept. 1939), attacked Finland (Nov. 1939), and took the Baltic states (July 1940). Mobile German forces staged *blitzkrieg* attacks during Apr.-June 1940, conquering neutral Denmark, Norway, and the Low Countries and defeating France; 350,000 British and French troops were evacuated at **Dunkirk**, France (May). The **Battle of Britain** (June-Dec. 1940) denied Germany air superiority. German-Italian campaigns won the Balkans by Apr. 1941. Three million Axis troops **invaded Russia** in June 1941, marching through Ukraine to the Caucasus, and through White Russia and the Baltic republics to Moscow and Leningrad.

Russian winter counterthrusts (1941-42 and 1942-43) stopped the German advance (**Stalingrad**, Sept. 1942-Feb. 1943). Sustaining great casualties, the Russians drove the Axis from all E Europe and the Balkans in the next two years. Invasions of N Africa (Nov. 1942), Italy (Sept. 1943), and **Normandy** (launched on D-Day, June 6, 1944) brought U.S., British, Free French, and allied troops to Germany by spring 1945. In Feb. 1945, the three Allied leaders, Winston **Churchill** (Britain), Joseph **Stalin** (USSR), and Franklin D. **Roosevelt** (U.S.), met in Yalta to discuss strategy and resolve political issues, including the postwar Allied occupation of Germany. Germany surrendered May 7, 1945.

The U.S. bombing of Hiroshima and Nagasaki, Japan, in 1945 demonstrated the deadly, destructive power of atomic weapons.

Atrocities. The war brought 20th-cent. cruelty to its peak. The Nazi regime systematically killed an estimated 5-6 million Jews, including some 3 million who died in death camps (e.g., **Auschwitz**). Gypsies, political opponents, people with mental or physical disabilities, homosexuals, and others deemed undesirable were also murdered by the Nazis, as were vast numbers of Slavs.

German bombs killed 70,000 British civilians. More than 100,000 Chinese civilians were killed by Japanese forces in the capture and occupation of Nanking. Severe retaliation by the Soviet army, E European partisans, Free French, and others took a heavy toll. U.S. and British bombing of Germany killed hundreds of thousands, as did U.S. bombing of Japan (80,000-200,000 at Hiroshima alone). Some 45 million people died in the war.

Settlement. The **United Nations** charter was signed in San Francisco on June 26, 1945, by 50 nations. The International Tribunal at **Nuremberg** convicted 22 German leaders for war crimes in Sept. 1946; 23 Japanese leaders were convicted in Nov. 1948. Postwar border changes included large gains in territory for the USSR, losses for Germany, a shift to the W in Polish borders, and minor losses for Italy. Communist regimes, supported by Soviet troops, took power in most of Eastern Europe, including Soviet-occupied Germany (GDR, a.k.a. East Germany, proclaimed Oct. 1949). Japan lost all overseas lands. Global developments involved establishing new economic coordinating bodies like the International Monetary Fund (1944) and the Universal Declaration of Human Rights (1948).

Recovery. Basic political and social changes were imposed on Japan and W Germany by the Western allies (Japan constitution adopted, Nov. 1946; W German basic law, May 1949). U.S. **Marshall Plan** aid ($12 bil, 1947-51) spurred W European economic recovery after a period of severe inflation and strikes

in Europe and the U.S. The British Labour Party introduced a national health service and nationalized basic industries in 1946.

Cold War. Western fears of further Soviet advances (Cominform formed in Oct. 1947; Czechoslovakia coup, Feb. 1948; Berlin blockade, Apr. 1948-Sept. 1949) led to the formation of **NATO**. Civil war in Greece and Soviet pressure on Turkey led to U.S. aid under the **Truman Doctrine** (Mar. 1947). Other anti-Communist security pacts were the Organization of American States (Apr. 1948) and the SE Asia Treaty Organization (Sept. 1954). A new wave of **Soviet purges** and repression intensified in the last years of Stalin's rule, extending to E Europe (Slansky trial in Czechoslovakia, 1951). Only Yugoslavia resisted Soviet control (expelled by Cominform, June 1948; U.S. aid, June 1949).

China, Korea. Communist forces emerged from World War II strengthened by the Soviet takeover of industrial Manchuria. In four years of fighting, the Kuomintang was driven from the mainland; the People's Republic of China was proclaimed Oct. 1, 1949. Korea was divided by USSR and U.S. occupation forces. Separate republics were proclaimed in the two zones in Aug.-Sept. 1948.

India. India and Pakistan became independent dominions on Aug. 15, 1947. Millions of Hindu and Muslim refugees were created by the partition. Riots (1946-47) took hundreds of thousands of lives. Mahatma **Gandhi** was assassinated in Jan. 1948. Burma became completely independent in Jan. 1948; Ceylon (later Sri Lanka) took dominion status in Feb.

Middle East. The UN approved partition of Palestine into Jewish and Arab states. **Israel** was proclaimed a state, May 14, 1948. Arabs rejected partition, but failed to defeat Israel in war (May 1948-July 1949). Immigration from Europe and the Middle East swelled Israel's Jewish population. British and French forces left Lebanon and Syria in 1946. Transjordan occupied most of Arab Palestine.

Southeast Asia. Communists and others fought against restoration of French rule in **Indochina** from 1946; a non-Communist government was recognized by France in Mar. 1949, but fighting continued. Both Indonesia and the Philippines became independent; the former in 1949 after four years of war with the Netherlands, the latter in 1946. Philippine economic and military ties with the U.S. remained strong; a Communist-led peasant rising was checked in 1948.

Arts. New York became the center of the world art market; **abstract expressionism** was the chief mode (Pollock from 1943, de Kooning from 1947). Literature and philosophy explored **existentialism** (Camus's *The Stranger*, 1942; Sartre's *Being and Nothingness*, 1943). Non-Western attempts to revive or create regional styles (Senghor's Négritude, Mishima's novels) were responses to global cultural influences. Radio and phonograph records spread American popular music (swing, bebop) around the world.

The Cold War Decade: 1950-59

Decolonization. The relatively peaceful decline of European political and military power in Asia and Africa accelerated in the 1950s. Nearly all of **N Africa** was freed by 1956, but France fought a bitter war to retain Algeria, with its large European minority, until 1962. **Ghana**, independent in 1957, led a parade of new black African nations (more than two dozen by 1962), which altered the political character of the UN. Ethnic disputes often exploded in the new nations after decolonization (UN troops in Cyprus, 1964; **Nigerian civil war**, 1967-70). Leaders of the new states, mostly sharing socialist ideologies, tried to create an Afro-Asian bloc (Bandung Conference, 1955), but Western economic influence and U.S. political ties remained strong (Baghdad Pact, 1955).

Trade. World trade volume soared, in an atmosphere of monetary stability assured by international accords (**Bretton Woods**, 1944). In Europe, economic integration advanced (**European Economic Community**, 1957; European Free Trade Association, 1960). Comecon (1949) coordinated the economies of Soviet-bloc countries. Global developments included transcontinental jet travel (first South Africa to Britain flight, 1952; introduction of term "jet lag," 1965) and the increasing spread of English in global business, sports, and transportation.

U.S. Economic growth produced an abundance of consumer goods (9.3 million motor vehicles sold, 1955). Suburban housing changed life patterns for middle and working classes (Levittown, NY, 1947-51). Pres. Dwight **Eisenhower**'s landslide election victories (1952, 1956) reflected consensus politics. A system of alliances and military bases bolstered U.S. influence on all continents. Trade and payments surpluses were balanced by overseas investments and foreign aid ($50 bil, 1950-59).

USSR. In the "thaw" after Stalin's death in 1953, relations with the West improved (evacuation of Vienna, Geneva summit conference, both 1955). Repression of scientific and cultural life eased, and many prisoners were freed culminating in **de-Stalinization** (1956). Nikita **Khrushchev**'s leadership aimed at consumer sector growth, but farm production lagged, despite the virgin lands program (from 1954). Soviet crushing of the 1956 Hungarian revolution, the 1960 U-2 spy plane episode, and other incidents renewed E-W tension and domestic curbs.

Eastern Europe. Resentment of Russian domination and Stalinist repression combined with nationalist, economic, and religious factors to produce periodic violence. E Berlin workers rioted (1953), Polish workers rioted in Poznan (June 1956), and a broad-based **revolution** broke out in **Hungary** (Oct. 1956). All were suppressed by Soviet force or threats (at least 7,000 dead in Hungary), but Poland was allowed to restore private ownership of farms, and a degree of personal and economic freedom returned to Hungary. Yugoslavia experimented with worker self-management and a market economy.

Korea. The 1945 division of Korea along the 38th parallel left industry in the N, which was organized into a militant regime and armed by the USSR. The S was politically disunited. More than 60,000 N Korean troops invaded the S on June 25, 1950. The U.S., backed by the UN Security Council, sent troops. **UN troops** reached the Chinese border in Nov. Some 200,000 Chinese troops crossed the Yalu R. and drove back UN forces. By spring 1951, battle lines had become stabilized near the original 38th parallel border, but heavy fighting continued. Finally, an armistice was signed on July 27, 1953. U.S. troops remained in the S, and U.S. economic and military aid continued. The war stimulated rapid economic recovery in Japan.

China. Starting in 1952, industry, agriculture, and social institutions were forcibly collectivized. In a massive purge, as many as several million people were executed as Kuomintang supporters or as class and political enemies. The **Great Leap Forward** (1958-60) unsuccessfully tried to force the pace of development by substituting labor for investment.

Southeast Asia. Ho Chi Minh's forces, aided by the USSR and the new Chinese Communist government, fought French and pro-French Vietnamese forces to a standstill and captured the strategic **Dien Bien Phu** camp in May 1954. The Geneva Agreements divided Vietnam in half pending elections (never held) and recognized Laos and Cambodia as independent. The U.S. aided the anti-Communist Republic of Vietnam in the S.

Middle East. Arab revolutions placed leftist, militantly nationalist regimes in power in Egypt (1952) and Iraq (1958). But Arab unity attempts failed (United Arab Republic joined Egypt, Syria, Yemen, 1958-61). Arab refusal to recognize Israel (Arab League economic blockade began Sept. 1951) led to a permanent **state of war**, with repeated incidents (Gaza, 1955). Israel occupied Sinai, and Britain and France took (Oct. 1956) the Suez Canal, but were replaced by the UN Emergency Force. The Mossadegh government in Iran nationalized (May 1951) the British-owned oil industry in May, but was overthrown (Aug. 1953) in a U.S.-aided coup.

Latin America. Argentinian dictator Juan **Perón**, in office 1946, crushed opposition and enforced land reform, some nationalization, welfare state measures, and curbs on the Roman Catholic Church. A Sept. 1955 coup deposed Perón. The 1952 revolution in Bolivia brought land reform, nationalization of tin mines, and improvement in the status of Native Americans, who nevertheless remained poor. The Batista regime in Cuba was overthrown (Jan. 1959) by Fidel **Castro**, who imposed a Communist dictatorship, aligned Cuba with the USSR, and improved education and health care. A U.S.-backed anti-Castro invasion (**Bay of Pigs**, Apr. 1961) was crushed. Self-government advanced in the British Caribbean.

Technology. Large outlays on research and development in the U.S. and the USSR focused on military applications (H-bomb in U.S., 1952; USSR, 1953; Britain, 1957; intercontinental missiles, late 1950s). Soviet launching of the **Sputnik** satellite (Oct. 4, 1957) spurred increases in U.S. science education funds (National Defense Education Act).

Literature and film. Alienation from social and literary conventions reached an extreme in the theater of the absurd (Beckett's *Waiting for Godot*, 1952), the "new novel" (Robbe-Grillet's *Voyeur*, 1955), and avant-garde film (Antonioni's *L'Avventura*, 1960). U.S. beatniks (Kerouac's *On the Road*, 1957) and others rejected the supposed conformism of Americans (Riesman's *The Lonely Crowd*, 1950).

Rising Expectations and New Protests: 1960-69

Global economy. The longest sustained economic boom on record spanned almost the entire decade in the capitalist world; the closely watched GNP figure doubled (1960-70) in the U.S., fueled by **Vietnam War**-related budget deficits. The **General Agreement on Tariffs and Trade** (1967) stimulated Western European prosperity, which spread to peripheral areas (Spain, Italy, E Germany). Japan became a top economic power. Foreign investment aided the industrialization of Brazil. There were limited Soviet economic reform attempts. Outside the Soviet zone the global economy was marked by the growing role of multinational corporations (3,000 in 1914; 6,000 by 1970). International nongovernmental organizations (NGOs) also multiplied rapidly (Amnesty International, 1961).

Reform and radicalization. Pres. John F. **Kennedy**, inaugurated 1961, emphasized youthful idealism and vigor; his assassination Nov. 22, 1963, was a national trauma. Political and social reform movements took root in U.S. and other countries. Blacks demonstrated nonviolently and with partial success against segregation and poverty (1963 March on Washington; 1964 **Civil Rights Act**), but some urban areas erupted in riots (Watts, 1965; Detroit, 1967; more than 100 cities following **Martin Luther King Jr.** assassination, Apr. 4, 1968). New concern for the poor (Harrington's *Other America*, 1963) helped lead to Pres. Lyndon Johnson's **"Great Society"** programs (Medicare, Water Quality Act, Higher Education Act, all 1965). Concern for the **environment** surged (Carson's *Silent Spring*, 1962).

Feminism revived as a cultural and political movement (Friedan's *Feminine Mystique*, 1963; National Organization for Women founded, 1966), and a movement for homosexual rights emerged (Stonewall riot in NYC, 1969). Pope John XXIII called the **Second Vatican Council** (1962-65), which liberalized Roman Catholic liturgy and some other aspects of Catholicism.

Opposition to U.S. involvement in Vietnam, especially among university students (**Moratorium** protest, Nov. 1969), turned violent (Weatherman Chicago riots, Oct. 1969). **New Left** and Marxist theories became popular, and membership in radical groups (Students for a Democratic Society, Black Panthers) increased. Maoist groups, especially in Europe, called for total transformation of society. In France, students sparked a nationwide strike affecting 10 million workers in May-June 1968.

China. China's revolutionary militancy under **Mao Zedong** led to border disputes and other conflict with the USSR under "revisionist" Khrushchev, starting in 1960. The **"Great Proletarian Cultural Revolution"** tried to impose a utopian egalitarian program in China and spread revolution abroad; political struggle, often violent, convulsed China in 1965-68.

Southeast Asia. Communist-led guerrillas aided by N Vietnam fought from 1960 against the S Vietnam government of Ngo Dinh Diem (killed 1963). The U.S. military role increased after the 1964 **Tonkin Gulf** incident. Laotian and Cambodian neutrality were threatened by Communist insurgencies, with N Vietnamese aid, and U.S. intrigues.

Developing world. A bloc of authoritarian leftist regimes among the newly independent nations came to dominate the conference of nonaligned nations (Belgrade, 1961; Cairo, 1964; Lusaka, 1970). Soviet political ties and military bases were established in Cuba, Egypt, Algeria, Guinea, and other countries. Some leaders were ousted in coups by pro-Western groups—Dem. Rep. of the Congo's Patrice Lumumba (killed 1961), Ghana's Kwame Nkrumah (exiled 1966), and Indonesia's Sukarno (effectively ousted in 1965 after a Communist coup failed).

The brief 1967 Arab-Israeli War, also known as the Six Day War, had far-reaching geopolitical ramifications.

Middle East. Arab-Israeli tension erupted into a brief war June 1967. Israel emerged from the war as a major regional power. Military shipments before and after the war increased Soviet influence in much of the Arab world. Most Arab states broke U.S. diplomatic ties, while Communist countries cut their ties to Israel. Intra-Arab disputes continued: Egypt and Saudi Arabia supported rival factions in a bloody Yemen civil war 1962-70; Lebanese troops fought Palestinian commandos 1969.

Eastern Europe. To stop the large-scale exodus of citizens, E German authorities built (Aug. 1961) a fortified **wall across Berlin** that enclosed West Berlin. Soviet sway in the Balkans was weakened by Albania's support of China (USSR broke ties in Dec. 1961) and Romania's assertion (1964) of limited autonomy. Liberalization (spring 1968) in Czechoslovakia was crushed with massive force by troops of five Warsaw Pact countries. W German treaties (1970) with the USSR and Poland facilitated transfer of German technology and confirmed postwar boundaries.

Arts and styles. The boundary between fine and popular arts was blurred to some extent by Pop Art (Warhol) and rock musicals (*Hair*, 1968). Informality and exaggeration prevailed in fashion (beards, miniskirts). A nonpolitical "counterculture" developed, rejecting traditional bourgeois life goals and personal habits, and use of marijuana and hallucinogens spread (**Woodstock** festival, Aug. 1969). **The Beatles** brought unprecedented sophistication to rock music.

Science. Achievements in space (**humans on the moon**, July 1969) and electronics (lasers, integrated circuits) encouraged a faith in scientific solutions to problems in agriculture ("green revolution"), medicine (heart transplants, 1967), and other areas. Harmful technology, it was believed, could be controlled (1963 Limited Test Ban Treaty, 1968 Nuclear Nonproliferation Treaty).

New Global Balances and Religious Revivals: 1970-79

U.S.: Caution and neoconservatism. A sluggish economy, energy shortages, and environmental problems contributed to a **"limits of growth"** philosophy. Suspicion of science and technology killed or delayed some projects (supersonic transport dropped, 1971). The Three Mile Island nuclear reactor accident (Mar. 1979) reinforced fears of nuclear energy.

There was some backlash against social change. School busing and racial quotas were opposed (Bakke decision, June 1978); Equal Rights Amendment for women languished; legislation aimed at protecting homosexuals was opposed.

Completion of Communist forces' takeover of **South Vietnam** (evacuation of U.S. civilians, Apr. 1975), revelations of Central Intelligence Agency misdeeds (Rockefeller Commission report, June 1975), and Watergate scandals (Nixon resigned in Aug. 1974) reduced faith in U.S. moral and material capacity to influence world affairs. Revelations of Soviet crimes (Solzhenitsyn's *Gulag Archipelago*, 1974) and Soviet intervention in Africa helped foster a revival of anti-Communist sentiment.

Economy sluggish. The 1960s boom faltered in the 1970s; a severe recession in the U.S. and Europe (1974-75) followed a huge oil price hike (Dec. 1973). Monetary instability (U.S. cut ties to gold in Aug. 1971), the decline of the dollar, and protectionist moves by industrial countries (1977-78) threatened trade. Business investment declined. Severe inflation plagued many countries (25% in Britain, 1975; 18% in U.S., 1979).

China readjusts. After the 1976 deaths of Mao Zedong and Zhou Enlai, pragmatists won the struggle for leadership. A nationwide purge of orthodox Maoists ensued, and the **Gang of Four**, led by Mao's widow, Chiang Ching, was arrested. The new leaders freed more than 100,000 political prisoners and reduced public adulation of Mao. Political and trade ties expanded Japan, Europe, and the U.S. in the late 1970s, as relations worsened with the USSR, Cuba, and Vietnam (four-week invasion by China, 1979). Ideological guidelines were reversed (bonuses to workers, Dec. 1977; exams for college entrance, Oct. 1977). Some restrictions on cultural expression were eased.

Europe. European unity moves (EEC-EFTA trade accord, 1972) faltered as economic problems appeared (Britain floated pound, 1972; France floated franc, 1974). Germany and Switzerland curbed guest workers from S Europe. Greece and Turkey quarreled over Cyprus and Aegean oil rights.

All non-Communist Europe was under democratic rule after free elections (June 1976) in **Spain** seven months after the death of Franco. The conservative, colonialist regime in **Portugal** was overthrown in Apr. 1974. In **Greece** the seven-year military dictatorship yielded power in 1974. The **British** Labour government imposed (1975) wage curbs and suspended nationalization schemes. Terrorism in **Germany** (1972 Munich Olympics killings) led to laws curbing some civil liberties. **French** "new philosophers" rejected leftist ideologies, and the Socialist-Communist coalition lost a 1978 election bid.

Religion and politics. The improvement in **Muslim** countries' political fortunes by the 1950s (with the exception of Central Asia under Soviet and Chinese rule) and the growth of Arab oil wealth were followed by a resurgence of traditional religious fervor. Libyan dictator Muammar al-**Qaddafi** mixed Islamic laws with socialism. The illegal Muslim Brotherhood in **Egypt** was accused of violence, while extreme groups bombed (1977) theaters to protest Western and secular values.

In **Turkey**, the National Salvation Party was the first Islamic group to share (1974) power since secularization in the 1920s. In **Iran**, Ayatollah Ruhollah **Khomeini** led a revolution that deposed the secular shah (Jan. 1979) and created an Islamic republic. Religiously motivated Muslims took part in an insurrection in **Saudi Arabia** that briefly seized (1979) the Grand Mosque in Mecca. Muslim puritan opposition to **Pakistan** Pres. Zulfikar Ali-Bhutto helped lead to his overthrow in July 1977. Muslim solidarity, however, could not prevent Pakistan's eastern province (**Bangladesh**) from declaring (Dec. 1971) independence after a bloody civil war.

Muslim and Hindu resentment of coerced sterilization in **India** helped defeat the Indira Gandhi government, and a coalition including religious Hindu parties replaced it (Mar. 1977). Muslims in the S **Philippines**, aided by Libya, rebelled against central rule from 1973. The Buddhist Soka Gakkai movement launched (1964) the Komeito party in **Japan**, which became a major opposition party in 1972 and 1976 elections.

Evangelical Protestant groups grew in the U.S. A revival of interest in Orthodox Christianity occurred among **Russian** intellectuals (Solzhenitsyn). The secularist **Israeli** Labor party, after decades of rule, was ousted in 1977 by conservatives led by Menachem Begin; religious militants founded settlements on the disputed West Bank, part of biblically promised Israel. Reform Judaism in U.S. revived many traditional practices.

Religious wars raged in **Northern Ireland** (Catholic vs. Protestant, 1969-97) and **Lebanon** (Christian vs. Muslim, 1975-90),

The Vietnam War, in which an estimated 2 million Vietnamese and 58,000 Americans died, also engulfed Laos and Cambodia in deadly violence.

while religious militancy complicated the Israel-Arab dispute (1973 Israel-Arab war). The Camp David Accords in 1978, negotiated by Egyptian Pres. Anwar al-Sadat, Israeli Prime Min. Menachem Begin, and U.S. Pres. Jimmy Carter, facilitated the landmark 1979 **Egypt-Israel peace treaty**, but increased militancy on the West Bank impeded further progress.

Latin America. Repressive conservative regimes strengthened their hold, with a violent coup against the elected (Sept. 1973) **Allende** government in **Chile**, military coup in **Argentina** (1976), and coups against reformist regimes in **Bolivia** (1971, 1979) and **Peru** (1976). In Central America, increasing liberal and leftist militancy led to the ouster (1979) of the **Somoza** regime of **Nicaragua** and to civil conflict in **El Salvador**.

Southeast Asia. Communist victories in Vietnam, Cambodia, and Laos by May 1975 led to new turmoil. **Pol Pot's** Khmer Rouge regime in **Cambodia** ordered millions to resettle in rural areas, in a program of forced labor and terrorism that cost more than 1 million lives (1975-79) and caused hundreds of thousands to flee. The Vietnamese invasion of Cambodia (1979) swelled the refugee population and contributed to widespread starvation.

Russian expansion. Soviet influence, checked in some countries (troops ousted by Egypt, 1972), was projected farther afield, often with the use of Cuban troops (Angola, 1975-89; Ethiopia, 1977-88). **Détente** with the West—1972 Berlin pact, 1972 strategic arms pact (**SALT**)—gave way to a more antagonistic relationship in the late 1970s, exacerbated by the Soviet invasion (1979) of **Afghanistan**.

Africa. The last remaining European colonies were granted independence (**Spanish Sahara**, 1976; **Djibouti**, 1977), and, after 10 years of civil war, a black government took over (1979) in **Zimbabwe** (Rhodesia); white domination remained in **South Africa**. European involvement in local wars (Russia in **Angola**, **Ethiopia**; France in **Chad**, **Zaire**, **Mauritania**) and the use of tens of thousands of Cuban troops were denounced by some African leaders. Ethnic or tribal clashes made Africa a locus of sustained warfare during the late 1970s.

End of the Cold War and Demand for Democracy: 1980-89

Global developments. International contacts accelerated thanks to new openness in China (1978) and USSR (1985); global consumerism was symbolized by the rapid spread of McDonald's restaurants (Japan, 1971; Russia, 1990).

USSR, Eastern Europe. The late 1980s saw the remaking of the Soviet state and the beginning of the disintegration of the Soviet empire. After the deaths of Gen. Sec. Leonid **Brezhnev** (1982) and two successors, the harsh treatment of dissent and restriction of emigration, and the Soviet invasion (Dec. 1979) of Afghanistan, Gen. Sec. Mikhail **Gorbachev** (in office 1985-91) promoted *glasnost* and *perestroika*—economic, political, and social reform. Supported by the Communist Party, he signed (Dec. 1987) the INF nuclear disarmament treaty. Military withdrawal from Afghanistan was completed in Feb. 1989, and the Soviet people chose (Mar. 1989) part of the new Congress of People's Deputies from competing candidates. By decade's end the **Cold War** appeared to be fading away.

In **Poland**, Solidarity, the labor union founded (1980) by Lech Walesa, was outlawed in 1982 but legalized in 1988, after years of unrest. Poland's first free election since the Communist takeover brought **Solidarity** victory (June 1989); Tadeusz Mazowiecki, a Walesa adviser, became prime minister in a government with the Communists. In fall 1989 the failure of Marxist economies in **Hungary**, **East Germany**, **Czechoslovakia**, **Bulgaria**, and **Romania** brought the collapse of the Communist monopoly and a demand for democracy. In a historic step, the **Berlin Wall** was opened in Nov. 1989.

U.S. The **"Reagan Years"** (1981-88) featured new economic policies via budget and tax cuts, deregulation, "junk bond" financing, leveraged buyouts, and mergers. However, there was a stock market crash (Oct. 1987), and federal budget deficits and the trade deficit increased. Foreign policy showed a **strong anti-Communist stance**, via increased defense spending, aid to anti-Communists in Central America, invasion of Cuba-threatened Grenada, and championing of the "Star Wars" missile defense program. Four Reagan-Gorbachev summits (1985-88) climaxed in the INF treaty (1987). The **Iran-Contra affair** (Oliver North testimony, July 1987) was a major political scandal.

Middle East. The Middle East remained militarily unstable, with sharp divisions along economic, political, racial, and religious lines. In **Iran**, the Islamic revolution of 1979 created a strong anti-U.S. stance (hostage crisis, Nov. 1979-Jan. 1981). In Sept. 1980, **Iraq** repudiated its border agreement with Iran and began major hostilities that led to an eight-year war in which hundreds of thousands were killed.

Libya's support for international terrorism induced the U.S. to close (May 1981) its diplomatic mission there and embargo (Mar. 1982) Libyan oil. Following an attack on a West Berlin disco frequented by U.S. military, U.S. bombed targets in Libya (Apr. 1986).

Israel affirmed (July 1980) all Jerusalem as its capital, destroyed (June 1981) an Iraqi atomic reactor, and invaded **Lebanon**, citing terrorism by the Palestine Liberation Organization; PLO withdrew from Lebanon after cease-fire. A **Palestinian uprising** began (Dec. 1987) in Israeli-occupied Gaza and spread to the West Bank; troops responded with force, killing 300 by the end of 1988, with 6,000 more in detention camps. Israeli withdrawal from Lebanon began in Feb. 1985 and ended in June 1985, as Lebanon continued to be torn by military and political conflict. Artillery duels (Mar.-Apr. 1989) between Christian East Beirut and Muslim West Beirut left 200 dead.

Latin America. In **Nicaragua**, the leftist Sandinista National Liberation Front, in power after the 1979 civil war, faced problems as a result of Nicaragua's military aid to leftist guerrillas in El Salvador and U.S. backing of antigovernment contras. The CIA admitted (1984) having directed the mining of Nicaraguan ports, and the U.S. sent humanitarian (1985) and military (1986) aid. Profits from U.S. **secret arms sales** to Iran were found (1987) diverted to contras. Cease-fire talks between the Sandinista government and contras came in 1988, and elections were held in Nicaragua in Feb. 1990.

In **El Salvador**, a military coup (Oct. 1979) failed to halt extremist terrorism. Archbishop Oscar Romero, advocate for poor, was assassinated in Mar. 1980; from Jan. to June some 4,000 civilians were killed in the civil unrest. In 1984, newly elected Pres. José Napoleon Duarte worked to stem human rights abuses, but violence continued. In **Chile**, Gen. Augusto Pinochet yielded the presidency after a democratic election (Dec. 1989) but remained as head of the army. He had ruled the country since 1973, imposing harsh measures against leftists and dissidents.

Africa. The 1980s saw continuing economic decline in virtually all African countries, a result of accelerating desertification, the world economic recession, heavy indebtedness to overseas creditors, rapid population growth, and political instability. Some 60 million Africans faced prolonged hunger in 1981. Much of Africa had one of the worst **droughts** ever in 1983, and by year's end, one-third of the population, or about 150 million, were near **famine**. Live Aid, a marathon rock concert, was presented in July 1985, and the U.S. and Western nations sent aid in Sept. 1985. Wars in Ethiopia and Sudan and military strife in several other nations continued. **HIV/AIDS** took a heavy toll.

The Chinese government responded to pro-democracy demonstrations in Tiananmen Square with force (1989).

Anti-apartheid sentiment gathered force in **South Africa**, with demonstrations meeting violent police response. White voters approved (Nov. 1983) the first constitution to give "Coloureds" (people of mixed-race background) and Asians a voice, while still excluding the black majority. The U.S. imposed economic sanctions in Aug. 1985, and 11 Western nations followed in Sept. Pres. P. W. **Botha** was succeeded (Sept. 1989) by F. W. **de Klerk**, who promised negotiation with the black population.

Asia and the Pacific. Benazir **Bhutto** became the first woman to lead a majority-Muslim nation as prime minister of **Pakistan** (Dec. 1988). The "people power" revolt in the **Philippines** ousted Ferdinand **Marcos** (Feb. 1986) after two decades as president; he was replaced by Corazon **Aquino**.

During the 1980s **China**'s Communist government and paramount leader **Deng** Xiaoping expanded commercial and technical ties to the West and the role of market forces. In Apr. 1989 student demonstrators camped out in **Tiananmen Square**, Beijing, in a peaceful call for political reform. Some 100,000 students and workers marched; at least 20 other cities saw protests. In response, martial law was imposed. Army troops crushed the demonstration in and around Tiananmen Square on June 3-4, with death toll estimates of 500-7,000, up to 10,000 dissidents arrested, and 31 people tried and executed. The conciliatory Communist Party chief was ousted;

the Politburo adopted (July 1989) reforms against official corruption.

Japan's relations with other nations, especially the U.S., were dominated by **trade imbalances** favoring Japan. Western Europe and the U.S. accused Japan of restrictive trade policies.

Europe. With the addition of Greece, Portugal, and Spain, the European Community became a common market of more than 300 million people. Margaret **Thatcher** became the first British prime minister in the 20th cent. to win a third consecutive term (1987). **France** elected (1981) its first socialist president, François **Mitterrand**, who was reelected in 1988. Elections in 1983 brought **Italy** its first socialist premier, Bettino **Craxi**.

International terrorism. With the 1979 **overthrow of the shah** of Iran and with instablity in the Middle East, terrorism became a prominent tactic. In 1979-81, Iranian militants held 52 **U.S. hostages in Iran** for 444 days. In 1983 a truck bomb exploded at U.S. Marine headquarters in Beirut, Lebanon, killing 241 Americans; almost simultaneously a few miles away, a truck bomb blew up a French paratrooper barracks, killing 58. The *Achille Lauro* cruise ship was hijacked in Oct. 1985, and an American passenger killed. Incidents rose to 700 in 1985 and to 1,000 in 1988. **Assassinated leaders** included Egypt's Pres. Anwar al-**Sadat** (1981), India's Prime Min. Indira **Gandhi** (1984), and Lebanese Prem. Rashid **Karami** (1987).

New Regional Tensions in a Post-Cold War World: 1990-99

Soviet Empire breakup. The breakup of the Soviet Union into 15 independent states began with declarations of independence by the Baltic republics of **Lithuania**, **Latvia**, and **Estonia** during an abortive coup against Mikhail **Gorbachev** (Aug. 1991). Other republics followed. In Dec. 1991, **Russia**, **Ukraine**, and **Belarus** declared the Soviet Union dead; Gorbachev resigned. The Warsaw Pact and the Council for Mutual Economic Assistance (Comecon) were disbanded. Most of the former Soviet republics joined in a loose confederation (**Commonwealth of Independent States**). People suffered severe economic hardship as Russia, under Pres. Boris **Yeltsin**, moved to reboot the economy under a free market system.

The Muslim republic of **Chechnya** declared independence from Russia, leading to an invasion by Russian troops (Dec. 1994). A cease-fire took hold in 1996, and Russians withdrew. In 1999 Russia forcibly suppressed Muslim insurgents in Dagestan and entered Chechnya, again fighting separatist rebels. Yeltsin resigned Dec. 31, 1999, to be replaced by Vladimir **Putin** (elected in his own right, Mar. 2000).

Europe. Yugoslavia broke apart, and hostilities ensued along ethnic and religious lines. **Croatia**, **Slovenia**, and **Macedonia** declared independence (1991), followed by **Bosnia-Herzegovina** (1992). **Serbia** and **Montenegro** remained as the republic of Yugoslavia. Bitter fighting followed, especially in Bosnia, where Serbs engaged in **ethnic cleansing** of the Muslim population; a peace plan (**Dayton accord**, 1995) was brokered by the U.S., with **NATO** responsible for policing its implementation. In spring 1999, NATO conducted a bombing campaign aimed at stopping Yugoslavia from driving out ethnic Albanians from the **Kosovo** region; under a June peace accord, NATO peacekeeping troops entered Kosovo.

The **two Germanys were reunited** after 45 years (Oct. 1990), to great jubilation, though economic stresses followed. Czechoslovakia broke apart peacefully (Jan. 1993) into the **Czech Republic** and **Slovakia**. Labor leader Lech **Walesa** was elected president of **Poland** (Dec. 1991). In Jan. 1994, NATO approved the **Partnership for Peace**, coordinating the defense of E and Central European countries, which Russia later joined. NATO signed a cooperation pact with **Russia** (May 1997) which allowed for NATO expansion into former Soviet-bloc countries. The Czech Republic, **Hungary**, and Poland became NATO members in Jan. 1999. Efforts toward European unity continued with adoption of a single market (Jan. 1993) and conversion of the European Community to the **European Union** as the **Maastricht Treaty** took effect (Nov. 1993). Agreement was reached for 11 EU members to adopt a common currency (**euro**) in Jan. 1999.

An intraparty revolt forced Margaret **Thatcher** out as prime minister of the **UK**, to be succeeded by John **Major**

(Nov. 1990); seven years later, Labour took power under Tony **Blair** (May 1997). The divorce of Prince **Charles and Diana**, followed by the death of Diana (Aug. 1997), made headlines. Talks on peace in **Northern Ireland** that included Sinn Fein, political arm of the **Irish Republican Army**, led to peace plan, approved in an all-Ireland vote (May 1998). In Dec. 1999, Northern Ireland was granted home rule. In **Scotland** voters overwhelmingly approved establishment of a regional legislature (1997), and in **Wales** voters narrowly approved establishment of a local assembly (1997).

Middle East. In Aug. 1990, **Iraq**'s Saddam Hussein ordered troops to invade **Kuwait**. A UN-approved international force, led by U.S., bombed Iraq (Jan. 1991) and launched a land attack, crushing the invasion; cease-fire agreed to, Apr. 1991. The UN extended **sanctions** on Iraq for failure to abide by cease-fire terms. Iraq's reported failure to cooperate with UN inspectors seeking to eliminate **weapons of mass destruction** led to airstrikes by the U.S. and Britain (1998).

Israel and the **PLO** signed a peace accord (Sept. 1993) providing for Palestinian self-government in the West Bank and Gaza Strip; Prime Min. Yitzhak **Rabin** and Foreign Min. Shimon **Peres** of Israel and Yasir **Arafat** of the PLO received the 1994 Nobel Peace Prize for their efforts. Six Arab nations relaxed boycott against Israel (1994), and Israel and **Jordan** signed a peace treaty (Oct. 1994). Rabin was assassinated (Nov. 1995) by an Israeli opponent of the peace process. Benjamin **Netanyahu** became prime minister (May 1996). Arafat was elected to the presidency of the Palestinian Authority (Jan. 1996).

South Africa abandoned apartheid and transitioned to a nonracial democratic government, with Nelson Mandela (pictured, with U.S. Pres. Bill Clinton) elected president in 1994.

Asia and the Pacific. Hong Kong was returned to **China** (July 1997) after 156 years as a British colony, and **Macao** reverted to China (Dec. 1999) after over 400 years of Portuguese rule. **Jiang** Zemin, general secretary of the Chinese Communist Party, assumed the additional post of president of China (Mar. 1993). China subsequently released from prison—and exiled— several well-known dissidents but continued to jail large numbers. In Nov. 1999 the U.S. and China signed a landmark pact normalizing trade relations.

After years of prosperity, **Thailand, Indonesia,** and **South Korea** in 1997 began to suffer economic reverses that had a worldwide ripple effect. All three received IMF bailout packages. In Indonesia, protests over mismanagement led to the resignation of Pres. **Suharto** (May 1998) after 32 years of rule. In a referendum (Aug. 1999), **East Timor** voted overwhelmingly for independence; pro-Indonesian militias rampaged, but a multinational **peacekeeping force** helped restore order (Sept. 1999). In South Korea, former dissident **Kim** Dae-jung was elected president (Dec. 1997).

In Japan members of a religious cult released the nerve gas sarin on **Tokyo subway,** killing 12 and injuring more than 5,500 (Mar. 1995). **Tamil** rebels continued their armed conflict in **Sri Lanka.** In **Afghanistan** the **Taliban,** an extreme Islamic fundamentalist group, gained control of Kabul (Sept. 1996) and, eventually, most of the country. In **North Korea,** longtime dictator **Kim Il Sung** died (July 1994), to be succeeded by son **Kim Jong Il.** In Oct. 1994 the country signed an agreement with the U.S. setting a timetable for North Korea to eliminate its **nuclear weapons program.** The country also suffered from severe drought and famine.

Indian forces repeatedly clashed with pro-independence demonstrators in the disputed Muslim region of **Kashmir,** exacerbating relations with **Pakistan.** India and Pakistan both conducted nuclear tests in 1998. Conflict between government and the military led to a bloodless coup in Pakistan (Oct. 1999).

Africa. South Africa's Pres. F. W. **de Klerk** released dissident black leader Nelson **Mandela** from prison (Feb. 1990) after 27 years. The white minority government **repealed apartheid** laws (1990, 1991). Mandela was elected president (Apr. 1994), and a new constitution became law (Dec. 1996). **Namibia** officially became independent in Mar. 1990, after almost 20 years under UN trusteeship. A 16-year civil war appeared to end in **Angola** (May 1991) when the government signed a peace accord with the rebel UNITA faction. In **Nigeria,** former Gen. Olusegun **Obasanjo** was elected (Feb. 1999) the country's first civilian leader in 15 years

Civil war broke out in **Liberia** (Dec. 1989) and lasted, with interruptions, through the 1990s and beyond, leaving hundreds of thousands dead. Factional fighting erupted in **Somalia** (Jan. 1991); a U.S.-led UN **peacekeeping force** failed to restore order and left (Mar. 1995) with no durable government in place. In **Algeria,** the army canceled parliamentary elections (Jan. 1992) after the Islamic party won a first round. Ensuing civil war left more than 150,000 dead; a peace and amnesty plan was approved in a Sept. 1999 referendum. Assassination of **Burundi**'s president (June 1993) renewed ethnic violence between Hutus and Tutsis there. A suspicious plane crash that killed the presidents of Burundi and Rwanda (Apr. 1994) led to new outbreak of carnage in **Rwanda,** where some 800,000 died, mostly Tutsis massacred by Hutu militias. The decades-long rule of **Mobutu** Sese Seko in **Zaire** came to an end (May 1997) at the hands of rebel forces led by Laurent **Kabila.** Kabila changed the country's name back to **Democratic Republic of the Congo**; conditions remained unstable

The World Health Organization reported (1995) that Africa accounted for 70% of **AIDS** cases worldwide.

North America. U.S. Pres. Bill **Clinton** (D) (elected 1992, 1996) proposed (Feb. 1998) first balanced federal budget in decades, promoted free trade and so-called welfare reform, and intervened in Bosnia. Impeached (Dec. 1998) by U.S. House on charges stemming from affair with intern, he was acquitted by the Senate. In **Canada,** Liberal Jean **Chrétien** became prime minister (Nov. 1993; reelected 1997). The new Canadian territory of **Nunavut,** a large area formerly part of Northwest Territories, was created (Apr. 1999). In **Mexico,** Ernesto **Zedillo** of the ruling PRI party was elected president (July 1994) after the party's first candidate was assassinated. The country soon faced a monetary crisis but recovered with the help of a 1995 U.S. bailout package.

The **North American Free Trade Agreement** (NAFTA), liberalizing trade between the U.S., Canada, and Mexico, went into effect Jan. 1, 1994. Trade deals and other globalization trends drew protests from free-trade opponents and anti-capitalists (**World Trade Org.** meeting, Nov.-Dec. 1999).

Central America and the Caribbean. In **Haiti,** Jean-Bertrand **Aristide** was elected president (Dec. 1990) but was ousted in a military coup after nine months; restored to office (Oct. 1994) through negotiations led by former U.S. Pres. Jimmy Carter. In **Nicaragua,** Violeta **Chamorro** defeated Sandinista Pres. Daniel **Ortega** in Feb. 1990 election. In **Panama,** U.S. troops overthrew Manuel **Noriega** (Dec. 1989). Noriega was captured Jan. 1990; he was convicted and jailed on drug-related charges in U.S. and later in France. On Dec. 31, 1999, Panama assumed full control of the **Panama Canal,** in accord with 1977 treaty with the U.S.

South America. Alberto **Fujimori,** elected president of **Peru** in June 1990, suppressed the constitution to pursue his economic agenda (1992); popular for reducing terrorism but condemned for human rights abuses, he was reelected in 1995. Leftist guerrillas took hostages at an ambassador's residence in Lima (Dec. 1996); one hostage killed during rescue operation (Apr. 1997). Peronist Pres. Carlos Saúl **Menem** served as **Argentina**'s president for much of the decade, imposing economic austerity.

Former Chilean Pres. Augusto **Pinochet** continued to head the army until Mar. 1998; he was arrested in London (Oct. 1998) and charged with human-rights violations but judged unfit for trial. In **Brazil,** Fernando Henrique **Cardoso** was elected president (Oct. 1994) and reelected in 1998 despite economic slump; the IMF announced a $42-bil aid package for the country (Nov. 1998). In **Venezuela** two coups were thwarted (1992); leftist coup leader Hugo **Chávez** was elected president in Dec. 1998.

Terrorism. The U.S. was a target of terrorism linked to radical Islam. A bomb exploded in garage beneath New York City's **World Trade Center,** killing six people (Feb. 1993). Bombs set off outside **U.S. embassies** in Kenya and Tanzania killed over 220 (Aug. 1998); U.S. retaliated with airstrikes at alleged terrorist-linked sites in Afghanistan and Sudan. In the U.S.'s deadliest instance of domestic terrorism, 168 people were killed in bombing of a federal building in **Oklahoma City,** OK (Apr. 1995), by anti-government extremists.

Science, technology, and environment. The powerful **Hubble Space Telescope** was launched in Apr. 1990. U.S. space shuttle *Atlantis* docked with the orbiting Russian space station *Mir* (June 1995) in first of several joint missions. In Nov. 1998 the first component for a new **International Space Station** was launched into space from **Kazakhstan.** Scottish scientists announced (Feb. 1997) the **cloning** of a sheep—the first mammal successfully cloned from a cell from an adult animal.

Tim **Berners-Lee** launched first **World Wide Web** server (1990). User-friendly graphical browsers (Mosaic, 1993; Netscape, 1994) and consumer-friendly Internet service providers followed, beginning a transformation of global communications and information access. Efforts to deal with **global climate change** intensified with tentative agreements adopted in Kyoto, Japan (Dec. 1997).

Globalization and Global Realignments: 2000-09

Terrorism. The decade saw a surge in terrorism associated with **radical Islam.** In Oct. 2000, 17 were killed aboard the **USS Cole** in Aden, **Yemen,** in a suicide bombing tied to **al-Qaeda,** a terrorist network based in Afghanistan. Terrorism reached a new level **Sept. 11, 2001,** when hijackers crashed two jetliners into the twin towers of the **World Trade Center** in New York City and another into the **Pentagon** outside Washington, DC, with a fourth crashing in a Pennsylvania field. The attacks, linked to al-Qaeda and its leader **Osama bin Laden,** destroyed both towers and killed nearly 3,000.

Among other incidents tied to Islamic radicals, a car bomb on the Indonesian island of **Bali** (Oct. 2002) killed over 200. **Commuter trains** were bombed in **Madrid**, Spain, killing about 200 (Mar. 2004). Subway trains and a bus were bombed in **London** (July 2005); 56 died. Explosions killed more than 180 on commuter trains in **Mumbai**, India (July 2006); also in Mumbai (Nov. 2008), terrorists launched coordinated attacks on sites frequented by foreigners, killing more than 160. **Chechen** separatist guerrillas were implicated in an attack on a **Moscow** movie theater (Oct. 2002; over 100 hostages died), bombings in Moscow's subways (Feb. 2004), suicide bombings on two planes (Aug. 2004; 90 died), and takeover of a school in Beslan (Sept. 2004; over 330 killed).

Global economic crisis. Rapid economic growth in **China** and other developing countries contrasted with sluggish rates in traditional economic powers. A global **recession**, beginning in late 2007, led to a **financial meltdown** (Sept. 2008). **Iceland**'s banking system collapsed (Oct. 2008), rescued by loans and austerity. **Dubai**'s state-controlled investment company was bailed out (Dec. 2009) by neighboring emirate Abu Dhabi. Soaring food and fuel prices led to unrest, including an attempted general strike in **Egypt** and riots in **Haiti** (Apr. 2008). **Austerity** measures spurred protests in several European countries.

War in Iraq and Afghanistan. The U.S., with the UK, invaded **Iraq** (Mar. 2003) to oust the regime of Saddam **Hussein**. Troops took control of Baghdad and other cities, and U.S. Pres. George W. **Bush** declared major combat ended by May, but insurgents caused continuing casualties. No **weapons of mass destruction**, cited as major grounds for the invasion, were found. Hussein was captured by U.S. troops (Dec. 2003) and convicted and executed by Iraqi authorities for crimes against humanity (Dec. 2006). Iraqis voted in elections for a transitional assembly (Jan. 2005), democratic constitution (Oct. 2005), and parliament (Dec. 2005); negotiations produced a Shiite coalition government under Prime Min. Nouri al-**Maliki** (May 2006). With **insurgent violence** intensifying, Bush announced (Jan. 2007) a **"surge"** of additional U.S. troops; casualties fell sharply, aided by a cease-fire with Shiite militias and a shift by minority Sunni away from support for al-Qaeda.

In **Afghanistan**, a U.S.-led military coalition ousted the **Taliban** regime. A transitional government was installed (Dec. 2001), but the Taliban remained strong as NATO assumed control of multinational forces in Aug. 2003. Afghans elected Hamid **Karzai** president (Nov. 2004). From 2007, Taliban and other Islamist militants stepped up insurgent activities, often operating from safe havens inside Pakistan. The U.S. increased its troop strength in Afghanistan (2009) and expanded use of **drones**.

Middle East. Suicide bombings by Palestinians and retaliation by Israelis escalated violence. Israel launched major **West Bank offensive** (Mar. 2002) and reoccupied much of the West Bank after briefly withdrawing. The U.S., Russia, UN, and EU initiated (Apr. 2003) a **"road map"** for peace negotiations; little progress was made. After Palestinian leader Yasir **Arafat** died (Nov. 2004), Mahmoud **Abbas** was elected in his place. The militant Palestinian party **Hamas** won a parliamentary majority over the long-ruling **Fatah** party (Jan. 2006).

Israel launched attacks on **Lebanon** (July 2006) after a raid into N Israel by Lebanon-based **Hezbollah** guerrillas; a cease-fire was declared a month later. In reaction to Hamas rocket and mortar attacks, Israel launched an offensive in the **Gaza Strip** (Dec. 2008), which killed an estimated 1,300 Palestinians. Prime Min. Ehud **Olmert**, in office from 2006 on, resigned amid corruption inquiries; Feb. 2009 elections led to a coalition government headed by conservative former Prime Min. Benjamin **Netanyahu**.

In **Yemen**, U.S. used **drones** to kill suspected al-Qaeda terrorists (Nov. 2002), and the government of Pres. Ali Abdullah **Saleh**, from 2004 onward, battled a growing insurgency from Shiite Houthi rebels, believed aided by Iran.

Asia. Gen. Pervez **Musharraf**, brought to power in a 1999 coup, assumed **Pakistan**'s presidency (June 2001). Following the Sept. 11, 2001, terrorist attacks in U.S., Pakistan agreed to help in fighting Taliban and al-Qaeda militants. After former Pakistani Prime Min. Benazir **Bhutto** was assassinated in a bombing (Dec. 2007), her party won parliamentary elections (Feb. 2008) and her widower, Asif Ali **Zardari**, was elected president (Sept. 2008). In May 2009, the government launched an offensive against Taliban insurgents in the Swat Valley.

Riots in the mostly Hindu **Indian** state of Gujarat (Feb.-Apr. 2002) left at least 790 Muslims and over 250 Hindus dead. Pakistan and **India** restored ties (May 2003) and declared cease-fire in disputed territory (Nov. 2003); relations remained tense. The UN Intl. Atomic Energy Agency (IAEA) censured **Iran** (Dec. 2003) for covering up aspects of its **nuclear** program; Iran continued enriching uranium in defiance of IAEA deadlines. Pres. Mahmoud **Ahmadinejad** was declared landslide winner in June 2009 Iranian elections widely perceived as rigged; massive **protests** were crushed. In **Kyrgyzstan**, protests (Mar. 2005) against election fraud brought down Pres. Askar **Akayev** in a **"tulip revolution."**

South Korean Pres. Kim Dae-jung and **North Korean** ruler Kim Jong Il agreed to seek peace at a summit (June 2000), but tensions rose after North Korea admitted to a **nuclear weapons** development program (Oct. 2002). At multination talks, North Korea agreed (Feb. 2007) to end its nuclear program in exchange for aid, but reneged, conducting tests Apr.-May 2009.

A **tsunami** (Dec. 2004) swept ashore, affecting Indian Ocean nations and leaving some 228,000 dead. **Earthquakes** struck Kashmir and other parts of Pakistan and India (Oct. 2005), killing nearly 80,000, and hit China's Sichuan province (May 2008), killing nearly 70,000. With the retirement of **China**'s Pres. Jiang Zemin, **Hu** Jintao was named Communist party chief (Nov. 2002) and president (Mar. 2003). In **Japan**, Liberal Democrats, in virtually uninterrupted power since the 1950s, were dispatched in parliamentary elections (Aug. 2009).

Myanmar's military junta cracked down on hundreds of thousands of protesters (Sept. 2007). Over 80,000 people were killed in a **cyclone** there (May 2008); the regime thwarted international aid. Battered by stepped-up government offensive, **Tamil** guerrillas in **Sri Lanka** ended (May 2009) their rebellion, which in 26 years had claimed at least 80,000 lives.

Europe. The **European Union** admitted 10 East European nations in May 2004; two more joined in Jan. 2007, for a total of 27 members. By 2008 the **euro** was the common currency in 15 EU nations. Voters in France and the Netherlands rejected a treaty to establish a new **EU constitution** (May-June 2005). A modified plan (called the **Treaty of Lisbon**) came into force (Dec. 2009) after Irish voters approved it (Oct. 2009).

In Oct. 2000, Yugoslav strongman Slobodan **Milosevic** yielded power after a disputed election; he went on trial at the Intl. Criminal Tribunal for the former Yugoslavia (Feb. 2002) for **war crimes** during 1990s Balkan conflicts but died (Mar. 2006) before a verdict. Former Bosnian Serb leader Radovan **Karadzic** was charged with war crimes in 2008 (convicted Mar. 2016). **Kosovo** unilaterally declared independence (Feb. 2008).

Germany elected its first East German and first woman chancellor (Nov. 2005) in Angela **Merkel**, a Christian Democrat.

A U.S.-led coalition ousted the Taliban regime from Afghanistan in late 2001, but insurgent violence grew and the U.S. sent a surge of 30,000 troops at the end of the decade.

Constitutionally barred from a third consecutive term as president, Russian leader Vladimir Putin (left) temporarily ceded the office to Dmitri Medvedev in 2008.

Rioting shook France's immigrant communities in 300 cities and towns (Nov. 2005).

British Prime Min. Tony **Blair** won reelection twice (2001, 2005) and stepped down in June 2007, succeeded by fellow Labourite Gordon **Brown**. **France** saw the election (May 2007) of conservative Nicolas **Sarkozy** as president and rejoined **NATO** military command (Apr. 2009) after more than 40 years. Vladimir **Putin**, in power in Russia since 1999, was constitutionally barred from a new presidential term in 2008; his protégé, Dmitri **Medvedev**, was elected (May 2008). In **Ukraine**, a tainted presidential runoff election (Nov. 2004) led to the country's **"orange revolution"**; a recount gave power to nationalist Viktor **Yushchenko**.

Africa. **Ethiopia** and **Eritrea** signed a peace treaty (Dec. 2000). Laurent **Kabila**, president of **Dem. Rep. of the Congo**, was assassinated (Jan. 2001). **Liberian** Pres. Charles **Taylor** went into exile (Aug. 2003) as part of a deal to end a 14-year civil war; other accords were reached aimed at ending civil wars in **Angola** (Apr. 2002) and **Côte d'Ivoire** (Jan. 2003).

A peace agreement in **Dem. Rep. of the Congo** (Apr. 2003) did not end violence there; the nation agreed to work with Rwanda to disarm Hutu rebels (Nov. 2007). In **Sudan** the Muslim-led government and rebels from the Christian south signed power-sharing agreement, Jan. 2005. Rebellion in the **Darfur** area of western Sudan led to large-scale violence. Arab militias (**janjaweed**), reportedly backed by the government, were accused of displacing over 2 mil people in acts bordering on **genocide**; by the end of 2009 over 300,000 had been killed. The Intl. Criminal Court issued an arrest warrant for Sudanese Pres. Omar al-**Bashir** for war crimes (Mar. 2009); he remained in power. Disputed elections sparked violence in **Kenya** (Jan. 2008) and **Zimbabwe** (Apr. 2008). Under Pres. Robert **Mugabe**, unemployment in Zimbabwe topped 90% and hyperinflation left the currency virtually worthless. **Guinea-Bissau**'s defense chief and then its president were assassinated in turn by rival groups (Mar. 2009).

Americas and the Caribbean. In Jan. 2001, George W. **Bush** (R) was inaugurated as **U.S.** president, after one of the closest elections in U.S. history. He pursued an active foreign policy that included wars in Afghanistan and Iraq and an aggressive anti-HIV/AIDS program in Africa. Democrats

claimed the White House with the Nov. 2008 election of Barack **Obama**, first-ever black U.S. president. The long-supreme **Institutional Revolutionary Party** lost power in **Mexico** with the election of two successive presidents from a center-right party, Vicente **Fox** and Felipe **Calderón** (July 2000, 2006). Calderón launched a crackdown on drug trafficking (Dec. 2006); from then through 2010, over 30,000 people were killed in violence fueled by **drug cartels**.

Leftists were in power in several Latin American countries. **Chile** was ruled by Socialist governments under Ricardo **Lagos** Escobar (from 2000) and Michelle **Bachelet** (from 2006). In **Brazil**, reformist candidate Luiz Inácio **Lula da Silva** won a runoff (Oct. 2002) to become president; reelected Oct. 2006. In **Venezuela**, populist Pres. Hugo **Chávez** regained power after a 48-hour coup (Dec. 2002) and consolidated it, in part through a referendum (Feb. 2009) that eliminated presidential term limits. Peronist **Nestor Kirchner** won election as president of **Argentina** (Apr. 2003); his wife, **Cristina Kirchner**, was elected (Oct. 2007) to succeed him. In **Bolivia**, Evo **Morales**, another leftist populist, won election as president (Dec. 2005) and passage of a new constitution (Jan. 2009). In **Honduras**, leftist leader Manuel **Zelaya** was elected president (Nov. 2005) but was ousted by the military (June 2009); conservative Porfirio (Pepe) **Lobo** was elected (Nov. 2009) to succeed him.

In **Peru**, right-wing Pres. Alberto **Fujimori** was reelected (May 2000) but fled the country; he was extradited (2007) and convicted on human rights and corruption charges. **Haiti** was wracked by antigovernment protests, leading to resignation of Jean-Bertrand **Aristide** in Feb. 2004; a UN peacekeeping mission was brought in Jan. **Canada**'s Liberal Party was defeated in Jan. 2006 elections; Conservative Stephen **Harper** became prime minister, heading a minority government. Pres. Fidel **Castro**, **Cuba**'s leader since 1959, ceded powers to his brother, **Raúl**, to undergo surgery (July 2006) and when he formally resigned in Feb. 2008.

Religion. Pope **John Paul II** died, Apr. 2005, after 26 years in the papacy; German Cardinal Joseph Ratzinger was elected as his successor, taking the name **Benedict XVI**. During the decade, reports of **sexual abuse** by Catholic priests and evidence of inaction by church officials emerged.

Science and technology. The U.S. **space shuttle** *Columbia* broke up on reentering Earth's atmosphere (Feb. 2003), killing all seven crew members. **NASA** landed two rovers, *Spirit* and *Opportunity*, on **Mars** (Jan. 2004), and verified presence of water ice there (June 2008); evidence of liquid water detected in 2015. **China** launched its first manned space flight, Oct. 2003. **Internet** penetration and access to technology expanded exponentially; online commerce, use of social media (Facebook, 2004; Twitter, 2006), mobile computing (iPhone, 2007), and file-sharing services became commonplace.

Environment and health. Under the **Kyoto Protocol**, which took effect Feb. 2005, most industrialized nations agreed to specific reductions in emissions of **greenhouse gases** linked to global warming. A NASA report (Jan. 2010) found that 2000-09 had the **warmest average global temperatures** since modern records began in the 1880s.

Worldwide **AIDS** estimates were revised (Nov. 2007) to show new infections had peaked in the late 1990s. An epidemic of **swine flu**, or influenza A (H1N1), broke out in **Mexico** (Apr. 2009) and spread, killing more than 18,000.

Searching for Resolutions: 2010-June 2016

Middle East. The Middle East continued to be a region of turmoil, with underlying conflicts unresolved. UN General Assembly granted nonmember observer state status to **Palestine** (Nov. 2012). Arab-Israeli **peace talks** resumed, July 2013, but foundered as **Fatah** and militant **Hamas** factions agreed (Apr. 2014) to aim at unification. **Israel** began airstrikes on **Gaza** (July 2014) after rocket attacks by Hamas-affiliated groups; at least 2,000 Palestinians and 60 Israeli soldiers were killed; cease-fire reached in Aug. 2014. **Hamas** remained in effective control of Gaza and conducted sporadic terrorist attacks. Prime

Min. Benjamin **Netanyahu** retained power in Israel after Mar. 2015 elections, forming a right-wing government.

Poverty, religious and ethnic conflict, and government corruption and repression fueled revolts that challenged entrenched regimes. In **Tunisia**, protests forced ouster of Pres. Zine al-Abidine **Ben Ali** (Jan. 2011); elections followed and a new constitution (Jan. 2014) recognized civil liberties. But the so-called **Arab Spring** also backfired. In **Egypt**, after mass demonstrations led to overthrow of longtime Pres. Hosni **Mubarak** (Feb. 2011), the new **Muslim Brotherhood**-dominated government (elected June 2012) fell in a military coup (July 2013); raids (over 600 killed, Aug. 2013) and mass arrests followed. Coup leader Abdel Fattah **al-Sisi** was elected president, May 2014. In **Yemen**, protests led to fall of the government (Nov. 2011); the new president, inaugurated 2012, eventually resigned (Jan. 2015) and fled after Shia **Houthi** rebels took over the capital city. A **Saudi**-led coalition of Arab states began a bombing campaign (Mar. 2015) against the Houthi, believed aided by Iran. Tentative truce reached between Houthi and exiled government, Apr. 2016. In **Libya**, insurgents with NATO military backing overthrew dictator Muammar al-**Qaddafi**, who was killed (Oct. 2011). Westerners faced dangers (U.S. consulate attack in **Benghazi**, Sept. 2012; multiple embassy closures), as the country became a battleground for rival Islamist factions (rebels took over **Tripoli**, Oct. 2014). Libya was a transit point for **refugees** and **migrants** crossing the central Mediterranean in overcrowded boats. In Jan.-June 2016, over 2,800 people drowned attempting to cross the Mediterranean.

In **Syria**, Pres. Bashar al-**Assad** launched an offensive against antigovernment protesters (beginning Mar. 2011), giving rise to **civil war**. After about 1,400 people were killed in chemical attacks (Aug. 2013) attributed to the regime, the government accepted Russian-backed plan for surrender of chemical weapons. Among several opposition forces, the so-called **Islamic State in Iraq and Syria (ISIS)** occupied a swath of territory in Syria, including **Palmyra** (May 2015-Mar. 2016), and neighboring Iraq. Despite partial cease-fire, Feb. 2016, fighting continued, with heavy civilian casualties from government airstrikes and insurgents' bombs. By early 2016 up to 400,000 or more had died in Syria, and more than 11 mil were displaced, with millions seeking refuge in other Mideast countries or Europe.

Concerns over **Iranian** power in the region were exacerbated by its nuclear development program. Election of relatively moderate cleric Hassan **Rouhani** as president (June 2013) raised hopes for reduced tensions. Negotiations (with five permanent UN Security Council nations plus Germany) led to final agreement (July 2015) for Iran to cut back nuclear development; in return sanctions were lifted (Jan. 2016). **Saudi Arabia** broke ties with Iran after Iranians burned Saudi embassy in Tehran following Saudi mass execution of 47 accused terrorists (Jan. 2016).

War in Iraq and Afghanistan. The last U.S. combat unit withdrew from **Iraq**, Aug. 2010, and the U.S. military left in Dec. 2011. Death toll, 2003-11: about 4,500 U.S. service members, 300 from allied countries, with Iraqi civilian deaths estimated at over 100,000. But sectarian violence accelerated, with government forces and Shia militia fighting insurgents, including **ISIS** militants. After taking **Fallujah** and **Mosul**, ISIS declared an Islamic caliphate (June 2014) and took **Ramadi**, May 2015. Within its territory ISIS imposed strict Islamic law, murdered minorities and resisters, and videotaped beheadings; the group also launched bombings of Iraqi civilians in Baghdad and elsewhere (close to 400 killed, Jan.-June 2016). Separatist Kurds controlled part of Iraq and fought ISIS on the ground; U.S., aided by other countries, conducted airstrikes and sent in advisers, and ISIS suffered reverses (lost Ramadi, Dec. 2015, and Fallujah, June 2016). Prime Min. Nouri al-**Maliki** lost leadership of Shiite party to Haider **al-Abadi**, who formed new government (Sept. 2014); protesters stormed **Baghdad**'s Green Zone, for the first time in Apr. 2016, citing corruption and mismanagement.

U.S. and NATO-led troops in **Afghanistan** reached about 140,000 by mid-2011, when drawdown began. Combat operations officially ended in Dec. 2014, but troops remained in support roles under Sept. 2014 agreement with new unity government headed by Ashraf **Ghani**. Death toll, 2001-14: over 2,300 U.S. troops, 1,100 other NATO forces. At least 21,000 civilians died (UN estimate, 2009-15 only). Fighting continued, with about 30% of the country in **Taliban** hands or at risk, as of early 2016; sporadic Taliban bombings were launched against civilians. Taliban leader Mullah Akhtar **Mansour** was killed in U.S. drone strike in Pakistan, May 2016.

Terrorism. **Terrorism** associated with radical Islam remained a global threat, responsible, in 2015 alone, for 28,300 deaths in 92 countries; 74% of deaths were in Iraq, Afghanistan, Nigeria, Syria, or Pakistan. **Al-Qaeda** leader Osama **bin Laden** was killed in a Pakistan raid by U.S. Special Forces (May 2011), but al-Qaeda remained entrenched along Afghan-Pakistan border and returned to S Afghanistan.

Al-Qaeda and rival **ISIS** group recruited followers and maintained or inspired affiliates globally. **Boko Haram**, responsible for thousands of deaths in W Africa, pledged allegiance to ISIS (Mar. 2015).

Among other incidents, **al-Shabab** militants linked to al-Qaeda were behind July 2010 bombings in Kampala, **Uganda** (more than 70 World Cup soccer watchers killed), Sept. 2013 shootings at a Nairobi, **Kenya**, shopping mall (close to 70 killed), and Apr. 2015 massacre at a college in Garissa, Kenya (nearly 150 killed). In **Yemen**, al-Qaeda in the Arabian Peninsula (**AQAP**) attacked a military parade rehearsal (May 2012; over 100 killed). Boko Haram fighters abducted over 200 schoolgirls in **Nigeria** (Apr. 2014); **Taliban** gunmen in **Pakistan** killed some 150 at a Peshawar school (Dec. 2014).

In other attacks, radicalized brothers originally from Chechnya set off bombs, killing three spectators and injuring some 260, at the **Boston Marathon** (Apr. 2013); in **Ottawa**, Canada, a Muslim gunman killed a sentry and attacked Parliament (Oct. 2014) before being shot dead. Attackers possibly linked to AQAP killed 17 in and around **Paris**, Jan. 2015, most at offices of the satirical magazine *Charlie Hebdo*; jihadists linked to ISIS murdered some 130 in or near Paris, Nov. 2015, and over 30 in and around **Brussels**, Mar. 2016. Terrorists launched attacks in **Tunisia** (Mar., June 2015; about 60 killed) and in **Turkey** at Ankara peace rally (Oct. 2015; over 100 killed) and at airport (June 2016; over 40 died). **Russian airliner** exploded over **Egypt** (Oct. 2015, killing 224); ISIS claimed responsibility. Shooters with apparent Islamic radical sympathies killed 14 at a **San Bernardino**, CA, workplace (Dec. 2015). In June 2016, 49 were killed in a mass shooting (the deadliest by a single shooter in modern U.S. history) at a gay nightclub in **Orlando**, FL.

An anti-Muslim right-wing extremist killed 77 people in rampage in **Norway**, July 2011.

Europe. The EU, with IMF help, provided loan packages to bail out **Greece** (beginning May 2010) and **Ireland** (Nov. 2010). A leftist Greek government, elected Jan. 2015, ultimately accepted a rescue plan, despite its rejection by Greek voters in a July 2015 referendum. The European Central Bank bailed out **Portugal** (May 2011); the EU provided a bank bailout for **Spain** (June 2012) and reached a bailout agreement with **Cyprus** (Mar. 2013). With large numbers of **migrants from Syria** and other war-torn countries seeking asylum in Europe, **EU** approved plan, Sept. 2015, aimed at relocating some 160,000 from heavily impacted Greece and Italy; it reached agreement with **Turkey** (Mar. 2016) for that country (hosting nearly 3 mil refugees) to limit outflow and accept new migrants held in Greece.

Conservatives returned to power in **Britain** under David **Cameron** (May 2010; reelected June 2015). But Cameron was repudiated, the UK faced uncertainty, and world markets were shaken after Britons, in a historic referendum (June 2016), voted to **leave the EU**. During **"Brexit"** campaign, pro-EU Labour MP Jo **Cox** was assassinated.

In **France**, socialist François **Hollande** defeated conservative Nicolas **Sarkozy** to become president (May 2012). Conservative former Prime Min. Recep Tayyip **Erdogan** was elected president of **Turkey** (Aug. 2014). Elections in **Poland** (May 2015) and **Denmark** (June 2015) put center-right parties in power.

Fleeing violence, overcrowded camps, or poverty in Northern Africa, the Middle East, and Afghanistan, millions of refugees and migrants sought refuge in Europe.

Amid accusations of corruption and voter fraud, Vladimir **Putin** won third term as **Russia**'s president (Mar. 2012), facing economy battered by falling oil prices. He strengthened ties to China (natural gas deal, May 2014) and intervened with airstrikes in Syria (Sept. 2015).

Pro-Russian Viktor **Yanukovich**, elected president of **Ukraine** in Feb. 2010, faced mass protests after he rebuffed EU integration; he fled the country (Feb. 2014). Claiming a danger to ethnic Russians, Putin sent troops to **Crimea** and, in Mar. 2014, annexed it. With pro-Russian separatists fighting for control of E Ukraine, apparently with Russian backing, pro-European moderate Petro **Poroshenko** was elected Ukraine's president (May 2014); he signed EU trade agreement, June 2014. Multinational talks led to fragile cease-fire, Feb. 2015; UN estimated in Mar. 2016 that at least 9,160 had died since the conflict started in Apr. 2014, with many more fleeing or internally displaced. In **Moldova**, stung by the 2014 disappearance of $1 bil from banks, the election of Pavel **Filip** as prime minister (Jan. 2016) stirred protests charging corruption.

Traditionally Catholic **Ireland** became (May 2015) the first country to legalize same-sex marriage by popular vote. Multiple press outlets released so-called **Panama Papers** (Apr. 2016), leaked legal documents showing how politicians and others concealed assets abroad. Included were leaders in **Argentina**, **Russia**, **Saudi Arabia**, **Ukraine**, **UK**, and **Iceland** (whose prime minister resigned under pressure). Unionized workers launched **strikes across France** (starting May 2016), protesting proposed labor market reforms.

Asia and the Pacific. An **earthquake** and tsunami (Mar. 2011) struck Japan, killing more than 16,000 and leading to meltdowns at nuclear reactors. Over 8,500 were killed in two earthquakes in **Nepal** (Apr.-May 2015). A **Malaysian airliner** en route to Beijing with 239 aboard veered off course and **vanished** (Mar. 2014).

Kyrgyzstan's president was ousted (Apr. 2010) after clashes with protesters left at least 85 dead; despite ethnic violence (up to 2,000 killed), a referendum passed a new constitution (June 2010), and a new president was elected (Oct. 2011). **North Korean** dictator **Kim Jong Il** died, Dec. 2011; was succeeded by son **Kim Jong Un**, who launched nuclear-bomb and missile tests, threatened U.S., and sought to consolidate power. **Myanmar**'s military-backed USDP party won nation's first free elections in 20 years (Nov. 2010) but lost (Nov. 2015) to the party of dissident leader Aung San **Suu Kyi**. **Rohingya** Muslim minority suffered persecution, with many internally displaced or fleeing by boat.

In **China**, Xi Jinping succeeded retiring **Hu** Jintao as Communist party chief (Nov. 2012) and president (Mar. 2013). The party retained firm control (**Hong Kong** pro-democracy protests, Sept.-Dec. 2014). After Chinese stocks fell 30%, China devalued its currency (Aug. 2015); another **sell-off** came in Jan. 2016. Signs of **slowdown** in China's economic growth rattled investors globally. In **Japan**, Liberal Democrats regained power in Dec. 2012 elections. The Hindu nationalist Bharatiya Janata party won a majority in May 2014 elections in **India;** Narendra **Modi** became prime minister. Anti-crime hardliner Rodrigo **Duterte** was elected **Philippines** president, May 2016.

Trans-Pacific Partnership (TPP) was signed Feb. 2016; intended to eliminate thousands of tariffs among 12 countries in or bordering on the Pacific.

Africa. Coups ousted **Niger**'s president (Feb. 2010) and ended elections in **Guinea-Bissau** (Apr. 2012); in both cases, civilian rule returned following new elections. In a referendum, southern Sudanese (mostly Christian or indigenous beliefs) voted overwhelmingly for separation from the north (mostly Arab Muslim), and **South Sudan** was granted independence as of July 2011. A leadership struggle led to **civil war** (some 10,000 dead; over 2.4 mil displaced); peace accord reached Aug. 2015, unity government formed Apr. 2016.

Low-level soldiers staged a coup in **Mali** (Mar. 2012). The junta ceded power to civilians, but Islamic rebels seized control in the north. French and West African forces intervened; a peace deal was reached (June 2013) but proved fragile. In **Burkina Faso**, Pres. Blaise **Campaoré**, in power for 27 years, fled amid protests (Oct. 2014); elections in Dec. 2015 brought in a new civilian government. In **Nigeria**, former dictator Muhammadu **Buhari**, elected president in Mar. 2015, made inroads against **Boko Haram** terrorists; economy was badly hurt by **falling oil prices**. Ethnic and political violence plagued **Burundi** in 2015, killing hundreds and displacing at least 250,000. An African Union court in Senegal (June 2016) convicted Hissène **Habré** of crimes against humanity while ruler of **Chad** in the 1980s.

An **Ebola** epidemic in W Africa (2014-15) caused over 11,000 deaths, mostly in Guinea, Liberia, and Sierra Leone.

Americas and the Caribbean. Poverty, unemployment, and gang violence spurred migrations from **El Salvador**, **Honduras**, other Latin American countries. **Haiti** was devastated by an **earthquake** (Jan. 2010) that killed more than 200,000 and a lingering **cholera** epidemic that left more than 9,000 dead by early 2016. **Canada**'s Conservatives, under Prime Min. Stephen **Harper**, won majority in May 2011 elections, but Liberals came back to win in Oct. 2015 under charismatic party leader Justin **Trudeau**. **Mexico**'s Institutional Revolutionary Party regained power with election of Enrique **Peña Nieto** (July 2012).

Several leftist regimes suffered reverses. In **Brazil**, Pres. Lula da Silva's chosen successor, Dilma **Rousseff**, won the presidency (Oct. 2010), but a corruption scandal and devastated economy led to mass protests and her suspension by the Senate (May 2016) and eventual impeachment trial. Brazil was also locus of the **Zika virus**, which spread to other countries in the Americas. In **Venezuela**, leftist Pres. Hugo **Chávez** died in Mar. 2013; his ally and elected successor Nicolás **Maduro** Moros declared a state of emergency (May 2016) as the economy collapsed, battered by plunging oil prices. **Argentine** voters ended 12 years of Peronist rule, choosing center-right candidate Mauricio **Macri** as president (Nov. 2015); debt repayment deal approved, Mar. 2016. **Peru**'s voters elected conservative Pedro Pablo **Kuczynski** president in June 2016.

After 52 years of fighting, **Colombian** government reached (June 2016) peace accord with Revolutionary Army of Colombia (**FARC**) guerrillas.

U.S. Pres. Barack **Obama**, reelected in Nov. 2012, stressed diplomacy in foreign policy—announced restoration of relations with **Cuba**, Dec. 2014; finalized **Iran** nuclear deal, July 2015; visited **Vietnam** (arms embargo ended) and **Hiroshima**, May 2016—but U.S. military remained involved in actions in Afghanistan, Syria, Iraq, and elsewhere.

Religion. Benedict XVI resigned after eight years as pope (Feb. 2013); Argentinean Cardinal Jorge Mario Bergoglio succeeded him, taking the name **Francis** and becoming the first pope from the Americas.

Science, technology, environment. After 30 years, NASA's space shuttle program ended with return of *Atlantis* to Earth (July 2011). NASA's rover *Curiosity* landed on **Mars** Aug. 2012; **China** landed unmanned *Yulu* rover on the **Moon** Dec. 2013. NASA's *New Horizons* space probe made flyby of **Pluto**, July 2015. Scientists, Feb. 2016, reported first-ever direct observation of **gravitational waves**, confirming an Einstein prediction.

Average global temperatures continued a rising trend, with 2015 the warmest year on record and 2016 on track to overtake it. Representatives of most developed and developing nations meeting in Paris (Dec. 2015), committed to individual plans for reducing **greenhouse gases** linked to climate change.

Pope Benedict XVI, the leader of the world's 1.1 billion Roman Catholics, resigned in 2013 and was succeeded by Pope Francis, the first pontiff from the Americas.

HISTORICAL FIGURES

Note: Information accurate as of Sept. 2016.

Ancient Greeks and Romans

Greeks

Aeschines, orator, 389-314 BCE
Aeschylus, dramatist, 525-456 BCE
Aesop, fableist, c. 620-c. 560 BCE
Alcibiades, politician, 450-404 BCE
Anacreon, poet, c. 582-c. 485 BCE
Anaxagoras, philosopher, c. 500-428 BCE
Anaximander, philosopher, 611-546 BCE
Anaximenes, philosopher, c. 570-500 BCE
Antiphon, speechwriter, c. 480-411 BCE
Apollonius, mathematician, c. 265-170 BCE
Archimedes, mathematician, 287-212 BCE
Aristophanes, dramatist, c. 448-380 BCE
Aristotle, philosopher, 384-322 BCE
Athenaeus, scholar, fl. c. 200
Callicrates, architect, fl. 5th cent. BCE
Callimachus, poet, c. 305-240 BCE
Cratinus, comic dramatist, 520-421 BCE
Democritus, philosopher, c. 460-370 BCE
Demosthenes, orator, 384-322 BCE
Diodorus, historian, fl. 20 BCE
Diogenes, philosopher, 372-c. 287 BCE
Dionysius, historian, d. c. 7 BCE
Empedocles, philosopher, c. 490-430 BCE
Epicharmus, dramatist, c. 530-440 BCE
Epictetus, philosopher, c. 55-c. 135
Epicurus, philosopher, 341-270 BCE
Eratosthenes, scientist, 276-194 BCE
Euclid, mathematician, fl. c. 300 BCE
Euripides, dramatist, c. 484-406 BCE
Galen, physician, 129-216
Heraclitus, philosopher, c. 540-c. 475 BCE
Herodotus, historian, c. 484-420 BCE

Hesiod, poet, 8th cent. BCE
Hippocrates, physician, c. 460-377 BCE
Homer, poet, fl. c. 8th cent. BCE
Isocrates, orator, 436-338 BCE
Menander, dramatist, 342-292 BCE
Parmenides, philosopher, c. 515-440 BCE
Pericles, statesman, c. 495-429 BCE
Phidias, sculptor, c. 500-435 BCE
Pindar, poet, c. 518-c. 438 BCE
Plato, philosopher, c. 428-347 BCE
Plutarch, biographer, c. 46-120
Polybius, historian, c. 200-c. 118 BCE
Praxiteles, sculptor, 400-330 BCE
Pythagoras, phil., math., c. 580-c. 500 BCE
Sappho, poet, c. 610-c. 580 BCE
Simonides, poet, 556-c. 468 BCE
Socrates, philosopher, 469-399 BCE
Solon, statesman, 640-560 BCE
Sophocles, dramatist, c. 496-406 BCE
Strabo, geographer, c. 63 BCE-24 CE
Thales, philosopher, c. 634-546 BCE
Themistocles, politician, c. 524-c. 460 BCE
Theocritus, poet, c. 310-250 BCE
Theophrastus, phil., c. 372-c. 287 BCE
Thucydides, historian, fl. 5th cent. BCE
Timon, philosopher, c. 320-c. 230 BCE
Xenophon, historian, c. 434-c. 355 BCE
Zeno, philosopher, c. 335-c. 263 BCE

Romans

Ammianus, historian, c. 330-395
Apuleius, satirist, c. 124-c. 170
Boethius, scholar, c. 480-524
Caesar, Julius, leader, 100-44 BCE

Catiline, politician, c. 108-62 BCE
Cato (Elder), statesman, 234-149 BCE
Catullus, poet, c. 84-54 BCE
Cicero, orator, 106-43 BCE
Claudian, poet, c. 370-c. 404
Ennius, poet, 239-170 BCE
Gellius, author, c. 130-c. 165
Horace, poet, 65-8 BCE
Juvenal, satirist, 60-127
Livy, historian, 59 BCE-17 CE
Lucan, poet, 39-65
Lucilius, poet, c. 180-c.102 BCE
Lucretius, poet, c. 99-c. 55 BCE
Martial, epigrammatist, c. 38-c. 103
Nepos, historian, c. 100-c. 25 BCE
Ovid, poet, 43 BCE-17 CE
Persius, satirist, 34-62
Plautus, dramatist, c. 254-c. 184 BCE
Pliny the Elder, scholar, 23-79
Pliny the Younger, author, 62-113
Quintilian, rhetorician, c. 35-c. 97
Sallust, historian, 86-34 BCE
Seneca, philosopher, 4 BCE-65 CE
Silius, poet, c. 25-101
Statius, poet, c. 45-c. 96
Suetonius, biographer, c. 69-c. 122
Tacitus, historian, 56-120
Terence, dramatist, 195/185-c. 159 BCE
Tibullus, poet, c. 55-c. 19 BCE
Vergil, poet, 70-19 BCE
Vitruvius, architect, fl. late 1st cent. BCE

Roman Rulers

From Romulus to the end of the Empire in the West (Rome). Rulers in the East sat in Constantinople and, for a brief period, in Nicaea, until the capture of Constantinople by the Turks in 1453, when Byzantium was succeeded by the Ottoman Empire.

The Kingdom

BCE
753 Romulus (Quirinus)
715 Numa Pompilius
673 Tullus Hostilius
641 Ancus Marcius
616 L. Tarquinius Priscus
579 Servius Tullius
534 L. Tarquinius Superbus

The Republic

509 Consulate established;
    Quaestorship instituted
498 Dictatorship introduced
494 Plebeian Tribunate created;
    Plebeian Aedileship created
444 Consular Tribunate organized
435 Censorship instituted
366 Praetorship established;
    Curule Aedileship created
362 Military Tribunate elected
326 Proconsulate introduced
311 Naval Duumvirate elected
217 Dictatorship of Fabius Maximus
133 Tribunate of Tiberius Gracchus
123 Tribunate of Gaius Gracchus
82 Dictatorship of Sulla
60 First Triumvirate formed
    (Caesar, Pompeius, Crassus)
47 Dictatorship of Caesar
43 Second Triumvirate formed
    (Octavianus, Antonius, Lepidus)

The Empire

27 Augustus (or Octavian)
CE
14 Tiberius
37 Caligula
41 Claudius
54 Nero
68 Galba
69 Otho; Vitellius; Vespasian,
    established Flavian Dynasty
79 Titus
81 Domitian, end of Flavian Dynasty

96 Nerva
98 Trajan
117 Hadrian
138 Antoninus Pius
161 Marcus Aurelius and Lucius Verus
169 Marcus Aurelius (alone)
177 Marcus Aurelius and Commodus
180 Commodus
193 Pertinax
193 Didius Julianus
193 Septimius Severus, founded
    Severan Dynasty
211 Caracalla and Geta
212 Caracalla (alone)
217 Macrinus
218 Elagabalus (or Heliogabalus)
222 Alexander Severus, end of dynasty
235 Maximinus (the Thracian)
238 Gordian I and Gordian II
238 Pupienus and Balbinus
238 Gordian III
244 Philip (the Arabian)
249 Decius
251 Gallus and Volusianus
253 Aemilian
253 Valerian and Gallienus
258 Gallienus (alone)
268 Claudius II (or Claudius Gothicus)
270 Quintillus
270 Aurelian
275 Tacitus
276 Florian
276 Probus
282 Carus
283 Carinus and Numerian
284 Diocletian
286 Diocletian and Maximian
305 Galerius and Constantius I
306 Galerius, Maximinus (or
    Maximinus Daia), Severus
307 Galerius, Maximinus (Daia),
    Constantine I, Licinius, Maxentius
311 Maximinus (Daia), Constantine I,
    Licinius, Maxentius

314 Constantine I, Licinius
324 Constantine I (the Great), first
    Christian emperor
337 Constantine II, Constans I,
    Constantius II
340 Constantius II and Constans I
353 Constantius II (alone)
361 Julian (the Apostate)
363 Jovian

West (Rome) and East (Constantinople)

364 Valentinian I (West),
    Valens (East)
367 Valentinian I with Gratian (W),
    Valens (E)
375 Gratian with Valentinian II (W),
    Valens (E)
379 Gratian with Valentinian II (W),
    Theodosius I (E)
383 Magnus Maximus and
    Valentinian II (W),
    Theodosius I (E)
388 Valentinian II (W), Theodosius I (E)
392 Eugenius (W), Theodosius I (E)
394 Theodosius I (the Great)
395 Honorius (W), Arcadius (E)
408 Honorius (W), Theodosius II (E)
423 Valentinian III (W),
    Theodosius II (E)
450 Valentinian III (W), Marcian (E)
455 Petronius Maximus (W),
    Marcian (E)
455 Avitus (W), Marcian (E)
457 Majorian (W), Leo I (E)
461 Libius Severus (W), Leo I (E)
467 Anthemius (W), Leo I (E)
472 Olybrius (W), Leo I (E)
473 Glycerius (W), Leo I (E)
474 Julius Nepos (W), Leo II (E)
475 Romulus Augustulus (W), Zeno (E)
476 End of Empire in W when Romulus
    Augustulus deposed by Germanic
    chief Odoacer, who was later
    murdered by King Theodoric of
    Ostrogoths, 493

Rulers of England and the United Kingdom

Reign began	England: Saxons and Danes	Age at death[1]
829	Egbert, king of Wessex, won allegiance of all English	NA
839	Ethelwulf, son, king of Wessex, Sussex, Kent, Essex	NA
858	Ethelbald, eldest son, displaced father in Wessex	NA
860	Ethelbert, 2nd son of Ethelwulf, united Kent and Wessex	NA
866	Ethelred I, 3rd son of Ethelwulf, king of Wessex, fought Danes	NA
871	Alfred (the Great), 4th son of Ethelwulf, defeated Danes, fortified London	52
899	Edward (the Elder), son, united English, claimed Scotland	55
924	Athelstan (the Glorious), eldest son, king of Mercia, Wessex	45
940	Edmund, 3rd son of Edward, king of Wessex, Mercia	25
946	Edred, 4th son of Edward	32
955	Edwy (the Fair), eldest son of Edmund, king of Wessex	18
959	Edgar (the Peaceful), 2nd son of Edmund, ruled all English	32
975	Edward (the Martyr), eldest son, murdered by stepmother	17
978; 1014[2]	Ethelred II (the Unready), 2nd son of Edgar, married Emma of Normandy	48
1016	Edmund II (Ironside), son, king of London	27
1016	Canute (the Dane), son of Sweyn, who conquered English territory; gave Wessex to Edmund II; married Emma, Ethelred II's widow	40
1035	Harold I (Harefoot), illegitimate son	NA
1040	Hardecanute, son of Canute by Emma, also king of Denmark	24
1042	Edward (the Confessor), son of Ethelred II, canonized 1161	62
1066	Harold II, brother-in-law, last Saxon king	44

Reign began	England: House of Normandy	Age at death[1]
1066	William I (the Conqueror), son of Duke Robert I of Normandy, defeated Harold II at Hastings	60
1087	William II (Rufus), 3rd son, killed by arrow while hunting in possible assassination	43
1100	Henry I (Beauclerc), youngest son of William I	67

Reign began	England: House of Blois	Age at death[1]
1135	Stephen, son of Adela, daughter of William I, and Count of Blois	50

Reign began	England: House of Plantagenet	Age at death[1]
1154	Henry II, son of Geoffrey Plantagenet (Angevin) by Matilda, daughter of Henry I	56
1189	Richard I (Coeur de Lion), son, crusader	42
1199	John (Lackland), son of Henry II, approved Magna Carta, 1215	50
1216	Henry III, son, acceded at 9, under regency until 1227	65
1272	Edward I (Longshanks), son	68
1307	Edward II, son, deposed by Parliament	43
1327	Edward III (of Windsor), son	65
1377	Richard II, grandson of Edward III, deposed	33

Reign began	England: House of Lancaster	Age at death[1]
1399	Henry IV (of Bolingbroke), son of John of Gaunt, duke of Lancaster, son of Edward III	47
1413	Henry V, son, victor over French at Agincourt	34
1422; 1470	Henry VI, son, overthrown by Edward IV in 1461 but was returned to throne in 1470. Deposed, died in Tower of London, 1471	49

Reign began	England: House of York	Age at death[1]
1461; 1471	Edward IV, great-great-grandson of Edward III, son of duke of York. Acclaimed king by Parliament, 1461. Driven into exile in 1470 but regained throne, 1471	40
1483	Edward V, son, murdered in Tower of London	13
1483	Richard III, brother of Edward IV, fell in battle at Bosworth Field against Henry Tudor	32

Reign began	England: House of Tudor	Age at death[1]
1485	Henry VII, son of Edmund Tudor, earl of Richmond, whose father had married Henry V's widow. Descended from Edward III through mother, Margaret Beaufort, via John of Gaunt. Married Elizabeth of York, eldest daughter of Edward IV, to unite Lancaster and York	53
1509	Henry VIII, 2nd son, by Elizabeth	56
1547	Edward VI, son, by Jane Seymour, his 3rd queen. Was persuaded by John Dudley to name Lady Jane Grey, his cousin and Dudley's daughter-in-law, his successor. Council of State proclaimed her queen, July 10, 1553, but she ruled only nine days before Mary Tudor overthrew her	16
1553	Mary I, daughter of Henry VIII, by his 1st wife, Catherine of Aragon	43
1558	Elizabeth I, daughter of Henry VIII, by his 2nd wife, Anne Boleyn	69

Reign began	Great Britain: House of Stuart	Age at death[1]
1603	James I (James VI of Scotland), son of Mary, Queen of Scots. First to call self king of Great Britain; this became official with Acts of Union, 1707	59
1625	Charles I, only surviving son of James I	48

Reign began	Great Britain: Commonwealth	Age at death[1]
1649	Declared upon execution of Charles I	—

Reign began	Great Britain: Protectorate	Age at death[1]
1653	Oliver Cromwell, served on Council of State, executive body of Commonwealth, following overthrow of monarchy. Named Lord Protector upon creation of Protectorate by 1653 Instrument of Government	59
1658	Richard Cromwell, 3rd son, resigned as Lord Protector amid civil war, 1659	86

Reign began	Great Britain: House of Stuart (restored)	Age at death[1]
1660	Charles II, eldest son of Charles I, acceded to throne by Restoration, died without issue	55
1685	James II, 2nd son of Charles I, deposed 1688	68
1689	William III, son of William, Prince of Orange, by Mary, daughter of Charles I. Offered joint rule of throne with wife by Parliament	51
1689	Mary II, eldest daughter of James II and wife of William III, died 1694	33
1702	Anne, 2nd daughter of James II, sister-in-law of William III, assumed throne on William's death	49

Reign began	United Kingdom of Great Britain[3]: House of Hanover	Age at death[1]
1714	George I, son of Elector of Hanover by Sophia, granddaughter of James I	67
1727	George II, only son, married Caroline of Brandenburg	77
1760	George III, grandson, married Charlotte of Mecklenburg	81
1820	George IV, eldest son, prince regent from Feb. 1811	67
1830	William IV, 3rd son of George III, married Adelaide of Saxe-Meiningen	71
1837	Victoria, daughter of Edward, 4th son of George III; married Prince Albert of Saxe-Coburg and Gotha, 1840	81

Reign began	United Kingdom of Great Britain[3]: House of Saxe-Coburg-Gotha	Age at death[1]
1901	Edward VII, eldest son, married Alexandra, Princess of Denmark	68

Reign began	United Kingdom of Great Britain[3]: House of Windsor[4]	Age at death[1]
1910	George V, 2nd son, married Princess Mary of Teck	70
1936	Edward VIII, eldest son, acceded Jan. 20, abdicated Dec. 11	77
1936	George VI, 2nd son of George V, married Lady Elizabeth Bowes-Lyon	56
1952	Elizabeth II, elder daughter, acceded Feb. 6	NA

NA = Age/birthdate not certain or not applicable. (1) Except where noted, year of death is the same year the next ruler's reign began. (2) King Sweyn I of Denmark invaded England in 1013 and declared himself king. Ethelred II reclaimed the throne upon Sweyn's death in 1014. (3) Officially the United Kingdom of Great Britain and Ireland after Act of Union 1801 and the United Kingdom of Great Britain and Northern Ireland after Anglo-Irish Treaty of 1921 (name formalized 1927). (4) Name adopted by proclamation of George V, July 17, 1917, because of anti-German feeling during World War I.

Rulers of Scotland

Reign began	Name	Reign began	Name
846	Kenneth I, first Scot to rule both Scots and Picts	1306	Robert I (the Bruce), victor at Bannockburn, 1314. Treaty with England and secured throne, 1328
1005	Malcolm II, son of Kenneth II	1329	David II, only surviving son
1034	Duncan I, grandson, first general ruler	1371	Robert II (the Steward), son of Robert I's daughter Marjorie
1040	Macbeth, seized kingdom, slain by Malcolm Canmore		and Walter, steward of Scotland. First of Stewart line
1057	Malcolm III (Canmore), eldest son of Duncan I	1390	Robert III, son
1093	Donald III (the Fair), younger brother	1406	James I, son, assassinated
1094	Duncan II, eldest son of Malcolm III by first wife	1437	James II, son
1095	Donald III (restored)	1460	James III, eldest son, possibly assassinated
1097	Edgar, 4th son of Malcolm III and Queen Margaret	1488	James IV, eldest son
1107	Alexander I, brother	1513	James V, eldest son, died at Battle of Flodden
1124	David I, brother	1542	Mary (Queen of Scots), daughter, became queen before
1153	Malcolm IV (the Maiden), grandson		she was 1 week old. Married Francis II (d. 1560), son of
1165	William (the Lion), brother		King Henry II of France, 1558. Married her cousin, Henry
1214	Alexander II, son		Stewart, Lord Darnley (d. 1567), 1565. Married James
1249	Alexander III, son		Hepburn, Earl of Bothwell, 1567. Imprisoned by her
1286	Margaret (Maid of Norway), granddaughter; died 1290 at age 8. (Interregnum, 1290-92)		cousin Elizabeth I of England, 1568; beheaded, 1587
1292	John Balliol, proclaimed king of Scotland by Edward I of England. (Interregnum, 1296-1306[1])	1567	James VI, son of Mary and Lord Darnley, became James I, king of England, on Elizabeth's death, 1603. (Legislative union of Scotland and England as United Kingdom of Great Britain not official until Acts of Union, 1707)

Note: Not all rulers before 1005 are shown. (1) Edward I decreed annexation of Scotland to England, 1296, after defeating Balliol in battle. William Wallace led resistance, 1297-1305.

Prime Ministers of the United Kingdom

Titles are given on first mention only. C = Conservative; La. = Labour; Li. = Liberal; P = Peelite; T = Tory; W = Whig.

Entered office	Name (party)	Entered office	Name (party)	Entered office	Name (party)
1721	Sir Robert Walpole (W)[1]	1827	George Canning (T)	1894	Archibald Primrose, 5th Earl of Rosebery (Li.)
1742	Spencer Compton, 1st Earl of Wilmington (W)	1827	Frederick John Robinson, Viscount Goderich (T)	1895	Robert Gascoyne-Cecil (C)
1743	Henry Pelham (W)	1828	Arthur Wellesley, 1st Duke of Wellington (T)	1902	Arthur James Balfour (C)
1754	Thomas Pelham-Holles, 1st Duke of Newcastle (W)	1830	Charles Grey, 2nd Earl Grey (W)	1905	Sir Henry Campbell-Bannerman (Li.)
1756	William Cavendish, 4th Duke of Devonshire (W)	1834	William Lamb, 2nd Viscount Melbourne (W)	1908	Herbert Henry Asquith (Li.[2])
1757	Thomas Pelham-Holles (W)	1834	Arthur Wellesley (T)	1916	David Lloyd George (Li.[2])
1762	John Stuart, 3rd Earl of Bute (T)	1834	Sir Robert Peel, 2nd Baronet (C)	1922	Andrew Bonar Law (C)
1763	George Grenville (W)	1835	William Lamb (W)	1923	Stanley Baldwin (C)
1765	Charles Watson-Wentworth, 2nd Marquess of Rockingham (W)	1841	Sir Robert Peel (C)	1924	Ramsay MacDonald (La.)
1766	William Pitt the Elder, 1st Earl of Chatham (W)	1846	John Russell, 1st Earl Russell (W)	1924	Stanley Baldwin (C)
		1852	Edward Stanley, 14th Earl of Derby (C)	1929	Ramsay MacDonald (La.[2])
1768	Augustus Henry Fitzroy, 3rd Duke of Grafton (W)	1852	George Hamilton Gordon, 4th Earl of Aberdeen (P[2])	1935	Stanley Baldwin (C[2])
1770	Lord Frederick North (T)	1855	Henry John Temple, 3rd Viscount Palmerston (W-Li.)	1937	Neville Chamberlain (C[2])
1782	Charles Watson-Wentworth (W)			1940	Winston Churchill (C[2])
1782	William Petty, 2nd Earl of Shelburne (W)	1858	Edward Stanley (C)	1945	Clement Attlee (La.)
		1859	Henry John Temple (W-Li.)	1951	Winston Churchill (C)
1783	William Cavendish-Bentinck, 3rd Duke of Portland (W[2])	1865	John Russell (Li.)	1955	Anthony Eden (C)
		1866	Edward Stanley (C)	1957	Harold Macmillan (C)
1783	William Pitt the Younger (T)	1868	Benjamin Disraeli (C)	1963	Alec Douglas-Home (C)
1801	Henry Addington (T)	1868	William E. Gladstone (Li.)	1964	Harold Wilson (La.)
1804	William Pitt the Younger (T)	1874	Benjamin Disraeli (C)	1970	Edward Heath (C)
1806	William Wyndham Grenville, 1st Baron Grenville (W)	1880	William E. Gladstone (Li.)	1974	Harold Wilson (La.)
		1885	Robert Gascoyne-Cecil, 3rd Marquess of Salisbury (C)	1976	James Callaghan (La.)
1807	William Cavendish-Bentinck (T)			1979	Margaret Thatcher (C)
1809	Spencer Perceval (T)	1886	William E. Gladstone (Li.)	1990	John Major (C)
1812	Robert Banks Jenkinson, 2nd Earl of Liverpool (T)	1886	Robert Gascoyne-Cecil (C)	1997	Tony Blair (La.)
		1892	William E. Gladstone (Li.)	2007	Gordon Brown (La.)
				2010	David Cameron (C[2])
				2016	Theresa May (C)

Note: Prime ministers prior to 1801 are for Great Britain. The Conservative Party was formed in 1834, an outgrowth of the Tory party. (1) Walpole is traditionally regarded as the first prime minister of Britain though the title was not commonly used then and did not become official until 1905. (2) Led a coalition government for all or part of time in office.

Prime Ministers of Canada

C = Conservative; Lib. = Liberal; PC = Progressive Conservative; U = Unionist

Entered office	Name (party)	Entered office	Name (party)	Entered office	Name (party)
1867	John A. Macdonald (C)	1921	W. L. Mackenzie King (Lib.)	1979	Joe Clark (PC)
1873	Alexander Mackenzie (Lib.)	1926[3]	Arthur Meighen (C)	1980	Pierre Trudeau (Lib.)
1878	John A. Macdonald (C)	1926	W. L. Mackenzie King (Lib.)	1984[3]	John Turner (Lib.)
1891	John Abbott (C)	1930	Richard Bedford Bennett (C)	1984	Brian Mulroney (PC)
1892	John Thompson (C)	1935	W. L. Mackenzie King (Lib.)	1993[4]	Kim Campbell (PC)
1894	Mackenzie Bowell (C)	1948	Louis St. Laurent (Lib.)	1993	Jean Chrétien (Lib.)
1896[1]	Charles Tupper (C)	1957	John G. Diefenbaker (PC)	2003	Paul Martin (Lib.)
1896	Wilfrid Laurier (Lib.)	1963	Lester B. Pearson (Lib.)	2006	Stephen Harper (C)
1911	Robert Borden (C/U)[2]	1968	Pierre Trudeau (Lib.)	2015	Justin Trudeau (Lib.)
1920	Arthur Meighen (U)				

1) May-July. (2) Conservative 1911-17, Unionist 1917-20. (3) June-Sept. (4) June-Nov.

Rulers of France

Caesar to Charlemagne

Julius Caesar subdued the Gauls, native tribes of Gaul (France), 58 to 51 BCE. The Romans ruled 500 years. The Franks, a Teutonic tribe, reached the Somme from the east c. 250 CE. By the 5th cent., the Merovingian Franks ousted the Romans. In 451, with the help of Visigoths, Burgundians, and others, they defeated Attila and the Huns at Châlons-sur-Marne.

Childeric I became leader of the Merovingians, 458. His son Clovis I, crowned 481, founded the dynasty. After defeating the Alemanni (Germans), 496, he was baptized a Christian and made Paris his capital. His line ruled until Childeric III was deposed, 751.

The West Merovingians were called Neustrians, the eastern Austrasians. Pepin of Herstal (687-714), major domus (head of the palace) of Austrasia, took over Neustria as dux (leader) of the Franks. Pepin's son, Charles, called Martel (the Hammer), defeated the Saracens at Tours-Poitiers, 732; was succeeded in 741 by his sons, Pepin the Short and Carloman (abdicated 747). Pepin deposed Childeric III and ruled as king until 768.

His son, Charlemagne, or Charles the Great (742-814), became king of the Franks, 768, with his brother Carloman (751-71). Charlemagne ruled France, Germany, parts of Italy, Spain, and Austria, and enforced Christianity. Crowned Emperor of the Romans by Pope Leo III in Rome, Dec. 25, 800. Succeeded by son, Louis I (the Pious), 814. At death, 840, Louis left empire to sons Lothair (Roman emperor), Pepin I (king of Aquitaine), Louis II (the German), and Charles II (the Bald, of France). They quarreled and, by the Treaty of Verdun, 843, divided the empire.

The date preceding each entry is year of accession.

Carolingian Dynasty

843 Charles II (the Bald), Roman emperor, 875
877 Louis II (the Stammerer), son
879 Louis III (d. 882), son, and brother Carloman
885 Charles III (the Fat), son of Louis the German, Roman emperor, 881
888 Eudes (Odo), elected by nobles
898 Charles III (the Simple), son of Louis II the Stammerer, defeated by Robert
922 Robert, brother of Eudes, killed in war
923 Rudolph (Raoul), duke of Burgundy
936 Louis IV, son of Charles III (the Simple)
954 Lothair, son, aged 13, defeated by Capet
986 Louis V (the Sluggard), left no heirs

House of Capet

987 Hugh Capet, son of Hugh the Great
996 Robert II (the Pious), son
1031 Henry I, son
1060 Philip I (the Fair), son
1108 Louis VI (the Fat), son
1137 Louis VII (the Younger), son
1180 Philip II (Augustus), son, crowned at Reims
1223 Louis VIII (the Lion), son
1226 Louis IX, son, arbitrated disputes with English King Henry III; led crusades, 1248 (captured in Egypt, 1250) and 1270, when he died of plague in Tunis. Canonized as St. Louis, 1297
1270 Philip III (the Hardy), son
1285 Philip IV (the Fair), son, king at 17
1314 Louis X (the Headstrong), son. His posthumous son, John I, lived and reigned only five days.
1316 Philip V (the Tall), brother of Louis X
1322 Charles IV (the Fair), brother of Louis X

House of Valois

1328 Philip VI (of Valois), grandson of Philip III
1350 John II (the Good), son, retired to England
1364 Charles V (the Wise), son
1380 Charles VI (the Beloved), son
1422 Charles VII (the Victorious), son. In 1429, Joan of Arc (Jeanne d'Arc) defeated English at Orleans and Patay and had Charles crowned at Reims, July 17. Joan was captured May 24, 1430, and executed May 30, 1431, at Rouen for heresy. Charles ordered her rehabilitation, effected 1455.
1461 Louis XI (the Cruel), son, civil reformer
1483 Charles VIII (the Affable), son
1498 Louis XII, great-grandson of Charles V
1515 Francis I, of Angouleme, nephew, son-in-law. Fought four major wars, was patron of the arts
1547 Henry II, son, killed at joust. Husband of Catherine de Médicis and lover of Diane de Poitiers. Catherine was daughter of Lorenzo de Medici. By marriage to Henry II, she became the mother of Francis II, Charles IX, Henry III, and Queen Margaret (Reine Margot), wife of Henry IV (of Navarre).

1559 Francis II, son. Betrothed in 1548 at age 4 to Mary, Queen of Scots, aged 6; they were married 1558. Francis died 1560, aged 16. Mary returned to rule Scotland, 1561.
1560 Charles IX, brother
1574 Henry III, brother, assassinated

House of Bourbon

1589 Henry IV (of Navarre), grandson of Queen Margaret of Navarre. Made enemies when he gave tolerance to Protestants by Edict of Nantes, 1598. Married Margaret of Valois, daughter of Henry II and Catherine de Médicis; was divorced. Married Marie de Médicis, 1600. She became regent upon Henry's assassination, 1610-17, for her son, Louis XIII; she was exiled by Richelieu, 1631.
1610 Louis XIII (the Just), son, married Anne of Austria. His chief minister (1622-42), Cardinal Richelieu, determined his policies.
1643 Louis XIV (the Sun King), son; was king 72 years. Until 1661, Anne of Austria was regent with Cardinal Mazarin as chief minister; Louis then ruled absolutely. Known for his lavish style and arts patronage, he exhausted a prosperous country in wars for thrones and territory.
1715 Louis XV (the Beloved), great-grandson. Married a Polish princess, lost Canada to the English. His favorite mistresses, Mme. de Pompadour and Mme. Du Barry, influenced policies. Mme. Pompadour's saying "Après moi, le déluge" (After me, the deluge) often incorrectly attributed to Louis XV
1774 Louis XVI, grandson, married Marie Antoinette, daughter of Empress Maria Therese of Austria. King and queen beheaded by Revolution, 1793. Their son, called Louis XVII, died in prison, never ruled

First Republic

1792 National Convention of the French Revolution
1795 Directory, under Viscount of Barras and others
1799 Consulate, Napoleon Bonaparte, first consul. Elected consul for life, 1802

First Empire

1804 Napoleon I (Napoleon Bonaparte), emperor. Josephine (de Beauharnais), empress, 1804-09; Marie Louise, empress, 1810-14. Son, Napoleon II (1811-32), titular king of Rome, later duke of Reichstadt, never ruled. Napoleon I abdicated 1814; died in exile, 1821.

House of Bourbon (restored)

1814 Louis XVIII, brother of Louis XVI, king
1824 Charles X, brother, reactionary, deposed by the July Revolution, 1830

House of Orleans

1830 Louis-Philippe (the Citizen King)

Second Republic

1848 Louis Napoleon Bonaparte, nephew of Napoleon I, president

Second Empire

1852 Napoleon III (Louis Napoleon Bonaparte), emperor; Eugenie (de Montijo), empress. Lost Franco-Prussian war, deposed 1870. Son, Prince Imperial (1856-79), died in Zulu War. Eugenie died 1920.

Third Republic

1871 Louis Adolphe Thiers (1797-1877), president
1873 Marshal Patrice M. de MacMahon (1808-93)
1879 Paul J. Grevy (1807-91)
1887 M. Sadi-Carnot (1837-94), assassinated
1894 Jean P. P. Casimir-Perier (1847-1907)
1895 François Felix Faure (1841-99)
1899 Emile Loubet (1838-1929)
1906 C. Armand Fallieres (1841-1931)
1913 Raymond Poincaré (1860-1934)
1920 Paul Deschanel (1856-1922)
1920 Alexandre Millerand (1859-1943)
1924 Gaston Doumergue (1863-1937)
1931 Paul Doumer (1857-1932), assassinated
1932 Albert Lebrun (1871-1950), resigned 1940

Vichy Regime

1940 Henri Philippe Petain (1856-1951), chief of state, 1940-44, under German armistice

Provisional Government

1944 Charles Andre J. M. de Gaulle (1890-1970)
1946 Felix Gouin (1884-1977)
1946 Georges Bidault (1899-1983)

Fourth Republic

1947 Vincent Auriol (1884-1966), president
1954 Rene Coty (1882-1962)

Fifth Republic

1959 Charles Andre J. M. De Gaulle (1890-1970), president
1969 Georges Pompidou (1911-74)
1974 Valéry Giscard d'Estaing (1926-)
1981 François Mitterrand (1916-96)
1995 Jacques Chirac (1932-)
2007 Nicolas Sarkozy (1955-)
2012 François Hollande (1954-)

Rulers of Middle Europe and Germany

Carolingian Dynasty

Charles I (the Great), or Charlemagne, made Roman emperor by pope in Rome, 800. Ruled France, Italy, and Middle Europe; established Ostmark (later Austria). Died 814.

Louis I (Ludwig) (the Pious), son, crowned co-emperor by Charlemagne, 813. Divided empire among sons. Died 840; sons fought for control.

Louis II (the German), son, succeeded to East Francia (Germany), 843-76, with Treaty of Verdun.

Charles III (the Fat), son, inherited Swabia, 876. With brothers' deaths, acquired East Francia and West Francia (France), reuniting empire. Crowned emperor by pope, 881; deposed 887.

Arnulf, nephew, 887-99, took over East Francia; partition of empire.

Louis IV (the Child), son, 900-11, last direct descendant of Charlemagne.

Conrad I, duke of Franconia, first elected German king, 911-18.

Saxon Dynasty; First Reich

Henry I (the Fowler), duke of Saxony, elected king 919-36.

Otto I (the Great), son, 936-73, crowned Holy Roman Emperor by pope, 962.

Otto II, son, 961-83, ruled with Otto I as king, then emperor, 967.

Otto III, son, 983-1002, crowned Holy Roman Emperor, 996.

Henry II (the Saint), great-grandson of Otto the Great, duke of Bavaria, 1002-24. Crowned emperor, 1014.

Salian Dynasty

Conrad II, 1024-39, elected king of Germany.

Henry III (the Black), son, 1039-56, deposed three popes; annexed Burgundy.

Henry IV, son, 1056-1106, with mother, Agnes of Poitou, as regent in early years. He and Pope Gregory VII tried to depose each other. Civil war lasted about 20 years.

Henry V, son, 1106-25, last of Salian Dynasty.

Lothair, duke of Saxony, elected king 1125-37. Crowned emperor in Rome, 1133.

Hohenstaufen Dynasty

Conrad III, duke of Franconia, 1138-52, in Second Crusade.

Frederick I (Barbarossa, Italian for "Redbeard"), nephew, 1152-90.

Henry VI, son, 1190-97, gained kingdom of Sicily through marriage.

Philip of Swabia, brother, 1197-1208. Otto IV, nephew of King Richard I of England, 1198-1215, was elected rival king. Philip's murder, in 1208, led to Otto's win in new election same year. Civil war followed before Otto was deposed, 1215.

Frederick II, son of Henry VI, elected 1212-50. Had earlier succeeded father as king of Sicily; crowned himself king of Jerusalem, 1229, in Sixth Crusade.

Conrad IV, son, 1250-54. Conquered Naples.

(Interregnum, 1254-73. Conradin, son of Conrad IV and last legitimate Hohenstaufen, defeated by Charles of Anjou—brother of King Louis IX of France—and executed, 1268. Rise of electors of German monarch.)

Transition

Rudolf I, of Hapsburg, 1273-91, defeated King Ottocar II of Bohemia, 1278. Bequeathed duchies of Austria and Styria to sons.

Adolf of Nassau, 1292-98, killed in war with Albert I.

Albert I, elder son of Rudolf I, 1298-1308, assassinated.

Henry VII, of Luxemburg, 1308-13. Gained Bohemia, 1310; crowned Holy Roman Emperor, 1312.

Louis IV, of Wittelsbach, 1314-46. Also elected was a son of Albert I, Frederick of Austria, whom Louis defeated in 1322. Rejected need for papal confirmation of elected German king.

Charles IV, of Luxemburg, grandson of Henry VII, 1346-78. Took Brandenburg.

Wenceslaus, son, 1378-1400; deposed.

Rupert, of Wittelsbach, elector palatine, 1400-10.

Sigismund, brother of Wenceslaus, 1410-37.

Hapsburg Dynasty

Albert II, duke of Austria, son-in-law of Sigismund, elected German king, 1438-39; king of Hungary and Holy Roman Emperor.

Frederick III, cousin, 1440-93, fought Turks.

Maximilian I, son, 1493-1519, archduke of Austria.

Charles V, grandson, 1519-58. King of Spain; assumed title of Holy Roman Emperor. Martin Luther, who had been excommunicated by pope, appeared at Diet of Worms, 1521. Charles attempted church reform and conciliation between Catholicism and Protestantism; abdicated.

Ferdinand I, brother, 1558-64; king of Hungary and Bohemia, 1526 (successive leaders through Maria Theresa will rule these lands as well).

Maximilian II, son, 1564-76.

Rudolf II, son, 1576-1612.

Matthias, brother, 1612-19.

Ferdinand II, grandson of Ferdinand I, 1619-37. Bohemian Protestants, unhappy with Ferdinand's support of Catholic Counter-Reformation, crowned Frederick V, elector palatine. Frederick became known as "Winter King" with defeat in battle, 1620; start of Thirty Years' War.

Ferdinand III, son, 1637-57. Treaties signed, 1648, in Peace of Westphalia ended war.

Leopold I, son, 1658-1705.

Joseph I, son, 1705-11.

Charles VI, brother, 1711-40; died without male heir.

Maria Theresa, daughter, 1740-80. Appointed husband, Francis Stephen of Lorraine, co-regent. Dispute over her inheritance led to War of the Austrian Succession. Charles VII, also known as Charles Albert, elected in opposition to Francis, 1742-45. After Charles's death, Maria Theresa obtained election of her husband as Holy Roman Emperor Francis I, 1745-65. Fought Seven Years' War with Frederick II of Prussia.

Hapsburg-Lorraine Dynasty

Joseph II, son, 1765-90, reformer. Ruled jointly with Maria Theresa until her death. Participated in first partition of Poland, with Prussia and Russia.

Leopold II, brother, 1790-92; king of Hungary and Bohemia.

Francis II, son, 1792-1806; king of Hungary and Bohemia. Proclaimed first emperor of Austria, 1804-35. Unsuccessfully fought against Napoleon; forced to abdicate, 1806, as Holy Roman Emperor, last use of title.

Ferdinand, son, 1835-48; emperor of Austria; king of Hungary and Bohemia. Abdicated in favor of nephew after revolution broke out in Vienna.

Austro-Hungarian Monarchy

Francis Joseph I, nephew, 1848-1916, emperor of Austria and king of Hungary. Defeated in Austro-Prussian War, 1866. Formed dual monarchy of Austria-Hungary, 1867. After Serbian nationalist assassinated Francis Joseph's nephew and heir, Archduke Francis Ferdinand, June 28, 1914, Austrian diplomacy precipitated World War I.

Charles I, grandnephew, 1916-18, last emperor of Austria and king of Hungary. Abdicated Nov. 1918; died in exile, 1922.

Second and Third Reichs

William I, brother of Frederick William IV, 1861-88, king of Prussia. Appointed Otto von Bismarck chancellor, 1862. Franco-Prussian War, also known as Franco-German War, 1870-71, unified German states. William proclaimed German emperor, 1871; beginning of Second Reich.

Frederick III, son, 1888.

William II, son, 1888-1918, led Germany into World War I. Abdicated Nov. 1918; died in exile in the Netherlands, 1941.

Germany adopted constitution at Weimar, July 1, 1919, setting up Weimar Republic. Presidents included Friedrich Ebert, 1919-25, and Paul von Hindenburg, 1925-34, field marshal in World War I. Hindenburg appointed Adolf Hitler chancellor, 1933, at beginning of Third Reich. Following Hindenburg's death, Hitler succeeded as Führer and chancellor, 1934-45, with dictatorial powers. Annexed Austria, 1938. Precipitated World War II, 1939-45. Hitler committed suicide, 1945.

Germany After 1945

After World War II, Germany was split between democratic West and Soviet-dominated East. West German chancellors: Konrad Adenauer, 1949-63; Ludwig Erhard, 1963-66; Kurt Georg Kiesinger, 1966-69; Willy Brandt, 1969-74; Helmut Schmidt, 1974-82; Helmut Kohl, 1982-90. East German Communist party leaders: Walter Ulbricht, 1950-71; Erich Honecker, 1971-89; Egon Krenz, 1989. (Berlin Wall fell, Nov. 1989.)

Germany reunited Oct. 3, 1990. Post-reunification chancellors: Helmut Kohl, 1990-98; Gerhard Schröder, 1998-2005; Angela Merkel, 2005- .

Rulers of Hungary

The first king of Hungary was Stephen I, of the Arpad Dynasty, 1000-38. Feuds followed his death.

Charles I, also known as Charles Robert, became king, 1308-42.

Louis I (the Great), son, 1342-82. Succeeded uncle Casimir III as ruler of Poland, 1370.

Mary, elder daughter, 1382-95, ruled with husband, Sigismund of Luxemburg, 1387-1437, who also became king of Bohemia, Germany and Holy Roman Emperor. Hedwig (Jadwiga), younger daughter of Louis I, became queen of Poland. (See **Rulers of Poland**.)

Albert II, duke of Austria, son-in-law of Sigismund, 1438-39. Also king of Germany and Holy Roman Emperor.

Vladislaus I, 1440-44, king of Poland.

Ladislaus V, posthumous son of Albert II, 1444-57, not crowned until 1453. Janos Hunyadi acted as governor under young king, 1446-52; fought Turks.

Matthias I (Corvinus), son of Janos Hunyadi, 1458-90. Shared title of king of Bohemia. Captured Vienna, 1485; annexed Styria, Carinthia.

Vladislaus II, 1490-1516, king of Bohemia.

Louis II, son, 1516-26. Died in Battle of Mohács against Suleiman (the Magnificent), head of Ottoman Empire.

Ferdinand I, of Austria, brother-in-law, and John I, also known as John Zapolya of Transylvania, elected rival kings. Suleiman claimed part of Hungary for Ottoman Empire. Hungary partitioned. (Refer to **Hapsburg Dynasty** for continuation.)

Rulers of Prussia

Nucleus of Prussia was the margravate of Brandenburg, an electorate of the Holy Roman Empire. Frederick VI, burgrave of Nuremberg, was made elector of Brandenburg, 1415. Rise of Hohenzollern Dynasty in territory that included Brandenburg and duchy of Prussia.

Frederick William (the Great Elector), 1640-88, elector of Brandenburg.

Frederick III, son, 1688-1713, elector of Brandenburg. Crowned Frederick I, king in Prussia, 1701.

Frederick William I, son, 1713-40.

Frederick II (the Great), son, 1740-86; military strategist who expanded Prussia's holdings.

Frederick William II, nephew, 1786-97.

Frederick William III, son, 1797-1840; Napoleonic Wars.

Frederick William IV, son, 1840-61. Revolution of 1848; constitution adopted, 1850. (Refer to **Second and Third Reichs** for continuation.)

Rulers of Poland

House of Piast

Mieszko I, c. 963-92, duke of Poland; Poland Christianized, 966. Expansion under three with name Boleslaus (reigns not consecutive): Boleslaus I (the Brave), son, 992-1025, crowned first king of Poland, 1025; Boleslaus II (the Bold), great-grandson, 1058-79, exiled after killing bishop of Krakow, Stanislaus (who became a patron saint of Poland); Boleslaus III (the Wry-Mouthed), nephew, 1102-38, divided Poland among four sons with oldest also in control of crown. Period of feudal division followed.

A Polish duke, Conrad of Masovia, asked the Teutonic Knights—a German military religious order—to crusade against Prussia, 1226. Teutonic Knights conquered lands; thereafter warred with Poland. Mongols/Tatars invaded Poland, 1241.

Vladislaus I, 1306-33, reunited most Polish territories; crowned king, 1320. Casimir III (the Great), son, 1333-70, developed economy, cultural life, foreign policy. No male heir. Succeeded by Louis I, nephew, 1370-82, who was also Louis I (the Great) of Hungary.

Jadwiga, daughter, 1384-99.

House of Jagiello

Vladislaus Jagiello, grand duke of Lithuania, married Jadwiga, 1386, and ruled jointly as Vladislaus II, 1386-1434. Poland and Lithuania united; Lithuania converted to Christianity. Defeated Teutonic Knights at Grunwald (Tannenberg), 1410.

Vladislaus III, son, 1434-44, also king of Hungary. Fought Turks; killed in Battle of Varna, 1444.

Casimir IV, brother, 1447-92, put son Vladislaus on throne of Bohemia and Hungary. Victorious over Teutonic Knights; signed treaty, 1466, after 13-year war.

John I, son, 1492-1501.

Alexander I, brother, 1501-05.

Sigismund I, brother, 1506-48, patronized sciences and arts; his and son's reign were golden age. Grand Master of Teutonic Order, Albert Hohenzollern, converted to Protestantism; secularized his state and made first duke of Prussia by Sigismund, 1525.

Sigismund II, son, 1548-72; Union of Lublin, 1569, established dual state of Poland and Lithuania. No male heir.

Elective Kings

Henry of Valois, 1573-74, first king elected by nobility. Left Poland to assume crown of France after brother's death. Interregnum.

Stephen Bathory, 1576-86, prince of Transylvania, married Anna, sister of Sigismund II. Fought Russians.

Sigismund III Vasa, nephew of Sigismund II and son of king of Sweden, 1587-1632. Fought to reclaim Swedish crown, which he'd lost because of his Catholicism; battled Russians and Turks.

Vladislaus IV Vasa, son, 1632-48.

John II Casimir Vasa, brother, 1648-68. Fought Cossacks, Swedish, Russians, Turks, Tatars; period of invasions known as "the Deluge."

Michael Korybut Wisniowiecki, 1669-73.

John III Sobieski, 1674-96, freed Vienna from besieging Turks, 1683.

Augustus II (the Strong), 1697-1733, elector of Saxony.

Augustus III, son, 1733-63, elector of Saxony.

Stanislaus II, 1764-95, last king. Encouraged reforms; first modern constitution in Europe, 1791. Poland lost territory to Russia, Austria, and Prussia in three partitions (1772, 1793, 1795). Thaddeus Kosciusko, American-Polish general, attempted unsuccessful insurrection, 1794.

Poland Under Foreign Rule

Grand duchy of Warsaw created by Napoleon I out of Prussian (formerly Polish) territory. Frederick Augustus I, king of Saxony, ruled grand duchy, 1807-15. Defeat of Napoleon led to Congress of Vienna, 1814-15; part of Poland claimed as kingdom by Russia. Polish uprisings against Russia (1830, 1863) and Austria (1846) repressed. Poland regained independence following World War I.

Second Republic

Jozef Pilsudski, 1918-22, head of state. Presidents: Gabriel Narutowicz, 1922, assassinated by extremist; Stanislaus Wojciechowski, 1922-26, resigned after coup d'état by Pilsudski; Ignacy Moscicki, 1926-39, ruled with Pilsudski (d. 1935) and Pilsudski's military colleagues as virtual dictator during what came to be known as Sanacja (meaning "cleansing" or "healing") regime.

Poland Under Foreign Occupation, Influence

After Hitler and Stalin signed nonaggression pact, Germany invaded Poland Sept. 1, 1939; Russia invaded Sept. 17. Polish government-in-exile was in France, then England. Vladislaus Raczkiewicz, 1939-47, president; Gen. Vladislaus Sikorski, 1939-43, and Stanislaus Mikolajczyk, 1943-44, prime ministers. Polish residents were sent to German concentration camps and Soviet labor camps; about 3 million Jewish Poles were killed in the Holocaust. Thousands of Polish prisoners of war, mostly military officers, massacred in Katyn Forest by Soviet secret police, 1940. Soviet-sponsored Polish Committee of National Liberation took formative role in new government, 1945, renamed Polish People's Republic in 1952. Communist Polish United Workers' Party ruled the country. Brief period of liberalization followed Stalin's death in 1953. Vladislaus Gomulka, 1956-70, and Edward Gierek, 1970-80, led country as first secretary of Polish United Workers' Party.

Election of Cardinal Karol Wojtyla, archbishop of Krakow, as pope (John Paul II) inspired Poles, 1978. Strikes in 1980 prompted creation of Solidarity, an independent trade union headed by Lech Walesa. Solidarity gained control of government in partly free elections, 1985.

Third Republic

Presidents: Lech Walesa, 1990-95; Aleksander Kwasniewski, 1995-2005; Lech Kaczynski, 2005-10, died in plane crash; Bronislaus Komorowski and Grzegorz Schetyna, acting, 2010; Komorowski, 2010-15; Andrzej Duda, 2015- .

Rulers of Denmark, Sweden, Norway

Denmark

Canute (the Great) ruled area that included England, Denmark, and Norway, 1016-35. Valdemar IV Atterdag reunited Denmark, 1361. Margaret I, daughter, married to Haakon VI, king of Norway, 1363. After Valdemar's death, Olaf, Margaret's infant son, made king of Denmark, 1375. He was also crowned king of Norway after death of Haakon, 1380. Following Olaf's death, 1387, Margaret served as regent of Denmark, Norway, and Sweden. She effected the Union of Kalmar of the three kingdoms, 1397. She had her grandnephew, Eric of Pomerania, crowned (she held actual power until her death, 1412).

Succeeding rulers were unable to enforce their claims on Sweden until Christian II, 1512-23, conquered the country, 1520. He was soon deposed; accession of Gustavus I as king of Sweden, 1523, ended Kalmar Union. Denmark continued to dominate Norway until the Napoleonic Wars when Frederick VI, 1808-39, allied with Napoleon I after Danish fleet was attacked by Britain, 1807. By 1814 treaty, Denmark was forced to cede Norway to Sweden.

Succession: House of Oldenborg (began with Christian I, 1448): Christian VIII, 1839-48; Frederick VII, son, 1848-63. House of Glücksborg: Christian IX, 1863-1906; Frederick VIII, son, 1906-12; Christian X, son, 1912-47; Frederick IX, son, 1947-72; Margrethe II, daughter, 1972- .

Sweden

Under King Magnus Ladulas, hereditary nobility established around 1280. Swedish nobles opposed to Albert of Mecklenburg accepted Margaret I, regent of Denmark, as ruler, 1389. Sweden joined Kalmar Union, 1397. After internal unrest, Sweden was conquered anew by Denmark's Christian II, 1520. Execution of Christian's opponents in "Stockholm Bloodbath" led to uprising under Gustavus Vasa, who was elected Swedish king, 1523-60. Gustavus established an independent kingdom with centralized power, state church, and hereditary throne.

Gustavus II Adolphus (Lion of the North), 1611-32, fought Russia, Poland, Germany; died in battle.

Later rulers: Christina, daughter, 1632-54, abdicated; Charles X Gustavus, cousin, 1654-60; Charles XI, son, 1660-97; Charles XII, son, 1697-1718; Ulrika Eleonora, sister, 1718-20, abdicated; Frederick I, of Hesse, husband, 1720-51; Adolphus Frederick, 1751-71; Gustavus III, son, 1771-92; Gustavus IV Adolphus, son, 1792-1809, deposed; Charles XIII, uncle, 1809-18. Charles XIV John (born Jean Baptiste Bernadotte, a general under Napoleon I), 1818-44, founded House of Bernadotte.

Succession: Oscar I, son, 1844-59; Charles XV, son, 1859-72; Oscar II, brother, 1872-1907; Gustavus V, son, 1907-50; Gustavus VI Adolf, son, 1950-73; Carl XVI Gustavus, grandson, 1973- .

Norway

Harald I (Fairhair) overcame rivals to become first king of Norway, c. 885-c. 933. Olaf II Haraldsson, 1015-28, Christianized country; became patron saint of Norway. Haakon V Magnusson, 1299-1319, died without male heir. His daughter Ingeborg was married to Erik, a son of the Norwegian king; their son Magnus VII Eriksson became ruler of Norway, 1319-55, and Sweden, 1319-63. Haakon VI Magnusson, son, 1355-80, married Margaret of Denmark. Olaf IV, son, became king of Norway, 1380-87, and Denmark, 1375-87, with mother as regent. Margaret took over rule upon his death, 1387. Union of Kalmar, 1397, united Norway, Denmark, and Sweden.

After Napoleonic Wars, Denmark ceded Norway to Sweden, 1814. A strong nationalist movement forced Sweden to recognize Norway as an independent kingdom under the Swedish kings. Norwegian constitution, adopted 1814, allowed for creation of the Storting (Norwegian parliament), which governed country domestically. In 1905, the union was dissolved. Prince Charles of Denmark elected king of Norway as Haakon VII, 1905-57; founded House of Glücksburg. Succession: Olav V, son, 1957-91; Harald V, son, 1991- .

Rulers of the Netherlands and Belgium

The Netherlands

William I, son of Prince William V of Orange, came to power after French rule ended in the Netherlands, 1813; crowned king with approval of Congress of Vienna, 1815. Started House of Orange-Nassau. Northern Netherlands was known as Holland. Belgians, in southern Netherlands, rebelled against the Dutch and seceded, Oct. 4, 1830. Dutch formally recognized Belgian independence, Apr. 19, 1839. William I abdicated, 1840.

Succession: William II, son, 1840-49; William III, son, 1849-90; Wilhelmina, daughter, 1890-1948; Juliana, daughter, 1948-80; Beatrix, daughter, 1980-2013; Willem-Alexander, son, 2013- .

Belgium

A national congress elected Prince Leopold of Saxe-Coburg as king. He took the throne July 21, 1831, as Leopold I.

Succession: Leopold II, son, 1865-1909; Albert I, nephew, 1909-34; Leopold III, son, 1934-51, in exile after Germany invaded Belgium, later abdicated; Prince Charles, brother, acted as regent 1944-50; Baudouin I, son of Leopold III, 1951-93; Albert II, brother, 1993-2013; Philippe, son, 2013- .

Rulers of Modern Italy

After the fall of Napoleon, the Congress of Vienna, 1814-15, restored Italy as a political patchwork, comprising the Kingdom of the Two Sicilies (Naples and Sicily), the Papal States, and smaller units. King Victor Emmanuel I of Savoy ruled Sardinia, Piedmont, and Genoa.

Victor Emmanuel I abdicated 1821. Charles Felix, brother, 1821-31, died without issue. Succeeded by Charles Albert, 1831-49; he abdicated upon defeat by the Austrians. Succeeded by Victor Emmanuel II, son, 1849-61. United Italy emerged under Camillo Benso di Cavour, prime minister of the Kingdom of Sardinia, 1852-61. Giuseppe Mazzini and Giuseppe Garibaldi were also figures in Risorgimento ("resurgence") period before Italy's unification.

In 1859, France forced Austria to cede Lombardy to Sardinia. In 1860, Garibaldi led more than 1,000 volunteers in a campaign against King Francis II of the Two Sicilies, taking Sicily and Naples. The House of Savoy subsequently annexed the Two Sicilies, Tuscany, Parma, Modena, Romagna, the Marches, and Umbria. Victor Emmanuel II assumed leadership of a united Kingdom of Italy, Mar. 17, 1861.

In 1866, Victor Emmanuel II allied with Prussia in the Austro-Prussian War and, with Prussia's victory, received Venetia. On Sept. 20, 1870, Italian troops entered Rome, ending the temporal power of the Roman Catholic Church. (The 1929 Lateran Treaty established papal sovereignty in Vatican City.)

Succession: Umberto I, son, 1878-1900, assassinated; Victor Emmanuel III, son, 1900-46; Umberto II, son, 1946, ruled a month. In 1919, Benito Mussolini helped found the nationalist Fasci di Combattimento (Fighting Leagues), or Fascists. After Mussolini organized March on Rome, 1922, Victor Emmanuel III agreed to a coalition government. Mussolini eventually became dictator (Il Duce). He entered World War II as an ally of Hitler, 1940. He was dismissed by the king, 1943; executed, 1945.

At a plebiscite, 1946, voters approved a republic. Prime minister Alcide de Gasperi was chief of state, 1945-53; Enrico de Nicola was provisional president. Successive presidents: Luigi Einaudi, 1948-55; Giovanni Gronchi, 1955-62; Antonio Segni, 1962-64; Giuseppe Saragat, 1964-71; Giovanni Leone, 1971-78; Alessandro Pertini, 1978-85; Francesco Cossiga, 1985-92; Oscar Luigi Scalfaro, 1992-99; Carlo Azeglio Ciampi, 1999-2006; Giorgio Napolitano, 2006-15; Sergio Mattarella, 2015- .

Rulers of Spain

From 8th to 11th centuries, Spain was dominated by the Moors (Muslims from North Africa of Arab and Berber origin). A number of small kingdoms—Aragon, Asturias, Castile, Catalonia, Leon, Navarre, and Valencia—undertook a Christian reconquest. In 1474, Isabella I became Queen of Castile and Leon. By the Catholic Monarchs' request, Pope Sixtus IV authorized the Inquisition, 1478. Isabella's husband, Ferdinand V, acceded to the throne of Aragon, 1479. Last Moorish kingdom, Granada, seized 1492. Spain sponsored Christopher Columbus, who led European exploration of New World, 1492. Isabella was succeeded by daughter, Joanna (the Mad), but Ferdinand acted as regent until his death, 1516.

Charles I, son of Joanna and grandson of Hapsburg Emperor Maximilian I, became Holy Roman Emperor as Charles V, 1520;

abdicated 1556. Philip II, son, 1556-98, inherited only part of empire. He conquered Portugal, fought against Ottoman Empire, sent Armada in unsuccessful invasion of England. Succession: Philip III, son, 1598-1621; Philip IV, son, 1621-65; Charles II, son, 1665-1700, no issue, left Spain to Philip of Anjou, grandson of Louis XIV of France. As Philip V, he was first of Bourbon dynasty in Spain, 1700-46 (his son Louis ruled briefly in 1724); Ferdinand VI, son, 1746-59; Charles III, brother, 1759-88; Charles IV, son, 1788-1808, abdicated.

Joseph Bonaparte made king of Spain, 1808-13, by his brother Napoleon. Ferdinand VII, son of Charles IV, 1808, 1814-33, lost American colonies except Cuba, Puerto Rico. Maria Christina of the Two Sicilies, wife, was regent until 1843 for Isabella II, daughter, who was driven into exile by revolution, 1868. Amadeo of Savoy elected king by the Cortes (parliament), 1870-73. First Republic, 1873-74. Alfonso XII, son of Isabella II, 1875-85; Alfonso XIII, posthumous son, 1901-31, with mother Maria Christina as regent before he assumed throne. Spain ceded territory after loss in Spanish-American War, 1898. Primo de Rivera ruled as dictator after military coup but was forced to resign after losing support, 1923-30. Alfonso agreed to exile without formal abdication. Monarchy abolished; Second Republic established with socialist backing. Presidents: Niceto Alcala Zamora, 1931-36; Manuel Azaña, 1936-39.

Revolt by military started Spanish Civil War, 1936-39. Gen. Francisco Franco ruled as head of Nationalist regime, 1939-73. Monarchy restored after 1947 referendum. Juan Carlos, grandson of Alfonso XIII, acceded to throne after Franco's death in 1975; abdicated, 2014. Felipe VI, son, 2014- .

Leaders in the South American Wars of Liberation

Francisco de Miranda, José de San Martín, and Simón Bolívar led early 19th-cent. struggles of South American nations to free themselves from Spain.

Miranda (1750-1816), a Venezuelan, served as an officer in the Spanish army. After a dispute with the army, he fled to the U.S., 1783, where he met leaders of the American Revolution. He traveled seeking support for South American independence from other world leaders. Miranda unsuccessfully attempted a revolt in Venezuela, 1806. Napoleon's invasion of Spain, 1808, prompted the start of a revolution in Venezuela. Miranda returned, 1810, and headed the revolution with dictatorial powers. Venezuela declared independence, 1811. Overcome by royalist forces, 1812, Miranda surrendered and was arrested; he died in a Spanish prison.

San Martín (1778-1850) was born in present-day Argentina. He served in Spanish campaigns in Europe until 1811. He returned to Argentina and joined the independence movement, 1812. In 1817, he invaded Chile through the Andean mountain passes. He and Bernardo O'Higgins defeated the Spanish at Chacabuco, 1817. Chile gained independence, 1819; O'Higgins became first director of Chile, 1817-23. In 1821, San Martín entered Lima and took the port of Callao; he became protector of an independent Peru.

Bolívar (1783-1830) was born into an aristocratic family in Venezuela. He served under Miranda until Miranda's surrender in 1812. Bolívar continued to fight; he captured Caracas and was named Liberator, 1813. But he was forced to flee by royalist forces, 1814. In 1817, Bolívar again fought for control of Venezuela. With Francisco de Paula Santander and José Antonio Páez, he defeated the Spanish at the Battle of Boyacá, 1819, freeing New Granada (present-day Colombia). New Granada, Venezuela, and the area that is now Panama and Ecuador were joined as the Republic of Colombia, or Gran Colombia, with Bolívar as president later that same year, though parts of the republic remained under Spanish control. He decisively defeated the Spanish in the Battle of Carabobo in Venezuela, 1821.

Antonio José de Sucre, Bolívar's chief lieutenant, overcame Spanish forces at the Battle of Pichincha in Ecuador, 1822. Bolívar convinced San Martín to resign as protector of Peru. Peru was declared independent after Bolívar and Sucre won the Battle of Junin, Aug. 1824, and Sucre triumphed at the Battle of Ayacucho, Dec. 1824.

Sucre organized Upper Peru as Republica Bolívar (now Bolivia), 1825, and acted as president in place of Bolívar, who wrote its constitution.

Civil strife caused the Colombian federation to break apart. Bolívar gave up the presidency, 1830.

Rulers of Russia; Leaders of the USSR and Russian Federation

The Varangian (Viking) prince Rurik is considered to be the first leader of the Russians; he established himself at Novgorod, c. 862 CE. His successor, Oleg, and those who followed Oleg ruled as princes of Kiev. Vladimir I, or Saint Vladimir, married sister of Byzantine emperor and converted to Christianity, 988. Yaroslav I (the Wise), brother, 1019-54, was important organizer and lawgiver; his daughters married kings of Norway, Hungary, and France. In 1169, Andrew Bogolyubsky conquered Kiev and began the line of Vladimir.

Daniel, a son of grand prince of Vladimir, Alexander Nevsky, was first to be called prince of Muscovy (Moscow), 1263-1303. Dmitri Ivanovich (Donskoi), prince of Moscow, defeated the Tatars at the Battle of Kulikovo, 1380. His successors were grand princes of Moscow. Ivan III (the Great), 1462-1505, achieved considerable territorial expansion.

Ivan III married Sofia Palaeologus, niece of the last Byzantine emperor. Succession: Vasily III, son. Ivan IV (the Terrible), son, crowned 1547 as Tsar of Russia. Fyodor I, son, reigned 1584-98, but his brother-in-law Boris Godunov had real control before becoming tsar himself, 1598-1605. After years of internal strife ("Time of Troubles"), the Russians united under 16-year-old Michael Romanov, distantly related to Ivan IV's first wife. He ruled 1613-45, establishing the Romanov line.

Tsars, or emperors, of Russia (Romanovs): Peter I (the Great), 1682-1725, with Ivan V, brother, as co-ruler, 1682-96. Catherine I, his widow, 1725-27. Peter II, grandson of Peter I, 1727-30. Anna, daughter of Ivan V and niece of Peter I, 1730-40. Ivan VI, nephew, 1740-41; deposed by Elizabeth, daughter of Peter I, 1741-62. Peter III, nephew, 1762; deposed by his wife, Catherine II (the Great), former princess of Anhalt Zerbst (Germany), 1762-96. Paul I, son, 1796-1801, assassinated. Alexander I, son, 1801-25, defeated Napoleon. Nicholas I, brother, 1825-55. Alexander II, son, 1855-81, assassinated. Alexander III, son, 1881-94. Nicholas II, son, 1894-1917, last tsar of Russia, was forced to abdicate by revolutionaries following losses to Germany in WWI. The tsar, empress, tsarevich (crown prince), and tsar's four daughters were murdered by the Bolsheviks, July 1918.

Premiers of provisional government: Prince Georgi Lvov, followed by Alexander Kerensky, 1917.

Union of Soviet Socialist Republics

Bolshevik Revolution, Nov. 7, 1917, (also known as the October Revolution, based on Russia's then use of the Julian calendar) removed Kerensky from power. Council of People's Commissars formed with Lenin (Vladimir Ilyich Ulyanov) as chair (or premier), 1917-24. Aleksei Rykov (executed 1938) and Vyacheslav M. Molotov held the office, but effective ruler was Joseph Stalin (Joseph Vissarionovich Dzhugashvili), general secretary of the Communist Party. Stalin was chair of the Council of People's Commissars from 1941 until his death in 1953. Succeeded by Georgi M. Malenkov, who also briefly served as general secretary of the Communist Party before being ousted from the position by Nikita S. Khrushchev. Malenkov was forced to resign as premier, 1955, and was expelled from the Communist Party, 1961. Nikolai A. Bulganin was premier, 1955-58, until his replacement by Khrushchev, 1958-64.

Leonid I. Brezhnev ousted Khrushchev as general secretary of the party, a post he held until his death in 1982. Aleksei N. Kosygin was premier, 1964-80. The Central Committee elected former KGB (state security) head Yuri V. Andropov general secretary, 1982-84. After Andropov's death, Konstantin U. Chernenko was chosen for the position, 1984-85. Upon Chernenko's death, he was succeeded by Mikhail Gorbachev. Gorbachev assumed the newly created position of president of the Soviet Union, 1990. Boris Yeltsin was sworn in July 1991 as the Russian Republic's first elected president. Under Yeltsin, Russia became a founding member of the Commonwealth of Independent States. Gorbachev resigned the presidency, Dec. 25, 1991, and the Soviet Union officially disbanded Dec. 31. Each of the 15 former Soviet constituent republics became independent.

Post-Soviet Russia

Presidents of the Russian Federation: Boris Yeltsin, 1991-99; Vladimir Putin, 2000-08; Dmitry Medvedev, 2008-12; Putin 2012- .

Rulers of China

Where dynastic dates overlap, the rulers or events referred to appeared in different areas of China.

Years in power	Dynasty/ruler(s)
c. 1994-c. 1766 BCE	Xia dynasty, first hereditary Chinese dynasty
c. 1766-c. 1045 BCE	Shang dynasty, first Chinese dynasty with historical records
c. 1045-771 BCE	Western Zhou dynasty, capital near present-day Xi'an
770-256 BCE	Eastern Zhou dynasty, new capital established at Luoyang. During Chunqiu (Spring and Autumn) period (722-481 BCE), Zhou began to lose authority. Period of the Warring States (403-221 BCE) involved major powers of Qi, Chu, Yan, Han, Zhao, Wei, and Qin
221-207 BCE	Qin dynasty, quasi-feudal states unified for first time. Prefectures and counties organized under central government with uniform laws and procedures
206 BCE-9 CE	Earlier, or Western Han dynasty, founded by rebel leader Liu Bang. Expansion under Emperor Wudi (born Liu Che), 140-87 BCE; civil service system established
9-23	Xin dynasty, established by Wang Mang, who deposed infant emperor for whom he was regent
25-220	Later, or Eastern Han dynasty
220-265[1]	Wei dynasty, established by son of Han general Cao Cao
221-263[1]	Shu Han dynasty in SW China
222-280[1]	Wu dynasty in SE China
265-317	Western Jin dynasty, established by Sima Yan, Wei dynasty general
317-420	Eastern Jin dynasty, established by prince of Sima family
420-589	Southern dynasties, four short-lived dynasties with capital at Jiankang (present-day Nanjing)
589-618	Sui dynasty, reunified China; established by Emperor Wendi (born Yang Jian), military appointee who usurped throne of non-Chinese Northern Zhou, 581
618-906	Tang dynasty, founded by Li Yuan (known as Emperor Gaozu of Tang), who led rebellion against the Sui. Notable rulers include former imperial concubine Empress Wu, 683-705; Xuanzong, 712-56
907-960	Five Dynasties. Period of disunion with short-lived dynasties in N; Ten Kingdoms (states) in S and W
907-1125	Liao dynasty, of Khitan Mongols, capital at Yanjing (present-day Beijing)
960-1126	Northern Song dynasty, established by military leader Zhao Kuangyin (Emperor Taizu), capital at Kaifeng
1122-1234	Jin dynasty, of Juchen people of Manchuria; drove Song out of N China
1127-1279	Southern Song dynasty, capital at Lin'an (present-day Hangzhou)
1279-1368	Yuan, or Mongol dynasty; Kublai Khan, grandson of Genghis Khan, high point of Mongol power
1368-1644	Ming dynasty, founded by Buddhist monk turned rebel general Zhu Yuanzhang. Country again under Chinese rule; capital in present-day Nanjing, then Beijing after Mongolian tribes' defeat
1644-1912	Qing, or Manchu dynasty, under rule of Manchu people. Height of power of Chinese empire to date. Last imperial dynasty; Emperor Xuantong, or Puyi, last emperor. Sun Yat-sen led revolution, 1911. Republic of China formed, 1912
1912-1949	Rep. of China, Gen. Yuan Shikai was first president. Power passed to provincial warlords upon his death, 1916. Gen. Chiang Kai-shek sought to reunify China under Kuomintang (Nationalist party), with new national government at Nanjing, 1928. War with Japan, then civil war, led to Nationalist authority collapse, Communist declaration of People's Rep. of China, 1949

(1) Also known as the period of the Three Kingdoms because of warfare between the Wei, Shu Han, and Wu dynasties.

Leaders of People's Republic of China

Name	Title/position, years in power
Mao Zedong	People's Rep. of China (PRC) Chairman, 1949-59; Chinese Communist Party (CCP) Chairman, 1949-76
Zhou Enlai	Premier, 1949-76
Liu Shaoqi	PRC Chairman, 1959-68; one-time Mao successor removed from power during Cultural Revolution (1966-76)
Lin Biao	Red Army commander designated Mao's successor, 1966; government reported his death in plane crash, 1971, after failed coup attempt
Hua Guofeng	Premier, 1976-80; CCP Chairman, 1976-81
Deng Xiaoping	"Paramount leader," 1977-97
Hu Yaobang	CCP General Secretary, 1980-87; CCP Chairman, 1981-82[1]
Zhao Ziyang	Premier, 1980-87; CCP General Secretary, 1987-89
Li Xiannian	President, 1983-88
Yang Shangkun	President, 1988-93
Li Peng	Premier, 1988-98
Jiang Zemin	CCP General Secretary, 1989-2002; President, 1993-2003
Zhu Rongji	Premier, 1998-2003
Hu Jintao	CCP General Secretary, 2002-12; President, 2003-13
Wen Jiabao	Premier, 2003-13
Xi Jinping	CCP General Secretary, 2012- ; President, 2013-
Li Keqiang	Premier, 2013-

(1) Position of CCP chairman was abolished in 1982, making the CCP general secretary the party's highest-ranking official.

Historical Periods of Japan

Years in power	Period	Founding event
c. 300-592	Yamato	Conquest of Yamato plain. Also called Tumulus, or Tomb, period for large mounds built during this time
592-710	Asuka	Accession of Empress Suiko; capital in Asuka region
710-794	Nara	Heijo (Nara) completed; capital moved to Nagaoka, 784
794-1185	Heian	Capital moved to Heian (present-day Kyoto) by Emperor Kammu
858-1160	Fujiwara	Fujiwara no Yoshifusa became regent for his grandson
1160-1185	Taira	Taira no Kiyomoro assumed control; Minamoto no Yoritomo defeated Taira, 1185
1192-1333	Kamakura	Yoritomo became shogun
1334-1392	Namboku	Emperor Godaigo returned to power in Kemmu Restoration; 1336 revolt drove him from Kyoto to establish Southern Court at Yoshino
1392-1573	Muromachi	Unification of Southern and Northern Courts
1467-1600	Sengoku	Onin War began; also known as Warring States period
1573-1603	Momoyama	Oda Nobunaga entered Kyoto, 1568, deposed last Ashikaga shogun, 1573. Tokugawa Ieyasu victor at Battle of Sekigahara, 1600
1603-1867	Edo	Ieyasu established Tokugawa shogunate, became shogun
1868-1912	Meiji	Meiji Restoration of imperial power, with Meiji (reign name of Mutsuhito) ascending throne; Charter Oath, 1868, led to Westernization
1912-1926	Taisho	Accession of Emperor Taisho (reign name of Yoshihito)
1926-1989	Showa	Accession of Emperor Hirohito (posthumous name Showa)
1989-	Heisei	Accession of Emperor Akihito

WORLD EXPLORATION AND GEOGRAPHY

Early Explorers of the Western Hemisphere

Genetic evidence suggests that beginning around 14,000 years before the present (BP), humans crossed the Bering Land Bridge between Siberia and Alaska and spread through the Americas, reaching S America's southern tip by c. 10,700 BP. The Anzick child (c. 12,600 BP), Kennewick Man (9,600-9,200 BP), and Luzia (11,500 BP) were some of these early arrivals. Modern Native Americans appear to be descended from peoples indigenous to N and Central Asia who arrived in subsequent waves. Remains from a burial in Brazil (8,000-10,000 BP) seem to suggest that some of those who crossed the land bridge may have originated in Africa.

Long before Europeans arrived, the Americas were populated mostly by hunter-gatherers and small-scale horticulturalists. Complex chiefdoms and state-level societies appeared in a few areas (SE U.S., Mesoamerica, coastal Chile). The earliest known state in the Americas spanned 700 sq mi across river valleys in coastal Peru between 3,500 and 500 BP.

The Norse, led by Leif Ericson, are usually credited as being the first Europeans to reach America, with at least five voyages occurring about 1000 CE to areas they called Helluland, Markland, and Vinland—possibly present-day Baffin Island, Labrador, and either Newfoundland or somewhere in New England. L'Anse aux Meadows, Newfoundland, is the only documented settlement, with evidence of a small village dating to c. 1000 CE.

Sustained contact between the hemispheres began with Christopher Columbus (born Cristoforo Colombo, c. 1451, near Genoa, Italy), who made four voyages to the New World under the authority of the Spanish monarchs. He left Spain, Aug. 3, 1492, with a fleet of three vessels—the *Niña*, *Pinta*, and *Santa María*—and 88 men, landing at San Salvador (Watlings Island, The Bahamas) on Oct. 12, 1492. He also visited Cuba, Hispaniola, and many smaller Caribbean islands, then populated by the Taíno. A second expedition in 1493, with 17 ships and 1,400 men, reached the island of Dominica in the Lesser Antilles; a third, in 1498, took Columbus to Trinidad and the adjacent S American coast. A fourth voyage reached Mexico, Honduras, Panama, and what he christened Santiago (the present-day island of Jamaica) in 1502.

In 1497 and 1499, Amerigo Vespucci (for whom the Americas are named), an Italian sailing for Spain, passed along the N and E coasts of S America. He was the first to claim these lands were previously unknown and not part of Asia. Some early explorations are listed below.

Year	Explorer	Nationality (sponsor, if different)	Area reached or explored
1497	John Cabot	Italian (English)	Newfoundland, possibly Nova Scotia
1497-98	Vasco da Gama	Portuguese	Cape of Good Hope (Africa), India
1499	Alonso de Ojeda	Spanish	Northern S Amer. coast, Venezuela
1500	Vicente Yañez Pinzón	Spanish	S American coast, Amazon R.
1500	Pedro Álvarez Cabral	Portuguese	Brazil
1501	Rodrigo de Bastidas	Spanish	Central America
1513	Vasco Núñez de Balboa	Spanish	Panama, Pacific Ocean
1513	Juan Ponce de León	Spanish	Florida, Yucatán Peninsula
1515	Juan de Solís	Spanish	Río de la Plata
1519	Alonso de Pineda	Spanish	Mouth of Mississippi R.
1519	Hernán Cortés	Spanish	Mexico
1519-20	Ferdinand Magellan	Portuguese (Spanish)	Straits of Magellan, Tierra del Fuego
1524	Giovanni da Verrazano	Italian (French)	Atlantic coast, incl. New York Harbor
1528	Álvar Núñez Cabeza de Vaca	Spanish	Texas coast and interior
1532	Francisco Pizarro	Spanish	Peru
1534	Jacques Cartier	French	Canada, Gulf of St. Lawrence
1536	Pedro de Mendoza	Spanish	Buenos Aires
1539	Francisco de Ulloa	Spanish	California coast
1539	Marcos de Niza	Italian (Spanish)	SW United States
1539-41	Hernando de Soto	Spanish	Mississippi R., near Memphis, TN
1540	Francisco de Coronado	Spanish	SW United States
1540	Hernando de Alarcón	Spanish	Colorado R.
1540	Garcia Lopez de Cárdenas	Spanish	Colorado, Grand Canyon
1541	Francisco de Orellana	Spanish	Amazon R.
1542	Juan Rodriguez Cabrillo	Portuguese (Spanish)	Western Mexico, San Diego Harbor
1565	Pedro Menéndez de Avilés	Spanish	St. Augustine, FL
1576	Sir Martin Frobisher	English	Frobisher Bay, Canada
1577-80	Sir Francis Drake	English	CA coast, on voyage around world
1582	Antonio de Espejo	Spanish	SW U.S. (New Mexico)
1584	Philip Amadas and Arthur Barlowe (for Raleigh)	English	Virginia
1585-87	Sir Walter Raleigh's men	English	Roanoke Isl., NC
1595	Sir Walter Raleigh	English	Orinoco R.
1603-09	Samuel de Champlain	French	Canadian interior, Lake Champlain
1607	John Smith	English	Atlantic coast
1609-10	Henry Hudson	English (Dutch)	Hudson R., Hudson Bay
1634	Jean Nicolet	French	Lake Michigan, Wisconsin
1673	Jacques Marquette and Louis Jolliet	French	Mississippi R., south to Arkansas
1682	René-Robert Cavelier, sieur de La Salle	French	Mississippi R., south to Gulf of Mexico
1727-29	Vitus Bering	Danish (Russian)	Bering Strait, Alaska
1789	Sir Alexander Mackenzie	Canadian	NW Canada
1804-06	Meriwether Lewis and William Clark	American	Missouri R., Rocky Mts., Columbia R.

Arctic Exploration

1596-97: Willem Barents (Dutch) touched Spitsbergen, 79°49′N, and rounded Novaya Zemlya, where he and crew were forced to winter ashore, first W Europeans to successfully do so in the Arctic.

1610: Henry Hudson (Eng.) explored Hudson Strait, Hudson Bay on search for Northwest Passage. After winter ashore, crew mutinied, 1611, and set him, his son, and some others adrift on small boat.

1733-43: Great Northern Expedition (Russ.), led by Vitus Bering (Dan./Russ.), surveyed Siberian Arctic coast. Bering had sailed through what would become known as Bering Strait, 1728, but this second expedition proved that Asia and North America were separate.

1827: William Edward Parry (Eng.), attempting to reach North Pole, made it to 82°45′N via sledge, setting record for farthest north.

1831: James Clark Ross (Eng.) was first to north magnetic pole.

1878-79: Baron Adolf Erik Nordenskiöld (Swed.) was first to navigate Northeast Passage—ocean route connecting Europe's North Sea to Pacific O.

1881-84: Adolphus Greely led 25-person U.S. expedition to Ellesmere Isl. as part of first Intl. Polar Year (1882-83). Only he and five others survived scurvy and starvation after relief ships failed to reach them.

1893-96: Fridtjof Nansen (Nor.) deliberately allowed *Fram* to become icebound and drift from New Siberian Isls. Leaving others in charge of ship, he tried polar dash in 1895 but only reached 86°14′N.

1903-06: Roald Amundsen (Nor.) was first to sail length of Northwest Passage—route linking Atlantic and Pacific via Canada's marine waterways.

1909: Robert E. Peary (U.S.) began dash for North Pole, Mar. 1, from Ellesmere Isl. Reportedly reached the pole, 90°N, Apr. 6, with Matthew Henson and four Inuit. Research suggests he may have fallen short of goal by c. 30-60 mi. (Dr. Frederick Cook [U.S.] claimed to have reached the North Pole in 1908.)

1926: Richard E. Byrd and Floyd Bennett (both U.S.) reputedly flew over North Pole, May 9. Amundsen, Lincoln Ellsworth (U.S.), and Umberto Nobile (Ital.) flew over North Pole May 12 in dirigible *Norge*.

1958: Nuclear-powered submarine USS *Nautilus* crossed the North Pole beneath the ice.

1968: Ralph Plaisted (U.S.) and three amateur explorers on snowmobiles became first independently confirmed surface expedition to reach North Pole.

1978: Naomi Uemura (Jpn.) became first person to reach the North Pole alone, traveling by dog sled in 54-day, 600-mi trek.

1982: Ranulph Fiennes (Eng.) and Charles Burton (S. Afr.-UK) reached the North Pole and became first to circle the Earth from pole to pole. They had reached the South Pole 16 months earlier. The 52,000-mi trek took three years at an est. cost of $18 mil.

1995: Richard Weber (Can.) and Mikhail Malakhov (Russ.) became first to North Pole and back without any mechanical assistance. The 940-mi trip on skis took 121 days.

Antarctic Exploration

Explorers have approached Antarctica since 1773-75, when Capt. James Cook (Eng.) reached 71°10′S. Fabian von Bellingshausen (Russ.) mapped the region on an expedition sponsored by Tsar Alexander I, 1819-21. In 1823, James Weddell (Brit.) reached 74°15′S and found the Weddell Sea.

First to announce existence of the continent of Antarctica was Charles Wilkes (U.S.), who followed the coast for 1,500 mi, 1840. Ross Ice Shelf was found by James Clark Ross (Brit.), 1841-42.

1895: Leonard Kristensen (Nor.) landed a party on Victoria Land, first ashore on main continental mass. C. E. Borchgrevink, a member of that party, returned in 1899 with a Brit. expedition, first to winter on Antarctica.

1901-04: Robert Falcon Scott (Eng.), commander of Brit. Natl. Antarctic Expedition, crossed Ross Ice Shelf to 82°17′S, farthest south then reached.

1911: Roald Amundsen (Nor.) with four men and dog teams were first to South Pole, Dec. 14. Scott and four companions reached South Pole on Jan. 17, 1912; they died on return trip.

1929: Richard E. Byrd (U.S.) crossed South Pole, Nov. 29, with three others on 1,600-mi airplane flight.

1934-35: Byrd led second expedition to Little America base camp, explored 450,000 sq mi, wintered alone at 80°08′S.

1935: Lincoln Ellsworth (U.S.) made first transcontinental crossing by air, flying south along E coast of Palmer Peninsula then across to Little America.

1946-48: Ronne Antarctic Research Expedition Cmdr. Finn Ronne determined Antarctic to be one continent with no strait between Weddell and Ross Seas.

1955-57: Supporting U.S. scientific efforts for Intl. Geophysical Year (IGY), the U.S. Navy's Operation Deep Freeze, led by Byrd, established five coastal stations and three interior stations; explored more than 1 mil sq mi in Wilkes Land.

1957-58: During the IGY, scientists from 12 countries conducted research within network of some 60 stations on Antarctica. Vivian E. Fuchs (Eng.) led 12-person Trans-Antarctic Expedition on first land crossing of Antarctica; completed in Mar. 1958 after traveling 2,158 mi in 99 days.

1959: Argentina, Australia, Belgium, Chile, France, Japan, New Zealand, Norway, South Africa, USSR, UK, and U.S. signed a treaty (in force 1961) affirming the use of Antarctica (specifically the area south of 60°S) "for peaceful purposes only." Territorial claims suspended.

1961-62: Scientists discovered Bentley Trench, running from Ross Ice Shelf into Marie Byrd Land, near the end of the Ellsworth Mts., toward Weddell Sea.

1985: Ocean Drilling Project finds that the ice sheets of E Antarctica are 37 mil years old, main W Antarctic ice sheet about 8 mil years old.

1991: Protocol to the Antarctic Treaty on Environmental Protection, or Madrid Protocol, adopted (in force 1998); it banned activities—except for scientific research—related to mineral resources.

1995: After a 1994 solo expedition to North Pole, Borge Ousland (Nor.) reached South Pole on skis, becoming first to reach both N and S Poles alone. He later became the first to traverse both Antarctica (1996-97) and the Arctic (2001) solo.

Volcanoes

Source: *Volcanoes of the World*, Geoscience Press; Global Volcanism Program, Smithsonian Institution, www.volcano.si.edu

Eruptions have been documented in about 550 volcanoes. More than half to three-quarters of historically active volcanoes can be found on the so-called **Ring of Fire**, which runs along the W coast of the Americas from the southern tip of Chile to Alaska, down the E coast of Asia from Kamchatka to Indonesia, and continues from New Guinea to New Zealand. The Ring of Fire marks boundaries between tectonic plates underlying the Pacific Ocean and the surrounding continents. Volcanic activity also occurs along rift zones like Iceland, where plates pull apart, or over hot spots such as Hawaii, where molten material rises from the mantle to Earth's crust. The majority of Earth's volcanism takes place at submarine rift zones, on the seafloor.

Notable Volcanic Eruptions

In approximately 5,700 BC, Mount Mazama, in southern Oregon, erupted violently, ejecting large amounts of ash and pumice and sending out pyroclastic flows (mixture of volcanic debris and gases). The top of the mountain collapsed, leaving a caldera about 6 mi across and 1 mi deep. This depression filled with water from rain and snow to form Crater Lake.

Date	Volcano	Est. deaths	Date	Volcano	Est. deaths
Aug. 24, 79 CE	Vesuvius, Italy	16,000[1]	Jan. 30, 1911	Taal, Philippines	1,400
1586	Kelut, Java, Indon.	10,000	June 6-8, 1912	Novarupta, AK, U.S.[5]	1
Dec. 15, 1631	Vesuvius, Italy	4,000	May 19, 1919	Kelut, Java, Indon.	5,000
Aug. 12, 1772	Papandayan, Java, Indon.	3,000	Jan. 17-21, 1951	Lamington, New Guinea	3,000
June 8, 1783	Laki, Iceland	9,350	May 18, 1980	St. Helens, WA, U.S.	57
May 21, 1792	Unzen, Japan	14,500	Mar. 28, 1982	El Chichón, Mexico	1,880
Apr. 10-12, 1815	Tambora, Sumbawa, Indon.	92,000[2]	Nov. 13, 1985	Nevado del Ruiz, Colombia	23,000
Aug. 26-27, 1883	Krakatau, Indon.	36,000[3]	Aug. 21, 1986	Lake Nyos, Cameroon	1,700[6]
Apr. 24, 1902	Santa María, Guatemala	1,000[4]	June 15, 1991	Pinatubo, Luzon, Philippines	800[7]
May 8, 1902	Pelée, Martinique	28,000			

(1) Heated mud and ash engulfed Pompeii, Herculaneum, and Stabiae with debris more than 60 ft deep. About 10% of the three towns' pop. were killed. (2) Of these, about 10,000 were directly related to the eruption. Released gases and particles altered the global climate, leading to additional deaths from starvation and disease when crops failed. (3) At least 2,000 died in pyroclastic flows, Aug. 26. Collapse of volcano, Aug. 27, sank most of island, killing over 3,000. Resulting tsunamis were responsible for the majority of deaths, in Java and Sumatra. (4) An additional 3,000 deaths due to a malaria outbreak are sometimes attributed to the eruption. (5) Biggest eruption of 20th cent. by volume. (6) Caused by release of massive amount of carbon dioxide from crater lake. (7) Of these, about 500 were associated with post-eruption lahars (volcanic mudflows).

Notable Active Volcanoes

Source: Global Volcanism Program, Smithsonian Inst.; Volcano Hazards Program, U.S. Geological Survey, U.S. Dept. of the Interior

Active volcanoes display a wide range of activity, including the production of ash plumes and seismic swarms. An eruption may involve the explosive ejection of fragmental material and escape of liquid lava. Year of a volcano's last known or confirmed eruption, as of June 2016, is given. Volcanoes are listed by height, which does not reflect eruptive magnitude. Submarine volcanoes are not included.

Volcano (latest eruption)	Location	Height (ft)
Africa		
Cameroon (2000)	Cameroon	13,435
Nyiragongo (2016)	Dem. Rep. of the Congo	11,385
Nyamuragira (2015)	Dem. Rep. of the Congo	10,033
Ol Doinyo Lengai (2013)	Tanzania	9,718
Fogo (2015)	Cape Verde Isls.	9,281
Piton de la Fournaise (2015)	Réunion Isl. (Fr.), Indian O.	8,635
Karthala (2007)	Comoros	7,746
Nabro (2012)	Eritrea	7,277
Antarctica		
Erebus (2016)	Ross Isl.	12,448
Belinda (2007)	Montagu Isl. (UK)	4,495
Asia and Oceania		
Ararat (1840)	Turkey	16,946
Klyuchevskoy (2016)	Kamchatka, Russia	15,597
Kerinci (2016)	Sumatra, Indon.	12,467
Fuji (1708)	Honshu, Japan	12,388
Rinjani (2015)	Lombok, Indon.	12,224
Semeru (2016)	Java, Indon.	12,060
Tolbachik (2013)	Kamchatka, Russia	11,847
Koryaksky (2009)	Kamchatka, Russia	11,253
Slamet (2014)	Java, Indon.	11,247
Shiveluch (2016)	Kamchatka, Russia	10,771
Raung (2015)	Java, Indon.	10,696
Dempo (2009)	Sumatra, Indon.	10,410
Ontake (2014)	Honshu, Japan	10,062
Merapi (2014)	Java, Indon.	9,738
Zhupanovsky (2016)	Kamchatka, Russia	9,511
Marapi (2015)	Sumatra, Indon.	9,485
Bezymianny (2013)	Kamchatka, Russia	9,455
Ruapehu (2007)	North Isl., New Zealand	9,177
Heard (2016)	Heard Isl., Australia	9,006
Changbaishan (1903)	China-North Korea	9,003
Papandayan (2002)	Java, Indon.	8,743
Talang (2007)	Sumatra, Indon.	8,520
Asama (2015)	Honshu, Japan	8,425
Dieng Volcanic Complex (2009)	Java, Indon.	8,415
Mayon (2014)	Luzon, Philippines	8,077
Sinabung (2016)	Sumatra, Indon.	8,071
Kanlaon (2016)	Negros, Philippines	7,989
Niigata-Yakeyama (1998)	Honshu, Japan	7,874
Kizimen (2013)	Kamchatka, Russia	7,657
Ulawun (2013)	Papua New Guinea	7,657
Tengger Caldera (2016)	Java, Indon.	7,641
Alaid (2016)	Kuril Isls., Russia	7,497
Chokai (1974)	Honshu, Japan	7,336
Galunggung (1984)	Java, Indon.	7,113
Tangkubanparahu (2013)	Java, Indon.	6,837
Tongariro (2012)	North Isl., New Zealand	6,490
Azuma (1977)	Honshu, Japan	6,394
Sangeang Api (2015)	Lesser Sunda Isls., Indon.	6,394
Nasu (1963)	Honshu, Japan	6,283
Bagana (2016)	Papua New Guinea	6,086
Karkar (2014)	Papua New Guinea	6,033
Chachadake (Tiatia) (1981)	Kunashir Isl., Japan-admin. by Russia	5,978
Bandai (1888)	Honshu, Japan	5,958
Manam (2016)	Papua New Guinea	5,928
Gorely (2010)	Kamchatka, Russia	5,902
Kuju (1996)	Kyushu, Japan	5,876
Soputan (2016)	Sulawesi, Indon.	5,856
Karangetang (Api Siau) (2016)	Siau Isl., Indon.	5,853
Chikurachki (2016)	Kuril Isls., Russia	5,843
Kelut (2014)	Java, Indon.	5,679
Adatara (1996)	Honshu, Japan	5,669
Batur (2000)	Bali, Indon.	5,633
Gamalama (2015)	Ternate, Indon.	5,627
Lewotobi (2014)	Flores Isl., Indon.	5,587
Kirishima (2011)	Kyushu, Japan	5,577
Egon (2008)	Flores, Indon.	5,449
Gamkonora (2007)	Halmahera, Indon.	5,364
Aso (2016)	Kyushu, Japan	5,223
Lokon-Empung (2015)	Sulawesi, Indon.	5,184
Bulusan (2016)	Luzon, Philippines	5,135
Karymsky (2016)	Kamchatka, Russia	4,964
Akan (2008)	Hokkaido, Japan	4,918
Aoba (2011)	Vanuatu	4,908
Sarychev Peak (2009)	Kuril Isls., Russia	4,908
Pinatubo (1993)	Luzon, Philippines	4,875
Hakoneyama (2015)	Honshu, Japan	4,718
Lewotolo (2012)	Lembata, Indon.	4,669
Lopevi (2007)	Vanuatu	4,636
Ambrym (2015)	Vanuatu	4,377

Volcano (latest eruption)	Location	Height (ft)
Central America and West Indies		
Tacaná (1986)	Mexico-Guatemala	13,333
Acatenango (1972)	Guatemala	13,045
Santa María (2016)	Guatemala	12,375
Fuego (2016)	Guatemala	12,346
Irazú (1994)	Costa Rica	11,260
Turrialba (2016)	Costa Rica	10,958
Poás (2014)	Costa Rica	8,885
Pacaya (2015)	Guatemala	8,373
Santa Ana (2005)	El Salvador	7,812
San Miguel (2016)	El Salvador	6,988
Rincón de la Vieja (2016)	Costa Rica	6,286
San Cristóbal (2016)	Nicaragua	5,725
Concepción (2011)	Nicaragua	5,577
Arenal (2010)	Costa Rica	5,479
Soufrière Guadeloupe (1977)	Guadeloupe (France)	4,813
Pelée (1932)	Martinique (France)	4,573
Momotombo (2016)	Nicaragua	4,255
North America		
Pico de Orizaba (1846)	Mexico	18,255
Popocatépetl (2016)	Mexico	17,802
Rainier (1894)	Washington	14,409
Shasta (1786)	California	14,163
Wrangell (2002)	Alaska	14,035
Colima (2016)	Mexico	12,631
Hood (1866)	Oregon	11,240
Spurr (1992)	Alaska	11,070
Lassen Peak (1917)	California	10,456
Redoubt (2009)	Alaska	10,197
Iliamna (1876)	Alaska	10,016
Shishaldin (2015)	Unimak Isl., Aleutians, AK	9,373
St. Helens (2008)	Washington	8,363
Veniaminof (2013)	Alaska	8,225
Pavlof (2016)	Alaska	8,179
Fourpeaked (2006)	Alaska	6,906
Katmai (1912)	Alaska	6,716
Makushin (1995)	Unalaska Isl., Aleutians, AK	5,906
Great Sitkin (1974)	Great Sitkin Isl., Aleutians, AK	5,709
Cleveland (2016)	Chuginadak Isl., Aleutians, AK	5,676
South America		
Llullaillaco (1877)	Chile-Argentina	22,110
San Pedro (1960)	Chile	20,161
Guallatiri (1960)	Chile	19,918
San José (1960)	Chile-Argentina	19,915
Sabancaya (2015)	Peru	19,577
Cotopaxi (2016)	Ecuador	19,393
El Misti (1985)	Peru	19,101
Ubinas (2016)	Peru	18,609
Tupungatito (1987)	Chile-Argentina	18,570
Láscar (2015)	Chile	18,346
Nevado del Huila (2012)	Colombia	17,598
Sangay (2016)	Ecuador	17,343
Nevado del Ruiz (2016)	Colombia	17,320
Irruputuncu (1995)	Chile-Bolivia	16,939
Tungurahua (2016)	Ecuador	16,480
Guagua Pichincha (2002)	Ecuador	15,696
Puracé (1977)	Colombia	15,256
Galeras (2014)	Colombia	14,029
Planchón-Peteroa (2011)	Chile	13,048
Lautaro (1979)	Chile	11,834
Reventador (2016)	Ecuador	11,686
Nevados de Chillán (2016)	Chile	10,538
Llaima (2009)	Chile	10,253
Europe		
Etna (2016)	Italy	10,925
Vesuvius (1944)	Italy	4,203
Stromboli (2013)	Italy	3,031
Mid-Atlantic		
La Palma (1971)	Canary Isls. (Spain)	7,959
Beerenberg (1985)	Jan Mayen (Norway)	6,841
Bardarbunga (2015)	Iceland	6,562
Grímsvötn (2011)	Iceland	5,640
Eyjafjallajökull (2010)	Iceland	5,417
Hekla (2000)	Iceland	4,888
Mid-Pacific		
Mauna Loa (1984)	Hawaii, HI	13,681
Haleakala (1750)	Maui, HI	10,023
Kilauea (2016)	Hawaii, HI	4,009

Mountains
North America
Source: U.S. Geological Survey, U.S. Dept. of the Interior; National Geodetic Survey, NOAA, U.S. Dept. of Commerce; Natural Resources Canada. Survey dates and elevation sources may differ.

Peak, state/prov., country	Height (ft)	Peak, state/prov., country	Height (ft)	Peak, state/prov., country	Height (ft)
Denali (fmr. McKinley), AK	20,310	Hunter, AK	14,573	Cameron, CO	14,238
Logan, Yukon, Canada	19,551	Browne Tower, AK	14,530	Shavano, CO	14,231
Pico de Orizaba, Mexico	18,619	Whitney, CA	14,505	Princeton, CO	14,204
St. Elias, AK-YT, U.S.-Can.	18,009	Alverstone, AK-YT, U.S.-Can.	14,500	Belford, CO	14,203
Popocatépetl, Mexico	17,802	University Peak, AK	14,470	Yale, CO	14,200
Foraker, AK	17,400	Elbert, CO	14,440	Crestone Needle, CO	14,197
Iztaccíhuatl, Mexico	17,154	Massive, CO	14,421	Bross, CO	14,172
Lucania, YT, Canada	17,146	Harvard, CO	14,421	Kit Carson, CO	14,165
King Peak, YT, Canada	16,972	Rainier, WA	14,410	Point Success, WA	14,164
Steele, YT, Canada	16,624	Williamson, CA	14,376	Shasta, CA	14,163
Bona, AK	16,500	Blanca Peak, CO	14,345	Wrangell, AK	14,163
Blackburn, AK	16,390	La Plata Peak, CO	14,336	Maroon Peak, CO	14,163
Sanford, AK	16,237	Uncompahgre Peak, CO	14,321	Tabeguache, CO	14,162
South Buttress, AK	15,885	Crestone Peak, CO	14,294	Oxford, CO	14,160
Wood, YT, Canada	15,873	Lincoln, CO	14,293	El Diente Peak, CO	14,159
Vancouver, AK-YT, U.S.-Can.	15,699	Castle Peak, CO	14,279	Sill, CA	14,159
Churchill, AK	15,638	Grays Peak, CO	14,278	Democrat, CO	14,155
Nevado de Toluca (Xinantécatl),		Antero, CO	14,276	Sneffels, CO	14,150
Mexico	15,350	Torreys Peak, CO	14,275	Capitol Peak, CO	14,130
Fairweather, AK-BC, U.S.-Can.	15,299	Quandary Peak, CO	14,271	Liberty Cap, WA	14,118
Macaulay, YT, Canada	15,299	Evans, CO	14,265	Pikes Peak, CO	14,115
Slaggard, YT, Canada	15,299	Longs Peak, CO	14,259	Snowmass, CO	14,099
Hubbard, AK-YT, U.S.-Can.	15,016	McArthur, YT, Canada	14,253	Russell, CA	14,094
Bear, AK	14,831	White Mountain Peak, CA	14,252	Eolus, CO	14,083
Walsh, YT, Canada	14,780	North Palisade, CA	14,248	Windom, CO	14,082
East Buttress, AK	14,730	Wilson, CO	14,246	Challenger Point, CO	14,081
Matlalcueyetl, Mexico	14,636				

Note: The highest point in the West Indies is Pico Duarte (10,417 ft), in the Dominican Republic.

Other Notable U.S. Mountains

Peak, state	Height (ft)	Peak, state	Height (ft)	Peak, state	Height (ft)
Gannett, WY	13,810	Adams, WA	12,281	Mitchell, NC	6,683
Grand Teton, WY	13,775	San Gorgonio, CA	11,503	Clingmans Dome, NC-TN	6,644
Kings, UT	13,518	Hood, OR	11,247	Washington, NH	6,289
Cloud, WY	13,171	Cleveland, MT	10,466	Rogers, VA	5,729
Wheeler, NM	13,167	Lassen, CA	10,461	Marcy, NY	5,343
Boundary, NV	13,146	Granite, CA	10,325	Katahdin, ME	5,269
Granite, MT	12,807	Guadalupe, TX	8,751	Spruce Knob, WV	4,863
Borah, ID	12,668	Olympus, WA	7,973	Mansfield, VT	4,395
Humphreys, AZ	12,637	Harney, SD	7,244	Black Mountain, KY	4,139

South America

Peak, country	Height (ft)	Peak, country	Height (ft)	Peak, country	Height (ft)
Aconcagua, Argentina	22,835	Coropuna, Peru	21,083	Solo, Argentina	20,492
Ojos del Salado, Arg.-Chile	22,595	Laudo, Argentina	20,997	Polleras, Argentina	20,456
Bonete, Argentina	22,546	Ancohuma, Bolivia	20,958	Pular, Chile	20,423
Tupungato, Argentina-Chile	22,310	Ausangate, Peru	20,945	Chani, Argentina	20,341
Pissis, Argentina	22,241	Toro, Argentina-Chile	20,932	Aucanquilcha, Chile	20,295
Mercedario, Argentina	22,211	Illampu, Bolivia	20,873	Juncal, Argentina-Chile	20,276
Huascarán, Peru	22,205	Tres Cruces, Argentina-Chile	20,853	Negro, Argentina	20,184
Llullaillaco, Argentina-Chile	22,109	Huandoy, Peru	20,852	Quela, Argentina	20,128
El Libertador, Argentina	22,047	Parinacota, Bolivia-Chile	20,768	Condoriri, Bolivia	20,095
Cachi, Argentina	22,047	Tortolas, Argentina-Chile	20,745	Palermo, Argentina	20,079
Yerupajá, Peru	21,765	Ampato, Peru	20,702	Solimana, Peru	20,068
Incahuasi, Argentina-Chile	21,720	Chimborazo, Ecuador	20,702	San Juan, Argentina-Chile	20,049
Galan, Argentina	21,654	El Condor, Argentina	20,669	Sierra Nevada, Argentina-Chile	20,023
El Muerto, Argentina-Chile	21,457	Salcantay, Peru	20,574	Antofalla, Argentina	20,013
Sajama, Bolivia	21,391	Huancarhuas, Peru	20,531	Marmolejo, Argentina-Chile	20,013
Nacimiento, Argentina	21,302	Famatina, Argentina	20,505	Chachani, Peru	19,931
Illimani, Bolivia	21,201	Pumasillo, Peru	20,492		

Africa

Peak, country	Height (ft)	Peak, country	Height (ft)	Peak, country	Height (ft)
Kilimanjaro, Tanzania	19,341	Karisimbi, Congo-Rwanda	14,787	Guna, Ethiopia	13,881
Kenya, Kenya	17,057	Tullu Dimtu, Ethiopia	14,360	Gughe, Ethiopia	13,780
Margherita Pk., Uganda-Congo	16,763	Elgon, Kenya-Uganda	14,178	Toubkal, Morocco	13,661
Meru, Tanzania	14,977	Batu, Ethiopia	14,131	Cameroon, Cameroon	13,435
Ras Dashen, Ethiopia	14,872				

Australia, New Zealand, SE Asian Islands

Peak, country	Height (ft)	Peak, country	Height (ft)	Peak, country	Height (ft)
Jaya, New Guinea, Indon.	16,024	Wilhelm, Papua New Guinea	14,793	Aoraki/Cook, New Zealand	12,218
Trikora, New Guinea, Indon.	15,585	Kinabalu, Malaysia	13,436	Semeru, Java, Indonesia	12,060
Mandala, New Guinea, Indon.	15,420	Kerinci, Sumatra, Indon.	12,467	Kosciusko, Australia	7,310

Height of Mount Everest

Mt. Everest, the world's highest mountain, was considered 29,002 ft when Edmund Hillary and Tenzing Norgay became the first to scale it, in 1953. In 1954, the Surveyor General of the Republic of India set the height at 29,028 ft, plus or minus 10 ft because of snow. In 1999, a team of climbers sponsored by Boston's Museum of Science and the National Geographic Society measured the height at the summit using satellite-based technology. The new measurement, of 29,035 ft, was accepted by other authorities, including the U.S. National Imagery and Mapping Agency.

Climbers typically ascend Everest on its north (Tibet) or south face (Nepal). By the end of the 2015 climbing season, which runs from April through May, about 4,093 climbers had made successful ascents while around 282 climbers had died in the attempt. Among the dead were 16 Sherpas killed in an avalanche triggered by falling ice Apr. 18, 2014. Concerns about additional avalanches, the increasing number of tourists on Everest, and fair worker compensation contributed to the decision by most tour operators to cancel the rest of the 2014 season on the south face. A 7.8-magnitude earthquake hit Nepal Apr. 25, 2015, triggering avalanches that swept through Everest Base Camp on the south side, killing 19. The 2015 season was canceled, making it the first year since 1974 that no one reached the top of Everest.

Europe

Peak, country	Height (ft)	Peak, country	Height (ft)	Peak, country	Height (ft)
Alps		Dent D'Herens, Switzerland	13,686	Schalihorn, Switzerland	13,040
		Breithorn, It.-Switzerland	13,665	Scerscen, Switzerland	13,028
Mont Blanc, France-Italy	15,771	Bishorn, Switzerland	13,645	Eiger, Switzerland	13,025
Dufourspitze (highest of Monte		Jungfrau, Switzerland	13,642	Jagerhorn, Switzerland	13,024
Rosa group), Switzerland	15,203	Ecrins, France	13,461	Rottalhorn, Switzerland	13,022
Dom, Switzerland	14,911	Monch, Switzerland	13,448	**Pyrenees**	
Liskamm, It.-Switzerland	14,852	Pollux, Switzerland	13,422		
Weisshorn, Switzerland	14,780	Schreckhorn, Switzerland	13,379	Aneto, Spain	11,168
Taschhorn, Switzerland	14,733	Ober Gabelhorn, Switzerland	13,330	Posets, Spain	11,073
Matterhorn, It.-Switzerland	14,692	Gran Paradiso, Italy	13,323	Perdido, Spain	11,007
Dent Blanche, Switzerland	14,293	Bernina, It.-Switzerland	13,284	Vignemale, France-Spain	10,820
Nadelhorn, Switzerland	14,196	Fiescherhorn, Switzerland	13,283	Long, Spain	10,479
Grand Combin, Switzerland	14,154	Grunhorn, Switzerland	13,266	Estats, Spain	10,304
Lenzpitze, Switzerland	14,088	Lauteraarhorn, Switzerland	13,261	Montcalm, Spain	10,105
Finsteraarhorn, Switzerland	14,022	Durrenhorn, Switzerland	13,238	**Caucasus (Europe-Asia)**	
Castor, Switzerland	13,865	Allalinhorn, Switzerland	13,213		
Zinalrothorn, Switzerland	13,849	Weissmies, Switzerland	13,199	Elbrus, Russia	18,510
Hohberghom, Switzerland	13,842	Lagginhorn, Switzerland	13,156	Shkhara, Georgia	17,064
Alphubel, Switzerland	13,799	Zupo, Switzerland	13,120	Dykh Tau, Russia	17,054
Rimpfischhom, Switzerland	13,776	Fletschhorn, Switzerland	13,110	Kashtan Tau, Russia	16,877
Aletschorn, Switzerland	13,763	Adlerhorn, Switzerland	13,081	Janqi, Georgia	16,565
Strahlhorn, Switzerland	13,747	Gletscherhorn, Switzerland	13,068	Kazbek, Georgia	16,558

Asia (Mainland)

Peak, country/region	Height (ft)	Peak, country/region	Height (ft)	Peak, country/region	Height (ft)
Everest, Nepal-Tibet	29,035	Tirich Mir, Pakistan	25,230	Badrinath, India	23,420
K2 (Godwin Austen), Kashmir	28,251	Makalu II, Nepal-Tibet	25,120	Nunkun, Kashmir	23,410
Kanchenjunga, India-Nepal	28,169	Minya Konka, China	24,900	Lenin Peak, Tajikistan	23,406
Lhotse I (Everest), Nepal-Tibet	27,923	Annapurna III, Nepal	24,786	Pyramid, India-Nepal	23,400
Makalu I, Nepal-Tibet	27,824	Kula Gangri, Bhutan-Tibet	24,784	Api, Nepal	23,399
Lhotse II (Everest), Nepal-Tibet	27,560	Changtse (Everest), Nepal-Tibet	24,780	Pauhunri, India-Tibet	23,385
Dhaulagiri, Nepal	26,795	Muztagh Ata, Xinjiang, China	24,757	Trisul, India	23,360
Manaslu I, Nepal	26,781	Skyang Kangri, Kashmir	24,750	Kangto, India-Tibet	23,260
Cho Oyu, Nepal-Tibet	26,750	Annapurna IV, Nepal	24,688	Nyenchen Thanglha, Tibet	23,255
Nanga Parbat, Kashmir	26,660	Ismail Samani Peak, Tajikistan	24,590	Trisuli, India	23,210
Annapurna I, Nepal	26,545	Jongsong Peak,		Pumori, Nepal-Tibet	23,190
Annapurna II, Nepal	26,545	India-Nepal-China	24,472	Dunagiri, India	23,184
Gasherbrum, Kashmir	26,470	Jengish Chokusu, Xinjiang,		Lombo Kangra, Tibet	23,165
Broad, Kashmir	26,400	China-Kyrgyzstan	24,406	Saipal, Nepal	23,100
Gosainthan, Nepal-Tibet	26,287	Sia Kangri, Kashmir	24,350	Macha Pucchare, Nepal	22,958
Gyachung Kang, Nepal-Tibet	25,910	Haramosh Peak, Pakistan	24,270	Khan Tengri, Kazakhstan-	
Disteghil Sar, Kashmir	25,868	Istoro Nal, Pakistan	24,240	Kyrgyzstan-Xinjiang, China	22,949
Himalchuli, Nepal	25,801	Kirat Chuli, India-Nepal	24,165	Numbar, Nepal	22,817
Nuptse (Everest), Nepal-Tibet	25,726	Chomo Lhari, Bhutan-Tibet	24,040	Kanjiroba, Nepal	22,580
Masherbrum, Kashmir	25,660	Chamlang, Nepal	24,012	Ama Dablam, Nepal	22,350
Nanda Devi, India	25,645	Kabru, India-Nepal	24,002	Cho Polu, Nepal	22,093
Rakaposhi, Kashmir	25,550	Alung Gangri, Tibet	24,000	Lingtren, Nepal-Tibet	21,972
Kamet, India-Tibet	25,447	Baltoro Kangri, Kashmir	23,990	Khumbutse, Nepal-Tibet	21,785
Namcha Barwa, Tibet	25,445	Mana, India	23,860	Hlako Gangri, Tibet	21,266
Gurla Mandhata, Tibet	25,355	Baruntse, Nepal	23,688	Grosvenor, China	21,190
Ulugh Muztagh, Xinjiang,		Nepal Peak, India-Nepal	23,500	Thagchhab Gangri, Tibet	20,970
China-Tibet	25,340	Amne Machin, China	23,490	Damavand, Iran	18,406
Kungur, Xinjiang, China	25,325	Gauri Sankar, Nepal-Tibet	23,440	Ararat, Turkey	16,854

Antarctica

Peak	Height (ft)	Peak	Height (ft)	Peak	Height (ft)
Vinson Massif	16,066	Sidley	13,720	Donaldson	12,894
Tyree	15,919	Ostenso	13,710	Ray	12,808
Shinn	15,750	Minto	13,668	Sellery	12,779
Gardner	15,375	Miller	13,650	Waterman	12,730
Epperly	15,100	Long Gables	13,620	Anne	12,703
Kirkpatrick	14,855	Dickerson	13,517	Press	12,566
Elizabeth	14,698	Giovinetto	13,412	Falla	12,549
Markham	14,290	Wade	13,400	Rucker	12,520
Bell	14,117	Fisher	13,386	Goldthwait	12,510
Mackellar	14,098	Fridtjof Nansen	13,350	Morris	12,500
Anderson	13,957	Wexler	13,202	Erebus	12,450
Bentley	13,934	Lister	13,200	Campbell	12,434
Kaplan	13,878	Shear	13,100	Don Pedro Christophersen	12,355
Andrew Jackson	13,750	Odishaw	13,008	Lysaght	12,326

Notable Islands and Their Areas

Figures are for total area in square miles. Boldface figures in parentheses show rank among the world's 10 largest individual islands. Only the largest islands in an island group are shown. Table does not include islands smaller than 10 sq mi in area. Canada's Manitoulin Island (1,068 sq mi), in Lake Huron, is the world's largest island in a freshwater lake.

Antarctica	
Adelaide	1,400
Alexander	16,700
Berkner	18,500
Roosevelt	2,900

Arctic Ocean	
Amund Ringnes, NU, Can.	2,029
Axel Heiberg, NU, Can.	16,671
Baffin, NU, Can. (5)	195,928
Banks, NT, Can.	27,038
Bathurst, NU, Can.	6,194
Bolshoy Lyakhovsky, Russia	1,776
Borden, NT-NU, Can.	1,079
Bylot, NU, Can.	4,273
Coats, NU, Can.	2,123
Cornwallis, NU, Can.	2,701
Devon, NU, Can.	21,331
Disko, Greenland, Denmark	3,312
Ellef Ringnes, NU, Can.	4,361
Ellesmere, NU, Can. (10)	75,767
Faddayevskiy, Russia	1,930
Franz Josef Land, Russia	8,000
Iturup (Etorofu), Russia	2,596
King William, NU, Can.	5,062
Kotelny, Russia	4,504
Mackenzie King, NT, Can.	1,949
Melville, NT-NU, Can.	16,274
Milne Land, Greenland, Den.	1,400
New Siberian Isls., Russia	14,500
Novaya Zemlya, Russia (2 isls.)	31,730
Prince Charles, NT, Can.	3,676
Prince Patrick, NT, Can.	6,119
Prince of Wales, NU, Can.	12,872
Severnaya Zemlya, Russia (tot. group)	14,175
Bol'shevik	4,368
Komsomolets	3,477
Oktyabr'skoy Revolyutsii	5,471
Somerset, NU, Can.	9,570
Southampton, NU, Can.	15,913
Svalbard, Norway (tot. group)	23,561
Nordaustlandet	5,410
Spitsbergen	14,546
Traill, Greenland, Denmark	1,300
Victoria, NT-NU, Can. (8)	83,897
Wrangel, Russia	2,937

Atlantic Ocean	
Anticosti, QC, Can.	3,066
Ascension, UK	35
Azores, Portugal (tot. group)	868
Faial	67
San Miguel	291
Bahama Isls. (tot. group)	5,382
Andros	2,300
Bermuda Isls., UK (tot. group)	21
Bioko Isl., Equatorial Guinea	785
Block Island, RI, U.S.	21
Cabo Verde	1,557
Canary Isls., Spain (tot. group)	2,807
Fuerteventura	688
Gran Canaria	592
Tenerife	795
Cape Breton, NS, Can.	3,981
Caviana, Pará, Brazil	1,918
Channel Isls., UK (tot. group)	75
Guernsey	24
Jersey	45
Falkland Isls., UK (tot. group)	4,700
East Falkland	2,550
West Falkland	1,750
Faroe Isls., Denmark	539
Great Britain, UK (9)	80,823
Greenland, Denmark (1)	836,330
Gurupá, Pará, Brazil	1,878
Hebrides, Scotland, UK	2,744
Iceland	39,958
Ireland, Ireland-UK	32,589
Isle of Man, UK	221
Isle of Wight, England, UK	147
Long Island, NY, U.S.	1,320
Madeira Isls., Portugal	306
Marajo, Brazil	15,444
Martha's Vineyard, MA, U.S.	89

Atlantic Ocean (cont.)	
Mount Desert, ME, U.S.	104
Nantucket, MA, U.S.	45
Newfoundland, Canada	42,031
Orkney Isls., Scotland, UK	383
Prince Edward Isl. (main), Can.	2,170
St. Helena, UK	47
Shetland Isls., Scotland, UK	555
Skye, Scotland, UK	647
South Georgia, UK	1,450
Tierra del Fuego, Chile-Arg.	18,800
Tristan da Cunha, UK	38

Baltic Sea	
Aland Isls., Finland	610
Bornholm, Denmark	227
Funen, Denmark	1,154
Gotland, Sweden	1,159
Zealand, Denmark	2,722

Caribbean Sea	
Antigua	108
Aruba, Netherlands	69
Barbados	166
Cayman Isls., UK (tot. group)	102
Cuba	40,285
Isle of Youth	934
Curaçao, Netherlands	171
Dominica	290
Guadeloupe, France	687
Hispaniola (Haiti and Dominican Rep.)	29,389
Jamaica	4,244
Martinique, France	436
Puerto Rico, U.S.	3,425
Tobago	116
Trinidad	1,864
Virgin Isls., UK	59
Virgin Isls., U.S.	134

East Indies	
Bali, Indonesia	2,171
Bangka, Indonesia	4,375
Borneo, Indonesia-Malaysia-Brunei (3)	290,321
Bougainville, Papua New Guinea	3,880
Buru, Indonesia	3,670
Celebes, Indonesia	69,000
Flores, Indonesia	5,500
Halmahera, Indonesia	6,865
Java (Jawa), Indonesia	48,900
Madura, Indonesia	2,113
Moluccas, Indonesia	32,307
New Britain, PNG	14,093
New Guinea, Indon.-PNG (2)	303,381
New Ireland, PNG	3,707
Seram, Indonesia	6,621
Sumatra, Indonesia (6)	182,543
Sumba, Indonesia	4,306
Sumbawa, Indonesia	5,965
Timor, Indon.–Timor-Leste	13,094
Yos Sudarsa, Indonesia	4,500

Indian Ocean	
Andaman Isls., India	2,500
Kerguelen, France	2,247
Madagascar (4)	226,917
Mauritius	720
Pemba, Tanzania	380
Réunion, France	970
Seychelles	176
Sri Lanka	25,332
Zanzibar, Tanzania	640

Mediterranean Sea	
Balearic Isls., Spain	1,927
Corfu, Greece	229
Corsica, France	3,369
Crete, Greece	3,189
Cyprus	3,572
Elba, Italy	86
Euboea, Greece	1,411
Malta	95
Rhodes, Greece	540
Sardinia, Italy	9,301
Sicily, Italy	9,926

Pacific Ocean	
Admiralty, AK, U.S.	1,709
Aleutian Isls., AK, U.S. (tot. group)	6,912
Adak	275
Amchitka	116
Attu	350
Kanaga	142
Kiska	106
Tanaga	195
Umnak	686
Unalaska	1,051
Unimak	1,571
Baranof, AK, U.S.	1,636
Chichagof, AK, U.S.	2,062
Chiloe, Chile	3,241
Diomede (Big), Russia	11
Easter Isl. (Rapa Nui), Chile	63
Fiji (tot. group)	7,056
Vanua Levu	2,242
Viti Levu	4,109
Galapagos Isls., Ecuador	3,043
Graham Isl., BC, Can.	2,456
Guadalcanal, Solomon Isls.	2,180
Guam, U.S.	210
Hainan, China	13,000
Hawaiian Isls., HI, U.S. (tot. group)	6,428
Hawaii	4,028
Oahu	597
Hong Kong, China	31
Hoste, Chile	1,590
Japan (tot. group)	145,936
Hokkaido	30,110
Honshu (7)	88,017
Kyushu	14,202
Okinawa	466
Shikoku	7,065
Kangaroo, South Australia	1,705
Kiritimati (Christmas), Kiribati	150
Kodiak, AK, U.S.	3,485
Kupreanof, AK, U.S.	1,084
Marquesas Isls., France	492
Marshall Islands	70
Melville, Northern Terr., Australia	2,234
Micronesia	271
New Caledonia, France	6,530
New Zealand (tot. group)	103,362
Chatham Isls.	372
North	44,075
South	58,076
Stewart	649
Northern Mariana Isls., U.S.	179
Nunivak, AK, U.S.	1,600
Palau	188
Philippines (tot. group)	115,831
Leyte	2,787
Luzon	40,680
Mindanao	36,775
Mindoro	3,690
Negros	4,907
Palawan	4,554
Panay	4,446
Samar	5,050
Prince of Wales, AK, U.S.	2,770
Revillagigedo, AK, U.S.	1,134
Riesco, Chile	1,973
St. Lawrence, AK, U.S.	1,780
Sakhalin, Russia	29,500
Samoa Isls. (tot. group)	1,177
American Samoa, U.S.	77
Savaii, Samoa	659
Tutuila, U.S.	55
Upolu, Samoa	432
Santa Catalina, CA, U.S.	75
Santa Ines, Chile	1,407
Tahiti, France	402
Taiwan (tot. group)	13,892
Jinmen Dao (Quemoy)	56
Tasmania, Australia	26,178
Tonga	288
Vancouver Isl., BC, Can.	12,079
Vanuatu	4,707
Wellington, Chile	2,549

Persian Gulf	
Bahrain	295

Notable Deserts of the World

Deserts are defined as regions of the Earth receiving less than 10 in. of precipitation annually, usually in combination with an evaporation rate exceeding precipitation.

In addition to areas listed below, the continent of Antarctica, with an area of about 5.4 mil sq mi (roughly doubled by ice in winter), is generally considered a desert. Annual precipitation averages 8 in. along the coast and far less in the deep interior; however, there is little evaporation.

Arabian (Eastern), 86,000 sq mi in Egypt between the Nile R. and Red Sea, extending south into Sudan
Atacama, 600-mi-long area rich in nitrate and copper deposits in northern Chile
Chihuahuan, 140,000 sq mi in TX, NM, AZ, and Mexico
Dasht-e Kavir, approx. 500 mi long by 200 mi wide in north-central Iran
Dasht-e Lut, approx. 300 mi long by 200 mi wide in south-central Iran
Death Valley, 3,300 sq mi in CA and NV
Gibson, 60,232 sq mi in the interior of western Australia
Gobi, 500,000 sq mi in Mongolia and China
Great Sandy, 103,186 sq mi in western Australia
Great Victoria, 134,653 sq mi in southwestern Australia
Kalahari, 275,000 sq mi in southern Africa
Kara Kum, 115,000 sq mi in Turkmenistan
Kyzyl Kum, 115,000 sq mi in Kazakhstan and Uzbekistan
Libyan, 425,000 sq mi in the Sahara, extending from Libya through southwestern Egypt into Sudan

Mojave, 15,000 sq mi in southern CA
Namib, long narrow area (varies 30-100 mi wide) extending 800 mi along SW coast of Africa
Nubian, 157,000 sq mi in the Sahara in northeastern Sudan
Painted Desert, section of high plateau in northern AZ extending 200 mi southeast from Grand Canyon
Patagonia, 300,000 sq mi in southern Argentina
Rub al-Khali (Empty Quarter), 225,000 sq mi in the S Arabian Peninsula
Sahara, 3,500,000 sq mi in N Africa, extending west to the Atlantic. Largest desert in the world
Sonoran, 70,000 sq mi in southwestern AZ and southeastern CA extending into NW Mexico
Syrian, 100,000 sq mi over much of northern Saudi Arabia, eastern Jordan, southern Syria, and western Iraq
Taklamakan, 140,000 sq mi in Xinjiang Prov., China
Tanami, 71,236 sq mi in northern Australia
Thar (Great Indian), 100,000-sq-mi area extending 400 mi along India-Pakistan border

Areas and Average Depths of Oceans, Seas, and Gulfs

Geographers and mapmakers recognize at least four major bodies of water: the Pacific, Atlantic, Indian, and Arctic Oceans. The Atlantic and Pacific Oceans are considered divided at the equator into N and S. The Arctic Ocean is the name for waters north of the continental landmasses in the region of the Arctic Circle. The International Hydrographic Organization delimited a fifth world ocean in 2000. The Southern Ocean extends from the coast of Antarctica north to 60°S latitude, encompassing portions of the Atlantic, Indian, and Pacific Oceans. A Woods Hole Oceanographic Institution study published in 2010 calculated a mean depth of 12,081 ft for the world's oceans.

Body of water	Area (sq mi)	Avg. depth (ft)	Body of water	Area (sq mi)	Avg. depth (ft)
Pacific Ocean	60,060,893	14,040	Sea of Japan	391,100	5,468
Atlantic Ocean	29,637,974	11,810	Hudson Bay	281,900	305
Indian Ocean	26,469,620	12,800	East China Sea	256,600	620
Southern Ocean	7,848,299	14,450	Andaman Sea	218,100	3,667
Arctic Ocean	5,427,052	4,300	Black Sea	196,100	3,906
South China Sea	2,688,429	4,802	Red Sea	174,900	1,764
Caribbean Sea	971,400	8,448	North Sea	164,900	308
Mediterranean Sea	969,100	4,926	Baltic Sea	147,500	180
Bering Sea	873,000	4,893	Yellow Sea	113,500	121
Gulf of Mexico	582,100	5,297	Persian Gulf	88,800	328
Sea of Okhotsk	537,500	3,192	Gulf of California	59,100	2,375

Principal Ocean Depths

Source: Intl. Hydrographic Org. (IHO); Intergovernmental Oceanographic Commission (IOC) of UNESCO; National Geospatial-Intelligence Agency, U.S. Dept. of Defense

Body of water	Location (lat.)	(long.)	Depth (meters)	(fathoms)	(feet)
Pacific Ocean					
Mariana Trench	11°22′ N	142°36′ E	10,994	6,012	36,069
Tonga Trench	23°16′ S	174°44′ W	10,800	5,906	35,433
Philippine Trench	10°38′ N	126°36′ E	10,057	5,499	32,995
Kermadec Trench	31°53′ S	177°21′ W	10,047	5,494	32,963
Bonin Trench	24°30′ N	143°24′ E	9,994	5,464	32,788
Kuril Trench	44°15′ N	150°34′ E	9,750	5,331	31,988
Izu Trench	31°05′ N	142°10′ E	9,695	5,301	31,808
New Britain Trench	06°19′ S	153°45′ E	8,940	4,888	29,331
Yap Trench	08°33′ N	138°02′ E	8,527	4,663	27,976
Japan Trench	36°08′ N	142°43′ E	8,412	4,600	27,599
Peru-Chile Trench	23°18′ S	71°14′ W	8,064	4,409	26,457
Palau Trench	07°52′ N	134°56′ E	8,054	4,404	26,424
Aleutian Trench	50°51′ N	177°11′ E	7,679	4,199	25,194
New Hebrides Trench	20°36′ S	168°37′ E	7,570	4,139	24,836
North Ryukyu Trench	24°00′ N	126°48′ E	7,181	3,927	23,560
Middle America Trench	14°02′ N	93°39′ W	6,662	3,643	21,857
Atlantic Ocean					
Puerto Rico Trench	19°55′ N	65°27′ W	8,605	4,705	28,232
South Sandwich Trench	55°42′ S	25°56′ W	8,325	4,552	27,313
Romanche Gap	0°13′ S	18°26′ W	7,728	4,226	25,354
Cayman Trench	19°12′ N	80°00′ W	7,535	4,120	24,721
Brazil Basin	09°10′ S	23°02′ W	6,119	3,346	20,076
Indian Ocean					
Java Trench	10°19′ S	109°58′ E	7,125	3,896	23,376
Ob' Trench	09°45′ S	67°18′ E	6,874	3,759	22,553
Diamantina Trench	35°50′ S	105°14′ E	6,602	3,610	21,660
Vema Trench	09°08′ S	67°15′ E	6,402	3,501	21,004
Agulhas Basin	45°20′ S	26°50′ E	6,195	3,387	20,325
Arctic Ocean					
Eurasia Basin	82°23′ N	19°31′ E	5,450	2,980	17,881
Mediterranean Sea					
Ionian Basin	36°32′ N	21°06′ E	5,150	2,816	16,896

Note: Greater depths have been reported in some areas but have not been officially confirmed by research vessels.

Major World Rivers

North American rivers are listed in a separate table.

River	Source or upper limit of length	Outflow	Length (mi)
Africa			
Chari	Bamingui-Bangoran region, Central African Republic	Lake Chad	650
Congo	Junction of Lualaba and Luvua Rivers, Dem. Rep. of Congo	Atlantic Ocean	2,720
Cubango (fmr. Okavango)	Central Angola	Okavango Delta	1,000
Gambia	Fouta Djallon Highlands, Guinea	Atlantic Ocean	700
Kasai	Central Angola	Congo River	1,100
Limpopo	Junction of Marico and Ngotwane Rivers, South Africa	Indian Ocean	1,100
Lualaba	Southeastern Dem. Rep. of Congo	Congo River	1,100
Niger	Fouta Djallon Highlands, Guinea	Gulf of Guinea	2,600
Nile	Luvironza River, Burundi	Mediterranean Sea	4,160
Orange	Maluti Mountains, northern Lesotho	Atlantic Ocean	1,300
Sénégal	Junction of Bafing and Bakoy Rivers, Mali	Atlantic Ocean	1,000
Ubangi	Junction of Uele and Bomu Rivers, Dem. Rep. of Congo	Congo River	700
Zambezi	Northwestern Zambia	Indian Ocean	1,700
Asia			
Amu Darya	Junction of Vakhsh and Panj Rivers, Afghanistan-Tajikistan	Aral Sea	1,660
Amur	Junction of Shilka and Argun Rivers, China-Russia	Tartar Strait	1,780
Angara	Lake Baikal, Russia	Yenisei River	1,150
Ayeyarwady (fmr. Irrawaddy)	Junction of Mali and Nmai Rivers, Myanmar	Andaman Sea	1,000
Brahmaputra	Kailas Range, Himalayas, southwestern Tibet	Bay of Bengal	1,800
Chang-Jiang	Tibetan Plateau, southwestern Qinghai, China	East China Sea	3,450
Euphrates	Junction of Kara (Sarasu) and Murat Rivers, Turkey	Shatt al-Arab	1,700
Ganges	Gangotri glacier, Himalayas, India	Bay of Bengal	1,560
Godavari	Western Ghats, Maharashtra, India	Bay of Bengal	900
Hsi (see Xi He)			
Huang-He	Kunlun Mountains, Qinghai, China	Yellow Sea	3,000
Indus	Kailas Range, Himalayas, Tibet	Arabian Sea	1,900
Irtysh	Kazakhstan-Russia	Ob River	2,650
Jordan	Junction of Dan, Banias, and Hazbani streams, Israel	Dead Sea	200
Kolyma	Kolyma and Cherskogo Ranges, Russia	Arctic Ocean	1,500
Krishna	Western Ghats, Maharashtra, India	Bay of Bengal	800
Kura	Northeastern Turkey	Caspian Sea	950
Lena	Western Baikal Range, Russia	Laptev Sea	2,648
Mekong	Eastern Tibetan Plateau, China	South China Sea	2,700
Narmada	Madhya Pradesh, India	Arabian Sea	775
Ob	Junction of Biya and Katun Rivers, Russia	Gulf of Ob	2,300
Salween	Eastern Tibet, China	Gulf of Martaban	1,750
Songhua Jiang	Changbai Mountains, Jilin, China	Amur River	1,150
Sungari (see Songhua Jiang)			
Sutlej	Kailas Range, Himalayas, Tibet	Indus River	900
Syr	Junction of Naryn and Kara Darya Rivers, Uzbekistan	Aral Sea	1,380
Tarim	Junction of Kashi and Yarkant Rivers, China	Lop Nor	1,300
Tigris	Taurus Mountains, Turkey	Shatt al-Arab	1,150
Xi He	Eastern Yunnan, China	South China Sea	1,250
Yamuna	Yamnotri glacier, Uttarakhand, India	Ganges River	850
Yangtze (see Chang-Jiang)			
Yellow (see Huang-He)			
Yenisei	Kyzyl, Tuva Republic, Russia	Kara Sea	2,500
Australia			
Darling	Eastern Highlands, NE New South Wales/SE Queensland	Murray River	1,703
Murray	Australian Alps, SE New South Wales	Southern Ocean	1,558
Murrumbidgee	Australian Alps, SE New South Wales	Murray River	923
Europe			
Buh, Southern	Podolian Upland, Ukraine	Black Sea	532
Buh, Western	Western Ukraine	Vistula River	500
Danube	Brege and Brigach Rivers, Black Forest, southwestern Germany	Black Sea	1,770
Dnieper	Valdai Hills, western Russia	Black Sea	1,420
Dniester	Carpathian Mountains, Ukraine	Black Sea	850
Don	SE of Tula, Russia	Sea of Azov	1,200
Drava	Carnic Alps, northern Italy	Danube River	450
Dvina, North	Near Veliki Ustyug, Vologda, Russia	White Sea	465
Dvina, West	Valdai Hills, Russia	Gulf of Riga	635
Ebro	Cantabrian Mountains, northern Spain	Mediterranean Sea	575
Elbe	Giant Mountains, northwestern Czech Republic	North Sea	725
Garonne	Central Pyrenees, Spain	Bay of Biscay	402
Kama	Ural Mountains, N of Kuliga, Russia	Volga River	1,260
Loire	Mt. Gerbier-de-Jonc, Vivrais Mountains, France	Atlantic Ocean	630
Marne	Langres Plateau, northeastern France	Seine River	325
Meuse	Langres Plateau, northeastern France	North Sea	560
Oder	Sudetes Mountains, northeastern Czech Republic	Baltic Sea	562
Oka	S of Orël, Russia	Volga River	925
Pechora	Northern Ural Mountains, Russia	Barents Sea	1,120
Po	Cottian Alps, Piedmont, northwestern Italy	Adriatic Sea	405
Rhine	Swiss Alps	North Sea	820

River	Source or upper limit of length	Outflow	Length (mi)
Rhône	Rhône glacier, northeastern Valais, Switzerland	Mediterranean Sea	505
Seine	Langres Plateau, northern Burgundy, France	English Channel	480
Shannon	Near Cuilcagh Mountain, northwestern Cavan County, Ireland	Atlantic Ocean	240
Tagus	E of Madrid, Spain	Atlantic Ocean	585
Thames	4 headstreams in the Cotswold Hills, Gloucestershire, England, UK	North Sea	215
Tiber	Etruscan Apennines, Italy	Tyrrhenian Sea	251
Tisza	N of Rakhiv, western Ukraine	Danube River	700
Ural	Southern Ural Mountains, northeastern Bashkortostan, Russia	Caspian Sea	1,580
Vistula (Wisla)	W Beskid range, Carpathian Mountains, southwestern Poland	Gulf of Gdansk	665
Volga	Valdai Hills, Smolensk, Russia	Caspian Sea	2,290
Weser	Junction of Fulda and Werra Rivers, Germany	North Sea	273
South America			
Amazon	Junction of Ucayali and Marañón Rivers, Andes Mountains, Peru	Atlantic Ocean	3,900
Araguaía	Serra das Araras, Goiás-Mato Grosso, Brazil	Tocantins River	1,100
Beni	Cordillera Real, La Paz, Bolivia	Madeira River	1,000
Caquetá-Japura	Andes Mountains, southwestern Colombia	Amazon River	1,750
Juruá	Cerros de Canchyuaya, eastern Peru	Amazon River	1,500
Madeira	Junction of Beni and Mamoré Rivers, Bolivia	Amazon River	2,100
Magdalena	Cordillera Central, southwestern Colombia	Caribbean Sea	1,000
Negro	Southeastern Colombia	Amazon River	1,400
Orinoco	Near Mt. Delgado Chalbaud, Guiana Highlands, S Venezuela	Atlantic Ocean	1,600
Paraguay	Central Mato Grosso highlands, Brazil	Paraná River	1,584
Paraná	Junction of Paranaíba and Rio Grande Rivers, SE Brazil	Rio de la Plata	2,485
Pilcomayo	E of Lake Poopó, Bolivia	Paraguay River	1,000
Purus	Andes Mountains, eastern Peru	Amazon River	2,100
Putumayo	Andes Mountains, southern Colombia	Amazon River	1,000
Rio de la Plata	Estuary of Paraná and Uruguay Rivers, Argentina-Uruguay	Atlantic Ocean	170
São Francisco	Serra de Canastra, southwestern Minas Gerais, Brazil	Atlantic Ocean	1,800
Tocantins	South-central Goiás, Brazil	Para River	1,640
Ucayali	Junction of Apurímac and Urubamba Rivers, eastern Peru	Marañón River	1,000
Uruguay	Southern Brazil	Rio de la Plata	1,000
Xingu	Central Mato Grosso, Brazil	Amazon River	1,230

Major Rivers in North America

River	Source or upper limit of length	Outflow	Length (mi)
Alabama	Gilmer County, GA	Mobile River	729
Albany	Lake St. Joseph, ON, Can.	James Bay	610
Allegheny	Potter County, PA	Ohio River	325
Altamaha-Ocmulgee	Junction of Yellow and South Rivers, Newton Co., GA	Atlantic Ocean	392
Apalachicola-Chattahoochee	Towns County, GA	Gulf of Mexico	524
Arkansas	Lake County, CO	Mississippi River	1,459
Assiniboine	Eastern Saskatchewan, Can.	Red River	450
Attawapiskat	Attawapiskat, ON, Can.	James Bay	465
Back (NT)	Contwoyto Lake, NT, Can.	Chantrey Inlet, Arctic Ocean	605
Big Black	Webster County, MS	Mississippi River	330
Brazos	Junction of Salt and Double Mountain Forks, Stonewall Co., TX	Gulf of Mexico	1,280
Canadian	Las Animas County, CO	Arkansas River	906
Cedar (IA)	Dodge County, MN	Iowa River	329
Cheyenne	Junction of Antelope Creek and Dry Fork, Converse Co., WY	Missouri River	290
Churchill, Labrador	Lake Ashuanipi, NL, Can.	Atlantic Ocean	532
Churchill, Manitoba	Methy Lake, SK, Can.	Hudson Bay	1,000
Cimarron	Colfax County, NM	Arkansas River	600
Colorado (AZ)	Rocky Mountain Natl. Park, CO	Gulf of California	1,450
Colorado (TX)	Dawson County, TX	Matagorda Bay	862
Columbia	Columbia Lake, BC, Can.	Pacific Ocean, Astoria, OR	1,243
Columbia, Upper	Columbia Lake, BC, Can.	Mouth of Snake River	890
Connecticut	Third Connecticut Lake, NH	Long Island Sound, CT	407
Coppermine	Lac de Gras, NT, Can.	Coronation Gulf, Arctic Ocean	525
Cumberland	Letcher County, KY	Ohio River	720
Delaware	Schoharie County, NY	Liston Point, Delaware Bay	390
Fraser	Near Mount Robson (on Continental Divide)	Strait of Georgia	850
Gila	Catron County, NM	Colorado River	649
Green (UT-WY)	Junction of Wells and Trail Creeks, Sublette County, WY	Colorado River	730
Hudson	Henderson Lake, Essex County, NY	Upper New York Bay	306
Illinois	St. Joseph County, IN	Mississippi River	420
James (ND-SD)	Wells County, ND	Missouri River	710
James (VA)	Junction of Jackson and Cowpasture Rivers, Botetourt Co., VA	Hampton Roads	340
Kanawha-New	Junction of North and South Forks of New River, NC	Ohio River	352
Kentucky	Junction of North and Middle Forks, Lee County, KY	Ohio River	259
Klamath	Lake Ewauna, Klamath Falls, OR	Pacific Ocean, Klamath, CA	250

River	Source or upper limit of length	Outflow	Length (mi)
Kootenay (Kootenai)	Rocky Mountains, BC, Can.	Columbia River	485
Koyukuk	Endicott Mountains, AK	Yukon River	470
Kuskokwim	Alaska Range	Kuskokwim Bay	724
Liard	Southern Yukon, AK	Mackenzie River	693
Little Missouri	Crook County, WY	Missouri River	560
Mackenzie	Great Slave Lake, NT, Can.	Arctic Ocean	2,635
Milk	Junction of North and South Forks, AB, Can.	Missouri River	625
Minnesota	Big Stone Lake, MN	Mississippi River	332
Mississippi	Lake Itasca, Clearwater County, MN	Gulf of Mexico	2,340
Mississippi-Missouri-Red Rock	Source of Red Rock, Beaverhead County, MT	Gulf of Mexico	3,710
Missouri	Junction of Jefferson, Madison, and Gallatin Rivers, Gallatin County, MT	Mississippi River	2,315
Missouri-Red Rock	Source of Red Rock, Beaverhead County, MT	Mississippi River	2,540
Mobile-Alabama-Coosa	Gilmer County, GA	Mobile Bay	774
Nelson	Lake Winnipeg, MB, Can.	Hudson Bay	410
Neosho	Morris County, KS	Arkansas River, OK	460
Niobrara	Niobrara County, WY	Missouri River, NE	431
North Canadian	Union County, NM	Canadian River, OK	800
North Platte	Junction of Grizzly and Little Grizzly Creeks, Jackson Co., CO	Platte River, NE	618
Ohio	Junction of Allegheny and Monongahela Rivers, Pittsburgh, PA	Mississippi River	981
Ohio-Allegheny	Potter County, PA	Mississippi River	1,310
Osage	East-central Kansas	Missouri River	500
Ottawa	Lake Capimitchigama, QC, Can.	St. Lawrence River	790
Ouachita	Polk County, AR	Black River	605
Peace	Junction of Finlay and Parsnip Rivers, BC, Can.	Slave River	1,210
Pearl	Neshoba County, MS	Gulf of Mexico	411
Pecos	Mora County, NM	Rio Grande	926
Pee Dee-Yadkin	Watauga County, NC	Winyah Bay	435
Pend Oreille-Clark Fork	Near Butte, MT	Columbia River	531
Platte	Junction of North Platte and South Platte Rivers, NE	Missouri River	310
Porcupine	Ogilvie Mountains, AK	Yukon River, AK	569
Potomac	Garrett County, MD	Chesapeake Bay	383
Powder	Junction of South and Middle Forks, WY	Yellowstone River	375
Red (River of the South)	Curry County, NM	Atchafalaya River, LA	1,290
Red River of the North	Junction of Otter Tail and Bois de Sioux Rivers, Wilkin Co., MN	Lake Winnipeg	545
Republican	Junction of North Fork and Arikaree Rivers, NE	Kansas River	445
Rio Grande (Rio Bravo)	San Juan County, CO	Gulf of Mexico	1,900
Roanoke	Junction of North and South Forks, Montgomery Co., VA	Albemarle Sound	380
Rock (IL-WI)	Dodge County, WI	Mississippi River	300
Sabine	Junction of South and Caddo Forks, Hunt Co., TX	Sabine Lake	380
Sacramento	Siskiyou County, CA	Suisun Bay	377
St. Francis	Iron County, MO	Mississippi River	425
St. John	Northwestern Maine	Bay of Fundy	418
St. Lawrence	Lake Ontario, NY-ON, Can.	Gulf of St. Lawrence, Atlantic Ocean	800
Saguenay	Lake St. John, QC, Can.	St. Lawrence River	434
Salmon (ID)	Custer County, ID	Snake River	420
San Joaquin	Junction of South and Middle Forks, Madera Co., CA	Suisun Bay	350
San Juan	Silver Lake, Archuleta County, CO	Colorado River	360
Santee-Wateree-Catawba	McDowell County, NC	Atlantic Ocean	538
Saskatchewan, North	Rocky Mountains, AB, Can.	Saskatchewan R.	800
Saskatchewan, South	Rocky Mountains, AB, Can.	Saskatchewan R.	865
Savannah	Junction of Seneca and Tugaloo Rivers, Anderson Co., SC	Atlantic Ocean, GA-SC	314
Severn (ON)	Sandy Lake, ON, Can.	Hudson Bay	610
Smoky Hill	Cheyenne County, CO	Kansas River, KS	540
Snake	Teton County, WY	Columbia River, WA	1,038
South Platte	Junction of South and Middle Forks, Park County, CO	Platte River	424
Susitna	Alaska Range	Cook Inlet	313
Susquehanna	Otsego Lake, Otsego County, NY	Chesapeake Bay	447
Tallahatchie	Tippah County, MS	Yazoo River	301
Tanana	Wrangell Mountains, AK	Yukon River	659
Tennessee	Junction of French Broad and Holston Rivers, TN	Ohio River	652
Tennessee-French Broad	Courthouse Creek, Transylvania County, NC	Ohio River	886
Tombigbee	Prentiss County, MS	Mobile River	525
Trinity	N of Dallas, TX	Galveston Bay	360
Usumacinta	Junction of Pasión and Chixoy Rivers, Guatemala	Bay of Campeche, Mex.	600
Wabash	Darke County, OH	Ohio River	512
Washita	Hemphill County, TX	Red River, OK	500
White (AR-MO)	Madison County, AR	Mississippi River	722
Willamette	Douglas County, OR	Columbia River	309
Wind-Bighorn	Junction of Wind and Little Wind Rivers, Fremont Co., WY (source of Wind R. is Togwotee Pass, Teton Co., WY)	Yellowstone River	338
Wisconsin	Lac Vieux Desert, Vilas County, WI	Mississippi River	430
Yellowstone	Park County, WY	Missouri River	682
Yukon	McNeil River, YT, Can.	Bering Sea	1,979

Major Natural Lakes of the World

Source: U.S. Geological Survey, U.S. Dept. of the Interior; Natural Resources Canada

A lake is generally defined as a body of water surrounded by land. By this definition some bodies of water that are called seas, such as the Caspian Sea and the Aral Sea, are really lakes. In the following table, the word "lake" is omitted when it is part of the name.

Name	Continent	Area (sq mi)	Length (mi)	Maximum depth (ft)	Elevation (ft)
Caspian Sea[1]	Asia-Europe	143,244	760	3,363	–92
Superior	North America	31,700	350	1,333	601
Victoria	Africa	26,828	209	270	3,720
Huron	North America	23,000	206	750	578
Michigan	North America	22,300	307	923	578
Tanganyika	Africa	12,700	420	4,823	2,534
Baikal	Asia	12,162	395	5,315	1,493
Great Bear	North America	12,096	192	1,463	512
Nyasa (Malawi)	Africa	11,150	360	2,280	1,550
Great Slave	North America	11,030	298	2,014	512
Erie	North America	9,910	241	210	569
Winnipeg	North America	9,416	266	200	712
Ontario	North America	7,340	193	802	243
Balkhash[1]	Asia	7,115	376	85	1,115
Ladoga	Europe	6,835	124	738	13
Maracaibo	South America	5,217	133	115	sea level
Aral Sea[1,2]	Asia	4,040	260	180	175
Onega	Europe	3,710	145	328	108
Eyre[1]	Australia	3,600[3]	90	4	–52
Titicaca	South America	3,200	122	922	12,500
Nicaragua	North America	3,100	102	230	102
Athabasca	North America	3,064	208	407	699
Reindeer	North America	2,568	143	720	1,106
Tonle Sap	Asia	2,500[3]	70	45	NA
Turkana (Rudolf)	Africa	2,473	154	240	1,230
Issyk Kul[1]	Asia	2,355	115	2,303	5,279
Torrens[1]	Australia	2,230[3]	130	NA[3]	92
Vänern	Europe	2,181	91	328	144
Nettilling	North America	2,140	67	(3)	98
Winnipegosis	North America	2,075	141	38	833
Albert	Africa	2,075	100	168	2,030
Nipigon	North America	1,872	72	540	853
Gairdner[1]	Australia	1,840[3]	90	NA[3]	112
Urmia[1]	Asia	1,815	90	49	4,177
Manitoba	North America	1,799	140	21	813
Chad	Africa	521[4]	175	24	787

NA = Not available. (1) Salt lake. (2) The diversion of its two feeder rivers since the 1960s has devastated the Aral—once the world's fourth-largest lake (26,000 sq mi) with length, max. depth, and elevation shown. By 2000, the Aral had effectively become three lakes, with the total area shown. (3) Subject to great seasonal variation. (4) Once fourth-largest lake in Africa (about 10,000 sq mi in the 1960s), Chad had shrunk to around 5% of its original size by 2006 as a result of irrigation and long-term drought.

The Great Lakes

Source: National Ocean Service, National Oceanic and Atmospheric Administration, U.S. Dept. of Commerce

The Great Lakes form the world's **largest freshwater body** (in surface area) and with their connecting waterways are the largest inland water transportation unit. Draining the north-central basin of the U.S., they enable shipping to get to the Atlantic via their outlet, the St. Lawrence R.; the Gulf of Mexico can be reached via the Illinois Waterway, between Lake Michigan and the Mississippi R. A third outlet connects with the Hudson R. and then the Atlantic via the New York State Barge Canal System. Illinois Waterway and NYS Barge Canal System traffic is limited to recreational boating and small shipping vessels.

Only Lake Michigan is wholly in the U.S.; the other lakes are shared with Canada. Ships move from the shores of Lake Superior to Whitefish Bay in the east, then through the Soo Locks in Sault Ste. Marie, MI, onto St. Mary's R. and into Lake Huron. To reach the Port of Indiana-Burns Harbor and South Chicago, IL, ships travel west from Lake Huron to Lake Michigan through the Straits of Mackinac. Low water datum is based on the International Great Lakes Datum (1985), with Rimouski, Quebec, as the reference zero point. The distance between Duluth, MN, and Lake Ontario's east end is 1,156 mi.

	Superior	Michigan	Huron	Erie	Ontario
Length (mi)	350	307	206	241	193
Breadth (mi)	160	118	183	57	53
Deepest soundings (ft)	1,333	923	750	210	802
Volume of water (cu mi)	2,935	1,180	850	116	393
Area (sq mi) water surface—U.S.	20,600	22,300	9,100	4,980	3,460
Canada	11,100	NA	13,900	4,930	3,880
Area (sq mi) entire drainage basin—U.S.	16,900	45,600	16,200	18,000	15,200
Canada	32,400	NA	35,500	4,720	12,100
Total area (sq mi), U.S. and Canada	**81,000**	**67,900**	**74,700**	**32,630**	**34,850**
Low water datum above mean water level at Rimouski, QC, avg. level (ft)	601.10	577.50	577.50	569.20	243.30
Latitude, N	46°25′	41°37′	43°00′	41°23′	43°11′
	49°00′	46°06′	46°17′	42°52′	44°15′
Longitude, W	84°22′	84°45′	79°43′	78°51′	76°03′
	92°06′	88°02′	84°45′	83°29′	79°53′
National boundary line (mi)	282.8	NA	260.8	251.5	174.6
U.S. shoreline (mainland only) (mi)	863	1,400	580	431	300

NA = Not applicable.

Notable Waterfalls

The magnitude of a waterfall is determined not only by height but also by volume and steadiness of flow, crest width, the angle of a drop, and the number of leaps it may make. A series of low falls over a considerable distance is known as a cascade. Waterfalls are highly variable and few authoritative figures exist. For more information and some alternative measurements, see the World Waterfall Database at www.worldwaterfalldatabase.com.

Estimated mean annual flow (ft³/sec): Niagara, 212,200; Paulo Afonso, 100,000; Iguazú, 61,000; Victoria, 35,400.

Height is total drop in feet in one or more leaps. If river name is not shown, it is the same as the waterfall. # = more than one leap; * = diminishes greatly seasonally; ** = reduces to a trickle or is dry for part of each year; R. = river; (C) = cascade.

Name, location	Height (ft)
Africa	
Angola-Namibia	
Ruacana, Cunene R.	352
Lesotho	
Maletsunyane*	630
South Africa	
Augrabies, Orange R.*	480
Tugela#	2,800
Tanzania-Zambia	
Kalambo*	704
Zimbabwe-Zambia	
Victoria, Zambezi R.*	343
Asia and Oceania	
Australia	
New South Wales	
Wentworth	614
Wollomombi	722
Queensland	
Tully**	984
Wallaman, Stony Creek	879
India	
Jog, Sharavati R.*	829
Sivasamudram	320
Japan	
Kegon, Lake Chuzenji*	350
New Zealand	
Helena	722
Sutherland, Arthur R.#	1,904
Europe	
Austria	
Gastein#	487
Krimml#	1,246
France	
Gavarnie*	1,385
Italy	
Toce (C)	470
Norway	
Mardalsfossen#**	2,154
Skykje**	984
Vetti, Morka-Koldedola R.	900

Name, location	Height (ft)
Sweden	
Handol#	345
Switzerland	
Giessbach (C)	984
Reichenbach#	394
Staubbach	974
Trümmelbach#	950
United Kingdom	
Glomach, Scotland	370
Pistyll Rhaeadr, Wales	240
North America	
Canada	
Alberta	
Panther, Nigel Creek	600
British Columbia	
Della#	1,444
Takakkaw, Daly Glacier#	992
Ontario	
Niagara (Horseshoe)	167
Québec	
Montmorency	276
United States	
Alabama	
Noccalula Falls	90
California	
Feather*	640
Yosemite National Park	
Bridalveil*	620
Illilouette*	370
Nevada, Merced R.*	594
Ribbon**	1,612
Silver Strand,	
Meadow Brook**	574
Vernal, Merced R.*	317
Yosemite#**	2,425
Colorado	
Seven Falls,	
S. Cheyenne Creek#	300
Hawaii	
Akaka, Kolekole Stream	420
Idaho	
Shoshone, Snake R.**	212

Name, location	Height (ft)
Kentucky	
Cumberland	68
Maryland	
Great, Potomac R. (C)*	76
Minnesota	
Minnehaha**	53
New Jersey	
Great, Passaic R.	70
New York	
Niagara (American)	120
Taughannock*	215
Oregon	
Multnomah#	620
Tennessee	
Fall Creek	256
Washington	
Colonial Creek	2,568
Sluiskin, Paradise R.	300
Snoqualmie**	268
Wisconsin	
Big Manitou, Black R. (C)*	165
Wyoming	
Tower	132
Yellowstone (lower)*	308
Yellowstone (upper)*	109
South America	
Argentina-Brazil	
Iguazú	269
Brazil	
Cachoeira da Fumaça*	1,312
Paulo Afonso, São Francisco R.	275
Colombia	
Tequendama, Bogota R.*	482
Ecuador	
Agoyan, Pastaza R.*	200
Guyana	
Kaieteur, Potaro R.	741
King George VI, Kamarang R.	1,600
Marina, Ipobe R.#	500
Venezuela	
Angel (Kerepakupai Merú),	
Churún#*	3,212
Cuquenan	2,000

Latitude and Longitude of World Cities

Source: National Geospatial-Intelligence Agency, U.S. Dept. of Defense

City, country	Lat. °	'	Long. °	'	City, country	Lat. °	'	Long. °	'
Athens, Greece	37	59 N	23	44 E	Manila, Philippines	14	35 N	121	0 E
Bangkok, Thailand	13	45 N	100	31 E	Mexico City, Mexico	19	26 N	99	8 W
Beijing, China	39	55 N	116	23 E	Moscow, Russia	55	45 N	37	36 E
Berlin, Germany	52	31 N	13	24 E	Mumbai (Bombay), India	18	59 N	72	50 E
Bogotá, Colombia	4	38 N	74	3 W	New Delhi, India	28	36 N	77	12 E
Buenos Aires, Argentina	34	35 S	58	40 W	Paris, France	48	52 N	2	20 E
Cairo, Egypt	30	4 N	31	17 E	Rio de Janeiro, Brazil	22	52 S	43	16 W
Jakarta, Indonesia	6	10 S	106	49 E	Rome, Italy	41	54 N	12	29 E
Jerusalem, Israel	31	45 N	35	0 E	Santiago, Chile	33	27 S	70	40 W
Johannesburg, South Africa	26	12 S	28	2 E	Seoul, South Korea	37	35 N	127	0 E
Kiev, Ukraine	50	26 N	30	31 E	Sydney, Australia	33	51 S	151	12 E
Lagos, Nigeria	6	35 N	3	45 E	Tehran, Iran	35	40 N	51	25 E
London, UK (Greenwich)	51	28 N	0	0	Tokyo, Japan	35	41 N	139	45 E

Highest and Lowest Continental Elevations

Continent	Highest point	Elev. (ft)	Continent	Lowest point	Ft below sea level
Asia	Everest, Nepal-Tibet	29,035	Antarctica	Bentley Subglacial Trench	8,383[1]
South America	Aconcagua, Argentina	22,835	Asia	Dead Sea, Israel-Jordan	1,339
North America	Denali (fmr. McKinley), Alaska	20,310	Africa	Lake Assal, Djibouti	509
Africa	Kilimanjaro, Tanzania	19,341	South America	Laguna del Carbón, Argentina	344
Europe	Elbrus, Russia	18,510	North America	Death Valley, California	282
Antarctica	Vinson Massif	16,066	Europe	Caspian Sea, Azer.-Kazakh.-Russ.	92
Australia	Kosciusko, New South Wales	7,310	Australia	Lake Eyre, South Australia	49

(1) Estimated level of the continental floor. Lower points that have yet to be discovered may exist beneath the ice.

Latitude, Longitude, and Elevation of U.S. and Canadian Cities

Source: U.S. geographic positions and altitudes provided by U.S. Geological Survey, U.S. Dept. of the Interior.
Canadian geographic positions and altitudes provided by Natural Resources Canada.

City, state/province	Lat. N °	′	″	Long. W °	′	″	Elev. (ft)	City, state/province	Lat. N °	′	″	Long. W °	′	″	Elev. (ft)
Albany, NY	42	39	9	73	45	22	149	Lincoln, NE	40	48	0	96	40	0	1,200
Albuquerque, NM	35	5	4	106	39	4	4,956	Little Rock, AR	34	44	47	92	17	23	333
Anchorage, AK	61	13	5	149	54	1	104	Los Angeles, CA	34	3	8	118	14	37	291
Annapolis, MD	38	58	42	76	29	32	43	Louisville, KY	38	15	15	85	45	34	466
Atlanta, GA	33	44	56	84	23	17	1,050								
Augusta, GA	33	28	15	81	58	29	141	Madison, WI	43	4	23	89	24	4	873
Augusta, ME	44	18	38	69	46	46	123	Manchester, NH	42	59	44	71	27	17	258
Austin, TX	30	16	2	97	44	35	489	Memphis, TN	35	8	58	90	2	56	260
								Miami, FL	25	46	27	80	11	37	8
Baltimore, MD	39	17	25	76	36	44	36	Milwaukee, WI	43	2	20	87	54	23	615
Baton Rouge, LA	30	27	3	91	9	16	46	Minneapolis, MN	44	58	48	93	15	50	830
Billings, MT	45	47	0	108	30	2	3,124	Mobile, AL	30	41	40	88	2	35	10
Birmingham, AL	33	31	14	86	48	9	610	Montgomery, AL	32	22	0	86	18	0	238
Bismarck, ND	46	48	30	100	47	1	1,695	Montpelier, VT	44	15	36	72	34	31	526
Boise, ID	43	36	49	116	12	12	2,699	Montréal, QC	45	31	0	73	39	0	221
Boston, MA	42	21	30	71	3	35	45								
Buffalo, NY	42	53	11	78	52	42	600	Nashville, TN	36	9	57	86	47	4	567
Burlington, VT	44	28	33	73	12	43	196	New Orleans, LA	29	57	17	90	4	30	1
								New York, NY	40	42	51	74	0	22	35
Calgary, AB	51	2	45	114	3	27	3,557	Newark, NJ	40	44	8	74	10	21	32
Carson City, NV	39	9	50	119	46	3	4,681	Nome, AK	64	30	4	165	24	23	37
Casper, WY	42	52	0	106	18	47	5,105								
Cedar Rapids, IA	42	0	30	91	38	39	808	Oklahoma City, OK	35	28	3	97	30	59	1,198
Charleston, SC	32	46	36	79	55	51	11	Olympia, WA	47	2	16	122	54	3	93
Charleston, WV	38	20	59	81	37	57	596	Omaha, NE	41	15	31	95	56	16	1,059
Charlotte, NC	35	13	38	80	50	35	762	Ottawa, ON	45	20	0	75	35	3	382
Charlottetown, PE	46	14	25	63	8	5	160	Overland Park, KS	38	58	56	94	40	15	1,084
Cheyenne, WY	41	8	24	104	49	13	6,087								
Chicago, IL	41	51	0	87	39	0	586	Philadelphia, PA	39	57	8	75	9	50	45
Churchill, MB	58	46	51	94	11	13	94	Phoenix, AZ	33	26	54	112	4	27	1,085
Cleveland, OH	41	29	58	81	41	43	653	Pierre, SD	44	22	6	100	21	3	1,479
Colorado Springs, CO	38	50	2	104	49	17	6,010	Pittsburgh, PA	40	26	26	79	59	45	766
Columbia, SC	34	0	3	81	2	5	300	Portland, OR	45	31	24	122	40	34	33
Columbus, OH	39	57	40	82	59	56	780	Providence, RI	41	49	26	71	24	46	9
Concord, NH	43	12	29	71	32	15	273	Provo, UT	40	14	2	111	39	31	4,551
Corpus Christi, TX	27	48	2	97	23	47	7								
								Québec, QC	46	49	0	71	13	0	244
Dallas, TX	32	46	59	96	48	24	421								
Denver, CO	39	44	21	104	59	5	5,277	Raleigh, NC	35	46	20	78	38	19	315
Des Moines, IA	41	36	2	93	36	33	873	Rapid City, SD	44	4	50	103	13	52	3,243
Detroit, MI	42	19	53	83	2	45	598	Regina, SK	50	27	17	104	36	24	1,894
Dover, DE	39	9	29	75	31	27	28	Reno, NV	39	31	47	119	48	50	4,505
Durham, NC	35	59	39	78	53	55	400	Richmond, VA	37	33	14	77	27	37	213
								Rochester, NY	43	9	17	77	36	56	504
Edmonton, AB	53	32	4	113	29	25	2,200								
El Paso, TX	31	45	31	106	29	13	3,717	Sacramento, CA	38	34	54	121	29	40	27
Eugene, OR	44	3	7	123	5	12	430	St. John's, NL	47	28	56	52	47	49	461
Evansville, IN	37	58	29	87	33	21	388	St. Louis, MO	38	37	38	90	11	52	464
								St. Paul, MN	44	56	34	93	5	36	789
Fairbanks, AK	64	50	16	147	42	59	445	Salem, OR	44	56	35	123	2	6	157
Fargo, ND	46	52	38	96	47	23	902	Salt Lake City, UT	40	45	39	111	53	28	4,265
Ft. Smith, AR	35	23	9	94	23	55	440	San Antonio, TX	29	25	27	98	29	37	649
Ft. Wayne, IN	41	7	50	85	7	44	810	San Diego, CA	32	42	55	117	9	26	63
Ft. Worth, TX	32	43	31	97	19	15	653	San Francisco, CA	37	46	30	122	25	10	54
Frankfort, KY	38	12	3	84	52	24	507	San Jose, CA	37	20	22	121	53	42	82
Fredericton, NB	45	56	43	66	40	0	67	San Juan, PR	18	27	59	66	6	21	26
								Santa Fe, NM	35	41	13	105	56	16	6,995
Greensboro, NC	36	4	21	79	47	31	827	Saskatoon, SK	52	8	23	106	41	10	1,653
Greenville, SC	34	51	9	82	23	38	984	Savannah, GA	32	5	1	81	5	59	20
Gulfport, MS	30	22	3	89	5	34	21	Seattle, WA	47	36	22	122	19	55	177
								Shreveport, LA	32	31	31	93	45	1	151
Halifax, NS	44	52	0	63	42	58	477	Sioux City, IA	42	30	0	96	24	1	1,201
Hamilton, ON	43	14	34	79	59	22	780	Sioux Falls, SD	43	33	0	96	42	1	1,473
Harrisburg, PA	40	16	25	76	53	4	332	Spokane, WA	47	39	35	117	25	45	1,732
Hartford, CT	41	45	49	72	41	6	29	Springfield, IL	39	48	6	89	38	37	600
Helena, MT	46	35	34	112	2	10	4,047								
Hilo, HI	19	43	47	155	5	24	59	Tacoma, WA	47	15	10	122	26	39	250
Honolulu, HI	21	18	25	157	51	30	17	Tampa, FL	27	56	51	82	27	30	15
Houston, TX	29	45	48	95	21	48	37	Topeka, KS	39	2	54	95	40	41	948
								Toronto, ON	43	44	30	79	22	24	251
Idaho Falls, ID	43	28	0	112	2	3	4,705	Trenton, NJ	40	13	1	74	44	35	61
Indianapolis, IN	39	46	6	86	9	29	720	Tucson, AZ	32	13	18	110	55	35	2,490
Iqaluit, NU	63	45	0	68	31	0	112	Tulsa, OK	36	9	14	95	59	34	721
Jackson, MS	32	17	56	90	11	5	280	Vancouver, BC	49	15	40	123	6	50	14
Jacksonville, FL	30	19	56	81	39	20	15	Victoria, BC	48	25	42	123	21	53	63
Jefferson City, MO	38	34	36	92	10	25	630	Virginia Beach, VA	36	51	11	75	58	41	11
Jersey City, NJ	40	43	41	74	4	40	34								
Juneau, AK	58	18	7	134	25	11	33	Washington, DC	38	53	42	77	2	11	24
								Whitehorse, YT	60	41	46	135	4	51	2,305
Kansas City, MO	39	5	59	94	34	43	898	Wichita, KS	37	41	32	97	20	15	1,302
Knoxville, TN	35	57	38	83	55	15	904	Wilmington, DE	39	44	45	75	32	48	91
								Wilmington, NC	34	13	33	77	56	41	36
Lansing, MI	42	43	57	84	33	20	853	Winnipeg, MB	49	53	4	97	8	47	783
Laredo, TX	27	30	23	99	30	27	415								
Las Vegas, NV	36	10	30	115	8	14	2,001	Yakima, WA	46	36	7	120	30	21	1,068
Lexington, KY	37	59	19	84	28	40	968	Yellowknife, NT	62	27	13	114	22	12	675

RELIGION

Religious Group Membership in the U.S.

Source: Todd M. Johnson, ed. *World Christian Database* (Leiden/Boston: Brill, Aug. 2016), except where indicated.

Figures are latest available from the source and generally are based on collected reports made by each denomination and include only persons affiliated with a congregation of the denomination. Reporting practices vary from one denomination to another, but generally include all members, not only full communicants. Religious groups with fewer than 40,000 members not generally shown. Broad religious groups indicated in **boldface** are estimates for adherents, based on self-identification in surveys and other data, and are updated on a continuing basis.

Group (congregations)	Members
African Methodist Episcopal Church (8,915)	2,697,000
African Methodist Episcopal Zion Church (3,305)	1,596,000
Agnosticism (NA)	**48,525,440**
American Baptist Assn. (1,720)	349,000
American Baptist Churches in the USA (5,724)	1,692,000
American Evangelistic Assn. (560)	270,000
Antiochian Orthodox Christian, North America (247)	450,000
Apostolic Assemblies of Christ Intl. (300)	45,600
Apostolic Assembly of the Faith in Christ Jesus (759)	90,000
Armenian Apostolic Church of America (37)	350,000
Armenian Church of North America (94)	370,000
Armenian Evangelical Union of Churches (58)	44,100
Assemblies of God Fellowship Intl. (853)	820,000
Assemblies of God USA (12,516)	3,102,000
Assemblies of the Lord Jesus Christ (300)	50,000
Associate Reformed Presbyterian Church (275)	48,700
Assn. of Faith Churches and Ministries (1,111)	202,000
Assn. of Free Lutheran Congregations (271)	44,500
Assn. of Intl. Gospel Assemblies (260)	270,000
Assyrian Church of the East (22)	114,000
Atheism (NA)	**2,812,893**
Baha'i Faith (NA)	**542,050**
Baptist Bible Fellowship Intl. (4,500)	1,669,000
Baptist General Conference (1,200)	180,000
Baptist Missionary Assn. of America (1,250)	230,000
Bible Way Churches of Our Lord Jesus Christ World-Wide (1,400)	340,000
Brethren in Christ Church (222)	46,300
Buddhism (NA)	**4,112,757**
Calvary Chapels Intl. (1,111)	500,000
Charismatic Episcopal Church of N. America (85)	40,000
Chinese Folk Religions[1] (NA)	**112,621**
Christian and Missionary Alliance (2,021)	432,471
Christian Brethren (Open) (1,200)	110,000
Christian Church (Disciples of Christ) (3,691)	658,869
Christian Churches and Churches of Christ (5,007)	1,174,000
Christian Congregation (1,550)	125,000
Christian Methodist Episcopal Church (3,592)	919,000
Christian Reformed Church in N. America (1,062)	269,000
Christianity (all)[2] (NA)	**250,598,198**
Church of Christ, Scientist (2,206)	848,000
Church of God (Anderson, IN) (2,305)	259,000
Church of God (Cleveland, OH) (6,542)	1,334,000
Church of God (Huntsville, AL) (1,645)	84,800
Church of God in Christ (22,401)	8,016,000
Church of God of Prophecy (1,841)	98,800
Church of Jesus Christ (655)	150,000
Church of Jesus Christ of Latter-day Saints (13,601)	6,144,582
Church of Our Lord Jesus Christ of Apostolic Faith (535)	650,000
Church of the Brethren (1,047)	152,000
Church of the Living God (170)	42,000
Church of the Nazarene (5,130)	793,000
Churches of Christ (Non-Instrumental) (13,067)	1,402,000
Churches of God General Conference (320)	40,000
Churches on the Rock Intl. (188)	206,000
Congregational Christian Churches (400)	67,000
Conservative Baptist Assn. of America (1,250)	245,000
Conservative Congregational Christian Conference (296)	42,296
Coptic Orthodox Church (170)	130,000
Covenant Ministries Intl. (31)	101,000
Cumberland Presbyterian Church (740)	76,500
Czechoslovak Hussite Church (38)	59,900
Elim Assemblies Fellowship (240)	41,000
Episcopal Church in the USA (5,007)	1,923,046
Ethiopian Orthodox Church in the USA (77)	80,200
Ethnoreligious[1] (NA)	**1,124,438**
Evangelical Covenant Church of America (850)	150,000
Evangelical Fellowship Intl. (270)	80,000
Evangelical Free Church of America (1,355)	396,000
Evangelical Lutheran Church in America (10,498)	4,603,000
Evangelical Presbyterian Church (271)	113,762
Evangelistic Messengers Assn. (556)	131,000
Faith Christian Fellowship Intl. (331)	230,000

Group (congregations)	Members
Free Methodist Church of North America (1,053)	75,586
Full Gospel Baptist Church Fellowship (500)	165,000
Full Gospel Fellowship of Churches and Ministers (1,273)	432,632
General Assn. of General Baptists (840)	98,000
General Assn. of Regular Baptist Churches (1,321)	132,700
General Conference of Mennonite Brethren Churches (464)	111,000
Global Network of Christian Ministries (270)	40,000
Grace Gospel Fellowship (Network of Ministers) (41)	44,300
Grace Intl. (102)	120,000
Greater Emmanuel Intl. Fellowship of Churches and Ministries (47)	47,800
Greek Orthodox Archdiocese of America (525)	1,500,000
Hinduism (NA)	**1,454,287**
Independent Assemblies Fellowship (457)	91,200
Independent Assemblies of God Intl. (300)	120,000
Independent Churches of the Latter Rain Revival (706)	70,400
Independent Fundamental Churches of America (630)	59,000
Indian Pentecostal Church of America (361)	220,000
Interdenominational Ministries Intl. (163)	45,600
Intl. Church of the Foursquare Gospel (1,971)	480,000
Intl. Churches of Christ (142)	45,000
Intl. Convention of Faith Ministries (410)	100,000
Intl. Council of Community Churches (137)	69,276
Intl. Evangelical Church (100)	50,000
Intl. Evangelism Crusades (65)	65,000
Intl. Fellowship of Faith Ministries (2,618)	261,000
Intl. Gospel Assemblies (655)	460,000
Intl. Ministers Forum (492)	170,000
Intl. Pentecostal Holiness Church (2,024)	330,054
Islam[3] (NA)	**4,384,916**
Jainism (NA)	**88,488**
Jehovah's Witnesses (12,995)	2,710,000
Jesus Is Lord Church (245)	40,700
Judaism[4] (NA)	**5,648,360**
Korean American Presbyterian Church (817)	81,500
Korean Full Gospel Churches of America (914)	293,000
Korean Presbyterian Church of America (1,793)	569,000
Latin American Council of Christian Churches (226)	117,000
Lighthouse Gospel Fellowship (425)	50,500
Living Faith Christian Centers (533)	53,200
Lutheran Church-Missouri Synod (6,138)	2,327,000
Malankara Orthodox Syrian Church of the East (92)	45,000
Mennonite Church USA (920)	140,000
Ministers Fellowship Intl. (723)	65,300
Missionary Church (361)	52,200
Missionary Gospel Church Intl. (750)	45,000
Moravian Church in America (170)	42,200
Natl. Assn. of Free Will Baptists (2,400)	233,000
Natl. Baptist Convention of America (12,300)	4,200,000
Natl. Baptist Convention, USA (40,000)	9,364,000
Natl. Baptist Evangelical Life and Soul Saving Assembly (287)	85,800
Natl. David Spiritual Temple of Christ (73)	67,900
Natl. Missionary Baptist Conv. of America (280)	449,000
Natl. Primitive Baptist Convention (1,565)	600,000
Native American Church of North America (400)	200,000
Network of Kingdom Churches (1,210)	291,000
Network of Restoration Churches (163)	40,700
New Apostolic Church USA (320)	50,000
New Religion[1] (NA)	**1,697,176**
North American Baptist Conference (422)	90,900
North American Old Roman Catholic Church (137)	65,200
Old Order Amish Mennonite Church (950)	115,000
Open Bible Standard Churches (330)	40,000
Orthodox Church in America (551)	2,700,000
Pentecostal Assemblies of the Apostolic Faith (77)	59,400
Pentecostal Assemblies of the World (1,650)	1,300,000
Pentecostal Church of God (1,134)	98,579
Pentecostal Churches of the Apostolic Faith (246)	72,000
Presbyterian Church (USA) (10,746)	2,749,000

Group (congregations)	Members
Presbyterian Church in America (1,365)........	377,000
Primitive Baptists (2,897)....................	132,000
Progressive Natl. Baptist Convention (1,200).....	2,087,000
Reformed Church in America (896)...........	250,938
Reorganized Church of Jesus Christ of Latter Day Saints (920)............................	175,000
Rhema Bible Churches (560)..............	170,000
Roman Catholic Church[5] (18,538).............	70,655,599
Romanian Orthodox Episcopal of America (37)..	105,000
Russian Orthodox Church Outside Russia (221)..	90,100
Salvation Army (1,228).....................	377,000
Serbian Orthodox Church in N. and S. America (123)...............................	68,760
Seventh-day Adventist Church (4,917).........	1,241,000
Shintoism (NA)	**64,989**
Sikhism (NA)............................	**360,386**
Southern Baptist Convention (45,854)..........	20,678,000
Spanish Christian Churches (346).............	85,100
Spiritism (NA)...........................	**233,477**
Taoism (or Daoism) (NA).................	**12,871**
Trinity Church Network (20).................	131,000
Unitarian Universalist Assn. (1,048)............	221,367
United Baptist Churches (410)..............	56,800
United Church of Christ (5,232).............	1,086,000
United Church of Jesus Christ (Apostolic) (114)...	131,000

Group (congregations)	Members
United Evangelical Churches (294)............	78,800
United Free Will Baptist Church (706)...........	104,000
United House of Prayer for All People (161)......	1,632,000
United Methodist Church (33,869)...........	7,526,642
United Pentecostal Church Intl. (4,748).........	830,000
Unity School of Christianity (661)..............	115,000
Universal Fellowship of Metropolitan Community Churches (220).........................	40,000
Victory Fellowship of Ministries (160)...........	57,000
Vineyard Churches (USA) (556)...............	189,000
Volunteers of America (300)...............	45,400
Way of the Cross Church of Christ (72).........	75,000
Wesleyan Church (1,716).....................	139,008
Willow Creek Assn. of Churches (2,000)........	400,000
Wisconsin Evangelical Lutheran Synod (1,259)...	378,196
Word of Faith Fellowship/Ministries (25).........	45,600
World Council of Independent Christian Churches (327)...............................	54,700
World Harvest Ministerial Alliance (163)..........	59,000
World Ministry Fellowship (290)...............	50,000
World Missionary Church (163)...............	40,700
World Salt (82)...........................	50,500
Worldwide Missionary Evangelism (231)........	45,600
Worldwide/Last Churches (220)..............	156,000
Zoroastrianism (NA).....................	**18,283**

(1) See definition in World Adherents table on p. 698. (2) 2016 estimate. Self-identified; affiliated Christians in the U.S. were estimated at 206,725,198 in 2016. (3) Other sources vary. The Council on American-Islamic Relations estimates a total of 2,000 mosques and 6-7 mil Muslims in the U.S. (4) Includes congregations of Jewish Reconstructionist Communities (about 90), Union of Orthodox Jewish Congregations of America (500), Other Orthodox congregations (1,200), Chabad (over 2,000) Union for Reform Judaism (850), and United Synagogue of Conservative Judaism (580). Among Jewish adherents in the U.S., about 35% classify themselves as Reform, 18% as Conservative, 10% as Orthodox, 2% as Reconstructionist, the rest as "just Jewish." Source: Ira M. Sheskin and Arnold Dashefsky, "United States Jewish Population, 2016," in *The American Jewish Year Book* (Dordrecht: Springer, 2016). (This source estimates the total American Jewish population at 6.85 mil.) (5) According to another estimate, by the U.S. Center for Research in the Apostolate, there were 81.6 mil self-identified Roman Catholics in the U.S. in 2015.

World Adherents of Religions by Continental Area, 2015

Source: *2016 Encyclopædia Britannica Book of the Year.* All adherents figures are midyear estimates, in thous.

Religion (no. of countries)	Africa	Asia	Europe	Latin America	Northern America	Oceania	World	% of world pop.
Baha'is (224).........	2,371	3,591	136	971	609	121	7,799	0.1%
Buddhists (152)	277	511,984	1,905	802	4,766	628	520,362	7.1
Chinese folk religionists (120).....	147	451,741	626	202	825	109	453,650	6.2
Christians (234)	565,079	378,934	580,488	581,674	277,667	28,793	2,412,635	32.9
Roman Catholics (234)	204,994	148,545	276,864	509,190	89,275	9,437	1,238,305	16.9
Protestants (231).....	213,790	95,138	94,055	64,200	60,906	13,011	541,100	7.4
Independents (231)...	122,460	151,508	15,217	54,899	72,416	2,066	418,566	5.7
Orthodox (137)......	51,714	18,716	202,554	1,120	7,900	1,068	283,072	3.9
Confucianists (17)......	21	8,377	16	510	—	53	8,468	0.1
Ethnoreligionists (146)..	101,756	157,242	1,167	3,818	1,284	401	265,668	3.6
Hindus (144).........	3,211	977,037	1,146	800	1,923	556	984,673	13.4
Jains (19)...........	109	5,619	20	2	105	3	5,858	0.1
Jews (146)	132	6,380	1,465	439	6,093	125	14,634	0.2
Muslims (214)........	484,829	1,162,911	45,774	1,689	5,471	621	1,701,295	23.2
Sunnis (212).......	477,481	959,717	43,598	1,238	3,783	512	1,486,329	20.3
Shiites (148)........	2,836	193,612	2,143	438	1,089	106	200,224	2.7
New religionists (121)...	217	61,047	654	1,944	2,488	123	66,472	0.9
Shintoists (8).........	—	2,753	—	8	66	—	2,827	—
Sikhs (64)...........	84	23,029	619	8	858	104	24,701	0.3
Spiritists (59)........	3	2	147	13,852	255	8	14,268	0.2
Taoists (6)..........	—	8,678	—	—	13	5	8,696	0.1
Zoroastrians (27)......	1	164	6	—	22	3	196	—
All religious adherents (234)..............	**1,158,237**	**3,759,489**	**634,169**	**606,209**	**302,445**	**31,653**	**6,492,202**	**88.6**
Nonreligious (233).....	8,002	625,355	108,954	23,880	58,683	7,706	832,580	11.4
Agnostics (233)......	7,350	510,357	94,275	20,828	54,924	7,130	694,864	9.5
Atheists (223).......	652	114,998	14,679	3,052	3,759	576	137,716	1.9

— = Less than 1,000 adherents or 0.05%. **Note:** Figures may not add up to totals due to rounding. "Religious adherents," or those who indicate attachment to religion, may or may not consider themselves as belonging to a particular religious denomination. Figures shown for adherents to specific religious groups are estimates generally based on self-definition as reported in censuses, surveys, and other data; these people may not all be actually affiliated with a particular congregation as members. Some individuals report attachment to more than one religious group, and subdivisions shown in this table are not necessarily exhaustive. Continental areas are as per UN demographic terminology; "Asia" is defined to include the former Soviet Central Asian states, while "Europe" includes all of Russia, extending to the Pacific coast. Figures in parentheses indicate the number of countries where the religion or type of belief has a significant following. **Buddhists** include Mahayana (72%), Theravada or Hinayana (25%), and Tantrayana (incl. Lamaists, Tibetans) (3%). **Chinese folk religionists** are followers of traditional Chinese religion; it may involve worship of local deities, ancestor veneration, Confucian ethics, divination, and Buddhist or Taoist elements, among other beliefs and practices. **Christians** are usually baptized members of a church belonging to one of the major Christian traditions shown here. Those characterized as Independents belong to sects or groups that consider themselves independent of historical mainstream institutionalized Christianity; these include groups such as Unitarians, Mormons, and Jehovah's Witnesses. **Confucianists** are followers of Confucius, mostly living in China or elsewhere in East/Southeast Asia. **Ethnoreligionists** are followers of local, tribal, animistic, or shamanistic religions, generally belonging to a single ethnic group. **Hindus** include Vaishnavites (38%); Shaivites (36%); and Shaktas, neo-Hindi, and reformed Hindi (26%). **New religionists** include followers of Asian new religions, neoreligious movements, radical new crisis religions, and syncretistic mass religions.

Episcopal Church Liturgical Colors and Calendar, 2016-20

The most common liturgical colors in the Episcopal Church are as follows: **White**—Christmas Day through first Sunday after Epiphany; Maundy Thursday (as an alternative to crimson at the Eucharist); from the Vigil of Easter to the Day of Pentecost (Whitsunday); Trinity Sunday; Feasts of the Lord (except Holy Cross Day); the Confession of St. Peter; the Conversion of St. Paul; St. Joseph; St. Mary Magdalene; St. Mary the Virgin; St. Michael and All Angels; All Saints' Day; St. John the Evangelist; memorials of other saints who were not martyred; Independence Day and Thanksgiving Day; weddings and funerals. **Red**—the Day of Pentecost; Holy Cross Day; feasts of apostles and evangelists (except those previously mentioned); feasts and memorials of martyrs (including Holy Innocents' Day). **Violet**—Advent and Lent. **Crimson** or oxblood (dark red)—Holy Week. **Green**—the seasons after Epiphany and after Pentecost. **Black**—optional alternative for funerals and Good Friday.

The days of fasting are Ash Wednesday and Good Friday. Other days of special devotion (penitence) include the 40 days of Lent. Ember days are days of prayer for the church's ministry. They fall on the Wednesday, Friday, and Saturday after the first Sunday in Lent, the Day of Pentecost, Holy Cross Day, and Dec. 13. Rogation Days, the three days before Ascension Day, are days of prayer for God's blessing on the crops, on commerce and industry, and for conservation of the Earth's resources.

Holy days and other variables	2016	2017	2018	2019	2020
Golden Number	3	4	5	6	7
Sunday Letter	C/B	A	G	F	E/D
Sundays after Epiphany	5	8	6	8	7
Ash Wednesday	Feb. 10	Mar. 1	Feb. 14	Mar. 6	Feb. 26
First Sunday in Lent	Feb. 14	Mar. 5	Feb. 18	Mar. 10	Mar. 1
Passion/Palm Sunday	Mar. 20	Apr. 9	Mar. 25	Apr. 14	Apr. 5
Good Friday	Mar. 25	Apr. 14	Mar. 30	Apr. 19	Apr. 10
Easter Day	Mar. 27	Apr. 16	Apr. 1	Apr. 21	Apr. 12
Ascension Day	May 5	May 25	May 10	May 30	May 21
Day of Pentecost	May 15	June 4	May 20	June 9	May 31
Trinity Sunday	May 22	June 11	May 27	June 16	June 7
Numbered Proper of 2 Pentecost	#4	#6	#4	#7	#6
First Sunday of Advent	Nov. 27	Dec. 3	Dec. 2	Dec. 1	Nov. 29

Greek Orthodox Movable Ecclesiastical Dates, 2016-20

Feast days and fasting days are determined annually on the basis of the date of Holy Pascha (Easter). This ecclesiastical cycle begins with the first day of the Triodion and ends with the Sunday of All Saints, a total of 18 weeks.

Holy days and observances	2016	2017	2018	2019	2020
Triodion begins	Feb. 21	Feb. 5	Jan. 28	Feb. 18	Feb. 9
1st Saturday of Souls	Mar. 5	Feb. 18	Feb. 10	Mar. 2	Feb. 22
Meat-Fare Sunday	Mar. 6	Feb. 19	Feb. 11	Mar. 3	Feb. 23
2nd Saturday of Souls	Mar. 12	Feb. 25	Feb. 17	Mar. 9	Feb. 29
Lent begins	Mar. 14	Feb. 27	Feb. 19	Mar. 11	Mar. 1
St. Theodore—3rd Saturday of Souls	Mar. 19	Mar. 4	Feb. 24	Mar. 16	Mar. 7
Sunday of Orthodoxy	Mar. 20	Mar. 5	Feb. 25	Mar. 17	Mar. 8
Saturday of Lazarus	Apr. 23	Apr. 8	Mar. 31	Apr. 20	Apr. 11
Palm Sunday	Apr. 24	Apr. 9	Apr. 1	Apr. 21	Apr. 12
Holy (Good) Friday	Apr. 29	Apr. 14	Apr. 6	Apr. 26	Apr. 17
Western Easter	Mar. 27	Apr. 16	Apr. 1	Apr. 21	Apr. 12
Orthodox Pascha (Easter)	May 1	Apr. 16	Apr. 8	Apr. 28	Apr. 19
Ascension	June 9	May 25	May 17	June 6	May 28
Saturday of Souls	June 18	June 3	May 26	June 15	June 6
Pentecost	June 19	June 4	May 27	June 16	June 7
All Saints	June 26	June 11	June 3	June 23	June 14
Fast of Holy Apostles (first day)	June 27	June 12	June 4	June 24	June 15

Jewish Holy Days, 5776-5780 (2015-20)

The Jewish calendar consists of 12 lunar months, alternating between 29 and 30 days. It is lunisolar and adjusts for the solar cycle by adding an extra month (Adar II) in the 3rd, 6th, 8th, 11th, 14th, 17th, and 19th years of a 19-year cycle. The calendar starts on the day of Creation, reckoned in the 2nd-3rd cent. BCE as Tishrei 1, 3,761 years before the common era.

The religious calendar begins with the month Nisan, from which all other months are counted, and the civil calendar with Tishrei. The months are 1) Nisan, 2) Iyar, 3) Sivan, 4) Tammuz, 5) Av (also Abh), 6) Elul, 7) Tishrei, 8) Cheshvan (also Marcheshvan), 9) Kislev, 10) Tevet (also Tebeth), 11) Shevat (also Shebhat), 12) Adar, and 12a) Adar Sheni (II), added in leap years.

All holidays listed below begin at sunset of the previous day and end at nightfall on the last day shown.

Holiday	Date on Jewish cal.	(5776) 2015-16		(5777) 2016-17		(5778) 2017-18		(5779) 2018-19		(5780) 2019-20	
Rosh Hashanah (New Year)	Tishrei 1	Sept. 14	Mon.	Oct. 3	Mon.	Sept. 21	Thu.	Sept. 10	Mon.	Sept. 30	Mon.
	Tishrei 2	Sept. 15	Tue.	Oct. 4	Tue.	Sept. 22	Fri.	Sept. 11	Tue.	Oct. 1	Tue.
Yom Kippur (Day of Atonement)	Tishrei 10	Sept. 23	Wed.	Oct. 12	Wed.	Sept. 30	Sat.	Sept. 19	Wed.	Oct. 9	Wed
Sukkot	Tishrei 15	Sept. 28	Mon.	Oct. 17	Mon.	Oct. 5	Thu.	Sept. 24	Mon.	Oct. 14	Mon.
	Tishrei 21	Oct. 4	Sun.	Oct. 23	Sun.	Oct. 11	Wed.	Sept. 30	Sun.	Oct. 20	Sun.
Shemini Atzeret	Tishrei 22	Oct. 5	Mon.	Oct. 24	Mon.	Oct. 12	Thu.	Oct. 1	Mon.	Oct. 21	Mon.
Simchat Torah	Tishrei 23	Oct. 6	Tue.	Oct. 25	Tue.	Oct. 13	Fri.	Oct. 2	Tue.	Oct. 22	Tue.
Hanukkah	Kislev 25	Dec. 7	Mon.	Dec. 25	Sun.	Dec. 13	Wed.	Dec. 3	Mon.	Dec. 23	Mon.
	Tevet 2 or 3	Dec. 14	Mon.	Jan. 1	Sun.	Dec. 20	Wed.	Dec. 10	Mon.	Dec. 30	Mon.
Purim	Adar 14	Mar. 24	Thu.	Mar. 12	Sun.	Mar. 1	Thu.	Mar. 21	Thu.	Mar. 10	Tue.
Pesach (Passover)	Nisan 15	Apr. 23	Sat.	Apr. 11	Tue.	Mar. 31	Sat.	Apr. 20	Sat.	Apr. 9	Thu.
	Nisan 22	Apr. 30	Sat.	Apr. 18	Tue.	Apr. 7	Sat.	Apr. 27	Sat.	Apr. 16	Thu.
Shavuot (Pentecost)	Sivan 6	June 12	Sun.	May 31	Wed.	May 20	Sun.	June 9	Sun.	May 29	Fri.
	Sivan 7	June 13	Mon.	June 1	Thu.	May 21	Mon.	June 10	Mon.	May 30	Sat.
Fast of the 9th of Av	Av 9	Aug. 14	Sun.*	Aug. 1	Tue.	July 22	Sun.*	Aug. 11	Sun.*	July 30	Thu.

* = Date changed to avoid Sabbath.

Hindu Festivals, 2016-20

There are various traditional lunisolar Hindu calendars. Most have similar names for the 12 lunar months, with days beginning at dawn or sunrise, but they differ in various ways, including the numbering of years and the starting point of months. The Indian civil (Saka) calendar, adopted in 1957, is solar-based, and begins Mar. 22 (Mar. 21 in leap years). The year 1939 on the Saka calendar begins Mar. 22, 2017. There are many Hindu holidays and festivals; some are observed only in certain regions. Below are three of the most widely observed.

Festival	2016	2017	2018	2019	2020
Maha Shivaratri (Night of Shiva)[1]	Mar. 8	Feb. 25	Feb. 14	Mar. 5	Feb. 22
Holi (Festival of Color)	Mar. 23	Mar. 13	Mar. 2	Mar. 21	Mar. 10
Diwali (Festival of Lights)	Oct. 30	Oct. 19	Nov. 7	Oct. 27	Nov. 14

(1) Begins the night of the previous day.

Islamic Holy Days, 1437-41 AH (late 2015-20)

The Islamic calendar is a strict lunar calendar reckoned from the year of the Hijra (anno Hegirae, or AH)—Muhammad's flight from Mecca to Medina, in 622 CE. Each year consists of 12 lunar months of 29 or 30 days beginning and ending with each new moon's visible crescent. Common years have 354 days; leap years have 355 days. Some Muslim countries employ a conventionalized calendar with the leap day added to the last month, Dhu'l-Hijja, but for religious purposes the leap date is taken into account by tracking each new moon sighting.

Holy days begin at sunset of the day previous to the day cited. The actual dates may vary slightly from what is shown below, depending on the locality and the times of actual moon sightings as determined by different authorities.

Holy day (date)	(1437) 2015-16	(1438) 2016-17	(1439) 2017-18	(1440) 2018-19	(1441) 2019-20
New Year's Day (Muharram 1)	Oct. 14, 2015	Oct. 2, 2016	Sept. 21, 2017	Sept. 12, 2018	Sept. 1, 2019
Ashura (Muharram 10)	Oct. 23, 2015	Oct. 11, 2016	Sept. 30, 2017	Sept. 21, 2018	Sept. 10, 2019
Mawlid (Rabi' I 12)	Dec. 23, 2015	Dec. 12, 2016	Dec. 1, 2017	Nov. 21, 2018	Nov. 10, 2019
Ramadan begins (Ramadan 1)	June 6, 2016	May 27, 2017	May 16, 2018	May 6, 2019	Apr. 24, 2020
Eid al-Fitr (Shawwal 1)	July 7, 2016	June 26, 2017	June 15, 2018	June 5, 2019	May 24, 2020
Eid al-Adha (Dhu'l-Hijja 10)	Sept. 12, 2016	Sept. 1, 2017	Aug. 22, 2018	Aug. 12, 2019	July 31, 2020

Ash Wednesday and Easter Sunday (Western Churches), 2001-2100

Year	Ash Wed.	Easter Sunday	Year	Ash Wed.	Easter Sunday	Year	Ash Wed.	Easter Sunday	Year	Ash Wed.	Easter Sunday	Year	Ash Wed.	Easter Sunday
2001	Feb. 28	Apr. 15	2021	Feb. 17	Apr. 4	2041	Mar. 6	Apr. 21	2061	Feb. 23	Apr. 10	2081	Feb. 12	Mar. 30
2002	Feb. 13	Mar. 31	2022	Mar. 2	Apr. 17	2042	Feb. 19	Apr. 6	2062	Feb. 8	Mar. 26	2082	Mar. 4	Apr. 19
2003	Mar. 5	Apr. 20	2023	Feb. 22	Apr. 9	2043	Feb. 11	Mar. 29	2063	Feb. 28	Apr. 15	2083	Feb. 17	Apr. 4
2004	Feb. 25	Apr. 11	2024	Feb. 14	Mar. 31	2044	Mar. 2	Apr. 17	2064	Feb. 20	Apr. 6	2084	Feb. 9	Mar. 26
2005	Feb. 9	Mar. 27	2025	Mar. 5	Apr. 20	2045	Feb. 22	Apr. 9	2065	Feb. 11	Mar. 29	2085	Feb. 28	Apr. 15
2006	Mar. 1	Apr. 16	2026	Feb. 18	Apr. 5	2046	Feb. 7	Mar. 25	2066	Feb. 24	Apr. 11	2086	Feb. 13	Mar. 31
2007	Feb. 21	Apr. 8	2027	Feb. 10	Mar. 28	2047	Feb. 27	Apr. 14	2067	Feb. 16	Apr. 3	2087	Mar. 5	Apr. 20
2008	Feb. 6	Mar. 23	2028	Mar. 1	Apr. 16	2048	Feb. 19	Apr. 5	2068	Mar. 7	Apr. 22	2088	Feb. 25	Apr. 11
2009	Feb. 25	Apr. 12	2029	Feb. 14	Apr. 1	2049	Mar. 3	Apr. 18	2069	Feb. 27	Apr. 14	2089	Feb. 16	Apr. 3
2010	Feb. 17	Apr. 4	2030	Mar. 6	Apr. 21	2050	Feb. 23	Apr. 10	2070	Feb. 12	Mar. 30	2090	Mar. 1	Apr. 16
2011	Mar. 9	Apr. 24	2031	Feb. 26	Apr. 13	2051	Feb. 15	Apr. 2	2071	Mar. 4	Apr. 19	2091	Feb. 21	Apr. 8
2012	Feb. 22	Apr. 8	2032	Feb. 11	Mar. 28	2052	Mar. 6	Apr. 21	2072	Feb. 24	Apr. 10	2092	Feb. 13	Mar. 30
2013	Feb. 13	Mar. 31	2033	Mar. 2	Apr. 17	2053	Feb. 19	Apr. 6	2073	Feb. 8	Mar. 26	2093	Feb. 25	Apr. 12
2014	Mar. 5	Apr. 20	2034	Feb. 22	Apr. 9	2054	Feb. 11	Mar. 29	2074	Feb. 28	Apr. 15	2094	Feb. 17	Apr. 4
2015	Feb. 18	Apr. 5	2035	Feb. 7	Mar. 25	2055	Mar. 3	Apr. 18	2075	Feb. 20	Apr. 7	2095	Mar. 9	Apr. 24
2016	Feb. 10	Mar. 27	2036	Feb. 27	Apr. 13	2056	Feb. 16	Apr. 2	2076	Mar. 4	Apr. 19	2096	Feb. 29	Apr. 15
2017	Mar. 1	Apr. 16	2037	Feb. 18	Apr. 5	2057	Mar. 7	Apr. 22	2077	Feb. 24	Apr. 11	2097	Feb. 13	Mar. 31
2018	Feb. 14	Apr. 1	2038	Mar. 10	Apr. 25	2058	Feb. 27	Apr. 14	2078	Feb. 16	Apr. 3	2098	Mar. 5	Apr. 20
2019	Mar. 6	Apr. 21	2039	Feb. 23	Apr. 10	2059	Feb. 12	Mar. 30	2079	Mar. 8	Apr. 23	2099	Feb. 25	Apr. 12
2020	Feb. 26	Apr. 12	2040	Feb. 15	Apr. 1	2060	Mar. 3	Apr. 18	2080	Feb. 21	Apr. 7	2100	Feb. 10	Mar. 28

Roman Catholic Church Hierarchy

The Roman Catholic Church is headed by the pope, or bishop of Rome. He is assisted and advised by members of the College of Cardinals. The church is governed through a central administrative body, the Roman Curia. Dioceses around the world are headed by bishops appointed by the pope; collectively they also play a part in leadership of the church as a whole.

The Papacy

Roman Catholics consider Peter the Apostle to have been the first bishop of Rome and first in a line of popes extending to the present. He is said to have arrived in Rome c. 42 CE and to have been martyred there c. 67; he was later canonized as a saint. Popes through history have had both religious and secular roles. The pope today is the head of state of Vatican City as well as leader of the church.

German-born Pope **Benedict XVI**, formerly Cardinal Joseph Ratzinger, who was elected in Apr. 2005, resigned effective Feb. 28, 2013, citing his age (85) and declining health. Assuming the title of supreme pontiff emeritus, he took up residence in a restored convent near the Vatican.

At a papal conclave in Mar. 2013, 115 cardinals from 48 countries chose Argentinean Cardinal Jorge Mario Bergoglio as pope. He took the name **Francis**, after St. Francis of Assisi (1182-1226), known for his life of poverty and devotion to the poor. Pope Francis was the first member of the Society of Jesus (Jesuits), a Roman Catholic order, to become pope, and the first born outside Europe since Syrian-born Gregory III, who died in 741.

Chronological List of Popes

Source: *Annuario Pontificio*

Table lists year of accession of each pope. * = antipope, an illegitimate claimant to the papal throne.

Year	Pope	Year	Pope	Year	Pope	Year	Pope	Year	Pope
NA	St. Peter	530	Boniface II	884	St. Adrian III	1102	Albert*	1431	Eugene IV
67	St. Linus	530	Dioscorus*	885	Stephen V (VI)	1105	Sylvester IV*	1439	Felix V*
76	St. Anacletus,	533	John II	891	Formosus	1118	Gelasius II	1447	Nicholas V
	or Cletus	535	St. Agapitus I	896	Boniface VI	1118	Gregory VIII*	1455	Callistus III
88	St. Clement I	536	St. Silverius, Martyr	896	Stephen VI (VII)	1119	Callistus II	1458	Pius II
97	St. Evaristus	537	Vigilius	897	Romanus	1124	Honorius II	1464	Paul II
105	St. Alexander I	556	Pelagius I	897	Theodore II	1124	Celestine II*	1471	Sixtus IV
115	St. Sixtus I	561	John III	898	John IX	1130	Innocent II	1484	Innocent VIII
125	St. Telesphorus	575	Benedict I	900	Benedict IV	1130	Anacletus II*	1492	Alexander VI
136	St. Hyginus	579	Pelagius II	903	Leo V	1138	Victor IV*	1503	Pius III
140	St. Pius I	590	St. Gregory I	903	Christopher*	1143	Celestine II	1503	Julius II
155	St. Anicetus	604	Sabinian	904	Sergius III	1144	Lucius II	1513	Leo X
166	St. Soter	607	Boniface III	911	Anastasius III	1145	Bl. Eugene III	1522	Adrian VI
175	St. Eleutherius	608	St. Boniface IV	913	Landus	1153	Anastasius IV	1523	Clement VII
189	St. Victor I	615	St. Deusdedit,	914	John X	1154	Adrian IV	1534	Paul III
199	St. Zephyrinus		or Adeodatus	928	Leo VI	1159	Alexander III	1550	Julius III
217	St. Callistus I	619	Boniface V	928	Stephen VII (VIII)	1159	Victor IV*	1555	Marcellus II
217	St. Hippolytus*	625	Honorius I	931	John XI	1164	Paschal III*	1555	Paul IV
222	St. Urban I	640	Severinus	936	Leo VII	1168	Callistus III*	1559	Pius IV
230	St. Pontian	640	John IV	939	Stephen VIII (IX)	1179	Innocent III*	1566	St. Pius V
235	St. Anterus	642	Theodore I	942	Marinus II	1181	Lucius III	1572	Gregory XIII
236	St. Fabian	649	St. Martin I, Martyr	946	Agapitus II	1185	Urban III	1585	Sixtus V
251	St. Cornelius	654	St. Eugene I	955	John XII	1187	Clement III	1590	Urban VII
251	Novatian*	657	St. Vitalian	963	Leo VIII	1187	Gregory VIII	1590	Gregory XIV
253	St. Lucius I	672	Adeodatus II	964	Benedict V	1191	Celestine III	1591	Innocent IX
254	St. Stephen I	676	Donus	965	John XIII	1198	Innocent III	1592	Clement VIII
257	St. Sixtus II	678	St. Agatho	973	Benedict VI	1216	Honorius III	1605	Leo XI
259	St. Dionysius	682	St. Leo II	974	Boniface VII*	1227	Gregory IX	1605	Paul V
269	St. Felix I	684	St. Benedict II	974	Benedict VII	1241	Celestine IV	1621	Gregory XV
275	St. Eutychian	685	John V	983	John XIV	1243	Innocent IV	1623	Urban VIII
283	St. Caius	686	Conon	984	Boniface VII*	1254	Alexander IV	1644	Innocent X
296	St. Marcellinus	687	Theodore*	985	John XV	1261	Urban IV	1655	Alexander VII
308	St. Marcellus I	687	Paschal*	996	Gregory V	1265	Clement IV	1667	Clement IX
309	St. Eusebius	687	St. Sergius I	997	John XVI*	1271	Bl. Gregory X	1670	Clement X
311	St. Melchiades	701	John VI	999	Sylvester II	1276	Bl. Innocent V	1676	Bl. Innocent XI
314	St. Sylvester I	705	John VII	1003	John XVII	1276	Adrian V	1689	Alexander VIII
336	St. Marcus	708	Sisinnius	1004	John XVIII	1276	John XXI	1691	Innocent XII
337	St. Julius I	708	Constantine	1009	Sergius IV	1277	Nicholas III	1700	Clement XI
352	Liberius	715	St. Gregory II	1012	Benedict VIII	1281	Martin IV	1721	Innocent XIII
355	Felix II*	731	St. Gregory III	1012	Gregory*	1285	Honorius IV	1724	Benedict XIII
366	St. Damasus I	741	St. Zachary	1024	John XIX	1288	Nicholas IV	1730	Clement XII
366	Ursinus*	752	Stephen II (III)[1]	1032	Benedict IX	1294	St. Celestine V	1740	Benedict XIV
384	St. Siricius	757	St. Paul I	1045	Sylvester III	1294	Boniface VIII	1758	Clement XIII
399	St. Anastasius I	767	Constantine*	1045	Benedict IX	1303	Bl. Benedict XI	1769	Clement XIV
401	St. Innocent I	768	Philip*	1045	Gregory VI	1305	Clement V	1775	Pius VI
417	St. Zosimus	768	Stephen III (IV)	1046	Clement II	1316	John XXII	1800	Pius VII
418	St. Boniface I	772	Adrian I	1047	Benedict IX	1328	Nicholas V*	1823	Leo XII
418	Eulalius*	795	St. Leo III	1048	Damasus II	1334	Benedict XII	1829	Pius VIII
422	St. Celestine I	816	Stephen IV (V)	1049	St. Leo IX	1342	Clement VI	1831	Gregory XVI
432	St. Sixtus III	817	St. Paschal I	1055	Victor II	1352	Innocent VI	1846	Pius IX
440	St. Leo I	824	Eugene II	1057	Stephen IX (X)	1362	Bl. Urban V	1878	Leo XIII
461	St. Hilary	827	Valentine	1058	Benedict X*	1370	Gregory XI	1903	St. Pius X
468	St. Simplicius	827	Gregory IV	1059	Nicholas II	1378	Urban VI	1914	Benedict XV
483	St. Felix III (II)	844	John*	1061	Alexander II	1378	Clement VII*	1922	Pius XI
492	St. Gelasius I	844	Sergius II	1061	Honorius II*	1389	Boniface IX	1939	Pius XII
496	Anastasius II	847	St. Leo IV	1073	St. Gregory VII	1394	Benedict XIII*	1958	St. John XXIII
498	St. Symmachus	855	Benedict III	1080	Clement III*	1404	Innocent VII	1963	Paul VI
498	Lawrence* (also in	855	Anastasius*	1086	Bl. Victor III	1406	Gregory XII	1978	John Paul I
	501-505)	858	St. Nicholas I	1088	Bl. Urban II	1409	Alexander V*	1978	St. John Paul II
514	St. Hormisdas	867	Adrian II	1099	Paschal II	1410	John XXIII*	2005	Benedict XVI
523	St. John I, Martyr	872	John VIII	1100	Theodoric*	1417	Martin V	2013	Francis
526	St. Felix IV (III)	882	Marinus I						

NA = Not available. Bl. = Blessed. (1) After St. Zachary, a Roman priest named Stephen was elected who died before assuming the papacy. Another Stephen was then elected to succeed Zachary as Stephen II. He is sometimes listed as Stephen III.

Pope Francis

Pope Francis was born Jorge Mario Bergoglio in Buenos Aires, Argentina, Dec. 17, 1936; his parents were Italian immigrants. He joined the Jesuits in 1958 and was ordained a priest in 1969. Bergoglio served as a parish priest, theology professor, college administrator, and head of the Jesuit province covering Argentina and Uruguay. Ordained a bishop in 1992, he was named archbishop of Buenos Aires in 1998 and made a cardinal in 2001. He was said to have placed second in the balloting for pope in 2005.

Soon after his election in 2013, Francis took steps to illustrate his commitment to the ideals of St. Francis; for example, he chose to live in a modest apartment, rather than in the elaborate papal suite overlooking St. Peter's Square. He approved measures for reform of the scandal-ridden Vatican Bank and established a commission to advise the church on clerical sex abuse. In June 2015, Francis released an encyclical focusing on consumerism, climate change, and the environment.

College of Cardinals

Members of the Sacred College of Cardinals are chosen by the pope to be his chief assistants and advisers in the administration of the church. Among their duties is the election of the pope.

In its present form, the College of Cardinals dates from the 12th century. The first cardinals, from about the 6th century, were deacons and priests of the leading churches of Rome and were bishops of neighboring dioceses. The title of cardinal was limited to members of the college in 1567. The number of cardinals was set at 70 in 1586. Pope John XXIII began to increase the number in 1959; however, the number eligible to participate in papal elections was limited to 120. Previous limitations were set aside by Pope John Paul II when he created new cardinals. In 1918, the Code of Canon Law specified that all cardinals must be priests. Pope John XXIII in 1962 ruled that cardinals must ordinarily be bishops. In 1971, Pope Paul VI decreed that at age 80, cardinals must retire from curial departments and offices and cannot be summoned to participate in papal elections.

As of Sept. 2016, there were 211 cardinals from 73 countries, of whom 111 from 57 countries remained eligible to vote.

North American Cardinals

Name	Office	Born	Named cardinal
Raymond L. Burke	Archbishop emeritus of St. Louis	1948	2010
Thomas C. Collins[1]	Archbishop of Toronto, ON, Canada	1947	2012
Daniel N. DiNardo[2]	Archbishop of Galveston-Houston	1949	2007
Timothy M. Dolan	Archbishop of New York	1950	2012
James M. Harvey	Archpriest of St. Paul Outside-the-Walls	1949	2012
William Henry Keeler[3]	Archbishop emeritus of Baltimore	1931	1994
Gérald Cyprien Lacroix	Archbishop of Québec, Canada	1957	2014
Bernard F. Law[3]	Archbishop emeritus of Boston	1931	1985
William Levada[3]	Archbishop emeritus of San Francisco	1936	2006
Javier Lozano Barragán[3]	Archbishop emeritus of Zacatecas, Mexico	1933	2003
Roger Mahony[3]	Archbishop emeritus of Los Angeles	1936	1991
Adam Joseph Maida[3]	Archbishop emeritus of Detroit	1930	1994
Theodore McCarrick[3]	Archbishop emeritus of Washington, DC	1930	2001
Edwin F. O'Brien	Grand Master of the Knights of the Holy Sepulcher	1939	2012
Sean O'Malley[4]	Archbishop of Boston	1944	2006
Marc Ouellet	Prefect, Congregation for Bishops; archbishop emeritus of Québec, Canada	1944	2003
Justin F. Rigali[3]	Archbishop emeritus of Philadelphia	1935	2003
Norberto Rivera Carrera[2]	Archbishop of Mexico City, Mexico	1942	1998
José Francisco Robles Ortega	Archbishop of Guadalajara, Mexico	1949	2007
Juan Sandoval Íñiguez[3]	Archbishop emeritus of Guadalajara, Mexico	1933	1994
James F. Stafford[3]	Archbishop emeritus of Denver	1932	1998
Alberto Suárez Inda	Archbishop of Morelia, Mexico	1939	2015
Donald W. Wuerl	Archbishop of Washington, DC	1940	2010

(1) Member, Commission of Cardinals Overseeing the Institute for Works of Religion (Vatican Bank). (2) Member, Council for the Economy. (3) Ineligible to vote in a papal conclave because of age. (4) Member, Council of Cardinals and Pres., Pontifical Commission for the Protection of Minors.

The Ten Commandments

In the Hebrew Bible (Old Testament) the Ten Commandments (also called the Decalogue, from the Greek meaning "ten words") were revealed by God to Moses on Mt. Sinai. They form the covenant between God and the Israelites and the moral code that is the basis for the Jewish and Christian religions. The Ten Commandments appear in two places in the Old Testament—Exodus 20:1-17 and Deuteronomy 5:6-21.

Most Protestant, Anglican, and Orthodox Christians follow Jewish tradition, as shown here, which considers the introduction ("I am the Lord ...") the first commandment and makes the prohibition against idolatry the second. Roman Catholic and Lutheran traditions combine I and II and split the last commandment into two that separately prohibit coveting of a neighbor's wife and of a neighbor's goods. This arrangement alters the numbering of the other commandments by one.

Following is the text as it appears in Exodus 20:1-17 in the King James version of the Bible [Roman numerals added]:

And God spake all these words, saying,

I. I *am* the LORD thy God, which have brought thee out of the land of Egypt, out of the house of bondage. Thou shalt have no other gods before me.

II. Thou shalt not make unto thee any graven image, or any likeness of *any thing* that *is* in heaven above, or that *is* in the earth beneath, or that *is* in the water under the earth. Thou shalt not bow down thyself to them, nor serve them: for I the LORD thy God *am* a jealous God, visiting the iniquity of the fathers upon the children unto the third and fourth *generation* of them that hate me; and shewing mercy unto thousands of them that love me, and keep my commandments.

III. Thou shalt not take the name of the LORD thy God in vain: for the LORD will not hold him guiltless that taketh his name in vain.

IV. Remember the sabbath day, to keep it holy. Six days shalt thou labour, and do all thy work: but the seventh day *is* the sabbath of the LORD thy God: *in it* thou shalt not do any work, thou, nor thy son, nor thy daughter, thy manservant, nor thy maidservant, nor thy cattle, nor thy stranger that *is* within thy gates: for *in* six days the LORD made heaven and earth, the sea, and all that in them *is*, and rested the seventh day: wherefore the LORD blessed the sabbath day, and hallowed it.

V. Honour thy father and thy mother: that thy days may be long upon the land which the LORD thy God giveth thee.

VI. Thou shalt not kill.

VII. Thou shalt not commit adultery.

VIII. Thou shalt not steal.

IX. Thou shalt not bear false witness against thy neighbour.

X. Thou shalt not covet thy neighbour's house, thou shalt not covet thy neighbour's wife, nor his manservant, nor his maidservant, nor his ox, nor his ass, nor any thing that *is* thy neighbour's.

Books of the Bible

Old Testament—Standard Protestant List				New Testament List		
Genesis	I Kings	Ecclesiastes	Obadiah	Matthew	Ephesians	Hebrews
Exodus	II Kings	Song of Solomon	Jonah	Mark	Philippians	James
Leviticus	I Chronicles	Isaiah	Micah	Luke	Colossians	I Peter
Numbers	II Chronicles	Jeremiah	Nahum	John	I Thessalonians	II Peter
Deuteronomy	Ezra	Lamentations	Habakkuk	Acts	II Thessalonians	I John
Joshua	Nehemiah	Ezekiel	Zephaniah	Romans	I Timothy	II John
Judges	Esther	Daniel	Haggai	I Corinthians	II Timothy	III John
Ruth	Job	Hosea	Zechariah	II Corinthians	Titus	Jude
I Samuel	Psalms	Joel	Malachi	Galatians	Philemon	Revelation
II Samuel	Proverbs	Amos				

The standard Protestant Old Testament consists of the same 39 books as in the Bible of Judaism, but the latter is organized differently. The Old Testament used by Roman Catholics has 7 additional deuterocanonical books, plus some additional parts of books. The 7 are **Tobit, Judith, Wisdom, Sirach (Ecclesiasticus), Baruch, I Maccabees,** and **II Maccabees**. Both Catholic and Protestant versions of the New Testament have 27 books with the same names.

Figures in the Hebrew Bible (Old Testament)

Aaron: First of Hebrew high priests; brother of Moses and Miriam.

Abel: Second son of Adam and Eve; slain by Cain.

Abraham: Founder of monotheism; patriarch; also called Abram.

Adam: First human according to Genesis.

Amos: Herdsman; prophesized against social injustice and oppression of the poor.

Bathsheba: Seduced by King David; mother of King Solomon.

Cain: First son of Adam and Eve; killed his brother Abel.

Cyrus: Persian ruler; sent Jews home from exile.

Daniel: Cast into lion's den for violating decree of King Darius; saved.

David: Israel's greatest king; shepherd, warrior, musician, psalmist.

Deborah: Prophet and judge; ruled over Israel.

Elijah: Great prophet; was victorious over the priests of the Phoenician god Baal.

Elisha: Prophet; successor to Elijah.

Esther: Jewish wife of the king of Persia; saved Jews from annihilation.

Eve: First woman according to Genesis.

Ezekiel: Visionary; prophesized hope to exiled Jews in Babylon.

Ezra: Great Jewish leader; rededicated worship and Torah law after exile.

Goliath: Giant Philistine warrior; slain by David.

Hannah: Childless; promised child to God; mother to the prophet Samuel.

Hosea: Enacted prophecy; asked God's forgiveness for Israel's unfaithfulness.

Isaac: Son of Abraham and Sarah; saved from sacrificial altar.

Isaiah: Highly educated prophet; avoided war with Assyria; Israel destroyed; Jerusalem survived.

Jacob: Son of Isaac; father of the Twelve Tribes; renamed "Israel" by angel.

Jeremiah: Confronted leaders and urged surrender to Babylon.

Jezebel: Phoenician queen of King Ahab; had Israelite prophets killed.

Job: "Blameless" man; allowed by God to lose family, health, and possessions in a test of his faith.

Jonah: Swallowed by a great fish; prophesied destruction of the city of Nineveh, averted when the people repented.

Jonathan: Son of King Saul; friend of David.

Joseph: Favorite of Jacob; interpreted Pharaoh's dreams; brought Hebrews to Egypt.

Joshua: Successor of Moses; led Hebrews into Canaan.

Josiah: Reformist king; repaired Solomon's Temple; restored worship; reintroduced Passover.

Leah: Matriarch; older sister of Rachel; Jacob's wife.

Micah: Prophet; predicted the end of war and beginning of peace.

Miriam: Prophet and great leader of the Hebrews; sister to Moses and Aaron.

Moses: Most important Hebrew prophet; leader of the Israelites; received the Torah.

Nathan: Prophet; confronted King David over his seduction of Bathsheba.

Nebuchadnezzar: Babylonian king; destroyed Jerusalem.

Nehemiah: Led Jews back to Jerusalem from Babylonian exile.

Noah: Man of great faith who, according to Genesis, saved his family and two of every living thing on Earth from a great flood.

Rachel: Matriarch; younger sister of Leah; Jacob's wife; Joseph's mother.

Rebecca: Matriarch; wife of Isaac; mother of Jacob.

Ruth: Moabite convert; ancestor of David.

Samson: Judge and military leader of Israel; possessed super-human strength.

Samuel: Prophet; anointed Saul king of Israel and later anointed David to succeed him.

Sarah: First matriarch of Israel; wife of Abraham; mother of Isaac.

Saul: First king of Israel; father of Jonathan.

Solomon: King of Israel at its zenith; known for great wisdom.

Zechariah: Prophet; encouraged rebuilding of Solomon's Temple destroyed by Babylonians.

Figures in the New Testament

Andrew: One of the Twelve Apostles; brother of Peter and former fisherman; one of the earlier disciples.

Barabbas: Imprisoned with Jesus; set free by Pilate on Passover.

Barnabas: Disciple of Jesus; closely connected with Paul.

Bartholomew: A lesser-known member of the Twelve Apostles; cheerful and prayed often.

Cornelius: Roman convert; defended by Peter, allowing Gentiles to become Christians.

Elizabeth: Mother of John the Baptist; relation of the Virgin Mary.

Gabriel: Archangel; appeared to the Virgin Mary to announce that she was to give birth to the Messiah.

Herod: May refer to Herod the Great, who ordered the death of children after Jesus's birth, or to his son, Herod, who had John the Baptist beheaded.

James: May refer to either of two apostles: James, son of Zebedee, brother of John the Apostle, or the lesser-known James, son of Alphaeus.

Jesus: Central figure of the Gospels; believed to be the Messiah and son of God; crucified by the Romans.

John (Apostle): Beloved disciple of Jesus; one of the Twelve Apostles; possible author of fourth Gospel; brother of James.

John (Baptist): Known as John the Baptist; important prophet and forerunner to Jesus; relation of the Virgin Mary.

Joseph: Husband of the Virgin Mary; descendant of King David.

Judas Iscariot: Betrayer of Jesus; prominent member of the Apostles; committed suicide.

Judas Thaddeus: One of the Twelve Apostles; also called Jude to distinguish him from Judas Iscariot.

Lazarus: Brother of the disciples Martha and Mary of Bethany; raised from the dead by Jesus at their request; possibly the same Lazarus who appears in Jesus's parable of the rich man.

Luke: Traditional author of the Gospel of Luke; possibly a follower of Paul.

Mark: Traditional author of the Gospel of Mark; possibly a disciple of Peter.

Mary, the mother of Jesus: Traditionally believed to be a virgin who conceived without sin; wife of Joseph.

Mary Magdalene: Important female disciple of Jesus; witness to his death and resurrection.

Matthew: One of the Twelve Apostles; possible author of the Gospel of Matthew; former tax collector.

Matthias: Often included on lists of the Twelve Apostles as the apostle who replaced Judas Iscariot after his betrayal.

Paul (Saul): Writer of nearly a quarter of the New Testament; a former persecutor of Christians, converted after a vision; played a significant role in spreading Christianity.

Peter: Considered the foremost of the Twelve Apostles; traditionally the first pope and "rock" of the Christian church; author of epistles; also called Simon and Simon Peter.

Philip: One of the Twelve; considered pragmatic and sensible.

Pilate, Pontius: A Roman prefect; played large role in the trial and crucifixion of Jesus.

Simon: One of the Twelve Apostles; known as "the Zealot" to distinguish from Simon Peter.

Stephen: Fervently preached that Jesus was the Messiah; stoned to death by angry mob, including Saul; important figure in Saul's conversion.

Thomas: One of the Twelve Apostles; known as "Doubting Thomas" because he did not believe Jesus was risen until he could touch him.

Timothy: A disciple closely connected with Paul; recipient of epistles.

Zacharias: Father of John the Baptist; husband of Elizabeth; struck dumb when he doubted his barren wife could become pregnant.

Major Christian Denominations:

Brackets indicate some features that tend to

Denomination	Origins	Organization	Authority	Special rites
Baptists	In radical Reformation, objections to infant baptism, demands for church and state separation; John Smyth, English Separatist, in 1609; Roger Williams, 1638, Providence, RI.	Congregational; each local church is autonomous.	Scripture; some Baptists, particularly in the South, interpret the Bible literally.	[Baptism, usually early teen years and after, by total immersion]; Lord's Supper.
Church of Christ (Disciples)	Among evangelical Presbyterians in KY (1804) and PA (1809), in distress over Protestant factionalism and decline of fervor; organized in 1832.	Congregational.	["Where the Scriptures speak, we speak; where the Scriptures are silent, we are silent."]	Adult baptism; Lord's Supper (weekly).
Episcopalians	Henry VIII separated English Catholic Church from Rome, 1534, for political reasons; Protestant Episcopal Church in U.S. founded in 1789.	[Diocesan bishops, in apostolic succession, are elected by parish representatives; the national Church is headed by General Convention and Presiding Bishop; part of the Anglican Communion.]	Scripture as interpreted by tradition, especially 39 Articles (1563); tri-annual convention of bishops, priests, and lay people.	Infant baptism, Eucharist, and other sacraments; sacrament taken to be symbolic, but as having real spiritual effect.
Jehovah's Witnesses	Founded in 1870 in PA by Charles Taze Russell; incorporated as Watch Tower Bible and Tract Society of PA, 1884; name Jehovah's Witnesses adopted in 1931.	A governing body located in NY coordinates worldwide activities; each congregation cared for by a body of elders; each Witness considered a minister.	The Bible.	Baptism by immersion; annual Lord's Meal ceremony.
Latter-day Saints (Mormons)	In a vision of the Father and the Son reported by Joseph Smith (1820s) in NY; Smith also reported receiving new scripture on golden tablets: the Book of Mormon.	Theocratic; 1st Presidency (church president, two counselors), 12 Apostles preside over international church; local congregations headed by lay priesthood leaders.	Revelation to living prophet (church president). The Bible, Book of Mormon, and other revelations to Smith and his successors.	Baptism at age 8; laying on of hands (which confers the gift of the Holy Ghost); Lord's Supper; temple rites: baptism for the dead, marriage for eternity, others.
Lutherans	Begun by Martin Luther in Wittenberg, Germany, in 1517; objection to Catholic doctrine of salvation and sale of indulgences; break complete, 1519.	Varies from congregational to episcopal; in U.S., a combination of regional synods and congregational polities is most common.	Scripture alone; the *Book of Concord* (1580), which includes the three Ecumenical Creeds, is subscribed to as a correct exposition of Scripture.	Infant baptism; Lord's Supper; Christ's true body and blood present "in, with, and under the bread and wine."
Methodists	Rev. John Wesley began movement in 1738, within Church of England; first U.S. denomination in Baltimore (1784).	Conference and superintendent system; [in United Methodist Church, general superintendents are bishops—not a priestly order, only an office—who are elected for life].	Scripture as interpreted by tradition, reason, and experience.	Baptism of infants or adults; Lord's Supper commanded; other rites: marriage, ordination, solemnization of personal commitments.
Orthodox	Developed in original Christian proselytizing; broke with Rome in 1054 after centuries of doctrinal disputes and diverging traditions.	Synods of bishops in autonomous, usually national, churches elect a patriarch, archbishop, or metropolitan; these men, as a group, are the heads of the church.	Scripture, tradition, and the first seven church councils up to Nicaea II in 787; bishops in council have authority in doctrine and policy.	Seven sacraments: infant baptism and anointing, Eucharist, ordination, penance, marriage, and anointing of the sick.
Pentecostal	In Topeka, KS (1901) and Los Angeles (1906), in reaction to perceived loss of evangelical fervor among Methodists and others.	Originally a movement, not a formal organization, Pentecostalism now has a variety of organized forms and continues also as a movement.	Scripture; individual charismatic leaders, the teachings of the Holy Spirit.	[Spirit baptism, especially as shown in "speaking in tongues"; healing and sometimes exorcism]; adult baptism; Lord's Supper.
Presbyterians	In 16th-cent. Calvinist reformation; differed with Lutherans over sacraments, church government; John Knox founded Scotch Presbyterian church about 1560.	[Highly structured representational system of ministers and lay persons (presbyters) in local, regional, and national bodies (synods).]	Scripture.	Infant baptism; Lord's Supper; bread and wine symbolize Christ's spiritual presence.
Roman Catholics	Traditionally, founded by Jesus who named St. Peter the first vicar; developed in early Christian proselytizing, especially after the conversion of imperial Rome in the 4th cent.	[Hierarchy with supreme power vested in pope elected by cardinals]; councils of bishops advise on matters of doctrine and policy.	[The pope, when speaking for the whole church in matters of faith and morals, and tradition (which is expressed in church councils and in part contained in Scripture).]	Mass; seven sacraments: baptism, reconciliation, Eucharist, confirmation, marriage, ordination, and anointing of the sick (unction).
United Church of Christ	[By ecumenical union, in 1957, of Congregationalists and Evangelical and Reformed, representing both Calvinist and Lutheran traditions.]	Congregational; a General Synod, representative of all congregations, sets general policy.	Scripture.	Infant baptism; Lord's Supper.

How Do They Differ?

distinguish a denomination sharply from others.

Practice	Ethics	Doctrine	Other	Denomination
Worship style varies from staid to evangelistic; extensive missionary activity.	Usually opposed to alcohol and tobacco; some tendency toward a perfectionist ethical standard.	[No creed; true church is of believers only, who are all equal.]	Believing no authority can stand between the believer and God, the Baptists are strong supporters of church and state separation.	**Baptists**
Tries to avoid any rite not considered part of the 1st-cent. church; some congregations may reject instrumental music.	Some tendency toward perfectionism; increasing interest in social action programs.	Simple New Testament faith; avoids any elaboration not firmly based on Scripture.	Highly tolerant in doctrinal and religious matters; strongly supportive of scholarly education.	**Church of Christ (Disciples)**
Formal, based on *Book of Common Prayer*, updated 1979; services range from austerely simple to highly liturgical.	Tolerant, sometimes permissive; some social action programs.	Scripture; the "historic creeds," which include the Apostles, Nicene, and Athanasian, and the *Book of Common Prayer*; ranges from Anglo-Catholic to low church, with Calvinist influences.	Strongly ecumenical, holding talks with many branches of Christendom.	**Episcopalians**
Meetings are held in Kingdom Halls and members' homes for study and worship; [extensive door-to-door visitations].	High moral code; stress on marital fidelity and family values; avoidance of tobacco and blood transfusions.	[God, by his first creation, Christ, will soon destroy all wickedness; 144,000 faithful ones will rule in heaven with Christ over others on a paradise earth.]	Total allegiance proclaimed only to God's kingdom or heavenly government by Christ; main periodical, *The Watchtower*, is available in over 200 languages.	**Jehovah's Witnesses**
Simple service with prayers, hymns, sermon; private temple ceremonies may be more elaborate.	Temperance; strict moral code; [tithing]; a strong work ethic with communal self-reliance; [strong missionary activity]; family emphasis.	Jesus Christ is the Son of God, the Eternal Father. Jesus's atonement saves all humans; those who are obedient to God's laws may become joint-heirs with Christ in God's kingdom.	Mormons believe theirs is the true church of Jesus Christ, restored by God through Joseph Smith. Official name: The Church of Jesus Christ of Latter-day Saints.	**Latter-day Saints (Mormons)**
Relatively simple, formal liturgy with emphasis on the sermon.	Generally conservative in personal and social ethics; doctrine of "two kingdoms" (worldly and holy) supports conservatism in secular affairs.	Salvation by grace alone through faith; Lutheranism has made major contributions to Protestant theology.	Though still somewhat divided along ethnic lines (German, Swedish, etc.), main divisions are between fundamentalists and liberals.	**Lutherans**
Worship style varies widely by denomination, local church, geography.	Originally pietist and perfectionist; always strong social activist elements.	No distinctive theological development; 25 articles abridged from Church of England's 39, not binding.	In 1968, The United Methodist Church was formed by the union of The Methodist Church and The Evangelical United Brethren Church.	**Methodists**
Elaborate liturgy, usually in the vernacular, though extremely traditional; the liturgy is the essence of Orthodoxy; veneration of icons.	Tolerant; little stress on social action; divorce, remarriage permitted in some cases; bishops are celibate; priests need not be.	Emphasis on Christ's resurrection, rather than crucifixion; the Holy Spirit proceeds from God the Father only.	Orthodox Church in America originally under Patriarch of Moscow, was granted autonomy in 1970; Greek Orthodox do not recognize this autonomy.	**Orthodox**
Loosely structured service with rousing hymns and sermons, culminating in spirit baptism.	Usually, emphasis on perfectionism, with varying degrees of tolerance.	Simple traditional beliefs, usually Protestant, with emphasis on the immediate presence of God in the Holy Spirit.	Once confined to lower-class "holy rollers," Pentecostalism now appears in mainline churches and has established middle-class congregations.	**Pentecostal**
A simple, sober service in which the sermon is central.	Traditionally, a tendency toward strictness, with firm church- and self-discipline; otherwise tolerant.	Emphasizes the sovereignty and justice of God; no longer dogmatic.	Although traces of belief in predestination (that God has foreordained salvation for the "elect") remain, this idea is no longer a central element in Presbyterianism.	**Presbyterians**
Relatively elaborate ritual centered on the Mass; also rosary recitation, novenas.	Traditionally strict but increasingly tolerant in practice; divorce and remarriage not accepted, but annulments sometimes granted; celibate clergy, except in Eastern rite.	Highly elaborated; salvation by merit gained through grace; dogmatic; special veneration of Mary, the mother of Jesus.	Relatively rapid change followed Vatican Council II; Mass now in vernacular instead of Latin; more stress on social action, tolerance, ecumenism.	**Roman Catholics**
Usually simple service with emphasis on the sermon.	Tolerant; some social action emphasis.	Standard Protestant; Statement of Faith (1959) is not binding.	Two main churches in the 1957 union represented earlier unions with small groups of almost every Protestant denomination.	**United Church of Christ**

Major Non-Christian Religions

Source: Baha'i reviewed by the Baha'i Community Relations Center; Islam reviewed by Natana Delong-Bas, Lecturer in Islamic Studies, Boston Coll.; Hinduism and Judaism reviewed by Anthony Padovano, PhD, STD, Prof. of Literature & Religious Studies, Ramapo College, NJ, Adj. Prof. of Theology, Fordham Univ.; Sikhism reviewed by The Sikh Coalition of New York, NY.

Islam

Founded: Muhammad received his first revelation in 610 CE.

Founder: Muhammad (c. 570-632 CE), the Prophet.

Sacred texts: Two texts constitute the Muslim sacred canon, the *Quran* (Koran) and the *Hadith*. The Quran provides the foundation for Islamic religion and culture. It is regarded as the final, perfect, and complete word of God as revealed to Muhammad over the course of his life. Received by Muhammad in the Arabic language, it is memorized in Arabic by adherents regardless of their native language. It is divided into 114 chapters of unequal length, the shortest containing only 3 verses, and the longest containing 286 verses. The Quran is the ultimate source of everything Islamic, from metaphysics to theology to sacred history, to ethics and law, to art. The Hadith, which describes Muhammad's actions, attitudes, and teachings, complements the Quran. Due to its long history of oral transmission, the Hadith's lessons are seen as somewhat vulnerable to human error. It is not said to contain God's unadulterated voice as is the Quran but functions as a powerful spiritual and behavioral code nonetheless.

Organization: Muhammad was both the last prophet and a statesman. Muslim leaders have often assumed both civil and moral functions within Islamic states. Within the larger community, there are cultural and national groups, held together by a common religious law, the *Sharia*. Muslims believe that God is the ultimate lawgiver and that human beings cannot devise laws that oppose divine laws. Still, the Sharia is approached differently in different parts of the Islamic world. Over the centuries, Sunnis have developed four major schools of law: the Hanafi, the Shafi'i, the Hanbali, and the Maliki. The Ja'fari is the most important and well-known Shiite school. Before the 20th century, religious scholars known as the *ulama* held much legal power. Judges (*qadis*) and law-interpreters (*muftis*) are people learned in religious law who lead congregational prayers in mosques and perform other religious duties.

Practice: Five duties (of both men and women), known as the Pillars of Islam, are regarded as cardinal in Islam and as central to the life of the Islamic community. In accordance with Islam's absolute commitment to monotheism, the first duty is the profession of faith (the *Shahadah*): "There is no God but Allah and Muhammad is His Prophet." A Muslim must profess this belief publicly at least once in his or her lifetime; it defines the membership of an individual in the Islamic community. The second duty is that of five daily prayers organized in intervals throughout the day: sunrise, early afternoon, late afternoon, immediately after sunset, and before midnight. During prayer, Muslims face the Kaaba, a small, cube-shaped structure in the courtyard of al-Haram (the "inviolate place"), at the Grand Mosque of Mecca in Saudi Arabia. All five prayers in Islam are congregational and are to be offered in a mosque, but they may be offered individually if one cannot be present with a congregation. Congregational prayer is required only at the early afternoon prayer on Friday for men. The third cardinal duty of a Muslim is to pay alms, or *zakat*, which should be 2.5% of one's total wealth. This was originally the tax levied by Muhammad on the wealthy members of the community, primarily to help the poor. Only when zakat has been paid is the rest of a Muslim's property considered purified and legitimate. The fourth duty is the fast of the lunar month of Ramadan. During the fasting month, one must abstain from eating, drinking, smoking, impure thoughts, and sexual intercourse from dawn until sunset, and feed at least one poor person, if able. The fifth duty is the pilgrimage to the Kaaba, known as the hajj, which a Muslim must undertake, with exceptions for poverty and ill health, at least once during his or her lifetime.

Divisions: There are two major groups: the majority Sunni (84% of the worldwide Muslim population) and the minority Shiites (14%). Sects first appeared in Islam at the time of Muhammad's death. The group that came to be known as Sunni accepted Abu Bakr, an early convert, as his successor (caliph), while a smaller number, which became the Shia, believed that Ali ibn Abi Talib, the son-in-law and first cousin of the prophet, should have become his successor (Imam). Imams are believed to interpret the Quran infallibly. **Shiites** fall into three major branches: Fivers, Seveners, and Twelvers, reflecting the number of Imams they recognize. Twelvers believe that the 12th Imam has lived an invisible existence since 874, and will return as the Mahdi (a messiah figure) who will usher in a 1,000-year reign of peace and justice. **Sufism** (mystical dimension of Islam) emphasizes personal relation to God and obedience informed by love of God; it is prevalent among both Sunni and Shiites.

Location: W Africa to Philippines, across a band including E Africa, Central Asia and western China, India, Malaysia, Indonesia. Islam has several million adherents in North America and about 30 mil in Europe.

Beliefs: Strictly monotheistic. God is creator of the universe, omnipotent, omniscient, just, forgiving, and merciful. God revealed the Quran to Muhammad to guide humanity to truth and justice. Those who sincerely "submit" (literal meaning of "Islam") to God attain salvation.

World's Largest Muslim Populations, 2015

Source: Todd M. Johnson, ed. *World Christian Database* (Leiden/Boston: Brill, Aug. 2016)

Rank	Country	Muslim population	% of country's pop.
1.	Indonesia	204,196,713	79.3%
2.	India	188,559,306	14.4
3.	Pakistan	181,979,196	96.3
4.	Bangladesh	142,984,909	88.8
5.	Nigeria	83,541,514	45.9
6.	Egypt	83,212,971	90.9
7.	Iran	78,186,405	98.8
8.	Turkey	77,359,475	98.3
9.	Algeria	39,072,210	98.5
10.	Sudan	36,677,279	91.2
11.	Iraq	35,751,268	98.2
12.	Morocco	34,263,024	99.7
13.	Ethiopia	34,170,578	34.4
14.	Afghanistan	32,474,108	99.8
15.	Saudi Arabia	29,038,123	92.1
16.	Uzbekistan	28,171,007	94.2
17.	Yemen	26,586,501	99.1
18.	China	22,702,416	1.6
19.	Niger	18,990,398	95.4
20.	Syria	17,210,453	93.0

Baha'i

Founded: Mid-19th century.

Founder: Mirza Husayn-Ali Nuri (1817-92), later known as Baha'u'llah (Arabic for "Glory of God").

Sacred texts: The writings of Baha'u'llah and of his herald the Bab (Siyyid Ali-Muhammad, 1819-50). The primary text is *Kitab-i-Aqdas* (Most Holy Book).

Organization: The Baha'i administrative system consists of elected nine-member councils at the local, national, and international levels. There are also more than 180 National Spiritual Assemblies and an elected, international governing body known as the Universal House of Justice.

Practice: Prayer, meditation, and fasting are key components of the Baha'i Faith. Work performed in a spirit of service to humanity is considered an important form of worship. The Baha'i Faith has no clergy and minimal ritual and congregational worship.

Divisions: In a religion in which unity is perhaps the central spiritual value, the Baha'i Faith has avoided separating into sects with differentiated theologies and practices.

Location: Worldwide.

Beliefs: God has progressively revealed His will and purpose through a series of Divine manifestations including Jesus, Buddha, Muhammad, Zoroaster, and Baha'u'llah. Baha'u'llah's teachings include the oneness of humanity, the equality of men and women, the harmony of science and religion, and the need to abandon all forms of prejudice and eliminate extremes of poverty and wealth.

Buddhism

Founded: About 525 BCE, reportedly near Benares, India.

Founder: Gautama Siddhartha (c. 563-483 BCE), the Buddha, who achieved enlightenment through intense meditation.

Sacred texts: The *Tripitaka*, a collection of the Buddha's teachings, rules of monastic life, and philosophical commentaries on the teachings; also a vast body of Buddhist teachings and commentaries, many of which are called *sutras*.

Organization: The basic institution is the *sangha*, or monastic order, through which traditions are passed down. Monastic life tends to be democratic and antiauthoritarian.

Practice: Varies widely according to the sect and ranges from austere meditation to magical chanting and elaborate temple rites. Many practices, such as exorcism of devils, reflect pre-Buddhist beliefs.

Divisions: A variety of sects grouped into three primary branches: Theravada, which emphasizes the importance of pure thought and deed; Mahayana (includes Zen and Sokagakkai), which ranges from philosophical schools to belief in the saving grace of higher beings or ritual practices and to practical meditative disciplines; and Vajrayana, or Tantrism, a combination of belief in ritual magic and sophisticated philosophy.

Location: Mainly in Asia, from Sri Lanka to Japan.

Beliefs: Life is suffering, and there is no ultimate reality behind it. The cycle of birth and rebirth continues because of desire and attachment to the unreal "self." Meditation and deeds will end the cycle and achieve Nirvana (nothingness, enlightenment).

Hinduism

Founded: About 1500 BCE by Aryans who migrated to India, where their Vedic religion intermixed with the practices and beliefs of the native peoples.

Sacred texts: The *Veda*, including the *Upanishads*, a collection of rituals and commentaries; a vast number of epic stories about gods, heroes, and saints, including the *Bhagavadgita*, a part of the *Mahabharata*, and the *Ramayana*.

Organization: None, strictly speaking. Generally, rituals should be performed or assisted by Brahmins, the priestly caste, but in practice, simpler rituals can be performed by anyone. Brahmins are the final judges of ritual purity, the vital element in Hindu life. Temples and religious organizations are usually presided over by Brahmins.

Practice: Primarily passage rites (e.g., initiation, marriage, death) and daily devotions. Of the public rites, the *puja*, a ceremonial dinner for a god, is the most common.

Divisions: There is no concept of orthodoxy in Hinduism, which presents a variety of sects. The three major living traditions are those devoted to the gods Vishnu and Shiva and to the goddess Shakti. Numerous folk beliefs and practices, often in amalgamation with the above groups, exist side by side with philosophical schools.

Location: Mainly India, Nepal, Malaysia, Guyana, Suriname, and Sri Lanka.

Beliefs: There is only one divine principle; the many gods are only aspects of that unity. Life in all its forms is an aspect of the divine, but it appears as a separation from the divine, a meaningless cycle of birth and rebirth (*samsara*)

determined by the purity or impurity of past deeds (*karma*). To improve one's karma or escape samsara by pure acts, thought, and/or devotion is the aim of every Hindu.

Judaism

Founded: About 2000 BCE.

Founder: Abraham is regarded as the founding patriarch.

Sacred texts: The five books of Moses (the Torah), the basic source of teachings.

Organization: Originally theocratic, Judaism has evolved into a congregational polity. The basic institution is the local synagogue or temple, operated by the congregation and led by a rabbi of their choice. Chief rabbis in France and Great Britain have authority only over those who accept it; in Israel, the two chief rabbis have civil authority in family law.

Practice: Among traditional practitioners, almost all areas of life are governed by strict discipline. Sabbath and holidays are marked by observances, and attendance at public worship is considered especially important. Chief annual observances are Passover, celebrating liberation of the Israelites from Egypt and marked by the Seder meal in homes, and the 10 days from Rosh Hashanah (New Year) to Yom Kippur (Day of Atonement), a period of penitence.

Divisions: Judaism is an unbroken spectrum from ultraconservative to ultraliberal, largely reflecting different points of view regarding the binding character of the prohibitions and duties—particularly the dietary and Sabbath observations—traditionally prescribed for the daily life of the Jew.

Location: Mainly in Israel and the U.S.

Beliefs: Strictly monotheistic. God is the creator and ruler of the universe. God established a particular relationship with the Hebrew people: by obeying a divine law God gave them, they would be a special witness to God's mercy and justice. Judaism stresses ethical behavior (and, among the traditional, careful ritual obedience) as true worship of God.

Sikhism

Founded: Late 15th century in South Asia.

Founder: Guru Nanak Dev ji, Sikhism's first Guru.

Sacred texts: The *Guru Granth Sahib* was compiled by the Sikh Gurus and contains their experiences of the Divine. It also contains writings by other saintly figures of different faiths.

Organization: Each Sikh must make her or his own spiritual journey and not depend on clergy. Congregational prayer led by both men and women takes place in local *Gurdwaras* ("doorway to the Guru"). Harmandir Sahib in Amritsar, Punjab (northern India), is the central place of worship.

Practice: Prayers are required in the morning, evening, and before sleeping. The most important mode of congregational prayer is the singing of hymns from the Guru Granth Sahib. The "Five Ks" are five articles of faith required of all Sikhs: *Kes* (uncut hair), *Kangha* (comb), *Kara* (steel bracelet), *Kirpan* (sword), and *Kaccha* (short pants).

Divisions: The last living Guru, Guru Gobind Singh (1666-1708) crystallized the practices and beliefs of the faith and determined that no future living Guru was needed. Today the religion is guided by joint sovereignty of Guru Granth and Guru Panth. Guru Granth is the Sikh scripture, as the spiritual manifestation of the Guru, while the Guru Panth is the collectivity of all initiated Sikhs worldwide, as the physical manifestation of the Guru.

Location: Many Sikhs have Punjabi backgrounds. The Punjab region was divided between India and Pakistan with the end of British rule.

Beliefs: Sikhism preaches a message of devotion, remembrance of God at all times, truthful living, equality between all human beings, and social justice, while denouncing what is considered superstition and blind ritualism. Sikhism is a monotheistic religion based on revelation.

LANGUAGE

New Words in English

The following words and definitions were provided by Merriam-Webster Inc., publishers of *Merriam-Webster's Collegiate Dictionary, Eleventh Edition*, released in 2003. The words are among those that the Merriam-Webster editors decided had achieved enough currency in English to be added to the latest printing of this edition.

baby bump: the enlarged abdomen of a pregnant woman

boy band: a small ensemble of males in their teens or twenties who play pop songs geared esp. to a young female audience

brain fog: a usu. temporary state of diminished mental capacity marked by inability to concentrate or to think or reason clearly

cringeworthy: so embarrassing, awkward, or upsetting as to cause one to cringe

crowdfunding: the practice of soliciting financial contributions from a large number of people esp. from the online community

crudo: a dish of sliced, seasoned, uncooked seafood often served with a sauce

derecho: a large fast-moving complex of thunderstorms with powerful straight-line winds that cause widespread destruction

dubstep: a type of electronic dance music having prominent bass lines and syncopated drum patterns

exoplanet: a planet orbiting a star that is not our Sun

fist pump: a celebratory gesture (as by a sports player) in which the fist is raised in front of the body and then quickly and vigorously drawn back

fracking: the injection of fluid into shale beds at high pressure in order to free up petroleum resources (such as oil or natural gas)

game pad: a device having buttons and a joystick that is used for controlling images in video games

Generation Y: the generation of Americans born in the 1980s and 1990s: the millennials

hashtag: a word or phrase preceded by the symbol # that classifies or categorizes the accompanying text (such as a tweet)

insource: to procure (as some goods or services needed by a business or organization) under contract with a domestic or in-house supplier

manscaping: the trimming or shaving of a man's body hair so as to enhance his appearance

motion capture: a technology for digitally recording specific movements of a person (as an actor) and translating them into computer-animated images

paywall: a system that prevents internet users from accessing certain web content without a paid subscription

pepita: the edible seed of a pumpkin or squash, often dried or toasted

plantar fasciitis: inflammation of the dense fibrous band of tissue of the sole of the foot that is marked esp. by heel or arch pain

selfie: an image of oneself taken by oneself using a digital camera esp. for posting on social networks

sous vide: relating to or denoting a method of cooking food slowly in a vacuum-sealed pouch at a low temperature so as to retain most of the juice and aroma

spoiler alert: a reviewer's warning that a plot spoiler is about to be revealed

steampunk: science fiction dealing with 19th-century societies dominated by historical or imagined steam-powered technology

terroir: the combination of factors including soil, climate, and sunlight that gives wine grapes their distinctive character

thumb drive: a small usu. rectangular device used for storing and transferring computer data

turducken: a boneless chicken stuffed into a boneless duck stuffed into a boneless turkey

unfriend: to remove (someone) from a list of designated friends on a person's social networking website

vodcast: a video podcast

voluntourism: the act or practice of doing volunteer work as needed in the community where one is vacationing

Words About Words

alliteration: repetition of same, initial consonant sounds of two or more words in sequence or in short intervals. Ex.: "I have **s**tood **s**till and **s**topped the **s**ound of feet." —Robert Frost, "Acquainted With the Night"

anagram: word or word sequence that is a rearrangement, typically clever, of letters in another word or word sequence. Ex.: The Leaning Tower of Pisa = I spot one giant flaw here.

assonance: repetition of same or similar vowel sounds in words located near each other. Ex.: "Gr**ee**n as a dr**ea**m, and d**ee**p as death." —Rupert Brooke, "The Old Vicarage, Grantchester"

back-formation: creation of a word from an existing word, whose forms seem to suggest that the previously existing word derived from the newer word. Ex.: The verb "edit" is a back-formation of the word "editor."

cliché: a saying or expression that has been used so often it has lost its effect. Ex.: work like a dog

euphemism: a mild, indirect expression used instead of a plainer one that might be harsh, unpleasant, or offensive. Ex.: restroom instead of toilet; pass away, or pass, instead of die

hyperbole: exaggeration for emphasis or effect. Ex.: "And fired the shot heard round the world." —Ralph Waldo Emerson, "Concord Hymn"

irony: deliberate use of an expression in which the literal or surface meaning is contrary to a hidden intended, often opposite meaning that can be inferred. Ex.: "Yet Brutus says he was ambitious; / And Brutus is an honorable man." —William Shakespeare, *Julius Caesar*

litotes: intentional understatement made by negating the opposite of what is meant. Ex.: This was no small matter.

metaphor: a stated equivalence between two dissimilar things or a reference to one thing rather than another, so as to imply a comparison. Ex.: "Life is a tale told by an idiot, full of sound and fury, signifying nothing." —William Shakespeare, *Macbeth*

metonymy: substitution of one word for another that it suggests. Ex.: The pen is mightier than the sword.

onomatopoeia: words that imitate the sounds they describe. Ex.: buzz, murmur

oxymoron: expression containing seemingly contradictory words. Ex.: deafening silence

palindrome: word or phrase that reads the same backward and forward. Ex: radar, Hannah, "Madam, I'm Adam"

paradox: a statement that is phrased to seem contradictory, odd, or opposed to common sense or expectation, while being presented as true. Ex.: "What a pity that youth must be wasted on the young." —George Bernard Shaw

personification: treatment of objects or abstractions as if they were persons. Ex.: "Because I could not stop for Death— / He kindly stopped for me." —Emily Dickinson, "Because I Could Not Stop for Death"

simile: a comparison between two dissimilar things using the words "like" or "as." Ex.: "My love is like a red, red rose" —Robert Burns, "A Red, Red Rose"

spoonerism: play on words in which the initial sounds of two or more words are transposed, creating different phrases whose meanings when compared can be humorous: blushing crow instead of crushing blow

synecdoche: a form of metonymy; the use of a part for the whole, or the whole for the part. Ex.: All hands on deck!

tautology: useless, often unwitting repetition of the same idea in different wording. Ex.: close proximity. In logic, a proposition that would be self-contradictory to deny. Ex.: All bachelors are male.

National Spelling Bee

The annual Scripps National Spelling Bee, conducted by The E.W. Scripps Company and other newspapers since 1941, was instituted by *The Courier-Journal* of Louisville, KY, in 1925. Students under 16 who are not beyond 8th grade are eligible to compete locally for a chance to advance to the national competition in Washington, DC. In 2016, for the third consecutive year, there was a tie for first place. Co-winners Jairam Hathwar, 13, from Painted Post, NY, and Nihar Janga, 11, from Austin, TX, spelled the last available words correctly.

Here are the last words given and spelled correctly at the National Spelling Bee in recent years.

Year	Word	Year	Word	Year	Word	Year	Word	Year	Word
1985	milieu	1992	lyceum	1999	logorrhea	2006	Ursprache	2013	knaidel
1986	odontalgia	1993	kamikaze	2000	demarche	2007	serrefine	2014	feuilleton
1987	staphylococci	1994	antediluvian	2001	succedaneum	2008	guerdon		stichomythia
1988	elegiacal	1995	xanthosis	2002	prospicience	2009	Laodicean	2015	scherenschnitte
1989	spoliator	1996	vivisepulture	2003	pococurante	2010	stromuhr		nunatak
1990	fibranne	1997	euonym	2004	autochthonous	2011	cymotrichous	2016	Feldenkrais
1991	antipyretic	1998	chiaroscurist	2005	appoggiatura	2012	guetapens		gesellschaft

Foreign Words and Phrases

A = Arabic; F = French; Ger = German; Gr = Greek; I = Italian; J = Japanese; L = Latin; R = Russian; S = Spanish; Y = Yiddish

ad hoc (L; ad-HOK): for the end or purpose at hand; impromptu

ad hominem (L; ad-HOH-mee-nem): argument that criticizes an opponent, often unfairly, rather than addressing an issue directly

al fresco (I; ahl-FRAYS-koh): outdoors

anime (J: A-nuh-may): Japanese-style animation

antebellum (L; AHN-teh-BEL-lum): pre-war

au courant (F; oh-koo-RAHN): up-to-date, fashionable

belles lettres (F; bel-LET-truh): writing aspiring to artistic merit

bête noire (F; bet-NWAHR): a thing or person viewed with particular dislike or fear

bildungsroman (Ger; BIL-doongs-roh-mahn): novel embodying coming-of-age story

bodega (S; boh-DAY-gah): grocery store

bon vivant (F; bon-vee-VAHN): a person with refined tastes, esp. for food and drink

bonhomie (F; boh-noh-MEE): friendliness

bourgeois (F; boo-ZHWAH): middle-class; materialistic

carte blanche (F; kahrt-BLANSH): full discretionary power

cause célèbre (F; kawz-suh-LEB): a notorious incident

chutzpah (Y, HUHTS-pah): audacity, nerve

comme il faut (F; cum-eel-FOH): proper; as it should be

contretemps (F; kon-truh-TAHN): awkward situation

coup de grâce (F; kooh-duh-GRAHS): the decisive final blow

cum laude/magna cum laude/summa cum laude (L; kuhm-LOU-day; MAG-na ... ; SOO-ma ...): with praise or honor/with great praise or honor/with the highest praise or honor

de facto (L; day-FAK-toh): in fact, if not by law

de jure (L; dee-JOOR-ee, day-YOOR-ay): by right or by law

de rigueur (F; duh-ree-GUR): required by convention or etiquette

détente (F; day-TAHNT): an easing of strained relations

deus ex machina (L; DAY-uhs-eks-MAH-keh-nah): person/event that provides a solution unexpectedly or suddenly, esp. (in literature) a contrived solution to a plot

doppelgänger (Ger; DAH-pul-gang-ur): a double or ghostly counterpart of a person

double entendre (F; DOO-blahn-TAHN-druh): expression with a double meaning, one meaning of which is often risqué

e pluribus unum (L; eh-PLOO-ree-boos-OO-noom): out of many, one (U.S. motto)

éminence grise (F; ay-meh-nahns-GREEZ): one who wields power behind the scenes

ennui (F; ah-NOOEE): boredom; world-weariness; annoyance

ersatz (Ger; EHR-zats): artificial; being a (usually inferior) substitute

ex post facto (L; eks-pohst-FAK-toh): retroactive(ly)

fait accompli (F; fayt-uh-kom-PLEE): an accomplished fact

fatwa (A; FAHT-wah): in Islam, a legal or religious decree

faux pas (F; foh-PAH): false step; breach of etiquette

habeas corpus (L; HAY-bee-ahs-KOR-pus): an order for a prisoner to be brought to court to challenge his or her detention

hoi polloi (Gr; hoy-puh-LOY): the masses

impresario (I; im-prah-SAH-ri-oh): manager, promoter, or sponsor of a musical or theatrical program or company

imprimatur (L; im-prah-MAH-toor): approval or official permission to print, esp. by the Roman Catholic church

in loco parentis (L; in-LOH-koh-puh-REN-tis): in place of parent

in medias res (L; in-MAY-dee-oos-rays): into the middle of things

intelligentsia (R; in-te-luh-JEN-see-uh): elite social class made up of intellectuals and educated people

ipso facto (L; ip-soh-FAK-toh): by that fact itself

je ne sais quoi (F; zhuh-nuh-say-KWAH): literally, "I don't know what"; the little something that eludes description

jihad (A; jih-HAHD): Islamic holy war; struggle in devotion to Islam

joie de vivre (F; zhwah-duh-VEEV-ruh): zest for life

kvetch (Y; Kuh-VETCH): complain, gripe

leitmotif (Ger; lyt-moh-TEEF): the central theme or idea, particularly in art and literature

mano a mano (S; MAH-noh-ah-MAH-noh): hand to hand; in direct combat

mea culpa (L; MAY-uh-CUL-puh): through my fault

mensch (Y; MENTSCH): an upright, noble, admirable person

modus operandi (L; MOH-duhs-op-uh-RAN-dee): method of operation

mujahedeen (A; moo-jah-ha-DEEN): Islamic holy warrior

noblesse oblige (F; noh-BLES-oh-BLEEZH): the obligation of nobility to help the less fortunate

nolo contendere (L; NOH-loh-kohn-TEN-duh-ree): a plea of no contest to charges, without admitting guilt

non compos mentis (L; non-KOM-puhs-MEN-tis): not of sound mind

non sequitur (L; non-SEH-kwi-tour): a conclusion that does not logically follow from what preceded it

nouveau riche (F; noo-voh-REESH): a newly rich person, esp. one who spends money conspicuously

ombudsman (Swedish; AHM-budz-muhn): person who receives, investigates, and settles complaints

par excellence (F; par-ek-seh-LANS): best of all; incomparable

persona non grata (L; per-SOH-nah-non-GRAH-tah): unwelcome person

pièce de résistance (F; pee-es-duh-ray-ZEES-tonz): the outstanding item in a series or group

prima facie (L; pry-muh-FAY-shee-ee; pry-muh-FAY-shuh): true at first glance; presumptively valid

pro bono (L; proh-BOH-noh): (work) donated for the public good

quid pro quo (L; kwid-proh-KWOH): something given or received for something else

raison d'être (F; RAY-zohnn-DET-ruh): reason for being

savoir faire (F; sav-wahr-FAIR): dexterity in social affairs

schadenfreude (Ger; SHAH-duhn-froy-deh): joy at another's misfortune

semper fidelis (L; SEM-puhr-fee-DAY-lis): always faithful

sobriquet (F; SOH-bri-kay): nickname or informal descriptive name for someone

sotto voce (I; sah-toh-VOH-chee); in a low voice

sui generis (L; soo-ee-JEN-er-is); unique; one of a kind

terra firma (L; TER-uh-FUR-muh): solid ground

verboten (Ger; ver-BOH-ten): forbidden

vis-à-vis (F; vee-zuh-VEE): compared with; with regard to

voir dire (F; vwar-DEER): examination by lawyers or judge to determine the suitability of a witness or a prospective juror

zeitgeist (Ger; ZITE-gyste): the general intellectual, moral, and cultural climate of an era

Names for Animal Young

calf: cattle, elephant, hippo, camel, others
cheeper: grouse, partridge, quail
chick: chicken, penguin, other birds
cockerel: rooster
codling, sprag: codfish
colt: horse, zebra (male)
cria: llama, alpaca
cub: lion, bear, shark, fox, others
cygnet: swan
duckling: duck
elver: eel
ephyra: jellyfish
eyas: hawk, others

fawn: deer, antelope
filly: horse, zebra (female)
fingerling, fry: fish generally
fledgling, nestling: birds generally
foal: horse, zebra, others
gosling: goose
heifer: cow
hoglet: hedgehog
joey: kangaroo, opossum, wombat
kid: goat
kit: beaver, rabbit, ferret, others
kitten: cat, other small mammals
lamb: sheep

larva: frog, sea urchin, insects generally
parr, smolt, grilse: salmon
piglet, shoat, farrow, suckling: pig
polliwog, tadpole: frog
poult: turkey
pullet: hen
pup: dog, fox, seal, rat, others
spat: oyster, other bivalves
spiderling: spider
spike, blinker, tinker: mackerel
squab: pigeon
whelp: dog, tiger, other carnivores
yearling: cattle, sheep, horse, others

Names for Animal Collectives

alligators: congregation
ants: army, colony, swarm
apes: shrewdness, troop
bears: sleuth, sloth
bees: colony, swarm, hive, grist
birds: flight, volery
buffalo: gang, obstinacy
butterflies: flutter
buzzards: wake
camels: caravan, flock, train
cats: clowder, cluster, pounce
cattle: drove
cheetahs: coalition
cockroaches: intrusion
cranes: sedge, siege
crocodiles: bask, nest, float
crows: murder, horde
dolphins: pod

doves: dule, pitying
ducks: brace, team
eagles: convocation, aerie
ferrets: business
finches: charm
fish: school, shoal
flamingos: stand, flamboyance
foxes: skulk
geese: flock, gaggle, skein
giraffes: corps, herd, tower
goats: tribe, trip
gorillas: band, troop, whoop
grasshoppers: cloud
hawks: cast, kettle
hedgehogs: array, prickle
hippopotamuses: bloat
horses: pair, team
hounds: cry, mute, pack

hyenas: cackle
iguanas: mess
jellyfish: smack
kangaroos: mob, troop
larks: exaltation
leopards: leap
lions: pride
locusts: plague, swarm
moles: labor
monkeys: troop
mules: barren, span
nightingales: watch
otters: romp
owls: parliament
oxen: yoke
peacocks: muster
pheasants: nest, nide, bouquet
ponies: string

raccoons: gaze
ravens: unkindness
rhinoceroses: crash
seals: pod
sheep: flock, drove, hurtle
snakes: nest
squirrels: dray, scurry
starlings: flock, murmuration
swans: bevy
tigers: streak
toads: knot
trout: hover
turkeys: rafter
turtles: bale
vultures: committee
whales: gam, herd, pod
woodchucks: fall
woodpeckers: descent
zebras: herd, zeal

Eponyms

(words named for people)

boycott: to avoid trade or dealings with, as a protest; after Charles C. Boycott, an English land agent in County Mayo, Ireland, ostracized in 1880 for refusing to reduce rents

derrick: a type of crane consisting of a boom connected to the base of an upright mast; after Derrick, early 17th-cent. English hangman who used a gallows that operated via cables and pulleys

draconian: harsh; after Draco, statesman who codified laws with severe punishments in Athens c. 621 BCE

gerrymander: to draw an election district in such a way as to favor a political party; after Elbridge Gerry, who created (1812) just such an election district (shaped like a salamander) during his governorship of Massachusetts

guillotine: a machine for beheading; after Joseph Guillotin, French physician who proposed its use in 1789 as more humane than hanging

Luddite: one who opposes new technology; from Ned Ludd, leader of a group of textile workers in England who destroyed machinery in the early 1800s

maudlin: excessively sentimental; from scriptural figure Mary Magdalene, who is often shown weeping in depictions

milquetoast: a timid, unassertive person; after Caspar Milquetoast, comic strip character created by American cartoonist Harold Tucker Webster in 1924

salmonella: bacteria that can cause infections when contaminated food or water is consumed; named after Daniel Elmer Salmon, American veterinarian and public health official

sandwich: two or more slices of bread with a filling in-between; after John Montagu, 4th Earl of Sandwich (1718-92), who supposedly ate these at the gaming table

shrapnel: originally, a projectile with lead balls designed to inflict maximum damage in explosions, later pieces of shell casings; from Henry Shrapnel (1761-1842), British artillery officer who designed the projectile

silhouette: an outline image; from Étienne de Silhouette (1709-67), a stingy French finance minister

Zamboni: an ice resurfacing machine; after American inventor Frank Zamboni, who owned an ice skating rink

Some Common Abbreviations and Acronyms

Acronyms are pronounceable words formed from first letters (or syllables) of other words. Some abbreviations below (e.g., AIDS, NATO) are thus acronyms. Some acronyms are words coined as abbreviations and written in lowercase (e.g., sonar, yuppie). Italicized words preceding parenthetical definitions below are Latin unless otherwise noted.

A: ampere
AA: Alcoholics Anonymous; Associate in Arts; administrative assistant
ABA: American Bar Association
AC: alternating current; air-conditioning
ACA: Affordable Care Act
ACLU: American Civil Liberties Union
AD: *anno Domini* (in the year of the Lord)
ADD: attention deficit disorder
AFL-CIO: American Federation of Labor and Congress of Industrial Organizations
AFSCME: American Federation of State, County, and Municipal Employees
AFT: American Federation of Teachers
AI: artificial intelligence
AIDS: acquired immune deficiency syndrome
ALA: American Library Association
a.m. or **AM:** *ante meridiem* (before noon)
AP: Associated Press
APO: army post office
APR: annual percentage rate
AQAP: al-Qaeda in the Arabian Peninsula
ARM: adjustable rate mortgage
ASCAP: American Society of Composers, Authors, and Publishers
ASCII: American Standard Code for Information Interchange
ATM: automated teller machine
Ave.: Avenue
AWOL: absent without leave
BA: Bachelor of Arts
bbl: barrel(s)
BC: before Christ
BCE: before Common, or Christian, Era
bpd: barrels per day
Brexit: British exit (from the EU)
BS: Bachelor of Science
Btu: British thermal unit(s)
BTW: by the way
bu: bushel(s)
BYOB: bring your own bottle
C: Celsius, centigrade
c.: *circa* (about); copyright
CAT: computerized axial tomography
CD: compact disc
CDC: Centers for Disease Control and Prevention; Community Development Corporation
CE: Common Era; Christian Era
CEO: chief executive officer
cf.: *confer* (compare)
CFO: chief financial officer
CIA: Central Intelligence Agency
COBRA: Consolidated Omnibus Budget Reconciliation Act (health insurance continuation)
COD: cash (or collect) on delivery
COL or **Col.:** Colonel
COLA: cost of living adjustment
COO: chief operating officer

CPA: certified public accountant
CPI: consumer price index
CPL or **Cpl.:** Corporal
CPR: cardiopulmonary resuscitation
CPU: central processing unit
CST: central standard time
CV: curriculum vitae
DA: district attorney
DC: direct current
DD: Doctor of Divinity
DDS: Doctor of Dental Surgery
DEA: Drug Enforcement Agency
DHS: Department of Homeland Security
DM: direct message
DMD: Doctor of Dental Medicine
DMZ: demilitarized zone
DNA: deoxyribonucleic acid
DNC: Democratic National Committee
DNR: do not resuscitate
DOA: dead on arrival
DOB: date of birth
DoD: Department of Defense
dpi: dots per inch
DPT: diphtheria, pertussis, tetanus
DUI: driving under the influence
DVD: digital video disc
DVM: Doctor of Veterinary Medicine
DWI: driving while intoxicated
ECB: European Central Bank
ed.: edited; edition; editor
EEG: electroencephalogram
e.g.: *exempli gratia* (for example)
EKG or **ECG:** electrocardiogram
EOE: equal opportunity employer
EP: extended play
EPA: Environmental Protection Agency
ERA: Equal Rights Amendment; earned run average
ESL: English as a second language
ESP: extrasensory perception
Esq.: Esquire
EST: eastern standard time
et al.: *et alii* (and others)
etc.: *et cetera* (and so forth)
EU: European Union
F: Fahrenheit
Fannie Mae: Federal National Mortgage Association
FAQ: frequently asked questions
FBI: Federal Bureau of Investigation
FDA: Food and Drug Administration
FDIC: Federal Deposit Insurance Corporation
FEC: Federal Election Commission
FEMA: Federal Emergency Management Agency
ff.: and those following
FICA: Federal Insurance Contributions Act (Social Security)
FIFA: Fédération Internationale de Football Association

fl.: *floruit* (flourished), used for historical figures when life dates uncertain
Freddie Mac: Federal Home Loan Mortgage Corporation
FTP: file transfer protocol
FWIW: for what it's worth
FY: fiscal year
FYI: for your information
GB: gigabyte(s)
GDP: gross domestic product
GED: general equivalency diploma
GMT: Greenwich mean time
GOP: Grand Old Party (Republican Party)
GPS: Global Positioning System
GTG: got to go
GUI: graphical user interface
ha: hectare
hazmat: HAZardous MATerial
HDTV: high-definition television
HIV: human immunodeficiency virus
HMO: health maintenance organization
HMS: His/Her Majesty's Ship (UK)
Hon.: the Honorable
HOV: high-occupancy vehicle
HRH: Her (His) Royal Highness (UK)
HTML: hypertext markup language
HTTP: hypertext transfer protocol
HUD: Department of Housing and Urban Development
HVAC: heating, ventilating, and air-conditioning
Hz: hertz
ibid.: *ibidem* (in the same place)
ICU: intensive care unit
i.e.: *id est* (that is)
IM: instant messaging
IMF: International Monetary Fund
IM(H)O: in my (humble) opinion
INS: Immigration and Naturalization Service
IPO: initial public offering
IQ: intelligence quotient
IRA: individual retirement account; Irish Republican Army
IRS: Internal Revenue Service
ISBN: International Standard Book Number
ISIL or **ISIS:** Islamic State of Iraq in the Levant, or of Iraq and Syria (two names for the extremist group that calls itself the Islamic State)
ISP: Internet service provider
IVF: in vitro fertilization
JD: *Juris Doctor* (Doctor of Law)
k: karat; **K:** Kelvin
kWh: kilowatt-hour(s)
laser: Light Amplification by Stimulated Emission of Radiation
lb: pound
LGBT: lesbian, gay, bisexual, and transgender
LLP: limited liability partnership

LMAO: laughing my ass off
loc. cit.: *loco citato* (in the place cited)
LOL: laughing out loud
LSAT: Law School Admission Test
LT or **Lt.:** Lieutenant
MA: Master of Arts
MB: megabyte(s)
MBA: Master of Business Administration
MCAT: Medical College Admission Test
MD: *Medicinae Doctor* (Doctor of Medicine)
MIA: missing in action
modem: MOdulator-DEModulator
MP: member of Parliament (UK)
mph: miles per hour
MRI: magnetic resonance imaging
ms, mss: manuscript(s)
MS: Master of Science; multiple sclerosis
MSG: monosodium glutamate
MST: mountain standard time
MVP: most valuable player
NA: not applicable; not available
NAACP: National Association for the Advancement of Colored People
NAFTA: North American Free Trade Agreement
NASA: National Aeronautics and Space Administration
NATO: North Atlantic Treaty Organization
NB or **n.b.:** *nota bene* (note carefully)
NCAA: National Collegiate Athletic Association
NEA: National Education Association
NIH: National Institutes of Health
NOW: National Organization for Women
NPR: National Public Radio
NRA: National Rifle Association
NSA: National Security Agency
obs.: obsolete
OECD: Organization for Economic Cooperation and Development
OED: Oxford English Dictionary
OMB: Office of Management and Budget
op., opp.: *opus* (work[s])
OPEC: Organization of Petroleum Exporting Countries
OTC: over-the-counter
oz: ounce

p., pp.: page(s)
PA: public address
PAC: political action committee
PC: personal computer; politically correct
PDA: personal digital assistant
PETA: People for the Ethical Treatment of Animals
PhD: *Philosophiae Doctor* (Doctor of Philosophy)
PIN: personal identification number
p.m. or **PM:** *post meridiem* (after noon)
POTUS: President of the United States
PPO: preferred provider organization, a type of health-care provider network
PS: *post scriptum* (postscript)
PST: Pacific standard time
pt: part(s); pint(s); point(s)
PVT or **Pvt.:** Private
QC: Queen's Council (UK)
QED: *quod erat demonstrandum* (which was to be demonstrated)
radar: RAdio Detecting And Ranging
RAM: random access memory
RCMP: Royal Canadian Mounted Police
REM: rapid eye movement
Rev.: Reverend
rev.: revised; reviewed
RIP: *requiescat in pace* (may he/she rest in peace)
RN: registered nurse
RNA: ribonucleic acid
RNC: Republican National Committee
ROFL: rolling on the floor laughing
ROM: read only memory
ROTC: Reserve Officers' Training Corps
rpm: revolutions per minute
RSVP: *répondez s'il vous plaît* (Fr.) (please reply)
SARS: severe acute respiratory syndrome
SASE: self-addressed stamped envelope
SEC: Securities and Exchange Commission
SETI: Search for Extraterrestrial Intelligence
SGT or **Sgt.:** Sergeant
SIDS: sudden infant death syndrome
SJ: Society of Jesus (Jesuits)

sonar: SOund NAvigation and Ranging
SOTU: State of the Union
SPCA: Society for the Prevention of Cruelty to Animals
SSI: Supplementary Security Income
St.: Saint; Street
STEM: science, technology, engineering, math
TB: tuberculosis; terabyte(s)
TBA/TBD: to be announced/determined
tbsp: tablespoon
TBT: Throwback Thursday
TEFL: teaching English as a foreign language
TGIF: thank God it's Friday
TPP: Trans-Pacific Partnership (trade agreement)
TSA: Transportation Security Administration
tsp: teaspoon
UFO: unidentified flying object
UPC: Universal Product Code
URL: Universal Resource Locator
USDA: United States Department of Agriculture
USS: United States ship
UTC: coordinated universal time
VA: Department of Veterans Affairs
var.: variant
VAT: value-added tax
VCR: videocassette recorder
viz: *videlicet* (namely)
VP: vice president
W: watt(s)
WHO: World Health Organization
WMD: weapon of mass destruction
WPM: words per minute
WTF: what the f--- [expletive]
WTO: World Trade Organization
WWW: World Wide Web
YMCA/YWCA: Young Men's/Women's Christian Association
YTD: year to date
yuppie: young urban professional
ZIP: zone improvement plan (U.S. Postal Service)

Top 10 First Names of Americans by Decade or Year of Birth

Source: U.S. Social Security Administration

All names are from Social Security card applications for births that occurred in the United States after 1879. Rankings are based on one spelling of the name; variant spellings and similar sounding names are considered separate names.

BOYS

Decade/Year	Names
1880-1889	John, William, James, George, Charles, Frank, Joseph, Henry, Robert, Thomas
1890-1899	John, William, James, George, Charles, Joseph, Frank, Robert, Edward, Henry
1900-1909	John, William, James, George, Charles, Robert, Joseph, Frank, Edward, Thomas
1910-1919	John, William, James, Robert, Joseph, George, Charles, Edward, Frank, Thomas
1920-1929	Robert, John, James, William, Charles, George, Joseph, Richard, Edward, Donald
1930-1939	Robert, James, John, William, Richard, Charles, Donald, George, Thomas, Joseph
1940-1949	James, Robert, John, William, Richard, David, Charles, Thomas, Michael, Ronald
1950-1959	Michael, David, James, John, Robert, Mark, William, Richard, Thomas, Jeffrey
1960-1969	Michael, David, John, James, Robert, Mark, William, Richard, Thomas, Jeffrey
1970-1979	Michael, Christopher, Jason, David, James, John, Robert, Brian, William, Matthew
1980-1989	Michael, Christopher, Matthew, Joshua, David, James, Daniel, Robert, John, Joseph
1990-1999	Michael, Christopher, Matthew, Joshua, Jacob, Nicholas, Andrew, Daniel, Tyler, Joseph
2000-2009	Jacob, Michael, Joshua, Matthew, Daniel, Christopher, Andrew, Ethan, Joseph, William
2015	Noah, Liam, Mason, Jacob, William, Ethan, James, Alexander, Michael, Benjamin

GIRLS

Decade/Year	Names
1880-1889	Mary, Anna, Emma, Elizabeth, Margaret, Minnie, Ida, Bertha, Clara, Alice
1890-1899	Mary, Anna, Margaret, Helen, Elizabeth, Ruth, Florence, Ethel, Emma, Marie
1900-1909	Mary, Helen, Margaret, Anna, Ruth, Elizabeth, Dorothy, Marie, Florence, Mildred
1910-1919	Mary, Helen, Dorothy, Margaret, Ruth, Mildred, Anna, Elizabeth, Frances, Virginia
1920-1929	Mary, Dorothy, Helen, Betty, Margaret, Ruth, Virginia, Doris, Mildred, Frances
1930-1939	Mary, Betty, Barbara, Shirley, Patricia, Dorothy, Joan, Margaret, Nancy, Helen
1940-1949	Mary, Linda, Barbara, Patricia, Carol, Sandra, Nancy, Sharon, Judith, Susan
1950-1959	Mary, Linda, Patricia, Susan, Deborah, Barbara, Debra, Karen, Nancy, Donna
1960-1969	Lisa, Mary, Susan, Karen, Kimberly, Patricia, Linda, Donna, Michelle, Cynthia
1970-1979	Jennifer, Amy, Melissa, Michelle, Kimberly, Lisa, Angela, Heather, Stephanie, Nicole
1980-1989	Jessica, Jennifer, Amanda, Ashley, Sarah, Stephanie, Melissa, Nicole, Elizabeth, Heather
1990-1999	Jessica, Ashley, Emily, Sarah, Samantha, Amanda, Brittany, Elizabeth, Taylor, Megan
2000-2009	Emily, Madison, Emma, Olivia, Hannah, Abigail, Isabella, Samantha, Elizabeth, Ashley
2015	Emma, Olivia, Sophia, Ava, Isabella, Mia, Abigail, Emily, Charlotte, Harper

Origins of Popular American Given Names

Source: World Almanac research

Some names are commonly used for either sex but are listed here under the more traditionally associated sex. Some names listed here have variant spellings that are not shown.

Boys

Aiden: Gaelic *Aodhan*, "little fire," from name of Celtic sun god
Alexander: Gr. *Alexandros*, "defender of man"
Andrew: Gr. *andreios*, "manly"
Anthony: Roman *Antonius*, possibly from Gr. *anthos*, "flower"
Benjamin: Heb. *Binyamin*, "son of the right hand"
Brandon: Eng. place name, "gorse-covered hill"
Brian: Irish, perhaps Celtic *Brigonos*, "high" or "noble"
Charles: Ger. *ceorl*, "free man"
Christopher: Gr. *Christophoros*, "bearing Christ"
Daniel: Heb. "God is my judge"
David: Heb. *Dodavehu*, perhaps "darling"
Edward: Old Eng. *Eadweard*, "wealth-guard"
Elijah: Heb. "the Lord is my God"
Ethan: Heb. "solid, firm"

Francis, Frank: Late Lat. *Franciscus*, "Frenchman"
George: Gr. *georgos*, "soil tiller," "farmer"
Henry: Ger. *Haimric*, "home-power"
Jack: nickname for or variant of John
Jacob: Heb. *Yaakov*, "God protects" or "supplanter"
James: Late Lat. *Iacomus*, form of Jacob
Jason: Gr. *Iason*, "healer"
Jayden: prob. from Jay (short form for many *J* names) and Hayden (Old Eng. "little hollow")
Jeffrey: Norman Fr., from Ger. *Gaufrid*, "land-peace," or *Gisfrid*, "pledge-peace"
John: Heb. *Yohanan*, "God is gracious"
Jonathan: Heb. "God has given"
José: Heb. and Aramaic *Yose*, variant of Joseph
Joseph: Heb. *Yosef*, "[God] shall add"
Joshua: Heb. *Yoshua*, "God saves"
Liam: Gaelic form of William
Logan: Scot. "little hollow"

Mark: Lat. *Marcus*, perhaps from Mars, Roman god of war
Mason: Fr. "stone worker," related to Old Eng. "work"
Matthew: Heb. *Mattathia*, "gift of God"
Michael: Heb. "who could ever be like God?"
Nathan: Heb. "God has given"; modern short form of Nathaniel or Jonathan
Nicholas: Gr. *Nikolaos*, "victory-people"
Noah: Heb. "rest"
Patrick: Lat. *Patricius*, "of noble origin"
Richard: Ger. "power-hardy"
Robert: Ger. *Hrodberht*, "fame-bright"
Ryan: prob. from Irish surname, Gaelic "king"
Samuel: Heb. *Shemuel*, "God heard"
Sean: Gaelic form of John
Steven: Gr. *stephanos*, "crown" or "garland"
Thomas: Aramaic "twin"
Tyler: Old Eng. *tigeler*, "tile layer"
William: Ger. *Wilhelm*, "will-helmet"

Girls

Abigail: Heb. "my father is joy"
Alexandra, Sandra: fem. forms of Alexander
Alexis: Gr. "helper" or "defender"
Alyssa: variant of Alicia (Eng., Sp.) or Alice (Eng., Fr.); may mean "noble"
Amanda: 17th-cent. invention from Lat. "lovable"
Amelia: Ger. "hard-working," or from Lat. *aemulus*, "striving"
Amy: Old Fr. *Amee*, "beloved"
Andrea: fem. form of Andrew
Angela: Gr. *angelos*, "messenger [of God]"
Anna: Lat., Gr. form of Hannah; variants include Ann (Eng.), Ana (Sp.), Anne (Eng., Fr., Ger.)
Ashley: Eng. place name, "ash grove"
Ava: prob. modern form of Eva, Lat. form of Heb. *Eve*
Barbara: Gr. *barbarus*, "foreign"
Carol, Charlotte: fem. forms of Charles
Chloe: Gr. "young shoot," "blooming"
Claire, Clara: Lat. *clarus*, "famous"
Deborah: Heb. "bee"
Dorothy: Gr. *Dorothea*, "gift of God"
Elizabeth: Heb. *Elisheba*, perhaps "God is my oath" or "God is good fortune"
Ella: prob. variant or nickname for Ellen, variant of Helen, or Eleanor
Emily: prob. derived from Amelia
Emma: Ger. *ermen*, "whole" or "entire"

Eve, Evelyn: Heb. "life-giving"
Grace: Lat. *gratia*, "grace," "blessing"
Hailey: Eng. place name, "hay clearing"
Hannah: Heb. "He [God] has favored me"
Harper: Old Eng. "harp player"
Heather: Middle Eng. *hathir*, "heather"
Isabella, Isabel: Lat., Sp. variant of Elizabeth
Jennifer: Cornish form of Welsh *Gwenhwyfar*, "fair-smooth"
Jessica: Shakesp. invention, prob. fem. form of *Jesse*, Heb. "God exists"
Judith: Heb. "Jewish woman"
Julia: fem. form of Julius, Roman family name, or Lat. "youthful"
Kaitlyn: American spelling of Caitlin, the Irish form of Katherine
Karen: Danish form of Katherine
Katherine: Egyptian *Aikaterine*, later modified to resemble Gr. *katharos*, "pure"
Kelly: Irish Gaelic *Ceallagh*, perhaps "churchgoer" or "bright-headed"
Kimberly: Eng. place name, "Cyneburgh's clearing"
Laura: Lat. *laurus*, "laurel"
Lily: for the flower, symbol of purity
Linda: Sp. "pretty" or Ger. "tender"
Lisa: nickname for Elizabeth
Madison: Middle Eng. surname, "son of Madeline or Maud"

Margaret: Gr. *margaron*, "pearl"
Maria, Marie, Mary: Lat., Fr., Eng. forms for Heb. *Maryam*, perhaps "seeress" or "wished-for child"
Megan: Welsh form of Margaret
Melissa: Gr. "bee"
Mia: Nordic or Ital., short for Maria, etc.
Michelle: Fr. fem. form of Michael
Nancy: medieval Eng. nickname for Agnes (Gr. *hagnos*, "holy"), later also for Ann
Natalie: Fr., from Lat. *natalia*, "birthday [of Christ]"
Nicole: Fr. fem. form of Nicholas
Olivia: Lat. *oliva*, "olive tree"
Patricia: Lat. fem. form of Patrick
Rachel: Heb. "ewe"
Rose, Rosa: for the flower, suggesting beauty
Ruth: Heb., perhaps "companion"
Samantha: colonial American invention, prob. combining Sam from Samuel with *-antha* from Gr. *anthos*, "flower"
Sarah: Heb. "princess"
Sharon: Biblical place name, Heb. "plain"
Sofia, Sophia: Gr. "wisdom"
Stephanie: Fr. fem. form of Steven
Susan: Eng. form of Heb. *Shoshana*, "lily"
Teresa: Sp., perhaps "woman from Therasia"
Victoria: Lat. *victoria*, "victory"

Words and Expressions in Common Languages

English	Arabic	Chinese[1]	French	German	Hebrew	Russian	Spanish
Hello/hi	Salam	Ni hao	Bonjour	Hallo	Shalom	Privet (informal)	Hola
Good morning	Sabah el kheer	Zao shang hao	Bonjour	Guten Morgen	Boker tov	Dobraye utra	Buenos días
Good night	Tosbeho 'ala khair	Wan an	Bonne nuit	Gute Nacht	Layla tov	Spakoynay noci	Buenas noches
Good-bye	Ma'a salama	Zai jian	Au revoir	Auf wiedersehen	Lehitraot	Da svidan'ya	Adiós
Please	Men fadlek	Qing	S'il vous plaît	Bitte	Bevakasha	Pazhalusta	Por favor
Thank you very much	Shokran jazeelan	Xie xie	Merci beaucoup	Danke schön	Toda raba	Spasiba	Muchas gracias
You're welcome	Al' afw	Huan ying	De rien/pas de quoi	Keine Ursache	Bevakasha	Pazhalusta	De nada
How are you?	Kaifa haloka?	Ni hao?	Comment allez-vous?	Wie geht's dir/Ihnen?	Ma shelomkha?	Kak dela?	Cómo estás?
I'm fine	Ana bekhair	Hen hao	Je vais bien	Mir geht's gut	Tov	Harasho	Estoy bien
I'm sorry	Aasef	Bao qian	Je suis désolé	Entschuldigung	Ani mamash mitstaer	Prastite	Lo siento
Excuse me	Alma'derah	Bao qian	Pardon	Darf ich mal vorbei?	Selikha	Izvinite	Perdone
yes	na'am	shi [it is so]	oui	ja	ken	da	si
no	laa	bu [not]	non	nein	lo	nyet	no
one	wahed	yi	un	eins	ekhad	adin	uno
two	ithnaan	er	deux	zwei	shenayim	dva	dos
three	thalatha	san	trois	drei	shelosha	tri	tres
four	arba'a	si	quatre	vier	arbaa	chityri	cuatro
five	khamsa	wu	cinq	fünf	khamisha	p'at	cinco

Note: Actual form or usage of some words and expressions may vary depending on dialect, grammar, or circumstances. Transliterations for languages not in Latin alphabet vary. (1) Mandarin.

Principal Languages of the World

Source: Lewis, M. Paul, Gary F. Simons, Charles D. Fennig (eds.). *Ethnologue: Languages of the World, 17th Edition.* www.ethnologue. com. As updated in 2016. Used by permission. © SIL International.

Languages shown in italics are macrolanguages, or language groups that are equivalent in some ways to individual languages. Each language group consists of a number of variants, which may be mutually unintelligible; these variants, when they have 2.5 mil speakers or more, will also appear in the larger table below, and occasionally have the same name as the macrolanguage. Numbers are estimates and count only speakers for whom the language is a first language, or mother tongue.

Languages Spoken by the Most People

Language	Speakers (mil)	Language	Speakers (mil)	Language	Speakers (mil)
Chinese[1]	1,302	Japanese	128	Turkish	71
Spanish	427	*Lahnda*[2]	117	Urdu	69
English	339	Javanese	84	Vietnamese	68
Arabic	267	Korean	77	Tamil	68
Hindi	260	German (Standard)	77	Italian	63
Portuguese	202	French	76	*Persian*	61
Bengali	189	Telugu	74	*Malay*	61
Russian	171	Marathi	72		

(1) Mandarin (897 mil speakers), Wu (80 mil), and Yue (63 mil) are included here under Chinese; not listed separately. (2) Includes Punjabi (Western), which by itself has 91 mil speakers.

Languages With at Least 2.5 Million Speakers

Primary country is country of origin, not necessarily the country where the most speakers reside (e.g., Portugal is the primary country for Portuguese, but more Portuguese speakers live in Brazil). Number of speakers is worldwide total for each language.

Primary country	Language	Countries	Speakers (mil)	Primary country	Language	Countries	Speakers (mil)
Afghanistan	Dari	2	10.7	Ethiopia	Amharic	2	21.8
	Pashto, Southern	4	9.0		*Oromo*	3	17.5
	Uzbek, Southern	2	4.2		Oromo, Borana-Arsi-Guji	3	8.9
Albania	*Albanian*	17	3.8		Oromo, Eastern	1	7.7
Algeria	Arabic, Algerian Spoken	2	28.8		Oromo, West Central	1	4.5
	Kabyle	1	5.6		Tigrigna	3	3.9
Angola	Umbundu	1	6.0		Sidamo	1	3.0
Armenia	Armenian	15	5.3	Finland	Finnish	3	5.4
Austria	Bavarian	4	14.1	France	French	53	75.9
Azerbaijan	Azerbaijani, North	4	9.5	Georgia	Georgian	3	4.3
Bangladesh	Bengali	4	189.1	Germany	German, Standard	26	76.9
	Rangpuri	2	15.0	Ghana	Akan	1	8.2
	Chittagonian	1	13.0		Ghanaian Pidgin English	1	5.0
	Sylheti	2	10.3		Éwé	2	4.2
Belarus	Belarusan	4	2.5	Greece	Greek	9	13.1
Botswana	Tswana	4	5.4	Guinea	Pular	4	7.4
Brazil	Hunsrik	1	3.0		*Mandingo*	7	3.6
Bulgaria	Bulgarian	8	7.9		Maninkakan, Eastern	3	3.0
Burkina Faso	Môoré	2	6.4	Haiti	Haitian Creole	2	7.7
Burundi	Rundi	1	10.7	Hungary	Hungarian	9	12.6
Cambodia	Khmer, Central	2	14.3	India	Hindi	4	260.1
China	*Chinese*	35	1,302.0		Telugu	2	74.2
	Chinese, Gan	1	897.1		Marathi	1	71.8
	Chinese, Hakka	13	80.1		Tamil	7	67.8
	Chinese, Huizhou	1	63.0		Gujarati	7	46.9
	Chinese, Jinyu	1	50.2		Bhojpuri	3	39.4
	Chinese, Mandarin	14	48.0		Kannada	1	37.7
	Chinese, Min Bei	2	46.1		Malayalam	1	34.3
	Chinese, Min Dong	6	36.6		Maithili	2	33.9
	Chinese, Min Nan	11	31.4		Punjabi, Eastern	3	29.3
	Chinese, Min Zhong	1	21.7		*Marwari*	3	19.7
	Chinese, Pu-Xian	3	14.9		Marwari	2	14.0
	Chinese, Wu	1	10.9		Merwari	1	13.3
	Chinese, Xiang	1	10.4		Mewari	1	12.8
	Chinese, Yue	12	9.1		Shekhawati	1	12.8
	Zhuang	2	7.7		Magahi	1	12.4
	Uyghur	4	3.4		Chhattisgarhi	1	9.5
	Hmong	9	3.1		Assamese	1	8.0
	Mongolian, Peripheral	2	2.6		Deccan	1	7.0
	Bouyei	2	2.6		*Rajasthani*	3	6.2
Congo, Dem. Rep. of	Luba-Kasai	1	6.3		Malvi	1	6.1
	Kongo	3	5.6		Wagdi	1	5.9
	Koongo	3	5.0		Kanauji	1	5.6
	Kituba	1	4.2		Haryanvi	1	5.6
Côte d'Ivoire	Baoulé	1	3.0		Varhadi-Nagpuri	1	5.5
Croatia	Croatian	8	5.6		Santhali	3	5.1
Czech Republic	Czech	7	10.6		*Konkani*	4	4.2
Denmark	Danish	6	5.5		Konkani, Goan	2	4.0
Egypt	Arabic, Egyptian Spoken	1	58.4		Indian Sign Language	2	3.9
	Arabic, Sa'idi Spoken	1	20.3		Kashmiri	2	3.8
					Lambadi	1	3.6

Primary country	Language	Countries	Speakers (mil)
India (cont.)	Dogri	1	3.3
	Mina	1	3.3
	Bhili	1	3.1
	Sadri	2	3.0
	Bundeli	1	3.0
	Awadhi	2	3.0
	Godwari	1	2.9
	Garhwali	1	2.9
	Bagheli	2	2.5
Indonesia	Javanese	3	84.3
	Banjar	2	34.0
	Indonesian	1	23.2
	Minangkabau	1	6.8
	Musi	1	5.5
	Sunda	1	5.0
	Madura	2	5.0
	Bugis	2	3.5
	Betawi	1	3.5
	Aceh	1	3.3
	Bali	1	3.1
Iran	*Persian*	30	60.6
	Persian, Iranian	6	51.6
	Kurdish, Southern	2	24.4
	Azerbaijani	15	15.0
	Azerbaijani, South	5	3.0
	Gilaki	1	2.8
Iraq	Arabic, Mesopotamian Spoken	4	25.4
	Arabic, North Mesopotamian Spoken	3	15.4
	Kurdish	27	8.7
	Kurdish, Central	2	7.3
Israel	Hebrew	1	4.8
Italy	Italian	13	63.4
	Venetian	4	7.9
	Napoletano-Calabrese	1	5.7
	Sicilian	1	4.7
	Lombard	2	3.9
Jamaica	Jamaican Creole English	3	3.0
Japan	Japanese	2	128.1
Jordan	Arabic, South Levantine Spoken	3	6.8
Kazakhstan	Kazakh	6	12.8
Kenya	Gikuyu	1	6.6
	Oluluyia	3	5.1
	Kalenjin	3	4.8
	Dholuo	2	4.2
	Kamba	1	3.9
Korea, South	Korean	7	77.3
Kuwait	Arabic, Gulf Spoken	10	6.8
Kyrgyzstan	Kyrgyz	5	4.6
Laos	Lao	3	3.3
Lesotho	Sotho, Southern	2	5.6
Libya	Arabic, Libyan Spoken	3	3.6
Lithuania	Lithuanian	2	3.0
Madagascar	*Malagasy*	6	18.1
	Malagasy, Plateau	2	7.5
Malawi	Chichewa	5	9.5
	Yao	4	2.5
Malaysia	*Malay*	16	60.6
	Malay	3	15.9
	Malay, Kedah	2	2.6
Mali	Bamanankan	2	4.1
Mauritania	Hassaniyya	7	3.8
Mongolia	*Mongolian*	7	6.0
	Mongolian, Halh	2	2.6
Morocco	Arabic, Moroccan Spoken	3	23.1
	Tachelhit	2	3.9
Mozambique	Makhuwa	1	3.2
Myanmar (Burma)	Burmese	1	32.9
	Shan	3	3.3
Nepal	*Nepali*	7	16.2
	Nepali	3	15.4
Netherlands	Dutch	7	22.0
Niger	Zarma	4	3.2
Nigeria	Hausa	9	26.9
	Fulfulde, Nigerian	3	19.0
	Yoruba	2	18.0
	Igbo	1	11.6

Primary country	Language	Countries	Speakers (mil)
Nigeria (cont.)	*Kanuri*	6	3.8
	Kanuri, Central	5	3.3
Norway	Norwegian	1	4.7
Pakistan	*Lahnda*	8	116.6
	Pahari-Potwari	2	90.5
	Punjabi, Western	2	68.6
	Saraiki	2	38.3
	Urdu	6	23.8
	Pushto	9	21.0
	Pashto, Central	1	20.1
	Pashto, Northern	3	8.7
	Sindhi	3	6.5
	Baluchi	8	3.6
	Balochi, Eastern	2	3.5
	Balochi, Southern	4	3.1
Paraguay	*Guarani*	5	5.0
	Guarani, Paraguayan	1	4.9
Peru	*Quechua*	6	7.7
Philippines	Tagalog	3	24.7
	Cebuano	1	15.8
	Ilocano	1	7.0
	Hiligaynon	1	5.8
	Bikol	1	3.8
	Bikol, Central	1	2.6
	Waray-Waray	1	2.5
Poland	Polish	9	39.8
Portugal	Portuguese	12	202.2
Romania	Romanian	6	23.7
Russia	Russian	17	171.4
	Tatar	4	5.2
Rwanda	Kinyarwanda	3	11.3
Saudi Arabia	*Arabic*	58	266.9
	Arabic, Hijazi Spoken	2	11.6
	Arabic, Najdi Spoken	4	6.0
Senegal	*Fulah*	20	23.7
	Pulaar	6	5.3
	Mandinka	3	4.4
Serbia	*Serbo-Croatian*	27	15.6
	Serbian	10	8.4
Slovakia	Slovak	8	5.1
Somalia	Somali	4	14.6
South Africa	Zulu	5	12.0
	Xhosa	2	8.2
	Afrikaans	6	7.2
	Tsonga	4	5.1
	Sotho, Northern	1	4.6
Spain	Spanish	31	426.5
	Catalan	4	4.1
Sri Lanka	Sinhala	2	14.2
Sudan	Arabic, Sudanese Spoken	3	17.0
Sweden	Swedish	2	9.2
Switzerland	German, Swiss	5	6.3
Syria	Arabic, North Levantine Spoken	2	25.9
Tajikistan	Tajiki	4	7.9
Tanzania	*Swahili*	16	15.8
	Swahili	8	15.7
	Sukuma	1	7.3
Thailand	Thai	2	20.5
	Thai, Northeastern	1	15.0
	Thai, Northern	2	6.0
	Thai, Southern	1	4.5
Tunisia	Arabic, Tunisian Spoken	1	11.4
Turkey	Turkish	8	71.4
	Kurdish, Northern	9	15.2
Turkmenistan	Turkmen	4	6.7
Uganda	Ganda	1	4.1
Ukraine	Ukrainian	9	34.6
United Kingdom	English	106	339.4
Uzbekistan	*Uzbek*	13	28.2
	Uzbek, Northern	6	24.0
Vietnam	Vietnamese	3	68.0
Yemen	Arabic, Sanaani Spoken	1	7.6
	Arabic, Ta'izzi-Adeni Spoken	2	7.0
Zambia	Bemba	2	4.1
Zimbabwe	Shona	3	10.8

BUILDINGS, BRIDGES, AND TUNNELS

100 Tallest Buildings in the World

Source: Phorio, phorio.com; Council on Tall Buildings and Urban Habitat (CTBUH), www.ctbuh.org

Only buildings that are completed or under construction and topped out as of Oct. 1, 2016, are shown here. Structures under construction and topped out architecturally are denoted by an asterisk (*). Year in parentheses is date of completion or projected completion. Height is generally measured from the lowest significant open-air pedestrian entrance to the architectural top, including penthouses, spires, and other decorative features that are an integral part of the design. Stories generally counted from street level. NA = Not available.

Building	Ht. (ft)	Stories
Burj Khalifa, Dubai, United Arab Emirates (2010)	2,717	163
Shanghai Tower, Shanghai, China (2015)	2,073	128
Makkah Royal Clock Tower Hotel, Mecca, Saudi Arabia (2013)	1,972	120
Ping An Finance Center, Shenzhen, China (2016)	1,965	115
*Lotte World Tower, Seoul, South Korea (2016)	1,819	123
One World Trade Center, New York, NY, U.S. (2014)	1,776	92
CTF Finance Centre, Guangzhou, China (2016)	1,739	111
Taipei 101, Taipei, Taiwan (2004)	1,667	101
Shanghai World Financial Center, Shanghai, China (2008)	1,614	101
International Commerce Centre, Hong Kong, China (2010)	1,588	108
*Changsha IFS Tower T1, Changsha, China (2017)	1,483	94
Petronas Tower I, Kuala Lumpur, Malaysia (1998)	1,483	88
Petronas Tower II, Kuala Lumpur, Malaysia (1998)	1,483	88
*Suzhou IFS, Suzhou, China (2017)	1,476	95
Zifeng Tower, Nanjing, China (2010)	1,476	66
Willis (formerly Sears) Tower, Chicago, IL, U.S. (1974)	1,451	108
KK100, Shenzhen, China (2011)	1,449	100
Guangzhou International Finance Center, Guangzhou, China (2010)	1,439	103
*Wuhan Center, Wuhan, China (2017)	1,437	88
Marina 101, Dubai, UAE (2016)	1,399	101
432 Park Avenue, New York, NY, U.S. (2016)	1,396	85
Trump International Hotel & Tower, Chicago, IL, U.S. (2009)	1,389	98
Jin Mao Tower, Shanghai, China (1999)	1,380	88
Princess Tower, Dubai, UAE (2012)	1,356	101
Al Hamra Tower, Kuwait City, Kuwait (2011)	1,354	80
Two International Finance Centre, Hong Kong, China (2003)	1,352	88
23 Marina, Dubai, UAE (2012)	1,289	90
CITIC Plaza, Guangzhou, China (1997)	1,280	80
*Capital Market Authority Headquarters, Riyadh, Saudi Arabia (2017)	1,260	77
Shun Hing Square, Shenzhen, China (1996)	1,260	69
*Eton Place Dalian Tower 1, Dalian, China (2016)	1,257	80
World Trade Center Abu Dhabi-The Residences, Abu Dhabi, UAE (2014)	1,251	88
Empire State Building, New York, NY, U.S. (1931)	1,250	102
Elite Residence, Dubai, UAE (2012)	1,248	87
Central Plaza, Hong Kong, China (1992)	1,227	78
*Vostok, Moscow, Russia (2016)	1,226	95
*Dalian International Trade Center, Dalian, China (2016)	1,214	86
*The Address The BLVD, Dubai, UAE (2016)	1,207	72
Bank of China Tower, Hong Kong, China (1990)	1,205	72
Bank of America Tower, New York, NY, U.S. (2009)	1,200	55
Almas Tower, Dubai, UAE (2008)	1,181	68
JW Marriott Marquis Hotel Dubai Tower 2, Dubai, UAE (2013)	1,166	82
JW Marriott Marquis Hotel Dubai Tower 1, Dubai, UAE (2012)	1,166	82
Emirates Office Tower, Dubai, UAE (2000)	1,163	54
OKO South Tower, Moscow, Russia (2015)	1,160	90
The Torch, Dubai, UAE (2011)	1,155	86
Forum 66 Tower 2, Shenyang, China (2015)	1,150	67
The Pinnacle, Guangzhou, China (2012)	1,149	60
Tuntex Sky Tower, Kaohsiung, Taiwan (1998)	1,140	85
Aon Center, Chicago, IL, U.S. (1973)	1,136	83
The Center, Hong Kong, China (1998)	1,135	73
John Hancock Center, Chicago, IL, U.S. (1969)	1,128	100
*Xiamen Cross-Strait Financial Centre, Xiamen, China (2017)	1,128	68
*Ahmed Abdul Rahim Al Attar Tower, Dubai, UAE (2017)	1,122	76
ADNOC Headquarters, Abu Dhabi, UAE (2015)	1,122	65
Mercury City Tower, Moscow, Russia (2013)	1,112	75
Chongqing World Financial Center, Chongqing, China (2015)	1,112	72
Wuxi International Finance Square, Wuxi, China (2014)	1,112	68
*Tianjin Modern City Office Tower, Tianjin, China (2016)	1,109	65
Tianjin World Financial Center, Tianjin, China (2011)	1,105	75
*DAMAC Residenze, Dubai, UAE (2017)	1,100	88
*Twin Towers Guiyang East Tower, Guiyang, China (2017)	1,099	74
*Twin Towers Guiyang West Tower, Guiyang, China (2017)	1,099	74
*Wilshire Grand Center, Los Angeles, CA, U.S. (2017)	1,099	73
Shanghai Shimao International Plaza, Shanghai, China (2006)	1,094	60
Rose Rayhaan by Rotana, Dubai, UAE (2007)	1,093	71
Minsheng Bank Building, Wuhan, China (2008)	1,087	68
*Ryugyong Hotel, Pyongyang, North Korea (NA)	1,083	105
China World Tower, Beijing, China (2009)	1,083	74
*Zhuhai St. Regis Hotel & Office Tower, Zhuhai, China (2017)	1,083	67
*Yuexiu Fortune Center Tower 1, Wuhan, China (2017)	1,083	66
*Hon Kwok City Centre, Shenzhen, China (2016)	1,081	80
Hanoi Landmark Tower, Hanoi, Vietnam (2012)	1,079	72
Longxi International Hotel, Jiangyin, China (2011)	1,076	72
Al Yaqoub Tower, Dubai, UAE (2013)	1,076	69
Wuxi Suning Plaza 1, Wuxi, China (2014)	1,076	68
The Index, Dubai, UAE (2010)	1,070	80
The Landmark, Abu Dhabi, UAE (2013)	1,063	72
Deji Plaza Phase 2, Nanjing, China (2013)	1,063	62
*Yantai Shimao No. 1 The Harbour, Yantai, China (2016)	1,060	59
Q1 Tower, Gold Coast, Australia (2005)	1,058	78
Wenzhou Trade Center, Wenzhou, China (2011)	1,056	68
*Guangxi Financial Plaza, Nanning, China (2016)	1,053	68
Burj Al Arab, Dubai, UAE (1999)	1,053	56
Nina Tower I, Hong Kong, China (2007)	1,051	80
Sinar Mas New Bund 1, Shanghai, China (2016)	1,048	66
Chrysler Building, New York, NY, U.S. (1930)	1,046	77
Global City Square, Guangzhou, China (2016)	1,046	67
New York Times Tower, New York, NY, U.S. (2007)	1,046	52
*Jiuzhou International Tower, Nanning, China (2017)	1,043	71
HHHR Tower, Dubai, UAE (2010)	1,042	72
*Chongqing IFS T1, Chongqing, China (2017)	1,037	62
*China World Trade Center Phase 3B, Beijing, China (2017)	1,037	59
*Changsha IFS Tower T2, Changsha, China (2017)	1,033	63
International Youth Cultural Centre Tower 1, Nanjing, China (2015)	1,032	68
Maha Nakhon, Bangkok, Thailand (2016)	1,031	75
Bank of America Plaza, Atlanta, GA, U.S. (1992)	1,023	55
Moi Center Tower A, Shenyang, China (2014)	1,020	75
US Bank Tower, Los Angeles, CA, U.S. (1990)	1,018	73
Ocean Heights, Dubai, UAE (2010)	1,017	83

Tallest Free-Standing Towers in the World

Source: Phorio, phorio.com; Council on Tall Buildings and Urban Habitat (CTBUH), www.ctbuh.org

Year is date of completion or projected completion. As of Oct. 1, 2016.

Tower	Ht. (ft)	Year
Tokyo Sky Tree, Tokyo, Japan	2,080	2012
Canton Tower, Guangzhou, China	1,969	2010
CN Tower, Toronto, ON, Canada	1,815	1976
Ostankino Tower, Moscow, Russia	1,772	1967
Oriental Pearl Television Tower, Shanghai, China	1,535	1995
Milad Tower, Tehran, Iran	1,427	2008
Manara Kuala Lumpur, Kuala Lumpur, Malaysia	1,379	1996
Tianjin Radio & TV Tower, Tianjin, China	1,362	1991
Central Radio & TV Tower, Beijing, China	1,347	1992
Henan Province Radio & Television Emission Tower, Zhengzhou, China	1,273	2010
Kiev TV Tower, Kiev, Ukraine	1,263	1974
Tashkent Tower, Tashkent, Uzbekistan	1,230	1985
Liberation Tower, Kuwait City, Kuwait	1,220	1996
Alma-Ata Tower, Almaty, Kazakhstan	1,217	1982
TV Tower, Riga, Latvia	1,208	1987
Berliner Fernsehturm, Berlin, Germany	1,207	1969
Stratosphere Tower, Las Vegas, NV, U.S.	1,149	1996
Lotus Tower, Colombo, Sri Lanka	1,148	2017
West Pearl Tower, Chengdu, China	1,112	2004
Macau Tower, Macau, China	1,109	2001
Europaturm, Frankfurt, Germany	1,106	1979

Tall Buildings in Selected North American Cities

Source: Phorio, phorio.com; Council on Tall Buildings and Urban Habitat (CTBUH), www.ctbuh.org

List includes freestanding towers and other structures that do not have stories and are not technically considered buildings. Structures still under construction as of Oct. 1, 2016, are denoted by an asterisk (*). Year in parentheses is date of completion or projected completion. Height is generally measured from the lowest significant open-air pedestrian entrance to the architectural top, including penthouses, spires, and other decorative features that are an integral part of the design. Stories generally counted from street level. NA = Not applicable/available.

Building/structure	Ht. (ft)	Stories
Atlanta, GA		
Bank of America Plaza (incl. spire), 600 Peachtree St. NE (1992)	1,023	55
SunTrust Plaza, 303 Peachtree St. NE (1993)[1]	867	60
One Atlantic Center, 1201 W. Peachtree St. (1987)	820	50
191 Peachtree Tower (1991)	770	50
Westin Peachtree Plaza, 210 Peachtree St. NW (1976)[2]	723	73
Georgia Pacific Tower, 133 Peachtree St. NE (1981)	697	51
Promenade II (incl. spire), 1230 Peachtree St. NE (1989)	691	40
AT&T Building, 675 W. Peachtree St. (1980)	677	47
Sovereign, 3344 Peachtree (2008)	665	48
1180 Peachtree (2006)	657	41
GLG Grand/Four Seasons Hotel, 75 14th St. NE (1992)	609	53
The Mansion on Peachtree, 3376 Peachtree Rd. NE (2008)	580	42
Atlantic, 270 17th St. NW (2009)	577	46
State of Georgia Building, 2 Peachtree St. NW (1967)[3]	556	44
Marriott Marquis, 265 Peachtree Center Ave. NE (1985)	554	52
Viewpoint, 855 Peachtree St. NE (2008)	501	36
(1) 902 ft incl. antenna. (2) 883 ft incl. antenna. (3) 599 ft incl. antenna.		
Austin, TX		
*The Independent, 301 West Ave. (2019)	688	58
Austonian, 200 Congress Ave. (2010)	683	56
*Fairmont Austin (incl. spire), 101 Red River St. (2017)	595	36
360 Condominiums (incl. spire), 360 Nueces St. (2008)	581	45
Frost Bank Tower, 401 N. Congress Ave. (2004)	516	33
Boston, MA		
200 Clarendon (1976)	790	62
Prudential Tower, 800 Boylston St. (1964)[1]	750	52
*Four Seasons Hotel and Private Residences, One Dalton Street (2019)	746	61
Millennium Tower, 426 Washington St. (2016)	685	55
Federal Reserve Bldg., 600 Atlantic Ave. (1978)	604	32
BNY Mellon Center at One Boston Place, 201 Washington St. (1970)	602	41
One International Place, 100 Oliver St. (1987)	600	46
100 Federal St. (1971)	591	37
One Financial Center, 10 Dewey Square (1984)	590	46
111 Huntington Ave. (2002)	564	36
Two International Place (1993)	538	35
One Post Office Square (1981)	525	40
1 Federal St. (1975)	520	38
Exchange Place, 53 State St. (1984)	510	39
Sixty State St. (1977)	509	38
1 Beacon St. (1972)	507	36
State Street Financial Center (incl. spire), 1 Lincoln St. (2003)	503	36
28 State St. (1970)	500	40
(1) 920 ft incl. antenna.		
Burnaby, BC, Canada		
*Solo District-Altus (2017)	616	49
*Brentwood One (2017)	611	53
*Brentwood Two (2017)	611	53
*4670 Assembly Way (2018)	535	57
Sovereign, 4509 Kingsway (2014)	511	45
Calgary, AB, Canada		
*Brookfield Place Tower One, 225 6th Ave. (2018)	810	56
The Bow, 510 Centre St. (2012)	779	57
*Telus Sky (2018)	729	59
Petro Canada Centre West Tower, 150 6th Ave. SW (1984)	705	53
Eighth Avenue Place East Tower, 8th Ave. and 5th St. SW (2011)	696	49
Bankers Hall West Tower, 888 3rd St. SW (2000)	645	50
Bankers Hall East Tower, 855 2nd St. SW (1989)	645	50
Calgary Tower, 101 9th Ave. SW (1967)	626	NA
Centennial Place 1 (incl. spire), 520 3rd Ave. SW (2010)	599	40
TransCanada Tower, 450 1st St. SW (2001)	581	38
Canterra Tower, 400 3rd Ave. SW (1988)	580	46
Eighth Avenue Place West Tower, 8th Ave. and 5th St. SW (2014)	580	40
Jamieson Place (incl. spires), 302 4th Ave. SW (2009)	568	38
First Canadian Centre, 350 7th Ave. SW (1982)	547	41
Western Canadian Place-North Tower, 707 6th St. SW (1983)	538	41
Canada Trust, Calgary Eatons Centre, 421 7th Ave. SW (1991)	530	40
City Centre I, 339 2nd Ave. SW (2016)	530	36

Building/structure	Ht. (ft)	Stories
Scotia Centre, 700 2nd St. SW (1976)	509	42
Nexen Building, 801 7th Ave. SW (1982)	500	37
Charlotte, NC		
Bank of America Corporate Center, 100 N. Tryon St. (1992)	871	60
Duke Energy Center, 534 S. Tryon St. (2010)	786	48
Hearst Tower, 214 N. Tryon St. (2002)	659	47
One Wells Fargo Center, 301 S. College St. (1988)	588	42
The Vue, 400 W. 5th St. (2010)	574	50
Bank of America Plaza, 101 S. Tryon St. (1974)	503	40
Chicago, IL		
Willis (fmr. Sears) Tower, 233 S. Wacker Dr. (1974)[1]	1,451	108
Trump International Hotel & Tower (incl. spire), 401 N. Wabash Ave. (2009)	1,389	98
*Vista Tower, 381 E. Wacker Dr. (2020)	1,186	98
Aon Center, 200 E. Randolph St. (1973)	1,136	83
John Hancock Center, 875 N. Michigan Ave. (1969)[2]	1,128	100
Franklin Center-North Tower (incl. spires), 227 W. Monroe St. (1989)	1,007	60
Two Prudential Plaza (incl. spire), 180 N. Stetson Ave. (1990)	995	64
311 S. Wacker Dr. (1990)	961	65
900 N. Michigan Ave. (1989)	871	66
Aqua, 225 N. Columbus Dr. (2009)	859	86
Water Tower Place, 845 N. Michigan Ave. (1976)	859	74
Chase Tower, 21 S. Clark St. (1969)	850	60
Park Tower, 800 N. Michigan Ave. (2000)	844	68
*One Bennett Park, 451 E. Grand Ave. (2018)	843	67
The Legacy at Millennium Park, 21-39 S. Wabash (2010)	818	73
300 N. LaSalle (2009)	785	60
3 First National Plaza, 70 W. Madison St. (1981)	767	57
Chicago Title & Trust Center, 161 N. Clark St. (1992)	756	50
Blue Cross HQ, 300 E. Randolph St. (2010)	744	54
*River Point, 444 W. Lake St. (2017)	732	50
Olympia Centre, 737 N. Michigan Ave. (1986)	731	63
One Museum Park, 1215 S. Prairie Ave. (2009)	726	62
*150 North Riverside (2017)	725	53
AMA Plaza, 330 N. Wabash Ave. (1973)	695	52
Waldorf Astoria Chicago, 940 N. Rush St. (2009)	686	60
111 S. Wacker Dr. (2005)	681	51
181 W. Madison St. (1990)	680	50
Hyatt Center, 71 S. Wacker Dr. (2005)	679	48
One Magnificent Mile, 980 N. Michigan Ave. (1983)	673	57
340 on the Park, 340 E. Randolph St. (2007)	672	64
United Bldg., 77 W. Wacker Dr. (1992)	668	49
UBS Tower, 1 N. Wacker Dr. (2001)	652	50
Daley Center, 55 W. Washington St. (1965)	648	31
55 E. Erie St. (2004)	647	56
Lake Point Tower, 505 N. Lake Shore Dr. (1968)	645	70
River East Center, 350 E. Illinois St. (2001)	644	58
Grand Plaza I (incl. spire), 540 N. State St. (2003)	641	57
155 N. Wacker Dr. (2009)	638	45
Leo Burnett Bldg., 35 W. Wacker Dr. (1989)	635	46
The Heritage at Millennium Park, 125 N. Wabash Ave. (2005)	631	57
NBC Tower (incl. spire), 455 N. Cityfront Plaza Dr. (1989)	627	37
353 N. Clark (2009)	623	44
OneEleven, 111 W. Wacker Dr. (2014)	616	58
Millennium Centre, 33 W. Ontario St. (2003)	610	58
Board of Trade (incl. statue), 141 W. Jackson Blvd. (1930)	609	44
Chicago Place, 700 N. Michigan Ave. (1991)	608	49
CNA Plaza, 325 S. Wabash St. (1972)	601	44
One Prudential Plaza, 130 E. Randolph St. (1955)[3]	601	41
Heller International Tower, 500 W. Monroe St. (1992)	600	45
One Madison Plaza, 200 W. Madison St. (1982)	599	44
The Grant, 201 E. Roosevelt Rd. (2010)	595	54
1000 Lake Shore Plaza (1964)	590	55
The Clare at Water Tower, 55 E. Pearson St. (2008)	589	52
Citigroup Center, 500 W. Madison St. (1987)	588	42
*Optima Chicago Center II, 220 E. Illinois St. (2018)	587	57
The Park Monroe, 65 E. Monroe St. (1972)	583	49
Crain Communications Bldg., 150 N. Michigan Ave. (1983)	582	41
North Pier Apts., 474 N. Lake Shore Dr. (1990)	581	61
Citadel Center, 131 S. Dearborn St. (2003)	580	39
The Fordham, 25 E. Superior St. (2003)	574	52
190 S. LaSalle St. (1987)	573	40
One South Dearborn (2005)	571	39
Onterie Center, 446 E. Ontario St. (1986)	570	58

Building/structure	Ht. (ft)	Stories
Loews North Park Drive, 455 North Park Dr. (2015)	569	51
*CNA Center, 151 N. Franklin St. (2018)	568	36
Chicago Temple, 77 W. Washington St. (1924)	568	23
Palmolive Building (incl. beacon), 919 N. Michigan Ave. (1929)	565	37
Marina City I, 300 N. State St. (1964)	562	61
Marina City II, 301 N. Dearborn St. (1964)	562	61
Kluczynski Federal Bldg., 230 S. Dearborn St. (1975)	562	42
Huron Plaza Apts., 30 E. Huron St. (1983)	560	56
Boeing International Headquarters, 100 N. Riverside Plz. (1990)	560	36
The Parkshore, 195 N. Harbor Dr. (1991)	556	56
North Harbor Tower, 175 N. Harbor Dr. (1988)	556	55
Civic Opera Bldg., 20 N. Wacker Dr. (1929)	555	45
Streeter Place, 351 E. Ohio St. (2009)	554	55
Harbor Point, 155 N. Harbor Dr. (1975)	554	54
Newberry Plaza, 1000 N. State St. (1974)	553	53
Michigan Plaza South, 205 N. Michigan Ave. (1985)	553	46
30 N. LaSalle St. (1975)	553	44
Pittsfield Building, 55 E. Washington St. (1927)	551	38
One S. Wacker Dr. (1982)	550	40
Park Millennium, 222 N. Columbus Dr. (2002)	544	57
AMLI River North, 401 N. Clark St. (2013)	543	49
Franklin Center-South Tower, 125 S. Franklin St. (1992)	538	35
The Pinnacle, 21 E. Huron St. (2004)	535	48
*465 North Park Drive (2018)	535	47
LaSalle National Bank, 135 S. LaSalle St. (1934)	535	45
Park Place Tower, 655 W. Irving Park Rd. (1971)	531	56
One N. LaSalle St. (1930)	530	48
The Elysees, 111 E. Chestnut St. (1973)	529	56
River Plaza, 405 N. Wabash St. (1977)	524	56
35 E. Wacker Drive (1927)	523	40
Kemper Building, 1 E. Wacker Dr. (1962)	522	41
Mather Tower, 75 E. Wacker Dr. (1928)	521	41
Chicago Mercantile Exchange, 10 S. Wacker Dr. (1987)	520	40
Chicago Mercantile Exchange, 30 S. Wacker Dr. (1983)	520	40
The Columbian, 1180 S. Michigan Ave. (2008)	517	47
*200 N. Michigan (2016)	517	44
191 N. Wacker Drive (2002)	516	37
401 E. Ontario St. (1990)	515	51
One Financial Place, 440 S. LaSalle St. (1985)	515	39
The Streeter, 345 E. Ohio St. (2006)	514	50
Park Tower Condominiums, 5415 N. Sheridan Rd. (1973)	513	54
600 North Lake Shore Drive-South Tower (2009)	513	47
LaSalle-Wacker Bldg., 221 N. LaSalle St. (1930)	512	41
Harris Bank III, 115 S. LaSalle St. (1974)	510	38
321 N. Clark St. (1987)	510	35
215 West, 215 W. Washington St. (2010)	509	50
400 E. Ohio St. (1982)	505	50
Carbide & Carbon Bldg., 230 N. Michigan Ave. (1929)	503	37
One Superior Place, 1 W. Superior St. (1999)	502	52
120 N. LaSalle St. (1992)	501	39
10 S. LaSalle St. (1986)	501	37
The Tides, 360 E. South Water St. (2008)	500	51
200 S. Wacker Drive (1981)	500	41

(1) 1,729 ft incl. antenna. (2) 1,499 ft incl. antenna. (3) 912 ft incl. antenna.

Cleveland, OH

Building/structure	Ht. (ft)	Stories
Key Tower (incl. spire), 127 Public Sq. (1991)	947	57
Terminal Tower, 50 Public Sq. (1928)[1]	708	52
200 Public Sq. (1985)	658	46
Tower at Erieview, 1301 E. 9th St. (1964)	529	40

(1) 771 ft incl. flagpole.

Columbus, OH

Building/structure	Ht. (ft)	Stories
James A. Rhodes State Office Tower, 30 E. Broad St. (1973)	624	41
Leveque-Lincoln Tower, 50 W. Broad St. (1927)	555	47
William Green Building, 30 W. Spring St. (1990)	530	33
Huntington Center, 41 S. High St. (1983)	512	37
Vern Riffe State Office Tower, 77 S. High St. (1988)	503	33

Dallas, TX

Building/structure	Ht. (ft)	Stories
Bank of America Plaza, 901 Main St. (1985)	921	72
Renaissance Tower (incl. spire), 1201 Elm St. (1974)	886	56
Comerica Bank Tower, 1717 Main St. (1987)	787	60
JPMorgan Chase Tower, 2200 Ross Ave. (1987)	738	55
Fountain Place, 1445 Ross Ave. (1986)	720	58
Trammel Crow Center, 2001 Ross Ave. (1984)	686	50
1700 Pacific Ave. (1983)	655	50
Thanksgiving Tower, 1600 Pacific Ave. (1982)	645	50
Energy Plaza, 1601 Bryan St. (1983)	629	49
Elm Place, 1401 Elm St. (1965)	628	52
Gables Republic Tower (incl. spire), 300 N. Ervay (1954)	602	36
Republic Center Tower II, 325 N. St. Paul (1964)	598	50
One AT&T Plaza, 208 S. Akard St. (1984)	580	37
Ross Tower, 500 N. Akard St. (1984)	579	45
Museum Tower, 2112 Flora St. (2013)	560	42
Cityplace Center East, 2711 N. Haskell Ave. (1989)	560	42
Reunion Tower, 300 Reunion Blvd. (1976)	560	NA
Sheraton Dallas Hotel Center Tower, 400 Olive St. (1959)	550	42
Mercantile Bldg. (incl. spire), 1700 Main St. (1943)	523	31
Bryan Tower, 2001 Bryan St. (1973)	512	40

Denver, CO

Building/structure	Ht. (ft)	Stories
Republic Plaza, 330 17th St. (1984)	714	56
1801 California St. (1982)	709	52
Wells Fargo Center, 1700 Lincoln Ave. (1983)	698	50
Four Seasons Hotel and Private Residences, 1111 14th St. (2010)	639	45
*1144 Fifteenth (2018)	617	40
1999 Broadway (1985)	544	43
707 17th St. (1981)	522	42
555 17th St. (1978)	507	40

Detroit, MI

Building/structure	Ht. (ft)	Stories
Marriott Hotel, Renaissance Center I (1977)[1]	727	70
One Detroit Center, 500 Woodward Ave. (1991)	619	43
Penobscot Building, 633 Griswold Ave. (1928)[2]	565	47
Renaissance Center 100 Tower (1976)	508	39
Renaissance Center 200 Tower (1976)	508	39
Renaissance Center 300 Tower (1976)	508	39
Renaissance Center 400 Tower (1976)	508	39

(1) 755 ft incl. antenna. (2) 665 ft incl. antenna.

Fort Worth, TX

Building/structure	Ht. (ft)	Stories
Burnett Plaza, 801 Cherry St. (1983)	567	40
D.R. Horton Tower, 301 Commerce St. (1984)	547	38
Carter Burgess Plaza, 777 Main St. (1982)	525	40

Hartford, CT

Building/structure	Ht. (ft)	Stories
City Place I, 185 Asylum St. (1980)	535	38
Travelers Tower, 26 Grove St. (1919)	527	24
Goodwin Square, 225 Asylum St. (1990)	522	30

Houston, TX

Building/structure	Ht. (ft)	Stories
JPMorganChase Tower, 600 Travis St. (1982)	1,002	75
Wells Fargo Plaza, 1000 Louisiana St. (1983)	992	71
Williams Tower, 2800 Post Oak Blvd. (1982)	901	64
Bank of America Center, 700 Louisiana St. (1983)	780	56
Texaco Heritage Plaza, 1111 Bagby St. (1987)	762	53
*609 Main at Texas (2017)	757	49
Enterprise Plaza, 1100 Louisiana St. (1980)[1]	756	55
Centerpoint Energy Plaza, 1111 Louisiana St. (1996)	741	53
1600 Smith St. (1984)	732	55
Fulbright Tower, 1301 McKinney St. (1982)	725	52
One Shell Plaza, 900 Louisiana St. (1970)[2]	714	50
1400 Smith St. (1983)	691	50
3 Allen Center, 333 Clay St. (1980)	685	50
LyondellBassell Tower, 1221 McKinney St. (1978)	678	47
First City Tower, 1001 Fannin St. (1984)	662	47
BG Group Place, 811 Main St. (2011)	632	46
San Felipe Plaza, 5847 San Felipe Blvd. (1984)	625	45
ExxonMobil Building, 800 Bell Ave. (1962)	606	44
1500 Louisiana St. (2002)	600	40
America General Center, 2929 Allen Pkwy. (1983)	590	42
Two Houston Center, 909 Fannin St. (1974)	579	40
San Jacinto Monument, La Porte (1939)	570	NA
Marathon Oil Tower, 5555 San Felipe Blvd. (1983)	562	41
Wedge International Tower, 1415 Louisiana St. (1983)	550	44
KBR Tower, 601 Jefferson St. (1973)	550	40
Memorial Hermann Tower (incl. spires), 929 Gessner Rd. (2009)	542	35
2929 Weslayan (2015)	533	40
Pennzoil Place I, 700 Milam St. (1976)	523	36
Pennzoil Place II, 700 Louisiana St. (1976)	523	36
Devon Energy Center, 1200 Smith St. (1978)	521	36
RRI Energy Plaza, 1000 Main St. (2003)	518	36
Total Plaza, 1201 Louisiana St. (1971)	518	35
The Huntington, 2121 Kirby Dr. (1982)	503	34
*Market Square Tower, 777 Preston St. (2017)	502	40
El Paso Energy Building, 1010 Milam St. (1962)	502	33
One Park Place, 1500 McKinney St. (2009)	501	37

(1) 782 ft incl. antenna. (2) 999 ft incl. antenna.

Indianapolis, IN

Building/structure	Ht. (ft)	Stories
Chase Tower, 111 Monument Cir. (1990)[1]	701	49
One America Tower, 200 N. Illinois St. (1982)	533	38
One Indiana Square, 200 N. Delaware St. (1970)	504	36

(1) 811 ft incl. antenna.

Jersey City, NJ

Building/structure	Ht. (ft)	Stories
*99 Hudson St. (2019)	889	76
30 Hudson St. (2004)	781	42
*URL Harborside Tower 1 (2016)	700	71
*J3 (2016)	574	53
101 Hudson St. (1992)	548	42
Trump Plaza I, 88 Morgan St. (2008)	532	55
Newport Tower, 525 Washington Blvd. (1990)	531	37
*90 Columbus (2018)	529	50
70 Columbus (2015)	529	50
Exchange Place Center, 10 Exchange Pl. (incl. spire) (1990)	516	32

Building/structure	Ht. (ft)	Stories
Hudson Green East Tower, 77 Hudson St. (2009)	509	48
Hudson Green West Tower, 77 Hudson St. (2010)	501	48

Las Vegas, NV

Building/structure	Ht. (ft)	Stories
Stratosphere Tower, 2000 Las Vegas Blvd. S. (1996)	1,149	NA
*Fontainebleau Resort Hotel, 2755 Las Vegas Blvd. S. (NA)	735	63
*Resorts World Las Vegas Tower I (2019)	674	57
The Palazzo, 3339 Las Vegas Blvd. S. (2007)	642	53
Encore at Wynn Las Vegas, 3145 Las Vegas Blvd. S. (2008)	631	52
Trump International Hotel and Tower 1, 3128 Las Vegas Blvd. S. (2008)	622	64
Wynn Las Vegas, 3145 Las Vegas Blvd. S. (2005)	613	45
Cosmopolitan Casino Spa Tower, Las Vegas Blvd. and Harmon Ave. (2010)	603	52
Cosmopolitan Beach Resort Tower, Las Vegas Blvd. and Harmon Ave. (2010)	603	50
Aria Resort and Casino (2009)	600	60
Planet Hollywood Towers, 3667 Las Vegas Blvd. S. (2009)	597	50
VDARA, 2551 W. Harmon Ave. (2009)	556	55
Eiffel Tower, Paris Hotel and Casino, 3645 Las Vegas Blvd. S. (1998)	540	NA
Mandarin Oriental Hotel Las Vegas, 3750 Las Vegas Blvd. S. (2009)	539	47
New York, New York Hotel and Casino, 3790 Las Vegas Blvd. S. (1997)	529	48
Palms Place, 4321 W. Flamingo Rd. (2008)	518	50
Bellagio Hotel and Casino, 3600 Las Vegas Blvd. S. (1998)	508	36
Sky Las Vegas, 2780 Las Vegas Blvd. S. (2007)	500	45

Los Angeles, CA

Building/structure	Ht. (ft)	Stories
*Wilshire Grand Center (2017)	1,099	73
US Bank Tower, 633 W. 5th St. (1990)	1,018	73
Aon Center, 707 Wilshire Blvd. (1974)	858	62
Two California Plaza, 350 S. Grand Ave. (1992)	750	52
Gas Company Tower, 555 W. 5th St. (1991)	749	52
Bank of America Plaza, 333 S. Hope St. (1975)	735	55
777 Tower, 777 S. Figueroa St. (1991)	725	53
Wells Fargo Tower, 333 S. Grand Ave. (1983)	723	54
Figueroa at Wilshire, 601 S. Figueroa St. (1989)	717	52
City National Tower, 555 S. Flower St. (1971)	699	52
Paul Hastings Tower, 515 S. Flower St. (1971)	699	52
*Oceanside Plaza Tower I (2018)	677	49
Ritz Carlton/Marriott Marquis Los Angeles, 900 W. Olympic Blvd. (2010)	667	54
*Metropolis Tower D (2019)	647	58
*820 Olive Street (2019)	637	49
Citigroup Center, 444 S. Flower St. (1979)	625	48
611 Place, 611 W. 6th St. (1967)	620	42
KPMG Tower, 355 S. Grand Ave. (1984)	606	45
One California Plaza, 300 S. Grand Ave. (1985)	578	42
Century Plaza Tower 1, 2029 Century Park East (1973)	571	44
Century Plaza Tower 2, 2049 Century Park East (1973)	571	44
Ernst & Young, LLP Plaza, 725 S. Figueroa St. (1986)	534	41
AIG-SunAmerica Ctr., 1999 Ave. of the Stars (1989)	533	39
*Oceanwide Plaza Tower II (2018)	530	40
*Oceanwide Plaza Tower III (2018)	530	40
TCW Tower, 865 S. Figueroa St. (1990)	517	37
Union Bank Plaza, 445 S. Figueroa St. (1968)	516	40
10 Universal City Plaza (1984)	506	36

Mexico City, Mexico

Building/structure	Ht. (ft)	Stories
Torre Reforma, Paseo de la Reforma 483 (2016)	804	57
*Chapultepec Uno, Reforma 509 (2018)	791	59
Torre BBVA Bancomer, Paseo de la Reforma 506 (2015)	771	50
*Torre Paradox, Av. Santa Fe 562 (2017)	768	62
Torre Mayor, Paseo de la Reforma 505 (2003)	738	55
Torre Ejecutiva Pemex, Marina Nacional 329 Col. Huasteca (1984)	693	51
Torre Altus, Paseo de los Laureles 416 (1999)	640	44
Torre Reforma Latino, Paseo de la Reforma 296 (2016)	607	46
Torre Latino Americana (incl. spire), Eje Central Lazaro Cardenas 2 (1956)	597	45
*Torre Cuarzo, Paseo de la Reforma 26 (2017)	591	40
*Miyana Tower 1 (2017)	577	43
World Trade Center, Montecito 38 Col. Napoles (1972)	565	50
Siroco Elite Residences, Av. Santa Fe 482 (2015)	561	43
Peninsula Tower, Av. Santa Fe 1240 (2014)	539	50
Torre Punta Reforma, Paseo de la Reforma 180 (2015)	537	37
Arcos Torre II, Paseo de los Tamarindos 400 (2008)	529	35
Arcos Torre I, Paseo de los Tamarindos 400 (1997)	529	35
Torre Diana, Rio Lerma 232 (2016)	519	33

Miami, FL

Building/structure	Ht. (ft)	Stories
*Panorama Tower, 1101 Brickell Ave. (2017)	822	80
Four Seasons Hotel & Tower, 1441 Brickell Ave. (2003)	789	64
Wachovia Financial Ctr., 200 S. Biscayne Blvd. (1983)	764	55
*Brickell Flatiron, 1001 S. Miami Ave. (2018)	734	64
*One Thousand Museum, 1000 Biscayne Blvd. (2018)	706	60
*Paramount Miami Worldcenter (2018)	699	55
Marquis, 1100 Biscayne Blvd. (2009)	679	63
Met 2 Office Tower, 200 SE 3rd St. (2010)	655	47
900 Biscayne Bay, 900 Biscayne Blvd. (2008)	650	63
*Echo Brickell, 1451 Brickell Ave. (2017)	637	60
*Brickell CityCentre Office Tower 3 (2018)	634	45
Mint at Riverfront, 90 SW 3rd St. (2009)	631	55
Infinity at Brickell, 60 W. 13th St. (2008)	630	52
Miami Tower, 100 SE 2nd St. (1987)	625	47
Marinablue, 888 Biscayne Blvd. (2007)	615	57
Plaza on Brickell Tower I, 901 Brickell Ave. (2007)	610	56
Epic Residences & Hotel, 300 Biscayne Blvd. Way (2009)	601	54
*One Paraiso, 620 NE 31st St. (2017)	601	53
*SLS Brickell, 1300 S. Miami Ave. (2016)	599	52
*SLS Lux Brickell, 801 S. Miami Ave. (2017)	595	57
Icon Brickell North Tower, 495 Brickell Ave. (2008)	586	58
Icon Brickell South Tower, 495 Brickell Ave. (2008)	586	58
Ten Museum Park, 1040 Biscayne Blvd. (2007)	585	50
*Solitair Brickell, 80 SW 8th St. (2017)	555	48
Paramount at Edgewater Square, 2066 N. Bayshore Dr. (2009)	555	47
50 Biscayne Blvd. (2007)	554	55
Quantum on the Bay South Tower, 1900 N. Bayshore Dr. (2008)	554	51
*Biscayne Beach, 701 NE 29th St. (2016)	550	51
*Brickell Heights North Tower, 850 S. Miami Ave. (2017)	549	52
*GranParaiso, 600 NE 31st St. (2017)	548	55
*ParaisoBay, 600 NE 31st St. (2017)	548	55
*1010 Brickell (2017)	548	50
Opera Tower, 1750 N. Bayshore Dr. (2007)	543	56
Viceroy, 495 Brickell Ave. (2009)	542	50
Vizcayne North Tower, 244 Biscayne Blvd. (2008)	538	49
Vizcayne South Tower, 244 Biscayne Blvd. (2008)	538	49
*Avant at Met Square, 340 SE 3rd St. (2017)	538	46
Quantum on the Bay North Tower, 1900 N. Bayshore Dr. (2008)	536	44
*Aria on the Bay, 1770 N. Bayshore Dr. (2017)	535	50
*Brickell Heights South Tower, 850 S. Miami Ave. (2017)	529	52
Jade at Brickell Bay, 1331 Brickell Bay Dr. (2004)	528	49
Plaza on Brickell Tower II, 901 Brickell Ave. (2007)	525	48
*North Squared, BrickellCityCentre (2018)	522	48
Santa Maria, 1643 Brickell Ave. (1997)	520	51
Rise, Brickell CityCentre (2016)	520	45
EAST, Miami, Brickell CityCentre, 89 SE 8th St. (2016)	516	41
The Ivy, 90-95 SW 3rd St. (2008)	512	45
Stephen P. Clark Center, 111 NW 1st St. (1985)	510	28
BrickellHouse, 1300 Brickell Bay Dr. (2014)	509	48
Reach, Brickell CityCentre (2016)	503	44
Met 2 Marriott Marquis, 200 SE 3rd St. (2010)	502	41
Wind, 330 S. Miami Ave. (2008)	501	41
*Paraiso Bayviews (2018)	500	44
1450 Brickell (2010)	500	34

Minneapolis, MN

Building/structure	Ht. (ft)	Stories
IDS Tower, 80 S. 8th St. (1973)[1]	792	55
Capella Tower, 225 S. 6th St. (1992)	776	56
Wells Fargo Center, 90 S. 7th St. (1988)	775	56
33 South Sixth St. (1983)	668	52
Campbell Mithun Tower, 222 S. 9th St. (1985)	582	42
US Bank Plaza I, 200 S. 6th St. (1981)	561	40
RBC Plaza, 60 S. 6th St. (1992)	539	40
Fifth Street Towers II, 150 S. 5th St. (1988)	504	36
(1) 910 ft incl. antenna.		

Monterrey, Mexico

Building/structure	Ht. (ft)	Stories
*Torre Koi, San Pedro Garza Garcia (2016)	906	67
*Metropolitan Center Torre III, San Pedro Garza Garcia (incl. spire) (2019)	755	56
Pabellon M (2015)	674	45
Torre Avalanz, San Pedro Garza Garcia (2000)	597	43
*Metropolitan Center Torre II, San Pedro Garza Garcia (2017)	594	52
Centro de Gobierno Plaza Civica (2010)	591	36
LIU East, San Pedro Garza Garcia (2013)	564	39
Torre Sofia, Av. Sofia 440, San Pedro Garza Garcia (2014)	520	40
Torre Helicon, San Pedro Garza Garcia (2012)	512	33

Montréal, QC, Canada

Building/structure	Ht. (ft)	Stories
1250 Boulevard Rene Levesque (incl. spire) (1992)	743	47
1000 Rue de la Gauchetiere (1992)	673	51
Tour de la Bourse, 800 Place Victoria (1964)	624	47
1 Place Villa Marie (1962)	616	43
La Tour CIBC, 1155 Rene Levesque Blvd. (1962)[1]	604	45
*L'Avenue (2017)	574	50
Montreal Tower (1987)	574	NA
*Tour Avenue des Canadiens (2016)	548	50
Tour McGill College, 1501 McGill College (1992)	519	38
(1) 740 ft incl. antenna.		

Building/structure	Ht. (ft)	Stories
New Orleans, LA		
One Shell Square, 701 Poydras St. (1972)	697	51
CapitalOne Center, 201 St. Charles Ave. (1985)...	645	53
Plaza Tower, 1001 Howard Ave. (1969)	531	45
Energy Centre, 1100 Poydras St. (1984)	530	39
New York, NY		
One World Trade Center (incl. spire) (2014) ...	1,776	94
*Central Park Tower, 217 West 57th St. (2019) ...	1,550	95
*111 W. 57th St. (2017)......................	1,438	80
432 Park Avenue (2015)......................	1,396	85
*30 Hudson Yards (2019)	1,268	73
Empire State Building, 350 5th Ave. (1931)[1]...	1,250	102
Bank of America (incl. spire), One Bryant Park (2009)	1,200	55
*Three World Trade Center, 175 Greenwich St. (2018)	1,079	69
*53 West 53rd St. (2018).....................	1,050	77
Chrysler Building (incl. spire), 405 Lexington Ave. (1930)...................................	1,046	77
New York Times Tower (incl. spire), 620 8th Ave. (2007)...................................	1,046	52
*3 Hudson Boulevard, 555 W. 34th St. (2019) ...	1,034	66
*35 Hudson Yards (2018)	1,009	72
One57, 157 W. 57th St. (2014)	1,005	75
*One Manhattan West, 401 9th Ave. (2019)	995	69
4 World Trade Center, 150 Greenwich St. (2014) ..	977	65
70 Pine (incl. spire) (1932)	952	67
*220 Central Park South (2017)	950	66
30 Park Place, 99 Church St. (2016)	937	67
The Trump Bldg., 40 Wall St. (1930)..........	927	71
Citigroup Center, 153 E. 53rd St. (1977).......	915	63
*15 Hudson Yards (2018)	914	70
10 Hudson Yards (2016).....................	878	50
New York by Gehry at Eight Spruce Street (2011)	870	76
Trump World Tower, 845 UN Plaza (2001)	861	72
Comcast Building, 30 Rockefeller Center (1933) ..	850	70
*One Manhattan Square, 250 South St. (2019) ...	847	72
*425 Park Avenue (2018)	847	42
56 Leonard Street (2016).....................	821	57
Cityspire Center, 150 W. 56th St. (1987)	814	75
28 Liberty (1961)	813	60
4 Times Square (1999)[2]	809	48
MetLife Building, 200 Park Ave. (1963)	808	59
Bloomberg Tower, 731 Lexington Ave. (2005)[3]..	806	54
*138 E. 50th St. (2019)......................	803	64
*111 Murray Street (2018)	792	58
Woolworth Building, 233 Broadway (1913)	792	57
*520 Park Avenue (2017)....................	781	52
*50 West, 50 West St. (2017).................	778	64
*45 East 22nd Street (2017)...................	778	63
*55 Hudson Yards (2017)	778	51
1 Worldwide Plaza, 935 8th Ave. (1989)	778	47
Carnegie Hall Tower, 152 W. 57th St. (1991).....	757	60
383 Madison Avenue (2001)	755	47
1717 Broadway (2013).......................	753	67
AXA Center, 787 7th Ave. (1985).............	752	51
One Penn Plaza, 250 W. 34th St. (1972)	750	57
1251 Avenue of the Americas (1971).........	750	54
Time Warner Center North Tower, 10 Columbus Cir. (2004)	749	55
Time Warner Center South Tower, 10 Columbus Cir. (2004)	749	55
Goldman Sachs HQ, 200 Murray St. (2010).....	749	44
60 Wall Street (1989).......................	745	55
One Astor Plaza, 1515 Broadway (1972).......	745	54
One Liberty Plaza, 165 Broadway (1972).......	743	54
7 World Trade Center (2006)	743	49
Twenty Exchange, 20 Exchange Pl. (1931)......	741	57
Three World Financial Center, 200 Vesey St. (1986)	739	51
*Roseland Tower, 242 W. 53rd St. (2018)	737	62
1540 Broadway (incl. spire) (1990)............	732	42
Times Square Tower, 1459 Broadway (2004)	726	47
Metropolitan Tower, 142 W. 57th St. (1985)......	716	68
*252 E. 57th Street (2017)...................	715	59
*100 E. 53rd Street (2017)..................	711	61
JPMorganChase World Headquarters, 270 Park Ave. (1960)	707	52
General Motors Building, 767 5th Ave. (1968)	705	50
*3 Manhattan West, 401 W. 31st St. (2017)	702	64
Metropolitan Life Tower, 1 Madison Ave. (1909) ..	700	50
500 5th Avenue (1931).......................	697	59
Americas Tower, 1177 Ave. of the Americas (1992)	692	48
Solow Building, 9 W. 57th St. (1974)	689	49
Marine Midland Building, 140 Broadway (1967)...	688	52
55 Water Street (1972).......................	687	53
277 Park Avenue (1963).....................	687	50
*The Beekman Hotel & Residences, 5 Beekman St. (2016)	687	47
1585 Broadway (1989).......................	685	42
Random House/Park Imperial, 1739 Broadway (2003)...................................	684	52
Four Seasons Hotel, 57 E. 57th St. (1993).......	682	52
Sky, 605 W. 42nd St. (2015)	676	61
McGraw-Hill Building, 1221 Ave. of the Americas (1972)...................................	674	51
Barclay Tower, 10 Barclay St. (2007)..........	673	56

Building/structure	Ht. (ft)	Stories
One Grand Central Place, 60 E. 42nd St. (1930)..	673	53
Citigroup Building, 1 Court Sq., Queens (1990)...	673	50
*One Seaport, 161 Maiden Ln. (2018)	670	60
Paramount Plaza, 1633 Broadway (1970)	670	48
Trump Tower, 725 5th Ave. (1982)............	664	58
Bank of New York Building, 1 Wall St. (1932)	654	50
Silver Towers East, 600 W. 42nd St. (2009)	653	58
Silver Towers West, 600 W. 42nd St. (2009)	653	58
599 Lexington Avenue (1986)	653	51
712 5th Avenue (1990)......................	650	53
Chanin Building, 122 E. 42nd St. (1929)	649	56
245 Park Avenue (1967).....................	648	47
550 Madison Avenue (1983)	647	37
*28 on 28th, 42-12 28th St., Queens (2017).....	646	58
Two World Financial Center, 225 Liberty St. (1986)	645	44
1095 Avenue of the Americas (1974)...........	645	43
570 Lexington Avenue (1931)	642	50
1 New York Plaza, 1 Water St. (1969)	640	50
1 MiMA Tower, 440 W. 42nd St. (2011)........	638	63
1 Dag Hammarskjold Plaza, 885 2nd Ave. (1972)	637	48
345 Park Avenue (1968).....................	634	44
Langham Place, 400 5th Ave. (2010)..........	632	58
Mercantile Bldg., 10 E. 40th St. (1929)........	632	48
W New York Downtown Hotel & Residences, 123 Washington St. (2010).................	631	57
Grace Plaza, 1114 Ave. of the Americas (1972) ..	630	50
Home Insurance Plaza, 59 Maiden Ln. (1966)....	630	44
101 Park Avenue (1982).....................	629	49
Central Park Place, 301 W. 57th St. (1988)	628	56
888 7th Avenue (1971)......................	628	45
Burlington House, 1345 Ave. of the Americas (1969)	625	50
Waldorf Astoria New York, 301 Park Ave. (1931)	625	47
Avalon Willoughby West, 100 Willoughby St., Brooklyn (2015)	624	57
Trump Palace, 200 E. 69th St. (1991)	623	54
One Madison Park, 20 E. 23rd St. (2010)	621	51
Olympic Tower, 645 5th Ave. (1976)	620	51
425 Fifth Avenue (2003).....................	618	55
The Epic, 125 W. 31st St. (2007)	615	58
919 3rd Avenue (1970)......................	615	47
Tower 49, 12 E. 49th St. (1985)..............	615	44
750 7th Avenue (incl. spire) (1989)	615	35
New York Life, 51 Madison Ave. (1928)........	615	33
Eventi, 851 6th Ave. (2010)	614	46
551 10th Avenue (2016).....................	612	52
Credit Lyonnais Building, 1301 Ave. of the Americas (1964).........................	609	46
*The Hub, 333 Schermerhorn St., Brooklyn (2016)	607	53
Baccarat Hotel & Residences, 20 W. 53rd St. (2014)...................................	605	47
The Orion, 350 W. 42nd St. (2006)	604	58
590 Madison Avenue (1983)	603	41
250 W. 55th Street (2013)	602	40
Eleven Times Square, 644 8th Ave. (2011)	601	40
1166 Avenue of the Americas (1974)...........	600	44
*43-22 Queens St., Queens (2018)	598	54
Hawthorn Park, 160 W. 62nd St. (2014)........	598	54
Hearst Magazine Tower, 959 8th Ave. (2006) ...	597	46
3 Lincoln Center, 160 W. 66th St. (1993)........	595	60
Celanese Building, 1211 Ave. of the Americas (1973)...................................	592	45
The London NYC, 151 W. 54th St. (1990)	590	54
*28-34 Jackson Ave., Queens (2018)...........	590	53
388 Bridge Street, Brooklyn (2014)	590	51
Thurgood Marshall U.S. Courthouse, 505 Pearl St. (1936)...................................	590	37
Museum Tower Apts., 21 W. 53rd St. (1985).....	589	52
The Millenium Hilton Hotel, 55 Church St. (1992)	588	58
Sky House, 11 E. 29th St. (2008).............	588	55
Time-Life Building, 1271 Ave. of the Americas (1959)...................................	587	48
Jacob K. Javits Federal Bldg., 26 Federal Plz. (1967)	587	41
W Times Square, 1567 Broadway (2000)	584	53
Trump International Hotel & Tower, 15 Columbus Cir. (1970).................	583	44
Stevens Tower, 1185 Ave. of the Americas (1971)	580	42
Municipal Building, 1 Centre St. (1914)	580	34
520 Madison Avenue (1981)	577	43
One World Financial Center, 200 Liberty St. (1985)	577	37
Merchandise Mart, 41 Madison Ave. (1973)......	576	42
Park Avenue Plaza, 55 E. 52nd St. (1981)......	575	44
300 Madison Avenue (2003)	575	38
Lehman Building, 745 7th Ave. (2001).........	575	38
One Financial Square, 33 Old Slip (1987)	575	37
Marriott Marquis Times Square, 1531 Broadway (1985)...................................	574	50
*118 Fulton Street (2018)	574	49
299 Park Avenue (1967).....................	574	42
5 Times Square, 590 7th Ave. (2002)..........	574	40
Socony Mobil Building, 150 E. 42nd St. (1956) ...	572	42
1290 Avenue of the Americas (1963)...........	571	43
780 3rd Avenue (1983)......................	570	49
600 3rd Avenue (1971)......................	570	42
*590 Fulton St., Brooklyn (2016)..............	568	51
450 Lexington Avenue (1991)	568	38

Building/structure	Ht. (ft)	Stories
Paramount Tower, 240 E. 39th St. (1998)	567	51
230 Park Avenue (1928)	565	35
New York Palace Hotel, 455 Madison Ave. (1980)	563	51
Continental Bank Building, 30 Broad St. (1932)	562	48
Park Avenue Tower, 65 E. 55th St. (1986)	561	36
Nelson Tower, 450 7th Ave. (1931)	560	46
Sherry-Netherland, 781 5th Ave. (1927)	560	40
623 5th Avenue (1990)	560	36
South Park Tower, 124 W. 60th St. (1986)	558	51
100 UN Plaza, 327 E. 48th St. (1986)	557	52
Continental Can, 633 3rd Ave. (1962)	557	39
*222 E. 44th Street (2018)	556	42
3 Park Avenue (1975)	556	42
Continental Center, 180 Maiden Ln. (1983)	555	41
Sperry & Hutchinson Bldg., 330 Madison Ave. (1964)	555	41
Equitable Building, 120 Broadway (1915)	555	38
Reuters Building, 3 Times Sq. (2001)[4]	555	30
Tower 111, 885 6th Ave. (2011)	554	48
The Belvedere, 10 E. 29th St. (1999)	554	48
Inmont Bldg., 1133 Ave. of the Americas (1970)	552	45
Downtown by Philippe Starck, 15 Broad St. (1927)	551	42
Hyatt Times Square, 135 W. 45th St. (2013)	550	53
Biltmore Tower, 267 W. 47th St. (2003)	550	51
Unisys Building, 605 3rd Ave. (1963)	550	44
2 Grand Central Tower, 140 E. 45th St. (1982)	550	43
The Tower at 15 Central Park West (2008)	550	35
AT&T Long Lines Building, 33 Thomas St. (1974)	550	29
50 UN Plaza, 345 E. 46th St. (2015)	548	44
Bankers Trust, 33 E. 48th St. (1971)	547	41
The Corinthian, 330 E. 38th St. (1988)	546	55
Transportation Building, 225 Broadway (1928)	546	44
MillenniumTower, 101 W. 67th St. (1995)	545	54
The Galleria, 117 E. 57th St. (1975)	544	56
2 Gold Street (2005)	543	51
220 Riverside Blvd. at Trump Place (2003)	542	49
17 State Street (1988)	542	41
Grand Central Plaza, 622 3rd Ave. (1973)	542	38
*American Copper Buildings West Tower, 626 1st Ave. (2017)	540	46
New York Telephone, 375 Pearl St. (1976)	540	42
1285 Avenue of the Americas (1960)	540	42
Ritz Tower, 109 E. 57th St. (1925)	540	41
14 Wall (1912)	540	29
Tribeca Tower, 105 Duane St. (1990)	537	53
Lefcourt Colonial Building, 295 Madison Ave. (1929)	537	45
The Encore, 175 W. 60th St. (2016)	533	48
1700 Broadway (1969)	533	41
Westin Hotel New York, 43rd St. and 8th Ave. (2002)	532	45
515 Park Avenue (1999)	532	43
DuMont Building, 515 Madison Ave. (1931)	532	42
The Brooklyner, 111 Lawrence St., Brooklyn (2010)	531	52
One East River Place, 525 E. 72nd St. (1989)	530	49
*21 West End Avenue (2016)	529	45
The Metropolis, 150 E. 44th St. (2001)	528	50
William Beaver House, 15 William St. (2010)	528	47
North American Plywood, 800 3rd Ave. (1972)	526	41
City Point Tower II, 336 Flatbush Ave. Ext., Brooklyn (2016)	525	46
Hotel Pierre, 2 E. 61st St. (1928)	525	44
767 3rd Avenue (1980)	525	39

(1) 1,455 ft incl. antenna. (2) 1,118 ft incl. antenna. (3) 941 ft incl. antenna. (4) 659 ft incl. antenna.

Philadelphia, PA

Building/structure	Ht. (ft)	Stories
*Comcast Innovation and Technology Center, 1800 Arch St. (2018)	1,121	59
Comcast Center, 1701 JFK Blvd. (2008)	974	57
One Liberty Place (incl. spire), 1650 Market St. (1987)	945	61
Two Liberty Place (incl. spire), 1601 Chestnut St. (1989)	848	58
Mellon Bank Center, 1735 Market St. (1990)	792	54
Three Logan, 1717 Arch St. (1991)	739	55
*FMC Tower at Cira Centre South (2017)	730	49
G. Fred DiBona Jr. Building, 1901 Market St. (1990)	625	45
*The W Philadelphia and Element, 1441 Chestnut St. (2018)	617	51
Commerce Square #2, 2001 Market St. (1992)	572	40
Commerce Square #1, 2005 Market St. (1990)	572	40
City Hall (incl. statue) (1901)	548	7
Residences at Ritz-Carlton, 1416 S. Penn Sq. (2009)	518	46
1818 Market St. (1974)	500	40

Pittsburgh, PA

Building/structure	Ht. (ft)	Stories
US Steel Tower, 600 Grant St. (1970)	841	64
One Mellon Bank Center, 500 Grant St. (1983)	725	54
One PPG Place (1984)	635	40
Fifth Avenue Place, 120 5th Ave. (1987)	616	32
One Oxford Centre, 301 Grant St. (1982)	615	46
Gulf Tower, 707 Grant St. (1932)	582	44
The Tower at PNC Plaza (2015)	545	33
University of Pittsburgh Cathedral of Learning, 4200 5th Ave. (1936)	535	42
3 Mellon Bank Center, 525 Wm. Penn Way (1951)	520	41
K&L Gates Center, 210 6th Ave. (1968)	511	39

Portland, OR

Building/structure	Ht. (ft)	Stories
Wells Fargo Center, 1300 SW 5th Ave. (1973)	546	40
U.S. Bancorp Tower, 111 SW 5th Ave. (1983)	536	42
Park Avenue West, 728 SW 9th Ave. (2016)	515	33
Koin Center, 222 SW Columbia St. (1984)	509	31

St. Louis, MO

Building/structure	Ht. (ft)	Stories
Gateway Arch (1965)	630	NA
Metropolitan Square Tower, 211 N. Broadway (1988)	593	42
AT&T Center, 900 Pine St. (1984)	588	44
Thomas F. Eagleton Federal Courthouse, 111 S. 10th St. (2000)	557	29

San Francisco, CA

Building/structure	Ht. (ft)	Stories
*Salesforce Tower, 415 Mission St. (2018)	1,070	61
Sutro Tower (1972)	977	NA
Transamerica Pyramid, 600 Montgomery St. (1972)	853	48
*181 Fremont (2017)	802	54
555 California St. (1969)	779	52
345 California Center (1986)	695	48
Millennium Tower, 301 Mission St. (2009)	645	58
One Rincon Hill South Tower, 425 First St. (2008)	605	54
*Park Tower at Transbay (2018)	605	43
101 California Street (1982)	600	48
50 Fremont Center (1985)	600	43
Chevron Tower, 575 Market St. (1975)	573	40
Four Embarcadero Center, 55 Clay St. (1984)	570	45
One Embarcadero Center, 355 Clay St. (1970)	569	45
44 Montgomery Street (1967)	565	43
Spear Tower, 1 Market St. (1976)	565	42
One Sansome Street (1984)	550	43
One Rincon Hill North Tower, 425 First St. (2014)	541	45
Shaklee Terrace Building, 444 Market St. (1982)	537	38
First Market Tower, 525 Market St. (1972)	529	38
McKesson Plaza, 1 Post St. (1969)	529	38
425 Market Street (1973)	524	38
Telsis Tower, 1 Montgomery St. (1982)	500	38

Seattle, WA

Building/structure	Ht. (ft)	Stories
Columbia Center, 701 5th Ave. (1985)	933	76
1201 Third Avenue Tower, 1201 3rd Ave. (1988)	772	55
Two Union Square, 601 Union St. (1989)	740	56
Seattle Municipal Tower, 700 5th Ave. (1990)	722	57
*The Mark, 811 5th Ave. (2017)	660	43
Safeco Plaza, 1001 4th Ave. (1969)	630	50
City Centre, 1420 5th Ave. (1989)	606	44
Space Needle, 203 6th Ave. (1962)	605	NA
Russell Investments Center, 1301 2nd Ave. (2006)	598	42
Wells Fargo Center, 999 3rd Ave. (1983)	574	47
*Madison Centre, 505 Madison St. (2017)	560	36
Bank of America Fifth Ave. Plz., 800 5th Ave. (1981)	543	42
901 5th Avenue (1973)	536	41
Amazon Tower I, 2021 7th Ave. (2016)	524	37
*Amazon Tower II, 2021 7th Ave. (2017)	521	37
*808 Howell (2018)	520	45
*Amazon Tower III, 2021 7th Ave. (2017)	520	37
Rainier Tower, 1301 5th Ave. (1977)	514	31
Fourth & Madison Building, 915 4th Ave. (2003)	512	40
1918 8th Avenue (2009)	500	36

Sunny Isles Beach, FL

Building/structure	Ht. (ft)	Stories
*Armani Residences, 18975 Collins Ave. (2018)	649	60
*Muse, 17141 Collins Ave. (2017)	649	47
Mansions at Acqualina, 17749 Collins Ave. (2015)	643	46
*Porsche Design Tower, 18555 Collins Ave. (2016)	641	57
*Jade Signature, 16901 Collins Ave. (2017)	636	55
Jade on the Beach Condominiums, 17001 Collins Ave. (2008)	574	51
Trump Royale, 18201 Collins Ave. (2008)	551	43
Trump Palace, 18101 Collins Ave. (2005)	551	43
Acqualina Ocean Residences, 17875 Collins Ave. (2004)	550	51
Jade Ocean, 17121 Collins Ave. (2009)	543	51

Tampa, FL

Building/structure	Ht. (ft)	Stories
Regions Building, 100 N. Tampa St. (1992)	579	42
Bank of America Plaza, 101 E. Kennedy Blvd. (1986)	577	42
One Tampa City Center, 201 N. Franklin St. (1981)	537	39
SunTrust Financial Center, 401 E. Jackson St. (1992)	525	36

Toronto, ON, Canada

Building/structure	Ht. (ft)	Stories
CN Tower, 310 Front St. West (1976)	1,815	NA
First Canadian Place, 100 King St. West (1975)[1]	978	72
Trump International Hotel & Tower (incl. spire), 325 Bay St. (2012)	908	63
Scotia Tower, 40 King St. West (1989)	902	68
Aura at College Park, 388 Yonge St. (2014)	892	78
Brookfield Place (incl. spire), 161 Bay St. (1990)	856	53
*Number One Bloor, 1 Bloor St. East (2016)	844	75
Commerce Court West, 199 Bay St. (1973)[2]	784	57
Ice Condos at York Centre 2, 16 York St. (2015)	768	67
*Harbour Plaza Residences East, 90 Harbour St. (2017)	764	66
*Eau de Soleil Sky Tower, 2183 Lake Shore Blvd. West, Etobicoke (2018)	749	66

Building/structure	Ht. (ft)	Stories
*Ten York (2017)	735	65
*Harbour Plaza Residences West, 90 Harbour St. (2017)	735	62
TD Centre-Toronto Dominion Bank Tower, 66 Wellington St. West (1967)	730	56
Bay-Adelaide Center West Tower, 335 Bay St. (2010)	704	52
Living Shangri-La Toronto, 180 University Ave. (2012)	702	65
Ritz-Carlton Hotel and Residences, 185 Wellington St. West (2011)	687	54
*Massey Tower, 199 Yonge St. (2018)	683	60
*The Residences of 488 University Avenue (2018)	679	55
BCE Place, Bay-Wellington Tower, 181 Bay St. (1991)	679	49
L Tower, 1 Front St. (2014)	673	58
*88 Scott Street (2017)	669	58
Four Seasons Private Residences West, 48 Yorkville Ave. (2012)	669	55
Ice Condos at York Centre 1, 16 York St. (2014)	663	57
*YC Condos, 460 Yonge St. (2019)	651	60
Bay-Adelaide Center East Tower, 40 Adelaide St. (2016)	643	44
*E Condos South, 8 Eglinton Ave. (2017)	642	58
*Wellesley on the Park, 11 Wellesley St. West (2017)	637	60
*22l21 Yonge (2019)	632	58
*EY Tower, 100 Adelaide St. West (2017)	617	40
RBC Centre, 155 Wellington St. West (2009)	607	42
*CASA II, 42 Charles St. East (2016)	605	57
U Condominiums East Tower, 50 St. Joseph St. (2016)	604	55
*One Yorkville (2019)	601	58
TD North Tower, 77 King St. West (1969)	600	46
*Lighthouse Tower Condominium, 132 Queens Quay East (2019)	598	48
Maple Leaf Square North Tower, 65 Bremmer Blvd. (2010)	595	54
*Eau de Soleil Water Tower, 2183 Lake Shore Blvd. West, Etobicoke (2018)	593	49
*CASA III, 50 Charles St. East (2017)	589	55
*INDX Condominiums, 70 Temperance St. (2016)	587	54
1 King West (2005)	578	51
*Teahouse Condominiums South, 501 Yonge St. (2019)	571	52
Success Tower 2, 33 Bay St. (2010)	569	55
One York Street (2016)	569	35
Royal Bank Plaza-South Tower, 200 Bay St. (1976)	567	41
Maple Leaf Square South Tower, 55 Bremmer Blvd. (2010)	562	50
*The Selby Condominiums, 592 Shelbourne St. (2019)	560	49
Hullmark Centre I, 4789 Yonge St. (2015)	557	45
*Lago at the Waterfront, 2151 Lake Shore Blvd. West, Etobicoke (2016)	550	49
44 Charles Street West (1974)	545	51
*Karma, 9 Grenville St. (2016)	544	50
Quantum 2, 2195 Yonge St. (2008)	541	51
Theatre Park, 224 King St. West (2015)	541	47
Residences @ College Park I, 763 Bay St. (2006)	535	51
Burano, 832 Bay St. (2012)	535	50
Success Tower 1, 18 Harbour St. (2011)	531	52
X2, 580 Jarvis St. (2015)	529	44
*FIVE, 606 Yonge St. (2016)	528	48
Three Hundred, 300 Front St. West (2014)	518	52
The Uptown, 35 Balmuto St. (2011)	518	48
Southcore Financial Centre Delta Hotel, 75 Lower Simcoe St. (2014)	515	47
Festival Tower, 330 King St. West (2011)	514	42
*King Blue by Greenland North Tower, 355 King St. (2018)	511	48
*87 Peter (2017)	505	49
U Condominiums West Tower, 50 St. Joseph St. (2015)	505	45
*Yonge + Rich, 25 Richmond St. East (2019)	504	45
TD South Tower, 79 Wellington St. West (1985)	504	39
35 Mariner (2005)	503	49
Westlake Village 1 (2017)	503	48
Montage, 20 Fort York Blvd. (2009)	502	48

(1) 1,116 ft incl. antenna. (2) 942 ft incl. antenna.

Tulsa, OK

Building/structure	Ht. (ft)	Stories
BOK Tower, 1 E. 2nd St. (1975)	667	52

Building/structure	Ht. (ft)	Stories
Cityplex Central Tower, 2448 E. 81st St. (1979)	648	60
First Place Tower, 15 E. 5th St. (1973)	516	40
Mid-Continent Tower, 401 S. Boston St. (1984)	513	36

Vancouver, BC, Canada

Building/structure	Ht. (ft)	Stories
Shangri-La Vancouver, 1120 W. Georgia St. (2009)	659	59
Trump International Hotel & Tower, 1153 W. Georgia (2016)	616	58
*Telus Garden Residential Tower (2016)	550	53
Hotel Georgia, 667 Howe St. (2012)	520	50

Other Tall Buildings in North America

Building/structure	City	Ht. (ft)	Stories
Devon Energy Center (2012)	Oklahoma City, OK	844	52
*Stantec Tower (2018)	Edmonton, AB, Can.	823	70
RSA Battle House Tower (incl. spire) (2007)	Mobile, AL.	745	35
Revel Hotel (2012)	Atlantic City, NJ	718	53
Hotel Riu Plaza Guadalajara (2011)	Guadalajara, Mex.	705	44
Great American Tower at Queen City Square (2011)	Cincinnati, OH	665	40
The Tower at First National Center (2002)	Omaha, NE.	634	45
801 Grand (1991)	Des Moines, IA	630	44
*Delta Hotel and Residences (2018)	Edmonton, AB, Can.	627	56
One Kansas City Place (incl. spire) (1988)	Kansas City, MO	623	42
Tower of the Americas (1968)	San Antonio, TX	622	NA
Bank of America Tower (1990)	Jacksonville, FL	617	42
AT&T Building (1994)	Nashville TN	617	33
Hyatt Regency Andares (2016)	Zapopan, Mex.	607	41
U.S. Bank Center (1973)	Milwaukee, WI.	601	42
Town Pavilion (1986)	Kansas City, MO	591	38
Erastus Corning II Twr. (1973)	Albany, NY	589	44
Niagara Falls Hilton Phase 2 (2009)	Niagara Falls, ON, Can.	581	58
Absolute World 56 (2012)	Mississauga, ON, Can.	576	56
Carew Tower (1931)[1]	Cincinnati, OH	574	49
*Torre NVBOLA (2017)	Puebla, Mex.	574	43
Concourse Corporate Ctr. V (incl. spire) (1988)	Sandy Springs, GA	570	34
*Northwestern Mutual Tower (2017)	Milwaukee, WI.	550	33
Torre Aura Altitude (2008)	Zapopan, Mex.	563	44
Blue Diamond Tower (2000)	Miami Beach, FL.	559	44
Green Diamond Tower (2000)	Miami Beach, FL.	559	44
Washington Monument (1884)	Washington, DC	555	NA
Concourse Corporate Ctr. VI (incl. spire) (1991)	Sandy Springs, GA	553	34
*Northwestern Mutual Tower (2017)	Milwaukee, WI.	550	33
400 West Market (1992)	Louisville, KY	549	35
Metropolitan Tower (1986)	Little Rock, AR	546	40
Marriott Rivercenter (incl. spires) (1988)	San Antonio, TX	546	38
RBC Plaza (incl. spire) (2008)	Raleigh, NC	538	32
Modis Tower (1975)	Jacksonville, FL	535	37
Transamerica Tower (1973)	Baltimore, MD.	529	40
One Seneca Tower (1970)	Buffalo NY.	529	38
Vehicle Assembly Bldg. (1965)	Cape Canaveral, FL	526	40
Harrah's Waterfront Tower (2008)	Atlantic City, NJ	525	44
*505 CST (2018)	Nashville, TN	524	45
Skylon (1965)	Niagara Falls, ON, Can.	520	NA
Absolute World 50 (2012)	Mississauga, ON, Can.	518	50
*3 Civic Plaza (2017)	Surrey, BC, Can.	516	50
Bank of America (1924)	Baltimore, MD.	509	37
The Westin Virginia Beach Town Center and Residences (2007)	Virginia Beach, VA	508	38
The Beach Club Tower 2 (2006)	Hallandale Beach, FL	505	50
Chase Tower (1971)	Oklahoma City, OK	500	36
One American Plaza (1991)	San Diego, CA	500	34

(1) 623 ft incl. antenna.

Selected Bridge Styles

Bridges support weight through tension (pulling), compression (pushing), or a combination of both. **Suspension** and **cable-stayed** bridges are characterized by cables under tension. While the deck of a suspension bridge hangs from suspenders, that of a cable-stayed bridge ties directly to a bridge tower. The elements of a **truss** form triangles, which distribute the forces of tension and compression. Truss bridges can thus carry more weight than beam bridges. Steel plates can be welded or bolted together to make a **plate girder**, a kind of beam. A common form is the **box girder**.

A bridge can have a **simple** configuration, whereby its load is supported at both ends. If a bridge is **continuous**, its load extends across multiple supports. In a **cantilever** configuration, structural elements (e.g., trusses or girders) supported at one end project out, or cantilever, to carry a span.

Notable North American Bridges

Source: World Almanac research; Office of Bridge Technology, Federal Highway Administration, U.S. Dept. of Transportation Asterisk (*) designates a bridge that carries railroads only. All other bridges carry roads or roads and rail unless otherwise noted. Year is date of completion or projected completion. Span of bridge is the distance between its main supports. As of mid-2016.

Suspension

Year	Bridge	Location	Main span (ft)
1964	Verrazano-Narrows	New York, NY	4,260
1937	Golden Gate	San Francisco Bay, CA	4,200
1957	Mackinac	Straits of Mackinac, MI	3,800
1931	George Washington	New York, NY-Fort Lee, NJ	3,500
1950/ 2007	Tacoma Narrows (twin)	Tacoma, WA	2,800
2003	Al Zampa Mem. (New Carquinez) (westbound)	Carquinez Strait, CA	2,388
1936	San Francisco-Oakland Bay (West Span)[1]	San Francisco-Yerba Buena Isl., CA	2,310
1939	Bronx-Whitestone	East R., New York, NY	2,300
1970	Pierre Laporte	Quebec City, QC, Can.	2,190
1951/ 68	Delaware Mem. (twin)	Pennsville, NJ-New Castle, DE	2,150
1957	Walt Whitman	Philadelphia, PA	2,000
1929	Ambassador	Detroit, MI-Windsor, ON, Can.	1,850
1961	Throgs Neck	New York, NY	1,801
1926	Benjamin Franklin	Phila., PA-Camden, NJ	1,750
1924	Bear Mountain	Hudson R., Peekskill, NY	1,632
1969	Claiborne Pell/Newport	Narragansett Bay, RI	1,600
1952/ 73	William Preston Lane Jr. Memorial (twin)	Sandy Point, MD.	1,600
1903	Williamsburg	East R., New York, NY	1,600
1883	Brooklyn	East R., New York, NY	1,596
1938	Lions Gate	Vancouver, BC, Can.	1,549
1963	Vincent Thomas	L.A. Harbor, CA	1,500
1930	Mid-Hudson	Poughkeepsie, NY	1,495
1909	Manhattan	East R., New York, NY	1,470
1955	Angus L. Macdonald	Halifax, NS, Can.	1,447
1970	A. Murray MacKay	Halifax, NS, Can.	1,400
1936	Triborough (Harlem R. Lift/Bronx Crossing/ East R. Suspension)	East R., New York, NY	1,380
2013	San Francisco-Oakland Bay (SAS)[2]	San Francisco Bay, CA.	1,263

Cantilever

Year	Bridge	Location	Main span (ft)
1917	Quebec	Quebec City, QC, Can.	1,800
1974	Commodore Barry	Chester, PA-Bridgeport, NJ	1,644
1958/ 88	Crescent City Connection (twin)	Mississippi R., New Orleans, LA	1,575
1995	Veterans Memorial	Gramercy, LA	1,460
1968	Baton Rouge	Mississippi R., LA	1,235
1955	Tappan Zee (I-287)	Hudson R., Tarrytown, NY	1,212
1930	Lewis and Clark	Longview, WA-Rainier, OR	1,200
1909	Queensboro	East R., New York, NY	1,182
1958	Carquinez (eastbound)	San Francisco Bay, CA.	1,100
1930	Jacques Cartier	Montreal, QC, Can.	1,097
1968	Isaiah D. Hart	Jacksonville, FL	1,088
1956	Richmond-San Rafael (twin)	San Francisco Bay, CA.	1,070
1963/ 80	Newburgh-Beacon (twin)	Hudson R., NY	1,000

Truss

Year	Bridge	Location	Main span (ft)
1966	Astoria-Megler (U.S. 101)	Columbia R., OR-WA	1,232
1976	Francis Scott Key	Baltimore, MD	1,200
1981	Ravenswood	Ohio R., Ravenswood, WV	902
1995	Taylor-Southgate, Ohio R.	Cincinnati, OH-Newport, KY	850
1943	Julien Dubuque (U.S. 20)	Mississippi R., IA-IL	845
1966	Charles Braga	Fall River, MA	840
1956	Shawneetown (KY 56) (twin)	Ohio R., IL-KY.	825
1953	John E. Mathews	Jacksonville, FL	810
1992	Cooper R.	Charleston, SC	800
1957	Kingston-Rhinecliff	Hudson R., NY	800
1950	Maurice J. Tobin	Boston, MA	800
1940	Gov. Nice Mem.	Newburg, MD-Dahlgren, VA.	800
1986	Rochester-Monaca	Rochester-Monaca, PA.	780
1973/ 88	Atchafalaya R. (U.S. 190) (twin)	Krotz Springs, LA	780
1988	Phil G. McDonald (Glade Creek)	Beckley, WV	784
1917	*Sciotoville RR (twin)	Sciotoville, OH-KY	775
1981	Sewickley	Sewickley, PA	750
1977	Jennings Randolph	Chester, WV-E. Liverpool, OH	750
1974	Carroll C. Cropper (I-275)	Ohio R., IN-KY	750
1940	Glover Cary	Ohio R., Owensboro, KY-IN	750

Year	Bridge	Location	Main span (ft)
1984	13th Street	Ohio R., Ashland, KY-OH	740
1959	Monaca-E. Rochester	Monaca-E. Rochester, PA	730
1976	Betsy Ross	Philadelphia, PA	729
2013	Milton-Madison (U.S. 421)	Ohio R., KY-IN	727
1967	Matthew E. Welsh	Ohio R., Mauckport, IN-KY	725
1994	Robert C. Byrd	Huntington, WV.	720
1971	Atchafalaya R. (LA 1)	Simmesport, LA	720
1962	U.S. 41 Twin	Ohio R., Evansville, IN-Henderson, KY	720
1929	Irvin S. Cobb (U.S. 45)	Ohio R., Brookport, IL-Paducah, KY	716
1970	Vanport	Vanport, PA	715
1962	Champlain	Montreal, QC, Can.	707
1973	Girard Point	Philadelphia, PA	700
1963	John F. Kennedy (I-65)	Ohio R., Louisville, KY-Jeffersonville, IN	700
1923	*Mears Mem., Tanana R.	Nenana, AK	700

Plate and Box Girder

Year	Bridge	Location	Main span (ft)
1997	Confederation[3]	Prince Edward Isl.-NB, Can.	820
2010	Kanawha R. (I-64)	S. Charleston-Dunbar, WV	760
1982	Jesse H. Jones Memorial	Houston, TX	750
1977	LA 27, Intracoastal Canal	Gibbstown, LA	750
1976	LA 82, Intracoastal Canal	Forked Isl., LA	750
1967	San Mateo-Hayward	San Francisco Bay, CA	750
1992	Jamestown-Verrazano	Narragansett Bay, RI.	674
2002	Vietnam Veterans Mem.	James R., Richmond, VA.	672
1986	Umatilla	Columbia R., OR-WA	660
1969	San Diego-Coronado (twin)	San Diego Bay, CA	660
2007	Benicia-Martinez (new)	Carquinez Strait, CA	659
1967	Poplar St./William L. Clay Sr.	Miss. R., St. Louis, MO-IL	647
1978	Stanislaus R.	Parrots Ferry, CA	640
1992/ 94	Acosta (twin)	Jacksonville, FL	630
1973	Loop 610/Sidney Sherman	Houston, TX	630
1981	Juneau-Douglas	Gastineau Channel, AK	620
1981	Glenn Jackson (I-205)	Columbia R., OR-WA.	600

Cable-Stayed

Year	Bridge	Location	Main span (ft)
2018	Gerald Desmond Replacement	Long Beach, CA	2,001
2012	Baluarte Bicentennial	Sinaloa-Durango states, Mex.	1,706
2011	John James Audubon	Pointe Coupee-West Feliciana, LA	1,583
2005	Arthur Ravenel Jr.	Charleston, SC.	1,546
2012	Port Mann	Vancouver, BC, Can.	1,542
1986	Alex Fraser	Vancouver, BC, Can.	1,526
2014	Stan Musial Veterans Memorial (I-70)	Miss. R., St. Louis, MO-IL	1,500
2010	U.S. 82, Mississippi R.	Greenville, MS-Lake Village, AR	1,378
1994	Clark	Alton, IL-MO.	1,360
1989	Dames Point	Jacksonville, FL	1,300
2003	Sidney Lanier	Brunswick, GA	1,250
1995	Fred Hartman	Houston Ship Channel, Baytown, TX.	1,250
2007	Veterans' Glass City Skyway	Maumee R., Toledo, OH	1,225
1983	Hale Boggs Memorial	Luling, LA	1,222
2017/ 18	New NY (I-287) (twin)	Hudson R., Tarrytown, NY	1,200
2002	William Natcher, Ohio R.	Owensboro, KY-IN	1,200
1987	Sunshine Skyway (I-275)	Tampa Bay, FL.	1,200
2012	Margaret Hunt Hill	Trinity R., Dallas, TX	1,197
1988	Tampico	Panuco R., Mex.	1,181
2006	Penobscot Narrows	Bucksport, ME	1,161
2003	Bill Emerson Memorial	Cape Girardeau, MO-IL.	1,150
1988	Skybridge[4]	Vancouver, BC, Can.	1,115
1991	Talmadge Memorial	Savannah, GA	1,100
2000	Maysville (Wm. H. Harsha)	Savannah, GA	1,050

Steel Arch

Year	Bridge	Location	Main span (ft)
1977	New River Gorge	Fayetteville, WV.	1,700
1931	Bayonne (Kill Van Kull)	Bayonne, NJ-New York, NY	1,675
1973	Fremont	Portland, OR	1,255
1964	Port Mann	Vancouver, BC, Can.	1,200
1967	Laviolette	Trois-Rivières, QC, Can.	1,100
1990	Roosevelt Lake	Roosevelt Lake, AZ	1,080

Year	Bridge	Location	Main span (ft)
1959	Glen Canyon	Page, AZ	1,028
1962	Lewiston-Queenston	NY-ON, Can.	1,001
1976	Perrine	Twin Falls, ID	993
1916	*Hell Gate	East R., New York, NY	978
1941	Rainbow	Niagara Falls, NY-ON, Can.	950
1997	Second Blue Water	Port Huron, MI-ON, Can.	922
1977	Moundsville	Ohio R., WV	912
1983/	Jefferson Barracks (I-255)		
92	(twin)	Mississippi R., IL-MO	910
1973	Hernando DeSoto (I-40)		
	(two spans)	Mississippi R., AR-TN	900
2008	Blennerhassett (U.S. 50)	Parkersburg, WV-OH	878
1936	Henry Hudson	Harlem R., New York, NY	840
1966	Bob Cummings Lincoln Trail	Ohio R., IN-KY	825
1978	I-57, Mississippi R.	Cairo, IL	821
1980	I-65, Mobile R.	Mobile, AL	800
1961	Sherman Minton (I-64)	IN-Louisville, KY	800
1978	I-470, Ohio R.	Wheeling, WV	780
1932	West End	Pittsburgh, PA	780
1971	Piscataqua R.	Portsmouth, NH-	
	(I-95 High Level)	Kittery, ME	756
1995	Navajo	Marble Canyon, AZ	726

Movable Bridges
Vertical Lift

Year	Bridge	Location	Main span (ft)
1959	*Arthur Kill	New York, NY-Elizabeth, NJ	558
1935	*Cape Cod Canal	Buzzards Bay, MA	544

Year	Bridge	Location	Main span (ft)
1896	*Delair	Pennsauken, NJ-Phila., PA	542
1937	Marine Pkwy. Hodges Mem.	Jamaica Bay, New York, NY	540
1931	Burlington-Bristol	Delaware R., NJ-PA	540
1908	*Burlington Northern RR[5]	Portland, OR.	516
1968	*Second Narrows Railway	Vancouver, BC, Can.	499
1911	*Armour-Swift-Burlington		
	(ABS)	Missouri R., Kansas City, MO	428

Bascule

Year	Bridge	Location	Main span (ft)
1940	Charles Berry Memorial	Lorain, OH	333
1917	Market St./Ch. John Ross	Chattanooga, TN	310
2003	SW 2nd Avenue	Miami, FL	302

Swing

Year	Bridge	Location	Main span (ft)
1927	Fort Madison (Santa Fe)	Mississippi R., IA	525
1952	George P. Coleman Mem.	Yorktown, VA	500
1991	SW Spokane St.	Seattle, WA	480
1899	*Illinois Central RR	Chicago, IL	479
1914	*Coos Bay RR	Coos Bay, OR	458
1913	East Haddam (Rt. 82)	Connecticut R., CT	456

Floating Pontoon[6]

Year	Bridge	Location	Main span (ft)
2016	New SR 520	Seattle, WA	7,709
1993	Lacey V. Murrow (I-90)	Seattle, WA	6,620
1961	Hood Canal (SR 104)	Kitsap Co.-	
		Jefferson Co., WA	6,521
1989	Homer M. Hadley (I-90)	Seattle, WA	5,811

Other Notable North American Bridges

Year	Bridge	Type	Location	Tot. length (ft)
1956/				
69	Lake Pontchartrain Causeway[7]	Twin concrete trestle	Metairie-Mandeville, LA	126,055
1979	Manchac Swamp	Twin concrete trestle	Manchac, LA	120,384
1973	Atchafalaya Basin (I-10)	Twin concrete trestle	Baton Rouge, LA	95,040
1982	Seven Mile (Overseas Hwy., U.S. 1)	Segmental concrete	Florida Keys	35,867
2009/				
11	I-10 Twin Spans	Twin concrete trestle	Slidell-New Orleans, LA	29,040
2002	Croatan Sound	Continuous post-tensioned girder	Manteo, NC	27,000
1993	Choctawhatchee Mid-Bay	Segmental concrete	Destin-Niceville, FL	19,265
1962	International	Arch truss	Sault Ste. Marie, MI-ON, Can.	9,278
2009	Walkway Over the Hudson[8]	Pedestrian	Poughkeepsie-Highland, NY	6,768
1874	Eads, Mississippi R.[9]	Steel arch	St. Louis, MO-IL	6,442
2013	San Francisco-Oakland Bay (Skyway)	Segmental concrete box girder	San Francisco Bay, CA	6,336
1987	Powder Point	Tropical hardwood	Duxbury, MA	2,200
1969	Silver Memorial, Ohio R.[10]	Cantilever	Pt. Pleasant, WV-OH	1,964
2010	Mike O'Callaghan-Pat Tillman Mem.			
	(U.S. 93)[11]	Concrete arch	Colorado R., AZ-NV	1,900
1994	Natchez Trace Parkway	Concrete arch	Franklin, TN	1,572
1901	Hartland[12]	Covered	St. John R., Hartland, NB, Can.	1,282

(1) Two complete bridges each 2,310-ft long, which share an anchor point. (2) Self-Anchored Suspension Span (SAS); the world's longest single-tower, self-anchored suspension bridge. (3) World's longest bridge crossing ice-covered water, with total length of 8 mi. (4) World's longest cable-stayed bridge carrying mass transit only. (5) Vertical lift replaced swing span in 1989. (6) Length listed is of bridge's floating section. (7) World's second-longest bridge over water, behind China's Qingdao Bay Bridge (25.8 mi or 136,417 ft). (8) Originally opened in 1889 as a railroad bridge. (9) World's first major structure made of alloy steel. (10) Replaced Silver Bridge, the collapse of which in 1967 led to the creation of National Bridge Inspection Standards in the U.S. (11) Longest single-span concrete arch in Western Hemisphere. (12) World's longest covered bridge.

Oldest U.S. Bridges in Continuous Use

Built in 1697, the stone-arch Frankford Ave. Bridge (U.S. 13) crosses Pennypack Creek in Philadelphia, PA. It consists of three spans and has a total length of 154 ft. The bridge was constructed as part of the King's Road, which connected Philadelphia to New York.

The oldest covered bridge, completed in 1829, is the double-span, 256-ft-long Bath-Haverhill Bridge, which spans the Ammonoosuc River between the towns of Bath and Haverhill, NH. The bridge was bypassed in 1999. It has since reopened to pedestrian traffic only.

Notable World Bridges

Source: World Almanac research

Year is date of completion or projected completion. Span of bridge is the distance between its main supports. As of mid-2016. NA = Not available.

Year	Bridge	Location	Main span (ft)
	Suspension		
1998	Akashi Kaikyo	Japan	6,532
2009	Xihoumen	China	5,413
1998	Storebælt (Great Belt, East Bridge)	Denmark	5,328
2016	Osman Gazi	Turkey	5,085
2012	Yi Sun-sin (Gwangyang)	South Korea	5,069
2005	Runyang Yangtze R. (south)	China	4,888
2012	Nanjing Fourth Yangtze R.	China	4,652
1981	Humber	England	4,625
2016	Yavuz Sultan Selim		
	(Third Bosphorus)	Turkey	4,619
1999	Jiangyin Yangtze R.	China	4,544
1997	Tsing Ma	China	4,518
2013	Hardanger	Norway	4,298
2007	Yangluo Yangtze R.	China	4,199
1997	Höga Kusten	Sweden	3,970
2016	Longjian	China	3,924
2012	Aizhai	China	3,858
2015	Ulsan Grand	South Korea	3,773
2017	Halogaland	Norway	3,756
2008	Huangpu	China	3,635
1988	Minami Bisan-Seto	Japan	3,609
1988	Fatih Sultan Mehmet (Bosphorus II)	Turkey	3,576

Year	Bridge	Location	Main span (ft)
2009	Baling R.	China	3,570
2012	Taizhou Yangtze R.[1]	China	3,543
1973	Bosphorus	Turkey	3,524
1999	Kurushima III	Japan	3,379
1999	Kurushima II	Japan	3,346
1966	Ponte 25 de Abril, Tagus R.	Portugal	3,323
1964	Forth Road	Scotland	3,300

(1) Two consecutive spans of equal length.

	Steel Arch		
NA	Sheikh Rashid bin Saeed Crossing	United Arab	
		Emirates	2,188
2009	Chaotianmen Yangtze R.	China	1,811
2003	Lupu	China	1,804
2012	Bosideng	China	1,739
1932	Sydney Harbour	Australia	1,650
2005	Wushan Yangtze R.	China	1,614
2018	Chenab (rail)[1]	India	1,532
2013	Xijiang (rail)	China	1,476
2007	Xinguang	China	1,404
2007	Caiyuanba	China	1,378
2010	Daning R.	China	1,312
2008	Hiroshima Airport	Japan	1,247

Year	Bridge	Location	Main span (ft)
1959	Sloboda	Croatia	1,224
2000	Yajisha	China	1,181
1962	Bridge of the Americas	Panama	1,128
1967	Zdakov	Czech Republic.	1,083
1961	Runcorn-Widnes	England	1,082
1935	Birchenough	Zimbabwe	1,080

(1) Will be world's highest rail bridge (1,178 ft) upon completion.

Concrete Arch

Year	Bridge	Location	Main span (ft)
1997	Wanxian Yangtze R.	China	1,378
2015	Nanpanjiang (rail)	China	1,365
1980	Krk I	Croatia	1,280
2016	Almonte Viaduct	Spain	1,260
2012	Zhaohua Jialing R.	China	1,194
1995	Jiangjiehe	China	1,083
2015	Tajo Railway	Spain	1,063
1996	Yongjiang	China	1,024
1964	Gladesville	Australia	1,000

Cantilever

Year	Bridge	Location	Main span (ft)
1890	Forth Rail[1]	Scotland	1,710
1974	Minato	Japan	1,673
1943	Rabindra Setu (Howrah)	India	1,500

(1) Two spans of equal length.

Plate and Box Girder

Year	Bridge	Location	Main span (ft)
2006	Shibanpo	China	1,083
1998	Stolmasundet	Norway	988
1974	Pres. Costa e Silva (Rio-Niterói)	Brazil	984
1998	Raftsund	Norway	978
1978	Neckar Valley Viaduct, Weitingen	Germany	863
1956	Branko's	Serbia	856
1989	Third	Brazil	853
1966	Zoobrücke	Germany	850

Cable-Stayed

Year	Bridge	Location	Main span (ft)
2012	Russky Island	Russia	3,622
2008	Sutong Yangtze R.	China	3,570
2009	Stonecutters	China	3,340
2009	Edong	China	3,038
1999	Tatara	Japan	2,920
1995	Normandy	France	2,808
2013	Jiujiang Yangtze R. Expressway	China	2,684
2010	Jingyue Yangtze R.	China	2,677

Year	Bridge	Location	Main span (ft)
2009	Incheon	South Korea	2,625
2012	Zolotoy Rog	Russia	2,418
2009	Shanghai Yangtze R.	China	2,395
2009	Minpu	China	2,323
2017	Queensferry	Scotland	2,132
2005	Third Nanjing Yangtze R.	China	2,126
2001	Second Nanjing Yangtze R.	China	2,060
2000	Third Wuhan Yangtze R. (Baishazhou)	China	2,028
2002	Qingzhou Minjiang R.	China	1,985
1993	Yangpu	China	1,975
1998	Meiko Chuo	Japan	1,936
1997	Xupu	China	1,936
2004	Rion-Antirion	Greece	1,837
2014	Bukhang	South Korea	1,772
1991	Skarnsund	Norway	1,739
1999	Shantou Queshi	China	1,699
1995	Tsurumi Tsubasa	Japan	1,673
2008	Tianxingzhou Yangtze R.	China	1,654
2012	Mokpo	South Korea	1,640
2007	Kanchanaphisek	Thailand	1,640
2002	Jingsha	China	1,640
2000	Øresund	Denmark-Sweden	1,608
1991	Ikuchi	Japan	1,608
1994	Higashi Kobe	Japan	1,591
2011	Geo Geum	South Korea	1,575
1998	Zhanjiang	China	1,575
1997	Ting Kau	China	1,558
1999	Seohae Grand	South Korea	1,542
1989	Yokohama Bay	Japan	1,509

Other Notable World Bridges[1]

Year	Bridge	Location	Main span (ft)
2011	Danyang-Kunshan Grand (rail)[2]	China	538,000
2000	Bang Na Espressway[3]	Thailand	180,446
2011	Qingdao Bay[4]	China	136,417
2007	Hangzhou Bay	China	118,000
2013	Jiashao	China	33,136
1978	Demerara Harbour (floating)	Guyana	6,074
1994	Nordhordland (floating)	Norway	4,088
1991	Ikitsuki[5]	Japan	1,312

(1) Length listed is total length of bridge unless otherwise noted. (2) World's longest bridge. (3) World's longest road bridge. (4) World's longest oversea bridge. (5) Length listed is of main span, world's longest continuous truss span.

World's Longest Railway Tunnels

Source: World Almanac research

Year is date of opening or projected opening unless otherwise noted. As of mid-2016.

Year	Tunnel	Location	Operating railway	Length (mi)
2016	Gotthard Base (twin)	Switzerland-Italy	Swiss Federal Railways (SBB)	35.4/35.5
1988	Seikan	Japan	Japan Railways Group	33.5
2016	Yulhyeon	South Korea	SR/Korea Railroad Corporation (Korail)	31.3
1994	English Channel (Chunnel) (twin)	UK-France	Eurotunnel	31.1
2007	Lötschberg Base (twin)	Switzerland	BLS Lötschbergbahn AG	21.0
2014	New Guanjiao	China	Qinghai-Tibet Railway Company	20.3
2007	Guadarrama (twin)	Spain	Renfe	17.6
2009	Taihang (twin)	China	China's Ministry of Railways	17.3
2005	Hakkoda	Japan	Japan Railways Group	16.4
2018	Guangzhou-Shenzhen-Hong Kong Express Rail Link (XRL), Hong Kong section	China	MTR Corporation	16.2
2002	Iwate-Ichinohe	Japan	Japan Railways Group	16.0
NA[1]	Pajares (twin)	Spain	Renfe	15.3
2015	Iiyama	Japan	Japan Railways Group	13.8
1982	Daishimizu	Japan	Japan Railways Group	13.8
2008-09	Geumjeong	South Korea	Korea Railroad Corporation (Korail)	12.6
2006	Wushaoling (twin)	China	China's Ministry of Railways	12.5
1906/22	Simplon No. 1 and 2	Switzerland-Italy	BLS Lötschbergbahn AG	12.3
1999	Vereina	Switzerland	Rhätische Bahn (RhB)	11.8
2007	High Speed 1 (Channel Tunnel Rail Link, or CTRL) (twin)	UK-France	London & Continental Railways (LCR)	11.8
1975	Shin-Kanmon (twin)	Japan	Japan Railways Group	11.6
1934	Apennine	Italy	Ferrovie dello Stato (FS)	11.5
2002	Qinling (twin)	China	China's Ministry of Railways	11.5
2006	Vaglia	Italy	Ferrovie dello Stato (FS)	10.4
2014	West Qinling (twin)	China	China's Ministry of Railways	10.3
1972	Rokko	Japan	Japan Railways Group	10.1

NA = Not available. (1) Tunnels have been dug but are not yet in operation.

Underwater Vehicular Tunnels in North America

Source: World Almanac research

(more than 5,000 ft in length; year is date of opening)

Year	Name	Location	Waterway	Length (ft)
1950	Brooklyn Battery (twin)	New York, NY	East River	9,117
1927	Holland (twin)	New York, NY-Jersey City, NJ	Hudson River	8,558/8,371
1937/45/57	Lincoln (center/north/south tubes)	New York, NY-Weehawken, NJ	Hudson River	8,216/7,482/8,006
1985	Fort McHenry (twin)	Baltimore, MD	Patapsco River	7,920
1957/76	Hampton Roads (twin)	Hampton, VA	Hampton Roads	7,479
1957	Baltimore Harbor (twin)	Baltimore, MD	Baltimore Harbor	7,392
1940	Queens Midtown (twin)	New York, NY	East River	6,414
1934	Sumner	Boston, MA	Boston Harbor	5,653
1964	Thimble Shoal	Northampton Co., VA	Chesapeake Bay	5,552
1964	Chesapeake Channel	Northampton Co., VA	Chesapeake Bay	5,237
1930	Detroit-Windsor	Detroit, MI-Windsor, ON, Canada	Detroit River	5,160
1961	Callahan	Boston, MA	Boston Harbor	5,070

Land Vehicular Tunnels in the U.S.

Source: World Almanac research; Federal Highway Administration, U.S. Dept. of Transportation
(3,400 ft or more in length)

Name	Location	Length (ft)	Name	Location	Length (ft)
Anton Anderson Memorial[1]. . .	Whittier, AK.	13,300	Lehigh (twin).	PA Turnpike,	4,461/
Edwin C. Johnson Memorial	I-70, Clear Creek Co.-			NE Extension	4,380
(eastbound).	Summit Co., CO	8,960	Blue Mountain (twin).	PA Turnpike	4,339
Eisenhower Memorial	I-70, Clear Creek Co.-		Wawona	Yosemite Natl. Pk., CA..	4,233
(westbound).	Summit Co., CO	8,939	Big Walker Mountain (twin). . .	Bland Co., VA.	4,229
Ted Williams[2]	MA Turnpike, Boston, MA	8,448	Squirrel Hill.	Pittsburgh, PA.	4,225
Thomas P. O'Neill Jr.	I-93, Boston, MA.	7,920	Tom Lantos/Devil's Slide		
Allegheny (twin)	PA Turnpike	6,070	(twin).	San Mateo Co., CA.	4,200
Liberty (twin).	Pittsburgh, PA.	5,920	Hanging Lake (twin)	Glenwood Canyon, CO. .	4,000
Zion-Mount Carmel.	Zion Natl. Park, UT. . . .	5,808	Caldecott (4 tubes).	Oakland, CA.	3,771/3,610/
East River Mountain (twin) . . .	I-77, Rocky Gap, VA-				3,610/3,389
	Bluefield, WV	5,412	Fort Pitt (twin)	Pittsburgh, PA.	3,614
Tuscarora Mountain (twin) . . .	PA Turnpike	5,326	Mount Baker	Seattle, WA.	3,456
Tetsuo Harano (twin)	H-3 Freeway, HI	5,165	Dingess.	Mingo Co., WV	3,400
Kittatinny Mountain (twin)	PA Turnpike	4,727	Mall.	Washington, DC	3,400
Cumberland Gap (twin)	U.S. 25E, KY-TN	4,600			

(1) Vehicles and trains take turns using the tunnel's one lane. (2) Total length of tunnel is 8,448 ft, 3,960 ft of which is underwater.

Major U.S. Dams and Reservoirs

Source: 2013 National Inventory of Dams, U.S. Army Corps of Engineers

Highest U.S. Dams

					Height		Year
Rank	Dam	River	State	Type	Feet	Meters	completed
1.	Oroville	Feather.	California	E	770	235	1968
2.	Hoover	Colorado.	Nevada.	A-G	730	221	1935
3.	Dworshak	N. Fork Clearwater	Idaho.	G	717	219	1973
4.	Glen Canyon.	Colorado.	Arizona	A	710	216	1963
5.	New Bullards Bar	North Yuba	California	A	645	197	1970
6.	Mossyrock	Cowlitz	Washington.	A	606	185	1968
7.	Shasta	Sacramento	California	G	602	183	1945
8.	Don Pedro	Tuolumne	California	E	585	178	1971
9.	New Melones	Stanislaus.	California	E-R	578	176	1979
10.	Hungry Horse	S. Fork Flathead.	Montana	A	564	172	1952

A = Arch; E = Embankment, earthfill; G = Gravity; R = Embankment, rockfill. **Note:** The height of a dam is the vertical distance between the original streambed or excavated foundation and the dam's crest, parapet wall, or maximum design water level. Tailings and other mining dams (i.e., dams built from the waste generated by mining operations) are not included in this list.

Largest U.S. Embankment Dams

				Volume		Year
				Cubic yards	Cubic meters	
Rank	Dam	River	State	(thousands)	(thousands)	completed
1.	Fort Peck	Missouri	Montana	125,628	96,049	1957
2.	Oahe.	Missouri	South Dakota	92,000	70,339	1966
3.	Oroville	Feather.	California	80,000	61,164	1968
4.	B. F. Sisk	San Luis Creek.	California	77,670	59,383	1967
5.	Garrison	Missouri	North Dakota	66,500	50,843	1953
6.	Scotts Flat	Deer Creek.	California	66,300	50,690	1948
7.	Cochiti.	Rio Grande	New Mexico	65,000	49,696	1975
8.	Herbert Hoover.	North New River Canal. . .	Florida.	54,700	41,821	1965
9.	Fort Randall	Missouri	South Dakota	50,200	38,381	1954
10.	Castaic	Castaic Creek.	California	44,000	33,640	1973

Note: An embankment dam is any dam constructed with excavated material, including earth, rocks, and mining or other industrial waste. (In contrast, gravity, arch, and buttress dams are generally made out of concrete or masonry.) The majority of the world's dams are embankment dams. All dams in this list are earthfill, or formed primarily out of layers of compacted earth.

Largest-Capacity U.S. Reservoirs

				Max. reservoir capacity		Year
				Acre feet	Cubic meters	
Rank	Dam	Reservoir	State	(thousands)	(thousands)	completed
1.	Hoover	Lake Mead	Nevada.	30,237	37,296,790	1935
2.	Glen Canyon.	Lake Powell	Arizona	29,875	36,850,270	1963
3.	Garrison	Lake Sakakawea	North Dakota	24,500	30,220,305	1953
4.	Oahe.	Lake Oahe	South Dakota	23,600	29,110,172	1966
5.	Fort Peck	Fort Peck Lake	Montana	19,100	23,559,503	1957
6.	Grand Coulee.	Lake Roosevelt	Washington.	9,562	11,794,553	1941
7.	Herbert Hoover.	Lake Okeechobee	Florida	8,519	10,508,032	1965
8.	Kentucky.	Kentucky Lake	Kentucky.	7,535	9,294,779	1944
9.	Sam Rayburn	Sam Rayburn Lake.	Texas	6,520	8,042,302	1965
10.	Wright Patman	Wright Patman Lake. . . .	Texas	6,505	8,023,799	1954

Note: A reservoir is a body of water created by a dam for storage. This water may serve a single or multiple purposes, such as irrigation, flood reduction, and electricity generation.

Major Dams and Reservoirs of the World

Source: World Register of Dams, Intl. Commission on Large Dams (ICOLD)
Asterisk (*) designates structure is planned or under construction as of mid-2016.

World's Highest Dams

Rank	Dam	Country	Meters	Feet
1.	*Rogun	Tajikistan	335	1,099
2.	*Bakhtiari	Iran	315	1,033
3.	*Jinping I.	China	305	1,001
4.	Nurek	Tajikistan	300	984
5.	*Lianghekou	China	295	968
6.	Xiaowan (Yunnan Gorge)	China	294	965
7.	Xiluodu	China	286	938
8.	Grande Dixence	Switzerland	285	935
9.	*Baihetan	China	277	909
10.	*Diamer-Bhasha	Pakistan	272	892
11.	Inguri	Georgia	272	892
12.	*Yusufeli	Turkey	270	886
13.	Chicoasén	Mexico	262	860
14.	Vajont	Italy	262	860
15.	Nuozhadu	China	262	860

Height above lowest formation

World's Largest Embankment Dams

Rank	Dam	Country	Volume cubic meters (thousands)
1.	Tarbela	Pakistan	129,200
2.	Fort Peck	U.S.	96,049
3.	Ataturk	Turkey	84,500
4.	Yacyreta	Argentina/Paraguay	81,000
5.	Tucurui	Brazil	80,865
6.	*Rogun	Tajikistan	75,500
7.	Oahe	U.S.	70,339
8.	Guri	Venezuela	70,000
9.	Parambikulam	India	69,165
10.	High Island West	China	67,000
11.	Gardiner	Canada	65,440
12.	Mangla	Pakistan	64,991
13.	Afsluitdijk	Netherlands	63,400
14.	Oroville	U.S.	61,164
15.	B. F. Sisk	U.S.	59,378

World's Largest-Capacity Reservoirs

Rank	Dam	Country	Max. capacity cubic meters (millions)
1.	Kariba	Zimbabwe/Zambia	180,600
2.	Bratsk	Russia	169,000
3.	High Aswan	Egypt	162,000
4.	Akosombo (Lake Volta)	Ghana	150,000
5.	Daniel-Johnson	Canada	141,851
6.	Guri	Venezuela	135,000
7.	W. A. C. Bennett	Canada	74,300
8.	Krasnoyarsk	Russia	73,300
9.	Zeya	Russia	68,400
10.	*Hidase	Ethiopia	63,000
11.	Robert-Bourassa (La Grande 2)	Canada	61,715
12.	La Grande 3	Canada	60,020
13.	Ust-Ilim	Russia	59,300
14.	Cutarm Creek	Canada	58,596
15.	Boguchany	Russia	58,200

World's Largest-Capacity Hydro Plants

Rank	Dam	Country	Installed capacity (MW)
1.	Sanxia (Three Gorges Dam)	China	22,500
2.	Itaipu	Brazil/Paraguay	14,000
3.	*Baihetan	China	14,000
4.	*Xiluodu	China	13,860
5.	*Belo Monte	Brazil	11,234
6.	Guri	Venezuela	10,000
7.	Tucuruí	Brazil	8,370
8.	Grand Coulee	U.S.	6,809
9.	Sayano-Shushenskaya	Russia	6,400
10.	Xiangjiaba	China	6,400
11.	Longtan	China	6,300
12.	Krasnoyarsk	Russia	6,000
13.	*Myitsone	Myanmar (Burma)	6,000
14.	Nuozhadu	China	5,850
15.	Robert-Bourassa	Canada	5,616

Timeline of Selected Architectural Styles and Structures

Asterisk (*) denotes part of a UNESCO World Heritage site.

Style and period	Location; characteristics; significant examples
Mesopotamian c. 3500-539 BCE	City-states of Sumer, Akkad, Babylon, Assyria (modern-day Iraq). Mud-brick rectangular temples on oval platforms with simple corbel vaults, later ziggurats. Painted terra-cotta mosaics and murals; carved reliefs on columns and walls. **Ziggurat of Nanna**, Ur (Muqayyar, Iraq), ordered by Ur-Nammu, c. 2100 BCE **Anu Ziggurat and White Temple**, Uruk (Warka, Iraq), c. 3000 BCE
Egyptian c. 3000-30 BCE	Along Nile R. Mud-brick and limestone tombs and massive, geometric pyramids, post-and-lintel construction. Highly decorative with colorful hieroglyphics, carvings, columns, obelisks, paintings, and sculpture. *****Stepped Pyramid of Pharaoh Djoser** (Saqqara, Egypt), by Imhotep, c. 2737-2717 BCE *****Great Pyramid of Khufu** (Giza, Egypt), c. 2250 BCE *****Great Temple of Amon-Ra** (Karnak, Egypt), c. 1530-300 BCE *****Mortuary Temple of Queen Hatshepsut**, Deir el-Bahari (Thebes, Egypt), by Senenmut, c. 1479-1458 BCE
Three Dynasties c. 2100-221 BCE	China. Single-level mud-brick or mud-smeared timber structures on earthen platforms with thatched roofs. Later, bracketed wooden-framed structures with brick-tiled floors, roofs with overhanging eaves. **City of Erlitou** (Yanshi, China), c. 1900-1500 BCE
Minoan c. 1800-1450 BCE	Crete. Palaces, tombs in monumental style adapted from Mesopotamia and Egypt. Multilevel stone palaces with large central court, no fortifications. Walls made of doors (*polythyron*); stone porticoes and lintels; wooden ceilings and columns; beehive-shaped tombs (*tholi*). **Palace at Knossos** (Heraklion, Crete, Greece), c. 1700 BCE
Mycenaean c. 1600-1100 BCE	Greece. Adapted Minoan style, with large stone masonry, huge walls, and fortified citadels with complex palaces (*megaron*). *****Treasury of Atreus** (Mycenae, Greece), c. 1250 BCE
Olmec c. 1200-400 BCE	Mexico Gulf Coast. Many religious structures, including stone temple-pyramids centered in cities; also large stone sculptures and mosaic pavement with natural and animistic themes. **Great Pyramid** (La Venta, Mexico), c. 800-400 BCE
Mayan c. 900 BCE-900 CE	Central America. Religious structures with plaster-surfaced stone temple-pyramids with stairs containing tombs. Decorative animistic and geometric relief sculptures, lintels, and stone monuments with hieroglyphics. *****Pyramid of the Magician** (Uxmal, Mexico), c. 700-910 CE *****North Acropolis** (Tikal, Guatemala), c. 200 BCE

Style and period	Location; characteristics; significant examples
Greek c. 750-323 BCE	Greek peninsula, Asia Minor, North Africa, western Mediterranean. Religious, civic buildings in monumental style, inspired by Egypt, based on strict rules of form and human proportion; many ornamental details. Marble and limestone structures (including rectangular temples) with pediment, colonnaded porticoes in diverse regional styles, defined by orders of architecture like Ionic, Doric, Corinthian. Most early buildings with timber supports; solid stone in later temples. ***Parthenon, Acropolis** (Athens, Greece), by Ictinus and Callicrates, 447-436 BCE ***Temple of Zeus** (Olympia, Greece), by Libon of Elis, mid-5th cent. BCE **Mausoleum of Halicarnassus** (Bodrum, Turkey), by Pythis, c. 353 BCE (destroyed) ***Temple of Apollo Epicurius** (Bassae, Greece), by Ictinus, c. 420 BCE
Achaemenid c. 550-334 BCE	Persian Empire (Eastern Mediterranean to Indus R.). Palatial complexes influenced by cultures absorbed by the empire; limestone and mud-brick complexes on raised stone terraces with ornamental stairways, rectangular pillared audience halls with porticoes and corner towers; pleasure gardens (*bâgh*) as focal point of architecture. ***Pasargadae** (Iran), founded by Cyrus II, after 547 BCE ***Persepolis** (Iran), founded by Darius I, around 518 BCE
Roman c. 500 BCE-400 CE	Roman Empire. Civic and religious structures with grandiose limestone brick and concrete construction in systematic, practical layout. Adapted Greek orders in many structures, including circular temples and large covered halls (basilica), but emphasized movement with rounded arches and domes, geometric vaults. ***Pantheon** (Rome, Italy), ordered by Emperor Hadrian, 118-128 CE ***Colosseum** (Rome, Italy), ordered by Emperor Vespasian, 70-82 CE ***Roman Forum** (Rome, Italy), 500s BCE-608 CE
Qin and Han c. 221 BCE-220 CE	China. Massive public works, palaces, tombs, and planned cities; systematic layout and design determined by divination techniques (geomancy). Multistoried timber palace complexes with gardens, courtyards laid along a long hall with a south-north axis for weather; decorative roof with overhanging eaves. ***The Great Wall** (China), ordered by Qin Shi Huang, 220 BCE-c. 1600 CE ***Mausoleum of the First Qin Emperor** (Xianyang [Xi'an], China), c. 210 BCE
Sassanian 226-651	Iran. Mud-brick, mortared rubble, and stone palaces on platforms. Tall, vaulted entry chambers with one open side (*iwans*). Three-aisled hall chambers covered with rudimentary barrel vaults. Parabolic domes abandoned for square courtyards in later Sassanian period. **Palace of Ardashir I** (Firuzabad, Iran), c. 224 **Taq-i Kisra** [Arch of Khosrau] (Ctesiphon, Iraq), c. 260 or c. 550
Byzantine 330-1453	Byzantine Empire, Italy, Russia. Religious structures with masonry construction based on Roman architecture, many salvaged pieces. Centralized cross-in-square layout, with large central dome supported by vaults. Highly decorative, with iconographic frescoes, glass mosaics. ***Hagia Sophia** (Istanbul, Turkey), by Anthemius and Isidorus, 532-37 ***St. Mark's Basilica** (Venice, Italy), ordered by Domenico Contarini, 1063-94
Sui and Tang 581-906	China. Includes influences from other cultures; geomancy used to enhance harmony and social status. Rectangular, multistory modular timber structures with interlinking corridors; single-eaved roofs with exposed beams. **Daming Palace** (Xi'an, China), 634 (destroyed) ***Hall of the Great Buddha**, Foguang Temple (Mount Wutai, China), ordered rebuilt by Xuan Zhong, 857
Early Islamic (Umayyad) 692-c. 1000	Syria, Middle East, North Africa, southern Spain. Mosques in adapted Sassanian style. Austere exteriors; simple columned halls with minarets and mihrabs (prayer niches), walled courtyards and gardens, onion domes. Highly decorative interiors with patterned marble, mosaics. ***Dome of the Rock** [Qubbat al-Sakhra] (Jerusalem), ordered by Abd al-Malik, 692 ***Great Mosque of Córdoba** (Spain), ordered by Abd al-Rahman I, 784-86
Khmer c. 880-1200s	Indochina. Hindu or Buddhist temple complexes, including brick, later sandstone beehive-shaped shrines with arches atop terraced temple "mountains" symbolizing Mount Meru, Hindu and Buddhist center of the universe, where the gods dwell. Concentric layout of structures mimics the cosmos, relating religious narrative in carved reliefs. ***Angkor Wat** (Cambodia), ordered by Suryavarman II, 12th cent.
Romanesque (Norman) c. 900s-1100s	Western Europe. Churches and monasteries in localized Roman style; many reused material from Roman structures. Austere, heavy, simple masonry construction with thick walls, concealed buttresses, small windows, barrel arches, and vaults. Churches like Roman basilica with arched central nave, lower side aisles, apse, transept formed Latin cross. Monumental art and ornaments with Christian narrative throughout, especially on façade and portals. ***Durham Cathedral** (England, UK), ordered by Bishop William de Saint-Calais, 1093-1133 ***Cathedral, Baptistery, and "Leaning" Tower** (Pisa, Italy), by various architects, begun in 1063, tower not completed until 1372
Gothic c. 1100s-1500s	France, Europe. Cathedrals meant to inspire spirituality with design like Roman basilica: pointed arches and spires that reach toward heavens, skeletal masonry, revealed structure like flying buttresses, ribbed vaults to allow better lighting, large stained-glass windows. **Abbey Church of Saint-Denis** (France), ordered by Abbot Suger, 1135-44 ***Cathedral of Notre-Dame** (Paris, France), ordered by Bishop Maurice de Sully, 1163-1351 ***Cologne Cathedral** (Cologne, Germany), ordered by Archbishop Konrad von Hochstaden, 1248-1880 ***St. Vitus Cathedral** (Prague, Czech Republic), by Matthias of Arras, later Peter Parler, 1344-1929
Yuan and Ming 1279-1644	China. Mongol-influenced timber and some brick structures influenced by geomancy. Emphasized monumental mass in low-lying, sprawling structures with simple rectangular pavilions, great halls, elaborate wooden latticework, carved and painted details. ***Forbidden City** (Beijing, China), ordered by Emperor Yongle, 1406-20
Renaissance 1420s-1520s	Italy. The rebirth or rediscovery of ancient Roman design, grounded in a scholarly approach to architecture. Followed rules of proportion in perspective and symmetry, classical orders, and simple but perfected geometric forms; emphasis on human scale. ***Pazzi Chapel** (Florence, Italy), by Filippo Brunelleschi, 1429-61 ***Palazzo Medici-Riccardi** (Florence, Italy), by Michelozzo di Bartolomeo, 1444-60 ***Tempietto San Pietro** (Rome, Italy), by Donato Bramante, 1502-10 ***Villa Almerico Capra, or La Rotonda** (near Vicenza, Italy), by Andrea Palladio, later Vincenzo Scamozzi, 1566-1610

Style and period	Location; characteristics; significant examples
Mughal 1526-1858	India. Monumental palaces and mosques blending Hindu and Islamic architecture. Sandstone with marble inlay; highly decorative, with semiprecious stones, vegetal and Koranic motifs. Formulaic four-part pleasure gardens (*charbâgh*), exemplified by grounds of Taj Mahal. ***Humayun's Tomb** (Delhi, India), by Sayyid Muhammad, 1562-72 ***Taj Mahal** (Agra, India), ordered by Emperor Shah Jahan, 1631-48
Baroque 1630s-1700s	Italy, later Western Europe. Elaborate and theatrical religious and civic structures, focused on dramatic overall effect. Complex geometric shapes and elaborate sculptures meant to be viewed from many angles. **St. Carlo alle Quattro Fontane** (Rome, Italy), by Francesco Borromini, 1638-41 ***Palace of Versailles** (Versailles, France), royal hunting lodge (built 1631-34) expanded under Louis XIV, 1661-1710 **Church of San Lorenzo** (Turin, Italy), by Guarino Guarini, 1666-79 **Church of St. John of Nepomuk, or Asamkirche** (Munich, Germany), by Cosmas Damian and Egid Quirin Asam, 1733-46
Rococo 1690s-1700s	Europe. Mostly interior, simplified but still fanciful Baroque designs; ornate with natural motifs, gold trim, light and creamy colors, asymmetrical designs, and unusual materials. ***Sanssouci Palace** (Potsdam, Germany), by Georg Wenzeslaus von Knobelsdorff, 1745-47
Neoclassicism 1750-1830	Europe, Americas. Civic, commercial, and religious structures; chaste, non-decorative designs in reaction to Baroque excess. Grounded in Enlightenment-era principles and simple, strict adherence to classic (Greek, Roman, Renaissance) forms and details. Palladian style in England, Federal style in U.S. **Chiswick House** (Chiswick, England, UK), by Richard Boyle, 1725-29 ***Monticello** (Charlottesville, VA), by Thomas Jefferson, 1768-1809
Neo-Gothic 1837-1900s	Britain, U.S. Civic, commercial, and religious structures utilizing Gothic forms in new commercial enterprises like railway stations and hotels. Traditional masonry façade disguised modern structural material like iron and glass. ***Westminster Palace** (London, England, UK), by Charles Barry and A.W.N. Pugin, 1840-47 **Hotel fronting St. Pancras Railway Station** (London, England, UK), by George Gilbert Scott, 1865-71
Arts and Crafts 1850s-1930s	England, U.S. Residential structures made of brick and other indigenous materials with pastoral and traditional elements like gabled roofs. Conceived as a reaction against homogenization of style following the Industrial Revolution. **Red House** (Bexley Heath, England, UK), by Philip Webb, 1859 **Tigbourne Court** (Surrey, England, UK), by Edwin Lutyens, 1898
Beaux-Arts 1870s-1930s	France, U.S. Grandiose, highly decorative style, using a mix of classical forms taught at the École des Beaux-Arts (School of Fine Arts) in Paris: columns, wall projections, elaborate rooftops, high-relief decoration. **Boston Public Library** (Boston, MA), by McKim, Mead, and White, 1888-95 **Grand Central Terminal** (New York, NY), by Reed & Stem and Warren & Wetmore, 1903-13
Art Nouveau 1884-1905	Europe (esp. Brussels, Belgium; France). Civic and residential structures using industrial products like metal and glass to mimic natural forms; airy, fluid, and ornate. ***Hôtel Tassel** (Brussels, Belgium), by Victor Horta, 1892-93 **Entrances to Métro (subway)** (Paris, France), by Hector Guimard, 1900
Prairie 1893-1917	U.S. Mostly residences, some civic buildings in adapted Arts and Crafts style. Inspired by American Midwest and small-town values. Frank Lloyd Wright most notable architect of the style. Buildings centered on chimney, with overhanging eaves and horizontal emphasis, long bands of windows. **Robie House** (Chicago, IL), by Frank Lloyd Wright, 1908-10 **National Farmer's Bank** (Owatonna, MN), by Louis Sullivan, 1906-08
Futurism 1913-14	Italy. Purely theoretical style that produced no actual structures. Emphasized concrete, glass, and steel construction; pure geometric forms and straight lines; and exposed structure and utilities. **La Città Nuova (The New City)** (sketches), by Antonio Sant'Elia, 1913
Constructivism 1914-20s	Russia, Europe. Public buildings based on socialist philosophies. Purely utilitarian industrial design, modern materials. **Rusakov Club** (Moscow, Russia), by Konstantin Melnikov, 1927-28
De Stijl 1917-31	Netherlands. Building and fixtures designed as a complete, sculpture-like piece of art; emphasis on primary colors, simple but asymmetrical geometry. Name is Dutch for "The Style." ***Schröder House** (Utrecht, Netherlands), by Gerrit Thomas Rietveld, 1924
Bauhaus 1919-33	Weimar Republic Germany. Art and design school founded by Walter Gropius with philosophy that the machine is the modern medium. Concrete, glass, and steel construction that united industrial crafts and fine arts with simple geometric forms and colors. ***Bauhaus** (Dessau, Germany), by Walter Gropius, 1925-26
International Style 1920s-70s	Asia, Europe, North America. Reinforced concrete and steel structures, mostly commercial buildings with some residences and civic structures. Post-and-slab construction meant walls no longer supported weight so façades could be continuous strip (ribbon) glass "curtain-walls" with modular interiors. Emphasis on simple forms; glass, marble, and stainless steel; minimal decoration. **Philadelphia Savings Fund Society Building** (Philadelphia, PA), by George Howe and William Lescaze, 1926-32 **Villa Savoye** (Poissy, France), by Le Corbusier, 1928-31 **Seagram Building** (New York, NY), by Ludwig Mies Van Der Rohe with Philip Johnson, 1954-58
Art Deco 1925-30s	Europe, U.S. Traditional, symmetric, elegant construction like Beaux-Arts whimsically mixed with modern styles like geometric forms and steel or chrome features. **Chrysler Building** (New York, NY), by William van Alen, 1928-30 **Empire State Building** (New York, NY), by Shreve, Lamb & Harmon, 1930-31
Postmodernism 1970s-present	Asia, Europe, North America. Playful reaction against generic, mainstream "orthodox modern architecture," according to Robert Venturi. Token references to traditional architectural elements like pediments or gables on houses; aim to present, Venturi wrote, "old clichés in new settings." **Vanna Venturi House** (Philadelphia, PA), by Robert Venturi, 1962 **Public Service Building** (Portland, OR), by Michael Graves, 1980-82

World Population Growth

The global population in ancient times can only be very roughly estimated, but there were perhaps 50 mil people in the world in 1000 BCE. The United Nations (UN) Population Division estimates a figure of 300 mil for 1 CE. This diagram shows estimated population growth since then.

Although different sources may provide varying estimates, they agree that the world's population began growing more rapidly in the 18th and 19th centuries and increased at an even greater rate in the 20th century. According to the UN, the total population reached 1 bil in 1804; rose to 2 bil 123 years later, in 1927; to 3 bil 33 years after that, in 1960; to 4 bil in 1974; to 5 bil in 1987; and to 6 bil in 1999.

The U.S. Census Bureau, which also issues estimates and projections, put the world population in mid-2016 at about 7.3 bil. It projects that the population will reach 8 bil by 2025.

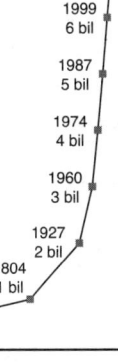

2011 7 bil
1999 6 bil
1987 5 bil
1974 4 bil
1960 3 bil
1927 2 bil
1804 1 bil
1500 500 mil
1250 400 mil
1 CE 300 mil

Area and Population of the World by Continent/Region

Source: International Data Base, International Programs Center, U.S. Census Bureau, U.S. Dept. of Commerce; *The World Factbook*, Central Intelligence Agency (CIA)

Continent/region	Land area (sq mi)	Land area (sq km)	% of Earth's land	1950	1975	2000	2016	% of world total, 2016	2025[1]
Asia	11,921,254	30,875,906	21.2	1,437,565,483	2,413,723,561	3,693,777,378	4,384,209,336	59.8	4,714,839,381
Africa	11,494,762	29,771,296	20.4	229,058,740	416,195,934	802,705,164	1,183,597,992	16.1	1,442,127,980
Europe[2]	8,559,255	22,168,368	15.2	547,140,324	678,635,710	730,523,121	746,610,224	10.2	750,004,442
N. America	7,879,373	20,407,482	14.0	165,945,185	238,783,486	313,388,332	359,492,293	4.9	385,028,748
Latin America[3]	7,762,306	20,104,280	13.8	165,442,794	320,629,690	517,756,498	623,286,710	8.5	673,313,198
Oceania	3,278,295	8,490,744	5.8	12,476,128	21,114,852	30,420,890	37,575,059	0.5	41,266,804
Antarctica[4]	5,405,430	14,000,000	9.6	NA	NA	NA	NA	NA	NA
World	56,300,674	145,818,075	100.0	2,557,628,654	4,089,083,233	6,088,571,383	7,334,771,614	100.0	8,006,580,553

NA = Not applicable. **Note:** Composition of geographical (continental) regions are as defined by the United Nations. Figures may not add up to totals due to rounding. (1) Projected. (2) Includes all of Russia. (3) Includes the Caribbean. (4) Antarctica has no indigenous inhabitants, though people are present at permanent and seasonal research stations.

Population of the World's Largest Urban Areas

Source: *World Urbanization Prospects: The 2014 Revision*, Dept. of Economic and Social Affairs, UN Population Division

Population figures are midyear estimates for urban agglomerations, i.e., whole metropolitan areas comprising an urban center and surrounding settlements of lower density. The UN releases an update every two years. Population counts for 2016 and 2030 are projections. Data may differ from figures elsewhere in *The World Almanac*. MMA = Major Metropolitan Area.

(ranked by mid-2016 population)

Rank	Urban area, country	1975	2000	2016	2030	1975-2000	2000-16	2016-30	Pop. of urban area as % of country's 2016 pop.
1.	Tokyo, Japan	26,615	34,450	38,140	37,190	29.4%	10.7%	-2.5%	30.1%
2.	Delhi, India	4,426	15,732	26,454	36,060	255.4	68.2	36.3	2.0
3.	Shanghai, China	5,627	13,959	24,484	30,751	148.1	75.4	25.6	1.7
4.	Mumbai (Bombay), India	7,082	16,367	21,357	27,797	131.1	30.5	30.2	1.6
5.	São Paulo, Brazil	9,614	17,014	21,297	23,444	77.0	25.2	10.1	10.4
6.	Beijing, China	4,828	10,162	21,240	27,706	110.5	109.0	30.4	1.5
7.	Mexico City, Mexico	10,734	18,457	21,157	23,865	71.9	14.6	12.8	16.7
8.	Kinki MMA (Osaka), Japan	16,298	18,660	20,337	19,976	14.5	9.0	-1.8	16.1
9.	Cairo, Egypt	6,450	13,626	19,128	24,502	111.3	40.4	28.1	22.2
10.	New York-Newark, NY-NJ, U.S.	15,880	17,813	18,604	19,885	12.2	4.4	6.9	5.7
11.	Dhaka, Bangladesh	2,221	10,285	18,237	27,374	363.1	77.3	50.1	11.2
12.	Karachi, Pakistan	3,989	10,032	17,121	24,838	151.5	70.7	45.1	9.0
13.	Buenos Aires, Argentina	8,745	12,407	15,334	16,956	41.9	23.6	10.6	36.1
14.	Kolkata (Calcutta), India	7,888	13,058	14,980	19,092	65.5	14.7	27.4	1.2
15.	Istanbul, Turkey	3,600	8,744	14,365	16,694	142.9	64.3	16.2	18.5
16.	Chongqing, China	2,545	7,863	13,744	17,380	209.0	74.8	26.5	1.0
17.	Lagos, Nigeria	1,890	7,281	13,661	24,239	285.2	87.6	77.4	7.2
18.	Manila, Philippines	4,999	9,962	13,131	16,756	99.3	31.8	27.6	12.7
19.	Guangzhou, Guangdong, China	1,698	7,330	13,070	17,574	331.7	78.3	34.5	0.9
20.	Rio de Janeiro, Brazil	7,733	11,307	12,981	14,174	46.2	14.8	9.2	6.3
21.	Los Angeles-Long Beach-Santa Ana, CA, U.S.	8,926	11,798	12,317	13,257	32.2	4.4	7.6	3.8
22.	Moscow, Russia	7,623	10,005	12,260	12,200	31.2	22.5	-0.5	8.7
23.	Kinshasa, Dem. Rep. of Congo	1,482	6,140	12,071	19,996	314.3	96.6	65.7	16.5
24.	Tianjin, China	3,527	6,670	11,558	14,655	89.1	73.3	26.8	0.8
25.	Paris, France	8,558	9,737	10,925	11,803	13.8	12.2	8.0	16.7
26.	Shenzhen, China	36	6,550	10,828	12,673	18,094.4	65.3	17.0	0.8
27.	Jakarta, Indonesia	4,813	8,390	10,483	13,812	74.3	24.9	31.8	4.1
28.	Bangalore, India	2,111	5,567	10,456	14,762	163.7	87.8	41.2	0.8
29.	London, UK	7,546	8,613	10,434	11,467	14.1	21.1	9.9	16.3
30.	Chennai (Madras), India	3,609	6,353	10,163	13,921	76.0	60.0	37.0	0.8

National Rankings by Population, Area, Population Density, 2016

Source: International Data Base, International Programs Center, U.S. Census Bureau, U.S. Dept. of Commerce; *The World Factbook*, Central Intelligence Agency (CIA)

Population figures are for midyear. The world had an estimated population of 7.3 bil in mid-2016. China was the most populous nation, with nearly one-fifth of the world total. A country's land area does not include inland water. Refer to Nations of the World for a country's total area. Population density is calculated using land area.

Largest Populations

Rank	Country	Population
1.	China[1]	1,373,541,278
2.	India	1,266,883,598
3.	United States	323,995,528
4.	Indonesia	258,316,051
5.	Brazil	205,823,665
6.	Pakistan	201,995,540
7.	Nigeria	186,053,386
8.	Bangladesh	171,696,855
9.	Russia	142,355,415
10.	Japan	126,702,133

Smallest Populations

Rank	Country	Population
1.	Vatican City[2]	1,000
2.	Nauru	9,591
3.	Tuvalu	10,959
4.	Palau	21,347
5.	Monaco	30,581
6.	San Marino	33,285
7.	Liechtenstein	37,937
8.	Saint Kitts and Nevis	52,329
9.	Marshall Islands	73,376
10.	Dominica	73,757

Largest Land Areas

Rank	Country	Area (sq mi)	Area (sq km)
1.	Russia	6,323,482	16,377,742
2.	China	3,600,947	9,326,410
3.	United States	3,531,905	9,147,593
4.	Canada	3,511,023	9,093,507
5.	Brazil	3,266,199	8,459,417
6.	Australia	2,966,153	7,682,300
7.	India	1,147,956	2,973,193
8.	Argentina	1,056,642	2,736,690
9.	Kazakhstan	1,042,360	2,699,700
10.	Algeria	919,595	2,381,741

Smallest Land Areas

Rank	Country	Area (sq mi)	Area (sq km)
1.	Vatican City	0.17	0.44
2.	Monaco	0.77	2
3.	Nauru	8	21
4.	Tuvalu	10	26
5.	San Marino	24	61
6.	Liechtenstein	62	160
7.	Marshall Islands	70	181
8.	Saint Kitts and Nevis	101	261
9.	Maldives	115	298
10.	Malta	122	316

Most Densely Populated

Rank	Country	Persons per sq mi	Persons per sq km
1.	Monaco	39,602.2	15,290.5
2.	Singapore	21,797.1	8,415.9
3.	Vatican City[2]	5,886.3	2,272.7
4.	Bahrain	4,699.1	1,814.3
5.	Bangladesh	3,416.3	1,319.0
6.	Maldives	3,415.3	1,318.7
7.	Malta	3,403.0	1,313.9
8.	Taiwan	1,883.9	727.4
9.	Barbados	1,755.7	677.9
10.	Mauritius	1,720.2	664.2

Least Densely Populated

Rank	Country	Persons per sq mi	Persons per sq km
1.	Mongolia	5.1	2.0
2.	Namibia	7.0	2.7
3.	Australia	7.8	3.0
4.	Iceland	8.7	3.4
5.	Mauritania	9.2	3.6
6.	Guyana	9.7	3.7
7.	Libya	9.6	3.7
8.	Suriname	9.7	3.8
9.	Botswana	10.1	3.9
10.	Canada	10.1	3.9

(1) Does not include mid-2016 population of Hong Kong (7,167,403) and Macao (597,425). (2) Population is for mid-2015.

Current Population and Projections for Countries and Other Areas

Source: International Data Base, International Programs Center, U.S. Census Bureau, U.S. Dept. of Commerce; *The World Factbook*, Central Intelligence Agency (CIA)

(midyear figures)

Country/area	2016	2025	2050	Country/area	2016	2025	2050
Afghanistan	33,332,025	41,117,073	63,795,418	Burundi	11,099,298	14,791,662	30,391,856
Albania	3,038,594	3,104,932	2,824,012	Cabo Verde	553,432	619,168	741,842
Algeria	40,263,711	45,841,317	55,444,735	Cambodia	15,957,223	18,037,946	22,338,891
American Samoa	54,194	53,316	49,308	Cameroon	24,360,803	30,508,842	51,912,309
Andorra	85,660	85,112	74,765	Canada	35,362,905	37,558,781	41,135,648
Angola	20,172,332	25,673,282	45,888,061	Cayman Islands	57,268	67,661	91,118
Anguilla	16,752	19,749	26,980	Central African			
Antigua and				Republic	5,507,257	6,637,613	10,338,863
Barbuda	93,581	103,830	122,930	Chad	11,852,462	13,914,726	20,473,601
Argentina	43,833,328	47,164,630	53,511,279	Chile	17,650,114	18,764,737	19,688,474
Armenia	3,051,250	2,961,175	2,468,311	China	1,373,541,278	1,407,006,788	1,301,627,048
Aruba	113,648	126,130	150,730	Colombia	47,220,856	51,194,904	56,227,630
Australia	22,992,654	25,053,669	29,012,740	Comoros	794,678	905,545	1,169,893
Austria	8,711,770	8,987,330	9,107,912	Congo, Dem.			
Azerbaijan	9,872,765	10,533,598	11,209,644	Rep. of	81,331,050	99,162,003	144,805,434
Bahamas, The	327,316	349,116	371,219	Congo Republic	4,852,412	5,947,999	10,201,971
Bahrain	1,378,904	1,579,899	1,847,072	Cook Islands	9,556	7,621	5,460
Bangladesh	171,696,855	197,673,655	250,155,274	Costa Rica	4,872,543	5,353,218	6,065,989
Barbados	291,495	297,015	282,041	Côte d'Ivoire	23,740,424	27,651,498	37,111,782
Belarus	9,570,376	9,325,020	8,339,664	Croatia	4,458,533	4,374,007	3,864,201
Belgium	11,409,077	12,037,746	12,772,233	Cuba	11,014,425	10,784,894	9,161,479
Belize	353,858	411,007	543,690	Curaçao	149,035	153,501	150,128
Benin	10,741,458	13,564,964	22,118,545	Cyprus	1,205,575	1,329,908	1,392,078
Bermuda	70,537	72,851	69,874	Czech Republic	10,660,932	10,696,842	10,209,638
Bhutan	750,125	820,143	951,873	Denmark	5,593,785	5,697,913	5,575,147
Bolivia	10,969,649	12,463,434	16,003,638	Djibouti	846,687	1,016,919	1,395,810
Bosnia and				Dominica	73,757	74,374	64,772
Herzegovina	3,861,912	3,787,402	3,216,039	Dominican Republic	10,606,865	11,702,846	13,690,264
Botswana	2,209,208	2,425,114	2,871,345	Ecuador	16,080,778	17,867,616	21,102,550
Brazil	205,823,665	218,259,140	232,304,177	Egypt	90,067,793	103,742,157	137,872,522
Brunei	436,620	498,756	638,157	El Salvador	6,156,670	6,288,430	6,181,181
Bulgaria	7,144,653	6,728,056	5,531,820	Equatorial Guinea	759,451	935,553	1,428,139
Burkina Faso	19,512,533	25,384,628	47,429,509	Eritrea	6,674,489	7,987,458	11,381,250

Country/area	2016	2025	2050
Estonia	1,258,545	1,182,920	923,335
Ethiopia	102,374,044	131,260,566	228,066,276
Faroe Islands	50,456	53,200	57,112
Fiji	915,303	956,003	1,013,636
Finland	5,498,211	5,630,882	5,475,753
France	66,836,154	68,860,292	69,484,481
French Polynesia	285,321	305,484	324,712
Gabon	1,738,541	2,063,339	3,229,741
Gambia, The	2,009,648	2,369,298	3,210,223
Gaza Strip	1,921,202	2,350,255	3,392,849
Georgia	4,928,052	4,929,789	4,714,548
Germany	80,722,792	79,226,209	71,541,906
Ghana	26,908,262	32,610,058	52,415,526
Gibraltar	29,328	29,753	28,423
Greece	10,773,253	10,670,697	10,035,935
Greenland	57,728	57,174	49,356
Grenada	111,219	114,741	114,205
Guam	162,742	176,770	201,610
Guatemala	15,189,958	17,564,073	22,995,434
Guernsey	66,297	67,710	66,521
Guinea	12,093,349	15,240,839	26,407,254
Guinea-Bissau	1,759,159	2,061,262	2,894,545
Guyana	735,909	781,231	878,028
Haiti	10,228,410	11,252,370	13,352,710
Honduras	8,893,259	10,143,828	12,948,839
Hong Kong	7,167,403	7,296,877	6,623,263
Hungary	9,874,784	9,615,020	8,489,811
Iceland	335,878	366,578	406,766
India	1,266,883,598	1,396,046,308	1,656,553,632
Indonesia	258,316,051	276,746,433	300,183,166
Iran	82,801,633	90,481,226	100,044,564
Iraq	38,146,025	47,656,612	76,519,418
Ireland	4,952,473	5,417,947	6,333,836
Isle of Man	88,195	92,606	92,840
Israel	8,174,527	9,305,235	12,364,874
Italy	62,007,540	62,591,055	61,415,852
Jamaica	2,970,340	3,151,611	3,554,571
Japan	126,702,133	123,385,521	107,209,536
Jersey	98,069	104,140	107,581
Jordan	8,185,384	8,320,007	11,411,275
Kazakhstan	18,360,353	19,809,426	22,237,156
Kenya	46,790,758	53,196,265	70,755,460
Kiribati	106,925	117,779	139,738
Korea, North	25,115,311	26,242,210	26,969,396
Korea, South	49,180,776	49,372,307	43,368,983
Kosovo	1,883,018	1,999,461	2,222,619
Kuwait	2,832,776	3,169,497	3,863,453
Kyrgyzstan	5,727,553	6,218,713	7,063,351
Laos	7,019,073	7,971,675	10,068,995
Latvia	1,965,686	1,772,796	1,249,812
Lebanon	6,237,738	5,396,843	5,621,049
Lesotho	1,953,070	1,970,540	1,920,225
Liberia	4,299,944	5,283,774	8,192,118
Libya	6,541,948	7,374,566	8,970,664
Liechtenstein	37,937	40,505	43,610
Lithuania	2,854,235	2,573,431	1,801,002
Luxembourg	582,291	680,527	864,238
Macau	597,425	630,434	620,184
Macedonia	2,100,025	2,119,511	1,990,728
Madagascar	24,430,325	30,182,920	45,807,534
Malawi	18,570,321	24,957,849	51,780,996
Malaysia	30,949,962	34,683,300	42,928,546
Maldives	392,960	388,681	444,429
Mali	17,467,108	22,533,811	38,395,414
Malta	415,196	421,239	395,639
Marshall Islands	73,376	83,203	103,092
Mauritania	3,677,293	4,425,089	6,536,272
Mauritius	1,348,242	1,412,384	1,441,100
Mexico	123,166,749	134,828,700	150,567,503
Micronesia	104,719	98,948	74,483
Moldova	3,510,485	3,176,863	2,261,208
Monaco	30,581	31,706	29,810
Mongolia	3,031,330	3,301,176	3,669,264
Montenegro	644,578	635,537	577,654
Montserrat	5,267	5,529	5,707
Morocco	33,655,786	36,484,418	42,026,448
Mozambique	25,930,150	32,306,018	58,998,457
Myanmar (Burma)	56,890,418	61,747,758	70,673,160
Namibia	2,224,786	2,283,845	2,149,815
Nauru	9,591	10,008	11,995
Nepal	32,111,345	36,622,606	45,984,605
Netherlands	17,016,967	17,572,113	17,906,594
New Caledonia	275,355	307,452	370,511
New Zealand	4,474,549	4,775,930	5,198,992
Nicaragua	5,966,798	6,493,913	7,233,620
Niger	18,638,600	24,618,828	44,221,854
Nigeria	186,053,386	230,570,741	391,296,754
Northern Mariana Islands	53,467	61,985	77,842

Country/area	2016	2025	2050
Norway	5,265,158	5,682,068	6,364,008
Oman	3,355,262	3,981,057	5,401,957
Pakistan	201,995,540	228,385,138	290,847,790
Palau	21,347	22,102	22,894
Panama	3,705,246	4,117,882	4,859,334
Papua New Guinea	6,791,317	7,823,210	10,110,027
Paraguay	6,862,812	7,602,853	8,840,105
Peru	30,741,062	33,283,408	36,943,693
Philippines	102,624,209	117,445,897	155,380,252
Poland	38,523,261	37,753,766	32,738,308
Portugal	10,833,816	10,806,202	9,933,334
Puerto Rico	3,578,056	3,476,473	2,984,291
Qatar	2,258,283	2,562,764	2,558,854
Romania	21,599,736	20,872,127	18,060,354
Russia	142,355,415	140,139,049	129,908,086
Rwanda	12,988,423	16,080,729	27,506,207
Saint Barthélemy	7,209	7,056	6,527
Saint Helena	7,813	7,888	7,296
Saint Kitts and Nevis	52,329	55,405	56,362
Saint Lucia	164,464	168,519	162,356
Saint Martin	31,949	33,048	34,601
Saint Pierre and Miquelon	5,595	5,030	3,516
Saint Vincent and the Grenadines	102,350	100,409	93,507
Samoa	198,926	210,369	245,010
San Marino	33,285	35,203	35,178
São Tomé and Príncipe	197,541	227,395	309,457
Saudi Arabia	28,160,273	31,877,311	40,250,628
Senegal	14,320,055	17,580,816	27,244,158
Serbia	7,143,921	6,845,638	5,869,146
Seychelles	93,186	98,843	100,391
Sierra Leone	6,018,888	7,500,140	13,593,862
Singapore	5,781,728	6,732,999	8,609,518
Sint Maarten	41,486	46,560	53,001
Slovakia	5,445,802	5,405,646	4,850,540
Slovenia	1,978,029	1,907,560	1,596,947
Solomon Islands	635,027	747,001	1,015,731
Somalia	10,817,354	13,274,251	22,626,120
South Africa	54,300,704	59,108,375	68,528,850
South Sudan	12,530,717	16,615,122	26,843,710
Spain	48,563,476	51,415,437	52,490,640
Sri Lanka	22,235,000	23,563,343	25,166,733
Sudan	36,729,501	42,733,103	59,129,521
Suriname	585,824	636,782	717,936
Swaziland	1,451,428	1,585,439	1,834,151
Sweden	9,880,604	10,587,441	12,011,256
Switzerland	8,179,294	8,665,531	9,539,097
Syria	17,185,170	24,537,876	31,225,740
Taiwan	23,464,787	23,642,264	20,834,040
Tajikistan	8,330,946	9,510,130	12,132,365
Tanzania	52,482,726	66,904,889	118,586,412
Thailand	68,200,824	69,588,429	66,063,997
Timor-Leste	1,261,072	1,539,173	2,191,749
Togo	7,756,937	9,741,450	16,583,950
Tonga	106,513	104,648	78,995
Trinidad and Tobago	1,220,479	1,183,838	1,023,741
Tunisia	11,134,588	11,849,537	12,180,271
Turkey	80,274,604	84,544,177	89,290,126
Turkmenistan	5,291,317	5,800,391	6,607,083
Turks and Caicos Islands	51,430	61,293	84,240
Tuvalu	10,959	11,819	13,423
Uganda	38,319,241	50,692,201	93,476,229
Ukraine	44,209,733	42,887,993	37,148,031
United Arab Emirates	5,927,482	7,063,346	8,018,904
United Kingdom	64,430,428	67,243,723	71,153,797
United States	323,995,528	347,334,912	398,328,349
Uruguay	3,351,016	3,431,610	3,495,238
Uzbekistan	29,473,614	31,823,964	35,116,374
Vanuatu	277,554	323,464	432,658
Vatican City[1]	1,000	NA	NA
Venezuela	29,680,303	33,188,608	40,255,592
Vietnam	95,261,021	102,458,828	111,173,583
Virgin Islands, British	34,232	41,324	59,618
Virgin Islands, U.S.	102,951	95,902	68,933
Wallis and Futuna	15,664	16,023	15,598
West Bank	2,839,777	3,328,248	4,376,251
Western Sahara	587,020	735,697	1,173,350
Yemen	27,392,779	32,822,216	46,080,625
Zambia	15,510,711	20,104,997	38,992,619
Zimbabwe	14,546,961	17,370,260	25,198,196
World[2]	7,334,771,614	8,006,580,553	9,408,141,302

NA = Not available. **Note:** Figures for countries do not include the population of any dependencies listed separately in this table. For example, China's population estimate and projections do not include Hong Kong or Macao. (1) Current pop. is as of 2015. (2) Total projected populations do not include countries for which projections were not available.

Countries Ranked by Gross Domestic Product and Per Capita GDP, 2015

Source: *The World Factbook*, Central Intelligence Agency (CIA)

Estimates of gross domestic product (GDP)—the value of all final goods and services that a country produced in a year—were made based on purchasing power parity exchange rates. Per capita GDP is calculated using the estimated population size as of July 1 in a given year. Data may differ from estimates made by the U.S. Bureau of Economic Analysis. GDP figures are for 2015 unless otherwise noted.

GDP (in mil)					Per capita GDP			
Highest		**Lowest**			**Highest**		**Lowest**	
1. China[1]	$19,390,000	1. Tuvalu	$37		1. Qatar	$132,100	1. Somalia[5]	$400
2. U.S.	17,950,000	2. Nauru	151		2. Luxembourg	99,000	2. Central African Republic	600
3. India	7,965,000	3. Marshall Islands	175		3. Liechtenstein[3]	89,400	3. Congo, Dem. Rep. of	800
4. Japan	4,830,000	4. Kiribati	203		4. Singapore	85,300	Burundi	800
5. Germany	3,841,000	5. Palau	272		5. Brunei	79,700	5. Liberia	900
6. Russia	3,718,000	6. Micronesia[2]	306		6. Monaco[4]	78,700	6. Malawi	1,100
7. Brazil	3,192,000	7. Tonga	526		7. Kuwait	70,200	Niger	1,100
8. Indonesia	2,842,000	8. São Tomé and Príncipe	658		8. Norway	68,400	8. Guinea	1,200
9. UK	2,679,000	9. Vanuatu	685		9. UAE	67,600	Mozambique	1,200
10. France	2,647,000	10. Dominica	763		10. Australia	65,400	10. Eritrea	1,300
11. Mexico	2,227,000	11. Samoa	1,000		11. San Marino	63,900	11. Comoros	1,500
12. Italy	2,171,000	12. Solomon Islands	1,146		12. Switzerland	58,600	Madagascar	1,500
13. South Korea	1,849,000	13. St. Vincent and the Grenadines	1,205		13. U.S.	55,800	Guinea-Bissau	1,500
14. Saudi Arabia	1,683,000	14. Comoros	1,214		14. Ireland	55,500	Togo	1,500
15. Canada	1,632,000	15. St. Kitts and Nevis	1,379		15. Saudi Arabia	53,600	15. Sierra Leone	1,600
16. Spain	1,615,000	16. Grenada	1,401		16. Bahrain	50,100	The Gambia	1,600
17. Turkey	1,589,000	17. San Marino	1,982		17. Netherlands	49,200	17. Burkina Faso	1,700
18. Australia	1,489,000	18. St. Lucia	2,030		18. Sweden	47,900	18. Haiti	1,800
19. Iran	1,371,000	19. Antigua and Barbuda	2,097		19. Austria	47,300	North Korea[5]	1,800
20. Thailand	1,108,000	20. Seychelles	2,417		20. Germany	46,900	Kiribati	1,800
							Ethiopia	1,800
							Rwanda	1,800

(1) Does not include Hong Kong ($414.6 bil GDP) or Macao ($65.4 bil GDP). (2) Supplemented by grant aid, averaging about $100 mil annually. (3) 2009 est. (4) 2013 est. (5) 2014 est.

Budget Deficits as Percent of GDP in Selected Countries, 1998-2016

Source: *OECD Economic Outlook*, Organisation for Economic Co-operation and Development (OECD)

Country	1998	2000	2005	2010	2011	2012	2013	2014	2015	2016
Australia	2.5%	1.5%	2.2%	−4.6%	−3.5%	−3.0%	−2.0%	−2.3%	−1.7%	−1.4%
Austria	−2.7	−2.0	−2.5	−4.5	−2.6	−2.2	−1.3	−2.7	−1.2	−1.6
Belgium	−0.9	−0.1	−2.6	−4.0	−4.1	−4.2	−3.0	−3.1	−2.6	−2.9
Brazil*	NA	−3.3	−3.5	−2.4	−2.5	−2.3	−3.0	−6.0	−10.4	−10.0
Canada	0.1	2.6	1.6	−4.7	−3.3	−2.5	−1.9	−0.5	−1.7	−2.2
China*	−1.5	−2.8	−0.9	−0.7	−0.1	0.1	−0.5	−0.6	−1.3	−1.8
Czech Republic	−4.6	−3.5	−3.1	−4.4	−2.7	−3.9	−1.3	−1.9	−0.4	−0.5
Denmark	−0.4	1.9	5.0	−2.7	−2.1	−3.5	−1.1	1.5	−2.1	−2.5
Estonia	−0.8	−0.1	1.1	0.2	1.2	−0.3	−0.2	0.8	0.4	−0.4
Finland	1.6	6.9	2.6	−2.6	−1.0	−2.2	−2.6	−3.2	−2.7	−2.4
France	−2.4	−1.3	−3.2	−6.8	−5.1	−4.8	−4.0	−4.0	−3.5	−3.4
Germany	−2.5	0.9	−3.4	−4.2	−1.0	−0.1	−0.1	0.3	0.7	0.3
Greece	−6.3	−4.1	−6.2	−11.2	−10.2	−8.8	−13.1	−3.7	−7.3	−1.9
Hungary	−7.4	−3.0	−7.8	−4.5	−5.4	−2.3	−2.6	−2.3	−2.0	−1.9
Iceland	−0.6	1.2	4.5	−9.8	−5.6	−3.7	−1.8	−0.1	−0.4	0.3
India*	−9.0	−9.5	−6.7	−7.1	−7.8	−6.9	−6.6	−6.9	−6.4	−6.1
Indonesia*	−1.4	−1.1	−0.5	−0.7	−1.1	−2.1	−2.4	−2.5	−2.3	−2.5
Ireland	2.0	4.9	1.6	−32.3	−12.6	−8.0	−5.7	−3.8	−2.3	−0.7
Israel	−6.9	−3.4	−4.2	−4.1	−3.4	−5.0	−4.2	−3.5	−2.9	−3.8
Italy	−3.0	−1.3	−4.2	−4.2	−3.5	−2.9	−2.9	−3.0	−2.6	−2.3
Japan	−10.3	−7.5	−4.8	−8.3	−8.8	−8.7	−8.5	−6.2	−5.4	−5.1
Korea, South	0.6	4.4	1.6	1.0	1.0	1.0	1.3	1.3	0.8	1.1
Latvia	0.0	−2.7	−0.4	−8.5	−3.4	−0.8	−0.9	−1.6	−1.3	−1.0
Lithuania*	−3.0	−3.2	−0.3	−6.9	−8.9	−3.1	−2.6	−0.7	−0.2	−0.8
Luxembourg	3.2	5.9	0.1	−0.7	0.5	0.3	0.8	1.7	1.2	1.3
Netherlands	−0.9	1.9	−0.3	−5.0	−4.3	−3.9	−2.4	−2.4	−1.8	−1.6
New Zealand	0.0	1.7	4.6	−7.1	−4.0	−2.1	−0.8	−0.1	−0.4	−0.2
Norway	3.3	15.1	14.8	11.0	13.4	13.8	10.8	8.7	5.7	3.2
Poland	−4.2	−3.0	−4.0	−7.5	−4.9	−3.7	−4.0	−3.3	−2.6	−2.6
Portugal	−4.4	−3.2	−6.2	−11.2	−7.4	−5.7	−4.8	−7.2	−4.4	−2.9
Russia*	NA	NA	5.6	−1.1	3.5	2.3	0.3	0.2	−3.6	−4.2
Slovakia	−5.2	−12.0	−2.9	−7.5	−4.1	−4.3	−2.7	−2.7	−3.0	−2.3
Slovenia	−2.3	−3.6	−1.3	−5.6	−6.7	−4.1	−15.0	−5.0	−2.9	−2.2
South Africa*	−5.3	−4.1	−2.4	−3.1	−3.0	−3.2	−3.3	−4.1	−3.9	−3.3
Spain	−2.9	−1.0	1.2	−9.4	−9.6	−10.4	−6.9	−5.9	−5.1	−3.7
Sweden	0.9	3.2	1.8	0.0	−0.1	−0.9	−1.4	−1.6	0.0	0.2
Switzerland	−1.9	−0.4	−1.2	0.3	0.8	0.2	−0.3	−0.2	−0.2	−0.4
United Kingdom	−0.2	1.1	−3.5	−9.7	−7.7	−8.3	−5.7	−5.6	−4.4	−3.8
United States	−0.4	0.8	−4.2	−12.2	−10.8	−9.0	−5.5	−5.1	−4.4	−4.3
OECD countries	−2.3	−0.4	−2.8	−7.9	−6.6	−5.8	−4.1	−3.6	−3.1	−2.9

* = Not an OECD member nation; excluded from OECD country total. NA = Not available. **Note:** 2015-16 figures are estimates.

Gold Reserves of Selected Central Banks and Governments, 1975-2015

Source: *International Financial Statistics*, International Monetary Fund (IMF)

(in mil fine troy ounces)

Year end	All countries	Canada	China[1]	France	Germany[2]	India	Italy	Japan	Nether-lands	Russia	Switzer-land	UK	U.S.
1975	1,179.1	22.0	NA	100.9	117.6	7.0	82.5	21.1	54.3	NA	83.2	21.0	274.7
1980	1,152.2	21.0	12.8	81.9	95.2	8.6	66.7	24.2	43.9	NA	83.3	18.8	264.3
1985	1,147.4	20.1	12.7	81.9	95.2	9.4	66.7	24.2	43.9	NA	83.3	19.0	262.7
1990	1,144.2	14.8	12.7	81.9	95.2	10.7	66.7	24.2	43.9	NA	83.3	18.9	261.9
1995	1,114.4	3.4	12.7	81.9	95.2	12.8	66.7	24.2	34.8	9.4	83.3	18.4	261.7
2000	1,066.0	1.2	12.7	97.2	111.5	11.5	78.8	24.5	29.3	12.4	77.8	15.7	261.6
2003	1,027.4	0.1	19.3	97.2	110.6	11.5	78.8	24.6	25.0	12.5	52.5	10.1	261.5
2004	1,010.7	0.1	19.3	96.0	110.4	11.5	78.8	24.6	25.0	12.4	43.5	10.0	261.6
2005	991.3	0.1	19.3	90.9	110.2	11.5	78.8	24.6	22.3	12.4	41.5	10.0	261.6
2006	979.6	0.1	19.3	87.4	110.0	11.5	78.8	24.6	20.6	12.9	41.5	10.0	261.5
2007	963.3	0.1	19.3	83.7	109.9	11.5	78.8	24.6	20.0	14.5	36.8	10.0	261.5
2008	963.9	0.1	19.3	80.1	109.7	11.5	78.8	24.6	19.7	16.7	33.4	10.0	261.5
2009	980.8	0.1	33.9	78.3	109.5	17.9	78.8	24.6	19.7	20.9	33.4	10.0	261.5
2010	991.5	0.1	33.9	78.3	109.3	17.9	78.8	24.6	19.7	25.4	33.4	10.0	261.5
2011	1,003.3	0.1	33.9	78.3	109.2	17.9	78.8	24.6	19.7	28.4	33.4	10.0	261.5
2012	1,018.6	0.1	33.9	78.3	109.0	17.9	78.8	24.6	19.7	30.8	33.4	10.0	261.5
2013	1,024.1	0.1	33.9	78.3	108.9	17.9	78.8	24.6	19.7	33.3	33.4	10.0	261.5
2014	1,029.8	0.1	33.9	78.3	108.8	17.9	78.8	24.6	19.7	38.8	33.4	10.0	261.5
2015	1,052.4	0.1	56.7	78.3	108.7	17.9	78.8	24.6	19.7	45.5	33.4	10.0	261.5

NA = Not available. (1) Figures are for mainland China only and do not include Hong Kong (0.07 mil oz t in 2015) or Macao. (2) West Germany prior to 1991.

Unemployment Rates in Selected Countries, 1970-2015

Source: *OECD Economic Outlook*, Organisation for Economic Co-operation and Development (OECD)

Year	U.S.	Australia	Canada	France	Germany	Italy	Japan	Netherlands	Sweden	UK
1970	5.0%	1.6%	5.7%	2.0%	NA	3.8%	1.2%	1.1%	2.0%	3.5%
1975	8.5	4.9	6.9	3.3	NA	4.1	1.9	4.6	2.1	4.5
1980	7.2	6.1	7.5	5.1	NA	5.4	2.0	4.8	2.6	6.8
1985	7.2	8.3	10.6	8.5	NA	8.3	2.6	10.6	3.6	11.4
1990	5.6	6.9	8.2	7.6	NA	8.8	2.1	6.9	2.1	7.1
1995	5.6	8.5	9.5	9.6	8.2%	11.2	3.1	8.2	10.5	8.6
1997	4.9	8.4	9.1	10.3	9.6	11.3	3.4	6.3	11.7	7.0
2000	4.0	6.3	6.8	8.2	7.9	10.0	4.7	3.6	6.7	5.5
2001	4.8	6.7	7.2	7.4	7.8	9.0	5.0	3.0	5.8	5.1
2002	5.8	6.4	7.7	7.5	8.6	8.5	5.4	3.6	6.0	5.2
2003	6.0	5.9	7.6	8.1	9.7	8.4	5.3	4.8	6.6	5.0
2004	5.5	5.4	7.2	8.5	10.3	8.0	4.7	5.7	7.4	4.8
2005	5.1	5.0	6.8	8.5	11.0	7.7	4.4	5.9	7.7	4.8
2006	4.6	4.8	6.3	8.5	10.0	6.8	4.1	5.0	7.1	5.4
2007	4.6	4.4	6.0	7.7	8.6	6.1	3.8	4.2	6.1	5.3
2008	5.8	4.2	6.1	7.1	7.4	6.7	4.0	3.7	6.2	5.7
2009	9.3	5.6	8.3	8.7	7.7	7.7	5.0	4.4	8.3	7.6
2010	9.6	5.2	8.0	8.9	7.0	8.3	5.0	5.0	8.6	7.9
2011	8.9	5.1	7.5	8.8	5.9	8.4	4.6	5.0	7.8	8.1
2012	8.1	5.2	7.3	9.4	5.4	10.7	4.3	5.8	8.0	8.0
2013	7.4	5.7	7.1	9.9	5.2	12.1	4.0	7.3	8.0	7.6
2014	6.2	6.1	6.9	9.9	5.0	12.6	3.6	7.4	7.9	6.2
2015	5.3	6.1	6.9	10.0	4.6	11.9	3.4	6.9	7.4	5.4

NA = Not available. **Note:** Labor market data are subject to differences in definitions across countries. Because of changes in methodology, some data may not be fully comparable over time.

Personal Tax Payments in Selected Countries, 2015

Source: *Taxing Wages*, Organisation for Economic Co-operation and Development (OECD)

Rates are averages for a single person without children at the income level of the average worker.

(as % of total gross earnings before taxes in U.S. dollars with equal purchasing power; ranked by total payment rate)

Country	Total payment rate[1]	Income tax	Employee soc. sec. contribs.	Gross earnings	Country	Total payment rate[1]	Income tax	Employee soc. sec. contribs.	Gross earnings
Belgium........	42.0%	28.1%	14.0%	$57,166	Australia	24.1%	24.1%	0.0%	$55,921
Germany.......	39.7	19.2	20.5	59,987	Poland.........	23.7	5.9	17.8	25,637
Denmark.......	36.1	36.1	0.0	54,013	United Kingdom	23.4	14.1	9.3	51,431
Austria	34.9	16.8	18.1	53,565	Canada	23.4	15.8	7.6	41,719
Hungary	34.5	16.0	18.5	24,308	Czech Republic	23.3	12.3	11.0	24,482
Slovenia	33.3	11.2	22.1	30,660	Slovakia	23.0	9.6	13.4	21,764
Italy...........	32.6	23.1	9.5	41,250	Japan	22.0	7.7	14.3	47,205
Finland........	30.9	22.7	8.3	47,503	Spain	21.5	15.1	6.4	39,529
Luxembourg	30.7	17.9	12.8	60,812	Ireland.........	19.7	15.7	4.0	41,054
Netherlands	29.9	16.7	13.3	60,867	Estonia	18.4	16.8	1.6	24,010
Iceland........	29.1	28.7	0.4	51,181	New Zealand ...	17.6	17.6	0.0	39,493
France.........	28.9	14.7	14.2	46,103	Switzerland.....	17.4	11.1	6.3	69,887
Norway	28.4	20.2	8.2	60,203	Israel..........	17.3	9.4	7.9	34,241
Portugal.......	28.3	17.3	11.0	29,692	South Korea	13.8	5.4	8.4	47,286
Turkey.........	27.5	12.5	15.0	25,926	Mexico	10.3	8.9	1.4	12,865
United States ...	25.6	18.0	7.7	50,964	Chile	7.0	0.0	7.0	19,338
Sweden........	24.7	17.7	7.0	46,678	**OECD**				
Greece	24.3	8.8	15.5	34,266	**countries[2] ...**	**25.5**	**15.7**	**9.8**	**42,088**

(1) Figures may not add up to totals due to rounding. (2) The 34 countries shown here.

Consumer Price Changes in Selected Countries, 1975-2015

Source: *International Financial Statistics*, International Monetary Fund (IMF)

(annual average % change)

Country	1975-80	1980-85	1985-90	1990-95	1995-2000	2000-05	2008-09	2009-10	2010-11	2011-12	2012-13	2013-14	2014-15
Canada.............	8.7%	7.5%	4.5%	2.3%	1.7%	2.3%	0.3%	1.8%	2.9%	1.5%	0.9%	1.9%	1.1%
China[1].............	NA	NA	NA	13.1	1.8	1.4	−0.7	3.3	5.4	2.6	2.6	2.0	1.4
France	10.5	9.7	3.1	2.2	1.2	1.9	0.1	1.5	2.1	2.0	0.9	0.5	0.04
Germany............	NA	NA	NA	2.8	1.3	1.5	0.3	1.1	2.1	2.0	1.5	0.9	0.2
Italy................	16.4	13.8	5.7	5.0	2.4	2.4	0.8	1.5	2.7	3.0	1.2	0.2	0.04
Japan	6.6	2.8	1.3	1.4	0.3	−0.4	−1.3	−0.7	−0.3	−0.03	0.4	2.7	0.8
Spain	18.6	12.2	6.5	5.2	2.6	3.2	−0.3	1.8	3.2	2.4	1.4	−0.1	−0.5
Sweden.............	10.5	9.0	6.2	4.2	0.5	1.5	−0.5	1.2	3.0	0.9	−0.04	−0.2	−0.05
Switzerland..........	2.3	4.3	2.5	3.2	0.7	0.8	−0.5	0.7	0.2	−0.7	−0.2	−0.01	−1.1
United Kingdom	NA	NA	NA	3.8	1.6	1.4	2.2	3.3	4.5	2.8	2.6	1.5	0.1
United States	8.9	5.5	4.0	3.1	2.5	2.6	−0.4	1.6	3.2	2.1	1.5	1.6	0.1
All countries	**11.3**	**15.0**	**16.1**	**19.2**	**6.0**	**3.7**	**2.4**	**3.6**	**4.8**	**3.8**	**3.6**	**3.2**	**2.8**

NA = Not available. (1) Figures for mainland China only and do not include Hong Kong (3.0% in 2014-15) or Macao (4.6% in 2014-15).

Number of Days Off Per Year in Selected Countries

Source: OECD Family Database, Organisation for Economic Co-operation and Development (OECD)

Entitlements are generally for full-time, full-year private-sector employees working a five-day week. The U.S. is the only OECD country without a national statute that entitles workers to a minimum number of days off per year.

Country	Paid days off[1]	Public holidays[2]	Total minimum days off	Country	Paid days off[1]	Public holidays[2]	Total minimum days off	Country	Paid days off[1]	Public holidays[2]	Total minimum days off
Australia	20	8	28	Germany....	20	9-13	29-33	Netherlands..	20	9	29
Austria	25	13	38	Greece	20	11	31	New Zealand	20	11	31
Belgium.....	20	10	30	Hungary	20	10	30	Norway	21	10	31
Bulgaria	20	12	32	Iceland	24	12	36	Poland......	20	12	32
Canada.....	10	9	19	Ireland......	20	9	29	Portugal	22	12	34
Chile	15	15	30	Israel.......	11	10	21	Romania.....	20	10	30
Costa Rica ..	10	11	21	Italy........	20	10	30	Slovakia	20	15	35
Croatia	20	13	33	Japan	10	15	25	Slovenia	20	12	32
Cyprus	20	NA	20	Korea,				Spain	22	14	36
Czech				South.....	15	15	30	Sweden.....	25	11	36
Republic ..	20	13	33	Latvia	20	12	32	Switzerland..	20	9	29
Denmark....	25	9	34	Lithuania....	20	11	31	Turkey......	12	NA	12
Estonia	20	10	30	Luxembourg	25	10	35	UK.........	28	9	37
Finland	25	11	36	Malta.......	24	14	38	U.S.	0	NA[3]	0
France	25	11	36	Mexico	6	7	13				

NA = Not applicable. (1) Statutory minimum. (2) Generally set at the national or federal level. May vary at the state level. In some countries, including the U.S., public holidays do not have to be given as paid leave. (3) The government designates 10 federal holidays per year, though private-sector employers decide how much paid leave to offer.

International Migrants by Destination and Origin, 2000, 2015

Source: Dept. of Economic and Social Affairs, UN Population Division

(number of international migrants in thousands)

Places hosting the most international migrants

	2015 Country/terr.	Number	2000 Country/terr.	Number
1.	U.S.	46,627.1	U.S.	34,814.1
2.	Germany......	12,005.7	Russia..........	11,900.3
3.	Russia........	11,643.3	Germany.......	8,992.6
4.	Saudi Arabia ...	10,185.9	India	6,411.3
5.	UK..........	8,543.1	France.........	6,278.7
6.	UAE	8,095.1	Ukraine........	5,527.1
7.	Canada.......	7,835.5	Canada........	5,511.0
8.	France........	7,784.4	Saudi Arabia	5,263.4
9.	Australia	6,763.7	UK............	4,730.2
10.	Spain	5,853.0	Australia	4,386.3
11.	Italy	5,788.9	Pakistan	4,181.9
12.	India	5,241.0	Kazakhstan	2,871.3
13.	Ukraine........	4,834.3	Iran	2,803.8
14.	Thailand	3,913.3	Hong Kong	2,669.1
15.	Pakistan	3,629.0	UAE	2,446.7
16.	Kazakhstan....	3,546.8	Italy	2,121.7
17.	South Africa ...	3,142.5	Côte d'Ivoire	1,994.1
18.	Jordan........	3,112.0	Jordan.........	1,927.8
19.	Turkey........	2,964.9	Israel..........	1,851.3
20.	Kuwait........	2,866.1	Japan	1,686.6
21.	Hong Kong	2,838.7	Spain	1,657.3
22.	Iran	2,726.4	Switzerland.....	1,570.8
23.	Singapore	2,543.6	Netherlands.....	1,556.3
24.	Malaysia	2,514.2	Argentina	1,540.2
25.	Switzerland....	2,438.7	Uzbekistan	1,405.3
26.	Côte d'Ivoire ...	2,175.4	Singapore	1,351.7
27.	Argentina	2,086.3	Turkey.........	1,281.0
28.	Japan	2,043.9	Malaysia	1,277.2
29.	Israel.........	2,011.7	Thailand	1,257.8
30.	Lebanon	1,997.8	Kuwait.........	1,127.6
	World 243,700.2		**World 172,703.3**	

Places of origin with the largest diaspora populations

	2015 Country/terr.	Number	2000 Country/terr.	Number
1.	India	15,575.7	Mexico	9,177.5
2.	Mexico	12,339.1	Puerto Rico.....	1,537.4
3.	Russia........	10,576.8	Philippines	1,369.1
4.	China[1]........	9,546.1	China[1].........	1,315.1
5.	Bangladesh....	7,205.4	India	1,022.6
6.	Pakistan	5,935.2	Vietnam	988.2
7.	Ukraine........	5,825.7	Cuba..........	872.7
8.	Philippines	5,316.3	South Korea	864.1
9.	Syria	5,011.5	Canada........	820.8
10.	UK...........	4,917.5	El Salvador	817.3
11.	Afghanistan....	4,843.1	Germany.......	706.7
12.	Poland........	4,449.8	Dom. Rep.......	687.7
13.	Kazakhstan....	4,075.7	UK............	677.8
14.	Germany......	4,045.4	Jamaica	553.8
15.	Indonesia	3,876.7	Colombia	509.9
16.	Palestine......	3,551.2	Guatemala	480.7
17.	Romania......	3,408.1	Italy	473.3
18.	Egypt	3,269.0	Poland.........	466.7
19.	Turkey........	3,114.5	Haiti	419.3
20.	U.S.	3,023.7	Portugal	378.7
21.	Italy..........	2,900.9	Japan	347.5
22.	Myanmar......	2,881.8	Russia.........	340.2
23.	Morocco	2,834.6	Ecuador	298.6
24.	Colombia	2,638.9	Iran	283.2
25.	Vietnam	2,558.7	Honduras	282.9
26.	South Korea ...	2,345.8	Peru	278.2
27.	Portugal	2,306.3	Ukraine........	275.2
28.	France........	2,146.0	Pakistan	223.5
29.	Somalia.......	1,998.8	Nicaragua......	220.3
30.	Uzbekistan	1,991.0	Brazil..........	212.4
	World 243,700.2		**World 172,703.3**	

(1) Not incl. Hong Kong or Macao.

Refugees and Other Populations of Concern, 2005-15

Source: *UNHCR Global Trends*, United Nations High Commissioner for Refugees (UNHCR)

Refugees are persons recognized under the 1951 UN Refugee Convention/1967 Protocol or the 1969 OAU (Org. of African Unity) Refugee Convention, those recognized in accordance with the UNHCR Statute, and persons granted or receiving protection. The UNHCR also extends assistance to internally displaced persons (IDPs), although they legally remain under their home country's protection. Stateless persons are not considered nationals under any state under the operation of its laws. Others of concern comprises persons who do not necessarily belong in any one category. Because of changes in classification and methodology, figures from 2005 are not fully comparable with figures for later years. Population as of year-end.

Category	2005	2008	2010	2012	2013	2014	2015	% change, 2014-15
Refugees	8,662,000	10,489,800	10,549,700	10,498,000	11,699,300	14,380,100	16,121,400	12.1%
Asylum-seekers (pending cases) . . .	802,100	825,800	837,500	942,800	1,164,400	1,796,200	3,219,900	79.3
Returned refugees[1] . .	1,105,600	603,800	197,700	525,900	414,600	126,900	201,400	58.7
IDPs	6,616,800	14,442,200	14,697,900	17,670,400	23,925,500	32,274,600	37,494,100	16.2
Returned IDPs[1]	519,400	1,361,400	2,923,300	1,545,400	1,356,200	1,822,700	2,317,300	27.1
Stateless persons	2,383,700	6,572,200	3,463,000	3,335,800	3,469,200	3,492,100	3,687,700	5.6
Others of concern	960,400	166,900	1,255,600	1,329,700	836,100	1,052,800	870,700	−17.3
Total	**21,050,000**	**34,462,100**	**33,924,700**	**35,848,000**	**42,865,300**	**54,945,400**	**63,912,700**	**16.3**

(1) Persons who have returned to their place of origin in that year.

Refugees and People in a Refugee-Like Situation, 2015

Source: *UNHCR Global Trends*, United Nations High Commissioner for Refugees (UNHCR)

Refugees are persons recognized under the 1951 UN Refugee Convention/1967 Protocol or the 1969 OAU (Org. of African Unity) Refugee Convention, those recognized in accordance with the UNHCR Statute, and persons granted or receiving protection. Persons outside of their country or territory of origin who face protection risks—but whose refugee status has not been ascertained—are described as being in a refugee-like situation. Only countries hosting 50,000 or more refugees and people in a refugee-like situation are shown; of those countries, only places originating 5,000 or more refugees and people in a refugee-like situation are given, in decreasing order. As of year-end.

Place of asylum	Origin of most refugees (excl. asylum seekers with pending cases)	Number
Africa		**4,811,365**
Algeria	Western Sahara	94,182
Burundi	Dem. Rep. of the Congo	53,363
Cameroon	Central African Republic, Nigeria	342,973
Chad	Sudan, Central African Republic, Nigeria	369,540
Congo, Dem. Rep. of the	Rwanda, Central African Republic, Burundi, South Sudan	383,095
Egypt	Syria, Palestinian[1], Sudan	212,500
Ethiopia	South Sudan, Somalia, Eritrea, Sudan	736,086
Kenya	Somalia, South Sudan, Ethiopia, Dem. Rep. of the Congo	553,912
Mauritania	Mali, Western Sahara	77,394
Niger	Nigeria, Mali	124,721
Rwanda	Dem. Rep. of the Congo, Burundi	144,737
South Africa	Somalia, Dem. Rep. of the Congo, Ethiopia, Congo Republic, Zimbabwe	121,645
South Sudan	Sudan, Dem. Rep. of the Congo	263,016
Sudan	South Sudan, Eritrea, Chad	309,639
Tanzania	Burundi, Dem. Rep. of the Congo	211,845
Uganda	Dem. Rep. of the Congo, South Sudan, Somalia, Burundi, Rwanda	477,187
Asia		**8,694,562**
Afghanistan	Pakistan	257,554
Bangladesh	Myanmar (Burma)	231,958
China	Vietnam	301,052
India	China, Sri Lanka, Myanmar (Burma), Afghanistan	201,381
Iran	Afghanistan, Iraq	979,437
Iraq	Syria, Turkey, Palestinian[1], Iran	277,701
Jordan	Syria, Iraq	664,118
Lebanon	Syria, Iraq	1,070,854
Malaysia	Myanmar (Burma)	94,166
Pakistan	Afghanistan	1,561,162
Thailand	Myanmar (Burma)	108,261
Turkey	Syria, Iraq, Iran	2,541,352
Yemen	Somalia, Ethiopia	267,173
Europe		**1,820,424**
Austria	Afghanistan, Russia, Syria	72,216
France	Sri Lanka, Russia, Dem. Rep. of the Congo, Serbia-Kosovo, Cambodia, Turkey, Vietnam, Laos, Guinea, Syria, Mauritania	273,126
Germany	Syria, Iraq, Afghanistan, Turkey, Iran, Eritrea, Serbia-Kosovo	316,115
Italy	Somalia, Afghanistan, Eritrea, Nigeria, Pakistan, Mali, Côte d'Ivoire	118,047
Netherlands	Somalia, Syria, Iraq, Eritrea, Afghanistan	88,536
Norway	Eritrea, Somalia, Afghanistan	50,389
Russia	Ukraine	314,506
Sweden	Syria, Iraq, Somalia, Eritrea, stateless[2], Afghanistan	169,520
Switzerland	Eritrea, Syria	73,336
United Kingdom	Iran, Eritrea, Afghanistan, Zimbabwe, Somalia, Syria, Pakistan, Sudan, Sri Lanka	123,067
Northern America		**409,090**
Canada	Colombia, China, Haiti, Sri Lanka, Pakistan, Mexico	135,888
United States	China, Haiti, El Salvador, Egypt, Ethiopia, Guatemala, Colombia, Nepal, Venezuela, Russia, Iraq, Syria, Iran	273,202
Latin America and the Caribbean		**337,698**
Ecuador	Colombia	121,535
Venezuela	Colombia	173,754
Oceania		**48,288**
TOTAL		**16,121,427**

(1) Number includes Palestinians under the UNHCR mandate only. (2) Persons not considered nationals under any state under the operation of its laws.

Internally Displaced Persons, 2015

Source: Internal Displacement Monitoring Centre, Norwegian Refugee Council

Internally displaced persons (IDPs) are people who have been forced to move due to conflict or disasters (e.g., earthquakes) but who have not crossed into another country. As such, they are not protected by international refugee law and legally remain under the protection of their home country. Estimates shown are of those displaced by conflict and violence only as of year-end 2015; they may comprise only registered IDPs or those displaced from a certain area of a country.

Country	Number	Country	Number	Country	Number
Afghanistan	1,174,000	Guatemala	251,000	Papua New Guinea	6,300
Armenia	<8,400	Honduras	174,000	Peru	60,000
Azerbaijan	564,000	India	612,000	Philippines	62,000
Bangladesh	426,000	Indonesia	6,100	Russia	27,000
Bosnia and Herzegovina	98,000	Iraq	3.3 mil	Senegal	24,000
Burundi	99,000	Kenya	309,000	Somalia	1.2 mil
Cameroon	124,000	Kosovo	17,000	South Sudan[3]	1.7 mil
Central African Republic	452,000	Lebanon	12,000	Sri Lanka	44,000
Chad	107,000	Libya	500,000	Sudan[3]	3.2 mil
Colombia[1]	6.3 mil	Macedonia	200	Syria	6.6 mil
Congo, Dem. Rep. of	1.5 mil	Mali	50,000	Thailand	35,000
Congo Republic	7,800	Mexico	287,000	Togo	3,000
Côte d'Ivoire	303,000	Myanmar (Burma)	644,000	Turkey	954,000
Cyprus	272,000	Nepal	50,000	Uganda	30,000
Egypt	78,000	Niger	153,000	Ukraine	1.7 mil
El Salvador	289,000	Nigeria	2.1 mil	Yemen	2.5 mil
Ethiopia	450,000	Pakistan	1.5 mil	**Total**	**40.8 mil**
Georgia	239,000	Palestine[2]	221,000		

(1) Cumulative since 1985. (2) Occupied Palestinian Territory. (3) Number does not incl. an est. 82,000 IDPs from Abyei Area, disputed territory between Sudan and South Sudan.

Mortality Rate by Cause of Death in Selected Nations, 2012

Source: World Health Organization (WHO)

(per 100,000 population; ranked by deaths from communicable, maternal, neonatal, and nutritional conditions)

Rank	Country	Communicable, maternal, neonatal, and nutritional conditions	Non-communicable diseases	Injuries	All causes
1.	Sierra Leone	1,327.4	963.5	149.5	2,440.4
2.	Central African Republic	1,212.1	550.8	107.9	1,870.9
3.	Lesotho	1,110.5	671.8	142.5	1,924.7
4.	Chad	1,070.9	712.6	114.5	1,897.9
5.	Mozambique	998.1	593.7	175.3	1,767.0
6.	Somalia	927.2	550.7	188.5	1,666.3
7.	Congo, Dem. Rep. of	920.7	724.4	137.1	1,782.2
8.	Swaziland	884.3	702.4	119.5	1,706.2
9.	Angola	873.3	768.4	137.8	1,779.4
10.	Guinea-Bissau	869.8	764.7	111.6	1,746.2
96.	Russia	73.8	790.3	102.8	966.9
121.	China	41.4	576.3	50.4	668.2
129.	Japan	33.9	244.2	40.5	318.6
133.	United States	31.3	412.8	44.2	488.4
138.	United Kingdom	28.5	358.8	21.5	408.8
149.	Canada	22.6	318.0	31.3	372.0
151.	Germany	21.6	365.1	23.0	409.7
153.	France	21.4	313.2	34.6	369.1
165.	Italy	15.5	303.6	20.1	339.2
170.	Austria	12.6	359.5	30.6	402.7

Global HIV/AIDS Status Report, 2015

Source: Joint United Nations Programme on HIV/AIDS (UNAIDS)

Between 2003—when the first global target in the treatment of HIV/AIDS was set—and 2015, the annual number of AIDS-related deaths dropped by 43%. That reduction was particularly notable among children, as pregnant women were increasingly able to access antiretroviral therapy. At the end of 2015, an estimated 46% of people living with HIV worldwide had access to antiretroviral therapy. While access to treatment has expanded, the risk of HIV infection remained high for certain groups, including sex workers, injecting drug users, transgender people, prisoners, and men who have sex with men. Laws allowing specifically for HIV criminalization existed in 72 countries as of mid-2016.

An estimated $187 billion was spent on the HIV/AIDS epidemic in 2000-14.

Current and New HIV/AIDS Cases and Deaths by Region, 2015

Source: Joint United Nations Programme on HIV/AIDS (UNAIDS)

Region	Number living with HIV/AIDS	Percent of world total[1]	New HIV infections	AIDS-related deaths
East and Southern Africa	19,000,000	51.8%	960,000	470,000
West and Central Africa	6,500,000	17.7	410,000	330,000
Asia and the Pacific	5,100,000	13.9	300,000	180,000
Western and Central Europe and North America . .	2,400,000	6.5	91,000	22,000
Latin America and the Caribbean	2,000,000	5.4	100,000	50,000
Eastern Europe and Central Asia	1,500,000	4.1	190,000	47,000
Middle East and North Africa	230,000	0.6	21,000	12,000
World[2]	**36,700,000**	**100.0**	**2,100,000**	**1,100,000**

(1) Population within a region living with HIV/AIDS as a percentage of population worldwide living with HIV/AIDS. (2) Figures may not add up to totals because of rounding.

Drinking Water and Sanitation, 2015

Source: World Health Organization (WHO) and United Nations Children's Fund (UNICEF)

In 2015, an estimated 91% of the world's population had access to improved drinking-water sources, although service and water quality were inconsistent. Meanwhile, the UN's Millennium Development Goal for access to improved sanitation (target 77%) has yet to be reached. As of 2015, only 68% of people worldwide used improved sanitation facilities. One in eight people still practiced open defecation. Those without access to improved sanitation are at increased risk of contracting a variety of infectious and parasitic diseases such as diarrhea, malaria, and hepatitis A.

The G7 countries have near-universal (99% or greater) access to improved water and sanitation. In comparison, while 97% of Russia's population had access to improved drinking-water sources, only 72% had access to improved sanitation in 2015. In China, the figures were 95% and 76%, respectively.

Lowest Access to Improved Sanitation Facilities, 2015

Source: World Health Organization (WHO) and United Nations Children's Fund (UNICEF)

Sanitation facilities are considered improved if they are private and not shared with other households, incl. sewer or septic system connections, ventilated improved pit latrines, and composting toilets.

(ranked by % of total pop. with access)

Rank	Country/area	% of pop. with access Total	Urban	Rural	Rank	Country/area	% of pop. with access Total	Urban	Rural
1.	South Sudan	6.7%	16.4%	4.5%	17.	Mozambique	20.5%	42.4%	10.1%
2.	Niger	10.9	37.9	4.6	18.	Guinea-Bissau	20.8	33.5	8.5
3.	Togo	11.6	24.7	2.9	19.	Central African Republic	21.8	43.6	7.2
4.	Madagascar	12.0	18.0	8.7	20.	Côte d'Ivoire	22.5	32.8	10.3
5.	Chad	12.1	31.4	6.5		Caucasus and Central Asia	95.9	96.3	95.7
6.	Sierra Leone	13.3	22.8	6.9		Eastern Asia	77.4	87.3	64.3
7.	Ghana	14.9	20.2	8.6		Latin America and the Caribbean	83.1	87.9	64.1
8.	Congo Republic	15.0	20.0	5.6		Northern Africa	89.5	92.2	86.1
9.	Tanzania	15.6	31.3	8.3		Oceania	35.5	75.9	23.2
10.	Eritrea	15.7	44.5	7.3		Southeastern Asia	72.2	80.8	64.3
11.	Liberia	16.9	28.0	5.9		Southern Asia	46.9	67.2	36.0
12.	Papua New Guinea	18.9	56.4	13.3		Sub-Saharan Africa	29.7	40.3	23.3
13.	Uganda	19.1	28.5	17.3		Western Asia	93.8	95.8	89.2
14.	Benin	19.7	35.6	7.3		Developed countries	95.6	96.8	91.4
15.	Burkina Faso	19.7	50.4	6.7		**World**	**67.6**	**82.2**	**50.5**
16.	Guinea	20.1	34.1	11.8					

Lowest Access to Improved Drinking-Water Sources, 2015

Source: World Health Organization (WHO) and United Nations Children's Fund (UNICEF)

Improved drinking-water sources protect from outside contamination and incl. household connections, public taps or standpipes, dug wells, and rainwater collection.

(ranked by % of total pop. with access)

Rank	Country/area	% of pop. with access Total	Urban	Rural	Rank	Country/area	% of pop. with access Total	Urban	Rural
1.	Papua New Guinea	40.0%	88.0%	32.8%	17.	Sierra Leone	62.6%	84.9%	47.8%
2.	Equatorial Guinea	47.9	72.5	31.5	18.	Togo	63.1	91.4	44.2
3.	Angola	49.0	75.4	28.2	19.	Kenya	63.2	81.6	56.8
4.	Chad	50.8	71.8	44.8	20.	Mongolia	64.4	66.4	59.2
5.	Mozambique	51.1	80.6	37.0		Caucasus and Central Asia	88.6	97.8	81.4
6.	Madagascar	51.5	81.6	35.3		Eastern Asia	95.6	97.6	93.0
7.	Congo, Dem. Rep. of	52.4	81.1	31.2		Latin America and the Caribbean	94.6	97.4	83.9
8.	Afghanistan	55.3	78.2	47.0		Northern Africa	92.8	94.9	90.2
9.	Tanzania	55.6	77.2	45.5		Oceania	55.7	94.2	44.1
10.	Ethiopia	57.3	93.1	48.6		Southeastern Asia	90.3	95.5	85.6
11.	Haiti	57.7	64.9	47.6		Southern Asia	92.5	95.5	91.0
12.	Eritrea	57.8	73.2	53.3		Sub-Saharan Africa	67.7	86.8	56.1
13.	Mauritania	57.9	58.4	57.1		Western Asia	94.6	96.5	90.1
14.	Niger	58.2	100.0	48.6		Developed countries	99.2	99.5	97.9
15.	Palestine	58.4	50.7	81.5		**World**	**90.9**	**96.4**	**84.5**
16.	South Sudan	58.7	66.7	56.9					

Foreign Development Aid Donors, 2014-15

Source: Development Assistance Committee (DAC), Organisation for Economic Co-operation and Development (OECD)
Listed below is the amount of official development assistance (ODA)—in the form of grants or loans—each DAC member country disbursed in a given year to developing countries. The numbers are net flows, or amounts disbursed less repayments on earlier loans. Both bilateral ODA (made directly to an aid recipient) and multilateral ODA (made to an agency like the World Bank) are included.

(ranked by size of ODA as % of 2015 gross national income [GNI]; 2015 figures are prelim.)

Rank	Donor	ODA as % of GNI 2014	2015	ODA in mil of current U.S. dollars 2014	2015	Rank	Donor	ODA as % of GNI 2014	2015	ODA in mil of current U.S. dollars 2014	2015
1.	Sweden.......	1.09%	1.41%	$6,232.72	$7,091.91	17.	Iceland	0.22%	0.24%	$37.33	$39.08
2.	Norway	1.00	1.05	5,085.94	4,277.76	18.	Japan	0.19	0.22	9,266.29	9,320.24
3.	Luxembourg ...	1.06	0.93	423.22	361.40	19.	Italy.........	0.19	0.21	4,009.18	3,844.41
4.	Denmark......	0.86	0.85	3,003.27	2,565.56	20.	United States ..	0.19	0.17	33,095.50	31,076.17
5.	Netherlands ...	0.64	0.76	5,572.97	5,812.62	21.	Portugal	0.19	0.16	430.23	305.73
6.	United Kingdom	0.70	0.71	19,305.70	18,699.94	22.	Slovenia	0.13	0.15	61.54	62.41
7.	Finland	0.59	0.56	1,634.57	1,291.53	23.	Greece	0.11	0.14	247.44	282.20
8.	Germany......	0.42	0.52	16,566.20	17,779.27	24.	South Korea ...	0.13	0.14	1,856.73	1,911.00
9.	Switzerland....	0.51	0.52	3,521.94	3,537.73	25.	Spain	0.13	0.13	1,876.83	1,603.77
10.	Belgium.......	0.46	0.42	2,448.02	1,894.38	26.	Czech Republic	0.11	0.12	212.15	201.62
11.	France........	0.37	0.37	10,620.32	9,225.98	27.	Poland........	0.09	0.10	451.84	442.35
12.	Ireland........	0.38	0.36	815.79	718.26	28.	Slovakia	0.09	0.10	83.21	85.77
13.	Austria	0.28	0.32	1,234.52	1,207.47	**Total DAC**		0.30	0.30	137,222.05	131,586.22
14.	Canada.......	0.24	0.28	4,240.04	4,287.22	**G7 countries**[1]		0.27	0.28	97,103.23	94,233.23
15.	Australia	0.31	0.27	4,382.42	3,222.45	**EU institutions**		NA	NA	16,451.10	13,848.01
16.	New Zealand...	0.27	0.27	506.14	437.99	**All donors**[2]		NA	NA	178,345.13	155,400.74

NA = Not applicable/available. (1) Canada, France, Germany, Italy, Japan, the UK, and the U.S. (2) Incl. countries not shown here.

Recipients of U.S. Official Development Assistance, 2013-14

Source: Development Assistance Committee (DAC), Organisation for Economic Co-operation and Development (OECD)

(net flows of official development assistance, or amounts disbursed less repayments on earlier loans, in mil of current U.S. dollars; ranked by 2014 numbers)

Rank	Country	2013	2014	Rank	Country	2013	2014
1.	Afghanistan...............	$1,694.07	$1,928.08	12.	Uganda..................	$459.08	$470.07
2.	Jordan...................	527.18	1,183.45	13.	Mozambique.............	541.17	395.38
3.	Kenya	893.63	807.37	14.	Congo, Dem. Rep. of the......	317.84	385.06
4.	South Sudan..............	410.12	796.07	15.	Iraq	483.82	356.59
5.	Pakistan	609.85	695.96	16.	Colombia	293.48	322.16
6.	Ethiopia.................	678.78	664.84	17.	Zambia	312.82	321.06
7.	Syria	765.72	644.27	18.	Haiti	400.48	312.44
8.	West Bank and Gaza Strip....	958.67	544.19	19.	Senegal	203.18	271.41
9.	South Africa	476.80	515.02	20.	Sudan...................	713.88	255.67
10.	Tanzania.................	734.88	509.01	**All developing countries**		26,360.31	27,509.84
11.	Nigeria	544.10	485.59				

Nuclear Powers of the World

As of Sept. 2016, eight countries were acknowledged nuclear weapons states: the **UK**, **France**, **China**, **India**, **Pakistan**, **Russia**, **North Korea**, and the **U.S. Israel** was presumed to have an arsenal. **South Africa** announced in 1993 that it had built six nuclear weapons and partially completed a seventh, but that they had all been dismantled. **Argentina** and **Brazil** established a joint inspection agency in the early 1990s after committing to the peaceful use of nuclear energy.

All of the more than 40 nations with the knowledge or technology to produce nuclear weapons have signed the Nuclear Non-Proliferation Treaty (NPT) with the exception of Israel, India, and Pakistan. After expelling Intl. Atomic Energy Agency (IAEA) inspectors in Dec. 2002, North Korea announced on Jan. 10, 2003, its withdrawal from the NPT effective the following day.

North Korea conducted at least five nuclear tests between 2006 and Sept. 2016. Analysts believe the country has sufficient weapons-grade plutonium for at least six bombs but lacks the means to deliver them via missile. North Korea is also suspected of attempting to enrich uranium. (Enriched uranium can be used as reactor fuel or in a nuclear weapon.)

Iran had argued that as an NPT signatory, it had a right to pursue the peaceful application of nuclear technology while the IAEA maintained the country had violated the NPT by withholding information. Iran continued its activities despite multiple UN Security Council resolutions against the transfer of nuclear technology to Iran and numerous international economic sanctions. Iranian president Hassan Rouhani, elected in June 2013, agreed to new talks. Iran and the so-called P5+1 (the five permanent members of the UN Security Council plus Germany) signed a Joint Comprehensive Plan of Action (JCPOA) July 14, 2015. Under the agreement, Iran would curb its ability to enrich uranium as well as reduce its current stockpile of the material. Iran's "breakout" time—the amount of time it would need to accumulate enough material for one nuclear bomb—would be increased to at least one year. After certifying that Iran had implemented key measures from the JCPOA, the IAEA lifted certain sanctions on Jan. 16, 2016 ("Implementation Day"). Iran was allowed to resume crude oil exports and to access assets that had been frozen overseas.

Estimated Numbers of Nuclear Weapons by Country, 1945-2016

Source: *Bulletin of the Atomic Scientists*; Carnegie Endowment for International Peace; Federation of American Scientists (FAS); Natural Resources Defense Council (NRDC); Nuclear Threat Initiative (NTI); Stockholm International Peace Research Institute (SIPRI)

Year	United States	USSR/Russia	United Kingdom	France	China	Israel[1]	India	Pakistan	Total[2]
1945	6	—	—	—	—	—	—	—	6
1950	369	5	—	—	—	—	—	—	374
1960	20,434	1,605	30	—	—	—	—	—	22,069
1970	26,662	11,643	280	36	75	8	—	—	38,696
1980	24,304	30,062	350	250	280	31	—	—	55,246
1990	21,004	37,000	300	505	430	53	—	—	59,239
2000	10,577	21,000	185	470	400	72	—	—	32,632
2010	9,400	12,300	225	300	240	60-80	60-80	70-90	22,400
2016	7,000	7,300	215	300	260	80	100-120	110-130	15,350

(1) Israel is widely presumed to have a nuclear stockpile although it has never confirmed nor denied its nuclear status. (2) Numbers may not add up to total due to rounding and uncertainty over size of stockpiles and operational status of warheads.

Nuclear Arms Treaties and Negotiations: A Historical Overview

Aug. 5, 1963: Partial (Limited) Test Ban Treaty signed by the UK, U.S., and USSR, went into effect Oct. 10, 1963. Prohibits parties from testing or participating in the testing of nuclear weapons in the atmosphere, in outer space, and under water.

July 1, 1968: Nuclear Non-Proliferation Treaty (NPT) opened to signatures, went into effect Mar. 5, 1970. With the UK, U.S., and USSR as major signers, the parties agree not to help non-nuclear nations get or make nuclear weapons, though such nations can pursue the peaceful application of nuclear energy.

On May 11, 1995, parties to the treaty voted to extend it indefinitely. As of Sept. 2016, 191 states were party to the treaty, not including North Korea, which withdrew in 2003. Israel, India, and Pakistan were not signatories.

May 26, 1972: The **Strategic Arms Limitation Talks (SALT I)** led to the signing of two agreements by the U.S. and USSR: the **Treaty on the Limitation of Anti-Ballistic Missile Systems** (or **ABM Treaty**) and an interim agreement. These agreements cap the numbers of intercontinental ballistic missile (ICBM) launchers and submarine-launched ballistic missile (SLBM) launchers.

July 3, 1974: Treaty on the Limitation of Underground Nuclear Weapon Tests (or **Threshold Test Ban Treaty**) signed by the U.S. and USSR. Limits underground testing of nuclear weapons to yields of 150 kilotons or less. On May 28, 1976, U.S. and Russia signed the **Peaceful Nuclear Explosions Treaty**, governing explosions outside weapons test sites. Both treaties entered into force Dec. 11, 1990.

June 18, 1979: Strategic Offensive Arms Limitation Treaty (or **SALT II**) signed by the U.S. and USSR. Limited each side to 2,400 missile launchers and heavy bombers; ceiling to apply until Jan. 1, 1985. Never ratified; superseded by START I.

Dec. 8, 1987: Intermediate-Range Nuclear Forces (INF) Treaty signed by the U.S. and USSR. Eliminates all U.S. and Soviet intermediate- and shorter-range nuclear missiles. For the first time, a treaty eliminated an entire category of nuclear weapons and established a comprehensive verification system. Entered into force June 1, 1988.

July 31, 1991: Strategic Arms Reduction Treaty (START I) signed by the USSR and U.S. to reduce long-range nuclear forces no later than seven years after the treaty entered into force. This was the first treaty to mandate reductions in so-called strategic nuclear weapons by the superpowers.

With the Soviet Union breakup in Dec. 1991, four former republics became independent nations with strategic nuclear arms: Russia, Ukraine, Kazakhstan, and Belarus. Under the **Lisbon Protocol** of May 1992, Ukraine, Kazakhstan, and Belarus agreed to accede to the NPT as non-nuclear-weapon states, to destroy or transfer their nuclear weapons to Russia, and to ratify START I. START I expired on Dec. 5, 2009.

Jan. 3, 1993: START II signed by the U.S. and Russia, ratified by the two on Jan. 26, 1996, and Apr. 14, 2000, respectively. Called for further reductions in their long-range nuclear arsenals. Both sides withdrew from the treaty before it went into force.

Sept. 24, 1996: Comprehensive Nuclear-Test-Ban Treaty (CTBT) signed by 71 countries, including the five nuclear-weapons states (China, France, Russia, UK, U.S.). The CTBT bans all nuclear explosions. It is intended to prevent the nuclear powers from developing more advanced weapons while limiting the ability of other states to acquire such devices. As of Sept. 2016, the CTBT had been signed by 183 nations. It had been ratified by 164 but not the U.S. or China. It will enter into force only after ratification by all Annex 2 states—the 44 states with nuclear technology capabilities at the time of the treaty's final negotiations. Only 36 have done so to date.

Dec. 13, 2001: The U.S. announced its intention to withdraw from the **ABM Treaty** in 180 days, arguing that it hindered the government in protecting itself from "future terrorist or rogue state missile attacks." Russia responded by withdrawing from **START II**, stating that U.S. withdrawal from the ABM Treaty effectively invalidated START II.

May 24, 2002: Strategic Offensive Reductions Treaty (SORT or Moscow Treaty) signed by the U.S. and Russia, entered into force June 1, 2003. Committed both countries to cutting nuclear arsenals to 1,700-2,200 warheads each by Dec. 31, 2012. SORT lapsed upon entry into force of the New START Treaty.

Apr. 8, 2010: New START Treaty signed by the U.S. and Russia, entered into force Feb. 5, 2011. It limits each country's arsenal of deployed strategic nuclear warheads to 1,550.

Major International Organizations

African Union (AU), inaugurated July 9, 2002, in Durban, South Africa, following disbanding of the Organization of African Unity (OAU). All of Africa's countries, with the exception of Morocco, make up its 54 members. (Morocco withdrew after the OAU admitted Western Sahara [Sahrawi Arab Dem. Rep.], a territory claimed by Morocco.) The AU is focused on achieving greater socioeconomic integration and unity among its member states. Its founding document authorized the organization to intervene to stop genocide, war crimes, or human rights abuses within individual member nations. **Headquarters:** Addis Ababa, Ethiopia. **Website:** www.au.int

Asia-Pacific Economic Cooperation (APEC), founded Nov. 1989 as a forum to further cooperation on trade and investment between nations of the region and the rest of the world. Its 21 members are Australia, Brunei, Canada, Chile, China, Hong Kong, Indonesia, Japan, Malaysia, Mexico, New Zealand, Papua New Guinea, Peru, Philippines, Russia, Singapore, South Korea, Taiwan, Thailand, the U.S., and Vietnam. **Secretariat:** Singapore. **Website:** www.apec.org

Association of Southeast Asian Nations (ASEAN), formed Aug. 8, 1967, to promote economic, social, and cultural cooperation and development among the states of Southeast Asia. Its members are Brunei, Cambodia, Indonesia, Laos, Malaysia, Myanmar, Philippines, Singapore, Thailand, and Vietnam. **Headquarters:** Jakarta, Indonesia. **Website:** www.asean.org

Caribbean Community and Common Market (CARICOM), established Aug. 1, 1973, to increase cooperation in economics, health, education, culture, science and technology, and tax administration, as well as the coordination of foreign policy. Its 15 members are Antigua and Barbuda, The Bahamas, Barbados, Belize, Dominica, Grenada, Guyana, Haiti, Jamaica, Montserrat, St. Kitts and Nevis, St. Lucia, St. Vincent and the Grenadines, Suriname, and Trinidad and Tobago. Anguilla, Bermuda, British Virgin Islands, Cayman Islands, and Turks and Caicos Islands are associate members. **Secretariat:** Georgetown, Guyana. **Website:** www.caricom.org

The Commonwealth, originally called the British Commonwealth of Nations, then the Commonwealth of Nations, in 1949, is an association of nations and dependencies, most part of the former British Empire. Queen Elizabeth II, the current British monarch, is the symbolic head of the Commonwealth. (The secretary-general is chosen by Commonwealth leaders.)

There are 53 independent, sovereign nations in the Commonwealth. Among them are the UK and 15 other nations recognizing the British monarch, represented by a governor-general, as their head of state. **Secretariat:** London, UK. **Website:** www.thecommonwealth.org

Commonwealth of Independent States (CIS), established in Dec. 1991 as an alliance of former Soviet constituent republics. Its members are Armenia, Azerbaijan, Belarus, Kazakhstan, Kyrgyzstan, Moldova, Russia, Tajikistan, and Uzbekistan; Turkmenistan and Ukraine are associate members. Georgia withdrew from the organization in 2009 following fighting with Russia over disputed territory. Policy is set through coordinating bodies such as the Council of the Heads of States and Council of the Heads of Governments. **Headquarters:** Minsk, Belarus. **Website:** www.cis.minsk.by or www.cisstat.com/eng/

European Free Trade Association (EFTA), created May 3, 1960, to promote free trade and economic integration. The European Economic Area (EEA) agreement, in force since 1994, set up a single market, with free flow of goods, services, capital, and labor, among EU nations and Iceland, Liechtenstein, and Norway, the EFTA members party to the EEA. Switzerland, the fourth EFTA member, has bilateral agreements with the EU. **Headquarters:** Geneva, Switzerland. **Website:** www.efta.int

European Union (EU), known as the European Community (EC) until 1993, aims to integrate economies, coordinate social developments, and foster political partnerships between member states. As of Jan. 1, 1993, there has been a single market, with no restrictions on the movement of people, goods, services, and money, within the EU.

The EU has its origins in such organizations as the European Coal and Steel Community (ECSC), established by the 1951 Treaty of Paris, and the European Economic Community (EEC, or Common Market) and European Atomic Energy Community (Euratom), created by the 1957 Treaties of Rome. A merger of the three communities' executives went into effect in 1967. As of Aug. 2016, there were 28 EU members: the 12 original members (Belgium, Denmark, France, Germany, Greece, Ireland, Italy, Luxembourg, Netherlands, Portugal, Spain, and UK); 3 that entered in 1995 (Austria, Finland, Sweden); 10 that joined in 2004 (Cyprus, Czech Republic, Estonia, Hungary, Latvia, Lithuania, Malta, Poland, Slovakia, Slovenia); 2 that joined in 2007 (Bulgaria, Romania); and 1 that joined in 2013 (Croatia). Albania, Macedonia, Montenegro, Serbia, and Turkey were candidate countries. The UK voted in June 2016 to leave the EU; once the country invokes Article 50 of the Lisbon Treaty, the EU and UK have two years to agree to terms of separation. All 79 member-states of the Africa, Caribbean, and Pacific Group of States (APC) with the exception of Cuba are affiliated with the EU under the Cotonou Agreement (for the 20-year period ending in 2020). **De facto capital:** Brussels, Belgium. **Website:** europa.eu

Leaders of the then-12 member nations signed the Treaty on European Union, also known as the Maastricht Treaty, on Feb. 7, 1992. It went into effect in 1993, committing the organization to launching a common currency, to establishing common foreign policies, and to taking a lead on social policy among other issues. The European Central Bank was established in 1998. In 1999, 11 of the then-15 EU countries began using the euro. By 2002, national currencies in those 11 countries and Greece were removed from circulation, leaving the euro as the only currency of legal tender. EU peacekeeping forces replaced NATO troops in Macedonia, 2003, the first such mission for the organization. A Treaty Establishing a Constitution for Europe was signed in 2004 by EU members but was never ratified.

Group of Eight (G8), forum of major industrialized countries. France, Germany, Italy, Japan, the UK, and the U.S. first met in 1975 as the Group of Six. Canada joined in 1976; Russia in 1998. The EU is represented at summits. In Mar. 2014, group members condemned Russia for its annexation of Crimea, a region of Ukraine. They boycotted a planned G8 summit in Russia and have met as the Group of Seven since June 2014.

International Criminal Police Organization (INTERPOL), created 1923 as the International Criminal Police Commission before changing its name in 1956, is the world's largest international police organization. There were 190 member nations as of Sept. 2016. **General Secretariat:** Lyon, France. **Website:** www.interpol.int

League of Arab States (Arab League), created Mar. 22, 1945. The League promotes economic, social, political, and military cooperation, mediates disputes, and represents Arab states in certain international negotiations. Its members are Algeria, Bahrain, Comoros, Djibouti, Egypt, Iraq, Jordan, Kuwait, Lebanon, Libya, Mauritania, Morocco, Oman, Palestine (considered an independent state by the League), Qatar, Saudi Arabia, Somalia, Sudan, Syria, Tunisia, United Arab Emirates, and Yemen. **Headquarters:** Cairo, Egypt. **Website:** www.lasportal.org

North Atlantic Treaty Organization (NATO), created with the signing of what is popularly known as the Washington Treaty Apr. 4, 1949 (in effect Aug. 24, 1949). Its 28 members as of Sept. 2016 are Albania, Belgium, Bulgaria, Canada, Croatia, Czech Republic, Denmark, Estonia, France, Germany, Greece, Hungary, Iceland, Italy, Latvia, Lithuania, Luxembourg, Netherlands, Norway, Poland, Portugal, Romania, Slovakia, Slovenia, Spain, Turkey, UK, and U.S.

Members agree to settle disputes by peaceful means, to develop their capacity to resist armed attack, to regard an attack on one as an attack on all, and to take necessary action to repel an attack under Article 51 of the UN Charter. **Headquarters:** Brussels, Belgium. **Website:** www.nato.int

NATO's military representatives include the Military Committee; International Military Staff, the committee's executive body; and the military command structure (Allied Command Operations and Allied Command Transformation). The North Atlantic Council is NATO's main political decision-making body.

With the end of the Cold War in the early 1990s, members put greater stress on political action and on creating a force that could rapidly deploy to local crises. By the mid-1990s, Russia and other former Soviet republics, among other countries, had joined with NATO in the so-called Partnership for Peace program, which provides for limited joint military exercises and peacekeeping missions. (NATO suspended cooperation with Russia, Apr. 2014, in response to Russia's conflict with Ukraine.) NATO also engages with countries through its Mediterranean Dialogue and Istanbul Cooperation Initiative.

A NATO-led multinational force was deployed to help keep the peace in Bosnia and Herzegovina in 1995. In 1999, a force was deployed in Kosovo. Following the Sept. 2001 terrorist attacks on the U.S., the NATO Council agreed to invoke for the first time Article 5 of the treaty, which stipulates mutual defense of alliance members. NATO assumed control of the International Security Assistance Force in Afghanistan (ISAF), Aug. 2003, marking the first time NATO led a mission outside Europe.

Organization of American States (OAS), which describes itself as the world's oldest regional organization, was officially formed by the signing of a charter on Apr. 30, 1948. Its four main pillars are democracy, human rights, security, and development.

The OAS's 35 members are Antigua and Barbuda, Argentina, The Bahamas, Barbados, Belize, Bolivia, Brazil, Canada, Chile, Colombia, Costa Rica, Cuba, Dominica, Dominican Republic, Ecuador, El Salvador, Grenada, Guatemala, Guyana, Haiti, Honduras, Jamaica, Mexico, Nicaragua, Panama, Paraguay, Peru, St. Kitts and Nevis, St. Lucia, St. Vincent and the Grenadines, Suriname, Trinidad and Tobago, U.S., Uruguay, and Venezuela. **Headquarters:** Washington, DC. **Website:** www.oas.org

Organization for Economic Cooperation and Development (OECD), established Dec. 14, 1960, to promote the economic and social welfare of member countries and to stimulate efforts for developing nations. Its 35 members, as of Sept. 2016, are Australia, Austria, Belgium, Canada, Chile, Czech Republic, Denmark, Estonia, Finland, France, Germany, Greece, Hungary, Iceland, Ireland, Israel, Italy, Japan, Latvia, Luxembourg, Mexico, Netherlands, New Zealand, Norway, Poland, Portugal, Slovakia, Slovenia, South Korea, Spain, Sweden, Switzerland, Turkey, UK, and the U.S. **Headquarters:** Paris, France. **Website:** www.oecd.org

Organization of Petroleum Exporting Countries (OPEC), created Sept. 14, 1960, by Iran, Iraq, Kuwait, Saudi Arabia, and Venezuela. This group made up of most but not all of the major petroleum exporting nations seeks to stabilize the oil market and set world oil prices by controlling production. In addition to the founding countries, members as of Sept. 2016 include Algeria, Angola, Ecuador, Gabon, Indonesia, Libya, Nigeria, Qatar, and United Arab Emirates. **Secretariat/headquarters:** Vienna, Austria. **Website:** www.opec.org

Organization for Security and Cooperation in Europe (OSCE), established in 1972 as the Conference on Security and Cooperation in Europe; current name adopted 1995. The group, formed by NATO and Warsaw Pact members, seeks improved East-West relations through a commitment to nonaggression and human rights, and cooperation in economics, science and technology, cultural exchange, and environmental protection. There were 57 member states as of Sept. 2016, making it the world's largest regional security organization. **Secretariat:** Vienna, Austria. **Website:** www.osce.org

United Nations

The 71st regular session of the United Nations General Assembly opened Sept. 13, 2016, attended by world leaders and other delegates from 193 nations. The UN headquarters is located on 18 acres, considered international territory, in New York, NY.

Proposals to establish an organization for maintenance of world peace led to the convening of the United Nations Conference on International Organization in San Francisco, Apr. 25-June 26, 1945, where the UN charter was drawn. It was signed June 26 by 50 nations and on Oct. 15 by Poland. It went into effect Oct. 24, 1945, upon ratification by the permanent members of the Security Council and a majority of the other signatories.

Purposes. To maintain international peace and security; to develop friendly relations among nations; to achieve international cooperation in solving economic, social, cultural, and humanitarian problems and in promoting respect for human rights and basic freedoms; to be a center for harmonizing the actions of nations in attaining these common ends.

Visitors to the UN. The UN headquarters is open every day except New Year's Day, Good Friday, Memorial Day, Independence Day, Eid al-Fitr, Labor Day, Eid al-Adha, Thanksgiving, and Christmas. It is closed to the public during the UN general debate and may also close on short notice at other times for meetings of heads of state and government. Guided one-hour tours are conducted on weekdays only. Tickets can be purchased online. A limited number of tickets for same-day tours may be sold on-site. Groups of 40 or more can reserve directly with the UN via their website. For safety reasons, children under 5 years of age are not admitted on tours. **Website:** visit.un.org

The UN Visitor Center, in the basement of the General Assembly Building, is the only area open to the public on weekends. It includes a bookstore, gift shops, and cafe. All visitors must first obtain a security pass to enter UN headquarters. Visitors age 18 and older must present a government-issued photo ID. Guided tours are also available at the UN's other headquarters, in Geneva, Switzerland; Vienna, Austria; and Nairobi, Kenya.

Six Main Organs of the United Nations

General Assembly. The General Assembly comprises representatives from all member nations. Each nation is entitled to one vote. The General Assembly regularly meets in Sept. for an annual session. A special session can be convoked at the request of the Security Council or a majority of UN members. Decisions on important issues, such as security, require a two-thirds majority of the General Assembly; a simple majority can decide other issues.

The General Assembly must approve the UN budget and apportion expenses among members. A member in arrears can lose its vote if the amount of arrears equals or exceeds the amount of the contributions due for the preceding two full years. **Website:** www.un.org/en/ga/

Security Council. The Security Council, which has primary responsibility within the UN for maintaining peace and security, consists of 15 members. Five members—China, France, Russia, United Kingdom, and the United States—have permanent seats. The remaining 10 are elected for two-year terms by the General Assembly. Nonpermanent members with terms expiring Dec. 31, 2016, are Angola, Malaysia, New Zealand, Spain, and Venezuela; those with terms expiring Dec. 31, 2017, are Egypt, Japan, Senegal, Ukraine, and Uruguay.

Any UN member may participate in Council discussions at its invitation. Decisions on procedural questions are made by an affirmative vote of nine members. On all other matters the affirmative vote of nine members must include the concurring votes of all permanent members (giving them veto power). The Security Council directs the various peacekeeping forces deployed throughout the world. **Website:** www.un.org/en/sc/

Secretariat. The Secretariat is responsible for the UN's day-to-day operations. It is headed by the secretary-general, who is the chief administrative officer of the UN. This person is appointed by the General Assembly, on the recommendation of the Security Council, for a five-year, renewable term. The secretary-general reports to the General Assembly and may bring to the attention of the Security Council any matter that threatens international peace. The Secretariat maintains an international staff of about 41,000. **Website:** www.un.org/en/sections/about-un/secretariat/

United Nations Secretaries General

Took office	Secretary, nation
1946	Trygve Lie, Norway
1953	Dag Hammarskjöld, Sweden
1961	U Thant, Burma (Myanmar)
1972	Kurt Waldheim, Austria
1982	Javier Pérez de Cuéllar, Peru
1992	Boutros Boutros-Ghali, Egypt
1997	Kofi Annan, Ghana
2007	Ban Ki-moon, South Korea

Economic and Social Council. The Economic and Social Council consists of 54 members elected by the General Assembly to overlapping three-year terms. The council is responsible for economic, social, and environmental matters. It meets with academics, non-governmental organizations, and private-sector representatives throughout the year. A month-long substantive session takes place each July. These sessions are alternately held in New York and Geneva, Switzerland. **Website:** www.un.org/ecosoc/

International Court of Justice (World Court). The International Court of Justice is the principal judicial organ of the UN. The Court has jurisdiction over cases that UN members or parties to the court's statute submit to it. In addition to rendering judgments, the Court gives advisory opinions.

The court's 15 judges are elected to nine-year terms by the General Assembly and the Security Council. No two judges come from the same nation, and they represent the world's principal legal systems. Once elected, the judges no longer act as representatives of a government. The Court remains permanently in session, except during vacations. All questions are decided by a majority. The International Court of Justice sits in The Hague, Netherlands. **Website:** www.icj-cij.org

Trusteeship Council. The Trusteeship Council, made up of the five permanent Security Council members, supervised the administration of UN trust territories. All 11 trust territories have since attained their right to self-determination. The Council formally suspended its work on Nov. 1, 1994, with Palau's independence.

The text of the **UN Charter** is online at www.un.org/en/charter-united-nations/.

Selected UN Programs and Funds, Specialized Agencies, and Related Organizations

UN programs and funds operate with voluntary funding. UN specialized agencies and related organizations are autonomous groups that have a functional relationship or working agreement with the UN. Their financing comes from voluntary and assessed contributions. The location in parentheses is the primary office or headquarters.

Food and Agriculture Org. (FAO) helps countries modernize farms, forests, and fisheries; improves food distribution; and raises levels of nutrition. (Rome, Italy) **Website:** www.fao.org

International Atomic Energy Agency (IAEA) promotes safe, peaceful uses of atomic energy. (Vienna, Austria) **Website:** www.iaea.org

International Civil Aviation Org. (ICAO) sets international civil aviation standards and regulations. (Montréal, Quebec, Canada) **Website:** www.icao.int

International Fund for Agricultural Development (IFAD) seeks to alleviate poverty in rural areas of developing countries. (Rome, Italy) **Website:** www.ifad.org

International Labor Org. (ILO) promotes decent and productive employment practices, the improvement of labor conditions, social security, and vocational training. (Geneva, Switzerland) **Website:** www.ilo.org

International Maritime Org. (IMO) seeks cooperation on technical matters affecting international shipping. (London, England, UK) **Website:** www.imo.org

International Monetary Fund (IMF) promotes international monetary cooperation, currency stabilization, and the expansion of international trade. (Washington, DC) **Website:** www.imf.org

International Telecommunication Union (ITU) regulates all aspects of global communication, including setting standards for radio, telegraph, telephone, and space radio-communications, and allocating radio frequencies. (Geneva, Switzerland) **Website:** www.itu.int

Office of the United Nations High Commissioner for Refugees (UNHCR) safeguards the rights of and provides essential assistance for refugees. (Geneva, Switzerland) **Website:** www.unhcr.org

United Nations Children's Fund (UNICEF) provides financial aid and development assistance to programs for children and mothers in developing countries. (New York, NY) **Website:** www.unicef.org

United Nations Educational, Scientific, and Cultural Org. (UNESCO) works to improve education around the world and to preserve historical and cultural sites. (Paris, France) **Website:** www.unesco.org

United Nations Industrial Development Org. (UNIDO) helps developing and transitional nations pursue sustainable industrial development while promoting international industrial cooperation. (Vienna, Austria) **Website:** www.unido.org

Universal Postal Union (UPU) facilitates international collaboration among postal service providers. (Berne, Switzerland) **Website:** www.upu.int

World Bank Group is focused on ending extreme poverty and promoting the sharing of prosperity worldwide. It encompasses five institutions. The **International Bank for Reconstruction and Development (IBRD)** provides loans and technical assistance for projects in developing member countries. The **International Development Assn. (IDA)** provides funds for development projects on concessional terms to the poorest countries. The IBRD and IDA make up the World Bank. The **International Finance Corp. (IFC)** promotes private-sector growth in developing countries; encourages the development of local capital markets; and stimulates the international flow of private capital. The **Multilateral Investment Guarantee Agency (MIGA)** promotes foreign direct investment in developing countries by guaranteeing investments from noncommercial political risks. The **International Center for Settlement of Investment Disputes (ICSID)** provides conciliation and arbitration services for disputes between foreign investors and host governments that arise out of an investment. (Washington, DC) **Website:** www.worldbank.org, www.ifc.org, www.miga.org

World Health Org. (WHO) responds to public-health emergencies and works to eradicate life-threatening diseases. (Geneva, Switzerland) **Website:** www.who.int

World Intellectual Property Org. (WIPO) protects literary, industrial, scientific, and artistic works through international cooperation. (Geneva, Switzerland) **Website:** www.wipo.int

World Meteorological Org. (WMO) coordinates the free exchange of world meteorological data. (Geneva, Switzerland) **Website:** www.wmo.int

World Tourism Org. (UNWTO) advocates for responsible, sustainable, and universally accessible tourism. (Madrid, Spain) **Website:** www.unwto.org

World Trade Org. (WTO) administers trade agreements and treaties between nations, attempts to settle disputes, and keeps track of trade measures and statistics. (Geneva, Switzerland) **Website:** www.wto.org

Ongoing UN Peacekeeping Missions, 2016

Source: Dept. of Peacekeeping Operations (DPKO), Dept. of Field Support, Dept. of Management; United Nations Secretariat
Unless otherwise noted, numbers are for peacekeeping operations only (not including political and peacebuilding missions), as of June 30, 2016, unless otherwise noted. Year given in graphic is the year each mission started.

Uniformed personnel (troops, police, and military observers) 101,280	Total personnel serving in 16 current peacekeeping operations 119,523
Countries contributing uniformed personnel 123	Approved budget for July 1, 2015-June 30, 2016 . . . . . $8.27 bil
Civilian personnel:	Peacekeeping operations since 1948 71
International (as of July 31, 2015) 5,256	Total fatalities in all peace operations since 1948 3,497
Local (as of July 31, 2015) 11,215	Est. total cost of operations, 1948 to June 30, 2010 . . . $69 bil

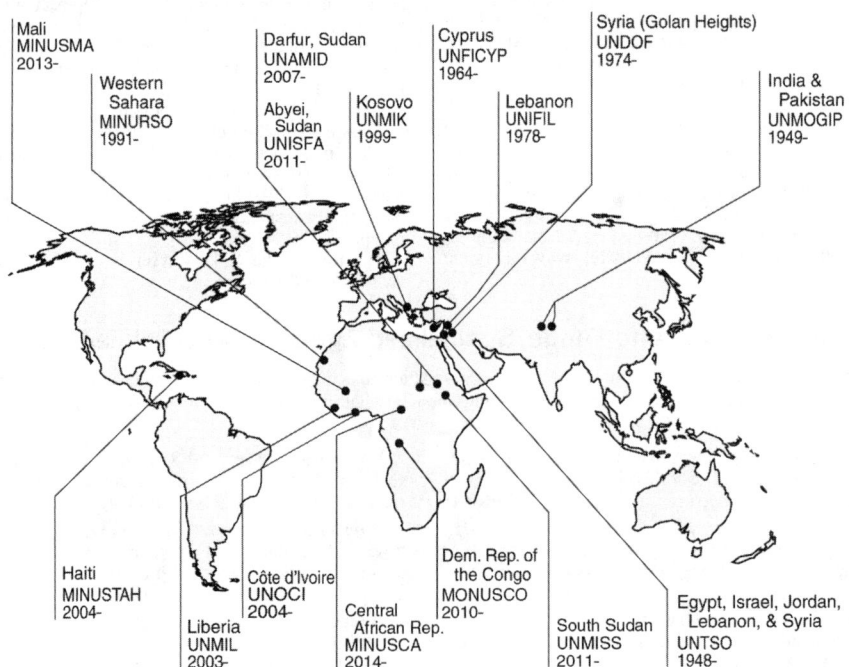

Mali MINUSMA 2013-
Western Sahara MINURSO 1991-
Darfur, Sudan UNAMID 2007-
Abyei, Sudan UNISFA 2011-
Kosovo UNMIK 1999-
Cyprus UNFICYP 1964-
Lebanon UNIFIL 1978-
Syria (Golan Heights) UNDOF 1974-
India & Pakistan UNMOGIP 1949-

Haiti MINUSTAH 2004-
Liberia UNMIL 2003-
Côte d'Ivoire UNOCI 2004-
Central African Rep. MINUSCA 2014-
Dem. Rep. of the Congo MONUSCO 2010-
South Sudan UNMISS 2011-
Egypt, Israel, Jordan, Lebanon, & Syria UNTSO 1948-

Roster of the United Nations

Listed below are the 193 members of the United Nations, with the years in which they were admitted (as of Sept. 2016). Vatican City (Holy See), Kosovo, and China (Taiwan)[1] are not members. Taiwan's repeated bids for UN membership have so far been unsuccessful. Palestine and Vatican City are non-member states of the UN with permanent observer status.

Member	Year	Member	Year	Member	Year	Member	Year
Afghanistan	1946	Dominica	1978	Libya	1955	Saint Vincent and the	
Albania	1955	Dominican Republic	1945	Liechtenstein	1990	Grenadines	1980
Algeria	1962	Ecuador	1945	Lithuania	1991	Samoa	1976
Andorra	1993	Egypt[4]	1945	Luxembourg	1945	San Marino	1992
Angola	1976	El Salvador	1945	Macedonia[2,7]	1993	São Tomé and Príncipe	1975
Antigua and Barbuda	1981	Equatorial Guinea	1968	Madagascar	1960	Saudi Arabia	1945
Argentina	1945	Eritrea	1993	Malawi	1964	Senegal	1960
Armenia	1992	Estonia	1991	Malaysia[8]	1957	Serbia[2,9]	2000
Australia	1945	Ethiopia	1945	Maldives	1965	Seychelles	1976
Austria	1955	Fiji	1970	Mali	1960	Sierra Leone	1961
Azerbaijan	1992	Finland	1955	Malta	1964	Singapore[8]	1965
Bahamas, The	1973	France	1945	Marshall Islands	1991	Slovakia[3]	1993
Bahrain	1971	Gabon	1960	Mauritania	1961	Slovenia[2]	1992
Bangladesh	1974	Gambia, The	1965	Mauritius	1968	Solomon Islands	1978
Barbados	1966	Georgia	1992	Mexico	1945	Somalia	1960
Belarus	1945	Germany[5]	1973	Micronesia	1991	South Africa[11]	1945
Belgium	1945	Ghana	1957	Moldova	1992	South Sudan[12]	2011
Belize	1981	Greece	1945	Monaco	1993	Spain	1955
Benin	1960	Grenada	1974	Mongolia	1961	Sri Lanka	1955
Bhutan	1971	Guatemala	1945	Montenegro[2,9]	2006	Sudan[12]	1956
Bolivia	1945	Guinea	1958	Morocco	1956	Suriname	1975
Bosnia and		Guinea-Bissau	1974	Mozambique	1975	Swaziland	1968
Herzegovina[2]	1992	Guyana	1966	Myanmar (Burma)	1948	Sweden	1946
Botswana	1966	Haiti	1945	Namibia	1990	Switzerland	2002
Brazil	1945	Honduras	1945	Nauru	1999	Syria[3]	1945
Brunei	1984	Hungary	1955	Nepal	1955	Tajikistan	1992
Bulgaria	1955	Iceland	1946	Netherlands	1945	Tanzania[13]	1961
Burkina Faso	1960	India	1945	New Zealand	1945	Thailand	1946
Burundi	1962	Indonesia[6]	1950	Nicaragua	1945	Timor-Leste	2002
Cabo Verde	1975	Iran	1945	Niger	1960	Togo	1960
Cambodia	1955	Iraq	1945	Nigeria	1960	Tonga	1999
Cameroon	1960	Ireland	1955	Norway	1945	Trinidad and Tobago	1962
Canada	1945	Israel	1949	Oman	1971	Tunisia	1956
Central African Rep.	1960	Italy	1955	Pakistan	1947	Turkey	1945
Chad	1960	Jamaica	1962	Palau	1994	Turkmenistan	1992
Chile	1945	Japan	1956	Panama	1945	Tuvalu	2000
China[1]	1945	Jordan	1955	Papua New Guinea	1975	Uganda	1962
Colombia	1945	Kazakhstan	1992	Paraguay	1945	Ukraine	1945
Comoros	1975	Kenya	1963	Peru	1945	United Arab Emirates	1971
Congo, Dem. Rep. of	1960	Kiribati	1999	Philippines	1945	United Kingdom	1945
Congo Republic	1960	Korea, North	1991	Poland	1945	United States	1945
Costa Rica	1945	Korea, South	1991	Portugal	1955	Uruguay	1945
Côte d'Ivoire	1960	Kuwait	1963	Qatar	1971	Uzbekistan	1992
Croatia[2]	1992	Kyrgyzstan	1992	Romania	1955	Vanuatu	1981
Cuba	1945	Laos	1955	Russia[10]	1945	Venezuela	1945
Cyprus	1960	Latvia	1991	Rwanda	1962	Vietnam	1977
Czech Republic[3]	1993	Lebanon	1945	Saint Kitts and Nevis	1983	Yemen[14]	1947
Denmark	1945	Lesotho	1966	Saint Lucia	1979	Zambia	1964
Djibouti	1977	Liberia	1945			Zimbabwe	1980

(1) The General Assembly (GA) voted in 1971 to expel the Chinese government in Taiwan and admit the government in Beijing. (2) The Socialist Federal Republic of Yugoslavia was an original UN member. After four of its six republics (Bosnia and Herzegovina, Croatia, Macedonia, and Slovenia) declared independence in 1991-92, the two remaining republics, Montenegro and Serbia, reconstituted as the Federal Republic of Yugoslavia. They sought to take over the former Yugoslavia's UN seat in 1992 but were expelled a few months later by GA vote. The Federal Republic of Yugoslavia was granted membership in 2000. In 2003, the country changed its name to Serbia and Montenegro. (3) Czechoslovakia, an original UN member from 1945 to 1992, was succeeded by both the Czech Republic and Slovakia in 1993. (4) Egypt and Syria were original UN members. In 1958, Egypt and Syria established the United Arab Republic and continued under a single UN membership. In 1961, Syria resumed separate membership following independence. (5) The Federal Republic of Germany and the German Democratic Republic became UN members in 1973. In 1990, the two formed one sovereign state. (6) Withdrew from the UN in 1965; rejoined in 1966. (7) Provisionally referred to as the former Yugoslav Republic of Macedonia within the UN pending settlement of Greece's objection to its constitutional name. (8) The Federation of Malaya joined the UN in 1957. In 1963, it changed its name to Malaysia following the accession of Singapore, Sabah, and Sarawak. Singapore became an independent UN member in 1965. (9) After Montenegro declared independence in 2006, the Republic of Serbia continued Serbia and Montenegro's UN membership. Montenegro was admitted to the UN as the Republic of Montenegro the same month. (10) The USSR was an original UN member. After the USSR's dissolution in 1991, Russia informed the UN it would continue the Soviet Union's membership in the Security Council and all other UN organs with the support of the Commonwealth of Independent States (comprising most of the former Soviet republics). (11) Readmitted in 1994. Its delegation had been suspended from participation in 1974 because of apartheid. (12) The Republic of South Sudan seceded from the Republic of the Sudan in 2011 and was admitted to the UN the same year. (13) Tanganyika was a UN member from 1961 and Zanzibar from 1963. The two countries united in 1964 to form the United Republic of Tanganyika and Zanzibar, which continued a single UN membership. It later changed its name to the United Republic of Tanzania. (14) The Yemen Arab Republic was admitted in 1947; the People's Democratic Republic of Yemen in 1967. In 1990, the two nations formed the Republic of Yemen.

U.S. Representatives to the United Nations, 1946-2016

The U.S. Permanent Representative to the United Nations is head of the U.S. Mission to the UN in New York. He or she is appointed by the president and confirmed by the Senate. This individual holds the rank and status of Ambassador Extraordinary and Plenipotentiary. Year given is the year each took office.

Year	Representative	Year	Representative	Year	Representative	Year	Representative
1946	Edward R. Stettinius Jr.	1968	James Russell Wiggins	1985	Vernon A. Walters	2001	John D. Negroponte
1946	Herschel V. Johnson (act.)	1969	Charles W. Yost	1989	Thomas R. Pickering	2004	John C. Danforth
1947	Warren R. Austin	1971	George H. W. Bush	1992	Edward J. Perkins	2005	Anne W. Patterson (act.)
1953	Henry Cabot Lodge Jr.	1973	John A. Scali	1993	Madeleine K. Albright		
1960	James J. Wadsworth	1975	Daniel P. Moynihan	1997	Bill Richardson	2005	John R. Bolton
1961	Adlai E. Stevenson	1976	William W. Scranton	1998	A. Peter Burleigh (act.)	2006	Alejandro D. Wolff (act.)
1965	Arthur J. Goldberg	1977	Andrew Young	1999	Richard C. Holbrooke	2007	Zalmay M. Khalilzad
1968	George W. Ball	1979	Donald McHenry	2001	James B. Cunningham (act.)	2009	Susan E. Rice
		1981	Jeane J. Kirkpatrick			2013	Samantha Power

International Criminal Court

The International Criminal Court (ICC) was created when 120 nations signed the Rome Statute on July 17, 1998. Its mission is to try individuals accused of genocide, war crimes, and crimes against humanity, which was undertaken in the past by temporary tribunals. The statute came into force on July 1, 2002. As of Aug. 2016, 124 nations were state parties to the Rome Statute of the ICC. China, Russia, and the U.S. have not yet signed or ratified the treaty.

The ICC, unlike the International Court of Justice (or World Court), is not part of the UN. It is an independent international agency with its own administration and budget, which is made up of funds from member states and voluntary contributions by other institutions, international groups, individuals, and corporations. It consists of 18 judges elected by state parties to nine-year, non-renewable terms. An absolute majority of these 18 judges elect three from among themselves to serve as president and first and second vice presidents. A Registry handles the non-judicial aspects of administration. The Office of the Prosecutor reviews, investigates, and prosecutes cases referred to it by a state or by the UN Security Council.

As of mid-2016, 23 cases in 10 situations had been brought before the ICC. Two situations were in the Central African Republic and one each in Côte d'Ivoire; Dem. Rep. of the Congo; Georgia; Kenya; Libya; Mali; Darfur, Sudan; and Uganda. It was conducting preliminary examinations in Afghanistan, Burundi, Colombia, Guinea, Iraq, Nigeria, Palestine, and Ukraine as well as on registered vessels of Comoros, Greece, and Cambodia. The court issued its first-ever conviction in Mar. 2012, when it found the warlord Thomas Lubanga Dyilo guilty of war crimes for his use of child soldiers in the Dem. Rep. of the Congo.

Though jurisdiction is limited to member nations, the ICC is a court of last resort. It may also initiate cases involving non-member nations if it deems the country's authorities have not taken steps to investigate or prosecute a case. The ICC is headquartered in The Hague, Netherlands, though it may sit elsewhere. **Website:** www.icc-cpi.int

Geneva Conventions

The Geneva Conventions are four international treaties governing the protection of civilians in times of war, the treatment of prisoners of war, and the care of the wounded and sick in the armed forces. The first convention, covering the sick and wounded in war, was concluded in Geneva, Switzerland, in 1864, at a conference convened by the Swiss government at the urging of the International Committee of the Red Cross. The convention was amended and expanded in 1906. In 1929, two more conventions covering the wounded and prisoners of war were signed. Outrage at the treatment of prisoners and civilians during WWII by some belligerents, notably Germany and Japan, prompted the conclusion, on Aug. 12, 1949, of four new conventions. Three of these restated and strengthened the previous conventions. The fourth codified general principles of international law governing the treatment of civilians in wartime.

The 1949 convention for civilians provided for special safeguards for wounded persons, children under 15 years of age, pregnant women, and the elderly. Discrimination on racial, religious, national, or political grounds was forbidden. Torture, collective punishment, reprisals, unwarranted destruction of property, and forced use of civilians for an occupier's armed forces were also prohibited. Also included was a pledge for the humane treatment, adequate feeding, and delivery of supplies to prisoners. They were not to be forced to disclose more than minimal information. Two additional protocols were adopted in June 1977 dealing with the protection of victims, especially civilians, in international and non-international armed conflicts. (A third protocol, adopted in 2005, created the Red Crystal emblem for use along with the Red Cross and Red Crescent.)

Most countries have formally accepted all or most of the humanitarian conventions as binding. However, there is no permanent international machinery in place to enforce these treaties.

Genocide

Source: Convention on the Prevention and Punishment of the Crime of Genocide, United Nations Treaty Series 277; Rome Statute of the International Criminal Court

The term "genocide" (which combines Greek and Latin roots to mean "murder of a race") was coined by Polish-Jewish lawyer Raphael Lemkin in 1944 to describe the intentional destruction or attempted destruction of a national, ethnic, racial, or religious group, whether in wartime or peacetime. Genocide is defined as killing members of a group, causing serious bodily harm to members of a group, or otherwise attempting to bring about a group's destruction, including efforts to prevent births or transfer children away from a group. Although the legal definition of genocide does not extend to political groups, the term is often used colloquially to refer to large-scale political violence.

The prohibition against genocide is part of customary international law and is codified in the Convention on the Prevention and Punishment of the Crime of Genocide, which entered into force on Jan. 12, 1951. As of Sept. 2016, 147 nations, including the U.S., were parties to it. Genocide is also prohibited by the domestic laws of many nations.

The first modern trials for genocide were conducted by the Allies after WWII. Although the charter of the Nuremberg Tribunal—the international court set up to try Nazi war criminals—did not use the term genocide, its definition of "crimes against humanity" included persecution on racial or religious grounds. More recently, the UN Security Council created ad hoc tribunals to try those responsible for genocide and other serious crimes in the former Yugoslavia and in Rwanda. The International Criminal Court (ICC) also has jurisdiction to try perpetrators of genocide. Sudanese Pres. Omar Hassan al-Bashir is the first person the ICC has charged with the crime of genocide, after the UN Security Council referred the situation in Darfur to the ICC prosecutor in Mar. 2005. The ICC issued two arrest warrants for Pres. Bashir, but the warrants remained unenforced as of Sept. 2016.

Examples of Genocides Since 1900

Year	Event	Location	Est. deaths
1915	Extermination of Armenians by the nationalist Young Turks	Turkey/Ottoman Empire	1,000,000+
1930s	Intentional infliction of famine on Ukraine	Soviet Union (Ukraine)	6,000,000-7,000,000
1933-45	Attempted destruction of European Jewry (Holocaust)	Europe	6,000,000
1975-79	Khmer Rouge campaign of extermination under Pol Pot[1]	Cambodia	1,500,000-2,000,000
1981-83	Army and paramilitary killings of indigenous Mayan during civil war	Guatemala	200,000+
1988	Anfal Campaign (named by the Iraqi government) against Iraqi Kurds	Iraq	100,000-200,000
1992-95	Ethnic killings during the breakup of Yugoslavia, chiefly Serbs against Bosnian Muslims (known as Bosniaks)	Bosnia-Herzegovina, Serbia, Croatia	200,000
1994	Hutu massacre of Tutsis	Rwanda	800,000
2003-present	Rebel group and government-backed Arab militia attacks on non-Arab southern tribes, black population[2]	Darfur region, Sudan	200,000-500,000

Note: Estimates based on historical evidence. The legal definition of "genocide" does not include politically motivated mass killings. Therefore, instances of mass violence against political or class enemies, such as Josef Stalin's purges of some 20 mil Soviets in the 1930s, and Mao Zedong's Cultural Revolution, which killed several million Chinese, are not included. (1) The mass killings during Cambodia's Khmer Rouge regime are often spoken of as genocide, though many of the murders were politically or class motivated. (2) In 2005, a UN commission concluded that although the "international offenses ... that have been committed in Darfur may be no less serious and heinous than genocide," it did not term the situation there a genocide.

NATIONS OF THE WORLD

As of mid-2016, there were **196 nations** in the world. This number includes three nations that are not United Nations (UN) members—Kosovo, Taiwan, and Vatican City (Holy See). Certain regions and territories can be found under the entry for their governing nation. **Sources:** FAOSTAT and AQUASTAT, Food and Agric. Org. of the UN (FAO); Global Health Observatory, World Health Organization (WHO); Intl. Data Base, U.S. Census Bureau; International Energy Statistics, Energy Information Admin., U.S. Dept. of Energy; *International Financial Statistics*, Intl. Monetary Fund (IMF); Joint UN Programme on HIV/AIDS (UNAIDS); *Key Indicators of the Labour Market*, International Labour Organization; *The Military Balance*, Intl. Inst. for Strategic Studies; *Oil & Gas Journal*, PennWell Corp.; *Trends in International Migrant Stock* and *World Urbanization Prospects*, Population Div., UN Dept. of Economic and Social Affairs; UN Educational, Scientific, and Cultural Org. (UNESCO); *UNWTO World Tourism Barometer* © World Tourism Org.; U.S. Dept. of State; WardsAuto Group, a div. of Penton; The World Bank; *The World Factbook*, Central Intelligence Agency (CIA); World Telecommunication/ICT Indicators Database, Intl. Telecommunication Union.

Note: Because of rounding or incomplete enumeration, percentages may not add up to 100%. FY = Fiscal year. NA = Not available/applicable. Figures are for years noted below unless otherwise indicated within a country's profile. **Population**, **age distrib.**, and **pop. density** are mid-2016 ests. **Growth** gives the avg. annual percent change in the pop. resulting from **births** and **deaths** at midyear 2016 as well as the flow of migrants into and out of a country. International **migrants**, including foreign-born citizens and refugees, as a percent of the total pop. is for 2015. Percent of total pop. living in **urban** areas, as defined by each country, are projections for mid-2016. **Languages** are ranked with those most widely spoken listed first. **Arable land** is given as percentage of country's land area. Pop. of **capitals** and **cities** are projected ests. for urban agglomerations as of mid-2016. **Defense budget** is for 2015, **active troops** for 2016. Selected **industries** are ranked by descending value of annual output. Selected **chief crops** are listed in descending order of importance. Total renewable **water** resources per inhabitant is for 2014. **Crude oil reserves** are as of Jan. 1, 2016; countries without this entry lack reserves. **Electricity prod.** indicates net, not gross, generated in 2013. **Labor force** percentages and **unemployment** (percentage of total labor force actively looking and available for work) are latest available. **Monetary unit** exchange rate is as of Sept. 2016. **GDP** data, for 2015, are based on purchasing power parity exchange rates; **per capita GDP** is calculated using a country's est. pop. size as of July 1 of given year. **GDP growth** is year-over-year. Value of **imports** and **exports**, calculated on an exchange rate basis, are from 2015; 2015 trade partners are listed in descending order of importance by percentage of total dollar value. **Tourism** is latest available receipts from intl. visitors; data not available for all countries. **Budget** calculated on an exchange rate basis, not purchasing power parity terms, is 2015 expenditures. **Inflation** is measured by the percent change in the consumer price index (or avg. consumer cost for certain goods and services) between 2014 and 2015. Total length of a country's **railway** network is the latest available. **Motor vehicle** statistics, for cars and comm. vehicles in operation based on registrations, are for 2015. The number of **airports** with paved, usable runways are as of 2013. Number of fixed-**telephone** subscriptions; **mobile**-cellular telephone subscriptions offering voice communications; and percentage of pop. accessing the **Internet**, regardless of device used, are for 2015. Active mobile-**broadband** subscriptions are for 2014. Total health **expend.** (both government and private) is given as a percentage of GDP in 2014. **Life expect.** is in avg. number of years at birth for persons born in 2016. **Infant mortality** measures the probability of a child dying between birth and exact age 1 in 2016. **Undernourished**, or the prevalence of undernourishment, is the probability in 2014-16 that a randomly selected person from the pop. does not consume enough calories for an active, healthy life. **HIV** prevalence is the percentage of a country's pop. of 15- to 49-year-olds living with HIV in 2015. **Education** and **literacy** rate ests. are latest available. Literacy measures the percent of the pop. age 15 and older able to read and write simple statements; some countries define as literate those who have completed certain schooling. **Embassy** addresses are for Wash., DC, area code (202). Current events as of Oct. 1, 2016.

See pages 473-88 for full-color maps and flags of all nations.

Afghanistan
Islamic Republic of Afghanistan

People: Population: 33,332,025. **Age distrib.:** <15: 41%; 65+: 2.6%. **Growth:** 2.3%. **Migrants:** 1.2%. **Pop. density:** 132.4 per sq mi, 51.1 per sq km. **Urban:** 27.1%. **Ethnic groups:** Pashtun, Tajik, Hazara, Uzbek, smaller numbers of 11 other constitutionally recognized ethnic groups. **Languages:** Afghan Persian or Dari, Pashto (both official); Turkic langs. (Uzbek, Turkmen); 30 minor langs. (Balochi, Pashai). **Religions:** Sunni Muslim 84.7%-89.7%, Shia Muslim 10%-15%.

Geography: Total area: 251,827 sq mi, 652,230 sq km; **Land area:** 251,827 sq mi, 652,230 sq km. **Location:** SW Asia, NW of Indian subcontinent. Pakistan on E, S; Iran on W; Turkmenistan, Uzbekistan, Tajikistan on N. NE tip touches China. **Topography:** Landlocked and mountainous, much of it over 4,000 ft above sea level. The Hindu Kush Mts. tower 16,000 ft above Kabul and reach a height of 25,000 ft to the E. Trade with Pakistan flows through the 35-mi-long Khyber Pass. Dry climate with extreme temperatures; large desert regions. **Arable land:** 11.9%. **Capital:** Kabul, 4,841,535.

Government: Type: Presidential Islamic republic. **Head of state and gov.:** Pres. Ashraf Ghani Ahmadzai; b. 1949; in office: Sept. 29, 2014; and Chief Exec. Abdullah Abdullah; b. 1960; in office: Sept. 29, 2014. **Local divisions:** 34 provinces. **Defense budget:** $3.2 bil. **Active troops:** 160,500.

Economy: Industries: small-scale prod. of bricks, textiles, soap, furniture, shoes, fertilizer, apparel, food prods. **Chief crops:** opium, wheat, fruits, nuts. **Natural resources:** nat. gas, petroleum, coal, copper, chromite, talc, barites, sulfur, lead, zinc, iron ore, salt, prec. and semiprec. stones. **Water:** 2,008 cu m per capita. **Electricity prod.:** 1 bil kWh. **Labor force:** agric. 78.6%, industry 5.7%, services 15.7%. **Unemployment:** 9.1%.

Finance: Monetary unit: Afghani (AFN) (66.64 = $1 U.S.). **GDP:** $62.3 bil; **per capita GDP:** $1,900; **GDP growth:** 1.5%. **Imports** (2013): $12.2 bil; Pakistan 38.6%, India 8.9%, U.S. 8.3%, Turkmenistan 6.2%, China 6%, Kazakhstan 5.9%. **Exports** (2013): $2.7 bil (not incl. illicit trade); India 42.2%, Pakistan 28.9%, Tajikistan 7.6%. **Tourism:** $84 mil. **Budget:** $6.6 bil. **Inflation:** -1.5%.

Transport: Motor vehicles: 49.5 per 1,000 pop. **Airports:** 23. **Communications: Telephone:** 0.3 per 100 pop. **Mobile:** 61.6 per 100 pop. **Broadband:** 3.2 per 100 pop. **Internet:** 8.3%.

Health: Expend.: 8.2%. **Life expect.:** 49.9 male; 52.7 female. **Births:** 38.3 per 1,000 pop. **Deaths:** 13.7 per 1,000 pop. **Infant mortality:** 112.8 per 1,000 live births. **Undernourished:** 26.8%. **HIV:** <0.1%.

Education: Compulsory: ages 7-15. **Literacy:** 38.2%. **Embassy:** 2341 Wyoming Ave. NW 20008; 483-6410. **Website:** www.president.gov.af/en

Afghanistan, occupying a favored invasion route since antiquity, has been variously known as Ariana or Bactria (in ancient times) and Khorasan (in the Middle Ages). Foreign empires alternated rule with local emirs and kings until the 18th cent., when a unified kingdom was established. In 1973, a military coup ushered in a republic.

Pro-Soviet leftists took power in a bloody 1978 coup. In Dec. 1979 the USSR began a massive airlift into Kabul and backed a new coup, leading to the installation of a more pro-Soviet leader. Soviet forces fanned out over Afghanistan and waged a protracted guerrilla war with Muslim rebels, in which some 15,000 Soviet troops reportedly died.

A UN-mediated agreement was signed Apr. 14, 1988, providing for withdrawal of Soviet troops, a neutral Afghan state, and repatriation of refugees. Afghan rebels rejected the pact. The Soviets completed their troop withdrawal Feb. 15, 1989; fighting between Afghan rebels and government forces ensued. Communist Pres. Najibullah resigned Apr. 16, 1992, as competing guerrilla forces advanced on Kabul. The rebels achieved power Apr. 28, ending 14 years of Soviet-backed regimes. More than 2 mil Afghans had been killed, and 6 mil had left the country since 1979.

Clashes between moderates and Islamic fundamentalist forces followed the rebel victory. Burhanuddin Rabbani, a guerrilla leader, became president June 28, 1992, but fierce fighting continued around Kabul and elsewhere. The Taliban, an insurgent radical-Islamist faction, captured Kabul in Sept. 1996. The Taliban executed Najibullah and empowered Islamic religious police to enforce strict Islamic codes of dress and behavior. Rabbani and other ousted leaders fled to the north.

Victories in the northern cities of Mazar-e Sharif, Aug. 8, 1998, and Taloqan, Aug. 8-11, gave the Taliban control over more than 90% of the country. On Aug. 20, U.S. cruise missiles struck SE of Kabul, hitting facilities the U.S. said were terrorist training camps run by Osama bin Laden. The UN imposed sanctions Nov. 14, 1999, when Afghanistan refused to turn over bin Laden to the U.S. for prosecution.

After the Sept. 11, 2001, attacks on the World Trade Center and Pentagon, the U.S., blaming bin Laden, demanded that the Taliban surrender him and shut down his al-Qaeda terrorist network. When the Taliban refused, the U.S., with British assistance, began bombing Afghanistan Oct. 7, as part of Operation Enduring Freedom (OEF).

Supported by the U.S., the opposition Northern Alliance recaptured Mazar-e Sharif Nov. 9 and took Kabul 4 days later; Taliban forces abandoned Kandahar, their last stronghold, to southern tribal fighters Dec. 7. A power-sharing agreement signed by four anti-Taliban factions, including the Northern Alliance, provided for an interim government headed by Hamid Karzai, a Pashtun tribal leader. The UN authorized a multinational security force Dec. 20, 2001.

Meeting June 13, 2002, in Kabul, a traditional council (*loya jirga*) chose Karzai to head a new transitional government. Although the U.S. announced the end of major combat operations in Afghanistan, May 1, 2003, resistance continued. NATO officially assumed control of peacekeeping forces—the Intl. Security Assistance Force (ISAF)—Aug. 11, 2003.

The most intense fighting in more than 4 years erupted Mar. 2006 with a new wave of attacks and other strikes by Taliban insurgents. Operating from sanctuaries in Pakistan, Islamist suicide bombers and Taliban insurgents stepped up their activities, 2007-11. Violence escalated in the run-up to the presidential election Aug. 20, 2009. With Karzai in the lead, a UN-backed commission ordered a recount, citing evidence of fraud; a Nov. runoff election was canceled when Karzai's lone opponent dropped out. Karzai was sworn in for a second term Nov. 19. After a decade-long manhunt, U.S. commandos killed bin Laden shortly after midnight May 2, 2011, in Abbottabad, Pakistan. Insurgents retaliated Aug. 6 by shooting down a helicopter, killing 30 Americans and 8 Afghans. Other violence included attacks Sept. 13, 2011, on the U.S. embassy and NATO headquarters in Kabul, as well as the assassination Sept. 20 of former Pres. Rabbani.

Between Jan. 2009 and June 2011, the number of U.S. troops in Afghanistan rose from about 36,000 to 101,000, while the number of allied foreign forces under ISAF increased from nearly 32,000 to more than 42,000. The U.S., June 22, 2011, outlined a timetable for drawing down troops and ending their combat role. Pres. Barack Obama announced, May 27, 2014, that by year's end most U.S. troops would be out of Afghanistan, with a residual force focusing on combating al-Qaeda and training and advising Afghan troops. The UN reported 3,701 civilian deaths from conflict in Afghanistan in 2014, 3,545 in 2015, and 1,601 Jan.-June 2016. About 2.7 mil Afghan refugees were living outside the country at the end of 2015, and 1.2 mil Afghans were internally displaced. OEF and ISAF officially ended Dec. 28, 2014; since Oct. 2001, 2,215 U.S. and 1,270 allied troops had been killed. The NATO-led Resolute Support mission (RSM) to aid Afghan forces began Jan. 1, 2015. As of June 2016, there were almost 13,000 RSM troops in Afghanistan, of which about 7,000 were from the U.S.; including other counterterrorism forces, total U.S. troop strength was about 9,800. Pres. Obama announced, July 6, that about 8,400 would remain until the end of his term in Jan. 2017.

The first round of elections for a new president was held Apr. 5, 2014. A June 14 runoff between the two top vote-getters—former Foreign Min. Abdullah Abdullah and former Finance Min. Ashraf Ghani Ahmadzai—was marred by allegations of electoral fraud. After an internationally supervised audit of all 8 mil runoff ballots, Ghani was declared the winner Sept. 21. Under a U.S.-brokered power-sharing agreement, he appointed Abdullah chief executive of the government. Fighting between government and Taliban forces continued in 2015-16, as did terrorist attacks in Kabul and other cities. By one estimate, Taliban forces controlled or were fighting for control in at least one-fifth of the country in early 2016. The government announced, July 29, 2015, that longtime Taliban leader Mohammad Omar had died in 2013. A U.S. drone strike in Pakistan, May 21, 2016, killed new Taliban leader Akhtar Muhammad Mansour; Haibatullah Akhundzada replaced Mansour. An affiliate of the Sunni extremist group ISIS, attracting Taliban defectors, staged attacks beginning in 2014 and gained control of areas in eastern Afghanistan. A suicide bombing in Kabul, July 23, 2016, for which ISIS claimed responsibility, killed at least 80 at a demonstration by a largely Shiite group. The U.S. announced, Aug. 12, that it had killed the ISIS leader in Afghanistan and Pakistan, Hafiz Saeed Khan, in a drone strike.

Albania
Republic of Albania

People: Population: 3,038,594. **Age distrib.:** <15: 18.4%; 65+: 11.6%. **Growth:** 0.3%. **Migrants:** 2%. **Pop. density:** 287.2 per sq mi, 110.9 per sq km. **Urban:** 58.4%. **Ethnic groups:** Albanian 82.6%. **Languages:** Albanian (official), Greek. **Religions:** Muslim 56.7%, Roman Catholic 10%, Orthodox 6.8%, atheist 2.5%.

Geography: Total area: 11,100 sq mi, 28,748 sq km; **Land area:** 10,578 sq mi, 27,398 sq km. **Location:** SE Europe, on SE coast of Adriatic Sea. Greece on S; Montenegro, Kosovo on N; Macedonia on E. **Topography:** Narrow coastal plain; hills and mountains covered with scrub forest, cut by small E-W rivers. **Arable land:** 22.5%. **Capital:** Tirana, 462,846.

Government: Type: Parliamentary republic. **Head of state:** Pres. Bujar Nishani; b. 1966; in office: July 24, 2012. **Head of gov.:** Prime Min. Edi Rama; b. 1964; in office: Sept. 15, 2013. **Local divisions:** 12 counties. **Defense budget:** $138 mil. **Active troops:** 8,000.

Economy: Industries: food and tobacco prods., textiles and clothing, lumber. **Chief crops:** wheat, corn, potatoes, vegetables, fruits, sugar beets, grapes. **Natural resources:** petroleum, nat. gas, coal, bauxite, chromite, copper, iron ore, nickel, salt, timber, hydropower. **Water:** 10,425 cu m per capita. **Crude oil reserves:**

0.2 bil bbls. **Electricity prod.:** 7 bil kWh. **Labor force:** agric. 41.8%, industry 11.4%, services 46.8%. **Unemployment:** 16.1%.

Finance: Monetary unit: Lek (ALL) (123.35 = $1 U.S.). **GDP:** $32.7 bil (unreported output may be as large as 50% of official GDP); **per capita GDP:** $11,900; **GDP growth:** 2.6%. **Imports:** $3.6 bil; Italy 33.4%, China 10%, Greece 9%, Turkey 6.7%, Germany 5.2%. **Exports:** $1 bil; Italy 42.8%, Kosovo 9.7%, U.S. 7.6%, China 6.1%, Greece 5.3%. **Tourism:** $1.5 bil. **Budget:** $3.5 bil. **Inflation:** 1.9%.

Transport: Railways: 421 mi. **Airports:** 4.

Communications: Telephone: 7.1 per 100 pop. **Mobile:** 106.4 per 100 pop. **Broadband:** 30.9 per 100 pop. **Internet:** 63.3%.

Health: Expend.: 5.9%. **Life expect.:** 75.7 male; 81.2 female. **Births:** 13.1 per 1,000 pop. **Deaths:** 6.7 per 1,000 pop. **Infant mortality:** 12.3 per 1,000 live births. **Undernourished:** <5%. **HIV:** NA.

Education: Compulsory: ages 6-14. **Literacy:** 97.6%.

Embassy: 2100 S St. NW 20008; 223-4942.

Website: www.kryeministria.al/en

Ancient Illyria was conquered by Romans, Slavs, and Turks (15th cent.); the Turks Islamized the population. Independent Albania was proclaimed in 1912; a republic was formed in 1920. King Zog I ruled 1925-39 until Italy invaded.

Communist partisans took over in 1944 and allied Albania with the USSR but broke with the USSR in 1960 over de-Stalinization. Billions of dollars in Chinese financial assistance was cut off in 1978 when Albania attacked China's policies. Large-scale purges of officials occurred during the 1970s.

Enver Hoxha, the nation's ruler for four decades, died Apr. 11, 1985. The new regime introduced some liberalization, including measures in 1990 providing for freedom to travel abroad.

Albania's former Communists were routed in elections Mar. 1992, amid economic collapse and social unrest. Sali Berisha was elected as the first non-Communist president since WWII. Berisha's party claimed a landslide victory in disputed parliamentary elections, May 26 and June 2, 1996. Public protests over the collapse of fraudulent investment schemes in Jan. 1997 led to armed rebellion. The UN Security Council, Mar. 28, authorized a 7,000-member force to restore order. Socialists and their allies won parliamentary elections, June 29 and July 6, and international peacekeepers pulled out by Aug. 11, 1997.

During NATO's air war against Yugoslavia, Mar.-June 1999, Albania hosted some 465,000 Kosovar refugees. A pro-Berisha coalition victory in July 3, 2005, elections ended eight years of Socialist rule. Albania became a full member of NATO Apr. 1, 2009. Socialists won June 23, 2013, parliamentary elections, and Edi Rama became the new prime min. The EU granted Albania official candidate status June 27, 2014. Membership negotiations were expected to include EU requests for reforms to reduce organized crime and political corruption. Pope Francis praised "peaceful and fruitful coexistence" between religious communities in Albania during a trip to Tirana, Sept. 21, 2014.

Algeria
People's Democratic Republic of Algeria

People: Population: 40,263,711. **Age distrib.:** <15: 29.1%; 65+: 5.5%. **Growth:** 1.8%. **Migrants:** 0.6%. **Pop. density:** 43.8 per sq mi, 16.9 per sq km. **Urban:** 71.3%. **Ethnic groups:** Arab-Berber 99%. **Languages:** Arabic (official), French (lingua franca), Berber or Tamazight (official), Berber dialects. **Religions:** Muslim (official; predom. Sunni) 99%.

Geography: Total area: 919,595 sq mi, 2,381,741 sq km; **Land area:** 919,595 sq mi, 2,381,741 sq km. **Location:** NW Africa, from Medit. Sea into Sahara. Morocco, Western Sahara on W; Mauritania, Mali, Niger on S; Libya, Tunisia on E. **Topography:** The Tell, on the coast, comprises fertile plains 50-100 mi wide with a moderate climate and adequate rain. Two major chains of Atlas Mts., running roughly E-W and reaching 7,000 ft, enclose a dry plateau region. Below lies the Sahara. **Arable land:** 3.1%. **Capital:** Algiers, 2,632,469. **Cities:** Oran, 868,209.

Government: Type: Presidential republic. **Head of state:** Pres. Abdelaziz Bouteflika; b. 1937; in office: Apr. 27, 1999. **Head of gov.:** Prime Min. Abdelmalek Sellal; b. 1948; in office: Sept. 3, 2012. **Local divisions:** 48 provinces. **Defense budget:** $10.8 bil. **Active troops:** 130,000.

Economy: Industries: petroleum, nat. gas, light industries, mining, electrical, petrochemical, food proc. **Chief crops:** wheat, barley, oats, grapes, olives, citrus, fruits. **Natural resources:** petroleum, nat. gas, iron ore, phosphates, uranium, lead, zinc. **Water:** 294 cu m per capita. **Crude oil reserves:** 12.2 bil bbls. **Electricity prod.:** 56 bil kWh. **Labor force:** agric. 10.8%, industry 30.9%, services 58.4%. **Unemployment:** 9.5%.

Finance: Monetary unit: Dinar (DZD) (109.18 = $1 U.S.). **GDP:** $578.7 bil; **per capita GDP:** $14,500; **GDP growth:** 3.7%. **Imports:** $52.7 bil; China 15.6%, France 14.3%, Italy 9.4%, Spain 7.4%, Germany 5.6%. **Exports:** $36.3 bil; Spain 18.8%, France

11.2%, U.S. 8.8%, Italy 8.7%, UK 7.1%, Brazil 5.2%. **Tourism:** $258 mil. **Budget:** $69 bil. **Inflation:** 4.8%.

Transport: Railways: 2,469 mi. **Motor vehicles:** 140.7 per 1,000 pop. **Airports:** 64.

Communications: Telephone: 8 per 100 pop. **Mobile:** 113 per 100 pop. **Broadband:** 20.8 per 100 pop. **Internet:** 38.2%.

Health: Expend.: 7.2%. **Life expect.:** 75.5 male; 78.2 female. **Births:** 23.0 per 1,000 pop. **Deaths:** 4.3 per 1,000 pop. **Infant mortality:** 20.3 per 1,000 live births. **Undernourished:** <5%. **HIV:** <0.1%.

Education: Compulsory: ages 6-15. **Literacy:** 79.6%.

Embassy: 2118 Kalorama Rd. NW 20008; 265-2800.

Website: www.algerianembassy.org or www.premier-ministre.gov.dz

Earliest known inhabitants were ancestors of Berbers, followed by Phoenicians, Romans, Vandals, and Arabs. Turkey ruled 1518-1830, when France took control. Large-scale European immigration followed. Arab nationalists launched a guerrilla war, 1954, that more than 400,000 French troops were unable to suppress. After French Pres. Charles de Gaulle came to power, 1958, colonial rule ended, nearly all Europeans left, and Algeria declared independence July 5, 1962. Ahmed Ben Bella ruled until 1965, when an army coup installed Col. Houari Boumedienne, a former guerrilla leader who held power until his death in 1978.

Hundreds died in antigovernment riots protesting economic hardship, Oct. 1988. The government canceled the Jan. 1992 elections and banned all nonreligious activities at Algeria's 10,000 mosques. Pres. Mohammed Boudiaf was assassinated June 29, 1992. Over the next seven years, Muslim fundamentalists attacked high-ranking officials, security forces, and foreigners; pro-government death squads were active.

Liamine Zeroual won the Nov. 16, 1995, presidential election. A new constitution banning Islamic political parties and increasing the president's powers passed in a Nov. 1996 referendum. Abdelaziz Bouteflika, who became president after a flawed Apr. 15, 1999, election, reconciled with rebels and won approval for an amnesty plan in a referendum, Sept. 16. Some 100 people died and thousands were injured in violent protests Apr.-June 2001, chiefly by Algeria's Berber minority. Bouteflika was reelected Apr. 8, 2004, though opponents charged fraud.

Under a reconciliation plan approved by referendum Sept. 2005, the government in Mar. 2006 began freeing Islamists jailed for their role in the 1990s civil war, which left up to 200,000 people dead and 8,000 "disappeared."

Radical Islamists bombed police stations in Oct. 2006 and Feb. 2007. A group known as al-Qaeda in the Islamic Maghreb (AQIM) carried out several suicide bombings throughout 2007, killing more than 100 people. A surge in AQIM violence in Aug. 2008 left another 100+ people dead.

Parliament, Nov. 12, 2008, amended the constitution to abolish presidential term limits, enabling Bouteflika to run for a third term. He claimed more than 90% of the vote in a 2009 election denounced as fraudulent by opposition parties. During Arab Spring uprisings in early 2011, Bouteflika's government suppressed street protests in Algiers, Feb. 12, and used oil revenues to raise salaries of teachers, police, and other discontented civil servants. The country's governing party, the Natl. Liberation Front, strengthened its hold on power in May 10, 2012, parliamentary elections that opposition groups called fraudulent. The 77-year-old Bouteflika won a fourth term as president with 81.5% of the vote in the Apr. 17, 2014, election, which some opposition parties boycotted. A Feb. 2016 constitutional amendment restored presidential term limits (two terms).

AQIM members protesting France's involvement in Mali seized the In Amenas gas facility Jan. 16, 2013, holding about 40 foreign workers hostage for 4 days and demanding the release of about 100 Islamist prisoners being held in Algeria. In the end, 38 hostages died, including 3 Americans, as well as some 29 militants at the hands of Algerian special forces attempting to liberate the facility. Algerian officials reported that security forces, May 19, 2015, had killed 21 Islamist extremists planning a terrorist attack on Algiers. AQIM claimed responsibility for a rocket-propelled grenade attack on the In Salah gas field, Mar. 18, 2016.

Andorra
Principality of Andorra

People: Population: 85,660. **Age distrib.:** <15: 14.7%; 65+: 15.1%. **Growth:** 0.1%. **Migrants:** 59.7%. **Pop. density:** 474.1 per sq mi, 183 per sq km. **Urban:** 84.6%. **Ethnic groups:** Andorran 49%, Spanish 24.6%, Portuguese 14.3%, French 3.9%. **Languages:** Catalan (official), French, Castilian, Portuguese. **Religions:** Roman Catholic (predom.).

Geography: Total area: 181 sq mi, 468 sq km; **Land area:** 181 sq mi, 468 sq km. **Location:** SW Europe, in Pyrenees Mts. Spain on S, France on N. **Topography:** High mountains and narrow valleys across country. **Arable land:** 6.2%. **Capital:** Andorra la Vella, 23,349 (2014).

Government: Type: Parliamentary democracy. **Heads of state:** President of France and Bishop of Urgell (Spain), as co-princes.

Head of gov.: Antoni Martí Petit; b. 1963; in office: May 12, 2011. **Local divisions:** 7 parishes. **Defense budget/active troops:** NA.

Economy: Industries: tourism (skiing), banking, timber, furniture. **Chief crops:** rye, wheat, barley, oats, vegetables, tobacco. **Natural resources:** hydropower, mineral water, timber, iron ore, lead. **Water:** 4,479 cu m per capita. **Labor force:** agric. 0.4%, industry 4.7%, services 94.9%. **Unemployment:** NA.

Finance: Monetary unit: Euro (EUR) (0.89 = $1 U.S.). **GDP** (2012): $3.2 bil; **per capita GDP** (2011): $37,200; **GDP growth** (2012): −1.6%. **Imports** (2012): $1.4 bil. **Exports** (2012): $70 mil. **Budget** (2012): $1 bil. **Inflation** (2011-12): 1.1%.

Transport: NA.

Communications: Telephone: 48 per 100 pop. **Mobile:** 88.1 per 100 pop. **Broadband:** 36.6 per 100 pop. **Internet:** 96.9%.

Health: Expend.: 8.1%. **Life expect.:** 80.6 male; 85.1 female. **Births:** 7.8 per 1,000 pop. **Deaths:** 7.1 per 1,000 pop. **Infant mortality:** 3.6 per 1,000 live births. **Undernourished:** <5%. **HIV:** NA.

Education: Compulsory: ages 6-15. **Literacy:** 100%.

Embassy: 2 UN Plz., 27th Fl., New York, NY 10017; (212) 750-8064.

Website: www.govern.ad

France and the bishop of Urgell held joint sovereignty over Andorra from 1278 to 1993. Voters chose to adopt a parliamentary system Mar. 14, 1993, although co-princes remain heads of state. Tourism, especially skiing, is an economic mainstay. For years, Andorra served as a tax haven, but it began reforms in 2008 and was removed by the OECD from its list of uncooperative tax havens, May 27, 2009. In Mar. 2015, the government seized control of Banca Privada d'Andorra (BPA) and arrested its chief executive after the U.S. Treasury Dept. accused BPA of facilitating money laundering on behalf of global criminal groups. Following his party's victory in Mar. 2015 elections, Antoni Martí Petit was reelected by the legislature as head of government.

Angola
Republic of Angola

People: Population: 20,172,332. **Age distrib.:** <15: 42.7%; 65+: 3%. **Growth:** 2.7%. **Migrants:** 0.4%. **Pop. density:** 41.9 per sq mi, 16.2 per sq km. **Urban:** 44.8%. **Ethnic groups:** Ovimbundu 37%, Kimbundu 25%, Bakongo 13%, mestico (mixed European/native African) 2%. **Languages:** Portuguese (official), Umbundu, Kikongo, Kimbundu, Chokwe. **Religions:** Roman Catholic 41.1%, Protestant 38.1%, none 12.3%.

Geography: Total area: 481,354 sq mi, 1,246,700 sq km; **Land area:** 481,354 sq mi, 1,246,700 sq km. **Location:** SW Africa on Atlantic coast. Namibia on S, Zambia on E, Dem. Rep. of the Congo on N; Cabinda, an exclave separated from rest of country by short Atlantic coast of Dem. Rep. of the Congo, borders Congo Rep. **Topography:** Mostly plateau 3,000-5,000 ft above sea level, rising from a narrow coastal strip. Temperate highland area in the W-central region, a desert in S, and a tropical rain forest in Cabinda. **Arable land:** 3.9%. **Capital:** Luanda, 5,737,475. **Cities:** Huambo, 1,337,366.

Government: Type: Presidential republic. **Head of state and gov.:** Pres. José Eduardo dos Santos; b. 1942; in office: Sept. 21, 1979. **Local divisions:** 18 provinces. **Defense budget:** $4.4 bil. **Active troops:** 107,000.

Economy: Industries: petroleum, diamonds, cement, metal prods, fish and food proc. **Chief crops:** bananas, sugarcane, coffee, sisal, corn, cotton, cassava, tobacco. **Natural resources:** petroleum, diamonds, iron ore, phosphates, copper, feldspar, gold, bauxite, uranium. **Water:** 5,931 cu m per capita. **Crude oil reserves:** 8.4 bil bbls. **Electricity prod.:** 5.8 bil kWh. **Labor force:** agric. 85%, industry and services 15%. **Unemployment:** 6.8%.

Finance: Monetary unit: Kwanza (AOA) (165.74 = $1 U.S.). **GDP:** $184.4 bil; **per capita GDP:** $7,300; **GDP growth:** 3%. **Imports:** $21.9 bil; China 22.1%, Portugal 13.8%, South Korea 11%, U.S. 6.9%, South Africa 5%. **Exports:** $37.4 bil; China 43.8%, India 9.6%, U.S. 7.7%, Spain 6.2%. **Tourism:** $1.6 bil. **Budget:** $41.8 bil. **Inflation:** 10.3%.

Transport: Railways: 1,772 mi. **Motor vehicles:** 7.2 per 1,000 pop. **Airports:** 31.

Communications: Telephone: 1.2 per 100 pop. **Mobile:** 60.8 per 100 pop. **Broadband:** 16.4 per 100 pop. **Internet:** 12.4%.

Health: Expend.: 3.3%. **Life expect.:** 54.8 male; 57.2 female. **Births:** 38.6 per 1,000 pop. **Deaths:** 11.3 per 1,000 pop. **Infant mortality:** 76.5 per 1,000 live births. **Undernourished:** 14.2%. **HIV:** 2.2%.

Education: Compulsory: ages 6-11. **Literacy:** 71.2%.

Embassy: 2100-2108 16th St. NW 20009; 785-1156.

Website: www.governo.gov.ao or www.angola.org

From the early centuries CE to 1500, Bantu tribes penetrated most of the region. Portuguese came in 1583, allied with the Bakongo kingdom in the north, and developed the slave trade. Large-scale colonization began in the 20th cent., when 400,000 Portuguese immigrated.

A guerrilla war, 1961-75, ended when Portugal granted Angola independence. Fighting then erupted among three rival rebel groups—the National Front, based in Zaire (now Dem. Rep. of the Congo); the Soviet-backed Popular Movement for the Liberation of Angola (MPLA); and the National Union for the Total Independence of Angola (UNITA), aided by the U.S. and South Africa. Cuban troops and Soviet aid helped the MPLA win control of most of the country by 1976, although fighting continued. The MPLA government and UNITA signed a peace accord May 1, 1991. Elections were held, Sept. 1992, but fighting again broke out when UNITA rejected the results. UNITA signed a new peace treaty with the government, Nov. 20, 1994, but the rebels were slow to demobilize. The UN Security Council voted, Aug. 28, 1997, to impose sanctions on UNITA. The UN ended its mission in Angola, Mar. 1999, as the civil war continued. The UN estimated that the war with UNITA had claimed some 1 mil lives and left another 2.5 mil people homeless by mid-2001. Government troops killed rebel leader Jonas Savimbi Feb. 22, 2002. UNITA agreed to a truce Apr. 4, 2002, ending the 27-year-long civil war. Separatist rebels in oil-rich Cabinda agreed to a cease-fire July 2006.

With proven petroleum reserves estimated at 9 bil barrels, Angola is among Africa's leading oil producers. Wealth is unevenly distributed. Half the population lacks access to health care, and the country's under-age-5 mortality rate in 2015, 157 per 1,000 live births, was the world's highest. The ruling MPLA claimed victory in voting Sept. 2008, in Angola's first parliamentary elections in 16 years. Parliament approved Jan. 21, 2010, a new constitution augmenting the power of MPLA leader José Eduardo dos Santos, Angola's president since 1979. The MPLA won flawed elections, Aug 31, 2012, giving Dos Santos another 5-year term.

Antigua and Barbuda

People: Population: 93,581. **Age distrib.:** <15: 23.4%; 65+: 7.8%. **Growth:** 1.2%. **Migrants:** 30.6%. **Pop. density:** 547.1 per sq mi, 211.2 per sq km. **Urban:** 23.4%. **Ethnic groups:** black 87.3%, mixed 4.7%, Hispanic 2.7%. **Languages:** English (official), Antiguan creole. **Religions:** Protestant 68.3% (incl. Anglican 17.6%, Seventh-day Adventist 12.4%, Pentecostal 12.2%, Moravian 8.3%), Roman Catholic 8.2%, none 5.9%.
Geography: Total area: 171 sq mi, 443 sq km (Antigua, 108 sq mi, 280 sq km; Barbuda, 62 sq mi, 161 sq km). **Land area:** 171 sq mi, 443 sq km. **Location:** E Caribbean. St. Kitts and Nevis to W, Guadeloupe (Fr.) to S. **Topography:** Mostly low-lying and limestone coral islands. Antigua is mostly hilly with an indented coast; Barbuda is a flat island with a large lagoon on W. **Arable land:** 9.1%. **Capital:** St. John's, 21,989 (2014).
Government: Type: Parliamentary democracy under constitutional monarchy. **Head of state:** Queen Elizabeth II, rep. by Gov.-Gen. Sir Rodney Williams; b. 1947; in office: Aug. 14, 2014. **Head of gov.:** Prime Min. Gaston Browne; b. 1967; in office: June 13, 2014. **Local divisions:** 6 parishes, 2 dependencies. **Defense budget:** $27 mil. **Active troops:** 180.
Economy: Industries: tourism, constr., light mfg. **Chief crops:** cotton, fruits, vegetables, bananas, coconuts. **Natural resources:** negligible. **Water:** 566 cu m per capita. **Electricity prod.:** 0.3 bil kWh. **Labor force:** agric. 7%, industry 11%, services 82%. **Unemployment:** NA.
Finance: Monetary unit: East Caribbean Dollar (XCD) (2.70 = $1 U.S.). **GDP:** $2.1 bil; **per capita GDP:** $23,600; **GDP growth:** 2.2%. **Imports:** $482.5 mil. **Exports:** $61 mil. **Tourism:** $333 mil. **Budget:** $217 mil. **Inflation:** 1%.
Transport: Airports: 2.
Communications: Telephone: 13.1 per 100 pop. **Mobile:** 137.2 per 100 pop. **Broadband:** 33 per 100 pop. **Internet:** 65.2%.
Health: Expend.: 5.5%. **Life expect.:** 74.4 male; 78.8 female. **Births:** 15.8 per 1,000 pop. **Deaths:** 5.7 per 1,000 pop. **Infant mortality:** 12.5 per 1,000 live births. **Undernourished:** NA. **HIV:** NA.
Education: Compulsory: ages 5-15. **Literacy:** 99%.
Embassy: 3216 New Mexico Ave. NW 20016; 362-5122.
Website: www.ab.gov.ag
Christopher Columbus landed on Antigua in 1493. The British colonized it in 1632. The British-associated state of Antigua achieved independence as Antigua and Barbuda on Nov. 1, 1981. Tourism accounts for almost 60% of GDP. The worldwide recession caused the economy to shrink in 2009-11. The economy also suffered after Robert Allen Stanford, a Texas businessman, was charged by U.S. authorities Feb. 17, 2009, with employing his Antigua-based Stanford Intl. Bank to conduct a fraudulent $7-bil investment scheme. He was convicted Mar. 6, 2012. With the economy still weak, the opposition Antigua and Barbuda Labour Party (ABLP) won an overwhelming victory in June 12, 2014, elections for the lower house of parliament, and ABLP leader Gaston Browne became prime minister.

Argentina
Argentine Republic

People: Population: 43,886,748. **Age distrib.:** <15: 24.7%; 65+: 11.5%. **Growth:** 0.9%. **Migrants:** 4.8%. **Pop. density:** 41.5 per sq mi, 16 per sq km. **Urban:** 91.9%. **Ethnic groups:** white (mostly Spanish and Italian) 97%, mestizo (mixed white/Amerindian), Amerindian, non-white groups 3%. **Languages:** Spanish (official), Italian, English, German, French, indigenous (Mapudungun, Quechua). **Religions:** nominally Roman Catholic 92%, Protestant 2%, Jewish 2%.
Geography: Total area: 1,073,518 sq mi, 2,780,400 sq km; **Land area:** 1,056,642 sq mi, 2,736,690 sq km. **Location:** Occupies most of southern S America. Chile on W; Bolivia, Paraguay on N; Brazil, Uruguay on NE. **Topography:** Andean, Central, Misiones, and Southern mountain ranges in W. Aconcagua (22,835 ft) is highest peak in Western Hemisphere. Heavily wooded plains called the Gran Chaco are E of Andes in the N; fertile, treeless Pampas in the central region. Patagonia, in S, is bleak and arid. Rio de la Plata, an estuary in NE, 170 by 140 mi, is mostly freshwater, from 2,485-mi Parana and 1,000-mi Uruguay Rivers. **Arable land:** 14.5%. **Capital:** Buenos Aires, 15,333,630. **Cities:** Córdoba, 1,518,997; Rosario, 1,395,035; Mendoza, 1,019,785.
Government: Type: Presidential republic. **Head of state and gov.:** Pres. Mauricio Macri; b. 1959; in office: Dec. 10, 2015. **Local divisions:** 23 provinces, 1 autonomous city. **Defense budget:** $6.5 bil. **Active troops:** 74,400.
Economy: Industries: food proc., motor vehicles, consumer durables, textiles, chemicals and petrochemicals. **Chief crops:** sunflower seeds, lemons, soybeans, grapes, corn, tobacco. **Natural resources:** lead, zinc, tin, copper, iron ore, manganese, petroleum, uranium. **Water:** 20,181 cu m per capita. **Crude oil reserves:** 2.4 bil bbls. **Electricity prod.:** 134 bil kWh. **Labor force:** agric. 5%, industry 23%, services 72%. **Unemployment:** 8.2%.
Finance: Monetary unit: Peso (ARS) (14.88 = $1 U.S.). **GDP:** $972 bil; **per capita GDP:** $22,600; **GDP growth:** 1.2%. **Imports:** $60.6 bil; Brazil 22.1%, U.S. 16.1%, China 15.4%, Germany 5.1%. **Exports:** $66 bil; Brazil 17%, China 8.6%, U.S. 5.9%. **Tourism:** $4.4 bil. **Budget:** $170.4 bil. **Inflation** (2012-13): 10.6%.
Transport: Railways: 22,939 mi. **Motor vehicles:** 329.4 per 1,000 pop. **Airports:** 161.
Communications: Telephone: 24 per 100 pop. **Mobile:** 143.9 per 100 pop. **Broadband:** 53.6 per 100 pop. **Internet:** 69.4%.
Health: Expend.: 4.8%. **Life expect.:** 74.0 male; 80.4 female. **Births:** 17.0 per 1,000 pop. **Deaths:** 7.5 per 1,000 pop. **Infant mortality:** 10.1 per 1,000 live births. **Undernourished:** <5%. **HIV:** 0.4%.
Education: Compulsory: ages 5-17. **Literacy:** 98.1%.
Embassy: 1600 New Hampshire Ave. NW 20009; 238-6400.
Website: www.argentina.gob.ar
Nomadic Indians roamed the Pampas when Spaniards arrived, 1515-16, led by Juan Díaz de Solís. Nearly all the Indians were killed by the late 19th cent. The colonists won independence, 1816. A long period of disorder ended in a strong centralized government.

Large-scale Italian, German, and Spanish immigration in the decades after 1880 spurred modernization. Social reforms were enacted in the 1920s, but military coups prevailed, 1930-46, until Gen. Juan Perón was elected president.

Perón, with his wife, Eva Duarte (d. 1952), introduced labor reforms but suppressed speech and press freedoms, closed religious schools, and ran the country into debt. A 1955 coup exiled Perón. A series of military and civilian regimes followed. Perón returned in 1973 and was again elected president. He died 10 months later. His wife and vice president, Isabel, succeeded him.

A military junta ousted Perón in 1976 amid charges of corruption. Under a continuing state of siege, the army conducted a "dirty war" against guerrillas and leftists. An estimated 30,000 people "disappeared."

Argentine troops seized control of the British-held Falkland Islands (Islas Malvinas) on Apr. 2, 1982. The British imposed an air and sea blockade around the Falklands. Fighting began May 1. British troops landed on East Falkland May 21. Argentine troops surrendered, June 14.

Democratic rule returned in 1983. On Dec. 9, 1985, five former junta members were found guilty of murder and human rights abuses during the "dirty war" period. Buenos Aires Mayor Fernando de la Rúa won the presidential election Oct. 24, 1999, but resigned in 2001 after a prolonged recession resulted in debt of more than $130 bil. Congress, Jan. 1, 2002, chose a Peronist, Eduardo Alberto Duhalde, to finish de la Rúa's term. Further economic decline and renewed protests led Duhalde, July 2, to schedule an early presidential election for Mar. 2003; another Peronist, Néstor Kirchner, took office May 25, 2003. A new IMF aid deal, approved Sept. 10, 2003, rescued Argentina from default.

The supreme court, June 14, 2005, overturned amnesty laws that had barred prosecution for "dirty war" crimes committed while the military ruled Argentina. Economic growth, 2004-05, allowed Argentina to repay its $9.57-bil debt to the IMF, Jan. 3, 2006.

Cristina Fernández de Kirchner ran as the Peronist candidate after her husband and was elected president Oct. 28, 2007. A candidate slate led by Néstor Kirchner was defeated in legislative elections June 2009, and the Peronists lost control of both houses of congress. Argentina became the first Latin American country to extend full marriage rights to same-sex couples in July 2010.

Néstor Kirchner died Oct. 27, 2010. Cristina Kirchner was reelected Oct. 23, 2011. In Nov. 2012, leaders of the nation's Jewish population charged the government with anti-Semitism for attempting to ease relations with Iran. On May 29, 2013, Argentine special prosecutor Alberto Nisman claimed that Iran was plotting to carry out terrorist attacks throughout Latin America. Nisman accused Cristina Kirchner of interfering with his investigation of Iranian involvement in a 1994 Jewish community center bombing in Buenos Aires that killed 85 people. Nisman was found dead in his home from a gunshot to the head Jan. 18, 2015. The accusations against Cristina Kirchner were formally dropped May 12, 2015, but a federal judge reopened the investigation Aug. 5, 2016. Former Pres. Carlos Saúl Menem, who had been convicted Mar. 8, 2013, of weapons smuggling during his 1989-99 term, went on trial, Aug. 6, 2015, on charges of interfering with the 1994 bombing investigation. In a separate trial, Menem was convicted, Dec. 1, 2015, on charges related to embezzlement of public funds. Defeating Peronist candidate Daniel Scioli in a runoff, Mauricio Macri of the center-right Republican Proposal Party was elected president Nov. 22, 2015. Cristina Kirchner was indicted, May 13, 2016, for allegedly interfering with the central bank to improve the value of the Argentine peso while president.

Buenos Aires Archbishop Jorge Mario Bergoglio was elected pope Mar. 13, 2013; he was the first Jesuit pope and the first pope from the Americas. He took the name Francis after advocate for the poor St. Francis of Assisi.

Armenia
Republic of Armenia

People: Population: 3,051,250. **Age distrib.:** <15: 19%; 65+: 11%. **Growth:** −0.2%. **Migrants:** 6.3%. **Pop. density:** 280.2 per sq mi, 108.2 per sq km. **Urban:** 62.6%. **Ethnic groups:** Armenian 98.1%, Yezidi (Kurd) 1.1%. **Languages:** Armenian (official), Kurdish. **Religions:** Armenian Apostolic 92.6%.

Geography: Total area: 11,484 sq mi, 29,743 sq km; **Land area:** 10,889 sq mi, 28,203 sq km. **Location:** SW Asia. Georgia on N, Azerbaijan on E, Iran on S, Turkey on W. **Topography:** Mountainous with many peaks above 10,000 ft. **Arable land:** 15.7%. **Capital:** Yerevan, 1,040,261.

Government: Type: Semi-presidential republic. **Head of state:** Pres. Serzh Sargsyan; b. 1954; in office: Apr. 9, 2008. **Head of gov.:** Prime Min. Karen Karapetyan; b. 1963; in office: Sept. 13, 2016. **Local divisions:** 11 provinces. **Defense budget:** $414 mil. **Active troops:** 44,800.

Economy: Industries: diamond proc., metal-cutting machine tools, forging and pressing machines, elec. motors, knitted wear. **Chief crops:** fruit (espec. grapes), vegetables. **Natural resources:** gold, copper, molybdenum, zinc, bauxite. **Water:** 2,574 cu m per capita. **Electricity prod.:** 7.3 bil kWh. **Labor force:** agric. 39%, industry 17%, services 44%. **Unemployment:** 17.1%.

Finance: Monetary unit: Dram (AMD) (474.75 = $1 U.S.). **GDP:** $25.3 bil; **per capita GDP:** $8,500; **GDP growth:** 3%. **Imports:** $3.1 bil; Russia 29.1%, China 9.7%, Germany 6.2%, Iran 6.1%. **Exports:** $1.5 bil; Russia 15.2%, China 11.1%, Germany 9.8%, Iraq 8.8%, Georgia 7.8%, Canada 7.6%, Bulgaria 5.3%, Iran 5.3%. **Tourism:** $936 mil. **Budget:** $2.8 bil. **Inflation:** 3.7%.

Transport: Railways: 485 mi (only partly operational). **Airports:** 10.

Communications: Telephone: 18.4 per 100 pop. **Mobile:** 115.1 per 100 pop. **Broadband:** 34.2 per 100 pop. **Internet:** 58.2%.

Health: Expend.: 4.5%. **Life expect.:** 71.4 male; 78.3 female. **Births:** 13.3 per 1,000 pop. **Deaths:** 9.4 per 1,000 pop. **Infant mortality:** 13.1 per 1,000 live births. **Undernourished:** 5.8%. **HIV:** 0.2%.

Education: Compulsory: ages 6-16. **Literacy:** 99.8%.
Embassy: 2225 R St. NW 20008; 319-1976.
Website: www.gov.am

Ancient Armenia extended into parts of what are now Turkey and Iran. Present-day Armenia was set up as a Soviet republic Apr. 2, 1921. It joined Georgian and Azerbaijan SSRs Mar. 12, 1922, to form the Transcaucasian SFSR, which became part of the USSR Dec. 30, 1922. Armenia became a constituent republic of the USSR Dec. 5, 1936. An earthquake struck Armenia Dec. 7, 1988; approximately 25,000 were killed.

Armenia declared independence Sept. 23, 1991, and became an independent state when the USSR disbanded Dec. 26, 1991. Nagorno-Karabakh, an enclave in Azerbaijan with an ethnic Armenian majority, seceded from Azerbaijan in 1988. A 1992-94 war that cost 30,000 lives ended in a cease-fire with Armenian forces in control. Voters in the breakaway region approved a pro-independence constitution Dec. 10, 2006, that was rejected by the EU and OSCE. Deadly clashes between Armenian and Azerbaijani forces occurred in 2015-16 in and near Nagorno-Karabakh; a cease-fire was announced Apr. 5, 2016.

Voters approved, July 5, 1995, a new constitution increasing presidential powers. Pres. Levon Ter-Petrosian won reelection

Sept. 22, 1996, amid claims of fraud. He resigned Feb. 3, 1998, and Robert Kocharian, a nationalist born in Nagorno-Karabak, won the presidency Mar. 30, 1998. Gunmen stormed Parliament Oct. 27, 1999, killing Prime Min. Vazgen Sarkissian and 7 others. Kocharian won a second term Mar. 5, 2003, in a runoff vote that observers viewed as flawed.

Prime Min. Serzh Sargsyan defeated Ter-Petrosian in a Feb. 19, 2008, presidential election and won reelection Feb. 18, 2013. Constitutional revisions approved in a Dec. 6, 2015, referendum transitioned the country's government to a parliamentary system as of 2018, with presidential powers reduced. Observers noted voting irregularities; the revisions could allow Sargsyan to retain power as prime min. Following the July 2016 takeover of a police compound and large-scale protests in Yerevan, Prime Min. Hovik Abrahamyan announced his resignation Sept. 8, 2016; Karen Karapetyan replaced him Sept. 13.

Armenia did not ratify an Oct. 2009 treaty it had approved with Turkey over the 1915-18 killing of more than 1 mil Armenians by Ottoman Turks, due to renewed friction between the countries in 2010. On Jan. 2, 2015, Armenia joined the new Russian-led Eurasian Economic Union.

Australia
Commonwealth of Australia

People: Population: 22,992,654. **Age distrib.:** <15: 17.8%; 65+: 15.8%. **Growth:** 1.1%. **Migrants:** 28.2%. **Pop. density:** 7.8 per sq mi, 3 per sq km. **Urban:** 89.6%. **Ethnic groups:** English 25.9%, Australian 25.4%, Irish 7.5%, Scottish 6.4%, Italian 3.3%, German 3.2%, Chinese 3.1%. **Languages:** English, Chinese, Italian, Arabic, Greek, Vietnamese. **Religions:** Protestant 30.1% (incl. Anglican 17.1%), Catholic 25.3%, other Christian 2.9%, Orthodox 2.8%, none 22.3%.

Geography: Total area: 2,988,902 sq mi, 7,741,220 sq km; **Land area:** 2,966,153 sq mi, 7,682,300 sq km. **Location:** SE of Asia. Surrounded by Indian O. on W and S, Pacific O. (Coral, Tasman Seas) in E. Tasmania lies 150 mi S of Victoria state, across Bass Strait. Nearest are Indonesia, Papua New Guinea on N; Solomons, Fiji, and New Zealand on E. **Topography:** An island continent. The Great Dividing Range along the E coast has Mt. Kosciusko (7,310 ft). The Western Plateau rises to 2,000 ft, with arid areas in the Great Sandy and Great Victoria Deserts. The NW part of Western Australia and Northern Terr. are arid and hot. The NE has heavy rainfall. Jungles in Cape York Peninsula. **Arable land:** 6%. **Capital:** Canberra, 430,876. **Cities:** Sydney, 4,539,598; Melbourne, 4,258,173; Brisbane, 2,237,853; Perth, 1,895,729; Adelaide, 1,264,982.

Government: Type: Parliamentary democracy under constitutional monarchy. **Head of state:** Queen Elizabeth II, rep. by Gov.-Gen. Sir Peter Cosgrove; b. 1947; in office: Mar. 28, 2014. **Head of gov.:** Prime Min. Malcolm Turnbull; b. 1954; in office: Sept. 15, 2015. **Local divisions:** 6 states, 2 territories. **Defense budget:** $22.8 bil. **Active troops:** 56,750.

Economy: Industries: mining, industrial and transp. equip., food proc., chemicals, steel. **Chief crops:** wheat, barley, sugarcane, fruits. **Natural resources:** bauxite, coal, iron ore, copper, tin, gold, silver, uranium, nickel, tungsten, rare earth elements, mineral sands, lead, zinc, diamonds, nat. gas, petroleum. **Water:** 20,527 cu m per capita. **Crude oil reserves:** 1.2 bil bbls. **Electricity prod.:** 238 bil kWh. **Labor force:** agric. 3.6%, industry 21.1%, services 75.3%. **Unemployment:** 6%.

Finance: Monetary unit: Dollar (AUD) (1.32 = $1 U.S.). **GDP:** $1.5 tril; **per capita GDP:** $65,400; **GDP growth:** 2.5%. **Imports:** $208.4 bil; China 23%, U.S. 11.2%, Japan 7.4%, South Korea 5.5%, Thailand 5.1%. **Exports:** $184.4 bil; China 32.2%, Japan 15.9%, South Korea 7.1%, U.S. 5.4%. **Tourism:** $29.4 bil. **Budget:** $451.4 bil. **Inflation:** 1.5%.

Transport: Railways: 22,971 mi. **Motor vehicles:** 753.5 per 1,000 pop. **Airports:** 349.

Communications: Telephone: 38 per 100 pop. **Mobile:** 132.8 per 100 pop. **Broadband:** 112.2 per 100 pop. **Internet:** 84.6%.

Health: Expend.: 9.4%. **Life expect.:** 79.8 male; 84.8 female. **Births:** 12.1 per 1,000 pop. **Deaths:** 7.2 per 1,000 pop. **Infant mortality:** 4.3 per 1,000 live births. **Undernourished:** <5%. **HIV:** 0.2%.

Education: Compulsory: ages 6-15. **Literacy:** 99%.
Embassy: 1601 Massachusetts Ave. NW 20036; 797-3000.
Website: www.australia.gov.au

Australia harbors many plant and animal species not found elsewhere, including kangaroos, koalas, platypuses, dingoes (wild dogs), Tasmanian devils, wombats, and barking and frilled lizards.

Capt. James Cook explored the eastern coast in 1770, when the continent and offshore islands were inhabited by Aborigines and other indigenous peoples. The first European settlers, beginning in 1788, were mostly convicts, soldiers, and government officials. By 1830, Britain had claimed the entire continent, and the immigration of free settlers accelerated. The Commonwealth was proclaimed Jan. 1, 1901. Northern Terr. was granted limited self-rule July 1, 1978.

State/territory, capital	Tot. area (sq mi)	Population (2015 est.)
New South Wales, Sydney	309,130	7,670,700
Victoria, Melbourne	87,806	5,996,400
Queensland, Brisbane	668,207	4,808,800
Western Australia, Perth	976,790	2,603,900
South Australia, Adelaide	379,725	1,702,800
Tasmania, Hobart	26,410	517,400
Australian Capital Terr., Canberra	910	393,000
Northern Terr., Darwin	520,902	244,000

Note: Pop. est. as of Dec. 31. (Source: Australian Bureau of Statistics.)

In a 1967 referendum, Australians voted to change parts of the country's constitution that discriminated against Aborigines. Racially discriminatory immigration policies ended in 1973, after 3 mil Europeans (half British) had entered since 1945.

Australia is among the top exporters of beef, lamb, wool, and wheat. Major mineral deposits have been developed, largely for export. Slumping commodity prices and reduced exports to China impacted the economy in 2016.

The Labor Party won a majority in Feb. 1983 general elections and was reelected in 1984, 1987, 1990, and 1993. Conservatives swept into power Mar. 2, 1996. Prime Min. John Howard retained power in the 1998, 2001, and 2004 elections.

Australia led an international peacekeeping force into Timor in Sept. 1999. In a referendum Nov. 6, voters rejected a proposal that would have made Australia a republic.

Australian troops fought in U.S.-led military operations in Afghanistan (2001) and Iraq (2003); about 175 Australian troops were in Afghanistan in mid-2016. Some 2,000 Australian peacekeepers began arriving in the Solomon Isls., July 24, 2003; nearly all were withdrawn by mid-2005. In race riots in Sydney suburbs, Dec. 11-12, 2005, thousands of youths assaulted people of Middle Eastern ancestry, who then retaliated. Australian troops were dispatched, 2006, to suppress disorder in the Solomon Isls. in Apr. and Timor in May. The last Australian troops in Timor returned home on Mar. 27, 2013. Australian warplanes, Oct. 1, 2014, joined the U.S.-led air campaign in Iraq against the Sunni extremist group ISIS. Beginning in late 2014, Australia sent about 500 military advisers to train and assist Iraqi armed forces. In Sept. 2015, Australia joined the U.S.-led air campaign against ISIS in Syria.

Kevin Rudd led the Labor Party to victory in parliamentary elections Nov. 24, 2007. After a series of policy missteps, Rudd was forced out June 24, 2010, by his deputy, Julia Gillard, who became Australia's first female prime minister. Inconclusive parliamentary elections Aug. 21 led to the formation of a minority government headed by Gillard. Downpours from Cyclone Tasha and other storms flooded Queensland in late Dec. 2010 and early Jan. 2011, with three-fourths of the state declared a disaster zone.

Prime Min. Gillard, Mar. 20, 2013, officially apologized for Australia's forced adoption policy (in effect late 1950s-70s), in which the state took the babies of single, teenage, or unfit mothers, often under duress, and gave them to childless married couples. Gillard resigned June 26 after being voted out as party leader. Former Prime Min. Rudd, who engineered Gillard's ouster, became premier once again. The conservatives won Sept. 7, 2013, elections, and Tony Abbott became prime min. Abbott announced, Sept. 9, 2015, that Australia would accept 12,000 refugees from the conflicts in Syria and Iraq. Malcolm Turnbull replaced Abbott as prime min., Sept. 15, after defeating him, Sept. 14, in an election for Liberal Party leader. Turnbull's Liberal/National Party coalition won a narrow victory in July 2, 2016, elections, but it failed to gain an upper house majority.

Australian External Territories

Norfolk Isl., area 14 sq mi, pop. (2014 est.) 2,210, was taken over, 1914. The soil is very fertile, suitable for citrus, bananas, and coffee. Many of the inhabitants are descended from Pitcairn Islanders who moved to Norfolk in 1856 after the British abandoned an attempted penal colony. Australia offered the island limited home rule in 1979 but revoked its autonomy in 2015. The island's legislative assembly was replaced by an elected regional council in 2016. **Website:** www.norfolkisland.gov.nf

The only inhabitants of **Coral Sea Isls.**, area <1.2 sq mi, are meteorological staff on Willis Isl.

Ashmore and Cartier Isls., area 1.9 sq mi, in the Indian O., came under Australian authority in 1934. **Heard Isl. and McDonald Isls.**, area 159 sq mi, are administered by the Australian Antarctic Division.

Cocos (Keeling) Isls. are 27 coral islands in the Indian O. about 1,833 mi NW of Australia. Area 5.4 sq mi; pop. (2014 est.) 596. The residents voted to become part of Australia, Apr. 1984.

Christmas Isl., area 52 sq mi, pop. (2014 est.) 1,530; 230 mi S of Java, was transferred by Britain in 1958. Phosphate mining is the main economic activity, though high-grade phosphate deposits are nearly depleted.

Australian Antarctic Territory was claimed by the UK and then transferred to Australian sovereignty in 1933. It comprises some 2.2 mil sq mi of territory S of 60th parallel S lat. between 45°E and 160°E (not incl. France's Adelie Coast) and between 136°E and 142°E.

Austria
Republic of Austria

People: Population: 8,711,770. **Age distrib.:** <15: 14%; 65+: 19.1%. **Growth:** 0.5%. **Migrants:** 17.5%. **Pop. density:** 273.7 per sq mi, 105.7 per sq km. **Urban:** 66%. **Ethnic groups:** Austrian 91.1%, former Yugoslav (incl. Croatians, Slovenes, Serbs, Bosniaks) 4%. **Languages:** German (official), Turkish, Serbian, Croatian (official in one state). **Religions:** Catholic 73.8%, Protestant 4.9%, Muslim 4.2%, none 12%.

Geography: Total area: 32,383 sq mi, 83,871 sq km; **Land area:** 31,832 sq mi, 82,445 sq km. **Location:** S Central Europe. Switzerland, Liechtenstein on W; Germany, Czech Rep. on N; Slovakia, Hungary on E; Slovenia, Italy on S. **Topography:** Primarily mountainous, with the Alps and foothills covering the western and southern provinces. The eastern provinces and Vienna are located in the Danube River Basin. **Arable land:** 16.4%. **Capital:** Vienna, 1,762,604.

Government: Type: Federal parliamentary republic. **Head of state:** Pres. Heinz Fischer; b. 1938; in office: July 8, 2004. **Head of gov.:** Chancellor Christian Kern; b. 1966; in office: May 17, 2016. **Local divisions:** 9 states. **Defense budget:** $2.1 bil. **Active troops:** 22,250.

Economy: Industries: constr., machinery, vehicles and parts, food, metals, chemicals, lumber, paper and paperboard. **Chief crops:** grains, potatoes, wine, fruit. **Natural resources:** oil, coal, lignite, timber, iron ore, copper, zinc, antimony, magnesite, tungsten, graphite, salt, hydropower. **Water:** 9,093 cu m per capita. **Crude oil reserves** (2015): 47.5 mil bbls. **Electricity prod.:** 61 bil kWh. **Labor force:** agric. 0.7%, industry 25.3%, services 74%. **Unemployment:** 5%.

Finance: Monetary unit: Euro (EUR) (0.89 = $1 U.S.). **GDP:** $404.3 bil; **per capita GDP:** $47,300; **GDP growth:** 0.9%. **Imports:** $139.8 bil; Germany 41.5%, Italy 6.3%, Switzerland 6%. **Exports:** $141.4 bil; Germany 29.4%, U.S. 6.4%, Italy 6.1%, Switzerland 5.7%. **Tourism:** $18.3 bil. **Budget:** $196.8 bil. **Inflation:** 0.9%.

Transport: Railways: 3,273 mi. **Motor vehicles:** 600.3 per 1,000 pop. **Airports:** 24.

Communications: Telephone: 42.2 per 100 pop. **Mobile:** 157.4 per 100 pop. **Broadband:** 67.2 per 100 pop. **Internet:** 83.9%.

Health: Expend.: 11.2%. **Life expect.:** 78.9 male; 84.3 female. **Births:** 9.5 per 1,000 pop. **Deaths:** 9.5 per 1,000 pop. **Infant mortality:** 3.4 per 1,000 live births. **Undernourished:** <5%. **HIV:** NA.

Education: Compulsory: ages 6-14. **Literacy:** 98%.

Embassy: 3524 International Ct. NW 20008; 895-6700.

Website: www.austria.gv.at

Rome conquered Austrian lands from Celtic tribes around 15 BCE. In 788 the territory was incorporated into Charlemagne's empire. By 1300, the House of Hapsburg had gained control; it added vast territories in all parts of Europe to the realm in the next few hundred years.

Austrian dominance of Germany was undermined in the 18th cent. and ended by Prussia by 1866. But the Congress of Vienna, 1815, confirmed Austrian control of a large empire in SE Europe consisting of Germans, Hungarians, Slavs, Italians, and others. The dual Austro-Hungarian monarchy was established in 1867, giving autonomy to Hungary and almost 50 years of peace.

World War I, which started after the June 28, 1914, assassination of Archduke Franz Ferdinand, the Hapsburg heir, by a Serbian nationalist, destroyed the empire. By 1918 Austria was reduced to a small republic, with the borders it has today.

Nazi Germany, ruled by the Austrian-born Adolf Hitler, annexed Austria Mar. 13, 1938. The republic was reestablished in 1945, under Allied occupation. Full independence and neutrality were restored in 1955. Austria joined the EU Jan. 1, 1995.

The right-wing, anti-immigrant Austrian Freedom Party (FPO) challenged the dominance of the Social Democratic Party (SPO) beginning in the late 1990s. However, the SPO won parliamentary elections in Oct. 2006, Sept. 2008, and Sept. 2013. Former Green Party leader Alexander Van der Bellen appeared to narrowly defeat FPO candidate Norbert Hofer in a May 22, 2016, presidential runoff election, but the Constitutional Court voided the result, citing voting irregularities. A new runoff scheduled for Oct. 2 was postponed to Dec. 4 after faulty adhesive on postal ballots was discovered.

Hundreds of thousands of migrants fleeing war and hardship in Syria and elsewhere entered Austria in 2015, many en route to Germany or elsewhere in N Europe; about 90,000 migrants applied for asylum in Austria in 2015. The government, Feb. 16, 2016, announced sharp limits on the number of migrants per day allowed to transit or apply for asylum. A law passed Apr. 27 made it easier for the government to deny asylum claims.

Azerbaijan
Republic of Azerbaijan

People: Population: 9,872,765. **Age distrib.:** <15: 22.8%; 65+: 6.5%. **Growth:** 0.9%. **Migrants:** 2.7%. **Pop. density:** 309.5 per sq mi, 119.5 per sq km. **Urban:** 54.9%. **Ethnic groups:** Azerbaijani

91.6%, Lezgian 2%. **Languages:** Azerbaijani (Azeri) (official), Russian, Armenian. **Religions:** Muslim (predom. Shia) 96.9%, Christian 3%.

Geography: Total area: 33,436 sq mi, 86,600 sq km; **Land area:** 31,903 sq mi, 82,629 sq km. **Location:** SW Asia. Russia, Georgia on N; Iran on S; Armenia on W; Caspian Sea on E. **Topography:** The Great Caucasus Mts. in N, Karabakh Upland in W border the Kur-Araz lowland. Arid climate except in subtropical SE. **Arable land:** 23.3%. **Capital:** Baku, 2,429,434.

Government: Type: Presidential republic. **Head of state:** Pres. Ilham Aliyev; b. 1961; in office: Oct. 31, 2003. **Head of gov.:** Prime Min. Artur Rasizade; b. 1935; in office: Nov. 4, 2003. **Local division:** 66 rayons, 11 cities. **Defense budget:** $1.7 bil. **Active troops:** 66,950.

Economy: Industries: petroleum and petroleum prods., nat. gas, oil field equip.; steel, iron ore; cement. **Chief crops:** fruit, vegetables, grain, rice. **Natural resources:** petroleum, nat. gas, iron ore, nonferrous metals, bauxite. **Water:** 3,555 cu m per capita. **Crude oil reserves:** 7 bil bbls. **Electricity prod.:** 22 bil kWh. **Labor force:** agric. 38.3%, industry 12.1%, services 49.6%. **Unemployment:** 5.2%.

Finance: Monetary unit: Manat (AZN) (1.66 = $1 U.S.). **GDP:** $169.4 bil; **per capita GDP:** $18,000; **GDP growth:** 1.1%. **Imports:** $8.4 bil; Russia 19.9%, Turkey 16.5%, UK 8.6%, Germany 6.6%, Italy 6.3%. **Exports:** $16.4 bil; Italy 26.3%, Germany 13.2%, Indonesia 7%, France 6.8%, Czech Republic 6%. **Tourism:** $2.3 bil. **Budget:** $17.9 bil. **Inflation:** 4.2%.

Transport: Railways: 1,285 mi. **Motor vehicles:** 144.3 per 1,000 pop. **Airports:** 30.

Communications: Telephone: 18.7 per 100 pop. **Mobile:** 111.3 per 100 pop. **Broadband:** 46.8 per 100 pop. **Internet:** 77%.

Health: Expend.: 6%. **Life expect.:** 69.5 male; 75.8 female. **Births:** 16.2 per 1,000 pop. **Deaths:** 7.1 per 1,000 pop. **Infant mortality:** 24.7 per 1,000 live births. **Undernourished:** <5%. **HIV:** 0.2%.

Education: Compulsory: ages 6-14. **Literacy:** 99.8%.
Embassy: 2741 34th St. NW 20008; 337-3500.
Website: www.president.az

Azerbaijan was home to Scythian tribes and part of the Roman Empire. Overrun by Turks in the 11th cent. and conquered by Russia in 1806 and 1813, it joined the USSR Dec. 30, 1922, and became a constituent republic in 1936. Azerbaijan gained independence when the Soviet Union disbanded Dec. 26, 1991.

Nagorno-Karabakh, an enclave with a majority population of ethnic Armenians, seceded from Azerbaijan in 1988, triggering a war between mostly Muslim Azerbaijan and mostly Christian Armenia, 1992-94, in which 30,000 lives were lost.

Voters approved a new constitution expanding presidential powers, Nov. 12, 1995. Pres. Haydar Aliyev, a pro-Russian former Communist, was reelected Oct. 11, 1998, but international monitors called the vote seriously flawed. The dying Pres. Aliyev named his son Ilham prime min. Aug. 4, 2003. The younger Aliyev won the Oct. 15, 2003, presidential election. International observers called the vote fraudulent. He responded to violent protests Oct. 16 by arresting hundreds of opposition leaders and their supporters. The opening May 25, 2005, of the Baku-Tbilisi-Ceyhan pipeline, providing an outlet for Azerbaijan's vast Caspian oil reserves, transformed the nation's economy. Construction began in 2014 on the second phase of a series of pipelines to carry natural gas from Caspian Sea deposits in Azerbaijan to Georgia, Turkey, Greece, Albania, and Italy.

Pres. Ilham Aliyev won a second term Oct. 15, 2008, but main opposition parties boycotted the election. A constitutional amendment abolishing presidential term limits was approved by referendum Mar. 18, 2009. Aliyev won a third term Oct. 9, 2013, in an election the OSCE said did not meet international standards.

The first European Games, organized by the European Olympic Committee, were held in Baku June 12-28, 2015—amid international criticism because of Azerbaijan's poor human rights record. Azerbaijan hosted its first Formula One Grand Prix auto race, in Baku, June 19, 2016. Low oil prices hurt the economy in 2015-16.

The Bahamas
Commonwealth of The Bahamas

People: Population: 327,316. **Age distrib.:** <15: 22.8%; 65+: 7.5%. **Growth:** 0.8%. **Migrants:** 15.3%. **Pop. density:** 84.7 per sq mi, 32.7 per sq km. **Urban:** 83%. **Ethnic groups:** black 90.6%, white 4.7%, black and white 2.1%. **Languages:** English (official), Creole (among Haitian immigrants). **Religions:** Protestant 69.9% (incl. Baptist 34.9%, Anglican 13.7%, Pentecostal 8.9%), Roman Catholic 12%, other Christian 13%.

Geography: Total area: 5,359 sq mi, 13,880 sq km; **Land area:** 3,865 sq mi, 10,010 sq km. **Location:** In Atlantic O., SE of Florida. U.S. is on W, Cuba to SW. **Topography:** Nearly 700 islands (30 inhabited) and over 2,000 cays in the W Atlantic O. extend 760 mi NW to SE. **Arable land:** 0.8%. **Capital:** Nassau, 266,765 (2014).

Government: Type: Parliamentary democracy under constitutional monarchy. **Head of state:** Queen Elizabeth II, rep. by

Gov.-Gen. Dame Marguerite Pindling; b. 1932; in office: July 8, 2014. **Head of gov.:** Prime Min. Perry Christie; b. 1943; in office: May 8, 2012. **Local divisions:** 31 districts. **Defense budget:** $102 mil. **Active troops:** 1,300.

Economy: Industries: tourism, banking, oil bunkering, maritime, transshipment, salt, rum. **Chief crops:** citrus, vegetables. **Natural resources:** salt, aragonite, timber. **Water:** 1,804 cu m per capita. **Electricity prod.:** 1.8 bil kWh. **Labor force:** agric. 3%, industry 11%, tourism 49%, other services 37%. **Unemployment:** 15.4%.

Finance: Monetary unit: Dollar (BSD) (1.00 = $1 U.S.). **GDP:** $9.2 bil; **per capita GDP:** $25,200; **GDP growth:** 0.5%. **Imports:** $2.7 bil; U.S. 22.3%, China 14.8%, Japan 9.5%, Poland 7.7%, South Korea 7.3%, Colombia 6.8%, Brazil 5.6%, Singapore 5.5%. **Exports:** $976.1 mil; Poland 26.3%, Côte d'Ivoire 20.9%, U.S. 15.9%, Dominican Republic 14.3%. **Tourism:** $2.3 bil. **Budget:** $1.8 bil. **Inflation:** 1.9%.

Transport: Motor vehicles: 411.9 per 1,000 pop. **Airports:** 24.
Communications: Telephone: 31.2 per 100 pop. **Mobile:** 80.3 per 100 pop. **Broadband:** NA. **Internet:** 78%.
Health: Expend.: 7.7%. **Life expect.:** 70.0 male; 74.8 female. **Births:** 15.4 per 1,000 pop. **Deaths:** 7.1 per 1,000 pop. **Infant mortality:** 11.7 per 1,000 live births. **Undernourished:** NA. **HIV:** 3.2%.

Education: Compulsory: ages 5-16. **Literacy:** 95%+.
Embassy: 2220 Massachusetts Ave. NW 20008; 319-2660.
Website: www.bahamas.gov.bs

Christopher Columbus first set foot in the New World on San Salvador (Watling Isl.) in 1492, when Arawak Indians inhabited the islands. British settlement began in 1647; the islands became a British colony in 1783. Internal self-government was granted in 1964; full independence within the Commonwealth was attained July 10, 1973. International banking and investment management have become major industries alongside tourism. The Progressive Liberal Party's Perry Christie, who was prime min. 2002-07, returned to the post after May 7, 2012, parliamentary elections, which saw the defeat of the Free Natl. Movement as the majority party.

Bahrain
Kingdom of Bahrain

People: Population: 1,378,904. **Age distrib.:** <15: 19.3%; 65+: 2.8%. **Growth:** 2.3%. **Migrants:** 51.1%. **Pop. density:** 4,699.1 per sq mi, 1,814.3 per sq km. **Urban:** 88.8%. **Ethnic groups:** Bahraini 46%, Asian 45.5%, other Arab 4.7%. **Languages:** Arabic (official), English, Farsi, Urdu. **Religions:** Muslim 70.3%, Christian 14.5%, Hindu 9.8%.

Geography: Total area: 293 sq mi, 760 sq km; **Land area:** 293 sq mi, 760 sq km. **Location:** SW Asia, in Persian Gulf. Saudi Arabia on W, Qatar on E. **Topography:** Bahrain Island and several adjacent, smaller islands, are flat, hot, and humid with little rain. **Arable land:** 2.1%. **Capital:** Manama, 425,062.

Government: Type: Constitutional monarchy. **Head of state:** King Hamad bin Isa al-Khalifa; b. 1950; in office: as emir Mar. 6, 1999; as king Feb. 14, 2002. **Head of gov.:** Prime Min. Khalifa bin Salman al-Khalifa; b. 1936; in office: 1971. **Local divisions:** 4 governorates. **Defense budget:** $1.5 bil. **Active troops:** 8,200.

Economy: Industries: petroleum proc. and refining, aluminum smelting, iron pelletization, fertilizers, Islamic and offshore banking. **Chief crops:** fruit, vegetables. **Natural resources:** oil, nat. gas, fish, pearls. **Water:** 84 cu m per capita. **Crude oil reserves:** 0.1 bil bbls. **Electricity prod.:** 14 bil kWh. **Labor force:** agric. 1%, industry 32%, services 67%. **Unemployment:** 3.9%.

Finance: Monetary unit: Dinar (BHD) (0.38 = $1 U.S.). **GDP:** $64.8 bil; **per capita GDP:** $50,100; **GDP growth:** 3.2%. **Imports:** $8.8 bil; Saudi Arabia 28.7%, U.S. 9.4%, China 7.4%, Japan 6.5%, Australia 5%. **Exports:** $14.1 bil; Saudi Arabia 3.6%, UAE 2.3%, U.S. 2.2%. **Tourism:** $1.2 bil. **Budget:** $9.3 bil. **Inflation:** 1.8%.

Transport: Motor vehicles: 460.9 per 1,000 pop. **Airports:** 4.
Communications: Telephone: 20.5 per 100 pop. **Mobile:** 185.3 per 100 pop. **Broadband:** 126.2 per 100 pop. **Internet:** 93.5%.
Health: Expend.: 5.0%. **Life expect.:** 76.7 male; 81.1 female. **Births:** 13.5 per 1,000 pop. **Deaths:** 2.7 per 1,000 pop. **Infant mortality:** 9.2 per 1,000 live births. **Undernourished:** NA. **HIV:** NA.

Education: Compulsory: ages 6-14. **Literacy:** 95.7%.
Embassy: 3502 International Dr. NW 20008; 342-0741.
Website: www.bahrain.bh

Long ruled by the Khalifa family, Bahrain was a British protectorate from 1861 to Aug. 15, 1971, when it regained independence. Pearls, shrimp, fruits, and vegetables were the mainstays of the economy until oil was discovered in 1932. Crude oil production has declined since the 1970s, but natural gas output has grown, and international banking has thrived.

Emir Hamad bin Isa al-Khalifa proclaimed himself king Feb. 14, 2002. Local elections in May 2002 marked the first time Bahraini women were allowed to vote and run for office. The monarchy suppressed Arab Spring demonstrations Feb.-Mar. 2011, aided by a Gulf Cooperation Council force of 1,600 led by Saudi Arabia. Protests, however, continued, largely by members of the country's Shiite majority against the mostly Sunni ruling elite. The government arrested opposition leaders and other critics, and a July 17, 2016, court ruling ordered the dissolution of a leading Shiite opposition group. A Nov. 2015 Human Rights Watch report accused the government of torturing detained dissidents. Forced labor and sexual exploitation of Asian and African immigrants also gained international attention. Beginning Sept. 23, 2014, Bahrain took part in U.S.-led airstrikes against Sunni extremists in Syria. A U.S. ban on military aid to Bahrain, imposed after suppression of Arab Spring protests, was lifted June 29, 2015.

Bangladesh
People's Republic of Bangladesh

People: Population: 156,186,882. **Age distrib.:** <15: 28.3%; 65+: 6%. **Growth:** 1.1%. **Migrants:** 0.9%. **Pop. density:** 3,107.6 per sq mi, 1,199.9 per sq km. **Urban:** 35%. **Ethnic groups:** Bengali 98%+. **Languages:** Bangla or Bengali (official). **Religions:** Muslim 89.1%, Hindu 10%.

Geography: Total area: 57,321 sq mi, 148,460 sq km; **Land area:** 50,259 sq mi, 130,170 sq km. **Location:** S Asia, on N bend of Bay of Bengal. India nearly surrounds country on W, N, E; Myanmar on SE. **Topography:** Mostly a low plain cut by the Ganges and Brahmaputra Rivers and their delta. Alluvial and marshy along the coast. Hilly only in the extreme SE and NE. Its tropical monsoon climate makes country among the rainiest in the world. **Arable land:** 59%. **Capital:** Dhaka, 18,237,104. **Cities:** Chittagong, 4,640,059; Khulna, 1,013,107.

Government: Type: Parliamentary republic. **Head of state:** Pres. Abdul Hamid; b. 1944; in office: Apr. 24, 2013. **Head of gov.:** Prime Min. Sheikh Hasina; b. 1947; in office: Jan. 6, 2009. **Local divisions:** 8 divisions. **Defense budget:** $2.2 bil. **Active troops:** 157,050.

Economy: Industries: jute, cotton, garments, paper, leather, fertilizer, iron and steel, cement, petroleum prods., tobacco, pharmaceuticals. **Chief crops:** rice, jute, tea, wheat, sugarcane, potatoes, tobacco, pulses, oilseeds, spices. **Natural resources:** nat. gas, timber, coal. **Water:** 7,621 cu m per capita. **Crude oil reserves** (2015): 28 mil bbls. **Electricity prod.:** 50 bil kWh. **Labor force:** agric. 47%, industry 13%, services 40%. **Unemployment:** 4.3%.

Finance: Monetary unit: Taka (BDT) (78.33 = $1 U.S.). **GDP:** $577 bil; **per capita GDP:** $3,600; **GDP growth:** 6.4%. **Imports:** $38.2 bil; China 22.4%, India 14.1%, Singapore 5.2%. **Exports:** $29.9 bil; U.S. 13.9%, Germany 12.9%, UK 8.9%, France 5%. **Tourism:** $153 mil. **Budget:** $27.5 bil. **Inflation:** 6.2%.

Transport: Railways: 1,529 mi. **Motor vehicles:** 3.4 per 1,000 pop. **Airports:** 16.

Communications: Telephone: 0.5 per 100 pop. **Mobile:** 83.4 per 100 pop. **Broadband:** 6.4 per 100 pop. **Internet:** 14.4%.

Health: Expend.: 2.8%. **Life expect.:** 71.0 male; 75.4 female. **Births:** 19.0 per 1,000 pop. **Deaths:** 5.3 per 1,000 pop. **Infant mortality:** 32.9 per 1,000 live births. **Undernourished:** 16.4%. **HIV:** <0.1%.

Education: Compulsory: ages 6-10. **Literacy:** 61.5%.
Embassy: 3510 International Dr. NW 20008; 244-0183.
Website: www.bangladesh.gov.bd

Muslim invaders conquered the formerly Hindu area in the 12th cent. British rule lasted from the 18th cent. to 1947, when East Bengal became part of Pakistan.

Opposing domination by West Pakistan, the Awami League, based in the East, won control of the National Assembly in 1971. Assembly sessions were postponed; riots broke out. Pakistani troops attacked, Mar. 25; Bangladesh independence was proclaimed the next day. In the ensuing civil war, 1 mil died and 10 mil fled to India. War between India and Pakistan broke out Dec. 3, 1971. Pakistan surrendered in the East on Dec. 16. Mujibur Rahman, known as Sheikh Mujib, became prime min.; he was killed in a coup Aug. 15, 1975.

Army rivals killed Pres. Ziaur Rahman in an unsuccessful coup attempt, May 1981. Vice Pres. Abdus Sattar assumed the presidency but was ousted in a coup led by army chief of staff Gen. H. M. Ershad, Mar. 1982. Ershad declared Bangladesh an Islamic Republic in 1988; a parliamentary system of government was adopted in 1991. A cyclone, Apr. 1991, killed over 131,000 people.

Political turmoil led to the resignation, Mar. 1996, of Prime Min. Khaleda Zia, the widow of Ziaur Rahman. Sheikh Mujib's daughter, known as Sheikh Hasina, led the country after the June 1996 election. Khaleda Zia returned to power following parliamentary elections, Oct. 1, 2001. Militant Islamists set off more than 400 small bombs in more than 50 cities and towns, Aug. 17, 2005, killing 3. Another wave of jihadist bombings killed 22, Nov. 29-Dec. 8, 2005. Bangladeshi economist Muhammad Yunus won the 2006 Nobel Peace Prize for using very small loans (microcredit) to help alleviate the nation's severe poverty.

Escalating political violence led Pres. Iajuddin Ahmed to declare a state of emergency Jan. 11, 2007. A military-backed caretaker government filed criminal charges against Khaleda Zia and Sheikh

Hasina but failed to force the two former prime ministers into exile. Cyclone Sidr struck Nov. 15, 2007, damaging more than 1.5 mil homes and leaving about 3,400 dead.

The Awami League triumphed in parliamentary elections Dec. 2008, and Sheikh Hasina was sworn in as prime min. Jan. 6, 2009, ending two years of emergency rule. She remained in office when her party won Jan. 5, 2014, elections marred by violence and low turnout.

A garment factory fire Nov. 24, 2012, outside Dhaka killed 112 workers. Rana Plaza, a building that housed garment factories, collapsed Apr. 24, 2013, killing more than 1,100 workers in the deadliest garment-factory disaster in world history. The owner of Rana Plaza was among 38 people formally charged, July 18, 2016, with murder in connection with the disaster. Security forces in Dhaka, July 1-2, 2015, arrested 12 people said to be affiliated with al-Qaeda, including a man who had claimed responsibility for the Feb. killing of a Bangladeshi-American blogger who had criticized Islamist extremists. Three other so-called secular bloggers had been killed by Aug. 2015. Assassinations of non-Muslims attributed to al-Qaeda or ISIS escalated in 2016. In an attack in Dhaka, July 1-2, for which ISIS claimed responsibility, 20 people inside a restaurant, mostly foreigners, were killed and others held hostage. Two police officers died before forces ended the takeover; five terrorist gunmen were killed. The suspected plotter of the attack was killed by police in a shootout, Aug. 27.

Barbados

People: Population: 291,495. **Age distrib.:** <15: 18.1%; 65+: 11.3%. **Growth:** 0.3%. **Migrants:** 12.1%. **Pop. density:** 1,755.7 per sq mi, 677.9 per sq km. **Urban:** 31.4%. **Ethnic groups:** black 92.4%, mixed 3.1%, white 2.7%. **Languages:** English (official), Bajan (English-based Creole). **Religions:** Protestant 66.4% (incl. Anglican 23.9%, other Pentecostal 19.5%), Roman Catholic 3.8%, none 20.6%.

Geography: Total area: 166 sq mi, 430 sq km; **Land area:** 166 sq mi, 430 sq km. **Location:** In Atlantic O., farthest E of West Indies. Nearest neighbors are St. Lucia and St. Vincent and the Grenadines to the W. **Topography:** Almost completely surrounded by coral reefs. Highest point is Mt. Hillaby (1,115 ft). **Arable land:** 25.6%. **Capital:** Bridgetown, 90,265 (2014).

Government: Type: Parliamentary democracy under constitutional monarchy. **Head of state:** Queen Elizabeth II, rep. by Gov.-Gen. Sir Elliot Belgrave; b. 1931; in office: June 1, 2012. **Head of gov.:** Prime Min. Freundel Stuart; b. 1951; in office: Oct. 23, 2010. **Local divisions:** 11 parishes, 1 city. **Defense budget:** $33 mil. **Active troops:** 610.

Economy: Industries: tourism, sugar, light mfg., component assembly for export. **Chief crops:** sugarcane, vegetables, cotton. **Natural resources:** petroleum, fish, nat. gas. **Water:** 282 cu m per capita. **Crude oil reserves** (2015): 2.5 mil bbls. **Other resources:** Fish. **Electricity prod.:** 1 bil kWh. **Labor force:** agric. 10%, industry 15%, services 75%. **Unemployment:** 12%.

Finance: Monetary unit: Dollar (BBD) (2.00 = $1 U.S.). **GDP:** $4.6 bil; **per capita GDP:** $16,600; **GDP growth:** 0.5%. **Imports:** $1.6 bil; Trinidad and Tobago 39%, U.S. 31.1%. **Exports:** $471.6 mil; Trinidad and Tobago 22.5%, U.S. 11.8%, St. Lucia 9.2%, St. Vincent and the Grenadines 5.7%. **Tourism:** $950 mil. **Budget:** $1.6 bil. **Inflation:** -1.1%.

Transport: Motor vehicles: 378.5 per 1,000 pop. **Airports:** 1.
Communications: Telephone: 54.6 per 100 pop. **Mobile:** 116.5 per 100 pop. **Broadband:** 106.8 per 100 pop. **Internet:** 76.1%.

Health: Expend.: 7.5%. **Life expect.:** 73.0 male; 77.7 female. **Births:** 11.8 per 1,000 pop. **Deaths:** 8.5 per 1,000 pop. **Infant mortality:** 10.5 per 1,000 live births. **Undernourished:** <5%. **HIV:** 1.6%.

Education: Compulsory: ages 5-15. **Literacy:** 99.7%.
Embassy: 2144 Wyoming Ave. NW 20008; 939-9200.
Website: www.gov.bb

Barbados was probably named by Portuguese sailors in reference to bearded fig trees. An English ship visited in 1605, and British settled on the uninhabited island in 1627. Slaves worked the sugarcane plantations until slavery was abolished in 1834. Self-rule came gradually, with full independence proclaimed Nov. 30, 1966. Tourism, banking, and manufacturing have surpassed the sugarcane industry in economic importance since the 1990s. The country signed an Economic and Technical Agreement with China, Aug. 24, 2012. A cumulative 604 suspected and 29 confirmed cases of Zika virus were reported since 2015 as of Oct. 2016.

Belarus
Republic of Belarus

People: Population: 9,570,376. **Age distrib.:** <15: 15.6%; 65+: 14.7%. **Growth:** -0.2%. **Migrants:** 11.4%. **Pop. density:** 122.2 per sq mi, 47.2 per sq km. **Urban:** 77%. **Ethnic groups:** Belarusian 83.7%, Russian 8.3%, Polish 3.1%. **Languages:** Russian,

Belarusian (both official). **Religions:** Orthodox 48.3%, Catholic 7.1%, non-believers 41.1%.

Geography: Total area: 80,155 sq mi, 207,600 sq km; **Land area:** 78,340 sq mi, 202,900 sq km. **Location:** Eastern Europe. Poland on W; Latvia, Lithuania on N; Russia on E; Ukraine on S. **Topography:** Landlocked country consisting mostly of hilly lowland with significant marsh areas in S. **Arable land:** 27.5%. **Capital:** Minsk, 1,925,067.

Government: Type: Presidential republic in name. **Head of state:** Pres. Aleksandr Lukashenko; b. 1954; in office: July 20, 1994. **Head of gov.:** Prime Min. Andrei Kobyakov; b. 1960; in office: Dec. 27, 2014. **Local divisions:** 6 provinces, 1 municipality. **Defense budget** (2013): $681 mil. **Active troops:** 48,000.

Economy: Industries: metal-cutting machine tools, tractors, trucks, earthmovers. **Chief crops:** grain, potatoes, vegetables, sugar beets, flax. **Natural resources:** timber, peat, oil, nat. gas, granite, dolomitic limestone, marl, chalk, sand, gravel, clay. **Water:** 6,097 cu m per capita. **Crude oil reserves:** 0.2 bil bbls. **Electricity prod.:** 30 bil kWh. **Labor force:** agric. 9.3%, industry 32.7%, services 58%. **Unemployment:** 5.9%.

Finance: Monetary unit: Ruble (BYN) (2.01 = $1 U.S.). **GDP:** $167.7 bil; **per capita GDP:** $17,700; **GDP growth:** –3.9%. **Imports:** $29.7 bil; Russia 56.6%, China 7.9%. **Exports:** $28.6 bil; Russia 39%, UK 11.2%, Ukraine 9.5%. **Tourism:** $734 mil. **Budget:** $22 bil. **Inflation:** 13.5%.

Transport: Railways: 3,435 mi. **Motor vehicles:** 365.2 per 1,000 pop. **Airports:** 33.

Communications: Telephone: 49 per 100 pop. **Mobile:** 123.6 per 100 pop. **Broadband:** 55 per 100 pop. **Internet:** 62.2%.

Health: Expend.: 5.7%. **Life expect.:** 67.2 male; 78.6 female. **Births:** 10.5 per 1,000 pop. **Deaths:** 13.3 per 1,000 pop. **Infant mortality:** 3.6 per 1,000 live births. **Undernourished:** <5%. **HIV:** 0.6%.

Education: Compulsory: ages 6-14. **Literacy:** 99.7%.

Embassy: 1619 New Hampshire Ave. NW 20009; 986-1604. **Website:** www.president.gov.by

Belarus became a constituent republic of the USSR in 1922. Overrun by German armies in 1941, Belarus was recaptured by Soviet troops in 1944. Following WWII, Belarus increased in area through Soviet annexation of part of NE Poland. Belarus declared independence Aug. 25, 1991, and became independent when the Soviet Union disbanded Dec. 26, 1991.

After a new constitution was adopted, Mar. 15, 1994, Aleksandr Lukashenko was elected president. Russia and Belarus signed a pact, Apr. 2, 1996, linking their political and economic systems. An authoritarian constitution enacted in Nov. gave Pres. Lukashenko vast new powers. Subsequently, Lukashenko retained office in 2001, 2006, 2010, and 2015 elections criticized as seriously flawed by Western observers. Lukashenko crushed protests that followed the Dec. 19, 2010, presidential election. Belarus, Russia, and Kazakhstan signed an agreement, May 29, 2014, to create a Eurasian Economic Union (EEU). The EEU came into existence Jan. 1, 2015, and Armenia and Kyrgyzstan joined in Jan. and May, respectively. Svetlana Alexievich of Belarus was awarded the Nobel Prize for literature, Oct. 8, 2015, in part for her nonfiction works, including oral histories about such recent events as the Chernobyl nuclear accident and the Soviet war in Afghanistan.

Belgium
Kingdom of Belgium

People: Population: 11,409,077. **Age distrib.:** <15: 17.1%; 65+: 18.4%. **Growth:** 0.7%. **Migrants:** 12.3%. **Pop. density:** 975.9 per sq mi, 376.8 per sq km. **Urban:** 97.9%. **Ethnic groups:** Flemish 58%, Walloon 31%, mixed or other 11%. **Languages:** Dutch, French, German (all official). **Religions:** Roman Catholic 75%, other (incl. Protestant) 25%.

Geography: Total area: 11,787 sq mi, 30,528 sq km; **Land area:** 11,690 sq mi, 30,278 sq km. **Location:** Western Europe, on North Sea. France on W and S, Luxembourg on SE, Germany on E, Netherlands on N. **Topography:** Mostly flat; trisected by the Scheldt and Meuse, major commercial rivers. The land becomes hilly and forested in the Ardennes region to the SE. **Arable land:** 26.9%. **Capital:** Brussels, 2,060,976. **Cities:** Antwerp, 997,723.

Government: Type: Federal parliamentary democracy under constitutional monarchy. **Head of state:** King Philippe; b. 1960; in office: July 21, 2013. **Head of gov.:** Prime Min. Charles Michel; b. 1975; in office: Oct. 11, 2014. **Local divisions:** 3 regions. **Defense budget:** $4 bil. **Active troops:** 30,800.

Economy: Industries: engineering and metal prods., motor vehicle assembly, transp. equip., scientific instruments, processed food and beverages. **Chief crops:** sugar beets, vegetables, fruits, grain, tobacco. **Natural resources:** constr. materials, silica sand, carbonates. **Water:** 1,620 cu m per capita. **Electricity prod.:** 76 bil kWh. **Labor force:** agric. 1.3%, industry 18.6%, services 80.1%. **Unemployment:** 8.5%.

Finance: Monetary unit: Euro (EUR) (0.89 = $1 U.S.). **GDP:** $494.1 bil; **per capita GDP:** $43,600; **GDP growth:** 1.4%. **Imports:** $280.3 bil; Netherlands 16.7%, Germany 12.7%, France 9.6%, U.S. 8.7%, UK 5.1%. **Exports:** $281.7 bil; Germany 16.9%, France 15.5%, Netherlands 11.4%, UK 8.8%, U.S. 6%, Italy 5%. **Tourism:** $11.7 bil. **Budget:** $239.4 bil. **Inflation:** 0.6%.

Transport: Railways: 2,232 mi. **Motor vehicles:** 572.9 per 1,000 pop. **Airports:** 26.

Communications: Telephone: 40.1 per 100 pop. **Mobile:** 115.7 per 100 pop. **Broadband:** 57.8 per 100 pop. **Internet:** 85.1%.

Health: Expend.: 10.6%. **Life expect.:** 78.4 male; 83.7 female. **Births:** 11.4 per 1,000 pop. **Deaths:** 9.7 per 1,000 pop. **Infant mortality:** 3.4 per 1,000 live births. **Undernourished:** <5%. **HIV:** NA.

Education: Compulsory: ages 6-17. **Literacy:** 99%.

Embassy: 3330 Garfield St. NW 20008; 333-6900. **Website:** www.belgium.be

Belgium derives its name from the Belgae, the first recorded inhabitants, probably Celts. The land was ruled for 1800 years by conquerors, including Rome, the Franks, Burgundy, Spain, Austria, and France. After 1815, Belgium was made a part of the Netherlands but became an independent constitutional monarchy in 1830.

King Leopold III surrendered to Germany, May 28, 1940. After WWII, he was forced to abdicate in favor of his son, King Baudouin. Baudouin was succeeded by his brother, Albert II, Aug. 9, 1993. Albert's son Philippe became king July 21, 2013.

The Flemings of northern Belgium speak Dutch, while the Walloons in the south speak French. The language difference is a source of controversy between the two groups. Parliament has passed measures transferring power from the central government to three regions—Wallonia, Flanders, and Brussels. Constitutional changes in 1993 made Belgium a federal state. After elections June 2007, rivalries between Flemings and Walloons created a 9-month political stalemate. June 2010 elections led to a political deadlock that ended when Elio Di Rupo became prime min. Dec. 2011. After May 25, 2014, elections in which Flemish nationalists made gains, Charles Michel was sworn in as prime min. Oct. 11, heading a center-right coalition government.

An Oct. 2014 government report stated that 350 Belgians had traveled to Syria to fight with Islamist extremists. Two suspects were killed Jan. 15, 2015, in a series of police raids in Belgium on alleged Islamist extremists. After evidence emerged that people living in Belgium planned and took part in terrorist attacks in France, Nov. 13, that killed 130, Belgian authorities, fearing similar attacks, closed the Brussels subway system for several days beginning Nov. 21, canceled public events, and urged Brussels residents to stay at home. In Mar. 22, 2016, attacks for which the Sunni extremist group ISIS claimed responsibility, 3 suicide bombers killed 32 others in a Brussels subway station and at the city's airport. Belgium announced, May 13, that it would join the U.S.-led bombing campaign against ISIS targets in Syria.

Belize

People: Population: 353,858. **Age distrib.:** <15: 34.4%; 65+: 3.8%. **Growth:** 1.8%. **Migrants:** 15%. **Pop. density:** 40.2 per sq mi, 15.5 per sq km. **Urban:** 43.8%. **Ethnic groups:** mestizo 52.9%, Creole 25.9%, Maya 11.3%, Garifuna 6.1%, East Indian 3.9%, Mennonite 3.6%. **Languages:** English (official), Spanish, Creole, Maya, German, Garifuna. **Religions:** Roman Catholic 40.1%, Protestant 31.5% (incl. Pentecostal 8.4%, Seventh-day Adventist 5.4%), other (incl. Baha'i, Buddhist, Hindu, Morman, Muslim, Rastafarian) 10.5%, none 15.5%.

Geography: Total area: 8,867 sq mi, 22,966 sq km; **Land area:** 8,805 sq mi, 22,806 sq km. **Location:** Eastern coast of Central America. Mexico on N, Guatemala on W and S. **Topography:** Swampy lowlands in N, Maya Mts. in S, coral reefs and cays near coast. Tropical climate. **Arable land:** 3.4%. **Capital:** Belmopan, 16,921 (2014).

Government: Type: Parliamentary democracy under constitutional monarchy. **Head of state:** Queen Elizabeth II, rep. by Gov.-Gen. Sir Colville Young; b. 1932; in office: Nov. 17, 1993. **Head of gov.:** Prime Min. Dean Barrow; b. 1951; in office: Feb. 8, 2008. **Local divisions:** 6 districts. **Defense budget:** $21 mil. **Active troops:** 1,050.

Economy: Industries: garment prod., food proc., tourism, constr. **Chief crops:** bananas, cacao, citrus, sugar. **Natural resources:** timber, fish, hydropower. **Water:** 60,479 cu m per capita. **Crude oil reserves** (2015): 6.7 mil bbls. **Electricity prod.:** 0.3 bil kWh. **Labor force:** agric. 10.2%, industry 18.1%, services 71.7%. **Unemployment:** 11.5%.

Finance: Monetary unit: Dollar (BZD) (1.98 = $1 U.S.). **GDP:** $3 bil; **per capita GDP:** $8,400; **GDP growth:** 1.5%. **Imports:** $964.4 mil; U.S. 26.6%, Mexico 11.7%, Cuba 10.2%, Guatemala 9%, China 7.5%, Trinidad and Tobago 5.6%. **Exports:** $580.7 mil; UK 30.8%, U.S. 18.7%, Nigeria 6.7%. **Tourism:** $408 mil. **Budget:** $550 mil. **Inflation:** –0.9%.

Transport: Motor vehicles: 108 per 1,000 pop. **Airports:** 6.

Communications: Telephone: 6 per 100 pop. **Mobile:** 48.9 per 100 pop. **Broadband:** 10.2 per 100 pop. **Internet:** 41.6%.

Health: Expend.: 5.8%. **Life expect.:** 67.2 male; 70.4 female. **Births:** 24.3 per 1,000 pop. **Deaths:** 6.0 per 1,000 pop. **Infant mortality:** 19.3 per 1,000 live births. **Undernourished:** 6.2%. **HIV:** 1.5%.

Education: Compulsory: ages 5-14. **Literacy:** 82.8%.

Embassy: 2535 Massachusetts Ave. NW 20008; 332-9636.

Website: www.belize.gov.bz

Belize (formerly British Honduras) was Britain's last colony on the American mainland; independence was achieved Sept. 21, 1981. Relations with neighboring Guatemala, which claims the southern half of Belize and its islands as its own territory, have improved in recent years. Belize has become a center for drug trafficking between Colombia and the U.S.

Benin
Republic of Benin

People: Population: 10,741,458. **Age distrib.:** <15: 43%; 65+: 2.8%. **Growth:** 2.8%. **Migrants:** 2.3%. **Pop. density:** 251.5 per sq mi, 97.1 per sq km. **Urban:** 44.4%. **Ethnic groups:** Fon and related 39.2%, Adja/related 15.2%, Yoruba/related 12.3%, Bariba/related 9.2%, Fulani/related 7%, Ottamari/related 6.1%, Yoa-Lokpa/related 4%, Dendi/related 2.5%. **Languages:** French (official), Fon, Yoruba, tribal langs. **Religions:** Catholic 27.1%, Muslim 24.4%, Vodoun 17.3%, Protestant 10.4%, none 6.5%.

Geography: Total area: 43,484 sq mi, 112,622 sq km; **Land area:** 42,711 sq mi, 110,622 sq km. **Location:** W Africa on Gulf of Guinea. Togo on W; Burkina Faso, Niger on N; Nigeria on E. **Topography:** Mostly flat and covered with dense vegetation. The coast is hot, humid, and rainy. **Arable land:** 23.9%. **Capital:** Porto-Novo (official), 268,057 (2014); Cotonou (seat), 686,024.

Government: Type: Presidential republic. **Head of state and gov.:** Pres. Patrice Talon; b. 1958; in office: Apr. 6, 2016. **Local divisions:** 12 departments. **Defense budget** (2014): $97 mil. **Active troops:** 6,950.

Economy: Industries: textiles, food proc., constr. materials, cement. **Chief crops:** cotton, corn, cassava, yams, beans, palm oil. **Natural resources:** offshore oil, limestone, marble, timber. **Water:** 2,426 cu m per capita. **Crude oil reserves** (2015): 8 mil bbls. **Electricity prod.:** 0.2 bil kWh. **Labor force:** NA. **Unemployment:** 1%.

Finance: Monetary unit: CFA Franc (XOF) (586.00 = $1 U.S.). **GDP:** $23 bil; **per capita GDP:** $2,100; **GDP growth:** 5.2%. **Imports:** $2.6 bil; China 42.2%, U.S. 8.9%, India 5.7%. **Exports:** $2 bil; India 24.8%, Gabon 15%, China 7.3%, Niger 6.1%, Bangladesh 5.1%, Nigeria 5%. **Tourism:** $151 mil. **Budget:** $1.9 bil. **Inflation:** 0.3%.

Transport: Railways: 272 mi. **Motor vehicles:** 3.4 per 1,000 pop. **Airports:** 1.

Communications: Telephone: 1.8 per 100 pop. **Mobile:** 85.6 per 100 pop. **Broadband:** 2.8 per 100 pop. **Internet:** 6.8%.

Health: Expend.: 4.6%. **Life expect.:** 60.5 male; 63.3 female. **Births:** 35.5 per 1,000 pop. **Deaths:** 8.0 per 1,000 pop. **Infant mortality:** 54.2 per 1,000 live births. **Undernourished:** 7.5%. **HIV:** 1.1%.

Education: Compulsory: ages 6-11. **Literacy:** 38.4%.

Embassy: 2124 Kalorama Rd. NW 20008; 232-6656.

Website: www.gouv.bj

The Kingdom of Abomey, rising to power in wars with neighboring kingdoms in the 17th cent., came under French domination in the late 19th cent., and was incorporated into French West Africa by 1904. Under the name Dahomey, the country gained independence Aug. 1, 1960; it became Benin in 1975. In the fifth coup since independence Col. Ahmed Kerekou took power in 1972; two years later he declared a socialist state with a Marxist-Leninist philosophy. In Dec. 1989, Kerekou announced Marxism-Leninism would no longer be the state ideology.

Boni Yayi, an economist, won a presidential runoff vote, Mar. 19, 2006, and was reelected Mar. 13, 2011. When Yayi stepped down after two terms, independent Patrice Talon won the presidential runoff election Mar. 20, 2016.

In June 2015, Benin agreed to join Nigeria, Chad, Cameroon, and Niger in contributing troops to a multinational force to fight the Islamist extremist group Boko Haram in northern Nigeria.

Bhutan
Kingdom of Bhutan

People: Population: 750,125. **Age distrib.:** <15: 26.3%; 65+: 6.2%. **Growth:** 1.1%. **Migrants:** 6.6%. **Pop. density:** 50.6 per sq mi, 19.5 per sq km. **Urban:** 39.4%. **Ethnic groups:** Ngalop or Bhote 50%, ethnic Nepalese (incl. Lhotsampa) 35%, indigenous or migrant tribes 15%. **Languages:** Sharchhopka, Dzongkha (official), Lhotshamkha. **Religions:** Lamaistic Buddhist 75.3%, Indian-and Nepalese-influenced Hinduism 22.1%.

Geography: Total area: 14,824 sq mi, 38,394 sq km; **Land area:** 14,824 sq mi, 38,394 sq km. **Location:** S Asia, in eastern Himalayan Mts. India (Sikkim state) on W and S, China on N. **Topography:** Very high mountains in the N, fertile valleys in the

center, and thick forests in the Duar Plain in the S. **Arable land:** 2.6%. **Capital:** Thimphu, 152,398 (2014).

Government: Type: Constitutional monarchy. **Head of state:** King Jigme Khesar Namgyel Wangchuk; b. 1980; in office: Dec. 14, 2006. **Head of gov.:** Prime Min. Tshering Tobgay; b. 1965; in office: July 27, 2013. **Local divisions:** 20 districts. **Defense budget/active troops:** NA.

Economy: Industries: cement, wood prods., processed fruits, alcoholic beverages, calcium carbide, tourism. **Chief crops:** rice, corn, root crops, citrus. **Natural resources:** timber, hydropower, gypsum, calcium carbonate. **Water:** 100,671 cu m per capita. **Electricity prod.:** 7.5 bil kWh. **Labor force:** agric. 57%, industry 21%, services 22%. **Unemployment:** 2.8%.

Finance: Monetary unit: Ngultrum (BTN) (66.78 = $1 U.S.). **GDP:** $6.4 bil; **per capita GDP:** $8,200; **GDP growth:** 7.7%. **Imports** (2013): $965 mil; India 72.3%, South Korea 6%. **Exports** (2013): $375 mil; India 83.8%, Hong Kong 10.8%. **Tourism:** $93 mil. **Budget:** $692.7 mil (nearly one-quarter financed by India's govt.). **Inflation:** 4.5%.

Transport: Airports: 2.

Communications: Telephone: 2.8 per 100 pop. **Mobile:** 87.1 per 100 pop. **Broadband:** 28.2 per 100 pop. **Internet:** 39.8%.

Health: Expend.: 3.6%. **Life expect.:** 69.1 male; 71.1 female. **Births:** 17.5 per 1,000 pop. **Deaths:** 6.6 per 1,000 pop. **Infant mortality:** 33.9 per 1,000 live births. **Undernourished:** NA. **HIV:** NA.

Education: Compulsory: NA. **Literacy:** 63.9%.

Permanent UN mission: 343 E. 43rd St., New York, NY 10017; (212) 661-0551.

Website: www.bhutan.gov.bt

The region came under Tibetan rule in the 16th cent. British influence grew in the 19th cent. A Buddhist monarchy was set up in 1907. After a 1910 treaty, Britain guided Bhutan's external affairs, while the country remained internally self-governing. Upon independence the treaty was revised, 1949, to allow India to assume Britain's role.

Isolated for much of its history, Bhutan has taken steps toward modernization. King Jigme Singye Wangchuk, in power since 1972, stepped down Dec. 14, 2006, in favor of his son, Jigme Khesar Namgyel Wangchuk. Multiparty parliamentary elections took place Mar. 24, 2008, and a new constitution was ratified July 18, making Bhutan a democratic constitutional monarchy. Tashi Chhozom became the first woman appointed to the country's supreme court, Aug. 3, 2012. The ruling party was defeated in July 13, 2013, parliamentary elections, with the opposition People's Democratic Party (PDP) winning 32 out of 47 seats.

Bolivia
Plurinational State of Bolivia

People: Population: 10,969,649. **Age distrib.:** <15: 32.4%; 65+: 5.2%. **Growth:** 1.5%. **Migrants:** 1.3%. **Pop. density:** 26.2 per sq mi, 10.1 per sq km. **Urban:** 68.9%. **Ethnic groups:** mestizo (mixed white/Amerindian) 68%, indigenous 20%, white 5%, cholo/chola 2%. **Languages:** Spanish, Quechua, Aymara, Guarani (all official). **Religions:** Roman Catholic 76.8%, Evangelical and Pentecostal 8.1%, Protestant 7.9%, none 5.5%.

Geography: Total area: 424,164 sq mi, 1,098,581 sq km; **Land area:** 418,265 sq mi, 1,083,301 sq km. **Location:** W central South America, in the Andes Mts. One of two landlocked countries in S America. Peru, Chile on W; Argentina, Paraguay on S; Brazil on E and N. **Topography:** The great central plateau, more than 500 mi long at an elevation of 12,000 ft, lies between two cordilleras having three of the highest peaks in S America. Lake Titicaca, on Peruvian border, is world's highest lake (12,500 ft) navigable by large boats. The E central region has semitropical forests; the llanos, or Amazon-Chaco lowlands, are in E. **Arable land:** 4.1%. **Capital:** La Paz (admin.), 1,834,047; Sucre (constitutional), 385,498. **Cities:** Santa Cruz, 2,181,105; Cochabamba, 1,272,930.

Government: Type: Presidential republic. **Head of state and gov.:** Pres. Juan Evo Morales Ayma; b. 1959; in office: Jan. 22, 2006. **Local divisions:** 9 departments. **Defense budget:** $435 mil. **Active troops:** 34,100.

Economy: Industries: mining, smelting, petroleum, food and beverages, tobacco, handicrafts, clothing. **Chief crops:** soybeans, quinoa, Brazil nuts, sugarcane, coffee, corn, rice, potatoes. **Natural resources:** tin, nat. gas, petroleum, zinc, tungsten, antimony, silver, iron, lead, gold, timber, hydropower. **Water:** 53,520 cu m per capita. **Crude oil reserves:** 0.2 bil bbls. **Other resources:** Timber. **Electricity prod.:** 7.7 bil kWh. **Labor force:** agric. 32%, industry 20%, services 47.9%. **Unemployment:** 2.7%.

Finance: Monetary unit: Boliviano (BOB) (6.87 = $1 U.S.). **GDP:** $74.4 bil; **per capita GDP:** $6,500; **GDP growth:** 4.8%. **Imports:** $10.4 bil; China 17.9%, Brazil 16.5%, Argentina 11.8%, U.S. 10.6%, Peru 6.2%, Japan 5.2%. **Exports:** $9.6 bil; Brazil 28.1%, Argentina 16.9%, U.S. 12.1%, Colombia 6.3%, China 5.3%. **Tourism:** $652 mil. **Budget:** $18 bil. **Inflation:** 4.1%.

Transport: Railways: 2,177 mi. **Motor vehicles:** 71.8 per 1,000 pop. **Airports:** 21.

Communications: Telephone: 8 per 100 pop. **Mobile:** 92.2 per 100 pop. **Broadband:** 28.1 per 100 pop. **Internet:** 45.1%.

Health: Expend.: 6.3%. **Life expect.:** 66.4 male; 72.1 female. **Births:** 22.4 per 1,000 pop. **Deaths:** 6.5 per 1,000 pop. **Infant mortality:** 36.4 per 1,000 live births. **Undernourished:** 15.9%. **HIV:** 0.3%.

Education: Compulsory: ages 4-17. **Literacy:** 95.1%.

Embassy: 3014 Massachusetts Ave. NW 20008; 483-4410.

Website: www.bolivia.gob.bo

The Incas conquered the region's earlier Indian inhabitants in the 13th cent. Spanish colonial rule began in the 1530s and lasted until Aug. 6, 1825. The country is named after independence fighter Simón Bolívar. In a series of wars, Bolivia lost its Pacific coast to Chile, the oil-bearing Chaco to Paraguay, and rubber-growing areas to Brazil, 1879-1935.

Economic unrest, especially among militant mine workers, led to continuing political instability. A reformist government under Victor Paz Estenssoro, 1951-64, nationalized tin mines and attempted to improve conditions for the Indian majority but was overthrown by a military junta. A series of coups and countercoups continued until constitutional government was restored in 1982.

U.S. pressure on the government to reduce production of coca, the raw material for cocaine, led to clashes between police and growers and increased anti-U.S. feeling in Bolivia, where chewing coca leaves is fairly common. Gen. Hugo Banzer Suárez, who ruled as a dictator, 1971-78, later governed as president, 1997-2001.

After an inconclusive presidential election June 2002, Congress chose Gonzalo Sánchez de Lozada, a U.S.-educated mining executive, as head of state. He quit Oct. 17, 2003, after indigenous Bolivians staged a month of antigovernment protests in which over 70 people died. His successor, Vice Pres. Carlos D. Mesa Gisbert, was embroiled in controversies over energy policy.

Leftist Juan Evo Morales Ayma won the presidential election, Dec. 2005. He nationalized the hydrocarbon sector and launched a land-redistribution program to benefit poor farmers. He faced resistance and demands for autonomy from leaders of Bolivia's relatively prosperous lowland provinces. Voters, Jan. 25, 2009, approved a new constitution strengthening the rights of Bolivia's indigenous majority and increasing federal control over the country's natural resources. Morales won a second term Dec. 6, 2009. His government nationalized major utility companies in 2012. Morales won reelection Oct. 12, 2014. A referendum measure that would have allowed him to seek a 4th term was defeated, Feb. 21, 2016. Miners protesting government regulation killed Bolivia's deputy interior minister, Aug. 25.

Bosnia and Herzegovina

People: Population: 3,861,912. **Age distrib.:** <15: 13.4%; 65+: 14%. **Growth:** –0.1%. **Migrants:** 0.9%. **Pop. density:** 195.4 per sq mi, 75.4 per sq km. **Urban:** 39.9%. **Ethnic groups:** Bosniak 50.1%, Serb 30.8%, Croat 15.4%. **Languages:** Bosnian, Croatian, Serbian (all official). **Religions:** Muslim 40%, Orthodox 31%, Roman Catholic 15%.

Geography: Total area: 19,767 sq mi, 51,197 sq km; **Land area:** 19,763 sq mi, 51,187 sq km. **Location:** Balkan Peninsula in SE Europe. Serbia, Montenegro on E and SE; Croatia on N and W. **Topography:** Hilly with some mountains. **Arable land:** 19.7%. **Capital:** Sarajevo, 315,759.

Government: Type: Parliamentary republic. **Heads of state:** Collective presidency with rotating leadership every 8 months. **Head of gov.:** Chairman of the Council of Ministers Denis Zvizdic; b. 1964; in office: Feb. 11, 2015. **Local divisions:** 2 first-order admin. divisions, 1 internationally supervised district. **Defense budget:** $192 mil. **Active troops:** 10,500.

Economy: Industries: steel, coal, iron ore, lead, zinc, manganese, bauxite, aluminum, motor vehicle assembly, textiles, tobacco prods. **Chief crops:** wheat, corn, fruits, vegetables. **Natural resources:** coal, iron ore, bauxite, copper, lead, zinc, chromite, cobalt, manganese, nickel, clay, gypsum, salt, sand, timber, hydropower. **Water:** 9,843 cu m per capita. **Electricity prod.:** 17 bil kWh. **Labor force:** agric. 19%; industry 30%; services 51%. **Unemployment:** 27.9%.

Finance: Monetary unit: Convertible Marka (BAM) (1.75 = $1 U.S.). **GDP:** $40.5 bil; **per capita GDP:** $10,500; **GDP growth:** 2.8%. **Imports:** $8.8 bil; Croatia 19.2%, Germany 13.8%, Slovenia 13.8%, Italy 10.9%, Austria 5.7%, Hungary 5.2%. **Exports:** $3.9 bil; Slovenia 16.5%, Italy 15.9%, Germany 12.1%, Croatia 11.5%, Austria 11.1%, Turkey 5.2%. **Tourism:** $656 mil. **Budget:** $7.6 bil. **Inflation** (2013-14): –0.9%.

Transport: Railways: 600 mi. **Airports:** 7.

Communications: Telephone: 20.2 per 100 pop. **Mobile:** 90.2 per 100 pop. **Broadband:** 27.8 per 100 pop. **Internet:** 65.1%.

Health: Expend.: 9.6%. **Life expect.:** 73.7 male; 80.0 female. **Births:** 8.8 per 1,000 pop. **Deaths:** 9.9 per 1,000 pop. **Infant mortality:** 5.6 per 1,000 live births. **Undernourished:** <5%. **HIV:** NA.

Education: Compulsory: ages 6-14. **Literacy:** 98.5%.

Embassy: 2109 E St. NW 20037; 337-1500.

Website: www.fbihvlada.gov.ba

Bosnia was ruled by Croatian kings c. 958 CE, and by Hungary 1000-1200. It became organized c. 1200 and later took control of Herzegovina. The kingdom disintegrated after 1391, with the southern part becoming the independent duchy of Herzegovina. It was conquered by Turks in 1463 and made a Turkish province. The area was placed under control of Austria-Hungary in 1878 and made part of the province of Bosnia and Herzegovina, which was formally annexed to Austria-Hungary, 1908. Bosnia became a province of Yugoslavia in 1918. It was reunited with Herzegovina as a federated republic under the 1946 Yugoslav constitution.

Bosnia and Herzegovina declared sovereignty Oct. 15, 1991. A referendum for independence was passed Feb. 29, 1992. Ethnic Serbs' opposition to the referendum spurred violent clashes and bombings. The U.S. and EU recognized the republic Apr. 7. Fierce three-way fighting continued between Bosnia's Serbs, Muslims, and Croats. Serb forces engaged in ethnic cleansing, killing thousands of Bosnian Muslims (Bosniaks) and expelling Muslims and other non-Serbs from areas under Bosnian Serb control. The capital, Sarajevo, was surrounded and besieged by Bosnian Serb forces. Muslims and Croats in Bosnia began a cease-fire Feb. 23, 1994, and signed an accord, Mar. 18, to create a Muslim-Croat confederation in Bosnia. However, by mid-1994, Bosnian Serbs controlled over 70% of the country.

As fighting continued in 1995, the balance of power shifted toward the Muslim-Croat alliance. Massive NATO airstrikes at Bosnian Serb targets beginning Aug. 30 triggered a new round of peace talks, and the siege of Sarajevo was lifted Sept. 15. The new talks produced an agreement to create autonomous regions within Bosnia, with the Serb region (Republika Srpska) constituting 49% of the country. A Croat-Muslim offensive in Sept. recaptured significant territory, leaving Bosnian Serbs in control of approximately half that percentage.

A Nov. 1995 peace agreement was signed in Paris, Dec. 14, 1995, by leaders of Bosnia, Croatia, and Serbia. Some 60,000 NATO troops (about 20,000 from the U.S.) moved in to police the accord. Meanwhile, a UN tribunal began bringing charges against suspected war criminals. Elections were held Sept. 14, 1996, for a 3-person collective presidency, for seats in a federal parliament, and for regional offices. In Dec. a revamped NATO Stabilization Force (SFOR) of over 30,000 members (more than 8,000 from the U.S.) received an 18-month mandate, which was later extended.

The UN tribunal found Radislav Krstic, a Bosnian Serb general, guilty Aug. 2, 2001, in connection with the genocide of thousands of Muslims at Srebrenica in 1995. An EU peacekeeping force (EUFOR), with 7,000 members, assumed responsibility from SFOR, Dec. 2, 2004. Accused of complicity in the Sarajevo and Srebrenica atrocities, former Bosnian Serb leader Radovan Karadzic was arrested in Serbia, July 21, 2008, and handed over to the UN tribunal at The Hague, Netherlands. He was convicted, Mar. 24, 2016, of genocide, war crimes, and crimes against humanity and sentenced to 40 years in prison. Also extradited to The Hague was Gen. Ratko Mladic, the former Bosnian Serb military commander accused of directing the Srebrenica massacre, who was arrested in Serbia May 26, 2011. He faced 11 counts of war crimes and crimes against humanity, 2 of them for genocide, in a trial that began May 16, 2012. On Dec. 12, 2012, Mladic's close associate Zdravko Tolimir was convicted of genocide and sentenced to life in prison; he died in prison Feb. 8, 2016. Serbian police, Mar. 18, 2015, arrested 8 men accused of killing more than 1,000 people during the Srebrenica massacre. EUFOR strength in Bosnia was about 600 troops in mid-2016.

Botswana
Republic of Botswana

People: Population: 2,209,208. **Age distrib.:** <15: 32.4%; 65+: 4.1%. **Growth:** 1.2%. **Migrants:** 7.1%. **Pop. density:** 10.1 per sq mi, 3.9 per sq km. **Urban:** 57.7%. **Ethnic groups:** Tswana or Setswana 79%, Kalanga 11%, Basarwa 3%, other (incl. Kgalagadi, white) 7%. **Languages:** Setswana, Sekalanga, Shekgalagadi, English (official). **Religions:** Christian 79.1%, Badimo 4.1%, none 15.2%.

Geography: Total area: 224,607 sq mi, 581,730 sq km; **Land area:** 218,816 sq mi, 566,730 sq km. **Location:** Southern Africa. Namibia on N and W, Zambia on N, Zimbabwe on NE, South Africa on S. **Topography:** The Kalahari Desert, supporting nomadic Bushmen (also known as the Basarwa or San people) and wildlife, spreads over SW. Swamplands and farming areas in N; rolling plains in E where livestock are grazed. **Arable land:** 0.5%. **Capital:** Gaborone, 246,562 (2014).

Government: Type: Parliamentary republic. **Head of state and gov.:** Pres. Seretse Khama Ian Khama; b. 1953; in office: Apr. 1, 2008. **Local divisions:** 10 districts, 6 town councils. **Defense budget:** $351 mil. **Active troops:** 9,000.

Economy: Industries: diamonds, copper, nickel, salt, soda ash, potash, coal, iron ore, silver. **Chief crops:** sorghum, maize, millet, beans, sunflowers, groundnuts. **Natural resources:** diamonds, copper, nickel, salt, soda ash, potash, coal, iron ore, silver. **Water:**

5,411 cu m per capita. **Electricity prod.:** 1.6 bil kWh. **Labor force:** NA. **Unemployment:** 18.2%.

Finance: Monetary unit: Pula (BWP) (10.86 = $1 U.S.). **GDP:** $34.8 bil; **per capita GDP:** $16,400; **GDP growth:** −0.3%. **Imports:** $7.3 bil. **Exports:** $6.7 bil. **Tourism:** $977 mil. **Budget:** $5.6 bil. **Inflation:** 3.1%.

Transport: Railways: 552 mi. **Motor vehicles:** 200.9 per 1,000 pop. **Airports:** 10.

Communications: Telephone: 7.8 per 100 pop. **Mobile:** 169 per 100 pop. **Broadband:** 49.7 per 100 pop. **Internet:** 27.5%.

Health: Expend.: 5.4%. **Life expect.:** 56.3 male; 52.6 female. **Births:** 20.7 per 1,000 pop. **Deaths:** 13.3 per 1,000 pop. **Infant mortality:** 8.6 per 1,000 live births. **Undernourished:** 24.1%. **HIV:** 22.2%.

Education: Free primary and junior secondary; not compulsory. **Literacy:** 88.2%.

Embassy: 1531-1533 New Hampshire Ave. NW 20036; 244-4990.

Website: www.gov.bw

First inhabited by Bushmen, then Bantus, the region became the British protectorate of Bechuanaland in 1886. The country became fully independent Sept. 30, 1966. Cattle raising and mining (diamonds, copper, nickel) have contributed to economic growth. Pres. Festus Mogae transferred power Apr. 1, 2008, to Seretse Khama Ian Khama, son of Botswana's independence leader and first president (1966-80), Sir Seretse Khama. In power since independence, the Botswana Democratic Party won legislative elections in 2009 and 2014, and each new National Assembly elected Ian Khama to a full 5-year term as president. The government outlawed commercial hunting in 2014, but poaching of big-game animals remained a problem.

Brazil
Federative Republic of Brazil

People: Population: 205,823,665. **Age distrib.:** <15: 22.8%; 65+: 8.1%. **Growth:** 0.8%. **Migrants:** 0.3%. **Pop. density:** 63.8 per sq mi, 24.6 per sq km. **Urban:** 85.9%. **Ethnic groups:** white 47.7%, mulatto (mixed white/black) 43.1%, black 7.6%. **Languages:** Portuguese (official). **Religions:** Roman Catholic 64.6%, Protestant 22.2% (incl. Adventist 6.5%), none 8%.

Geography: Total area: 3,287,957 sq mi, 8,515,770 sq km; **Land area:** 3,227,096 sq mi, 8,358,140 sq km. **Location:** Occupies E half of South America. French Guiana, Suriname, Guyana, Venezuela on N; Colombia, Peru, Bolivia, Paraguay, on W; Argentina, Uruguay on S. **Topography:** Atlantic coastline stretches 4,603 mi. Heavily wooded Amazon basin covers N half of country. Its network of rivers is navigable for 15,814 mi. The Amazon itself flows 2,093 mi in Brazil. The NE region is semiarid scrubland, heavily settled and poor. Almost half of pop. resides in S central region. Most major cities are in the narrow coastal belt. Almost the entire country has a tropical or semitropical climate. **Arable land:** 9.1%. **Capital:** Brasília, 4,235,298. **Cities:** São Paulo, 21,296,830; Rio de Janeiro, 12,981,382; Belo Horizonte, 5,765,974.

Government: Type: Federal presidential republic. **Head of state and gov.:** Pres. Michel Temer; b. 1940; in office: May 12, 2016. **Local divisions:** 26 states, 1 federal district. **Defense budget:** $24.3 bil. **Active troops:** 334,500.

Economy: Industries: textiles, shoes, chemicals, cement, lumber, iron ore, tin, steel, aircraft, motor vehicles and parts. **Chief crops:** coffee, soybeans, wheat, rice, corn, sugarcane, cocoa, citrus. **Natural resources:** bauxite, gold, iron ore, manganese, nickel, phosphates, platinum, tin, rare earth elements, uranium, petroleum, hydropower, timber. **Water:** 41,603 cu m per capita. **Crude oil reserves:** 16.2 bil bbls. **Electricity prod.:** 534 bil kWh. **Labor force:** agric. 15.7%, industry 13.3%, services 71%. **Unemployment:** 6.8%.

Finance: Monetary unit: Real (BRL) (3.24 = $1 U.S.). **GDP:** $3.2 tril; **per capita GDP:** $15,600; **GDP growth:** −3.8%. **Imports:** $174.2 bil; China 17.9%, U.S. 15.6%, Germany 6.1%, Argentina 6%. **Exports:** $189.1 bil; China 18.6%, U.S. 12.7%, Argentina 6.7%, Netherlands 5.3%. **Tourism:** $5.8 bil. **Budget:** $641.2 bil. **Inflation:** 9%.

Transport: Railways: 17,733 mi. **Motor vehicles:** 208.2 per 1,000 pop. **Airports:** 698.

Communications: Telephone: 21.4 per 100 pop. **Mobile:** 126.6 per 100 pop. **Broadband:** 78.1 per 100 pop. **Internet:** 59.1%.

Health: Expend.: 8.3%. **Life expect.:** 70.2 male; 77.5 female. **Births:** 14.3 per 1,000 pop. **Deaths:** 6.6 per 1,000 pop. **Infant mortality:** 18.0 per 1,000 live births. **Undernourished:** <5%. **HIV:** 0.6%.

Education: Compulsory: ages 4-17. **Literacy:** 92.6%.

Embassy: 3006 Massachusetts Ave. NW 20008; 238-2700.

Website: www.brasil.gov.br

Pedro Álvares Cabral, a Portuguese navigator, is generally credited as the first European to reach Brazil, in 1500. The country was thinly settled by various Indian tribes. Only a few survive today, mostly in the Amazon Basin.

In the next centuries, Portuguese colonists gradually pushed inland, bringing along large numbers of African slaves. (Slavery was not abolished until 1888.) The king of Portugal, fleeing Napoleon's army, moved the seat of government to Brazil in 1808. Brazil thereupon became a kingdom under Dom Joao VI. After Joao VI returned to Portugal, his son Pedro proclaimed Brazil's independence, Sept. 7, 1822, and was crowned emperor. The second emperor, Dom Pedro II, was deposed in 1889, and a republic proclaimed.

A military junta took control in 1930; Getulio Vargas assumed dictatorial power. The military forced him out in 1945. A democratic regime prevailed 1945-64, during which time the capital was moved from Rio de Janeiro to Brasília. Military-backed governments ruled Brazil for the next 20 years. Censorship was imposed, and the opposition was suppressed.

By the 1990s, Brazil had one of the world's largest economies. Income is unevenly distributed, however, and more than one-fifth of Brazilians live in poverty. Despite protective environmental legislation, development has destroyed much of the Amazon ecosystem.

Democratic presidential elections held in 1985 brought back civilian rule. Fernando Collor de Mello was elected president, Dec. 1989. In Sept. 1992, Collor was charged with corruption. He resigned, Dec. 29, as his Senate impeachment trial was beginning.

A new civil code guaranteeing legal equality for women was enacted Aug. 15, 2001. Luiz Inácio Lula da Silva, a union leader and reformer, won a presidential runoff, Oct. 2002. Brazil's space program launched its first rocket into space Oct. 23, 2004.

A top aide to Pres. Lula resigned June 16, 2005, amid allegations the ruling party bribed legislators for votes; he and two others involved in the scandal were found guilty and sentenced to upwards of 40 years in prison Oct.-Nov. 2012. Despite scandals, Lula won a second presidential term, Oct. 2006. The nation reported huge offshore oil finds in 2007-08. Lula's former chief of staff, Dilma Rousseff, won a runoff election Oct. 31, 2010, to become Brazil's first woman president. She narrowly won reelection in an Oct. 26, 2014, runoff.

After public transportation fares were raised June 1, 2013, demonstrations began in São Paulo June 6 and quickly spread to other cities; fares were lowered June 20. Demonstrators also protested a lack of public services, government corruption, and the expected high costs of Pope Francis's 2013 visit, the 2014 men's soccer World Cup, and the 2016 Summer Olympics.

A $3-bil bribery and corruption scandal involving Petrobras (the national oil company), Pres. Rousseff's Workers' Party, and high-level government officials led to the resignations of Petrobras's top executives in Feb. 2015 and to arrests, in Nov. 2014 and June 2015, of business executives at Petrobras subcontractors. The Workers' Party's former treasurer was convicted of bribery and sentenced, Sept. 21, 2015, to more than 15 years in prison. A similar scandal involved Electrobras, the government's electric utility company. Former Pres. Lula was ordered, July 29, 2016, to stand trial for allegedly obstructing the Petrobras investigation and, Sept. 20, to stand trial on bribery charges. José Dirceu, Lula's former chief of staff, was sentenced, May 18, 2016, to 23 years in prison for money laundering and other Petrobras-related offenses.

With Brazil suffering an economic downturn (real GDP declined 3.8% in 2015), the lower house of Congress, Apr. 17, 2016, charged Pres. Rousseff with illegally manipulating the federal budget to conceal the size of the deficit. The Senate suspended her from office, May 12; her Senate impeachment trial, Aug. 25-31, ended with her conviction and removal from office. Former Vice Pres. Michel Temer (a centrist and political rival who had been acting president since May 12) succeeded Rousseff.

Responding to a widespread Zika virus outbreak and related cases of microcephaly, Brazil declared a public health emergency, Nov. 11, 2015. As of Aug. 2016, health officials had confirmed more than 1,800 microcephaly cases; more than 250,000 confirmed or suspected Zika infections had occurred. Amid concerns about Zika, high crime rates in host city Rio de Janeiro, and the inadequacy of preparations, the 2016 Olympics were held Aug. 5-21 without major incidents; 85,000 police and military personnel provided security.

Brunei
Brunei Darussalam

People: Population: 436,620. **Age distrib.:** <15: 23.5%; 65+: 4.5%. **Growth:** 1.6%. **Migrants:** 24.3%. **Pop. density:** 214.8 per sq mi, 82.9 per sq km. **Urban:** 77.5%. **Ethnic groups:** Malay 65.7%, Chinese 10.3%, other indigenous 3.4%. **Languages:** Malay (official), English, Chinese. **Religions:** Muslim (official) 78.8%, Christian 8.7%, Buddhist 7.8%, other (incl. indigenous beliefs) 4.7%.

Geography: Total area: 2,226 sq mi, 5,765 sq km; **Land area:** 2,033 sq mi, 5,265 sq km. **Location:** SE Asia, on the N coast of the island of Borneo. It is surrounded on its landward side by the Malaysian state of Sarawak. **Topography:** Narrow coastal plain with mountains in E, hilly lowlands in W. Swamps in W and NE. Tropical climate. **Arable land:** 0.9%. **Capital:** Bandar Seri Begawan, 14,025 (2014).

Government: Type: Absolute monarchy or sultanate. **Head of state and gov.:** Sultan and Prime Min. Sir Hassanal Bolkiah

Mu'izzaddin Waddaulah; b. 1946; in office: Jan. 1, 1984 (sultan since Oct. 5, 1967). **Local divisions:** 4 districts. **Defense budget:** $396 mil. **Active troops:** 7,000.

Economy: Industries: petroleum, petroleum refining, liquefied nat. gas, constr. **Chief crops:** rice, vegetables, fruits. **Natural resources:** petroleum, nat. gas, timber. **Water:** 20,085 cu m per capita. **Crude oil reserves:** 1.1 bil bbls. **Electricity prod.:** 4.1 bil kWh. **Labor force:** agric. 4.2%, industry 62.8%, services 33%. **Unemployment:** 3.8%.

Finance: Monetary unit: Dollar (BND) (1.36 = $1 U.S.). **GDP:** $33.2 bil; **per capita GDP:** $79,700; **GDP growth:** −0.2%. **Imports:** $4.8 bil; Singapore 27.9%, China 25.3%, Malaysia 12.4%, UK 10.6%. **Exports:** $7.1 bil; Japan 35.9%, South Korea 14.8%, Thailand 10.8%, India 9.8%, New Zealand 5.6%, Australia 5%. **Tourism:** $92 mil. **Budget:** $5.5 bil. **Inflation:** −0.4%.

Transport: Motor vehicles: 707.3 per 1,000 pop. **Airports:** 1. **Communications: Telephone:** 9 per 100 pop. **Mobile:** 108.1 per 100 pop. **Broadband:** 6.3 per 100 pop. **Internet:** 71.2%.

Health: Expend.: 2.7%. **Life expect.:** 74.8 male; 79.6 female. **Births:** 17.2 per 1,000 pop. **Deaths:** 3.6 per 1,000 pop. **Infant mortality:** 9.9 per 1,000 live births. **Undernourished:** <5%. **HIV:** NA.

Education: Compulsory: ages 6-14. **Literacy:** 96.7%.

Embassy: 3520 International Ct. NW 20008; 237-1838.

Website: www. brunei.gov.bn

The Sultanate of Brunei was a powerful state in the early 16th cent., with authority over all of the island of Borneo as well as parts of the Sulu Islands and the Philippines. In 1888, a treaty placed the state under the protection of Great Britain.

Brunei became a fully sovereign and independent state on Jan. 1, 1984. The country fielded female athletes for the first time at the 2012 Summer Olympics. Brunei began enacting, May 1, 2014, a new penal code based on Islamic law. If fully implemented in future years, the code would make theft punishable by whipping or limb amputation, and adultery and gay sex would become capital crimes. Brunei outlawed public Christmas celebrations and displays in 2015.

Bulgaria
Republic of Bulgaria

People: Population: 7,144,653. **Age distrib.:** <15: 14.5%; 65+: 19%. **Growth:** −0.6%. **Migrants:** 1.4%. **Pop. density:** 170.6 per sq mi, 65.9 per sq km. **Urban:** 74.3%. **Ethnic groups:** Bulgarian 76.9%, Turkish 8%, Roma 4.4%. **Languages:** Bulgarian (official), Turkish, Roma. **Religions:** Eastern Orthodox 59.4%, Muslim 7.8%, none 3.7%.

Geography: Total area: 42,811 sq mi, 110,879 sq km; **Land area:** 41,888 sq mi, 108,489 sq km. **Location:** SE Europe, in E Balkan Peninsula on Black Sea. Romania on N; Serbia, Macedonia on W; Greece, Turkey on S. **Topography:** The Stara Planina (Balkan) Mts. stretch E-W across the center of country, with the Danubian plain on N, the Rhodope Mts. on SW, and Thracian Plain on SE. **Arable land:** 32%. **Capital:** Sofia, 1,230,102.

Government: Type: Parliamentary republic. **Head of state:** Pres. Rosen Plevneliev; b. 1964; in office: Jan. 22, 2012. **Head of gov.:** Prime Min. Boyko Borisov; b. 1959; in office: Nov. 7, 2014. **Local divisions:** 28 provinces. **Defense budget:** $600 mil. **Active troops:** 31,300.

Economy: Industries: electricity, gas, water; food, beverages, tobacco; machinery and equip. **Chief crops:** vegetables, fruits, tobacco, wine, wheat, barley, sunflowers, sugar beets. **Natural resources:** bauxite, copper, lead, zinc, coal, timber. **Water:** 2,979 cu m per capita. **Crude oil reserves** (2015): 15 mil bbls. **Electricity prod.:** 39 bil kWh. **Labor force:** agric. 7%, industry 30.1%, services 62.9%. **Unemployment:** 11.6%.

Finance: Monetary unit: Lev (BGN) (1.75 = $1 U.S.). **GDP:** $133.9 bil; **per capita GDP:** $19,100; **GDP growth:** 3%. **Imports:** $27.7 bil; Germany 12.9%, Russia 12%, Italy 7.6%, Romania 6.8%, Turkey 5.7%. **Exports:** $24.3 bil; Germany 12.5%, Italy 9.2%, Turkey 8.5%, Romania 8.2%, Greece 6.5%. **Tourism:** $3.1 bil. **Budget:** $19.1 bil. **Inflation:** −0.1%.

Transport: Railways: 3,178 mi. **Motor vehicles:** 486.3 per 1,000 pop. **Airports:** 57.

Communications: Telephone: 23.3 per 100 pop. **Mobile:** 129.3 per 100 pop. **Broadband:** 66.4 per 100 pop. **Internet:** 56.7%.

Health: Expend.: 8.4%. **Life expect.:** 71.2 male; 78.0 female. **Births:** 8.8 per 1,000 pop. **Deaths:** 14.5 per 1,000 pop. **Infant mortality:** 8.5 per 1,000 live births. **Undernourished:** <5%. **HIV:** NA.

Education: Compulsory: ages 5-15. **Literacy:** 98.4%.

Embassy: 1621 22nd St. NW 20008; 387-0174.

Website: www.government.bg

Bulgaria was settled by Slavs in the 6th cent. Turkic Bulgars arrived in the 7th cent., merged with the Slavs, became Christians by the 9th cent., and set up powerful empires in the 10th and 12th cents. Ottomans took over in 1396 and ruled for nearly 500 years.

An 1876 revolt led to an independent kingdom in 1908. Bulgaria expanded after the first Balkan War but lost its Aegean coastline

in WWI, when it sided with Germany. Bulgaria joined the Axis in WWII but withdrew in 1944. Communists took power with Soviet aid; the monarchy was abolished Sept. 8, 1946.

On Nov. 10, 1989, Communist Party leader and head of state Todor Zhivkov resigned after 35 years. In Jan. 1990, Parliament voted to revoke the constitutionally guaranteed dominant role of the Communist Party. A new constitution took effect July 13, 1991.

Bulgaria became a full member of NATO, Apr. 2, 2004, and entered the EU, Jan. 1, 2007. Restrictions on Bulgarians' right to work in nine other EU nations ended Jan. 1, 2014.

A terrorist blew up a bus carrying Israeli tourists, July 18, 2012, leaving 5 Israelis, the Bulgarian bus driver, and the bomber dead. An investigation ending Feb. 5, 2013, blamed the attack on the Muslim militant group Hezbollah, which denied involvement. The identity of the bomber, a Lebanese-French citizen, was determined by DNA evidence in July 2014.

Worsening economic conditions in 2012-13 inspired protests that led Prime Min. Boyko Borisov to submit his government's resignation Feb. 20, 2013. No clear winner emerged from May 12 elections. Parliament elected Plamen Oresharski, with no party affiliation, prime min. May 29. Amid a banking crisis, Oresharski resigned July 23, 2014. After Oct. 5 elections, Borisov again became prime min., Nov. 7, 2014. Construction began in 2015 on the second phase of a security fence along the Turkish border, intended to stop Middle Eastern, SW Asian, and African migrants from entering Bulgaria; about 30,000 entered in 2015. The U.S. announced, June 25, 2015, that it would send rotating contingents of about 150 Marines to Bulgaria, as part of an effort to deter Russian aggression.

Burkina Faso

People: Population: 19,512,533. **Age distrib.:** <15: 45%; 65+: 2.4%. **Growth:** 3%. **Migrants:** 3.9%. **Pop. density:** 184.6 per sq mi, 71.3 per sq km. **Urban:** 30.7%. **Ethnic groups:** Mossi 52.5%, Fulani 8.4%, Gurma 6.8%, Bobo 4.8%, Gurunsi 4.5%, Senufo 4.4%, Bissa 3.9%, Lobi 2.5%, Dagara 2.4%. **Languages:** French (official), native African Sudanic-family langs. **Religions:** Muslim 61.6%, Catholic 23.2%, traditional/animist 7.3%, Protestant 6.7%.

Geography: Total area: 105,869 sq mi, 274,200 sq km; **Land area:** 105,715 sq mi, 273,800 sq km. **Location:** W Africa, S of the Sahara. Mali on NW; Niger on NE; Benin, Togo, Ghana, Côte d'Ivoire on S. **Topography:** Landlocked in the savanna region of W Africa. The N is arid, hot, and thinly populated. **Arable land:** 22.7%. **Capital:** Ouagadougou, 2,923,474.

Government: Type: Presidential republic. **Head of state:** Pres. Roch Marc Christian Kaboré; b. 1957; in office: Dec. 29, 2015. **Head of gov.:** Prime Min. Paul Kaba Thieba; b. 1960; in office: Jan. 6, 2016. **Local divisions:** 13 regions. **Defense budget** $151 mil. **Active troops:** 11,200.

Economy: Industries: cotton lint, beverages, agric. proc., soap, cigarettes, textiles. **Chief crops:** cotton, peanuts, shea nuts, sesame, sorghum, millet, corn, rice. **Natural resources:** manganese, limestone, marble, gold, phosphates, pumice, salt. **Water:** 746 cu m per capita. **Electricity prod.:** 0.7 bil kWh. **Labor force:** agric. 90%, industry and services 10%. **Unemployment:** 3.1%.

Finance: Monetary unit: CFA Franc (XOF) (586.00 = $1 U.S.). **GDP:** $30.9 bil; **per capita GDP:** $1,700; **GDP growth:** 4%. **Imports:** $2.5 bil; Côte d'Ivoire 23.1%, France 11.1%, Togo 7.5%. **Exports:** $2.2 bil; Switzerland 53.3%, India 14.5%. **Tourism:** $135 mil. **Budget:** $2.5 bil. **Inflation:** 1%.

Transport: Railways: 386 mi. **Motor vehicles:** 14.6 per 1,000 pop. **Airports:** 2.

Communications: Telephone: 0.4 per 100 pop. **Mobile:** 80.6 per 100 pop. **Broadband:** 9.6 per 100 pop. **Internet:** 11.4%.

Health: Expend.: 5.0%. **Life expect.:** 53.4 male; 57.6 female. **Births:** 41.6 per 1,000 pop. **Deaths:** 11.5 per 1,000 pop. **Infant mortality:** 73.8 per 1,000 live births. **Undernourished:** 20.7%. **HIV:** 0.8%.

Education: Compulsory: ages 6-15. **Literacy:** 37.7%.

Embassy: 2340 Massachusetts Ave. NW 20008; 332-5577.

Website: www.gouvernement.gov.bf or burkina-usa.org

The Mossi people entered Burkina Faso in the 11th-13th cents. Their kingdoms ruled until they were defeated by the Mali and Songhai empires. French control came by 1896, but Upper Volta (renamed Burkina Faso on Aug. 4, 1984) was not established as a separate territory until 1947. Independence came Aug. 5, 1960; a pro-French government was elected. The military seized power in 1980. A 1987 coup brought to power military officers including Blaise Compaoré, who became sole ruler by 1989. Pres. Compaoré most recently won reelection Nov. 21, 2010. Violent protests in 2014 against economic hardship and attempts to amend the constitution to allow Compaoré to run again led to his resignation Oct. 31. Civilian Michel Kafando became interim president Nov. 18, 2014. The Presidential Security Regiment (RSP), loyal to Compaoré, ousted Kafando, Sept. 16, 2015. An agreement negotiated by the Econ. Community of West African States restored Kafando, Sept. 23, and provided for Nov. 29, 2015, elections; former Prime Min. Roch Marc Christian Kaboré of the center-left People's Movement for Progress party was elected president. An attack by

Islamist extremists on a café and two hotels in Ouagadougou the night of Jan. 15-16, 2016, left 30 people dead, many of them foreigners; 3 attackers were killed, and 3 escaped.

Burma
See Myanmar.

Burundi
Republic of Burundi

People: Population: 11,099,298. **Age distrib.:** <15: 45.6%; 65+: 2.6%. **Growth:** 3.3%. **Migrants:** 2.6%. **Pop. density:** 1,119.4 per sq mi, 432.2 per sq km. **Urban:** 12.4%. **Ethnic groups:** Hutu (Bantu) 85%, Tutsi (Hamitic) 14%. **Languages:** Kirundi, French (both official). **Religions:** Catholic 62.1%, Protestant 23.9%, Muslim 2.5%.

Geography: Total area: 10,745 sq mi, 27,830 sq km; **Land area:** 9,915 sq mi, 25,680 sq km. **Location:** Central Africa. Rwanda on N, Dem. Rep. of the Congo on W, Tanzania on E and S. **Topography:** Mostly grassy highland, with mountains reaching 8,900 ft. The southernmost source of the White Nile is located in Burundi. Lake Tanganyika is the second deepest lake in the world (max. depth 4,823 ft). **Arable land:** 46.7%. **Capital:** Bujumbura, 797,121.

Government: Type: Presidential republic. **Head of state and gov.:** Pres. Pierre Nkurunziza; b. 1963; in office: Aug. 26, 2005. **Local divisions:** 18 provinces. **Defense budget:** $62 mil. **Active troops:** 20,000.

Economy: Industries: light consumer goods, assembly of imported components, public works constr., food proc. **Chief crops:** coffee, cotton, tea, corn, sorghum, sweet potatoes, bananas, cassava. **Natural resources:** nickel, uranium, rare earth oxides, peat, cobalt, copper, platinum, vanadium, hydropower, niobium, tantalum, gold, tin, tungsten, kaolin, limestone. **Water:** 1,122 cu m per capita. **Electricity prod.:** 0.2 bil kWh. **Labor force:** agric. 93.6%, industry 2.3%, services 4.1%. **Unemployment:** 6.9%.

Finance: Monetary unit: Franc (BIF) (1,653.90 = $1 U.S.). **GDP:** $7.7 bil; **per capita GDP:** $800; **GDP growth:** –4.1%. **Imports:** $815.1 mil; Kenya 15%, Saudi Arabia 14%, Belgium 9.9%, Tanzania 8.3%, Uganda 7.3%, China 7.1%. **Exports:** $96.6 mil; Germany 12.3%, Pakistan 10.7%, Dem. Rep. of the Congo 10.7%, Uganda 8.1%, Sweden 7.8%, U.S. 7.1%, Belgium 6.3%. **Tourism:** $4 mil. **Budget:** $1 bil. **Inflation:** 5.6%.

Transport: Motor vehicles: 6.3 per 1,000 pop. **Airports:** 1. **Communications: Telephone:** 0.2 per 100 pop. **Mobile:** 46.2 per 100 pop. **Broadband:** NA. **Internet:** 4.9%.

Health: Expend.: 7.5%. **Life expect.:** 58.8 male; 62.3 female. **Births:** 41.7 per 1,000 pop. **Deaths:** 9.0 per 1,000 pop. **Infant mortality:** 60.4 per 1,000 live births. **Undernourished:** NA. **HIV:** 1.0%.

Education: Compulsory: NA. **Literacy:** 85.5%.

Embassy: 2233 Wisconsin Ave. NW, Ste. 408, 20007; 342-2574.

Website: presidence.gov.bi or www.burundiembassydc-usa.org

The pygmy Twa were the first inhabitants, followed by Bantu Hutus, who were conquered in the 16th cent. by the Tutsi (Watusi), probably from Ethiopia. Germany gained control in 1899. Belgium took over in 1916, successively exercising a League of Nations mandate and UN trusteeship over Ruanda-Urundi (now the two countries of Rwanda and Burundi). Burundi became independent July 1, 1962.

An unsuccessful Hutu rebellion in 1972-73 left 10,000 Tutsi and 150,000 Hutu dead. Over 100,000 Hutu fled to Tanzania and Zaire (now Dem. Rep. of the Congo). In the 1980s, Burundi's Tutsi-dominated regime pledged itself to ethnic reconciliation and democratic reform. In the nation's first democratic presidential election, June 1993, a Hutu, Melchior Ndadaye, was elected. He was killed in an attempted coup, Oct. 21, 1993. At least 150,000 Burundians died in ethnic conflicts over the next three years. Pres. Cyprien Ntaryamira, elected Jan. 1994, and the president of Rwanda were killed when missiles shot down their plane, Apr. 6. The incident sparked massive carnage in Rwanda; violence in Burundi, initially far more limited, intensified in 1995. Ethnic strife continued after a military coup, July 25, 1996. Most warring groups signed a draft peace treaty, Aug. 2000. Two coup attempts were suppressed in 2001. A power-sharing government headed by Pierre Buyoya was sworn in Nov. 1, 2001, but clashes with rebels continued.

Domitien Ndayizeye, a Hutu, became president Apr. 2003. The UN Security Council authorized, May 2004, a peacekeeping force (ONUB) for Burundi. Approval of a power-sharing constitution by referendum, Feb. 28, 2005, paved the way for local and parliamentary elections. Chosen by parliament, Pierre Nkurunziza, former leader of a Hutu rebel group, became president Aug. 2005. ONUB was succeeded by the UN Integrated Office in Burundi (BINUB), 2007-10, and by the UN Office in Burundi (BNUB), 2011-14, both intended to assist with political transition. Under a reconciliation accord reached Dec. 4, 2008, remaining Hutu rebels began to demobilize. Candidates opposing Nkurunziza dropped

out of the June 2010 presidential election, claiming the vote was rigged. The government was accused of ordering extrajudicial killings, 2010-11.

Violent protests against Nkurunziza's Apr. 2015 decision to seek reelection led to a postponement of 2015 presidential voting from June 26 to July 21. A May 13 attempted military coup was put down. Several opposition parties boycotted the election, won by Nkurunziza. Ongoing political violence and government repression resulted in at least several hundred deaths by mid-2016. From Apr. 2015 to Sept. 2016, about 300,000 refugees fled the country.

Cabo Verde
Republic of Cabo Verde

People: Population: 553,432. **Age distrib.:** <15: 29.6%; 65+: 5.1%. **Growth:** 1.4%. **Migrants:** 2.9%. **Pop. density:** 355.4 per sq mi, 137.2 per sq km. **Urban:** 66.2%. **Ethnic groups:** Creole (mulatto) 71%, African 28%. **Languages:** Portuguese (official), Crioulo (Portuguese/West African blend). **Religions:** Roman Catholic 77.3%, Protestant 3.7%, none 10.8%.

Geography: Total area: 1,557 sq mi, 4,033 sq km; **Land area:** 1,557 sq mi, 4,033 sq km. **Location:** In Atlantic O., off W tip of Africa. Nearest neighbors are Mauritania, Senegal to E. **Topography:** 15 Cabo Verde islands, volcanic in origin (active crater on Fogo). Landscape is eroded and stark, with vegetation mostly in interior valleys. **Arable land:** 13.6%. **Capital:** Praia, 144,648 (2014).

Government: Type: Parliamentary republic. **Head of state:** Pres. Jorge Carlos Fonseca; b. 1950; in office: Sept. 9, 2011. **Head of gov.:** Prime Min. José Ulisses Correia e Silva; b. 1962; in office: Apr. 22, 2016. **Local divisions:** 22 municipalities. **Defense budget:** $10 mil. **Active troops:** 1,200.

Economy: Industries: food and beverages, fish proc., shoes and garments, salt mining, ship repair. **Chief crops:** bananas, corn, beans, sweet potatoes, sugarcane, coffee, peanuts. **Natural resources:** salt, basalt rock, limestone, kaolin, fish, clay, gypsum. **Water:** 576 cu m per capita. **Electricity prod.:** 0.3 bil kWh. **Labor force:** NA. **Unemployment:** 9.2%.

Finance: Monetary unit: Escudo (CVE) (98.95 = $1 U.S.). **GDP:** $3.4 bil; **per capita GDP:** $6,500; **GDP growth:** 1.8%. **Imports:** $797.8 mil; Portugal 29.9%, Australia 26.4%, Netherlands 11.2%, Spain 5.6%, China 5.6%. **Exports:** $192.7 mil; Australia 83%, Spain 8.6%. **Tourism:** $351 mil. **Budget:** $489.9 mil. **Inflation:** 0.1%.

Transport: Airports: 9.

Communications: Telephone: 11.5 per 100 pop. **Mobile:** 127.2 per 100 pop. **Broadband:** 51.3 per 100 pop. **Internet:** 43%.

Health: Expend.: 4.8%. **Life expect.:** 69.8 male; 74.5 female. **Births:** 20.2 per 1,000 pop. **Deaths:** 6.1 per 1,000 pop. **Infant mortality:** 22.7 per 1,000 live births. **Undernourished:** 9.4%. **HIV:** 1.0%.

Education: Compulsory: ages 6-15. **Literacy:** 88.5%.

Embassy: 3415 Massachusetts Ave. NW 20007; 965-6820.

Website: www.governo.cv

The first Portuguese colonists landed in 1462; African slaves were brought soon after, and most Cabo Verdeans descend from both groups. Independence for Cabo Verde (known as Cape Verde until Oct. 2013) came July 5, 1975. Antonio Mascarenhas Monteiro won the nation's first free presidential election Feb. 17, 1991; he was reelected without opposition five years later. Pres. Pedro Pires served two 5-year terms, 2001-11. Jorge Carlos Fonseca won a presidential runoff election Aug. 21, 2011; he easily won reelection, Oct. 2, 2016. Remittances from Cabo Verdean emigrants are a major source of income.

Cambodia
Kingdom of Cambodia

People: Population: 15,957,223. **Age distrib.:** <15: 31.2%; 65+: 4.1%. **Growth:** 1.6%. **Migrants:** 0.5%. **Pop. density:** 234.1 per sq mi, 90.4 per sq km. **Urban:** 20.9%. **Ethnic groups:** Khmer 90%, Vietnamese 5%. **Language:** Khmer (official). **Religions:** Buddhist (official) 96.9%, Muslim 1.9%.

Geography: Total area: 69,898 sq mi, 181,035 sq km; **Land area:** 68,153 sq mi, 176,515 sq km. **Location:** SE Asia, on Indochina Peninsula. Thailand on W and N, Laos on NE, Vietnam on E. **Topography:** The central area, formed by the Mekong R. basin and Tonle Sap Lake, is level. Hills and mountains in SE; long escarpment in NW separates the country from Thailand. **Arable land:** 23.5%. **Capital:** Phnom Penh, 1,778,782.

Government: Type: Parliamentary constitutional monarchy. **Head of state:** King Norodom Sihamoni; b. 1953; in office: Oct. 29, 2004. **Head of gov.:** Prime Min. Hun Sen; b. 1952; in office: Jan. 14, 1985. **Local divisions:** 24 provinces, 1 municipality. **Defense budget (2014):** $446 mil. **Active troops:** 124,300.

Economy: Industries: tourism, garments, constr., rice milling, fishing, wood and wood prods., rubber, cement, gem mining, textiles. **Chief crops:** rice, rubber, corn, vegetables, cashews, cassava. **Natural resources:** oil and gas, timber, gemstones, iron ore, manganese, phosphates. **Water:** 30,562 cu m per capita.

Electricity prod.: 1.7 bil kWh. Labor force: agric. 48.7%, industry 19.9%, services 31.5%. Unemployment: 0.4%.

Finance: Monetary unit: Riel (KHR) (4,053.00 = $1 U.S.). GDP: $54.2 bil; per capita GDP: $3,500; GDP growth: 6.9%. Imports: $10.65 bil; Thailand 28.5%, China 22%, Vietnam 16.3%, Hong Kong 6%, Singapore 5.6%. Exports: $7.867 bil; U.S. 23.1%, UK 8.8%, Germany 8.2%, Japan 7.4%, Canada 6.7%, China 5.1%, Vietnam 5%, Thailand 4.9%, Netherlands 4.1%. Tourism: $3.1 bil. Budget: $3.7 bil. Inflation: 1.2%.

Transport: Railways: 399 mi (under restoration). Airports: 6. Communications: Telephone: 1.6 per 100 pop. Mobile: 133 per 100 pop. Broadband: 14 per 100 pop. Internet: 19%.

Health: Expend.: 5.7%. Life expect.: 62.0 male; 67.1 female. Births: 23.4 per 1,000 pop. Deaths: 7.6 per 1,000 pop. Infant mortality: 48.7 per 1,000 live births. Undernourished: 14.2%. HIV: 0.6%.

Education: Compulsory: NA. Literacy: 78.3%.
Embassy: 4530 16th St. NW 20011; 726-7742.
Website: cnv.org.kh

Early kingdoms dating from that of Funan in the 1st cent. CE culminated in the great Khmer empire that flourished from the 9th cent. to the 13th, encompassing present-day Thailand, Cambodia, Laos, and southern Vietnam. The peripheral areas were lost to invading Siamese and Vietnamese. France established a protectorate in 1863. Independence came in 1953.

Prince Norodom Sihanouk, king (1941-55) and head of state from 1960, tried to maintain neutrality during the Vietnam War. The U.S. bombed Cambodia, 1969-73, targeting suspected border sanctuaries of Vietnamese insurgents.

In 1970, pro-U.S. Prem. Lon Nol seized power, demanded removal of 40,000 North Vietnamese troops, and abolished the monarchy. Sihanouk formed a government-in-exile in Beijing. Open war began between Nol's government and Communist Khmer Rouge guerrillas, led by Pol Pot and supported by Vietnam and China. The U.S. provided Nol with heavy military and economic aid.

Khmer Rouge forces captured Phnom Penh Apr. 17, 1975. Cities were depopulated with the stated goal of making Cambodia a classless agrarian society; Cambodians were executed or forced to work on cooperative farms. An estimated 1.7 mil people died in "killing fields" or from other hardships under Khmer Rouge rule, 1975-79.

Severe border fighting broke out with Vietnam in 1978 and developed into a full-fledged Vietnamese invasion. Formation of a Vietnamese-backed government was announced, Jan. 8, 1979, one day after Phnom Penh was seized. Thousands of refugees fled to Thailand; widespread starvation was reported. Vietnamese troops remained in Cambodia during the 1980s, meeting resistance from Khmer Rouge guerrillas. Vietnam withdrew nearly all its troops by Sept. 1989.

Following 1993 UN-sponsored elections in Cambodia, two leading parties agreed to share power in an interim government. On Sept. 21, the National Assembly adopted a constitution reestablishing a monarchy, and Sihanouk became king. The Khmer Rouge boycotted the elections and opposed the new government. The insurgency weakened and splintered by 1996.

Co-Prime Min. Hun Sen staged a coup July 5, 1997, ousting his rival, Prince Norodom Ranariddh. Pol Pot was denounced by his former comrades at a show trial, July 25, 1997, and sentenced to house arrest; he died Apr. 15, 1998. Sihanouk abdicated because of poor health and was succeeded, Oct. 2004, by his son Norodom Sihamoni.

Hun Sen's party retained power through a series of flawed elections. A UN-backed war crimes tribunal convicted a former prison warden known as Duch July 2010 for overseeing the killing and torture of more than 14,000 inmates under the Khmer Rouge. Two Khmer Rouge leaders were convicted of murder, crimes against humanity, and other charges, Aug. 7, 2014, and sentenced to life in prison.

Unsafe working conditions led to two factory collapses May 16, 2013, outside of Phnom Penh and in Tream Tbal that killed four workers. In June 2014, as many as 200,000 Cambodians working in Thailand repatriated after a Thai military coup raised fears of a crackdown on illegal migrants.

Cameroon
Republic of Cameroon

People: Population: 24,360,803. Age distrib.: <15: 42.6%; 65+: 3.2%. Growth: 2.6%. Migrants: 1.6%. Pop. density: 133.5 per sq mi, 51.5 per sq km. Urban: 54.9%. Ethnic groups: Cameroon Highlander 31%, Equatorial Bantu 19%, Kirdi 11%, Fulani 10%, Northwestern Bantu 8%, Eastern Nigritic 7%. Languages: English, French (both official); 24 major African lang. groups. Religions: Catholic 38.4%, Protestant 26.3%, Muslim 20.9%, animist 5.6%.

Geography: Total area: 183,568 sq mi, 475,440 sq km; Land area: 182,514 sq mi, 472,710 sq km. Location: Between W and central Africa. Nigeria on NW; Chad, Central African Republic on E; Congo Rep., Gabon, Equatorial Guinea on S. Topography: Low coastal plain with rain forests in S; plateaus in center lead to forested mountains in W, including Mt. Cameroon (13,435 ft). Grasslands in N, marshes around Lake Chad. Arable land: 13.1%. Capital: Yaoundé, 3,203,778. Cities: Douala, 3,050,792.

Government: Type: Presidential republic. Head of state: Pres. Paul Biya; b. 1933; in office: Nov. 6, 1982. Head of gov.: Prime Min. Philemon Yang; b. 1947; in office: June 30, 2009. Local divisions: 10 regions. Defense budget: $355 mil. Active troops: 14,200.

Economy: Industries: petroleum prod. and refining, aluminum prod., food proc., light consumer goods, textiles, lumber. Chief crops: coffee, cocoa, cotton, rubber, bananas, oilseed, grains, cassava. Natural resources: petroleum, bauxite, iron ore, timber, hydropower. Water: 12,127 cu m per capita. Crude oil reserves: 0.2 bil bbls. Electricity prod.: 6.7 bil kWh. Labor force: agric. 70%, industry 13%, services 17%. Unemployment: 4.3%.

Finance: Monetary unit: Central African CFA Franc (XAF) (586.00 = $1 U.S.). GDP: $72.6 bil; per capita GDP: $3,100; GDP growth: 5.9%. Imports: $6.159 bil; China 27.9%, Nigeria 13.9%, France 10.9%, Belgium 4.1%. Exports: $5.283 bil; China 16.7%, India 15.7%, Spain 6.2%, Belgium 6.1%, France 6.1%, Portugal 5.6%, Netherlands 5%, Italy 5%. Tourism: $576 mil. Budget: $5.4 bil. Inflation: 2.7%.

Transport: Railways: 613 mi. Motor vehicles: 15.5 per 1,000 pop. Airports: 11.

Communications: Telephone: 4.5 per 100 pop. Mobile: 71.8 per 100 pop. Broadband: 0.0 per 100 pop. Internet: 20.7%.

Health: Expend.: 4.1%. Life expect.: 57.1 male; 59.9 female. Births: 35.8 per 1,000 pop. Deaths: 9.8 per 1,000 pop. Infant mortality: 52.2 per 1,000 live births. Undernourished: 9.9%. HIV: 4.5%.

Education: Compulsory: ages 6-11. Literacy: 75%.
Embassy: 3400 International Dr. NW 20008; 265-8790.
Website: www.spm.gov.cm

Portuguese sailors were the first Europeans to reach Cameroon, in the 15th cent. The European and American slave trade was very active in the area. German control lasted from 1884 to 1916, when France and Britain divided the territory, for which they later received League of Nations mandates and UN trusteeships. French Cameroon became independent Jan. 1, 1960; one part of British Cameroon joined Nigeria in 1961 while the other part joined Cameroon. Pres. Paul Biya has retained power since 1982 in a series of elections that were boycotted by opposition parties or disputed as fraudulent. Rising food and fuel costs and discontent with Biya's continued rule sparked antigovernment riots Feb. 23-29, 2008. The legislature, controlled by Biya loyalists, voted Apr. 2008 to abolish presidential term limits introduced in 1996.

More than a dozen French citizens were kidnapped during 2013, allegedly in retaliation for France's intervention in Mali, and taken to Nigeria by the Nigerian-based jihadist group Boko Haram. Kidnappings and attacks by Boko Haram in Cameroon continued in 2014-16. Beginning in 2015, Cameroon troops fought in Nigeria against Boko Haram forces. The White House announced, Oct. 14, 2015, that about 300 U.S. troops would be sent to Cameroon to assist government forces fighting Boko Haram.

Canada

People: Population: 35,362,905. Age distrib.: <15: 15.4%; 65+: 18.2%. Growth: 0.7%. Migrants: 21.8%. Pop. density: 10.1 per sq mi, 3.9 per sq km. Urban: 82%. Ethnic groups: Canadian 32.2%, English 19.8%, French 15.5%, Scottish 14.4%, Irish 13.8%, German 9.8%, Italian 4.5%, Chinese 4.5%, N. Amer. Indian 4.2%. Languages: English, French (both official). Religions: Catholic 39%, Protestant 20.3%, Muslim 3.2%, none 23.9%.

Geography: Total area: 3,855,103 sq mi, 9,984,670 sq km; Land area: 3,511,023 sq mi, 9,093,507 sq km. Location: Extends 3,426 mi E-W and S from the North Pole to the U.S. Topography: Its seacoast includes 36,356 mi of mainland and 115,133 mi of islands, including the Arctic islands almost from Greenland to near the Alaskan border. Generally temperate, though varies from freezing winter cold to blistering summer heat. Arable land: 5%. Capital: Ottawa, 1,345,857 (figure is for Ottawa-Gatineau census metro area). Cities: Toronto, 6,082,916; Montréal, 4,014,245; Vancouver, 2,523,379; Calgary, 1,364,900; Edmonton, 1,297,527; Québec City, 813,865; Winnipeg, 765,850; Halifax, 407,969; Victoria, 359,225.

Government: Type: Federal parliamentary democracy under constitutional monarchy. Head of state: Queen Elizabeth II, rep. by Gov.-Gen. David Johnston; b. 1941; in office: Oct. 1, 2010. Head of gov.: Prime Min. Justin Trudeau; b. 1971; in office: Nov. 4, 2015. Local divisions: 10 provinces, 3 territories. Defense budget: $14 bil. Active troops: 66,000.

Economy: Industries: transp. equip., chemicals, minerals, food prods., wood and paper prods., fish prods. Chief crops: wheat, barley, oilseed, tobacco, fruits, vegetables. Natural resources: iron ore, nickel, zinc, copper, gold, lead, rare earth elements, molybdenum, potash, diamonds, silver, fish, timber, wildlife, coal, petroleum, nat. gas, hydropower. Water: 80,746 cu m per capita. Crude oil reserves: 170.9 bil bbls. Electricity prod.: 641 bil kWh.

Canada's Provinces and Territories

Province/territory	Joined confed.	Tot. area (sq mi)	Population (2015 est.)	Capital	Premier	Party	In office
Alberta	1905	255,541	4,196,457	Edmonton	Rachel Notley	New Democratic	2015
British Columbia	1871	364,764	4,683,139	Victoria	Christy Clark	Liberal	2011
Manitoba.	1870	250,116	1,293,378	Winnipeg	Brian Pallister	Prog. Cons.	2016
New Brunswick	1867	28,150	753,871	Fredericton	Brian Gallant	Liberal	2014
Newfoundland and Labrador	1949	156,453	527,756	St. John's	Dwight Ball	Liberal	2015
Nova Scotia	1867	21,345	943,002	Halifax	Stephen McNeil	Liberal	2013
Ontario	1867	415,598	13,792,052	Toronto	Kathleen Wynne	Liberal	2013
Prince Edward Island	1873	2,185	146,447	Charlottetown	Wade MacLauchlan	Liberal	2015
Québec.	1867	595,391	8,263,600	Québec	Philippe Couillard	Liberal	2014
Saskatchewan	1905	251,366	1,133,637	Regina	Brad Wall	Saskatchewan	2007
Northwest Territories[1].	1871	519,734	44,088	Yellowknife	Bob McLeod	Nonpartisan	2011
Nunavut[1,2].	1999	808,185	36,919	Iqaluit	Peter Taptuna	Independent	2013
Yukon[1]	1898	186,272	37,428	Whitehorse	Darrell Pasloski	Yukon	2011

Note: Pop. est. as of July 1. (Source: Statistics Canada.) (1) Territories also have federally appointed commissioners to represent federal interests. (2) Territory created in 1999 from eastern portion of Northwest Territories.

Labor force: agric. 2%, mfg. 13%, constr. 6%, services 76%, other 3%. **Unemployment:** 6.9%.

Finance: Monetary unit: Dollar (CAD) (1.31 = $1 U.S.). **GDP:** $1.6 tril; **per capita GDP:** $45,600; **GDP growth:** 1.2%. **Imports:** $440.9 bil; U.S. 53.1%, China 12.2%, Mexico 5.8%. **Exports:** $428.3 bil; U.S. 76.7%. **Tourism:** $16 bil. **Budget:** $614.1 bil. **Inflation:** 1.1%.

Transport: Railways: 48,425 mi. **Motor vehicles:** 661.4 per 1,000 pop. **Airports:** 523.

Communications: Telephone: 44.3 per 100 pop. **Mobile:** 81.9 per 100 pop. **Broadband:** 59.8 per 100 pop. **Internet:** 88.5%.

Health: Expend.: 10.5%. **Life expect.:** 79.2 male; 84.6 female. **Births:** 10.3 per 1,000 pop. **Deaths:** 8.5 per 1,000 pop. **Infant mortality:** 4.6 per 1,000 live births. **Undernourished:** <5%. **HIV:** NA.

Education: Compulsory: ages 6-15. **Literacy:** 99%.

Embassy: 501 Pennsylvania Ave. NW 20001; 682-1740.

Website: www.canada.ca

French explorer Jacques Cartier, who reached the Gulf of St. Lawrence in 1534, is generally regarded as Canada's founder. But English seaman John Cabot sighted Newfoundland in 1497, and Vikings are believed to have reached the Atlantic coast centuries before either explorer. The French pioneered Canadian settlement, establishing Quebec City (1608) and Montréal (1642) and declaring New France a colony in 1663.

Britain acquired Acadia (later Nova Scotia) in 1717 and defeated French forces in Canada to gain control of Quebec (1759) and the rest of New France in 1763. The French, through the Quebec Act of 1774, retained rights to their language, religion, and civil law. The British presence in Canada increased during the American Revolution when many colonials, calling themselves United Empire Loyalists, moved north to Canada. Fur traders and explorers led Canadians westward across the continent. Sir Alexander Mackenzie reached the Pacific in 1793 and scrawled on a rock, "From Canada by land."

In Upper and Lower Canada (later called Ontario and Quebec) and in the Maritimes, legislative assemblies were formed in the 18th cent. Upper Canada was involved in the War of 1812, a conflict between Great Britain and the U.S. that ended in a stalemate in 1814.

In 1837 political agitation for a more democratic government culminated in rebellions in Upper and Lower Canada and the union of the two into the colony of Canada in 1839. The union lasted until the 1867 British North America Act (now known as the Constitution Act, 1867) launched the Dominion of Canada, consisting of Ontario, Quebec, and the former colonies of Nova Scotia and New Brunswick.

The British North America Act, which was the basis for the country's written constitution, established a federal system of government modeled on the British parliament and cabinet structure under the crown. Canada was proclaimed a self-governing dominion within the British Empire in 1931. The Constitution Act, 1982, gave Canada the right to amend its constitution, thereby severing its last legislative link with Britain.

Failure in 1990 of the so-called Meech Lake Accord, which would have assured constitutional protection for Quebec's efforts to preserve its French language and culture, sparked a separatist revival in Quebec. The Charlottetown agreement, calling for constitutional changes, such as recognition of Quebec as a "distinct society" within the Canadian confederation, was defeated by a national referendum Oct. 1992.

The North American Free Trade Agreement among Canada, Mexico, and the U.S. went into effect Jan. 1, 1994. A Quebec referendum on secession held Oct. 1995 was defeated. On Jan. 7, 1998, the government apologized to indigenous peoples for 150 years of mistreatment and pledged to set up a "healing fund." Nunavut ("Our Land"), carved from the Northwest Territories as a homeland for the Inuit, was established Apr. 1, 1999.

Victory by the Liberals in national elections Nov. 27, 2000, made Jean Chrétien the first Canadian prime min. in over 50 years to head a third successive majority government. Canada sent troops and warships to aid the U.S.-led coalition in Afghanistan beginning Oct. 2001; 157 Canadian troops had been killed in Afghanistan by the time Canada's combat mission ended July 7, 2011.

Chrétien retired Dec. 12, 2003, and Paul Martin became prime min. The Liberals won only 135 of 308 seats in parliamentary elections June 28, 2004, and Martin became head of a minority government. Same-sex marriage (already permitted in 8 of 10 provinces) became legal throughout the country July 2005.

Twelve years of Liberal Party rule ended when Conservatives won 124 seats to the Liberals' 103 in parliamentary elections, Jan. 23, 2006. Conservative leader Stephen Harper took office Feb. 6 as head of a minority government. Police and intelligence officials in the Toronto area, June 2-3, 2006, arrested and charged 17 people with plotting terrorist attacks in Canada. The supreme court, Feb. 23, 2007, unanimously struck down a law under which foreign-born terrorism suspects had been indefinitely detained without charge.

Prime Min. Harper remained the head of a minority government after 2008 elections, but Harper's Conservatives gained a parliamentary majority (166 seats) in federal elections May 2, 2011. Elections Oct. 19, 2015, returned Liberals to power (184 seats), and Justin Trudeau, son of former Prime Min. Pierre Trudeau, became prime min.

The Canadian government approved, Dec. 7, 2012, a $15-bil takeover of the energy company Nexen by China Natl. Offshore Oil and the acquisition of Progress Energy Resources of Canada by the Malaysian state-owned oil-and-gas company Petronas. Improved technology has facilitated extracting oil from Alberta's tar sands. The Canadian government's 2014 conditional approval of a new oil pipeline from Alberta to British Columbia was overturned by a federal court, June 30, 2016. Pres. Barack Obama announced, Nov. 6, 2015, that the U.S. government would not approve the building of the Keystone XL pipeline, which would have carried Alberta tar-sands oil through the central U.S. to the Gulf of Mexico.

On Oct. 22, 2014, a terrorist gunman in Ottawa, apparently inspired by the Islamist extremist group ISIS, killed a soldier at the Canadian War Memorial and opened fire in the Parliament building before being shot to death. Two days earlier in Montréal, a terrorist with apparently similar motivation ran down two soldiers with his car, killing one, before being fatally shot. Canada joined the U.S.-led campaign of airstrikes against ISIS forces in Iraq (Nov. 2, 2014) and Syria (Apr. 8, 2015). The Trudeau government ended airstrikes Feb. 15, 2016, but continued other military assistance to the anti-ISIS campaign. Under a resettlement program begun in Nov. 2015, Canada had admitted more than 31,000 Syrian refugees by late Sept. 2016.

Central African Republic

People: Population: 5,507,257. **Age distrib.:** <15: 40.3%; 65+: 3.5%. **Growth:** 2.1%. **Migrants:** 1.7%. **Pop. density:** 22.9 per sq mi, 8.8 per sq km. **Urban:** 40.3%. **Ethnic groups:** Baya 33%, Banda 27%, Mandjia 13%, Sara 10%, Mboum 7%, M'Baka 4%, Yakoma 4%. **Languages:** French (official), Sangho (lingua franca and national lang.), tribal langs. **Religions:** indigenous beliefs 35%, Protestant 25%, Roman Catholic 25%, Muslim 15%.

Geography: Total area: 240,535 sq mi, 622,984 sq km; **Land area:** 240,535 sq mi, 622,984 sq km. **Location:** Central Africa. Chad on N, Cameroon on W, Congo Republic and Dem. Rep. of the Congo on S, South Sudan and Sudan on E. **Topography:** Mostly rolling plateau, avg. elevation 2,000 ft, with rivers draining S to the Congo and N to Lake Chad. Open, well-watered savanna covers most of area, with an arid area in NE and tropical rain forest in SW. **Arable land:** 2.9%. **Capital:** Bangui, 807,825.

Government: Type: Presidential republic. **Head of state:** Pres. Faustin-Archange Touadéra; b. 1957; in office: Mar. 30, 2016.

Head of gov.: Prime Min. Simplice Sarandji; b. 1955; in office: Apr. 2, 2016. **Local divisions:** 14 prefectures, 2 economic prefectures, 1 commune. **Defense budget** (2013): $52 mil. **Active troops:** 7,150.

Economy: Industries: gold, diamond mining; logging; brewing; sugar refining. **Chief crops:** cotton, coffee, tobacco, cassava, yams, millet, corn, bananas. **Natural resources:** diamonds, uranium, timber, gold, oil, hydropower. **Water:** 28,776 cu m per capita. **Electricity prod.:** 0.2 bil kWh. **Labor force:** NA. **Unemployment:** 7.4%.

Finance: Monetary unit: Central African CFA Franc (XAF) (586.00 = $1 U.S.). **GDP:** $3 bil; **per capita GDP:** $600; **GDP growth:** 4.3%. **Imports:** $264.9 mil; Norway 39.5%, France 6.8%. **Exports:** $172.8 mil; Norway 52.2%, China 14.1%, Dem. Rep. of the Congo 8.3%. **Tourism:** $11 mil. **Budget:** $253.4 mil. **Inflation:** 37.1%.

Transport: Motor vehicles: 1 per 1,000 pop. **Airports:** 2.

Communications: Telephone: 0.02 per 100 pop. **Mobile:** 20.4 per 100 pop. **Broadband** (2012): 0.2 per 100 pop. **Internet:** 4.6%.

Health: Expend.: 4.2%. **Life expect.:** 51.0 male; 53.7 female. **Births:** 34.7 per 1,000 pop. **Deaths:** 13.5 per 1,000 pop. **Infant mortality:** 88.4 per 1,000 live births. **Undernourished:** 47.7%. **HIV:** 3.7%.

Education: Compulsory: NA. **Literacy:** 36.8%.

Embassy: 2704 Ontario Rd. 20009; 483-7800.

Website: www.rcawashington.org or www.state.gov/p/af/ci/car/

Various Bantu peoples migrated through the region for centuries before French control was asserted in the late 19th cent., when the region was named Ubangi-Shari. Independence was attained Aug. 13, 1960.

Pres. Jean-Bedel Bokassa, who seized power in a 1965 military coup, proclaimed himself constitutional emperor of the renamed Central African Empire Dec. 1976. Bokassa's rule was characterized by ruthless authoritarianism and human rights violations. He was ousted in a bloodless coup aided by the French government, Sept. 20, 1979. In 1981, Gen. André Kolingba became head of state in another bloodless coup. Elections in Aug. and Sept. 1993 led to civilian rule under Pres. Ange-Félix Patassé.

Patassé was ousted Mar. 15, 2003, by rebels under former army chief François Bozizé. Bozizé won a presidential runoff election May 8, 2005, but insurgent activity by Patassé loyalists and others continued in the north. A national peace conference, Dec. 8-20, 2008, enabled the installation of a unity government Jan. 19, 2009. Pres. Bozizé won reelection Jan. 23, 2011, but was ousted when the largely Muslim rebel group Seleka, led by Michel Djotodia, seized the capital Mar. 24, 2013. Djotodia declared himself president. Bozizé supporters and Christian militias clashed with pro-Djotodia and Muslim fighters, resulting in thousands of deaths and more than 850,000 internally displaced persons and refugees by the end of 2014. A National Transitional Council elected Catherine Samba-Panza interim pres. Jan. 20, 2014, and other African nations, France, and the EU sent peacekeeping troops. A UN peacekeeping force (MINUSCA) was authorized Apr. 10, 2014, and about 12,150 MINUSCA uniformed personnel were in the country as of Aug. 31, 2016. UNICEF reported, Mar. 2016, over 100 mostly underage women alleged sexual abuse by peacekeepers, 2013-15. France announced, July 13, 2016, it would withdraw the last of its peacekeeping troops in Oct. Faustin-Archange Touadéra, a Christian, won a UN-supervised presidential runoff election, Feb. 14, 2016. Muslim-Christian violence continued.

crops: cotton, sorghum, millet, peanuts, sesame, corn, rice, potatoes, onions, cassava. **Natural resources:** petroleum, uranium, natron, kaolin, fish, gold, limestone, sand and gravel, salt. **Water:** 3,256 cu m per capita. **Crude oil reserves:** 1.5 bil bbls. **Electricity prod.:** 0.2 bil kWh. **Labor force:** agric. 80%, industry and services 20%. **Unemployment:** 7%.

Finance: Monetary unit: Central African CFA Franc (XAF) (586.00 = $1 U.S.). **GDP:** $30.5 bil; **per capita GDP:** $2,600; **GDP growth:** 1.8%. **Imports:** $3.3 bil; France 16.5%, China 14.2%, Cameroon 11%, U.S. 6.4%, India 6%, Belgium 5.7%. **Exports:** $4.1 bil; U.S. 58.5%, India 13.3%, Japan 11.3%. **Budget:** $2.7 bil. **Inflation:** 3.7%.

Transport: Airports: 9.

Communications: Telephone: 0.1 per 100 pop. **Mobile:** 40.2 per 100 pop. **Broadband:** 0.0 per 100 pop. **Internet:** 2.7%.

Health: Expend.: 3.6%. **Life expect.:** 49.0 male; 51.5 female. **Births:** 36.1 per 1,000 pop. **Deaths:** 14.0 per 1,000 pop. **Infant mortality:** 87.0 per 1,000 live births. **Undernourished:** 34.4%. **HIV:** 2.0%.

Education: Compulsory: ages 6-15. **Literacy:** 40%.

Embassy: 2401 Massachusetts Ave. NW 20008; 652-1312.

Website: www.gouvernement.td or www.state.gov/p/af/ci/cd/

Chad was the site of Paleolithic and Neolithic cultures before the Sahara Desert formed. A succession of kingdoms and Arab slave traders dominated Chad until France took control around 1900. Independence came Aug. 11, 1960. Northern Muslim rebels fought animist and Christian southern government and French troops from 1966.

Rebel forces, led by Hissène Habré, captured the capital and forced Pres. Goukouni Oueddei to flee the country in June 1982. In Dec. 1990, a Libyan-supported insurgent group, the Patriotic Salvation Movement, overthrew Habré, who went into exile in Senegal. After approval of a new constitution Mar. 1996, Chad's first multiparty presidential election was held in June and July.

Oil began flowing July 15, 2003, through a 665-mi pipeline that allows landlocked Chad to export via Cameroon. Pres. Idriss Déby Itno won a third term, May 3, 2006, in an election boycotted by major opposition groups. Violence along the Sudan border escalated during the year, as Sudanese *janjaweed* militias and Chadian rebels attacked civilians, and Darfur rebels preyed on refugee camps. Between 140 and 700 civilians died in N'Djaména, Feb. 2-5, 2008, as more than 2,000 Chadian rebels stormed the capital and clashed with government troops in a failed coup attempt.

On Jan. 15, 2010, Chad and Sudan signed an accord aimed at normalizing relations and suppressing cross-border activities by rebel groups. Established in 2007, a UN peacekeeping force (MINURCAT) completed its mandate Dec. 31, 2010. More than 300,000 Sudanese refugees were living in Chad as of Apr. 30, 2016. Pres. Déby won reelection for a fifth term, Apr. 10, 2016.

After Islamist groups took over northern Mali and imposed a repressive regime in late 2012, Chad contributed roughly 2,000 soldiers to aid French, Malian, and other African forces in a military intervention. On Apr. 15, 2013, the Chadian government announced it would begin pulling its troops out of Mali. Chadian troops in 2015-16 fought Boko Haram Islamist extremists in Nigeria. Boko Haram fighters and suicide bombers staged attacks in Chad.

Former Pres. Habré, accused of killing and torturing thousands of opponents in the 1980s, was arrested in Senegal June 30, 2013. The Extraordinary African Chambers (created within Senegal's court system) convicted Habré of crimes against humanity, torture, and rape, May 30, 2016, and sentenced him to life in prison.

Chad
Republic of Chad

People: Population: 11,852,462. **Age distrib.:** <15: 43.6%; 65+: 3%. **Growth:** 1.9%. **Migrants:** 3.7%. **Pop. density:** 24.4 per sq mi, 9.4 per sq km. **Urban:** 22.6%. **Ethnic groups:** Sara 25.9%, Arab 12.6%, Kanembu/Bornu/Buduma 8.3%, Wadai/Maba/Masalit/Mimi 7%, Gorane 6.8%, Masa/Musseye/Musgum 4.7%. **Languages:** French, Arabic (both official); Sara; 120+ langs. and dialects. **Religions:** Muslim 58.4%, Catholic 18.5%, Protestant 16.1%, animist 4%.

Geography: Total area: 495,755 sq mi, 1,284,000 sq km; **Land area:** 486,180 sq mi, 1,259,200 sq km. **Location:** Central N Africa. Libya on N; Niger, Nigeria, Cameroon on W; Central African Republic on S; Sudan on E. **Topography:** Wooded savanna, steppe, and desert in the S; part of the Sahara in the N. Southern rivers flow N to Lake Chad, surrounded by marshland. **Arable land:** 3.9%. **Capital:** N'Djamena, 1,310,206.

Government: Type: Presidential republic. **Head of state:** Pres. Idriss Déby Itno; b. 1952; in office: Dec. 4, 1990. **Head of gov.:** Prime Min. Albert Pahimi Padacke; b. 1966; in office: Feb. 15, 2016. **Local divisions:** 23 regions. **Defense budget** (2013): $209 mil. **Active troops:** 30,350.

Economy: Industries: oil, cotton textiles, brewing, natron (sodium carbonate), soap, cigarettes, constr. materials. **Chief**

Chile
Republic of Chile

People: Population: 17,650,114. **Age distrib.:** <15: 20.3%; 65+: 10.5%. **Growth:** 0.8%. **Migrants:** 2.6%. **Pop. density:** 61.5 per sq mi, 23.7 per sq km. **Urban:** 89.7%. **Ethnic groups:** white and non-indigenous 88.9%, Mapuche 9.1%. **Languages:** Spanish (official), English, indigenous. **Religions:** Roman Catholic 66.7%, Evangelical or Protestant 16.4%, none 11.5%.

Geography: Total area: 291,933 sq mi, 756,102 sq km; **Land area:** 287,187 sq mi, 743,812 sq km. **Location:** W coast of southern S America. Peru on N, Bolivia on NE, Argentina on E. **Topography:** Andes Mts., with some of world's highest peaks, on E border; on W is 2,650-mi Pacific coast. Width varies 100-250 mi. Atacama Desert in N. **Arable land:** 1.8%. **Capital:** Santiago, 6,543,879. **Cities:** Valparaíso (seat of natl. legislature) 912,627; Concepción, 826,633.

Government: Type: Presidential republic. **Head of state and gov.:** Pres. Michelle Bachelet Jeria; b. 1951; in office: Mar. 11, 2014. **Local divisions:** 15 regions. **Defense budget:** $3.5 bil. **Active troops:** 64,750.

Economy: Industries: copper, lithium, other minerals; foodstuffs, fish proc.; iron and steel; wood and wood prods.; transp. equip.; cement; textiles. **Chief crops:** grapes, apples, pears, onions, wheat, corn, oats, peaches, garlic, asparagus, beans.

Natural resources: copper, timber, iron ore, nitrates, prec. metals, molybdenum, hydropower. **Water:** 51,432 cu m per capita. **Crude oil reserves:** 0.2 bil bbls. **Electricity prod.:** 70 bil kWh. **Labor force:** agric. 13.2%, industry 23%, services 63.9%. **Unemployment:** 6.4%.

Finance: Monetary unit: Peso (CLP) (681.40 = $1 U.S.). **GDP:** $422.4 bil; **per capita GDP:** $23,500; **GDP growth:** 2.1%. **Imports:** $56 bil; China 23.4%, U.S. 18.8%, Brazil 7.8%. **Exports:** $61.8 bil; China 26.3%, U.S. 13.2%, Japan 8.5%, South Korea 6.5%. **Tourism:** $2.4 bil. **Budget:** $56.3 bil. **Inflation:** 4.3%.

Transport: Railways: 4,525 mi. **Motor vehicles:** 245.5 per 1,000 pop. **Airports:** 90.

Communications: Telephone: 19.2 per 100 pop. **Mobile:** 129.5 per 100 pop. **Broadband:** 50.5 per 100 pop. **Internet:** 64.3%.

Health: Expend.: 7.8%. **Life expect.:** 75.7 male; 81.9 female. **Births:** 13.7 per 1,000 pop. **Deaths:** 6.1 per 1,000 pop. **Infant mortality:** 6.7 per 1,000 live births. **Undernourished:** <5%. **HIV:** 0.3%.

Education: Compulsory: ages 6-17. **Literacy:** 96.6%.

Embassy: 1732-1736 Massachusetts Ave. NW 20036; 785-1746.

Website: www.gob.cl

Northern Chile was under Inca rule before the Spanish conquest, 1536-40. The southern Araucanian Indians resisted until the late 19th cent. Independence was gained 1810-18 under José de San Martin and Bernardo O'Higgins; the latter, as supreme director 1817-23, sought social and economic reforms until deposed. Chile defeated Peru and Bolivia in 1836-39 and 1879-84, gaining mineral-rich northern land.

In 1970, Salvador Allende Gossens, a Marxist, became president with a narrow plurality of the popular vote. His government improved conditions for the poor, but property seizures by left-wing extremists, poorly planned socialist economic programs, and a destabilization campaign backed by the U.S. led to political and financial chaos. A military junta seized power Sept. 11, 1973. With the presidential palace under attack, Allende refused to surrender; a 2011 autopsy confirmed police reports that he killed himself. The junta, headed by Gen. Augusto Pinochet Ugarte, implemented plans to privatize the economy and "exterminate Marxism." Repression continued into the 1980s.

In Dec. 1989 voters elected a civilian president, although Pinochet continued to head the army until Mar. 10, 1998. In Mar. 1994, a Chilean human rights group estimated that more than 3,100 people were killed or "disappeared" during Pinochet's rule. Efforts to prosecute him failed when courts in Britain and Chile declared him mentally unfit to stand trial.

Ricardo Lagos Escobar, Chile's first Socialist president since the 1973 coup, took office Mar. 11, 2000. Chile and the U.S. signed a free trade accord June 6, 2003. Michelle Bachelet Jeria, also a Socialist, won a runoff election Jan. 2006 and took office in Mar. as Chile's first woman president. Pinochet died Dec. 10, 2006.

Billionaire businessman Sebastián Piñera Echenique, a conservative, won a presidential runoff election Jan. 2010. A powerful earthquake and tsunami, Feb. 27, 2010, killed at least 521 people and caused up to $30 bil in property damage. Chile successfully rescued 33 miners trapped for 10 weeks 2,300 ft underground after a cave-in at the San José Mine Aug. 5, 2010. A prison fire Dec. 8 in Santiago killed at least 81 inmates. Chile's economy was growing at a 6.6% annual rate in mid-2011, but lagging wages sparked labor protests against the Piñera government that continued into 2012 and spread to the student population. Bachelet won a presidential runoff election Dec. 15, 2013. She made major cabinet changes in May 2015 in the wake of an economic slowdown and corruption scandals. Civil unions between same-sex couples became legal in Chile, Oct. 22, 2015.

Tierra del Fuego is the largest (18,800 sq mi) island in the archipelago of the same name at the southern tip of S America, an area of majestic mountains, tortuous channels, and high winds. It was visited 1520 by Magellan and named Land of Fire because of its many Indian bonfires. Part of the island is in Chile, part in Argentina. Punta Arenas, on a mainland peninsula, is a center of sheep raising and the world's southernmost city; Puerto Williams is the southernmost settlement.

China
People's Republic of China

(Statistical data do not include Hong Kong or Macao.)

People: Population: 1,373,541,278. **Age distrib.:** <15: 17.1%; 65+: 10.3%. **Growth:** 0.4%. **Migrants:** 0.1%. **Pop. density:** 381.4 per sq mi, 147.3 per sq km. **Urban:** 56.8%. **Ethnic groups:** Han Chinese 91.6%, other (incl. Hui, Manchu, Uighur, Miao, Yi, Tujia, Tibetan, Mongol, Dong, Buyei, Yao, Bai, Korean, Hani, Li, Kazakh, Dai) 7.1%. **Languages:** Standard Chinese or Mandarin (official; Putonghua, based on Beijing dialect), Yue (Cantonese), Wu (Shanghainese), Minbei (Fuzhou), Minnan (Hokkien-Taiwanese), Xiang, Gan. **Religions:** officially atheist; folk religion 21.9%, Buddhist 18.2%, Christian 5.1%, unaffiliated 52.2%.

Geography: Total area: 3,705,407 sq mi, 9,596,960 sq km; **Land area:** 3,600,947 sq mi, 9,326,410 sq km. **Location:** Occupies most of the habitable mainland of E Asia. Mongolia on N; Russia on NE and NW; Kazakhstan, Kyrgyzstan, Tajikistan, Afghanistan, Pakistan on W; India, Nepal, Bhutan, Myanmar, Laos, Vietnam on S; North Korea on NE. **Topography:** Two-thirds of territory is mountainous or desert. The Da Xing'an Ling Mts. in N separate Manchuria and Mongolia. Other ranges incl. the Tien Shan in Xinjiang and the Himalayan and Kunlun Mts. in the SW and in Tibet. The eastern half of China is one of the world's best-watered lands with three great river systems: the Chang (Yangtze), Huang (Yellow), and Xi. **Arable land:** 11.3%. **Capital:** Beijing, 21,240,005. **Cities:** Shanghai, 24,483,789; Chongqing, 13,744,348; Guangzhou, Guangdong, 13,069,954; Tianjin, 11,558,414; Shenzhen, 10,828,252; Wuhan, 7,979,081; Chengdu, 7,820,492; Nanjing, Jiangsu, 7,609,306; Dongguan, 7,468,539; Foshan, 7,089,402.

Government: Type: Communist state. **Head of state:** Pres. Xi Jinping; b. 1953; in office: Mar. 14, 2013 (gen. sec. of Communist Party since Nov. 15, 2012). **Head of gov.:** Prem. Li Keqiang; b. 1955; in office: Mar. 15, 2013. **Local divisions:** 22 provinces (not incl. Taiwan), 5 autonomous regions, 4 municipalities, special admin. regions of Hong Kong (as of July 1, 1997) and Macao (as of Dec. 20, 1999). **Defense budget:** $145.8 bil. **Active troops:** 2,333,000.

Economy: Industries: mining and ore proc., iron, steel, aluminum, other metals, coal; machine building; armaments; textiles and apparel; petroleum; cement; chemicals; fertilizers; consumer prods.; food proc.; transp. equip.; telecom equip. **Chief crops:** rice, wheat, potatoes, corn, peanuts, tea, millet, barley, apples, cotton, oilseed. **Natural resources:** coal, iron ore, petroleum, nat. gas, mercury, tin, tungsten, antimony, manganese, molybdenum, vanadium, magnetite, aluminum, lead, zinc, rare earth elements, uranium. **Water:** 2,018 cu m per capita. **Crude oil reserves:** 25.1 bil bbls. **Electricity prod.:** 5.2 tril kWh. **Labor force:** agric. 33.6%, industry 30.3%, services 36.1%. **Unemployment:** 4.7%.

Finance: Monetary unit: Yuan Renminbi (CNY) (6.67 = $1 U.S.). **GDP:** $19.4 tril; **per capita GDP:** $14,100; **GDP growth:** 6.9%. **Imports:** $1.6 tril; South Korea 10.9%, U.S. 9%, Japan 8.9%, Germany 5.5%. **Exports:** $2.3 tril; U.S. 18%, Hong Kong 14.6%, Japan 6%. **Tourism:** $114.1 bil. **Budget:** $2.7 tril. **Inflation:** 1.4%.

Transport: Railways: 118,850 mi. **Motor vehicles:** 115.8 per 1,000 pop. **Airports:** 463.

Communications: Telephone: 16.5 per 100 pop. **Mobile:** 93.2 per 100 pop. **Broadband:** 41.8 per 100 pop. **Internet:** 50.3%.

Health: Expend.: 5.6%. **Life expect.:** 73.5 male; 77.9 female. **Births:** 12.4 per 1,000 pop. **Deaths:** 7.7 per 1,000 pop. **Infant mortality:** 12.2 per 1,000 live births. **Undernourished:** 9.3%. **HIV:** NA.

Education: Compulsory: ages 6-14. **Literacy:** 96.4%.

Embassy: 3505 International Pl. NW 20008; 495-2000.

Website: www.english.gov.cn

Remains of various humanlike creatures who lived as early as several hundred thousand years ago have been found in many parts of China. Neolithic agricultural settlements dotted the Huang (Yellow) R. basin from about 5000 BCE. Their language, religion, and art were the sources of later Chinese civilization.

Bronze metallurgy reached a peak and Chinese pictographic writing, similar to today's, was in use in the more developed culture of the Shang Dynasty (c. 1766 BCE-c. 1045 BCE), which ruled much of North China.

A succession of dynasties and interdynastic warring kingdoms ruled China for the next 3,000 years. They expanded Chinese political and cultural domination to the south and west, and developed a technologically and culturally advanced society that was unaffected by foreign rule (Mongols in the Yuan Dynasty, 1279-1368, and Manchus in the Qing Dynasty, 1644-1912).

Rebellions in the 19th cent. left tens of millions dead. Russia, Japan, Britain, and other powers exercised political and economic control in large parts of the country. China became a republic Jan. 1, 1912, following the Wuchang Uprising inspired by Dr. Sun Yat-sen, founder of the Kuomintang (Nationalist) party. By 1928, the Kuomintang, led by Chiang Kai-shek, succeeded in nominal reunification of China. About the same time, a bloody purge of Communists from the ranks of the Kuomintang fomented hostilities.

For over 50 years, 1894-1945, China was involved in conflicts with Japan. In 1895, China ceded Korea, Taiwan, and other areas. On Sept. 18, 1931, Japan seized the Northeastern Provinces (Manchuria) and set up a puppet state called Manchukuo. Taking advantage of Chinese dissension, Japan invaded China proper July 7, 1937. On Nov. 20 the retreating Nationalist government moved its capital to Chongqing (Chungking) from Nanking (Nanjing), which Japanese troops then ravaged Dec. 13.

From 1939 the Sino-Japanese War (1937-45) became part of the broader world conflict. After its defeat in World War II, Japan relinquished China. Within China, conflicts involving the Kuomintang, Communists, and other factions resumed. China came under the domination of Communist armies, 1949-50. The Kuomintang government fled to Taiwan, Dec. 8, 1949.

The People's Republic of China was proclaimed in Beijing (Peking) Oct. 1, 1949, under Mao Zedong. China and the USSR signed a 30-year treaty of "friendship, alliance, and mutual assistance," Feb. 15, 1950. The U.S. refused to recognize the new regime. On Nov. 26, 1950, the People's Republic sent armies into Korea against U.S. troops and forced a stalemate in the Korean War.

Frequent drastic changes in policy and violent factionalism 1949-52 interfered with economic development. In 1957, Mao admitted an estimated 800,000 people had been executed 1949-54; opponents claimed much higher figures. The Great Leap Forward, 1958-60, tried to accelerate economic development through intensive labor on huge new rural communes and emphasis on ideological purity. Many resisted, and the program was largely abandoned.

By the 1960s, relations with the USSR deteriorated over disagreements on borders, ideology, and leadership of world Communism. The USSR canceled aid accords. The Great Proletarian Cultural Revolution, 1965, an attempt to instruct a new generation in revolutionary principles, resulted in massive purges. Millions of urban teenagers were relocated to rural areas. By 1968 the movement had run its course; many purged officials returned to office in subsequent years, and several ideological reforms were gradually weakened.

On Oct. 25, 1971, the UN General Assembly ousted the Taiwan government from the UN and seated the People's Republic in its place. The U.S. had supported the mainland's admission but opposed Taiwan's expulsion.

U.S. Pres. Richard Nixon visited China Feb. 21-28, 1972, on invitation from Prem. Zhou Enlai, ending years of antipathy between the two nations. China and the U.S. opened liaison offices in each other's capitals, May-June 1973. The U.S., Dec. 15, 1978, formally recognized the People's Republic of China as the sole legal government of China; diplomatic relations between the two were established, Jan. 1, 1979.

Mao died Sept. 9, 1976. By 1978, Vice Prem. Deng Xiaoping had consolidated power, succeeding Mao as "paramount leader" of China. The new ruling group modified Maoist policies in education, culture, and industry, and sought better ties with non-Communist countries. By the mid-1980s, China had enacted far-reaching economic reforms, deemphasizing centralized planning and incorporating market-oriented incentives.

Some 100,000 students and workers marched in Beijing to demand political reforms, May 4, 1989. As the unrest spread, martial law was imposed, May 20. Troops entered Beijing, June 3-4, and crushed the pro-democracy protests, as tanks and armored personnel carriers rolled through Tiananmen Square. It is estimated that hundreds died and thousands were injured, and hundreds of students and workers were arrested.

Deng Xiaoping died Feb. 19, 1997, leaving Jiang Zemin in control as president. Hong Kong reverted to Chinese sovereignty July 1, 1997. Portugal returned Macao to China Dec. 20, 1999.

Hu Jintao was named Communist Party general secretary at the 16th party congress, Nov. 2002, and elected president by the 10th National People's Congress, Mar. 2003. With the successful launch and recovery, Oct. 15-16, 2003, of the *Shenzhou 5* spacecraft, China became the third nation (after the U.S. and USSR) to send a person into space. In Dec. 2013, China became the third nation to reach the Moon with a spacecraft that made a soft landing.

China's industries, exports, and oil demand have increased rapidly since the 1980s. China became the world's largest producer and consumer of coal. In part to diversify energy production, China completed construction in 2006 of the world's largest hydroelectric dam, the Three Gorges Dam on the Yangtze R. However, the burning of fossil fuels has caused severe air pollution. After negotiations with the U.S., China pledged, Nov. 11, 2014, that its CO_2 emissions would peak and then begin to decline no later than 2030 and that 20% of its energy would come from non-fossil fuel sources by that year. China announced, Sept. 3, 2016, that it had ratified the agreement to limit climate change negotiated in Paris in Dec. 2015.

A powerful earthquake rocked Sichuan prov. May 12, 2008, leaving 69,226 people dead and 17,923 missing. China hosted the Summer Olympics, held in Beijing, Aug. 8-24, 2008. The Nobel Peace Prize was awarded Oct. 8, 2010, to Liu Xiaobo, a human rights activist who had received an 11-year prison sentence in 2009. Xi Jinping was chosen Communist Party general secretary and China's new leader, and Li Keqiang the country's prime min. Nov. 15, 2012.

Western computer security experts Jan.-Feb. 2010 blamed hackers in China for cyberattacks on Google and at least 30 other firms. Hackers in China were suspected in two attacks on U.S. government computer systems in 2015; personal data on tens of millions of people was stolen. At a White House meeting, Sept. 25, 2015, Xi and U.S. Pres. Barack Obama reached a general agreement on refraining from cybertheft.

Periods of rapid growth made China the world's second-largest economy by 2010, behind the U.S. China's economy subsequently slowed. GDP growth was under 8% annually 2012-14 and under 7% in 2015, compared to double-digit gains for most years since the 1980s. After a run-up in prices, shares on China's two largest stock exchanges (Shanghai and Shenzhen) plunged, losing about one-third of their value June 12-July 31, 2015. Further sharp selloffs occurred later in 2015 and in early 2016. To boost the economy, China devalued its currency, lowered interest rates, and increased infrastructure spending. The presidents of China and Taiwan held a summit meeting in Singapore, Nov. 7, 2015, the first such meeting since the founding of the People's Republic. The international Permanent Court of Arbitration in The Hague, July 12, 2016, rejected China's claim to most of the South China Sea as territorial waters and ruled that China's building of artificial islands—in some cases militarized—in the disputed area violated international law.

China has occupied the **Paracel Isls.**, in the South China Sea, since 1974. Taiwan and Vietnam also claim the resource-rich islands. The **Spratly Isls.** are similarly in dispute, with small military forces from those three countries, Malaysia, and the Philippines occupying different areas.

Autonomous Regions

Guangxi Zhuang is in SE China, bounded on the N by Guizhou and Hunan provinces, E and S by Guangdong, on the SW by Vietnam, and on the W by Yunnan. It produces rice in the river valleys and has valuable forest products. Pop. (2010): 46,026,629. Capital: Nanning.

Inner Mongolia was organized by the People's Republic in 1947. Its boundaries have undergone frequent changes, reaching its greatest extent in 1956 (and restored in 1979), with an area of 454,600 sq mi, allegedly in order to dilute the minority Mongol population. Chinese settlers outnumber the Mongols more than 10 to 1. Pop. (2010) 24,706,321. Capital: Hohhot.

Ningxia Hui, in N central China, is about 60,000 sq mi. Pop. (2010) 6,301,350. Capital: Yinchuan. The climate is mostly semi-arid, with desert areas in the N. The Huang He (Yellow R.) flows across the N, furnishing water for irrigation. Coal is mined in the E. The majority of the population is Han; the Hui (Chinese Muslims) constitute about one-third of the population. The region experienced a significant population boom, 1950-80.

Xinjiang Uighur, in Central Asia, is 635,900 sq mi, pop. (2010) 21,813,334 (75% Uighurs, a Turkic Muslim group, with a heavy Han Chinese increase in recent years). Capital: Urumqi. It is China's richest region in strategic minerals. China has moved to suppress Uighur cultural and religious practices and to crack down on Uighur separatists, whom Beijing regards as terrorists. A protest march July 5, 2009, by Uighurs in Urumqi led to violent clashes with Han Chinese; at least 197 people (mostly Han) were killed in riots. Unrest and domestic terrorist attacks continued, including truck bombings in Urumqi May 22, 2014, that killed more than 40 people. The government's crackdown included the June 16 execution of 13 people convicted of terrorism-related crimes. Violence in Yarkand July 28 left almost 100 people dead. An apparent separatist attack at a coal mine, Sept. 18, 2015, left about 50 dead.

Tibet, 471,700 sq mi, is a thinly populated region of high plateaus and massive mountains, the Himalayas on the S, the Kunluns on the N. High passes connect with India and Nepal; roads lead into China proper. Capital: Lhasa. Avg. elevation is 15,000 ft. Jiachan, 15,870 ft, is believed to be the highest inhabited town on Earth. Agriculture is primitive. Pop. (2010) 3,002,166 (of whom about 500,000 are Chinese). Another 4 mil Tibetans form the majority of the population of vast adjacent areas that have long been incorporated into China.

China ruled all of Tibet from the 18th cent. Independence came in 1911, but China reasserted control in 1951, and a Communist government was installed in 1953. Serfdom was abolished, but all land remained collectivized. A Tibetan uprising within China in 1956 spread to Lhasa in 1959. The rebellion was crushed by Chinese troops, and Buddhism was almost totally suppressed. The Dalai Lama and 100,000 Tibetans fled to India. Efforts by Chinese authorities to halt peaceful demonstrations by Tibetan monks led to anti-Chinese riots in Lhasa, Mar. 14, 2008; the Chinese government sent troops into Tibet to crush dissent, sparking international protests. Protests (including more than 140 self-immolations, 2009-16) and government repression of dissent continued in subsequent years.

Hong Kong

Hong Kong (Xianggang), located at the mouth of the Zhu Jiang (Pearl R.) in SE China, 90 mi S of Guangzhou, was a British dependency from 1842 until July 1, 1997, when it became a Special Administrative Region of China. Its nucleus is Hong Kong Isl., 31 sq mi, occupied by the British in 1841 and formally ceded to them in 1842, on which is located the seat of government. Opposite is Kowloon Peninsula, 3 sq mi, and Stonecutters Isl., added to the territory in 1860. An additional 355 sq mi known as the New Territories, a mainland area and islands, were leased from China, 1898, for 99 years. Area 428 sq mi (total); 414 sq mi (land); pop. (2016 est.) 7,167,403. **Website:** www.gov.hk

Hong Kong is a major trade and banking center. Per capita GDP, $56,700 (2015 est.), is among the highest in the world. Principal industries are textiles and apparel, tourism, electronics, shipbuilding, iron and steel, fishing, cement, and small manufactures. Tourism receipts in 2015 were $35.9 bil. Hong Kong's spinning mills are among the world's best. Outside of the public sector, the labor force is engaged in the following sectors: wholesale and retail trade, restaurants, and hotels 53.3%; community and social services 17.1%; financing, insurance, and real estate 12.5%; transp. and communications 10.1%; manufacturing 3.8%; and construction 2.8%.

Hong Kong harbor was long an important British naval station and one of the world's great transshipment ports. The colony often provided refuge for exiles from mainland China. It was occupied by Japan during WWII.

From 1949 to 1962, Hong Kong absorbed more than 1 mil refugees fleeing Communist China. Starting in the 1950s, cheap labor led to a boom in light manufacturing, while liberal tax policies attracted foreign investment. Hong Kong became one of the wealthiest, most productive areas in the Far East.

With the end of the 99-year lease on the New Territories drawing near, Britain and China signed an agreement, Dec. 19, 1984, under which all of Hong Kong was to be returned to China in 1997; under this agreement Hong Kong was to be allowed to keep its capitalist system for 50 years. Following the transfer of government, Hong Kong retained its street names and its currency, the Hong Kong dollar, but without the queen's picture. Cantonese (a Chinese dialect) and English remained official languages.

Hundreds of thousands of Hong Kong residents protested July 1, 2003, a proposed anti-subversion law; the bill was withdrawn Sept. 5. Another mass march, July 1, 2004, protested Beijing's refusal to allow greater freedom. Leung Chun-ying, whose close ties to China became an issue during the campaign, was elected chief executive Mar. 2012 by a committee of 1,200 members. Large pro-democracy protests took place July-Dec. 2014, opposing Chinese plans to restrict candidate selection for a proposed direct election of the chief executive in 2017. Hong Kong's Legislative Council, June 18, 2015, rejected the direct-election plan because of limitations on the openness of candidate selection. Six of the 2014 pro-democracy activists won seats on the Legislative Council in Sept. 4, 2016, elections.

Macao

Macao, area of 11 sq mi, is a peninsula and two small islands at the mouth of the Xi (Pearl) R. in China. It was established as a Portuguese trading colony in 1557. In 1849, Portugal claimed sovereignty over the territory; this claim was accepted by China in an 1887 treaty. Portugal granted broad autonomy in 1976. Under a 1987 agreement, Macao reverted to China Dec. 20, 1999. As in the case of Hong Kong, the Chinese government guaranteed Macao it would not interfere in its way of life and capitalist system for a period of 50 years. Tourism is the fastest-growing economic sector. Tourism receipts in 2015 were $31.3 bil. Per capita GDP was $98,200 (2015 est.). The labor force is occupied in the following areas: gambling 25.9%, restaurants and hotels 15%, wholesale and retail trade 12.4%, construction 9.8%, public sector 7.1%, transp. and communications 4.4%, manufacturing 2.5%, and financial services 2.6%. Pop. (2016 est.) 597,425. **Website:** portal.gov.mo

Colombia
Republic of Colombia

People: Population: 47,220,856. **Age distrib.:** <15: 24.6%; 65+: 7.2%. **Growth:** 1%. **Migrants:** 0.3%. **Pop. density:** 117.7 per sq mi, 45.5 per sq km. **Urban:** 76.7%. **Ethnic groups:** mestizo and white 84.2%, Afro-Colombian (incl. mulatto, Raizal, Palenquero) 10.4%, Amerindian 3.4%. **Language:** Spanish (official). **Religions:** Roman Catholic 90%.

Geography: Total area: 439,736 sq mi, 1,138,910 sq km; **Land area:** 401,044 sq mi, 1,038,700 sq km. **Location:** NW corner of S America. Panama on NW, Ecuador and Peru on S, Brazil and Venezuela on E. **Topography:** Three Andes ranges—Western, Central, and Eastern Cordilleras—run N-S. The eastern range consists mostly of high tablelands. The Magdalena R. rises in the Andes, flows N to Caribbean through a rich alluvial plain. Sparsely settled plains in E are drained by Orinoco and Amazon systems. **Arable land:** 1.5%. **Capital:** Bogotá, 9,968,232. **Cities:** Medellín, 3,971,785; Cali, 2,681,843; Barranquilla, 2,008,589.

Government: Type: Presidential republic. **Head of state and gov.:** Pres. Juan Manuel Santos Calderón; b. 1951; in office: Aug. 7, 2010. **Local divisions:** 32 departments, 1 capital district. **Defense budget:** $9.9 bil. **Active troops:** 296,750.

Economy: Industries: textiles, food proc., oil, clothing and footwear, beverages, chemicals, cement. **Chief crops:** coffee, cut flowers, bananas, rice, tobacco, corn, sugarcane, cocoa beans, oilseed, vegetables. **Natural resources:** petroleum, nat. gas, coal, iron ore, nickel, gold, copper, emeralds, hydropower. **Water:**

48,933 cu m per capita. **Crude oil reserves:** 2.3 bil bbls. **Electricity prod.:** 56 bil kWh. **Labor force:** agric. 17%, industry 21%, services 62%. **Unemployment:** 10.1%.

Finance: Monetary unit: Peso (COP) (2,980.70 = $1 U.S.). **GDP:** $667.4 bil; **per capita GDP:** $13,800; **GDP growth:** 3.1%. **Imports:** $56.1 bil; U.S. 28.8%, China 18.6%, Mexico 7.1%. **Exports:** $48.5 bil; U.S. 27.5%, Panama 7.2%, China 5.2%. **Tourism:** $4.2 bil. **Budget:** $86.8 bil. **Inflation:** 5%.

Transport: Railways: 1,330 mi. **Motor vehicles:** 103.2 per 1,000 pop. **Airports:** 121.

Communications: Telephone: 14.4 per 100 pop. **Mobile:** 115.7 per 100 pop. **Broadband:** 45.1 per 100 pop. **Internet:** 55.9%.

Health: Expend.: 7.2%. **Life expect.:** 72.6 male; 79.0 female. **Births:** 16.3 per 1,000 pop. **Deaths:** 5.4 per 1,000 pop. **Infant mortality:** 14.1 per 1,000 live births. **Undernourished:** 8.8%. **HIV:** 0.5%.

Education: Compulsory: ages 5-14. **Literacy:** 94.6%.

Embassy: 1724 Massachusetts Ave. NW 20036; 387-8338.

Website: wp.presidencia.gov.co

Spain subdued the local Indian kingdoms (Funza, Tunja) by the 1530s and ruled Colombia and neighboring areas as New Granada for 300 years. Independence was won by 1819. Venezuela and Ecuador broke away in 1829-30, and Panama withdrew in 1903.

In the 20th and early 21st cent., Colombia was plagued by rural and urban violence. "La Violencia" of 1948-58 claimed 200,000 lives. Guerrilla warfare and terrorist attacks by leftist rebels, including the Revolutionary Armed Forces of Colombia (FARC), began in the 1960s. Violence by right-wing paramilitary groups became widespread by the 1980s. Government activity against drug cartels sparked retaliation killings of politicians and judges. The FARC engaged in drug trafficking and kidnappings for ransom to finance its operations. The violence led to an internally displaced population estimated by UNHCR at 6.7 mil in early 2016.

Álvaro Uribe Vélez, a hardliner, won a presidential election May 2002. A wave of guerrilla violence as he took office led Uribe to declare a state of unrest Aug. 12, and police powers were increased as part of a new government offensive. Uribe easily won reelection, May 2006. Key political figures, including major allies of Uribe, were arrested in 2007 on charges of colluding with paramilitary death squads. Former Defense Min. Juan Manuel Santos Calderón won a presidential runoff election June 2010; he was reelected June 15, 2014. Peace talks with the FARC began in Norway Oct. 2012 and shifted to Havana, Cuba. The government and the FARC signed a cease-fire agreement, June 23, 2016, and a peace accord, Sept. 26, providing for FARC disarmament and reintegration of FARC members into civilian life. However, in an Oct. 2, 2016, referendum, Colombian voters narrowly rejected the accord, with many apparently believing it treated FARC members too leniently.

Since 2000, the U.S. has provided billions of dollars to Colombia to reduce farming of coca (used to make cocaine) and combat the drug trade. The Colombian government, May 14, 2015, halted a U.S.-backed program of aerial spraying of coca crops because of concerns the herbicide used could cause cancer. The government announced, Apr. 18, 2016, that herbicide use would resume—but with ground rather than aerial spraying.

Comoros
Union of the Comoros

People: Population: 794,678. **Age distrib.:** <15: 40.1%; 65+: 3.9%. **Growth:** 1.7%. **Migrants:** 1.6%. **Pop. density:** 920.9 per sq mi, 355.6 per sq km. **Urban:** 28.4%. **Ethnic groups:** Antalote, Cafre, Makoa, Oimatsaha, Sakalava. **Languages:** Arabic, French, Shikomoro (Swahili/Arabic blend) (all official). **Religions:** Sunni Muslim 98%, Roman Catholic 2%.

Geography: Total area: 863 sq mi, 2,235 sq km; **Land area:** 863 sq mi, 2,235 sq km. **Location:** 3 islands—Grande Comore (Njazidja), Anjouan (Nzwani), and Moheli (Mwali)—in the Mozambique Channel between NW Madagascar and SE Africa. Nearest neighbor is Mozambique on W. **Topography:** Of volcanic origin; an active volcano on Grande Comore. **Arable land:** 34.9%. **Capital:** Moroni, 55,872 (2014).

Government: Type: Federal presidential republic. **Head of state and gov.:** Pres. Azali Assoumani; b. 1959; in office: May 26, 2016. **Local divisions:** 3 islands, 4 municipalities. **Defense budget/active troops:** NA.

Economy: Industries: fishing, tourism, perfume distillation. **Chief crops:** vanilla, cloves, ylang-ylang, coconuts, bananas, cassava. **Natural resources:** fish. **Water:** 1,522 cu m per capita. **Electricity prod.** (2012): 43 mil kWh. **Labor force:** agric. 80%, industry and services 20%. **Unemployment:** 6.5%.

Finance: Monetary unit: Franc (KMF) (439.50 = $1 U.S.). **GDP:** $1.2 bil; **per capita GDP:** $1,500; **GDP growth:** 1%. **Imports:** $188.2 mil; China 18.9%, Pakistan 16.2%, France 14.7%, UAE 11.3%, India 6.4%. **Exports:** $18.6 mil; India 28.7%, France 17%, Germany 8.7%, Saudi Arabia 7.1%, Singapore 6.6%, Netherlands

6.1%, Mauritius 5.3%. **Tourism:** $51 mil. **Budget:** $147.3 mil. **Inflation:** –8.1%.
Transport: Airports: 4.
Communications: Telephone: 3.1 per 100 pop. **Mobile:** 54.8 per 100 pop. **Broadband** (2012): 0.0 per 100 pop. **Internet:** 7.5%.
Health: Expend.: 6.8%. **Life expect.:** 61.9 male; 66.6 female. **Births:** 26.9 per 1,000 pop. **Deaths:** 7.4 per 1,000 pop. **Infant mortality:** 61.8 per 1,000 live births. **Undernourished:** NA. **HIV:** NA.
Education: Compulsory: ages 6-11. **Literacy:** 78.1%.
Permanent UN Mission: 866 UN Plz., Ste. 418, New York, NY 10017; (212) 750-1637.
Website: www.state.gov/p/af/ci/cn/
France acquired the islands from Muslim sultans, 1841-1909. The islands became a French overseas territory in 1947. In a 1974 referendum, all islands favored independence except Mayotte. The French National Assembly decided to allow each island to decide its own fate. The Comore Chamber of Deputies declared independence July 6, 1975, with Ahmed Abdallah as president. In a 1976 referendum, Mayotte voted to remain French.

A leftist regime that seized power from Abdallah in 1975 was deposed in a pro-French 1978 coup in which he regained the presidency. In Nov. 1989, Pres. Abdallah was assassinated; soon after, a multiparty system was instituted. A Sept. 1995 military coup, assisted by French mercenaries, ousted Pres. Said Mohamed Djohar. French troops invaded, Oct. 4, and forced coup leaders to surrender.

Anjouan and Moheli seceded from the Comoros in 1997. Unrest on Grande Comore culminated in a military coup, Apr. 1999. Anjouan endorsed secession in a disputed vote Jan. 2000. A constitution adopted in a referendum Dec. 2001 that went into effect the following year reunited Anjouan and Moheli with Grande Comore, granting each a semi-autonomous status and its own president.

Irregularities marred the Apr. 2002 runoff election for national president, won by Azali Assoumani, who led the 1999 coup. Ahmed Abdallah Mohamed Sambi won a presidential runoff vote, May 2006. After each of the three islands elected its own president in 2007, Col. Mohamed Bacar refused to relinquish power in Anjouan when the central government ruled his election illegal; he fled when Comorian and African Union troops took control of the island, Mar. 2008. Sambi's Vice Pres. Ikililou Dhoinine won a runoff election for national president Dec. 2010. Assoumani was again elected president in an Apr. 10, 2016, runoff.

Congo
Democratic Republic of the Congo

(The Democratic Republic of the Congo [formerly Zaire], now commonly called Congo or DRC, is also known as Congo-Kinshasa. The Republic of the Congo, commonly called Congo Republic, is also known as Congo-Brazzaville.)
People: Population: 81,331,050. **Age distrib.:** <15: 42.2%; 65+: 2.6%. **Growth:** 2.4%. **Migrants:** 0.7%. **Pop. density:** 92.9 per sq mi, 35.9 per sq km. **Urban:** 43%. **Ethnic groups:** 200+ groups, majority Bantu. Four largest tribes (Mongo, Luba, Kongo [all Bantu], and Mangbetu-Azande [Hamitic]) 45%. **Languages:** French (official), Lingala (lingua franca trade lang.), Kingwana (Kiswahili or Swahili dialect), Kikongo, Tshiluba. **Religions:** Roman Catholic 50%, Protestant 20%, Kimbanguist 10%, Muslim 10%, other (incl. syncretic sects, indigenous beliefs) 10%.
Geography: Total area: 905,355 sq mi, 2,344,858 sq km; **Land area:** 875,312 sq mi, 2,267,048 sq km. **Location:** Central Africa. Congo Republic on W; Central African Republic, South Sudan on N; Uganda, Rwanda, Burundi, Tanzania on E; Zambia, Angola on S. **Topography:** Includes the bulk of the Congo R. basin. Central region is a low-lying plateau covered by rain forest. Mountainous terraces in the W, savannas in the S and SE, grasslands toward the N, and Ruwenzori Mts. on the E. A short strip of territory borders the Atlantic O. **Arable land:** 3.1%. **Capital:** Kinshasa, 12,070,741. **Cities:** Lubumbashi, 2,096,939; Mbuji-Mayi, 2,096,846.
Government: Type: Semi-presidential republic. **Head of state:** Pres. Joseph Kabila; b. 1971; in office: Jan. 26, 2001. **Head of gov.:** Prime Min. Augustin Matata Ponyo Mapon; b. 1964; in office: Apr. 18, 2012. **Local divisions:** 26 provinces, 1 city. **Defense budget:** $738 mil. **Active troops:** 134,250.
Economy: Industries: mining, mineral proc., consumer prods., metal prods., processed foods and beverages, timber, cement. **Chief crops:** coffee, sugar, palm oil, rubber, tea, cotton, cocoa, quinine, cassava, bananas, plantains, peanuts, root crops, corn, fruits. **Natural resources:** cobalt, copper, niobium, tantalum, petroleum, diamonds, gold, silver, zinc, manganese, tin, uranium, coal, hydropower, timber. **Water:** 16,605 cu m per capita. **Crude oil reserves:** 0.2 bil bbls. **Electricity prod.:** 8.5 bil kWh. **Labor force:** NA. **Unemployment:** 8%.
Finance: Monetary unit: Franc (CDF) (965.00 = $1 U.S.). **GDP:** $62.9 bil; **per capita GDP:** $800; **GDP growth:** 7.7%.

Imports: $12.3 bil; China 20.6%, South Africa 17.7%, Zambia 12.3%, Belgium 6.9%, Zimbabwe 5.1%. **Exports:** $12.4 bil; China 43.5%, Zambia 25%. **Tourism:** $0.4 mil. **Budget:** $6.8 bil. **Inflation** (2012-13): 1.6%.
Transport: Railways: 2,490 mi. **Motor vehicles:** 24.3 per 1,000 pop. **Airports:** 26.
Communications: Telephone (2012): 0.1 per 100 pop. **Mobile:** 53 per 100 pop. **Broadband:** 7.9 per 100 pop. **Internet:** 3.8%.
Health: Expend.: 4.3%. **Life expect.:** 55.8 male; 58.9 female. **Births:** 34.2 per 1,000 pop. **Deaths:** 9.9 per 1,000 pop. **Infant mortality:** 69.8 per 1,000 live births. **Undernourished:** NA. **HIV:** 0.8%.
Education: Compulsory: ages 6-11. **Literacy:** 77.2%.
Embassy: 1100 Connecticut Ave. NW, Ste. 725, 20036; 234-7690.
Website: www.presidentrdc.cd
The earliest inhabitants of Congo may have been the pygmies, followed by Bantus from the east and Nilotic tribes from the north. The large Bantu Bakongo kingdom ruled much of Congo and Angola when Portuguese explorers visited in the 15th cent.

Leopold II, king of the Belgians, formed an international group to exploit the Congo region in 1876. In 1877, British explorer Henry M. Stanley traveled the Congo R, and in 1878 he returned to organize the region and win over the indigenous leaders. The Conference of Berlin, 1884-85, established the Congo Free State with Leopold as king and chief owner. The colony became known as the Belgian Congo in 1908 when Leopold sold it to the Belgian government. Millions of Congolese rubber plantation workers were exploited and died under brutal European rule between 1880 and 1920.

Belgian and Congolese leaders agreed Jan. 27, 1960, that Congo would become independent in June. In the first general elections, May 31, Patrice Lumumba's party won a plurality in the National Assembly. The Republic of the Congo was proclaimed June 30. Europeans and others fled widespread violence. The UN Security Council, Aug. 9, called on Belgium to withdraw its troops and sent a UN contingent. Lumumba was dismissed as premier in Sept. and murdered Jan. 17, 1961. The last UN troops left the Congo June 30, 1964.

In late 1965, Gen. Joseph D. Mobutu was named president. He later changed his name to Mobutu Sese Seko and ruled as a dictator. The country became the Democratic Republic of the Congo (1966) and the Republic of Zaire (1971). Under Mobutu, economic decline and government corruption plagued the country. He retained power despite mounting international pressure and internal opposition.

During 1994, Zaire was inundated with refugees from the massive ethnic bloodshed in Rwanda. Ethnic violence spread to eastern Zaire in 1996. In Oct., militant Hutus, who dominated in the refugee camps, fought rebels (mostly Tutsis) in Zaire, precipitating intervention by government troops. As a result of the fighting, Rwandan refugees abandoned the camps; hundreds of thousands returned to Rwanda, while hundreds of thousands more were dispersed throughout eastern Zaire. The rebels, led by Gen. Laurent Kabila—a former Marxist and longtime opponent of Mobutu—began to move west across Zaire. On May 17, 1997, Kabila's troops entered Kinshasa, and Mobutu went into exile. The country again became the Dem. Rep. of the Congo. Mobutu died Sept. 7 in Morocco.

Kabila, who ruled by decree, alienated UN officials, international aid donors, and former allies. Rebels assisted by Rwanda and Uganda threatened Kinshasa in Aug. 1998 but were turned back with help from Angola, Namibia, and Zimbabwe. Rebel groups agreed to a cease-fire, Aug. 31, 1999, but the truce was widely violated. Kabila was assassinated Jan. 16, 2001, and was succeeded by his son Joseph.

The estimated death toll from the civil war and related causes was 3.3 mil through Nov. 2002. By then, Rwanda and Uganda had agreed to pull out their remaining troops. A power-sharing accord signed Apr. 2, 2003, led to the installation of a new Congolese government in July. A new constitution won legislative approval May 13, 2005. A UN peacekeeping force (MONUC), established in 1999, oversaw July 2006 elections. Kabila defeated former rebel leader Jean-Pierre Bemba in a presidential runoff election, Oct. 2006.

Hundreds reportedly died in Kinshasa, Mar. 22-23, 2007, in clashes between security forces and a militia loyal to Bemba, who fled to Europe. He was arrested in Belgium May 24, 2008. Held responsible for atrocities committed by his forces in the Central African Rep. in 2002-03, Bemba was convicted of war crimes and crimes against humanity, Mar. 21, 2016, by the Intl. Criminal Court (ICC) at The Hague and sentenced, June 21, to 18 years in prison. A peace deal with militia groups in eastern Congo, including one led by Tutsi rebel Gen. Laurent Nkunda, was signed Jan. 23, 2008, but Nkunda launched a new offensive Aug. 28; Rwandan authorities arrested him Jan. 2009.

Kabila was reelected, Nov. 28, 2011. A June 2011 study estimated that more than 1,000 women were raped in Congo every day. The ICC convicted Congolese warlord Thomas Lubanga Dyilo Mar. 2012 of war crimes for conscripting child soldiers during the country's civil war. The ICC, May 23, 2014, sentenced rebel leader Germain Katanga to 12 years in prison in connection with a 2003 massacre of more than 200 villagers.

The MONUC peacekeeping mission, reconstituted and renamed MONUSCO as of July 1, 2010, included more than 18,600 uniformed personnel as of Aug. 31, 2016. Eleven African nations signed a peace plan Feb. 24, 2013, designed to end the violence in Congo. Rebel leader Bosco Ntaganda surrendered in Rwanda Mar. 18, 2013, to face charges of war crimes and crimes against humanity; his trial at the ICC began Sept. 2, 2015. A peace agreement with the M23 militia group was reached in Dec. 2013. About 8,000 rebels laid down their arms by mid-Jan. 2014, but other fighters remained active. With Kabila legally required to leave office in Dec. 2016, violent protests that left dozens dead erupted in Kinshasa in Sept. after the government announced plans to delay the next presidential election.

Congo Republic
Republic of the Congo

(Congo Republic, officially Republic of the Congo, is also known as Congo-Brazzaville. The Democratic Republic of the Congo [formerly Zaire], now commonly called Congo or DRC, is also known as Congo-Kinshasa.)

People: Population: 4,852,412. **Age distrib.:** <15: 41.5%; 65+: 3%. **Growth:** 2.1%. **Migrants:** 8.5%. **Pop. density:** 36.8 per sq mi, 14.2 per sq km. **Urban:** 65.8%. **Ethnic groups:** Kongo 48%, Sangha 20%, M'Bochi 12%, Teke 17%, European, other 3%. **Languages:** French (official); Lingala, Monokutuba (lingua franca trade langs.); many local langs., dialects (Kikongo most widespread). **Religions:** Roman Catholic 33.1%, Awakening Churches/Christian Revival 22.3%, Protestant 19.9%, none 11.3%.

Geography: Total area: 132,047 sq mi, 342,000 sq km; **Land area:** 131,854 sq mi, 341,500 sq km. **Location:** W central Africa. Gabon and Cameroon on W, Central African Republic on N, Dem. Rep. of the Congo on E, Angola on SW. **Topography:** Thick forests across much of country. A coastal plain leads to the fertile Niari Valley. The Congo R. basin consists of flood plains in the lower portion and savanna in the upper. **Arable land:** 1.6%. **Capital:** Brazzaville, 1,949,265.

Government: Type: Presidential republic. **Head of state:** Pres. Denis Sassou-Nguesso; b. 1943; in office: Oct. 25, 1997. **Head of gov.:** Prime Min. Clément Mouamba; in office Apr. 23, 2016. **Local divisions:** 12 departments. **Defense budget** (2013): $367 mil. **Active troops:** 10,000.

Economy: Industries: petroleum extraction, cement, lumber, brewing, sugar, palm oil. **Chief crops:** cassava, sugar, rice, corn, peanuts, vegetables, coffee, cocoa. **Natural resources:** petroleum, timber, potash, lead, zinc, uranium, copper, phosphates, gold, magnesium, nat. gas, hydropower. **Water:** 180,087 cu m per capita. **Crude oil reserves:** 1.6 bil bbls. **Electricity prod.:** 1.7 bil kWh. **Labor force:** NA. **Unemployment:** 6.5%.

Finance: Monetary unit: Central African CFA Franc (XAF) (586.00 = $1 U.S.). **GDP:** $29.4 bil; **per capita GDP:** $6,700; **GDP growth:** 2.5%. **Imports:** $3.8 bil; China 20.3%, France 14.2%, South Korea 9.8%. **Exports:** $5.9 bil; China 42.1%, Italy 16.9%. **Tourism:** $38 mil. **Budget:** $4.7 bil. **Inflation:** 5.1%.

Transport: Railways: 317 mi. **Motor vehicles:** 16.8 per 1,000 pop. **Airports:** 8.

Communications: Telephone: 0.4 per 100 pop. **Mobile:** 111.7 per 100 pop. **Broadband:** 10.8 per 100 pop. **Internet:** 7.6%.

Health: Expend.: 5.2%. **Life expect.:** 58.1 male; 60.6 female. **Births:** 35.1 per 1,000 pop. **Deaths:** 9.7 per 1,000 pop. **Infant mortality:** 56.4 per 1,000 live births. **Undernourished:** 30.5%. **HIV:** NA.

Education: Compulsory: ages 6-15. **Literacy:** 79.3%.
Embassy: 1720 16th St. NW 20009; 726-5500.
Website: www.sassou.cg or www.ambacongo-us.org

The Loango kingdom flourished in the 15th cent., as did the Anzico kingdom of the Batekes; by the late 17th cent. they had weakened. By 1885, France controlled the region. The Republic of the Congo gained independence Aug. 15, 1960.

After trade unions sparked a 1963 coup, the country adopted a Marxist-Leninist stance, with the USSR and China vying for influence. France remained a dominant trade partner and source of technical assistance, and French-owned private enterprise retained a major economic role. In 1970, the country was renamed People's Republic of the Congo. Since the 1980s, oil has dominated the economy.

In 1990, Marxism was renounced and opposition parties were legalized. In 1991 the country's name was changed back to Rep. of the Congo, and a new constitution was approved. A democratically elected government came into office in 1992. Factional fighting broke out in Brazzaville, June 1997. Troops loyal to former Marxist dictator Denis Sassou-Nguesso took control of the city Oct. 15, 1997; he claimed lopsided victories in 2002 and 2009 presidential elections. After 2015 constitutional changes allowed him to run again, Sassou-Nguesso was reelected Mar. 20, 2016; the U.S. and EU criticized the fairness of the election. Violence between government forces and opposition militias erupted in the weeks after voting, and opposition leaders were arrested.

Costa Rica
Republic of Costa Rica

People: Population: 4,872,543. **Age distrib.:** <15: 22.8%; 65+: 7.5%. **Growth:** 1.2%. **Migrants:** 8.8%. **Pop. density:** 247.2 per sq mi, 95.4 per sq km. **Urban:** 77.7%. **Ethnic groups:** white or mestizo 83.6%, mulato 6.7%, indigenous 2.4%. **Languages:** Spanish (official), English. **Religions:** Roman Catholic 76.3%, Evangelical 13.7%, none 3.2%.

Geography: Total area: 19,730 sq mi, 51,100 sq km; **Land area:** 19,714 sq mi, 51,060 sq km. **Location:** Central America. Nicaragua on N, Panama on S. **Topography:** Tropical lowlands by the Caribbean. The interior plateau, at an elevation of about 4,000 ft, is temperate. **Arable land:** 4.5%. **Capital:** San José, 1,182,767.

Government: Type: Presidential republic. **Head of state and gov.:** Pres. Luis Guillermo Solís Rivera; b. 1958; in office: May 8, 2014. **Local divisions:** 7 provinces. **Defense budget:** $439 mil (paramilitary budget). **Active troops:** No armed forces. 9,800 paramilitary-style police only.

Economy: Industries: medical equip., food proc., textiles and clothing, constr. materials, fertilizer, plastic prods. **Chief crops:** bananas, pineapples, coffee, melons, ornamental plants, sugar, corn, rice, beans, potatoes. **Natural resources:** hydropower. **Water:** 23,502 cu m per capita. **Electricity prod.:** 10 bil kWh. **Labor force:** agric. 14%, industry 22%, services 64%. **Unemployment:** 8.3%.

Finance: Monetary unit: Colon (CRC) (546.00 = $1 U.S.). **GDP:** $74.9 bil; **per capita GDP:** $15,500; **GDP growth:** 3.7%. **Imports:** $15.4 bil; U.S. 45.3%, China 9.8%, Mexico 7.1%. **Exports:** $9.8 bil; U.S. 33.6%, China 6.2%. **Tourism:** $3.3 bil. **Budget:** $10.6 bil. **Inflation:** 0.8%.

Transport: Railways: 173 mi (not in current use though some sections rehabilitated). **Motor vehicles:** 223 per 1,000 pop. **Airports:** 47.

Communications: Telephone: 17.2 per 100 pop. **Mobile:** 150.7 per 100 pop. **Broadband:** 86.9 per 100 pop. **Internet:** 59.8%.

Health: Expend.: 9.3%. **Life expect.:** 75.9 male; 81.4 female. **Births:** 15.7 per 1,000 pop. **Deaths:** 4.6 per 1,000 pop. **Infant mortality:** 8.3 per 1,000 live births. **Undernourished:** <5%. **HIV:** 0.3%.

Education: Compulsory: ages 5-14. **Literacy:** 97.6%.
Embassy: 2114 S St. NW 20008; 234-2945.
Website: presidencia.go.cr

Guaymi Indians inhabited the area when Spaniards arrived, 1502. Independence came in 1821. Costa Rica seceded from the Central American Federation in 1838. Since the civil war of 1948-49, free political institutions have been preserved.

Costa Rica, still a largely agricultural country, has achieved a relatively high standard of living, and land ownership is widespread. Tourism is an important source of revenue. Nobel Peace Prize-winner Óscar Arias Sánchez, president 1986-90, won a second term in a close election, Feb. 5, 2006. An election victory Feb. 7, 2010, made ruling party candidate Laura Chinchilla Miranda the nation's first female president. Luis Guillermo Solís Rivera of the opposition Citizen Action Party won an Apr. 6, 2014, runoff election and was sworn in as president May 8, 2014.

Côte d'Ivoire
Republic of Côte d'Ivoire

People: Population: 23,740,424. **Age distrib.:** <15: 37.5%; 65+: 3.4%. **Growth:** 1.9%. **Migrants:** 9.6%. **Pop. density:** 193.4 per sq mi, 74.7 per sq km. **Urban:** 54.9%. **Ethnic groups:** Akan 32.1%, Voltaique or Gur 15%, Northern Mande 12.4%, Krou 9.8%, Southern Mande 9%, other (incl. European, Lebanese descent) 21.2%. **Languages:** French (official), 60 native dialects (Dioula most widely spoken). **Religions:** Muslim 40.2%, Catholic 19.4%, Evangelical 19.3%, animist or no religion 12.8%.

Geography: Total area: 124,504 sq mi, 322,463 sq km; **Land area:** 122,782 sq mi, 318,003 sq km. **Location:** S coast of W Africa. Liberia, Guinea on W; Mali, Burkina Faso on N; Ghana on E. **Topography:** Forests cover W half of country. A sparse inland plain leads to low mountains in NW. **Arable land:** 9.1%. **Capital:** Yamoussoukro (official), 258,962 (2014); Abidjan (de facto), 5,019,689.

Government: Type: Presidential republic. **Head of state:** Pres. Alassane Ouattara; b. 1942; in office: Apr. 11, 2011 (sworn in Dec. 4, 2010). **Head of gov.:** Prime Min. Daniel Kablan Duncan; b. 1943; in office: Nov. 21, 2012. **Local divisions:** 12 districts, 2 autonomous districts. **Defense budget:** $846 mil. **Active troops:** 25,000.

Economy: Industries: foodstuffs, beverages, wood prods., oil refining, gold mining, truck and bus assembly, textiles, fertilizer. **Chief crops:** coffee, cocoa beans, bananas, palm kernels, corn, rice, cassava, sweet potatoes, sugar, cotton, rubber. **Natural resources:** petroleum, nat. gas, diamonds, manganese, iron ore, cobalt, bauxite, copper, gold, nickel, tantalum, silica sand, clay, cocoa beans, coffee, palm oil, hydropower. **Water:** 3,706 cu m per capita. **Crude oil reserves:** 0.1 bil bbls. **Electricity prod.:** 7 bil kWh. **Labor force:** agric. 68%. **Unemployment:** 4%.

Finance: Monetary unit: CFA Franc (XOF) (586.00 = $1 U.S.). **GDP:** $78.6 bil; **per capita GDP:** $3,300; **GDP growth:** 8.6%. **Imports:** $9.2 bil; Nigeria 21.8%, China 14.4%, France 11.3%, Bahamas 5%. **Exports:** $11.9 bil; U.S. 8.5%, Netherlands 6.2%, France 5.6%, Germany 5.6%, Nigeria 5.5%, Burkina Faso 5.5%, Belgium 5.3%. **Tourism:** $181 mil. **Budget:** $7.1 bil. **Inflation:** 1.2%.

Transport: Railways: 410 mi. **Motor vehicles:** 25.1 per 1,000 pop. **Airports:** 7.

Communications: Telephone: 1.3 per 100 pop. **Mobile:** 119.3 per 100 pop. **Broadband:** 24.6 per 100 pop. **Internet:** 21%.

Health: Expend.: 5.7%. **Life expect.:** 57.5 male; 59.9 female. **Births:** 28.2 per 1,000 pop. **Deaths:** 9.5 per 1,000 pop. **Infant mortality:** 57.2 per 1,000 live births. **Undernourished:** 13.3%. **HIV:** 3.2%.

Education: Compulsory: NA. **Literacy:** 43.3%. **Embassy:** 2424 Massachusetts Ave. NW 20008; 797-0300. **Website:** www.gouv.ci

A French protectorate from 1842, Côte d'Ivoire became independent in 1960. The name was officially changed from Ivory Coast, Oct. 1985.

Students and workers protested, Feb. 1990, demanding the ouster of longtime Pres. Félix Houphouët-Boigny. Côte d'Ivoire held its first multiparty presidential election Oct. 1990, which Houphouët-Boigny won. He died Dec. 7, 1993. The National Assembly named as successor Henri Konan Bédié. He was reelected Oct. 1995 but was ousted in a military coup Dec. 24, 1999. The coup leader, Robert Guéi, lost a presidential vote Oct. 2000 but claimed victory anyway. After mass protests, he fled, and Laurent Gbagbo became president. Guéi was killed in Abidjan Sept. 19, 2002.

Agreement on power sharing was reached in Mar. 2003, and Gbagbo and former rebel leaders declared an end to their war July 5. The country remained divided, however. Rebels held the north and government forces controlled the south. Under a new accord reached Mar. 2007, rebel leader Guillaume Soro became prime min.

After apparently losing a presidential runoff election, Nov. 28, 2010, to former Prime Min. Alassane Ouattara, Gbagbo clung to power. A violent power struggle followed, claiming several thousand lives and displacing at least 1 mil people. Ouattara loyalists captured Gbagbo in Abidjan, Apr. 2011. Human Rights Watch reported June 2 that after taking power, Ouattara's troops killed at least 149 suspected Gbagbo supporters. In 2013 and 2014 reports, Amnesty Intl. accused the army and its allies of killing and torturing Gbagbo loyalists. Ouattara won reelection Oct. 25, 2015. A UN peacekeeping mission (UNOCI), authorized since 2004, had about 2,800 uniformed personnel in Côte d'Ivoire as of Aug. 31, 2016. The ICC, June 12, 2014, ordered Gbagbo to stand trial for crimes against humanity; his trial began Jan. 28, 2016. His wife, Simone Gbagbo, was sentenced, Mar. 10, 2015, by a Côte d'Ivoire court to 20 years in prison for her role in the violence that followed the 2010 election; another trial, for crimes against humanity, began May 31, 2016. In attacks, Mar. 13, 2016, for which al-Qaeda in the Islamic Maghreb claimed responsibility, gunmen killed 19 people and wounded more than 30 at 3 resort hotels in Grand-Bassam.

Croatia
Republic of Croatia

People: Population: 4,313,707. **Age distrib.:** <15: 14.2%; 65+: 18.8%. **Growth:** −0.5%. **Migrants:** 13.6%. **Pop. density:** 199.6 per sq mi, 77.1 per sq km. **Urban:** 59.3%. **Ethnic groups:** Croat 90.4%, Serb 4.4%, other (incl. Bosniak, Hungarian, Slovene, Czech, Roma) 4.4%. **Languages:** Croatian (official), Serbian. **Religions:** Roman Catholic 86.3%, Orthodox 4.4%, not religious or atheist 3.8%.

Geography: Total area: 21,851 sq mi, 56,594 sq km; **Land area:** 21,612 sq mi, 55,974 sq km. **Location:** SE Europe, on the Balkan Peninsula. Slovenia, Hungary on N; Bosnia and Herzegovina, Serbia, Montenegro on E. **Topography:** Flat plains in NE; highlands, low mts. along Adriatic. **Arable land:** 15.7%. **Capital:** Zagreb, 687,299.

Government: Type: Parliamentary republic. **Head of state:** Pres. Kolinda Grabar-Kitarovic; b. 1968; in office: Feb. 19, 2015. **Head of gov.:** Interim Prime Min. Tihomir Oreskovic; b. 1966; in office: June 16, 2016. **Local divisions:** 20 counties, 1 city with special county status. **Defense budget:** $674 mil. **Active troops:** 16,550.

Economy: Industries: chemicals and plastics, machine tools, fabricated metal, electronics. **Chief crops:** wheat, corn, barley, sugar beets, sunflowers, rapeseed, alfalfa, clover, vegetables, fruits, grapes for wine. **Natural resources:** oil, coal, bauxite, iron ore, calcium, gypsum, nat. asphalt, silica, mica, clays, salt, hydropower. **Water:** 24,882 cu m per capita. **Crude oil reserves:** 0.1 bil bbls. **Electricity prod.:** 13 bil kWh. **Labor force:** agric. 1.9%, industry 27.6%, services 70.4%. **Unemployment:** 16.7%.

Finance: Monetary unit: Kuna (HRK) (6.65 = $1 U.S.). **GDP:** $91.1 bil; **per capita GDP:** $21,600; **GDP growth:** 1.6%. **Imports:** $19.3 bil; Germany 15.5%, Italy 13.1%, Slovenia 10.7%, Austria 9.2%, Hungary 7.8%. **Exports:** $12.2 bil; Italy 13.4%, Slovenia 12.5%, Germany 11.4%, Bosnia and Herzegovina 9.9%, Austria 6.6%. **Tourism:** $8.8 bil. **Budget:** $22.9 bil. **Inflation:** −0.5%.

Transport: Railways: 1,691 mi. **Motor vehicles:** 370.5 per 1,000 pop. **Airports:** 24.

Communications: Telephone: 34.7 per 100 pop. **Mobile:** 103.8 per 100 pop. **Broadband:** 68.5 per 100 pop. **Internet:** 69.8%.

Health: Expend.: 7.8%. **Life expect.:** 72.7 male; 79.2 female. **Births:** 9.0 per 1,000 pop. **Deaths:** 12.1 per 1,000 pop. **Infant mortality:** 9.5 per 1,000 live births. **Undernourished:** <5%. **HIV:** NA.

Education: Compulsory: ages 7-14. **Literacy:** 99.3%. **Embassy:** 2343 Massachusetts Ave. NW 20008; 588-5899. **Website:** vlada.gov.hr

From the 7th cent. the area was inhabited by Croats, a south Slavic people. It was formed into a kingdom under Tomislav in 924, and joined with Hungary in 1102. The Croats became westernized and separated from Slavs under Austro-Hungarian influence. Croatia united with other Yugoslav areas to proclaim the Kingdom of Serbs, Croats, and Slovenes in 1918. A nominally independent state between 1941 and 1945, it became a constituent republic of Yugoslavia in the 1946 constitution.

On June 25, 1991, Croatia declared independence from Yugoslavia. Fighting began between ethnic Serbs and Croats. The Serbs gained control of some Croatian territory, but Croatian troops recaptured most of the Serb-held territory Aug. 1995. A peace accord was signed in Dec. The last Serb-held enclave, E Slavonia, was returned to Croatia in 1998. Croatia became a full NATO member Apr. 1, 2009, and joined the EU July 1, 2013.

Former Croatian Gen. Ante Gotovina was convicted by a UN tribunal Apr. 15, 2011, of war crimes against Serbs committed in the mid-1990s; the conviction was overturned on appeal, Nov. 16, 2012. A UN tribunal convicted six Croats May 29, 2013, for ethnic cleansing of Bosnians during the 1990s. Conservative Kolinda Grabar-Kitarovic narrowly won a runoff election, Jan. 11, 2015, to become Croatia's first woman president. A conservative coalition—formed after Nov. 2015 parliamentary elections—collapsed in June 2016. Conservative parties again won the most seats in Sept. 11, 2016, elections and began negotiations on a new coalition.

Beginning Sept. 2015, tens of thousands of Middle Eastern, SW Asian, and African refugees and other migrants—most trying to reach N Europe—entered Croatia from Serbia. Croatia announced that as of Mar. 9, 2016, it would block virtually all migrants from transiting through the country.

Cuba
Republic of Cuba

People: Population: 11,179,995. **Age distrib.:** <15: 16.7%; 65+: 14.6%. **Growth:** −0.3%. **Migrants:** 0.1%. **Pop. density:** 263.7 per sq mi, 101.8 per sq km. **Urban:** 77.2%. **Ethnic groups:** white 64.1%, mestizo 26.6%, black 9.3%. **Languages:** Spanish (official). **Religions:** Roman Catholic (nominally, prior to 1959 revolution) 85%.

Geography: Total area: 42,803 sq mi, 110,860 sq km; **Land area:** 42,402 sq mi, 109,820 sq km. **Location:** In Caribbean, westernmost of West Indies. The Bahamas, U.S. to N; Mexico to W; Jamaica to S; Haiti to E. **Topography:** Coastline is about 2,500 mi. The N coast is steep and rocky, the S coast low and marshy. Low hills and fertile valleys cover more than half the country. Three mountain ranges. **Arable land:** 29.7%. **Capital:** Havana, 2,128,932.

Government: Type: Communist state. **Head of state and gov.:** Pres. Raúl Castro Ruz; b. 1931; in office: Feb. 24, 2008 (acting from July 31, 2006). **Local divisions:** 15 provinces, 1 special municipality. **Defense troops:** NA. **Active troops:** 49,000.

Economy: Industries: petroleum, nickel, cobalt, pharmaceuticals, tobacco, constr., steel, cement, agric. machinery, sugar. **Chief crops:** sugar, tobacco, citrus, coffee, rice, potatoes, beans. **Natural resources:** cobalt, nickel, iron ore, chromium, copper, salt, timber, silica, petroleum. **Water:** 3,347 cu m per capita. **Crude oil reserves:** 0.1 bil bbls. **Electricity prod.:** 18 bil kWh. **Labor force:** agric. 18%, industry 10%, services 72%. **Unemployment:** 3.3%.

Finance: Monetary unit: Peso (CUP) (26.50 = $1 U.S.). **GDP** (2014): $128.5 bil; **per capita GDP** (2010): $10,200; **GDP growth** (2014): 1.3%. **Imports:** $15.2 bil; Venezuela 31.8%, China 17.6%, Spain 10%. **Exports:** $4.4 bil; Canada 17.8%, Venezuela 13.9%, China 13.1%, Netherlands 6.4%, Spain 5.4%. **Tourism:** $2.4 bil. **Budget:** $2.9 bil. **Inflation:** 4.4%.

Transport: Railways: 5,148 mi. **Motor vehicles:** 44 per 1,000 pop. **Airports:** 64.

Communications: Telephone: 11.5 per 100 pop. **Mobile:** 29.7 per 100 pop. **Broadband:** 0.0 per 100 pop. **Internet:** 31.1%.
Health: Expend.: 11.1%. **Life expect.:** 76.4 male; 81.1 female. **Births:** 10.8 per 1,000 pop. **Deaths:** 8.6 per 1,000 pop. **Infant mortality:** 4.5 per 1,000 live births. **Undernourished:** <5%. **HIV:** 0.3%.
Education: Compulsory: ages 6-14. **Literacy:** 99.7%.
Embassy: 2630 16th St. NW 20009; 797-8518.
Website: www.cubagob.cu

Some 50,000 indigenous people lived in Cuba when Christopher Columbus reached it in 1492. Its name derives from the Indian word Cubanacan. Except for British occupation of Havana, 1762-63, Cuba remained Spanish until 1898. A slave-based sugar plantation economy developed from the 18th cent. Sugar remains a leading agricultural product. Spain failed to deliver on rights guaranteed in 1878, prompting a full-scale liberation movement under Jose Martí in 1895.

The Spanish-American War began Apr. 1898 with the sinking of the USS *Maine* in Havana harbor. Spain lost the war and gave up all claims to Cuba. U.S. troops withdrew in 1902, but under 1903 and 1934 agreements, the U.S. continued to lease a site at Guantánamo Bay in the SE as a naval base. U.S. and other foreign investors dominated the economy. In 1952, former Pres. Fulgencio Batista established a dictatorship, which grew increasingly harsh and corrupt. Fidel Castro began a rebellion in 1956. Batista fled Jan. 1, 1959, and Castro took power, becoming premier Feb. 16.

Government-instituted economic and social changes failed to restore promised liberties. Opponents were imprisoned or executed. Some 700,000 Cubans emigrated in the first years after Castro's takeover, mostly to the U.S. By 1960, all banks and industrial companies had been nationalized, including over $1-bil worth of U.S.-owned properties, mostly without compensation. U.S. economic sanctions became a complete trade embargo under legislation passed by Congress in 1961. The U.S. broke diplomatic relations with Cuba in Jan. 1961.

In Apr. 1961, some 1,400 Cubans, trained and backed by the U.S. Central Intelligence Agency, unsuccessfully tried to overthrow the regime. On Oct. 22, 1962, U.S. Pres. John F. Kennedy ordered a naval blockade around Cuba and demanded that Soviet-installed nuclear missiles be withdrawn. The crisis ended Oct. 28 when Soviet Prem. Nikita S. Khrushchev agreed to withdraw the missiles; the U.S. ended the blockade, pledged not to invade Cuba, and removed its own missiles from Turkey.

In 1977, Cuba and the U.S. agreed to exchange diplomats without restoring full ties. In 1978 and 1980, the U.S. agreed to accept political prisoners released by Cuba, some of whom were criminals and mental patients. A 1987 agreement provided for 20,000 Cubans to emigrate to the U.S. each year; Cuba agreed to take back some 2,500 jailed in the U.S. since 1980. Cuba's support for left-wing regimes and liberation movements in Central America, Africa, and the Caribbean contributed to poor relations with the U.S.

Cuba's economy, hobbled by U.S. sanctions and dependent on aid from other Communist countries, was shaken by the collapse of the Communist bloc in the late 1980s. Stiffer trade sanctions enacted by the U.S. in 1992 made things worse. Antigovernment demonstrations in Aug. 1994 prompted Castro to loosen emigration restrictions. A new U.S.-Cuba accord in Sept. ended the exodus of "boat people" after more than 30,000 had left Cuba. The U.S. also announced May 1995 it would admit 20,000 Cuban refugees held at Guantánamo but would return additional refugees to Cuba.

The U.S. imposed additional sanctions after Cuba, Feb. 1996, shot down two aircraft operated by anti-Castro exiles. Cuba blamed exile groups for bombings at Havana tourist hotels, July-Sept. 1997.

On July 31, 2006, the ailing Fidel Castro yielded power to his 75-year-old brother Raúl, who served as acting president until formally succeeding Feb. 24, 2008. The U.S. in 2009 eased restrictions on remittances and family travel to Cuba. The Cuban government announced, Sept. 2010, economic restructuring plans involving cutting more than 500,000 public jobs. A Communist Party conference, Apr. 2011, confirmed Raúl Castro as first secretary and approved economic reforms, including an expansion of private property rights and private ownership of some small businesses.

The U.S., Jan. 11, 2002, began using its naval base at Guantánamo Bay to detain prisoners captured in Afghanistan. The indefinite detention and aggressive interrogation of Guantánamo prisoners were criticized by human rights groups. U.S. Pres. Barack Obama signed, Jan. 22, 2009, an executive order calling for the closure of the Guantánamo detention center within a year; however, 61 detainees were still held there as of Sept. 30, 2016.

Landmark migration rules were enacted Jan. 14, 2013, allowing Cubans to remain overseas longer without forfeiting their Cuban residency. Legislation to encourage foreign investment was adopted in Mar. 2014. Pres. Obama announced, Dec. 17, 2014, that the U.S. would restore full diplomatic relations with Cuba. Following the announcement, some travel and economic restrictions were eased. Relations were formally resumed July 20, 2015. In Mar. 2016, Obama became the first U.S. president to visit Cuba since the Communist takeover. Scheduled U.S. commercial flights to Cuba, suspended in the early 1960s, resumed Aug. 31, 2016.

Cyprus
Republic of Cyprus

People: Population: 1,205,575. **Age distrib.:** <15: 15.6%; 65+: 11.8%. **Growth:** 1.4%. **Migrants:** 16.8%. **Pop. density:** 337.9 per sq mi, 130.5 per sq km. **Urban:** 66.8%. **Ethnic groups:** Greek 98.8% (govt.-controlled area only). **Languages:** Greek, Turkish (both official); English; Romanian; Russian; Bulgarian. **Religions:** Orthodox Christian 89.1%, Roman Catholic 2.9%, Protestant/ Anglican 2%.
Geography: Total area: 3,572 sq mi, 9,251 sq km; **Land area:** 3,568 sq mi, 9,241 sq km. **Location:** Eastern Mediterranean Sea, off Turkish coast. Nearest neighbors are Turkey to N, Syria and Lebanon to E. **Topography:** Two mountain ranges run E-W, separated by a wide, fertile plain. **Arable land:** 8.6%. **Capital:** Nicosia (Lefkosia), 251,142 (2014).
Government: Type: Presidential democracy. **Head of state and gov.:** Pres. Nicos Anastasiades; b. 1946; in office: Feb. 28, 2013. **Local divisions:** 6 districts. **Defense budget:** $355 mil. **Active troops:** 12,000 (3,500 in territory where govt. does not exercise effective control).
Economy: Industries: tourism, food and beverage proc., cement and gypsum, ship repair and refurb., textiles, light chemicals, metal prods. **Chief crops:** citrus, vegetables, barley, grapes, olives, vegetables. **Natural resources:** copper, pyrites, asbestos, gypsum, timber, salt, marble, clay earth pigment. **Water:** 670 cu m per capita. **Electricity prod.:** 4 bil kWh. **Labor force:** agric. 3.8%, industry 15.2%, services 81%. **Unemployment:** 15.6%.
Finance: Monetary unit: Euro (EUR) (0.89 = $1 U.S.). **GDP:** $28.1 bil; **per capita GDP:** $32,800; **GDP growth:** 1.6%. **Imports** (2014): $6.8 bil; Greece 25.7%, UK 9.1%, Italy 8%, Germany 7.5%, Israel 5.5%. **Exports** (2014): $1.8 bil; Greece 10.9%, Ireland 10.2%, UK 7.2%, Israel 6%. **Tourism:** $2.5 bil. **Budget:** $7.9 bil. **Inflation:** –2.1%.
Transport: Motor vehicles: 581.7 per 1,000 pop. **Airports:** 13.
Communications: Telephone: 27.8 per 100 pop. **Mobile:** 95.4 per 100 pop. **Broadband:** 42.1 per 100 pop. **Internet:** 71.7%.
Health: Expend.: 7.4%. **Life expect.:** 75.8 male; 81.6 female. **Births:** 11.4 per 1,000 pop. **Deaths:** 6.7 per 1,000 pop. **Infant mortality:** 8.1 per 1,000 live births. **Undernourished:** <5%. **HIV:** NA.
Education: Compulsory: ages 6-14. **Literacy:** 99.1%.
Embassy: 2211 R St. NW 20008; 462-5772.
Website: www.cyprus.gov.cy

The Ottoman Empire held Cyprus, 1571-1878, until it yielded control to Britain. Agitation for *enosis* (union) with Greece, which the Turkish minority opposed, increased after WWII and led to violence in 1955-56. In 1959, Britain, Greece, Turkey, and Cypriot leaders approved a plan for an independent republic, with constitutional guarantees for the Turkish minority and permanent division of offices on an ethnic basis.

Archbishop Makarios III was elected president, and full independence became final Aug. 16, 1960. Communal strife led the UN to send a peacekeeping force (UNFICYP) in 1964; its mandate was repeatedly renewed, and more than 1,000 UNFICYP uniformed personnel were in Cyprus as of Aug. 31, 2016.

The Cypriot National Guard, led by officers from the Greek army, seized the government July 15, 1974. On July 20, Turkey invaded the island; Greece mobilized its forces but did not intervene. By Aug. 16, Turkish forces had occupied the northeastern 40% of the island.

Turkish Cyprus opened its border with Greek Cyprus Apr. 23, 2003, for the first time since partition. In separate referendums Apr. 2004, 65% of Turkish Cypriot voters accepted a UN-sponsored reunification plan, but 76% of Greek Cypriots rejected it. Still divided, Cyprus became a full member of the EU on May 1, 2004. It began using the euro as its currency in 2008. Dimitris Christofias won a 2008 runoff election, becoming the country's first Communist president. In a runoff election Feb. 24, 2013, the conservative candidate and head of the Democratic Rally party, Nicos Anastasiades, was voted Cyprus's new president.

In part because Cypriot banks held large amounts of Greek bonds, Cyprus suffered a banking crisis in 2013. The outline of a Cyprus bailout package was agreed upon Mar. 5, 2013, by the Intl. Monetary Fund, the European Central Bank, and eurozone countries. In exchange for $13 bil in IMF and EU assistance, Cyprus agreed to stringent banking reforms and economic austerity measures. Those with deposits of more than 100,000 euros in Cypriot banks lost some or all the money above that amount to help finance the restructuring of the banking system. Cyprus's GDP shrank in 2012, 2013, and 2014. Modest growth (1.6%) returned in 2015, but the unemployment rate remained above 15%.

Turkish Republic of Northern Cyprus

A declaration of independence was announced by Turkish-Cypriot leader Rauf Denktash, Nov. 15, 1983. The state is not internationally recognized but has trade relations with some countries. Denktash was succeeded as president by Mehmet Ali Talat (2005-10) and Dervis Eroglu (2010-15). Political moderate Mustafa Akinci defeated Eroglu in an Apr. 26, 2015, presidential runoff election. Akinci and Anastasiades met in May, and a new round of

UN-sponsored reunification talks began in June 2015. Area 1,295 sq mi; pop. (2011 census) 286,257, nearly all Turkish. Capital: Nicosia (Lefkosia). Local divisions: 5 districts. Active troops: 3,500. **Website:** www.kktcb.org

Czechia
Czech Republic

(As of May 17, 2016, the country's official short form name in English was Czechia.)
People: Population: 10,660,932. **Age distrib.:** <15: 15.1%; 65+: 18.5%. **Growth:** 0.1%. **Migrants:** 3.8%. **Pop. density:** 357.4 per sq mi, 138 per sq km. **Urban:** 73%. **Ethnic groups:** Czech 64.3%, Moravian 5%. **Languages:** Czech (official), Slovak. **Religions:** Roman Catholic 10.4%, none 34.5%.

Geography: Total area: 30,451 sq mi, 78,867 sq km; **Land area:** 29,825 sq mi, 77,247 sq km. **Location:** E central Europe. Poland on N, Germany on N and W, Austria on S, Slovakia on E and SE. **Topography:** Bohemia, in W, is a plateau surrounded by mountains; Moravia is hilly. **Arable land:** 40.8%. **Capital:** Prague, 1,324,403.

Government: Type: Parliamentary republic. **Head of state:** Pres. Milos Zeman; b. 1944; in office: Mar. 8, 2013. **Head of gov.:** Prime Min. Bohuslav Sobotka; b. 1971; in office: Jan. 29, 2014. **Local divisions:** 13 regions, 1 capital city. **Defense budget:** $1.8 bil. **Active troops:** 21,700.

Economy: Industries: motor vehicles, metallurgy, machinery and equip., glass, armaments. **Chief crops:** wheat, potatoes, sugar beets, hops, fruit. **Natural resources:** coal, kaolin, clay, graphite, timber. **Water:** 1,247 cu m per capita. **Crude oil reserves** (2015): 15 mil bbls. **Electricity prod.:** 81 bil kWh. **Labor force:** agric. 2.6%, industry 37.4%, services 60%. **Unemployment:** 6.2%.

Finance: Monetary unit: Koruna (CZK) (24.14 = $1 U.S.). **GDP:** $332.5 bil; **per capita GDP:** $31,600; **GDP growth:** 4.2%. **Imports:** $124 bil; Germany 30%, Poland 9%, China 8.3%, Slovakia 6.6%, Netherlands 5%. **Exports:** $133.8 bil; Germany 32.4%, Slovakia 9%, Poland 5.8%, UK 5.3%, France 5.1%. **Tourism:** $6 bil. **Budget:** $75.6 bil. **Inflation:** 0.3%.

Transport: Railways: 5,979 mi. **Motor vehicles:** 543.7 per 1,000 pop. **Airports:** 41.

Communications: Telephone: 18.1 per 100 pop. **Mobile:** 129.2 per 100 pop. **Broadband:** 62.8 per 100 pop. **Internet:** 81.3%.

Health: Expend.: 7.4%. **Life expect.:** 75.7 male; 81.8 female. **Births:** 9.5 per 1,000 pop. **Deaths:** 10.4 per 1,000 pop. **Infant mortality:** 2.6 per 1,000 live births. **Undernourished:** <5%. **HIV:** NA.

Education: Compulsory: ages 6-14. **Literacy:** 99%.
Embassy: 3900 Spring of Freedom St. NW 20008; 274-9100.
Website: www.czech.cz

Bohemia and Moravia were part of the Great Moravian Empire in the 9th cent. and later became part of the Holy Roman Empire. Under the kings of Bohemia, Prague in the 14th cent. was the cultural center of Central Europe. Bohemia and Hungary became part of Austria-Hungary.

In 1914-18, Thomas G. Masaryk and Eduard Benes formed a provisional government with the support of Slovak leaders, including Milan Stefanik. They proclaimed the Republic of Czechoslovakia Oct. 28, 1918.

By 1938, Nazi Germany had generated disaffection among German-speaking citizens in Sudetenland and demanded its cession. British Prime Min. Neville Chamberlain signed with Adolf Hitler at Munich, Sept. 30, 1938, an agreement to the cession, with a guarantee of peace by Hitler and Italian dictator Benito Mussolini. Germany occupied Sudetenland Oct. 1-2. Hitler on Mar. 15, 1939, dissolved Czechoslovakia, made protectorates of Bohemia and Moravia, and supported the autonomy of Slovakia, proclaimed independent Mar. 14, 1939.

Soviet troops with some Czechoslovak contingents entered eastern Czechoslovakia in 1944 and reached Prague in May 1945; Benes returned as president. In May 1946 elections, the Communist Party won 38% of the votes. In Feb. 1948, the Communists seized power in advance of scheduled elections. The country was renamed the Czechoslovak Socialist Republic. A harsh Stalinist period followed; all opposition was suppressed.

In Jan. 1968 a liberalization movement spread through Czechoslovakia. Long-time Stalinist ruler Antonin Novotny was deposed; the democrat Slovak Alexander Dubcek succeeded him. In July, the USSR and 4 Warsaw Pact nations demanded an end to liberalization. On Aug. 20, the Soviet, Polish, East German, Hungarian, and Bulgarian armies invaded Czechoslovakia. Despite demonstrations and riots by students and workers, press censorship was imposed and liberal leaders were ousted. On Apr. 17, 1969, Dubcek resigned as Communist Party leader and was succeeded by Gustav Husak. Censorship was tightened, and the Communist Party expelled a third of its members.

More than 700 leading Czechoslovak intellectuals and former party leaders signed a human rights manifesto in 1977, called Charter 77, prompting a renewed crackdown by the regime.

The police crushed a massive protest in Prague, Nov. 17, 1989. As protesters demanded free elections, the Communist Party leadership resigned Nov. 24; millions went on strike Nov. 27.

On Dec. 10, 1989, the first cabinet in 41 years without a Communist majority took power; Vaclav Havel, playwright and human rights campaigner, was chosen president, Dec. 29. In Mar. 1990 the country was officially renamed the Czech and Slovak Federal Republic. A Slovak-led coalition blocked Havel's bid to win reelection July 1992.

Slovakia declared sovereignty, July 17, 1992. Czech and Slovak leaders agreed, July 23, on a plan for a peaceful division of Czechoslovakia. It split into two separate states—the Czech Republic and Slovakia—Jan. 1, 1993. Havel was elected president of the Czech Republic on Jan. 26. The country became a full member of NATO in 1999.

Vaclav Klaus replaced the retiring Havel, 2003. The nation became a full EU member May 1, 2004. Inconclusive parliamentary elections, June 2006, led to a political deadlock, after which a minority center-right government took office Sept. 2006. Center-right parties made a strong showing in May 2010 parliamentary elections. In the country's first direct presidential election, former Social Democrat prime min. Milos Zeman was elected with more than 55% of the vote in a runoff election Jan. 26, 2013.

Heavy rains in early June 2013 caused massive flooding throughout central Europe; parts of Prague were submerged where the Vitava R. overflowed its banks. On June 4, the prime min. declared a state of emergency throughout the country.

A corruption scandal erupted June 13, 2013, with a police raid on government offices and the arrests of seven parliamentarians, including the prime min.'s closest aide, causing Prime Min. Petr Necas to resign June 17. After Oct. 2013 elections, Social Democrat Bohuslav Sobotka, who had campaigned on increasing government spending to boost the economy, became prime min. Jan. 29, 2014.

Denmark
Kingdom of Denmark

People: Population: 5,593,785. **Age distrib.:** <15: 16.6%; 65+: 19%. **Growth:** 0.2%. **Migrants:** 10.1%. **Pop. density:** 341.4 per sq mi, 131.8 per sq km. **Urban:** 87.8%. **Ethnic groups:** Scandinavian, Inuit, Faroese, German, Turkish, Iranian, Somali. **Languages:** Danish, Faroese, Greenlandic, English (predominant second lang.). **Religions:** Evangelical Lutheran (official) 80%, Muslim 4%.

Geography: Total area: 16,639 sq mi, 43,094 sq km; **Land area:** 16,384 sq mi, 42,434 sq km. **Location:** Northern Europe, separating North and Baltic Seas. Germany on S, Norway on NW, Sweden on NE. **Topography:** Consists of the Jutland Peninsula and about 500 islands, 100 inhabited. Land is flat or gently rolling. **Arable land:** 56.7%. **Capital:** Copenhagen, 1,281,289.

Government: Type: Parliamentary constitutional monarchy. **Head of state:** Queen Margrethe II; b. 1940; in office: Jan. 14, 1972. **Head of gov.:** Prime Min. Lars Loekke Rasmussen; b. 1964; in office: June 28, 2015. **Local divisions:** 5 regions. **Defense budget:** $3.5 bil. **Active troops:** 17,200.

Economy: Industries: iron, steel, nonferrous metals, chemicals, food proc., machinery and transp. equip., textiles and clothing, electronics, constr., furniture and other wood prods. **Chief crops:** barley, wheat, potatoes, sugar beets. **Natural resources:** petroleum, nat. gas, fish, salt, limestone, chalk, stone, gravel and sand. **Water:** 1,058 cu m per capita. **Crude oil reserves:** 0.6 bil bbls. **Electricity prod.:** 34 bil kWh. **Labor force:** agric. 2.6%, industry 20.3%, services 77.1%. **Unemployment:** 6.6%.

Finance: Monetary unit: Krone (DKK) (6.65 = $1 U.S.). **GDP:** $258.7 bil; **per capita GDP:** $45,700; **GDP growth:** 1.2%. **Imports:** $83.8 bil; Germany 20.4%, Sweden 12.3%, Netherlands 8.1%, China 7.3%, Norway 6.1%. **Exports:** $94.1 bil; Germany 17.8%, Sweden 11.6%, U.S. 8.4%, Norway 6.3%, UK 6.3%. **Tourism:** $6.6 bil. **Budget:** $170.9 bil. **Inflation:** 0.5%.

Transport: Railways: 1,636 mi. **Motor vehicles:** 509.1 per 1,000 pop. **Airports:** 28.

Communications: Telephone: 29.9 per 100 pop. **Mobile:** 128.3 per 100 pop. **Broadband:** 115.8 per 100 pop. **Internet:** 96.3%.

Health: Expend.: 10.8%. **Life expect.:** 77.0 male; 82.0 female. **Births:** 10.4 per 1,000 pop. **Deaths:** 10.3 per 1,000 pop. **Infant mortality:** 4.0 per 1,000 live births. **Undernourished:** <5%. **HIV:** NA.

Education: Compulsory: ages 6-15. **Literacy:** 99%.
Embassy: 3200 Whitehaven St. NW 20008; 234-4300.
Website: www.denmark.dk

Most of the Viking raiders in the early Middle Ages were Danes. The Danish kingdom was a major power until the 17th cent., when it lost its land in southern Sweden. Norway was separated in 1815, and Schleswig-Holstein in 1864. Northern Schleswig was returned in 1920. Nazi Germany occupied Denmark, Apr. 1940-May 1945, but Danes helped more than 7,200 Jews escape to safety in Sweden, Sept. 1943. Voters ratified the Maastricht Treaty, enabling Denmark to join the EU, in May 1993.

The Danish newspaper *Jyllands-Posten* published, Sept. 30, 2005, cartoon images of the prophet Muhammad, offensive to Muslims; the caricatures, republished elsewhere, triggered violent protests and a boycott of Danish products in Islamic countries in early 2006. Danish police raids broke up alleged Islamist bomb plots Sept. 2006 and Sept. 2007. A car bomb blast linked to al-Qaeda killed 8 people outside Denmark's embassy in Islamabad, Pakistan, June 2, 2008.

A left-wing coalition won Sept. 2011 parliamentary elections, and Helle Thorning-Schmidt, a Social Democrat, became Denmark's first female prime min. Oct. 3. A bill granting marriage rights to same-sex couples was voted into law, June 7, 2012. A center-right coalition returned to power in June 2015 elections in which the anti-immigration Danish People's Party won 21% of the vote. In 2015, about 21,000 migrants from the Middle East and elsewhere applied for asylum in Denmark. A Jan. 26, 2016, law allowed the government to seize the assets of arriving asylum seekers.

The **Faroe Islands** in the N Atlantic, about 300 mi NW of the Shetlands, and 850 mi from Denmark proper, 18 inhabited, have an area of 538 sq mi and pop. (2016 est.) of 50,456. They are an administrative division of Denmark, self-governing in most matters. Capital: Torshavn; pop. (2014 est.) 20,646. Fish is a primary export. **Website:** www.government.fo

Greenland (Kalaallit Nunaat)

Greenland, an island between the North Atlantic and the Arctic Oceans, is separated from the North American continent by Davis Strait and Baffin Bay. Total area is 836,330 sq mi, about 81% of which is ice-capped. Most of the island is a lofty plateau 9,000-10,000 ft in elevation. The average thickness of the cap is 1,000 ft. Scientists point to accelerated melting of Greenland's ice sheet in recent years as evidence of global warming. The pop. (2016 est.) was 57,728. About 88% of the pop. in 2010 were Inuit. Under the 1953 Danish constitution the colony became an integral part of the realm with representatives in the Folketing (Danish legislature). The Danish parliament, 1978, approved home rule for Greenland, effective May 1, 1979. With home rule, Greenlandic place names came into official use. The technically correct name for Greenland is Kalaallit Nunaat. The official name for its capital is Nuuk (2014 est. pop., 16,911), rather than Godthab. The labor force is distributed as follows: agric. 13.9%, industry 19.2%, services 67%. Fish is the principal export (about 89% of exports in 2010). Other natural resources include coal, iron ore, lead, zinc, molybdenum, diamonds, gold, and platinum. **Website:** naalakkersuisut.gl

Djibouti
Republic of Djibouti

People: Population: 846,687. **Age distrib.:** <15: 31.7%; 65+: 3.7%. **Growth:** 2.2%. **Migrants:** 12.7%. **Pop. density:** 94.6 per sq mi, 36.5 per sq km. **Urban:** 77.4%. **Ethnic groups:** Somali 60%, Afar 35%, other (incl. French, Arab, Ethiopian, Italian) 5%. **Languages:** French, Arabic (both official); Somali; Afar. **Religions:** Muslim 94%, Christian 6%.

Geography: Total area: 8,958 sq mi, 23,200 sq km; **Land area:** 8,950 sq mi, 23,180 sq km. **Location:** E coast of Africa, separated from Arabian Peninsula by strategically vital strait of Bab el-Mandeb. Eritrea on NW, Ethiopia on W and SW, Somalia on SE. **Topography:** Low coastal plain with mountains behind and an interior plateau. Arid, sandy, and desolate. Hot and dry climate. **Arable land:** 0.1%. **Capital:** Djibouti, 535,469.

Government: Type: Semi-presidential republic. **Head of state:** Pres. Ismail Omar Guelleh; b. 1947; in office: May 8, 1999. **Head of gov.:** Prime Min. Abdoulkader Kamil Mohamed; b. 1951; in office: Apr. 1, 2013. **Local divisions:** 6 districts. **Defense budget** (2013): $11 mil. **Active troops:** 10,450.

Economy: Industries: constr., agric. proc., shipping. **Chief crops:** fruits, vegetables. **Natural resources:** potential geothermal power, gold, clay, granite, limestone, marble, salt, diatomite, gypsum, pumice, petroleum. **Water:** 338 cu m per capita. **Electricity prod.:** 0.4 bil kWh. **Labor force:** NA. **Unemployment:** NA.

Finance: Monetary unit: Franc (DJF) (176.88 = $1 U.S.). **GDP:** $3.1 bil. **per capita GDP:** $3,200; **GDP growth:** 6.5%. **Imports:** $983.9 mil; China 42.1%, Saudi Arabia 14.3%, Indonesia 5.9%. **Exports:** $141.6 mil; Somalia 79.5%, U.S. 5.4%. **Tourism:** $21 mil. **Budget:** $792.9 mil. **Inflation** (2013-14): 2.9%.

Transport: Railways: 62 mi (largely inoperable; Djibouti segment of railway jointly controlled with Ethiopia). **Airports:** 3. **Communications: Telephone:** 2.6 per 100 pop. **Mobile:** 34.7 per 100 pop. **Broadband:** 3.2 per 100 pop. **Internet:** 11.9%.

Health: Expend.: 10.6%. **Life expect.:** 60.7 male; 65.8 female. **Births:** 23.6 per 1,000 pop. **Deaths:** 7.6 per 1,000 pop. **Infant mortality:** 47.2 per 1,000 live births. **Undernourished:** 15.9%. **HIV:** 1.6%.

Education: Compulsory: ages 6-15. **Literacy:** NA. **Embassy:** 1156 15th St. NW, Ste. 515, 20005; 331-0270. **Website:** www.presidence.dj

France gained control of the territory in stages between 1862 and 1900. As French Somaliland, it became an overseas French territory in 1945; in 1967 it was renamed the French Territory of the Afars and the Issas. Ethiopia and Somalia renounced their claims to the area, but each accused the other of trying to gain control. There were clashes between Afars (ethnically related to

Ethiopians) and Issas (related to Somalis) in 1976. Immigrants from both countries continued to enter Djibouti until independence on June 27, 1977.

Post-independence economic support has come from France, Arab countries, the U.S., and China. A peace accord Dec. 1994 ended a 3-year Afar rebel uprising. Drought in 2007-11 devastated crops and livestock. Protests associated with the Arab Spring broke out in late Jan. 2011 demanding the resignation of Pres. Ismail Omar Guelleh. Authorities suppressed the protests, and Guelleh won a third term in an Apr. 2011 election boycotted by the main opposition. The U.S. announced, May 5, 2014, the signing of a new 20-year lease for its military base in Djibouti, used for anti-terrorism and other military operations in the Middle East and Africa. After signing a 10-year lease with the Guelleh government, China began construction, Apr. 18, 2016, of a naval base in Djibouti. Guelleh won a fourth term in disputed Apr. 8, 2016, elections.

Dominica
Commonwealth of Dominica

People: Population: 73,757. **Age distrib.:** <15: 21.8%; 65+: 10.9%. **Growth:** 0.2%. **Migrants:** 9.2%. **Pop. density:** 254.4 per sq mi, 98.2 per sq km. **Urban:** 69.8%. **Ethnic groups:** black 86.6%, mixed 9.1%, indigenous 2.9%. **Languages:** English (official), French patois. **Religions:** Roman Catholic 61.4%, Protestant 28.6% (incl. Evangelical 6.7%, Seventh-day Adventist 6.1%), none 6.1%.

Geography: Total area: 290 sq mi, 751 sq km; **Land area:** 290 sq mi, 751 sq km. **Location:** E Caribbean, most northerly Windward Isl. Guadeloupe to N, Martinique to S (both French terr.). **Topography:** Central ridge runs N-S, terminating in cliffs. Volcanic in origin, with numerous thermal springs. **Arable land:** 8%. **Capital:** Roseau, 14,994 (2014).

Government: Type: Parliamentary republic. **Head of state:** Pres. Charles A. Savarin; b. 1943; in office: Oct. 2, 2013. **Head of gov.:** Prime Min. Roosevelt Skerrit; b. 1972; in office: Jan. 8, 2004. **Local divisions:** 10 parishes. **Defense budget/active troops:** NA.

Economy: Industries: soap, coconut oil, tourism, copra, furniture, cement blocks, shoes. **Chief crops:** bananas, citrus, mangoes, root crops, coconuts, cocoa. **Natural resources:** timber, hydropower. **Water:** 2,752 cu m per capita. **Electricity prod.** (2012): 96.5 mil kWh. **Labor force:** agric. 40%, industry 32%, services 28%. **Unemployment:** NA.

Finance: Monetary unit: East Caribbean Dollar (XCD) (2.70 = $1 U.S.). **GDP:** $763 mil; **per capita GDP:** $10,700; **GDP growth:** –4.3%. **Imports:** $182.9 mil; Japan 42%, Trinidad and Tobago 17%, U.S. 11.9%, China 6%. **Exports:** $39.4 mil; Japan 38.1%, Jamaica 19%, Antigua and Barbuda 10.4%, Trinidad and Tobago 6.2%. **Tourism:** $128 mil. **Budget:** $148.1 mil. **Inflation:** –0.8%.

Transport: Airports: 2.
Communications: Telephone: 20.8 per 100 pop. **Mobile:** 106.3 per 100 pop. **Broadband:** 4.1 per 100 pop. **Internet:** 67.6%.

Health: Expend.: 5.5%. **Life expect.:** 74.0 male; 80.1 female. **Births:** 15.2 per 1,000 pop. **Deaths:** 7.9 per 1,000 pop. **Infant mortality:** 10.9 per 1,000 live births. **Undernourished:** NA. **HIV:** NA.

Education: Compulsory: ages 5-16. **Literacy:** NA. **Embassy:** 1001 19th St. N, Ste. 1200, Arlington, VA 22209; (571) 527-1370.
Website: www.dominica.gov.dm

A British colony since 1805, Dominica was granted self-government in 1967. Independence was achieved Nov. 3, 1978.

Hurricane David struck, Aug. 30, 1979, devastating the island and destroying the banana plantations, Dominica's economic mainstay. Coups were attempted in 1980 and 1981. Prime Min. Pierre Charles died Jan. 6, 2004, and was succeeded by Roosevelt Skerrit. Charles A. Savarin was sworn in as Dominica's eighth pres., Oct. 2, 2013. Tropical storm Erika, Aug. 27, 2015, killed 30 and caused widespread damage.

Dominican Republic

People: Population: 10,606,865. **Age distrib.:** <15: 27.1%; 65+: 7.4%. **Growth:** 1.2%. **Migrants:** 3.9%. **Pop. density:** 568.5 per sq mi, 219.5 per sq km. **Urban:** 79.8%. **Ethnic groups:** mixed 73%, white 16%, black 11%. **Languages:** Spanish (official). **Religions:** Roman Catholic 95%.

Geography: Total area: 18,792 sq mi, 48,670 sq km; **Land area:** 18,656 sq mi, 48,320 sq km. **Location:** W Indies, sharing isl. of Hispaniola with Haiti on W, Puerto Rico (U.S.) to E. **Topography:** The Cordillera Central range crosses center, rising to over 10,000 ft, highest in the Caribbean. Cibao Valley to N. **Arable land:** 16.6%. **Capital:** Santo Domingo, 3,019,989.

Government: Type: Presidential republic. **Head of state and gov.:** Pres. Danilo Medina Sánchez; b. 1951; in office: Aug. 16, 2012. **Local divisions:** 10 regions. **Defense budget:** $446 mil. **Active troops:** 56,050.

Economy: Industries: tourism, sugar proc., gold mining, textiles, cement, tobacco. **Chief crops:** cocoa, tobacco, sugarcane, coffee, cotton, rice, beans, potatoes, corn, bananas. **Natural**

resources: nickel, bauxite, gold, silver. **Water:** 2,232 cu m per capita. **Electricity prod.:** 14 bil kWh. **Labor force:** agric. 14.4%, industry 20.8%, services 64.7%. **Unemployment:** 15%.

Finance: Monetary unit: Peso (DOP) (45.97 = $1 U.S.). **GDP:** $149.7 bil; **per capita GDP:** $15,000; **GDP growth:** 7%. **Imports:** $15.3 bil; U.S. 41.9%, China 9.2%, Venezuela 5.6%. **Exports:** $9.6 bil; U.S. 42.5%, Haiti 16.5%, Canada 8.1%. **Tourism:** $6.2 bil. **Budget:** $11.7 bil. **Inflation:** 0.8%.

Transport: Railways: 308 mi. **Motor vehicles:** 151 per 1,000 pop. **Airports:** 16.

Communications: Telephone: 12.3 per 100 pop. **Mobile:** 82.6 per 100 pop. **Broadband:** 30.1 per 100 pop. **Internet:** 51.9%.

Health: Expend.: 4.4%. **Life expect.:** 75.9 male; 80.5 female. **Births:** 18.6 per 1,000 pop. **Deaths:** 4.6 per 1,000 pop. **Infant mortality:** 18.1 per 1,000 live births. **Undernourished:** 12.3%. **HIV:** 1.0%.

Education: Compulsory: ages 5-13. **Literacy:** 92.5%.

Embassy: 1715 22nd St. NW 20008; 332-6280.

Website: www.presidencia.gov.do

Carib and Arawak Indians inhabited the island of Hispaniola when Christopher Columbus landed in 1492. The city of Santo Domingo, founded 1496, is the oldest European settlement in the Western Hemisphere.

France took over the western third of the island (now Haiti) in 1697 and Santo Domingo in 1795. Spain returned intermittently 1803-21, as several native republics came and went. Haiti ruled again, 1822-44; Spanish occupation occurred 1861-63. U.S. Marines occupied the country 1916-24.

In 1930, Gen. Rafael Leonidas Trujillo Molina was elected president. The brutal Trujillo era ended with his assassination in 1961. Pres. Joaquín Balaguer, appointed by Trujillo in 1960, resigned under pressure in 1962.

Juan Bosch, elected president in the first free elections in 38 years, was overthrown in 1963. On Apr. 24, 1965, Bosch's followers and others, including a few Communists, launched a revolt. Four days later U.S. Marines intervened against pro-Bosch forces. A provisional government supervised a June 1966 election in which Balaguer defeated Bosch. Balaguer remained in office for most of the next 28 years, but his May 1994 reelection was widely denounced as fraudulent. He called for new elections but did not run, and Leonel Fernández Reyna was elected June 1996. The leftist candidate, Hipólito Mejía, won a presidential vote in 2000. After a banking scandal and soaring inflation, Fernández defeated Mejía in 2004, and he was reelected in 2008. Danilo Medina Sánchez, Fernández's ally, was elected in 2012 and reelected in 2016.

The Constitutional Court ruled, Sept. 23, 2013, that people born in the Dominican Rep. after 1929 to undocumented immigrant parents were not entitled to Dominican citizenship. The decision affected perhaps 200,000 people or more, most of Haitian descent. May 2014 legislation provided a path to citizenship for such people if they completed an application process by June 17, 2015; most did not. In 2015, the government also required undocumented immigrants—estimated at more than 500,000, most of them Haitian—to register by June 17 or face deportation; about half had not registered by the deadline. The government did not immediately begin large-scale deportations, but tens of thousands of Haitians left the country. A Zika virus outbreak resulted in about 5,500 confirmed or suspected cases by late Sept. 2016.

Ecuador
Republic of Ecuador

People: Population: 16,080,778. **Age distrib.:** <15: 27.5%; 65+: 7.2%. **Growth:** 1.3%. **Migrants:** 2.4%. **Pop. density:** 150.4 per sq mi, 58.1 per sq km. **Urban:** 64%. **Ethnic groups:** mestizo (mixed Amerindian/white) 71.9%, Montubio 7.4%, Amerindian 7%, white 6.1%, Afroecuadorian 4.3%. **Languages:** Spanish (Castilian) (official), Quechua. **Religions:** Roman Catholic 74%, Evangelical 10.4%, atheist 7.9%.

Geography: Total area: 109,484 sq mi, 283,561 sq km; **Land area:** 106,889 sq mi, 276,841 sq km. **Location:** NW S America, on Pacific coast, astride the equator. Colombia on N, Peru on E and S. **Topography:** Two Andes ranges run N-S, splitting country into 3 zones: hot, humid lowlands on coast; temperate highlands between ranges; and rainy, tropical lowlands to E. **Arable land:** 4.8%. **Capital:** Quito, 1,754,057. **Cities:** Guayaquil, 2,756,100.

Government: Type: Presidential republic. **Head of state and gov.:** Pres. Rafael Correa; b. 1963; in office: Jan. 15, 2007. **Local divisions:** 24 provinces. **Defense budget:** $1.9 bil. **Active troops:** 40,250.

Economy: Industries: petroleum, food proc., textiles, wood prods., chemicals. **Chief crops:** bananas, coffee, cocoa, rice, potatoes, cassava, plantains, sugarcane. **Natural resources:** petroleum, fish, timber, hydropower. **Water:** 27,403 cu m per capita. **Crude oil reserves:** 8.3 bil bbls. **Electricity prod.:** 22 bil kWh. **Labor force:** agric. 27.8%, industry 17.8%, services 54.4%. **Unemployment:** 4.6%.

Finance: Monetary unit: U.S. Dollar (USD) (1.00 = $1 U.S.). **GDP:** $183.4 bil; **per capita GDP:** $11,300; **GDP growth:** 0%.

Imports: $20.9 bil; U.S. 27.1%, China 15.3%, Colombia 8.3%. **Exports:** $18.4 bil; U.S. 39.5%, Chile 6.2%, Peru 5.1%. **Tourism:** $1.6 bil. **Budget:** $39.8 bil. **Inflation:** 4%.

Transport: Railways: 600 mi. **Motor vehicles:** 98.6 per 1,000 pop. **Airports:** 104.

Communications: Telephone: 15.5 per 100 pop. **Mobile:** 79.4 per 100 pop. **Broadband:** 30.9 per 100 pop. **Internet:** 48.9%.

Health: Expend.: 9.2%. **Life expect.:** 73.8 male; 79.9 female. **Births:** 18.2 per 1,000 pop. **Deaths:** 5.1 per 1,000 pop. **Infant mortality:** 16.9 per 1,000 live births. **Undernourished:** 10.9%. **HIV:** 0.3%.

Education: Compulsory: ages 3-17. **Literacy:** 94.5%.

Embassy: 2535 15th St. NW 20009; 234-7200.

Website: www.presidencia.gob.ec

The region, which was the northern Inca empire, was conquered by Spain in 1533. Liberation forces defeated the Spanish May 24, 1822, near Quito. Ecuador became part of the Great Colombia Republic but seceded, May 13, 1830.

Ecuadoran indigenous peoples, demanding greater rights, staged protests in the 1990s. A border war with Peru flared Jan. 26-Mar. 1, 1995. Elected president, July 1996, Abdalá Bucaram—a populist known as El Loco, or "The Crazy One"—imposed stiff price increases and other austerity measures. His rising unpopularity and erratic behavior led the National Congress, Feb. 1997, to dismiss him for "mental incapacity."

Jamil Mahuad Witt won a presidential runoff election July 1998. In Sept. 1998 and Mar. 1999 he imposed emergency measures to cope with a continuing economic crisis. Opposed by Indian groups and military leaders, he was ousted Jan. 2000, and succeeded by Vice Pres. Gustavo Noboa Bejarano. Noboa enacted a plan introduced by Mahuad to replace the sucre with the U.S. dollar as Ecuador's currency. Lucio Gutiérrez Borbúa, a leader in the 2000 coup, won a presidential runoff Nov. 2002.

Gutiérrez imposed economic austerity measures, purged opponents from the supreme court, Dec. 2004, and then dissolved the court, Apr. 15, 2005. With street protests rising, Congress ousted Gutiérrez Apr. 20, and Vice Pres. Alfredo Palacio González became president. In May 2006, Ecuador took over oil assets belonging to U.S.-based Occidental Petroleum.

Rafael Correa, a left-wing economist, won a presidential runoff vote Nov. 2006. He won voter approval, Apr. 2007, to convene an assembly to rewrite the constitution. The revised constitution was approved in a national referendum Sept. 2008. Early in his term, when oil revenues were high, he boosted development spending and aid to poor families; later, as oil prices dropped, he restricted imports to prevent an outflow of dollars and, Dec. 2008, allowed Ecuador to default on part of its $10 bil foreign debt.

Correa, reelected Apr. 2009, pressured foreign oil companies in 2010 to renegotiate contracts to increase the government's share of mineral revenues. A confrontation Sept. 30, 2010, between Correa and rebellious police officers led to a shootout between government troops and police; 5 people were killed and at least 38 wounded. An Ecuadoran judge Feb. 14, 2011, ordered Chevron (which had absorbed Texaco in 2001) to pay $9.5 bil to clean up oil pollution from Texaco operations in Ecuador, 1965-92; Chevron disputed the ruling and opposed collection efforts in courts in various countries. Ecuador granted asylum, Aug. 16, 2012, to Julian Assange, the founder of WikiLeaks. Assange had been in Ecuador's UK embassy in London since June 19, avoiding extradition to Sweden from Britain. He remained in the embassy as of Sept. 2016.

Correa was reelected Feb. 17, 2013, becoming Ecuador's longest-serving president. Beginning in 2013, his government encouraged new exploration for oil and other mineral resources in the Amazon. During a July 2015 visit to Ecuador, Pope Francis called for increased protection of the Amazon and its indigenous peoples. A 7.8 magnitude earthquake off the northern coast, Apr. 16, 2016, killed at least 660 and left some 28,000 homeless.

The **Galápagos Islands**, pop. (2008 est.) 30,000, about 600 mi to the W, are the home of huge tortoises and other unusual animals. The oil tanker *Jessica* ran aground Jan. 16, 2001, off San Cristóbal Isl., spilling some 185,000 gallons of fuel.

Egypt
Arab Republic of Egypt

People: Population: 94,666,993. **Age distrib.:** <15: 33.2%; 65+: 4.2%. **Growth:** 2.5%. **Migrants:** 0.5%. **Pop. density:** 246.3 per sq mi, 95.1 per sq km. **Urban:** 43.2%. **Ethnic groups:** Egyptian 99.6%. **Languages:** Arabic (official), English and French widely understood by educated classes. **Religions:** Muslim (predom. Sunni) 90%, Christian (most Coptic Orthodox) 10%.

Geography: Total area: 386,662 sq mi, 1,001,450 sq km; **Land area:** 384,345 sq mi, 995,450 sq km. **Location:** NE corner of Africa. Libya on W; Sudan on S; Israel, Gaza Strip on E. **Topography:** Almost entirely desolate and barren with hills and mountains in E and along Nile. Most people live in 550-mi-long Nile Valley. **Arable land:** 2.8%. **Capital:** Cairo, 19,127,890. **Cities:** Alexandria, 4,862,891.

Government: Type: Presidential republic. **Head of state:** Pres. Abdel Fattah al-Sisi; b. 1954; in office: June 8, 2014. **Head of gov.:** Prime Min. Sherif Ismail; b. 1955; in office: Sept. 19, 2015. **Local divisions:** 27 governorates. **Defense budget:** $6.4 bil. **Active troops:** 438,500.

Economy: Industries: textiles, food proc., tourism, chemicals, pharmaceuticals, hydrocarbons, constr., cement, metals, light manufactures. **Chief crops:** cotton, rice, corn, wheat, beans, fruits, vegetables. **Natural resources:** petroleum, nat. gas, iron ore, phosphates, manganese, limestone, gypsum, talc, asbestos, lead, rare earth elements, zinc. **Water:** 637 cu m per capita. **Crude oil reserves:** 4.4 bil bbls. **Electricity prod.:** 159 bil kWh. **Labor force:** agric. 29.2%, industry 23.5%, services 47.3%. **Unemployment:** 13.2%.

Finance: Monetary unit: Pound (EGP) (8.88 = $1 U.S.). **GDP:** $1 tril; **per capita GDP:** $11,800; **GDP growth:** 4.2%. **Imports:** $57.9 bil; China 13%, Germany 7.7%, U.S. 5.9%. **Exports:** $20.9 bil; Saudi Arabia 9.1%, Italy 7.5%, Turkey 5.8%, UAE 5.1%, U.S. 5.1%. **Tourism:** $6.1 bil. **Budget:** $111.5 bil. **Inflation:** 10.4%.

Transport: Railways: 3,160 mi. **Motor vehicles:** 58.8 per 1,000 pop. **Airports:** 72.

Communications: Telephone: 7.4 per 100 pop. **Mobile:** 111 per 100 pop. **Broadband:** 43.5 per 100 pop. **Internet:** 35.9%.

Health: Expend.: 5.6%. **Life expect.:** 71.4 male; 74.2 female. **Births:** 30.3 per 1,000 pop. **Deaths:** 4.7 per 1,000 pop. **Infant mortality:** 19.7 per 1,000 live births. **Undernourished:** <5%. **HIV:** <0.1%.

Education: Compulsory: ages 6-17. **Literacy:** 75.8%.

Embassy: 3521 International Ct. NW 20008; 895-5400.

Website: www.egypt.gov.eg

Archaeological records of ancient Egyptian civilization date back to 4000 BCE. A unified kingdom arose around 3200 BCE and extended south into Nubia and as far north as Syria. A high culture of rulers and priests was built on an economic base of serfdom, fertile soil, and annual flooding of the Nile.

Imperial decline facilitated conquest by Asian invaders (Hyksos, Assyrians). The last native dynasty fell in 341 BCE to the Persians, who were in turn replaced by Greeks (Alexander and the Ptolemies), Romans, Byzantines, and Arabs, who introduced Islam and the Arabic language. The ancient Egyptian language is preserved only in Coptic Christian liturgy.

Egypt was ruled as part of larger Islamic empires for many centuries. Britain intervened in Egypt in 1882 and ruled the country as a protectorate, 1914-22. A 1936 treaty strengthened Egyptian autonomy, but Britain retained bases in Egypt and a condominium over Sudan. When the state of Israel was proclaimed in 1948, Egypt joined other Arab nations invading Israel and was defeated. In 1951 Egypt abrogated the 1936 treaty; Sudan became independent in 1956.

A July 1952 uprising overthrew King Farouk and established a republic. Lt. Col. Gamal Abdel Nasser rose to power, becoming premier in 1954 and president in 1956. Nasser pushed construction of Egypt's Aswan High Dam, completed in 1970.

After guerrilla raids across its border, Israel invaded Egypt's Sinai Peninsula, Oct. 29, 1956. Egypt rejected a cease-fire demand by Britain and France; on Oct. 31 the two nations dropped bombs and on Nov. 5-6 landed forces. Egypt and Israel accepted a UN cease-fire; fighting ended Nov. 7. Subsequently, a UN Emergency Force guarded the border. Full-scale war with Israel broke out again, June 5, 1967; before it ended under a UN cease-fire June 10, Israel had captured Gaza and the Sinai Peninsula and taken control of the E bank of the Suez Canal.

Nasser died Sept. 28, 1970, and was replaced by Vice Pres. Anwar Sadat. In a surprise attack Oct. 6, 1973, Egyptian forces crossed the Suez Canal into the Sinai. (At the same time, Syrian forces attacked Israelis on the Golan Heights.) Israel counterattacked, crossed the canal, and surrounded Suez City. A UN cease-fire took effect Oct. 24. Under an agreement signed Jan. 1974, Israeli forces withdrew from the canal's W bank; limited numbers of Egyptian forces occupied a strip along the E bank. A second accord was signed in 1975, with Israel yielding Sinai oil fields.

Pres. Sadat's surprise visit to Jerusalem, Nov. 1977, opened the prospect of peace with Israel. On Mar. 26, 1979, Egypt and Israel signed a formal peace treaty, ending 30 years of war and establishing diplomatic relations. On Oct. 6, 1981, Muslim extremists within the army assassinated Pres. Sadat, who was succeeded by Hosni Mubarak. Israel returned control of the Sinai to Egypt in Apr. 1982.

Egyptian security forces battled Islamist violence in the 1990s and early 2000s. On Nov. 17, 1997, near Luxor, Muslim extremists killed 58 foreign tourists and 4 Egyptians. Bombs Oct. 7, 2004, in and near Taba, a Sinai tourist site popular with Israelis, killed at least 35 people. Another 88 people were killed in bombings July 23, 2005, at Sharm el Sheikh, a Red Sea resort city.

Mubarak easily won reelection in Sept. 2005. Suicide bombings at the Sinai resort town of Dahab, Apr. 24, 2006, killed at least 18 people; security forces May 9 killed Nasser Khamis al-Mallahi,

leader of the group blamed for the Taba, Sharm el Sheikh, and Dahab attacks. Constitutional amendments expanding presidential powers were approved Mar. 2007.

Following 18 days of mass protests in which at least 846 people died in clashes between Arab Spring dissidents and Mubarak loyalists, Mubarak surrendered power Feb. 11, 2011. A transitional military regime prepared for elections and charged Mubarak and associates with corruption and abuse of power. Mubarak was convicted June 2, 2012, in connection with the 2011 deaths of protesters and sentenced to life in prison. The verdict was overturned on appeal Jan. 13, 2013, and the charges were dismissed Nov. 29, 2014. However, a judge ordered, June 4, 2015, that Mubarak stand trial again. Mubarak had been convicted of separate corruption charges, May 21, 2014; after that conviction was overturned, Mubarak was re-tried, convicted May 9, 2015, and sentenced to three years in prison.

Islamist candidate Mohammed Morsi of the Muslim Brotherhood was declared winner of the presidential election, June 2012. Morsi overhauled the country's military leadership Aug. 12. On Oct. 8, 2012, he pardoned select political prisoners detained during the Arab Spring uprising. At least 110 people were injured in violent clashes between Morsi supporters and opponents Oct. 12, and additional conflicts erupted Nov. 23 after Morsi announced an edict interpreted as a power-grab. The proposal of a new Islamist constitution prompted demonstrations throughout Dec.; it passed Dec. 23, 2012.

The military forced Morsi out of office July 3, 2013, and his supporters protested continuously in Cairo and other cities. The military cracked down violently on these encampments Aug. 14. More than 600 protesters and at least 40 police officers died in confrontations. The military outlawed the Muslim Brotherhood as a terrorist organization Dec. 25, 2013. Under a new constitution approved in a Jan. 2014 referendum, former Gen. Abdel Fattah al-Sisi, one of the leaders in ousting Morsi, won a May presidential election. Violence between Morsi supporters and security forces continued, causing hundreds of deaths on both sides. Muslim Brotherhood leader Mohamed Badie was sentenced to death June 21, 2014, in connection with July 2013 violence; the sentence was reduced to life in prison Aug. 30, 2014. In a separate case, Morsi and Badie were sentenced to death May 16, 2015. Morsi had been sentenced to 20 years in prison, Apr. 21, 2015, in a trial related to Dec. 2012 street violence. In 2013-16, Islamist militants battled security forces and seized territory in the northern Sinai. Terrorist attacks occurred at major tourist sites in Luxor and Giza in June 2015. All 224 passengers and crew were killed when a Russian airliner crashed in the Sinai, Oct. 31, 2015, apparently after a bomb onboard exploded; Sinai Province, an ISIS-affiliated Islamist group, claimed responsibility. Egypt announced, Aug. 4, 2016, that it had killed Sinai Province's leader in an airstrike. An EgyptAir flight from Paris to Cairo crashed in the Mediterranean, May 19, 2016, killing all 66 onboard; a fire apparently caused the plane to break up in midair. As the number of migrants trying to reach Europe by crossing the Mediterranean from Egypt increased in 2016, more than 200 people were confirmed dead after a ship capsized near the Egyptian coast Sept. 21.

The Suez Canal, 103 mi long, links the Mediterranean and Red Seas. It was built by a French corporation 1859-69, but Britain obtained controlling interest in 1875. On July 26, 1956, Egypt nationalized the canal.

El Salvador
Republic of El Salvador

People: Population: 6,156,670. **Age distrib.:** <15: 26.6%; 65+: 7.3%. **Growth:** 0.3%. **Migrants:** 0.7%. **Pop. density:** 769.5 per sq mi, 297.1 per sq km. **Urban:** 67.2%. **Ethnic groups:** mestizo 86.3%, white 12.7%. **Languages:** Spanish (official), Nawat. **Religions:** Roman Catholic 57.1%, Protestant 21.2%, none 16.8%.

Geography: Total area: 8,124 sq mi, 21,041 sq km; **Land area:** 8,000 sq mi, 20,721 sq km. **Location:** Central America. Guatemala on W, Honduras on N. **Topography:** A hot Pacific coastal plain in S rises to a cooler plateau and valley region, densely populated. The N is mountainous with many volcanoes. **Arable land:** 35.2%. **Capital:** San Salvador, 1,101,502.

Government: Type: Presidential republic. **Head of state and gov.:** Pres. Salvador Sánchez Cerén; b. 1944; in office: June 1, 2014. **Local divisions:** 14 departments. **Defense budget:** $150 mil. **Active troops:** 24,500.

Economy: Industries: food proc., beverages, petroleum, chemicals, fertilizer, textiles, furniture, light metals. **Chief crops:** coffee, sugar, corn, rice, beans, oilseed, cotton, sorghum. **Natural resources:** hydropower, geothermal power, petroleum. **Water:** 4,288 cu m per capita. **Electricity prod.:** 6.1 bil kWh. **Labor force:** agric. 21%, industry 20%, services 58%. **Unemployment:** 6.2%.

Finance: Monetary unit: Colon (SVC) (8.75 = $1 U.S.). **GDP:** $53 bil; **per capita GDP:** $8,300; **GDP growth:** 2.4%. **Imports:** $9.2 bil; U.S. 39.4%, Guatemala 9.6%, China 8.1%, Mexico 7.4%,

Honduras 5.7%. **Exports:** $4.5 bil; U.S. 47.1%, Honduras 13.9%, Guatemala 13.6%, Nicaragua 6.6%. **Tourism:** $817 mil. **Budget:** $5.9 bil. **Inflation:** –0.7%.

Transport: Railways: 8 mi. **Motor vehicles:** 42.5 per 1,000 pop. **Airports:** 5.

Communications: Telephone: 14.7 per 100 pop. **Mobile:** 145.3 per 100 pop. **Broadband:** 34.4 per 100 pop. **Internet:** 26.9%.

Health: Expend.: 6.8%. **Life expect.:** 71.4 male; 78.1 female. **Births:** 16.3 per 1,000 pop. **Deaths:** 5.7 per 1,000 pop. **Infant mortality:** 17.3 per 1,000 live births. **Undernourished:** 12.4%. **HIV:** 0.5%.

Education: Compulsory: ages 7-15. **Literacy:** 87.6%.

Embassy: 1400 16th St. NW, Ste. 100, 20036; 265-9671.

Website: www.presidencia.gob.sv

El Salvador became independent of Spain in 1821, and of the Central American Federation in 1839.

A military coup overthrew Pres. Carlos Humberto Romero in 1979, but a new military-civilian junta failed to quell a rebellion by leftist insurgents, armed by Cuba and Nicaragua. Right-wing death squads organized to eliminate suspected leftists killed thousands in the 1980s. The Reagan administration supported the government with military aid. After taking the lives of some 75,000 people (with thousands more "disappeared"), the 12-year civil war ended Jan. 16, 1992, as the government and leftist rebels signed a formal peace treaty. Rightist legislators passed a sweeping amnesty, Mar. 20, 1993, for civil war atrocities, but the Supreme Court struck down the law, July 13, 2016.

Members of the right-wing ARENA party held the presidency from 1989 to 2009. Mauricio Funes, a leftist, won the 2009 presidential election. His vice pres., Salvador Sánchez Cerén, a former rebel commander, narrowly won the 2014 election. Since late 2013, thousands of undocumented immigrants from El Salvador have been caught trying to enter the U.S. from Mexico; most were unaccompanied children or children with their mothers, fleeing widespread gang violence. Government officials advised women, Jan. 2016, not to become pregnant for two years to avoid birth defects associated with the spread of the Zika virus; there were more than 11,000 Zika cases as of Sept. 2016.

Equatorial Guinea
Republic of Equatorial Guinea

People: Population: 759,451. **Age distrib.:** <15: 40.1%; 65+: 4%. **Growth:** 2.5%. **Migrants:** 1.3%. **Pop. density:** 70.1 per sq mi, 27.1 per sq km. **Urban:** 40.1%. **Ethnic groups:** Fang 85.7%, Bubi 6.5%, Mdowe 3.6%. **Languages:** Spanish, French (both official); Fang; Bubi. **Religions:** nominally Christian and predom. Roman Catholic, pagan practices.

Geography: Total area: 10,831 sq mi, 28,051 sq km; **Land area:** 10,831 sq mi, 28,051 sq km. **Location:** Bioko Isl. off W Africa coast in Gulf of Guinea. Rio Muni, mainland enclave, has Gabon on S, Cameroon on E and N. **Topography:** Bioko Isl. consists of 2 volcanic mountains and connecting valley. Rio Muni, with over 90% of area, has coastal plain and low hills. **Arable land:** 4.3%. **Capital:** Malabo, 145,077 (2014).

Government: Type: Presidential republic. **Head of state:** Pres. Teodoro Obiang Nguema Mbasogo; b. 1942; in office: Aug. 3, 1979. **Head of gov.:** Prime Min. Francisco Pascual Eyegue Obama Asue; in office: June 23, 2016. **Local divisions:** 7 provinces. **Defense budget** (2013): $8 mil. **Active troops:** 1,320.

Economy: Industries: petroleum, nat. gas, sawmilling. **Chief crops:** coffee, cocoa, rice, yams, cassava, bananas, palm oil nuts. **Natural resources:** petroleum, nat. gas, timber, gold, bauxite, diamonds, tantalum, sand and gravel, clay. **Water:** 30,766 cu m per capita. **Crude oil reserves:** 1.1 bil bbls. **Electricity prod.** (2012): 100 mil kWh. **Labor force:** NA. **Unemployment:** 7.9%.

Finance: Monetary unit: Central African CFA Franc (XAF) (586.00 = $1 U.S.). **GDP:** $25.4 bil; **per capita GDP:** $31,800; **GDP growth:** –12.2%. **Imports:** $4.1 bil; Netherlands 16.9%, Spain 16.3%, China 14.9%, U.S. 8.9%, Côte d'Ivoire 6%. **Exports:** $9.2 bil; China 16.6%, South Korea 15.1%, Spain 9%, Brazil 8.2%, Netherlands 6.8%, South Africa 6.6%, India 5.8%, UK 5.7%, France 5.7%. **Budget:** $3.6 bil. **Inflation:** 11.7%.

Transport: Airports: 6.

Communications: Telephone: 1.4 per 100 pop. **Mobile:** 66.7 per 100 pop. **Broadband:** 0.0 per 100 pop. **Internet:** 21.3%.

Health: Expend.: 3.8%. **Life expect.:** 63.1 male; 65.4 female. **Births:** 32.8 per 1,000 pop. **Deaths:** 8.0 per 1,000 pop. **Infant mortality:** 67.2 per 1,000 live births. **Undernourished:** NA. **HIV:** 4.9%.

Education: Compulsory: ages 7-12. **Literacy:** 95.2%.

Embassy: 2020 16th St. NW 20009; 518-5700.

Website: www.guineaecuatorialpress.com or www.state.gov/p/af/ci/ek/

Fernando Po (now Bioko) Island was reached by Portugal in the late 15th cent. and ceded to Spain in 1778. Independence came Oct. 12, 1968. Anti-Spanish riots erupted in 1969 in Rio Muni province on the mainland.

Masie Nguema Biyogo, a mainlander, became president for life in 1972. His reign, among the most brutal in Africa, left the nation bankrupt; most of the nation's 7,000 Europeans emigrated. He was ousted in a military coup, Aug. 1979. Teodoro Obiang Nguema Mbasogo, leader of the coup, became president. Multiparty presidential elections held in 1996, 2002, 2009, and 2016 were seriously flawed.

The economy is heavily dependent on oil exports. There have been allegations of government misuse of oil revenue, and poverty remains widespread. Human Rights Watch (HRW) reported in 2012 that the Obiang regime "regularly tortures and arbitrarily detains" suspected dissidents. A referendum on constitutional reforms was overwhelmingly approved Nov. 2011, but HRW reported voter fraud and intimidation. The government planned to move its capital to a newly built city, Oyala, financing construction with oil sales.

Eritrea
State of Eritrea

People: Population: 5,869,869. **Age distrib.:** <15: 40.7%; 65+: 3.9%. **Growth:** 0.8%. **Migrants:** 0.3%. **Pop. density:** 150.5 per sq mi, 58.1 per sq km. **Urban:** 23.1%. **Ethnic groups:** Tigrinya 55%, Tigre 30%, Saho 4%, Kunama 2%, Rashaida 2%, Bilen 2%, other (Afar, Beni Amir, Nera) 5%. **Languages:** Tigrinya, Arabic, English (all official); Tigre; Kunama; Afar. **Religions:** Muslim, Coptic Christian, Roman Catholic, Protestant.

Geography: Total area: 45,406 sq mi, 117,600 sq km; **Land area:** 38,996 sq mi, 101,000 sq km. **Location:** E Africa, on SW coast of Red Sea. Sudan on W, Ethiopia on S, Djibouti on SE. **Topography:** Includes many islands of the Dahlak Archipelago. Low coastal plains in N, mountain range with peaks to 9,000 ft in N. **Arable land:** 6.8%. **Capital:** Asmara, 835,140.

Government: Type: Presidential republic. **Head of state and gov.:** Pres. Isaias Afworki; b. 1946; in office: June 8, 1993. **Local divisions:** 6 regions. **Defense budget** (2013): $78 mil. **Active troops:** 201,750.

Economy: Industries: food proc., beverages, clothing and textiles, light mfg. **Chief crops:** sorghum, lentils, vegetables, corn, cotton, tobacco, sisal. **Natural resources:** gold, potash, zinc, copper, salt, fish. **Water:** 1,399 cu m per capita. **Electricity prod.:** 0.3 bil kWh. **Labor force:** agric. 80%, industry and services 20%. **Unemployment:** 7.2%.

Finance: Monetary unit: Nakfa (ERN) (10.47 = $1 U.S.). **GDP:** $8.7 bil; **per capita GDP:** $1,300; **GDP growth:** 4.8%. **Imports:** $1.2 bil. **Exports:** $510.9 mil. **Budget:** $2 bil. **Inflation:** 9%.

Transport: Railways: 190 mi. **Airports:** 4.

Communications: Telephone: 1 per 100 pop. **Mobile:** 7 per 100 pop. **Broadband:** 0.0 per 100 pop. **Internet:** 1.1%.

Health: Expend.: 3.3%. **Life expect.:** 62.4 male; 67.5 female. **Births:** 30.1 per 1,000 pop. **Deaths:** 7.3 per 1,000 pop. **Infant mortality:** 45.6 per 1,000 live births. **Undernourished:** NA. **HIV:** 0.6%.

Education: Compulsory: NA. **Literacy:** 73.8%.

Embassy: 1708 New Hampshire Ave. NW 20009; 319-1991.

Website: www.shabait.com or www.state.gov/p/af/ci/er/

Eritrea was part of the Ethiopian kingdom of Aksum. It was an Italian colony from 1890 to 1941, when it was captured by the British. Following a period of British and UN supervision, Eritrea was awarded to Ethiopia as part of a federation in 1952. Ethiopia annexed Eritrea as a province in 1962. After a 31-year struggle, Eritrea formally declared its independence May 24, 1993. A constitution was ratified in 1997 but not implemented.

A border war with Ethiopia that erupted in June 1998 intensified in May 2000, as Ethiopian troops plunged into western Eritrea; a cease-fire signed June 18 provided for a UN peacekeeping force (UNMEE) to patrol a buffer zone on Eritrean territory. A peace treaty was signed Dec. 12, 2000.

A 2007 UN report accused Eritrea of aiding an Islamic insurgency in Somalia. Citing Eritrean obstruction of UNMEE activities, the UN Security Council ended the peacekeeping mission July 2008. Many thousands have fled repressive conditions in Eritrea, including defections by the national soccer team during tournaments in Kenya, Dec. 2009, and Uganda, Dec. 2012. Four Eritrean athletes sought asylum in the UK during the 2012 Summer Olympics in London. A coup attempt against Pres. Isaias Afworki failed, Jan. 21, 2013. A UN commission's final report, issued June 8, 2016, concluded that the government was committing widespread human rights violations. Tens of thousands of Eritreans were among migrants reaching Southern Europe by boat 2014-16.

Estonia
Republic of Estonia

People: Population: 1,258,545. **Age distrib.:** <15: 16.1%; 65+: 19.5%. **Growth:** –0.5%. **Migrants:** 15.4%. **Pop. density:** 76.9 per sq mi, 29.7 per sq km. **Urban:** 67.5%. **Ethnic groups:** Estonian

68.7%, Russian 24.8%. **Languages:** Estonian (official), Russian. **Religions:** Orthodox 16.2%, Lutheran 9.9%, none 54.1%.

Geography: Total area: 17,463 sq mi, 45,228 sq km; **Land area:** 16,366 sq mi, 42,388 sq km. **Location:** Eastern Europe, bordering Baltic Sea and Gulf of Finland. Russia on E, Latvia on S. **Topography:** Marshy lowland with numerous lakes and swamps. Elongated hills show evidence of former glaciation. More than 800 islands on Baltic coast. **Arable land:** 14.9%. **Capital:** Tallinn, 390,509.

Government: Type: Parliamentary republic. **Head of state:** Pres. Toomas Hendrik Ilves; b. 1953; in office: Oct. 9, 2006. **Head of gov.:** Prime Min. Taavi Rxivas; b. 1979; in office: Mar. 26, 2014. **Local divisions:** 15 counties. **Defense budget:** $449 mil. **Active troops:** 5,750.

Economy: Industries: food, engineering, electronics, wood and wood prods., textiles, information tech., telecom. **Chief crops:** grain, potatoes, vegetables. **Natural resources:** oil shale, peat, rare earth elements, phosphorite, clay, limestone, sand, dolomite, sea mud. **Water:** 9,756 cu m per capita. **Electricity prod.:** 13 bil kWh. **Labor force:** agric. 3.9%, industry 28.4%, services 67.7%. **Unemployment:** 7.7%.

Finance: Monetary unit: Euro (EUR) (0.89 = $1 U.S.). **GDP:** $37.6 bil; **per capita GDP:** $28,600; **GDP growth:** 1.1%. **Imports:** $14.4 bil; Finland 14.5%, Germany 11%, Lithuania 9%, Sweden 8.5%, Latvia 8.3%, Poland 7.4%, Russia 6.1%, Netherlands 5.5%. **Exports:** $13.4 bil; Sweden 18.8%, Finland 16%, Latvia 10.4%, Russia 6.7%, Lithuania 5.9%, Germany 5.2%. **Tourism:** $1.5 bil. **Budget:** $8.7 bil. **Inflation:** –0.5%.

Transport: Railways: 743 mi. **Airports:** 13.

Communications: Telephone: 30.3 per 100 pop. **Mobile:** 148.7 per 100 pop. **Broadband:** 117 per 100 pop. **Internet:** 88.4%.

Health: Expend.: 6.4%. **Life expect.:** 71.9 male; 81.7 female. **Births:** 10.3 per 1,000 pop. **Deaths:** 12.5 per 1,000 pop. **Infant mortality:** 3.8 per 1,000 live births. **Undernourished:** <5%. **HIV:** NA.

Education: Compulsory: ages 7-15. **Literacy:** 99.8%.

Embassy: 2131 Massachusetts Ave. NW 20008; 588-0101.

Website: www.eesti.ee

Estonia, a province of imperial Russia before World War I, was independent between World Wars I and II. The USSR conquered it in 1940 and incorporated it as the Estonian SSR. Estonia, Aug. 20, 1991, declared independence, which the Soviet Union recognized Sept. 1991. The first free elections in over 50 years were held Sept. 20, 1992. The last occupying Russian troops departed Aug. 31, 1994.

Estonia became a full member of the EU and NATO, 2004, and adopted the euro, 2011. The government accused Russia of orchestrating a cyberattack against Estonia's computer network in Apr.-May 2007. Amid growing discontent over austerity policies, Prime Min. Andrus Ansip was replaced, Mar. 26, 2014, by Taavi Rõivas, who formed a center-left government. His Reform Party won the most votes in Mar. 1, 2015, elections. NATO leaders, at a July 2016 summit, agreed to station troops in Estonia to deter Russian aggression.

Ethiopia
Federal Democratic Republic of Ethiopia

People: Population: 102,374,044. **Age distrib.:** <15: 43.7%; 65+: 2.9%. **Growth:** 2.9%. **Migrants:** 1.1%. **Pop. density:** 265.1 per sq mi, 102.4 per sq km. **Urban:** 19.9%. **Ethnic groups:** Oromo 34.4%, Amhara 27%, Somali 6.2%, Tigray 6.1%, Sidama 4%, Gurage 2.5%, Welaita 2.3%. **Languages:** Oromo (official in one state); Amharic (official nationally); Somali, Tigrigna (both official in one state each); Sidamo; Wolaytta; Gurage. **Religions:** Ethiopian Orthodox 43.5%, Muslim 33.9%, Protestant 18.5%, traditional 2.7%.

Geography: Total area: 426,373 sq mi, 1,104,300 sq km; **Land area:** 386,102 sq mi, 1,000,000 sq km. **Location:** E Africa. Sudan, South Sudan on W; Kenya on S; Somalia, Djibouti on E; Eritrea on N. **Topography:** A central plateau, 6,000-10,000 ft high, rises to mountains near the Great Rift Valley, cutting in from SW. Blue Nile and other rivers cross the plateau, which descends to plains on W and SE. **Arable land:** 15.1%. **Capital:** Addis Ababa, 3,316,220.

Government: Type: Federal parliamentary republic. **Head of state:** Pres. Mulatu Teshome Wirtu; in office: Oct. 7, 2013. **Head of gov.:** Prime Min. Hailemariam Desalegn; b. 1965; in office: Sept. 21, 2012. **Local divisions:** 9 states (ethnically based), 2 self-governing administrations. **Defense budget:** $399 mil. **Active troops:** 138,000.

Economy: Industries: food proc., beverages, textiles, leather, garments, chemicals, metals proc., cement. **Chief crops:** cereals, coffee, oilseed, cotton, sugarcane, vegetables, khat, cut flowers. **Natural resources:** gold, platinum, copper, potash, nat. gas, hydropower. **Water:** 1,227 cu m per capita. **Crude oil reserves** (2015): 430 bbls. **Electricity prod.:** 8.6 bil kWh. **Labor force:** agric. 85%, industry 5%, services 10%. **Unemployment:** 5.2%.

Finance: Monetary unit: Birr (ETB) (22.13 = $1 U.S.). **GDP:** $161.6 bil; **per capita GDP:** $1,800; **GDP growth:** 10.2%. **Imports:** $10.7 bil; China 20.4%, U.S. 9.2%, Saudi Arabia 6.5%. **Exports:** $3.8 bil; Switzerland 14.3%, China 11.7%, U.S. 9.5%,

Netherlands 8.8%, Saudi Arabia 5.9%, Germany 5.7%. **Tourism:** $394 mil. **Budget:** $11 bil. **Inflation:** 10.1%.

Transport: Railways: 423 mi (Ethiopian segment of Addis Ababa-Djibouti railroad). **Motor vehicles:** 1.6 per 1,000 pop. **Airports:** 17.

Communications: Telephone: 0.9 per 100 pop. **Mobile:** 42.8 per 100 pop. **Broadband:** 7.5 per 100 pop. **Internet:** 11.6%.

Health: Expend.: 4.9%. **Life expect.:** 59.8 male; 64.7 female. **Births:** 36.9 per 1,000 pop. **Deaths:** 7.9 per 1,000 pop. **Infant mortality:** 51.1 per 1,000 live births. **Undernourished:** 32%. **HIV:** NA.

Education: Compulsory: NA. **Literacy:** 49%.

Embassy: 3506 International Dr. NW 20008; 364-1200.

Website: www.ethiopia.gov.et

Ethiopian culture was influenced by Egypt and Greece. Italy invaded the region in 1880, but Ethiopia maintained its independence until the Italian invasion of 1936. British forces freed the country in 1941.

A series of droughts in the 1970s killed hundreds of thousands. An army mutiny, strikes, and student demonstrations led to the 1974 dethronement of Ethiopia's last emperor, Haile Selassie I, ending his 58-year reign; he died a prisoner of the ruling junta, known as the Dergue, 1975. The junta dissolved parliament, abolished the monarchy, established a socialist state, redistributed land, curbed the influence of the Coptic Church, and violently suppressed opposition.

The regime, torn by bloody coups, faced uprisings by tribal and political groups aided in part by Sudan and Somalia. Ties with the U.S., once a major ally, deteriorated, while cooperation accords were signed with the USSR in 1977. In 1978, Soviet advisers and Cuban troops helped defeat Somali forces. Ethiopia and Somalia signed a peace agreement in 1988. A worldwide relief effort began in 1984, as an extended drought precipitated famine; up to 1 mil people died as a result.

The Ethiopian People's Revolutionary Democratic Front (EPRDF), an umbrella group of six rebel armies, launched a major push against government forces in 1991, prompting Pres. Mengistu Haile Mariam's resignation. The EPRDF set up a transitional government. Ethiopia's first multiparty general elections were held in 1995.

Eritrea, a province on the Red Sea, declared its independence May 24, 1993. Fighting along the border with Eritrea, which erupted in 1998, intensified in May 2000, as Ethiopian forces entered Eritrean territory; a peace treaty was signed Dec. 12. The war displaced 350,000 Ethiopians.

The ruling EPRDF won parliamentary elections May 2005. In July 2006, Ethiopia sent troops into Somalia in response to advances by Islamist militias there. Tried in absentia, former Pres. Mengistu was convicted of genocide Dec. 12, 2006. Drought and other food supply disruptions occurred 2008-09. Ethiopia withdrew troops from Somalia Jan. 2009. The EPRDF dominated 2010 parliamentary elections, though the opposition contested the results. When Prime Min. Meles Zenawi died Aug. 2012, the EPRDF's Hailemariam Desalegn became prime min. Ethiopian troops joined an African Union peacekeeping force in Somalia in Jan. 2014. As of May 31, 2016, Ethiopia housed about 738,000 refugees, the largest numbers being from Somalia and South Sudan. The EPRDF won every seat in May 24, 2015, parliamentary elections. Pres. Barack Obama visited Ethiopia, July 2015, the first sitting U.S. president to do so. Drought again caused severe food shortages, 2015-16.

Ethiopia began construction, Apr. 2, 2013, of the Grand Renaissance Dam (Hidase) across the Blue Nile. The dam, which will be Africa's largest when completed (scheduled for 2017), raised concerns in Egypt and Sudan over loss of water resources.

Fiji
Republic of Fiji

People: Population: 915,303. **Age distrib.:** <15: 27.9%; 65+: 6.3%. **Growth:** 0.6%. **Migrants:** 1.5%. **Pop. density:** 129.7 per sq mi, 50.1 per sq km. **Urban:** 54.1%. **Ethnic groups:** iTaukei (predom. Melanesian with Polynesian admixture; name for original, native settlers of Fiji) 56.8%, Indian 37.5%, other (European, part European, other Pac. Islanders, Chinese) 4.5%. **Languages:** English, Fijian (both official); Hindustani. **Religions:** Protestant 45% (incl. Methodist 34.6%), Hindu 27.9%, Roman Catholic 9.1%, Muslim 6.3%.

Geography: Total area: 7,056 sq mi, 18,274 sq km; **Land area:** 7,056 sq mi, 18,274 sq km. Viti Levu, largest island of group, has over half the total land area. **Location:** Western S Pacific O. Nearest neighbors are Vanuatu to W, Tonga to E. **Topography:** 322 isls. (about 110 inhabited), many mountainous, with tropical forests and large fertile areas. **Arable land:** 9%. **Capital:** Suva, 176,397 (2014).

Government: Type: Parliamentary republic. **Head of state:** Pres. George Konrote; b. 1947; in office: Nov. 12, 2015. **Head of gov.:** Prime Min. Voreqe "Frank" Bainimarama; b. 1954; in office: Sept. 22, 2014 (acting from Jan. 5, 2007). **Local divisions:** 14 provinces, 1 dependency. **Defense budget:** $55 mil. **Active troops:** 3,500.

Economy: Industries: tourism, sugar, clothing, copra. **Chief crops:** sugarcane, coconuts, cassava, rice, sweet potatoes, bananas. **Natural resources:** timber, fish, gold, copper, hydropower. **Water:** 32,003 cu m per capita. **Electricity prod.:** 0.9 bil kWh. **Labor force:** agric. 70%, industry and services 30%. **Unemployment:** 7.9%.

Finance: Monetary unit: Dollar (FJD) (2.07 = $1 U.S.). **GDP:** $8 bil; **per capita GDP:** $9,000; **GDP growth:** 4.3%. **Imports:** $2.3 bil; China 16.2%, South Korea 15.7%, New Zealand 14%, Australia 13.4%, Singapore 8.7%, France 7%. **Exports:** $1.2 bil; U.S. 13.4%, Australia 10.2%, Samoa 6.7%, Tonga 5.9%. **Tourism:** $749 mil. **Budget:** $1.2 bil. **Inflation:** 1.4%.

Transport: Railways: 371 mi. **Motor vehicles:** 194.4 per 1,000 pop. **Airports:** 4.

Communications: Telephone: 8.1 per 100 pop. **Mobile:** 108.2 per 100 pop. **Broadband:** 42.3 per 100 pop. **Internet:** 46.3%.

Health: Expend.: 4.5%. **Life expect.:** 70.0 male; 75.5 female. **Births:** 19.0 per 1,000 pop. **Deaths:** 6.1 per 1,000 pop. **Infant mortality:** 9.7 per 1,000 live births. **Undernourished:** <5%. **HIV:** NA.

Education: Compulsory: NA. **Literacy:** NA.

Embassy: 1707 L St. NW, Ste. 200, 20036; 466-8320.

Website: www.fiji.gov.fj

A British colony since 1874, Fiji became independent Oct. 10, 1970. Cultural differences between the Indian community (mostly descendants of contract laborers brought to the islands in the 19th cent.) and indigenous Fijians have led to political tensions. More than 100,000 Indians left Fiji after a 1987 coup deposed an Indian-majority government.

Fiji's first Indian prime minister, Mahendra Chaudhry, and other government officials were taken captive May 19, 2000, by indigenous Fijian gunmen led by George Speight, culminating in a military takeover, May 29, led by Frank Bainimarama. Release of the last remaining hostages in July 2000 coincided with the installation of an interim military-backed government. Speight was convicted of treason and sentenced to life in prison in 2002. Prime Min. Laisenia Qarase headed an elected civilian government, 2001-06, but was ousted in a military coup Dec. 5, 2006. Bainimarama took office as interim prime min. After a court ruled in 2009 that the 2006 coup was illegal, Pres. Ratu Josefa Iloilo abrogated the constitution, dissolved the judiciary, and reappointed Interim Prime Min. Bainimarama. In July, Bainimarama promised a new constitution and legislative elections. He accepted a draft constitution released Mar. 22, 2013, and he retained office in democratic elections Sept. 17, 2014. The Commonwealth, Sept. 26, 2014, reinstated Fiji's membership, which had been suspended since the 2006 coup; U.S. sanctions were lifted Oct. 2014. Cyclone Winston, a Category 5 storm, killed 44 and caused widespread damage when it struck, Feb. 20, 2016.

Finland
Republic of Finland

People: Population: 5,498,211. **Age distrib.:** <15: 16.4%; 65+: 20.7%. **Growth:** 0.4%. **Migrants:** 5.7%. **Pop. density:** 46.9 per sq mi, 18.1 per sq km. **Urban:** 84.4%. **Ethnic groups:** Finn 93.4%, Swede 5.6%. **Languages:** Finnish, Swedish (both official). **Religions:** Lutheran 73.8%, other or none 25.1%.

Geography: Total area: 130,559 sq mi, 338,145 sq km; **Land area:** 117,304 sq mi, 303,815 sq km. **Location:** Northern Europe. Norway on N, Sweden on W, Russia on E. **Topography:** Flat with low hills and many lakes in S and center. The N has mountainous areas 3,000-4,000 ft above sea level. **Arable land:** 7.3%. **Capital:** Helsinki, 1,189,821.

Government: Type: Parliamentary republic. **Head of state:** Pres. Sauli Niinistö; b. 1948; in office: Mar. 1, 2012. **Head of gov.:** Prime Min. Juha Sipilä; b. 1961; in office: May 29, 2015. **Local divisions:** 19 regions. **Defense budget:** $3.0 bil. **Active troops:** 22,200.

Economy: Industries: metals and metal prods., electronics, machinery and scientific instruments, shipbuilding, pulp and paper, foodstuffs. **Chief crops:** barley, wheat, sugar beets, potatoes. **Natural resources:** timber, iron ore, copper, lead, zinc, chromite, nickel, gold, silver, limestone. **Water:** 19,989 cu m per capita. **Electricity prod.:** 68 bil kWh. **Labor force:** agric. and forestry 4.4%; industry 15.5%; constr. 7.1%; commerce 21.3%; finance, insurance, and business services 13.3%; transp. and communications 9.9%; public services 28.5%. **Unemployment:** 8.6%.

Finance: Monetary unit: Euro (EUR) (0.89 = $1 U.S.). **GDP:** $225 bil; **per capita GDP:** $41,100; **GDP growth:** 0.4%. **Imports:** $58.1 bil; Germany 17%, Sweden 16%, Russia 11%, Netherlands 9.1%. **Exports:** $66.9 bil; Germany 13.9%, Sweden 10.1%, U.S. 7%, Netherlands 6.6%, Russia 5.9%, UK 5.2%. **Tourism:** $2.8 bil. **Budget:** $137.3 bil (central govt. budget). **Inflation:** -0.2%.

Transport: Railways: 3,678 mi. **Motor vehicles:** 700.3 per 1,000 pop. **Airports:** 74.

Communications: Telephone: 9.8 per 100 pop. **Mobile:** 135.5 per 100 pop. **Broadband:** 138.5 per 100 pop. **Internet:** 92.7%.

Health: Expend.: 9.7%. **Life expect.:** 77.9 male; 84.0 female. **Births:** 10.7 per 1,000 pop. **Deaths:** 9.9 per 1,000 pop. **Infant mortality:** 2.5 per 1,000 live births. **Undernourished:** <5%. **HIV:** NA.

Education: Compulsory: ages 7-16. **Literacy:** 100%.

Embassy: 3301 Massachusetts Ave. NW 20008; 298-5800.

Website: valtioneuvosto.fi

Early Finns may have migrated from the Ural region and other areas about 6,000 years ago. Swedish settlers brought the country into Sweden, 1154 to 1809, when Finland became an autonomous grand duchy of the Russian Empire. On Dec. 6, 1917, Finland declared its independence, and in 1919 it became a republic. On Nov. 30, 1939, the Soviet Union invaded, and Finland was forced to cede 16,173 sq mi of territory. After World War II, further cessions were exacted. In 1948, Finland signed a treaty of mutual assistance with the USSR that was renegotiated as a cooperation agreement with Russia, effective July 11, 1992, after the dissolution of the USSR, Dec. 26, 1991.

Finland entered the EU Jan. 1, 1995. Former Pres. Martti Ahtisaari was awarded the Nobel Peace Prize, Oct. 10, 2008, for mediating international conflicts. The conservative Sauli Niinistö won the 2012 presidential election. Juha Sipilä's Center Party won the most seats in Apr. 19, 2015, parliamentary elections; he formed a center-right government. About 32,000 refugees and other migrants applied for asylum in Finland in 2015. The government announced, Jan. 28, 2016, it would deport rejected asylum applicants, and Finland concluded border security agreements with Russia, Mar. 2016, to reduce migrant crossings.

Aland, or Ahvenanmaa, an autonomous, Swedish-speaking province, is a group of small islands, 590 sq mi, in the Gulf of Bothnia, 25 mi from Sweden, 15 mi from Finland. Mariehamn is the chief port and seat of government. **Website:** www.aland.ax

France
French Republic

People: Population: 66,836,154. **Age distrib.:** <15: 18.6%; 65+: 19.1%. **Growth:** 0.4%. **Migrants:** 12.1%. **Pop. density:** 270.3 per sq mi, 104.4 per sq km. **Urban:** 79.8%. **Ethnic groups:** Celtic and Latin with Teutonic, Slavic, North African, Indochinese, Basque minorities. **Languages:** French (official); rapidly declining regional dialects and langs. (Provençal, Breton, Alsatian, Corsican, Catalan, Basque, Flemish). **Religions:** Christian (overwhelmingly Roman Catholic) 63%-66%, Muslim 7%-9%, none 23%-28%. France maintains a tradition of secularism.

Geography: Total area: 248,573 sq mi, 643,801 sq km; **Land area:** 247,270 sq mi, 640,427 sq km. **Location:** Western Europe, between Atlantic O. and Medit. Sea. Spain, Andorra, Monaco on S; Italy, Switzerland, Germany on E; Luxembourg, Belgium on N. **Topography:** A wide plain covers more than half of the country, in N and W, drained to W by Seine, Loire, Garonne Rivers. The Alps (Mt. Blanc is tallest in W Europe at 15,771 ft), the lower Jura range, and forested Vosges are in E. The Rhone flows from Lake Geneva to Mediterranean. Pyrenees are on SW border. **Arable land:** 33.4%. **Capital:** Paris, 10,925,231. **Cities:** Lyon, 1,621,561; Marseille-Aix-en-Provence, 1,615,603; Lille, 1,030,344.

Government: Type: Semi-presidential republic. **Head of state:** Pres. François Hollande; b. 1954; in office: May 15, 2012. **Head of gov.:** Prime Min. Manuel Valls; b. 1962; in office: Mar. 31, 2014. **Local divisions:** 13 metropolitan regions, 5 overseas regions. **Defense budget:** $46.8 bil. **Active troops:** 208,950.

Economy: Industries: machinery, chemicals, automobiles, metallurgy, aircraft, electronics, textiles, food proc., tourism. **Chief crops:** wheat, cereals, sugar beets, potatoes, wine grapes. **Natural resources:** coal, iron ore, bauxite, zinc, uranium, antimony, arsenic, potash, feldspar, fluorspar, gypsum, timber, fish. **Water:** 3,277 cu m per capita. **Crude oil reserves:** 0.1 bil bbls. **Other resources:** Timber, dairy. **Electricity prod.:** 539 bil kWh. **Labor force:** agric. 3%, industry 21.3%, services 75.7%. **Unemployment:** 9.9%.

Finance: Monetary unit: Euro (EUR) (0.89 = $1 U.S.). **GDP:** $2.6 tril; **per capita GDP:** $41,200; **GDP growth:** 1.1%. **Imports:** $539 bil; Germany 19.5%, Belgium 10.7%, Italy 7.7%, Netherlands 7.5%, Spain 6.8%, U.S. 5.5%, China 5.4%. **Exports:** $509.1 bil; Germany 15.9%, Spain 7.3%, U.S. 7.2%, Italy 7.1%, UK 7.1%, Belgium 6.8%. **Tourism:** $45.9 bil. **Budget:** $1.4 tril. **Inflation:** 0.04%.

Transport: Railways: 18,417 mi. **Motor vehicles:** 580.8 per 1,000 pop. **Airports:** 294.

Communications: Telephone: 59.9 per 100 pop. **Mobile:** 102.6 per 100 pop. **Broadband:** 66.2 per 100 pop. **Internet:** 84.7%.

Health: Expend.: 11.5%. **Life expect.:** 78.7 male; 85.1 female. **Births:** 12.3 per 1,000 pop. **Deaths:** 9.3 per 1,000 pop. **Infant mortality:** 3.3 per 1,000 live births. **Undernourished:** <5%. **HIV:** NA.

Education: Compulsory: ages 6-16. **Literacy:** 99%.

Embassy: 4101 Reservoir Rd. NW 20007; 944-6000.

Website: www.gouvernement.fr

Julius Caesar conquered Celtic Gaul 58-51 BCE; Romans ruled for 500 years. Under Charlemagne, Frankish rule extended over much of Europe. After his death, France emerged as one of the successor kingdoms.

The monarchy was overthrown in the French Revolution (1789-93) and succeeded by the First Republic, followed by the First Empire under Napoleon I (1804-15), a monarchy (1814-48), the Second Republic (1848-52), the Second Empire (1852-70), the Third Republic (1871-1946), the Fourth Republic (1946-58), and the Fifth Republic (1958-present).

France suffered severe losses in people and wealth in WWI (1914-18) when it was invaded by Germany. By the Treaty of Versailles, 1919, France exacted return of Alsace and Lorraine, provinces seized by Germany in 1871 after it defeated France in the Franco-Prussian War. During WWII (1939-45), Germany invaded France in May 1940 and signed an armistice with a government based in Vichy. After the Allies liberated France in 1944, Gen. Charles de Gaulle became head of the provisional government, serving until 1946. De Gaulle again became premier in 1958, during a crisis over Algeria, and obtained voter approval for a new constitution, ushering in the Fifth Republic. He then became president.

France withdrew from Indochina in 1954 and from Morocco and Tunisia in 1956. Most of its remaining African territories, including Algeria, were freed 1958-62.

In May 1968, students in Paris and other centers rioted, battled police, and were joined by workers who launched nationwide strikes. De Gaulle resigned from office in Apr. 1969, after losing a nationwide referendum on constitutional reform. Georges Pompidou was elected to succeed him. After Pompidou's death, in 1974, Valery Giscard d'Estaing was elected president; he continued his predecessors' conservative policies.

In 1981, France elected Socialist François Mitterrand president. Under Mitterrand the government nationalized five major industries and most private banks. After 1986, however, when rightists won a narrow victory in the National Assembly, Mitterrand chose conservative Jacques Chirac as premier. During a two-year period of "cohabitation," France pursued a privatization program, selling many state-owned companies. During Mitterrand's second 7-year term starting in 1988, he appointed first a Socialist as premier, then a conservative after the center-right won a large majority in 1993 legislative elections.

Chirac won the 1995 presidency in a runoff election. He cut government spending to meet budgetary goals for the introduction of the euro. With unemployment at nearly 13%, leftist parties won a decisive victory in 1997 legislative elections, resulting in a new period of cohabitation. Chirac easily won the 2002 presidential election in a runoff, and his center-right allies won parliamentary elections. Parliament gave final approval in 2004 to a law barring the wearing of Islamic head scarves and other religious symbols in public schools.

Displeased with sluggish economic growth, high unemployment, and budget cuts in entitlement programs, voters rejected, 2005, a proposed EU constitution supported by the Chirac government. A state of emergency was declared Nov. 8 after 12 days of riots that began in Paris and spread to some 300 French cities and towns; rioters were mainly young immigrants from N and W Africa.

The conservative Nicolas Sarkozy won the 2007 presidential runoff election. Sarkozy responded to the global recession, Dec. 2008, with a $33-bil economic stimulus plan; measures announced Feb. 2009, following labor protests, added $3.3 bil in aid for lower-income people. With France's economy still struggling, the Socialist François Hollande won a presidential runoff over Sarkozy in 2012, and the Socialist Party won an absolute majority in parliamentary elections. Hollande, May 18, 2013, signed a bill that legalized same-sex marriage and allowed gay couples to adopt children. After a weak showing by Socialists in Mar. 2014 municipal elections and with the economy still sluggish, Prime Min. Jean-Marc Ayrault was replaced by centrist Socialist Manuel Valls. In European Parliament elections May 25, 2014, the far-right National Front was the largest vote-getter, with 25%.

France, a founding NATO member, formally returned to the alliance's military command structure Apr. 2009 after 43 years. In Dec. 2014, France withdrew its last troops deployed with NATO forces in Afghanistan. France participated in military operations that ousted Libyan leader Muammar al-Qaddafi, Aug. 23, 2011. In 2014-16, France took part in the U.S.-led campaign of airstrikes in Iraq against the Sunni extremist group ISIS. In Sept. 2015, France began airstrikes against ISIS targets in Syria. French troops entered the conflict between government forces in Mali and Islamist militants Jan. 11, 2013; they pushed the militants out of most seized territory. France maintained a counterterrorism force in the region, consisting of about 3,500 troops in mid-2016.

On Jan. 7, 2015, two French gunmen of Algerian descent attacked the Paris offices of the magazine *Charlie Hebdo*, which had published satirical images of Muhammad. The gunmen, who claimed affiliation with al-Qaeda in the Arabian Peninsula, killed 12 people, including magazine staff and police officers, before fleeing. They were killed in a shootout with police, Jan. 9. In coordinated attacks in Paris, a third gunman, who claimed loyalty to ISIS, fatally shot a police officer Jan. 8 and killed 4 people and took hostages at a kosher supermarket Jan. 9, before being killed by police. On the night of Nov. 13, 2015, in coordinated attacks in and near Paris

for which ISIS claimed responsibility, terrorist gunmen and suicide bombers killed 130. Most victims were killed by gunmen in Paris's Bataclan concert hall or outside restaurants. In a July 14, 2016, attack ISIS claimed to have inspired, a Tunisian-born French resident drove a truck through a Bastille Day fireworks crowd in Nice, killing 86 people before he was fatally shot by police; by Sept. 30, 2016, more than a dozen suspects linked to the attacker had been arrested.

France ratified, June 15, 2016, a global agreement to reduce greenhouse gas emissions negotiated at a UN climate conference in Paris, Dec. 2015.

The island of **Corsica**, in the Mediterranean W of Italy and N of Sardinia, is a territorial collectivity and region of France comprising two departments. It elects 2 senators and 3 deputies to the French Parliament. Area 3,369 sq mi; pop. (2014 est.) 323,092. The capital is Ajaccio, birthplace of Napoleon I. Violence by Corsican separatist groups, especially in the 1980s and 1990s, hurt tourism, a leading industry. Corsicans rejected, 51%-49%, a limited autonomy plan in a referendum July 6, 2003. Violence by criminal gangs has been widespread in recent years. **Website:** www.corse.fr

French Overseas Departments

French Guiana is on the NE coast of South America with Suriname on the W and Brazil on the E and S. Its area is 35,135 sq mi (total), 34,421 sq mi (land); pop. (2014 est.) 250,377. Guiana sends one senator and two deputies to the French Parliament. Guiana is administered by a prefect and has a Council General of 16 elected members; capital is Cayenne.

The famous penal colony, Devil's Island, was phased out between 1938 and 1951. The European Space Agency maintains a satellite-launching center (established by France in 1964) in the city of Kourou.

Immense forests of rich timber cover 88% of the land. Fishing (especially shrimp), forestry, and gold mining are the most important industries. Natural resources include petroleum, kaolin, niobium, tantalum, and clay.

Guadeloupe, in the West Indies' Leeward Islands, consists of two large islands, Basse-Terre and Grande-Terre, separated by the Salt R., plus Marie Galante and the Saintes group to the S and, to the N, Desirade. A French possession since 1635, the department is represented in the French Parliament; administration consists of a prefect (governor) as well as an elected general and regional councils.

Area of the islands is 525 sq mi; pop. (2014 est., incl. St. Barthélemy, St. Martin) 403,750, mainly descendants of slaves; capital is Basse-Terre (2014 est. pop: 55,295) on Basse-Terre Island. The land is fertile; sugar, rum, and bananas are exported. Tourism is an important industry. International tourism receipts in 2013 were $671 mil.

Martinique, the northernmost of the Windward Islands, in the West Indies, has been a possession since 1635, and a department since Mar. 1946. It is represented in the French Parliament by 2 senators and 4 deputies. The island was the birthplace of Napoleon's first wife, Empress Josephine.

It has an area of 425 sq mi (total), 409 sq mi (land); pop. (2014 est.) 381,326, mostly descendants of slaves. The capital is Fort-de-France; pop. (2014 est.) 85,817. It is a popular tourist stop; 2014 international tourism receipts were $483 mil. The chief exports are rum, bananas, and petroleum products. **Website:** www.collectivitedemartinique.mq

Mayotte, claimed by Comoros and administered by France, voted in 1976 to become a territorial collectivity of France. An island NW of Madagascar, area is 144 sq mi, pop. (2012 est.) 216,000. The capital is Mamoudzou; pop. (2014 est.) 5,715. In a Mar. 29, 2009, referendum, 95% of voters endorsed a plan under which Mayotte became an overseas department of France as of Mar. 31, 2011.

Réunion is a volcanic island in the Indian O. about 420 mi E of Madagascar, and has belonged to France since 1665. Area, 972 sq mi (total), 968 sq mi (land); pop. (2014 est.) 844,994, 30% of French extraction. Capital: Saint-Denis; pop. (2014 est.) 143,617. The chief export is sugar. International tourism receipts in 2014 were $387 mil. It elects 5 deputies, 3 senators to the French Parliament. **Website:** www.regionreunion.com

French Overseas Territorial Collectivities

French Polynesia, comprises 130 islands widely scattered among 5 archipelagos in the S Pacific; administered by a Council of Ministers (headed by a president). Territorial Assembly and the Council have headquarters at Papeete, on Tahiti, one of the Society Islands (which include the Windward Isls. and Leeward Isls.) Two deputies and a senator are elected to the French Parliament.

Other groups are the Marquesas Isls.; the Tuamotu Archipelago the Gambier Isls.; and the Austral, or Tubuai, Isls.

Total area of the islands administered from Tahiti is 1,609 sq mi (total), 1,478 sq mi (land); pop. (2016 est.) 285,321. Tahiti is mountainous with a productive coastline bearing coconuts, citrus, pineapples, and vanilla. Tourism is the largest industry.

Tahiti was visited by Capt. James Cook in 1769 and by Capt Bligh in the *Bounty*, 1788-89. Its beauty impressed Herman

Melville, Paul Gauguin, and Charles Darwin. A coalition favoring independence for French Polynesia within 20 years gained control of the territorial assembly after elections May 23, 2004. An anti-independence party won May 5, 2013, elections. A UN General Assembly resolution May 17, 2013, called on France to grant French Polynesia independence. A 2013-14 Zika virus outbreak affected about 28,000 people.

St. Pierre and Miquelon became a territorial collectivity in 1985. It consists of two groups of rocky islands near the SW coast of Newfoundland, inhabited by fishermen. Fish products are the chief export. The St. Pierre group has an area of 10 sq mi; Miquelon, 83 sq mi. Total pop. (2016 est.) 5,595. Capital: Saint-Pierre; pop. (2014 est.) 5,459. Both Mayotte and St. Pierre and Miquelon elect a deputy and a senator to the French Parliament.

St. Barthélemy and **St. Martin**, both formerly part of Guadeloupe, voted for secession in 2003 and became overseas territorial collectivities in 2007. Total area 10 sq mi and 21 sq mi; total pop. (2016 est.) 7,209 and 31,949 respectively.

The territorial collectivity of **Wallis and Futuna** comprises two island groups in the SW Pacific S of Tuvalu, N of Fiji, and W of Western Samoa. It became an overseas territory July 29, 1961. The islands have a total area of 55 sq mi and pop. (2016 est.) of 15,664. Alofi, attached to Futuna, is uninhabited. Capital: Mata-Utu; pop. (2014 est.) 1,064. Chief exports are copra, chemicals, and construction materials. A senator and a deputy are elected to the French Parliament.

Overseas Territory and Special Collectivity

The territory of the **French Southern and Antarctic Lands** comprises island groups in the Indian O. Area: 2,991 sq mi (total), 2,960 sq mi (land).

The U.S. does not recognize French claim to Adelie Land, an area of about 193,051 sq mi on Antarctica. Adelie, reached 1840, has a 185-mi coastline and tapers 1,240 mi inland to the S Pole. It has a research station. There are two glaciers: Ninnis, 22 mi wide, 99 mi long, and Mentz, 11 mi by 140 mi.

The Indian O. groups are as follows: Kerguelen Archipelago, visited 1772, consists of one large and 300 small islands. The chief is 87 mi long, 74 mi wide, and has Mt. Ross (6,429 ft). Principal research station is Port-aux-Français. There are seals, blue whales, coal, peat, semiprecious stones. Crozet Archipelago, reached 1772, covers 136 sq mi. Eastern Island rises to 6,560 ft. Volcanic Saint Paul, in southern Indian O., has warm springs. Amsterdam Island is nearby; both produce cod and rock lobster. Military garrisons and meteorological stations are located on the Scattered Isls.

The special collectivity of **New Caledonia** and Dependencies is a group of islands in the Pacific O. about 1,115 mi E of Australia and approx. the same distance NW of New Zealand. Dependencies are the Loyalty Isls., Isle of Pines, Belep Archipelago, and Huon Isls.

The largest island, New Caledonia, is 6,530 sq mi. Total area of the territory is 7,172 sq mi (total), 7,056 sq mi (land); pop. (2016 est.) 275,355. The group was acquired by France in 1853.

The territory is administered by a High Commissioner. There is a popularly elected Territorial Congress. Two deputies and a senator are elected to the French Parliament. Capital: Nouméa; pop. (2014 est.) 181,002.

Mining is the chief industry. New Caledonia is one of the world's largest nickel producers. Chrome, iron, cobalt, manganese, silver, gold, lead, and copper are also found. Agric. products include yams, sweet potatoes, potatoes, cassava, corn, and coconuts.

In 1987, New Caledonian voters chose by referendum to remain within the Republic. French and Melanesians (Kanaks) clashed in 1988. An agreement Apr. 21, 1998, between France and rival New Caledonian factions specified a 15- to 20-year period of shared sovereignty and a referendum on independence no later than 2018. Parties favoring remaining part of France won a majority in May 11, 2014, Territorial Congress elections. **Website:** www.gouv.nc

Gabon
Gabonese Republic

People: Population: 1,738,541. **Age distrib.:** <15: 42%; 65+: 3.8%. **Growth:** 1.9%. **Migrants:** 15.6%. **Pop. density:** 17.5 per sq mi, 6.7 per sq km. **Urban:** 87.4%. **Ethnic groups:** Bantu tribes, incl. four major groupings (Fang, Bapounou, Nzebi, Obamba). **Languages:** French (official), Fang, Myene, Nzebi, Bapounou/Eschira, Bandjabi. **Religions:** Catholic 41.9%, Protestant 13.7%, other Christian 32.4%, Muslim 6.4%.

Geography: Total area: 103,347 sq mi, 267,667 sq km; **Land area:** 99,486 sq mi, 257,667 sq km. **Location:** Atlantic coast of W central Africa. Equatorial Guinea, Cameroon on N; Congo Republic on E and S. **Topography:** Heavily forested, consisting of coastal lowlands; plateaus in N, E, and S; mountains in N, SE, and center. The Ogooue R. system covers most of Gabon. **Arable land:** 1.3%. **Capital:** Libreville, 720,091.

Government: Type: Presidential republic. **Head of state:** Pres. Ali Bongo Ondimba; b. 1959; in office: Oct. 16, 2009. **Head of gov.:**

Prime Min. Daniel Ona Ondo; b. 1945; in office: Jan. 25, 2014. **Local divisions:** 9 provinces. **Defense budget:** $197 mil. **Active troops:** 4,700.

Economy: Industries: petroleum extraction and refining; manganese, gold; chemicals, ship repair, food and beverages. **Chief crops:** cocoa, coffee, sugar, palm oil, rubber. **Natural resources:** petroleum, nat. gas, diamonds, niobium, manganese, uranium, gold, timber, iron ore, hydropower. **Water:** 96,232 cu m per capita. **Crude oil reserves:** 2 bil bbls. **Electricity prod.:** 2.3 bil kWh. **Labor force:** agric. 60%, industry 15%, services 25%. **Unemployment:** 19.7%.

Finance: Monetary unit: Central African CFA Franc (XAF) (586.00 = $1 U.S.). **GDP:** $34.6 bil; **per capita GDP:** $18,600; **GDP growth:** 4%. **Imports:** $2.4 bil; China 21.4%, France 19.6%, U.S. 6.5%. **Exports:** $5.6 bil; China 15.5%, Italy 7.3%, Trinidad and Tobago 7.2%, Australia 7%, Spain 6.3%, South Korea 5.4%, Netherlands 5%. **Budget:** $3.9 bil. **Inflation:** 0.6%.

Transport: Railways: 403 mi. **Airports:** 14.

Communications: Telephone: 1.1 per 100 pop. **Mobile:** 168.9 per 100 pop. **Broadband:** 0.0 per 100 pop. **Internet:** 23.5%.

Health: Expend.: 3.4%. **Life expect.:** 51.6 male; 52.5 female. **Births:** 34.3 per 1,000 pop. **Deaths:** 13.1 per 1,000 pop. **Infant mortality:** 45.1 per 1,000 live births. **Undernourished:** <5%. **HIV:** 3.8%.

Education: Compulsory: ages 6-15. **Literacy:** 83.2%.

Embassy: 2034 20th St. NW 20009; 797-1000.

Website: www.gouvernement.ga or www.state.gov/p/af/ci/gb/

France established control over the region in the second half of the 19th cent. Gabon became independent Aug. 17, 1960. Backed by France, Pres. Albert-Bernard Bongo (later Omar Bongo Ondimba) ruled the country 1967-2009, greatly enriching himself and his family. A multiparty political system was introduced in 1990. Bongo's reelection victories in 1993, 1998, and 2003 were faulted by international observers. After he died June 8, 2009, his son Ali Bongo Ondimba claimed victory in the disputed 2009 presidential election. Bongo was declared the winner of the Aug. 27, 2016, presidential election. Violent protests followed, and the opposition rejected the result as fraudulent. However, the Constitutional Court confirmed the result in Sept. 2016.

Gabon has abundant natural resources (including oil) and is one of the most prosperous African countries, although there is extreme income inequality.

The Gambia
Islamic Republic of The Gambia

People: Population: 2,009,648. **Age distrib.:** <15: 37.9%; 65+: 3.4%. **Growth:** 2.1%. **Migrants:** 9.7%. **Pop. density:** 514.3 per sq mi, 198.6 per sq km. **Urban:** 60.2%. **Ethnic groups:** Mandinka/Jahanka 33.8%, Fulani/Tukulur/Lorobo 22.1%, Wollof 12.2%, Jola/Karoninka 10.9%, Serahuleh 7%, Serere 3.2%, Manjago 2.1%. **Languages:** English (official), Mandinka, Wolof, Fula, other indigenous vernaculars. **Religions:** Muslim 95.7%, Christian 4.2%.

Geography: Total area: 4,363 sq mi, 11,300 sq km; **Land area:** 3,907 sq mi, 10,120 sq km. **Location:** Atlantic coast near W tip of Africa. Surrounded on 3 sides by Senegal. **Topography:** Narrow strip of land on each side of lower Gambia R. **Arable land:** 43.5%. **Capital:** Banjul, 518,736.

Government: Type: Presidential republic. **Head of state and gov.:** Pres. Yahya Jammeh; b. 1965; in office: Oct. 18, 1996. **Local divisions:** 5 divisions, 1 city. **Defense budget** (2013): $10 mil. **Active troops:** 800.

Economy: Industries: peanuts, fish, hides, tourism, beverages, agric. machinery assembly. **Chief crops:** rice, millet, sorghum, peanuts, corn, sesame, cassava, palm kernels. **Natural resources:** fish, clay, silica sand, titanium, tin, zircon. **Water:** 4,018 cu m per capita. **Electricity prod.:** 0.3 bil kWh. **Labor force:** agric. 75%, industry 19%, services 6%. **Unemployment:** 7%.

Finance: Monetary unit: Dalasi (GMD) (42.34 = $1 U.S.). **GDP:** $3.3 bil; **per capita GDP:** $1,600; **GDP growth:** 4.4%. **Imports:** $310 mil; China 34.2%, Brazil 8.1%, Senegal 6.9%, India 5.7%. **Exports:** $102.5 mil; China 47.5%, India 27.2%, France 5.9%. **Tourism:** $88 mil. **Budget:** $324.4 mil. **Inflation** (2013-14): 5.9%.

Transport: Airports: 1.

Communications: Telephone: 2.3 per 100 pop. **Mobile:** 131.3 per 100 pop. **Broadband:** 8 per 100 pop. **Internet:** 17.1%.

Health: Expend.: 7.3%. **Life expect.:** 62.5 male; 67.3 female. **Births:** 30.1 per 1,000 pop. **Deaths:** 7.1 per 1,000 pop. **Infant mortality:** 62.0 per 1,000 live births. **Undernourished:** 5.3%. **HIV:** 1.8%.

Education: Compulsory: ages 7-15. **Literacy:** 55.6%.

Embassy: 2233 Wisconsin Ave. NW, Ste. 240, 20007; 785-1399.

Website: statehouse.gov.gm

The peoples of The Gambia were at one time associated with the West African empires of Ghana, Mali, and Songhai. The area became Britain's first African possession in 1588.

Independence came Feb. 18, 1965; republic status within the Commonwealth was achieved in 1970. The country suffered from severe famine in the 1970s. Senegambia, a confederation with Senegal, lasted from 1982 to 1989.

On July 22, 1994, after 24 years in power, Pres. Dawda K. Jawara was deposed in a bloodless coup by a military officer, Yahya Jammeh. Jammeh barred political activity, detained potential opponents, and governed by decree. Despite a nominal return to constitutional government in 1996, Jammeh retained a tight grip on power. He won a fourth 5-year term in 2011. The Gambia withdrew from the Commonwealth, Oct. 2013. Jammeh proclaimed the country an Islamic republic, Dec. 2015. With per capita GDP of about $1,600 in 2015, The Gambia is one of the world's poorest countries.

Georgia

People: Population: 4,928,052. **Age distrib.:** <15: 17.9%; 65+: 15.8%. **Growth:** –0.1%. **Migrants:** 4.2%. **Pop. density:** 183.1 per sq mi, 70.7 per sq km. **Urban:** 53.8%. **Ethnic groups:** Georgian 83.8%, Azeri 6.5%, Armenian 5.7%. **Languages:** Georgian (official), Russian, Armenian, Azeri, Abkhaz (official in Abkhazia). **Religions:** Orthodox Christian (official) 83.9%, Muslim 9.9%, Armenian-Gregorian 3.9%.

Geography: Total area: 26,911 sq mi, 69,700 sq km; **Land area:** 26,911 sq mi, 69,700 sq km. **Location:** SW Asia, on E coast of Black Sea. Russia on N and NE, Turkey and Armenia on S, Azerbaijan on SE. **Topography:** Main range of Caucasus Mts. in NE separates country from Russia. **Arable land:** 6.5%. **Capital:** Tbilisi, 1,145,475.

Government: Type: Semi-presidential republic. **Head of state:** Pres. Giorgi Margvelashvili; b. 1969; in office: Nov. 17, 2013. **Head of gov.:** Prime Min. Giorgi Kvirikashvili; b. 1967; in office: Dec. 30, 2015. **Local divisions:** 9 regions, 1 city, 2 autonomous republics. **Defense budget:** $307 mil. **Active troops:** 20,650.

Economy: Industries: steel, machine tools, elec. appliances, mining, chemicals, wood prods., wine. **Chief crops:** citrus, grapes, tea, hazelnuts, vegetables. **Natural resources:** timber, hydropower, manganese, iron ore, copper, minor coal and oil deposits. **Water:** 15,832 cu m per capita. **Crude oil reserves** (2015): 35 mil bbls. **Electricity prod.:** 9.9 bil kWh. **Labor force:** agric. 55.6%, industry 8.9%, services 35.5%. **Unemployment:** 13.4%.

Finance: Monetary unit: Lari (GEL) (2.29 = $1 U.S.). **GDP:** $35.6 bil; **per capita GDP:** $9,600; **GDP growth:** 2.8%. **Imports:** $7.5 bil; Turkey 17.2%, Russia 8.1%, China 7.6%, Azerbaijan 7%, Ireland 5.9%, Ukraine 5.9%, Germany 5.6%. **Exports:** $3.5 bil; Azerbaijan 10.9%, Bulgaria 9.7%, Turkey 8.4%, Armenia 8.2%, Russia 7.4%, China 5.7%. **Tourism:** $1.9 bil. **Budget:** $4.3 bil. **Inflation:** 4%.

Transport: Railways: 847 mi. **Airports:** 18.

Communications: Telephone: 22.1 per 100 pop. **Mobile:** 129 per 100 pop. **Broadband:** 21.8 per 100 pop. **Internet:** 45.2%.

Health: Expend.: 7.4%. **Life expect.:** 72.1 male; 80.6 female. **Births:** 12.5 per 1,000 pop. **Deaths:** 10.9 per 1,000 pop. **Infant mortality:** 15.6 per 1,000 live births. **Undernourished:** 7.4%. **HIV:** 0.4%.

Education: Compulsory: ages 6-14. **Literacy:** 99.8%.

Embassy: 1824-1826 R St. NW 20008; 387-2390.

Website: www.gov.ge

The region, which contained the ancient kingdoms of Colchis and Iberia, was Christianized in the 4th cent. and conquered by Arabs in the 8th cent. Annexed by Russia in 1801, Georgia was forcibly incorporated into the USSR in 1922.

Georgia declared independence Apr. 9, 1991, and became an independent country when the Soviet Union disbanded Dec. 26. After a power struggle, former Soviet Foreign Min. Eduard A. Shevardnadze became president. He survived several coup attempts and won reelection in 1995 and 2000. Parliamentary elections Nov. 2, 2003, denounced as fraudulent by opposition groups and international observers, sparked massive antigovernment protests, causing Shevardnadze to resign Nov. 23. Opposition leader Mikhail Saakashvili won the 2004 presidential election. He survived an apparent assassination attempt along with U.S. Pres. George W. Bush in Tbilisi May 10, 2005. He suppressed an alleged coup plot Sept. 6, 2006, and cracked down violently on antigovernment protests and imposed a state of emergency, Nov. 7-16, 2007. He called early elections, Jan. 2008, which he won. Giorgi Margvelashvili of the recently formed Georgian Dream coalition, which won 2012 parliamentary elections, was elected president Oct. 27, 2013. Irakli Garibashvili of Georgian Dream became prime min., Nov. 20, 2013, a post with greatly increased powers under constitutional revisions. Giorgi Kvirikashvili, also of Georgian Dream, became prime min., Dec. 30, 2015. Georgia signed an economic cooperation agreement with the EU, June 27, 2014. Saakashvili (then living in the U.S.) was charged, July 28, 2014, with abuse of power in connection with the suppression of the Nov. 2007 protests. He was stripped of his Georgian citizenship, Dec. 2015, after he was given Ukrainian citizenship and appointed governor of Ukraine's Odessa region in May 2015.

Since independence, secessionist movements in the enclaves of South Ossetia and Abkhazia, supported by Russia, have rejected the Tbilisi government. Open warfare between Georgia and Russia erupted when Saakashvili sent troops, Aug. 7, 2008, to suppress insurgent activity in Tskhinvali, the South Ossetian capital. Russia, Aug. 8-9, dispatched forces to South Ossetia and Abkhazia and attacked key Georgian cities. A cease-fire signed Aug. 15-16 called for withdrawal of Russian forces from Georgia proper, but allowed thousands of Russian troops to remain in the breakaway regions. Russia, Aug. 2008, formally recognized South Ossetia and Abkhazia's independence; almost all other nations have not extended recognition. South Ossetia Pres. Leonid Tibilov, who won a runoff election in Apr. 2012, signed a military cooperation treaty with Russia, Mar. 18, 2015. Raul Khajimba won an Aug. 2014 presidential election in Abkhazia; he signed a new cooperation agreement with Russia, Nov. 24, 2014.

Germany
Federal Republic of Germany

People: Population: 80,722,792. **Age distrib.:** <15: 12.8%; 65+: 21.8%. **Growth:** –0.2%. **Migrants:** 14.9%. **Pop. density:** 599.6 per sq mi, 231.5 per sq km. **Urban:** 75.5%. **Ethnic groups:** German 91.5%, Turkish 2.4%, other (largely Greek, Italian, Polish, Russian, Serbo-Croatian, Spanish) 6.1%. **Languages:** German (official); Danish, Frisian, Sorbian, Romany (all official minority langs.). **Religions:** Protestant 34%, Roman Catholic 34%, Muslim 3.7%.

Geography: Total area: 137,847 sq mi, 357,022 sq km; **Land area:** 134,623 sq mi, 348,672 sq km. **Location:** Central Europe. Denmark on N; Netherlands, Belgium, Luxembourg, France on W; Switzerland, Austria on S; Czech Rep., Poland on E. **Topography:** Flat in N, hilly in center and W, and mountainous in Bavaria in the S. Chief rivers are Elbe, Weser, Ems, Rhine, and Main, all flowing toward North Sea, and Danube, flowing toward Black Sea. **Arable land:** 34.1%. **Capital:** Berlin, 3,578,459. **Cities:** Hamburg, 1,838,850; Munich, 1,453,604; Cologne, 1,041,936.

Government: Type: Federal parliamentary republic. **Head of state:** Pres. Joachim Gauck; b. 1940; in office: Mar. 18, 2012. **Head of gov.:** Chancellor Angela Merkel; b. 1954; in office: Nov. 22, 2005. **Local divisions:** 16 states. **Defense budget:** $36.7 bil. **Active troops:** 178,600.

Economy: Industries: iron, steel, coal, cement, chemicals, machinery, vehicles, machine tools, electronics, automobiles, food and beverages. **Chief crops:** potatoes, wheat, barley, sugar beets, fruit, cabbages. **Natural resources:** coal, lignite, nat. gas, iron ore, copper, nickel, uranium, potash, salt, constr. materials, timber. **Water:** 1,909 cu m per capita. **Crude oil reserves:** 0.1 bil bbls. **Electricity prod.:** 591 bil kWh. **Labor force:** agric. 1.6%, industry 24.6%, services 73.8%. **Unemployment:** 5%.

Finance: Monetary unit: Euro (EUR) (0.89 = $1 U.S.). **GDP:** $3.8 tril; **per capita GDP:** $46,900; **GDP growth:** 1.5%. **Imports:** $983.9 bil; Netherlands 13.7%, France 7.6%, China 7.3%, Belgium 6%, Italy 5.2%, Poland 5%. **Exports:** $1.3 tril; U.S. 9.6%, France 8.6%, UK 7.5%, Netherlands 6.6%, China 6%. **Tourism:** $36.9 bil. **Budget:** $1.5 tril. **Inflation:** 0.2%.

Transport: Railways: 27,010 mi. **Motor vehicles:** 598.9 per 1,000 pop. **Airports:** 318.

Communications: Telephone: 54.9 per 100 pop. **Mobile:** 116.7 per 100 pop. **Broadband:** 63.6 per 100 pop. **Internet:** 87.6%.

Health: Expend.: 11.3%. **Life expect.:** 78.4 male; 83.1 female. **Births:** 8.5 per 1,000 pop. **Deaths:** 11.6 per 1,000 pop. **Infant mortality:** 3.4 per 1,000 live births. **Undernourished:** <5%. **HIV:** NA.

Education: Compulsory: ages 6-17. **Literacy:** 99%.

Embassy: 4645 Reservoir Rd. NW, 20037; 298-4000.

Website: www.deutschland.de

Julius Caesar defeated Germanic tribes, 55 and 53 BCE, but Roman expansion north of the Rhine was stopped in 9 CE. Charlemagne, ruler of the Franks, consolidated Saxon, Bavarian, Rhenish, Frankish, and other lands; after him the eastern part became the German Empire. The Thirty Years' War, 1618-48, split Germany into small principalities and kingdoms.

Otto von Bismarck, Prussian chancellor, formed the North German Confederation, 1867. In 1870 Bismarck maneuvered Napoleon III into declaring war. After the quick defeat of France, Bismarck formed the German Empire and on Jan. 18, 1871, in Versailles, proclaimed King Wilhelm I of Prussia the German emperor (Deutscher kaiser).

The German Empire reached its peak before WWI in 1914, with 208,780 sq mi, plus overseas colonies. After losing the war in 1918, Germany ceded Alsace-Lorraine to France, West Prussia and Posen (Poznan) province to Poland, and part of Schleswig to Denmark. It lost all colonies and the ports of Memel and Danzig.

Republic of Germany, 1919-33, adopted the Weimar constitution; met reparation payments and elected Friedrich Ebert and Gen. Paul von Hindenburg presidents.

Third Reich, 1933-45: Adolf Hitler led the National Socialist German Workers' (Nazi) party after WWI. Pres. von Hindenburg named Hitler chancellor in 1933; on Aug. 3, 1934, the day after

Hindenburg's death, the cabinet joined the offices of president and chancellor and made Hitler *führer* (leader). Hitler abolished freedom of speech and assembly, and began a long series of persecutions culminating in the murder of millions of Jews and others.

He repudiated the Versailles treaty and reparations agreements, remilitarized the Rhineland (1936), and annexed Austria (Anschluss, 1938). At Munich he made an agreement with British Prime Min. Neville Chamberlain, which permitted Germany to annex part of Czechoslovakia. He signed a nonaggression treaty with the USSR, 1939, and declared war on Poland Sept. 1, 1939, precipitating WWII. With total defeat near, Hitler committed suicide in Berlin Apr. 1945. The victorious Allies voided all acts and annexations of Hitler's Reich.

Germany was sectioned into four zones of occupation, administered by the Allied Powers (U.S., USSR, UK, and France). The USSR took control of many E German states. The territory E of the so-called Oder-Neisse line was assigned to, and later annexed by, Poland. The USSR annexed Northern East Prussia (now Kaliningrad). Greater Berlin, within but not part of the Soviet zone, was administered by the four occupying powers under the Allied Command. In 1948 the USSR withdrew, established its single command in East Berlin, and cut off supplies. The Western Allies utilized a gigantic airlift to bring food to West Berlin, 1948-49.

In 1949, two separate German states were established. In May the zones administered by the Western Allies became West Germany; in Oct. the Soviet sector became East Germany. West Berlin was considered a West German enclave, a status the Soviet bloc disputed.

East Germany. The German Democratic Republic (East Germany) was proclaimed in the Soviet sector of Berlin Oct. 7, 1949. It was declared fully sovereign in 1954, but Soviet troops remained.

Coincident with the entrance of West Germany into the European defense community in 1952, the East German government decreed a prohibited zone 3 mi deep along its 600-mi border with West Germany and cut Berlin's telephone system in two. East Germany also erected a fortified wall dividing Berlin in 1961, after over 3 mil East Germans had fled to the West. The oppressive Communist regime maintained control through the state security police, known as the Stasi.

By the early 1970s, the economy of East Germany was highly industrialized, and the nation was credited with the highest standard of living among Warsaw Pact countries. Growth slowed in the late 1970s because of shortages of natural resources and labor and huge debt. Comparison with the lifestyle in the West caused many young people to emigrate.

In the late 1980s the government firmly resisted following the USSR's policy of openness (*glasnost*) but was faced with nationwide demonstrations demanding reform. Pres. Erich Honecker, in office since 1976, was forced to resign Oct. 18, 1989. On Nov. 9, the East German government announced its decision to open the border with the West, signaling the end of the Berlin Wall. On Aug. 23, 1990, the East German parliament agreed to reunite with West Germany.

West Germany. The Federal Republic of Germany (West Germany) was proclaimed May 23, 1949, in Bonn. The occupying powers—the U.S., Britain, and France—restored civil status, Sept. 21. The Western Allies ended the state of war with Germany in 1951, while the USSR did so in 1955. The powers lifted controls, and the republic became fully independent May 5, 1955.

Dr. Konrad Adenauer, a Christian Democrat, was made chancellor 1949 and was reelected 1953, 1957, 1961. Willy Brandt, heading a coalition of Social Democrats and Free Democrats, became chancellor 1969 and pursued a policy of *Ostpolitik*, or rapprochement with East Germany and the USSR. Brandt resigned May 1974 after a spy scandal. Terrorist acts on German soil in the 1970s included activities of the Baader-Meinhof gang, also known as the Red Army Faction, and the murder of Israeli athletes by Palestinian commandos at the Olympic Games in Munich, Sept. 5, 1972.

Helmut Kohl became chancellor in 1982 and led Christian Democrats to victory in 1983 and 1987.

Unified Germany. In May 1990, NATO ministers voted to make the united Germany a full member of NATO and barred the new Germany from having its own nuclear, chemical, or biological weapons. The merger of the two Germanys took place Oct. 3, and the first all-German elections since 1932 were held Dec. 2, with West German Chancellor Helmut Kohl confirmed as leader of the unified nation. Eastern Germany received over $1 tril in public and private funds from western Germany, 1990-95. In 1991, Berlin again became Germany's official capital; the Bundestag (parliament) relocated from Bonn to Berlin in 1999. Unemployment hit a postwar high of 12.6% in Jan. 1998. The Christian Democrats lost parliamentary elections, Sept. 27, 1998, and Gerhard Schröder, of the Social Democratic Party (SPD), became chancellor. The Christian Democrats, led by Angela Merkel, won a razor-thin plurality in 2005 parliamentary elections, and she became chancellor Nov. 22, heading a "grand coalition" that included the SPD.

Responding to the global recession, the government passed a 50-bil euro economic stimulus plan in early 2009. Merkel led a center-right coalition to victory in 2009 national elections. After an earthquake and tsunami in Japan caused a nuclear disaster, the Merkel government announced May 2011 that it would close Germany's 17 nuclear power plants by 2022. Merkel and then-French Pres. Nicolas Sarkozy led the international response to the European debt crisis involving Greece in late 2009, followed by Ireland, Portugal, Italy, and Spain; debtor nations were required to adopt stern austerity measures in return for aid. Although new recessions in several austerity-bound countries caused some eurozone nations to doubt Germany's strategy, Merkel's government again took a hard line in new debt negotiations with Greece in 2015, requiring further austerity measures in exchange for additional bailout funds.

A report released Jan 19, 2013, contained information from more than 1,100 people describing themselves as victims of child sexual abuse perpetrated by German Catholic priests over the course of several years. The Constitutional Court in Karlsruhe, the nation's highest court, affirmed Feb. 19, 2013, gay couples' right to adopt children.

Merkel's Christian Democrats won Sept. 22, 2013, parliamentary elections but fell short of a majority. She formed a new coalition, including the SPD, in Dec. Germany was the destination in 2015 for many migrants reaching Europe after fleeing war or hardship in the Middle East, SW Asia, or Africa; it also received large numbers of migrants from the Balkans. An estimated 1.1 mil migrants arrived in 2015, and more than 476,000 applied for asylum. Almost 362,000 additional migrants applied for asylum Jan.-June. 2016. Germany provided temporary care, set up expedited procedures for asylum applicants, and began repatriating migrants judged not to be refugees. In Jan. 2016, Germany declared Algeria, Morocco, and Tunisia "safe" countries, providing a basis for rejecting asylum applications, and delayed family reunification for asylum recipients. In Apr., the government announced new requirements for asylum seekers to learn the German language and culture. Germany played a key role in negotiating a Mar. 2016 EU-Turkey agreement to stem the flow of migrants to Europe. In two attacks in Bavaria that may have been inspired by ISIS, an Afghan migrant wounded 5 people with a knife and ax, July 18, 2016, and a Syrian suicide bomber wounded 15, July 24. In an unrelated incident, an 18-year-old gunman killed 9 at and near a Munich shopping mall, July 22, before fatally shooting himself.

Helgoland, an island of 0.66 sq mi in the North Sea, was taken from Denmark by a British naval force in 1807 and ceded to Germany in 1890. The island was surrendered to the UK, May 23, 1945, and returned to then-West Germany, Mar. 1, 1952.

Ghana
Republic of Ghana

People: Population: 26,908,262. **Age distrib.:** <15: 38.2%; 65+: 4.2%. **Growth:** 2.2%. **Migrants:** 1.5%. **Pop. density:** 306.3 per sq mi, 118.3 per sq km. **Urban:** 54.7%. **Ethnic groups:** Akan 47.5%, Mole-Dagbon 16.6%, Ewe 13.9%, Ga-Dangme 7.4%, Gurma 5.7%, Guan 3.7%, Grusi 2.5%. **Languages:** Asante, Ewe, Fante, Boron, Dagomba, Dangme, Dagarte, Kokomba, Akyem, Ga, English (official). **Religions:** Christian 71.2% (incl. Pentecostal/Charismatic 28.3%, Protestant 18.4%, Catholic 13.1%), Muslim 17.6%, traditional 5.2%, none 5.2%.

Geography: Total area: 92,098 sq mi, 238,533 sq km; **Land area:** 87,851 sq mi, 227,533 sq km. **Location:** S coast of W Africa. Côte d'Ivoire on W, Burkina Faso on N, Togo on E. **Topography:** Mostly low fertile plains and scrubland, cut by rivers and by the artificial Lake Volta. **Arable land:** 20.7%. **Capital:** Accra, 2,315,819. **Cities:** Kumasi, 2,717,586.

Government: Type: Presidential republic. **Head of state and gov.:** Pres. John Dramani Mahama; b. 1958; in office: July 24, 2012. **Local divisions:** 10 regions. **Defense budget:** $248 mil. **Active troops:** 15,500.

Economy: Industries: mining, lumbering, light mfg., aluminum smelting, food proc., cement, small comm. shipbuilding. **Chief crops:** cocoa, rice, cassava, peanuts, corn, shea nuts, bananas. **Natural resources:** gold, timber, industrial diamonds, bauxite, manganese, fish, rubber, hydropower, petroleum, silver, salt, limestone. **Water:** 2,050 cu m per capita. **Crude oil reserves:** 0.7 bil bbls. **Electricity prod.:** 13 bil kWh. **Labor force:** agric. 44.7%, industry 14.4%, services 40.9%. **Unemployment:** 2.4%.

Finance: Monetary unit: Cedi (GHS) (3.94 = $1 U.S.). **GDP:** $114.7 bil; **per capita GDP:** $4,300; **GDP growth:** 3.5%. **Imports:** $13.4 bil; China 32.6%, Nigeria 14%, Netherlands 5.5%, U.S. 5.4%. **Exports:** $10.8 bil; India 25.2%, Switzerland 12.2%, China 10.6%, France 5.7%. **Tourism:** $897 mil. **Budget:** $10.8 bil. **Inflation:** 17.1%.

Transport: Railways: 588 mi. **Motor vehicles:** 8 per 1,000 pop. **Airports:** 7.

Communications: Telephone: 1 per 100 pop. **Mobile:** 129.7 per 100 pop. **Broadband:** 59.8 per 100 pop. **Internet:** 23.5%.

Health: Expend.: 3.6%. **Life expect.:** 64.1 male; 69.1 female. **Births:** 30.8 per 1,000 pop. **Deaths:** 7.1 per 1,000 pop. **Infant mortality:** 36.3 per 1,000 live births. **Undernourished:** <5%. **HIV:** 1.6%.

Education: Compulsory: ages 4-14. **Literacy:** 76.6%.
Embassy: 3512 International Dr. NW 20008; 686-4520.

Website: www.ghana.gov.gh

Named for an African empire along the Niger R., 400-1240 CE, Ghana was ruled by Britain for 113 years as the Gold Coast. The UN in 1956 approved merger with the British Togoland trust territory. Independence came Mar. 6, 1957, and republic status within the Commonwealth in 1960.

Pres. Kwame Nkrumah built hospitals and schools and promoted development projects but ran the country into debt, jailed opponents, and was accused of corruption. A 1964 referendum gave Nkrumah dictatorial powers and set up a one-party socialist state. A police-army coup overthrew Nkrumah in 1966. Elections were held in 1969, but four further coups occurred in 1972, 1978, 1979, and 1981. A new constitution, allowing multiparty politics, was approved in Apr. 1992. Former coup leader Jerry Rawlings won the 1996 presidential election. Kofi Annan, a career UN diplomat from Ghana, served as UN sec.-gen., 1997-2006.

Opposition leader John Agyekum Kufuor won a 2000 runoff vote and was sworn in Jan. 7, 2001, marking Ghana's first peaceful transfer of power from one elected president to another. He was reelected in 2004. John Atta Mills won a 2008 runoff election. A major offshore oil and gas find was announced June 2007; the Jubilee field, estimated to hold recoverable oil reserves of 1.5 bil barrels, began production Dec. 2010. When Mills died in 2012, Vice Pres. John Dramani Mahama replaced him. Mahama won a full term in Dec. 2012 elections.

Greece
Hellenic Republic

People: Population: 10,773,253. **Age distrib.:** <15: 13.9%; 65+: 20.7%. **Growth:** −0.03%. **Migrants:** 11.3%. **Pop. density:** 213.6 per sq mi, 82.5 per sq km. **Urban:** 78.3%. **Ethnic groups:** Greek 93%, foreign citizen 7%. (Greece does not collect ethnicity data.) **Languages:** Greek (official). **Religions:** Greek Orthodox (official) 98%, Muslim 1.3%.

Geography: Total area: 50,949 sq mi, 131,957 sq km; **Land area:** 50,443 sq mi, 130,647 sq km. **Location:** S end of Balkan Peninsula in SE Europe. Albania, Macedonia, Bulgaria on N; Turkey on E. **Topography:** About three-quarters is non-arable, with mountains in all areas incl. N-S Pindus Mts. Heavily indented coastline is 9,385 mi long. About 2,000 islands, only 169 inhabited, among them Crete, Rhodes, Milos, Kerkira (Corfu), Chios, Lesbos, Samos, Euboea, Delos, Mykonos. **Arable land:** 19.8%. **Capital:** Athens, 3,046,479. **Cities:** Thessaloniki, 733,717.

Government: Type: Parliamentary republic. **Head of state:** Pres. Prokopis Pavlopoulos; b. 1950; in office: Mar. 13, 2015. **Head of gov.:** Prime Min. Alexis Tsipras; b. 1974; in office: Sept. 21, 2015. **Local divisions:** 13 regions, 1 autonomous monastic state. **Defense budget:** $4.7 bil. **Active troops:** 142,950.

Economy: Industries: tourism, food and tobacco proc., textiles, chemicals, metal prods. **Chief crops:** wheat, corn, barley, sugar beets, olives, tomatoes, wine, tobacco, potatoes. **Natural resources:** lignite, petroleum, iron ore, bauxite, lead, zinc, nickel, magnesite, marble, salt. **Water:** 6,244 cu m per capita. **Crude oil reserves** (2015): 10 mil bbls. **Electricity prod.:** 55 bil kWh. **Labor force:** agric. 12.6%, industry 15%, services 72.4%. **Unemployment:** 26.3%.

Finance: Monetary unit: Euro (EUR) (0.89 = $1 U.S.). **GDP:** $286 bil; **per capita GDP:** $26,400; **GDP growth:** −0.2%. **Imports:** $47.2 bil; Germany 10.7%, Italy 8.4%, Russia 7.9%, Iraq 7%, China 5.9%, Netherlands 5.5%. **Exports:** $25.3 bil; Italy 11.2%, Germany 7.3%, Turkey 6.6%, Cyprus 5.9%, Bulgaria 5.2%. **Tourism:** $15.7 bil. **Budget:** $60.2 bil. **Inflation:** −1.7%.

Transport: Railways: 1,583 mi. **Motor vehicles:** 599.2 per 1,000 pop. **Airports:** 68.

Communications: Telephone: 46.5 per 100 pop. **Mobile:** 114 per 100 pop. **Broadband:** 41 per 100 pop. **Internet:** 66.8%.

Health: Expend.: 8.1%. **Life expect.:** 77.9 male; 83.3 female. **Births:** 8.5 per 1,000 pop. **Deaths:** 11.2 per 1,000 pop. **Infant mortality:** 4.6 per 1,000 live births. **Undernourished:** <5%. **HIV:** 0.3%.

Education: Compulsory: ages 6-14. **Literacy:** 95.3%.

Embassy: 2217 Massachusetts Ave. NW 20008; 939-1300.

Website: www.primeminister.gov.gr

The achievements of ancient Greece in art, architecture, science, mathematics, philosophy, drama, literature, and democracy became legacies for succeeding ages. Greece reached the height of its power, particularly in the Athenian city-state, in the 5th cent. BCE. Greece fell under Roman rule in the 2nd and 1st cents. BCE. In the 4th cent. CE, it became part of the Byzantine Empire and, after the fall of Constantinople to the Turks in 1453, part of the Ottoman Empire.

Greece won its war of independence from Turkey, 1821-29, and became a kingdom. A republic was established 1924; the monarchy was restored, 1935. In Oct. 1940, Greece rejected an ultimatum from Italy, but the country was defeated and occupied by German, Italian, and Bulgarian forces. By the end of 1944 the invaders withdrew. Communist resistance forces were overcome by Royalist and British troops. A plebiscite restored the monarchy.

Communists waged guerrilla war 1947-49 against the government but were defeated with the aid of the U.S. A period of reconstruction and rapid development followed, mainly with conservative governments under Prem. Constantine Karamanlis. The Center Union, led by Georgios Papandreou, won elections in 1963 and 1964, but King Constantine forced Papandreou to resign. A period of political maneuvers ended with Col. George Papadopoulos's military takeover Apr. 1967. King Constantine tried to reverse the consolidation of the harsh dictatorship Dec. 1967, but failed and fled to Italy. Papadopoulos was ousted Nov. 1973.

Greek army officers serving in the Cyprus National Guard staged a coup on the island July 15, 1974. Turkey invaded Cyprus a week later, precipitating the collapse of the Greek junta. Democratic government returned, and in 1975 the monarchy was abolished.

The 1981 electoral victory of the Panhellenic Socialist Movement (Pasok) of Andreas Papandreou (Georgios's son) substantially changed Greece's internal and external policies. A scandal contributed to the 1989 defeat of the Socialists at the polls. Papandreou, who was acquitted Jan. 1992 of corruption charges, led the Socialists to a comeback victory in 1993 general elections. The Socialists retained power in 1996 and 2000 elections.

The conservative New Democracy (ND) party won 2004 parliamentary elections, and Konstantinos (Costas) Karamanlis became prime min. Beset by scandals and an ailing economy, Karamanlis called early elections for Oct. 4, 2009, won by Pasok under the leadership of the U.S.-born George A. Papandreou (Andreas's son). The IMF and eurozone countries agreed in 2010 on a 110-bil euro loan package to prevent Greece from defaulting on its debt; in return, Greek leaders implemented an austerity plan. As the debt crisis continued, parliament passed, amid violent anti-austerity protests, new austerity measures, Feb. 2012, to obtain a second, 130-bil euro bailout in Mar. The conservative, pro-bailout Antonis Samaras of ND became prime min., June 2012. The government agreed on a plan for 13.5 bil euros in budget cuts and austerity measures Sept. 27, touching off renewed violent protests but paving the way for the Intl. Monetary Fund, European Central Bank, and eurozone members (known as the troika) to release 43.7 bil euros in bailout funds Nov. 26. Recession and austerity measures, 2007-13, caused Greece's GDP to shrink by 26%. Campaigning against austerity, the leftist Syriza party won Jan. 25, 2015, elections. Syriza's Alexis Tsipras became prime min. and negotiated with the troika on a third bailout needed by mid-2015 to avert default. Resisting new austerity measures, Tsipras called a July 5 referendum in which Greek voters decisively rejected the austerity terms. The government closed Greek banks, which were running out of money, June 29-July 20, 2015. Negotiations with the troika after the referendum produced an 86-bil euro bailout agreement (final approval came Aug. 19) with tougher austerity terms than previously proposed—including further tax increases and pension cuts, sales of government assets, deregulation of the economy, and banking system reform. Seeking a renewed mandate, Tsipras resigned Aug. 20 and called elections for Sept. 20; Syriza won, and Tsipras again became prime min., Sept. 21.

In 2015, Greece was the most common entry point for undocumented migrants from the Middle East, SW Asia, and Africa trying to reach the EU. More than 850,000 migrants arrived in Greece in 2015, and more than 165,000 Jan.-Sept. 2016; the leading country of origin was Syria. Under an EU-Turkey agreement, effective Mar. 20, 2016, Greece could return to Turkey undocumented migrants arriving by boat from that country, and Turkey pledged to crack down on smugglers engaged in human trafficking. Most migrants reaching Greece tried to continue to N Europe, and new arrivals declined after the Turkey agreement. However, several countries closed their borders to migrants traveling north. In Sept. 2016, more than 60,000 migrants were living in refugee camps in Greece.

Grenada

People: Population: 111,219. **Age distrib.:** <15: 24.2%; 65+: 9.8%. **Growth:** 0.5%. **Migrants:** 6.6%. **Pop. density:** 837.4 per sq mi, 323.3 per sq km. **Urban:** 35.6%. **Ethnic groups:** African descent 89.4%, mixed 8.2%. **Languages:** English (official), French patois. **Religions:** Roman Catholic 44.6%, Protestant 43.5% (incl. Anglican 11.5%, Pentecostal 11.3%, Seventh-day Adventist 10.5%), none 3.6%.

Geography: Total area: 133 sq mi, 344 sq km; **Land area:** 133 sq mi, 344 sq km. **Location:** In Caribbean, 90 mi N of Venezuela. Trinidad and Tobago to S, St. Vincent and the Grenadines to N. **Topography:** Main island is mountainous. Country also comprised of Carriacou and Petit Martinique Isls. **Arable land:** 8.8%. **Capital:** St. George's, 37,822 (2014).

Government: Type: Parliamentary democracy. **Head of state:** Queen Elizabeth II, rep. by Gov.-Gen. Cecile La Grenade; b. 1952; in office: May 7, 2013. **Head of gov.:** Prime Min. Keith Mitchell; b. 1946; in office: Feb. 20, 2013. **Local divisions:** 6 parishes, 1 dependency. **Defense budget/active troops:** NA.

Economy: Industries: food and beverages, textiles, light assembly operations, tourism, constr. **Chief crops:** bananas, cocoa, nutmeg, mace, citrus, avocados, root crops, sugarcane, corn, vegetables. **Natural resources:** timber, deepwater harbors. **Water:** 1,873 cu m per capita. **Electricity prod.:** 0.2 bil kWh. **Labor force:** agric. 11%, industry 20%, services 69%. **Unemployment:** NA.

Finance: Monetary unit: East Caribbean Dollar (XCD) (2.70 = $1 U.S.). **GDP:** $1.4 bil; **per capita GDP:** $13,100; **GDP growth:** 4.6%. **Imports:** $310.4 mil; Trinidad and Tobago 49.6%, U.S. 16.4%. **Exports:** $43.8 mil; Nigeria 44.7%, St. Lucia 10.8%, Antigua and Barbuda 7.3%, St. Kitts and Nevis 6.6%, Dominica 6.6%, U.S. 5.8%. **Tourism:** $137 mil. **Budget** (2012 est.): $230.9 mil. **Inflation:** –0.6%.

Transport: Airports: 3.

Communications: Telephone: 25.3 per 100 pop. **Mobile:** 112.3 per 100 pop. **Broadband:** 1.2 per 100 pop. **Internet:** 53.8%.

Health: Expend.: 6.1%. **Life expect.:** 71.7 male; 77.1 female. **Births:** 15.8 per 1,000 pop. **Deaths:** 8.1 per 1,000 pop. **Infant mortality:** 9.9 per 1,000 live births. **Undernourished:** NA. **HIV:** NA.

Education: Compulsory: ages 5-16. **Literacy:** NA. **Embassy:** 1701 New Hampshire Ave. NW 20009; 265-2561.

Website: www.gov.gd

Christopher Columbus sighted Grenada in 1498. The first European settlers were French, 1650. The island was held alternately by France and England until final British occupation, 1784. Grenada became fully independent Feb. 7, 1974, during a general strike.

On Oct. 14, 1983, a military coup ousted Prime Min. Maurice Bishop, who was put under house arrest, later freed by supporters, rearrested, and executed Oct. 19. U.S. forces, with a token force from six area nations, invaded Grenada, Oct. 25. Resistance from the Grenadian army and Cuban advisors was quickly overcome, and U.S. troops left Grenada in June 1985.

Hurricane Ivan slammed into Grenada, Sept. 7, 2004, killing 39 people and damaging an estimated 90% of the buildings on the island. The New National Party won all 15 seats available in general elections Feb. 19, 2013, and Keith Mitchell became prime min.

Guatemala
Republic of Guatemala

People: Population: 15,189,958. **Age distrib.:** <15: 35%; 65+: 4.4%. **Growth:** 1.8%. **Migrants:** 0.5%. **Pop. density:** 367.1 per sq mi, 141.8 per sq km. **Urban:** 52%. **Ethnic groups:** mestizo or Ladino (mixed Amerindian/Spanish) and European 59.4%, K'iche 9.1%, Kaqchikel 8.4%, Mam 7.9%, Q'eqchi 6.3%, other Mayan 8.6%. **Languages:** Spanish (official), Amerindian langs. (23 officially recognized). **Religions:** Roman Catholic, Protestant, indigenous Mayan beliefs.

Geography: Total area: 42,042 sq mi, 108,889 sq km; **Land area:** 41,374 sq mi, 107,159 sq km. **Location:** Central America. Mexico on N and, El Salvador on S, Honduras and Belize on E. **Topography:** Central highland and mountain areas bordered by a narrow Pacific coast and lowlands and fertile river valleys on the Caribbean. Numerous volcanoes in S, more than half a dozen over 11,000 ft. **Arable land:** 9.4%. **Capital:** Guatemala City, 2,994,428.

Government: Type: Presidential republic. **Head of state and gov.:** Pres. Jimmy Ernesto Morales; b. 1969; in office: Jan. 14, 2016. **Local divisions:** 22 departments. **Defense budget:** $275 mil. **Active troops:** 18,050.

Economy: Industries: sugar, textiles and clothing, furniture, chemicals, petroleum, metals, rubber, tourism. **Chief crops:** sugarcane, corn, bananas, coffee, beans, cardamom. **Natural resources:** petroleum, nickel, rare woods, fish, chicle, hydropower. **Water:** 7,826 cu m per capita. **Crude oil reserves:** 0.1 bil bbls. **Electricity prod.:** 9.7 bil kWh. **Labor force:** agric. 31.2%, industry 14.4%, services 54.4%. **Unemployment:** 2.9%.

Finance: Monetary unit: Quetzal (GTQ) (7.55 = $1 U.S.). **GDP:** $125.9 bil; **per capita GDP:** $7,700; **GDP growth:** 4.1%. **Imports:** $17.6 bil; U.S. 38.3%, China 13.4%, Mexico 11.8%. **Exports:** $10.7 bil; U.S. 34.9%, El Salvador 8.4%, Honduras 7.3%, Nicaragua 5%. **Tourism:** $1.6 bil. **Budget:** $8.7 bil. **Inflation:** 2.4%.

Transport: Railways: 497 mi. **Motor vehicles:** 124.2 per 1,000 pop. **Airports:** 16.

Communications: Telephone: 10.6 per 100 pop. **Mobile:** 111.5 per 100 pop. **Broadband:** 9.4 per 100 pop. **Internet:** 27.1%.

Health: Expend.: 6.2%. **Life expect.:** 70.3 male; 74.4 female. **Births:** 24.5 per 1,000 pop. **Deaths:** 4.7 per 1,000 pop. **Infant mortality:** 22.0 per 1,000 live births. **Undernourished:** 15.6%. **HIV:** 0.6%.

Education: Compulsory: ages 6-15. **Literacy:** 79.1%. **Embassy:** 2220 R St. NW 20008; 745-4953.

Website: www.guatemala.gob.gt

A Mayan Indian empire flourished in present-day Guatemala for over 1,000 years before Spaniards came. Guatemala was a Spanish colony 1524-1821. A republic was established in 1839.

In 1954, the U.S. Central Intelligence Agency engineered the overthrow of elected Pres. Jacobo Arbenz Guzmán, a left-wing reformer. Since then, the country has experienced a variety of military and civilian governments and periods of insurgency, repression, paramilitary violence, and civil war. After military coups in 1982 and 1983, the nation returned to civilian rule in 1986.

The Guatemalan government and leftist rebels signed a peace accord Dec. 29, 1996. During more than 35 years of armed conflict, some 200,000 people were killed or "disappeared" (and are presumed dead); most casualties were attributed to the government and its paramilitary allies. Gen. Efraín Ríos Montt, dictator for 17 months, 1982-83, was found guilty of genocide and sentenced to 80 years in prison May 10, 2013, but the Constitutional Court overturned his conviction May 20 and ruled that part of his trial had to be repeated.

Former Pres. Alfonso Portillo was extradited to the U.S. May 24, 2013, to be tried for money laundering; he pleaded guilty and was sentenced May 22, 2014, to nearly six years in prison. Drug trafficking, arms smuggling, police corruption, and one of the world's highest homicide rates posed threats to national stability. Apparently seeking safety from drug-related and other violence, Guatemalans made up a sizable portion of the tens of thousands of undocumented immigrant children—some with their mothers, many traveling unaccompanied—detained trying to enter the U.S. from Mexico in late 2013 and 2014. A new surge in such immigration began in late 2015.

Pres. Otto Pérez Molina's vice president, Roxana Baldetti, resigned and the president dismissed other officials, May 2015, following bribery and corruption scandals; Baldetti was arrested Aug. 21, 2015. Following large-scale protests, Pérez Molina resigned Sept. 2, was jailed Sept. 3, and was ordered to stand trial on bribery, corruption, and conspiracy charges Sept. 8. Former TV comedian Jimmy Ernesto Morales Cabrera won a runoff election for president Oct. 25, 2015.

Guinea
Republic of Guinea

People: Population: 12,093,349. **Age distrib.:** <15: 41.7%; 65+: 3.7%. **Growth:** 2.6%. **Migrants:** 1.8%. **Pop. density:** 127.5 per sq mi, 49.2 per sq km. **Urban:** 37.7%. **Ethnic groups:** Fulani (Peul) 33.9%, Malinke 31.1%, Soussou 19.1%, Guerze 6%, Kissi 4.7%, Toma 2.6%. **Languages:** French (official), ethnic group-specific langs. **Religions:** Muslim 86.7%, Christian 8.9%.

Geography: Total area: 94,926 sq mi, 245,857 sq km; **Land area:** 94,872 sq mi, 245,717 sq km. **Location:** Atlantic coast of W Africa. Guinea-Bissau, Senegal, Mali on N; Côte d'Ivoire on E; Liberia, Sierra Leone on S. **Topography:** Narrow coastal belt leads to mountainous middle region, source of the Gambia, Senegal, and Niger Rivers. Upper Guinea, farther inland, is cooler upland. The SE is forested. **Arable land:** 12.6%. **Capital:** Conakry, 1,988,702.

Government: Type: Presidential republic. **Head of state:** Pres. Alpha Condé; b. 1938; in office: Dec. 21, 2010. **Head of gov.:** Prime Min. Mamady Youla; in office: Dec. 26, 2015. **Local divisions:** 7 regions, 1 governorate. **Defense budget** (2013): $40 mil. **Active troops:** 9,700.

Economy: Industries: bauxite, gold, diamonds, iron ore; light mfg.; agric. proc. **Chief crops:** rice, coffee, pineapples, mangoes, palm kernels, cocoa, cassava, bananas, potatoes. **Natural resources:** bauxite, iron ore, diamonds, gold, uranium, hydropower, fish, salt. **Water:** 17,924 cu m per capita. **Electricity prod.:** 1 bil kWh. **Labor force:** agric. 76%, industry and services 24%. **Unemployment:** 1.8%.

Finance: Monetary unit: Franc (GNF) (7,350.24 = $1 U.S.). **GDP:** $15 bil; **per capita GDP:** $1,200; **GDP growth:** 0.1%. **Imports:** $1.9 bil; China 20.3%, Netherlands 5.4%. **Exports:** $1.8 bil; India 22.5%, Spain 8.2%, Ireland 7.3%, Germany 6.2%, Belgium 5.5%, Ukraine 5.3%. **Tourism:** $1 mil. **Budget:** $2.1 bil. **Inflation:** 8.2%.

Transport: Railways: 411 mi. **Airports:** 4.

Communications: Telephone (2011): 0.2 per 100 pop. **Mobile:** 87.2 per 100 pop. **Broadband** (2012): 0.0 per 100 pop. **Internet:** 4.7%.

Health: Expend.: 5.6%. **Life expect.:** 59.0 male; 62.2 female. **Births:** 35.4 per 1,000 pop. **Deaths:** 9.2 per 1,000 pop. **Infant mortality:** 51.7 per 1,000 live births. **Undernourished:** 16.4%. **HIV:** 1.6%.

Education: Compulsory: ages 7-12. **Literacy:** 30.5%. **Embassy:** 2112 Leroy Pl. NW 20008; 986-4300.

Website: www.presidence.gov.gn or www.state.gov/p/af/ci/gv/

Guinea, a French colony, attained independence Oct. 2, 1958. Sékou Touré, Guinea's first president (1958-84), turned to Communist nations for support and set up a one-party state. Thousands of opponents were jailed and tortured, and many were killed in the 1970s after an unsuccessful Portuguese invasion.

The military took control in a bloodless coup after the Mar. 1984 death of Touré. A new constitution was approved in 1991, but movement toward democracy was slow. Gen. Lansana Conté, the incumbent, won a long-awaited presidential election in Dec. 1993, which outside monitors called flawed. Conté suppressed an army mutiny in Conakry, Feb. 2-3, 1996, and won reelection in 1998. Fighting in early 2001 along the border with Liberia and Sierra Leone created a refugee crisis in Guinea; voluntary repatriation of more than 51,000 Liberian refugees was largely completed in 2007.

Major opposition parties boycotted the 2003 presidential election, in which the ailing Conté won 95.6% of the vote. More than 120 died in Jan.-Feb. 2007 strikes and protests that pressured Conté to name a new prime min. from a union-leader approved list; protests followed Prime Min. Lansana Kouyate's ouster by Conté in May 2008. After Conté's death Dec. 22, a military junta took power, calling itself the National Council for Democracy and Development. More than 150 people were reportedly killed Sept. 28, 2009, when Guinean troops fired into a crowd of about 50,000 antigovernment protesters in Conakry. After an assassination attempt Dec. 3, 2009, by a former aide left Pres. Moussa Dadis Camara seriously wounded, Vice Pres. Sékouba Konaté became interim head of state. Presidential elections June-Nov. 2010 brought a civilian government headed by Alpha Condé to power Dec. 21. Condé won reelection, Oct. 11, 2015. Seeking to revive the struggling economy, Condé named business executive Mamady Youla prime min., Dec. 26.

The largest known outbreak of Ebola virus disease (EVD) began in Guinea in Dec. 2013, spread rapidly to Liberia and Sierra Leone, and caused thousands of deaths 2014-15. WHO lifted its public health emergency in West Africa, Mar. 29, 2016. As of May 8, 2016, WHO recorded 28,616 EVD cases in the 3 heavily affected countries (including 3,814 in Guinea) and 11,310 deaths (2,544 in Guinea). Guinea declared an end to the epidemic there, June 1.

Guinea-Bissau
Republic of Guinea-Bissau

People: Population: 1,759,159. **Age distrib.:** <15: 39.3%; 65+: 3.4%. **Growth:** 1.9%. **Migrants:** 1.2%. **Pop. density:** 162 per sq mi, 62.6 per sq km. **Urban:** 50.1%. **Ethnic groups:** Fulani 28.5%, Balanta 22.5%, Mandinga 14.7%, Papel 9.1%, Manjaco 8.3%, Beafada 3.5%, Mancanha 3.1%, Bijago 2.1%. **Languages:** Crioulo, Portuguese (official), French, English. **Religions:** Muslim 45.1%, Christian 22.1%, animist 14.9%.

Geography: Total area: 13,948 sq mi, 36,125 sq km; **Land area:** 10,857 sq mi, 28,120 sq km. **Location:** Atlantic coast of W Africa. **Senegal** on N, **Guinea** on E and S. **Topography:** A swampy coastal plain covers most of country. Low savanna region to E. **Arable land:** 10.7%. **Capital:** Bissau, 511,524.

Government: Type: Semi-presidential republic. **Head of state:** Pres. José Mário Vaz; b. 1957; in office: June 23, 2014. **Head of gov.:** Prime Min. Baciro Dja; b. 1973; in office: May 27, 2016. **Local divisions:** 9 regions. **Defense budget** (2013): $26 mil. **Active troops:** 4,450.

Economy: Industries: agric. prods. proc., beer, soft drinks. **Chief crops:** rice, corn, beans, cassava, cashew nuts, peanuts, palm kernels, cotton. **Natural resources:** fish, timber, phosphates, bauxite, clay, granite, limestone, unexploited petroleum deposits. **Water:** 17,028 cu m per capita. **Electricity prod.** (2012): 50 mil kWh. **Labor force:** agric. 82%, industry and services 18%. **Unemployment:** 6.9%.

Finance: Monetary unit: CFA Franc (XOF) (586.00 = $1 U.S.). **GDP:** $2.7 bil; **per capita GDP:** $1,500; **GDP growth:** 4.8%. **Imports:** $218.2 mil; Portugal 27.1%, Senegal 12.8%, China 6.5%, Spain 5.5%. **Exports:** $198.2 mil; India 63.5%, Nigeria 20.3%, China 5.7%, Togo 5.6%. **Tourism:** $21 mil. **Budget:** $185.2 mil. **Inflation:** 1.4%.

Transport: Airports: 2.
Communications: Telephone (2009): 0.3 per 100 pop. **Mobile:** 69.3 per 100 pop. **Broadband:** 0.0 per 100 pop. **Internet:** 3.5%.
Health: Expend.: 5.6%. **Life expect.:** 48.6 male; 52.7 female. **Births:** 32.9 per 1,000 pop. **Deaths:** 14.1 per 1,000 pop. **Infant mortality:** 87.5 per 1,000 live births. **Undernourished:** 20.7%. **HIV:** NA.
Education: Compulsory: ages 6-14. **Literacy:** 59.8%.
Permanent UN Mission: 336 E. 45th St., 13th Fl., New York, NY 10017; (212) 896-8311.
Website: www.gov.gw or www.state.gov/p/af/ci/pu/

Portuguese mariners explored the area in the mid-15th cent.; the slave trade flourished in the 17th and 18th cents., and colonization began in the 19th. Independence came Sept. 10, 1974, ending 13 years of guerrilla warfare against the Portuguese regime.

A Nov. 1980 coup gave army chief João Bernardo Vieira absolute power. Vieira eventually initiated political liberalization; multiparty elections were held in 1994. A 1998 army uprising triggered a civil war, with Senegal and Guinea aiding the Vieira regime. After a peace accord signed Nov. 2 broke down, rebel troops ousted Vieira on May 7, 1999.

Civilian rule returned with 1999-2000 elections, but top military officers staged a coup Sept. 14, 2003. Vieira won a presidential runoff election, July 24, 2005. A group of soldiers murdered Vieira, Mar. 2, 2009. Political violence continued as the 2009 presidential election approached; the ruling party candidate, Malam Bacai

Sanhá, won a runoff vote July 26. He died Jan. 9, 2012. A military coup Apr. 12 derailed a runoff election scheduled for Apr. 29. The military appointed Manuel Serifo Nhamadjo to lead a transitional government. Drug trafficking increased substantially, with the support of the military. The U.S. arrested and indicted former navy chief Rear Adm. José Américo Bubo Na Tchuto on drug charges Apr. 2013; armed forces head Gen. Antonio Injai was indicted in absentia. Na Tchuto pleaded guilty, May 13, 2014. Former Finance Min. José Mário Vaz won a May 18, 2014, presidential runoff. His appointment of a new prime min., effective May 27, 2016, was protested by the party (the PAIGC) with a legislative majority.

Guyana
Cooperative Republic of Guyana

People: Population: 735,909. **Age distrib.:** <15: 27.1%; 65+: 5.8%. **Growth:** 0.2%. **Migrants:** 2%. **Pop. density:** 9.7 per sq mi, 3.7 per sq km. **Urban:** 28.7%. **Ethnic groups:** East Indian 43.5%, black (African) 30.2%, mixed 16.7%, Amerindian 9.1%. **Languages:** English (official), Guyanese Creole, Amerindian langs., Indian langs., Chinese. **Religions:** Protestant 30.5% (incl. Pentecostal 16.9%), Hindu 28.4%, Roman Catholic 8.1%, Muslim 7.2%, none 4.3%.

Geography: Total area: 83,000 sq mi, 214,969 sq km; **Land area:** 76,004 sq mi, 196,849 sq km. **Location:** N coast of S America. **Venezuela** on W, **Brazil** on S, **Suriname** on E. **Topography:** Dense tropical forests cover much of land. A grassy savanna divides it from flat coastal area, where 90% of the pop. lives, with its rich alluvial soil. **Arable land:** 2.1%. **Capital:** Georgetown, 123,852 (2014).

Government: Type: Parliamentary republic. **Head of state:** Pres. David Arthur Granger; b. 1945; in office: May 16, 2015. **Head of gov.:** Prime Min. Moses Nagamootoo; b. 1947; in office: May 19, 2015. **Local divisions:** 10 regions. **Defense budget:** $40 mil. **Active troops:** 3,400.

Economy: Industries: bauxite, sugar, rice milling, timber, textiles. **Chief crops:** sugarcane, rice, edible oils. **Natural resources:** bauxite, gold, diamonds, timber, shrimp, fish. **Water:** 353,279 cu m per capita. **Electricity prod.:** 0.9 bil kWh. **Labor force:** NA. **Unemployment:** 11.1%.

Finance: Monetary unit: Dollar (GYD) (203.20 = $1 U.S.). **GDP:** $5.8 bil; **per capita GDP:** $7,500; **GDP growth:** 3%. **Imports:** $1.7 bil; U.S. 24.6%, Trinidad and Tobago 24.1%, China 10.8%, Suriname 9.5%. **Exports:** $1.1 bil; U.S. 33.5%, Canada 17.9%, UK 6.7%. **Tourism:** $79 mil. **Budget:** $940 mil. **Inflation:** −1%.

Transport: Motor vehicles: 84.9 per 1,000 pop. **Airports:** 11.
Communications: Telephone: 19.1 per 100 pop. **Mobile:** 67.2 per 100 pop. **Broadband:** 0.2 per 100 pop. **Internet:** 38.2%.
Health: Expend.: 5.3%. **Life expect.:** 65.4 male; 71.5 female. **Births:** 15.5 per 1,000 pop. **Deaths:** 7.4 per 1,000 pop. **Infant mortality:** 31.5 per 1,000 live births. **Undernourished:** 10.6%. **HIV:** 1.5%.
Education: Compulsory: ages 6-14. **Literacy:** 87.5%.
Embassy: 2490 Tracy Pl. NW 20008; 265-6900.
Website: www.gina.gov.gy

Guyana became a Dutch possession in the 17th cent., but sovereignty passed to Britain in 1815. Indentured servants from India soon outnumbered African slaves. Guyana became independent May 26, 1966.

The Port Kaituma ambush of U.S. Rep. Leo J. Ryan and others investigating mistreatment of American followers of the Rev. Jim Jones's Peoples Temple cult triggered a mass suicide-execution of 911 cultists at their commune in Jonestown, Nov. 18, 1978.

The People's National Congress, the party in power since Guyana became independent, was voted out of office with the election of Cheddi Jagan in Oct. 1992. When Pres. Jagan died Mar. 6, 1997, Prime Min. Samuel Hinds succeeded him. Jagan's widow, Janet, became prime min. Mar. 17. She won the presidency in a disputed election Dec. 15. She resigned because of ill health Aug. 1999 and was succeeded by Bharrat Jagdeo. He won reelection in 2001 and 2006. Donald Ramotar, the candidate of Jagdeo's party, was elected president in 2011. Ramotar suspended parliament, Nov. 10, 2014, to prevent a no-confidence vote; an opposition coalition won a 1-seat majority over Ramotar's party in May 11, 2015, elections, and coalition leader David Granger became president, May 16.

Haiti
Republic of Haiti

People: Population: 10,485,800. **Age distrib.:** <15: 33.4%; 65+: 4.1%. **Growth:** 1.7%. **Migrants:** 0.4%. **Pop. density:** 985.4 per sq mi, 380.5 per sq km. **Urban:** 59.8%. **Ethnic groups:** black 95%, mulatto and white 5%. **Languages:** French, Creole (both official). **Religions:** Roman Catholic (official) 54.7%, Protestant 28.5% (incl. Baptist 15.4%), voodoo (official) 2.1%, none 10.2%.

Geography: Total area: 10,714 sq mi, 27,750 sq km; **Land area:** 10,641 sq mi, 27,560 sq km. **Location:** In Caribbean; occupies western third of isl. of Hispaniola. **Dominican Republic** on E, **Cuba** to W. **Topography:** About two-thirds is mountainous. Much of rest is semiarid. Coastal areas are warm and moist. **Arable land:** 38.8%. **Capital:** Port-au-Prince, 2,507,309.

Government: Type: Semi-presidential republic. **Head of state:** Interim Pres. Jocelerme Privert; b. 1954; in office: Feb. 14, 2016. **Head of gov.:** Prime Min. Enex Jean-Charles; b. 1960; in office: Mar. 28, 2016. **Local divisions:** 10 departments. **Defense budget:** NA. **Active troops:** 70; UN mission MINUSTAH in country since 2004.

Economy: Industries: textiles, sugar refining, flour milling, cement, light assembly of imported parts. **Chief crops:** coffee, mangoes, cocoa, sugarcane, rice, corn, sorghum. **Natural resources:** bauxite, copper, calcium carbonate, gold, marble, hydropower. **Water:** 1,310 cu m per capita. **Electricity prod.:** 1 bil kWh. **Labor force:** agric. 38.1%, industry 11.5%, services 50.4%. **Unemployment:** 6.8%.

Finance: Monetary unit: Gourde (HTG) (64.72 = $1 U.S.). **GDP:** $18.8 bil; **per capita GDP:** $1,800; **GDP growth:** 1%. **Imports:** $3.4 bil; Dominican Republic 35.3%, U.S. 24.5%, Netherlands Antilles 9.4%, China 9.4%. **Exports:** $1 bil; U.S. 85.3%. **Tourism:** $609 mil. **Budget:** $2.2 bil. **Inflation:** 9%.

Transport: Motor vehicles: 8.6 per 1,000 pop. **Airports:** 4. **Communications: Telephone:** 0.4 per 100 pop. **Mobile:** 69.9 per 100 pop. **Broadband:** NA. **Internet:** 12.2%.

Health: Expend.: 7.6%. **Life expect.:** 61.2 male; 66.4 female. **Births:** 23.3 per 1,000 pop. **Deaths:** 7.7 per 1,000 pop. **Infant mortality:** 48.2 per 1,000 live births. **Undernourished:** 53.4%. **HIV:** 1.7%.

Education: Compulsory: ages 6-11. **Literacy:** 60.7%.
Embassy: 2311 Massachusetts Ave. NW 20008; 332-4090.
Website: primature.gouv.ht or www.haiti.org

Haiti, visited by Christopher Columbus in 1492 and a French colony from 1697, attained its independence, 1804, following a rebellion led by former slave Toussaint L'Ouverture. After a period of political violence, the U.S. occupied the country 1915-34.

François Duvalier, known as Papa Doc, was elected president in 1957; in 1964 he was named president for life. Upon his death in 1971, he was succeeded by his son, Jean Claude Duvalier, known as Baby Doc. Following weeks of unrest, Jean Claude fled Haiti aboard a U.S. Air Force jet Feb. 7, 1986. His departure ended the Duvalier family's brutal 28-year dictatorship, but political violence, government corruption, poverty, AIDS and other health problems, and deteriorating environmental quality have continued to plague Haiti.

Jean-Bertrand Aristide was elected president in 1990, but the military arrested and expelled him from the country in Sept. 1991. The U.S. Coast Guard intercepted some 35,000 Haitian refugees as they tried to enter the U.S., 1991-92. Most were returned to Haiti. There was a new upsurge of refugees starting in late 1993.

The UN authorized in 1994 an invasion of Haiti by a multinational force. With U.S. troops already en route, a full-scale invasion was averted, Sept. 18, when military leaders agreed to step down. Aristide returned to Haiti and was restored to office Oct. 15. A UN peacekeeping force exercised responsibility in Haiti from 1995 to 1997. Aristide transferred power to his elected successor, René Préval, in 1996.

At least 140 people died and over 160,000 were left homeless when Hurricane Georges struck Haiti Sept. 22, 1998. Aristide won the 2000 presidency in an election boycotted by opposition groups. An armed uprising in early 2004 and pressure from France and the U.S. toppled Aristide, who went into exile Feb. 29. A U.S.-led contingent, sent in after the upheaval, yielded authority June 1, 2004, to a UN stabilization force (MINUSTAH). MINUSTAH uniformed personnel numbered about 4,700 as of Aug. 31, 2016.

Flooding in late May 2004 killed more than 1,000 people, and more than 2,400 were killed in Tropical Storm Jeanne in Sept. Préval was reelected in 2006. Skyrocketing prices for food imports sparked riots and mass protests in Apr. 2008. A succession of hurricanes and tropical storms (Fay, Gustav, Hanna, Ike), Aug.-Sept. 2008, left more than 550 Haitians dead and up to 1 mil homeless.

An earthquake Jan. 12, 2010, near Port-au-Prince caused cataclysmic damage. More than 220,000 people (including nearly 100 UN peacekeepers) were killed, at least 300,000 were injured, and more than 1.5 mil were left homeless. With the central government paralyzed a massive international relief effort saw mixed results. As of Mar. 31, 2016, more than 6 years after the earthquake, over 62,000 Haitians were still living in displacement camps. A cholera epidemic, which began soon after the 2010 earthquake, had infected almost 779,000 and killed more than 9,300 by Apr. 2016; an internal 2016 UN study concluded UN peacekeepers had brought the disease into the country. A Doctors Without Borders study reported in 2016 that the death toll was likely significantly underestimated early in the epidemic.

After the first round of presidential balloting Nov. 28, 2010, Michel Martelly, an entertainer, was declared ineligible for the second round. Violent protests, allegations of electoral fraud, and diplomatic pressure from the U.S. and other nations gained him a place in the runoff Mar. 20, 2011, which he won. After allegations of widespread fraud in the Oct. 25, 2015, first-round election for a new president, an electoral commission nullified the results and ruled that the balloting should be held again Oct. 9, 2016.

Interim Pres. Jocelerme Privert, appointed by parliament, took office in Feb. 2016 after Martelly's term expired. The re-vote was postponed, Oct. 5, 2016, after Hurricane Matthew caused flooding, widespread damage, and an estimated 500-1,000 deaths.

Honduras
Republic of Honduras

People: Population: 8,893,259. **Age distrib.:** <15: 33.6%; 65+: 4.2%. **Growth:** 1.6%. **Migrants:** 0.3%. **Pop. density:** 205.9 per sq mi, 79.5 per sq km. **Urban:** 55.3%. **Ethnic groups:** mestizo (mixed Amerindian/European) 90%, Amerindian 7%, black 2%. **Languages:** Spanish (official), Amerindian dialects. **Religions:** Roman Catholic 97%, Protestant 3%.

Geography: Total area: 43,278 sq mi, 112,090 sq km; **Land area:** 43,201 sq mi, 111,890 sq km. **Location:** Central America. Guatemala on W; El Salvador, Nicaragua on S. **Topography:** Caribbean coast is 500 mi long. Pacific coast, on Gulf of Fonseca, is 40 mi long. Mountainous, with wide fertile valleys and rich forests. **Arable land:** 9.1%. **Capital:** Tegucigalpa, 1,145,547.

Government: Type: Presidential republic. **Head of state and gov.:** Pres. Juan Orlando Hernandez Alvarado; b. 1968; in office: Jan. 27, 2014. **Local divisions:** 18 departments. **Defense budget:** $249 mil. **Active troops:** 10,700.

Economy: Industries: sugar, coffee, woven and knit apparel, wood prods., cigars. **Chief crops:** bananas, coffee, citrus, corn, African palm. **Natural resources:** timber, gold, silver, copper, lead, zinc, iron ore, antimony, coal, fish, hydropower. **Water:** 11,413 cu m per capita. **Electricity prod.:** 7.8 bil kWh. **Labor force:** agric. 39.2%, industry 20.9%, services 39.8%. **Unemployment:** 3.9%.

Finance: Monetary unit: Lempira (HNL) (22.83 = $1 U.S.). **GDP:** $41.1 bil; **per capita GDP:** $4,900; **GDP growth:** 3.6%. **Imports:** $10.9 bil; U.S. 35.2%, China 13.6%, Guatemala 9.2%, Mexico 6.6%, El Salvador 5.1%. **Exports:** $7.8 bil; U.S. 36%, Germany 8.7%, El Salvador 8.5%, Guatemala 6%, Nicaragua 5.6%. **Tourism:** $650 mil. **Budget:** $4.2 bil. **Inflation:** 3.2%.

Transport: Railways: 434 mi. **Motor vehicles:** 18.5 per 1,000 pop. **Airports:** 13.
Communications: Telephone: 5.9 per 100 pop. **Mobile:** 95.5 per 100 pop. **Broadband:** 16.3 per 100 pop. **Internet:** 20.4%.

Health: Expend.: 8.7%. **Life expect.:** 69.5 male; 72.8 female. **Births:** 22.8 per 1,000 pop. **Deaths:** 5.2 per 1,000 pop. **Infant mortality:** 17.7 per 1,000 live births. **Undernourished:** 12.2%. **HIV:** 0.4%.

Education: Compulsory: ages 6-14. **Literacy:** 88.4%.
Embassy: 3007 Tilden St. NW, Ste. 4-M, 20008; 966-2604.
Website: www.presidencia.gob.hn

Mayan civilization flourished in Honduras in the 1st millennium CE. Columbus arrived in 1502. Honduras became independent after freeing itself from Spain, 1821, and from the Fed. of Central America, 1838.

In 1975, the army ousted Gen. Oswaldo Lopez Arellano, president for most of the time since 1963, over charges of pervasive bribery by United Brands Co. of the U.S. An elected civilian government took power in 1982.

Already one of the poorest countries in the Western Hemisphere, Honduras was devastated in late Oct. 1998 by Hurricane Mitch, which killed at least 5,600 people and caused more than $850 mil in damage to crops and livestock.

Ricardo Maduro, a businessman who pledged to crack down on crime, won the 2001 presidency. He was succeeded by Manuel Zelaya Rosales of the opposition Liberal Party, who won the 2005 presidential election. After the military ousted Zelaya in June 2009, Porfirio "Pepe" Lobo of the conservative National Party defeated Liberal Party nominee Elvin Santos in the Nov. 2009 presidential election. National Party candidate Juan Orlando Hernández won the Nov. 2013 presidential election.

Northern Honduras has become a major transshipment point for illegal drugs being smuggled from South America to the U.S. Drug-gang violence and other crime apparently contributed to a significant increase in migrants, including thousands of children traveling alone or with their mothers, trying to enter the U.S. along the Mexican border, 2013-14; a new surge in such undocumented immigration began in late 2015. Environmental and indigenous rights activist Berta Cáceres was shot to death in her home, Mar. 3, 2016. Nelson García, a colleague of Cáceres, was fatally shot Mar. 15, and another, Lesbia Janeth Urquía, was found murdered July 6, 2016.

Hungary

People: Population: 9,874,784. **Age distrib.:** <15: 14.8%; 65+: 18.7%. **Growth:** –0.2%. **Migrants:** 4.6%. **Pop. density:** 285.4 per sq mi, 110.2 per sq km. **Urban:** 71.7%. **Ethnic groups:** Hungarian 85.6%, Roma 3.2%. **Languages:** Hungarian (official), English, German. **Religions:** Roman Catholic 37.2%, Calvinist 11.6%, none 18.2%.

Geography: Total area: 35,918 sq mi, 93,028 sq km; **Land area:** 34,598 sq mi, 89,608 sq km. **Location:** E central Europe. Ukraine, Slovakia on N; Austria on W; Slovenia, Croatia, Serbia on S; Romania on E. **Topography:** Danube R. forms Slovak border in NW, then swings S to bisect the country. Eastern half of Hungary is mainly a great fertile plain, the Alfold. Hilly in W and N. **Arable land:** 48.6%. **Capital:** Budapest, 1,712,054.

Government: Type: Parliamentary republic. **Head of state:** Pres. János Áder; b. 1959; in office: May 10, 2012. **Head of gov.:** Prime Min. Viktor Orbán; b. 1963; in office: May 29, 2010. **Local divisions:** 19 counties, 23 cities with county rights, 1 capital city. **Defense budget:** $879 mil. **Active troops:** 26,500.

Economy: Industries: mining, metallurgy, constr. materials, processed foods, textiles, chemicals (espec. pharmaceuticals), motor vehicles. **Chief crops:** wheat, corn, sunflower seeds, potatoes, sugar beets. **Natural resources:** bauxite, coal, nat. gas. **Water:** 10,553 cu m per capita. **Crude oil reserves** (2015): 27.2 mil bbls. **Electricity prod.:** 29 bil kWh. **Labor force:** agric. 7.1%, industry 29.7%, services 63.2%. **Unemployment:** 7.8%.

Finance: Monetary unit: Forint (HUF) (276.66 = $1 U.S.). **GDP:** $258.4 bil; **per capita GDP:** $26,200; **GDP growth:** 2.9%. **Imports:** $92.9 bil; Germany 25.8%, China 6.7%, Austria 6.6%, Poland 5.5%, Slovakia 5.3%, France 5%. **Exports:** $97.6 bil; Germany 28%, Romania 5.4%, Slovakia 5.1%, Austria 5%. **Tourism:** $5.3 bil. **Budget** (2016 est.): $59.4 bil. **Inflation:** −0.1%.

Transport: Railways: 5,001 mi. **Motor vehicles:** 367.9 per 1,000 pop. **Airports:** 20.

Communications: Telephone: 31.2 per 100 pop. **Mobile:** 118.9 per 100 pop. **Broadband:** 34 per 100 pop. **Internet:** 72.8%.

Health: Expend.: 7.4%. **Life expect.:** 72.2 male; 79.8 female. **Births:** 9.1 per 1,000 pop. **Deaths:** 12.8 per 1,000 pop. **Infant mortality:** 5.0 per 1,000 live births. **Undernourished:** <5%. **HIV:** NA.

Education: Compulsory: ages 6-13. **Literacy:** 99.4%. **Embassy:** 3910 Shoemaker St. NW 20008; 362-6730. **Website:** www.kormany.hu

Earliest settlers, chiefly Slav and Germanic, were overrun by Magyars from the east. Stephen I (997-1038) was made king by Pope Sylvester II in 1000 CE. The country suffered repeated Turkish invasions in the 15th-17th cents. After the Turks were defeated, 1686-97, Austria dominated, but Hungary obtained concessions, and regained internal independence in 1867 under a dual monarchy with the emperor of Austria. Defeated with the Central Powers at the end of WWI in 1918, Hungary lost Transylvania to Romania, Croatia and Bacska to Yugoslavia, and Slovakia and Carpatho-Ruthenia to Czechoslovakia. All had large Hungarian minorities. A republic under Michael Karolyi and a Bolshevist revolt under Bela Kun were followed by a vote for a monarchy in 1920 with Adm. Nicholas Horthy as regent.

Hungary allied with Germany before WWII and was allowed to annex, 1938-41, most of its lost territories. Russian troops captured the country, 1944-45. By terms of an armistice with the Allied powers, Hungary agreed to return to its borders of 1937.

A republic was declared Feb. 1, 1946. In 1947 a hard-line Communist, pro-Soviet government was installed. Demonstrations against Communist rule developed into open revolt in 1956. Soviet forces launched a massive attack Nov. 4 against Budapest. About 200,000 persons fled the country. Thousands were arrested and executed.

Major economic reforms were launched early in 1968, switching from a central planning system to one based on market forces and profit. In 1989 Parliament legalized freedom of assembly and association as Hungary shifted away from Communism. In Oct. the Communist Party was formally dissolved. The last Soviet troops left June 19, 1991. Hungary became a full member of NATO in 1999 and of the EU in 2004.

The IMF, EU, and World Bank agreed Oct. 2008 to extend $25.1 bil to rescue Hungary's economy, battered by a global financial crisis. With the nation still reeling from recession, the center-right Fidesz party ousted the Socialists in 2010 parliamentary elections. Parliament approved Apr. 2011 a fiscally and socially conservative constitution that went into force Jan. 1, 2012. Fidesz retained its majority in Apr. 6, 2014, elections. Hungary was a major transit route in 2015 for migrants from the Balkans, SW Asia, the Middle East, and Africa trying to reach N Europe. More than 411,000 migrants entered or tried to enter Hungary in 2015, almost all before the end of Oct., by which time Hungary had built more than 300 mi of security fencing along its southern borders with Serbia and Croatia. With migrant crossings into Hungary increasing again by Mar. 2016 (100+ people daily), the government declared a state of emergency Mar. 9 and deployed thousands of troops at its southern borders. In an Oct. 2, 2016, referendum, not binding because of low turnout, Hungarian voters rejected mandatory participation in EU refugee resettlement programs.

Iceland
Republic of Iceland

People: Population: 335,878. **Age distrib.:** <15: 20.4%; 65+: 14.1%. **Growth:** 1.2%. **Migrants:** 11.4%. **Pop. density:** 8.7 per sq mi, 3.4 per sq km. **Urban:** 94.2%. **Ethnic groups:** homogeneous mix of Norse-Celt descendants 94%, foreign origin 6%. **Languages:** Icelandic, English, Nordic langs., German. **Religions:** Evangelical Lutheran Church of Iceland (official) 73.8%, Roman Catholic 3.6%, Reykjavik Free Church 2.9%, none 5.6%.

Geography: Total area: 39,769 sq mi, 103,000 sq km; **Land area:** 38,707 sq mi, 100,250 sq km. **Location:** Isl. at N end of Atlantic O. Nearest neighbor is Greenland (Den.) to W. **Topography:** Recent volcanic origin. Three-quarters of surface is wasteland: glaciers, lakes, a lava desert, geysers, and hot springs. The climate is moderated by the Gulf Stream. **Arable land:** 1.2%. **Capital:** Reykjavík, 184,171 (2014).

Government: Type: Parliamentary republic. **Head of state:** Pres. Gudni Thorlacius Johannesson; b. 1968; in office: Aug. 1, 2016. **Head of gov.:** Prime Min. Sigurdur Ingi Johannsson; b. 1962; in office: Apr. 7, 2016. **Local divisions:** 8 regions. **Defense budget:** $34 mil (Coast Guard budget). **Active troops:** No armed forces; 200 paramilitary. Relies on NATO allies for air policing and defense.

Economy: Industries: tourism, fish proc., aluminum smelting, ferrosilicon prod., geothermal power, hydropower. **Chief crops:** potatoes, carrots, green vegetables. **Natural resources:** fish, hydropower, geothermal power, diatomite. **Water:** 516,090 cu m per capita. **Electricity prod.:** 17 bil kWh. **Labor force:** agric. 4.8%, industry 22.2%, services 73%. **Unemployment:** 5%.

Finance: Monetary unit: Krona (ISK) (115.82 = $1 U.S.). **GDP:** $15.2 bil; **per capita GDP:** $46,100; **GDP growth:** 4%. **Imports:** $4.6 bil; Norway 10.1%, Germany 8.6%, China 7.9%, U.S. 7.9%, Denmark 7.1%, Netherlands 5.9%, Brazil 5.8%, UK 5%. **Exports:** $4.4 bil; Netherlands 26.1%, Spain 11.5%, UK 11.6%, Germany 7.4%, France 5.7%, U.S. 5.7%. **Tourism:** $1.6 bil. **Budget:** $6.9 bil. **Inflation:** 1.6%.

Transport: Motor vehicles: 771.3 per 1,000 pop. **Airports:** 7.

Communications: Telephone: 49.9 per 100 pop. **Mobile:** 114 per 100 pop. **Broadband:** 85.3 per 100 pop. **Internet:** 98.2%.

Health: Expend.: 8.9%. **Life expect.:** 80.9 male; 85.3 female. **Births:** 13.8 per 1,000 pop. **Deaths:** 6.3 per 1,000 pop. **Infant mortality:** 2.1 per 1,000 live births. **Undernourished:** <5%. **HIV:** NA.

Education: Compulsory: ages 6-15. **Literacy:** 99%. **Embassy:** 2900 K St. NW, Ste. 509, 20007; 265-6653. **Website:** www.iceland.is

Iceland was an independent republic from 930 to 1262, when it joined with Norway. Its language has maintained its purity for 1,000 years. The Althing, or assembly, established in 930, is the world's oldest surviving parliament. Danish rule lasted 1380-1918; the last ties with the Danish crown were severed in 1941.

A 55-year U.S. military presence in Iceland ended with the closure of the Keflavík naval air station in Sept. 2006. Iceland's banking system and currency collapsed amid the global financial crisis in Oct. 2008. More than $10 bil in loans from the IMF and European governments restored financial stability; austerity measures were imposed, and the nation entered a deep recession. Political unrest sparked by soaring inflation and unemployment led to the Feb. 2009 installation of a center-left government, which swept to victory in Apr. 25 elections. A major eruption Apr. 14, 2010, of the Eyjafjallajökull volcano disrupted European air traffic for six days. The governing coalition lost Apr. 28, 2013, parliamentary elections, in which center-right parties came to power. Prime Min. Sigmundur David Gunnlaugsson resigned, Apr. 5, 2016, after "Panama Papers," leaked from a Panamanian law firm, revealed that he and his wife had bought a company in the British Virgin Islands, apparently kept secret to avoid conflict-of-interest allegations.

India
Republic of India

People: Population: 1,266,883,598. **Age distrib.:** <15: 27.7%; 65+: 6.1%. **Growth:** 1.2%. **Migrants:** 0.4%. **Pop. density:** 1,103.6 per sq mi, 426.1 per sq km. **Urban:** 33.1%. **Ethnic groups:** Indo-Aryan 72%, Dravidian 25%, Mongoloid and other 3%. **Languages:** Hindi (most widely spoken); 14 other official langs. (incl. Bengali, Telugu, Marathi, Tamil, Urdu, Gujarati); English (subsidiary official lang.; crucial for natl., political, commercial communication); Hindustani (variant of Hindi/Urdu widely spoken throughout N). **Religions:** Hindu 79.8%, Muslim 14.2%.

Geography: Total area: 1,269,219 sq mi, 3,287,263 sq km; **Land area:** 1,147,956 sq mi, 2,973,193 sq km. **Location:** Occupies most of Indian subcontinent in S Asia. Pakistan on W; China, Nepal, Bhutan on N; Myanmar, Bangladesh on E. **Topography:** The Himalayan Mts., highest in world, stretch across northern borders. The Ganges Plain below is among the world's most densely populated regions. The climate varies from tropical heat in S to near-Arctic cold in N. Rajasthan Desert is NW. NE Assam Hills get 400 in. of rain a year. **Arable land:** 52.8%. **Capital:** New Delhi, 26,453,827 (figure is for Delhi National Capital Region). **Cities:** Mumbai (Bombay), 21,357,362; Kolkata (Calcutta), 14,980,232; Bangalore, 10,456,055; Chennai (Madras), 10,162,822; Hyderabad, 9,217,613; Ahmadabad, 7,570,528.

Government: Type: Federal parliamentary republic. **Head of state:** Pres. Pranab Mukherjee; b. 1935; in office: July 25, 2012. **Head of gov.:** Prime Min. Narendra Modi; b. 1950; in office: May 26, 2014. **Local divisions:** 29 states, 7 union territories. **Defense budget:** $48 bil. **Active troops:** 1,346,000.

Economy: Industries: textiles, chemicals, food proc., steel, transp. equip., cement, mining, petroleum, machinery, software, pharmaceuticals. **Chief crops:** rice, wheat, oilseed, cotton, jute, tea, sugarcane, lentils, onions, potatoes. **Natural resources:** coal, iron ore, manganese, mica, bauxite, rare earth elements, titanium ore, chromite, nat. gas, diamonds, petroleum, limestone. **Water:** 1,458 cu m per capita. **Crude oil reserves:** 5.7 bil bbls. **Electricity prod.:** 1.1 tril kWh. **Labor force:** agric. 49%, industry 20%, services 31%. **Unemployment:** 3.6%.

Finance: Monetary unit: Rupee (INR) (66.78 = $1 U.S.). **GDP:** $8 tril; **per capita GDP:** $6,200; **GDP growth:** 7.3%. **Imports:** $432.3 bil; China 15.4%, UAE 5.5%, Saudi Arabia 5.4%, Switzerland 5.3%, U.S. 5.1%. **Exports:** $287.6 bil; U.S. 15.2%, UAE 11.4%. **Tourism:** $21 bil. **Budget:** $326.2 bil. **Inflation:** 4.9%.

Transport: Railways: 42,579 mi. **Motor vehicles:** 33.4 per 1,000 pop. **Airports:** 253.

Communications: Telephone: 2 per 100 pop. **Mobile:** 78.8 per 100 pop. **Broadband:** 5.5 per 100 pop. **Internet:** 26%.

Health: Expend.: 4.7%. **Life expect.:** 67.3 male; 69.8 female. **Births:** 19.3 per 1,000 pop. **Deaths:** 7.3 per 1,000 pop. **Infant mortality:** 40.5 per 1,000 live births. **Undernourished:** 15.2%. **HIV:** NA.

Education: Compulsory: ages 6-13. **Literacy:** 72.2%.

Embassy: 2107 Massachusetts Ave. NW 20008; 939-7000.

Website: india.gov.in

India has one of the oldest civilizations in the world. Excavations trace the Indus Valley civilization back for at least 5,000 years. Paintings in the mountain caves of Ajanta, richly carved temples, the Taj Mahal in Agra, and the Kutab Minar in Delhi are among treasured relics of the past.

Aryan tribes, speaking Sanskrit, invaded from the NW around 1500 BCE. Asoka ruled most of the Indian subcontinent in the 3rd cent. BCE and established Buddhism. But Hinduism revived and eventually predominated. Under the Guptas, 4th-6th cent. CE, science, literature, and the arts enjoyed a golden age. Arab invaders established a Muslim foothold in the west in the 8th cent., and Turkish Muslims gained control of North India by 1200. The Mughal emperors ruled 1526-1857.

Vasco da Gama established Portuguese trading posts 1498-1503. The Dutch followed. The British East India Co. sent Capt. William Hawkins, 1609, to get concessions from the Mughal emperor for spices and textiles. Operating as the East India Co., the British gained control of most of India. The British parliament assumed political direction; under Lord Bentinck, 1828-35, rule by rajahs (princes) was curbed. After the Sepoy troops mutinied, 1857-58, the British supported the native rulers.

Nationalism grew after WWI. The Indian National Congress and the Muslim League demanded constitutional reform. A leader emerged in Mohandas K. Gandhi (called Mahatma, or Great Soul) (b. Oct. 2, 1869), who advocated self-rule, nonviolence, and an end to caste discrimination against "untouchables." In 1930 he launched a program of civil disobedience, boycotting British goods and rejecting taxes without representation. He was assassinated Jan. 30, 1948.

In 1935, Britain gave India a constitution providing a bicameral federal congress. Muhammad Ali Jinnah, head of the Muslim League, sought creation of a Muslim nation, Pakistan.

The British government partitioned British India into the dominions of India and Pakistan. India became a member of the UN in 1945, a self-governing member of the Commonwealth in 1947, and a democratic republic, Jan. 26, 1950. More than 12 mil Hindu and Muslim refugees crossed the India-Pakistan borders in 1947; about 200,000 were killed in communal fighting.

After Pakistan troops began attacks on Bengali separatists in East Pakistan, Mar. 25, 1971, some 10 mil refugees fled to India. India and Pakistan went to war Dec. 3, 1971, on both the east and west fronts. Pakistan troops, Dec. 16, surrendered in the east, which became Bangladesh; Pakistan agreed to a cease-fire in the west Dec. 17.

Indira Gandhi, India's prime minister since Jan. 1966, invoked emergency powers in June 1975. Thousands of opponents were arrested and press censorship imposed. These and other actions, including population control through forced vasectomies, were widely resented. Opposition parties, united in the Janata coalition, won the 1977 elections.

Gandhi became prime minister for the second time in 1980. She was assassinated by two of her Sikh bodyguards Oct. 31, 1984, in response to the government suppression in June 1984 of a Sikh uprising in Punjab, which included an assault on the Golden Temple at Amritsar, the holiest Sikh shrine. Widespread rioting followed the assassination; thousands of Sikhs were killed and some 50,000 left homeless. Rajiv, Indira Gandhi's son, replaced her as prime minister. A gas leak at a Union Carbide chemical plant in Bhopal, Dec. 1984, eventually killed some 14,000 people.

Many died in religious, ethnic, and political conflicts during the late 1980s and early '90s. To suppress the Sikh insurgency in Punjab, Indian government troops attacked the Golden Temple again in 1988. Rajiv Gandhi was swept from office in 1989 amid charges of incompetence and corruption; he was assassinated May 21, 1991, while campaigning to regain power. Nationwide riots followed the destruction of a 16th-cent. mosque by Hindu militants in Dec. 1992. Ethnic clashes in Assam, in NW India, killed thousands

in Feb. 1993. Bombs jolted Mumbai and Kolkata, Mar. 12-19, killing over 300.

India's first president from the lowest caste, K. R. Narayanan, took office July 1997. India conducted a series of nuclear tests in mid-May 1998, raising tensions with Pakistan. India blamed Pakistani-sponsored terrorist groups for an Oct. 1, 2001, suicide attack on the state legislature in Jammu and Kashmir (see below), in which at least 40 people died, and a Dec. 13 assault on the Indian parliament in New Delhi that left 13 people dead. Hindu-Muslim clashes in Gujarat Feb.-Mar. 2002 claimed more than 700 lives; 11 people were convicted, June 2, 2016, of murdering 69 Muslims during the Gujarat violence.

Led by Rajiv Gandhi's Italian-born widow, Sonia, the Congress Party won the most seats in 2004 parliamentary elections. When Hindu nationalists objected to her candidacy, she chose not to become prime minister, and Manmohan Singh, a Sikh economist, took office instead.

The Indian Ocean tsunami of Dec. 26, 2004, left more than 10,700 people dead, some 5,600 missing, and over 647,000 displaced. Islamic extremists set off 7 bombs on commuter trains in Mumbai, July 11, 2006, killing some 200 people; 12 men were convicted, Sept. 11, 2015, of murder or other charges in connection with the bombings. The unmanned *Chandrayaan-1*, India's first lunar survey mission, was launched into space Oct. 22, 2008.

Ten Pakistanis linked to the Kashmir militant group Lashkar-e-Taiba stormed luxury hotels, a railway station, a Jewish center, and other sites in Mumbai, Nov. 26, 2008; by the time Indian army commandos took control three days later, the attackers had slaughtered 163 people. Nine of the terrorists were also killed. Convicted of murder and of waging war against India, the lone surviving gunman, Ajmal Kasab, was executed by hanging Nov. 20, 2012.

In 2009 parliamentary elections, Prime Min. Manmohan Singh's United Progressive Alliance, headed by the Congress party, gained a resounding victory. A triple bombing in Mumbai July 13, 2011, killed 26 people and injured about 140; 11 were killed when a bomb exploded Sept. 7 outside the High Court in New Delhi. Electricity blackouts July 30-31, 2012, left 670 mil people without power.

Several rapes in New Delhi in Nov.-Dec. 2012 prompted outrage and large protests for their mishandling by police and government inaction. Tougher laws against sexual violence were passed Feb. 4, 2013. The Hindu nationalist Bharatiya Janata party won a large majority in Apr.-May 2014 parliamentary elections; Narendra Modi became prime min. The Supreme Court, July 9, 2015, ordered the national government to take over the investigation of a large-scale corruption scandal in Madhya Pradesh, involving bribery, cheating, and falsification of results on school admission tests; since 2013, about 2,000 people had been arrested. Development of high-tech industries has propelled rapid economic growth since the 1990s; hundreds of millions have emerged from extreme poverty, although distribution of wealth remains highly uneven. Since 2011, India has had the world's third-largest GDP, after the U.S. and China. To combat climate change, the government released a plan, Oct. 1, 2015, for reducing the rate of growth in India's carbon emissions and generating 40% of electricity from non-fossil-fuel sources by 2030. On Oct. 2, 2016, India ratified the UN climate change agreement negotiated in Paris, Dec. 2015.

Sikkim, bordered by Tibet, Bhutan, and Nepal, formerly British protected, became a protectorate of India in 1950. Area 2,740 sq mi; pop. (2011 census) 610,577; capital is Gangtok. In Sept. 1974, India's parliament voted to make Sikkim an associate Indian state, absorbing it into India.

Kashmir is a predominantly Muslim region in the NW that borders India, Pakistan, Afghanistan, and China. Muslim rule of the previously Hindu kingdom began in 1341; after almost 200 years under the Mughals, the area was incorporated into British India in 1846. Fighting broke out in the region between India and Pakistan in 1947 following independence from Britain. A cease-fire was negotiated by the UN Jan. 1, 1949; it gave Pakistan control of one-third of the area as Azad Kashmir, in the W and NW, and India the remaining two-thirds, as the Indian state of Jammu and Kashmir. Area 85,806 sq mi; pop. (2011 census) 12,541,302. Capitals: Srinagar (summer), pop. (2014 est.) 1,393,580; Jammu (winter), pop. (2014 est.) 667,261. Fighting in the area resumed during the 1965 and 1971 wars with Pakistan. China occupied about 14,000 sq mi in the Ladakh district after a war with India in 1962.

In the 1990s, India's decision to impose central government rule triggered clashes between Indian army troops and separatist fighters. India charged Pakistan with aiding the separatists; fighting was especially heavy in May-June 1999. A cease-fire between Indian and Pakistani troops along the line of control took effect Nov. 2003. Some breaches have occurred, and fighting between Indian forces and Islamic militants has continued. Estimates of conflict-related deaths since 1989 range from 40,000 to over 80,000. A powerful earthquake Oct. 8, 2005, killed about 80,000 and left up to 3 mil homeless in Pakistani-held Kashmir and northern Pakistan. Violent protests, in which more than 80 had died by late Sept., followed the July 8, 2016, killing by Indian security forces of Kashmiri rebel leader Burhan Wani; 19 Indian soldiers were killed in a militant attack on an army base Sept. 18, 2016.

France, 1952-54, peacefully yielded to India its five colonies, former French India: Pondicherry, Karikal, Mahe, and Yanaon were merged to become Pondicherry, now Puducherry, area 185 sq mi; pop. (2011 census) 1,247,953. The colony of Chandernagor was incorporated into the state of West Bengal.

Indonesia
Republic of Indonesia

People: Population: 258,316,051. **Age distrib.:** <15: 25.4%; 65+: 6.8%. **Growth:** 0.9%. **Migrants:** 0.1%. **Pop. density:** 369.3 per sq mi, 142.6 per sq km. **Urban:** 54.5%. **Ethnic groups:** Javanese 40.1%, Sundanese 15.5%, Malay 3.7%, Batak 3.6%, Madurese 3%, Betawi 2.9%, Minangkabau 2.7%, Buginese 2.7%, Bantenese 2%. **Languages:** Bahasa Indonesia (official; modified form of Malay), English, Dutch, local dialects (Javanese most widely spoken). **Religions:** Muslim 87.2%, Christian 7%, Roman Catholic 2.9%.

Geography: Total area: 735,358 sq mi, 1,904,569 sq km; **Land area:** 699,451 sq mi, 1,811,569 sq km. **Location:** Archipelago SE of Asian mainland along the equator. Malaysia on N, Papua New Guinea on E, Timor-Leste on S. **Topography:** Comprises 17,508 islands (about 6,000 inhabited), including Java, Sumatra, Kalimantan (most of Borneo), Sulawesi (Celebes), and West Irian (Irian Jaya, the W half of New Guinea). Also Bangka, Billiton, Madura, Bali, Timor. Cooler climate in mountains and plateaus on the major isls.; tropical lowlands. **Arable land:** 13%. **Capital:** Jakarta, 10,483,109. **Cities:** Surabaya, 2,877,647; Bandung, 2,578,414; Medan, 2,229,915.

Government: Type: Presidential republic. **Head of state and gov.:** Pres. Joko Widodo; b. 1961; in office: Oct. 20, 2014. **Local divisions:** 31 provinces, 1 autonomous province, 1 special region, 1 national capital district. **Defense budget:** $7.6 bil. **Active troops:** 395,500.

Economy: Industries: petroleum and nat. gas, textiles, automotive, elec. appliances, apparel, footwear, mining, cement, medical instruments and appliances. **Chief crops:** rubber, palm oil, forest prods., cocoa, coffee, medicinal herbs. **Natural resources:** petroleum, tin, nat. gas, nickel, timber, bauxite, copper, coal, gold, silver. **Water:** 7,839 cu m per capita. **Crude oil reserves:** 3.7 bil bbls. **Electricity prod.:** 206 bil kWh. **Labor force:** agric. 38.9%, industry 13.2%, services 47.9%. **Unemployment:** 6.2%.

Finance: Monetary unit: Rupiah (IDR) (13,270.00 = $1 U.S.). **GDP:** $2.8 tril; **per capita GDP:** $11,100; **GDP growth:** 4.8%. **Imports:** $138.4 bil; China 20.6%, Singapore 12.6%, Japan 9.3%, Malaysia 6%, South Korea 5.9%, Thailand 5.7%, U.S. 5.3%. **Exports:** $152.5 bil; Japan 12%, U.S. 10.8%, China 10%, Singapore 8.4%, India 7.8%, South Korea 5.1%, Malaysia 5.1%. **Tourism:** $10.7 bil. **Budget:** $142.8 bil. **Inflation:** 6.4%.

Transport: Railways: 5,070 mi (only partly operational). **Motor vehicles:** 90.2 per 1,000 pop. **Airports:** 186.

Communications: Telephone: 8.8 per 100 pop. **Mobile:** 132.3 per 100 pop. **Broadband:** 34.7 per 100 pop. **Internet:** 22%.

Health: Expend.: 2.9%. **Life expect.:** 70.1 male; 75.5 female. **Births:** 16.4 per 1,000 pop. **Deaths:** 6.4 per 1,000 pop. **Infant mortality:** 23.5 per 1,000 live births. **Undernourished:** 7.6%. **HIV:** 0.5%.

Education: Compulsory: ages 7-15. **Literacy:** 95.4%.

Embassy: 2020 Massachusetts Ave. NW 20036; 775-5200.

Website: www.indonesia.go.id

Hindu and Buddhist civilization from India reached Indonesia nearly 2,000 years ago, taking root especially in Java. Islam spread along the maritime trade routes in the 15th cent., and became predominant by the 16th cent. The Dutch replaced the Portuguese as the area's most important European trade power in the 17th cent., securing territorial control over Java by 1750. The outer islands were subdued in the early 20th cent.

Following Japanese occupation, 1942-45, nationalists led by Sukarno and Hatta declared independence. The Netherlands ceded sovereignty in 1949. A republic was declared, Aug. 17, 1950, with Sukarno as president. Irian Jaya, on New Guinea, remained under Dutch control but was transferred by the UN to Indonesia in 1963; it became the provinces of Papua and West Papua in the early 2000s. Several thousand people in West Papua were arrested, May-June 2016, during demonstrations calling for a referendum on independence.

Sukarno suspended parliament in 1960 and was named president for life in 1963. He made close alliances with Communist governments. In Sept. 1965 an attempted coup was successfully put down, but Sukarno was forced to cede power to the army, led by Gen. Suharto, who became acting president in 1967 and ruled Indonesia for the next 31 years. The regime blamed the coup on the Communist Party; more than 300,000 alleged Communists were killed in army-initiated massacres.

Parliament reelected Suharto to a seventh consecutive 5-year term in 1998, as a severe economic downturn focused public anger on nepotism, cronyism, and corruption in the Suharto regime. Price increases in May sparked mass protests and then mob violence in Jakarta and other cities, claiming some 500 lives. Suharto resigned May 21 and was succeeded by his vice president, Bacharuddin

Jusuf Habibie. Abdurrahman Wahid, leader of Indonesia's largest Muslim organization, was elected president in 1999. In Aug. 2000, under pressure from the legislature, he agreed to share power with Vice Pres. Megawati Sukarnoputri, the daughter of the late Pres. Sukarno. Charging Wahid with incompetence and corruption, the legislature ousted him July 23, 2001, and Megawati became Indonesia's first woman president.

Clashes between Muslims and Christians in the Maluku (Molucca) Isls., 1999-2002, claimed about 5,000 lives. East Timor, a former Portuguese colony that Indonesia invaded in Dec. 1975 and controlled until Oct. 1999, became a fully independent country May 20, 2002, as Timor-Leste. Separatists in Aceh, NW Sumatra, fought against government troops during the 1980s through early 2000s. A peace agreement granting Aceh greater autonomy was signed Aug. 15, 2005.

Investigators blamed the Islamic terrorist group Jemaah Islamiyah, an al-Qaeda affiliate, for bombings that killed 202 people, mostly foreign tourists, at nightclubs in Bali, Oct. 12, 2002, and 12 people at a Marriott hotel in Jakarta, Aug. 5, 2003. A car bomb attack outside the Australian embassy in Jakarta, Sept. 9, 2004, killed 9 people. Susilo Bambang Yudhoyono, a retired general, defeated Megawati in a 2004 direct presidential runoff vote.

A massive earthquake off NW Sumatra, Dec. 26, 2004, triggered tsunamis that wreaked havoc in the Indian Ocean region. The death toll in Indonesia alone exceeded 125,000, not counting almost 40,000 missing. On Java, an earthquake, May 27, 2006, killed 5,800.

Faced with falling oil production, Indonesia left OPEC in 2008. Pres. Yudhoyono won a second 5-year term July 8, 2009. Suicide bombings at two Jakarta hotels July 17 left nine people dead. Police confirmed Sept. 17 that Noordin Muhammad Top, suspected of plotting the Jakarta attacks and other terrorist bombings, had been killed in a shootout.

The General Elections Commission, July 22, 2014, declared populist Jakarta governor Joko Widodo the presidential election winner over former general Prabowo Subianto. All 162 people aboard an AirAsia Indonesia flight were killed, Dec. 28, 2014, when the plane, en route from Surabaya, Indonesia, to Singapore, crashed into the Java Sea near Borneo.

Assaults by terrorist gunmen and bombers in Jakarta, Jan. 14, 2016, left 8 dead, including 4 attackers; ISIS claimed responsibility. Security forces, July 18, killed the suspected terrorist leader known as Santoso, whose group had declared allegiance to ISIS. Rainforest destruction and air pollution from fires to clear areas for agriculture have been major environmental problems in recent years. A Sept. 2016 study estimated that especially severe pollution from 2015 fires may have caused more than 100,000 premature deaths in Indonesia and neighboring countries.

Iran
Islamic Republic of Iran

People: Population: 82,801,633. **Age distrib.:** <15: 23.7%; 65+: 5.4%. **Growth:** 1.2%. **Migrants:** 3.4%. **Pop. density:** 140 per sq mi, 54.1 per sq km. **Urban:** 73.9%. **Ethnic groups:** Persian, Azeri, Kurd, Lur, Baloch, Arab, Turkmen and Turkic tribes. **Languages:** Persian (official), Azeri Turkic and Turkic dialects, Kurdish, Gilaki and Mazandarani, Luri, Balochi, Arabic. **Religions:** Muslim (official) 99.4% (Shia 90%-95%, Sunni 5%-10%).

Geography: Total area: 636,372 sq mi, 1,648,195 sq km; **Land area:** 591,352 sq mi, 1,531,595 sq km. **Location:** Between the Middle East and S Asia. Iraq, Turkey on W; Armenia, Azerbaijan, Turkmenistan on N; Afghanistan, Pakistan on E. **Topography:** Interior highlands and plains surrounded by high mountains, up to 18,000 ft. Large salt deserts cover much of area, though there are oases and forests. Most of pop. inhabits N and NW. **Arable land:** 9.1%. **Capital:** Tehran, 8,515,571. **Cities:** Mashhad, 3,088,072.

Government: Type: Theocratic republic. **Religious head:** Ayatollah Sayyed Ali Khamenei; b. 1939; in office: June 4, 1989. **Head of state and gov.:** Pres. Hassan Rouhani; b. 1948; in office: Aug. 4, 2013. **Local divisions:** 31 provinces. **Defense budget** (2014): $15.9 bil. **Active troops:** 523,000.

Economy: Industries: petroleum, petrochemicals, gas, fertilizers, caustic soda, textiles, cement and other constr. materials. **Chief crops:** wheat, rice, other grains, sugar beets, sugarcane, fruits, nuts, cotton. **Natural resources:** petroleum, nat. gas, coal, chromium, copper, iron ore, lead, manganese, zinc, sulfur. **Water:** 1,732 cu m per capita. **Crude oil reserves:** 157.5 bil bbls. **Electricity prod.:** 254 bil kWh. **Labor force:** agric. 16.3%, industry 35.1%, services 48.6%. **Unemployment:** 12.8%.

Finance: Monetary unit: Rial (IRR) (30,093.00 = $1 U.S.). **GDP:** $1.4 tril; **per capita GDP:** $17,300; **GDP growth:** 0%. **Imports:** $70.6 bil; UAE 39.6%, China 22.4%. **Exports:** $79 bil; China 22.2%, India 9.9%, Turkey 8.4%. **Tourism:** $3.5 bil. **Budget:** $70.1 bil. **Inflation:** 13.7%.

Transport: Railways: 5,271 mi. **Motor vehicles:** 59.6 per 1,000 pop. **Airports:** 140.

Communications: Telephone: 38.3 per 100 pop. **Mobile:** 93.4 per 100 pop. **Broadband:** 10.7 per 100 pop. **Internet:** 44.1%.

Health: Expend.: 6.9%. **Life expect.:** 69.8 male; 73.1 female. **Births:** 17.8 per 1,000 pop. **Deaths:** 5.9 per 1,000 pop. **Infant mortality:** 37.1 per 1,000 live births. **Undernourished:** <5%. **HIV:** 0.1%.

Education: Compulsory: ages 6-13. **Literacy:** 87.2%.

Permanent UN mission: 622 Third Ave., 34th Fl., New York, NY 10017; (212) 687-2020.

Website: www.president.ir

Ancestors of inhabitants of Iran, formerly known as Persia, came from the east during the second millennium BCE; they were an Indo-European group related to the Aryans of India. In 549 BCE, Cyrus the Great united the Medes and Persians in the Persian Empire; he conquered Babylonia in 538 BCE, and restored Jerusalem to the Jews. Alexander the Great conquered Persia in 333 BCE, but Persians regained independence in the next century under the Parthians, themselves succeeded by Sassanian Persians in 226 CE. Arabs brought Islam to Persia in the 7th cent., replacing the indigenous Zoroastrian faith. After Persian political and cultural autonomy was reasserted in the 9th cent., arts and sciences flourished.

Turks and Mongols ruled Persia in turn from the 11th cent. to 1502, when Ismael I established the Iranian Safavid dynasty and made Shiite Islam the official religion. The dynasty lasted until 1722. The British and Russian empires vied for influence in the 19th cent.; Britain severed Afghanistan from Iran in 1857.

Reza Khan, a military officer, became prime min., 1923, and shah in 1925. He began modernization, curbed foreign influence, and officially changed the country's name from Persia to Iran in 1935. Fearing the shah's Axis sympathies, British and Soviet troops forced him to abdicate, 1941; he was succeeded by his son, Mohammad Reza Pahlavi. The U.S. Central Intelligence Agency had a major role in the ouster, 1953, of Prime Min. Muhammad Mossadegh, who had nationalized the oil industry.

With U.S. backing, the shah brought economic and social change to Iran (White Revolution), but repression of opposition groups grew severe. Violent protests in 1978 eventually forced the shah to depart, Jan. 16, 1979. Shiite leader Ayatollah Ruhollah Khomeini, exiled by the shah in 1963, returned to Tehran, Feb. 1. Pro-Khomeini forces defeated government troops, Feb 11. Khomeini established an Islamic theocracy.

Iranian militants seized the U.S. embassy in Tehran Nov. 4, 1979, and took hostages, including 62 Americans. Despite international condemnations and U.S. efforts, including an abortive Apr. 1980 rescue attempt, the crisis continued. The U.S. broke diplomatic relations with Iran, Apr. 7. The shah died in Egypt, July 27. The hostage drama ended Jan. 20, 1981, when an accord, involving the release of frozen Iranian assets, was reached.

A dispute over the Shatt al-Arab waterway between Iran and Iraq led to a long and costly war between the two countries, 1980-88, killing hundreds of thousands of people. In Nov. 1986 it became known that the U.S., which had generally sided with Iraq during the war, had secretly shipped arms to Iran to gain that country's help in obtaining the release of U.S. hostages held in Lebanon. The revelation sparked a major scandal in the U.S. A U.S. Navy warship shot down an Iranian airliner, July 3, 1988, after mistaking it for an F-14 fighter jet; all 290 aboard died.

An earthquake struck northern Iran June 21, 1990, killing more than 45,000 and leaving 400,000 homeless. Some 1 mil Kurdish refugees fled from Iraq to Iran following the Persian Gulf War of 1991. To curb Iran's alleged support for international terrorism, the U.S. in 1996 authorized sanctions on foreign companies that invested there.

Mohammad Khatami, a moderate Shiite Muslim cleric, was elected president in 1997. During the next three years, hard-line Islamists clashed, sometimes violently, with reformers, who won a majority in 2000 parliamentary elections. Inviting rapprochement with Iran, the U.S. eased some sanctions Mar. 18. Khatami was reelected in 2001 but continued to face resistance from religious conservatives.

An earthquake Dec. 26, 2003, in Bam, SE Iran, killed about 26,000 people. After the Guardian Council, dominated by religious conservatives, disqualified some 2,400 reformist candidates, hardliners won legislative elections Feb. 20, 2004.

The religiously conservative mayor of Tehran, Mahmoud Ahmadinejad, defeated former Pres. Hashemi Rafsanjani in a 2005 runoff election. U.S. Pres. George W. Bush's administration accused Iran of seeking to build nuclear weapons, aiding Shiite militias opposing government forces in the U.S.-led war in Iraq (2003-11), and supplying rockets to Hezbollah fighters in Lebanon for use against Israel.

Seeking to halt Iran's uranium-enrichment program, the UN Security Council imposed sanctions, Dec. 2006, and toughened them, Mar. 2007. After the Guardian Council disqualified about 1,700 reformist candidates, conservative allies of Ahmadinejad won parliamentary elections Mar.-Apr. 2008. Further talks on nuclear enrichment ended in deadlock July 20, and the U.S. imposed additional sanctions Sept. 10.

Ahmadinejad won the 2009 presidential election. His main opponent, former Prime Min. Mir Hussein Moussavi, claimed the vote count was fraudulent. Huge protests by Moussavi supporters

in Tehran and other major cities were crushed. Tensions with the U.S. and European governments were heightened in late Sept. 2009 by disclosures that Iran had been secretly enriching uranium at an underground site near Qom, and by Iranian tests of medium-range missiles capable of reaching Israel or U.S. and European bases in the Persian Gulf region. Iran agreed in Oct. to allow international inspection of the Qom site and to other nuclear safeguards.

The UN and U.S. toughened sanctions, June-July 2010, but did not object when loading of uranium fuel began in Aug. at Iran's Russian-built Bushehr nuclear power plant. Iran blamed Israel, the U.S., and other Western powers for carrying out cyberattacks against the country's nuclear facilities and for assassinating Iranian scientists. In Dec. 2010, the U.S. announced new sanctions. Iran announced, Jan. 2012, it was enriching uranium at its underground Fordo nuclear facility; more international sanctions followed.

The moderate cleric Hassan Rouhani was elected president June 14, 2013. An interim agreement was reached Nov. 24, 2013, under which Iran pledged to limit some aspects of its nuclear program and allow wider international inspections in exchange for the temporary lifting of some sanctions. Negotiations toward a longer-term accord produced a 15-year agreement—signed July 14, 2015, by the U.S., UK, France, Germany, Russia, China, Iran, and the EU—for Iran to limit and partly dismantle its nuclear program and submit to international inspections in return for the lifting of most sanctions in stages. Sanctions were eased Jan. 16, 2016, after the Intl. Atomic Energy Agency reported Iran was complying with the agreement. Pro-Rouhani reformers won the largest bloc of seats in Feb. and Apr. 2016 parliamentary elections.

Playing a role in regional conflicts, Iran supported the Syrian government with military aid, 2012-16, in its civil war; provided military assistance to Iraqi Shiite militia forces combating ISIS Sunni extremist fighters in Iraq, 2014-16; and aided Houthi rebels in Yemen's civil war, 2014-16.

Iraq
Republic of Iraq

People: Population: 38,146,025. **Age distrib.:** <15: 39.9%; 65+: 3.4%. **Growth:** 2.9%. **Migrants:** 1%. **Pop. density:** 225.9 per sq mi, 87.2 per sq km. **Urban:** 69.6%. **Ethnic groups:** Arab 75%-80%; Kurdish 15%-20%; Turkoman, Assyrian, other 5%. **Languages:** Arabic, Kurdish (both official); Turkmen, Assyrian (both official in areas); Armenian. **Religions:** Muslim (official) 99% (Shia 60%-65%, Sunni 32%-37%).

Geography: Total area: 169,235 sq mi, 438,317 sq km; **Land area:** 168,868 sq mi, 437,367 sq km. **Location:** Middle East, occupying most of historic Mesopotamia. Jordan, Syria on W; Turkey on N; Iran on E; Kuwait, Saudi Arabia on S. **Topography:** Mostly an alluvial plain, including the Tigris and Euphrates Rivers, descending from mountains in N to desert in SW. Persian Gulf region is marshland. **Arable land:** 11.5%. **Capital:** Baghdad, 6,810,608. **Cities:** Mosul, 1,748,949; Erbil, 1,200,443; Basra, 1,041,037; Sulaimaniya, 1,040,862.

Government: Type: Federal parliamentary republic. **Head of state:** Pres. Fuad Masum; b. 1938; in office: July 24, 2014. **Head of gov.:** Prime Min. Haider al-Abadi; b. 1952; in office: Sept. 8, 2014. **Local divisions:** 18 governorates, 1 region (Kurdistan Regional Govt.). **Defense budget:** $21.1 bil. **Active troops:** 64,000.

Economy: Industries: petroleum, chemicals, textiles, leather, constr. materials, food proc., fertilizer, metal fabrication/proc. **Chief crops:** wheat, barley, rice, vegetables, dates, cotton. **Natural resources:** petroleum, nat. gas, phosphates, sulfur. **Water:** 2,467 cu m per capita. **Crude oil reserves:** 143.1 bil bbls. **Electricity prod.:** 69 bil kWh. **Labor force:** agric. 21.6%, industry 18.7%, services 59.8%. **Unemployment:** 16.4%.

Finance: Monetary unit: Dinar (IQD) (1,162.50 = $1 U.S.). **GDP:** $544.1 bil; **per capita GDP:** $15,500; **GDP growth:** 2.4%. **Imports:** $42.9 bil; Turkey 20.7%, Syria 19.6%, China 19.2%. **Exports:** $54.7 bil; China 22.6%, India 21.1%, South Korea 11.2%, U.S. 7.8%, Italy 6.7%, Greece 6%. **Tourism:** $1.6 bil. **Budget:** $86.6 bil. **Inflation:** -1.2%.

Transport: Railways: 1,412 mi. **Motor vehicles:** 53.2 per 1,000 pop. **Airports:** 72.

Communications: Telephone: 5.6 per 100 pop. **Mobile:** 93.8 per 100 pop. **Broadband:** NA. **Internet:** 17.2%.

Health: Expend.: 5.5%. **Life expect.:** 72.6 male; 77.2 female. **Births:** 30.9 per 1,000 pop. **Deaths:** 3.8 per 1,000 pop. **Infant mortality:** 37.5 per 1,000 live births. **Undernourished:** 22.8%. **HIV:** NA.

Education: Compulsory: ages 6-11. **Literacy:** 79.7%.

Embassy: 3421 Massachusetts Ave. NW 20007; 742-1600.

Website: www.pmo.iq

The Tigris-Euphrates valley, formerly called Mesopotamia, was the site of one of the earliest civilizations in the world. Mesopotamia ceased to be a separate entity after Persian, Greek, and Arab conquests. The Arabs founded Baghdad, from where the caliph ruled a vast Islamic empire in the 8th and 9th cents. Mongol and Turkish conquests led to a decline in the region's population, economy, cultural life, and irrigation system.

Britain secured a League of Nations mandate over Iraq after WWI. Independence under a king came in 1932. Rebellious army officers killed King Faisal II, July 1958, and established a leftist, pan-Arab republic. The Baath Arab Socialist Party increasingly dominated successive regimes. A Baath leader, Saddam Hussein, became president in 1979. He ruled as a dictator for more than two decades, repressing Iraq's Kurds and Shiites. Israeli planes destroyed a nuclear reactor near Baghdad in 1981, claiming it could be used to produce nuclear weapons.

After skirmishing intermittently for 10 months over the sovereignty of the disputed Shatt al-Arab waterway dividing the two countries, Iraq and Iran entered into open warfare on Sept. 22, 1980. Iran repulsed early Iraqi advances, producing a long and costly stalemate; hundreds of thousands of Iraqis lost their lives during the 8-year conflict. Hussein used poison gas against Iraqi Kurds in 1988, killing more than 5,000 people in Halabja, the first mass use of poison gas against civilians since the Holocaust.

Iraq invaded Kuwait in 1990. Backed by the UN, a U.S.-led coalition launched air and missile attacks on Iraq, Jan. 16, 1991, and began a ground attack to retake Kuwait Feb. 23. Iraqi forces showed little resistance and were defeated in four days. Some 175,000 Iraqis were taken prisoner, and Iraqi casualties were estimated at over 85,000. As part of the cease-fire agreement, Iraq agreed to scrap all poison gas and germ weapons and allow UN observers to inspect the sites. UN trade sanctions would remain in effect until Iraq complied with all terms.

Iraqi cooperation with UN weapons inspection teams was intermittent throughout the 1990s. Standoffs over inspections led to diplomatic crises 1997-98, culminating in intensive U.S. and British aerial bombardment of Iraqi military targets, Dec. 16-19, 1998. After two years of sporadic activity, U.S. and British warplanes struck sites near Baghdad mid-Feb. 2001.

Despite opposition from some countries, including France, Germany, and Russia, a U.S.-led coalition invaded Iraq Mar. 19, 2003. By Apr. 6 the British controlled Basra and other areas in the south, and the U.S. entered Baghdad Apr. 7. Hussein disappeared, the Iraqi government collapsed, and most of Iraq's armed forces dissolved into the civilian population. On May 1, U.S. Pres. George W. Bush declared the end of major combat. Searches failed to find chemical, biological, or nuclear weapons that the U.S. and other countries claimed Iraq had stockpiled.

The U.S.-led Coalition Provisional Authority was unable to maintain order in the weeks following Hussein's fall. Reconstruction efforts were hampered by guerrilla attacks from Baath remnants, Islamic extremists, and others. U.S. troops killed two of Hussein's sons, Uday and Qusay, July 22, 2003, in Mosul. Saddam Hussein was captured in an underground hideout mid-Dec. 2003; tried and convicted for committing crimes against humanity in the 1980s, he was executed Dec. 30, 2006.

Photographs released in Apr. 2004 showed instances of physical abuse and sexual humiliation of Iraqi inmates by U.S. military personnel at Baghdad's Abu Ghraib prison in 2003. The images sparked widespread condemnation and U.S. criminal proceedings against some individuals.

On June 28, 2004, U.S. authorities transferred sovereignty to a transitional Iraqi government. Despite insurgent threats, an estimated 8 mil people in Iraq, mostly Shiites and Kurds, cast ballots Jan. 30, 2005, for a transitional national assembly. The assembly elected Jalal Talabani, a Kurd, as president; Ibrahim al-Jaafari, a Shiite, became prime min. Insurgents launched new waves of attacks. Rumors of a suicide bomber set off a stampede by Shiite pilgrims in northern Baghdad Aug. 31, killing close to 1,000 people. The U.S. blamed Jordanian militant Abu Musab al-Zarqawi, leader of al-Qaeda in Iraq, for directing a series of kidnappings, beheadings, and suicide bombings. He was killed by a U.S. airstrike, June 2006.

A new government elected in legislative elections Dec. 15, 2005, was installed May 20, 2006, headed by Shiite leader Nouri Kamel al-Maliki. The Iraqi civilian death toll averaged more than 2,800 per month in 2006.

A 2007 "surge" elevated U.S. troop strength from 132,000 in Jan. to 171,000 in Oct. U.S. troop deaths in 2007 totaled 899 (the highest for any year since the war began), but military and civilian casualties began dropping after mid-2007. Contributing to the reduction in violence were a cease-fire by Shiite militias and a shift by Sunni clan leaders against al-Qaeda in Iraq.

A Nov. 2008 agreement called for all U.S. forces to leave Iraq by Dec. 31, 2011. Legislative elections in 2010 brought gains by the Iraqi coalition headed by former Prime Min. Iyad Allawi, a Shiite who had campaigned as a secularist to win widespread Sunni support. On Aug. 31, Pres. Barack Obama formally declared an end to the U.S. combat role, and Operation Iraqi Freedom was succeeded by Operation New Dawn. More than 9 months of political deadlock ended when Prime Min. Maliki was sworn in for a second term Dec. 21, heading a unity government that included Shiite, Sunni, and Kurdish factions.

U.S. troops completed their withdrawal from Iraq Dec. 15, 2011. From Mar. 2003 through Dec. 2011, more than 4,486 U.S.

service members died in operations in Iraq; another 32,000 were wounded. British troop losses totaled 179; other allies, 139. More than 115,000 Iraqi civilians and over 10,000 police and security forces were killed. U.S. budgeted costs of the Iraq war exceeded $820 bil for the 2003-12 period.

Tensions manifested between Sunnis and Shiites after the U.S. departure. The Sunni insurgent group al-Qaeda in Iraq was blamed for ongoing violence; in periodic assaults throughout 2012, 4,573 civilians were killed. Violence accelerated; the UN reported Jan. 1, 2014, that violent attacks killed 8,868 people in Iraq during 2013, including at least 7,818 civilians. In 2014, 12,282 civilians were killed according to UN estimates, the highest death toll since 2006-07.

In parliamentary elections Apr. 30, 2014, Maliki's coalition won the largest bloc of seats. Parliament elected, July 24, Kurdish politician Fuad Masum as the country's new president. On Aug. 11, Masum named Shiite Haider al-Abadi, of Maliki's Dawa Party, to be prime min.

In Dec. 2013, the Sunni extremist Islamic State in Iraq and Syria (ISIS) began crossing from Syria into Iraq and seizing territory, including the city of Fallujah (Jan. 2014). The ISIS offensive intensified beginning in June 2014. The group took control of large areas of northern and central Iraq, including the cities of Mosul (Iraq's second-largest) and Tikrit, where ISIS killed 1,700 captured Shiite soldiers. ISIS imposed Islamic law, with harsh punishments, in areas it controlled while suppressing, killing, and sexually assaulting civilians who were non-Sunni Muslims or members of the Yazidi sect and other religious minorities. The U.S., later joined by European and other allies, began, Aug. 8, airstrikes against ISIS targets; the U.S. provided military aid to Iraqi government forces and Kurdish fighters opposing ISIS, including ground troops to serve as advisers and trainers beginning in mid-2014. A series of troop increases announced through Sept. 2016 brought the total number of U.S. advisers to more than 5,000.

Forces fighting ISIS in 2015-16 included government troops, Shiite militias (often backed by Iran), Sunni tribal militias, and Kurdish troops. Kurdish fighters made gains in northern Iraq, and government and Shiite forces completed recapturing Tikrit, Apr. 1, 2015. Ramadi, capital of Anbar province, captured by ISIS May 17, 2015, was retaken by government forces Dec. 28, 2015. Fallujah was retaken by government forces June 26, 2016. According to a June 2016 U.S. estimate, ISIS had lost 47% of the Iraqi territory it had captured. As it lost territory, ISIS increased terrorist bombings in Baghdad and other cities, often targeting Shiite areas. UN estimates put all conflict-related civilian deaths at 7,515 in 2015 and 4,446 in Jan.-Sept. 2016. A truck bombing, July 3, 2016, in Baghdad for which ISIS claimed responsibility killed more than 300 people.

Ireland

People: Population: 4,952,473. **Age distrib.:** <15: 21.5%; 65+: 12.8%. **Growth:** 1.2%. **Migrants:** 15.9%. **Pop. density:** 186.2 per sq mi, 71.9 per sq km. **Urban:** 63.5%. **Ethnic groups:** Irish 84.5%, other white 9.8%. **Languages:** English (official; predominant), Irish (Gaelic or Gaeilge) (official; spoken mainly on western coast). **Religions:** Roman Catholic 84.7%, Church of Ireland 2.7%, none 5.7%.

Geography: Total area: 27,133 sq mi, 70,273 sq km; **Land area:** 26,596 sq mi, 68,883 sq km. **Location:** Atlantic O. just W of Great Britain. Northern Ireland (UK) on E. **Topography:** Central plateau surrounded by isolated groups of hills and mountains. Heavily indented Atlantic coastline. **Arable land:** 16.2%. **Capital:** Dublin, 1,184,771.

Government: Type: Parliamentary republic. **Head of state:** Pres. Michael D. Higgins; b. 1941; in office: Nov. 11, 2011. **Head of gov.:** Prime Min. Enda Kenny; b. 1951; in office: Mar. 9, 2011. **Local divisions:** 28 counties, 3 cities. **Defense budget:** $993 mil. **Active troops:** 9,100.

Economy: Industries: pharmaceuticals, chemicals, computer hardware and software, food prods., beverages and brewing, medical devices. **Chief crops:** barley, potatoes, wheat. **Natural resources:** nat. gas, peat, copper, lead, zinc, silver, barite, gypsum, limestone, dolomite. **Water:** 11,092 cu m per capita. **Electricity prod.:** 24 bil kWh. **Labor force:** agric. 5%, industry 19%, services 76%. **Unemployment:** 11.6%.

Finance: Monetary unit: Euro (EUR) (0.89 = $1 U.S.). **GDP:** $257.4 bil; **per capita GDP:** $55,500; **GDP growth:** 7.8%. **Imports:** $81.4 bil; UK 32.5%, U.S. 14%, France 10.2%, Germany 9.3%. **Exports:** $140.4 bil; U.S. 23.7%, UK 13.8%, Belgium 13.2%, Germany 6.6%, Switzerland 5.5%. **Tourism:** $4.8 bil. **Budget:** $84.1 bil. **Inflation:** −0.3%.

Transport: Railways: 2,011 mi. **Motor vehicles:** 492.2 per 1,000 pop. **Airports:** 16.

Communications: Telephone: 40.9 per 100 pop. **Mobile:** 103.7 per 100 pop. **Broadband:** 81 per 100 pop. **Internet:** 80.1%.

Health: Expend.: 7.8%. **Life expect.:** 78.5 male; 83.2 female. **Births:** 14.5 per 1,000 pop. **Deaths:** 6.5 per 1,000 pop. **Infant mortality:** 3.7 per 1,000 live births. **Undernourished:** <5%. **HIV:** NA.

Education: Compulsory: ages 6-15. **Literacy:** 99%.
Embassy: 2234 Massachusetts Ave. NW 20008; 462-3939.
Website: www.gov.ie

Celtic tribes invaded the islands about the 4th cent. BCE; their Gaelic culture and literature flourished in the 5th cent. CE, the same century in which St. Patrick converted the Irish to Christianity. Norse invasions began in the 8th cent., ending with defeat of the Danes by the Irish King Brian Boru in 1014. English invasions started in the 12th cent. For over 700 years the Anglo-Irish struggle continued with bitter rebellions and savage repressions. In the Irish Potato Famine, failure of the staple potato crop, 1845-49, caused 1 mil deaths from starvation and related diseases; up to 2 mil people emigrated, many to the U.S.

The Easter Monday Rebellion in 1916 failed but was followed by guerrilla warfare and harsh reprisals by British troops called the Black and Tans. The Dail Eireann (Irish parliament) reaffirmed independence in Jan. 1919. The British offered dominion status to Ulster (6 counties) and southern Ireland (26 counties) Dec. 1921. The constitution of the Irish Free State, a British dominion, was adopted Dec. 11, 1922. Northern Ireland remained part of the UK (see United Kingdom—Northern Ireland).

A new constitution adopted by plebiscite came into operation Dec. 29, 1937. It declared the name of the state Eire in the Irish language (Ireland in the English) and declared it a sovereign democratic state. On Dec. 21, 1948, the country was declared a republic rather than a dominion and withdrew from the Commonwealth. The British Parliament recognized both actions, 1949, but the six northeastern counties remained in the UK.

Irish governments have favored peaceful unification of all Ireland and cooperated with Britain against terrorist groups. After negotiators in Northern Ireland approved a peace settlement on Good Friday, Apr. 10, 1998, voters in the Irish Republic endorsed the accord, on May 22, and the Irish gave up their constitution's territorial claims on the north.

Expansion of educational opportunities and foreign investment in high-tech industries in the 1990s boosted Ireland's prosperity. Ireland's first woman president, Mary Robinson, resigned Sept. 1997, to become UN high commissioner for human rights, 1997-2002. She was succeeded as president by Mary McAleese, the first person from Northern Ireland to hold the office.

Responding to a growing scandal over abusive Catholic clergy in Ireland, Pope Benedict XVI issued a public apology to victims and their families Mar. 2010.

To aid Ireland's banks and prevent default after a 2008-10 financial crisis, EU finance ministers approved, Nov. 2010, an 85-bil euro emergency loan package that obligated Ireland to impose unpopular austerity measures. Fianna Fáil, the party that had dominated Irish politics since the 1930s, suffered a crushing defeat in Feb. 2011 elections, and Enda Kenny, leader of the opposition Fine Gael, became prime minister. Lawmakers voted, July 11, 2013, to legalize abortion when a woman's pregnancy jeopardizes her life. In a national referendum, May 22, 2015, voters approved changing the constitution to legalize same-sex marriage. After inconclusive elections, Feb. 26, 2016, and negotiations with Fianna Fáil, which officially remained in opposition, Kenny continued as prime minister, heading a minority government.

Israel
State of Israel

People: Population: 8,174,527. **Age distrib.:** <15: 27.7%; 65+: 11.1%. **Growth:** 1.5%. **Migrants:** 24.9%. **Pop. density:** 1,041.4 per sq mi, 402.1 per sq km. **Urban:** 92.2%. **Ethnic groups:** Jewish (Israel-born 74.4%, Europe/America/Oceania-born 17.4%, Africa-born 5.1%, Asia-born 3.1%) 75%, non-Jewish (mostly Arab) 25%. **Languages:** Hebrew, Arabic (both official); English. **Religions:** Jewish 75%, Muslim 17.5%, Christian 2%.

Geography: Total area: 8,019 sq mi, 20,770 sq km; **Land area:** 7,849 sq mi, 20,330 sq km. **Location:** Middle East, on E end of Mediterranean Sea. Lebanon on N; Syria, West Bank, Jordan on E; Gaza Strip, Egypt on W. **Topography:** The Mediterranean coastal plain is fertile and well-watered. Judean Plateau in center. Semidesert Negev region extends to apex at head of Gulf of Aqaba. The E border drops sharply into the Jordan Rift Valley, which incl. Lake Tiberias (Sea of Galilee) and the Dead Sea (1,339 ft below sea level), lowest point in Asia. **Arable land:** 13.2%. **Capital:** Jerusalem, 849,932. **Cities:** Tel Aviv-Jaffa, 3,661,189; Haifa, 1,105,057.

Government: Type: Parliamentary democracy. **Head of state:** Pres. Reuven Rivlin; b. 1939; in office: July 27, 2014. **Head of gov.:** Prime Min. Benjamin Netanyahu; b. 1949; in office: Mar. 31, 2009. **Local divisions:** 6 districts. **Defense budget:** $18.6 bil. **Active troops:** 176,500.

Economy: Industries: high-tech prods. (incl. aviation, communications, computer-aided design and manufactures, medical electronics, fiber optics), wood and paper prods. **Chief crops:** citrus, vegetables, cotton. **Natural resources:** timber, potash, copper ore, nat. gas, phosphate rock, magnesium bromide, clays, sand. **Water:** 221 cu m per capita. **Crude oil reserves** (2015):

14 mil bbls. **Electricity prod.:** 56 bil kWh. **Labor force:** agric. 1.1%, industry 17.3%, services 81.6%. **Unemployment:** 6.1%.

Finance: Monetary unit: Shekel (ILS) (3.77 = $1 U.S.). **GDP:** $281.9 bil; **per capita GDP:** $33,700; **GDP growth:** 2.6%. **Imports:** $58.8 bil; U.S. 13%, China 9.3%, Switzerland 7.1%, Germany 6.1%, Belgium 5.3%. **Exports:** $56.4 bil; U.S. 27.5%, Hong Kong 8%, UK 6.1%. **Tourism:** $5.4 bil. **Budget:** $82.1 bil. **Inflation:** −0.6%.

Transport: Railways: 777 mi. **Motor vehicles:** 367.7 per 1,000 pop. **Airports:** 29.

Communications: Telephone: 43.1 per 100 pop. **Mobile:** 133.5 per 100 pop. **Broadband:** 52.2 per 100 pop. **Internet:** 78.9%.

Health: Expend.: 7.8%. **Life expect.:** 80.6 male; 84.4 female. **Births:** 18.3 per 1,000 pop. **Deaths:** 5.2 per 1,000 pop. **Infant mortality:** 3.5 per 1,000 live births. **Undernourished:** <5%. **HIV:** NA.

Education: Compulsory: ages 5-17. **Literacy:** 97.8%.
Embassy: 3514 International Dr. NW 20008; 364-5500.
Website: www.gov.il

Occupying the southwest corner of the ancient Fertile Crescent, Israel contains some of the oldest known evidence of agriculture and of primitive town life. The Hebrews probably arrived early in the 2nd millennium BCE. Under King David and his successors (c. 1000 BCE-597 BCE), Judaism was developed and secured. After conquest by Babylonians, Persians, and Greeks, an independent Jewish kingdom was revived, 168 BCE, but Rome took over in the next century, suppressed Jewish revolts in 70 CE and 135 CE, and renamed Judea Palestine, after the earlier coastal inhabitants, the Philistines.

Arab invaders conquered Palestine in 636. The Arabic language and Islam prevailed within a few centuries, but a Jewish minority remained. The land was ruled from the 11th cent. as a part of non-Arab empires by Seljuks, Mamluks, and Ottomans (with a Crusader interval, 1098-1291).

After four centuries of Ottoman rule, the land was taken in 1917 by Britain, which pledged in the Balfour Declaration to support a Jewish homeland there. In 1920 a British Palestine Mandate was recognized; in 1922 the land east of the Jordan R. was detached.

Jewish immigration, begun in the late 19th cent., swelled in the 1930s and 1940s with refugees from Nazi Germany and survivors of the Holocaust; heavy Arab immigration from Syria and Lebanon also occurred. Arab opposition to Jewish immigration turned violent in 1920, 1921, 1929, and 1936. The UN General Assembly voted in 1947 to partition Palestine into an Arab and a Jewish state. Britain withdrew in May 1948.

Israel was declared independent May 14, 1948; Arabs rejected partition. Egypt, Jordan, Syria, Lebanon, Iraq, and Saudi Arabia invaded but failed to destroy the Jewish state, which gained territory. Separate armistices with the Arab nations were signed in 1949; Jordan occupied the West Bank, Egypt occupied Gaza. Neither granted Palestinian autonomy.

After persistent terrorist raids, Israel invaded Egypt's Sinai, Oct. 29, 1956, aided briefly by British and French forces. A UN cease-fire was arranged Nov. 6.

An uneasy truce between Israel and the Arab countries lasted until 1967, when Egypt reoccupied the Gaza Strip and closed the Gulf of Aqaba to Israeli shipping. In the Six-Day War, starting June 5, the Israelis took the Gaza Strip, occupied the Sinai Peninsula to the Suez Canal, and captured East Jerusalem, Syria's Golan Heights, and Jordan's West Bank. Together, the West Bank and Gaza comprise the Palestinian territories, now represented by the Palestinian Authority.

Egypt and Syria attacked Israel, Oct. 6, 1973 (Yom Kippur, the most solemn day in the Jewish calendar). Israel counterattacked, driving the Syrians back, and crossed the Suez Canal. A cease-fire took effect Oct. 24 and a UN peacekeeping force arrived. Under a 1974 disengagement agreement, Israel withdrew from the canal's west bank. Israeli forces raided Entebbe, Uganda, in 1976 and rescued 103 hostages who had been seized by Arab and German terrorists.

Israel's prime ministers, including David Ben-Gurion, Golda Meir, and Yitzhak Rabin, pursued a moderate socialist program, 1948-77. In 1977, the conservative opposition, led by Menachem Begin, was voted into office for the first time. Egypt's Pres. Anwar al-Sadat visited Jerusalem in 1977, and on Mar. 26, 1979, Egypt and Israel signed a formal peace treaty, ending 30 years of war. Israel returned the Sinai to Egypt in 1982.

Israeli forces invaded Lebanon, June 6, 1982, to destroy Palestine Liberation Organization (PLO) strongholds. After massive Israeli bombing of West Beirut, the PLO agreed to evacuate the city. Israeli troops entered West Beirut after newly elected Lebanese Pres. Bashir Gemayel was assassinated on Sept. 14. Israel drew widespread condemnation when Lebanese Christian forces, Sept. 16, entered two West Beirut refugee camps and slaughtered hundreds of Palestinians.

In 1989, violence escalated over the Israeli military occupation of the West Bank and Gaza Strip. In a series of uprisings known as the first intifada, Palestinian protesters defied Israeli troops, who forcibly retaliated. During the Persian Gulf War, 1991, Iraq fired Scud missiles at Israel.

Ongoing peace talks led to historic agreements between Israel and the PLO, Sept. 1993. The PLO recognized Israel's right to exist; Israel recognized the PLO as the Palestinians' representative. The two sides then signed, Sept. 13, an agreement (known as the Oslo Accord) for limited Palestinian self-rule in the West Bank and Gaza. A follow-up Sept. 1995 agreement (Oslo II) essentially divided the West Bank into areas under Israeli or Palestinian control. Israel and Jordan signed, July 25, 1994, in Washington, DC, a declaration ending their 46-year state of war.

Arab and Jewish extremists repeatedly challenged the peace process. On Nov. 4, 1995, an Orthodox Jewish Israeli assassinated Labor Party Prime Min. Yitzhak Rabin as he left a peace rally in Tel Aviv. Support for Rabin's successor, Shimon Peres, was shaken by a series of suicide bombings and rocket attacks against Israel by Islamic militants. Emphasizing security issues, the candidate of the conservative Likud bloc, Benjamin Netanyahu, was elected prime minister on May 29, 1996.

Under an interim accord brokered by Pres. Bill Clinton and signed by Netanyahu and PLO leader Yasir Arafat at the White House, Oct. 23, 1998, Israel yielded more West Bank territory to the Palestinians, in exchange for new security guarantees. Full implementation did not begin until Sept. 1999. In the interim, Netanyahu lost to the Labor candidate, Ehud Barak, in the May 1999, election.

Israel pulled virtually all its troops out of southern Lebanon in May 2000. Marathon summit talks in the U.S. between Barak and Arafat, July 11-25, failed. A second intifada began in late Sept. in Israel and the Palestinian territories. Barak called new elections for prime minister but lost Feb. 2001 to Ariel Sharon, a hardliner. The bloodshed intensified during the summer, as Palestinian suicide bombers attacked Israeli civilians, and Israel struck at Palestinian-controlled territory attempting to assassinate suspected terrorists.

Israel launched a major West Bank offensive Mar. 29, 2002, two days after a suicide bomber killed 26 Israeli Jews at a Passover celebration in Netanya. A U.S.-sponsored "road map" to Middle East peace, unveiled Apr. 2003, made little headway.

Sharon's decision to pull all Israeli settlers and troops out of Gaza, approved by the cabinet Feb. 2005, led Israeli politics to be realigned. When right-wing Likud members opposed the plan, Sharon and Deputy Prime Min. Ehud Olmert broke with them and formed the centrist Kadima Party. Sharon suffered a massive stroke Jan. 4, 2006. Olmert became prime minister, led Kadima to victory in Mar. elections, and formed a broad coalition government.

Clashes in mid-2006 along the Gaza and Lebanon borders rapidly escalated into full-scale war. By Aug. 14, when a UN-sponsored cease-fire took hold, the estimated death toll from the war included nearly 1,150 Lebanese, almost 200 Gaza Palestinians, and 150 Israelis. Olmert, targeted in multiple corruption inquiries, announced his resignation July 30, 2008. (He was acquitted of bribery charges, July 10, 2012, but convicted after a retrial, Mar. 30, 2015. While that conviction was being appealed, Olmert began serving, Feb. 15, 2016, a 19-month sentence for a separate Mar. 31, 2014, bribery conviction.) After a campaign overshadowed by a three-week war between Israel and Hamas, both Kadima and Likud fell far short of a majority in Feb. 2009 elections. On Mar. 31, Netanyahu became prime min. for a second time.

Israel's relations with allies were strained when senior Hamas commander Mahmoud al-Mabhouh was killed Jan. 2010 in Dubai, allegedly by agents of the Israeli spy agency Mossad. There was further criticism of the Israeli government after its Mar. 2010 announcement that it would build 1,600 homes in Ramat Shlomo (a Jewish settlement in mostly Arab East Jerusalem), and later in the spring, when Israeli commandos killed nine Turkish pro-Palestinian activists in clashes May 31 on board the *Mavi Marmara*, part of a flotilla seeking to break Israel's blockade of Gaza. Turkish-Israeli relations, downgraded by Turkey after the *Mavi Marmara* incident, were normalized under an agreement signed June 28, 2016.

Israel clashed with Palestinians in Gaza Oct.-Nov. 2012. In retaliation for the Gaza attacks, the hacker collective Anonymous launched cyberattacks on Israel before a cease-fire was declared Nov. 21, 2012.

Netanyahu's right-wing Likud-Yisrael Beiteinu political bloc narrowly won Jan. 22, 2013, parliamentary elections. Likud won the largest bloc of seats in Mar. 17, 2015, elections, and Netanyahu assembled a new coalition government.

Conflict between Israel and Hamas escalated in 2014. Rocket attacks from Gaza into Israel increased beginning in June. Israel blamed Hamas for the June 12 kidnapping and killing of 3 Israeli teenagers in the West Bank. Israel launched air and artillery attacks on targets in Gaza, including suspected missile launch sites, and Hamas intensified rocket attacks on Israel. Israeli ground forces entered Gaza July 17, in part to destroy tunnels used to infiltrate fighters into Israel. Israeli ground and air attacks caused high civilian casualties, for which international criticism mounted. Israel pulled out ground troops Aug. 5. Fighting resumed intermittently (rockets, artillery, airstrikes) when a 3-day cease-fire ended

Aug. 8. An Israeli airstrike, Aug. 21, killed 3 top Hamas commanders. A new cease-fire was agreed Aug. 26. By that time, more than 2,100 Palestinians were estimated to have died in the conflict, and Israel reported 64 soldiers and 5 civilians killed.

In 2015-16, tensions between Israelis and Palestinians remained high. Attacks by Palestinians and countermeasures by security forces resulted in the deaths of more than 30 Israelis and about 200 Palestinians in the 9 months ending June 30, 2016.

Tensions between Iran and Israel have grown over Iran's nuclear program, which Israel sees as an existential threat. An agreement to limit Iran's nuclear program, signed July 14, 2015, after U.S.-led negotiations, was criticized by Netanyahu as inadequate to prevent Iran's developing nuclear weapons.

Palestinian Territories

The Palestinian territories comprise the Gaza Strip, often called Gaza, and the West Bank, both occupied by Israel in 1967. Since 1996 the Palestinian Authority has been responsible for civil government in the territories. Elected president Jan. 20, 1996, PLO leader Yasir Arafat headed the Palestinian Authority until his death Nov. 11, 2004. Mahmoud Abbas, who had succeeded Arafat as PLO chairman and leader of the Fatah faction, was elected president Jan. 2005. (Abbas resigned as PLO chairman Aug. 22, 2015.) A victory by Hamas militants in Jan. 2006 legislative elections led to a power struggle with Abbas, who favored a negotiated settlement with Israel. In bitter fighting, Hamas ousted Fatah from Gaza, June 2007, but Abbas retained power in the West Bank. Fatah and Hamas reached a reconciliation agreement Apr. 27, 2011, and announced Feb. 6, 2012, that Abbas would lead an interim unity government. However, Fatah-Hamas tensions increased in 2013. A new reconciliation agreement was completed Apr. 2014; a unity government sworn in June 2, 2014, was unable to exert effective authority in Gaza. In a 2011 UN speech, Abbas sought full UN membership for an independent Palestinian state; the General Assembly voted, Nov. 29, 2012, to make Palestine a non-member observer state. Speaking at the UN Sept. 30, 2015, Abbas said the Palestinian Authority would no longer be bound by the Oslo Accords and other power-sharing agreements with Israel, which he alleged had violated such agreements and was an "occupying power."

The **Gaza Strip** extends NE from the Sinai Peninsula for 25 mi, with the Mediterranean Sea to the W and Israel to the E. The Palestinian Authority is responsible for civil government. Nearly all the inhabitants are Palestinian Arabs, more than 35% of whom live in refugee camps. Area 139 sq mi; pop. (2016 est.) 1,753,327.

Israel captured Gaza from Egypt in the 1967 war. It remained under Israeli occupation until May 1994, when the Israeli Defense Forces withdrew. Agreements between Israel and the PLO in 1993 and 1994 provided for interim self-rule in Gaza, but Israel retained control over security. Israel forcibly evacuated all 9,000 Jewish settlers from Gaza by Aug. 22, 2005, and the last remaining Israeli soldiers pulled out Sept. 12. Israel established a fortified barrier on its Gaza border to block Palestinian infiltrators.

After the Hamas takeover, Israel declared Gaza a "hostile entity," Sept. 19, 2007, and intensified military and economic pressures. Hamas thwarted an Israeli blockade, Jan. 2008, blowing up part of the border wall between Gaza and Egypt. Retaliating for Hamas rocket and mortar attacks, Israel launched an aerial assault and ground offensive in Gaza, Dec. 2008-Jan. 2009. A UN report issued in 2009 found evidence of war crimes committed by both sides. After the *Mavi Marmara* incident, Israel June 2010 eased some restrictions on the flow of goods to Gaza. Egypt's new Islamist govt. lifted the blockade along its Gaza border May 28, 2011. However, Egypt's subsequent military government re-closed the border in 2013 and sought to destroy tunnels dug by Hamas to bring military and other equipment into Gaza. Egypt briefly reopened the Gaza border several times in 2015, in part to allow in materials for reconstruction after the 2014 conflict.

Members of the Israeli Air Force, Oct. 31, 2012, assassinated Hamas's military chief, Ahmed al-Jabari, in the Gaza Strip.

The **West Bank** is located W of the Jordan R. and Dead Sea, bounded by Jordan on the E and by Israel on the N, W, and S. The Palestinian Authority administers several major cities, but Israel retains control over much land, including Jewish settlements. Total area 2,263 sq mi, land area 2,178 sq mi; pop. (2016 est.) 2,697,687. The Palestinian Authority's National Security Force is a paramilitary organization of about 56,000 that maintains internal security in the West Bank.

In June 2002 the Israeli government began building a controversial security barrier in the West Bank to restrict Palestinian access to Israel and reduce infiltration by suicide bombers. In a nonbinding ruling, July 9, 2004, the World Court said the barrier violated international law. Israel has continued to allow the expansion of Jewish settlements on the West Bank, despite U.S. government calls for a settlement freeze; as of Dec. 31, 2015, more than 400,000 Jewish settlers were living in the West Bank (not including East Jerusalem, which Israel annexed in 1967).

Italy
Italian Republic

People: Population: 62,007,540. **Age distrib.:** <15: 13.7%; 65+: 21.4%. **Growth:** 0.2%. **Migrants:** 9.7%. **Pop. density:** 546 per sq mi, 210.8 per sq km. **Urban:** 69.1%. **Ethnic groups:** Italian (incl. small clusters of German-, French-, and Slovene-Italians in N; Albanian- and Greek-Italians in S). **Languages:** Italian (official), German, French, Slovene. **Religions:** Christian (overwhelmingly Roman Catholic) 80%, atheist and agnostic 20%.

Geography: Total area: 116,348 sq mi, 301,340 sq km; **Land area:** 113,568 sq mi, 294,140 sq km. **Location:** Southern Europe, jutting into Mediterranean Sea. France on W; Switzerland, Austria on N; Slovenia on E. **Topography:** Long boot-shaped peninsula, with Apennine Mts. running its length, extending SE from the Alps into Mediterranean, with islands of Sicily and Sardinia offshore. The alluvial Po Valley drains most of N. Rest of the country is rugged and mountainous, except for intermittent coastal plains like the Campania S of Rome. **Arable land:** 23.2%. **Capital:** Rome, 3,737,750. **Cities:** Milan, 3,104,243; Naples, 2,197,731; Turin, 1,768,777.

Government: Type: Parliamentary republic. **Head of state:** Pres. Sergio Mattarella; b. 1941; in office: Feb. 3, 2015. **Head of gov.:** Prime Min. Matteo Renzi; b. 1975; in office: Feb. 22, 2014. **Local divisions:** 20 regions (5 autonomous). **Defense budget:** $21.6 bil. **Active troops:** 174,500.

Economy: Industries: tourism, machinery, iron and steel, chemicals, food proc., textiles, motor vehicles, clothing, footwear. **Chief crops:** fruits, vegetables, grapes, potatoes, sugar beets, soybeans, grain, olives. **Natural resources:** coal, mercury, zinc, potash, marble, barite, asbestos, pumice, fluorspar, feldspar, pyrite (sulfur), nat. gas and crude oil reserves, fish. **Water:** 3,199 cu m per capita. **Crude oil reserves:** 0.6 bil bbls. **Electricity prod.:** 273 bil kWh. **Labor force:** agric. 3.9%, industry 28.3%, services 67.8%. **Unemployment:** 12.5%.

Finance: Monetary unit: Euro (EUR) (0.89 = $1 U.S.). **GDP:** $2.2 tril; **per capita GDP:** $35,700; **GDP growth:** 0.8%. **Imports:** $389.2 bil; Germany 15.4%, France 8.7%, China 7.7%, Netherlands 5.6%, Spain 5%. **Exports:** $454.6 bil; Germany 12.3%, France 10.3%, U.S. 8.7%, UK 5.4%. **Tourism:** $39.7 bil. **Budget:** $930.5 bil. **Inflation:** 0.04%.

Transport: Railways: 12,540 mi. **Motor vehicles:** 682.9 per 1,000 pop. **Airports:** 98.

Communications: Telephone: 33.1 per 100 pop. **Mobile:** 151.3 per 100 pop. **Broadband:** 70.9 per 100 pop. **Internet:** 65.6%.

Health: Expend.: 9.3%. **Life expect.:** 79.6 male; 85.0 female. **Births:** 8.7 per 1,000 pop. **Deaths:** 10.3 per 1,000 pop. **Infant mortality:** 3.3 per 1,000 live births. **Undernourished:** <5%. **HIV:** 0.4%.

Education: Compulsory: ages 6-17. **Literacy:** 99%.
Embassy: 3000 Whitehaven St. NW 20008; 612-4400.
Website: www.governo.it

Rome emerged as the major power in Italy after 500 BCE, dominating the Etruscans to the north and Greeks to the south. Under the Empire, which lasted until the 5th cent. CE, Rome ruled most of Western Europe, the Balkans, the Middle East, and North Africa. After Rome fell, Italy became a patchwork of kingdoms, principalities, and city-states until reunified, 1870.

The Fascist leader Benito Mussolini came to power, 1922, and aligned Italy with Nazi Germany in WWII. After Fascism was overthrown in 1943, Italy declared war on Germany and Japan and contributed to the Allied victory. It surrendered conquered lands and lost its colonies. Mussolini was killed by partisans Apr. 28, 1945. Victor Emmanuel III abdicated May 9, 1946; his son Humbert II was king until June 10, when Italy became a republic after a referendum, June 2-3. In the postwar decades, Italy had a succession of short-lived governments.

Christian Democratic leader and former Prime Min. Aldo Moro was abducted and murdered in 1978 by Red Brigade terrorists. The wave of left-wing political violence, including other kidnappings and assassinations, continued into the 1980s.

In Mar. 1994 voting, right-wing parties won a majority, dislodging Italy's long-powerful Christian Democratic Party. Italy led a 7,000-member peacekeeping force in Albania, Apr.-Aug. 1997, and contributed 2,000 troops to the NATO-led security force (KFOR) that entered Kosovo in June 1999.

Supporters of Silvio Berlusconi, a multibillionaire media magnate, won the 2001 parliamentary elections. Berlusconi backed American-led military operations in Afghanistan (2001) and Iraq (2003). As of mid-2016, 945 Italian troops were serving with the NATO mission in Afghanistan.

A coalition of center-left parties led by Romano Prodi scored a narrow win over Berlusconi in 2006 parliamentary voting; Berlusconi returned at the head of a center-right coalition after Apr. 2008 elections. An earthquake in the Abruzzo region of central Italy Apr. 6, 2009, battered the town of L'Aquila, killing more than 300 people. Sluggish economic growth and rising public debt raised investors' concerns about Italy's financial stability. Berlusconi

resigned Nov. 12, 2011, and Mario Monti, an economist, succeeded him Nov. 16. Italy's economic problems worsened, and its public debt reached nearly 2 tril euros by Aug. 30, 2012. After Feb. 25, 2013, elections, a coalition government was announced Apr. 27, 2013, with Enrico Letta of the center-left Democratic Party as prime minister. After leading an intra-party revolt, Matteo Renzi replaced Letta, Feb. 22, 2014, promising political reforms and initiatives to revive the economy.

A Milan court, June 24, 2013, found Berlusconi guilty of paying for sex with a minor and using his office to cover it up. An appeals court overturned the verdict, July 18, 2014, a decision upheld by the Supreme Court, Mar. 10, 2015. Berlusconi was sentenced, Apr. 15, 2014, to community service, following a 2012 conviction for tax fraud. He was convicted, July 8, 2015, of bribing a senator.

An estimated 170,000 African, Middle Eastern, and SW Asian migrants fleeing violence and economic hardship crossed the Mediterranean from North Africa to Italy in 2014. More than 150,000 arrived in 2015, and more than 130,000 in Jan.-Sept. 2016. Thousands died trying to make the crossing, often in unseaworthy boats; Italian ships, as well other EU vessels, engaged in rescue operations that saved thousands.

Legalization of civil unions between same-sex couples won final parliamentary approval, May 11, 2016. A 6.2 magnitude earthquake, Aug. 24, 2016, killed at least 290 and caused heavy damage in Amatrice and other central Italy towns.

Sicily, 9,927 sq mi, pop. (2014 est.) 5,094,937, is an island 180 by 120 mi, seat of an autonomous region that embraces the island of Pantelleria, 32 sq mi, and the Lipari group, 44 sq mi, including 2 active volcanoes: Vulcano (1,637 ft) and Stromboli (3,031 ft). From prehistoric times Sicily has been settled by various peoples; a Greek state had its capital at Syracuse. Rome took Sicily from Carthage 215 BCE. Mt. Etna, a 10,925-ft active volcano, is its tallest peak.

Sardinia, 9,301 sq mi, pop. (2014 est.) 1,663,859, lies in the Mediterranean, 115 mi W of Italy and 7½ mi S of Corsica. It is 160 mi long, 68 mi wide, and mountainous, with mining of coal, zinc, lead, copper. In 1720, Sardinia was added to the possessions of the Dukes of Savoy in Piedmont and Savoy to form the Kingdom of Sardinia. Elba, 86 sq mi, lies 6 mi W of Tuscany. Napoleon I lived in exile on Elba 1814-15.

Jamaica

People: Population: 2,970,340. **Age distrib.:** <15: 27.6%; 65+: 7.9%. **Growth:** 0.7%. **Migrants:** 0.8%. **Pop. density:** 710.3 per sq mi, 274.2 per sq km. **Urban:** 55%. **Ethnic groups:** black 92.1%, mixed 6.1%. **Languages:** English, English patois. **Religions:** Protestant 64.8% (incl. Seventh-day Adventist 12%, Pentecostal 11%), none 21.3%.

Geography: Total area: 4,244 sq mi, 10,991 sq km; **Land area:** 4,182 sq mi, 10,831 sq km. **Location:** W Indies. Cuba to N, Haiti to E. **Topography:** Four-fifths of country is covered by mountains. **Arable land:** 11.1%. **Capital:** Kingston, 589,287.

Government: Type: Parliamentary democracy under constitutional monarchy. **Head of state:** Queen Elizabeth II, rep. by Gov.-Gen. Sir Patrick Allen; b. 1951; in office: Feb. 26, 2009. **Head of gov.:** Prime Min. Andrew Holness; b. 1972; in office: Mar. 3, 2016. **Local divisions:** 14 parishes. **Defense budget:** $119 mil. **Active troops:** 3,450.

Economy: Industries: tourism, bauxite/alumina, agric. proc., light manufactures, rum, cement, metal, paper, chem. prods., telecom. **Chief crops:** sugarcane, bananas, coffee, citrus, yams, ackees, vegetables. **Natural resources:** bauxite, gypsum, limestone. **Water:** 3,874 cu m per capita. **Electricity prod.:** 3.9 bil kWh. **Labor force:** agric. 17%, industry 19%, services 64%. **Unemployment:** 13.2%.

Finance: Monetary unit: Dollar (JMD) (126.90 = $1 U.S.). **GDP:** $24.7 bil; **per capita GDP:** $8,800; **GDP growth:** 1.1%. **Imports:** $4.1 bil; U.S. 32.6%, Venezuela 12.4%, China 12%, Trinidad and Tobago 11.1%. **Exports:** $1.2 bil; U.S. 24.4%, Canada 16.5%, Russia 9.3%, Netherlands 8.9%, Iceland 7.2%, UK 6.5%. **Tourism:** $2.4 bil. **Budget:** $3.8 bil. **Inflation:** 3.7%.

Transport: Motor vehicles: 63.6 per 1,000 pop. **Airports:** 11.
Communications: Telephone: 9 per 100 pop. **Mobile:** 111.5 per 100 pop. **Broadband:** 33.1 per 100 pop. **Internet:** 43.2%.

Health: Expend.: 5.4%. **Life expect.:** 72.0 male; 75.3 female. **Births:** 18.0 per 1,000 pop. **Deaths:** 6.7 per 1,000 pop. **Infant mortality:** 13.1 per 1,000 live births. **Undernourished:** 7.9%. **HIV:** 1.6%.

Education: Compulsory: ages 6-11. **Literacy:** 88.5%.
Embassy: 1520 New Hampshire Ave. NW 20036; 452-0660.
Website: jis.gov.jm

Jamaica was visited by Christopher Columbus, 1494, and ruled by Spain (under whom Arawak Indians died out) until seized by Britain, 1655. Jamaica won independence Aug. 6, 1962. The island's rich musical innovations include ska and reggae. Rastafarianism is an influential religious movement.

In 1974 Jamaica sought an increase in taxes paid by U.S. and Canadian bauxite mines. The socialist government acquired 50%

ownership of the companies' Jamaican interests in 1976. Rudimentary welfare state measures were passed. Relations with the U.S. improved in the 1980s when Jamaican politics entered a more conservative phase.

Portia Simpson-Miller, leader of the People's National Party (PNP), became Jamaica's first female prime min., Mar. 30, 2006. The opposition Jamaica Labour Party (JLP) won the parliamentary elections of Sept. 3, 2007. While trying to arrest alleged gang leader Christopher (Dudus) Coke, police and soldiers clashed with residents in a section of Kingston in May 2010, leaving 76 people dead. Coke surrendered June 22, 2010. Extradited to the U.S., he pleaded guilty to racketeering charges in 2011. The PNP won Dec. 2011 elections; Simpson-Miller again became prime min. After Simpson-Miller implemented unpopular austerity measures to obtain IMF financial assistance, the JLP won Feb. 25, 2016, elections; Andrew Holness became prime min.

Japan

People: Population: 126,702,133. **Age distrib.:** <15: 13%; 65+: 27.3%. **Growth:** –0.2%. **Migrants:** 1.6%. **Pop. density:** 900.3 per sq mi, 347.6 per sq km. **Urban:** 93.9%. **Ethnic groups:** Japanese 98.5%, Korean 0.5%. **Languages:** Japanese. **Religions:** Shintoism 79.2%, Buddhism 66.8% (many people observe both).

Geography: Total area: 145,914 sq mi, 377,915 sq km; **Land area:** 140,728 sq mi, 364,485 sq km. Consists of 4 main islands: Honshu ("mainland"), 87,805 sq mi; Hokkaido, 30,144 sq mi; Kyushu, 14,114 sq mi; Shikoku, 7,049 sq mi. **Location:** Archipelago off E coast of Asia. Russia to N, N. Korea and S. Korea to W. **Topography:** Deeply indented coast. The northern islands are continuation of the Sakhalin Mts. China's Kunlun range continues into southern islands. The ranges meet in Japanese Alps. Group of mostly extinct or inactive volcanoes, incl. Mt. Fuji (Fujiyama) (12,388 ft), cross Honshu E-W in a vast transverse fissure. **Arable land:** 11.6%. **Capital:** Tokyo, 38,139,625 (figure is for Major Metro area). **Cities:** Kinki Major Metro Area (MMA) (Osaka), 20,336,527; Chukyo MMA (Nagoya), 9,434,239; Kitakyushu-Fukuoka MMA, 5,493,841; Shizuoka-Hamamatsu MMA, 3,492,520; Sapporo, 2,564,367; Hiroshima, 2,180,100; Sendai, 2,070,513.

Government: Type: Parliamentary constitutional monarchy. **Head of state:** Emperor Akihito; b. 1933; in office: Jan. 7, 1989. **Head of gov.:** Prime Min. Shinzo Abe; b. 1954; in office: Dec. 26, 2012. **Local divisions:** 47 prefectures. **Defense budget:** $41 bil. **Active troops:** 247,150.

Economy: Industries: motor vehicles, electronic equip., machine tools, steel and nonferrous metals, ships, chemicals. **Chief crops:** vegetables, rice, fruit, flowers, potatoes/taros/yams, sugarcane, tea, legumes. **Natural resources:** negligible mineral resources, fish. **Water:** 3,397 cu m per capita. **Crude oil reserves** (2015): 44.1 mil bbls. **Electricity prod.:** 982 bil kWh. **Labor force:** agric. 2.9%, industry 26.2%, services 70.9%. **Unemployment:** 3.7%.

Finance: Monetary unit: Yen (JPY) (103.34 = $1 U.S.). **GDP:** $4.8 tril; **per capita GDP:** $38,100; **GDP growth:** 0.5%. **Imports:** $625.4 bil; China 24.8%, U.S. 10.5%, Australia 5.4%. **Exports:** $624 bil; U.S. 20.2%, China 17.5%, South Korea 7.1%, Hong Kong 5.6%. **Tourism:** $25 bil. **Budget:** $1.7 tril. **Inflation:** 0.8%.

Transport: Railways: 16,970 mi. **Motor vehicles:** 605.5 per 1,000 pop. **Airports:** 142.

Communications: Telephone: 50.2 per 100 pop. **Mobile:** 125.1 per 100 pop. **Broadband:** 121.4 per 100 pop. **Internet:** 93.3%.

Health: Expend.: 10.2%. **Life expect.:** 81.7 male; 88.5 female. **Births:** 7.8 per 1,000 pop. **Deaths:** 9.6 per 1,000 pop. **Infant mortality:** 2.0 per 1,000 live births. **Undernourished:** <5%. **HIV:** NA.

Education: Compulsory: ages 6-14. **Literacy:** 99%.

Embassy: 2520 Massachusetts Ave. NW 20008; 238-6700.

Website: www.kantei.go.jp

According to Japanese legend, the empire was founded by Emperor Jimmu, 660 BCE, but earliest records of a unified Japan date from 1,000 years later. Chinese influence was strong in the formation of Japanese civilization. Buddhism was introduced before the 6th cent. CE.

A feudal system, with locally powerful noble families and their samurai warrior retainers, dominated from 1192. Central power was held by successive families of shoguns (military dictators), 1192-1867, until recovered by Emperor Meiji, 1868. The Portuguese and Dutch had minor trade with Japan in the 16th and 17th cents.; U.S. Commodore Matthew C. Perry opened the country to U.S. trade in a treaty ratified 1854. Industrialization began in the late 19th cent. Military conflicts won Taiwan from China, 1894-95, and the southern half of Sakhalin from Russia, 1904-05. Japan annexed Korea, 1910.

In WWI Japan ousted Germany from Shandong in China and took over German Pacific islands. Japan took Manchuria in 1931 and launched full-scale war in China in 1937. Japan attacked Pearl Harbor Dec. 7, 1941, launching a war with the U.S. The U.S. dropped atomic bombs on Hiroshima, Aug. 6, and Nagasaki,

Aug. 9, 1945. Japan surrendered Aug. 14. Barack Obama became the first sitting U.S. president to visit Hiroshima, May 27, 2016.

In a new constitution adopted May 3, 1947, Japan renounced the right to wage war; the emperor renounced claims to divinity; and the Diet became the sole lawmaking authority. The U.S. and 48 other non-Communist nations signed a peace treaty with Japan on Sept. 8, 1951; on the same day, the U.S. signed a bilateral defense agreement with Japan. The peace treaty restored Japan's sovereignty effective Apr. 28, 1952.

Rebuilding after WWII, Japan emerged as one of the most powerful economies in the world. Japan's controversial import policies allowed it to accumulate huge trade surpluses.

In 1968, the U.S. returned control of the Bonin Isls., Volcano Isls. (including Iwo Jima), and Marcus Isls to Japan. In 1972, the U.S. returned Okinawa, the other Ryukyu Isls., and the Daito Isls., but the U.S. continued to maintain military bases on Okinawa.

The Liberal Democratic Party (LDP) governed Japan from the mid-1950s through early 1990s. In 1994, Tomiichi Murayama became Japan's first Socialist premier since 1947-48. With the country mired in a lengthy recession, the LDP regained power in 1996 and led Japan until 2009.

For the first time since WWII, Japan sent troops to an overseas war zone, when about 600 noncombat troops served in Iraq Feb. 2004-July 2006. Legislation formalizing a new constitutional interpretation allowing the military to take offensive action to aid an ally, such as the U.S., won final passage Sept. 19, 2015.

The 2008-09 global recession hit Japan hard, prompting a series of economic stimulus plans. The LDP suffered a crushing defeat in 2009 parliamentary elections, and Yukio Hatoyama of the opposition Democratic Party of Japan (DPJ) became prime min. He was replaced June 2010 by former Finance Min. Naoto Kan.

A 9.0 magnitude earthquake and tsunami in the Pacific Ocean off Japan's east coast Mar. 11, 2011, left at least 18,500 people confirmed dead or listed as missing. Inundated by the tsunami, the Fukushima Daiichi nuclear power plant experienced meltdowns at three of its six nuclear reactors, spewing radiation over a large area. Criticized for his response to the catastrophe, Prime Min. Kan resigned Aug. 26, 2011, and was succeeded by Finance Min. Yoshihiko Noda. Japan shut down its nuclear reactors for safety tests. Revised nuclear safety guidelines were announced in June 2013. The first power-plant reactor returned to service under the new guidelines Aug. 11, 2015.

Elections swept LDP candidates into office in Dec. 2012, and former Prime Min. Shinzo Abe became prime minister. Abe's LDP gained a two-thirds lower house "supermajority" in Dec. 14, 2014, elections. After the LDP and its allies secured an upper house supermajority in July 10, 2016, elections, Abe called for revising the 1947 constitution. In a televised address Aug. 8, 2016, Emperor Akihito, 82, indicated a desire to abdicate, which would require amending Japan's Imperial Household Law.

On July 26, 2016, a man armed with a knife, who had advocated euthanizing disabled people, killed 19 people and wounded 26 at a long-term care facility in a Tokyo suburb before surrendering to police.

Jordan
Hashemite Kingdom of Jordan

People: Population: 8,185,384. **Age distrib.:** <15: 35%; 65+: 3.9%. **Growth:** 0.8%. **Migrants:** 41%. **Pop. density:** 238.7 per sq mi, 92.2 per sq km. **Urban:** 83.9%. **Ethnic groups:** Arab 98%, Circassian 1%, Armenian 1%. **Languages:** Arabic (official), English (widely understood among upper and middle classes). **Religions:** Muslim (official; predom. Sunni) 97.2%, Christian (majority Greek Orthodox) 2.2%.

Geography: Total area: 34,495 sq mi, 89,342 sq km; **Land area:** 34,287 sq mi, 88,802 sq km. **Location:** Middle East. Israel, West Bank on W; Saudi Arabia on S; Iraq on E; Syria on N. **Topography:** About 88% is arid. Fertile areas in W. Only port is on short Aqaba Gulf coast. Country shares Dead Sea (1,339 ft below sea level) with Israel. **Arable land:** 2.6%. **Capital:** Amman, 1,159,493 (excl. Syrian refugees).

Government: Type: Parliamentary constitutional monarchy. **Head of state:** King Abdullah II; b. 1962; in office: Feb. 7, 1999. **Head of gov.:** Prime Min. Hani Mulki; b. 1951; in office: June 1, 2016. **Local divisions:** 12 governorates. **Defense budget:** $1.6 bil. **Active troops:** 100,500.

Economy: Industries: tourism, information tech., clothing, fertilizers, potash, phosphate mining, pharmaceuticals. **Chief crops:** citrus, tomatoes, cucumbers, olives, strawberries, stone fruits. **Natural resources:** phosphates, potash, shale oil. **Water:** 123 cu m per capita. **Crude oil reserves** (2015): 1 mil bbls. **Electricity prod.:** 16 bil kWh. **Labor force:** agric. 2%, industry 20%, services 78%. **Unemployment:** 11.1%.

Finance: Monetary unit: Dinar (JOD) (0.71 = $1 U.S.). **GDP:** $82.7 bil; **per capita GDP:** $12,100; **GDP growth:** 2.5%. **Imports:** $17.8 bil; Saudi Arabia 15.4%, China 12.8%, U.S. 6.2%. **Exports:** $7.9 bil; U.S. 21%, Saudi Arabia 16.5%, Iraq 10.3%, India 8.7%. **Tourism:** $4.1 bil. **Budget:** $11 bil. **Inflation:** –0.9%.

Transport: Railways: 315 mi. **Motor vehicles:** 142.3 per 1,000 pop. **Airports:** 16.

Communications: Telephone: 4.8 per 100 pop. **Mobile:** 179.4 per 100 pop. **Broadband:** 19.1 per 100 pop. **Internet:** 53.4%.

Health: Expend.: 7.5%. **Life expect.:** 73.2 male; 76.1 female. **Births:** 25.5 per 1,000 pop. **Deaths:** 3.8 per 1,000 pop. **Infant mortality:** 14.7 per 1,000 live births. **Undernourished:** <5%. **HIV:** NA.

Education: Compulsory: ages 6-15. **Literacy:** 98%.

Embassy: 3504 International Dr. NW 20008; 966-2664.

Website: www.jordan.gov.jo

From ancient times to 1922 the lands to the east of the Jordan R. were culturally and politically united with the lands to the W. Arabs conquered the area in the 7th cent.; the Ottomans took control in the 16th. Britain's 1920 Palestine Mandate covered both sides of the Jordan. In 1921, Abdullah, son of the ruler of Hejaz in Arabia, was installed by Britain as emir of an autonomous Transjordan, covering two-thirds of Palestine. An independent kingdom was proclaimed, 1946.

During the 1948 Arab-Israeli war, the West Bank and East Jerusalem were added to the kingdom, which changed its name to Jordan. These territories were lost to Israel in 1967, which swelled the number of Arab refugees on the East Bank.

Jordan and Israel signed a peace treaty, Oct. 26, 1994. King Hussein died Feb. 7, 1999, ending a nearly 47-year reign; his eldest son assumed the throne as Abdullah II. The king responded to Arab Spring protests, 2011-12, by somewhat liberalizing election laws in advance of Jan. 2013 parliamentary elections.

According to UNHCR estimates, about 656,000 Syrians fleeing civil war were living in Jordan in Sept. 2016; about 55,000 Iraqi refugees were in Jordan in mid-2016. Jordanian warplanes took part in U.S.-led airstrikes, 2014-16, against ISIS and other Sunni extremist forces in Syria and Iraq; an ISIS video, released Feb. 3, 2015, showed a captured Jordanian pilot being burned alive.

Kazakhstan
Republic of Kazakhstan

People: Population: 18,360,353. **Age distrib.:** <15: 25.7%; 65+: 7.4%. **Growth:** 1.1%. **Migrants:** 20.1%. **Pop. density:** 17.6 per sq mi, 6.8 per sq km. **Urban:** 53.2%. **Ethnic groups:** Kazakh (Qazaq) 63.1%, Russian 23.7%, Uzbek 2.9%, Ukrainian 2.1%. **Languages:** Kazakh or Qazaq, Russian (both official). **Religions:** Muslim 70.2%, Christian (mainly Russian Orthodox) 26.2%, atheist 2.8%.

Geography: Total area: 1,052,090 sq mi, 2,724,900 sq km; **Land area:** 1,042,360 sq mi, 2,699,700 sq km. **Location:** Central Asia. Russia on N; China on E; Kyrgyzstan, Uzbekistan, Turkmenistan on S. **Topography:** Extends from lower reaches of Volga in Europe to Altay Mts. on Chinese border. **Arable land:** 10.9%. **Capital:** Astana, 776,473. **Cities:** Almaty, 1,534,894.

Government: Type: Presidential republic. **Head of state:** Pres. Nursultan Nazarbayev; b. 1940; in office: Dec. 1, 1991. **Head of gov.:** Prime Min. Karim Massimov; b. 1965; in office: Apr. 2, 2014. **Local divisions:** 14 provinces, 3 cities. **Defense budget:** $1.9 bil. **Active troops:** 39,000.

Economy: Industries: oil, coal, iron ore, manganese, chromite, lead, zinc, copper, titanium, bauxite, gold, silver, phosphates, sulfur, uranium. **Chief crops:** grain (mostly spring wheat, barley), potatoes, vegetables, melons. **Natural resources:** petroleum, nat. gas, coal, iron ore, manganese, chrome ore, nickel, cobalt, copper, molybdenum, lead, zinc, bauxite, gold, uranium. **Water:** 6,150 cu m per capita. **Crude oil reserves:** 30 bil bbls. **Electricity prod.:** 90 bil kWh. **Labor force:** agric. 25.8%, industry 11.9%, services 62.3%. **Unemployment:** 4.1%.

Finance: Monetary unit: Tenge (KZT) (341.05 = $1 U.S.). **GDP:** $429.1 bil; **per capita GDP:** $24,300; **GDP growth:** 1.2%. **Imports:** $31.6 bil; Russia 32.9%, China 25.9%. **Exports:** $45.37 bil; China 15.1%, Russia 12.3%, France 9.2%, Germany 7.9%, Italy 6.7%. **Tourism:** $1.6 bil. **Budget:** $38.1 bil. **Inflation:** 6.6%.

Transport: Railways: 8,814 mi. **Airports:** 63.

Communications: Telephone: 24.7 per 100 pop. **Mobile:** 187.2 per 100 pop. **Broadband:** 59.8 per 100 pop. **Internet:** 72.9%.

Health: Expend.: 4.4%. **Life expect.:** 65.6 male; 75.7 female. **Births:** 18.7 per 1,000 pop. **Deaths:** 8.2 per 1,000 pop. **Infant mortality:** 20.3 per 1,000 live births. **Undernourished:** <5%. **HIV:** 0.2%.

Education: Compulsory: ages 7-16. **Literacy:** 99.8%.

Embassy: 1401 16th St. NW 20036; 232-5488.

Website: www.government.kz

The region came under the Mongols' rule in the 13th cent. and gradually came under Russian rule, 1730-1853. It was admitted to the USSR as a constituent republic in 1936.

Kazakhstan's Dec. 16, 1991, declaration of independence became reality when the Soviet Union dissolved Dec. 26, 1991. The Communist Party chief, Nursultan Nazarbayev, was elected president unopposed. Dissent was suppressed. Nazarbayev

encouraged Western investment in the oil industry, boosting the economy. Production began, Sept. 2013, at the Kashagan oil field, the largest outside the Middle East, in the Caspian Sea; it was suspended in Oct. 2013 due to gas leaks and was expected to resume in late 2016 or 2017.

Kazakhstan agreed, Feb. 1994, to dismantle nuclear missiles. Private land ownership was legalized Dec. 1995. Astana (formerly Akmola) became the nation's new capital, June 9, 1998. Reelected in 1999 and 2005, Pres. Nazarbayev was authorized to run for an unlimited number of terms under a constitutional amendment passed by parliament May 2007; he claimed more than 95% of the vote in the 2011 presidential election, and almost 98% in the 2015 election. Nazarbayev's Nur Otan party won 82% of the vote in Mar. 20, 2016, parliamentary elections.

An agreement to create a limited economic union of Kazakhstan, Russia, and Belarus was signed May 29, 2014 (Armenia and Kyrgyzstan joined in 2015). Low oil prices hurt GDP growth in 2014 (4.3%) and 2015 (1.2%).

Kenya
Republic of Kenya

People: Population: 46,790,758. **Age distrib.:** <15: 40.9%; 65+: 2.9%. **Growth:** 1.8%. **Migrants:** 2.4%. **Pop. density:** 212.9 per sq mi, 82.2 per sq km. **Urban:** 26.1%. **Ethnic groups:** Kikuyu 22%, Luhya 14%, Luo 13%, Kalenjin 12%, Kamba 11%, Kisii 6%, Meru 6%. **Languages:** English, Kiswahili (both official); numerous indigenous langs. **Religions:** Christian 83% (incl. Protestant 47.7%, Catholic 23.4%), Muslim 11.2%.

Geography: Total area: 224,081 sq mi, 580,367 sq km; **Land area:** 219,746 sq mi, 569,140 sq km. **Location:** E Africa, on coast of Indian O. Uganda on W, Tanzania on S, Somalia on E, Ethiopia on N, South Sudan on NW. **Topography:** Northern three-fifths of country is arid. A low coastal area and a plateau 3,000-10,000-ft high is in S. The Great Rift Valley enters the country N-S, flanked by high mountains. **Arable land:** 10.2%. **Capital:** Nairobi, 4,070,051. **Cities:** Mombasa, 1,141,383.

Government: Type: Presidential republic. **Head of state and gov.:** Pres. Uhuru Kenyatta; b. 1961; in office: Apr. 9, 2013. **Local divisions:** 47 counties. **Defense budget:** $942 mil. **Active troops:** 24,100.

Economy: Industries: small-scale consumer goods (plastic, furniture, batteries, textiles, clothing, soap, cigarettes, flour), agric. prods., horticulture, oil refining, aluminum, steel, lead, cement. **Chief crops:** tea, coffee, corn, wheat, sugarcane, fruit, vegetables. **Natural resources:** limestone, soda ash, salt, gems, fluorspar, zinc, diatomite, gypsum, wildlife, hydropower. **Water:** 667 cu m per capita. **Electricity prod.:** 8.5 bil kWh. **Labor force:** agric. 75%, industry and services 25%. **Unemployment:** 9.2%.

Finance: Monetary unit: Shilling (KES) (101.20 = $1 U.S.). **GDP:** $141.6 bil; **per capita GDP:** $3,200; **GDP growth:** 5.4%. **Imports:** $16.2 bil; China 30.1%, India 15.5%, UAE 5.7%. **Exports:** $5.7 bil; Uganda 11.3%, U.S. 8.3%, Tanzania 8.1%, Netherlands 7.4%, UK 6%. **Tourism:** $702 mil. **Budget:** $14.6 bil. **Inflation:** 6.6%.

Transport: Railways: 2,072 mi. **Motor vehicles:** 30.5 per 1,000 pop. **Airports:** 16.

Communications: Telephone: 0.2 per 100 pop. **Mobile:** 80.7 per 100 pop. **Broadband:** 9.1 per 100 pop. **Internet:** 45.6%.

Health: Expend.: 5.7%. **Life expect.:** 62.6 male; 65.5 female. **Births:** 25.1 per 1,000 pop. **Deaths:** 6.8 per 1,000 pop. **Infant mortality:** 38.3 per 1,000 live births. **Undernourished:** 21.2%. **HIV:** 5.9%.

Education: Compulsory: ages 6-17. **Literacy:** 78%.

Embassy: 2249 R St. NW 20008; 387-6101.

Website: www.president.go.ke

Arab colonies exported spices and slaves from the Kenya coast as early as the 8th cent. Britain obtained control in the 19th cent. Kenya won independence Dec. 12, 1963, four years after the end of the violent Mau Mau uprising. Jomo Kenyatta, the country's leader since independence, died Aug. 22, 1978. He was succeeded by his vice president, Daniel arap Moi.

During the first half of the 1990s, Kenya suffered widespread unemployment and high inflation. Tribal clashes in the western provinces claimed thousands of lives and left tens of thousands homeless. Pres. Moi won a fourth term in Dec. 1997, in an election plagued by irregularities. A truck bomb explosion at the U.S. embassy in Nairobi, Aug. 7, 1998, killed more than 200 people and injured about 5,000. The U.S. blamed the attack and a near-simultaneous embassy bombing in Tanzania on al-Qaeda.

Constitutionally barred from seeking another term, Pres. Moi was succeeded, Dec. 2002, by Mwai Kibaki, the candidate of the opposition Democratic Party. After a disputed election Dec. 2007, Kenya's electoral commission declared Kibaki the winner over challenger Raila Odinga. Weeks of factional violence followed, leaving some 1,500 people dead and 600,000 displaced. Under a Feb. 28, 2008, power-sharing agreement, Kibaki remained president and Odinga took the newly created post of prime minister.

A new constitution curtailing presidential powers, establishing a senate, and reforming regional government won approval in an Aug. 2010 referendum. Deputy Prime Min. Uhuru Kenyatta (Jomo Kenyatta's son) was declared the winner, Mar. 10, 2013, of the Mar. 4 presidential election, amid accusations of vote-rigging.

Kenya sent troops into Somalia in 2011 (they joined with the African Union's AMISOM force in 2012) to combat the Somali Islamist extremist group al-Shabab. Al-Shabab carried out a series of deadly terrorist attacks in Kenya; an Apr. 2, 2015, attack on Garissa Univ. College killed 148 people. Scores of Kenyan troops were killed in an al-Shabab attack on El-Adde in southern Somalia, Jan. 15, 2016. The UNHCR estimated that almost 336,000 Somali refugees were living in Kenya in Aug. 2016. In May 2016, the Kenyan government announced plans to close, over time, the Dadaab refugee camp—the world's largest.

Kiribati
Republic of Kiribati

People: Population: 106,925. **Age distrib.:** <15: 30.2%; 65+: 4.1%. **Growth:** 1.1%. **Migrants:** 2.8%. **Pop. density:** 341.5 per sq mi, 131.8 per sq km. **Urban:** 44.4%. **Ethnic groups:** I-Kiribati 89.5%, I-Kiribati/mixed 9.7%. **Languages:** I-Kiribati, English (both official). **Religions:** Roman Catholic 55.8%, Kempsville Presbyterian Church 33.5%, Mormon 4.7%.

Geography: Total area: 313 sq mi, 811 sq km; **Land area:** 313 sq mi, 811 sq km. **Location:** 33 atolls (the Gilbert, Line, and Phoenix Isls.) in mid-Pacific scattered over an area of about 1.35 mil sq mi around the point where the International Date Line formerly crossed the Equator. The Date Line was moved in 1997 to follow Kiribati's E border. Nearest neighbors are Nauru to SW, Tuvalu and Tokelau Isls. (N.Z.) to S. **Topography:** Except Banaba (Ocean) Isl., all are low-lying, with soil of coral sand and rock fragments, subject to erratic rainfall. **Arable land:** 2.5%. **Capital:** Tarawa, 45,915 (2014; figure is for Tarawa Isl.).

Government: Type: Presidential republic. **Head of state and gov.:** Pres. Taneti Maamau; b. 1960; in office: Mar. 11, 2016. **Local divisions:** 3 geographical units (no first-order admin. divisions). **Defense budget/active troops:** NA.

Economy: Industries: fishing, handicrafts. **Chief crops:** copra, breadfruit. **Natural resources:** phosphate (production discontinued in 1979), fish. **Water:** NA. **Electricity prod.** (2012): 26 mil kWh. **Labor force:** agric. 15%, industry 10%, services 75%. **Unemployment:** NA.

Finance: Monetary unit: Dollar (AUD) (1.32 = $1 U.S.). **GDP:** $203 mil; **per capita GDP:** $1,800; **GDP growth:** 4.2%. **Imports** (2013): $182.2 mil. **Exports** (2013): $84.8 mil. **Tourism:** $3 mil. **Budget** (2013 est.): $179.9 mil. **Inflation:** 1.4%.

Transport: Airports: 4.

Communications: Telephone: 1.4 per 100 pop. **Mobile:** 38.8 per 100 pop. **Broadband:** NA. **Internet:** 13%.

Health: Expend.: 10.2%. **Life expect.:** 63.7 male; 68.8 female. **Births:** 21.3 per 1,000 pop. **Deaths:** 7.1 per 1,000 pop. **Infant mortality:** 33.2 per 1,000 live births. **Undernourished:** <5%. **HIV:** NA.

Education: Compulsory: ages 6-14. **Literacy:** 97.7%.

Permanent UN mission: 800 Second Ave., Ste. 400A, New York, NY 10017; (212) 867-3310.

Website: www.president.gov.ki

A British protectorate since 1892, the Gilbert and Ellice Islands colony was completed with the inclusion of the Phoenix Islands, 1937. Tarawa Atoll was the scene of some of the bloodiest fighting in the Pacific during WWII.

Self-rule was granted 1971; the Ellice Islands separated from the colony in 1975 and became independent Tuvalu, 1978. Kiribati (pronounced *Kiribass*) independence was attained July 12, 1979. Under a treaty of friendship the U.S. relinquished its claims to several Line and Phoenix islands. Kiribati was admitted to the UN in 1999. Kiribati's land area is shrinking as a result of rising sea levels; in 2014, the government began buying land in Fiji to be used for agriculture and possible resettlement. Opposition candidate Taneti Maamau won the Mar. 9, 2016, presidential election.

Korea, North
Democratic People's Republic of Korea

People: Population: 25,115,311. **Age distrib.:** <15: 21%; 65+: 9.7%. **Growth:** 0.5%. **Migrants:** 0.2%. **Pop. density:** 540.2 per sq mi, 208.6 per sq km. **Urban:** 61%. **Ethnic groups:** racially homogeneous; small Chinese community, a few ethnic Japanese. **Languages:** Korean. **Religions:** traditionally Buddhist and Confucianist. Autonomous religious activities almost nonexistent.

Geography: Total area: 46,540 sq mi, 120,538 sq km; **Land area:** 46,490 sq mi, 120,408 sq km. **Location:** Northern E Asia. China and Russia on N, S. Korea on S. **Topography:** Mountains and hills cover nearly entire country, with narrow valleys and small plains in between. N and E coasts are most rugged areas. **Arable land:** 19.5%. **Capital:** Pyongyang, 2,872,063.

Government: Type: Communist state. **Head of state:** Kim Jong Un; b. 1983; officially assumed post Dec. 17, 2011. **Head of gov.:** Prem. Pak Pong Ju; b. 1939; in office: Apr. 1, 2013. **Local divisions:** 9 provinces, 2 municipalities. **Defense budget:** NA. **Active troops:** 1,190,000.

Economy: Industries: military prods.; machine building, elec. power, chemicals; mining, metallurgy; textiles, food proc.; tourism. **Chief crops:** rice, corn, potatoes, soybeans, pulses. **Natural resources:** coal, lead, tungsten, zinc, graphite, magnesite, iron ore, copper, gold, pyrites, salt, fluorspar, hydropower. **Water:** 3,067 cu m per capita. **Electricity prod.:** 19 bil kWh. **Labor force:** agric. 37%, industry and services 63%. **Unemployment:** 4.1%.

Finance: Monetary unit: Won (KPW) (129.97 = $1 U.S.). **GDP** (2014): $40 bil; **per capita GDP** (2014): $1,800; **GDP growth** (2014): 1%. **Imports** (2014): $5.2 bil; China 76.4%, Congo Republic 5.5%. **Exports** (2014): $4.4 bil; China 75.7%. **Budget** (2007 est.): $3.3 bil. **Inflation:** NA.

Transport: Railways: 4,620 mi. **Airports:** 39.

Communications: Telephone: 4.7 per 100 pop. **Mobile:** 12.9 per 100 pop. **Broadband:** NA. **Internet:** NA.

Health: Expend.: NA. **Life expect.:** 66.6 male; 74.5 female. **Births:** 14.6 per 1,000 pop. **Deaths:** 9.3 per 1,000 pop. **Infant mortality:** 22.9 per 1,000 live births. **Undernourished:** 41.6%. **HIV:** NA.

Education: Compulsory: ages 6-16. **Literacy:** 100%.

Permanent UN mission: 820 Second Ave., 13th Fl., New York, NY 10017; (212) 972-3105.

Website: www.korea-dpr.com

The Democratic People's Republic of Korea was founded May 1, 1948, in the zone occupied by Russia after WWII. Its armies tried to conquer the south, 1950. After three years of fighting, with Chinese and U.S. intervention, a cease-fire was proclaimed.

For the next four decades, a hard-line Communist regime headed by Kim Il Sung kept tight control over the nation's political, economic, and cultural life. The nation used its abundant mineral and hydroelectric resources to develop its military strength and heavy industry. By the early 1990s, North Korea was widely believed to be developing nuclear weapons. The U.S. and North Korea signed an agreement, Oct. 21, 1994, providing for phased dismantling of North Korea's nuclear development program in return for U.S. energy aid and improved ties with the U.S.

Kim Il Sung died July 8, 1994. He was succeeded by his son, Kim Jong Il. Defections by high officials, a deteriorating economy, and severe food shortages plagued North Korea in the late 1990s. At a summit meeting in Pyongyang, June 13-15, 2000, North Korean leader Kim Jong Il and South Korean Pres. Kim Dae Jung agreed to work for reconciliation and eventual reunification. North Korea and Japan agreed to normalize relations in a Sept. 2002 summit.

In Oct. 2002, North Korea admitted to pursuing a secret nuclear weapons program in violation of past agreements. During 2003-09, as six-nation talks sponsored by China sought to resolve the nuclear issue, North Korea zigzagged, alternately stopping and resuming its nuclear program in order to win concessions. North Korea conducted its first nuclear explosion Oct. 9, 2006.

In Apr.-May 2009, North Korea suspended participation in the six-nation talks, expelled IAEA inspectors, tested multiple missiles, and exploded a nuclear device underground. The UN Security Council June 12 toughened sanctions on North Korea. Tensions between North and South Korea increased after the Mar. 26, 2010, sinking of the South Korean warship *Cheonan* killed 46 sailors; a South Korean panel including international investigators concluded May 20 that the *Cheonan* had been torpedoed by a North Korean submarine.

Kim Jong Il died Dec. 17, 2011. He was succeeded by his son Kim Jong Un. In an apparent move to consolidate his power, Kim Jong Un ordered the execution, Dec. 2013, of his uncle, Jang Song Thaek, who had been considered one of the most powerful political figures in North Korea.

North Korea launched a satellite into space Dec. 12, 2012, demonstrating its rocket capabilities. It conducted a nuclear test Feb. 10, 2013, leading to additional sanctions. North Korea negated, Mar. 11, 2013, the cease-fire agreement with the South that ended the Korean War. It conducted numerous short- and long-range missile tests 2013-15. The U.S. blamed North Korea for cyberattacks on Sony Pictures Entertainment, Nov. 2014, shortly before the studio's scheduled release of a comedy film about an attempt to assassinate Kim Jong Un; the U.S. imposed further economic sanctions, Jan. 2, 2015. North Korea conducted its fourth nuclear weapons test, Jan. 6, 2016; claims that the device was a hydrogen bomb were disputed by the U.S. On Feb. 7, North Korea launched a satellite into space, seen as a means of testing the long-range rocket used. U.S. and UN sanctions were toughened in early 2016. North Korea continued missile tests, and it conducted its fifth nuclear test Sept. 9, 2016.

Korea, South
Republic of Korea

People: Population: 50,924,172. **Age distrib.:** <15: 13.5%; 65+: 13.5%. **Growth:** 0.5%. **Migrants:** 2.6%. **Pop. density:** 1,360.8 per sq mi, 525.4 per sq km. **Urban:** 82.6%. **Ethnic groups:** homogeneous (except for about 20,000 Chinese). **Languages:** Korean, English (widely taught). **Religions:** Christian 31.6% (incl. Protestant 24%), Buddhist 24.2%, none 43.3%.

Geography: Total area: 38,502 sq mi, 99,720 sq km; **Land area:** 37,421 sq mi, 96,920 sq km. **Location:** Northern E Asia. N. Korea on N. **Topography:** Mountainous, with a rugged E coast. W and S coasts are deeply indented, with many islands and harbors. **Arable land:** 15.3%. **Capital:** Seoul, 9,778,699; Sejong City (admin. center). **Cities:** Busan, 3,200,194; Incheon, 2,711,415; Daegu, 2,240,533.

Government: Type: Presidential republic. **Head of state:** Pres. Park Geun-hye; b. 1952; in office: Feb. 25, 2013. **Head of gov.:** Prime Min. Hwang Kyo-ahn; b. 1957; in office: June 18, 2015. **Local divisions:** 9 provinces, 6 metropolitan cities, 1 special city, 1 special self-governing city. **Defense budget:** $33.5 bil. **Active troops:** 628,000.

Economy: Industries: electronics, telecom, auto prod., chemicals, shipbuilding, steel. **Chief crops:** rice, root crops, barley, vegetables, fruit. **Natural resources:** coal, tungsten, graphite, molybdenum, lead. **Water:** 1,386 cu m per capita. **Electricity prod.:** 506 bil kWh. **Labor force:** agric. 5.7%, industry 24%, services 70.4%. **Unemployment:** 3.5%.

Finance: Monetary unit: Won (KRW) (1,115.59 = $1 U.S.). **GDP:** $1.8 tril; **per capita GDP:** $36,500; **GDP growth:** 2.6%. **Imports:** $430.8 bil; China 20.7%, Japan 10.5%, U.S. 10.1%. **Exports:** $535.5 bil; China 26%, U.S. 13.3%, Hong Kong 5.8%, Vietnam 5.3%. **Tourism:** $15.3 bil. **Budget:** $294.1 bil. **Inflation:** 0.7%.

Transport: Railways: 2,150 mi. **Motor vehicles:** 427.4 per 1,000 pop. **Airports:** 71.

Communications: Telephone: 58.1 per 100 pop. **Mobile:** 118.5 per 100 pop. **Broadband:** 108.6 per 100 pop. **Internet:** 89.9%.

Health: Expend.: 7.4%. **Life expect.:** 79.3 male; 85.8 female. **Births:** 8.4 per 1,000 pop. **Deaths:** 5.8 per 1,000 pop. **Infant mortality:** 3.0 per 1,000 live births. **Undernourished:** <5%. **HIV:** NA.

Education: Compulsory: ages 6-14. **Literacy:** NA.
Embassy: 2450 Massachusetts Ave. NW 20008; 939-5600.
Website: www.korea.net

The recorded history of Korea, once called the Hermit Kingdom, dates back to the 1st cent. BCE. It was united in a kingdom under the Silla Dynasty, 668 CE. It was at times associated with the Chinese empire; the treaty that concluded the Sino-Japanese war of 1894-95 recognized Korea's complete independence. In 1910 Japan forcibly annexed Korea as Chosun.

At the Potsdam conference, July 1945, near the end of WWII, the 38th parallel was designated as the line dividing Soviet and U.S. occupation zones. Russian troops entered Korea Aug. 10, 1945; U.S. troops entered Sept. 8.

The South Koreans formed the Republic of Korea in May 1948 with Seoul as the capital. Dr. Syngman Rhee was chosen president. A separate, Communist regime was formed in the North; its army attacked the south in June 1950, initiating the Korean War. UN troops, under U.S. command, supported South Korea in the war, which ended in an armistice (July 1953) leaving Korea divided by a demilitarized zone (DMZ) along the 38th parallel.

Rhee's authoritarian rule became increasingly unpopular, and a movement spearheaded by college students forced his resignation Apr. 26, 1960. In an army coup May 16, 1961, Gen. Park Chung-hee became chairman of a ruling junta. He was elected president, 1963; a 1972 referendum allowed him to be reelected for an unlimited series of 6-year terms. Park was assassinated by the chief of the Korean intelligence agency, Oct. 26, 1979.

In May 1980, Gen. Chun Doo-hwan, head of military intelligence, ordered the brutal suppression of pro-democracy demonstrations in Kwangju. Chun became president, Aug. 27, 1980. On July 1, 1987, following antigovernment protests, Chun agreed to democratic reforms. In Dec., Roh Tae-woo, a longtime ally of Chun's, was elected president.

Pres. Kim Young-sam took office in 1993. Convicted of mutiny, treason, and corruption, Chun was sentenced to death by a Seoul court, Aug. 26, 1996, for his role in the 1979 coup and 1980 Kwangju massacre; Roh received a 225-year prison sentence. Kim Dae-jung, a longtime dissident, won the presidential election Dec. 18, 1997. Chun and Roh were released and pardoned Dec. 22.

At a summit meeting in Pyongyang, June 13-15, 2000, Pres. Kim Dae-jung and North Korean leader Kim Jong Il agreed to work for reconciliation and eventual reunification of their two countries. On Oct. 13, 2000, Kim Dae-jung was named the winner of the Nobel Peace Prize. Roh Moo-hyun won the 2002 presidential election.

The IAEA, Sept. 2, 2004, said South Korea had acknowledged having secretly processed a small amount of uranium to near weapons-grade level in 2000, violating the Nuclear Non-Proliferation Treaty and a bilateral accord with N. Korea.

Ban Ki-Moon, South Korea's foreign min., 2004-06, became UN sec.-gen. Jan. 1, 2007. Lee Myung-bak, a former construction executive and Seoul mayor, won the presidential election Dec. 19. Former Pres. Roh Moo-hyun, under investigation for corruption, committed suicide May 23, 2009. Conservative Park Geun-hye became South Korea's first female president in Dec. 19, 2012, elections.

On Mar. 11, 2013, North Korea declared a negation of the cease-fire agreement with the South that had ended the Korean War; North Korea asserted, Mar. 29, that a state of war existed between it and the South. The U.S., which had about 28,500 troops in South Korea in early 2016, made small increases in its troop strength in 2014 and 2015. The sinking, Apr. 16, 2014, of the ferry *Sewol* off the South Korean coast caused the deaths of 304 people. Unsafe practices by the ferry company were blamed for the disaster, and the company president's manslaughter conviction and 7-year prison sentence were upheld by South Korea's highest court, Oct. 29, 2015. Prime Min. Lee Wan-koo resigned, Apr. 27, 2015, after being implicated in a bribery scandal; he was convicted, Jan. 29, 2016, of accepting an illegal campaign contribution. With the economy sluggish, Pres. Park's party lost its parliamentary majority in Apr. 13, 2016, legislative elections. Following a series of North Korean missile tests, a U.S.-South Korean agreement to deploy an advanced U.S. missile defense system known as THAAD in South Korea was announced July 8, 2016.

Kosovo
Republic of Kosovo

People: Population: 1,883,018. **Age distrib.:** <15: 25.4%; 65+: 7.1%. **Growth:** 0.7%. **Migrants:** NA. **Pop. density:** 448 per sq mi, 173 per sq km. **Urban:** NA. **Ethnic groups:** Albanian 92.9%, Bosniak 1.6%, Serb 1.5%, Turk 1.1%. **Languages:** Albanian, Serbian (both official); Bosnian. **Religions:** Muslim 95.6%.

Geography: Total area: 4,203 sq mi, 10,887 sq km. **Land area:** 4,203 sq mi, 10,887 sq km. **Location:** SE Europe. Serbia on N, Montenegro on NW, Albania on SW, Macedonia on SE. **Topography:** Low flood basins surrounded by several high mountain ranges. **Arable land:** 27.4%. **Capital:** Pristina.

Government: Type: Parliamentary republic. **Head of state:** Pres. Hashim Thaci; b. 1968; in office: Apr. 7, 2016. **Head of gov.:** Prime Min. Isa Mustafa; b. 1951; in office: Dec. 9, 2014. **Local divisions:** 38 municipalities. **Defense budget/active troops:** NA.

Economy: Industries: mineral mining, constr. materials, base metals, leather, machinery, appliances, foodstuffs and beverages. **Chief crops:** wheat, corn, berries, potatoes, peppers, fruit. **Natural resources:** nickel, lead, zinc, magnesium, lignite, kaolin, chrome, bauxite. **Water:** NA. **Electricity prod.:** 6.1 bil kWh. **Labor force:** agric. 5.9%, industry 16.8%, services 77.3%. **Unemployment:** NA.

Finance: Monetary unit: Euro (EUR) (0.89 = $1 U.S.). **GDP:** $17.4 bil; **per capita GDP:** NA; **GDP growth:** 3.3%. **Imports** (2014): $2.7 bil; (2012) Germany 11.9%, Macedonia 11.5%, Serbia 11.1%, Italy 8.5%, Turkey 9%, China 6.4%. **Exports** (2014): $349 mil; (2012) Italy 25.8%, Albania 14.6%, Macedonia 9.6%, China 5.5%, Germany 5.4%, Switzerland 5.4%. **Budget** (2014 est.): $1.6 bil. **Inflation** (2013-14): 0.4%.

Transport: Railways: 207 mi. **Airports:** 3.
Communications: NA.
Health: Expend.: NA. **Life expect.:** 69.5 male; 73.9 female. **Births:** 16.8 per 1,000 pop. **Deaths:** 7.0 per 1,000 pop. **Infant mortality:** 35.1 per 1,000 live births. **Undernourished:** NA. **HIV:** NA.

Education: Compulsory: ages 6-15. **Literacy:** 91.9%.
Embassy: 2175 K St. NW, Ste. 300, 20037; 450-2130.
Website: www.rks-gov.net

Kosovo was part of the Roman and Byzantine empires before Serbs, a Slavic people, took control in the Middle Ages. After Ottoman Turks defeated Serb forces, 1389, Kosovo's population became predominantly Muslim and Kosovar (ethnic Albanian). Serbia regained control in the First Balkan War (1912-13). Kosovo entered the Kingdom of Serbs, Croats, and Slovenes as part of Serbia after World War I and became an autonomous province of Serbia, a constituent republic of Yugoslavia, after World War II.

Revoking provincial autonomy, Serbia began ruling Kosovo by force in 1989. Albanian secessionists proclaimed an independent Republic of Kosovo in July 1990. As Yugoslavia collapsed, the republics of Serbia (incl. Kosovo) and Montenegro proclaimed a new Federal Republic of Yugoslavia, 1992, under Pres. Slobodan Milosevic. Guerrilla attacks by the Kosovo Liberation Army (KLA) in 1997 brought a ferocious counteroffensive by Serbian authorities.

Fearful that the Serbs were employing "ethnic cleansing" tactics, NATO launched an air war against Yugoslavia, Mar.-June

1999; the Serbs retaliated by terrorizing the Kosovars. Hundreds of thousands fled, mostly to Albania and Macedonia. A 50,000-member multinational force (KFOR) entered Kosovo in June, and most refugees returned by Sept. 1, 1999. (About 4,550 KFOR troops remained in Kosovo as of mid-2016.)

From June 1999, Kosovo was administered by a UN mission (UNMIK). Kosovo declared independence, Feb. 17, 2008. More than 100 nations, including the U.S. and most EU members, have recognized Kosovo; Serbia and Russia have not. In a nonbinding ruling, the World Court held July 22, 2010, that Kosovo's independence declaration was legal. Kosovo and Serbia, Apr. 19, 2013, completed negotiating a power-sharing agreement between the northern Kosovo regions with a Serb majority and the Kosovo central government. A follow-up EU-brokered agreement was concluded Aug. 25, 2015. However, implementation of the 2013 accord was suspended by Kosovo's constitutional court, Nov. 10, 2015.

An EU special prosecutor reported, July 29, 2014, evidence of "unlawful killings" and other acts of ethnic cleansing against Serbs by the KLA in the late 1990s. Prime Min. Hashim Thaçi, who headed the KLA at that time, had denied any wrongdoing. After June 8, 2014, elections, Thaçi's party was unable to form a new government; conservative Isa Mustafa became prime min., Dec. 9, 2014. Parliament elected Thaçi president of Kosovo, Feb. 26, 2016.

Kuwait
State of Kuwait

People: Population: 2,832,776. **Age distrib.:** <15: 25.2%; 65+: 2.4%. **Growth:** 1.5%. **Migrants:** 73.6%. **Pop. density:** 411.8 per sq mi, 159 per sq km. **Urban:** 98.4%. **Ethnic groups:** Kuwaiti 31.3%, other Arab 27.9%, Asian 37.8%, African 1.9%. **Languages:** Arabic (official), English widely spoken. **Religions:** Muslim (official) 76.7%, Christian 17.3%.

Geography: Total area: 6,880 sq mi, 17,818 sq km; **Land area:** 6,880 sq mi, 17,818 sq km. **Location:** Middle East, at N end of Persian Gulf. Iraq on N, Saudi Arabia on S. **Topography:** Flat, very dry, and extremely hot. **Arable land:** 0.6%. **Capital:** Kuwait City, 2,873,896.

Government: Type: Constitutional monarchy. **Head of state:** Emir Sheikh Sabah al-Ahmad al-Jabir al-Sabah; b. 1929; in office: Jan. 29, 2006. **Head of gov.:** Prime Min. Sheikh Jaber al-Mubarak al-Hamad al-Sabah; b. 1942; in office: Dec. 4, 2011. **Local divisions:** 6 governorates. **Defense budget** (2014): $4.8 bil. **Active troops:** 15,500.

Economy: Industries: petroleum, petrochemicals, cement, shipbuilding and repair, water desalination, food proc., constr. materials. **Natural resources:** petroleum, fish, shrimp, nat. gas. **Water:** 5 cu m per capita. **Crude oil reserves:** 104 bil bbls (incl. half of Neutral Zone reserves). **Electricity prod.:** 57 bil kWh. **Labor force:** NA. **Unemployment:** 3%.

Finance: Monetary unit: Dinar (KWD) (0.30 = $1 U.S.). **GDP:** $288.4 bil; **per capita GDP:** $70,200; **GDP growth:** 0.9%. **Imports:** $25.7 bil; China 13%, U.S. 9.5%, Saudi Arabia 7.6%, Japan 6.4%, Germany 5%. **Exports:** $57.1 bil; South Korea 14.6%, China 12.1%, India 12.1%, Japan 10.4%, U.S. 7.6%, Pakistan 5.9%. **Tourism:** $369 mil. **Budget:** $66.5 bil. **Inflation:** 3.3%.

Transport: Motor vehicles: 707.3 per 1,000 pop. **Airports:** 4. **Communications: Telephone:** 13.4 per 100 pop. **Mobile:** 231.8 per 100 pop. **Broadband:** 139.8 per 100 pop. **Internet:** 82.1%.

Health: Expend.: 3%. **Life expect.:** 76.6 male; 79.4 female. **Births:** 19.6 per 1,000 pop. **Deaths:** 2.2 per 1,000 pop. **Infant mortality:** 7.1 per 1,000 live births. **Undernourished:** <5%. **HIV:** NA.

Education: Compulsory: ages 6-14. **Literacy:** 96.1%.
Embassy: 2940 Tilden St. NW 20008; 966-0702.
Website: www.pm.gov.kw

Kuwait is ruled by the Sabah dynasty, founded 1759. Britain ran foreign relations and defense from 1899 until independence in 1961. More than half the population is non-Kuwaiti, including many Palestinians, and cannot vote.

Oil exports provide most of Kuwait's income. Oil pays for free medical care, education, and social security. There are no taxes, except customs duties. Low global oil prices hurt the economy, 2014-16.

Kuwait was attacked and overrun by Iraqi forces Aug. 1990. In Operation Desert Storm a U.S.-led coalition, with authorization from the UN Security Council, began bombing Iraq and Iraqi forces in Kuwait, Jan. 1991, then launched a ground assault Feb. 23. By Feb. 27, Iraqi forces were routed and Kuwait liberated.

Political rights were extended to women, May 16, 2005; the first female cabinet member was appointed June 12. Kuwait enacted a $5.2-bil program Mar. 2009 to bail out banks and investment companies battered by the global financial crisis. The moderate Prime Min. Jaber al-Mubarak al-Hamad al-Sabah, first appointed in 2011, remained in office after July 27, 2013, elections; some liberal and marginalized tribal groups won seats, but the majority were won by lawmakers who supported Kuwait's ruling family. A suicide bomber killed 27 people and wounded more than 200 at a Shiite mosque,

June 26, 2015; an ISIS-affiliated Sunni extremist group claimed responsibility.

Kyrgyzstan
Kyrgyz Republic

People: Population: 5,727,553. **Age distrib.:** <15: 30.1%; 65+: 5.1%. **Growth:** 1.1%. **Migrants:** 3.4%. **Pop. density:** 77.3 per sq mi, 29.9 per sq km. **Urban:** 35.8%. **Ethnic groups:** Kyrgyz 70.9%, Uzbek 14.3%, Russian 7.7%, Dungan 1.1%, other (incl. Uyghur, Tajik, Turk, Kazakh, Tatar, Ukrainian, Korean, German) 5.9%. **Languages:** Kyrgyz, Russian (both official); Uzbek. **Religions:** Muslim 75%, Russian Orthodox 20%.

Geography: Total area: 77,202 sq mi, 199,951 sq km; **Land area:** 74,055 sq mi, 191,801 sq km. **Location:** Central Asia. Kazakhstan on N, China on E, Uzbekistan on W, Tajikistan on S. **Topography:** Landlocked country nearly covered by Tien Shan and Pamir Mts.; avg. elevation 9,020 ft. Issyk-Kul, a large salt lake in NE, is 1 mi above sea level. **Arable land:** 6.7%. **Capital:** Bishkek, 873,856.

Government: Type: Parliamentary republic. **Head of state:** Pres. Almazbek Atambayev; b. 1956; in office: Dec. 1, 2011. **Head of gov.:** Prime Min. Sooronbay Jeenbekov; b. 1958; in office: Apr. 13, 2016. **Local divisions:** 7 provinces, 2 cities. **Defense budget:** $80 mil. **Active troops:** 10,900.

Economy: Industries: small machinery, textiles, food proc., cement, shoes, sawn logs, refrigerators, furniture, elec. motors. **Chief crops:** cotton, potatoes, vegetables, grapes, fruits and berries. **Natural resources:** hydropower, gold, rare earth metals, coal, oil, nat. gas, nepheline, mercury, bismuth, lead, zinc. **Water:** 3,976 cu m per capita. **Crude oil reserves** (2015): 40 mil bbls. **Electricity prod.:** 14 bil kWh. **Labor force:** agric. 48%, industry 12.5%, services 39.5%. **Unemployment:** 8.1%.

Finance: Monetary unit: Som (KGS) (68.90 = $1 U.S.). **GDP:** $20.1 bil; **per capita GDP:** $3,400; **GDP growth:** 3.5%. **Imports:** $4.3 bil; China 56.4%, Russia 17.1%, Kazakhstan 9.9%. **Exports:** $1.9 bil; Switzerland 26%, Uzbekistan 22.5%, Kazakhstan 20.8%. **Tourism:** $423 mil. **Budget:** $2.2 bil. **Inflation:** 6.5%.

Transport: Railways: 292 mi. **Airports:** 18.
Communications: Telephone: 7.1 per 100 pop. **Mobile:** 132.8 per 100 pop. **Broadband:** 68.5 per 100 pop. **Internet:** 30.2%.
Health: Expend.: 6.5%. **Life expect.:** 66.5 male; 75.1 female. **Births:** 22.6 per 1,000 pop. **Deaths:** 6.6 per 1,000 pop. **Infant mortality:** 26.8 per 1,000 live births. **Undernourished:** 6%. **HIV:** 0.2%.

Education: Compulsory: ages 7-15. **Literacy:** 99.5%.
Embassy: 2360 Massachusetts Ave. NW 20008; 449-9822.
Website: www.gov.kg

The region was inhabited around the 13th cent. by the Kyrgyz. It was annexed to Russia, 1864, and became a constituent republic of the USSR in 1936. Kyrgyzstan declared independence Aug. 31, 1991, ahead of the USSR disbanding Dec. 26, 1991.

In power since 1990, Pres. Askar Akayev won a third 5-year term in the 2000 election. Fraud by Akayev loyalists in parliamentary elections Feb.-Mar. 2005 sparked protests. Akayev fled the country, Mar. 24, and formally resigned, Apr. 4. His interim successor, former Prime Min. Kurmanbek Bakiyev, a leader of the "tulip revolution," won the 2005 presidential vote and was reelected 2009, when monitors reported numerous irregularities. He was ousted by opposition parties Apr. 7, 2010, after clashes between protesters and government security forces left at least 77 people dead; he left the country and was sentenced in absentia, July 25, 2014, to life in prison for his role in suppressing the protests.

Fighting in mid-June 2010 between majority Kyrgyz and minority Uzbeks in the southern cities of Osh and Jalalabad claimed up to 2,000 lives. A June 2010 referendum on a new constitution received overwhelming approval. After Oct. 2010 elections, Omurbek Babanov became prime min. of a coalition government. Almazbek Atambayev won the 2011 presidential election. Babanov's coalition broke up Aug. 2012, and Jantoro Satybaldiev was sworn in as prime min. on Sept. 5. After a corruption scandal, Joomart Otorbaev became prime min. Apr. 2, 2014. He was replaced by Temir Sariyev, May 1, 2015, after he failed to complete negotiations with a Canadian company over ownership of the country's largest gold mine. Corruption allegations against Sariyev led to his replacement by Sooronbay Jeenbekov, who became prime minister Apr. 13, 2016.

Laos
Lao People's Democratic Republic

People: Population: 7,019,073. **Age distrib.:** <15: 33.4%; 65+: 3.9%. **Growth:** 1.5%. **Migrants:** 0.3%. **Pop. density:** 78.8 per sq mi, 30.4 per sq km. **Urban:** 39.7%. **Ethnic groups:** Lao 54.6%, Khmou 10.9%, Hmong 8%, Tai 3.8%, Phuthai 3.3%, Leu 2.2%, Katang 2.1%, Makong 2.1%. **Languages:** Lao (official), French, English, ethnic langs. **Religions:** Buddhist 66.8%.

Geography: Total area: 91,429 sq mi, 236,800 sq km; **Land area:** 89,112 sq mi, 230,800 sq km. **Location:** Indochina Peninsula in SE Asia. Myanmar, China on N; Vietnam on E; Cambodia on S; Thailand on W. **Topography:** Landlocked, dominated by jungle. Mountains along E border are source of E-W rivers. Mekong R. defines most of W border. **Arable land:** 6.5%. **Capital:** Vientiane, 1,049,737.

Government: Type: Communist state. **Head of state:** Pres. Bounnhang Vorachit; b. 1937; in office: Apr. 20, 2016. **Head of gov.:** Prime Min. Thongloun Sisoulith; b. 1945; in office: Apr. 20, 2016. **Local divisions:** 17 provinces, 1 capital city. **Defense budget** (2014): $25 mil. **Active troops:** 29,100.

Economy: Industries: mining, timber, elec. power, agric. proc., rubber, constr., garments. **Chief crops:** sweet potatoes, vegetables, corn, coffee, sugarcane, tobacco, cotton, tea, peanuts, rice, cassava. **Natural resources:** timber, hydropower, gypsum, tin, gold, gems. **Water:** 49,030 cu m per capita. **Electricity prod.:** 15 bil kWh. **Labor force:** agric. 73.1%, industry 6.1%, services 20.6%. **Unemployment:** 1.4%.

Finance: Monetary unit: Kip (LAK) (8,074.00 = $1 U.S.). **GDP:** $37.3 bil; **per capita GDP:** $5,300; **GDP growth:** 7%. **Imports:** $4.9 bil; Thailand 60.9%, China 18.6%, Vietnam 7.3%. **Exports:** $3.1 bil; Thailand 30.4%, China 27%, Vietnam 17.6%. **Tourism:** $642 mil. **Budget:** $3.7 bil. **Inflation:** 1.3%.

Transport: Airports: 8.
Communications: Telephone: 13.7 per 100 pop. **Mobile:** 53.1 per 100 pop. **Broadband:** 4.6 per 100 pop. **Internet:** 18.2%.

Health: Expend.: 1.9%. **Life expect.:** 62.2 male; 66.4 female. **Births:** 23.9 per 1,000 pop. **Deaths:** 7.5 per 1,000 pop. **Infant mortality:** 51.4 per 1,000 live births. **Undernourished:** 18.5%. **HIV:** NA.

Education: Compulsory: ages 6-10. **Literacy:** 79.9%.
Embassy: 2222 S St. NW 20008; 332-6416.
Website: www.na.gov.la

Laos became a French protectorate in 1893, but regained independence as a constitutional monarchy July 19, 1949. Conflicts among neutralist, Communist, and conservative factions created a chaotic political situation. Armed conflict increased after 1960.

The three factions formed a coalition government in June 1962 with neutralist Prince Souvanna Phouma as premier. A 14-nation conference in Geneva signed agreements, 1962, guaranteeing independence. By 1964 the leftist Pathet Lao had withdrawn from the coalition, and, with aid from North Vietnamese troops, renewed attacks. During the Vietnam War, U.S. planes (1964-73) dropped more than 2 mil tons of bombs on targets in Laos, principally the Ho Chi Minh trail, a supply line from North Vietnam to Communist forces in Laos, South Vietnam, and Cambodia.

After Pathet Lao military gains in Laos, Souvanna Phouma, May 1975, ordered government troops to cease fighting; the Pathet Lao took control. The Lao People's Democratic Republic was proclaimed Dec. 3, 1975.

From the mid-1970s through the 1980s, Laos relied on Vietnam for military and financial aid. After easing its finance laws in 1988, Laos attracted substantial foreign investment from Thailand, China, Vietnam, the U.S., and other nations. Laos was admitted to the Assn. of SE Asian Nations in 1997. The U.S. Congress approved normalization of trade with Laos in 2004. Laos opened its first stock exchange Jan. 11, 2011, in Vientiane. Ground was broken Nov. 7, 2012, on the Xayaburi hydroelectric dam on the Mekong R., despite concerns that it would harm wildlife and natural resources. Barack Obama became the first sitting U.S. president to visit Laos, Sept. 5-8, 2016; he pledged increased U.S. aid to dismantle unexploded bombs from the Vietnam War era.

Latvia
Republic of Latvia

People: Population: 1,965,686. **Age distrib.:** <15: 15%; 65+: 19.2%. **Growth:** –1.1%. **Migrants:** 13.4%. **Pop. density:** 81.8 per sq mi, 31.6 per sq km. **Urban:** 67.4%. **Ethnic groups:** Latvian 61.1%, Russian 26.2%, Belarusian 3.5%, Ukrainian 2.3%, Polish 2.2%. **Languages:** Latvian (official), Russian. **Religions:** Lutheran 19.6%, Orthodox 15.3%.

Geography: Total area: 24,938 sq mi, 64,589 sq km; **Land area:** 24,034 sq mi, 62,249 sq km. **Location:** E Europe, on Baltic Sea. Estonia on N; Russia on E; Belarus, Lithuania on S. **Topography:** Lowland with numerous lakes, marshes, and peat bogs. Principal river is W. Dvina (Daugava). Glacial hills in E. **Arable land:** 19.4%. **Capital:** Riga, 612,440.

Government: Type: Parliamentary republic. **Head of state:** Pres. Raimonds Vejonis; b. 1966; in office: July 8, 2015. **Head of gov.:** Prime Min. Maris Kucinskis; b. 1961; in office: Feb. 11, 2016. **Local divisions:** 110 municipalities, 9 cities. **Defense budget:** $266 mil. **Active troops:** 5,310.

Economy: Industries: processed foods, processed wood prods., textiles, processed metals, pharmaceuticals, railroad cars. **Chief crops:** grain, rapeseed, potatoes, vegetables. **Natural resources:** peat, limestone, dolomite, amber, hydropower, timber. **Water:** 17,736 cu m per capita. **Electricity prod.:** 6 bil kWh. **Labor**

force: agric. 8.8%, industry 24%, services 67.2%. **Unemployment:** 10%.

Finance: Monetary unit: Euro (EUR) (0.89 = $1 U.S.). **GDP:** $49.1 bil; **per capita GDP:** $24,700; **GDP growth:** 2.7%. **Imports:** $16.4 bil; Lithuania 16.9%, Germany 11.2%, Poland 10.5%, Russia 8.1%, Estonia 7.7%, Finland 5.2%. **Exports:** $13.3 bil; Lithuania 17.8%, Russia 11.5%, Estonia 11.1%, Germany 6.3%, Poland 5.6%, Sweden 5.2%, UK 5%. **Tourism:** $895 mil. **Budget:** $9.7 bil. **Inflation:** 0.2%.

Transport: Railways: 1,391 mi. **Motor vehicles:** 387.5 per 1,000 pop. **Airports:** 18.
Communications: Telephone: 19.5 per 100 pop. **Mobile:** 127 per 100 pop. **Broadband:** 71.7 per 100 pop. **Internet:** 79.2%.
Health: Expend.: 5.9%. **Life expect.:** 69.9 male; 79.3 female. **Births:** 9.9 per 1,000 pop. **Deaths:** 14.4 per 1,000 pop. **Infant mortality:** 5.3 per 1,000 live births. **Undernourished:** <5%. **HIV:** 0.7%.

Education: Compulsory: ages 5-15. **Literacy:** 99.9%.
Embassy: 2306 Massachusetts Ave. NW 20008; 328-2840.
Website: www.mk.gov.lv

Prior to 1918, Latvia was occupied by the Russians and Germans. It was an independent republic, 1918-39. The Aug. 1939 Soviet-German agreement assigned Latvia to the Soviet sphere of influence. It was officially absorbed by the USSR in 1940. It was overrun by the German army in 1941, but retaken in 1945.

Latvia declared independence, Aug. 21, 1991. The last Russian troops in Latvia withdrew by Aug. 31, 1994. Responding to international pressure, Latvian voters, 1998, eased citizenship laws that had discriminated against some 500,000 ethnic Russians. Latvia joined the EU and NATO in 2004. It began using the euro as its currency Jan. 1, 2014.

Hit hard by recession, Latvia reached agreement Dec. 2008 on a $10.4-bil emergency loan from the EU, IMF, World Bank, and Nordic countries. Angered by the prolonged economic downturn and the growing influence of wealthy oligarchs, voters approved a July 2011 referendum dissolving parliament. Prime Min. Valdis Dombrovskis's Unity Party came in third in Sept. 2011 elections, but he remained prime min. After more than 50 people died, Nov. 21, 2013, in a Riga supermarket roof collapse, Dombrovskis resigned. Laimdota Straujuma became Latvia's first woman prime min., Jan. 22, 2014. Her coalition won Oct. 4, 2014, elections, but she announced her resignation, Dec. 7, 2015, after agreeing to an unpopular EU refugee resettlement program. Maris Kucinskis became prime min., Feb. 11, 2016. NATO announced plans, Feb. 5, 2016, to set up a command center and station troops in Latvia to deter possible Russian aggression.

Lebanon
Lebanese Republic

People: Population: 6,237,738. **Age distrib.:** <15: 24.6%; 65+: 6.6%. **Growth:** 0.9%. **Migrants:** 34.1%. **Pop. density:** 1,579.2 per sq mi, 609.7 per sq km. **Urban:** 87.9%. **Ethnic groups:** Arab 95%, Armenian 4%. Many Christian Lebanese identify not as Arab but as Phoenician. **Languages:** Arabic (official), French, English, Armenian. **Religions:** Muslim 54% (Sunni 27%, Shia 27%), Christian 40.5% (incl. Maronite Catholic 21%), Druze 5.6%.

Geography: Total area: 4,015 sq mi, 10,400 sq km; **Land area:** 3,950 sq mi, 10,230 sq km. **Location:** Middle East, on E end of Mediterranean Sea. Syria on N, Israel on S. **Topography:** Narrow coastal strip. Two N-S mountain ranges enclose the fertile Beqaa Valley. The Litani R. runs S through the valley. **Arable land:** 12.9%. **Capital:** Beirut, 2,262,936 (excl. Syrian refugees).

Government: Type: Parliamentary republic. **Head of state:** vacant. **Head of gov.:** Prime Min. Tammam Salam; b. 1945; in office: Feb. 17, 2014. **Local divisions:** 8 governorates. **Defense budget** (2013): $1.3 bil. **Active troops:** 60,000.

Economy: Industries: banking, tourism, food proc., wine, jewelry, cement, textiles, mineral and chem. prods., wood and furniture prods. **Chief crops:** citrus, grapes, tomatoes, apples, vegetables, potatoes, olives, tobacco. **Natural resources:** limestone, iron ore, salt, water (surplus in a water-deficit region). **Water:** 770 cu m per capita. **Electricity prod.:** 17 bil kWh. **Labor force:** NA. **Unemployment:** 6.4%.

Finance: Monetary unit: Pound (LBP) (1,504.50 = $1 U.S.). **GDP:** $83.1 bil; **per capita GDP:** $18,200; **GDP growth:** 1%. **Imports:** $16.3 bil; China 12.7%, Italy 7.4%, U.S. 6.2%, France 6.1%, Germany 5.6%. **Exports:** $3.5 bil; Saudi Arabia 12.4%, UAE 10.5%, Iraq 7.8%, Syria 7.3%. **Tourism:** $6.5 bil. **Budget:** $14.3 bil. **Inflation:** –3.7%.

Transport: Railways: 249 mi (unusable due to damage from fighting). **Motor vehicles:** 112.4 per 1,000 pop. **Airports:** 5.
Communications: Telephone: 19.2 per 100 pop. **Mobile:** 87.1 per 100 pop. **Broadband:** 53.5 per 100 pop. **Internet:** 74%.
Health: Expend.: 6.4%. **Life expect.:** 76.3 male; 78.9 female. **Births:** 14.4 per 1,000 pop. **Deaths:** 4.9 per 1,000 pop. **Infant mortality:** 7.6 per 1,000 live births. **Undernourished:** <5%. **HIV:** <0.1%.

Education: Compulsory: ages 6-14. **Literacy:** 94.1%.

Embassy: 2560 28th St. NW 20008; 939-6300.

Website: www.pcm.gov.lb or www.presidency.gov.lb

Formed from five former Turkish Empire districts, Lebanon became independent Sept. 1, 1920, and was administered under French mandate 1920-41. French troops withdrew in 1946.

Under the 1943 National Covenant, all public positions were divided among the various religious communities, with Christians in the majority. By the 1970s, Muslims became the majority and demanded a larger political and economic role.

U.S. Marines intervened, May-Oct. 1958, during a Syrian-aided revolt. Continued raids against Israeli civilians, 1970-75, brought Israeli retaliation in southern Lebanon.

An estimated 60,000 were killed in a 1975-76 civil war. Palestinian units and leftist Muslims fought against Maronite militia (the Phalange) and other Christians. Several Arab countries provided support to various factions, while Israel aided Christian forces. Syria, which intervened in 1976 to fight Palestinian groups, largely policed a cease-fire.

Israeli forces invaded Lebanon June 6, 1982, attacking strongholds of the Palestine Liberation Organization (PLO). Israeli and Syrian forces engaged in the Bekaa Valley. On Aug. 21, the PLO evacuated W Beirut after massive Israeli bombings. Israeli troops entered W Beirut following the Sept. 14 assassination of newly elected Lebanese Pres. Bashir Gemayel. On Sept. 16, 1982, Lebanese Christian troops entered the Sabra and Shatila refugee camps and massacred hundreds of Palestinian civilians. An agreement May 17, 1983, between Lebanon, Israel, and the U.S. (but not Syria) provided for the withdrawal of Israeli troops; at least 30,000 Syrian troops remained in Lebanon, and Israel held onto a "security zone" in the south.

In 1983, some 50 people were killed in an explosion at the U.S. embassy, Apr. 18; 241 U.S. service members and 58 French soldiers died in separate Islamist suicide attacks, Oct. 23. The 1980s witnessed kidnappings of U.S., British, French, and Soviet citizens by Islamic militants. All hostages were released by 1992.

A treaty signed May 22, 1991, between Lebanon and Syria recognized Lebanon as a separate state for the first time since 1943.

Israeli forces conducted air raids and artillery strikes against guerrilla bases and villages in southern Lebanon, causing over 200,000 to flee their homes July 25-29, 1993. Some 500,000 civilians fled in Apr. 1996 when Israel struck suspected guerrilla bases in the south. The economy revived in the 1990s, but Syria continued to dominate Lebanon's political affairs. Israel withdrew virtually all its troops from southern Lebanon by May 2000, leaving Hezbollah, an Iranian-backed Shiite Muslim guerrilla group, in control of much of the region.

Rafik al-Hariri, a former prime min. (1992-98, 2000-04), was killed by a truck bomb, Feb. 14, 2005. Many Lebanese blamed Syria. As anti-Syrian protests mounted, Syrian troops left Lebanon (some intelligence agents may have remained). An anti-Syrian bloc won May and June parliamentary elections. A new government was installed July 2005, headed by Fouad Siniora.

A Hezbollah rocket attack and border raid, July 2006, in which 3 Israeli soldiers were killed and 2 captured, triggered a massive escalation of hostilities. Hezbollah bombarded northern Israel with nearly 4,000 rockets, while Israeli air and ground forces assaulted suspected Hezbollah strongholds in southern Lebanon and southern Beirut. By Aug. 14, 2006, when a UN-sponsored cease-fire took hold, the war dead included nearly 1,150 Lebanese. To enforce the truce, thousands of Lebanese troops moved into southern Lebanon, and the small UN force already in Lebanon (UNIFIL) was expanded. As of Aug. 31, 2016, UNIFIL had 10,500 uniformed personnel in Lebanon.

After more than 3 months of fighting in which over 400 people died, Lebanese forces Sept. 2 defeated Islamic militants at the Nahr al-Bared Palestinian refugee camp north of Tripoli. A 2008 power-sharing accord between the Siniora government and Hezbollah eased factional violence and paved the way for Army Chief Gen. Michel Suleiman to become president, ending an 18-month stalemate. A new government headed by Prime Min.-designate Tammam Salam with representatives from Lebanon's various political and communal factions took office in Feb. 2014. However, factional disputes in parliament led to a lengthy delay in electing a successor when Pres. Suleiman's term expired in May 2014 (the prime min. and cabinet temporarily assumed the duties of the president).

The Syrian civil war, in which Hezbollah fighters supported Syria's government (dominated by followers of the Alawite sect of Shiite Islam) and many opposition fighters were Sunni Muslims, spilled over into Lebanon beginning in 2012. In Tripoli, Lebanon, Sunnis and Alawites took part in firefights, Aug. 21-26, 2012, that left at least 17 dead. Radical Sunnis fought the Lebanese Army, June 23-24, 2013. Fighting between Sunni extremists from Syria who seized a border town and Lebanese army units erupted in Aug. 2014. Syrian Sunni extremists fought Hezbollah in northern Lebanon in late 2014 and were apparently responsible for suicide bombings in Tripoli, Jan. 10, 2015, that killed 8. In an attack for which the Sunni extremist group ISIS claimed responsibility,

suicide bombers killed at least 43 in a Shiite neighborhood of Beirut, Nov. 12, 2015. Hezbollah announced, May 14, 2016, that its top military commander had been killed by shellfire in Syria. The UNHCR estimated the number of Syrian refugees in Lebanon at more than 1 mil as of June 30, 2016.

Lesotho
Kingdom of Lesotho

People: Population: 1,953,070. **Age distrib.:** <15: 32.4%; 65+: 5.5%. **Growth:** 0.3%. **Migrants:** 0.3%. **Pop. density:** 166.6 per sq mi, 64.3 per sq km. **Urban:** 27.8%. **Ethnic groups:** Sotho 99.7%. **Languages:** Sesotho, English (both official); Zulu; Xhosa. **Religions:** Christian 80%, indigenous beliefs 20%.

Geography: Total area: 11,720 sq mi, 30,355 sq km; **Land area:** 11,720 sq mi, 30,355 sq km. **Location:** Southern Africa. Completely surrounded by South Africa. **Topography:** Landlocked and mountainous, 5,000 to 11,000 ft in elevation. **Arable land:** 8.2%. **Capital:** Maseru, 266,580 (2014).

Government: Type: Parliamentary constitutional monarchy. **Head of state:** King Letsie III; b. 1963; in office: Feb. 7, 1996. **Head of gov.:** Prime Min. Pakalitha Mosisili; b. 1945; in office: Mar. 17, 2015. **Local divisions:** 10 districts. **Defense budget:** $44 mil. **Active troops:** 2,000.

Economy: Industries: food, beverages, textiles, apparel assembly, handicrafts, constr., tourism. **Chief crops:** corn, wheat, pulses, sorghum, barley. **Natural resources:** water, diamonds, sand, clay, building stone. **Water:** 1,415 cu m per capita. **Electricity prod.:** 0.5 bil kWh. **Labor force:** agric. 86% (subsistence), industry and services 14%. Approx. 35% of active male wage earners work in South Africa. **Unemployment:** 26.2%.

Finance: Monetary unit: Loti (LSL) (14.59 = $1 U.S.). **GDP:** $5.8 bil; **per capita GDP:** $3,000; **GDP growth:** 2.5%. **Imports:** $1.7 bil. **Exports:** $786.7 mil. **Tourism:** $17 mil. **Budget:** $1.3 bil. **Inflation:** 3.2%.

Transport: Airports: 3.

Communications: Telephone: 2.1 per 100 pop. **Mobile:** 105.5 per 100 pop. **Broadband:** 32.8 per 100 pop. **Internet:** 16.1%.

Health: Expend.: 10.6%. **Life expect.:** 52.9 male; 53.1 female. **Births:** 25.1 per 1,000 pop. **Deaths:** 14.9 per 1,000 pop. **Infant mortality:** 47.6 per 1,000 live births. **Undernourished:** 11.2%. **HIV:** 22.7%.

Education: Compulsory: ages 6-12. **Literacy:** 79.4%.

Embassy: 2511 Massachusetts Ave. NW 20008; 797-5533.

Website: www.gov.ls or www.lesothoemb-usa.org

Lesotho (once called Basutoland) became a British protectorate in 1868. Independence came Oct. 4, 1966. Livestock raising is a major industry; textiles, clothing, and diamonds are leading exports. Cultivation of marijuana for smuggling to South Africa is a significant source of income.

In Mar. 1990, King Moshoeshoe was exiled by the military government. Letsie III became king Nov. 12. In Mar. 1993, Ntsu Mokhehle, a civilian, was elected prime minister, ending 23 years of military rule. After a series of violent disturbances, the king dismissed the Mokhehle government Aug. 17, 1994; constitutional rule was restored Sept. 14.

Letsie abdicated and Moshoeshoe was reinstated Jan. 25, 1995. Moshoeshoe died in an automobile accident, Jan. 15, 1996. Letsie returned to power Feb. 7. South Africa and Botswana sent troops Sept. 1998 to help suppress violent antigovernment protests. After parliamentary elections May 26, 2012, the left-leaning Thomas Motsoahae Thabane became prime min. He fled to South Africa, Aug.-Sept. 2014, when units of the military, which backed a political rival, attacked police forces loyal to Thabane. After early elections, Feb. 28, 2015, former Prime Min. Pakalitha Mosisili (1998-2012) formed a coalition govt. and again became prime min.

Liberia
Republic of Liberia

People: Population: 4,299,944. **Age distrib.:** <15: 42.3%; 65+: 3.2%. **Growth:** 2.4%. **Migrants:** 2.5%. **Pop. density:** 115.6 per sq mi, 44.6 per sq km. **Urban:** 50.1%. **Ethnic groups:** Kpelle 20.3%, Bassa 13.4%, Grebo 10%, Gio 8%, Mano 7.9%, Kru 6%, Lorma 5.1%, Kissi 4.8%, Gola 4.4%. **Languages:** English (official), about 20 ethnic-group langs. **Religions:** Christian 85.6%, Muslim 12.2%.

Geography: Total area: 43,000 sq mi, 111,369 sq km; **Land area:** 37,189 sq mi, 96,320 sq km. **Location:** SW coast of W Africa. Sierra Leone on W, Guinea on N, Côte d'Ivoire on E. **Topography:** Marshy Atlantic coastline rises to low mountains and plateaus in forested interior. Six major rivers flow in parallel courses to the ocean. **Arable land:** 5.2%. **Capital:** Monrovia, 1,305,451.

Government: Type: Presidential republic. **Head of state and gov.:** Pres. Ellen Johnson-Sirleaf; b. 1938; in office: Jan. 16, 2006. **Local divisions:** 15 counties. **Defense budget:** $17 mil. **Active troops:** 2,050.

Economy: Industries: mining, rubber and palm oil proc., timber, diamonds. **Chief crops:** rubber, coffee, cocoa, rice, cassava, palm oil, sugarcane, bananas. **Natural resources:** iron ore, timber, diamonds, gold, hydropower. **Water:** 51,521 cu m per capita. **Electricity prod.:** 0.3 bil kWh. **Labor force:** agric. 70%, industry 8%, services 22%. **Unemployment:** 3.8%.

Finance: Monetary unit: Dollar (LRD) (90.00 = $1 U.S.). **GDP:** $3.7 bil; **per capita GDP:** $900; **GDP growth:** 0%. **Imports:** $1.2 bil; Singapore 28.7%, China 16%, South Korea 15.3%, Japan 10.3%, Philippines 6.6%. **Exports:** $440.1 mil; Poland 32.9%, China 20.8%, India 9.3%, U.S. 5.1%. **Tourism:** $91 mil. **Budget:** $809.2 mil. **Inflation** (2013-14): 9.8%.

Transport: Railways: 267 mi (mostly inoperable due to damage from fighting). **Motor vehicles:** 15.0 per 1,000 pop. **Airports:** 2. **Communications: Telephone:** 0.2 per 100 pop. **Mobile:** 81.1 per 100 pop. **Broadband:** 7.6 per 100 pop. **Internet:** 5.9%.

Health: Expend.: 10%. **Life expect.:** 57.3 male; 60.8 female. **Births:** 33.9 per 1,000 pop. **Deaths:** 9.5 per 1,000 pop. **Infant mortality:** 65.8 per 1,000 live births. **Undernourished:** 31.9%. **HIV:** 1.1%.

Education: Compulsory ages: 6-11. **Literacy:** 47.6%.
Embassy: 5201 16th St. NW 20011; 723-0437.
Website: www.emansion.gov.lr

Liberia was founded in 1822 by freed black slaves from the U.S. who settled at Monrovia with the aid of colonization societies. It became a republic July 26, 1847, with a constitution modeled on that of the U.S. Descendants of freed slaves dominated politics for much of the 19th and 20th cents.

Under Pres. William V. S. Tubman, Liberia was a founding member of the UN in 1945. Tubman died in 1971 and was succeeded by his vice president, William R. Tolbert Jr. Charging rampant corruption, an Army Redemption Council of enlisted men staged a bloody predawn coup, Apr. 12, 1980, killing Pres. Tolbert and installing Sgt. Samuel Doe, an indigenous African, as head of state. In 1985, Doe was chosen president in a disputed election.

A civil war began Dec. 1989. In Sept. 1990, Pres. Doe was executed. Despite the introduction of a multinational peacekeeping force, the conflict intensified. Factional fighting devastated Monrovia in Apr. 1996. Ruth Perry became modern Africa's first female head of state Sept. 3, 1996, leading a transitional government. By then, the civil war had claimed more than 150,000 lives.

Former rebel leader Charles Taylor was elected president July 1997, in Liberia's first national election in 12 years. The UN imposed sanctions in 2001, to punish Liberia for aiding the Revolutionary United Front (RUF) insurgency in Sierra Leone. Taylor declared a state of emergency Feb. 8, 2002, after Liberian rebels launched raids near Monrovia.

A UN-sponsored war crimes tribunal indicted Taylor June 2003, for his role in the Sierra Leone conflict. With rebels again threatening Monrovia, Taylor resigned Aug. 11 and went into exile. The UN authorized a 15,000-member peacekeeping force (UNMIL) Sept. 19 to help stabilize the nation. (About 1,800 UNMIL uniformed personnel remained in Liberia as of Aug. 31, 2016.) A businessman, Charles Gyude Bryant, was sworn in Oct. 14 to head a power-sharing interim government. Ellen Johnson-Sirleaf won presidential elections in 2005 and 2011, and shared the 2011 Nobel Peace Prize with two other women. Captured in 2006 while trying to flee Nigeria, Charles Taylor went to trial at The Hague in 2007. He was convicted in 2012 of 11 counts of aiding and abetting war crimes and crimes against humanity, and sentenced to 50 years in prison May 30.

Liberia was seriously affected by an Ebola virus epidemic that began in Guinea in Dec. 2013. WHO declared the outbreak over in Liberia, May 9, 2015; minor flare-ups followed, but were contained. By June 2016, 10,678 Liberian cases had been reported, and 4,810 had died.

Libya

People: Population: 6,541,948. **Age distrib.:** <15: 26.2%; 65+: 4.2%. **Growth:** 1.8%. **Migrants:** 12.3%. **Pop. density:** 9.6 per sq mi, 3.7 per sq km. **Urban:** 78.8%. **Ethnic groups:** Berber and Arab 97%, other (incl. Greek, Maltese, Italian, Egyptian, Pakistani, Turk, Indian, Tunisian) 3%. **Languages:** Arabic (official), Italian, English, Berber. **Religions:** Muslim (official; virtually all Sunni) 96.6%, Christian 2.7%.

Geography: Total area: 679,362 sq mi, 1,759,540 sq km; **Land area:** 679,362 sq mi, 1,759,540 sq km. **Location:** Mediterranean coast of N Africa. Tunisia, Algeria on W; Niger, Chad on S; Sudan, Egypt on E. **Topography:** Desert and semidesert regions cover 92% of land with low mountains in N, higher mountains in S, and a narrow coastal zone. **Arable land:** 1%. **Capital:** Tripoli (Tarabulus), 1,128,104.

Government: Type: In transition. **Head of state and gov.:** Prime Min. Abdullah al-Thinni leads a govt. in eastern Libya; in office: Mar. 11, 2014. Prime Min. Faiez Mustafa Serraj is head of the internationally backed Government of National Accord; in office: Jan. 25, 2016. **Local divisions:** 22 districts. **Defense budget** (2013): $4.7 bil. **Active troops:** NA.

Economy: Industries: petroleum, petrochemicals, aluminum, iron and steel, food proc., textiles, handicrafts, cement. **Chief crops:** wheat, barley, olives, dates, citrus, vegetables, peanuts, soybeans. **Natural resources:** petroleum, nat. gas, gypsum. **Water:** 112 cu m per capita. **Crude oil reserves:** 48.4 bil bbls. **Electricity prod.:** 28 bil kWh. **Labor force:** agric. 17%, industry 23%, services 59%. **Unemployment:** 19.2%.

Finance: Monetary unit: Dinar (LYD) (1.38 = $1 U.S.). **GDP:** $92.6 bil; **per capita GDP:** $14,600; **GDP growth:** -6.4%. **Imports:** $11.2 bil; China 14.8%, Italy 12.9%, Turkey 11.1%, Tunisia 6.5%, France 6.1%. **Exports:** $10.5 bil; Italy 32%, Germany 11.3%, China 8%, France 8%, Spain 5.6%, Netherlands 5.4%, Syria 5.3%. **Tourism:** $60 mil. **Budget:** $24.9 bil. **Inflation** (2012-13): 2.6%.

Transport: Motor vehicles: 424.1 per 1,000 pop. **Airports:** 68. **Communications: Telephone:** 10 per 100 pop. **Mobile:** 157 per 100 pop. **Broadband:** NA. **Internet:** 19%.

Health: Expend.: 5%. **Life expect.:** 74.7 male; 78.3 female. **Births:** 17.8 per 1,000 pop. **Deaths:** 3.6 per 1,000 pop. **Infant mortality:** 11.1 per 1,000 live births. **Undernourished:** NA. **HIV:** NA.

Education: Compulsory: ages 6-14. **Literacy:** 91.4%.
Embassy: 2600 Virginia Ave. NW, Ste. 400, 20037; 944-9601.
Website: www.pm.gov.ly or www.embassyoflibyadc.org

First settled by Berbers, Libya was ruled in succession by Carthage, Rome, the Vandals, and the Ottomans. Italy ruled from 1912, and Britain and France after WWII. Libya became an independent constitutional monarchy Jan. 2, 1952. In 1969 a junta led by Col. Muammar al-Qaddafi seized power.

Under Qaddafi's dictatorship, dissent was suppressed and wars were waged with Egypt and Chad. During the 1980s, Libya was accused of promoting terrorism, such as the Apr. 5, 1986, bombing of a West Berlin nightclub, which killed 3, including a U.S. serviceman. The U.S. responded by attacking what it called "terrorist-related targets" in Libya, Apr. 14, including Qaddafi's barracks.

Libyan agents were accused of planting bombs that blew up Pan Am Flight 103 over Lockerbie, Scotland, killing 270 people Dec. 21, 1988, and French UTA Flight 772 over Niger, killing 170 people Sept. 19, 1989. The UN imposed sanctions in 1992 for Libya's failure to cooperate in the Lockerbie and UTA cases.

Libya agreed in 2003 to renounce terrorism and settle compensation cases for the families of the Lockerbie and UTA bombing victims. The UN lifted sanctions in Sept., and in Dec., Libya renounced nuclear, chemical, and biological weapons and long-range missiles. The U.S. ended most economic sanctions Apr. 2004 and restored full diplomatic relations May 2006. Abdel Basset Ali al-Megrahi, a former Libyan agent sentenced to life in prison in 2001 for his role in the Lockerbie bombing, was freed by Scottish authorities on humanitarian grounds Aug. 20, 2009; he died in Tripoli, May 20, 2012.

Arab Spring rebels fought Qaddafi's forces throughout the spring of 2011. With diplomatic backing from the Arab League and the UN Security Council, NATO forces imposed an arms embargo and no-fly zone against Qaddafi. Aided by NATO, rebels took control of Tripoli Aug. 23, 2011, and began governing. Rebels killed Qaddafi Oct. 20, 2011. Ansar al-Shariah terrorists attacked the U.S. consulate in Benghazi Sept. 11, 2012, killing Ambassador J. Christopher Stephens and three others. The U.S. captured, June 15, 2014, the alleged leader of the attack, Ahmed Abu Khattala; he was indicted for murder, Oct. 14, 2014.

Violence between Islamists, rival militia groups, and pro-government forces intensified in 2013-14, and conflict continued in 2015-16. Parliamentary elections marred by violence were held June 25, 2014. The new parliament met in Tobruk because of militia control of Tripoli, where an Islamist coalition had set up a rival government. A UN-backed Government of National Accord (GNA) was formed in Jan. 2016. The GNA had taken control of most government ministries in Tripoli by Apr. from the rival Islamist government. ISIS seized territory in Libya and, by early 2016, controlled the city of Surt (Sirte) and about 150 mi of the Mediterranean coast, as well as areas extending inland. An offensive by pro-GNA and other militia forces had retaken most ISIS territory by mid-2016, and these forces, aided by U.S. airstrikes and special operations troops, recaptured almost all of Surt by Aug. 30.

Liechtenstein
Principality of Liechtenstein

People: Population: 37,937. **Age distrib.:** <15: 15.4%; 65+: 17%. **Growth:** 0.8%. **Migrants:** 62.6%. **Pop. density:** 614.1 per sq mi, 237.1 per sq km. **Urban:** 14.3%. **Ethnic groups:** Liechtensteiner 66.3%. **Languages:** German (official). **Religions:** Roman Catholic (official) 75.9%, Protestant Reformed 6.5%, Muslim 5.4%, none 5.4%.

Geography: Total area: 62 sq mi, 160 sq km; **Land area:** 62 sq mi, 160 sq km. **Location:** Central Europe, in Alps. Switzerland on W, Austria on E. **Topography:** Rhine Valley occupies one-third of country, Alps in the rest. **Arable land:** 16.3%. **Capital:** Vaduz, 5,321 (2014).

Government: Type: Constitutional monarchy. **Head of state:** Prince Hans-Adam II; b. 1945; in office: Nov. 13, 1989. **Head of gov.:** Prime Min. Adrian Hasler; b. 1964; in office: Mar. 27,

2013. **Local divisions:** 11 communes. **Defense budget/active troops:** NA.

Economy: Industries: electronics, metal mfg., dental prods., ceramics, pharmaceuticals, food prods., precision instruments. **Chief crops:** wheat, barley, corn, potatoes. **Natural resources:** hydroelectric potential. **Water:** NA. **Labor force:** agric. 0.8%, industry 39.4%, services 59.9%. **Unemployment:** NA.

Finance: Monetary unit: Franc (CHF) (0.98 = $1 U.S.). **GDP** (2009): $3.2 bil; **per capita GDP** (2009): $89,400; **GDP growth** (2012): 1.8%. **Imports** (2012): $2.1 bil. **Exports** (2012): $3.8 bil. Data excl. trade with Switzerland. **Budget** (2012 est.): $890.4 mil. **Inflation** (2012-13): −0.2%.

Transport: Railways: 6 mi (owned by Austrian Railway System).

Communications: Telephone: 45.9 per 100 pop. **Mobile:** 108.8 per 100 pop. **Broadband:** NA. **Internet:** 96.6%.

Health: Expend.: NA. **Life expect.:** 79.7 male; 84.6 female. **Births:** 10.4 per 1,000 pop. **Deaths:** 7.3 per 1,000 pop. **Infant mortality:** 4.3 per 1,000 live births. **Undernourished:** <5%. **HIV:** NA.

Education: Compulsory: ages 6-14. **Literacy:** 100%.

Embassy: 2900 K St. NW, Ste. 602B, 20007; 331-0590.

Website: www.liechtenstein.li

Liechtenstein became sovereign in 1806. It is united with Switzerland by a customs and monetary union. Many workers commute daily from Austria, Switzerland, and Germany.

On Aug. 15, 2004, Prince Hans-Adam II assigned day-to-day responsibilities for running the country to his son, Crown Prince Alois. Long regarded as a tax haven, Liechtenstein took steps, 2008-13, to ease banking secrecy laws that had impeded international tax fraud investigations. A referendum to abolish the prince's power to veto referendums was defeated July 1, 2012.

Lithuania
Republic of Lithuania

People: Population: 2,854,235. **Age distrib.:** <15: 14.9%; 65+: 19.4%. **Growth:** −1.1%. **Migrants:** 4.7%. **Pop. density:** 117.9 per sq mi, 45.5 per sq km. **Urban:** 66.5%. **Ethnic groups:** Lithuanian 84.1%, Polish 6.6%, Russian 5.8%. **Languages:** Lithuanian (official), Russian, Polish. **Religions:** Roman Catholic 77.2%, Russian Orthodox 4.1%, none 6.1%.

Geography: Total area: 25,212 sq mi, 65,300 sq km; **Land area:** 24,201 sq mi, 62,680 sq km. **Location:** Eastern Europe, on SE coast of Baltic. Latvia on N; Belarus on E, S; Poland, Russia on W. **Topography:** Lowland with hills in W and S. Many small lakes and rivers with marshes espec. in N and W. **Arable land:** 36.5%. **Capital:** Vilnius, 515,018.

Government: Type: Semi-presidential republic. **Head of state:** Pres. Dalia Grybauskaite; b. 1956; in office: July 12, 2009. **Head of gov.:** Prime Min. Algirdas Butkevicius; b. 1958; in office: Nov. 26, 2012. **Local divisions:** 60 municipalities. **Defense budget:** $474 mil. **Active troops:** 16,400.

Economy: Industries: metal-cutting machine tools, elec. motors, TVs, refrigerators and freezers, petroleum refining, shipbuilding, furniture. **Chief crops:** grain, potatoes, sugar beets, flax, vegetables. **Natural resources:** peat, amber. **Water:** 8,513 cu m per capita. **Crude oil reserves** (2015): 12 mil bbls. **Electricity prod.:** 3.4 bil kWh. **Labor force:** agric. 7.9%, industry 19.6%, services 72.5%. **Unemployment:** 11.3%.

Finance: Monetary unit: Euro (EUR) (0.89 = $1 U.S.). **GDP:** $82.4 bil; **per capita GDP:** $28,400; **GDP growth:** 1.6%. **Imports:** $34 bil; Russia 16.9%, Germany 11.5%, Poland 10.3%, Latvia 7.6%, Netherlands 5.1%. **Exports:** $30.9 bil; Russia 13.7%, Latvia 9.8%, Poland 9.7%, Germany 7.8%, Estonia 5.3%. **Tourism:** $1.1 bil. **Budget:** $14 bil. **Inflation:** −0.9%.

Transport: Railways: 1,099 mi. **Motor vehicles:** 727 per 1,000 pop. **Airports:** 22.

Communications: Telephone: 18.7 per 100 pop. **Mobile:** 139.5 per 100 pop. **Broadband:** 58.6 per 100 pop. **Internet:** 71.4%.

Health: Expend.: 6.6%. **Life expect.:** 69.5 male; 80.6 female. **Births:** 10.0 per 1,000 pop. **Deaths:** 14.5 per 1,000 pop. **Infant mortality:** 3.8 per 1,000 live births. **Undernourished:** <5%. **HIV:** NA.

Education: Compulsory: ages 7-15. **Literacy:** 99.8%.

Embassy: 2622 16th St. NW 20009; 234-5860.

Website: lrvk.lrv.lt

Lithuania, briefly occupied by the German army, 1914-18, was annexed by the Soviet Union until 1919. In 1939 it rejoined the Soviet sphere of influence and was annexed by the USSR Aug. 3, 1940.

Lithuania declared its independence from the Soviet Union Mar. 11, 1990; its independence was ratified by the Soviet Union Sept. 1991. The country became a full member of NATO and the EU in 2004; it began using the euro as its currency, Jan. 1, 2015. A plummeting economy spurred popular discontent and brought a rightward shift in parliamentary and presidential elections, 2008-09. The center-left Social Democrats won Oct. 2012 parliamentary

elections. Running as an independent and focusing on national security, Pres. Dalia Grybauskaite won reelection in a May 25, 2014, runoff.

Luxembourg
Grand Duchy of Luxembourg

People: Population: 582,291. **Age distrib.:** <15: 16.8%; 65+: 15%. **Growth:** 2.1%. **Migrants:** 44%. **Pop. density:** 583.2 per sq mi, 225.2 per sq km. **Urban:** 90.4%. **Ethnic groups:** Luxembourger 54.1%, Portuguese 16.4%, French 7%, Italian 3.5%, Belgian 3.3%, German 2.3%. Groups by nationality. **Languages:** Luxembourgish (national lang.), French, German (all official admin. and judicial langs.); Portuguese. **Religions:** Roman Catholic 87%, other (incl. Protestant, Jewish, Muslim) 13%.

Geography: Total area: 998 sq mi, 2,586 sq km; **Land area:** 998 sq mi, 2,586 sq km. **Location:** Western Europe. Belgium on W, France on S, Germany on E. **Topography:** Heavy forests (Ardennes) cover N. Low, open plateau in S. **Arable land:** 24.1%. **Capital:** Luxembourg, 106,680 (2014).

Government: Type: Constitutional monarchy. **Head of state:** Grand Duke Henri; b. 1955; in office: Oct. 7, 2000. **Head of gov.:** Prime Min. Xavier Bettel; b. 1973; in office: Dec. 4, 2013. **Local divisions:** 12 cantons **Defense budget:** $215 mil. **Active troops:** 900.

Economy: Industries: banking and financial services; constr.; real estate services; iron, metals, steel; information tech.; telecom; cargo transp. and logistics. **Chief crops:** grapes, barley, oats, potatoes, wheat, fruits. **Natural resources:** iron ore (no longer exploited). **Water:** 6,172 cu m per capita. **Electricity prod.:** 1.3 bil kWh. **Labor force:** agric. 1.1%, industry 20%, services 78.9%. **Unemployment:** 6.1%.

Finance: Monetary unit: Euro (EUR) (0.89 = $1 U.S.). **GDP:** $55.7 bil; **per capita GDP:** $99,000; **GDP growth:** 4.5%. **Imports:** $21.9 bil; Belgium 27.6%, Germany 22.9%, China 11.7%, France 9.5%, U.S. 8.4%. **Exports:** $20.9 bil; Germany 22.1%, Belgium 16.7%, France 16.6%. **Tourism:** $4.2 bil. **Budget:** $23.7 bil. **Inflation:** 0.5%.

Transport: Railways: 171 mi. **Motor vehicles:** 746.3 per 1,000 pop. **Airports:** 1.

Communications: Telephone: 51 per 100 pop. **Mobile:** 148.5 per 100 pop. **Broadband:** 111.3 per 100 pop. **Internet:** 97.3%.

Health: Expend.: 6.9%. **Life expect.:** 79.8 male; 84.9 female. **Births:** 11.4 per 1,000 pop. **Deaths:** 7.3 per 1,000 pop. **Infant mortality:** 3.4 per 1,000 live births. **Undernourished:** <5%. **HIV:** NA.

Education: Compulsory: ages 4-15. **Literacy:** 100%.

Embassy: 2200 Massachusetts Ave. NW 20008; 265-4171.

Website: www.gouvernement.lu

Luxembourg, founded about 963, was ruled by Burgundy, Spain, Austria, and France from 1448 to 1815. It left the Germanic Confederation in 1866. Overrun by Germany in two world wars, Luxembourg ended its neutrality in 1948, when a customs union with Belgium and the Netherlands was adopted. Luxembourg was one of the six founding members (1951) of what became the European Union.

After Oct. 20, 2013, elections, Liberal Party leader Xavier Bettel became prime min. The Chamber of Deputies, June 18, 2014, legalized same-sex marriage. Bettel, May 15, 2015, became the first EU government head to marry a same-sex partner. Two former PricewaterhouseCooper employees were convicted of theft, June 29, 2016, for leaking documents in 2014 indicating that hundreds of multinational corporations had reached tax-avoidance agreements with the Luxembourg government; both received suspended sentences and small fines.

Macedonia
Republic of Macedonia

People: Population: 2,100,025. **Age distrib.:** <15: 17.3%; 65+: 13.1%. **Growth:** 0.2%. **Migrants:** 6.3%. **Pop. density:** 213.9 per sq mi, 82.6 per sq km. **Urban:** 57.2%. **Ethnic groups:** Macedonian 64.2%, Albanian 25.2%, Turkish 3.9%, Roma 2.7%. **Languages:** Macedonian, Albanian (both official); Turkish. **Religions:** Macedonian Orthodox 64.8%, Muslim 33.3%.

Geography: Total area: 9,928 sq mi, 25,713 sq km; **Land area:** 9,820 sq mi, 25,433 sq km. **Location:** SE Europe. Bulgaria on E, Greece on S, Albania on W, Serbia on N. **Topography:** Landlocked, mostly mountainous with deep river valleys, 3 large lakes. Country is bisected by Vardar R. **Arable land:** 16.4%. **Capital:** Skopje, 504,031.

Government: Type: Parliamentary republic. **Head of state:** Pres. Gjorge Ivanov; b. 1960; in office: May 12, 2009. **Head of gov.:** Prime Min. Emil Dimitriev; b. 1979; in office: Jan. 18, 2016. **Local divisions:** 70 municipalities, 1 city. **Defense budget:** $108 mil. **Active troops:** 8,000.

Economy: Industries: food proc., beverages, textiles, chemicals, iron, steel, cement, energy, pharmaceuticals. **Chief crops:** grapes, tobacco, vegetables, fruits. **Natural resources:** iron ore, copper, lead, zinc, chromite, manganese, nickel, tungsten, gold, silver, asbestos, gypsum, timber. **Water:** 3,080 cu m per capita. **Electricity prod.:** 5.8 bil kWh. **Labor force:** agric. 18.3%, industry 29.1%, services 52.6%. **Unemployment:** 27.9%.

Finance: Monetary unit: Denar (MKD) (55.08 = $1 U.S.). **GDP:** $29 bil (may not reflect country's large informal sector); **per capita GDP:** $14,000; **GDP growth:** 3.7%. **Imports:** $6.2 bil; Germany 15.9%, UK 13.6%, Greece 10.9%, Serbia 8.7%, Bulgaria 6.7%, Turkey 5.5%. **Exports:** $3.9 bil; Germany 33.2%, Kosovo 11.5%, Bulgaria 5.1%. **Tourism:** $267 mil. **Budget:** $3.1 bil. **Inflation:** −0.3%.

Transport: Railways: 434 mi. **Airports:** 8.

Communications: Telephone: 17.7 per 100 pop. **Mobile:** 105.4 per 100 pop. **Broadband:** 47.7 per 100 pop. **Internet:** 70.4%.

Health: Expend.: 6.5%. **Life expect.:** 73.6 male; 79.0 female. **Births:** 11.5 per 1,000 pop. **Deaths:** 9.1 per 1,000 pop. **Infant mortality:** 7.5 per 1,000 live births. **Undernourished:** <5%. **HIV:** NA.

Education: Compulsory: ages 6-14. **Literacy:** 97.8%. **Embassy:** 2129 Wyoming Ave. NW 20008; 667-0501. **Website:** www.vlada.mk

Muslim Turks ruled Macedonia from 1389 to 1912. In 1913, the area was incorporated into Serbia, which in 1918 became part of the Kingdom of Serbs, Croats, and Slovenes (later Yugoslavia). In 1946, Macedonia became a constituent republic of Yugoslavia.

Macedonia declared its independence Sept. 8, 1991, and was admitted to the UN in 1993. Greece, which objected to Macedonia's use of what it considered a Hellenic name, imposed a trade blockade; the countries agreed to normalize relations Sept. 13, 1995. However, Greece continued to block Macedonia's bid to join NATO.

By the end of NATO's air war against Yugoslavia, Mar.-June 1999, Macedonia had a Kosovar refugee population of more than 250,000; over 90% had been repatriated by Sept. 1.

Ethnic Albanian guerrillas launched an offensive Mar. 2001 in NW Macedonia. An accord signed Aug. 13 paved the way for a NATO peacekeeping force. A law broadening the rights of ethnic Albanians was enacted Jan. 2002.

Gjorge Ivanov won a presidential runoff vote Apr. 5, 2009, and was reelected Apr. 27, 2014. After a government wiretapping and corruption scandal, Prime Min. Nikola Gruevski resigned Jan. 15, 2016. New elections were postponed following protests, after Pres. Ivanov, Apr. 12, pardoned potential targets of the wiretapping investigation. Ivanov revoked the pardons June 6, and a July 20 agreement among political parties paved the way for Dec. elections. In 2015 and early 2016, tens of thousands of migrants from the Middle East and SW Asia who landed in Greece tried to cross Macedonia on their way to N Europe. After building razor-wire border fencing and taking other steps to restrict the flow of migrants, Macedonia announced, Mar. 9, 2016, that its border with Greece was closed to migrants, and it used troops and tear gas to enforce the closure.

Madagascar
Republic of Madagascar

People: Population: 24,430,325. **Age distrib.:** <15: 40.2%; 65+: 3.3%. **Growth:** 2.5%. **Migrants:** 0.1%. **Pop. density:** 108.8 per sq mi, 42 per sq km. **Urban:** 35.7%. **Ethnic groups:** Malayo-Indonesian (Merina and related Betsileo), Cotiers (mixed African/Malayo-Indonesian/Arab ancestry), French, Indian, Creole, Comoran. **Languages:** French, Malagasy (both official); English. **Religions:** Christian, indigenous beliefs, Muslim.

Geography: Total area: 226,658 sq mi, 587,041 sq km; **Land area:** 224,534 sq mi, 581,540 sq km. **Location:** In Indian O., off SE coast of Africa. Comoro Isls. to NW, Mozambique to W. **Topography:** Humid coastal strip in E, fertile valleys in mountainous center plateau region, and a wider coastal strip on W. **Arable land:** 6%. **Capital:** Antananarivo, 2,738,588.

Government: Type: Semi-presidential republic. **Head of state:** Pres. Hery Rajaonarimampianina; b. 1958; in office: Jan. 25, 2014. **Head of gov.:** Prime Min. Olivier Mahafaly Solonandrasana; b. 1964; in office: Apr. 13, 2016. **Local divisions:** 6 provinces. **Defense budget:** $57 mil. **Active troops:** 13,500.

Economy: Industries: meat proc., seafood, soap, beer, leather, sugar, textiles, glassware, cement, auto assembly. **Chief crops:** coffee, vanilla, sugarcane, cloves, cocoa, rice, cassava, beans, bananas, peanuts. **Natural resources:** graphite, chromite, coal, bauxite, rare earth elements, salt, quartz, tar sands, semiprec. stones, mica, fish, hydropower. **Water:** 13,906 cu m per capita. **Electricity prod.:** 2 bil kWh. **Labor force:** NA. **Unemployment:** 3.6%.

Finance: Monetary unit: Ariary (MGA) (3,020.00 = $1 U.S.). **GDP:** $35.4 bil; **per capita GDP:** $1,500; **GDP growth:** 3%. **Imports:** $3 bil; China 24.8%, France 10.3%, Bahrain 5.6%, India 5.5%. **Exports:** $2.4 bil; France 15.2%, U.S. 12.7%, China 7.1%, South Africa 5.9%, Japan 5.5%, Netherlands 5.4%, Germany 5.1%, Belgium 5%. **Tourism:** $574 mil. **Budget:** $2.9 bil. **Inflation:** 7.4%.

Transport: Railways: 519 mi. **Motor vehicles:** 12.6 per 1,000 pop. **Airports:** 26.

Communications: Telephone: 1 per 100 pop. **Mobile:** 46 per 100 pop. **Broadband:** 6.1 per 100 pop. **Internet:** 4.2%.

Health: Expend.: 3%. **Life expect.:** 64.4 male; 67.4 female. **Births:** 32.1 per 1,000 pop. **Deaths:** 6.7 per 1,000 pop. **Infant mortality:** 42.4 per 1,000 live births. **Undernourished:** 33%. **HIV:** 0.4%.

Education: Compulsory: ages 6-10. **Literacy:** 64.7%. **Embassy:** 2374 Massachusetts Ave. NW 20008; 265-5525. **Website:** www.primature.gov.mg

Madagascar was settled 2,000 years ago by Malayan-Indonesian people, whose descendants still predominate. A unified kingdom ruled in the 18th and 19th cent. The island became a French protectorate, 1885, and a colony, 1896. Independence came June 26, 1960.

Discontent with inflation and French domination led to a coup in 1972. The new regime nationalized French-owned financial interests, closed French bases and a U.S. space-tracking station, and obtained Chinese aid. The government conducted a program of arrests, expulsion of foreigners, and repression of strikes in 1979.

In 1990, Madagascar ended a ban on multiparty politics that had existed since 1975. Albert Zafy won the 1993 presidential election, ending the 17-year rule of Adm. Didier Ratsiraka, but was impeached and removed from office in 1996.

Marc Ravalomanana won a contentious presidential election over Ratsiraka Dec. 2001 and was reelected in 2006. A power struggle between Ravalomanana and the military-backed Andry Rajoelina culminated in Rajoelina's installation as head of a transitional regime, Mar. 17, 2009. Postponed presidential elections were finally held in late 2013, and won by Hery Rajaonarimampianina. Parliamentary elections were also held Dec. 10, 2013. With economic and living conditions unimproved, Rajaonarimampianina changed prime ministers in Jan. 2015 and Apr. 2016.

Malawi
Republic of Malawi

People: Population: 18,570,321. **Age distrib.:** <15: 46.5%; 65+: 2.7%. **Growth:** 3.3%. **Migrants:** 1.2%. **Pop. density:** 511.2 per sq mi, 197.4 per sq km. **Urban:** 16.5%. **Ethnic groups:** Chewa 32.6%, Lomwe 17.6%, Yao 13.5%, Ngoni 11.5%, Tumbuka 8.8%, Nyanja 5.8%, Sena 3.6%, Tonga 2.1%. **Languages:** English (official), Chichewa (common), Chinyanja, Chiyao, Chitumbuka, Chilomwe, Chinkhonde. **Religions:** Christian 82.6%, Muslim 13%.

Geography: Total area: 45,747 sq mi, 118,484 sq km; **Land area:** 36,324 sq mi, 94,080 sq km. **Location:** SE Africa. Zambia on W, Mozambique on S and E, Tanzania on N. **Topography:** 560 mi N-S along Lake Nyasa (Lake Malawi), most of which belongs to Malawi. High plateaus and mountains line the Rift Valley along length of nation. **Arable land:** 40.3%. **Capital:** Lilongwe, 945,072.

Government: Type: Presidential republic. **Head of state and gov.:** Pres. Arthur Peter Mutharika; b. 1940; in office: May 31, 2014. **Local divisions:** 28 districts. **Defense budget:** $36 mil. **Active troops:** 5,300.

Economy: Industries: tobacco, tea, sugar, sawmill prods., cement, consumer goods. **Chief crops:** tobacco, sugarcane, cotton, tea, corn, potatoes, cassava, sorghum, pulses, groundnuts, Macadamia nuts. **Natural resources:** limestone; hydropower; unexploited deposits of uranium, coal, bauxite. **Water:** 1,004 cu m per capita. **Electricity prod.:** 1.9 bil kWh. **Labor force:** agric. 90%, industry and services 10%. **Unemployment:** 7.5%.

Finance: Monetary unit: Kwacha (MWK) (711.91 = $1 U.S.). **GDP:** $20.4 bil; **per capita GDP:** $1,100; **GDP growth:** 3%. **Imports:** $2.7 bil; South Africa 26.4%, China 16.7%, India 12%, Zambia 10.3%, Tanzania 6%. **Exports:** $1.2 bil; Belgium 15.8%, Zimbabwe 12%, India 6.9%, South Africa 6.2%, U.S. 6%, Russia 5.6%. **Tourism:** $31 mil. **Budget:** $1.4 bil. **Inflation:** 21.9%.

Transport: Railways: 477 mi. **Motor vehicles:** 2 per 1,000 pop. **Airports:** 7.

Communications: Telephone: 0.3 per 100 pop. **Mobile:** 35.3 per 100 pop. **Broadband:** 4.1 per 100 pop. **Internet:** 9.3%.

Health: Expend.: 11.4%. **Life expect.:** 59.2 male; 63.2 female. **Births:** 41.3 per 1,000 pop. **Deaths:** 8.1 per 1,000 pop. **Infant mortality:** 44.8 per 1,000 live births. **Undernourished:** 20.7%. **HIV:** 9.1%.

Education: Compulsory: NA. **Literacy:** 66%. **Embassy:** 2408 Massachusetts Ave. NW 20008; 721-0270. **Website:** www.malawi.gov.mw

Bantus came to the land in the 16th cent., Arab slavers in the 19th. The area became the British protectorate Nyasaland in 1891. It became independent July 6, 1964, and a republic in 1966. After three decades as a one-party state under Pres. Hastings Kamuzu Banda, Malawi adopted a new constitution and, in multiparty elections held May 17, 1994, chose a new leader, Bakili Muluzi.

Bingu wa Mutharika, candidate of the ruling United Democratic Front, won a disputed 2004 presidential election. An effort by his former political allies to impeach him was halted by Malawi's Constitutional Court, Oct. 2005. Mutharika won reelection May 2009.

Joyce Banda became Malawi's first female pres. after the death of Mutharika Apr. 5, 2012. Banda finished third in May 20-22, 2014, presidential elections. After her attempt to nullify the result was blocked in court, Peter Mutharika was declared the winner. Heavy rains produced widespread flooding in Jan. 2015 that killed hundreds and left more than 200,000 displaced. El Niño-related drought left up to 8 mil in need of food aid in 2016.

Malaysia

People: Population: 30,949,962. **Age distrib.:** <15: 28.2%; 65+: 5.9%. **Growth:** 1.4%. **Migrants:** 8.3%. **Pop. density:** 243.9 per sq mi, 94.2 per sq km. **Urban:** 75.4%. **Ethnic groups:** Malay 50.1%, Chinese 22.6%, indigenous 11.8%, Indian 6.7%, noncitizen 8.2%. **Languages:** Bahasa Malaysia (official), English, Chinese, Tamil, Telugu, Malayalam, Panjabi, Thai. **Religions:** Muslim (official) 61.3%, Buddhist 19.8%, Christian 9.2%, Hindu 6.3%.

Geography: Total area: 127,355 sq mi, 329,847 sq km; **Land area:** 126,895 sq mi, 328,657 sq km. **Location:** SE tip of Asia, plus N coast of the island of Borneo. Thailand, Brunei on N; Indonesia on S. **Topography:** Most of W is covered by tropical jungle, including a central mountain range that runs N-S through the peninsula. Marshy W coast, sandy E coast. Wide swampy coastal plain with interior jungles and mountains in E. **Arable land:** 2.9%. **Capital:** Kuala Lumpur, 7,046,886. Putrajaya is referred to as the admin. center of the federal govt. **Cities:** Johor Bahru, 932,925.

Government: Type: Federal constitutional monarchy. **Head of state:** Paramount Ruler Tuanku Abdul Halim Mu'adzam Shah; b. 1927; in office: Apr. 11, 2012. **Head of gov.:** Prime Min. Najib Razak; b. 1953; in office: Apr. 3, 2009. **Local divisions:** 13 states, 1 federal territory. **Defense budget:** $4.7 bil. **Active troops:** 109,000.

Economy: Industries: rubber and palm oil proc. and mfg., petroleum and nat. gas, light mfg., pharmaceuticals, medical tech., logging. **Chief crops:** palm oil, rubber, cocoa, rice, pepper. **Natural resources:** tin, petroleum, timber, copper, iron ore, nat. gas, bauxite. **Water:** 19,122 cu m per capita. **Crude oil reserves:** 3.6 bil bbls. **Electricity prod.:** 131 bil kWh. **Labor force:** agric. 11%, industry 36%, services 53%. **Unemployment:** 2%.

Finance: Monetary unit: Ringgit (MYR) (4.09 = $1 U.S.). **GDP:** $815.6 bil; **per capita GDP:** $26,300; **GDP growth:** 5%. **Imports:** $174.7 bil; China 18.8%, Singapore 12%, U.S. 8.1%, Japan 7.8%, Thailand 6.1%. **Exports:** $203.8 bil; Singapore 13.9%, China 13%, Japan 9.5%, U.S. 9.4%, Thailand 5.7%. **Tourism:** $17.6 bil. **Budget:** $64.3 bil. **Inflation:** 2.1%.

Transport: Railways: 1,149 mi. **Motor vehicles:** 413.4 per 1,000 pop. **Airports:** 39.

Communications: Telephone: 14.3 per 100 pop. **Mobile:** 143.9 per 100 pop. **Broadband:** 58.3 per 100 pop. **Internet:** 71.1%.

Health: Expend.: 4.2%. **Life expect.:** 72.2 male; 78.0 female. **Births:** 19.4 per 1,000 pop. **Deaths:** 5.1 per 1,000 pop. **Infant mortality:** 12.9 per 1,000 live births. **Undernourished:** <5%. **HIV:** 0.4%.

Education: Compulsory: ages 6-11. **Literacy:** 94.6%.

Embassy: 3516 International Ct. NW 20008; 572-9700.

Website: www.malaysia.gov.my

European traders visited in the 16th cent.; Britain established control in 1867. Malaysia was created Sept. 16, 1963. It included Malaya (which gained independence in 1957 after the suppression of Communist rebels), plus the formerly British Singapore, Sabah (N Borneo), and Sarawak (NW Borneo). Singapore was separated in 1965.

Malaysia has abundant natural resources, though rainforest destruction has become a major environmental problem. Work on a federal administrative center at Putrajaya, south of Kuala Lumpur, was completed in 1999; it is linked by rail with Kuala Lumpur's city center and Cyberjaya, a hub for high-tech manufacturing and research.

Recession and scandals plagued Malaysia as National Front leader Najib Razak took over the premiership in 2009. Tuanku Abdul Halim Mu'adzam Shah was chosen in 2011 to serve as the paramount ruler for a second 5-year term, more than 35 years after his first (1970-75). In a close election (deemed fraudulent by the opposition), May 5, 2013, the governing coalition was returned to power.

A Malaysia Airlines flight to Beijing, carrying 239 passengers and crew, lost contact with air traffic control Mar. 8, 2014, shortly after takeoff from Kuala Lumpur and was presumed lost in the Indian Ocean. Part of a wing from the plane was found on Réunion, July 2015, and other debris was subsequently found elsewhere. On July 17, 2014, a Malaysia Airlines flight from Amsterdam to Kuala Lumpur was shot down by a missile over eastern Ukraine, killing all 298 people onboard. An international team of investigators concluded, Sept. 2016, that the missile was Russian made and had been fired from an area controlled by pro-Russian separatists.

Beginning in 2015, Malaysian authorities (as well as officials in the U.S. and other countries) investigated possible misappropriation of billions of dollars from a development fund, and more than $700 mil in transfers to bank accounts controlled by Prime Min. Najib, who denied wrongdoing. The Malaysian government inquiry

was closed, Jan. 2016, after concluding no laws were broken. The U.S. Justice Dept., July 2016, initiated legal action to seize more than $1 bil worth of assets purchased with funds that passed through U.S. banks. A security law enacted Dec. 3, 2015, gave the government sweeping powers to conduct surveillance and searches and to suppress protests.

Maldives
Republic of Maldives

People: Population: 392,960. **Age distrib.:** <15: 21.2%; 65+: 4.4%. **Growth:** -0.1%. **Migrants:** 25.9%. **Pop. density:** 3,415.3 per sq mi, 1,318.7 per sq km. **Urban:** 46.5%. **Ethnic groups:** South Indian, Sinhalese, Arab. **Languages:** Dhivehi (official), English (spoken by most govt. officials). **Religions:** Sunni Muslim (official).

Geography: Total area: 115 sq mi, 298 sq km; **Land area:** 115 sq mi, 298 sq km. **Location:** In Indian O. Nearest neighbor is India to NE. **Topography:** 19 atolls with 1,190 islands, 200 inhabited. None of the islands are over 5 sq mi in area; all are nearly flat. **Arable land:** 13%. **Capital:** Male, 156,427 (2014).

Government: Type: Presidential republic. **Head of state and gov.:** Pres. Abdulla Yameen Abdul Gayoom; b. 1959; in office: Nov. 17, 2013. **Local divisions:** 7 provinces, 1 municipality. **Defense budget/active troops:** NA.

Economy: Industries: tourism, fish proc., shipping, boat building, coconut proc., woven mats, rope. **Chief crops:** coconuts, corn, sweet potatoes. **Natural resources:** fish. **Water:** 82 cu m per capita. **Electricity prod.:** 0.3 bil kWh. **Labor force:** agric. 15%, industry 15%, services 70%. **Unemployment:** 11.6%.

Finance: Monetary unit: Rufiyaa (MVR) (15.08 = $1 U.S.). **GDP:** $5.2 bil; **per capita GDP:** $14,900; **GDP growth:** 1.9%. **Imports** (2014): $2 bil; UAE 18.3%, Singapore 13.8%, China 10.6%, India 10.4%, Malaysia 6.9%, Sri Lanka 5.5%. **Exports** (2014): $300.9 mil; Thailand 17.9%, France 12.1%, Germany 10.7%, U.S. 9.6%, Italy 6.8%, UK 6.4%, Sri Lanka 5.8%. **Tourism:** $2.6 bil. **Budget** (2014 est.): $1.1 bil. **Inflation:** 1%.

Transport: Airports: 7.

Communications: Telephone: 6.1 per 100 pop. **Mobile:** 206.7 per 100 pop. **Broadband:** 48.9 per 100 pop. **Internet:** 54.5%.

Health: Expend.: 13.7%. **Life expect.:** 73.3 male; 78.0 female. **Births:** 16.0 per 1,000 pop. **Deaths:** 3.9 per 1,000 pop. **Infant mortality:** 22.9 per 1,000 live births. **Undernourished:** 5.2%. **HIV:** NA.

Education: Compulsory: NA. **Literacy:** 99.3%.

Embassy: 800 Second Ave., Ste. 400E, New York, NY 10017; (212) 599-6195.

Website: www.presidencymaldives.gov.mv

A British protectorate since 1887, the nation achieved independence July 26, 1965; long a sultanate, the Maldives became a republic in 1968. Rising sea levels threaten the country, which comprises small, low-lying coral islands.

The Indian Ocean tsunami of Dec. 26, 2004, killed at least 82 people and displaced more than 21,600 in the Maldives. Pres. Maumoon Abdul Gayoom, in office 1978-2008, lost a 2008 runoff vote to pro-democracy leader and former political prisoner Mohamed (Anni) Nasheed. Following protests over the arrest of a judge, Nasheed resigned Feb. 2012. He ran for president Sept. 7, 2013, and won 45% of the vote, not enough to avoid a runoff. The Supreme Court canceled the runoff Sept. 24. In new elections Nov. 9, 2013, Nasheed won 47% but lost the Nov. 16 runoff to Abdulla Yameen Abdul Gayoom (the former president's half-brother). Nasheed, Mar. 2015, was convicted on terrorism charges and sentenced to 13 years in prison in connection with his 2012 actions against the judge; the conviction and sentence were upheld by the Supreme Court, June 27, 2016, by which time Nasheed had received political asylum in the UK. Former Vice Pres. Ahmed Adeeb was convicted, June 9, 2016, of attempting to assassinate Pres. Yameen in 2015.

Mali
Republic of Mali

People: Population: 17,467,108. **Age distrib.:** <15: 47.3%; 65+: 3%. **Growth:** 3%. **Migrants:** 2.1%. **Pop. density:** 37.1 per sq mi, 14.3 per sq km. **Urban:** 40.7%. **Ethnic groups:** Bambara 34.1%, Fulani (Peul) 14.7%, Sarakole 10.8%, Senufo 10.5%, Dogon 8.9%, Malinke 8.7%, Bobo 2.9%. **Languages:** French (official), Bambara, 12 other national langs. **Religions:** Muslim 94.8%, Christian 2.4%.

Geography: Total area: 478,841 sq mi, 1,240,192 sq km; **Land area:** 471,118 sq mi, 1,220,190 sq km. **Location:** Interior of W Africa. Mauritania, Senegal on W; Guinea, Côte d'Ivoire, Burkina Faso on S; Niger on E; Algeria on N. **Topography:** Landlocked grassy plain in upper basins of the Senegal and Niger Rivers, extending N into the Sahara. **Arable land:** 5.3%. **Capital:** Bamako, 2,651,066.

Government: Type: Semi-presidential republic. **Head of state:** Pres. Ibrahim Boubacar Keita; b. 1945; in office: Sept. 4, 2013

Head of gov.: Prime Min. Modibo Keita; b. 1942; in office: Jan. 8, 2015. **Local divisions:** 8 regions, 1 district. **Defense budget:** $469 mil. **Active troops:** 6,000.

Economy: Industries: food proc., constr., phosphate and gold mining. **Chief crops:** cotton, millet, rice, corn, vegetables, peanuts. **Natural resources:** gold, phosphates, kaolin, salt, limestone, uranium, gypsum, granite, hydropower. **Water:** 6,818 cu m per capita. **Electricity prod.:** 1.4 bil kWh. **Labor force:** agric. 80%, industry and services 20%. **Unemployment:** 8.1%.

Finance: Monetary unit: CFA Franc (XOF) (586.00 = $1 U.S.). **GDP:** $35.8 bil; **per capita GDP:** $2,200; **GDP growth:** 6.1%. **Imports:** $2.9 bil; Côte d'Ivoire 9.9%, France 9.5%, Senegal 7.7%, China 7%. **Exports:** $2.2 bil; Switzerland 48.7%, China 9.4%, India 9.1%, Bangladesh 8%. **Tourism:** $212 mil. **Budget:** $2.8 bil. **Inflation:** 1.4%.

Transport: Railways: 368 mi. **Motor vehicles:** 1.7 per 1,000 pop. **Airports:** 8.

Communications: Telephone: 1 per 100 pop. **Mobile:** 139.6 per 100 pop. **Broadband:** 11.3 per 100 pop. **Internet:** 10.3%.

Health: Expend.: 6.9%. **Life expect.:** 53.9 male; 57.7 female. **Births:** 44.4 per 1,000 pop. **Deaths:** 12.6 per 1,000 pop. **Infant mortality:** 100.0 per 1,000 live births. **Undernourished:** <5%. **HIV:** 1.3%.

Education: Compulsory: ages 6-14. **Literacy:** 33.1%. **Embassy:** 2130 R St. NW 20008; 332-2249.

Website: primature.gov.ml

Until the 15th cent. the area was part of the great Mali Empire. Timbuktu (Tombouctou) was a center of Islamic study. French rule was secured, 1898. The Sudanese Rep. and Senegal became independent as the Mali Federation in 1960, but Senegal withdrew, and the Sudanese Rep. was renamed Mali.

A coup toppled a socialist regime led, 1960-68, by Pres. Modibo Keita. Famine struck in 1973-74, killing as many as 100,000 people. Drought conditions returned in the 1980s.

The military, Mar. 1991, overthrew Pres. Moussa Traoré, who had ruled since 1968. Oumar Konare, a coup leader, was elected president, 1992. The government and a Tuareg rebel group signed a peace accord in 1994, but Taureg separatists remained active in the north. Twice condemned to death for crimes committed in office, Traoré had his sentences commuted to life imprisonment in 1997 and 1999; he was pardoned in 2002.

Amadou Toumani Touré, who led the 1991 coup, was elected president in 2002 and reelected 2007. After a Mar. 2012 coup, an interim government led by Pres. Dioncounda Traoré took office Apr. 12. The coup enabled Islamist rebels, who had allied themselves with the separatists, to seize control of the country's north. France entered the fight against the Islamists Jan. 10, 2013, and West African regional forces joined them Jan 17. The Islamists were pushed out of most of the territory they had seized. The UN Stabilization Mission in Mali (MINUSMA) was approved Apr. 25, 2013; it included almost 12,000 uniformed personnel as of Aug. 31, 2016. Ibrahim Boubacar Keita was elected president Aug. 11, 2013. Attacks by Taureg separatists, as well as fighting against Islamists, continued in 2014 and early 2015. A new peace agreement with separatists was signed June 20, 2015. Islamist extremist attacks continued; gunmen killed 20 people at a Bamako hotel, Nov. 20, 2015, and killed 17 Malian soldiers in a July 2016 attack. France maintained about 3,500 troops across five countries in the region as of mid-2016.

Malta
Republic of Malta

People: Population: 415,196. **Age distrib.:** <15: 15%; 65+: 19.1%. **Growth:** 0.3%. **Migrants:** 9.9%. **Pop. density:** 3,403 per sq mi, 1,313.9 per sq km. **Urban:** 95.5%. **Ethnic groups:** Maltese (descendants of ancient Carthaginians and Phoenicians with Italian, other Mediterranean stock). **Languages:** Maltese, English (both official). **Religions:** Roman Catholic (official) 90%+.

Geography: Total area: 122 sq mi, 316 sq km; **Land area:** 122 sq mi, 316 sq km. Island of Malta is 95 sq mi. Gozo, 26 sq mi, and Comino, 1 sq mi, are other islands in group. **Location:** Center of Mediterranean Sea. Nearest neighbor is Italy to N. **Topography:** Heavily indented coastline. Low hills cover interior. **Arable land:** 28%. **Capital:** Valletta, 197,447 (2014).

Government: Type: Parliamentary republic. **Head of state:** Pres. Marie-Louise Coleiro Preca; b. 1958; in office: Apr. 4, 2014. **Head of gov.:** Prime Min. Joseph Muscat; b. 1974; in office: Mar. 11, 2013. **Local divisions:** 68 localities. **Defense budget:** $56 mil. **Active troops:** 1,950.

Economy: Industries: tourism, electronics, shipbuilding and repair, constr., food and beverages, pharmaceuticals, footwear. **Chief crops:** potatoes, cauliflower, grapes, wheat, barley, tomatoes, citrus, cut flowers, green peppers. **Natural resources:** limestone, salt. **Water:** 121 cu m per capita. **Electricity prod.:** 2.1 bil kWh. **Labor force:** agric. 1.7%, industry 18.3%, services 80%. **Unemployment:** 5.9%.

Finance: Monetary unit: Euro (EUR) (0.89 = $1 U.S.). **GDP:** $15.4 bil; **per capita GDP:** $35,900; **GDP growth:** 5.4%. **Imports:**

$6.7 bil; Italy 23%, Netherlands 8.4%, UK 7.5%, Germany 6.8%, Canada 6.1%. **Exports:** $3.9 bil; Germany 13.3%, France 10.2%, Hong Kong 7.4%, Singapore 7.3%, UK 6.4%, U.S. 5.8%, Italy 5.6%. **Tourism:** $1.4 bil. **Budget:** $3.4 bil. **Inflation:** 1.1%.

Transport: Motor vehicles: 784.9 per 1,000 pop. **Airports:** 1.

Communications: Telephone: 53.4 per 100 pop. **Mobile:** 129.3 per 100 pop. **Broadband:** 49.7 per 100 pop. **Internet:** 76.2%.

Health: Expend.: 9.8%. **Life expect.:** 78.0 male; 82.8 female. **Births:** 10.1 per 1,000 pop. **Deaths:** 9.2 per 1,000 pop. **Infant mortality:** 3.5 per 1,000 live births. **Undernourished:** <5%. **HIV:** NA.

Education: Compulsory: ages 5-15. **Literacy:** 94.1%. **Embassy:** 2017 Connecticut Ave. NW 20008; 462-3611.

Website: www.gov.mt

Malta was ruled by Phoenicians, Romans, Arabs, Normans, the Knights of Malta, France, and Britain (since 1814). It became independent Sept. 21, 1964. Malta became a republic in 1974. The last British forces withdrew, Apr. 1, 1979.

From 1971 to 1987 and again from 1996 to 1998, Malta was governed by the socialist Labour Party; the Nationalist Party, which pressed for Malta's entry into the EU, held office 1987-96 and won parliamentary elections in 1998, 2003, and 2008. Malta became a full member of the EU May 1, 2004. The Labour Party returned to power as a result of Mar. 9, 2013, elections.

Marshall Islands
Republic of the Marshall Islands

People: Population: 73,376. **Age distrib.:** <15: 35.5%; 65+: 3.8%. **Growth:** 1.6%. **Migrants:** 6.2%. **Pop. density:** 1,050 per sq mi, 405.4 per sq km. **Urban:** 72.9%. **Ethnic groups:** Marshallese 92.1%, mixed Marshallese 5.9%. **Languages:** Marshallese, English (both official). **Religions:** Protestant 54.8%, Assembly of God 25.8%, Roman Catholic 8.4%, Bukot nan Jesus 2.8%.

Geography: Total area: 70 sq mi, 181 sq km; **Land area:** 70 sq mi, 181 sq km. **Location:** In N Pacific O.; made up of two 800-mi-long parallel chains of coral atolls. Nearest neighbors are Micronesia to W, Nauru and Kiribati to S. **Topography:** Low coral limestone and sand islands. **Arable land:** 11.1%. **Capital:** Majuro, 30,861 (2014).

Government: Type: Presidential republic in free association with U.S. **Head of state and gov.:** Pres. Hilda C. Heine; b. 1951; in office: Jan. 28, 2016. **Local divisions:** 24 municipalities. **Defense budget/active troops:** NA.

Economy: Industries: copra, tuna proc., tourism, craft items. **Chief crops:** coconuts, tomatoes, melons, taro, breadfruit, fruits. **Natural resources:** coconut prods., marine prods., deep-seabed minerals. **Water:** NA. **Labor force:** agric. 11%, industry 16.3%, services 72.7%. **Unemployment:** NA.

Finance: Monetary unit: U.S. Dollar (USD) (1.00 = $1 U.S.). **GDP:** $175 mil; **per capita GDP:** $3,200; **GDP growth:** 1.6%. **Imports** (2013): $133.7 mil. **Exports** (2013): $53.7 mil. **Tourism:** $5 mil. **Budget** (2013 est.): $113.9 mil. **Inflation:** -4%.

Transport: Airports: 4.

Communications: Telephone (2014): 4.5 per 100 pop. **Mobile:** 29.2 per 100 pop. **Broadband:** NA. **Internet:** 19.3%.

Health: Expend.: 17.1%. **Life expect.:** 70.9 male; 75.4 female. **Births:** 25.0 per 1,000 pop. **Deaths:** 4.2 per 1,000 pop. **Infant mortality:** 20.0 per 1,000 live births. **Undernourished:** NA. **HIV:** NA.

Education: Compulsory: ages 5-13. **Literacy:** 98.3%. **Embassy:** 2433 Massachusetts Ave. NW, 1st Fl., 20008; 234-5414.

Website: www.rmiparliament.org

The Marshall Islands were a German possession until WWI and were administered by Japan between the World Wars. After WWII, they were administered by the U.S. as part of the UN Trust Territory of the Pacific Islands. During 1946-58, Bikini and Enewetak Atolls were used as test sites for U.S. nuclear weapons.

The Compact of Free Association, ratified by the U.S. in 1986, gave the islands their independence. In the compact, the U.S. agreed to provide financial aid to the islands, maintain their defense, and compensate victims of nuclear testing; it was renewed Dec. 2003. Droughts in 2013 and 2016 prompted Pres. Barack Obama to sign disaster declarations, making the Marshall Islands eligible for U.S. relief funds. Elected by parliament, Jan. 27, 2016, Hilda Heine became the country's first female president. Made up of low-lying atolls, the Marshall Islands is considered highly vulnerable to rising sea levels resulting from climate change.

Mauritania
Islamic Republic of Mauritania

People: Population: 3,677,293. **Age distrib.:** <15: 38.9%; 65+: 3.7%. **Growth:** 2.2%. **Migrants:** 3.4%. **Pop. density:** 9.2 per sq mi, 3.6 per sq km. **Urban:** 60.4%. **Ethnic groups:** black Moor (Arab-speaking slaves, former slaves, and their descendants of African origin, enslaved by white Moors) 40%, white Moor (Arab-Berber descent) 30%, black African (non-Arabic speaking) 30%. **Languages:** Arabic (official and national); Pulaar, Soninke, Wolof (all national langs.); French. **Religions:** Muslim (official) 100%.

Geography: Total area: 397,955 sq mi, 1,030,700 sq km; **Land area:** 397,955 sq mi, 1,030,700 sq km. **Location:** NW Africa. Western Sahara on N; Algeria, Mali on E; Senegal on S. **Topography:** Fertile Senegal R. valley in S gives way to wide central region of sandy plains and scrub trees. N is arid and extends into the Sahara. **Arable land:** 0.4%. **Capital:** Nouakchott, 990,342.

Government: Type: Presidential republic. **Head of state:** Pres. Mohamed Ould Abdel Aziz; b. 1956; in office: Aug. 5. 2009. **Head of gov.:** Prime Min. Yahya Ould Hademinein; b. 1953; in office: Aug. 21, 2014. **Local divisions:** 15 regions. **Defense budget** (2013): $150 mil. **Active troops:** 15,850.

Economy: Industries: fish proc., oil prod., mining. **Chief crops:** dates, millet, sorghum, rice, corn. **Natural resources:** iron ore, gypsum, copper, phosphate, diamonds, gold, oil, fish. **Water:** 2,802 cu m per capita. **Crude oil reserves** (2015): 20 mil bbls. **Electricity prod.:** 0.8 bil kWh. **Labor force:** agric. 50%, industry 2%, services 48%. **Unemployment:** 31%.

Finance: Monetary unit: Ouguiya (MRO) (353.00 = $1 U.S.). **GDP:** $16.3 bil; **per capita GDP:** $4,400; **GDP growth:** 1.9%. **Imports:** $2.1 bil; China 25.5%, Algeria 8.4%, France 6.3%, Morocco 5.1%. **Exports:** $1.7 bil; China 32.7%, Switzerland 11.1%, Spain 8.6%, Italy 6.7%, Côte d'Ivoire 6.6%, Japan 5.7%. **Tourism:** $36 mil. **Budget:** $2.2 bil. **Inflation:** 0.5%.

Transport: Railways: 452 mi. **Motor vehicles:** 7.6 per 1,000 pop. **Airports:** 9.

Communications: Telephone: 1.3 per 100 pop. **Mobile:** 89.3 per 100 pop. **Broadband:** 14.4 per 100 pop. **Internet:** 15.2%.

Health: Expend.: 3.8%. **Life expect.:** 60.7 male; 65.4 female. **Births:** 30.9 per 1,000 pop. **Deaths:** 8.1 per 1,000 pop. **Infant mortality:** 53.3 per 1,000 live births. **Undernourished:** 5.6%. **HIV:** 0.6%.

Education: Compulsory: ages 6-11. **Literacy:** 52.1%.
Embassy: 2129 Leroy Pl. NW 20008; 232-5700.
Website: primature.gov.mr

A French protectorate from 1903, Mauritania became independent Nov. 28, 1960. It annexed the south of former Spanish Sahara (now Morocco-claimed Western Sahara) in 1976 but renounced its claim to the region after signing a peace treaty with the Saharan guerrillas of the Polisario Front, 1979.

Maaouiya Ould Sid Ahmed Taya took power in a military coup in 1984. Taya, a U.S. ally, was toppled in a bloodless coup in 2005. During Jan.-June 2006, up to 10,000 people tried to emigrate in handmade boats from Mauritania to Spain's Canary Islands; more than 1,700 died. Civilian rule was restored, 2006-07, but a 2008 military coup toppled the elected government. The coup leader, Gen. Mohamed Ould Abdel Aziz, won disputed presidential elections in 2009 and 2014. Security concerns, including a rising threat from al-Qaeda in the Islamic Maghreb, led the U.S. Peace Corps to remove its volunteers from Mauritania in Aug. 2009. In 2013, U.S. Special Operations troops began providing training and equipment to Mauritanian counterterrorism forces, to help combat Islamic extremists.

Major oil finds have recently been developed. Slavery, repeatedly abolished, continues to exist but appears to be declining. Legislation mandating prison terms for slaveholders was enacted in 2007 and strengthened in 2015. The Global Slavery Index estimated that 43,000 Mauritanians lived under conditions of servitude in 2016.

Mauritius
Republic of Mauritius

People: Population: 1,348,242. **Age distrib.:** <15: 20.4%; 65+: 9.2%. **Growth:** 0.6%. **Migrants:** 2.2%. **Pop. density:** 1,720.2 per sq mi, 664.2 per sq km. **Urban:** 39.5%. **Ethnic groups:** Indo-Mauritian 68%, Creole 27%, Sino-Mauritian 3%, Franco-Mauritian 2%. **Languages:** Creole, Bhojpuri, French, English (official). **Religions:** Hindu 48.5%, Roman Catholic 26.3%, Muslim 17.3%.

Geography: Total area: 788 sq mi, 2,040 sq km; **Land area:** 784 sq mi, 2,030 sq km. **Location:** In Indian O., 500 mi E of Madagascar, its nearest neighbor. **Topography:** A volcanic island nearly surrounded by coral reefs. A central plateau is encircled by peaks. **Arable land:** 36.9%. **Capital:** Port Louis, 135,496 (2014).

Government: Type: Parliamentary republic. **Head of state:** Pres. Ameenah Gurib-Fakim; b. 1959; in office: June 5, 2015. **Head of gov.:** Prime Min. Sir Anerood Jugnauth; b. 1930; in office: Dec. 15, 2014. **Local divisions:** 9 districts, 3 dependencies. **Defense budget:** $240 mil. **Active troops:** No standing armed forces; 2,500 paramilitary. Special Mobile Force and coast guard provide security.

Economy: Industries: food proc. (largely sugar milling), textiles, clothing, mining, chemicals, metal prods. **Chief crops:** sugarcane, tea, corn, potatoes, bananas, pulses. **Natural resources:**

fish. **Water:** 2,161 cu m per capita. **Electricity prod.:** 2.7 bil kWh. **Labor force:** agric. and fishing 9%; constr. and industry 30%; transp. and communication 7%; trade, restaurants, hotels 22%; finance 6%; other services 25%. **Unemployment:** 7.7%.

Finance: Monetary unit: Rupee (MUR) (35.06 = $1 U.S.). **GDP:** $24.6 bil; **per capita GDP:** $19,500; **GDP growth:** 3.4%. **Imports:** $4.6 bil; India 18.7%, China 17.8%, France 7.1%, South Africa 6.5%. **Exports:** $2.8 bil; UK 13.2%, UAE 12.4%, France 11.9%, U.S. 10.7%, South Africa 8.6%, Madagascar 6.5%, Italy 5.4%. **Tourism:** $1.4 bil. **Budget:** $2.6 bil. **Inflation:** 1.3%.

Transport: Motor vehicles: 174.5 per 1,000 pop. **Airports:** 2.
Communications: Telephone: 30.3 per 100 pop. **Mobile:** 140.6 per 100 pop. **Broadband:** 31.8 per 100 pop. **Internet:** 50.1%.

Health: Expend.: 4.8%. **Life expect.:** 72.2 male; 79.2 female. **Births:** 13.1 per 1,000 pop. **Deaths:** 7.0 per 1,000 pop. **Infant mortality:** 10.0 per 1,000 live births. **Undernourished:** <5%. **HIV:** 0.9%.

Education: Compulsory: ages 5-15. **Literacy:** 90.6%.
Embassy: 1709 N St. NW 20036; 244-1491.
Website: www.govmu.org

Mauritius was uninhabited when settled in 1638 by the Dutch, who introduced sugarcane. France took over in 1721, bringing African slaves. Britain ruled from 1810 to Mar. 12, 1968, bringing Indian workers for the sugar plantations.

Mauritius formally severed its association with the British crown Mar. 12, 1992. Since 2006, Mauritius has topped the Ibrahim Index of African Governance as the best-governed African country.

Mexico
United Mexican States

People: Population: 123,166,749. **Age distrib.:** <15: 27.3%; 65+: 6.9%. **Growth:** 1.2%. **Migrants:** 0.9%. **Pop. density:** 164.1 per sq mi, 63.4 per sq km. **Urban:** 79.5%. **Ethnic groups:** mestizo (Amerindian-Spanish) 62%, predom. Amerindian 21%, Amerindian 7%. **Languages:** Spanish, indigenous langs. (incl. Mayan, Nahuatl). **Religions:** Roman Catholic 82.7%, none 4.7%.

Geography: Total area: 758,449 sq mi, 1,964,375 sq km; **Land area:** 750,561 sq mi, 1,943,945 sq km. **Location:** Southern N America. U.S. on N, Guatemala and Belize on S. **Topography:** The Sierra Madre Occidental Mts. run NW-SE near the W coast; the Sierra Madre Oriental Mts. are near Gulf of Mexico. They join S of Mexico City. In between lies a dry central plateau (5,000-8,000 ft) with temperate vegetation. Coastal lowlands are tropical. About 45% of land is arid. **Arable land:** 11.8%. **Capital:** Mexico City, 21,157,173. **Cities:** Guadalajara, 4,919,655; Monterrey, 4,588,893; Puebla, 3,032,056; Toluca de Lerdo, 2,207,353; Tijuana, 2,031,874.

Government: Type: Federal presidential republic. **Head of state and gov.:** Pres. Enrique Peña Nieto; b. 1966; in office: Dec. 1, 2012. **Local divisions:** 31 states, 1 federal district. **Defense budget:** $6.1 bil. **Active troops:** 277,150.

Economy: Industries: food and beverages, tobacco, chemicals, iron and steel, petroleum, mining, textiles, clothing, motor vehicles. **Chief crops:** corn, wheat, soybeans, rice, beans, cotton, coffee, fruit, tomatoes. **Natural resources:** petroleum, silver, copper, gold, lead, zinc, nat. gas, timber. **Water:** 3,637 cu m per capita. **Crude oil reserves:** 9.7 bil bbls. **Electricity prod.:** 281 bil kWh. **Labor force:** agric. 13.4%, industry 24.1%, services 61.9%. **Unemployment:** 4.9%.

Finance: Monetary unit: Peso (MXN) (18.81 = $1 U.S.). **GDP:** $2.2 tril; **per capita GDP:** $17,500; **GDP growth:** 2.5%. **Imports:** $434.8 bil; U.S. 47.3%, China 17.7%. **Exports:** $430.9 bil; U.S. 81.1%. **Tourism:** $17.5 bil. **Budget:** $300.5 bil. **Inflation:** 2.7%.

Transport: Railways: 9,562 mi. **Motor vehicles:** 304.1 per 1,000 pop. **Airports:** 243.

Communications: Telephone: 15.9 per 100 pop. **Mobile:** 85.3 per 100 pop. **Broadband:** 37.5 per 100 pop. **Internet:** 57.4%.

Health: Expend.: 6.3%. **Life expect.:** 73.1 male; 78.8 female. **Births:** 18.5 per 1,000 pop. **Deaths:** 5.3 per 1,000 pop. **Infant mortality:** 11.9 per 1,000 live births. **Undernourished:** <5%. **HIV:** 0.2%.

Education: Compulsory: ages 4-17. **Literacy:** 94.5%.
Embassy: 1911 Pennsylvania Ave. NW 20006; 728-1600.
Website: www.gob.mx

Mexico was the site of advanced civilizations. The Mayans, an agricultural people, moved up from Yucatan, built huge stone pyramids and invented a calendar. The Toltecs were overcome by the Aztecs, who founded Tenochtitlan 1325 CE, now Mexico City. Hernán Cortés, Spanish conquistador, destroyed the Aztec empire, 1519-21. After three centuries of Spanish rule the people revolted under Fr. Miguel Hidalgo y Costilla, 1810, Fr. Morelos y Pavón, 1812, and Gen. Agustín Iturbide, who made himself emperor as Agustín I, 1822. A republic was declared in 1823.

Mexican territory extended into the present American SW and California. Texas established a republic in 1836, and Mexico lost lands north of the Rio Grande during the U.S.-Mexican War, 1846-48.

The French supported an Austrian archduke on the Mexican throne as Maximilian I, 1864-67. He was deposed in an uprising led by Benito Juárez. Dictatorial rule by Porfirio Díaz, president 1877-80, 1884-1911, led to a period of rebellion and factional fighting. A new constitution in 1917 brought reform.

The Institutional Revolutionary Party (PRI) dominated politics from 1929 until the late 1990s. Radical opposition, including some guerrilla activity, was contained by strong measures. Gains in agriculture, industry, and social services were achieved, but poverty remained widespread. Vast oil reserves were discovered, 1970s-80s. Mexico signed the North American Free Trade Agreement (NAFTA) with the U.S. and Canada in 1992; it took effect Jan. 1, 1994.

After guerrillas of the Zapatista National Liberation Army (EZLN) rebelled Jan. 1994, a tentative peace accord was reached Mar. 2. The presidential candidate of the governing PRI, Luis Donaldo Colosio Murrieta, was assassinated at a political rally in Tijuana, Mar. 23. The new PRI candidate, Ernesto Zedillo Ponce de León, won election Aug. 21, 1994.

An austerity plan and pledges of aid from the U.S. saved Mexico's currency from collapse in early 1995. Popular Revolutionary Army guerrillas launched coordinated attacks on government targets in Aug. 1996. In 1997 elections, the PRI lost a congressional majority for the first time since 1929.

In the 2000 presidential election, the PRI lost for the first time in over 7 decades; the winner, Vicente Fox Quesada of the National Action Party (PAN), took office Dec. 1, 2000. The PAN candidate, conservative Felipe Calderón Hinojosa, won the 2006 presidential election. Despite a government crackdown on drug cartels, drug-related violence intensified. The cumulative death toll in the drug war exceeded 47,500, Dec. 2006-Sept. 2012. Enrique Peña Nieto (PRI) won the 2012 presidential election. He continued the policy of using federal troops to combat drug gangs. Notorious drug-gang leader Joaquín Guzmán Loera, known as El Chapo, was captured, Feb. 22, 2014. He escaped from Mexico's highest-security prison, July 11, 2015, but was recaptured, Jan. 8, 2016. Peña Nieto passed 2013 constitutional changes intended to bring greater competition to key industries, including oil, telecommunications, and broadcasting. Congress gave final approval to new regulations, Aug. 2014, opening the oil industry (nationalized in 1938) to foreign companies and other private investment. The Supreme Court, June 3, 2015, declared unconstitutional state laws barring gay couples from marrying, in effect legalizing same-sex marriage nationwide.

Micronesia
Federated States of Micronesia

People: Population: 104,719. **Age distrib.:** <15: 30.8%; 65+: 3.7%. **Growth:** –0.5%. **Migrants:** 2.6%. **Pop. density:** 386.4 per sq mi, 149.2 per sq km. **Urban:** 22.5%. **Ethnic groups:** Chuukese/Mortlockese 49.3%, Pohnpeian 29.8%, Kosraean 6.3%, Yapese 5.7%, Yap outer islander 5.1%. **Languages:** English (official), Chuukese, Kosrean, Pohnpeian, Yapese, Ulithian, Woleaian, Nukuoro, Kapingamarangi. **Religions:** Roman Catholic 54.7%, Protestant 41.1% (incl. Congregational 38.5%).

Geography: Total area: 271 sq mi, 702 sq km; **Land area:** 271 sq mi, 702 sq km. **Location:** Consists of 607 islands in four major island groups in W Pacific O. **Topography:** Mountainous islands and coral atolls; volcanic outcroppings on Pohnpei, Kosrae, and Truk. Tropical climate. **Arable land:** 2.9%. **Capital:** Palikir, 6,821 (2014).

Government: Type: Federal republic in free association with U.S. **Head of state and gov.:** Pres. Peter M. Christian; b. 1948; in office: May 11, 2015. **Local divisions:** 4 states. **Defense budget/active troops:** NA.

Economy: Industries: tourism, constr., specialized aquaculture, craft items. **Chief crops:** taro, yams, coconuts, bananas, cassava, kava, Kosraen citrus, betel nuts, black pepper. **Natural resources:** timber, marine prods., deep-seabed minerals, phosphate. **Water:** NA. **Labor force:** agric. 0.9%, industry 5.2%, services 93.9%. Two-thirds of labor force are govt. employees. **Unemployment:** NA.

Finance: Monetary unit: U.S. Dollar (USD) (1.00 = $1 U.S.). **GDP:** $306 mil (supplemented by grant aid, avg. about $100 mil annually); **per capita GDP:** $3,000; **GDP growth:** –0.2%. **Imports** (2013): $258.5 mil. **Exports** (2013): $88.3 mil. **Tourism:** $25 mil. **Budget** (FY12/13 est.): $192.1 mil. **Inflation:** –1%.

Transport: Airports: 6.

Communications: Telephone: 6.5 per 100 pop. **Mobile** (2013): 30.3 per 100 pop. **Broadband:** NA. **Internet:** 31.5%.

Health: Expend.: 13.7%. **Life expect.:** 70.8 male; 75.0 female. **Births:** 20.3 per 1,000 pop. **Deaths:** 4.2 per 1,000 pop. **Infant mortality:** 20.5 per 1,000 live births. **Undernourished:** NA. **HIV:** NA.

Education: Compulsory: ages 6-14. **Literacy:** 90.4%.
Embassy: 1725 N St. NW 20036; 223-4383.
Website: micronesia.fm

Micronesia, formerly known as the Caroline Islands, was ruled successively by Spain, Germany, Japan, and the U.S. The nation gained independence under a compact of free association with the U.S., Nov. 1986, and was admitted to the UN in 1991. Micronesian officials have repeatedly warned of the dangers to their country of rising sea levels linked to global climate change.

Moldova
Republic of Moldova

People: Population: 3,510,485. **Age distrib.:** <15: 18%; 65+: 12.2%. **Growth:** 3.5%. **Migrants:** –1%. **Pop. density:** 276.4 per sq mi, 106.7 per sq km. **Urban:** 45.1%. **Ethnic groups:** Moldovan 75.8%, Ukrainian 8.4%, Russian 5.9%, Gagauz 4.4%, Romanian 2.2%. **Languages:** Moldovan (official; virtually the same as Romanian), Romanian, Russian, Ukrainian, Gagauz. **Religions:** Orthodox 93.3%.

Geography: Total area: 13,070 sq mi, 33,851 sq km; **Land area:** 12,699 sq mi, 32,891 sq km. **Location:** Eastern Europe. Romania on W; Ukraine on N, E, and S. **Topography:** Landlocked; mainly hilly plains with steppelands in S near Black Sea. **Arable land:** 55.2%. **Capital:** Chişinău, 729,999.

Government: Type: Parliamentary republic. **Head of state:** Pres. Nicolae Timofti; b. 1948; in office: Mar. 23, 2012. **Head of gov.:** Prime Min. Pavel Filip; b. 1966; in office: Jan. 20, 2016. **Local divisions:** 32 raions, 3 municipalities, 2 territorial units (1 autonomous). **Defense budget:** $23 mil. **Active troops:** 5,350.

Economy: Industries: sugar, vegetable oil, food proc., agric. machinery, foundry equip., refrigerators and freezers. **Chief crops:** vegetables, fruits, grapes, grain, sugar beets, sunflower seeds, tobacco. **Natural resources:** lignite, phosphorites, gypsum, limestone. **Water:** 3,015 cu m per capita. **Electricity prod.:** 5.5 bil kWh. **Labor force:** agric. 30.5%, industry 12.2%, services 57.3%. **Unemployment:** 3.4%.

Finance: Monetary unit: Leu (MDL) (19.68 = $1 U.S.). **GDP:** $17.8 bil; **per capita GDP:** $5,000; **GDP growth:** –1.1%. **Imports:** $4 bil; Russia 22.7%, Romania 18.1%, Ukraine 11.5%, Germany 7%. **Exports:** $2 bil; Romania 23.1%, Italy 10.2%, Turkey 9.4%, Russia 8.1%, Germany 6.6%, Belarus 6.5%. **Tourism:** $210 mil. **Budget:** $2.5 bil (natl. public budget). **Inflation:** 9.7%.

Transport: Railways: 728 mi. **Airports:** 5.

Communications: Telephone: 35 per 100 pop. **Mobile:** 108 per 100 pop. **Broadband:** 49.4 per 100 pop. **Internet:** 49.8%.

Health: Expend.: 10.3%. **Life expect.:** 66.9 male; 74.8 female. **Births:** 11.8 per 1,000 pop. **Deaths:** 12.6 per 1,000 pop. **Infant mortality:** 12.3 per 1,000 live births. **Undernourished:** <5%. **HIV:** 0.6%.

Education: Compulsory: ages 7-15. **Literacy:** 99.2%.
Embassy: 2101 S St. NW 20008; 667-1130.
Website: www.moldova.md

In 1918, Romania annexed all of Bessarabia, west of the Dniester R, that Russia had acquired from Turkey in 1812 by the Treaty of Bucharest. In 1924, the Soviet Union established the Moldavian Autonomous Soviet Socialist Republic on the eastern bank of the Dniester R (Trans-Dniester region). It was merged with the Romanian-speaking districts of Bessarabia in 1940 to form the Moldavian SSR. During WWII, Romania, allied with Germany, occupied the area. It was recaptured by the USSR in 1944. Moldova declared independence Aug. 27, 1991, prior to the dissolution of the USSR Dec. 26, 1991.

Fighting erupted Mar. 1992 in the Trans-Dniester region between Moldovan security forces and Slavic separatists—ethnic Russians and ethnic Ukrainians—who feared Moldova's merging with neighboring Romania. In a 1994 plebiscite, voters in Moldova supported independence, without unification with Romania. Defying the Moldovan government, voters in the breakaway Trans-Dniester region held legislative elections and approved a separatist constitution in 1995. A peace accord with Trans-Dniester separatists was signed in Moscow in 1997. In a 2006 referendum, Trans-Dniester voters overwhelmingly supported independence from Moldova and eventual union with Russia.

A fragile coalition of pro-Western parties won Moldova's parliamentary elections in 2009 and 2010. The pro-Western Nicolae Timofti, elected by parliament, became president in 2012. Moldova and the EU signed an Association Agreement, June 27, 2014. Pro-Western parties won a narrow majority in Nov. 30, 2014, parliamentary elections. A banking scandal involving the disappearance of about $1 bil in bad loans, 2010-14, caused political turmoil. Chiril Gaburici and Valeriu Strelet each served as prime min. for a few months in 2015 before being forced out of office. Pavel Filip became prime min., Jan. 20, 2016, pledging to fight corruption and improve the economy. The Constitutional Court ruled, Mar. 4, that Moldova's president should be directly elected; parliament scheduled the election for Oct. 30, 2016.

Monaco
Principality of Monaco

People: Population: 30,581. **Age distrib.:** <15: 11.1%; 65+: 31.3%. **Growth:** 0.2%. **Migrants:** 55.8%. **Pop. density:** 39,602.2 per sq mi, 15,290.5 per sq km. **Urban:** 100%. **Ethnic groups:** French (official) 47%, Monegasque 16%, Italian 16%. **Languages:** French (official), English, Italian, Monegasque. **Religions:** Roman Catholic (official) 90%.

Geography: Total area: 0.77 sq mi, 2 sq km; **Land area:** 0.77 sq mi, 2 sq km. **Location:** NW Mediterranean coast. France to W, N, and E. **Topography:** Principality rises from port up to Monaco-Ville on a high promontory. **Arable land:** 0%. **Capital:** Monaco.

Government: Type: Constitutional monarchy. **Head of state:** Prince Albert II; b. 1958; in office: Apr. 6, 2005. **Head of gov.:** Min. of State Serge Telle; b. 1955; in office: Feb. 1, 2016. **Local divisions:** no first-order admin. divisions. **Defense budget/active troops:** NA.

Economy: Industries: banking, insurance, tourism, constr. **Water:** NA. **Labor force:** industry 16.1%, services 83.9%. **Unemployment:** NA.

Finance: Monetary unit: Euro (EUR) (0.89 = $1 U.S.). **GDP** (2013): $6.8 bil; **per capita GDP** (2013): $78,700; **GDP growth** (2013): 9.3%. **Imports** (2011): $1.2 bil; (2013) Europe 70.4%, Asia 20.8%. **Exports** (2011): $1.1 bil; (2013) Europe 73.2%, Africa 14.6%, America 5.2%. Full customs integration with France. Also participates in EU market system through customs union with France. **Budget** (2011 est.): $1.1 bil. **Inflation** (2009-10): 1.5%.

Transport: NA.

Communications: Telephone: 128.1 per 100 pop. **Mobile:** 88.8 per 100 pop. **Broadband:** 63.2 per 100 pop. **Internet:** 93.4%.

Health: Expend.: 4.3%. **Life expect.:** 85.6 male; 93.5 female. **Births:** 6.6 per 1,000 pop. **Deaths:** 9.6 per 1,000 pop. **Infant mortality:** 1.8 per 1,000 live births. **Undernourished:** <5%. **HIV:** NA.

Education: Compulsory: ages 6-16. **Literacy:** 99%.

Embassy: 3400 International Dr. NW, Ste. 2K-100, 20008; 234-1530.

Website: www.gouv.mc

An independent principality for over 300 years, Monaco has belonged to the House of Grimaldi since 1297, except during the French Revolution. It was placed under the protectorate of Sardinia in 1815, and under France, 1861. The Prince of Monaco was an absolute ruler until the 1911 constitution. Monaco was admitted to the UN in 1993. Monaco is noted for its climate, scenery, casinos, and Formula One Grand Prix auto race. Prince Rainier III, who ruled Monaco from 1949 and turned it into one of Europe's top tourist spots, died in 2005 and was succeeded by his son, Albert II.

Mongolia

People: Population: 3,031,330. **Age distrib.:** <15: 26.9%; 65+: 4.2%. **Growth:** 1.3%. **Migrants:** 0.6%. **Pop. density:** 5.1 per sq mi, 2 per sq km. **Urban:** 72.8%. **Ethnic groups:** Khalkh 81.9%, Kazak 3.8%, Dorvod 2.7%, Bayad 2.1%. **Languages:** Khalkha Mongol (official), Turkic, Russian. **Religions:** Buddhist 53%, Muslim 3%, Shamanist 2.9%, none 38.6%.

Geography: Total area: 603,909 sq mi, 1,564,116 sq km; **Land area:** 599,831 sq mi, 1,553,556 sq km. **Location:** E Central Asia. Russia on N, China on E, W, and S. **Topography:** Mostly high plateau with mountains, salt lakes, and vast grasslands. Gobi Desert in S. **Arable land:** 0.4%. **Capital:** Ulaanbaatar, 1,420,605.

Government: Type: Semi-presidential republic. **Head of state:** Pres. Tsakhiagiin Elbegdorj; b. 1963; in office: June 18, 2009. **Head of gov.:** Prime. Min. Chimed Saikhanbileg; b. 1958; in office: Nov. 21, 2014. **Local divisions:** 21 provinces, 1 municipality. **Defense budget:** $93 mil. **Active troops:** 10,000.

Economy: Industries: constr. and constr. materials, mining, oil, food and beverages, animal prods. proc., cashmere and natural fiber mfg. **Chief crops:** wheat, barley, vegetables, forage crops. **Natural resources:** oil, coal, copper, molybdenum, tungsten, phosphates, tin, nickel, zinc, fluorspar, gold, silver, iron. **Water:** 11,761 cu m per capita. **Electricity prod.:** 4.6 bil kWh. **Labor force:** agric. 28.6%, industry 21%, services 50.4%. **Unemployment:** 4.8%.

Finance: Monetary unit: Tugrik (MNT) (2,178.00 = $1 U.S.). **GDP:** $36.1 bil; **per capita GDP:** $12,100; **GDP growth:** 2.3%. **Imports:** $3.9 bil; China 39.9%, Russia 28.4%, Japan 6.4%, South Korea 6.2%. **Exports:** $5.3 bil; China 84%, Switzerland 9%. **Tourism:** $205 mil. **Budget:** $3.4 bil. **Inflation:** 5.8%.

Transport: Railways: 1,128 mi. **Airports:** 15.

Communications: Telephone: 8.7 per 100 pop. **Mobile:** 105 per 100 pop. **Broadband:** 57.6 per 100 pop. **Internet:** 21.4%.

Health: Expend.: 4.7%. **Life expect.:** 65.4 male; 74.1 female. **Births:** 19.6 per 1,000 pop. **Deaths:** 6.3 per 1,000 pop. **Infant mortality:** 21.8 per 1,000 live births. **Undernourished:** 20.5%. **HIV:** <0.1%.

Education: Compulsory: ages 6-17. **Literacy:** 98.4%.

Embassy: 2833 M St. NW 20007; 333-7117.

Website: www.president.mn

One of the world's oldest countries, Mongolia reached the zenith of its power in the 13th cent. when Genghis Khan and his successors conquered all of China and extended their influence as far west as Hungary and Poland. In later centuries, the empire dissolved and Mongolia became a province of China.

With the advent of the 1911 Chinese revolution, Mongolia, with Russian backing, declared its independence. A Communist regime was established, 1921. The Mongolian People's Revolutionary Party (MPRP) yielded its monopoly on power, 1990. A new constitution took effect, 1992.

Mongolia sent troops to U.S.-led operations in Afghanistan (2001); as of June 2016, 120 remained. Riots followed 2008 parliamentary elections, won by the ruling MPRP. In 2009 presidential voting, former Prime Min. Tsakhiagiin Elbergdorj of the Democratic Party (DP) defeated incumbent Pres. Nambaryn Enkhbayar of the MPRP (renamed the Mongolian People's Party, or MPP, in 2010). A 2012 legislative election gave the DP the most seats in parliament, and Norov Altankhuyag became prime min. Aug. 9. Elbergdorj was reelected June 27, 2013. With the economy slumping, Altankhuyag was replaced by Chimed Saikhanbileg (also DP), Nov. 21, 2014. Low commodity prices and reduced exports to China caused the economy to remain sluggish, and the MPP won a large majority in June 29, 2016, parliamentary elections.

Montenegro

People: Population: 644,578. **Age distrib.:** <15: 15.1%; 65+: 14.8%. **Growth:** −0.4%. **Migrants:** 13.2%. **Pop. density:** 124.1 per sq mi, 47.9 per sq km. **Urban:** 64.2%. **Ethnic groups:** Montenegrin 45%, Serbian 28.7%, Bosniak 8.7%, Albanian 4.9%, Muslim 3.3%. **Languages:** Serbian, Montenegrin (official), Bosnian, Albanian, Serbo-Croat. **Religions:** Orthodox 72.1%, Muslim 19.1%, Catholic 3.4%.

Geography: Total area: 5,333 sq mi, 13,812 sq km; **Land area:** 5,194 sq mi, 13,452 sq km. **Location:** Balkan Peninsula in SE Europe. Bosnia and Herzegovina on N and W, Serbia on E, Albania on SE, Croatia on W. **Topography:** Mostly rugged and mountainous, with few arable regions, mostly along the Zeta R. Highly indented narrow coastline. **Arable land:** 0.6%. **Capital:** Podgorica, 164,999 (2014).

Government: Type: Parliamentary republic. **Head of state:** Pres. Filip Vujanovic; b. 1954; in office: Apr. 6, 2008. **Head of gov.:** Prime. Min. Milo Djukanovic; b. 1962; in office: Dec. 4, 2012. **Local divisions:** 23 municipalities. **Defense budget:** $68 mil. **Active troops:** 2,080.

Economy: Industries: steelmaking, aluminum, agric. proc., consumer goods, tourism. **Chief crops:** tobacco, potatoes, citrus fruits, olives, grapes. **Natural resources:** bauxite, hydroelectricity. **Water:** NA. **Electricity prod.:** 3.8 bil kWh. **Labor force:** agric. 5.3%, industry 17.9%, services 76.8%. **Unemployment:** 19.1%.

Finance: Monetary unit: Euro (EUR) (0.89 = $1 U.S.). **GDP:** $10 bil; **per capita GDP:** $16,100; **GDP growth:** 4.1%. **Imports** (2014): $2 bil; (2012) Serbia 29.3%, Greece 8.7%, China 7.1%. **Exports** (2014): $370.2 mil; (2012) Croatia 22.7%, Serbia 22.7%, Slovenia 7.8%. **Tourism:** $902 mil. **Budget** (2014 est.): $1.6 bil. **Inflation:** 1.5%.

Transport: Railways: 155 mi. **Airports:** 5.

Communications: Telephone: 24.8 per 100 pop. **Mobile:** 162.2 per 100 pop. **Broadband:** 31 per 100 pop. **Internet:** 64.6%.

Health: Expend.: 6.4%. **Life expect.:** 75.6 male; 81.8 female. **Births:** 10.2 per 1,000 pop. **Deaths:** 9.6 per 1,000 pop. **Infant mortality:** 8.5 per 1,000 live births. **Undernourished:** <5%. **HIV:** NA.

Education: Compulsory: ages 6-14. **Literacy:** 98.7%.

Embassy: 1610 New Hampshire Ave. NW 20009; 234-6108.

Website: www.gov.me

Part of the medieval Serbian Kingdom, Montenegro preserved its autonomy for centuries because of its mountainous terrain. After WWI, it was part of the Kingdom of Serbs, Croats, and Slovenes, later renamed Yugoslavia. Italian forces occupied parts of Montenegro during WWII. In 1945, with the establishment of a federal Yugoslavia under Communist rule, Montenegro became one of six constituent republics.

In Apr. 1992, after four other republics had declared independence, Montenegro and Serbia reconstituted themselves as the Federal Republic of Yugoslavia. Because of its ties with Serbia, Montenegro was a target of NATO airstrikes during the Kosovo war, Mar.-June 1999. The republic sought closer ties with the West, however, and worked to reduce its political and economic dependence on Serbia. After an independence referendum narrowly passed, Montenegro declared independence June 3, 2006, and was admitted as a UN member June 28. It applied, Dec. 15 2008, to join the EU. NATO, May 19, 2016, formally invited Montenegro to join the alliance.

Morocco
Kingdom of Morocco

People: Population: 33,655,786. **Age distrib.:** <15: 26.1%; 65+: 6.6%. **Growth:** 1%. **Migrants:** 0.3%. **Pop. density:** 195.3 per sq mi, 75.4 per sq km. **Urban:** 60.7%. **Ethnic groups:** Arab-Berber 99%. **Languages:** Arabic (official), Berber langs. (incl. Tamazight [official]), French (lang. of business, govt., diplomacy). **Religions:** Muslim (official; virtually all Sunni) 99%.

Geography: Total area: 172,414 sq mi, 446,550 sq km; **Land area:** 172,317 sq mi, 446,300 sq km. **Location:** NW coast of Africa. Western Sahara on S, Algeria on E, Spain to N. **Topography:** Consists of 5 natural regions: mountain ranges (Riff in N, Middle Atlas, Upper Atlas, and Anti-Atlas); rich plains in W; alluvial plains in SW; well-cultivated plateaus in center; pre-Sahara arid zone extending from SE. **Arable land:** 18%. **Capital:** Rabat, 2,003,764. **Cities:** Dar-el-Beida (Casablanca), 3,544,498.

Government: Type: Parliamentary constitutional monarchy. **Head of state:** King Mohammed VI; b. 1963; in office: July 30, 1999. **Head of gov.:** Prime Min. Abdelilah Benkirane; b. 1954; in office: Nov. 29, 2011. **Local divisions:** 11 regions (recognized; not incl. claimed region in territory of disputed Western Sahara). **Defense budget:** $3.3 bil. **Active troops:** 195,800.

Economy: Industries: automotive parts, phosphate mining and proc., food proc., aerospace, food proc., leather goods. **Chief crops:** barley, wheat, citrus fruits, grapes, vegetables, olives. **Natural resources:** phosphates, iron ore, manganese, lead, zinc, fish, salt. **Water:** 844 cu m per capita. **Crude oil reserves** (2015): 680 bbls. **Electricity prod.:** 26 bil kWh. **Labor force:** agric. 39.1%, industry 20.3%, services 40.5%. **Unemployment:** 10.2%.

Finance: Monetary unit: Dirham (MAD) (9.74 = $1 U.S.). **GDP:** $273.5 bil; **per capita GDP:** $8,200; **GDP growth:** 4.5%. **Imports:** $37.3 bil; Spain 13.9%, France 12.4%, China 8.5%, U.S. 6.5%, Germany 5.8%, Italy 5.5%. **Exports:** $21.2 bil; Spain 22.1%, France 19.7%. **Tourism:** $6 bil. **Budget:** $29 bil. **Inflation:** 1.6%.

Transport: Railways: 1,284 mi. **Motor vehicles:** 107.5 per 1,000 pop. **Airports:** 31.

Communications: Telephone: 6.5 per 100 pop. **Mobile:** 126.9 per 100 pop. **Broadband:** 26.8 per 100 pop. **Internet:** 57.1%.

Health: Expend.: 5.9%. **Life expect.:** 73.8 male; 80.1 female. **Births:** 18.0 per 1,000 pop. **Deaths:** 4.8 per 1,000 pop. **Infant mortality:** 22.7 per 1,000 live births. **Undernourished:** <5%. **HIV:** 0.1%.

Education: Compulsory: ages 6-14. **Literacy:** 71.7%.

Embassy: 1601 21st St. NW 20009; 462-7980.

Website: www.maroc.ma

Berbers were the region's original inhabitants, followed by Carthaginians and Romans. Arabs conquered it in 683. In the 11th and 12th cents., a Berber empire ruled all NW Africa and most of Spain from Morocco.

Part of Morocco came under Spanish rule in the 19th cent.; France controlled the rest in the early 20th. Tribal uprisings lasted from 1911 to 1933. Independence was achieved Mar. 2, 1956. Tangier, an internationalized seaport, was incorporated into Morocco, 1956. Ifni, a Spanish enclave, was ceded in 1969.

King Hassan II assumed the throne in 1961, reigning until his death in 1999; he was succeeded by his eldest son. A bicameral legislature was established in 1997.

Five terrorist attacks in Casablanca May 16, 2003, left 45 people dead, including 12 suicide bombers; the government blamed Salafia Jihadia, an al-Qaeda-linked group. Following a series of suicide bombings in 2007, the government stepped up its campaign against militant Islamists. Following Arab Spring street demonstrations Feb.-Mar. 2011, the monarchy implemented modest constitutional reforms. Throughout 2011, Moroccans staged protests of what they saw as social injustices, including persistent unemployment, unjust detentions, and lack of free speech. The moderate Islamist Justice and Development Party won a plurality in Nov. 25, 2011, parliamentary elections, and Abdelilah Benkirane was named prime min. On Feb. 4, 2016, Morocco opened the first phase of what will be the world's largest concentrated solar power plant when completed (scheduled for 2018).

Western Sahara

Western Sahara, formerly the protectorate of Spanish Sahara, is bounded on the N by Morocco, the NE by Algeria, the E and S by Mauritania, and the W by the Atlantic O. Phosphates are the major resource. Area 102,703 sq mi; pop. (2016 est.) 587,020. Capital is Laayoune; pop. (2014 est.) 262,360. Half of the labor force is employed in agriculture, the other half in industry and services.

Spain withdrew in Feb. 1976. On Apr. 14, 1976, Morocco annexed over 70,000 sq mi, with the remainder annexed by Mauritania. The Polisario Front guerrilla movement, which proclaimed the region independent Feb. 27, launched attacks with Algerian support. After Mauritania signed a treaty with Polisario Aug. 5, 1979, Morocco occupied Mauritania's portion of Western Sahara.

After years of bitter fighting, Morocco controlled the main urban areas, but Polisario guerrillas moved freely in the vast, sparsely populated deserts. The two sides implemented a cease-fire in 1991, when a UN peacekeeping force (MINURSO) was established with a mandate to prepare for a referendum on self-determination as early as 1992; as of Aug. 31, 2016, MINURSO had more than 200 uniformed personnel in Western Sahara. A referendum had still not been held.

Mozambique
Republic of Mozambique

People: Population: 25,930,150. **Age distrib.:** <15: 44.9%; 65+: 2.9%. **Growth:** 2.5%. **Migrants:** 0.8%. **Pop. density:** 85.4 per sq mi, 33 per sq km. **Urban:** 32.5%. **Ethnic groups:** African (incl. Makhuwa, Tsonga, Lomwe, Sena) 99.66%. **Languages:** Emakhuwa, Portuguese (official), Xichangana, Cisena, Elomwe, Echuwabo, other Mozambican langs. **Religions:** Roman Catholic 28.4%, Muslim 17.9%, Zionist Christian 15.5%, Protestant 12.2% (incl. Pentecostal 10.9%), none 18.7%.

Geography: Total area: 308,642 sq mi, 799,380 sq km; **Land area:** 303,623 sq mi, 786,380 sq km. **Location:** SE coast of Africa. Tanzania on N; Malawi, Zambia, Zimbabwe on W; South Africa, Swaziland on S. **Topography:** Coastal lowlands comprise nearly half the country with plateaus rising in steps to mountains along western border. **Arable land:** 7.2%. **Capital:** Maputo, 1,203,089. **Cities:** Matola, 976,955.

Government: Type: Presidential republic. **Head of state and gov.:** Pres. Filipe Jacinto Nyusi; b. 1959; in office: Jan. 15, 2015. **Local divisions:** 10 provinces, 1 city. **Defense budget:** $152 mil. **Active troops:** 11,200.

Economy: Industries: aluminum, petroleum prods., chemicals, textiles, cement, glass, asbestos, tobacco, food, beverages. **Chief crops:** cotton, cashew nuts, sugarcane, tea, cassava, corn, coconuts, sisal, citrus and tropical fruits, potatoes, sunflowers. **Natural resources:** coal, titanium, nat. gas, hydropower, tantalum, graphite. **Water:** 7,760 cu m per capita. **Electricity prod.:** 15 bil kWh. **Labor force:** agric. 81%, industry 6%, services 13%. **Unemployment:** 22.6%.

Finance: Monetary unit: Metical (MZN) (73.01 = $1 U.S.). **GDP:** $33.2 bil; **per capita GDP:** $1,200; **GDP growth:** 6.3%. **Imports:** $7.1 bil; South Africa 26.8%, China 19.3%, India 13.9%. **Exports:** $3.6 bil; South Africa 24.9%, China 10.2%, Italy 8.9%, India 8.9%, Belgium 7.9%. **Tourism:** $193 mil. **Budget:** $5.8 bil. **Inflation:** 3.6%.

Transport: Railways: 2,975 mi. **Motor vehicles:** 3.4 per 1,000 pop. **Airports:** 21.

Communications: Telephone: 0.3 per 100 pop. **Mobile:** 74.2 per 100 pop. **Broadband:** 3 per 100 pop. **Internet:** 9%.

Health: Expend.: 7%. **Life expect.:** 52.6 male; 54.1 female. **Births:** 38.3 per 1,000 pop. **Deaths:** 11.9 per 1,000 pop. **Infant mortality:** 67.9 per 1,000 live births. **Undernourished:** 25.3%. **HIV:** 10.5%.

Education: Compulsory: NA. **Literacy:** 58.8%.

Embassy: 1525 New Hampshire Ave. NW 20036; 293-7146.

Website: www.portaldogoverno.gov.mz

The first Portuguese post on the Mozambique coast was established in 1505 on the trade route to Asia. Mozambique became independent June 25, 1975, after a 10-year war against the Portuguese. The 1974 revolution in Portugal paved the way for an orderly transfer of power to Frelimo (Front for the Liberation of Mozambique).

The Frelimo government, headed by Pres. Samora Machel, a former guerrilla commander, gradually transitioned to a Communist system. Most of the country's whites emigrated. In the 1980s, severe drought and civil war caused famine and heavy loss of life. Pres. Machel was killed in a plane crash just inside the South African border, Oct. 19, 1986. Frelimo formally abandoned Marxist-Leninism in 1989, and a new constitution, effective Nov. 30, 1990, established multiparty elections and a free-market economy.

A 1992 peace agreement ended hostilities between the government and the Mozambique National Resistance (Renamo), which became the main opposition party. Repatriation of 1.7 mil Mozambican refugees ended June 1995.

In Feb.-Mar. 2000, heavy floods claimed more than 600 lives and devastated the economy. Another flood crisis, Jan.-Mar. 2008, claimed some 700 lives and displaced 650,000 people.

Frelimo retained its hold on power under Pres. Joaquim Chissano (1986-2005) and his successor, Pres. Armando Guebuza, elected in 2004, reelected in 2009. Frelimo candidate Filipe Jacinto Nyusi won the Oct. 15, 2014, presidential election, and the party won almost 60% of the seats in legislative elections the same day. Clashes between government forces and Renamo, which had begun in 2013, intensified in 2015-16.

Abundant energy resources have the potential to increase economic growth. Natural gas reserves were estimated at 100 tril cu ft (third-largest in Africa) as of 2016. Oil exploration continued.

Myanmar
(Burma)
Union of Myanmar

People: Population: 56,890,418. **Age distrib.:** <15: 25.8%; 65+: 5.5%. **Growth:** 1%. **Migrants:** 0.1%. **Pop. density:** 225.5 per sq mi, 87.1 per sq km. **Urban:** 34.6%. **Ethnic groups:** Burman 68%, Shan 9%, Karen 7%, Rakhine 4%, Chinese 3%, Indian 2%, Mon 2%. **Languages:** Burmese (official). **Religions:** Buddhist 87.9%, Christian 6.2%, Muslim 4.3%.

Geography: Total area: 261,228 sq mi, 676,578 sq km; **Land area:** 252,321 sq mi, 653,508 sq km. **Location:** Between S and SE Asia, on Bay of Bengal. Bangladesh, India on W; China, Laos, Thailand on E. **Topography:** Surrounding mountains on W, N, and E. Dense forests cover much of nation. N-S rivers provide habitable valleys, especially the Irrawaddy, navigable for 900 mi. Tropical monsoon climate. **Arable land:** 16.5%. **Capital:** Yangon (Rangoon), 4,903,507; Nay Pyi Taw (admin.), 1,045,178. **Cities:** Mandalay, 1,196,235.

Government: Type: Parliamentary republic. **Head of state and gov.:** Pres. Htin Kyaw; b. 1946; in office: Mar. 30, 2016. **Local divisions:** 7 regions, 7 states, 1 union territory. **Defense budget:** $2.2 bil. **Active troops:** 406,000.

Economy: Industries: agric. proc.; wood and wood prods.; copper, tin, tungsten, iron; cement, constr. materials; pharmaceuticals. **Chief crops:** rice, pulses, beans, sesame, groundnuts, sugarcane. **Natural resources:** petroleum, timber, tin, antimony, zinc, copper, tungsten, lead, coal, marble, limestone, prec. stones, nat. gas, hydropower. **Water:** 21,671 cu m per capita. **Crude oil reserves:** 0.1 bil bbls. **Electricity prod.:** 12 bil kWh. **Labor force:** agric. 70%, industry 7%, services 23%. **Unemployment:** 3.3%.

Finance: Monetary unit: Kyat (MMK) (1,208.00 = $1 U.S.). **GDP:** $283.5 bil; **per capita GDP:** $5,500; **GDP growth:** 7%. **Imports:** $12.6 bil; China 42.2%, Thailand 18.5%, Singapore 11%. **Exports:** $9.8 bil; China 37.7%, Thailand 25.6%, India 7.7%, Japan 6.2%. Import/export figures grossly underestimated due to value of goods smuggled into and out of Thailand, China, Malaysia, and India. **Tourism:** $1.6 bil. **Budget:** $4.5 bil. **Inflation:** 10.8%.

Transport: Railways: 3,126 mi. **Motor vehicles:** 0.6 per 1,000 pop. **Airports:** 36.

Communications: Telephone: 1 per 100 pop. **Mobile:** 76.7 per 100 pop. **Broadband:** 14.9 per 100 pop. **Internet:** 21.8%.

Health: Expend.: 2.3%. **Life expect.:** 64.2 male; 69.2 female. **Births:** 18.2 per 1,000 pop. **Deaths:** 7.9 per 1,000 pop. **Infant mortality:** 42.2 per 1,000 live births. **Undernourished:** 14.2%. **HIV:** 0.8%.

Education: Compulsory: ages 5-9. **Literacy:** 93.1%.

Embassy: 2300 S St. NW 20008; 332-3344.

Website: www.president-office.gov.mm

The Burmese arrived from Tibet before the 9th cent., displacing earlier cultures, and a Buddhist monarchy was established by the 11th cent. Burma was conquered by China's Mongol dynasty in 1272, then ruled by the Shan people as a Chinese tributary until the 16th cent. Britain subjugated Burma in three wars, 1824-84, and ruled the country as part of India until 1937, when Burma became self-governing. Full independence was achieved Jan. 4, 1948.

Gen. Ne Win dominated politics from 1962 to 1988, first as military ruler, then as constitutional president, advancing policies that increased economic socialization and international isolation. In 1987, the UN granted Burma, once the richest nation in SE Asia, less-developed status. Ne Win resigned July 1988, following anti-government riots. In Sept., the military seized power, under Gen. Saw Maung. In 1989 the country's name was changed to Myanmar.

Although the main opposition party won a decisive victory in 1990 multiparty elections, the military refused to surrender power. A key opposition leader, Aung San Suu Kyi, was held under house arrest, 1989-95, 2000-02, and 2003-10. The regime's poor human rights record and continued harassment of Suu Kyi and her supporters led to U.S.-imposed sanctions.

In late Sept. 2007, thousands of Buddhist monks led mass protests in Yangon; security forces cracked down by raiding monasteries, arresting monks, and firing on demonstrators. On Sept. 25, the U.S. announced tougher sanctions. Cyclone Nargis, May 2-3, 2008, left at least 84,537 people dead, with an estimated 53,836 missing.

After the military dominated Nov. 2010 parliamentary elections, the ruling council was dissolved and an initially nominal civilian government returned, Mar. 30, 2011. Suu Kyi's National League for Democracy (NLD) won 43 of 45 parliamentary seats in an Apr. 1, 2012, election, and Suu Kyi traveled to Oslo, Norway, to accept the Nobel Peace Prize (awarded in absentia in 1991). The EU, Apr. 23, and U.S., May 17, suspended most sanctions. Myanmar's government announced Aug. 28, 2012, the removal of more than 2,000 names from the country's notorious blacklist of those banned from entering or leaving the country. In 2015, Myanmar became the 191st country to sign the Chemical Weapons Convention banning such weapons. The NLD won a majority of seats in Nov. 8, 2015, parliamentary elections. Htin Kyaw of the NLD was elected president by the parliament, Mar. 15, 2016. Suu Kyi, constitutionally barred from the presidency, assumed the newly created post of state counsellor, Apr. 6, 2016, becoming the country's de facto leader. At a White House meeting with Suu Kyi, Sept. 14, 2016, Pres. Barack Obama announced the U.S. would lift all remaining sanctions against Myanmar.

Violence against Rohingya Muslims in the northwest that began in 2012 killed hundreds and drove hundreds of thousands from their homes. The Rohingya are not recognized as citizens by the government, which as of mid-2016 was confining more than 100,000 in camps. Almost 100,000 Rohingya fled by boat, 2014-15, seeking asylum in other SE Asian countries; smugglers reportedly often exploited and abused refugees. Meeting with a UN official, June 20, 2016, Suu Kyi reiterated the government's nonrecognition policy.

Namibia
Republic of Namibia

People: Population: 2,436,469. **Age distrib.:** <15: 37.4%; 65+: 4%. **Growth:** 2%. **Migrants:** 3.8%. **Pop. density:** 7.7 per sq mi, 3 per sq km. **Urban:** 47.6%. **Ethnic groups:** black 87.5%, white 6%, mixed 6.5%. Ovambo tribe about 50% of pop.; Kavangos tribe 9%. **Languages:** Oshiwambo langs., Nama/Damara, Afrikaans (common), Otjiherero langs., Kavango langs., Caprivi langs., English (official). **Religions:** Christian 80%-90% (Lutheran 50%+), indigenous beliefs 10%-20%.

Geography: Total area: 318,261 sq mi, 824,292 sq km; **Land area:** 317,874 sq mi, 823,290 sq km. **Location:** Southern Africa on Atlantic coast. Angola on N; Botswana, Zambia on E; South Africa on S. **Topography:** Three distinct regions incl. Namib Desert along the Atlantic, a mountainous central plateau with woodland savanna, and Kalahari Desert in E. True forests found in NE. Four rivers but little other surface water. **Arable land:** 1%. **Capital:** Windhoek, 380,289.

Government: Type: Presidential republic. **Head of state and gov.:** Pres. Hage Geingob; b. 1941; in office: Mar. 21, 2015. **Local divisions:** 14 regions. **Defense budget:** $574 mil. **Active troops:** 9,200.

Economy: Industries: meatpacking, fish proc., dairy prods., pasta, beverages, mining. **Chief crops:** millet, sorghum, peanuts, grapes. **Natural resources:** diamonds, copper, uranium, gold, silver, lead, tin, lithium, cadmium, tungsten, zinc, salt, hydropower, fish. **Water:** 16,230 cu m per capita. **Electricity prod.:** 1.3 bil kWh. **Labor force:** agric. 31%, industry 14%, services 54% (formal sector only). About two-thirds of rural population rely on subsistence agric. **Unemployment:** 18.6%.

Finance: Monetary unit: Dollar (NAD) (14.59 = $1 U.S.). **GDP:** $25.3 bil; **per capita GDP:** $11,400; **GDP growth:** 4.5%. **Imports:** $7.2 bil. **Exports:** $5 bil. **Tourism:** $409 mil. **Budget:** $5.3 bil. **Inflation:** 3.4%.

Transport: Railways: 1,633 mi. **Motor vehicles:** 120.2 per 1,000 pop. **Airports:** 19.

Communications: Telephone: 7.6 per 100 pop. **Mobile:** 102.1 per 100 pop. **Broadband:** 35.5 per 100 pop. **Internet:** 22.3%.

Health: Expend.: 8.9%. **Life expect.:** 62.1 male; 65.1 female. **Births:** 27.9 per 1,000 pop. **Deaths:** 8.1 per 1,000 pop. **Infant mortality:** 36.4 per 1,000 live births. **Undernourished:** 42.3%. **HIV:** 13.3%.

Education: Compulsory: ages 7-13. **Literacy:** 90.8%.

Embassy: 1605 New Hampshire Ave. NW 20009; 986-0540.

Website: www.gov.na

Namibia was declared a German protectorate in 1890 and officially called South-West Africa. South Africa seized the territory in 1915 during WWI; the League of Nations gave South Africa a mandate over the territory in 1920. In 1966, the Marxist South-West Africa People's Organization (SWAPO) launched a guerrilla war for independence. The UN General Assembly named the area Namibia in 1968.

After many years of guerrilla warfare, South Africa, Angola, and Cuba signed a U.S.-mediated agreement Dec. 22, 1988, to end South African administration of Namibia and provide for a ceasefire and transition to independence, in accordance with a 1978 UN plan. A separate accord between Cuba and Angola provided for a phased withdrawal of Cuban troops from Namibia. A constitution providing for multiparty government was adopted Feb. 9, 1990, and Namibia gained independence Mar. 21.

Walvis Bay, the principal deepwater port, under South African administration since 1922, was returned to Namibia in 1994. Separatist violence flared in the Caprivi Strip in the late 1990s. SWAPO, the leading political group since independence, dominated presidential and parliamentary elections, Nov. 28, 2014. Severe drought led Pres. Hage Geingob to declare a state of emergency, June 29, 2016.

SPORTS

FINAL FIVE Aly Raisman, Madison Kocian, Laurie Hernandez, Simone Biles, and Gabrielle Douglas worked together to claim Olympic gold for the U.S. in the women's gymnastics team event at the Games in Rio de Janeiro, Brazil, Aug. 9, 2016.

HISTORY REPEATING U.S. swimmer Michael Phelps further entrenched his status as the most decorated Olympian of all time in 2016, winning five gold medals and a silver to bring his career total to 28 medals, of which 23 were gold.

THREE-PEAT Jamaica's Usain Bolt became the first men's sprinter ever to win gold in the 100-m and 200-m events at three straight Olympic Games in 2016.

22 AND COUNTING Serena Williams defeated Angelique Kerber in London July 9, 2016, to claim her 7th Wimbledon singles title and 22nd career Grand Slam title.

SPORTS

'BAMA DYNASTY

Heisman-winner Derrick Henry and the Crimson Tide defeated Clemson, 45-40, to claim the College Football Playoff National Championship Jan. 11, 2016, and Alabama's fourth title in the last seven seasons.

EXCLUSIVE CLUB'S NEWEST MEMBER

Ichiro Suzuki claimed his 3,000th MLB-career hit Aug. 7, 2016; he was the first player from Japan—where he had 1,278 hits in nine seasons that were not counted toward his MLB record—to reach the milestone.

DEFENSE DOES IT Veteran quarterback Peyton Manning and the Denver Broncos won Super Bowl 50 Feb. 7, 2016, 24-10, over the Carolina Panthers; Manning retired the next month.

UNDERDOG TRIUMPHS The unheralded Leicester City club beat 5,000-to-1 odds to win their first English Premier League soccer championship in May 2016, 132 years after the club was founded.

BUZZER BEATER Villanova claimed the NCAA men's basketball championship Apr. 4, 2016, edging out a 77-74 win over North Carolina at the buzzer.

CLEVELAND LOVES LEBRON Cleveland celebrated LeBron James and the Cavaliers' NBA championship with a victory parade June 22, 2016, marking the city's first major pro sports championship in 52 years.

NO SURPRISES Breanna Stewart led UConn over Syracuse, 82-51, to the Huskies' fourth consecutive NCAA women's title Apr. 5, 2016, and Stewart's unprecedented fourth award as the most outstanding player of the Final Four.

RECORD RESET Stephen Curry and the Golden State Warriors won their 73rd game of the regular season Apr. 13, 2016, eclipsing the 20-year-old NBA record for regular-season wins.

ARTS

CATCHING 'EM ALL *Pokémon Go* players used smartphones to catch Pokémon in the hit augmented-reality game released July 6, 2016.

VERDICT'S IN Sarah Paulson and Sterling K. Brown won Emmy Awards for playing Marcia Clark and Christopher Darden in FX's *The People v. O.J. Simpson*, which also won the Emmy for best limited series Sept. 18, 2016.

IN FORMATION Beyoncé's album *Lemonade* and its accompanying 60-minute film won 8 awards out of 11 nominations at MTV's Video Music Awards Aug. 28, 2016.

"ONE LAST TIME" *Hamilton* creator and star Lin-Manuel Miranda took his final curtain call with the wildly successful Broadway musical July 9, 2016; the show won 11 Tony Awards.

PEOPLE

AILES OUSTED After former Fox News personality Gretchen Carlson charged Fox News CEO Roger Ailes with sexual harassment, Ailes was forced to resign his post July 21, 2016, ending a 20-year tenure as the head of the influential cable channel.

TAKE A KNEE Beginning in the 2016 preseason, San Francisco 49ers quarterback Colin Kaepernick (right) touched off a storm of controversy by refusing to stand for the national anthem in protest of "a country that oppresses black people and people of color." Dozens of other pro athletes followed suit with similar protests.

GOING, GOING, GONE After 67 seasons with the franchise, iconic Dodgers play-by-play announcer Vin Scully broadcast his last home game in Los Angeles, Sept. 25, 2016.

I'LL MISS YOU!

MONEY TALKS The U.S. Treasury announced Apr. 20, 2016, that Harriet Tubman, the abolitionist and former slave, would replace Pres. Andrew Jackson on the face of the $20 bill as part of a major redesign of U.S. currency.

END OF AN ERA? Japanese Emperor Akihito Aug. 8, 2016, publicly indicated that he wished to abdicate as the nation's monarch.

FAREWELLS

EDWARD ALBEE
Mar. 12, 1928-Sept. 16, 2016

MUHAMMAD ALI
Jan. 17, 1942-June 3, 2016

DAVID BOWIE
Jan. 8, 1947-Jan. 10, 2016

NATALIE COLE
Feb. 6, 1950-Dec. 31, 2015

PATTY DUKE
Dec. 14, 1946-Mar. 29, 2016

ZAHA HADID
Oct. 31, 1950-Mar. 31, 2016

MERLE HAGGARD
Apr. 6, 1937-Apr. 6, 2016

GORDIE HOWE
Mar. 31, 1928-June 10, 2016

HARPER LEE
Apr. 28, 1926-Feb. 19, 2016

GARRY MARSHALL
Nov. 13, 1934-July 19, 2016

ARNOLD PALMER
Sept. 10, 1929-Sept. 25, 2016

SHIMON PERES
Aug. 2, 1923-Sept. 28, 2016

PRINCE
June 7, 1958-Apr. 21, 2016

NANCY REAGAN
July 6, 1921-Mar. 6, 2016

ALAN RICKMAN
Feb. 21, 1946-Jan. 14, 2016

DORIS ROBERTS
Nov. 4, 1925-Apr. 17, 2016

MORLEY SAFER
Nov. 8, 1931-May 19, 2016

ANTONIN SCALIA
Mar. 11, 1936-Feb. 13, 2016

PHYLLIS SCHLAFLY
Aug. 15, 1924-Sept. 5, 2016

GARRY SHANDLING
Nov. 29, 1949-Mar. 24, 2016

PAT SUMMITT
June 14, 1952-June 28, 2016

ABE VIGODA
Feb. 24, 1921-Jan. 26, 2016

ELIE WIESEL
Sept. 30, 1928-July 2, 2016

GENE WILDER
June 11, 1933-Aug. 29, 2016

SCIENCE & TECHNOLOGY

EINSTEIN THEORY CONFIRMED 100 years after Albert Einstein predicted the existence of gravitational waves, researchers reported twice in 2016 that they had finally succeeded in observing the creation of gravitational waves by the merging of black holes, as simulated here.

SHOW'S OVER After years of criticism from animal rights activists, the theme park company SeaWorld announced Mar. 17, 2016, that it would cease breeding killer whales and phase out its orca shows.

SPACE ODYSSEY NASA astronaut Scott Kelly and Russian cosmonaut Mikhail Kornienko returned to Earth Mar. 1, 2016, after spending a NASA-record 340 days on the International Space Station.

ROCKET RETURNS SpaceX's Falcon 9 rocket achieved a milestone Apr. 8, 2016, when it delivered its payload into space, then returned and successfully landed its CRS-8 first stage on a drone ship.

Nauru
Republic of Nauru

People: Population: 9,591. **Age distrib.:** <15: 31.9%; 65+: 2.4%. **Growth:** 0.5%. **Migrants:** 31.1%. **Pop. density:** 1,182.9 per sq mi, 456.7 per sq km. **Urban:** 100%. **Ethnic groups:** Nauruan 58%, other Pac. Islander 26%, Chinese 8%, European 8%. **Languages:** Nauruan (official), English (used in govt. and commerce). **Religions:** Protestant 60.4% (incl. Nauru Congregational 35.7%, Assembly of God 13%), Roman Catholic 33%.
Geography: Total area: 8.1 sq mi, 21 sq km; **Land area:** 8.1 sq mi, 21 sq km. **Location:** In W Pacific O. just S of equator. Nearest neighbor is Kiribati to E. **Topography:** Mostly a plateau bearing high-grade phosphate deposits, surrounded by a sandy shore and coral reef in concentric rings. **Arable land:** 0%. **Capital:** None official; govt. offices in Yaren district.
Government: Type: Parliamentary republic. **Head of state and gov.:** Pres. Baron Waqa; b. 1959; in office: June 11, 2013. **Local divisions:** 14 districts. **Defense budget/active troops:** NA.
Economy: Industries: phosphate mining, offshore banking, coconut prods. **Chief crops:** coconuts. **Natural resources:** phosphates, fish. **Water:** NA. **Electricity prod.** (2012): 25 mil kWh. **Labor force:** phosphate mining, public admin., education, transportation. **Unemployment:** NA.
Finance: Monetary unit: Australian Dollar (AUD) (1.32 = $1 U.S.). **GDP:** $150.8 mil; **per capita GDP:** $14,800; **GDP growth:** 8%. **Imports** (2013): $143.1 mil. **Exports** (2013): $125 mil. **Budget** (2010 est.): $51.8 mil. **Inflation:** 8%.
Transport: Airports: 1.
Communications: Telephone (2009): 18.9 per 100 pop. **Mobile** (2012): 67.8 per 100 pop. **Broadband:** NA. **Internet** (2011): 54%.
Health: Expend.: 3.3%. **Life expect.:** 63.0 male; 70.5 female. **Births:** 24.4 per 1,000 pop. **Deaths:** 5.9 per 1,000 pop. **Infant mortality:** 7.9 per 1,000 live births. **NA. HIV:** NA.
Education: Compulsory: ages 4-17. **Literacy:** NA.
Permanent UN mission: 801 2nd Ave., 3rd Fl., New York, NY 10017; (212) 937-0074.
Website: www.naurugov.nr
The British reached the island in 1798, but it was annexed to the German Empire in 1886. After WWI, Australia administered Nauru under a League of Nations mandate. Japan occupied the island during WWII. In 1947 Nauru was made a UN trust territory, administered by Australia. It became an independent republic Jan. 31, 1968.
Phosphate exports provided Nauru with per capita revenues that were among the highest in the Third World. Phosphate reserves, however, are nearly depleted, and environmental damage from strip mining has been severe. Lax banking practices have made Nauru a haven for money laundering. Rising sea levels linked to global climate change have eroded Nauru's coastline. A Nov. 20, 2012, Amnesty Intl. report found inhumane living conditions at Australia's detention center on Nauru for refugees and undocumented immigrants who had sought to enter Australia by boat. An Australian government report, released Mar. 20, 2015, confirmed allegations of sexual and physical abuse of detainees by staff. Two detainees conducted self-immolation protests, one fatal, Apr.-May 2016.

Nepal
Federal Democratic Republic of Nepal

People: Population: 29,033,914. **Age distrib.:** <15: 30.9%; 65+: 5%. **Growth:** 1.2%. **Migrants:** 1.8%. **Pop. density:** 524.6 per sq mi, 202.5 per sq km. **Urban:** 19%. **Ethnic groups:** Chhettri 16.6%, Brahman-Hill 12.2%, Magar 7.1%, Tharu 6.6%, Tamang 5.8%, Newar 5%, Kami 4.8%, Muslim 4.4%, Yadav 4%, Rai 2.3%, Gurung 2%. **Languages:** Nepali (official), Maithali, Bhojpuri, Tharu, Tamang, Newar, Magar, Bajjika, Urdu. **Religions:** Hindu 81.3%, Buddhist 9%, Muslim 4.4%, Kirant 3.1%.
Geography: Total area: 56,827 sq mi, 147,181 sq km; **Land area:** 55,348 sq mi, 143,351 sq km. **Location:** Astride Himalaya Mts. China on N, India on S. **Topography:** The Himalayas across the N, hill country with fertile valleys across the center. S border region is part of flat, subtropical Ganges Plain. **Arable land:** 14.7%. **Capital:** Kathmandu, 1,224,098.
Government: Type: Federal parliamentary republic. **Head of state:** Pres. Bidhya Devi Bhandari; b. 1961; in office: Oct. 29, 2015. **Head of gov.:** Prime Min. Pushpa Kamal Dahal (Prachanda); b. 1954; in office: Aug. 4, 2016. **Local divisions:** 14 zones. **Defense budget:** $324 mil. **Active troops:** 95,750.
Economy: Industries: tourism, carpets, textiles; small rice, jute, sugar, oilseed mills; cigarettes, cement, brick prod. **Chief crops:** pulses, rice, corn, wheat, sugarcane, jute, root crops. **Natural resources:** quartz, water, timber, hydropower, lignite, copper, cobalt, iron ore. **Water:** 7,372 cu m per capita. **Electricity prod.:** 3.6 bil kWh. **Labor force:** agric. 69%, industry 12%, services 19%. **Unemployment:** 2.7%.
Finance: Monetary unit: Rupee (NPR) (107.19 = $1 U.S.). **GDP:** $70.1 bil; **per capita GDP:** $2,500; **GDP growth:** 3.4%. **Imports:** $8.6 bil; India 61.4%, China 15.4%. **Exports:** $924.2 mil; India 61.2%, U.S. 9.4%. **Tourism:** $480 mil. **Budget:** $4.2 bil. **Inflation:** 7.9%.

Transport: Railways: 33 mi. **Airports:** 11.
Communications: Telephone: 3 per 100 pop. **Mobile:** 96.7 per 100 pop. **Broadband:** 17.4 per 100 pop. **Internet:** 17.6%.
Health: Expend.: 5.8%. **Life expect.:** 70.1 male; 71.3 female. **Births:** 19.9 per 1,000 pop. **Deaths:** 5.7 per 1,000 pop. **Infant mortality:** 28.9 per 1,000 live births. **Undernourished:** 7.8%. **HIV:** 0.2%.
Education: Compulsory: NA. **Literacy:** 64.7%.
Embassy: 2131 Leroy Pl. NW 20008; 667-4550.
Website: nepal.gov.np
Nepal was originally a group of principalities, with the Gurkha principality becoming dominant about 1769. In 1951 King Tribhubana Bir Bikram, member of the Shah family, ended the system of rule by hereditary premiers of the Ranas family, who had kept the kings virtual prisoners, and established a cabinet system of government. Polygamy, child marriage, and the caste system were officially abolished in 1963. Political parties were legalized in 1990.
Nine members of Nepal's royal family, including King Birendra and Queen Aishwarya, died in a June 1, 2001, massacre. The killings were blamed on a 10th family member, Crown Prince Dipendra, who reportedly shot himself that night and died 3 days later, allowing Birendra's brother Gyanendra Bir Bikram Shah Dev to take the throne.
Citing the government's failure to stop a Maoist insurgency, King Gyanendra assumed absolute authority, Feb. 1, 2005, but after protests, he agreed, Apr. 24, 2006, to reinstate parliament. A new government, led by Prime Min. Girija Prasad Koirala, signed a peace accord with Maoist rebels Nov. 21 ending a decade-long civil war that claimed 13,000 lives. Maoists joined an interim parliament Jan. 2007 and entered the cabinet Apr. 1. A constituent assembly voted May 2008 to abolish the monarchy and make Nepal a republic. Maoist Baburam Bhattarai became prime min. Aug. 29, 2011. Bhattarai dissolved parliament May 27, 2012, when the deadline for a new constitution passed. Maoists suffered a defeat in Nov. 19, 2013, elections, in which moderate parties won the largest blocs.
The new constitution, establishing a federal system with seven states, was adopted Sept. 20, 2015. Protests beginning in Sept., largely by ethnic and religious groups fearing loss of autonomy, left more than 40 people dead and caused severe fuel shortages when roads from India were blocked. Khadga Prasad Oli, leader of a non-Maoist Communist party, was elected prime min. by parliament, Oct. 11, 2015. Bidhya Devi Bhandari (of Oli's party) was elected by parliament, Oct. 28, 2015, as Nepal's first female president. After Oli, facing a no-confidence vote, resigned, parliament elected former prime min. (2008-09) and Maoist party leader Pushpa Kamal Dahal to replace him, Aug. 3, 2016.
A magnitude 7.8 earthquake near Kathmandu, Apr. 25, 2015, killed more than 8,000 people and displaced 2.8 mil. Historic temples and other sites were heavily damaged. A second quake, May 12, brought the combined death toll to over 8,600.

Netherlands
Kingdom of the Netherlands

People: Population: 17,016,967. **Age distrib.:** <15: 16.6%; 65+: 18.4%. **Growth:** 0.4%. **Migrants:** 11.7%. **Pop. density:** 1,300.4 per sq mi, 502.1 per sq km. **Urban:** 91%. **Ethnic groups:** Dutch 78.6%, EU 5.8%, Turkish 2.4%, Indonesian 2.2%, Moroccan 2.2%, Surinamese 2.1%. **Languages:** Dutch (official). **Religions:** Roman Catholic 28%, Protestant 19% (incl. Dutch Reformed 9%, Protestant Church of The Netherlands, 7%), none 42%.
Geography: Total area: 16,040 sq mi, 41,543 sq km; **Land area:** 13,086 sq mi, 33,893 sq km. **Location:** NW Europe on North Sea. Germany on E, Belgium on S. **Topography:** Land is flat with avg. elevation of 37 ft above sea level; much of land reclaimed and protected by some 1,500 mi of dikes. **Arable land:** 30.8%. **Capital:** Amsterdam, 1,098,684; s-Gravenhage (The Hague) (seat), 653,477. **Cities:** Rotterdam, 994,469.
Government: Type: Parliamentary constitutional monarchy. **Head of state:** King Willem-Alexander; b. 1967; in office: Apr. 30, 2013. **Head of gov.:** Prime Min. Mark Rutte; b. 1967; in office: Oct. 14, 2010. **Local divisions:** 12 provinces. **Defense budget:** $8.9 bil. **Active troops:** 36,050.
Economy: Industries: agroindustries, metal and engineering prods., elec. machinery and equip., chemicals. **Chief crops:** grains, potatoes, sugar beets, fruits, vegetables. **Natural resources:** nat. gas, petroleum, peat, limestone, salt, sand and gravel. **Water:** 5,377 cu m per capita. **Crude oil reserves:** 0.1 bil bbls. **Electricity prod.:** 93 bil kWh. **Labor force:** agric. 1.8%, industry 17%, services 81.2%. **Unemployment:** 6.9%.
Finance: Monetary unit: Euro (EUR) (0.89 = $1 U.S.). **GDP:** $832.6 bil; **per capita GDP:** $49,200; **GDP growth:** 1.9%. **Imports:** $404.6 bil; Germany 14.7%, China 14.5%, Belgium 8.2%, U.S. 8.1%, UK 5.1%. **Exports:** $488.3 bil; Germany 24.5%, Belgium 11.1%, UK 9.3%, France 8.4%. **Tourism:** $13.2 bil. **Budget:** $351.8 bil. **Inflation:** 0.6%.
Transport: Railways: 2,003 mi. **Motor vehicles:** 554.4 per 1,000 pop. **Airports:** 23.
Communications: Telephone: 41.3 per 100 pop. **Mobile:** 123.5 per 100 pop. **Broadband:** 69.1 per 100 pop. **Internet:** 93.1%.

Health: Expend.: 10.9%. **Life expect.:** 79.2 male; 83.6 female. **Births:** 10.9 per 1,000 pop. **Deaths:** 8.8 per 1,000 pop. **Infant mortality:** 3.6 per 1,000 live births. **Undernourished:** <5%. **HIV:** NA.

Education: Compulsory: ages 5-16. **Literacy:** 99%.
Embassy: 4200 Linnean Ave. NW 20008; 244-5300.
Website: www.government.nl

Julius Caesar conquered the region in 55 BCE, when it was inhabited by Celtic and Germanic tribes. After the empire of Charlemagne fell apart, the Netherlands (Holland, Belgium, Flanders) split among counts, dukes, and bishops, passed to Burgundy and thence to Spain. William the Silent, prince of Orange, led a confederation of the northern provinces, called Estates, in the Union of Utrecht, 1579; in 1581 they repudiated allegiance to Spain. The rise of the Dutch republic to naval, economic, and artistic eminence came in the 17th cent.

After a period of French hegemony, 1795-1813, the Congress of Vienna in 1815 formed a kingdom of the Netherlands, including Belgium, under William I. In 1830, the Belgians seceded and formed a separate kingdom.

The Netherlands maintained its neutrality in WWI but was invaded during WWII and occupied by Germany, 1940-45. In 1949, after several years of fighting, the Netherlands granted independence to Indonesia.

The murder May 6, 2002, of right-wing populist leader Pim Fortuyn, 9 days before legislative elections, marked the first political assassination in modern Dutch history. Filmmaker Theo van Gogh was killed by an Islamic extremist Nov. 2, 2004. On Apr. 30, 2009, the national Queen's Day holiday, an attempted assassination of Queen Beatrix and other royal family members resulted in the deaths of 7 bystanders and the would-be assassin. The anti-Islamic, right-wing Freedom Party, headed by Geert Wilders, gained in parliamentary elections June 2010. Prime Min. Mark Rutte resigned Apr. 23, 2012, after failing to pass a budget in line with EU requirements, but Rutte's pro-business Liberal party won a majority of seats in parliamentary elections held Sept. 2012. Queen Beatrix, 75, abdicated the throne to her son, Willem-Alexander, Apr. 30, 2013. A Malaysia Airlines flight from Amsterdam to Kuala Lumpur was shot down over eastern Ukraine, July 17, 2014; nearly 200 Dutch passport holders were among the 298 killed.

Dutch Dependencies

Constitutional changes effective Oct. 10, 2010, dissolved the political entity known as the Netherlands Antilles, which consisted of two island groups in the West Indies. **Curaçao** (area 171 sq mi), near the coast of Venezuela, and **Sint Maarten** (13 sq mi), SE of Puerto Rico, were elevated to the status of autonomous countries. Bonaire, Saba, and Sint Eustatius became special municipalities. The northern two-thirds of St. Maarten is a French overseas territorial collectivity (St. Martin). St. Maarten suffered extensive damage from Hurricane Luis, Sept. 1995. Pop. of Curaçao, 149,035 (2016 est.); that of its capital, Willemstad, 144,730 (2014 est.). Sint Maarten, pop. 41,486 (2016 est.); capital is Philipsburg, pop. 46,085 (2014 est.). The principal industry is the refining of crude oil from Venezuela. Tourism and shipbuilding are other important industries. International tourism receipts in 2014 were $635 mil for Curaçao, $914 mil for Sint Maarten. Per capita GDP of Sint Maarten was $66,800 (2014 est.). **Websites:** www.gobiernu.cw (Curaçao); www.sintmaartengov.org (St. Maarten)

Aruba, about 26 mi west of Curaçao, was separated from the Netherlands Antilles on Jan. 1, 1986; it is an autonomous component of the Netherlands, with a status similar to Curaçao and St. Maarten. Area: 69 sq mi; pop. (2016 est.) 113,648. Capital: Oranjestad; pop. (2014 est.) 29,041. Chief industries are oil refining and tourism. International tourism receipts in 2015 were $1.7 bil. **Website:** www.kabga.aw

New Zealand

People: Population: 4,474,549. **Age distrib.:** <15: 19.8%; 65+: 14.9%. **Growth:** 0.8%. **Migrants:** 23%. **Pop. density:** 43.8 per sq mi, 16.9 per sq km. **Urban:** 86.3%. **Ethnic groups:** European 71.2%, Maori 14.1%, Asian 11.3%, Pacific peoples 7.6%. Respondents could identify more than one ethnic group. **Languages:** English (de facto official), Maori (de jure official), Samoan. **Religions:** Christian 44.3% (incl. Catholic 11.6%, Anglican 10.8%), no religion 38.5%.

Geography: Total area: 103,799 sq mi, 268,838 sq km; **Land area:** 102,138 sq mi, 264,537 sq km. **Location:** SW Pacific O. Nearest neighbors are Australia to W, Fiji and Tonga to N. **Topography:** Two main islands (North and South Isls.) are hilly and mountainous. The E coasts consist of fertile plains, incl. Canterbury Plains on South Isl. Volcanic plateau in center of North Isl. Glaciers and 15 peaks over 10,000 ft on South Isl. **Arable land:** 2.1%. **Capital:** Wellington, 385,899. **Cities:** Auckland, 1,360,422.

Government: Type: Parliamentary democracy under constitutional monarchy. **Head of state:** Queen Elizabeth II, rep. by Gov.-Gen. Sir Jeremiah "Jerry" Mateparae; b. 1954; in office: Aug. 31, 2011. **Head of gov.:** Prime Min. John Key; b. 1961; in office: Nov. 19, 2008. **Local divisions:** 16 regions, 1 territory. **Defense budget:** $2.4 bil. **Active troops:** 8,950.

Economy: Industries: agric., forestry, fishing, logs and wood prods., mfg., mining, constr., financial services, real estate services, tourism. **Chief crops:** fruit, vegetables, wine, wheat, barley. **Natural resources:** nat. gas, iron ore, sand, coal, timber, hydropower, gold, limestone. **Water:** 72,201 cu m per capita. **Crude oil reserves:** 0.1 bil bbls. **Electricity prod.:** 43 bil kWh. **Labor force:** agric. 7%, industry 19%, services 74%. **Unemployment:** 5.6%.

Finance: Monetary unit: Dollar (NZD) (1.37 = $1 U.S.). **GDP:** $168.2 bil; **per capita GDP:** $36,200; **GDP growth:** 3.4%. **Imports:** $35.3 bil; China 19.4%, Australia 11.8%, U.S. 11.7%, Japan 6.6%. **Exports:** $34.3 bil; China 17.5%, Australia 16.9%, U.S. 11.8%, Japan 6%. **Tourism:** $8.9 bil. **Budget:** $73.3 bil. **Inflation:** 0.3%.

Transport: Railways: 2,565 mi. **Motor vehicles:** 769 per 1,000 pop. **Airports:** 39.

Communications: Telephone: 40.2 per 100 pop. **Mobile:** 121.8 per 100 pop. **Broadband:** 92.7 per 100 pop. **Internet:** 88.2%.

Health: Expend.: 11%. **Life expect.:** 79.1 male; 83.3 female. **Births:** 13.3 per 1,000 pop. **Deaths:** 7.4 per 1,000 pop. **Infant mortality:** 4.5 per 1,000 live births. **Undernourished:** <5%. **HIV:** NA.

Education: Compulsory: ages 6-15. **Literacy:** 99%.
Embassy: 37 Observatory Cir. NW 20008; 328-4800.
Website: www.govt.nz

New Zealand comprises North Island, 43,911 sq mi; South Island, 58,084 sq mi; Stewart Island, 649 sq mi; Chatham Isls., 373 sq mi; and several groups of smaller islands. The Maori, a Polynesian group from the eastern Pacific, reached New Zealand before and during the 14th cent. The first European to sight New Zealand was Dutch navigator Abel Janszoon Tasman. The Maori refused to allow him to land. British Capt. James Cook explored the coasts, 1769-70.

British sovereignty was proclaimed and Maori land rights were recognized in the Treaty of Waitangi, 1840, with organized settlement beginning the same year. Representative institutions were granted in 1853. The Maori Wars, or New Zealand Wars, ended in 1870 with British victory. The colony became a dominion in 1907 and gained full independence in 1947.

A progressive tradition in politics began in the 19th cent., when New Zealand was known for social experimentation. Much of the nation's economy has been deregulated since the 1980s. Jenny Shipley of the National Party became the nation's first female prime min., Dec. 8, 1997. The Labour Party, led by Helen Clark, won general elections, Nov. 27, 1999, and July 27, 2002.

Prostitution was legalized June 2003. In July, New Zealand contributed troops to the Australian-led force in the Solomon Islands. A measure establishing a supreme court and ending appeals to the UK Privy Council passed Oct. 14. A major settlement of Maori land claims dating from the 19th cent. was signed June 25, 2008.

An explosion Nov. 19, 2010, at the Pike River coal mine on South Island killed 29 men. A Christchurch earthquake, Feb. 22, 2011, killed 181 people and caused damage estimated at $11 bil to the central business district. Prime Min. John Key's handling of these and other disasters bolstered the popularity of his National Party (in office since 2008), and it was returned to power in elections Nov. 26, 2011. New Zealand legalized same-sex marriage in a 77-44 parliamentary vote Apr. 17, 2013. Key's National Party won a majority of seats in Sept. 20, 2014, parliamentary elections. Key announced, Feb. 24, 2015, that New Zealand would send 143 troops to Iraq to help train Iraqi forces fighting the Islamist extremist group ISIS.

In 1965, the **Cook Islands** (area: 91 sq mi; 2016 est. pop.: 9,556), halfway between New Zealand and Hawaii, became self-governing. New Zealand retains responsibility for defense and foreign affairs. **Niue** (area: 100 sq mi; 2014 est. pop.: 1,190) attained the same status in 1974; it lies about 675 mi W of Cook Isls. Cyclone Heta devastated Niue Jan. 6, 2004. **Tokelau** (area: 4.6 sq mi; 2014 est. pop.: 1,337) comprises three atolls 300 mi N of Samoa. Two referendums on Tokelau self-government, held Feb. 13-15, 2006, and Oct. 20-24, 2007, failed to gain the required two-third majority. **Ross Dependency**, administered by New Zealand since 1923, comprises 160,000 sq mi of Antarctic territory. **Website:** www.cook-islands.gov.ck; www.gov.nu; www.tokelau.org.nz

Nicaragua
Republic of Nicaragua

People: Population: 5,966,798. **Age distrib.:** <15: 27.9%; 65+: 5.1%. **Growth:** 1%. **Migrants:** 0.7%. **Pop. density:** 128.8 per sq mi, 49.7 per sq km. **Urban:** 59.1%. **Ethnic groups:** mestizo (mixed Amerindian/white) 69%, white 17%, black 9%, Amerindian 5%. **Languages:** Spanish (official), Miskito, Mestizo on Carib. coast. **Religions:** Roman Catholic 58.5%, Protestant 23.2% (incl. Evangelical 21.6%), none 15.7%.

Geography: Total area: 50,336 sq mi, 130,370 sq km; **Land area:** 46,328 sq mi, 119,990 sq km. **Location:** Central America. Honduras on N, Costa Rica on S. **Topography:** Both Caribbean and Pacific coasts are over 200 mi long. Cordillera Mts., with many volcanic peaks, run NW-SE through middle of country. **Arable land:** 12.5%. **Capital:** Managua, 963,195.

Government: Type: Presidential republic. **Head of state and gov.:** Pres. Daniel Ortega Saavedra; b. 1945; in office: Jan. 10, 2007. **Local divisions:** 15 departments, 2 autonomous regions. **Defense budget:** $72 mil. **Active troops:** 12,000.

Economy: Industries: food proc., chemicals, machinery and metal prods., knit and woven apparel, petroleum refining and distrib. **Chief crops:** coffee, bananas, sugarcane, rice, corn, tobacco, cotton, sesame, soya, beans. **Natural resources:** gold, silver, copper, tungsten, lead, zinc, timber, fish. **Water:** 27,047 cu m per capita. **Electricity prod.:** 4.2 bil kWh. **Labor force:** agric. 31%, industry 18%, services 50%. **Unemployment:** 5.3%.

Finance: Monetary unit: Cordoba (NIO) (28.86 = $1 U.S.). **GDP:** $31.3 bil; **per capita GDP:** $5,000; **GDP growth:** 4.5%. **Imports:** $5.9 bil; U.S. 19.9%, Mexico 14.9%, China 10.6%, Venezuela 7%, Costa Rica 7%, El Salvador 5.7%, Guatemala 5.6%, Netherlands Antilles 5.5%. **Exports:** $4.5 bil; U.S. 56.5%, Mexico 10.7%, Venezuela 5.4%. **Tourism:** $529 mil. **Budget:** $2.4 bil. **Inflation:** 4%.

Transport: Motor vehicles: 52 per 1,000 pop. **Airports:** 12. **Communications: Telephone:** 5.7 per 100 pop. **Mobile:** 116.1 per 100 pop. **Broadband:** 1.4 per 100 pop. **Internet:** 19.7%.

Health: Expend.: 9%. **Life expect.:** 71.1 male; 75.5 female. **Births:** 17.9 per 1,000 pop. **Deaths:** 5.1 per 1,000 pop. **Infant mortality:** 19.0 per 1,000 live births. **Undernourished:** 16.6%. **HIV:** 0.3%.

Education: Compulsory: ages 6-11. **Literacy:** 82.5%.
Embassy: 1627 New Hampshire Ave. NW 20009; 939-6570.
Website: www.asamblea.gob.ni

Nicaragua, inhabited by various Indian tribes, was conquered by Spain in 1552. After gaining independence from Spain, 1821, Nicaragua was united for a short period with Mexico, then with the United Provinces of Central America, before becoming an independent republic, 1838. U.S. Marines occupied the country at times in the early 20th cent., the last time from 1926 to 1933.

Gen. Anastasio Somoza Debayle held the presidency 1967-72, 1974-79. Martial law was imposed in Dec. 1974, after officials were kidnapped by Marxist Sandinista guerrillas. Nationwide antigovernment strikes touched off a civil war, 1978, which ended when Somoza fled Nicaragua and the Sandinistas took control of Managua, July 1979. Somoza was assassinated in Paraguay, Sept. 17, 1980.

Relations with the U.S. were strained as a result of Nicaragua's aid to leftist guerrillas in El Salvador and U.S. backing of anti-Sandinista contra guerrilla groups, which fought the Sandinista government throughout the 1980s. In 1985 the U.S. House rejected Pres. Ronald Reagan's request for military aid to the contras. The subsequent diversion of funds to the contras from the proceeds of a secret arms sale to Iran caused a major scandal in the U.S.

In a stunning upset, Violeta Barrios de Chamorro defeated Sandinista leader Daniel Ortega Saavedra in national elections, Feb. 25, 1990. The conservative Arnoldo Alemán Lacayo defeated Ortega in the Oct. 1996 presidential election.

Drought and a drop in coffee prices precipitated an economic crisis in 2001. Enrique Bolaños Geyer, a conservative businessman, won the presidency that year. Convicted Dec. 7, 2003, on corruption charges, former Pres. Alemán received a $10-mil fine and a 20-year sentence. Ortega won the Nov. 2006 presidential election and cultivated ties with Venezuela and Iran, which offered Nicaragua financial assistance. He was reelected Nov. 6, 2011. The Sandinista-controlled legislature gave final approval, Jan. 28, 2014, to constitutional changes removing presidential term limits. Amid protests by environmentalists and other opponents of the project, preliminary construction work began, Dec. 2014, on a 170+-mi canal across Nicaragua by a Chinese consortium.

Niger
Republic of Niger

People: Population: 18,638,600. **Age distrib.:** <15: 49.3%; 65+: 2.6%. **Growth:** 3.2%. **Migrants:** 1%. **Pop. density:** 38.1 per sq mi, 14.7 per sq km. **Urban:** 19%. **Ethnic groups:** Hausa 53.1%, Zarma/Songhai 21.2%, Tuareg 11%, Fulani (Peul) 6.5%, Kanuri 5.9%. **Languages:** French (official), Hausa, Djerma. **Religions:** Muslim 80%, other (incl. indigenous beliefs and Christian) 20%.

Geography: Total area: 489,191 sq mi, 1,267,000 sq km; **Land area:** 489,076 sq mi, 1,266,700 sq km. **Location:** Interior of N Africa. Libya, Algeria on N; Mali, Burkina Faso on W; Benin, Nigeria on S; Chad on E. **Topography:** Mostly arid desert and mountains. Narrow savanna in S and Niger R. basin in the SW. **Arable land:** 12.6%. **Capital:** Niamey, 1,124,974.

Government: Type: Semi-presidential republic. **Head of state:** Pres. Mahamadou Issoufou; b. 1952; in office: Apr. 7, 2011. **Head of gov.:** Prime Min. Brigi Rafini; b. 1953; in office: Apr. 7, 2011. **Local divisions:** 7 regions, 1 capital district. **Defense budget** (2013): $72 mil. **Active troops:** 5,300.

Economy: Industries: uranium mining, petroleum, cement, brick, soap, textiles, food proc., chemicals, slaughterhouses. **Chief crops:** cowpeas, cotton, peanuts, millet, sorghum, cassava, rice. **Natural resources:** uranium, coal, iron ore, tin, phosphates, gold, molybdenum, gypsum, salt, petroleum. **Water:** 1,711 cu m per capita. **Crude oil reserves:** 0.2 bil bbls. **Electricity prod.:**

0.4 bil kWh. **Labor force:** agric. 90%, industry 6%, services 4%. **Unemployment:** 5.1%.

Finance: Monetary unit: CFA Franc (XOF) (586.00 = $1 U.S.). **GDP:** $19.1 bil; **per capita GDP:** $1,100; **GDP growth:** 4%. **Imports:** $2.2 bil; France 12%, China 10.4%, Nigeria 9.5%, French Polynesia 9%, Togo 6.1%, Belgium 5.3%, Côte d'Ivoire 5.3%. **Exports:** $1.4 bil; France 53.1%, Nigeria 20.3%, China 13.8%. **Tourism:** $90 mil. **Budget:** $2.2 bil. **Inflation:** 1%.

Transport: Motor vehicles: 12.2 per 1,000 pop. **Airports:** 10. **Communications: Telephone:** 0.6 per 100 pop. **Mobile:** 46.5 per 100 pop. **Broadband** (2012): 0.6 per 100 pop. **Internet:** 2.2%.

Health: Expend.: 5.8%. **Life expect.:** 54.3 male; 56.8 female. **Births:** 44.8 per 1,000 pop. **Deaths:** 12.1 per 1,000 pop. **Infant mortality:** 82.8 per 1,000 live births. **Undernourished:** 9.5%. **HIV:** 0.5%.

Education: Compulsory: NA. **Literacy:** 19.1%.
Embassy: 2204 R St. NW 20008; 483-4224.
Website: www.gouv.ne

Niger was part of ancient and medieval African empires. European explorers reached the area in the late 18th cent. The French colony of Niger was established 1900-22 after the defeat of Tuareg fighters, who had invaded the area from the north a century before. The country became independent Aug. 3, 1960.

In 1993, Niger held its first free and open elections since independence; an opposition leader, Mahamane Ousmane, won the presidency. A peace accord Apr. 24, 1995, ended a Tuareg rebellion that began in 1990. After a coup, Jan. 27, 1996, the military retained control. On Apr. 9, 1999, Gen. Ibrahim Bare Mainassara, president since 1996, was assassinated. Elections held Oct. 17 and Nov. 24, 1999, under a new constitution, restored civilian rule.

One of the world's poorest countries, Niger experienced severe food shortages in 2005 after locusts and drought ruined the grain harvest. Popularly elected in 1999 and 2004, Pres. Mamadou Tandja invoked emergency powers in 2009, seeking to remain in office for a third 5-year term. He was overthrown by a military junta Feb. 18, 2010. Civilian rule returned following Jan.-Mar. 2011 elections. Pres. Mahamadou Issoufou won reelection in a Mar. 20, 2016, runoff.

Terrorist attacks in Niger by an al-Qaeda-linked group, May 23, 2013, killed 21 soldiers and 5 of the bombers. Beginning in Feb. 2015, the Nigeria-based Islamist extremist group Boko Haram staged attacks in southern Niger. Niger's parliament approved, Feb. 9, sending troops into Nigeria to fight Boko Haram. The UNHCR estimated 50,000 people fled an area in SE Niger after a Boko Haram attack on the town of Bosso, beginning June 3, 2016, left dozens of Niger soldiers dead.

Nigeria
Federal Republic of Nigeria

People: Population: 186,053,386. **Age distrib.:** <15: 42.8%; 65+: 3.1%. **Growth:** 2.4%. **Migrants:** 0.7%. **Pop. density:** 529.1 per sq mi, 204.3 per sq km. **Urban:** 48.6%. **Ethnic groups:** 250+ ethnic groups. Most populous, politically influential: Hausa and Fulani 29%, Yoruba 21%, Igbo (Ibo) 18%, Ijaw 10%, Kanuri 4%, Ibibio 3.5%, Tiv 2.5%. **Languages:** English (official), Hausa, Yoruba, Igbo (Ibo), Fulani, 500+ indigenous langs. **Religions:** Muslim 50%, Christian 40%, indigenous beliefs 10%.

Geography: Total area: 356,669 sq mi, 923,768 sq km; **Land area:** 351,649 sq mi, 910,768 sq km. **Location:** S coast of W Africa. Benin on W, Niger on N, Chad and Cameroon on E. **Topography:** 4 E-W regions: a coastal mangrove swamp, a tropical rain forest, a plateau of savanna and open woodland, and semi-desert in N. **Arable land:** 37.3%. **Capital:** Abuja, 2,586,112. **Cities:** Lagos, 13,661,426; Kano, 3,675,716; Ibadan, 3,243,072; Port Harcourt, 2,464,947.

Government: Type: Federal presidential republic. **Head of state and gov.:** Pres. Muhammadu Buhari; b. 1942; in office: May 29, 2015. **Local divisions:** 36 states, 1 territory. **Defense budget:** $1.9 bil. **Active troops:** 80,000.

Economy: Industries: crude oil, coal, tin, columbite; rubber prods., wood; hides and skins, textiles, cement and other constr. materials. **Chief crops:** cocoa, peanuts, cotton, palm oil, corn, rice, sorghum, millet, cassava, yams, rubber. **Natural resources:** nat. gas, petroleum, tin, iron ore, coal, limestone, niobium, lead, zinc. **Water:** 1,571 cu m per capita. **Crude oil reserves:** 37.1 bil bbls. **Electricity prod.:** 27 bil kWh. **Labor force:** agric. 70%, industry 10%, services 20%. **Unemployment:** 7.5%.

Finance: Monetary unit: Naira (NGN) (305.00 = $1 U.S.). **GDP:** $1.1 tril; **per capita GDP:** $6,100; **GDP growth:** 2.7%. **Imports:** $48.4 bil; China 25.7%, U.S. 6.4%, Netherlands 6.3%. **Exports:** $50.7 bil; India 18.2%, Netherlands 8.5%, Spain 8.2%, Brazil 8.2%, South Africa 7.8%, France 5.2%. **Tourism:** $404 mil. **Budget:** $23.1 bil. **Inflation:** 9%.

Transport: Railways: 2,360 mi. **Motor vehicles:** 8.2 per 1,000 pop. **Airports:** 40.

Communications: Telephone: 0.1 per 100 pop. **Mobile:** 82.2 per 100 pop. **Broadband:** 11.7 per 100 pop. **Internet:** 47.4%.

Health: Expend.: 3.7%. **Life expect.:** 52.4 male; 54.5 female. **Births:** 37.3 per 1,000 pop. **Deaths:** 12.7 per 1,000 pop. **Infant mortality:** 71.2 per 1,000 live births. **Undernourished:** 7%. **HIV:** NA.

Education: Compulsory: ages 6-14. **Literacy:** 59.6%.
Embassy: 3519 International Ct. NW 20008; 986-8400.
Website: services.gov.ng

Early cultures in Nigeria date back to at least 700 BCE. From the 12th to the 14th cent., more advanced cultures developed in the Yoruba area, at Ife, and in the north, where Muslim influence prevailed. Portuguese and British slavers appeared in the 15th-16th cent. Britain seized Lagos, 1861, and gradually extended control inland until 1900. Nigeria became independent Oct. 1, 1960, and a republic Oct. 1, 1963.

On May 30, 1967, the Eastern Region seceded, proclaiming itself the Republic of Biafra, plunging the country into civil war. Casualties were estimated at over 1 mil, including many Biafrans (mostly Igbos) who died of starvation despite international relief efforts. The secessionists capitulated Jan. 12, 1970.

Nigeria emerged as one of the world's leading oil exporters in the 1970s, but much of the revenue has been squandered through corruption and mismanagement. Oil spills have polluted much of the Niger Delta region.

After 13 years of military rule, the nation made a peaceful return to civilian government Oct. 1979. Military rule resumed Dec. 31, 1983. An interim civilian government (in office Aug. 26, 1993) was ousted Nov. 17, 1993, in a coup led by Gen. Sani Abacha. His brutal rule ended June 8, 1998, when he died of an apparent heart attack. Abacha's successor, Gen. Abdulsalam Abubakar, promised elections and a return to civilian rule. Olusegun Obasanjo won the presidential vote Feb. 27, 1999, to lead Nigeria's first civilian government in 15 years.

The imposition of strict Islamic law in northern states led to clashes, Jan.-Mar. 2000, in which at least 800 people died. Fighting between Muslims and Christians Sept. 7-12 and Oct. 13-14, 2001, claimed an est. 600 lives. At least 1,000 people were killed Jan. 27, 2002, when an army weapons depot in Lagos exploded. Christian militia members massacred about 630 Muslims at Yelwa, central Nigeria, May 2, 2004. Obasanjo's chosen successor, Umaru Musa Yar'Adua, won a presidential election, Apr. 21, 2007, marred by violence and described as "not credible" by international monitors. After prolonged illness, Yar'Adua died May 5, 2010, and was succeeded by Vice Pres. Goodluck Jonathan, a southern Christian. After he won reelection Apr. 16, 2011, over Muhammadu Buhari, a northern-based Muslim, riots in 12 northern provinces left more than 800 people dead.

Boko Haram, a radical Islamist group based in NE Nigeria that seeks to establish an Islamist state, began terrorist attacks in 2009 against government forces and civilian targets. When Islamists gained control of a number of towns, Pres. Jonathan declared a state of emergency in the NE May 14, 2013. Boko Haram violence and seizures of territory escalated in 2014 and continued in 2015. In a message released Mar. 7, 2015, the group claimed allegiance to ISIS. Boko Haram also staged attacks in neighboring Chad, Cameroon, and Niger; troops from those countries fought Boko Haram in Nigeria beginning in 2015. Vowing tougher action against Boko Haram, Buhari defeated Jonathan in the Mar. 28-29, 2015, presidential election. Subsequent government offensives retook a significant portion of the territory Boko Haram had seized, but in 2016, the group continued to control areas of NE Nigeria and stage deadly attacks against civilians and security forces. The Council on Foreign Relations estimated that, by mid-2016, more than 28,000 people had been killed as a result of Boko Haram attacks, clashes with security forces, and related actions by security forces. The UNHCR estimated that 187,000 Nigerian refugees were in Niger, Cameroon, and Chad in mid-2016, and more than 2 mil Nigerians were internally displaced.

In NW Nigeria, Dec. 2015, hundreds of members of a Shiite group, the Islamic Movement in Nigeria, were killed by security forces. A Judicial Commission of Inquiry report, released Aug. 1, 2016, concluded that soldiers involved should be prosecuted.

Norway
Kingdom of Norway

People: Population: 5,265,158. **Age distrib.:** <15: 18%; 65+: 16.5%. **Growth:** 1.1%. **Migrants:** 14.2%. **Pop. density:** 44.8 per sq mi, 17.3 per sq km. **Urban:** 80.7%. **Ethnic groups:** Norwegian (incl. Sami) 94.4%, other European 3.6%. **Languages:** Bokmal Norwegian, Nynorsk Norwegian (both official); Sami (official in 9 municipalities). **Religions:** Church of Norway (Evangelical Lutheran official) 82.1%.
Geography: Total area: 125,021 sq mi, 323,802 sq km; **Land area:** 117,484 sq mi, 304,282 sq km. **Location:** W part of Scandinavian peninsula in NW Europe (extends farther N than any European land). Sweden, Finland, Russia on E. **Topography:** Highly indented coast lined with tens of thousands of islands. Mountains and plateaus cover most of country, which is only 33% forested. **Arable land:** 2.2%. **Capital:** Oslo, 1,002,450.
Government: Type: Parliamentary constitutional monarchy. **Head of state:** King Harald V; b. 1937; in office: Jan. 17, 1991. **Head of gov.:** Prime Min. Erna Solberg; b. 1961; in office: Oct. 16, 2013. **Local divisions:** 19 counties. **Defense budget:** $5.5 bil. **Active troops:** 23,550.
Economy: Industries: petroleum and gas, shipping, fishing, aquaculture, food proc., shipbuilding, pulp and paper prods. **Chief**

crops: barley, wheat, potatoes. **Natural resources:** petroleum, nat. gas, iron ore, copper, lead, zinc, titanium, pyrites, nickel, fish, timber, hydropower. **Water:** 75,417 cu m per capita. **Crude oil reserves:** 5.1 bil bbls. **Electricity prod.:** 132 bil kWh. **Labor force:** agric. 2.7%, industry 18.3%, services 79%. **Unemployment:** 3.4%.
Finance: Monetary unit: Krone (NOK) (8.32 = $1 U.S.). **GDP:** $356.2 bil; **per capita GDP:** $68,400; **GDP growth:** 1.6%. **Imports:** $72 bil; Sweden 12%, Germany 11.8%, China 10.9%, UK 6.7%, U.S. 6.6%, Denmark 6%. **Exports:** $106.2 bil; UK 22.2%, Germany 17.9%, Netherlands 10.2%, France 6.6%, Sweden 6.1%, Belgium 5%. **Tourism:** $5 bil. **Budget:** $193.9 bil. **Inflation:** 2.2%.
Transport: Railways: 2,641 mi. **Motor vehicles:** 612.3 per 1,000 pop. **Airports:** 67.
Communications: Telephone: 20 per 100 pop. **Mobile:** 113.6 per 100 pop. **Broadband:** 93.0 per 100 pop. **Internet:** 96.8%.
Health: Expend.: 9.7%. **Life expect.:** 79.8 male; 83.9 female. **Births:** 12.2 per 1,000 pop. **Deaths:** 8.1 per 1,000 pop. **Infant mortality:** 2.5 per 1,000 live births. **Undernourished:** <5%. **HIV:** NA.
Education: Compulsory: ages 6-15. **Literacy:** 100%.
Embassy: 2720 34th St. NW 20008; 333-6000.
Website: www.regjeringen.no

The first ruler of Norway was Harald the Fairhaired, who came to power in 872 CE. Between 800 and 1000, Norway's Vikings raided and occupied widely dispersed parts of Europe. The country was united with Denmark, 1381-1814, and with Sweden, 1814-1905. In 1905, the country became independent with Prince Charles of Denmark as king.

Norway remained neutral during WWI. In WWII, Germany attacked Norway Apr. 9, 1940, and held it until liberation May 8, 1945. The country abandoned its neutrality after the war and joined NATO. In a referendum Nov. 28, 1994, Norwegian voters rejected European Union membership.

Abundant hydroelectric resources (accounting for more than 90% of electricity production) have provided a base for industrialization, giving Norway one of the highest living standards in the world. The country is a leading producer and exporter of crude oil, with extensive reserves in the North Sea, and natural gas production has increased in recent years. Norway has used oil revenue to build up the world's largest sovereign wealth fund (more than $800 bil as of 2016).

A right-wing extremist, Anders Behring Breivik, confessed to killing 8 people with a car bomb in central Oslo and murdering another 69 at an island camp sponsored by the Labor Party's youth wing July 22, 2011. He was sentenced Aug. 24, 2012, to 21 years in prison, the maximum sentence. Parliament voted June 18, 2013, to make military service compulsory for women as well as men. Rightist parties, including the anti-immigration Progress Party, won the most seats in Sept. 9, 2013, elections; Conservative Party leader Erna Solberg became prime min. In 2015, about 31,000 migrants from the Middle East, SW Asia, and Africa applied for asylum in Norway, including thousands who entered Norway from Russia, many by bicycle.

Svalbard is a group of mountainous islands in the Arctic O., area 23,956 sq mi, pop. (2014 est.), 1,872. The largest, Spitsbergen (formerly called West Spitsbergen), 14,546 sq mi, seat of the governor, is about 370 mi N of Norway. By the 1920 Svalbard Treaty (in force 1925), major European powers recognized Norway's sovereignty over the archipelago.

Jan Mayen, area 146 sq mi, is a volcanic island located about 565 mi W-NW of Norway; it was annexed in 1929. The only people on Jan Mayen are military personnel and researchers. Norway operates a research station on volcanic **Bouvet Isl.**, area 19 sq mi, in the South Atlantic O., about midway between South Africa and Antarctica. The UK waived its claim to the island in 1928.

Oman
Sultanate of Oman

People: Population: 3,355,262. **Age distrib.:** <15: 30.1%; 65+: 3.4%. **Growth:** 2.1%. **Migrants:** 41.1%. **Pop. density:** 28.1 per sq mi, 10.8 per sq km. **Urban:** 78.1%. **Ethnic groups:** Arab, Baluchi, South Asian (Indian, Pakistani, Sri Lankan, Bangladeshi), African. **Languages:** Arabic (official), English, Baluchi, Urdu, Indian dialects. **Religions:** Muslim (official; majority Ibadhi) 85.9%, Christian 6.5%, Hindu 5.5%.
Geography: Total area: 119,499 sq mi, 309,500 sq km; **Land area:** 119,499 sq mi, 309,500 sq km. **Location:** SE coast of Arabian peninsula. United Arab Emirates, Saudi Arabia, Yemen on W. **Topography:** A narrow coastal plain, a range of barren mountains reaching 9,900 ft, and a wide, stony, mostly waterless plateau, avg. elevation 1,000 ft. An exclave at the tip of the Musandam peninsula controls access to the Persian Gulf. **Arable land:** 0.1%. **Capital:** Muscat, 865,547.
Government: Type: Absolute monarchy. **Head of state and gov.:** Sultan Qaboos bin Said al-Said; b. 1940; in office: July 23, 1970 (also prime min. since 1972). **Local divisions:** 11 governorates. **Defense budget:** $9.9 bil. **Active troops:** 42,600.
Economy: Industries: crude oil prod. and refining, nat. and liquefied nat. gas prod., constr., cement, copper, steel, chemicals, optic fiber. **Chief crops:** dates, limes, bananas, alfalfa,

vegetables. **Natural resources:** petroleum, copper, asbestos, marble, limestone, chromium, gypsum, nat. gas. **Water:** 312 cu m per capita. **Crude oil reserves:** 5.3 bil bbls. **Electricity prod.:** 26 bil kWh. **Labor force:** NA. **Unemployment:** 7.2%.

Finance: Monetary unit: Rial (OMR) (0.38 = $1 U.S.). **GDP:** $171.4 bil; **per capita GDP:** $44,600; **GDP growth:** 4.1%. **Imports:** $25.1 bil; UAE 29.5%, Japan 10.2%, U.S. 7.5%, China 6.7%, India 6.3%. **Exports:** $39.1 bil; China 35.4%, UAE 15.2%, South Korea 6.8%, Saudi Arabia 5.8%. **Tourism:** $1.4 bil. **Budget:** $36.6 bil. **Inflation:** 0.1%.

Transport: Motor vehicles: 197.5 per 1,000 pop. **Airports:** 13. **Communications: Telephone:** 10.5 per 100 pop. **Mobile:** 159.9 per 100 pop. **Broadband:** 73.7 per 100 pop. **Internet:** 74.2%.

Health: Expend.: 3.6%. **Life expect.:** 73.5 male; 77.5 female. **Births:** 24.3 per 1,000 pop. **Deaths:** 3.3 per 1,000 pop. **Infant mortality:** 13.2 per 1,000 live births. **Undernourished:** <5%. **HIV:** NA.

Education: Compulsory: NA. **Literacy:** 94%.

Embassy: 2535 Belmont Rd. NW 20008; 387-1980.

Website: www.oman.om

Oman was originally called Muscat and Oman. A long history of rule by other lands, including Portugal in the 16th cent., ended with the ouster of the Persians in 1744. By the early 19th cent., Muscat and Oman controlled much of the Persian and Pakistan coasts.

British influence was confirmed in a 1951 treaty, and Britain helped suppress an uprising by traditionally rebellious interior tribes against control by Muscat in the 1950s.

On July 23, 1970, Sultan Said bin Taimur was overthrown by his son, Sultan Qaboos bin Said al-Said, who changed the nation's name to Sultanate of Oman. Petroleum and natural gas are major sources of income. Oman has strong military and economic ties to the U.S. but also has favorable relations with Iran. Sultan Qaboos shuffled his cabinet after Arab Spring protests Feb. 2011 and expanded the powers of the Majlis al-Shura, the lower house of parliament, Oct. 20, 2011.

Pakistan
Islamic Republic of Pakistan

People: Population: 201,995,540. **Age distrib.:** <15: 32%; 65+: 4.4%. **Growth:** 1.5%. **Migrants:** 1.9%. **Pop. density:** 678.7 per sq mi, 262 per sq km. **Urban:** 39.2%. **Ethnic groups:** Punjabi 44.7%, Pashtun (Pathan) 15.4%, Sindhi 14.1%, Saraiki 8.4%, Muhajir 7.6%, Balochi 3.6%. **Languages:** Punjabi, Sindhi, Saraiki, Pashto or Pashtu, Urdu (official), Balochi, Hindko, English (official; lingua franca of elite and most govt. ministries). **Religions:** Muslim (official) 96.4% (Sunni 85%-90%, Shia 10%-15%).

Geography: Total area: 307,374 sq mi, 796,095 sq km; **Land area:** 297,637 sq mi, 770,875 sq km. **Location:** W part of S Asia. Iran on W, Afghanistan and China on N, India on E. **Topography:** The Indus R. rises in the Hindu Kush and Himalaya Mts. in the N, then flows 1,000 mi into Arabian Sea. Thar Desert, Eastern Plains flank Indus Valley. **Arable land:** 39.5%. **Capital:** Islamabad, 1,433,221. **Cities:** Karachi, 17,121,434; Lahore, 8,989,549; Faisalabad, 3,676,778; Rawalpindi, 2,581,511; Gujranwala, 2,192,727; Multan, 1,969,451; Hyderabad, 1,812,077; Peshawar, 1,787,365.

Government: Type: Federal parliamentary republic. **Head of state:** Pres. Mamnoon Hussain; b. 1940; in office: Sept. 9, 2013. **Head of gov.:** Prime Min. Nawaz Sharif; b. 1949; in office: June 5, 2013. **Local divisions:** 4 provinces, 1 territory, 1 capital territory; 2 admin. entities in Pakistan-administered part of disputed Jammu and Kashmir region. **Defense budget:** $7.5 bil. **Active troops:** 643,800.

Economy: Industries: textiles and apparel, food proc., pharmaceuticals, constr. materials, paper prods., fertilizer, shrimp. **Chief crops:** cotton, wheat, rice, sugarcane, fruits, vegetables. **Natural resources:** nat. gas, limited petroleum, poor quality coal, iron ore, copper, salt, limestone. **Water:** 1,306 cu m per capita. **Crude oil reserves:** 0.4 bil bbls. **Electricity prod.:** 93 bil kWh. **Labor force:** agric. 43.7%, industry 22.4%, services 33.9%. **Unemployment:** 5.2%.

Finance: Monetary unit: Rupee (PKR) (104.45 = $1 U.S.). **GDP:** $931 bil; **per capita GDP:** $5,000; **GDP growth:** 4.2%. **Imports:** $45.8 bil; China 28.2%, Saudi Arabia 10.9%, UAE 10.8%, Kuwait 5.6%. **Exports:** $23.7 bil; U.S. 13.1%, UAE 9.1%, Afghanistan 9.1%, China 8.8%, UK 5.3%. **Tourism:** $315 mil. **Budget** (FY2015 est.): $53.1 bil. **Inflation:** 2.5%.

Transport: Railways: 7,383 mi. **Motor vehicles:** 15.8 per 1,000 pop. **Airports:** 108.

Communications: Telephone: 1.6 per 100 pop. **Mobile:** 66.9 per 100 pop. **Broadband:** 5.1 per 100 pop. **Internet:** 18%.

Health: Expend.: 2.6%. **Life expect.:** 65.8 male; 69.8 female. **Births:** 22.3 per 1,000 pop. **Deaths:** 6.4 per 1,000 pop. **Infant mortality:** 53.9 per 1,000 live births. **Undernourished:** 22%. **HIV:** <0.1%.

Education: Compulsory: ages 5-16. **Literacy:** 56.4%.

Embassy: 3517 International Ct. NW 20008; 243-6500.

Website: www.pakistan.gov.pk

Pakistan shares the 5,000-year history of the India-Pakistan subcontinent. At present-day Harappa and Mohenjo Daro, the Indus Valley civilization, with large cities and elaborate irrigation systems, flourished c. 4,000-2,500 BCE. Aryan invaders from the northwest conquered the region around 1,500 BCE, forging the Vedic civilization that dominated the region for over a thousand years. The first Arab invasion, 712 CE, introduced Islam. Present-day Pakistan and India were part of the Mughal Empire from 1526 to 1857. Muslim power faded by the end of the 19th cent. as the British gained control.

Muhammad Ali Jinnah (1876-1948) was the principal architect of Pakistan. When the British withdrew Aug. 14, 1947, India's Islamic majority acquired self-government as Pakistan, with dominion status in the Commonwealth. Pakistan was divided into West Pakistan and East Pakistan, nearly 1,000 mi apart on opposite sides of India. Kashmir, a predominantly Muslim region divided between Pakistan and India, has remained a source of conflict between the two countries.

Rioting and strikes broke out in the East after Pakistan's government, Mar. 1, 1971, postponed the constituent assembly, dominated by supporters of regional autonomy for East Pakistan. Armed conflict between East and West lasted from Mar. to Dec. 1971, with India siding with Easterners, who proclaimed the independent nation of Bangladesh. Thousands were killed, and some 10 mil Easterners fled to India. Full-scale war erupted between India and Pakistan, but Pakistan troops in the East surrendered Dec. 16; Pakistan agreed to a cease-fire in the West Dec. 17. On July 3, 1972, Pakistan and India signed a pact agreeing to troop withdrawals and peaceful conflict resolution.

Dec. 1970 elections brought Zulfikar Ali Bhutto to the presidency Dec. 20, 1971. Bhutto was overthrown in a military coup July 1977. Convicted of complicity in a 1974 political murder, he was executed Apr. 4, 1979. Millions of Afghan refugees flooded into Pakistan after the USSR invaded Afghanistan Dec. 1979. During 2002-10, some 3.6 mil refugees were repatriated, but with conflict in Afghanistan continuing, almost 1.6 mil Afghan refugees were living in Pakistan in mid-2016.

Pres. Mohammad Zia ul-Haq was killed when his plane exploded in Aug. 1988. Following Nov. elections, Benazir Bhutto, daughter of Zulfikar Ali Bhutto, became prime min., making her the first elected woman leader of a Muslim nation. She was accused of corruption and dismissed by the president, Aug. 1990. Bhutto returned to power Oct. 1993 but was dismissed Nov. 1996 amid further corruption charges. Responding to India's nuclear weapons tests, Pakistan conducted its own tests in 1998; the U.S. imposed economic sanctions on both countries.

Prime Min. Nawaz Sharif fired, Oct. 1999, army chief Gen. Pervez Musharraf, whose supporters staged a bloodless coup. Musharraf assumed the presidency June 20, 2001. Following the Sept. 11, 2001, terrorist attacks on the U.S., Pres. Musharraf pledged cooperation with the U.S. in fighting Taliban and al-Qaeda militants within Pakistan and in neighboring Afghanistan. In return, the U.S. waived its 1998 sanctions and offered Pakistan financial aid and debt relief. A referendum Apr. 30, 2002, extended Musharraf's rule for five years; many observers called the vote rigged. Musharraf Feb. 5, 2004, pardoned Pakistan's top nuclear scientist, Abdul Qadeer Khan, who admitted to selling atomic secrets to Iran, Libya, and North Korea. An earthquake that rocked Pakistan and the Pakistani-held region of Kashmir Oct. 8, 2005, killed about 80,000 people.

Musharraf's grip weakened in 2007, as his efforts to oust Pakistan's chief justice sparked mass pro-democracy demonstrations. He retained the presidency in an electoral-college vote Oct. 6, 2007, after his main opponents boycotted the election. More than 140 people died Oct. 18 when suicide bombers struck a convoy carrying Benazir Bhutto from the Karachi airport after she spent more than eight years in exile. Musharraf imposed emergency rule Nov. 3 and suspended the constitution while Pakistan's supreme court debated the constitutionality of his reelection. Musharraf gave up his army post Nov. 25, was sworn in as civilian president the next day, and lifted emergency rule Dec. 16. Bhutto was assassinated Dec. 27, 2007, after a rally in Rawalpindi.

Headed by Bhutto's widower, Asif Ali Zardari, the Pakistan Peoples Party led in parliamentary elections Feb. 18, 2008. Musharraf resigned Aug. 18 under threat of impeachment, and Zardari became president Sept. 9. Amid deteriorating security, U.S. and Pakistani forces clashed with the Taliban near the Afghan border, and Islamists carried out new suicide attacks. The government announced Feb. 16, 2009, a truce conceding de facto control of the strategic Swat Valley to the Taliban, but in May, government forces launched an offensive that reclaimed most of the region; the fighting displaced nearly 2 mil civilians. Catastrophic floods and monsoon rains, July-Aug. 2010, inundated one-fifth of Pakistan, leaving more than 1,750 people dead and displacing up to 20 mil.

A decade-long international manhunt came to an end shortly after midnight May 2, 2011, when U.S. commandos killed al-Qaeda leader Osama bin Laden in Abbottabad. The raid, carried out by helicopter from Jalalabad, Afghanistan, was launched without prior warning to Pakistani authorities.

In the worst industrial accident in Pakistan's history, nearly 300 died in a fire that consumed a factory complex in Karachi Sept. 12, 2012. On Oct. 9, 2012, 15-year-old Malala Yousafzai, who advocated for education rights for girls in Pakistan, was shot by the

Taliban, sparking worldwide outrage. After treatment at a British hospital, she resumed her work on behalf of children's rights, for which she shared the 2014 Nobel Peace Prize. The Pakistan military announced, Sept. 12, 2014, that 10 people had been arrested in connection with the shooting; 2 were convicted in Apr. 2015.

Musharraf returned to Pakistan Mar. 24, 2013, to attempt a political comeback. He was indicted in connection with Benazir Bhutto's assassination, Aug. 20, 2013, and charged with treason, Mar. 31, 2014, but he was allowed to leave the country, Mar. 18, 2016. Former Prime Min. Nawaz Sharif was returned to office with May 11, 2013, elections. Mamnoon Hussain won the presidential election July 30, 2013. A terrorist attack on a Peshawar school, Dec. 16, 2014, left about 150 dead. In 2007-14, an estimated 7,500 people died in terrorist attacks. Fighting between Pakistani forces and Islamic extremists resulted in more than 17,000 fatalities, 2007-14.

Terrorist attacks and conflict between Islamic extremists and Pakistani forces, sometimes supported by U.S. drone strikes, continued in 2015-16. A suicide bomber killed about 70 people in a Lahore park, Mar. 27, 2016; a Taliban offshoot group claimed responsibility. An Aug. 8 suicide bombing at a hospital in Quetta killed more than 70; both a Taliban offshoot and ISIS claimed responsibility. Attacks on health workers administering polio vaccine intensified in 2012, in part because of allegations the CIA used vaccination programs as a cover to gather intelligence. The attacks continued in 2016, although increased security for the workers was reducing the number of attacks and new polio cases.

Palau
Republic of Palau

People: Population: 21,347. **Age distrib.:** <15: 19.9%; 65+: 7.7%. **Growth:** 0.4%. **Migrants:** 26.6%. **Pop. density:** 120.5 per sq mi, 46.5 per sq km. **Urban:** 87.6%. **Ethnic groups:** Palauan (Micronesian with Malayan/Melanesian admixtures) 72.5%, Filipino 16.3%, other Asian 3.4%, other Micronensian 2.4%. **Languages:** Palauan (official on most islands), English (official), Filipino. **Religions:** Roman Catholic 49.4%, Protestant 30.9%, Modekngei (indigenous to Palau) 8.7%.

Geography: Total area: 177 sq mi, 459 sq km; **Land area:** 177 sq mi, 459 sq km. **Location:** Archipelago (26 islands, more than 300 islets) in W Pacific O., about 530 mi SE of the Philippines. Micronesia to E, Indonesia to S. **Topography:** A mountainous main island and low coral atolls, usually fringed with large barrier reefs. **Arable land:** 2.2%. **Capital:** Ngerulmud.

Government: Type: Presidential republic in free association with U.S. **Head of state and gov.:** Pres. Tommy Remengesau; b. 1956; in office: Jan. 17, 2013. **Local divisions:** 16 states. **Defense budget/active troops:** NA.

Economy: Industries: tourism, craft items, constr., garment making. **Chief crops:** coconuts, copra, cassava, sweet potatoes. **Natural resources:** forests, minerals (espec. gold), marine prods., deep-seabed minerals. **Water:** NA. **Labor force:** agric. 20%. **Unemployment:** NA.

Finance: Monetary unit: U.S. Dollar (USD) (1.00 = $1 U.S.). **GDP:** $272 mil (incl. U.S. subsidy); **per capita GDP:** $15,100; **GDP growth:** 9.4%. **Imports** (2014): $177.7 mil. **Exports** (2014): $19.1 mil. **Tourism:** $127 mil. **Budget** (2012 est.): $97.5 mil. **Inflation:** 2.2%.

Transport: Airports: 1.
Communications: Telephone: 33.8 per 100 pop. **Mobile:** 111.5 per 100 pop. **Broadband:** NA. **Internet** (2004): 27%.

Health: Expend.: 9%. **Life expect.:** 69.9 male; 76.5 female. **Births:** 11.2 per 1,000 pop. **Deaths:** 8.0 per 1,000 pop. **Infant mortality:** 10.9 per 1,000 live births. **Undernourished:** NA. **HIV:** NA.

Education: Compulsory: ages 6-17. **Literacy:** 99.5%.
Embassy: 1701 Pennsylvania Ave. NW, Ste. 300, 20036; 452-6814.
Website: palaugov.pw

Spain acquired the Palau Islands, 1886, and sold them to Germany, 1899. Japan seized them in 1914. U.S. forces occupied the islands in 1944; in 1947, they became part of the U.S.-administered UN Trust Territory of the Pacific Islands. In 1981, Palau became an autonomous republic. It ratified a compact of free association with the U.S. in 1993 and became an independent nation, Oct. 1, 1994. Oct. 2015 legislation provided for the creation of a 193,000 sq mi marine sanctuary, in which fishing and mineral development would be prohibited.

Panama
Republic of Panama

People: Population: 3,705,246. **Age distrib.:** <15: 26.7%; 65+: 8.2%. **Growth:** 1.3%. **Migrants:** 4.7%. **Pop. density:** 129.1 per sq mi, 49.8 per sq km. **Urban:** 66.9%. **Ethnic groups:** mestizo (mixed Amerindian/white) 65%, Native American (incl. Ngabe 7.6%, Kuna 2.4%) 12.3%, black or African descent 9.2%, mulatto 6.8%, white 6.7%. **Languages:** Spanish (official), indigenous langs. **Religions:** Roman Catholic 85%, Protestant 15%.

Geography: Total area: 29,120 sq mi, 75,420 sq km; **Land area:** 28,703 sq mi, 74,340 sq km. **Location:** Central America.

Costa Rica on W, Colombia on E. **Topography:** Two mountain ranges run length of isthmus. Tropical rain forests cover the Caribbean coast and E. **Arable land:** 7.6%. **Capital:** Panama City, 1,708,239.

Government: Type: Presidential republic. **Head of state and gov.:** Pres. Juan Carlos Varela; b. 1963; in office: July 1, 2014. **Local divisions:** 10 provinces, 3 indigenous territories. **Defense budget:** $656 mil. **Active troops:** No armed forces. 12,000 paramilitary only.

Economy: Industries: constr., brewing, cement and other constr. materials, sugar milling. **Chief crops:** bananas, rice, corn, coffee, sugarcane, vegetables. **Natural resources:** copper, mahogany forests, shrimp, hydropower. **Water:** 35,454 cu m per capita. **Electricity prod.:** 8.7 bil kWh. **Labor force:** agric. 17%, industry 18.6%, services 64.4%. **Unemployment:** 4.3%.

Finance: Monetary unit: Balboa (PAB) (1.00 = $1 U.S.). **GDP:** $87.2 bil; **per capita GDP:** $21,800; **GDP growth:** 5.8%. **Imports:** $23.3 bil; U.S. 25.9%, China 9.6%, Mexico 5.1%. **Exports:** $15.9 bil; U.S. 19.7%, Germany 13.2%, Costa Rica 7.7%, China 5.9%. Import/export figures incl. Colón Free Zone. **Tourism:** $4.2 bil. **Budget:** $11.4 bil. **Inflation:** 0.1%.

Transport: Railways: 48 mi. **Motor vehicles:** 170.5 per 1,000 pop. **Airports:** 57.
Communications: Telephone: 15.6 per 100 pop. **Mobile:** 174.2 per 100 pop. **Broadband:** 29.5 per 100 pop. **Internet:** 51.2%.

Health: Expend.: 8%. **Life expect.:** 75.8 male; 81.6 female. **Births:** 18.1 per 1,000 pop. **Deaths:** 4.9 per 1,000 pop. **Infant mortality:** 10.1 per 1,000 live births. **Undernourished:** 9.5%. **HIV:** 0.7%.

Education: Compulsory: ages 6-14. **Literacy:** 95%.
Embassy: 2862 McGill Ter. NW 20007; 483-1407.
Website: www.presidencia.gob.pa

The coast of Panama was sighted by Rodrigo de Bastidas, sailing with Columbus for Spain in 1501, and was visited by Columbus in 1502. Vasco Núñez de Balboa crossed the isthmus and "discovered" the Pacific Ocean, Sept. 13, 1513. Spanish colonies were ravaged by Francis Drake, 1572-95, and Henry Morgan, 1668-71. Morgan destroyed the old city of Panama, which was founded in 1519. Freed from Spain, Panama joined Colombia in 1821.

Panama declared independence from Colombia Nov. 3, 1903, and granted use, occupation, and control of the Canal Zone to the U.S. Feb. 26, 1904. The U.S.-built Panama Canal opened Aug. 15, 1914. A 1978 treaty provided for a gradual takeover by Panama of the canal. The U.S. handed over control Dec. 31, 1999. A $5.3-bil project to expand the Panama Canal was approved by national referendum Oct. 22, 2006. Construction began Sept. 3, 2007; the first ship crossed the canal's new wider channel June 26, 2016.

Pres. Eric Arturo Delvalle was ousted by the National Assembly, Feb. 26, 1988, after he tried to fire Gen. Manuel Antonio Noriega, who was under a U.S. indictment on drug charges. U.S. troops invaded Panama Dec. 20, 1989, and Noriega surrendered Jan. 3, 1990. After two decades in a U.S. prison, Noriega was extradited to France Apr. 26, 2010; he was convicted of money laundering July 7 and received a 7-year sentence. France extradited him to Panama, Dec. 11, 2011, to serve a 20-year sentence for human rights violations. Juan Carlos Varela of the Panameñista Party won the May 4, 2014, presidential election. Information published beginning Apr. 3, 2016, from "Panama Papers" documents—leaked from a Panama City law firm—linked public officials and others in various countries to offshore bank accounts and companies created to conceal wealth or avoid taxes.

Papua New Guinea
Independent State of Papua New Guinea

People: Population: 6,791,317. **Age distrib.:** <15: 33.9%; 65+: 4.2%. **Growth:** 1.8%. **Migrants:** 0.3%. **Pop. density:** 38.8 per sq mi, 15 per sq km. **Urban:** 13%. **Ethnic groups:** Melanesian, Papuan, Negrito, Micronesian, Polynesian. **Languages:** Tok Pisin, English, Hiri Motu (all official); some 836 indigenous langs. (most spoken by fewer than 1,000). **Religions:** Protestant 69.4% (incl. Evangelical Lutheran 19.5%, United Church 11.5%, Seventh-day Adventist 10%), Roman Catholic 27%.

Geography: Total area: 178,704 sq mi, 462,840 sq km; **Land area:** 174,850 sq mi, 452,860 sq km. **Location:** SE Asia; E half of island of New Guinea and about 600 nearby islands. Indonesia on W, Australia on S. **Topography:** Thickly forested mountains cover much of center, with lowlands along the coasts. Incl. some islands of Bismarck and Solomon groups, such as Admiralty Isls., New Ireland, New Britain, and Bougainville. **Arable land:** 0.7%. **Capital:** Port Moresby, 352,625.

Government: Type: Parliamentary democracy under constitutional monarchy. **Head of state:** Queen Elizabeth II, rep. by Gov.-Gen. Sir Michael Ogio; b. 1942; in office: Feb. 25, 2011. **Head of gov.:** Prime Min. Peter O'Neill; b. 1965; in office: Aug. 2, 2011. **Local divisions:** 20 provinces, 1 autonomous region, 1 district. **Defense budget:** $100 mil. **Active troops:** 1,900.

Economy: Industries: copra crushing, palm oil proc., plywood prod., wood chip prod., mining, crude oil and petroleum prods.

Chief crops: coffee, cocoa, copra, palm kernels, tea, sugar, rubber, sweet potatoes. **Natural resources:** gold, copper, silver, nat. gas, timber, oil, fisheries. **Water:** 105,132 cu m per capita. **Crude oil reserves:** 0.2 bil bbls. **Electricity prod.:** 3.2 bil kWh. **Labor force:** agric. 85%. **Unemployment:** 2.5%.

Finance: Monetary unit: Kina (PGK) (3.17 = $1 U.S.). **GDP:** $20.5 bil; **per capita GDP:** $2,700; **GDP growth:** 9%. **Imports:** $3.3 bil; Australia 25.9%, China 20%, Singapore 12.6%, Malaysia 7.2%. **Exports:** $8.7 bil; Japan 17.4%, Australia 15.9%, China 12.1%. **Tourism:** $3 mil. **Budget:** $5.6 bil. **Inflation:** 6%. **Transport: Motor vehicles:** 21.6 per 1,000 pop. **Airports:** 21. **Communications: Telephone:** 2 per 100 pop. **Mobile:** 46.6 per 100 pop. **Broadband:** NA. **Internet:** 7.9%.

Health: Expend.: 4.3%. **Life expect.:** 65.0 male; 69.5 female. **Births:** 24.0 per 1,000 pop. **Deaths:** 6.5 per 1,000 pop. **Infant mortality:** 37.4 per 1,000 live births. **Undernourished:** NA. **HIV:** 0.8%.

Education: Compulsory: NA. **Literacy:** 63.4%.

Embassy: 1779 Massachusetts Ave. NW, Ste. 805, 20036; 745-3680.

Website: www.pm.gov.pg

Human remains dating back at least 10,000 years have been found in the interior of New Guinea. European colonization began in the 19th cent., when the Dutch took control of the island's western half (now part of Indonesia). The southern half of eastern New Guinea was claimed by Britain in 1884 and transferred to Australia in 1905. Germany claimed the northern half in 1884, but Australia captured it in WWI, receiving a League of Nations mandate and later a UN trusteeship. The two territories were administered jointly after 1949; gained self-government Dec. 1, 1973; and became independent Sept. 16, 1975.

Secessionist rebels clashed with government forces on Bougainville 1988-97, claiming some 20,000 lives. A Bougainville autonomy agreement was signed Aug. 30, 2001. Sir Michael Somare, the nation's first prime min. (1975-80, 1982-85), regained the office in 2002 and was reelected by parliament Aug. 13, 2007. Somare took indefinite medical leave Apr. 2011; parliament, Aug. 2, elected Peter O'Neill as permanent replacement, but the Supreme Court, Dec. 12, ruled that action illegal. After June-July 2012 parliamentary elections, the new parliament elected O'Neill prime min., Aug. 3, 2012. O'Neill's refusal to answer 2014 corruption charges prompted weeks of protests in 2016. Police fired on student demonstrators, June 8, seriously wounding 8; a student was killed during a later protest.

The Supreme Court, Apr. 26, 2016, ruled illegal Australia's detention center on Manus Island for migrants intercepted trying to reach Australia by boat; the Papua New Guinea and Australian governments announced, Aug. 17, that the center would be closed.

The country has extensive energy resources. After the initial phase of a natural gas pipeline project was completed, shipments of liquefied natural gas through a new processing and shipping facility near Port Moresby began in May 2014.

Paraguay
Republic of Paraguay

People: Population: 6,862,812. **Age distrib.:** <15: 25%; 65+: 6.9%. **Growth:** 1.2%. **Migrants:** 2.4%. **Pop. density:** 44.7 per sq mi, 17.3 per sq km. **Urban:** 59.9%. **Ethnic groups:** mestizo (mixed Spanish/Amerindian) 95%. **Languages:** Spanish, Guaraní (both official). **Religions:** Roman Catholic 89.6%, Protestant 6.2%.

Geography: Total area: 157,048 sq mi, 406,752 sq km; **Land area:** 153,399 sq mi, 397,302 sq km. **Location:** Landlocked country in central S America. Bolivia on N, Argentina on S, Brazil on E. **Topography:** Paraguay R. bisects country. Fertile plains, wooded slopes, grasslands to E. Gran Chaco plain, with marshes and scrub trees, to W. Extreme W is arid. **Arable land:** 11.3%. **Capital:** Asunción, 2,405,588.

Government: Type: Presidential republic. **Head of state and gov.:** Pres. Horacio Cartes; b. 1956; in office: Aug. 15, 2013. **Local divisions:** 17 departments, 1 capital city. **Defense budget:** $322 mil. **Active troops:** 10,650.

Economy: Industries: sugar, cement, textiles, beverages, wood prods., steel. **Chief crops:** cotton, sugarcane, soybeans, corn, wheat, tobacco, cassava, fruits, vegetables. **Natural resources:** hydropower, timber, iron ore, manganese, limestone. **Water:** 58,412 cu m per capita. **Electricity prod.:** 60 bil kWh. **Labor force:** agric. 26.5%, industry 18.5%, services 55%. **Unemployment:** 4.5%.

Finance: Monetary unit: Guarani (PYG) (5,519.00 = $1 U.S.). **GDP:** $61 bil; **per capita GDP:** $8,700; **GDP growth:** 3%. **Imports:** $9.6 bil; Brazil 25.4%, China 23.7%, Argentina 14.8%, U.S. 7.9%. **Exports:** $8.4 bil; Brazil 31.7%, Russia 9.1%, Chile 7.1%, Argentina 7%. **Tourism:** $484 mil. **Budget:** $6.2 bil. **Inflation:** 3.1%.

Transport: Railways: 19 mi. **Motor vehicles:** 67.8 per 1,000 pop. **Airports:** 15.

Communications: Telephone: 5.5 per 100 pop. **Mobile:** 105.4 per 100 pop. **Broadband:** 4.2 per 100 pop. **Internet:** 44.4%.

Health: Expend.: 9.8%. **Life expect.:** 74.5 male; 80.0 female. **Births:** 16.5 per 1,000 pop. **Deaths:** 4.7 per 1,000 pop. **Infant mortality:** 19.4 per 1,000 live births. **Undernourished:** 10.4%. **HIV:** 0.4%.

Education: Compulsory: ages 6-14. **Literacy:** 95.5%.

Embassy: 2400 Massachusetts Ave. NW 20008; 483-6960.

Website: www.presidencia.gov.py

Guaraní Indians preceded Europeans in Paraguay, which was visited by Sebastian Cabot in 1527 and became a Spanish possession in 1535. Paraguay gained independence from Spain in 1811. It lost half its population and much of its territory to Brazil, Uruguay, and Argentina in the War of the Triple Alliance, 1865-70. Large areas were won from Bolivia in the Chaco War, 1932-35. Gen. Alfredo Stroessner held the presidency 1954-89, until his ouster in a military coup.

Power struggles ensued between civilian and military leaders, 1993-97. The assassination of Vice Pres. Luis María Argaña, Mar. 23, 1999, was widely attributed to Pres. Raúl Cubas Grau and triggered protests and an impeachment vote; Cubas resigned Mar. 28 and was succeeded by Senate leader Luis Angel González Macchi. An attempted military coup was suppressed May 18, 2000.

Mass protests over the depressed economy led to the proclamation of a state of emergency July 15, 2002. Nicanor Duarte Frutos of the conservative Colorado Party won the presidency, Apr. 27, 2003.

Paraguayan authorities blamed a leftist group for the Sept. 2004 kidnapping and subsequent murder of Cecilia Cubas, daughter of former Pres. Cubas. Fernando Lugo, a former Catholic cleric known as the "bishop of the poor," won a presidential election Apr. 20, 2008, ending over six decades of Colorado rule. On June 22, 2012, Lugo was removed from office after his handling of a dispute between landless peasants and police left 17 dead June 15. Colorado candidate Horacio Cartes, a former tobacco magnate, was elected president Apr. 21, 2013. Pope Francis visited Paraguay, July 10-12, 2015; in public remarks he urged combating corruption and drug trafficking.

Peru
Republic of Peru

People: Population: 30,741,062. **Age distrib.:** <15: 26.6%; 65+: 7.2%. **Growth:** 1%. **Migrants:** 0.3%. **Pop. density:** 62.2 per sq mi, 24 per sq km. **Urban:** 78.9%. **Ethnic groups:** Amerindian 45%; mestizo (mixed Amerindian/white) 37%; white 15%; black, Japanese, Chinese, other 3%. **Languages:** Spanish, Quechua, Aymara (all official). **Religions:** Roman Catholic 81.3%, Evangelical 12.5%, none 2.9%.

Geography: Total area: 496,225 sq mi, 1,285,216 sq km; **Land area:** 494,209 sq mi, 1,279,996 sq km. **Location:** Pacific coast of S America. Ecuador, Colombia on N; Brazil, Bolivia on E; Chile on S. **Topography:** An arid coastal strip, 10-100 mi wide. The Andes cover one-quarter of land area. The uplands are well-watered, as are the eastern slopes reaching the Amazon Basin, which covers half of country. **Arable land:** 3.2%. **Capital:** Lima, 10,072,359. **Cities:** Arequipa, 861,622.

Government: Type: Presidential republic. **Head of state and gov:** Pres. Pedro Pablo Kuczynski; b. 1938; in office July 28, 2016. **Local divisions:** 25 regions, 1 province. **Defense budget:** $2.3 bil. **Active troops:** 81,000.

Economy: Industries: mining, refining of minerals; steel, metal fabrication; petroleum extraction and refining, nat. gas and nat. gas liquefaction; fishing and fish proc., cement, glass, textiles. **Chief crops:** artichokes, asparagus, avocados, blueberries, coffee, cocoa, cotton, sugarcane, rice, potatoes, corn, plantains, grapes, oranges and other fruits, coca, tomatoes, barley, medicinal plants, quinoa. **Natural resources:** copper, silver, gold, petroleum, timber, fish, iron ore, coal, phosphate, potash, hydropower, nat. gas. **Water:** 59,916 cu m per capita. **Crude oil reserves:** 0.7 bil bbls. **Electricity prod.:** 42 bil kWh. **Labor force:** agric. 25.8%, industry 17.4%, services 56.8%. **Unemployment:** 4.2%.

Finance: Monetary unit: Sol (PEN) (3.38 = $1 U.S.). **GDP:** $389.1 bil; **per capita GDP:** $12,200; **GDP growth:** 3.3%. **Imports:** $39 bil; China 22.7%, U.S. 20.7%, Brazil 5.1%. **Exports:** $36.4 bil; China 22.1%, U.S. 15.2%, Switzerland 8.1%, Canada 7%. **Tourism:** $3.3 bil. **Budget:** $63.3 bil. **Inflation:** 3.6%.

Transport: Railways: 1,152 mi. **Motor vehicles:** 71.2 per 1,000 pop. **Airports:** 59.

Communications: Telephone: 9.3 per 100 pop. **Mobile:** 109.9 per 100 pop. **Broadband:** 13.7 per 100 pop. **Internet:** 40.9%.

Health: Expend.: 5.5%. **Life expect.:** 71.7 male; 75.9 female. **Births:** 18.0 per 1,000 pop. **Deaths:** 6.0 per 1,000 pop. **Infant mortality:** 19.0 per 1,000 live births. **Undernourished:** 7.5%. **HIV:** 0.3%.

Education: Compulsory: ages 5-16. **Literacy:** 94.4%.

Embassy: 1700 Massachusetts Ave. NW 20036; 833-9860.

Website: www.peru.gob.pe

The powerful Inca Empire had its seat at Cuzco in the Andes and covered much of S America. A civil war had weakened the empire when Spaniard Francisco Pizarro began raiding Peru for its wealth, 1532. In 1533 he executed the Inca ruler, Atahualpa, and enslaved the people.

José de San Martín captured Lima from the Spanish in 1821; Simón Bolívar routed Spanish forces in 1824, and for much of the 19th cent., the country was governed by military leaders. Chile defeated Peru in the War of the Pacific, 1879-83. Right-wing groups allied with the military and the leftist APRA party vied for power in the first half of the 20th cent.

Peru returned to democratic leadership in 1980 but was plagued by economic problems and by leftist Shining Path (Sendero Luminoso) guerrillas. Conflict between guerrillas and government troops, 1980-2000, killed more than 69,000 people, mostly Andean Indians.

Elected president in June 1990, Alberto Fujimori, the son of Japanese immigrants, dissolved the National Congress, suspended parts of the constitution, and initiated press censorship, Apr. 1992. The leader of Shining Path was captured Sept. 12. Fujimori won reelection in 1995 and 2000, but his repressive antiterrorism tactics drew international criticism.

Scandals involving top aide and intelligence chief Vladimiro Montesinos led Fujimori to resign Nov. 20, 2000; instead of accepting his resignation, Congress ousted him as "morally unfit." Montesinos was captured in Venezuela June 23, 2001; extradited to Peru, he was convicted in a series of criminal trials. Fujimori was arrested in Chile, Nov. 7, 2005, and extradited to Peru, Sept. 22, 2007. He was convicted in three separate proceedings, 2007-09, on charges that included complicity in a paramilitary death squad's killing of at least 25 people, 1991-92. He was convicted, Jan. 8, 2015, of misusing public funds during his 2000 campaign.

Alan García, whose first term as president, 1985-90, ended with the country facing hyperinflation and guerrilla war, won a presidential runoff election June 4, 2006. In a presidential runoff June 5, 2011, Ollanta Humala Tasso, a leftist former military officer, defeated Keiko Fujimori, daughter of jailed former Pres. Fujimori. Former Finance Min. Pedro Pablo Kuczynski narrowly defeated Keiko Fujimori in a June 5, 2016, presidential runoff.

Philippines
Republic of the Philippines

People: Population: 102,624,209. **Age distrib.:** <15: 33.7%; 65+: 4.4%. **Growth:** 1.6%. **Migrants:** 0.2%. **Pop. density:** 891.4 per sq mi, 344.2 per sq km. **Urban:** 44.3%. **Ethnic groups:** Tagalog 28.1%, Cebuano 13.1%, Ilocano 9%, Bisaya/Binisaya 7.6%, Hiligaynon Ilonggo 7.5%, Bikol 6%, Waray 3.4%. **Languages:** Filipino (based on Tagalog), English (both official); 8 major dialects (incl. Tagalog). **Religions:** Catholic 82.9% (incl. Roman Catholic 80.9%), Muslim 5%, Evangelical 2.8%, Iglesia ni Kristo 2.3%.

Geography: Total area: 115,831 sq mi, 300,000 sq km; **Land area:** 115,124 sq mi, 298,170 sq km. **Location:** Archipelago in SE Asia. Malaysia, Indonesia on S; Taiwan on N. **Topography:** Comprises some 7,107 islands stretching 1,100 mi N-S. About 95% of area and pop. are on 11 largest islands, which are mountainous, except for the heavily indented coastlines and central plain on Luzon. **Arable land:** 18.7%. **Capital:** Manila, 13,131,483 (figure is for natl. capital region). **Cities:** Davao City, 1,661,721; Cebu City, 965,363; Zamboanga City, 959,378.

Government: Type: Presidential republic. **Head of state and gov.:** Pres. Rodrigo Roa Duterte; b. 1945; in office: June 30, 2016. **Local divisions:** 80 provinces, 39 chartered cities. **Defense budget:** $2.2 bil. **Active troops:** 125,000.

Economy: Industries: electronics assembly, garments, footwear, pharmaceuticals, chemicals, wood prods., food proc. **Chief crops:** sugarcane, coconuts, rice, corn, bananas, cassava, pineapples, mangoes. **Natural resources:** timber, petroleum, nickel, cobalt, silver, gold, salt, copper. **Water:** 4,757 cu m per capita. **Crude oil reserves:** 0.1 bil bbls. **Electricity prod.:** 72 bil kWh. **Labor force:** agric. 29%, industry 16%, services 55%. **Unemployment:** 7.1%.

Finance: Monetary unit: Peso (PHP) (46.68 = $1 U.S.). **GDP:** $741 bil; **per capita GDP:** $7,300; **GDP growth:** 5.8%. **Imports:** $66.7 bil; China 16.2%, U.S. 10.8%, Japan 9.6%, Singapore 7%, South Korea 6.5%, Thailand 6.4%. **Exports:** $58.7 bil; Japan 21.1%, U.S. 15%, China 10.9%, Hong Kong 10.6%, Singapore 6.2%. **Tourism:** $5.3 bil. **Budget:** $47.8 bil. **Inflation:** 1.4%.

Transport: Railways: 618 mi. **Motor vehicles:** 35.3 per 1,000 pop. **Airports:** 89.

Communications: Telephone: 3 per 100 pop. **Mobile:** 118.1 per 100 pop. **Broadband:** 28 per 100 pop. **Internet:** 40.7%.

Health: Expend.: 4.7%. **Life expect.:** 65.7 male; 72.9 female. **Births:** 24.0 per 1,000 pop. **Deaths:** 6.1 per 1,000 pop. **Infant mortality:** 21.9 per 1,000 live births. **Undernourished:** 13.5%. **HIV:** <0.1%.

Education: Compulsory: ages 5-17. **Literacy:** 96.6%.

Embassy: 1600 Massachusetts Ave. NW 20036; 467-9300.

Website: www.gov.ph

Originally inhabited by Malay peoples, the archipelago was visited by Magellan, 1521. The Spanish founded Manila, 1571. Spain ceded the islands, named for King Philip II of Spain, to the U.S. for $20 mil, 1898, following the Spanish-American War. U.S. troops suppressed a guerrilla uprising in a brutal war, 1899-

1905. Japan attacked the Philippines Dec. 8, 1941, and occupied the islands during WWII. Independence was proclaimed, July 4, 1946. A republic was established.

The repressive and corrupt regime of Pres. Ferdinand Marcos and his wife, Imelda, was in place 1965-86. The assassination of prominent opposition leader Benigno S. Aquino Jr., Aug. 21, 1983, sparked calls for Marcos's resignation. Marcos defeated Corazon Aquino, widow of the slain opposition leader, Feb. 16, 1986, in an allegedly fraudulent election. Mass protests and international pressure forced Marcos to flee the country Feb. 25, and Aquino became president.

Her government was plagued by a weak economy, widespread poverty, Communist and Muslim insurgencies, and lukewarm military support; an attempted coup Dec. 1, 1989, was defeated. Fidel Ramos won the May 1992 presidential election. The U.S. vacated the Subic Bay Naval Station in late 1992, ending its long military presence. However, a 2014 agreement gave U.S. forces increased access to Philippines bases. Some Muslim separatist guerrillas refused to abide by a cease-fire agreement signed Jan. 30, 1994, so a new treaty providing for expansion and development of an autonomous Muslim region on Mindanao was signed Sept. 2, 1996; the rebellion had claimed more than 120,000 lives since 1972.

Joseph (Erap) Estrada, a former movie actor, won the presidential election, May 11, 1998, but was impeached on bribery and corruption charges Nov. 13, 2000. Vice Pres. Gloria Macapagal Arroyo became president Jan. 20, 2001. Pres. Arroyo won reelection May 10, 2004. Former Pres. Estrada was convicted, Sept. 12, 2007, of taking more than $85 mil in bribes and kickbacks while in office; Pres. Arroyo pardoned him Oct. 25. Benigno "NoyNoy" Aquino III, the son of former Pres. Aquino (who died Aug. 1, 2009), defeated Estrada in the May 10, 2010, presidential election. Former Pres. Arroyo, who was serving in Congress, was arrested Oct. 4, 2012, on corruption charges. The Supreme Court, citing insufficient evidence, ordered, July 19, 2016, that she be released.

The government, Oct. 15, 2012, signed a new peace deal with Muslim rebels on Mindanao; violence had persisted after the 1996 accord. Yet another peace agreement, providing for a large measure of autonomy for Mindanao, was signed by the government and Moro Islamic Liberation Front, Mar. 27, 2014. The Abu Sayyaf Islamist guerrilla group rejected the accord. Abu Sayyaf, which claimed allegiance to ISIS, staged a number of kidnappings of foreigners; two Canadian hostages were beheaded, in Apr. and June 2016.

Congress voted, Dec. 17, 2012, to provide free contraceptives at health clinics, despite objections from many of the nation's Catholics. Typhoon Haiyan, with winds up to 195 mph, struck the Philippines Nov. 8, 2013, killing more than 6,200 people and displacing over 4 mil. Vowing a tough crackdown on drug crime, Rodrigo Duterte was elected president, May 9, 2016. As of Sept. 30, 2016, perhaps as many as 3,000 drug suspects had been killed by police or vigilantes since Duterte took office, including 1,120 acknowledged police killings. By Sept., about 687,000 drug users or dealers turned themselves in to police; some 15,000 were arrested. Duterte's government completed a new cease-fire agreement with Communist rebels, Aug. 26, 2016.

Poland
Republic of Poland

People: Population: 38,523,261. **Age distrib.:** <15: 14.7%; 65+: 16.3%. **Growth:** -0.1%. **Migrants:** 1.6%. **Pop. density:** 327.9 per sq mi, 126.6 per sq km. **Urban:** 60.5%. **Ethnic groups:** Polish 96.9%. **Languages:** Polish (official). **Religions:** Catholic 87.2%.

Geography: Total area: 120,728 sq mi, 312,685 sq km; **Land area:** 117,474 sq mi, 304,255 sq km. **Location:** On Baltic Sea in E central Europe. Germany on W; Czech Rep., Slovakia on S; Lithuania, Belarus, Ukraine on E; Russia on N. **Topography:** Mostly lowlands forming part of the Northern European Plain. The Carpathian Mts. along S border rise to 8,200 ft. **Arable land:** 35.2%. **Capital:** Warsaw, 1,726,836. **Cities:** Kraków, 760,226.

Government: Type: Parliamentary republic. **Head of state:** Pres. Andrzej Duda; b. 1972; in office: Aug. 6, 2015. **Head of gov.:** Prime Min. Beata Szydło; b. 1963; in office: Nov. 16, 2015. **Local divisions:** 16 provinces. **Defense budget:** $10.3 bil. **Active troops:** 99,300.

Economy: Industries: machine building, iron and steel, coal mining, chemicals, shipbuilding, food proc., glass, beverages, textiles. **Chief crops:** potatoes, fruits, vegetables, wheat. **Natural resources:** coal, sulfur, copper, nat. gas, silver, lead, salt, amber. **Water:** 1,567 cu m per capita. **Crude oil reserves:** 0.1 bil bbls. **Electricity prod.:** 160 bil kWh. **Labor force:** agric. 12.6%, industry 30.4%, services 57%. **Unemployment:** 9.2%.

Finance: Monetary unit: Zloty (PLN) (3.90 = $1 U.S.). **GDP:** $1 tril; **per capita GDP:** $26,500; **GDP growth:** 3.6%. **Imports:** $187.5 bil; Germany 27.6%, China 7.5%, Russia 7.2%, Netherlands 5.9%, Italy 5.2%. **Exports:** $190.2 bil; Germany 27.1%, UK 6.8%, Czech Republic 6.6%, France 5.5%. **Tourism:** $9.7 bil. **Budget:** $90.2 bil. **Inflation:** -1%.

Transport: Railways: 12,326 mi. **Motor vehicles:** 633.6 per 1,000 pop. **Airports:** 87.

Communications: Telephone: 11.1 per 100 pop. **Mobile:** 148.7 per 100 pop. **Broadband:** 62.3 per 100 pop. **Internet:** 68%.
Health: Expend.: 6.4%. **Life expect.:** 73.7 male; 81.7 female.
Births: 9.6 per 1,000 pop. **Deaths:** 10.3 per 1,000 pop. **Infant mortality:** 4.5 per 1,000 live births. **Undernourished:** <5%. **HIV:** NA.
Education: Compulsory: ages 6-17. **Literacy:** 99.8%.
Embassy: 2640 16th St. NW 20009; 234-3800.
Website: www.poland.gov.pl

Slavic tribes in the area were converted to Latin Christianity in the 10th cent. Poland was a great power from the 14th to the 17th cent. In three partitions (1772, 1793, 1795) it was apportioned among Prussia, Russia, and Austria. Overrun by the Austro-German armies in WWI, it declared its independence on Nov. 11, 1918, and was recognized as independent by the Treaty of Versailles, June 28, 1919. Large territories to the east were taken in a war with Russia, 1921.

Germany and the USSR invaded Poland Sept. 1939 and divided the country. During the war, Nazis killed some 6 mil Polish citizens, half of them Jews. In compensation for territory ceded to the USSR when the war ended, Poland received German territory comprising Silesia, Pomerania, West Prussia, and part of East Prussia. Communists, who aligned themselves with the USSR, dominated the 1947 election.

In 12 years of rule by Stalinists, large estates were abolished, industries nationalized, schools secularized, and Roman Catholic prelates jailed. Farm production fell off. Harsh working conditions caused a riot in Poznan, June 28-29, 1956. A new Politburo, committed to a more independent Polish Communism, was named Oct. 1956, with Wladyslaw Gomulka as first secretary of the party. Collectivization of farms was ended. Gomulka agreed to increase religious liberty.

In Dec. 1970 workers in port cities rioted because of price rises and new incentive wage rules. On Dec. 20 Gomulka resigned as party leader; he was succeeded by Edward Gierek. The rules were dropped and price rises revoked.

Independent trade union Solidarity gained strength in the 1980s, organizing strikes and making bold demands. Led by Lech Walesa, Solidarity helped to win political and economic reforms, including free elections, in an Apr. 5, 1989, accord. Candidates endorsed by Solidarity swept the parliamentary elections, June 4. Walesa became president Dec. 22, 1990.

A radical economic program designed to transform the economy into a free-market system led to inflation, unemployment, and a return to the political left in 1993 parliamentary elections. A former Communist, Aleksander Kwasniewski, defeated Walesa in the 1995 presidential election and was reelected 5 years later. A new constitution was approved by referendum May 25, 1997. Poland became a full member of NATO, Mar. 12, 1999, and entered the European Union May 1, 2004. At a July 2016 NATO summit in Warsaw, the alliance agreed to permanently station troops in Poland and other Eastern European countries bordering Russia.

Lech Kaczynski of the conservative Law and Justice (PiS) party won a presidential runoff election Oct. 23, 2005. In July 2006 he appointed his twin brother, Jaroslaw, as prime min. The center-right Civic Platform party, led by Donald Tusk, won parliamentary elections Oct. 21, 2007. Pres. Lech Kaczynski and many senior Polish government officials were among the 96 passengers and crew killed in a plane crash Apr. 10, 2010, near Smolensk, Russia. Parliament Speaker Bronislaw Komorowski, an ally of Prime Min. Tusk, became acting president; he won a full term July 4, 2010. Parliament Speaker Ewa Kopacz became prime min. Sept. 22, 2014, when Tusk was selected president of the European Council. Komorowski was narrowly defeated for reelection by Andrzej Duda of PiS in a May 24, 2015, runoff. PiS won a majority of seats in Oct. 25, 2015, parliamentary elections; Beata Szydlo of PiS became prime min.

Portugal
Portuguese Republic

People: Population: 10,833,816. **Age distrib.:** <15: 15.5%; 65+: 19.1%. **Growth:** 0.1%. **Migrants:** 8.1%. **Pop. density:** 306.8 per sq mi, 118.4 per sq km. **Urban:** 64%. **Ethnic groups:** homogeneous Mediterranean stock. **Languages:** Portuguese, Mirandese (both official). **Religions:** Roman Catholic 81%, none 6.8%.
Geography: Total area: 35,556 sq mi, 92,090 sq km; **Land area:** 35,317 sq mi, 91,470 sq km. **Location:** SW extreme of Europe. Spain on N, E. **Topography:** Tajus R. bisects country NE-SW. N is cool and rainy, mountainous. S is drier, with warm climate and rolling plains. **Arable land:** 12.2%. **Capital:** Lisbon, 2,901,521. **Cities:** Porto, 1,303,977.
Government: Type: Semi-presidential republic. **Head of state:** Pres. Marcelo Rebelo de Sousa; b. 1948; in office: Mar. 9, 2016. **Head of gov.:** Prime Min. António Costa; b. 1961; in office Nov. 24, 2015. **Local divisions:** 18 districts, 2 autonomous regions. **Defense budget:** $2.2 bil. **Active troops:** 32,850.
Economy: Industries: textiles, clothing, footwear, wood and cork, paper and pulp, chemicals, lubricants, automobiles and auto parts, base metals. **Chief crops:** grain, potatoes, tomatoes,

olives, grapes. **Natural resources:** fish, forests (cork), iron ore, copper, zinc, tin, tungsten, silver, gold, uranium, marble, clay, gypsum, salt, hydropower. **Water:** 7,478 cu m per capita. **Electricity prod.:** 48 bil kWh. **Labor force:** agric. 8.6%, industry 23.9%, services 67.5%. **Unemployment:** 14.2%.
Finance: Monetary unit: Euro (EUR) (0.89 = $1 U.S.). **GDP:** $289.8 bil; **per capita GDP:** $27,800; **GDP growth:** 1.5%. **Imports:** $66.4 bil; Spain 32.9%, Germany 12.9%, France 7.4%, Italy 5.4%, Netherlands 5.1%. **Exports:** $57.2 bil; Spain 25%, France 12.1%, Germany 11.8%, UK 6.7%, U.S. 5.2%. **Tourism:** $12.6 bil. **Budget:** $96.8 bil. **Inflation:** 0.5%.
Transport: Railways: 1,911 mi. **Motor vehicles:** 521.9 per 1,000 pop. **Airports:** 43.
Communications: Telephone: 44.1 per 100 pop. **Mobile:** 110.4 per 100 pop. **Broadband:** 45.3 per 100 pop. **Internet:** 68.6%.
Health: Expend.: 9.5%. **Life expect.:** 76.1 male; 82.8 female.
Births: 9.1 per 1,000 pop. **Deaths:** 11.1 per 1,000 pop. **Infant mortality:** 4.4 per 1,000 live births. **Undernourished:** <5%. **HIV:** NA.
Education: Compulsory: ages 6-14. **Literacy:** 95.4%.
Embassy: 2012 Massachusetts Ave. NW 20036; 328-8610.
Website: www.portugal.gov.pt

Portugal, an independent state since the 12th cent., was a kingdom until a 1910 revolution drove out King Manoel II and a republic was proclaimed. Beginning in 1932, Prime Min. Antonio de Oliveira Salazar headed a repressive government. Illness forced his retirement in Sept. 1968.

On Apr. 25, 1974, a military junta led by Gen. Antonio de Spinola seized the government; Spinola became president. The new government granted independence to Guinea-Bissau, Mozambique, Cabo Verde, Angola, and São Tomé and Príncipe. Portugal returned Macao to China on Dec. 20, 1999.

With the economy lagging, Socialists led by Jóse Sócrates gained a parliamentary majority in 2005 and held onto a plurality in 2009. After Portugal was given a 78-bil-euro bailout package from international lenders to avert default, the center-right Social Democratic Party, headed by Pedro Passos Coelho, won parliamentary elections June 2011. Austerity cuts caused widespread protests in Nov. 2012; the Constitutional Court ruled Apr. 5, 2013, that many of the cuts were illegal. Portugal completed loan repayments and exited the bailout program in May 2014. Passos Coelho lost his parliamentary majority in Oct. 4, 2015, elections. Leading an anti-austerity leftist coalition, Socialist António Costa became prime min., Nov. 24, 2015.

Azores Isls., in the Atlantic, 740 mi W of Portugal, have an area of 868 sq mi and a pop. (2014 est.) of 246,353. A 1951 agreement gave the U.S. rights to use defense facilities in the Azores. The **Madeira Isls.**, 350 mi off the NW coast of Africa, have an area of 306 sq mi and a pop. (2014 est.) of 258,686. Both groups were offered partial autonomy in 1976.

Qatar
State of Qatar

People: Population: 2,258,283. **Age distrib.:** <15: 12.6%; 65+: 0.9%. **Growth:** 2.6%. **Migrants:** 75.5%. **Pop. density:** 504.8 per sq mi, 194.9 per sq km. **Urban:** 99.3%. **Ethnic groups:** Arab 40%, Indian 18%, Pakistani 18%, Iranian 10%. **Languages:** Arabic (official), English. **Religions:** Muslim 77.5%, Christian 8.5%.
Geography: Total area: 4,473 sq mi, 11,586 sq km; **Land area:** 4,473 sq mi, 11,586 sq km. **Location:** Middle East, occupying peninsula on W coast of Persian Gulf. Saudi Arabia on S. **Topography:** Mostly flat desert with some limestone ridges; scarce vegetation. **Arable land:** 1.2%. **Capital:** Doha (Ad-Dawhah), 734,407.
Government: Type: Absolute monarchy. **Head of state:** Emir Sheikh Tamim bin Hamad al-Thani; b. 1980; in office: June 25, 2013. **Head of gov.:** Prime Min. Sheikh Abdullah bin Nasser bin Khalifa al-Thani; b. 1959; in office: June 26, 2013. **Local divisions:** 7 municipalities. **Defense budget** (2013): $4.4 bil. **Active troops:** 11,800.
Economy: Industries: liquefied nat. gas, crude oil prod. and refining, ammonia, fertilizers, petrochemicals, steel reinforcing bars. **Chief crops:** fruits, vegetables. **Natural resources:** petroleum, nat. gas, fish. **Water:** 26 cu m per capita. **Crude oil reserves:** 25.2 bil bbls. **Electricity prod.:** 33 bil kWh. **Labor force:** NA. **Unemployment:** 0.3%.
Finance: Monetary unit: Riyal (QAR) (3.64 = $1 U.S.). **GDP:** $319.8 bil; **per capita GDP:** $132,100; **GDP growth:** 3.3%. **Imports:** $37.2 bil; U.S. 13.7%, France 10.1%, UK 9.1%, UAE 7.9%, Germany 7.7%, China 7.4%, Japan 5%. **Exports:** $77.7 bil; South Korea 18.3%, Japan 18.2%, India 12.4%, UAE 8.8%, China 7.5%. **Tourism:** $5 bil. **Budget:** $68.7 bil. **Inflation:** 1.9%.
Transport: Motor vehicles: 172 per 1,000 pop. **Airports:** 4.
Communications: Telephone: 18.2 per 100 pop. **Mobile:** 153.6 per 100 pop. **Broadband:** 106.3 per 100 pop. **Internet:** 92.9%.
Health: Expend.: 2.2%. **Life expect.:** 76.7 male; 80.8 female.
Births: 9.7 per 1,000 pop. **Deaths:** 1.5 per 1,000 pop. **Infant mortality:** 6.2 per 1,000 live births. **Undernourished:** NA. **HIV:** NA.
Education: Compulsory: ages 6-14. **Literacy:** 97.8%.
Embassy: 2555 M St. NW 20037; 274-1600.
Website: portal.www.gov.qa

Qatar was under Bahrain's control until the Ottoman Turks took power, 1872 to 1915. In a treaty signed 1916, Qatar gave Great Britain responsibility for its defense and foreign relations. Qatar declared itself independent, Sept. 1, 1971. Crown Prince Hamad bin Khalifa al-Thani ousted his father, Emir Khalifa bin Hamad al-Thani, June 27, 1995. In municipal elections held Mar. 8, 1999, women participated for the first time as candidates and voters. Sheikh Hamad bin Khalifa al-Thani abdicated in favor of his son, Sheikh Tamim bin Hamad al-Thani, June 25, 2013.

Qatar, a major producer and exporter of oil and natural gas, is one of the world's wealthiest nations per capita. Regular flights in and out of Doha's new Hamad Intl. Airport began in May 2014. Military ties with the U.S. have been expanding. Camp As-Sayliyah, a base near Doha, served as a command center for the U.S.-led invasion of Iraq, Mar. 2003. A 10-yr. defense cooperation agreement was signed, Dec. 10, 2013. Qatar provided support for U.S.-led airstrikes, beginning Sept. 2014, against Sunni extremists in Syria. Qatar joined Saudi-led airstrikes, beginning Mar. 2015, against Shiite Houthi rebels in Yemen.

Romania

People: Population: 21,599,736. **Age distrib.:** <15: 14.4%; 65+: 16.1%. **Growth:** −0.3%. **Migrants:** 1.2%. **Pop. density:** 243.3 per sq mi, 94 per sq km. **Urban:** 54.7%. **Ethnic groups:** Romanian 83.4%, Hungarian 6.1%, Roma 3.1%. **Languages:** Romanian (official), Hungarian. **Religions:** Eastern Orthodox 81.9%, Protestant 6.4%, Roman Catholic 4.3%.

Geography: Total area: 92,043 sq mi, 238,391 sq km; **Land area:** 88,761 sq mi, 229,891 sq km. **Location:** SE Europe, on the Black Sea. Moldova on E, Ukraine on N, Hungary and Serbia on W, Bulgaria on S. **Topography:** The Carpathian Mts. surround the N central Transylvanian plateau. The lower reaches of the Danube river system flow through plains S and E of the mountains. **Arable land:** 38%. **Capital:** Bucharest, 1,865,107.

Government: Type: Semi-presidential republic. **Head of state:** Pres. Klaus Iohannis; b. 1959; in office: Dec. 21, 2014. **Head of gov.:** Prime Min. Dacian Ciolos; b. 1969; in office: Nov. 17, 2015. **Local divisions:** 41 counties, 1 municipality. **Defense budget:** $2.5 bil. **Active troops:** 70,500.

Economy: Industries: elec. machinery and equip., auto assembly, textiles and footwear, light machinery, metallurgy, chemicals, food proc. **Chief crops:** wheat, corn, barley, sugar beets, sunflower seeds, potatoes, grapes. **Natural resources:** petroleum (reserves declining), timber, nat. gas, coal, iron ore, salt, hydropower. **Water:** 10,866 cu m per capita. **Crude oil reserves:** 0.6 bil bbls. **Electricity prod.:** 53 bil kWh. **Labor force:** agric. 28.3%, industry 28.9%, services 42.8%. **Unemployment:** 7%.

Finance: Monetary unit: Leu (RON) (3.98 = $1 U.S.). **GDP:** $413.8 bil; **per capita GDP:** $20,800; **GDP growth:** 3.7%. **Imports:** $63.1 bil; Germany 19.8%, Italy 10.9%, Hungary 8%, France 5.6%. **Exports:** $54.5 bil; Germany 19.8%, Italy 12.5%, France 6.8%, Hungary 5.4%. **Tourism:** $1.7 bil. **Budget:** $61 bil. **Inflation:** −0.6%.

Transport: Railways: 7,002 mi. **Motor vehicles:** 279.6 per 1,000 pop. **Airports:** 26.

Communications: Telephone: 19.8 per 100 pop. **Mobile:** 107.1 per 100 pop. **Broadband:** 49.4 per 100 pop. **Internet:** 55.8%.

Health: Expend.: 5.6%. **Life expect.:** 71.7 male; 78.8 female. **Births:** 9.0 per 1,000 pop. **Deaths:** 11.9 per 1,000 pop. **Infant mortality:** 9.6 per 1,000 live births. **Undernourished:** <5%. **HIV:** NA.

Education: Compulsory: ages 7-16. **Literacy:** 98.8%. **Embassy:** 1607 23rd St. NW 20008; 332-4846. **Website:** www.gov.ro

Romania's earliest known people merged with invading Proto-Thracians, preceding by centuries the Dacians. Rome occupied the Dacian kingdom, 106-271 CE; people and language were Romanized. The Turkey-dominated principalities of Wallachia and Moldavia were united in 1859, became Romania in 1861, and gained recognition as an independent kingdom, 1881.

After WWI, Romania acquired Bessarabia, Bukovina, Transylvania, and Banat. In 1940 it ceded Bessarabia and Northern Bukovina to the USSR, part of southern Dobrudja to Bulgaria, and northern Transylvania to Hungary. In 1941, Prem. Marshal Ion Antonescu led Romania in support of Germany against the USSR. He was overthrown in 1944, and Romania joined the Allies. After occupation by Soviet troops, a People's Republic was proclaimed, Dec. 30, 1947.

On Aug. 22, 1965, a new constitution proclaimed Romania a socialist republic. The domestic policies of Pres. Nicolae Ceausescu were repressive. All industry was state-owned, and state farms and cooperatives owned almost all arable land. Ceausescu's security forces fired on antigovernment demonstrators, Dec. 1989, killing hundreds, but when the army sided with the protesters, his regime fell. Charged with genocide and abuse of power, Ceausescu and his wife were executed Dec. 25, 1989.

A new constitution providing for a multiparty system took effect Dec. 8, 1991. Many of Romania's state-owned companies were privatized in 1996. Romania became a full NATO member in 2004. It entered the European Union Jan. 1, 2007; restrictions on Romanians' right to work in 9 other EU countries ended Jan. 1, 2014. The IMF and other donors agreed to provide a $27-bil loan Mar. 25, 2009, to rescue the country from the global recession. Romania, a firm U.S. ally, pulled its remaining troops out of Iraq July 2009. Romanian soldiers served with NATO-led forces in Afghanistan; almost 600 remained as of June 2016. Social Democrat Victor-Viorel Ponta became prime min. May 7, 2012. He ran for president in 2014 but lost the Nov. 16 runoff to Klaus Iohannis. Prime Min. Ponta went on trial, Sept. 21, 2015, on charges including money laundering and tax evasion while he worked as a lawyer in 2007-08. Large protests, blaming government incompetence for the deaths of more than 60 in a Bucharest nightclub fire, Oct. 30, 2015, led to Ponta's resignation, Nov. 4, 2015; Dacian Ciolos became prime min.

Russia
Russian Federation

People: Population: 142,355,415. **Age distrib.:** <15: 16.9%; 65+: 13.9%. **Growth:** −0.1%. **Migrants:** 8.1%. **Pop. density:** 22.5 per sq mi, 8.7 per sq km. **Urban:** 74.1%. **Ethnic groups:** Russian 77.7%, Tatar 3.7%. **Languages:** Russian (official), Tatar. **Religions:** Russian Orthodox 15%-20%, Muslim 10%-15%.

Geography: Total area: 6,601,668 sq mi, 17,098,242 sq km; **Land area:** 6,323,482 sq mi, 16,377,742 sq km, more than 76% of total area of the former USSR and the largest country in the world. **Location:** Stretches from Eastern Europe across N Asia to the Pacific O. Finland, Norway, Estonia, Latvia, Belarus, Ukraine on W; Georgia, Azerbaijan, Kazakhstan, China, Mongolia, N. Korea on S; Kaliningrad exclave bordered by Poland on the S, Lithuania on the N and E. **Topography:** Every type of climate except distinctly tropical. European portion is low plain, grassy in S, wooded in N, with Ural Mts. on E, and Caucasus Mts. on S. Urals stretch N-S for 2,500 mi. Asiatic portion is vast plain, with mountains on S and in E; tundra covers extreme N with forest belt below; plains, marshes in W, desert in SW. **Arable land:** 7.5%. **Capital:** Moscow, 12,259,631. **Cities:** Saint Petersburg, 5,001,238; Novosibirsk, 1,497,989; Yekaterinburg, 1,381,308; Nizhniy Novgorod, 1,200,208; Kazan, 1,163,070; Samara, 1,161,536; Omsk, 1,160,612; Chelyabinsk, 1,159,798.

Government: Type: Semi-presidential federation. **Head of state:** Pres. Vladimir Putin; b. 1952; in office: May 7, 2012. **Head of gov.:** Prime Min. Dmitri Medvedev; b. 1965; in office: May 8, 2012. **Local divisions:** 46 provinces (oblasts), 21 republics, 4 autonomous okrugs, 9 krays, 2 federal cities, 1 autonomous oblast. **Defense budget:** $51.6 bil. **Active troops:** 798,000.

Economy: Industries: coal, oil, gas, chemicals, metals; machine building; defense (incl. radar, missile prod.); shipbuilding; road, rail transp. equip.; communications equip.; agric. machinery, tractors, constr. equip. **Chief crops:** grain, sugar beets, sunflower seeds, vegetables, fruits. **Natural resources:** oil, nat. gas, coal, minerals, rare earth elements, timber. Climate, terrain, and distance are obstacles to exploitation of resources. **Water:** 31,543 cu m per capita. **Crude oil reserves:** 80 bil bbls. **Electricity prod.:** 999 bil kWh. **Labor force:** agric. 9.4%, industry 27.6%, services 63%. **Unemployment:** 5.1%.

Finance: Monetary unit: Ruble (RUB) (65.89 = $1 U.S.). **GDP:** $3.7 tril; **per capita GDP:** $25,400; **GDP growth:** −3.7%. **Imports:** $197.3 bil; China 19.2%, Germany 11.2%, U.S. 6.4%. **Exports:** $337.8 bil; Netherlands 11.9%, China 8.3%, Germany 7.4%, Italy 6.5%, Turkey 5.6%. **Tourism:** $8.5 bil. **Budget:** $251.6 bil. **Inflation:** 15.5%.

Transport: Railways: 54,157 mi. **Motor vehicles:** 344 per 1,000 pop. **Airports:** 594.

Communications: Telephone: 25.7 per 100 pop. **Mobile:** 160 per 100 pop. **Broadband:** 65.9 per 100 pop. **Internet:** 73.4%.

Health: Expend.: 7.1%. **Life expect.:** 65.0 male; 76.8 female. **Births:** 11.3 per 1,000 pop. **Deaths:** 13.6 per 1,000 pop. **Infant mortality:** 6.9 per 1,000 live births. **Undernourished:** <5%. **HIV:** NA.

Education: Compulsory: ages 6-15. **Literacy:** 99.7%. **Embassy:** 2650 Wisconsin Ave. NW 20007; 298-5700. **Website:** www.government.ru

Slavic tribes began migrating into Russia from the W in the 5th cent. The first Russian state, centered in Novgorod and Kiev, was founded by Scandinavian chieftains in the 9th cent. In the 13th cent., Mongols overran the country. It recovered under the grand dukes and princes of Muscovy, or Moscow, and by 1480 freed itself from the Mongols. Ivan the Terrible was proclaimed Tsar, 1547. Peter the Great (1682-1725) extended the domain and, in 1721, founded the Russian empire. Western ideas and the beginnings of modernization spread through the empire in the 19th and early 20th cent.

Military reverses in the 1905 war with Japan and in WWI led to the breakdown of the Tsarist regime. The 1917 Revolution began in Mar. with a series of sporadic strikes for higher wages by factory workers. A provisional democratic government under Prince Georgi Lvov was established but a second provisional government, under Alexander Kerensky, followed in May. Vladimir Ilyich Lenin, Nov. 7, overthrew the Kerensky government and the freely elected Constituent Assembly in a Communist coup.

Soviet Union. Lenin's death Jan. 21, 1924, led to an internal power struggle won by Joseph Stalin. His brutal tactics, including purge trials, mass executions, and exile to work camps, resulted in millions of deaths.

Despite a Germany-USSR non-aggression pact signed in Aug. 1939, Germany invaded the Soviet Union, June 1941. Russian winter counterthrusts, 1941-42 and 1942-43; victory at Stalingrad (now Volgograd), Feb. 2, 1943 (2 mil total casualties); and resistance to the siege of Leningrad (now St. Petersburg) stopped the German advance. Russian armies drove the Germans from Eastern Europe and the Balkans in the next two years.

After WWII, Communists took over in countries throughout the region, extending the Soviet sphere of influence. The USSR and the U.S., the world's leading nuclear superpowers, became Cold War rivals. After Stalin died, Mar. 5, 1953, Nikita Khrushchev gained power and denounced Stalin, 1956, beginning "de-Stalinization."

Under Khrushchev the open antagonism of Poles and Hungarians toward Moscow's domination was suppressed in 1956. He aided the Cuban revolution under Fidel Castro but withdrew Soviet missiles from Cuba during a confrontation with U.S. Pres. John Kennedy, Sept.-Oct. 1962. Khrushchev was deposed, Oct. 1964, and replaced by Leonid I. Brezhnev. In Aug. 1968, Soviet forces invaded Czechoslovakia, crushing liberalization there.

Massive Soviet military aid to North Vietnam in the late 1960s and early 1970s helped ensure Communist victories throughout Indochina. In Dec. 1979, Soviet forces entered Afghanistan to support a pro-Soviet regime against U.S.-supported Muslim resistance fighters. In Apr. 1988, the Soviets agreed to withdraw their troops, ending a futile 8-year war.

Mikhail Gorbachev was chosen Communist Party gen. sec., Mar. 1985. In 1987 he initiated a program of political and economic reforms through openness (*glasnost*) and restructuring (*perestroika*). Gorbachev faced economic problems as well as ethnic and nationalist unrest in the republics. A coup by Communist hardliners Aug. 1991 was foiled with help from Russian Republic Pres. Boris Yeltsin. On Aug. 24, Gorbachev resigned as leader of the Communist Party. Several republics declared their independence, including Russia, Ukraine, and Kazakhstan. On Aug. 29, the Soviet Parliament voted to suspend all activities of the Communist Party. The Soviet Union officially broke up Dec. 26, 1991, ending the 74-year domination of the Communist Party.

Russian Federation. Under Pres. Yeltsin, Russia took steps toward privatization, which caused inflation and a severe economic downturn. In June 1992, Yeltsin and U.S. Pres. George H. W. Bush agreed to massive arms reductions. Yeltsin prevailed in a power struggle with the Congress of People's Deputies, which was dominated by former Communists, and in a referendum Dec. 12, 1993, a new constitution was approved. Russian troops fought rebels in the breakaway republic of Chechnya Dec. 1994-Aug. 1996, when a peace accord temporarily ended the conflict. On May 27, 1997, Yeltsin signed a founding act, pledging cooperation with NATO and paving the way for NATO to admit Eastern European nations.

Russia's economic crisis deepened in the late 1990s, heightening tensions between parliament and Pres. Yeltsin, who had been reelected in 1996. An Aug. 1999 operation to suppress Islamic rebels in the republic of Dagestan reignited the war in neighboring Chechnya, where Russia launched a full-scale assault. Yeltsin unexpectedly resigned Dec. 31, 1999, naming Prime Min. Vladimir Putin as his interim successor. Putin won presidential elections Mar. 2000. Putin's allies won legislative elections, Dec. 2003, and the president was reelected Mar. 2004.

A bomb in Grozny, May 9, 2004, killed Chechnya's pro-Moscow president, Akhmad Kadyrov. In another terrorist act linked to the Chechnya conflict, two passenger planes exploded in midair after taking off from Moscow Aug. 24, killing 90 people. Chechen rebels, Sept. 1, 2004, seized control of a school in Beslan, North Ossetia, taking more than 1,100 hostages. Russian troops stormed the school Sept. 3; more than 330 people died, including 186 children. Putin cited the terrorist threat Sept. 13 in proposing a government overhaul that tightened his control over parliament and regional officeholders. Russian forces killed Chechen rebel leader Aslan Maskhadov, Mar. 8, 2005, and Chechen guerrilla leader Shamil Basayev, organizer of the terrorist attack at Beslan, July 10, 2006.

Constitutionally barred from seeking another term, Pres. Putin backed his protégé Prime Min. Dmitri Medvedev, who won the presidential election Mar. 2, 2008. Medvedev named Putin as prime min. A long-simmering conflict with Georgia erupted into open warfare Aug. 7-16. Russia dispatched troops to support secessionists in the enclaves of South Ossetia and Abkhazia and launched assaults on strategic Georgian cities; a cease-fire left thousands of Russian troops in the breakaway regions, which Pres. Medvedev recognized as independent, Aug. 26, 2008.

An economic boom fueled by oil and gas sales stalled in late 2008. The global financial crisis and a drop in oil prices led to turmoil in Russian financial markets.

Russia declared, Apr. 16, 2009, that it had ended counterterrorism operations in Chechnya; from June through Aug., there was an upsurge of insurgent violence in Chechnya and neighboring Dagestan and Ingushetia. Female suicide bombers from Dages-

tan struck two Moscow subway stations Mar. 29, 2010, killing 40 people. A bombing at a Moscow airport Jan. 24, 2011, killed 37.

With U.S.-Russia relations strained since the 2008 Georgia war, Medvedev and Pres. Barack Obama Apr. 8, 2010, signed a nuclear arms reduction treaty known as New START, which the U.S. Senate ratified Dec. 22. In Dec. 2011 parliamentary elections, Putin's party, United Russia, failed to garner 50% of the vote. Putin nonetheless won 64% of the vote in the Mar. 4, 2012, presidential election, though there were claims of fraud. Medvedev again became prime min. Three members of the anti-Putin punk-protest band Pussy Riot were convicted of hooliganism Aug. 17, 2012, despite international criticism; the last two women were released from jail in Dec. 2013. Putin signed a law, June 30, 2013, effectively making it illegal to advocate publicly for gay rights. The Putin administration granted one-year asylum to U.S. National Security Agency whistleblower Edward Snowden Aug. 1, 2013—extended for three years Aug. 1, 2014.

Sochi, Russia, hosted the 2014 Winter Olympics Feb. 7-23, 2014. Although suicide bombings in Volgograd, for which Dagestan separatists claimed responsibility, killed 34, Dec. 29-30, 2013, there were no major security incidents at the Games.

After Ukraine's pro-Russian president was removed from office Feb. 22, 2014, Russia sent troops into Ukraine's Crimean Peninsula and annexed Crimea Mar. 18. Russia also apparently provided military equipment and troops to pro-Russian separatists in eastern Ukraine fighting Ukrainian government forces beginning in Apr. 2014. The U.S. and EU imposed several rounds of economic sanctions to protest Russia's Ukraine policies. Sanctions and low prices for Russian oil exports hurt the economy in 2015 (–3.7% GDP change) and 2016.

Russia supported Pres. Bashar al-Assad in Syria's civil war (2011-). In Sept. 2015, Russia sent combat aircraft, other military equipment, and troops to Syria, and it began, Sept. 30, airstrikes against forces, including ISIS, fighting the Assad regime. An ISIS-affiliated group claimed responsibility for planting a bomb on a Russian airliner that crashed in Egypt, Oct. 31, 2015, killing all 224 onboard. Putin announced, Mar. 14, 2016, that Russia would withdraw the "main part" of its forces from Syria, but airstrikes against anti-Assad forces continued.

More than 100 Russian athletes were barred from the 2016 Summer Olympics after the World Anti-Doping Agency presented evidence of a widespread state-sponsored program to provide athletes with banned performance-enhancing drugs and falsify drug tests to conceal such usage. In Sept. 18, 2016, parliamentary elections, United Russia won a majority of the vote and of seats.

Rwanda
Republic of Rwanda

People: Population: 12,988,423. **Age distrib.:** <15: 41.5%; 65+: 2.6%. **Growth:** 2.5%. **Migrants:** 3.8%. **Pop. density:** 1,363.7 per sq mi, 526.5 per sq km. **Urban:** 29.8%. **Ethnic groups:** Hutu (Bantu) 84%, Tutsi (Hamitic) 15%. **Languages:** Kinyarwanda (universal Bantu vernacular), French, English (all official). **Religions:** Roman Catholic 49.5%, Protestant 39.4% (incl. Adventist 12.2%), none 3.6%.

Geography: Total area: 10,169 sq mi, 26,338 sq km; **Land area:** 9,524 sq mi, 24,668 sq km. **Location:** E central Africa. Uganda on N, Dem. Rep. of the Congo on W, Burundi on S, Tanzania on E. **Topography:** Grassy uplands and hills cover most of country, with chain of volcanoes in NW. Nile R. source is in headwaters of the Kagera (Akagera) R. **Arable land:** 47.9%. **Capital:** Kigali, 1,293,312.

Government: Type: Presidential republic. **Head of state:** Pres. Paul Kagame; b. 1957; in office: Apr. 22, 2000 (de facto from Mar. 24). **Head of gov.:** Prime Min. Anastase Murekezi; b. 1952; in office: July 24, 2014. **Local divisions:** 4 provinces, 1 city. **Defense budget:** $91 mil. **Active troops:** 33,000.

Economy: Industries: cement, agric. prods., small-scale beverages, soap, furniture, shoes, plastic goods, textiles, cigarettes. **Chief crops:** coffee, tea, pyrethrum (insecticide made from chrysanthemums), bananas, beans, sorghum, potatoes. **Natural resources:** gold, tin ore, tungsten ore, methane, hydropower. **Water:** 1,146 cu m per capita. **Electricity prod.:** 0.4 bil kWh. **Labor force:** agric. 90%, industry and services 10%. **Unemployment:** 0.6%.

Finance: Monetary unit: Franc (RWF) (799.62 = $1 U.S.). **GDP:** $20.4 bil; **per capita GDP:** $1,800; **GDP growth:** 6.9%. **Imports:** $1.9 bil; Uganda 15.7%, Kenya 11.8%, India 8.7%, China 8.7%, UAE 8.6%, Russia 6.6%, Tanzania 5.1%. **Exports:** $726.1 mil; Dem. Rep. of the Congo 19.8%, U.S. 10.8%, China 10.3%, Swaziland 7.9%, Malaysia 7%, Pakistan 6.2%, Germany 5.9%, Thailand 5.5%. **Tourism:** $305 mil. **Budget:** $2.3 bil. **Inflation:** 2.5%.

Transport: Airports: 4.

Communications: Telephone: 0.1 per 100 pop. **Mobile:** 70.5 per 100 pop. **Broadband:** 11.1 per 100 pop. **Internet:** 18%.

Health: Expend.: 7.5%. **Life expect.:** 58.5 male; 61.7 female. **Births:** 33.3 per 1,000 pop. **Deaths:** 8.8 per 1,000 pop. **Infant mortality:** 56.8 per 1,000 live births. **Undernourished:** 31.6%. **HIV:** 2.9%.

Education: Compulsory: ages 7-12. **Literacy:** 71.2%.

Embassy: 1875 Connecticut Ave. NW, Ste. 540, 20009; 232-2882.

Website: www.gov.rw

For centuries, the Tutsi dominated the Hutu majority. A civil war broke out in 1959 and Tutsi power was ended. Many Tutsi went into exile. Rwanda, which had been part of the Belgian UN trusteeship of Rwanda-Urundi, became independent July 1, 1962.

A large-scale massacre of Tutsi occurred in 1963. Hutu rivalries led to a bloodless coup July 1973 in which Hutu army officer Juvénal Habyarimana took power. After an invasion and coup attempt by Tutsi exiles in 1990, a multiparty democracy was established.

Renewed ethnic strife led to an Aug. 1993 peace accord between the government and rebels of the Tutsi-led Rwandan Patriotic Front (RPF). But after Habyarimana and Burundi Pres. Cyprien Ntaryamira were killed Apr. 6, 1994, in a suspicious plane crash, violence broke out. More than 1 mil may have died in massacres, mostly of Tutsi by Hutu militias, and in civil warfare as the RPF sought power. About 2 mil Tutsi and Hutu fled to camps in Zaire (now Dem. Rep. of the Congo, or DRC) and other countries; many died of disease. French troops under a UN mandate moved into SW Rwanda June 23 to establish a safe zone. The RPF claimed victory, installing a government led by a moderate Hutu president in July. French troops pulled out Aug. 22. A UN peacekeeping mission ended Mar. 8, 1996. More than 1 mil refugees, mostly Hutu, returned to Rwanda in Nov.-Dec. 1996.

Former Prime Min. Jean Kambanda pleaded guilty to genocide, May 1, 1998, before the UN-backed Intl. Criminal Tribunal for Rwanda (ICTR); he received a life sentence Sept. 4, 1998. RPF leader Maj. Gen. Paul Kagame became Rwanda's first Tutsi president Apr. 22, 2000.

Rwandans approved a new constitution, May 26, 2003, and reelected Pres. Kagame, Aug. 25. Rwanda cut diplomatic ties with France Nov. 24, 2006, after a French judge linked Kagame to the 1994 deaths of Habyarimana and Ntaryamira. The country restored relations with France, Nov. 2009, when Rwanda also joined the Commonwealth.

Accused of being one of the architects of the 1994 genocide, Col. Theoneste Bagosora was convicted and sentenced by the ICTR, Dec. 18, 2008, to life in prison (later reduced to 35 years). A Rwandan court Jan. 20, 2009, sentenced former Justice Min. Agnes Ntamabyariro to life in prison for her role in inciting the massacres. Up to 4,000 Rwandan troops fought that month alongside Congolese forces against Hutu militias in eastern DRC. After a campaign criticized as repressive by human rights groups, Pres. Kagame won reelection Aug. 9, 2010.

Steady economic growth beginning in 2003 was accompanied by U.S. military and medical aid. An Oct. 17, 2012, UN report found that the Rwanda military was backing the mostly-Tutsi M23 rebel troops in the DRC. The U.S. announced on Dec. 2013 that it was sanctioning Rwanda for its support of M23 by withholding military funding. After successful offensives by UN troops in the DRC against M23 and the Hutu militia known as the Democratic Forces for the Liberation of Rwanda (FDLR), some 200 FDLR members laid down their arms in June 2014. More than 73,000 DRC refugees were living in Rwanda as of Aug. 2016. Political unrest in Burundi beginning in early 2015 caused tens of thousands to flee to Rwanda, which hosted more than 80,000 Burundian refugees as of Aug. 2016. Shortly before the ICTR ceased operations, Dec. 31, 2015, one of its most-wanted fugitives, Ladislas Ntaganzwa, was arrested by Interpol in the DRC. His genocide trial in Rwanda began Apr. 4, 2016.

Saint Kitts and Nevis
Federation of Saint Kitts and Nevis

People: Population: 52,329. **Age distrib.:** <15: 20.6%; 65+: 8.3%. **Growth:** 0.8%. **Migrants:** 13.4%. **Pop. density:** 519.3 per sq mi, 200.5 per sq km. **Urban:** 32.2%. **Ethnic groups:** predominantly black; some British, Portuguese, Lebanese. **Languages:** English (official). **Religions:** Anglican, other Protestant, Roman Catholic.

Geography: Total area: 101 sq mi, 261 sq km; **Land area:** 101 sq mi, 261 sq km. **Location:** In N part of the Leeward group of Lesser Antilles in E Caribbean Sea. Antigua and Barbuda to E. **Topography:** Forested volcanic slopes on St. Kitts; beaches rising to central peak on Nevis. Tropical climate moderated by sea breezes. **Arable land:** 19.2%. **Capital:** Basseterre, 14,149 (2014).

Government: Type: Federal parliamentary democracy under constitutional monarchy. **Head of state:** Queen Elizabeth II, rep. by Gov.-Gen. Samuel W. T. Seaton; in office: Sept. 1, 2015. **Head of gov.:** Prime Min. Timothy Harris; b. 1964; in office: Feb. 16, 2015. **Local divisions:** 14 parishes. **Defense budget/active troops:** NA.

Economy: Industries: tourism, cotton, salt, copra, clothing, footwear, beverages. **Chief crops:** sugarcane, rice, yams, vegetables, bananas. **Water:** 432 cu m per capita. **Electricity prod.:** 0.2 bil kWh. **Labor force:** NA. **Unemployment:** NA.

Finance: Monetary unit: East Caribbean Dollar (XCD) (2.70 = $1 U.S.). **GDP:** $1.4 bil; **per capita GDP:** $24,600; **GDP growth:** 6.6%. **Imports:** $240.3 mil; U.S. 37.7%, Trinidad and Tobago 22.7%. **Exports:** $61.3 mil; U.S. 44.4%, Poland 14.6%, Bangladesh 10.1%. **Tourism:** $109 mil. **Budget:** $259.3 mil. **Inflation:** −2.3%.

Transport: Railways: 31 mi. **Airports:** 2.

Communications: Telephone: 35.7 per 100 pop. **Mobile:** 131.8 per 100 pop. **Broadband:** 6.4 per 100 pop. **Internet:** 75.7%. **Health: Expend.:** 5.1%. **Life expect.:** 73.3 male; 78.2 female. **Births:** 13.3 per 1,000 pop. **Deaths:** 7.1 per 1,000 pop. **Infant mortality:** 8.6 per 1,000 live births. **Undernourished:** NA. **HIV:** NA. **Education:** Compulsory: ages 5-16. **Literacy:** 98%. **Embassy:** 1001 19th St. N, Ste. 1221, Arlington, VA 22209. **Website:** www.gov.kn

St. Kitts (formerly St. Christopher; known by indigenous peoples as Liamuiga) and Nevis were reached by Columbus in 1493. They were settled by Britain in 1623 (ownership was disputed with France until 1713). The colony achieved self-government as an Associated State of the UK in 1967, becoming independent, Sept. 19, 1983. A secession referendum on Nevis, Aug. 10, 1998, fell short of the two-thirds majority required. Twenty years of Labour Party governments ended when an opposition coalition won a majority of seats in Feb. 16, 2015, legislative elections.

Saint Lucia

People: Population: 164,464. **Age distrib.:** <15: 20.3%; 65+: 11.2%. **Growth:** 0.3%. **Migrants:** 6.9%. **Pop. density:** 702.9 per sq mi, 271.4 per sq km. **Urban:** 18.5%. **Ethnic groups:** black/African descent 85.3%, mixed 10.9%, East Indian 2.2%. **Languages:** English (official), French patois. **Religions:** Roman Catholic 61.5%, Protestant 25.5% (incl. Seventh-day Adventist 10.4%), none 5.9%.

Geography: Total area: 238 sq mi, 616 sq km; **Land area:** 234 sq mi, 606 sq km. **Location:** E Caribbean, second largest of Windward Isls. Martinique (Fr.) to N, St. Vincent to S. **Topography:** Mountainous, volcanic in origin; Soufrière Volcanic Centre in S. Wooded mountains run N-S. **Arable land:** 4.9%. **Capital:** Castries, 22,186 (2014).

Government: Type: Parliamentary democracy under constitutional monarchy. **Head of state:** Queen Elizabeth II, rep. by Gov.-Gen. Dame Pearlette Louisy; b. 1946; in office: Sept. 17, 1997. **Head of gov.:** Prime Min. Allen Chastanet; in office: June 7, 2016. **Local divisions:** 10 districts. **Defense budget/active troops:** NA.

Economy: Industries: tourism, clothing, electronic components assembly, beverages, corrugated cardboard boxes, lime proc. **Chief crops:** bananas, coconuts, vegetables, citrus, root crops, cocoa. **Natural resources:** forests, beaches, pumice, mineral springs. **Water:** 1,622 cu m per capita. **Electricity prod.:** 0.4 bil kWh. **Labor force:** agric. 21.7%, industry 24.7%, services 53.6%. **Unemployment:** NA.

Finance: Monetary unit: East Caribbean Dollar (XCD) (2.70 = $1 U.S.). **GDP:** $2 bil; **per capita GDP:** $11,700; **GDP growth:** 1.6%. **Imports:** $540.6 mil; Brazil 34.9%, U.S. 25.7%, Trinidad and Tobago 14.4%, Colombia 10.9%. **Exports:** $207 mil; Dominican Republic 25.1%, U.S. 15.9%, Suriname 9.1%, Antigua and Barbuda 7%, Dominica 6.8%, Trinidad and Tobago 6.3%, Barbados 6.1%. **Tourism:** $373 mil. **Budget** (2011 est.): $222.2 mil. **Inflation:** −1%.

Transport: Airports: 2.

Communications: Telephone: 18.9 per 100 pop. **Mobile:** 101.5 per 100 pop. **Broadband:** 29.8 per 100 pop. **Internet:** 52.4%.

Health: Expend.: 6.7%. **Life expect.:** 75.0 male; 80.7 female. **Births:** 13.5 per 1,000 pop. **Deaths:** 7.6 per 1,000 pop. **Infant mortality:** 11.2 per 1,000 live births. **Undernourished:** NA. **HIV:** NA. **Education:** Compulsory: ages 5-14. **Literacy:** NA. **Embassy:** 1629 K St. NW, Ste. 1250, 20006; 364-6792. **Website:** www.govt.lc

St. Lucia, ceded to Britain by France with the Treaty of Paris, 1814, gained independence Feb. 22, 1979. Investigation results announced Mar. 8, 2015, by Prime Min. Kenny Anthony found that 12 suspected criminals were put on a "death list" and killed by police in 2010-11. Pledging a tax cut and resolution of the police scandal, the conservative United Workers Party (UWP) defeated Anthony's Labor Party in June 6, 2016, elections; UWP leader Allen Chastanet became prime min.

Saint Vincent and the Grenadines

People: Population: 102,350. **Age distrib.:** <15: 21.8%; 65+: 9.1%. **Growth:** −0.3%. **Migrants:** 4.2%. **Pop. density:** 681.5 per sq mi, 263.1 per sq km. **Urban:** 50.9%. **Ethnic groups:** black 66%, mixed 19%, East Indian 6%, European 4%, Carib Amerindian 2%. **Languages:** English, French patois. **Religions:** Protestant 75% (Anglican 47%, Methodist 28%), Roman Catholic 13%, other (incl. Hindu, Seventh-day Adventist, other Protestant) 12%.

Geography: Total area: 150 sq mi, 389 sq km; **Land area:** 150 sq mi, 389 sq km. **Location:** E Caribbean; St. Vincent (133 sq mi) and the northern islets of the Grenadines form a part of Windward chain. St. Lucia to N, Barbados to E, Grenada to S. **Topography:** St. Vincent is volcanic, with a ridge of thickly wooded mountains running its length. **Arable land:** 12.8%. **Capital:** Kingstown, 27,314 (2014).

Government: Type: Parliamentary democracy under constitutional monarchy. **Head of state:** Queen Elizabeth II, rep. by Gov.-Gen. Sir Frederick Ballantyne; b. 1936; in office: Sept. 2, 2002. **Head of gov.:** Prime Min. Ralph Gonsalves; b. 1946; in office: Mar. 29, 2001. **Local divisions:** 6 parishes. **Defense budget/active troops:** NA.

Economy: Industries: tourism, food proc., cement, furniture, clothing, starch. **Chief crops:** bananas, coconuts, sweet potatoes, spices. **Natural resources:** hydropower. **Water:** 913 cu m per capita. **Electricity prod.:** 0.1 bil kWh. **Labor force:** agric. 26%, industry 17%, services 57%. **Unemployment:** NA.

Finance: Monetary unit: East Caribbean Dollar (XCD) (2.70 = $1 U.S.). **GDP:** $1.2 bil; **per capita GDP:** $11,000; **GDP growth:** 1.6%. **Imports:** $320.7 mil; Trinidad and Tobago 29.3%, U.S. 17.2%, Singapore 8.7%, China 8%, Barbados 6%, Poland 5.5%. **Exports:** $49.8 mil; Trinidad and Tobago 18.9%, St. Lucia 14.8%, Barbados 12.3%, Dominica 9.7%, Grenada 9.3%, Antigua and Barbuda 8.4%, Poland 7.1%. **Tourism:** $104 mil. **Budget:** $222.2 mil. **Inflation:** −1.7%.

Transport: Airports: 5.

Communications: Telephone: 22.7 per 100 pop. **Mobile:** 103.7 per 100 pop. **Broadband:** 34.4 per 100 pop. **Internet:** 51.8%.

Health: Expend.: 8.6%. **Life expect.:** 73.3 male; 77.4 female. **Births:** 13.4 per 1,000 pop. **Deaths:** 7.3 per 1,000 pop. **Infant mortality:** 12.3 per 1,000 live births. **Undernourished:** 6.2%. **HIV:** NA.

Education: Compulsory: ages 5-16. **Literacy:** 88%.

Embassy: 1001 N. 19th St., Ste. 1242, Arlington, VA 22209; 364-6730.

Website: www.gov.vc

Columbus landed on St. Vincent on Jan. 22, 1498 (St. Vincent's Day). Britain and France both laid claim to the island in the 17th and 18th cent.; the Treaty of Versailles, 1783, ceded it to Britain. Associated State status was granted 1969; independence was attained Oct. 27, 1979.

Samoa
Independent State of Samoa

People: Population: 198,926. **Age distrib.:** <15: 32%; 65+: 5.6%. **Growth:** 0.6%. **Migrants:** 2.6%. **Pop. density:** 182.6 per sq mi, 70.5 per sq km. **Urban:** 19%. **Ethnic groups:** Samoan 92.6%, Euronesian (European/Polynesian) 7%. **Languages:** Samoan (Polynesian) (official), English. **Religions:** Protestant 57.4% (incl. Congregationalist 31.8%, Methodist 13.7%), Roman Catholic 19.4%, Mormon 15.2%.

Geography: Total area: 1,093 sq mi, 2,831 sq km; **Land area:** 1,089 sq mi, 2,821 sq km. **Location:** S Pacific O. Nearest neighbors are Fiji to SW, Tonga to S. **Topography:** Main islands, Savaii (659 sq mi) and Upolu (432 sq mi), both ruggedly mountainous. Small islands of Manono and Apolima. **Arable land:** 2.8%. **Capital:** Apia, 36,946 (2014).

Government: Type: Parliamentary republic. **Head of state:** Tui Atua Tupua Tamasese Efi; b. 1938; in office: June 20, 2007. **Head of gov.:** Prime Min. Tuilaepa Sailele Malielegaoi; b. 1945; in office: Nov. 23, 1998. **Local divisions:** 11 districts. **Defense budget/ active troops:** NA.

Economy: Industries: food proc., building materials, auto parts. **Chief crops:** coconuts, nonu, bananas, taro, yams, coffee, cocoa. **Natural resources:** hardwood forests, fish, hydropower. **Water:** NA. **Electricity prod.:** 0.1 bil kWh. **Labor force:** agric. 65%. **Unemployment:** NA.

Finance: Monetary unit: Tala (WST) (2.58 = $1 U.S.). **GDP:** $1 bil; **per capita GDP:** $5,200; **GDP growth:** 1.7%. **Imports** (2013): $325.3 mil; Fiji 22.6%, New Zealand 18.8%, China 15.8%, South Korea 7.9%, Australia 6%, U.S. 5.6%, Singapore 5.2%. **Exports** (2013): $24 mil; American Samoa 57.1%, Australia 17.2%. **Tourism:** $137 mil. **Budget:** $234.8 mil. **Inflation:** 0.7%.

Transport: Airports: 1.

Communications: Telephone: 5.6 per 100 pop. **Mobile:** 58.5 per 100 pop. **Broadband:** 16.4 per 100 pop. **Internet:** 25.4%.

Health: Expend.: 7.2%. **Life expect.:** 70.8 male; 76.8 female. **Births:** 20.6 per 1,000 pop. **Deaths:** 5.3 per 1,000 pop. **Infant mortality:** 19.0 per 1,000 live births. **Undernourished:** <5%. **HIV:** NA.

Education: Compulsory: ages 5-12. **Literacy:** 99%.

Embassy: 800 Second Ave., 4th Fl., New York, NY 10017; (212) 599-6196.

Website: www.samoagovt.ws

Samoa (formerly Western Samoa) was a German colony, 1899 to 1914, when New Zealand landed troops and took over. It became a New Zealand mandate under the League of Nations and, in 1945, a New Zealand UN Trusteeship. An elected local government took office in Oct. 1959, and the country became fully independent Jan. 1, 1962. Malietoa Tanumafili II, head of state since independence, was succeeded by Tuiatua Tupua Tamasese Efi. In 2011, Samoa moved west of the Intl. Date Line to reduce time differences with Australia and New Zealand. "Panama Papers" documents showed, in 2016, that the law firm from which the files leaked had set up thousands of shell companies in Samoa.

San Marino
Republic of San Marino

People: Population: 33,285. **Age distrib.:** <15: 15.5%; 65+: 19.3%. **Growth:** 0.8%. **Migrants:** 14.8%. **Pop. density:** 1,413.2

per sq mi, 545.7 per sq km. **Urban:** 94.2%. **Ethnic groups:** Sammarinese, Italian. **Languages:** Italian. **Religions:** Roman Catholic.

Geography: Total area: 24 sq mi, 61 sq km; **Land area:** 24 sq mi, 61 sq km. **Location:** Completely surrounded by Italy, in N center of that country, near Adriatic coast. **Topography:** On slopes of Mt. Titano. **Arable land:** 16.7%. **Capital:** San Marino, 4,197 (2014).

Government: Type: Parliamentary republic. **Heads of state:** Two captains regent, elected by parliament from among its members, to 6-month term. **Head of gov.:** Sec. of State for Foreign and Political Affairs Pasquale Valentini; b. 1953; in office: Dec. 5, 2012. **Local divisions:** 9 municipalities. **Defense budget/active troops:** NA.

Economy: Industries: tourism, banking, textiles, electronics, ceramics, cement, wine. **Chief crops:** wheat, grapes, corn, olives. **Natural resources:** building stone. **Water:** NA. **Labor force:** agric. 0.2%, industry 33.5%, services 66.3%. **Unemployment:** NA.

Finance: Monetary unit: Euro (EUR) (0.89 = $1 U.S.). **GDP:** $2 bil; **per capita GDP:** $63,900; **GDP growth:** 1%. **Imports** (2011): $2.6 bil; (2012) Italy 81.8%. **Exports** (2011): $3.8 bil; (2012) Italy 82.3%. **Budget** (2011 est.): $713.1 mil. **Inflation** (2013-14): 1.1%.

Transport: NA.

Communications: Telephone: 52 per 100 pop. **Mobile:** 115.2 per 100 pop. **Broadband:** NA. **Internet** (2011): 49.6%.

Health: Expend.: 6.1%. **Life expect.:** 80.7 male; 86.1 female. **Births:** 8.6 per 1,000 pop. **Deaths:** 8.6 per 1,000 pop. **Infant mortality:** 4.4 per 1,000 live births. **Undernourished:** <5%. **HIV:** NA.

Education: Compulsory: ages 6-15. **Literacy:** 96%.

Embassy: 1711 N St. NW, 2nd Fl., 20036; 223-2418.

Website: www.sanmarino.sm

San Marino claims to be the world's oldest republic, having been founded in the 4th cent. It has had a treaty of friendship with Italy since 1862. A Communist-led coalition ruled 1947-57; a similar coalition ruled 1978-86. The broad-based San Marino Common Good coalition won parliamentary elections Nov. 11, 2012.

São Tomé and Príncipe
Democratic Republic of São Tomé and Príncipe

People: Population: 197,541. **Age distrib.:** <15: 42.5%; 65+: 2.8%. **Growth:** 1.8%. **Migrants:** 1.3%. **Pop. density:** 530.7 per sq mi, 204.9 per sq km. **Urban:** 65.6%. **Ethnic groups:** mestico, angolares (descendants of Angolan slaves), forros (descendants of freed slaves), servicais (contract laborers fr. Angola, Mozambique, Cabo Verde), tongas (children of servicais born on islands), Europeans (primarily Portuguese), Asians (mostly Chinese). **Languages:** Portuguese (official), Forro, Cabo Verdian, French, Angolar, English. **Religions:** Catholic 55.7%, Adventist 4.1%, Assembly of God 3.4%, New Apostolic 2.9%, none 21.2%.

Geography: Total area: 372 sq mi, 964 sq km; **Land area:** 372 sq mi, 964 sq km. **Location:** Gulf of Guinea about 125 mi off W central Africa. Gabon, Equatorial Guinea to E. **Topography:** Part of an extinct volcano chain; lush forests and croplands. **Arable land:** 9.1%. **Capital:** São Tomé, 71,294 (2014).

Government: Type: Semi-presidential republic. **Head of state:** Pres. Evaristo Carvalho; b. 1941; in office: Sept. 3, 2016. **Head of gov.:** Prime Min. Patrice Emery Trovoada; b. 1936; in office: Nov. 29, 2014. **Local divisions:** 2 provinces. **Defense budget/ active troops:** NA.

Economy: Industries: light constr., textiles, soap, beer, fish proc., timber. **Chief crops:** cocoa, coconuts, palm kernels, copra, cinnamon, pepper, coffee, bananas, papayas, beans. **Natural resources:** fish, hydropower. **Water:** 11,456 cu m per capita. **Electricity prod.** (2012): 65 mil kWh. **Labor force:** Pop. mainly engaged in subsistence agric. and fishing; shortage of skilled workers. **Unemployment:** NA.

Finance: Monetary unit: Dobra (STD) (21,997.00 = $1 U.S.). **GDP:** $658 mil; **per capita GDP:** $3,200; **GDP growth:** 4%. **Imports:** $138.7 mil; Portugal 65.1%, China 8%, Gabon 7.3%. **Exports:** $18.1 mil; Netherlands 29.2%, Belgium 22.4%, Spain 15.5%, U.S. 6.6%, Nigeria 5.1%. **Tourism:** $56 mil. **Budget:** $101.3 mil. **Inflation:** 5.2%.

Transport: Airports: 2.

Communications: Telephone: 3.5 per 100 pop. **Mobile:** 65.1 per 100 pop. **Broadband:** NA. **Internet:** 25.8%.

Health: Expend.: 8.4%. **Life expect.:** 63.6 male; 66.3 female. **Births:** 33.3 per 1,000 pop. **Deaths:** 7.0 per 1,000 pop. **Infant mortality:** 46.6 per 1,000 live births. **Undernourished:** 6.6%. **HIV:** NA.

Education: Compulsory: ages 6-11. **Literacy:** 91.7%.

Permanent UN mission: 675 Third Ave., Ste. 1807, New York, NY 10017; (212) 651-8116.

Website: www.state.gov/p/af/ci/tp/

The Portuguese discovered the islands in 1471 and brought the first inhabitants—convicts and exiled Jews. Sugarcane planting was replaced by the slave trade as the chief economic activity until coffee and cocoa were introduced in the 19th century.

Portugal agreed, 1974, to turn the colony over to the Gabon-based Movement for the Liberation of São Tomé and Príncipe; its East German-trained leader, Manuel Pinto da Costa, became the country's first president. Independence came July 12, 1975. Democratic reforms were instituted in 1987. In 1991, Miguel Trovoada won the first free presidential election. Trovoada defeated Pinto da Costa in a presidential runoff election July 21, 1996.

Fradique de Menezes, a wealthy cocoa exporter, beat Pinto da Costa in July 29, 2001, presidential elections and was reelected July 30, 2006. After the Independent Democratic Action (ADI) party won legislative elections Aug. 1, 2010, Patrice Trovoada (son of the former president) became prime min. Pinto da Costa returned to power after a presidential runoff vote Aug. 7, 2011. The National Assembly elected Gabriel Arcanjo Ferreira da Costa prime min. Dec. 2012, but Trovoada again became prime min. after ADI won Oct. 12, 2014, legislative elections. Evaristo Carvalho of ADI unseated the incumbent in an Aug. 7, 2016, presidential runoff boycotted by Pinto da Costa, who claimed electoral fraud in the July 17 first round. The country, long one of the world's poorest, has sought to develop oil deposits in the Gulf of Guinea.

Saudi Arabia
Kingdom of Saudi Arabia

People: Population: 28,160,273. **Age distrib.:** <15: 26.6%; 65+: 3.3%. **Growth:** 1.5%. **Migrants:** 32.3%. **Pop. density:** 33.9 per sq mi, 13.1 per sq km. **Urban:** 83.3%. **Ethnic groups:** Arab 90%, Afro-Asian 10%. **Languages:** Arabic (official). **Religions:** Muslim (official). Citizens are 85%-90% Sunni and 10%-15% Shia; non-Muslims are not allowed Saudi citizenship.

Geography: Total area: 830,000 sq mi, 2,149,690 sq km; **Land area:** 830,000 sq mi, 2,149,690 sq km. **Location:** Occupies most of Arabian Peninsula in Middle East. Kuwait, Iraq, Jordan on N; Yemen, Oman on S; UAE, Qatar on E. **Topography:** Bordered by Red Sea on W. Highlands in W slope as barren desert to the Persian Gulf on E. **Arable land:** 1.4%. **Capital:** Riyadh, 6,539,712. **Cities:** Jiddah, 4,161,242; Mecca, 1,798,803; Medina, 1,302,641; Ad-Dammam, 1,085,383.

Government: Type: Absolute monarchy. **Head of state and gov.:** King Salman bin Abdul Aziz; b. 1924; in office: Jan. 23, 2015. **Local divisions:** 13 provinces. **Defense budget:** $81.9 bil. **Active troops:** 227,000.

Economy: Industries: crude oil prod., petroleum refining, basic petrochemicals, ammonia, industrial gases, caustic soda, cement, fertilizer. **Chief crops:** wheat, barley, tomatoes, melons, dates, citrus. **Natural resources:** petroleum, nat. gas, iron ore, gold, copper. **Water:** 76 cu m per capita. **Crude oil reserves:** 269.1 bil bbls (incl. half of Neutral Zone reserves). **Electricity prod.:** 267 bil kWh. **Labor force:** agric. 6.7%, industry 21.4%, services 71.9%. **Unemployment:** 5.6%.

Finance: Monetary unit: Riyal (SAR) (3.75 = $1 U.S.). **GDP:** $1.7 tril; **per capita GDP:** $53,600; **GDP growth:** 3.4%. **Imports:** $156.9 bil; China 13.9%, U.S. 12.6%, Germany 7.1%, South Korea 6.1%. **Exports:** $224.6 bil; China 13.1%, Japan 10.9%, U.S. 9.6%, India 9.6%, South Korea 8.5%. **Tourism:** $10.1 bil. **Budget:** $318 bil. **Inflation:** 2.2%.

Transport: Railways: 856 mi. **Motor vehicles:** 243.9 per 1,000 pop. **Airports:** 82.

Communications: Telephone: 12.5 per 100 pop. **Mobile:** 176.6 per 100 pop. **Broadband:** 99 per 100 pop. **Internet:** 69.6%.

Health: Expend.: 4.7%. **Life expect.:** 73.2 male; 77.4 female. **Births:** 18.4 per 1,000 pop. **Deaths:** 3.3 per 1,000 pop. **Infant mortality:** 13.6 per 1,000 live births. **Undernourished:** <5%. **HIV:** NA.

Education: Compulsory: ages 6-14. **Literacy:** 94.8%.

Embassy: 601 New Hampshire Ave. NW 20037; 342-3800.

Website: www.saudi.gov.sa

Before Muhammad, Arabia was divided among numerous warring tribes and small kingdoms. Muhammad united it in the early 7th cent. His successors conquered the entire Near East and North Africa, bringing Islam and the Arabic language. But Arabia soon returned to its former status.

Nejd, in central Arabia, long an independent state and center of the Wahhabi sect, fell under Turkish rule in the 18th cent. Ibn Saud, founder of the Saudi dynasty, overthrew the Turks, 1913. He captured Hasa, a Turkish province in eastern Arabia, also 1913; the Hejaz region in western Arabia, 1925; and most of Asir, in SW Arabia, by 1926. The discovery of oil in the 1930s transformed the nation. The Hejaz contains the holy cities of Islam—Medina and Mecca. About 2-3 mil Muslims make the *hajj* (pilgrimage) to Mecca annually.

Ibn Saud reigned until his death, Nov. 1953. Subsequent kings have been his sons. The king exercises authority with a Council of Ministers. The Islamic religious code is the law of the land. Alcohol and public entertainments are restricted; women have an inferior legal status.

Saudi Arabia has often allied itself with and purchased arms from the U.S. and other Western nations. Saudi units, nevertheless, fought against Western ally Israel in the 1948 and 1973 Arab-Israeli wars. Beginning with the 1967 Arab-Israeli war, Saudi Arabia gave large annual financial gifts to Egypt, Syria, Jordan, and Palestinian groups. Saudi Arabia played a leading role in the 1973-74 Arab oil embargo against the U.S. and other nations.

After Iraq invaded Kuwait, Aug. 2, 1990, Saudi Arabia accepted the Kuwait royal family and more than 400,000 Kuwaiti refugees.

Western and Arab troops also deployed on Saudi soil before and during the 1991 Persian Gulf War.

When 15 of the 19 al-Qaeda hijackers who carried out the Sept. 11, 2001, attacks on the U.S. were found to be Saudi, some in the U.S. blamed the Saudi government for allowing Muslim extremism to flourish in Saudi Arabia. Alarmed at guerrilla attacks that killed more than 100 people, mostly foreigners, in Saudi Arabia, 2003-04, the Saudis worked with the U.S. to increase antiterrorist activities. The U.S. completed a pullout of its combat forces from Saudi Arabia, Sept. 2003.

Islamist candidates on a "golden list" circulated by conservative clerics fared well in Feb.-Apr. 2005 municipal council elections, the country's first since 1963; women were barred from voting. Just before male-only Sept. 2011 municipal elections, King Abdullah announced that women would be allowed to vote and run for office in future elections; women won 20 of 2,106 elective council seats in voting Dec. 12, 2015. In 2012, Saudi women athletes competed in the Olympics for the first time. King Abdullah decreed, Jan. 11, 2013, that women would be permitted to hold 30 of the 150 seats on the government's advisory Shura council. Abdullah died, Jan. 23, 2015, and was succeeded by his half-brother Salman.

Middle East Respiratory Syndrome (MERS), a viral disease, was first recognized in Saudi Arabia in 2012. As of Sept. 1, 2016, the Saudi Ministry of Health reported 1,449 total cases since the outbreak began; 609 had died. MERS had spread to more than 25 other countries by mid-2016.

Hoping to contain Arab Spring uprisings, a Saudi-led Gulf Cooperation Council force suppressed protests in Bahrain Mar. 14, 2011. Saudi Arabia supplied weapons to anti-government rebels in Syria's civil war. Beginning Sept. 23, 2014, Saudi warplanes participated in U.S.-led airstrikes against ISIS and other Sunni extremists in Syria. ISIS claimed responsibility for terrorist attacks inside Saudi Arabia in 2014-16, and the government arrested thousands of alleged ISIS supporters. Saudi Arabia led a 10-nation Sunni coalition that began airstrikes, Mar. 25, 2015, against Shiite Houthi rebels in Yemen, causing high civilian casualties; a ceasefire as of Apr. 10, 2016, reduced the level of violence, but Saudi airstrikes intensified after peace talks stalled in Aug.

Low oil prices reduced government revenue in 2015 and 2016, leading to estimated annual budget deficits of close to $100 bil. King Salman announced, Apr. 25, 2016, a plan for economic diversification and privatization by the year 2030. Salaries and benefits of government employees were cut, Sept. 26, 2016.

Senegal
Republic of Senegal

People: Population: 14,320,055. **Age distrib.:** <15: 41.8%; 65+: 3%. **Growth:** 2.4%. **Migrants:** 1.7%. **Pop. density:** 192.6 per sq mi, 74.4 per sq km. **Urban:** 44.1%. **Ethnic groups:** Wolof 38.7%, Pular 26.5%, Serer 15%, Mandinka 4.2%, Jola 4%, Soninke 2.3%. **Languages:** French (official), Wolof, Pulaar, Jola, Mandinka. **Religions:** Muslim (mostly four main Sufi brotherhoods) 95.4%, Christian (mostly Roman Catholic) 4.2%.

Geography: Total area: 75,955 sq mi, 196,722 sq km; **Land area:** 74,336 sq mi, 192,530 sq km. **Location:** W extreme of Africa. Mauritania on N, Mali on E, Guinea and Guinea-Bissau on S; surrounds The Gambia on three sides. **Topography:** Mostly low rolling plains, rising somewhat in SE. Swamp and jungles in SW. **Arable land:** 16.9%. **Capital:** Dakar, 3,653,028.

Government: Type: Presidential republic. **Head of state:** Pres. Macky Sall; b. 1961; in office: Apr. 2, 2012. **Head of gov.:** Prime Min. Mohammed Abdallah Boun Dionne; in office: July 6, 2014. **Local divisions:** 14 regions. **Defense budget:** $216 mil. **Active troops:** 13,600.

Economy: Industries: agric. and fish proc., phosphate mining, fertilizer prod., petroleum refining, zircon and gold mining, constr. materials, ship constr. and repair. **Chief crops:** peanuts, millet, corn, sorghum, rice, cotton, tomatoes, green vegetables. **Natural resources:** fish, phosphates, iron ore. **Water:** 2,576 cu m per capita. **Electricity prod.:** 3.4 bil kWh. **Labor force:** agric. 77.5%, industry and services 22.5%. **Unemployment:** 10%.

Finance: Monetary unit: CFA Franc (XOF) (586.00 = $1 U.S.). **GDP:** $36.7 bil; **per capita GDP:** $2,500; **GDP growth:** 6.5%. **Imports:** $4.7 bil; France 17.9%, China 10%, Nigeria 8.7%, India 5.6%. **Exports:** $2.3 bil; Mali 12.8%, Switzerland 9.7%, India 5.9%, Côte d'Ivoire 5.3%, China 5.1%. **Tourism:** $423 mil. **Budget:** $4 bil. **Inflation:** 0.1%.

Transport: Railways: 563 mi. **Airports:** 9.

Communications: Telephone: 2 per 100 pop. **Mobile:** 99.9 per 100 pop. **Broadband:** 23.7 per 100 pop. **Internet:** 21.7%.

Health: Expend.: 4.7%. **Life expect.:** 59.7 male; 63.8 female. **Births:** 34.0 per 1,000 pop. **Deaths:** 8.3 per 1,000 pop. **Infant mortality:** 50.3 per 1,000 live births. **Undernourished:** 10%. **HIV:** 0.5%.

Education: Compulsory: ages 6-16. **Literacy:** 55.6%.

Embassy: 2215 M St. NW 20007; 234-0540.

Website: www.gouv.sn

Portuguese settlers arrived in the 15th cent., but French control grew from the 17th cent. The last independent Muslim state was subdued in 1893. Senegal became an independent republic

Aug. 20, 1960, but French political and economic influence remained strong. Senegambia, a loose confederation of Senegal and The Gambia, was established in 1982 but dissolved seven years later.

Forty years of Socialist Party rule ended when Abdoulaye Wade, leader of the Senegalese Democratic Party (PDS), won a presidential runoff election, Mar. 19, 2000. A Senegalese ferry capsized off the coast of The Gambia Sept. 26, 2002, killing at least 1,863 people. A peace accord signed Dec. 30, 2004, with separatists in Cassamance Province, S Senegal, sought to end a 22-year insurgency. Pres. Wade was reelected Feb. 25, 2007, but lost his bid for a third term Mar. 26, 2012, to Macky Sall, his former prime min. Wade's son Karim, the PDS's candidate for the next presidential election, was convicted on corruption charges and sentenced to six years in prison, Mar. 23, 2015; he was pardoned by Sall, June 24, 2016.

Serbia
Republic of Serbia

People: Population: 7,143,921. **Age distrib.:** <15: 14.6%; 65+: 18%. **Growth:** –0.5%. **Migrants:** 9.1% (incl. Kosovo). **Pop. density:** 238.8 per sq mi, 92.2 per sq km. **Urban:** 55.7% (incl. Kosovo). **Ethnic groups:** Serb 83.3%, Hungarian 3.5%, Romany 2.1%, Bosniak 2%. **Languages:** Serbian (official), Hungarian. **Religions:** Serbian Orthodox 84.6%, Catholic 5%, Muslim 3.1%.

Geography: Total area: 29,913 sq mi, 77,474 sq km; **Land area:** 29,913 sq mi, 77,474 sq km. **Location:** Balkan Peninsula in SE Europe. Croatia, Bosnia and Herzegovina on W; Hungary on N; Romania, Bulgaria on E; Montenegro, Albania, Macedonia on S. **Topography:** Terrain varies widely, with fertile plains drained by Danube and other rivers in E, limestone basins in N, mountains and hills in SE. **Arable land:** 37.7%. **Capital:** Belgrade, 1,182,686.

Government: Type: Parliamentary republic. **Head of state:** Pres. Tomislav Nikolic; b. 1952; in office: June 11, 2012. **Head of gov.:** Prime Min. Aleksandar Vucic; b. 1970; in office: Apr. 27, 2014. **Local divisions:** 119 municipalities, 26 cities (39 municipalities, 6 cities in Vojvodina). **Defense budget:** $592 mil. **Active troops:** 28,150.

Economy: Industries: automobiles, base metals, furniture, food proc., machinery, chemicals, sugar, tires. **Chief crops:** wheat, maize, sunflowers, sugar beets, grapes/wine, fruits (raspberries, apples, sour cherries), vegetables. **Natural resources:** oil, gas, coal, iron ore, copper, zinc, antimony, chromite, gold, silver, magnesium, pyrite, limestone, marble, salt. **Water:** 18,326 cu m per capita. **Crude oil reserves:** 0.1 bil bbls. **Electricity prod.:** 37 bil kWh. **Labor force:** agric. 21.9%, industry 15.6%, services 62.5%. **Unemployment:** 22.2%.

Finance: Monetary unit: Dinar (RSD) (110.09 = $1 U.S.). **GDP:** $97.5 bil; **per capita GDP:** $13,700; **GDP growth:** 0.7%. **Imports:** $17.2 bil; Germany 12.4%, Italy 10.6%, Russia 9.6%, China 8.5%. **Exports:** $12.8 bil; Italy 16.2%, Germany 12.6%, Bosnia and Herzegovina 8.7%, Romania 5.6%, Russia 5.4%. **Tourism:** $1 bil. **Budget:** $16.4 bil (consolidated; incl. central and local govt. budgets). **Inflation:** 1.4%.

Transport: Railways: 2,366 mi. **Motor vehicles:** 284.5 per 1,000 pop. **Airports:** 10.

Communications: Telephone: 36.5 per 100 pop. **Mobile:** 120.5 per 100 pop. **Broadband:** 61.1 per 100 pop. **Internet:** 65.3%.

Health: Expend.: 10.4%. **Life expect.:** 72.6 male; 78.5 female. **Births:** 9.0 per 1,000 pop. **Deaths:** 13.6 per 1,000 pop. **Infant mortality:** 5.9 per 1,000 live births. **Undernourished:** <5%. **HIV:** NA.

Education: Compulsory: ages 7-14. **Literacy:** 98%.

Embassy: 2233 Wisconsin Ave. NW, Ste. 410, 20007; 332-0333.

Website: www.srbija.gov.rs

Serbia was a vassal principality of Turkey from 1389 to 1878, when the Treaty of Berlin established it as an independent kingdom. After the Balkan wars, Serbia annexed Old Serbia and Macedonia, 1913.

When the Austro-Hungarian empire collapsed after WWI, the Kingdom of Serbs, Croats, and Slovenes—Yugoslavia after 1929—was formed from the provinces of Croatia, Dalmatia, Bosnia, Herzegovina, Slovenia, Vojvodina, and the independent state of Montenegro.

After Nazi Germany's occupation 1941-45, Yugoslavia became a federal republic, headed by Josip Broz, a Communist, known as Marshal Tito. He rejected Stalin's dictatorship and accepted economic and military aid from the West. After Tito died in 1980, Yugoslavia held together for a decade before breaking apart. During 1991-95, Serbia, under Pres. Slobodan Milosevic, supported ethnic Serb fighters in Croatia and in Bosnia and Herzegovina, which had declared independence. The republics of Serbia and Montenegro proclaimed a new Federal Republic of Yugoslavia, Apr. 17, 1992. The UN imposed sanctions on the newly reconstituted Yugoslavia to end the bloodshed in Bosnia.

A peace agreement was reached in 1995. A UN-backed war crimes tribunal began in May 1996 to try suspects from the former Yugoslavia. Mass protests erupted when Milosevic refused to accept opposition victories in local elections, Nov. 17; non-Communist governments took office in Belgrade and other cities,

Feb. 1997. Barred from running for a third term as Serbian president, Milosevic had himself inaugurated as president of Yugoslavia, July 23, 1997.

Serbian efforts to suppress a secessionist movement in Kosovo led in Mar.-June 1999 to a war with the U.S. and its NATO allies; they accused Milosevic of pursuing a policy of ethnic cleansing against the predominantly Muslim Kosovars (ethnic Albanians). NATO stationed a multinational force in Kosovo, which was placed under UN administration.

Milosevic initially refused to accept defeat by opposition leader Vojislav Kostunica in a 2000 presidential election but resigned Oct. 6 after mass demonstrations. Kostunica was sworn in the next day. Charged with corruption and abuse of power, Milosevic surrendered to Serbian authorities Apr. 1, 2001. He was extradited June 28 to The Hague, Netherlands, where a UN tribunal had indicted him for war crimes. His trial began Feb. 12, 2002. He was found dead in prison Mar. 11, 2006, before a verdict was reached.

A pact to reconstitute Yugoslavia as a new union of Serbia and Montenegro took effect Feb. 4, 2003. Zoran Djindjic, premier of the Republic of Serbia, was assassinated Mar. 12 in Belgrade, triggering a roundup of more than 4,500 people associated with organized crime and the Milosevic regime. Serbia's union with Montenegro disintegrated in 2006. Montenegrins voted for separation in a referendum May 21, and Montenegro became an independent republic June 3.

Kosovo declared independence from Serbia Feb. 17, 2008, but Serbia refused to recognize the new country. Following parliamentary elections in Serbia May 11, a pro-Western government under Mirko Cvetkovic took office July 7. To meet a requirement for EU membership, Serbia arrested, in 2008, former Bosnian Serb leader Radovan Karadzic, who was extradited to the Intl. Criminal Court in The Hague on charges of genocide and crimes against humanity; Karadzic was convicted and sentenced to 40 years in prison, Mar. 24, 2016. Serbia's parliament passed a resolution Mar. 31, 2010, apologizing for the 1995 massacre of 8,000 Bosnian Muslims (Bosniaks) by Bosnian Serbs at Srebrenica. Ratko Mladic, the former Bosnian Serb military commander accused of directing the Srebrenica massacre, was arrested in Serbia, May 2011, and sent to The Hague. His trial began May 16, 2012. Serbia attained EU candidate status, Mar. 1, 2012. Tomislav Nikolic, an advocate for EU membership, was elected president May 20. After reaching an EU-brokered power-sharing deal with Kosovo Apr. 19, 2013, Serbia began accession negotiations for EU membership Jan. 21, 2014. Aleksandar Vucic, who favors EU membership, became prime min. following Mar. 16, 2014, elections; he retained office after his party's victory in Apr. 24, 2016, elections.

Serbia estimated that 600,000 refugees and other migrants, largely from the Middle East and SW Asia, passed through the country in 2015, most en route to Northern Europe. More than 90,000 entered Jan. 1-Mar. 9, 2016, when the government essentially closed Serbia's borders. However, by the end of Aug., the UNHCR estimated that an additional 25,000 migrants had entered Serbia.

Vojvodina (8,304 sq mi) is a nominally autonomous province in northern Serbia with a pop. (2011 census) of 1,931,809, mostly Serbian. The capital is Novi Sad. Website: www.vojvodina.gov.rs.

Seychelles
Republic of Seychelles

People: Population: 93,186. **Age distrib.:** <15: 20.2%; 65+: 7.5%. **Growth:** 0.8%. **Migrants:** 13.3%. **Pop. density:** 530.4 per sq mi, 204.8 per sq km. **Urban:** 54.2%. **Ethnic groups:** mixed French, African, Indian, Chinese, and Arab. **Languages:** Seychellois Creole, English, French (all official). **Religions:** Roman Catholic 76.2%, Protestant 10.6%.

Geography: Total area: 176 sq mi, 455 sq km; **Land area:** 176 sq mi, 455 sq km. **Location:** In Indian O. 700 mi NE of Madagascar. Nearest neighbors are Madagascar and Somalia on NW. **Topography:** Archipelago of over 116 islands. One group is composed of coral; the Mahe group of isls., predominantly mountainous, is granite. **Arable land:** 0.2%. **Capital:** Victoria, 26,062 (2014).

Government: Type: Presidential republic. **Head of state and gov.:** Pres. James Michel; b. 1944; in office: Apr. 14, 2004. **Local divisions:** 25 admin. districts. **Defense budget** (2013): $13 mil. **Active troops:** 420.

Economy: Industries: fishing, tourism, beverages. **Chief crops:** coconuts, cinnamon, vanilla, sweet potatoes, cassava, copra, bananas. **Natural resources:** fish, cinnamon trees. **Water:** NA. **Electricity prod.:** 0.3 bil kWh. **Labor force:** agric. 3%, industry 23%, services 74%. **Unemployment:** NA.

Finance: Monetary unit: Rupee (SCR) (13.04 = $1 U.S.). **GDP:** $2.4 bil; **per capita GDP:** $26,300; **GDP growth:** 4.4%. **Imports:** $1.1 bil; Saudi Arabia 22.5%, Spain 11.1%, Singapore 7.4%. **Exports:** $450.6 mil; France 18.2%, UK 17.8%, Mauritius 10%, Japan 9.2%, Italy 7.7%. **Tourism:** $392 mil. **Budget:** $423.7 mil. **Inflation:** 4%.

Transport: Airports: 7.

Communications: Telephone: 22.8 per 100 pop. **Mobile:** 158.1 per 100 pop. **Broadband:** 12.7 per 100 pop. **Internet:** 58.1%.

Health: Expend.: 3.4%. **Life expect.:** 70.2 male; 79.4 female. **Births:** 13.9 per 1,000 pop. **Deaths:** 6.9 per 1,000 pop. **Infant mortality:** 10.2 per 1,000 live births. **Undernourished:** NA. **HIV:** NA. **Education:** Compulsory: ages 6-15. **Literacy:** 95.3%.
Permanent UN mission: 800 Second Ave., Ste. 400G, New York, NY 10017; (212) 972-1785.
Website: www.egov.sc

The islands were occupied by France in 1768 and seized by Britain in 1794. Ruled as part of Mauritius from 1814, Seychelles became a separate colony in 1903 and declared independence June 29, 1976. The tourism industry has been a major driver of economic growth since independence. The country's first president was ousted in a 1977 coup by socialist leader France Albert René. A new constitution, approved June 1993, provided for a multiparty state. René resigned Apr. 14, 2004. Vice Pres. James Michel succeeded him and won 2006 and 2011 elections. Michel's Dec. 2015 reelection, by 193 votes, was upheld by the Constitutional Court, Mar. 31, 2016.

Sierra Leone
Republic of Sierra Leone

People: Population: 6,018,888. **Age distrib.:** <15: 41.9%; 65+: 3.7%. **Growth:** 2.4%. **Migrants:** 1.4%. **Pop. density:** 217.7 per sq mi, 84 per sq km. **Urban:** 40.3%. **Ethnic groups:** Temne 35%, Mende 31%, Limba 8%, Kono 5%, Kriole or Krio (descendants of freed Jamaican slaves) 2%, Mandingo 2%, Loko 2%, other (incl. Liberian refugees; small numbers of Europeans, Lebanese, Pakistanis, Indians) 15%. **Languages:** English (official), Mende (principal vernacular in S), Temne (principal vernacular in N), Krio (English-based Creole, a lingua franca). **Religions:** Muslim 60%, indigenous beliefs 30%, Christian 10%.
Geography: Total area: 27,699 sq mi, 71,740 sq km; **Land area:** 27,653 sq mi, 71,620 sq km. **Location:** W coast of W Africa. Guinea on N and E, Liberia on S. **Topography:** Mangrove swamps in heavily indented, 210-mi coastline. Wooded hills rise to a plateau and mountains in E. **Arable land:** 21.9%. **Capital:** Freetown, 1,029,157.
Government: Type: Presidential republic. **Head of state and gov.:** Pres. Ernest Bai Koroma; b. 1953; in office: Sept. 17, 2007. **Local divisions:** 3 provinces, 1 area. **Defense budget:** $13 mil. **Active troops:** 8,500.
Economy: Industries: diamond mining, iron ore, rutile and bauxite mining, small-scale mfg. (beverages, textiles, footwear). **Chief crops:** rice, coffee, cocoa, palm kernels, palm oil, peanuts, cashews. **Natural resources:** diamonds, titanium ore, bauxite, iron ore, gold, chromite. **Water:** 24,795 cu m per capita. **Electricity prod.:** 0.2 bil kWh. **Labor force:** agric. 61.1%, services 33.4%. **Unemployment:** 3.3%.
Finance: Monetary unit: Leone (SLL) (5,575.00 = $1 U.S.). **GDP:** $10 bil; **per capita GDP:** $1,600; **GDP growth:** –21.5%. **Imports:** $929.3 mil; China 23%, India 7.9%, U.S. 6.4%, Netherlands 5.1%. **Exports:** $533.3 mil; China 31.1%, Belgium 27.6%, Romania 11.3%, U.S. 7.2%. **Tourism:** $35 mil. **Budget:** $737.3 mil. **Inflation:** 8%.
Transport: Motor vehicles: 3.7 per 1,000 pop. **Airports:** 1.
Communications: Telephone: 0.3 per 100 pop. **Mobile:** 89.5 per 100 pop. **Broadband:** NA. **Internet:** 2.5%.
Health: Expend.: 11.1%. **Life expect.:** 55.6 male; 60.9 female. **Births:** 36.7 per 1,000 pop. **Deaths:** 10.6 per 1,000 pop. **Infant mortality:** 70.0 per 1,000 live births. **Undernourished:** 22.3%. **HIV:** 1.3%.
Education: Compulsory: ages 6-14. **Literacy:** 48.4%.
Embassy: 1701 19th St. NW 20009; 939-9261.
Website: www.statehouse.gov.sl

The British founded Freetown, 1787, as a haven for freed slaves. Full independence arrived Apr. 27, 1961. A one-party state was established by referendum in 1978.

Mutinous soldiers ousted Pres. Joseph Momoh, Apr. 30, 1992. A coup, Jan. 16, 1996, paved the way for multiparty elections and a return to civilian rule. A peace accord, signed Nov. 30 with the Revolutionary United Front (RUF), brought a temporary halt to a civil war that had claimed over 10,000 lives in five years.

A coup on May 25, 1997, was met with international opposition. Nigeria's military restored Pres. Ahmad Tejan Kabbah to power on Mar. 10, 1998, but RUF rebels mounted a guerrilla counteroffensive, killing thousands of civilians and mutilating thousands more. A power-sharing agreement between the Kabbah government and the RUF, July 1999, was maintained by a UN mission (UNAMSIL). The accord collapsed in early May 2000, as RUF guerrillas took more than 500 UN peacekeepers hostage. Rebel leader Foday Sankoh was captured in Freetown, May 17. The hostages were freed by the end of May. A UN-sponsored disarmament program in 2001 reduced the level of violence. The Sierra Leone Special Court was created in 2002 to try war crimes that had occurred after Nov. 1996. Government and rebel leaders declared an official end to the war Jan. 18; more than 50,000 people had died in the conflict. Kabbah won the May 14 presidential election.

Sankoh, an indicted war criminal, died in UN custody, July 29, 2003. Opposition leader Ernest Bai Koroma won a presidential runoff vote, Sept. 8, 2007. Three former RUF leaders were convicted of war crimes, Feb. 25, 2009. A cholera epidemic swept through the country in 2012; about 23,000 cases were reported, killing about 300. Koroma won reelection Nov. 17, 2012. An Ebola virus epidemic that began in Guinea in Dec. 2013 caused 14,124 cases and 3,956 deaths in Sierra Leone by Mar. 29, 2016.

Singapore
Republic of Singapore

People: Population: 5,781,728. **Age distrib.:** <15: 12.9%; 65+: 9.2%. **Growth:** 1.9%. **Migrants:** 45.4%. **Pop. density:** 21,797.1 per sq mi, 8,415.9 per sq km. **Urban:** 100%. **Ethnic groups:** Chinese 74.2%, Malay 13.3%, Indian 9.2%. **Languages:** Mandarin, English, Malay, Tamil (all official); Hokkien; Cantonese; Teochew. **Religions:** Buddhist 33.9%, Muslim 14.3%, Taoist 11.3%, Catholic 7.1%, Hindu 5.2%, none 16.4%.
Geography: Total area: 269 sq mi, 697 sq km; **Land area:** 265 sq mi, 687 sq km. **Location:** Off tip of Malayan Peninsula in SE Asia. Nearest neighbors are Malaysia on N, Indonesia on S. **Topography:** Flat, formerly swampy island with 40 nearby islets. **Arable land:** 0.8%. **Capital:** Singapore, 5,717,082.
Government: Type: Parliamentary republic. **Head of state:** Pres. Tony Tan Keng Yam; b. 1940; in office: Sept. 1, 2011. **Head of gov.:** Prime Min. Lee Hsien Loong; b. 1952; in office: Aug. 12, 2004. **Local divisions:** none. **Defense budget:** $9.7 bil. **Active troops:** 72,500.
Economy: Industries: electronics, chemicals, financial services, oil drilling equip., petroleum refining, rubber proc. and prods, proc. food and beverages. **Chief crops:** orchids, vegetables. **Natural resources:** fish, deepwater ports. **Water:** 107 cu m per capita. **Electricity prod.:** 44 bil kWh. **Labor force** (excl. nonresidents): agric. 1.3%, industry 14.8%, services 83.9%. **Unemployment:** 3%.
Finance: Monetary unit: Dollar (SGD) (1.36 = $1 U.S.). **GDP:** $471.9 bil; **per capita GDP:** $85,300; **GDP growth:** 2%. **Imports:** $294.2 bil; China 14.2%, U.S. 11.2%, Malaysia 11.2%, Japan 6.3%, South Korea 6.1%. **Exports:** $384.6 bil; China 13.7%, Hong Kong 11.5%, Malaysia 10.8%, Indonesia 8.2%, U.S. 6.9%. **Tourism:** $16.7 bil. **Budget:** $45.5 bil (incl. operational and development expenditures). **Inflation:** –0.5%.
Transport: Motor vehicles: 143.3 per 1,000 pop. **Airports:** 9.
Communications: Telephone: 36 per 100 pop. **Mobile:** 146.1 per 100 pop. **Broadband:** 156.1 per 100 pop. **Internet:** 82.1%.
Health: Expend.: 4.9%. **Life expect.:** 82.3 male; 87.8 female. **Births:** 8.4 per 1,000 pop. **Deaths:** 3.5 per 1,000 pop. **Infant mortality:** 2.4 per 1,000 live births. **Undernourished:** NA. **HIV:** NA.
Education: Compulsory: ages 6-11. **Literacy:** 96.8%.
Embassy: 3501 International Pl. NW 20008; 537-3100.
Website: www.gov.sg

Founded in 1819 by Sir Thomas Stamford Raffles, Singapore was a British colony until 1959, when it became autonomous within the Commonwealth. On Sept. 16, 1963, it joined with Malaya, Sarawak, and Sabah to form the Federation of Malaysia. Tensions between Malayans, dominant in the federation, and ethnic Chinese, dominant in Singapore, led to an accord under which Singapore became a separate nation, Aug. 9, 1965.

Singapore is one of the world's largest ports and a major manufacturing, banking, and commerce center with high standards in health, education, and housing. Immigrant workers from elsewhere in Asia hold many low-paying jobs. The government, dominated by the People's Action Party (PAP), has taken strong actions to keep order and suppress dissent.

Singapore's first prime min., Lee Kuan Yew (in office 1959-90), credited with building the country's strong economy, died Mar. 23, 2015. His son, Lee Hsien Loong, took office as prime min., Aug. 12, 2004. The PAP won a landslide victory in Sept. 11, 2015, parliamentary elections.

Slovakia
Slovak Republic

People: Population: 5,445,802. **Age distrib.:** <15: 15.1%; 65+: 14.9%. **Growth:** 0.01%. **Migrants:** 3.3%. **Pop. density:** 293.2 per sq mi, 113.2 per sq km. **Urban:** 53.5%. **Ethnic groups:** Slovak 80.7%, Hungarian 8.5%, Roma 2%. **Languages:** Slovak (official), Hungarian, Roma. **Religions:** Roman Catholic 62%, Protestant 8.2%, Greek Catholic 3.8%, none 13.4%.
Geography: Total area: 18,933 sq mi, 49,035 sq km; **Land area:** 18,573 sq mi, 48,105 sq km. **Location:** E central Europe. Poland on N, Hungary on S, Austria and Czech Rep. on W, Ukraine on E. **Topography:** Carpathian Mts. in N, fertile Danube plain in S. **Arable land:** 29%. **Capital:** Bratislava, 398,143.
Government: Type: Parliamentary republic. **Head of state:** Pres. Andrej Kiska; b. 1963; in office: June 15, 2014. **Head of gov.:** Prime Min. Robert Fico; b. 1964; in office: Apr. 4, 2012. **Local divisions:** 8 regions. **Defense budget:** $924 mil. **Active troops:** 15,850.
Economy: Industries: automobiles; metal and metal prods.; electricity, gas, coke, oil, nuclear fuel; chemicals, synthetic fibers, wood and paper prods.; machinery. **Chief crops:** grains, potatoes, sugar beets, hops, fruit. **Natural resources:** lignite, iron ore, copper and manganese ore, salt. **Water:** 9,233 cu m per capita. **Crude oil reserves** (2015): 9 mil bbls. **Electricity prod.:** 26 bil

kWh. **Labor force:** agric. 4.2%, industry 22.6%, services 73.2%. **Unemployment:** 13.3%.

Finance: Monetary unit: Euro (EUR) (0.89 = $1 U.S.). **GDP:** $161 bil; **per capita GDP:** $29,700; **GDP growth:** 3.6%. **Imports:** $53.3 bil; Germany 19.4%, Czech Republic 17.4%, Austria 9.1%, Hungary 6.3%, Poland 6.3%, South Korea 5.5%, Russia 5.2%. **Exports:** $56.4 bil; Germany 22.7%, Czech Republic 12.5%, Poland 8.5%, Austria 5.7%, Hungary 5.7%, France 5.6%, UK 5.5%. **Tourism:** $2.4 bil. **Budget:** $18.2 bil. **Inflation:** −0.3%.

Transport: Railways: 2,252 mi. **Motor vehicles:** 426.3 per 1,000 pop. **Airports:** 21.

Communications: Telephone: 15.9 per 100 pop. **Mobile:** 122.3 per 100 pop. **Broadband:** 59.5 per 100 pop. **Internet:** 85%.

Health: Expend.: 8.1%. **Life expect.:** 73.5 male; 80.9 female. **Births:** 9.8 per 1,000 pop. **Deaths:** 9.8 per 1,000 pop. **Infant mortality:** 5.2 per 1,000 live births. **Undernourished:** <5%. **HIV:** NA.

Education: Compulsory: ages 6-15. **Literacy:** NA.

Embassy: 3523 International Ct. NW 20008; 237-1054.

Website: www.government.gov.sk

Slovakia was originally settled by Illyrian, Celtic, and Germanic tribes and was incorporated into Great Moravia in the 9th cent. It became part of Hungary in the 11th cent. Overrun by Czech Hussites in the 15th cent., it was restored to Hungarian rule in 1526. The Slovaks disassociated themselves from Hungary after WWI and joined the Czechs of Bohemia to form the Republic of Czechoslovakia, Oct. 28, 1918.

Germany invaded Czechoslovakia, 1939, and declared Slovakia independent. Slovakia rejoined Czechoslovakia in 1945. Czechoslovakia split into two separate states—the Czech Republic and Slovakia—on Jan. 1, 1993.

Slovakia joined the EU and NATO in 2004. The country adopted the euro currency Jan. 1, 2009. Slovakia's economy was battered in the global recession 2008-09. GDP growth returned beginning in 2010. In Mar. 10, 2012, legislative elections, Robert Fico's social-democratic party, Smer, won a majority (83 of 150 seats). Fico ran for president in 2014 but lost a Mar. 29 runoff election to former businessman Andrej Kiska. Smer won the most seats but lost its majority in Mar. 5, 2016, elections in which far-right, anti-immigration parties made gains; Fico remained prime min., heading a coalition government.

Slovenia
Republic of Slovenia

People: Population: 1,978,029. **Age distrib.:** <15: 13.3%; 65+: 19%. **Growth:** −0.3%. **Migrants:** 11.4%. **Pop. density:** 254.2 per sq mi, 98.2 per sq km. **Urban:** 49.6%. **Ethnic groups:** Slovene 83.1%, Serb 2%, Croat 1.8%. **Languages:** Slovenian (official), Serbo-Croatian. **Religions:** Catholic 57.8%, none 10.1%.

Geography: Total area: 7,827 sq mi, 20,273 sq km; **Land area:** 7,780 sq mi, 20,151 sq km. **Location:** SE Europe. Italy on W, Austria on N, Hungary on NE, Croatia on SE, S. **Topography:** Mostly hilly; more than half forested. **Arable land:** 8.6%. **Capital:** Ljubljana, 278,903 (2014).

Government: Type: Parliamentary republic. **Head of state:** Pres. Borut Pahor; b. 1963; in office: Dec. 22, 2012. **Head of gov.:** Prime Min. Miro Cerar; b. 1963; in office: Sept. 18, 2014. **Local divisions:** 201 municipalities, 11 urban municipalities. **Defense budget:** $447 mil. **Active troops:** 7,600.

Economy: Industries: ferrous metallurgy and aluminum prods., lead and zinc smelting, electronics (incl. military), trucks, automobiles, elec. power equip., wood prods. **Chief crops:** hops, wheat, coffee, corn, apples, pears. **Natural resources:** lignite, lead, zinc, building stone, hydropower, forests. **Water:** 15,411 cu m per capita. **Electricity prod.:** 15 bil kWh. **Labor force:** agric. 8.3%, industry 30.8%, services 60.9%. **Unemployment:** 9.5%.

Finance: Monetary unit: Euro (EUR) (0.89 = $1 U.S.). **GDP:** $64 bil; **per capita GDP:** $31,000; **GDP growth:** 2.9%. **Imports:** $27.1 bil; Germany 16.5%, Italy 13.6%, Austria 10.2%, China 5.5%, Croatia 5.1%. **Exports:** $28.1 bil; Germany 19.1%, Italy 10.6%, Austria 8%, Croatia 6.8%. **Tourism:** $2.5 bil. **Budget:** $18.6 bil. **Inflation:** −0.5%.

Transport: Railways: 764 mi. **Motor vehicles:** 594.3 per 1,000 pop. **Airports:** 7.

Communications: Telephone: 36.2 per 100 pop. **Mobile:** 113.2 per 100 pop. **Broadband:** 46.7 per 100 pop. **Internet:** 73.1%.

Health: Expend.: 9.2%. **Life expect.:** 74.6 male; 82.0 female. **Births:** 8.3 per 1,000 pop. **Deaths:** 11.5 per 1,000 pop. **Infant mortality:** 4.0 per 1,000 live births. **Undernourished:** <5%. **HIV:** NA.

Education: Compulsory: ages 6-14. **Literacy:** 99.7%.

Embassy: 2410 California St. NW 20008; 386-6610.

Website: www.vlada.si

The Slovenes settled in their current territory during the 6th to 8th cent. They fell under German domination in the 9th cent. Modern Slovenian political history began after 1848 when the Slovenes, divided among several Austrian provinces, began their struggle for unification. In 1918 a majority of Slovenes became part of the Kingdom of Serbs, Croats, and Slovenes, later renamed Yugoslavia.

Slovenia declared independence June 25, 1991; joined the UN May 22, 1992; attained full membership in the EU and NATO in 2004; and adopted the euro Jan. 1, 2007. In July 13, 2014, National Assembly elections, a new party (named the Modern Center Party as of Mar. 7, 2015) headed by Miro Cerar won the most seats, and Cerar became prime min. After Hungary, Oct. 2015, blocked migrants and refugees (many from the Middle East and SW Asia) trying to reach N Europe, large numbers entered Slovenia. After building border fencing and restricting border crossings, Slovenia announced, Mar. 8, 2016, it was essentially closing its border. About 474,000 migrants entered Slovenia Oct. 1, 2015-Mar. 8, 2016.

Solomon Islands

People: Population: 635,027. **Age distrib.:** <15: 35.1%; 65+: 4.2%. **Growth:** 2%. **Migrants:** 0.4%. **Pop. density:** 58.8 per sq mi, 22.7 per sq km. **Urban:** 22.8%. **Ethnic groups:** Melanesian 95.3%, Polynesian 3.1%. **Languages:** Melanesian pidgin (lingua franca in much of country), English (official), 120 indigenous langs. **Religions:** Protestant 73.4% (incl. Church of Melanesia 31.9%, South Sea Evangelical 17.1%, Seventh-day Adventist 11.7%, United Church 10.1%), Roman Catholic 19.6%.

Geography: Total area: 11,157 sq mi, 28,896 sq km; **Land area:** 10,805 sq mi, 27,986 sq km. **Location:** Melanesian Archipelago in W Pacific O. Nearest neighbor is Papua New Guinea to W. **Topography:** 10 large volcanic, rugged islands; 4 groups of smaller islands. **Arable land:** 0.7%. **Capital:** Honiara, 73,302 (2014).

Government: Type: Parliamentary democracy under constitutional monarchy. **Head of state:** Queen Elizabeth II, rep. by Gov.-Gen. Sir Frank Ofagioro Kabui; in office: July 7, 2009. **Head of gov.:** Prime Min. Manasseh Sogavare; b. 1955; in office: Dec. 9, 2014. **Local divisions:** 9 provinces, 1 city. **Defense budget/active troops:** NA.

Economy: Industries: fish (tuna), mining, timber. **Chief crops:** cocoa, coconuts, palm kernels, rice, fruit. **Natural resources:** fish, forests, gold, bauxite, phosphates, lead, zinc, nickel. **Water:** 76,594 cu m per capita. **Electricity prod.** (2012): 85 mil kWh. **Labor force:** agric. 75%, industry 5%, services 20%. **Unemployment:** 3.9%.

Finance: Monetary unit: Dollar (SBD) (7.79 = $1 U.S.). **GDP:** $1.1 bil; **per capita GDP:** $1,900; **GDP growth:** 3.3%. **Imports** (2012): $446 mil; Australia 24.7%, China 18.4%, Malaysia 6.3%, Singapore 5.8%. **Exports** (2012): $493.1 mil; China 61.7%, India 5.9%, Italy 5.9%. **Tourism:** $47 mil. **Budget:** $440.7 mil. **Inflation:** −0.6%.

Transport: Airports: 1.

Communications: Telephone: 1.3 per 100 pop. **Mobile:** 72.7 per 100 pop. **Broadband:** 13 per 100 pop. **Internet:** 10%.

Health: Expend.: 5.1%. **Life expect.:** 72.7 male; 78.1 female. **Births:** 25.3 per 1,000 pop. **Deaths:** 3.8 per 1,000 pop. **Infant mortality:** 15.2 per 1,000 live births. **Undernourished:** 11.3%. **HIV:** NA.

Education: Compulsory: none. **Literacy:** 84.1%.

Permanent UN Mission: 800 Second Ave., Ste. 400L, New York, NY 10017; (212) 599-6192.

Website: www.pmc.gov.sb

The Solomon Isls. were sighted 1568 by an expedition from Peru. Britain established a protectorate in the 1890s over most of the group, inhabited by Melanesians. The islands saw major WWII battles. They achieved self-government, Jan. 2, 1976, and formal independence, July 7, 1978.

A coup attempt, June 5, 2000, sparked factional fighting in Honiara. To restore order after three years of lawlessness, a 2,225-member intervention force, led by Australia and authorized by the Pacific Isls. Forum, provided security 2003-05.

Following Apr. 2006 elections, parliament's choice of Snyder Rini as prime min. led to two days of rioting in Honiara over alleged influence-buying by the ethnic Chinese business community. Rini resigned Apr. 26, 2006, rather than face a no-confidence vote. Prime Min. Danny Philip, who was elected Aug. 25, 2010, dismissed finance min. Gordon Darcy Lilo and was forced to resign when a number of MPs abandoned the government in protest. The parliament then elected Lilo prime min., Nov. 16, 2011. Former prime min. Manasseh Sogavare (2000-01, 2006-07) again became head of government following Nov. 19, 2014, parliamentary elections.

Somalia
Federal Republic of Somalia

People: Population: 10,817,354. **Age distrib.:** <15: 43.4%; 65+: 2.2%. **Growth:** 1.9%. **Migrants:** 0.2%. **Pop. density:** 44.7 per sq mi, 17.2 per sq km. **Urban:** 40%. **Ethnic groups:** Somali 85%, Bantu and other non-Somali 15%. **Languages:** Somali, Arabic (both official); Italian; English. **Religions:** Sunni Muslim (Islam) (official).

Geography: Total area: 246,201 sq mi, 637,657 sq km; **Land area:** 242,216 sq mi, 627,337 sq km. **Location:** Eastern horn of Africa. Djibouti, Ethiopia, Kenya on W. **Topography:** Coastline extends for 1,700 mi. Hills cover the N; center and S are flat. **Arable land:** 1.8%. **Capital:** Mogadishu, 2,264,850.

Government: Type: Federal parliamentary republic. **Head of state:** Pres. Hassan Sheikh Mohamud; b. 1955; in office: Sept. 10, 2012. **Head of gov.:** Prime Min. Omar Abdirashid Ali Sharmarke; in office: Dec. 24, 2014. **Local divisions:** 18 regions. **Defense budget:** NA. **Active troops:** 17,000.

Economy: Industries: light industries incl. sugar refining, textiles, wireless communication. **Chief crops:** bananas, sorghum, corn, coconuts, rice, sugarcane, mangoes, sesame seeds, beans. **Natural resources:** uranium, largely unexploited reserves of iron ore, tin, gypsum, bauxite, copper, salt, nat. gas. **Water:** 1,363 cu m per capita. **Electricity prod.:** 0.3 bil kWh. **Labor force:** agric. 71%, industry and services 29%. **Unemployment:** 6.9%.

Finance: Monetary unit: Shilling (SOS) (579.49 = $1 U.S.). **GDP** (2014): $4.4 bil; **per capita GDP** (2014): $400; **GDP growth** (2010): 2.6%. **Imports** (2014): $3.5 bil; Djibouti 18.7%, India 16.5%, China 11.8%, Oman 8.7%, Kenya 6.1%. **Exports** (2014): $819 mil; UAE 45.7%, Yemen 19.7%, Oman 15.9%. **Budget** (2014 est.): $151.1 mil. **Inflation:** NA.

Transport: Airports: 6.

Communications: Telephone: 0.5 per 100 pop. **Mobile:** 52.5 per 100 pop. **Broadband:** NA. **Internet:** 1.8%.

Health: Expend.: NA. **Life expect.:** 50.3 male; 54.5 female. **Births:** 40.0 per 1,000 pop. **Deaths:** 13.3 per 1,000 pop. **Infant mortality:** 96.6 per 1,000 live births. **Undernourished:** NA. **HIV:** 0.5%.

Education: Compulsory: NA. **Literacy:** NA.

Embassy: 1705 Desales St., Ste. 300, 20036; 296-0570.

Website: www.villasomalia.gov.so or www.state.gov/p/af/ci/so/

British Somaliland (present-day N Somalia) was formed in the 19th cent., as was Italian Somaliland (now central and S Somalia). Italy lost its African colonies in WWII. British Somaliland gained independence, June 26, 1960, and by prearrangement, merged, July 1, with the UN Trust Territory of Somalia to create the independent Somali Republic.

On Oct. 15, 1969, Somalia's first civilian president, Abdirashid Ali Sharmarke, was assassinated. Six days later, Maj. Gen. Muhammad Siad Barre led a military coup. In 1970, he declared the country a socialist state—the Somali Democratic Republic.

Somalia has laid claim to Ogaden, the huge eastern region of Ethiopia, peopled mostly by Somalis. Some 11,000 Cuban troops with Soviet arms defeated Somali army troops and ethnic Somali rebels in Ethiopia, 1978. As many as 1.5 mil refugees entered Somalia. Guerrilla fighting in Ogaden continued until 1988, when a peace agreement was reached with Ethiopia.

Fighting in Mogadishu led Siad Barre to flee the capital, Jan. 1991. Fighting between rival factions caused 40,000 casualties, 1991-92, and by mid-1992 the civil war, drought, and banditry combined to produce a famine that threatened some 1.5 mil people.

U.S. troops and the UN worked to safeguard food delivery, 1991-93, resulting in significant U.S. and other casualties; a failed mission Oct. 3-4, 1993, left 18 U.S. troops and more than 500 Somalis dead. The U.S. withdrew its peacekeeping forces Mar. 25, 1994.

When the last UN troops pulled out, Mar. 3, 1995, armed factions controlled different regions. A joint police force in the capital could not stop the continued violence and food shortages. A peace deal Jan. 29, 2004, led to the Aug. 22 inauguration of a transitional parliament, Somalia's first legislature in 13 years. Meeting in Nairobi, Kenya, the parliament chose Abdullahi Yusuf Ahmed as president; he was sworn in Oct. 14.

Because Mogadishu was held by his rivals, Pres. Yusuf moved, July 26, 2005, to make his transitional capital at Jowhar; an interim parliament convened Feb. 26, 2006, at Baidoa. On June 5, an Islamist militia took over Mogadishu, defeating U.S.-backed secular warlords. The Islamists, calling themselves the Supreme Islamic Courts Council, held much of the central and southern regions.

With aid from Ethiopian troops, transitional govt. forces recaptured Mogadishu in Dec. 2006. The UN Security Council authorized, Feb. 20, 2007, an African Union peacekeeping mission to Somalia (AMISOM). An upsurge of fighting in Mogadishu, Feb.-Apr., killed hundreds of people and caused 350,000 to flee. Bombings and kidnappings escalated in 2007-08; the violence forced international aid workers to pull out, worsening a humanitarian crisis. Many of the attacks on transitional authorities and their allies were blamed on al-Shabab, an al-Qaeda ally.

After Pres. Yusuf resigned Dec. 29, 2008, the transitional parliament, meeting in Djibouti Jan. 31, 2009, elected a moderate Islamist, Sheikh Sharif Sheikh Ahmed. Meanwhile, pirates carried out more than 200 attacks off the Horn of Africa in 2009. Pirates and Islamist insurgents continued to disrupt famine relief efforts in 2010-11. Pressured by AMISOM forces, al-Shabab pulled out of Mogadishu, Aug. 6, 2011, but continued to control much of southern Somalia. Somali leaders met in Feb. 2012 in Garowe, Somalia, and signed Feb. 18 the Garowe II Principles, which established the conditions to install the caretaker government sworn in Aug. 20. The new parliament elected activist-professor Hassan Sheik Mohamud president Sept. 10, 2012. Bombings and other attacks by al-Shabab, in Mogadishu and elsewhere, continued. In 2014, al-Shabab attacked the parliament building and presidential palace in Mogadishu and assassinated several members of parliament. Al-Shabab leader Ahmed Abdi Godane was killed by a U.S. airstrike Sept. 1, 2014, and U.S. drone strikes killed

other high-ranking members of the group, 2014-15. AMISOM and Somali forces had pushed al-Shabab out of major towns by mid-2015. However, the group's terrorist attacks continued, killing more than 150 in early 2016, and it retook some towns. A U.S. airstrike, Mar. 5, 2016, killed an estimated 150 al-Shabab fighters, and U.S. special operations troops assisted AMISOM forces (totaling more than 22,000 uniformed personnel in 2016). Al-Shabab attacks intensified as Somalia prepared for late 2016 indirect parliamentary and presidential elections.

South Africa
Republic of South Africa

People: Population: 54,300,704. **Age distrib.:** <15: 28.3%; 65+: 5.6%. **Growth:** 1%. **Migrants:** 5.8%. **Pop. density:** 115.8 per sq mi, 44.7 per sq km. **Urban:** 65.3%. **Ethnic groups:** black African 80.2%, colored (South African term for persons of mixed-race ancestry) 8.8%, white 8.4%, Indian/Asian 2.5%. **Languages:** IsiZulu, IsiXhosa, Afrikaans, English, Sepedi, Setswana, Sesotho, Xitsonga, siSwati, Tshivenda, isiNdebele (all official). **Religions:** Protestant 36.6% (incl. Zionist Christian 11.1%), Catholic 7.1%, none 15.1%.

Geography: Total area: 470,693 sq mi, 1,219,090 sq km; **Land area:** 468,909 sq mi, 1,214,470 sq km. **Location:** Southern extreme of Africa. Namibia, Botswana, Zimbabwe on N; Mozambique, Swaziland on E; surrounds Lesotho. **Topography:** Large interior plateau reaches close to the country's 1,739-mi coastline. Few major rivers or lakes. Rainfall is sparse in W, more plentiful in E. **Arable land:** 10.3%. **Capital:** Pretoria (admin.), 2,125,465; Cape Town (legis.), 3,697,912; Bloemfontein (judicial), 510,106. **Cities:** Johannesburg, 9,615,976; Durban, 2,913,685; Port Elizabeth, 1,185,796; Vereeniging, 1,163,557.

Government: Type: Parliamentary republic. **Head of state and gov.:** Pres. Jacob Zuma; b. 1942; in office: May 9, 2009. **Local divisions:** 9 provinces. **Defense budget:** $3.5 bil. **Active troops:** 67,200.

Economy: Industries: mining (platinum, gold, chromium), auto assembly, metalworking, machinery, textiles, iron and steel, chemicals, fertilizer, foodstuffs. **Chief crops:** corn, wheat, sugarcane, fruits, vegetables. **Natural resources:** gold, chromium, antimony, coal, iron ore, manganese, nickel, phosphates, tin, rare earth elements, uranium, gem diamonds, platinum, copper, vanadium, salt, nat. gas. **Water:** 942 cu m per capita. **Crude oil reserves** (2015): 15 mil bbls. **Electricity prod.:** 238 bil kWh. **Labor force:** agric. 4%, industry 18%, services 66%. **Unemployment:** 25.1%.

Finance: Monetary unit: Rand (ZAR) (14.59 = $1 U.S.). **GDP:** $723.5 bil; **per capita GDP:** $13,200; **GDP growth:** 1.3%. **Imports:** $86.8 bil; China 17.6%, Germany 11.2%, U.S. 6.7%, Nigeria 5%. **Exports:** $85.1 bil; China 11.3%, U.S. 7.3%, Germany 6%, Namibia 5.2%, Botswana 5.2%. **Tourism:** $8.2 bil. **Budget:** $98.3 bil. **Inflation:** 4.6%.

Transport: Railways: 13,040 mi. **Motor vehicles:** 185.4 per 1,000 pop. **Airports:** 144.

Communications: Telephone: 7.7 per 100 pop. **Mobile:** 159.3 per 100 pop. **Broadband:** 46.7 per 100 pop. **Internet:** 51.9%.

Health: Expend.: 8.8%. **Life expect.:** 61.6 male; 64.6 female. **Births:** 20.5 per 1,000 pop. **Deaths:** 9.6 per 1,000 pop. **Infant mortality:** 32.0 per 1,000 live births. **Undernourished:** <5%. **HIV:** 19.2%.

Education: Compulsory: ages 7-15. **Literacy:** 94.6%.

Embassy: 3051 Massachusetts Ave. NW 20008; 232-4400.

Website: www.gov.za

Bushmen and KhoiKhoi were the original inhabitants. Bantus, including Zulu, Xhosa, Swazi, and Sotho, occupied the area from northeastern to southern South Africa before the 17th cent.

The Dutch settled the Cape of Good Hope area, beginning in the 17th cent. Britain seized the Cape, 1806. Many Dutch trekked north and founded two republics, Transvaal and Orange Free State. Diamonds were discovered, 1867, and gold, 1886. The Dutch (Boers) resented encroachments by the British and others; the Anglo-Boer War followed, 1899-1902. Britain won and created, May 31, 1910, the Union of South Africa, incorporating two British colonies (Cape and Natal) with Transvaal and Orange Free State. After a referendum, the Union became the Republic of South Africa, May 31, 1961, and withdrew from the Commonwealth (it rejoined in 1994).

Daniel Malan's National Party election in 1948 made the policy of separate development of the races, or apartheid, official. Under apartheid, blacks were severely restricted to certain occupations and paid less than whites for similar work. Only whites could vote or run for public office. Persons of Asian Indian ancestry and those of mixed race ("coloureds") had limited political rights.

Protests against apartheid were suppressed. At Sharpeville on Mar. 21, 1960, government troops killed 69 black protesters. At least 600 persons, mostly Bantus, were killed in 1976 anti-apartheid riots. In 1986, Nobel Peace Prize winner Bishop Desmond Tutu called for Western nations to apply sanctions against South Africa to force an end to apartheid. Pres. P. W. Botha offered blacks an advisory role in government starting in Apr. On May 19, South Africa attacked three neighboring countries—Zimbabwe, Botswana, Zambia—striking at guerrilla strongholds of the anti-apartheid African National Congress (ANC).

Some 2 mil South African black workers staged a strike, June 6-8, 1988. Pres. Botha, head of the government since 1978, resigned Aug. 14, 1989, and was replaced by F. W. de Klerk. In 1990 the government lifted its ban on the ANC. Anti-apartheid leader Nelson Mandela was freed Feb. 11 after more than 27 years in prison. In Feb. 1991, Pres. de Klerk pledged to end apartheid laws.

In 1993 negotiators agreed on basic principles for a new democratic constitution. South Africa's partially self-governing black territories, or "homelands," were incorporated into a national system of 9 provinces. The ANC won elections Apr. 26-29, 1994, making Mandela president. The predominantly-Zulu Inkatha Freedom Party won control of the legislature in a mainly Zulu province. By then, fighting between the ANC and Inkatha (aided, during the apartheid era, by South African defense forces) had killed more than 14,000 people in the Zulu region.

A post-apartheid constitution became law Dec. 10, 1996. The ANC won elections, June 2, 1999, and ANC leader Thabo Mbeki became president. South Africa, Nov. 30, 2006, became the first African country to legalize same-sex marriage.

After Mbeki's former deputy president, Jacob Zuma, defeated him in a power struggle for the ANC leadership, Mbeki resigned his presidency, Sept. 21, 2008. Zuma became president after Apr. 22, 2009, elections. Mandela died Dec. 5, 2013. Despite corruption charges, Zuma was reelected president by the National Assembly, May 21, 2014, following an ANC victory in May 7 parliamentary elections.

Thousands of miners struck for better wages at the Lonmin platinum mine near Marikana, Aug. 10, 2012. Protests at the mine left at least 10 dead, before police officers opened fire on protesters Aug. 16, killing 34. A strike-ending wage agreement was reached Sept. 18. A five-month strike in 2014 against Lonmin, Anglo American Platinum, and Impala Platinum Holdings ended in June with a wage increase for 70,000 union workers. With platinum prices depressed in 2015, Lonmin and Anglo American announced plans to close or sell some mines.

Hurt by continuing corruption allegations and a weak economy, the ANC won 54% of the vote nationwide—a sharp drop in support—and lost control of major cities including Pretoria and Port Elizabeth in Aug. 3, 2016, municipal elections.

South Sudan
Republic of South Sudan

People: Population: 12,530,717. **Age distrib.:** <15: 44.9%; 65+: 2.1%. **Growth:** 3.9%. **Migrants:** 6.7%. **Pop. density:** 50.4 per sq mi, 19.4 per sq km. **Urban:** 19%. **Ethnic groups:** Dinka 35.8%; Nuer 15.6%; Shilluk, Azande, Bari, Kakwa, Kuku, Murle, Mandari, Didinga, Ndogo, Bviri, Lndi, Anuak, Bongo, Lango, Dungotona, Acholi. **Languages:** English (official), Arabic (incl. Juba, Sudanese variants). **Religions:** animist, Christian.

Geography: Total area: 248,777 sq mi, 644,329 sq km. **Location:** NE Africa. Sudan on N, Uganda and Kenya on S, Ethiopia on E, Central African Rep. and Dem. Rep. of the Congo on W. **Topography:** The White Nile R. flows N through center of country and feeds the Sudd, a swampy area occupying more than 15% of the country's center; it is one of the world's largest wetlands. **Arable land:** NA. **Capital:** Juba, 336,232.

Government: Type: Presidential republic. **Head of state and gov.:** Pres. Salva Kiir Mayardit; b. 1951; in office: July 9, 2011. **Local divisions:** 10 states. **Defense budget:** $1.3 bil. **Active troops:** 185,000.

Economy: Chief crops: sorghum, maize, rice, millet, wheat, gum arabic, sugarcane, mangoes, papayas, bananas, sweet potatoes, sunflower seeds, cotton, sesame seeds, cassava. **Natural resources:** hydropower, gold, diamonds, petroleum, hardwoods, limestone, iron ore, copper, chromium ore, zinc, tungsten, mica, silver. **Water:** 4,011 cu m per capita. **Labor force:** Vast majority of pop. relies on subsistence agriculture. **Unemployment:** NA.

Finance: Monetary unit: Pound (SSP) (56.98 = $1 U.S.). **GDP:** $23.7 bil; **per capita GDP:** $2,000; **GDP growth:** -0.2%. **Budget** (FY 2013 est.): $2.3 bil. **Inflation:** 50.2%.

Transport: Railways: 154 mi. **Airports:** 3.

Communications: Telephone (2012): 0.001 per 100 pop. **Mobile:** 23.9 per 100 pop. **Broadband:** 1.3 per 100 pop. **Internet:** 17.9%.

Health: Expend.: 2.7%. **Life expect.:** 59.7 male; 62.7 female. **Births:** 36.2 per 1,000 pop. **Deaths:** 8.0 per 1,000 pop. **Infant mortality:** 64.6 per 1,000 live births. **Undernourished:** NA. **HIV:** 2.5%.

Education: Compulsory: ages 6-13. **Literacy:** 32%.
Embassy: 1015 31st St. NW, 3rd Fl., 20007; 293-7940.
Website: www.goss.org

South Sudan was a region of the Republic of the Sudan when that country became independent in 1956. Northerners (mostly Arab Muslims) dominated, while southerners (mostly black Africans who practiced Christianity or traditional religions) were marginalized. Southern Anya Nya rebels waged war against the north, 1955-72, until an agreement was reached offering regional self-government for the south. Oil was discovered in the south in 1978.

Civil war broke out again in 1983, with southern rebels led by the Sudan People's Liberation Movement (SPLM). Fighting and related famine cost an estimated 2 mil lives and displaced millions of southerners. A peace accord was signed in 2005. A power-sharing agreement offered autonomy for southern Sudan and allowed for an independence referendum.

Almost 99% of southern Sudanese who voted in the referendum, Jan. 9-15, 2011, supported secession. The UN Security Council, July 8, authorized a peacekeeping force (UNMISS) for the area. South Sudan attained full independence July 9, 2011. The country faced challenges of poverty and factional conflict.

Pres. Salva Kiir fired Vice Pres. Riek Machar, July 23, 2013. Heavy fighting broke out in Juba in Dec. 2013 between government troops and rebels led by Machar. Forces of Kiir and Machar (who belong to different ethnic groups) battled throughout the country in 2014-15, killing tens of thousands and displacing more than 2 mil. Kiir and Machar signed a peace accord Aug. 2015, although a number of cease-fire violations occurred. Machar returned to Juba and resumed the vice presidency in Apr. 2016 but fled the country, Aug. 17; a new round of heavy fighting began July 7. UNMISS had 12,000 troops in South Sudan as of July 31, 2016. An Aug. 12 UN Security Council Resolution authorized an additional 4,000 troops focused on protecting civilians. The UN estimated in Aug. that almost 5 mil South Sudanese faced severe hunger.

Spain
Kingdom of Spain

People: Population: 48,563,476. **Age distrib.:** <15: 15.4%; 65+: 17.9%. **Growth:** 0.8%. **Migrants:** 12.7%. **Pop. density:** 252.1 per sq mi, 97.3 per sq km. **Urban:** 79.8%. **Ethnic groups:** mixed Mediterranean/Nordic. **Languages:** Castilian Spanish (official); Catalan, Galician, Basque (all official in areas). **Religions:** Roman Catholic 94%.

Geography: Total area: 195,124 sq mi, 505,370 sq km; **Land area:** 192,657 sq mi, 498,980 sq km. **Location:** SW Europe. Portugal on W; France, Andorra on N; Morocco to S. **Topography:** High, arid plateau broken by mountain ranges and river valleys in interior. The NW is heavily watered, the S has lowlands and a Medit. climate. **Arable land:** 25.1%. **Capital:** Madrid, 6,263,907. **Cities:** Barcelona, 5,308,600.

Government: Type: Parliamentary constitutional monarchy. **Head of state:** King Felipe VI; b. 1968; in office: June 19, 2014. **Head of gov.:** Prime Min. Mariano Rajoy; b. 1955; in office: Dec. 21, 2011. **Local divisions:** 17 semi-autonomous communities, 2 autonomous cities. **Defense budget:** $10.8 bil. **Active troops:** 122,000.

Economy: Industries: textiles and apparel (incl. footwear), food and beverages, metals and metal manufactures, chemicals, shipbuilding, automobiles, machine tools, tourism. **Chief crops:** grain, vegetables, olives, wine grapes, sugar beets, citrus. **Natural resources:** coal, lignite, iron ore, copper, lead, zinc, uranium, tungsten, mercury, pyrites, magnesite, fluorspar, gypsum, sepiolite, kaolin, potash, hydropower. **Water:** 2,418 cu m per capita. **Crude oil reserves:** 0.2 bil bbls. **Electricity prod.:** 267 bil kWh. **Labor force:** agric. 2.9%; industry 15%; services 58.4%. **Unemployment:** 24.7%.

Finance: Monetary unit: Euro (EUR) (0.89 = $1 U.S.). **GDP:** $1.6 tril; **per capita GDP:** $34,800; **GDP growth:** 3.2%. **Imports:** $298.3 bil; Germany 14.4%, France 11.7%, China 7.1%, Italy 6.5%, Netherlands 5%. **Exports:** $277.3 bil; France 15.7%, Germany 11%, Italy 7.4%, UK 7.4%, Portugal 7.1%. **Tourism:** $56.5 bil. **Budget:** $527.9 bil. **Inflation:** -0.5%.

Transport: Railways: 10,005 mi. **Motor vehicles:** 570.4 per 1,000 pop. **Airports:** 99.

Communications: Telephone: 40.6 per 100 pop. **Mobile:** 107.9 per 100 pop. **Broadband:** 77.1 per 100 pop. **Internet:** 78.7%.

Health: Expend.: 9%. **Life expect.:** 78.7 male; 84.9 female. **Births:** 9.4 per 1,000 pop. **Deaths:** 9.1 per 1,000 pop. **Infant mortality:** 3.3 per 1,000 live births. **Undernourished:** <5%. **HIV:** 0.4%.

Education: Compulsory: ages 6-15. **Literacy:** 98.1%.
Embassy: 2375 Pennsylvania Ave. NW 20037; 452-0100.
Website: www.lamoncloa.gob.es

Settled by Iberians, Basques, and Celts, Spain was successively ruled (wholly or in part) by Carthage, Rome, and the Visigoths. Muslims invaded Iberia from N Africa in 711. Reconquest of the peninsula by Christians from the N laid the foundations of modern Spain. In 1469 the kingdoms of Aragon and Castile were united by the marriage of Ferdinand II and Isabella I. Moorish rule ended with the fall of Granada, 1492, the year Spain's large Jewish community was expelled.

Spain established a colonial empire after Columbus's 1492 "discovery" of America. Cortés conquered Mexico, and Pizarro conquered Peru. Spain also controlled the Netherlands and parts of Italy and Germany. Spain lost its American colonies in the early 19th cent. and Cuba, the Philippines, and Puerto Rico during the Spanish-American War, 1898.

Primo de Rivera became dictator, 1923. King Alfonso XIII revoked the dictatorship, 1930, but was forced into exile in 1931. A republic was proclaimed, which disestablished the church, curtailed its privileges, and secularized education. A Popular Front of socialists, Communists, republicans, and anarchists governed 1936-39.

Army officers under Francisco Franco revolted, 1936. Some 500,000 to 1 mil died before the war's end, Mar. 28, 1939. Franco was named *caudillo*, leader of the nation. Spain was officially neutral in WWII, but its cordial relations with fascist countries prompted its exclusion from the UN until 1955.

After Franco's death, Nov. 20, 1975, Prince Juan Carlos became king. In free elections, June 1977, moderates and democratic socialists won the most votes. The king thwarted a 1981 coup attempt by right-wing military officers. The Socialist Workers' Party (PSOE), under Felipe González Márquez, won four consecutive general elections, 1982-93, but lost to a coalition of conservative and regional parties, 1996. Conservative Prime Min. José María Aznar, who won a parliamentary majority in the 2000 election, supported the U.S.-led invasion of Iraq, Mar. 2003.

Islamic extremists bombed four commuter trains in central Madrid, Mar. 11, 2004, killing 191 people. The PSOE won elections three days later, and Socialist leader José Luis Rodríguez Zapatero, who became prime min. Apr. 17, removed all 1,300 Spanish troops from Iraq. Spain legalized same-sex marriage in 2005.

Prime Min. Zapatero won a second term in 2008. Spain's banking, building, and tourism industries suffered during the worldwide financial crisis; in May 2010, as the budget deficit mounted, the government introduced austerity measures to reassure international lenders. Mariano Rajoy's conservative Popular Party (PP) won Nov. 2011 elections. Spain received a 100-bil-euro EU bailout for its ailing banks in 2012. Spain's unemployment rate surpassed 26% in 2013. GDP began growing in 2014, after five years of decline; unemployment dipped slightly by 2015.

Juan Carlos abdicated in favor of his son, who became King Felipe VI, June 19, 2014. Felipe's sister, Princess Cristina, was indicted, Dec. 22, 2014, for tax fraud in connection with alleged embezzlement of public funds by her husband. Testimony in her trial concluded June 22, 2016.

Hurt by corruption scandals, the PP lost its majority in Dec. 20, 2015, legislative elections. Rajoy, unable to form a coalition government, remained prime min. in a caretaker capacity. When elections were repeated, June 26, 2016, the PP again fell short of a majority.

Catalonia and the **Basque Country** were granted autonomy, Jan. 1980, following overwhelming approval in home-rule referendums. But Basque extremists pushed for independence. The Basque separatist group ETA carried out bombings that killed about 830 since 1968. ETA declared a cease-fire effective Mar. 24, 2006, after which Spain agreed to formal peace talks. Negotiations broke down after ETA exploded a car bomb at the Madrid airport, Dec. 30, 2006, killing two. ETA declared a new unilateral cease-fire Oct. 20, 2011. In Catalonia, voters approved a plan for expanded home-rule, June 18, 2006. Catalonia held a nonbinding Nov. 9, 2014, referendum in which more than 80% of voters favored independence. Separatist parties won a majority of seats in Catalonia's regional parliamentary elections Sept. 27, 2015. A measure passed by the regional parliament in Nov. 2015 to begin separation was declared unconstitutional, Dec. 2, by Spain's Constitutional Court; a similar July 2016 measure was suspended by the court, Aug. 1. **Website:** web.gencat.cat

The **Balearic Isls.** in the W Mediterranean, 1,927 sq mi, is an autonomous community of Spain; the islands include Majorca (Mallorca; capital Palma de Mallorca), Minorca, Cabrera, Ibiza, and Formentera. The **Canary Isls.**, 2,807 sq mi, another autonomous community in the Atlantic W of Morocco, includes the islands of Tenerife, Palma, Gomera, Hierro, Grand Canary, Fuerteventura, and Lanzarote; Las Palmas and Santa Cruz are thriving ports. More than 1,700 people died trying to get from Mauritania to the Canary Isls. in rickety boats, Jan.-June 2006.

Ceuta and **Melilla**, small Spanish enclaves on Morocco's Mediterranean coast, gained limited autonomy in Sept. 1994. In 2014-15, thousands of African and Middle Eastern migrants seeking to reach European-controlled territory crossed the borders between Morocco and the enclaves. New fencing and other security measures reduced border crossings, but the number of migrants entering with forged passports had increased by 2016.

Spain has sought the return of Gibraltar, in British hands since 1704.

Sri Lanka
Democratic Socialist Republic of Sri Lanka

People: Population: 22,235,000. **Age distrib.:** <15: 24.3%; 65+: 9.4%. **Growth:** 0.8%. **Migrants:** 0.2%. **Pop. density:** 891 per sq mi, 344 per sq km. **Urban:** 18.4%. **Ethnic groups:** Sinhalese 74.9%, Sri Lankan Tamil 11.2%, Sri Lankan Moor 9.2%, Indian Tamil 4.2%. **Languages:** Sinhala (official and national), Tamil (national), English (commonly used in govt.). **Religions:** Buddhist (official) 70.2%, Hindu 12.6%, Muslim 9.7%, Roman Catholic 6.1%.

Geography: Total area: 25,332 sq mi, 65,610 sq km; **Land area:** 24,954 sq mi, 64,630 sq km. **Location:** Indian O. off SE coast of India. **Topography:** Coastal area and N half are flat; S central area is hilly and mountainous. **Arable land:** 20.7%. **Capital:** Colombo, 709,451; Sri Jayewardenepura Kotte (legis.), 127,534 (2014).

Government: Type: Presidential republic. **Head of state and gov.:** Pres. Maithripala Sirisena; b. 1951; in office: Jan. 9, 2015. **Local divisions:** 9 provinces. **Defense budget:** $1.9 bil. **Active troops:** 160,900.

Economy: Industries: rubber, tea, coconuts, tobacco and other agric. commodities proc.; telecom, insurance, banking; tourism, shipping; clothing, textiles; cement, petroleum refining. **Chief crops:** rice, sugarcane, grains, pulses, oilseed, spices, vegetables, fruit, tea, rubber, coconuts. **Natural resources:** limestone, graphite, mineral sands, gems, phosphates, clay, hydropower. **Water:** 2,549 cu m per capita. **Electricity prod.:** 12 bil kWh. **Labor force:** agric. 28.4%, industry 25.7%, services 45.9%. **Unemployment:** 4.6%.

Finance: Monetary unit: Rupee (LKR) (145.43 = $1 U.S.). **GDP:** $223 bil; **per capita GDP:** $10,600; **GDP growth:** 5.2%. **Imports:** $20.1 bil; India 24.6%, China 20.6%, UAE 7.1%, Singapore 5.9%, Japan 5.7%. **Exports:** $11.3 bil; U.S. 26.1%, UK 9%, India 7.2%. **Tourism:** $3 bil. **Budget:** $15.4 bil. **Inflation:** 0.9%.

Transport: Railways: 899 mi. **Motor vehicles:** 50.6 per 1,000 pop. **Airports:** 15.

Communications: Telephone: 12 per 100 pop. **Mobile:** 112.8 per 100 pop. **Broadband:** 13 per 100 pop. **Internet:** 30%.

Health: Expend.: 3.5%. **Life expect.:** 73.3 male; 80.4 female. **Births:** 15.5 per 1,000 pop. **Deaths:** 6.2 per 1,000 pop. **Infant mortality:** 8.6 per 1,000 live births. **Undernourished:** 22%. **HIV:** <0.1%. **Education:** Compulsory: ages 5-13. **Literacy:** 92.6%. **Embassy:** 3025 Whitehaven St. NW 20008; 483-4025. **Website:** www.gov.lk

The island was known to the ancient world as Taprobane (Greek for copper-colored) and later as Serendip (from Arabic). Colonists from N India subdued the indigenous Veddahs about 543 BCE; their descendants, the Buddhist Sinhalese, still form most of the population. Hindu descendants of Tamil immigrants from S India account for about one-fifth of the population.

Parts were occupied by the Portuguese in 1505 and the Dutch in 1658. The British seized the island in 1796. It became an independent member of the Commonwealth as Ceylon in 1948 before changing its name to Sri Lanka May 22, 1972.

Prime Min. Solomon W. R. D. Bandaranaike was assassinated Sept. 25, 1959. His widow, Sirimavo Bandaranaike, served as prime min. 1960-65, 1970-77, 1994-2000. In the 1970s, thousands of ultra-leftists were executed, while massive land reform and nationalization of foreign-owned plantations took place.

Tensions between Sinhalese and Tamil separatists erupted in the early 1980s and turned into a 20-year civil war that killed more than 60,000; another 20,000, mostly young Tamils, "disappeared" while in government custody.

Pres. Ranasinghe Premadasa was assassinated May 1, 1993, by a Tamil rebel. Mrs. Bandaranaike's daughter, Chandrika Bandaranaike Kumaratunga, became prime min. after Aug. 1994 general elections. Elected president Nov. 9, Kumaratunga appointed her mother prime min. Kumaratunga won a second 6-year term Dec. 21, 1999. In failing health, Mrs. Bandaranaike resigned Aug. 10 and died Oct. 10, 2000. A truce intended to bring an end to the civil war was signed Feb. 22, 2002. More than 31,000 died in the Dec. 26, 2004, Indian Ocean tsunami.

Prime Min. Mahinda Rajapaksa of the United People's Freedom Alliance won the 2005 presidential election and was reelected in 2010. Thousands died during three years of fighting among government forces, paramilitary groups, and Tamil rebels beginning in Dec. 2005. About 7,000 noncombatants were killed Jan. 20-May 7, 2009. Tamil leader Vellupillai Prabhakaran was killed May 18-19, 2009, and Pres. Rajapaksa formally declared victory. Maithripala Sirisena defeated Rajapaksa in the Jan. 8, 2015, presidential election. The governing coalition defeated Rajapaksa's coalition in Aug. 17 parliamentary elections. A Sept. 16, 2015, UN report documented numerous human rights violations by both sides in Sri Lanka's civil war, including widespread torture of detainees by government security forces. WHO announced, Sept. 5, 2016, that Sri Lanka had eradicated the disease malaria.

Sudan
Republic of the Sudan

(Pre-2012 data and communications statistics include South Sudan, which became independent July 9, 2011.)

People: Population: 36,729,501. **Age distrib.:** <15: 39.4%; 65+: 3.2%. **Growth:** 1.7%. **Migrants:** 1.3%. **Pop. density:** 51.1 per sq mi, 19.7 per sq km. **Urban:** 34%. **Ethnic groups:** Sudanese Arab (approx. 70%), Fur, Beja, Nuba, Fallata. **Languages:** Arabic, English (both official); Nubian; Ta Bedawie; Fur. **Religions:** Sunni Muslim, small Christian minority.

Geography: Total area: 718,723 sq mi, 1,861,484 sq km. **Location:** E end of Sahara desert zone. Egypt on N; Libya, Chad, Central African Republic on W; South Sudan on S; Ethiopia, Eritrea on E. **Topography:** The N consists of Libyan Desert in W and the mountainous Nubia Desert in E, with narrow Nile Valley between. Large rainy areas with fields, pastures, and forests in center. The S has rich soil, heavy rain. **Arable land:** 15.7%. **Capital:** Khartoum, 5,264,922.

Government: Type: Presidential republic. **Head of state and gov.:** Pres. Gen. Omar Hassan Ahmad al-Bashir; b. 1944; in office: Oct. 16, 1993 (de facto since June 30, 1989). **Local divisions:** 18 states. **Defense budget** (2013): $1.9 bil. **Active troops:** 244,300.

Economy: Industries: oil, cotton ginning, textiles, cement, edible oils, sugar, soap distilling, shoes, petroleum refining, pharmaceuticals. **Chief crops:** cotton, groundnuts, sorghum, millet, wheat, gum arabic, sugarcane, cassava, mangoes, papayas, bananas, sweet potatoes, sesame seeds. **Natural resources:** petroleum; small reserves of iron ore, copper, chromium ore, zinc, tungsten, mica, silver, gold; hydropower. **Water:** 940 cu m per capita. **Crude oil reserves:** 5 bil bbls (incl. South Sudan). **Electricity prod.:** 11 bil kWh (incl. South Sudan). **Labor force:** agric. 80%, industry 7%, services 13%. **Unemployment:** 14.8%.

Finance: Monetary unit: Pound (SDG) (6.07 = $1 U.S.). **GDP:** $167 bil; **per capita GDP:** $4,300; **GDP growth:** 3.5%. **Imports:** $8.3 bil; China 26.3%, UAE 10%, India 9%, Egypt 5.6%. **Exports:** $4.4 bil; UAE 32%, China 16.2%, Saudi Arabia 15.5%. **Tourism:** $949 mil. **Budget:** $9.8 bil. **Inflation:** 16.9%.

Transport: Railways: 4,506 mi. **Motor vehicles:** 3.1 per 1,000 pop. **Airports:** 16.

Communications: Telephone: 0.3 per 100 pop. **Mobile:** 70.5 per 100 pop. **Broadband:** 27.2 per 100 pop. **Internet:** 26.6%.

Health: Expend.: 8.4%. **Life expect.:** 62.0 male; 66.3 female. **Births:** 28.5 per 1,000 pop. **Deaths:** 7.5 per 1,000 pop. **Infant mortality:** 50.2 per 1,000 live births. **Undernourished:** NA. **HIV:** 0.3%.

Education: Compulsory: 6-13. **Literacy:** 58.6%.

Embassy: 2210 Massachusetts Ave. NW 20008; 338-8565.

Website: www.presidency.gov.sd

Northern Sudan, ancient Nubia, was settled by Egyptians in antiquity. The population was converted to Coptic Christianity in the 6th cent. Arab conquests brought Islam to the area in the 15th cent. In the 1820s, Egypt took over Sudan, defeating the last of the earlier empires, including the Fung. In the 1880s, Muhammad Ahmad, who called himself the Mahdi (leader of the faithful), and his followers, the dervishes, led a revolution. An Anglo-Egyptian force crushed the Mahdi's successors, 1898.

Sudan gained independence Jan. 1, 1956. In 1969, a Revolutionary Council took power, led by authoritarian Pres. Gaafar al-Nimeiry. He was overthrown, Apr. 6, 1985. Sudan held its first democratic parliamentary elections in 18 years in 1986. Brig. Omar Hassan Ahmad al-Bashir staged a bloodless military coup, June 30, 1989. He became president in 1993.

During 1955-72 and 1983-2005, rebels in the south (primarily Christians and followers of traditional religions) fought against government domination by mostly Arab-Muslim northern Sudan. War and related famine cost an estimated 2 mil lives. An accord ended the rebellion Jan. 9, 2005.

A rebellion in the Darfur region of western Sudan caused a new crisis, 2003-11. Marauding Arab militias, the *janjaweed*, reportedly acting in collusion with Sudanese government troops, looted and burned homes in Darfur and killed many African villagers. More than 7,000 African Union peacekeepers were ineffectual. Rebel and militia activities in Sudan and Chad led to border clashes and further attacks on civilians. By Sept. 2009, the Darfur war had killed about 300,000 people and displaced another 2.7 mil. A joint UN-African Union force of up to 26,000 peacekeepers (UNMIS) was deployed Aug. 2007-July 2011.

The Intl. Criminal Court in The Hague, Netherlands, issued two arrest warrants for Pres. Bashir—one in 2009 for war crimes and other crimes against humanity in Darfur, and another in 2010 for genocide. Bashir defied the calls for his arrest. In Apr. 2010 and Apr. 2015, he won new 5-year terms in elections not deemed credible and largely boycotted by the opposition.

After southern Sudanese voted overwhelmingly for secession, Jan. 9-15, 2011, South Sudan attained full independence July 9. Border disputes between Sudan and South Sudan ensued. Conflict in Darfur flared up again in 2014-16, including attacks on civilians by pro-government militias; hundreds of thousands of people were displaced. Government bombings of rebel-held areas in the southern South Kordofan and Blue Nile states caused high civilian casualties.

Suriname
Republic of Suriname

People: Population: 585,824. **Age distrib.:** <15: 25.2%; 65+: 5.9%. **Growth:** 1.1%. **Migrants:** 8.6%. **Pop. density:** 9.7 per sq mi, 3.8 per sq km. **Urban:** 66%. **Ethnic groups:** Hindustani or East Indian (descended fr. 19th-cent. emigrants fr. northern India) 37%, Creole (mixed white/black) 31%, Javanese 15%, Maroon (descendants of escaped African slaves) 10%, Amerindian 2%, Chinese 2%. **Languages:** Dutch (official), English (widely spoken), Sranang Tongo (Surinamese), Caribbean Hindustani, Javanese. **Religions:** Hindu 27.4%, Protestant (predom. Moravian) 25.2%, Roman Catholic 22.8%, Muslim 19.6%, indigenous beliefs 5%. **Geography: Total area:** 63,251 sq mi, 163,820 sq km. **Land area:** 60,232 sq mi, 156,000 sq km. **Location:** N shore of S America. Guyana on W, Brazil on S, French Guiana on E. **Topography:** Flat Atlantic coast, where dikes permit agriculture. Inland is forest belt. To S, hills cover three-fourths of country. **Arable land:** 0.4%. **Capital:** Paramaribo, 234,483 (2014).

Government: Type: Presidential republic. **Head of state and gov.:** Pres. Désiré Delano Bouterse; b. 1945; in office: Aug. 12, 2010. **Local divisions:** 10 districts. **Defense budget** (2013): $49 mil. **Active troops:** 1,840.

Economy: Industries: bauxite and gold mining, alumina prod., oil, lumber, food proc., fishing. **Chief crops:** rice, bananas, palm kernels, coconuts, plantains, peanuts. **Natural resources:** timber, hydropower, fish, kaolin, shrimp, bauxite, gold; small amounts of nickel, copper, platinum, iron ore. **Water:** 182,320 cu m per capita. **Crude oil reserves:** 0.1 bil bbls. **Electricity prod.:** 1.5 bil kWh. **Labor force:** agric. 11.2%, industry 19.5%, services 69.3%. **Unemployment:** 5.6%.

Finance: Monetary unit: Dollar (SRD) (7.39 = $1 U.S.). **GDP:** $9.1 bil; **per capita GDP:** $16,300; **GDP growth:** 3%. **Imports:** $2.1 bil; U.S. 26.8%, Netherlands 14.3%, China 12.2%. **Exports:** $1.8 bil; Switzerland 21.8%, UAE 14.5%, India 13.9%, Belgium 9.7%, U.S. 8.9%, France 8.1%, Canada 6.6%. **Tourism:** $88 mil. **Budget:** $1.5 bil. **Inflation:** 6.9%.

Transport: Motor vehicles: 246 per 1,000 pop. **Airports:** 6.

Communications: Telephone: 15.5 per 100 pop. **Mobile:** 180.7 per 100 pop. **Broadband:** 71.6 per 100 pop. **Internet:** 42.8%.

Health: Expend.: 5.7%. **Life expect.:** 69.8 male; 74.8 female. **Births:** 16.0 per 1,000 pop. **Deaths:** 6.1 per 1,000 pop. **Infant mortality:** 25.3 per 1,000 live births. **Undernourished:** 8%. **HIV:** 1.1%.

Education: Compulsory: ages 7-12. **Literacy:** 95.5%.

Embassy: 4301 Connecticut Ave. NW, Ste. 460, 20008; 244-7488.

Website: www.gov.sr or www.surinameembassy.org

The Netherlands acquired Suriname in 1667 from Britain. The 1954 Dutch constitution raised the colony to a level of equality with the Netherlands and the Netherlands Antilles. Independence was granted Nov. 25, 1975. Some 40% of the population (mostly E Indians, who opposed independence) immigrated to the Netherlands before independence.

Désiré "Dési" Bouterse, who masterminded coups in 1982 and 1990, was elected president by parliament, July 19, 2010. Bouterse had been convicted in absentia in the Netherlands, 1999, for drug trafficking. Named by the U.S. as a transshipment point for cocaine, Suriname signed the UN-supported Container Control Programme (CCP), Aug. 23, 2012, to improve inspection of shipping containers in its ports. Bouterse's son Dino, arrested in Panama in a sting operation and extradited to the U.S. in 2013, pleaded guilty, Aug. 29, 2014, to drug trafficking and terrorism charges; he was sentenced, Mar. 10, 2015, to 16 years in prison. Bouterse was elected by parliament to a new 5-year term as president, July 14, 2015. Suriname was one of the countries affected by the Zika virus outbreak that began in summer 2015.

Swaziland
Kingdom of Swaziland

People: Population: 1,451,428. **Age distrib.:** <15: 35.5%; 65+: 3.9%. **Growth:** 1.1%. **Migrants:** 2.5%. **Pop. density:** 218.5 per sq mi, 84.4 per sq km. **Urban:** 21.3%. **Ethnic groups:** African 97%, European 3%. **Languages:** English (used in govt.), siSwati (both official). **Religions:** Zionist (blend of Christianity/indigenous ancestral worship) 40%, Roman Catholic 20%, Muslim 10%, other (incl. Anglican, Baha'i, Methodist, Mormon, Jewish) 30%. **Geography: Total area:** 6,704 sq mi, 17,364 sq km; **Land area:** 6,643 sq mi, 17,204 sq km. **Location:** Southern Africa, near Indian O. coast. South Africa on N, W, S; Mozambique on E. **Topography:** Descends W-E in broad belts, becoming more arid in low veld region, then rising to plateau in E. **Arable land:** 10.2%. **Capital:** Mbabane (admin.), 65,990 (2014); Lobamba (legis.).

Government: Type: Absolute monarchy. **Head of state:** King Mswati III; b. 1968; in office: Apr. 25, 1986. **Head of gov.:** Prime Min. Barnabas Sibusiso Dlamini; b. 1942; in office: Oct. 23, 2008. **Local divisions:** 4 districts. **Defense budget/active troops:** NA.

Economy: Industries: coal, forestry, sugar, soft drink concentrates, textiles and apparel. **Chief crops:** sugarcane, cotton, corn, tobacco, rice, citrus, pineapples, sorghum, peanuts. **Natural resources:** asbestos, coal, clay, cassiterite, hydropower, forests, small gold and diamond deposits, quarry stone, talc. **Water:** 3,504 cu m per capita. **Electricity prod.:** 0.6 bil kWh. **Labor force:** agric. 70%. **Unemployment:** 22.3%.

Finance: Monetary unit: Lilangeni (SZL) (14.59 = $1 U.S.). **GDP:** $10.9 bil; **per capita GDP:** $8,500; **GDP growth:** 1.7%. **Imports:** $1.6 bil. **Exports:** $1.6 bil. **Tourism:** $15 mil. **Budget:** $1.3 bil. **Inflation:** 5%.

Transport: Railways: 187 mi. **Airports:** 2.

Communications: Telephone: 3.3 per 100 pop. **Mobile:** 73.2 per 100 pop. **Broadband** (2012): 12 per 100 pop. **Internet:** 30.4%.

Health: Expend.: 9.3%. **Life expect.:** 52.2 male; 51.0 female. **Births:** 24.3 per 1,000 pop. **Deaths:** 13.4 per 1,000 pop. **Infant mortality:** 50.4 per 1,000 live births. **Undernourished:** 26.8%. **HIV:** 28.8%.

Education: Compulsory: ages 6-12. **Literacy:** 87.5%.

Embassy: 1712 New Hampshire Ave. NW 20009; 234-5002.

Website: www.gov.sz

The royal house of Swaziland traces back 400 years. The Zulus drove the Swazis, a Bantu people, to Swaziland from lands to the N, 1820. Britain and Transvaal (later part of South Africa) later guaranteed their autonomy, and Britain assumed control after 1903. Independence came Sept. 6, 1968. In 1973, the king repealed the constitution and assumed full powers.

A new constitution banning political parties took effect Oct. 13, 1978. Under a revised constitution effective Feb. 8, 2006, nonpartisan parliamentary elections were permitted. An attempt failed in 2012 to unite pro-democracy groups under the People's United Democratic Movement (PUDEMO), which had been outlawed as a terrorist group in 2008. An AIDS crisis and the huge gap between rich and poor have fueled student and labor unrest in recent years. The UN reported July 30, 2013, that AIDS-related deaths had fallen sharply due to the use of antiretroviral therapy; as of 2015, almost 30% of people ages 15-49 were HIV positive. PUDEMO leader Mario Masuku, arrested on terrorism charges May 1, 2014, was released on bail July 14, 2015.

Sweden
Kingdom of Sweden

People: Population: 9,880,604. **Age distrib.:** <15: 17.3%; 65+: 20.1%. **Growth:** 0.8%. **Migrants:** 16.8%. **Pop. density:** 62.4 per sq mi, 24.1 per sq km. **Urban:** 86%. **Ethnic groups:** Swedes with Finnish and Sami minorities. Foreign-born or first-gen. immigrants: Finn, Yugoslav, Dane, Norwegian, Greek, Turk. **Languages:** Swedish (official). **Religions:** Lutheran 87%.

Geography: Total area: 173,860 sq mi, 450,295 sq km; **Land area:** 158,431 sq mi, 410,335 sq km. **Location:** Scandinavian Peninsula in N Europe. Norway on W, Denmark on S (across Kattegat strait), Finland on E. **Topography:** Mountains along NW border cover 25% of Sweden. Flat or rolling terrain with several large lakes across central and southern areas. **Arable land:** 6.4%. **Capital:** Stockholm, 1,507,407.

Government: Type: Parliamentary constitutional monarchy. **Head of state:** King Carl XVI Gustaf; b. 1946; in office: Sept. 15, 1973. **Head of gov.:** Prime Min. Stefan Löfven; b. 1957; in office: Oct. 3, 2014. **Local divisions:** 21 counties. **Defense budget:** $5.3 bil. **Active troops:** 29,750.

Economy: Industries: iron and steel, precision equip. (bearings, radio and phone parts, armaments), wood pulp and paper prods., processed foods, motor vehicles. **Chief crops:** barley, wheat, sugar beets. **Natural resources:** iron ore, copper, lead, zinc, gold, silver, tungsten, uranium, arsenic, feldspar, timber, hydropower. **Water:** 17,793 cu m per capita. **Electricity prod.:** 149 bil kWh. **Labor force:** agric. 2%, industry 12%, services 86%. **Unemployment:** 8%.

Finance: Monetary unit: Krona (SEK) (8.56 = $1 U.S.). **GDP:** $473.4 bil; **per capita GDP:** $47,900; **GDP growth:** 4.1%. **Imports:** $133.2 bil; Germany 17.9%, Netherlands 8.1%, Norway 7.8%, Denmark 7.7%, China 6%, UK 5.5%. **Exports:** $151.1 bil; Norway 10.3%, Germany 10.3%, U.S. 7.7%, UK 7.2%, Denmark 6.8%, Finland 6.7%, Netherlands 5.2%. **Tourism:** $12.2 bil. **Budget:** $256.1 bil. **Inflation:** −0.05%.

Transport: Railways: 7,404 mi. **Motor vehicles:** 539.7 per 1,000 pop. **Airports:** 149.

Communications: Telephone: 36.7 per 100 pop. **Mobile:** 130.4 per 100 pop. **Broadband:** 116.3 per 100 pop. **Internet:** 90.6%.

Health: Expend.: 11.9%. **Life expect.:** 80.2 male; 84.1 female. **Births:** 12.0 per 1,000 pop. **Deaths:** 9.4 per 1,000 pop. **Infant mortality:** 2.6 per 1,000 live births. **Undernourished:** <5%. **HIV:** NA.

Education: Compulsory: ages 7-15. **Literacy:** 99%. **Embassy:** 2900 K St. NW 20007; 467-2600. **Website:** sweden.se

The Swedes have lived in present-day Sweden for at least 5,000 years. Gothic tribes from Sweden played a major role in the disintegration of the Roman Empire. Other Swedes helped create the first Russian state in the 9th cent. The Swedes were Christianized from the 11th cent., and a strong centralized monarchy developed. The Riksdag, the first European parliament to represent all classes of society, was first called in 1435.

A revolt led by Gustavus I in 1521-23 freed Sweden from Danish rule (dating from 1397); he built up the government and military and established the Lutheran Church. In the 17th cent. Sweden was a major European power, gaining most of the Baltic seacoast. The Napoleonic wars, 1799-1815, in which Sweden acquired Norway (it became independent 1905), were the last in which Sweden participated. Armed neutrality was maintained in both world wars.

The Social Democratic Party (SAP) has governed Sweden for most of the period since World War II. Prime Min. Olof Palme was shot to death in Stockholm, Feb. 28, 1986. Sweden entered the EU, Jan. 1, 1995. A center-right alliance led by Fredrik Reinfeldt defeated the SAP in Sept. 2006 elections. Parliament voted Apr. 1, 2009, to legalize same-sex marriage. Reinfeldt's bloc won a renewed mandate in Sept. 2010 parliamentary elections. The SAP won the largest bloc of seats in Sept. 14, 2014, parliamentary elections, in which the anti-immigration Sweden Democrats won 13% of the vote and 49 seats. The SAP's Stefan Löfven became prime min., heading a center-left minority government, Oct. 3. Parliament approved, May 25, 2016, a defense cooperation agreement with NATO. A Sweden-U.S. defense cooperation agreement was signed June 8, 2016.

Almost 163,000 migrants, mostly from the Middle East, SW Asia, and Africa, applied for asylum in Sweden in 2015, and about 20,000 in Jan.-Sept. 2016. Legislation tightening asylum rules

was enacted June 21, 2016. The government did not grant asylum to more than 26,000 applicants in 2015 and estimated that more than 96,000 other applicants would be rejected by 2018.

Switzerland
Swiss Confederation

People: Population: 8,179,294. **Age distrib.:** <15: 15.1%; 65+: 18%. **Growth:** 0.7%. **Migrants:** 29.4%. **Pop. density:** 529.6 per sq mi, 204.5 per sq km. **Urban:** 74%. **Ethnic groups:** German 65%, French 18%, Italian 10%. **Languages:** German, French, Italian, Romansch (all official); English; Portuguese; Albanian; Serbo-Croatian; Spanish. **Religions:** Roman Catholic 38.2%, Protestant 26.9%, other Christian 5.6%, Muslim 5%, none 21.4%.

Geography: Total area: 15,937 sq mi, 41,277 sq km; **Land area:** 15,443 sq mi, 39,997 sq km. **Location:** In Alps Mts. in central Europe. France on W; Italy on S; Liechtenstein, Austria on E; Germany on N. **Topography:** The Alps cover 60% of land area; the Jura, near France, 10%. The midlands run NE-SW in-between. **Arable land:** 10.2%. **Capital:** Bern, 359,810. **Cities:** Zürich, 1,259,403; Geneva, 564,688.

Government: Type: Federal republic (formally a confederation). **Head of state and gov.:** President chosen on rotating basis from among 7-member Federal Council for 1-year term. **Local divisions:** 26 cantons. **Defense budget:** $4.8 bil. **Active troops:** 20,800.

Economy: Industries: machinery, chemicals, watches, textiles, precision instruments, tourism, banking, insurance. **Chief crops:** grains, fruits, vegetables. **Natural resources:** timber, salt. **Water:** 6,447 cu m per capita. **Electricity prod.:** 65 bil kWh. **Labor force:** agric. 3.4%, industry 23.4%, services 73.2%. **Unemployment:** 4.5%.

Finance: Monetary unit: Franc (CHF) (0.98 = $1 U.S.). **GDP:** $482.3 bil; **per capita GDP:** $58,600; **GDP growth:** 0.9%. **Imports:** $214.8 bil; Germany 20.7%, UK 12.8%, U.S. 8.1%, Italy 7.8%, France 6.7%, China 5.1%. **Exports:** $270.6 bil; Germany 14.2%, U.S. 10.6%, Hong Kong 8.7%, India 7.3%, China 6.9%, France 6.1%, Italy 5.4%. **Tourism:** $16.2 bil. **Budget:** $220.8 bil (federal, cantonal, and municipal). **Inflation:** −1.1%.

Transport: Railways: 3,512 mi. **Motor vehicles:** 605.5 per 1,000 pop. **Airports:** 40.

Communications: Telephone: 50.3 per 100 pop. **Mobile:** 142 per 100 pop. **Broadband:** 76.6 per 100 pop. **Internet:** 88%.

Health: Expend.: 11.7%. **Life expect.:** 80.3 male; 85.0 female. **Births:** 10.5 per 1,000 pop. **Deaths:** 8.2 per 1,000 pop. **Infant mortality:** 3.6 per 1,000 live births. **Undernourished:** <5%. **HIV:** NA.

Education: Compulsory: ages 4-15. **Literacy:** 99%. **Embassy:** 2900 Cathedral Ave. NW 20008; 745-7900. **Website:** www.ch.ch

Switzerland, the former Roman province of Helvetia, traces its modern history to 1291, when three cantons created a defensive league. Other cantons were subsequently admitted to the Swiss Confederation, which obtained its independence from the Holy Roman Empire through the Peace of Westphalia (1648). The cantons were joined under a federal constitution in 1848.

Switzerland has maintained an armed neutrality since 1815 and has not been involved in a foreign war since 1515. It is the seat of many UN and other international agencies but only became a full UN member on Sept. 10, 2002.

Switzerland is a world banking center. The government announced, Mar. 1997, a $4.7-bil fund to compensate victims of the Nazi Holocaust and other catastrophes. Swiss banks agreed Aug. 12, 1998, to pay $1.25 bil in reparations. A June 2002 referendum decriminalized abortion. Two more referendums in 2005 harmonized travel, asylum, law enforcement, and labor policies with the EU; more rights for same-sex couples were also endorsed June 5, 2005.

The Swiss government bailed out the troubled banking giant UBS during the international financial crisis in Oct. 2008. U.S. tax authorities pressured UBS Jan. 2009 to close some 19,000 hidden offshore accounts and to disclose in Aug. data on accounts for over 4,400 U.S. clients. In a Nov. 2009 referendum reflecting rising anti-Muslim sentiment, voters approved a constitutional ban on construction of new minarets on mosques. In a Feb. 9, 2014, referendum, voters narrowly approved a measure requiring government quotas limiting immigration within three years. Switzerland officially opened the Gotthard Base Tunnel, the world's longest railway tunnel, June 1, 2016; it extends for 35 mi under the Alps in southern Switzerland.

Syria
Syrian Arab Republic

People: Population: 17,185,170. **Age distrib.:** <15: 31.9%; 65+: 4.1%. **Growth:** 1.6%. **Migrants:** 4.7%. **Pop. density:** 242.4 per sq mi, 93.6 per sq km. **Urban:** 58.1%. **Ethnic groups:** Arab 90.3%, Kurd, Armenian, and other 9.7%. **Languages:** Arabic (official), Kurdish, Armenian, Aramaic, Circassian, French, English. **Religions:** Muslim 87% (official; incl. Sunni 74%; Alawi, Ismaili, Shia 13%), Christian 10%, Druze 3%.

Geography: Total area: 71,498 sq mi, 185,180 sq km; **Land area:** 70,900 sq mi, 183,630 sq km. (500 sq mi of area is occupied by Israel.) **Location:** Middle East, at E end of Medit. Sea. Lebanon, Israel on W; Jordan on S; Iraq on E; Turkey on N. **Topography:** A short Medit. coastline stretches E and S with fertile lowlands and plains, alternating with mountains and large desert areas. **Arable land:** 25.4%. **Capital:** Damascus (Dimashq), 2,586,032 (excl. refugees and internally displaced persons). **Cities:** Aleppo (Halab), 3,641,048; Homs (Hims), 1,694,918; Hamah, 1,297,160. (Figures for Homs and Hamah excl. refugees and internally displaced persons.)

Government: Type: Presidential republic; highly authoritarian regime. **Head of state:** Pres. Bashar al-Assad; b. 1965; in office: July 17, 2000. **Head of gov.:** Prime Min. Imad Muhammad Dib Khamis; b. 1961; in office: June 22, 2016. **Local divisions:** 14 provinces. **Defense budget:** NA. **Active troops:** 130,500.

Economy: Industries: petroleum, textiles, food proc., beverages, tobacco, phosphate rock mining, cement. **Chief crops:** wheat, barley, cotton, lentils, chickpeas, olives, sugar beets. **Natural resources:** petroleum, phosphates, chrome and manganese ores, asphalt, iron ore, rock salt, marble, gypsum, hydropower. **Water:** 908 cu m per capita. **Crude oil reserves:** 2.5 bil bbls. **Electricity prod.:** 25 bil kWh. **Labor force:** agric. 17%, industry 16%, services 67%. **Unemployment:** 10.8%.

Finance: Monetary unit: Pound (SYP) (214.38 = $1 U.S.). **GDP** (2014): $55.8 bil; **per capita GDP** (2011): $5,100; **GDP growth:** −9.9%. **Imports:** $6.6 bil; Saudi Arabia 27.9%, UAE 13.7%, Iran 10.1%, Turkey 9%, Iraq 8.3%, China 6.1%. **Exports:** $1.8 bil; Iraq 64.7%, Saudi Arabia 11.2%, Kuwait 7.1%, UAE 6.1%. **Tourism:** $6.2 bil. **Budget:** $5.7 bil (govt. projections for FY2016). **Inflation** (2015): 33.6%.

Transport: Railways: 1,275 mi. **Motor vehicles:** 127.8 per 1,000 pop. **Airports:** 29.

Communications: Telephone: 18.3 per 100 pop. **Mobile:** 62.4 per 100 pop. **Broadband:** 5.7 per 100 pop. **Internet:** 30%.

Health: Expend.: 3.3%. **Life expect.:** 72.5 male; 77.4 female. **Births:** 21.7 per 1,000 pop. **Deaths:** 4.0 per 1,000 pop. **Infant mortality:** 15.2 per 1,000 live births. **Undernourished:** NA. **HIV:** NA.

Education: Compulsory: ages 6-14. **Literacy:** 86.3%.
Embassy: 2215 Wyoming Ave. NW 20008; 232-6313.
Website: www.egov.sy

Syria was the center of the Seleucid Empire but later was absorbed into the Roman and Arab empires. Ottoman rule prevailed for four cents., until the end of WWI.

The state of Syria was formed from former Turkish districts, separated by the Treaty of Sevres, 1920, and divided into the states of Syria and Greater Lebanon. Both were administered under a French League of Nations mandate, 1920-41. The occupying French proclaimed Syria a republic Sept. 16, 1941; independence came Apr. 17, 1946. Syria joined the Arab invasion of Israel in 1948.

Syria belonged to the United Arab Republic from Feb. 1958 to Sept. 1961. The Socialist Baath party seized power Mar. 1963 and became the only legal party. The Alawite minority has dominated the government (Alawism is a sect of Shiite Islam).

In the June 1967 Arab-Israeli war, Israel seized and occupied the Golan Heights, from which Syria had shelled Israeli settlements. On Oct. 6, 1973, Syria and Egypt attacked Israel but failed to recapture the Golan Heights. Syrian troops entered Lebanon in 1976, during the Lebanese civil war, and remained a strong presence in the country. They fought Palestinian guerrillas and, later, Christian militiamen. Syria sided with Iran during the Iran-Iraq War, 1980-88.

Thousands died in the city of Hama Feb. 1982 when government troops crushed a Muslim Brotherhood uprising. Following Israel's invasion of Lebanon, June 6, 1982, Israeli planes destroyed 17 Syrian antiaircraft missile batteries in the Bekaa Valley, June 9, and some 25 Syrian planes. Israel and Syria agreed to a cease-fire June 11.

Hafez al-Assad, president of Syria since 1971, died June 10, 2000, and was succeeded by his son Bashar al-Assad. Israeli planes hit an alleged terrorist camp near Damascus Oct. 4, 2003. The U.S. imposed limited sanctions on Syria, May 11, 2004. Syria aided fighters of the Lebanon-based Shiite group Hezbollah in their conflict with Israel and gave about 180,000 Lebanese temporary refuge when Israeli forces targeted Hezbollah, July-Aug. 2006. On Sept. 6, 2007, Israel bombed a secret site in N Syria where the Israelis believed Syria and North Korea were developing a nuclear facility; both countries denied the claim.

The Assad regime used troops and tanks during Arab Spring demonstrations in Mar. 2011, but the confrontations escalated into outright rebellion. The Intl. Committee of the Red Cross declared the conflict a civil war, July 15, 2012. A number of armed opposition groups fought Assad's forces and each other for control of territory. The Natl. Coalition for Syrian Revolutionary and Opposition Forces was formed Nov. 11, 2012; it gained international support, but its leadership was not recognized by many rebel groups. Hezbollah forces fought on the side of the Assad government, which was also backed by Iran. The U.S., Aug. 18, 2011, called on Assad to step down and imposed new economic sanctions.

International intelligence communities announced, May 2013, increasing evidence that Assad's forces had used chemical and biological weapons. The EU May 28 lifted an arms embargo prohibiting weapons shipments to rebel fighters, and U.S. Pres. Barack Obama, June 13, decided to supply military support to rebel groups. A chemical attack on an opposition-controlled Damascus suburb Aug. 21, 2013, killed more than 1,400. Assad and the rebels accused each other of the attack. Russian and U.S. negotiators reached an agreement with Syria requiring the Assad government to relinquish chemical weapons; the agreement was reinforced by a UN Security Council resolution Sept. 27, 2013. Inspectors arrived in Syria Oct. 1, and the last known covered chemical weapons were believed to have been removed June 23, 2014. The UN received allegations that Assad's forces were using chlorine gas (not removable under the 2013 agreement because it has nonmilitary purposes) as a chemical weapon; an Aug. 24, 2016, UN report confirmed two such uses.

As heavy fighting continued, by summer 2014, the Sunni extremist group ISIS (Islamic State in Iraq and Syria) controlled large areas in eastern and northern Syria. Beginning the night of Sept. 22-23, 2014, the U.S. conducted air and cruise missile strikes against ISIS and other Islamist extremist groups in Syria, supported by several Middle East countries and European and other allies. Russia, which backed Assad, sent warplanes to Syria in Sept. 2015 and began its own air campaign, Sept. 30, against anti-government forces. Russia announced, Mar. 14, 2016, that it would remove the "main part" of its forces from Syria, but Russian airstrikes continued, helping the Assad regime regain control of some areas. Syrian Kurdish and other rebel forces, with support from U.S. airstrikes and special operations troops, retook some territory in northern and eastern Syria from ISIS, 2015-16. Turkish tanks and ground troops entered Syria, Aug. 24, 2016, to support non-Kurdish rebels. The first of several rounds of UN-mediated peace talks between the Assad government and some rebel groups began in Geneva, Switzerland, Jan. 29, 2016. A partial cease-fire, beginning Feb. 27, 2016, reduced casualties for a time but failed to hold. The city of Aleppo was the scene of intense airstrikes and other fighting, with high civilian casualties.

Estimates of the total death toll in Syria's civil war since Mar. 2011 varied widely; the Syrian Center for Policy Research released an estimate of 470,000 in Feb. 2016. The UNHCR reported the number of Syrian refugees in Turkey, the Middle East, and North Africa at more than 4.8 mil as of Sept. 2016. More than 1 mil Syrians applied for asylum in Europe, Apr. 2011-July 2016. As of Aug. 31, 2016, the U.S. had admitted 12,000 Syrian refugees since the civil war began. More than 6 mil people were displaced within Syria as of Sept. 2016.

Taiwan

People: Population: 23,464,787. **Age distrib.:** <15: 13.1%; 65+: 13.1%. **Growth:** 0.2%. **Migrants:** NA. **Pop. density:** 1,883.9 per sq mi, 727.4 per sq km. **Urban:** NA. **Ethnic groups:** Taiwanese (incl. Hakka) 84%, mainland Chinese 14%, indigenous 2%. **Languages:** Mandarin Chinese (official), Taiwanese (Min), Hakka dialects. **Religions:** mixture of Buddhist and Taoist 93%, Christian 4.5%.

Geography: Total area: 13,892 sq mi, 35,980 sq km; **Land area:** 12,456 sq mi, 32,260 sq km. **Location:** Off SE coast of China, between E and S China Seas. **Topography:** A mountain range forms backbone of island. The eastern half is very steep and craggy; western slope is flat, fertile, and well cultivated. **Arable land:** 16.8%. **Capital:** Taipei, 2,668,633. **Cities:** Kaohsiung, 1,524,893; Taichung, 1,241,279.

Government: Type: Semi-presidential republic. **Head of state:** Pres. Tsai Ing-wen; b. 1956; in office: May 20, 2016. **Head of gov.:** Prem. Lin Chuan; b. 1951; in office: May 20, 2016. **Local divisions:** 13 counties, 3 cities, 6 special municipalities. **Defense budget:** $10.3 bil. **Active troops:** 215,000.

Economy: Industries: electronics, communications and information tech. prods., petroleum refining, chemicals, textiles, iron and steel, machinery, cement, food proc. **Chief crops:** rice, vegetables, fruit, tea, flowers. **Natural resources:** coal, nat. gas, limestone, marble, asbestos. **Water:** NA. **Crude oil reserves** (2015): 2.4 mil bbls. **Electricity prod.:** 233 bil kWh. **Labor force:** agric. 5%, industry 36%, services 59%. **Unemployment:** 3.8%.

Finance: Monetary unit: New Dollar (TWD) (31.72 = $1 U.S.). **GDP:** $1.1 tril; **per capita GDP:** $46,800; **GDP growth:** 0.7%. **Imports:** $228.6 bil; (2012) Japan 17.6%, China 16.1%, U.S. 9.5%. **Exports:** $284.9 bil; (2012) China 27.1%, Hong Kong 13.2%, U.S. 10.3%, Japan 6.4%. **Tourism:** $14.4 bil. **Budget:** $83.5 bil. **Inflation:** −0.3%.

Transport: Railways: 992 mi. **Motor vehicles:** 327.9 per 1,000 pop. **Airports:** 35.

Communications: Telephone: 59.7 per 100 pop. **Mobile:** 127.3 per 100 pop. **Broadband:** NA. **Internet:** 88%.

Health: Expend.: NA. **Life expect.:** 77.0 male; 83.5 female. **Births:** 8.4 per 1,000 pop. **Deaths:** 7.3 per 1,000 pop. **Infant mortality:** 4.4 per 1,000 live births. **Undernourished:** NA. **HIV:** NA.

Education: Compulsory: ages 6-14. **Literacy:** 98.5%.

Taipei Economic and Cultural Representative Office: 4201 Wisconsin Ave. NW 20016; 895-1800.
Website: www.taiwan.gov.tw

Large-scale immigration from China began in the 17th cent. The island came under mainland control after an interval of Dutch rule, 1620-62. Japan ruled Taiwan (also called Formosa), 1895-1945. The Kuomintang (Chinese Nationalist Party) government fled to Taiwan in 1949 and established the Republic of China under Chiang Kai-shek, who ruled until his death in 1975. The U.S. provided military aid to deter a Communist invasion.

In 1971, the UN expelled Taiwan as a member and recognized the mainland government. The U.S. acknowledged the People's Republic of China, Dec. 15, 1978, and severed ties with Taiwan. However, the U.S. and Taiwan have continued a strong trading relationship and maintain contact via quasi-official agencies.

Land reform, government planning, U.S. aid and investment, and free universal education brought advances in industry, agriculture, and living standards. In 1987 martial law was lifted after 38 years, and in 1991 the 43 years of emergency rule ended. Taiwan held its first direct presidential election Mar. 23, 1996. An earthquake on Sept. 21, 1999, killed more than 2,300 people.

Five decades of Kuomintang rule ended when Chen Shui-bian, leader of the pro-independence Democratic Progressive Party (DPP), won the Mar. 2000 presidential election. Chen was wounded in an apparent assassination attempt Mar. 19, 2004, one day before he won a second term as president. Promising increased cooperation with China, Kuomintang candidate Ma Ying-jeou won the presidential election, Mar. 22, 2008, and was reelected Jan. 14, 2012. Former Pres. Chen was convicted of corruption and sentenced to life in prison, Sept. 11, 2009.

Since 1949, the People's Republic has considered Taiwan a rebel province of the mainland; in 1991, the Kuomintang dropped its claim to be the sole government of both. The first formal talks between representatives of Taiwan and China were held Feb. 11, 2014. The first summit meeting, between Ma and Chinese Pres. Xi Jinping, took place in Singapore, Nov. 7, 2015. Concern over recent Kuomintang pro-China policies helped the DPP win sweeping victories in Jan. 16, 2016, presidential and legislative elections. The DPP's Tsai Ing-wen became Taiwan's first female president.

The Penghu Isls. (Pescadores), 49 sq mi, pop. (2011 est.) 96,597, lie between Taiwan and the mainland. Kinmen, fmr. Quemoy, pop. (2011 est.) 99,691, and Matsu, pop. (2011 est.) 10,106, lie just off the mainland.

Tajikistan
Republic of Tajikistan

People: Population: 8,330,946. **Age distrib.:** <15: 32.6%; 65+: 3.2%. **Growth:** 1.7%. **Migrants:** 3.2%. **Pop. density:** 152.5 per sq mi, 58.9 per sq km. **Urban:** 26.9%. **Ethnic groups:** Tajik 84.3%, Uzbek (incl. Lakai, Kongrat, Katagan, Barlos, Yuz) 13.8%, other (incl. Kyrgyz, Russian, Turkmen, Tatar, Arab) 2%. **Languages:** Tajik (official), Russian (used in govt. and business). **Religions:** Sunni Muslim 85%, Shia Muslim 5%.
Geography: Total area: 55,637 sq mi, 144,100 sq km; **Land area:** 54,637 sq mi, 141,510 sq km. **Location:** Central Asia. Uzbekistan on N and W, Kyrgyzstan on N, China on E, Afghanistan on S. **Topography:** Mountainous; contains the Pamirs, Trans-Alai mountain system. **Arable land:** 6.1%. **Capital:** Dushanbe, 844,859.
Government: Type: Presidential republic. **Head of state:** Pres. Emomali Rahmon; b. 1952; in office: Nov. 6, 1994. **Head of gov.:** Prime Min. Qohir Rasulzoda; b. 1961; in office: Nov. 23, 2013. **Local divisions:** 2 provinces, 1 autonomous province, 1 capital region, 1 district under republic admin. **Defense budget:** $152 mil. **Active troops:** 8,800.
Economy: Industries: aluminum, cement, vegetable oil. **Chief crops:** cotton, grain, fruits, grapes, vegetables. **Natural resources:** hydropower, petroleum, uranium, mercury, brown coal, lead, zinc, antimony, tungsten, silver, gold. **Water:** 2,583 cu m per capita. **Crude oil reserves** (2015): 12 mil bbls. **Electricity prod.:** 17 bil kWh. **Labor force:** agric. 46.5%, industry 10.7%, services 42.8%. **Unemployment:** 10.9%.
Finance: Monetary unit: Somoni (TJS) (7.87 = $1 U.S.). **GDP:** $23.3 bil; **per capita GDP:** $2,700; **GDP growth:** 3%. **Imports:** $3.2 bil; China 42.3%, Russia 17.9%, Kazakhstan 13.1%. **Exports:** $555.6 mil; Turkey 19.7%, Kazakhstan 17.6%, Switzerland 13.7%, Iran 8.7%, Afghanistan 7.5%, Russia 5.3%. **Budget:** $2.5 bil. **Inflation:** 5.7%.
Transport: Railways: 423 mi. **Airports:** 17.
Communications: Telephone: 5.3 per 100 pop. **Mobile:** 98.6 per 100 pop. **Broadband:** NA. **Internet:** 19%.
Health: Expend.: 6.9%. **Life expect.:** 64.6 male; 71.0 female. **Births:** 23.8 per 1,000 pop. **Deaths:** 6.1 per 1,000 pop. **Infant mortality:** 32.8 per 1,000 live births. **Undernourished:** 33.2%. **HIV:** 0.3%.
Education: Compulsory: ages 7-15. **Literacy:** 99.8%.
Embassy: 1005 New Hampshire Ave. NW 20037; 223-6090.
Website: www.president.tj

Societies were settled in the region from about 3000 BCE. Invaders have included Iranians, Arabs (who converted the population to Islam), Mongols, Uzbeks, Afghans, and Russians. The USSR gained control 1918-25, making the region a part of the Uzbek SSR until the Tajik SSR was proclaimed, 1929.

Tajikistan declared independence Sept. 9, 1991. Factional fighting led to the installation of a pro-Communist regime, Jan. 1993. A new constitution establishing a presidential system was approved by referendum in 1994.

An estimated 55,000 died in clashes between Muslim rebels and loyalist troops (supported by Russia) by mid-1997, despite a series of peace accords. Constitutional changes including legalization of Islamic political parties were approved by referendum in 1999. Pres. Imomali Rakhmonov, first elected in 1994, won a Nov. 1999 election called a farce by human-rights observers. Leading opposition groups boycotted the Nov. 2006 election, again won by Rakhmonov (who changed his name to Rakhmon in 2007). He won the Nov. 2013 election with 84% of the vote. Constitutional changes approved by referendum, May 22, 2016, allowed Rakhmon to serve an unlimited number of terms.

Poverty and corruption are widespread. Much of the nation's income is supplied by international donors and by remittances from Tajiks working in Kazakhstan and Russia, though a new Russian law in 2015 restricted the ability of Tajiks to work in Russia legally. After rebels murdered a Tajik general in the semiautonomous province of Gorno-Badakhshan, July 21, 2012, the army attacked and killed about 30 militants July 24; 17 government troops died. A former warlord surrendered Aug. 13, 2012, in exchange for a troop withdrawal from the region.

Tanzania
United Republic of Tanzania

People: Population: 52,482,726. **Age distrib.:** <15: 44.1%; 65+: 3%. **Growth:** 2.8%. **Migrants:** 0.5%. **Pop. density:** 153.5 per sq mi, 59.2 per sq km. **Urban:** 32.3%. **Ethnic groups:** African 99% (of which 95% are Bantu consisting of 130+ tribes). **Languages:** Kiswahili or Swahili, English (primary lang. of commerce, admin., higher ed.) (both official); Arabic (widely spoken in Zanzibar). **Religions:** Christian 61.4%, Muslim 35.2%; almost entirely Muslim on Zanzibar.
Geography: Total area: 365,755 sq mi, 947,300 sq km; **Land area:** 342,009 sq mi, 885,800 sq km. **Location:** Coast of E Africa. Kenya, Uganda on N; Rwanda, Burundi, Dem. Rep. of the Congo on W; Zambia, Malawi, Mozambique on S. **Topography:** Hot, arid central plateau surrounded by lake region in W. Temperate highlands in N and S; coastal plains. Mt. Kilimanjaro (19,341 ft) is highest in Africa. **Arable land:** 15.2%. **Capital:** Dodoma (official; National Assembly meets here), 227,762 (2014). **Cities:** Dar es Salaam (exec. branch offices), 5,408,669.
Government: Type: Presidential republic. **Head of state and gov.:** Pres. John Magufuli; b. 1959; in office: Nov. 5, 2015. **Local divisions:** 30 regions. **Defense budget:** $424 mil. **Active troops:** 27,000.
Economy: Industries: agric. proc.; mining; salt, soda ash; cement, oil refining, shoes, apparel, wood prods., fertilizer. **Chief crops:** coffee, sisal, tea, cotton, pyrethrum (insecticide made from chrysanthemums), cashews, tobacco, cloves, corn, wheat, cassava. **Natural resources:** hydropower, tin, phosphates, iron ore, coal, diamonds, gems, gold, nat. gas, nickel. **Water:** 1,800 cu m per capita. **Electricity prod.:** 5.3 bil kWh. **Labor force:** agric. 80%, industry and services 20%. **Unemployment:** 3.1%.
Finance: Monetary unit: Shilling (TZS) (2,181.00 = $1 U.S.). **GDP:** $138.5 bil; **per capita GDP:** $2,900; **GDP growth:** 7%. **Imports:** $10.5 bil; China 34.7%, India 13.5%. **Exports:** $5.4 bil; India 21.4%, China 8.1%, Japan 5.1%. **Tourism:** $2.2 bil. **Budget:** $8.4 bil. **Inflation:** 5.6%.
Transport: Railways: 2,838 mi. **Motor vehicles:** 1.8 per 1,000 pop. **Airports:** 10.
Communications: Telephone: 0.3 per 100 pop. **Mobile:** 75.9 per 100 pop. **Broadband:** 3 per 100 pop. **Internet:** 5.4%.
Health: Expend.: 5.6%. **Life expect.:** 60.8 male; 63.6 female. **Births:** 36.0 per 1,000 pop. **Deaths:** 7.8 per 1,000 pop. **Infant mortality:** 41.2 per 1,000 live births. **Undernourished:** 32.1%. **HIV:** 4.7%.
Education: Compulsory: ages 7-13. **Literacy:** 80.4%.
Embassy: 1232 22nd St. NW 20037; 939-6125.
Website: www.tanzania.go.tz

Arab colonization and slaving in Tanganyika began in the 8th cent.; Portuguese sailors explored the coast around 1500. Other Europeans followed.

In 1885 Germany established German East Africa, of which Tanganyika formed the bulk. Under Britain, it became a League of Nations mandate and after 1946, a UN trust territory. It became independent, Dec. 9, 1961, and a republic within the Commonwealth a year later.

Zanzibar, the Isle of Cloves, has an area of 640 sq mi and lies 23 mi off mainland Tanzania. The island of Pemba, area 380 sq mi, is 25 mi to the NE. Ethnic groups in Zanzibar include Arabs and Africans. Zanzibar and Pemba produce most of the world's supply of cloves and clove oil.

Zanzibar was for centuries the center for Arab slave traders. Portugal ruled the region for two centuries until ousted by Arabs around 1700. Zanzibar became a British Protectorate in 1890; independence came Dec. 10, 1963. Revolutionary forces overthrew the Sultan, Jan. 12, 1964. The new government ousted

Western diplomats and journalists, slaughtered thousands of Arabs, and nationalized farms.

The Republic of Tanganyika and the Republic of Zanzibar joined to form the United Republic of Tanzania, Apr. 26, 1964. Zanzibar retains internal self-government.

Until resigning as president in 1985, Julius K. Nyerere, a former Tanganyikan independence leader, dominated Tanzania's single-party government, which emphasized government planning and economic control. A multiparty system was established in 1992, and the economy was privatized in the 1990s.

A bomb at the U.S. embassy in Dar es Salaam, Aug. 7, 1998, killed 11 people and injured at least 70 others. The U.S. blamed the attack and a near-simultaneous embassy bombing in Kenya on Islamic terrorists associated with Osama bin Laden.

Jakaya Mrisho Kikwete of the ruling Chama Cha Mapinduzi (CCM), won the Dec. 2005, presidential election; he was reelected to a second 5-year term Oct. 2010. Large natural gas deposits have been discovered in recent years; estimated recoverable gas reserves totaled more than 55 tril cubic ft by 2016. CCM candidate John Magufuli won the Oct. 25, 2015, presidential election. Zanzibar regional elections the same day were annulled because of voting irregularities and rerun Mar. 20, 2016; the CCM incumbent won Zanzibar's presidency in voting boycotted by the opposition.

Thailand
Kingdom of Thailand

People: Population: 68,200,824. **Age distrib.:** <15: 17.2%; 65+: 10.2%. **Growth:** 0.3%. **Migrants:** 5.8%. **Pop. density:** 345.7 per sq mi, 133.5 per sq km. **Urban:** 51.5%. **Ethnic groups:** Thai 95.9%, Burmese 2%. **Languages:** Thai (official), English (secondary lang. of elite). **Religions:** Buddhist (official) 93.6%, Muslim 4.9%.

Geography: Total area: 198,117 sq mi, 513,120 sq km; **Land area:** 197,256 sq mi, 510,890 sq km. **Location:** On Indochinese and Malayan peninsulas in SE Asia. Myanmar on W and N, Laos on N, Cambodia on E, Malaysia on S. **Topography:** A plateau dominates NE third of Thailand, dropping to fertile alluvial valley of Chao Phraya R. in center. Forested mountains with narrow fertile valleys are in N. Rain forests cover S peninsula region. **Arable land:** 32.9%. **Capital:** Bangkok (Krung Thep), 9,444,184. **Cities:** Samut Prakan, 1,979,998.

Government: Type: Constitutional monarchy. **Head of state:** In transition. **Head of gov.:** Prime Min. Prayuth Chan-ocha; b. 1954; in office: Aug. 24, 2014. **Local divisions:** 76 provinces, 1 municipality. **Defense budget:** $5.4 bil. **Active troops:** 360,850.

Economy: Industries: tourism, textiles and garments, agric. proc., beverages, tobacco, cement, light mfg. (jewelry, elec. appliances, computers and parts, integrated circuits, furniture). **Chief crops:** rice, cassava, rubber, corn, sugarcane, coconuts, palm oil, pineapples. **Natural resources:** tin, rubber, nat. gas, tungsten, tantalum, timber, lead, fish, gypsum, lignite, fluorite. **Water:** 6,454 cu m per capita. **Crude oil reserves:** 0.4 bil bbls. **Electricity prod.:** 157 bil kWh. **Labor force:** agric. 32.2%, industry 16.7%, services 51.1%. **Unemployment:** 0.9%.

Finance: Monetary unit: Baht (THB) (34.61 = $1 U.S.). **GDP:** $1.1 tril; **per capita GDP:** $16,100; **GDP growth:** 2.8%. **Imports:** $196.4 bil; China 20.3%, Japan 15.4%, U.S. 6.9%, Malaysia 5.9%. **Exports:** $214.8 bil; U.S. 11.2%, China 11.1%, Japan 9.4%, Hong Kong 5.5%. **Tourism:** $44.6 bil. **Budget:** $80.5 bil. **Inflation:** –0.9%.

Transport: Railways: 2,529 mi. **Motor vehicles:** 227.9 per 1,000 pop. **Airports:** 63.

Communications: Telephone: 7.9 per 100 pop. **Mobile:** 125.8 per 100 pop. **Broadband:** 79.9 per 100 pop. **Internet:** 39.3%.

Health: Expend.: 6.5%. **Life expect.:** 71.5 male; 78.0 female. **Births:** 11.1 per 1,000 pop. **Deaths:** 7.9 per 1,000 pop. **Infant mortality:** 9.4 per 1,000 live births. **Undernourished:** 7.4%. **HIV:** 1.1%.

Education: Compulsory: ages 6-14. **Literacy:** 94%.

Embassy: 1024 Wisconsin Ave. NW 20007; 944-3600.

Website: www.thaigov.go.th

Thais began migrating from southern China during the 11th cent. and established a unified Thai kingdom, 1350. Known as Siam until 1939, Thailand is the only country in SE Asia never colonized by Europeans. King Mongkut and his son King Chulalongkorn, ruling successively from 1851 to 1910, modernized the country and signed trade treaties with Britain and France. A bloodless revolution in 1932 limited the monarchy. Thailand was an ally of Japan during WWII and of the U.S. during the postwar period. For decades, the military had a dominant role in governing the country.

An economic downturn forced Thailand to seek more than $15 bil in emergency international loans, Aug. 1997. A new constitution won legislative approval Sept. 27. By the end of the 1990s, according to UN estimates, more than 750,000 people in Thailand had HIV/AIDS, with 143,000 new infections in 1991 alone. A nationwide prevention campaign reduced the number of new HIV infections; in 2015 about 440,000 people were living with HIV/AIDS.

Beginning in 2004, security forces tried to suppress a Muslim insurgency in southern Thailand. By mid-2016, more than 6,500 people, mostly civilians, had been killed in insurgent attacks and actions by security forces.

Following elections in Jan. 2001, Thaksin Shinawatra became prime min. A military junta took power in a bloodless coup Sept. 19, 2006. Thaksin supporters won Dec. 2007 elections, and Samak Sundaravej became prime min. after civilian rule was restored Jan. 22, 2008. Thailand's Constitutional Court ousted Samak in Sept., and Thaksin's brother-in-law Somchai Wongsawat became prime min. Sept. 18. But a Constitutional Court ruling, Dec. 2, barred him from politics and dissolved his People Power Party because of electoral fraud.

Mass protests by Thaksin supporters, known as Red Shirts, led the government to declare a state of emergency in Bangkok, Apr. 12-24, 2009. On Feb. 26, 2010, Thailand's Supreme Court ordered the seizure of about $1.4 bil of Thaksin's family assets. Thaksin supporters staged mass rallies in Bangkok. After the Red Shirts began to build a fortified compound in Bangkok, a crackdown by Thai security forces May 14-19, 2010, left more than 90 people dead. Thaksin's sister, Yingluck Shinawatra, became Thailand's first female prime min. after parliamentary elections July 3, 2011. On May 7, 2014, she was removed from office by the Constitutional Court, and the military seized power in a May 22 coup. An interim legislature, with a majority of military members, was appointed July 31; it named coup leader Gen. Prayuth Chan-ocha as prime min. Aug. 21, 2014.

A 2015 investigation resulted in charges against dozens, including government and military officials, for involvement in human trafficking; the charges related to smuggling by boat, abusing, holding for ransom, and selling as slave laborers migrants from Myanmar and Bangladesh. A bombing at the Erawan shrine in Bangkok, Aug. 17, 2015, killed 20. Thai police arrested two suspects, Aug. 29 and Sept. 1, said to be Uighur militants; in July, Thailand had deported more than 100 Uighur migrants to China. In an Aug. 7, 2016, referendum (opposition campaigning had been barred), voters approved a military-drafted new constitution and a companion measure that would effectively dilute the power of any one political party and increase the military's role in selecting prime ministers after a return to civilian rule. A series of 11 bombings, Aug. 11-12, 2016, mainly in tourist areas, killed four and injured dozens.

King Bhumibol, monarch since June 1946, died Oct. 13, 2016; crown prince Maha Vajiralongkorn was expected to succeed him.

Timor-Leste
(East Timor)
Democratic Republic of Timor-Leste

People: Population: 1,261,072. **Age distrib.:** <15: 41.4%; 65+: 3.8%. **Growth:** 2.4%. **Migrants:** 0.9%. **Pop. density:** 219.6 per sq mi, 84.8 per sq km. **Urban:** 33.4%. **Ethnic groups:** Austronesian (Malayo-Polynesian), Papuan, small Chinese minority. **Languages:** Tetum, Portuguese (both official); Indonesian; English; about 16 indigenous langs. **Religions:** Roman Catholic 96.9%.

Geography: Total area: 5,743 sq mi, 14,874 sq km. **Land area:** 5,743 sq mi, 14,874 sq km. **Location:** E half of Timor Isl. in SW Pacific O. Indonesia on W half of island. **Topography:** Rugged terrain, rising to 9,721 ft at Mt. Ramelau. **Arable land:** 10.4%. **Capital:** Dili, 228,136 (2014).

Government: Type: Semi-presidential republic. **Head of state:** Pres. Taur Matan Ruak; b. 1956; in office: May 20, 2012. **Head of gov.:** Prime Min. Rui Maria de Araújo; b. 1964; in office: Feb. 16, 2015. **Local divisions:** 13 admin. districts. **Defense budget:** $73 mil. **Active troops:** 1,330.

Economy: Industries: printing, soap mfg., handicrafts, woven cloth. **Chief crops:** coffee, rice, corn, cassava, sweet potatoes, soybeans, cabbages, mangoes, bananas, vanilla. **Natural resources:** gold, petroleum, nat. gas, manganese, marble. **Water:** 6,932 cu m per capita. **Electricity prod.:** 0 kWh. **Labor force:** agric. 64%, industry 10%, services 26%. **Unemployment:** 4.7%.

Finance: Monetary unit: U.S. Dollar (USD) (1.00 = $1 U.S.). **GDP:** $6.6 bil; **per capita GDP:** $5,600; **GDP growth:** 4.3%. **Imports** (2014): $764.2 mil. **Exports** (2014): $15.5 mil. **Tourism:** $51 mil. **Budget:** $2.1 bil. **Inflation:** 0.6%.

Transport: Airports: 2.

Communications: Telephone: 0.2 per 100 pop. **Mobile:** 117.4 per 100 pop. **Broadband:** NA. **Internet:** 13.4%.

Health: Expend.: 1.5%. **Life expect.:** 66.5 male; 69.7 female. **Births:** 33.8 per 1,000 pop. **Deaths:** 6.0 per 1,000 pop. **Infant mortality:** 36.3 per 1,000 live births. **Undernourished:** 26.9%. **HIV:** NA.

Education: Compulsory: ages 6-14. **Literacy:** 64.1%.

Embassy: 4201 Connecticut Ave. NW, Ste. 504, 20008; 966-3202.

Website: timor-leste.gov.tl

The collapse of Portuguese rule in East Timor led to factional fighting, Aug. 1975, and an invasion by Indonesia in Dec. Indonesia annexed East Timor as a 27th province in 1976. In over two decades, more than 200,000 Timorese died due to civil war, famine, and persecution by Indonesian authorities. In a referendum held Aug. 1999 under UN auspices, Timorese voted overwhelmingly for independence but were then terrorized by pro-Indonesian militias. An international peacekeeping force entered in Sept.; a UN interim administration formally took command Oct. 26, 1999. Pro-independence forces won elections for a constituent assembly Aug. 2001. Xanana Gusmão, a former guerrilla leader, won the presidential election Apr. 2002. As Timor-Leste, the territory became independent May 20 and entered the UN Sept. 27.

José Ramos-Horta, a Nobel Peace Prize laureate, won a presidential runoff vote May 2007. After inconclusive parliamentary elections June 30, Ramos-Horta chose Gusmão as prime min. The Gusmão-supported independent candidate, Taur Matan Ruak, became president in a May 2012 runoff election. Gusmão's party won a majority of seats in the July parliamentary election, and he became prime min. of a coalition government in Aug. The UN peacekeeping mission ended Dec. 31, 2012. Beginning in 2005, much of East Timor's budget consisted of revenue from offshore oil and natural gas deposits. Lower oil prices in 2014-16 and indications that gas reserves could be less than previously estimated, even as the government tapped the energy-revenue fund for infrastructure and other projects, were troubling signs for the country's struggling economy. Gusmão resigned Feb. 6, 2015, to pave the way for restructuring; he was replaced as prime min. five days later by opposition figure Rui Maria de Araújo.

Togo
Togolese Republic

People: Population: 7,756,937. **Age distrib.:** <15: 40.4%; 65+: 3.4%. **Growth:** 2.7%. **Migrants:** 3.8%. **Pop. density:** 369.4 per sq mi, 142.6 per sq km. **Urban:** 40.5%. **Ethnic groups:** African (37 tribes; largest and most important are Ewe, Mina, Kabre) 99%. **Languages:** French (official, lang. of commerce), Ewe and Mina (in S), Kabye and Dagomba (in N). **Religions:** indigenous beliefs 51%, Christian 29%, Muslim 20%.
Geography: Total area: 21,925 sq mi, 56,785 sq km; **Land area:** 20,998 sq mi, 54,385 sq km. **Location:** S coast of W Africa. Ghana on W, Burkina Faso on N, Benin on E. **Topography:** Hills running SW-NE split Togo into two savanna plains regions. **Arable land:** 48.7%. **Capital:** Lomé, 984,904.
Government: Type: Presidential republic. **Head of state:** Pres. Faure Gnassingbé; b. 1966; in office: May 4, 2005. **Head of gov.:** Prime Min. Komi Klassou; b. 1960; in office: June 5, 2015. **Local divisions:** 5 regions. **Defense budget:** $71 mil. **Active troops:** 8,550.
Economy: Industries: phosphate mining, agric. proc., cement, handicrafts, textiles, beverages. **Chief crops:** coffee, cocoa, cotton, yams, cassava, corn, beans, rice, millet, sorghum. **Natural resources:** phosphates, limestone, marble. **Water:** 2,012 cu m per capita. **Electricity prod.:** 0.1 bil kWh. **Labor force:** agric. 65%, industry 5%, services 30%. **Unemployment:** 6.9%.
Finance: Monetary unit: CFA Franc (XOF) (586.00 = $1 U.S.). **GDP:** $10.9 bil; **per capita GDP:** $1,500; **GDP growth:** 5.3%. **Imports:** $3 bil; China 22.9%, Belgium 20.3%, Netherlands 11.9%, France 6.6%. **Exports:** $1.9 bil; India 14.3%, Burkina Faso 11.1%, China 11.1%, Lebanon 10%, Benin 9.4%, Ghana 8.8%, Nigeria 6%, Niger 5.8%. **Tourism:** $125 mil. **Budget:** $1.2 bil. **Inflation:** 1.8%.
Transport: Railways: 353 mi. **Motor vehicles:** 25.4 per 1,000 pop. **Airports:** 2.
Communications: Telephone: 0.7 per 100 pop. **Mobile:** 64.9 per 100 pop. **Broadband:** 4.1 per 100 pop. **Internet:** 7.1%.
Health: Expend.: 5.3%. **Life expect.:** 62.3 male; 67.7 female. **Births:** 33.7 per 1,000 pop. **Deaths:** 7.1 per 1,000 pop. **Infant mortality:** 43.7 per 1,000 live births. **Undernourished:** 11.4%. **HIV:** 2.4%.
Education: Compulsory: ages 6-15. **Literacy:** 66.5%.
Embassy: 2208 Massachusetts Ave. NW 20008; 234-4212.
Website: www.primature.gouv.tg or www.state.gov/p/af/ci/to/

Togoland was administered by Germany and then by France and Britain. The French sector became the republic of Togo Apr. 27, 1960. In office since 1967, Pres. Gnassingbé Eyadéma was Africa's longest-serving head of state until his death Feb. 5, 2005. His son, Faure Gnassingbé, was installed as president, but African leaders pressured Togo to hold an election, which Gnassingbé won Apr. 24. Opposition parties disputed the result, and protests led to violent clashes in Lomé.

After a shootout at his home Apr. 12, 2009, former Defense Min. Kpatcha Gnassingbé, the president's brother, was arrested and accused of plotting a coup. Pres. Gnassingbé won reelection Mar. 4, 2010, to a second 5-year term. Weeks of antigovernment protest led Prime Min. Gilbert Fossoun Houngbo to resign, July 13, 2012, and a new government was formed. Legislative elections were held July 25, 2013, with the ruling party maintaining its majority and the opposition claiming voting irregularities. Pres. Gnassingbé won a third term in Apr. 25, 2015, elections; the opposition disputed the result. Gnassingbé appointed a new prime min., former Education Min. Komi Klassou, June 5, 2015.

Tonga
Kingdom of Tonga

People: Population: 106,513. **Age distrib.:** <15: 34.5%; 65+: 6.3%. **Growth:** -0.01%. **Migrants:** 5.4%. **Pop. density:** 384.8 per sq mi, 148.6 per sq km. **Urban:** 23.8%. **Ethnic groups:** Tongan 96.6%. **Languages:** Tongan, English (both official). **Religions:**

Protestant 64.9% (incl. Free Wesleyan Church 37.3%, Free Church of Tonga 11.4%), Mormon 16.8%, Roman Catholic 15.6%.
Geography: Total area: 288 sq mi, 747 sq km; **Land area:** 277 sq mi, 717 sq km. **Location:** Western S Pacific O. Nearest neighbors are Fiji to NW, Samoa to NE. **Topography:** Comprises 170 volcanic and coral islands, 36 inhabited. **Arable land:** 22.2%. **Capital:** Nuku'alofa, 24,998 (2014).
Government: Type: Constitutional monarchy. **Head of state:** King Tupou VI; b. 1959; in office: Mar. 18, 2012. **Head of gov.:** Prime Min. 'Akilisi Pohiva; b. 1941; in office: Dec. 30, 2014. **Local divisions:** 5 island divisions. **Defense budget/active troops:** NA.
Economy: Industries: tourism, constr., fishing. **Chief crops:** squash, coconuts, copra, bananas, vanilla beans, cocoa, coffee, sweet potatoes, cassava, taro, kava. **Natural resources:** fish. **Water:** NA. **Electricity prod.** (2012): 48 mil kWh. **Labor force:** agric. 27.5%, industry 27.5%, services 45.1%. **Unemployment:** NA.
Finance: Monetary unit: Pa'anga (TOP) (2.24 = $1 U.S.). **GDP:** $526 mil; **per capita GDP:** $5,100; **GDP growth:** 2.6%. **Imports:** $151.9 mil; Fiji 37.7%, New Zealand 21.2%, China 14.2%, U.S. 6.4%. **Exports:** $29.4 mil; Japan 15.9%, U.S. 15.4%, Fiji 12.7%, New Zealand 12.5%, South Korea 11%, Samoa 10.7%, Australia 7.5%, American Samoa 6.8%. **Tourism:** $45 mil. **Budget:** $146.3 mil. **Inflation:** -1%.
Transport: Airports: 1.
Communications: Telephone: 12.4 per 100 pop. **Mobile:** 65.6 per 100 pop. **Broadband:** 19.3 per 100 pop. **Internet:** 45%.
Health: Expend.: 5.2%. **Life expect.:** 74.7 male; 77.8 female. **Births:** 22.6 per 1,000 pop. **Deaths:** 4.9 per 1,000 pop. **Infant mortality:** 11.6 per 1,000 live births. **Undernourished:** NA. **HIV:** NA.
Education: Compulsory: ages 4-18. **Literacy:** 99.4%.
Permanent UN mission: 250 E. 51st St., New York, NY 10022; (917) 369-1025.
Website: www.gov.to

First inhabited by ancestors of Polynesians c. 2000 BCE, Tonga was visited by the Dutch in the early 17th cent. and by British explorer James Cook in the 1770s. A series of civil wars ended, 1845, with establishment of the Tupou dynasty. In 1900, Tonga became a British protectorate. Tonga gained independence June 1970 and joined the Commonwealth. It joined the UN in 1999. George Tupou VI became king Mar. 18, 2012, following the death of his brother, who had introduced reforms. Elections in Nov. 2010 gave the country its first democratically elected parliament, reducing the monarch's powers. With the economy sluggish, almost two-thirds of directly elected members were voted out of office in Nov. 27, 2014, elections.

Trinidad and Tobago
Republic of Trinidad and Tobago

People: Population: 1,220,479. **Age distrib.:** <15: 19.3%; 65+: 10.2%. **Growth:** -0.2%. **Migrants:** 3.7%. **Pop. density:** 616.4 per sq mi, 238 per sq km. **Urban:** 8.4%. **Ethnic groups:** East Indian 35.4%, African 34.2%, mixed-other 15.3%, mixed African/East Indian 7.7%. **Languages:** English (official), Caribbean Hindustani, French, Spanish, Chinese. **Religions:** Protestant 32.1% (incl. Pentecostal/Evangelical/Full Gospel 12%), Roman Catholic 21.6%, Hindu 18.2%, Muslim 5%.
Geography: Total area: 1,980 sq mi, 5,128 sq km; **Land area:** 1,980 sq mi, 5,128 sq km. **Location:** In Caribbean, off E coast of Venezuela. **Topography:** Three low mountain ranges cross Trinidad E-W, with a well-watered plain between N and central ranges. Parts of E and W coasts are swamps. Tobago, 116 sq mi, lies 20 mi NE. **Arable land:** 4.9%. **Capital:** Port of Spain, 34,387 (2014).
Government: Type: Parliamentary republic. **Head of state:** Pres. Anthony Carmona; b. 1953; in office: Mar. 18, 2013. **Head of gov.:** Prime Min. Keith Rowley; b. 1949; in office: Sept. 8, 2015. **Local divisions:** 9 regions, 3 boroughs, 2 cities, 1 ward. **Defense budget:** $443 mil. **Active troops:** 4,050.
Economy: Industries: petroleum and petroleum prods., liquefied nat. gas, methanol, ammonia, urea, steel prods., beverages. **Chief crops:** cocoa, dasheen, pumpkin, cassava, tomatoes, cucumbers, eggplant, hot pepper, pommecythere, coconut water. **Natural resources:** petroleum, nat. gas, asphalt. **Water:** 2,824 cu m per capita. **Crude oil reserves:** 0.7 bil bbls. **Electricity prod.:** 8.9 bil kWh. **Labor force:** agric. 3.8%; mfg., mining, and quarrying 12.8%; constr. and utilities 20.4%; services 62.9%. **Unemployment:** 4%.
Finance: Monetary unit: Dollar (TTD) (6.67 = $1 U.S.). **GDP:** $44.3 bil; **per capita GDP:** $32,600; **GDP growth:** -1.8%. **Imports:** $7.6 bil; U.S. 35.6%, China 6.8%, Gabon 6.6%. **Exports:** $8.7 bil; U.S. 26.3%, Argentina 12%, Brazil 6.6%, Chile 5.3%, Dominican Republic 5.2%, Barbados 5%. **Tourism:** $450 mil. **Budget:** $9.8 bil. **Inflation:** 4.7%.
Transport: Motor vehicles: 321 per 1,000 pop. **Airports:** 2.
Communications: Telephone: 21.1 per 100 pop. **Mobile:** 157.7 per 100 pop. **Broadband:** 28.3 per 100 pop. **Internet:** 69.2%.
Health: Expend.: 5.9%. **Life expect.:** 69.9 male; 75.9 female. **Births:** 13.1 per 1,000 pop. **Deaths:** 8.7 per 1,000 pop. **Infant mortality:** 23.0 per 1,000 live births. **Undernourished:** 7.4%. **HIV:** 1.2%.

Education: Compulsory: ages 6-11. **Literacy:** 99%.
Embassy: 1708 Massachusetts Ave. NW 20036; 467-6490.
Website: www.ttconnect.gov.tt

Christopher Columbus sighted Trinidad in 1498. It became a British possession in 1802; in the 1800s tens of thousands of indentured servants and their families were brought from India to work in agriculture. Trinidad and Tobago won independence Aug. 31, 1962. It became a republic in 1976.

The nation, among the most prosperous in the Caribbean, produces oil and natural gas; it also refines and exports Middle Eastern oil.

In July 1990, some 120 Muslim extremists captured the Parliament building and TV station and took about 50 hostages, including Prime Min. Arthur N. R. Robinson. After a six-day siege, the rebels surrendered.

Basdeo Panday, in office 1995-2001, was the nation's first prime min. of Indian ancestry. The country's first female prime min., Kamla Persad-Bissessar, leader of the People's Partnership coalition, took office May 26, 2010. After her coalition lost Sept. 7, 2015, elections, Keith Rowley of the People's National Movement became prime min., Sept. 9.

Tunisia
Republic of Tunisia

People: Population: 11,134,588. **Age distrib.:** <15: 23%; 65+: 8.2%. **Growth:** 0.9%. **Migrants:** 0.5%. **Pop. density:** 185.6 per sq mi, 71.7 per sq km. **Urban:** 67%. **Ethnic groups:** Arab 98%. **Languages:** Arabic (official), French (used in commerce), Berber (Tamazight). **Religions:** Muslim (official; Sunni) 99.1%.

Geography: Total area: 63,170 sq mi, 163,610 sq km; **Land area:** 59,985 sq mi, 155,360 sq km. **Location:** N coast of Africa. Algeria on W, Libya on E. **Topography:** The N is wooded and fertile. Grazing lands and orchards are in central coastal plains. The S is arid, approaching Sahara Desert. **Arable land:** 18.4%. **Capital:** Tunis, 2,010,125.

Government: Type: Parliamentary republic. **Head of state:** Pres. Béji Caïd Essebsi; b. 1926; in office: Dec. 31, 2014. **Head of gov.:** Prime Min. Youssef Chahed; b. 1975; in office: Aug. 27, 2016. **Local divisions:** 24 governorates. **Defense budget** (2014): $926 mil. **Active troops:** 35,800.

Economy: Industries: petroleum, mining, tourism, textiles, footwear, agribusiness, beverages. **Chief crops:** olives, olive oil, grain, tomatoes, citrus, sugar beets, dates, almonds. **Natural resources:** petroleum, phosphates, iron ore, lead, zinc, salt. **Water:** 410 cu m per capita. **Crude oil reserves:** 0.4 bil bbls. **Electricity prod.:** 16 bil kWh. **Labor force:** agric. 14.8%, industry 33.2%, services 51.7%. **Unemployment:** 13.3%.

Finance: Monetary unit: Dinar (TND) (2.21 = $1 U.S.). **GDP:** $127 bil; **per capita GDP:** $11,400; **GDP growth:** 0.8%. **Imports:** $19.4 bil; France 19.4%, Italy 16.4%, Algeria 8.2%, Germany 7.4%, China 6%. **Exports:** $14.7 bil; France 28.5%, Italy 17.2%, Germany 10.9%, Libya 6.1%. **Tourism:** $1.4 bil. **Budget:** $12.8 bil. **Inflation:** 4.9%.

Transport: Railways: 1,350 mi (only partly operational). **Motor vehicles:** 135.2 per 1,000 pop. **Airports:** 15.

Communications: Telephone: 8.4 per 100 pop. **Mobile:** 129.9 per 100 pop. **Broadband:** 47.6 per 100 pop. **Internet:** 48.5%.

Health: Expend.: 7%. **Life expect.:** 74.0 male; 78.4 female. **Births:** 16.4 per 1,000 pop. **Deaths:** 6.0 per 1,000 pop. **Infant mortality:** 21.6 per 1,000 live births. **Undernourished:** <5%. **HIV:** <0.1%.

Education: Compulsory: ages 6-14. **Literacy:** 81.1%.
Embassy: 1515 Massachusetts Ave. NW 20005; 862-1850.
Website: www.tunisie.gov.tn or www.pm.gov.tn

Site of ancient Carthage and a former Barbary state under the suzerainty of Turkey, Tunisia became a protectorate of France, May 12, 1881. The nation became independent Mar. 20, 1956, and ended the monarchy the following year. Habib Bourguiba, an independence leader, served as president until 1987, when he was deposed by his prime min., Zine al-Abidine Ben Ali, who then won five presidential elections, 1989-2009, all tightly controlled.

Arab Spring protests, which began Dec. 2010, ousted Ben Ali, Jan. 14, 2011, and also forced the removal of Prime Min. Mohamed Ghannouchi. Moncef Marzouki of the secular center-left Congress for the Republic party became interim president, Dec. 13, 2011, but real power lay with Prime Min. Hamadi Jebali, an Islamist leader of the moderate Ennahda party, which won Oct. 2011 elections. Jebali resigned Feb. 19, 2013, after failing to institute promised reforms. After a new constitution was approved, Jan. 26, 2014, the secular Nida Tunis party won the most seats in Oct. 26, 2014, legislative elections; independent Habib Essid became prime min. Nida Tunis leader Beji Caid Essebsi was elected pres., Dec. 21, 2014. Essid lost a no-confidence vote, July 30, 2016, and Youssef Chahed of Nida Tunis became prime min., Aug. 27.

Three Islamist extremist gunmen attacked a museum in Tunis, Mar. 18, 2015, killing 22. A gunman killed 38 foreign tourists at a resort hotel in Sousse, June 26. ISIS claimed responsibility for the Sousse attack and a suicide bombing in Tunis, Nov. 24, 2015, that left 12 victims dead. A sharp drop in tourism hurt the economy. More than 30 Islamist fighters were killed, Mar. 7, 2016, in

unsuccessful attacks on an army post and police station near the Libyan border.

Turkey
Republic of Turkey

People: Population: 80,274,604. **Age distrib.:** <15: 25.1%; 65+: 7.3%. **Growth:** 0.9%. **Migrants:** 3.8%. **Pop. density:** 270.1 per sq mi, 104.3 per sq km. **Urban:** 73.9%. **Ethnic groups:** Turkish 70%-75%, Kurdish 18%. **Languages:** Turkish (official), Kurdish. **Religions:** Muslim (mostly Sunni) 99.8%.

Geography: Total area: 302,535 sq mi, 783,562 sq km; **Land area:** 297,157 sq mi, 769,632 sq km. **Location:** Asia Minor, stretching into continental Europe; borders on Medit. and Black Seas. Bulgaria, Greece on W; Georgia, Armenia on N; Iran on E; Iraq, Syria on S. **Topography:** Center has wide plateaus with hot, dry summers and cold winters. High mountains ring the interior on all but W, with more than 20 peaks over 10,000 ft. Rolling plains in W; mild, fertile coastal plains in S and W. **Arable land:** 26.7%. **Capital:** Ankara, 4,852,163. **Cities:** Istanbul, 14,365,329; Izmir, 3,090,176; Bursa, 1,973,832; Adana, 1,879,021; Gaziantep, 1,567,228.

Government: Type: Parliamentary republic. **Head of state:** Pres. Recep Tayyip Erdogan; b. 1954; in office: Aug. 28, 2014. **Head of gov.:** Prime Min. Binali Yildirim; b. 1955; in office: May 22, 2016. **Local divisions:** 81 provinces. **Defense budget:** $8.3 bil. **Active troops:** 510,600.

Economy: Industries: textiles, food proc., autos, electronics, mining, steel, petroleum, constr., lumber, paper. **Chief crops:** tobacco, cotton, grain, olives, sugar beets, hazelnuts, pulses, citrus. **Natural resources:** coal, iron ore, copper, chromium, antimony, mercury, gold, barite, borate, strontium, emery, feldspar, limestone, magnesite, marble, perlite, pumice, pyrites (sulfur), clay, hydropower. **Water:** 2,690 cu m per capita. **Crude oil reserves:** 0.3 bil bbls. **Electricity prod.:** 226 bil kWh. **Labor force:** agric. 25.5%, industry 26.2%, services 48.4%. **Unemployment:** 9.2%.

Finance: Monetary unit: Lira (TRY) (2.96 = $1 U.S.). **GDP:** $1.6 tril; **per capita GDP:** $20,400; **GDP growth:** 3.8%. **Imports:** $204.3 bil; China 12%, Germany 10.3%, Russia 9.9%, U.S. 5.4%, Italy 5.1%. **Exports:** $153.6 bil; Germany 9.3%, UK 7.3%, Iraq 5.9%. **Tourism:** $26.6 bil. **Budget:** $187.4 bil. **Inflation:** 7.7%.

Transport: Railways: 7,461 mi. **Motor vehicles:** 192.9 per 1,000 pop. **Airports:** 91.

Communications: Telephone: 15 per 100 pop. **Mobile:** 96 per 100 pop. **Broadband:** 42.7 per 100 pop. **Internet:** 53.7%.

Health: Expend.: 5.4%. **Life expect.:** 72.5 male; 77.3 female. **Births:** 16.0 per 1,000 pop. **Deaths:** 5.9 per 1,000 pop. **Infant mortality:** 18.2 per 1,000 live births. **Undernourished:** <5%. **HIV:** NA.

Education: Compulsory: ages 6-17. **Literacy:** 95.7%.
Embassy: 2525 Massachusetts Ave. NW 20008; 612-6700.
Website: www.tccb.gov.tr

Ancient inhabitants of Turkey were among the world's first agriculturalists. Such civilizations as the Hittite, Phrygian, and Lydian flourished in Asiatic Turkey (Asia Minor), as did much of Greek civilization. After the fall of Rome in the 5th cent., Constantinople (now Istanbul) was the capital of the Byzantine Empire for 1,000 years. It fell in 1453 to Ottoman Turks, who ruled a vast empire for over 400 years.

Just before WWI, Turkey, or the Ottoman Empire, ruled what is now Syria, Lebanon, Iraq, Jordan, Israel, Saudi Arabia, Yemen, and islands in the Aegean Sea. Turkey joined Germany and Austria in WWI, and its defeat resulted in the loss of territory and the fall of the sultanate. A secular republic was established Oct. 29, 1923. The first pres., Mustafa Kemal (later Kemal Ataturk), led Turkey until his death in 1938.

Turkey kept neutral during most of WWII. The country became a full member of NATO in 1952. Military coups overthrew civilian governments in 1960 and 1980. Turkey invaded nearby Cyprus July 20, 1974, to prevent that country from uniting with Greece, and Cyprus was divided into Greek and Turkish zones.

Turkey joined the U.S.-led force that ousted Iraq from Kuwait, 1991. Millions of Iraqi Kurdish refugees fled to Turkey's SE border region after the war. Turkish offensives in Kurdish areas of Turkey caused heavy casualties among separatist guerrillas and civilians. Kurdish militants raided Turkish diplomatic missions in some 25 Western European cities, June 24, 1993.

Tansu Ciller became Turkey's first woman prime min. July 5, 1993. The Islamic Welfare Party gained strength in the 1990s, and in June 1996, a coalition with Ciller's True Path Party was formed. The pro-Islamic government resigned June 18, 1997, under pressure from the military, which stepped up its campaign against Islamic fundamentalism in 1998.

Kurdish rebel leader Abdullah Öcalan was captured Feb. 15, 1999, and convicted of terrorism June 29. His organization, the Kurdistan Workers' Party (PKK), announced in 1999 that it would abandon its 14-year-old insurgency. Violence continued at a lower level, however, including attacks by both the PKK and Turkish forces.

Earthquakes in Apr. and Nov. 1999 killed over 17,000 people. The Islamic Justice and Development Party (AKP) led by Recep Tayyip Erdogan won Nov. 3, 2002, parliamentary elections.

Erdogan became prime min., May 14, 2003. After Erdogan's party scored a landslide win in 2007 elections, parliament chose an Islamic politician, Abdullah Gül, as president. Turkish voters in 2010 gave resounding approval to constitutional changes favored by the Islamic government.

The AKP gained a third consecutive general election victory in June 2011. Demonstrations in Istanbul's Taksim Square in 2013 over plans to replace Gezi Park became protests against Erdogan. Force was used, June 15, to clear Gezi Park, and protests began to die down in July. A coal mine explosion in Soma, May 13, 2014, killed 301 and prompted anti-government protests. Erdogan nevertheless won an Aug. 10 election to become Turkey's first popularly elected president. Foreign Min. Ahmet Davutoglu, an Erdogan ally, replaced him as prime min. The AKP failed to win a majority of seats in June 7, 2015, parliamentary elections. Erdogan called new elections for Nov. 1, in which the AKP regained its majority. After policy disagreements with Erdogan, Prime Min. Davutoglu resigned and was replaced by Binali Yildirim in May 2016.

During Syria's civil war (2011-), Turkey became a haven for Syrian refugees (more than 2.7 mil as of Sept. 2016). Turkey was also a major transit route for hundreds of thousands of Syrian and other migrants trying to reach Europe. Under a Turkey-EU agreement, effective Mar. 20, 2016, Turkey pledged to crack down on smugglers ferrying migrants to Greece and take back migrants reaching the EU. The EU pledged to accelerate Turkey's application for membership, provide up to 6 bil euros to help Turkey care for refugees, and resettle up to 72,000 Syrians from Turkish refugee camps. Migrant crossings dropped sharply but began increasing somewhat by Sept. 2016.

Attacks beginning in Sept. 2014 by the Sunni extremist group ISIS against Kurdish areas in N Syria sent tens of thousands of Syrian Kurds across the border into Turkey. Turkish government forces launched a new offensive against the PKK in SE Turkey, beginning in mid-2015, and Kurdish extremists staged terrorist attacks in Ankara and other cities, 2015-16. Syrian Kurdish forces, including some apparently affiliated with the PKK, retook territory in N Syria in 2015-16. Turkey began artillery and airstrikes against ISIS forces in N Syria, July 23-24, 2015. It also began airstrikes, July 24, against PKK strongholds in N Iraq and later launched attacks on Syrian Kurdish fighters said to be affiliated with the PKK. Turkey agreed, July 2015, to allow U.S. warplanes to use bases in Turkey to attack ISIS targets in Syria.

A number of terrorist attacks attributed to ISIS took place in Turkey in 2015-16. Suicide bombings at Istanbul's main airport, June 28, 2016, killed at least 45. On Aug. 20, a suicide bomber killed at least 54 at a wedding in a Kurdish town in SE Turkey, near the Syrian border. Turkish ground forces entered Syria, Aug. 24, to help non-Kurdish rebels capture territory from ISIS, while preventing Syrian Kurds from taking it.

A coup attempt against Erdogan by elements of the military, July 15-16, 2016, was put down by loyal military units. The abortive coup left at least 230 dead, and more than 40,000 soldiers, government officials, and civilians (including journalists) were detained. Intensifying an ongoing crackdown on dissent, the government closed more than 100 media outlets and suspended tens of thousands of judges, government officials, and teachers. The government blamed the coup on Muslim cleric Fethullah Gülen, living in the U.S.; most of those detained or suspended were suspected followers of his movement or the PKK.

Turkmenistan

People: Population: 5,291,317. **Age distrib.:** <15: 25.9%; 65+: 4.6%. **Growth:** 1.1%. **Migrants:** 3.7%. **Pop. density:** 29.2 per sq mi, 11.3 per sq km. **Urban:** 50.4%. **Ethnic groups:** Turkmen 85%, Uzbek 5%, Russian 4%. **Languages:** Turkmen (official), Russian, Uzbek. **Religions:** Muslim 89%, Eastern Orthodox 9%.

Geography: Total area: 188,456 sq mi, 488,100 sq km; **Land area:** 181,441 sq mi, 469,930 sq km. **Location:** Central Asia. Kazakhstan on N; Uzbekistan on N and E; Afghanistan, Iran on S. **Topography:** Kara Kum Desert occupies 80% of country. Bordered on W by Caspian Sea. **Arable land:** 4.1%. **Capital:** Ashgabat, 756,719.

Government: Type: Presidential republic; highly authoritarian. **Head of state and gov.:** Pres. Gurbanguly Berdymukhammedov; b. 1957; in office: Feb. 14, 2007 (acting from Dec. 21, 2006). **Local divisions:** 5 provinces, 1 independent city. **Defense budget** (2013): $612 mil. **Active troops:** 36,500.

Economy: Industries: nat. gas, oil, petroleum prods., textiles, food proc. **Chief crops:** cotton, grain, melons. **Natural resources:** petroleum, nat. gas, sulfur, salt. **Water:** 4,609 cu m per capita. **Crude oil reserves:** 0.6 bil bbls. **Electricity prod.:** 18 bil kWh. **Labor force:** agric. 48.2%, industry 14%, services 37.8%. **Unemployment:** 10.5%.

Finance: Monetary unit: Manat (TMT) (3.50 = $1 U.S.). **GDP:** $88.6 bil; **per capita GDP:** $16,400; **GDP growth:** 6.5%. **Imports:** $14.8 bil; Turkey 24.9%, Russia 12.3%, China 10.9%, UAE 9.1%, Kazakhstan 5.1%. **Exports:** $21 bil; China 68.5%. **Budget:** $6.5 bil. **Inflation:** 5.5%.

Transport: Railways: 1,852 mi. **Airports:** 21.
Communications: Telephone: 12.1 per 100 pop. **Mobile:** 145.9 per 100 pop. **Broadband:** NA. **Internet:** 15%.

Health: Expend.: 2.1%. **Life expect.:** 67.1 male; 73.3 female. **Births:** 19.3 per 1,000 pop. **Deaths:** 6.1 per 1,000 pop. **Infant mortality:** 35.5 per 1,000 live births. **Undernourished:** <5%. **HIV:** NA.

Education: Compulsory: ages 6-17. **Literacy:** 99.7%.
Embassy: 2207 Massachusetts Ave. NW 20008; 588-1500.
Website: www.turkmenistan.gov.tm

The region has been inhabited by Turkic tribes since the 10th cent. It became part of Russian Turkestan in 1881, and a constituent republic of the USSR in 1925. Turkmenistan declared independence Oct. 27, 1991, and became an independent state when the USSR disbanded Dec. 26, 1991.

Turkmenistan has extensive natural gas reserves and also oil reserves. Political power centers on the former Communist Party apparatus and authoritarian leadership. Gurbanguly Berdymukhammedov won the Feb. 2007 presidential election, considered fraudulent by international observers. He was reelected with 97% of the vote, Feb. 12, 2012. The country's one-party system officially ended, Aug. 21, 2012. A draft constitution that received final approval Sept. 14, 2016, essentially allowed Berdymukhammedov to serve as president for life.

Tuvalu

People: Population: 10,959. **Age distrib.:** <15: 29.3%; 65+: 5.8%. **Growth:** 0.9%. **Migrants:** 1.4%. **Pop. density:** 1,091.7 per sq mi, 421.5 per sq km. **Urban:** 60.6%. **Ethnic groups:** Polynesian 96%, Micronesian 4%. **Languages:** Tuvaluan, English (both official); Samoan. **Religions:** Protestant 98.4% (incl. Church of Tuvalu [Congregationalist] 97%).

Geography: Total area: 10 sq mi, 26 sq km; **Land area:** 10 sq mi, 26 sq km. **Location:** 9 islands forming NW-SE chain 360 mi long in SW Pacific O. Nearest neighbors are Kiribati to NE, Fiji to S. **Topography:** All low-lying atolls, no more than 15 ft above sea level, composed of coral reefs. **Arable land:** 0%. **Capital:** Funafuti, 5,816 (2014).

Government: Type: Parliamentary democracy under constitutional monarchy. **Head of state:** Queen Elizabeth II, rep. by Gov.-Gen. Sir Iakoba Taeia Italeli; in office: Apr. 16, 2010. **Head of gov.:** Prime Min. Enele Sopoaga; b. 1956; in office: Aug. 5, 2013. **Local divisions:** 7 island councils, 1 town council. **Defense budget/active troops:** NA.

Economy: Industries: fishing. **Chief crops:** coconuts. **Natural resources:** fish. **Water:** NA. **Labor force:** Pop. makes living mainly through exploitation of the sea, reefs, and atolls and from wages sent home by those abroad (mostly phosphate industry workers and sailors). **Unemployment:** NA.

Finance: Monetary unit: Australian Dollar (AUD) (1.32 = $1 U.S.). **GDP:** $37 mil; **per capita GDP:** $3,400; **GDP growth:** 2.6%. **Imports** (2013): $136.5 mil. **Exports** (2010): $600,000. **Tourism:** $2 mil. **Budget** (2013 est.): $32.5 mil. **Inflation:** 3.3%.

Transport: NA.
Communications: Telephone: 20.2 per 100 pop. **Mobile:** 40.3 per 100 pop. **Broadband:** NA. **Internet:** 42.7%.

Health: Expend.: 16.5%. **Life expect.:** 64.3 male; 68.8 female. **Births:** 23.8 per 1,000 pop. **Deaths:** 8.6 per 1,000 pop. **Infant mortality:** 29.9 per 1,000 live births. **Undernourished:** NA. **HIV:** NA.

Education: Compulsory: ages 7-14. **Literacy:** NA.
Permanent UN Mission: 800 Second Ave., Ste. 400D, New York, NY 10017; (212) 490-0534.
Website: www.state.gov/p/eap/ci/tv/

The Ellice Islands separated from the British Gilbert and Ellice Islands Colony in 1975 and became Tuvalu; independence came Oct. 1, 1978. In 2000, Tuvalu joined the United Nations. A major drought that began in Nov. 2010 obliged the government to declare a state of emergency Sept. 28, 2011. Prime Min. Enele Sopoaga, in office since Aug. 5, 2013, formed a new government after Mar. 31, 2015, elections. Rising sea levels due to climate change are threatening to submerge the tiny island nation.

Uganda
Republic of Uganda

People: Population: 38,319,241. **Age distrib.:** <15: 48.3%; 65+: 2%. **Growth:** 3.2%. **Migrants:** 1.9%. **Pop. density:** 503.5 per sq mi, 194.4 per sq km. **Urban:** 16.4%. **Ethnic groups:** Baganda 16.9%, Banyankole 9.5%, Basoga 8.4%, Bakiga 6.9%, Iteso 6.4%, Langi 6.1%, Acholi 4.7%, Bagisu 4.6%, Lugbara 4.2%, Bunyoro 2.7%. **Languages:** English (official), Ganda or Luganda (most widely used Niger-Congo lang.). **Religions:** Protestant 42% (incl. Anglican 35.9%), Roman Catholic 41.9%, Muslim 12.1%.

Geography: Total area: 93,065 sq mi, 241,038 sq km; **Land area:** 76,101 sq mi, 197,100 sq km. **Location:** E Central Africa. South Sudan on N, Dem. Rep. of the Congo on W, Rwanda and Tanzania on S, Kenya on E. **Topography:** Mostly high plateau 3,000-6,000 ft high, with Ruwenzori Range in W (Mt. Margherita, 16,763 ft), volcanoes in SW. NE is arid, W and SW rainy. Lakes Victoria, Edward, Albert form much of borders. **Arable land:** 34.4%. **Capital:** Kampala, 2,011,948.

Government: Type: Presidential republic. **Head of state and gov.:** Pres. Yoweri Kaguta Museveni; b. 1944; in office: Jan. 29, 1986. **Local divisions:** 111 districts, 1 capital city. **Defense budget:** $362 mil. **Active troops:** 45,000.

Economy: Industries: sugar, brewing, tobacco, cotton textiles, cement, steel prod. **Chief crops:** coffee, tea, cotton, tobacco, cassava, potatoes, corn, millet, pulses, cut flowers. **Natural resources:** copper, cobalt, hydropower, limestone, salt, gold. **Water:** 1,540 cu m per capita. **Crude oil reserves:** 2.5 bil bbls. **Electricity prod.:** 3.9 bil kWh. **Labor force:** agric. 40%, industry 10%, services 50%. **Unemployment:** 3.8%.

Finance: Monetary unit: Shilling (UGX) (3,368.00 = $1 U.S.). **GDP:** $79.9 bil; **per capita GDP:** $2,000; **GDP growth:** 5%. **Imports:** $4.6 bil; Kenya 16.4%, UAE 15.5%, India 13.4%, China 13.1%. **Exports:** $2.8 bil; Rwanda 10.7%, UAE 9.9%, Dem. Rep. of the Congo 9.8%, Kenya 9.7%, Italy 5.8%. **Tourism:** $1.2 bil. **Budget:** $4.3 bil. **Inflation:** 5.2%.

Transport: Railways: 773 mi. **Motor vehicles:** 10.9 per 1,000 pop. **Airports:** 5.

Communications: Telephone: 0.8 per 100 pop. **Mobile:** 50.4 per 100 pop. **Broadband:** 14.7 per 100 pop. **Internet:** 19.2%.

Health: Expend.: 7.2%. **Life expect.:** 54.0 male; 56.9 female. **Births:** 43.4 per 1,000 pop. **Deaths:** 10.4 per 1,000 pop. **Infant mortality:** 57.6 per 1,000 live births. **Undernourished:** 25.5%. **HIV:** 7.1%.

Education: Compulsory: ages 6-12. **Literacy:** 73.8%.

Embassy: 5911 16th St. NW 20011; 726-0416.

Website: www.statehouse.go.ug

Britain obtained a protectorate over Uganda in 1894. The country became independent Oct. 9, 1962, and a republic within the Commonwealth a year later. In 1967, the traditional kingdoms, including the powerful Buganda state, were abolished.

Gen. Idi Amin seized power from Prime Min. Milton Obote in 1971. During his 8-year dictatorship, he was responsible for the deaths of up to 300,000 of his opponents. In 1972 he expelled nearly all of Uganda's 45,000 Asians. Tanzanian troops and Ugandan exiles and rebels ousted Amin, Apr. 11, 1979.

Obote, president from Dec. 1980, was ousted in a military coup July 1985. Guerrilla war and rampant human rights abuses had plagued Uganda under Obote's regime.

Conditions improved after Yoweri Museveni took power in Jan. 1986. In 1993 the Buganda and other traditional monarchies were restored for ceremonial purposes. Uganda helped Laurent Kabila seize power in the Dem. Rep. of the Congo (DRC; formerly Zaire) in 1997 but sent troops in 1998 to aid insurgents seeking his ouster. A withdrawal accord was signed Sept. 2002.

Pres. Museveni won reelection in 2001, 2006, 2011, and 2016; his political opponents, the U.S., and the EU considered the elections flawed.

The rebel Lord's Resistance Army (LRA), led by Joseph Kony, began an insurgency against the Museveni government in 1986 and abducted tens of thousands of children to serve as soldiers and sex slaves. According to UN estimates, the LRA, 1987-2012, killed more than 100,000 people and displaced some 2.5 mil in Uganda and neighboring countries. Peace talks brokered by Sudan began July 2006, and LRA violence in Uganda diminished. A cease-fire accord was signed Feb. 23, 2008, by which time the LRA had largely moved its activities to the DRC and Central African Rep. (CAR). On Apr. 3, 2013, the U.S. offered a $5-mil reward for information leading to the capture of Kony, who had been charged with war crimes and crimes against humanity by the International Criminal Court in 2005. As of mid-2016, he remained at large, and LRA violence and kidnappings in the DRC and CAR continued.

Suicide bombings July 11, 2010, killed 76 people watching a World Cup soccer match on outdoor video screens in Kampala. Al-Shabab, a Somali al-Qaeda-linked Islamist group, claimed responsibility.

The UNHCR estimated that more than 217,000 refugees from conflicts in the DRC were living in Uganda as of Aug. 31, 2016. More than 370,000 refugees from South Sudan's civil war were in Uganda as of Sept. 21, 2016. Legislation strengthening penalties for homosexual sex, signed by Museveni Feb. 24, 2014, was struck down on technical grounds by a Uganda court Aug. 1, 2014; however, homosexual sex remained illegal, and persecution based on sexual orientation reportedly remained widespread.

Ukraine

People: Population: 44,209,733. **Age distrib.:** <15: 15.5%; 65+: 16%. **Growth:** –0.4%. **Migrants:** 10.8%. **Pop. density:** 197.6 per sq mi, 76.3 per sq km. **Urban:** 69.9%. **Ethnic groups:** Ukrainian 77.8%, Russian 17.3%. **Languages:** Ukrainian (official), Russian. **Religions:** Orthodox (incl. Ukrainian Orthodox-Kyiv Patriarchate, Ukrainian Orthodox-Moscow Patriarchate, Ukrainian Greek Catholic).

Geography: Total area: 233,032 sq mi, 603,550 sq km; **Land area:** 223,681 sq mi, 579,330 sq km. **Location:** Eastern Europe. Belarus on N; Russia on NE and E; Moldova, Romania on SW; Hungary, Slovakia, Poland on W. **Topography:** Part of E European plain with arable black soil. Carpathians in the SW, Crimean chain in the S. **Arable land:** 56.1%. **Capital:** Kiev, 2,965,625. **Cities:** Kharkiv, 1,437,753; Odesa, 1,010,558.

Government: Type: Semi-presidential republic. **Head of state:** Pres. Petro Poroshenko; b. 1965; in office: June 7, 2014. **Head of gov.:** Prime Min. Volodymyr Groysman; b. 1978; in office: Apr. 14, 2016. **Local divisions:** 24 provinces, 2 municipalities, 1 autonomous republic. **Defense budget:** $3.9 bil. **Active troops:** 204,000.

Economy: Industries: coal, elec. power, metals, machinery and transp. equip., chemicals, food proc. **Chief crops:** grain, sugar beets, sunflower seeds, vegetables. **Natural resources:** iron ore, coal, manganese, nat. gas, oil, salt, sulfur, graphite, titanium, magnesium, kaolin, nickel, mercury, timber. **Water:** 3,911 cu m per capita. **Crude oil reserves:** 0.4 bil bbls. **Electricity prod.:** 181 bil kWh. **Labor force:** agric. 5.8%, industry 26.5%, services 67.8%. **Unemployment:** 7.7%.

Finance: Monetary unit: Hryvnia (UAH) (26.60 = $1 U.S.). **GDP:** $339.5 bil; **per capita GDP:** $7,500; **GDP growth:** –9.9%. **Imports:** $37.2 bil; Russia 20%, Germany 10.4%, China 10.1%, Belarus 6.5%, Poland 6.2%. **Exports:** $35 bil; Russia 12.7%, Turkey 7.3%, China 6.3%, Egypt 5.5%, Italy 5.2%, Poland 5.2%. **Tourism:** $1.1 bil. **Budget:** $29.4 bil (planned and consolidated). **Inflation:** 48.7%.

Transport: Railways: 13,504 mi. **Motor vehicles:** 213.8 per 1,000 pop. **Airports:** 108.

Communications: Telephone: 21.6 per 100 pop. **Mobile:** 144 per 100 pop. **Broadband:** 7.5 per 100 pop. **Internet:** 49.3%.

Health: Expend.: 7.1%. **Life expect.:** 67.1 male; 76.9 female. **Births:** 10.5 per 1,000 pop. **Deaths:** 14.4 per 1,000 pop. **Infant mortality:** 8.0 per 1,000 live births. **Undernourished:** <5%. **HIV:** 0.9%.

Education: Compulsory: ages 6-16. **Literacy:** 99.8%.

Embassy: 3350 M St. NW 20007; 349-2920.

Website: www.kmu.gov.ua

Ukrainians' Slavic ancestors inhabited the region well before the 1st cent. CE. In the 9th cent., the princes of Kiev established a strong state called Kievan Rus, which included much of present-day Ukraine. Internal conflicts led to the disintegration of the Ukrainian state by the 13th cent. Mongol rule was supplanted by Poland and Lithuania in the 14th and 15th cent. The N Black Sea coast and Crimea came under Turkish control in 1478. Ukrainian Cossacks, starting in the late 16th cent., rebelled against the occupiers of Ukraine: Russia, Poland, and Turkey.

An independent Ukrainian National Republic was proclaimed on Jan. 22, 1918. But in 1921, Ukraine's neighbors occupied and divided Ukrainian territory. In 1922, Ukraine became a constituent republic of the USSR. In 1932-33, the Soviet government engineered a famine in eastern Ukraine, and 6-7 mil Ukrainians died. During WWII the Ukrainian nationalist underground fought Nazi and Soviet forces. Over 5 mil Ukrainians died in the war. The reoccupation of Ukraine by Soviet troops in 1944 brought a renewed wave of repression.

The world's worst nuclear power plant disaster occurred in Chernobyl, Ukraine, in Apr. 1986; many thousands were killed or disabled as a result of the radiation leak.

Ukrainian independence was restored, Dec. 1991, with the Soviet Union's dissolution. Following a 1994 accord with Russia and the U.S., Ukraine's large nuclear arsenal was transferred to Russia for destruction.

President since 1994, Leonid Kuchma attempted to engineer the 2004 election of his handpicked successor, the Russian-backed Prime Min. Viktor Yanukovych. When Yanukovych was declared the winner in Nov., supporters of his main challenger, former Prime Min. Viktor Yushchenko, called the election fraudulent and staged massive protests (the Orange Revolution); the vote was annulled. An election rerun Dec. 26 gave Yushchenko the victory. Yushchenko's party fared poorly in Mar. 2006 parliamentary elections, and Yanukovych returned as prime min. in Aug.

Following Sept. 2007 elections, Yulia Tymoshenko, a former Orange Revolution ally of Yushchenko, became prime min. but lost the presidential election to Yanukovych in Feb. 2010. Tymoshenko was convicted in Oct. 2011 of abusing her powers as prime min. She was released from prison in Feb. 2014.

Large anti-Yanukovych protests began in Nov. 2013, following his decision not to sign a free trade pact with the EU. After dozens were killed in violent protests in Kiev, Feb. 18-20, 2014, parliament removed Yanukovych from office, Feb. 22. Pro-EU candidate Petro Poroshenko won a May 25, 2014, presidential election. Signing and ratification of the EU agreement were completed June 27 and Sept. 16. Pro-EU parties won a majority of seats in parliamentary elections, Oct. 26, 2014. Hurt by his perceived failure reduce corruption, Prime Min. Arseniy Yatsenyuk resigned and was replaced by Volodymyr Groysman in Apr. 2016.

Aiding pro-Russian separatists, Russian forces entered Crimea in Mar., and Russia annexed the region Mar. 18, 2014. Fighting began in Apr. 2014 in eastern Ukraine between Ukrainian forces and pro-Russian separatists, widely reported to be aided by Russian military equipment and troops. Separatists apparently shot down a Malaysia Airlines commercial flight over eastern Ukraine, July 17, 2014, killing all 298 on board. A Feb. 12, 2015, cease-fire reduced violence somewhat, but fighting continued despite subsequent cease-fires. The UN reported that as of Aug. 15, 2016, the death toll in Ukraine's civil war was at least 9,578. The UNHCR estimated that as of Aug. 2016, more than 2 mil people were internally displaced or had become refugees.

United Arab Emirates

People: Population: 5,927,482. **Age distrib.:** <15: 20.9%; 65+: 1%. **Growth:** 2.5%. **Migrants:** 88.4%. **Pop. density:** 183.6

per sq mi, 70.9 per sq km. **Urban:** 85.8%. **Ethnic groups:** Emirati 19%, other Arab and Iranian 23%, South Asian 50%, other expatriates (incl. Westerner, East Asian) 8%. Less than 20% of pop. are UAE citizens. **Languages:** Arabic (official), Persian, English, Hindi, Urdu. **Religions:** Muslim (official) 76%, Christian 9%.

Geography: Total area: 32,278 sq mi, 83,600 sq km; **Land area:** 32,278 sq mi, 83,600 sq km. **Location:** Middle East, on S shore of the Persian Gulf. Saudi Arabia on W and S, Oman on E. **Topography:** A barren, flat coastal plain gives way to uninhabited sand dunes on S. Hajar Mts. in E. **Arable land:** 0.4%. **Capital:** Abu Dhabi, 1,178,594. **Cities:** Dubai, 2,503,700; Sharjah, 1,332,418.

Government: Type: Federation of monarchies. **Head of state:** Pres. Sheikh Khalifa bin Zayed al Nahyan; b. 1948; in office: Nov. 3, 2004. **Head of gov.:** Prime Min. Sheikh Muhammad bin Rashid al-Maktum; b. 1949; in office: Jan. 5, 2006. **Local divisions:** 7 emirates: Abu Dhabi, Ajman, Dubai, Fujaira, Ras al-Khaimah, Sharjah, Umm al-Qaiwain. **Defense budget** (2013): $13.9 bil. **Active troops:** 63,000.

Economy: Industries: petroleum and petrochemicals, fishing, aluminum, cement, fertilizers, commercial ship repair, constr. materials. **Chief crops:** dates, vegetables, watermelons. **Natural resources:** petroleum, nat. gas. **Water:** 16 cu m per capita. **Crude oil reserves:** 97.8 bil bbls. **Electricity prod.:** 105 bil kWh. **Labor force:** agric. 7%, industry 15%, services 78%. **Unemployment:** 3.6%.

Finance: Monetary unit: Dirham (AED) (3.67 = $1 U.S.). **GDP:** $647.8 bil; **per capita GDP:** $67,600; **GDP growth:** 3.9%. **Imports:** $248.2 bil; China 15.5%, India 12.7%, U.S. 9.6%, Germany 6.8%. **Exports:** $323.8 bil; Iran 14.5%, Japan 9.8%, India 9.2%. **Tourism:** $16 bil. **Budget:** $119.8 bil (not incl. emirate-level spending in Abu Dhabi and Dubai). **Inflation** (2013-14): 2.3%.

Transport: Motor vehicles: 441.6 per 1,000 pop. **Airports:** 25. **Communications: Telephone:** 23.1 per 100 pop. **Mobile:** 187.3 per 100 pop. **Broadband:** 114 per 100 pop. **Internet:** 91.2%. **Health: Expend.:** 3.6%. **Life expect.:** 74.8 male; 80.2 female. **Births:** 15.3 per 1,000 pop. **Deaths:** 2.0 per 1,000 pop. **Infant mortality:** 10.3 per 1,000 live births. **Undernourished:** <5%. **HIV:** NA. **Education:** Compulsory: ages 6-11. **Literacy:** 93%. **Embassy:** 3522 International Ct. NW 20008; 243-2400. **Website:** www.government.ae

The 7 "Trucial Sheikdoms" gave Britain control of defense and foreign relations in the 19th cent. They merged to become an independent state Dec. 2, 1971. Oil revenues have made the UAE one of the world's wealthiest countries. Foreigners make up most of the work force.

International banking, investment, and construction boomed during the late 1990s and early 2000s. But Dubai, hurt by the global recession beginning in 2008, accepted up to $9.5 bil in government loans to help a state-controlled investment company avoid default. Beginning in Sept. 2014, UAE warplanes took part in U.S.-led airstrikes against ISIS in Syria. The UAE was part of a Saudi-led coalition conducting airstrikes, beginning Mar. 25, 2015, against Shiite Houthi rebels in Yemen. UAE ground troops fought in Yemen, beginning in mid-2015; the UAE announced the end of their combat operations, June 15, 2016.

United Kingdom
United Kingdom of Great Britain and Northern Ireland

People: Population: 64,430,428. **Age distrib.:** <15: 17.4%; 65+: 17.9%. **Growth:** 0.5%. **Migrants:** 13.2%. **Pop. density:** 689.8 per sq mi, 266.3 per sq km. **Urban:** 82.8%. **Ethnic groups:** white 87.2%, black/African/Caribbean/black British 3%, Asian/Asian British: Indian 2.3%. **Languages:** English; Scots, Scottish Gaelic, Welsh, Irish (all recognized regional langs.). **Religions:** Christian (incl. Anglican, Roman Catholic, Presbyterian, Methodist) 59.5%, Muslim 4.4%, none 25.7%.

Geography: Total area: 94,058 sq mi, 243,610 sq km; **Land area:** 93,410 sq mi, 241,930 sq km. **Location:** Off NW coast of Europe, across English Channel, Strait of Dover, North Sea. Ireland to W, France to SE. **Topography:** England is mostly rolling land, rising to Uplands of southern Scotland. Lowlands in center of Scotland, granite highlands in N. British Isles have milder climate than N Europe due to Gulf Stream and ample rainfall. Severn, 220 mi., and Thames, 215 mi, are longest rivers. **Arable land:** 25.9%. **Capital:** London, 10,434,035. **Cities:** Manchester, 2,667,779; Birmingham (West Midlands), 2,532,642; Leeds and Bradford (West Yorkshire), 1,943,813.

Government: Type: Parliamentary constitutional monarchy. **Head of state:** Queen Elizabeth II; b. 1926; in office: Feb. 6, 1952. **Head of gov.:** Prime Min. Theresa May; b. 1956; in office: July 13, 2016. **Local divisions:** 232 local authorities (England: 152; Wales: 22; Scotland: 32; Northern Ireland: 11; 15 other dependent areas.). **Defense budget:** $56.2 bil. **Active troops:** 154,700.

Economy: Industries: machine tools, elec. power equip., automation equip., railroad equip., shipbuilding, aircraft, motor vehicles and parts, electronics and communications equip. **Chief crops:** cereals, oilseed, potatoes, vegetables. **Natural resources:** coal, petroleum, nat. gas, iron ore, lead, zinc, gold, tin, limestone, salt, clay, chalk, gypsum, potash, silica sand, slate. **Water:** 2,271 cu

m per capita. **Crude oil reserves:** 2.8 bil bbls. **Electricity prod.:** 332 bil kWh. **Labor force:** agric. 1.3%, industry 15.2%, services 83.5%. **Unemployment:** 6.3%.

Finance: Monetary unit: Pound (GBP) (0.75 = $1 U.S.). **GDP:** $2.7 tril; **per capita GDP:** $41,200; **GDP growth:** 2.2%. **Imports:** $617.1 bil; Germany 14.8%, China 9.8%, U.S. 9.2%, Netherlands 7.5%, France 5.8%, Belgium 5%. **Exports:** $442 bil; U.S. 14.6%, Germany 10.1%, Switzerland 7%, China 6%, France 5.9%, Netherlands 5.8%, Ireland 5.5%. **Tourism:** $42.4 bil. **Budget:** $1.2 tril. **Inflation:** 0.1%.

Transport: Railways: 10,462 mi. **Motor vehicles:** 596.4 per 1,000 pop. **Airports:** 271.

Communications: Telephone: 52.6 per 100 pop. **Mobile:** 125.8 per 100 pop. **Broadband:** 98.7 per 100 pop. **Internet:** 92%. **Health: Expend.:** 9.1%. **Life expect.:** 78.5 male; 83.0 female. **Births:** 12.1 per 1,000 pop. **Deaths:** 9.4 per 1,000 pop. **Infant mortality:** 4.3 per 1,000 live births. **Undernourished:** <5%. **HIV:** NA. **Education:** Compulsory: ages 5-15. **Literacy:** 99%. **Embassy:** 3100 Massachusetts Ave. NW 20008; 588-6500. **Website:** www.gov.uk

The United Kingdom of Great Britain and Northern Ireland comprises England, Wales, Scotland, and Northern Ireland.

Queen and Royal Family. The ruling sovereign is Elizabeth II of the House of Windsor, elder daughter of King George VI. She succeeded to the throne Feb. 6, 1952, and was crowned June 2, 1953. She was married Nov. 20, 1947, to Lt. Philip Mountbatten (b. June 10, 1921), former Prince of Greece. He was created Duke of Edinburgh, and given the title H.R.H., Nov. 19, 1947; he was named Prince of the United Kingdom and Northern Ireland Feb. 22, 1957. Prince Charles Philip Arthur George (b. Nov. 14, 1948) is the Prince of Wales and heir apparent. His first son, William Philip Arthur Louis (b. June 21, 1982), is second in line to the throne. William's son, George Alexander Louis (b. July 22, 2013), is third in line; William's daughter, Charlotte Elizabeth Diana (b. May 2, 2015), is fourth in line.

Parliament is the UK's legislative body, with certain powers over dependent units. It consists of two houses. The House of Commons has 650 members, elected by direct ballot and divided as follows: England, 533; Wales, 40; Scotland, 59; Northern Ireland, 18. The House of Lords (Sept. 2016) comprised 810 members: 91 hereditary peers, 693 life peers, and 26 archbishops and bishops of the Church of England.

Resources and Industries. Great Britain is a major global trade and financial services center. As of 2015, service industries accounted for almost 80% of GDP; industry, almost 20%; agriculture, less than 1%. Manufacturing, historically important since the Industrial Revolution, has declined in economic significance, while finance, centered in London, has grown in importance. Coal production, also historically important, has declined by more than 90% since 1970. Large oil and gas fields have been found in the North Sea, and commercial oil production began in 1975. However, proved reserves are declining, and the country has been a net energy importer since 2005. The world's largest offshore wind farm, the London Array in the North Sea, opened July 4, 2013.

Religion and Education. The Church of England is Protestant Episcopal. The queen is its temporal head, with rights of appointments to archbishoprics, bishoprics, and other offices. There are two provinces, Canterbury and York, each headed by an archbishop. Westminster Abbey (1050-1760) is the site of coronations and the tombs of Elizabeth I, Mary, Queen of Scots, kings, poets, and the Unknown Warrior. Celebrated British universities Oxford and Cambridge each date to the 13th cent.

History. Recent research indicates that Britain was separated from the European continent at least 200,000 years ago by a catastrophic flood that created the English Channel. Migrants across the Channel included the Celts, who arrived 2,500 to 3,000 years ago. Their language survives in Welsh and Gaelic enclaves.

England was part of the Roman Empire 43-410 CE, after which waves of Jutes, Angles, and Saxons arrived from German lands, followed by Danish raiders from the 8th through 11th cent. French-speaking Normans invaded in 1066, uniting the country with their dominions in France.

Opposition by nobles to royal authority forced King John to agree to the Magna Carta in 1215, a guarantee of rights and the rule of law. In the ensuing decades, the foundations of the parliamentary system were laid.

English dynastic claims to large parts of France led to the Hundred Years War, 1338-1453, an unsuccessful campaign. A long civil war, the War of the Roses, 1455-85, ended with the establishment of the Tudor monarchy. The economy prospered over long periods of domestic peace unmatched in continental Europe. The Church of England separated from the authority of the pope, 1534.

During the reign of Queen Elizabeth I, 1558-1603, England became a major naval power, leading to the founding of colonies in the New World and the expansion of trade with Europe and Asia. Scotland and England shared a single monarch after James VI of Scotland was crowned James I of England in 1603.

A struggle between Parliament and the Stuart kings led to a civil war, 1642-49, and the establishment of a republic under the Puritan Oliver Cromwell. The monarchy was restored in 1660, but the Glorious Revolution of 1688 confirmed the sovereignty of Parliament: a Bill of Rights was granted 1689. Scotland was united with England after the ratification of the Articles of Union of Scotland and England, May 1707.

Technological and entrepreneurial innovations led to the Industrial Revolution in the 18th cent. The 13 N American colonies were lost but replaced by growing empires in Canada, India, Australia, and elsewhere. Britain's role in the defeat of Napoleon, 1815, strengthened its position as the leading world power.

The limited extension of voting rights in 1832, 1867, and 1884; the formation of trade unions; and the development of universal public education were among the social changes that accompanied the spread of industrialization and urbanization in the 19th cent. (Men gained full voting rights in 1918 and women in 1928.) Large parts of Africa and Asia were added to the empire during the reign of Queen Victoria, 1837-1901.

Though victorious in WWI, Britain suffered huge casualties and economic dislocation. Ireland became independent in 1921, and independence movements became active in India and other colonies. The country suffered major bombing damage in WWII but rallied behind Prime Min. Winston Churchill and held off Germany until Allied victory was achieved, 1945.

In the postwar period, Britain lost its world leadership position to other powers. Labour governments passed socialist programs nationalizing some basic industries and expanding social security. In 1973, the UK joined the European Economic Community, which became the European Union (EU). Prime Min. Margaret Thatcher's Conservative governments, 1979-90, fostered private enterprise and began denationalization of key industries. Her Conservative successor, John Major, held power 1990-97. The Channel Tunnel linking Britain to the Continent was opened May 6, 1994.

The 1997 victory by the Labour Party made Tony Blair, 43, Britain's youngest prime min. since 1812. Diana, Princess of Wales, died in a car crash in Paris, Aug. 31. Britain played a leading role in the NATO air war against Yugoslavia, Mar.-June 1999, and contributed 12,000 troops to the multinational Kosovo security force.

After the Sept. 11 attacks on the U.S., the UK participated, beginning in 2001, in the Afghanistan war, maintaining as many as 9,500 troops in the country. About 450 remained as of June 2016, and British troops had suffered more than 450 fatalities since the war started. Blair, reelected in June 2001, committed British troops to the U.S.-led invasion of Iraq, Mar.-Apr. 2003. UK forces, which numbered 46,000 at the height of combat operations, almost entirely pulled out by mid-2009; 179 had died. Parliament approved British airstrikes against ISIS forces in Iraq (Sept. 26, 2014) and in Syria (Dec. 2, 2015).

In May 2005 elections, Blair became the first Labour prime min. to win 3 consecutive terms. Suicide bombings on 3 London underground trains and a bus, July 7, 2005, left 56 people dead and hundreds injured; police identified the bombers as 4 British Muslim men (3 of Pakistani origin).

Blair was succeeded by Gordon Brown, June 2007. Responding Oct. 13, 2008, to the worldwide financial crisis, Prime Min. Brown initiated a plan to partially nationalize three of Britain's largest banks and support them with a capital infusion of up to $63 bil.

In the wake of Britain's deepest recession since WWII, voters rejected the Labour Party in May 2010 parliamentary elections. Conservatives and Liberal Democrats formed a coalition government; Conservative leader David Cameron became prime min. Cameron responded to the fiscal crisis with austerity measures meant to rein in debt. The government reported Oct. 25, 2012, that London's hosting of the Olympics, July 27-Aug. 12, 2012, helped the economy recover from its double-dip recession during the third quarter of 2012. Justin Welby was installed Feb. 4, 2013, as the new Archbishop of Canterbury, the head of the Church of England. Parliament voted in favor of same-sex marriage July 16, 2013. The Conservatives won a House of Commons majority in May 7, 2015, elections. Tens of thousands of migrants to Europe from Africa, the Middle East, and SW Asia in 2015 tried to enter Britain. More than 37,000 were intercepted, Jan.-July, trying to cross via the Channel Tunnel; crossings declined after Britain and France agreed, Aug. 20, on increased security measures at the French end of the tunnel. Anti-immigrant sentiment contributed to a 51.9%-48.1% referendum vote, June 23, 2016, favoring Britain's exit from the EU ("Brexit"). Cameron, who had campaigned for "remain," announced, June 24, that he would resign as prime min. Conservative Theresa May replaced him, July 13, pledging to begin Brexit negotiations with the EU—with key issues including continued UK access to EU markets and continued EU immigration to the UK.

When Cyprus gained independence, the UK retained the sovereign base areas of **Akrotiri** and **Dhekelia** (98 sq mi total) on the island.

Wales

The Principality of Wales in western Britain has an area of 8,019 sq mi and a population (2014 est.) of 3,092,036. Cardiff is the capital, pop. (2014 est., city proper) 354,300.

A 1979 referendum rejected, 4-1, the creation of an elected Welsh assembly; a similar proposal passed by a thin margin on Sept. 18, 1997, and the first elections for the 60-seat assembly were held in 1997.

Early Anglo-Saxon invaders drove Celtic peoples into the mountains of Wales, where they developed a distinct nationality. Members of the ruling house of Gwynedd in the 13th cent. fought

England but were crushed, 1283. Edward of Caernarvon, son of Edward I of England, was created Prince of Wales, 1301. **Website:** gov.wales

Scotland

Scotland occupies the northern 37% of the main British island, and the Hebrides, Orkney, Shetland, and smaller islands. Length 275 mi, breadth approx. 150 mi, area 30,414 sq mi, pop. (2014 est.) 5,347,600.

The Lowlands, a belt of land approx. 60 mi wide from the Firth of Clyde to the Firth of Forth, divide the farming region of the Southern Uplands from the granite Highlands of the N; they contain 75% of the population and most of the industry. The Highlands, famous for hunting and fishing, have been opened to industry by many hydroelectric power stations.

Edinburgh, pop. (2014 est., city proper) 492,680, is the capital. Glasgow, pop. (2014 est., city proper) 599,650, is Scotland's greatest commercial city. It is a major port and shipbuilding center and has developed a services-based economy in the 21st cent., including financial services, healthcare, and engineering. Aberdeen, pop. (2014 est., city proper) 228,990, NE of Edinburgh, is a major port, center of granite industry, fish-processing, and North Sea oil exploration. Dundee, pop. (2014 est., city proper) 148,260, NE of Edinburgh, is an industrial and fish-processing center.

History. Scotland was called Caledonia by the Romans who battled early Celtic tribes and occupied southern areas from the 1st to the 4th cent. Missionaries from Britain introduced Christianity in the 4th cent.; St. Columba, an Irish monk, converted most of Scotland in the 6th cent.

The Kingdom of Scotland was founded in 1018. William Wallace and Robert Bruce both defeated English armies 1297 and 1314, respectively. In 1603, James VI of Scotland, son of Mary, Queen of Scots, succeeded to the English throne as James I, and effected the Union of the Crowns. In 1707 Scotland received representation in the British Parliament, resulting from the union of formerly separate Parliaments. A 1997 proposal to create a regional legislature with limited taxing authority passed by a landslide. In 2011 elections for the 129-seat parliament, the pro-independence Scottish National Party (SNP) won a majority. In a referendum on independence Sept. 18, 2014, 55% of Scottish voters opposed separating from the UK. The SNP remained in power but lost its majority in May 5, 2016, parliamentary elections.

Memorials of Robert Burns, Sir Walter Scott, John Knox, and Mary, Queen of Scots, draw many tourists, as do the beauties of the Trossachs, Loch Katrine, Loch Lomond, and abbey ruins.

Industries. Engineering products are a key industry, with growing emphasis on office machinery, autos, electronics, and other consumer goods. Oil discoveries offshore in the North Sea stimulated onshore support industries.

Scotland produces fine woolens, worsteds, tweeds, silks, fine linens, and jute. It is known for its special breeds of cattle and sheep. Commercial fishing is an important industry. Whisky is a major export.

The Hebrides are a group of about 500 islands, 100 inhabited, off the W coast. The **Inner Hebrides** include Skye, Mull, and Iona, the last famous for the arrival of St. Columba, 563 CE. The **Outer Hebrides** include Lewis and Harris. Industries include sheep raising and weaving. The approx. 70 **Orkney Isls.** are to the NE. The capital is Kirkwall, on Pomona Isl. Fish curing, sheep raising, and weaving are occupations. NE of Orkney are the 200 **Shetland Isls.,** 24 inhabited, home of Shetland ponies. Orkney and Shetland are centers for the North Sea oil industry. **Website:** www.gov.scot

Northern Ireland

Northern Ireland was constituted in 1920 from 6 of the 9 counties of Ulster, the NE corner of Ireland. Area 5,452 sq mi, pop. (2014 est.) 1,840,500. Capital and chief industrial center, Belfast, pop. (2014 est., local govt. dist.) 336,800.

Industries. Shipbuilding, including large tankers, has long been an important industry, centered in Belfast, the largest port. Linen is manufactured, along with apparel, rope, and twine. Growing diversification has added engineering products, synthetic fibers, and electronics. Major farm products include livestock, poultry, potatoes, and dairy foods.

Government and History. An act of the British Parliament, 1920, divided Northern from Southern Ireland, each with a parliament and government. When Ireland became a dominion, 1921, and later a republic, Northern Ireland chose to remain a part of the UK.

During 1968-69, Roman Catholics, then comprising about one-third of the population, claimed discrimination against them in voting rights, housing, and employment. Violence and terrorism intensified, involving branches of the Irish Republican Army (IRA; outlawed in the Irish Republic), Protestant groups, police, and British troops. Between 1969 and 2001, more than 3,500 were killed in sectarian violence in Northern Ireland, Ireland, England, and elsewhere. For most of this period, the Northern Ireland parliament was suspended, and Britain imposed direct rule.

A settlement reached on Good Friday, Apr. 10, 1998, and approved May 22 by voters in Northern Ireland and the Irish Republic, restored home rule and election of a 108-member assembly with safeguards for minority rights. Both Ireland and

Great Britain agreed to relinquish constitutional claims on Northern Ireland. Elections to the assembly were held June 25. IRA dissidents seeking to derail the agreement detonated a bomb at Omagh Aug. 15 that killed 29 people and injured over 330.

London transferred authority to a Northern Ireland power-sharing government in 1999. Delays in IRA disarmament led to renewed suspensions of self-government. The IRA July 2005 renounced violence and ordered all units to disarm. The British responded by reducing their military presence in the region. On Sept. 26, an international monitoring group reported that the IRA had apparently scrapped its entire arsenal. The Northern Ireland legislature, suspended for 3½ years, reconvened May 15, 2006.

Religion and Education. Northern Ireland is about 58% Protestant, 42% Roman Catholic. Education is compulsory between the ages of 5 and 16 years. **Website:** www.northernireland.gov.uk

Channel Islands

The Channel Islands, area 75 sq mi, off the NW coast of France, the only parts of the former Dukedom of Normandy belonging to England, are Jersey, Guernsey, and the dependencies of Guernsey—Alderney, Brecqhou, Herm, Jethou, Lihou, and Sark. The Bailiwicks of **Jersey**, area 45 sq mi, pop. (2016 est.) 98,069, and **Guernsey**, area 30 sq mi, pop. (2016 est.) 66,297, have separate legal existences and lieutenant governors named by the Crown. The islands were the only British soil occupied by German troops in WWII. **Websites:** www.gov.je; www.gov.gg

Isle of Man

The Isle of Man, area 221 sq mi, pop. (2016 est.) 88,195, is in the Irish Sea, 20 mi from Scotland, 30 mi from Cumberland. It is rich in lead and iron. The island has its own laws and a lieutenant governor appointed by the Crown. The Tynwald (legislature) consists of the Legislative Council, partly elected, and House of Keys, elected. Capital: Douglas; pop. (2011 census, city proper) 27,938. Farming, tourism, and fishing (kippers, scallops) are chief occupations. Man is famous for the Manx tailless cat. **Website:** www.gov.im

Gibraltar

A dependency on the S coast of Spain, Gibraltar guards the entrance to the Mediterranean. The Rock of Gibraltar has been in British possession since 1704. It is 2.5 mi long, 0.75 of a mi wide, and 1,396 ft in height, with a total area of 2.5 sq mi; a narrow isthmus connects it with the mainland. Pop. (2016 est.) 29,328.

Gibraltar has historically been an object of contention between Britain and Spain. In 1967, residents voted almost unanimously to remain under British rule. A new constitution, May 30, 1969, increased Gibraltarian control of domestic affairs (the UK continues to handle defense and internal security matters). The border, closed by Spain in 1969, was fully reopened in Feb. 1985. A UN General Assembly resolution requested Britain to end Gibraltar's colonial status by Oct. 1, 1996. Gibraltar voters rejected a plan for the UK and Spain to share sovereignty, Nov. 7, 2002. Residents approved a new constitution Nov. 30, 2006. Tensions have continued between Britain and Spain over the question of territorial control. **Website:** www.gibraltar.gov.gi

British West Indies

Swinging in a vast arc from the coast of Venezuela NE, then N and NW toward Puerto Rico are the Leeward Isls., forming a coral and volcanic barrier sheltering the Caribbean from the open Atlantic. Many of the islands are self-governing British possessions. Universal suffrage was instituted 1951-54; ministerial systems were set up 1956-60.

The Leeward Isls. still associated with the UK are **Montserrat**, area 39 sq mi, pop. (2016 est.) 5,267, capital Plymouth; the **British Virgin Isls.**, 58 sq mi, pop. (2016 est.) 34,232, capital Road Town (2014 est. pop., 13,102); and **Anguilla**, the most northerly of Leeward Isls., 35 sq mi, pop. (2016 est.) 16,752, capital The Valley (2014 est. pop., 1,039). Montserrat has been devastated by the Soufrière Hills volcano, which began erupting July 18, 1995.

The three **Cayman Isls.**, a dependency, lie S of Cuba, NW of Jamaica. Pop. (2016 est.) 57,268, most of it on Grand Cayman. It is a free port; in the 1970s Grand Cayman became a tax-free refuge for foreign funds and branches of many Western banks were opened there. International tourism receipts in 2014 were $565 mil. Total area 102 sq mi. Capital: George Town; pop. (2014 est.) 30,603.

The **Turks and Caicos Isls.** are a dependency at the SE end of the Bahama Islands. Of about 40 islands, only 8 are inhabited; area 366 sq mi, pop. (2016 est.) 51,430; capital Grand Turk. Salt, shellfish, and conch shells are the main exports.

Bermuda

Bermuda is a British dependency governed by a royal governor and an assembly, dating from 1620, the oldest legislative body among British dependencies. Capital: Hamilton; pop. (2014 est.) 10,334. It is a group of about 150 small islands of coral formation, 20 inhabited, comprising 21 sq mi in the western Atlantic, 580 mi E of N. Carolina. Pop. (2016) 70,537 (about 54% of African descent). Pop. density is high.

Tourism is the major industry; tourism receipts in 2014 were $403 mil. Bermuda is also a haven for the offshore insurance industry. Exports include petroleum products, medicine. GDP per capita in 2013 was $85,700. In a referendum Aug. 15, 1995, voters rejected independence by nearly a 3-to-1 majority. Hurricane Fabian, the most potent storm to reach Bermuda in 50 years, struck Sept. 5, 2003; four people were missing and presumed dead, and damage was estimated at over $300 mil. **Website:** www.gov.bm

South Atlantic Territories

The **Falkland Isls.**, a dependency, lie 300 mi E of the Strait of Magellan at the southern end of S America.

The Falklands include 2 large islands and about 200 smaller ones, area 4,700 sq mi, pop. (2014) 3,361, capital Stanley. The licensing of foreign fishing vessels has become the major source of revenue. Sheep-grazing is a main industry; wool is the principal export. There are indications of large oil and gas deposits. Argentina claims the islands as Islas Malvinas; 97% of inhabitants are of British origin. Argentina invaded the islands Apr. 2, 1982. The British responded by sending a task force to the area, landing their main force on the Falklands, May 21, and forcing an Argentine surrender at Port Stanley, June 14. A pact resuming commercial air service with Argentina was signed July 14, 1999. **Website:** www.falklands.gov.fk

British Antarctic Territory, S of 60° S lat., formerly a dependency of the Falkland Isls., was made a separate colony in 1962 and includes the South Shetland Isls., the South Orkney Isls., and the Antarctic Peninsula. A chain of meteorological stations is maintained.

South Georgia and the **South Sandwich Isls.**, formerly administered by the Falklands Isls., became a separate dependency in 1985. Total area of 1,507 sq mi. South Georgia, with no permanent population, is about 800 mi SE of the Falklands; the South Sandwich Isls. are uninhabited, about 470 mi SE of South Georgia. **Website:** www.gov.gs

St. Helena, an island 1,200 mi off the W coast of Africa and 1,800 mi E of S America, 47 sq mi and pop. (2016 est.) 7,813. Flax, lace, and rope-making are the chief industries. After Napoleon Bonaparte was defeated at Waterloo the Allies exiled him to St. Helena, where he lived from Oct. 16, 1815, to his death, May 5, 1821. Capital: Jamestown; pop. (2014 est.) 638. **Website:** www.sainthelena.gov.sh

Tristan da Cunha is the principal island in a group of islands of volcanic origin, total area 38 sq mi, halfway between the Cape of Good Hope and S America. A volcanic peak 6,760 ft high erupted in 1961. The 262 inhabitants were removed to England, but most returned in 1963. The islands are dependencies of St. Helena. Pop. (2010 est.): 265.

Ascension is an island of volcanic origin, 34 sq mi in area, 700 mi NW of St. Helena, through which it is administered. It is a communications relay center for Britain, and has a U.S. satellite tracking center. Pop. (2010) was 884, half of them communications workers. The island is noted for sea turtles. **Website:** www. ascension-island.gov.ac

British Indian Ocean Territory (BIOT)

Formed Nov. 1965, with islands formerly dependencies of Mauritius or Seychelles: the Chagos Archipelago (including Diego Garcia), Aldabra, Farquhar, and Des Roches. The latter three were transferred to Seychelles, which became independent in 1976. Total area 21,004 sq mi, land area 23 sq mi. The Chagos civilian population was removed by the UK in the 1970s to make way for expansion of the U.S. military base on Diego Garcia. A UN tribunal ruled, Mar. 2015, that the UK acted illegally in creating a BIOT marine protected area without adequately consulting with Mauritius.

Pacific Ocean Territories

Pitcairn Isl. is in the Pacific, halfway between S America and Australia. The island was discovered in 1767 by Philip Carteret but was not inhabited until 23 years later when the mutineers of the *Bounty* landed there. Pop. (2014 est.) 48; descendants of mutineers and their Tahitian wives. It is administered by a British High Commissioner in New Zealand and a local Council. The uninhabited islands of Henderson, Ducie, and Oeno are in the Pitcairn group, area 18 sq mi. **Website:** www.government.pn

United States

United States of America

(Figures for U.S. may differ elsewhere in The World Almanac.*)*

People: Population: 323,995,528. *The World Almanac.*) **Age distrib.:** <15: 18.8%; 65+: 15.3%. **Growth:** 0.8%. **Migrants:** 14.5%. **Pop. density:** 91.7 per sq mi, 35.4 per sq km. **Urban:** 81.8%. **Ethnic groups:** white 79.96%, black 12.85%, Asian 4.43%. About 15.1% of pop. is Hispanic (any race). **Languages:** English, Spanish, other Indo-European langs., Asian and Pacific island langs. **Religions:** Protestant 51.3%, Roman Catholic 23.9%, unaffiliated 12.1%, none 4%.

Geography: Total area: 3,796,742 sq mi, 9,833,517 sq km; **Land area:** 3,531,905 sq mi, 9,147,593 sq km. (Area is for 50 states and DC only.) **Location:** Primarily N America. Canada on N, Mexico on S; Pacific on W, Atlantic on E. **Topography:** Vast central plain, mountains in W, hills and low mountains in E. **Arable land:** 16.6%. **Capital:** Washington, DC, 5,013,304.

Government: Type: Federal presidential republic. **Head of state and gov.:** Pres. Barack Obama; b. 1961; in office: Jan. 20,

2009. **Local divisions:** 50 states, 1 district. **Defense budget:** $596.8 bil. **Active troops:** 1,381,250.

Economy: Industries: petroleum, steel, motor vehicles, aerospace, telecom, chemicals, electronics, food proc., consumer goods, lumber, mining. **Chief crops:** wheat, corn, other grains, fruits, vegetables, cotton. **Natural resources:** coal, copper, lead, molybdenum, phosphates, rare earth elements, uranium, bauxite, gold, iron, mercury, nickel, potash, silver, tungsten, zinc, petroleum, nat. gas, timber. **Water:** 9,538 cu m per capita. **Crude oil reserves** (2015): 39.9 bil bbls. **Electricity prod.:** 4.1 tril kWh. **Labor force** (excl. unemployed): farming, forestry, fishing 0.7%; mfg., extraction, transp., crafts 20.3%; managerial, professional, technical 37.3%; sales and office 24.2%; other services 17.6%. **Unemployment:** 6.2%.

Finance: Monetary unit: Dollar (USD) (1.00 = $1 U.S.). **GDP:** $18 tril; **per capita GDP:** $55,800; **GDP growth:** 2.4%. **Imports:** $2.3 tril; China 21.5%, Canada 13.2%, Mexico 13.2%, Japan 5.9%, Germany 5.5%. **Exports:** $1.6 tril; Canada 18.6%, Mexico 15.7%, China 7.7%. **Tourism:** $178.3 bil. **Budget:** $3.7 tril (excl. approx. $2.3 tril of social benefits). **Inflation:** 0.1%.

Transport: Railways: 182,412 mi. **Motor vehicles:** 846.9 per 1,000 pop. **Airports:** 5,054.

Communications: Telephone: 37.5 per 100 pop. **Mobile:** 117.6 per 100 pop. **Broadband:** 97.9 per 100 pop. **Internet:** 74.6%.

Health: Expend.: 17.1%. **Life expect.:** 77.5 male; 82.1 female. **Births:** 12.5 per 1,000 pop. **Deaths:** 8.2 per 1,000 pop. **Infant mortality:** 5.8 per 1,000 live births. **Undernourished:** <5%. **HIV:** NA.

Education: Compulsory: ages 6-17. **Literacy:** 99%.

Website: www.usa.gov

See also U.S. History chapter; Chronology of the Year's Events.

Uruguay
Oriental Republic of Uruguay

People: Population: 3,351,016. **Age distrib.:** <15: 20.4%; 65+: 14.1%. **Growth:** 0.3%. **Migrants:** 2.1%. **Pop. density:** 49.6 per sq mi, 19.1 per sq km. **Urban:** 95.5%. **Ethnic groups:** white 88%, mestizo 8%, black 4%. **Languages:** Spanish (official), Portunol, Brazilero. **Religions:** Roman Catholic 47.1%, nondenominational 23.2%, atheist or agnostic 17.2%, non-Catholic Christians 11.1%.

Geography: Total area: 68,037 sq mi, 176,215 sq km; **Land area:** 67,574 sq mi, 175,015 sq km. **Location:** Southern S America, on Atlantic O. Argentina on W, Brazil on N. **Topography:** Rolling, grassy plains and hills, well-watered by rivers flowing W to Uruguay R. **Arable land:** 13.3%. **Capital:** Montevideo, 1,716,162.

Government: Type: Presidential republic. **Head of state and gov.:** Pres. Tabaré Vázquez; b. 1940; in office: Mar. 1, 2015. **Local divisions:** 19 departments. **Defense budget:** $517 mil. **Active troops:** 24,650.

Economy: Industries: food proc., elec. machinery, transp. equip., petroleum prods., textiles, chemicals, beverages. **Chief crops:** soybeans, rice, wheat. **Natural resources:** hydropower, minor minerals, fish. **Water:** 50,175 cu m per capita. **Electricity prod.:** 11 bil kWh. **Labor force:** agric. 13%, industry 14%, services 73%. **Unemployment:** 7%.

Finance: Monetary unit: Peso (UYU) (28.54 = $1 U.S.). **GDP:** $71.4 bil; **per capita GDP:** $21,500; **GDP growth:** 1.5%. **Imports:** $9.8 bil; Brazil 18.2%, China 17.4%, Argentina 12.6%, U.S. 9.1%. **Exports:** $7.7 bil; China 15%, Brazil 14.4%, U.S. 6.5%. **Tourism:** $1.8 bil. **Budget:** $17.7 bil. **Inflation:** 8.7%.

Transport: Railways: 1,020 mi. **Motor vehicles:** 286.3 per 1,000 pop. **Airports:** 11.

Communications: Telephone: 32.3 per 100 pop. **Mobile:** 160.2 per 100 pop. **Broadband:** 59.8 per 100 pop. **Internet:** 64.6%.

Health: Expend.: 8.6%. **Life expect.:** 74.1 male; 80.5 female. **Births:** 13.0 per 1,000 pop. **Deaths:** 9.4 per 1,000 pop. **Infant mortality:** 8.5 per 1,000 live births. **Undernourished:** <5%. **HIV:** 0.5%.

Education: Compulsory: ages 4-17. **Literacy:** 98.4%.

Embassy: 1913 I St. NW 20006; 331-1313.

Website: portal.gub.uy

Spanish settlers began to supplant the indigenous Charrua Indians in 1624. Portuguese from Brazil arrived later, but Uruguay was attached to the Spanish Viceroyalty of Rio de la Plata in the 18th cent. Rebels fought against Spain beginning in 1810, with independence declared Aug. 25, 1825. To suppress Tupamaro guerrilla activities, a repressive military regime took power in 1973. Constitutional government was restored in 1985.

José (Pepe) Mujica, a former guerrilla who transformed his Marxist Tupamaro movement into a mainstream political party, won a presidential runoff election Nov. 2009. Legislation legalizing same-sex marriage was signed into law May 3, 2013. A law passed in Dec. 2013 made Uruguay the first country to legalize marijuana nationwide. Former Pres. (2005-10) Tabaré Vázquez, the candidate of Mujica's Broad Front coalition, won a presidential runoff election, Nov. 30, 2014.

Uzbekistan
Republic of Uzbekistan

People: Population: 29,473,614. **Age distrib.:** <15: 24.2%; 65+: 5.1%. **Growth:** 0.9%. **Migrants:** 3.9%. **Pop. density:** 179.4 per sq mi, 69.3 per sq km. **Urban:** 36.5%. **Ethnic groups:** Uzbek 80%, Russian 5.5%, Tajik 5%, Kazakh 3%, Karakalpak 2.5%. **Languages:** Uzbek (official), Russian, Tajik. **Religions:** Muslim (mostly Sunni) 88%, Eastern Orthodox 9%.

Geography: Total area: 172,742 sq mi, 447,400 sq km; **Land area:** 164,248 sq mi, 425,400 sq km. **Location:** Central Asia. Kazakhstan on N and W; Kyrgyzstan, Tajikistan on E; Afghanistan, Turkmenistan on S. **Topography:** Mostly plains and desert. **Arable land:** 10.3%. **Capital:** Tashkent, 2,263,764.

Government: Type: Presidential republic; highly authoritarian. **Head of state:** Prime Min. Mirziyaev was named interim president Sept. 8, 2016. **Head of gov.:** Prime Min. Shavkat Mirziyaev; b. 1957; in office: Dec. 11, 2003. **Local divisions:** 12 provinces, 1 autonomous republic, 1 city. **Defense budget** (2013): $1.6 bil. **Active troops:** 48,000.

Economy: Industries: textiles, food proc., machine building, metallurgy, mining, hydrocarbon extraction, chemicals. **Chief crops:** cotton, vegetables, fruits, grain. **Natural resources:** nat. gas, petroleum, coal, gold, uranium, silver, copper, lead, zinc, tungsten, molybdenum. **Water:** 1,635 cu m per capita. **Crude oil reserves:** 0.6 bil bbls. **Electricity prod.:** 52 bil kWh. **Labor force:** agric. 25.9%, industry 13.2%, services 60.9%. **Unemployment:** 10.6%.

Finance: Monetary unit: Som (UZS) (2,989.63 = $1 U.S.). **GDP:** $187.9 bil; **per capita GDP:** $6,100; **GDP growth:** 8%. **Imports:** $13.5 bil; China 20.8%, Russia 20.8%, South Korea 12%, Kazakhstan 10.8%. **Exports:** $13.5 bil; Switzerland 25.8%, China 17.6%, Kazakhstan 14.2%, Turkey 9.9%, Russia 8.4%, Bangladesh 6.9%. **Tourism:** $121 mil. **Budget:** $19.7 bil. **Inflation:** 8.5%.

Transport: Railways: 2,265 mi. **Motor vehicles:** 76.9 per 1,000 pop. **Airports:** 33.

Communications: Telephone: 8.4 per 100 pop. **Mobile:** 73.3 per 100 pop. **Broadband** (2012): 20.7 per 100 pop. **Internet:** 42.8%.

Health: Expend.: 5.8%. **Life expect.:** 70.7 male; 77.0 female. **Births:** 16.9 per 1,000 pop. **Deaths:** 5.3 per 1,000 pop. **Infant mortality:** 18.6 per 1,000 live births. **Undernourished:** <5%. **HIV:** 0.2%.

Education: Compulsory: ages 7-18. **Literacy:** 100%.

Embassy: 1746 Massachusetts Ave. NW 20036; 293-6803.

Website: www.gov.uz

The region was overrun by the Mongols under Genghis Khan in 1220. In the 14th cent., Uzbekistan became the center of a native Timurid empire. In later centuries Muslim feudal states emerged. Russian military conquest began in the 19th cent. The Uzbek SSR became a Soviet republic in 1925.

Uzbekistan gained independence when the Soviet Union disbanded Dec. 26, 1991, and was led by the authoritarian government of a former Communist, Islam A. Karimov.

Attacks by Islamic militants, Mar.-July 2004, killed more than 50 people. In June 2004, Russia's OAO Lukoil signed a $1-bil deal to develop Uzbekistan's natural gas fields.

After armed dissidents at Andizhan, east Uzbekistan, attacked government buildings and freed hundreds of prisoners, May 2005, Uzbek security forces killed many rebels and unarmed demonstrators. Karimov then launched a general crackdown on human rights activists. Irritated by U.S. human rights pressures, Karimov ordered the U.S. to vacate an airbase used to support operations in Afghanistan; the U.S. pullout was completed Nov. 21. Meeting in Moscow a week earlier, Karimov and Russian Pres. Vladimir Putin signed a military cooperation agreement.

Karimov remained in office following the formal expiration of his presidential term Jan. 22, 2007; despite a two-term limit under the constitution, he ran for a third term Dec. 23 and won with an 88.1% majority. Karimov won a fourth term, with 90.4% of the vote, Mar. 29, 2015. The government announced, Sept. 2, 2016, that Karimov had died. Parliament, Sept. 8, selected Prime Min. Shavkat Mirziyaev as interim president, pending Dec. 4 elections.

Vanuatu
Republic of Vanuatu

People: Population: 277,554. **Age distrib.:** <15: 36.1%; 65+: 3.9%. **Growth:** 1.9%. **Migrants:** 1.2%. **Pop. density:** 59 per sq mi, 22.8 per sq km. **Urban:** 26.4%. **Ethnic groups:** Ni-Vanuatu 97.6%. **Languages:** 100+ local langs. Bislama (creole), English, French (all official). **Religions:** Protestant 70% (incl. Presbyterian 27.9%, Anglican 15.1%, Seventh-day Adventist 12.5%), Roman Catholic 12.4%.

Geography: Total area: 4,706 sq mi, 12,189 sq km; **Land area:** 4,706 sq mi, 12,189 sq km. **Location:** SW Pacific, 1,200 mi NE of Brisbane, Australia. Fiji to E, Solomon Isls. to NW. **Topography:** Dense forest with narrow coastal strips of cultivated land. **Arable land:** 1.6%. **Capital:** Port-Vila, 52,542 (2014).

Government: Type: Parliamentary republic. **Head of state:** Pres. Baldwin Lonsdale; in office: Sept. 22, 2014. **Head of gov.:** Prime Min. Charlot Salwai; b. 1963; in office: Feb. 11, 2016. **Local divisions:** 6 provinces. **Defense budget/active troops:** NA.

Economy: Industries: food and fish freezing, wood proc., meat canning. **Chief crops:** copra, coconuts, cocoa, coffee, taro, yams, fruits, vegetables. **Natural resources:** manganese, hardwood forests, fish. **Water:** 37,793 cu m per capita. **Electricity prod.** (2012): 53 mil kWh. **Labor force:** agric. 65%, industry 5%, services 30%. **Unemployment:** NA.

Finance: Monetary unit: Vatu (VUV) (105.90 = $1 U.S.). **GDP:** $685 mil; **per capita GDP:** $2,500; **GDP growth:** −0.8%. **Imports:**

$314.1 mil; China 16.7%, Australia 14.6%, Japan 13.9%, Singapore 10%, Fiji 9.3%, New Zealand 8.3%, New Caledonia 5.2%. **Exports:** $38.3 mil; Japan 35.1%, Turkey 10.5%, Thailand 8.7%, China 8.2%, Venezuela 5.9%, UK 5.6%. **Tourism:** $257 mil. **Budget:** $182.7 mil. **Inflation:** 2.5%.

Transport: Motor vehicles: 58 per 1,000 pop. **Airports:** 3.

Communications: Telephone: 1.8 per 100 pop. **Mobile:** 66.2 per 100 pop. **Broadband:** 26.2 per 100 pop. **Internet:** 22.4%.

Health: Expend.: 5%. **Life expect.:** 71.8 male; 75.1 female. **Births:** 24.5 per 1,000 pop. **Deaths:** 4.1 per 1,000 pop. **Infant mortality:** 15.1 per 1,000 live births. **Undernourished:** 6.4%. **HIV:** NA.

Education: Compulsory: none. **Literacy:** 85.1%.

Permanent UN mission: 800 Second Ave., Ste. 400C, New York, NY 10017; (212) 661-4303.

Website: parliament.gov.vu

The Anglo-French condominium of the New Hebrides, administered jointly since 1906, became the independent Republic of Vanuatu on July 30, 1980. Vanuatu is located in the Ring of Fire, a zone with frequent earthquakes and volcanic eruptions. Cyclone Pam battered Vanuatu, Mar. 13, 2015, destroying 96% of the country's crops and leaving 267,000 people in need of emergency shelter; the official death toll was 11. The speaker and 13 other members of parliament were convicted, Oct. 9, 2015, of accepting bribes in 2014 in exchange for voting no-confidence in the prime min.

Vatican City
The Holy See (Vatican City State)

People: Population (2015): 1,000. **Migrants:** 100%. **Pop. density** (2015): 5,886.3 per sq mi, 2,272.7 per sq km. **Urban:** 100%. **Ethnic groups:** Italian, Swiss, other. **Languages:** Italian, Latin, French. **Religions:** Roman Catholic.

Geography: Total area: 0.17 sq mi, 0.44 sq km; **Land area:** 0.17 sq mi, 0.44 sq km. **Location:** Within the city of Rome, completely surrounded by Italy. **Arable land:** 0%.

Economy: Industries: printing; coins, medals, postage stamps prod.; mosaics, staff uniforms; worldwide banking, financial activities. **Natural resources:** none. **Water:** NA. **Labor force:** Essentially services with small amount of industry; nearly all dignitaries, priests, nuns, guards, and approx. 3,000 lay workers live outside the Vatican.

Finance: Monetary unit: Euro (EUR) (0.89 = $1 U.S.). **GDP:** NA; **per capita GDP:** NA. **Budget** (2011): $326.4 mil.

Health: Undernourished: <5%.

Apostolic Nunciature: 3339 Massachusetts Ave. NW 20008; 333-7121.

Website: www.vatican.va

The popes for many centuries, with brief interruptions, held temporal sovereignty over mid-Italy (the so-called Papal States), comprising an area of some 16,000 sq mi, with a population in the 19th cent. of more than 3 mil. This territory was incorporated in the new Kingdom of Italy (1861), the sovereignty of the pope being confined to the palaces of the Vatican and the Lateran in Rome and the villa of Castel Gandolfo, by an Italian law, May 13, 1871.

A Treaty of Conciliation, a concordat, and a financial convention were signed Feb. 11, 1929, by Cardinal Gasparri and Prem. Mussolini. The documents established the independent state of Vatican City and gave the Roman Catholic Church special status in Italy. The treaty (Lateran Agreement) was incorporated into Italy's Constitution (Article 7) in 1947. Italy and the Vatican signed an agreement in 1984 eliminating Roman Catholicism as the state religion and ending required religious education in Italian schools.

Vatican City includes the Basilica of Saint Peter, the Vatican Palace and Museum covering over 13 acres, the Vatican gardens, and neighboring buildings between Viale Vaticano and the church. Thirteen buildings in Rome, outside the boundaries, which house congregations or officers necessary for the administration of the Holy See, enjoy extraterritorial rights.

The legal system is based on the code of canon law, the apostolic constitutions, and laws especially promulgated for Vatican City by the pope.

Citing health problems, Pope Benedict XVI, elected Apr. 19, 2005, announced he would resign Feb. 11, 2013, the first pontiff to do so since 1415. He became Pope Emeritus Feb. 28. Cardinal Jorge Mario Bergoglio, from Argentina, was elected Mar. 13, taking the name of Francis. Pope Francis became the first Latin American and the first Jesuit pope. In an encyclical issued June 18, 2015, Francis called for action to stem environmental destruction and climate change. The Vatican signed a treaty June 26, 2015, formalizing its recognition of Palestine as a state.

Venezuela
Bolivarian Republic of Venezuela

People: Population: 30,912,302. **Age distrib.:** <15: 27.7%; 65+: 6.8%. **Growth:** 1.3%. **Migrants:** 4.5%. **Pop. density:** 90.8 per sq mi, 35 per sq km. **Urban:** 89%. **Ethnic groups:** Spanish, Italian, Portuguese, Arab, German, African, indigenous. **Languages:** Spanish (official), indigenous dialects. **Religions:** nominally Roman Catholic 96%.

Geography: Total area: 352,144 sq mi, 912,050 sq km; **Land area:** 340,561 sq mi, 882,050 sq km. **Location:** Carib. coast of S America. Colombia on W, Brazil on S, Guyana on E. **Topography:** Plains, called *llanos*, extend between Andes Mts. and Orinoco Delta. Orinoco stretches 1,600 mi and drains 80% of country. **Arable land:** 3.1%. **Capital:** Caracas, 2,923,130. **Cities:** Maracaibo, 2,229,333; Valencia, 1,757,107; Maracay, 1,186,158; Barquisimeto, 1,044,377.

Government: Type: Federal presidential republic. **Head of state and gov.:** Pres. Nicolás Maduro Moros; b. 1962; in office: Apr. 19, 2013. **Local divisions:** 23 states, 1 capital district, 1 federal dependency consisting of 11 fed.-controlled island groups. **Defense budget:** $1.2 bil. **Active troops:** 115,000.

Economy: Industries: agric. prods., livestock, raw materials, machinery and equip., transp. equip., constr. materials, medical equip., pharmaceuticals. **Chief crops:** corn, sorghum, sugarcane, rice, bananas, vegetables, coffee. **Natural resources:** petroleum, nat. gas, iron ore, gold, bauxite, hydropower, diamonds. **Water:** 42,594 cu m per capita. **Crude oil reserves:** 300 bil bbls. **Electricity prod.:** 120 bil kWh. **Labor force:** agric. 7.3%, industry 21.8%, services 70.9%. **Unemployment:** 8.6%.

Finance: Monetary unit: Bolivar (VEF) (9.98 = $1 U.S.). **GDP:** $515.7 bil; **per capita GDP:** $16,700; **GDP growth:** –5.7%. **Imports:** $33.4 bil; U.S. 18.4%, China 15.3%, Brazil 9.7%, Colombia 5.9%. **Exports:** $47.5 bil; U.S. 26.6%, India 13.7%, China 11.7%, Cuba 6.4%. **Tourism:** $643 mil. **Budget:** $348.3 bil. **Inflation:** 109.7%.

Transport: Railways: 278 mi. **Motor vehicles:** 120.2 per 1,000 pop. **Airports:** 127.

Communications: Telephone: 24.9 per 100 pop. **Mobile:** 93 per 100 pop. **Broadband:** 43.9 per 100 pop. **Internet:** 61.9%.

Health: Expend.: 5.3%. **Life expect.:** 72.7 male; 78.9 female. **Births:** 19.2 per 1,000 pop. **Deaths:** 5.2 per 1,000 pop. **Infant mortality:** 12.5 per 1,000 live births. **Undernourished:** <5%. **HIV:** 0.5%.

Education: Compulsory: ages 3-17. **Literacy:** 95.4%.

Embassy: 1099 30th St. NW 20007; 342-2214.

Website: www.gobiernoenlinea.ve or eeuu.embajada.gob.ve

Columbus first set foot on the South American continent on the peninsula of Paria, Aug. 1498. Alonso de Ojeda, 1499, called the land Venezuela, or Little Venice, because the Indians had houses on stilts. Spanish colonialists dominated Venezuela until Simón Bolívar's victory near Carabobo in June 1821. The republic was formed after secession from the Colombian Federation in 1830. Military strongmen ruled Venezuela for much of its history. Since 1959, the country has had democratically elected governments.

Venezuela has the world's largest crude oil reserves, and oil accounts for more than 95% of export earnings and almost half of government revenues. The government, Jan. 1, 1976, nationalized the oil industry. Attempts to reduce dependence on the hydrocarbon sector have met with limited success. The country has large reserves of natural gas.

Two attempted coups were thwarted by loyalist troops in Feb. and Nov. 1992. Pres. Carlos Andrés Pérez was removed from office on corruption charges, May 1993, and convicted, May 1996, of mismanaging a $17-mil secret government fund.

A 1992 coup leader, Hugo Chávez, who ran as a populist, was elected president Dec. 1998. That month, voters approved a new constitution greatly increasing his powers.

Popular among the poor, Chávez alienated middle- and upper-class Venezuelans with economic and political reforms, and his foreign policy antagonized the U.S. Chávez was forced to relinquish power, Apr. 12, 2002, but when an interim government suspended democratic institutions, Chávez loyalists rebelled, and the president reclaimed his office Apr. 14.

Chávez countered U.S. attempts to isolate him by solidifying ties with Latin American leftist leaders and with Iran and Russia. With the economy surging, he won the Dec. 2006 presidential election. On Jan. 31, 2007, the legislature granted him the power to rule by decree. Venezuelan voters approved constitutional changes abolishing presidential term limits Feb. 15, 2009. Suffering from cancer, Chávez won reelection, Oct. 7, 2012. He died Mar. 5, 2013, before he could be sworn in. Vice Pres. Nicolás Maduro Moros became interim president and won a narrow victory in Apr. 14, 2013, elections. With the economy hurt by low oil prices and tight currency and price controls, GDP declined 3.9% in 2014 and 5.7% in 2015. The 2015 inflation rate was an est. 121.7%, and shortages of food, medicine, and other goods were widespread. Large anti-Maduro protests, Feb.-June 2014, were met with a harsh crackdown; more than 40 people, mostly protesters, were killed. The Maduro government arrested a number of opposition figures in 2014-15. Opposition leader Leopoldo López was convicted, Sept. 10, 2015, of inciting violence and sentenced to more than 13 years in prison. The government, Aug. 2015, closed border crossings with Colombia, in part to crack down on smuggling. A Venezuelan-Colombian agreement on reopening the border was announced, Aug. 11, 2016. An opposition coalition won Dec. 6, 2015, legislative elections. Looting and sometimes violent demonstrations, protesting food and electricity shortages and calling for Maduro's removal, became widespread in 2016. Maduro declared a 60-day state of emergency, Jan. 15—renewed repeatedly for 60 days at a time—and in July put the military in charge of food distribution.

Vietnam
Socialist Republic of Vietnam

People: Population: 95,261,021. **Age distrib.:** <15: 23.8%; 65+: 6%. **Growth:** 1%. **Migrants:** 0.1%. **Pop. density:** 795.7 per sq mi, 307.2 per sq km. **Urban:** 34.2%. **Ethnic groups:** Kinh (Viet) 85.7%. **Languages:** Vietnamese (official), English, French, Chinese, Khmer. **Religions:** Buddhist 7.9%, Catholic 6.6%, none 81.8%.

Geography: Total area: 127,881 sq mi, 331,210 sq km; **Land area:** 119,719 sq mi, 310,070 sq km. **Location:** SE Asia, on E coast of Indochinese Peninsula. China on N; Laos, Cambodia on W. **Topography:** Long and narrow, with 1,400-mi coast. Densely settled Red R. Valley in N; narrow coastal plains in center; wide, often marshy Mekong R. Delta in S. Semi-arid plateaus and barren mountains, with some stretches of tropical rain forest, in rest of country. **Arable land:** 20.7%. **Capital:** Hanoi, 3,790,214. **Cities:** Ho Chi Minh City, 7,498,237; Can Tho, 1,241,608; Hai Phòng, 1,110,298.

Government: Type: Communist state. **Head of state:** Pres. Tran Dai Quang; b. 1956; in office: Apr. 2, 2016. **Head of gov.:** Prime Min. Nguyen Xuan Phuc; b. 1954; in office: Apr. 7, 2016. **Local divisions:** 58 provinces, 5 municipalities. **Defense budget** (2013): $4 bil. **Active troops:** 482,000.

Economy: Industries: food proc., garments, shoes, machine-building, mining, coal, steel, cement, chemical fertilizer. **Chief crops:** rice, coffee, rubber, tea, pepper, soybeans, cashews, sugarcane, peanuts, bananas. **Natural resources:** phosphates, coal, manganese, rare earth elements, bauxite, chromate, offshore oil and gas deposits, timber, hydropower. **Water:** 9,461 cu m per capita. **Crude oil reserves:** 4.4 bil bbls. **Electricity prod.:** 122 bil kWh. **Labor force:** agric. 48%, industry 21%, services 31%. **Unemployment:** 2.3%.

Finance: Monetary unit: Dong (VND) (22,295.00 = $1 U.S.). **GDP:** $552.3 bil; **per capita GDP:** $6,000; **GDP growth:** 6.7%. **Imports:** $150.4 bil; China 34.1%, South Korea 14.3%, Singapore 6.5%, Japan 6.4%, Hong Kong 5.1%. **Exports:** $158.7 bil; U.S. 21.2%, China 13.3%, Japan 8.4%, South Korea 5.5%. **Tourism:** $7.3 bil. **Budget:** $47.4 bil. **Inflation:** 0.9%.

Transport: Railways: 1,616 mi. **Motor vehicles:** 4.5 per 1,000 pop. **Airports:** 38.

Communications: Telephone: 6.3 per 100 pop. **Mobile:** 130.6 per 100 pop. **Broadband:** 31 per 100 pop. **Internet:** 52.7%.

Health: Expend.: 7.1%. **Life expect.:** 70.9 male; 76.2 female. **Births:** 15.7 per 1,000 pop. **Deaths:** 5.9 per 1,000 pop. **Infant mortality:** 17.8 per 1,000 live births. **Undernourished:** 11%. **HIV:** 0.5%.

Education: Compulsory: ages 5-14. **Literacy:** 94.5%.

Embassy: 1233 20th St. NW, Ste. 400, 20036; 861-0737. **Website:** vietnam.gov.vn

Settled by Viets from central China, Vietnam was held by China, 111 BCE-939 CE, and was a vassal state during subsequent periods. Conquest by France began in 1858 and ended in 1884 with the protectorates of Tonkin and Annam in the N and the colony of Cochin-China in the S.

Japan occupied Vietnam in 1940. Several groups formed the Vietminh (Independence) League, headed by Communist guerrilla leader Ho Chi Minh. In Aug. 1945, the Vietminh forced out Bao Dai, former emperor of Annam and head of a Japan-sponsored regime. France, seeking to reestablish colonial control, unsuccessfully battled Communist and nationalist forces, 1946-54.

Separate states formed in N. and S. Vietnam, with Communists under Ho Chi Minh (backed by Russia and China) controlling N. Vietnam and a non-Communist government (backed by the U.S.) controlling S. Vietnam. N. Vietnam aided Vietcong guerrillas who sought to take over S. Vietnam. U.S. troops and the S. Vietnamese army fought N. Vietnamese and Vietcong forces, including in border areas of Laos and Cambodia. Casualties of the war were as follows—combat deaths: U.S. 47,434 (Aug. 4, 1964-Jan. 27, 1973); S. Vietnam more than 200,000; other allied forces 5,225. Total U.S. fatalities numbered more than 58,000. Vietnamese civilian casualties were more than 1 mil. The war displaced more than 6.5 mil in S. Vietnam.

A never-implemented cease-fire agreement was signed in Paris Jan. 27, 1973, by the U.S., N. and S. Vietnam, and the Vietcong. The last U.S. troops left Vietnam Mar. 27, 1973. S. Vietnam surrendered Apr. 30, 1975. N. Vietnam assumed control. The country was officially reunited July 2, 1976.

Among the unstable conditions that persisted in the region, heavy fighting with Cambodia took place, 1977-80. China cut off economic aid when 140,000 ethnic Chinese fled discrimination in Vietnam. Reacting to Vietnam's 1979 invasion of Cambodia, China attacked four Vietnamese border provinces, Feb. 1979.

Vietnam announced in 1987 reforms aimed at reducing central control of the economy. The U.S. ended, Feb. 1994, a 19-year embargo on trade with Vietnam. The U.S. extended full diplomatic recognition to Vietnam July 11, 1995. In Aug. 2012, the U.S. began cleaning up the herbicide Agent Orange, used to clear forests during the Vietnam War. In a move apparently aimed at countering China's growing power in the South China Sea region, the U.S., Oct. 2, 2014, eased its embargo on lethal arms sales to Vietnam. During a visit to Vietnam, U.S. Pres. Barack Obama announced, May 23, 2016, that the embargo would be completely lifted. Vietnam was one of the 12 nations that signed, Feb. 4, 2016, the

Trans-Pacific Partnership trade agreement (which required ratification before it could take effect).

Yemen
Republic of Yemen

People: Population: 27,392,779. **Age distrib.:** <15: 40.5%; 65+: 2.7%. **Growth:** 2.4%. **Migrants:** 1.3%. **Pop. density:** 134.4 per sq mi, 51.9 per sq km. **Urban:** 35.2%. **Ethnic groups:** predominantly Arab; Afro-Arab, South Asian, European. **Languages:** Arabic (official). **Religions:** Muslim 99.1% (official; Sunni 65%, Shia 35%).

Geography: Total area: 203,850 sq mi, 527,968 sq km; **Land area:** 203,850 sq mi, 527,968 sq km. **Location:** Middle East, on S coast of the Arabian Peninsula. Saudi Arabia on N, Oman on E. **Topography:** Sandy coastal strip; well-watered fertile mountains in interior. **Arable land:** 2.4%. **Capital:** Sanaa, 3,094,124. **Cities:** Aden, 909,577.

Government: Type: In transition. **Head of state:** Pres. Abd Rabbuh Mansur Hadi; b. 1950; in office: Feb. 25, 2012. **Head of gov.:** Prime Min. Ahmed Obaid bin Daghr; in office: Apr. 3, 2016. **Local divisions:** 22 governorates. **Defense budget** (2014): $1.9 bil. **Active troops:** 10,000-20,000. (20,000-30,000 insurgent forces in territory where govt. does not exercise effective control.)

Economy: Industries: crude oil prod. and petroleum refining, small-scale prod. of cotton textiles and leather goods, food proc., handicrafts, aluminum prods. **Chief crops:** grains, fruits, vegetables, pulses, khat, coffee, cotton. **Natural resources:** petroleum; fish; rock salt; marble; small deposits of coal, gold, lead, nickel, copper. **Water:** 78 cu m per capita. **Crude oil reserves:** 3 bil bbls. **Electricity prod.:** 8 bil kWh. **Labor force:** Most people employed in agric. and herding; services, constr., industry, and commerce account for less than one-fourth of labor force. **Unemployment:** 17.4%.

Finance: Monetary unit: Rial (YER) (249.95 = $1 U.S.). **GDP:** $75.5 bil; **per capita GDP:** $2,700; **GDP growth:** −28.1%. **Imports:** $5.5 bil; UAE 20.9%, China 14.3%, Saudi Arabia 9.8%, Kuwait 7.4%. **Exports:** $1.4 bil; China 24.5%, UAE 16.5%, South Korea 10%, Saudi Arabia 9.9%, Kuwait 9.1%, India 8.5%. **Tourism:** $1 bil. **Budget:** $5.9 bil. **Inflation** (2015): 30%.

Transport: Motor vehicles: 29.2 per 1,000 pop. **Airports:** 17.

Communications: Telephone: 4.7 per 100 pop. **Mobile:** 68 per 100 pop. **Broadband** (2012): 0.2 per 100 pop. **Internet:** 25.1%.

Health: Expend.: 5.6%. **Life expect.:** 63.4 male; 67.8 female. **Births:** 29.2 per 1,000 pop. **Deaths:** 6.1 per 1,000 pop. **Infant mortality:** 47.4 per 1,000 live births. **Undernourished:** 26.1%. **HIV:** <0.1%.

Education: Compulsory: ages 6-14. **Literacy:** 70%.

Embassy: 2319 Wyoming Ave. NW 20008; 965-4760. **Website:** www.yemen.gov.ye or www.yemenembassy.org

Yemen's territory once was part of the ancient biblical Kingdom of Sheba, or Saba. Yemen became independent in 1918, after centuries of Ottoman Turkish rule.

Imam Yahya ibn Muhammad ruled, 1904-48, and after his assassination was succeeded by his son, Imam Ahmed, 1948-62. Army officers headed by Brig. Gen. Abdullah al-Salal declared the country the Yemen Arab Republic, Sept. 1962. Ahmed's heir, the Imam Mohamad al-Badr, fled to the mountains where tribesmen joined royalist forces, aided by the Saudi monarchy. Fighting between royalists and republicans killed about 150,000 people until hostilities ended in 1970.

South Yemen, formed from the British colony of Aden and the British protectorate of South Arabia, became independent Nov. 1967. A Marxist state and a Soviet ally, it took the name People's Democratic Republic of Yemen in 1970. More than 300,000 Yemenis fled from the S to the N after independence, contributing to two decades of hostility between the two states.

The two countries were formally united May 21, 1990, but regional clan-based rivalries led to full-scale civil war in 1994. Secessionists declared a breakaway state in South Yemen, May 21, 1994, but northern troops captured the former southern capital of Aden in July. A new constitution was approved Sept. 28.

While on a refueling stop in Aden, Oct. 12, 2000, the destroyer U.S.S. *Cole* was bombed, killing 17 Americans; the U.S. blamed the attack on terrorists associated with al-Qaeda leader Osama bin Laden.

Clashes beginning in June 2004 between Yemeni government forces and Shiite rebels led by an anti-U.S. cleric, Hussein al-Houthi, left more than 200 people dead. The government announced Sept. 10 that Yemeni troops had killed al-Houthi.

During 2007-10, Shiite rebels in the northwest, secessionists in the south, Sunni militants in the east affiliated with al-Qaeda in the Arabian Peninsula (AQAP), and pirates in coastal waters challenged Yemeni government authority. In 2011, Arab Spring demonstrators demanded Pres. Ali Abdullah Saleh's resignation. Saleh was severely wounded June 3 in a rocket attack on the presidential compound in Sanaa. Vice Pres. Abd Rabbuh Mansur Hadi became acting president. Anwar al-Awlaki, a U.S. citizen and radical Muslim cleric linked to several plots against the U.S., was killed Sept. 30, 2011, by a U.S. missile in northern Yemen. Saleh effectively ceded power Nov. 23, 2011. Hadi officially became president in uncontested Feb. 2012 elections but failed to stabilize the country. The U.S. continued air attacks against AQAP; a drone strike June 9, 2015, killed the group's leader, Nasser al-Wuhayshi. Shiite rebels known as Houthis took over Sanaa in Sept. 2014 and gained control of much of western Yemen. Fierce fighting for other areas occurred. A coalition of Sunni nations led by Saudi Arabia, which backed Hadi, began, Mar. 25, 2015, airstrikes against Houthi forces, who were aided by Iran and joined by Yemeni military units loyal to Saleh. Airstrikes and other fighting caused high civilian casualties. AQAP seized control of parts of southern Yemen but was driven out of some areas in 2016. The Sunni extremist group ISIS staged deadly terrorist bombings, mainly against Shiite targets, in 2015-16. A UN-brokered cease-fire, in effect Apr. 10, 2016, somewhat reduced the level of conflict, which intensified again in Aug. when UN-sponsored peace talks were suspended. A UN official estimated, Aug. 30, 2016, that at least 10,000 people had died in Yemen's civil war since Mar. 2015. As of July 31, 2016, about 2.8 mil people were internally displaced; more than 180,000 Yemeni refugees were living in nearby countries as of Sept. 15.

Zambia
Republic of Zambia

People: Population: 15,510,711. **Age distrib.:** <15: 46.1%; 65+: 2.4%. **Growth:** 2.9%. **Migrants:** 0.8%. **Pop. density:** 54 per sq mi, 20.9 per sq km. **Urban:** 41.4%. **Ethnic groups:** Bemba 21%, Tonga 13.6%, Chewa 7.4%, Lozi 5.7%, Nsenga 5.3%, Tumbuka 4.4%, Ngoni 4%, Lala 3.1%, Kaonde 2.9%, Namwanga 2.8%, Lunda (northwestern) 2.6%, Mambwe 2.5%, Luvale 2.2%, Lamba 2.1%. **Languages:** Bantu langs. (incl. Bembe, Nyanja, Tonga, Lozi, Chewa, Nsenga, Tumbuka); English (official). **Religions:** Protestant 75.3%, Roman Catholic 20.2%.
Geography: Total area: 290,587 sq mi, 752,618 sq km; **Land area:** 287,028 sq mi, 743,398 sq km. **Location:** S central Africa. Dem. Rep. of the Congo on N; Tanzania, Malawi, Mozambique on E; Zimbabwe, Namibia on S; Angola on W. **Topography:** Mostly high plateau with thick forests, drained by several important rivers, including the Zambezi. **Arable land:** 5%. **Capital:** Lusaka, 2,285,349.
Government: Type: Presidential republic. **Head of state and gov.:** Pres. Edgar Lungu; b. 1956; in office: Jan. 25, 2015. **Local divisions:** 10 provinces. **Defense budget:** $435 mil. **Active troops:** 15,100.
Economy: Industries: copper mining and proc., emerald mining, constr., foodstuffs, beverages, chemicals, textiles, fertilizer, horticulture. **Chief crops:** corn, sorghum, rice, peanuts, sunflower seeds, vegetables, flowers, tobacco, cotton, sugarcane, cassava, coffee. **Natural resources:** copper, cobalt, zinc, lead, coal, emeralds, gold, silver, uranium, hydropower. **Water:** 6,464 cu m per capita. **Electricity prod.:** 13 bil kWh. **Labor force:** agric. 85%, industry 6%, services 9%. **Unemployment:** 13.3%.
Finance: Monetary unit: Kwacha (ZMW) (9.65 = $1 U.S.). **GDP:** $62.7 bil; **per capita GDP:** $3,900; **GDP growth:** 3.6%. **Imports:** $6.8 bil; South Africa 34.5%, Dem. Rep. of the Congo 18.2%, Kenya 9.7%, China 7.2%. **Exports:** $6.3 bil; China 25.5%, Dem. Rep. of the Congo 13%, South Africa 6.4%. **Tourism:** $642 mil. **Budget:** $5.2 bil. **Inflation:** 10.1%.
Transport: Railways: 1,942 mi (incl. 1,156 mi of Tanzania-Zambia Railway Authority). **Motor vehicles:** 22 per 1,000 pop. **Airports:** 8.
Communications: Telephone: 0.7 per 100 pop. **Mobile:** 74.5 per 100 pop. **Broadband:** 1 per 100 pop. **Internet:** 21%.
Health: Expend.: 5%. **Life expect.:** 50.8 male; 54.1 female. **Births:** 41.8 per 1,000 pop. **Deaths:** 12.4 per 1,000 pop. **Infant mortality:** 62.9 per 1,000 live births. **Undernourished:** 47.8%. **HIV:** 12.9%.
Education: Compulsory: NA. **Literacy:** 85.1%.
Embassy: 2200 R St. NW 20008; 265-9717.
Website: www.zambia.gov.zm
Ruled by the British as Northern Rhodesia, the country became the independent republic of Zambia within the Commonwealth Oct. 24, 1964. Independence leader Kenneth Kaunda governed as president, 1964-91. A Zambian government corporation in 1970 took over 51% of two foreign-owned copper-mining companies. Privately held land and other enterprises were nationalized in 1975. In the 1980s and 1990s, lowered copper prices hurt the economy and severe drought caused famine.
Oct. 1991 elections brought an end to Kaunda's one-party rule. The new government sought to sell state enterprises, including the copper industry. Pres. Frederick Chiluba won reelection Nov. 1996. In 2001, Chiluba endorsed Levy Patrick Mwanawasa, who won a disputed Dec. election. Food shortages threatened more than 2 mil Zambians in 2002; the government refused to distribute shipments of U.S. grain because it was genetically modified. Mwanawasa won a second term in 2006. Accused of embezzling state funds as president, Chiluba was ordered to pay $58 mil by a British court, June 2007; he was acquitted by a Zambian court, Aug. 2009, of misusing $500,000 in public money.
Pres. Mwanawasa died Aug. 19, 2008. Vice Pres. Rupiah Banda became acting pres. He narrowly won the presidency in

the Oct. 2008 election but lost to opposition leader Michael Sata Sept. 2011. Sata died in office, Oct. 28, 2014. Edgar Lungu of Sata's Patriotic Front party narrowly won a Jan. 2015 special election. Lungu narrowly won a new term in Aug. 11, 2016, elections that his main opponent claimed were marred by fraud.
The country has made progress in treating HIV/AIDS, but the disease afflicted 1.2 mil Zambians as of 2015. Drought and low copper prices again hurt the economy in 2016.

Zimbabwe
Republic of Zimbabwe

People: Population: 14,546,961. **Age distrib.:** <15: 37.8%; 65+: 3.5%. **Growth:** 2.2%. **Migrants:** 2.6%. **Pop. density:** 97.4 per sq mi, 37.6 per sq km. **Urban:** 32.3%. **Ethnic groups:** African (predom. Shona; Ndebele is second-largest ethnic group) 99.4%. **Languages:** Shona, Ndebele (both official and most widely spoken); English (official, used in business), 13 official minority langs. **Religions:** Protestant 75.9% (incl. Apostolic 38%, Pentecostal 21.1%), Roman Catholic 8.4%, none 6.1%.
Geography: Total area: 150,872 sq mi, 390,757 sq km; **Land area:** 149,362 sq mi, 386,847 sq km. **Location:** Southern Africa. Zambia on N, Botswana on W, South Africa on S, Mozambique on E. **Topography:** High plateau rising to mountains on E border, sloping down on other borders. **Arable land:** 10.3%. **Capital:** Harare, 1,511,181.
Government: Type: Semi-presidential republic. **Head of state and gov.:** Pres. Robert Gabriel Mugabe; b. 1924; in office: Dec. 31, 1987. **Local divisions:** 8 provinces, 2 cities with provincial status. **Defense budget:** $379 mil. **Active troops:** 29,000.
Economy: Industries: mining, steel, wood prods., cement, chemicals, fertilizer, clothing and footwear, foodstuffs, beverages. **Chief crops:** tobacco, corn, cotton, wheat, coffee, sugarcane, peanuts. **Natural resources:** coal, chromium ore, asbestos, gold, nickel, copper, iron ore, vanadium, lithium, tin, platinum group metals. **Water:** 1,282 cu m per capita. **Electricity prod.:** 9.2 bil kWh. **Labor force:** agric. 66%, industry 10%, services 24%. **Unemployment:** 5.4%.
Finance: Monetary unit: Dollar (ZWD) (361.90 = $1 U.S.). **GDP:** $28.1 bil; **per capita GDP:** $2,100; **GDP growth:** 1.5%. **Imports:** $5.2 bil; South Africa 48.1%, China 12.1%, India 5.2%. **Exports:** $3.3 bil; China 27.8%, Dem. Rep. of the Congo 14%, Botswana 12.5%, South Africa 7.6%. **Tourism:** $827 mil. **Budget (2014):** $4.6 bil. **Inflation:** −2.4%.
Transport: Railways: 2,129 mi. **Motor vehicles:** 40.6 per 1,000 pop. **Airports:** 17.
Communications: Telephone: 2.2 per 100 pop. **Mobile:** 84.8 per 100 pop. **Broadband:** 39.2 per 100 pop. **Internet:** 16.4%.
Health: Expend.: 6.4%. **Life expect.:** 57.3 male; 58.7 female. **Births:** 31.9 per 1,000 pop. **Deaths:** 9.9 per 1,000 pop. **Infant mortality:** 25.9 per 1,000 live births. **Undernourished:** 33.4%. **HIV:** 14.7%.
Education: Compulsory: ages 6-12. **Literacy:** 86.9%.
Embassy: 1608 New Hampshire Ave. NW 20009; 332-7100.
Website: www.zim.gov.zw
Britain took over the area as Southern Rhodesia in 1923 from the British South Africa Co. (which, under Cecil Rhodes, had conquered it by 1897) and granted internal self-government. A 1961 constitution restricted voting to keep whites in power.
On Nov. 11, 1965, Prime Min. Ian D. Smith unilaterally declared independence. Britain termed the act illegal and demanded that the country (known as Rhodesia until 1980) enfranchise the black African majority. The UN imposed sanctions and, in May 1968, a trade embargo, as black nationalists launched guerrilla attacks.
After the country held its first universal-franchise election, Apr. 21, 1979, all parties accepted a cease-fire, Dec. 5. The country changed its name to Zimbabwe upon independence, Apr. 18, 1980. Robert Mugabe, the nation's first prime min., became executive president in 1987.
From the late 1990s, Mugabe's rule became increasingly repressive. A land redistribution campaign triggered violent attacks in Apr. 2000 against some white farmers. (Whites made up less than 1% of the population but had held 70% of the land.) Production of corn, the nation's food staple, subsequently declined sharply. Mugabe, relying on fraud and intimidation, international observers claimed, won the Mar. 9-11, 2002, presidential election. In May 2005, Mugabe launched Operation Murambatsvina ("Drive out rubbish"), razing shanty dwellings and illegal street markets in urban areas and leaving some 700,000 people homeless. During 2006-08, inflation soared to a yearly rate of more than 100,000%; inflation eased after the U.S. dollar and other foreign currencies became legal tender beginning in 2009.
Mugabe clung to power after a widely discredited 2008 presidential election. Opposition groups, Jan. 18, 2013, condemned an increasing crackdown on Mugabe's critics. In the July 31, 2013, presidential election, Mugabe was once again declared the winner.
The July 2015 killing of a lion named Cecil, allegedly lured out of a national park to be shot, sparked international outrage. Drought caused food shortages in 2016. Police cracked down on strikes and widespread demonstrations protesting deteriorating economic conditions.

SPORTS HIGHLIGHTS, 2016

Retirements and perennial favorites dominated sports in 2016, an eventful year in which Cleveland finally took home a championship, Americans dominated the Games in Rio, and the Chicago Cubs won the World Series for the first time since 1908.

Alabama took its customary place in the **College Football Playoff National Championship**, and won the national title for the fourth time in seven seasons. The game, held Jan. 11 at Univ. of Phoenix Stadium in Glendale, AZ, was a thriller between the Crimson Tide and Clemson Tigers. With 10:34 left in the fourth quarter, Alabama rallied to tie at 24-24, then surprised the Tigers with a successful onside kick and scored touchdowns on each of its next three possessions to put the game out of reach. 'Bama's Heisman Trophy-winner Derrick Henry rushed for 158 yards and three TDs.

Peyton Manning capped off his 18-year NFL career with his second championship, but it was the Denver defense, not Manning's offensive contributions, that propelled the Broncos to victory over the Carolina Panthers in **Super Bowl 50**, Feb. 7 at Levi's Stadium in Santa Clara, CA. Von Miller, the game's MVP, twice took the ball from Carolina quarterback Cam Newton, the regular season MVP, to set up Denver's only two touchdowns. The Orange Crush defense sacked Newton seven times, led by Miller (2.5) and linebacker DeMarcus Ware (2). Manning, who retired a month later, became the first quarterback to win Super Bowls with two teams.

A game-tying three-pointer by North Carolina's Marcus Paige with 4.7 seconds left looked like it was going to send the **NCAA men's basketball championship** into overtime, Apr. 4, at Houston's NRG Stadium. But Villanova's Kris Jenkins countered with an even more unlikely three-pointer that gave the Wildcats a 77-74 victory, and the school's first championship in 31 years. Senior guard Ryan Arcidiacono, who averaged 15.5 points and 73% shooting during the Final Four, was named the tournament's most outstanding player. Villanova's 95-51 victory over Oklahoma in the semifinal game was the largest margin of victory in Final Four history.

The Univ. of Connecticut cruised to its fourth straight **NCAA women's basketball championship**, Apr. 5 at Bankers Life Fieldhouse in Indianapolis, IN. The win gave head coach Geno Auriemma his 11th title, surpassing UCLA's legendary John Wooden for most ever Div. I basketball titles. The Lady Huskies put up a perfect 38-0 record, extending a 75-game unbeaten streak dating back to Nov. 2014. UConn walloped its tournament opponents by a minimum of 21 points. Senior forward Breanna Stewart became the first player ever to win the most outstanding player award four years in a row.

Defending champion Jordan Spieth held a five-stroke lead going into the back nine on the final day of the **Masters Championship** Apr. 10 in Augusta, GA. But he suffered an epic collapse, bogeying the 10th and 11th holes and hitting two balls into Rae's Creek on 12. Unheralded Englishman Danny Willett took advantage of Spieth's misfortune to become the first European to wear the green jacket since 1999. American Dustin Johnson also won his first major with a three-stroke victory in the **U.S. Open**, June 19 at Oakmont Country Club in Oakmont, PA. Sweden's Henrik Stenson shot a record 20-under-par to become the first Scandinavian to win a major with his victory at the **British Open**, July 14-17 at Scotland's Royal Troon Golf Club. American Jimmy Walker won his first major at the **PGA Championship**, July 28-31 at Baltusrol Golf Club in Springfield, NJ.

Perennial also-rans Leicester City May 2 clinched the **English Premier League**'s 2015-16 title, the first championship in the club's 132-year history. The Foxes began the season as 5,000-1 longshots but lost just three Premier League games all season to finish first.

Nyquist became the fourth consecutive favorite to win the **Kentucky Derby** at Churchill Downs in Louisville, KY, May 7. He held off Exaggerator by 1¼ lengths to extend his undefeated record to 8-0. But there would be no Triple Crown, as Exaggerator won the rematch two weeks later at the **Preakness Stakes** by 3½ lengths on a sloppy track at Pimlico Race Course in Baltimore, MD. Nyquist didn't run in the **Belmont Stakes** June 11 at Belmont Park in Elmont, NY, and Exaggerator, the favorite, faded down the stretch and finished 11th. Creator, a 16-1 longshot, nosed out the 9-1 Destin in a photo finish.

No Canadian hockey team reached the playoffs in 2016, ensuring that the NHL's **Stanley Cup** would go to an American squad for the 22nd consecutive season. The Pittsburgh Penguins won their fourth title in franchise history, defeating the San Jose Sharks in six games June 12. Forward Sidney Crosby won the Conn Smythe Trophy, awarded to the most valuable player in the playoffs.

The Golden State Warriors and unanimous regular season MVP Stephen Curry set a record for most wins during an NBA season with 73 but failed to cap it off with an **NBA Championship**. After rallying from a 3-1 deficit against Oklahoma City in the Western Conference Finals, Golden State blew a 3-1 lead against the Cleveland Cavaliers in a rematch of the 2015 Championship, losing Game 7, 93-89, on their home court June 19. LeBron James, an Ohio native who began his career with the Cavaliers, averaged 29.7 points and 11.3 rebounds and was named the Finals MVP. Cleveland claimed its first NBA title ever and its first championship in any major pro sport since the Browns won the NFL championship in 1964 (in the pre-Super-Bowl era).

Three of the NBA's all-time greats called it quits in 2016: Laker Kobe Bryant, who carried on a much-hyped season-long farewell tour; San Antonio's Tim Duncan, who released a simple statement on the team's website after the end of the season; and Minnesota's Kevin Garnett, who announced his retirement after 21 NBA seasons a month before the 2016-17 season began.

Serbia's Novak Djokovic equaled the 2015 accomplishment of Serena Williams by holding all four major tennis titles at once. Djokovic won Wimbledon and the U.S. Open in 2015, then bested Scotland's Andy Murray in both the **Australian Open** on Jan. 31 and the **French Open** on June 5. Murray went on July 10 to win **Wimbledon**, where Djokovic was upset in the third round. Djokovic returned to form in the **U.S. Open**, reaching the finals, but fell, Sept. 11, to Switzerland's Stan Wawrinka.

Defending champion Serena Williams fell to Germany's Angelique Kerber at the **Australian Open** in Melbourne, Jan. 30, and to Spain's Garbiñe Muguruza June 4 at the **French Open**. Williams defeated Kerber in a rematch at **Wimbledon**, July 9; it was her 22nd Grand Slam singles title, equaling the mark set by Steffi Graf. Kerber rose to number one in the rankings with a **U.S. Open** victory Sept. 10 over the Czech Republic's Karolina Pliskova. On June 8, the International Tennis Federation banned former Maria Sharapova for two years (reduced Oct. 4 to 15 months) after she tested positive for the heart drug meldonium. The drug, which Sharapova claimed to have been taking for years, was added to the World Anti-Doping Agency's list of prohibited substances in Jan. 2016.

The U.S. dominated the 2016 **Summer Olympics** Aug. 5-21, 2016, in Rio de Janeiro, Brazil, winning 121 medals, outpacing second-place finisher China (70 medals). Thirty-one-year-old U.S. swimmer Michael Phelps won five golds and a silver to raise his lifetime medal total to 28; his 19-year-old teammate Katie Ledecky won four golds and a silver and was the most decorated woman athlete at the Games. Jamaican sprinter Usain Bolt became the first man in history to complete a triple-triple: winning gold in the 100-m run, the 200-m run, and the 4x100-m relay in three consecutive Olympics.

The Chicago Cubs won the World Series for the first time in 108 years, defeating the Cleveland Indians in seven tumultuous games. The Cubs also dominated **Major League Baseball**'s regular season, winning 103 games, and beat the NL West champion L.A. Dodgers in the National League Championship Series for their first pennant since 1945. They were joined in the postseason by the NL East leading Washington Nationals and the two NL wild card teams: the San Francisco Giants and NY Mets. Two teams from the AL East, the Toronto Blue Jays and the Baltimore Orioles, squared off in the American League wild card game. The Texas Rangers cruised to an AL West division title, the Boston Red Sox won the East, and former Red Sox manager Terry Francona captured the Central with Cleveland, then won the ALCS over Toronto. The Miami Marlins saw their wild card hopes slip away in the last week of the season when their 24-year-old ace, José Fernández, was killed in a boating accident.

Baseball also witnessed a slew of high-profile departures. The NY Yankees suddenly jettisoned Alex Rodriguez on Aug. 12; the team's aging first baseman Mark Teixeira retired at season's end. David Ortiz hit 38 homers in his farewell season with the Boston Red Sox. Announcer Vin Scully called it a career after 67 years of broadcasting Dodger games, an unprecedented tenure that dated back to the team's days in Brooklyn.

WORLD ALMANAC EDITORS' PICKS: BEST TEAMS THAT DIDN'T WIN IT ALL

The Golden State Warriors' loss in the 2016 NBA Finals completed a neat irony. In each of the four major U.S. sports, the team with the all-time record for most victories in a regular season didn't win the sport's championship that year. They all earned the dubious distinction of being the best teams that didn't win it all.

1906 Chicago Cubs (116-36)
Lost to: Chicago White Sox in World Series

Not yet lovable losers, these Cubs were the beginning of a short-lived dynasty that included World Series wins in 1907 and 1908. Future Hall-of-Famers Joe Tinker, Johnny Evers, and player-manager Frank Chance combined for double plays immortalized in verse, and third baseman Harry Steinfeldt led the National League in hits and RBIs. Mordecai "Three-Finger" Brown won 26 games and a season ERA of 1.04. Chicago still holds the MLB modern record for the highest winning percentage (.763). The World Series that year was a crosstown affair. But the Cubs gave up their home field advantage, losing all three home games at their West Side Grounds—Wrigley Field was built in 1914, and the Cubs moved there in 1916—en route to a 4-2 World Series loss.

1980 Soviet Union Olympic Hockey Team
Lost to: U.S. National Team (eventual champion)

The "Miracle on Ice" at the 1980 Olympics in Lake Placid, NY, wouldn't have been so unbelievable if the Soviets hadn't been the Cold War hockey equivalent of the Dream Team. A year prior, the USSR team had beaten a team of NHL All-Stars. Just two weeks before their fated Olympic matchup, the Soviets trounced the Americans (who were mostly college players), 10-3, at an exhibition game at Madison Square Garden in New York City. The U.S.'s medal-round victory, 4-3, over the Soviets at Lake Placid Feb. 22, 1980, was the highlight of the Olympics that year for American fans. (Few recall that the team still had to beat Finland two days later to win gold.)

1990-91 UNLV Men's Basketball (27-0)
Lost to: Duke Univ. (eventual champion) in Final Four

The 1990-91 UNLV Runnin' Rebels returned a squad little changed from the 1989-90 team that cruised to an NCAA title, winning the final game over Duke by a record 30 points. Four of UNLV's starting five were top picks in the 1991 NBA draft—Larry Johnson (#1 overall), Stacey Augmon (9th), Greg Anthony (12th), and George Ackles (29th). Playing in the Big West Conference, the Rebels faced only one top-10-ranked opponent all year prior to the NCAA tournament: no. 2 Arkansas, who fell 112-105 in Feb. But on Mar. 30, the Rebels came up against no. 6 Duke, who finally upset the defending champs, 79-77, in a Final Four rematch.

1995-96 Detroit Red Wings (62-13-7)
Lost to: Colorado (eventual champion) in Conference Finals

After getting swept by New Jersey in the Stanley Cup Finals the year prior, Detroit played the 1995-96 season with something to prove. After a 4-3-2 start, the Red Wings acquired center Igor Larionov, who completed a "Russian Five" with Sergei Fedorov, Vyacheslav Kozlov, Viacheslav Fetisov, and Vladimir Konstantinov. Together they played a Soviet style of hockey in which positions were fluid. It worked to perfection: Fedorov notched 39 goals and 68 assists; Kozlov, 36 and 37, respectively; Larionov, 21 and 50; Konstantinov, 14 and 20; and Fetisov, 7 and 35. In the playoffs, though, the Red Wings struggled to get past lowly Winnipeg and then needed a double-OT Game 7 win to dispatch St. Louis. They scored 11 goals in two wins against Colorado in the conference finals, but only 5 goals in their four decisive losses.

2001 Seattle Mariners (116-46)
Lost to: NY Yankees in ALCS
Eventual champion: Arizona Diamondbacks

Seattle's 2001 lineup initially seemed to lack firepower, with Carlos Guillen filling in for Texas-bound Alex Rodriguez and Japanese import Ichiro Suzuki considered somewhat of an unknown quantity. But these new-look Mariners won 31 of their first 40 games, energized by eventual batting title-winner Suzuki and 37 homers from 2nd baseman Bret Boone. Standing between the Mariners and the World Series were the NY Yankees, who three years earlier had gone 114-48. The nucleus of that team was seeking its fourth straight championship. In the ALCS, Seattle's bats went cold, scoring just two runs in each of the first two home games. They exploded for 14 runs in Game 3 but dropped the next two games.

2005 USC Football (12-0)
Lost to: Univ. of Texas in 2006 Rose Bowl/BCS National Championship Game

The defending national champions—including 2004 and 2005 Heisman winners Matt Leinart and Reggie Bush—steamrolled their opponents all season, averaging more than 500 yards of total offense per game. USC was riding a 34-game winning streak when they met Texas in the Rose Bowl, the site of the year's national title game, and practically a home game for the L.A.-centered team. The Trojans put up 38 points, but they could not stop Texas's Vince Young, who threw for 267 yards and ran for 200, capped by an 8-yard mad dash on fourth down for the winning touchdown as the Longhorns won, 41-38. (In 2010, USC was forced to vacate all 12 wins from the 2005 season when an NCAA investigation found that Bush had received improper benefits.)

2007 New England Patriots (16-0)
Lost to: NY Giants in Super Bowl XLII

The Tom Brady-led Patriots offense broke records (since eclipsed) for touchdowns (75) and points scored (589). The Patriots beat other teams by an average of 20 points per win. In the first eight games of the season, they scored at least 34 points per game and never gave up more than 28. They finished the regular season a perfect 16-0 with a comeback win over the NY Giants, 38-35. After easy playoff wins against Jacksonville and San Diego, New England once again faced the Giants in Super Bowl XLII in a defensive struggle. New York's ball-control offense kept Tom Brady on the sidelines for much of the first quarter, and its defense sacked him five times. Some saw the Giants' 17-14 victory as the Patriots' just deserts for the team's involvement in the Spygate scandal, in which they were fined $250,000 for illegally videotaping opponents' defensive signals.

2013-14 Notre Dame Women's Basketball (37-0)
Lost to: Univ. of Connecticut in NCAA Finals

Notre Dame head coach Muffet McGraw has established a women's basketball dynasty in South Bend, coaching her teams to the NCAA tournament for 21 years straight. But the Fighting Irish have had the misfortune of playing at the same time as Geno Auriemma's juggernaut at UConn, winners of the last four NCAA tournaments. Notre Dame lost to UConn in the 2013 Final Four, then the two teams, both undefeated, faced off again in the 2014 finals. The Fighting Irish kept the game close, trailing 45-38 at halftime, but ultimately succumbed, 79-58. McGraw's teams have lost just eight games in the past four seasons without winning a single championship.

2014-15 Univ. of Kentucky Men's Basketball (31-0)
Lost to: Univ. of Wisconsin in Final Four
Eventual Champion: Duke Univ.

Despite the decampments of the previous season's freshmen stars Julius Randle and James Young to the NBA, the 2014-15 Wildcats came out even stronger, bludgeoning their first 12 opponents (all nonconference) by double digits. The team struggled only twice against its SEC opponents, needing OT to get wins against Mississippi and Texas A&M (2OT). The no. 1-seed Wildcats dispatched their first three NCAA tournament opponents in similar fashion, but after a squeaker against no. 8 Notre Dame, Kentucky met its match in no. 3 Wisconsin. Trailing 60-56 with less than five minutes to play, the Badgers went on an 8-0 run on their way to a 71-64 victory.

2015-16 Golden State Warriors (73-9)
Lost to: Cleveland Cavaliers in NBA Finals

The defending NBA champions won their first 24 games for the fastest start in league history and didn't lose at home until Apr. 1, ending a 54-game streak dating back to Jan. 31, 2015. Led by Stephen Curry and Klay Thompson, the team tallied 1,077 three-pointers for the season. Curry smashed the NBA season record for three-pointers (286, held by him) with an incredible 402 and became the first unanimous MVP in NBA history. Golden State breezed to easy wins in the first two playoff rounds, but they needed to rally from 3-1 down against Oklahoma City to make the finals. This time it was the Warriors who couldn't hold a big lead, as Cleveland became the first team ever to rebound from a 3-1 deficit in the NBA Finals.

OLYMPIC GAMES

2016 Summer Olympic Games
Rio de Janeiro, Brazil, Aug. 5-21, 2016

Familiar names dominated the XXXI Summer Olympics in Rio de Janeiro, Brazil. The first-ever Games in South America set records for number of athletes (11,544) and nations participating (206, plus teams composed of refugees and of independent athletes). Thirty-two venues hosted 306 events in 28 different sports.

U.S. swimmer Michael Phelps won five gold medals and one silver, bringing the 31-year-old's career haul to 28 (including 23 gold medals) over four Olympiads. Fellow U.S. swimmer Katie Ledecky was the most decorated female athlete in Rio, with four golds and one silver, along with two new Olympic records. Hungary's Katinka Hosszú also set two new Olympic records on her way to three gold medals and one silver.

The U.S. excelled in women's gymnastics, cruising to the team gold medal behind the performances of 19-year-old Simone Biles and 22-year-old Aly Raisman. Biles and Raisman finished 1-2 in both the floor exercise and the individual all-around competitions; Biles also captured gold in the vault and bronze on the balance beam.

Jamaica's Usain Bolt defended his title as the world's fastest human, and completed an unprecedented feat, becoming the first man in history to win the 100-m run, the 200-m run, and the 4x100-m relay in three consecutive Olympics. South Africa's Wayde van Niekerk broke Michael Johnson's 17-year-old world record in the 400-m run.

Brazil's national team won its first-ever gold medal in soccer, avenging the 7-1 shellacking the team suffered against Germany in the 2014 World Cup semifinals, also played in Brazil. The medal win in the country's favorite sport was also a balm for months of speculation about whether Brazil could pull off staging the Games. Even in the last days before competition began, concerns lingered about public safety, incomplete facilities and arenas, water quality for the sailing and canoeing events, and the threat of Zika virus.

Less than a month before the Games began, the World Anti-Doping Agency released evidence of a comprehensive state-run doping program in Russia, and recommended banning all Russian athletes from the Games. The International Olympic Committee took a less punitive stance, and ultimately cleared more than two-thirds of Russia's contingent to compete at Rio.

2016 Summer Olympic Games: Final Medal Standings

Country	G	S	B	T	Country	G	S	B	T	Country	G	S	B	T
United States ..	46	37	38	121	Colombia	3	2	3	8	Independent Olympic Athletes.....	1	0	1	2
China	26	18	26	70	Iran	3	1	4	8	Algeria	0	2	0	2
Great Britain . . .	27	23	17	67	Serbia........	2	4	2	8	Ireland........	0	2	0	2
Russia........	19	18	19	56	Turkey........	1	3	4	8	India	0	1	1	2
Germany......	17	10	15	42	Ethiopia.......	1	2	5	8	Mongolia	0	1	1	2
France........	10	18	14	42	Switzerland....	3	2	2	7	Israel.........	0	0	2	2
Japan	12	8	21	41	North Korea ...	2	3	2	7	Fiji...........	1	0	0	1
Australia	8	11	10	29	Georgia	2	1	4	7	Jordan........	1	0	0	1
Italy.........	8	12	8	28	Greece	3	1	2	6	Kosovo	1	0	0	1
Canada.......	4	3	15	22	Belgium.......	2	2	2	6	Puerto Rico....	1	0	0	1
South Korea ...	9	3	9	21	Thailand	2	2	2	6	Singapore.....	1	0	0	1
Netherlands ...	8	7	4	19	Romania......	1	1	3	5	Tajikistan......	1	0	0	1
Brazil.........	7	6	6	19	Malaysia	0	4	1	5	Burundi.......	0	1	0	1
New Zealand ..	4	9	5	18	Mexico	0	3	2	5	Grenada......	0	1	0	1
Azerbaijan.....	1	7	10	18	Argentina	3	1	0	4	Niger.........	0	1	0	1
Spain	7	4	6	17	Slovakia	2	2	0	4	Philippines	0	1	0	1
Kazakhstan....	3	5	9	17	Armenia	1	3	0	4	Qatar	0	1	0	1
Hungary	8	3	4	15	Slovenia	1	2	1	4	Austria	0	0	1	1
Denmark......	2	6	7	15	Lithuania......	0	1	3	4	Dominican Rep.	0	0	1	1
Kenya	6	6	1	13	Norway	0	0	4	4	Estonia	0	0	1	1
Uzbekistan	4	2	7	13	Indonesia	1	2	0	3	Finland	0	0	1	1
Jamaica	6	3	2	11	Taiwan	1	0	2	3	Moldova	0	0	1	1
Cuba.........	5	2	4	11	Bulgaria	0	1	2	3	Morocco	0	0	1	1
Sweden.......	2	6	3	11	Venezuela.....	0	1	2	3	Nigeria	0	0	1	1
Ukraine.......	2	5	4	11	Egypt	0	0	3	3	Portugal	0	0	1	1
Poland	2	3	6	11	Tunisia	0	0	3	3	Trinidad and Tobago	0	0	1	1
Croatia	5	3	2	10	Bahrain.......	1	1	0	2	UAE	0	0	1	1
South Africa ...	2	6	2	10	Vietnam	1	1	0	2					
Czech Republic	1	2	7	10	The Bahamas..	1	0	1	2					
Belarus.......	1	4	4	9	Côte d'Ivoire ...	1	0	1	2					

2016 Summer Olympic Medal Winners

Archery
Men's Individual: G–Ku Bon-chan, South Korea; S–Jean-Charles Valladont, France; B–Brady Ellison, U.S.
Women's Individual: G–Chang Hye-jin, South Korea; S–Lisa Unruh, Germany; B–Ki Bo-bae, South Korea.
Men's Team: G–South Korea; S–U.S.; B–Australia.
Women's Team: G–South Korea; S–Russia; B–Taiwan.

Badminton
Men's Singles: G–Chen Long, China; S–Chong Wei Lee, Malaysia; B–Viktor Axelsen, Denmark.
Men's Doubles: G–Fu Haifeng & Zhang Nan, China; S–V Shem Goh & Wee Kiong Tan, Malaysia; B–Marcus Ellis & Chris Langridge, Great Britain.
Women's Singles: G–Carolina Marín, Spain; S–P. V. Sindhu, India; B–Nozomi Okuhara, Japan.
Women's Doubles: G–Misaki Matsutomo & Ayaka Takahashi, Japan; S–Christinna Pedersen & Kamilla Rytter Juhl, Denmark; B–Jung Kyung-eun & Shin Seung-chan, South Korea.

Mixed Doubles: G–Tontowi Ahmad & Liliyana Natsir, Indonesia; S–Peng Soon Chan & Liu Ying Goh, Malaysia; B–Zhang Nan & Zhao Yunlei, China.

Basketball
Men: G–U.S.; S–Serbia; B–Spain.
Women: G–U.S.; S–Spain; B–Serbia.

Beach Volleyball
Men: G–Alison Cerutti & Bruno Oscar Schmidt, Brazil; S–Daniele Lupo & Paolo Nicolai, Italy; B–Alexander Brouwer & Robert Meeuwsen, Netherlands.
Women: G–Laura Ludwig & Kira Walkenhorst, Germany; S–Agatha Bednarczuk & Bárbara Seixas de Freitas, Brazil; B–April Ross & Kerri Walsh Jennings, U.S.

Boxing
Men
Light Flyweight (46-49 kg/101-108 lbs): G–Hasanboy Dusmatov, Uzbekistan; S–Yuberjén Herney Martínez, Colombia; B–Nico Miguel Hernández, U.S; B–Joahnys Argilagos, Cuba.

Flyweight (52 kg/115 lbs): G–Shakhobidin Zoirov, Uzbekistan; S–Misha Aloian, Russia; B–Yoel Finol, Venezuela; B–Hu Jianguan, China.

Bantamweight (56 kg/123 lbs): G–Robeisy Ramírez, Cuba; S–Shakur Stevenson, U.S.; B–Murodjon Akhmadaliev, Uzbekistan; B–Vladimir Nikitin, Russia.

Lightweight (60 kg/132 lbs): G–Robson Conceição, Brazil; S–Sofiane Oumiha, France; B–Otgondalai Dorjnyambuu, Mongolia; B–Lázaro Jorge Álvarez, Cuba.

Light Welterweight (64 kg/141 lbs): G–Fazliddin Gaibnazarov, Uzbekistan; S–Lorenzo Sotomayor Collazo, Azerbaijan; B–Vitaly Dunaytsev, Russia; B–Artem Harutyunyan, Germany.

Welterweight (69 kg/152 lbs): G–Daniyar Yeleussinov, Kazakhstan; S–Shakhram Giyasov, Uzbekistan; B–Souleymane Diop Cissokho, France; B–Mohammed Rabii, Morocco.

Middleweight (75 kg/165 lbs): G–Arlen López, Cuba; S–Bektemir Melikuziev, Uzbekistan; B–Misael Uziel Rodríguez, Mexico; B–Kamran Shakhsuvarly, Azerbaijan.

Light Heavyweight (81 kg/179 lbs): G–Julio César La Cruz, Cuba; S–Adilbek Niyazymbetov, Kazakhstan; B–Mathieu Albert Daniel Bauderlique, France; B–Joshua Buatsi, Great Britain.

Heavyweight (91 kg/201 lbs): G–Evgeny Tishchenko, Russia; S–Vassiliy Levit, Kazakhstan; B–Erislandy Savón, Cuba; B–Rustam Tulaganov, Uzbekistan.

Super Heavyweight (91+ kg/201+ lbs): G–Tony Yoka, France; S–Joe Joyce, Great Britain; B–Ivan Dychko, Kazakhstan; B–Filip Hrgovic, Croatia.

Women

Flyweight (48-51 kg/106-112 lbs): G–Nicola Adams, Great Britain; S–Sarah Ourahmoune, France; B–Ren Cancan, China; B–Ingrit Valencia, Colombia.

Lightweight (57-60 kg/126-132 lbs): G–Estelle Mossely, France; S–Yin Junhua, China; B–Anastasiia Beliakova, Russia; B–Mira Potkonen, Finland.

Middleweight (69-75 kg/152-165 lbs): G–Claressa Shields, U.S.; S–Nouchka Fontijn, Netherlands; B–Li Qian, China; B–Dariga Shakimova, Kazakhstan.

Canoe/Kayak—Slalom

Canoe Single Men: G–Denis Gargaud Chanut, France; S–Matej Benus, Slovakia; B–Takuya Haneda, Japan.

Canoe Double Men: G–Ladislav Skantár & Peter Skantár, Slovakia; S–David Florence & Richard Hounslow, Great Britain; B–Gauthier Klauss & Matthieu Péché, France.

Kayak Men: G–Joseph Clarke, Great Britain; S–Peter Kauzer, Slovenia; B–Jirí Prskavec, Czech Republic.

Kayak Women: G–Maialen Chourraut, Spain; S–Luuka Jones, New Zealand; B–Jessica Fox, Australia.

Canoe/Kayak—Sprint

Men

Canoe Single 200-m: G–Iurii Cheban, Ukraine; S–Valentin Demyanenko, Azerbaijan; B–Isaquias Queiroz dos Santos, Brazil.

Canoe Single 1000-m: G–Sebastian Brendel, Germany; S–Isaquias Queiroz dos Santos, Brazil; B–Serghei Tarnovschi, Moldova.

Canoe Double 1000-m: G–Sebastian Brendel & Jan Vandrey, Germany; S–Erlon de Souza Silva & Isaquias Queiroz dos Santos, Brazil; B–Dmytro Ianchuk & Taras Mishchuk, Ukraine.

Kayak Single 200-m: G–Liam Heath, Great Britain; S–Maxime Beaumont, France; B–Saúl Craviotto, Spain; B–Ronald Rauhe, Germany.

Kayak Single 1000-m: G–Marcus Walz, Spain; S–Josef Dostál, Czech Republic; B–Roman Anoshkin, Russia.

Kayak Double 200-m: G–Saúl Craviotto & Cristian Toro, Spain; S–Liam Heath & Jon Schofield, Great Britain; B–Aurimas Lankas & Edvians Ramanauskas, Lithuania.

Kayak Double 1000-m: G–Marcus Gross & Max Rendschmidt, Germany; S–Marko Tomicevic & Milenko Zoric, Serbia; B–Lachlan Tame & Ken Wallace, Australia.

Kayak Four 1000-m: G–Germany; S–Slovakia; B–Czech Republic.

Women

Kayak Single 200-m: G–Lisa Carrington, New Zealand; S–Marta Walczykiewicz, Poland; B–Inna Osipenko-Rodomska, Azerbaijan.

Kayak Single 500-m: G–Danuta Kozák, Hungary; S–Emma Jorgensen, Denmark; B–Lisa Carrington, New Zealand.

Kayak Double 500-m: G–Danuta Kozák & Gabriella Szabó, Hungary; S–Tina Dietze & Franziska Weber, Germany; B–Beata Mikolajczyk & Karolina Naja, Poland.

Kayak Four 500-m: G–Hungary; S–Germany; B–Belarus.

Cycling—BMX

Men: G–Connor Fields, U.S.; S–Jelle van Gorkom, Netherlands; B–Carlos Alberto Ramirez Yepes, Colombia.

Women: G–Mariana Pajón, Colombia; S–Alise Post, U.S.; B–Stefany Hernandez, Venezuela.

Cycling—Mountain Bike

Men's Cross-country: G–Nino Schurter, Switzerland; S–Jaroslav Kulhavy, Czech Republic; B–Carlos Coloma Nicolas, Spain.

Women's Cross-country: G–Jenny Rissveds, Sweden; S–Maja Wloszczowska, Poland; B–Catharine Pendrel, Canada.

Cycling—Road

Men's Road Race: G–Greg van Avermaet, Belgium; S–Jakob Fuglsang, Denmark; B–Rafal Majka, Poland.

Men's Individual Time Trial: G–Fabian Cancellara, Switzerland; S–Tom Dumoulin, Netherlands; B–Christopher Froome, Great Britain.

Women's Road Race: G–Anna van der Breggen, Netherlands; S–Emma Johansson, Sweden; B–Elisa Longo Borghini, Italy.

Women's Individual Time Trial: G–Kristin Armstrong, U.S.; S–Olga Zabelinskaya, Russia; B–Anna van der Breggen, Netherlands.

Cycling—Track

Men

Sprint: G–Jason Kenny, Great Britain; S–Callum Skinner, Great Britain; B–Denis Dmitriev, Russia.

Team Sprint: G–Great Britain; S–New Zealand; B–France.

Keirin: G–Jason Kenny, Great Britain; S–Matthijs Buchli, Netherlands; B–Azizulhasni Awang, Malaysia.

Team Pursuit: G–Great Britain; S–Australia; B–Denmark.

Omnium: G–Elia Viviani, Italy; S–Mark Cavendish, Great Britain; B–Lasse Norman Hansen, Denmark.

Women

Sprint: G–Kristina Vogel, Germany; S–Rebecca James, Great Britain; B–Katy Marchant, Great Britain.

Team Sprint: G–China; S–Russia; B–Germany.

Keirin: G–Elis Ligtlee, Netherlands; S–Rebecca James, Great Britain; B–Anna Meares, Australia.

Team Pursuit: G–Great Britain; S–United States; B–Canada.

Omnium: G–Laura Trott, Great Britain; S–Sarah Hammer, U.S.; B–Jolien D'hoore, Belgium.

Diving

Men

Springboard: G–Cao Yuan, China; S–Jack Laugher, Great Britain; B–Patrick Hausding, Germany.

Platform: G–Chen Aisen, China; S–Germán Sánchez, Mexico; B–David Boudia, U.S.

Synchronized Springboard: G–Jack Laugher & Chris Mears, Great Britain; S–Sam Dorman & Mike Hixon, U.S.; B–Cao Yuan & Qin Kai, China.

Synchronized Platform: G–Lin Yue & Chen Aisen, China; S–David Boudia & Steele Johnson, U.S.; B–Thomas Daley & Daniel Goodfellow, Great Britain.

Women

Springboard: G–Shi Tingmao, China; S–He Zi, China; B–Tania Cagnotto, Italy.

Platform: G–Ren Qian, China; S–Si Yajie, China; B–Meaghan Benfeito, Canada.

Synchronized Springboard: G–Wu Minxia & Shi Tingmao, China; S–Tania Cagnotto & Francesca Dallapè, Italy; B–Maddison Keeney & Anabelle Smith, Australia.

Synchronized Platform: G–Chen Ruolin & Liu Huixia, China; S–Jun Hoong Cheong & Pandelela Rinong Pamg, Malaysia; B–Meaghan Benfeito & Roseline Filion, Canada.

Equestrian

Eventing Individual: G–Michael Jung, Germany; S–Astier Nicolas, France; B–Phillip Dutton, U.S.

Eventing Team: G–France; S–Germany; B–Australia.

Dressage Individual: G–Charlotte Dujardin, Great Britain; S–Isabell Werth, Germany; B–Kristina Bröring-Sprehe, Germany.

Dressage Team: G–Germany; S–Great Britain; B–U.S.

Jumping Individual: G–Nick Skelton, Great Britain; S–Peder Fredricson, Sweden; B–Eric Lamaze, Canada.

Jumping Team: G–France; S–U.S.; B–Germany.

Fencing

Men

Foil Individual: G–Daniele Garozzo, Italy; S–Alexander Massialas, U.S.; B–Timur Safin, Russia.
Épée Individual: G–Park Sang-young, South Korea; S–Géza Imre, Hungary; B–Gauthier Grumier, France.
Sabre Individual: G–Áron Szilágyi, Hungary; S–Daryl Homer, U.S.; B–Kim Jung-hwan, South Korea.
Foil Team: G–Russia; S–France; B–U.S.
Épée Team: G–France; S–Italy; B–Hungary.

Women

Foil Individual: G–Inna Deriglazova, Russia; S–Elisa di Francisca, Italy; B–Inès Boubakri, Tunisia.
Épée Individual: G–Emese Szász, Hungary; S–Rossella Fiamingo, Italy; B–Sun Yiwen, China.
Sabre Individual: G–Yana Egorian, Russia; S–Sofya Velikaya, Russia; B–Olga Kharlan, Ukraine.
Épée Team: G–Romania; S–China; B–Russia.
Sabre Team: G–Russia; S–Ukraine; B–U.S.

Field Hockey

Men: G–Argentina; S–Belgium; B–Germany.
Women: G–Great Britain; S–Netherlands; B–Germany.

Golf

Men's Individual Stroke Play: G–Justin Rose, Great Britain; S–Henrik Stenson, Sweden; B–Matt Kuchar, U.S.
Women's Individual Stroke Play: G–Park Inbee, South Korea; S–Lydia Ko, New Zealand; B–Feng Shanshan, China.

Gymnastics—Artistic

Men

Individual All-Around: G–Kohei Uchimura, Japan; S–Oleg Verniaiev, Ukraine; B–Max Whitlock, Great Britain.
Floor Exercise: G–Max Whitlock, Great Britain; S–Diego Hypólito, Brazil; B–Arthur Mariano, Brazil.
Pommel Horse: G–Max Whitlock, Great Britain; S–Louis Smith, Great Britain; B–Alexander Naddour, U.S.
Rings: G–Eleftherios Petrounias, Greece; S–Arthur Zanetti, Brazil; B–Denis Abliazin, Russia.
Vault: G–Ri Se Gwang, North Korea; S–Denis Abliazin, Russia; B–Kenzo Shirai, Japan.
Parallel Bars: G–Oleg Verniaiev, Ukraine; S–Danell Leyva, U.S.; B–David Belyavskiy, Russia.
Horizontal Bar: G–Fabian Hambüchen, Germany; S–Danell Leyva, U.S.; B–Nile Wilson, Great Britain.
Team: G–Japan; S–Russia; B–China.

Women

Individual All-Around: G–Simone Biles, U.S.; S–Alexandra Raisman, U.S.; B–Aliya Mustafina, Russia.
Vault: G–Simone Biles, U.S.; S–Maria Paseka, Russia; B–Giulia Steingruber, Switzerland.
Uneven Bars: G–Aliya Mustafina, Russia; S–Madison Kocian, U.S.; B–Sophie Scheder, Germany.
Balance Beam: G–Sanne Wevers, Netherlands; S–Lauren Hernandez, U.S.; B–Simone Biles, U.S.
Floor Exercise: G–Simone Biles, U.S.; S–Alexandra Raisman, U.S.; B–Amy Tinkler, Great Britain.
Team: G–U.S.; S–Russia; B–China.

Gymnastics—Rhythmic

Individual All-Around: G–Margarita Mamun, Russia; S–Yana Kudryavtseva, Russia; B–Ganna Rizatdinova, Ukraine.
Group All-Around: G–Russia; S–Spain; B–Bulgaria.

Gymnastics—Trampoline

Men: G–Uladzislau Hancharou, Belarus; S–Dong Dong, China; B–Gao Lei, China.
Women: G–Rosannagh Maclennan, Canada; S–Bryony Page, Great Britain; B–Li Dan, China.

Handball

Men: G–Denmark; S–France; B–Germany.
Women: G–Russia; S–France; B–Norway.

Judo

Men

60 kg/132 lbs: G–Beslan Mudranov, Russia; S–Yeldos Smetov, Kazakhstan; B–Diyorbek Urozboev, Uzbekistan; B–Naohisa Takato, Japan.
66 kg/146 lbs: G–Fabio Basile, Italy; S–An Baul, South Korea; B–Rishod Sobirov, Uzbekistan; B–Masashi Ebinuma, Japan.
73 kg/161 lbs: G–Shohei Ono, Japan; S–Rustam Orujov, Azerbaijan; B–Lasha Shavdatuashvili, Georgia; B–Dirk van Tichelt, Belgium.
81 kg/179 lbs: G–Khasan Khalmurzaev, Russia; S–Travis Stevens, U.S.; B–Sergiu Toma, United Arab Emirates; B–Takanori Nagase, Japan.

90 kg/198 lbs: G–Mashu Baker, Japan; S–Varlam Liparteliani, Georgia; B–Cheng Xunzhao, China; B–Gwak Dong-han, South Korea.
100 kg/220 lbs: G–Lukás Krpálek, Czech Republic; S–Elmar Gasimov, Azerbaijan; B–Ryunosuke Haga, Japan; B–Cyrille Maret, France.
100+ kg/220+ lbs: G–Teddy Riner, France; S–Hisayoshi Harasawa, Japan; B–Or Sasson, Israel; B–Rafael Silva, Brazil.

Women

48 kg/106 lbs: G–Paula Pareto, Argentina; S–Jeong Bo-kyeong, South Korea; B–Otgontsetseg Galbadrakh, Kazakhstan; B–Ami Kondo, Japan.
52 kg/115 lbs: G–Majlinda Kelmendi, Kosovo; S–Odette Giufrida, Italy; B–Misato Nakamura, Japan; B–Natalia Kuziutina, Russia.
57 kg/126 lbs: G–Rafaela Silva, Brazil; S–Sumiya Dorjsuren, Mongolia; B–Telma Monteiro, Portugal; B–Kaori Matsumoto, Japan.
63 kg/139 lbs: G–Tina Trstenjak, Slovenia; S–Clarisse Agbegnenou, France; B–Yarden Gerbi, Israel; B–Anicka van Emden, Netherlands.
70 kg/154 lbs: G–Haruka Tachimoto, Japan; S–Yuri Alvear, Colombia; B–Laura Vargas Koch, Germany; B–Sally Conway, Great Britain.
78 kg/172 lbs: G–Kayla Harrison, U.S.; S–Audrey Tcheuméo, France; B–Mayra Aguiar, Brazil; B–Anamari Velensek, Slovenia.
78+ kg/172+ lbs: G–Émilie Andéol, France; S–Idalys Ortiz, Cuba; B–Kanae Yamabe, Japan; B–Yu Song, China.

Modern Pentathlon

Men: G–Alexander Lesun, Russia; S–Pavlo Tymoshchenko, Ukraine; B–Ismael Marcelo Hernandez Uscanga, Mexico.
Women: G–Chloe Esposito, Australia; S–Élodie Clouvel, France; B–Oktawia Nowacka, Poland.

Rowing

Men

Single Sculls: G–Mahé Drysdale, New Zealand; S–Damir Martin, Croatia; B–Ondrej Synek, Czech Republic.
Double Sculls: G–Martin Sinkovic & Valent Sinkovic, Croatia; S–Mindaugas Griskonis & Saulius Ritter, Lithuania; B–Kjetil Borch & Olaf Tufte, Norway.
Pair: G–Hamish Bond & Eric Murray, New Zealand; S–Lawrence Brittain & Shaun Keeling, South Africa; B–Giovanni Abagnale & Marco di Costanzo, Italy.
Four: G–Great Britain; S–Australia; B–Italy.
Lightweight Double Sculls: G–Jérémie Azou & Pierre Houin, France; S–Gary O'Donovan & Paul O'Donovan, Ireland; B–Kristoffer Brun & Are Strandli, Norway.
Lightweight Four: G–Switzerland; S–Denmark; B–France.
Quadruple Sculls: G–Germany; S–Australia; B–Estonia.
Eight: G–Great Britain; S–Germany; B–Netherlands.

Women

Single Sculls: G–Kimberley Brennan, Australia; S–Genevra Stone, U.S.; B–Duan Jingli, China.
Double Sculls: G–Magdalena Fularczyk-Kozlowska & Natalia Madaj, Poland; S–Katherine Grainger & Victoria Thornley, Great Britain; B–Milda Valciukaite & Donata Vistartaite, Lithuania.
Pair: G–Helen Glover & Heather Stanning, Great Britain; S–Genevieve Behrent & Rebecca Scown, New Zealand; B–Anne Andersen & Hedvig Rasmussen, Denmark.
Lightweight Double Sculls: G–Maaike Head & Ilse Paulis, Netherlands; S–Lindsay Jennerich & Patricia Obee, Canada; B–Huang Wenyi & Pan Feihong, China.
Quadruple Sculls: G–Germany; S–Netherlands; B–Poland.
Eight: G–U.S.; S–Great Britain; B–Romania.

Rugby Sevens

Men: G–Fiji; S–Great Britain; B–South Africa.
Women: G–Australia; S–New Zealand; B–Canada.

Sailing

RS:X Men: G–Dorian van Rijsselberghe, Netherlands; S–Nick Dempsey, Great Britain; B–Pierre le Coq, France.
RS:X Women: G–Charline Picon, France; S–Chen Peina, China; B–Stefaniya Elfutina, Russia.
Laser Men: G–Tom Burton, Australia; S–Tonci Stipanovic, Croatia; B–Sam Meech, New Zealand.
Laser Radial Women: G–Marit Bouwmeester, Netherlands; S–Annalise Murphy, Ireland; B–Anne-Marie Rindom, Denmark.
Finn Men: G–Giles Scott, Great Britain; S–Vasilij Zbogar, Slovenia; B–Caleb Paine, U.S.
470 Men: G–Sime Fantela & Igor Marenic, Croatia; S–Mathew Belcher & Will Ryan, Australia; B–Pavlos Kagialis & Panagiotis Mantis, Greece.
470 Women: G–Saskia Clark & Hannah Mills, Great Britain; S–Jo Aleh & Polly Powrie, New Zealand; B–Hélène Defrance & Camille Lecointre, France.
49er Men: G–Peter Burling & Blair Tuke, New Zealand; S–Iain Jensen & Nathan Outteridge, Australia; B–Erik Heil & Thomas Ploessel, Germany.

49er FX Women: G–Martine Grael & Kahena Kunze, Brazil; S–Alex Maloney & Molly Meech, New Zealand; B–Jena Hansen & Katja Steen Salskov-Iversen, Denmark.

Nacra 17 Mixed: G–Cecilia Carranza Saroli & Santiago Lange, Argentina; S–Lisa Darmanin & Jason Waterhouse, Australia; B–Tanja Frank & Thomas Zajac, Austria.

Shooting

Men

50-m Rifle 3 Positions: G–Niccolò Campriani, Italy; S–Sergey Kamenskiy, Russia; B–Alexis Raynaud, France.

50-m Rifle Prone: G–Henri Junghaenel, Germany; S–Kim Jong-hyun, South Korea; B–Kirill Grigorian, Russia.

10-m Air Rifle: G–Niccolò Campriani, Italy; S–Serhiy Kulish, Ukraine; B–Vladimir Maslennikov, Russia.

50-m Pistol: G–Jin Jong-oh, South Korea; S–Xuân Vinh Hoàng, Vietnam; B–Kim Song Guk, North Korea.

25-m Rapid Fire Pistol: G–Christian Reitz, Germany; S–Jean Quiquampoix, France; B–Li Yuehong, China.

10-m Air Pistol: G–Xuân Vinh Hoàng, Vietnam; S–Felipe Almeida Wu, Brazil; B–Pang Wei, China.

Trap: G–Josip Glasnovic, Croatia; S–Giovanni Pellielo, Italy; B–Edward Ling, Great Britain.

Double Trap: G–Fehaid Aldeehani, Independent Olympic Athletes; S–Marco Innocenti, Italy; B–Steven Scott, Great Britain.

Skeet: G–Gabriele Rossetti, Italy; S–Marcus Svensson, Sweden; B–Abdullah Alrashidi, Independent Olympic Athletes.

Women

50-m Rifle 3 Positions: G–Barbara Engleder, Germany; S–Zhang Binbin, China; B–Du Li, China.

10-m Air Rifle: G–Virginia Thrasher, U.S.; S–Du Li, China; B–Yi Siling, China.

25-m Pistol: G–Anna Korakaki, Greece; S–Monika Karsch, Germany; B–Heidi Diethelm Gerber, Switzerland.

10-m Air Pistol: G–Zhang Mengxue, China; S–Vitalina Batsarashkina, Russia; B–Anna Korakaki, Greece.

Trap: G–Catherine Skinner, Australia; S–Natalie Rooney, New Zealand; B–Corey Cogdell, U.S.

Skeet: G–Diana Bacosi, Italy; S–Chiara Cainero, Italy; B–Kimberly Rhode, U.S.

Soccer

Men: G–Brazil; S–Germany; B–Nigeria.

Women: G–Germany; S–Sweden; B–Canada.

Swimming

Men

50-m Freestyle: G–Anthony Ervin, U.S.; S–Florent Manaudou, France; B–Nathan Adrian, U.S.

100-m Freestyle: G–Kyle Chalmers, Australia; S–Pieter Timmers, Belgium; B–Nathan Adrian, U.S.

200-m Freestyle: G–Sun Yang, China; S–Chad le Clos, South Africa; B–Conor Dwyer, U.S.

400-m Freestyle: G–Mack Horton, Australia; S–Sun Yang, China; B–Gabriele Detti, Italy.

1500-m Freestyle: G–Gregorio Paltrinieri, Italy; S–Connor Jaeger, U.S.; B–Gabriele Detti, Italy.

100-m Backstroke: G–Ryan Murphy, U.S.; S–Xu Jiayu, China; B–David Plummer, U.S.

200-m Backstroke: G–Ryan Murphy, U.S.; S–Mitchell Larkin, Australia; B–Evgeny Rylov, Russia.

100-m Breaststroke: G–Adam Peaty, Great Britain; S–Cameron van der Burgh, South Africa; B–Cody Miller, U.S.

200-m Breaststroke: G–Dmitriy Balandin, Kazakhstan; S–Josh Prenot, U.S.; B–Anton Chupkov, Russia.

100-m Butterfly: G–Joseph Schooling, Singapore; S–László Cseh, Hungary; B–Michael Phelps, U.S.; S–Chad le Clos, South Africa.

200-m Butterfly: G–Michael Phelps, U.S.; S–Masato Sakai, Japan; B–Tamás Kenderesi, Hungary.

200-m Individual Medley: G–Michael Phelps, U.S.; S–Kosuke Hagino, Japan; B–Wang Shun, China.

400-m Individual Medley: G–Kosuke Hagino, Japan; S–Chase Kalisz, U.S.; B–Daiya Seto, Japan.

10-km marathon: G–Ferry Weertman, Netherlands; S–Spiros Gianniotis, Greece; B–Marc-Antoine Olivier, France.

4x100-m Freestyle Relay: G–U.S.; S–France; B–Australia.

4x200-m Freestyle Relay: G–U.S.; S–Great Britain; B–Japan.

4x100-m Medley Relay: G–U.S.; S–Great Britain; B–Australia.

Women

50-m Freestyle: G–Pernille Blume, Denmark; S–Simone Manuel, U.S.; B–Aliaksandra Herasimenia, Belarus.

100-m Freestyle: G–Penny Oleksiak, Canada; G–Simone Manuel, U.S.; B–Sarah Sjöström, Sweden.

200-m Freestyle: G–Katie Ledecky, U.S.; S–Sarah Sjöström, Sweden; B–Emma McKeon, Australia.

400-m Freestyle: G–Katie Ledecky, U.S.; S–Jazz Carlin, Great Britain; B–Leah Smith, U.S.

800-m Freestyle: G–Katie Ledecky, U.S.; S–Jazz Carlin, Great Britain; B–Boglárka Kapás, Hungary.

100-m Backstroke: G–Katinka Hosszú, Hungary; S–Kathleen Baker, U.S.; B–Kylie Masse, Canada; B–Fu Yuanhui, China.

200-m Backstroke: G–Maya DiRado, U.S.; S–Katinka Hosszú, Hungary; B–Hilary Caldwell, Canada.

100-m Breaststroke: G–Lilly King, U.S.; S–Yulia Efimova, Russia; B–Catherine Meili, U.S.

200-m Breaststroke: G–Rie Kaneto, Japan; S–Yulia Efimova, Russia; B–Shi Jinglin, China.

100-m Butterfly: G–Sarah Sjöström, Sweden; S–Penny Oleksiak, Canada; B–Dana Vollmer, U.S.

200-m Butterfly: G–Mireia Belmonte, Spain; S–Madeline Groves, Australia; B–Natsumi Hoshi, Japan.

200-m Individual Medley: G–Katinka Hosszú, Hungary; S–Siobhan-Marie O'Connor, Great Britain; B–Madeline Dirado, U.S.

400-m Individual Medley: G–Katinka Hosszú, Hungary; S–Madeline Dirado, U.S.; B–Mireia Belmonte, Spain.

10km marathon: G–Sharon van Rouwendaal, Netherlands; S–Rachele Bruni, Italy; B–Poliana Okimoto, Brazil.

4x100-m Freestyle Relay: G–Australia; S–U.S.; B–Canada.

4x200-m Freestyle Relay: G–U.S.; S–Australia; B–Canada.

4x100-m Medley Relay: G–U.S.; S–Australia; B–Denmark.

Synchronized Swimming

Duets: G–Natalia Ishchenko & Svetlana Romashina, Russia; S–Huang Xuechen & Sun Wenyan, China; B–Yukiko Inui & Risako Mitsui, Japan.

Teams: G–Russia; S–China; B–Japan.

Table Tennis

Men's Singles: G–Ma Long, China; S–Zhang Jike, China; B–Jun Mizutani, Japan.

Women's Singles: G–Ding Ning, China; S–Li Xiaoxia, China; B–Kim Song I, North Korea.

Men's Team: G–China; S–Japan; B–Germany.

Women's Team: G–China; S–Germany; B–Japan.

Taekwondo

Men

58 kg/128 lbs: G–Zhao Shuai, China; S–Tawin Hanprab, Thailand; B–Kim Tae-hun, South Korea; B–Luisito Pie, Dominican Republic.

68 kg/150 lbs: G–Ahmad Abughaush, Jordan; S–Alexey Denisenko, Russia; B–Joel González Bonilla, Spain; B–Lee Dae-hoon, South Korea.

80 kg/176 lbs: G–Cheick Sallah Junior Cisse, Côte d'Ivoire; S–Lutalo Muhammad, Great Britain; B–Oussama Oueslati, Tunisia; B–Milad Beigi Harchegani, Azerbaijan.

80+ kg/176+ lbs: G–Radik Isaev, Azerbaijan; S–Abdoulrazak Issoufou Alfaga, Niger; B–Cha Dong-min, South Korea; B–Maicon Siqueira, Brazil.

Women

49 kg/108 lbs: G–Kim So-hui, South Korea; S–Tijana Bogdanovic, Serbia; B–Patimat Abakarova, Azerbaijan; B–Panipak Wongpattanakit, Thailand.

57 kg/126 lbs: G–Jade Jones, Great Britain; S–Eva Calvo Gomez, Spain; B–Hedaya Wahba, Egypt; B–Kimia Alizadeh Zenoorin, Iran.

67 kg/148 lbs: G–Oh Hye-ri, South Korea; S–Haby Niaré, France; B–Nur Tatar, Turkey; B–Ruth Marie Christelle Gbagbi, Côte d'Ivoire.

67+ kg/148+ lbs: G–Zheng Shuyin, China; S–Maria Espinoza, Mexico; B–Jackie Galloway, U.S.; B–Bianca Walkden, Great Britain.

Tennis

Men's Singles: G–Andy Murray, Great Britain; S–Juan Martín del Potro, Argentina; B–Kei Nishikori, Japan.

Men's Doubles: G–Marc López & Rafael Nadal, Spain; S–Florin Mergea & Horia Tecau, Romania; B–Steve Johnson & Jack Sock, U.S.

Women's Singles: G–Mónica Puig, Puerto Rico; S–Angelique Kerber, Germany; B–Petra Kvitová, Czech Republic.

Women's Doubles: G–Ekaterina Makarova & Elena Vesnina, Russia; S–Timea Bacsinszky & Martina Hingis, Switzerland; B–Lucie Safárová & Barbora Strycová, Czech Republic.

Mixed Doubles: G–Bethanie Mattek-Sands & Jack Sock, U.S.; S–Venus Williams & Rajeev Ram, U.S.; B–Lucie Hradecká & Radek Stepánek, Czech Republic.

Track and Field

Men

100-m: G–Usain Bolt, Jamaica; S–Justin Gatlin, U.S.; B–Andre de Grasse, Canada.

200-m: G–Usain Bolt, Jamaica; S–Andre de Grasse, Canada; B–Christophe Lemaitre, France.

400-m: G–Wayde van Niekerk, South Africa; S–Kirani James, Grenada; B–Lashawn Merritt, U.S.

800-m: G–David Lekuta Rudisha, Kenya; S–Taoufik Makhloufi, Algeria; B–Clayton Murphy, U.S.

1500-m: G–Matthew Centrowitz, U.S.; S–Taoufik Makhloufi, Algeria; B–Nicholas Willis, New Zealand.

5000-m: G–Mo Farah, Great Britain; S–Paul Kipkemoi Chelimo, U.S.; B–Hagos Gebrhiwet, Ethiopia.

10,000-m: G–Mo Farah, Great Britain; S–Paul Kipngetich Tanui, Kenya; B–Tamirat Tola, Ethiopia.

Marathon: G–Eliud Kipchoge, Kenya; S–Feyisa Lilesa, Ethiopia; B–Galen Rupp, U.S.

3000-m Steeplechase: G–Conseslus Kipruto, Kenya; S–Evan Jager, U.S.; B–Mahiedine Mekhissi, France.

110-m Hurdles: G–Omar McLeod, Jamaica; S–Orlando Ortega, Spain; B–Dimitri Bascou, France.

400-m Hurdles: G–Kerron Clement, U.S.; S–Boniface Mucheru Tumuti, Kenya; B–Yasmani Copello, Turkey.

High Jump: G–Derek Drouin, Canada; S–Mutaz Essa Barshim, Qatar; B–Bohdan Bondarenko, Ukraine.

Pole Vault: G–Thiago Braz da Silva, Brazil; S–Renaud Lavillenie, France; B–Sam Kendricks, U.S.

Long Jump: G–Jeff Henderson, U.S.; S–Luvo Manyonga, South Africa; B–Greg Rutherford, Great Britain.

Triple Jump: G–Christian Taylor, U.S.; S–Will Claye, U.S.; B–Dong Bin, China.

Shot Put: G–Ryan Crouser, U.S.; S–Joe Kovacs, U.S.; B–Tomas Walsh, New Zealand.

Discus Throw: G–Christoph Harting, Germany; S–Piotr Malachowski, Poland; B–Daniel Jasinski, Germany.

Hammer Throw: G–Dilshod Nazarov, Tajikistan; S–Ivan Tsikhan, Belarus; B–Wojciech Nowicki, Poland.

Javelin Throw: G–Thomas Röhler, Germany; S–Julius Yego, Kenya; B–Keshorn Walcott, Trinidad and Tobago.

Decathlon: G–Ashton Eaton, U.S.; S–Kévin Mayer, France; B–Damian Warner, Canada.

20-km Walk: G–Wang Zhen, China; S–Cai Zelin, China; B–Dane Bird-Smith, Australia.

50-km Walk: G–Matej Tóth, Slovakia; S–Jared Tallent, Australia; B–Hirooki Arai, Japan.

4x100-m Relay: G–Jamaica; S–Japan; B–Canada.

4x400-m Relay: G–U.S.; S–Jamaica; B–The Bahamas.

Women

100-m: G–Elaine Thompson, Jamaica; S–Tori Bowie, U.S.; B–Shelly-Ann Fraser-Pryce, Jamaica.

200-m: G–Elaine Thompson, Jamaica; S–Dafne Schippers, Netherlands; B–Tori Bowie, U.S.

400-m: G–Shaunae Miller, The Bahamas; S–Allyson Felix, U.S.; B–Shericka Jackson, Jamaica.

800-m: G–Caster Semenya, South Africa; S–Francine Niyonsaba, Burundi; B–Margaret Nyairera Wambui, Kenya.

1500-m: G–Faith Chepngetich Kipyegon, Kenya; S–Genzebe Dibaba, Ethiopia; B–Jennifer Simpson, U.S.

5000-m: G–Vivian Cheruiyot, Kenya; S–Hellen Onsando Obiri, Kenya; B–Almaz Ayana, Ethiopia.

10,000-m: G–Almaz Ayana, Ethiopia; S–Vivian Jepkemoi Cheruiyot, Kenya; B–Tirunesh Dibaba, Ethiopia.

Marathon: G–Jemima Jelagat Sumgong, Kenya; S–Eunice Jepkirui Kirwa, Bahrain; B–Mare Dibaba, Ethiopia.

3000-m Steeplechase: G–Ruth Jebet, Bahrain; S–Hyvin Kiyeng Jepkemoi, Kenya; B–Emma Coburn, U.S.

100-m Hurdles: G–Brianna Rollins, U.S.; S–Nia Ali, U.S.; B–Kristi Castlin, U.S.

400-m Hurdles: G–Dalilah Muhammad, U.S.; S–Sara Slott Petersen, Denmark; B–Ashley Spencer, U.S.

High Jump: G–Ruth Beitia, Spain; S–Mirela Demireva, Bulgaria; B–Blanka Vlasic, Croatia.

Pole Vault: G–Ekateríni Stefanídi, Greece; S–Sandi Morris, U.S.; B–Eliza McCartney, New Zealand.

Long Jump: G–Tianna Bartoletta, U.S.; S–Brittney Reese, U.S.; B–Ivana Spanovic, Serbia.

Triple Jump: G–Caterine Ibargüen, Colombia; S–Yulimar Rojas, Venezuela; B–Olga Rypakova, Kazakhstan.

Shot Put: G–Michelle Carter, U.S.; S–Valerie Adams, New Zealand; B–Anita Marton, Hungary.

Discus Throw: G–Sandra Perkovic, Croatia; S–Mélina Robert-Michon, France; B–Denia Caballero, Cuba.

Hammer Throw: G–Anita Wlodarczyk, Poland; S–Zhang Wenxiu, China; B–Sophie Hitchon, Great Britain.

Javelin Throw: G–Sara Kolak, Croatia; S–Sunette Viljoen, South Africa; B–Barbora Spotáková, Czech Republic.

Heptathlon: G–Nafissatou Thiam, Belgium; S–Jessica Ennis-Hill, Great Britain; B–Brianne Theisen Eaton, Canada.

20-km Walk: G–Liu Hong, China; S–María Guadalupe González Gonzalez, Mexico; B–Lü Xiuzhi, China.

4x100-m Relay: G–U.S.; S–Jamaica; B–Great Britain.

4x400-m Relay: G–U.S.; S–Jamaica; B–Great Britain.

Triathlon

Men: G–Alistair Brownlee, Great Britain; S–Jonathan Brownlee, Great Britain; B–Henri Schoeman, South Africa.

Women: G–Gwen Jorgensen, U.S.; S–Nicola Spirig Hug, Switzerland; B–Vicky Holland, Great Britain.

Volleyball (Indoor)

Men: G–Brazil; S–Italy; B–U.S.

Women: G–China; S–Serbia; B–U.S.

Water Polo

Men: G–Serbia; S–Croatia; B–Italy.

Women: G–U.S.; S–Italy; B–Russia.

Weightlifting

Men

56 kg/123 lbs: G–Long Qingquan, China; S–Om Yun Chol, North Korea; B–Sinphet Kruaithong, Thailand.

62 kg/137 lbs: G–Óscar Albeiro Figueroa Mosquera, Colombia; S–Eko Yuli Irawan, Indonesia; B–Farkhad Kharki, Kazakhstan.

69 kg/152 lbs: G–Shi Zhiyong, China; S–Daniyar Ismayilov, Turkey; B–Luis Javier Mosquera Lozano, Colombia.

77 kg/170 lbs: G–Nijat Rahimov, Kazakhstan; S–Lyu Xiaojun, China; B–Mohamed Mahmoud, Egypt.

85 kg/187 lbs: G–Kianoush Rostami, Iran; S–Tian Tao, China; B–Gabriel Sincraian, Romania.

94 kg/207 lbs: G–Sohrab Moradi, Iran; S–Vadzim Straltsou, Belarus; B–Aurimas Didzbalis, Lithuania.

105 kg/231 lbs: G–Ruslan Nurudinov, Uzbekistan; S–Simon Martirosyan, Armenia; B–Alexandr Zaichikov, Kazakhstan.

105+ kg/231+ lbs: G–Lasha Talakhadze, Georgia; S–Gor Minasyan, Armenia; B–Irakli Turmanidze, Georgia.

Women

48 kg/106 lbs: G–Sopita Tanasan, Thailand; S–Sri Wahyuni Agustiani, Indonesia; B–Hiromi Miyake, Japan.

53 kg/117 lbs: G–Hsu Shu-Ching, Taiwan; S–Hidilyn Diaz, Philippines; B–Yoon Jin-hee, South Korea.

58 kg/128 lbs: G–Sukanya Srisurat, Thailand; S–Pimsiri Sirikaew, Thailand; B–Kuo Hsing-Chun, Taiwan.

63 kg/139 lbs: G–Deng Wei, China; S–Choe Hyo Sim, North Korea; B–Karina Goricheva, Kazakhstan.

69 kg/152 lbs: G–Xiang Yanmei, China; S–Zhazira Zhapparkul, Kazakhstan; B–Sara Ahmed, Egypt.

75 kg/165 lbs: G–Rim Jong Sim, North Korea; S–Darya Naumava, Belarus; B–Lidia Valentin Perez, Spain.

75+ kg/165+ lbs: G–Meng Suping, China; S–Kim Kuk Hyang, North Korea; B–Sarah Elizabeth Robles, U.S.

Wrestling

Men

Greco-Roman 59 kg/130 lbs: G–Ismael Borrero Molina, Cuba; S–Shinobu Ota, Japan; B–Elmurat Tasmuradov, Uzbekistan; B–Stig-André Berge, Norway.

Greco-Roman 66 kg/146 lbs: G–Davor Stefanek, Serbia; S–Migran Arutyunyan, Armenia; B–Shmagi Bolkvadze, Georgia; B–Rasul Chunayev, Azerbaijan.

Greco-Roman 75 kg/165 lbs: G–Roman Vlasov, Russia; S–Mark Overgaard Madsen, Denmark; B–Saeid Morad Abdvali, Iran; B–Kim Hyeon-woo, South Korea.

Greco-Roman 85 kg/187 lbs: G–Davit Chakvetadze, Russia; S–Zhan Beleniuk, Ukraine; B–Denis Maksymilian Kudla, Germany; B–Javid Hamzatau, Belarus.

Greco-Roman 98 kg/216 lbs: G–Artur Aleksanyan, Armenia; S–Yasmany Daniel Lugo Cabrera, Cuba; B–Ghasem Gholamreza Rezaei, Iran; B–Cenk Ildem, Turkey.

Greco-Roman 130 kg/287 lbs: G–Mijaín López Núñez, Cuba; S–Riza Kayaalp, Turkey; B–Sabah Shariati, Azerbaijan; B–Sergey Semenov, Russia.

Freestyle 57 kg/126 lbs: G–Vladimer Khinchegashvili, Georgia; S–Rei Higuchi, Japan; B–Haji Aliyev, Azerbaijan; B–Hassan Sabzali Rahimi, Iran.

Freestyle 65 kg/143 lbs: G–Soslan Ramonov, Russia; S–Toghrul Asgarov, Azerbaijan; B–Ikhtiyor Navruzov, Uzbekistan; B–Frank Chamizo Marquez, Italy.

Freestyle 74 kg/163 lbs: G–Hassan Aliazam Yazdanicharati, Iran; S–Aniuar Geduev, Russia; B–Jabrayil Hasanov, Azerbaijan; B–Soner Demirtas, Turkey.

Freestyle 86 kg/190 lbs: G–Abdulrashid Sadulaev, Russia; S–Selim Yasar, Turkey; B–Sharif Sharifov, Azerbaijan; B–J'den Cox, U.S.

Freestyle 97 kg/214 lbs: G–Kyle Frederick Snyder, U.S.; S–Khetag Goziumov, Azerbaijan; B–Magomed Idrisovitch Ibragimov, Uzbekistan; B–Albert Saritov, Romania.

Freestyle 125 kg/276 lbs: G–Taha Akgül, Turkey; S–Komeil Nemat Ghasemi, Iran; B–Geno Petriashvili, Georgia; B–Ibrahim Saidau, Belarus.

Women

48 kg/106 lbs: G–Eri Tosaka, Japan; S–Mariya Stadnik, Azerbaijan; B–Sun Yanan, China; B–Elitsa Atanasova Yankova, Bulgaria.

Freestyle 53 kg/117 lbs: G–Helen Louise Maroulis, U.S.; S–Saori Yoshida, Japan; B–Sofia Magdalena Mattsson, Sweden; B–Natalya Sinishin, Azerbaijan.

Freestyle 58 kg/128 lbs: G–Kaori Icho, Japan; S–Valeriia Koblova Zholobova, Russia; B–Sakshi Malik, India; B–Marwa Amri, Tunisia.

Freestyle 63 kg/139 lbs: G–Risako Kawai, Japan; S–Maryia Mamashuk, Belarus; B–Monika Ewa Michalík, Poland; B–Yekaterina Larionova, Kazakhstan.

Freestyle 69 kg/152 lbs: G–Sara Dosho, Japan; S–Natalia Vorobeva, Russia; B–Elmira Syzdykova, Kazakhstan; B–Anna Jenny Fransson, Sweden.

Freestyle 75 kg/165 lbs: G–Erica Elizabeth Wiebe, Canada; S–Guzel Manyurova, Kazakhstan; B–Ekaterina Bukina, Russia; B–Zhang Fengliu, China.

Summer Olympic Games Champions, 1896-2016

* = Olympic record; (w) wind-aided; times are shown in hour:minute:sec.

The 1980 games were boycotted by 62 nations, including the U.S. The 1984 games were boycotted by the USSR and most Eastern bloc nations. East and West Germany competed separately, 1968-88. The 1992 Unified Team consisted of 12 former Soviet republics. The 1992 Independent Olympic Participants (IOP) were from Serbia, Montenegro, and Macedonia.

Not all sports are listed here, and many events are omitted, even within listed sports, particularly if the event has not been held in more recent Games. Point systems for scoring events have changed many times. Points shown are those under the point system in use at the time.

Basketball

Men
1936	United States, Canada, Mexico
1948	United States, France, Brazil
1952	United States, USSR, Uruguay
1956	United States, USSR, Uruguay
1960	United States, USSR, Brazil
1964	United States, USSR, Brazil
1968	United States, Yugoslavia, USSR
1972	USSR, United States, Cuba
1976	United States, Yugoslavia, USSR
1980	Yugoslavia, Italy, USSR
1984	United States, Spain, Yugoslavia

Men
1988	USSR, Yugoslavia, United States
1992	United States, Croatia, Lithuania
1996	United States, Yugoslavia, Lithuania
2000	United States, France, Lithuania
2004	Argentina, Italy, United States
2008	United States, Spain, Argentina
2012	United States, Spain, Russia
2016	United States, Serbia, Spain

Women
1976	USSR, United States, Bulgaria
1980	USSR, Bulgaria, Yugoslavia

Women
1984	United States, South Korea, China
1988	United States, Yugoslavia, USSR
1992	Unified Team, China, United States
1996	United States, Brazil, Australia
2000	United States, Australia, Brazil
2004	United States, Australia, Russia
2008	United States, Australia, Russia
2012	United States, France, Australia
2016	United States, Spain, Serbia

Boxing—Men

Weight class limits have changed many times since the first Olympic boxing events were held in 1904. The limits shown were used in the 2016 Olympic Games. The Super Heavyweight class was known as Heavyweight 1904-80.

Lt. Flyweight (49 kg/108 lbs)
1968	Francisco Rodriguez, Venezuela
1972	Gyorgy Gedo, Hungary
1976	Jorge Hernandez, Cuba
1980	Shamil Sabyrov, USSR
1984	Paul Gonzalez, United States
1988	Ivailo Hristov, Bulgaria
1992	Rogelio Marcelo, Cuba
1996	Daniel Petrov, Bulgaria
2000	Brahim Asloum, France
2004	Yan Bhartelemy Varela, Cuba
2008	Zou Shiming, China
2012	Zou Shiming, China
2016	Hasanboy Dusmatov, Uzbekistan

Flyweight (52 kg/115 lbs)
1904	George Finnegan, United States
1920	Frank Di Gennara, United States
1924	Fidel LaBarba, United States
1928	Antal Kocsis, Hungary
1932	Istvan Enekes, Hungary
1936	Willi Kaiser, Germany
1948	Pascual Perez, Argentina
1952	Nathan Brooks, United States
1956	Terence Spinks, Great Britain
1960	Gyula Török, Hungary
1964	Fernando Atzori, Italy
1968	Ricardo Delgado, Mexico
1972	Georgi Kostadinov, Bulgaria
1976	Leo Randolph, United States
1980	Peter Lesov, Bulgaria
1984	Steve McCrory, United States
1988	Kim Kwang-sun, S. Korea
1992	Choi Chol Su, N. Korea
1996	Maikro Romero, Cuba
2000	Wijan Ponlid, Thailand
2004	Yuriorkis Gamboa Toledano, Cuba
2008	Somjit Jongjohor, Thailand
2012	Robeisy Ramírez, Cuba
2016	Shakhobidin Zoirov, Uzbekistan

Bantamweight (56 kg/123 lbs)
1904	Oliver Kirk, United States
1908	A. Henry Thomas, Great Britain
1920	Clarence Walker, South Africa
1924	William Smith, South Africa
1928	Vittorio Tamagnini, Italy
1932	Horace Gwynne, Canada
1936	Ulderico Sergo, Italy
1948	Tibor Csik, Hungary
1952	Pentti Hamalainen, Finland
1956	Wolfgang Behrendt, E. Germany
1960	Oleg Grigoryev, USSR
1964	Takao Sakurai, Japan
1968	Valery Sokolov, USSR
1972	Orlando Martinez, Cuba
1976	Gu Yong Ju, N. Korea
1980	Juan Hernandez, Cuba
1984	Maurizio Stecca, Italy
1988	Kennedy McKinney, United States
1992	Joel Casamayor, Cuba
1996	Istvan Kovacs, Hungary

Bantamweight (56 kg/123 lbs)
2000	Guillermo Rigondeaux, Cuba
2004	Guillermo Rigondeaux, Cuba
2008	Badar-Uugan Enkhbat, Mongolia
2012	Luke Campbell, Great Britain
2016	Robeisy Ramírez, Cuba

Featherweight (57 kg/125 lbs)
1904	Oliver Kirk, United States
1908	Richard Gunn, Great Britain
1920	Paul Fritsch, France
1924	John Fields, United States
1928	Lambertus van Klaveren, Netherlands
1932	Carmelo Robledo, Argentina
1936	Oscar Casanovas, Argentina
1948	Ernesto Formenti, Italy
1952	Jan Zachara, Czechoslovakia
1956	Vladimir Safronov, USSR
1960	Francesco Musso, Italy
1964	Stanislav Stephashkin, USSR
1968	Antonio Roldan, Mexico
1972	Boris Kousnetsov, USSR
1976	Angel Herrera, Cuba
1980	Rudi Fink, E. Germany
1984	Meldrick Taylor, United States
1988	Giovanni Parisi, Italy
1992	Andreas Tews, Germany
1996	Somluck Kamsing, Thailand
2000	Bekzat Sattarkhanov, Kazakhstan
2004	Alexei Tichtchenko, Russia
2008	Vasyl Lomachenko, Ukraine

Lightweight (60 kg/132 lbs)
1904	Harry Spanger, United States
1908	Frederick Grace, Great Britain
1920	Samuel Mosberg, United States
1924	Hans Nielsen, Denmark
1928	Carlo Orlandi, Italy
1932	Lawrence Stevens, South Africa
1936	Imre Harangi, Hungary
1948	Gerald Dreyer, South Africa
1952	Aureliano Bolognesi, Italy
1956	Richard McTaggart, Great Britain
1960	Kazimierz Pazdzior, Poland
1964	Jozef Grudzien, Poland
1968	Ronald Harris, United States
1972	Jan Szczepanski, Poland
1976	Howard Davis, United States
1980	Angel Herrera, Cuba
1984	Pernell Whitaker, United States
1988	Andreas Zülow, E. Germany
1992	Oscar De La Hoya, United States
1996	Hocine Soltani, Algeria
2000	Mario Kindelan, Cuba
2004	Mario Kindelan, Cuba
2008	Alexey Tishchenko, Russia
2012	Vasyl Lomachenko, Ukraine
2016	Robson Conceição, Brazil

Lt. Welterweight (64 kg/141 lbs)
1952	Charles Adkins, United States
1956	Vladimir Yengibaryan, USSR

Lt. Welterweight (64 kg/141 lbs)
1960	Bohumil Nemecek, Czechoslovakia
1964	Jerzy Kulej, Poland
1968	Jerzy Kulej, Poland
1972	Ray Seales, United States
1976	Ray Leonard, United States
1980	Patrizio Oliva, Italy
1984	Jerry Page, United States
1988	Viatcheslav Janovski, USSR
1992	Hector Vinent, Cuba
1996	Hector Vinent, Cuba
2000	Mahamadkadyz Abdullaev, Uzbekistan
2004	Manus Boonjumnong, Thailand
2008	Felix Diaz, Dominican Republic
2012	Rosniel Iglesias, Cuba
2016	Fazliddin Gaibnazarov, Uzbekistan

Welterweight (69 kg/152 lbs)
1904	Albert Young, United States
1920	Albert Schneider, Canada
1924	Jean Delarge, Belgium
1928	Edward Morgan, New Zealand
1932	Edward Flynn, United States
1936	Sten Suvio, Finland
1948	Julius Torma, Czechoslovakia
1952	Zygmunt Chychia, Poland
1956	Nicolae Linca, Romania
1960	Giovanni Benvenuti, Italy
1964	Marian Kasprzyk, Poland
1968	Manfred Wolke, E. Germany
1972	Emilio Correa, Cuba
1976	Jochen Bachfeld, E. Germany
1980	Andres Aldama, Cuba
1984	Mark Breland, United States
1988	Robert Wangila, Kenya
1992	Michael Carruth, Ireland
1996	Oleg Saitov, Russia
2000	Oleg Saitov, Russia
2004	Artayev Bakhtiyar, Kazakhstan
2008	Bakhyt Sarsekbayev, Kazakhstan
2012	Serik Sapiyev, Kazakhstan
2016	Daniyar Yeleussinov, Kazakhstan

Lt. Middleweight (71 kg/156 lbs)
1952	Laszlo Papp, Hungary
1956	Laszlo Papp, Hungary
1960	Wilbert McClure, United States
1964	Boris Lagutin, USSR
1968	Boris Lagutin, USSR
1972	Dieter Kottysch, W. Germany
1976	Jerzy Rybicki, Poland
1980	Armando Martinez, Cuba
1984	Frank Tate, United States
1988	Park Si-hun, S. Korea
1992	Juan Lemus, Cuba
1996	David Reid, United States
2000	Yermakhan Ibraimov, Kazakhstan

Middleweight (75 kg/165 lbs)
1904	Charles Mayer, United States
1908	John Douglas, Great Britain
1920	Harry Mallin, Great Britain
1924	Harry Mallin, Great Britain

Middleweight (75 kg/165 lbs)

1928	Piero Toscani, Italy
1932	Carmen Barth, United States
1936	Jean Despeaux, France
1948	Laszlo Papp, Hungary
1952	Floyd Patterson, United States
1956	Gennady Schatkov, USSR
1960	Edward Crook, United States
1964	Valery Popenchenko, USSR
1968	Christopher Finnegan, Great Britain
1972	Vyacheslav Lemechev, USSR
1976	Michael Spinks, United States
1980	Jose Gomez, Cuba
1984	Shin Joon-sup, S. Korea
1988	Henry Maske, E. Germany
1992	Ariel Hernandez, Cuba
1996	Ariel Hernandez, Cuba
2000	Jorge Gutierrez, Cuba
2004	Gaydarbek Gaydarbekov, Russia
2008	James Degale, Great Britain
2012	Ryota Murata, Japan
2016	Arlen López, Cuba

Lt. Heavyweight (81 kg/179 lbs)

1920	Edward Eagan, United States
1924	Harry Mitchell, Great Britain
1928	Victor Avendaño, Argentina
1932	David Carstens, South Africa
1936	Roger Michelot, France
1948	George Hunter, South Africa

Lt. Heavyweight (81 kg/179 lbs)

1952	Norvel Lee, United States
1956	James Boyd, United States
1960	Cassius Clay, United States
1964	Cosimo Pinto, Italy
1968	Dan Poznyak, USSR
1972	Mate Parlov, Yugoslavia
1976	Leon Spinks, United States
1980	Slobodan Kacar, Yugoslavia
1984	Anton Josipovic, Yugoslavia
1988	Andrew Maynard, United States
1992	Torsten May, Germany
1996	Vassili Jirov, Kazakhstan
2000	Alexander Lebziak, Russia
2004	Andre Ward, United States
2008	Zhang Xiaoping, China
2012	Yegor Mekhontsev, Russia
2016	Julio César la Cruz, Cuba

Heavyweight (91 kg/201 lbs)

1984	Henry Tillman, United States
1988	Ray Mercer, United States
1992	Felix Savon, Cuba
1996	Felix Savon, Cuba
2000	Felix Savon, Cuba
2004	Odlanier Solis Fonte, Cuba
2008	Rakhim Chakhkiev, Russia
2012	Oleksandr Usik, Ukraine
2016	Evgeny Tishchenko, Russia

Super Heavyweight (91+ kg/201+ lbs)

1904	Samuel Berger, United States
1908	Albert Oldham, Great Britain
1920	Ronald Rawson, Great Britain
1924	Otto von Porat, Norway
1928	Arturo Rodriguez Jurado, Argentina
1932	Santiago Lovell, Argentina
1936	Herbert Runge, Germany
1948	Rafael Iglesias, Argentina
1952	H. Edward Sanders, United States
1956	T. Peter Rademacher, United States
1960	Franco De Piccoli, Italy
1964	Joe Frazier, United States
1968	George Foreman, United States
1972	Teofilo Stevenson, Cuba
1976	Teofilo Stevenson, Cuba
1980	Teofilo Stevenson, Cuba
1984	Tyrell Biggs, United States
1988	Lennox Lewis, Canada
1992	Roberto Balado, Cuba
1996	Vladimir Klitchko, Ukraine
2000	Audley Harrison, Great Britain
2004	Alexander Povetkin, Russia
2008	Roberto Cammarelle, Italy
2012	Anthony Joshua, Great Britain
2016	Tony Yoka, France

Boxing—Women

Flyweight (51 kg/112 lbs)

2012	Nicola Adams, Great Britain
2016	Nicola Adams, Great Britain

Lightweight (60 kg/132 lbs)

2012	Katie Taylor, Ireland
2016	Estelle Mossely, France

Middleweight (75 kg/165 lbs)

2012	Claressa Shields, United States
2016	Claressa Shields, United States

Gymnastics—Men

Floor Exercise

1932	István Pelle, Hungary
1936	Georges Miez, Switzerland
1948	Ferenc Pataki, Hungary
1952	William Thoresson, Sweden
1956	Valentin Muratov, USSR
1960	Nobuyuki Aihara, Japan
1964	Franco Menichelli, Italy
1968	Sawao Kato, Japan
1972	Nikolay Andrianov, USSR
1976	Nikolay Andrianov, USSR
1980	Roland Brückner, E. Germany
1984	Li Ning, China
1988	Serguei Kharikov, USSR
1992	Li Xiaoshuang, China
1996	Ioannis Melissanidis, Greece
2000	Igors Vihrovs, Latvia
2004	Kyle Shewfelt, Canada
2008	Zou Kai, China
2012	Zou Kai, China
2016	Max Whitlock, Great Britain

Horizontal Bar

1896	Hermann Weingärtner, Germany
1904	Anton Heida, United States; Edward Hennig, United States (tie)
1924	Leon Stukelj, Yugoslavia
1928	Georges Miez, Switzerland
1932	Dallas Denver Bixler, United States
1936	Aleksanteri Saarvala, Finland
1948	Josef Stadler, Switzerland
1952	Jakob "Jack" Günthard, Switzerland
1956	Takashi Ono, Japan
1960	Takashi Ono, Japan
1964	Boris Shakhlin, USSR
1968	Akinori Nakayama, Japan; Mikhail Voronin, USSR (tie)
1972	Mitsuo Tsukahara, Japan
1976	Mitsuo Tsukahara, Japan
1980	Stoyan Deltchev, Bulgaria
1984	Shinji Morisue, Japan
1988	Vladimir Artemov, USSR; Valeri Lioukine, USSR (tie)
1992	Trent Dimas, United States
1996	Andreas Wecker, Germany
2000	Alexei Nemov, Russia
2004	Igor Cassina, Italy

Horizontal Bar

2008	Zou Kai, China
2012	Epke Zonderland, Netherlands
2016	Fabian Hambüchen, Germany

Individual All-Around

1900	Gustave Sandras, France
1904	Julius Lenhart, United States
1908	G. Alberto Braglia, Italy
1912	G. Alberto Braglia, Italy
1920	Giorgio Zampori, Italy
1924	Leon Stukelj, Yugoslavia
1928	Georges Miez, Switzerland
1932	Romeo Neri, Italy
1936	Karl-Alfred Schwarzmann, Germany
1948	Veikko Huhtanen, Finland
1952	Viktor Ivanovich Chukarin, USSR
1956	Viktor Ivanovich Chukarin, USSR
1960	Boris Shakhlin, USSR
1964	Yukio Endo, Japan
1968	Sawao Kato, Japan
1972	Sawao Kato, Japan
1976	Nikolay Andrianov, USSR
1980	Aleksandr Dityatin, USSR
1984	Koji Gushiken, Japan
1988	Vladimir Artemov, USSR
1992	Vitaly Scherbo, Unified Team (Belarus)
1996	Li Xiaoshuang, China
2000	Alexei Nemov, Russia
2004	Paul Hamm, United States
2008	Yang Wei, China
2012	Kohei Uchimura, Japan
2016	Kohei Uchimura, Japan

Parallel Bars

1896	Alfred Flatow, Germany
1904	George Eyser, United States
1924	August Güttinger, Switzerland
1928	Ladislav Vacha, Czechoslovakia
1932	Romeo Neri, Italy
1936	Konrad Frey, Germany
1948	Michael Reusch, Switzerland
1952	Hans Eugster, Switzerland
1956	Viktor Ivanovich Chukarin, USSR
1960	Boris Shakhlin, USSR
1964	Yukio Endo, Japan

Parallel Bars

1968	Akinori Nakayama, Japan
1972	Sawao Kato, Japan
1976	Sawao Kato, Japan
1980	Aleksandr Tkachev, USSR
1984	Bart Conner, United States
1988	Vladimir Artemov, USSR
1992	Vitaly Scherbo, Unified Team (Belarus)
1996	Roustam Sharipov, Ukraine
2000	Li Xiaopeng, China
2004	Valeri Goncharov, Ukraine
2008	Li Xiaopeng, China
2012	Feng Zhe, China
2016	Oleg Verniaiev, Ukraine

Pommel Horse

1896	Louis Zutter, Switzerland
1904	Anton Heida, United States
1924	Josef Wilhelm, Switzerland
1928	Hermann Hänggi, Switzerland
1932	István Pelle, Hungary
1936	Konrad Frey, Germany
1948	Paavo Johannes Aaltonen, Finland; Veikko Huhtanen, Finland; Heikki Savolainen, Finland (tie)
1952	Viktor Ivanovich Chukarin, USSR
1956	Boris Shakhlin, USSR
1960	Eugen Georg Oskar Ekman, Finland; Boris Shakhlin, USSR (tie)
1964	Miroslav Cerar, Yugoslavia
1968	Miroslav Cerar, Yugoslavia
1972	Viktor Klimenko, USSR
1976	Zoltan Magyar, Hungary
1980	Zoltan Magyar, Hungary
1984	Li Ning, China; Peter Glen Vidmar, United States (tie)
1988	Dmitri Bilozerchev, USSR; Zsolt Borkai, Hungary; Lubomir Geraskov, Bulgaria (tie)
1992	Pae Gil Su, N. Korea; Vitaly Scherbo, Unified Team (Belarus) (tie)
1996	Li Donghua, Switzerland
2000	Marius Daniel Urzica, Romania

Pommel Horse

2004	Teng Haibin, China
2008	Xiao Qin, China
2012	Krisztián Berki, Hungary
2016	Max Whitlock, Great Britain

Rings

1896	Ioannis Mitropoulos, Greece
1904	Hermann Glass, United States
1924	Francesco Martino, Italy
1928	Leon Stukelj, Yugoslavia
1932	George Julipus Gulack, United States
1936	Alois Hudec, Czechoslovakia
1948	Karl Frei, Switzerland
1952	Grant Shaginyan, USSR
1956	Albert Azaryan, USSR
1960	Albert Azaryan, USSR
1964	Takuji Hayata, Japan
1968	Akinori Nakayama, Japan
1972	Akinori Nakayama, Japan
1976	Nikolay Andrianov, USSR
1980	Aleksandr Dityatin, USSR
1984	Koji Gushiken, Japan; Li Ning, China (tie)
1988	Holger Behrendt, E. Germany; Dmitri Bilozerchev, USSR (tie)
1992	Vitaly Scherbo, Unified Team (Belarus)
1996	Juri Chechi, Italy
2000	Szilveszter Csollany, Hungary
2004	Dimosthenis Tampakos, Greece
2008	Chen Yibing, China

Rings

2012	Arthur Zanetti, Brazil
2016	Eleftherios Petrounias, Greece

Team Competition

1904	United States, United States, United States
1908	Sweden, Norway, Finland
1912	Italy, Hungary, Great Britain
1920	Italy, Belgium, France
1924	Italy, France, Switzerland
1928	Switzerland, Czechoslovakia, Yugoslavia
1932	Italy, United States, Finland
1936	Germany, Switzerland, Finland
1948	Finland, Switzerland, Hungary
1952	USSR, Switzerland, Finland
1956	USSR, Japan, Finland
1960	Japan, USSR, Italy
1964	Japan, USSR, Unified Team of Germany
1968	Japan, USSR, E. Germany
1972	Japan, USSR, E. Germany
1976	Japan, USSR, E. Germany
1980	USSR, E. Germany, Hungary
1984	United States, China, Japan
1988	USSR, E. Germany, Japan
1992	Unified Team, China, Japan
1996	Russia, China, Ukraine
2000	China, Ukraine, Russia
2004	Japan, United States, Romania
2008	China, Japan, United States
2012	China, Japan, Great Britain
2016	Japan, Russia, China

Vault

1896	Carl Schumann, Germany
1904	George Eyser, United States; Anton Heida, United States (tie)
1924	Frank Kriz, United States
1928	Eugen Mack, Switzerland
1932	Savino Guglielmetti, Italy
1936	Karl-Alfred Schwarzmann, Germany
1948	Paavo Johannes Aaltonen, Finland
1952	Viktor Ivanovich Chukarin, USSR
1956	Helmut Bantz, Unified Team of Germany; Valentin Muratov, USSR (tie)
1960	Takashi Ono, Japan; Boris Shakhlin, USSR (tie)
1964	Haruhiro Yamashita, Japan
1968	Mikhail Voronin, USSR
1972	Klaus Köste, E. Germany
1976	Nikolay Andrianov, USSR
1980	Nikolay Andrianov, USSR
1984	Lou Yun, China
1988	Lou Yun, China
1992	Vitaly Scherbo, Unified Team (Belarus)
1996	Alexei Nemov, Russia
2000	Gervasio Deferr, Spain
2004	Gervasio Deferr, Spain
2008	Leszek Blanik, Poland
2012	Yang Hak-seon, South Korea
2016	Ri Se Gwang, North Korea

Gymnastics—Women

Balance Beam

1952	Nina Bocharova, USSR
1956	Agnes Keleti, Hungary
1960	Eva Vechtova-Bosakova, Czechoslovakia
1964	Vera Caslavska, Czechoslovakia
1968	Natalya Kuchinskaya, USSR
1972	Olga Korbut, USSR
1976	Nadia Comaneci, Romania
1980	Nadia Comaneci, Romania
1984	Ecaterina Szabo, Romania; Simona Pauca, Romania (tie)
1988	Daniela Silivas, Romania
1992	Tatiana Lyssenko, Unified Team (Ukraine)
1996	Shannon Miller, United States
2000	Liu Xuan, China
2004	Catalina Ponor, Romania
2008	Shawn Johnson, United States
2012	Deng Linlin, China
2016	Sanne Wevers, Netherlands

Floor Exercise

1952	Agnes Keleti, Hungary
1956	Agnes Keleti, Hungary; Larisa Latynina, USSR (tie)
1960	Larisa Latynina, USSR
1964	Larisa Latynina, USSR
1968	Vera Caslavska, Czechoslovakia; Larisa Petrik, USSR (tie)
1972	Olga Korbut, USSR
1976	Nelli Kim, USSR
1980	Nelli Kim, USSR; Nadia Comaneci, Romania (tie)
1984	Ecaterina Szabo, Romania
1988	Daniela Silivas, Romania
1992	Lavinia Corina Milosovici, Romania
1996	Lilia Podkopayeva, Ukraine
2000	Elena Zamolodchikova, Russia
2004	Catalina Ponor, Romania
2008	Sandra Izbasa, Romania
2012	Aly Raisman, United States
2016	Simone Biles, United States

Individual All-Around

1952	Mariya Gorokhovskaya, USSR
1956	Larisa Latynina, USSR
1960	Larisa Latynina, USSR
1964	Vera Caslavska, Czechoslovakia
1968	Vera Caslavska, Czechoslovakia
1972	Lyudmila Turisheva, USSR
1976	Nadia Comaneci, Romania
1980	Elena Davydova, USSR
1984	Mary-Lou Retton, United States
1988	Elena Shushunova, USSR
1992	Tatiana Goutsou, Unified Team (Ukraine)
1996	Lilia Podkopayeva, Ukraine
2000	Simona Amanar, Romania
2004	Carly Patterson, United States
2008	Nastia Liukin, United States
2012	Gabby Douglas, United States
2016	Simone Biles, United States

Team Competition

1928	Netherlands, Italy, Great Britain
1936	Germany, Czechoslovakia, Hungary
1948	Czechoslovakia, Hungary, United States
1952	USSR, Hungary, Czechoslovakia
1956	USSR, Hungary, Romania
1960	USSR, Czechoslovakia, Romania
1964	USSR, Czechoslovakia, Japan
1968	USSR, Czechoslovakia, E. Germany
1972	USSR, E. Germany, Hungary
1976	USSR, Romania, E. Germany
1980	USSR, Romania, E. Germany
1984	Romania, United States, China
1988	USSR, Romania, E. Germany
1992	Unified Team, Romania, United States
1996	United States, Russia, Romania
2000	Romania, Russia, United States
2004	Romania, United States, Russia
2008	China, United States, Romania

Team Competition

2012	United States, Russia, Romania
2016	United States, Russia, China

Uneven Bars

1952	Margit Korondi, Hungary
1956	Agnes Keleti, Hungary
1960	Polina Astakhova, USSR
1964	Polina Astakhova, USSR
1968	Vera Caslavska, Czechoslovakia
1972	Karin Janz, E. Germany
1976	Nadia Comaneci, Romania
1980	Maxi Gnauck, E. Germany
1984	Julianne McNamara, United States; Yan-Hong Ma, China (tie)
1988	Daniela Silivas, Romania
1992	Lu Li, China
1996	Svetlana Khorkina, Russia
2000	Svetlana Khorkina, Russia
2004	Emilie LePennec, France
2008	He Kexin, China
2012	Aliya Mustafina, Russia
2016	Aliya Mustafina, Russia

Vault

1952	Ekaterina Kalinchuk, USSR
1956	Larisa Latynina, USSR
1960	Margarita Nikolaeva, USSR
1964	Vera Caslavska, Czechoslovakia
1968	Vera Caslavska, Czechoslovakia
1972	Karin Janz, E. Germany
1976	Nelli Kim, USSR
1980	Natalia Shaposhnikova, USSR
1984	Ecaterina Szabo, Romania
1988	Svetlana Boginskaya, USSR
1992	Henrietta Onodi, Hungary; Lavinia Milosovici, Romania (tie)
1996	Simona Amanar, Romania
2000	Elena Zamolodchikova, Russia
2004	Monica Rosu, Romania
2008	Hong Un Jong, N. Korea
2012	Sandra Izbaşa, Romania
2016	Simone Biles, United States

Soccer

Men

1900	Great Britain, France, Belgium
1904	Canada, United States, United States
1908	Great Britain, Denmark, Netherlands
1912	Great Britain, Denmark, Netherlands
1920	Belgium, Spain, Netherlands
1924	Uruguay, Switzerland, Sweden

Men

1928	Uruguay, Argentina, Italy
1936	Italy, Austria, Norway
1948	Sweden, Yugoslavia, Denmark
1952	Hungary, Yugoslavia, Sweden
1956	USSR, Yugoslavia, Bulgaria
1960	Yugoslavia, Denmark, Hungary

Men

1964	Hungary, Czechoslovakia, Unified Team of Germany
1968	Hungary, Bulgaria, Japan
1972	Poland; Hungary, E. Germany (tie for bronze)
1976	E. Germany, Poland, USSR

Men			**Men**			**Women**	
1980	Czechoslovakia, E. Germany, USSR		2000	Cameroon, Spain, Chile		1996	United States, China, Norway
1984	France, Brazil, Yugoslavia		2004	Argentina, Paraguay, Italy		2000	Norway, United States, Germany
1988	USSR, Brazil, W. Germany		2008	Argentina, Nigeria, Brazil		2004	United States, Brazil, Germany
1992	Spain, Poland, Ghana		2012	Mexico, Brazil, South Korea		2008	United States, Brazil, Germany
1996	Nigeria, Argentina, Brazil		2016	Brazil, Germany, Nigeria		2012	United States, Japan, Canada
						2016	Germany, Sweden, Canada

Swimming and Diving—Men

50-Meter Freestyle — Time

1988	Matt Biondi, United States	0:22.14
1992	Aleksandr Popov, Unified Team	0:21.91
1996	Aleksandr Popov, Russia	0:22.13
2000	Anthony Ervin, United States	0:21.98
	Gary Hall Jr., United States (tie)	0:21.98
2004	Gary Hall Jr., United States	0:21.93
2008	Cesar Cielo Filho, Brazil	0:21.30*
2012	Florent Manaudou, France	0:21.34
2016	Anthony Ervin, United States	0:21.40

100-Meter Freestyle — Time

1896	Alfred Hajos, Hungary	1:22.2
1904	Zoltan de Halmay, Hungary (100 yds)	1:02.8
1908	Charles Daniels, United States	1:05.6
1912	Duke P. Kahanamoku, United States	1:03.4
1920	Duke P. Kahanamoku, United States	1:01.4
1924	Johnny Weissmuller, United States	0:59.0
1928	Johnny Weissmuller, United States	0:58.6
1932	Yasuji Miyazaki, Japan	0:58.2
1936	Ferenc Csik, Hungary	0:57.6
1948	Wally Ris, United States	0:57.3
1952	Clark Scholes, United States	0:57.4
1956	Jon Henricks, Australia	0:55.4
1960	John Devitt, Australia	0:55.2
1964	Don Schollander, United States	0:53.4
1968	Mike Wenden, Australia	0:52.2
1972	Mark Spitz, United States	0:51.22
1976	Jim Montgomery, United States	0:49.99
1980	Jorg Woithe, E. Germany	0:50.40
1984	Ambrose "Rowdy" Gaines, United States	0:49.80
1988	Matt Biondi, United States	0:48.63
1992	Aleksandr Popov, Unified Team	0:49.02
1996	Aleksandr Popov, Russia	0:48.74
2000	Pieter van den Hoogenband, Netherlands	0:48.30
2004	Pieter van den Hoogenband, Netherlands	0:48.17
2008	Alain Bernard, France	0:47.21
2012	Nathan Adrian, United States	0:47.52
2016	Kyle Chalmers, Australia	0:47.58

200-Meter Freestyle — Time

1968	Mike Wenden, Australia	1:55.2
1972	Mark Spitz, United States	1:52.78
1976	Bruce Furniss, United States	1:50.29
1980	Sergei Kopliakov, USSR	1:49.81
1984	Michael Gross, W. Germany	1:47.44
1988	Duncan Armstrong, Australia	1:47.25
1992	Yevgeny Sadovyi, Unified Team	1:46.70
1996	Danyon Loader, New Zealand	1:47.63
2000	Pieter van den Hoogenband, Netherlands	1:45.35
2004	Ian Thorpe, Australia	1:44.71
2008	Michael Phelps, United States	1:42.96*
2012	Yannick Agnel, France	1:43.14
2016	Sun Yang, China	1:44.65

400-Meter Freestyle — Time

1904	C. M. Daniels, United States (440 yds)	6:16.2
1908	Henry Taylor, Great Britain	5:36.8
1912	George Hodgson, Canada	5:24.4
1920	Norman Ross, United States	5:26.8
1924	Johnny Weissmuller, United States	5:04.2
1928	Albert Zorilla, Argentina	5:01.6
1932	Clarence Crabbe, United States	4:48.4
1936	Jack Medica, United States	4:44.5
1948	William Smith, United States	4:41.0
1952	Jean Boiteux, France	4:30.7
1956	Murray Rose, Australia	4:27.3
1960	Murray Rose, Australia	4:18.3
1964	Don Schollander, United States	4:12.2
1968	Mike Burton, United States	4:09.0
1972	Brad Cooper, Australia	4:00.27
1976	Brian Goodell, United States	3:51.93
1980	Vladimir Salnikov, USSR	3:51.31
1984	George DiCarlo, United States	3:51.23
1988	Ewe Dassler, E. Germany	3:46.95
1992	Yevgeny Sadovyi, Unified Team	3:45.00
1996	Danyon Loader, New Zealand	3:47.97
2000	Ian Thorpe, Australia	3:40.59
2004	Ian Thorpe, Australia	3:43.10
2008	Park Tae-hwan, S. Korea	3:41.86

400-Meter Freestyle — Time

2012	Sun Yang, China	3:40.14*
2016	Mack Horton, Australia	3:41.55

1500-Meter Freestyle — Time

1908	Henry Taylor, Great Britain	22:48.4
1912	George Hodgson, Canada	22:00.0
1920	Norman Ross, United States	22:23.2
1924	Johnny Charlton, Australia	20:06.6
1928	Arne Borg, Sweden	19:51.8
1932	Kusuo Kitamura, Japan	19:12.4
1936	Noboru Terada, Japan	19:13.7
1948	James McLane, United States	19:18.5
1952	Ford Konno, United States	18:30.3
1956	Murray Rose, Australia	17:58.9
1960	Jon Konrads, Australia	17:19.6
1964	Robert Windle, Australia	17:01.7
1968	Mike Burton, United States	16:38.9
1972	Mike Burton, United States	15:52.58
1976	Brian Goodell, United States	15:02.40
1980	Vladimir Salnikov, USSR	14:58.27
1984	Michael O'Brien, United States	15:05.20
1988	Vladimir Salnikov, USSR	15:00.40
1992	Kieren Perkins, Australia	14:43.48
1996	Kieren Perkins, Australia	14:56.40
2000	Grant Hackett, Australia	14:48.33
2004	Grant Hackett, Australia	14:43.40
2008	Oussama Mellouli, Tunisia	14:40.84
2012	Sun Yang, China	14:31.02*
2016	Gregorio Paltrinieri, Italy	14:34.57

100-Meter Backstroke — Time

1904	Walter Brack, Germany (100 yds)	1:16.8
1908	Arno Bieberstein, Germany	1:24.6
1912	Harry Hebner, United States	1:21.2
1920	Warren Kealoha, United States	1:15.2
1924	Warren Kealoha, United States	1:13.2
1928	George Kojac, United States	1:08.2
1932	Masaji Kiyokawa, Japan	1:08.6
1936	Adolph Kiefer, United States	1:05.9
1948	Allen Stack, United States	1:06.4
1952	Yoshi Oyakawa, United States	1:05.4
1956	David Thiele, Australia	1:02.2
1960	David Thiele, Australia	1:01.9
1968	Roland Matthes, E. Germany	0:58.7
1972	Roland Matthes, E. Germany	0:56.58
1976	John Naber, United States	0:55.49
1980	Bengt Baron, Sweden	0:56.33
1984	Rick Carey, United States	0:55.79
1988	Daichi Suzuki, Japan	0:55.05
1992	Mark Tewksbury, Canada	0:53.98
1996	Jeff Rouse, United States	0:54.10
2000	Lenny Krayzelburg, United States	0:53.72
2004	Aaron Peirsol, United States	0:54.06
2008	Aaron Peirsol, United States	0:52.54
2012	Matt Grevers, United States	0:52.16
2016	Ryan Murphy, United States	0:51.97*

200-Meter Backstroke — Time

1964	Jed Graef, United States	2:10.3
1968	Roland Matthes, E. Germany	2:09.6
1972	Roland Matthes, E. Germany	2:02.82
1976	John Naber, United States	1:59.19
1980	Sandor Wladar, Hungary	2:01.93
1984	Rick Carey, United States	2:00.23
1988	Igor Polianski, USSR	1:59.37
1992	Martin Lopez-Zubero, Spain	1:58.47
1996	Brad Bridgewater, United States	1:58.54
2000	Lenny Krayzelburg, United States	1:56.76
2004	Aaron Peirsol, United States	1:54.95
2008	Ryan Lochte, United States	1:53.94
2012	Tyler Clary, United States	1:53.41*
2016	Ryan Murphy, United States	1:53.62

100-Meter Breaststroke — Time

1968	Don McKenzie, United States	1:07.79
1972	Nobutaka Taguchi, Japan	1:04.94
1976	John Hencken, United States	1:03.11
1980	Duncan Goodhew, Great Britain	1:03.44
1984	Steve Lundquist, United States	1:01.65
1988	Adrian Moorhouse, Great Britain	1:02.04
1992	Nelson Diebel, United States	1:01.50

100-Meter Breaststroke

		Time
1996	Fred Deburghgraeve, Belgium	1:00.60
2000	Domenico Fioravanti, Italy	1:00.46
2004	Kosuke Kitajima, Japan	1:00.08
2008	Kosuke Kitajima, Japan	0:58.91
2012	Cameron van der Burgh, South Africa	0:58.46
2016	Adam Peaty, Great Britain	0:57.13*

200-Meter Breaststroke

		Time
1908	Frederick Holman, Great Britain	3:09.2
1912	Walter Bathe, Germany	3:01.8
1920	Haken Malmroth, Sweden	3:04.4
1924	Robert Skelton, United States	2:56.6
1928	Yoshiyuki Tsuruta, Japan	2:48.8
1932	Yoshiyuki Tsuruta, Japan	2:45.4
1936	Tetsuo Hamuro, Japan	2:41.5
1948	Joseph Verdeur, United States	2:39.3
1952	John Davies, Australia	2:34.4
1956	Masura Furukawa, Japan	2:34.7
1960	William Mulliken, United States	2:37.4
1964	Ian O'Brien, Australia	2:27.8
1968	Felipe Munoz, Mexico	2:28.7
1972	John Hencken, United States	2:21.55
1976	David Wilkie, Great Britain	2:15.11
1980	Robertas Zhulpa, USSR	2:15.85
1984	Victor Davis, Canada	2:13.34
1988	Jozsef Szabo, Hungary	2:13.52
1992	Mike Barrowman, United States	2:10.16
1996	Norbert Rozsa, Hungary	2:12.57
2000	Domenico Fioravanti, Italy	2:10.87
2004	Kosuke Kitajima, Japan	2:09.44
2008	Kosuke Kitajima, Japan	2:07.64
2012	Dániel Gyurta, Hungary	2:07.28
2016	Dmitriy Balandin, Kazakhstan	2:07.46

100-Meter Butterfly

		Time
1968	Doug Russell, United States	0:55.9
1972	Mark Spitz, United States	0:54.27
1976	Matt Vogel, United States	0:54.35
1980	Par Arvidsson, Sweden	0:54.92
1984	Michael Gross, W. Germany	0:53.08
1988	Anthony Nesty, Suriname	0:53.00
1992	Pablo Morales, United States	0:53.32
1996	Denis Pankratov, Russia	0:52.27
2000	Lars Froelander, Sweden	0:52.00
2004	Michael Phelps, United States	0:51.25
2008	Michael Phelps, United States	0:50.58
2012	Michael Phelps, United States	0:51.21
2016	Joseph Schooling, Singapore	0:50.39*

200-Meter Butterfly

		Time
1956	William Yorzyk, United States	2:19.3
1960	Michael Troy, United States	2:12.8
1964	Kevin J. Berry, Australia	2:06.6
1968	Carl Robie, United States	2:08.7
1972	Mark Spitz, United States	2:00.70
1976	Mike Bruner, United States	1:59.23
1980	Sergei Fesenko, USSR	1:59.76
1984	Jon Sieben, Australia	1:57.04
1988	Michael Gross, W. Germany	1:56.94
1992	Mel Stewart, United States	1:56.26
1996	Denis Pankratov, Russia	1:56.51
2000	Tom Malchow, United States	1:55.35
2004	Michael Phelps, United States	1:54.04
2008	Michael Phelps, United States	1:52.03*
2012	Chad le Clos, South Africa	1:52.96
2016	Michael Phelps, United States	1:53.36

200-Meter Individual Medley

		Time
1968	Charles Hickcox, United States	2:12.0
1972	Gunnar Larsson, Sweden	2:07.17
1984	Alex Baumann, Canada	2:01.42
1988	Tamas Darnyi, Hungary	2:00.17
1992	Tamas Darnyi, Hungary	2:00.76
1996	Attila Czene, Hungary	1:59.91
2000	Massimiliano Rosolino, Italy	1:58.98
2004	Michael Phelps, United States	1:57.14
2008	Michael Phelps, United States	1:54.23*
2012	Michael Phelps, United States	1:54.27
2016	Michael Phelps, United States	1:54.66

400-Meter Individual Medley

		Time
1964	Dick Roth, United States	4:45.4
1968	Charles Hickcox, United States	4:48.4
1972	Gunnar Larsson, Sweden	4:31.98
1976	Rod Strachan, United States	4:23.68
1980	Aleksandr Sidorenko, USSR	4:22.89
1984	Alex Baumann, Canada	4:17.41
1988	Tamas Darnyi, Hungary	4:14.75
1992	Tamas Darnyi, Hungary	4:14.23
1996	Tom Dolan, United States	4:14.90
2000	Tom Dolan, United States	4:11.76

400-Meter Individual Medley

		Time
2004	Michael Phelps, United States	4:08.26
2008	Michael Phelps, United States	4:03.84*
2012	Ryan Lochte, United States	4:05.18
2016	Kosuke Hagino, Japan	4:06.05

4x100-Meter Freestyle Relay

		Time
1964	United States	3:31.2
1968	United States	3:31.7
1972	United States	3:26.42
1984	United States	3:19.03
1988	United States	3:16.53
1992	United States	3:16.74
1996	United States	3:15.41
2000	Australia	3:13.67
2004	South Africa	3:13.17
2008	United States	3:08.24*
2012	France	3:09.93
2016	United States	3:09.02

4x200-Meter Freestyle Relay

		Time
1908	Great Britain	10:55.6
1912	Australasia (Australia and New Zealand)	10:11.6
1920	United States	10:04.4
1924	United States	9:53.4
1928	United States	9:36.2
1932	Japan	8:58.4
1936	Japan	8:51.5
1948	United States	8:46.0
1952	United States	8:31.1
1956	Australia	8:23.6
1960	United States	8:10.2
1964	United States	7:52.1
1968	United States	7:52.33
1972	United States	7:35.78
1976	United States	7:23.22
1980	USSR	7:23.50
1984	United States	7:15.69
1988	United States	7:12.51
1992	Unified Team	7:11.95
1996	United States	7:14.84
2000	Australia	7:07.05
2004	United States	7:07.33
2008	United States	6:58.56*
2012	United States	6:59.70
2016	United States	7:00.66

4x100-Meter Medley Relay

		Time
1960	United States	4:05.4
1964	United States	3:58.4
1968	United States	3:54.9
1972	United States	3:48.16
1976	United States	3:42.22
1980	Australia	3:45.70
1984	United States	3:39.30
1988	United States	3:36.93
1992	United States	3:36.93
1996	United States	3:34.84
2000	United States	3:33.73
2004	United States	3:30.68
2008	United States	3:29.34
2012	United States	3:29.35
2016	United States	3:27.95*

10-Kilometer Marathon

		Time
2008	Maarten van der Weijden, Netherlands	1:51:51.6
2012	Oussama Mellouli, Tunisia	1:49:55.1
2016	Ferry Weertman, Netherlands	1:52:59.8

Platform Diving

		Points
1904	Dr. G. E. Sheldon, United States	112.75
1908	Hjalmar Johansson, Sweden	183.75
1912	Erik Adlerz, Sweden	73.94
1920	Clarence Pinkston, United States	100.67
1924	Albert White, United States	97.46
1928	Pete Desjardins, United States	98.74
1932	Harold Smith, United States	124.80
1936	Marshall Wayne, United States	113.58
1948	Sammy Lee, United States	130.05
1952	Sammy Lee, United States	156.28
1956	Joaquin Capilla, Mexico	152.44
1960	Robert Webster, United States	165.56
1964	Robert Webster, United States	148.58
1968	Klaus Dibiasi, Italy	164.18
1972	Klaus Dibiasi, Italy	504.12
1976	Klaus Dibiasi, Italy	600.51
1980	Falk Hoffmann, E. Germany	835.65
1984	Greg Louganis, United States	710.91
1988	Greg Louganis, United States	638.61
1992	Sun Shuwei, China	677.31
1996	Dmitri Sautin, Russia	692.34
2000	Tian Liang, China	724.53
2004	Hu Jia, China	748.08
2008	Matthew Mitcham, Australia	537.95

Platform Diving	Points
2012 David Boudia, United States	568.65
2016 Chen Aisen, China	545.35

Springboard Diving	Points
1908 Albert Zurner, Germany	85.50
1912 Paul Guenther, Germany	79.23
1920 Louis Kuehn, United States	675.40
1924 Albert White, United States	97.46
1928 Pete Desjardins, United States	185.04
1932 Michael Galitzen, United States	161.38
1936 Richard Degener, United States	163.57
1948 Bruce Harlan, United States	163.64
1952 David Browning, United States	205.29
1956 Robert Clotworthy, United States	159.56
1960 Gary Tobian, United States	170.00
1964 Kenneth Sitzberger, United States	159.90
1968 Bernie Wrightson, United States	170.15
1972 Vladimir Vasin, USSR	594.09
1976 Phil Boggs, United States	619.52
1980 Aleksandr Portnov, USSR	905.02
1984 Greg Louganis, United States	754.41
1988 Greg Louganis, United States	730.80

Springboard Diving	Points
1992 Mark Lenzi, United States	676.53
1996 Xiong Ni, China	701.46
2000 Xiong Ni, China	708.72
2004 Peng Bo, China	787.30
2008 He Chong, China	572.90
2012 Ilya Zakharov, Russia	555.90
2016 Cao Yuan, China	547.60

Synchronized Platform Diving	Points
2004 Tian Liang & Yang Jinghui, China	383.88
2008 Lin Yue & Huo Liang, China	468.18
2012 Cao Yuan & Zhang Yanquan, China	486.78
2016 Chen Aisen & Lin Yue, China	496.98

Synchronized Springboard Diving	Points
2004 Nikolaos Siranidis & Thomas Bimis, Greece	353.34
2008 Wang Feng & Qin Kai, China	469.08
2012 Luo Yutong & Qin Kai, China	477.00
2016 Jack Laugher & Chris Mears, Great Britain	454.32

Swimming and Diving—Women

50-Meter Freestyle	Time
1988 Kristin Otto, E. Germany	0:25.49
1992 Yang Wenyi, China	0:24.76
1996 Amy Van Dyken, United States	0:24.87
2000 Inge de Bruijn, Netherlands	0:24.32
2004 Inge de Bruijn, Netherlands	0:24.58
2008 Britta Steffen, Germany	0:24.06
2012 Ranomi Kromowidjojo, Netherlands	0:24.05*
2016 Pernille Blume, Denmark	0:24.07

100-Meter Freestyle	Time
1912 Fanny Durack, Australia	1:22.2
1920 Ethelda Bleibtrey, United States	1:13.6
1924 Ethel Lackie, United States	1:12.4
1928 Albina Osipowich, United States	1:11.0
1932 Helene Madison, United States	1:06.8
1936 Hendrika Mastenbroek, Netherlands	1:05.9
1948 Greta Andersen, Denmark	1:06.3
1952 Katalin Szoke, Hungary	1:06.8
1956 Dawn Fraser, Australia	1:02.0
1960 Dawn Fraser, Australia	1:01.2
1964 Dawn Fraser, Australia	0:59.5
1968 Jan Henne, United States	1:00.0
1972 Sandra Neilson, United States	0:58.59
1976 Kornelia Ender, E. Germany	0:55.65
1980 Barbara Krause, E. Germany	0:54.79
1984 Carrie Steinseifer, United States	0:55.92
Nancy Hogshead, United States (tie)	0:55.92
1988 Kristin Otto, E. Germany	0:54.93
1992 Zhuang Yong, China	0:54.64
1996 Li Jingyi, China	0:54.50
2000 Inge de Bruijn, Netherlands	0:53.83
2004 Jodie Henry, Australia	0:53.84
2008 Britta Steffen, Germany	0:53.12
2012 Ranomi Kromowidjojo, Netherlands	0:53.00
2016 Simone Manuel, United States; Penny Oleksiak, Canada (tie)	0:52.70*

200-Meter Freestyle	Time
1968 Debbie Meyer, United States	2:10.5
1972 Shane Gould, Australia	2:03.56
1976 Kornelia Ender, E. Germany	1:59.26
1980 Barbara Krause, E. Germany	1:58.33
1984 Mary Wayte, United States	1:59.23
1988 Heike Friedrich, E. Germany	1:57.65
1992 Nicole Haislett, United States	1:57.90
1996 Claudia Poll, Costa Rica	1:58.16
2000 Susan O'Neill, Australia	1:58.24
2004 Camelia Potec, Romania	1:58.03
2008 Federica Pellegrini, Italy	1:54.82
2012 Allison Schmitt, United States	1:53.61*
2016 Katie Ledecky, United States	1:53.73

400-Meter Freestyle	Time
1924 Martha Norelius, United States	6:02.2
1928 Martha Norelius, United States	5:42.8
1932 Helene Madison, United States	5:28.5
1936 Hendrika Mastenbroek, Netherlands	5:26.4
1948 Ann Curtis, United States	5:17.8
1952 Valerie Gyenge, Hungary	5:12.1
1956 Lorraine Crapp, Australia	4:54.6
1960 Chris von Saltza, United States	4:50.6
1964 Virginia Duenkel, United States	4:43.3
1968 Debbie Meyer, United States	4:31.8
1972 Shane Gould, Australia	4:19.44

400-Meter Freestyle	Time
1976 Petra Thuemer, E. Germany	4:09.89
1980 Ines Diers, E. Germany	4:08.76
1984 Tiffany Cohen, United States	4:07.10
1988 Janet Evans, United States	4:03.85
1992 Dagmar Hase, Germany	4:07.18
1996 Michelle Smith, Ireland	4:07.25
2000 Brooke Bennett, United States	4:05.80
2004 Laure Manaudou, France	4:05.34
2008 Rebecca Adlington, Great Britain	4:03.22
2012 Camille Muffat, France	4:01.45
2016 Katie Ledecky, United States	3:56.46*

800-Meter Freestyle	Time
1968 Debbie Meyer, United States	9:24.0
1972 Keena Rothhammer, United States	8:53.68
1976 Petra Thuemer, E. Germany	8:37.14
1980 Michelle Ford, Australia	8:28.90
1984 Tiffany Cohen, United States	8:24.95
1988 Janet Evans, United States	8:20.20
1992 Janet Evans, United States	8:25.52
1996 Brooke Bennett, United States	8:27.89
2000 Brooke Bennett, United States	8:19.67
2004 Ai Shibata, Japan	8:24.54
2008 Rebecca Adlington, Great Britain	8:14.10
2012 Katie Ledecky, United States	8:14.63
2016 Katie Ledecky, United States	8:04.79*

100-Meter Backstroke	Time
1924 Sybil Bauer, United States	1:23.2
1928 Marie Braun, Netherlands	1:22.0
1932 Eleanor Holm, United States	1:19.4
1936 Dina Senff, Netherlands	1:18.9
1948 Karen Harup, Denmark	1:14.4
1952 Joan Harrison, South Africa	1:14.3
1956 Judy Grinham, Great Britain	1:12.9
1960 Lynn Burke, United States	1:09.3
1964 Cathy Ferguson, United States	1:07.7
1968 Kaye Hall, United States	1:06.2
1972 Melissa Belote, United States	1:05.78
1976 Ulrike Richter, E. Germany	1:01.83
1980 Rica Reinisch, E. Germany	1:00.86
1984 Theresa Andrews, United States	1:02.55
1988 Kristin Otto, E. Germany	1:00.89
1992 Krisztina Egerszegi, Hungary	1:00.68
1996 Beth Botsford, United States	1:01.19
2000 Diana Mocanu, Romania	1:00.21
2004 Natalie Coughlin, United States	1:00.37
2008 Natalie Coughlin, United States	0:58.96
2012 Missy Franklin, United States	0:58.33
2016 Katinka Hosszú, Hungary	0:58.45

200-Meter Backstroke	Time
1968 Pokey Watson, United States	2:24.8
1972 Melissa Belote, United States	2:19.19
1976 Ulrike Richter, E. Germany	2:13.43
1980 Rica Reinisch, E. Germany	2:11.77
1984 Jolanda De Rover, Netherlands	2:12.38
1988 Krisztina Egerszegi, Hungary	2:09.29
1992 Krisztina Egerszegi, Hungary	2:07.06
1996 Krisztina Egerszegi, Hungary	2:07.83
2000 Diana Mocanu, Romania	2:08.16
2004 Kirsty Coventry, Zimbabwe	2:09.19
2008 Kirsty Coventry, Zimbabwe	2:05.24
2012 Missy Franklin, United States	2:04.06*
2016 Maya DiRado, United States	2:05.99

100-Meter Breaststroke

Year	Champion	Time
1968	Djurdjica Bjedov, Yugoslavia	1:15.8
1972	Cathy Carr, United States	1:13.58
1976	Hannelore Anke, E. Germany	1:11.16
1980	Ute Geweniger, E. Germany	1:10.22
1984	Petra Van Staveren, Netherlands	1:09.88
1988	Tania Dangalakova, Bulgaria	1:07.95
1992	Yelena Rudkovskaya, Unified Team (Bel.)	1:08.00
1996	Penny Heyns, South Africa	1:07.73
2000	Megan Quann, United States	1:07.05
2004	Luo Xuejuan, China	1:06.64
2008	Leisel Jones, Australia	1:05.17
2012	Rūta Meilutytė, Lithuania	1:05.47
2016	Lilly King, United States	1:04.93*

200-Meter Breaststroke

Year	Champion	Time
1924	Lucy Morton, Great Britain	3:33.2
1928	Hilde Schrader, Germany	3:12.6
1932	Clare Dennis, Australia	3:06.3
1936	Hideko Maehata, Japan	3:03.6
1948	Nelly Van Vliet, Netherlands	2:57.2
1952	Eva Szekely, Hungary	2:51.7
1956	Ursula Happe, Germany	2:53.1
1960	Anita Lonsbrough, Great Britain	2:49.5
1964	Galina Prozumenschikova, USSR	2:46.4
1968	Sharon Wichman, United States	2:44.4
1972	Beverly Whitfield, Australia	2:41.71
1976	Marina Koshevaia, USSR	2:33.35
1980	Lina Kachushite, USSR	2:29.54
1984	Anne Ottenbrite, Canada	2:30.38
1988	Silke Hoerner, E. Germany	2:26.71
1992	Kyoko Iwasaki, Japan	2:26.65
1996	Penny Heyns, South Africa	2:25.41
2000	Agnes Kovacs, Hungary	2:24.35
2004	Amanda Beard, United States	2:23.37
2008	Rebecca Soni, United States	2:20.22
2012	Rebecca Soni, United States	2:19.59*
2016	Rie Kaneto, Japan	2:20.30

100-Meter Butterfly

Year	Champion	Time
1956	Shelley Mann, United States	1:11.0
1960	Carolyn Schuler, United States	1:09.5
1964	Sharon Stouder, United States	1:04.7
1968	Lynn McClements, Australia	1:05.5
1972	Mayumi Aoki, Japan	1:03.34
1976	Kornelia Ender, E. Germany	1:00.13
1980	Caren Metschuck, E. Germany	1:00.42
1984	Mary T. Meagher, United States	0:59.26
1988	Kristin Otto, E. Germany	0:59.00
1992	Qian Hong, China	0:58.62
1996	Amy Van Dyken, United States	0:59.13
2000	Inge de Bruijn, Netherlands	0:56.61
2004	Petria Thomas, Australia	0:57.72
2008	Lisbeth Trickett, Australia	0:56.73
2012	Dana Vollmer, United States	0:55.98
2016	Sarah Sjöström, Sweden	0:55.48*

200-Meter Butterfly

Year	Champion	Time
1968	Ada Kok, Netherlands	2:24.7
1972	Karen Moe, United States	2:15.57
1976	Andrea Pollack, E. Germany	2:11.41
1980	Ines Geissler, E. Germany	2:10.44
1984	Mary T. Meagher, United States	2:06.90
1988	Kathleen Nord, E. Germany	2:09.51
1992	Summer Sanders, United States	2:08.67
1996	Susan O'Neill, Australia	2:07.76
2000	Misty Hyman, United States	2:05.88
2004	Otylia Jedrzejczak, Poland	2:06.05
2008	Liu Zige, China	2:04.18
2012	Jiao Liuyang, China	2:04.06*
2016	Mireia Belmonte, Spain	2:04.85

200-Meter Individual Medley

Year	Champion	Time
1968	Claudia Kolb, United States	2:24.7
1972	Shane Gould, Australia	2:23.07
1984	Tracy Caulkins, United States	2:12.64
1988	Daniela Hunger, E. Germany	2:12.59
1992	Lin Li, China	2:11.65
1996	Michelle Smith, Ireland	2:13.93
2000	Yana Klochkova, Ukraine	2:10.68
2004	Yana Klochkova, Ukraine	2:11.14
2008	Stephanie Rice, Australia	2:08.45
2012	Ye Shiwen, China	2:07.57
2016	Katinka Hosszú, Hungary	2:06.58*

400-Meter Individual Medley

Year	Champion	Time
1964	Donna de Varona, United States	5:18.7
1968	Claudia Kolb, United States	5:08.5
1972	Gail Neall, Australia	5:02.97
1976	Ulrike Tauber, E. Germany	4:42.77
1980	Petra Schneider, E. Germany	4:36.29
1984	Tracy Caulkins, United States	4:39.24
1988	Janet Evans, United States	4:37.76
1992	Krisztina Egerszegi, Hungary	4:36.54
1996	Michelle Smith, Ireland	4:39.18
2000	Yana Klochkova, Ukraine	4:33.59
2004	Yana Klochkova, Ukraine	4:34.83
2008	Stephanie Rice, Australia	4:29.45
2012	Ye Shiwen, China	4:28.43
2016	Katinka Hosszú, Hungary	4:26.36*

4x100-Meter Freestyle Relay

Year	Champion	Time
1912	Great Britain	5:52.8
1920	United States	5:11.6
1924	United States	4:58.8
1928	United States	4:47.6
1932	United States	4:38.0
1936	Netherlands	4:36.0
1948	United States	4:29.2
1952	Hungary	4:24.4
1956	Australia	4:17.1
1960	United States	4:08.9
1964	United States	4:03.8
1968	United States	4:02.5
1972	United States	3:55.19
1976	United States	3:44.82
1980	East Germany	3:42.71
1984	United States	3:43.43
1988	East Germany	3:40.63
1992	United States	3:39.46
1996	United States	3:39.29
2000	United States	3:36.61
2004	Australia	3:35.94
2008	Netherlands	3:33.76
2012	Australia	3:33.15
2016	Australia	3:30.65*

4x200-Meter Freestyle Relay

Year	Champion	Time
1996	United States	7:59.87
2000	United States	7:57.80
2004	United States	7:53.42
2008	Australia	7:44.31
2012	United States	7:42.92*
2016	United States	7:43.03

4x100-Meter Medley Relay

Year	Champion	Time
1960	United States	4:41.1
1964	United States	4:33.9
1968	United States	4:28.3
1972	United States	4:20.75
1976	East Germany	4:07.95
1980	East Germany	4:06.67
1984	United States	4:08.34
1988	East Germany	4:03.74
1992	United States	4:02.54
1996	United States	4:02.88
2000	United States	3:58.30
2004	Australia	3:57.32
2008	Australia	3:52.69
2012	United States	3:52.05*
2016	United States	3:53.13

10-Kilometer Marathon

Year	Champion	Time
2008	Larisa Ilchenko, Russia	1:59:27.7
2012	Éva Risztov, Hungary	1:57:38.2
2016	Sharon van Rouwendaal, Netherlands	1:56:32.1

Platform Diving

Year	Champion	Points
1912	Greta Johansson, Sweden	39.90
1920	Stefani Fryland-Clausen, Denmark	34.60
1924	Caroline Smith, United States	33.20
1928	Elizabeth B. Pinkston, United States	31.60
1932	Dorothy Poynton, United States	40.26
1936	Dorothy Poynton Hill, United States	33.93
1948	Victoria M. Draves, United States	68.87
1952	Patricia McCormick, United States	79.37
1956	Patricia McCormick, United States	84.85
1960	Ingrid Kramer, Germany	91.28
1964	Lesley Bush, United States	99.80
1968	Milena Duchkova, Czechoslovakia	109.59
1972	Ulrika Knape, Sweden	390.00
1976	Elena Vaytsekhouskaya, USSR	406.59
1980	Martina Jaschke, E. Germany	596.25
1984	Zhou Jihong, China	435.51
1988	Xu Yanmei, China	445.20
1992	Fu Mingxia, China	461.43
1996	Fu Mingxia, China	521.58
2000	Laura Wilkinson, United States	543.75
2004	Chantelle Newbery, Australia	590.31

Platform Diving	Points
2008 Chen Ruolin, China	447.70
2012 Chen Ruolin, China	422.30
2016 Ren Qian, China	439.25

Springboard Diving	Points
1920 Aileen Riggin, United States	539.90
1924 Elizabeth Becker, United States	474.50
1928 Helen Meany, United States	78.62
1932 Georgia Coleman United States	87.52
1936 Marjorie Gestring, United States	89.27
1948 Victoria M. Draves, United States	108.74
1952 Patricia McCormick, United States	147.30
1956 Patricia McCormick, United States	142.36
1960 Ingrid Kramer, Germany	155.81
1964 Ingrid Engel-Kramer, Germany	145.00
1968 Sue Gossick, United States	150.77
1972 Micki King, United States	450.03
1976 Jenni Chandler, United States	506.19
1980 Irina Kalinina, USSR	725.91
1984 Sylvie Bernier, Canada	530.70

Springboard Diving	Points
1988 Gao Min, China	580.23
1992 Gao Min, China	572.40
1996 Fu Mingxia, China	547.68
2000 Fu Mingxia, China	609.42
2004 Guo Jingjing, China	633.15
2008 Guo Jingjing, China	415.35
2012 Wu Minxia, China	414.00
2016 Shi Tingmao, China	406.05

Synchronized Platform Diving	Points
2004 Lao Lishi & Li Ting, China	352.14
2008 Wang Xin & Chen Ruolin, China	363.54
2012 Chen Ruolin & Wang Hao, China	368.40
2016 Chen Ruolin & Liu Huixia, China	354.00

Synchronized Springboard Diving	Points
2004 Wu Minxia & Guo Jingjing, China	336.90
2008 Guo Jingjing & Wu Minxia, China	343.50
2012 He Zi & Wu Minxia, China	346.20
2016 Wu Minxia & Shi Tingmao, China	345.60

Tennis

Men's Singles

1896 John Boland, Great Britain
1900 Hugh Lawrence Doherty, Great Britain
1904 Beals Coleman Wright, United States
1908 Josiah George Ritchie, Great Britain
1912 Charles Lyndhurst Winslow, South Africa
1920 Louis Raymond, South Africa
1924 Vincent Richards, United States
1988 Miloslav Mecir, Czechoslovakia
1992 Marc Rosset, Switzerland
1996 Andre Agassi, United States
2000 Eugueni Kafelnikov, Russia
2004 Nicolas Massu, Chile
2008 Rafael Nadal, Spain
2012 Andy Murray, Great Britain
2016 Andy Murray, Great Britain

Men's Doubles

1896 John Boland, Great Britain & Friedrick Traun, Germany
1900 Hugh Lawrence Doherty & Reginald Frank Doherty, Great Britain
1904 Edgar Welch Leonard & Beals Coleman Wright, U.S.
1908 George Whiteside Hillyard & Reginald Frank Doherty, Great Britain
1912 Harry Austin Kitson & Charles Lyndhurst Winslow, South Africa
1920 Oswald Graham Noel Turnbull & Maxwell Woosnam, Great Britain
1924 Vincent Richards & Francis Townsend Hunter, U.S.
1988 Kenneth Flach & Robert A. Seguso, United States
1992 Boris Becker & Michael Stich, Germany
1996 Mark Woodforde & Todd Woodbridge, Australia
2000 Sebastien Lareau & Daniel Nestor, Canada
2004 Fernando Gonzales & Nicolas Massu, Chile

Men's Doubles

2008 Roger Federer & Stanislas Wawrinka, Switzerland
2012 Mike Bryan & Bob Bryan, United States
2016 Marc López & Rafael Nadal, Spain

Women's Singles

1900 Charlotte Cooper, Great Britain
1908 Dorothy Katherine Chambers, Great Britain
1912 Marguerite Broquedis, France
1920 Suzanne Lenglen, France
1924 Helen Wills, United States
1988 Steffi Graf, W. Germany
1992 Jennifer Capriati, United States
1996 Lindsay Davenport, United States
2000 Venus Williams, United States
2004 Justine Henin-Hardenne, Belgium
2008 Elena Dementieva, Russia
2012 Serena Williams, United States
2016 Mónica Puig, Puerto Rico

Women's Doubles

1920 Winifred Margaret McNair & Kathleen McKane, Great Britain
1924 Hazel Virginia Wightman & Helen Wills, United States
1988 Pam Shriver & Zina Garrison, United States
1992 Gigi Fernandez & Mary Joe Fernandez, United States
1996 Gigi Fernandez & Mary Joe Fernandez, United States
2000 Venus Williams & Serena Williams, United States
2004 Ting Li & Tian Tian Sun, China
2008 Serena Williams & Venus Williams, United States
2012 Serena Williams & Venus Williams, United States
2016 Ekaterina Makarova & Elena Vesnina, Russia

Mixed Doubles

2012 Victoria Azarenka & Max Mirnyi, Belarus
2016 Bethanie Mattek-Sands & Jack Sock, United States

Track and Field—Men

100-Meter Run	Time
1896 Thomas Burke, United States	0:12.0
1900 Francis Jarvis, United States	0:11.0
1904 Archie Hahn, United States	0:11.0
1908 Reginald Walker, South Africa	0:10.8
1912 Ralph Craig, United States	0:10.8
1920 Charles Paddock, United States	0:10.8
1924 Harold Abrahams, Great Britain	0:10.6
1928 Percy Williams, Canada	0:10.8
1932 Eddie Tolan, United States	0:10.3
1936 Jesse Owens, United States	0:10.3
1948 Harrison Dillard, United States	0:10.3
1952 Lindy Remigino, United States	0:10.4
1956 Bobby Morrow, United States	0:10.5
1960 Armin Hary, Germany	0:10.2
1964 Bob Hayes, United States	0:10.0
1968 Jim Hines, United States	0:09.95
1972 Valery Borzov, USSR	0:10.14
1976 Hasely Crawford, Trinidad	0:10.06
1980 Allan Wells, Great Britain	0:10.25
1984 Carl Lewis, United States	0:09.99
1988 Carl Lewis, United States	0:09.92
1992 Linford Christie, Great Britain	0:09.96
1996 Donovan Bailey, Canada	0:09.84
2000 Maurice Greene, United States	0:09.87

100-Meter Run	Time
2004 Justin Gatlin, United States	0:09.85
2008 Usain Bolt, Jamaica	0:09.69
2012 Usain Bolt, Jamaica	0:09.63*
2016 Usain Bolt, Jamaica	0:09.81

200-Meter Run	Time
1900 Walter Tewksbury, United States	0:22.2
1904 Archie Hahn, United States	0:21.6
1908 Robert Kerr, Canada	0:22.6
1912 Ralph Craig, United States	0:21.7
1920 Allan Woodring, United States	0:22.0
1924 Jackson Scholz, United States	0:21.6
1928 Percy Williams, Canada	0:21.8
1932 Eddie Tolan, United States	0:21.2
1936 Jesse Owens, United States	0:20.7
1948 Mel Patton, United States	0:21.1
1952 Andrew Stanfield, United States	0:20.7
1956 Bobby Morrow, United States	0:20.6
1960 Livio Berruti, Italy	0:20.5
1964 Henry Carr, United States	0:20.3
1968 Tommie Smith, United States	0:19.83
1972 Valery Borzov, USSR	0:20.00
1976 Donald Quarrie, Jamaica	0:20.23
1980 Pietro Mennea, Italy	0:20.19
1984 Carl Lewis, United States	0:19.80

200-Meter Run

		Time
1988	Joe DeLoach, United States	0:19.75
1992	Mike Marsh, United States	0:20.01
1996	Michael Johnson, United States	0:19.32
2000	Konstantinos Kenteris, Greece	0:20.09
2004	Shawn Crawford, United States	0:19.79
2008	Usain Bolt, Jamaica	0:19.30*
2012	Usain Bolt, Jamaica	0:19.32
2016	Usain Bolt, Jamaica	0:19.78

400-Meter Run

		Time
1896	Thomas Burke, United States	0:54.2
1900	Maxwell Long, United States	0:49.4
1904	Harry Hillman, United States	0:49.2
1908	Wyndham Halswelle, Gr. Brit. (walkover)	0:50.0
1912	Charles Reidpath, United States	0:48.2
1920	Bevil Rudd, South Africa	0:49.6
1924	Eric Liddell, Great Britain	0:47.6
1928	Ray Barbuti, United States	0:47.8
1932	William Carr, United States	0:46.2
1936	Archie Williams, United States	0:46.5
1948	Arthur Wint, Jamaica	0:46.2
1952	George Rhoden, Jamaica	0:45.9
1956	Charles Jenkins, United States	0:46.7
1960	Otis Davis, United States	0:44.9
1964	Michael Larrabee, United States	0:45.1
1968	Lee Evans, United States	0:43.86
1972	Vincent Matthews, United States	0:44.66
1976	Alberto Juantorena, Cuba	0:44.26
1980	Viktor Markin, USSR	0:44.60
1984	Alonzo Babers, United States	0:44.27
1988	Steve Lewis, United States	0:43.87
1992	Quincy Watts, United States	0:43.50
1996	Michael Johnson, United States	0:43.49
2000	Michael Johnson, United States	0:43.84
2004	Jeremy Wariner, United States	0:44.00
2008	LaShawn Merritt, United States	0:43.75
2012	Kirani James, Grenada	0:43.94
2016	Wayde van Niekerk, South Africa	0:43.03*

800-Meter Run

		Time
1896	Edwin Flack, Australia	2:11.0
1900	Alfred Tysoe, Great Britain	2:01.2
1904	James Lightbody, United States	1:56.0
1908	Mel Sheppard, United States	1:52.8
1912	James "Ted" Meredith, United States	1:51.9
1920	Albert Hill, Great Britain	1:53.4
1924	Douglas Lowe, Great Britain	1:52.4
1928	Douglas Lowe, Great Britain	1:51.8
1932	Thomas Hampson, Great Britain	1:49.8
1936	John Woodruff, United States	1:52.9
1948	Mal Whitfield, United States	1:49.2
1952	Mal Whitfield, United States	1:49.2
1956	Tom Courtney, United States	1:47.7
1960	Peter Snell, New Zealand	1:46.3
1964	Peter Snell, New Zealand	1:45.1
1968	Ralph Doubell, Australia	1:44.3
1972	Dave Wottle, United States	1:45.9
1976	Alberto Juantorena, Cuba	1:43.50
1980	Steve Ovett, Great Britain	1:45.40
1984	Joaquim Cruz, Brazil	1:43.00
1988	Paul Ereng, Kenya	1:43.45
1992	William Tanui, Kenya	1:43.66
1996	Vebjørn Rodal, Norway	1:42.58
2000	Nils Schumann, Germany	1:45.08
2004	Yuriy Borzakovskiy, Russia	1:44.45
2008	Wilfred Bungei, Kenya	1:44.65
2012	David Lekuta Rudisha, Kenya	1:40.91*
2016	David Lekuta Rudisha, Kenya	1:42.15

1500-Meter Run

		Time
1896	Edwin Flack, Australia	4:33.2
1900	Charles Bennett, Great Britain	4:06.2
1904	James Lightbody, United States	4:05.4
1908	Mel Sheppard, United States	4:03.4
1912	Arnold Jackson, Great Britain	3:56.8
1920	Albert Hill, Great Britain	4:01.8
1924	Paavo Nurmi, Finland	3:53.6
1928	Harry Larva, Finland	3:53.2
1932	Luigi Beccali, Italy	3:51.2
1936	Jack Lovelock, New Zealand	3:47.8
1948	Henry Eriksson, Sweden	3:49.8
1952	Joseph Barthel, Luxembourg	3:45.2
1956	Ron Delany, Ireland	3:41.2
1960	Herb Elliott, Australia	3:35.6
1964	Peter Snell, New Zealand	3:38.1

1500-Meter Run

		Time
1968	Kipchoge Keino, Kenya	3:34.91
1972	Pekka Vasala, Finland	3:36.33
1976	John Walker, New Zealand	3:39.17
1980	Sebastian Coe, Great Britain	3:38.4
1984	Sebastian Coe, Great Britain	3:32.53
1988	Peter Rono, Kenya	3:35.96
1992	Fermin Cacho Ruiz, Spain	3:40.12
1996	Noureddine Morceli, Algeria	3:35.78
2000	Noah Ngeny, Kenya	3:32.07*
2004	Hicham El Guerrouj, Morocco	3:34.18
2008	Asbel Kiprop, Kenya[1]	3:33.11
2012	Taoufik Makhloufi, Algeria	3:34.08
2016	Matthew Centrowitz, United States	3:50.00

(1) Originally won by Rashid Ramzi, Bahrain, who was stripped of the gold in 2009 due to doping.

3000-Meter Steeplechase

		Time
1920	Percy Hodge, Great Britain	10:00.4
1924	Ville Ritola, Finland	9:33.6
1928	Toivo Loukola, Finland	9:21.8
1932	Volmari Iso-Hollo, Finland (about 3,450 m; extra lap by error)	10:33.4
1936	Volmari Iso-Hollo, Finland	9:03.8
1948	Tore Sjöstrand, Sweden	9:04.6
1952	Horace Ashenfelter, United States	8:45.4
1956	Chris Brasher, Great Britain	8:41.2
1960	Zdzislaw Krzyszkowiak, Poland	8:34.2
1964	Gaston Roelants, Belgium	8:30.8
1968	Amos Biwott, Kenya	8:51.0
1972	Kipchoge Keino, Kenya	8:23.64
1976	Anders Garderud, Sweden	8:08.02
1980	Bronislaw Malinowski, Poland	8:09.7
1984	Julius Korir, Kenya	8:11.80
1988	Julius Kariuki, Kenya	8:05.51
1992	Matthew Birir, Kenya	8:08.84
1996	Joseph Keter, Kenya	8:07.12
2000	Reuben Kosgei, Kenya	8:21.43
2004	Ezekiel Kemboi, Kenya	8:05.81
2008	Brimin Kiprop Kirpruto, Kenya	8:10.34
2012	Ezekiel Kemboi, Kenya	8:18.56
2016	Conseslus Kipruto, Kenya	8:03.28*

5000-Meter Run

		Time
1912	Hannes Kolehmainen, Finland	14:36.6
1920	Joseph Guillemot, France	14:55.6
1924	Paavo Nurmi, Finland	14:31.2
1928	Ville Ritola, Finland	14:38.0
1932	Lauri Lehtinen, Finland	14:30.0
1936	Gunnar Höckert, Finland	14:22.2
1948	Gaston Reiff, Belgium	14:17.6
1952	Emil Zatopek, Czechoslovakia	14:06.6
1956	Vladimir Kuts, USSR	13:39.6
1960	Murray Halberg, New Zealand	13:43.4
1964	Bob Schul, United States	13:48.8
1968	Mohamed Gammoudi, Tunisia	14:05.0
1972	Lasse Viren, Finland	13:26.4
1976	Lasse Viren, Finland	13:24.76
1980	Miruts Yifter, Ethiopia	13:20.91
1984	Said Aouita, Morocco	13:05.59
1988	John Ngugi, Kenya	13:11.70
1992	Dieter Baumann, Germany	13:12.52
1996	Venuste Niyongabo, Burundi	13:07.96
2000	Millon Wolde, Ethiopia	13:35.49
2004	Hicham El Guerrouj, Morocco	13:14.39
2008	Kenenisa Bekele, Ethiopia	12:57.82*
2012	Mo Farah, Great Britain	13:41.66
2016	Mo Farah, Great Britain	13:03.30

10,000-Meter Run

		Time
1912	Hannes Kolehmainen, Finland	31:20.8
1920	Paavo Nurmi, Finland	31:45.8
1924	Ville Ritola, Finland	30:23.2
1928	Paavo Nurmi, Finland	30:18.8
1932	Janusz Kusocinski, Poland	30:11.4
1936	Ilmari Salminen, Finland	30:15.4
1948	Emil Zatopek, Czechoslovakia	29:59.6
1952	Emil Zatopek, Czechoslovakia	29:17.0
1956	Vladimir Kuts, USSR	28:45.6
1960	Pyotr Bolotnikov, USSR	28:32.2
1964	Billy Mills, United States	28:24.4
1968	Naftali Temu, Kenya	29:27.4
1972	Lasse Viren, Finland	27:38.4
1976	Lasse Viren, Finland	27:40.38
1980	Miruts Yifter, Ethiopia	27:42.7
1984	Alberto Cova, Italy	27:47.54

10,000-Meter Run	Time
1988 Brahim Boutayeb, Morocco	27:21.46
1992 Khalid Skah, Morocco	27:46.70
1996 Haile Gebrselassie, Ethiopia	27:07.34
2000 Haile Gebrselassie, Ethiopia	27:18.20
2004 Kenenisa Bekele, Ethiopia	27:05.10
2008 Kenenisa Bekele, Ethiopia	27:01.17*
2012 Mo Farah, Great Britain	27:30.42
2016 Mo Farah, Great Britain	27:05.17

Marathon	Time
1896 Spyridon Louis, Greece	2:58:50
1900 Michel Theato, France	2:59:45.0
1904 Thomas Hicks, United States	3:28:53.0
1908 John Hayes, United States	2:55:18.4
1912 Kenneth McArthur, South Africa	2:36:54.8
1920 Hannes Kolehmainen, Finland	2:32:35.8
1924 Albin Stenroos, Finland	2:41:22.6
1928 Boughera El Ouafi, France	2:32.57
1932 Juan Zabala, Argentina	2:31:36
1936 Kee-chung Sohn, Japan[1]	2:29:19.2
1948 Delfo Cabrera, Argentina	2:34:51.6
1952 Emil Zatopek, Czechoslovakia	2:23:03.2
1956 Alain Mimoun, France	2:25:00.0
1960 Abebe Bikila, Ethiopia	2:15:16.2
1964 Abebe Bikila, Ethiopia	2:12:11.2
1968 Mamo Wolde, Ethiopia	2:20:26.4
1972 Frank Shorter, United States	2:12:19.8
1976 Waldemar Cierpinski, E. Germany	2:09:55.0
1980 Waldemar Cierpinski, E. Germany	2:11:03.0
1984 Carlos Lopes, Portugal	2:09:21
1988 Gelindo Bordin, Italy	2:10:32
1992 Hwang Young-cho, S. Korea	2:13:23
1996 Josia Thugwane, South Africa	2:12:36
2000 Gezahegne Abera, Ethiopia	2:10:11
2004 Stefano Baldini, Italy	2:10:55
2008 Samuel Kamau Wansiru, Kenya	2:06:32*
2012 Stephen Kiprotich, Uganda	2:08:01
2016 Eliud Kipchoge, Kenya	2:08:44

(1) Korean runner who competed under Japanese name Kitei Son.

4x100-Meter Relay	Time
1912 Great Britain	0:42.4
1920 United States	0:42.2
1924 United States	0:41.0
1928 United States	0:41.0
1932 United States	0:40.0
1936 United States	0:39.8
1948 United States	0:40.6
1952 United States	0:40.1
1956 United States	0:39.5
1960 Germany (U.S. disqualified)	0:39.5
1964 United States	0:39.0
1968 United States	0:38.24
1972 United States	0:38.19
1976 United States	0:38.33
1980 USSR	0:38.26
1984 United States	0:37.83
1988 USSR (U.S. disqualified)	0:38.19
1992 United States	0:37.40
1996 Canada	0:37.69
2000 United States	0:37.61
2004 Great Britain	0:38.07
2008 Jamaica	0:37.10
2012 Jamaica	0:36.84*
2016 Jamaica	0:37.27

4x400-Meter Relay	Time
1908 United States	3:29.4
1912 United States	3:16.6
1920 Great Britain	3:22.2
1924 United States	3:16.0
1928 United States	3:14.2
1932 United States	3:08.2
1936 Great Britain	3:09.0
1948 United States	3:10.4
1952 Jamaica	3:03.9
1956 United States	3:04.8
1960 United States	3:02.2
1964 United States	3:00.7
1968 United States	2:56.16
1972 Kenya	2:59.8
1976 United States	2:58.65
1980 USSR	3:01.1
1984 United States	2:57.91
1988 United States	2:56.16

4x400-Meter Relay	Time
1992 United States	2:55.74
1996 United States	2:55.99
2000 Nigeria[1]	2:58.68
2004 United States	2:55.91
2008 United States	2:55.39*
2012 The Bahamas	2:56.72
2016 United States	2:57.30

(1) Originally won by the U.S. but awarded to Nigeria in 2012 after U.S. team member Antonio Pettigrew admitted to doping.

20-Kilometer Walk	Time
1956 Leonid Spirin, USSR	1:31:27.4
1960 Vladimir Golubnichy, USSR	1:34:07.2
1964 Kenneth Matthews, Great Britain	1:29:34.0
1968 Vladimir Golubnichy, USSR	1:33:58.4
1972 Peter Frenkel, E. Germany	1:26:42.4
1976 Daniel Bautista, Mexico	1:24:40.6
1980 Maurizio Damilano, Italy	1:23:35.5
1984 Ernesto Canto, Mexico	1:23:13
1988 Jozef Pribilinec, Czechoslovakia	1:19.57
1992 Daniel Plaza Montero, Spain	1:21:45
1996 Jefferson Perez, Ecuador	1:20:07
2000 Robert Korzeniowski, Poland	1:18:59
2004 Ivano Brugnetti, Italy	1:19:40
2008 Valeriy Borchin, Russia	1:19:01
2012 Chen Ding, China	1:18.46*
2016 Wang Zhen, China	1:19.44

50-Kilometer Walk	Time
1932 Thomas "Tommy" Green, Great Britain	4:50.10
1936 Harold Whitlock, Great Britain	4:30:41.4
1948 John Ljunggren, Sweden	4:41.52
1952 Giuseppe Dordoni, Italy	4:28:07.8
1956 Norman Read, New Zealand	4:30:42.8
1960 Donald Thompson, Great Britain	4:25:30
1964 Abdon Pamich, Italy	4:11:12.4
1968 Christoph Höhne, E. Germany	4:20:13.6
1972 Bernd Kannenberg, W. Germany	3:56:11.6
1980 Hartwig Gauder, E. Germany	3:49:24.0
1984 Raul Gonzalez, Mexico	3:47:26
1988 Vyacheslav Ivanenko, USSR	3:38.29
1992 Andrey Perlov, Unified Team	3:50:13
1996 Robert Korzeniowski, Poland	3:43:30
2000 Robert Korzeniowski, Poland	3:42:22
2004 Robert Korzeniowski, Poland	3:38:46
2008 Alex Schwazer, Italy	3:37:09
2012 Jared Tallent, Australia[1]	3:36:53
2016 Matej Tóth, Slovakia	3:40:58

(1) Russia's Sergey Kirdyapkin was stripped of the gold medal in 2016 for doping.

110-Meter Hurdles	Time
1896 Thomas Curtis, United States	0:17.6
1900 Alvin Kraenzlein, United States	0:15.4
1904 Frederick Schule, United States	0:16.0
1908 Forrest Smithson, United States	0:15.0
1912 Frederick Kelly, United States	0:15.1
1920 Earl Thomson, Canada	0:14.8
1924 Daniel Kinsey, United States	0:15.0
1928 Sydney Atkinson, South Africa	0:14.8
1932 George Saling, United States	0:14.6
1936 Forrest Towns, United States	0:14.2
1948 William Porter, United States	0:13.9
1952 Harrison Dillard, United States	0:13.7
1956 Lee Calhoun, United States	0:13.5
1960 Lee Calhoun, United States	0:13.8
1964 Hayes Jones, United States	0:13.6
1968 Willie Davenport, United States	0:13.33
1972 Rod Milburn, United States	0:13.24
1976 Guy Drut, France	0:13.30
1980 Thomas Munkelt, E. Germany	0:13.39
1984 Roger Kingdom, United States	0:13.20
1988 Roger Kingdom, United States	0:12.98
1992 Mark McKoy, Canada	0:13.12
1996 Allen Johnson, United States	0:12.95
2000 Anier Garcia, Cuba	0:13.00
2004 Liu Xiang, China	0:12.91*
2008 Dayron Robles, Cuba	0:12.93
2012 Aries Merritt, United States	0:12.92
2016 Omar McLeod, Jamaica	0:13.05

400-Meter Hurdles	Time
1900 Walter Tewksbury, United States	0:57.6
1904 Harry Hillman, United States	0:53.0
1908 Charles Bacon, United States	0:55.0
1920 Frank Loomis, United States	0:54.0

400-Meter Hurdles	Time
1924 F. Morgan Taylor, United States	0:52.6
1928 Lord Burghley, Great Britain	0:53.4
1932 Bob Tisdall, Ireland	0:51.7
1936 Glenn Hardin, United States	0:52.4
1948 Roy Cochran, United States	0:51.1
1952 Charles Moore, United States	0:50.8
1956 Glenn Davis, United States	0:50.1
1960 Glenn Davis, United States	0:49.3
1964 Rex Cawley, United States	0:49.6
1968 David Hemery, Great Britain	0:48.12
1972 John Akii-Bua, Uganda	0:47.82
1976 Edwin Moses, United States	0:47.64
1980 Volker Beck, E. Germany	0:48.70
1984 Edwin Moses, United States	0:47.75
1988 Andre Phillips, United States	0:47.19
1992 Kevin Young, United States	0:46.78
1996 Derrick Adkins, United States	0:47.54
2000 Angelo Taylor, United States	0:47.50
2004 Félix Sánchez, Dominican Republic	0:47.63
2008 Angelo Taylor, United States	0:47.25
2012 Félix Sánchez, Dominican Republic	0:47.63
2016 Kerron Clement, United States	0:47.73

Note: Event not held in 1912.

Discus Throw	Dist.	
1896 Robert Garrett, United States	29.15m	(95' 7")
1900 Rudolf Bauer, Hungary	36.04m	(118' 3")
1904 Martin Sheridan, United States	39.28m	(128' 10")
1908 Martin Sheridan, United States	40.89m	(134' 1")
1912 Armas Taipale, Finland	45.21m	(148' 3")
1920 Elmer Niklander, Finland	44.68m	(146' 7")
1924 Clarence "Bud" Houser, U.S.	46.15m	(151' 4")
1928 Clarence "Bud" Houser, U.S.	47.32m	(155' 3")
1932 John Anderson, United States	49.49m	(162' 4")
1936 Ken Carpenter, United States	50.48m	(165' 7")
1948 Adolfo Consolini, Italy	52.78m	(173' 2")
1952 Sim Iness, United States	55.03m	(180' 6")
1956 Al Oerter, United States	56.36m	(184' 11")
1960 Al Oerter, United States	59.18m	(194' 2")
1964 Al Oerter, United States	61.00m	(200' 1")
1968 Al Oerter, United States	64.78m	(212' 6")
1972 Ludvik Danek, Czechoslovakia	64.40m	(211' 3")
1976 Mac Wilkins, United States	67.50m	(221' 5")
1980 Viktor Rashchupkin, USSR	66.64m	(218' 8")
1984 Rolf Dannenberg, W. Germany	66.60m	(218' 6")
1988 Jürgen Schult, E. Germany	68.82m	(225' 9")
1992 Romas Ubartas, Lithuania	65.12m	(213' 8")
1996 Lars Riedel, Germany	69.40m	(227' 8")
2000 Virgilijus Alekna, Lithuania	69.30m	(227' 4")
2004 Virgilijus Alekna, Lithuania	69.89m	(228' 9¾")*
2008 Gerd Kanter, Estonia	68.82m	(225' 9½")
2012 Robert Harting, Germany	68.27m	(224')
2016 Christoph Harting, Germany	68.37m	(224' 3¾")

Hammer Throw	Dist.	
1900 John Flanagan, United States	49.73m	(163' 1")
1904 John Flanagan, United States	51.23m	(168' 1")
1908 John Flanagan, United States	51.92m	(170' 4")
1912 Matt McGrath, United States	54.74m	(179' 7")
1920 Pat Ryan, United States	52.875m	(173' 5¾")
1924 Fred Tootell, United States	53.295m	(174' 10")
1928 Patrick O'Callaghan, Ireland	51.39m	(168' 7")
1932 Patrick O'Callaghan, Ireland	53.92m	(176' 11")
1936 Karl Hein, Germany	56.49m	(185' 4")
1948 Imre Németh, Hungary	56.07m	(183' 11½")
1952 József Csérmák, Hungary	60.34m	(197' 11")
1956 Harold Connolly, United States	63.19m	(207' 3")
1960 Vasily Rudenkov, USSR	67.10m	(202' 0")
1964 Romuald Klim, USSR	69.74m	(228' 10")
1968 Gyula Zsivótzky, Hungary	73.36m	(240' 8")
1972 Anatoly Bondarchuk, USSR	75.50m	(247' 8")
1976 Yuri Sedykh, USSR	77.52m	(254' 4")
1980 Yuri Sedykh, USSR	81.80m	(268' 4")
1984 Juha Tiainen, Finland	78.08m	(256' 2")
1988 Sergei Litvinov, USSR	84.80m	(278' 2")*
1992 Andrey Abduvaliyev, Unified Team	82.54m	(270' 9")
1996 Balázs Kiss, Hungary	81.24m	(266' 6")
2000 Szymon Ziolkowski, Poland	80.02m	(262' 6")
2004 Koji Murofushi, Japan	82.91m	(272')
2008 Primoz Kozmus, Slovenia	82.02m	(269' 1")
2012 Krisztián Pars, Hungary	80.59m	(264' 5")
2016 Dilshod Nazarov, Tajikistan	78.68m	(258' 1¾")

High Jump	Height	
1896 Ellery Clark, United States	1.81m	(5' 11¼")
1900 Irving Baxter, United States	1.90m	(6' 2¾")

High Jump	Height	
1904 Samuel Jones, United States	1.80m	(5' 11")
1908 Harry Porter, United States	1.90m	(6' 2¾")
1912 Alma Richards, United States	1.93m	(6' 4")
1920 Richmond Landon, United States	1.94m	(6' 4¼")
1924 Harold Osborn, United States	1.98m	(6' 6")
1928 Robert "Bob" King, United States	1.94m	(6' 4¼")
1932 Duncan McNaughton, Canada	1.97m	(6' 5½")
1936 Cornelius Johnson, United States	2.03m	(6' 8")
1948 John Winter, Australia	1.98m	(6' 6")
1952 Walter Davis, United States	2.04m	(6' 8¼")
1956 Charles Dumas, United States	2.12m	(6' 11½")
1960 Robert Shavlakadze, USSR	2.16m	(7' 1")
1964 Valery Brumel, USSR	2.18m	(7' 1¾")
1968 Dick Fosbury, United States	2.24m	(7' 4¼")
1972 Jüri Tarmak, USSR	2.23m	(7' 3¾")
1976 Jacek Wszola, Poland	2.25m	(7' 4½")
1980 Gerd Wessig, E. Germany	2.36m	(7' 8¾")
1984 Dietmar Mögenburg, W. Germany	2.35m	(7' 8½")
1988 Gennadi Avdeyenko, USSR	2.38m	(7' 9¾")
1992 Javier Sotomayor, Cuba	2.34m	(7' 8")
1996 Charles Austin, United States	2.39m	(7' 10")*
2000 Sergey Kliugin, Russia	2.35m	(7' 8½")
2004 Stefan Holm, Sweden	2.36m	(7' 8¾")
2008 Andrey Silnov, Russia	2.36m	(7' 8¾")
2012 Ivan Ukhov, Russia	2.38m	(7' 9¾")
2016 Derek Drouin, Canada	2.38m	(7' 9¾")

Javelin Throw	Dist.	
1908 Eric Lemming, Sweden	54.82m	(179' 10")
1912 Eric Lemming, Sweden	60.64m	(198' 11")
1920 Jonni Myyrä, Finland	65.78m	(215' 9¾")
1924 Jonni Myyrä, Finland	62.96m	(206' 7")
1928 Erik Lundkvist, Sweden	66.60m	(218' 6")
1932 Matti Järvinen, Finland	72.71m	(238' 6½")
1936 Gerhard Stöck, Germany	71.84m	(235' 8")
1948 Kaj Tapio Rautavaara, Finland	69.77m	(228' 11")
1952 Cy Young, United States	73.78m	(242' 1")
1956 Egil Danielsen, Norway	85.71m	(281' 2½")
1960 Viktor Tsybulenko, USSR	84.64m	(277' 8")
1964 Pauli Nevala, Finland	82.66m	(271' 2")
1968 Janis Lusis, USSR	90.10m	(295' 7")
1972 Klaus Wolfermann, W. Germany	90.48m	(296' 10")
1976 Miklós Németh, Hungary	94.58m	(310' 4")
1980 Dainis Kula, USSR	91.20m	(299' 2")
1984 Arto Härkönen, Finland	86.76m	(284' 8")
1988 Tapio Korjus, Finland	84.28m	(276' 6")
1992 Jan Zelezny, Czechoslovakia	89.66m	(294' 2")
1996 Jan Zelezny, Czech Republic	88.16m	(289' 3")
2000 Jan Zelezny, Czech Republic	90.17m	(295' 9½")
2004 Andreas Thorkildsen, Norway	86.50m	(283' 10")
2008 Andreas Thorkildsen, Norway	90.57m	(297' 1¾")
2012 Keshorn Walcott, Trinidad & Tobago	84.58m	(277' 6")
2016 Thomas Röhler, Germany	90.30m	(296' 3")

Long Jump	Dist.	
1896 Ellery Clark, United States	6.35m	(20' 10")
1900 Alvin Kraenzlein, United States	7.18m	(23' 6¾")
1904 Meyer Prinstein, United States	7.34m	(24' 1")
1908 Frank Irons, United States	7.48m	(24' 6½")
1912 Albert Gutterson, United States	7.60m	(24' 11¼")
1920 William Petersson, Sweden	7.15m	(23' 5½")
1924 William DeHart Hubbard, U.S.	7.45m	(24' 5¼")
1928 Ed Hamm, United States	7.73m	(25' 4½")
1932 Edward Gordon, United States	7.64m	(25' ¾")
1936 Jesse Owens, United States	8.06m	(26' 5½")
1948 Willie Steele, United States	7.82m	(25' 8")
1952 Jerome Biffle, United States	7.57m	(24' 10")
1956 Gregory Bell, United States	7.83m	(25' 8¼")
1960 Ralph Boston, United States	8.12m	(26' 7¾")
1964 Lynn Davies, Great Britain	8.07m	(26' 5¾")
1968 Bob Beamon, United States	8.90m	(29' 2½")*
1972 Randy Williams, United States	8.24m	(27' ½")
1976 Arnie Robinson, United States	8.35m	(27' 4¾")
1980 Lutz Dombrowski, E. Germany	8.54m	(28' ¼")
1984 Carl Lewis, United States	8.54m	(28' ¼")
1988 Carl Lewis, United States	8.72m	(28' 7½")
1992 Carl Lewis, United States	8.67m	(28' 5½")
1996 Carl Lewis, United States	8.50m	(27' 10¾")
2000 Ivan Pedroso, Cuba	8.55m	(28' ¾")
2004 Dwight Phillips, United States	8.59m	(28' 2¼")
2008 Irving Jahir Saladino Aranda, Panama	8.34m	(27' 4¼")
2012 Greg Rutherford, Great Britain	8.31m	(27' 3¼")
2016 Jeff Henderson, United States	8.38m	(27' 6")

	Pole Vault	Height	
1896	William Welles Hoyt, United States	3.30m	(10' 10")
1900	Irving Baxter, United States	3.30m	(10' 10")
1904	Charles Dvorak, United States	3.50m	(11' 6")
1908	Edward Cooke, United States	3.71m	(12' 2")
	Alfred Gilbert, United States (tie)	3.71m	(12' 2")
1912	Harry Stoddard Babcock, U.S.	3.95m	(12' 11½")
1920	Frank Foss, United States	4.09m	(13' 5")
1924	Lee Barnes, United States	3.95m	(12' 11½")
1928	Sabin Carr, United States	4.20m	(13' 9¼")
1932	Bill Miller, United States	4.31m	(14' 1¾")
1936	Earle Meadows, United States	4.35m	(14' 3¼")
1948	Guinn Smith, United States	4.30m	(14' 1¼")
1952	Robert Richards, United States	4.55m	(14' 11¼")
1956	Robert Richards, United States	4.56m	(14' 11½")
1960	Don Bragg, United States	4.70m	(15' 5")
1964	Fred Hansen, United States	5.10m	(16' 8¾")
1968	Bob Seagren, United States	5.40m	(17' 8½")
1972	Wolfgang Nordwig, E. Germany	5.50m	(18' ½")
1976	Tadeusz Slusarski, Poland	5.50m	(18' ½")
1980	Wladyslaw Kozakiewicz, Poland	5.78m	(18' 11½")
1984	Pierre Quinon, France	5.75m	(18' 10¼")
1988	Sergei Bubka, USSR	5.90m	(19' 4¼")
1992	Maksim Tarasov, Unified Team	5.80m	(19' ¼")
1996	Jean Galfione, France	5.92m	(19' 5")
2000	Nick Hysong, United States	5.90m	(19' 4¼")
2004	Timothy Mack, United States	5.95m	(19' 6¼")
2008	Steve Hooker, Australia	5.96m	(19' 6¾")
2012	Renaud Lavillenie, France	5.97m	(19' 7")*
2016	Thiago Braz da Silva, Brazil	6.03m*	(19' 9½")*

	Shot Put	Dist.	
1896	Robert Garrett, United States	11.22m	(36' 9¾")
1900	Richard Sheldon, United States	14.10m	(46' 3¼")
1904	Ralph Rose, United States	14.81m	(48' 7")
1908	Ralph Rose, United States	14.21m	(46' 7½")
1912	Pat McDonald, United States	15.34m	(50' 4")
1920	Ville Pörhölä, Finland	14.81m	(48' 7¼")
1924	Clarence "Bud" Houser, United States	14.99m	(49' 2¼")
1928	John Kuck, United States	15.87m	(52' ¾")
1932	Leo Sexton, United States	16.00m	(52' 6")
1936	Hans Woellke, Germany	16.20m	(53' 1¾")
1948	Wilbur Thompson, United States	17.12m	(56' 2")
1952	W. Parry O'Brien, United States	17.41m	(57' 1½")
1956	W. Parry O'Brien, United States	18.57m	(60' 11¼")
1960	Bill Nieder, United States	19.68m	(64' 6¾")
1964	Dallas Long, United States	20.33m	(66' 8½")
1968	Randy Matson, United States	20.54m	(67' 4¾")
1972	Wladyslaw Komar, Poland	21.18m	(69' 6")
1976	Udo Beyer, E. Germany	21.05m	(69' ¾")
1980	Vladimir Kiselyov, USSR	21.35m	(70' ½")
1984	Alessandro Andrei, Italy	21.26m	(69' 9")
1988	Ulf Timmermann, E. Germany	22.47m	(73' 8¾")
1992	Michael Stulce, United States	21.70m	(71' 2½")
1996	Randy Barnes, United States	21.62m	(70' 11¼")
2000	Arsi Harju, Finland	21.29m	(69' 10¼")
2004	Adam Nelson, United States[1]	21.16m	(69' 5¼")
2008	Tomasz Majewski, Poland	21.51m	(70' 6¾")
2012	Tomasz Majewski, Poland	21.89m	(71' 9¾")
2016	Ryan Crouser, United States	22.52m*	(73' 10½")*

(1) Originally won by Yuriy Bilonog, Ukraine, who was stripped of the gold in 2012 due to doping.

	Triple Jump	Dist.	
1896	James Connolly, United States	13.71m	(44' 11¾")
1900	Meyer Prinstein, United States	14.47m	(47' 5¾")
1904	Meyer Prinstein, United States	14.35m	(47' 1")
1908	Tim Ahearne, Gr. Brit.-Ireland	14.92m	(48' 11½")
1912	Gustaf Lindblom, Sweden	14.76m	(48' 5")
1920	Vilho Tuulos, Finland	14.505m	(47' 7")
1924	Anthony Winter, Australia	15.525m	(50' 11¼")
1928	Mikio Oda, Japan	15.21m	(49' 11")
1932	Chuhei Nambu, Japan	15.72m	(51' 7")
1936	Naoto Tajima, Japan	16.00m	(52' 6")
1948	Arne Ahman, Sweden	15.40m	(50' 6¼")
1952	Adhemar Ferreira da Silva, Brazil	16.22m	(53' 2¾")
1956	Adhemar Ferreira da Silva, Brazil	16.35m	(53' 7¾")
1960	Jozef Schmidt, Poland	16.81m	(55' 1½")
1964	Jozef Schmidt, Poland	16.85m	(55' 3½")
1968	Viktor Saneyev, USSR	17.39m	(57' ¾")
1972	Viktor Saneyev, USSR	17.35m	(56' 11¼")
1976	Viktor Saneyev, USSR	17.29m	(56' 8¾")
1980	Jaak Uudmäe, USSR	17.35m	(56' 11")
1984	Al Joyner, United States	17.26m	(56' 7½")
1988	Khristo Markov, Bulgaria	17.61m	(57' 9½")
1992	Mike Conley, United States	18.17m	(59' 7½")(w)
1996	Kenny Harrison, United States	18.09m	(59' 4¼")*
2000	Jonathan Edwards, Great Britain	17.71m	(58' 1¼")
2004	Christian Olsson, Sweden	17.79m	(58' 4½")
2008	Nelson Evora, Portugal	17.67m	(57' 11¾")
2012	Christian Taylor, United States	17.81m	(58' 5¼")
2016	Christian Taylor, United States	17.86m	(58' 7¼")

	Decathlon	Points
1904	Thomas F. Kiely, Ireland	6,036
1912	Jim Thorpe, United States[1]	8,412.995
1920	Helge Lovland, Norway	6,804.355
1924	Harold Osborn, United States	7,710.775
1928	Paavo Yrjölä, Finland	8,053.29
1932	James Bausch, United States	8,462.23
1936	Glenn Morris, United States	7,900
1948	Robert Mathias, United States	7,139
1952	Robert Mathias, United States	7,887
1956	Milton Campbell, United States	7,937
1960	Rafer Johnson, United States	8,392
1964	Willi Holdorf, Germany	7,887
1968	Bill Toomey, United States	8,193
1972	Nikolai Avilov, USSR	8,454
1976	Bruce Jenner, United States	8,618
1980	Daley Thompson, Great Britain	8,495
1984	Daley Thompson, Great Britain	8,797
1988	Christian Schenk, E. Germany	8,488
1992	Robert Zmelik, Czechoslovakia	8,611
1996	Dan O'Brien, United States	8,824
2000	Erki Nool, Estonia	8,641
2004	Roman Sebrle, Czech Republic	8,893
2008	Bryan Clay, United States	8,791
2012	Ashton Eaton, United States	8,869
2016	Ashton Eaton, United States	8,893*

Note: Event not held in 1908. (1) Thorpe had been stripped of his medal for playing pro baseball prior to the Olympics. The Intl. Olympic Committee in 1982 posthumously restored his decathlon and pentathlon gold medals.

Track and Field—Women

	100-Meter Run	Time
1928	Elizabeth Robinson, United States	0:12.2
1932	Stella Walsh, Poland	0:11.9
1936	Helen Stephens, United States	0:11.5
1948	Fanny Blankers-Koen, Netherlands	0:11.9
1952	Marjorie Jackson, Australia	0:11.5
1956	Betty Cuthbert, Australia	0:11.5
1960	Wilma Rudolph, United States	0:11.0
1964	Wyomia Tyus, United States	0:11.4
1968	Wyomia Tyus, United States	0:11.08
1972	Renate Stecher, E. Germany	0:11.07
1976	Annegret Richter, W. Germany	0:11.08
1980	Lyudmila Kondratyeva, USSR	0:11.06
1984	Evelyn Ashford, United States	0:10:97
1988	Florence Griffith-Joyner, United States	0:10.54*
1992	Gail Devers, United States	0:10.82
1996	Gail Devers, United States	0:10.94
2000	No winner[1]	NA
2004	Yuliya Nesterenko, Belarus	0:10.93
2008	Shelly-Ann Fraser, Jamaica	0:10.78
2012	Shelly-Ann Fraser-Pryce, Jamaica	0:10.75
2016	Elaine Thompson, Jamaica	0:10.71

(1) Marion Jones, U.S., was stripped of her gold medal in 2007 due to doping; the Intl. Olympic Committee declined to award the medal to the runner-up, who was also suspected of doping.

	200-Meter Run	Time
1948	Fanny Blankers-Koen, Netherlands	0:24.4
1952	Marjorie Jackson, Australia	0:23.7
1956	Betty Cuthbert, Australia	0:23.4
1960	Wilma Rudolph, United States	0:24.0
1964	Edith McGuire, United States	0:23.0
1968	Irena Szewinska, Poland	0:22.5
1972	Renate Stecher, E. Germany	0:22.40
1976	Bärbel Eckert, E. Germany	0:22.37
1980	Bärbel Wöckel, E. Germany	0:22.03
1984	Valerie Brisco-Hooks, United States	0:21.81
1988	Florence Griffith-Joyner, United States	0:21.34*

200-Meter Run	Time
1992 Gwen Torrence, United States	0:21.81
1996 Marie-Jose Perec, France	0:22.12
2000 Pauline Davis-Thompson, The Bahamas[1]	0:22.27
2004 Veronica Campbell, Jamaica	0:22.05
2008 Veronica Campbell-Brown, Jamaica	0:21.74
2012 Allyson Felix, United States	0:21.88
2016 Elaine Thompson, Jamaica	0:21.78

(1) Originally won by Marion Jones, U.S., who was stripped of the gold in 2007 due to doping.

400-Meter Run	Time
1964 Betty Cuthbert, Australia	0:52.0
1968 Colette Besson, France	0:52.0
1972 Monika Zehrt, E. Germany	0:51.08
1976 Irena Szewinska, Poland	0:49.29
1980 Marita Koch, E. Germany	0:48.88
1984 Valerie Brisco-Hooks, United States	0:48.83
1988 Olga Bryzgina, USSR	0:48.65
1992 Marie-Jose Perec, France	0:48.83
1996 Marie-Jose Perec, France	0:48.25*
2000 Cathy Freeman, Australia	0:49.11
2004 Tonique Williams-Darling, The Bahamas	0:49.41
2008 Christine Ohuruogu, Great Britain	0:49.62
2012 Sanya Richards-Ross, United States	0:49.55
2016 Shaunae Miller, The Bahamas	0:49.44

800-Meter Run	Time
1928 Lina Radke, Germany	2:16.8
1960 Lyudmila Shevtsova, USSR	2:04.3
1964 Ann Packer, Great Britain	2:01.1
1968 Madeline Manning, United States	2:00.9
1972 Hildegard Falck, W. Germany	1:58.55
1976 Tatyana Kazankina, USSR	1:54.94
1980 Nadezhda Olizarenko, USSR	1:53.43*
1984 Doina Melinte, Romania	1:57.60
1988 Sigrun Wodars, E. Germany	1:56.10
1992 Ellen Van Langen, Netherlands	1:55.54
1996 Svetlana Masterkova, Russia	1:57.73
2000 Maria Mutola, Mozambique	1:56.15
2004 Kelly Holmes, Great Britain	1:56.38
2008 Pamela Jelimo, Kenya	1:54.87
2012 Mariya Savinova, Russia	1:56.19
2016 Caster Semenya, South Africa	1:55.28

1500-Meter Run	Time
1972 Lyudmila Bragina, USSR	4:01.04
1976 Tatyana Kazankina, USSR	4:05.48
1980 Tatyana Kazankina, USSR	3:56.06
1984 Gabriella Dorio, Italy	4:03.25
1988 Paula Ivan, Romania	3:53.96*
1992 Hassiba Boulmerka, Algeria	3:55.30
1996 Svetlana Masterkova, Russia	4:00.83
2000 Nouria Merah-Benida, Algeria	4:05.10
2004 Kelly Holmes, Great Britain	3:57.90
2008 Nancy Jebet Langat, Kenya	4:00.23
2012 Gamze Bulut, Turkey[1]	4:10.40
2016 Faith Chepngetich Kipyegon, Kenya	4:08.92

(1) Turkey's Asli Cakir Alpetkin was stripped of the gold medal in 2016 for doping.

3000-Meter Run	Time
1984 Maricica Puica, Romania	8:35.96
1988 Tatyana Samolenko, USSR	8:26.53*
1992 Elena Romanova, Unified Team	8:46.04

3000-Meter Steeplechase	Time
2008 Gulnara Galkina-Samitova, Russia	8:58.81*
2012 Habiba Ghribi, Tunisia[1]	9:08.37
2016 Ruth Jebet, Bahrain	8:59.75

(1) Russia's Yuliya Zaripova was stripped of the gold medal in 2016 for doping.

5000-Meter Run	Time
1996 Wang Junxia, China	14:59.88
2000 Gabriela Szabo, Romania	14:40.79
2004 Meseret Defar, Ethiopia	14:45.65
2008 Tirunesh Dibaba, Ethiopia	15:41.40
2012 Meseret Defar, Ethiopia	15:04.25
2016 Vivian Cheruiyot, Kenya	14:26.17*

10,000-Meter Run	Time
1988 Olga Boldarenko, USSR	31:05.21
1992 Derartu Tulu, Ethiopia	31:06.02
1996 Fernanda Ribeiro, Portugal	31:01.63

10,000-Meter Run	Time
2000 Derartu Tulu, Ethiopia	30:17.49
2004 Xing Huina, China	30:24.36
2008 Tirunesh Dibaba, Ethiopia	29:54.66
2012 Tirunesh Dibaba, Ethiopia	30:20.75
2016 Almaz Ayana, Ethiopia	29:17.45*

Marathon	Time
1984 Joan Benoit, United States	2:24:52
1988 Rosa Mota, Portugal	2:25:40
1992 Valentina Yegorova, Unified Team	2:32:41
1996 Fatuma Roba, Ethiopia	2:26:05
2000 Naoko Takahashi, Japan	2:23:14
2004 Mizuki Noguchi, Japan	2:26:20
2008 Constantina Tomescu, Romania	2:26:44
2012 Tiki Gelana, Ethiopia	2:23:07*
2016 Jemima Jelagat Sumgong, Kenya	2:24:04

4x100-Meter Relay	Time
1928 Canada	0:48.4
1932 United States	0:46.9
1936 United States	0:46.9
1948 Netherlands	0:47.5
1952 United States	0:45.9
1956 Australia	0:44.5
1960 United States	0:44.5
1964 Poland	0:43.6
1968 United States	0:42.8
1972 West Germany	0:42.81
1976 East Germany	0:42.55
1980 East Germany	0:41.60
1984 United States	0:41.65
1988 United States	0:41.98
1992 United States	0:42.11
1996 United States	0:41.95
2000 The Bahamas	0:41.95
2004 Jamaica	0:41.73
2008 Russia	0:42.31
2012 United States	0:40.82*
2016 United States	0:41.01

4x400-Meter Relay	Time
1972 East Germany	3:23.0
1976 East Germany	3:19.23
1980 USSR	3:20.2
1984 United States	3:18.29
1988 USSR	3:15.18*
1992 Unified Team	3:20.20
1996 United States	3:20.91
2000 United States[1]	3:22.62
2004 United States[2]	3:19.01
2008 United States	3:18.54
2012 United States	3:16.87
2016 United States	3:19.06

(1) Due to team member Marion Jones's doping, the U.S. was stripped of the victory in 2008, but Jones's teammates won an appeal in 2010 to have their medals restored. (2) Team member Crystal Cox was stripped of her gold medal due to doping.

20-Kilometer Walk	Time
2000 Wang Liping, China	1:29:05
2004 Athanasia Tsoumeleka, Greece	1:29:12
2008 Olga Kaniskina, Russia	1:26:31
2012 Elena Lashmanova, Russia	1:25:02*
2016 Liu Hong, China	1:28:35

100-Meter Hurdles	Time
1972 Annelie Ehrhardt, E. Germany	0:12.59
1976 Johanna Schaller, E. Germany	0:12.77
1980 Vera Komisova, USSR	0:12.56
1984 Benita Fitzgerald-Brown, United States	0:12.84
1988 Yordanka Donkova, Bulgaria	0:12.38
1992 Paraskevi Patoulidou, Greece	0:12.64
1996 Ludmila Engquist, Sweden	0:12.58
2000 Olga Shishigina, Kazakhstan	0:12.65
2004 Joanna Hayes, United States	0:12.37
2008 Dawn Harper, United States	0:12.54
2012 Sally Pearson, Australia	0:12.35*
2016 Brianna Rollins, United States	0:12.48

400-Meter Hurdles	Time
1984 Nawal El Moutawakel, Morocco	0:54.61
1988 Debra Flintoff-King, Australia	0:53.17
1992 Sally Gunnell, Great Britain	0:53.23

400-Meter Hurdles

		Time
1996	Deon Hemmings, Jamaica	0:52.82
2000	Irina Privalova, Russia	0:53.02
2004	Faní Halkia, Greece	0:52.82
2008	Melaine Walker, Jamaica	0:52.64*
2012	Natalya Antyukh, Russia	0:52.70
2016	Dalilah Muhammad, United States	0:53.13

Discus Throw

		Dist.	
1928	Halina Konopacka, Poland	39.62m	(130' 0")
1932	Lillian Copeland, United States	40.58m	(133' 2")
1936	Gisela Mauermayer, Germany	47.63m	(156' 3")
1948	Micheline Ostermeyer, France	41.92m	(137' 6")
1952	Nina Ponomareva, USSR	51.42m	(168' 8")
1956	Olga Fikotová, Czechoslovakia	53.69m	(176' 1¾")
1960	Nina Ponomareva, USSR	55.10m	(180' 9")
1964	Tamara Press, USSR	57.27m	(187' 10¾")
1968	Lia Manoliu, Romania	58.28m	(191' 2")
1972	Faina Melnik, USSR	66.62m	(218' 7")
1976	Evelin Jahl, E. Germany	69.00m	(226' 4")
1980	Evelin Jahl, E. Germany	69.96m	(229' 6")
1984	Ria Stalman, Netherlands	65.36m	(214' 5")
1988	Martina Hellmann, E. Germany	72.30m	(237' 2")*
1992	Maritza Martén, Cuba	70.06m	(229' 10")
1996	Ilke Wyludda, Germany	69.66m	(228' 6")
2000	Ellina Zvereva, Belarus	68.40m	(224' 5")
2004	Natalya Sadova, Russia	67.02m	(219' 8¾")
2008	Stephanie Brown Trafton, U.S.	64.74m	(212' 4¾")
2012	Sandra Perkovic, Croatia	69.11m	(226' 9")
2016	Sandra Perkovic, Croatia	69.21m	(227' ¾")

Hammer Throw

		Dist.	
2000	Kamila Skolimowska, Poland	71.16m	(233' 5¾")
2004	Olga Kuzenkova, Russia	75.02m	(246' 1")
2008	Aksana Miankova, Belarus	76.34m	(250' 5½")
2012	Tatyana Lysenko, Russia	78.18m	(256' 6")
2016	Anita Wlodarczyk, Poland	82.29m	(269' 11¾")*

High Jump

		Height	
1928	Ethel Catherwood, Canada	1.59m	(5' 2½")
1932	Jean Shiley, United States	1.67m	(5' 5½")
1936	Ibolya Csák, Hungary	1.60m	(5' 3")
1948	Alice Coachman, United States	1.68m	(5' 6")
1952	Esther Brand, South Africa	1.67m	(5' 5¾")
1956	Mildred McDaniel, United States	1.76m	(5' 9¼")
1960	Iolanda Balas, Romania	1.85m	(6' ¾")
1964	Iolanda Balas, Romania	1.90m	(6' 2¾")
1968	Miloslava Rezková, Czech.	1.82m	(5' 11½")
1972	Ulrike Meyfarth, W. Germany	1.92m	(6' 3½")
1976	Rosemarie Ackermann, E. Germany	1.93m	(6' 4")
1980	Sara Simeoni, Italy	1.97m	(6' 5½")
1984	Ulrike Meyfarth, W. Germany	2.02m	(6' 7½")
1988	Louise Ritter, United States	2.03m	(6' 8")
1992	Heike Henkel, Germany	2.02m	(6' 7½")
1996	Stefka Kostadinova, Bulgaria	2.05m	(6' 8¾")
2000	Yelena Yelesina, Russia	2.01m	(6' 7")
2004	Yelena Slesarenko, Russia	2.06m	(6' 9")*
2008	Tia Hellebaut, Belgium	2.05m	(6' 8¾")
2012	Anna Chicherova, Russia	2.05m	(6' 8¾")
2016	Ruth Beitia, Spain	1.97m	(6' 5½")

Javelin Throw

		Dist.	
1932	"Babe" Didrikson, United States	43.68m	(143' 4")
1936	Tilly Fleischer, Germany	45.18m	(148' 3")
1948	Herma Bauma, Austria	45.57m	(149' 6")
1952	Dana Zátopková, Czechoslovakia	50.47m	(165' 7")
1956	Inese Jaunzeme, USSR	53.86m	(176' 8")
1960	Elvira Ozolina, USSR	55.98m	(183' 8")
1964	Mihaela Penes, Romania	60.54m	(198' 7")
1968	Angéla Németh, Hungary	60.36m	(198' 0")
1972	Ruth Fuchs, E. Germany	63.88m	(209' 7")
1976	Ruth Fuchs, E. Germany	65.94m	(216' 4")
1980	Maria Colón, Cuba	68.40m	(224' 5")
1984	Tessa Sanderson, Great Britain	69.56m	(228' 2")
1988	Petra Felke, E. Germany	74.68m	(245' 0")
1992	Silke Renk, Germany	68.34m	(224' 2")
1996	Heli Rantanen, Finland	67.94m	(222' 11")

Javelin Throw

		Dist.	
2000	Trine Hattestad, Norway	68.91m	(226' 1")
2004	Osleidys Menendez, Cuba	71.53m	(234' 8")*
2008	Barbora Spotáková, Czech Republic	71.42m	(234' ¾")
2012	Barbora Spotáková, Czech Republic	69.55m	(228' 2¼")
2016	Sara Kolak, Croatia	66.18m	(217' 1½")

Note: New records were kept after javelin was modified in 1999.

Long Jump

		Dist.	
1948	Olga Gyarmati, Hungary	5.69m	(18' 8")
1952	Yvette Williams, New Zealand	6.24m	(20' 5¼")
1956	Elzbieta Krzesinska, Poland	6.35m	(20' 10")
1960	Vera Krepkina, USSR	6.37m	(20' 10¾")
1964	Mary Rand, Great Britain	6.76m	(22' 2¼")
1968	Viorica Viscopoleanu, Romania	6.82m	(22' 4½")
1972	Heidemarie Rosendahl, W. Germany	6.78m	(22' 3")
1976	Angela Voigt, E. Germany	6.72m	(22' ¾")
1980	Tatyana Kolpakova, USSR	7.06m	(23' 2")
1984	Anisoara Cusmir-Stanciu, Romania	6.96m	(22' 10")
1988	Jackie Joyner-Kersee, United States	7.40m	(24' 3½")*
1992	Heike Drechsler, Germany	7.14m	(23' 5¼")
1996	Chioma Ajunwa, Nigeria	7.12m	(23' 4¼")
2000	Heike Drechsler, Germany	6.99m	(22' 11¼")
2004	Tatyana Lebedeva, Russia	7.07m	(23' 2½")
2008	Maurren Higa Maggi, Brazil	7.04m	(23' 1¼")
2012	Brittney Reese, United States	7.12m	(23' 4¼")
2016	Tianna Bartoletta, United States	7.17m	(23' 6¼")

Pole Vault

		Height	
2000	Stacy Dragila, United States	4.60m	(15' 1")
2004	Elena Isinbaeva, Russia	4.91m	(16' 1¼')
2008	Elena Isinbaeva, Russia	5.05m	(16' 6¾")
2012	Jennifer Suhr, United States	4.75m	(15' 7")
2016	Ekateríni Stefanídi, Greece	4.85m	(15' 11")

Shot Put

		Dist.	
1948	Micheline Ostermeyer, France	13.75m	(45' 1½")
1952	Galina Zybina, USSR	15.28m	(50' 1½")
1956	Tamara Tyshkevich, USSR	16.59m	(54' 5¼")
1960	Tamara Press, USSR	17.32m	(56' 10")
1964	Tamara Press, USSR	18.14m	(59' 6¼")
1968	Margitta Gummel, E. Germany	19.61m	(64' 4")
1972	Nadezhda Chizhova, USSR	21.03m	(69' 0")
1976	Ivanka Khristova, Bulgaria	21.16m	(69' 5¼")
1980	Ilona Slupianek, E. Germany	22.41m	(73' 6¼")*
1984	Claudia Losch, W. Germany	20.48m	(67' 2")
1988	Natalya Lisovskaya, USSR	22.24m	(72' 11¾")
1992	Svetlana Krivelyova, Unified Team	21.06m	(69' 1¼")
1996	Astrid Kumbernuss, Germany	20.56m	(67' 5½")
2000	Yanina Karolchik, Belarus	20.56m	(67' 5½")
2004	Yumileidi Cumbá, Cuba	19.59m	(64' 3¼")
2008	Valerie Vili, New Zealand	20.56m	(67' 5½")
2012	Valerie Adams, New Zealand	20.70m	(67' 11")
2016	Michelle Carter, United States	20.63m	(67' 8¼")

Triple Jump

		Dist.	
1996	Inessa Kravets, Ukraine	15.33m	(50' 3½")
2000	Tereza Marinova, Bulgaria	15.20m	(49' 10½")
2004	Francoise Mbango Etone, Cameroon	15.30m	(50' 2¼")
2008	Francoise Mbango Etone, Cameroon	15.39m	(50' 6")*
2012	Olga Rypakova, Kazakhstan	14.98m	(49' 1¾")
2016	Caterine Ibargüen, Colombia	15.17m	(49' 9¼")

Heptathlon

		Points
1984	Glynis Nunn, Australia	6,390
1988	Jackie Joyner-Kersee, United States	7,291*
1992	Jackie Joyner-Kersee, United States	7,044
1996	Ghada Shouaa, Syria	6,780
2000	Denise Lewis, Great Britain	6,584
2004	Carolina Kluft, Sweden	6,952
2008	Nataliia Dobrynska, Ukraine	6,733
2012	Jessica Ennis, Great Britain	6,955
2016	Nafissatou Thiam, Belgium	6,810

Paralympic Games

More than 4,300 athletes from 159 countries met at the XV Paralympic Summer Games, held Sept. 7-18, 2016, in Rio de Janeiro, Brazil. A total of 529 gold medals were awarded in 23 sports. China claimed 239 medals, outpacing Great Britain (147), Ukraine (117) and the United States (115). China also placed first in the number of gold medals, with 107.

The first Olympic Games for athletes with an impairment were held in Rome after the 1960 Summer Olympics; use of the name "paralympic" began with the 1964 games in Tokyo. The Paralympics are held by the Olympic host country in the same year and usually the same city and venue or venues. In 1976, the first Winter Paralympics were held in Ornskoldsvik, Sweden.

The XI Paralympic Winter Games were held Mar. 7-16, 2014, in Sochi, Russia. More than 500 athletes from 45 nations competed in five sports. Russia dominated the total medal count with 80, followed by Ukraine, with 25 medals, and the U.S., with 18.

General Olympic Information

The modern Olympic Games, first held in Athens, Greece, in 1896, were the result of efforts by Baron Pierre de Coubertin, a French educator, to promote interest in education and culture and to foster better international understanding through love of athletics. His inspiration was the ancient Greek Olympic Games, most notable of the four Panhellenic celebrations. The games were combined patriotic, religious, and athletic festivals held every four years. The first such recorded festival was held in 776 BCE, when the Greeks began to keep their calendar by "Olympiads," or four-year spans between the games.

Coubertin enlisted 14 nations to send athletes to the first modern Olympics. Now athletes from more than 200 nations and territories compete in the Summer Olympics. The Winter Olympic Games, started in 1924, draw competitors from about 80 countries and territories.

Symbol: Five rings or circles, linked to represent the sporting friendship of all peoples. They also symbolize five geographic areas—Africa, America, Asia, Australia, and Europe. Each ring is a different color—blue, yellow, black, green, and red—which, with the color white, represent the colors of the world's flags.

Flag: The five-ring symbol on a plain white background.

Creed: "The most important thing in the Olympic Games is not to win but to take part, just as the most important thing in life is not the triumph but the struggle. The essential thing is not to have conquered but to have fought well."

Motto: Citius, Altius, Fortius. ("Faster, higher, stronger" in Latin)

Oath: "In the name of all the competitors I promise that we shall take part in these Olympic Games, respecting and abiding by the rules which govern them, committing ourselves to a sport without doping and without drugs, in the true spirit of sportsmanship, for the glory of sport and the honor of our teams."

Flame: The modern version of the flame was adopted in 1936. The torch used to kindle it is first lit by the sun's rays in Olympia, Greece, then carried to the site of the Games by relays of runners. Ships and planes are used when necessary.

Winter Olympic Games Sites, 1924-2022

1924 Chamonix, France	**1956** Cortina d'Ampezzo, Italy	**1980** Lake Placid, NY, U.S.	**2006** Turin, Italy
1928 St. Moritz, Switzerland	**1960** Squaw Valley, CA, U.S.	**1984** Sarajevo, Yugoslavia	**2010** Vancouver, BC, Canada
1932 Lake Placid, NY, U.S.	**1964** Innsbruck, Austria	**1988** Calgary, AB, Canada	
1936 Garmisch-Partenkirchen, Germany	**1968** Grenoble, France	**1992** Albertville, France	**2014** Sochi, Russia
1948 St. Moritz, Switzerland	**1972** Sapporo, Japan	**1994** Lillehammer, Norway	**2018** PyeongChang, South Korea
1952 Oslo, Norway	**1976** Innsbruck, Austria	**1998** Nagano, Japan	
		2002 Salt Lake City, UT, U.S.	**2022** Beijing, China

Summer Olympic Games Sites, 1896-2020

1896 Athens, Greece	**1928** Amsterdam, Netherlands	**1968** Mexico City, Mexico	**1996** Atlanta, GA, U.S.
1900 Paris, France	**1932** Los Angeles, CA, U.S.	**1972** Munich, W. Germany	**2000** Sydney, Australia
1904 St. Louis, MO, U.S.	**1936** Berlin, Germany	**1976** Montreal, QC, Canada	**2004** Athens, Greece
1906 Athens, Greece*	**1948** London, England, UK	**1980** Moscow, USSR	**2008** Beijing, China
1908 London, England, UK	**1952** Helsinki, Finland	**1984** Los Angeles, CA, U.S.	**2012** London, England, UK
1912 Stockholm, Sweden	**1956** Melbourne, Australia	**1988** Seoul, South Korea	**2016** Rio de Janeiro, Brazil
1920 Antwerp, Belgium	**1960** Rome, Italy	**1992** Barcelona, Spain	**2020** Tokyo, Japan
1924 Paris, France	**1964** Tokyo, Japan		

*Games not recognized by International Olympic Committee. **Note:** Games VI (1916), XII (1940), and XIII (1944) were not celebrated.

2014 Winter Olympic Games

Sochi, Russia, Feb. 7-23, 2014

More than 2,800 athletes from 88 nations met in Sochi, Russia, to compete in a record 98 events in the XXII Olympic Winter Games Feb. 7-23, 2014. Host nation Russia won 33 medals, including 13 gold, to top the final medal count, followed by the United States, Norway, and Canada.

Meryl Davis and Charlie White became the first Americans ever to win gold in ice dancing, but the figure skating events were mostly dominated by Russia, which claimed gold in the women's, pairs, and team events. Russia's former Olympic champion Yevgeny Plushenko bowed out of the men's competition just before the short program, citing a back injury, and Yuzuru Hanyu of Japan won men's gold.

Eighteen-year-old American Mikaela Shiffrin became the youngest Olympian ever to win a gold medal in slalom. Canada won both ice hockey events, with the Canadian women defeating the U.S. in dramatic overtime fashion for the gold.

Twelve new medal events debuted at the Sochi Games, including a figure skating mixed team event, women's ski jumping, ski slopestyle and halfpipe, and snowboard slopestyle and parallel slalom.

2014 Winter Olympic Games: Final Medal Standings

Country	G	S	B	T	Country	G	S	B	T	Country	G	S	B	T
Russia	13	11	9	33	Switzerland	6	3	2	11	Finland	1	3	1	5
United States	9	7	12	28	China	3	4	2	9	Great Britain	1	1	2	4
Norway	11	5	10	26	South Korea	3	3	2	8	Latvia	0	2	2	4
Canada	10	10	5	25	Czech Republic	2	4	2	8	Australia	0	2	1	3
Netherlands	8	7	9	24	Slovenia	2	2	4	8	Ukraine	1	0	1	2
Germany	8	6	5	19	Japan	1	4	3	8	Slovakia	1	0	0	1
Austria	4	8	5	17	Italy	0	2	6	8	Croatia	0	1	0	1
France	4	4	7	15	Belarus	5	0	1	6	Kazakhstan	0	0	1	1
Sweden	2	7	6	15	Poland	4	1	1	6	**Total**	99	97	99	295

Winter Olympic Games Champions, 1924-2014

The 1980 games were boycotted by 62 nations, including the U.S. The 1984 games were boycotted by the USSR and most Eastern bloc nations. East and West Germany competed separately, 1968-88. In 1992, the Unified Team represented the former Soviet republics of Russia, Ukraine, Belarus, Kazakhstan, and Uzbekistan. Times are shown in hour:minute:sec.

Alpine Skiing

Men's Downhill

		Time
1948	Henri Oreiller, France	2:55.0
1952	Zeno Colo, Italy	2:30.8
1956	Toni Sailer, Austria	2:52.2
1960	Jean Vuarnet, France	2:06.0
1964	Egon Zimmermann, Austria	2:18.16
1968	Jean-Claude Killy, France	1:59.85
1972	Bernhard Russi, Switzerland	1:51.43
1976	Franz Klammer, Austria	1:45.73
1980	Leonhard Stock, Austria	1:45.50
1984	Bill Johnson, United States	1:45.49
1988	Pirmin Zurbriggen, Switzerland	1:59.63
1992	Patrick Ortlieb, Austria	1:50.37
1994	Tommy Moe, United States	1:45.75
1998	Jean-Luc Cretier, France	1:50.11
2002	Fritz Strobl, Austria	1:39.13
2006	Antoine Deneriaz, France	1:48.80
2010	Didier Defago, Switzerland	1:54.31
2014	Matthias Mayer, Austria	2:06.23

Men's Giant Slalom

		Time
1952	Stein Eriksen, Norway	2:25.0
1956	Toni Sailer, Austria	3:00.1
1960	Roger Staub, Switzerland	1:48.3
1964	Francois Bonlieu, France	1:46.71
1968	Jean-Claude Killy, France	3:29.28
1972	Gustavo Thoeni, Italy	3:09.62
1976	Heini Hemmi, Switzerland	3:26.97
1980	Ingemar Stenmark, Sweden	2:40.74
1984	Max Julen, Switzerland	2:41.18
1988	Alberto Tomba, Italy	2:06.37
1992	Alberto Tomba, Italy	2:06.98
1994	Markus Wasmeier, Germany	2:52.46
1998	Hermann Maier, Austria	2:38.51
2002	Stephan Eberharter, Austria	2:23.28
2006	Benjamin Raich, Austria	2:35.00
2010	Carlo Janka, Switzerland	2:37.83
2014	Ted Ligety, United States	2:45.29

Men's Slalom

		Time
1948	Edi Reinalter, Switzerland	2:10.3
1952	Othmar Schneider, Austria	2:00.0
1956	Toni Sailer, Austria	3:14.7
1960	Ernst Hinterseer, Austria	2:08.9
1964	Josef Stiegler, Austria	2:11.13
1968	Jean-Claude Killy, France	1:39.73
1972	Francisco Fernandez-Ochoa, Spain	1:49.27
1976	Piero Gros, Italy	2:03.29
1980	Ingemar Stenmark, Sweden	1:44.26
1984	Phil Mahre, United States	1:39.41
1988	Alberto Tomba, Italy	1:39.47
1992	Finn Christian Jagge, Norway	1:44.39
1994	Thomas Stangassinger, Austria	2:02.02
1998	Hans-Petter Buraas, Norway	1:49.31
2002	Jean-Pierre Vidal, France	1:41.06
2006	Benjamin Raich, Austria	1:43.14
2010	Giuliano Razzoli, Italy	1:39.32
2014	Mario Matt, Austria	1:41.84

Men's Super Combined

		Time
1936	Franz-Pfnuer, Germany	99.25 (pts.)
1948	Henri Oreiller, France	3.27 (pts.)
1988	Hubert Strolz, Austria	36.55 (pts.)
1992	Josef Polig, Italy	14.58 (pts.)
1994	Lasse Kjus, Norway	3:17.53
1998	Mario Reiter, Austria	3:08.06
2002	Kjetil Andre Aamodt, Norway	3:17.56
2006	Ted Ligety, United States	3:09.35
2010	Bode Miller, United States	2:44.92
2014	Sandro Viletta, Switzerland	2:45.20

Note: In 2010, a one-day super combined event replaced the traditional two-day combined event.

Men's Super Giant Slalom

		Time
1988	Franck Piccard, France	1:39.66
1992	Kjetil Andre Aamodt, Norway	1:13.04
1994	Markus Wasmeier, Germany	1:32.53
1998	Hermann Maier, Austria	1:34.82

Men's Super Giant Slalom

		Time
2002	Kjetil Andre Aamodt, Norway	1:21.58
2006	Kjetil Andre Aamodt, Norway	1:30.65
2010	Aksel Lund Svindal, Norway	1:30.34
2014	Kjetil Jansrud, Norway	1:18.14

Women's Downhill

		Time
1948	Hedi Schlunegger, Switzerland	2:28.3
1952	Trude Beiser-Jochum, Austria	1:47.1
1956	Madeleine Berthod, Switzerland	1:40.7
1960	Heidi Biebl, Germany	1:37.6
1964	Christl Haas, Austria	1:55.39
1968	Olga Pall, Austria	1:40.87
1972	Marie-Theres Nadig, Switzerland	1:36.68
1976	Rosi Mittermaier, W. Germany	1:46.16
1980	Annemarie Moser-Proell, Austria	1:37.52
1984	Michela Figini, Switzerland	1:13.36
1988	Marina Kiehl, W. Germany	1:25.86
1992	Kerrin Lee-Gartner, Canada	1:52.55
1994	Katja Seizinger, Germany	1:35.93
1998	Katja Seizinger, Germany	1:28.89
2002	Carole Montillet, France	1:39.56
2006	Michaela Dorfmeister, Austria	1:56.49
2010	Lindsey Vonn, United States	1:44.19
2014	Tina Maze, Slovenia	1:41.57
	Dominique Gisin, Switzerland (tie)	1:41.57

Women's Giant Slalom[1]

		Time
1952	Andrea Mead Lawrence, United States	2:06.8
1956	Ossi Reichert, Germany	1:56.5
1960	Yvonne Ruegg, Switzerland	1:39.9
1964	Marielle Goitschel, France	1:52.24
1968	Nancy Greene, Canada	1:51.97
1972	Marie-Theres Nadig, Switzerland	1:29.90
1976	Kathy Kreiner, Canada	1:29.13
1980	Hanni Wenzel, Liechtenstein	2:41.66
1984	Debbie Armstrong, United States	2:20.98
1988	Vreni Schneider, Switzerland	2:06.49
1992	Pernilla Wiberg, Sweden	2:12.74
1994	Deborah Compagnoni, Italy	2:30.97
1998	Deborah Compagnoni, Italy	2:50.59
2002	Janica Kostelic, Croatia	2:30.01
2006	Julia Mancuso, United States	2:09.19
2010	Viktoria Rebensburg, Germany	2:27.11
2014	Tina Maze, Slovenia	2:36.87

(1) Beginning in 1980, the event time combined two runs.

Women's Slalom

		Time
1948	Gretchen Fraser, United States	1:57.2
1952	Andrea Mead Lawrence, United States	2:10.6
1956	Renee Colliard, Switzerland	1:52.3
1960	Anne Heggtveit, Canada	1:49.6
1964	Christine Goitschel, France	1:29.86
1968	Marielle Goitschel, France	1:25.86
1972	Barbara Ann Cochran, United States	1:31.24
1976	Rosi Mittermaier, W. Germany	1:30.54
1980	Hanni Wenzel, Liechtenstein	1:25.09
1984	Paoletta Magoni, Italy	1:36.47
1988	Vreni Schneider, Switzerland	1:36.69
1992	Petra Kronberger, Austria	1:32.68
1994	Vreni Schneider, Switzerland	1:56.01
1998	Hilde Gerg, Germany	1:32.40
2002	Janica Kostelic, Croatia	1:46.10
2006	Anja Paerson, Sweden	1:29.04
2010	Maria Riesch, Germany	1:42.89
2014	Mikaela Shiffrin, United States	1:44.54

Women's Super Combined

		Time
1936	Christl Cranz, Germany	97.06 (pts.)
1948	Trude Beiser-Jochum, Austria	6.58 (pts.)
1988	Anita Wachter, Austria	29.25 (pts.)
1992	Petra Kronberger, Austria	2.55 (pts.)
1994	Pernilla Wiberg, Sweden	3:05.16
1998	Katja Seizinger, Germany	2:40.74
2002	Janica Kostelic, Croatia	2:43.28

Women's Super Combined

		Time
2006	Janica Kostelic, Croatia.	2:51.08
2010	Maria Riesch, Germany	2:09.14
2014	Maria Hoefl-Riesch, Germany	2:34.62

Note: In 2010, a one-day super combined event replaced the traditional two-day combined event.

Women's Super Giant Slalom

		Time
1988	Sigrid Wolf, Austria.	1:19.03
1992	Deborah Compagnoni, Italy	1:21.22
1994	Diann Roffe (Steinrotter), United States.	1:22.15
1998	Picabo Street, United States	1:18.02
2002	Daniela Ceccarelli, Italy	1:13.59
2006	Michaela Dorfmeister, Austria	1:32.47
2010	Andrea Fischbacher, Austria	1:20.14
2014	Anna Fenninger, Austria.	1:25.52

Bobsledding
(Driver in parentheses.)

Two-Man Bobsled

		Time
1932	United States (Hubert Stevens)	8:14.74
1936	United States (Ivan Brown).	5:29.29
1948	Switzerland (Felix Endrich).	5:29.20
1952	Germany (Andreas Ostler).	5:24.54
1956	Italy (Dalla Costa).	5:30.14
1964	Great Britain (Anthony Nash).	4:21.90
1968	Italy (Eugenio Monti).	4:41.54
1972	W. Germany (Wolfgang Zimmerer)	4:57.07
1976	E. Germany (Meinhard Nehmer)	3:44.42
1980	Switzerland (Erich Schaerer)	4:09.36
1984	E. Germany (Wolfgang Hoppe)	3:25.56
1988	USSR (Janis Kipours).	3:54.19
1992	Switzerland (Gustav Weber).	4:03.26
1994	Switzerland (Gustav Weber).	3:30.81
1998	Canada (Pierre Lueders)	3:37.24
	Italy (Guenther Huber) (tie).	3:37.24
2002	Germany II (Christoph Langen)	3:10.11
2006	Germany (Andre Lange).	3:43.38
2010	Germany (Andre Lange).	3:26.65
2014	Russia (Alexander Zubkov)	3:45.39

Four-Man Bobsled

		Time
1924	Switzerland (Eduard Scherrer)	5:45.54
1928	United States (William Fiske) (5-man)	3:20.50
1932	United States (William Fiske).	7:53.68
1936	Switzerland (Pierre Musy)	5:19.85
1948	United States (Francis Tyler)	5:20.10
1952	Germany (Andreas Ostler).	5:07.84
1956	Switzerland (Franz Kapus)	5:10.44
1964	Canada (Victor Emery).	4:14.46
1968	Italy (Eugenio Monti) (2 heats)	2:17.39
1972	Switzerland (Jean Wicki)	4:43.07
1976	E. Germany (Meinhard Nehmer)	3:40.43
1980	E. Germany (Meinhard Nehmer)	3:59.92
1984	E. Germany (Wolfgang Hoppe)	3:20.22
1988	Switzerland (Ekkehard Fasser)	3:47.51
1992	Austria (Ingo Appelt).	3:53.90
1994	Germany (Wolfgang Hoppe).	3:27.28
1998	Germany II (Christoph Langen)	2:39.41
2002	Germany II (Andre Lange)	3:07.51
2006	Germany (Andre Lange).	3:40.42
2010	United States (Steven Holcomb)	3:24.46
2014	Russia (Alexander Zubkov)	3:40.60

Two-Woman Bobsled

		Time
2002	United States II (Jill Bakken)	1:37.76
2006	Germany (Sandra Kiriasis)	3:49.98
2010	Canada (Kaillie Humphries)	3:32.28
2014	Canada (Kaillie Humphries)	3:50.61

Cross-Country Skiing

Men's Individual Sprint

		Time
2002	Tor Arne Hetland, Norway (1.5 km)	2:56.9
2006	Bjoern Lind, Sweden (1.3 km)	2:26.5
2010	Nikita Kriukov, Russia	3:36.3
2014	Ola Vigen Hattestad, Norway.	3:38.39

Men's 10 Kilometers

		Time
1992	Vegard Ulvang, Norway	27:36.0
1994	Bjoern Daehlie, Norway	24:20.1
1998	Bjoern Daehlie, Norway	27:24.5
2002	Thomas Alsgaard, Norway.	49:48.9
	Frode Estil, Norway (tie)[1]	49:48.9

(1) Both awarded gold after Johann Muehlegg of Spain was stripped of gold for a drug offense.

Men's 15 Kilometers

		Time
1924	Thorleif Haug, Norway	1:14:31
1928	Johan Grottumsbraaten, Norway	1:37:01
1932	Sven Utterstrom, Sweden	1:23:07
1936	Erik-August Larsson, Sweden	1:14:38
1948	Martin Lundstrom, Sweden	1:13:50
1952	Hallgeir Brenden, Norway	1:01:34
1956	Hallgeir Brenden, Norway	0:49:39.0
1960	Haakon Brusveen, Norway.	0:51:55.5
1964	Eero Maentyranta, Finland.	0:50:54.1
1968	Harald Groenningen, Norway.	0:47:54.2
1972	Sven-Ake Lundback, Sweden	0:45:28.24
1976	Nikolai Balukov, USSR.	0:43:58.47
1980	Thomas Wassberg, Sweden	0:41:57.63
1984	Gunde Svan, Sweden	0:41:25.6
1988	Mikhail Deviatiarov, USSR.	0:41:18.9
1992	Bjoern Daehlie, Norway	0:38:01.9
1994	Bjoern Daehlie, Norway	0:35:48.8
1998	Thomas Alsgaard, Norway.	1:07:01.7
2002	Andrus Veerpalu, Estonia.	0:37:07.4
2006	Andrus Veerpalu, Estonia.	0:38:01.3
2010	Dario Cologna, Switzerland	0:33:36.3
2014	Dario Cologna, Switzerland	0:38:29.7

Note: Approx. 18-km course 1924-52.

Men's 30-Kilometer Pursuit

		Time
1956	Veikko Hakulinen, Finland	1:44:06.0
1964	Eero Maentyranta, Finland	1:30:50.7
1968	Franco Nones, Italy	1:35:39.2
1972	Vyacheslav Vedenine, USSR.	1:36:31.15
1976	Sergei Saveliev, USSR	1:30:29.38
1980	Nikolai Zimyatov, USSR.	1:27:02.80
1984	Nikolai Zimyatov, USSR.	1:28:56.3
1988	Aleksei Prokourorov, USSR.	1:24:26.3
1992	Vegard Ulvang, Norway	1:22:27.8
1994	Thomas Alsgaard, Norway.	1:12:26.4
1998	Mika Myllylae, Finland	1:33:55.8
2002	Christian Hoffmann, Austria[1]	1:11:31.0
2006	Eugeni Dementiev, Russia	1:17:00.8
2010	Marcus Hellner, Sweden	1:15:11.4

(1) Awarded gold after Johann Muehlegg of Spain was stripped of gold for a drug offense.

Men's Skiathlon

		Time
2014	Dario Cologna, Switzerland	1:08:15.4

Men's 50-Kilometer Mass Start

		Time
1924	Thorleif Haug, Norway	3:44:32.0
1928	Per Erik Hedlund, Sweden.	4:52:03.0
1932	Veli Saarinen, Finland	4:28:00.0
1936	Elis Wiklund, Sweden.	3:30:11.0
1948	Nils Karlsson, Sweden	3:47:48.0
1952	Veikko Hakulinen, Finland	3:33:33.0
1956	Sixten Jernberg, Sweden.	2:50:27.0
1960	Kalevi Hamalainen, Finland	2:59:06.3
1964	Sixten Jernberg, Sweden.	2:43:52.6
1968	Ole Ellefsaeter, Norway	2:28:45.8
1972	Paal Tyldum, Norway	2:43:14.75
1976	Ivar Formo, Norway	2:37:30.05
1980	Nikolai Zimyatov, USSR.	2:27:24.60
1984	Thomas Wassberg, Sweden	2:15:55.8
1988	Gunde Svan, Sweden	2:04:30.9
1992	Bjoern Daehlie, Norway	2:03:41.5
1994	Vladimir Smirnov, Kazakhstan	2:07:20.3
1998	Bjoern Daehlie, Norway	2:05:08.2
2002	Mikhail Ivanov, Russia	2:06:20.8
2006	Giorgio di Centa, Italy.	2:06:11.8
2010	Petter Northug, Norway	2:05:35.5
2014	Alexander Legkov, Russia	1:46:55.2

Men's 4x10-Kilometer Relay

Year	Champions	Time
1936	Finland, Norway, Sweden	2:41:33.0
1948	Sweden, Finland, Norway	2:32:08.0
1952	Finland, Norway, Sweden	2:20:16.0
1956	USSR, Finland, Sweden	2:15:30.0
1960	Finland, Norway, USSR	2:18:45.6
1964	Sweden, Finland, USSR	2:18:34.6
1968	Norway, Sweden, Finland	2:08:33.5
1972	USSR, Norway, Switzerland	2:04:47.94
1976	Finland, Norway, USSR	2:07:59.72
1980	USSR, Norway, Finland	1:57:03.46
1984	Sweden, USSR, Finland	1:55:06.30
1988	Sweden, USSR, Czechoslovakia	1:43:58.60
1992	Norway, Italy, Finland	1:39:26.00
1994	Italy, Norway, Finland	1:41:15.00
1998	Norway, Italy, Finland	1:40:55.70
2002	Norway, Italy, Germany	1:32:45.5
2006	Italy, Germany, Sweden	1:43:45.7
2010	Sweden, Norway, Czech Republic	1:45:05.4
2014	Sweden, Russia, France	1:28:42.0

Men's Team Sprint

Year	Champions	Time
2006	Bjoern Lind & Thobias Fredriksson, Sweden	17:02.9
2010	Oeystein Pettersen & Petter Northug, Norway	19:01.0
2014	Sami Jauhojaervi & Iivo Niskanen, Finland	23:14.89

Women's Individual Sprint

Year	Champions	Time
2002	Julia Tchepalova, Russia (1.5 km)	3:10.6
2006	Chandra Crawford, Canada (1.1 km)	2:12.3
2010	Marit Bjoergen, Norway	3:39.2
2014	Maiken Caspersen Falla, Norway	2:35.49

Women's 5 Kilometers

Year	Champion	Time
1964	Claudia Boyarskikh, USSR	17:50.5
1968	Toini Gustafsson, Sweden	16:45.2
1972	Galina Koulacova, USSR	17:00.50
1976	Helena Takalo, Finland	15:48.69
1980	Raisa Smetanina, USSR	15:06.92
1984	Marja-Liisa Haemaelainen, Finland	17:04.0
1988	Marjo Matikainen, Finland	15:04.0
1992	Marjut Lukkarinen, Finland	14:13.8
1994	Ljubov Egorova, Russia	14:08.8
1998	Larissa Lazutina, Russia	17:37.9
2002	Beckie Scott, Canada[1]	25:09.9

(1) Awarded gold after Olga Danilova of Russia was stripped of gold and Larissa Lazutina of Russia was stripped of silver for drug offenses.

Women's 10 Kilometers

Year	Champion	Time
1952	Lydia Wideman, Finland	41:40.0
1956	Lyubov Kosyreva, USSR	38:11.0
1960	Maria Gusakova, USSR	39:46.6
1964	Claudia Boyarskikh, USSR	40:24.3
1968	Toini Gustafsson, Sweden	36:46.5
1972	Galina Koulacova, USSR	34:17.82
1976	Raisa Smetanina, USSR	30:13.41
1980	Barbara Petzold, E. Germany	30:31.54
1984	Marja-Liisa Haemaelainen, Finland	31:44.2
1988	Vida Ventsene, USSR	30:08.3
1992	Lyubov Egorova, Unified Team	25:53.7
1994	Lyubov Egorova, Russia	27:30.1
1998	Larissa Lazutina, Russia	46.06.9
2002	Bente Skari, Norway	28:05.6
2006	Kristina Smigun, Estonia	27:51.4
2010	Charlotte Kalla, Sweden	24:58.4
2014	Justyna Kowalczyk, Poland	28:17.8

Women's 15-Kilometer Pursuit

Year	Champion	Time
1992	Lyubov Egorova, Unified Team	42:20.8
1994	Manuela Di Centa, Italy	39:44.5
1998	Olga Danilova, Russia	46:55.4
2002	Stefania Belmondo, Italy	39:54.4
2006	Kristina Smigun, Estonia	42:48.7
2010	Marit Bjoergen, Norway	39:58.1

Women's Skiathlon

Year	Champion	Time
2014	Marit Bjoergen, Norway	38:33.6

Women's 30-Kilometer Mass Start

Year	Champion	Time
1992	Stefania Belmondo, Italy	1:22:30.1
1994	Manuela Di Centa, Italy	1:25:41.6
1998	Julija Tchepalova, Russia	1:22:01.5
2002	Gabriella Paruzzi, Italy	1:30:57.1
2006	Katerina Neumannova, Czech Republic	1:22:25.4
2010	Justyna Kowalczyk, Poland	1:30:33.7
2014	Marit Bjoergen, Norway	1:11:05.2

Women's 4x5-Kilometer Relay

Year	Champions	Time
1956	Finland, USSR, Sweden (15 km)	1:09:01.0
1960	Sweden, USSR, Finland (15 km)	1:04:21.4
1964	USSR, Sweden, Finland (15 km)	0:59:20.2
1968	Norway, Sweden, USSR (15 km)	0:57:30.0
1972	USSR, Finland, Norway (15 km)	0:48:46.15
1976	USSR, Finland, E. Germany	1:07:49.75
1980	E. Germany, USSR, Norway	1:02:11.1
1984	Norway, Czechoslovakia, Finland	1:06:49.7
1988	USSR, Norway, Finland	0:59:51.1
1992	United Team, Norway, Italy	0:59:34.8
1994	Russia, Norway, Italy	0:57:12.5
1998	Russia, Norway, Italy	0:55:13.5
2002	Germany, Norway, Switzerland	0:49:30.6
2006	Russia, Germany, Italy	0:54:47.7
2010	Norway, Germany, Finland	0:55:19.5
2014	Sweden, Finland, Germany	0:53:02.7

Women's Team Sprint

Year	Champions	Time
2006	Lina Andersson & Anna Dahlberg, Sweden	16:36.9
2010	Evi Sachenbacher-Stehle & Claudia Nystad, Germany	18:03.7
2014	Marit Bjoergen & Ingvild Flugstad Oestberg, Norway	16:04.05

Curling

Men

Year	Medalists
1998	Switzerland, Canada, Norway
2002	Norway, Canada, Switzerland
2006	Canada, Finland, United States
2010	Canada, Norway, Switzerland
2014	Canada, Great Britain, Sweden

Women

Year	Medalists
1998	Canada, Denmark, Sweden
2002	Britain, Switzerland, Canada
2006	Sweden, Switzerland, Canada
2010	Sweden, Canada, China
2014	Canada, Sweden, Great Britain

Figure Skating

Men's Singles

1908[1]	Ulrich Salchow, Sweden
1920[1]	Gillis Grafstrom, Sweden
1924	Gillis Grafstrom, Sweden
1928	Gillis Grafstrom, Sweden
1932	Karl Schaefer, Austria
1936	Karl Schaefer, Austria
1948	Richard Button, United States
1952	Richard Button, United States
1956	Hayes Alan Jenkins, United States
1960	David W. Jenkins, United States
1964	Manfred Schnelldorfer, Germany
1968	Wolfgang Schwartz, Austria
1972	Ondrej Nepela, Czechoslovakia
1976	John Curry, Great Britain
1980	Robin Cousins, Great Britain
1984	Scott Hamilton, United States
1988	Brian Boitano, United States
1992	Viktor Petrenko, Unified Team (Ukraine)
1994	Aleksei Urmanov, Russia
1998	Ilya Kulik, Russia
2002	Alexei Yagudin, Russia
2006	Yevgeny Plushenko, Russia
2010	Evan Lysacek, United States
2014	Yuzuru Hanyu, Japan

(1) Event held during Summer Olympic Games.

Women's Singles

1908[1]	Madge Syers, Great Britain
1920[1]	Magda Julin-Mauroy, Sweden
1924	Herma von Szabo-Planck, Austria
1928	Sonja Henie, Norway

Women's Singles

1932	Sonja Henie, Norway
1936	Sonja Henie, Norway
1948	Barbara Ann Scott, Canada
1952	Jeanette Altwegg, Great Britain
1956	Tenley Albright, United States
1960	Carol Heiss, United States
1964	Sjoukje Dijkstra, Netherlands
1968	Peggy Fleming, United States
1972	Beatrix Schuba, Austria
1976	Dorothy Hamill, United States
1980	Anett Poetzsch, E. Germany
1984	Katarina Witt, E. Germany
1988	Katarina Witt, E. Germany
1992	Kristi Yamaguchi, United States
1994	Oksana Baiul, Ukraine
1998	Tara Lipinski, United States
2002	Sarah Hughes, United States
2006	Shizuka Arakawa, Japan
2010	Kim Yu-na, South Korea
2014	Adelina Sotnikova, Russia

(1) Event held during Summer Olympic Games.

Pairs

1908[1]	Anna Hubler & Heinrich Burger, Germany
1920[1]	Ludovika Jakobsson & Walter Jakobsson, Finland
1924	Helene Engelman & Alfred Berger, Austria
1928	Andree Joly & Pierre Brunet, France
1932	Andree Joly & Pierre Brunet, France
1936	Maxi Herber & Ernst Baier, Germany
1948	Micheline Lannoy & Pierre Baugniet, Belgium
1952	Ria Falk & Paul Falk, Germany
1956	Elisabeth Schwartz & Kurt Oppelt, Austria
1964	Ludmila Beloussova & Oleg Protopopov, USSR
1968	Ludmila Beloussova & Oleg Protopopov, USSR
1972	Irina Rodnina & Alexei Ulanov, USSR
1976	Irina Rodnina & Aleksandr Zaitzev, USSR
1980	Irina Rodnina & Aleksandr Zaitzev, USSR
1984	Elena Valova & Oleg Vassiliev, USSR
1988	Ekaterina Gordeeva & Sergei Grinkov, USSR
1992	Natalia Mishkutienok & Artur Dimitriev, Unified Team
1994	Ekaterina Gordeeva & Sergei Grinkov, Russia
1998	Oksana Kazakova & Artur Dmitriev, Russia
2002	Elena Berezhnaya & Anton Sikharulidze, Russia; Jamie Sale & David Pelletier, Canada (tie)
2006	Tatyana Totmianina & Maxim Marinin, Russia
2010	Shen Xue & Zhao Hongbo, China
2014	Tatiana Volosozhar & Maxim Trankov, Russia

(1) Event held during Summer Olympic Games.

Ice Dancing

1976	Ludmila Pakhomova & Aleksandr Gorschkov, USSR
1980	Natalya Linichuk & Gennadi Karponosov, USSR
1984	Jayne Torvill & Christopher Dean, Great Britain
1988	Natalia Bestemianova & Andrei Bukin, USSR
1992	Marina Klimova & Sergei Ponomarenko, Unified Team
1994	Pasha Grishuk & Evgeny Platov, Russia
1998	Pasha Grishuk & Evgeny Platov, Russia
2002	Marina Anissina & Gwendal Peizerat, France
2006	Tatyana Navka & Roman Kostomarov, Russia
2010	Tessa Virtue & Scott Moir, Canada
2014	Meryl Davis & Charlie White, United States

Mixed Team

2014	Russia, Canada, United States

Freestyle Skiing

Men's Aerials		Points
1994	Andreas Schoenbaechler, Switzerland	234.67
1998	Eric Bergoust, United States	255.64
2002	Ales Valenta, Czech Republic	257.02
2006	Xiaopeng Han, China	250.77
2010	Alexei Grishin, Belarus	248.41
2014	Anton Kushnir, Belarus	134.50

Men's Moguls		Points
1992	Edgar Grospiron, France	25.81
1994	Jean-Luc Brassard, Canada	27.24
1998	Jonny Moseley, United States	26.93

Men's Moguls		Points
2002	Janne Lahtela, Finland	27.97
2006	Dale Begg-Smith, Australia	26.77
2010	Alex Bilodeau, Canada	26.75
2014	Alex Bilodeau, Canada	26.31

Men's Ski Cross

2010	Michael Schmid, Switzerland
2014	Jean Frederic Chapuis, France

Men's Ski Halfpipe		Points
2014	David Wise, United States	92.00

Men's Ski Slopestyle		Points
2014	Joss Christensen, United States	95.80

Women's Aerials		Points
1994	Lina Tcherjazova, Uzbekistan	166.84
1998	Nikki Stone, United States	193.00
2002	Alisa Camplin, Australia	193.47
2006	Evelyne Leu, Switzerland	202.55
2010	Lydia Lassila, Australia	214.74
2014	Alla Tsuper, Belarus	98.01

Women's Moguls		Points
1992	Donna Weinbrecht, United States	23.69
1994	Stine Lise Hattestad, Norway	25.97
1998	Tae Satoya, Japan	25.06
2002	Kari Traa, Norway	25.94
2006	Jennifer Heil, Canada	26.50
2010	Hannah Kearney, United States	26.63
2014	Justine Dufour-Lapointe, Canada	22.44

Women's Ski Cross

2010	Ashleigh McIvor, Canada
2014	Marielle Thompson, Canada

Women's Ski Halfpipe		Points
2014	Maddie Bowman, United States	89.00

Women's Ski Slopestyle		Points
2014	Dara Howell, Canada	94.20

Ice Hockey

Men

1920[1]	Canada, United States, Czechoslovakia
1924	Canada, United States, Great Britain
1928	Canada, Sweden, Switzerland
1932	Canada, United States, Germany
1936	Great Britain, Canada, United States
1948	Canada, Czechoslovakia, Switzerland
1952	Canada, United States, Sweden
1956	USSR, United States, Canada
1960	United States, Canada, USSR
1964	USSR, Sweden, Czechoslovakia
1968	USSR, Czechoslovakia, Canada
1972	USSR, United States, Czechoslovakia
1976	USSR, Czechoslovakia, W. Germany
1980	United States, USSR, Sweden
1984	USSR, Czechoslovakia, Sweden
1988	USSR, Finland, Sweden
1992	Unified Team, Canada, Czechoslovakia
1994	Sweden, Canada, Finland
1998	Czech Republic, Russia, Finland
2002	Canada, United States, Russia
2006	Sweden, Finland, Czech Republic
2010	Canada, United States, Finland
2014	Canada, Sweden, Finland

(1) Event held during Summer Olympic Games.

Women

1998	United States, Canada, Finland
2002	Canada, United States, Sweden
2006	Canada, Sweden, United States
2010	Canada, United States, Finland
2014	Canada, United States, Switzerland

Luge

Men's Singles		Time
1964	Thomas Keohler, E. Germany	3:27.77
1968	Manfred Schmid, Austria	2:52.48
1972	Wolfgang Scheidel, E. Germany	3:27.58

Men's Singles	Time
1976	Detlef Guenther, E. Germany	3:27.688
1980	Bernhard Glass, E. Germany	2:54.796
1984	Paul Hildgartner, Italy	3:04.258
1988	Jens Mueller, E. Germany	3:05.548
1992	Georg Hackl, Germany	3:02.363
1994	Georg Hackl, Germany	3:21.571
1998	Georg Hackl, Germany	3:18.436
2002	Armin Zoeggeler, Italy	2:57.941
2006	Armin Zoeggeler, Italy	3:26.088
2010	Felix Loch, Germany	3:13.085
2014	Felix Loch, Germany	3:27.526

Men's Doubles	Time
1964	Austria	1:41.62
1968	E. Germany	1:35.85
1972	Italy, E. Germany (tie)	1:28.35
1976	E. Germany	1:25.604
1980	E. Germany	1:19.331
1984	W. Germany	1:23.620
1988	E. Germany	1:31.940
1992	Germany	1:32.053
1994	Italy	1:36.720
1998	Germany	1:41.105
2002	Germany	1:26.082
2006	Austria	1:34.497
2010	Austria	1:22.705
2014	Germany	1:38.933

Women's Singles	Time
1964	Ortun Enderlein, Germany	3:24.67
1968	Erica Lechner, Italy	2:28.66
1972	Anna M. Muller, E. Germany	2:59.18
1976	Margit Schumann, E. Germany	2:50.621
1980	Vera Zozulya, USSR	2:36.537
1984	Steffi Martin, E. Germany	2:46.570
1988	Steffi Walter, E. Germany	3:03.973
1992	Doris Neuner, Austria	3:06.696
1994	Gerda Weissensteiner, Italy	3:15.517
1998	Silke Kraushaar, Germany	3:23.779
2002	Sylke Otto, Germany	2:52.464
2006	Sylke Otto, Germany	3:07.979
2010	Tatjana Huefner, Germany	2:46.524
2014	Natalie Geisenberger, Germany	3:19.768

Mixed Team Relay	Time
2014	Germany, Russia, Latvia	2:45.649

Nordic Combined

Men's Individual

1924	Thorleif Haug, Norway
1928	Johan Grottumsbraaten, Norway
1932	Johan Grottumsbraaten, Norway
1936	Oddbjorn Hagen, Norway
1948	Heikki Hasu, Finland
1952	Simon Slattvik, Norway
1956	Sverre Stenersen, Norway
1960	Georg Thoma, W. Germany
1964	Tormod Knutsen, Norway
1968	Franz Keller, W. Germany
1972	Ulrich Wehling, E. Germany
1976	Ulrich Wehling, E. Germany
1980	Ulrich Wehling, E. Germany
1984	Tom Sandberg, Norway
1988	Hippolyt Kempf, Switzerland
1992	Fabrice Guy, France
1994	Fred Barre Lundberg, Norway
1998	Bjarte Engen Vik, Norway
2002	Samppa Lajunen, Finland
2006	Georg Hettich, Germany

Men's 10-Kilometer Large Hill

2010	Bill Demong, United States
2014	Joergen Graabak, Norway

Men's 10-Kilometer Normal Hill

2010	Jason Lamy Chappuis, France
2014	Eric Frenzel, Germany

Men's Team 4x5-Kilometer Relay	
1988	W. Germany, Switzerland, Austria
1992	Japan, Norway, Austria
1994	Japan, Norway, Switzerland
1998	Norway, Finland, France
2002	Finland, Germany, Austria
2006	Austria, Germany, Finland
2010	Austria, United States, Germany
2014	Norway, Germany, Austria

Ski Jumping

Men's Normal Hill	Points
1964	Veikko Kankkonen, Finland	229.9
1968	Jiri Raska, Czechoslovakia	216.5
1972	Yukio Kasaya, Japan	244.2
1976	Hans-Georg Aschenbach, E. Germany	252.0
1980	Toni Innauer, Austria	266.3
1984	Jens Weissflog, E. Germany	215.2
1988	Matti Nykaenen, Finland	230.5
1992	Ernst Vettori, Austria	222.8
1994	Espen Bredesen, Norway	282.0
1998	Jani Soininen, Finland	234.5
2002	Simon Ammann, Switzerland	269.0
2006	Lars Bystoel, Norway	266.5
2010	Simon Ammann, Switzerland	276.5
2014	Kamil Stoch, Poland	278.0

Men's Large Hill	Points
1924	Jacob Tullin Thams, Norway	18.960
1928	Alfred Andersen, Norway	19.208
1932	Birger Ruud, Norway	228.1
1936	Birger Ruud, Norway	232.0
1948	Petter Hugsted, Norway	228.1
1952	Arnfinn Bergmann, Norway	226.0
1956	Antti Hyvarinen, Finland	227.0
1960	Helmut Recknagel, E. Germany	227.2
1964	Toralf Engan, Norway	230.7
1968	Vladimir Beloussov, USSR	231.3
1972	Wojciech Fortuna, Poland	219.9
1976	Karl Schnabl, Austria	234.8
1980	Jouko Tormanen, Finland	271.0
1984	Matti Nykaenen, Finland	231.2
1988	Matti Nykaenen, Finland	224.0
1992	Toni Nieminen, Finland	239.5
1994	Jens Weissflog, Germany	274.5
1998	Kazuyoshi Funaki, Japan	272.3
2002	Simon Ammann, Switzerland	281.4
2006	Thomas Morgenstern, Austria	276.9
2010	Simon Ammann, Switzerland	283.6
2014	Kamil Stoch, Poland	278.7

Men's Team	Points
1988	Finland, Yugoslavia, Norway	634.4
1992	Finland, Austria, Czechoslovakia	644.4
1994	Germany, Japan, Austria	970.1
1998	Japan, Germany, Austria	933.0
2002	Germany, Finland, Slovenia	974.1
2006	Austria, Finland, Norway	984.0
2010	Austria, Germany, Norway	1,107.9
2014	Germany, Austria, Japan	1,041.1

Women's Normal Hill	Points
2014	Carina Vogt, Germany	247.4

Snowboarding

Men's Halfpipe	Points
1998	Gian Simmen, Switzerland	85.2
2002	Ross Powers, United States	46.1
2006	Shaun White, United States	46.8
2010	Shaun White, United States	48.4
2014	Iouri Podladtchikov, Switzerland	94.75

Men's Parallel Giant Slalom	
1998	Ross Rebagliati, Canada
2002	Philipp Schoch, Switzerland
2006	Philipp Schoch, Switzerland

Men's Parallel Giant Slalom
2010   Jasey Jay Anderson, Canada
2014   Vic Wild, Russia
Note: In 2002, the Giant Slalom became the Parallel Giant Slalom.

Men's Parallel Slalom
2014   Vic Wild, Russia

Men's Slopestyle	Points
2014 Sage Kotsenburg, United States	93.50

Men's Snowboard Cross
2006   Seth Wescott, United States
2010   Seth Wescott, United States
2014   Pierre Vaultier, France

Women's Halfpipe	Points
1998 Nicola Thost, Germany	74.6
2002 Kelly Clark, United States	47.9
2006 Hannah Teter, United States	46.4
2010 Torah Bright, Australia	45.0
2014 Kaitlyn Farrington, United States	91.75

Women's Parallel Giant Slalom
1998   Karine Ruby, France
2002   Isabelle Blanc, France
2006   Daniela Meuli, Switzerland
2010   Nicolien Sauerbreij, Netherlands
2014   Patrizia Kummer, Switzerland
Note: In 2002, the Giant Slalom became the Parallel Giant Slalom.

Women's Parallel Slalom
2014   Julia Dujmovits, Austria

Women's Slopestyle	Points
2014 Jamie Anderson, United States	95.25

Women's Snowboard Cross
2006   Tanja Frieden, Switzerland
2010   Maelle Ricker, Canada
2014   Eva Samkova, Czech Republic

Speed Skating
*Olympic record

Men's 500 Meters	Time
1924 Charles Jewtraw, United States	0:44.0
1928 C. Thunberg, Finland; B. Evensen, Norway (tie)	0:43.4
1932 John A. Shea, United States	0:43.4
1936 Ivar Ballangrud, Norway	0:43.4
1948 Finn Helgesen, Norway	0:43.1
1952 Kenneth Henry, United States	0:43.2
1956 Evgeniy Grishin, USSR	0:40.2
1960 Evgeniy Grishin, USSR	0:40.2
1964 Terry McDermott, United States	0:40.1
1968 Erhard Keller, W. Germany	0:40.3
1972 Erhard Keller, W. Germany	0:39.44
1976 Evgeny Kulikov, USSR	0:39.17
1980 Eric Heiden, United States	0:38.03
1984 Sergei Fokichev, USSR	0:38.19
1988 Uwe-Jens Mey, E. Germany	0:36.45
1992 Uwe-Jens Mey, Germany	0:37.14
1994 Aleksandr Golubev, Russia	0:36.33
1998 Hiroyasu Shimizu, Japan	0:35.59
2002 Casey FitzRandolph, United States	0:34.42*
2006 Joey Cheek, United States	0:34.82
2010 Mo Tae-bum, S. Korea	0:34.906
2014 Michel Mulder, Netherlands	0:69.312

Note: In 2014, results include the total of two 500-km race times.

Men's 1000 Meters	Time
1976 Peter Mueller, United States	1:19.32
1980 Eric Heiden, United States	1:15.18
1984 Gaetan Boucher, Canada	1:15.80
1988 Nikolai Guiliaev, USSR	1:13.03
1992 Olaf Zinke, Germany	1:14.85
1994 Dan Jansen, United States	1:12.43
1998 Ids Postma, Netherlands	1:10.64
2002 Gerard van Velde, Netherlands	1:07.18*
2006 Shani Davis, United States	1:08.89
2010 Shani Davis, United States	1:08.94
2014 Stefan Groothuis, Netherlands	1:08.39

Men's 1500 Meters	Time
1924 Clas Thunberg, Finland	2:20.8
1928 Clas Thunberg, Finland	2:21.1
1932 John A. Shea, United States	2:57.5
1936 Charles Mathiesen, Norway	2:19.2
1948 Sverre Farstad, Norway	2:17.6
1952 Hjalmar Andersen, Norway	2:20.4
1956 Y. Grishin, USSR; Y. Mikhailov, USSR (tie)	2:08.6
1960 R. Aas, Norway; Y. Grishin, USSR (tie)	2:10.4
1964 Ants Anston, USSR	2:10.3
1968 Cornetis Verkerk, Netherlands	2:03.4
1972 Ard Schenk, Netherlands	2:02.96
1976 Jan Egil Storholt, Norway	1:59.38
1980 Eric Heiden, United States	1:55.44
1984 Gaetan Boucher, Canada	1:58.36
1988 Andre Hoffmann, E. Germany	1:52.06
1992 Johann Koss, Norway	1:54.81
1994 Johann Koss, Norway	1:51.29
1998 Aadne Sondral, Norway	1:47.87
2002 Derek Parra, United States	1:43.95*
2006 Enrico Fabris, Italy	1:45.97
2010 Mark Tuitert, Netherlands	1:45.57
2014 Zbigniew Brodka, Poland	1:45.006

Men's 5000 Meters	Time
1924 Clas Thunberg, Finland	8:39.0
1928 Ivar Ballangrud, Norway	8:50.5
1932 Irving Jaffee, United States	9:40.8
1936 Ivar Ballangrud, Norway	8:19.6
1948 Reidar Liaklev, Norway	8:29.4
1952 Hjalmar Andersen, Norway	8:10.6
1956 Boris Shilkov, USSR	7:48.7
1960 Viktor Kosichkin, USSR	7:51.3
1964 Knut Johannesen, Norway	7:38.4
1968 F. Anton Maier, Norway	7:22.4
1972 Ard Schenk, Netherlands	7:23.61
1976 Sten Stensen, Norway	7:24.48
1980 Eric Heiden, United States	7:02.29
1984 Tomas Gustafson, Sweden	7:12.28
1988 Tomas Gustafson, Sweden	6:44.63
1992 Geir Karlstad, Norway	6:59.97
1994 Johann Koss, Norway	6:34.96
1998 Gianni Romme, Netherlands	6:22.20
2002 Jochem Uytdehaage, Netherlands	6:14.66
2006 Chad Hedrick, United States	6:14.68
2010 Sven Kramer, Netherlands	6:14.60
2014 Sven Kramer, Netherlands	6:10.76*

Men's 10,000 Meters	Time
1924 Julius Skutnabb, Finland	18:04.8
1928 Event not held because of thawing of ice	
1932 Irving Jaffee, United States	19:13.6
1936 Ivar Ballangrud, Norway	17:24.3
1948 Ake Seyffarth, Sweden	17:26.3
1952 Hjalmar Andersen, Norway	16:45.8
1956 Sigvard Ericsson, Sweden	16:35.9
1960 Knut Johannesen, Norway	15:46.6
1964 Jonny Nilsson, Sweden	15:50.1
1968 Jonny Hoeglin, Sweden	15:23.6
1972 Ard Schenk, Netherlands	15:01.35
1976 Piet Kleine, Netherlands	14:50.59
1980 Eric Heiden, United States	14:28.13
1984 Igor Malkov, USSR	14:39.90
1988 Tomas Gustafson, Sweden	13:48.20
1992 Bart Veldkamp, Netherlands	14:12.12
1994 Johann Koss, Norway	13:30.55
1998 Gianni Romme, Netherlands	13:15.33
2002 Jochem Uytdehaage, Netherlands	12:58.92
2006 Bob de Jong, Netherlands	13:01.57
2010 Lee Seung-hoon, S. Korea	12:58.55
2014 Jorrit Bergsma, Netherlands	12:44.45*

Men's Team Pursuit

		Time
2006	Italy, Canada, Netherlands	3:44.46
2010	Canada, United States, Netherlands	3:41.37
2014	Netherlands, S. Korea, Poland	3:37.71*

Women's 500 Meters

		Time
1960	Helga Haase, Germany	0:45.9
1964	Lydia Skoblikova, USSR	0:45.0
1968	Ludmila Titova, USSR	0:46.1
1972	Anne Henning, United States	0:43.33
1976	Sheila Young, United States	0:42.76
1980	Karin Enke, E. Germany	0:41.78
1984	Christa Rothenburger, E. Germany	0:41.02
1988	Bonnie Blair, United States	0:39.10
1992	Bonnie Blair, United States	0:40.33
1994	Bonnie Blair, United States	0:39.25
1998	Catriona Le May-Doan, Canada	0:38.21
2002	Catriona Le May Doan, Canada	0:37.30
2006	Svetlana Zhurova, Russia	0:38.23
2010	Lee Sang-hwa, S. Korea	0:37.850
2014	Lee Sang-hwa, S. Korea	0:74.70*

Note: In 2014, results include the total of two 500-km race times.

Women's 1000 Meters

		Time
1960	Klara Guseva, USSR	1:34.1
1964	Lydia Skoblikova, USSR	1:33.2
1968	Carolina Geijssen, Netherlands	1:32.6
1972	Monika Pflug, W. Germany	1:31.40
1976	Tatiana Averina, USSR	1:28.43
1980	Natalya Petruseva, USSR	1:24.10
1984	Karin Enke, E. Germany	1:21.61
1988	Christa Rothenburger, E. Germany	1:17.65
1992	Bonnie Blair, United States	1:21.90
1994	Bonnie Blair, United States	1:18.74
1998	Marianne Timmer, Netherlands	1:16.51
2002	Chris Witty, United States	1:13.83*
2006	Marianne Timmer, Netherlands	1:16.05
2010	Christine Nesbitt, Canada	1:16.56
2014	Zhang Hong, China	1:14.02

Women's 1500 Meters

		Time
1960	Lydia Skoblikova, USSR	2:52.2
1964	Lydia Skoblikova, USSR	2:22.6
1968	Kaija Mustonen, Finland	2:22.4
1972	Dianne Holum, United States	2:20.85
1976	Galina Stepanskaya, USSR	2:16.58
1980	Anne Borckink, Netherlands	2:10.95
1984	Karin Enke, E. Germany	2:03.42
1988	Yvonne van Gennip, Netherlands	2:00.68
1992	Jacqueline Boerner, Germany	2:05.87
1994	Emese Hunyady, Austria	2:02.19
1998	Marianne Timmer, Netherlands	1:57.58
2002	Anni Friesinger, Germany	1:54.02
2006	Cindy Klassen, Canada	1:55.27
2010	Ireen Wust, Netherlands	1:56.89
2014	Jorien Ter Mors, Netherlands	1:53.51*

Women's 3000 Meters

		Time
1960	Lydia Skoblikova, USSR	5:14.3
1964	Lydia Skoblikova, USSR	5:14.9
1968	Johanna Schut, Netherlands	4:56.2
1972	Christina Baas-Kaiser, Netherlands	4:52.14
1976	Tatiana Averina, USSR	4:45.19
1980	Bjoerg Eva Jensen, Norway	4:32.13
1984	Andrea Schoene, E. Germany	4:24.79
1988	Yvonne van Gennip, Netherlands	4:11.94
1992	Gunda Niemann, Germany	4:19.90
1994	Svetlana Bazhanova, Russia	4:17.43
1998	Gunda Niemann-Stirnemann, Germany	4:07.29
2002	Claudia Pechstein, Germany	3:57.70*
2006	Ireen Wust, Netherlands	4:02.43
2010	Martina Sablikova, Czech Republic	4:02.53
2014	Ireen Wust, Netherlands	4:00.34

Women's 5000 Meters

		Time
1988	Yvonne van Gennip, Netherlands	7:14.13
1992	Gunda Niemann, Germany	7:31.57

Women's 5000 Meters

		Time
1994	Claudia Pechstein, Germany	7:14.37
1998	Claudia Pechstein, Germany	6:59.61
2002	Claudia Pechstein, Germany	6:46.91*
2006	Clara Hughes, Canada	6:59.07
2010	Martina Sablikova, Czech Republic	6:50.91
2014	Martina Sablikova, Czech Republic	6:51.54

Women's Team Pursuit

		Time
2006	Germany, Canada, Russia	3:01.25
2010	Germany, Japan, Poland	3:02.82
2014	Netherlands, Poland, Russia	2:58.05*

Speed Skating (Short Track)
*Olympic record

Men's 500 Meters

		Time
1998	Takafumi Nishitani, Japan	0:42.862
2002	Marc Gagnon, Canada	0:41.802
2006	Apolo Anton Ohno, United States	0:41.935
2010	Charles Hamelin, Canada	0:40.981
2014	Victor An, Russia	0:41.312

Men's 1000 Meters

		Time
1992	Kim Ki-hoon, S. Korea	1:30.76
1994	Kim Ki-hoon, S. Korea	1:34.57
1998	Kim Dong-sung, S. Korea	1:32.375
2002	Steven Bradbury, Australia	1:29.109
2006	Ahn Hyun-soo, S. Korea	1:26.739
2010	Lee Jung-su, S. Korea	1:23.747*
2014	Victor An, Russia	1:25.325

Men's 1500 Meters

		Time
2002	Apolo Anton Ohno, United States	2:18.541
2006	Ahn Hyun-soo, S. Korea	2:25.341
2010	Lee Jung-su, S. Korea	2:17.611
2014	Charles Hamelin, Canada	2:14.985

Men's 5000-Meter Relay

		Time
1992	S. Korea, Canada, Japan	7:14.02
1994	Italy, United States, Australia	7:11.74
1998	Canada, S. Korea, China	7:06.075
2002	Canada, Italy, China	6:51.579
2006	S. Korea, Canada, United States	6:43.376*
2010	Canada, S. Korea, United States	6:44.224
2014	Russia, United States, China	6:42.100*

Women's 500 Meters

		Time
1992	Cathy Turner, United States	0:47.04
1994	Cathy Turner, United States	0:45.98
1998	Annie Perreault, Canada	0:46.568
2002	Yang Yang (A), China	0:44.187
2006	Wang Meng, China	0:44.345
2010	Wang Meng, China	0:43.048
2014	Li Jianrou, China	0:45.263

Women's 1000 Meters

		Time
1998	Chun Lee-kyung, S. Korea	1:42.776
2002	Yang Yang (A), China	1:36.391
2006	Jin Sun-yu, S. Korea	1:32.859
2010	Wang Meng, China	1:29.213
2014	Park Seung-hi, China	1:30.761

Women's 1500 Meters

		Time
2002	Ko Gi-hyun, S. Korea	2:31.581
2006	Jin Sun-yu, S. Korea	2:23.494
2010	Zhou Yang, China	2:16.993*
2014	Zhou Yang, China	2:19.140

Women's 3000-Meter Relay

		Time
1992	Canada, United States, Unified Team	4:36.62
1994	S. Korea, Canada, United States	4:26.64
1998	S. Korea, China, Canada	4:16.26
2002	S. Korea, China, Canada	4:12.793
2006	S. Korea, Canada, Italy	4:17.040
2010	China, Canada, United States	4:06.610*
2014	S. Korea, Canada, Italy	4:09.498

COLLEGE FOOTBALL

2015 CFP Championship: Alabama Outlasts Clemson

No. 2-ranked Alabama Crimson Tide defeated the No. 1 Clemson Tigers, 45-40, Jan. 11, 2016, in Glendale, AZ, for 'Bama's fourth national title in seven years. Heisman-winning Tide running back Derrick Henry ran for 158 yards and three touchdowns as head coach Nick Saban claimed his fifth career national title and fourth title with Alabama. The Tigers led the game, 24-21, after three quarters but were outscored 24-16 in a wild fourth quarter.

Clemson handily defeated No. 4-ranked Oklahoma in the College Football Playoff (CFP) semifinal Orange Bowl, 37-17, to reach the national title game. Alabama reached the CFP championship with a dominating semifinal Cotton Bowl victory, 38-0, over No. 3 Michigan State.

The NCAA Football Bowl Subdivision (FBS) College Football Playoff replaced the Bowl Championship Series (BCS) at the end of the 2014 regular season. The four-team CFP consists of a semifinal round (rotating among the following six bowl games: Sugar, Rose, Orange, Cotton, Peach, and Fiesta) and a championship game played on a Monday night. A committee ranks 25 teams for the playoffs and selected other bowl games at the end of the regular season, using guidelines that include strength of schedule, head-to-head results, and won-loss records; preference is given to conference champions.

National College Football Champions, 1936-2015

A four-team College Football Playoff has determined the champion since the 2014 season. The Bowl Championship Series (BCS) National Championship game (BCS No. 1 vs. BCS No. 2) determined the NCAA's Football Bowl Subdivision (Div. I-A) official champion in 1998-2013. Years preceding 1998 show the unofficial champion(s), as selected by the AP poll of writers and a separate poll of coaches. Where the polls disagreed, both teams are listed with the AP winner first. The AP poll started in 1936, the coaches poll in 1950.

Year	Champion(s)	Year	Champion(s)	Year	Champion(s)	Year	Champion(s)	Year	Champion(s)
1936	Minnesota	1953	Maryland	1969	Texas	1984	Brigham Young	2000	Oklahoma
1937	Pittsburgh	1954	Ohio St./UCLA	1970	Nebraska/Texas	1985	Oklahoma	2001	Miami (FL)
1938	Texas Christian	1955	Oklahoma	1971	Nebraska	1986	Penn St.	2002	Ohio St.
1939	Texas A&M	1956	Oklahoma	1972	USC	1987	Miami (FL)	2003	LSU/USC
1940	Minnesota	1957	Auburn/Ohio St.	1973	Notre Dame/	1988	Notre Dame	2004	Vacated[1]
1941	Minnesota	1958	LSU		Alabama	1989	Miami (FL)	2005	Texas
1942	Ohio St.	1959	Syracuse	1974	Oklahoma/USC	1990	Colorado/GA Tech	2006	Florida
1943	Notre Dame	1960	Minnesota	1975	Oklahoma	1991	Miami (FL)/Wash.	2007	LSU
1944	Army	1961	Alabama	1976	Pittsburgh	1992	Alabama	2008	Florida
1945	Army	1962	USC	1977	Notre Dame	1993	Florida St.	2009	Alabama
1946	Notre Dame	1963	Texas	1978	Alabama/USC	1994	Nebraska	2010	Auburn
1947	Notre Dame	1964	Alabama	1979	Alabama	1995	Nebraska	2011	Alabama
1948	Michigan	1965	Alabama/Mich. St.	1980	Georgia	1996	Florida	2012	Alabama
1949	Notre Dame	1966	Notre Dame	1981	Clemson	1997	Mich./Nebraska	2013	Florida St.
1950	Oklahoma	1967	USC	1982	Penn St.	1998	Tennessee	2014	Ohio St.
1951	Tennessee	1968	Ohio St.	1983	Miami (FL)	1999	Florida St.	2015	Alabama
1952	Michigan St.								

(1) The BCS's Presidential Oversight Committee vacated USC's 2004 championship due to rules violations.

2015 Final Rankings

College Football Playoff Rankings		Associated Press Poll		USA Today Coaches Poll	
Rank, team	**Rank, team**	**Rank, team**	**Rank, team**	**Rank, team**	**Rank, team**
1. Clemson	14. Michigan	1. Alabama	14. Florida State	1. Alabama	14. Florida State
2. Alabama	15. Oregon	2. Clemson	15. North Carolina	2. Clemson	15. North Carolina
3. Michigan State	16. Oklahoma State	3. Stanford	16. LSU	3. Stanford	16. Utah
4. Oklahoma	17. Baylor	4. Ohio State	17. Utah	4. Ohio State	17. LSU
5. Iowa	18. Houston	5. Oklahoma	18. Navy	5. Oklahoma	18. Navy
6. Stanford	19. Florida	6. Michigan State	19. Oregon	6. Michigan State	19. Oklahoma Stat
7. Ohio State	20. LSU	7. TCU	20. Oklahoma State	7. TCU	20. Oregon
8. Notre Dame	21. Navy	8. Houston	21. Wisconsin	8. Houston	21. Wisconsin
9. Florida State	22. Utah	9. Iowa	22. Tennessee	9. Mississippi	22. Northwestern
10. North Carolina	23. Tennessee	10. Mississippi	23. Northwestern	10. Iowa	23. Tennessee
11. TCU	24. Temple	11. Notre Dame	24. Western	11. Michigan	24. Georgia
12. Mississippi	25. USC	12. Michigan	Kentucky	12. Notre Dame	25. Florida
13. Northwestern		13. Baylor	25. Florida	13. Baylor	

Note: College Football Playoff ranking is as of Dec. 6, 2015, prior to bowl games and playoffs. Final AP and USA Today polls are as of Jan. 12, 2016 (after all bowls and championship game).

Annual Results of Major Bowl Games

Date indicates year the game was played; bowl games are generally played in late Dec. or early Jan. CFP = College Football Playoff semifinal game.

Rose Bowl Results, 1902-2016

1902	(Jan.) Michigan 49, Stanford 0	1933	USC 35, Pittsburgh 0	1951	Michigan 14, California 6
1916	Washington St. 14, Brown 0	1934	Columbia 7, Stanford 0	1952	Illinois 40, Stanford 7
1917	Oregon 14, Pennsylvania 0	1935	Alabama 29, Stanford 13	1953	USC 7, Wisconsin 0
1918-19	Service teams	1936	Stanford 7, SMU 0	1954	Michigan St. 28, UCLA 20
1920	Harvard 7, Oregon 6	1937	Pittsburgh 21, Washington 0	1955	Ohio St. 20, USC 7
1921	California 28, Ohio St. 0	1938	California 13, Alabama 0	1956	Michigan St. 17, UCLA 14
1922	Washington & Jefferson 0,	1939	USC 7, Duke 3	1957	Iowa 35, Oregon St. 19
	California 0	1940	USC 14, Tennessee 0	1958	Ohio St. 10, Oregon 7
1923	USC 14, Penn St. 3	1941	Stanford 21, Nebraska 13	1959	Iowa 38, California 12
1924	Navy 14, Washington 14	1942	Oregon St. 20, Duke 16	1960	Washington 44, Wisconsin 8
1925	Notre Dame 27, Stanford 10	1943	Georgia 9, UCLA 0	1961	Washington 17, Minnesota 7
1926	Alabama 20, Washington 19	1944	USC 29, Washington 0	1962	Minnesota 21, UCLA 3
1927	Alabama 7, Stanford 7	1945	USC 25, Tennessee 0	1963	USC 42, Wisconsin 37
1928	Stanford 7, Pittsburgh 6	1946	Alabama 34, USC 14	1964	Illinois 17, Washington 7
1929	Georgia Tech 8, California 7	1947	Illinois 45, UCLA 14	1965	Michigan 34, Oregon St. 7
1930	USC 47, Pittsburgh 14	1948	Michigan 49, USC 0	1966	UCLA 14, Michigan St. 12
1931	Alabama 24, Washington St. 0	1949	Northwestern 20, California 14	1967	Purdue 14, USC 13
1932	USC 21, Tulane 12	1950	Ohio St. 17, California 14	1968	USC 14, Indiana 3

1969	Ohio St. 27, USC 16	1985	USC 20, Ohio St. 17	2001	Washington 34, Purdue 24
1970	USC 10, Michigan 3	1986	UCLA 45, Iowa 28	2002	Miami (FL) 37, Nebraska 14
1971	Stanford 27, Ohio St. 17	1987	Arizona St. 22, Michigan 15	2003	Oklahoma 34, Washington St. 14
1972	Stanford 13, Michigan 12	1988	Michigan St. 20, USC 17	2004	USC 28, Michigan 14
1973	USC 42, Ohio St. 17	1989	Michigan 22, USC 14	2005	Texas 38, Michigan 37
1974	Ohio St. 42, USC 21	1990	USC 17, Michigan 10	2006	Texas 41, USC 38
1975	USC 18, Ohio St. 17	1991	Washington 46, Iowa 34	2007	USC 32, Michigan 18
1976	UCLA 23, Ohio St. 10	1992	Washington 34, Michigan 14	2008	USC 49, Illinois 17
1977	USC 14, Michigan 6	1993	Michigan 38, Washington 31	2009	USC 38, Penn St. 24
1978	Washington 27, Michigan 20	1994	Wisconsin 21, UCLA 16	2010	Ohio St. 26, Oregon 17
1979	USC 17, Michigan 10	1995	Penn St. 38, Oregon 20	2011	TCU 21, Wisconsin 19
1980	USC 17, Ohio St. 16	1996	USC 41, Northwestern 32	2012	Oregon 45, Wisconsin 38
1981	Michigan 23, Washington 6	1997	Ohio St. 20, Arizona St. 17	2013	Stanford 20, Wisconsin 14
1982	Washington 28, Iowa 0	1998	Michigan 21, Washington St. 16	2014	Michigan St. 24, Stanford 20
1983	UCLA 24, Michigan 14	1999	Wisconsin 38, UCLA 31	2015	Oregon 59, Florida St. 20 (CFP)
1984	UCLA 45, Illinois 9	2000	Wisconsin 17, Stanford 9	2016	Stanford 45, Iowa 16

Orange Bowl Results, 1935-2015

1935	(Jan.) Bucknell 26, Miami (FL) 0	1963	Alabama 17, Oklahoma 0	1992	Miami (FL) 22, Nebraska 0
1936	Catholic U. 20, Mississippi 19	1964	Nebraska 13, Auburn 7	1993	Florida St. 27, Nebraska 14
1937	Duquesne 13, Mississippi St. 12	1965	Texas 21, Alabama 17	1994	Florida St. 18, Nebraska 16
1938	Auburn 6, Michigan St. 0	1966	Alabama 39, Nebraska 28	1995	Nebraska 24, Miami (FL) 17
1939	Tennessee 17, Oklahoma 0	1967	Florida 27, Georgia Tech 12	1996	Florida St. 31, Notre Dame 26
1940	Georgia Tech 21, Missouri 7	1968	Oklahoma 26, Tennessee 24	1996	(Dec.) Nebraska 41,
1941	Mississippi St. 14,	1969	Penn St. 15, Kansas 14		Virginia Tech 21
	Georgetown 7	1970	Penn St. 10, Missouri 3	1998	(Jan.) Nebraska 42,
1942	Georgia 40, TCU 26	1971	Nebraska 17, LSU 12		Tennessee 17
1943	Alabama 37, Boston College 21	1972	Nebraska 38, Alabama 6	1999	Florida 31, Syracuse 10
1944	LSU 19, Texas A&M 14	1973	Nebraska 40, Notre Dame 6	2000	Michigan 35, Alabama 34 (OT)
1945	Tulsa 26, Georgia Tech 12	1974	Penn St. 16, LSU 9	2001	Oklahoma 13, Florida St. 2
1946	Miami (FL) 13, Holy Cross 6	1975	Notre Dame 13, Alabama 11	2002	Florida 56, Maryland 23
1947	Rice 8, Tennessee 0	1976	Oklahoma 14, Michigan 6	2003	USC 38, Iowa 17
1948	Georgia Tech 20, Kansas 14	1977	Ohio St. 27, Colorado 10	2004	Miami (FL) 16, Florida St. 14
1949	Texas 41, Georgia 28	1978	Arkansas 31, Oklahoma 6	2005	USC 55, Oklahoma 19
1950	Santa Clara 21, Kentucky 13	1979	Oklahoma 31, Nebraska 24	2006	Penn St. 26, Florida St. 23
1951	Clemson 15, Miami (FL) 14	1980	Oklahoma 24, Florida St. 7		(3 OT)
1952	Georgia Tech 17, Baylor 14	1981	Oklahoma 18, Florida St. 17	2007	Louisville 24, Wake Forest 13
1953	Alabama 61, Syracuse 6	1982	Clemson 22, Nebraska 15	2008	Kansas 24, Virginia Tech 21
1954	Oklahoma 7, Maryland 0	1983	Nebraska 21, LSU 20	2009	Virginia Tech 20, Cincinnati 7
1955	Duke 34, Nebraska 7	1984	Miami (FL) 31, Nebraska 30	2010	Iowa 24, Georgia Tech 14
1956	Oklahoma 20, Maryland 6	1985	Washington 28, Oklahoma 17	2011	Stanford 40, Virginia Tech 12
1957	Colorado 27, Clemson 21	1986	Oklahoma 25, Penn St. 10	2012	West Virginia 70, Clemson 33
1958	Oklahoma 48, Duke 21	1987	Oklahoma 42, Arkansas 8	2013	Florida St. 31, Northern Illinois 10
1959	Oklahoma 21, Syracuse 6	1988	Miami (FL) 20, Oklahoma 14	2014	Clemson 40, Ohio St. 35
1960	Georgia 14, Missouri 0	1989	Miami (FL) 23, Nebraska 3	2014	(Dec.) Georgia Tech 49,
1961	Missouri 21, Navy 14	1990	Notre Dame 21, Colorado 6		Mississippi St. 34
1962	LSU 25, Colorado 7	1991	Colorado 10, Notre Dame 9	2015	Clemson 37, Oklahoma 17 (CFP)

Sugar Bowl Results, 1935-2016

1935	(Jan.) Tulane 20, Temple 14	1962	Alabama 10, Arkansas 3	1990	Miami (FL) 33, Alabama 25
1936	TCU 3, LSU 2	1963	Mississippi 17, Arkansas 13	1991	Tennessee 23, Virginia 22
1937	Santa Clara 21, LSU 14	1964	Alabama 12, Mississippi 7	1992	Notre Dame 39, Florida 28
1938	Santa Clara 6, LSU 0	1965	LSU 13, Syracuse 10	1993	Alabama 34, Miami (FL) 13
1939	TCU 15, Carnegie Tech 7	1966	Missouri 20, Florida 18	1994	Florida 41, West Virginia 7
1940	Texas A&M 14, Tulane 13	1967	Alabama 34, Nebraska 7	1995	Florida St. 23, Florida 17
1941	Boston College 19, Tennessee 13	1968	LSU 20, Wyoming 13	1995	(Dec.) Virginia Tech 28, Texas 10
1942	Fordham 2, Missouri 0	1969	Arkansas 16, Georgia 2	1997	(Jan.) Florida 52, Florida St. 20
1943	Tennessee 14, Tulsa 7	1970	Mississippi 27, Arkansas 22	1998	Florida St. 31, Ohio St. 14
1944	Georgia Tech 20, Tulsa 18	1971	Tennessee 34, Air Force 13	1999	Ohio St. 24, Texas A&M 14
1945	Duke 29, Alabama 26	1972	Oklahoma 40, Auburn 22	2000	Florida St. 46, Virginia Tech 29
1946	Oklahoma A&M 33,	1972	(Dec.) Oklahoma 14, Penn St. 0	2001	Miami (FL) 37, Florida 20
	St. Mary's (CA) 13	1973	Notre Dame 24, Alabama 23	2002	LSU 47, Illinois 34
1947	Georgia 20, N. Carolina 10	1974	Nebraska 13, Florida 10	2003	Georgia 26, Florida St. 13
1948	Texas 27, Alabama 7	1975	Alabama 13, Penn St. 6	2004	LSU 21, Oklahoma 14
1949	Oklahoma 14, N. Carolina 6	1977	(Jan.) Pittsburgh 27, Georgia 3	2005	Auburn 16, Virginia Tech 13
1950	Oklahoma 35, LSU 0	1978	Alabama 35, Ohio St. 6	2006	West Virginia 38, Georgia 35
1951	Kentucky 13, Oklahoma 7	1979	Alabama 14, Penn St. 7	2007	LSU 41, Notre Dame 14
1952	Maryland 28, Tennessee 13	1980	Alabama 24, Arkansas 9	2008	Georgia 41, Hawaii 10
1953	Georgia Tech 24, Mississippi 7	1981	Georgia 17, Notre Dame 10	2009	Utah 31, Alabama 17
1954	Georgia Tech 42, West Virginia 19	1982	Pittsburgh 24, Georgia 20	2010	Florida 51, Cincinnati 24
1955	Navy 21, Mississippi 0	1983	Penn St. 27, Georgia 23	2011	Ohio St. 31, Arkansas 26
1956	Georgia Tech 7, Pittsburgh 0	1984	Auburn 9, Michigan 7	2012	Michigan 23, Virginia Tech 20
1957	Baylor 13, Tennessee 7	1985	Nebraska 28, LSU 10	2013	Louisville 33, Florida 23
1958	Mississippi 39, Texas 7	1986	Tennessee 35, Miami (FL) 7	2014	Oklahoma 45, Alabama 31
1959	LSU 7, Clemson 0	1987	Nebraska 30, LSU 15	2015	Ohio St. 42, Alabama 35 (CFP)
1960	Mississippi 21, LSU 0	1988	Syracuse 16, Auburn 16	2016	Mississippi 48, Oklahoma St. 20
1961	Mississippi 14, Rice 6	1989	Florida St. 13, Auburn 7		

Other Bowl Results, Dec. 2015-Jan. 2016

Bowl games are generally played in late Dec. or early Jan. CFP = College Football Playoff semifinal game.

Alamo Bowl, San Antonio, TX: TCU 47, Oregon 41 (3 OT)

Arizona Bowl, Tucson, AZ: Nevada 28, Colorado St. 23

Armed Forces Bowl, Ft. Worth, TX: California 55, Air Force 36

Bahamas Bowl, Nassau, Bahamas: Western Michigan 45, Middle Tennessee St. 31

Belk Bowl, Charlotte, NC: Mississippi St. 51, North Carolina St. 28

Birmingham Bowl, Birmingham, AL: Auburn 31, Memphis 10

Boca Raton Bowl, Boca Raton, FL: Toledo 32, Temple 17

Cactus Bowl, Phoenix, AZ: West Virginia 43, Arizona St. 42

Camellia Bowl, Montgomery, AL: Appalachian St. 31, Ohio 29

Citrus Bowl, Orlando, FL: Michigan 41, Florida 7

Cotton Bowl, Arlington, TX: Alabama 38, Michigan St. 0 (CFP)

Cure Bowl, Orlando, FL: San Jose St. 27, Georgia St. 16

Fiesta Bowl, Glendale, AZ: Ohio St. 44, Notre Dame 28

Foster Farms Bowl, Santa Clara, CA: Nebraska 37, UCLA 29

GoDaddy Bowl, Mobile, AL: Georgia Southern 58, Bowling Green 27

Hawaii Bowl, Honolulu, HI: San Diego St. 42, Cincinnati 7

Heart of Dallas Bowl, Dallas, TX: Washington 44, Southern Mississippi 31

Holiday Bowl, San Diego, CA: Wisconsin 23, USC 21

Independence Bowl, Shreveport, LA: Virginia Tech 55, Tulsa 52

Las Vegas Bowl, Las Vegas, NV: Utah 35, BYU 28

Liberty Bowl, Memphis, TN: Arkansas 45, Kansas St. 23

Miami Beach Bowl, Miami, FL: Western Kentucky 45, South Florida 35

Military Bowl, Annapolis, MD: Navy 44, Pittsburgh 28

Music City Bowl, Nashville, TN: Louisville 27, Texas A&M 21

New Mexico Bowl, Albuquerque, NM: Arizona 45, New Mexico 37

New Orleans Bowl, New Orleans, LA: Louisiana Tech 47, Arkansas St. 28

Outback Bowl, Tampa, FL: Tennessee 45, Northwestern 6

Peach Bowl, Atlanta, GA: Houston 38, Florida St. 24

Pinstripe Bowl, Bronx, NY: Duke 44, Indiana 41 (OT)

Poinsettia Bowl, San Diego, CA: Boise St. 55, Northern Illinois 7

Potato Bowl, Boise, ID: Akron 23, Utah St. 21

Quick Lane Bowl, Detroit, MI: Minnesota 21, Central Michigan 14

Russell Athletic Bowl, Orlando, FL: Baylor 49, North Carolina 38

St. Petersburg Bowl, St. Petersburg, FL: Marshall 16, Connecticut 10

Sun Bowl, El Paso, TX: Washington St. 20, Miami (FL) 14

TaxSlayer (fmr. Gator) Bowl, Jacksonville, FL: Georgia 24, Penn St. 17

Texas Bowl, Houston, TX: LSU 56, Texas Tech 27

All-Time NCAA Bowl Subdivision (FBS) Statistical Leaders

Career Rushing Yards

Player, team	Yrs	Carries	Yds	Avg
Ron Dayne, Wisconsin	1996-99	1,115	6,397	5.74
Ricky Williams, Texas	1995-98	1,011	6,279	6.21
Tony Dorsett, Pittsburgh ...	1973-76	1,074	6,082	5.66
DeAngelo Williams, Memphis	2002-05	969	6,026	6.22
Charles White, USC	1976-79	1,023	5,598	5.47

Career Rushing Yards/Game (min. 2,500 yds)

Player, team	Yrs	Carries	Yds	Avg/game
Ed Marinaro, Cornell	1969-71	918	4,715	174.6
O. J. Simpson, USC	1967-68	621	3,124	164.4
Herschel Walker, Georgia ..	1980-82	994	5,259	159.4
Garrett Wolfe, N. Illinois....	2004-06	807	5,164	156.5
LeShon Johnson, N. Illinois	1992-93	592	3,314	150.6

Career Passing Yards

Player, team	Yrs	Comp/att	Yds
Case Keenum, Houston ...	2007-11	1,546/2,229	19,217
Timmy Chang, Hawaii	2000-04	1,388/2,436	17,072
Landry Jones, Oklahoma...	2009-12	1,388/2,183	16,646
Graham Harrell, Texas Tech	2005-08	1,403/2,010	15,793
Ty Detmer, BYU	1988-91	958/1,530	15,031

Career Receiving Yards

Player, team	Yrs	Rec	Yds	Avg
Trevor Insley, Nevada	1996-99	298	5,005	16.8
Ryan Broyles, Oklahoma...	2008-11	349	4,586	13.1
Justin Hardy, E. Carolina..	2011-14	387	4,541	11.7
Marcus Harris, Wyoming...	1993-96	259	4,518	17.4
Rashaun Woods, Oklahoma St.	2000-03	293	4,414	15.1

Note: As of end of 2015 season. Prior to 2002, postseason games were not included in NCAA final football statistics or records. All postseason games were included for the 2002 season and thereafter. Career rushing yards per game rankings do not include active players.

All-Time NCAA Bowl Subdivision (FBS) Team Won-Lost Records

Team	Yrs	W	L	T	Games	Pct.
Notre Dame	127	892	313	42	1,247	0.732
Michigan	136	925	331	36	1,292	0.730
Boise St. (1996) ...	48	417	159	2	578	0.723
Ohio St.[1]	126	875	320	53	1,248	0.722
Oklahoma	121	861	319	53	1,233	0.720
Alabama[1]	121	864	326	43	1,233	0.718
Texas	123	886	353	33	1,272	0.710
USC[1]	122	813	333	54	1,200	0.700
Nebraska	126	880	368	40	1,288	0.699
Penn St.	129	856	382	42	1,280	0.685
Tennessee	119	820	371	53	1,244	0.680
Florida St.[1]	69	522	241	17	780	0.680

Team	Yrs	W	L	T	Games	Pct.
LSU	122	770	404	47	1,221	0.650
Georgia Southern (2014)	52	373	199	10	582	0.649
Georgia	122	787	413	54	1,254	0.649
Appalachian St. (2014)	86	587	326	29	942	0.639
Miami (FL)	90	604	347	19	970	0.632
Florida	109	701	404	40	1,145	0.630
Auburn	123	741	427	47	1,215	0.629
Arizona St.	103	595	375	24	994	0.611
Washington......	126	703	440	50	1,193	0.610

Note: As of end of 2015 season. Includes records as senior college only. Bowl and playoff games are included, and each tie game is computed as half won and half lost. Teams must have been in Div. I for at least 25 years to qualify. Year in parentheses indicates the first year of FBS membership, that is, reclassification to Bowl Subdivision (FBS) (formerly Division I-A). Tiebreaker rule began with 1996 season. (1) Record adjusted by action of the NCAA Committee on Infractions.

Heisman Trophy Winners, 1935-2015

The Heisman Memorial Trophy is awarded annually to the nation's outstanding college football player by the Downtown Athletic Club.

Year	Winner, school, position
1935	Jay Berwanger, Chicago, HB
1936	Larry Kelley, Yale, E
1937	Clinton Frank, Yale, HB
1938	David O'Brien, Texas Christian, QB
1939	Nile Kinnick, Iowa, HB
1940	Tom Harmon, Michigan, HB
1941	Bruce Smith, Minnesota, HB
1942	Frank Sinkwich, Georgia, HB
1943	Angelo Bertelli, Notre Dame, QB
1944	Leslie Horvath, Ohio St., QB
1945	Felix Blanchard, Army, FB
1946	Glenn Davis, Army, HB
1947	John Lujack, Notre Dame, QB
1948	Doak Walker, SMU, HB
1949	Leon Hart, Notre Dame, E
1950	Vic Janowicz, Ohio St., HB
1951	Richard Kazmaier, Princeton, HB
1952	Billy Vessels, Oklahoma, HB
1953	John Lattner, Notre Dame, HB
1954	Alan Ameche, Wisconsin, FB
1955	Howard Cassady, Ohio St., HB
1956	Paul Hornung, Notre Dame, QB
1957	John Crow, Texas A&M, HB
1958	Pete Dawkins, Army, HB
1959	Billy Cannon, LSU, HB
1960	Joe Bellino, Navy, HB
1961	Ernest Davis, Syracuse, HB

Year	Winner, school, position
1962	Terry Baker, Oregon St., QB
1963	Roger Staubach, Navy, QB
1964	John Huarte, Notre Dame, QB
1965	Mike Garrett, USC, HB
1966	Steve Spurrier, Florida, QB
1967	Gary Beban, UCLA, QB
1968	O. J. Simpson, USC, RB
1969	Steve Owens, Oklahoma, RB
1970	Jim Plunkett, Stanford, QB
1971	Pat Sullivan, Auburn, QB
1972	Johnny Rodgers, Nebraska, RB-WR
1973	John Cappelletti, Penn St., RB
1974	Archie Griffin, Ohio St., RB
1975	Archie Griffin, Ohio St., RB
1976	Tony Dorsett, Pittsburgh, RB
1977	Earl Campbell, Texas, RB
1978	Billy Sims, Oklahoma, RB
1979	Charles White, USC, RB
1980	George Rogers, S. Carolina, RB
1981	Marcus Allen, USC, RB
1982	Herschel Walker, Georgia, RB
1983	Mike Rozier, Nebraska, RB
1984	Doug Flutie, Boston College, QB
1985	Bo Jackson, Auburn, RB
1986	Vinny Testaverde, Miami (FL), QB
1987	Tim Brown, Notre Dame, WR
1988	Barry Sanders, Oklahoma St., RB

Year	Winner, school, position
1989	Andre Ware, Houston, QB
1990	Ty Detmer, BYU, QB
1991	Desmond Howard, Michigan, WR
1992	Gino Torretta, Miami (FL), QB
1993	Charlie Ward, Florida St., QB
1994	Rashaan Salaam, Colorado, RB
1995	Eddie George, Ohio St., RB
1996	Danny Wuerffel, Florida, QB
1997	Charles Woodson, Michigan, CB
1998	Ricky Williams, Texas, RB
1999	Ron Dayne, Wisconsin, RB
2000	Chris Weinke, Florida St., QB
2001	Eric Crouch, Nebraska, QB
2002	Carson Palmer, USC, QB
2003	Jason White, Oklahoma, QB
2004	Matt Leinart, USC, QB
2005	Reggie Bush, USC, RB[1]
2006	Troy Smith, Ohio St., QB
2007	Tim Tebow, Florida, QB
2008	Sam Bradford, Oklahoma, QB
2009	Mark Ingram, Alabama, RB
2010	Cam Newton, Auburn, QB
2011	Robert Griffin III, Baylor, QB
2012	Johnny Manziel, Texas A&M, QB
2013	Jameis Winston, Florida St., QB
2014	Marcus Mariota, Oregon, QB
2015	Derrick Henry, Alabama, RB

(1) Bush forfeited the trophy voluntarily Sept. 14, 2010, following revelations of NCAA rules violations while Bush was at USC.

College Football Coach of the Year, 1935-2015

The Coach of the Year has been selected by the American Football Coaches Assn. (AFCA) since 1935 as well as the Football Writers Assn. of America (FWAA) since 1957. When polls disagree, both winners are indicated.

1935 Lynn Waldorf, Northwestern	1967 John Pont, Indiana	1993 Barry Alvarez, Wisconsin (AFCA);
1936 Dick Harlow, Harvard	1968 Joe Paterno, Penn St. (AFCA);	Terry Bowden, Auburn (FWAA)
1937 Edward Mylin, Lafayette	Woody Hayes, Ohio St. (FWAA)	1994 Tom Osborne, Nebraska (AFCA);
1938 Bill Kern, Carnegie Tech	1969 Bo Schembechler, Michigan	Rich Brooks, Oregon (FWAA)
1939 Eddie Anderson, Iowa	1970 Charles McClendon, LSU &	1995 Gary Barnett, Northwestern
1940 Clark Shaughnessy, Stanford	Darrell Royal, Texas (AFCA);	1996 Bruce Snyder, Arizona St.
1941 Frank Leahy, Notre Dame	Alex Agase, Northwestern (FWAA)	1997 Mike Price, Washington St.
1942 Bill Alexander, Georgia Tech	1971 Paul "Bear" Bryant, Alabama (AFCA);	1998 Phillip Fulmer, Tennessee
1943 Amos Alonzo Stagg, Pacific (CA)	Bob Devaney, Nebraska (FWAA)	1999 Frank Beamer, Virginia Tech
1944 Carroll Widdoes, Ohio St.	1972 John McKay, USC	2000 Bob Stoops, Oklahoma
1945 Bo McMillin, Indiana	1973 Paul "Bear" Bryant, Alabama (AFCA);	2001 Larry Coker, Miami (FL) &
1946 Earl "Red" Blaik, Army	Johnny Majors, Pittsburgh (FWAA)	Ralph Friedgen, Maryland (AFCA);
1947 Fritz Crisler, Michigan	1974 Grant Teaff, Baylor	Ralph Friedgen, Maryland (FWAA)
1948 Bennie Oosterbaan, Michigan	1975 Frank Kush, Arizona St. (AFCA);	2002 Jim Tressel, Ohio St.
1949 Bud Wilkinson, Oklahoma	Woody Hayes, Ohio St. (FWAA)	2003 Pete Carroll, USC (AFCA);
1950 Charlie Caldwell, Princeton	1976 Johnny Majors, Pittsburgh	Nick Saban, LSU (FWAA)
1951 Chuck Taylor, Stanford	1977 Don James, Washington (AFCA);	2004 Tommy Tuberville, Auburn (AFCA);
1952 Biggie Munn, Michigan St.	Lou Holtz, Arkansas (FWAA)	Urban Meyer, Utah (FWAA)
1953 Jim Tatum, Maryland	1978 Joe Paterno, Penn St.	2005 Joe Paterno, Penn St. (AFCA);
1954 Henry "Red" Sanders, UCLA	1979 Earle Bruce, Ohio St.	Charlie Weis, Notre Dame (FWAA)
1955 Duffy Daugherty, Michigan St.	1980 Vince Dooley, Georgia	2006 Jim Grobe, Wake Forest (AFCA);
1956 Bowden Wyatt, Tennessee	1981 Danny Ford, Clemson	Greg Schiano, Rutgers (FWAA)
1957 Woody Hayes, Ohio St.	1982 Joe Paterno, Penn St.	2007 Mark Mangino, Kansas
1958 Paul Dietzel, LSU	1983 Ken Hatfield, Air Force (AFCA);	2008 Kyle Whittingham, Utah (AFCA);
1959 Ben Schwartzwalder, Syracuse	Howard Schnellenberger,	Nick Saban, Alabama (FWAA)
1960 Murray Warmath, Minnesota	Miami (FL) (FWAA)	2009 Gary Patterson, TCU
1961 Paul "Bear" Bryant, Alabama (AFCA);	1984 LaVell Edwards, Brigham Young	2010 Chip Kelly, Oregon
Darrell Royal, Texas (FWAA)	1985 Fisher De Berry, Air Force	2011 Les Miles, LSU (AFCA);
1962 John McKay, USC	1986 Joe Paterno, Penn St.	Mike Gundy, Oklahoma St. (FWAA)
1963 Darrell Royal, Texas	1987 Dick MacPherson, Syracuse	2012 Brian Kelly, Notre Dame
1964 Ara Parseghian, Notre Dame &	1988 Don Nehlen, W. Virginia (AFCA);	2013 David Cutcliffe, Duke (AFCA);
Frank Broyles, Arkansas (AFCA);	Lou Holtz, Notre Dame (FWAA)	Gus Malzahn, Auburn (FWAA)
Ara Parseghian, Notre Dame (FWAA)	1989 Bill McCartney, Colorado	2014 Gary Patterson, TCU
1965 Tommy Prothro, UCLA (AFCA);	1990 Bobby Ross, Georgia Tech	2015 Dabo Swinney, Clemson (AFCA);
Duffy Daugherty, Mich. St. (FWAA)	1991 Don James, Washington	Kirk Ferentz, Iowa (FWAA)
1966 Tom Cahill, Army	1992 Gene Stallings, Alabama	

NCAA Div. I-A (FBS) Football Conference Champions, 1995-2015

American Athletic
2013 UCF
2014 UCF, Cincinnati,
    Memphis
2015 Houston

Atlantic Coast
1995 Virginia, Florida St.
1996 Florida St.
1997 Florida St.
1998 Florida St.,
    Georgia Tech
1999 Florida St.
2000 Florida St.
2001 Maryland
2002 Florida St.
2003 Florida St.
2004 Virginia Tech
2005 Florida St.
2006 Wake Forest
2007 Virginia Tech
2008 Virginia Tech
2009 Georgia Tech
2010 Virginia Tech
2011 Clemson
2012 Florida St.
2013 Florida St.
2014 Florida St.
2015 Clemson

Big Ten
1995 Northwestern
1996 Northwestern,
    Ohio St.
1997 Michigan
1998 Michigan, Ohio St.,
    Wisconsin
1999 Wisconsin
2000 Michigan,
    Northwestern,
    Purdue
2001 Illinois
2002 Iowa, Ohio St.
2003 Michigan

2004 Iowa, Michigan
2005 Ohio St., Penn St.
2006 Ohio St.
2007 Ohio St.
2008 Ohio St., Penn St.
2009 Ohio St.
2010 Michigan St., Ohio
    St., Wisconsin
2011 Wisconsin
2012 Wisconsin
2013 Michigan St.
2014 Ohio St.
2015 Michigan St.

Big 12
1996 Texas
1997 Nebraska
1998 Texas A&M
1999 Nebraska
2000 Oklahoma
2001 Colorado
2002 Oklahoma
2003 Kansas St.
2004 Oklahoma
2005 Texas
2006 Oklahoma
2007 Oklahoma
2008 Oklahoma
2009 Texas
2010 Oklahoma
2011 Oklahoma St.
2012 Kansas St.
2013 Baylor
2014 Baylor, TCU
2015 Oklahoma

Conference USA
1996 Houston,
    Southern Miss
1997 Southern Miss
1998 Tulane
1999 Southern Miss
2000 Louisville
2001 Louisville

2002 Cincinnati, TCU
2003 Southern Miss
2004 Louisville
2005 Tulsa
2006 Houston
2007 UCF
2008 East Carolina
2009 East Carolina
2010 UCF
2011 Southern Miss
2012 Tulsa
2013 Rice
2014 Marshall
2015 Western Kentucky

Mid-American
1995 Toledo
1996 Ball St.
1997 Marshall
1998 Marshall
1999 Marshall
2000 Marshall
2001 Toledo
2002 Marshall
2003 Miami (OH)
2004 Toledo
2005 Akron
2006 Central Michigan
2007 Central Michigan
2008 Buffalo
2009 Central Michigan
2010 Miami (OH)
2011 Northern Illinois
2012 Northern Illinois
2013 Bowling Green
2014 Northern Illinois
2015 Bowling Green

Mountain West
1999 BYU, Colorado
    St., Utah
2000 Colorado St.
2001 BYU
2002 Colorado St.

2003 Utah
2004 Utah
2005 TCU
2006 BYU, TCU
2007 BYU
2008 Utah
2009 TCU
2010 TCU
2011 TCU
2012 Boise St., Fresno
    St., San Diego St.
2013 Fresno St.
2014 Boise St.
2015 San Diego St.

Pac-12
1995 USC, Washington
1996 Arizona St.
1997 UCLA,
    Washington St.
1998 UCLA
1999 Stanford
2000 Oregon, Oregon
    St., Washington
2001 Oregon
2002 USC,
    Washington St.
2003 USC
2004 USC
2005 USC
2006 California, USC
2007 Arizona St., USC
2008 USC
2009 Oregon
2010 Oregon
2011 Oregon
2012 Stanford
2013 Stanford
2014 Oregon
2015 Stanford

Southeastern
1995 Florida
1996 Florida

1997 Tennessee
1998 Tennessee
1999 Alabama
2000 Florida
2001 LSU
2002 Georgia
2003 LSU
2004 Auburn
2005 Georgia
2006 Florida
2007 LSU
2008 Florida
2009 Alabama
2010 Auburn
2011 LSU
2012 Alabama
2013 Auburn
2014 Alabama
2015 Alabama

Sun Belt
2001 Mid. Tenn. St.,
    North Texas
2002 North Texas
2003 North Texas
2004 North Texas
2005 Arkansas St.,
    LA-Lafayette,
    LA-Monroe
2006 Mid. Tenn. St.,
    Troy
2007 Florida Atlantic,
    Troy
2008 Troy
2009 Troy
2010 Florida Intl., Troy
2011 Arkansas St.
2012 Arkansas St.
2013 Arkansas St.,
    LA-Lafayette
2014 Georgia
    Southern
2015 Arkansas St.

Selected NCAA Division I Teams

(Conferences and coaches listed are as of June 2016.)

Team	Nickname	Team colors	Conference	Basketball coach	Football coach
Air Force	Falcons	Blue & silver	Mountain West	Dave Pilipovich	Troy Calhoun
Akron	Zips	Blue & gold	Mid-American	Keith Dambrot	Terry Bowden
Alabama	Crimson Tide	Crimson & white	Southeastern	Avery Johnson	Nick Saban
Appalachian State	Mountaineers	Black & gold	Sun Belt	Jim Fox	Scott Satterfield
Arizona	Wildcats	Cardinal & navy	Pac-12	Sean Miller	Rich Rodriguez
Arizona State	Sun Devils	Maroon & gold	Pac-12	Bobby Hurley	Todd Graham
Arkansas	Razorbacks	Cardinal & white	Southeastern	Mike Anderson	Bret Bielema
Arkansas State	Red Wolves	Scarlet & black	Sun Belt	Grant McCasland	Blake Anderson
Army	Black Knights	Black, gold, & gray	Independent#	Jimmy Allen	Jeff Monken
Auburn	Tigers	Burnt orange & navy blue	Southeastern	Bruce Pearl	Gus Malzahn
Ball State	Cardinals	Cardinal & white	Mid-American	James Whitford	Mike Neu
Baylor	Bears	Green & gold	Big 12	Scott Drew	Jim Grobe
Boise State	Broncos	Blue & orange	Mountain West	Leon Rice	Bryan Harsin
Boston College	Eagles	Maroon & gold	Atlantic Coast	Jim Christian	Steve Addazio
Bowling Green	Falcons	Orange & brown	Mid-American	Michael Huger	Mike Jinks
Brigham Young (BYU)	Cougars	Dark blue & white	Independent#	Dave Rose	Kalani Sitake
Brown*	Bears	Brown, red, & white	Ivy League	Mike Martin	Phil Estes
Butler	Bulldogs	Blue & white	Pioneer League#	Chris Holtmann	Jeff Voris
California	Golden Bears	Blue & gold	Pac-12	Cuonzo Martin	Sonny Dykes
Central Michigan	Chippewas	Maroon & gold	Mid-American	Keno Davis	John Bonamego
Cincinnati	Bearcats	Red & black	American Athletic	Mick Cronin	Tommy Tuberville
Citadel*	Bulldogs	Citadel blue & white	Southern	Duggar Baucom	Brent Thompson
Clemson	Tigers	Tiger orange & regalia	Atlantic Coast	Brad Brownell	Dabo Swinney
Colgate*	Raiders	Maroon & white	Patriot League	Matt Langel	Dan Hunt
Colorado	Buffaloes	Silver, black, & gold	Pac-12	Tad Boyle	Mike MacIntyre
Colorado State	Rams	Green & gold	Mountain West	Larry Eustachy	Mike Bobo
Columbia*	Lions	Columbia blue & white	Ivy League	Jim Engles	Al Bagnoli
Connecticut	Huskies	National flag blue & white	American Athletic	Kevin Ollie	Bob Diaco
Cornell*	Big Red	Carnelian red & white	Ivy League	Brian Earl	David Archer
Dartmouth*	Big Green	Dartmouth green & white	Ivy League	David McLaughlin	Buddy Teevens
Delaware*	Fightin' Blue Hens	Blue & gold	Colonial Athletic	Martin Ingelsby	Dave Brock
Duke	Blue Devils	Duke blue & white	Atlantic Coast	Mike Krzyzewski	David Cutcliffe
East Carolina	Pirates	Purple & gold	American Athletic	Jeff Lebo	Scottie Montgomery
Eastern Illinois*	Panthers	Blue & gray	Ohio Valley	Jay Spoonhour	Kim Dameron
Eastern Kentucky*	Colonels	Maroon & white	Ohio Valley	Dan McHale	Mark Elder
Eastern Michigan	Eagles	Green & white	Mid-American	Rob Murphy	Chris Creighton
Eastern Washington*	Eagles	Red & white	Big Sky	Jim Hayford	Beau Baldwin
Florida	Gators	Orange & blue	Southeastern	Mike White	Jim McElwain
Florida A&M*	Rattlers	Orange & green	Mid-Eastern Athletic	Byron Samuels	Alex Wood
Florida State	Seminoles	Garnet & gold	Atlantic Coast	Leonard Hamilton	Jimbo Fisher
Fresno State	Bulldogs	Red & blue	Mountain West	Rodney Terry	Tim DeRuyter
Furman*	Paladins	Purple & white	Southern	Niko Medved	Bruce Fowler
Georgia	Bulldogs	Red & black	Southeastern	Mark Fox	Kirby Smart
Georgia Southern	Eagles	Blue & white	Sun Belt	Mark Byington	Tyson Summers
Georgia Tech	Yellow Jackets	Old gold & white	Atlantic Coast	Josh Pastner	Paul Johnson
Harvard*	Crimson	Crimson, black, & white	Ivy League	Tommy Amaker	Tim Murphy
Hawaii	Rainbow Warriors	Green, black, white, silver	Mountain West#	Eran Ganot	Nick Rolovich
Holy Cross*	Crusaders	Royal purple	Patriot League	Bill Carmody	Tom Gilmore
Houston	Cougars	Scarlet & white	American Athletic	Kelvin Sampson	Tom Herman
Howard*	Bison	Blue & white	Mid-Eastern Athletic	Kevin Nickelberry	Gary Harrell
Idaho	Vandals	Silver & vandal gold	Sun Belt	Don Verlin	Paul Petrino
Illinois	Fighting Illini	Orange & blue	Big Ten	John Groce	Lovie Smith
Illinois State*	Redbirds	Red & white	Missouri Valley	Dan Muller	Brock Spack
Indiana	Hoosiers	Cream & crimson	Big Ten	Tom Crean	Kevin Wilson
Indiana State*	Sycamores	Royal blue & white	Missouri Valley	Greg Lansing	Mike Sanford
Iowa	Hawkeyes	Black & gold	Big Ten	Fran McCaffery	Kirk Ferentz
Iowa State	Cyclones	Cardinal & gold	Big 12	Steve Prohm	Matt Campbell
Jackson State*	Tigers	Blue & white	Southwestern Athletic	Wayne Brent	Tony Hughes
James Madison*	Dukes	Purple & gold	Colonial Athletic	Louis Rowe	Mike Houston
Kansas	Jayhawks	Crimson & blue	Big 12	Bill Self	David Beaty
Kansas State	Wildcats	Purple & white	Big 12	Bruce Weber	Bill Snyder
Kent State	Golden Flashes	Navy blue & gold	Mid-American	Rob Senderoff	Paul Haynes
Kentucky	Wildcats	Blue & white	Southeastern	John Calipari	Mark Stoops
Lafayette*	Leopards	Maroon & white	Patriot League	Fran O'Hanlon	Frank Tavani
Lehigh*	Mountain Hawks	Brown & white	Patriot League	Brett Reed	Andy Coen
Liberty*	Flames	Red, white, & blue	Big South	Ritchie McKay	Turner Gill
Louisiana State (LSU)	Fighting Tigers	Purple & gold	Southeastern	Johnny Jones	Les Miles
Louisiana Tech	Bulldogs	Red & blue	Conference USA	Eric Konkol	Skip Holtz
Louisiana-Lafayette	Ragin' Cajuns	Vermilion & white	Sun Belt	Bob Marlin	Mark Hudspeth
Louisiana-Monroe	Warhawks	Maroon & gold	Sun Belt	Keith Richard	Matt Viator
Louisville	Cardinals	Red & black	Atlantic Coast	Rick Pitino	Bobby Petrino
Maine*	Black Bears	Blue & white	Colonial Athletic#	Bob Walsh	Joe Harasymiak
Marshall	Thundering Herd	Kelly green & white	Conference USA	Dan D'Antoni	Doc Holliday
Maryland	Terrapins	Red, white, black, gold	Big Ten	Mark Turgeon	D. J. Durkin
Massachusetts	Minutemen	Maroon & white	Mid-American#	Derek Kellogg	Mark Whipple
Memphis	Tigers	Blue & gray	American Athletic	Tubby Smith	Mike Norvell
Miami (Florida)	Hurricanes	Orange & green	Atlantic Coast	Jim Larrañaga	Mark Richt
Miami (Ohio)	RedHawks	Red & white	Mid-American	John Cooper	Chuck Martin
Michigan	Wolverines	Maize & blue	Big Ten	John Beilein	Jim Harbaugh
Michigan State	Spartans	Green & white	Big Ten	Tom Izzo	Mark Dantonio
Mid. Tennessee State	Blue Raiders	Royal blue & white	Conference USA	Kermit Davis	Rick Stockstill
Minnesota	Golden Gophers	Maroon & gold	Big Ten	Richard Pitino	Tracy Claeys
Mississippi	Rebels	Cardinal red & navy blue	Southeastern	Andy Kennedy	Hugh Freeze
Mississippi State	Bulldogs	Maroon & white	Southeastern	Ben Howland	Dan Mullen

Team	Nickname	Team colors	Conference	Basketball coach	Football coach
Missouri	Tigers	Old gold & black	Southeastern	Kim Anderson	Barry Odom
Montana*	Grizzlies	Maroon & silver	Big Sky	Travis DeCuire	Bob Stitt
Montana State*	Bobcats	Blue & gold	Big Sky	Brian Fish	Jeff Choate
Morgan State*	Bears	Blue & orange	Mid-Eastern Athletic	Todd Bozeman	Fred Farrier
Murray State*	Racers	Navy & gold	Ohio Valley	Matt McMahon	Mitch Stewart
Navy	Midshipmen	Navy blue & gold	American Athletic#	Ed DeChellis	Ken Niumatalolo
Nebraska	Cornhuskers	Scarlet & cream	Big Ten	Tim Miles	Mike Riley
Nevada	Wolf Pack	Silver & blue	Mountain West	Eric Musselman	Brian Polian
Nevada-Las Vegas (UNLV)	Rebels	Scarlet & gray	Mountain West	Marvin Menzies	Tony Sanchez
New Hampshire*	Wildcats	Blue & white	Colonial Athletic#	Bill Herrion	Sean McDonnell
New Mexico	Lobos	Cherry & silver	Mountain West	Craig Neal	Bob Davie
New Mexico State	Aggies	Crimson & white	Western Athletic	Paul Weir	Doug Martin
Nicholls State*	Colonels	Red & gray	Southland	Richie Riley	Tim Rebowe
North Carolina	Tar Heels	Carolina blue & white	Atlantic Coast	Roy Williams	Larry Fedora
North Carolina State	Wolfpack	Red & white	Atlantic Coast	Mark Gottfried	Dave Doeren
North Texas	Mean Green	Green & white	Conference USA	Tony Benford	Seth Littrell
Northern Illinois	Huskies	Cardinal & black	Mid-American	Mark Montgomery	Rod Carey
Northern Iowa*	Panthers	Purple & old gold	Missouri Valley	Ben Jacobson	Mark Farley
Northwestern	Wildcats	Purple & white	Big Ten	Chris Collins	Pat Fitzgerald
Northwestern State*	Demons	Purple, white, & orange	Southland	Mike McConathy	Jay Thomas
Notre Dame	Fighting Irish	Blue & gold	Independent#	Mike Brey	Brian Kelly
Ohio	Bobcats	Hunter green & white	Mid-American	Saul Phillips	Frank Solich
Ohio State	Buckeyes	Scarlet & gray	Big Ten	Thad Matta	Urban Meyer
Oklahoma	Sooners	Crimson & cream	Big 12	Lon Kruger	Bob Stoops
Oklahoma State	Cowboys	Orange & black	Big 12	Brad Underwood	Mike Gundy
Oregon	Ducks	Green & yellow	Pac-12	Dana Altman	Mark Helfrich
Oregon State	Beavers	Orange & black	Pac-12	Wayne Tinkle	Gary Andersen
Penn State	Nittany Lions	Blue & white	Big Ten	Patrick Chambers	James Franklin
Pennsylvania*	Quakers	Red & blue	Ivy League	Steve Donahue	Ray Priore
Pittsburgh	Panthers	Gold & blue	Atlantic Coast	Kevin Stallings	Pat Narduzzi
Princeton*	Tigers	Orange & black	Ivy League	Mitch Henderson	Bob Surace
Purdue	Boilermakers	Old gold & black	Big Ten	Matt Painter	Darrell Hazell
Rhode Island*	Rams	Keaney blue, navy blue, & white	Colonial Athletic#	Dan Hurley	Jim Fleming
Rice	Owls	Blue & gray	Conference USA	Mike Rhoades	David Bailiff
Richmond*	Spiders	Red & blue	Colonial Athletic#	Chris Mooney	Danny Rocco
Rutgers	Scarlet Knights	Scarlet	Big Ten	Steve Pikiell	Chris Ash
Sam Houston State*	Bearkats	Orange & white	Southland	Jason Hooten	K. C. Keeler
San Diego State	Aztecs	Scarlet & black	Mountain West	Steve Fisher	Rocky Long
San Jose State	Spartans	Gold, white, & blue	Mountain West	Dave Wojcik	Ron Caragher
South Carolina	Gamecocks	Garnet & black	Southeastern	Frank Martin	Will Muschamp
South Carolina State*	Bulldogs	Garnet & blue	Mid-Eastern Athletic	Murray Garvin	Oliver Pough
South Florida	Bulls	Green & gold	American Athletic	Orlando Antigua	Willie Taggart
Southeast Missouri State*	Redhawks	Red, black, & white	Ohio Valley	Rick Ray	Tom Matukewicz
Southern California (USC)	Trojans	Cardinal & gold	Pac-12	Andy Enfield	Clay Helton
Southern Illinois*	Salukis	Maroon & white	Missouri Valley	Barry Hinson	Nick Hill
Southern Methodist (SMU)	Mustangs	Red & blue	American Athletic	Larry Brown	Chad Morris
Southern Mississippi	Golden Eagles	Black & gold	Conference USA	Doc Sadler	Jay Hopson
Stanford	Cardinal	Cardinal & white	Pac-12	Jerod Haase	David Shaw
Stephen F. Austin*	Lumberjacks	Purple & white	Southland	Kyle Keller	Clint Conque
Syracuse	Orange	Orange	Atlantic Coast	Jim Boeheim	Dino Babers
Temple	Owls	Cherry & white	American Athletic	Fran Dunphy	Matt Rhule
Tennessee	Volunteers	Orange & white	Southeastern	Rick Barnes	Butch Jones
Tennessee State*	Tigers	Reflex blue & white	Ohio Valley	Dana Ford	Rod Reed
Tennessee Tech*	Golden Eagles	Purple & gold	Ohio Valley	Steve Payne	Marcus Satterfield
Texas	Longhorns	Burnt orange & white	Big 12	Jamie Dixon	Charlie Strong
Texas A&M	Aggies	Maroon & white	Southeastern	Billy Kennedy	Kevin Sumlin
Texas Christian (TCU)	Horned Frogs	Purple & white	Big 12	Jamie Dixon	Gary Patterson
Texas Southern*	Tigers	Maroon & gray	Southwestern Athletic	Mike Davis	Michael Haywood
Texas State*	Bobcats	Maroon & gold	Sun Belt	Danny Kaspar	Everett Withers
Texas Tech	Red Raiders	Scarlet & black	Big 12	Chris Beard	Kliff Kingsbury
Toledo	Rockets	Midnight blue & gold	Mid-American	Tod Kowalczyk	Jason Candle
Troy	Trojans	Cardinal, silver, & black	Sun Belt	Phil Cunningham	Neal Brown
Tulane	Green Wave	Olive green & sky blue	American Athletic	Mike Dunleavy Sr.	Willie Fritz
Tulsa	Golden Hurricane	Old gold, royal blue, & crimson	American Athletic	Frank Haith	Philip Montgomery
UCLA	Bruins	Blue & gold	Pac-12	Steve Alford	Jim Mora
Utah	Utes	Crimson & white	Pac-12	Larry Krystkowiak	Kyle Whittingham
Utah State	Aggies	Navy blue & white	Mountain West	Tim Duryea	Matt Wells
UTEP (Texas-El Paso)	Miners	Dark blue, orange, & silver	Conference USA	Tim Floyd	Sean Kugler
Vanderbilt	Commodores	Black & gold	Southeastern	Bryce Drew	Derek Mason
Villanova*	Wildcats	Blue & white	Colonial Athletic#	Jay Wright	Andy Talley
Virginia	Cavaliers	Orange & blue	Atlantic Coast	Tony Bennett	Bronco Mendenhall
Virginia Tech	Hokies	Chicago maroon & burnt orange	Atlantic Coast	Buzz Williams	Justin Fuente
Wake Forest	Demon Deacons	Old gold & black	Atlantic Coast	Danny Manning	Dave Clawson
Washington	Huskies	Purple & gold	Pac-12	Lorenzo Romar	Chris Peterson
Washington State	Cougars	Crimson & gray	Pac-12	Ernie Kent	Mike Leach
Weber State*	Wildcats	Purple & white	Big Sky	Randy Rahe	Jay Hill
West Virginia	Mountaineers	Old gold & blue	Big 12	Bob Huggins	Dana Holgorsen
Western Illinois*	Leathernecks	Purple & gold	Missouri Valley#	Billy Wright	Charlie Fisher
Western Kentucky	Hilltoppers	Red & white	Conference USA	Rick Stansbury	Jeff Brohm
Western Michigan	Broncos	Brown & gold	Mid-American	Steve Hawkins	P. J. Fleck
Wisconsin	Badgers	Cardinal & white	Big Ten	Greg Gard	Paul Chryst
Wyoming	Cowboys	Brown & gold	Mountain West	Allen Edwards	Craig Bohl
Yale*	Elis, Bulldogs	Yale blue & white	Ivy League	James Jones	Tony Reno
Youngstown State*	Penguins	Red & white	Missouri Valley#	Jerry Slocum	Bo Pelini

* = Football Championship Subdivision (FCS) team (formerly known as I-AA). # = Team competes in conference listed in football but not in basketball.

COLLEGE BASKETBALL

2016 Men's NCAA Tournament: Villanova Beats North Carolina at Buzzer

The Villanova Wildcats beat the Univ. of North Carolina Tar Heels, 77-74, at NRG Stadium in Houston, TX, to claim the NCAA Men's Division I national basketball title Apr. 4, 2016. Tar Heels senior guard Marcus Paige hit a three-pointer with less than five seconds left to tie the game, but Wildcats junior forward Kris Jenkins answered with a three at the buzzer for the win. Villanova senior point guard Ryan Arcidiacono scored 16 points before setting Jenkins up for the game-winning shot and was named the Final Four's most outstanding player.

NCAA Men's Basketball Division I Champions, 1943-2016

Year	Champion	Winning coach	Final opponent	Score	Most outstanding player	Site
1943	Wyoming	Everett Shelton	Georgetown	46-34	Ken Sailors, Wyoming	New York, NY
1944	Utah	Vadal Peterson	Dartmouth	42-40[1]	Arnold Ferrin, Utah	New York, NY
1945	Oklahoma St.[2]	Henry Iba	NYU	49-45	Bob Kurland, Oklahoma St.	New York, NY
1946	Oklahoma St.[2]	Henry Iba	North Carolina	43-40	Bob Kurland, Oklahoma St.	New York, NY
1947	Holy Cross	Alvin Julian	Oklahoma	58-47	George Kaftan, Holy Cross	New York, NY
1948	Kentucky	Adolph Rupp	Baylor	58-42	Alex Groza, Kentucky	New York, NY
1949	Kentucky	Adolph Rupp	Oklahoma St.	46-36	Alex Groza, Kentucky	Seattle, WA
1950	CCNY	Nat Holman	Bradley	71-68	Irwin Dambrot, CCNY	New York, NY
1951	Kentucky	Adolph Rupp	Kansas St.	68-58	Bill Spivey, Kentucky	Minneapolis, MN
1952	Kansas	Forrest Allen	St. John's (NY)	80-63	Clyde Lovellette, Kansas	Seattle, WA
1953	Indiana	Branch McCracken	Kansas	69-68	B. H. Born, Kansas	Kansas City, MO
1954	La Salle	Kenneth Loeffler	Bradley	92-76	Tom Gola, La Salle	Kansas City, MO
1955	San Francisco	Phil Woolpert	La Salle	77-63	Bill Russell, San Francisco	Kansas City, MO
1956	San Francisco	Phil Woolpert	Iowa	83-71	Hal Lear, Temple	Evanston, IL
1957	North Carolina	Frank McGuire	Kansas	54-53[1]	Wilt Chamberlain, Kansas	Kansas City, MO
1958	Kentucky	Adolph Rupp	Seattle	84-72	Elgin Baylor, Seattle	Louisville, KY
1959	California	Pete Newell	West Virginia	71-70	Jerry West, West Virginia	Louisville, KY
1960	Ohio St.	Fred Taylor	California	75-55	Jerry Lucas, Ohio St.	San Francisco, CA
1961	Cincinnati	Edwin Jucker	Ohio St.	70-65[1]	Jerry Lucas, Ohio St.	Kansas City, MO
1962	Cincinnati	Edwin Jucker	Ohio St.	71-59	Paul Hogue, Cincinnati	Louisville, KY
1963	Loyola (IL)	George Ireland	Cincinnati	60-58[1]	Art Heyman, Duke	Louisville, KY
1964	UCLA	John Wooden	Duke	98-83	Walt Hazzard, UCLA	Kansas City, MO
1965	UCLA	John Wooden	Michigan	91-80	Bill Bradley, Princeton	Portland, OR
1966	UTEP[3]	Don Haskins	Kentucky	72-65	Jerry Chambers, Utah	College Park, MD
1967	UCLA	John Wooden	Dayton	79-64	Lew Alcindor[4], UCLA	Louisville, KY
1968	UCLA	John Wooden	North Carolina	78-55	Lew Alcindor[4], UCLA	Los Angeles, CA
1969	UCLA	John Wooden	Purdue	92-72	Lew Alcindor[4], UCLA	Louisville, KY
1970	UCLA	John Wooden	Jacksonville	80-69	Sidney Wicks, UCLA	College Park, MD
1971	UCLA	John Wooden	Villanova*	68-62	Howard Porter, Villanova*	Houston, TX
1972	UCLA	John Wooden	Florida St.	81-76	Bill Walton, UCLA	Los Angeles, CA
1973	UCLA	John Wooden	Memphis[5]	87-66	Bill Walton, UCLA	St. Louis, MO
1974	North Carolina St.	Norm Sloan	Marquette	76-64	David Thompson, NC State	Greensboro, NC
1975	UCLA	John Wooden	Kentucky	92-85	Richard Washington, UCLA	San Diego, CA
1976	Indiana	Bob Knight	Michigan	86-68	Kent Benson, Indiana	Philadelphia, PA
1977	Marquette	Al McGuire	North Carolina	67-59	Butch Lee, Marquette	Atlanta, GA
1978	Kentucky	Joe Hall	Duke	94-88	Jack Givens, Kentucky	St. Louis, MO
1979	Michigan St.	Jud Heathcote	Indiana St.	75-64	Magic Johnson, Michigan St.	Salt Lake City, UT
1980	Louisville	Denny Crum	UCLA*	59-54	Darrell Griffith, Louisville	Indianapolis, IN
1981	Indiana	Bob Knight	North Carolina	63-50	Isiah Thomas, Indiana	Philadelphia, PA
1982	North Carolina	Dean Smith	Georgetown	63-62	James Worthy, N. Carolina	New Orleans, LA
1983	North Carolina St.	Jim Valvano	Houston	54-52	Hakeem Olajuwon, Houston	Albuquerque, NM
1984	Georgetown	John Thompson	Houston	84-75	Patrick Ewing, Georgetown	Seattle, WA
1985	Villanova	Rollie Massimino	Georgetown	66-64	Ed Pinckney, Villanova	Lexington, KY
1986	Louisville	Denny Crum	Duke	72-69	Pervis Ellison, Louisville	Dallas, TX
1987	Indiana	Bob Knight	Syracuse	74-73	Keith Smart, Indiana	New Orleans, LA
1988	Kansas	Larry Brown	Oklahoma	83-79	Danny Manning, Kansas	Kansas City, MO
1989	Michigan	Steve Fisher	Seton Hall	80-79[1]	Glen Rice, Michigan	Seattle, WA
1990	UNLV	Jerry Tarkanian	Duke	103-73	Anderson Hunt, UNLV	Denver, CO
1991	Duke	Mike Krzyzewski	Kansas	72-65	Christian Laettner, Duke	Indianapolis, IN
1992	Duke	Mike Krzyzewski	Michigan	71-51	Bobby Hurley, Duke	Minneapolis, MN
1993	North Carolina	Dean Smith	Michigan	77-71	Donald Williams, N. Carolina	New Orleans, LA
1994	Arkansas	Nolan Richardson	Duke	76-72	Corliss Williamson, Arkansas	Charlotte, NC
1995	UCLA	Jim Harrick	Arkansas	89-78	Ed O'Bannon, UCLA	Seattle, WA
1996	Kentucky	Rick Pitino	Syracuse	76-67	Tony Delk, Kentucky	E. Rutherford, NJ
1997	Arizona	Lute Olson	Kentucky	84-79[1]	Miles Simon, Arizona	Indianapolis, IN
1998	Kentucky	Tubby Smith	Utah	78-69	Jeff Sheppard, Kentucky	San Antonio, TX
1999	Connecticut	Jim Calhoun	Duke	77-74	Richard Hamilton, Connecticut	St. Petersburg, FL
2000	Michigan St.	Tom Izzo	Florida	89-76	Mateen Cleaves, Michigan St.	Indianapolis, IN
2001	Duke	Mike Krzyzewski	Arizona	82-72	Shane Battier, Duke	Minneapolis, MN
2002	Maryland	Gary Williams	Indiana	64-52	Juan Dixon, Maryland	Atlanta, GA
2003	Syracuse	Jim Boeheim	Kansas	81-78	Carmelo Anthony, Syracuse	New Orleans, LA
2004	Connecticut	Jim Calhoun	Georgia Tech	82-73	Emeka Okafor, Connecticut	San Antonio, TX
2005	North Carolina	Roy Williams	Illinois	75-70	Sean May, N. Carolina	St. Louis, MO
2006	Florida	Billy Donovan	UCLA	73-57	Joakim Noah, Florida	Indianapolis, IN
2007	Florida	Billy Donovan	Ohio St.	84-75	Corey Brewer, Florida	Atlanta, GA
2008	Kansas	Bill Self	Memphis	75-68[1]	Mario Chalmers, Kansas	San Antonio, TX
2009	North Carolina	Roy Williams	Michigan St.	89-72	Wayne Ellington, N. Carolina	Detroit, MI
2010	Duke	Mike Krzyzewski	Butler	61-59	Kyle Singler, Duke	Indianapolis, IN
2011	Connecticut	Jim Calhoun	Butler	53-41	Kemba Walker, Connecticut	Houston, TX
2012	Kentucky	John Calipari	Kansas	67-59	Anthony Davis, Kentucky	New Orleans, LA
2013	Louisville	Rick Pitino	Michigan	82-76	Luke Hancock, Louisville	Atlanta, GA
2014	Connecticut	Kevin Ollie	Kentucky	60-54	Shabazz Napier, Connecticut	Arlington, TX
2015	Duke	Mike Krzyzewski	Wisconsin	68-63	Tyus Jones, Duke	Indianapolis, IN
2016	Villanova	Jay Wright	North Carolina	77-74	Ryan Arcidiacono, Villanova	Houston, TX

* = Declared ineligible after the tournament. (1) Overtime. (2) Then known as Oklahoma A&M. (3) Then known as Texas Western. (4) Changed name to Kareem Abdul-Jabbar in 1971. (5) Then known as Memphis State.

2016 Men's NCAA Basketball Tournament

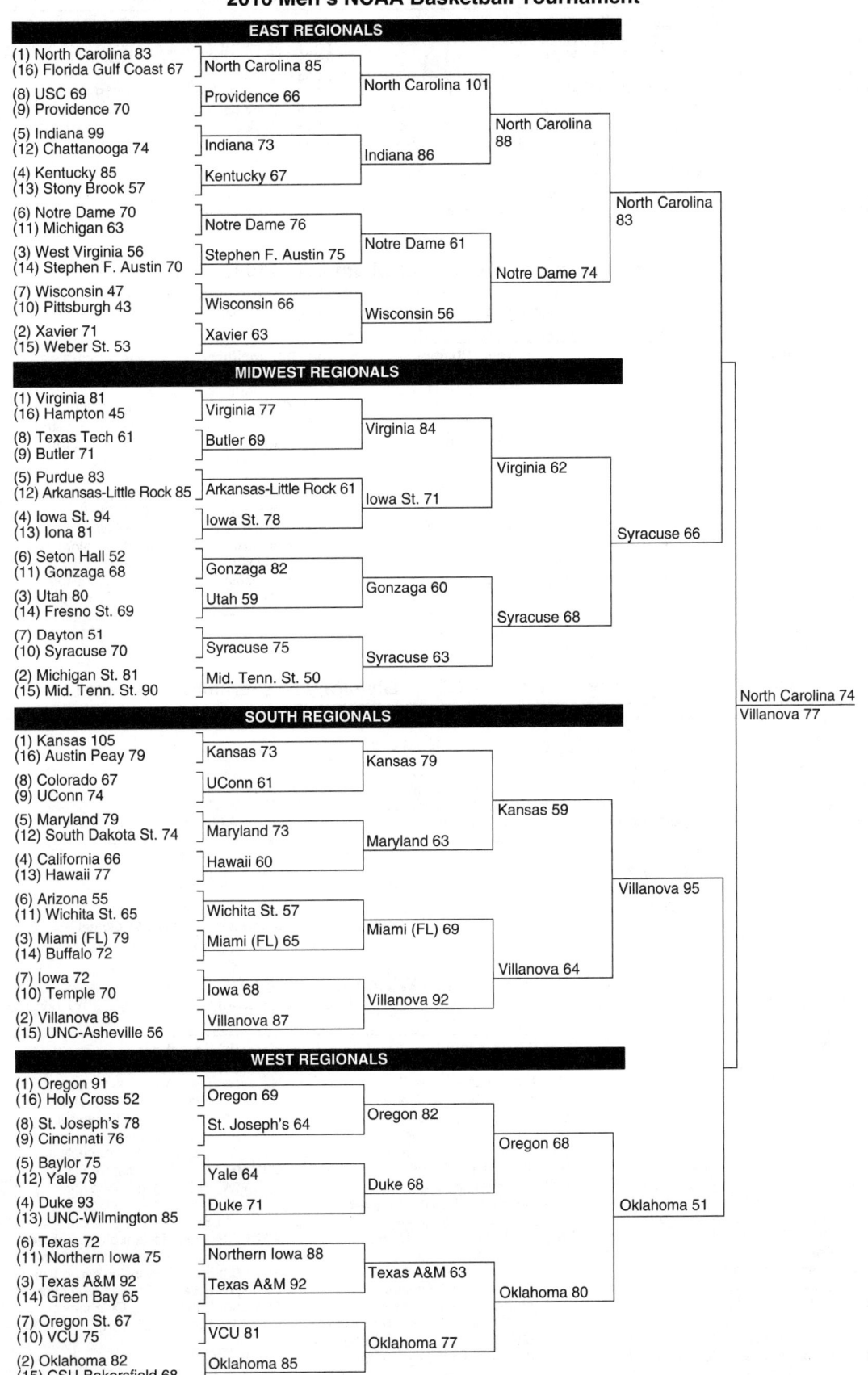

EAST REGIONALS

(1) North Carolina 83
(16) Florida Gulf Coast 67 — North Carolina 85
(8) USC 69
(9) Providence 70 — Providence 66
North Carolina 101
(5) Indiana 99
(12) Chattanooga 74 — Indiana 73
(4) Kentucky 85
(13) Stony Brook 57 — Kentucky 67
Indiana 86
North Carolina 88
(6) Notre Dame 70
(11) Michigan 63 — Notre Dame 76
(3) West Virginia 56
(14) Stephen F. Austin 70 — Stephen F. Austin 75
Notre Dame 61
North Carolina 83
(7) Wisconsin 47
(10) Pittsburgh 43 — Wisconsin 66
(2) Xavier 71
(15) Weber St. 53 — Xavier 63
Wisconsin 56
Notre Dame 74

MIDWEST REGIONALS

(1) Virginia 81
(16) Hampton 45 — Virginia 77
(8) Texas Tech 61
(9) Butler 71 — Butler 69
Virginia 84
(5) Purdue 83
(12) Arkansas-Little Rock 85 — Arkansas-Little Rock 61
(4) Iowa St. 94
(13) Iona 81 — Iowa St. 78
Iowa St. 71
Virginia 62
(6) Seton Hall 52
(11) Gonzaga 68 — Gonzaga 82
(3) Utah 80
(14) Fresno St. 69 — Utah 59
Gonzaga 60
Syracuse 66
(7) Dayton 51
(10) Syracuse 70 — Syracuse 75
(2) Michigan St. 81
(15) Mid. Tenn. St. 90 — Mid. Tenn. St. 50
Syracuse 63
Syracuse 68

SOUTH REGIONALS

(1) Kansas 105
(16) Austin Peay 79 — Kansas 73
(8) Colorado 67
(9) UConn 74 — UConn 61
Kansas 79
(5) Maryland 79
(12) South Dakota St. 74 — Maryland 73
(4) California 66
(13) Hawaii 77 — Hawaii 60
Maryland 63
Kansas 59
(6) Arizona 55
(11) Wichita St. 65 — Wichita St. 57
(3) Miami (FL) 79
(14) Buffalo 72 — Miami (FL) 65
Miami (FL) 69
Villanova 95
(7) Iowa 72
(10) Temple 70 — Iowa 68
(2) Villanova 86
(15) UNC-Asheville 56 — Villanova 87
Villanova 92
Villanova 64

WEST REGIONALS

(1) Oregon 91
(16) Holy Cross 52 — Oregon 69
(8) St. Joseph's 78
(9) Cincinnati 76 — St. Joseph's 64
Oregon 82
(5) Baylor 75
(12) Yale 79 — Yale 64
(4) Duke 93
(13) UNC-Wilmington 85 — Duke 71
Duke 68
Oregon 68
(6) Texas 72
(11) Northern Iowa 75 — Northern Iowa 88
(3) Texas A&M 92
(14) Green Bay 65 — Texas A&M 92
Texas A&M 63
Oklahoma 51
(7) Oregon St. 67
(10) VCU 75 — VCU 81
(2) Oklahoma 82
(15) CSU-Bakersfield 68 — Oklahoma 85
Oklahoma 77
Oklahoma 80

North Carolina 74
Villanova 77

All-Time Winningest Men's NCAA Division I Basketball Teams

Team	Yrs	Won	Lost	Pct.	Team	Yrs	Won	Lost	Pct.	Team	Yrs	Won	Lost	Pct.
Kentucky	113	2,205	682	0.764	Notre Dame . .	111	1,819	984	0.649	Arkansas.	93	1,621	917	0.639
N. Carolina. . .	106	2,173	774	0.737	VCU	46	895	485	0.649	Weber State . .	54	1,004	572	0.637
Kansas.	118	2,186	836	0.723	St. John's (NY)	109	1,803	980	0.648	Cincinnati	115	1,727	997	0.634
UNLV	58	1,223	503	0.709	Villanova.	96	1,681	916	0.647	Missouri State	104	1,619	944	0.632
Duke	111	2,087	864	0.707	Utah	108	1,759	966	0.646	Memphis.	95	1,502	877	0.631
Syracuse . . .	115	1,943	865	0.692	Illinois	111	1,744	958	0.645	Purdue	118	1,720	1,011	0.630
UCLA.	97	1,818	819	0.689	Murray State . .	91	1,570	866	0.644	Texas	110	1,739	1,032	0.628
Louisville	102	1,778	892	0.666	Connecticut. . .	113	1,666	922	0.644	UAB	38	759	454	0.626
W. Kentucky. .	97	1,733	884	0.662	Temple	120	1,870	1,037	0.643	BYU	114	1,764	1,059	0.625
Arizona	111	1,737	918	0.654	Indiana	116	1,783	1,003	0.640	NC State.	104	1,677	1,025	0.621

Note: Through 2015-16 season; winningest teams by percentage. Minimum 25 years as Div. I program.

National Invitation Tournament Champions, 1938-2015

The National Invitation Tournament (NIT), first played in 1938, is the oldest U.S. basketball tournament. The first National Collegiate Athletic Association (NCAA) national championship tournament was played one year later. In Aug. 2005, the NCAA agreed to purchase the NIT from the five New York City-area colleges that had run the NIT.

Year	Champion	Year	Champion	Year	Champion	Year	Champion	Year	Champion
1938	Temple	1954	Holy Cross	1970	Marquette	1986	Ohio State	2002	Memphis
1939	Long Island Univ.	1955	Duquesne	1971	North Carolina	1987	Southern Miss	2003	St. John's (NY)
1940	Colorado	1956	Louisville	1972	Maryland	1988	Connecticut	2004	Michigan
1941	Long Island Univ.	1957	Bradley	1973	Virginia Tech	1989	St. John's (NY)	2005	South Carolina
1942	West Virginia	1958	Xavier (OH)	1974	Purdue	1990	Vanderbilt	2006	South Carolina
1943	St. John's (NY)	1959	St. John's (NY)	1975	Princeton	1991	Stanford	2007	West Virginia
1944	St. John's (NY)	1960	Bradley	1976	Kentucky	1992	Virginia	2008	Ohio State
1945	DePaul	1961	Providence	1977	St. Bonaventure	1993	Minnesota	2009	Penn State
1946	Kentucky	1962	Dayton	1978	Texas	1994	Villanova	2010	Dayton
1947	Utah	1963	Providence	1979	Indiana	1995	Virginia Tech	2011	Wichita State
1948	St. Louis	1964	Bradley	1980	Virginia	1996	Nebraska	2012	Stanford
1949	San Francisco	1965	St. John's (NY)	1981	Tulsa	1997	Michigan	2013	Baylor
1950	CCNY	1966	Brigham Young	1982	Bradley	1998	Minnesota	2014	Minnesota
1951	Brigham Young	1967	Southern Illinois	1983	Fresno State	1999	California	2015	Stanford
1952	La Salle	1968	Dayton	1984	Michigan	2000	Wake Forest	2016	George
1953	Seton Hall	1969	Temple	1985	UCLA	2001	Tulsa		Washington

Most Coaching Victories in Men's NCAA Division I Basketball Tournament

Coach, school(s), first/latest appearance	Wins	Tournaments	Championships
Mike Krzyzewski, Duke, 1984/2016.	90	32	5
Roy Williams; Kansas, North Carolina; 1990/2016.	70	26	2
Dean Smith, North Carolina, 1967/1997	65	27	2
Jim Boeheim, Syracuse, 1977/2016.	57	32	1
Rick Pitino; Boston Univ., Providence, Kentucky, Louisville; 1983/2015.	53	20	2
Jim Calhoun; Northeastern, Connecticut; 1981/2012.	49	22	3
John Wooden, UCLA, 1950/1975	47	16	10
Tom Izzo, Michigan St., 1998/2016.	46	19	1
Lute Olson; Iowa, Arizona; 1979/2007.	46	27	1
Bob Knight; Indiana, Texas Tech; 1973/2007.	45	28	3
Denny Crum, Louisville, 1972/2000.	42	23	2

Note: Through 2016 tournament. Coaches active in 2015-16 season in bold. Some records adjusted for vacated victories.

John R. Wooden Award Winners, 1977-2016

Awarded to the nation's outstanding men's college basketball player by the Los Angeles Athletic Club since 1977; awarded under the same name to women since 2004.

Year	Player, school	Year	Player, school	Year	Player, school
1977	Marques Johnson, UCLA	1996	Marcus Camby, Massachusetts	2009	(M) Blake Griffin, Oklahoma
1978	Phil Ford, North Carolina	1997	Tim Duncan, Wake Forest		(W) Maya Moore, Connecticut
1979	Larry Bird, Indiana State	1998	Antawn Jamison, North Carolina	2010	(M) Evan Turner, Ohio State
1980	Darrell Griffith, Louisville	1999	Elton Brand, Duke		(W) Tina Charles, Connecticut
1981	Danny Ainge, Brigham Young	2000	Kenyon Martin, Cincinnati	2011	(M) Jimmer Fredette, Brigham Young
1982	Ralph Sampson, Virginia	2001	Shane Battier, Duke		(W) Maya Moore, Connecticut
1983	Ralph Sampson, Virginia	2002	Jay Williams, Duke	2012	(M) Anthony Davis, Kentucky
1984	Michael Jordan, North Carolina	2003	T. J. Ford, Texas		(W) Brittney Griner, Baylor
1985	Chris Mullin, St. John's (NY)	2004	(M) Jameer Nelson, St. Joseph's	2013	(M) Trey Burke, Michigan
1986	Walter Berry, St. John's (NY)		(W) Alana Beard, Duke		(W) Brittney Griner, Baylor
1987	David Robinson, Navy	2005	(M) Andrew Bogut, Utah	2014	(M) Doug McDermott, Creighton
1988	Danny Manning, Kansas		(W) Seimone Augustus, LSU		(W) Chiney Ogwumike, Stanford
1989	Sean Elliott, Arizona	2006	(M) J. J. Redick, Duke	2015	(M) Frank Kaminsky, Wisconsin
1990	Lionel Simmons, La Salle		(W) Seimone Augustus, LSU		(W) Breanna Stewart, Connecticut
1991	Larry Johnson, UNLV	2007	(M) Kevin Durant, Texas	2016	(M) Buddy Hield, Oklahoma
1992	Christian Laettner, Duke		(W) Candace Parker, Tennessee		(W) Breanna Stewart, Connecticut
1993	Calbert Cheaney, Indiana	2008	(M) Tyler Hansbrough, N. Carolina		
1994	Glenn Robinson, Purdue		(W) Candace Parker, Tennessee		
1995	Ed O'Bannon, UCLA				

2016 Women's NCAA Basketball Tournament

BRIDGEPORT REGIONAL

(1) Connecticut 101
(16) Robert Morris 49
— Connecticut 97
(8) Seton Hall 76
(9) Duquesne 97
— Duquesne 51
Connecticut 98

(5) Mississippi St. 60
(12) Chattanooga 50
— Mississippi St. 74
(4) Michigan St. 74
(13) Belmont 60
— Michigan St. 72
Mississippi St. 38
Connecticut 86

(6) South Florida 48
(11) Colorado St. 45
— South Florida 67
(3) UCLA 66
(14) Hawaii 50
— UCLA 72
UCLA 64

(7) BYU 69
(10) Missouri 78
— Missouri 55
(2) Texas 86
(15) Alabama St. 42
— Texas 73
Texas 72
Texas 65

Connecticut 80

DALLAS REGIONAL

(1) Baylor 89
(16) Idaho 59
— Baylor 84
(8) St. John's (NY) 57
(9) Auburn 68
— Auburn 52
Baylor 78

(5) Florida St. 72
(12) Mid. Tenn. St. 55
— Florida St. 74
(4) Texas A&M 74
(13) Missouri St. 65
— Texas A&M 56
Florida St. 58
Baylor 57

(6) DePaul 97
(11) James Madison 67
— DePaul 73
(3) Louisville 87
(14) Central Arkansas 60
— Louisville 72
DePaul 71

(7) Oklahoma St. 54
(10) St. Bonaventure 65
— St. Bonaventure 40
(2) Oregon St. 73
(15) Troy 31
— Oregon St. 69
Oregon St. 83
Oregon St. 60

Oregon St. 51

Connecticut 82
Syracuse 51

LEXINGTON REGIONAL

(1) Notre Dame 95
(16) North Carolina A&T 61
— Notre Dame 87
(8) Georgia 58
(9) Indiana 62
— Indiana 70
Notre Dame 84

(5) Miami (FL) 71
(12) South Dakota St. 74
— South Dakota St. 65
(4) Stanford 85
(13) San Francisco 58
— Stanford 66
Stanford 90
Stanford 76

(6) Oklahoma 61
(11) Purdue 45
— Oklahoma 58
(3) Kentucky 85
(14) UNC Asheville 31
— Kentucky 79
Kentucky 72

(7) Washington 65
(10) Pennsylvania 53
— Washington 74
(2) Maryland 74
(15) Iona 58
— Maryland 65
Washington 85
Washington 85

Washington 59

SIOUX FALLS REGIONAL

(1) South Carolina 77
(16) Jacksonville 41
— South Carolina 73
(8) George Washington 51
(9) Kansas St. 56
— Kansas St. 47
South Carolina 72

(5) Florida 59
(12) Albany (NY) 61
— Albany (NY) 59
(4) Syracuse 73
(13) Army 56
— Syracuse 76
Syracuse 80
Syracuse 89

(6) West Virginia 74
(11) Princeton 65
— West Virginia 81
(3) Ohio St. 88
(14) Buffalo 69
— Ohio St. 88
Ohio St. 62

(7) Tennessee 59
(10) Green Bay 53
— Tennessee 75
(2) Arizona St. 74
(15) New Mexico St. 52
— Arizona St. 64
Tennessee 78
Tennessee 67

Syracuse 80

2016 Women's NCAA Tournament: UConn and Stewart Make History

The Univ. of Connecticut Huskies easily defeated the Syracuse Orange in a 82-51 victory Apr. 5, 2016, at Bankers Life Fieldhouse in Indianapolis, IN, to claim the Women's Division I basketball title for a record fourth consecutive year. Head coach Geno Auriemma, who has never lost a national title game, claimed his eleventh championship, surpassing UCLA men's coaching legend John Wooden. Senior Breanna Stewart scored 24 points with 10 rebounds and was named the Final Four's most outstanding player for the fourth straight year.

NCAA Women's Basketball Division I Champions, 1982-2016

Year	Champion	Winning coach	Final opponent	Score	Most outstanding player	Site
1982	Louisiana Tech	Sonja Hogg	Cheyney	76-62	Janice Lawrence, LA Tech	Norfolk, VA
1983	USC	Linda Sharp	Louisiana Tech	69-67	Cheryl Miller, USC	Norfolk, VA
1984	USC	Linda Sharp	Tennessee	72-61	Cheryl Miller, USC	Los Angeles, CA
1985	Old Dominion	Marianne Stanley	Georgia	70-65	Tracy Claxton, Old Dominion	Austin, TX
1986	Texas	Jody Conradt	USC	97-81	Clarissa Davis, Texas	Lexington, KY
1987	Tennessee	Pat Summitt	Louisiana Tech	67-44	Tonya Edwards, Tennessee	Austin, TX
1988	Louisiana Tech	Leon Barmore	Auburn	56-54	Erica Westbrooks, LA Tech	Tacoma, WA
1989	Tennessee	Pat Summitt	Auburn	76-60	Bridgette Gordon, Tennessee	Tacoma, WA
1990	Stanford	Tara VanDerveer	Auburn	88-81	Jennifer Azzi, Stanford	Knoxville, TN
1991	Tennessee	Pat Summitt	Virginia	70-67 (OT)	Dawn Staley, Virginia	New Orleans, LA
1992	Stanford	Tara VanDerveer	W. Kentucky	78-62	Molly Goodenbour, Stanford	Los Angeles, CA
1993	Texas Tech	Marsha Sharp	Ohio St.	84-82	Sheryl Swoopes, Texas Tech	Atlanta, GA
1994	North Carolina	Sylvia Hatchell	Louisiana Tech	60-59	Charlotte Smith, North Carolina	Richmond, VA
1995	Connecticut	Geno Auriemma	Tennessee	70-64	Rebecca Lobo, Connecticut	Minneapolis, MN
1996	Tennessee	Pat Summitt	Georgia	83-65	Michelle Marciniak, Tennessee	Charlotte, NC
1997	Tennessee	Pat Summitt	Old Dominion	68-59	Chamique Holdsclaw, Tennessee	Cincinnati, OH
1998	Tennessee	Pat Summitt	Louisiana Tech	93-75	Chamique Holdsclaw, Tennessee	Kansas City, MO
1999	Purdue	Carolyn Peck	Duke	62-45	Ukari Figgs, Purdue	San Jose, CA
2000	Connecticut	Geno Auriemma	Tennessee	71-52	Shea Ralph, Connecticut	Philadelphia, PA
2001	Notre Dame	Muffet McGraw	Purdue	68-66	Ruth Riley, Notre Dame	St. Louis, MO
2002	Connecticut	Geno Auriemma	Oklahoma	82-70	Swin Cash, Connecticut	San Antonio, TX
2003	Connecticut	Geno Auriemma	Tennessee	73-68	Diana Taurasi, Connecticut	Atlanta, GA
2004	Connecticut	Geno Auriemma	Tennessee	70-61	Diana Taurasi, Connecticut	New Orleans, LA
2005	Baylor	Kim Mulkey-Robertson	Michigan State	84-62	Sophia Young, Baylor	Indianapolis, IN
2006	Maryland	Brenda Frese	Duke	78-75 (OT)	Laura Harper, Maryland	Boston, MA
2007	Tennessee	Pat Summitt	Rutgers	59-46	Candace Parker, Tennessee	Cleveland, OH
2008	Tennessee	Pat Summitt	Stanford	64-48	Candace Parker, Tennessee	Tampa Bay, FL
2009	Connecticut	Geno Auriemma	Louisville	76-54	Tina Charles, Connecticut	St. Louis, MO
2010	Connecticut	Geno Auriemma	Stanford	53-47	Maya Moore, Connecticut	San Antonio, TX
2011	Texas A&M	Gary Blair	Notre Dame	76-70	Danielle Adams, Texas A&M	Indianapolis, IN
2012	Baylor	Kim Mulkey	Notre Dame	80-61	Brittney Griner, Baylor	Denver, CO
2013	Connecticut	Geno Auriemma	Louisville	93-60	Breanna Stewart, Connecticut	New Orleans, LA
2014	Connecticut	Geno Auriemma	Notre Dame	79-58	Breanna Stewart, Connecticut	Nashville, TN
2015	Connecticut	Geno Auriemma	Notre Dame	63-53	Breanna Stewart, Connecticut	Tampa, FL
2016	Connecticut	Geno Auriemma	Syracuse	82-51	Breanna Stewart, Connecticut	Indianapolis, IN

Wade Trophy Winners, 1978-2016

Awarded by the National Assn. for Girls and Women in Sport and the Women's Basketball Coaches Assn. (WBCA) to the best college women's basketball player in terms of character, leadership, and player performance.

Year	Player, school	Year	Player, school	Year	Player, school
1978	Carol Blazejowski, Montclair St.	1991	Daedra Charles, Tennessee	2004	Alana Beard, Duke
1979	Nancy Lieberman, Old Dominion	1992	Susan Robinson, Penn St.	2005	Seimone Augustus, LSU
1980	Nancy Lieberman, Old Dominion	1993	Karen Jennings, Nebraska	2006	Seimone Augustus, LSU
1981	Lynette Woodard, Kansas	1994	Carol Ann Shudlick, Minnesota	2007	Candace Parker, Tennessee
1982	Pam Kelly, Louisiana Tech	1995	Rebecca Lobo, Connecticut	2008	Candice Wiggins, Stanford
1983	LaTaunya Pollard, Long Beach St.	1996	Jennifer Rizzotti, Connecticut	2009	Maya Moore, Connecticut
1984	Janice Lawrence, Louisiana Tech	1997	DeLisha Milton, Florida	2010	Maya Moore, Connecticut
1985	Cheryl Miller, USC	1998	Ticha Penicheiro, Old Dominion	2011	Maya Moore, Connecticut
1986	Kamie Ethridge, Texas	1999	Stephanie White-McCarty, Purdue	2012	Brittney Griner, Baylor
1987	Shelly Pennefeather, Villanova	2000	Edwina Brown, Texas	2013	Brittney Griner, Baylor
1988	Teresa Weatherspoon, Louisiana Tech	2001	Jackie Stiles, SW Missouri St.	2014	Odyssey Sims, Baylor
1989	Clarissa Davis, Texas	2002	Sue Bird, Connecticut	2015	Breanna Stewart, Connecticut
1990	Jennifer Azzi, Stanford	2003	Diana Taurasi, Connecticut	2016	Breanna Stewart, Connecticut

NCAA Men's Baseball Division I Champions, 1947-2016

Year	Champion	Year	Champion	Year	Champion	Year	Champion	Year	Champion
1947	California	1961	USC	1975	Texas	1989	Wichita St.	2003	Rice
1948	USC	1962	Michigan	1976	Arizona	1990	Georgia	2004	Cal St. Fullerton
1949	Texas	1963	USC	1977	Arizona St.	1991	LSU	2005	Texas
1950	Texas	1964	Minnesota	1978	USC	1992	Pepperdine	2006	Oregon St.
1951	Oklahoma	1965	Arizona St.	1979	Cal St. Fullerton	1993	LSU	2007	Oregon St.
1952	Holy Cross	1966	Ohio St.	1980	Arizona	1994	Oklahoma	2008	Fresno St.
1953	Michigan	1967	Arizona St.	1981	Arizona St.	1995	Cal St. Fullerton	2009	LSU
1954	Missouri	1968	USC	1982	Miami (FL)	1996	LSU	2010	South Carolina
1955	Wake Forest	1969	Arizona St.	1983	Texas	1997	LSU	2011	South Carolina
1956	Minnesota	1970	USC	1984	Cal St. Fullerton	1998	USC	2012	Arizona
1957	California	1971	USC	1985	Miami (FL)	1999	Miami (FL)	2013	UCLA
1958	USC	1972	USC	1986	Arizona	2000	LSU	2014	Vanderbilt
1959	Oklahoma St.	1973	USC	1987	Stanford	2001	Miami (FL)	2015	Virginia
1960	Minnesota	1974	USC	1988	Stanford	2002	Texas	2016	Coastal Carolina

NCAA Women's Softball Division I Champions, 1982-2016

Year	Champion	Year	Champion	Year	Champion	Year	Champion	Year	Champion
1982	UCLA	1989	UCLA	1996	Arizona	2003	UCLA	2010	UCLA
1983	Texas A&M	1990	UCLA	1997	Arizona	2004	UCLA	2011	Arizona St.
1984	UCLA	1991	Arizona	1998	Fresno St.	2005	Michigan	2012	Alabama
1985	UCLA	1992	UCLA	1999	UCLA	2006	Arizona	2013	Oklahoma
1986	Cal St. Fullerton	1993	Arizona	2000	Oklahoma	2007	Arizona	2014	Florida
1987	Texas A&M	1994	Arizona	2001	Arizona	2008	Arizona St.	2015	Florida
1988	UCLA	1995	UCLA	2002	California	2009	Washington	2016	Oklahoma

NCAA Men's Hockey Division I Champions, 1948-2016

Year	Champion	Year	Champion	Year	Champion	Year	Champion	Year	Champion
1948	Michigan	1962	Michigan Tech	1976	Minnesota	1990	Wisconsin	2004	Denver
1949	Boston College	1963	North Dakota	1977	Wisconsin	1991	North Michigan	2005	Denver
1950	Colorado College	1964	Michigan	1978	Boston Univ.	1992	Lake Superior St.	2006	Wisconsin
1951	Michigan	1965	Michigan Tech	1979	Minnesota	1993	Maine	2007	Michigan St.
1952	Michigan	1966	Michigan St.	1980	North Dakota	1994	Lake Superior St.	2008	Boston College
1953	Michigan	1967	Cornell	1981	Wisconsin	1995	Boston Univ.	2009	Boston Univ.
1954	Rensselaer	1968	Denver	1982	North Dakota	1996	Michigan	2010	Boston College
1955	Michigan	1969	Denver	1983	Wisconsin	1997	North Dakota	2011	Minnesota Duluth
1956	Michigan	1970	Cornell	1984	Bowling Green	1998	Michigan	2012	Boston College
1957	Colorado College	1971	Boston Univ.	1985	Rensselaer	1999	Maine	2013	Yale
1958	Denver	1972	Boston Univ.	1986	Michigan St.	2000	North Dakota	2014	Union College
1959	North Dakota	1973	Wisconsin	1987	North Dakota	2001	Boston College	2015	Providence
1960	Denver	1974	Minnesota	1988	Lake Superior St.	2002	Minnesota	2016	North Dakota
1961	Denver	1975	Michigan Tech	1989	Harvard	2003	Minnesota		

NCAA Women's Hockey Champions, 2001-16

Year	Champion	Year	Champion	Year	Champion	Year	Champion	Year	Champion
2001	Minnesota Duluth	2005	Minnesota	2008	Minnesota Duluth	2011	Wisconsin	2014	Clarkson Univ.
2002	Minnesota Duluth	2006	Wisconsin	2009	Wisconsin	2012	Minnesota	2015	Minnesota
2003	Minnesota Duluth	2007	Wisconsin	2010	Minnesota Duluth	2013	Minnesota	2016	Minnesota
2004	Minnesota								

NCAA Division I Lacrosse Champions, 1982-2016

Year	Men	Women	Year	Men	Women	Year	Men	Women
1982	North Carolina	Massachusetts	1994	Princeton	Princeton	2006	Virginia	Northwestern
1983	Syracuse	Delaware	1995	Syracuse	Maryland	2007	Johns Hopkins	Northwestern
1984	Johns Hopkins	Temple	1996	Princeton	Maryland	2008	Syracuse	Northwestern
1985	Johns Hopkins	New Hampshire	1997	Princeton	Maryland	2009	Syracuse	Northwestern
1986	North Carolina	Maryland	1998	Princeton	Maryland	2010	Duke	Maryland
1987	Johns Hopkins	Penn St.	1999	Virginia	Maryland	2011	Virginia	Northwestern
1988	Syracuse	Temple	2000	Syracuse	Maryland	2012	Loyola (MD)	Northwestern
1989	Syracuse	Penn St.	2001	Princeton	Maryland	2013	Duke	North Carolina
1990	Syracuse[1]	Harvard	2002	Syracuse	Princeton	2014	Duke	Maryland
1991	North Carolina	Virginia	2003	Virginia	Princeton	2015	Denver	Maryland
1992	Princeton	Maryland	2004	Syracuse	Virginia	2016	North Carolina	North Carolina
1993	Syracuse	Virginia	2005	Johns Hopkins	Northwestern			

Note: NCAA Championships began in 1971 for men, in 1982 for women. (1) Vacated due to an NCAA rules violation.

NCAA Division I Soccer Champions, 1982-2015

Year	Men	Women	Year	Men	Women	Year	Men	Women
1982	Indiana	North Carolina	1993	Virginia	North Carolina	2005	Maryland	Portland
1983	Indiana	North Carolina	1994	Virginia	North Carolina	2006	UC Santa Barbara	North Carolina
1984	Clemson	North Carolina	1995	Wisconsin	Notre Dame			
1985	UCLA	George Mason	1996	St. John's (NY)	North Carolina	2007	Wake Forest	USC
1986	Duke	North Carolina	1997	UCLA	North Carolina	2008	Maryland	North Carolina
1987	Clemson	North Carolina	1998	Indiana	Florida	2009	Virginia	North Carolina
1988	Indiana	North Carolina	1999	Indiana	North Carolina	2010	Akron	Notre Dame
1989	Santa Clara; Virginia (tie)	North Carolina	2000	Connecticut	North Carolina	2011	North Carolina	Stanford
			2001	North Carolina	Santa Clara	2012	Indiana	North Carolina
1990	UCLA	North Carolina	2002	UCLA	Portland	2013	Notre Dame	UCLA
1991	Virginia	North Carolina	2003	Indiana	North Carolina	2014	Virginia	Florida St.
1992	Virginia	North Carolina	2004	Indiana	Notre Dame	2015	Stanford	Penn St.

Note: NCAA Championships began in 1959 for men, in 1982 for women.

NCAA Division I Wrestling Champions, 1964-2016

Year	Champion	Year	Champion	Year	Champion	Year	Champion	Year	Champion
1964	Oklahoma St.	1975	Iowa	1986	Iowa	1997	Iowa	2007	Minnesota
1965	Iowa St.	1976	Iowa	1987	Iowa St.	1998	Iowa	2008	Iowa
1966	Oklahoma St.	1977	Iowa St.	1988	Arizona St.	1999	Iowa	2009	Iowa
1967	Michigan St.	1978	Iowa	1989	Oklahoma St.	2000	Iowa	2010	Iowa
1968	Oklahoma St.	1979	Iowa	1990	Oklahoma St.	2001	Minnesota	2011	Penn St.
1969	Iowa St.	1980	Iowa	1991	Iowa	2002	Minnesota	2012	Penn St.
1970	Iowa St.	1981	Iowa	1992	Iowa	2003	Oklahoma St.	2013	Penn St.
1971	Oklahoma St.	1982	Iowa	1993	Iowa	2004	Oklahoma St.	2014	Penn St.
1972	Iowa St.	1983	Iowa	1994	Oklahoma St.	2005	Oklahoma St.	2015	Ohio St.
1973	Iowa St.	1984	Iowa	1995	Iowa	2006	Oklahoma St.	2016	Penn St.
1974	Oklahoma	1985	Iowa	1996	Iowa				

FOOTBALL

NFL 2015: Broncos Win in a Season of Changes

The end-of-season attention was on Peyton Manning and westward franchise moves, but much of the 2015 NFL focus was on the Carolina Panthers' near-perfect regular season and the continuing "Deflategate" saga. The Panthers won their first 14 games before losing to the Atlanta Falcons, 20-13, in Week 16. Carolina quarterback Cam Newton, voted the regular season Most Valuable Player, passed for 3,837 yards and 35 touchdowns, with an additional 10 rushing touchdowns, to lead a Carolina offense that averaged more than 31 points per game.

Newton passed for 335 yards and 2 touchdowns and added a pair of rushing TDs as Carolina advanced to Super Bowl 50 with a 49-15 victory over the Arizona Cardinals in the NFC Championship game Jan. 24, 2016, at Bank of America Stadium in Charlotte, NC. Cardinals QB Carson Palmer passed for 4,671 yards in the regular season, second in the NFC behind New Orleans Saints QB Drew Brees (4,870 yards).

Brees ranked fourth in all-time passing yards with 60,903, and Denver's Peyton Manning surpassed Brett Favre (71,838) for most career passing yards in NFL history (71,940). The Super Bowl 50 champion Manning announced his retirement Mar. 7, 2016, after 18 years (14 with Indianapolis), 4 trips to the Super Bowl, and a record 5 NFL MVP awards. Manning, who missed the entire 2011 season following spinal fusion surgery, was injured for a portion of the 2015 season and shared QB duties with Brock Osweiler. Manning benefited from the Broncos' league-leading defense that allowed only 283.1 overall yards per game.

Denver's defense played a key role against the visiting New England Patriots in the AFC Championship game Jan. 24, 2016, intercepting Tom Brady twice in a 20-18 win at Sports Authority Field at Mile High Stadium in Denver, CO. The Patriots won their seventh consecutive AFC East division title as Brady led the league with 36 touchdown passes. Before the season began, Brady was suspended for four games for "violating the NFL policy on the integrity of the game"—the consequences of his alleged knowledge of underinflated footballs having been used in the 2014 AFC Championship game. But a federal judge voided the suspension in Sept. 2015, allowing Brady to play the entire season. The league appealed the judge's ruling in Oct., and a federal appeals court reinstated the suspension in Apr. 2016 and declined to revisit the decision in July. Brady announced July 15, 2016, that he would not appeal the decision to the U.S. Supreme Court and would sit out the first four games of the 2016 season.

The NFL announced Jan. 12, 2016, that the team owners had approved the St. Louis Rams' relocation to Los Angeles, the franchise's earlier home (1946-94). The Rams were expected to play at the L.A. Coliseum until a new stadium in the suburb of Inglewood was completed. The San Diego Chargers have until Jan. 2017 to decide if they want to relocate to Los Angeles; should they decline, the Oakland Raiders would be given the option to join the Rams in L.A.

NFL Final Standings, 2015
(playoff seeding in parentheses)

AMERICAN FOOTBALL CONFERENCE

	W	L	T	Pct	PF	PA	Div
East Division							
New England (2)....	12	4	0	.750	465	315	4-2
NY Jets...........	10	6	0	.625	387	314	3-3
Buffalo...........	8	8	0	.500	379	359	4-2
Miami	6	10	0	.375	310	389	1-5
North Division							
Cincinnati (3)	12	4	0	.750	419	279	5-1
*Pittsburgh (6)......	10	6	0	.625	423	319	3-3
Baltimore	5	11	0	.313	328	401	3-3
Cleveland	3	13	0	.188	278	432	1-5
South Division							
Houston (4).......	9	7	0	.563	339	313	5-1
Indianapolis	8	8	0	.500	333	408	4-2
Jacksonville	5	11	0	.313	376	448	2-4
Tennessee	3	13	0	.188	299	423	1-5
West Division							
Denver (1)........	12	4	0	.750	355	296	4-2
*Kansas City (5)	11	5	0	.688	405	287	5-1
Oakland	7	9	0	.438	359	399	3-3
San Diego	4	12	0	.250	320	398	0-6

*Wild card qualifier for playoffs. **Note:** Denver wins tiebreaker over New England for no. 1 seed based on head-to-head win percentage; New England wins tiebreaker over Cincinnati for no. 2 seed based on best win percentage in common games. Pittsburgh wins tiebreaker over NY Jets for no. 6 seed based on best win percentage in common games.

NATIONAL FOOTBALL CONFERENCE

	W	L	T	Pct	PF	PA	Div
East Division							
Washington (4)	9	7	0	.563	388	379	4-2
Philadelphia	7	9	0	.438	377	430	3-3
NY Giants.........	6	10	0	.375	420	442	2-4
Dallas	4	12	0	.250	275	374	3-3
North Division							
Minnesota (3)	11	5	0	.688	365	302	5-1
*Green Bay (5)	10	6	0	.625	368	323	3-3
Detroit............	7	9	0	.438	358	400	3-3
Chicago	6	10	0	.375	335	397	1-5
South Division							
Carolina (1).......	15	1	0	.938	500	308	5-1
Atlanta	8	8	0	.500	339	345	1-5
New Orleans.......	7	9	0	.438	408	476	3-3
Tampa Bay	6	10	0	.375	342	417	3-3
West Division							
Arizona (2)	13	3	0	.813	489	313	4-2
*Seattle (6)	10	6	0	.625	423	277	3-3
St. Louis	7	9	0	.438	280	330	4-2
San Francisco......	5	11	0	.313	238	387	1-5

*Wild card qualifier for playoffs. **Note:** Green Bay wins tiebreaker over Seattle for no. 5 seed based on head-to-head win percentage.

NFL Playoffs, 2015

AFC Wild Card Games: Kansas City 30, Houston 0; Pittsburgh 18, Cincinnati 16
NFC Wild Card Games: Seattle 10, Minnesota 9; Green Bay 35, Washington 18
AFC Divisional Playoff Games: New England 27, Kansas City 20; Denver 23, Pittsburgh 16

NFC Divisional Playoff Games: Arizona 26, Green Bay 20 (OT); Carolina 31, Seattle 24
AFC Championship Game: Denver 20, New England 18
NFC Championship Game: Carolina 49, Arizona 15
Super Bowl 50: Denver 24, Carolina 10

Super Bowl 50: Denver 24, Carolina 10

The Denver Broncos defeated the Carolina Panthers, 24-10, in Super Bowl 50 on Feb. 7, 2016, at Levi's Stadium in Santa Clara, CA. The Broncos defense recorded seven sacks and forced four turnovers, stifling Carolina's challenge. Denver linebacker Von Miller recorded 2½ sacks and was voted Super Bowl MVP. Denver's Peyton Manning notched just 13 completions and 141 passing yards and was, at 39, the oldest quarterback ever to start in a Super Bowl. Denver claimed its third Super Bowl win and first since 1999. Carolina dropped its second Super Bowl in as many appearances.

Carolina's Cam Newton, the regular season MVP, passed for 265 yards with an interception and 2 fumbles. Miller sacked Newton at the Carolina 15-yard line and forced a fumble that gave Denver a quick 10-0 lead in the first quarter. The Panthers cut the lead to 10-7 in the second quarter in their only touchdown of the game, but Denver, which managed just 194 yards of offense against a strong Panthers defense, maintained its lead throughout on three field goals by Brandon McManus. The game was put out of reach late in the fourth quarter with a 3-play, 4-yard Denver scoring drive that was set up by another Miller sack.

Quarters

Team	1	2	3	4	Final
Carolina	0	7	0	3	10
Denver	10	3	3	8	24

Total attendance: 71,088
Game length: 3:43

Scoring

Denver: Brandon McManus, 34-yard field goal
Denver: Malik Jackson, fumble recovery in end zone (McManus PAT)
Carolina: Jonathan Stewart, 1-yard run (Graham Gano PAT)
Denver: McManus, 33-yard field goal
Denver: McManus, 30-yard field goal
Carolina: Gano, 39-yard field goal
Denver: C. J. Anderson, 2-yard run (Bennie Fowler pass from Peyton Manning for 2-point conversion)

Individual Statistics

Rushing

Carolina: Cam Newton, 6-45; Stewart, 12-29; Fozzy Whittaker, 4-26; Mike Tolbert, 5-18.
Denver: Anderson, 23-90; Ronnie Hillman, 5-0.

Passing

Carolina: Newton, 18-41, 265 yards, 0 TD, 1 int.; Ted Ginn Jr., 0-0, 0 yards, 0 TD, 0 int.
Denver: Manning, 13-23, 141 yards, 0 TD, 1 int.

Receiving

Carolina: Corey Brown, 4-80; Ginn, 4-74; Greg Olsen, 4-41; Devin Funchess, 2-40; Jerricho Cotchery, 2-17; Whittaker, 1-14; Stewart, 1- −1.
Denver: Emmanuel Sanders, 6-83; Andre Caldwell, 1-22; Owen Daniels, 1-18; Anderson, 4-10; Demaryius Thomas, 1-8.

Team Statistics

	Panthers	Broncos
First downs	21	11
Total net yards	315	194
Rushes-yards	27-118	28-90
Passing yards, net	197	104
Punt returns-yards	3-2	1-61
Kickoff returns-yards	2-42	2-42
Interception returns-yards	1-19	1- −3
Field goals made-attempts	1-2	3-3
Pass attempts-completions-interceptions	41-18-1	23-13-1
Sacked-yards lost	7-68	5-37
Punts-average	7-45.0	8-45.9
Fumbles-lost	4-3	3-1
Penalties-yards	12-102	6-51
Time of possession	32:47	27:13

NFL Individual Leaders: American Football Conference, 2015

(* = rookie)

PASSING

Player, team	Att	Comp	Pct comp	Yds	Yds/Att	Long	TD	Pct TD	Int	Rating
Andy Dalton, Cincinnati	386	255	66.1	3,250	8.4	80T	25	6.5	7	106.2
Tom Brady, New England	624	402	64.4	4,770	7.6	76T	36	5.8	7	102.2
Tyrod Taylor, Buffalo	380	242	63.7	3,035	8.0	63	20	5.3	6	99.4
Alex Smith, Kansas City	470	307	65.3	3,486	7.4	80T	20	4.3	7	95.4
Ben Roethlisberger, Pittsburgh	469	319	68.0	3,938	8.4	69T	21	4.5	16	94.5
Philip Rivers, San Diego	661	437	66.1	4,792	7.2	80T	29	4.4	13	93.8
Josh McCown, Cleveland	292	186	63.7	2,109	7.2	56	12	4.1	4	93.3
*Marcus Mariota, Tennessee	370	230	62.2	2,818	7.6	61T	19	5.1	10	91.5
Brian Hoyer, Houston	369	224	60.7	2,606	7.1	49	19	5.1	7	91.4
Derek Carr, Oakland	573	350	61.1	3,987	7.0	68T	32	5.6	13	91.1
Ryan Tannehill, Miami	586	363	61.9	4,208	7.2	54T	24	4.1	12	88.7
Blake Bortles, Jacksonville	606	355	58.6	4,428	7.3	90T	35	5.8	18	88.2
Ryan Fitzpatrick, NY Jets	562	335	59.6	3,905	6.9	69T	31	5.5	15	88.0

RUSHING YARDS

Player, team	Yds	Att	Avg	Long	TD
Chris Ivory, NY Jets	1,070	247	4.3	58	7
Latavius Murray, Oakland	1,066	266	4.0	54	6
Frank Gore, Indianapolis	967	260	3.7	37T	6
DeAngelo Williams, Pittsburgh	907	200	4.5	55	11
LeSean McCoy, Buffalo	895	203	4.4	48T	3
Lamar Miller, Miami	872	194	4.5	85T	8
Ronnie Hillman, Denver	863	207	4.2	72T	7
Jeremy Hill, Cincinnati	794	223	3.6	38T	11
*T.J. Yeldon, Jacksonville	740	182	4.1	45	2
Giovani Bernard, Cincinnati	730	154	4.7	28	2

RECEPTIONS

Player, team	Rec	Yds	Avg	Long	TD
Antonio Brown, Pittsburgh	136	1,834	13.5	59	10
DeAndre Hopkins, Houston	111	1,521	13.7	61T	11
Jarvis Landry, Miami	110	1,157	10.5	50T	4
Brandon Marshall, NY Jets	109	1,502	13.8	69T	14
Demaryius Thomas, Denver	105	1,304	12.4	72T	6
Delanie Walker, Tennessee	94	1,088	11.6	61T	6
Jeremy Maclin, Kansas City	87	1,088	12.5	61	8
A.J. Green, Cincinnati	86	1,297	15.1	80T	10
Michael Crabtree, Oakland	85	922	10.8	38T	9
Eric Decker, NY Jets	80	1,027	12.8	35	12
Allen Robinson, Jacksonville	80	1,400	17.5	90T	14
Danny Woodhead, San Diego	80	755	9.4	61	6

INTERCEPTIONS

Player, team	No.	Yds	Avg	Long	TD
Reggie Nelson, Cincinnati	8	115	14.4	37	0
*Marcus Peters, Kansas City	8	280	35.0	90T	2
Marcus Williams, NY Jets	6	45	7.5	21	0
Mike Adams, Indianapolis	5	63	12.6	38	1
Reshad Jones, Miami	5	104	20.8	42	2
Darrelle Revis, NY Jets	5	48	9.6	24	0
Charles Woodson, Oakland	5	22	4.4	11	0
David Amerson, Oakland	4	28	7.0	24T	1
Vontae Davis, Indianapolis	4	6	1.5	6	0
Brent Grimes, Miami	4	20	5.0	17	0
Andre Hal, Houston	4	54	13.5	31T	1
Davon House, Jacksonville	4	21	5.3	15	0
Dwight Lowery, Indianapolis	4	96	24.0	69T	1
Logan Ryan, New England	4	39	9.8	25	0

SCORING—KICKERS

Player, team	PAT	FG	Long	Pts
Stephen Gostkowski, New England	52/52	33/36	57	151
Cairo Santos, Kansas City	39/41	30/37	53	129
Justin Tucker, Baltimore	29/29	33/40	52	128
Brandon McManus, Denver	35/36	30/35	57	125
Mike Nugent, Cincinnati	48/49	23/28	52	117
Chris Boswell, Pittsburgh	26/27	29/32	51	113

SCORING—NON-KICKERS

Player, team (position)	TD	Rush	Rec	2-Pt	Pts
Brandon Marshall, NY Jets (WR)	14	0	14	0	84
Allen Robinson, Jacksonville (WR)	14	0	14	0	84
Tyler Eifert, Cincinnati (TE)	13	0	13	0	78
Jeremy Hill, Cincinnati (RB)	12	11	1	1	74
Eric Decker, NY Jets (WR)	12	0	12	0	72
Antonio Brown, Pittsburgh (WR)	11	1**	10	2	70
DeAndre Hopkins, Houston (WR)	11	0	11	1	68
DeAngelo Williams, Pittsburgh (RB)	11	11	0	1	68

** = Punt return.

KICKOFF RETURNS

Player, team	No.	Yds	Avg	Long	TD
*Quan Bray, Indianapolis	21	570	27.1	60	0
Taiwan Jones, Oakland	31	829	26.7	70	0
Knile Davis, Kansas City	24	603	25.1	54	0
Damien Williams, Miami	21	457	21.8	37	0

PUNTING

Player, team	No.	Yds	Long	Avg
Pat McAfee, Indianapolis	85	4,052	63	47.7
*Matt Darr, Miami	92	4,380	70	47.6
Brett Kern, Tennessee	88	4,175	61	47.4
Shane Lechler, Houston	95	4,497	64	47.3
Sam Koch, Baltimore	74	3,454	67	46.7
Andy Lee, Cleveland	70	3,270	67	46.7

PUNT RETURNS

Player, team	No.	Yds	Avg	Long	TD
Danny Amendola, New England	23	276	12.0	82	0
Travis Benjamin, Cleveland. . . .	28	324	11.6	78T	1
*Kaelin Clay, Baltimore	23	244	10.6	82T	1
Jarvis Landry, Miami	36	356	9.9	69T	1
Antonio Brown, Pittsburgh	22	212	9.6	71T	1
Dexter McCluster, Tennessee. .	24	217	9.0	37	0

SACKS

Player, team	No.
J.J. Watt, Houston	17.5
Khalil Mack, Oakland	15.0
Carlos Dunlap, Cincinnati	13.5
Chandler Jones, New England	12.5
Whitney Mercilus, Houston	12.0
Muhammad Wilkerson, NY Jets	12.0
Geno Atkins, Cincinnati	11.0
Von Miller, Denver	11.0
Melvin Ingram, San Diego	10.5
Jabaal Sheard, New England	8.0

NFL Individual Leaders: National Football Conference, 2015

(* = rookie)

PASSING

Player, team	Att	Comp	Pct comp	Yds	Yds/Att	Long	TD	Pct TD	Int	Rating
Russell Wilson, Seattle	483	329	68.1	4,024	8.3	80T	34	7.0	8	110.1
Carson Palmer, Arizona	537	342	63.7	4,671	8.7	68	35	6.5	11	104.6
Kirk Cousins, Washington.	543	379	69.8	4,166	7.7	78T	29	5.3	11	101.6
Drew Brees, New Orleans	627	428	68.3	4,870	7.8	80T	32	5.1	11	101.0
Cam Newton, Carolina	495	296	59.8	3,837	7.8	74T	35	7.1	10	99.4
Matthew Stafford, Detroit	592	398	67.2	4,262	7.2	57	32	5.4	13	97.0
Eli Manning, NY Giants	618	387	62.6	4,432	7.2	87T	35	5.7	14	93.6
Aaron Rodgers, Green Bay.	572	347	60.7	3,821	6.7	65T	31	5.4	8	92.7
Jay Cutler, Chicago.	483	311	64.4	3,659	7.6	87T	21	4.3	11	92.3
Matt Ryan, Atlanta	614	407	66.3	4,591	7.5	70T	21	3.4	16	89.0
Teddy Bridgewater, Minnesota	447	292	65.3	3,231	7.2	52	14	3.1	9	88.7
Sam Bradford, Philadelphia	532	346	65.0	3,725	7.0	78T	19	3.6	14	86.4
Blaine Gabbert, San Francisco.	282	178	63.1	2,031	7.2	71T	10	3.5	7	86.2
*Jameis Winston, Tampa Bay	535	312	58.3	4,042	7.6	68	22	4.1	15	84.2

RUSHING YARDS

Player, team	Yds	Att	Avg	Long	TD
Adrian Peterson, Minnesota	1,485	327	4.5	80T	11
Doug Martin, Tampa Bay	1,402	288	4.9	84	6
*Todd Gurley, St. Louis	1,106	229	4.8	71T	10
Darren McFadden, Dallas.	1,089	239	4.6	50	3
Devonta Freeman, Atlanta	1,056	265	4.0	39	11
Jonathan Stewart, Carolina	989	242	4.1	44	6
Matt Forte, Chicago	898	218	4.1	27	4
Rashad Jennings, NY Giants . . .	863	195	4.4	38T	3
*Thomas Rawls, Seattle	830	147	5.6	69T	4
Chris Johnson, Arizona.	814	196	4.2	62	3

Player, team (position)	TD	Rush	Rec	2-Pt	Pts
Odell Beckham, NY Giants (WR) . .	13	0	13	0	78
*David Johnson, Arizona (RB)	13	9**	4	0	78
Adrian Peterson, Minnesota (RB). .	11	11	0	0	66
Jordan Reed, Washington (TE). . . .	11	0	11	0	66
** = One kickoff return.					

RECEPTIONS

Player, team	Rec	Yds	Avg	Long	TD
Julio Jones, Atlanta.	136	1,871	13.8	70T	8
Larry Fitzgerald, Arizona.	109	1,215	11.1	44	9
Odell Beckham, NY Giants.	96	1,450	15.1	87T	13
Golden Tate, Detroit	90	813	9.0	43	6
Calvin Johnson, Detroit.	88	1,214	13.8	57	9
Jordan Reed, Washington	87	952	10.9	32	11
Jordan Matthews, Philadelphia . .	85	997	11.7	78T	8
Brandin Cooks, New Orleans . . .	84	1,138	13.5	71T	9
Theo Riddick, Detroit	80	697	8.7	34	3
Randall Cobb, Green Bay	79	829	10.5	53T	6

KICKOFF RETURNS

Player, team	No.	Yds	Avg	Long	TD
Cordarrelle Patterson, Minnesota . .	32	1,019	31.8	101T	2
*Ameer Abdullah, Detroit	37	1,077	29.1	104	0
Dwayne Harris, NY Giants	22	631	28.7	100T	1
Benny Cunningham, St. Louis	25	714	28.6	102	0
*David Johnson, Arizona.	22	598	27.2	108T	1
*Tyler Lockett, Seattle	33	852	25.8	105T	1

INTERCEPTIONS

Player, team	No.	Yds	Avg	Long	TD
Kurt Coleman, Carolina	7	89	12.7	36T	1
Trumaine Johnson, St. Louis	7	136	19.4	58T	1
Rashad Johnson, Arizona.	5	14	2.8	11	0
Tyrann Mathieu, Arizona.	5	92	18.4	33T	1
Earl Thomas, Seattle	5	67	13.4	32	0
Thomas Davis, Carolina	4	22	5.5	22	0
Luke Kuechly, Carolina	4	48	12.0	32T	1
Josh Norman, Carolina.	4	110	27.5	46T	2
Glover Quin, Detroit	4	77	19.3	31T	1

PUNTING

Player, team	No.	Yds	Long	Avg
Johnny Hekker, St. Louis	96	4,601	68	47.9
Matt Bosher, Atlanta	58	2,735	69	47.2
Donnie Jones, Philadelphia	86	4,038	64	47.0
Tress Way, Washington	70	3,224	64	46.1
Sam Martin, Detroit.	80	3,679	66	46.0
Jon Ryan, Seattle	68	3,105	73	45.7
Thomas Morstead, New Orleans . .	56	2,551	58	45.6

SCORING—KICKERS

Player, team	PAT	FG	Long	Pts
Graham Gano, Carolina	56/59	30/36	52	146
Chandler Catanzaro, Arizona	53/58	28/31	47	137
Blair Walsh, Minnesota.	33/37	34/39	54	135
Josh Brown, NY Giants	44/45	30/32	53	134
Robbie Gould, Chicago	28/29	33/39	55	127
Steven Hauschka, Seattle.	40/44	29/31	54	127

PUNT RETURNS

Player, team	No.	Yds	Avg	Long	TD
Darren Sproles, Philadelphia	38	446	11.7	89T	2
Ted Ginn, Carolina	27	277	10.3	37	0
Dwayne Harris, NY Giants	34	341	10.0	80T	1
Bobby Rainey, Tampa Bay	29	288	9.9	58	0
*Tyler Lockett, Seattle.	40	379	9.5	66	1
*Marcus Murphy, New Orleans	28	261	9.3	74T	1
Marcus Sherels, Minnesota	34	311	9.1	65T	1

SCORING—NON-KICKERS

Player, team (position)	TD	Rush	Rec	2-Pt	Pts
Doug Baldwin, Seattle (WR)	14	0	14	0	84
Devonta Freeman, Atlanta (RB) . . .	14	11	3	0	84

SACKS

Player, team	No.
Ezekiel Ansah, Detroit	14.5
Aaron Donald, St. Louis	11.0
Kawann Short, Carolina	11.0
Julius Peppers, Green Bay	10.5
Everson Griffen, Minnesota	10.5
Michael Bennett, Seattle.	10.0
Cameron Jordan, New Orleans	10.0
Robert Ayers, NY Giants	9.5
Ryan Kerrigan, Washington	9.5
Fletcher Cox, Philadelphia	9.5

Super Bowl, 1967-2016

The Super Bowl was created as a condition of the merger between the American Football League (AFL, formed in 1959) and National Football League (NFL, formed in 1920). Announced June 8, 1966, the merger agreement stipulated that the leagues would play separate regular season schedules through the 1969 season but meet after each in an AFL-NFL Championship Game, unofficially dubbed the Super Bowl. The first Super Bowl, played at the Memorial Coliseum in Los Angeles on Jan. 15, 1967, did not sell out, unlike every Super Bowl game since. Each player on the victorious Green Bay Packers earned $15,000 for the win; the defeated Kansas City Chiefs each collected $7,500.

No.	Year	Winner	Opponent	Winning coach	Site
I	1967	*Green Bay Packers, 35	Kansas City Chiefs, 10	Vince Lombardi	Memorial Coliseum, Los Angeles, CA
II	1968	Green Bay Packers, 33	*Oakland Raiders, 14	Vince Lombardi	Orange Bowl, Miami, FL
III	1969	*NY Jets, 16	Baltimore Colts, 7	Weeb Ewbank	Orange Bowl, Miami, FL
IV	1970	Kansas City Chiefs, 23	*Minnesota Vikings, 7	Hank Stram	Tulane Stadium, New Orleans, LA
V	1971	Baltimore Colts, 16	*Dallas Cowboys, 13	Don McCafferty	Orange Bowl, Miami, FL
VI	1972	Dallas Cowboys, 24	*Miami Dolphins, 3	Tom Landry	Tulane Stadium, New Orleans, LA
VII	1973	*Miami Dolphins, 14	Washington Redskins, 7	Don Shula	Memorial Coliseum, Los Angeles, CA
VIII	1974	*Miami Dolphins, 24	Minnesota Vikings, 7	Don Shula	Rice Stadium, Houston, TX
IX	1975	*Pittsburgh Steelers, 16	Minnesota Vikings, 6	Chuck Noll	Tulane Stadium, New Orleans, LA
X	1976	Pittsburgh Steelers, 21	*Dallas Cowboys, 17	Chuck Noll	Orange Bowl, Miami, FL
XI	1977	*Oakland Raiders, 32	Minnesota Vikings, 14	John Madden	Rose Bowl, Pasadena, CA
XII	1978	*Dallas Cowboys, 27	Denver Broncos, 10	Tom Landry	Superdome, New Orleans, LA
XIII	1979	Pittsburgh Steelers, 35	*Dallas Cowboys, 31	Chuck Noll	Orange Bowl, Miami, FL
XIV	1980	Pittsburgh Steelers, 31	*L.A. Rams, 19	Chuck Noll	Rose Bowl, Pasadena, CA
XV	1981	Oakland Raiders, 27	*Philadelphia Eagles, 10	Tom Flores	Superdome, New Orleans, LA
XVI	1982	*San Francisco 49ers, 26	Cincinnati Bengals, 21	Bill Walsh	Silverdome, Pontiac, MI
XVII	1983	Washington Redskins, 27	*Miami Dolphins, 17	Joe Gibbs	Rose Bowl, Pasadena, CA
XVIII	1984	*L.A. Raiders, 38	Washington Redskins, 9	Tom Flores	Tampa Stadium, Tampa, FL
XIX	1985	*San Francisco 49ers, 38	Miami Dolphins, 16	Bill Walsh	Stanford Stadium, Stanford, CA
XX	1986	*Chicago Bears, 46	New England Patriots, 10	Mike Ditka	Superdome, New Orleans, LA
XXI	1987	NY Giants, 39	*Denver Broncos, 20	Bill Parcells	Rose Bowl, Pasadena, CA
XXII	1988	*Washington Redskins, 42	Denver Broncos, 10	Joe Gibbs	Jack Murphy Stadium, San Diego, CA
XXIII	1989	*San Francisco 49ers, 20	Cincinnati Bengals, 16	Bill Walsh	Joe Robbie Stadium, Miami, FL
XXIV	1990	San Francisco 49ers, 55	*Denver Broncos, 10	George Seifert	Superdome, New Orleans, LA
XXV	1991	NY Giants, 20	*Buffalo Bills, 19	Bill Parcells	Tampa Stadium, Tampa, FL
XXVI	1992	*Washington Redskins, 37	Buffalo Bills, 24	Joe Gibbs	Metrodome, Minneapolis, MN
XXVII	1993	Dallas Cowboys, 52	*Buffalo Bills, 17	Jimmy Johnson	Rose Bowl, Pasadena, CA
XXVIII	1994	*Dallas Cowboys, 30	Buffalo Bills, 13	Jimmy Johnson	Georgia Dome, Atlanta, GA
XXIX	1995	*San Francisco 49ers, 49	San Diego Chargers, 26	George Seifert	Joe Robbie Stadium, Miami, FL
XXX	1996	*Dallas Cowboys, 27	Pittsburgh Steelers, 17	Barry Switzer	Sun Devil Stadium, Tempe, AZ
XXXI	1997	Green Bay Packers, 35	*New England Patriots, 21	Mike Holmgren	Superdome, New Orleans, LA
XXXII	1998	Denver Broncos, 31	*Green Bay Packers, 24	Mike Shanahan	Qualcomm Stadium, San Diego, CA
XXXIII	1999	Denver Broncos, 34	*Atlanta Falcons, 19	Mike Shanahan	Pro Player Stadium, Miami, FL
XXXIV	2000	*St. Louis Rams, 23	Tennessee Titans, 16	Dick Vermeil	Georgia Dome, Atlanta, GA
XXXV	2001	Baltimore Ravens, 34	*NY Giants, 7	Brian Billick	Raymond James Stadium, Tampa, FL
XXXVI	2002	New England Patriots, 20	*St. Louis Rams, 17	Bill Belichick	Superdome, New Orleans, LA
XXXVII	2003	*Tampa Bay Buccaneers, 48	Oakland Raiders, 21	Jon Gruden	Qualcomm Stadium, San Diego, CA
XXXVIII	2004	New England Patriots, 32	*Carolina Panthers, 29	Bill Belichick	Reliant Stadium, Houston, TX
XXXIX	2005	New England Patriots, 24	*Philadelphia Eagles, 21	Bill Belichick	Alltel Stadium, Jacksonville, FL
XL	2006	Pittsburgh Steelers, 21	*Seattle Seahawks, 10	Bill Cowher	Ford Field, Detroit, MI
XLI	2007	Indianapolis Colts, 29	*Chicago Bears, 17	Tony Dungy	Dolphin Stadium, Miami Gardens, FL
XLII	2008	*NY Giants, 17	New England Patriots, 14	Tom Coughlin	Univ. of Phoenix Stadium, Glendale, AZ
XLIII	2009	Pittsburgh Steelers, 27	**Arizona Cardinals, 23	Mike Tomlin	Raymond James Stadium, Tampa, FL
XLIV	2010	*New Orleans Saints, 31	Indianapolis Colts, 17	Sean Payton	Sun Life Stadium, Miami Gardens, FL
XLV	2011	**Green Bay Packers, 31	Pittsburgh Steelers, 25	Mike McCarthy	Cowboys Stadium, Arlington, TX
XLVI	2012	NY Giants, 21	**New England Patriots, 17	Tom Coughlin	Lucas Oil Stadium, Indianapolis, IN
XLVII	2013	**Baltimore Ravens, 34	San Francisco 49ers, 31	John Harbaugh	Mercedes-Benz Superdome, New Orleans, LA
XLVIII	2014	**Seattle Seahawks, 43	Denver Broncos, 8	Pete Carroll	MetLife Stadium, East Rutherford, NJ
XLIX	2015	New England Patriots, 28	**Seattle Seahawks, 24	Bill Belichick	Univ. of Phoenix Stadium, Glendale, AZ
50 (L)	2016	Denver Broncos, 24	**Carolina Panthers, 10	Gary Kubiak	Levi's Stadium, Santa Clara, CA

* = Team won the coin toss and elected to receive. ** = Team won the coin toss and elected to receive in the second half.

Super Bowl Sites, 2017-21

No.	Site	Date	No.	Site	Date
LI	NRG Stadium, Houston, TX	Feb. 5, 2017	LIV	New Miami Stadium, Miami Gardens, FL	Feb. 2, 2020
LII	U.S. Bank Stadium, Minneapolis, MN. . . .	Feb. 4, 2018	LV	Inglewood, CA	Feb. 7, 2021
LIII	Mercedes-Benz Stadium, Atlanta, GA. . . .	Feb. 3, 2019			

Super Bowl MVPs, 1967-2016

Year	Most valuable player, team	Year	Most valuable player, team	Year	Most valuable player, team
1967	Bart Starr, Green Bay	1984	Marcus Allen, L.A. Raiders	2001	Ray Lewis, Baltimore
1968	Bart Starr, Green Bay	1985	Joe Montana, San Francisco	2002	Tom Brady, New England
1969	Joe Namath, NY Jets	1986	Richard Dent, Chicago	2003	Dexter Jackson, Tampa Bay
1970	Len Dawson, Kansas City	1987	Phil Simms, NY Giants	2004	Tom Brady, New England
1971	Chuck Howley, Dallas	1988	Doug Williams, Washington	2005	Deion Branch, New England
1972	Roger Staubach, Dallas	1989	Jerry Rice, San Francisco	2006	Hines Ward, Pittsburgh
1973	Jake Scott, Miami	1990	Joe Montana, San Francisco	2007	Peyton Manning, Indianapolis
1974	Larry Csonka, Miami	1991	Ottis Anderson, NY Giants	2008	Eli Manning, NY Giants
1975	Franco Harris, Pittsburgh	1992	Mark Rypien, Washington	2009	Santonio Holmes, Pittsburgh
1976	Lynn Swann, Pittsburgh	1993	Troy Aikman, Dallas	2010	Drew Brees, New Orleans
1977	Fred Biletnikoff, Oakland	1994	Emmitt Smith, Dallas	2011	Aaron Rodgers, Green Bay
1978	Randy White, Harvey Martin; Dallas	1995	Steve Young, San Francisco	2012	Eli Manning, NY Giants
1979	Terry Bradshaw, Pittsburgh	1996	Larry Brown, Dallas	2013	Joe Flacco, Baltimore
1980	Terry Bradshaw, Pittsburgh	1997	Desmond Howard, Green Bay	2014	Malcolm Smith, Seattle
1981	Jim Plunkett, Oakland	1998	Terrell Davis, Denver	2015	Tom Brady, New England
1982	Joe Montana, San Francisco	1999	John Elway, Denver	2016	Von Miller, Denver
1983	John Riggins, Washington	2000	Kurt Warner, St. Louis		

Super Bowl Single-Game Statistical Leaders

PASSING YARDS

Player, team	Year	Att/comp	Yds	TD
Kurt Warner, St. Louis	2000	45/24	414	2
Kurt Warner, Arizona	2009	43/31	377	3
Kurt Warner, St. Louis	2002	44/28	365	1
Donovon McNabb, Philadelphia	2005	51/30	357	3
Joe Montana, San Francisco	1989	36/23	357	2

PASSING TOUCHDOWNS

Player, team	Year	Att/comp	Yds	TD
Steve Young, San Francisco	1995	36/24	325	6
Joe Montana, San Francisco	1990	29/22	297	5
Tom Brady, New England	2015	50/37	328	4
Troy Aikman, Dallas	1993	30/22	273	4
Doug Williams, Washington	1988	29/18	340	4
Terry Bradshaw, Pittsburgh	1979	30/17	318	4

RECEIVING YARDS

Player, team	Year	Rec	Yds	TD
Jerry Rice, San Francisco	1989	11	215	1
Ricky Sanders, Washington	1988	9	193	2
Isaac Bruce, St. Louis	2000	6	162	1

SCORING

Player, team	Year	Pts	
Terrell Davis, Denver	1998	18	(3 TDs)
Jerry Rice, San Francisco	1995	18	(3 TDs)
Ricky Watters, San Francisco	1995	18	(3 TDs)
Jerry Rice, San Francisco	1990	18	(3 TDs)
Roger Craig, San Francisco	1985	18	(3 TDs)
Don Chandler, Green Bay	1968	15	(4 FGs, 3 PATs)
Kevin Butler, Chicago Bears	1986	14	(3 FGs, 5 PATs)
Ray Wersching, San Francisco	1982	14	(4 FGs, 2 PATs)

RUSHING YARDS

Player, team	Year	Att	Yds	TD
Timmy Smith, Washington	1988	22	204	2
Marcus Allen, L.A. Raiders	1984	20	191	2
John Riggins, Washington	1983	38	166	1

First-Round Selections in the 2016 NFL Draft

Held Apr. 28-30, 2016.

Team	Player	Pos.	College
1. L.A. Rams[1]	Jared Goff	QB	California
2. Philadelphia Eagles[2]	Carson Wentz	QB	North Dakota St.
3. San Diego Chargers	Joey Bosa	DE	Ohio St.
4. Dallas Cowboys	Ezekiel Elliott	RB	Ohio St.
5. Jacksonville Jaguars	Jalen Ramsey	CB	Florida St.
6. Baltimore Ravens	Ronnie Stanley	OT	Notre Dame
7. San Francisco 49ers	DeForest Buckner	DE	Oregon
8. Tennessee Titans[3]	Jack Conklin	OT	Michigan St.
9. Chicago Bears[4]	Leonard Floyd	LB	Georgia
10. NY Giants	Eli Apple	CB	Ohio St.
11. Tampa Bay Buccaneers[5]	Vernon Hargreaves	CB	Florida
12. New Orleans Saints	Sheldon Rankins	DT	Louisville
13. Miami Dolphins[6]	Laremy Tunsil	OT	Mississippi
14. Oakland Raiders	Karl Joseph	S	West Virginia
15. Cleveland Browns[7]	Corey Coleman	WR	Baylor
16. Detroit Lions	Taylor Decker	OT	Ohio St.
17. Atlanta Falcons	Keanu Neal	SS	Florida
18. Indianapolis Colts	Ryan Kelly	C	Alabama
19. Buffalo Bills	Shaq Lawson	DE	Clemson
20. NY Jets	Darron Lee	LB	Ohio St.
21. Houston Texans[8]	Will Fuller	WR	Notre Dame
22. Washington Redskins[9]	Josh Doctson	WR	TCU
23. Minnesota Vikings	Laquon Treadwell	WR	Mississippi
24. Cincinnati Bengals	William Jackson III	CB	Houston
25. Pittsburgh Steelers	Artie Burns	CB	Miami
26. Denver Broncos[10]	Paxton Lynch	QB	Memphis
27. Green Bay Packers	Kenny Clark	DT	UCLA
28. San Francisco 49ers[11]	Joshua Garnett	OG	Stanford
30. Arizona Cardinals	Robert Nkemdiche	DT	Mississippi
31. Carolina Panthers	Vernon Butler	DT	Louisiana Tech
32. Seattle Seahawks[12]	Germain Ifedi	OG	Texas A&M

(1) From Titans. (2) From Browns. (3) From Browns through Eagles, Dolphins. (4) From Buccaneers. (5) From Bears. (6) From Eagles. (7) From Titans through Rams. (8) From Redskins. (9) From Texans. (10) From Seahawks. (11) From Chiefs. (12) From Broncos.

Number One NFL Draft Choices, 1960-2016

Year	Team	Player, pos., college	Year	Team	Player, pos., college
1960	L.A. Rams	Billy Cannon, HB, LSU	1967	Baltimore Colts	Bubba Smith, DE, Michigan St.
1961	Minnesota	Tommy Mason, HB, Tulane	1968	Minnesota	Ron Yary, OT, USC
1962	Washington	Ernie Davis, HB, Syracuse	1969	Buffalo	O. J. Simpson, RB, USC
1963	L.A. Rams	Terry Baker, QB, Oregon St.	1970	Pittsburgh	Terry Bradshaw, QB, LA Tech
1964	San Francisco	Dave Parks, E, Texas Tech	1971	New England	Jim Plunkett, QB, Stanford
1965	NY Giants	Tucker Frederickson, RB, Auburn	1972	Buffalo	Walt Patulski, DE, Notre Dame
1966	Atlanta	Tommy Nobis, LB, Texas	1973	Houston	John Matuszak, DE, Tampa

Year	Team	Player, pos., college
1974	Dallas	Ed "Too Tall" Jones, DE, Tenn. St.
1975	Atlanta	Steve Bartkowski, QB, California
1976	Tampa Bay	Lee Roy Selmon, DE, Oklahoma
1977	Tampa Bay	Ricky Bell, RB, USC
1978	Houston	Earl Campbell, RB, Texas
1979	Buffalo	Tom Cousineau, LB, Ohio St.
1980	Detroit	Billy Sims, RB, Oklahoma
1981	New Orleans	George Rogers, RB, S. Carolina
1982	New England	Kenneth Sims, DT, Texas
1983	Baltimore Colts	John Elway, QB, Stanford
1984	New England	Irving Fryar, WR, Nebraska
1985	Buffalo	Bruce Smith, DE, Virginia Tech
1986	Tampa Bay	Bo Jackson, RB, Auburn
1987	Tampa Bay	Vinny Testaverde, QB, Miami (FL)
1988	Atlanta	Aundray Bruce, LB, Auburn
1989	Dallas	Troy Aikman, QB, UCLA
1990	Indianapolis	Jeff George, QB, Illinois
1991	Dallas	Russell Maryland, DL, Miami (FL)
1992	Indianapolis	Steve Emtman, DL, Washington
1993	New England	Drew Bledsoe, QB, Washington St.
1994	Cincinnati	Dan Wilkinson, DT, Ohio St.
1995	Cincinnati	Ki-Jana Carter, RB, Penn State

Year	Team	Player, pos., college
1996	NY Jets	Keyshawn Johnson, WR, USC
1997	St. Louis	Orlando Pace, OT, Ohio St.
1998	Indianapolis	Peyton Manning, QB, Tennessee
1999	Cleveland	Tim Couch, QB, Kentucky
2000	Cleveland	Courtney Brown, DE, Penn State
2001	Atlanta	Michael Vick, QB, Virginia Tech
2002	Houston	David Carr, QB, Fresno St.
2003	Cincinnati	Carson Palmer, QB, USC
2004	San Diego	Eli Manning, QB, Mississippi
2005	San Francisco	Alex D. Smith, QB, Utah
2006	Houston	Mario Williams, DE, NC State
2007	Oakland	JaMarcus Russell, QB, LSU
2008	Miami	Jake Long, OT, Michigan
2009	Detroit	Matthew Stafford, QB, Georgia
2010	St. Louis	Sam Bradford, QB, Oklahoma
2011	Carolina	Cam Newton, QB, Auburn
2012	Indianapolis	Andrew Luck, QB, Stanford
2013	Kansas City	Eric Fisher, OT, Central Michigan
2014	Houston	Jadeveon Clowney, DE, S. Carolina
2015	Tampa Bay	Jameis Winston, QB, Florida St.
2016	L.A. Rams	Jared Goff, QB, California

American Football League Champions, 1960-69

Year	Eastern (W-L-T)	Western (W-L-T)	Championship
1960	Houston Oilers (10-4-0)	L.A. Chargers (10-4-0)	Houston 24, L.A. 16
1961	Houston Oilers (10-3-1)	San Diego Chargers (12-2-0)	Houston 10, San Diego 3
1962	Houston Oilers (11-3-0)	Dallas Texans (11-3-0)	Dallas 20, Houston 17 (2 OT)
1963	Boston Patriots (7-6-1)[1]	San Diego Chargers (11-3-0)	San Diego 51, Boston 10
1964	Buffalo Bills (12-2-0)	San Diego Chargers (8-5-1)	Buffalo 20, San Diego 7
1965	Buffalo Bills (10-3-1)	San Diego Chargers (9-2-3)	Buffalo 23, San Diego 0
1966	Buffalo Bills (9-4-1)	Kansas City Chiefs (11-2-1)	Kansas City 31, Buffalo 7
1967	Houston Oilers (9-4-1)	Oakland Raiders (13-1-0)	Oakland 40, Houston 7
1968	NY Jets (11-3-0)	Oakland Raiders (12-2-0)[2]	NY Jets 27, Oakland 23
1969	NY Jets (10-4-0)	Oakland Raiders (12-1-1)	Kansas City 17, Oakland 7[3]

(1) Defeated conference champion Buffalo Bills in divisional playoff. (2) Defeated conference champion Kansas City Chiefs in divisional playoff. (3) Kansas City Chiefs defeated NY Jets, and Oakland Raiders defeated Houston Oilers in divisional playoffs.

National Football League Champions, 1933-69

Year	Eastern (W-L-T)	Western (W-L-T)	Championship
1933	NY Giants (11-3-0)	Chicago Bears (10-2-1)	Chicago Bears 23, NY Giants 21
1934	NY Giants (8-5-0)	Chicago Bears (13-0-0)	NY Giants 30, Chicago Bears 13
1935	NY Giants (9-3-0)	Detroit Lions (7-3-2)	Detroit 26, NY Giants 7
1936	Boston Redskins (7-5-0)	Green Bay Packers (10-1-1)	Green Bay 21, Boston 6
1937	Washington Redskins (8-3-0)	Chicago Bears (9-1-1)	Washington 28, Chicago Bears 21
1938	NY Giants (8-2-1)	Green Bay Packers (8-3-0)	NY Giants 23, Green Bay 17
1939	NY Giants (9-1-1)	Green Bay Packers (9-2-0)	Green Bay 27, NY Giants 0
1940	Washington Redskins (9-2-0)	Chicago Bears (8-3-0)	Chicago Bears 73, Washington 0
1941	NY Giants (8-3-0)	Chicago Bears (10-1-0)[1]	Chicago Bears 37, NY Giants 9
1942	Washington Redskins (10-1-0)	Chicago Bears (11-0-0)	Washington 14, Chicago Bears 6
1943	Washington Redskins (6-3-1)[1]	Chicago Bears (8-1-1)	Chicago Bears, 41, Washington 21
1944	NY Giants (8-1-1)	Green Bay Packers (8-2-0)	Green Bay 14, NY Giants 7
1945	Washington Redskins (8-2-0)	Cleveland Rams (9-1-0)	Cleveland Rams 15, Washington 14
1946	NY Giants (7-3-1)	Chicago Bears (8-2-1)	Chicago Bears 24, NY Giants 14
1947	Philadelphia Eagles (8-4-0)[1]	Chicago Cardinals (9-3-0)	Chicago Cardinals 28, Philadelphia 21
1948	Philadelphia Eagles (9-2-1)	Chicago Cardinals (11-1-0)	Philadelphia 7, Chicago Cardinals 0
1949	Philadelphia Eagles (11-1-0)	L.A. Rams (8-2-2)	Philadelphia 14, L.A. Rams 0
1950	Cleveland Browns (10-2-0)[1]	L.A. Rams (9-3-0)[1]	Cleveland 30, L.A. Rams 28
1951	Cleveland Browns (11-1-0)	L.A. Rams (8-4-0)	L.A. Rams 24, Cleveland Browns 17
1952	Cleveland Browns (8-4-0)	Detroit Lions (9-3-0)[1]	Detroit 17, Cleveland Browns 7
1953	Cleveland Browns (11-1-0)	Detroit Lions (10-2-0)	Detroit 17, Cleveland Browns 16
1954	Cleveland Browns (9-3-0)	Detroit Lions (9-2-1)	Cleveland Browns 56, Detroit 10
1955	Cleveland Browns (9-2-1)	L.A. Rams (8-3-1)	Cleveland Browns 38, L.A. Rams 14
1956	NY Giants (8-3-1)	Chicago Bears (9-2-1)	NY Giants 47, Chicago Bears 7
1957	Cleveland Browns (9-2-1)	Detroit Lions (8-4-0)[1]	Detroit 59, Cleveland Browns 14
1958	NY Giants (9-3-0)[1]	Baltimore Colts (9-3-0)	Baltimore 23, NY Giants 17[2]
1959	NY Giants (10-2-0)	Baltimore Colts (9-3-0)	Baltimore 31, NY Giants 16
1960	Philadelphia Eagles (10-2-0)	Green Bay Packers (8-4-0)	Philadelphia 17, Green Bay 13
1961	NY Giants (10-3-1)	Green Bay Packers (11-3-0)	Green Bay 37, NY Giants 0
1962	NY Giants (12-2-0)	Green Bay Packers (13-1-0)	Green Bay 16, NY Giants 7
1963	NY Giants (11-3-0)	Chicago Bears (11-1-2)	Chicago 14, NY Giants 10
1964	Cleveland Browns (10-3-1)	Baltimore Colts (12-2-0)	Cleveland Browns 27, Baltimore 0
1965	Cleveland Browns (11-3-0)	Green Bay Packers (10-3-1)[1]	Green Bay 23, Cleveland Browns 12
1966	Dallas Cowboys (10-3-1)	Green Bay Packers (12-2-0)	Green Bay 34, Dallas 27
1967	Dallas Cowboys (9-5-0)	Green Bay Packers (9-4-1)	Green Bay 21, Dallas 17
1968	Cleveland Browns (10-4-0)	Baltimore Colts (13-1-0)	Baltimore 34, Cleveland Browns 0
1969	Cleveland Browns (10-3-1)	Minnesota Vikings (12-2-0)	Minnesota 27, Cleveland Browns 7

Note: Conference title games preceded NFL Championship from 1967-69. (1) Won divisional or conference playoff. (2) Won at 8:15 of sudden death overtime period.

NFL Divisional Champions and Wild Cards, 1970-95

The American Football League and National Football League officially merged in 1966. At the beginning of the 1970 season, the two leagues became the AFC and NFC conferences in the new NFL. Regular-season (W-L-T) records are in parentheses.

AMERICAN FOOTBALL CONFERENCE

Year	Eastern	Central	Western	Wild card
1970	Baltimore Colts (11-2-1)	Cincinnati Bengals (8-6-0)	Oakland Raiders (8-4-2)	Miami Dolphins (10-4-0)
1971	Miami Dolphins (10-3-1)	Cleveland Browns (9-5-0)	Kansas City Chiefs (10-3-1)	Baltimore Colts (10-4-0)
1972	Miami Dolphins (14-0-0)	Pittsburgh Steelers (11-3-0)	Oakland Raiders (10-3-1)	Cleveland Browns (10-4-0)
1973	Miami Dolphins (12-2-0)	Cincinnati Bengals (10-4-0)	Oakland Raiders (9-4-1)	Pittsburgh Steelers (10-4-0)
1974	Miami Dolphins (11-3-0)	Pittsburgh Steelers (10-3-1)	Oakland Raiders (12-2-0)	Buffalo Bills (9-5-0)
1975	Baltimore Colts (10-4-0)	Pittsburgh Steelers (12-2-0)	Oakland Raiders (11-3-0)	Cincinnati Bengals (11-3-0)
1976	Baltimore Colts (11-3-0)	Pittsburgh Steelers (10-4-0)	Oakland Raiders (13-1-0)	New England Patriots (11-3-0)
1977	Baltimore Colts (10-4-0)	Pittsburgh Steelers (9-5-0)	Denver Broncos (12-2-0)	Oakland Raiders (11-3-0)
1978	New England Patriots (11-5-0)	Pittsburgh Steelers (14-2-0)	Denver Broncos (10-6-0)	Houston Oilers (10-6-0) Miami Dolphins (11-5-0)
1979	Miami Dolphins (10-6-0)	Pittsburgh Steelers (12-4-0)	San Diego Chargers (12-4-0)	Houston Oilers (11-5-0) Denver Broncos (10-6-0)
1980	Buffalo Bills (11-5-0)	Cleveland Browns (11-5-0)	San Diego Chargers (11-5-0)	Houston Oilers (11-5-0) Oakland Raiders (11-5-0)
1981	Miami Dolphins (11-4-1)	Cincinnati Bengals (12-4-0)	San Diego Chargers (10-6-0)	Buffalo Bills (10-6-0) NY Jets (10-5-1)
1982	Strike abbreviated season. See note.			
1983	Miami Dolphins (12-4-0)	Pittsburgh Steelers (10-6-0)	L.A. Raiders (12-4-0)	Denver Broncos (9-7-0) Seattle Seahawks (9-7-0)
1984	Miami Dolphins (14-2-0)	Pittsburgh Steelers (9-7-0)	Denver Broncos (13-3-0)	L.A. Raiders (11-5-0) Seattle Seahawks (12-4-0)
1985	Miami Dolphins (12-4-0)	Cleveland Browns (8-8-0)	L.A. Raiders (12-4-0)	New England Patriots (11-5-0) NY Jets (11-5-0)
1986	New England Patriots (11-5-0)	Cleveland Browns (12-4-0)	Denver Broncos (11-5-0)	Kansas City Chiefs (10-6-0) NY Jets (10-6-0)
1987	Indianapolis Colts (9-6-0)	Cleveland Browns (10-5-0)	Denver Broncos (10-4-1)	Houston Oilers (9-6-0) Seattle Seahawks (9-6-0)
1988	Buffalo Bills (12-4-0)	Cincinnati Bengals (12-4-0)	Seattle Seahawks (9-7-0)	Cleveland Browns (10-6-0) Houston Oilers (10-6-0)
1989	Buffalo Bills (9-7-0)	Cleveland Browns (9-6-1)	Denver Broncos (11-5-0)	Houston Oilers (9-7-0) Pittsburgh Steelers (9-7-0)
1990	Buffalo Bills (13-3-0)	Cincinnati Bengals (9-7-0)	L.A. Raiders (12-4-0)	Houston Oilers (9-7-0) Kansas City Chiefs (10-6-0) Miami Dolphins (12-4-0)
1991	Buffalo Bills (13-3-0)	Houston Oilers (11-5-0)	Denver Broncos (12-4-0)	Kansas City Chiefs (10-6-0) L.A. Raiders (9-7-0) NY Jets (8-8-0)
1992	Miami Dolphins (11-5-0)	Pittsburgh Steelers (11-5-0)	San Diego Chargers (11-5-0)	Buffalo Bills (11-5-0) Houston Oilers (10-6-0) Kansas City Chiefs (10-6-0)
1993	Buffalo Bills (12-4-0)	Houston Oilers (12-4-0)	Kansas City Chiefs (11-5-0)	Denver Broncos (9-7-0) L.A. Raiders (10-6-0) Pittsburgh Steelers (9-7-0)
1994	Miami Dolphins (10-6-0)	Pittsburgh Steelers (12-4-0)	San Diego Chargers (11-5-0)	Cleveland Browns (11-5-0) Kansas City Chiefs (9-7-0) New England Patriots (10-6-0)
1995	Buffalo Bills (10-6-0)	Pittsburgh Steelers (11-5-0)	Kansas City Chiefs (13-3-0)	Miami Dolphins (9-7-0) Indianapolis Colts (9-7-0) San Diego Chargers (9-7-0)

NATIONAL FOOTBALL CONFERENCE

Year	Eastern	Central	Western	Wild card
1970	Dallas Cowboys (10-4-0)	Minnesota Vikings (12-2-0)	San Francisco 49ers (10-3-1)	Detroit Lions (10-4-0)
1971	Dallas Cowboys (11-3-0)	Minnesota Vikings (11-3-0)	San Francisco 49ers (9-5-0)	Washington Redskins (9-4-1)
1972	Washington Redskins (11-3-0)	Green Bay Packers (10-4-0)	San Francisco 49ers (8-5-1)	Dallas Cowboys (10-4-0)
1973	Dallas Cowboys (10-4-0)	Minnesota Vikings (12-2-0)	L.A. Rams (12-2-0)	Washington Redskins (10-4-0)
1974	St. Louis Cardinals (10-4-0)	Minnesota Vikings (10-4-0)	L.A. Rams (10-4-0)	Washington Redskins (10-4-0)
1975	St. Louis Cardinals (11-3-0)	Minnesota Vikings (12-2-0)	L.A. Rams (12-2-0)	Dallas Cowboys (10-4-0)
1976	Dallas Cowboys (11-3-0)	Minnesota Vikings (11-2-1)	L.A. Rams (10-3-1)	Washington Redskins (10-4-0)
1977	Dallas Cowboys (12-2-0)	Minnesota Vikings (9-5-0)	L.A. Rams (10-4-0)	Chicago Bears (9-5-0)
1978	Dallas Cowboys (12-4-0)	Minnesota Vikings (8-7-1)	L.A. Rams (12-4-0)	Atlanta Falcons (9-7-0) Philadelphia Eagles (9-7-0)
1979	Dallas Cowboys (11-5-0)	Tampa Bay Buccaneers (10-6-0)	L.A. Rams (9-7-0)	Chicago Bears (10-6-0) Philadelphia Eagles (11-5-0)
1980	Philadelphia Eagles (12-4-0)	Minnesota Vikings (9-7-0)	Atlanta Falcons (12-4-0)	Dallas Cowboys (12-4-0) L.A. Rams (11-5-0)
1981	Dallas Cowboys (12-4-0)	Tampa Bay Buccaneers (9-7-0)	San Francisco 49ers (13-3-0)	NY Giants (9-7-0) Philadelphia Eagles (10-6-0)
1982	Strike abbreviated season. See note.			
1983	Washington Redskins (14-2-0)	Detroit Lions (9-7-0)	San Francisco 49ers (10-6-0)	Dallas Cowboys (12-4-0) L.A. Rams (9-7-0)
1984	Washington Redskins (11-5-0)	Chicago Bears (10-6-0)	San Francisco 49ers (15-1-0)	L.A. Rams (10-6-0) NY Giants (9-7-0)
1985	Dallas Cowboys (10-6-0)	Chicago Bears (15-1-0)	L.A. Rams (11-5-0)	NY Giants (10-6-0) San Francisco 49ers (10-6-0)
1986	NY Giants (14-2-0)	Chicago Bears (14-2-0)	San Francisco 49ers (10-5-1)	L.A. Rams (10-6-0) Washington Redskins (12-4-0)

Year				
1987	Washington Redskins (11-4-0)	Chicago Bears (11-4-0)	San Francisco 49ers (13-2-0)	Minnesota Vikings (8-7-0) / New Orleans Saints (12-3-0)
1988	Philadelphia Eagles (10-6-0)	Chicago Bears (12-4-0)	San Francisco 49ers (10-6-0)	L.A. Rams (10-6-0) / Minnesota Vikings (11-5-0)
1989	NY Giants (12-4-0)	Minnesota Vikings (10-6-0)	San Francisco 49ers (14-2-0)	L.A. Rams (11-5-0) / Philadelphia Eagles (11-5-0)
1990	NY Giants (13-3-0)	Chicago Bears (11-5-0)	San Francisco 49ers (14-2-0)	New Orleans Saints (8-8-0) / Philadelphia Eagles (10-6-0) / Washington Redskins (10-6-0)
1991	Washington Redskins (14-2-0)	Detroit Lions (12-4-0)	New Orleans Saints (11-5-0)	Atlanta Falcons (10-6-0) / Chicago Bears (11-5-0) / Dallas Cowboys (11-5-0)
1992	Dallas Cowboys (13-3-0)	Minnesota Vikings (11-5-0)	San Francisco 49ers (14-2-0)	New Orleans Saints (12-4-0) / Philadelphia Eagles (11-5-0) / Washington Redskins (9-7-0)
1993	Dallas Cowboys (12-4-0)	Detroit Lions (10-6-0)	San Francisco 49ers (10-6-0)	Green Bay Packers (9-7-0) / Minnesota Vikings (9-7-0) / NY Giants (11-5-0)
1994	Dallas Cowboys (12-4-0)	Minnesota Vikings (10-6-0)	San Francisco 49ers (13-3-0)	Chicago Bears (9-7-0) / Detroit Lions (9-7-0) / Green Bay Packers (9-7-0)
1995	Dallas Cowboys (12-4-0)	Green Bay Packers (11-5-0)	San Francisco 49ers (11-5-0)	Philadelphia Eagles (10-6-0) / Detroit Lions (10-6-0) / Atlanta Falcons (9-7-0)

Note: A strike shortened the 1982 season from 16 to 9 games. The top eight teams in each conference played in a tournament to determine the conference champion.

NFL Playoff Results, 1996-2015

Year	Conference	Division	Winner (W-L-T)	Playoffs[1]	Year
1996	American	Eastern	New England Patriots (11-5-0)	Jacksonville* 30, Denver 27	1996
		Central	Pittsburgh Steelers (10-6-0)	New England 28, Pittsburgh 3	
		Western	Denver Broncos (13-3-0)	New England 20, Jacksonville* 6	
	National	Eastern	Dallas Cowboys (10-6-0)	Green Bay 35, San Francisco* 14	
		Central	Green Bay Packers (13-3-0)	Carolina 26, Dallas 17	
		Western	Carolina Panthers (12-4-0)	Green Bay 30, Carolina 13	
1997	American	Eastern	New England Patriots (10-6-0)	Pittsburgh 7, New England 6	1997
		Central	Pittsburgh Steelers (11-5-0)	Denver* 14, Kansas City 10	
		Western	Kansas City Chiefs (13-3-0)	Denver* 24, Pittsburgh 21	
	National	Eastern	NY Giants (10-5-1)	San Francisco 38, Minnesota* 22	
		Central	Green Bay Packers (13-3-0)	Green Bay 21, Tampa Bay* 7	
		Western	San Francisco 49ers (13-3-0)	Green Bay 23, San Francisco 10	
1998	American	Eastern	NY Jets (12-4-0)	Denver 38, Miami* 3	1998
		Central	Jacksonville Jaguars (11-5-0)	NY Jets 34, Jacksonville 24	
		Western	Denver Broncos (14-2-0)	Denver 23, NY Jets 10	
	National	Eastern	Dallas Cowboys (10-6-0)	Atlanta 20, San Francisco* 18	
		Central	Minnesota Vikings (15-1-0)	Minnesota 41, Arizona* 21	
		Western	Atlanta Falcons (14-2-0)	Atlanta 30, Minnesota 27 (OT)	
1999	American	Eastern	Indianapolis Colts (13-3-0)	Jacksonville 62, Miami* 7	1999
		Central	Jacksonville Jaguars (14-2-0)	Tennessee* 19, Indianapolis 16	
		Western	Seattle Seahawks (9-7-0)	Tennessee* 33, Jacksonville 14	
	National	Eastern	Washington Redskins (10-6-0)	Tampa Bay 14, Washington 13	
		Central	Tampa Bay Buccaneers (11-5-0)	St. Louis 49, Minnesota* 37	
		Western	St. Louis Rams (13-3-0)	St. Louis 11, Tampa Bay 6	
2000	American	Eastern	Miami Dolphins (11-5-0)	Oakland 27, Miami 0	2000
		Central	Tennessee Titans (13-3-0)	Baltimore* 24, Tennessee 10	
		Western	Oakland Raiders (12-4-0)	Baltimore* 16, Oakland 3	
	National	Eastern	NY Giants (12-4-0)	Minnesota 34, New Orleans 16	
		Central	Minnesota Vikings (11-5-0)	NY Giants 20, Philadelphia* 10	
		Western	New Orleans Saints (10-6-0)	NY Giants 41, Minnesota 0	
2001	American	Eastern	New England Patriots (11-5-0)	New England 16, Oakland 13 (OT)	2001
		Central	Pittsburgh Steelers (13-3-0)	Pittsburgh 27, Baltimore* 10	
		Western	Oakland Raiders (10-6-0)	New England 24, Pittsburgh 17	
	National	Eastern	Philadelphia Eagles (11-5-0)	Philadelphia 33, Chicago 19	
		Central	Chicago Bears (13-3-0)	St. Louis 45, Green Bay* 17	
		Western	St. Louis Rams (14-2-0)	St. Louis 29, Philadelphia 24	
2002	American	East	NY Jets (9-7-0)		2002
		North	Pittsburgh Steelers (10-5-1)	Oakland 30, NY Jets 10	
		South	Tennessee Titans (11-5-0)	Tennessee 34, Pittsburgh 31 (OT)	
		West	Oakland Raiders (11-5-0)	Oakland 41, Tennessee 24	
	National	East	Philadelphia Eagles (12-4-0)		
		North	Green Bay Packers (12-4-0)	Philadelphia 20, Atlanta* 6	
		South	Tampa Bay Buccaneers (12-4-0)	Tampa Bay 31, San Francisco 6	
		West	San Francisco 49ers (10-6-0)	Tampa Bay 27, Philadelphia 10	

Year	Conference	Division	Winner (W-L-T)	Playoffs[1]	Year
2003	American	East	New England Patriots (14-2-0)		2003
		North	Baltimore Ravens (10-6-0)	Indianapolis 38, Kansas City 31	
		South	Indianapolis Colts (12-4-0)	New England 17, Tennessee* 14	
		West	Kansas City Chiefs (13-3-0)	New England 24, Indianapolis 14	
	National	East	Philadelphia Eagles (12-4-0)		
		North	Green Bay Packers (10-6-0)	Carolina 29, St. Louis 23 (2 OT)	
		South	Carolina Panthers (11-5-0)	Philadelphia 20, Green Bay 17 (OT)	
		West	St. Louis Rams (12-4-0)	Carolina 14, Philadelphia 3	
2004	American	East	New England Patriots (14-2-0)		2004
		North	Pittsburgh Steelers (15-1-0)	Pittsburgh 20, NY Jets* 17 (OT)	
		South	Indianapolis Colts (12-4-0)	New England 20, Indianapolis 3	
		West	San Diego Chargers (12-4-0)	New England 41, Pittsburgh 27	
	National	East	Philadelphia Eagles (13-3-0)		
		North	Green Bay Packers (10-6-0)	Atlanta 47, St. Louis* 17	
		South	Atlanta Falcons (11-5-0)	Philadelphia 27, Minnesota* 14	
		West	Seattle Seahawks (9-7-0)	Philadelphia 27, Atlanta 10	
2005	American	East	New England Patriots (10-6-0)		2005
		North	Cincinnati Bengals (11-5-0)	Denver 27, New England 13	
		South	Indianapolis Colts (14-2-0)	Pittsburgh* 21, Indianapolis 18	
		West	Denver Broncos (13-3-0)	Pittsburgh* 34, Denver 17	
	National	East	NY Giants (11-5-0)		
		North	Chicago Bears (11-5-0)	Seattle 20, Washington* 10	
		South	Tampa Bay Buccaneers (11-5-0)	Carolina* 29, Chicago 21	
		West	Seattle Seahawks (13-3-0)	Seattle 34, Carolina* 14	
2006	American	East	New England Patriots (12-4-0)		2006
		North	Baltimore Ravens (13-3-0)	Indianapolis 15, Baltimore 6	
		South	Indianapolis Colts (12-4-0)	New England 24, San Diego 21	
		West	San Diego Chargers (14-2-0)	Indianapolis 38, New England 34	
	National	East	Philadelphia Eagles (10-6-0)		
		North	Chicago Bears (13-3-0)	New Orleans 27, Philadelphia 24	
		South	New Orleans Saints (10-6-0)	Chicago 27, Seattle 24 (OT)	
		West	Seattle Seahawks (9-7-0)	Chicago 39, New Orleans 14	
2007	American	East	New England Patriots (16-0-0)		2007
		North	Pittsburgh Steelers (10-6-0)	New England 31, Jacksonville* 20	
		South	Indianapolis Colts (13-3-0)	San Diego 28, Indianapolis 24	
		West	San Diego Chargers (11-5-0)	New England 21, San Diego 12	
	National	East	Dallas Cowboys (13-3-0)		
		North	Green Bay Packers (13-3-0)	Green Bay 42, Seattle 20	
		South	Tampa Bay Buccaneers (9-7-0)	NY Giants* 21, Dallas 17	
		West	Seattle Seahawks (10-6-0)	NY Giants* 23, Green Bay 20 (OT)	
2008	American	East	Miami Dolphins (11-5-0)		2008
		North	Pittsburgh Steelers (12-4-0)	Baltimore* 13, Tennessee 10	
		South	Tennessee Titans (13-3-0)	Pittsburgh 35, San Diego 24	
		West	San Diego Chargers (8-8-0)	Pittsburgh 23, Baltimore* 14	
	National	East	NY Giants (12-4-0)		
		North	Minnesota Vikings (10-6-0)	Arizona 33, Carolina 13	
		South	Carolina Panthers (12-4-0)	Philadelphia* 23, NY Giants 11	
		West	Arizona Cardinals (9-7-0)	Arizona 32, Philadelphia* 25	
2009	American	East	New England Patriots (10-6-0)		2009
		North	Cincinnati Bengals (10-6-0)	Indianapolis 20, Baltimore* 3	
		South	Indianapolis Colts (14-2-0)	NY Jets* 17, San Diego 14	
		West	San Diego Chargers (13-3-0)	Indianapolis 30, NY Jets* 17	
	National	East	Dallas Cowboys (11-5-0)		
		North	Minnesota Vikings (12-4-0)	New Orleans 45, Arizona 14	
		South	New Orleans Saints (13-3-0)	Minnesota 34, Dallas 3	
		West	Arizona Cardinals (10-6-0)	New Orleans 31, Minnesota 28 (OT)	
2010	American	East	New England Patriots (14-2-0)		2010
		North	Pittsburgh Steelers (12-4-0)	Pittsburgh 31, Baltimore* 24	
		South	Indianapolis Colts (10-6-0)	NY Jets* 28, New England 21	
		West	Kansas City Chiefs (10-6-0)	Pittsburgh 24, NY Jets* 19	
	National	East	Philadelphia Eagles (10-6-0)		
		North	Chicago Bears (11-5-0)	Green Bay* 48, Atlanta 21	
		South	Atlanta Falcons (13-3-0)	Chicago 35, Seattle 24	
		West	Seattle Seahawks (7-9-0)	Green Bay* 21, Chicago 14	
2011	American	East	New England Patriots (13-3-0)		2011
		North	Baltimore Ravens (12-4-0)	New England 45, Denver 10	
		South	Houston Texans (10-6-0)	Baltimore 20, Houston 13	
		West	Denver Broncos (8-8-0)	New England 23, Baltimore 20	
	National	East	NY Giants (9-7-0)		
		North	Green Bay Packers (15-1-0)	San Francisco 36, New Orleans 32	
		South	New Orleans (13-3-0)	NY Giants 37, Green Bay 20	
		West	San Francisco (13-3-0)	NY Giants 20, San Francisco 17 (OT)	

Year	Conference	Division	Winner (W-L-T)	Playoffs[1]	Year
2012	American	East	New England Patriots (12-4-0)		2012
		North	Baltimore Ravens (10-6-0)	Baltimore 38, Denver 35 (2 OT)	
		South	Houston Texans (12-4-0)	New England 41, Houston 28	
		West	Denver Broncos (13-3-0)	Baltimore 28, New England 13	
	National	East	Washington Redskins (10-6-0)		
		North	Green Bay Packers (11-5-0)	San Francisco 45, Green Bay 31	
		South	Atlanta Falcons (13-3-0)	Atlanta 30, Seattle* 28	
		West	San Francisco 49ers (11-4-1)	San Francisco 28, Atlanta 24	
2013	American	East	New England Patriots (12-4-0)		2013
		North	Cincinnati Bengals (11-5-0)	New England 43, Indianapolis 22	
		South	Indianapolis Colts (11-5-0)	Denver 24, San Diego* 17	
		West	Denver Broncos (13-3-0)	Denver 26, New England 16	
	National	East	Philadelphia Eagles (10-6-0)		
		North	Green Bay Packers (8-7-1)	Seattle 23, New Orleans* 15	
		South	Carolina Panthers (12-4-0)	San Francisco* 23, Carolina 10	
		West	Seattle Seahawks (13-3-0)	Seattle 23, San Francisco* 17	
2014	American	East	New England Patriots (12-4-0)		2014
		North	Pittsburgh Steelers (11-5-0)	New England 35, Baltimore* 31	
		South	Indianapolis Colts (11-5-0)	Indianapolis 24, Denver 13	
		West	Denver Broncos (12-4-0)	New England 45, Indianapolis 7	
	National	East	Dallas Cowboys (12-4-0)		
		North	Green Bay Packers (12-4-0)	Seattle 31, Carolina 17	
		South	Carolina Panthers (7-8-1)	Green Bay 26, Dallas 21	
		West	Seattle Seahawks (12-4-0)	Seattle 28, Green Bay 22 (OT)	
2015	American	East	New England Patriots (12-4-0)	New England 27, Kansas City* 20	2015
		North	Cincinnati Bengals (12-4-0)	Denver 23, Pittsburgh* 16	
		South	Houston Texans (9-7-0)	Denver 20, New England 18	
		West	Denver Broncos (12-4-0)		
	National	East	Washington Redskins (9-7-0)	Arizona 26, Green Bay* 20 (OT)	
		North	Minnesota Vikings (11-5-0)	Carolina 31, Seattle* 24	
		South	Carolina Panthers (15-1-0)	Carolina 49, Arizona 15	
		West	Arizona Cardinals (13-3-0)		

*Wild card team. (1) Only the final two conference playoff rounds are shown.

American Football Conference Leaders, 1960-2015

(American Football League, 1960-69)

PASSING (BASED ON QB RATING POINTS)							RECEPTIONS			
Player, team	Rating	Att	Comp	Yds	TD	Year	Player, team	Rec	Yds	TD
Jack Kemp, L.A. Chargers	NA	406	211	3,018	20	1960	Lionel Taylor, Denver	92	1,235	12
George Blanda, Houston	NA	362	187	3,330	36	1961	Lionel Taylor, Denver	100	1,176	4
Len Dawson, Dallas Texans	NA	310	189	2,759	29	1962	Lionel Taylor, Denver	77	908	4
Tobin Rote, San Diego	NA	286	170	2,510	20	1963	Lionel Taylor, Denver	78	1,101	10
Len Dawson, Kansas City	NA	354	199	2,879	30	1964	Charley Hennigan, Houston	101	1,546	8
John Hadl, San Diego	NA	348	174	2,798	20	1965	Lionel Taylor, Denver	85	1,131	6
Len Dawson, Kansas City	NA	284	159	2,527	26	1966	Lance Alworth, San Diego	73	1,383	13
Daryle Lamonica, Oakland	NA	425	220	3,228	30	1967	George Sauer, NY Jets	75	1,189	6
Len Dawson, Kansas City	NA	224	131	2,109	17	1968	Lance Alworth, San Diego	68	1,312	10
Greg Cook, Cincinnati	NA	197	106	1,854	15	1969	Lance Alworth, San Diego	64	1,003	4
Daryle Lamonica, Oakland	NA	356	179	2,516	22	1970	Marlin Briscoe, Buffalo	57	1,036	8
Bob Griese, Miami	NA	263	145	2,089	19	1971	Fred Biletnikoff, Oakland	61	929	9
Earl Morrall, Miami	NA	150	83	1,360	11	1972	Fred Biletnikoff, Oakland	58	802	7
Ken Stabler, Oakland	88.3	260	163	1,997	14	1973	Fred Willis, Houston	57	371	1
Ken Anderson, Cincinnati	95.7	328	213	2,667	18	1974	Lydell Mitchell, Baltimore Colts	72	544	2
Ken Anderson, Cincinnati	93.9	377	228	3,169	21	1975	Reggie Rucker, Cleveland	60	770	3
							Lydell Mitchell, Baltimore Colts	60	554	4
Ken Stabler, Oakland	103.4	291	194	2,737	27	1976	MacArthur Lane, Kansas City	66	686	1
Bob Griese, Miami	87.8	307	180	2,252	22	1977	Lydell Mitchell, Baltimore Colts	71	620	4
Terry Bradshaw, Pittsburgh	84.7	368	207	2,915	28	1978	Steve Largent, Seattle	71	1,168	8
Dan Fouts, San Diego	82.6	530	332	4,082	24	1979	Joe Washington, Baltimore Colts	82	750	3
Brian Sipe, Cleveland	91.4	554	337	4,132	30	1980	Kellen Winslow, San Diego	89	1,290	9
Ken Anderson, Cincinnati	98.4	479	300	3,754	29	1981	Kellen Winslow, San Diego	88	1,075	10
Ken Anderson, Cincinnati	95.3	309	218	2,495	12	1982	Kellen Winslow, San Diego	54	721	6
Dan Marino, Miami	96.0	296	173	2,210	20	1983	Todd Christensen, L.A. Raiders	92	1,247	12
Dan Marino, Miami	108.9	564	362	5,084	48	1984	Ozzie Newsome, Cleveland	89	1,001	5
Ken O'Brien, NY Jets	96.2	488	297	3,888	25	1985	Lionel James, San Diego	86	1,027	6
Dan Marino, Miami	92.5	623	378	4,746	44	1986	Todd Christensen, L.A. Raiders	95	1,153	8
Bernie Kosar, Cleveland	95.4	389	241	3,033	22	1987	Al Toon, NY Jets	68	976	5
Boomer Esiason, Cincinnati	97.4	388	223	3,572	28	1988	Al Toon, NY Jets	93	1,067	5
Boomer Esiason, Cincinnati	92.1	455	258	3,525	28	1989	Andre Reed, Buffalo	88	1,312	9
Jim Kelly, Buffalo	101.2	346	219	2,829	24	1990	Haywood Jeffires, Houston	74	1,048	8
							Drew Hill, Houston	74	1,019	5
Jim Kelly, Buffalo	97.6	474	304	3,844	33	1991	Haywood Jeffires, Houston	100	1,181	7
Warren Moon, Houston	89.3	346	224	2,521	18	1992	Haywood Jeffires, Houston	90	913	9
John Elway, Denver	92.8	551	348	4,030	25	1993	Reggie Langhorne, Indianapolis	85	1,038	3
Dan Marino, Miami	89.2	615	385	4,453	30	1994	Ben Coates, New England	96	1,174	7
Jim Harbaugh, Indianapolis	100.7	314	200	2,575	17	1995	Carl Pickens, Cincinnati	99	1,234	17
John Elway, Denver	89.2	466	287	3,328	26	1996	Carl Pickens, Cincinnati	100	1,180	12
Mark Brunell, Jacksonville	91.2	435	264	3,281	18	1997	Tim Brown, Oakland	104	1,408	5
Vinny Testaverde, NY Jets	101.6	421	259	3,256	29	1998	O. J. McDuffie, Miami	90	1,050	7
Peyton Manning, Indianapolis	90.7	533	331	4,135	26	1999	Jimmy Smith, Jacksonville	116	1,636	6
Brian Griese, Denver	102.9	336	216	2,688	19	2000	Marvin Harrison, Indianapolis	102	1,413	14
Rich Gannon, Oakland	95.5	549	361	3,828	27	2001	Rod Smith, Denver	113	1,343	11
Chad Pennington, NY Jets	104.2	399	275	3,120	22	2002	Marvin Harrison, Indianapolis	143	1,722	11
Steve McNair, Tennessee	100.4	400	250	3,215	24	2003	LaDainian Tomlinson, San Diego	100	725	4
Peyton Manning, Indianapolis	121.1	497	336	4,557	49	2004	Tony Gonzalez, Kansas City	102	1,258	7

PASSING (BASED ON QB RATING POINTS) / RECEPTIONS

Player, team	Rating	Att	Comp	Yds	TD	Year	Player, team	Rec	Yds	TD
Peyton Manning, Indianapolis	104.1	453	305	3,747	28	2005	Chad Johnson, Cincinnati	97	1,432	9
Peyton Manning, Indianapolis	101.0	557	362	4,397	31	2006	Andre Johnson, Houston	103	1,147	5
Tom Brady, New England	117.2	578	398	4,806	50	2007	Wes Welker, New England	112	1,175	8
							T.J. Houshmandzadeh, Cincinnati	112	1,143	12
Philip Rivers, San Diego	105.5	478	312	4,009	34	2008	Andre Johnson, Houston	115	1,575	8
Philip Rivers, San Diego	104.4	486	317	4,254	28	2009	Wes Welker, New England	123	1,348	4
Tom Brady, New England	111.0	492	324	3,900	36	2010	Reggie Wayne, Indianapolis	111	1,355	6
Tom Brady, New England	105.6	611	401	5,235	39	2011	Wes Welker, New England	122	1,569	9
Peyton Manning, Denver	105.8	583	400	4,659	37	2012	Wes Welker, New England	118	1,354	6
Peyton Manning, Denver	115.1	659	450	5,477	55	2013	Antonio Brown, Pittsburgh	110	1,499	8
Ben Roethlisberger, Pittsburgh	103.3	608	408	4,952	32	2014	Antonio Brown, Pittsburgh	129	1,698	13
Andy Dalton, Cincinnati	106.2	386	255	3,250	25	2015	Antonio Brown, Pittsburgh	136	1,834	10

SCORING / RUSHING YARDS

Player, team	TD	XPM	FGM	Pts	Year	Player, team	Yds	Att	TD
Gene Mingo, Denver	6	33	18	123	1960	Abner Haynes, Dallas Texans	875	156	9
Gino Cappelletti, Boston	8	48	17	147	1961	Billy Cannon, Houston	948	200	6
Gene Mingo, Denver	4	32	27	137	1962	Cookie Gilchrist, Buffalo	1,096	214	13
Gino Cappelletti, Boston	2	35	22	113	1963	Clem Daniels, Oakland	1,099	215	3
Gino Cappelletti, Boston	7	36	25	155	1964	Cookie Gilchrist, Buffalo	981	230	6
Gino Cappelletti, Boston	9	27	17	132	1965	Paul Lowe, San Diego	1,121	222	7
Gino Cappelletti, Boston	6	35	16	119	1966	Jim Nance, Boston	1,458	299	11
George Blanda, Oakland	0	56	20	116	1967	Jim Nance, Boston	1,216	269	7
Jim Turner, NY Jets	0	43	34	145	1968	Paul Robinson, Cincinnati	1,023	238	8
Jim Turner, NY Jets	0	33	32	129	1969	Dickie Post, San Diego	873	182	6
Jan Stenerud, Kansas City	0	26	30	116	1970	Floyd Little, Denver	901	209	3
Garo Yepremian, Miami	0	33	28	117	1971	Floyd Little, Denver	1,133	284	6
Bobby Howfield, NY Jets	0	40	27	121	1972	O. J. Simpson, Buffalo	1,251	292	6
Roy Gerela, Pittsburgh	0	36	29	123	1973	O. J. Simpson, Buffalo	2,003	332	12
Roy Gerela, Pittsburgh	0	33	20	93	1974	Otis Armstrong, Denver	1,407	263	9
O. J. Simpson, Buffalo	23	0	0	138	1975	O. J. Simpson, Buffalo	1,817	329	16
Toni Linhart, Baltimore Colts	0	49	20	109	1976	O. J. Simpson, Buffalo	1,503	290	8
Errol Mann, Oakland	0	39	20	99	1977	Mark van Eeghen, Oakland	1,273	324	7
Pat Leahy, NY Jets	0	41	22	107	1978	Earl Campbell, Houston	1,450	302	13
John Smith, New England	0	46	23	115	1979	Earl Campbell, Houston	1,697	368	19
John Smith, New England	0	51	26	129	1980	Earl Campbell, Houston	1,934	373	13
Jim Breech, Cincinnati	0	49	22	115	1981	Earl Campbell, Houston	1,376	361	10
Nick Lowery, Kansas City	0	37	26	115					
Marcus Allen, L.A. Raiders	14	0	0	84	1982	Freeman McNeil, NY Jets	786	151	6
Gary Anderson, Pittsburgh	0	38	27	119	1983	Curt Warner, Seattle	1,449	335	13
Gary Anderson, Pittsburgh	0	45	24	117	1984	Earnest Jackson, San Diego	1,179	296	8
Gary Anderson, Pittsburgh	0	40	33	139	1985	Marcus Allen, L.A. Raiders	1,759	380	11
Tony Franklin, New England	0	44	32	140	1986	Curt Warner, Seattle	1,481	319	13
Jim Breech, Cincinnati	0	25	24	97	1987	Eric Dickerson, L.A. Rams-Ind.	1,288*	283	6
Scott Norwood, Buffalo	0	33	32	129	1988	Eric Dickerson, Indianapolis	1,659	388	14
David Treadwell, Denver	0	39	27	120	1989	Christian Okoye, Kansas City	1,480	370	12
Nick Lowery, Kansas City	0	37	34	139	1990	Thurman Thomas, Buffalo	1,297	271	11
Pete Stoyanovich, Miami	0	28	31	121	1991	Thurman Thomas, Buffalo	1,407	288	7
Pete Stoyanovich, Miami	0	34	30	124	1992	Barry Foster, Pittsburgh	1,690	390	11
Jeff Jaeger, L.A. Raiders	0	27	35	132	1993	Thurman Thomas, Buffalo	1,315	355	6
John Carney, San Diego	0	33	34	135	1994	Chris Warren, Seattle	1,545	333	9
Norm Johnson, Pittsburgh	0	39	34	141	1995	Curtis Martin, New England	1,487	368	14
Cary Blanchard, Indianapolis	0	27	36	135	1996	Terrell Davis, Denver	1,538	345	13
Mike Hollis, Jacksonville	0	41	31	134	1997	Terrell Davis, Denver	1,750	369	15
Steve Christie, Buffalo	0	41	33	140	1998	Terrell Davis, Denver	2,008	392	21
Mike Vanderjagt, Indianapolis	0	43	34	145	1999	Edgerrin James, Indianapolis	1,553	369	13
Matt Stover, Baltimore	0	30	35	135	2000	Edgerrin James, Indianapolis	1,709	387	13
Mike Vanderjagt, Indianapolis	0	41	28	125	2001	Priest Holmes, Kansas City	1,555	327	8
Priest Holmes, Kansas City	24	0	0	144	2002	Ricky Williams, Miami	1,853	383	16
Priest Holmes, Kansas City	27	0	0	162	2003	Jamal Lewis, Baltimore	2,066	387	14
Adam Vinatieri, New England	0	48	31	141	2004	Curtis Martin, NY Jets	1,697	371	12
Shayne Graham, Cincinnati	0	47	28	131	2005	Larry Johnson, Kansas City	1,750	336	20
LaDainian Tomlinson, San Diego	31	0	0	186	2006	LaDainian Tomlinson, San Diego	1,815	348	28
Randy Moss, New England	23	0	0	138	2007	LaDainian Tomlinson, San Diego	1,474	315	15
Stephen Gostkowski, New England	0	40	36	148	2008	Thomas Jones, NY Jets	1,312	290	13
Nate Kaeding, San Diego	0	50	32	146	2009	Chris Johnson, Tennessee	2,006	358	14
Sebastian Janikowski, Oakland	0	43	33	142	2010	Arian Foster, Houston	1,616	327	16
Stephen Gostkowski, New England	0	59	28	143	2011	Maurice Jones-Drew, Jacksonville	1,606	343	8
Stephen Gostkowski, New England	0	66	29	153	2012	Jamaal Charles, Kansas City	1,509	285	5
Stephen Gostkowski, New England	0	44	38	158	2013	Jamaal Charles, Kansas City	1,287	259	12
Stephen Gostkowski, New England	0	51	35	156	2014	Le'Veon Bell, Pittsburgh	1,361	290	8
Stephen Gostkowski, New England	0	52	33	151	2015	Chris Ivory, NY Jets	1,070	247	7

*Includes 277 yards after being traded to NFC; 1,011 yards led AFC. NA = Not applicable/available. **Note:** Passer ratings for years prior to 1973 were determined by different measures and are not directly comparable to current passer ratings.

National Football Conference Leaders, 1960-2015
(National Football League, 1960-69)

PASSING (BASED ON QB RATING POINTS)

Player, team	Rating	Att	Comp	Yds	TD	Year
Milt Plum, Cleveland	NA	250	151	2,297	21	1960
Milt Plum, Cleveland	NA	302	177	2,416	18	1961
Bart Starr, Green Bay	NA	285	178	2,438	12	1962
Y. A. Tittle, NY Giants	NA	367	221	3,145	36	1963
Bart Starr, Green Bay	NA	272	163	2,144	15	1964
Rudy Bukich, Chicago	NA	312	176	2,641	20	1965
Bart Starr, Green Bay	NA	251	156	2,257	14	1966
Sonny Jurgensen, Washington	NA	508	288	3,747	31	1967
Earl Morrall, Baltimore Colts	NA	317	182	2,909	26	1968
Sonny Jurgensen, Washington	NA	442	274	3,102	22	1969
John Brodie, San Francisco	NA	378	223	2,941	24	1970
Roger Staubach, Dallas	NA	211	126	1,882	15	1971
Norm Snead, NY Giants	NA	325	196	2,307	17	1972
Roger Staubach, Dallas	94.6	286	179	2,428	23	1973
Sonny Jurgensen, Washington	94.5	167	107	1,185	11	1974
Fran Tarkenton, Minnesota	91.8	425	273	2,994	25	1975
James Harris, L.A. Rams	89.6	158	91	1,460	8	1976
Roger Staubach, Dallas	87.0	361	210	2,620	18	1977
Roger Staubach, Dallas	84.9	413	231	3,190	25	1978
Roger Staubach, Dallas	92.3	461	267	3,586	27	1979
Ron Jaworski, Philadelphia	91.0	451	257	3,529	27	1980
Joe Montana, San Francisco	88.4	488	311	3,565	19	1981
Joe Theismann, Washington	91.3	252	161	2,033	13	1982
Steve Bartkowski, Atlanta	97.6	432	274	3,167	22	1983
Joe Montana, San Francisco	102.9	432	279	3,630	28	1984
Joe Montana, San Francisco	91.3	494	303	3,653	27	1985
Tommy Kramer, Minnesota	92.6	372	208	3,000	24	1986
Joe Montana, San Francisco	102.1	398	266	3,054	31	1987
Wade Wilson, Minnesota	91.5	332	204	2,746	15	1988
Joe Montana, San Francisco	112.4	386	271	3,521	26	1989
Phil Simms, NY Giants	92.7	311	184	2,284	15	1990
Steve Young, San Francisco	101.8	279	180	2,517	17	1991
Steve Young, San Francisco	107.0	402	268	3,465	25	1992
Steve Young, San Francisco	101.5	462	314	4,023	29	1993
Steve Young, San Francisco	112.8	461	324	3,969	35	1994
Brett Favre, Green Bay	99.5	570	359	4,413	38	1995
Steve Young, San Francisco	97.2	316	214	2,410	14	1996
Steve Young, San Francisco	104.7	356	241	3,029	19	1997
Randall Cunningham, Minnesota	106.0	425	259	3,704	34	1998
Kurt Warner, St. Louis	109.2	499	325	4,353	41	1999
Trent Green, St. Louis	101.8	240	145	2,063	16	2000
Kurt Warner, St. Louis	101.4	546	375	4,830	36	2001
Brad Johnson, Tampa Bay	92.9	451	281	3,049	22	2002
Daunte Culpepper, Minnesota	96.4	454	295	3,479	25	2003
Daunte Culpepper, Minnesota	110.9	548	379	4,717	39	2004
Matt Hasselbeck, Seattle	98.2	449	294	3,459	24	2005
Drew Brees, New Orleans	96.2	554	356	4,418	26	2006
Tony Romo, Dallas	97.4	520	335	4,211	36	2007
Kurt Warner, Arizona	96.9	598	401	4,583	30	2008
Drew Brees, New Orleans	109.6	514	363	4,388	34	2009
Aaron Rodgers, Green Bay	101.2	475	312	3,922	28	2010
Aaron Rodgers, Green Bay	122.5	502	343	4,643	45	2011
Aaron Rodgers, Green Bay	108.0	552	371	4,295	39	2012
Nick Foles, Philadelphia	119.2	317	203	2,891	27	2013
Tony Romo, Dallas	113.2	435	304	3,705	34	2014
Russell Wilson, Seattle	110.1	483	329	4,024	34	2015

RECEPTIONS

Year	Player, team	Rec	Yds	TD
1960	Raymond Berry, Baltimore Colts	74	1,298	10
1961	Jim Phillips, L.A. Rams	78	1,092	5
1962	Bobby Mitchell, Washington	72	1,384	11
1963	Bobby Joe Conrad, St. Louis Cardinals	73	967	10
1964	Johnny Morris, Chicago	93	1,200	10
1965	Dave Parks, San Francisco	80	1,344	12
1966	Charley Taylor, Washington	72	1,119	12
1967	Charley Taylor, Washington	70	990	9
1968	Clifton McNeil, San Francisco	71	994	7
1969	Dan Abramowicz, New Orleans	73	1,015	7
1970	Dick Gordon, Chicago	71	1,026	13
1971	Bob Tucker, NY Giants	59	791	4
1972	Harold Jackson, Philadelphia	62	1,048	4
1973	Harold Carmichael, Philadelphia	67	1,116	9
1974	Charles Young, Philadelphia	63	696	3
1975	Chuck Foreman, Minnesota	73	691	9
1976	Drew Pearson, Dallas	58	806	6
1977	Ahmad Rashad, Minnesota	51	681	2
1978	Rickey Young, Minnesota	88	704	5
1979	Ahmad Rashad, Minnesota	80	1,156	9
1980	Earl Cooper, San Francisco	83	567	4
1981	Dwight Clark, San Francisco	85	1,105	4
1982	Dwight Clark, San Francisco	60	913	5
1983	Roy Green, St. Louis Cardinals	78	1,227	14
	Charlie Brown, Washington	78	1,225	8
	Earnest Gray, NY Giants	78	1,139	5
1984	Art Monk, Washington	106	1,372	7
1985	Roger Craig, San Francisco	92	1,016	6
1986	Jerry Rice, San Francisco	86	1,570	15
1987	J. T. Smith, St. Louis Cardinals	91	1,117	8
1988	Henry Ellard, L.A. Rams	86	1,414	10
1989	Sterling Sharpe, Green Bay	90	1,423	12
1990	Jerry Rice, San Francisco	100	1,502	13
1991	Michael Irvin, Dallas	93	1,523	8
1992	Sterling Sharpe, Green Bay	108	1,461	13
1993	Sterling Sharpe, Green Bay	112	1,274	11
1994	Cris Carter, Minnesota	122	1,256	7
1995	Herman Moore, Detroit	123	1,686	14
1996	Jerry Rice, San Francisco	108	1,254	8
1997	Herman Moore, Detroit	104	1,293	8
1998	Frank Sanders, Arizona	89	1,145	3
1999	Muhsin Muhammad, Carolina	96	1,253	8
2000	Muhsin Muhammad, Carolina	102	1,183	6
2001	Keyshawn Johnson, Tampa Bay	106	1,266	1
2002	Randy Moss, Minnesota	106	1,347	7
2003	Torry Holt, St. Louis	117	1,696	12
2004	Joe Horn, New Orleans	94	1,399	11
	Torry Holt, St. Louis	94	1,372	10
2005	Steve Smith, Carolina	103	1,563	12
	Larry Fitzgerald, Arizona	103	1,409	10
2006	Mike Furrey, Detroit	98	1,086	6
2007	Larry Fitzgerald, Arizona	100	1,409	10
2008	Larry Fitzgerald, Arizona	96	1,431	12
2009	Steve Smith, NY Giants	107	1,220	7
2010	Roddy White, Atlanta	115	1,389	10
2011	Roddy White, Atlanta	100	1,296	8
2012	Calvin Johnson, Detroit	122	1,964	5
2013	Pierre Garcon, Washington	113	1,346	5
2014	Julio Jones, Atlanta	104	1,593	6
2015	Julio Jones, Atlanta	136	1,871	8

SCORING

Player, team	TD	XPM	FGM	Pts	Year
Paul Hornung, Green Bay	15	41	15	176	1960
Paul Hornung, Green Bay	10	41	15	146	1961
Jim Taylor, Green Bay	19	0	0	114	1962
Don Chandler, NY Giants	0	52	18	106	1963
Lenny Moore, Baltimore Colts	20	0	0	120	1964
Gale Sayers, Chicago	22	0	0	132	1965
Bruce Gossett, L.A. Rams	0	29	28	113	1966
Jim Bakken, St. Louis Cardinals	0	36	27	117	1967
Leroy Kelly, Cleveland	20	0	0	120	1968
Fred Cox, Minnesota	0	43	26	121	1969
Fred Cox, Minnesota	0	35	30	125	1970
Curt Knight, Washington	0	27	29	114	1971
Chester Marcol, Green Bay	0	29	33	128	1972

RUSHING YARDS

Year	Player, team	Yds	Att	TD
1960	Jim Brown, Cleveland	1,257	215	9
1961	Jim Brown, Cleveland	1,408	305	8
1962	Jim Taylor, Green Bay	1,474	272	19
1963	Jim Brown, Cleveland	1,863	291	12
1964	Jim Brown, Cleveland	1,446	280	7
1965	Jim Brown, Cleveland	1,544	289	17
1966	Gale Sayers, Chicago	1,231	229	8
1967	Leroy Kelly, Cleveland	1,205	235	11
1968	Leroy Kelly, Cleveland	1,239	248	16
1969	Gale Sayers, Chicago	1,032	236	8
1970	Larry Brown, Washington	1,125	237	5
1971	John Brockington, Green Bay	1,105	216	4
1972	Larry Brown, Washington	1,216	285	8

Player, team	TD	XPM	FGM	Pts	Year	Player, team	Yds	Att	TD
David Ray, L.A. Rams	0	40	30	130	1973	John Brockington, Green Bay	1,144	265	3
Chester Marcol, Green Bay	0	19	25	94	1974	Lawrence McCutcheon, L.A. Rams	1,109	236	3
Chuck Foreman, Minnesota	22	0	0	132	1975	Jim Otis, St. Louis Cardinals	1,076	269	5
Mark Moseley, Washington	0	31	22	97	1976	Walter Payton, Chicago	1,390	311	13
Walter Payton, Chicago	16	0	0	96	1977	Walter Payton, Chicago	1,852	339	14
Frank Corral, L.A. Rams	0	31	29	118	1978	Walter Payton, Chicago	1,395	333	11
Mark Moseley, Washington	0	39	25	114	1979	Walter Payton, Chicago	1,610	369	14
Ed Murray, Detroit	0	35	27	116	1980	Walter Payton, Chicago	1,460	317	6
Ed Murray, Detroit	0	46	25	121	1981	George Rogers, New Orleans	1,674	378	13
Rafael Septien, Dallas	0	40	27	121					
Wendell Tyler, L.A. Rams	13	0	0	78	1982	Tony Dorsett, Dallas	745	177	5
Mark Moseley, Washington	0	62	33	161	1983	Eric Dickerson, L.A. Rams	1,808	390	18
Ray Wersching, San Francisco	0	56	25	131	1984	Eric Dickerson, L.A. Rams	2,105	379	14
Kevin Butler, Chicago	0	51	31	144	1985	Gerald Riggs, Atlanta	1,719	397	10
Kevin Butler, Chicago	0	36	28	120	1986	Eric Dickerson, L.A. Rams	1,821	404	11
Jerry Rice, San Francisco	23	0	0	138	1987	Charles White, L.A. Rams	1,374	324	11
Mike Cofer, San Francisco	0	40	27	121	1988	Herschel Walker, Dallas	1,514	361	5
Mike Cofer, San Francisco	0	49	29	136	1989	Barry Sanders, Detroit	1,470	280	14
Chip Lohmiller, Washington	0	41	30	131	1990	Barry Sanders, Detroit	1,304	255	13
Chip Lohmiller, Washington	0	56	31	149	1991	Emmitt Smith, Dallas	1,563	365	12
Morten Andersen, New Orleans	0	33	29	120	1992	Emmitt Smith, Dallas	1,713	373	18
Chip Lohmiller, Washington	0	30	30	120					
Jason Hanson, Detroit	0	28	34	130	1993	Emmitt Smith, Dallas	1,486	283	9
Fuad Reveiz, Minnesota	0	30	34	132	1994	Barry Sanders, Detroit	1,883	331	7
Emmitt Smith, Dallas	22	0	0	132					
Emmitt Smith, Dallas	25	0	0	150	1995	Emmitt Smith, Dallas	1,773	377	25
John Kasay, Carolina	0	34	37	145	1996	Barry Sanders, Detroit	1,553	307	11
Richie Cunningham, Dallas	0	24	34	126	1997	Barry Sanders, Detroit	2,053	335	11
Gary Anderson, Minnesota	0	59	35	164	1998	Jamal Anderson, Atlanta	1,846	410	14
Jeff Wilkins, St. Louis	0	64	20	124	1999	Stephen Davis, Washington	1,405	290	17
Marshall Faulk, St. Louis	26	0	0	160	2000	Robert Smith, Minnesota	1,521	295	7
Marshall Faulk, St. Louis	21	0	0	128	2001	Stephen Davis, Washington	1,432	356	5
Jay Feely, Atlanta	0	42	32	138	2002	Deuce McAllister, New Orleans	1,388	325	13
Jeff Wilkins, St. Louis	0	46	39	163	2003	Ahman Green, Green Bay	1,883	355	15
David Akers, Philadelphia	0	41	27	122	2004	Shaun Alexander, Seattle	1,696	353	16
Shaun Alexander, Seattle	28	0	0	168	2005	Shaun Alexander, Seattle	1,880	370	27
Robbie Gould, Chicago	0	47	32	143	2006	Frank Gore, San Francisco	1,695	312	8
Mason Crosby, Green Bay	0	48	31	141	2007	Adrian Peterson, Minnesota	1,341	238	12
David Akers, Philadelphia	0	45	33	144	2008	Adrian Peterson, Minnesota	1,760	363	10
David Akers, Philadelphia	0	43	32	139	2009	Steven Jackson, St. Louis	1,416	324	4
David Akers, Philadelphia	0	47	32	143	2010	Michael Turner, Atlanta	1,371	334	12
David Akers, San Francisco	0	34	44	166	2011	Michael Turner, Atlanta	1,340	301	11
Lawrence Tynes, NY Giants	0	46	33	145	2012	Adrian Peterson, Minnesota	2,097	348	12
Steven Hauschka, Seattle	0	44	33	143	2013	LeSean McCoy, Philadelphia	1,607	314	9
Cody Parkey, Philadelphia	0	54	32	150	2014	DeMarco Murray, Dallas	1,845	392	13
Graham Gano, Carolina	0	56	30	146	2015	Adrian Peterson, Minnesota	1,485	327	11

Note: Passer ratings for years prior to 1973 were determined by different measures and are not directly comparable to current passer ratings.

NFL Most Valuable Player, 1957-2015

The Most Valuable Player is one of many awards given out annually by the Associated Press according to the results of balloting by a nationwide panel of media. Many other organizations give out annual awards honoring the NFL's best players.

Year	Player, team	Year	Player, team	Year	Player, team
1957	Jim Brown, Cleveland	1978	Terry Bradshaw, Pittsburgh	1998	Terrell Davis, Denver
1958	Jim Brown, Cleveland	1979	Earl Campbell, Houston	1999	Kurt Warner, St. Louis
1959	Charley Conerly, NY Giants	1980	Brian Sipe, Cleveland	2000	Marshall Faulk, St. Louis
1960	Norm Van Brocklin, Philadelphia	1981	Ken Anderson, Cincinnati	2001	Kurt Warner, St. Louis
1961	Paul Hornung, Green Bay	1982	Mark Moseley, Washington	2002	Rich Gannon, Oakland
1962	Jim Taylor, Green Bay	1983	Joe Theismann, Washington	2003	Peyton Manning, Indianapolis;
1963	Y. A. Tittle, NY Giants	1984	Dan Marino, Miami		Steve McNair, Tennessee
1964	Johnny Unitas, Baltimore	1985	Marcus Allen, Los Angeles	2004	Peyton Manning, Indianapolis
1965	Jim Brown, Cleveland	1986	Lawrence Taylor, NY Giants	2005	Shaun Alexander, Seattle
1966	Bart Starr, Green Bay	1987	John Elway, Denver	2006	LaDainian Tomlinson, San Diego
1967	Johnny Unitas, Baltimore	1988	Boomer Esiason, Cincinnati	2007	Tom Brady, New England
1968	Earl Morrall, Baltimore	1989	Joe Montana, San Francisco	2008	Peyton Manning, Indianapolis
1969	Roman Gabriel, Los Angeles	1990	Joe Montana, San Francisco	2009	Peyton Manning, Indianapolis
1970	John Brodie, San Francisco	1991	Thurman Thomas, Buffalo	2010	Tom Brady, New England
1971	Alan Page, Minnesota	1992	Steve Young, San Francisco	2011	Aaron Rodgers, Green Bay
1972	Larry Brown, Washington	1993	Emmitt Smith, Dallas	2012	Adrian Peterson, Minnesota
1973	O. J. Simpson, Buffalo	1994	Steve Young, San Francisco	2013	Peyton Manning, Denver
1974	Ken Stabler, Oakland	1995	Brett Favre, Green Bay	2014	Aaron Rodgers, Green Bay
1975	Fran Tarkenton, Minnesota	1996	Brett Favre, Green Bay	2015	Cam Newton, Carolina
1976	Bert Jones, Baltimore	1997	Brett Favre, Green Bay;		
1977	Walter Payton, Chicago		Barry Sanders, Detroit		

All-Time Professional (NFL and AFL) Football Records

(at end of 2015 season; * = active in 2015; (a) includes AFL statistics; ** = 2-pt conversions scored)

All-Time Defensive Leaders

Interceptions, career: 81, Paul Krause, Washington-Minnesota, 1964-79.

Interceptions, season: 14, Dick "Night Train" Lane, L.A. Rams, 1952.

Interception touchdowns, career: 12, Rod Woodson, Pittsburgh-San Francisco-Baltimore Ravens-Oakland, 1987-2003.

Interception touchdowns, season: 4; Ken Houston, Houston, 1971; Jim Kearney, Kansas City, 1972; Eric Allen, Philadelphia, 1993.

Sacks, career (since 1982): 200.0, Bruce Smith, Buffalo-Washington, 1985-2003.

Sacks, season (since 1982): 22.5, Michael Strahan, NY Giants, 2001.

All-Time Scoring Leaders by Points

Player	Yrs	TD	PAT	FG	Total
Morten Andersen	25	0	849	565	2,544
Gary Anderson	23	0	820	538	2,434
Adam Vinatieri*......	20	0	742	503	2,253
Jason Hanson	21	0	665	495	2,150
John Carney	23	0	628	478	2,062
Matt Stover	19	0	591	471	2,004
George Blanda (a) ...	26	9	943	335	2,002
Jason Elam.........	17	0	675	436	1,983
John Kasay.........	20	0	587	461	1,970
Norm Johnson	18	0	638	366	1,736
David Akers........	16	0	563	386	1,721
Nick Lowery	18	0	562	383	1,711
Jan Stenerud (a)....	19	0	580	373	1,699
Ryan Longwell	15	0	604	361	1,687
Sebastian Janikowski*	16	0	520	385	1,675
Phil Dawson*	17	1	447	386	1,611

Points, season: 186, LaDainian Tomlinson, San Diego, 2006 (31 TDs).
Points, game: 40, Ernie Nevers, Chicago Cardinals vs. Chicago Bears, Nov. 28, 1929 (6 TDs, 4 PATs).
Touchdowns, season: 31, LaDainian Tomlinson, San Diego, 2006.
Touchdowns, game: 6; Ernie Nevers, Chicago Cardinals vs. Chicago Bears, Nov. 28, 1929 (6 rushing); Dub Jones, Cleveland Browns vs. Chicago Bears, Nov. 25, 1951 (4 rushing, 2 pass receptions); Gale Sayers, Chicago Bears vs. San Francisco, Dec. 12, 1965 (4 rushing, 1 pass reception, 1 punt return).

All-Time Scoring Leaders by Touchdowns

Player	Yrs	Rush	Rec	Ret	TD
Jerry Rice	20	10	197	1	208
Emmitt Smith	15	164	11	0	175
LaDainian Tomlinson ..	11	145	17	0	162
Randy Moss	14	0	156	1	157
Terrell Owens	15	3	153	0	156
Marcus Allen	16	123	21	1	145
Marshall Faulk	12	100	36	0	136
Cris Carter	16	0	130	1	131
Marvin Harrison	13	0	128	0	128
Jim Brown...........	9	106	20	0	126
Walter Payton	13	110	15	0	125
John Riggins.........	14	104	12	0	116
Lenny Moore.........	12	63	48	2	113
Shaun Alexander	9	100	12	0	112
Tony Gonzalez	17	0	111	0	111
Barry Sanders........	10	99	10	0	109

Points after TD, season: 75, Matt Prater, Denver, 2013.
Consecutive points after TD: 463, Stephen Gostkowski, New England, 2006-15.
Field goals, career: 565, Morten Andersen, New Orleans-Atlanta-NY Giants-Kansas City-Minnesota-Atlanta, 1982-2007.
Field goals, season: 44, David Akers, San Francisco, 2011.
Field goals, game: 8, Rob Bironas, Tennessee vs. Houston, Oct. 21, 2007.
Longest field goal: 64 yards, Matt Prater, Denver vs. Tennessee, Dec. 8, 2013.

All-Time Rushing Leaders

(ranked by rushing yards; * = active in 2015)

Player	Yrs	Att	Yds	Avg	Long	TD
Emmitt Smith	15	4,409	18,355	4.2	75T	164
Walter Payton	13	3,838	16,726	4.4	76	110
Barry Sanders......	10	3,062	15,269	5.0	85	99
Curtis Martin	11	3,518	14,101	4.0	70T	90
LaDainian Tomlinson	11	3,174	13,684	4.3	85T	145
Jerome Bettis	13	3,479	13,662	3.9	71T	91
Eric Dickerson......	11	2,996	13,259	4.4	85T	90
Tony Dorsett	12	2,936	12,739	4.3	99T	77
Jim Brown.........	9	2,359	12,312	5.2	80T	106
Marshall Faulk	12	2,836	12,279	4.3	71T	100
Edgerrin James	11	3,028	12,246	4.0	72	80
Marcus Allen.......	16	3,022	12,243	4.1	61T	123
Franco Harris	13	2,949	12,120	4.1	75T	91
Thurman Thomas ...	13	2,877	12,074	4.2	80T	65
Frank Gore*	11	2,702	12,040	4.5	80T	70
Fred Taylor	13	2,534	11,695	4.6	80T	66
Adrian Peterson*....	9	2,381	11,675	4.9	82T	97
Steven Jackson*.....	11	2,743	11,388	4.2	59T	68
John Riggins.......	14	2,916	11,352	3.9	66T	104
Corey Dillon	10	2,618	11,241	4.3	96T	82

Yards gained, season: 2,105, Eric Dickerson, L.A. Rams, 1984.
Yards gained, game: 296, Adrian Peterson, Minnesota vs. San Diego, Nov. 4, 2007.
Rushing TDs, career: 164, Emmitt Smith, Dallas-Arizona, 1990-2004.
Rushing TDs, season: 28, LaDainian Tomlinson, San Diego, 2006.
Rushing TDs, game: 6, Ernie Nevers, Chicago Cardinals vs. Chicago Bears, Nov. 28, 1929.
Rushing attempts, game: 45, Jamie Morris, Washington vs. Cincinnati, Dec. 17, 1988 (OT).
Longest run from scrimmage: 99 yards (TD), Tony Dorsett, Dallas vs. Minnesota, Jan. 3, 1983.

All-Time Receiving Leaders

(ranked by number of receptions; * = active in 2015)

Player	Yrs	No.	Yds	Avg	Long	TD
Jerry Rice	20	1,549	22,895	14.8	96T	197
Tony Gonzalez	17	1,325	15,127	11.4	73T	111
Marvin Harrison	13	1,102	14,580	13.2	80T	128
Cris Carter	16	1,101	13,899	12.6	80T	130
Tim Brown.........	17	1,094	14,934	13.7	80T	100
Terrell Owens	15	1,078	15,934	14.8	98T	153
Reggie Wayne	14	1,070	14,345	13.4	80	82
Andre Johnson*	13	1,053	14,100	13.4	77T	68
Isaac Bruce	16	1,024	15,208	14.9	80T	91
Jason Witten*	13	1,020	11,215	11.0	69	60
Larry Fitzgerald*....	12	1,018	13,366	13.1	80T	98
Anquan Boldin*.....	13	1,009	13,195	13.1	79T	74
Hines Ward	14	1,000	12,083	12.1	85T	85
Randy Moss	14	982	15,292	15.6	82T	156
Steve Smith Sr.* ...	15	961	13,932	14.5	80T	76
Andre Reed	16	951	13,198	13.9	83T	87
Derrick Mason	15	943	12,061	12.8	79T	66
Art Monk...........	16	940	12,721	13.5	79T	68
Torry Holt	11	920	13,382	14.5	85T	74
Wes Welker*	12	903	9,924	11.0	99T	50

Yards gained, career: 22,895, Jerry Rice, San Francisco-Oakland-Seattle, 1985-2004.
Yards gained, season: 1,964, Calvin Johnson, Detroit, 2012.
Yards gained, game: 336, Willie "Flipper" Anderson, L.A. Rams vs. New Orleans, Nov. 26, 1989 (OT).
Pass receptions, season: 143, Marvin Harrison, Indianapolis, 2002.
Pass receptions, game: 21, Brandon Marshall, Denver vs. Indianapolis, Dec. 13, 2009.
Touchdown receptions, career: 197, Jerry Rice, San Francisco-Oakland-Seattle, 1985-2004.
Touchdown receptions, season: 23, Randy Moss, New England, 2007.
Touchdown receptions, game: 5; Bob Shaw, Chicago Cardinals vs. Baltimore Colts, Oct. 2, 1950; Kellen Winslow, San Diego vs. Oakland, Nov. 22, 1981; Jerry Rice, San Francisco vs. Atlanta, Oct. 14, 1990.

All-Time Passing Leaders

(minimum 1,500 attempts; ranked by quarterback rating points; * = active in 2015)

Player	Yrs	Att	Comp	Yds	TD	Int	Pts[1]
Aaron Rodgers* ...	11	4,047	2,633	32,399	257	65	104.1
Russell Wilson*	4	1,735	1,123	13,974	106	34	101.8
Tony Romo*	12	4,331	2,826	34,154	247	117	97.1
Steve Young	15	4,149	2,667	33,124	232	107	96.8
Peyton Manning* ..	17	9,380	6,125	71,940	539	251	96.5
Tom Brady*.......	16	7,792	4,953	58,028	428	150	96.4
Drew Brees*	15	8,085	5,365	60,903	428	205	95.8
Philip Rivers*	12	5,339	3,462	41,447	281	135	95.5
Ben Roethlisberger*	12	5,423	3,476	42,995	272	147	94.0
Kurt Warner	12	4,070	2,666	32,344	208	128	93.7
Joe Montana.......	15	5,391	3,409	40,551	273	139	92.3
Matt Ryan*	8	4,530	2,915	32,757	202	107	90.9
Chad Pennington ..	11	2,471	1,632	17,823	102	64	90.1
Matt Schaub*	12	3,271	2,092	24,851	133	90	89.1
Andy Dalton*	5	2,497	1,556	18,008	124	73	88.4
Cam Newton*	5	2,418	1,440	18,263	117	64	88.3
Carson Palmer* ...	12	5,443	3,413	40,036	259	166	88.1
Daunte Culpepper..	11	3,199	2,016	24,153	149	106	87.8
Jeff Garcia	11	3,676	2,264	25,537	161	83	87.5
Dan Marino.......	17	8,358	4,967	61,361	420	252	86.4

(1) Rating points based on performances in the following categories: percentage of completions, percentage of touchdown passes, percentage of interceptions, and average gain per pass attempt.

Yards gained, career: 71,940, Peyton Manning, Indianapolis-Denver, 1998-2015.
Yards gained, season: 5,477, Peyton Manning, Denver, 2013.
Yards gained, game: 554, Norm Van Brocklin, L.A. Rams vs. NY Yanks, Sept. 28, 1951 (27 completions in 41 attempts).
Touchdowns passing, career: 539, Peyton Manning, Indianapolis-Denver, 1998-2015.
Touchdowns passing, season: 55, Peyton Manning, Denver, 2013.
Touchdowns passing, game: 7; Sid Luckman, Chicago Bears vs. NY Giants, Nov. 14, 1943; Adrian Burk, Philadelphia vs.

Washington, Oct. 17, 1954; George Blanda, Houston vs. NY Titans, Nov. 19, 1961; Y. A. Tittle, NY Giants vs. Washington, Oct. 28, 1962; Joe Kapp, Minnesota vs. Baltimore Colts, Sept. 28, 1969; Peyton Manning, Denver vs. Baltimore, Sept. 5, 2013; Nick Foles, Philadelphia vs. Oakland, Nov. 3, 2013; Drew Brees, New Orleans vs. NY Giants, Nov. 1, 2015.
Passes completed, career: 6,300, Brett Favre, Atlanta-Green Bay-NY Jets-Minnesota, 1991-2010.
Passes completed, season: 468, Drew Brees, New Orleans, 2011.
Passes completed, game: 45, Drew Bledsoe, New England vs. Minnesota, Nov. 13, 1994 (OT).

National Football League Franchise Origins
(Team: founding year, league. Home stadium location; subsequent history.)

Arizona Cardinals: 1920, American Professional Football Association (APFA)[1]. Chicago, 1920-59; St. Louis, 1960-87; Tempe, AZ, 1988-2005; Glendale, AZ, 2006-present.
Atlanta Falcons: 1966, NFL. Atlanta, 1966-present.
Baltimore Ravens: 1996, NFL. Baltimore, 1996-present.
Buffalo Bills: 1960, American Football League (AFL)[2]. Buffalo, 1960-72; Orchard Park, NY, 1973-present.
Carolina Panthers: 1995, NFL. Clemson, SC, 1995; Charlotte, NC, 1996-present.
Chicago Bears: 1920, APFA. Decatur, IL, 1920; Chicago, 1921-present.
Cincinnati Bengals: 1968, AFL. Cincinnati, 1968-present.
Cleveland Browns: 1946, All-America Football Conference (AAFC)[3]. Cleveland, 1946-95; 1999-present.
Dallas Cowboys: 1960, NFL. Dallas, 1960-70; Irving, TX, 1971-2008; Arlington, TX, 2009-present.
Denver Broncos: 1960, AFL. Denver, 1960-present.
Detroit Lions: 1930, NFL. Portsmouth, OH, 1930-33; Detroit, 1934-74; Pontiac, MI, 1975-2001; Detroit, 2002-present.
Green Bay Packers: 1921, APFA. Green Bay, WI, 1921-present.
Houston Texans: 2002, NFL. Houston, 2002-present.
Indianapolis Colts: 1953, NFL[3]. Baltimore, 1953-83; Indianapolis, 1984-present.
Jacksonville Jaguars: 1995, NFL. Jacksonville, FL, 1995-present.
Kansas City Chiefs: 1960, AFL. Dallas, 1960-62; Kansas City, MO, 1963-present.
L.A. Rams: 1937, NFL. Cleveland, 1936-45; Los Angeles, 1946-79; Anaheim, CA, 1980-94; St. Louis, 1995-2015; L.A., 2016-present.

Miami Dolphins: 1966, AFL. Miami, 1966-2002; Miami Gardens, FL, 2003-present.
Minnesota Vikings: 1961, NFL. Bloomington, MN, 1961-81; Minneapolis, 1982-present.
New England Patriots: 1960, AFL. Boston, 1960-70; Foxborough, MA, 1971-present.
New Orleans Saints: 1967, NFL. New Orleans, 1967-2004; Baton Rouge and San Antonio, 2005; New Orleans, 2006-present.
NY Giants: 1925, NFL. New York, NY, 1925-73; 1975; New Haven, CT, 1973-74; E. Rutherford, NJ, 1976-present.
NY Jets: 1960, AFL. New York, NY, 1960-83; E. Rutherford, NJ, 1984-present.
Oakland Raiders: 1960, AFL. San Francisco, 1960-61; Oakland, CA, 1962-81; Los Angeles, 1982-94; Oakland, CA, 1995-present.
Philadelphia Eagles: 1933, NFL. Philadelphia, 1933-present.
Pittsburgh Steelers: 1933, NFL. Pittsburgh, 1933-present.
San Diego Chargers: 1960, AFL. Los Angeles, 1960; San Diego, 1961-present.
San Francisco 49ers: 1946, AAFC. San Francisco, 1946-present.
Seattle Seahawks: 1976, NFL. Seattle, 1976-present.
Tampa Bay Buccaneers: 1976, NFL. Tampa, 1976-present.
Tennessee Titans: 1960, AFL. Houston, 1960-96; Memphis, 1997; Nashville, 1998-present.
Washington Redskins: 1932, NFL. Boston, 1932-36; Washington, DC, 1937-96; Landover, MD, 1997-present.

(1) The American Professional Football Association (APFA) was formed in 1920 to standardize the rules of professional football. In 1922, the name was changed to the National Football League (NFL). (2) The most successful of four leagues called the American Football League, or AFL (1926; 1936-37; 1940-41; 1960-69). Congress approved an NFL/AFL merger in 1966. Baltimore, Cleveland, and Pittsburgh agreed to join the 10 incoming AFL teams to form the American Football Conference. The NFL began play in 1970 with 26 teams. (3) The All-America Football Conference (AAFC), 1946-49. In 1950, three of its teams joined the NFL (Baltimore, Cleveland, and San Francisco). The Baltimore franchise failed, but the NFL awarded the city a second one, also called the Colts, in 1953.

NFL Stadiums
(**A** = A-Turf Titan, **D** = DD Grassmaster (grass), **F** = FieldTurf, **G** = Grass, **N** = Natural grass,
S = Synthetic, **SM** = Sportexe Momentum, **SS** = Sportfield Softtop)

Team: stadium, location, surface (year built)	Capacity[1]	Team: stadium, location, surface (year built)	Capacity[1]
Bears: Soldier Field[2], Chicago, IL, N (1924)	61,500	**Giants:** MetLife Stadium[8], E. Rutherford, NJ, F (2010)	82,500
Bengals: Paul Brown Stadium, Cincinnati, OH, S (2000)	65,515	**Jaguars:** EverBank Field[9], Jacksonville, FL, G (1995)	67,246
Bills: Ralph Wilson Stadium, Orchard Park, NY, A (1973)	73,079	**Jets:** MetLife Stadium[8], E. Rutherford, NJ, F (2010)	82,500
Broncos: Sports Authority Field at Mile High[3], Denver, CO, N (2001)	76,125	**Lions:** Ford Field, Detroit, MI, F (2002)	65,000
Browns: FirstEnergy Stadium[4], Cleveland, OH, G (1999)	67,431	**Packers:** Lambeau Field[10], Green Bay, WI, D (1957)	80,750
Buccaneers: Raymond James Stadium, Tampa, FL, G (1998)	65,890	**Panthers:** Bank of America Stadium[11], Charlotte, NC, G (1996)	73,778
Cardinals: University of Phoenix Stadium, Glendale, AZ, G (2006)	63,400	**Patriots:** Gillette Stadium, Foxborough, MA, F (2002)	68,756
Chargers: Qualcomm Stadium[5], San Diego, CA, G (1967)	71,500	**Raiders:** O.co Coliseum[12], Oakland, CA, G (1966)	56,063
Chiefs: Arrowhead Stadium, Kansas City, MO, G (1972; fully renovated 2010)	76,416	**Rams:** Los Angeles Memorial Coliseum, Los Angeles, CA, G (1923)	93,607
Colts: Lucas Oil Stadium, Indianapolis, IN, F (2008)	63,000	**Ravens:** M&T Bank Stadium[13], Baltimore, MD, SM (1998)	71,008
Cowboys: AT&T Stadium[6], Arlington, TX, SS (2009)	80,000	**Redskins:** FedExField[14], Landover, MD, N (1997)	82,000
Dolphins: Sun Life Stadium[7], Miami Gardens, FL, G (1987)	64,982	**Saints:** Mercedes-Benz Superdome[15], New Orleans, LA, G (1975)	73,000
Eagles: Lincoln Financial Field, Philadelphia, PA, N (2003)	69,596	**Seahawks:** CenturyLink Field[16], Seattle, WA, F (2002)	67,000
Falcons: Georgia Dome, Atlanta, GA, F (1992)	71,228	**Steelers:** Heinz Field, Pittsburgh, PA, N (2001)	68,400
49ers: Levi's Stadium, Santa Clara, CA, N (2014)	68,500	**Texans:** NRG Stadium[17], Houston, TX, G (2002)	71,795
		Titans: Nissan Stadium[18], Nashville, TN, N (1999)	69,143
		Vikings: U.S. Bank Stadium, Minneapolis, MN, F (2016)	66,200

(1) As of the start of the 2015 season. (2) Renovation in 2002 replaced interior of stadium. (3) Formerly INVESCO Field at Mile High (2001-11). (4) Formerly Cleveland Browns Stadium (1999-2012). (5) Formerly San Diego Stadium (1967-80); San Diego Jack Murphy Stadium (1981-97). (6) Formerly Cowboys Stadium (2009-12). (7) Formerly Joe Robbie Stadium (1987-96); Pro Player Stadium (1996-2005); Land Shark Stadium (2009). (8) Formerly New Meadowlands Stadium (2010-11). (9) Formerly ALLTEL Stadium (1997-2007); Jacksonville Municipal Stadium (1946-97, 2007-09). (10) Formerly City Stadium (1957-65). Renovation completed in 2003 added 11,625 seats. (11) Formerly Ericsson Stadium (1996-2003). (12) Formerly Oakland-Alameda County Coliseum (1966-98); Network Associates Coliseum (1998-2004); McAfee Stadium (2004-08); Oakland Coliseum (2008-11). (13) Formerly PSINet Stadium (1998-2002); Ravens Stadium (2002-03). (14) Formerly Jack Kent Cooke Stadium (1997-99). (15) Formerly Louisiana Superdome (1975-2011). (16) Formerly Seahawks Stadium (2002-04); Qwest Field (2004-11). (17) Formerly Reliant Stadium (2002-13). (18) Formerly Adelphia Coliseum (1999-2002); The Coliseum (2002-06); LP Field (2006-15).

Pro Football Hall of Fame, Canton, OH

(Asterisk indicates member elected in Feb. 2016 and inducted Aug. 6, 2016.)

Herb Adderley	Tony Dorsett	Jimmy Johnson	Joe Montana	O. J. Simpson
Troy Aikman	John "Paddy" Driscoll	John Henry Johnson	Warren Moon	Mike Singletary
George Allen	Bill Dudley	Charlie Joiner	Lenny Moore	Jackie Slater
Larry Allen	*Tony Dungy	David "Deacon" Jones	Marion Motley	Bruce Smith
Marcus Allen	Glen "Turk" Edwards	Stan Jones	Mike Munchak	Emmitt Smith
Lance Alworth	Carl Eller	Walter Jones	Anthony Muñoz	Jackie Smith
Doug Atkins	John Elway	Henry Jordan	George Musso	*Ken Stabler
Morris "Red" Badgro	Weeb Ewbank	Sonny Jurgensen	Bronko Nagurski	John Stallworth
Lem Barney	Marshall Faulk	Jim Kelly	Joe Namath	*Dick Stanfel
Cliff Battles	*Brett Favre	Leroy Kelly	Earle "Greasy" Neale	Bart Starr
Sammy Baugh	Tom Fears	Cortez Kennedy	Ernie Nevers	Roger Staubach
Chuck Bednarik	Jim Finks	Walt Kiesling	Ozzie Newsome	Ernie Stautner
Bert Bell	Ray Flaherty	Frank "Bruiser" Kinard	Ray Nitschke	Jan Stenerud
Bobby Bell	Len Ford	Paul Krause	Chuck Noll	Dwight Stephenson
Raymond Berry	Dr. Daniel Fortmann	Earl "Curly" Lambeau	Leo Nomellini	Michael Strahan
Elvin Bethea	Dan Fouts	Jack Lambert	Jonathan Ogden	Hank Stram
Jerome Bettis	Benny Friedman	Tom Landry	Merlin Olsen	Ken Strong
Charles Bidwill	Frank Gatski	Dick "Night Train" Lane	Jim Otto	Joe Stydahar
Fred Biletnikoff	Bill George	Jim Langer	Steve Owen	Lynn Swann
George Blanda	Joe Gibbs	Willie Lanier	*Orlando Pace	Fran Tarkenton
Mel Blount	Frank Gifford	Steve Largent	Alan Page	Charley Taylor
Terry Bradshaw	Sid Gillman	Yale Lary	Bill Parcells	Jim Taylor
Derrick Brooks	Otto Graham	Dante Lavelli	Clarence "Ace" Parker	Lawrence "LT" Taylor
Bob Brown	Harold "Red" Grange	Bobby Layne	Jim Parker	Derrick Thomas
Jim Brown	Bud Grant	Dick LeBeau	Walter Payton	Emmitt Thomas
Paul Brown	Darrell Green	Alphonse "Tuffy"	Joe Perry	Thurman Thomas
Roosevelt Brown	Joe Greene	Leemans	Pete Pihos	Jim Thorpe
Tim Brown	*Kevin Greene	Marv Levy	Bill Polian	Mick Tingelhoff
Willie Brown	Forrest Gregg	Bob Lilly	Fritz Pollard	Andre Tippett
Junious "Buck"	Bob Griese	Floyd Little	John Randle	Y. A. Tittle
Buchanan	Russ Grimm	Larry Little	Hugh "Shorty" Ray	George Trafton
Nick Buoniconti	Lou Groza	James Lofton	Andre Reed	Charley Trippi
Dick Butkus	Ray Guy	Vince Lombardi	Dan Reeves	Emlen Tunnell
Jack Butler	Joe Guyon	Howie Long	Mel Renfro	Clyde "Bulldog" Turner
Earl Campbell	George Halas	Ronnie Lott	Jerry Rice	Johnny Unitas
Tony Canadeo	Charles Haley	Sid Luckman	Les Richter	Gene Upshaw
Joe Carr	Jack Ham	Roy "Link" Lyman	John Riggins	Norm Van Brocklin
Harry Carson	Dan Hampton	Tom Mack	Jim Ringo	Steve Van Buren
Cris Carter	Chris Hanburger	John Mackey	Willie Roaf	Doak Walker
Dave Casper	John Hannah	John Madden	Dave Robinson	Bill Walsh
Guy Chamberlin	*Marvin Harrison	Tim Mara	Andy Robustelli	Paul Warfield
Jack Christiansen	Bob Hayes	Wellington Mara	Art Rooney	Bob Waterfield
Earl "Dutch" Clark	Mike Haynes	Gino Marchetti	Dan Rooney	Mike Webster
George Connor	Mel Hein	Dan Marino	Pete Rozelle	Randy White
Jim Conzelman	Ted Hendricks	George Preston Marshall	Ed Sabol	Reggie White
Lou Creekmur	Wilbur "Pete" Henry	Curtis Martin	Bob St. Clair	Dave Wilcox
Larry Csonka	Arnold Herber	Bruce Mathews	Barry Sanders	Aeneas Williams
Curley Culp	Bill Hewitt	Ollie Matson	Charlie Sanders	Bill Willis
Al Davis	Gene Hickerson	Don Maynard	Deion Sanders	Larry Wilson
Willie Davis	Clarke Hinkle	George McAfee	Warren Sapp	Ralph Wilson Jr.
Dermontti Dawson	Elroy "Crazylegs" Hirsch	Mike McCormack	Gale Sayers	Kellen Winslow
Len Dawson	Paul Hornung	Randall McDaniel	Joe Schmidt	Alex Wojciechowicz
Fred Dean	Ken Houston	Tommy McDonald	Tex Schramm	Ron Wolf
*Edward DeBartolo Jr.	Robert "Cal" Hubbard	Hugh McElhenny	Junior Seau	Willie Wood
Joe DeLamielleure	Sam Huff	Johnny "Blood" McNally	Lee Roy Selmon	Rod Woodson
Richard Dent	Claude Humphrey	Mike Michalske	Shannon Sharpe	Rayfield Wright
Eric Dickerson	Lamar Hunt	Wayne Millner	Billy Shaw	Ron Yary
Dan Dierdorf	Don Hutson	Bobby Mitchell	Art Shell	Steve Young
Mike Ditka	Michael Irvin	Ron Mix	Will Shields	Jack Youngblood
Chris Doleman	Rickey Jackson	Art Monk	Don Shula	Gary Zimmerman
Art Donovan				

All-Time NFL Coaching Victories

(at end of 2015 season; ranked by overall career wins; * = active in 2015)

			Regular Season				Overall			
Coach	Team	Yrs	W	L	T	Pct	W	L	T	Pct
Don Shula	Baltimore Colts, Dolphins	33	328	156	6	.677	347	173	6	.666
George Halas	Bears	40	318	148	31	.682	324	151	31	.682
Tom Landry	Cowboys	29	250	162	6	.607	270	178	6	.603
Bill Belichick*	Browns, Patriots	21	223	113	0	.664	246	123	0	.667
Earl "Curly" Lambeau	Packers, Chicago Cardinals, Redskins	33	226	132	22	.631	229	134	22	.631
Chuck Noll	Steelers	23	193	148	1	.566	209	156	1	.572
Marty Schottenheimer	Browns, Chiefs, Redskins, Chargers	21	200	126	1	.613	205	139	1	.596
Dan Reeves	Broncos, Giants, Falcons	23	190	165	2	.535	201	174	2	.536
Chuck Knox	L.A. Rams, Bills, Seahawks	22	186	147	1	.558	193	158	1	.550
Bill Parcells	Giants, Patriots, Jets, Cowboys	19	172	130	1	.569	183	138	1	.570
Tom Coughlin*	Jaguars, Giants	20	170	150	0	.531	182	157	0	.537
Mike Shanahan	L.A. Raiders, Broncos, Redskins	20	170	138	0	.552	178	144	0	.553
Jeff Fisher*	Houston/Tennessee Oilers, Titans, St. Louis Rams	21	169	156	1	.520	174	162	1	.518
Mike Holmgren	Packers, Seahawks	17	161	111	0	.592	174	122	0	.588
Andy Reid*	Eagles, Chiefs	17	161	110	1	.594	172	121	1	.587
Joe Gibbs	Redskins	16	154	94	0	.621	171	101	0	.629
Paul Brown	Browns, Bengals	21	166	100	6	.624	170	108	6	.612
Bud Grant	Vikings	18	158	96	5	.621	168	108	5	.608
Bill Cowher	Steelers	15	149	90	1	.623	161	99	1	.619
Marv Levy	Chiefs, Bills	17	143	112	0	.561	154	120	0	.562

Note: Official NFL records do not include All-America Football Conference statistics.

BASEBALL

Playoff Results, 2016

American League

American League Wild Card Game: Toronto 5, Baltimore 2.

American League Division Series (ALDS): Toronto defeated Texas, 3 games to 0; Cleveland defeated Boston, 3 games to 0.

American League Championship Series (ALCS): Cleveland defeated Toronto, 4 games to 1.

National League

National League Wild Card Game: San Francisco 3, NY Mets 0.

National League Division Series (NLDS): Chicago defeated San Francisco, 3 games to 1; L.A. defeated Washington, 3 games to 2.

National League Championship Series (NLCS): Chicago defeated L.A., 4 games to 2.

World Series, 2016: Chicago Cubs Defeat Cleveland in Seven Games

After a hard-fought seven games, the Chicago Cubs became World Series champions for the first time since 1908. The World Series concluded in a dramatic 8-7, 10-inning victory over the Cleveland Indians in Game 7, Nov. 2, 2016, at Progressive Field in Cleveland, OH. Ben Zobrist's RBI double in the 10th inning scored pinch-runner Albert Almora Jr. and broke a 6-6 tie after a 17-minute rain delay between the 9th and 10th innings. Cleveland had tied the game 6-6 in the 8th on a 2-run homer by Rajai Davis off reliever Aroldis Chapman. Zobrist, who also won the 2015 World Series with the Kansas City Royals, batted .357 and was named the 2016 World Series Most Valuable Player.

Chicago won the last three games of the series after a 3-1 start against Cleveland, which was seeking its first title since 1948. Cubs starter Jon Lester and Chapman kept Chicago alive in Game 5, a 3-2 Cubs win Oct. 30 at Wrigley Field in Chicago. The comeback continued in Game 6 on Nov. 1 in Cleveland as shortstop Addison Russell tied a single-game World Series record with six RBI, including a grand-slam home run. Cleveland right-hander Corey Kluber struck out nine as the Indians won the series opener, 6-0, Oct. 25 at Progressive Field. Chicago's Kyle Schwarber, who missed all but two games during the season due to injury, had two hits and two RBI in a 5-1 victory in Game 2, Oct. 26. Four Cleveland pitchers—starter Josh Tomlin and relievers Andrew Miller, Bryan Shaw, and Cody Allen combined on a 1-0 shutout win in Game 3, Oct. 28, when the series moved to Chicago for the first World Series game at Wrigley Field since 1945. It was Cleveland's major-league-record fifth shutout of the 2016 postseason. Kluber won his second game in Game 4, a 7-2 victory Oct. 29 at Wrigley.

Game 1

Oct. 25 at Progressive Field, Cleveland, OH. Attendance: 38,091.

	1	2	3	4	5	6	7	8	9	R	H	E
Chicago Cubs	0	0	0	0	0	0	0	0	0	0	7	0
Cleveland Indians	2	0	0	1	0	0	0	3	X	6	10	0

Winning pitcher: Corey Kluber
Losing pitcher: Jon Lester

Game 2

Oct. 26 at Progressive Field, Cleveland, OH. Attendance: 38,172.

	1	2	3	4	5	6	7	8	9	R	H	E
Chicago Cubs	1	0	1	0	3	0	0	0	0	5	9	0
Cleveland Indians	0	0	0	0	0	1	0	0	0	1	4	2

Winning pitcher: Jake Arrieta
Losing pitcher: Trevor Bauer

Game 3

Oct. 28 at Wrigley Field, Chicago, IL. Attendance: 41,703.

	1	2	3	4	5	6	7	8	9	R	H	E
Cleveland Indians	0	0	0	0	0	0	1	0	0	1	8	1
Chicago Cubs	0	0	0	0	0	0	0	0	0	0	5	0

Winning pitcher: Andrew Miller
Losing pitcher: Carl Edwards Jr.
Save: Cody Allen

Game 4

Oct. 29 at Wrigley Field, Chicago, IL. Attendance: 41,706.

	1	2	3	4	5	6	7	8	9	R	H	E
Cleveland Indians	0	2	1	0	0	1	3	0	0	7	10	0
Chicago Cubs	1	0	0	0	0	0	0	1	0	2	7	2

Winning pitcher: Corey Kluber
Losing pitcher: John Lackey

Game 5

Oct. 30 at Wrigley Field, Chicago, IL. Attendance: 41,711.

	1	2	3	4	5	6	7	8	9	R	H	E
Cleveland Indians	0	1	0	0	0	1	0	0	0	2	6	1
Chicago Cubs	0	0	0	3	0	0	0	0	X	3	7	0

Winning pitcher: Jon Lester
Losing pitcher: Trevor Bauer
Save: Aroldis Chapman

Game 6

Nov. 1 at Progressive Field, Cleveland, OH. Attendance: 38,116.

	1	2	3	4	5	6	7	8	9	R	H	E
Chicago Cubs	3	0	4	0	0	0	0	0	2	9	13	0
Cleveland Indians	0	0	0	1	1	0	0	0	1	3	6	1

Winning pitcher: Jake Arrieta
Losing pitcher: Josh Tomlin

Game 7

Nov. 2 at Progressive Field, Cleveland, OH. Attendance: 38,104.

	1	2	3	4	5	6	7	8	9	10	R	H	E
Chicago Cubs	1	0	0	2	2	1	0	0	0	2	8	13	3
Cleveland Indians	0	0	1	0	2	0	0	3	0	1	7	11	1

Winning pitcher: Aroldis Chapman
Losing pitcher: Bryan Shaw
Save: Mike Montgomery

Major League Baseball, 2016: At Long Last, Cubs Win

Both the Chicago Cubs and Cleveland Indians spent decades chasing a World Series title. The Cubs ultimately won a memorable seven-game series over the Indians for their third World Series title in franchise history and first in 108 years. The Cubs won an MLB-best 103 games during the season before claiming their first National League pennant and trip to the Fall Classic since 1945.

The Cubs beat the wild-card San Francisco Giants in the NL Division Series and dropped two of the first three NL Championship Series games to the L.A. Dodgers before reeling off three straight wins. Kyle Hendricks and Aroldis Chapman combined on a two-hit shutout in Game 6 as the Cubs beat the Dodgers 5-0, Oct. 22, 2016, at Wrigley Field in Chicago. Jon Lester, who earned the Game 5 NLCS win, and Javier Baez (.318 batting average, seven hits, five RBI) were named co-MVPs of the championship series. Lester (19-5) was one of four Cubs pitchers in 2016 with at least 15 wins. Hendricks led all MLB starters with a 2.13 ERA, and Jake Arrieta (18-8) threw his second career no-hitter in a 16-0 win over the Reds, Apr. 21, 2016, in Cincinnati. Sluggers Kris Bryant (39 home runs, 102 RBI) and Anthony Rizzo (32 HR, 109 RBI) led the Chicago offense.

The Dodgers won their fourth straight NL West crown and came back to beat the Washington Nationals in five games in the NLDS. Dodgers ace starter Clayton Kershaw got the final two outs in relief to save L.A.'s 4-3 win over the Nationals in Game 5 Oct. 13 in Washington, DC. The Dodgers' legendary play-by-play announcer Vin Scully retired at the end of the season after 67 years. Nationals right-hander Max Scherzer topped the NL with 20 wins and 284 strikeouts and led Washington (95-67) to the NL East title. Miami Marlins outfielder Ichiro Suzuki, Aug. 7, reached the 3,000 career-hit milestone when he tripled at Coors Field in Denver, CO. But Miami was dealt a tragic blow when 24-year-old star pitcher José Fernández died in a boating accident Sept. 25.

Cleveland manager Terry Francona guided the team to their first American League title since 1997 by defeating the wild-card Toronto Blue Jays in five games in the AL Championship Series. Relief pitcher Andrew Miller, who recorded a save and 14 strikeouts in four ALCS appearances, was named series MVP. The Blue Jays reached the ALCS by belting eight homers in a three-game ALDS sweep of Texas. The Rangers won an AL-high 95 games; Cleveland (94-67) won the AL Central and swept the AL East champion Boston Red Sox in the ALDS. Boston's David Ortiz, a 20-year veteran who announced he would retire at season's end, hit 38 home runs, tied for the league lead with 127 RBI and ended with 541 career RBI.

The Baltimore Orioles topped the majors with 253 home runs, and the Orioles' Mark Trumbo led the majors with 47 home runs. Houston's Jose Altuve won his second career American League batting title with a .338 average and led the majors with 216 hits. Colorado's DJ LeMahieu won the NL batting crown (.348) and teammate Nolan Arenado led the majors with 133 RBI and tied Milwaukee's Chris Carter for the NL lead with 41 home runs. The NY Yankees in August released veteran third baseman Alex Rodriguez, who retired with 696 career home runs (fourth all-time).

National League Final Standings, 2016

(* = wild card)

Eastern Division

Team	W	L	PCT	GB	Home	Road	vs. East	vs. Central	vs. West	vs. AL
Washington.......	95	67	.586	—	50-31	45-36	51-25	17-16	15-18	12-8
NY Mets*	87	75	.537	8	44-37	43-38	40-36	22-10	13-21	12-8
Miami	79	82	.491	15.5	40-40	39-42	32-43	21-13	20-12	6-14
Philadelphia	71	91	.438	24	37-44	34-47	30-46	12-21	18-15	11-9
Atlanta	68	93	.422	26.5	31-50	37-43	36-39	13-20	11-22	8-12

Central Division

Team	W	L	PCT	GB	Home	Road	vs. East	vs. Central	vs. West	vs. AL
Chicago Cubs......	103	58	.640	—	57-24	46-34	19-14	50-25	19-14	15-5
St. Louis	86	76	.531	17.5	38-43	48-33	17-16	42-34	19-14	8-12
Pittsburgh	78	83	.484	25	38-42	40-41	14-19	33-42	22-11	9-11
Milwaukee........	73	89	.451	30.5	41-40	32-49	16-17	31-45	15-18	11-9
Cincinnati	68	94	.420	35.5	38-43	30-51	14-19	33-43	16-17	5-15

Western Division

Team	W	L	PCT	GB	Home	Road	vs. East	vs. Central	vs. West	vs. AL
L.A. Dodgers.......	91	71	.562	—	53-28	38-43	19-13	19-15	43-33	10-10
San Francisco*.....	87	75	.537	4	45-36	42-39	17-16	17-16	45-31	8-12
Colorado.........	75	87	.463	16	42-39	33-48	20-14	11-21	35-41	9-11
Arizona..........	69	93	.426	22	33-48	36-45	18-15	13-20	33-43	5-15
San Diego........	68	94	.420	23	39-42	29-52	14-19	14-19	34-42	6-14

American League Final Standings, 2016

(* = wild card)

Eastern Division

Team	W	L	PCT	GB	Home	Road	vs. East	vs. Central	vs. West	vs. NL
Boston	93	69	.574	—	47-34	46-35	43-33	15-18	21-12	14-6
Baltimore*........	89	73	.549	4	50-31	39-42	40-36	23-9	12-22	14-6
Toronto*.........	89	73	.549	4	46-35	43-38	40-36	18-15	18-15	13-7
NY Yankees	84	78	.519	9	48-33	36-45	35-41	21-12	20-13	8-12
Tampa Bay	68	94	.420	25	36-45	32-49	32-44	11-23	15-17	10-10

Central Division

Team	W	L	PCT	GB	Home	Road	vs. East	vs. Central	vs. West	vs. NL
Cleveland	94	67	.584	—	53-28	41-39	14-18	49-26	18-16	13-7
Detroit...........	86	75	.534	8	45-35	41-40	19-15	38-37	16-16	13-7
Kansas City	81	81	.500	13.5	47-34	34-47	15-17	46-30	10-24	10-10
Chicago White Sox ..	78	84	.481	16.5	45-36	33-48	19-14	32-44	18-15	9-11
Minnesota........	59	103	.364	35.5	30-51	29-52	10-24	24-52	17-15	8-12

Western Division

Team	W	L	PCT	GB	Home	Road	vs. East	vs. Central	vs. West	vs. NL
Texas	95	67	.586	—	53-28	42-39	16-17	19-14	47-29	13-7
Seattle	86	76	.531	9	44-37	42-39	19-13	16-18	38-38	13-7
Houston	84	78	.519	11	43-38	41-40	15-18	17-16	41-35	11-9
L.A. Angels	74	88	.457	21	40-41	34-47	13-21	17-15	35-41	9-11
Oakland	69	93	.426	26	34-47	35-46	16-17	17-16	29-47	7-13

National League Statistics, 2016

Individual statistics. Players recording fewer than 150 at-bats (batters) or fewer than 70 innings or 10 saves (pitchers) are not listed here. * = changed teams within NL during season; entry includes statistics for more than one team. # = changed teams to or from AL during season; entry includes only NL statistics. Team Batting and Team Pitching include players not shown separately.

Team Batting

Team	AVG	AB	R	H	HR	RBI
Colorado Rockies	.275	5,614	845	1,544	204	805
Miami Marlins.	.263	5,547	655	1,460	128	626
Arizona Diamondbacks. .	.261	5,665	752	1,479	190	709
San Francisco Giants . . .	.258	5,565	715	1,437	130	675
Pittsburgh Pirates	.257	5,542	729	1,426	153	696
Chicago Cubs.	.256	5,503	808	1,409	199	767
Cincinnati Reds	.256	5,487	716	1,403	164	678
Washington Nationals . .	.256	5,490	763	1,403	203	735
St. Louis Cardinals	.255	5,548	779	1,415	225	745
Atlanta Braves	.255	5,514	649	1,404	122	615
Los Angeles Dodgers . . .	.249	5,518	725	1,376	189	680
New York Mets	.246	5,459	671	1,342	218	649
Milwaukee Brewers.	.244	5,330	671	1,299	194	641
Philadelphia Phillies	.240	5,434	610	1,305	161	574
San Diego Padres	.235	5,419	686	1,275	177	654

Team Pitching

Team	ERA	IP	H	BB	SO	SV
Chicago Cubs.	3.15	1,459.2	1,125	495	1,441	38
Washington Nationals. . .	3.51	1,459.2	1,272	468	1,476	46
New York Mets	3.57	1,447.0	1,397	439	1,396	55
San Francisco Giants . . .	3.65	1,460.1	1,334	439	1,309	43
Los Angeles Dodgers . . .	3.70	1,453.0	1,266	464	1,510	47
Miami Marlins.	4.05	1,435.0	1,358	595	1,379	55
St. Louis Cardinals	4.08	1,448.1	1,432	475	1,290	38
Milwaukee Brewers.	4.08	1,434.1	1,450	532	1,175	46
Pittsburgh Pirates	4.21	1,450.2	1,490	533	1,232	51
San Diego Padres	4.43	1,440.0	1,425	569	1,222	35
Atlanta Braves	4.51	1,447.2	1,414	547	1,227	39
Philadelphia Phillies	4.63	1,437.0	1,468	466	1,299	43
Colorado Rockies	4.91	1,429.1	1,532	547	1,223	37
Cincinnati Reds	4.91	1,442.0	1,457	636	1,241	28
Arizona Diamondbacks. .	5.09	1,451.1	1,563	603	1,318	31

Arizona Diamondbacks

Batters	AVG	AB	R	H	HR	RBI	SO	SB
Jean Segura	.319	637	102	203	20	64	101	33
Paul Goldschmidt . .	.297	579	106	172	24	95	150	32
Brandon Drury	.282	461	59	130	16	53	100	1
Phil Gosselin.	.277	220	26	61	2	13	46	3
Chris Owings	.277	437	52	121	5	49	87	21
Yasmany Tomas . . .	.272	530	72	144	31	83	136	2
Welington Castillo. .	.264	416	41	110	14	68	121	2
Michael Bourn# . . .	.261	329	43	86	3	30	83	13
David Peralta	.251	171	23	43	4	15	42	2
Jake Lamb	.249	523	81	130	29	91	154	6
Rickie Weeks Jr. . .	.239	180	29	43	9	27	54	5
Nick Ahmed.	.218	284	26	62	4	20	58	5

Pitchers	ERA	W	L	IP	H	BB	SO	SV
Brad Ziegler#	2.82	2	3	38.1	41	15	27	18
Zach Greinke	4.37	13	7	158.2	161	41	134	0
Randall Delgado . . .	4.44	5	2	75.0	77	36	68	0
Robbie Ray	4.90	8	15	174.1	185	71	218	0
Archie Bradley	5.02	8	9	141.2	154	67	143	0
Patrick Corbin	5.15	5	13	155.2	177	66	131	1
Braden Shipley	5.27	4	5	70.0	80	28	43	0
Shelby Miller	6.15	3	12	101.0	127	42	70	0
Zack Godley	6.39	5	4	74.2	86	25	60	0

Manager: Chip Hale

Atlanta Braves

Batters	AVG	AB	R	H	HR	RBI	SO	SB
Freddie Freeman . .	.302	589	102	178	34	91	171	6
Ender Inciarte	.291	522	85	152	3	29	68	16
Adonis Garcia	.273	532	65	145	14	65	93	3
Tyler Flowers.	.270	281	27	76	8	41	91	0
Nick Markakis	.269	599	67	161	13	89	101	0
Matt Kemp*	.268	623	89	167	35	108	156	1
Jeff Francoeur*	.254	307	33	78	7	34	90	2
Jace Peterson	.254	350	45	89	7	29	69	5
Kelly Johnson*	.247	304	25	75	10	34	65	4
Chase d'Arnaud . . .	.245	233	24	57	1	21	50	9
Erick Aybar#	.242	335	27	81	2	26	59	3
Mallex Smith	.238	189	28	45	3	22	48	16
A.J. Pierzynski	.219	247	15	54	2	23	29	1
Gordon Beckham*. .	.212	245	25	52	5	31	52	1

Pitchers	ERA	W	L	IP	H	BB	SO	SV
Jim Johnson	3.06	2	6	64.2	57	20	68	20
Julio Teheran	3.21	7	10	188.0	157	41	167	0
Mike Foltynewicz . .	4.31	9	5	123.1	125	35	111	0
Arodys Vizcaino . . .	4.42	1	4	38.2	37	26	50	10
Matt Wisler	5.00	7	13	156.2	159	49	115	1
Bud Norris*	5.10	6	10	113.0	116	49	102	0
Aaron Blair	7.59	2	7	70.0	82	34	46	0

Manager: Fredi González, Brian Snitker

Chicago Cubs

Batters	AVG	AB	R	H	HR	RBI	SO	SB
Kris Bryant	.292	603	121	176	39	102	154	8
Anthony Rizzo	.292	583	94	170	32	109	108	3
Willson Contreras . .	.282	252	33	71	12	35	67	2
Dexter Fowler	.276	456	84	126	13	48	124	13
Javier Baez	.273	421	50	115	14	59	108	12
Ben Zobrist	.272	523	94	142	18	76	82	6
Matt Szczur	.259	185	30	48	5	24	39	2
Addison Russell . . .	.238	525	67	125	21	95	135	5
Jorge Soler	.238	227	37	54	12	31	66	0
Jason Heyward	.230	530	61	122	7	49	93	11
David Ross	.229	166	24	38	10	32	54	0
Miguel Montero	.216	241	33	52	8	33	58	1

Pitchers	ERA	W	L	IP	H	BB	SO	SV
Aroldis Chapman#. .	1.01	1	1	26.2	12	10	46	16
Kyle Hendricks	2.13	16	8	190.0	142	44	170	0
Jon Lester.	2.44	19	5	202.2	154	52	197	0
Jake Arrieta	3.10	18	8	197.1	138	76	190	0
John Lackey	3.35	11	8	188.1	146	53	180	0
Hector Rondon	3.53	2	3	51.0	42	8	58	18
Jason Hammel	3.83	15	10	166.2	148	53	144	0

Manager: Joe Maddon

Cincinnati Reds

Batters	AVG	AB	R	H	HR	RBI	SO	SB
Joey Votto	.326	556	101	181	29	97	120	8
Jose Peraza	.324	241	25	78	3	25	33	21
Brandon Phillips . . .	.291	550	74	160	11	64	68	14
Scott Schebler	.265	257	36	68	9	40	59	2
Billy Hamilton	.260	411	69	107	3	17	93	58
Tucker Barnhart . . .	.257	377	34	97	7	51	72	1
Ivan De Jesus Jr. . .	.253	221	21	56	1	20	51	3
Zack Cozart	.252	464	67	117	16	50	84	4
Jay Bruce*	.250	539	74	135	33	99	126	4
Eugenio Suarez . . .	.248	565	78	140	21	70	155	11
Ramon Cabrera . . .	.246	171	11	42	3	23	30	1
Adam Duvall	.241	552	85	133	33	103	164	6
Tyler Holt.	.235	179	21	42	0	13	48	4

Pitchers	ERA	W	L	IP	H	BB	SO	SV
Raisel Iglesias	2.53	3	2	78.1	63	26	83	6
Anthony DeSclafani	3.28	9	5	123.1	120	30	105	0
Dan Straily	3.76	14	8	191.1	154	73	162	0
Brandon Finnegan	3.98	10	11	172.0	150	84	145	0
Blake Wood	3.99	6	5	76.2	72	38	81	1
Tony Cingrani	4.14	2	5	63.0	54	37	49	17
John Lamb	6.43	1	7	70.0	84	31	58	0

Manager: Bryan Price

Colorado Rockies

Batters	AVG	AB	R	H	HR	RBI	SO	SB
DJ LeMahieu	.348	552	104	192	11	66	80	11
Charlie Blackmon . .	.324	578	111	187	29	82	102	17

Batters	AVG	AB	R	H	HR	RBI	SO	SB
David Dahl	.315	222	42	70	7	24	59	5
Carlos Gonzalez	.298	584	87	174	25	100	129	2
Nolan Arenado	.294	618	116	182	41	133	103	2
Mark Reynolds	.282	393	61	111	14	53	112	1
Trevor Story	.272	372	67	101	27	72	130	8
Daniel Descalso	.264	250	38	66	8	38	56	3
Nick Hundley	.260	289	30	75	10	48	65	0
Tony Wolters	.259	205	27	53	3	30	53	4
Gerardo Parra	.253	368	45	93	7	39	73	6
Ryan Raburn	.220	223	30	49	9	30	80	0
Cristhian Adames	.218	225	25	49	2	17	47	2

Pitchers	ERA	W	L	IP	H	BB	SO	SV
Tyler Anderson	3.54	5	6	114.1	119	28	99	0
Chris Rusin	3.74	3	5	84.1	82	23	69	0
Tyler Chatwood	3.87	12	9	158.0	147	70	117	0
Jon Gray	4.61	10	10	168.0	153	59	185	0
Jake McGee	4.73	2	3	45.2	56	16	38	15
Chad Bettis	4.79	14	8	186.0	204	59	138	0
Carlos Estevez	5.24	3	7	55.0	50	28	59	11
Jorge De La Rosa	5.51	8	9	134.0	157	63	108	0

Manager: Walt Weiss

Los Angeles Dodgers

Batters	AVG	AB	R	H	HR	RBI	SO	SB
Corey Seager	.308	627	105	193	26	72	133	3
Adrian Gonzalez	.285	568	69	162	18	90	117	0
Justin Turner	.275	556	79	153	27	90	107	4
Carlos Ruiz*	.264	201	21	53	3	15	33	3
Yasiel Puig	.263	334	45	88	11	45	74	5
Josh Reddick#	.258	155	20	40	2	9	22	3
Howie Kendrick	.255	487	65	124	8	40	96	10
Chase Utley	.252	512	79	129	14	52	115	2
Joc Pederson	.246	406	64	100	25	68	130	6
Yasmani Grandal	.228	390	49	89	27	72	116	1
Trayce Thompson	.225	236	31	53	13	32	66	5
A.J. Ellis*	.216	171	11	37	2	22	31	2
Enrique Hernandez	.190	216	25	41	7	18	64	2

Pitchers	ERA	W	L	IP	H	BB	SO	SV
Clayton Kershaw	1.69	12	4	149.0	97	11	172	0
Kenley Jansen	1.83	3	2	68.2	35	11	104	47
Joe Blanton	2.48	7	2	80.0	55	26	80	0
Pedro Baez	3.04	3	2	74.0	52	22	83	0
Julio Urias	3.39	5	2	77.0	81	31	84	0
Kenta Maeda	3.48	16	11	175.2	150	50	179	0
Ross Stripling	3.96	5	9	100.0	96	30	74	0
Scott Kazmir	4.56	10	6	136.1	133	52	134	0
Bud Norris*	5.10	6	10	113.0	116	49	102	0

Manager: Dave Roberts

Miami Marlins

Batters	AVG	AB	R	H	HR	RBI	SO	SB
Martin Prado	.305	600	70	183	8	75	69	2
J.T. Realmuto	.303	509	60	154	11	48	100	12
Christian Yelich	.298	578	78	172	21	98	138	9
Ichiro Suzuki	.291	327	48	95	1	22	42	10
Derek Dietrich	.279	351	39	98	7	42	84	1
Dee Gordon	.268	325	47	87	1	14	55	30
Marcell Ozuna	.266	557	75	148	23	76	115	0
Justin Bour	.264	280	35	74	15	51	56	0
Jeff Francoeur*	.254	307	33	78	7	34	90	2
Miguel Rojas	.247	194	27	48	1	14	27	2
Giancarlo Stanton	.240	413	56	99	27	74	140	0
Adeiny Hechavarria	.236	508	52	120	3	38	73	1
Chris Johnson	.222	243	20	54	5	24	78	0

Pitchers	ERA	W	L	IP	H	BB	SO	SV
David Phelps	2.28	7	6	86.2	61	38	114	4
A.J. Ramos	2.81	1	4	64.0	52	35	73	40
Kyle Barraclough	2.85	6	3	72.2	45	44	113	0
José Fernández	2.86	16	8	182.1	149	55	253	0
Fernando Rodney*	3.44	2	4	65.1	54	37	74	25
Adam Conley	3.85	8	6	133.1	125	62	124	0
Paul Clemens*	4.04	4	5	71.1	72	31	53	0
Tom Koehler	4.33	9	13	176.2	176	83	147	0
Colin Rea*	4.82	5	5	102.2	102	44	80	0

Pitchers	ERA	W	L	IP	H	BB	SO	SV
Wei-Yin Chen	4.96	5	5	123.1	134	24	100	0
Justin Nicolino	4.99	3	6	79.1	96	20	37	0
Andrew Cashner*	5.25	5	11	132.0	142	60	112	0
Edwin Jackson*	5.89	5	7	84.0	92	41	61	0
Jose Urena	6.13	4	9	83.2	91	29	58	1

Managers: Don Mattingly

Milwaukee Brewers

Batters	AVG	AB	R	H	HR	RBI	SO	SB
Ryan Braun	.305	511	80	156	30	91	98	16
Jonathan Lucroy#	.299	338	48	101	13	50	70	5
Jonathan Villar	.285	589	92	168	19	63	174	62
Aaron Hill#	.283	254	34	72	8	29	43	4
Hernan Perez	.272	404	50	110	13	56	94	34
Scooter Gennett	.263	498	58	131	14	56	114	8
Domingo Santana	.256	246	34	63	11	32	91	2
Keon Broxton	.242	207	28	50	9	19	88	23
Chris Carter	.222	549	84	122	41	94	206	3
Orlando Arcia	.219	201	21	44	4	17	47	8
Kirk Nieuwenhuis	.209	335	38	70	13	44	133	8
Ramon Flores	.205	249	18	51	2	19	58	3
Martin Maldonado	.202	208	21	42	8	21	56	1

Pitchers	ERA	W	L	IP	H	BB	SO	SV
Tyler Thornburg	2.15	8	5	67.0	38	25	90	13
Jeremy Jeffress#	2.22	2	2	44.2	45	11	35	27
Carlos Torres	2.73	3	3	82.1	65	30	78	2
Junior Guerra	2.81	9	3	121.2	94	43	100	0
Zach Davies	3.97	11	7	163.1	166	38	135	0
Chase Anderson	4.39	9	11	151.2	155	53	120	0
Matt Garza	4.51	6	8	101.2	117	36	70	0
Jimmy Nelson	4.62	8	16	179.1	186	86	140	0
Wily Peralta	4.86	7	11	127.2	152	43	93	0

Managers: Craig Counsell

New York Mets

Batters	AVG	AB	R	H	HR	RBI	SO	SB
Neil Walker	.282	412	57	116	23	55	84	3
Yoenis Cespedes	.280	479	72	134	31	86	108	3
Asdrubal Cabrera	.280	521	65	146	23	62	103	5
Wilmer Flores	.267	307	38	82	16	49	48	1
Jose Reyes	.267	255	45	68	8	24	49	9
James Loney	.265	343	30	91	9	34	37	0
Jay Bruce*	.250	539	74	135	33	99	126	4
Kelly Johnson*	.247	304	25	75	10	34	65	4
Travis d'Arnaud	.247	251	27	62	4	15	50	0
Curtis Granderson	.237	545	88	129	30	59	130	4
Lucas Duda	.229	153	20	35	7	23	36	0
Rene Rivera	.222	185	12	41	6	26	54	0
Michael Conforto	.220	304	38	67	12	42	89	2
Alejandro De Aza	.205	234	31	48	6	25	67	4

Pitchers	ERA	W	L	IP	H	BB	SO	SV
Addison Reed	1.97	4	2	77.2	60	13	91	1
Jeurys Familia	2.55	3	4	77.2	63	31	84	51
Noah Syndergaard	2.60	14	9	183.2	168	43	218	0
Jacob deGrom	3.04	7	8	148.0	142	36	143	0
Steven Matz	3.40	9	8	132.1	129	31	129	0
Bartolo Colon	3.43	15	8	191.2	200	32	128	0
Hansel Robles	3.48	6	4	77.2	69	36	85	1
Matt Harvey	4.86	4	10	92.2	111	25	76	0
Logan Verrett	5.20	3	8	91.2	100	43	66	0
Jonathon Niese*	5.50	8	7	121.0	145	47	88	0

Manager: Terry Collins

Philadelphia Phillies

Batters	AVG	AB	R	H	HR	RBI	SO	SB
Cesar Hernandez	.294	547	67	161	6	39	116	17
Odubel Herrera	.286	583	87	167	15	49	134	25
Carlos Ruiz*	.264	201	21	53	3	15	33	3
Tommy Joseph	.257	315	47	81	21	47	75	1
Maikel Franco	.255	581	67	148	25	88	106	1
Andres Blanco	.253	190	26	48	4	21	41	2
Cameron Rupp	.252	389	36	98	16	54	114	1

Batters	AVG	AB	R	H	HR	RBI	SO	SB
Peter Bourjos	.251	355	40	89	5	23	91	6
Freddy Galvis	.241	584	61	141	20	67	136	17
A.J. Ellis*........	.216	171	11	37	2	22	31	2
Cody Asche	.213	197	22	42	4	18	54	3
Aaron Altherr.......	.197	198	23	39	4	22	69	7
Ryan Howard	.196	331	35	65	25	59	114	0
Tyler Goeddel	.192	213	17	41	4	16	52	3

Pitchers	ERA	W	L	IP	H	BB	SO	SV
Hector Neris	2.58	4	4	80.1	59	30	102	2
Jerad Eickhoff....	3.65	11	14	197.1	187	42	167	0
Jeremy Hellickson...	3.71	12	10	189.0	173	45	154	0
David Hernandez ...	3.84	3	4	72.2	77	32	80	1
Vince Velasquez....	4.12	8	6	131.0	129	45	152	0
Aaron Nola	4.78	6	9	111.0	116	29	121	0
Jeanmar Gomez	4.85	3	5	68.2	78	22	47	37
Adam Morgan	6.04	2	11	113.1	141	29	95	0

Managers: Pete Mackanin

Pittsburgh Pirates

Batters	AVG	AB	R	H	HR	RBI	SO	SB
Starling Marte......	.311	489	71	152	9	46	104	47
Josh Harrison	.283	487	57	138	4	59	76	19
David Freese	.270	437	63	118	13	55	142	0
Sean Rodriguez	.270	300	49	81	18	56	102	2
John Jaso	.268	380	45	102	8	42	74	0
Francisco Cervelli ...	.264	326	42	86	1	33	72	6
Gregory Polanco....	.258	527	79	136	22	86	119	17
Andrew McCutchen..	.256	598	81	153	24	79	143	6
Jordy Mercer....	.256	519	66	133	11	59	83	1
Jung Ho Kang......	.255	318	45	81	21	62	79	3
Matt Joyce.........	.242	231	45	56	13	42	67	1

Pitchers	ERA	W	L	IP	H	BB	SO	SV
Mark Melancon*	1.64	2	2	71.1	52	12	65	47
Tony Watson.......	3.06	2	5	67.2	52	20	58	15
Jameson Taillon ...	3.38	5	4	104.0	99	17	85	0
Gerrit Cole	3.88	7	10	116.0	131	36	98	0
Felipe Rivero*	4.09	1	6	77.0	66	33	92	1
Chad Kuhl.........	4.20	5	4	70.2	73	20	53	0
Juan Nicasio.......	4.50	10	7	118.0	117	45	138	0
Ryan Vogelsong ...	4.81	3	7	82.1	80	40	61	0
Jeff Locke	5.44	9	8	127.1	151	44	73	0
Francisco Liriano# ..	5.46	6	11	113.2	115	69	116	0
Jonathon Niese*....	5.50	8	7	121.0	145	47	88	0

Manager: Clint Hurdle

San Diego Padres

Batters	AVG	AB	R	H	HR	RBI	SO	SB
Jon Jay	.291	347	49	101	2	26	78	2
Yangervis Solarte ...	.286	405	55	116	15	71	63	1
Matt Kemp*.........	.268	623	89	167	35	108	156	1
Wil Myers	.259	599	99	155	28	94	160	28
Alex Dickerson	.257	253	39	65	10	37	44	5
Melvin Upton Jr.# ...	.256	344	46	88	16	45	106	20
Travis Jankowski....	.245	335	53	82	2	12	100	30
Alexei Ramirez#	.240	421	33	101	5	41	56	6
Adam Rosales	.229	214	37	49	13	35	88	4
Christian								
Bethancourt ...	.228	193	20	44	6	25	56	1
Ryan Schimpf	.217	276	48	60	20	51	105	1
Brett Wallace.......	.189	217	19	41	6	20	83	0
Derek Norris	.186	415	50	77	14	42	139	9

Pitchers	ERA	W	L	IP	H	BB	SO	SV
Drew Pomeranz# ...	2.47	8	7	102.0	67	41	115	0
Brad Hand	2.92	4	4	89.1	63	36	111	1
Fernando Rodney* ..	3.44	2	4	65.1	54	37	74	25
Paul Clemens*	4.04	4	5	71.1	72	31	53	0
Brandon Maurer	4.52	0	5	69.2	65	23	72	13
Christian Friedrich...	4.80	5	12	129.1	131	52	100	0
Colin Rea*	4.82	5	5	102.2	102	44	80	0
Andrew Cashner* ...	5.25	5	11	132.0	142	60	112	0
Luis Perdomo	5.71	9	10	146.2	187	46	105	0
Edwin Jackson*	5.89	5	7	84.0	92	41	61	0
Carlos Villanueva ...	5.96	2	2	74.0	89	14	61	1

Managers: Andy Green

San Francisco Giants

Batters	AVG	AB	R	H	HR	RBI	SO	SB
Hunter Pence	.289	395	58	114	13	57	95	1
Buster Posey	.288	539	82	155	14	80	68	6
Angel Pagan........	.277	495	71	137	12	55	66	15
Brandon Belt.......	.275	542	77	149	17	82	148	0
Brandon Crawford...	.275	553	67	152	12	84	115	7
Eduardo Nunez#.....	.269	182	24	49	4	20	30	13
Denard Span	.266	572	70	152	11	53	79	12
Conor Gillaspie.....	.262	191	24	50	6	25	28	1
Matt Duffy#	.253	257	32	65	4	21	40	4
Joe Panik	.239	464	67	111	10	62	47	5
Trevor Brown.......	.237	173	17	41	5	19	39	0
Gregor Blanco	.224	241	28	54	1	18	51	6
Gordon Beckham*...	.212	245	25	52	5	31	52	1

Pitchers	ERA	W	L	IP	H	BB	SO	SV
Madison Bumgarner	2.74	15	9	226.2	179	54	251	0
Johnny Cueto	2.79	18	5	219.2	195	45	198	0
Santiago Casilla ...	3.57	2	5	58.0	50	19	65	31
Jeff Samardzija.....	3.81	12	11	203.1	190	54	167	0
Albert Suarez	4.29	3	5	84.0	84	26	54	0
Josh Osich	4.71	1	3	36.1	31	19	25	0
Jake Peavy	5.54	5	9	118.2	134	36	102	0
Matt Cain	5.64	4	8	89.1	103	32	72	0

Manager: Bruce Bochy

St. Louis Cardinals

Batters	AVG	AB	R	H	HR	RBI	SO	SB
Yadier Molina	.307	534	56	164	8	58	63	3
Aledmys Diaz	.300	404	71	121	17	65	60	4
Greg Garcia	.276	214	33	59	3	17	50	1
Stephen Piscotty....	.273	582	86	159	22	85	133	7
Matt Carpenter	.271	473	81	128	21	68	108	0
Jhonny Peralta	.260	289	37	75	8	29	56	0
Matt Adams........	.249	297	37	74	16	54	81	0
Matt Holliday.......	.246	382	48	94	20	62	71	0
Jedd Gyorko	.243	400	58	97	30	59	96	0
Randal Grichuk.....	.240	446	66	107	24	68	141	5
Kolten Wong	.240	313	39	75	5	23	52	7
Jeremy Hazelbaker..	.235	200	35	47	12	28	64	5
Tommy Pham	.226	159	26	36	9	17	71	2
Brandon Moss	.225	413	66	93	28	67	141	1

Pitchers	ERA	W	L	IP	H	BB	SO	SV
Seung Hwan Oh	1.92	6	3	79.2	55	18	103	19
Carlos Martinez	3.04	16	9	195.1	169	70	174	0
Trevor Rosenthal....	4.46	2	4	40.1	48	29	56	14
Adam Wainwright ...	4.62	13	9	198.2	220	59	161	0
Jaime Garcia	4.67	10	13	171.2	179	57	150	0
Mike Leake	4.69	9	12	176.2	203	30	125	0
Michael Wacha	5.09	7	7	138.0	159	45	114	0

Manager: Mike Matheny

Washington Nationals

Batters	AVG	AB	R	H	HR	RBI	SO	SB
Daniel Murphy	.347	531	88	184	25	104	57	5
Trea Turner	.342	307	53	105	13	40	59	33
Wilson Ramos	.307	482	58	148	22	80	79	0
Anthony Rendon....	.270	567	91	153	20	85	117	12
Jayson Werth	.244	525	84	128	21	69	139	5
Bryce Harper	.243	506	84	123	24	86	117	21
Clint Robinson	.235	196	16	46	5	26	38	0
Michael Taylor.....	.231	221	28	51	7	16	77	14
Ryan Zimmerman....	.218	427	60	93	15	46	104	4
Ben Revere........	.217	350	44	76	2	24	34	14
Danny Espinosa	.209	516	66	108	24	72	174	9

Pitchers	ERA	W	L	IP	H	BB	SO	SV
Mark Melancon*	1.64	2	2	71.1	52	12	65	47
Tanner Roark	2.83	16	10	210.0	173	73	172	0
Max Scherzer	2.96	20	7	228.1	165	56	284	0
Joe Ross..........	3.43	7	5	105.0	108	29	93	0
Stephen Strasburg...	3.60	15	4	147.2	119	44	183	0
Felipe Rivero*......	4.09	1	6	77.0	66	33	92	1
Jonathan Papelbon..	4.37	2	4	35.0	37	14	31	19
Gio Gonzalez	4.57	11	11	177.1	179	59	171	0

Manager: Dusty Baker

American League Statistics, 2016

Individual statistics. Players recording fewer than 150 at-bats (batters) or fewer than 70 innings or 10 saves (pitchers) are not listed here. * = Changed teams within AL during season; entry includes statistics for more than one team. # = Changed teams to or from NL during season; entry includes only AL statistics. Team Batting and Team Pitching include players not shown separately.

Team Batting

Team	AVG	AB	R	H	HR	RBI
Boston Red Sox	.282	5,670	878	1,598	208	836
Detroit Tigers	.267	5,526	750	1,476	211	719
Texas Rangers	.262	5,525	765	1,446	215	746
Cleveland Indians	.262	5,484	777	1,435	185	733
Kansas City Royals. . .	.261	5,552	675	1,450	147	640
Los Angeles Angels . .	.260	5,431	717	1,410	156	686
Seattle Mariners	.259	5,583	768	1,446	223	735
Chicago White Sox . . .	.257	5,550	686	1,428	168	656
Baltimore Orioles	.256	5,524	744	1,413	253	710
New York Yankees. . . .	.252	5,458	680	1,378	183	647
Minnesota Twins	.251	5,618	722	1,409	200	690
Toronto Blue Jays	.248	5,479	759	1,358	221	728
Houston Astros	.247	5,545	724	1,367	198	689
Oakland Athletics	.246	5,500	653	1,352	169	634
Tampa Bay Rays.	.243	5,481	672	1,333	216	647

Team Pitching

Team	ERA	IP	H	BB	SO	SV
Toronto Blue Jays	3.78	1,459.1	1,340	461	1,314	43
Cleveland Indians	3.84	1,445.0	1,330	461	1,398	37
Seattle Mariners	4.00	1,457.0	1,410	460	1,318	49
Boston Red Sox	4.00	1,439.2	1,342	490	1,362	43
Houston Astros	4.06	1,468.0	1,441	453	1,396	44
Chicago White Sox . . .	4.10	1,446.2	1,422	521	1,270	43
New York Yankees. . . .	4.16	1,428.1	1,358	444	1,393	48
Tampa Bay Rays.	4.20	1,426.1	1,395	491	1,357	42
Kansas City Royals. . .	4.21	1,440.0	1,433	517	1,287	41
Baltimore Orioles	4.22	1,432.0	1,408	545	1,248	54
Detroit Tigers	4.24	1,428.0	1,417	462	1,232	47
Los Angeles Angels . .	4.28	1,421.1	1,480	498	1,136	29
Texas Rangers	4.37	1,443.0	1,441	534	1,154	56
Oakland Athletics	4.51	1,433.1	1,459	464	1,188	42
Minnesota Twins	5.08	1,443.0	1,617	479	1,191	26

Baltimore Orioles

Batters	AVG	AB	R	H	HR	RBI	SO	SB
Hyun Soo Kim	.302	305	36	92	6	22	51	1
Manny Machado . . .	.294	640	105	188	37	96	120	0
Steve Pearce*	.288	264	35	76	13	35	54	0
J.J. Hardy.	.269	405	43	109	9	48	68	0
Joey Rickard	.268	257	32	69	5	19	54	4
Jonathan Schoop. . .	.267	615	82	164	25	82	137	1
Adam Jones	.265	619	86	164	29	83	115	2
Mark Trumbo	.256	613	94	157	47	108	170	2
Pedro Alvarez.	.249	337	43	84	22	49	97	1
Matt Wieters.	.243	423	48	103	17	66	85	1
Nolan Reimold.	.222	203	25	45	6	15	62	1
Chris Davis	.221	566	99	125	38	84	219	1
Ryan Flaherty	.217	157	16	34	3	15	48	2

Pitchers	ERA	W	L	IP	H	BB	SO	SV
Zach Britton	0.54	2	1	67.0	38	18	74	47
Brad Brach	2.05	10	4	79.0	57	25	92	2
Mychal Givens.	3.13	8	2	74.2	59	36	96	0
Vance Worley.	3.53	2	2	86.2	84	35	56	1
Kevin Gausman	3.61	9	12	179.2	183	47	174	0
Chris Tillman	3.77	16	6	172.0	155	66	140	0
Dylan Bundy	4.02	10	6	109.2	109	42	104	0
Tyler Wilson	5.27	4	6	94.0	110	24	55	0
Wade Miley*	5.37	9	13	166.0	187	49	137	0
Yovani Gallardo	5.42	6	8	118.0	126	61	85	0
Ubaldo Jimenez. . . .	5.44	8	12	142.1	150	72	125	1
Mike Wright	5.79	3	4	74.2	81	26	50	0

Manager: Buck Showalter

Boston Red Sox

Batters	AVG	AB	R	H	HR	RBI	SO	SB
Mookie Betts	.318	672	122	214	31	113	80	26
Dustin Pedroia	.318	633	105	201	15	74	73	7
David Ortiz.	.315	537	79	169	38	127	86	2
Sandy Leon	.310	252	36	78	7	35	66	0
Xander Bogaerts . . .	.294	652	115	192	21	89	123	13
Hanley Ramirez	.286	549	81	157	30	111	120	9
Chris Young	.276	203	29	56	9	24	50	4
Jackie Bradley Jr. . .	.267	558	94	149	26	87	143	9
Brock Holt	.255	290	45	74	7	34	58	4
Travis Shaw	.242	480	63	116	16	71	133	5
Christian Vazquez . .	.227	172	21	39	1	12	39	0

Pitchers	ERA	W	L	IP	H	BB	SO	SV
Rick Porcello	3.15	22	4	223.0	193	32	189	0
Steven Wright	3.33	13	6	156.2	138	57	127	0
Craig Kimbrel	3.40	2	6	53.0	28	30	83	31

Team Pitching

Pitchers	ERA	W	L	IP	H	BB	SO	SV
David Price	3.99	17	9	230.0	227	50	228	0
Eduardo Rodriguez. .	4.71	3	7	107.0	99	40	100	0
Clay Buchholz.	4.78	8	10	139.1	130	55	93	0

Manager: John Farrell

Chicago White Sox

Batters	AVG	AB	R	H	HR	RBI	SO	SB
Melky Cabrera	.296	591	70	175	14	86	69	2
Jose Abreu	.293	624	67	183	25	100	125	0
Adam Eaton	.284	619	91	176	14	59	115	14
Tim Anderson	.283	410	57	116	9	30	117	10
Tyler Saladino	.282	298	33	84	8	38	62	11
Justin Morneau.	.261	203	16	53	6	25	52	0
Austin Jackson	.254	181	24	46	0	18	39	2
Brett Lawrie.	.248	351	35	87	12	36	109	7
Avisail Garcia	.245	413	59	101	12	51	115	4
Todd Frazier	.225	590	89	133	40	98	163	15
Alex Avila	.213	169	19	36	7	11	78	0
Dioner Navarro*	.207	304	26	63	6	35	71	1
Carlos Sanchez	.208	154	15	32	4	21	42	0
J.B. Shuck.	.205	224	27	46	4	14	21	3

Pitchers	ERA	W	L	IP	H	BB	SO	SV
Nate Jones	2.29	5	3	70.2	48	15	80	3
Jose Quintana	3.20	13	12	208.0	192	50	181	0
Chris Sale.	3.34	17	10	226.2	190	45	233	0
David Robertson. . . .	3.47	5	3	62.1	53	32	75	37
Miguel Gonzalez	3.73	5	8	135.0	132	35	95	0
Carlos Rodon	4.04	9	10	165.0	176	54	168	0
James Shields#	6.77	4	12	114.1	139	55	78	0

Manager: Robin Ventura

Cleveland Indians

Batters	AVG	AB	R	H	HR	RBI	SO	SB
Jose Ramirez	.312	565	84	176	11	76	62	22
Francisco Lindor	.301	604	99	182	15	78	88	19
Tyler Naquin	.296	321	52	95	14	43	112	6
Lonnie Chisenhall. . .	.286	385	43	110	8	57	70	6
Jason Kipnis	.275	610	91	168	23	82	146	15
Brandon Guyer*	.266	293	39	78	9	32	55	3
Abraham Almonte . . .	.264	182	24	48	1	22	42	8
Carlos Santana	.259	582	89	151	34	87	99	5
Rajai Davis	.249	454	74	113	12	48	106	43
Mike Napoli	.239	557	92	133	34	101	194	5
Coco Crisp*	.231	446	54	103	13	55	78	10
Juan Uribe	.206	238	19	49	7	25	49	0
Roberto Perez	.183	153	14	28	3	17	44	0
Yan Gomes	.167	251	22	42	9	34	69	0

Pitchers	ERA	W	L	IP	H	BB	SO	SV
Andrew Miller*......	1.45	10	1	74.1	42	9	123	12
Dan Otero.........	1.53	5	1	70.2	54	10	57	1
Cody Allen	2.51	3	5	68.0	41	27	87	32
Corey Kluber.......	3.14	18	9	215.0	170	57	227	0
Carlos Carrasco	3.32	11	8	146.1	134	34	150	0
Danny Salazar	3.87	11	6	137.1	121	63	161	0
Trevor Bauer	4.26	12	8	190.0	179	70	168	0
Josh Tomlin........	4.40	13	9	174.0	187	20	118	0

Manager: Terry Francona

Pitchers	ERA	W	L	IP	H	BB	SO	SV
Wade Davis	1.87	2	1	43.1	33	16	47	27
Kelvin Herrera.....	2.75	2	6	72.0	57	12	86	12
Danny Duffy	3.51	12	3	179.2	163	42	188	0
Ian Kennedy	3.68	11	11	195.2	173	66	184	0
Yordano Ventura	4.45	11	12	186.0	190	78	144	0
Dillon Gee.........	4.68	8	9	125.0	146	37	89	0
Edinson Volquez	5.37	10	11	189.1	217	76	139	0
Chris Young........	6.19	3	9	88.2	104	43	94	1

Manager: Ned Yost

Detroit Tigers

Batters	AVG	AB	R	H	HR	RBI	SO	SB
Miguel Cabrera.....	.316	595	92	188	38	108	116	0
Cameron Maybin ...	.315	349	65	110	4	43	69	15
J.D. Martinez.......	.307	460	69	141	22	68	128	1
Victor Martinez	.289	553	65	160	27	86	90	0
Ian Kinsler.........	.288	618	117	178	28	83	115	14
Nick Castellanos....	.285	411	54	117	18	58	111	1
Jose Iglesias.......	.255	467	57	119	4	32	50	7
Justin Upton.......	.246	570	81	140	31	87	179	9
Bobby Wilson*	.237	228	25	54	7	33	64	0
Andrew Romine	.236	174	21	41	2	16	38	8
James McCann.....	.221	344	31	76	12	48	109	0
Mike Aviles	.210	167	17	35	1	6	27	2
Jarrod Saltalamacchia ...	.171	246	30	42	12	38	104	0

Pitchers	ERA	W	L	IP	H	BB	SO	SV
Alex Wilson........	2.96	4	0	73.0	68	21	49	0
Justin Verlander	3.04	16	9	227.2	171	57	254	0
Michael Fulmer.....	3.06	11	7	159.0	136	42	132	0
Francisco Rodriguez	3.24	3	4	58.1	45	21	52	44
Matt Boyd	4.53	6	5	97.1	97	29	82	0
Jordan Zimmermann	4.87	9	7	105.1	118	26	66	0
Mike Pelfrey	5.07	4	10	119.0	160	46	56	0
Anibal Sanchez.....	5.87	7	13	153.1	171	53	135	0

Manager: Brad Ausmus

Los Angeles Angels

Batters	AVG	AB	R	H	HR	RBI	SO	SB
Mike Trout	.315	549	123	173	29	100	137	30
Yunel Escobar......	.304	517	68	157	5	39	67	0
Andrelton Simmons	.281	448	48	126	4	44	38	10
C.J. Cron..........	.278	407	51	113	16	69	75	2
Kole Calhoun	.271	594	91	161	18	75	118	2
Albert Pujols	.268	593	71	159	31	119	75	4
Johnny Giavotella ...	.260	346	44	90	6	31	39	4
Jefry Marte	.252	258	38	65	15	44	59	2
Gregorio Petit	.245	204	21	50	2	17	51	1
Jett Bandy	.234	209	23	49	8	25	38	1
Rafael Ortega	.232	185	24	43	1	16	23	8
Cliff Pennington....	.209	172	18	36	3	10	55	1
Carlos Perez.......	.209	268	25	56	5	31	49	1

Pitchers	ERA	W	L	IP	H	BB	SO	SV
Matt Shoemaker	3.88	9	13	160.0	166	30	143	0
Ricky Nolasco*.....	4.42	8	14	197.2	202	44	144	0
Jhoulys Chacin#....	4.68	5	6	117.1	124	47	92	0
Hector Santiago* ...	4.70	13	10	182.0	169	79	144	0
Jered Weaver	5.06	12	12	178.0	209	51	103	0

Manager: Mike Scioscia

Houston Astros

Batters	AVG	AB	R	H	HR	RBI	SO	SB
Jose Altuve........	.338	640	108	216	24	96	70	30
Carlos Correa......	.274	577	76	158	20	96	139	13
Alex Bregman......	.264	201	31	53	8	34	52	2
George Springer....	.261	644	116	168	29	82	178	9
Luis Valbuena	.260	292	38	76	13	40	81	1
Marwin Gonzalez ...	.254	484	55	123	13	51	118	12
Evan Gattis........	.251	447	58	112	32	72	127	2
Tyler White	.217	249	24	54	8	28	65	1
Carlos Gomez*.....	.231	411	45	95	13	53	136	18
Jason Castro.......	.210	329	41	69	11	32	123	2
Jake Marisnick	.209	287	40	60	5	21	83	10
Colby Rasmus	.206	369	38	76	15	54	121	4

Pitchers	ERA	W	L	IP	H	BB	SO	SV
Chris Devenski	2.16	4	4	108.1	79	20	104	1
Will Harris........	2.25	1	2	64.0	52	15	69	12
Lance McCullers....	3.22	6	5	81.0	80	45	106	0
Luke Gregerson	3.28	4	3	57.2	38	18	67	15
Scott Feldman*.....	3.97	7	4	77.0	87	19	56	0
Ken Giles	4.11	2	5	65.2	60	25	102	15
Collin McHugh	4.34	13	10	184.2	206	54	177	0
Mike Fiers........	4.48	11	8	168.2	187	42	134	0
Dallas Keuchel	4.55	9	12	168.0	168	48	144	0
Doug Fister	4.64	12	13	180.1	195	62	115	0

Manager: A. J. Hinch

Minnesota Twins

Batters	AVG	AB	R	H	HR	RBI	SO	SB
Eduardo Nunez#....	.296	371	49	110	12	47	58	27
Jorge Polanco......	.282	245	24	69	4	27	46	4
Robbie Grossman..	.280	332	49	93	11	37	96	2
Eddie Rosario......	.269	335	52	90	10	32	91	5
Brian Dozier	.268	615	104	165	42	99	138	18
Juan Centeno	.261	176	16	46	3	25	38	0
Joe Mauer.........	.261	494	68	129	11	49	93	2
Trevor Plouffe	.260	319	35	83	12	47	60	1
Kurt Suzuki.......	.258	345	34	89	8	49	48	0
Danny Santana.....	.240	233	29	56	2	14	55	12
Eduardo Escobar ...	.236	352	32	83	6	37	72	1
Miguel Sano.......	.236	437	57	103	25	66	178	1
Max Kepler	.235	396	52	93	17	63	93	6
Kennys Vargas	.230	152	27	35	10	20	57	0
Oswaldo Arcia#*.....	.229	157	15	36	6	19	65	1
Byron Buxton	.225	298	44	67	10	38	118	10
Byung-ho Park	.191	215	28	41	12	24	80	1

Pitchers	ERA	W	L	IP	H	BB	SO	SV
Brandon Kintzler....	3.15	0	2	54.1	59	8	35	17
Ervin Santana......	3.38	7	11	181.1	168	53	149	0
Ryan Pressly.......	3.70	6	7	75.1	79	23	67	1
Ricky Nolasco*.....	4.42	8	14	197.2	202	44	144	0
Hector Santiago* ...	4.70	13	10	182.0	169	79	144	0
Michael Tonkin	5.02	3	2	71.2	80	24	80	0
Kyle Gibson	5.07	6	11	147.1	175	55	104	0
Tyler Duffey	6.43	9	12	133.0	167	32	114	0

Manager: Paul Molitor

Kansas City Royals

Batters	AVG	AB	R	H	HR	RBI	SO	SB
Paulo Orlando......	.302	457	52	138	5	43	105	14
Lorenzo Cain	.287	397	56	114	9	56	84	14
Whit Merrifield.....	.283	311	44	88	2	29	72	8
Jarrod Dyson	.278	299	46	83	1	25	39	30
Cheslor Cuthbert ...	.274	475	49	130	12	46	96	2
Eric Hosmer	.266	605	80	161	25	104	132	5
Kendrys Morales ...	.263	558	65	147	30	93	120	0
Alcides Escobar	.261	637	57	166	7	55	96	17
Salvador Pérez	.247	514	57	127	22	64	119	0
Billy Burns*........	.235	311	39	73	0	13	37	17
Alex Gordon	.220	445	62	98	17	40	148	8
Brett Eibner*	.193	187	21	36	6	22	50	0

New York Yankees

Batters	AVG	AB	R	H	HR	RBI	SO	SB
Gary Sanchez......	.299	201	34	60	20	42	57	1
Carlos Beltran*.....	.295	552	73	163	29	93	101	1
Billy Butler*.......	.284	250	27	71	5	35	42	0
Didi Gregorius......	.276	562	68	155	20	70	82	7
Starlin Castro	.270	577	63	156	21	70	118	4
Jacoby Ellsbury	.263	551	71	145	9	56	84	20
Brett Gardner	.261	547	80	143	7	41	106	16
Ronald Torreyes ...	.258	155	20	40	1	12	20	2
Chase Headley.....	.253	467	58	118	14	51	118	8
Rob Refsnyder	.250	152	25	38	0	12	30	2
Brian McCann	.242	429	56	104	20	58	99	1
Austin Romine	.242	165	17	40	4	26	31	1

Batters	AVG	AB	R	H	HR	RBI	SO	SB
Aaron Hicks	.217	327	32	71	8	31	68	3
Mark Teixeira	.204	387	43	79	15	44	105	2
Alex Rodriguez	.200	225	19	45	9	31	67	3

Pitchers	ERA	W	L	IP	H	BB	SO	SV
Andrew Miller*	1.45	10	1	74.1	42	9	123	12
Aroldis Chapman#	2.01	3	0	31.1	20	8	44	20
Masahiro Tanaka	3.07	14	4	199.2	179	36	165	0
Dellin Betances	3.08	3	6	73.0	54	28	126	12
CC Sabathia	3.91	9	12	179.2	172	65	152	0
Luis Cessa	4.35	4	4	70.1	64	14	46	0
Nathan Eovaldi	4.76	9	8	124.2	123	40	97	0
Michael Pineda	4.82	6	12	175.2	184	53	207	0
Ivan Nova#	4.90	7	6	97.1	107	25	75	1
Luis Severino	5.83	3	8	71.0	78	25	66	0

Manager: Joe Girardi

Oakland Athletics

Batters	AVG	AB	R	H	HR	RBI	SO	SB
Ryon Healy	.305	269	36	82	13	37	60	0
Josh Reddick#	.296	243	33	72	8	28	34	5
Danny Valencia	.287	471	72	135	17	51	115	1
Billy Butler*	.284	250	27	71	5	35	42	0
Jed Lowrie	.263	338	30	89	2	27	65	0
Yonder Alonso	.253	482	52	122	7	56	74	3
Stephen Vogt	.251	490	54	123	14	56	83	0
Khris Davis	.247	555	85	137	42	102	166	1
Jake Smolinski	.238	290	28	69	7	27	44	1
Marcus Semien	.238	568	72	135	27	75	139	10
Billy Burns*	.235	311	39	73	0	13	37	17
Coco Crisp*	.231	446	54	103	13	55	78	10
Brett Eibner*	.193	187	21	36	6	22	50	0
Chris Coghlan#	.146	158	14	23	5	14	47	1

Pitchers	ERA	W	L	IP	H	BB	SO	SV
Rich Hill#	2.25	9	3	76.0	55	28	90	0
Ryan Dull	2.42	5	5	74.1	50	15	73	3
Ryan Madson	3.62	6	7	64.2	63	20	49	30
Sean Manaea	3.86	7	9	144.2	135	37	124	0
Kendall Graveman	4.11	10	11	186.0	196	47	108	0
Zach Neal	4.24	2	4	76.0	72	6	27	2
Sonny Gray	5.69	5	11	117.0	133	42	94	0
Daniel Mengden	6.50	2	9	72.0	83	33	71	0

Manager: Bob Melvin

Seattle Mariners

Batters	AVG	AB	R	H	HR	RBI	SO	SB
Robinson Cano	.298	655	107	195	39	103	100	0
Nelson Cruz	.287	589	96	169	43	105	159	2
Norichika Aoki	.283	417	63	118	4	28	45	7
Kyle Seager	.278	597	89	166	30	99	108	3
Ketel Marte	.259	437	55	113	1	33	84	11
Dae-Ho Lee	.253	292	33	74	14	49	74	0
Seth Smith	.249	378	62	94	16	63	89	0
Leonys Martin	.247	518	72	128	15	47	149	24
Franklin Gutierrez	.246	248	33	61	14	39	85	1
Adam Lind	.239	401	48	96	20	58	89	0
Shawn O'Malley	.229	210	24	48	2	17	59	6
Chris Iannetta	.210	295	23	62	7	24	83	0
Mike Zunino	.207	164	16	34	12	31	65	0

Pitchers	ERA	W	L	IP	H	BB	SO	SV
Edwin Diaz	2.79	0	4	51.2	45	15	88	18
Steve Cishek	2.81	4	6	64.0	44	21	76	25
James Paxton	3.79	6	7	121.0	134	24	117	0
Felix Hernandez	3.82	11	8	153.1	138	65	122	0
Hisashi Iwakuma	4.12	16	12	199.0	218	46	147	0
Taijuan Walker	4.22	8	11	134.1	129	37	119	0
Nathan Karns	5.15	6	2	94.1	95	45	101	1
Wade Miley*	5.37	9	13	166.0	187	49	137	0

Manager: Scott Servais

Tampa Bay Rays

Batters	AVG	AB	R	H	HR	RBI	SO	SB
Steve Pearce*	.288	264	35	76	13	35	54	0
Evan Longoria	.273	633	81	173	36	98	144	0
Nick Franklin	.270	174	18	47	6	26	42	6
Brandon Guyer*	.266	293	39	78	9	32	55	3
Logan Forsythe	.264	511	76	135	20	52	127	6
Tim Beckham	.247	198	25	49	5	16	67	2

Batters	AVG	AB	R	H	HR	RBI	SO	SB
Steven Souza Jr.	.247	430	58	106	17	49	159	7
Kevin Kiermaier	.246	366	55	90	12	37	74	21
Corey Dickerson	.245	510	57	125	24	70	134	0
Brad Miller	.243	548	73	133	30	81	149	6
Logan Morrison	.238	353	45	84	14	43	89	4
Bobby Wilson*	.237	228	25	54	7	33	64	0
Oswaldo Arcia#	.229	157	15	36	6	19	65	1
Desmond Jennings	.200	200	22	40	7	20	58	2
Mikie Mahtook	.195	185	16	36	3	11	68	0
Curt Casali	.186	226	23	42	8	25	82	0

Pitchers	ERA	W	L	IP	H	BB	SO	SV
Alex Colome	1.91	2	4	56.2	43	15	71	37
Blake Snell	3.54	6	8	89.0	93	51	98	0
Jake Odorizzi	3.69	10	6	187.2	170	54	166	0
Erasmo Ramirez	3.77	7	11	90.2	90	26	63	2
Chris Archer	4.02	9	19	201.1	183	67	233	0
Matt Moore#	4.08	7	7	130.0	125	40	109	0
Matt Andriese	4.37	8	8	127.2	131	25	109	1
Drew Smyly	4.88	7	12	175.1	174	49	167	0

Manager: Kevin Cash

Texas Rangers

Batters	AVG	AB	R	H	HR	RBI	SO	SB
Elvis Andrus	.302	506	75	153	8	69	70	24
Adrian Beltre	.300	583	89	175	32	104	66	1
Carlos Beltran*	.295	552	73	163	29	93	101	1
Ian Desmond	.285	625	107	178	22	86	160	21
Jonathan Lucroy#	.276	152	19	42	11	31	30	0
Rougned Odor	.271	605	89	164	33	88	135	14
Nomar Mazara	.266	516	59	137	20	64	112	0
Ryan Rua	.258	240	40	62	8	22	76	9
Shin-Soo Choo	.242	178	27	43	7	17	46	6
Jurickson Profar	.239	272	35	65	5	20	61	2
Bobby Wilson*	.237	228	25	54	7	33	64	0
Mitch Moreland	.233	460	49	107	22	60	118	1
Carlos Gomez*	.231	411	45	95	13	53	136	18
Prince Fielder	.212	326	29	69	8	44	63	0
Delino DeShields	.209	182	36	38	4	13	54	8

Pitchers	ERA	W	L	IP	H	BB	SO	SV
Sam Dyson	2.43	3	2	70.1	63	23	55	38
Cole Hamels	3.32	15	5	200.2	185	77	200	0
Yu Darvish	3.41	7	5	100.1	81	31	132	0
Colby Lewis	3.71	6	5	116.1	103	28	73	0
Martin Perez	4.39	10	11	198.2	205	76	103	0
Derek Holland	4.95	7	9	107.1	116	35	67	0
A.J. Griffin	5.07	7	4	119.0	116	46	107	0
Shawn Tolleson	7.68	2	2	36.1	53	10	29	11

Manager: Jeff Banister

Toronto Blue Jays

Batters	AVG	AB	R	H	HR	RBI	SO	SB
Devon Travis	.300	410	54	123	11	50	87	4
Josh Donaldson	.284	577	122	164	37	99	119	7
Darwin Barney	.269	279	35	75	4	19	48	2
Kevin Pillar	.266	548	59	146	7	53	90	14
Edwin Encarnacion	.263	601	99	158	42	127	138	2
Troy Tulowitzki	.254	492	54	125	24	79	101	1
Michael Saunders	.253	490	70	124	24	57	157	1
Ezequiel Carrera	.248	270	47	67	6	23	70	7
José Bautista	.234	423	68	99	22	69	103	2
Russell Martin	.231	455	62	105	20	74	148	2
Justin Smoak	.217	299	33	65	14	34	112	1
Dioner Navarro*	.207	304	26	63	6	35	71	1
Ryan Goins	.186	183	13	34	3	12	48	1

Pitchers	ERA	W	L	IP	H	BB	SO	SV
Roberto Osuna	2.68	4	3	74.0	55	14	82	36
Aaron Sanchez	3.00	15	2	192.0	161	63	161	0
J.A. Happ	3.18	20	4	195.0	168	60	163	0
Marco Estrada	3.48	9	9	176.0	132	65	165	0
Scott Feldman*	3.97	7	4	77.0	87	19	56	0
Marcus Stroman	4.37	9	10	204.0	209	54	166	0
R.A. Dickey	4.46	10	15	169.2	169	63	126	0

Manager: John Gibbons

Major League Leaders, 2016
National League

Batting Average: DJ LeMahieu, Colorado, .348; Daniel Murphy, Washington, .347; Joey Votto, Cincinnati, .326; Charlie Blackmon, Colorado, .324; Jean Segura, Arizona, .319.
Runs Scored: Kris Bryant, Chicago Cubs, 121; Nolan Arenado, Colorado, 116; Charlie Blackmon, Colorado, 111; Paul Goldschmidt, Arizona, 106; Corey Seager, L.A. Dodgers, 105.
Runs Batted In: Nolan Arenado, Colorado, 133; Anthony Rizzo, Chicago Cubs, 109; Matt Kemp, Atlanta, 108; Daniel Murphy, Washington, 104; Adam Duvall, Cincinnati, 103.
Hits: Jean Segura, Arizona, 203; Corey Seager, L.A. Dodgers, 193; DJ LeMahieu, Colorado, 192; Charlie Blackmon, Colorado, 187; Daniel Murphy, Washington, 184.
Doubles: Daniel Murphy, Washington, 47; Freddie Freeman, Atlanta, 43; Anthony Rizzo, Chicago Cubs, 43; Carlos Gonzalez, Colorado, 42; Brandon Belt, San Francisco, 41; Jean Segura, Arizona, 41.
Triples: Brandon Crawford, San Francisco, 11; Cesar Hernandez, Philadelphia, 11; Chris Owings, Arizona, 11; Jake Lamb, Arizona, 9; Brandon Belt, San Francisco, 8; DJ LeMahieu, Colorado, 8; Trea Turner, Washington, 8.

Home Runs: Nolan Arenado, Colorado, 41; Chris Carter, Milwaukee, 41; Kris Bryant, Chicago Cubs, 39; Matt Kemp, Atlanta, 35; Freddie Freeman, Atlanta, 34.
Stolen Bases: Jonathan Villar, Milwaukee, 62; Billy Hamilton, Cincinnati, 58; Starling Marte, Pittsburgh, 47; Hernan Perez, Milwaukee, 34; Jean Segura, Arizona, 33; Trea Turner, Washington, 33.
Pitching Wins: Max Scherzer, Washington, 20; Jon Lester, Chicago Cubs, 19; Jake Arrieta, Chicago Cubs, 18; Johnny Cueto, San Francisco, 18; José Fernández, Miami, 16; Kyle Hendricks, Chicago Cubs, 16; Kenta Maeda, L.A. Dodgers, 16; Carlos Martinez, St. Louis, 16; Tanner Roark, Washington, 16.
Earned Run Average: Kyle Hendricks, Chicago Cubs, 2.13; Jon Lester, Chicago Cubs, 2.44, Noah Syndergaard, NY Mets, 2.60; Madison Bumgarner, San Francisco, 2.74; Johnny Cueto, San Francisco, 2.79.
Strikeouts: Max Scherzer, Washington, 284; José Fernández, Miami, 253; Madison Bumgarner, San Francisco, 251; Robbie Ray, Arizona, 218; Noah Syndergaard, NY Mets, 218.
Saves: Jeurys Familia, NY Mets, 51; Kenley Jansen, L.A. Dodgers, 47; Mark Melancon, Washington, 47; A.J. Ramos, Miami, 40; Jeanmar Gomez, Philadelphia, 37.

American League

Batting Average: Jose Altuve, Houston, .338; Mookie Betts, Boston, .318; Dustin Pedroia, Boston, .318; Miguel Cabrera, Detroit, .316; Mike Trout, L.A. Angels, .315; David Ortiz, Boston, .315.
Runs Scored: Mike Trout, L.A. Angels, 123; Mookie Betts, Boston, 122; Josh Donaldson, Toronto, 122; Ian Kinsler, Detroit, 117; George Springer, Houston, 116.
Runs Batted In: Edwin Encarnacion, Toronto, 127; David Ortiz, Boston, 127; Albert Pujols, L.A. Angels, 119; Mookie Betts, Boston, 113; Hanley Ramirez, Boston, 111.
Hits: Jose Altuve, Houston, 216; Mookie Betts, Boston, 214; Dustin Pedroia, Boston, 201; Robinson Cano, Seattle, 195; Xander Bogaerts, Boston, 192.
Doubles: David Ortiz, Boston, 48; Jose Ramirez, Cleveland, 46; Jose Altuve, Houston, 42; Mookie Betts, Boston, 42; Melky Cabrera, Chicago White Sox, 42.
Triples: Adam Eaton, Chicago White Sox, 9; Jarrod Dyson, Kansas City, 8; Elvis Andrus, Texas, 7; Jackie Bradley Jr., Boston, 7; Tim Anderson, Chicago White Sox, 6; Byron Buxton, Minnesota, 6; Alcides Escobar, Kansas City, 6; Brett Gardner, NY Yankees, 6; Brad Miller, Tampa Bay, 6.

Home Runs: Mark Trumbo, Baltimore, 47; Nelson Cruz, Seattle, 43; Khris Davis, Oakland, 42; Brian Dozier, Minnesota, 42; Edwin Encarnacion, Toronto, 42.
Stolen Bases: Rajai Davis, Cleveland, 43; Jose Altuve, Houston, 30; Jarrod Dyson, Kansas City, 30; Mike Trout, L.A. Angels, 30; Eduardo Nunez, Minnesota, 27.
Pitching Wins: Rick Porcello, Boston, 22; J. A. Happ, Toronto, 20; Corey Kluber, Cleveland, 18; David Price, Boston, 17; Chris Sale, Chicago White Sox, 17.
Earned Run Average: Aaron Sanchez, Toronto, 3.00; Justin Verlander, Detroit, 3.04; Masahiro Tanaka, NY Yankees, 3.07; Corey Kluber, Cleveland, 3.14; Rick Porcello, Boston, 3.15.
Strikeouts: Justin Verlander, Detroit, 254; Chris Archer, Tampa Bay, 233; Chris Sale, Chicago White Sox, 233; David Price, Boston, 228; Corey Kluber, Cleveland, 227.
Saves: Zach Britton, Baltimore, 47; Francisco Rodriguez, Detroit, 44; Sam Dyson, Texas, 38; Alex Colome, Tampa Bay, 37; David Robertson, Chicago White Sox, 37.

All-Time Major League Single-Season Leaders

Source: www.mlb.com; * = Active in 2016 season; records for "modern" era beginning in 1901.

Home Runs

Barry Bonds (2001)	73
Mark McGwire (1998)	70
Sammy Sosa (1998)	66
Mark McGwire (1999)	65
Sammy Sosa (2001)	64

Runs Scored

Babe Ruth (1921)	177
Lou Gehrig (1936)	167
Lou Gehrig (1931)	163
Babe Ruth (1928)	163
Chuck Klein (1930)	158
Babe Ruth (1920, 1927)	158

Hits

Ichiro Suzuki* (2004)	262
George Sisler (1920)	257
Lefty O'Doul (1929)	254
Bill Terry (1930)	254
Al Simmons (1925)	253
Rogers Hornsby (1922)	250
Chuck Klein (1930)	250

Runs Batted In

Hack Wilson (1930)	191
Lou Gehrig (1931)	184
Hank Greenberg (1937)	183
Jimmie Foxx (1938)	175
Lou Gehrig (1927)	175

Batting Average

Rogers Hornsby (1924)	.424
Napoleon Lajoie (1901)	.421
George Sisler (1922)	.420
Ty Cobb (1911)	.420
Ty Cobb (1912)	.410

Stolen Bases

Rickey Henderson (1982)	130
Lou Brock (1974)	118
Vince Coleman (1985)	110
Vince Coleman (1987)	109
Rickey Henderson (1983)	108

Walks (Batter)

Barry Bonds (2004)	232
Barry Bonds (2002)	198
Barry Bonds (2001)	177
Babe Ruth (1923)	170
Mark McGwire (1998)	162
Ted Williams (1947, 1949)	162

Strikeouts (Batter)

Mark Reynolds* (2009)	223
Adam Dunn (2012)	222
Chris Davis* (2016)	219
Chris Carter* (2013)	212
Mark Reynolds* (2010)	211

Earned Run Average

Dutch Leonard (1914)	0.96
Mordecai "Three Finger" Brown (1906)	1.04
Bob Gibson (1968)	1.12
Christy Mathewson (1909)	1.14
Walter Johnson (1913)	1.14

Wins

Jack Chesbro (1904)	41
Ed Walsh (1908)	40
Christy Mathewson (1908)	37
Walter Johnson (1913)	36
Joe McGinnity (1904)	35

Strikeouts

Nolan Ryan (1973)	383
Sandy Koufax (1965)	382
Randy Johnson (2001)	372
Nolan Ryan (1974)	367
Randy Johnson (1999)	364

Saves

Francisco Rodriguez* (2008)	62
Bobby Thigpen (1990)	57
Eric Gagne (2003)	55
John Smoltz (2002)	55
Trevor Hoffman (1998)	53
Randy Myers (1993)	53
Mariano Rivera (2004)	53

All-Time Major League Leaders

Source: www.mlb.com; * = Active in 2016 season; career records for players in "modern" era beginning in 1901 may include statistics from preceding years.

Games
Pete Rose	3,562
Carl Yastrzemski	3,308
Hank Aaron	3,298
Rickey Henderson	3,081
Ty Cobb	3,035
Eddie Murray	3,026
Stan Musial	3,026
Cal Ripken Jr.	3,001
Willie Mays	2,992
Barry Bonds	2,986

At Bats
Pete Rose	14,053
Hank Aaron	12,364
Carl Yastrzemski	11,988
Cal Ripken Jr.	11,551
Ty Cobb	11,429
Eddie Murray	11,336
Derek Jeter	11,195
Robin Yount	11,008
Dave Winfield	11,003
Stan Musial	10,972

Runs Batted In
Hank Aaron	2,297
Babe Ruth	2,213
Alex Rodriguez*	2,086
Barry Bonds	1,996
Lou Gehrig	1,995
Stan Musial	1,951
Ty Cobb	1,938
Jimmie Foxx	1,922
Eddie Murray	1,917
Willie Mays	1,903

Runs
Rickey Henderson	2,295
Ty Cobb	2,246
Barry Bonds	2,227
Hank Aaron	2,174
Babe Ruth	2,174
Pete Rose	2,165
Willie Mays	2,062
Alex Rodriguez*	2,021
Stan Musial	1,949
Derek Jeter	1,923

Stolen Bases
Rickey Henderson	1,406
Lou Brock	938
Billy Hamilton	912
Ty Cobb	892
Tim Raines	808
Vince Coleman	752
Eddie Collins	745
Arlie Latham	739
Max Carey	738
Honus Wagner	722

Triples
Sam Crawford	309
Ty Cobb	297
Honus Wagner	252
Jake Beckley	243
Roger Connor	233
Tris Speaker	222
Fred Clarke	220
Dan Brouthers	205
Joe Kelley	194
Paul Waner	191

Batting Average
Ty Cobb	.367
Rogers Hornsby	.358
Joe Jackson	.356
Ed Delahanty	.346
Tris Speaker	.345
Ted Williams	.344
Billy Hamilton	.344
Dan Brouthers	.342
Babe Ruth	.342
Harry Heilmann	.342

Walks (Batter)
Barry Bonds	2,558
Rickey Henderson	2,190
Babe Ruth	2,062
Ted Williams	2,019
Joe Morgan	1,865
Carl Yastrzemski	1,845
Jim Thome	1,747
Mickey Mantle	1,733
Mel Ott	1,708
Frank Thomas	1,667

Strikeouts
Nolan Ryan	5,714
Randy Johnson	4,875
Roger Clemens	4,672
Steve Carlton	4,136
Bert Blyleven	3,701
Tom Seaver	3,640
Don Sutton	3,574
Gaylord Perry	3,534
Walter Johnson	3,508
Greg Maddux	3,371

Saves
Mariano Rivera	652
Trevor Hoffman	601
Lee Smith	478
Francisco Rodriguez*	430
John Franco	424
Billy Wagner	422
Dennis Eckersley	390
Joe Nathan*	377
Jonathan Papelbon*	368
Jeff Reardon	367

Shutouts
Walter Johnson	110
Grover Alexander	90
Christy Mathewson	79
Cy Young	76
Eddie Plank	69
Warren Spahn	63
Nolan Ryan	61
Tom Seaver	61
Bert Blyleven	60
Don Sutton	58

Losses
Cy Young	316
Nolan Ryan	292
Walter Johnson	279
Phil Niekro	274
Gaylord Perry	265
Don Sutton	256
Jack Powell	254
Eppa Rixey	251
Bert Blyleven	250
Robin Roberts	245
Warren Spahn	245

All-Time Home Run Leaders

Source: www.mlb.com; * = Active in 2016 season.

Player	HR	Player	HR	Player	HR	Player	HR
Barry Bonds	762	Manny Ramirez	555	Fred McGriff	493	Jason Giambi	440
Hank Aaron	755	Mike Schmidt	548	Stan Musial	475	Paul Konerko	439
Babe Ruth	714	David Ortiz*	541	Willie Stargell	475	Andre Dawson	438
Alex Rodriguez*	696	Mickey Mantle	536	Carlos Delgado	473	Juan Gonzalez	434
Willie Mays	660	Jimmie Foxx	534	Chipper Jones	468	Andruw Jones	434
Ken Griffey	630	Willie McCovey	521	Dave Winfield	465	Cal Ripken Jr.	431
Jim Thome	612	Frank Thomas	521	Jose Canseco	462	Mike Piazza	427
Sammy Sosa	609	Ted Williams	521	Adam Dunn	462	Billy Williams	426
Albert Pujols*	591	Ernie Banks	512	Carl Yastrzemski	452	Carlos Beltran*	421
Frank Robinson	586	Eddie Mathews	512	Jeff Bagwell	449	Darrell Evans	414
Mark McGwire	583	Mel Ott	511	Vladimir Guerrero	449	Alfonso Soriano	412
Harmon Killebrew	573	Gary Sheffield	509	Miguel Cabrera*	446	Mark Teixeira*	409
Rafael Palmeiro	569	Eddie Murray	504	Adrian Beltre*	445	Duke Snider	407
Reggie Jackson	563	Lou Gehrig	493	Dave Kingman	442		

Players With 3,000 Major League Hits

Source: www.mlb.com; * = Active in 2016 season.

Player	Hits	Player	Hits	Player	Hits	Player	Hits
Pete Rose	4,256	Paul Molitor	3,319	Robin Yount	3,142	Ichiro Suzuki*	3,030
Ty Cobb	4,191	Eddie Collins	3,314	Tony Gwynn	3,141	Lou Brock	3,023
Hank Aaron	3,771	Willie Mays	3,283	Alex Rodriguez*	3,115	Rafael Palmeiro	3,020
Stan Musial	3,630	Eddie Murray	3,255	Dave Winfield	3,110	Cap Anson	3,011
Tris Speaker	3,515	Nap Lajoie	3,252	Craig Biggio	3,060	Wade Boggs	3,010
Derek Jeter	3,465	Cal Ripken Jr.	3,184	Rickey Henderson	3,055	Al Kaline	3,007
Honus Wagner	3,430	George Brett	3,154	Rod Carew	3,053	Roberto Clemente	3,000
Carl Yastrzemski	3,419	Paul Waner	3,152				

50 Home Run Club

Only Barry Bonds and Mark McGwire hit 70 or more home runs in a season. Five players—including Babe Ruth and Roger Maris—hit 60 or more, a feat Sammy Sosa accomplished for the third time in 2001.

HR	Player, team	Year	HR	Player, team	Year
73	Barry Bonds, San Francisco Giants	2001	54	Alex Rodriguez, NY Yankees	2007
70	Mark McGwire, St. Louis Cardinals	1998	54	Babe Ruth, NY Yankees	1920
66	Sammy Sosa, Chicago Cubs	1998	54	Babe Ruth, NY Yankees	1928
65	Mark McGwire, St. Louis Cardinals	1999	53	Chris Davis, Baltimore Orioles	2013
64	Sammy Sosa, Chicago Cubs	2001	52	George Foster, Cincinnati Reds	1977
63	Sammy Sosa, Chicago Cubs	1999	52	Mickey Mantle, NY Yankees	1956
61	Roger Maris, NY Yankees	1961	52	Willie Mays, San Francisco Giants	1965
60	Babe Ruth, NY Yankees	1927	52	Mark McGwire, Oakland A's	1996
59	Babe Ruth, NY Yankees	1921	52	Alex Rodriguez, Texas Rangers	2001
58	Jimmie Foxx, Philadelphia Athletics	1932	52	Jim Thome, Cleveland Indians	2002
58	Hank Greenberg, Detroit Tigers	1938	51	Cecil Fielder, Detroit Tigers	1990
58	Ryan Howard, Philadelphia Phillies	2006	51	Andruw Jones, Atlanta Braves	2005
58	Mark McGwire, Oakland A's/St. Louis Cardinals	1997	51	Ralph Kiner, Pittsburgh Pirates	1947
57	Luis Gonzalez, Arizona Diamondbacks	2001	51	Willie Mays, NY Giants	1955
57	Alex Rodriguez, Texas Rangers	2002	51	Johnny Mize, NY Giants	1947
56	Ken Griffey Jr., Seattle Mariners	1997	50	Brady Anderson, Baltimore Orioles	1996
56	Ken Griffey Jr., Seattle Mariners	1998	50	Albert Belle, Cleveland Indians	1995
56	Hack Wilson, Chicago Cubs	1930	50	Prince Fielder, Milwaukee Brewers	2007
54	José Bautista, Toronto Blue Jays	2010	50	Jimmie Foxx, Boston Red Sox	1938
54	Ralph Kiner, Pittsburgh Pirates	1949	50	Sammy Sosa, Chicago Cubs	2000
54	Mickey Mantle, NY Yankees	1961	50	Greg Vaughn, San Diego Padres	1998
54	David Ortiz, Boston Red Sox	2006			

Pitchers With 300 Major League Wins

Source: www.mlb.com

Pitcher	Wins	Pitcher	Wins	Pitcher	Wins	Pitcher	Wins
Cy Young	511	Charles "Kid" Nichols	361	Eddie Plank	326	Charley Radbourn	309
Walter Johnson	417	Greg Maddux	355	Nolan Ryan	324	Mickey Welch	307
Grover Alexander	373	Roger Clemens	354	Don Sutton	324	Tom Glavine	305
Christy Mathewson	373	Tim Keefe	342	Phil Niekro	318	Randy Johnson	303
Warren Spahn	363	Steve Carlton	329	Gaylord Perry	314	Robert "Lefty" Grove	300
James "Pud" Galvin	361	John Clarkson	328	Tom Seaver	311	Early "Gus" Wynn	300

Official Major League Perfect Games Since 1901

Date	Pitcher	Teams	Date	Pitcher	Teams
5/5/1904	Cy Young	Boston 3 vs. Phil. 0 (AL)	7/28/1994	Kenny Rogers	Texas 4 vs. California 0 (AL)
10/2/1908	Addie Joss	Clev. 1 vs. Chicago 0 (AL)	5/17/1998	David Wells	NY 4 vs. Minn. 0 (AL)
4/30/1922	Charlie Robertson	Chicago 2 vs. Detroit 0 (AL)	7/18/1999	David Cone	NY 6 vs. Montréal 0 (AL)
10/8/1956	Don Larsen	NY 2 (AL) vs. Brooklyn 0* (NL)	5/18/2004	Randy Johnson	Arizona 2 vs. Atlanta 0 (NL)
6/21/1964	Jim Bunning	Phil. 6 vs. NY 0 (NL)	7/23/2009	Mark Buehrle	Chicago 5 vs. Tampa Bay 0 (AL)
9/9/1965	Sandy Koufax	L.A. 1 vs. Chicago 0 (NL)	5/9/2010	Dallas Braden	Oakland 4 vs. Tampa Bay 0 (AL)
5/8/1968	Jim "Catfish" Hunter	Oakland 4 vs. Minn. 0 (AL)	5/29/2010	Roy Halladay	Phil. 1 vs. Florida 0 (NL)
5/15/1981	Len Barker	Clev. 3 vs. Toronto 0 (AL)	4/21/2012	Philip Humber	Chicago 4 vs. Seattle 0 (AL)
9/30/1984	Mike Witt	California 1 vs. Texas 0 (AL)	6/13/2012	Matt Cain	S.F. 10 vs. Houston 0 (NL)
9/16/1988	Tom Browning	Cincinnati 1 vs. L.A. 0 (NL)	8/15/2012	Felix Hernandez	Seattle 1 vs. Tampa Bay 0 (AL)
7/28/1991	Dennis Martinez	Montréal 2 vs. L.A. 0 (NL)			

* = World Series game. **Note:** Two pre-1901 National League pitchers are also credited with perfect games. Within one week in 1880, Lee Richmond (June 12, Worcester 1, Cleveland 0) and John "Monte" Ward (June 17, Providence 5, Buffalo 0) each threw a perfect game.

Most Career Major League No-Hitters

No.	Pitcher	No.	Pitcher
7	Nolan Ryan	2	Jake Arrieta, Homer Bailey, Mark Buehrle, Jim Bunning, Steve Busby, Carl Erskine, Bob
4	Sandy Koufax		Forsch, Pud Galvin, Roy Halladay, Ken Holtzman, Randy Johnson, Addie Joss, Dutch
3	Larry Corcoran,		Leonard, Tim Lincecum, Jim Maloney, Christy Mathewson, Hideo Nomo, Allie Reynolds,
	Bob Feller,		Max Scherzer, Frank Smith, Warren Spahn, Bill Stoneman, Virgil Trucks, Johnny Vander
	Cy Young		Meer, Justin Verlander, Ed Walsh, Don Wilson

Home Run Leaders by Season, 1901-2016

* = All-time single-season record for league since beginning of "modern" era in 1901.

	National League			American League	
Year	Player, team	HR	Year	Player, team	HR
1901	Sam Crawford, Cincinnati	16	1901	Napoleon Lajoie, Philadelphia	14
1902	Thomas Leach, Pittsburgh	6	1902	Socks Seybold, Philadelphia	16
1903	James Sheckard, Brooklyn	9	1903	Buck Freeman, Boston	13
1904	Harry Lumley, Brooklyn	9	1904	Harry Davis, Philadelphia	10
1905	Fred Odwell, Cincinnati	9	1905	Harry Davis, Philadelphia	8
1906	Timothy Jordan, Brooklyn	12	1906	Harry Davis, Philadelphia	12
1907	David Brain, Boston	10	1907	Harry Davis, Philadelphia	8
1908	Timothy Jordan, Brooklyn	12	1908	Sam Crawford, Detroit	7
1909	Red Murray, New York	7	1909	Ty Cobb, Detroit	9
1910	Fred Beck, Boston; Frank Schulte, Chicago	10	1910	Jake Stahl, Boston	10
1911	Frank Schulte, Chicago	21	1911	J. Franklin Baker, Philadelphia	11
1912	Henry Zimmerman, Chicago	14	1912	J. Franklin Baker, Phil.; Tris Speaker, Boston	10
1913	Gavvy Cravath, Philadelphia	19	1913	J. Franklin Baker, Philadelphia	12
1914	Gavvy Cravath, Philadelphia	19	1914	J. Franklin Baker, Philadelphia	9
1915	Gavvy Cravath, Philadelphia	24	1915	Robert Roth, Chicago-Cleveland	7
1916	Dave Robertson, NY; Fred "Cy" Williams, Chi.	12	1916	Wally Pipp, New York	12
1917	Gavvy Cravath, Phil.; Dave Robertson, NY	12	1917	Wally Pipp, New York	9

National League			American League		
Year	Player, team	HR	Year	Player, team	HR
1918	Gavvy Cravath, Philadelphia	8	1918	Babe Ruth, Boston; Tilly Walker, Philadelphia	11
1919	Gavvy Cravath, Philadelphia	12	1919	Babe Ruth, Boston	29
1920	Cy Williams, Philadelphia	15	1920	Babe Ruth, New York	54
1921	George Kelly, New York	23	1921	Babe Ruth, New York	59
1922	Rogers Hornsby, St. Louis	42	1922	Ken Williams, St. Louis	39
1923	Cy Williams, Philadelphia	41	1923	Babe Ruth, New York	41
1924	Jacques Fournier, Brooklyn	27	1924	Babe Ruth, New York	46
1925	Rogers Hornsby, St. Louis	39	1925	Bob Meusel, New York	33
1926	Hack Wilson, Chicago	21	1926	Babe Ruth, New York	47
1927	Hack Wilson, Chicago; Cy Williams, Philadelphia	30	1927	Babe Ruth, New York	60
1928	Hack Wilson, Chicago; Jim Bottomley, St. Louis	31	1928	Babe Ruth, New York	54
1929	Chuck Klein, Philadelphia	43	1929	Babe Ruth, New York	46
1930	Hack Wilson, Chicago	56	1930	Babe Ruth, New York	49
1931	Chuck Klein, Philadelphia	31	1931	Lou Gehrig, New York; Babe Ruth, New York	46
1932	Chuck Klein, Philadelphia; Mel Ott, New York	38	1932	Jimmie Foxx, Philadelphia	58
1933	Chuck Klein, Philadelphia	28	1933	Jimmie Foxx, Philadelphia	48
1934	Rip Collins, St. Louis; Mel Ott, New York	35	1934	Lou Gehrig, New York	49
1935	Walter Berger, Boston	34	1935	Jimmie Foxx, Phil.; Hank Greenberg, Detroit	36
1936	Mel Ott, New York	33	1936	Lou Gehrig, New York	49
1937	Joe Medwick, St. Louis; Mel Ott, New York	31	1937	Joe DiMaggio, New York	46
1938	Mel Ott, New York	36	1938	Hank Greenberg, Detroit	58
1939	John Mize, St. Louis	28	1939	Jimmie Foxx, Boston	35
1940	John Mize, St. Louis	43	1940	Hank Greenberg, Detroit	41
1941	Dolph Camilli, Brooklyn	34	1941	Ted Williams, Boston	37
1942	Mel Ott, New York	30	1942	Ted Williams, Boston	36
1943	Bill Nicholson, Chicago	29	1943	Rudy York, Detroit	34
1944	Bill Nicholson, Chicago	33	1944	Nick Etten, New York	22
1945	Tommy Holmes, Boston	28	1945	Vern Stephens, St. Louis	24
1946	Ralph Kiner, Pittsburgh	23	1946	Hank Greenberg, Detroit	44
1947	Ralph Kiner, Pittsburgh; John Mize, New York	51	1947	Ted Williams, Boston	32
1948	Ralph Kiner, Pittsburgh; John Mize, New York	40	1948	Joe DiMaggio, New York	39
1949	Ralph Kiner, Pittsburgh	54	1949	Ted Williams, Boston	43
1950	Ralph Kiner, Pittsburgh	47	1950	Al Rosen, Cleveland	37
1951	Ralph Kiner, Pittsburgh	42	1951	Gus Zernial, Chicago-Philadelphia	33
1952	Ralph Kiner, Pittsburgh; Hank Sauer, Chicago	37	1952	Larry Doby, Cleveland	32
1953	Ed Mathews, Milwaukee	47	1953	Al Rosen, Cleveland	43
1954	Ted Kluszewski, Cincinnati	49	1954	Larry Doby, Cleveland	32
1955	Willie Mays, New York	51	1955	Mickey Mantle, New York	37
1956	Duke Snider, Brooklyn	43	1956	Mickey Mantle, New York	52
1957	Hank Aaron, Milwaukee	44	1957	Roy Sievers, Washington	42
1958	Ernie Banks, Chicago	47	1958	Mickey Mantle, New York	42
1959	Ed Mathews, Milwaukee	46	1959	Rocky Colavito, Clev.; Harmon Killebrew, Wash.	42
1960	Ernie Banks, Chicago	41	1960	Mickey Mantle, New York	40
1961	Orlando Cepeda, San Francisco	46	1961	Roger Maris, New York	61*
1962	Willie Mays, San Francisco	49	1962	Harmon Killebrew, Minnesota	48
1963	Hank Aaron, Milwaukee; Willie McCovey, S.F.	44	1963	Harmon Killebrew, Minnesota	45
1964	Willie Mays, San Francisco	47	1964	Harmon Killebrew, Minnesota	49
1965	Willie Mays, San Francisco	52	1965	Tony Conigliaro, Boston	32
1966	Hank Aaron, Atlanta	44	1966	Frank Robinson, Baltimore	49
1967	Hank Aaron, Atlanta	39	1967	Harmon Killebrew, Minn.; Carl Yastrzemski, Boston	44
1968	Willie McCovey, San Francisco	36	1968	Frank Howard, Washington	44
1969	Willie McCovey, San Francisco	45	1969	Harmon Killebrew, Minnesota	49
1970	Johnny Bench, Cincinnati	45	1970	Frank Howard, Washington	44
1971	Willie Stargell, Pittsburgh	48	1971	Bill Melton, Chicago	33
1972	Johnny Bench, Cincinnati	40	1972	Dick Allen, Chicago	37
1973	Willie Stargell, Pittsburgh	44	1973	Reggie Jackson, Oakland	32
1974	Mike Schmidt, Philadelphia	36	1974	Dick Allen, Chicago	32
1975	Mike Schmidt, Philadelphia	38	1975	Reggie Jackson, Oak.; George Scott, Milw.	36
1976	Mike Schmidt, Philadelphia	38	1976	Graig Nettles, New York	32
1977	George Foster, Cincinnati	52	1977	Jim Rice, Boston	39
1978	George Foster, Cincinnati	40	1978	Jim Rice, Boston	46
1979	Dave Kingman, Chicago	48	1979	Gorman Thomas, Milwaukee	45
1980	Mike Schmidt, Philadelphia	48	1980	Reggie Jackson, New York; Ben Oglivie, Milw.	41
1981	Mike Schmidt, Philadelphia	31	1981	Tony Armas, Oakland; Dwight Evans, Boston; Bobby Grich, Cal.; Eddie Murray, Baltimore	22
1982	Dave Kingman, New York	37	1982	Gorman Thomas, Milw.; Reggie Jackson, Cal.	39
1983	Mike Schmidt, Philadelphia	40	1983	Jim Rice, Boston	39
1984	Dale Murphy, Atlanta; Mike Schmidt, Philadelphia	36	1984	Tony Armas, Boston	43
1985	Dale Murphy, Atlanta	37	1985	Darrell Evans, Detroit	40
1986	Mike Schmidt, Philadelphia	37	1986	Jesse Barfield, Toronto	40
1987	Andre Dawson, Chicago	49	1987	Mark McGwire, Oakland	49
1988	Darryl Strawberry, New York	39	1988	Jose Canseco, Oakland	42
1989	Kevin Mitchell, San Francisco	47	1989	Fred McGriff, Toronto	36
1990	Ryne Sandberg, Chicago	40	1990	Cecil Fielder, Detroit	51
1991	Howard Johnson, New York	38	1991	Jose Canseco, Oakland; Cecil Fielder, Detroit	44
1992	Fred McGriff, San Diego	35	1992	Juan Gonzalez, Texas	43
1993	Barry Bonds, San Francisco	46	1993	Juan Gonzalez, Texas	46
1994	Matt Williams, San Francisco	43	1994	Ken Griffey Jr., Seattle	40
1995	Dante Bichette, Colorado	40	1995	Albert Belle, Cleveland	50
1996	Andres Galarraga, Colorado	47	1996	Mark McGwire, Oakland	52
1997[1]	Larry Walker, Colorado	49	1997[1]	Ken Griffey Jr., Seattle	56
1998	Mark McGwire, St. Louis	70	1998	Ken Griffey Jr., Seattle	56
1999	Mark McGwire, St. Louis	65	1999	Ken Griffey Jr., Seattle	48
2000	Sammy Sosa, Chicago	50	2000	Troy Glaus, Anaheim	47
2001	Barry Bonds, San Francisco	73*	2001	Alex Rodriguez, Texas	52
2002	Sammy Sosa, Chicago	49	2002	Alex Rodriguez, Texas	57
2003	Jim Thome, Philadelphia	47	2003	Alex Rodriguez, Texas	47
2004	Adrian Beltre, Los Angeles	48	2004	Manny Ramirez, Boston	43
2005	Andruw Jones, Atlanta	51	2005	Alex Rodriguez, New York	48

National League			American League		
Year	Player, team	HR	Year	Player, team	HR
2006	Ryan Howard, Philadelphia	58	2006	David Ortiz, Boston	54
2007	Prince Fielder, Milwaukee	50	2007	Alex Rodriguez, New York	54
2008	Ryan Howard, Philadelphia	48	2008	Miguel Cabrera, Detroit	37
2009	Albert Pujols, St. Louis	47	2009	Carlos Peña, Tampa Bay; Mark Teixeira, New York	39
2010	Albert Pujols, St. Louis	42	2010	José Bautista, Toronto	54
2011	Matt Kemp, Los Angeles	39	2011	José Bautista, Toronto	43
2012	Ryan Braun, Milwaukee	41	2012	Miguel Cabrera, Detroit	44
2013	Pedro Alvarez, Pitt.; Paul Goldschmidt, Arizona	36	2013	Chris Davis, Baltimore	53
2014	Giancarlo Stanton, Miami	37	2014	Nelson Cruz, Baltimore	40
2015	Nolan Arenado, Colorado; Bryce Harper, Washington	42	2015	Chris Davis, Baltimore	47
2016	Nolan Arenado, Colorado; Chris Carter, Milwaukee	41	2016	Mark Trumbo, Baltimore	47

(1) In 1997, Mark McGwire hit 58 home runs, 34 with the Oakland Athletics (AL) and 24 with the St. Louis Cardinals (NL).

Batting Champions by Season, 1901-2016

* = All-time single-season record for league since beginning of "modern" era in 1901.

National League			American League		
Year	Player, team	AVG	Year	Player, team	AVG
1901	Jesse C. Burkett, St. Louis	.376	1901[1]	Napoleon Lajoie, Philadelphia	.426*
1902	Clarence Beaumont, Pittsburgh	.357	1902	Ed Delahanty, Washington	.376
1903	Honus Wagner, Pittsburgh	.355	1903	Napoleon Lajoie, Cleveland	.357
1904	Honus Wagner, Pittsburgh	.349	1904	Napoleon Lajoie, Cleveland	.382
1905	James Seymour, Cincinnati	.377	1905	Elmer Flick, Cleveland	.308
1906	Honus Wagner, Pittsburgh	.339	1906	George Stone, St. Louis	.358
1907	Honus Wagner, Pittsburgh	.350	1907	Ty Cobb, Detroit	.350
1908	Honus Wagner, Pittsburgh	.354	1908	Ty Cobb, Detroit	.324
1909	Honus Wagner, Pittsburgh	.339	1909	Ty Cobb, Detroit	.377
1910	Sherwood Magee, Philadelphia	.331	1910[2]	Ty Cobb, Detroit	.385
1911	Honus Wagner, Pittsburgh	.334	1911	Ty Cobb, Detroit	.420
1912	Henry Zimmerman, Chicago	.372	1912	Ty Cobb, Detroit	.410
1913	Jacob Daubert, Brooklyn	.350	1913	Ty Cobb, Detroit	.390
1914	Jacob Daubert, Brooklyn	.329	1914	Ty Cobb, Detroit	.368
1915	Larry Doyle, New York	.320	1915	Ty Cobb, Detroit	.369
1916	Hal Chase, Cincinnati	.339	1916	Tris Speaker, Cleveland	.386
1917	Edd Roush, Cincinnati	.341	1917	Ty Cobb, Detroit	.383
1918	Zach Wheat, Brooklyn	.335	1918	Ty Cobb, Detroit	.382
1919	Edd Roush, Cincinnati	.321	1919	Ty Cobb, Detroit	.384
1920	Rogers Hornsby, St. Louis	.370	1920	George Sisler, St. Louis	.407
1921	Rogers Hornsby, St. Louis	.397	1921	Harry Heilmann, Detroit	.394
1922	Rogers Hornsby, St. Louis	.401	1922	George Sisler, St. Louis	.420
1923	Rogers Hornsby, St. Louis	.384	1923	Harry Heilmann, Detroit	.403
1924	Rogers Hornsby, St. Louis	.424*	1924	Babe Ruth, New York	.378
1925	Rogers Hornsby, St. Louis	.403	1925	Harry Heilmann, Detroit	.393
1926	Eugene Hargrave, Cincinnati	.353	1926	Henry Manush, Detroit	.378
1927	Paul Waner, Pittsburgh	.380	1927	Harry Heilmann, Detroit	.398
1928	Rogers Hornsby, Boston	.387	1928	Goose Goslin, Washington	.379
1929	Lefty O'Doul, Philadelphia	.398	1929	Lew Fonseca, Cleveland	.369
1930	Bill Terry, New York	.401	1930	Al Simmons, Philadelphia	.381
1931	Chick Hafey, St. Louis	.349	1931	Al Simmons, Philadelphia	.390
1932	Lefty O'Doul, Brooklyn	.368	1932	Dale Alexander, Detroit-Boston	.367
1933	Chuck Klein, Philadelphia	.368	1933	Jimmie Foxx, Philadelphia	.356
1934	Paul Waner, Pittsburgh	.362	1934	Lou Gehrig, New York	.363
1935	Arky Vaughan, Pittsburgh	.385	1935	Buddy Myer, Washington	.349
1936	Paul Waner, Pittsburgh	.373	1936	Luke Appling, Chicago	.388
1937	Joe Medwick, St. Louis	.374	1937	Charlie Gehringer, Detroit	.371
1938	Ernie Lombardi, Cincinnati	.342	1938	Jimmie Foxx, Boston	.349
1939	John Mize, St. Louis	.349	1939	Joe DiMaggio, New York	.381
1940	Debs Garms, Pittsburgh	.355	1940	Joe DiMaggio, New York	.352
1941	Pete Reiser, Brooklyn	.343	1941	Ted Williams, Boston	.406
1942	Ernie Lombardi, Boston	.330	1942	Ted Williams, Boston	.356
1943	Stan Musial, St. Louis	.357	1943	Luke Appling, Chicago	.328
1944	Dixie Walker, Brooklyn	.357	1944	Lou Boudreau, Cleveland	.327
1945	Phil Cavarretta, Chicago	.355	1945	George Stirnweiss, New York	.309
1946	Stan Musial, St. Louis	.365	1946	Mickey Vernon, Washington	.353
1947	Harry Walker, St. Louis-Phil.	.363	1947	Ted Williams, Boston	.343
1948	Stan Musial, St. Louis	.376	1948	Ted Williams, Boston	.369
1949	Jackie Robinson, Brooklyn	.342	1949	George Kell, Detroit	.343
1950	Stan Musial, St. Louis	.346	1950	Billy Goodman, Boston	.354
1951	Stan Musial, St. Louis	.355	1951	Ferris Fain, Philadelphia	.344
1952	Stan Musial, St. Louis	.336	1952	Ferris Fain, Philadelphia	.327
1953	Carl Furillo, Brooklyn	.344	1953	Mickey Vernon, Washington	.337
1954	Willie Mays, New York	.345	1954	Roberto Avila, Cleveland	.341
1955	Richie Ashburn, Philadelphia	.338	1955	Al Kaline, Detroit	.340
1956	Hank Aaron, Milwaukee	.328	1956	Mickey Mantle, New York	.353
1957	Stan Musial, St. Louis	.351	1957	Ted Williams, Boston	.388
1958	Richie Ashburn, Philadelphia	.350	1958	Ted Williams, Boston	.328
1959	Hank Aaron, Milwaukee	.355	1959	Harvey Kuenn, Detroit	.353
1960	Dick Groat, Pittsburgh	.325	1960	Pete Runnels, Boston	.320
1961	Roberto Clemente, Pittsburgh	.351	1961	Norm Cash, Detroit	.361
1962	Tommy Davis, Los Angeles	.346	1962	Pete Runnels, Boston	.326
1963	Tommy Davis, Los Angeles	.326	1963	Carl Yastrzemski, Boston	.321
1964	Roberto Clemente, Pittsburgh	.339	1964	Tony Oliva, Minnesota	.323
1965	Roberto Clemente, Pittsburgh	.329	1965	Tony Oliva, Minnesota	.321
1966	Matty Alou, Pittsburgh	.342	1966	Frank Robinson, Baltimore	.316
1967	Roberto Clemente, Pittsburgh	.357	1967	Carl Yastrzemski, Boston	.326
1968	Pete Rose, Cincinnati	.335	1968	Carl Yastrzemski, Boston	.301
1969	Pete Rose, Cincinnati	.348	1969	Rod Carew, Minnesota	.332
1970	Rico Carty, Atlanta	.366	1970	Alex Johnson, California	.329

National League		American League	
Year **Player, team**	**AVG**	**Year** **Player, team**	**AVG**
1971 Joe Torre, St. Louis	.363	1971 Tony Oliva, Minnesota	.337
1972 Billy Williams, Chicago	.333	1972 Rod Carew, Minnesota	.318
1973 Pete Rose, Cincinnati	.338	1973 Rod Carew, Minnesota	.350
1974 Ralph Garr, Atlanta	.353	1974 Rod Carew, Minnesota	.364
1975 Bill Madlock, Chicago	.354	1975 Rod Carew, Minnesota	.359
1976 Bill Madlock, Chicago	.339	1976 George Brett, Kansas City	.333
1977 Dave Parker, Pittsburgh	.338	1977 Rod Carew, Minnesota	.388
1978 Dave Parker, Pittsburgh	.334	1978 Rod Carew, Minnesota	.333
1979 Keith Hernandez, St. Louis	.344	1979 Fred Lynn, Boston	.333
1980 Bill Buckner, Chicago	.324	1980 George Brett, Kansas City	.390
1981 Bill Madlock, Pittsburgh	.341	1981 Carney Lansford, Boston	.336
1982 Al Oliver, Montréal	.331	1982 Willie Wilson, Kansas City	.332
1983 Bill Madlock, Pittsburgh	.323	1983 Wade Boggs, Boston	.361
1984 Tony Gwynn, San Diego	.351	1984 Don Mattingly, New York	.343
1985 Willie McGee, St. Louis	.353	1985 Wade Boggs, Boston	.368
1986 Tim Raines, Montréal	.334	1986 Wade Boggs, Boston	.357
1987 Tony Gwynn, San Diego	.370	1987 Wade Boggs, Boston	.363
1988 Tony Gwynn, San Diego	.313	1988 Wade Boggs, Boston	.366
1989 Tony Gwynn, San Diego	.336	1989 Kirby Puckett, Minnesota	.339
1990 Willie McGee, St. Louis	.335	1990 George Brett, Kansas City	.329
1991 Terry Pendleton, Atlanta	.319	1991 Julio Franco, Texas	.341
1992 Gary Sheffield, San Diego	.330	1992 Edgar Martinez, Seattle	.343
1993 Andres Galarraga, Colorado	.370	1993 John Olerud, Toronto	.363
1994 Tony Gwynn, San Diego	.394	1994 Paul O'Neill, New York	.359
1995 Tony Gwynn, San Diego	.368	1995 Edgar Martinez, Seattle	.356
1996 Tony Gwynn, San Diego	.353	1996 Alex Rodriguez, Seattle	.358
1997 Tony Gwynn, San Diego	.372	1997 Frank Thomas, Chicago	.347
1998 Larry Walker, Colorado	.363	1998 Bernie Williams, New York	.339
1999 Larry Walker, Colorado	.379	1999 Nomar Garciaparra, Boston	.357
2000 Todd Helton, Colorado	.372	2000 Nomar Garciaparra, Boston	.372
2001 Larry Walker, Colorado	.350	2001 Ichiro Suzuki, Seattle	.350
2002 Barry Bonds, San Francisco	.370	2002 Manny Ramirez, Boston	.349
2003 Albert Pujols, St. Louis	.359	2003 Bill Mueller, Boston	.326
2004 Barry Bonds, San Francisco	.362	2004 Ichiro Suzuki, Seattle	.372
2005 Derrek Lee, Chicago	.335	2005 Michael Young, Texas	.331
2006 Freddy Sanchez, Pittsburgh	.344	2006 Joe Mauer, Minnesota	.347
2007 Matt Holliday, Colorado	.340	2007 Magglio Ordoñez, Detroit	.363
2008 Chipper Jones, Atlanta	.364	2008 Joe Mauer, Minnesota	.328
2009 Hanley Ramirez, Florida	.342	2009 Joe Mauer, Minnesota	.365
2010 Carlos Gonzalez, Colorado	.336	2010 Josh Hamilton, Texas	.359
2011 Jose Reyes, New York	.337	2011 Miguel Cabrera, Detroit	.344
2012 Buster Posey, San Francisco	.336	2012 Miguel Cabrera, Detroit	.330
2013 Michael Cuddyer, Colorado	.331	2013 Miguel Cabrera, Detroit	.348
2014 Justin Morneau, Colorado	.319	2014 Jose Altuve, Houston	.341
2015 Dee Gordon, Miami	.333	2015 Miguel Cabrera, Detroit	.338
2016 DJ LeMahieu, Colorado	.348	2016 Jose Altuve, Houston	.338

(1) Napoleon Lajoie's 1901 batting average varies in historical records from .421 to .426. (2) Some baseball researchers have concluded that Ty Cobb actually hit .382 in 1910 while Napoleon Lajoie, Cleveland, hit .383.

Earned Run Average Leaders by Season, 1977-2016

National League				American League			
Year **Pitcher, team**	**G**	**IP**	**ERA**	**Year** **Pitcher, team**	**G**	**IP**	**ERA**
1977 John Candelaria, Pittsburgh	33	230.2	2.34	1977 Frank Tanana, California	31	241.1	2.54
1978 Craig Swan, New York	29	207.1	2.43	1978 Ron Guidry, New York	35	273.2	1.74
1979 J. R. Richard, Houston	38	292.1	2.71	1979 Ron Guidry, New York	33	236.1	2.78
1980 Don Sutton, Los Angeles	32	212.1	2.20	1980 Rudy May, New York	41	175.1	2.46
1981 Nolan Ryan, Houston	21	149.0	1.69	1981 Sammy Stewart, Baltimore	29	112.1	2.32
1982 Steve Rogers, Montréal	35	277.0	2.40	1982 Rick Sutcliffe, Cleveland	34	216.0	2.96
1983 Atlee Hammaker, San Francisco	23	172.1	2.25	1983 Rick Honeycutt, Texas	25	174.2	2.42
1984 Alejandro Peña, Los Angeles	28	199.1	2.48	1984 Mike Boddicker, Baltimore	34	261.1	2.79
1985 Dwight Gooden, New York	35	276.2	1.53	1985 Dave Stieb, Toronto	36	265.0	2.48
1986 Mike Scott, Houston	37	275.1	2.22	1986 Roger Clemens, Boston	33	254.0	2.48
1987 Nolan Ryan, Houston	34	211.2	2.76	1987 Jimmy Key, Toronto	36	261.0	2.76
1988 Joe Magrane, St. Louis	24	165.1	2.18	1988 Allan Anderson, Minnesota	30	202.1	2.45
1989 Scott Garrelts, San Francisco	30	193.1	2.28	1989 Bret Saberhagen, Kansas City	36	262.1	2.16
1990 Danny Darwin, Houston	48	162.2	2.21	1990 Roger Clemens, Boston	31	228.1	1.93
1991 Dennis Martinez, Montréal	31	222.0	2.39	1991 Roger Clemens, Boston	35	271.1	2.62
1992 Bill Swift, San Francisco	30	164.2	2.08	1992 Roger Clemens, Boston	32	246.2	2.41
1993 Greg Maddux, Atlanta	36	267.0	2.36	1993 Kevin Appier, Kansas City	34	238.2	2.56
1994 Greg Maddux, Atlanta	25	202.0	1.56	1994 Steve Ontiveros, Oakland	27	115.1	2.65
1995 Greg Maddux, Atlanta	28	209.2	1.63	1995 Randy Johnson, Seattle	30	214.1	2.48
1996 Kevin Brown, Florida	32	233.0	1.89	1996 Juan Guzman, Toronto	27	187.2	2.93
1997 Pedro Martinez, Montréal	31	241.1	1.90	1997 Roger Clemens, Toronto	34	264.0	2.05
1998 Greg Maddux, Atlanta	34	251.0	2.22	1998 Roger Clemens, Toronto	33	234.2	2.65
1999 Randy Johnson, Arizona	35	271.2	2.48	1999 Pedro Martinez, Boston	31	213.1	2.07
2000 Kevin Brown, Los Angeles	33	230.0	2.58	2000 Pedro Martinez, Boston	29	217.0	1.74
2001 Randy Johnson, Arizona	35	249.2	2.49	2001 Freddy Garcia, Seattle	34	238.2	3.05
2002 Randy Johnson, Arizona	35	260.0	2.32	2002 Pedro Martinez, Boston	30	199.1	2.26
2003 Jason Schmidt, San Francisco	29	207.2	2.34	2003 Pedro Martinez, Boston	29	186.2	2.22
2004 Jake Peavy, San Diego	27	166.1	2.27	2004 Johan Santana, Minnesota	34	228.0	2.61
2005 Roger Clemens, Houston	32	211.1	1.87	2005 Kevin Millwood, Cleveland	30	192.0	2.86
2006 Roy Oswalt, Houston	33	220.2	2.98	2006 Johan Santana, Minnesota	34	233.2	2.77
2007 Jake Peavy, San Diego	34	223.1	2.54	2007 John Lackey, Los Angeles	33	224.0	3.01
2008 Johan Santana, New York	34	234.1	2.53	2008 Cliff Lee, Cleveland	31	223.1	2.54
2009 Chris Carpenter, St. Louis	28	192.2	2.24	2009 Zack Greinke, Kansas City	33	229.1	2.16
2010 Josh Johnson, Florida	28	183.2	2.30	2010 Felix Hernandez, Seattle	34	249.2	2.27
2011 Clayton Kershaw, Los Angeles	33	233.1	2.28	2011 Justin Verlander, Detroit	34	251.0	2.40
2012 Clayton Kershaw, Los Angeles	33	227.2	2.53	2012 David Price, Tampa Bay	31	211.0	2.56
2013 Clayton Kershaw, Los Angeles	33	236.0	1.83	2013 Anibal Sanchez, Detroit	29	182.0	2.57
2014 Clayton Kershaw, Los Angeles	27	198.1	1.77	2014 Felix Hernandez, Seattle	34	236.0	2.14
2015 Zack Greinke, Los Angeles	32	222.2	1.66	2015 David Price, Detroit-Toronto	32	220.1	2.45
2016 Kyle Hendricks, Chicago	31	190.0	2.13	2016 Aaron Sanchez, Toronto	30	192.0	3.00

Strikeout Leaders by Season, 1901-2016

* = All-time single-season record for league since beginning of "modern" era in 1901.

	National League			American League	
Year	Pitcher, team	SO	Year	Pitcher, team	SO
1901	Noodles Hahn, Cincinnati	239	1901	Cy Young, Boston	158
1902	Vic Willis, Boston	225	1902	Rube Waddell, Philadelphia	210
1903	Christy Mathewson, New York	267	1903	Rube Waddell, Philadelphia	302
1904	Christy Mathewson, New York	212	1904	Rube Waddell, Philadelphia	349
1905	Christy Mathewson, New York	206	1905	Rube Waddell, Philadelphia	287
1906	Fred Beebe, Chicago-St. Louis	171	1906	Rube Waddell, Philadelphia	196
1907	Christy Mathewson, New York	178	1907	Rube Waddell, Philadelphia	232
1908	Christy Mathewson, New York	259	1908	Ed Walsh, Chicago	269
1909	Orval Overall, Chicago	205	1909	Frank Smith, Chicago	177
1910	Earl Moore, Philadelphia	185	1910	Walter Johnson, Washington	313
1911	Rube Marquard, New York	237	1911	Ed Walsh, Chicago	255
1912	Grover Alexander, Philadelphia	195	1912	Walter Johnson, Washington	303
1913	Tom Seaton, Philadelphia	168	1913	Walter Johnson, Washington	243
1914	Grover Alexander, Philadelphia	214	1914	Walter Johnson, Washington	225
1915	Grover Alexander, Philadelphia	241	1915	Walter Johnson, Washington	203
1916	Grover Alexander, Philadelphia	167	1916	Walter Johnson, Washington	228
1917	Grover Alexander, Philadelphia	200	1917	Walter Johnson, Washington	188
1918	Hippo Vaughn, Chicago	148	1918	Walter Johnson, Washington	162
1919	Hippo Vaughn, Chicago	141	1919	Walter Johnson, Washington	147
1920	Grover Alexander, Chicago	173	1920	Stan Coveleski, Cleveland	133
1921	Burleigh Grimes, Brooklyn	136	1921	Walter Johnson, Washington	143
1922	Dazzy Vance, Brooklyn	134	1922	Urban Shocker, St. Louis	149
1923	Dazzy Vance, Brooklyn	197	1923	Walter Johnson, Washington	130
1924	Dazzy Vance, Brooklyn	262	1924	Walter Johnson, Washington	158
1925	Dazzy Vance, Brooklyn	221	1925	Lefty Grove, Philadelphia	116
1926	Dazzy Vance, Brooklyn	140	1926	Lefty Grove, Philadelphia	194
1927	Dazzy Vance, Brooklyn	184	1927	Lefty Grove, Philadelphia	174
1928	Dazzy Vance, Brooklyn	200	1928	Lefty Grove, Philadelphia	183
1929	Pat Malone, Chicago	166	1929	Lefty Grove, Philadelphia	170
1930	Bill Hallahan, St. Louis	177	1930	Lefty Grove, Philadelphia	209
1931	Bill Hallahan, St. Louis	159	1931	Lefty Grove, Philadelphia	175
1932	Dizzy Dean, St. Louis	191	1932	Red Ruffing, New York	190
1933	Dizzy Dean, St. Louis	199	1933	Lefty Gomez, New York	163
1934	Dizzy Dean, St. Louis	195	1934	Lefty Gomez, New York	158
1935	Dizzy Dean, St. Louis	190	1935	Tommy Bridges, Detroit	163
1936	Van Lingle Mungo, Brooklyn	238	1936	Tommy Bridges, Detroit	175
1937	Carl Hubbell, New York	159	1937	Lefty Gomez, New York	194
1938	Clay Bryant, Chicago	135	1938	Bob Feller, Cleveland	240
1939	Claude Passeau, Philadelphia-Chicago; Bucky Walters, Cincinnati	137	1939	Bob Feller, Cleveland	246
1940	Kirby Higbe, Philadelphia	137	1940	Bob Feller, Cleveland	261
1941	John Vander Meer, Cincinnati	202	1941	Bob Feller, Cleveland	260
1942	John Vander Meer, Cincinnati	186	1942	Tex Hughson, Boston; Bobo Newsom, Washington	113
1943	John Vander Meer, Cincinnati	174	1943	Allie Reynolds, Cleveland	151
1944	Bill Voiselle, New York	161	1944	Hal Newhouser, Detroit	187
1945	Preacher Roe, Pittsburgh	148	1945	Hal Newhouser, Detroit	212
1946	Johnny Schmitz, Cincinnati	135	1946	Bob Feller, Cleveland	348
1947	Ewell Blackwell, Cincinnati	193	1947	Bob Feller, Cleveland	196
1948	Harry Brecheen, St. Louis	149	1948	Bob Feller, Cleveland	164
1949	Warren Spahn, Boston	151	1949	Virgil Trucks, Detroit	153
1950	Warren Spahn, Boston	191	1950	Bob Lemon, Cleveland	170
1951	Warren Spahn, Boston; Don Newcombe, Brooklyn	164	1951	Vic Raschi, New York	164
1952	Warren Spahn, Boston	183	1952	Allie Reynolds, New York	160
1953	Robin Roberts, Philadelphia	198	1953	Billy Pierce, Chicago	186
1954	Robin Roberts, Philadelphia	185	1954	Bob Turley, Baltimore	185
1955	Sam Jones, Chicago	198	1955	Herb Score, Cleveland	245
1956	Sam Jones, Chicago	176	1956	Herb Score, Cleveland	263
1957	Jack Sanford, Philadelphia	188	1957	Early Wynn, Cleveland	184
1958	Sam Jones, St. Louis	225	1958	Early Wynn, Chicago	179
1959	Don Drysdale, Los Angeles	242	1959	Jim Bunning, Detroit	201
1960	Don Drysdale, Los Angeles	246	1960	Jim Bunning, Detroit	201
1961	Sandy Koufax, Los Angeles	269	1961	Camilo Pascual, Minnesota	221
1962	Don Drysdale, Los Angeles	232	1962	Camilo Pascual, Minnesota	206
1963	Sandy Koufax, Los Angeles	306	1963	Camilo Pascual, Minnesota	202
1964	Bob Veale, Pittsburgh	250	1964	Al Downing, New York	217
1965	Sandy Koufax, Los Angeles	382*	1965	Sam McDowell, Cleveland	325
1966	Sandy Koufax, Los Angeles	317	1966	Sam McDowell, Cleveland	225
1967	Jim Bunning, Philadelphia	253	1967	Jim Lonborg, Boston	246
1968	Bob Gibson, St. Louis	268	1968	Sam McDowell, Cleveland	283
1969	Ferguson Jenkins, Chicago	273	1969	Sam McDowell, Cleveland	279
1970	Tom Seaver, New York	283	1970	Sam McDowell, Cleveland	304
1971	Tom Seaver, New York	289	1971	Mickey Lolich, Detroit	308
1972	Steve Carlton, Philadelphia	310	1972	Nolan Ryan, California	329
1973	Tom Seaver, New York	251	1973	Nolan Ryan, California	383*
1974	Steve Carlton, Philadelphia	240	1974	Nolan Ryan, California	367
1975	Tom Seaver, New York	243	1975	Frank Tanana, California	269
1976	Tom Seaver, New York	235	1976	Nolan Ryan, California	327
1977	Phil Niekro, Atlanta	262	1977	Nolan Ryan, California	341
1978	J. R. Richard, Houston	303	1978	Nolan Ryan, California	260

National League Year	Pitcher, team	SO	American League Year	Pitcher, team	SO
1979	J. R. Richard, Houston	313	1979	Nolan Ryan, California	223
1980	Steve Carlton, Philadelphia	286	1980	Len Barker, Cleveland	187
1981	Fernando Valenzuela, Los Angeles	180	1981	Len Barker, Cleveland	127
1982	Steve Carlton, Philadelphia	286	1982	Floyd Bannister, Seattle	209
1983	Steve Carlton, Philadelphia	275	1983	Jack Morris, Detroit	232
1984	Dwight Gooden, New York	276	1984	Mark Langston, Seattle	204
1985	Dwight Gooden, New York	268	1985	Bert Blyleven, Cleveland-Minnesota	206
1986	Mike Scott, Houston	306	1986	Mark Langston, Seattle	245
1987	Nolan Ryan, Houston	270	1987	Mark Langston, Seattle	262
1988	Nolan Ryan, Houston	228	1988	Roger Clemens, Boston	291
1989	Jose DeLeon, St. Louis	201	1989	Nolan Ryan, Texas	301
1990	David Cone, New York	233	1990	Nolan Ryan, Texas	232
1991	David Cone, New York	241	1991	Roger Clemens, Boston	241
1992	John Smoltz, Atlanta	215	1992	Randy Johnson, Seattle	241
1993	Jose Rijo, Cincinnati	227	1993	Randy Johnson, Seattle	308
1994	Andy Benes, San Diego	189	1994	Randy Johnson, Seattle	204
1995	Hideo Nomo, Los Angeles	236	1995	Randy Johnson, Seattle	294
1996	John Smoltz, Atlanta	276	1996	Roger Clemens, Boston	257
1997	Curt Schilling, Philadelphia	319	1997	Roger Clemens, Toronto	292
1998	Curt Schilling, Philadelphia	300	1998	Roger Clemens, Toronto	271
1999	Randy Johnson, Arizona	364	1999	Pedro Martinez, Boston	313
2000	Randy Johnson, Arizona	347	2000	Pedro Martinez, Boston	284
2001	Randy Johnson, Arizona	372	2001	Hideo Nomo, Boston	220
2002	Randy Johnson, Arizona	334	2002	Pedro Martinez, Boston	239
2003	Kerry Wood, Chicago	266	2003	Esteban Loaiza, Chicago	207
2004	Randy Johnson, Arizona	290	2004	Johan Santana, Minnesota	265
2005	Jake Peavy, San Diego	216	2005	Johan Santana, Minnesota	238
2006	Aaron Harang, Cincinnati	216	2006	Johan Santana, Minnesota	245
2007	Jake Peavy, San Diego	240	2007	Scott Kazmir, Tampa Bay	239
2008	Tim Lincecum, San Francisco	265	2008	A. J. Burnett, Toronto	231
2009	Tim Lincecum, San Francisco	261	2009	Justin Verlander, Detroit	269
2010	Tim Lincecum, San Francisco	231	2010	Jered Weaver, Los Angeles	233
2011	Clayton Kershaw, Los Angeles	248	2011	Justin Verlander, Detroit	250
2012	R.A. Dickey, New York	230	2012	Justin Verlander, Detroit	239
2013	Clayton Kershaw, Los Angeles	232	2013	Yu Darvish, Texas	277
2014	Johnny Cueto, Cincinnati; Stephen Strasburg, Washington	242	2014	David Price, Tampa Bay-Detroit	271
2015	Clayton Kershaw, Los Angeles	301	2015	Chris Sale, Chicago	274
2016	Max Scherzer, Washington	284	2016	Justin Verlander, Detroit	254

Cy Young Award Winners, 1956-2015

Year	Pitcher, team	Year	Pitcher, team	Year	Pitcher, team
1956	Don Newcombe, Brooklyn	1980	(NL) Steve Carlton, Philadelphia	1997	(NL) Pedro Martinez, Montréal
1957	Warren Spahn, Milwaukee		(AL) Steve Stone, Baltimore		(AL) Roger Clemens, Toronto
1958	Bob Turley, NY Yankees	1981	(NL) Fernando Valenzuela, L.A.	1998	(NL) Tom Glavine, Atlanta
1959	Early Wynn, Chicago White Sox		(AL) Rollie Fingers, Milwaukee		(AL) Roger Clemens, Toronto
1960	Vernon Law, Pittsburgh	1982	(NL) Steve Carlton, Philadelphia	1999	(NL) Randy Johnson, Arizona
1961	Whitey Ford, NY Yankees		(AL) Pete Vuckovich, Milwaukee		(AL) Pedro Martinez, Boston
1962	Don Drysdale, L.A. Dodgers	1983	(NL) John Denny, Philadelphia	2000	(NL) Randy Johnson, Arizona
1963	Sandy Koufax, L.A. Dodgers		(AL) LaMarr Hoyt, Chicago		(AL) Pedro Martinez, Boston
1964	Dean Chance, L.A. Angels	1984	(NL) Rick Sutcliffe, Chicago	2001	(NL) Randy Johnson, Arizona
1965	Sandy Koufax, L.A. Dodgers		(AL) Willie Hernandez, Detroit		(AL) Roger Clemens, NY
1966	Sandy Koufax, L.A. Dodgers	1985	(NL) Dwight Gooden, NY	2002	(NL) Randy Johnson, Arizona
1967	(NL) Mike McCormick, S.F.		(AL) Bret Saberhagen, Kansas City		(AL) Barry Zito, Oakland
	(AL) Jim Lonborg, Boston	1986	(NL) Mike Scott, Houston	2003	(NL) Eric Gagne, L.A.
1968	(NL) Bob Gibson, St. Louis		(AL) Roger Clemens, Boston		(AL) Roy Halladay, Toronto
	(AL) Denny McLain, Detroit	1987	(NL) Steve Bedrosian, Phil.	2004	(NL) Roger Clemens, Houston
1969	(NL) Tom Seaver, NY		(AL) Roger Clemens, Boston		(AL) Johan Santana, Minnesota
	(AL) Denny McLain, Detroit; Mike Cuellar, Baltimore	1988	(NL) Orel Hershiser, L.A.	2005	(NL) Chris Carpenter, St. Louis
			(AL) Frank Viola, Minnesota		(AL) Bartolo Colon, L.A.
1970	(NL) Bob Gibson, St. Louis	1989	(NL) Mark Davis, San Diego	2006	(NL) Brandon Webb, Arizona
	(AL) Jim Perry, Minnesota		(AL) Bret Saberhagen, Kansas City		(AL) Johan Santana, Minnesota
1971	(NL) Ferguson Jenkins, Chicago	1990	(NL) Doug Drabek, Pittsburgh	2007	(NL) Jake Peavy, San Diego
	(AL) Vida Blue, Oakland		(AL) Bob Welch, Oakland		(AL) CC Sabathia, Cleveland
1972	(NL) Steve Carlton, Philadelphia	1991	(NL) Tom Glavine, Atlanta	2008	(NL) Tim Lincecum, S.F.
	(AL) Gaylord Perry, Cleveland		(AL) Roger Clemens, Boston		(AL) Cliff Lee, Cleveland
1973	(NL) Tom Seaver, NY	1992	(NL) Greg Maddux, Chicago	2009	(NL) Tim Lincecum, S.F.
	(AL) Jim Palmer, Baltimore		(AL) Dennis Eckersley, Oakland		(AL) Zack Greinke, Kansas City
1974	(NL) Mike Marshall, L.A.	1993	(NL) Greg Maddux, Atlanta	2010	(NL) Roy Halladay, Philadelphia
	(AL) Jim "Catfish" Hunter, Oakland		(AL) Jack McDowell, Chicago		(AL) Felix Hernandez, Seattle
1975	(NL) Tom Seaver, NY	1994	(NL) Greg Maddux, Atlanta	2011	(NL) Clayton Kershaw, L.A.
	(AL) Jim Palmer, Baltimore		(AL) David Cone, Kansas City		(AL) Justin Verlander, Detroit
1976	(NL) Randy Jones, San Diego	1995	(NL) Greg Maddux, Atlanta	2012	(NL) R.A. Dickey, NY
	(AL) Jim Palmer, Baltimore		(AL) Randy Johnson, Seattle		(AL) David Price, Tampa Bay
1977	(NL) Steve Carlton, Philadelphia	1996	(NL) John Smoltz, Atlanta	2013	(NL) Clayton Kershaw, L.A.
	(AL) Sparky Lyle, NY		(AL) Pat Hentgen, Toronto		(AL) Max Scherzer, Detroit
1978	(NL) Gaylord Perry, San Diego			2014	(NL) Clayton Kershaw, L.A.
	(AL) Ron Guidry, NY				(AL) Corey Kluber, Cleveland
1979	(NL) Bruce Sutter, Chicago			2015	(NL) Jake Arrieta, Chicago
	(AL) Mike Flanagan, Baltimore				(AL) Dallas Keuchel, Houston

Most Valuable Players, 1931-2015

As selected by the Baseball Writers' Assn. of America. Prior to 1931, MVP honors were named by various sources.

National League

Year	Player, team	Year	Player, team	Year	Player, team
1931	Frank Frisch, St. Louis	1961	Frank Robinson, Cincinnati	1988	Kirk Gibson, Los Angeles
1932	Chuck Klein, Philadelphia	1962	Maury Wills, Los Angeles	1989	Kevin Mitchell, San Francisco
1933	Carl Hubbell, New York	1963	Sandy Koufax, Los Angeles	1990	Barry Bonds, Pittsburgh
1934	Dizzy Dean, St. Louis	1964	Ken Boyer, St. Louis	1991	Terry Pendleton, Atlanta
1935	Gabby Hartnett, Chicago	1965	Willie Mays, San Francisco	1992	Barry Bonds, Pittsburgh
1936	Carl Hubbell, New York	1966	Roberto Clemente, Pittsburgh	1993	Barry Bonds, San Francisco
1937	Joe Medwick, St. Louis	1967	Orlando Cepeda, St. Louis	1994	Jeff Bagwell, Houston
1938	Ernie Lombardi, Cincinnati	1968	Bob Gibson, St. Louis	1995	Barry Larkin, Cincinnati
1939	Bucky Walters, Cincinnati	1969	Willie McCovey, San Francisco	1996	Ken Caminiti, San Diego
1940	Frank McCormick, Cincinnati	1970	Johnny Bench, Cincinnati	1997	Larry Walker, Colorado
1941	Dolph Camilli, Brooklyn	1971	Joe Torre, St. Louis	1998	Sammy Sosa, Chicago
1942	Mort Cooper, St. Louis	1972	Johnny Bench, Cincinnati	1999	Chipper Jones, Atlanta
1943	Stan Musial, St. Louis	1973	Pete Rose, Cincinnati	2000	Jeff Kent, San Francisco
1944	Martin Marion, St. Louis	1974	Steve Garvey, Los Angeles	2001	Barry Bonds, San Francisco
1945	Phil Cavarretta, Chicago	1975	Joe Morgan, Cincinnati	2002	Barry Bonds, San Francisco
1946	Stan Musial, St. Louis	1976	Joe Morgan, Cincinnati	2003	Barry Bonds, San Francisco
1947	Bob Elliott, Boston	1977	George Foster, Cincinnati	2004	Barry Bonds, San Francisco
1948	Stan Musial, St. Louis	1978	Dave Parker, Pittsburgh	2005	Albert Pujols, St. Louis
1949	Jackie Robinson, Brooklyn	1979	Keith Hernandez, St. Louis;	2006	Ryan Howard, Philadelphia
1950	Jim Konstanty, Philadelphia		Willie Stargell, Pittsburgh	2007	Jimmy Rollins, Philadelphia
1951	Roy Campanella, Brooklyn	1980	Mike Schmidt, Philadelphia	2008	Albert Pujols, St. Louis
1952	Hank Sauer, Chicago	1981	Mike Schmidt, Philadelphia	2009	Albert Pujols, St. Louis
1953	Roy Campanella, Brooklyn	1982	Dale Murphy, Atlanta	2010	Joey Votto, Cincinnati
1954	Willie Mays, New York	1983	Dale Murphy, Atlanta	2011	Ryan Braun, Milwaukee
1955	Roy Campanella, Brooklyn	1984	Ryne Sandberg, Chicago	2012	Buster Posey, San Francisco
1956	Don Newcombe, Brooklyn	1985	Willie McGee, St. Louis	2013	Andrew McCutchen,
1957	Hank Aaron, Milwaukee	1986	Mike Schmidt, Philadelphia		Pittsburgh
1958	Ernie Banks, Chicago	1987	Andre Dawson, Chicago	2014	Clayton Kershaw, Los Angeles
1959	Ernie Banks, Chicago			2015	Bryce Harper, Washington
1960	Dick Groat, Pittsburgh				

American League

Year	Player, team	Year	Player, team	Year	Player, team
1931	Lefty Grove, Philadelphia	1959	Nellie Fox, Chicago	1988	Jose Canseco, Oakland
1932	Jimmie Foxx, Philadelphia	1960	Roger Maris, New York	1989	Robin Yount, Milwaukee
1933	Jimmie Foxx, Philadelphia	1961	Roger Maris, New York	1990	Rickey Henderson, Oakland
1934	Mickey Cochrane, Detroit	1962	Mickey Mantle, New York	1991	Cal Ripken Jr., Baltimore
1935	Hank Greenberg, Detroit	1963	Elston Howard, New York	1992	Dennis Eckersley, Oakland
1936	Lou Gehrig, New York	1964	Brooks Robinson, Baltimore	1993	Frank Thomas, Chicago
1937	Charlie Gehringer, Detroit	1965	Zoilo Versalles, Minnesota	1994	Frank Thomas, Chicago
1938	Jimmie Foxx, Boston	1966	Frank Robinson, Baltimore	1995	Mo Vaughn, Boston
1939	Joe DiMaggio, New York	1967	Carl Yastrzemski, Boston	1996	Juan Gonzalez, Texas
1940	Hank Greenberg, Detroit	1968	Denny McLain, Detroit	1997	Ken Griffey Jr., Seattle
1941	Joe DiMaggio, New York	1969	Harmon Killebrew, Minnesota	1998	Juan Gonzalez, Texas
1942	Joe Gordon, New York	1970	John "Boog" Powell, Baltimore	1999	Ivan Rodriguez, Texas
1943	Spurgeon "Spud" Chandler,	1971	Vida Blue, Oakland	2000	Jason Giambi, Oakland
	New York	1972	Dick Allen, Chicago	2001	Ichiro Suzuki, Seattle
1944	Hal Newhouser, Detroit	1973	Reggie Jackson, Oakland	2002	Miguel Tejada, Oakland
1945	Hal Newhouser, Detroit	1974	Jeff Burroughs, Texas	2003	Alex Rodriguez, Texas
1946	Ted Williams, Boston	1975	Fred Lynn, Boston	2004	Vladimir Guerrero, Anaheim
1947	Joe DiMaggio, New York	1976	Thurman Munson, New York	2005	Alex Rodriguez, New York
1948	Lou Boudreau, Cleveland	1977	Rod Carew, Minnesota	2006	Justin Morneau, Minnesota
1949	Ted Williams, Boston	1978	Jim Rice, Boston	2007	Alex Rodriguez, New York
1950	Phil Rizzuto, New York	1979	Don Baylor, California	2008	Dustin Pedroia, Boston
1951	Yogi Berra, New York	1980	George Brett, Kansas City	2009	Joe Mauer, Minnesota
1952	Bobby Shantz, Philadelphia	1981	Rollie Fingers, Milwaukee	2010	Josh Hamilton, Texas
1953	Al Rosen, Cleveland	1982	Robin Yount, Milwaukee	2011	Justin Verlander, Detroit
1954	Yogi Berra, New York	1983	Cal Ripken Jr., Baltimore	2012	Miguel Cabrera, Detroit
1955	Yogi Berra, New York	1984	Willie Hernandez, Detroit	2013	Miguel Cabrera, Detroit
1956	Mickey Mantle, New York	1985	Don Mattingly, New York	2014	Mike Trout, Los Angeles
1957	Mickey Mantle, New York	1986	Roger Clemens, Boston	2015	Josh Donaldson, Toronto
1958	Jackie Jensen, Boston	1987	George Bell, Toronto		

Rookie of the Year, 1949-2015

(as selected by the Baseball Writers' Assn. of America)

1947: Jackie Robinson, Brooklyn, 1B (combined selection); 1948: Alvin Dark, Boston (NL), SS (combined selection).

National League

Year	Player, team, position	Year	Player, team, position	Year	Player, team, position
1949	Don Newcombe, Brooklyn, P	1956	Frank Robinson, Cincinnati, OF	1963	Pete Rose, Cincinnati, 2B
1950	Sam Jethroe, Boston, OF	1957	Jack Sanford, Philadelphia, P	1964	Richie Allen, Philadelphia, 3B
1951	Willie Mays, NY, OF	1958	Orlando Cepeda, San Francisco, 1B	1965	Jim Lefebvre, L.A., 2B
1952	Joe Black, Brooklyn, P	1959	Willie McCovey, San Francisco, 1B	1966	Tommy Helms, Cincinnati, 2B
1953	Jim Gilliam, Brooklyn, 2B	1960	Frank Howard, L.A., OF	1967	Tom Seaver, NY, P
1954	Wally Moon, St. Louis, OF	1961	Billy Williams, Chicago, OF	1968	Johnny Bench, Cincinnati, C
1955	Bill Virdon, St. Louis, OF	1962	Ken Hubbs, Chicago, 2B	1969	Ted Sizemore, L.A., 2B

Year	Player, team, position	Year	Player, team, position	Year	Player, team, position
1970	Carl Morton, Montréal, P	1985	Vince Coleman, St. Louis, OF	2001	Albert Pujols, St. Louis, OF
1971	Earl Williams, Atlanta, C	1986	Todd Worrell, St. Louis, P	2002	Jason Jennings, Colorado, P
1972	Jon Matlack, NY, P	1987	Benito Santiago, San Diego, C	2003	Dontrelle Willis, Florida, P
1973	Gary Matthews, San Francisco, OF	1988	Chris Sabo, Cincinnati, 3B	2004	Jason Bay, Pittsburgh, OF
1974	Bake McBride, St. Louis, OF	1989	Jerome Walton, Chicago, OF	2005	Ryan Howard, Philadelphia, 1B
1975	John Montefusco, San Francisco, P	1990	Dave Justice, Atlanta, 1B	2006	Hanley Ramirez, Florida, SS
1976	Butch Metzger, San Diego, P; Pat Zachry, Cincinnati, P	1991	Jeff Bagwell, Houston, 1B	2007	Ryan Braun, Milwaukee, 3B
		1992	Eric Karros, L.A., 1B	2008	Geovany Soto, Chicago, C
1977	Andre Dawson, Montréal, OF	1993	Mike Piazza, L.A., C	2009	Chris Coghlan, Florida, OF
1978	Bob Horner, Atlanta, 3B	1994	Raul Mondesi, L.A., OF	2010	Buster Posey, San Francisco, C
1979	Rick Sutcliffe, L.A., P	1995	Hideo Nomo, L.A., P	2011	Craig Kimbrel, Atlanta, P
1980	Steve Howe, L.A., P	1996	Todd Hollandsworth, L.A., OF	2012	Bryce Harper, Washington, OF
1981	Fernando Valenzuela, L.A., P	1997	Scott Rolen, Philadelphia, 3B	2013	José Fernández, Miami, P
1982	Steve Sax, L.A., 2B	1998	Kerry Wood, Chicago, P	2014	Jacob deGrom, NY, P
1983	Darryl Strawberry, NY, OF	1999	Scott Williamson, Cincinnati, P	2015	Kris Bryant, Chicago, 3B
1984	Dwight Gooden, NY, P	2000	Rafael Furcal, Atlanta, SS		

American League

Year	Player, team, position	Year	Player, team, position	Year	Player, team, position
1949	Roy Sievers, St. Louis, OF	1972	Carlton Fisk, Boston, C	1994	Bob Hamelin, Kansas City, DH
1950	Walt Dropo, Boston, 1B	1973	Al Bumbry, Baltimore, OF	1995	Marty Cordova, Minnesota, OF
1951	Gil McDougald, NY, 3B	1974	Mike Hargrove, Texas, 1B	1996	Derek Jeter, NY, SS
1952	Harry Byrd, Philadelphia, P	1975	Fred Lynn, Boston, OF	1997	Nomar Garciaparra, Boston, SS
1953	Harvey Kuenn, Detroit, SS	1976	Mark Fidrych, Detroit, P	1998	Ben Grieve, Oakland, OF
1954	Bob Grim, NY, P	1977	Eddie Murray, Baltimore, DH	1999	Carlos Beltran, Kansas City, OF
1955	Herb Score, Cleveland, P	1978	Lou Whitaker, Detroit, 2B	2000	Kazuhiro Sasaki, Seattle, P
1956	Luis Aparicio, Chicago, SS	1979	John Castino, Minnesota, 3B; Alfredo Griffin, Toronto, SS	2001	Ichiro Suzuki, Seattle, OF
1957	Tony Kubek, NY, IF-OF			2002	Eric Hinske, Toronto, 3B
1958	Albie Pearson, Washington, OF	1980	Joe Charboneau, Cleveland, OF	2003	Angel Berroa, Kansas City, SS
1959	Bob Allison, Washington, OF	1981	Dave Righetti, NY, P	2004	Bobby Crosby, Oakland, SS
1960	Ron Hansen, Baltimore, SS	1982	Cal Ripken Jr., Baltimore, SS	2005	Huston Street, Oakland, P
1961	Don Schwall, Boston, P	1983	Ron Kittle, Chicago, OF	2006	Justin Verlander, Detroit, P
1962	Tom Tresh, NY, IF-OF	1984	Alvin Davis, Seattle, 1B	2007	Dustin Pedroia, Boston, 2B
1963	Gary Peters, Chicago, P	1985	Ozzie Guillen, Chicago, SS	2008	Evan Longoria, Tampa Bay, 3B
1964	Tony Oliva, Minnesota, OF	1986	Jose Canseco, Oakland, OF	2009	Andrew Bailey, Oakland, P
1965	Curt Blefary, Baltimore, OF	1987	Mark McGwire, Oakland, 1B	2010	Neftali Feliz, Texas, P
1966	Tommie Agee, Chicago, OF	1988	Walt Weiss, Oakland, SS	2011	Jeremy Hellickson, Tampa Bay, P
1967	Rod Carew, Minnesota, 2B	1989	Gregg Olson, Baltimore, P	2012	Mike Trout, L.A., OF
1968	Stan Bahnsen, NY, P	1990	Sandy Alomar Jr., Cleveland, C	2013	Wil Myers, Tampa Bay, OF
1969	Lou Piniella, Kansas City, OF	1991	Chuck Knoblauch, Minnesota, 2B	2014	Jose Abreu, Chicago, 1B
1970	Thurman Munson, NY, C	1992	Pat Listach, Milwaukee, SS	2015	Carlos Correa, Houston, SS
1971	Chris Chambliss, Cleveland, 1B	1993	Tim Salmon, California, OF		

Major League Pennant Winners, 1901-75

	National League						American League				
Year	Winner	W	L	PCT	Manager	Year	Winner	W	L	PCT	Manager
1901	Pittsburgh	90	49	.647	Clarke	1901	Chicago	83	53	.610	Griffith
1902	Pittsburgh	103	36	.741	Clarke	1902	Philadelphia	83	53	.610	Mack
1903	Pittsburgh	91	49	.650	Clarke	1903	Boston	91	47	.659	Collins
1904	New York	106	47	.693	McGraw	1904	Boston	95	59	.617	Collins
1905	New York	105	48	.686	McGraw	1905	Philadelphia	92	56	.622	Mack
1906	Chicago	116	36	.763	Chance	1906	Chicago	93	58	.616	Jones
1907	Chicago	107	45	.704	Chance	1907	Detroit	92	58	.613	Jennings
1908	Chicago	99	55	.643	Chance	1908	Detroit	90	63	.588	Jennings
1909	Pittsburgh	110	42	.724	Clarke	1909	Detroit	98	54	.645	Jennings
1910	Chicago	104	50	.675	Chance	1910	Philadelphia	102	48	.680	Mack
1911	New York	99	54	.647	McGraw	1911	Philadelphia	101	50	.669	Mack
1912	New York	103	48	.682	McGraw	1912	Boston	105	47	.691	Stahl
1913	New York	101	51	.664	McGraw	1913	Philadelphia	96	57	.627	Mack
1914	Boston	94	59	.614	Stallings	1914	Philadelphia	99	53	.651	Mack
1915	Philadelphia	90	62	.592	Moran	1915	Boston	101	50	.669	Carrigan
1916	Brooklyn	94	60	.610	Robinson	1916	Boston	91	63	.591	Carrigan
1917	New York	98	56	.636	McGraw	1917	Chicago	100	54	.649	Rowland
1918	Chicago	84	45	.651	Mitchell	1918	Boston	75	51	.595	Barrow
1919	Cincinnati	96	44	.686	Moran	1919	Chicago	88	52	.629	Gleason
1920	Brooklyn	93	61	.604	Robinson	1920	Cleveland	98	56	.636	Speaker
1921	New York	94	59	.614	McGraw	1921	New York	98	55	.641	Huggins
1922	New York	93	61	.604	McGraw	1922	New York	94	60	.610	Huggins
1923	New York	95	58	.621	McGraw	1923	New York	98	54	.645	Huggins
1924	New York	93	60	.608	McGraw	1924	Washington	92	62	.597	Harris
1925	Pittsburgh	95	58	.621	McKechnie	1925	Washington	96	55	.636	Harris
1926	St. Louis	89	65	.578	Hornsby	1926	New York	91	63	.591	Huggins
1927	Pittsburgh	94	60	.610	Bush	1927	New York	110	44	.714	Huggins
1928	St. Louis	95	59	.617	McKechnie	1928	New York	101	53	.656	Huggins
1929	Chicago	98	54	.645	McCarthy	1929	Philadelphia	104	46	.693	Mack
1930	St. Louis	92	62	.597	Street	1930	Philadelphia	102	52	.662	Mack
1931	St. Louis	101	53	.656	Street	1931	Philadelphia	107	45	.704	Mack
1932	Chicago	90	64	.584	Hornsby, Grimm	1932	New York	107	47	.695	McCarthy

National League / American League

Year	Winner	W	L	PCT	Manager	Year	Winner	W	L	PCT	Manager
1933	New York	91	61	.599	Terry	1933	Washington	99	53	.651	Cronin
1934	St. Louis	95	58	.621	Frisch	1934	Detroit	101	53	.656	Cochrane
1935	Chicago	100	54	.649	Grimm	1935	Detroit	93	58	.616	Cochrane
1936	New York	92	62	.597	Terry	1936	New York	102	51	.667	McCarthy
1937	New York	95	57	.625	Terry	1937	New York	102	52	.662	McCarthy
1938	Chicago	89	63	.586	Grimm, Hartnett	1938	New York	99	53	.651	McCarthy
1939	Cincinnati	97	57	.630	McKechnie	1939	New York	106	45	.702	McCarthy
1940	Cincinnati	100	53	.654	McKechnie	1940	Detroit	90	64	.584	Baker
1941	Brooklyn	100	54	.649	Durocher	1941	New York	101	53	.656	McCarthy
1942	St. Louis	106	48	.688	Southworth	1942	New York	103	51	.669	McCarthy
1943	St. Louis	105	49	.682	Southworth	1943	New York	98	56	.636	McCarthy
1944	St. Louis	105	49	.682	Southworth	1944	St. Louis	89	65	.578	Sewell
1945	Chicago	98	56	.636	Grimm	1945	Detroit	88	65	.575	O'Neill
1946	St. Louis	98	58	.628	Dyer	1946	Boston	104	50	.675	Cronin
1947	Brooklyn	94	60	.610	Shotton	1947	New York	97	57	.630	Harris
1948	Boston	91	62	.595	Southworth	1948	Cleveland	97	58	.626	Boudreau
1949	Brooklyn	97	57	.630	Shotton	1949	New York	97	57	.630	Stengel
1950	Philadelphia	91	63	.591	Sawyer	1950	New York	98	56	.636	Stengel
1951	New York	98	59	.624	Durocher	1951	New York	98	56	.636	Stengel
1952	Brooklyn	96	57	.627	Dressen	1952	New York	95	59	.617	Stengel
1953	Brooklyn	105	49	.682	Dressen	1953	New York	99	52	.656	Stengel
1954	New York	97	57	.630	Durocher	1954	Cleveland	111	43	.721	Lopez
1955	Brooklyn	98	55	.641	Alston	1955	New York	96	58	.623	Stengel
1956	Brooklyn	93	61	.604	Alston	1956	New York	97	57	.630	Stengel
1957	Milwaukee	95	59	.617	Haney	1957	New York	98	56	.636	Stengel
1958	Milwaukee	92	62	.597	Haney	1958	New York	92	62	.597	Stengel
1959	Los Angeles	88	68	.564	Alston	1959	Chicago	94	60	.610	Lopez
1960	Pittsburgh	95	59	.617	Murtaugh	1960	New York	97	57	.630	Stengel
1961	Cincinnati	93	61	.604	Hutchinson	1961	New York	109	53	.673	Houk
1962	San Francisco	103	62	.624	Dark	1962	New York	96	66	.593	Houk
1963	Los Angeles	99	63	.611	Alston	1963	New York	104	57	.646	Houk
1964	St. Louis	93	69	.574	Keane	1964	New York	99	63	.611	Berra
1965	Los Angeles	97	65	.599	Alston	1965	Minnesota	102	60	.630	Mele
1966	Los Angeles	95	67	.586	Alston	1966	Baltimore	97	63	.606	Bauer
1967	St. Louis	101	60	.627	Schoendienst	1967	Boston	92	70	.568	Williams
1968	St. Louis	97	65	.599	Schoendienst	1968	Detroit	103	59	.636	Smith
1969	New York	100	62	.617	Hodges	1969	Baltimore	109	53	.673	Weaver
1970	Cincinnati	102	60	.630	Anderson	1970	Baltimore	108	54	.667	Weaver
1971	Pittsburgh	97	65	.599	Murtaugh	1971	Baltimore	101	57	.639	Weaver
1972	Cincinnati	95	59	.617	Anderson	1972	Oakland	93	62	.600	Williams
1973	New York	82	79	.509	Berra	1973	Oakland	94	68	.580	Williams
1974	Los Angeles	102	60	.630	Alston	1974	Oakland	90	72	.556	Dark
1975	Cincinnati	108	54	.667	Anderson	1975	Boston	95	65	.594	Johnson

Major League Pennant Winners, 1976-2016

National League

Year	East winner	W	L	PCT	Manager	West winner	W	L	PCT	Manager	Pennant winner
1976	Philadelphia	101	61	.623	Ozark	Cincinnati	102	60	.630	Anderson	Cincinnati
1977	Philadelphia	101	61	.623	Ozark	Los Angeles	98	64	.605	Lasorda	Los Angeles
1978	Philadelphia	90	72	.556	Ozark	Los Angeles	95	67	.586	Lasorda	Los Angeles
1979	Pittsburgh	98	64	.605	Tanner	Cincinnati	90	71	.559	McNamara	Pittsburgh
1980	Philadelphia	91	71	.562	Green	Houston	93	70	.571	Virdon	Philadelphia
1981(a)	Philadelphia	34	21	.618	Green	Los Angeles	36	21	.632	Lasorda	(c)
1981(b)	Montréal	30	23	.566	Williams, Fanning	Houston	33	20	.623	Virdon	Los Angeles
1982	St. Louis	92	70	.568	Herzog	Atlanta	89	73	.549	Torre	St. Louis
1983	Philadelphia	90	72	.556	Corrales, Owens	Los Angeles	91	71	.562	Lasorda	Philadelphia
1984	Chicago	96	65	.596	Frey	San Diego	92	70	.568	Williams	San Diego
1985	St. Louis	101	61	.623	Herzog	Los Angeles	95	67	.586	Lasorda	St. Louis
1986	New York	108	54	.667	Johnson	Houston	96	66	.593	Lanier	New York
1987	St. Louis	95	67	.586	Herzog	San Francisco	90	72	.556	Craig	St. Louis
1988	New York	100	60	.625	Johnson	Los Angeles	94	67	.584	Lasorda	Los Angeles
1989	Chicago	93	69	.574	Zimmer	San Francisco	92	70	.568	Craig	San Francisco
1990	Pittsburgh	95	67	.586	Leyland	Cincinnati	91	71	.562	Piniella	Cincinnati
1991	Pittsburgh	98	64	.605	Leyland	Atlanta	94	68	.580	Cox	Atlanta
1992	Pittsburgh	96	66	.593	Leyland	Atlanta	98	64	.605	Cox	Atlanta
1993	Philadelphia	97	65	.599	Fregosi	Atlanta	104	58	.642	Cox	Philadelphia

Year	Division	Winner	W	L	PCT	Manager	Playoffs	Pennant winner
1994(d)	East	Montréal	74	40	.649	Alou	—	—
	Central	Cincinnati	66	48	.579	Johnson		
	West	Los Angeles	58	56	.509	Lasorda		
1995	East	Atlanta	90	54	.625	Cox	Atlanta 3, Colorado* 1	Atlanta
	Central	Cincinnati	85	59	.590	Johnson	Cincinnati 3, Los Angeles 0	
	West	Los Angeles	78	66	.542	Lasorda	Atlanta 4, Cincinnati 0	
1996	East	Atlanta	96	66	.593	Cox	Atlanta 3, Los Angeles* 0	Atlanta
	Central	St. Louis	88	74	.543	La Russa	St. Louis 3, San Diego 0	
	West	San Diego	91	71	.562	Bochy	Atlanta 4, St. Louis 3	

Year	Division	Winner	W	L	PCT	Manager	Playoffs	Pennant winner
1997	East	Atlanta	101	61	.623	Cox	Atlanta 3, Houston 0	Florida*
	Central	Houston	84	78	.519	Dierker	Florida* 3, San Francisco 0	(Leyland)
	West	San Francisco	90	72	.556	Baker	Florida* 4, Atlanta 2	
1998	East	Atlanta	106	56	.654	Cox	Atlanta 3, Chicago* 0	San Diego
	Central	Houston	102	60	.630	Dierker	San Diego 3, Houston 1	
	West	San Diego	98	64	.605	Bochy	San Diego 4, Atlanta 2	
1999	East	Atlanta	103	59	.636	Cox	Atlanta 3, Houston 1	Atlanta
	Central	Houston	97	65	.599	Dierker, Galante	New York* 3, Arizona 1	
	West	Arizona	100	62	.617	Showalter	Atlanta 4, New York* 2	
2000	East	Atlanta	95	67	.586	Cox	St. Louis 3, Atlanta 0	New York*
	Central	St. Louis	95	67	.586	La Russa	New York* 3, San Francisco 1	(Valentine)
	West	San Francisco	97	65	.599	Baker	New York* 4, St. Louis 1	
2001	East	Atlanta	88	74	.543	Cox	Atlanta 3, Houston 0	Arizona
	Central	Houston	93	69	.574	Dierker	Arizona 3, St. Louis* 2	
	West	Arizona	92	70	.568	Brenly	Arizona 4, Atlanta 1	
2002	East	Atlanta	101	59	.631	Cox	St. Louis 3, Arizona 0	San Francisco*
	Central	St. Louis	97	65	.599	La Russa	San Francisco* 3, Atlanta 2	(Baker)
	West	Arizona	98	64	.605	Brenly	San Francisco* 4, St. Louis 1	
2003	East	Atlanta	101	61	.623	Cox	Chicago 3, Atlanta 2	Florida*
	Central	Chicago	88	74	.543	Baker	Florida* 3, San Francisco 1	(McKeon)
	West	San Francisco	100	61	.621	Alou	Florida* 4, Chicago 3	
2004	East	Atlanta	96	66	.593	Cox	Houston* 3, Atlanta 2	St. Louis
	Central	St. Louis	105	57	.648	La Russa	St. Louis 3, Los Angeles 1	
	West	Los Angeles	93	69	.574	Tracy	St. Louis 4, Houston* 3	
2005	East	Atlanta	90	72	.556	Cox	St. Louis 3, San Diego 0	Houston*
	Central	St. Louis	100	62	.617	La Russa	Houston* 3, Atlanta 1	(Garner)
	West	San Diego	82	80	.506	Bochy	Houston* 4, St. Louis 2	
2006	East	New York	97	65	.599	Randolph	New York 3, Los Angeles* 0	St. Louis
	Central	St. Louis	83	78	.516	La Russa	St. Louis 3, San Diego 1	
	West	San Diego	88	74	.543	Bochy	St. Louis 4, New York 3	
2007	East	Philadelphia	89	73	.549	Manuel	Colorado* 3, Philadelphia 0	Colorado*
	Central	Chicago	85	77	.525	Piniella	Arizona 3, Chicago 0	(Hurdle)
	West	Arizona	90	72	.556	Melvin	Colorado* 4, Arizona 0	
2008	East	Philadelphia	92	70	.568	Manuel	Philadelphia 3, Milwaukee* 1	Philadelphia
	Central	Chicago	97	64	.602	Piniella	Los Angeles 3, Chicago 0	
	West	Los Angeles	84	78	.519	Torre	Philadelphia 4, Los Angeles 1	
2009	East	Philadelphia	93	69	.574	Manuel	Philadelphia 3, Colorado* 1	Philadelphia
	Central	St. Louis	91	71	.562	La Russa	Los Angeles 3, St. Louis 0	
	West	Los Angeles	95	67	.586	Torre	Philadelphia 4, Los Angeles 1	
2010	East	Philadelphia	97	65	.599	Manuel	San Francisco 3, Atlanta* 1	San Francisco
	Central	Cincinnati	91	71	.562	Baker	Philadelphia 3, Cincinnati 0	
	West	San Francisco	92	70	.568	Bochy	San Francisco 4, Philadelphia 2	
2011	East	Philadelphia	102	60	.630	Manuel	Milwaukee 3, Arizona 2	St. Louis*
	Central	Milwaukee	96	66	.593	Roenicke	St. Louis* 3, Philadelphia 2	(La Russa)
	West	Arizona	94	68	.580	Gibson	St. Louis* 4, Milwaukee 2	
2012	East	Washington	98	64	.605	Johnson	#St. Louis* 6, Atlanta* 3	San Francisco
	Central	Cincinnati	97	65	.599	Baker	St. Louis* 3, Washington 2	
	West	San Francisco	94	68	.580	Bochy	San Francisco 3, Cincinnati 2	
							San Francisco 4, St. Louis* 3	
2013	East	Atlanta	96	66	.593	González	#Pittsburgh* 6, Cincinnati* 2	St. Louis
	Central	St. Louis	97	65	.599	Matheny	St. Louis 3, Pittsburgh* 2	
	West	Los Angeles	92	70	.568	Mattingly	Los Angeles 3, Atlanta 1	
							St. Louis 4, Los Angeles 2	
2014	East	Washington	96	66	.593	Williams	#San Francisco* 8, Pittsburgh* 0	San Francisco*
	Central	St. Louis	90	72	.556	Matheny	San Francisco* 3, Washington 1	(Bochy)
	West	Los Angeles	94	68	.580	Mattingly	St. Louis 3, Los Angeles 1	
							San Francisco* 4, St. Louis 1	
2015	East	New York	90	72	.556	Collins	#Chicago* 4, Pittsburgh* 0	New York
	Central	St. Louis	100	62	.617	Matheny	Chicago* 3, St. Louis 1	
	West	Los Angeles	92	70	.568	Mattingly	New York 3, Los Angeles 2	
							New York 4, Chicago* 0	
2016	East	Washington	95	67	.586	Baker	#San Francisco* 3, New York* 0	Chicago
	Central	Chicago	103	58	.640	Maddon	Chicago 3, San Francisco* 1	
	West	Los Angeles	91	71	.562	Roberts	Los Angeles 3, Washington 2	
							Chicago 4, Los Angeles 2	

American League

Year	East winner	W	L	PCT	Manager	West winner	W	L	PCT	Manager	Pennant winner
1976	New York	97	62	.610	Martin	Kansas City	90	72	.556	Herzog	New York
1977	New York	100	62	.617	Martin	Kansas City	102	60	.630	Herzog	New York
1978	New York	100	63	.613	Martin, Lemon	Kansas City	92	70	.568	Herzog	New York
1979	Baltimore	102	57	.642	Weaver	California	88	74	.543	Fregosi	Baltimore
1980	New York	103	59	.636	Howser	Kansas City	97	65	.599	Frey	Kansas City
1981(a)	New York	34	22	.607	Michael	Oakland	37	23	.617	Martin	(c)
1981(b)	Milwaukee	31	22	.585	Rodgers	Kansas City	30	23	.566	Frey, Howser	New York
1982	Milwaukee	95	67	.586	Rodgers, Kuenn	California	93	69	.574	Mauch	Milwaukee
1983	Baltimore	98	64	.605	Altobelli	Chicago	99	63	.611	La Russa	Baltimore
1984	Detroit	104	58	.642	Anderson	Kansas City	84	78	.519	Howser	Detroit
1985	Toronto	99	62	.615	Cox	Kansas City	91	71	.562	Howser	Kansas City
1986	Boston	95	66	.590	McNamara	California	92	70	.568	Mauch	Boston
1987	Detroit	98	64	.605	Anderson	Minnesota	85	77	.525	Kelly	Minnesota
1988	Boston	89	73	.549	McNamara, Morgan	Oakland	104	58	.642	La Russa	Oakland
1989	Toronto	89	73	.549	Williams, Gaston	Oakland	99	63	.611	La Russa	Oakland
1990	Boston	88	74	.543	Morgan	Oakland	103	59	.636	La Russa	Oakland
1991	Toronto	91	71	.562	Gaston, Tenace	Minnesota	95	67	.586	Kelly	Minnesota
1992	Toronto	96	66	.593	Gaston	Oakland	96	66	.593	La Russa	Toronto
1993	Toronto	95	67	.586	Gaston	Chicago	94	68	.580	Lamont	Toronto

Year	Division	Winner	W	L	PCT	Manager	Playoffs	Pennant winner
1994(d)	East	New York	70	43	.619	Showalter	—	—
	Central	Chicago	67	46	.593	Lamont		
	West	Texas	52	62	.456	Kennedy		
1995	East	Boston	86	58	.597	Kennedy	Cleveland 3, Boston 0	Cleveland
	Central	Cleveland	100	44	.694	Hargrove	Seattle 3, New York* 2	
	West	Seattle	79	66	.545	Piniella	Cleveland 4, Seattle 2	
1996	East	New York	92	70	.568	Torre	Baltimore* 3, Cleveland 1	New York
	Central	Cleveland	99	62	.615	Hargrove	New York 3, Texas 1	
	West	Texas	90	72	.556	Oates	New York 4, Baltimore* 1	
1997	East	Baltimore	98	64	.605	Johnson	Baltimore 3, Seattle 1	Cleveland
	Central	Cleveland	86	75	.534	Hargrove	Cleveland 3, New York* 2	
	West	Seattle	90	72	.556	Piniella	Cleveland 4, Baltimore 2	
1998	East	New York	114	48	.704	Torre	New York 3, Texas 0	New York
	Central	Cleveland	89	73	.549	Hargrove	Cleveland 3, Boston* 1	
	West	Texas	88	74	.543	Oates	New York 4, Cleveland 2	
1999	East	New York	98	64	.605	Torre	New York 3, Texas 0	New York
	Central	Cleveland	97	65	.599	Hargrove	Boston* 3, Cleveland 2	
	West	Texas	95	67	.586	Oates	New York 4, Boston* 1	
2000	East	New York	87	74	.540	Torre	New York 3, Oakland 2	New York
	Central	Chicago	95	67	.586	Manuel	Seattle* 3, Chicago 0	
	West	Oakland	91	70	.565	Howe	New York 4, Seattle* 2	
2001	East	New York	95	65	.594	Torre	Seattle 3, Cleveland 2	New York
	Central	Cleveland	91	71	.562	Manuel	New York 3, Oakland* 2	
	West	Seattle	116	46	.716	Piniella	New York 4, Seattle 1	
2002	East	New York	103	58	.640	Torre	Anaheim* 3, New York 1	Anaheim*
	Central	Minnesota	94	67	.584	Gardenhire	Minnesota 3, Oakland 2	(Scioscia)
	West	Oakland	103	59	.636	Howe	Anaheim* 4, Minnesota 1	
2003	East	New York	101	61	.623	Torre	New York 3, Minnesota 1	New York
	Central	Minnesota	90	72	.556	Gardenhire	Boston* 3, Oakland 2	
	West	Oakland	96	66	.593	Macha	New York 4, Boston* 3	
2004	East	New York	101	61	.623	Torre	New York 3, Minnesota 1	Boston*
	Central	Minnesota	92	70	.568	Gardenhire	Boston* 3, Anaheim 0	(Francona)
	West	Anaheim	92	70	.568	Scioscia	Boston* 4, New York 3	
2005	East	New York	95	67	.586	Torre	Chicago 3, Boston* 0	Chicago
	Central	Chicago	99	63	.611	Guillen	Los Angeles 3, New York 2	
	West	Los Angeles	95	67	.586	Scioscia	Chicago 4, Los Angeles 1	
2006	East	New York	97	65	.599	Torre	Oakland 3, Minnesota 0	Detroit*
	Central	Minnesota	96	66	.593	Gardenhire	Detroit* 3, New York 1	(Leyland)
	West	Oakland	93	69	.574	Macha	Detroit* 4, Oakland 0	
2007	East	Boston	96	66	.593	Francona	Boston 3, Los Angeles 0	Boston
	Central	Cleveland	96	66	.593	Wedge	Cleveland 3, New York* 1	
	West	Los Angeles	94	68	.580	Scioscia	Boston 4, Cleveland 3	
2008	East	Tampa Bay	97	65	.599	Maddon	Tampa Bay 3, Chicago 1	Tampa Bay
	Central	Chicago	89	74	.546	Guillen	Boston* 3, Los Angeles 1	
	West	Los Angeles	100	62	.617	Scioscia	Tampa Bay 4, Boston* 3	
2009	East	New York	103	59	.636	Girardi	New York 3, Minnesota 0	New York
	Central	Minnesota	87	76	.534	Gardenhire	Los Angeles 3, Boston* 0	
	West	Los Angeles	97	65	.599	Scioscia	New York 4, Los Angeles 2	
2010	East	Tampa Bay	96	66	.593	Maddon	New York* 3, Minnesota 0	Texas
	Central	Minnesota	94	68	.580	Gardenhire	Texas 3, Tampa Bay 2	
	West	Texas	90	72	.556	Washington	Texas 4, New York* 2	
2011	East	New York	97	65	.599	Girardi	Detroit 3, New York 2	Texas
	Central	Detroit	95	67	.586	Leyland	Texas 3, Tampa Bay* 1	
	West	Texas	96	66	.593	Washington	Texas 4, Detroit 2	
2012	East	New York	95	67	.586	Girardi	#Baltimore* 5, Texas* 1	Detroit
	Central	Detroit	88	74	.543	Leyland	New York 3, Baltimore* 2	
	West	Oakland	94	68	.580	Melvin	Detroit 3, Oakland 2	
							Detroit 4, New York 0	
2013	East	Boston	97	65	.599	Farrell	#Tampa Bay* 4, Cleveland* 0	Boston
	Central	Detroit	93	69	.574	Leyland	Boston 3, Tampa Bay* 1	
	West	Oakland	96	66	.593	Melvin	Detroit 3, Oakland 2	
							Boston 4, Detroit 2	
2014	East	Baltimore	96	66	.593	Showalter	#Kansas City* 9, Oakland* 8	Kansas City*
	Central	Detroit	90	72	.556	Ausmus	Kansas City* 3, Los Angeles 0	(Yost)
	West	Los Angeles	98	64	.605	Scioscia	Baltimore 3, Detroit 0	
							Kansas City* 4, Baltimore 0	
2015	East	Toronto	93	69	.574	Gibbons	#Houston* 3, New York* 0	Kansas City
	Central	Kansas City	95	67	.586	Yost	Kansas City 3, Houston* 2	
	West	Texas	88	74	.543	Banister	Toronto 3, Texas 2	
							Kansas City 4, Toronto 2	
2016	East	Boston	93	69	.574	Farrell	#Toronto* 5, Baltimore* 2	Cleveland
	Central	Cleveland	94	67	.584	Francona	Toronto* 3, Texas 0	
	West	Texas	95	67	.586	Banister	Cleveland 3, Boston 0	
							Cleveland 4, Toronto* 1	

* = Wild-card team. If pennant winner is wild-card team, manager's name is given in parentheses. # = Single-game wild card playoff (debuted in 2012). (a) First half. (b) Second half. (c) Montréal, L.A., NY Yankees, and Oakland won the divisional playoffs. (d) In Aug. 1994, a players' strike began that caused the cancellation of the remainder of the season, the playoffs, and the World Series. Teams listed as division "winners" for 1994 were leading their divisions at the time of the strike.

World Series Results, 1903-2016

1903 Boston AL 5, Pittsburgh NL 3	
1904 No series	
1905 New York NL 4, Philadelphia AL 1	
1906 Chicago AL 4, Chicago NL 2	
1907 Chicago NL 4, Detroit AL 0, 1 tie	
1908 Chicago NL 4, Detroit AL 1	
1909 Pittsburgh NL 4, Detroit AL 3	
1910 Philadelphia AL 4, Chicago NL 1	
1911 Philadelphia AL 4, New York NL 2	
1912 Boston AL 4, New York NL 3, 1 tie	
1913 Philadelphia AL 4, New York NL 1	
1914 Boston NL 4, Philadelphia AL 0	
1915 Boston AL 4, Philadelphia NL 1	
1916 Boston AL 4, Brooklyn NL 1	
1917 Chicago AL 4, New York NL 2	
1918 Boston AL 4, Chicago NL 2	
1919 Cincinnati NL 5, Chicago AL 3	
1920 Cleveland AL 5, Brooklyn NL 2	
1921 New York NL 5, New York AL 3	
1922 New York NL 4, New York AL 0, 1 tie	
1923 New York AL 4, New York NL 2	
1924 Washington AL 4, New York NL 3	
1925 Pittsburgh NL 4, Washington AL 3	
1926 St. Louis NL 4, New York AL 3	
1927 New York AL 4, Pittsburgh NL 0	
1928 New York AL 4, St. Louis NL 0	
1929 Philadelphia AL 4, Chicago NL 1	
1930 Philadelphia AL 4, St. Louis NL 2	
1931 St. Louis NL 4, Philadelphia AL 3	
1932 New York AL 4, Chicago NL 0	
1933 New York NL 4, Washington AL 1	
1934 St. Louis NL 4, Detroit AL 3	
1935 Detroit AL 4, Chicago NL 2	
1936 New York AL 4, New York NL 2	
1937 New York AL 4, New York NL 1	
1938 New York AL 4, Chicago NL 0	
1939 New York AL 4, Cincinnati NL 0	
1940 Cincinnati NL 4, Detroit AL 3	

1941 New York AL 4, Brooklyn NL 1
1942 St. Louis NL 4, New York AL 1
1943 New York AL 4, St. Louis NL 1
1944 St. Louis NL 4, St. Louis AL 2
1945 Detroit AL 4, Chicago NL 3
1946 St. Louis NL 4, Boston AL 3
1947 New York AL 4, Brooklyn NL 3
1948 Cleveland AL 4, Boston NL 2
1949 New York AL 4, Brooklyn NL 1
1950 New York AL 4, Philadelphia NL 0
1951 New York AL 4, New York NL 2
1952 New York AL 4, Brooklyn NL 3
1953 New York AL 4, Brooklyn NL 2
1954 New York NL 4, Cleveland AL 0
1955 Brooklyn NL 4, New York AL 3
1956 New York AL 4, Brooklyn NL 3
1957 Milwaukee NL 4, New York AL 3
1958 New York AL 4, Milwaukee NL 3
1959 Los Angeles NL 4, Chicago AL 2
1960 Pittsburgh NL 4, New York AL 3
1961 New York AL 4, Cincinnati NL 1
1962 New York AL 4, San Francisco NL 3
1963 Los Angeles NL 4, New York AL 0
1964 St. Louis NL 4, New York AL 3
1965 Los Angeles NL 4, Minnesota AL 3
1966 Baltimore AL 4, Los Angeles NL 0
1967 St. Louis NL 4, Boston AL 3
1968 Detroit AL 4, St. Louis NL 3
1969 New York NL 4, Baltimore AL 1
1970 Baltimore AL 4, Cincinnati NL 1
1971 Pittsburgh NL 4, Baltimore AL 3
1972 Oakland AL 4, Cincinnati NL 3
1973 Oakland AL 4, New York NL 3
1974 Oakland AL 4, Los Angeles NL 1
1975 Cincinnati NL 4, Boston AL 3
1976 Cincinnati NL 4, New York AL 0
1977 New York AL 4, Los Angeles NL 2
1978 New York AL 4, Los Angeles NL 2

1979 Pittsburgh NL 4, Baltimore AL 3
1980 Philadelphia NL 4, Kansas City AL 2
1981 Los Angeles NL 4, New York AL 2
1982 St. Louis NL 4, Milwaukee AL 3
1983 Baltimore AL 4, Philadelphia NL 1
1984 Detroit AL 4, San Diego NL 1
1985 Kansas City AL 4, St. Louis NL 3
1986 New York NL 4, Boston AL 3
1987 Minnesota AL 4, St. Louis NL 3
1988 Los Angeles NL 4, Oakland AL 1
1989 Oakland AL 4, San Francisco NL 0
1990 Cincinnati NL 4, Oakland AL 0
1991 Minnesota AL 4, Atlanta NL 3
1992 Toronto AL 4, Atlanta NL 2
1993 Toronto AL 4, Philadelphia NL 2
1994 No series due to strike
1995 Atlanta NL 4, Cleveland AL 2
1996 New York AL 4, Atlanta NL 2
1997 Florida NL 4, Cleveland AL 3
1998 New York AL 4, San Diego NL 0
1999 New York AL 4, Atlanta NL 0
2000 New York AL 4, New York NL 1
2001 Arizona NL 4, New York AL 3
2002 Anaheim AL 4, San Francisco NL 3
2003 Florida NL 4, New York AL 2
2004 Boston AL 4, St. Louis NL 0
2005 Chicago AL 4, Houston NL 0
2006 St. Louis NL 4, Detroit AL 1
2007 Boston AL 4, Colorado NL 0
2008 Philadelphia NL 4, Tampa Bay AL 1
2009 New York AL 4, Philadelphia NL 2
2010 San Francisco NL 4, Texas AL 1
2011 St. Louis NL 4, Texas AL 3
2012 San Francisco NL 4, Detroit AL 0
2013 Boston AL 4, St. Louis NL 2
2014 San Fran. NL 4, Kansas City AL 3
2015 Kansas City AL 4, New York NL 1
2016 Chicago NL 4, Cleveland AL 3

World Series Most Valuable Player, 1955-2016

Year	Player, position, team
1955	Johnny Podres, P, Brooklyn
1956	Don Larsen, P, NY (AL)
1957	Lew Burdette, P, Milwaukee (NL)
1958	Bob Turley, P, NY (AL)
1959	Larry Sherry, P, Los Angeles (NL)
1960[1]	Bobby Richardson, 2B, NY (AL)
1961	Whitey Ford, P, NY (AL)
1962	Ralph Terry, P, NY (AL)
1963	Sandy Koufax, P, Los Angeles (NL)
1964	Bob Gibson, P, St. Louis
1965	Sandy Koufax, P, Los Angeles (NL)
1966	Frank Robinson, OF, Baltimore
1967	Bob Gibson, P, St. Louis
1968	Mickey Lolich, P, Detroit
1969	Donn Clendenon, 1B, NY (NL)
1970	Brooks Robinson, 3B, Baltimore
1971	Roberto Clemente, OF, Pittsburgh
1972	Gene Tenace, C, Oakland
1973	Reggie Jackson, OF, Oakland
1974	Rollie Fingers, P, Oakland
1975	Pete Rose, 3B, Cincinnati
1976	Johnny Bench, C, Cincinnati

Year	Player, position, team
1977	Reggie Jackson, OF, NY (AL)
1978	Bucky Dent, SS, NY (AL)
1979	Willie Stargell, 1B, Pittsburgh
1980	Mike Schmidt, 3B, Philadelphia
1981	Ron Cey, 3B, Los Angeles (NL); Pedro Guerrero, OF, Los Angeles; Steve Yeager, C, Los Angeles
1982	Darrell Porter, C, St. Louis
1983	Rick Dempsey, C, Baltimore
1984	Alan Trammell, SS, Detroit
1985	Bret Saberhagen, P, Kansas City
1986	Ray Knight, 3B, NY (NL)
1987	Frank Viola, P, Minnesota
1988	Orel Hershiser, P, Los Angeles (NL)
1989	Dave Stewart, P, Oakland
1990	Jose Rijo, P, Cincinnati
1991	Jack Morris, P, Minnesota
1992	Pat Borders, C, Toronto
1993	Paul Molitor, DH, Toronto
1994	No series due to strike
1995	Tom Glavine, P, Atlanta
1996	John Wetteland, P, NY (AL)

Year	Player, position, team
1997	Livan Hernandez, P, Florida
1998	Scott Brosius, 3B, NY (AL)
1999	Mariano Rivera, P, NY (AL)
2000	Derek Jeter, SS, NY (AL)
2001	Curt Schilling, P, Arizona; Randy Johnson, P, Arizona
2002	Troy Glaus, 3B, Anaheim
2003	Josh Beckett, P, Florida
2004	Manny Ramirez, OF, Boston
2005	Jermaine Dye, OF, Chicago (AL)
2006	David Eckstein, SS, St. Louis
2007	Mike Lowell, 3B, Boston
2008	Cole Hamels, P, Philadelphia
2009	Hideki Matsui, DH, NY (AL)
2010	Edgar Renteria, SS, San Francisco
2011	David Freese, 3B, St. Louis
2012	Pablo Sandoval, 3B, San Francisco
2013	David Ortiz, DH, Boston
2014	Madison Bumgarner, P, San Francisco
2015	Salvador Pérez, C, Kansas City
2016	Ben Zobrist, OF, Chicago (NL)

Note: World Series canceled in 1994 due to strike. (1) Richardson won the MVP although Pittsburgh beat New York.

World Series Won-Lost Records, by Franchise

Since beginning of "modern" era in 1901. Figures represent overall Series wins, not individual games.

Team	Wins	Losses	Team	Wins	Losses
New York Yankees	27	13	Florida Marlins	2	0
St. Louis Cardinals	11	8	Toronto Blue Jays	2	0
Philadelphia/Kansas City/Oakland A's	9	5	Kansas City Royals	2	2
Boston Red Sox	8	4	New York Mets	2	3
New York/San Francisco Giants	8	12	Cleveland Indians	2	4
Brooklyn/Los Angeles Dodgers	6	12	Philadelphia Phillies	2	5
Pittsburgh Pirates	5	2	Arizona Diamondbacks	1	0
Cincinnati Reds	5	4	L.A./California/Anaheim/L.A. Angels	1	0
Detroit Tigers	4	7	Colorado Rockies	0	1
Chicago White Sox	3	2	Houston Astros	0	1
Washington Senators/Minnesota Twins	3	3	Seattle Pilots/Milwaukee Brewers	0	1
St. Louis Browns/Baltimore Orioles	3	4	Tampa Bay Rays	0	1
Boston/Milwaukee/Atlanta Braves	3	6	San Diego Padres	0	2
Chicago Cubs	3	8	Texas Rangers	0	2

All-Time World Series Career Leaders
(through 2016)

Batting Leaders

Batter (min. 50 PA)	H	AB	AVG	Batter (min. 50 PA)	H	AB	AVG
1. David Ortiz	20	44	.455	6. Hal McRae	18	45	.400
2. Pablo Sandoval	20	47	.426	7. Lou Brock	34	87	.391
3. Johnny "Pepper" Martin	23	55	.418	8. Marquis Grissom	30	77	.390
4. Paul Molitor	23	55	.418	9. Thurman Munson	25	67	.373
5. Lance Berkman	16	39	.410	10. George Brett	19	51	.373

Games Played
Yogi Berra 75
Mickey Mantle 65
Elston Howard 54
Hank Bauer 53
Gil McDougald 53
Phil Rizzuto 52
Joe DiMaggio 51
Frankie Frisch 50
Pee Wee Reese 44
Roger Maris 41
Babe Ruth 41

Hits
Yogi Berra 71
Mickey Mantle 59
Frankie Frisch 58
Joe DiMaggio 54
Derek Jeter 50
Hank Bauer 46
Pee Wee Reese 46
Gil McDougald 45
Phil Rizzuto 45
Lou Gehrig 43

Runs
Mickey Mantle 42
Yogi Berra 41
Babe Ruth 37
Derek Jeter 32
Lou Gehrig 30
Joe DiMaggio 27
Roger Maris 26
Elston Howard 25
Gil McDougald 23
Jackie Robinson 22

Runs Batted In
Mickey Mantle 40
Yogi Berra 39
Lou Gehrig 35
Babe Ruth 33
Joe DiMaggio 30
Bill Skowron 29
Duke Snider 26

Home Runs
Mickey Mantle 18
Babe Ruth 15
Yogi Berra 12
Duke Snider 11
Lou Gehrig 10
Reggie Jackson 10
Joe DiMaggio 8
Frank Robinson 8
Bill Skowron 8

Stolen Bases
Lou Brock 14
Eddie Collins 14
Frank Chance 10
Dave Lopes 10
Phil Rizzuto 10
Frankie Frisch 9
Kenny Lofton 9
Honus Wagner 9
Johnny Evers 8

Pitching Leaders

Games Pitched		Wins		Strikeouts		Saves	
Mariano Rivera	24	Whitey Ford	10	Whitey Ford	94	Mariano Rivera	11
Whitey Ford	22	Bob Gibson	7	Bob Gibson	92	Rollie Fingers	6
Mike Stanton	20	Allie Reynolds	7	Allie Reynolds	62	Johnny Murphy	4
Rollie Fingers	16	Red Ruffing	7	Sandy Koufax	61	Robb Nen	4
Jeff Nelson	16	Chief Bender	6	Red Ruffing	61	Allie Reynolds	4
Allie Reynolds	15	Lefty Gomez	6	Chief Bender	59	John Wetteland	4
Bob Turley	15	Waite Hoyt	6	George Earnshaw	56	Roy Face	3
Clay Carroll	14	Three Finger Brown	5	Andy Pettitte	56	Neftali Feliz	3
Clem Labine	13	Jack Coombs	5	John Smoltz	52	Firpo Marberry	3
Andy Pettitte	13	Catfish Hunter	5	Roger Clemens	49	Will McEnaney	3
Mark Wohlers	13	Christy Mathewson	5	Waite Hoyt	49	Tug McGraw	3
Jeremy Affeldt	12	Herb Pennock	5	Christy Mathewson	48	Jonathan Papelbon	3
Waite Hoyt	12	Andy Pettitte	5	Bob Turley	46	Herb Pennock	3
Catfish Hunter	12	Vic Raschi	5			Troy Percival	3
Ryan Madson	12					Sergio Romo	3
Art Nehf	12					Kent Tekulve	3
						Todd Worrell	3

All-Star Baseball Games, 1933-2016

Year	Winner, score	Host team	Year	Winner, score	Host team	Year	Winner, score	Host team
1933*	American, 4-2	Chicago (AL)	1960*	National, 6-0	New York (AL)	1988	American, 2-1	Cincinnati
1934*	American, 9-7	New York (NL)	1961*	National, 5-4[3]	San Francisco	1989	American, 5-3	California
1935*	American, 4-1	Cleveland	1961*	Called–rain, 1-1	Boston	1990	American, 2-0	Chicago (NL)
1936*	National, 4-3	Boston (NL)	1962*	National, 3-1	Washington	1991	American, 4-2	Toronto
1937*	American, 8-3	Washington	1962*	American, 9-4	Chicago (NL)	1992	American, 13-6	San Diego
1938*	National, 4-1	Cincinnati	1963*	National, 5-3	Cleveland	1993	American, 9-3	Baltimore
1939*	American, 3-1	New York (AL)	1964*	National, 7-4	New York (NL)	1994	National, 8-7[3]	Pittsburgh
1940*	National, 4-0	St. Louis (NL)	1965*	National, 6-5	Minnesota	1995	National, 3-2	Texas
1941*	American, 7-5	Detroit	1966*	National, 2-1[3]	St. Louis	1996	National, 6-0	Philadelphia
1942	American, 3-1	New York (NL)	1967*	National, 2-1[4]	California	1997	American, 3-1	Cleveland
1943	American, 5-3	Philadelphia (AL)	1968	National, 1-0	Houston	1998	American, 13-8	Colorado
1944	National, 7-1	Pittsburgh	1969*	National, 9-3	Washington	1999	American, 4-1	Boston
1945	Not played		1970	National, 5-4[2]	Cincinnati	2000	American, 6-3	Atlanta
1946*	American, 12-0	Boston (AL)	1971	American, 6-4	Detroit	2001	American, 4-1	Seattle
1947*	American, 2-1	Chicago (NL)	1972	National, 4-3[3]	Atlanta	2002	Tie, 7-7[6]	Milwaukee
1948*	American, 5-2	St. Louis (AL)	1973	National, 7-1	Kansas City	2003	American, 7-6[7]	Chicago (AL)
1949*	American, 11-7	Brooklyn	1974	National, 7-2	Pittsburgh	2004	American, 9-4	Houston
1950*	National, 4-3[1]	Chicago (AL)	1975	National, 6-3	Milwaukee	2005	American, 7-5	Detroit
1951*	National, 8-3	Detroit	1976	National, 7-1	Philadelphia	2006	American, 3-2	Pittsburgh
1952*	National, 3-2	Philadelphia (NL)	1977	National, 7-5	New York (AL)	2007	American, 5-4	San Francisco
1953*	National, 5-1	Cincinnati	1978	National, 7-3	San Diego	2008	American, 4-3[4]	New York (AL)
1954*	American, 11-9	Cleveland	1979	National, 7-6	Seattle	2009	American, 4-3	St. Louis
1955*	National, 6-5[2]	Milwaukee	1980	National, 4-2	Los Angeles (NL)	2010	National, 3-1	Los Angeles (AL)
1956*	National, 7-3	Washington	1981	National, 5-4	Cleveland	2011	National, 5-1	Arizona
1957*	American, 6-5	St. Louis	1982	National, 4-1	Montréal	2012	National, 8-0	Kansas City
1958*	American, 4-3	Baltimore	1983	American, 13-3	Chicago (AL)	2013	American, 3-0	New York (NL)
1959*	National, 5-4	Pittsburgh	1984	National, 3-1	San Francisco	2014	American, 5-3	Minnesota
1959*	American, 5-3	Los Angeles (NL)	1985	National, 6-1	Minnesota	2015	American, 6-3	Cincinnati
1960*	National, 5-3	Kansas City	1986	American, 3-2	Houston	2016	American, 4-2	San Diego
			1987	National, 2-0[5]	Oakland			

* = Day game. **Note:** Two all-star games played 1959-62 to help increase players' pension fund. (1) 14 innings. (2) 12 innings. (3) 10 innings. (4) 15 innings. (5) 13 innings. (6) Commissioner's decision—game called in 11th inning when both teams ran out of pitchers. (7) Under rule change beginning in 2003, league winning All-Star game earned World Series home-field advantage.

MLB Stadiums, 2016

Team	Stadium (year opened)	Surface	LF	Center	RF	Seating capacity[1]
Arizona Diamondbacks	Chase Field (1998)	Grass	330	407	335	48,519
Atlanta Braves	Turner Field (1997)	Grass	335	400	330	49,393
Chicago Cubs	Wrigley Field (1914)	Grass	355	400	353	42,495
Cincinnati Reds	Great American Ball Park (2003)	Grass	328	404	325	42,319
Colorado Rockies	Coors Field (1995)	Grass	347	415	350	50,480
Los Angeles Dodgers	Dodger Stadium (1962)	Grass	330	395	330	56,000
Miami Marlins	Marlins Park (2012)	Grass	344	407	335	37,422
Milwaukee Brewers	Miller Park (2001)	Grass	344	400	345	41,900
New York Mets	Citi Field (2009)	Grass	335	408	330	41,922
Philadelphia Phillies	Citizens Bank Park (2004)	Grass	329	401	330	43,651
Pittsburgh Pirates	PNC Park at North Shore (2001)	Grass	325	399	320	38,362
St. Louis Cardinals	Busch Stadium (2006)	Grass	336	400	335	45,538
San Diego Padres	Petco Park (2004)	Grass	336	396	322	40,162
San Francisco Giants	AT&T Park (2000)	Grass	339	399	309	41,915
Washington Nationals	Nationals Park (2008)	Grass	336	402	335	41,313
Baltimore Orioles	Oriole Park at Camden Yards (1992)	Grass	333	400	318	45,971
Boston Red Sox	Fenway Park (1912)	Grass	310	390	302	37,497[2]
Chicago White Sox	U.S. Cellular Field (1991)	Grass	330	400	335	40,615
Cleveland Indians	Progressive Field (1994)	Grass	325	405	325	35,225
Detroit Tigers	Comerica Park (2000)	Grass	345	420	330	41,297
Houston Astros	Minute Maid Park (2000)	Grass	315	435	326	41,676
Kansas City Royals	Kauffman Stadium (1973)	Grass	330	410	330	37,903
Los Angeles Angels	Angel Stadium of Anaheim (1966)	Grass	347	396	348	45,493
Minnesota Twins	Target Field (2010)	Grass	339	404	328	38,871
New York Yankees	Yankee Stadium (2009)	Grass	318	408	314	49,469
Oakland Athletics	Oakland Coliseum (1968)	Grass	330	400	330	35,067
Seattle Mariners	Safeco Field (1999)	Grass	331	401	326	47,943
Tampa Bay Rays	Tropicana Field (1990)	Astroturf	315	404	322	31,042
Texas Rangers	Globe Life Park in Arlington (1994)	Grass	332	400	325	48,114
Toronto Blue Jays	Rogers Centre (1989)	Astroturf	328	400	328	49,282

(1) As of 2016 season. (2) For day games; night game capacity is 37,949.

Major League Franchise Shifts and Additions

1953: Boston Braves (NL) became Milwaukee Braves.
1954: St. Louis Browns (AL) became Baltimore Orioles.
1955: Philadelphia Athletics (AL) became Kansas City Athletics.
1958: New York Giants (NL) became San Francisco Giants.
1958: Brooklyn Dodgers (NL) became L.A. Dodgers.
1961: Washington Senators (AL) became Minnesota Twins.
1961: L.A. Angels enfranchised by the AL.
1961: Washington Senators enfranchised by the AL, replacing the former Washington club, whose franchise moved to Minneapolis-St. Paul.
1962: Houston Colt .45's enfranchised by the NL.
1962: New York Mets enfranchised by the NL.
1966: Milwaukee Braves (NL) became Atlanta Braves.
1968: Kansas City Athletics (AL) became Oakland Athletics.

1969: Kansas City Royals and Seattle Pilots enfranchised by the AL; Montréal Expos and San Diego Padres enfranchised by the NL.
1970: Seattle Pilots (AL) became Milwaukee Brewers.
1971: Washington Senators (AL) became Texas Rangers (Dallas-Fort Worth area).
1977: Toronto Blue Jays and Seattle Mariners enfranchised by the AL.
1993: Colorado Rockies (Denver) and Florida Marlins (Miami) enfranchised by the NL.
1998: Tampa Bay Devil Rays began play in the AL; Arizona Diamondbacks (Phoenix) began play in the NL (both teams enfranchised in 1995). Milwaukee Brewers moved from the AL to the NL.
2005: Montréal Expos (NL) became Washington Nationals.
2013: Houston Astros moved from the NL to the AL.

Little League World Series, 1950-2016

The Little League World Series is played annually in Williamsport, PA.

Year	Winning team; opponent	Score	Year	Winning team; opponent	Score
1950	Houston, TX; Bridgeport, CT	2-1	1984	South Korea; Altamonte Springs, FL	6-2
1951	Stamford, CT; Austin, TX	3-0	1985	Seoul, South Korea; Mexicali, Mexico	7-1
1952	Norwalk, CT; Monongahela, PA	4-3	1986	Tainan Park, Taiwan; Tucson, AZ	12-0
1953	Birmingham, AL; Schenectady, NY	1-0	1987	Hualien, Taiwan; Irvine, CA	21-1
1954	Schenectady, NY; Colton, CA	7-5	1988	Taichung, Taiwan; Pearl City, HI	10-0
1955	Morrisville, PA; Merchantville, NJ	4-3	1989	Trumbull, CT; Kaohsiung, Taiwan	5-2
1956	Roswell, NM; Delaware, NJ	3-1	1990	Tainan County, Taiwan; Shippensburg, PA	9-0
1957	Mexico; La Mesa, CA	4-0	1991	Taichung, Taiwan; Danville, CA	11-0
1958	Mexico; Kankakee, IL	10-1	1992	Long Beach, CA; Mindanao, Philippines	6-0[1]
1959	Hamtramck, MI; Auburn, CA	12-0	1993	Long Beach, CA; David, Panama	3-2
1960	Levittown, PA; Ft. Worth, TX	5-0	1994	Maracaibo, Venezuela; Northridge, CA	4-3
1961	El Cajon, CA; El Campo, TX	4-2	1995	Tainan, Taiwan; Spring, TX	17-3
1962	San Jose, CA; Kankakee, IL	3-0	1996	Kaohsiung, Taiwan; Cranston, RI	13-3
1963	Granada Hills, CA; Stratford, CT	2-1	1997	Guadalupe, Mexico; Mission Viejo, CA	5-4
1964	Staten Island, NY; Monterrey, Mexico	4-0	1998	Toms River, NJ; Kashima, Japan	12-9
1965	Windsor Locks, CT; Stoney Creek, ON, Canada	3-1	1999	Osaka, Japan; Phenix City, AL	5-0
1966	Houston, TX; W. New York, NJ	8-2	2000	Maracaibo, Venezuela; Bellaire, TX	3-2
1967	Tokyo, Japan; Chicago, IL	4-1	2001	Tokyo, Japan; Apopka, FL	2-1
1968	Osaka, Japan; Richmond, VA	1-0	2002	Louisville, KY; Sendai, Japan	1-0
1969	Taipei, Taiwan; Santa Clara, CA	5-0	2003	Tokyo, Japan; Boynton Beach, FL	10-1
1970	Wayne, NJ; Campbell, CA	2-0	2004	Willemstad, Curaçao; Thousand Oaks, CA	5-2
1971	Tainan, Taiwan; Gary, IN	12-3	2005	Ewa Beach, HI; Willemstad, Curaçao	7-6
1972	Taipei, Taiwan; Hammond, IN	6-0	2006	Columbus, GA; Kawaguchi City, Japan	2-1
1973	Tainan City, Taiwan; Tucson, AZ	12-0	2007	Warner Robins, GA; Tokyo, Japan	3-2
1974	Kaohsiung, Taiwan; Red Bluff, CA	12-1	2008	Waipahu, HI; Matamoros, Mexico	12-3
1975	Lakewood, NJ; Tampa, FL	4-3	2009	Chula Vista, CA; Taoyuan, Taiwan	6-3
1976	Tokyo, Japan; Campbell, CA	10-3	2010	Tokyo, Japan; Waipahu, HI	4-1
1977	Kaohsiung, Taiwan; El Cajon, CA	7-2	2011	Huntington Beach, CA; Hamamatsu, Japan	2-1
1978	Taipei, Taiwan; Danville, CA	11-1	2012	Tokyo, Japan; Goodlettsville, TN	12-2
1979	Taipei, Taiwan; Campbell, CA	2-1	2013	Tokyo, Japan; Chula Vista, CA	6-4
1980	Taipei, Taiwan; Tampa, FL	4-3	2014	Seoul, South Korea; Chicago, IL	8-4
1981	Taichung, Taiwan; Tampa, FL	4-2	2015	Tokyo, Japan; Lewisberry, PA	18-11
1982	Kirkland, WA; Taiwan	6-0	2016	Endwell, NY; Seoul, South Korea	2-1
1983	Marietta, GA; Dominican Republic	3-1			

(1) Philippines won 15-4 but was disqualified for using ineligible players. Long Beach was awarded title by forfeit 6-0 (1 run per inning).

Manager of the Year, 1986-2015

1986 (NL) Hal Lanier, Houston	1996 (NL) Bruce Bochy, San Diego	2006 (NL) Joe Girardi, Florida
(AL) John McNamara, Boston	(AL) Joe Torre, NY;	(AL) Jim Leyland, Detroit
1987 (NL) Buck Rodgers, Montréal	Johnny Oates, Texas	2007 (NL) Bob Melvin, Arizona
(AL) Sparky Anderson, Detroit	1997 (NL) Dusty Baker, San Francisco	(AL) Eric Wedge, Cleveland
1988 (NL) Tommy Lasorda, L.A.	(AL) Davey Johnson, Baltimore	2008 (NL) Lou Piniella, Chicago
(AL) Tony La Russa, Oakland	1998 (NL) Larry Dierker, Houston	(AL) Joe Maddon, Tampa Bay
1989 (NL) Don Zimmer, Chicago	(AL) Joe Torre, NY	2009 (NL) Jim Tracy, Colorado
(AL) Frank Robinson, Baltimore	1999 (NL) Jack McKeon, Cincinnati	(AL) Mike Scioscia, L.A.
1990 (NL) Jim Leyland, Pittsburgh	(AL) Jimy Williams, Boston	2010 (NL) Bud Black, San Diego
(AL) Jeff Torborg, Chicago	2000 (NL) Dusty Baker, San Francisco	(AL) Ron Gardenhire, Minnesota
1991 (NL) Bobby Cox, Atlanta	(AL) Jerry Manuel, Chicago	2011 (NL) Kirk Gibson, Arizona
(AL) Tom Kelly, Minnesota	2001 (NL) Larry Bowa, Philadelphia	(AL) Joe Maddon, Tampa Bay
1992 (NL) Jim Leyland, Pittsburgh	(AL) Lou Piniella, Seattle	2012 (NL) Davey Johnson, Washington
(AL) Tony La Russa, Oakland	2002 (NL) Tony La Russa, St. Louis	(AL) Bob Melvin, Oakland
1993 (NL) Dusty Baker, San Francisco	(AL) Mike Scioscia, Anaheim	2013 (NL) Clint Hurdle, Pittsburgh
(AL) Gene Lamont, Chicago	2003 (NL) Jack McKeon, Florida	(AL) Terry Francona, Cleveland
1994 (NL) Felipe Alou, Montréal	(AL) Tony Pena, Kansas City	2014 (NL) Matt Williams, Washington
(AL) Buck Showalter, NY	2004 (NL) Bobby Cox, Atlanta	(AL) Buck Showalter, Baltimore
1995 (NL) Don Baylor, Colorado	(AL) Buck Showalter, Texas	2015 (NL) Joe Maddon, Chicago
(AL) Lou Piniella, Seattle	2005 (NL) Bobby Cox, Atlanta	(AL) Jeff Banister, Texas
	(AL) Ozzie Guillen, Chicago	

National Baseball Hall of Fame and Museum, Cooperstown, NY

= Player chosen in first year of eligibility (five seasons after retirement) or earlier. * = 2016 inductee.

#Aaron, Hank
Alexander, Grover
Alomar, Roberto
Alston, Walt
Anderson, George
Anson, Cap
Aparicio, Luis
Appling, Luke
Ashburn, Richie
Averill, Earl
Baker, Frank "Home Run"
Bancroft, Dave
#Banks, Ernie
Barlick, Al
Barrow, Edward G.
Beckley, Jake
Bell, James "Cool Papa"
#Bench, Johnny
Bender, Charles "Chief"
Berra, Lawrence "Yogi"
Biggio, Craig
Blyleven, Bert
#Boggs, Wade
Bottomley, Jim
Boudreau, Lou
Bresnahan, Roger
#Brett, George
#Brock, Lou
Brouthers, Dan
Brown, Mordecai
Brown, Ray
Brown, Willard
Bulkeley, Morgan C.
Bunning, Jim
Burkett, Jesse C.
Campanella, Roy
#Carew, Rod
Carey, Max
#Carlton, Steve
Carter, Gary
Cartwright, Alexander
Cepeda, Orlando
Chadwick, Henry
Chance, Frank
Chandler, Albert "Happy"
Charleston, Oscar
Chesbro, John
Chylak, Nestor
Clarke, Fred
Clarkson, John
#Clemente, Roberto
Cobb, Ty[1]
Cochrane, Mickey
Collins, Eddie
Collins, James
Combs, Earle
Comiskey, Charles A.
Conlan, John "Jocko"
Connolly, Thomas H.
Connor, Roger
Cooper, Andy
Coveleski, Stan
Cox, Bobby

Crawford, Sam
Cronin, Joe
Cummings, W. A. "Candy"
Cuyler, Hazen "Kiki"
Dandridge, Ray
Davis, George
Dawson, Andre
Day, Leon
Dean, Jay Hanna "Dizzy"
Delahanty, Ed
Dickey, Bill
Dihigo, Martín
#DiMaggio, Joe
#Doby, Larry
Doerr, Bobby
Dreyfuss, Barney
Drysdale, Don
Duffy, Hugh
Durocher, Leo
#Eckersley, Dennis
Evans, Billy
Evers, John
Ewing, Buck
Faber, Urban "Red"
#Feller, Bob
Ferrell, Rick
Fingers, Rollie
Fisk, Carlton
Flick, Elmer H.
Ford, Whitey
Foster, Andrew "Rube"
Foster, Bill
Fox, Nellie
Foxx, Jimmie
Frick, Ford
Frisch, Frank
Galvin, James "Pud"
#Gehrig, Lou
Gehringer, Charles
#Gibson, Bob
Gibson, Josh
Giles, Warren
Gillick, Pat
#Glavine, Tom
Gomez, Lefty
Gordon, Joe
Goslin, Leon "Goose"
Gossage, Rich
Grant, Frank
Greenberg, Hank
*#Griffey, Ken, Jr.
Griffith, Clark
Grimes, Burleigh
Grove, Lefty
#Gwynn, Tony
Hafey, Charles "Chick"
Haines, Jesse
Hamilton, Bill
Hanlon, Ned
Harridge, Will
Harris, Bucky
Hartnett, Gabby
Harvey, Doug

Heilmann, Harry
#Henderson, Rickey
Herman, Billy
Herzog, Whitey
Hill, Pete
Hooper, Harry
Hornsby, Rogers
Hoyt, Waite
Hubbard, Cal
Hubbell, Carl
Huggins, Miller
Hulbert, William
Hunter, James "Catfish"
Irvin, Monte
#Jackson, Reggie
Jackson, Travis
Jenkins, Ferguson
Jennings, Hugh
Johnson, Byron "Ban"
#Johnson, Randy
Johnson, Walter[1]
Johnson, William "Judy"
Joss, Addie
#Kaline, Al
Keefe, Timothy
Keeler, William
Kell, George
Kelley, Joe
Kelly, George
Kelly, King
Killebrew, Harmon
Kiner, Ralph
Klein, Chuck
Klem, Bill
#Koufax, Sandy
Kuhn, Bowie
La Russa, Tony
Lajoie, Napoleon
Landis, Kenesaw M.
Larkin, Barry
Lasorda, Tommy
Lazzeri, Tony
Lemon, Bob
Leonard, Buck
Lindstrom, Fred
Lloyd, Pop
Lombardi, Ernie
Lopez, Al
Lyons, Ted
Mack, Connie
Mackey, James "Biz"
MacPhail, Larry
MacPhail, Lee
Madden, Bill
#Maddux, Greg
Manley, Effa
#Mantle, Mickey
Manush, Henry
Maranville, Walter
Marichal, Juan
Marquard, Rube
#Martinez, Pedro
Mathews, Eddie

Mathewson, Christy[1]
#Mays, Willie
Mazeroski, Bill
McCarthy, Joe
McCarthy, Thomas
#McCovey, Willie
McGinnity, Joe
McGowan, Bill
McGraw, John
McKechnie, Bill
McPhee, John "Bid"
Medwick, Joe
Mendez, Jose
Mize, Johnny
#Molitor, Paul
#Morgan, Joe
#Murray, Eddie
#Musial, Stan
Newhouser, Hal
Nichols, Kid
Niekro, Phil
O'Day, Hank
O'Malley, Walter
O'Rourke, Jim
Ott, Mel
Paige, Satchel
#Palmer, Jim
Pennock, Herb
Perez, Tony
Perry, Gaylord
*Piazza, Mike
Plank, Ed
Pompez, Alex
Posey, Cum(berland)
#Puckett, Kirby
Radbourn, Charlie
Reese, Pee Wee
Rice, Jim
Rice, Sam
Rickey, Branch
#Ripken, Cal, Jr.
Rixey, Eppa
Rizzuto, Phil "Scooter"
Roberts, Robin
#Robinson, Brooks
#Robinson, Frank
#Robinson, Jackie
Robinson, Wilbert
Rogan, Joe "Bullet"
Roush, Edd
Ruffing, Red
Ruppert, Jacob
Rusie, Amos
#Ruth, Babe[1]
#Ryan, Nolan
Sandberg, Ryne
Santo, Ron
Santop, Louis
Schalk, Ray
#Schmidt, Mike
Schoendienst, Red
#Seaver, Tom

Selee, Frank
Sewell, Joe
Simmons, Al
Sisler, George
Slaughter, Enos
Smith, Hilton
#Smith, Ozzie
#Smoltz, John
Snider, Duke
Southworth, Billy
#Spahn, Warren
Spalding, Albert
Speaker, Tris
#Stargell, Willie
Stearnes, Norman
Stengel, Casey
Sutter, Bruce
Suttles, George "Mule"
Sutton, Don
Taylor, Ben
Terry, Bill
#Thomas, Frank
Thompson, Sam
Tinker, Joe
Torre, Joe
Torriente, Cristobal
Traynor, Harold J. "Pie"
Vance, Arthur "Dazzy"
Vaughan, Joseph "Arky"
Veeck, Bill
Waddell, Rube
Wagner, Honus[1]
Wallace, Roderick
Walsh, Ed
Waner, Lloyd
Waner, Paul
Ward, John
Weaver, Earl
Weiss, George
Welch, Mickey
Wells, Willie
Wheat, Zach
White, Deacon
White, Sol
Wilhelm, Hoyt
Wilkinson, J. L.
Williams, Billy
Williams, Dick
Williams, Joe
#Williams, Ted
Willis, Vic
Wilson, Hack
Wilson, Jud
#Winfield, Dave
Wright, George
Wright, Harry
Wynn, Early
#Yastrzemski, Carl
Yawkey, Tom
Young, Cy
Youngs, Ross
#Yount, Robin

(1) Player inducted in 1936, the year the Hall of Fame began.

BASKETBALL

Cleveland Dethrones Record-Setting Golden State for 2016 NBA Title

The Cleveland Cavaliers won their first NBA championship in dramatic fashion, becoming the first team ever to overcome a 3-games-to-1 deficit to beat the defending-champion Golden State Warriors in 7 games. Hometown Cav star LeBron James scored 27 points and added 11 rebounds and 11 assists in their deciding 93-89 victory in Game 7, June 19, 2016, at Oracle Arena in Oakland, CA. James and guard Kyrie Irving kept Cleveland alive in Game 5 as each scored 41 points in a 112-97 victory June 13 in Oakland. James, who averaged 29.7 points per game in the Finals and was voted Finals Most Valuable Player, had another 41-point effort in Game 6, a 115-101 win on June 16 at Quicken Loans Arena in Cleveland, OH. In his sixth consecutive NBA Finals (and second since returning to Cleveland from Miami in 2014), LeBron led the Cavaliers to the city's first major professional sports title since the Cleveland Browns won the 1964 NFL championship.

Golden State, which won an NBA-record 73 games during the 2015-16 season, came back from a 3-1 deficit in the Western Conference finals against the Oklahoma City Thunder. Warriors guard Stephen Curry scored 46 en route to a 125-104 win over visiting Memphis to claim win number 73 in their last regular season game Apr. 13. The victory broke the previous mark of 72-10, set by the Chicago Bulls in 1995-96. Golden State also set a league mark with 24 straight wins to start a season. Curry was the first unanimous winner as league MVP, setting a regular-season record for three-point field goals made (402), breaking his own mark of 286 set in 2014-15. Golden State's feat overshadowed San Antonio's franchise-record 67-win season, which included an NBA record-tying 40-1 record at home. The Spurs then fell in six games to Oklahoma City in the Western Conference semifinals.

The 2015-16 season was the last for 18-time All-Star guard Kobe Bryant, who retired after 20 seasons with the L.A. Lakers and finished third all-time in points (33,643). Bryant set an NBA record for most points in a player's final game on Apr. 13 when he poured in 60 in a season-ending, 101-96 win over the Utah Jazz in Los Angeles. After the season ended, San Antonio Spurs legend and two-time NBA MVP Tim Duncan retired July 11, 2016, after 19 seasons and 5 NBA championships, all with San Antonio.

NBA Final Standings, 2015-16

(playoff seeding in parentheses)

Eastern Conference

Atlantic Division	W	L	PCT	GB
Toronto Raptors (2)	56	26	.683	—
Boston Celtics (5)	48	34	.585	8
NY Knicks	32	50	.390	24
Brooklyn Nets	21	61	.256	35
Philadelphia 76ers	10	72	.122	46

Central Division	W	L	PCT	GB
Cleveland Cavaliers (1)	57	25	.695	—
Indiana Pacers (7)	45	37	.549	12
Detroit Pistons (8)	44	38	.537	13
Chicago Bulls	42	40	.512	15
Milwaukee Bucks	33	49	.402	24

Southeast Division	W	L	PCT	GB
Miami Heat (3)	48	34	.585	—
Atlanta Hawks (4)	48	34	.585	—
Charlotte Hornets (6)	48	34	.585	—
Washington Wizards	41	41	.500	7
Orlando Magic	35	47	.427	13

Western Conference

Northwest Division	W	L	PCT	GB
Oklahoma City Thunder (3)	55	27	.671	—
Portland Trail Blazers (5)	44	38	.537	11
Utah Jazz	40	42	.488	15
Denver Nuggets	33	49	.402	22
Minnesota Timberwolves	29	53	.354	26

Pacific Division	W	L	PCT	GB
Golden State Warriors (1)	73	9	.890	—
L.A. Clippers (4)	53	29	.646	20
Sacramento Kings	33	49	.402	40
Phoenix Suns	23	59	.280	50
L.A. Lakers	17	65	.207	56

Southwest Division	W	L	PCT	GB
San Antonio Spurs (2)	67	15	.817	—
Dallas Mavericks (6)	42	40	.512	25
Memphis Grizzlies (7)	42	40	.512	25
Houston Rockets (8)	41	41	.500	26
New Orleans Pelicans	30	52	.366	37

Note: Miami won the Southeast Division due to a better head-to-head record (5-3) over Atlanta (4-4) and Charlotte (3-5); Atlanta earned the no. 4 seed due to a better head-to-head record (6-2) over Boston (3-4) and Charlotte (2-5); Dallas earned the no. 6 seed due to a better head-to-head record (3-1) over Memphis.

NBA Playoff Results, 2016

Eastern Conference
Cleveland defeated Detroit, 4 games to 0
Atlanta defeated Boston, 4 games to 2
Miami defeated Charlotte, 4 games to 3
Toronto defeated Indiana, 4 games to 3
Cleveland defeated Atlanta, 4 games to 0
Toronto defeated Miami, 4 games to 3
Cleveland defeated Toronto, 4 games to 2

Western Conference
Golden State defeated Houston, 4 games to 1
San Antonio defeated Memphis, 4 games to 0
Oklahoma City defeated Dallas, 4 games to 1
Portland defeated L.A. Clippers, 4 games to 2
Golden State defeated Portland, 4 games to 1
Oklahoma City defeated San Antonio, 4 games to 2
Golden State defeated Oklahoma City, 4 games to 3

Championship
Cleveland defeated Golden State, 4 games to 3 (89-104, 77-110, 120-90, 97-108, 112-97, 115-101, 93-89)

NBA Regular Season Individual Highs, 2015-16

Minutes, game: 57, Marcus Morris, Detroit v. Chicago, Dec. 18 (4 OT)

Points, game: 60, Kobe Bryant, L.A. Lakers v. Utah, Apr. 13

Field goals, game: 24, Anthony Davis, New Orleans v. Detroit, Feb. 21

Field goal attempts, game: 50, Kobe Bryant, L.A. Lakers v. Utah, Apr. 13

3-pointers, game: 12, Stephen Curry, Golden State v. Oklahoma City, Feb. 27 (OT)

3-pt. attempts, game: 21, Kobe Bryant, L.A. Lakers v. Utah, Apr. 13

Free throws, game: 24, DeMar DeRozan, Toronto v. Portland, Mar. 4

Free throw attempts, game: 36, Andre Drummond, Detroit v. Houston, Jan. 20

Rebounds, game: 29, Andre Drummond, Detroit v. Indiana, Nov. 3

Assists, game: 20, Rajon Rondo, Sacramento v. Charlotte, Nov. 23 (OT); Sacramento v. Charlotte, Jan. 25 (2 OT)

Steals, game: 8, Robert Covington, Philadelphia v. Houston, Nov. 27; Ricky Rubio, Minnesota v. New York, Dec. 16; Pablo Prigioni, L.A. Clippers v. Miami, Jan. 13; James Harden, Houston v. Utah, Mar. 23

Blocks, game: 11, Hassan Whiteside, Miami v. Denver, Jan. 15

Minutes played, season: 3,125, James Harden, Houston

Off. rebounds, season: 395, Andre Drummond, Detroit

Def. rebounds, season: 803, Andre Drummond, Detroit

Personal fouls, season: 258, Giannis Antetokuonmpo, Milwaukee

NBA Finals MVP, 1969-2016

Year	Player, team	Year	Player, team	Year	Player, team
1969	Jerry West, L.A. Lakers	1985	Kareem Abdul-Jabbar, L.A. Lakers	2001	Shaquille O'Neal, L.A. Lakers
1970	Willis Reed, New York			2002	Shaquille O'Neal, L.A. Lakers
1971	Lew Alcindor (Kareem Abdul-Jabbar), Milwaukee	1986	Larry Bird, Boston	2003	Tim Duncan, San Antonio
		1987	Magic Johnson, L.A. Lakers	2004	Chauncey Billups, Detroit
1972	Wilt Chamberlain, L.A. Lakers	1988	James Worthy, L.A. Lakers	2005	Tim Duncan, San Antonio
1973	Willis Reed, New York	1989	Joe Dumars, Detroit	2006	Dwyane Wade, Miami
1974	John Havlicek, Boston	1990	Isiah Thomas, Detroit	2007	Tony Parker, San Antonio
1975	Rick Barry, Golden State	1991	Michael Jordan, Chicago	2008	Paul Pierce, Boston
1976	Jo Jo White, Boston	1992	Michael Jordan, Chicago	2009	Kobe Bryant, L.A. Lakers
1977	Bill Walton, Portland	1993	Michael Jordan, Chicago	2010	Kobe Bryant, L.A. Lakers
1978	Wes Unseld, Washington	1994	Hakeem Olajuwon, Houston	2011	Dirk Nowitzki, Dallas
1979	Dennis Johnson, Seattle	1995	Hakeem Olajuwon, Houston	2012	LeBron James, Miami
1980	Magic Johnson, L.A. Lakers	1996	Michael Jordan, Chicago	2013	LeBron James, Miami
1981	Cedric Maxwell, Boston	1997	Michael Jordan, Chicago	2014	Kawhi Leonard, San Antonio
1982	Magic Johnson, L.A. Lakers	1998	Michael Jordan, Chicago	2015	Andre Iguodala, Golden State
1983	Moses Malone, Philadelphia	1999	Tim Duncan, San Antonio	2016	LeBron James, Cleveland
1984	Larry Bird, Boston	2000	Shaquille O'Neal, L.A. Lakers		

NBA Finals All-Time Statistical Leaders

(At the end of the 2016 NBA Finals. * = Active in 2015-16 season. Minimum 10 games played.)

Scoring average	GP	FG	FT	PTS	AVG	Scoring average	GP	FG	FT	PTS	AVG
Rick Barry	10	138	87	363	36.3	Hakeem Olajuwon	17	187	91	467	27.5
Michael Jordan	35	438	258	1,176	33.6	*LeBron James	40	405	201	1,079	27.0
Jerry West	55	612	455	1,679	30.5	Elgin Baylor	44	442	277	1,161	26.4
Shaquille O'Neal	30	340	185	865	28.8	Julius Erving	22	216	128	561	25.5
Bob Pettit	25	241	227	709	28.4	*Kobe Bryant	37	333	223	937	25.3

Games Played		Rebounds		Assists	
Bill Russell	70	Bill Russell	1,718	Magic Johnson	584
Sam Jones	64	Wilt Chamberlain	862	Bob Cousy	400
Kareem Abdul-Jabbar	56	Elgin Baylor	593	Bill Russell	315
Jerry West	55	Kareem Abdul-Jabbar	507	Jerry West	306
Tom Heinsohn	52	Tom Heinsohn	473	*LeBron James	289

NBA Most Valuable Player, 1956-2016

Year	Player, team	Year	Player, team	Year	Player, team
1956	Bob Pettit, St. Louis	1977	Kareem Abdul-Jabbar, L.A. Lakers	1997	Karl Malone, Utah
1957	Bob Cousy, Boston	1978	Bill Walton, Portland	1998	Michael Jordan, Chicago
1958	Bill Russell, Boston	1979	Moses Malone, Houston	1999	Karl Malone, Utah
1959	Bob Pettit, St. Louis	1980	Kareem Abdul-Jabbar, L.A. Lakers	2000	Shaquille O'Neal, L.A. Lakers
1960	Wilt Chamberlain, Philadelphia	1981	Julius Erving, Philadelphia	2001	Allen Iverson, Philadelphia
1961	Bill Russell, Boston	1982	Moses Malone, Houston	2002	Tim Duncan, San Antonio
1962	Bill Russell, Boston	1983	Moses Malone, Philadelphia	2003	Tim Duncan, San Antonio
1963	Bill Russell, Boston	1984	Larry Bird, Boston	2004	Kevin Garnett, Minnesota
1964	Oscar Robertson, Cincinnati	1985	Larry Bird, Boston	2005	Steve Nash, Phoenix
1965	Bill Russell, Boston	1986	Larry Bird, Boston	2006	Steve Nash, Phoenix
1966	Wilt Chamberlain, Philadelphia	1987	Magic Johnson, L.A. Lakers	2007	Dirk Nowitzki, Dallas
1967	Wilt Chamberlain, Philadelphia	1988	Michael Jordan, Chicago	2008	Kobe Bryant, L.A. Lakers
1968	Wilt Chamberlain, Philadelphia	1989	Magic Johnson, L.A. Lakers	2009	LeBron James, Cleveland
1969	Wes Unseld, Baltimore	1990	Magic Johnson, L.A. Lakers	2010	LeBron James, Cleveland
1970	Willis Reed, New York	1991	Michael Jordan, Chicago	2011	Derrick Rose, Chicago
1971	Lew Alcindor (Abdul-Jabbar), Milw.	1992	Michael Jordan, Chicago	2012	LeBron James, Miami
1972	Kareem Abdul-Jabbar, Milwaukee	1993	Charles Barkley, Phoenix	2013	LeBron James, Miami
1973	Dave Cowens, Boston	1994	Hakeem Olajuwon, Houston	2014	Kevin Durant, Oklahoma City
1974	Kareem Abdul-Jabbar, Milwaukee	1995	David Robinson, San Antonio	2015	Stephen Curry, Golden State
1975	Bob McAdoo, Buffalo	1996	Michael Jordan, Chicago	2016	Stephen Curry, Golden State
1976	Kareem Abdul-Jabbar, L.A. Lakers				

NBA Scoring Leaders, 1947-2016

(Average points per game; 58 games minimum in 2015-16; prior season minimums vary.)

Year	Player, team	PTS	AVG	Year	Player, team	PTS	AVG
1947	Joe Fulks, Philadelphia	1,389	23.2	1968	Dave Bing, Detroit	2,142	27.1
1948	Max Zaslofsky, Chicago	1,007	21.0	1969	Elvin Hayes, San Diego	2,327	28.4
1949	George Mikan, Minneapolis	1,698	28.3	1970	Jerry West, L.A. Lakers	2,309	31.2
1950	George Mikan, Minneapolis	1,865	27.4	1971	Lew Alcindor (Kareem Abdul-Jabbar), Milw.	2,596	31.7
1951	George Mikan, Minneapolis	1,932	28.4	1972	Kareem Abdul-Jabbar, Milwaukee	2,822	34.8
1952	Paul Arizin, Philadelphia	1,674	25.4	1973	Nate Archibald, Kansas City-Omaha	2,719	34.0
1953	Neil Johnston, Philadelphia	1,564	22.3	1974	Bob McAdoo, Buffalo	2,261	30.6
1954	Neil Johnston, Philadelphia	1,759	24.4	1975	Bob McAdoo, Buffalo	2,831	34.5
1955	Neil Johnston, Philadelphia	1,631	22.7	1976	Bob McAdoo, Buffalo	2,427	31.1
1956	Bob Pettit, St. Louis	1,849	25.7	1977	Pete Maravich, New Orleans	2,273	31.1
1957	Paul Arizin, Philadelphia	1,817	25.6	1978	George Gervin, San Antonio	2,232	27.2
1958	George Yardley, Detroit	2,001	27.8	1979	George Gervin, San Antonio	2,365	29.6
1959	Bob Pettit, St. Louis	2,105	29.2	1980	George Gervin, San Antonio	2,585	33.1
1960	Wilt Chamberlain, Philadelphia	2,707	37.6	1981	Adrian Dantley, Utah	2,452	30.7
1961	Wilt Chamberlain, Philadelphia	3,033	38.4	1982	George Gervin, San Antonio	2,551	32.3
1962	Wilt Chamberlain, Philadelphia	4,029	50.4	1983	Alex English, Denver	2,326	28.4
1963	Wilt Chamberlain, San Francisco	3,586	44.8	1984	Adrian Dantley, Utah	2,418	30.6
1964	Wilt Chamberlain, San Francisco	2,948	36.9	1985	Bernard King, New York	1,809	32.9
1965	Wilt Chamberlain, San Francisco-Phil.	2,534	34.7	1986	Dominique Wilkins, Atlanta	2,366	30.3
1966	Wilt Chamberlain, Philadelphia	2,649	33.5	1987	Michael Jordan, Chicago	3,041	37.1
1967	Rick Barry, San Francisco	2,775	35.6	1988	Michael Jordan, Chicago	2,868	35.0

Year	Player, team	PTS	AVG	Year	Player, team	PTS	AVG
1989	Michael Jordan, Chicago	2,633	32.5	2003	Tracy McGrady, Orlando	2,407	32.1
1990	Michael Jordan, Chicago	2,753	33.6	2004	Tracy McGrady, Orlando	1,878	28.0
1991	Michael Jordan, Chicago	2,580	31.5	2005	Allen Iverson, Philadelphia	2,302	30.7
1992	Michael Jordan, Chicago	2,404	30.1	2006	Kobe Bryant, L.A. Lakers	2,832	35.4
1993	Michael Jordan, Chicago	2,541	32.6	2007	Kobe Bryant, L.A. Lakers	2,430	31.6
1994	David Robinson, San Antonio	2,383	29.8	2008	LeBron James, Cleveland	2,250	30.0
1995	Shaquille O'Neal, Orlando	2,315	29.3	2009	Dwyane Wade, Miami	2,386	30.2
1996	Michael Jordan, Chicago	2,491	30.4	2010	Kevin Durant, Oklahoma City	2,472	30.1
1997	Michael Jordan, Chicago	2,431	29.6	2011	Kevin Durant, Oklahoma City	2,161	27.7
1998	Michael Jordan, Chicago	2,357	28.7	2012	Kevin Durant, Oklahoma City	1,850	28.0
1999	Allen Iverson, Philadelphia	1,284	26.8	2013	Carmelo Anthony, New York	1,920	28.7
2000	Shaquille O'Neal, L.A. Lakers	2,344	29.7	2014	Kevin Durant, Oklahoma City	2,593	32.0
2001	Allen Iverson, Philadelphia	2,207	31.1	2015	Russell Westbrook, Oklahoma City	1,886	28.1
2002	Allen Iverson, Philadelphia	1,883	31.4	2016	Stephen Curry, Golden State	2,375	30.1

NBA Champions, 1947-2016

Year	Eastern champion	Western champion	Champion	Winning coach	Opponent
1947	Washington Capitols	Chicago Stags	Philadelphia	Ed Gottlieb	Chicago
1948	Philadelphia Warriors	St. Louis Bombers	Baltimore	Buddy Jeannette	Philadelphia
1949	Washington Capitols	Rochester	Minneapolis	John Kundla	Washington
1950[1]	Syracuse	Indianapolis	Minneapolis	John Kundla	Syracuse
1951	Philadelphia Warriors	Minneapolis	Rochester	Lester Harrison	New York
1952	Syracuse	Rochester	Minneapolis	John Kundla	New York
1953	New York	Minneapolis	Minneapolis	John Kundla	New York
1954	New York	Minneapolis	Minneapolis	John Kundla	Syracuse
1955	Syracuse	Ft. Wayne	Syracuse	Al Cervi	Ft. Wayne
1956	Philadelphia Warriors	Ft. Wayne	Philadelphia	George Senesky	Ft. Wayne
1957	Boston	St. Louis	Boston	Red Auerbach	St. Louis
1958	Boston	St. Louis	St. Louis	Alex Hannum	Boston
1959	Boston	St. Louis	Boston	Red Auerbach	Minneapolis
1960	Boston	St. Louis	Boston	Red Auerbach	St. Louis
1961	Boston	St. Louis	Boston	Red Auerbach	St. Louis
1962	Boston	L.A. Lakers	Boston	Red Auerbach	L.A. Lakers
1963	Boston	L.A. Lakers	Boston	Red Auerbach	L.A. Lakers
1964	Boston	San Francisco	Boston	Red Auerbach	San Francisco
1965	Boston	L.A. Lakers	Boston	Red Auerbach	L.A. Lakers
1966	Philadelphia	L.A. Lakers	Boston	Red Auerbach	L.A. Lakers
1967	Philadelphia	San Francisco	Philadelphia	Alex Hannum	San Francisco
1968	Philadelphia	St. Louis	Boston	Bill Russell	L.A. Lakers
1969	Baltimore	L.A. Lakers	Boston	Bill Russell	L.A. Lakers
1970	New York	Atlanta	New York	Red Holzman	L.A. Lakers

Year	Atlantic	Central	Midwest	Pacific	Champion	Winning coach	Opponent
1971	New York	Baltimore	Milwaukee	L.A. Lakers	Milwaukee	Larry Costello	Baltimore
1972	Boston	Baltimore	Milwaukee	L.A. Lakers	L.A. Lakers	Bill Sharman	New York
1973	Boston	Baltimore	Milwaukee	L.A. Lakers	New York	Red Holzman	L.A. Lakers
1974	Boston	Capital	Milwaukee	L.A. Lakers	Boston	Tom Heinsohn	Milwaukee
1975	Boston	Washington	Chicago	Golden State	Golden State	Al Attles	Washington
1976	Boston	Cleveland	Milwaukee	Golden State	Boston	Tom Heinsohn	Phoenix
1977	Philadelphia	Houston	Denver	L.A. Lakers	Portland	Jack Ramsay	Philadelphia
1978	Philadelphia	San Antonio	Denver	Portland	Washington	Dick Motta	Seattle
1979	Washington	San Antonio	Kansas City	Seattle	Seattle	Len Wilkens	Washington
1980	Boston	Atlanta	Milwaukee	L.A. Lakers	L.A. Lakers	Paul Westhead	Philadelphia
1981	Boston	Milwaukee	San Antonio	Phoenix	Boston	Bill Fitch	Houston
1982	Boston	Milwaukee	San Antonio	L.A. Lakers	L.A. Lakers	Pat Riley	Philadelphia
1983	Philadelphia	Milwaukee	San Antonio	L.A. Lakers	Philadelphia	Billy Cunningham	L.A. Lakers
1984	Boston	Milwaukee	Utah	L.A. Lakers	Boston	K. C. Jones	L.A. Lakers
1985	Boston	Milwaukee	Denver	L.A. Lakers	L.A. Lakers	Pat Riley	Boston
1986	Boston	Milwaukee	Houston	L.A. Lakers	Boston	K. C. Jones	Houston
1987	Boston	Atlanta	Dallas	L.A. Lakers	L.A. Lakers	Pat Riley	Boston
1988	Boston	Detroit	Denver	L.A. Lakers	L.A. Lakers	Pat Riley	Detroit
1989	New York	Detroit	Utah	L.A. Lakers	Detroit	Chuck Daly	L.A. Lakers
1990	Philadelphia	Detroit	San Antonio	L.A. Lakers	Detroit	Chuck Daly	Portland
1991	Boston	Chicago	San Antonio	Portland	Chicago	Phil Jackson	L.A. Lakers
1992	Boston	Chicago	Utah	Portland	Chicago	Phil Jackson	Portland
1993	New York	Chicago	Houston	Phoenix	Chicago	Phil Jackson	Phoenix
1994	New York	Atlanta	Houston	Seattle	Houston	Rudy Tomjanovich	New York
1995	Orlando	Indiana	San Antonio	Phoenix	Houston	Rudy Tomjanovich	Orlando
1996	Orlando	Chicago	San Antonio	Seattle	Chicago	Phil Jackson	Seattle
1997	Miami	Chicago	Utah	Seattle	Chicago	Phil Jackson	Utah
1998	Miami	Chicago	Utah	L.A. Lakers	Chicago	Phil Jackson	Utah
1999	Miami	Indiana	San Antonio	Portland	San Antonio	Gregg Popovich	New York
2000	Miami	Indiana	Utah	L.A. Lakers	L.A. Lakers	Phil Jackson	Indiana
2001	Philadelphia	Milwaukee	San Antonio	L.A. Lakers	L.A. Lakers	Phil Jackson	Philadelphia
2002	New Jersey	Detroit	San Antonio	Sacramento	L.A. Lakers	Phil Jackson	New Jersey
2003	New Jersey	Detroit	San Antonio	Sacramento	San Antonio	Gregg Popovich	New Jersey
2004	New Jersey	Indiana	Minnesota	L.A. Lakers	Detroit	Larry Brown	L.A. Lakers

Year	Atlantic	Central	Southeast	Northwest	Pacific	Southwest	Champion	Winning coach	Opponent
2005	Boston	Detroit	Miami	Seattle	Phoenix	San Antonio	San Antonio	Gregg Popovich	Detroit
2006	New Jersey	Detroit	Miami	Denver	Phoenix	San Antonio	Miami	Pat Riley	Dallas
2007	Toronto	Detroit	Miami	Utah	Phoenix	Dallas	San Antonio	Gregg Popovich	Cleveland
2008	Boston	Detroit	Orlando	Utah	L.A. Lakers	New Orleans	Boston	Glenn "Doc" Rivers	L.A. Lakers
2009	Boston	Cleveland	Orlando	Denver	L.A. Lakers	San Antonio	L.A. Lakers	Phil Jackson	Orlando
2010	Boston	Cleveland	Orlando	Denver	L.A. Lakers	Dallas	L.A. Lakers	Phil Jackson	Boston
2011	Boston	Chicago	Miami	OK City	L.A. Lakers	San Antonio	Dallas	Rick Carlisle	Miami
2012	Boston	Chicago	Miami	OK City	L.A. Lakers	San Antonio	Miami	Erik Spoelstra	OK City
2013	New York	Indiana	Miami	OK City	L.A. Clippers	San Antonio	Miami	Erik Spoelstra	San Antonio
2014	Toronto	Indiana	Miami	OK City	L.A. Clippers	San Antonio	San Antonio	Gregg Popovich	Miami
2015	Toronto	Cleveland	Atlanta	Portland	Golden State	Houston	Golden State	Steve Kerr	Cleveland
2016	Toronto	Cleveland	Miami	Oklahoma City	Golden State	San Antonio	Cleveland	Tyronn Lue	Golden State

(1) The newly formed NBA combined the 11-team BAA (Basketball Assn. of Amer.) and six NBL (Natl. Basketball League) teams in the 1949-50 season and had three divisions for one year. The Minneapolis Lakers were co-champions of the soon-defunct Central Division.

All-NBA and All-Defensive Teams, 2015-16

	All-NBA Team			All-Defensive Team	
First Team	**Second Team**	**Position**	**First Team**	**Second Team**	
LeBron James, Cleveland	Kevin Durant, Oklahoma City	**Forward**	Kawhi Leonard, San Antonio	Paul Millsap, Atlanta	
Kawhi Leonard, San Antonio	Draymond Green, Golden State	**Forward**	Draymond Green, Golden State	Paul George, Indiana	
DeAndre Jordan, L.A. Clippers	DeMarcus Cousins, Sacramento	**Center**	DeAndre Jordan, L.A. Clippers	Hassan Whiteside, Miami	
Stephen Curry, Golden State	Chris Paul, L.A. Clippers	**Guard**	Avery Bradley, Boston	Tony Allen, Memphis	
Russell Westbrook, Oklahoma City	Damian Lillard, Portland	**Guard**	Chris Paul, L.A. Clippers	Jimmy Butler, Chicago	

NBA Statistical Leaders, 2015-16

(* = rookie)

To qualify for averaged categories, player must be on pace to play 58 games in an 82-game season.

Scoring Average

Player, team	GP	FG	FT	PTS	AVG
Stephen Curry, Golden State	79	805	363	2,375	30.1
James Harden, Houston	82	710	720	2,376	29.0
Kevin Durant, Oklahoma City	72	698	447	2,029	28.2
DeMarcus Cousins, Sacramento	65	601	476	1,748	26.9
LeBron James, Cleveland	76	737	359	1,920	25.3
Damian Lillard, Portland	75	618	414	1,879	25.1
Anthony Davis, New Orleans	61	560	326	1,481	24.3
Russell Westbrook, Oklahoma City	80	656	465	1,878	23.5
DeMar DeRozan, Toronto	78	614	555	1,830	23.5
Paul George, Indiana	81	605	454	1,874	23.1

Rebounds per Game

Player, team	GP	OFF	DEF	TOT	AVG
Andre Drummond, Detroit	81	395	803	1,198	14.8
DeAndre Jordan, L.A. Clippers	77	267	792	1,059	13.8
Hassan Whiteside, Miami	73	238	627	865	11.8
Dwight Howard, Houston	71	238	597	835	11.8
DeMarcus Cousins, Sacramento	65	158	589	747	11.5
Pau Gasol, Chicago	72	155	638	793	11.0
Rudy Gobert, Utah	61	208	460	668	11.0
*Karl-Anthony Towns, Minnesota	82	228	629	857	10.5
Anthony Davis, New Orleans	61	130	497	627	10.3
Julius Randle, L.A. Lakers	81	172	657	829	10.2

3-Point Field Goal Percentage
(Minimum 82 3-point field goals made)

Player, team	3-FGM	3-FGA	PCT
J.J. Redick, L.A. Clippers	200	421	.475
Stephen Curry, Golden State	402	886	.454
Kawhi Leonard, San Antonio	129	291	.443
Jerryd Bayless, Milwaukee	101	231	.437
Doug McDermott, Chicago	110	259	.425
Klay Thompson, Golden State	276	650	.425
Jared Dudley, Washington	100	238	.420
CJ McCollum, Portland	197	472	.417
Chandler Parsons, Dallas	104	251	.414
Jose Calderon, New York	84	203	.414

Assists per Game

Player, team	GP	AST	APG
Rajon Rondo, Sacramento	72	839	11.7
Russell Westbrook, Oklahoma City	80	834	10.4
John Wall, Washington	77	789	10.2
Chris Paul, L.A. Clippers	74	738	10.0
Ricky Rubio, Minnesota	76	658	8.7
James Harden, Houston	82	612	7.5
Draymond Green, Golden State	81	598	7.4
LeBron James, Cleveland	76	514	6.8
Damian Lillard, Portland	75	512	6.8
Stephen Curry, Golden State	79	527	6.7

Field Goal Percentage
(Minimum 300 field goals made)

Player, team	FGM	FGA	PCT
DeAndre Jordan, L.A. Clippers	357	508	.703
Dwight Howard, Houston	372	600	.620
Hassan Whiteside, Miami	413	682	.606
Enes Kanter, Oklahoma City	414	719	.576
Marcin Gortat, Washington	433	764	.567
Jonas Valanciunas, Toronto	303	536	.565
Kenneth Faried, Denver	349	626	.558
*Karl-Anthony Towns, Minnesota	625	1,153	.542
Robin Lopez, New York	357	662	.539
Gorgui Dieng, Minnesota	308	579	.532

Steals per Game

Player, team	GP	STL	AVG
Stephen Curry, Golden State	79	169	2.14
Ricky Rubio, Minnesota	76	162	2.13
Kyle Lowry, Toronto	77	158	2.05
Chris Paul, L.A. Clippers	74	152	2.05
Russell Westbrook, Oklahoma City	80	163	2.04
Trevor Ariza, Houston	81	160	1.98
Rajon Rondo, Sacramento	72	141	1.96
John Wall, Washington	77	145	1.88
Paul George, Indiana	81	152	1.88
Monta Ellis, Indiana	81	150	1.85

Free Throw Percentage
(Minimum 125 free throws made)

Player, team	FTM	FTA	PCT
Stephen Curry, Golden State	363	400	.908
Jamal Crawford, L.A. Clippers	245	271	.904
Kevin Durant, Oklahoma City	447	498	.898
Chris Paul, L.A. Clippers	294	328	.896
Dirk Nowitzki, Dallas	250	280	.893
Damian Lillard, Portland	414	464	.892
Kevin Martin, Minnesota-San Antonio	153	172	.890
J.J. Redick, L.A. Clippers	182	205	.888
Khris Middleton, Milwaukee	277	312	.888
Kyrie Irving, Cleveland	169	191	.885

Blocked Shots per Game

Player, team	GP	BLK	AVG
Hassan Whiteside, Miami	73	269	3.68
DeAndre Jordan, L.A. Clippers	77	177	2.30
Rudy Gobert, Utah	61	135	2.21
Anthony Davis, New Orleans	61	125	2.05
Pau Gasol, Chicago	72	146	2.03
Serge Ibaka, Oklahoma City	78	148	1.90
*Kristaps Porzingis, New York	72	134	1.86
Paul Millsap, Atlanta	81	139	1.72
Brook Lopez, Brooklyn	73	124	1.70
*Karl-Anthony Towns, Minnesota	82	138	1.68

NBA Defensive Player of the Year, 1983-2016

Year	Player, team	Year	Player, team	Year	Player, team
1983	Sidney Moncrief, Milwaukee	1995	Dikembe Mutombo, Denver	2006	Ben Wallace, Detroit
1984	Sidney Moncrief, Milwaukee	1996	Gary Payton, Seattle	2007	Marcus Camby, Denver
1985	Mark Eaton, Utah	1997	Dikembe Mutombo, Atlanta	2008	Kevin Garnett, Boston
1986	Alvin Robertson, San Antonio	1998	Dikembe Mutombo, Atlanta	2009	Dwight Howard, Orlando
1987	Michael Cooper, L.A. Lakers	1999	Alonzo Mourning, Miami	2010	Dwight Howard, Orlando
1988	Michael Jordan, Chicago	2000	Alonzo Mourning, Miami	2011	Dwight Howard, Orlando
1989	Mark Eaton, Utah	2001	Dikembe Mutombo, Philadelphia-	2012	Tyson Chandler, New York
1990	Dennis Rodman, Detroit		Atlanta	2013	Marc Gasol, Memphis
1991	Dennis Rodman, Detroit	2002	Ben Wallace, Detroit	2014	Joakim Noah, Chicago
1992	David Robinson, San Antonio	2003	Ben Wallace, Detroit	2015	Kawhi Leonard, San Antonio
1993	Hakeem Olajuwon, Houston	2004	Ron Artest, Indiana	2016	Kawhi Leonard, San Antonio
1994	Hakeem Olajuwon, Houston	2005	Ben Wallace, Detroit		

NBA Rookie of the Year, 1953-2016

Year	Player, team	Year	Player, team	Year	Player, team
1953	Don Meineke, Ft. Wayne	1974	Ernie DiGregorio, Buffalo	1996	Damon Stoudamire, Toronto
1954	Ray Felix, Baltimore	1975	Jamaal Wilkes, Golden State	1997	Allen Iverson, Philadelphia
1955	Bob Pettit, Milwaukee	1976	Alvan Adams, Phoenix	1998	Tim Duncan, San Antonio
1956	Maurice Stokes, Rochester	1977	Adrian Dantley, Buffalo	1999	Vince Carter, Toronto
1957	Tom Heinsohn, Boston	1978	Walter Davis, Phoenix	2000	Elton Brand, Chicago;
1958	Woody Sauldsberry, Philadelphia	1979	Phil Ford, Kansas City		Steve Francis, Houston
1959	Elgin Baylor, Minneapolis	1980	Larry Bird, Boston	2001	Mike Miller, Orlando
1960	Wilt Chamberlain, Philadelphia	1981	Darrell Griffith, Utah	2002	Pau Gasol, Memphis
1961	Oscar Robertson, Cincinnati	1982	Buck Williams, New Jersey	2003	Amar'e Stoudemire, Phoenix
1962	Walt Bellamy, Chicago	1983	Terry Cummings, San Diego	2004	LeBron James, Cleveland
1963	Terry Dischinger, Chicago	1984	Ralph Sampson, Houston	2005	Emeka Okafor, Charlotte
1964	Jerry Lucas, Cincinnati	1985	Michael Jordan, Chicago	2006	Chris Paul, New Orl./OK City
1965	Willis Reed, New York	1986	Patrick Ewing, New York	2007	Brandon Roy, Portland
1966	Rick Barry, San Francisco	1987	Chuck Person, Indiana	2008	Kevin Durant, Seattle
1967	Dave Bing, Detroit	1988	Mark Jackson, New York	2009	Derrick Rose, Chicago
1968	Earl Monroe, Baltimore	1989	Mitch Richmond, Golden State	2010	Tyreke Evans, Sacramento
1969	Wes Unseld, Baltimore	1990	David Robinson, San Antonio	2011	Blake Griffin, L.A. Clippers
1970	Lew Alcindor (Abdul-Jabbar),	1991	Derrick Coleman, New Jersey	2012	Kyrie Irving, Cleveland
	Milwaukee	1992	Larry Johnson, Charlotte	2013	Damian Lillard, Portland
1971	Dave Cowens, Boston;	1993	Shaquille O'Neal, Orlando	2014	Michael Carter-Williams,
	Geoff Petrie, Portland	1994	Chris Webber, Golden State		Philadelphia
1972	Sidney Wicks, Portland	1995	Grant Hill, Detroit;	2015	Andrew Wiggins, Minnesota
1973	Bob McAdoo, Buffalo		Jason Kidd, Dallas	2016	Karl-Anthony Towns, Minnesota

NBA Sixth Man Award, 1983-2016

Year	Player, team	Year	Player, team	Year	Player, team
1983	Bobby Jones, Philadelphia	1995	Anthony Mason, New York	2006	Mike Miller, Memphis
1984	Kevin McHale, Boston	1996	Toni Kukoc, Chicago	2007	Leandro Barbosa, Phoenix
1985	Kevin McHale, Boston	1997	John Starks, New York	2008	Manu Ginobili, San Antonio
1986	Bill Walton, Boston	1998	Danny Manning, Phoenix	2009	Jason Terry, Dallas
1987	Ricky Pierce, Milwaukee	1999	Darrell Armstrong, Orlando	2010	Jamal Crawford, Atlanta
1988	Roy Tarpley, Dallas	2000	Rodney Rogers, Phoenix	2011	Lamar Odom, L.A. Lakers
1989	Eddie Johnson, Phoenix	2001	Aaron McKie, Philadelphia	2012	James Harden, Oklahoma City
1990	Ricky Pierce, Milwaukee	2002	Corliss Williamson, Detroit	2013	J.R. Smith, New York
1991	Detlef Schrempf, Indiana	2003	Bobby Jackson, Sacramento	2014	Jamal Crawford, L.A. Clippers
1992	Detlef Schrempf, Indiana	2004	Antawn Jamison, Dallas	2015	Lou Williams, Toronto
1993	Clifford Robinson, Portland	2005	Ben Gordon, Chicago	2016	Jamal Crawford, L.A. Clippers
1994	Dell Curry, Charlotte				

NBA Player Draft First-Round Picks, 2016

(June 23, 2016)

Team	Player, position, school/team	Team	Player, position, school/team
1. Philadelphia	Ben Simmons, Forward, LSU	15. Denver[7]	Juan Hernangómez, Forward, Estudiantes, Spain
2. L.A. Lakers	Brandon Ingram, Forward, Duke	16. Boston[8]	Guerschon Yabusele, Forward, Rouen, France
3. Boston[1]	Jaylen Brown, Forward, California	17. Memphis	Wade Baldwin IV, Guard, Vanderbilt
4. Phoenix	Dragan Bender, Forward, Maccabi Tel Aviv, Israel	18. Detroit	Henry Ellenson, Forward, Marquette
5. Minnesota	Kris Dunn, Guard, Providence	19. Denver[9]	Malik Beasley, Guard, Florida State
6. New Orleans	Buddy Hield, Guard, Oklahoma	20. Indiana[10]	Caris LeVert, Guard, Michigan
7. Denver[2]	Jamal Murray, Guard, Kentucky	21. Atlanta	DeAndre' Bembry, Guard, Saint Joseph's
8. Sacramento[3]	Marquese Chriss, Forward, Washington	22. Charlotte[11]	Malachi Richardson, Guard, Syracuse
9. Toronto[4]	Jakob Poeltl, Center, Utah	23. Boston	Ante Zizic, Center, Cibona, Croatia
10. Milwaukee	Thon Maker, Forward, Orangeville Prep/ Athlete Institute, Canada	24. Philadelphia[12]	Timothe Luwawu, Guard, Mega Leks, Serbia
11. Orlando[5]	Domantas Sabonis, Forward, Gonzaga	25. L.A. Clippers	Brice Johnson, Forward, North Carolina
12. Utah[6]	Taurean Prince, Forward, Baylor	26. Philadelphia[13]	Furkan Korkmaz, Guard, Efes, Turkey
13. Phoenix[3]	Georgios Papagiannis, Center, Panathinaikos, Greece	27. Toronto	Pascal Siakam, Forward, New Mexico State
14. Chicago	Denzel Valentine, Guard, Michigan State	28. Phoenix[3,14]	Skal Labissiere, Forward, Kentucky
		29. San Antonio	Dejounte Murray, Guard, Washington
		30. Golden State	Damian Jones, Center, Vanderbilt

(1) From Brooklyn. (2) From New York. (3) Sacramento traded No. 8 pick to Phoenix for selections No. 13 and 28. (4) From Denver via New York. (5) Rights traded to Oklahoma City. (6) Rights traded to Atlanta. (7) From Houston. (8) From Dallas. (9) From Portland. (10) Rights traded to Brooklyn. (11) Rights traded to Sacramento. (12) From Miami via Cleveland. (13) From Oklahoma City via Denver and Cleveland. (14) From Cleveland via Boston.

Number-One First-Round NBA Draft Picks, 1966-2016

Year	Team	Player, school/team	Year	Team	Player, school/team
1966	New York	Cazzie Russell, Michigan	1984	Houston	Hakeem Olajuwon, Houston
1967	Detroit	Jimmy Walker, Providence	1985	New York	Patrick Ewing, Georgetown
1968	San Diego	Elvin Hayes, Houston	1986	Cleveland	Brad Daugherty, North Carolina
1969	Milwaukee	Lew Alcindor (Kareem Abdul-Jabbar), UCLA	1987	San Antonio	David Robinson, Navy
1970	Detroit	Bob Lanier, St. Bonaventure	1988	L.A. Clippers	Danny Manning, Kansas
1971	Cleveland	Austin Carr, Notre Dame	1989	Sacramento	Pervis Ellison, Louisville
1972	Portland	LaRue Martin, Loyola-Chicago	1990	New Jersey	Derrick Coleman, Syracuse
1973	Philadelphia	Doug Collins, Illinois State	1991	Charlotte	Larry Johnson, UNLV
1974	Portland	Bill Walton, UCLA	1992	Orlando	Shaquille O'Neal, LSU
1975	Atlanta	David Thompson[1], NC State	1993	Orlando	Chris Webber[2], Michigan
1976	Houston	John Lucas, Maryland	1994	Milwaukee	Glenn Robinson, Purdue
1977	Milwaukee	Kent Benson, Indiana	1995	Golden State	Joe Smith, Maryland
1978	Portland	Mychal Thompson, Minnesota	1996	Philadelphia	Allen Iverson, Georgetown
1979	L.A. Lakers	Earvin "Magic" Johnson, Michigan State	1997	San Antonio	Tim Duncan, Wake Forest
1980	Golden State	Joe Barry Carroll, Purdue	1998	L.A. Clippers	Michael Olowokandi, Pacific (CA)
1981	Dallas	Mark Aguirre, DePaul	1999	Chicago	Elton Brand, Duke
1982	L.A. Lakers	James Worthy, North Carolina	2000	New Jersey	Kenyon Martin, Cincinnati
1983	Houston	Ralph Sampson, Virginia	2001	Washington	Kwame Brown, Glynn Academy (HS)
			2002	Houston	Yao Ming, Shanghai Sharks (China)

Year	Team	Player, school/team	Year	Team	Player, school/team
2003	Cleveland	LeBron James, St. Vincent-St. Mary (HS)	2010	Washington	John Wall, Kentucky
2004	Orlando	Dwight Howard, Southwest Atlanta Christian Academy (HS)	2011	Cleveland	Kyrie Irving, Duke
			2012	New Orleans	Anthony Davis, Kentucky
2005	Milwaukee	Andrew Bogut, Utah	2013	Cleveland	Anthony Bennett, UNLV
2006	Toronto	Andrea Bargnani, Benetton Treviso (Italy)	2014	Cleveland	Andrew Wiggins, Kansas
2007	Portland	Greg Oden, Ohio State	2015	Minnesota	Karl-Anthony Towns, Kentucky
2008	Chicago	Derrick Rose, Memphis	2016	Philadelphia	Ben Simmons, LSU
2009	L.A. Clippers	Blake Griffin, Oklahoma			

HS = High school. (1) Signed with Denver of the American Basketball Association (ABA). (2) Traded to Golden State for rights to Anfernee Hardaway and three future first-round draft choices.

All-Time NBA Statistical Leaders

(At the end of the 2015-16 season. * = Active in 2015-16 season.)

Scoring Average
(Minimum 400 games or 10,000 points)

	GP	PTS	AVG
Michael Jordan	1,072	32,292	30.1
Wilt Chamberlain	1,045	31,419	30.1
*Kevin Durant	641	17,566	27.4
Elgin Baylor	846	23,149	27.4
*LeBron James	987	26,833	27.2
Jerry West	932	25,192	27.0
Allen Iverson	914	24,368	26.7
Bob Pettit	792	20,880	26.4
George Gervin	791	20,708	26.2
Oscar Robertson	1,040	26,710	25.7

Field Goal Percentage
(Minimum 2,000 field goals made)

	FGM	FGA	PCT
*DeAndre Jordan	2,075	3,097	67.0
Artis Gilmore	5,732	9,570	59.9
*Tyson Chandler	3,209	5,432	59.1
Shaquille O'Neal	11,330	19,457	58.2
*Dwight Howard	5,600	9,624	58.2
Mark West	2,528	4,356	58.0
*Amir Johnson	2,126	3,703	57.4
Darryl Dawkins	3,477	6,079	57.2
Steve Johnson	2,841	4,965	57.2
James Donaldson	3,105	5,442	57.1

Free Throw Percentage
(Minimum 1,200 free throws made)

	FTM	FTA	PCT
Steve Nash	3,060	3,384	90.4
Mark Price	2,135	2,362	90.4
*Stephen Curry	1,668	1,850	90.2
Rick Barry	3,818	4,243	90.0
Peja Stojakovic	2,237	2,500	89.5
Ray Allen	4,398	4,920	89.4
Chauncey Billups	4,496	5,029	89.4
Calvin Murphy	3,445	3,864	89.2
Scott Skiles	1,548	1,741	88.9
Reggie Miller	6,237	7,026	88.8
*J.J. Redick	1,241	1,398	88.8

3-Point Field Goal Percentage
(Minimum 250 3-point field goals made)

	3-FGM	3-FGA	PCT
Steve Kerr	726	1,599	45.4
*Stephen Curry	1,593	3,590	44.4
Hubert Davis	728	1,651	44.1
Drazen Petrovic	255	583	43.7
Jason Kapono	457	1,054	43.4
*Steve Novak	574	1,331	43.1
Tim Legler	260	603	43.1
*Kyle Korver	1,887	4,395	42.9
Steve Nash	1,685	3,939	42.8
B.J. Armstrong	436	1,026	42.5
*Anthony Morrow	766	1,804	42.5

Minutes Played

Kareem Abdul-Jabbar	57,446
Karl Malone	54,852
*Kevin Garnett	50,418
Jason Kidd	50,111
Elvin Hayes	50,000
*Kobe Bryant	48,637
Wilt Chamberlain	47,859
John Stockton	47,764
Reggie Miller	47,619
*Tim Duncan	47,368

Field Goals Attempted

Kareem Abdul-Jabbar	28,307
Karl Malone	26,210
*Kobe Bryant	26,200
Michael Jordan	24,537
Elvin Hayes	24,272
John Havlicek	23,930
Wilt Chamberlain	23,497
*Dirk Nowitzki	21,922
Dominique Wilkins	21,589
*Kevin Garnett	21,142

Points

Kareem Abdul-Jabbar	38,387
Karl Malone	36,928
*Kobe Bryant	33,643
Michael Jordan	32,292
Wilt Chamberlain	31,419
*Dirk Nowitzki	29,491
Shaquille O'Neal	28,596
Moses Malone	27,409
Elvin Hayes	27,313
Hakeem Olajuwon	26,946

Games Played

Robert Parish	1,611
Kareem Abdul-Jabbar	1,560
John Stockton	1,504
Karl Malone	1,476
*Kevin Garnett	1,462
Kevin Willis	1,424
*Tim Duncan	1,392
Jason Kidd	1,391
Reggie Miller	1,389
Clifford Robinson	1,380

Field Goals Made

Kareem Abdul-Jabbar	15,837
Karl Malone	13,528
Wilt Chamberlain	12,681
Michael Jordan	12,192
*Kobe Bryant	11,719
Shaquille O'Neal	11,330
Elvin Hayes	10,976
Hakeem Olajuwon	10,749
Alex English	10,659
John Havlicek	10,513

Rebounds

Wilt Chamberlain	23,924
Bill Russell	21,620
Kareem Abdul-Jabbar	17,440
Elvin Hayes	16,279
Moses Malone	16,212
*Tim Duncan	15,091
Karl Malone	14,968
Robert Parish	14,715
*Kevin Garnett	14,662
Nate Thurmond	14,464

Personal Fouls

Kareem Abdul-Jabbar	4,657
Karl Malone	4,578
Robert Parish	4,443
Charles Oakley	4,421
Hakeem Olajuwon	4,383
Buck Williams	4,267
Elvin Hayes	4,193
Clifford Robinson	4,175
Kevin Willis	4,172
Shaquille O'Neal	4,146
Otis Thorpe	4,146

3-Point Field Goals Attempted

Ray Allen	7,429
Reggie Miller	6,486
*Paul Pierce	5,773
*Jason Terry	5,724
Jason Kidd	5,701
*Kobe Bryant	5,546
*Jamal Crawford	5,539
*Vince Carter	5,189
*Joe Johnson	4,928
Chauncey Billups	4,725

Assists

John Stockton	15,806
Jason Kidd	12,091
Steve Nash	10,335
Mark Jackson	10,334
Magic Johnson	10,141
Oscar Robertson	9,887
Isiah Thomas	9,061
Gary Payton	8,966
*Andre Miller	8,524
Rod Strickland	7,987

Blocked Shots

Hakeem Olajuwon	3,830
Dikembe Mutombo	3,289
Kareem Abdul-Jabbar	3,189
Mark Eaton	3,064
*Tim Duncan	3,020
David Robinson	2,954
Patrick Ewing	2,894
Shaquille O'Neal	2,732
Tree Rollins	2,542
Robert Parish	2,361

3-Point Field Goals Made

Ray Allen	2,973
Reggie Miller	2,560
*Jason Terry	2,169
*Paul Pierce	2,128
Jason Kidd	1,988
*Vince Carter	1,937
*Jamal Crawford	1,933
*Kyle Korver	1,887
*Joe Johnson	1,832
Chauncey Billups	1,830

Steals

John Stockton	3,265
Jason Kidd	2,684
Michael Jordan	2,514
Gary Payton	2,445
Maurice Cheeks	2,310
Scottie Pippen	2,307
Clyde Drexler	2,207
Hakeem Olajuwon	2,162
Alvin Robertson	2,112
Karl Malone	2,085

NBA Coach of the Year, 1963-2016

Year	Coach, team	Year	Coach, team	Year	Coach, team
1963	Harry Gallatin, St. Louis	1981	Jack McKinney, Indiana	1999	Mike Dunleavy, Portland
1964	Alex Hannum, San Francisco	1982	Gene Shue, Washington	2000	Glenn "Doc" Rivers, Orlando
1965	Red Auerbach, Boston	1983	Don Nelson, Milwaukee	2001	Larry Brown, Philadelphia
1966	Dolph Schayes, Philadelphia	1984	Frank Layden, Utah	2002	Rick Carlisle, Detroit
1967	Johnny Kerr, Chicago	1985	Don Nelson, Milwaukee	2003	Gregg Popovich, San Antonio
1968	Richie Guerin, St. Louis	1986	Mike Fratello, Atlanta	2004	Hubie Brown, Memphis
1969	Gene Shue, Baltimore	1987	Mike Schuler, Portland	2005	Mike D'Antoni, Phoenix
1970	Red Holzman, New York	1988	Doug Moe, Denver	2006	Avery Johnson, Dallas
1971	Dick Motta, Chicago	1989	Cotton Fitzsimmons, Phoenix	2007	Sam Mitchell, Toronto
1972	Bill Sharman, L.A. Lakers	1990	Pat Riley, L.A. Lakers	2008	Byron Scott, New Orleans
1973	Tom Heinsohn, Boston	1991	Don Chaney, Houston	2009	Mike Brown, Cleveland
1974	Ray Scott, Detroit	1992	Don Nelson, Golden State	2010	Scott Brooks, Oklahoma City
1975	Phil Johnson, Kansas City-Omaha	1993	Pat Riley, New York	2011	Tom Thibodeau, Chicago
1976	Bill Fitch, Cleveland	1994	Lenny Wilkens, Atlanta	2012	Gregg Popovich, San Antonio
1977	Tom Nissalke, Houston	1995	Del Harris, L.A. Lakers	2013	George Karl, Denver
1978	Hubie Brown, Atlanta	1996	Phil Jackson, Chicago	2014	Gregg Popovich, San Antonio
1979	Cotton Fitzsimmons, Kansas City	1997	Pat Riley, Miami	2015	Mike Budenholzer, Atlanta
1980	Bill Fitch, Boston	1998	Larry Bird, Indiana	2016	Steve Kerr, Golden State

National Basketball Association Franchise Origins

Team, founding year (in NBA, Basketball Assn. of Amer. [BAA], or Amer. Basketball Assn. [ABA]), location, and subsequent history. Neutral sites and arena sites in the same metropolitan area not listed separately.

Atlanta Hawks: 1949, NBA, as Tri-Cities Blackhawks, 1949-51, Moline, IL. Milwaukee Hawks, 1951-55; St. Louis Hawks, 1955-68; Atlanta Hawks, 1968-present.
Boston Celtics: 1946, BAA, Boston, 1946-present.
Brooklyn Nets: 1967, ABA, as New Jersey Americans, 1967-68, Teaneck, NJ. New York Nets, 1968-77; New Jersey Nets, 1977-2012; Brooklyn Nets, 2012-present.
Charlotte Hornets: 2004, NBA, as Charlotte Bobcats, 2004-14, Charlotte, NC. Charlotte Hornets, 2014-present.
Chicago Bulls: 1966, NBA, Chicago, 1966-present.
Cleveland Cavaliers: 1970, NBA, Cleveland, OH, 1970-present.
Dallas Mavericks: 1980, NBA, Dallas, TX, 1980-present.
Denver Nuggets: 1967, ABA, as Denver Rockets, 1967-74, Denver, CO. Denver Nuggets, 1974-present.
Detroit Pistons: 1948, BAA, as Ft. Wayne Pistons, 1948-57, Ft. Wayne, IN. Detroit Pistons, 1957-present.
Golden State Warriors: 1946, BAA, as Philadelphia Warriors, 1946-62, Philadelphia, PA. San Francisco Warriors, 1962-71; Golden State Warriors, 1971-present, Oakland, CA.
Houston Rockets: 1967, NBA, as San Diego Rockets, 1967-71, San Diego, CA. Houston Rockets, 1971-present.
Indiana Pacers: 1967, ABA, Indianapolis, IN, 1974-present.
L.A. Clippers: 1970, NBA, as Buffalo Braves, 1970-78, Buffalo, NY. San Diego Clippers, 1978-84; L.A. Clippers, 1984-present.
L.A. Lakers: 1948, BAA, as Minneapolis Lakers, 1948-60, Minneapolis, MN. L.A. Lakers, 1960-present.
Memphis Grizzlies: 1995, NBA, as Vancouver Grizzlies, 1995-2001, Vancouver, BC, Canada. Memphis Grizzlies, 2001-present.
Miami Heat: 1988, NBA, Miami, FL, 1988-present.

Milwaukee Bucks: 1968, NBA, Milwaukee, WI, 1968-present.
Minnesota Timberwolves: 1989, NBA, Minneapolis, MN, 1989-present.
New Orleans Pelicans: 1988, NBA, as Charlotte Hornets, 1988-2002, Charlotte, NC. New Orleans Hornets, 2002-13 (Hornets played most home games in Oklahoma City, 2005-07, as city repaired Hurricane Katrina damage); New Orleans Pelicans, 2013-present.
New York Knicks: 1946, BAA, New York, NY, 1946-present.
Oklahoma City Thunder: 1967, NBA, as Seattle SuperSonics, 1967-2008, Seattle, WA. Oklahoma City Thunder, 2008-present.
Orlando Magic: 1989, NBA, Orlando, FL, 1989-present.
Philadelphia 76ers: 1949, NBA, as Syracuse Nationals, 1949-63, Syracuse, NY. Philadelphia 76ers, 1963-present.
Phoenix Suns: 1968, NBA, Phoenix, AZ, 1968-present.
Portland Trail Blazers: 1970, NBA, Portland, OR, 1970-present.
Sacramento Kings: 1948, BAA, as Rochester Royals, 1948-57, Rochester, NY. Cincinnati Royals, 1957-72; Kansas City-Omaha Kings, 1972-75; Kansas City Kings, 1975-85; Sacramento Kings, 1985-present.
San Antonio Spurs: ABA, as Dallas Chaparrals, 1967-73, Dallas, TX. San Antonio Spurs, 1973-present.
Toronto Raptors: 1995, NBA, Toronto, ON, Canada, 1995-present.
Utah Jazz: 1974, NBA, as New Orleans Jazz, 1974-79, New Orleans, LA. Utah Jazz, 1979-present, Salt Lake City.
Washington Wizards: 1961, NBA, as Chicago Packers, 1961-62, Chicago. Chicago Zephyrs, 1962-63; Baltimore Bullets, 1963-73; Capital Bullets, 1973-74, Landover, MD; Washington Bullets, 1974-97; Washington Wizards, 1997-present.

NBA Home Courts

Team	Name (year built)	Capacity[1]	Team	Name (year built)	Capacity[1]
Atlanta	Philips Arena (1999)	18,047	Miami	AmericanAirlines Arena (1999)	19,600
Boston	TD Garden[2] (1995)	18,624	Milwaukee	BMO Harris Bradley Center[6] (1988)	18,717
Brooklyn	Barclays Center[3] (2012)	17,732	Minnesota	Target Center (1990)	19,356
Charlotte	Time Warner Cable Arena (2005)	19,077	New Orleans	Smoothie King Center[7] (1999)	16,867
Chicago	United Center (1994)	20,917	New York	Madison Square Garden (IV) (1968)	19,812
Cleveland	Quicken Loans Arena (1994)	20,562	Oklahoma City	Chesapeake Energy Arena[8] (2002)	18,203
Dallas	American Airlines Center (2001)	19,200	Orlando	Amway Center (2010)	18,846
Denver	Pepsi Center (1999)	19,155	Philadelphia	Wells Fargo Center[9] (1996)	20,328
Detroit	The Palace of Auburn Hills (1988)	21,165	Phoenix	Talking Stick Resort Arena[10] (1992)	18,055
Golden State	Oracle Arena[4] (1966)	19,596	Portland	Moda Center[11] (1995)	19,441
Houston	Toyota Center (2003)	18,055	Sacramento	Sleep Train Arena[12] (1988)	17,317
Indiana	Bankers Life Fieldhouse[5] (1999)	18,165	San Antonio	AT&T Center[13] (2002)	18,460
L.A. Clippers	Staples Center (1999)	19,060	Toronto	Air Canada Centre (1999)	19,800
L.A. Lakers	Staples Center (1999)	18,997	Utah	Vivint Smart Home Arena[14] (1991)	19,911
Memphis	FedExForum (2004)	18,119	Washington	Verizon Center[15] (1997)	20,356

(1) At the end of the 2015-16 season. (2) FleetCenter, 1995-2005; TD Banknorth Garden, 2005-09. (3) The New Jersey Nets relocated to Brooklyn prior to the 2012-13 season. (4) Oakland Coliseum Arena, 1966-96; Arena in Oakland, 1997-2006. (5) Conseco Fieldhouse, 1999-2011. (6) Bradley Center, 1988-2012. (7) New Orleans Arena, 1999-2014; because of damage to New Orleans Arena due to Hurricane Katrina, the Hornets played 35 games in the Ford Center in Oklahoma City, OK, 3 games in New Orleans Arena, and 3 games at other locations during the 2005-06 season; in 2006-07, the Hornets played 35 games at the Ford Center and 6 games in New Orleans Arena. (8) Ford Center, 2008-11; the Seattle SuperSonics relocated to Oklahoma City prior to the 2008-09 season. (9) CoreStates Center, 1996-98; First Union Center, 1998-2003; Wachovia Center, 2003-10. (10) America West Arena, 1992-2006; US Airways Center, 2006-15. (11) The Rose Garden, 1995-2013. (12) ARCO Arena, 1988-2011; Power Balance Pavilion, 2011-12. (13) SBC Center, 2002-06. (14) Delta Center, 1991-2006; EnergySolutions Arena, 2006-15. (15) MCI Center, 1997-2006.

All-Time NBA Regular Season Coaching Victories
(At the end of the 2015-16 season, ranked by wins. * = Active in 2015-16 season.)

Coach	W	L	PCT	Coach	W	L	PCT	Coach	W	L	PCT
Don Nelson	1,335	1,063	.557	Rick Adelman	1,042	749	.582	John MacLeod	707	657	.518
Lenny Wilkens	1,332	1,155	.536	Bill Fitch	944	1,106	.460	Red Holzman	696	603	.536
Jerry Sloan	1,221	803	.603	Red Auerbach	938	479	.662	Mike Fratello	667	548	.549
Pat Riley	1,210	694	.636	Dick Motta	935	1,017	.479	*Rick Carlisle	661	471	.584
*George Karl	1,175	824	.588	Jack Ramsay	864	783	.525	Flip Saunders	654	592	.525
Phil Jackson	1,155	485	.704	Cotton Fitzsimmons	832	775	.518	Chuck Daly	638	437	.593
Larry Brown	1,098	904	.548	Gene Shue	784	861	.477	Doug Moe	628	529	.543
*Gregg Popovich	1,089	485	.692	*Glenn "Doc" Rivers	753	553	.577	Mike Dunleavy	613	716	.461

Naismith Memorial Basketball Hall of Fame
(Located in Springfield, MA. * = 2016 inductee. + = Enshrined as both a player and coach.)

Players

Abdul-Jabbar, Kareem · Archibald, Nate · Arizin, Paul · Barkley, Charles · Barlow, Thomas · Barry, Rick · Baylor, Elgin · *Beaty, Zelmo · Beckman, John · Bellamy, Walt · Belov, Sergei · Bing, Dave · Bird, Larry · Blazejowski, Carol · Borgmann, Bennie · Bradley, Bill · Brennan, Joseph · Brown, Roger · Cervi, Al · Chamberlain, Wilt · Cooper, Charles · Cooper, Cynthia · Cosic, Kresimir · Cousy, Bob · Cowens, Dave · Crawford, Joan · Cunningham, Billy · Curry, Denise · Dalipagic, Drazen · Dampier, Louis · Daniels, Mel · Dantley, Adrian · Davies, Bob · DeBernardi, Forrest · DeBusschere, Dave · Dehnert, Henry "Dutch" · Donovan, Anne · Drexler, Clyde · Dumars, Joe · Edwards, Teresa · Endacott, Paul · English, Alex · Erving, Julius · Ewing, Patrick · Foster, Bud · Frazier, Walt · Friedman, Max · Fulks, Joe · Gale, Lauren · Gallatin, Harry · Gates, William "Pop" · Gervin, George · Gilmore, Artis · Gola, Tom · Goodrich, Gail · Greer, Hal · Gruenig, Robert "Ace" · Guerin, Richard · Hagan, Cliff · Hanson, Victor · Harris-Stewart, Lusia · Havlicek, John · Hawkins, Cornelius "Connie" · Hayes, Elvin · Haynes, Marques · Haywood, Spencer · +Heinsohn, Tom · Holman, Nat · Houbregs, Bob · Howell, Bailey · Hyatt, Chuck · Isaacs, John · Issel, Dan · *Iverson, Allen · Jeannette, Harry "Buddy" · Johnson, Dennis · Johnson, Earvin "Magic" · Johnson, Gus · Johnson, William · Johnston, Neil · Jones, K. C. · Jones, Sam · Jordan, Michael · King, Bernard · Krause, Ed "Moose" · Kurland, Bob · Lanier, Bob · Lapchick, Joe · Leslie, Lisa · Lieberman, Nancy · Lovellette, Clyde · Lucas, Jerry · Luisetti, Angelo "Hank" · Macauley, Ed · Malone, Karl · Malone, Moses · Maravich, Pete · Marcari, Hortencia · Marciulionis, Sarunas · Martin, Slater · McAdoo, Bob · McClain, Katrina · McCracken, Emmett "Branch" · McCracken, Jack · McDermott, Bobby · McGuire, Dick · McHale, Kevin · Meneghin, Dino · Meyers, Ann · Mikan, George · Mikkelsen, Vern · Miller, Cheryl · Miller, Reggie · *Ming, Yao · Monroe, Earl · Mourning, Alonzo · Mullin, Chris · Murphy, Calvin · Murphy, Charles "Stretch" · Mutombo, Dikembe · Olajuwon, Hakeem · *O'Neal, Shaquille · Page, Harlan "Pat" · Parish, Robert · Payton, Gary · Pereira, Maciel "Ubiratan" · Petrovic, Drazen · Pettit, Bob · Phillip, Andy · Pippen, Scottie · Pollard, Jim · *Posey, Cumberland · Ramsey, Frank · Reed, Willis · Richmond, Mitch · Risen, Arnie · Robertson, Oscar · Robinson, David · Rodgers, Guy · Rodman, Dennis · Roosma, John · Russell, Bill · Russell, John "Honey" · Sabonis, Arvydas · Sampson, Ralph · Sanders, Tom "Satch" · Schayes, Adolph · Schmidt, Ernest · Schmidt, Oscar "Jack" · Schommer, John · Sedran, Barney · Semjonova, Uljana · *Sharman, Bill · Staley, Dawn · Steinmetz, Chris · Stockton, John · Stokes, Maurice · *Swoopes, Sheryl · Tatum, Reece "Goose" · Thomas, Isiah · Thompson, David · Thompson, John · Thurmond, Nate · Twyman, Jack · Unseld, Wes · Vandivier, Robert "Fuzzy" · Wachter, Ed · Walker, Chet · Walton, Bill · Wanzer, Bobby · West, Jerry · White, Jo Jo · White, Nera · +Wilkens, Lenny · Wilkes, Jamaal · Wilkins, Dominique · Woodard, Lynette · +Wooden, John · Worthy, James · Yardley, George

Coaches

Alexeeva, Lidia · Allen, Forrest C. "Phog" · Anderson, Harold · Auerbach, Arnold "Red" · Auriemma, Geno · Barmore, Leon · Barry, Justin "Sam" · Blood, Ernest · Boeheim, Jim · Brown, Larry · Calhoun, Jim · Calipari, John · Cann, Howard · Carlson, Clifford · Carnesecca, Lou · Carnevale, Ben · Carril, Pete · Case, Everett · Chancellor, Van · Chaney, John · Conradt, Jody · Crum, Denzil "Denny" · Daly, Chuck · Dean, Everett · Diaz-Miguel, Antonio · Diddle, Edgar · Drake, Bruce · Ferrandiz, Pedro · Gaines, Clarence · Gamba, Sandro · Gardner, James "Jack" · Gaze, Lindsay · Gill, Amory "Slats" · Gomelsky, Aleksandr · Gunter, Sue · Hannum, Alex · Harshman, Marv · Haskins, Don · Hatchell, Sylvia · +Heinsohn, Tom · Hickey, Edgar · Hobson, Howard · Holzman, William "Red" · Hurley, Bob, Sr. · Iba, Hank · *Izzo, Tom · Jackson, Phil · Julian, Alvin · Keaney, Frank · Keogan, George · Knight, Bob · Krzyzewski, Mike · Kundla, John · Lambert, Ward · Leonard, Bob · Lewis, Guy V. · Litwack, Harry · Loeffler, Kenneth · Lonborg, Arthur "Dutch" · Magee, Herb · McCutchan, Arad · McGuire, Al · McGuire, Frank · *McLendon, John · Meanwell, Dr. Walter · Meyer, Ray · Miller, Ralph · Moore, Billie · Nelson, Don · Newell, Pete · Nikolic, Aleksandar · Novosel, Mirko · Olson, Robert "Lute" · Pitino, Rick · Ramsay, John "Jack" · Richardson, Nolan · Riley, Pat · Rubini, Cesare · Rupp, Adolph · Rush, Cathy · Sachs, Leonard · +Sharman, Bill · Shelton, Everett · Sloan, Jerry · Smith, Dean · Stringer, C. Vivian · Summitt, Pat · Tarkanian, Jerry · Taylor, Fred · Thompson, John R. · VanDerveer, Tara · Wade, Margaret · Watts, Stan · +Wilkens, Lenny · Williams, Gary · Williams, Roy · Winter, Tex · +Wooden, John · Woolpert, Phil · Wootten, Morgan · Yow, Kay

Teams

1960 USA Men's Olympic Team · 1966 Texas Western · 1972-73-74 Immaculata Univ. · 1992 USA Men's Olympic "Dream Team" · All American Red Heads · Buffalo Germans First Team · Harlem Globetrotters · New York Renaissance · Original Celtics

Referees

Bavetta, Dick · Enright, James · *Garretson, Darell · Hepbron, George · Hoyt, George · Kennedy, Matthew · Leith, Lloyd · Mihalik, Zigmund "Red" · Nichols, Hank · Nucatola, John · Quigley, Ernest · Rudolph, Marvin "Mendy" · Shirley, J. Dallas · Strom, Earl · Tobey, David · Walsh, David

Contributors

Abbott, Senda Berenson · Barksdale, Don · Bee, Clair · Biasone, Danny · Brown, Hubert "Hubie" · Brown, Walter · Bunn, John · Buss, Jerry · Clifton, Nat · Colangelo, Jerry · Davidson, Bill · Douglas, Bob · Duer, Al · Embry, Wayne · Fagan, Cliff · Fisher, Harry · Fleisher, Larry · Gavitt, David · Gottlieb, Edward · Granik, Russ · Gulick, Dr. Luther · Harrison, Lester · Hearn, Francis "Chick" · Henderson, E. B. · Hepp, Dr. Ferenc · Hickox, Edward · Hinkle, Tony · Irish, Edward "Ned" · Jones, R. William · Kennedy, Walter · Knight, Phil · Lemon, Meadowlark · Liston, Emil · Lloyd, Earl · McLendon, John · Mokray, Bill · Morgan, Ralph · Morgenweck, Frank · Naismith, Dr. James · Newton, C. M. · O'Brien, John · O'Brien, Larry · Olsen, Harold · Podoloff, Maurice · Porter, Henry V. · Raveling, George · Reid, William · *Reinsdorf, Jerry · Ripley, Elmer · St. John, Lynn · Saperstein, Abe · Schabinger, Arthur "Red" · Stagg, Alonzo · Stankovic, Boris · Steitz, Edward · Stern, David · Taylor, Chuck · Teague, Bertha · Tower, Oswald · Trester, Arthur · Wells, Clifford · Wilke, Lou · Zollner, Fred

Los Angeles Sparks Win 2016 WNBA Championship

In the WNBA's 20th season, the Los Angeles Sparks beat the defending-champion Minnesota Lynx in five games to win their first league title since 2002. Nneka Ogwumike's field goal with 3.1 seconds left lifted the Sparks to a 77-76 Game 5 win, Oct. 20, 2016, at Target Center in Minneapolis, MN. Sparks veteran Candace Parker scored 28 points with 12 rebounds in Game 5 and earned WNBA Finals MVP.

WNBA Coach of the Year Cheryl Reeve led Minnesota to a franchise-record 28 wins and its fifth WNBA Finals appearance in the last six years. Nneka Ogwumike was named regular season Most Valuable Player, averaging 19.7 points and 9.1 rebounds per game with a league-best .665 field goal percentage.

WNBA Final Standings, 2016

(playoff seeds in parentheses; top eight teams by PCT advance, regardless of conference; top two seeds receive a bye to the semifinals)

Eastern Conference	W	L	PCT	GB	Western Conference	W	L	PCT	GB
New York Liberty (3)	21	13	.618	—	Minnesota Lynx (1)	28	6	.824	—
Chicago Sky (4)	18	16	.529	3	Los Angeles Sparks (2)	26	8	.765	2
Indiana Fever (5)	17	17	.500	4	Seattle Storm (7)	16	18	.471	12
Atlanta Dream (6)	17	17	.500	4	Phoenix Mercury (8)	16	18	.471	12
Connecticut Sun	14	20	.412	7	Dallas Wings	11	23	.324	17
Washington Mysitcs	13	21	.382	8	San Antonio Stars	7	27	.206	21

Note: Indiana earned the no. 5 seed over Atlanta due to a better head-to-head record; Seattle earned the no. 7 seed over Phoenix due to a better head-to-head record.

WNBA Playoff Results, 2016

First Round (single elimination)
(8) Phoenix 89, (5) Indiana 78
(6) Atlanta 94, (7) Seattle 85

Second Round (single elimination)
(8) Phoenix 101, (3) New York 94
(4) Chicago 108, (6) Atlanta 98

Semifinals (best-of-five)
(1) Minnesota defeated (8) Phoenix, 3 games to 0
(2) Los Angeles defeated (4) Chicago, 3 games to 1

WNBA Championship

Los Angeles defeated Minnesota, 3 games to 2 (78-76, 60-79, 92-75, 79-85, 77-76), in the best-of-five series.

All-WNBA Teams, 2016

First team	Position	Second team	Position
Nneka Ogwumike, Los Angeles	Forward	Angel McCoughtry, Atlanta	Forward
Elena Delle Donne, Chicago	Forward	Breanna Stewart, Seattle	Forward
Tina Charles, New York	Center	Sylvia Fowles, Minnesota	Center
Maya Moore, Minnesota	Guard	Diana Taurasi, Phoenix	Guard
Sue Bird, Seattle	Guard	Jewell Loyd, Seattle	Guard

WNBA Statistical Leaders, 2016

Minutes played: 1,179, Breanna Stewart, Seattle; Elizabeth Williams, Atlanta
Total points: 688, Tina Charles, New York
Points per game: 21.5, Tina Charles, New York
Field goal pct.: .665, Nneka Ogwumike, Los Angeles
3-point field goal pct.: .448, Emma Meesseman, Washington

Free throw pct.: .938, Shenise Johnson, Indiana
Rebounds: 317, Tina Charles, New York; Breanna Stewart, Seattle
Assists: 196, Sue Bird, Seattle
Steals: 62, Tamika Catchings, Indiana
Blocks: 107, Brittney Griner, Phoenix

WNBA Champions, 1997-2016

Year	Eastern champion	Western champion	Champion	Winning coach	Opponent
	Regular Season		Playoffs		
1997	Houston Comets	Phoenix Mercury	Houston	Van Chancellor	New York
1998	Cleveland Rockers	Houston Comets	Houston	Van Chancellor	Phoenix
1999	New York Liberty	Houston Comets	Houston	Van Chancellor	New York
2000	New York Liberty	Los Angeles Sparks	Houston	Van Chancellor	New York
2001	Cleveland Rockers	Los Angeles Sparks	Los Angeles	Michael Cooper	Charlotte
2002	New York Liberty	Los Angeles Sparks	Los Angeles	Michael Cooper	New York
2003	Detroit Shock	Los Angeles Sparks	Detroit	Bill Laimbeer	Los Angeles
2004	Connecticut Sun	Los Angeles Sparks	Seattle	Anne Donovan	Connecticut
2005	Connecticut Sun	Sacramento Monarchs	Sacramento	John Whisenant	Connecticut
2006	Connecticut Sun	Los Angeles Sparks	Detroit	Bill Laimbeer	Sacramento
2007	Detroit Shock	Phoenix Mercury	Phoenix	Paul Westhead	Detroit
2008	Detroit Shock	San Antonio Silver Stars	Detroit	Bill Laimbeer	San Antonio
2009	Indiana Fever	Phoenix Mercury	Phoenix	Corey Gaines	Indiana
2010	Washington Mystics	Seattle Storm	Seattle	Brian Agler	Atlanta
2011	Indiana Fever	Minnesota Lynx	Minnesota	Cheryl Reeve	Atlanta
2012	Connecticut Sun	Minnesota Lynx	Indiana	Lin Dunn	Minnesota
2013	Chicago Sky	Minnesota Lynx	Minnesota	Cheryl Reeve	Atlanta
2014	Atlanta Dream	Phoenix Mercury	Phoenix	Sandy Brondello	Chicago
2015	New York Liberty	Minnesota Lynx	Minnesota	Cheryl Reeve	Indiana
2016	New York Liberty	Minnesota Lynx	Los Angeles	Brian Agler	Minnesota

WNBA Finals MVP, 1997-2016

Year	Player, team	Year	Player, team	Year	Player, team
1997	Cynthia Cooper, Houston	2004	Betty Lennox, Seattle	2011	Seimone Augustus, Minnesota
1998	Cynthia Cooper, Houston	2005	Yolanda Griffith, Sacramento	2012	Tamika Catchings, Indiana
1999	Cynthia Cooper, Houston	2006	Deanna Nolan, Detroit	2013	Maya Moore, Minnesota
2000	Cynthia Cooper, Houston	2007	Cappie Pondexter, Phoenix	2014	Diana Taurasi, Phoenix
2001	Lisa Leslie, Los Angeles	2008	Katie Smith, Detroit	2015	Sylvia Fowles, Minnesota
2002	Lisa Leslie, Los Angeles	2009	Diana Taurasi, Phoenix	2016	Candace Parker, Los Angeles
2003	Ruth Riley, Detroit	2010	Lauren Jackson, Seattle		

WNBA Most Valuable Player, 1997-2016

Year	Player, team	Year	Player, team	Year	Player, team
1997	Cynthia Cooper, Houston	2004	Lisa Leslie, Los Angeles	2011	Tamika Catchings, Indiana
1998	Cynthia Cooper, Houston	2005	Sheryl Swoopes, Houston	2012	Tina Charles, Connecticut
1999	Yolanda Griffith, Sacramento	2006	Lisa Leslie, Los Angeles	2013	Candace Parker, Los Angeles
2000	Sheryl Swoopes, Houston	2007	Lauren Jackson, Seattle	2014	Maya Moore, Minnesota
2001	Lisa Leslie, Los Angeles	2008	Candace Parker, Los Angeles	2015	Elena Delle Donne, Chicago
2002	Sheryl Swoopes, Houston	2009	Diana Taurasi, Phoenix	2016	Nneka Ogwumike, Los Angeles
2003	Lauren Jackson, Seattle	2010	Lauren Jackson, Seattle		

WNBA Rookie of the Year, 1997-2016

Year	Player, team	Year	Player, team	Year	Player, team
1997	No award	2004	Diana Taurasi, Phoenix	2011	Maya Moore, Minnesota
1998	Tracy Reid, Charlotte	2005	Temeka Johnson, Washington	2012	Nneka Ogwumike, Los Angeles
1999	Chamique Holdsclaw, Washington	2006	Seimone Augustus, Minnesota	2013	Elena Delle Donne, Chicago
2000	Betty Lennox, Minnesota	2007	Armintie Price, Chicago	2014	Chiney Ogwumike, Connecticut
2001	Jackie Stiles, Portland	2008	Candace Parker, Los Angeles	2015	Jewell Loyd, Seattle
2002	Tamika Catchings, Indiana	2009	Angel McCoughtry, Atlanta	2016	Breanna Stewart, Seattle
2003	Cheryl Ford, Detroit	2010	Tina Charles, Connecticut		

WNBA Scoring Leaders, 1997-2016

(Average points per game; 24 games or 480 point minimum, 2004-16; prior season minimums vary.)

Year	Player, team	PTS	AVG	Year	Player, team	PTS	AVG
1997	Cynthia Cooper, Houston	621	22.2	2007	Lauren Jackson, Seattle	739	23.8
1998	Cynthia Cooper, Houston	680	22.7	2008	Diana Taurasi, Phoenix	820	24.1
1999	Cynthia Cooper, Houston	686	22.1	2009	Diana Taurasi, Phoenix	631	20.4
2000	Sheryl Swoopes, Houston	643	20.7	2010	Diana Taurasi, Phoenix	702	22.6
2001	Katie Smith, Minnesota	739	23.1	2011	Diana Taurasi, Phoenix	692	21.6
2002	Chamique Holdsclaw, Washington	397	19.9	2012	Angel McCoughtry, Atlanta	514	21.4
2003	Lauren Jackson, Seattle	698	21.2	2013	Angel McCoughtry, Atlanta	711	21.5
2004	Lauren Jackson, Seattle	634	20.5	2014	Maya Moore, Minnesota	812	23.9
2005	Sheryl Swoopes, Houston	614	18.6	2015	Elena Delle Donne, Chicago	725	23.4
2006	Diana Taurasi, Phoenix	860	25.3	2016	Tina Charles, New York	688	21.5

WNBA Rebounding Leaders, 1997-2016

(Average rebounds per game; 24 games or 240 rebounds minimum, 2004-16; prior season minimums vary.)

Year	Player, team	REB	RPG	Year	Player, team	REB	RPG
1997	Lisa Leslie, Los Angeles	266	9.5	2007	Lauren Jackson, Seattle	300	9.7
1998	Lisa Leslie, Los Angeles	285	10.2	2008	Candace Parker, Los Angeles	313	9.5
1999	Yolanda Griffith, Sacramento	329	11.3	2009	Candace Parker, Los Angeles	244	9.8
2000	Natalie Williams, Utah	336	11.6	2010	Tina Charles, Connecticut	398	11.7
2001	Yolanda Griffith, Sacramento	357	11.2	2011	Tina Charles, Connecticut	374	11.0
2002	Chamique Holdsclaw, Washington	232	11.6	2012	Tina Charles, Connecticut	345	10.5
2003	Chamique Holdsclaw, Washington	294	10.9	2013	Sylvia Fowles, Chicago	369	11.5
2004	Lisa Leslie, Los Angeles	336	9.9	2014	Courtney Paris, Tulsa	347	10.2
2005	Cheryl Ford, Detroit	322	9.8	2015	Courtney Paris, Tulsa	317	9.3
2006	Cheryl Ford, Detroit	363	11.3	2016	Tina Charles, New York	317	9.9

WNBA Assist Leaders, 1997-2016

(Average assists per game; 24 games or 140 assists minimum, 2004-16; prior season minimums vary.)

Year	Player, team	AST	APG	Year	Player, team	AST	APG
1997	Teresa Weatherspoon, New York	172	6.1	2007	Becky Hammon, San Antonio	140	5.0
1998	Ticha Penicheiro, Sacramento	224	7.5	2008	Lindsay Whalen, Connecticut	166	5.4
1999	Ticha Penicheiro, Sacramento	226	7.1	2009	Sue Bird, Seattle	179	5.8
2000	Ticha Penicheiro, Sacramento	236	7.9	2010	Ticha Penicheiro, Los Angeles	220	6.9
2001	Ticha Penicheiro, Sacramento	172	7.5	2011	Lindsay Whalen, Minnesota	199	5.9
2002	Ticha Penicheiro, Sacramento	192	8.0	2012	Lindsay Whalen, Minnesota	178	5.4
2003	Ticha Penicheiro, Sacramento	229	6.7	2013	Danielle Robinson, San Antonio	168	6.7
2004	Nikki Teasley, Los Angeles	207	6.1	2014	Diana Taurasi, Phoenix	185	5.6
2005	Sue Bird, Seattle	176	5.9	2015	Courtney Vandersloot, Chicago	198	5.8
2006	Nikki Teasley, Washington	183	5.4	2016	Sue Bird, Seattle	196	5.8

All-Time WNBA Statistical Leaders

(At the end of the 2016 season. * = Active in 2016 season.)

Scoring Average
(minimum 100 games)

Player	G	PTS	AVG	Player	G	PTS	AVG
Cynthia Cooper	124	2,601	21.0	*Maya Moore	203	3,784	18.6
*Elena Delle Donne	105	2,155	20.5	*Tina Charles	230	4,101	17.8
*Diana Taurasi	367	7,311	19.9	*Cappie Pondexter	357	6,312	17.7
*Angel McCoughtry	256	4,990	19.5	*Seimone Augustus	293	5,131	17.5
Lauren Jackson	317	6,007	18.9	*Candace Parker	229	4,001	17.5

Points

Tina Thompson	7,488
*Tamika Catchings	7,380
*Diana Taurasi	7,311
Katie Smith	6,452
*Cappie Pondexter	6,312
Lisa Leslie	6,263
Lauren Jackson	6,007
Becky Hammon	5,841
DeLisha Milton-Jones	5,571
Katie Douglas	5,563

Rebounds

*Tamika Catchings	3,316
Lisa Leslie	3,307
Tina Thompson	3,070
Taj McWilliams-Franklin	3,013
*Rebekkah Brunson	2,986
DeLisha Milton-Jones	2,574
*Swin Cash	2,521
Michelle Snow	2,482
Lauren Jackson	2,447
Yolanda Griffith	2,444

Assists

Ticha Penicheiro	2,599
*Sue Bird	2,411
*Lindsay Whalen	2,159
Becky Hammon	1,708
*Diana Taurasi	1,576
*Tamika Catchings	1,488
Shannon Johnson	1,424
*Cappie Pondexter	1,400
Temeka Johnson	1,382
Teresa Weatherspoon	1,338

3-Point Field Goals Made

Katie Smith	906
*Diana Taurasi	900
Becky Hammon	829
Tina Thompson	748
*Sue Bird	736
Katie Douglas	727
*Tamika Catchings	606
Kara Lawson	584
Nicole Powell	580
*Ivory Latta	492

Steals

*Tamika Catchings	1,074
Ticha Penicheiro	764
Sheryl Swoopes	657
Katie Douglas	623
DeLisha Milton-Jones	619
*Jia Perkins	597
*Alana Beard	583
*Sue Bird	581
Taj McWilliams-Franklin	580
Tully Bevilaqua	573

Blocked Shots

Margo Dydek	877
Lisa Leslie	822
Lauren Jackson	586
Tangela Smith	557
Tammy Sutton-Brown	555
Ruth Riley	505
*Sylvia Fowles	465
Taj McWilliams-Franklin	443
*Brittney Griner	422
*Candace Parker	413

HOCKEY

Pittsburgh Penguins Win 2016 Stanley Cup

Sidney Crosby and the Pittsburgh Penguins captured the 2016 Stanley Cup title over the San Jose Sharks in a 3-1, Game 6 win June 12, 2016, at SAP Center in San Jose, CA. Crosby had a pair of assists in the deciding game and won the Conn Smythe Trophy as playoff MVP. San Jose's Joe Pavelski led all playoff scorers with 14 goals as the Sharks reached their first-ever Stanley Cup Final. Mike Sullivan, who had replaced Mike Johnston as Pittsburgh's head coach in Dec. 2015, guided the team to win 14 of its last 16 regular season games and its fourth Stanley Cup in franchise history.

Before toppling Tampa Bay in seven games in the Eastern Conference finals, Pittsburgh won a six-game, Eastern Conference semifinal over Washington, which had taken the Presidents' Trophy with a league-best 120 points. Alex Ovechkin led the Capitals with an NHL-high 50 goals and goalie Braden Holtby tied Martin Brodeur's single-season record for most wins by a goaltender (48).

The NHL's new 3-on-3 overtime format (three skaters per team plus goalie for the five-minute OT period) reduced total shootouts in the regular season to 107, the fewest since the shootout rule was introduced in 2005-06.

Final NHL Standings, 2015-16

(* = clinched playoff berth)

Standings are determined by total points, then by the number of games won excluding games won in a shootout (regulation plus overtime wins, or the number in the ROW column). Teams tied at the end of regulation time are each awarded one point. An additional point is awarded to the overtime or shootout winner.

The top three finishers in each division qualify for the first 12 playoff seeds. Two additional wild-card playoff spots are awarded in each conference to the next two highest-placed finishers, regardless of division.

Eastern Conference

Atlantic Division	W	L	OT	GF	GA	PTS	ROW
*Florida Panthers	47	26	9	239	203	103	40
*Tampa Bay Lightning	46	31	5	227	201	97	43
*Detroit Red Wings	41	30	11	211	224	93	39
Boston Bruins	42	31	9	240	230	93	38
Ottawa Senators	38	35	9	236	247	85	32
Montréal Canadiens	38	38	6	221	236	82	33
Buffalo Sabres	35	36	11	201	222	81	33
Toronto Maple Leafs	29	42	11	198	246	69	23

Metropolitan Division	W	L	OT	GF	GA	PTS	ROW
*Washington Capitals	56	18	8	252	193	120	52
*Pittsburgh Penguins	48	26	8	245	203	104	44
*New York Rangers	46	27	9	236	217	101	43
*New York Islanders	45	27	10	232	216	100	40
*Philadelphia Flyers	41	27	14	214	218	96	38
Carolina Hurricanes	35	31	16	198	226	86	33
New Jersey Devils	38	36	8	184	208	84	36
Columbus Blue Jackets	34	40	8	219	252	76	28

Western Conference

Central Division	W	L	OT	GF	GA	PTS	ROW
*Dallas Stars	50	23	9	267	230	109	48
*St. Louis Blues	49	24	9	224	201	107	44
*Chicago Blackhawks	47	26	9	235	209	103	46
*Nashville Predators	41	27	14	228	215	96	37
*Minnesota Wild	38	33	11	216	206	87	35
Colorado Avalanche	39	39	4	216	240	82	35
Winnipeg Jets	35	39	8	215	239	78	32

Pacific Division	W	L	OT	GF	GA	PTS	ROW
*Anaheim Ducks	46	25	11	218	192	103	43
*Los Angeles Kings	48	28	6	225	195	102	46
*San Jose Sharks	46	30	6	241	210	98	42
Arizona Coyotes	35	39	8	209	245	78	34
Calgary Flames	35	40	7	231	260	77	33
Vancouver Canucks	31	38	13	191	243	75	26
Edmonton Oilers	31	43	8	203	245	70	27

Stanley Cup Playoff Results, 2016

Eastern Conference

Washington defeated Philadelphia, 4 games to 2
Pittsburgh defeated NY Rangers, 4 games to 1
Tampa Bay defeated Detroit, 4 games to 1
NY Islanders defeated Florida, 4 games to 2
Pittsburgh defeated Washington, 4 games to 2
Tampa Bay defeated NY Islanders, 4 games to 1
Pittsburgh defeated Tampa Bay, 4 games to 3

Western Conference

Nashville defeated Anaheim, 4 games to 3
San Jose defeated Los Angeles, 4 games to 1
Dallas defeated Minnesota, 4 games to 2
St. Louis defeated Chicago, 4 games to 3
San Jose defeated Nashville, 4 games to 3
St. Louis defeated Dallas, 4 games to 3
San Jose defeated St. Louis, 4 games to 2

Stanley Cup Final

Pittsburgh defeated San Jose, 4 games to 2 (3-2, 2-1 [OT], 2-3 [OT], 3-1, 2-4, 3-1)

Stanley Cup Champions, 1927-2016

Year	Champion	Coach	Final opponent	Year	Champion	Coach	Final opponent
1927	Ottawa	Dave Gill	Boston	1956	Montréal	Toe Blake	Detroit
1928	NY Rangers	Lester Patrick	Montréal	1957	Montréal	Toe Blake	Boston
			Maroons	1958	Montréal	Toe Blake	Boston
1929	Boston	Art Ross	NY Rangers	1959	Montréal	Toe Blake	Toronto
1930	Montréal Canadiens	Cecil Hart	Boston	1960	Montréal	Toe Blake	Toronto
1931	Montréal Canadiens	Cecil Hart	Chicago	1961	Chicago	Rudy Pilous	Detroit
1932	Toronto	Dick Irvin	NY Rangers	1962	Toronto	Punch Imlach	Chicago
1933	NY Rangers	Lester Patrick	Toronto	1963	Toronto	Punch Imlach	Detroit
1934	Chicago	Tommy Gorman	Detroit	1964	Toronto	Punch Imlach	Detroit
1935	Montréal Maroons	Tommy Gorman	Toronto	1965	Montréal	Toe Blake	Chicago
1936	Detroit	Jack Adams	Toronto	1966	Montréal	Toe Blake	Detroit
1937	Detroit	Jack Adams	NY Rangers	1967	Toronto	Punch Imlach	Montréal
1938	Chicago	Bill Stewart	Toronto	1968	Montréal	Toe Blake	St. Louis
1939	Boston	Art Ross	Toronto	1969	Montréal	Claude Ruel	St. Louis
1940	NY Rangers	Frank Boucher	Toronto	1970	Boston	Harry Sinden	St. Louis
1941	Boston	Cooney Weiland	Detroit	1971	Montréal	Al MacNeil	Chicago
1942	Toronto	Hap Day	Detroit	1972	Boston	Tom Johnson	NY Rangers
1943	Detroit	Jack Adams	Boston	1973	Montréal	Scotty Bowman	Chicago
1944	Montréal	Dick Irvin	Chicago	1974	Philadelphia	Fred Shero	Boston
1945	Toronto	Hap Day	Detroit	1975	Philadelphia	Fred Shero	Buffalo
1946	Montréal	Dick Irvin	Boston	1976	Montréal	Scotty Bowman	Philadelphia
1947	Toronto	Hap Day	Montréal	1977	Montréal	Scotty Bowman	Boston
1948	Toronto	Hap Day	Detroit	1978	Montréal	Scotty Bowman	Boston
1949	Toronto	Hap Day	Detroit	1979	Montréal	Scotty Bowman	NY Rangers
1950	Detroit	Tommy Ivan	NY Rangers	1980	NY Islanders	Al Arbour	Philadelphia
1951	Toronto	Joe Primeau	Montréal	1981	NY Islanders	Al Arbour	Minnesota
1952	Detroit	Tommy Ivan	Montréal	1982	NY Islanders	Al Arbour	Vancouver
1953	Montréal	Dick Irvin	Boston	1983	NY Islanders	Al Arbour	Edmonton
1954	Detroit	Tommy Ivan	Montréal	1984	Edmonton	Glen Sather	NY Islanders
1955	Detroit	Jimmy Skinner	Montréal	1985	Edmonton	Glen Sather	Philadelphia

Year	Champion	Coach	Final opponent	Year	Champion	Coach	Final opponent
1986	Montréal	Jean Perron	Calgary	2002	Detroit	Scotty Bowman	Carolina
1987	Edmonton	Glen Sather	Philadelphia	2003	New Jersey	Pat Burns	Anaheim
1988	Edmonton	Glen Sather	Boston	2004	Tampa Bay	John Tortorella	Calgary
1989	Calgary	Terry Crisp	Montréal	2005	No competition (labor dispute; season canceled)		
1990	Edmonton	John Muckler	Boston	2006	Carolina	Peter Laviolette	Edmonton
1991	Pittsburgh	Bob Johnson	Minnesota	2007	Anaheim	Randy Carlyle	Ottawa
1992	Pittsburgh	Scotty Bowman	Chicago	2008	Detroit	Mike Babcock	Pittsburgh
1993	Montréal	Jacques Demers	Los Angeles	2009	Pittsburgh	Dan Bylsma	Detroit
1994	NY Rangers	Mike Keenan	Vancouver	2010	Chicago	Joel Quenneville	Philadelphia
1995	New Jersey	Jacques Lemaire	Detroit	2011	Boston	Claude Julien	Vancouver
1996	Colorado	Marc Crawford	Florida	2012	Los Angeles	Darryl Sutter	New Jersey
1997	Detroit	Scotty Bowman	Philadelphia	2013	Chicago	Joel Quenneville	Boston
1998	Detroit	Scotty Bowman	Washington	2014	Los Angeles	Darryl Sutter	NY Rangers
1999	Dallas	Ken Hitchcock	Buffalo	2015	Chicago	Joel Quenneville	Tampa Bay
2000	New Jersey	Larry Robinson	Dallas	2016	Pittsburgh	Mike Sullivan	San Jose
2001	Colorado	Bob Hartley	New Jersey				

Most NHL Goals in a Season

Player	Team	Season	Goals	Player	Team	Season	Goals
Wayne Gretzky	Edmonton	1981-82	92	Jari Kurri	Edmonton	1984-85	71
Wayne Gretzky	Edmonton	1983-84	87	Mario Lemieux	Pittsburgh	1987-88	70
Brett Hull	St. Louis	1990-91	86	Bernie Nicholls	Los Angeles	1988-89	70
Mario Lemieux	Pittsburgh	1988-89	85	Brett Hull	St. Louis	1991-92	70
Phil Esposito	Boston	1970-71	76	Mike Bossy	NY Islanders	1978-79	69
Alexander Mogilny	Buffalo	1992-93	76	Mario Lemieux	Pittsburgh	1992-93	69
Teemu Selanne	Winnipeg	1992-93	76	Mario Lemieux	Pittsburgh	1995-96	69
Wayne Gretzky	Edmonton	1984-85	73	Phil Esposito	Boston	1973-74	68
Brett Hull	St. Louis	1989-90	72	Mike Bossy	NY Islanders	1980-81	68
Wayne Gretzky	Edmonton	1982-83	71	Jari Kurri	Edmonton	1985-86	68

All-Time Regular Season Scoring Leaders

(Through end of 2015-16 season. * = active in 2015-16 season.)

Player	Goals	Assists	Points	Player	Goals	Assists	Points	Player	Goals	Assists	Points
Wayne Gretzky	894	1,963	2,857	Mario Lemieux	690	1,033	1,723	Teemu Selanne	684	773	1,457
Mark Messier	694	1,193	1,887	Joe Sakic	625	1,016	1,641	Bryan Trottier	524	901	1,425
*Jaromir Jagr	749	1,119	1,868	Phil Esposito	717	873	1,590	Adam Oates	341	1,079	1,420
Gordie Howe	801	1,049	1,850	Ray Bourque	410	1,169	1,579	Doug Gilmour	450	964	1,414
Ron Francis	549	1,249	1,798	Mark Recchi	577	956	1,533	Dale Hawerchuk	518	891	1,409
Marcel Dionne	731	1,040	1,771	Paul Coffey	396	1,135	1,531	Jari Kurri	601	797	1,398
Steve Yzerman	692	1,063	1,755	Stan Mikita	541	926	1,467	Luc Robitaille	668	726	1,394

Hart Memorial Trophy (MVP), 1927-2016

Year	Player, team	Year	Player, team	Year	Player, team
1927	Herb Gardiner, Montréal Canadiens	1957	Gordie Howe, Detroit	1987	Wayne Gretzky, Edmonton
1928	Howie Morenz, Montréal Canadiens	1958	Gordie Howe, Detroit	1988	Mario Lemieux, Pittsburgh
1929	Roy Worters, NY Americans	1959	Andy Bathgate, NY Rangers	1989	Wayne Gretzky, Los Angeles
1930	Nels Stewart, Montréal Maroons	1960	Gordie Howe, Detroit	1990	Mark Messier, Edmonton
1931	Howie Morenz, Montréal Canadiens	1961	Bernie Geoffrion, Montréal	1991	Brett Hull, St. Louis
1932	Howie Morenz, Montréal Canadiens	1962	Jacques Plante, Montréal	1992	Mark Messier, NY Rangers
1933	Eddie Shore, Boston	1963	Gordie Howe, Detroit	1993	Mario Lemieux, Pittsburgh
1934	Aurel Joliat, Montréal Canadiens	1964	Jean Beliveau, Montréal	1994	Sergei Fedorov, Detroit
1935	Eddie Shore, Boston	1965	Bobby Hull, Chicago	1995	Eric Lindros, Philadelphia
1936	Eddie Shore, Boston	1966	Bobby Hull, Chicago	1996	Mario Lemieux, Pittsburgh
1937	Babe Siebert, Montréal Canadiens	1967	Stan Mikita, Chicago	1997	Dominik Hasek, Buffalo
1938	Eddie Shore, Boston	1968	Stan Mikita, Chicago	1998	Dominik Hasek, Buffalo
1939	Toe Blake, Montréal	1969	Phil Esposito, Boston	1999	Jaromir Jagr, Pittsburgh
1940	Ebbie Goodfellow, Detroit	1970	Bobby Orr, Boston	2000	Chris Pronger, St. Louis
1941	Bill Cowley, Boston	1971	Bobby Orr, Boston	2001	Joe Sakic, Colorado
1942	Tom Anderson, Brooklyn Americans	1972	Bobby Orr, Boston	2002	Jose Theodore, Montréal
1943	Bill Cowley, Boston	1973	Bobby Clarke, Philadelphia	2003	Peter Forsberg, Colorado
1944	Babe Pratt, Toronto	1974	Phil Esposito, Boston	2004	Martin St. Louis, Tampa Bay
1945	Elmer Lach, Montréal	1975	Bobby Clarke, Philadelphia	2006	Joe Thornton, San Jose
1946	Max Bentley, Chicago	1976	Bobby Clarke, Philadelphia	2007	Sidney Crosby, Pittsburgh
1947	Maurice Richard, Montréal	1977	Guy Lafleur, Montréal	2008	Alexander Ovechkin, Washington
1948	Buddy O'Connor, NY Rangers	1978	Guy Lafleur, Montréal	2009	Alexander Ovechkin, Washington
1949	Sid Abel, Detroit	1979	Bryan Trottier, NY Islanders	2010	Henrik Sedin, Vancouver
1950	Chuck Rayner, NY Rangers	1980	Wayne Gretzky, Edmonton	2011	Corey Perry, Anaheim
1951	Milt Schmidt, Boston	1981	Wayne Gretzky, Edmonton	2012	Evgeni Malkin, Pittsburgh
1952	Gordie Howe, Detroit	1982	Wayne Gretzky, Edmonton	2013	Alexander Ovechkin, Washington
1953	Gordie Howe, Detroit	1983	Wayne Gretzky, Edmonton	2014	Sidney Crosby, Pittsburgh
1954	Al Rollins, Chicago	1984	Wayne Gretzky, Edmonton	2015	Carey Price, Montréal
1955	Ted Kennedy, Toronto	1985	Wayne Gretzky, Edmonton	2016	Patrick Kane, Chicago
1956	Jean Beliveau, Montréal	1986	Wayne Gretzky, Edmonton		

Conn Smythe Trophy (MVP in Playoffs), 1965-2016

Year	Player, team	Year	Player, team	Year	Player, team
1965	Jean Beliveau, Montréal	1977	Guy Lafleur, Montréal	1989	Al MacInnis, Calgary
1966	Roger Crozier, Detroit	1978	Larry Robinson, Montréal	1990	Bill Ranford, Edmonton
1967	Dave Keon, Toronto	1979	Bob Gainey, Montréal	1991	Mario Lemieux, Pittsburgh
1968	Glenn Hall, St. Louis	1980	Bryan Trottier, NY Islanders	1992	Mario Lemieux, Pittsburgh
1969	Serge Savard, Montréal	1981	Butch Goring, NY Islanders	1993	Patrick Roy, Montréal
1970	Bobby Orr, Boston	1982	Mike Bossy, NY Islanders	1994	Brian Leetch, NY Rangers
1971	Ken Dryden, Montréal	1983	Billy Smith, NY Islanders	1995	Claude Lemieux, New Jersey
1972	Bobby Orr, Boston	1984	Mark Messier, Edmonton	1996	Joe Sakic, Colorado
1973	Yvan Cournoyer, Montréal	1985	Wayne Gretzky, Edmonton	1997	Mike Vernon, Detroit
1974	Bernie Parent, Philadelphia	1986	Patrick Roy, Montréal	1998	Steve Yzerman, Detroit
1975	Bernie Parent, Philadelphia	1987	Ron Hextall, Philadelphia	1999	Joe Nieuwendyk, Dallas
1976	Reggie Leach, Philadelphia	1988	Wayne Gretzky, Edmonton	2000	Scott Stevens, New Jersey

Year	Player, team	Year	Player, team	Year	Player, team
2001	Patrick Roy, Colorado	2007	Scott Niedermayer, Anaheim	2012	Jonathan Quick, Los Angeles
2002	Nicklas Lidstrom, Detroit	2008	Henrik Zetterberg, Detroit	2013	Patrick Kane, Chicago
2003	Jean-Sebastien Giguere, Anaheim	2009	Evgeni Malkin, Pittsburgh	2014	Justin Williams, Los Angeles
2004	Brad Richards, Tampa Bay	2010	Jonathan Toews, Chicago	2015	Duncan Keith, Chicago
2006	Cam Ward, Carolina	2011	Tim Thomas, Boston	2016	Sidney Crosby, Pittsburgh

Calder Memorial Trophy (Rookie of the Year), 1933-2016

Year	Player, team	Year	Player, team	Year	Player, team
1933	Carl Voss, Detroit	1961	Dave Keon, Toronto	1989	Brian Leetch, NY Rangers
1934	Russ Blinco, Montréal Maroons	1962	Bobby Rousseau, Montréal	1990	Sergei Makarov, Calgary
1935	Dave Schriner, NY Americans	1963	Kent Douglas, Toronto	1991	Ed Belfour, Chicago
1936	Mike Karakas, Chicago	1964	Jacques Laperrière, Montréal	1992	Pavel Bure, Vancouver
1937	Syl Apps, Toronto	1965	Roger Crozier, Detroit	1993	Teemu Selanne, Winnipeg
1938	Cully Dahlstrom, Chicago	1966	Brit Selby, Toronto	1994	Martin Brodeur, New Jersey
1939	Frank Brimsek, Boston	1967	Bobby Orr, Boston	1995	Peter Forsberg, Quebec
1940	Kilby MacDonald, NY Rangers	1968	Derek Sanderson, Boston	1996	Daniel Alfredsson, Ottawa
1941	John Quilty, Montréal	1969	Danny Grant, Minnesota	1997	Bryan Berard, NY Islanders
1942	Grant Warwick, NY Rangers	1970	Tony Esposito, Chicago	1998	Sergei Samsonov, Boston
1943	Gaye Stewart, Toronto	1971	Gilbert Perreault, Buffalo	1999	Chris Drury, Colorado
1944	Gus Bodnar, Toronto	1972	Ken Dryden, Montréal	2000	Scott Gomez, New Jersey
1945	Frank McCool, Toronto	1973	Steve Vickers, NY Rangers	2001	Evgeni Nabokov, San Jose
1946	Edgar Laprade, NY Rangers	1974	Denis Potvin, NY Islanders	2002	Dany Heatley, Atlanta
1947	Howie Meeker, Toronto	1975	Eric Vail, Atlanta	2003	Barret Jackman, St. Louis
1948	Jim McFadden, Detroit	1976	Bryan Trottier, NY Islanders	2004	Andrew Raycroft, Boston
1949	Pentti Lund, NY Rangers	1977	Willi Plett, Atlanta	2006	Alexander Ovechkin, Washington
1950	Jack Gelineau, Boston	1978	Mike Bossy, NY Islanders	2007	Evgeni Malkin, Pittsburgh
1951	Terry Sawchuk, Detroit	1979	Bobby Smith, Minnesota	2008	Patrick Kane, Chicago
1952	Bernie Geoffrion, Montréal	1980	Ray Bourque, Boston	2009	Steve Mason, Columbus
1953	Gump Worsley, NY Rangers	1981	Peter Stastny, Quebec	2010	Tyler Myers, Buffalo
1954	Camille Henry, NY Rangers	1982	Dale Hawerchuk, Winnipeg	2011	Jeff Skinner, Carolina
1955	Ed Litzenberger, Chicago	1983	Steve Larmer, Chicago	2012	Gabriel Landeskog, Colorado
1956	Glenn Hall, Detroit	1984	Tom Barrasso, Buffalo	2013	Jonathan Huberdeau, Florida
1957	Larry Regan, Boston	1985	Mario Lemieux, Pittsburgh	2014	Nathan MacKinnon, Colorado
1958	Frank Mahovlich, Toronto	1986	Gary Suter, Calgary	2015	Aaron Ekblad, Florida
1959	Ralph Backstrom, Montréal	1987	Luc Robitaille, Los Angeles	2016	Artemi Panarin, Chicago
1960	Bill Hay, Chicago	1988	Joe Nieuwendyk, Calgary		

Lady Byng Memorial Trophy (Most Gentlemanly Player), 1925-2016

Year	Player, team	Year	Player, team	Year	Player, team
1925	Frank Nighbor, Ottawa	1956	Earl Reibel, Detroit	1986	Mike Bossy, NY Islanders
1926	Frank Nighbor, Ottawa	1957	Andy Hebenton, NY Rangers	1987	Joe Mullen, Calgary
1927	Billy Burch, NY Americans	1958	Camille Henry, NY Rangers	1988	Mats Naslund, Montréal
1928	Frank Boucher, NY Rangers	1959	Alex Delvecchio, Detroit	1989	Joe Mullen, Calgary
1929	Frank Boucher, NY Rangers	1960	Don McKenney, Boston	1990	Brett Hull, St. Louis
1930	Frank Boucher, NY Rangers	1961	Red Kelly, Toronto	1991	Wayne Gretzky, Los Angeles
1931	Frank Boucher, NY Rangers	1962	Dave Keon, Toronto	1992	Wayne Gretzky, Los Angeles
1932	Joe Primeau, Toronto	1963	Dave Keon, Toronto	1993	Pierre Turgeon, NY Islanders
1933	Frank Boucher, NY Rangers	1964	Ken Wharram, Chicago	1994	Wayne Gretzky, Los Angeles
1934	Frank Boucher, NY Rangers	1965	Bobby Hull, Chicago	1995	Ron Francis, Pittsburgh
1935	Frank Boucher, NY Rangers	1966	Alex Delvecchio, Detroit	1996	Paul Kariya, Anaheim
1936	Doc Romnes, Chicago	1967	Stan Mikita, Chicago	1997	Paul Kariya, Anaheim
1937	Marty Barry, Detroit	1968	Stan Mikita, Chicago	1998	Ron Francis, Pittsburgh
1938	Gordie Drillon, Toronto	1969	Alex Delvecchio, Detroit	1999	Wayne Gretzky, NY Rangers
1939	Clint Smith, NY Rangers	1970	Phil Goyette, St. Louis	2000	Pavol Demitra, St. Louis
1940	Bobby Bauer, Boston	1971	John Bucyk, Boston	2001	Joe Sakic, Colorado
1941	Bobby Bauer, Boston	1972	Jean Ratelle, NY Rangers	2002	Ron Francis, Carolina
1942	Syl Apps, Toronto	1973	Gil Perreault, Buffalo	2003	Alexander Mogilny, Toronto
1943	Max Bentley, Chicago	1974	John Bucyk, Boston	2004	Brad Richards, Tampa Bay
1944	Clint Smith, Chicago	1975	Marcel Dionne, Detroit	2006	Pavel Datsyuk, Detroit
1945	Bill Mosienko, Chicago	1976	Jean Ratelle, NYR-Boston	2007	Pavel Datsyuk, Detroit
1946	Toe Blake, Montréal	1977	Marcel Dionne, Los Angeles	2008	Pavel Datsyuk, Detroit
1947	Bobby Bauer, Boston	1978	Butch Goring, Los Angeles	2009	Pavel Datsyuk, Detroit
1948	Buddy O'Connor, NY Rangers	1979	Bob MacMillan, Atlanta	2010	Martin St. Louis, Tampa Bay
1949	Bill Quackenbush, Detroit	1980	Wayne Gretzky, Edmonton	2011	Martin St. Louis, Tampa Bay
1950	Edgar Laprade, NY Rangers	1981	Rick Kehoe, Pittsburgh	2012	Brian Campbell, Florida
1951	Red Kelly, Detroit	1982	Rick Middleton, Boston	2013	Martin St. Louis, Tampa Bay
1952	Sid Smith, Toronto	1983	Mike Bossy, NY Islanders	2014	Ryan O'Reilly, Colorado
1953	Red Kelly, Detroit	1984	Mike Bossy, NY Islanders	2015	Jiri Hudler, Calgary
1954	Red Kelly, Detroit	1985	Jari Kurri, Edmonton	2016	Anze Kopitar, Los Angeles
1955	Sid Smith, Toronto				

James Norris Memorial Trophy (Outstanding Defenseman), 1954-2016

Year	Player, team	Year	Player, team	Year	Player, team
1954	Red Kelly, Detroit	1975	Bobby Orr, Boston	1995	Paul Coffey, Detroit
1955	Doug Harvey, Montréal	1976	Denis Potvin, NY Islanders	1996	Chris Chelios, Chicago
1956	Doug Harvey, Montréal	1977	Larry Robinson, Montréal	1997	Brian Leetch, NY Rangers
1957	Doug Harvey, Montréal	1978	Denis Potvin, NY Islanders	1998	Rob Blake, Los Angeles
1958	Doug Harvey, Montréal	1979	Denis Potvin, NY Islanders	1999	Al MacInnis, St. Louis
1959	Tom Johnson, Montréal	1980	Larry Robinson, Montréal	2000	Chris Pronger, St. Louis
1960	Doug Harvey, Montréal	1981	Randy Carlyle, Pittsburgh	2001	Nicklas Lidstrom, Detroit
1961	Doug Harvey, Montréal	1982	Doug Wilson, Chicago	2002	Nicklas Lidstrom, Detroit
1962	Doug Harvey, NY Rangers	1983	Rod Langway, Washington	2003	Nicklas Lidstrom, Detroit
1963	Pierre Pilote, Chicago	1984	Rod Langway, Washington	2004	Scott Niedermayer, New Jersey
1964	Pierre Pilote, Chicago	1985	Paul Coffey, Edmonton	2006	Nicklas Lidstrom, Detroit
1965	Pierre Pilote, Chicago	1986	Paul Coffey, Edmonton	2007	Nicklas Lidstrom, Detroit
1966	Jacques Laperrière, Montréal	1987	Ray Bourque, Boston	2008	Nicklas Lidstrom, Detroit
1967	Harry Howell, NY Rangers	1988	Ray Bourque, Boston	2009	Zdeno Chara, Boston
1968	Bobby Orr, Boston	1989	Chris Chelios, Montréal	2010	Duncan Keith, Chicago
1969	Bobby Orr, Boston	1990	Ray Bourque, Boston	2011	Nicklas Lidstrom, Detroit
1970	Bobby Orr, Boston	1991	Ray Bourque, Boston	2012	Erik Karlsson, Ottawa
1971	Bobby Orr, Boston	1992	Brian Leetch, NY Rangers	2013	P. K. Subban, Montréal
1972	Bobby Orr, Boston	1993	Chris Chelios, Chicago	2014	Duncan Keith, Chicago
1973	Bobby Orr, Boston	1994	Ray Bourque, Boston	2015	Erik Karlsson, Ottawa
1974	Bobby Orr, Boston			2016	Drew Doughty, Los Angeles

Art Ross Trophy (Point-Scoring Leader), 1947-2016

Year	Player, team	Year	Player, team	Year	Player, team
1947	Max Bentley, Chicago	1970	Bobby Orr, Boston	1993	Mario Lemieux, Pittsburgh
1948	Elmer Lach, Montréal	1971	Phil Esposito, Boston	1994	Wayne Gretzky, Los Angeles
1949	Roy Conacher, Chicago	1972	Phil Esposito, Boston	1995	Jaromir Jagr, Pittsburgh
1950	Ted Lindsay, Detroit	1973	Phil Esposito, Boston	1996	Mario Lemieux, Pittsburgh
1951	Gordie Howe, Detroit	1974	Phil Esposito, Boston	1997	Mario Lemieux, Pittsburgh
1952	Gordie Howe, Detroit	1975	Bobby Orr, Boston	1998	Jaromir Jagr, Pittsburgh
1953	Gordie Howe, Detroit	1976	Guy Lafleur, Montréal	1999	Jaromir Jagr, Pittsburgh
1954	Gordie Howe, Detroit	1977	Guy Lafleur, Montréal	2000	Jaromir Jagr, Pittsburgh
1955	Bernie Geoffrion, Montréal	1978	Guy Lafleur, Montréal	2001	Jaromir Jagr, Pittsburgh
1956	Jean Beliveau, Montréal	1979	Bryan Trottier, NY Islanders	2002	Jarome Iginla, Calgary
1957	Gordie Howe, Detroit	1980	Marcel Dionne, Los Angeles	2003	Peter Forsberg, Colorado
1958	Dickie Moore, Montréal	1981	Wayne Gretzky, Edmonton	2004	Martin St. Louis, Tampa Bay
1959	Dickie Moore, Montréal	1982	Wayne Gretzky, Edmonton	2006	Joe Thornton, San Jose
1960	Bobby Hull, Chicago	1983	Wayne Gretzky, Edmonton	2007	Sidney Crosby, Pittsburgh
1961	Bernie Geoffrion, Montréal	1984	Wayne Gretzky, Edmonton	2008	Alexander Ovechkin, Washington
1962	Bobby Hull, Chicago	1985	Wayne Gretzky, Edmonton	2009	Evgeni Malkin, Pittsburgh
1963	Gordie Howe, Detroit	1986	Wayne Gretzky, Edmonton	2010	Henrik Sedin, Vancouver
1964	Stan Mikita, Chicago	1987	Wayne Gretzky, Edmonton	2011	Daniel Sedin, Vancouver
1965	Stan Mikita, Chicago	1988	Mario Lemieux, Pittsburgh	2012	Evgeni Malkin, Pittsburgh
1966	Bobby Hull, Chicago	1989	Mario Lemieux, Pittsburgh	2013	Martin St. Louis, Tampa Bay
1967	Stan Mikita, Chicago	1990	Wayne Gretzky, Los Angeles	2014	Sidney Crosby, Pittsburgh
1968	Stan Mikita, Chicago	1991	Wayne Gretzky, Los Angeles	2015	Jamie Benn, Dallas
1969	Phil Esposito, Boston	1992	Mario Lemieux, Pittsburgh	2016	Patrick Kane, Chicago

Vezina Trophy (Outstanding Goalie), 1927-2016

Before 1982, awarded to the goalie or goalies who played a minimum of 25 games for the team that allowed the fewest goals; since 1982, awarded to the most outstanding goalie, as determined by a vote of NHL general managers.

Year	Player, team	Year	Player, team	Year	Player, team
1927	George Hainsworth, Montréal Canadiens	1956	Jacques Plante, Montréal	1985	Pelle Lindbergh, Philadelphia
1928	George Hainsworth, Montréal Canadiens	1957	Jacques Plante, Montréal	1986	John Vanbiesbrouck, NY Rangers
1929	George Hainsworth, Montréal Canadiens	1958	Jacques Plante, Montréal	1987	Ron Hextall, Philadelphia
		1959	Jacques Plante, Montréal	1988	Grant Fuhr, Edmonton
		1960	Jacques Plante, Montréal	1989	Patrick Roy, Montréal
		1961	Johnny Bower, Toronto	1990	Patrick Roy, Montréal
1930	Tiny Thompson, Boston	1962	Jacques Plante, Montréal	1991	Ed Belfour, Chicago
1931	Roy Worters, NY Americans	1963	Glenn Hall, Chicago	1992	Patrick Roy, Montréal
1932	Charlie Gardiner, Chicago	1964	Charlie Hodge, Montréal	1993	Ed Belfour, Chicago
1933	Tiny Thompson, Boston	1965	Sawchuk, Bower; Toronto	1994	Dominik Hasek, Buffalo
1934	Charlie Gardiner, Chicago	1966	Lorne Worsley, Hodge; Montréal	1995	Dominik Hasek, Buffalo
1935	Lorne Chabot, Chicago	1967	Hall, Denis DeJordy; Chicago	1996	Jim Carey, Washington
1936	Tiny Thompson, Boston	1968	Worsley, Rogatien Vachon; Montréal	1997	Dominik Hasek, Buffalo
1937	Normie Smith, Detroit	1969	Hall, Plante; St. Louis	1998	Dominik Hasek, Buffalo
1938	Tiny Thompson, Boston	1970	Tony Esposito, Chicago	1999	Dominik Hasek, Buffalo
1939	Frank Brimsek, Boston	1971	Ed Giacomin, Gilles Villemure; NY Rangers	2000	Olaf Kolzig, Washington
1940	Dave Kerr, NY Rangers			2001	Dominik Hasek, Buffalo
1941	Turk Broda, Toronto	1972	Esposito, Gary Smith; Chicago	2002	Jose Theodore, Montréal
1942	Frank Brimsek, Boston	1973	Ken Dryden, Montréal	2003	Martin Brodeur, New Jersey
1943	Johnny Mowers, Detroit	1974	Bernie Parent, Philadelphia; Tony Esposito, Chicago	2004	Martin Brodeur, New Jersey
1944	Bill Durnan, Montréal			2006	Miikka Kiprusoff, Calgary
1945	Bill Durnan, Montréal	1975	Bernie Parent, Philadelphia	2007	Martin Brodeur, New Jersey
1946	Bill Durnan, Montréal	1976	Ken Dryden, Montréal	2008	Martin Brodeur, New Jersey
1947	Bill Durnan, Montréal	1977	Dryden, Michel Larocque; Montréal	2009	Tim Thomas, Boston
1948	Turk Broda, Toronto	1978	Dryden, Larocque; Montréal	2010	Ryan Miller, Buffalo
1949	Bill Durnan, Montréal	1979	Dryden, Larocque; Montréal	2011	Tim Thomas, Boston
1950	Bill Durnan, Montréal	1980	Bob Sauve, Don Edwards; Buffalo	2012	Henrik Lundqvist, NY Rangers
1951	Al Rollins, Toronto	1981	Richard Sevigny, Larocque, Denis Herron; Montréal	2013	Sergei Bobrovsky, Columbus
1952	Terry Sawchuk, Detroit			2014	Tuukka Rask, Boston
1953	Terry Sawchuk, Detroit	1982	Bill Smith, NY Islanders	2015	Carey Price, Montréal
1954	Harry Lumley, Toronto	1983	Pete Peeters, Boston	2016	Braden Holtby, Washington
1955	Terry Sawchuk, Detroit	1984	Tom Barrasso, Buffalo		

NHL Home Ice

Team	Name (year built)	Capacity[1]	Team	Name (year built)	Capacity[1]
Anaheim	Honda Center[2] (1993)	17,174	Montréal	Le Centre Bell[10] (1996)	21,287
Arizona	Gila River Arena[3] (2003)	17,125	Nashville	Bridgestone Arena[11] (1997)	17,113
Boston	TD Garden[4] (1995)	17,565	New Jersey	Prudential Center (2007)	16,592
Buffalo	First Niagara Center[5] (1996)	19,070	NY Islanders	Barclays Center (2015)	15,795
Calgary	Scotiabank Saddledome[6] (1983)	19,289	NY Rangers	Madison Square Garden (1968)	18,006
Carolina	PNC Arena[7] (1999)	18,680	Ottawa	Canadian Tire Centre[12] (1996)	18,533
Chicago	United Center (1994)	19,717	Philadelphia	Wells Fargo Center[13] (1996)	19,541
Colorado	Pepsi Center (1999)	18,007	Pittsburgh	CONSOL Energy Center (2010)	18,387
Columbus	Nationwide Arena (2000)	18,144	St. Louis	Scottrade Center[14] (1994)	19,150
Dallas	American Airlines Center (2001)	18,532	San Jose	SAP Center at San Jose[15] (1993)	17,562
Detroit	Joe Louis Arena (1979)	20,027	Tampa Bay	Amalie Arena[16] (1996)	19,204
Edmonton	Rexall Place[8] (1974)	16,839	Toronto	Air Canada Centre (1999)	18,819
Florida	BB&T Center[9] (1998)	15,720	Vancouver	Rogers Arena[17] (1995)	18,870
Los Angeles	STAPLES Center (1999)	18,230	Washington	Verizon Center[18] (1997)	18,506
Minnesota	Xcel Energy Center (2000)	17,954	Winnipeg	MTS Centre (2004)	15,294

(1) At the end of the 2015-16 season. (2) The Arrowhead Pond of Anaheim, 1993-2006. (3) Glendale Arena, 2003-06; Jobing.com Arena, 2006-14. (4) FleetCenter, 1995-2005; TD Banknorth Garden, 2005-09. (5) Marine Midland Arena, 1996-99; HSBC Arena, 1999-2011. (6) Olympic Saddledome, 1983-96; Canadian Airlines Saddledome, 1996-2000; Pengrowth Saddledome, 2000-10. (7) Raleigh Entertainment and Sports Arena, 1999-2002; RBC Center, 2002-11. (8) Northlands Coliseum, 1974-79; Edmonton Col., 1979-98; Skyreach Centre, 1998-2003. (9) National Car Rental Center, 1998-2002; Office Depot Center, 2002-05; BankAtlantic Center, 2005-12. (10) Le Centre Molson, 1996-2002. (11) Nashville Arena, 1997-99; Gaylord Entertainment Center, 1999-2007; Sommet Center, 2007-10. (12) Corel Centre, 1996-2006; Scotiabank Place, 2006-13. (13) CoreStates Center, 1996-98; First Union Center, 1998-2003; Wachovia Center, 2003-10. (14) Kiel Center, 1994-2000; Savvis Center, 2000-06. (15) San Jose Arena, 1993-2001; Compaq Center, 2001-02; HP Pavilion at San Jose, 2002-13. (16) Ice Palace, 1996-2002; St. Pete Times Forum, 2002-12; Tampa Bay Times Forum, 2012-14. (17) General Motors Place, 1995-2010. (18) MCI Center, 1997-2006.

SOCCER

Portland Timbers Win First MLS Cup

A pair of early goals carried the Portland Timbers to a 2-1 MLS Cup victory over the Columbus Crew Dec. 6, 2015, at MAPFRE Stadium in Columbus, OH. Portland's Diego Valeri scored just 27 seconds into the match and was voted MLS Cup MVP. The Timbers, who joined the league in 2011, reached the MLS Cup by defeating FC Dallas on aggregate in the Western Conference finals.

Columbus reached the MLS Cup by beating the NY Red Bulls, who won the Supporters' Shield in 2015 with MLS's best overall record. New York's Jesse Marsch was voted 2015 MLS Coach of the Year, and the Red Bulls' Luis Robles won MLS Goalkeeper of the Year. Toronto FC forward Sebastian Giovinco won the 2015 MLS Golden Boot and MVP awards after setting a single-season record for combined goals (22) and assists (16).

Major League Soccer expanded to 20 teams in 2015 with the addition of New York City FC and Orlando City SC. Chivas USA (Southern California) ceased operations following the 2014 season.

Major League Soccer (MLS) Cup Results, 1996-2015

Year	Winner	Final opponent	Score	Site	MVP
1996	DC United	Los Angeles Galaxy	3-2 (OT)	Foxborough, MA	Marco Etcheverry
1997	DC United	Colorado Rapids	2-1	Washington, DC	Jaime Moreno
1998	Chicago Fire	DC United	2-0	Pasadena, CA	Peter Nowak
1999	DC United	Los Angeles Galaxy	2-0	Foxborough, MA	Ben Olsen
2000	Kansas City Wizards	Chicago Fire	1-0	Washington, DC	Tony Meola
2001	San Jose Earthquakes	Los Angeles Galaxy	2-1 (OT)	Columbus, OH	Dwayne De Rosario
2002	Los Angeles Galaxy	New England Revolution	1-0 (OT)	Foxborough, MA	Carlos Ruiz
2003	San Jose Earthquakes	Chicago Fire	4-2	Carson, CA	Landon Donovan
2004	DC United	Kansas City Wizards	3-2	Carson, CA	Alecko Eskandarian
2005	Los Angeles Galaxy	New England Revolution	1-0 (OT)	Frisco, TX	Guillermo Ramírez
2006	Houston Dynamo	New England Revolution	1-1 (4-3)*	Frisco, TX	Brian Ching
2007	Houston Dynamo	New England Revolution	2-1	Washington, DC	Dwayne De Rosario
2008	Columbus Crew	New York Red Bulls	3-1	Carson, CA	Guillermo Barros Schelotto
2009	Real Salt Lake	Los Angeles Galaxy	1-1 (5-4)*	Seattle, WA	Nick Rimando
2010	Colorado Rapids	FC Dallas	2-1 (OT)	Toronto, ON, Canada	Conor Casey
2011	Los Angeles Galaxy	Houston Dynamo	1-0	Carson, CA	Landon Donovan
2012	Los Angeles Galaxy	Houston Dynamo	3-1	Carson, CA	Omar Gonzalez
2013	Sporting Kansas City	Real Salt Lake	1-1 (7-6)*	Kansas City, KS	Aurelien Collin
2014	Los Angeles Galaxy	New England Revolution	2-1 (OT)	Carson, CA	Robbie Keane
2015	Portland Timbers	Columbus Crew	2-1	Columbus, OH	Diego Valeri

* = Match decided in penalty kicks (shootout score in parentheses). OT = Overtime.

Major League Soccer Final Standings, 2015

(Does not include playoff games.)

Eastern Conference	W	L	T	PTS	GF	GA	GD	Western Conference	W	L	T	PTS	GF	GA	GD
New York Red Bulls..	18	10	6	60	62	43	19	FC Dallas	18	10	6	60	52	39	13
Columbus Crew SC..	15	11	8	53	58	53	5	Vancouver Whitecaps							
Montréal Impact	15	13	6	51	48	44	4	FC..	16	13	5	53	45	36	9
D.C. United	15	13	6	51	43	45	-2	Portland Timbers.....	15	11	8	53	41	39	2
New England								Seattle Sounders FC..	15	13	6	51	44	36	8
Revolution.......	14	12	8	50	48	47	1	LA Galaxy..........	14	11	9	51	56	46	10
Toronto FC	15	15	4	49	58	58	0	Sporting Kansas City..	14	11	9	51	48	45	3
Orlando City SC....	12	14	8	44	46	56	-10	San Jose Earthquakes	13	13	8	47	41	39	2
New York City FC ...	10	17	7	37	49	58	-9	Houston Dynamo	11	14	9	42	42	49	-7
Philadelphia Union ..	10	17	7	37	42	55	-13	Real Salt Lake	11	15	8	41	38	48	-10
Chicago Fire	8	20	6	30	43	58	-15	Colorado Rapids.....	9	15	10	37	33	43	-10

Major League Soccer Scoring Leaders, 2015

Player	Club	GP	Goals	Player	Club	GP	Goals
Sebastian Giovinco.....	Toronto	33	22	Bradley Wright-Phillips ..	New York Red Bulls	34	17
Kei Kamara..........	Columbus	32	22	Fanendo Adi	Portland	33	16
Robbie Keane.........	Los Angeles	24	20	Chris Wondolowski.....	San Jose.............	31	16
David Villa...........	New York City FC	30	18	Obafemi Martins.......	Seattle	21	15
Cyle Larin	Orlando..............	27	17	Jozy Altidore.........	Toronto	25	13

Landon Donovan MLS Most Valuable Player Award, 1996-2015

(Honda MLS Most Valuable Player Award, 1996-2007; Volkswagen MLS Most Valuable Player Award, 2007-14)

Year	Most valuable player, team	Year	Most valuable player, team
1996	Carlos Valderrama, Tampa Bay Mutiny	2006	Christian Gómez, DC United
1997	Preki, Kansas City Wizards	2007	Luciano Emilio, DC United
1998	Marco Etcheverry, DC United	2008	Guillermo Barros Schelotto, Columbus Crew
1999	Jason Kreis, Dallas Burn	2009	Landon Donovan, L.A. Galaxy
2000	Tony Meola, Kansas City Wizards	2010	David Ferreira, FC Dallas
2001	Alex Pineda Chacón, Miami Fusion	2011	Dwayne De Rosario, DC United
2002	Carlos Ruiz, L.A. Galaxy	2012	Chris Wondolowski, San Jose Earthquakes
2003	Preki, Kansas City Wizards	2013	Mike Magee, Chicago Fire
2004	Amado Guevara, New York/New Jersey MetroStars	2014	Robbie Keane, L.A. Galaxy
2005	Taylor Twellman, New England Revolution	2015	Sebastian Giovinco, Toronto FC

Western New York Flash Win 2016 National Women's Soccer League Title

The Western New York Flash won their first-ever NWSL Championship by defeating the Washington Spirit, 3-2, on penalty kicks after the teams played to a 2-2 draw, Oct. 9, 2016, at BBVA Compass Stadium in Houston, TX. Lynn Williams scored the game-tying goal in the 124th minute, and goalkeeper Sabrina D'Angelo earned match MVP with three saves during the penalty shootout. Williams, who earned regular season MVP honors, scored twice in the Flash's 4-3 (OT) win over Portland Thorns FC in their semifinal playoff Oct. 2. Washington earned its first trip to the league championship with a 2-1 overtime win over the Chicago Red Stars, Sept. 30.

Women's Professional Soccer Champions

Year	Winner	Final opponent	Score	Site	MVP
		Women's United Soccer Association champions			
2001	Bay Area CyberRays	Atlanta Beat	3-3 (4-2)*	Foxborough, MA	Julie Murray
2002	Carolina Courage	Washington Freedom	3-2	Atlanta, GA	Birgit Prinz
2003	Washington Freedom	Atlanta Beat	2-1	San Diego, CA	Abby Wambach
		Women's Professional Soccer champions			
2009	Sky Blue FC	Los Angeles Sol	1-0	Carson, CA	Heather O'Reilly
2010	FC Gold Pride	Philadelphia Independence	4-0	Hayward, CA	Marta
2011	Western New York Flash	Philadelphia Independence	1-1 (5-4)*	Rochester, NY	Christine Sinclair
		National Women's Soccer League champions			
2013	Portland Thorns FC	Western New York Flash	2-0	Rochester, NY	Tobin Heath
2014	FC Kansas City	Seattle Reign FC	2-1	Tukwila, WA	Lauren Holiday
2015	FC Kansas City	Seattle Reign FC	1-0	Portland, OR	Amy Rodriguez
2016	Western New York Flash	Washington Spirit	2-2 (3-2)*	Houston, TX	Sabrina D'Angelo

* = Match decided on penalty kicks (shootout score in parentheses). **Note:** The Women's United Soccer Association (WUSA) folded in 2003. Women's Professional Soccer (WPS) stopped operating in 2012, suspending its fourth season. In Apr. 2013, the National Women's Soccer League (NWSL) began play with eight teams competing: Boston Breakers, Chicago Red Stars, FC Kansas City, Portland Thorns FC, Seattle Reign FC, Sky Blue FC (New York/New Jersey), Washington Spirit, and Western New York Flash. The Houston Dash began play as an NWSL expansion team for the 2014 season; Orlando joined the league in 2016.

U.S. Wins 2015 World Cup in Japan Rematch

The U.S. women's soccer team won the 2015 World Cup with a 5-2 victory over Japan July 5, 2015, at BC Place Stadium in Vancouver, BC, Canada. Veteran midfielder Carli Lloyd scored three goals in the first 16 minutes—the first-ever hat trick in a women's FIFA World Cup final match—as the U.S. captured its third World Cup title. Lloyd, who won the Golden Ball award as the tournament's top player, complemented a strong U.S. defense that allowed only three goals; U.S. goalkeeper Hope Solo won the Golden Glove as best goalie. Lloyd tied Germany's Celia Sasic with six goals and one assist in the tournament, but Sasic won the Golden Boot award as top scorer based on fewer minutes played.

Canada served as host of the 2015 tournament, which was contested in six venues throughout the country. All of the stadiums featured artificial turf, the first time that all Women's World Cup matches were played on such surfaces. Prior to the tournament, a group of players concerned over gender equity, increased injury risk, and excessive heat while playing on turf filed a lawsuit against FIFA and the Canadian Soccer Assn. but eventually dropped it.

Women's World Cup Results, 2015

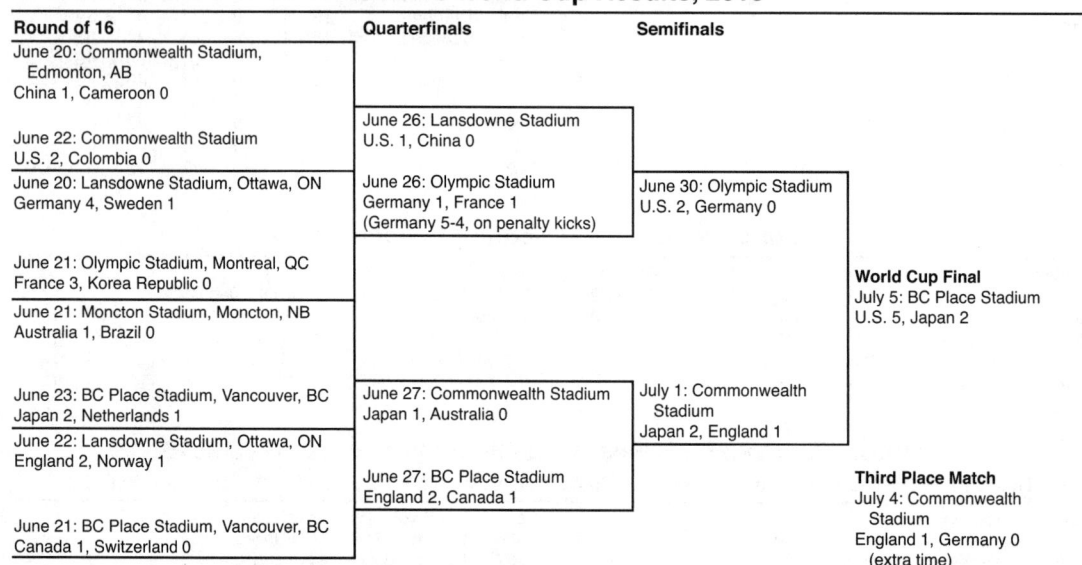

Round of 16

June 20: Commonwealth Stadium, Edmonton, AB
China 1, Cameroon 0

June 22: Commonwealth Stadium
U.S. 2, Colombia 0

June 20: Lansdowne Stadium, Ottawa, ON
Germany 4, Sweden 1

June 21: Olympic Stadium, Montreal, QC
France 3, Korea Republic 0

June 21: Moncton Stadium, Moncton, NB
Australia 1, Brazil 0

June 23: BC Place Stadium, Vancouver, BC
Japan 2, Netherlands 1

June 22: Lansdowne Stadium, Ottawa, ON
England 2, Norway 1

June 21: BC Place Stadium, Vancouver, BC
Canada 1, Switzerland 0

Quarterfinals

June 26: Lansdowne Stadium
U.S. 1, China 0

June 26: Olympic Stadium
Germany 1, France 1
(Germany 5-4, on penalty kicks)

June 27: Commonwealth Stadium
Japan 1, Australia 0

June 27: BC Place Stadium
England 2, Canada 1

Semifinals

June 30: Olympic Stadium
U.S. 2, Germany 0

July 1: Commonwealth Stadium
Japan 2, England 1

World Cup Final
July 5: BC Place Stadium
U.S. 5, Japan 2

Third Place Match
July 4: Commonwealth Stadium
England 1, Germany 0
(extra time)

Women's World Cup Results, 1991-2015

Year	Winner	Final opponent	Score	Site	Year	Winner	Final opponent	Score	Site
1991	U.S.	Norway	2-1	China	2007	Germany	Brazil	2-0	China
1995	Norway	Germany	2-0	Sweden	2011	Japan	U.S.	2-2 (3-1)*	Germany
1999	U.S.	China	0-0 (5-4)*	Pasadena, CA, U.S.	2015	U.S.	Japan	5-2	Canada
2003	Germany	Sweden	2-1#	Carson, CA, U.S.					

* = Match decided in penalty kicks (shootout score in parentheses). # = Match decided in extra time.

Germany Defeats Argentina for 2014 Men's World Cup Title

Germany won its fourth FIFA World Cup title July 13, 2014, with a dramatic goal in extra time, defeating Argentina, 1-0, at the Estádio do Maracanã in Rio de Janeiro, Brazil. Mario Götze, who entered the match for Germany in the 88th min., scored in the 113th min. Thomas Müller led Germany with five goals in the tournament, and teammate Manuel Neuer won the Golden Glove as the tournament's top goalkeeper. Argentina's Lionel Messi earned the Golden Ball as the competition's best player, and James Rodriguez of Colombia won the Golden Boot as top scorer with six goals in five games. After exceeding expectations somewhat in the so-called Group of Death, the U.S. team fell July 1, 2-1, to Belgium in the Round of 16.

Men's World Cup Results, 1930-2014

Year	Winner	Final opponent	Score	Site	Year	Winner	Final opponent	Score	Site
1930	Uruguay	Argentina	4-2	Uruguay	1978	Argentina	Netherlands	3-1#	Argentina
1934	Italy	Czechoslovakia	2-1#	Italy	1982	Italy	W. Germany	3-1	Spain
1938	Italy	Hungary	4-2	France	1986	Argentina	W. Germany	3-2	Mexico
1950	Uruguay	Brazil	2-1	Brazil	1990	W. Germany	Argentina	1-0	Italy
1954	W. Germany	Hungary	3-2	Switzerland	1994	Brazil	Italy	0-0 (3-2)*	U.S.
1958	Brazil	Sweden	5-2	Sweden	1998	France	Brazil	3-0	France
1962	Brazil	Czechoslovakia	3-1	Chile	2002	Brazil	Germany	2-0	Japan/S. Korea
1966	England	W. Germany	4-2#	England	2006	Italy	France	1-1 (5-3)*	Germany
1970	Brazil	Italy	4-1	Mexico	2010	Spain	Netherlands	1-0#	South Africa
1974	W. Germany	Netherlands	2-1	W. Germany	2014	Germany	Argentina	1-0#	Brazil

* = Match decided in penalty kicks (shootout score in parentheses). # = Match decided in extra time.

UEFA Champions League Results, 1956-2016

Year	Winner	Final opponent	Score	Year	Winner	Final opponent	Score
1956	Real Madrid	Reims	4-3	1986	Steaua	FC Barcelona	0-0 (2-0)*
1957	Real Madrid	Fiorentina	2-0	1987	Porto	Bayern Munich	2-1
1958	Real Madrid	AC Milan	3-2#	1988	PSV	Benfica	0-0 (6-5)*
1959	Real Madrid	Reims	2-0	1989	AC Milan	Steaua	4-0
1960	Real Madrid	Eintracht Frankfurt	7-3	1990	AC Milan	Benfica	1-0
1961	Benfica	FC Barcelona	3-2	1991	Crvena Zvezda	Marseille	0-0 (5-3)*
1962	Benfica	Real Madrid	5-3	1992	FC Barcelona	Sampdoria	1-0#
1963	AC Milan	Benfica	2-1	1993	Marseille	AC Milan	1-0
1964	Inter Milan	Real Madrid	3-1	1994	AC Milan	FC Barcelona	4-0
1965	Inter Milan	Benfica	1-0	1995	Ajax	AC Milan	1-0
1966	Real Madrid	Partizan	2-1	1996	Juventus	Ajax	1-1 (4-2)*
1967	Celtic	Inter Milan	2-1	1997	Borussia Dortmund	Juventus	3-1
1968	Manchester United	Benfica	4-1#	1998	Real Madrid	Juventus	1-0
1969	AC Milan	Ajax	4-1	1999	Manchester United	Bayern Munich	2-1
1970	Feyenoord	Celtic	2-1#	2000	Real Madrid	Valencia	3-0
1971	Ajax	Panathinaikos	2-0	2001	Bayern Munich	Valencia	1-1 (5-4)*
1972	Ajax	Inter Milan	2-0	2002	Real Madrid	Leverkusen	2-1
1973	Ajax	Juventus	1-0	2003	AC Milan	Juventus	0-0 (3-2)*
1974	Bayern Munich	Atlético Madrid	5-1[1]	2004	Porto	Monaco	3-0
1975	Bayern Munich	Leeds United	2-0	2005	Liverpool	AC Milan	3-3 (3-2)*
1976	Bayern Munich	St-Étienne	1-0	2006	FC Barcelona	Arsenal	2-1
1977	Liverpool	Borussia Mönchengladbach	3-1	2007	AC Milan	Liverpool	2-1
1978	Liverpool	Club Brugge	1-0	2008	Manchester United	Chelsea	1-1 (6-5)*
1979	Nottingham Forest	Malmö	1-0	2009	FC Barcelona	Manchester United	2-0
1980	Nottingham Forest	Hamburg SV	1-0	2010	Inter Milan	Bayern Munich	2-0
1981	Liverpool	Real Madrid	1-0	2011	FC Barcelona	Manchester United	3-1
1982	Aston Villa	Bayern Munich	1-0	2012	Chelsea	Bayern Munich	1-1 (4-3)*
1983	Hamburg SV	Juventus	1-0	2013	Bayern Munich	Borussia Dortmund	2-1
1984	Liverpool	AS Roma	1-1 (4-2)*	2014	Real Madrid	Atlético Madrid	4-1#
1985	Juventus	Liverpool	1-0	2015	FC Barcelona	Juventus	3-1
				2016	Real Madrid	Atlético Madrid	1-1 (5-3)*

* = Match decided in penalty kicks (shootout score in parentheses). # = Match decided in extra time. (1) Aggregate score. First game 1-1; second, 4-0.

UEFA European Football Championships, 1960-2016

The final rounds of the 2016 Union of European Football Associations (UEFA) European Championships were hosted by France and opened June 10, 2016, when the host country defeated Romania, 2-1, at Stade de France in Saint-Denis. France advanced to the Euro 2016 final match against Portugal, but Portugal prevailed, 1-0, in extra time on a goal by Éder in the 109th minute July 10 at Stade de France. Portugal had reached the final with a 2-0 victory over Wales on July 6 at Stade de Lyon in Lyon. France had defeated Germany, 2-0, in the other semifinal match July 7 at Stade Vélodrome in Marseilles. France's Antoine Griezmann was voted player of the tournament, with six goals and two assists.

Year	Winner	Final opponent	Score	Site	Year	Winner	Final opponent	Score	Site
1960	USSR	Yugoslavia	2-1#	France	1992	Denmark	Germany	2-0	Sweden
1964	Spain	USSR	2-1	Spain	1996	Germany	Czech Rep.	2-1#	England
1968	Italy	Yugoslavia	2-0	Italy	2000	France	Italy	2-1#	Belgium/Neth.
1972	W. Germany	USSR	3-0	Belgium	2004	Greece	Portugal	1-0	Portugal
1976	Czechoslovakia	W. Germany	2-2 (5-3)*	Yugoslavia	2008	Spain	Germany	1-0	Austria/Switz.
1980	W. Germany	Belgium	2-1	Italy	2012	Spain	Italy	4-0	Poland/Ukr.
1984	France	Spain	2-0	France	2016	Portugal	France	1-0#	France
1988	Netherlands	USSR	2-0	W. Germany					

* = Match decided in penalty kicks (shootout score in parentheses). # = Match decided in extra time.

Selected European Soccer League Champions, 1950-2016

Season	England: Premier League[1]	Spain: La Liga	Italy: Serie A	Germany: Bundesliga[2]
1949-50	Portsmouth FC	Atlético Madrid	Juventus	VfB Stuttgart
1950-51	Tottenham Hotspur	Atlético Madrid	AC Milan	Kaiserslautern
1951-52	Manchester United	FC Barcelona	Juventus	VfB Stuttgart
1952-53	Arsenal	FC Barcelona	Inter Milan	Kaiserslautern
1953-54	Wolverhampton Wanderers	Real Madrid	Inter Milan	Hannoverscher SV 96
1954-55	Chelsea	Real Madrid	AC Milan	Rot-Weiss Essen
1955-56	Manchester United	Athletic Bilbao	Fiorentina	Borussia Dortmund
1956-57	Manchester United	Real Madrid	AC Milan	Borussia Dortmund
1957-58	Wolverhampton Wanderers	Real Madrid	Juventus	Schalke 04
1958-59	Wolverhampton Wanderers	FC Barcelona	AC Milan	Eintracht Frankfurt
1959-60	Burnley FC	FC Barcelona	Juventus	Hamburg SV
1960-61	Tottenham Hotspur	Real Madrid	Juventus	FC Nuremberg
1961-62	Ipswich Town	Real Madrid	AC Milan	FC Cologne
1962-63	Everton	Real Madrid	Inter Milan	Borussia Dortmund
1963-64	Liverpool	Real Madrid	Bologna	FC Cologne
1964-65	Manchester United	Real Madrid	Inter Milan	Werder Bremen
1965-66	Liverpool	Atlético Madrid	Inter Milan	TSV 1860 Munich
1966-67	Manchester United	Real Madrid	Juventus	Eintracht Braunschweig
1967-68	Manchester City	Real Madrid	AC Milan	FC Nuremberg
1968-69	Leeds United	Real Madrid	Fiorentina	Bayern Munich
1969-70	Everton	Atlético Madrid	Cagliari	Borussia Mönchengladbach
1970-71	Arsenal	Valencia	Inter Milan	Borussia Mönchengladbach
1971-72	Derby County	Real Madrid	Juventus	Bayern Munich
1972-73	Liverpool	Atlético Madrid	Juventus	Bayern Munich
1973-74	Leeds United	FC Barcelona	Lazio	Bayern Munich
1974-75	Derby County	Real Madrid	Juventus	Borussia Mönchengladbach
1975-76	Liverpool	Real Madrid	Torino	Borussia Mönchengladbach
1976-77	Liverpool	Atlético Madrid	Juventus	Borussia Mönchengladbach
1977-78	Nottingham Forest	Real Madrid	Juventus	FC Cologne
1978-79	Liverpool	Real Madrid	AC Milan	Hamburg SV
1979-80	Liverpool	Real Madrid	Inter Milan	Bayern Munich
1980-81	Aston Villa	Real Sociedad	Juventus	Bayern Munich
1981-82	Liverpool	Real Sociedad	Juventus	Hamburg SV
1982-83	Liverpool	Athletic Bilbao	AS Roma	Hamburg SV
1983-84	Liverpool	Athletic Bilbao	Juventus	VfB Stuttgart
1984-85	Everton	FC Barcelona	Verona	Bayern Munich
1985-86	Liverpool	Real Madrid	Juventus	Bayern Munich
1986-87	Everton	Real Madrid	Napoli	Bayern Munich
1987-88	Liverpool	Real Madrid	AC Milan	Werder Bremen
1988-89	Arsenal	Real Madrid	Inter Milan	Bayern Munich
1989-90	Liverpool	Real Madrid	Napoli	Bayern Munich
1990-91	Arsenal	FC Barcelona	Sampdoria	FC Kaiserslautern
1991-92	Leeds United	FC Barcelona	AC Milan	VfB Stuttgart
1992-93	Manchester United	FC Barcelona	AC Milan	Werder Bremen
1993-94	Manchester United	FC Barcelona	AC Milan	Bayern Munich
1994-95	Blackburn Rovers	Real Madrid	Juventus	Borussia Dortmund
1995-96	Manchester United	Atlético Madrid	AC Milan	Borussia Dortmund
1996-97	Manchester United	Real Madrid	Juventus	Bayern Munich
1997-98	Arsenal	FC Barcelona	Juventus	FC Kaiserslautern
1998-99	Manchester United	FC Barcelona	AC Milan	Bayern Munich
1999-2000	Manchester United	Deportivo Coruña	Lazio	Bayern Munich
2000-01	Manchester United	Real Madrid	AS Roma	Bayern Munich
2001-02	Arsenal	Valencia	Juventus	Borussia Dortmund
2002-03	Manchester United	Real Madrid	Juventus	Bayern Munich
2003-04	Arsenal	Valencia	AC Milan	Werder Bremen
2004-05	Chelsea	FC Barcelona	None[3]	Bayern Munich
2005-06	Chelsea	FC Barcelona	Inter Milan[3]	Bayern Munich
2006-07	Manchester United	Real Madrid	Inter Milan	VfB Stuttgart
2007-08	Manchester United	Real Madrid	Inter Milan	Bayern Munich
2008-09	Manchester United	FC Barcelona	Inter Milan	VfL Wolfsburg
2009-10	Chelsea	FC Barcelona	Inter Milan	Bayern Munich
2010-11	Manchester United	FC Barcelona	AC Milan	Borussia Dortmund
2011-12	Manchester City	Real Madrid	Juventus	Borussia Dortmund
2012-13	Manchester United	FC Barcelona	Juventus	Bayern Munich
2013-14	Manchester City	Atlético Madrid	Juventus	Bayern Munich
2014-15	Chelsea	FC Barcelona	Juventus	Bayern Munich
2015-16	Leicester City	FC Barcelona	Juventus	Bayern Munich

(1) Football League champions are listed prior to 1992-93 season, when the Premier League formed. (2) Regional champions are listed prior to 1963-64 season, when National Bundesliga formed. (3) Juventus was stripped of two titles in 2006 because of match-fixing.

FIFA Confederations Cup, 2013

Brazil won its third straight Confederations Cup title with a 3-0 victory over Spain June 30, 2013, at Maracanã Stadium in Rio de Janeiro, Brazil. Fred scored twice in the championship and Neymar, who won the Golden Ball as the tournament's top player, added his fourth goal of the tournament in the 44th minute.

FIFA Confederations Cup Results, 1997-2013

The FIFA Confederations Cup, now held every four years, is a tournament contested by six continental champions, the World Cup winner, and the host country.

Year	Winner	Final opponent	Score	Third place	Fourth place	Site
1997	Brazil	Australia	6-0	Czech Republic	Uruguay	Saudi Arabia
1999	Mexico	Brazil	4-3	U.S.	Saudi Arabia	Mexico
2001	France	Japan	1-0	Australia	Brazil	S. Korea/Japan
2003	France	Cameroon	1-0	Turkey	Colombia	France
2005	Brazil	Argentina	4-1	Germany	Mexico	Germany
2009	Brazil	U.S.	3-2	Spain	South Africa	South Africa
2013	Brazil	Spain	3-0	Italy	Uruguay	Brazil

GOLF

Men's All-Time Major Professional Championship Leaders

Through Sept. 2016. * = Active PGA player in 2016; (a) = amateur.

Player	Masters	U.S. Open	British Open	PGA	Total
Jack Nicklaus	1963, '65-'66, '72, '75, '86	1962, '67, '72, '80	1966, '70, '78	1963, '71, '73, '75, '80	18
Tiger Woods*	1997, 2001-02, '05	2000, '02, '08	2000, '05-'06	1999-2000, '06-'07	14
Walter Hagen	—	1914, '19	1922, '24, '28-'29	1921, '24-'27	11
Ben Hogan	1951, '53	1948, '50-'51, '53	1953	1946, '48	9
Gary Player	1961, '74, '78	1965	1959, '68, '74	1962, '72	9
Tom Watson	1977, '81	1982	1975, '77, '80, '82-'83	—	8
Bobby Jones (a)	—	1923, '26, '29-'30	1926-27, '30	—	7
Arnold Palmer	1958, '60, '62, '64	1960	1961-62	—	7
Gene Sarazen	1935	1922, '32	1932	1922-23, '33	7
Sam Snead	1949, '52, '54	—	1946	1942, '49, '51	7
Harry Vardon	—	1900	1896, '98-'99, 1903, '11, '14	—	7
Nick Faldo	1989-90, '96	—	1987, '90, '92	—	6
Lee Trevino	—	1968, '71	1971-72	1974, '84	6

Professional Golfers' Association Leading Money Winners, 1946-2016

Year	Player	Earnings	Year	Player	Earnings	Year	Player	Earnings
1946	Ben Hogan	$42,556	1970	Lee Trevino	$157,037	1994	Nick Price	$1,499,927
1947	Jimmy Demaret	27,936	1971	Jack Nicklaus	244,490	1995	Greg Norman	1,654,959
1948	Ben Hogan	32,112	1972	Jack Nicklaus	320,542	1996	Tom Lehman	1,780,159
1949	Sam Snead	31,593	1973	Jack Nicklaus	308,362	1997	Tiger Woods	2,066,833
1950	Sam Snead	35,758	1974	Johnny Miller	353,201	1998	David Duval	2,591,031
1951	Lloyd Mangrum	26,088	1975	Jack Nicklaus	298,149	1999	Tiger Woods	6,616,585
1952	Julius Boros	37,032	1976	Jack Nicklaus	266,438	2000	Tiger Woods	9,188,321
1953	Lew Worsham	34,002	1977	Tom Watson	310,653	2001	Tiger Woods	5,687,777
1954	Bob Toski	65,819	1978	Tom Watson	362,429	2002	Tiger Woods	6,912,625
1955	Julius Boros	63,121	1979	Tom Watson	462,636	2003	Vijay Singh	7,573,907
1956	Ted Kroll	72,835	1980	Tom Watson	530,808	2004	Vijay Singh	10,905,166
1957	Dick Mayer	65,835	1981	Tom Kite	375,699	2005	Tiger Woods	10,628,024
1958	Arnold Palmer	42,607	1982	Craig Stadler	446,462	2006	Tiger Woods	9,941,563
1959	Art Wall Jr.	53,167	1983	Hal Sutton	426,668	2007	Tiger Woods	10,867,052
1960	Arnold Palmer	75,262	1984	Tom Watson	476,260	2008	Vijay Singh	6,601,094
1961	Gary Player	64,540	1985	Curtis Strange	542,321	2009	Tiger Woods	10,508,163
1962	Arnold Palmer	81,448	1986	Greg Norman	653,296	2010	Matt Kuchar	4,910,477
1963	Arnold Palmer	128,230	1987	Curtis Strange	925,941	2011	Luke Donald	6,683,214
1964	Jack Nicklaus	113,284	1988	Curtis Strange	1,147,644	2012	Rory McIlroy	8,047,952
1965	Jack Nicklaus	140,752	1989	Tom Kite	1,395,278	2013	Tiger Woods	8,553,439
1966	Billy Casper	121,944	1990	Greg Norman	1,165,477	2014	Rory McIlroy	8,280,096
1967	Jack Nicklaus	188,998	1991	Corey Pavin	979,430	2015	Jordan Spieth	12,030,465
1968	Billy Casper	205,168	1992	Fred Couples	1,344,188	2016	Dustin Johnson	9,365,185
1969	Frank Beard	164,707	1993	Nick Price	1,478,557			

Note: The PGA tour introduced a new split season format in Oct. 2013, which concluded with the FedEx Cup in Sept. 2014. From 2014 on, year shown is the one in which season ended.

Masters Golf Tournament Winners, 1940-2016

First contested in 1934 as Augusta National Invitation Tournament (name changed in 1939); not played, 1943-45.

Year	Winner	Year	Winner	Year	Winner	Year	Winner	Year	Winner
1940	Jimmy Demaret	1959	Art Wall Jr.	1974	Gary Player	1989	Nick Faldo	2002	Tiger Woods
1941	Craig Wood	1960	Arnold Palmer	1975	Jack Nicklaus	1990	Nick Faldo	2003	Mike Weir
1942	Byron Nelson	1961	Gary Player	1976	Ray Floyd	1991	Ian Woosnam	2004	Phil Mickelson
1946	Herman Keiser	1962	Arnold Palmer	1977	Tom Watson	1992	Fred Couples	2005	Tiger Woods
1947	Jimmy Demaret	1963	Jack Nicklaus	1978	Gary Player	1993	Bernhard Langer	2006	Phil Mickelson
1948	Claude Harmon	1964	Arnold Palmer	1979	Fuzzy Zoeller	1994	José María Olazábal	2007	Zach Johnson
1949	Sam Snead	1965	Jack Nicklaus	1980	Seve Ballesteros			2008	Trevor Immelman
1950	Jimmy Demaret	1966	Jack Nicklaus	1981	Tom Watson	1995	Ben Crenshaw	2009	Angel Cabrera
1951	Ben Hogan	1967	Gay Brewer Jr.	1982	Craig Stadler	1996	Nick Faldo	2010	Phil Mickelson
1952	Sam Snead	1968	Bob Goalby	1983	Seve Ballesteros	1997	Tiger Woods	2011	Charl Schwartzel
1953	Ben Hogan	1969	George Archer	1984	Ben Crenshaw	1998	Mark O'Meara	2012	Bubba Watson
1954	Sam Snead	1970	Billy Casper	1985	Bernhard Langer	1999	José María Olazábal	2013	Adam Scott
1955	Cary Middlecoff	1971	Charles Coody	1986	Jack Nicklaus			2014	Bubba Watson
1956	Jack Burke	1972	Jack Nicklaus	1987	Larry Mize	2000	Vijay Singh	2015	Jordan Spieth
1957	Doug Ford	1973	Tommy Aaron	1988	Sandy Lyle	2001	Tiger Woods	2016	Danny Willett
1958	Arnold Palmer								

U.S. Open Winners, 1940-2016

First contested in 1895; not played, 1942-45.

Year	Winner	Year	Winner	Year	Winner	Year	Winner	Year	Winner
1940	Lawson Little	1959	Billy Casper	1974	Hale Irwin	1989	Curtis Strange	2003	Jim Furyk
1941	Craig Wood	1960	Arnold Palmer	1975	Lou Graham	1990	Hale Irwin	2004	Retief Goosen
1946	Lloyd Mangrum	1961	Gene Littler	1976	Jerry Pate	1991	Payne Stewart	2005	Michael Campbell
1947	Lew Worsham	1962	Jack Nicklaus	1977	Hubert Green	1992	Tom Kite	2006	Geoff Ogilvy
1948	Ben Hogan	1963	Julius Boros	1978	Andy North	1993	Lee Janzen	2007	Angel Cabrera
1949	Cary Middlecoff	1964	Ken Venturi	1979	Hale Irwin	1994	Ernie Els	2008	Tiger Woods
1950	Ben Hogan	1965	Gary Player	1980	Jack Nicklaus	1995	Corey Pavin	2009	Lucas Glover
1951	Ben Hogan	1966	Billy Casper	1981	David Graham	1996	Steve Jones	2010	Graeme McDowell
1952	Julius Boros	1967	Jack Nicklaus	1982	Tom Watson	1997	Ernie Els	2011	Rory McIlroy
1953	Ben Hogan	1968	Lee Trevino	1983	Larry Nelson	1998	Lee Janzen	2012	Webb Simpson
1954	Ed Furgol	1969	Orville Moody	1984	Fuzzy Zoeller	1999	Payne Stewart	2013	Justin Rose
1955	Jack Fleck	1970	Tony Jacklin	1985	Andy North	2000	Tiger Woods	2014	Martin Kaymer
1956	Cary Middlecoff	1971	Lee Trevino	1986	Ray Floyd	2001	Retief Goosen	2015	Jordan Spieth
1957	Dick Mayer	1972	Jack Nicklaus	1987	Scott Simpson	2002	Tiger Woods	2016	Dustin Johnson
1958	Tommy Bolt	1973	Johnny Miller	1988	Curtis Strange				

British Open Winners, 1946-2016

Officially called the Open Championship. First contested in 1860; not played, 1940-45.

Year Winner	Year Winner	Year Winner	Year Winner	Year Winner
1946 Sam Snead	1961 Arnold Palmer	1975 Tom Watson	1989 Mark Calcavecchia	2003 Ben Curtis
1947 Fred Daly	1962 Arnold Palmer	1976 Johnny Miller	1990 Nick Faldo	2004 Todd Hamilton
1948 Henry Cotton	1963 Bob Charles	1977 Tom Watson	1991 Ian Baker-Finch	2005 Tiger Woods
1949 Bobby Locke	1964 Tony Lema	1978 Jack Nicklaus	1992 Nick Faldo	2006 Tiger Woods
1950 Bobby Locke	1965 Peter Thomson	1979 Seve Ballesteros	1993 Greg Norman	2007 Padraig Harrington
1951 Max Faulkner	1966 Jack Nicklaus	1980 Tom Watson	1994 Nick Price	2008 Padraig Harrington
1952 Bobby Locke	1967 Roberto de Vicenzo	1981 Bill Rogers	1995 John Daly	2009 Stewart Cink
1953 Ben Hogan	1968 Gary Player	1982 Tom Watson	1996 Tom Lehman	2010 Louis Oosthuizen
1954 Peter Thomson	1969 Tony Jacklin	1983 Tom Watson	1997 Justin Leonard	2011 Darren Clarke
1955 Peter Thomson	1970 Jack Nicklaus	1984 Seve Ballesteros	1998 Mark O'Meara	2012 Ernie Els
1956 Peter Thomson	1971 Lee Trevino	1985 Sandy Lyle	1999 Paul Lawrie	2013 Phil Mickelson
1957 Bobby Locke	1972 Lee Trevino	1986 Greg Norman	2000 Tiger Woods	2014 Rory McIlroy
1958 Peter Thomson	1973 Tom Weiskopf	1987 Nick Faldo	2001 David Duval	2015 Zach Johnson
1959 Gary Player	1974 Gary Player	1988 Seve Ballesteros	2002 Ernie Els	2016 Henrik Stenson
1960 Kel Nagle				

PGA Championship Winners, 1940-2016

First contested in 1916; not played, 1943.

Year Winner	Year Winner	Year Winner	Year Winner	Year Winner
1940 Byron Nelson	1957 Lionel Hebert	1972 Gary Player	1987 Larry Nelson	2002 Rich Beem
1941 Victor Ghezzi	1958 Dow Finsterwald	1973 Jack Nicklaus	1988 Jeff Sluman	2003 Shaun Micheel
1942 Sam Snead	1959 Bob Rosburg	1974 Lee Trevino	1989 Payne Stewart	2004 Vijay Singh
1944 Bob Hamilton	1960 Jay Hebert	1975 Jack Nicklaus	1990 Wayne Grady	2005 Phil Mickelson
1945 Byron Nelson	1961 Jerry Barber	1976 Dave Stockton	1991 John Daly	2006 Tiger Woods
1946 Ben Hogan	1962 Gary Player	1977 Lanny Wadkins	1992 Nick Price	2007 Tiger Woods
1947 Jim Ferrier	1963 Jack Nicklaus	1978 John Mahaffey	1993 Paul Azinger	2008 Padraig Harrington
1948 Ben Hogan	1964 Bob Nichols	1979 David Graham	1994 Nick Price	2009 Y.E.Yang
1949 Sam Snead	1965 Dave Marr	1980 Jack Nicklaus	1995 Steve Elkington	2010 Martin Kaymer
1950 Chandler Harper	1966 Al Geiberger	1981 Larry Nelson	1996 Mark Brooks	2011 Keegan Bradley
1951 Sam Snead	1967 Don January	1982 Ray Floyd	1997 Davis Love III	2012 Rory McIlroy
1952 James Turnesa	1968 Julius Boros	1983 Hal Sutton	1998 Vijay Singh	2013 Jason Dufner
1953 Walter Burkemo	1969 Ray Floyd	1984 Lee Trevino	1999 Tiger Woods	2014 Rory McIlroy
1954 Melvin Harbert	1970 Dave Stockton	1985 Hubert Green	2000 Tiger Woods	2015 Jason Day
1955 Doug Ford	1971 Jack Nicklaus	1986 Bob Tway	2001 David Toms	2016 Jimmy Walker
1956 Jack Burke				

FedEx Cup Winners, 2007-16

The FedEx Cup, a season-long, $10-mil competition with points awarded by finishing rank in each tournament, divides the PGA Tour into a regular season consisting of 43 events, combined with a 4-event playoff that ends with the Tour Championship.

Year Winner	Year Winner	Year Winner	Year Winner	Year Winner
2007 Tiger Woods	2009 Tiger Woods	2011 Bill Haas	2013 Henrik Stenson	2015 Jordan Spieth
2008 Vijay Singh	2010 Jim Furyk	2012 Brandt Snedeker	2014 Billy Horschel	2016 Rory McIlroy

Women's All-Time Major Professional Championship Leaders

Through Oct. 2016. * = Active in 2016 LPGA season.

Player	ANA Inspiration[1]	KPMG Women's PGA[2]	U.S. Women's Open	Women's British Open[3]	Titleholders[4]	Western Open[5]	Total
Patty Berg	—	—	1946	—	1937-39, '48, '53, '55, '57	1941, '43, '48, '51, '55, '57-'58	15
Mickey Wright	—	1958, '60-'61, '63	1958-59, '61, '64	—	1961-62	1962-63, '66	13
Louise Suggs	—	1957	1949, '52	—	1946, '54, '56, '59	1946-47, '49, '53	11
Annika Sorenstam	2001-02, '05	2003-05	1995-96, 2006	2003	—	—	10
Babe Zaharias	—	—	1948, '50, '54	—	1947, '50, '52	1940, '44-'45, '50	10
Betsy Rawls	—	1959, '69	1951, '53, '57, '60	—	—	1952, '59	8
Juli Inkster*	1984, '89	1999-2000	1999, 2002	1984	—	—	7
Karrie Webb*	2000, '06	2001	2000-01	1999, 2002	—	—	7
Inbee Park*	2013	2013-15	2008, '13	2015	—	—	7

(1) Formerly the Nabisco Dinah Shore (1982-99), the Nabisco Championship (2000-01), and the Kraft Nabisco Championship (2002-14); designated major in 1983. (2) Formerly the LPGA Championship (1955-2014). (3) In 2001, the British Open replaced the du Maurier Classic as the LPGA's fourth major; wins in column prior to 2001 are for the Peter Jackson (1979-82) or du Maurier (1983-2000) Classic. (4) Titleholders Championship was a major, 1937-72. (5) Western Open was a major, 1930-67.

Ladies Professional Golf Association Leading Money Winners, 1954-2015

Year	Player	Earnings	Year	Player	Earnings	Year	Player	Earnings
1954	Patty Berg	$16,011	1975	Sandra Palmer	$76,374	1996	Karrie Webb	$1,002,000
1955	Patty Berg	16,492	1976	Judy Rankin	150,734	1997	Annika Sorenstam	1,236,789
1956	Marlene Hagge	20,235	1977	Judy Rankin	122,890	1998	Annika Sorenstam	1,092,748
1957	Patty Berg	16,272	1978	Nancy Lopez	189,814	1999	Karrie Webb	1,591,959
1958	Beverly Hanson	12,639	1979	Nancy Lopez	197,489	2000	Karrie Webb	1,876,853
1959	Betsy Rawls	26,774	1980	Beth Daniel	231,000	2001	Annika Sorenstam	2,105,868
1960	Louise Suggs	16,892	1981	Beth Daniel	206,998	2002	Annika Sorenstam	2,863,904
1961	Mickey Wright	22,236	1982	JoAnne Carner	310,400	2003	Annika Sorenstam	2,029,506
1962	Mickey Wright	21,641	1983	JoAnne Carner	291,404	2004	Annika Sorenstam	2,544,707
1963	Mickey Wright	31,269	1984	Betsy King	266,771	2005	Annika Sorenstam	2,588,240
1964	Mickey Wright	29,800	1985	Nancy Lopez	416,472	2006	Lorena Ochoa	2,592,872
1965	Kathy Whitworth	28,658	1986	Pat Bradley	492,021	2007	Lorena Ochoa	4,364,994
1966	Kathy Whitworth	33,517	1987	Ayako Okamoto	466,034	2008	Lorena Ochoa	2,763,193
1967	Kathy Whitworth	32,937	1988	Sherri Turner	350,851	2009	Jiyai Shin	1,807,334
1968	Kathy Whitworth	48,379	1989	Betsy King	654,132	2010	Na Yeon Choi	1,871,166
1969	Carol Mann	49,152	1990	Beth Daniel	863,578	2011	Yani Tseng	2,921,713
1970	Kathy Whitworth	30,235	1991	Pat Bradley	763,118	2012	Inbee Park	2,287,080
1971	Kathy Whitworth	41,181	1992	Dottie Mochrie	693,335	2013	Inbee Park	2,456,619
1972	Kathy Whitworth	65,063	1993	Betsy King	595,992	2014	Stacy Lewis	2,539,039
1973	Kathy Whitworth	82,864	1994	Laura Davies	687,201	2015	Lydia Ko	2,800,802
1974	JoAnne Carner	87,094	1995	Annika Sorenstam	666,533			

ANA Inspiration Winners, 1983-2016

Event began in 1972 and was designated a major championship in 1983. Formerly the Colgate Dinah Shore (1972-81), the Nabisco Dinah Shore (1982-99), the Nabisco Championship (2000-01), and the Kraft Nabisco Championship (2002-14).

Year	Winner	Year	Winner	Year	Winner	Year	Winner	Year	Winner
1983	Amy Alcott	1990	Betsy King	1997	Betsy King	2004	Grace Park	2011	Stacy Lewis
1984	Juli Inkster	1991	Amy Alcott	1998	Pat Hurst	2005	Annika Sorenstam	2012	Sun Young Yoo
1985	Alice Miller	1992	Dottie Pepper	1999	Dottie Pepper	2006	Karrie Webb	2013	Inbee Park
1986	Pat Bradley	1993	Helen Alfredsson	2000	Karrie Webb	2007	Morgan Pressel	2014	Lexi Thompson
1987	Betsy King	1994	Donna Andrews	2001	Annika Sorenstam	2008	Lorena Ochoa	2015	Brittany Lincicome
1988	Amy Alcott	1995	Nanci Bowen	2002	Annika Sorenstam	2009	Brittany Lincicome	2016	Lydia Ko
1989	Juli Inkster	1996	Patty Sheehan	2003	P. Meunier-Lebouc	2010	Yani Tseng		

KPMG Women's PGA Championship Winners, 1955-2016

Formerly LPGA Championship (1955-2014).

Year	Winner	Year	Winner	Year	Winner	Year	Winner	Year	Winner
1955	Beverly Hanson	1968	Sandra Post	1981	Donna Caponi	1993	Patty Sheehan	2005	Annika Sorenstam
1956	Marlene Hagge	1969	Betsy Rawls	1982	Jan Stephenson	1994	Laura Davies	2006	Se Ri Pak
1957	Louise Suggs	1970	Shirley Englehorn	1983	Patty Sheehan	1995	Kelly Robbins	2007	Suzann Pettersen
1958	Mickey Wright	1971	Kathy Whitworth	1984	Patty Sheehan	1996	Laura Davies	2008	Yani Tseng
1959	Betsy Rawls	1972	Kathy Ahern	1985	Nancy Lopez	1997	Christa Johnson	2009	Anna Nordqvist
1960	Mickey Wright	1973	Mary Mills	1986	Pat Bradley	1998	Se Ri Pak	2010	Cristie Kerr
1961	Mickey Wright	1974	Sandra Haynie	1987	Jane Geddes	1999	Juli Inkster	2011	Yani Tseng
1962	Judy Kimball	1975	Kathy Whitworth	1988	Sherri Turner	2000	Juli Inkster	2012	Shanshan Feng
1963	Mickey Wright	1976	Betty Burfeindt	1989	Nancy Lopez	2001	Karrie Webb	2013	Inbee Park
1964	Mary Mills	1977	Chako Higuchi	1990	Beth Daniel	2002	Se Ri Pak	2014	Inbee Park
1965	Sandra Haynie	1978	Nancy Lopez	1991	Meg Mallon	2003	Annika Sorenstam	2015	Inbee Park
1966	Gloria Ehret	1979	Donna Caponi	1992	Betsy King	2004	Annika Sorenstam	2016	Brooke Henderson
1967	Kathy Whitworth	1980	Sally Little						

U.S. Women's Open Winners, 1946-2016

Year	Winner	Year	Winner	Year	Winner	Year	Winner	Year	Winner
1946	Patty Berg	1961	Mickey Wright	1975	Sandra Palmer	1989	Betsy King	2003	Hilary Lunke
1947	Betty Jameson	1962	Murle Lindstrom	1976	JoAnne Carner	1990	Betsy King	2004	Meg Mallon
1948	Babe Zaharias	1963	Mary Mills	1977	Hollis Stacy	1991	Meg Mallon	2005	Birdie Kim
1949	Louise Suggs	1964	Mickey Wright	1978	Hollis Stacy	1992	Patty Sheehan	2006	Annika Sorenstam
1950	Babe Zaharias	1965	Carol Mann	1979	Jerilyn Britz	1993	Lauri Merten	2007	Cristie Kerr
1951	Betsy Rawls	1966	Sandra Spuzich	1980	Amy Alcott	1994	Patty Sheehan	2008	Inbee Park
1952	Louise Suggs	1967	Catherine Lacoste	1981	Pat Bradley	1995	Annika Sorenstam	2009	Eun-Hee Ji
1953	Betsy Rawls	1968	Susie Berning	1982	Janet Alex	1996	Annika Sorenstam	2010	Paula Creamer
1954	Babe Zaharias	1969	Donna Caponi	1983	Jan Stephenson	1997	Alison Nicholas	2011	So Yeon Ryu
1955	Fay Crocker	1970	Donna Caponi	1984	Hollis Stacy	1998	Se Ri Pak	2012	Na Yeon Choi
1956	Kathy Cornelius	1971	JoAnne Carner	1985	Kathy Baker	1999	Juli Inkster	2013	Inbee Park
1957	Betsy Rawls	1972	Susie Berning	1986	Jane Geddes	2000	Karrie Webb	2014	Michelle Wie
1958	Mickey Wright	1973	Susie Berning	1987	Laura Davies	2001	Karrie Webb	2015	In Gee Chun
1959	Mickey Wright	1974	Sandra Haynie	1988	Liselotte Neumann	2002	Juli Inkster	2016	Brittany Lang
1960	Betsy Rawls								

Women's British Open Winners, 1979-2016

First contested as the Ladies' British Open in 1976; became the LPGA's fourth major championship in 2001, replacing the du Maurier Classic. Winners listed are for the Peter Jackson (1979-82) and du Maurier (1983-2000) Classic.

Year	Winner	Year	Winner	Year	Winner	Year	Winner	Year	Winner
1979	Amy Alcott	1987	Jody Rosenthal	1995	Jenny Lidback	2003	Annika Sorenstam	2010	Yani Tseng
1980	Pat Bradley	1988	Sally Little	1996	Laura Davies	2004	Karen Stupples	2011	Yani Tseng
1981	Jan Stephenson	1989	Tammie Green	1997	Colleen Walker	2005	Jeong Jang	2012	Jiyai Shin
1982	Sandra Haynie	1990	Cathy Johnston	1998	Brandie Burton	2006	Sherri Steinhauer	2013	Stacy Lewis
1983	Hollis Stacy	1991	Nancy Scranton	1999	Karrie Webb	2007	Lorena Ochoa	2014	Mo Martin
1984	Juli Inkster	1992	Sherri Steinhauer	2000	Meg Mallon	2008	Jiyai Shin	2015	Inbee Park
1985	Pat Bradley	1993	Brandie Burton	2001	Se Ri Pak	2009	Catriona Matthew	2016	Ariya Jutanugarn
1986	Pat Bradley	1994	Martha Nause	2002	Karrie Webb				

Evian Championship, 2013-16

Began in 1994 as the Evian Masters; became the LPGA's fifth major tournament in 2013, when it was renamed the Evian Championship.

Year	Winner	Year	Winner	Year	Winner	Year	Winner
2013	Suzann Pettersen	2014	Hyo Joo Kim	2015	Lydia Ko	2016	In Gee Chun

Ryder Cup, 1927-2016

The Ryder Cup began in 1927 as a biennial team competition between pro male golfers from the U.S. and Great Britain. The British team was expanded in 1973 to include players from Ireland and in 1979 to golfers from the rest of Europe.

Year	Winner, score	Year	Winner, score	Year	Winner, score	Year	Winner, score
1927	U.S., 9½-2½	1957	Great Britain, 7½-4½	1977	U.S., 12½-7½	1997	Europe, 14½-13½
1929	Great Britain, 7-5	1959	U.S., 8½-3½	1979	U.S., 17-11	1999	U.S., 14½-13½
1931	U.S., 9-3	1961	U.S., 14½-9½	1981	U.S., 18½-9½	2002	Europe, 15½-12½
1933	Great Britain, 6½-5½	1963	U.S., 23-9	1983	U.S., 14½-13½	2004	Europe, 18½-9½
1935	U.S., 9-3	1965	U.S., 19½-12½	1985	Europe, 16½-11½	2006	Europe, 18½-9½
1937	U.S., 8-4	1967	U.S., 23½-8½	1987	Europe, 15-13	2008	U.S., 16½-11½
1947	U.S., 11-1	1969	Draw, 16-16	1989	Draw, 14-14	2010	Europe, 14½-13½
1949	U.S., 7-5	1971	U.S., 18½-13½	1991	U.S., 14½-13½	2012	Europe, 14½-13½
1951	U.S., 9½-2½	1973	U.S., 19-13	1993	U.S., 15-13	2014	Europe, 16½-11½
1953	U.S., 6½-5½	1975	U.S., 21-11	1995	Europe, 14½-13½	2016	U.S., 17-11
1955	U.S., 8-4						

Solheim Cup, 1990-2015

The Solheim Cup began in 1990 as a biennial team competition between pro women golfers from the U.S. and Europe.

Year	Winner, score	Year	Winner, score	Year	Winner, score	Year	Winner, score
1990	U.S., 11½-4½	1998	U.S., 16-12	2005	U.S., 15½-12½	2011	Europe, 15-13
1992	Europe, 11½-6½	2000	Europe, 14½-11½	2007	U.S., 16-12	2013	Europe, 18-10
1994	U.S., 13-7	2002	U.S., 15½-12½	2009	U.S., 16-12	2015	U.S., 14½-13½
1996	U.S., 17-11	2003	Europe, 17½-10½				

TENNIS

Australian Open Champions, 1969-2016

First contested 1905 for men, 1922 for women. Became an open championship in 1969. Two tournaments held in 1977, in Jan. and Dec. No tournament held in 1986.

Men's Singles

Year	Champion	Final opponent
1969	Rod Laver	Andrés Gimeno
1970	Arthur Ashe	Dick Crealy
1971	Ken Rosewall	Arthur Ashe
1972	Ken Rosewall	Mal Anderson
1973	John Newcombe	Onny Parun
1974	Jimmy Connors	Phil Dent
1975	John Newcombe	Jimmy Connors
1976	Mark Edmondson	John Newcombe
1977	Roscoe Tanner	Guillermo Vilas
	Vitas Gerulaitis	John Lloyd
1978	Guillermo Vilas	John Marks
1979	Guillermo Vilas	John Sadri
1980	Brian Teacher	Kim Warwick
1981	Johan Kriek	Steve Denton
1982	Johan Kriek	Steve Denton
1983	Mats Wilander	Ivan Lendl
1984	Mats Wilander	Kevin Curren
1985	Stefan Edberg	Mats Wilander
1987	Stefan Edberg	Pat Cash
1988	Mats Wilander	Pat Cash
1989	Ivan Lendl	Miloslav Mecir
1990	Ivan Lendl	Stefan Edberg
1991	Boris Becker	Ivan Lendl
1992	Jim Courier	Stefan Edberg
1993	Jim Courier	Stefan Edberg
1994	Pete Sampras	Todd Martin
1995	Andre Agassi	Pete Sampras
1996	Boris Becker	Michael Chang
1997	Pete Sampras	Carlos Moya
1998	Petr Korda	Marcelo Rios
1999	Yevgeny Kafelnikov	Thomas Enqvist
2000	Andre Agassi	Yevgeny Kafelnikov
2001	Andre Agassi	Arnaud Clement
2002	Thomas Johansson	Marat Safin
2003	Andre Agassi	Rainer Schuettler
2004	Roger Federer	Marat Safin
2005	Marat Safin	Lleyton Hewitt
2006	Roger Federer	Marcos Baghdatis
2007	Roger Federer	Fernando Gonzalez
2008	Novak Djokovic	Jo-Wilfried Tsonga
2009	Rafael Nadal	Roger Federer
2010	Roger Federer	Andy Murray
2011	Novak Djokovic	Andy Murray
2012	Novak Djokovic	Rafael Nadal
2013	Novak Djokovic	Andy Murray
2014	Stanislas Wawrinka	Rafael Nadal
2015	Novak Djokovic	Andy Murray
2016	Novak Djokovic	Andy Murray

Women's Singles

Year	Champion	Final opponent
1969	Margaret Smith Court	Billie Jean King
1970	Margaret Smith Court	Kerry Melville Reid
1971	Margaret Smith Court	Evonne Goolagong
1972	Virginia Wade	Evonne Goolagong
1973	Margaret Smith Court	Evonne Goolagong
1974	Evonne Goolagong	Chris Evert
1975	Evonne Goolagong	Martina Navratilova
1976	Evonne Goolagong Cawley	Renata Tomanova
1977	Kerry Reid	Dianne Balestrat
	Evonne Goolagong Cawley	Helen Gourlay
1978	Chris O'Neil	Betsy Nagelsen
1979	Barbara Jordan	Sharon Walsh
1980	Hana Mandlikova	Wendy Turnbull
1981	Martina Navratilova	Chris Evert Lloyd
1982	Chris Evert Lloyd	Martina Navratilova
1983	Martina Navratilova	Kathy Jordan
1984	Chris Evert Lloyd	Helena Sukova
1985	Martina Navratilova	Chris Evert Lloyd
1987	Hana Mandlikova	Martina Navratilova
1988	Steffi Graf	Chris Evert
1989	Steffi Graf	Helena Sukova
1990	Steffi Graf	Mary Joe Fernandez
1991	Monica Seles	Jana Novotna
1992	Monica Seles	Mary Joe Fernandez
1993	Monica Seles	Steffi Graf
1994	Steffi Graf	Arantxa Sánchez Vicario
1995	Mary Pierce	Arantxa Sánchez Vicario
1996	Monica Seles	Anke Huber
1997	Martina Hingis	Mary Pierce
1998	Martina Hingis	Conchita Martínez
1999	Martina Hingis	Amélie Mauresmo
2000	Lindsay Davenport	Martina Hingis
2001	Jennifer Capriati	Martina Hingis
2002	Jennifer Capriati	Martina Hingis
2003	Serena Williams	Venus Williams
2004	Justine Henin-Hardenne	Kim Clijsters
2005	Serena Williams	Lindsay Davenport
2006	Amélie Mauresmo	Justine Henin-Hardenne
2007	Serena Williams	Maria Sharapova
2008	Maria Sharapova	Ana Ivanovic
2009	Serena Williams	Dinara Safina
2010	Serena Williams	Justine Henin
2011	Kim Clijsters	Li Na
2012	Victoria Azarenka	Maria Sharapova
2013	Victoria Azarenka	Li Na
2014	Li Na	Dominika Cibulkova
2015	Serena Williams	Maria Sharapova
2016	Angelique Kerber	Serena Williams

French Open (Roland Garros) Champions, 1968-2016

First contested 1891 for men, 1897 for women. Became an open championship in 1968.

Men's Singles

Year	Champion	Final opponent
1968	Ken Rosewall	Rod Laver
1969	Rod Laver	Ken Rosewall
1970	Jan Kodes	Zeljko Franulovic
1971	Jan Kodes	Ilie Nastase
1972	Andrés Gimeno	Patrick Proisy
1973	Ilie Nastase	Nikki Pilic
1974	Björn Borg	Manuel Orantes
1975	Björn Borg	Guillermo Vilas
1976	Adriano Panatta	Harold Solomon
1977	Guillermo Vilas	Brian Gottfried
1978	Björn Borg	Guillermo Vilas
1979	Björn Borg	Victor Pecci
1980	Björn Borg	Vitas Gerulaitis
1981	Björn Borg	Ivan Lendl
1982	Mats Wilander	Guillermo Vilas
1983	Yannick Noah	Mats Wilander
1984	Ivan Lendl	John McEnroe
1985	Mats Wilander	Ivan Lendl
1986	Ivan Lendl	Mikael Pernfors
1987	Ivan Lendl	Mats Wilander
1988	Mats Wilander	Henri Leconte
1989	Michael Chang	Stefan Edberg
1990	Andres Gomez	Andre Agassi
1991	Jim Courier	Andre Agassi
1992	Jim Courier	Petr Korda
1993	Sergi Bruguera	Jim Courier
1994	Sergi Bruguera	Alberto Berasategui
1995	Thomas Muster	Michael Chang
1996	Yevgeny Kafelnikov	Michael Stich
1997	Gustavo Kuerten	Sergi Bruguera
1998	Carlos Moya	Alex Corretja
1999	Andre Agassi	Andrei Medvedev
2000	Gustavo Kuerten	Magnus Norman
2001	Gustavo Kuerten	Alex Corretja
2002	Albert Costa	Juan Carlos Ferrero
2003	Juan Carlos Ferrero	Martin Verkerk
2004	Gaston Gaudio	Guillermo Coria
2005	Rafael Nadal	Mariano Puerta
2006	Rafael Nadal	Roger Federer
2007	Rafael Nadal	Roger Federer
2008	Rafael Nadal	Roger Federer
2009	Roger Federer	Robin Soderling
2010	Rafael Nadal	Robin Soderling
2011	Rafael Nadal	Roger Federer
2012	Rafael Nadal	Novak Djokovic
2013	Rafael Nadal	David Ferrer
2014	Rafael Nadal	Novak Djokovic
2015	Stan Wawrinka	Novak Djokovic
2016	Novak Djokovic	Andy Murray

Women's Singles

Year	Champion	Final opponent
1968	Nancy Richey	Ann Jones
1969	Margaret Smith Court	Ann Jones
1970	Margaret Smith Court	Helga Niessen
1971	Evonne Goolagong	Helen Gourlay
1972	Billie Jean King	Evonne Goolagong
1973	Margaret Smith Court	Chris Evert
1974	Chris Evert	Olga Morozova
1975	Chris Evert	Martina Navratilova
1976	Sue Barker	Renata Tomanova
1977	Mima Jausovec	Florenta Mihai
1978	Virginia Ruzici	Mima Jausovec
1979	Chris Evert Lloyd	Wendy Turnbull
1980	Chris Evert Lloyd	Virginia Ruzici
1981	Hana Mandlikova	Sylvia Hanika
1982	Martina Navratilova	Andrea Jaeger

Year	Champion	Final opponent	Year	Champion	Final opponent
1983	Chris Evert Lloyd	Mima Jausovec	2000	Mary Pierce	Conchita Martínez
1984	Martina Navratilova	Chris Evert Lloyd	2001	Jennifer Capriati	Kim Clijsters
1985	Chris Evert Lloyd	Martina Navratilova	2002	Serena Williams	Venus Williams
1986	Chris Evert Lloyd	Martina Navratilova	2003	Justine Henin-Hardenne	Kim Clijsters
1987	Steffi Graf	Martina Navratilova	2004	Anastasia Myskina	Elena Dementieva
1988	Steffi Graf	Natalia Zvereva	2005	Justine Henin-Hardenne	Mary Pierce
1989	Arantxa Sánchez Vicario	Steffi Graf	2006	Justine Henin-Hardenne	Svetlana Kuznetsova
1990	Monica Seles	Steffi Graf	2007	Justine Henin	Ana Ivanovic
1991	Monica Seles	Arantxa Sánchez Vicario	2008	Ana Ivanovic	Dinara Safina
1992	Monica Seles	Steffi Graf	2009	Svetlana Kuznetsova	Dinara Safina
1993	Steffi Graf	Mary Joe Fernandez	2010	Francesca Schiavone	Samantha Stosur
1994	Arantxa Sánchez Vicario	Mary Pierce	2011	Li Na	Francesca Schiavone
1995	Steffi Graf	Arantxa Sánchez Vicario	2012	Maria Sharapova	Sara Errani
1996	Steffi Graf	Arantxa Sánchez Vicario	2013	Serena Williams	Maria Sharapova
1997	Iva Majoli	Martina Hingis	2014	Maria Sharapova	Simona Halep
1998	Arantxa Sánchez Vicario	Monica Seles	2015	Serena Williams	Lucie Safarova
1999	Steffi Graf	Martina Hingis	2016	Garbiñe Muguruza	Serena Williams

Wimbledon Champions, 1925-2016

First contested 1877 for men, 1884 for women. Became an open championship in 1968. Not held 1940-45.

Men's Singles

Year	Champion	Final opponent
1925	René Lacoste	Jean Borotra
1926	Jean Borotra	Howard Kinsey
1927	Henri Cochet	Jean Borotra
1928	René Lacoste	Henri Cochet
1929	Henri Cochet	Jean Borotra
1930	Bill Tilden	Wilmer Allison
1931	Sidney B. Wood	Francis X. Shields
1932	Ellsworth Vines	Henry Austin
1933	Jack Crawford	Ellsworth Vines
1934	Fred Perry	Jack Crawford
1935	Fred Perry	Gottfried von Cramm
1936	Fred Perry	Gottfried von Cramm
1937	Donald Budge	Gottfried von Cramm
1938	Donald Budge	Henry Austin
1939	Bobby Riggs	Elwood Cooke
1946	Yvon Petra	Geoff E. Brown
1947	Jack Kramer	Tom P. Brown
1948	Bob Falkenburg	John Bromwich
1949	Ted Schroeder	Jaroslav Drobny
1950	Budge Patty	Frank Sedgman
1951	Dick Savitt	Ken McGregor
1952	Frank Sedgman	Jaroslav Drobny
1953	Vic Seixas	Kurt Nielsen
1954	Jaroslav Drobny	Ken Rosewall
1955	Tony Trabert	Kurt Nielsen
1956	Lew Hoad	Ken Rosewall
1957	Lew Hoad	Ashley Cooper
1958	Ashley Cooper	Neale Fraser
1959	Alex Olmedo	Rod Laver
1960	Neale Fraser	Rod Laver
1961	Rod Laver	Chuck McKinley
1962	Rod Laver	Martin Mulligan
1963	Chuck McKinley	Fred Stolle
1964	Roy Emerson	Fred Stolle
1965	Roy Emerson	Fred Stolle
1966	Manuel Santana	Dennis Ralston
1967	John Newcombe	Wilhelm Bungert
1968	Rod Laver	Tony Roche
1969	Rod Laver	John Newcombe
1970	John Newcombe	Ken Rosewall
1971	John Newcombe	Stan Smith
1972	Stan Smith	Ilie Nastase
1973	Jan Kodes	Alex Metreveli
1974	Jimmy Connors	Ken Rosewall
1975	Arthur Ashe	Jimmy Connors
1976	Björn Borg	Ilie Nastase
1977	Björn Borg	Jimmy Connors
1978	Björn Borg	Jimmy Connors
1979	Björn Borg	Roscoe Tanner
1980	Björn Borg	John McEnroe
1981	John McEnroe	Björn Borg
1982	Jimmy Connors	John McEnroe
1983	John McEnroe	Chris Lewis
1984	John McEnroe	Jimmy Connors
1985	Boris Becker	Kevin Curren
1986	Boris Becker	Ivan Lendl
1987	Pat Cash	Ivan Lendl
1988	Stefan Edberg	Boris Becker
1989	Boris Becker	Stefan Edberg
1990	Stefan Edberg	Boris Becker
1991	Michael Stich	Boris Becker
1992	Andre Agassi	Goran Ivanisevic
1993	Pete Sampras	Jim Courier
1994	Pete Sampras	Goran Ivanisevic
1995	Pete Sampras	Boris Becker
1996	Richard Krajicek	MaliVai "Mai" Washington

Year	Champion	Final opponent
1997	Pete Sampras	Cedric Pioline
1998	Pete Sampras	Goran Ivanisevic
1999	Pete Sampras	Andre Agassi
2000	Pete Sampras	Patrick Rafter
2001	Goran Ivanisevic	Patrick Rafter
2002	Lleyton Hewitt	David Nalbandian
2003	Roger Federer	Mark Philippoussis
2004	Roger Federer	Andy Roddick
2005	Roger Federer	Andy Roddick
2006	Roger Federer	Rafael Nadal
2007	Roger Federer	Rafael Nadal
2008	Rafael Nadal	Roger Federer
2009	Roger Federer	Andy Roddick
2010	Rafael Nadal	Tomas Berdych
2011	Novak Djokovic	Rafael Nadal
2012	Roger Federer	Andy Murray
2013	Andy Murray	Novak Djokovic
2014	Novak Djokovic	Roger Federer
2015	Novak Djokovic	Roger Federer
2016	Andy Murray	Milos Raonic

Women's Singles

Year	Champion	Final opponent
1925	Suzanne Lenglen	Joan Fry
1926	Kathleen McKane Godfree	Lili de Alvarez
1927	Helen Wills	Lili de Alvarez
1928	Helen Wills	Lili de Alvarez
1929	Helen Wills	Helen H. Jacobs
1930	Helen Wills Moody	Elizabeth Ryan
1931	Cilly Aussem	Hilde Krahwinkel
1932	Helen Wills Moody	Helen H. Jacobs
1933	Helen Wills Moody	Dorothy Round
1934	Dorothy Round	Helen H. Jacobs
1935	Helen Wills Moody	Helen H. Jacobs
1936	Helen H. Jacobs	Hilde Krahwinkel Sperling
1937	Dorothy Round	Jadwiga Jedrzejowska
1938	Helen Wills Moody	Helen H. Jacobs
1939	Alice Marble	Kay Stammers
1946	Pauline Betz	Louise Brough
1947	Margaret Osborne	Doris Hart
1948	Louise Brough	Doris Hart
1949	Louise Brough	Margaret Osborne duPont
1950	Louise Brough	Margaret Osborne duPont
1951	Doris Hart	Shirley Fry
1952	Maureen Connolly	Louise Brough
1953	Maureen Connolly	Doris Hart
1954	Maureen Connolly	Louise Brough
1955	Louise Brough	Beverly Fleitz
1956	Shirley Fry	Angela Buxton
1957	Althea Gibson	Darlene Hard
1958	Althea Gibson	Angela Mortimer
1959	Maria Bueno	Darlene Hard
1960	Maria Bueno	Sandra Reynolds
1961	Angela Mortimer	Christine Truman
1962	Karen Hantze-Susman	Vera Sukova
1963	Margaret Smith	Billie Jean Moffitt
1964	Maria Bueno	Margaret Smith
1965	Margaret Smith	Maria Bueno
1966	Billie Jean King	Maria Bueno
1967	Billie Jean King	Ann Haydon Jones
1968	Billie Jean King	Judy Tegart
1969	Ann Haydon Jones	Billie Jean King
1970	Margaret Smith Court	Billie Jean King
1971	Evonne Goolagong	Margaret Smith Court
1972	Billie Jean King	Evonne Goolagong
1973	Billie Jean King	Chris Evert
1974	Chris Evert	Olga Morozova
1975	Billie Jean King	Evonne Goolagong Cawley

Year	Champion	Final opponent	Year	Champion	Final opponent
1976	Chris Evert	Evonne Goolagong Cawley	1996	Steffi Graf	Arantxa Sánchez Vicario
1977	Virginia Wade	Betty Stove	1997	Martina Hingis	Jana Novotna
1978	Martina Navratilova	Chris Evert	1998	Jana Novotna	Nathalie Tauziat
1979	Martina Navratilova	Chris Evert Lloyd	1999	Lindsay Davenport	Steffi Graf
1980	Evonne Goolagong Cawley	Chris Evert Lloyd	2000	Venus Williams	Lindsay Davenport
			2001	Venus Williams	Justine Henin
1981	Chris Evert Lloyd	Hana Mandlikova	2002	Serena Williams	Venus Williams
1982	Martina Navratilova	Chris Evert Lloyd	2003	Serena Williams	Venus Williams
1983	Martina Navratilova	Andrea Jaeger	2004	Maria Sharapova	Serena Williams
1984	Martina Navratilova	Chris Evert Lloyd	2005	Venus Williams	Lindsay Davenport
1985	Martina Navratilova	Chris Evert Lloyd	2006	Amélie Mauresmo	Justine Henin-Hardenne
1986	Martina Navratilova	Hana Mandlikova	2007	Venus Williams	Marion Bartoli
1987	Martina Navratilova	Steffi Graf	2008	Venus Williams	Serena Williams
1988	Steffi Graf	Martina Navratilova	2009	Serena Williams	Venus Williams
1989	Steffi Graf	Martina Navratilova	2010	Serena Williams	Vera Zvonareva
1990	Martina Navratilova	Zina Garrison	2011	Petra Kvitova	Maria Sharapova
1991	Steffi Graf	Gabriela Sabatini	2012	Serena Williams	Agnieszka Radwanska
1992	Steffi Graf	Monica Seles	2013	Marion Bartoli	Sabine Lisicki
1993	Steffi Graf	Jana Novotna	2014	Petra Kvitova	Eugenie Bouchard
1994	Conchita Martínez	Martina Navratilova	2015	Serena Williams	Garbiñe Muguruza
1995	Steffi Graf	Arantxa Sánchez Vicario	2016	Serena Williams	Angelique Kerber

U.S. Open Champions, 1925-2016

First contested 1881 for men, 1887 for women. The former U.S. National Championship became an open championship in 1968.

Men's Singles

Year	Champion	Final opponent
1925	Bill Tilden	William Johnston
1926	René Lacoste	Jean Borotra
1927	René Lacoste	Bill Tilden
1928	Henri Cochet	Francis Hunter
1929	Bill Tilden	Francis Hunter
1930	John Doeg	Francis X. Shields
1931	Ellsworth Vines	George Lott
1932	Ellsworth Vines	Henri Cochet
1933	Fred Perry	John Crawford
1934	Fred Perry	Wilmer Allison
1935	Wilmer Allison	Sidney Wood
1936	Fred Perry	Don Budge
1937	Don Budge	Gottfried von Cramm
1938	Don Budge	C. Gene Mako
1939	Bobby Riggs	S. Welby Van Horn
1940	Don McNeill	Bobby Riggs
1941	Bobby Riggs	F. L. Kovacs
1942	F. R. Schroeder Jr.	Frank Parker
1943	Joseph Hunt	Jack Kramer
1944	Frank Parker	Bill Talbert
1945	Frank Parker	Bill Talbert
1946	Jack Kramer	Tom Brown Jr.
1947	Jack Kramer	Frank Parker
1948	Pancho Gonzales	Eric Sturgess
1949	Pancho Gonzales	F. R. Schroeder Jr.
1950	Arthur Larsen	Herbert Flam
1951	Frank Sedgman	E. Victor Seixas Jr.
1952	Frank Sedgman	Gardnar Mulloy
1953	Tony Trabert	E. Victor Seixas Jr.
1954	E. Victor Seixas Jr.	Rex Hartwig
1955	Tony Trabert	Ken Rosewall
1956	Ken Rosewall	Lewis Hoad
1957	Malcolm Anderson	Ashley Cooper
1958	Ashley Cooper	Malcolm Anderson
1959	Neale A. Fraser	Alejandro Olmedo
1960	Neale A. Fraser	Rod Laver
1961	Roy Emerson	Rod Laver
1962	Rod Laver	Roy Emerson
1963	Rafael Osuna	F. A. Froehling III
1964	Roy Emerson	Fred Stolle
1965	Manuel Santana	Cliff Drysdale
1966	Fred Stolle	John Newcombe
1967	John Newcombe	Clark Graebner
1968	Arthur Ashe	Tom Okker
1969	Rod Laver	Tony Roche
1970	Ken Rosewall	Tony Roche
1971	Stan Smith	Jan Kodes
1972	Ilie Nastase	Arthur Ashe
1973	John Newcombe	Jan Kodes
1974	Jimmy Connors	Ken Rosewall
1975	Manuel Orantes	Jimmy Connors
1976	Jimmy Connors	Björn Borg
1977	Guillermo Vilas	Jimmy Connors
1978	Jimmy Connors	Björn Borg
1979	John McEnroe	Vitas Gerulaitis
1980	John McEnroe	Björn Borg
1981	John McEnroe	Björn Borg
1982	Jimmy Connors	Ivan Lendl
1983	Jimmy Connors	Ivan Lendl
1984	John McEnroe	Ivan Lendl
1985	Ivan Lendl	John McEnroe

Year	Champion	Final opponent
1986	Ivan Lendl	Miloslav Mecir
1987	Ivan Lendl	Mats Wilander
1988	Mats Wilander	Ivan Lendl
1989	Boris Becker	Ivan Lendl
1990	Pete Sampras	Andre Agassi
1991	Stefan Edberg	Jim Courier
1992	Stefan Edberg	Pete Sampras
1993	Pete Sampras	Cedric Pioline
1994	Andre Agassi	Michael Stich
1995	Pete Sampras	Andre Agassi
1996	Pete Sampras	Michael Chang
1997	Patrick Rafter	Greg Rusedski
1998	Patrick Rafter	Mark Philippoussis
1999	Andre Agassi	Todd Martin
2000	Marat Safin	Pete Sampras
2001	Lleyton Hewitt	Pete Sampras
2002	Pete Sampras	Andre Agassi
2003	Andy Roddick	Juan Carlos Ferrero
2004	Roger Federer	Lleyton Hewitt
2005	Roger Federer	Andre Agassi
2006	Roger Federer	Andy Roddick
2007	Roger Federer	Novak Djokovic
2008	Roger Federer	Andy Murray
2009	Juan Martin del Potro	Roger Federer
2010	Rafael Nadal	Novak Djokovic
2011	Novak Djokovic	Rafael Nadal
2012	Andy Murray	Novak Djokovic
2013	Rafael Nadal	Novak Djokovic
2014	Marin Cilic	Kei Nishikori
2015	Novak Djokovic	Roger Federer
2016	Stan Wawrinka	Novak Djokovic

Women's Singles

Year	Champion	Final opponent
1925	Helen Willis	Kathleen McKane
1926	Molla B. Mallory	Elizabeth Ryan
1927	Helen Wills	Betty Nuthall
1928	Helen Wills	Helen H. Jacobs
1929	Helen Wills	Phoebe Holcroft-Watson
1930	Betty Nuthall	Anna McCune Harper
1931	Helen Wills Moody	E. B. Whittingstall
1932	Helen H. Jacobs	Carolin A. Babcock
1933	Helen H. Jacobs	Helen Wills Moody
1934	Helen H. Jacobs	Sarah H. Palfrey
1935	Helen H. Jacobs	Sarah Palfrey Fabyan
1936	Alice Marble	Helen H. Jacobs
1937	Anita Lizana	Jadwiga Jedrzejowska
1938	Alice Marble	Nancye Wynne
1939	Alice Marble	Helen H. Jacobs
1940	Alice Marble	Helen H. Jacobs
1941	Sarah Palfrey Cooke	Pauline Betz
1942	Pauline Betz	Louise Brough
1943	Pauline Betz	Louise Brough
1944	Pauline Betz	Margaret Osborne
1945	Sarah Palfrey Cooke	Pauline Betz
1946	Pauline Betz	Patricia Canning
1947	Louise Brough	Margaret Osborne
1948	Margaret Osborne duPont	Louise Brough
1949	Margaret Osborne duPont	Doris Hart
1950	Margaret Osborne duPont	Doris Hart
1951	Maureen Connolly	Shirley Fry
1952	Maureen Connolly	Doris Hart
1953	Maureen Connolly	Doris Hart

Year	Champion	Final opponent	Year	Champion	Final opponent
1954	Doris Hart	Louise Brough	1984	Martina Navratilova	Chris Evert Lloyd
1955	Doris Hart	Patricia Ward	1985	Hana Mandlikova	Martina Navratilova
1956	Shirley Fry	Althea Gibson	1986	Martina Navratilova	Helena Sukova
1957	Althea Gibson	Louise Brough	1987	Martina Navratilova	Steffi Graf
1958	Althea Gibson	Darlene Hard	1988	Steffi Graf	Gabriela Sabatini
1959	Maria Bueno	Christine Truman	1989	Steffi Graf	Martina Navratilova
1960	Darlene Hard	Maria Bueno	1990	Gabriela Sabatini	Steffi Graf
1961	Darlene Hard	Ann Haydon	1991	Monica Seles	Martina Navratilova
1962	Margaret Smith	Darlene Hard	1992	Monica Seles	Arantxa Sánchez Vicario
1963	Maria Bueno	Margaret Smith	1993	Steffi Graf	Helena Sukova
1964	Maria Bueno	Carole Graebner	1994	Arantxa Sánchez Vicario	Steffi Graf
1965	Margaret Smith	Billie Jean Moffitt	1995	Steffi Graf	Monica Seles
1966	Maria Bueno	Nancy Richey	1996	Steffi Graf	Monica Seles
1967	Billie Jean King	Ann Haydon Jones	1997	Martina Hingis	Venus Williams
1968	Virginia Wade	Billie Jean King	1998	Lindsay Davenport	Martina Hingis
1969	Margaret Smith Court	Nancy Richey	1999	Serena Williams	Martina Hingis
1970	Margaret Smith Court	Rosemary Casals	2000	Venus Williams	Lindsay Davenport
1971	Billie Jean King	Rosemary Casals	2001	Venus Williams	Serena Williams
1972	Billie Jean King	Kerry Melville	2002	Serena Williams	Venus Williams
1973	Margaret Smith Court	Evonne Goolagong	2003	Justine Henin-Hardenne	Kim Clijsters
1974	Billie Jean King	Evonne Goolagong	2004	Svetlana Kuznetsova	Elena Dementieva
1975	Chris Evert	Evonne Goolagong Cawley	2005	Kim Clijsters	Mary Pierce
1976	Chris Evert	Evonne Goolagong Cawley	2006	Maria Sharapova	Justine Henin-Hardenne
1977	Chris Evert	Wendy Turnbull	2007	Justine Henin	Svetlana Kuznetsova
1978	Chris Evert	Pam Shriver	2008	Serena Williams	Jelena Jankovic
1979	Tracy Austin	Chris Evert Lloyd	2009	Kim Clijsters	Caroline Wozniacki
1980	Chris Evert Lloyd	Hana Mandlikova	2010	Kim Clijsters	Vera Zvonareva
1981	Tracy Austin	Martina Navratilova	2011	Samantha Stosur	Serena Williams
1982	Chris Evert Lloyd	Hana Mandlikova	2012	Serena Williams	Victoria Azarenka
1983	Martina Navratilova	Chris Evert Lloyd	2013	Serena Williams	Victoria Azarenka
			2014	Serena Williams	Caroline Wozniacki
			2015	Flavia Pennetta	Roberta Vinci
			2016	Angelique Kerber	Karolina Pliskova

Davis Cup, 1950-2015

The Davis Cup began in 1900 as a competition between the U.S. and Great Britain and later expanded to include other countries.

Year	Result	Year	Result	Year	Result
1950	Australia 4, U.S. 1	1972	U.S. 3, Romania 2	1994	Sweden 4, Russia 1
1951	Australia 3, U.S. 2	1973	Australia 5, U.S. 0	1995	U.S. 3, Russia 2
1952	Australia 4, U.S. 1	1974	South Africa (default by India)	1996	France 3, Sweden 2
1953	Australia 3, U.S. 2	1975	Sweden 3, Czechoslovakia 2	1997	Sweden 5, U.S. 0
1954	U.S. 3, Australia 2	1976	Italy 4, Chile 1	1998	Sweden 4, Italy 1
1955	Australia 5, U.S. 0	1977	Australia 3, Italy 1	1999	Australia 3, France 2
1956	Australia 5, U.S. 0	1978	U.S. 4, Great Britain 1	2000	Spain 3, Australia 1
1957	Australia 3, U.S. 2	1979	U.S. 5, Italy 0	2001	France 3, Australia 2
1958	U.S. 3, Australia 2	1980	Czechoslovakia 4, Italy 1	2002	Russia 3, France 2
1959	Australia 3, U.S. 2	1981	U.S. 3, Argentina 1	2003	Australia 3, Spain 1
1960	Australia 4, Italy 1	1982	U.S. 4, France, 1	2004	Spain 3, U.S. 2
1961	Australia 5, Italy 0	1983	Australia 3, Sweden 2	2005	Croatia 3, Slovakia 2
1962	Australia 5, Mexico 0	1984	Sweden 4, U.S. 1	2006	Russia 3, Argentina 2
1963	U.S. 3, Australia 2	1985	Sweden 3, W. Germany 2	2007	U.S. 4, Russia 1
1964	Australia 3, U.S. 2	1986	Australia 3, Sweden 2	2008	Spain 3, Argentina 1
1965	Australia 4, Spain 1	1987	Sweden 5, India 0	2009	Spain 5, Czech Republic 0
1966	Australia 4, India 1	1988	W. Germany 4, Sweden 1	2010	Serbia 3, France 2
1967	Australia 4, Spain 1	1989	W. Germany 4, Sweden 2	2011	Spain 3, Argentina 1
1968	U.S. 4, Australia 1	1990	U.S. 3, Australia 2	2012	Czech Republic 3, Spain 2
1969	U.S. 5, Romania 0	1991	France 3, U.S. 1	2013	Czech Republic 3, Serbia 2
1970	U.S. 5, W. Germany 0	1992	U.S. 3, Switzerland 1	2014	Switzerland 3, France 1
1971	U.S. 3, Romania 2	1993	Germany 4, Australia 1	2015	Great Britain 3, Belgium 1

Note: The challenge round format, which guaranteed the previous year's winner a spot in the finals at home, was eliminated in 1972.

All-Time Grand Slam Singles Titles Leaders

Men	Australian Open	French Open[1]	Wimbledon	U.S. Open	Total
Roger Federer*	2004, '06-'07, '10	2009	2003-07, '09, '12	2004-08	17
Rafael Nadal*	2009	2005-08, '10-'14	2008, '10	2010, '13	14
Pete Sampras	1994, '97	—	1993-95, 1997-2000	1990, '93, '95-'96, 2002	14
Novak Djokovic*	2008, '11-'13, '15-'16	2016	2011, '14-'15	2011, '15	12
Roy Emerson	1961, '63-'67	1963, '67	1964-65	1961, '64	12
Björn Borg	—	1974-75, '78-'81	1976-80	—	11
Rod Laver	1960, '62, '69	1962, '69	1961-62, '68-'69	1962, '69	11
Bill Tilden	—	—	1920-21, '30	1920-25, '29	10
Andre Agassi	1995, 2000, '01, '03	1999	1992	1994, '99	8
Jimmy Connors	1974	—	1974, '82	1974, '76, '78, '82-'83	8
Ivan Lendl	1989-90	1984, '86-'87	—	1985-87	8
Fred Perry	1934	1935	1934-36	1933-34, '36	8
Ken Rosewall	1953, '55, '71-'72	1953, '68	—	1956, '70	8

Women	Australian Open	French Open[1]	Wimbledon	U.S. Open	Total
Margaret Smith Court	1960-66, '69-'71, '73	1962, '64, '69-'70, '73	1963, '65, '70	1962, '65, '69-'70, '73	24
Steffi Graf	1988-90, '94	1987-88, '93, '95-'96, '99	1988-89, '91-'93, '95-'96	1988-89, '93, '95-'96	22
Serena Williams*	2003, '05, '07, '09-'10, '15	2002, '13, '15	2002-03, '09-'10, '12, '15-'16	1999, 2002, '08, '12-'14	22
Helen Wills Moody	—	1928-30, '32	1927-30, '32-'33, '35, '38	1923-25, '27-'29, '31	19
Chris Evert	1982, '84	1974-75, '79-'80, '83, '85-'86	1974, '76, '81	1975-78, '80, '82	18
Martina Navratilova	1981, '83, '85	1982, '84	1978-79, '82-'87, '90	1983-84, '86-'87	18
Billie Jean King	1968	1972	1966-68, '72-'73, '75	1967, '71-'72, '74	12
Suzanne Lenglen	—	1920-23, '25-'26	1919-23, '25	—	12
Maureen Connolly	1953	1953-54	1952-54	1951-53	9
Monica Seles	1991-93, '96	1990-92	—	1991-92	9

* = player active in 2016. (1) Prior to 1925, French Open entry was limited to members of French clubs.

AUTO RACING

Indianapolis 500 Winners, 1911-2016

At Indianapolis Motor Speedway in Indianapolis, IN. Not held 1917-18, 1942-45. * = Race record.

Year	Driver(s), car[1]	Avg. mph	Year	Driver(s), car[1]	Avg. mph
1911	Ray Harroun, Marmon	74.602	1967	A. J. Foyt, Coyote-Ford	151.207
1912	Joe Dawson, National	78.719	1968	Bobby Unser, Eagle-Offy	152.882
1913	Jules Goux, Peugeot	75.933	1969	Mario Andretti, Hawk-Ford	156.867
1914	Rene Thomas, Delage	82.474	1970	Al Unser, P.J. Colt-Ford	155.749
1915	Ralph DePalma, Mercedes	89.840	1971	Al Unser, P.J. Colt-Ford	157.735
1916	Dario Resta, Peugeot	84.001	1972	Mark Donohue, McLaren-Offy	162.962
1919	Howdy Wilcox, Peugeot	88.050	1973	Gordon Johncock, Eagle-Offy	159.036
1920	Gaston Chevrolet, Frontenac	88.618	1974	Johnny Rutherford, McLaren-Offy	158.589
1921	Tommy Milton, Frontenac	89.621	1975	Bobby Unser, Eagle-Offy	149.213
1922	Jimmy Murphy, Duesenberg-Miller	94.484	1976	Johnny Rutherford, McLaren-Offy	148.725
1923	Tommy Milton, Miller	90.954	1977	A. J. Foyt, Coyote-Foyt	161.331
1924	L. L. Corum/Joe Boyer, Duesenberg	98.234	1978	Al Unser, Lola-Cosworth	161.363
1925	Peter DePaolo, Duesenberg	101.127	1979	Rick Mears, Penske-Cosworth	158.899
1926	Frank Lockhart, Miller	95.904	1980	Johnny Rutherford, Chaparral-Cosworth	142.862
1927	George Souders, Duesenberg	97.545	1981	Bobby Unser, Penske-Cosworth	139.184
1928	Louis Meyer, Miller	99.482	1982	Gordon Johncock, Wildcat-Cosworth	162.029
1929	Ray Keech, Miller	97.585	1983	Tom Sneva, March-Cosworth	162.117
1930	Billy Arnold, Summers-Miller	100.448	1984	Rick Mears, March-Cosworth	163.612
1931	Louis Schneider, Stevens-Miller	96.629	1985	Danny Sullivan, March-Cosworth	152.982
1932	Fred Frame, Wetteroth-Miller	104.144	1986	Bobby Rahal, March-Cosworth	170.722
1933	Louis Meyer, Miller	104.162	1987	Al Unser, March-Cosworth	162.175
1934	Bill Cummings, Miller	104.863	1988	Rick Mears, Penske-Chevy Indy V8	144.809
1935	Kelly Petillo, Wetteroth-Offy	106.240	1989	Emerson Fittipaldi, Penske-Chevy Indy V8	167.581
1936	Louis Meyer, Stevens-Miller	109.069	1990	Arie Luyendyk, Lola-Chevy Indy V8	185.981
1937	Wilbur Shaw, Shaw-Offy	113.580	1991	Rick Mears, Penske-Chevy Indy V8	176.457
1938	Floyd Roberts, Wetteroth-Miller	117.200	1992	Al Unser Jr., Galmer-Chevy Indy V8A	134.477
1939	Wilbur Shaw, Maserati	115.035	1993	Emerson Fittipaldi, Penske-Chevy Indy V8C	157.207
1940	Wilbur Shaw, Maserati	114.277	1994	Al Unser Jr., Penske-Mercedes Benz	160.872
1941	Floyd Davis/Mauri Rose, Wetteroth-Offy	115.117	1995	Jacques Villeneuve, Reynard-Ford Cosworth XB	153.616
1946	George Robson, Adams-Sparks	114.820	1996	Buddy Lazier, Reynard-Ford Cosworth XB	147.956
1947	Mauri Rose, Deidt-Offy	116.338	1997	Arie Luyendyk, G Force-Aurora	145.827
1948	Mauri Rose, Deidt-Offy	119.814	1998	Eddie Cheever Jr., Dallara-Aurora	145.155
1949	Bill Holland, Deidt-Offy	121.327	1999	Kenny Brack, Dallara-Aurora	153.176
1950	Johnnie Parsons, Kurtis-Offy	124.002	2000	Juan Pablo Montoya, G Force-Oldsmobile	167.607
1951	Lee Wallard, Kurtis-Offy	126.244	2001	Helio Castroneves, Dallara-Oldsmobile	141.574
1952	Troy Ruttman, Kuzma-Offy	128.922	2002	Helio Castroneves, Dallara-Chevrolet	166.499
1953	Bill Vukovich, KK500A-Offy	127.740	2003	Gil de Ferran, G Force-Toyota	156.291
1954	Bill Vukovich, KK500A-Offy	130.840	2004	Buddy Rice, G Force-Honda	138.518
1955	Bob Sweikert, KK500D-Offy	128.209	2005	Dan Wheldon, Dallara-Honda	157.603
1956	Pat Flaherty, Watson-Offy	128.490	2006	Sam Hornish Jr., Dallara-Honda	157.085
1957	Sam Hanks, Salih-Offy	135.601	2007	Dario Franchitti, Dallara-Honda	151.774
1958	Jimmy Bryan, Salih-Offy	133.791	2008	Scott Dixon, Dallara-Honda	143.567
1959	Rodger Ward, Watson-Offy	135.857	2009	Helio Castroneves, Dallara-Honda	150.318
1960	Jim Rathmann, Watson-Offy	138.767	2010	Dario Franchitti, Dallara-Honda	161.623
1961	A. J. Foyt, Trevis-Offy	139.130	2011	Dan Wheldon, Dallara-Honda	170.265
1962	Rodger Ward, Watson-Offy	140.293	2012	Dario Franchitti, Dallara-Honda	167.734
1963	Parnelli Jones, Watson-Offy	143.137	2013	Tony Kanaan, Dallara-Chevrolet	187.433*
1964	A. J. Foyt, Watson-Offy	147.350	2014	Ryan Hunter-Reay, Dallara-Honda	186.563
1965	Jim Clark, Lotus-Ford	150.686	2015	Juan Pablo Montoya, Dallara-Chevrolet	161.341
1966	Graham Hill, Lola-Ford	144.317	2016	Alexander Rossi, Dallara-Honda	166.634

Note: The race was less than 500 mi in the following years: 1916 (300 mi), 1926 (400 mi), 1950 (345 mi), 1973 (332.5 mi), 1975 (435 mi), 1976 (255 mi), 2004 (450 mi), 2007 (415 mi). (1) Chassis-engine.

IndyCar Series Champions, 1996-2016

A breakaway group of Championship Auto Racing Teams (CART) drivers began the Indy Racing League (IRL) in 1994; it awarded its first championship in 1996. Known as the IndyCar Series in 2003-11 and as IndyCar from 2011 on. Merged with Champ Car World Series, 2008, under the IndyCar name.

Year	Driver	Year	Driver	Year	Driver	Year	Driver	Year	Driver
1996	Scott Sharp; Buzz Calkins (tie)	2000	Buddy Lazier	2005	Dan Wheldon	2009	Dario Franchitti	2013	Scott Dixon
1997	Tony Stewart	2001	Sam Hornish Jr.	2006	Sam Hornish Jr.	2010	Dario Franchitti	2014	Will Power
1998	Kenny Brack	2002	Sam Hornish Jr.	2007	Dario Franchitti	2011	Dario Franchitti	2015	Scott Dixon
1999	Greg Ray	2003	Scott Dixon	2008	Scott Dixon	2012	Ryan Hunter-Reay	2016	Simon Pagenaud
		2004	Tony Kanaan						

Champ Car World Series Winners, 1959-2007

Known as U.S. Auto Club, 1959-78; Championship Auto Racing Teams (CART), 1979-2003; Champ Car World Series, 2004-07. The Vanderbilt Cup became the series championship trophy in 2000. Merged with Indy Racing League (now IndyCar) in 2008.

Year	Driver	Year	Driver	Year	Driver	Year	Driver	Year	Driver
1959	Rodger Ward	1969	Mario Andretti	1979	Rick Mears	1989	Emerson Fittipaldi	1999	Juan Montoya
1960	A. J. Foyt	1970	Al Unser	1980	Johnny Rutherford	1990	Al Unser Jr.	2000	Gil de Ferran
1961	A. J. Foyt	1971	Joe Leonard	1981	Rick Mears	1991	Michael Andretti	2001	Gil de Ferran
1962	Rodger Ward	1972	Joe Leonard	1982	Rick Mears	1992	Bobby Rahal	2002	Cristiano da Matta
1963	A. J. Foyt	1973	Roger McCluskey	1983	Al Unser	1993	Nigel Mansell	2003	Paul Tracy
1964	A. J. Foyt	1974	Bobby Unser	1984	Mario Andretti	1994	Al Unser Jr.	2004	Sébastien Bourdais
1965	Mario Andretti	1975	A. J. Foyt	1985	Al Unser	1995	Jacques Villeneuve	2005	Sébastien Bourdais
1966	Mario Andretti	1976	Gordon Johncock	1986	Bobby Rahal	1996	Jimmy Vasser	2006	Sébastien Bourdais
1967	A. J. Foyt	1977	Tom Sneva	1987	Bobby Rahal	1997	Alex Zanardi	2007	Sébastien Bourdais
1968	Bobby Unser	1978	Tom Sneva	1988	Danny Sullivan	1998	Alex Zanardi		

NASCAR Sprint Cup Series Champions, 1949-2015

Known as Strictly Stock, 1949; Grand National, 1950-70; Winston Cup, 1971-2003; and Sprint Cup, 2004-present.

Year	Driver	Year	Driver	Year	Driver	Year	Driver	Year	Driver
1949	Red Byron	1963	Joe Weatherly	1977	Cale Yarborough	1990	Dale Earnhardt	2003	Matt Kenseth
1950	Bill Rexford	1964	Richard Petty	1978	Cale Yarborough	1991	Dale Earnhardt	2004	Kurt Busch
1951	Herb Thomas	1965	Ned Jarrett	1979	Richard Petty	1992	Alan Kulwicki	2005	Tony Stewart
1952	Tim Flock	1966	David Pearson	1980	Dale Earnhardt	1993	Dale Earnhardt	2006	Jimmie Johnson
1953	Herb Thomas	1967	Richard Petty	1981	Darrell Waltrip	1994	Dale Earnhardt	2007	Jimmie Johnson
1954	Lee Petty	1968	David Pearson	1982	Darrell Waltrip	1995	Jeff Gordon	2008	Jimmie Johnson
1955	Tim Flock	1969	David Pearson	1983	Bobby Allison	1996	Terry Labonte	2009	Jimmie Johnson
1956	Buck Baker	1970	Bobby Isaac	1984	Terry Labonte	1997	Jeff Gordon	2010	Jimmie Johnson
1957	Buck Baker	1971	Richard Petty	1985	Darrell Waltrip	1998	Jeff Gordon	2011	Tony Stewart
1958	Lee Petty	1972	Richard Petty	1986	Dale Earnhardt	1999	Dale Jarrett	2012	Brad Keselowski
1959	Lee Petty	1973	Benny Parsons	1987	Dale Earnhardt	2000	Bobby Labonte	2013	Jimmie Johnson
1960	Rex White	1974	Richard Petty	1988	Bill Elliott	2001	Jeff Gordon	2014	Kevin Harvick
1961	Ned Jarrett	1975	Richard Petty	1989	Rusty Wallace	2002	Tony Stewart	2015	Kyle Busch
1962	Joe Weatherly	1976	Cale Yarborough						

NASCAR Sprint Cup Series Rookie of the Year, 1958-2015

Year	Driver	Year	Driver	Year	Driver	Year	Driver	Year	Driver
1958	Shorty Rollins	1970	Bill Dennis	1982	Geoff Bodine	1994	Jeff Burton	2005	Kyle Busch
1959	Richard Petty	1971	Walter Ballard	1983	Sterling Marlin	1995	Ricky Craven	2006	Denny Hamlin
1960	David Pearson	1972	Larry Smith	1984	Rusty Wallace	1996	Johnny Benson	2007	Juan Montoya
1961	Woodie Wilson	1973	Lennie Pond	1985	Ken Schrader	1997	Mike Skinner	2008	Regan Smith
1962	Tom Cox	1974	Earl Ross	1986	Alan Kulwicki	1998	Kenny Irwin	2009	Joey Logano
1963	Billy Wade	1975	Bruce Hill	1987	Davey Allison	1999	Tony Stewart	2010	Kevin Conway
1964	Doug Cooper	1976	Skip Manning	1988	Ken Bouchard	2000	Matt Kenseth	2011	Andy Lally
1965	Sam McQuagg	1977	Ricky Rudd	1989	Dick Trickle	2001	Kevin Harvick	2012	Stephen Leicht
1966	James Hylton	1978	Ronnie Thomas	1990	Rob Moroso	2002	Ryan Newman	2013	Ricky Stenhouse Jr.
1967	Donnie Allison	1979	Dale Earnhardt	1991	Bobby Hamilton	2003	Jamie McMurray	2014	Kyle Larson
1968	Pete Hamilton	1980	Jody Ridley	1992	Jimmy Hensley	2004	Kasey Kahne	2015	Brett Moffitt
1969	Dick Brooks	1981	Ron Bouchard	1993	Jeff Gordon				

Daytona 500 Winners, 1959-2016

At Daytona International Speedway in Daytona Beach, FL.

Year	Driver, car	Avg. mph	Year	Driver, car	Avg. mph	Year	Driver, car	Avg. mph
1959	Lee Petty, Oldsmobile	135.521	1980	Buddy Baker, Oldsmobile	177.602	2000	Dale Jarrett, Ford	155.669
1960	Junior Johnson, Chevrolet	124.740	1981	Richard Petty, Buick	169.651	2001	Michael Waltrip, Chevrolet	161.783
1961	Marvin Panch, Pontiac	149.601	1982	Bobby Allison, Buick	153.991	2002	Ward Burton, Dodge	142.971
1962	Fireball Roberts, Pontiac	152.529	1983	Cale Yarborough, Pontiac	155.979	2003	Michael Waltrip, Chevrolet	133.870
1963	Tiny Lund, Ford	151.566	1984	Cale Yarborough, Chevrolet	150.994	2004	Dale Earnhardt Jr., Chevrolet	156.345
1964	Richard Petty, Plymouth	154.334	1985	Bill Elliott, Ford	172.265	2005	Jeff Gordon, Chevrolet	135.173
1965	Fred Lorenzen, Ford	141.539	1986	Geoff Bodine, Chevrolet	148.124	2006	Jimmie Johnson, Chevrolet	142.667
1966	Richard Petty, Plymouth	160.627	1987	Bill Elliott, Ford	176.263	2007	Kevin Harvick, Chevrolet	149.335
1967	Mario Andretti, Ford	146.926	1988	Bobby Allison, Buick	137.531	2008	Ryan Newman, Dodge	152.672
1968	Cale Yarborough, Mercury	143.251	1989	Darrell Waltrip, Chevrolet	148.466	2009	Matt Kenseth, Ford	132.816
1969	LeeRoy Yarbrough, Ford	157.950	1990	Derrike Cope, Chevrolet	165.761	2010	Jamie McMurray, Chevrolet	137.284
1970	Pete Hamilton, Plymouth	149.601	1991	Ernie Irvan, Chevrolet	148.148	2011	Trevor Bayne, Ford	130.326
1971	Richard Petty, Plymouth	144.462	1992	Davey Allison, Ford	160.256	2012	Matt Kenseth, Ford	140.256
1972	A. J. Foyt, Mercury	161.550	1993	Dale Jarrett, Chevrolet	154.972	2013	Jimmie Johnson, Chevrolet	159.250
1973	Richard Petty, Dodge	157.205	1994	Sterling Marlin, Chevrolet	156.931	2014	Dale Earnhardt Jr., Chevrolet	145.290
1974	Richard Petty, Dodge	140.894	1995	Sterling Marlin, Chevrolet	141.710	2015	Joey Logano, Ford	161.939
1975	Benny Parsons, Chevrolet	153.649	1996	Dale Jarrett, Ford	154.308	2016	Denny Hamlin, Toyota	157.549
1976	David Pearson, Mercury	152.181	1997	Jeff Gordon, Chevrolet	148.295			
1977	Cale Yarborough, Chevrolet	153.218	1998	Dale Earnhardt, Chevrolet	172.712			
1978	Bobby Allison, Ford	159.730	1999	Jeff Gordon, Chevrolet	161.551			
1979	Richard Petty, Oldsmobile	143.977						

Note: The race was less than 500 mi in the following years: 1965 (332.5 mi), 1966 (495 mi), 1974 (450 mi), 2003 (272.5 mi), 2009 (380 mi).

Coca-Cola 600 Winners, 1960-2016

At Charlotte Motor Speedway in Concord, NC. Known as the World 600, 1960-85. * = Rain-shortened.

Year	Driver, car	Avg. mph	Year	Driver, car	Avg. mph	Year	Driver, car	Avg. mph
1960	Joe Lee Johnson, Chevrolet	107.735	1978	Darrell Waltrip, Chevrolet	138.355	1997	Jeff Gordon, Chevrolet	136.745*
1961	David Pearson, Pontiac	111.633	1979	Darrell Waltrip, Chevrolet	136.674	1998	Jeff Gordon, Chevrolet	136.424
1962	Nelson Stacy, Ford	125.552	1980	Benny Parsons, Chevrolet	119.265	1999	Jeff Burton, Ford	151.367
1963	Fred Lorenzen, Ford	132.418	1981	Bobby Allison, Buick	129.326	2000	Matt Kenseth, Ford	142.640
1964	Jim Paschal, Plymouth	125.772	1982	Neil Bonnett, Ford	130.058	2001	Jeff Burton, Ford	138.107
1965	Fred Lorenzen, Ford	121.722	1983	Neil Bonnett, Ford	140.707	2002	Mark Martin, Ford	137.729
1966	Marvin Panch, Plymouth	135.042	1984	Bobby Allison, Buick	129.233	2003	Jimmie Johnson, Chevrolet	126.198*
1967	Jim Paschal, Plymouth	135.832	1985	Darrell Waltrip, Chevrolet	141.807	2004	Jimmie Johnson, Chevrolet	142.763
1968	Buddy Baker, Dodge	104.207*	1986	Dale Earnhardt, Chevrolet	140.406	2005	Jimmie Johnson, Chevrolet	114.698
1969	LeeRoy Yarbrough, Mercury	134.361	1987	Kyle Petty, Ford	131.483	2006	Kasey Kahne, Dodge	128.840
1970	Donnie Allison, Ford	129.680	1988	Darrell Waltrip, Chevrolet	124.460	2007	Casey Mears, Chevrolet	130.222
1971	Bobby Allison, Mercury	140.422	1989	Darrell Waltrip, Chevrolet	144.077	2008	Kasey Kahne, Dodge	135.772
1972	Buddy Baker, Dodge	142.255	1990	Rusty Wallace, Pontiac	137.650	2009	David Reutimann, Toyota	120.899*
1973	Buddy Baker, Dodge	134.890	1991	Davey Allison, Ford	138.951	2010	Kurt Busch, Dodge	144.966
1974	David Pearson, Mercury	135.720	1992	Dale Earnhardt, Chevrolet	132.980	2011	Kevin Harvick, Chevrolet	132.414
1975	Richard Petty, Dodge	145.327	1993	Dale Earnhardt, Chevrolet	145.504	2012	Kasey Kahne, Chevrolet	155.687
1976	David Pearson, Mercury	137.352	1994	Jeff Gordon, Chevrolet	139.445	2013	Kevin Harvick, Chevrolet	130.521
1977	Richard Petty, Dodge	137.676	1995	Bobby Labonte, Chevrolet	151.952	2014	Jimmie Johnson, Chevrolet	145.484
			1996	Dale Jarrett, Ford	147.581	2015	Carl Edwards, Toyota	147.803
						2016	Martin Truex Jr., Toyota	160.655

Brickyard 400 Winners, 1994-2016

At Indianapolis Motor Speedway in Indianapolis, IN.

Year	Driver, car	Avg. mph	Year	Driver, car	Avg. mph	Year	Driver, car	Avg. mph
1994	Jeff Gordon, Chevrolet	131.977	2002	Bill Elliott, Dodge	125.033	2010	Jamie McMurray, Chevrolet	136.054
1995	Dale Earnhardt, Chevrolet	155.206	2003	Kevin Harvick, Chevrolet	134.554	2011	Paul Menard, Chevrolet	140.762
1996	Dale Jarrett, Ford	139.508	2004	Jeff Gordon, Chevrolet	115.037	2012	Jimmie Johnson, Chevrolet	137.680
1997	Ricky Rudd, Ford	130.814	2005	Tony Stewart, Chevrolet	118.782	2013	Ryan Newman, Chevrolet	153.485
1998	Jeff Gordon, Chevrolet	126.772	2006	Jimmie Johnson, Chevrolet	137.182	2014	Jeff Gordon, Chevrolet	150.297
1999	Dale Jarrett, Ford	148.194	2007	Tony Stewart, Chevrolet	117.379	2015	Kyle Busch, Toyota	131.656
2000	Bobby Labonte, Pontiac	155.912	2008	Jimmie Johnson, Chevrolet	115.117	2016	Kyle Busch, Toyota	128.940
2001	Jeff Gordon, Chevrolet	130.790	2009	Jimmie Johnson, Chevrolet	145.882			

Bass Pro Shops NRA Night Race Winners, 1961-2016

At Bristol Motor Speedway in Bristol, TN. Known as the Volunteer 500, 1961-75, '78-'79; Volunteer 400, 1976-77; Busch 500, 1980-90; Bud 500, 1991-93; Goody's 500, 1994-99; goracing.com 500, 2000; Sharpie 500, 2001-09; Irwin Tools, 2010-15. * = Rain-shortened.

Year	Driver, car	Avg. mph	Year	Driver, car	Avg. mph	Year	Driver, car	Avg. mph
1961	Jack Smith, Pontiac	68.373	1980	Cale Yarborough, Chevrolet	86.973	1999	Dale Earnhardt, Chevrolet	91.276
1962	Bobby Johns, Pontiac	73.320	1981	Darrell Waltrip, Buick	84.723	2000	Rusty Wallace, Ford	85.394
1963	Fred Lorenzen, Ford	74.844	1982	Darrell Waltrip, Buick	94.318	2001	Tony Stewart, Pontiac	85.106
1964	Fred Lorenzen, Ford	78.044	1983	Darrell Waltrip, Chevrolet	89.430*	2002	Jeff Gordon, Chevrolet	77.097
1965	Ned Jarrett, Ford	61.826	1984	Terry Labonte, Chevrolet	85.365	2003	Kurt Busch, Ford	77.421
1966	Paul Goldsmith, Plymouth	77.963	1985	Dale Earnhardt, Chevrolet	81.388	2004	Dale Earnhardt Jr.,	
1967	Richard Petty, Plymouth	78.705	1986	Darrell Waltrip, Chevrolet	86.934		Chevrolet	88.538
1968	David Pearson, Ford	76.310	1987	Dale Earnhardt, Chevrolet	90.373	2005	Matt Kenseth, Ford	84.678
1969	David Pearson, Ford	79.737	1988	Dale Earnhardt, Chevrolet	78.775	2006	Matt Kenseth, Ford	90.025
1970	Bobby Allison, Dodge	84.880	1989	Darrell Waltrip, Chevrolet	85.554	2007	Carl Edwards, Ford	89.006
1971	Charlie Glotzbach,		1990	Ernie Irvan, Chevrolet	91.782	2008	Carl Edwards, Ford	91.581
	Chevrolet	101.074	1991	Alan Kulwicki, Ford	82.028	2009	Kyle Busch, Toyota	84.820
1972	Bobby Allison, Chevrolet	92.735	1992	Darrell Waltrip, Chevrolet	91.198	2010	Kyle Busch, Toyota	99.071
1973	Benny Parsons, Chevrolet	91.342	1993	Mark Martin, Ford	88.172	2011	Brad Keselowski, Dodge	96.753
1974	Cale Yarborough, Chevrolet	75.430	1994	Rusty Wallace, Ford	91.363	2012	Denny Hamlin, Ford	84.402
1975	Richard Petty, Dodge	97.016	1995	Terry Labonte, Chevrolet	81.979	2013	Matt Kenseth, Toyota	90.279
1976	Cale Yarborough, Chevrolet	99.175	1996	Rusty Wallace, Ford	91.267	2014	Joey Logano, Ford	92.965
1977	Cale Yarborough, Chevrolet	79.726	1997	Dale Jarrett, Ford	80.013	2015	Joey Logano, Ford	96.890
1978	Cale Yarborough, Olds.	88.628	1998	Mark Martin, Ford	86.949	2016	Kevin Harvick, Chevrolet	77.968
1979	Darrell Waltrip, Chevrolet	91.493						

NASCAR Sprint All-Star Race Winners, 1985-2016

At Charlotte Motor Speedway in Concord, NC. Known as The Winston, 1985-93, 1997-2003; The Winston Select, 1994-96; and Nextel All-Star Challenge, 2004-07.

Year	Driver, car	Year	Driver, car	Year	Driver, car
1985	Darrell Waltrip, Chevrolet	1996	Michael Waltrip, Ford	2007	Kevin Harvick, Chevrolet
1986	Bill Elliott, Ford	1997	Jeff Gordon, Chevrolet	2008	Kasey Kahne, Dodge
1987	Dale Earnhardt, Chevrolet	1998	Mark Martin, Ford	2009	Tony Stewart, Chevrolet
1988	Terry Labonte, Chevrolet	1999	Terry Labonte, Chevrolet	2010	Kurt Busch, Dodge
1989	Rusty Wallace, Pontiac	2000	Dale Earnhardt Jr., Chevrolet	2011	Carl Edwards, Ford
1990	Dale Earnhardt, Chevrolet	2001	Jeff Gordon, Chevrolet	2012	Jimmie Johnson, Chevrolet
1991	Davey Allison, Ford	2002	Ryan Newman, Ford	2013	Jimmie Johnson, Chevrolet
1992	Davey Allison, Ford	2003	Jimmie Johnson, Chevrolet	2014	Jamie McMurray, Chevrolet
1993	Dale Earnhardt, Chevrolet	2004	Matt Kenseth, Ford	2015	Denny Hamlin, Toyota
1994	Geoffrey Bodine, Ford	2005	Mark Martin, Ford	2016	Joey Logano, Ford
1995	Jeff Gordon, Chevrolet	2006	Jimmie Johnson, Chevrolet		

Formula One World Drivers' Champions, 1950-2015

Awarded by the Fédération Internationale de l'Automobile (FIA); champions determined through a series of Grand Prix races.

Year	Driver, country	Year	Driver, country	Year	Driver, country
1950	Giuseppe "Nino" Farina, Italy	1972	Emerson Fittipaldi, Brazil	1994	Michael Schumacher, Germany
1951	Juan Manuel Fangio, Argentina	1973	Jackie Stewart, Scotland, UK	1995	Michael Schumacher, Germany
1952	Alberto Ascari, Italy	1974	Emerson Fittipaldi, Brazil	1996	Damon Hill, England, UK
1953	Alberto Ascari, Italy	1975	Niki Lauda, Austria	1997	Jacques Villeneuve, Canada
1954	Juan Manuel Fangio, Argentina	1976	James Hunt, England, UK	1998	Mika Hakkinen, Finland
1955	Juan Manuel Fangio, Argentina	1977	Niki Lauda, Austria	1999	Mika Hakkinen, Finland
1956	Juan Manuel Fangio, Argentina	1978	Mario Andretti, United States	2000	Michael Schumacher, Germany
1957	Juan Manuel Fangio, Argentina	1979	Jody Scheckter, South Africa	2001	Michael Schumacher, Germany
1958	Mike Hawthorn, England, UK	1980	Alan Jones, Australia	2002	Michael Schumacher, Germany
1959	Jack Brabham, Australia	1981	Nelson Piquet, Brazil	2003	Michael Schumacher, Germany
1960	Jack Brabham, Australia	1982	Keke Rosberg, Finland	2004	Michael Schumacher, Germany
1961	Phil Hill, United States	1983	Nelson Piquet, Brazil	2005	Fernando Alonso, Spain
1962	Graham Hill, England, UK	1984	Niki Lauda, Austria	2006	Fernando Alonso, Spain
1963	Jim Clark, Scotland, UK	1985	Alain Prost, France	2007	Kimi Raikkonen, Finland
1964	John Surtees, England, UK	1986	Alain Prost, France	2008	Lewis Hamilton, England, UK
1965	Jim Clark, Scotland, UK	1987	Nelson Piquet, Brazil	2009	Jenson Button, England, UK
1966	Jack Brabham, Australia	1988	Ayrton Senna, Brazil	2010	Sebastian Vettel, Germany
1967	Denis Hulme, New Zealand	1989	Alain Prost, France	2011	Sebastian Vettel, Germany
1968	Graham Hill, England, UK	1990	Ayrton Senna, Brazil	2012	Sebastian Vettel, Germany
1969	Jackie Stewart, Scotland, UK	1991	Ayrton Senna, Brazil	2013	Sebastian Vettel, Germany
1970	Jochen Rindt, Austria	1992	Nigel Mansell, England, UK	2014	Lewis Hamilton, England, UK
1971	Jackie Stewart, Scotland, UK	1993	Alain Prost, France	2015	Lewis Hamilton, England, UK

24 Hours of Le Mans Race, 2016

Porsche unexpectedly won the 84th running of the 24 Hours of Le Mans at Circuit de la Sarthe in Le Mans, France, June 18-19, 2016. The No. 5 Toyota TS050-Hybrid led the race with one lap left when the car, driven by Kazuki Nakajima of Japan, stopped after reporting a loss of power. The No. 5 Toyota restarted but took longer than the maximum six minutes to complete the lap so it was officially listed as not classified and missed the podium. The surprising incident resulted in a record 18th victory for Porsche. Driving the No 2. Porsche 919 Hybrid, France's Romain Dumas, Neel Jani of Switzerland, and Germany's Marc Lieb completed 384 laps. The No. 6 Toyota TS050-Hybrid finished second, and the No. 8 Audi R18 took third.

BOXING

There are many boxing governing bodies, including the World Boxing Assn. (WBA; known as the National Boxing Assn. [NBA] until 1962), World Boxing Council (WBC), International Boxing Fed. (IBF), World Boxing Org., U.S. Boxing Assn., N. American Boxing Fed., and European Boxing Union. All have their own champions and divisions.

Boxing Champions by Class

Class (weight limit)	WBA Champion	WBC Champion	IBF Champion
Heavyweight (none)	Vacant	Deontay Wilder, U.S.	Anthony Joshua, UK
Cruiserweight (200 lbs)	Denis Lebedev, Russia[1] Beibut Shumenov, Kazakhstan Yunier Dorticos, Cuba[2]	Tony Bellew, UK	Denis Lebedev, Russia
Light Heavyweight (175 lbs)	Sergey Kovalev, Russia[1] Nathan Cleverly, UK Dmitry Bivol, Russia[2]	Adonis Stevenson, Canada	Sergey Kovalev, Russia
Super Middleweight (168 lbs)	Felix Sturm, Germany[1] Giovanni De Carolis, Italy	Badou Jack, Sweden	James DeGale, UK
Middleweight (160 lbs)	Gennady Golovkin, Kazakhstan[1] Daniel Jacobs, U.S. Alfonso Blanco, Venezuela[2]	Gennady Golovkin, Kazakhstan	Gennady Golovkin, Kazakhstan
Super Welterweight/ Jr. Middleweight (154 lbs)	Erislandy Lara, Cuba[1] Jack Culcay, Germany	Jermell Charlo, U.S.	Jermall Charlo, U.S.
Welterweight (147 lbs)	Keith Thurman, U.S. David Avanesyan, Russia[2]	Danny Garcia, U.S.	Kell Brook, UK
Super Lightweight/ Jr. Welterweight (140 lbs)	Ricky Burns, UK	Terence Crawford, U.S.	Eduard Troyanovsky, Russia
Lightweight (135 lbs)	Jorge Linares, Venezuela	Dejan Zlaticanin, Montenegro	Robert Easter Jr., U.S.
Super Featherweight/ Jr. Lightweight (130 lbs)	Jezreel Corrales, Panama[1] Jason Sosa, U.S.	Francisco Vargas, Mexico	Jose Pedraza, U.S.
Featherweight (126 lbs)	Carl Frampton, UK[1] Jesus Andres Cuellar, Argentina Carlos Zambrano, Peru[2]	Gary Russell Jr., U.S. Oscar Escandon, Colombia[2]	Lee Selby, Wales
Super Bantamweight/ Jr. Featherweight (122 lbs)	Guillermo Rigondeaux, Cuba[1] Nehomar Cermeño, Venezuela Moises Flores, Mexico[2]	Hozumi Hasegawa, Japan	Jonathan Guzman, Dominican Republic
Bantamweight (118 lbs)	Rau'shee Warren, U.S.[1] Jamie McDonnell, UK Zhanat Zhakiyanov, Kazakhstan[2]	Shinsuke Yamanaka, Japan	Lee Haskins, UK
Super Flyweight/ Jr. Bantamweight (115 lbs)	Luis Concepcion, Panama	Roman Gonzalez, Nicaragua	Jerwin Ancajas, Philippines
Flyweight (112 lbs)	Kazuto Ioka, Japan Stamp Kiatniwat, Thailand[2]	Vacant	John Riel Casimero, Philippines
Jr. Flyweight (108 lbs)	Ryoichi Taguchi, Japan	Ganigan Lopez, Mexico	Akira Yaegashi, Japan
Strawweight/ Mini Flyweight (105 lbs)	Knockout CP Freshmart, Thailand	Wanheng Menayothin, Thailand	Jose Argumedo, Mexico

Note: As of Oct. 19, 2016. (1) Super champion. (2) Interim champion.

Ring Champions by Years

* = Abandoned/relinquished the title or was stripped of it. IBF champions listed only for heavyweight division. International Boxing Hall of Fame inductees in *italics*. For years with multiple champions, boxers are listed according to date of earliest title bout.

Heavyweights

1882-92	*John L. Sullivan*[1]	1978-79	*Muhammad Ali* (WBA*)[5]	1996	*Mike Tyson* (WBA/WBC*)
1892-97	*James J. Corbett*[2]	1978-83	*Larry Holmes* (WBC*)[6]	1996-97	Michael Moorer (IBF)
1897-99	*Bob Fitzsimmons*	1979-80	John Tate (WBA)	1996-99	Evander Holyfield (WBA/IBF)
1899-1905	*James J. Jeffries*[3]	1980-82	Mike Weaver (WBA)	1997-99	Lennox Lewis (WBC)
1905-06	Marvin Hart	1982-83	Michael Dokes (WBA)	1999-2001	*Lennox Lewis* (WBA*/WBC/IBF)
1906-08	*Tommy Burns*	1983-84	Gerrie Coetzee (WBA)	2000-01	Evander Holyfield (WBA)
1908-15	*Jack Johnson*	1983-85	*Larry Holmes* (IBF)[6]	2001-03	John Ruiz (WBA)
1915-19	*Jess Willard*	1984	Tim Witherspoon (WBC)	2001	Hasim Rahman (WBC/IBF)
1919-26	*Jack Dempsey*	1984-86	Pinklon Thomas (WBC)	2001-02	*Lennox Lewis* (IBF*)
1926-28	*Gene Tunney*[*]	1984-85	Greg Page (WBA)	2001-04	*Lennox Lewis* (WBC)
1928-30	Vacant	1985-86	Tony Tubbs (WBA)	2002-06	Chris Byrd (IBF)
1930-32	*Max Schmeling*	1985-87	*Michael Spinks* (IBF*)	2003	Roy Jones Jr. (WBA*)
1932-33	*Jack Sharkey*	1986	Tim Witherspoon (WBA);	2004-05	John Ruiz (WBA)[7];
1933-34	Primo Carnera		Trevor Berbick (WBC)		Vitali Klitschko (WBC*)
1934-35	*Max Baer*	1986-87	*Mike Tyson* (WBC); James	2005-06	Hasim Rahman (WBC)
1935-37	*James J. Braddock*		"Bonecrusher" Smith (WBA)	2005-07	Nicolai Valuev (WBA)
1937-49	*Joe Louis*[*]	1987	Tony Tucker (IBF)	2006-15	Wladimir Klitschko (IBF)
1949-51	*Ezzard Charles*	1987-90	*Mike Tyson* (WBA/WBC/IBF)	2006-08	Oleg Maskaev (WBC)
1951-52	*Joe Walcott*	1990	James "Buster" Douglas	2007-08	Ruslan Chagaev (WBA)
1952-56	*Rocky Marciano*[*]		(WBA/WBC/IBF)	2008	Samuel Peter (WBC)
1956-59	*Floyd Patterson*	1990-92	Evander Holyfield	2008-09	Nikolai Valuev (WBA)
1959-60	*Ingemar Johansson*		(WBA/WBC/IBF)	2008-13	Vitali Klitschko (WBC)
1960-62	*Floyd Patterson*	1992-93	*Riddick Bowe* (WBA/WBC*/IBF)	2009-11	David Haye (WBA)
1962-64	*Sonny Liston*	1992-94	Lennox Lewis (WBC)	2011-15	Wladimir Klitschko (WBA)
1964-67	*Cassius Clay (Muhammad Ali)*[*4]	1993-94	Evander Holyfield (WBA/IBF)	2014-15	Bermane Stiverne (WBC)
1968-70	*Jimmy Ellis*[4]	1994	Michael Moorer (WBA/IBF)	2015-	Deontay Wilder (WBC)
1970-73	*Joe Frazier*	1994-95	Oliver McCall (WBC)	2015-16	Tyson Fury (WBA*)
1973-74	*George Foreman*	1995	George Foreman (WBA*/IBF*)	2015	Tyson Fury (IBF*)
1974-78	*Muhammad Ali*	1995-96	Bruce Seldon (WBA);	2016	Charles Martin (IBF)
1978	Leon Spinks (WBA/WBC*)[5];		Frank Bruno (WBC)	2016-	Anthony Joshua (IBF)
	Ken Norton (WBC)	1995	Frans Botha (IBF*)		

(1) London Prize Ring (bare-knuckle champion). (2) First Marquis of Queensberry champion. (3) Jeffries vacated title (1905) and designated Marvin Hart and Jack Root as logical contenders. Hart def. Root in 12 rounds (1905); in turn was def. by Tommy Burns (1906), who claimed the title. Jack Johnson def. Burns (1908) and was recognized as champ. Johnson won the title by defeating Jeffries in the latter's attempted comeback (1910). (4) Title declared vacant by the WBA and others in 1967 after Ali refused military induction for religious reasons during the Vietnam War. Joe Frazier recognized as champ by six states, Mexico, and S. America. Jimmy Ellis won a tournament for the WBA title. (5) After Spinks beat Ali for the WBA title, the WBC recognized Ken Norton as champ. Ali def. Spinks in 1978 rematch for WBA title and retired in 1979. (6) Relinquished WBC title in Dec. 1983 to fight as champ of the new IBF. (7) James Toney def. Ruiz Apr. 30, 2005, to claim the title, but it was rescinded when Toney tested positive for steroids.

Light Heavyweights

Years	Champion	Years	Champion	Years	Champion
1903	Jack Root; George Gardner	1978	Mate Parlov (WBC)	1995-96	Fabrice Tiozzo (WBC*)
1903-05	Bob Fitzsimmons	1978-79	Mike Rossman (WBA);	1996-97	Roy Jones Jr. (WBC)
1905-12	Philadelphia Jack O'Brien*		Marvin Johnson (WBC)	1997	Montell Griffin (WBC);
1912-16	Jack Dillon	1979	Victor Galindez (WBA)		Darius Michalczewski (WBA*);
1916-20	Battling Levinsky	1979-81	Matthew Saad Muhammad (WBC)		Roy Jones Jr. (WBC)
1920-22	Georges Carpentier	1979-80	Marvin Johnson (WBA)	1997-98	Lou Del Valle (WBA)
1922-23	Battling Siki	1980-81	Eddie Mustafa Muhammad (WBA)	1998-2003	Roy Jones Jr. (WBA*/WBC*)
1923-25	Mike McTigue	1981-85	Michael Spinks (WBA)	2003	Mehdi Sahnoune (WBA);
1925-26	Paul Berlenbach	1981-83	Dwight Muhammed-Qawi Braxton (WBC)		Silvio Branco (WBA);
1926-27	Jack Delaney*	1983-85	Michael Spinks (WBC*)		Antonio Tarver (WBC)
1927-29	Tommy Loughran*	1985-86	J. B. Williamson (WBC)	2003-04	Roy Jones Jr. (WBA/WBC*)
1930-34	Maxie Rosenbloom	1986-87	Marvin Johnson (WBA);	2004	Antonio Tarver (WBA/WBC*)
1934-35	Bob Olin		Dennis Andries (WBC)	2004-06	Fabrice Tiozzo (WBA)
1935-39	John Henry Lewis*	1987	Thomas Hearns (WBC*)	2005-07	Tomasz Adamek (WBC)
1939	Melio Bettina	1987	Leslie Stewart (WBA)	2006-07	Silvio Branco (WBA)
1939-41	Billy Conn*	1987-91	Virgil Hill (WBA)	2007-08	Chad Dawson (WBC)
1941	Anton Christoforidis (NBA)	1987-88	Don Lalonde (WBC)	2007	Stipe Drews (WBA);
1941-48	Gus Lesnevich	1988	Sugar Ray Leonard (WBC*)		Danny Green (WBA)
1948-50	Freddie Mills	1989	Dennis Andries (WBC)	2008-09	Hugo Hernan Garay (WBA);
1950-52	Joey Maxim	1989-90	Jeff Harding (WBC)		Adrian Diaconu (WBC)
1952-62	Archie Moore	1990-91	Dennis Andries (WBC)	2009-11	Jean Pascal (WBC)
1962-63	Harold Johnson	1991-92	Thomas Hearns (WBA)	2009-10	Gabriel Campillo (WBA)
1963-65	Willie Pastrano	1991-94	Jeff Harding (WBC)	2010-14	Beibut Shumenov (WBA)
1965-66	Jose Torres	1992	Iran Barkley (WBA*)	2011-12	Bernard Hopkins (WBC)
1966-68	Dick Tiger	1992-97	Virgil Hill (WBA)	2012-13	Chad Dawson (WBC)
1968-74	Bob Foster*	1994-95	Mike McCallum (WBC)	2013-	Adonis Stevenson (WBC)
1974-77	John Conteh (WBC)			2014	Bernard Hopkins (WBA)
1974-78	Victor Galindez (WBA)			2014-	Sergey Kovalev (WBA)
1977-78	Miguel Cuello (WBC)				

Middleweights

Years	Champion	Years	Champion	Years	Champion
1884-91	Jack "Nonpareil" Dempsey	1958	"Sugar" Ray Robinson	1992-93	Reggie Johnson (WBA)
1891-97	Bob Fitzsimmons*	1959	Gene Fullmer (NBA);	1993-95	Gerald McClellan (WBC*)
1897-1907	Tommy Ryan*		"Sugar" Ray Robinson (NY)	1993-94	John David Jackson (WBA)
1907-08	Stanley Ketchel; Billy Papke	1960	Gene Fullmer (NBA);	1994-95	Jorge Castro (WBA)
1908-10	Stanley Ketchel		Paul Pender (NY/MA)	1995	Julian Jackson (WBC)
1911-13	Vacant	1961	Gene Fullmer (NBA);	1995-96	Quincy Taylor (WBC);
1913	Frank Klaus; George Chip		Terry Downes (NY/MA/Europe)		Shinji Takehara (WBA)
1914-17	Al McCoy	1962	Gene Fullmer;	1996-98	Keith Holmes (WBC)
1917-20	Mike O'Dowd		Paul Pender (NY/MA*);	1996-97	William Joppy (WBA)
1920-23	Johnny Wilson		Dick Tiger (NBA)	1997	Julio Cesar Green (WBA)
1923-26	Harry Greb	1963	Dick Tiger (universal)	1998-2001	William Joppy (WBA)
1926	Theodore "Tiger" Flowers	1963-65	Joey Giardello	1998-99	Hassine Cherifi (WBC)
1926-31	Mickey Walker	1965-66	Dick Tiger	1999-2001	Keith Holmes (WBC)
1931-32	William "Gorilla" Jones (NBA)	1966-67	Emile Griffith	2001	Felix Trinidad (WBA)
1932-37	Marcel Thil	1967	Nino Benvenuti	2001-05	Bernard Hopkins (WBC/WBA)
1938	Al Hostak (NBA);	1967-68	Emile Griffith	2005-06	Jermain Taylor (WBA)
	Solly Krieger (NBA)	1968-70	Nino Benvenuti	2005-07	Jermain Taylor (WBC)
1939-40	Al Hostak (NBA)	1970-77	Carlos Monzon*	2006-07	Javier Castillejo (WBA)[1]
1940-47	Tony Zale	1977-78	Rodrigo Valdez	2007-12	Felix Sturm (WBA)
1947-48	Rocky Graziano	1978-79	Hugo Corro	2007-10	Kelly Pavlik (WBC)
1948	Tony Zale; Marcel Cerdan	1979-80	Vito Antuofermo	2009-11	Sebastian Zbik (WBC)
1949-51	Jake LaMotta	1980	Alan Minter	2010	Sergio Martinez (WBC)
1951	"Sugar" Ray Robinson;	1980-87	"Marvelous" Marvin Hagler	2011-12	Julio Cesar Chavez Jr. (WBC)
	Randy Turpin	1987	Sugar Ray Leonard (WBC*)	2012	Daniel Geale (WBA*)
1951-52	"Sugar" Ray Robinson*	1987-89	Sumbu Kalambay (WBA)	2012-14	Sergio Martinez (WBC)
1953-55	Carl "Bobo" Olson	1987-88	Thomas Hearns (WBC)	2012-	Gennady Golovkin (WBA)
1955-57	"Sugar" Ray Robinson	1988-89	Iran Barkley (WBC)	2014-15	Miguel Cotto (WBC)
1957	Gene Fullmer;	1989-90	Roberto Duran (WBC*)	2015-16	Saul Alvarez (WBC*)
	"Sugar" Ray Robinson	1989-90	Mike McCallum (WBA)	2016-	Gennady Golovkin (WBC)
1957-58	Carmen Basilio	1990-93	Julian Jackson (WBC)		

(1) Castillejo lost title to Mariano Carrera Dec. 2, 2006, but regained it Feb. 23, 2007, after Carrera tested positive for steroids.

Welterweights

Years	Champion	Years	Champion	Years	Champion
1892-94	"Mysterious" Billy Smith	1933	Young Corbett III;	1966-69	Curtis Cokes
1894-96	Tommy Ryan		Jimmy McLarnin	1969-70	Jose Napoles
1896	Kid McCoy*	1934	Barney Ross;	1970-71	Billy Backus
1900	Rube Ferns;		Jimmy McLarnin	1971-75	Jose Napoles
	Matty Matthews	1935-38	Barney Ross	1975-76	Angel Espada (WBA);
1901	Rube Ferns	1938-40	Henry Armstrong		John Stracey (WBC)
1901-04	Joe Walcott	1940-41	Fritzie Zivic	1976-79	Carlos Palomino (WBC)
1904-06	Dixie Kid; Joe Walcott	1941-46	Fred Cochrane	1976-80	Jose "Pipino" Cuevas (WBA)
1906	William "Honey" Mellody	1946	Marty Servo*	1979	Wilfred Benitez (WBC)
1907-11	Mike Sullivan	1946-51	"Sugar" Ray Robinson*[1]	1979-80	Sugar Ray Leonard (WBC)
1911-15	Vacant	1951	Johnny Bratton (NBA)	1980	Roberto Duran (WBC)
1915-16	Ted Lewis	1951-54	Kid Gavilan	1980-81	Thomas Hearns (WBA)
1916-17	Jack Britton	1954-55	Johnny Saxton	1980-82	Sugar Ray Leonard (WBC*/WBA*)
1917-19	Ted Lewis	1955	Tony De Marco	1983-85	Donald Curry (WBA);
1919-22	Jack Britton	1955-56	Carmen Basilio		Milton McCrory (WBC)
1922-26	Mickey Walker	1956	Johnny Saxton	1985-86	Donald Curry (WBC)
1926-27	Pete Latzo	1956-57	Carmen Basilio*	1986-87	Lloyd Honeyghan (WBC)
1927-29	Joe Dundee	1958	Virgil Akins	1987	Mark Breland (WBA)
1929-30	Jackie Fields	1958-60	Don Jordan	1987-88	Marlon Starling (WBA);
1930	Jack Thompson;	1960-61	Benny Paret		Jorge Vaca (WBC)
	Tommy Freeman	1961	Emile Griffith	1988-89	Tomas Molinares (WBA*);
1931	Tommy Freeman;	1961-62	Benny Paret		Lloyd Honeyghan (WBC)
	Jack Thompson;	1962-63	Emile Griffith	1989-90	Marlon Starling (WBC);
	Lou Brouillard	1963	Luis Rodriguez		Mark Breland (WBA)
1932	Jackie Fields	1963-66	Emile Griffith*		

1990-91	Maurice Blocker (WBC);	2000	*Oscar De La Hoya* (WBC*)	2008	Antonio Margarito (WBA)
	Aaron Davis (WBA)	2000-02	Shane Mosley (WBC)	2008-11	Andre Berto (WBC)
1991-92	Meldrick Taylor (WBA)	2001-02	Andrew Lewis (WBA)	2009	Shane Mosley (WBA)
1991	Simon Brown (WBC)	2002-03	Vernon Forrest (WBC)	2009-12	Vyacheslav Senchenko (WBA)
1991-93	Buddy McGirt (WBC)	2002	Ricardo Mayorga (WBA)	2011	Victor Ortiz (WBC)
1992-94	Crisanto Espana (WBA)	2003	Ricardo Mayorga (WBA/WBC)	2011-15	Floyd Mayweather Jr. (WBC*)
1993-97	*Pernell Whitaker* (WBC)	2003-05	Cory Spinks (WBA/WBC)	2012-13	Paulie Malignaggi (WBA)
1994-98	Ike Quartey (WBA*)	2005-06	Zab Judah (WBA/WBC)	2013	Adrien Broner (WBA);
1997-99	*Oscar De La Hoya* (WBC*)	2006	Carlos Baldomir (WBC);		Marcos Maidana (WBA)
1998-	James Page (WBA*)		Ricky Hatton (WBA)	2014-15	Floyd Mayweather Jr. (WBA*)
2000		2006-08	Floyd Mayweather Jr. (WBC);	2016-	Danny Garcia (WBC)
1999-	*Felix Trinidad* (WBC*)		Miguel Cotto (WBA)	2016-	Keith Thurman (WBA)
2000					

(1) Robinson gained the title by defeating Tommy Bell in an elimination agreed to by the New York Commission and the National Boxing Association. Both claimed Robinson waived his title when he won the middleweight crown from Jake LaMotta in 1951.

Lightweights

1896-99	George *"Kid" Lavigne*	1970	*Ismael Laguna*	1993-98	Orzubek Nazarov (WBA)
1899-1902	Frank Erne	1970-72	Ken Buchanan (WBA)	1996-97	Jean-Baptiste Mendy (WBC)
1902-08	*Joe Gans*	1971-72	Pedro Carrasco (WBC)	1997-98	Steve Johnston (WBC)
1908-10	*Oscar "Battling" Nelson*	1972	Mando Ramos (WBC)	1998-99	Jean-Baptiste Mendy (WBA);
1910-12	*Ad Wolgast*	1972-79	*Roberto Duran* (WBA*)		Cesar Bazan (WBC)
1912-14	*Willie Ritchie*	1972	Chango Carmona (WBC)	1999-2000	Steve Johnston (WBC)
1914-17	*Freddie Welsh*	1972-74	Rodolfo Gonzalez (WBC)	1999	Julian Lorcy (WBA);
1917-25	*Benny Leonard**	1974-76	Ishimatsu Suzuki (WBC)		Stefano Zoff (WBA)
1925	Jimmy Goodrich;	1976-78	Esteban De Jesus (WBC)	1999-2000	Gilberto Serrano (WBA)
	Rocky Kansas	1979-81	Jim Watt (WBC)	2000-01	Takanori Hatakeyama (WBA)
1926-30	*Sammy Mandell*	1979-80	Ernesto España (WBA)	2000-02	Jose Luis Castillo (WBC)
1930	Al Singer; *Tony Canzoneri*	1980-81	Hilmer Kenty (WBA)	2001	Julien Lorcy (WBA)
1930-33	*Tony Canzoneri*	1981	Sean O'Grady (WBA);	2001-02	Raul Balbi (WBA)
1933-35	*Barney Ross**		Claude Noel (WBA)	2002-03	Leonard Dorin (WBA)
1935-36	*Tony Canzoneri*	1981-83	Alexis Arguello (WBC*)	2002-04	Floyd Mayweather Jr. (WBC)
1936-38	*Lou Ambers*	1981-82	Arturo Frias (WBA)	2004	Lakva Sim (WBA)
1938	*Henry Armstrong*	1982-84	Ray Mancini (WBA)	2004-05	Jose Luis Castillo (WBA)
1939	*Lou Ambers*	1983-84	Edwin Rosario (WBC)	2004-08	Juan Diaz (WBA)
1940	*Lew Jenkins*	1984-86	Livingstone Bramble (WBA)	2005-06	Diego Corrales (WBC)
1941-43	*Sammy Angott*	1984-85	Jose Luis Ramirez (WBC)	2006	Joel Casamayor (WBC)
1944	*Sammy Angott* (NBA);	1985-86	*Hector "Macho" Camacho*	2006-08	David Diaz (WBC)
	Juan Zurita (NBA)		(WBC)	2008	Nate Campbell (WBA);
1945-51	*Ike Williams*	1986-87	Edwin Rosario (WBA)		Manny Pacquiao (WBC)
	(NBA; later universal)	1987-88	*Julio Cesar Chavez* (WBA);	2009-12	Juan Manuel Marquez (WBA*)
1951-52	*James Carter*		Jose Luis Ramirez (WBC)	2009-10	Edwin Valero (WBC)
1952	Lauro Salas; *James Carter*	1988-89	*Julio Cesar Chavez*	2010-11	Humberto Soto (WBC*)
1953-54	*James Carter*		(WBA/WBC)	2011-12	Antonio DeMarco (WBC)
1954	Paddy De Marco; *James Carter*	1989-90	Edwin Rosario (WBA);	2012-14	Adrien Broner (WBC*)
1955	*James Carter*; Bud Smith		*Pernell Whitaker* (WBC)	2013-15	Richard Abril (WBA*)
1956	Bud Smith; *Joe Brown*	1990	Juan Nazario (WBA)	2014	Omar Figueroa (WBC*)
1956-62	*Joe Brown*	1990-92	*Pernell Whitaker* (WBC*/WBA*)	2014-15	Jorge Linares (WBC)
1962-65	*Carlos Ortiz*	1992	Joey Gamache (WBA)	2015	Darleys Perez (WBA)
1965	*Ismael Laguna*	1992-96	Miguel Angel Gonzalez (WBC*)	2015-16	Anthony Crolla (WBA)
1965-68	*Carlos Ortiz*	1992-93	Tony Lopez (WBA)	2016-	Dejan Zlaticanin (WBC)
1968-69	Carlos Teo Cruz	1993	Dingaan Thobela (WBA)	2016-	Jorge Linares (WBA)
1969-70	Mando Ramos				

Featherweights

1892-1900	*George Dixon* (disputed)	1970-72	Kuniaki Shibata (WBC)	1995-99	Luisito Espinosa (WBC)
1900-01	*Terry McGovern*;	1971-72	Antonio Gomez (WBA)	1996-98	Wilfredo Vasquez (WBA*)
	*Young Corbett II**	1972	Clemente Sanchez (WBC*)	1998	Freddie Norwood (WBA)
1901-12	*Abe Attell*	1972-74	Ernesto Marcel (WBA*)	1998-99	Antonio Cermeno (WBA)
1912-23	*Johnny Kilbane*	1972-73	Jose Legra (WBC)	1999	Cesar Soto (WBC)
1923	*Eugene Criqui*	1973-74	*Eder Jofre* (WBC*)	1999-2000	Freddie Norwood (WBA)
1923-25	*Johnny Dundee**	1974	*Ruben Olivares* (WBA)	1999	*Naseem Hamed* (WBC*)
1925-27	Louis *"Kid" Kaplan**	1974-75	*Bobby Chacon* (WBC)	2000-01	Guty Espadas Jr. (WBC)
1927-28	Benny Bass; *Tony Canzoneri*	1974-76	*Alexis Arguello* (WBA*)	2000-03	Derrick Gainer (WBA)
1928-29	Andre Routis	1975	*Ruben Olivares* (WBC)	2001-04	Erik Morales (WBC)[1]
1929-32	*Battling Battalino**	1975-76	David Kotey (WBC)	2003-05	Juan Manuel Marquez (WBA*)
1932-34	Tommy Paul (NBA)	1976-80	*Danny "Little Red"*	2004-06	In-Jin Chi (WBC)
1933-36	*Freddie Miller*		*Lopez* (WBC)	2005-13	Chris John (WBA)
1936-37	*Petey Sarron*	1977	Rafael Ortega (WBA)	2006	Takashi Koshimoto (WBC);
1937-38	*Henry Armstrong**	1977-78	Cecilio Lastra (WBA)		Rodolfo Lopez (WBC)
1938-40	Joey Archibald	1978-85	Eusebio Pedroza (WBA)	2006-07	In-Jin Chi (WBC)
1940-41	Harry Jeffra	1980-82	*Salvador Sanchez* (WBC)	2007-08	Jorge Linares (WBC*)
1941	Joey Archibald	1982-84	Juan LaPorte (WBC)	2008	Oscar Larios (WBC)
1941-42	*Chalky Wright*	1984	*Wilfredo Gomez* (WBC)	2009	Takahiro Ao (WBC)
1942-48	*Willie Pep*	1984-88	*Azumah Nelson* (WBC)	2009-10	Elio Rojas (WBC)
1948-49	*Sandy Saddler*	1985-86	*Barry McGuigan* (WBA)	2010-11	Hozumi Hasegawa (WBC)
1949-50	*Willie Pep*	1986-87	Steve Cruz (WBA)	2011-12	Jhonny Gonzalez (WBC)
1950-57	*Sandy Saddler**	1987-91	Antonio Esparragoza (WBA)	2012-13	Daniel Ponce de León (WBC)
1957-59	Hogan "Kid" Bassey	1988-90	*Jeff Fenech* (WBC*)	2013	Abner Mares (WBC)
1959-63	Davey Moore	1990-91	Marcos Villasana (WBC)	2013-15	Jhonny Gonzalez (WBC)
1963-64	*Ultiminio "Sugar" Ramos*	1991-93	Park Yung Kyun (WBA);	2013-14	Simpiwe Vetyeka (WBA)
1964-67	*Vicente Saldivar**		Paul Hodkinson (WBC)	2014	Nonito Donaire (WBA)
1968	Raul Rojas (WBA)	1993	Goyo Vargas (WBC)	2014-15	Nicholas Walters (WBA*)
1968-69	Jose Legra (WBC)	1993-95	Kevin Kelley (WBC)	2015-	Gary Russell Jr. (WBC)
1968-71	Shozo Saijyo (WBA)	1993-96	Eloy Rojas (WBA)	2015-	Jesus Andres Cuellar (WBA)
1969-70	Johnny Famechon (WBC)	1995	Alejandro Gonzalez (WBC);		
1970	*Vicente Saldivar* (WBC)		Manuel Medina (WBC)		

(1) Marco Antonio Barrera won unanimous decision over Morales, June 22, 2002, but refused WBC title. Morales regained WBC title with unanimous decision over Paulie Ayala, Nov. 16, 2002. Morales moved to Jr. Lightweight div. in 2004.

International Boxing Hall of Fame Inductees, 2016

Source: International Boxing Hall of Fame, 1 Hall of Fame Dr., Canastota, NY 13032. www.ibhof.com

Modern: Hector "Macho" Camacho (79-6-3, 38 KO), Lupe Pintor (56-14-2, 42 KO), Hilario Zapata (43-10-1, 15 KO).

Old-Timer: Petey Sarron (102-23-12, 25 KO, 10 ND).

Non-Participant: Whitey Esneault, trainer; Harold Lederman, boxing judge; Marc Ratner, fmr. exec. dir., Nevada State Athletic Commission.

Observer: Jerry Izenberg, journalist; Col. Bob Sheridan, broadcaster.

Title-Changing Heavyweight Championship Bouts, 1889-2016

1889: July 8, John L. Sullivan def. Jake Kilrain, 75, Richburg, MS.

1892: Sept. 7, James J. Corbett def. John L. Sullivan, 21, New Orleans.

1897: Mar. 17, Bob Fitzsimmons def. James J. Corbett, 14, Carson City, NV.

1899: June 9, James J. Jeffries def. Bob Fitzsimmons, 11, Coney Island, NY. (Jeffries retired as champion in 1905.)

1905: July 3, Marvin Hart KOd Jack Root, 12, Reno, NV. (James J. Jeffries refereed, gave title to Hart. Jack O'Brien also claimed the title.)

1906: Feb. 23, Tommy Burns def. Marvin Hart, 20, Los Angeles.

1908: Dec. 26, Jack Johnson def. Tommy Burns, 14, Sydney, Australia. (Police halted contest.)

1915: Apr. 5, Jess Willard KOd Jack Johnson, 26, Havana, Cuba.

1919: July 4, Jack Dempsey KOd Jess Willard, Toledo, OH. (Willard failed to answer bell for 4th round.)

1926: Sept. 23, Gene Tunney def. Jack Dempsey, 10, Philadelphia. (Tunney retired as champion in 1928.)

1930: June 12, Max Schmeling def. Jack Sharkey on a foul, 4, New York City. (Resulted in the election of a successor to Gene Tunney.)

1932: June 21, Jack Sharkey def. Max Schmeling, 15, NYC.

1933: June 29, Primo Carnera KOd Jack Sharkey, 6, NYC.

1934: June 14, Max Baer KOd Primo Carnera, 11, NYC.

1935: June 13, James J. Braddock def. Max Baer, 15, NYC.

1937: June 22, Joe Louis KOd James J. Braddock, 8, Chicago. (Louis retired as champion in 1949.)

1949: June 22, Ezzard Charles def. Joe Walcott, 15, Chicago; NBA recognition only.

1951: July 18, Joe Walcott KOd Ezzard Charles, 7, Pittsburgh.

1952: Sept. 23, Rocky Marciano KOd Joe Walcott, 13, Philadelphia. (Marciano retired as champion in 1956.)

1956: Nov. 30, Floyd Patterson KOd Archie Moore, 5, Chicago.

1959: June 26, Ingemar Johansson KOd Floyd Patterson, 3, NYC.

1960: June 20, Floyd Patterson KOd Ingemar Johansson, 5, NYC.

1962: Sept. 25, Sonny Liston KOd Floyd Patterson, 1, Chicago.

1964: Feb. 25, Cassius Clay (Muhammad Ali) KOd Sonny Liston, 7, Miami Beach, FL. (In 1967, Ali was stripped of his title by the WBA and others for refusing military service.)

1970: Feb. 16, Joe Frazier KOd Jimmy Ellis, 5, NYC. (Frazier def. Ali, 15, NYC, on Mar. 8, 1971, in "Fight of the Century.")

1973: Jan. 22, George Foreman KOd Joe Frazier, 2, Kingston, Jamaica.

1974: Oct. 30, Muhammad Ali KOd George Foreman, 8, Kinshasa, Zaire (billed as the "Rumble in the Jungle").

1978: Feb. 15, Leon Spinks def. Muhammad Ali, 15, Las Vegas (WBC recognized Ken Norton as champion after Spinks refused to fight him before his rematch with Ali); June 9, (WBC) Larry Holmes def. Ken Norton, 15, Las Vegas; Sept. 15, (WBA) Muhammad Ali def. Leon Spinks, 15, New Orleans. (Ali retired as champion in 1979.)

1979: Oct. 20, (WBA) John Tate def. Gerrie Coetzee, 15, Pretoria, South Africa.

1980: Mar. 31, (WBA) Mike Weaver KOd John Tate, 15, Knoxville, TN.

1982: Dec. 10, (WBA) Michael Dokes KOd Mike Weaver, 1, Las Vegas.

1983: Sept. 23, (WBA) Gerrie Coetzee KOd Michael Dokes, 10, Richfield, OH; in Dec., Larry Holmes relinquished the WBC title and was named champion of the newly formed IBF.

1984: Mar. 9, (WBC) Tim Witherspoon def. Greg Page, 12, Las Vegas; Aug. 31, (WBC) Pinklon Thomas def. Tim Witherspoon, 12, Las Vegas; Dec. 1, (WBA) Greg Page KOd Gerrie Coetzee, 8, Sun City, Bophuthatswana, South Africa.

1985: Apr. 29, (WBA) Tony Tubbs def. Greg Page, 15, Buffalo, NY; Sept. 21, (IBF) Michael Spinks def. Larry Holmes, 15, Las Vegas (Spinks relinquished title in Feb. 1987).

1986: Jan. 17, (WBA) Tim Witherspoon def. Tony Tubbs, 15, Atlanta; Mar. 22, (WBC) Trevor Berbick def. Pinklon Thomas, 12, Miami; Nov. 22, (WBC) Mike Tyson KOd Trevor Berbick, 2, Las Vegas; Dec. 12, (WBA) James "Bonecrusher" Smith KOd Tim Witherspoon, 1, NYC.

1987: Mar. 7, (WBA) Mike Tyson def. James "Bonecrusher" Smith, 12, Las Vegas; May 30, (IBF) Tony Tucker KOd James "Buster" Douglas, 10, Las Vegas; Aug. 1, (IBF) Mike Tyson def. Tony Tucker, 12, Las Vegas. (Tyson became undisputed champion.)

1990: Feb. 11, (WBA/WBC/IBF) James "Buster" Douglas KOd Mike Tyson, 10, Tokyo, Japan; Oct. 25, (WBA/WBC/IBF) Evander Holyfield KOd James "Buster" Douglas, 3, Las Vegas.

1992: Nov. 13, (WBA/WBC/IBF) Riddick Bowe def. Evander Holyfield, 12, Las Vegas; in Dec., Lennox Lewis was named WBC champion after Bowe relinquished the WBC title rather than fight Lewis.

1993: Nov. 6, (WBA/IBF) Evander Holyfield def. Riddick Bowe, 12, Las Vegas.

1994: Apr. 22, (WBA/IBF) Michael Moorer def. Evander Holyfield, 12, Las Vegas; Sept. 24, (WBC) Oliver McCall KOd Lennox Lewis, 2, London, Eng.; Nov. 5, (WBA/IBF) George Foreman KOd Michael Moorer, 10, Las Vegas.

1995: In Mar., George Foreman was stripped of his WBA title for refusing to fight challenger Tony Tucker; in June, Foreman relinquished his IBF title rather than submit to a rematch with Axel Schulz; Apr. 8, (WBA) Bruce Seldon TKOd Tony Tucker, 7, Las Vegas; Sept. 2, (WBC) Frank Bruno def. Oliver McCall, 12, London, Eng.; Dec. 9, (IBF) Frans Botha def. Axel Schulz, 12, Stuttgart, Germany (Botha was subsequently stripped of title after testing positive for a steroid).

1996: Mar. 16, (WBC) Mike Tyson KOd Frank Bruno, 3, Las Vegas; June 22, (IBF) Michael Moorer def. Axel Schulz, 12, Dortmund, Germany; Sept. 7, (WBA) Mike Tyson KOd Bruce Seldon, 1, Las Vegas (Tyson was subsequently stripped of WBC title after refusing to fight Lennox Lewis); Nov. 9, (WBA) Evander Holyfield KOd Mike Tyson, 11, Las Vegas.

1997: Feb. 7, (WBC) Lennox Lewis TKOd Oliver McCall, 5, Las Vegas; Nov. 8, (IBF) Evander Holyfield def. Michael Moorer, 8, Las Vegas.

1999: Nov. 13, (IBF) Lennox Lewis def. Evander Holyfield, 12, Las Vegas. (Lewis became undisputed champion.)

2000: In Apr., Lennox Lewis was stripped of his WBA title after refusing to fight challenger John Ruiz; Aug. 12, (WBA) Evander Holyfield def. John Ruiz, 12, Las Vegas.

2001: Mar. 3, (WBA) John Ruiz def. Evander Holyfield, 12, Las Vegas; Apr. 22, (WBC/IBF) Hasim Rahman KOd Lennox Lewis, 5, Brakpan, South Africa; Nov. 17, (WBC/IBF) Lennox Lewis KOd Hasim Rahman, 4, Las Vegas.

2002: In Sept., Lennox Lewis relinquished his IBF title; Dec. 14, (IBF) Chris Byrd def. Evander Holyfield, 12, Atlantic City, NJ.

2003: Mar. 1, (WBA) Roy Jones Jr. def. John Ruiz, 12, Las Vegas.

2004: Feb. 20, (WBA) John Ruiz gained title when Roy Jones Jr. relinquished it; Apr. 24, (WBC) Vitali Klitschko TKOd Corrie Sanders, 8, Los Angeles, CA, to win title vacated by retirement of Lennox Lewis in Feb.

2005: Apr. 30, (WBA) James Toney def. John Ruiz, 12, NYC (title was returned to Ruiz after Toney tested positive for steroids); Nov. 9, (WBC) Hasim Rahman gained title when Vitali Klitschko retired due to an injury; Dec. 17, (WBA) Nikolai Valuev def. John Ruiz, 12, Berlin, Germany.

2006: Apr. 22, (IBF) Wladimir Klitschko TKOd Chris Byrd, 7, Mannheim, Germany; Aug. 12, (WBC) Oleg Maskaev TKOd Hasim Rahman, 12, Las Vegas.

2007: Apr. 14, (WBA) Ruslan Chagaev def. Nikolai Valuev, 12, Stuttgart, Germany. (An injured Chagaev was named champion in recess, July 2008.)

2008: Mar. 8, (WBC) Samuel Peter TKOd Oleg Maskaev, 6, Cancun, Mexico; Aug. 30, (WBA) Nikolai Valuev def. John Ruiz, 12, Berlin, Germany; Oct. 11, (WBC) Vitali Klitschko TKOd Samuel Peter, 8, Berlin, Germany.

2009: Nov. 7, (WBA) David Haye def. Nikolai Valuev, 12, Nuremberg, Germany.

2011: July 2, (WBA) Wladimir Klitschko def. David Haye, 12, Hamburg, Germany.

2014: May 10, (WBC) Bermane Stiverne TKOd Chris Arreola, 6, Los Angeles, CA, to win title vacated in Dec. 2013.

2015: Jan. 17, (WBC) Deontay Wilder def. Bermane Stiverne, 12, Las Vegas; Nov. 28 (WBA/IBF) Tyson Fury def. Wladimir Klitschko, 12, Dusseldorf, Germany; in Dec., Fury was stripped of IBF title for refusing to fight mandatory challenger Vyacheslav Glazkov.

2016: Jan. 16, (IBF) Charles Martin TKOd Vyacheslav Glazkov, 3, Brooklyn, NY; Apr. 9, (IBF) Anthony Joshua KOd Charles Martin, 2, London, Eng., UK.

THOROUGHBRED RACING
Triple Crown Winners

The Kentucky Derby, Preakness Stakes, and Belmont Stakes make up the Triple Crown. Since 1920, colts have carried 126 lbs in Triple Crown events; fillies, 121 lbs.

Year	Horse	Jockey	Trainer	Year	Horse	Jockey	Trainer
1919	Sir Barton	J. Loftus	H. G. Bedwell	1946	Assault	W. Mehrtens	M. Hirsch
1930	Gallant Fox	E. Sande	J. Fitzsimmons	1948	Citation	E. Arcaro	H. A. Jones
1935	Omaha	W. Sanders	J. Fitzsimmons	1973	Secretariat	R. Turcotte	L. Laurin
1937	War Admiral	C. Kurtsinger	G. Conway	1977	Seattle Slew	J. Cruguet	W. H. Turner Jr.
1941	Whirlaway	E. Arcaro	B. A. Jones	1978	Affirmed	S. Cauthen	L. S. Barrera
1943	Count Fleet	J. Longden	G. D. Cameron	2015	American Pharoah	V. Espinoza	B. Baffert

Kentucky Derby Winners, 1875-2016

Churchill Downs, Louisville, KY; inaug. 1875. Distance: 1-1/4 mi; 1-1/2 mi until 1896. 3-year-olds. Best time: 1:59-2/5, Secretariat (1973); 2016 time: 2:01.31. (Until 2001, times were measured in fifths of a second.)

Year	Horse	Jockey	Year	Horse	Jockey	Year	Horse	Jockey
1875	Aristides	O. Lewis	1923	Zev	E. Sande	1970	Dust Commander	M. Manganello
1876	Vagrant	R. Swim	1924	Black Gold	J. D. Mooney	1971	Canonero II	G. Avila
1877	Baden Baden	W. Walker	1925	Flying Ebony	E. Sande	1972	Riva Ridge	R. Turcotte
1878	Day Star	J. Carter	1926	Bubbling Over	A. Johnson	1973	Secretariat	R. Turcotte
1879	Lord Murphy	C. Schauer	1927	Whiskery	L. McAtee	1974	Cannonade	A. Cordero
1880	Fonso	G. Lewis	1928	Reigh Count	C. Lang	1975	Foolish Pleasure	J. Vasquez
1881	Hindoo	J. McLaughlin	1929	Clyde Van Dusen	L. McAtee	1976	Bold Forbes	A. Cordero
1882	Apollo	B. Hurd	1930	Gallant Fox	E. Sande	1977	Seattle Slew	J. Cruguet
1883	Leonatus	W. Donohue	1931	Twenty Grand	C. Kurtsinger	1978	Affirmed	S. Cauthen
1884	Joe Cotton	I. Murphy	1932	Burgoo King	E. James	1979	Spectacular Bid	R. Franklin
1885	Joe Cotton	E. Henderson	1933	Brokers Tip	D. Meade	1980	Genuine Risk[1]	J. Vasquez
1886	Ben Ali	P. Duffy	1934	Cavalcade	M. Garner	1981	Pleasant Colony	J. Velasquez
1887	Montrose	I. Lewis	1935	Omaha	W. Saunders	1982	Gato del Sol	E. Delahoussaye
1888	Macbeth II	G. Covington	1936	Bold Venture	I. Hanford	1983	Sunny's Halo	E. Delahoussaye
1889	Spokane	T. Kiley	1937	War Admiral	C. Kurtsinger	1984	Swale	L. Pincay
1890	Riley	I. Murphy	1938	Lawrin	E. Arcaro	1985	Spend a Buck	A. Cordero
1891	Kingman	I. Murphy	1939	Johnstown	J. Stout	1986	Ferdinand	W. Shoemaker
1892	Azra	A. Clayton	1940	Gallahadion	C. Bierman	1987	Alysheba	C. McCarron
1893	Lookout	E. Kunze	1941	Whirlaway	E. Arcaro	1988	Winning Colors[1]	G. Stevens
1894	Chant	F. Goodale	1942	Shut Out	W. Wright	1989	Sunday Silence	P. Valenzuela
1895	Halma	J. Perkins	1943	Count Fleet	J. Longden	1990	Unbridled	C. Perret
1896	Ben Brush	W. Simms	1944	Pensive	C. McCreary	1991	Strike the Gold	C. Antley
1897	Typhoon II	F. Garner	1945	Hoop Jr.	E. Arcaro	1992	Lil E. Tee	P. Day
1898	Plaudit	W. Simms	1946	Assault	W. Mehrtens	1993	Sea Hero	J. Bailey
1899	Manuel	F. Taral	1947	Jet Pilot	E. Guerin	1994	Go for Gin	C. McCarron
1900	Lieut. Gibson	J. Boland	1948	Citation	E. Arcaro	1995	Thunder Gulch	G. Stevens
1901	His Eminence	J. Winkfield	1949	Ponder	S. Brooks	1996	Grindstone	J. Bailey
1902	Alan-a-Dale	J. Winkfield	1950	Middleground	W. Boland	1997	Silver Charm	G. Stevens
1903	Judge Himes	H. Booker	1951	Count Turf	C. McCreary	1998	Real Quiet	K. Desormeaux
1904	Elwood	F. Prior	1952	Hill Gail	E. Arcaro	1999	Charismatic	C. Antley
1905	Agile	J. Martin	1953	Dark Star	H. Moreno	2000	Fusaichi Pegasus	K. Desormeaux
1906	Sir Huon	R. Troxler	1954	Determine	R. York	2001	Monarchos	J. Chavez
1907	Pink Star	A. Minder	1955	Swaps	W. Shoemaker	2002	War Emblem	V. Espinoza
1908	Stone Street	A. Pickens	1956	Needles	D. Erb	2003	Funny Cide	J. Santos
1909	Wintergreen	V. Powers	1957	Iron Liege	W. Hartack	2004	Smarty Jones	S. Elliot
1910	Donau	F. Herbert	1958	Tim Tam	I. Valenzuela	2005	Giacomo	M. Smith
1911	Meridian	G. Archibald	1959	Tomy Lee	W. Shoemaker	2006	Barbaro	E. Prado
1912	Worth	C. Shilling	1960	Venetian Way	W. Hartack	2007	Street Sense	C. Borel
1913	Donerail	R. Goose	1961	Carry Back	J. Sellers	2008	Big Brown	K. Desormeaux
1914	Old Rosebud	J. McCabe	1962	Decidedly	W. Hartack	2009	Mine That Bird	C. Borel
1915	Regret[1]	J. Notter	1963	Chateaugay	B. Baeza	2010	Super Saver	C. Borel
1916	George Smith	J. Loftus	1964	Northern Dancer	W. Hartack	2011	Animal Kingdom	J. Velazquez
1917	Omar Khayyam	C. Borel	1965	Lucky Debonair	W. Shoemaker	2012	I'll Have Another	M. Gutierrez
1918	Exterminator	W. Knapp	1966	Kauai King	D. Brumfield	2013	Orb	J. Rosario
1919	Sir Barton	J. Loftus	1967	Proud Clarion	R. Ussery	2014	California Chrome	V. Espinoza
1920	Paul Jones	T. Rice	1968	Forward Pass[2]	I. Valenzuela	2015	American Pharoah	V. Espinoza
1921	Behave Yourself	C. Thompson	1969	Majestic Prince	W. Hartack	2016	Nyquist	M. Gutierrez
1922	Morvich	A. Johnson						

Note: Two jockeys have won the Kentucky Derby five times: Eddie Arcaro and Bill Hartack. Willie Shoemaker won four times. Seven jockeys won three times: Isaac Murphy, Earle Sande, Angel Cordero, Gary Stevens, Kent Desormeaux, Calvin Borel, and Victor Espinoza. (1) Regret, Genuine Risk, and Winning Colors are the only fillies to have won the Derby. (2) Dancer's Image came in first but was disqualified after tests disclosed that the horse had run with a prohibited painkilling drug in his system. All wagers were paid on Dancer's Image, but Forward Pass was awarded the first-place money.

Fastest Winning Times for the Kentucky Derby

Until 2001, Kentucky Derby times were measured in fifths of a second.

Time	Horse	Jockey	Year	Time	Horse	Jockey	Year
1 min., 59-2/5 s.	Secretariat	Ron Turcotte	1973	2 min., 1.19 s.	Funny Cide	Jose Santos	2003
1 min., 59.97 s.	Monarchos	Jorge Chavez	2001	2 min., 1-1/5 s.	Thunder Gulch	Gary Stevens	1995
2 min.	Northern Dancer	Bill Hartack	1964		Affirmed	Steve Cauthen	1978
2 min., 1/5 s.	Spend a Buck	Angel Cordero Jr.	1985		Lucky Debonair	Bill Shoemaker	1965
2 min., 2/5 s.	Decidedly	Bill Hartack	1962	2 min., 1.31 s.	Nyquist	Mario Gutierrez	2016
2 min., 3/5 s.	Proud Clarion	Robert Ussery	1967	2 min., 1-2/5 s.	Barbaro	Edgar Prado	2006
2 min., 1 s.	Fusaichi Pegasus	Kent Desormeaux	2000		Whirlaway	Eddie Arcaro	1941
	Grindstone	Jerry Bailey	1996	2 min., 1-3/5 s.	Bold Forbes	Angel Cordero Jr.	1976
2 min., 1.13 s.	War Emblem	Victor Espinoza	2002		Hill Gail	Eddie Arcaro	1952
2 min., 1.19 s.	Funny Cide	Jose Santos	2003		Middleground	William Boland	1950

Preakness Stakes Winners, 1873-2016

Pimlico Race Course, Baltimore, MD; inaug. 1873. Distance: 1-3/16 mi. 3-year-olds. * = Horses ran in two divisions. Best time: 1:53, Secretariat (1973); 2016 time: 1:58.31.

Year	Horse	Jockey	Year	Horse	Jockey	Year	Horse	Jockey
1873	Survivor	G. Barbee	1924	Nellie Morse	J. Merimee	1971	Canonero II	G. Avila
1874	Culpepper	M. Donohue	1925	Coventry	C. Kummer	1972	Bee Bee Bee	E. Nelson
1875	Tom Ochiltree	L. Hughes	1926	Display	J. Malben	1973	Secretariat	R. Turcotte
1876	Shirley	G. Barbee	1927	Bostonian	A. Abel	1974	Little Current	M. Rivera
1877	Cloverbrook	C. Holloway	1928	Victorian	R. Workman	1975	Master Derby	D. McHargue
1878	Duke of Magenta	C. Holloway	1929	Dr. Freeland	L. Schaefer	1976	Elocutionist	J. Lively
1879	Harold	L. Hughes	1930	Gallant Fox	E. Sande	1977	Seattle Slew	J. Cruguet
1880	Grenada	L. Hughes	1931	Mate	G. Ellis	1978	Affirmed	S. Cauthen
1881	Saunterer	W. Costello	1932	Burgoo King	E. James	1979	Spectacular Bid	R. Franklin
1882	Vanguard	W. Costello	1933	Head Play	C. Kurtsinger	1980	Codex	A. Cordero
1883	Jacobus	G. Barbee	1934	High Quest	R. Jones	1981	Pleasant Colony	J. Velasquez
1884	Knight of Ellerslie	S. Fisher	1935	Omaha	W. Saunders	1982	Aloma's Ruler	J. Kaenel
1885	Tecumseh	J. McLaughlin	1936	Bold Venture	G. Woolf	1983	Deputed	
1886	The Bard	S. Fisher	1937	War Admiral	C. Kurtsinger		Testamony	D. Miller
1887	Dunboyne	W. Donohue	1938	Dauber	M. Peters	1984	Gate Dancer	A. Cordero
1888	Refund	F. Littlefield	1939	Challedon	G. Seabo	1985	Tank's Prospect	P. Day
1889	Buddhist	G. Anderson	1940	Bimelech	F. A. Smith	1986	Snow Chief	A. Solis
1890	Montague	W. Martin	1941	Whirlaway	E. Arcaro	1987	Alysheba	C. McCarron
1894	Assignee	F. Taral	1942	Alsab	B. James	1988	Risen Star	E. Delahoussaye
1895	Belmar	F. Taral	1943	Count Fleet	J. Longden	1989	Sunday Silence	P. Valenzuela
1896	Margrave	H. Griffin	1944	Pensive	C. McCreary	1990	Summer Squall	P. Day
1897	Paul Kauvar	C. Thorpe	1945	Polynesian	W. D. Wright	1991	Hansel	J. Bailey
1898	Sly Fox	W. Simms	1946	Assault	W. Mehrtens	1992	Pine Bluff	C. McCarron
1899	Half Time	R. Clawson	1947	Faultless	D. Dodson	1993	Prairie Bayou	M. Smith
1900	Hindus	H. Spencer	1948	Citation	E. Arcaro	1994	Tabasco Cat	P. Day
1901	The Parader	F. Landry	1949	Capot	T. Atkinson	1995	Timber Country	P. Day
1902	Old England	L. Jackson	1950	Hill Prince	E. Arcaro	1996	Louis Quatorze	P. Day
1903	Flocarline	W. Gannon	1951	Bold	E. Arcaro	1997	Silver Charm	G. Stevens
1904	Bryn Mawr	E. Hildebrand	1952	Blue Man	C. McCreary	1998	Real Quiet	K. Desormeaux
1905	Cairngorm	W. Davis	1953	Native Dancer	E. Guerin	1999	Charismatic	C. Antley
1906	Whimsical	W. Miller	1954	Hasty Road	J. Adams	2000	Red Bullet	J. Bailey
1907	Don Enrique	G. Mountain	1955	Nashua	E. Arcaro	2001	Point Given	G. Stevens
1908	Royal Tourist	E. Dugan	1956	Fabius	W. Hartack	2002	War Emblem	V. Espinoza
1909	Effendi	W. Doyle	1957	Bold Ruler	E. Arcaro	2003	Funny Cide	J. Santos
1910	Layminster	R. Estep	1958	Tim Tam	I. Valenzuela	2004	Smarty Jones	S. Elliot
1911	Watervale	E. Dugan	1959	Royal Orbit	W. Harmatz	2005	Afleet Alex	J. Rose
1912	Colonel Holloway	C. Turner	1960	Bally Ache	R. Ussery	2006	Bernardini	J. Castellano
1913	Buskin	J. Butwell	1961	Carry Back	J. Sellers	2007	Curlin	R. Albarado
1914	Holiday	A. Schuttinger	1962	Greek Money	J. L. Rotz	2008	Big Brown	K. Desormeaux
1915	Rhine Maiden	D. Hoffman	1963	Candy Spots	W. Shoemaker	2009	Rachel Alexandra	C. Borel
1916	Damrosch	L. McAtee	1964	Northern Dancer	W. Hartack	2010	Lookin at Lucky	M. Garcia
1917	Kalitan	E. Haynes	1965	Tom Rolfe	R. Turcotte	2011	Shackleford	J. Castanon
1918*	War Cloud	J. Loftus	1966	Kauai King	D. Brumfield	2012	I'll Have Another	M. Gutierrez
	Jack Hare Jr.	C. Peak	1967	Damascus	W. Shoemaker	2013	Oxbow	G. Stevens
1919	Sir Barton	J. Loftus	1968	Forward Pass	I. Valenzuela	2014	California Chrome	V. Espinoza
1920	Man o' War	C. Kummer	1969	Majestic Prince	W. Hartack	2015	American Pharoah	V. Espinoza
1921	Broomspun	F. Coltiletti	1970	Personality	E. Belmonte	2016	Exaggerator	K. Desormeaux
1922	Pillory	L. Morris						
1923	Vigil	B. Marinelli						

Belmont Stakes Winners, 1867-2016

Belmont Park, Elmont, NY; inaug. 1867. Distance: 1-1/2 mi. 3-year-olds. Best time: 2:24, Secretariat (1973); 2016 time: 2:28.51.

Year	Horse	Jockey	Year	Horse	Jockey	Year	Horse	Jockey
1867	Ruthless	J. Gilpatrick	1900	Ildrim	N. Turner	1935	Omaha	W. Saunders
1868	General Duke	R. Swim	1901	Commando	H. Spencer	1936	Granville	J. Stout
1869	Fenian	C. Miller	1902	Masterman	J. Bullman	1937	War Admiral	C. Kurtsinger
1870	Kingfisher	W. Dick	1903	Africander	J. Bullman	1938	Pasteurized	J. Stout
1871	Harry Bassett	W. Miller	1904	Delhi	G. Odom	1939	Johnstown	J. Stout
1872	Joe Daniels	J. Rowe	1905	Tanya	E. Hildebrand	1940	Bimelech	F. A. Smith
1873	Springbok	J. Rowe	1906	Burgomaster	L. Lyne	1941	Whirlaway	E. Arcaro
1874	Saxon	G. Barbee	1907	Peter Pan	G. Mountain	1942	Shut Out	E. Arcaro
1875	Calvin	R. Swim	1908	Colin	J. Notter	1943	Count Fleet	J. Longden
1876	Algerine	W. Donohue	1909	Joe Madden	E. Dugan	1944	Bounding Home	G. L. Smith
1877	Cloverbrook	C. Holloway	1910	Sweep	J. Butwell	1945	Pavot	E. Arcaro
1878	Duke of Magenta	L. Hughes	1913	Prince Eugene	R. Troxler	1946	Assault	W. Mehrtens
1879	Spendthrift	S. Evans	1914	Luke McLuke	M. Buxton	1947	Phalanx	R. Donoso
1880	Grenada	L. Hughes	1915	The Finn	G. Byrne	1948	Citation	E. Arcaro
1881	Saunterer	T. Costello	1916	Friar Rock	E. Haynes	1949	Capot	T. Atkinson
1882	Forester	J. McLaughlin	1917	Hourless	J. Butwell	1950	Middleground	W. Boland
1883	George Kinney	J. McLaughlin	1918	Johren	F. Robinson	1951	Counterpoint	D. Gorman
1884	Panique	J. McLaughlin	1919	Sir Barton	J. Loftus	1952	One Count	E. Arcaro
1885	Tyrant	P. Duffy	1920	Man o' War	C. Kummer	1953	Native Dancer	E. Guerin
1886	Inspector B.	J. McLaughlin	1921	Grey Lag	E. Sande	1954	High Gun	E. Guerin
1887	Hanover	J. McLaughlin	1922	Pillory	C. H. Miller	1955	Nashua	E. Arcaro
1888	Sir Dixon	J. McLaughlin	1923	Zev	E. Sande	1956	Needles	D. Erb
1889	Eric	W. Hayward	1924	Mad Play	E. Sande	1957	Gallant Man	W. Shoemaker
1890	Burlington	S. Barnes	1925	American Flag	A. Johnson	1958	Cavan	P. Anderson
1891	Foxford	E. Garrison	1926	Crusader	A. Johnson	1959	Sword Dancer	W. Shoemaker
1892	Patron	W. Hayward	1927	Chance Shot	E. Sande	1960	Celtic Ash	W. Hartack
1893	Comanche	W. Simms	1928	Vito	C. Kummer	1961	Sherluck	B. Baeza
1894	Henry of Navarre	W. Simms	1929	Blue Larkspur	M. Garner	1962	Jaipur	W. Shoemaker
1895	Belmar	F. Taral	1930	Gallant Fox	E. Sande	1963	Chateaugay	B. Baeza
1896	Hastings	H. Griffin	1931	Twenty Grand	C. Kurtsinger	1964	Quadrangle	M. Ycaza
1897	Scottish Chieftain	J. Scherrer	1932	Faireno	T. Malley	1965	Hail to All	J. Sellers
1898	Bowling Brook	F. Littlefield	1933	Hurryoff	M. Garner	1966	Amberoid	W. Boland
1899	Jean Bereaud	R. R. Clawson	1934	Peace Chance	W. D. Wright	1967	Damascus	W. Shoemaker

Year	Horse	Jockey	Year	Horse	Jockey	Year	Horse	Jockey
1968	Stage Door Johnny	H. Gustines	1985	Creme Fraiche	E. Maple	2001	Point Given	G. Stevens
1969	Arts and Letters	B. Baeza	1986	Danzig Connection	C. McCarron	2002	Sarava	E. Prado
1970	High Echelon	J. L. Rotz	1987	Bet Twice	C. Perret	2003	Empire Maker	J. Bailey
1971	Pass Catcher	W. Blum	1988	Risen Star	E. Delahoussaye	2004	Birdstone	E. Prado
1972	Riva Ridge	R. Turcotte	1989	Easy Goer	P. Day	2005	Afleet Alex	J. Rose
1973	Secretariat	R. Turcotte	1990	Go and Go	M. Kinane	2006	Jazil	F. Jara
1974	Little Current	M. Rivera	1991	Hansel	J. Bailey	2007	Rags to Riches	J. Velazquez
1975	Avatar	W. Shoemaker	1992	A.P. Indy	E. Delahoussaye	2008	Da' Tara	A. Garcia
1976	Bold Forbes	A. Cordero	1993	Colonial Affair	J. Krone	2009	Summer Bird	K. Desormeaux
1977	Seattle Slew	J. Cruguet	1994	Tabasco Cat	P. Day	2010	Drosselmeyer	M. Smith
1978	Affirmed	S. Cauthen	1995	Thunder Gulch	G. Stevens	2011	Ruler On Ice	J. Valdivia Jr.
1979	Coastal	R. Hernandez	1996	Editor's Note	R. Douglas	2012	Union Rags	J. Velazquez
1980	Temperence Hill	E. Maple	1997	Touch Gold	C. McCarron	2013	Palace Malice	M. Smith
1981	Summing	G. Martens	1998	Victory Gallop	G. Stevens	2014	Tonalist	J. Rosario
1982	Conquistador Cielo	L. Pincay	1999	Lemon Drop Kid	J. Santos	2015	American Pharoah	V. Espinoza
1983	Caveat	L. Pincay	2000	Commendable	P. Day	2016	Creator	I. Ortiz Jr.
1984	Swale	L. Pincay						

Annual Leading Jockey by Earnings, 1957-2015

Total purses earned by all horses that jockey raced in year listed; does not reflect what jockey earned.

Year	Jockey	Earnings	Year	Jockey	Earnings	Year	Jockey	Earnings
1957	Bill Hartack	$3,060,501	1977	Steve Cauthen	$6,151,750	1997	Jerry D. Bailey	$18,320,743
1958	Willie Shoemaker	2,961,693	1978	Darrel McHargue	6,029,885	1998	Gary Stevens	19,622,855
1959	Willie Shoemaker	2,843,133	1979	Laffit Pincay Jr.	8,193,535	1999	Pat Day	18,092,845
1960	Willie Shoemaker	2,123,961	1980	Chris McCarron	7,663,300	2000	Pat Day	17,479,838
1961	Willie Shoemaker	2,690,819	1981	Chris McCarron	8,397,604	2001	Jerry D. Bailey	22,597,720
1962	Willie Shoemaker	2,916,844	1982	Angel Cordero Jr.	9,483,590	2002	Jerry D. Bailey	19,271,814
1963	Willie Shoemaker	2,526,925	1983	Angel Cordero Jr.	10,116,697	2003	Jerry D. Bailey	23,354,960
1964	Willie Shoemaker	2,649,553	1984	Chris McCarron	12,045,813	2004	John R. Velazquez	22,220,261
1965	Braulio Baeza	2,582,702	1985	Laffit Pincay Jr.	13,353,299	2005	John R. Velazquez	20,799,923
1966	Braulio Baeza	2,951,022	1986	Jose Santos	11,329,297	2006	Garrett K. Gomez	20,122,592
1967	Braulio Baeza	3,088,888	1987	Jose Santos	12,375,433	2007	Garrett K. Gomez	22,800,074
1968	Braulio Baeza	2,835,108	1988	Jose Santos	14,877,298	2008	Garrett K. Gomez	23,344,351
1969	Jorge Velasquez	2,542,315	1989	Jose Santos	13,838,389	2009	Garrett K. Gomez	18,536,105
1970	Laffit Pincay Jr.	2,626,526	1990	Gary Stevens	13,881,198	2010	Ramon A. Dominguez	16,911,880
1971	Laffit Pincay Jr.	3,784,377	1991	Chris McCarron	14,441,083	2011	Ramon A. Dominguez	20,267,032
1972	Laffit Pincay Jr.	3,225,827	1992	Kent Desormeaux	14,193,006	2012	Ramon A. Dominguez	25,584,852
1973	Laffit Pincay Jr.	4,093,492	1993	Mike Smith	14,024,815	2013	Javier Castellano	26,214,007
1974	Laffit Pincay Jr.	4,251,060	1994	Mike Smith	15,979,820	2014	Javier Castellano	25,056,464
1975	Braulio Baeza	3,695,198	1995	Jerry D. Bailey	16,311,876	2015	Javier Castellano	28,120,767
1976	Angel Cordero Jr.	4,709,500	1996	Jerry D. Bailey	19,465,376			

Breeders' Cup World Thoroughbred Championships, 1984-2016

The Breeders' Cup began in 1984 and through 2006, consisted of seven races at one track on one day. In 2007, it expanded to two days, and three new races debuted: Filly and Mare Sprint, Juvenile Turf, and Dirt. In 2008, a "Ladies' Day" for fillies and several more races debuted: Turf Sprint, Marathon (eliminated in 2014), and Juvenile Fillies Turf. In 2011, the Juvenile Sprint debuted; it was eliminated in 2013.

Classic
Distance: 1-1/4 mi.

Year	Horse	Jockey	Year	Horse	Jockey	Year	Horse	Jockey
1984	Wild Again	P. Day	1995	Cigar	J. Bailey	2006	Invasor	F. Jara
1985	Proud Truth	J. Velasquez	1996	Alphabet Soup	C. McCarron	2007	Curlin	R. Albarado
1986	Skywalker	L. Pincay Jr.	1997	Skip Away	M. Smith	2008	Raven's Pass	F. Dettori
1987	Ferdinand	W. Shoemaker	1998	Awesome Again	P. Day	2009	Zenyatta	M. Smith
1988	Alysheba	C. McCarron	1999	Cat Thief	P. Day	2010	Blame	G. Gomez
1989	Sunday Silence	C. McCarron	2000	Tiznow	C. McCarron	2011	Drosselmeyer	M. Smith
1990	Unbridled	P. Day	2001	Tiznow	C. McCarron	2012	Fort Larned	B. Hernandez
1991	Black Tie Affair	J. Bailey	2002	Volponi	J. Santos	2013	Mucho Macho Man	G. Stevens
1992	A.P. Indy	E. Delahoussaye	2003	Pleasantly Perfect	A. Solis	2014	Bayern	M. Garcia
1993	Arcangues	J. Bailey	2004	Ghostzapper	J. Castellano	2015	American Pharoah	V. Espinoza
1994	Concern	J. Bailey	2005	Saint Liam	J. Bailey	2016	Arrogate	M. Smith

Juvenile
Distance: 1-1/16 mi, 1986 and since 1988; 1 mi, 1984-85, 1987.

Year	Horse	Jockey	Year	Horse	Jockey	Year	Horse	Jockey
1984	Chief's Crown	D. MacBeth	1995	Unbridled's Song	M. Smith	2006	Street Sense	C. Borel
1985	Tasso	L. Pincay Jr.	1996	Boston Harbor	J. Bailey	2007	War Pass	C. Velasquez
1986	Capote	L. Pincay Jr.	1997	Favorite Trick	P. Day	2008	Midshipman	G. Gomez
1987	Success Express	J. Santos	1998	Answer Lively	J. Bailey	2009	Vale of York	A. Ajtebi
1988	Is It True	L. Pincay Jr.	1999	Anees	G. Stevens	2010	Uncle Mo	J. Velazquez
1989	Rhythm	C. Perret	2000	Macho Uno	J. Bailey	2011	Hansen	R. Dominguez
1990	Fly So Free	J. Santos	2001	Johannesburg	M. Kinane	2012	Shanghai Bobby	R. Napravnik
1991	Arazi	P. Valenzuela	2002	Vindication	M. Smith	2013	New Year's Day	M. Garcia
1992	Gilded Time	C. McCarron	2003	Action This Day	D. Flores	2014	Texas Red	K. Desormeaux
1993	Brocco	G. Stevens	2004	Wilko	F. Dettori	2015	Nyquist	M. Gutierrez
1994	Timber Country	P. Day	2005	Stevie Wonderboy	G. Gomez	2016	Classic Empire	J. Leparoux

Juvenile Fillies
Distance: 1-1/16 mi, 1986 and since 1988; 1 mi, 1984-85, 1987. Outstandingly won the 1984 race by disqualification.

Year	Horse	Jockey	Year	Horse	Jockey	Year	Horse	Jockey
1984	Outstandingly	W. Guerra	1996	Storm Song	C. Perret	2007	Indian Blessing	G. Gomez
1985	Twilight Ridge	J. Velasquez	1997	Countess Diana	S. Sellers	2008	Stardom Bound	M. Smith
1986	Brave Raj	P. Valenzuela	1998	Silverbulletday	G. Stevens	2009	She Be Wild	J. Leparoux
1987	Epitome	P. Day	1999	Cash Run	J. Bailey	2010	Awesome Feather	J. Sanchez
1988	Open Mind	A. Cordero Jr.	2000	Caressing	J. Velazquez	2011	My Miss Aurelia	C. Nakatani
1989	Go for Wand	R. Romero	2001	Tempera	D. Flores	2012	Beholder	G. Gomez
1990	Meadow Star	J. Santos	2002	Storm Flag Flying	J. Velazquez	2013	Ria Antonia	J. Castellano
1991	Pleasant Stage	E. Delahoussaye	2003	Halfbridled	J. Krone	2014	Take Charge Brandi	V. Espinoza
1992	Eliza	P. Valenzuela	2004	Sweet Catomine	C. Nakatani			
1993	Phone Chatter	L. Pincay Jr.	2005	Folklore	E. Prado	2015	Songbird	M. Smith
1994	Flanders	P. Day	2006	Dreaming of Anna	R. Douglas	2016	Champagne Room	M. Gutierrez
1995	My Flag	J. Bailey						

Sprint
Distance: 6 furlongs.

Year	Horse	Jockey	Year	Horse	Jockey	Year	Horse	Jockey
1984	Eillo	C. Perret	1995	Desert Stormer	K. Desormeaux	2006	Thor's Echo	C. Nakatani
1985	Precisionist	C. McCarron	1996	Lit de Justice	C. Nakatani	2007	Midnight Lute	G. Gomez
1986	Smile	J. Vasquez	1997	Elmhurst	C. Nakatani	2008	Midnight Lute	G. Gomez
1987	Very Subtle	P. Valenzuela	1998	Reraise	C. Nakatani	2009	Dancing in Silks	J. Rosario
1988	Gulch	A. Cordero Jr.	1999	Artax	J. Chaves	2010	Big Drama	E. Coa
1989	Dancing Spree	A. Cordero Jr.	2000	Kona Gold	A. Solis	2011	Amazombie	M. Smith
1990	Safely Kept	C. Perret	2001	Squirtle Squirt	J. Bailey	2012	Trinniberg	W. Martinez
1991	Sheikh Albadou	P. Eddery	2002	Orientate	J. Bailey	2013	Secret Circle	M. Garcia
1992	Thirty Slews	E. Delahoussaye	2003	Cajun Beat	C. Velasquez	2014	Work All Week	C. Geroux
1993	Cardmania	E. Delahoussaye	2004	Speightstown	J. Velazquez	2015	Runhappy	E. Prado
1994	Cherokee Run	M. Smith	2005	Silver Train	E. Prado	2016	Drefong	M. Garcia

Mile

Year	Horse	Jockey	Year	Horse	Jockey	Year	Horse	Jockey
1984	Royal Heroine	F. Toro	1995	Ridgewood Pearl	J. Murtagh	2006	Miesque's Approval	E. Castro
1985	Cozzene	W. Guerra	1996	Da Hoss	G. Stevens	2007	Kip Deville	C. Velasquez
1986	Last Tycoon	Y. St.-Martin	1997	Spinning World	C. Asmussan	2008	Goldikova	O. Peslier
1987	Miesque	F. Head	1998	Da Hoss	J. Velazquez	2009	Goldikova	O. Peslier
1988	Miesque	F. Head	1999	Silic	C. Nakatani	2010	Goldikova	O. Peslier
1989	Steinlen	J. Santos	2000	War Chant	G. Stevens	2011	Court Vision	R. Albarado
1990	Royal Academy	L. Piggott	2001	Val Royal	J. Valdivia Jr.	2012	Wise Dan	J. Velazquez
1991	Opening Verse	P. Valenzuela	2002	Domedriver	T. Thulliez	2013	Wise Dan	J. Lezcano
1992	Lure	M. Smith	2003	Six Perfections	J. Bailey	2014	Karakatonie	S. Pasquier
1993	Lure	M. Smith	2004	Singletary	D. Flores	2015	Tepin	J. Leparoux
1994	Barathea	F. Dettori	2005	Artie Schiller	G. Gomez	2016	Tourist	J. Rosario

Distaff
Distance: 1-1/8 mi since 1988; 1-1/4 mi, 1984-87; race known as Ladies' Classic, 2008-12.

Year	Horse	Jockey	Year	Horse	Jockey	Year	Horse	Jockey
1984	Princess Rooney	E. Delahoussaye	1995	Inside Information	M. Smith	2006	Round Pond	E. Prado
1985	Life's Magic	A. Cordero Jr.	1996	Jewel Princess	C. Nakatani	2007	Ginger Punch	R. Bejarano
1986	Lady's Secret	P. Day	1997	Ajina	M. Smith	2008	Zenyatta	M. Smith
1987	Sacahuista	R. Romero	1998	Escena	G. Stevens	2009	Life Is Sweet	G. Gomez
1988	Personal Ensign	R. Romero	1999	Beautiful Pleasure	J. Chaves	2010	Unrivaled Belle	K. Desormeaux
1989	Bayakoa	L. Pincay Jr.	2000	Spain	V. Espinoza	2011	Royal Delta	J. Lezcano
1990	Bayakoa	L. Pincay Jr.	2001	Unbridled Elaine	P. Day	2012	Royal Delta	M. Smith
1991	Dance Smartly	P. Day	2002	Azeri	M. Smith	2013	Beholder	G. Stevens
1992	Paseana	C. McCarron	2003	Adoration	P. Valenzuela	2014	Untapable	R. Napravnik
1993	Hollywood Wildcat	E. Delahoussaye	2004	Ashado	J. Velazquez	2015	Stopchargingmaria	J. Castellano
1994	One Dreamer	G. Stevens	2005	Pleasant Home	C. Velasquez	2016	Beholder	G. Stevens

Turf
Distance: 1-1/2 mi.

Year	Horse	Jockey	Year	Horse	Jockey	Year	Horse	Jockey
1984	Lashkari	Y. St.-Martin	1995	Northern Spur	C. McCarron	2006	Red Rocks	F. Dettori
1985	Pebbles	P. Eddery	1996	Pilsudski	W. Swinburn	2007	English Channel	J. Velasquez
1986	Manila	J. Santos	1997	Chief Bearhart	J. Santos	2008	Conduit	R. Moore
1987	Theatrical	P. Day	1998	Buck's Boy	S. Sellers	2009	Conduit	R. Moore
1988	Great Communicator	R. Sibille	1999	Daylami	F. Dettori	2010	Dangerous Midge	F. Dettori
			2000	Kalanisi	J. Murtagh	2011	St Nicholas Abbey	J. O'Brien
1989	Prized	E. Delahoussaye	2001	Fantastic Light	F. Dettori	2012	Little Mike	R. Dominguez
1990	In the Wings	G. Stevens	2002	High Chaparral	M. Kinane	2013	Magician	R. Moore
1991	Miss Alleged	E. Legrix	2003	(tie) High Chaparral	M. Kinane	2014	Main Sequence	J. Velazquez
1992	Fraise	P. Valenzuela		Johar	A. Solis	2015	Found	R. Moore
1993	Kotashaan	K. Desormeaux	2004	Better Talk Now	R. Dominguez	2016	Highland Reel	S. Heffernan
1994	Tikkanen	M. Smith	2005	Shirocco	C. Soumillon			

Eclipse Awards, 2015

The Eclipse Awards, honoring the Horse of the Year and other champions of thoroughbred racing, began in 1971 and are sponsored by the *Daily Racing Form*, the National Thoroughbred Racing Association, and the National Turf Writers Assn.

Horse of the Year: American Pharoah
2-year-old male: Nyquist
2-year-old female: Songbird
3-year-old male: American Pharoah
3-year-old female: Stellar Wind
Older male (4+ years old): Honor Code

Older female (4+ years old): Beholder
Male sprinter: Runhappy
Female sprinter: La Verdad
Male turf horse: Big Blue Kitten
Female turf horse: Tepin
Steeplechase horse: Dawalan

Trainer: Bob Baffert
Jockey: Javier Castellano
Apprentice jockey: Tyler Gaffalione
Breeder: Zayat Stables
Owner: Zayat Stables

HARNESS RACING
Harness Horse of the Year, 1947-2015
Chosen by the U.S. Trotting Assn. and the U.S. Harness Writers Assn.

Year	Horse	Year	Horse	Year	Horse	Year	Horse
1947	Victory Song	1965	Bret Hanover	1982	Cam Fella	1999	Moni Maker
1948	Rodney	1966	Bret Hanover	1983	Cam Fella	2000	Gallo Blue Chip
1949	Good Time	1967	Nevele Pride	1984	Fancy Crown	2001	Bunny Lake
1950	Proximity	1968	Nevele Pride	1985	Nihilator	2002	Real Desire
1951	Pronto Don	1969	Nevele Pride	1986	Forrest Skipper	2003	No Pan Intended
1952	Good Time	1970	Fresh Yankee	1987	Mack Lobell	2004	Rainbow Blue
1953	Hi Lo's Forbes	1971	Albatross	1988	Mack Lobell	2005	Rocknroll Hanover
1954	Stenographer	1972	Albatross	1989	Matt's Scooter	2006	Glidemaster
1955	Scott Frost	1973	Sir Dalrae	1990	Beach Towel	2007	Donato Hanover
1956	Scott Frost	1974	Delmonica Hanover	1991	Precious Bunny	2008	Somebeachsomewhere
1957	Torpid	1975	Savoir	1992	Artsplace	2009	Muscle Hill
1958	Emily's Pride	1976	Keystone Ore	1993	Staying Together	2010	Rock N Roll Heaven
1959	Bye Bye Byrd	1977	Green Speed	1994	Cam's Card Shark	2011	San Pail
1960	Adios Butler	1978	Abercrombie	1995	CR Kay Suzie	2012	Chapter Seven
1961	Adios Butler	1979	Niatross	1996	Continental Victory	2013	Bee a Magician
1962	Su Mac Lad	1980	Niatross	1997	Malabar Man	2014	JK She'salady
1963	Speedy Scot	1981	Fan Hanover	1998	Moni Maker	2015	Wiggle It Jiggleit
1964	Bret Hanover						

Hambletonian Winners (3-year-old trotters), 1965-2016

Year	Horse	Driver	Year	Horse	Driver	Year	Horse	Driver
1965	Egyptian Candor	D. Cameron	1983	Duenna	S. Dancer	2000	Yankee Paco	T. Ritchie
1966	Kerry Way	F. Ervin	1984	Historic Freight	B. Webster	2001	Scarlet Knight	S. Melander
1967	Speedy Streak	D. Cameron	1985	Prakas	B. O'Donnell	2002	Chip Chip Hooray	E. Ledford
1968	Nevele Pride	S. Dancer	1986	Nuclear Kosmos	U. Thoresen	2003	Amigo Hall	M. Lachance
1969	Lindy's Pride	H. Beissinger	1987	Mack Lobell	J. Campbell	2004	Windsong's Legacy	T. Smedshammer
1970	Timothy T	J. Simpson Sr.	1988	Armbro Goal	J. Campbell	2005	Vivid Photo	R. Hammer
1971	Speedy Crown	H. Beissinger	1989	Park Avenue Joe	R. Waples	2006	Glidemaster	J. Campbell
1972	Super Bowl	S. Dancer	1990	Harmonious	J. Campbell	2007	Donato Hanover	R. Pierce
1973	Flirth	R. Baldwin	1991	Giant Victory	J. Moiseyev	2008	Deweycheatumnhowe	R. Schnittker
1974	Christopher T	B. Haughton	1992	Alf Palema	M. McNicholl	2009	Muscle Hill	B. Sears
1975	Bonefish	S. Dancer	1993	American Winner	R. Pierce	2010	Muscle Massive	R. Pierce
1976	Steve Lobell	B. Haughton	1994	Victory Dream	M. Lachance	2011	Broad Bahn	G. Brennan
1977	Green Speed	B. Haughton	1995	Tagliabue	J. Campbell	2012	Market Share	T. Tetrick
1978	Speedy Somolli	H. Beissinger	1996	Continental Victory	M. Lachance	2013	Royalty For Life	B. Sears
1979	Legend Hanover	G. Sholty	1997	Malabar Man	M. Burroughs	2014	Trixton	J. Takter
1980	Burgomeister	B. Haughton	1998	Muscles Yankee	J. Campbell	2015	Pinkman	B. Sears
1981	Shiaway St. Pat	R. Remmen	1999	Self Possessed	M. Lachance	2016	Marion Marauder	S. Zeron
1982	Speed Bowl	T. Haughton						

BOWLING
Professional Bowlers Association Tournament of Champions, 1965-2016

Year	Winner	Year	Winner	Year	Winner	Year	Winner
1965	Billy Hardwick	1978	Earl Anthony	1990	Dave Ferraro	2005	Steve Jaros
1966	Wayne Zahn	1979	George Pappas	1991	David Ozio	2006	Chris Barnes
1967	Jim Stefanich	1980	Wayne Webb	1992	Marc McDowell	2007	Tommy Jones
1968	Dave Davis	1981	Steve Cook	1993	George Branham III	2008	Michael Haugen Jr.
1969	Jim Godman	1982	Mike Durbin	1994	Norm Duke	2009	Patrick Allen
1970	Don Johnson	1983	Joe Berardi	1996	Dave D'Entremont	2010	Kelly Kulick
1971	Johnny Petraglia	1984	Mike Durbin	1997	John Gant	2011	Mika Koivuniemi
1972	Mike Durbin	1985	Mark Williams	1998	Bryan Goebel	2012	Sean Rash
1973	Jim Godman	1986	Marshall Holman	1999	Jason Couch	2013	Pete Weber
1974	Earl Anthony	1987	Pete Weber	2000	Jason Couch	2014	Jason Belmonte
1975	Dave Davis	1988	Mark Williams	2002	Jason Couch	2015	Jason Belmonte
1976	Marshall Holman	1989	Del Ballard Jr.	2003	Patrick Healey Jr.	2016	Jesper Svensson
1977	Mike Berlin						

Note: No tournament held in 2001 or 2004.

Professional Bowlers Association Leading Money Winners, 1962-2016

Total winnings from tournaments only. For 2000-13, year shown is year the PBA season ended. As of Aug. 12, 2016.

Year	Bowler	Earnings	Year	Bowler	Earnings	Year	Bowler	Earnings
1962	Don Carter	$49,972	1980	Wayne Webb	$116,700	1998	Walter Ray Williams Jr.	$238,225
1963	Dick Weber	46,333	1981	Earl Anthony	164,735	1999	Parker Bohn III	240,912
1964	Bob Strampe	33,592	1982	Earl Anthony	134,760	2000	Norm Duke	143,325
1965	Dick Weber	47,674	1983	Earl Anthony	135,605	2002	Parker Bohn III	245,200
1966	Wayne Zahn	54,720	1984	Mark Roth	158,712	2003	Walter Ray Williams Jr.	419,700
1967	Dave Davis	54,165	1985	Mike Aulby	201,200	2004	Mika Koivuniemi	238,590
1968	Jim Stefanich	67,377	1986	Walter Ray Williams Jr.	145,550	2005	Patrick Allen	350,740
1969	Billy Hardwick	64,160	1987	Pete Weber	175,491	2006	Tommy Jones	301,700
1970	Mike McGrath	52,049	1988	Brian Voss	225,485	2007	Doug Kent	200,530
1971	Johnny Petraglia	85,065	1989	Mike Aulby	298,237	2008	Norm Duke	176,855
1972	Don Johnson	56,648	1990	Amleto Monacelli	204,775	2009	Norm Duke	199,130
1973	Don McCune	69,000	1991	David Ozio	225,585	2010	Walter Ray Williams Jr.	152,670
1974	Earl Anthony	99,585	1992	Marc McDowell	174,215	2011	Mika Koivuniemi	333,040
1975	Earl Anthony	107,585	1993	Walter Ray Williams Jr.	296,370	2012	Sean Rash	140,250
1976	Earl Anthony	110,833	1994	Norm Duke	273,753	2013	Sean Rash	248,317
1977	Mark Roth	105,583	1995	Mike Aulby	219,792	2014	Jason Belmonte	163,778
1978	Mark Roth	134,500	1996	Walter Ray Williams Jr.	241,330	2015	Jason Belmonte	178,542
1979	Mark Roth	124,517	1997	Walter Ray Williams Jr.	240,544	2016	Anthony Simonsen	91,775

World Chess Champions, 1886-2016
Source: U.S. Chess Federation, International Chess Federation (FIDE)
Official world champions since the title was first used. As of Oct. 2016.

Years	Champion, country	Years	Champion, country
1886-94	Wilhelm Steinitz, Austria	1972-75	Bobby Fischer, U.S.[2]
1894-1921	Emanuel Lasker, Germany	1975-85	Anatoly Karpov, USSR
1921-27	Jose R. Capablanca, Cuba	1985-2000	Garry Kasparov, USSR/Russia[3,4]
1927-35	Alexander Alekhine, France	1993-99	Anatoly Karpov, Russia (FIDE)[3]
1935-37	Max Euwe, Netherlands	1999-2000	Alexander Khalifman, Russia (FIDE)
1937-46	Alexander Alekhine, France[1]	2000-02	Viswanathan Anand, India (FIDE)
1948-57	Mikhail Botvinnik, USSR	2000-06	Vladimir Kramnik, Russia (classical)[4]
1957-58	Vassily Smyslov, USSR	2002-04	Ruslan Ponomariov, Ukraine (FIDE)
1958-59	Mikhail Botvinnik, USSR	2004-05	Rustam Kasimdzhanov, Uzbekistan (FIDE)
1960-61	Mikhail Tal, USSR	2005-06	Veselin Topalov, Bulgaria (FIDE)[5]
1961-63	Mikhail Botvinnik, USSR	2006-07	Vladimir Kramnik, Russia[5]
1963-69	Tigran Petrosian, USSR	2007-13	Viswanathan Anand, India
1969-72	Boris Spassky, USSR	2013-	Magnus Carlsen, Norway

(1) After Alekhine died in 1946, the title was vacant until 1948, when Botvinnik won the first world championship event sanctioned by FIDE. (2) Defaulted championship after refusing to accept FIDE rules for a championship match, Apr. 1975. (3) Kasparov broke with FIDE, Feb. 26, 1993. FIDE stripped Kasparov of his FIDE title Mar. 23. Kasparov defeated Nigel Short (UK) in a world championship match played Sept.-Oct. 1993 under the auspices of the Professional Chess Association (PCA), a new organization the two had founded. FIDE held a championship match between Anatoly Karpov (Russia) and Jan Timman (Netherlands), which Karpov won in Nov. 1993. The PCA folded in 1995, but Kasparov was still considered the "classical" world champion. (That is, he defended his title against challengers; FIDE matches are arranged differently.) (4) In Nov. 2000, Kramnik defeated Kasparov for the classical world championship title. (5) Kramnik, the classical world champion since 2000, unified the chess titles by defeating Topalov on Oct. 13, 2006, at a world championship match.

U.S. and World Figure Skating Championships, 1952-2016

U.S. Champions			World Champions	
Men's winner	Women's winner	Year	Men's winner, country	Women's winner, country
Dick Button	Tenley Albright	1952	Dick Button, U.S.	Jacqueline du Bief, France
Hayes Jenkins	Tenley Albright	1953	Hayes Jenkins, U.S.	Tenley Albright, U.S.
Hayes Jenkins	Tenley Albright	1954	Hayes Jenkins, U.S.	Gundi Busch, W. Germany
Hayes Jenkins	Tenley Albright	1955	Hayes Jenkins, U.S.	Tenley Albright, U.S.
Hayes Jenkins	Tenley Albright	1956	Hayes Jenkins, U.S.	Carol Heiss, U.S.
David Jenkins	Carol Heiss	1957	David Jenkins, U.S.	Carol Heiss, U.S.
David Jenkins	Carol Heiss	1958	David Jenkins, U.S.	Carol Heiss, U.S.
David Jenkins	Carol Heiss	1959	David Jenkins, U.S.	Carol Heiss, U.S.
David Jenkins	Carol Heiss	1960	Alain Giletti, France	Carol Heiss, U.S.
Bradley Lord	Laurence Owen	1961	No competition[1]	No competition[1]
Monty Hoyt	Barbara Roles Pursley	1962	Don Jackson, Canada	Sjoukje Dijkstra, Netherlands
Tommy Litz	Lorraine Hanlon	1963	Don McPherson, Canada	Sjoukje Dijkstra, Netherlands
Scott Allen	Peggy Fleming	1964	Manfred Schnelldorfer, W. Germany	Sjoukje Dijkstra, Netherlands
Gary Visconti	Peggy Fleming	1965	Alain Calmat, France	Petra Burka, Canada
Scott Allen	Peggy Fleming	1966	Emmerich Danzer, Austria	Peggy Fleming, U.S.
Gary Visconti	Peggy Fleming	1967	Emmerich Danzer, Austria	Peggy Fleming, U.S.
Tim Wood	Peggy Fleming	1968	Emmerich Danzer, Austria	Peggy Fleming, U.S.
Tim Wood	Janet Lynn	1969	Tim Wood, U.S.	Gabriele Seyfert, E. Germany
Tim Wood	Janet Lynn	1970	Tim Wood, U.S.	Gabriele Seyfert, E. Germany
John Misha Petkevich	Janet Lynn	1971	Ondrej Nepela, Czechoslovakia	Beatrix Schuba, Austria
Ken Shelley	Janet Lynn	1972	Ondrej Nepela, Czechoslovakia	Beatrix Schuba, Austria
Gordon McKellen Jr.	Janet Lynn	1973	Ondrej Nepela, Czechoslovakia	Karen Magnussen, Canada
Gordon McKellen Jr.	Dorothy Hamill	1974	Jan Hoffmann, E. Germany	Christine Errath, E. Germany
Gordon McKellen Jr.	Dorothy Hamill	1975	Sergei Volkov, USSR	Dianne de Leeuw, Neth.
Terry Kubicka	Dorothy Hamill	1976	John Curry, UK	Dorothy Hamill, U.S.
Charles Tickner	Linda Fratianne	1977	Vladimir Kovalev, USSR	Linda Fratianne, U.S.
Charles Tickner	Linda Fratianne	1978	Charles Tickner, U.S.	Anett Poetzsch, E. Germany
Charles Tickner	Linda Fratianne	1979	Vladimir Kovalev, USSR	Linda Fratianne, U.S.
Charles Tickner	Linda Fratianne	1980	Jan Hoffmann, E. Germany	Anett Poetzsch, E. Germany
Scott Hamilton	Elaine Zayak	1981	Scott Hamilton, U.S.	Denise Biellmann, Switzerland
Scott Hamilton	Rosalynn Sumners	1982	Scott Hamilton, U.S.	Elaine Zayak, U.S.
Scott Hamilton	Rosalynn Sumners	1983	Scott Hamilton, U.S.	Rosalynn Sumners, U.S.
Scott Hamilton	Rosalynn Sumners	1984	Scott Hamilton, U.S.	Katarina Witt, E. Germany
Brian Boitano	Tiffany Chin	1985	Aleksandr Fadeev, USSR	Katarina Witt, E. Germany
Brian Boitano	Debi Thomas	1986	Brian Boitano, U.S.	Debi Thomas, U.S.
Brian Boitano	Jill Trenary	1987	Brian Orser, Canada	Katarina Witt, E. Germany
Brian Boitano	Debi Thomas	1988	Brian Boitano, U.S.	Katarina Witt, E. Germany
Christopher Bowman	Jill Trenary	1989	Kurt Browning, Canada	Midori Ito, Japan
Todd Eldredge	Jill Trenary	1990	Kurt Browning, Canada	Jill Trenary, U.S.
Todd Eldredge	Tonya Harding	1991	Kurt Browning, Canada	Kristi Yamaguchi, U.S.
Christopher Bowman	Kristi Yamaguchi	1992	Viktor Petrenko, Ukraine	Kristi Yamaguchi, U.S.
Scott Davis	Nancy Kerrigan	1993	Kurt Browning, Canada	Oksana Baiul, Ukraine
Scott Davis	Vacant[2]	1994	Elvis Stojko, Canada	Yuka Sato, Japan
Todd Eldredge	Nicole Bobek	1995	Elvis Stojko, Canada	Chen Lu, China
Rudy Galindo	Michelle Kwan	1996	Todd Eldredge, U.S.	Michelle Kwan, U.S.
Todd Eldredge	Tara Lipinski	1997	Elvis Stojko, Canada	Tara Lipinski, U.S.
Todd Eldredge	Michelle Kwan	1998	Alexei Yagudin, Russia	Michelle Kwan, U.S.
Michael Weiss	Michelle Kwan	1999	Alexei Yagudin, Russia	Maria Butyrskaya, Russia
Michael Weiss	Michelle Kwan	2000	Alexei Yagudin, Russia	Michelle Kwan, U.S.
Timothy Goebel	Michelle Kwan	2001	Yevgeny Plushenko, Russia	Michelle Kwan, U.S.
Todd Eldredge	Michelle Kwan	2002	Alexei Yagudin, Russia	Irina Slutskaya, Russia
Michael Weiss	Michelle Kwan	2003	Yevgeny Plushenko, Russia	Michelle Kwan, U.S.
Johnny Weir	Michelle Kwan	2004	Yevgeny Plushenko, Russia	Shizuka Arakawa, Japan
Johnny Weir	Michelle Kwan	2005	Stephane Lambiel, Switzerland	Irina Slutskaya, Russia
Johnny Weir	Sasha Cohen	2006	Stephane Lambiel, Switzerland	Kimmie Meissner, U.S.
Evan Lysacek	Kimmie Meissner	2007	Brian Joubert, France	Miki Ando, Japan
Evan Lysacek	Mirai Nagasu	2008	Jeffrey Buttle, Canada	Mao Asada, Japan
Jeremy Abbott	Alissa Czisny	2009	Evan Lysacek, U.S.	Yuna Kim, South Korea
Jeremy Abbott	Rachael Flatt	2010	Daisuke Takahashi, Japan	Mao Asada, Japan
Ryan Bradley	Alissa Czisny	2011	Patrick Chan, Canada	Miki Ando, Japan
Jeremy Abbott	Ashley Wagner	2012	Patrick Chan, Canada	Carolina Kostner, Italy
Max Aaron	Ashley Wagner	2013	Patrick Chan, Canada	Yuna Kim, South Korea
Jeremy Abbott	Gracie Gold	2014	Yuzuru Hanyu, Japan	Mao Asada, Japan
Jason Brown	Ashley Wagner	2015	Javier Fernandez, Spain	Elizaveta Tuktamysheva, Russia
Adam Rippon	Gracie Gold	2016	Javier Fernandez, Spain	Evgenia Medvedeva, Russia

(1) Competition canceled after 18-member U.S. team died in plane crash en route. (2) Tonya Harding was stripped of the title for her involvement in an attack on rival Nancy Kerrigan.

Alpine Skiing Men's World Cup Champions, 1967-2016

Year	Champion, country	Year	Champion, country	Year	Champion, country
1967	Jean Claude Killy, France	1984	Pirmin Zurbriggen, Switzerland	2001	Hermann Maier, Austria
1968	Jean Claude Killy, France	1985	Marc Girardelli, Luxembourg	2002	Stephan Eberharter, Austria
1969	Karl Schranz, Austria	1986	Marc Girardelli, Luxembourg	2003	Stephan Eberharter, Austria
1970	Karl Schranz, Austria	1987	Pirmin Zurbriggen, Switzerland	2004	Hermann Maier, Austria
1971	Gustavo Thoeni, Italy	1988	Pirmin Zurbriggen, Switzerland	2005	Bode Miller, U.S.
1972	Gustavo Thoeni, Italy	1989	Marc Girardelli, Luxembourg	2006	Benjamin Raich, Austria
1973	Gustavo Thoeni, Italy	1990	Pirmin Zurbriggen, Switzerland	2007	Aksel Lund Svindal, Norway
1974	Piero Gros, Italy	1991	Marc Girardelli, Luxembourg	2008	Bode Miller, U.S.
1975	Gustavo Thoeni, Italy	1992	Paul Accola, Switzerland	2009	Aksel Lund Svindal, Norway
1976	Ingemar Stenmark, Sweden	1993	Marc Girardelli, Luxembourg	2010	Carlo Janka, Switzerland
1977	Ingemar Stenmark, Sweden	1994	Kjetil Andre Aamodt, Norway	2011	Ivica Kostelic, Croatia
1978	Ingemar Stenmark, Sweden	1995	Alberto Tomba, Italy	2012	Marcel Hirscher, Austria
1979	Peter Luescher, Switzerland	1996	Lasse Kjus, Norway	2013	Marcel Hirscher, Austria
1980	Andreas Wenzel, Liechtenstein	1997	Luc Alphand, France	2014	Marcel Hirscher, Austria
1981	Phil Mahre, U.S.	1998	Hermann Maier, Austria	2015	Marcel Hirscher, Austria
1982	Phil Mahre, U.S.	1999	Lasse Kjus, Norway	2016	Marcel Hirscher, Austria
1983	Phil Mahre, U.S.	2000	Hermann Maier, Austria		

Alpine Skiing Women's World Cup Champions, 1967-2016

Year	Champion, country	Year	Champion, country	Year	Champion, country
1967	Nancy Greene, Canada	1984	Erika Hess, Switzerland	2001	Janica Kostelic, Croatia
1968	Nancy Greene, Canada	1985	Michela Figini, Switzerland	2002	Michaela Dorfmeister, Austria
1969	Gertrud Gabl, Austria	1986	Maria Walliser, Switzerland	2003	Janica Kostelic, Croatia
1970	Michele Jacot, France	1987	Maria Walliser, Switzerland	2004	Anja Paerson, Sweden
1971	Annemarie Proell, Austria	1988	Michela Figini, Switzerland	2005	Anja Paerson, Sweden
1972	Annemarie Proell, Austria	1989	Vreni Schneider, Switzerland	2006	Janica Kostelic, Croatia
1973	Annemarie Proell, Austria	1990	Petra Kronberger, Austria	2007	Nicole Hosp, Austria
1974	Annemarie Proell, Austria	1991	Petra Kronberger, Austria	2008	Lindsey Vonn, U.S.
1975	Annemarie Proell, Austria	1992	Petra Kronberger, Austria	2009	Lindsey Vonn, U.S.
1976	Rose Mittermaier, W. Germany	1993	Anita Wachter, Austria	2010	Lindsey Vonn, U.S.
1977	Lise-Marie Morerod, Switzerland	1994	Vreni Schneider, Switzerland	2011	Maria Höfl-Riesch, Germany
1978	Hanni Wenzel, Liechtenstein	1995	Vreni Schneider, Switzerland	2012	Lindsey Vonn, U.S.
1979	Annemarie Proell Moser, Austria	1996	Katja Seizinger, Germany	2013	Tina Maze, Slovenia
1980	Hanni Wenzel, Liechtenstein	1997	Pernilla Wiberg, Sweden	2014	Anna Fenninger, Austria
1981	Marie-Theres Nadig, Switzerland	1998	Katja Seizinger, Germany	2015	Anna Fenninger, Austria
1982	Erika Hess, Switzerland	1999	Alexandra Meissnitzer, Austria	2016	Lara Gut, Switzerland
1983	Tamara McKinney, U.S.	2000	Renate Goetschl, Austria		

Tour de France, 2016

The UK's Chris Froome won the Tour de France for the third time in four years in the 103rd edition of cycling's premier race July 24, 2016. The first stage of the 2,187-mi (3,519-km) Tour de France began July 2 in Mont-Saint-Michel, France. The final and 21st stage concluded on the streets of Paris, where Froome claimed victory in 89 hr., 4 min., 48 sec., followed by France's Romain Bardet, 4 min., 5 sec. behind, and Colombia's Nairo Quintana, 4 min., 21 sec. behind. Australian Adam Yates won the white jersey as the best rider under age 25 in the Tour de France, and Poland's Rafal Majka won the polka dot jersey as the best climber. Slovakian Peter Sagan won the green jersey as the points leader for the fifth straight year.

The 2017 Tour de France is scheduled to be held July 1-23. Its route will take cyclists from Düsseldorf, Germany, to Paris.

Tour de France Winners, 1903-2016

The Tour de France was first held in 1903. Sixty cyclists began the 1,509-mi (2,428-km) race at Montgeron, a suburb of Paris, and 21 cyclists finished the six-stage race 17 days later in Paris. The race route changes every year. Race not held, 1915-18, 1940-46.

Year	Winner, country	Year	Winner, country	Year	Winner, country
1903	Maurice Garin, France	1949	Fausto Coppi, Italy	1983	Laurent Fignon, France
1904	Henri Cornet, France	1950	Ferdi Kübler, Switzerland	1984	Laurent Fignon, France
1905	Louis Trousselier, France	1951	Hugo Koblet, Switzerland	1985	Bernard Hinault, France
1906	René Pottier, France	1952	Fausto Coppi, Italy	1986	Greg LeMond, U.S.
1907	Lucien Petit-Breton, France	1953	Louison Bobet, France	1987	Stephen Roche, Ireland
1908	Lucien Petit-Breton, France	1954	Louison Bobet, France	1988	Pedro Delgado, Spain
1909	François Faber, Luxembourg	1955	Louison Bobet, France	1989	Greg LeMond, U.S.
1910	Octave Lapize, France	1956	Roger Walkowiak, France	1990	Greg LeMond, U.S.
1911	Gustave Garrigou, France	1957	Jacques Anquetil, France	1991	Miguel Indurain, Spain
1912	Odile Defraye, Belgium	1958	Charly Gaul, Luxembourg	1992	Miguel Indurain, Spain
1913	Philippe Thys, Belgium	1959	Federico Bahamontes, Spain	1993	Miguel Indurain, Spain
1914	Philippe Thys, Belgium	1960	Gastone Nencini, Italy	1994	Miguel Indurain, Spain
1919	Firmin Lambot, Belgium	1961	Jacques Anquetil, France	1995	Miguel Indurain, Spain
1920	Philippe Thys, Belgium	1962	Jacques Anquetil, France	1996	Bjarne Riis, Denmark
1921	Léon Scieur, Belgium	1963	Jacques Anquetil, France	1997	Jan Ullrich, Germany
1922	Firmin Lambot, Belgium	1964	Jacques Anquetil, France	1998	Marco Pantani, Italy
1923	Henri Pélissier, France	1965	Felice Gimondi, Italy	1999	Vacant[1]
1924	Ottavio Bottecchia, Italy	1966	Lucien Aimar, France	2000	Vacant[1]
1925	Ottavio Bottecchia, Italy	1967	Roger Pingeon, France	2001	Vacant[1]
1926	Lucien Buysse, Belgium	1968	Jan Janssen, Netherlands	2002	Vacant[1]
1927	Nicolas Frantz, Luxembourg	1969	Eddy Merckx, Belgium	2003	Vacant[1]
1928	Nicolas Frantz, Luxembourg	1970	Eddy Merckx, Belgium	2004	Vacant[1]
1929	Maurice Dewaele, Belgium	1971	Eddy Merckx, Belgium	2005	Vacant[1]
1930	André Leducq, France	1972	Eddy Merckx, Belgium	2006	Óscar Pereiro, Spain[2]
1931	Antonin Magne, France	1973	Luis Ocaña, Spain	2007	Alberto Contador, Spain
1932	André Leducq, France	1974	Eddy Merckx, Belgium	2008	Carlos Sastre, Spain
1933	Georges Speicher, France	1975	Bernard Thévenet, France	2009	Alberto Contador, Spain
1934	Antonin Magne, France	1976	Lucien Van Impe, Belgium	2010	Andy Schleck, Luxembourg[3]
1935	Romain Maes, Belgium	1977	Bernard Thévenet, France	2011	Cadel Evans, Australia
1936	Sylvère Maes, Belgium	1978	Bernard Hinault, France	2012	Bradley Wiggins, UK
1937	Roger Lapépie, France	1979	Bernard Hinault, France	2013	Chris Froome, UK
1938	Gino Bartali, Italy	1980	Joop Zoetemelk, Netherlands	2014	Vincenzo Nibali, Italy
1939	Sylvère Maes, Belgium	1981	Bernard Hinault, France	2015	Chris Froome, UK
1947	Jean Robic, France	1982	Bernard Hinault, France	2016	Chris Froome, UK
1948	Gino Bartali, Italy				

(1) Lance Armstrong, U.S., was stripped of his seven Tour titles Oct. 22, 2012, in accordance with World Anti-Doping Code; Armstrong had dropped his fight against doping charges Aug. 23, 2012. (2) Floyd Landis, U.S., was stripped of the 2006 title, Sept. 20, 2007, for doping. Landis lost a final appeal of the ruling June 30, 2008. (3) Alberto Contador, Spain, was stripped of the 2010 title, Feb. 6, 2012, for doping.

Swimming World Records

Long course (50-m pools only) records, as of Sept. 2016. All times in minutes:seconds. * = Record pending ratification.

Men's Records

Freestyle

Distance	Record	Holder	Nationality	Location	Date
50 meters	0:20.91	César Cielo Filho	Brazil	São Paulo, Brazil	Dec. 18, 2009
100 meters	0:46.91	César Cielo Filho	Brazil	Rome, Italy	July 30, 2009
200 meters	1:42.00	Paul Biedermann	Germany	Rome, Italy	July 28, 2009
400 meters	3:40.07	Paul Biedermann	Germany	Rome, Italy	July 26, 2009
800 meters	7:32.12	Zhang Lin	China	Rome, Italy	July 29, 2009
1,500 meters	14:31.02	Yang Sun	China	London, England, UK	Aug. 4, 2012

Backstroke

Distance	Record	Holder	Nationality	Location	Date
50 meters	0:24.04	Liam Tancock	UK	Rome, Italy	Aug. 2, 2009
100 meters	0:51.85*	Ryan Murphy	U.S.	Rio de Janeiro, Brazil	Aug. 13, 2016
200 meters	1:51.92	Aaron Peirsol	U.S.	Rome, Italy	July 31, 2009

Breaststroke

Distance	Record	Holder	Nationality	Location	Date
50 meters	0:26.42	Adam Peaty	UK	Kazan, Russia	Aug. 4, 2015
100 meters	0:57.13*	Adam Peaty	UK	Rio de Janeiro, Brazil	Aug. 7, 2016
200 meters	2:07.01	Akihiro Yamaguchi	Japan	Gifu, Japan	Sept. 15, 2012

Butterfly

Distance	Record	Holder	Nationality	Location	Date
50 meters	0:22.43	Rafael Muñoz	Spain	Malaga, Spain	Apr. 5, 2009
100 meters	0:49.82	Michael Phelps	U.S.	Rome, Italy	Aug. 1, 2009
200 meters	1:51.51	Michael Phelps	U.S.	Rome, Italy	July 29, 2009

Individual medley

Distance	Record	Holder	Nationality	Location	Date
200 meters	1:54.00	Ryan Lochte	U.S.	Shanghai, China	July 28, 2011
400 meters	4:03.84	Michael Phelps	U.S.	Beijing, China	Aug. 10, 2008

Freestyle relay

Distance	Record	Holder	Nationality	Location	Date
400 m (4×100)	3:08.24	Phelps, Weber-Gale, Jones, Lezak	U.S.	Beijing, China	Aug. 11, 2008
800 m (4×200)	6:58.55	Phelps, Berens, Walters, Lochte	U.S.	Rome, Italy	July 31, 2009

Medley relay

Distance	Record	Holder	Nationality	Location	Date
400 m (4×100)	3:27.28	Peirsol, Shanteau, Phelps, Walters	U.S.	Rome, Italy	Aug. 2, 2009

Women's Records

Freestyle

Distance	Record	Holder	Nationality	Location	Date
50 meters	0:23.73	Britta Steffen	Germany	Rome, Italy	Aug. 2, 2009
100 meters	0:52.07	Britta Steffen	Germany	Rome, Italy	July 31, 2009
200 meters	1:52.98	Federica Pellegrini	Italy	Rome, Italy	July 29, 2009
400 meters	3:56.46*	Katie Ledecky	U.S.	Rio de Janeiro, Brazil	Aug. 7, 2016
800 meters	8:04.79*	Katie Ledecky	U.S.	Rio de Janeiro, Brazil	Aug. 12, 2016
1,500 meters	15:25.48	Katie Ledecky	U.S.	Kazan, Russia	Aug. 4, 2015

Backstroke

Distance	Record	Holder	Nationality	Location	Date
50 meters	0:27.06	Zhao Jing	China	Rome, Italy	July 30, 2009
100 meters	0:58.12	Gemma Spofforth	UK	Rome, Italy	July 28, 2009
200 meters	2:04.06	Missy Franklin	U.S.	London, England, UK	Aug. 3, 2012

Breaststroke

Distance	Record	Holder	Nationality	Location	Date
50 meters	0:29.48	Ruta Meilutyte	Lithuania	Barcelona, Spain	Aug. 3, 2013
100 meters	1:04.35	Ruta Meilutyte	Lithuania	Barcelona, Spain	July 29, 2013
200 meters	2:19.11	Rikke Moller Pedersen	Denmark	Barcelona, Spain	Aug. 1, 2013

Butterfly

Distance	Record	Holder	Nationality	Location	Date
50 meters	0:24.43	Sarah Sjöström	Sweden	Boras, Sweden	July 5, 2014
100 meters	0:55.48*	Sarah Sjöström	Sweden	Rio de Janeiro, Brazil	Aug. 7, 2016
200 meters	2:01.81	Liu Zige	China	Jinan, China	Oct. 21, 2009

Individual medley

Distance	Record	Holder	Nationality	Location	Date
200 meters	2:06.12	Katinka Hosszú	Hungary	Kazan, Russia	Aug. 3, 2015
400 meters	4:26.36*	Katinka Hosszú	Hungary	Rio de Janeiro, Brazil	Aug. 6, 2016

Freestyle relay

Distance	Record	Holder	Nationality	Location	Date
400 m (4×100)	3:30.65*	Campbell, McKeon, Elmslie, Campbell	Australia	Rio de Janeiro, Brazil	Aug. 6, 2016
800 m (4×200)	7:42.08	Yang, Zhu, Liu, Pang	China	Rome, Italy	July 30, 2009

Medley relay

Distance	Record	Holder	Nationality	Location	Date
400 m (4×100)	3:52.05	Franklin, Soni, Vollmer, Schmitt	U.S.	London, England, UK	Aug. 4, 2012

World Track and Field Outdoor Records

The International Association of Athletics Federations (IAAF), the world body of track and field, recognizes only records in metric distances, except for the mile. As of Sept. 2016.

Men's Records

Running

Event	Record	Holder	Nationality	Location	Date
100 meters	9.58 s.	Usain Bolt	Jamaica	Berlin, Germany	Aug. 16, 2009
200 meters	19.19 s.	Usain Bolt	Jamaica	Berlin, Germany	Aug. 20, 2009
400 meters	43.03 s.	Wayde Van Niekerk	South Africa	Rio de Janeiro, Brazil	Aug. 14, 2016
800 meters	1 min., 40.91 s.	David Lekuta Rudisha	Kenya	London, England, UK	Aug. 9, 2012
1,000 meters	2 min., 11.96 s.	Noah Ngeny	Kenya	Rieti, Italy	Sept. 5, 1999
1,500 meters	3 min., 26.00 s.	Hicham El Guerrouj	Morocco	Rome, Italy	July 14, 1998
1 mile	3 min., 43.13 s.	Hicham El Guerrouj	Morocco	Rome, Italy	July 7, 1999
2,000 meters	4 min., 44.79 s.	Hicham El Guerrouj	Morocco	Berlin, Germany	Sept. 7, 1999
3,000 meters	7 min., 20.67 s.	Daniel Komen	Kenya	Rieti, Italy	Sept. 1, 1996
3,000-meter stpl.	7 min., 53.63 s.	Saif Saaeed Shaheen	Qatar	Brussels, Belgium	Sept. 3, 2004
5,000 meters	12 min., 37.35 s.	Kenenisa Bekele	Ethiopia	Hengelo, Netherlands	May 31, 2004
10,000 meters	26 min., 17.53 s.	Kenenisa Bekele	Ethiopia	Brussels, Belgium	Aug. 26, 2005
20,000 meters	56 min., 26.00 s.	Haile Gebrselassie	Ethiopia	Ostrava, Czech Rep.	June 27, 2007
25,000 meters	1 hr., 12 min., 25.4 s.	Moses Cheruiyot Mosop	Kenya	Eugene, OR	June 3, 2011
Marathon	2 hr., 2 min., 57 s.	Dennis Kimetto	Kenya	Berlin, Germany	Sept. 28, 2014
110-meter hurdles	12.80 s.	Aries Merritt	U.S.	Brussels, Belgium	Sept. 7, 2012
400-meter hurdles	46.78 s.	Kevin Young	U.S.	Barcelona, Spain	Aug. 6, 1992
400 m (4×100)	36.84 s.	Carter, Frater, Blake, Bolt	Jamaica	London, England, UK	Aug. 11, 2012
800 m (4×200)	1 min., 18.63 s.	Ashmeade, Weir, Brown, Blake	Jamaica	Nassau, The Bahamas	May 24, 2014
1,600 m (4×400)	2 min., 54.29 s.	Valmon, Watts, Reynolds, Johnson	U.S.	Stuttgart, Germany	Aug. 22, 1993
3,200 m (4×800)	7 min., 2.43 s.	Mutua, Yiampoy, Kombich, Bungei	Kenya	Brussels, Belgium	Aug. 25, 2006

Field Events

Event	Record	Holder	Nationality	Location	Date
High jump	2.45 m (8' ½")	Javier Sotomayor	Cuba	Salamanca, Spain	July 27, 1993
Long jump	8.95 m (29' 4½")	Mike Powell	U.S.	Tokyo, Japan	Aug. 30, 1991
Triple jump	18.29 m (60' ¼")	Jonathan Edwards	UK	Gothenburg, Sweden	Aug. 7, 1995
Pole vault	6.14 m (20' 1¾")	Sergey Bubka	Ukraine	Sestriere, Italy	July 31, 1994
Discus	74.08 m (243' 0")	Jürgen Schult	E. Germany	Neubrandenburg, E. Germany	June 6, 1986
Hammer	86.74 m (284' 7")	Yuriy Sedykh	USSR	Stuttgart, W. Germany	Aug. 30, 1986
Javelin	98.48 m (323' 1")	Jan Zelezný	Czech Rep.	Jena, W. Germany	May 25, 1996
Shot put	23.12 m (75' 10¼")	Randy Barnes	U.S.	Westwood, CA	May 20, 1990
Decathlon	9,045 pts.	Ashton Eaton	U.S.	Beijing, China	Aug. 29, 2015

Women's Records

Running

Event	Record	Holder	Nationality	Location	Date
100 meters	10.49 s.	Florence Griffith-Joyner	U.S.	Indianapolis, IN.	July 16, 1988
200 meters	21.34 s.	Florence Griffith-Joyner	U.S.	Seoul, S. Korea	Sept. 29, 1988
400 meters	47.60 s.	Marita Koch	E. Germany	Canberra, Australia	Oct. 6, 1985
800 meters	1 min., 53.28 s.	Jarmila Kratochvílová	Czechoslovakia	Munich, W. Germany	July 26, 1983
1,000 meters	2 min., 28.98 s.	Svetlana Masterkova	Russia	Brussels, Belgium	Aug. 23, 1996
1,500 meters	3 min., 50.07 s.	Genzebe Dibaba	Ethiopia	Fontvieille, Monaco	July 17, 2015
1 mile	4 min., 12.56 s.	Svetlana Masterkova	Russia	Zürich, Switzerland	Aug. 14, 1996
2,000 meters	5 min., 25.36 s.	Sonia O'Sullivan	Ireland	Edinburgh, Scotland, UK	July 8, 1994
3,000 meters	8 min., 6.11 s.	Wang Junxia	China	Beijing, China	Sept. 13, 1993
3,000-meter stpl.	8 min., 52.78 s.	Ruth Jebet	Kenya-Bahrain	Paris, France	Aug. 27, 2016
5,000 meters	14 min., 11.15 s.	Tirunesh Dibaba	Ethiopia	Oslo, Norway	June 6, 2008
10,000 meters	29 min., 17.45 s.	Almaz Ayana	Ethiopia	Rio de Janeiro, Brazil	Aug. 12, 2016
20,000 meters	1 hr., 5 min., 26.6 s.	Tegla Loroupe	Kenya	Borgholzhausen, Germany	Sept. 3, 2000
Marathon	2 hr., 15 min., 25.0 s.	Paula Radcliffe	UK	London, England, UK	Apr. 13, 2003
100-meter hurdles	12.20 s.	Kendra Harrison	U.S.	London, England, UK	July 22, 2016
400-meter hurdles	52.34 s.	Yuliya Pechenkina	Russia	Tula, Russia	Aug. 8, 2003
400 m (4×100)	40.82 s.	Madison, Felix, Knight, Jeter	U.S.	London, England, UK	Aug. 10, 2012
800 m (4×200)	1 min., 27.46 s.	Jenkins, Colander, Perry, Jones	U.S.	Philadelphia, PA.	Apr. 29, 2000
1,600 m (4×400)	3 min., 15.17 s.	Ledovskaya, Nazarova, Pinigina, Bryzgina	USSR	Seoul, S. Korea	Oct. 1, 1988
3,200 m (4×800)	7 min., 50.17 s.	Olizarenko, Gurina, Borisova, Podyalovskaya	USSR	Moscow, USSR	Aug. 5, 1984

Field Events

Event	Record	Holder	Nationality	Location	Date
High jump	2.09 m (6' 10¼")	Stefka Kostadinova	Bulgaria	Rome, Italy	Aug. 30, 1987
Long jump	7.52 m (24' 8¼")	Galina Chistyakova	USSR	Leningrad, Russia	June 11, 1988
Triple jump	15.50 m (50' 10¼")	Inessa Kravets	Ukraine	Gothenburg, Sweden	Aug. 10, 1995
Pole vault	5.06 m (16' 7¾")	Yelena Isinbaeva	Russia	Zürich, Switzerland	Aug. 28, 2009
Discus	76.80 m (252' 0")	Gabriele Reinsch	E. Germany	Neubrandenburg, E. Germany	July 9, 1988
Hammer	82.98 m (272' 3")	Anita Wlodarczyk	Poland	Warsaw, Poland	Aug. 28, 2016
Javelin	72.28 m (237' 1¾")	Barbora Spotáková	Czech Rep.	Stuttgart, Germany	Sept. 13, 2008
Shot put	22.63 m (74' 3")	Natalya Lisovskaya	USSR	Moscow, Russia	June 7, 1987
Heptathlon	7,291 pts.	Jackie Joyner-Kersee	U.S.	Seoul, S. Korea	Sept. 24, 1988

Iditarod Trail Sled Dog Race, 2016

Dallas Seavey won the 44th annual Iditarod Trail Sled Dog Race to Nome, AK, Mar. 15, 2016. It was the fourth victory in five years for the 29-year-old Seavey, who finished the 964-mi course along the northern route to Nome. At 8 days, 11 hr., 20 min., and 16 sec., Seavey's total race time was the fastest in Iditarod history. The race's ceremonial start in Anchorage was shortened due to a lack of snow. The 2017 race was scheduled to begin Mar. 4 in Anchorage and follow the 987-mi southern route.

Westminster Kennel Club Best-In-Show Dogs, 1985-2016

Year	Best-in-Show winner, breed
1985	Ch. Braeburn's Close Encounter, Scottish Terrier
1986	Ch. Marjetta's National Acclaim, Pointer
1987	Ch. Covy Tucker Hill's Manhattan, German Shepherd Dog
1988	Ch. Great Elms Prince Charming II, Pomeranian
1989	Ch. Royal Tudor's Wild As The Wind, Doberman Pinscher
1990	Ch. Wendessa Crown Prince, Pekingese
1991	Ch. Whisperwind On A Carousel, Poodle (Standard)
1992	Ch. Registry's Lonesome Dove, Fox Terrier (Wire)
1993	Ch. Salilyn's Condor, Spaniel (English Springer)
1994	Ch. Chidley Willum The Conqueror, Norwich Terrier
1995	Ch. Gaelforce Post Script, Scottish Terrier
1996	Ch. Clussexx Country Sunrise, Spaniel (Clumber)
1997	Ch. Parsifal Di Casa Netzer, Standard Schnauzer
1998	Ch. Fairewood Frolic, Norwich Terrier
1999	Ch. Loteki Supernatural Being, Papillon
2000	Ch. Salilyn 'N Erin's Shameless, Spaniel (English Springer)
2001	Ch. Special Times Just Right, Bichon Frise

Year	Best-in-Show winner, breed
2002	Ch. Surrey Spice Girl, Poodle (Miniature)
2003	Ch. Torums Scarf Michael, Kerry Blue Terrier
2004	Ch. Darbydale's All Rise PouCh. Cove, Newfoundland
2005	Ch. Kan-Point's VJK Autumn Roses, Pointer (German Shorthaired)
2006	Ch. Rocky Top's Sundance Kid, Bull Terrier (Colored)
2007	Ch. Felicity's Diamond Jim, Spaniel (English Springer)
2008	Ch. K-Run's Park Me In First, Beagle (15 Inch)
2009	Ch. Clussexx Three D Grinchy Glee, Spaniel (Sussex)
2010	Ch. Roundtown Mercedes Of Maryscot, Scottish Terrier
2011	GCh. Foxcliffe Hickory Wind, Scottish Deerhound
2012	GCh. Palacegarden Malachy, Pekingese
2013	GCh. Banana Joe V Tani Kazari, Affenpinscher
2014	GCh. Afterall Painting The Sky, Fox Terrier (Wire)
2015	Ch. Tashtins Lookin For Trouble, Beagle (15 Inch)
2016	GCH Vjk-Myst Garbonita's California Journey, Pointer (German Shorthaired)

MARATHONS
World Marathon Majors Cycle Winners, 2006-16

The organizers of five marathons (Berlin, Boston, Chicago, London, and New York) agreed Jan. 23, 2006, to form a series called the World Marathon Majors. Tokyo joined the series in 2013. Marathoners are awarded points relative to their finish in each race in the series and in the Olympic and Intl. Assn. of Athletics Federations World Championships marathons when applicable. The number of races and time period encompassed by each series varies.

Cycle	Men's winner, country	Women's winner, country	Cycle	Men's winner, country	Women's winner, country
I: 2006-07	Robert Kipkoech Cheruiyot, Kenya	Gete Wami, Ethiopia	V: 2010-11	Emmanuel Mutai, Kenya	Liliya Shobukhova, Russia
II: 2007-08	Martin Lel, Kenya	Gete Wami, Ethiopia	VI: 2011-12	Geoffrey Mutai, Kenya	Mary Keitany, Kenya
III: 2008-09	Samuel Wanjiru, Kenya	Irina Mikitenko, Germany	VII: 2012-13	Tsegaye Kebede, Ethiopia	Priscah Jeptoo, Kenya
IV: 2009-10	Samuel Wanjiru, Kenya	Liliya Shobukhova, Russia	VIII: 2013-14	Wilson Kipsang, Kenya	Edna Kiplagat, Kenya[1]
			IX: 2015-16	Eliud Kipchoge, Kenya	Mary Keitany, Kenya

(1) Kenya's Rita Jeptoo ended the 2013-14 season ranked first but tested positive for a banned substance in Sept. 2014.

Boston Marathon Winners, 1972-2016

All times in hour:minute:second format. * = Course record.

Men's winner, country	Time	Year	Women's winner, country	Time
Olavi Suomalainen, Finland	2:15:39	1972	Nina Kuscsik, U.S.	3:10:26
Jon Anderson, U.S.	2:16:03	1973	Jacqueline Hansen, U.S.	3:05:59
Neil Cusack, Ireland	2:13:39	1974	Michiko Gorman, U.S.	2:47:11
Bill Rodgers, U.S.	2:09:55	1975	Liane Winter, West Germany	2:42:24
Jack Fultz, U.S.	2:20:19	1976	Kim Merritt, U.S.	2:47:10
Jerome Drayton, Canada	2:14:46	1977	Michiko Gorman, U.S.	2:48:33
Bill Rodgers, U.S.	2:10:13	1978	Gayle S. Barron, U.S.	2:44:52
Bill Rodgers, U.S.	2:09:27	1979	Joan Benoit, U.S.	2:35:15
Bill Rodgers, U.S.	2:12:11	1980	Jacqueline Gareau, Canada	2:34:28
Toshihiko Seko, Japan	2:09:26	1981	Allison Roe, New Zealand	2:26:46
Alberto Salazar, U.S.	2:08:52	1982	Charlotte Teske, West Germany	2:29:33
Greg Meyer, U.S.	2:09:00	1983	Joan Benoit, U.S.	2:22:43
Geoff Smith, England, UK	2:10:34	1984	Lorraine Moller, New Zealand	2:29:28
Geoff Smith, England, UK	2:14:05	1985	Lisa Larsen Weidenbach, U.S.	2:34:06
Robert de Castella, Australia	2:07:51	1986	Ingrid Kristiansen, Norway	2:24:55
Toshihiko Seko, Japan	2:11:50	1987	Rosa Mota, Portugal	2:25:21
Ibrahim Hussein, Kenya	2:08:43	1988	Rosa Mota, Portugal	2:24:30
Abebe Mekonnen, Ethiopia	2:09:06	1989	Ingrid Kristiansen, Norway	2:24:33
Gelindo Bordin, Italy	2:08:19	1990	Rosa Mota, Portugal	2:25:24
Ibrahim Hussein, Kenya	2:11:06	1991	Wanda Panfil, Poland	2:24:18
Ibrahim Hussein, Kenya	2:08:14	1992	Olga Markova, Russia	2:23:43
Cosmas Ndeti, Kenya	2:09:33	1993	Olga Markova, Russia	2:25:27
Cosmas Ndeti, Kenya	2:07:15	1994	Uta Pippig, Germany	2:21:45
Cosmas Ndeti, Kenya	2:09:22	1995	Uta Pippig, Germany	2:25:11
Moses Tanui, Kenya	2:09:15	1996	Uta Pippig, Germany	2:27:12
Lameck Aguta, Kenya	2:10:34	1997	Fatuma Roba, Ethiopia	2:26:23
Moses Tanui, Kenya	2:07:34	1998	Fatuma Roba, Ethiopia	2:23:21
Joseh Chebet, Kenya	2:09:52	1999	Fatuma Roba, Ethiopia	2:23:25
Elijah Lagat, Kenya	2:09:47	2000	Catherine Ndereba, Kenya	2:26:11
Lee Bong-ju, South Korea	2:09:43	2001	Catherine Ndereba, Kenya	2:23:53
Rodgers Rop, Kenya	2:09:02	2002	Margaret Okayo, Kenya	2:20:43
Robert Kipkoech Cheruiyot, Kenya	2:10:11	2003	Svetlana Zakharova, Russia	2:25:20
Timothy Cherigat, Kenya	2:10:37	2004	Catherine Ndereba, Kenya	2:24:27
Hailu Negussie, Ethiopia	2:11:45	2005	Catherine Ndereba, Kenya	2:25:13
Robert Kipkoech Cheruiyot, Kenya	2:07:14	2006	Rita Jeptoo, Kenya	2:23:38
Robert Kipkoech Cheruiyot, Kenya	2:14:13	2007	Lidiya Grigoryeva, Russia	2:29:18
Robert Kipkoech Cheruiyot, Kenya	2:07:46	2008	Dire Tune, Ethiopia	2:25:25
Deriba Merga, Ethiopia	2:08:42	2009	Salina Kosgei, Kenya	2:32:16
Robert Kiprono Cheruiyot, Kenya	2:05:52	2010	Teyba Erkesso, Ethiopia	2:26:11
Geoffrey Mutai, Kenya	2:03:02*	2011	Caroline Kilel, Kenya	2:22:36
Wesley Korir, Kenya	2:12:40	2012	Sharon Cherop, Kenya	2:31:50
Lelisa Desisa, Ethiopia	2:10:22	2013	Rita Jeptoo, Kenya	2:26:25
Meb Keflezighi, U.S.	2:08:37	2014	Rita Jeptoo, Kenya	2:18:57*
Lelisa Desisa, Ethiopia	2:09:17	2015	Caroline Rotich, Kenya	2:24:55
Lemi Berhanu Hayle, Ethiopia	2:12:45	2016	Atsede Baysa, Ethiopia	2:29:19

Boston Marathon Winners, 1897-1971

The first Boston Marathon was held in 1897. Women were officially accepted into the race in 1972. Times in hr.:min.:sec. format.

Year	Winner, state/country	Time	Year	Winner, state/country	Time
1897	John J. McDermott, New York	2:55:10	1935	John A. Kelley, Massachusetts	2:32:07
1898	Ronald J. MacDonald, Canada	2:42:00	1936	Ellison M. Brown, Rhode Island	2:33:40
1899	Lawrence Brignolia, Massachusetts	2:54:38	1937	Walter Young, Canada	2:33:20
1900	John Caffery, Canada	2:39:44	1938	Leslie S. Pawson, Rhode Island	2:35:34
1901	John Caffery, Canada	2:29:23	1939	Ellison M. Brown, Rhode Island	2:28:51
1902	Sammy Mellor, New York	2:43:12	1940	Gerard Cote, Canada	2:28:28
1903	John Lorden, Massachusetts	2:41:29	1941	Leslie S. Pawson, Rhode Island	2:30:38
1904	Michael Spring, New York	2:38:04	1942	Joe Smith, Massachusetts	2:26:51
1905	Frederick Lorz, New York	2:38:25	1943	Gerard Cote, Canada	2:28:25
1906	Tim Ford, Massachusetts	2:45:45	1944	Gerard Cote, Canada	2:31:50
1907	Thomas Longboat, Canada	2:24:24	1945	John A. Kelley, Massachusetts	2:30:40
1908	Thomas Morrissey, New York	2:25:43	1946	Stylianos Kyriakides, Greece	2:29:27
1909	Henri Renaud, New Hampshire	2:53:36	1947	Yun Bok Suh, Korea	2:25:39
1910	Fred Cameron, Canada	2:28:52	1948	Gerard Cote, Canada	2:31:02
1911	Clarence DeMar, Massachusetts	2:21:39	1949	Karl Leandersson, Sweden	2:31:50
1912	Michael Ryan, New York	2:21:18	1950	Kee Yong Ham, Korea	2:32:39
1913	Fritz Carlson, Minnesota	2:25:14	1951	Shigeki Tanaka, Japan	2:27:45
1914	James Duffy, Canada	2:25:14	1952	Doroteo Flores, Guatamela	2:31:53
1915	Edouard Fabre, Canada	2:31:41	1953	Keizo Yamada, Japan	2:18:51
1916	Arthur Roth, Massachusetts	2:27:16	1954	Veikko Karvonen, Finland	2:20:39
1917	Bill Kennedy, New York	2:28:37	1955	Hideo Hamamura, Japan	2:18:22
1918	Military relay, Camp Devens	2:29:53	1956	Antti Viskari, Finland	2:14:14
1919	Carl Linder, Massachusetts	2:29:13	1957	John J. Kelley, Connecticut	2:20:05
1920	Peter Trivoulides, New York	2:29:31	1958	Franjo Mihalic, Yugoslavia	2:25:54
1921	Frank Zuna, New York	2:18:57	1959	Eino Oksanen, Finland	2:22:42
1922	Clarence DeMar, Massachusetts	2:18:10	1960	Paavo Kotila, Finland	2:20:54
1923	Clarence DeMar, Massachusetts	2:23:47	1961	Eino Oksanen, Finland	2:23:39
1924	Clarence DeMar, Massachusetts	2:29:40	1962	Eino Oksanen, Finland	2:23:48
1925	Charles Mellor, Illinois	2:33:00	1963	Aurele Vandendriessche, Belgium	2:18:58
1926	John C. Miles, Canada	2:25:40	1964	Aurele Vandendriessche, Belgium	2:19:59
1927	Clarence DeMar, Massachusetts	2:40:22	1965	Morio Shigematsu, Japan	2:16:33
1928	Clarence DeMar, Massachusetts	2:37:07	1966	Kenji Kemihara, Japan	2:17:11
1929	John C. Miles, Canada	2:33:08	1967	David McKenzie, New Zealand	2:15:45
1930	Clarence DeMar, Massachusetts	2:34:48	1968	Amby Burfoot, Connecticut	2:22:17
1931	James P. Henigan, Massachusetts	2:46:45	1969	Yoshiaki Unetani, Japan	2:13:49
1932	Paul DeBruyn, Germany	2:33:36	1970	Ron Hill, England, UK	2:10:30
1933	Leslie S. Pawson, Rhode Island	2:31:01	1971	Alvaro Mejia, Colombia	2:18:45
1934	Dave Komonen, Canada	2:32:53			

New York City Marathon Winners, 1970-2016

All times in hour:minute:second format. * = Course record. Race not held, 2012.

Men's winner, country	Time	Year	Women's winner, country	Time
Gary Muhrcke, U.S.	2:31:38	1970	No finisher	—
Norman Higgins, U.S.	2:22:54	1971	Beth Bonner, U.S.	2:55:22
Sheldon Karlin, U.S.	2:27:52	1972	Nina Kuscsik, U.S.	3:08:41
Tom Fleming, U.S.	2:19:25	1973	Nina Kuscsik, U.S.	2:57:07
Norbert Sander, U.S.	2:26:30	1974	Katherine Switzer, U.S.	3:07:29
Tom Fleming, U.S.	2:19:27	1975	Kim Merritt, U.S.	2:46:14
Bill Rodgers, U.S.	2:10:10	1976	Miki Gorman, U.S.	2:39:11
Bill Rodgers, U.S.	2:11:28	1977	Miki Gorman, U.S.	2:43:10
Bill Rodgers, U.S.	2:12:12	1978	Grete Waitz, Norway	2:32:30
Bill Rodgers, U.S.	2:11:42	1979	Grete Waitz, Norway	2:27:33
Alberto Salazar, U.S.	2:09:41	1980	Grete Waitz, Norway	2:25:42
Alberto Salazar, U.S.	2:08:13	1981	Allison Roe, New Zealand	2:25:29
Alberto Salazar, U.S.	2:09:29	1982	Grete Waitz, Norway	2:27:14
Rod Dixon, New Zealand	2:08:59	1983	Grete Waitz, Norway	2:27:00
Orlando Pizzolato, Italy	2:14:53	1984	Grete Waitz, Norway	2:29:30
Orlando Pizzolato, Italy	2:11:34	1985	Grete Waitz, Norway	2:28:34
Gianni Poli, Italy	2:11:06	1986	Grete Waitz, Norway	2:28:06
Ibrahim Hussein, Kenya	2:11:01	1987	Priscilla Welch, England, UK	2:30:17
Steve Jones, Wales, UK	2:08:20	1988	Grete Waitz, Norway	2:28:07
Juma Ikangaa, Tanzania	2:08:01	1989	Ingrid Kristiansen, Norway	2:25:30
Douglas Wakiihuri, Kenya	2:12:39	1990	Wanda Panfil, Poland	2:30:45
Salvador Garcia, Mexico	2:09:28	1991	Liz McColgan, Scotland, UK	2:27:32
Willie Mtolo, South Africa	2:09:29	1992	Lisa Ondieki, Australia	2:24:40
Andres Espinosa, Mexico	2:10:04	1993	Uta Pippig, Germany	2:26:24
German Silva, Mexico	2:11:21	1994	Tegla Loroupe, Kenya	2:27:37
German Silva, Mexico	2:11:00	1995	Tegla Loroupe, Kenya	2:28:06
Giacomo Leone, Italy	2:09:54	1996	Anuta Catuna, Romania	2:28:43
John Kagwe, Kenya	2:08:12	1997	F. Rochat-Moser, Switzerland	2:28:43
John Kagwe, Kenya	2:08:45	1998	Franca Fiacconi, Italy	2:25:17
Joseph Chebet, Kenya	2:09:14	1999	Adriana Fernandez, Mexico	2:25:06
Abdelkader El Mouaziz, Morocco	2:10:09	2000	Ludmila Petrova, Russia	2:25:45
Tesfaye Jifar, Ethiopia	2:07:43	2001	Margaret Okayo, Kenya	2:24:21
Rodgers Rop, Kenya	2:08:07	2002	Joyce Chepchumba, Kenya	2:25:56
Martin Lel, Kenya	2:10:30	2003	Margaret Okayo, Kenya	2:22:31*
Hendrik Ramaala, South Africa	2:09:28	2004	Paula Radcliffe, England, UK	2:23:10
Paul Tergat, Kenya	2:09:30	2005	Jelena Prokopcuka, Latvia	2:24:41
Marilson Gomes dos Santos, Brazil	2:09:58	2006	Jelena Prokopcuka, Latvia	2:25:05
Martin Lel, Kenya	2:09:04	2007	Paula Radcliffe, England, UK	2:23:09
Marilson Gomes dos Santos, Brazil	2:08:43	2008	Paula Radcliffe, England, UK	2:23:56
Meb Keflezighi, U.S.	2:09:15	2009	Derartu Tulu, Ethiopia	2:28:52
Gebre Gebrmariam, Ethiopia	2:08:14	2010	Edna Kiplagat, Kenya	2:28:20
Geoffrey Mutai, Kenya	2:05:06*	2011	Firehiwot Dado, Ethiopia	2:23:15
Geoffrey Mutai, Kenya	2:08:24	2013	Priscah Jeptoo, Kenya	2:25:07
Wilson Kipsang, Kenya	2:10:59	2014	Mary Keitany, Kenya	2:25:07
Stanley Biwott, Kenya	2:10:34	2015	Mary Keitany, Kenya	2:24:25
Ghirmay Ghebreslassie, Eritrea	2:07:51	2016	Mary Keitany, Kenya	2:24:26

Other Marathon Results, 2016

Los Angeles Marathon: Feb. 14. Men: Weldon Kirui, Kenya, 2:13:06. Women: Nataliya Lehonkova, Ukraine, 2:30:40.
Tokyo Marathon: Feb. 28. Men: Feyisa Lilesa, Ethiopia, 2:06:56. Women: Helah Kiprop, 2:21:27.
Paris Marathon: Apr. 3. Men: Cyprian Kotut, Kenya, 2:07:11. Women: Visiline Jepkesho, Kenya, 2:25:53.
Rotterdam Marathon: Apr. 10. Men: Marius Kipserem, Kenya, 2:06:11. Women: Letebrhan Haylay Gebreslasea, Ethiopia, 2:26:15.

London Marathon: Apr. 24. Men: Eliud Kipchoge, Kenya, 2:03:05. Women: Jemima Sumgong, Kenya, 2:22:58.
Berlin Marathon: Sept. 25. Men: Kenenisa Bekele, Ethiopia, 2:03:03. Women: Aberu Kebede, Ethiopia, 2:20:45.
Chicago Marathon: Oct. 9. Men: Abel Kirui, Kenya, 2:11:23. Women: Florence Kiplagat, Kenya, 2:21:32.

Ironman Triathlon World Championships, 1978-2016

The Ironman Triathlon World Championship—a 2.4-mi ocean swim, 112-mi bike ride, and 26.2-mi run—is held annually in Kailua-Kona, HI. All times in hour:minute:second format. * = Course record.

Men's winner, country	Time	Year	Women's winner, country	Time
Gordon Haller, U.S.	11:46:58	**1978**	No finisher	—
Tom Warren, U.S.	11:15:56	**1979**	Lyn Lemaire, U.S.	12:55:00
Dave Scott, U.S.	9:24:33	**1980**	Robin Beck, U.S.	11:21:24
John Howard, U.S.	9:38:29	**1981**	Linda Sweeney, U.S.	12:00:32
Dave Scott, U.S.	9:08:23	**1982**	Julie Leach, U.S.	10:54:08
Dave Scott, U.S.	9:05:57	**1983**	Sylviane Puntous, Canada	10:43:36
Dave Scott, U.S.	8:54:20	**1984**	Sylviane Puntous, Canada	10:25:13
Scott Tinley, U.S.	8:50:54	**1985**	Joanne Ernst, U.S.	10:25:22
Dave Scott, U.S.	8:28:37	**1986**	Paula Newby-Fraser, Zimbabwe	9:49:14
Dave Scott, U.S.	8:34:13	**1987**	Erin Baker, New Zealand	9:35:25
Scott Molina, U.S.	8:31:00	**1988**	Paula Newby-Fraser, Zimbabwe	9:01:01
Mark Allen, U.S.	8:09:15	**1989**	Paula Newby-Fraser, Zimbabwe	9:00:56
Mark Allen, U.S.	8:28:17	**1990**	Erin Baker, New Zealand	9:13:42
Mark Allen, U.S.	8:18:32	**1991**	Paula Newby-Fraser, Zimbabwe	9:07:52
Mark Allen, U.S.	8:09:08	**1992**	Paula Newby-Fraser, Zimbabwe	8:55:28
Mark Allen, U.S.	8:07:45	**1993**	Paula Newby-Fraser, Zimbabwe	8:58:23
Greg Welch, Australia	8:20:27	**1994**	Paula Newby-Fraser, Zimbabwe	9:20:14
Mark Allen, U.S.	8:20:34	**1995**	Karen Smyers, U.S.	9:16:46
Luc Van Lierde, Belgium	8:04:08	**1996**	Paula Newby-Fraser, Zimbabwe	9:06:49
Thomas Hellriegel, Germany	8:33:01	**1997**	Heather Fuhr, Canada	9:31:43
Peter Reid, Canada	8:24:20	**1998**	Natascha Badmann, Switzerland	9:24:16
Luc Van Lierde, Belgium	8:17:17	**1999**	Lori Bowden, U.S.	9:13:02
Peter Reid, Canada	8:21:01	**2000**	Natascha Badmann, Switzerland	9:26:16
Timothy Deboom, U.S.	8:31:18	**2001**	Natascha Badmann, Switzerland	9:28:37
Timothy Deboom, U.S.	8:29:56	**2002**	Natascha Badmann, Switzerland	9:07:54
Peter Reid, Canada	8:22:35	**2003**	Lori Bowden, Canada	9:11:55
Normann Stadler, Germany	8:33:29	**2004**	Natascha Badmann, Switzerland[1]	9:50:04
Faris al-Sultan, Germany	8:14:17	**2005**	Natascha Badmann, Switzerland	9:09:30
Normann Stadler, Germany	8:11:56	**2006**	Michellie Jones, Australia	9:18:31
Chris McCormack, Australia	8:15:34	**2007**	Chrissie Wellington, UK	9:08:45
Craig Alexander, Australia	8:17:45	**2008**	Chrissie Wellington, UK	9:06:23
Craig Alexander, Australia	8:20:21	**2009**	Chrissie Wellington, UK	8:54:02
Chris McCormack, Australia	8:10:37	**2010**	Mirinda Carfrae, Australia	8:58:36
Craig Alexander, Australia	8:03:56*	**2011**	Chrissie Wellington, UK	8:55:08
Pete Jacobs, Australia	8:18:37	**2012**	Leanda Cave, U.S.	9:15:54
Frederik Van Lierde, Belgium	8:12:29	**2013**	Mirinda Carfrae, Australia	8:52:14
Sebastian Kienle, Germany	8:14:18	**2014**	Mirinda Carfrae, Australia	9:00:55
Jan Frodeno, Germany	8:14:40	**2015**	Daniela Ryf, Switzerland	8:57:57
Jan Frodeno, Germany	8:06:30	**2016**	Daniela Ryf, Switzerland	8:46:46*

(1) First-place finisher Nina Kraft, Germany, admitted to using performance-enhancing drugs and was disqualified, Nov. 15, 2004.

James E. Sullivan Award Winners, 1930-2015

The James E. Sullivan Award, named after the former president of the Amateur Athletic Union (AAU), is given annually by the AAU to the American athlete who "by his or her performance, example, and influence as an amateur, has done the most during the year to advance the cause of sportsmanship."

Year	Winner	Sport	Year	Winner	Sport	Year	Winner	Sport
1930	Bobby Jones	Golf	1963	John Pennel	Track	1993	Charlie Ward	Football, basketball
1931	Barney Berlinger	Track	1964	Don Schollander	Swimming			
1932	Jim Bausch	Track	1965	Bill Bradley	Basketball	1994	Dan Jansen	Speed skating
1933	Glenn Cunningham	Track	1966	Jim Ryun	Track			
1934	Bill Bonthron	Track	1967	Randy Matson	Track	1995	Bruce Baumgartner	Wrestling
1935	Lawson Little	Golf	1968	Debbie Meyer	Swimming	1996	Michael Johnson	Track
1936	Glenn Morris	Track	1969	Bill Toomey	Track	1997	Peyton Manning	Football
1937	Don Budge	Tennis	1970	John Kinsella	Swimming	1998	Chamique Holdsclaw	Basketball
1938	Don Lash	Track	1971	Mark Spitz	Swimming	1999	Coco Miller and	
1939	Joe Burk	Rowing	1972	Frank Shorter	Track		Kelly Miller	Basketball
1940	Greg Rice	Track	1973	Bill Walton	Basketball	2000	Rulon Gardner	Wrestling
1941	Leslie MacMitchell	Track	1974	Rick Wohlhutter	Track	2001	Michelle Kwan	Figure skating
1942	Cornelius Warmerdam	Track	1975	Tim Shaw	Swimming			
1943	Gilbert Dodds	Track	1976	Bruce Jenner	Track	2002	Sarah Hughes	Figure skating
1944	Ann Curtis	Swimming	1977	John Naber	Swimming			
1945	Doc Blanchard	Football	1978	Tracy Caulkins	Swimming	2003	Michael Phelps	Swimming
1946	Arnold Tucker	Football	1979	Kurt Thomas	Gymnastics	2004	Paul Hamm	Gymnastics
1947	John Kelly Jr.	Rowing	1980	Eric Heiden	Speed skating	2005	J. J. Redick	Basketball
1948	Robert Mathias	Track				2006	Jessica Long	Swimming (paralympics)
1949	Dick Button	Skating	1981	Carl Lewis	Track			
1950	Fred Wilt	Track	1982	Mary Decker	Track	2007	Tim Tebow	Football
1951	Rev. Robert Richards	Track	1983	Edwin Moses	Track	2008	Shawn Johnson	Gymnastics
1952	Horace Ashenfelter	Track	1984	Greg Louganis	Diving	2009	Amy Palmiero-Winters	Ultra-marathon
1953	Dr. Sammy Lee	Diving	1985	Joan Benoit Samuelson	Marathon	2010	Evan Lysacek	Figure skating
1954	Mal Whitfield	Track						
1955	Harrison Dillard	Track	1986	Jackie Joyner-Kersee	Track	2011	Andrew Rodriguez	Football
1956	Patricia McCormick	Diving	1987	Jim Abbott	Baseball	2012	Missy Franklin	Swimming
1957	Bobby Joe Morrow	Track	1988	Florence Griffith Joyner	Track	2013	John Urschel	Football
1958	Glenn Davis	Track	1989	Janet Evans	Swimming	2014	Ezekiel Elliott	Football
1959	Parry O'Brien	Track	1990	John Smith	Wrestling	2015	Keenan Reynolds	Football
1960	Rafer Johnson	Track	1991	Mike Powell	Track		Breanna Stewart	Basketball
1961	Wilma Rudolph Ward	Track	1992	Bonnie Blair	Speed skating			
1962	James Beatty	Track						

America's Cup Yacht Race, 1851-2013

Competition for the America's Cup grew out of a yachting race during the London Exposition of 1851. The race covered an approximately 60-mi course around the Isle of Wight. The prize was a cup donated by the Royal Yacht Squadron of England. It became known as the America's Cup after the New York Yacht Club won the race with the ship *America*. Prior to 1983, all yachts are American unless otherwise noted.

Year	Result (score)
1851	America
1870	Magic defeated Cambria, England (1-0)
1871	Columbia (first three races) and Sappho (last two races) defeated Livonia, England (4-1)
1876	Madeline defeated Countess of Dufferin, Canada (2-0)
1881	Mischief defeated Atalanta, Canada (2-0)
1885	Puritan defeated Genesta, England (2-0)
1886	Mayflower defeated Galatea, England (2-0)
1887	Volunteer defeated Thistle, Scotland (2-0)
1893	Vigilant defeated Valkyrie II, England (3-0)
1895	Defender defeated Valkyrie III, England (3-0)
1899	Columbia defeated Shamrock, England (3-0)
1901	Columbia defeated Shamrock II, England (3-0)
1903	Reliance defeated Shamrock III, England (3-0)
1920	Resolute defeated Shamrock IV, England (3-2)
1930	Enterprise defeated Shamrock V, England (4-0)
1934	Rainbow defeated Endeavour, England (4-2)
1937	Ranger defeated Endeavour II, England (4-0)
1958	Columbia defeated Sceptre, England (4-0)
1962	Weatherly defeated Gretel, Australia (4-1)

Year	Result (score)
1964	Constellation defeated Sovereign, England (4-0)
1967	Intrepid defeated Dame Pattie, Australia (4-0)
1970	Intrepid defeated Gretel II, Australia (4-1)
1974	Courageous defeated Southern Cross, Australia (4-0)
1977	Courageous defeated Australia, Australia (4-0)
1980	Freedom defeated Australia, Australia (4-1)
1983	Australia II, Australia, defeated Liberty, U.S. (4-3)
1987	Stars & Stripes, U.S., defeated Kookaburra III, Aust. (4-0)
1988	Stars & Stripes, U.S., defeated New Zealand, NZ (2-0)
1992	America[3], U.S., defeated Il Moro di Venezia, Italy (4-1)
1995	Team New Zealand, NZ, defeated Young America, U.S. (5-0)
2000	Team New Zealand, NZ, defeated Luna Rossa, Italy (5-0)
2003	Alinghi, Switzerland, defeated Team New Zealand, NZ (5-0)
2007	Alinghi, Switzerland, defeated Emirates Team New Zealand, NZ (5-2)
2010	BMW Oracle Racing, U.S., defeated Alinghi 5, Switzerland (2-0)
2013	Oracle Team USA, U.S., defeated Emirates Team New Zealand, NZ (9-8)

Rifle and Pistol Individual Championships, 2016

Source: National Rifle Association (NRA)

NRA Bianchi Cup National Action Pistol Championship

Action Pistol: Doug Koenig, Hamberg, PA, 1920-183X
Woman Action Pistol: Tiffany Piper, New Zealand, 1904-15X

Junior Action Pistol: Tim Yackley, Portage, WI, 1898-125X

National Outdoor Rifle and Pistol Championships

Pistol: Philip Hemphill, Brandon, MS, 2598-107X
Civilian Pistol: John Zurek, Alpine, AZ, 2595-89X
Woman Pistol: Brenda Silva, Snowflake, AZ, 2514-73X
Smallbore Rifle Prone: Mark Delcotto, Lexington, KY, 6398-529X
Smallbore Rifle Metric Position: SSG George Norton, USA, Phenix City, AL, 4730-262X

High Power Rifle: Norman Houle, West Warwick, RI, 2383-130X
Woman High Power Rifle: Brooke Culpepper, Sharpsburg, GA, 2368-86X
High Power Rifle Long Range: John Whidden, Nashville, GA, 1240-77X
Woman High Power Rifle Long Range: Hanne Brantner, Cypress, TX, 1214-47X

National Indoor Rifle and Pistol Championships

Smallbore Rifle Conventional Position: Nicholas Stolarow, Folsom, CA, 797-12X
Woman Smallbore Rifle Conventional Position: Alaina Sims, Live Oak, CA, 792-11X
Smallbore Rifle Metric Position: Morgan Phillips, Salisbury, MD, 1170
Woman Smallbore Rifle Metric Position: Cassidy Fairman, Indiana, PA, 1135
Air Rifle: Katie Zaun, Buffalo, ND, 589
Woman Air Rifle: Calista Smoyer, Slatington, PA, 585
Conventional Pistol: Jack Adams, Chillicothe, OH, 894-39X

Woman Conventional Pistol: Brenda Silva, Snowflake, AZ, 881-27X
International Free Pistol: Cody Owsley, Tonganoxie, KS, 549
Woman International Free Pistol: Susan Brown, Kimberly, ID, 501
International Standard Pistol: John Bickar, Menlo Park, CA, 581
Woman International Standard Pistol: Kathy Chatterton, Glen Rock, NJ, 541
Air Pistol: Dan Brown, Twin Falls, ID, 570
Woman Air Pistol: Sandra Uptagraft, Phenix City, AL, 569

Pro Rodeo Cowboys Association All-Around Champions, 1977-2015

Year	Winner, hometown	Earnings	Year	Winner, hometown	Earnings
1977	Tom Ferguson, Miami, OK	$76,730	1997	Dan Mortensen, Manhattan, MT	$184,559
1978	Tom Ferguson, Miami, OK	103,734	1998	Ty Murray, Stephenville, TX	264,673
1979	Tom Ferguson, Miami, OK	96,272	1999	Fred Whitfield, Hockley, TX	217,819
1980	Paul Tierney, Rapid City, SD	105,568	2000	Joe Beaver, Huntsville, TX	225,396
1981	Jimmie Cooper, Monument, NM	105,862	2001	Cody Ohl, Stephensville, TX.	296,419
1982	Chris Lybbert, Coyote, CA	123,709	2002	Trevor Brazile, Anson, TX	273,997
1983	Roy Cooper, Durant, OK	153,391	2003	Trevor Brazile, Anson, TX	294,839
1984	Dee Pickett, Caldwell, ID	122,618	2004	Trevor Brazile, Decatur, TX	253,170
1985	Lewis Feild, Elk Ridge, UT	130,347	2005	Ryan Jarrett, Summerville, GA	263,665
1986	Lewis Feild, Elk Ridge, UT	166,042	2006	Trevor Brazile, Decatur, TX	329,924
1987	Lewis Feild, Elk Ridge, UT	144,335	2007	Trevor Brazile, Decatur, TX	425,115
1988	Dave Appleton, Arlington, TX	121,546	2008	Trevor Brazile, Decatur, TX	419,868
1989	Ty Murray, Odessa, TX	134,806	2009	Trevor Brazile, Decatur, TX	346,779
1990	Ty Murray, Stephenville, TX	213,772	2010	Trevor Brazile, Decatur, TX	507,921
1991	Ty Murray, Stephenville, TX	244,230	2011	Trevor Brazile, Decatur, TX	337,601
1992	Ty Murray, Stephenville, TX	225,992	2012	Trevor Brazile, Decatur, TX	298,626
1993	Ty Murray, Stephenville, TX	297,896	2013	Trevor Brazile, Decatur, TX	426,010
1994	Ty Murray, Stephenville, TX	246,170	2014	Trevor Brazile, Decatur, TX	494,369
1995	Joe Beaver, Huntsville, TX	141,753	2015	Trevor Brazile, Decatur, TX	518,011
1996	Joe Beaver, Huntsville, TX	166,103			

GENERAL INDEX

Note: Page numbers in boldface indicate key reference. Page numbers in italics indicate photo or illustration captions.

QUICK REFERENCE INDEX

For complete index, see pages 980-1007.